Social Register®
1997

VOL. CXI

November, 1996

SOCIAL REGISTER ASSOCIATION

381 PARK AVENUE SOUTH, NEW YORK, N.Y. 10016

ISBN 0 940281 10 4

The Social Register is issued in November and its accuracy is maintained by a Summer Edition (including Dilatory Domiciles and a list of Yachts and Their Owners) which is issued in May.

The Social Register records the full names and addresses of members of prominent families grouped together, any change of address, the clubs to which they belong, and the birth, marriage or death of each person as it may occur.

Names of Juniors MISSES $\begin{Bmatrix} 12 \text{ to } 17 \\ 14 \text{ to } 20 \end{Bmatrix}$ appear under the names of
MSRS adult members of their families.

If the married name you are seeking has escaped your memory and you can recall the maiden name, reference to the Married Maidens will then indicate the present name.

CLUB ABBREVIATIONS

Certain clubs in various cities have similar names. If a person belongs to one of these clubs, yet lives *in another state, or is listed with a foreign address,* the club abbreviation will be followed by these city designations.

b	—	Boston	ch	— Chicago	dy —	Dayton	po	—	Portland, OR	sf	— San Francisco
bf	—	Buffalo	cl	— Cleveland	n	—	New York	pt	—	Pittsburgh	sl	— St Louis
bl	—	Baltimore	cn	— Cincinnati	no	—	New Orleans	px	—	Phoenix	w	— Washington
bm	—	Birmingham, AL	cs	— Charleston, SC	p	—	Philadelphia	sa	—	San Antonio	wl	— Wilmington

A	Argyle	Bm	Badminton	Cm	Commercial
Ac	Acorn	Btc	Bath & Tennis	Cnt	Contemporary
AF	Armée Française	Btn	Badminton & Tennis	Co	Corinthians
Aga	Agamenticus Yacht	BtP	Bath & Tennis (Palm Beach)	Coa	Colonial Order of the Acorn
Al	Algonquin	Buf	Buffalo Yacht	Cos	Cosmos
An	Army & Navy	Bur	Burlingame Country	Cp	Society of California Pioneers
At	Athelstan	Bv	Bellerive Country	Cry	Corinthian Yacht
Au	Ausable	Bvl	Beverly Yacht	Cs	Cosmopolitan
Ayc	Annapolis Yacht	Bz	Ye Buz Fuz	Csh	Cold Spring Harbor Beach
B	The Brook	C	Century Association	Cspa	Colonial Society of PA
BA	British Army	Cas	Casino	Ct	City Tavern
Bcs	Bathing Corporation of Southampton	Cc	Society of the Cincinnati	Cts	The Courts
Bf	Buffalo	Cda	Colonial Dames of America	Cv	Chagrin Valley Hunt
Bg	Baltusrol Golf	Chi	Chilton	Cvc	Chevy Chase
Bgt	Bedford Golf & Tennis	Cho	Chicago	Cw	Society of Colonial Wars
Bgy	Bogey	Chr	Church	Cy	Country
Bhm	Bohemian	Ck	Creek	Cyc	Chicago Yacht
Bhy	Bar Harbor Yacht	Cly	Colony	D	Dedham Country & Polo

Colleges
(Abbreviations for Those Most Frequently Cited)

Aht	Amherst	Ken	Kenyon	Smu	Southern Methodist U
Ant	Antioch	Laf	Lafayette	Stan	Stanford
Aub	Auburn	LakeF	Lake Forest	Sth	Smith
Bab	Babson	Leh	Lehigh	StLaw	St Lawrence U
B'gton	Bennington	Man'vl	Manhattanville	Susq	Susquehanna U
BMr	Bryn Mawr	Mid	Middlebury	Swb	Sweet Briar
Bnd	Barnard	Mit	Massachusetts Institute of Technology	Swth	Swarthmore
Bow	Bowdoin	MtH	Mt Holyoke	Tul	Tulane
Br	Brown	NCar	U of North Carolina	Ty	Trinity
Buck	Bucknell	Ncmb	Newcomb College	U	Union
Cal	U of California	NotreD	Notre Dame	USA	US Military Academy
Ch	U of Chicago	Nu	New York U	USAF	US Air Force Academy
Cl	Columbia U	Nw	Northwestern	USCG	US Coast Guard Academy
Colg	Colgate	Ober	Oberlin	USN	US Naval Academy
Cr	Cornell	OWes	Ohio Wesleyan	V	Vassar
Denis	Denison	P	Princeton	Va	U of Virginia
Dth	Dartmouth	Pa	U of Pennsylvania	Van	Vanderbilt
F&M	Franklin & Marshall	Rdc	Radcliffe	WakeF	Wake Forest
Gchr	Goucher	Rens	Rensselaer Poly Tech	Wes	Wesleyan
Geo	Georgetown	RISD	Rhode Island School of Design	Wheat	Wheaton
GeoW	George Washington	Rm	Randolph-Macon	W&L	Washington & Lee
H	Harvard	RMWmn	Randolph-Macon Woman's College	W&M	William & Mary
Ham	Hamilton	Rut	Rutgers U	Wms	Williams
Hav	Haverford	Skd	Skidmore	Ws	Wellesley
Hlns	Hollins	SL	Sarah Lawrence	Y	Yale
JHop	Johns Hopkins				

NOTE

The order observed in listing abbreviations within an entry is: College (Mrs.); Clubs (Mr.); Societies (Mr.); Clubs (Mrs.); Societies (Mrs.); College Clubs (Mr. and Mrs.); College (Mr.). If a college abbreviation is followed by a period (.), membership in that university's local club is indicated.

The yacht symbol ⚓ included in a listing indicates that reference should be made to the Summer Edition which will contain a full listing of yachts and their owners as well as particulars.

The subscription is $96.00 per annum and includes the Winter Edition, the Summer Edition, Dilatory Domiciles and the *Social Register Observer*.

The listings of Births, Marriages and Deaths now appear in the *Social Register Observer*.

1997

A

Aalde MR & MRS Heilo (Brander—Sumner—Joan de B Mirc)
Mds.Ne.Cly.Dar.Dll.Cda . . .of
☎ (212) 752-3118 . . 345 E 57 St, Apt 1B, New York, NY *10022*
☎ (011-52-69) 16-50-48 . . Doña Elvira 223, Fracc El Cid, Mazatlán,
Sinaloa, Mexico

Aall MR & MRS Christian H (Ely—Sally Sample) SL'48.Grenoble'34 . . of
☎ (212) 838-0800 . . 825 Fifth Av, New York, NY *10021*
☎ (808) 923-2202 . . 3049 La Pietra Circle, Honolulu, HI *96815*

Abbett MRS Alice G (Alice B Gordon) Pg.Fcg.
☎ (412) 681-0974 . . 932 S Aiken Av, Pittsburgh, PA *15232-2212*

Abbett MR Taylor G—Pg.Denis'89
☎ (412) 681-0974 . . 932 S Aiken Av, Pittsburgh, PA *15232-2212*

Abbey MR & MRS Clifford L (Clare M Luce) OreSt'69
☎ (415) 928-7675 . . 1150 Greenwich St, San Francisco, CA *94109*

Abbey MR & MRS Paul R (Constance E Norweb) CtCol'74.Un.Kt.Woos'73
☎ (216) 974-0532 . . 9150 Little Mountain Rd, Kirtland Hills,
OH *44060*

Abbot MR & MRS John (Susan B Sharples) Cc.H'39 . | ☎ (011-39-75)
MISS Posy S . . . . | 9413719
| Castello Di Polgeto,
| 06019 Umbértide,
| Perugia, Italy

Abbot MISS Sarah W
☎ (508) 448-2205 . . 3 Highland Rd, Groton, MA *01450*

Abbott MRS Alice Reid (Alice F Reid) | ☎ (317) 743-4374
CtCol'69.Ne'74 . . . . | 220 W Stadium Av,
MISS Laurel S—at Yale . . . . | West Lafayette, IN
JUNIORS MISS Sally N . . . . | *47906*

Abbott MRS Charles C (Louise Slocum) . . . . | ☎ (860) 974-0543
MISS Margaret E—at 130 Brush Neck Av, | ''Spring Farm''
Warwick, RI *02886* . . . . | Pomfret Center, CT
| *06259*

Abbott MR & MRS Christopher C (Lexanne Johnson)
Stan'79.Pa'84.Ec.Sm.Ny.Myc.StLaw'80
☎ (508) 526-8589 . . 1 Proctor St, Manchester, MA *01944*

Abbott MR & MRS Clinton S JR (Mary L Robertson) | ☎ (847) 446-3716
Minn'49.Ih.Y'47 . . . . | 465 Cedar St,
MISS Kathryn C . . . . | Winnetka, IL *60093*

Abbott MR & MRS Gordon JR (Katharine O | ☎ (508) 526-4436
Stanley-Brown) V'49.Ec.Myc.Tv.Chi.H'50. | ''Glass Head''
Mass'90 . . . . | 3 Tuck's Point Rd,
MISS Alexandra G—Conn'89 . . . . | Manchester, MA
| *01944*

Abbott MRS Henry Paul (Elizabeth L Knight) . . . . . | ☎ (904) 285-3085
DR Anthony A—P'62—at ☎ (954) 786-1442 | 9740 Deer Run Dv,
4451 NE 25 Av, Lighthouse Point, FL *33064* . . | Ponte Vedra Beach,
| FL *32082*

Abbott MR & MRS James K (Mary L Althans) | ☎ (561) 393-0316
Denis'57.Cwr'59 . . . . | 1000 Spanish River
MISS Julia K—at ☎ (216) 581-0396 | Rd, Apt 2C,
644 Tuney Rd, Cleveland, OH *44146* . . . . | Boca Raton, FL
| *33432*

Abbott MR & MRS James S 3d (Mary M Torrance) It.May.Ofp.Cw.
☎ (216) 449-2274 . . Hill Creek Lane, Gates Mills, OH *44040*

Abbott MR & MRS James S 4th (Nancy A Hamilton) Woos'92.Ofp.Woos'91
☎ (216) 423-3875 . . PO Box 171, 1795 Epping Rd, Gates Mills,
OH *44040*

Abbott MRS John A (Diana A Ballin) Ws'37
☎ (617) 860-0473 . . Brookhaven C351, 1010 Waltham St, Lexington,
MA *02173*

Abbott MISS Katrina S (Gordon JR) . . . . Married at Manchester, MA
Lummis MR Benjamin R (John M) . . . . Jun 29'96

Abbott MRS R Tucker (Edy—vonder Heyden— | ☎ (407) 725-2260
Cecelia R White) . . . . | 2208 S Colonial Dv,
MISS Erika vonder Heyden—at U of Cal | Melbourne, FL
Berkeley . . . . | *32901*

Abdulrazak MR & MRS Fawzi (Caroline D Wendell) | ☎ (617) 926-5731
Gchr'68.Ncd.Bagd'67 . . . . | 4 Sheldon Rd,
MISS Caroline Earle—H'95 . . . . | Watertown, MA
MISS Nadia Wendell—at Winsor . . . . | *02172*

Abeel MISS Daphne (Thomas—Ehrlich—Daphne Abeel) Bnd'59.Cl'64
☎ (617) 491-3410 . . 148 Pleasant St, Cambridge, MA *02139*

Abeel MR James S
☎ (508) 462-7824 . . Rte 11, Box 316, Newburyport, MA *01950*

Abeel MR & MRS Neilson (Robertson—Victoria A Bryer) Bnd'63.Nu'65.Hl.Cl'62 . . . .
MISS Maud A—Ober'92.H'95—at
☎ (212) 316-2085 . . 132 W 109 St, New York, NY *10025*. . . . .
MR Neilson JR—Reed'90 . . . .
MISS Isabel A Robertson—Ober'89—at
☎ (415) 626-3885 . . 671 Ashbury St, San Francisco, CA *94117* . . . .
MR Samuel D Robertson—Bard'92 . . . .
☎ (503) 222-3895
1325 NW Flanders St, Portland, OR *97209-2619*

Abel MR & MRS John A (Sarah E Hunter) Vh.
☎ (510) 531-6852 . . 161 Estates Dv, Piedmont, CA *94611*

Abel MR & MRS Robert B (Mary Beth H Turner) Cda.Nw'53 . . . .
MR William T—at U of Miami Law . . . .
MR Taylor D—at U of Fla . . . .
☎ (941) 349-0687
333 Givens St, Siesta Key, Sarasota, FL *34242*

Abel MR & MRS Robert B JR (Stephanie M Clark) SoFla'84
☎ (415) 485-4491 . . 11 Tern Court, San Rafael, CA *94901*

Abele MR & MRS John E (Mary L Seton) Aht'59 . . .
MISS Jennifer L . . . .
MR Christopher S . . . .
MR Alexander T . . . .
☎ (508) 369-6343
101 Fairhaven Hill, Concord, MA *01742*

Abeles MR & MRS Charles C (Mehitable Mackay-Smith) VPI'56.Va'59.Mt.H'52.Va'58 . .
MISS Damaris S—Duke'86 . . . .
MISS Jessica A K—at U of Va . . . .
MR Nathaniel C—Va'85 . . . .
☎ (202) 333-3356
4531 Dexter St NW, Washington, DC *20007*

Abeles MRS Charles T (Sally P Taylor)
☎ (757) 423-3952 . . 1307 Daniel Av, Norfolk, VA *23505*

Abell MISS Alice O'M . . see R A Marks

Abell MR Charles L 3d . . see R A Marks

Abell MR Edward S G . . see R A Marks

Abell MRS Elizabeth P (Elizabeth A Phelps) Denis'57 . . . .
MISS Kimberly S—Mich'88 . . . .
MISS Hilary A—P'90 . . . .
MR Glenn B . . . .
☎ (941) 954-2360
101 Gulfstream Av, Apt 4F, Sarasota, FL *34236*

Abell MISS Ishtar J (Fulton—Whitehead—Stallings —Ishtar J Abell) . . . .
MISS Leasha C Fulton . . . .
☎ (540) 474-2507
''High Meadow'' PO Box 44, Hightown, VA *24465*

Abell MISS Mary Carroll—Gchr'46
☎ (603) 786-9573 . . ''Red Fox Hill'' RD 1, Rumney, NH *03266*

Abell MR & MRS Richard Bender (Lucia del C Lombana-Cadavid) Ct.Cw.Rv.Sar.StJ.Wt.Ll. Fw.Coa.Cc.Ht.Cspa.GeoW'66.GeoW'74 . . . . . .
MISS Rachel M C . . . .
MR Christian A L . . . .
☎ (703) 780-4934
8209 Chancery Court, Alexandria, VA *22308-1514*

Abell MR & MRS William S (Patricia E O'Callaghan) MaryMt'35.Cvc.Evg.Geo'36
☎ (301) 652-2518 . . 8101 Connecticut Av, Chevy Chase, MD *20815*

Abels MRS Robert S (Dorothy V Nevills) Buf.St.G.
☎ (716) 884-9235 . . 12 Soldiers Place, Buffalo, NY *14222*

Abercrombie CAPT (RET) & MRS Daniel W (MacMullan—White— Rachel M Horak) USN.Cvc.Y'38
☎ (941) 261-4430 . . 1285 Gulf Shore Blvd N, Apt 8C, Naples, FL *34102*

Aberg MR & MRS Charles P (Elizabeth Goodman) Sth'46.Y'41.Y'47 . . of
☎ (214) 526-6853 . . 3521 Arrowhead Dv, Dallas, TX *75204*
302 W 12 St, Apt 1B, New York, NY *10014*

Aberg MR & MRS Peter Martin (Susan M Correale) Bost'77.Kas'79
☎ (214) 739-5679 . . 3009 Bryn Mawr Dv, Dallas, TX *75225*

Abernethy MR & MRS Samuel F (Carolyn Gibbons) DU'70.Rc.Rcp.StA.P.'65 ⚓
☎ (914) 962-0099 . . 3 Maple Dv, Rye, NY *10580*

Abrahams MR James F (Richard T) . . . . Married at Chicago, IL
Wilbur MISS Holli (Scott) . . . . Jly 14'96

Abrahams MRS Jeanine M (Jeanine S Miller) MtH'69 . . . .
MR Matthew S—Wms'96 . . . .
☎ (303) 388-4776
1601 Fairfax St, Denver, CO *80220-1323*

Abrahams MASTER Jordan James (gg—MRS Charles Duncan Miller) . . . . .
Born at Denver, CO Jly 24'95

Abrahamson MR & MRS Eric S (Donna-Moore Bowman) Bur.Cal'83
☎ (415) 776-8087 . . 1230 Clay St, Apt 301, San Francisco, CA *94108*

Abreu MR & MRS Jean Claude (Mann—Farr—Georgiana W Manly) . . of
☎ (212) 794-9877 . . 315 E 72 St, New York, NY *10021*
☎ (011-33-1) 42-22-52-80 . . 55 rue de Verneuil, 75007 Paris, France

Abreu MR Miguel . . see MRS R W Davenport

Absher MR & MRS B Steven (Sarah R Reid) Wit'80.Tenn'83.WakeF'78.Tenn'84
☎ (423) 694-8816 . . 1012 Bretton Ridge Lane, Knoxville, TN *37919*

Achelis MR David T
☎ (212) 757-6527 . . 38 W 56 St, New York, NY *10019*

Acheson MR & MRS Christopher (Sheryl L Benson) Rol'72.Va'71 . . . .
JUNIORS MISS Karen E . . . .
☎ (503) 274-9416
2431 SW Sherwood Dv, Portland, OR *97201*

Acheson MR & MRS David (Jane Hickman) Ken'37.Cl'40.Y'42 . . . .
MISS Sophie—Scripps'71—at ☎ (203) 255-1349
6 Post Office Lane, Greens Farms, CT *06436* . .
☎ (860) 767-2220
20 Benson Lane, PO Box 511, Essex, CT *06426*

Acheson MR & MRS David C (Patricia J Castles) BMr'46.Mt.Yn.Y'43.H'48
☎ (202) 462-8664 . . 2700 Calvert St NW, Washington, DC *20008*

Acheson MISS Jane—V'30
☎ (212) 753-8320 . . 200 E 66 St, New York, NY *10021-6728*

Acheson MRS Marcus W 3d (BRNSS Cecilia von Schilling)
☎ (516) 723-3518 . . 21 Hampton Bays Dv, Hampton Bays, NY *11946-0270*

Achilles MISS Daphne F
221 E 78 St, New York, NY *10021*

Achilles MR & MRS Jonathan N (Nancy S Gerrity) Skd'79.Sth'82
☎ (540) 635-8832 . . 40 Old Browntown Lane, Box 723, Flint Hill, VA *22627*

Acker MR Lewis S—Bost'64
☎ (914) 688-5757 . . Box 81, Chichester, NY *12416*

Ackerman MR Allan D—Dth'68.H'74 . . . .
MISS Mary F—H'92 . . . .
MR Samuel K—at RI Sch of Design . . . .
☎ (773) 871-8681
905 W Willow St, Chicago, IL *60614*

Ackerman MR & MRS Asche (Susan Vail)
StLaw'82.Tex'84.Menlo'80.Hous'84
☎ (713) 622-4917 . . 3859 Chevy Chase Dv, Houston, TX *77019-3013*

Ackerman MR Bradley D . . . . Married at Pebble Beach, CA
Wilkens MISS Jannell . . . . Jly 19'96

Ackerman MR Jay R . . . . Married at Philadelphia, PA
Jefferson MISS Elizabeth . . . . Sep 7'96

Ackerman MR & MRS Jay R (Elizabeth Jefferson)
☎ (212) 758-9723 . . 30 E 62 St, New York, NY *10021*

Ackerman MR Marion S—Nyc.Hl.Yn.Wms'48.Y'52
☎ (713) 850-7560 . . 3711 San Felipe St, Apt 3B, Houston, TX *77027*

Ackerman MASTER Ross Asche (Asche) . . . . Born Jly 18'96

Ackerman MR & MRS Warren 3d (Cynthia R Melcher) . . . . | ☎ (203) 966-3829 1179 Smith Ridge
MR Warren 4th—at 127 W 92 St, New York, NY *10025* . . . . | Rd, New Canaan, CT *06840*
MR Robert G . . . . |
JUNIORS MR Casey M . . . . |

Acklen CAPT Robert L JR—USA.Cc.StJ.Snc.Lm.
TexA&M'67.Tex'73.NTex'89
☎ (214) 696-1783 . . 3132 Westminster Av, Dallas, TX *75205-1425*

Acquavella MISS Eleanor H . . see MRS H B Perlberg

Acton MR & MRS David (Young—Jane E Thomas)
Wils'51.Me.Cspa.Y.'55.Pa'60
☎ (610) 649-5254 . . 233 Righters Mill Rd, Gladwyne, PA *19035*

Acton MISS Lauren D—Ithaca'82
☎ (610) 644-6662 . . 1404 Mountainview Dv, Wayne, PA *19087*

Acton MR Paul B (David) . . . . Married at Wayne, PA
Tyson MISS Melissa C (Harrison S JR) . . . . Jan 6'96

Adair MR Jerald D JR—Tul'91
☎ (610) 992-9820 . . 560 American Av, Apt A409, King of Prussia, PA *19406*

Adair MRS John A (Carroll—Grace L Shumway) V'42.Chi.Ncd.
☎ (617) 235-3701 . . 131 Coolidge House, 75 Grove St, Wellesley, MA *02181*

Adam MR & MRS K Bruce (Anne P Ellice)
Swb'62.Mo.Leh'61 . . . . | ☎ (908) 782-3754 33 Pleasant Run Rd,
MISS Aubrey C—Swb'89 . . . . | Flemington, NJ *08822*

Adam MR & MRS Laszlo (Eleanor J Furlaud)
Ant'73.Cl'78.Rc.Mds.B.P'73 . . of
☎ (212) 316-5091 . . 370 Central Park W, Apt 613, New York, NY *10025*
☎ (516) 329-1097 . . 26 Pondview Lane, East Hampton, NY *11937*

Adamoski MR & MRS Gary J (Leila Werlein) Ch'79.Fy.Purd'72.Nw'74.Ill'82
☎ (773) 472-0453 . . 1216 W Montana St, Chicago, IL *60614*

Adams MR Alexander D . . see MISS C A Phillips

Adams MR & MRS Andrew M (Charlotte M Whann) Va'91.Col'85.CalSt'88
1107 Arabella St, New Orleans, LA *70115*

Adams MR Ansel (Virginia Best)
☎ (408) 624-2558 . . 181 Van Ess Way, Carmel, CA *93923*

Adams MR & MRS Anthony L (Louise de C Rambo) Rcn.Ng.B.So.H'67
☎ (203) 532-0408 . . Hardscrabble Rd, Greenwich, CT *06831*

Adams MR & MRS Benjamin C (Jennifer L Goldsmith) Bow'90.Tufts'88
☎ (212) 689-7787 . . 333 E 34 St, New York, NY *10016*

Adams MRS Braman B (Marjorie A McPherson) Cly.
☎ (203) 869-6198 . . 435 Lake Av, Greenwich, CT *06830*

Adams MR & MRS Brian R M (Willoughby G E Meyns) Aht'83.Rich'91
☎ (804) 359-1810 . . 4202 Park Av, Richmond, VA *23221*

Adams MR Brinton H . . see R A MacDonnell

Adams MRS Burnham (Goldsborough—Caroline J Crittenden) Ncd.Dar.
☎ (310) 823-1854 . . 229 Rees St, Playa Del Rey, CA *90293*

Adams MISS Caroline C . . see R A MacDonnell

Adams MR & MRS Charles A (Phyllis J Petersen)
Ariz'73.Ariz'72 . . . . | ☎ (602) 996-0816 11202 N 50 St,
JUNIORS MISS Katharine A . . . . | Scottsdale, AZ *85254*

Adams MR & MRS Charles C 3d (Leith McLean) Ny. | ☎ (212) UN1-2223 210 E 68 St,
LT Christopher W D—USNR.Ny.Ken'84—at | New York, NY
☎ (310) 395-5086 . . 621 San Vicente Blvd, | *10021-6031*
Apt 303, Santa Monica, CA *90402-1812* . . . . . . |
MR Charles C 4th—Ken'87—at |
☎ (310) 395-5086 . . 621 San Vicente Blvd, |
Apt 303, Santa Monica, CA *90402-1812* . . . . . . |

Adams MR & MRS Charles F (Penati—Beatrice Dabney) Sm.D.Cy.B.Ny.Plg.Cc.Cw.Ds.H'32 ⚓ | ☎ (508) 785-0071 Box 308,
MR Giannotto Penati . . . . | 195 Dedham St, Dover, MA *02030-0308*

Adams MR & MRS Charles S 3d (Elise T Dewey) Vt'83
☎ (301) 229-6877 . . 5008 Worthington Dv, Bethesda, MD *20816-2747*

Adams MR D Nelson—Y'32.H'35
☎ (212) RE7-8095 . . 137 E 66 St, New York, NY *10021*

Adams MR & MRS Daniel N JR (Siglow—Camilla A Sloat) Colg'62 . . . . | ☎ (203) 938-2102 Winsome Farm,
MR Daniel N 3d—at Providence, RI . . . . | 92 Marchant Rd,
MR Bryan G—at Trinity . . . . | West Redding, CT
MR Jesse W Siglow JR—KeeSt'92—at | *06896*
Tampa, FL . . . . |
MR Zachary H Siglow—at Storrs, CT . . . . . . |

Adams MRS Daniel P (Adelaide B Koop) Bm.Cly.Dc.Dh.Ncd.Dar.Myf . . .of
☎ (203) 762-7003 . . 39 Old Huckleberry Rd, Wilton, CT *06897*
☎ (212) 371-5995 . . 200 E 66 St, New York, NY *10021*

Adams MR & MRS Dayton W JR (Shelley A West)
CalSt'68.ArizSt'83.TexTech'63.AGSIM'67
☎ (602) 991-9288 . . 5027 Crestview Dv, Paradise Valley, AZ *85253*

Adams MISS Elizabeth C . . see MRS C P Carden

Adams MRS F Dennette (Achtmeyer—Virginia Albert) Carl'42.Cy.
☎ (617) 277-9122 . . 80 Craftsland Rd, Chestnut Hill, MA *02167*

Adams MRS F Jackson (Frances M Jackson) V'20
☎ (802) 485-3177 . . Mayo, 27 Vine St, Northfield, VT *05663*

Adams MRS Frances E—Pa'72.Cwr'78
☎ (413) 549-9948 . . 14 Aloha Dv, Hadley, MA *01035*

Adams MR & MRS Frederick B (Metz—Slater—PRCSSE Marie Louise de Croy) Gr.C.Y'32
☎ (011-33-1) 42-60-46-16 . . 208 rue de Rivoli, 75001 Paris, France

Adams MR & MRS G Lawrence (Kate D Brandon) Ncd.Dar.Miss'37
☎ (601) 442-2047 . . ''Oakland'' 9 Oakhurst Dv, Natchez, MS *39120*

Adams MRS (REV) Hope H (Hope H Howlett) . . . . Married at Hartford, CT
Eakins REV William J . . . . May 11'96

Adams MR Hugh T—Chr.Plg.Ne.StJ.P.'35
☎ (212) PL9-5627 . . 435 E 52 St, New York, NY *10022*

Adams MR Hughlett M . . see MRS J R Webster

Adams DR & MRS James L (Player—Marian B Leib)
Stan'64.CalTech'52.Stan'60 . . . . | ☎ (415) 324-0200
MR Robert L—Stan'86.Stan'88—at | 740 Santa Ynez St,
1325 Bryant St, Palo Alto, CA *94301* . . . . | Stanford, CA *94305*
 MISS Elizabeth C Player—Ty'93—at
 ☎ (415) 462-1139 . . 505 Hawthorne St,
 Palo Alto, CA *94301* . . . .
 MR Samuel L Player—Wes'91—at
 ☎ (415) 321-3528 . . 200 Waverly St, Apt 1,
 Menlo Park, CA *94025* . . . .
Adams MR & MRS John (Mary Ellen Noonan) Rm.Csn.Cl'50
 ☎ (908) 291-2894 . . 2 Tan Vat Rd, Locust, NJ *07760*
Adams MR & MRS John B (Rumsey—Roebling—Martha A Osborne)
Cw.Cda.Ga'42
 ☎ (912) 598-1758 . . 4 Ramshorn Court, Savannah, GA *31411*
Adams MR & MRS John Brooks (Lisa I Liebmann) SL'76.Cl'79.SL'75.Nu'78
 ☎ (212) 580-7887 . . 26 W 74 St, Apt 9, New York, NY *10023*
Adams MRS John Q (Nancy Motley) . . . . | ☎ (508) 785-0573
MISS Margery L . . . . | 17 Wilsondale St,
 | Dover, MA *02030*
Adams MR & MRS John Q JR (Anne C Daughaday) On.Cas.Ncd.Wms'39
 ☎ (561) 546-4124 . . ''Seascape'' PO Box 604, Hobe Sound,
 FL *33475*
Adams MR & MRS John W (Mary M Pierce) Cy.P'57.H'60
 ☎ (617) 326-6989 . . 743 High St, Dedham, MA *02026*
Adams MRS John W JR (Edith R Harris) Ty'85
 ☎ (617) 449-1639 . . 27 Concord St, Needham, MA *02192*
Adams MISS Judith
 ☎ (011-44-1584) 872758 . . 41 Broad St, Ludlow, Shropshire
 SY8 1NL, England
Adams MISS Julia L (Samuel) . . . . Married at Manchester, MA
 Richardson MR Paul J (late Donald) . . . . Jly 6'96
Adams MISS Martha L—ArizSt'70.Sl.
 ☎ (305) 294-3433 . . PO Box 4122, Key West, FL *33041*
Adams DR & MRS Michael (Jeanne V Falk) | ☎ (209) 431-7355
Fresno'61.Stan'94.Fresno'61.Wash'67 . . . . | 1772 W Alluvial
MISS Sarah J—Nu'88 . . . . | Av, Fresno, CA
MR Matthew—Pom'89 . . . . | *93711*
Adams MR Mitchell—Sm.H'66.H'69
 ☎ (617) 326-2081 . . 447 Westfield St, Dedham, MA *02026*
Adams DR P Evans—Sa.Rv.Pa'45
 Wanamaker House 25D, 2020 Walnut St, Philadelphia, PA *19103*
Adams MISS P Lee Hamilton—Woos'89.Bost'95
 ☎ (617) 887-2528 . . 27 Pembroke St, Apt 1, Chelsea, MA *02150*
Adams MR & MRS Peter B (Sharon K Pruett) | ☎ (617) 259-9042
Tv.Norw'66.Bost'74 . . . . | Baker Farm,
MR Charles F . . . . | Lincoln, MA *01773*
JUNIORS MR Reid B . . . . |
JUNIORS MR Jarrett M . . . . |
Adams DR & MRS Reuben Homer JR (Lindalyn Bennett) Smu'48.Duke'53
 ☎ (214) 521-0689 . . 4440 Westway Av, Dallas, TX *75205*
Adams MR & MRS Richard M (Caroline C Hollingsworth) H'53
 ☎ (617) 227-0983 . . 7 W Cedar St, Boston, MA *02108*
Adams MR & MRS Samuel (Cornelia Van R Thayer) H'79.Sm.Ec.H.'50
 ☎ (508) 526-1257 . . 11 University Lane, Manchester, MA *01944*

Adams MRS Scarritt (Beatrice M Agnew) Wash'43
 ☎ (441) 236-6040 . . ''Springfield'' 1 Pointfinger Rd, Paget DV 04,
 Bermuda
Adams MR & MRS Stirling S (Rosamond Hodges) | ☎ (561) 231-2127
H'33 . . . . | 230 John's Island
MR Stirling S JR—at Pittsford Common, RR 3, | Dv, Vero Beach, FL
Box 3130-22, Pittsford, VT *05763* . . . . | *32963*
MR W Woodward—Box 727, Millbrook, NY |
12545 . . . . |
Adams MR & MRS Thatcher M (Lilian R Stubbs) . . . | ☎ (441) 295-5093
MR John T—Rby.Ty'79.Y'82 . . . . | ''Coral Hill'' Shaw
 | Wood Crescent,
 | Pembroke HM 01,
 | Bermuda
Adams MR & MRS Thomas B (Ramelle F Cochrane) Sm.Tv.H'33
 ☎ (617) 259-8350 . . 37 Baker Farm, Lincoln, MA *01773*
Adams MRS Thomas E (Caroline Cecil) Evg.
 ☎ (561) 585-4207 . . 65 Curlew Rd, Point Manalapan, FL *33462*
Adams MR & MRS Warren S 2d (Wheeler—Clinton—Romaine Bristow)
Unn.Rcn.Mto.Plg.StJ.Cly.Srb.Cda.Pn.P'30.H'34.Nu'41
 ☎ (512) 338-0923 . . 6901 Ladera Norte, Austin, TX *78731*
Adams MRS Weston W (Gordon—Nancy E Atkins) Chi.Ey . . .of
 ☎ (617) 267-0540 . . 330 Beacon St, Boston, MA *02116*
 ☎ (617) 631-1677 . . 67 Harbor Av, Marblehead, MA *01945*
Adams MR & MRS Weston W JR (M Juliette Gross) | ☎ (617) 631-1731
Chi. . . . . | 67 Harbor Av,
MR Weston W 3d . . . . | Marblehead, MA
MR Walker B—at 1336 N Cleaver St, Chicago, IL | *01945*
60622 . . . . |
Adams MR & MRS William Carter (Una L Kauffman) Duke'29
 ☎ (412) 363-3100 . . 201 S Winebiddle St, Pittsburgh, PA *15224*
Adams MR & MRS William E (Jeannine L Earnshaw) Pa'54.W.P'53
 ☎ (508) 359-4717 . . 40 Flintlock Lane, Medfield, MA *02052*
Adamson MR Ames—Lm.CUNY'86 . . of
 ☎ (201) 217-0287 . . 244—1 St, Jersey City, NJ *07302*
 ''Thornburg'' Rte 22, West Exeter, NY *13491*
Adamson SIR Campbell & LADY (Chandler— | ☎ (011-44-171)
Josephine L Lloyd) Cl'56.Cly.Camb'42 . . . . | 223-2421
 MISS Hilary K Chandler . . . . | 13 Henning St,
 MR Logan M Chandler—Pa'82.Nw'86. | London SW11 3DR,
 Pa'93—at ☎ (212) 570-4196 . . 205 E 78 St, | England
 New York, NY *10021* . . . . |
Adamson MR & MRS Gary (Millicent W Ames) SWMoSt'59.Drury'59
 ☎ (314) 241-3589 . . 1827 Rutger St, St Louis, MO *63104*
Adamson MISS Helen M (Kimberling—Helen M Adamson)
 ☎ (504) 392-9508 . . 4439 Woodland Dv, Apt D, New Orleans,
 LA *70131*
Adamson MR & MRS L Talbot (Storey—Mary S Kennedy) Gm.Fw.P'44
 ☎ (610) 687-8116 . . 684 Wetherby Lane, Devon, PA *19333*
Adamson MISS Margaret L—RockyMt'79
 1257 Monroe St, Denver, CO *80206*
Adamson MR Talbot Scott—Emer'91
 ☎ (212) 861-8368 . . 155 E 84 St, Apt 1A, New York, NY *10028*
Adamson MR & MRS William JR (Keyser—Helen H | ☎ (941) 676-5310
Angier) P'44. . . . . | Box 832,
 MR W McHenry Keyser—at Shelbourne, VT | Lake Wales, FL
 05482 . . . . | *33859-0832*

Adcock MR & MRS Eugene D (Brown—Ziluca—Jeanie A Renchard)
Sth'59.Wayne'50.KendSchDsgn'55
☎ (970) 963-0103 . . 0278 Ronce Lane, Carbondale, CO *81623*

Adda MR & MRS Michael E S (Judith B Henderson) | ☎ (011-44-171)
CtCol'70.Camb'64 . . . . | 352-8442
JUNIORS MISS Alexia M E . . . . | 2 Hobury St,
JUNIORS MR Gavin J E . . . . | London SW10 0JD,
JUNIORS MR Benjamin R L . . . . | England

Addington MISS Elinor H (late Keene H 2d) . . . Married at Lake Forest, IL
Jannotta MR Ross H (Edgar D) . . . . Jun 22'96

Addington MRS Keene H 2d (Hodgkins—Constance | ☎ (847) 234-3143
E Goldsmith) Sr.On.Ct.Cho.Cnt. . . . . | 877 Woodbine
MR Brooks H—Denis'94—at ☎ (312) 335-9762 | Place, Lake Forest,
1835 N Hudson St, Chicago, IL *60614* . . . . | IL *60045*

Addington MR Keene H 3d—Rc.
2214 N Halsted St, Chicago, IL *60614*

Addison MR & MRS Christopher C (Sylvia McN Ripley) GeoW'80.GeoW'74
☎ (202) 625-2762 . . 2811—34 Place NW, Washington, DC *20007-1406*

Addison MR & MRS Francis G 3d (Sherrard C Marthinson) Sl.W&L'47
☎ (202) 338-6442 . . 1525—29 St NW, Washington, DC *20007*

Addison MRS Joseph JR (Grace Landes) Ct.
☎ (202) FE7-9042 . . 3612 S St NW, Washington, DC *20007*

Adelizzi MR & MRS Robert Frederick (Thomasine S | ☎ (619) 222-2028
Lane) SCal'58.Sdy.Dth'57.SanDiego'62 . . . . | 511 San Fernando
MISS Judith A—SCal'90.AGSIM'95 . . . . | St, San Diego, CA
MR James F—Dth'94 . . . . | *92106*

Adibi DR & MRS Siamak A (Joan W Foedisch) | of ☎ (412)621-9400
Ws'62.BMr'63.Bost'64.CarnM'84.Pg.Eyc. | 1154 Wightman St,
JHop'55.Jef'59.Mit'63 . . . . | Pittsburgh, PA
MISS Elise W—Swth'88.Pa'94—at 54 E 3 St, | *15217-1050*
Apt 10, New York, NY *10003* . . . . | ☎ (508) 627-4807
MISS Jennifer J—Br'92—at 54 E 3 St, Apt 10, | Star Rte 109,
New York, NY *10003* . . . . | Edgartown, MA
MR Camron F—Box 4221, Grand Junction, CO | *02539*
81502 . . . . |

Adler MR & MRS Allen (Frances F L Beatty) V'70.Cl'81.Ncd.P'67.H'70
☎ (212) 288-8516 . . 800 Park Av, New York, NY *10021*

Adler MRS Francis H (Emily Anne MacDonald) Bvr'44.Pc.
☎ (215) 984-8862 . . Cathedral Village E102, 600 E Cathedral Rd,
Philadelphia, PA *19128*

Adler MRS Kurt H (Nancy G Miller) SL'64 . . . . | ☎ (415) 459-3270
JUNIORS MISS Sabrina S M . . . . | 7 Allen Lane,
| Box 1446, Ross, CA
| *94957*

Adler MR & MRS Mark A (Nancy J Clark) StJ'61 . . . | ☎ (301) OL6-2991
MR Clark A—Wes'91 . . . . | 4617 De Russey
JUNIORS MR M Winter . . . . | P'kway,
| Chevy Chase, MD
| *20815*

Adleta MR & MRS Edward Jackson (Brussell—Linda D Bardin)
Bay'70.Tex'60
☎ (214) 528-6400 . . 5445 Oxford Av, Dallas, TX *75205*

Adriance MR & MRS H Benson 2d (Alexandra J Lyde)
Box 1, North Sandwich, NH *03259*

Adriance MRS William A (Johnson—Winifred Van Sickle)
☎ (706) 724-1450 . . St John Towers, Apt 1501, 724 Green St, Augusta,
GA *30901*

Adsit MR & MRS Willcox B (Harriet J McNulty) Wms'30
☎ (941) 676-2859 . . Mountain Lake, Box 832, Lake Wales, FL *33859*

Aeed MR & MRS Frederick M (Chaunci G Chick) Ariz'68.ArizSt'61.Ariz'68
☎ (602) 944-1333 . . 14 E Orangewood Av, Phoenix, AZ *85020*

Aertsen MISS Elizabeth W
☎ (215) 732-6972 . . 225 S 18 St, Apt 1002, Philadelphia, PA *19103*

Aertsen MR & MRS Guilliaem 4th (Margaret P | ☎ (617) 267-1184
Campbell) H'70 . . . . | 175 W Brookline St,
JUNIORS MISS Frances W . . . . | Boston, MA *02118*

Aertsen MR John G
☎ (802) 492-3322 . . Spring Lake Ranch, Cuttingsville, VT *05738*

Affel MR & MRS Herman A (Eugenia G Burnett) | ☎ (215) CH7-9529
Swb'42.Ac.Pc.Mit'41 . . . . | 315 Rex Av,
MR Lee B—HWSth'84 . . . . | Philadelphia, PA
| *19118*

Affoumado MR & MRS Seth J (Caroline T Cory) Dick'86.RochTech'84
☎ (415) 386-1775 . . 347—21 Av, Apt 3, San Francisco, CA *94121*

Agar MR & MRS J H Michael (Virginia C Pratt) | ☎ (610) 995-0773
Wh'lck'64.Geo'60.H'72 . . . . | 970 Weadley Rd,
MISS Elizabeth S . . . . | Radnor, PA *19087*
MR Carter P—Ty'94—at 1438 Third Av, |
New York, NY *10028* . . . . |
MR Trevor M—at Hawaii Pacific . . . . |

Agate MRS Williams J (Kathleen McGusty)
☎ (610) 584-3831 . . Meadowood at Worcester, 132 Bluebird Crossing,
Lansdale, PA *19446*

Agate MR & MRS Williams J JR (Martha W Sheble)
Denis'81.Un.Pc.Gettys'80
☎ (215) 247-1104 . . 179 Hillcrest Av, Philadelphia, PA *19118*

Agee MR Willard Curtis—St.Va'63
1534 Oxford Rd, Charlottesville, VA *22903*

Agnew MRS Cornelius R (Dorothea H Sowers)
☎ (203) 869-1368 . . 636 Steamboat Rd, Apt 2D, Greenwich, CT *06830*

Agnew MR & MRS David P (Hope L Coombe) Ln.P'48
☎ (203) 869-6279 . . 2 Echo Lane, Greenwich, CT *06830*

Agnew MR & MRS Donald (Shields—Rebecca W Tenney)
Unn.Pr.Evg.P'28.H'31
☎ (561) 546-2001 . . PO Box 188, Hobe Sound, FL *33475*

Agnew MR & MRS James Q (Barbara L Rossiter) W&L'50
☎ (804) 740-8049 . . 8912 Brieryle Rd, Richmond, VA *23229*

Agnew MISS Jennifer S—P'90
☎ (303) 871-0488 . . 379 S Pennsylvania St, Denver, CO *80209*

Agnew MR & MRS Rudolph I J (Whitney Warren)
☎ (011-44-171) 730-1252 . . 64 Eaton Terr, London SW1W 8TZ,
England

Agnew MRS Seth M (Nancy Longley) Ws'50
☎ (617) 237-3696 . . 204 Grove St, Wellesley, MA *02181*

Aguirre MR & MRS Javier (Laura Linardi) Paris'71.Cly.Madrid'72 . . of
☎ (212) 472-7547 . . 44 E 67 St, New York, NY *10021*
☎ (516) 726-5030 . . ''Pheasant Hill'' 60 Schwenk Rd, Water Mill,
NY *11976*

Ahearne MR & MRS John J (Elizabeth W Horne) Mid'82.Cas.StN'83
☎ (773) 935-0952 . . 2424 N Surrey Court, Chicago, IL *60614*

Ahern MR & MRS F Gregory (Vivian M Spencer) Msq.Nrr.Srb.Br'74 . . of
☎ (617) 461-1196 . . 9 Marsh St, Dedham, MA *02026*
☎ (401) 847-4050 . . ''Chastellux'' Chastellux Av, Newport, RI *02840*

Ahlander MRS Judd (Portner—Leslie Judd)
☎ (941) 346-7509 . . 601 Venice Lane, Sarasota, FL *34242*

Ahlefeldt MRS Benedict (Alette Moltke) Cs . . .of
☎ (914) 277-5386 . . 228A Heritage Hills, Somers, NY *10589*
☎ (212) 348-3719 . . 111 E 85 St, New York, NY *10028*

Ahlheim MRS Carl F (Eleanor Van Allen) Ers'31
☎ (716) 883-4480 . . 35 Hodge Av, Buffalo, NY *14222*

Ahmanson MR & MRS Robert H (Kathleen M Holser) Cal'50.Cal'49
☎ (213) 930-1179 . . 150 S Hudson Place, Los Angeles, CA *90004*

Ahn MR & MRS Sangwoo (Alison Donald) ☎ (203) 869-4875
Ln.Wms'60.Y'63 . . . . 106 Patterson Av,
MISS Laura . . . . Greenwich, CT
MISS Ginger *06830*

Ahn MR Woodrow—Y'92
☎ (212) 628-8404 . . 30 E 68 St, New York, NY *10021*

Aidinoff MR M Bernard—C.Mt.Mich'50.H.'53
☎ (212) 369-6887 . . 1136 Fifth Av, New York, NY *10128*

Aigeltinger MR & MRS John F (Virginia R Lander) ☎ (610) MU8-4770
Pa'42 . . . . 308 Midland Av,
MISS Virginia R . . . . Wayne, PA *19087*
MISS Barbara C . . . . |

Aiken MRS Douglas S (Mary A Bennett)
824 Pinetree Circle, Apt 21, Thousand Oaks, CA *91360*

Aiken MR & MRS Isaac M JR (Louise I McNeel) Ga'51.Va'47
☎ (912) 638-4723 . . 123 E 15 St, PO Box 30095, Sea Island, GA *31561*

Aiken MR & MRS R Kenneth (Sara J Ledes) ☎ (703) 533-8330
Col'84.AmU'90.Cda.QUNIre'83 . . . . 2842 W George
MR Kenneth D—Loughb'95—at London, England Mason Rd,
Falls Church, VA
22042

Aimers MR John L—McG'74
☎ (416) 975-2608 . . 49 St Clair Av W, Apt 505, Toronto,
Ontario M4V 1K6, Canada

Ainslie MR & MRS Michael L (Braga—Suzanne B Hooker)
Bnd'75.Ri.Van'65
☎ (203) 869-3154 . . 476 Lake Av, Greenwich, CT *06830*

Ainsworth MR & MRS Bertram J L (Hoes—Louise W Hutcheson)
☎ (203) 259-6869 . . 4720 Congress St, Fairfield, CT *06430*

Aitchison MISS Beatrice—Gchr'28.JHop'33.Ore'37.Gchr'79
☎ (202) 244-1430 . . 3001 Veazey Terr NW, Apt 534, Washington,
DC *20008-5402*

Aitken MR & MRS Russell B (McAlpin—Roosevelt—Irene E Boyd)
Nrr.L.Srb.Evg.BtP.Cly.StJ.Cda.Dc.
☎ (212) BU8-5697 . . 990 Fifth Av, New York, NY *10021*

Akabane DR & MRS Yoshiharu (Cynthia Miller) SUNY'70.H'67
☎ (617) 595-5543 . . 76 Sargent Rd, Swampscott, MA *01904*

Ake MRS Roscoe C (Beatrice C Williams)
☎ (505) 835-1849 . . PO Box 624, Socorro, NM *87801*

Akers MR Christopher G . . see MISS (REV) L P Tower

Akin MISS Gwendolyn . . see MRS O L Thorne

Akin MR & MRS John (Margaret F Wendt) Sth'65.StLaw'62
☎ (206) 329-2403 . . 302 Maiden Lane E, Seattle, WA *98112*

Alatas MRS Madeleine DeG L H (Madeleine DeG ☎ (011-44-171)
Livingston Hammond) SL'74.Pa'82 351-4375
MR Mishal . . . . 42 Slaidburn St,
London SW10 0JW,
England

Albano MRS Salvatore A (Stillman—Spier—Frances D Johnson)
Cly.Ncd.Ht.
☎ (212) 288-2040 . . 135 E 71 St, New York, NY *10021*

Alberts MRS Lee Winfield (Nathalie Fowler) ☎ (847) 381-1530
Ch'45.Cho.Ncd. 229 Donlea Rd,
MISS Anne B . . . . Barrington, IL
60010

Albright MR & MRS Craig H (Susannah F Robins)
☎ (415) 327-3535 . . 709 College Av, Menlo Park, CA *94025*

Albright DR & MRS Nile L (M Lee Lawrence) H'61 . | ☎ (617) 566-1105
MISS Tara L . . . . 282 Newton St,
MR Lars . . . . Brookline, MA
02146

Albrittain MRS James S (Andrea C Robinson) . . . . Married at
Fishers Island, NY
Ross MR H Lawrence 3d (Henry L JR) . . . . Jly 27'96

Alcock MR & MRS George L JR (Louise S Bachelder) Ws'78.Sar.Ne'62
☎ (617) 894-9469 . . 105 Cherry Brook Rd, Weston, MA *02193*

Alcorn MR Richard L—M.
☎ (610) 644-7847 . . "Hawthorne" 521 Leopard Rd, Berwyn, PA *19312*

Alcorn MRS William Neely JR (Anna Hacker) Ncd.
☎ (610) 584-3934 . . Meadowood at Worcester, 53 Pine Croft, Lansdale,
PA *19446*

Alcott COL & MRS Henry S (Mary J Charlton) | ☎ (612) 825-9585
USA.Minn'72.Web'86.FlaIT'89 . . . . | 4636 Oakland Av S,
MISS Catherine A . . . . Minneapolis, MN
MR Michael B *55407*

Alcott MR & MRS Leverett C (Marlene M McCoy) | ☎ (513) 232-7111
Cin'73.Minn'69 . . . . 7150 Goldengate
JUNIORS MISS Laura M . . . . Dv, Cincinnati, OH
JUNIORS MR Leverett M *45244*

Alden MR & MRS John J W (Llewellyn P Hall) | ☎ (902) 542-9541
Sth'57.Bow'56.H'59.Y'69 . . . . 76 Highland Av,
MISS Mary S—Col'88—at 810 Jones St, Apt 207, Wolfville,
San Francisco, CA *94109* . . . . Nova Scotia
MISS Sarah L P—at 2385 SW 23 Terr, B0P 1X0, Canada
Garage Apt, Miami, FL *33145* . . . . |

Aldrich MR & MRS Alexander (Watts—Phyllis | ☎ (518) 587-5026
Williamson) Rdc'60.C.H.'50 . . . . 104 Union Av,
MISS Sarah F—at Brown . . . . Saratoga Springs,
MR William C—at Georgetown . . . . NY *12866*

Aldrich MR & MRS John Winthrop (Middleton— | ☎ (914) 758-5895
Katharine D Ryan) SL'64.Hn.H'65 . . . . "Good Hap"
MISS Margaret L—at Columbia . . . . Barrytown, NY
MISS Katharine D—at U of Tex Austin *12507*
  MISS Laura D R Middleton—Sth'86.
  Wash'87.AmU'94—at ☎ (202) 328-3721
  3000 Connecticut Av NW, Washington, DC
  20008 . . . .
  MR Daniel T Middleton—Stan'87—at
  ☎ (415) 567-7841 . . 601 Van Ness Av,
San Francisco, CA *94102* . . . . |

Aldrich MRS Nelson W (Frances E Turner) Chi.
☎ (617) 329-0210 . . 10 Longwood Dv, Westwood, MA *02090*

Aldrich MRS Richard Chanler (Susan K Cutler) .... | ☎ (914) 758-9961
MR & MRS Richard (Anna Olbrychtowicz) | "Rokeby"
Warsaw'68.H'62—☎ (914) 758-8693 .... | Barrytown, NY
MISS Alexandra W—☎ (914) 758-8693 .... | *12507*

Aldrich MR & MRS Richard R (Kirsten J Schabacker) Bnd'88.Nw'89
345 E 80 St, Apt 19B, New York, NY *10021*

Aldrich MR & MRS Richard Steere (Frances Daggett) Mt.K.Cly.Y'45 .. of
☎ (401) 273-8308 .. 199 Hope St, Providence, RI *02906*
☎ (508) 994-6101 .. 1 Featherbed Lane, Nonquitt, MA *02748*

Aldworth MR & MRS Edward K (Finnell—Boak—Grace D Vogel)
☎ (505) 989-7669 .. Box 2666, Santa Fe, NM *87504*

Alessio MR & MRS Marco D (Kimberly E Amory) SanDiego'87.SanDiego'84
☎ (619) 456-1146 .. 410 Belvedere St, La Jolla, CA *92037*

Alexander MRS Annalita (Annalita Marsigli) | ☎ (212) 787-2422
Bnd'61.Cly. .... | 173 Riverside Dv,
MR Henry C 4th .... | New York, NY
| *10024*

Alexander MR Brooke—Un.Cc.P'35
☎ (212) 289-9218 .. 65 E 96 St, New York, NY *10128*

Alexander MR & MRS Charles T (Leary—Susan Lee Tessman) Rv.Temp'68
☎ (610) 520-0948 .. 405 Fishers Rd, Bryn Mawr, PA *19010*

Alexander DR & MRS Dave A JR (Beth V Callaway) Van'76.Van'72.Van'76
☎ (615) 377-9600 .. 104 Vaughn Rd, Nashville, TN *37221*

Alexander MR & MRS David D (Elizabeth A Rand) | ☎ (314) 993-3863
Mar'vil'89 .... | 18 Glen Abbey Dv,
JUNIORS MISS Elisabeth B .... | St Louis, MO *63131*

Alexander MR & MRS David G (Margaretha E | ☎ (212) 722-3926
Barczyk) StA.Cly.Pace'69 .... | 1133 Park Av,
MISS Natasha D—Wheat'92.Dc. .... | New York, NY
| *10128*

Alexander MR & MRS Donald C (Margaret Savage)
Van'44.Nyc.Cvc.Mt.Yn.Y'42.H'48
☎ (202) 338-1333 .. 2801 New Mexico Av NW, PH-2, Washington,
DC *20007*

Alexander DR & MRS E Pendleton (S Ramsey Murray)
Briar'77.Gi.Ayc.SCal'75
☎ (410) 224-3062 .. 6 Weems Creek Dv, Annapolis, MD *21401-1125*

Alexander MR & MRS Edward T (Claudia J Spicer) | ☎ (610) 644-8890
DU'67.VillaN'73.DavEl'69 .... | 144 Conestoga Rd,
MISS Katherine T .... | Malvern, PA *19355*
MR Joshua E ....
JUNIORS MISS Rebecca G .... |

Alexander MISS Elizabeth W—Y'82
☎ (213) 874-9633 .. 6740 Whitley Terr, Los Angeles, CA *90068*

Alexander MR & MRS Frederick B JR (Dorothy Schierenberg) V'31
☎ (214) 369-5946 .. 4730 Irvin Simmons Dv, Dallas, TX *75229*

Alexander DR & MRS J David (Catharine B Coleman)
Rhodes'56.C.Bhm.Rhodes'54.Ox'57
☎ (909) 624-7848 .. 807 N College Av, Claremont, CA *91711-3923*

Alexander DR & MRS J Deaver (Flood—Susanna | ☎ (561) 793-8594
Boylston Bolton) P'45.Pa'47 .... | 204C La Quinta,
MISS Helen C .... | 13368 Polo Rd W,
MISS Caroline R—A. .... | West Palm Beach,
MISS Henrietta K. .... | FL *33414*
MISS Dorothy D ....
MR John D JR ....

Alexander MR J Forsyth—Me.Rv.P'38.H'42
☎ (215) 984-8819 .. Cathedral Village D204, 600 E Cathedral Rd,
Philadelphia, PA *19128*

Alexander MR & MRS J Heywood (Beatrice M Sanderson)
Sth'53.Kt.Pn.P'51.H'53
☎ (603) 466-3881 .. Randolph Hill Rd, Randolph, NH *03570*

Alexander MR & MRS James M (Martha A O'Reilly) Pars'79.Y'73.H'75
☎ (713) 529-0133 .. 1419 Kirby Dv, Houston, TX *77019*

Alexander MR & MRS John S (G Elizabeth Bakewell)
UMiami'57.UMiami'48
☎ (904) 893-9352 .. Rte 19, Box 1098, Tallahassee, FL *32308*

Alexander CDR (RET) & MRS John W (Theresa M | ☎ (703) 478-6745
Pietropaoli) USN.CathU'72.Mo'71 .... | 12026 Heather
JUNIORS MR Richard J .... | Down Dv, Herndon,
| VA *20170*

Alexander MISS Julia M (J David) .... Married at Claremont, CA
Marciari MR John J (Harold) .... Aug 17'96

Alexander MR & MRS Lee C (E Ann Goff) | ☎ (516) 922-7358
Pr.Purd'48 .... | Box 549, Remsen's
MISS Olivia—LakeF'74.Ford'89 .... | Lane, Oyster Bay,
MR Neal—Ark'81.Ark'83 .... | NY *11771*

Alexander MR & MRS Quentin (Elisabeth S Hadden)
Un.Kt.Tv.Cv.Pk.Sar.Pa'41 .. of
☎ (216) 423-4763 .. "Eutrophia Farm" 2657 River Rd, Chagrin Falls,
OH *44022*
☎ (561) 278-9345 .. 901 S Ocean Blvd, Delray Beach, FL *33483*

Alexander MR & MRS William B 5th (Sarajane P | ☎ (202) 234-3694
Smith) Cvc.Me.Cry.Rv.Ll.StA.Pn.P'41........ | 1834 Kenyon St
MR William B 6th—Cvc.StA.Rv.Ll.StLaw'91. | NW, Washington,
GeoW'95 .... | DC *20010-2619*

Alexander MR & MRS DeWitt L JR (Hubbard—Gerrity—Kristin C Kuhns)
Swb'70.Unn.Eh.Shcc.DU'71
☎ (908) 234-2689 .. Box 367, Far Hills, NJ *07931*

Alexandre MRS J Henry (Sturges—Post—Olivia D Wheeler) Cda.
☎ (212) 288-9455 .. 55 E 72 St, New York, NY *10021-4149*

Alexandre MRS L Jerome (Patton—Margot L Edwards) .... Died at
Greenville, SC Jun 23'96

Alexandre MR Lawrence .... Died at
Bryn Mawr, PA Apr 28'96

Alexandre MRS Lawrence (Beverly Burger) Gm.
☎ (610) 687-1527 .. 590 Cricket Lane, Radnor, PA *19087*

Alexandre MRS P Hill (Priscilla B Hill) .... | ☎ (908) 766-6437
MISS Priscilla H .... | 84 Dryden Rd,
JUNIORS MISS Anthony D................. | Bernardsville, NJ
| *07924*

Alford MR & MRS Bryant K (Susanne S Hall) | ☎ (908) 273-3049
Wh'lck'68.BaldW'68 .... | 26 Hawthorne Place,
MR Jonathan L—StLaw'96 .... | Summit, NJ *07901*
MR Stuart K—at Lafayette ....

Alford MR & MRS C Douglas (U Britt Jönsson) SanDiego'84.Sdy.Cal'63
☎ (619) 223-3318 .. 3445 Xenophon St, San Diego, CA *92106*

Alford MRS J Edwin (Mary-Louise Kittinger) St.G.
☎ (716) 885-7475 .. 33 Gates Circle, Buffalo, NY *14209*

Alford MR & MRS J Keith (Wende S Adams) Buf.St.G.Syr'64
☎ (716) 835-1411 .. 228 Woodbridge Av, Buffalo, NY *14214*

Alford MR & MRS Michael R (Shannon E Cronan) | ☎ (202) 882-4888
Bost'70.Y'67 . . . . | 4800 Blagden Av
MR Samuel M . . . . | NW, Washington,
JUNIORS MISS Marisa G . . . . | DC 20011
Alford MR & MRS Robertson F (M Paige Cartmell) Myf.Y'40
☎ (860) 542-1647 . . 34 Laurel Way, Norfolk, CT 06058
Alford MR & MRS W Stewart (Mary W Randall) | ☎ (215) CH2-3291
Pc.Rm'64 . . . . | 79 E Bells Mill Rd,
MR J Winslow—Aht'91 . . . . | Philadelphia, PA
MR Joseph S—at Conn Coll . . . . | 19118-2614
Alfriend MR & MRS J Hunter (Barbara Berean) JHop'59
☎ (410) 669-3645 . . 128 W Lanvale St, Baltimore, MD 21217
Alger MISS Roxana S . . see H Robinson JR
Alig MRS de Vaulogé (Katharine de Vaulogé)
☎ (908) 234-1946 . . Larger Cross Rd, PO Box 751, Far Hills,
NJ 07931
Alig MR Wallace Baird—P'43
☎ (011-34-1) 266-5170 . . Calle de Felipe III 6, Plaza Mayor,
28012 Madrid, Spain
Allan MR & MRS David L (Catharine Bonsall) ArizSt'70.Vh.Va'68
☎ (818) 584-1411 . . 1201 Arden Rd, Pasadena, CA 91106
Allan MRS J Hamilton (Offutt—Agnes de B Edelen) . . . . Died at
Charlottesville, VA Feb 17'96
Allard MR & MRS Herbert K (Catherine C Curtis) Ec.H'48
☎ (508) 526-7733 . . 25 Masconomo St, Manchester-By-The-Sea,
MA 01944
Alleman DR & MRS H Edward JR (Richardsson— | of ☎ (561)844-7520
Joan I Keary) Rc.T.Snc.Rv.Ll.Chr.P'46.H'49. | "Eden Run"
Pace'85 . . . . | 991 N Lake Way,
MR Jonathan E F—Menlo'92—at | Palm Beach, FL
☎ (212) 486-0631 . . 447 E 57 St, New York, NY | 33480
10022 . . . . | ☎ (212) 427-7474
MR Peter K Richardsson | 47 E 88 St,
MR Richard K Richardsson—at Pratt Inst . . . | New York, NY
MR Richmond H Richardsson . . . . | 10128
Allen MRS A Christine (Peipers—Zetterberg—Caplow—A Christine Allen)
Col'66.Cly.Cda.
☎ (212) 595-8790 . . 101 W 79 St, Apt 27A, New York, NY 10024
☎ (908) 234-9034 . . "Corner House" 1641 Larger Cross Rd, Far Hills,
NJ 07931
Allen MR & MRS A Clinton 3d (Lawson Prince) | ☎ (617) 449-3365
B.Ny.Un.Hn.H.'67 . . . . | 710 South St,
MISS Samantha L—at Harvard . . . . | Needham, MA
MISS Walker P—at Harvard . . . . | 02192
MISS Lawson K . . . . |
Allen MR A William B (Armin B) . . . . Married at East Greenwich, RI
Loats MISS Sara T (Thomas) . . . . Apr 17'95
Allen MISS Alice (Groves—Donald—Alice Allen) | ☎ (212) 772-2255
Dar. . . . . | 320 E 72 St,
MISS Helen . . . . | New York, NY
| 10021
Allen MR Armin B—K.Nrr.Srb.Pa'69
☎ (212) 517-4854 . . 50 E 72 St, New York, NY 10021
Allen MR & MRS Arthur Yorke (Towner—Mary Stewart Hammond)
Gchr'68.Err.Ny.Plg.C.Cly.P'58
☎ (212) 289-6264 . . 1095 Park Av, New York, NY 10128

Allen MR Barton B (late David C) . . . . Married at Pittsfield, MA
Mester MISS Marianne S (Robert C) . . . . Jun 29'96
Allen MR & MRS Barton B (Marianne S Mester) LakeF'96.LakeF'93
☎ (508) 255-2006 . . 646 Shore Rd, South Orleans, MA 02662
Allen MRS Bertram S (Dickinson—Carolyn G Huntoon) Me.Ncd.
☎ (610) 525-6412 . . Tedwyn 507, 840 Montgomery Av, Bryn Mawr,
PA 19010
Allen MR & MRS Bruce R (Patricia R Northrup) Y'70
Box 2953, Morada Rd, Taos, NM 87571
Allen MR C Edmonds 3d—Pl.W&L'64.W&L'67
☎ (212) 355-3324 . . 405 E 54 St, New York, NY 10022
Allen MRS Carolyn G (Carolyn G Pile) . . . . | ☎ (401) 849-6109
JUNIORS MISS Ashley G . . . . | 140 Greene Lane,
JUNIORS MR Christian T—at St George's . . . . . . | Middletown, RI
| 02842
Allen MISS Carolyn Y
☎ (212) RE7-1142 . . 116 E 66 St, New York, NY 10021
Allen MR & MRS Charles C JR (Cynthia P Hayward) Cy.Lc.Nd.P'45
☎ (314) 994-1336 . . 10 Little Lane, St Louis, MO 63124
Allen MR & MRS Charles E G (Kristin A Rae) Nw'88.Exeter'84
☎ (212) 734-6944 . . 340 E 66 St, Apt 6K, New York, NY 10021
Allen MRS Charles H (Ann Bullard) Ncd.
☎ (415) 461-3302 . . 501 Via Casitas, Apt 811, Greenbrae, CA 94904
Allen MISS Charlotte
via Giacinto Carini 9, 90144 Palermo, Italy
Allen MR Christopher D (Philip D) . . . . Married at Chestnut Hill, PA
Griswold MISS Eliza T (Frank T 3d) . . . . Jun 8'96
Allen MR & MRS Christopher D (Eliza T Griswold) P'95.Rc.Ln.Shcc.H'92
☎ (212) 443-5564 . . 240 Mercer St, Apt 1504, New York, NY 10012
Allen MR & MRS Christopher J L (Victoria S Pulling)
V'93.Cl'96.Rc.T.Pr.An.Cr'86.Nu'92
☎ (212) 369-6708 . . 1775 York Av, Apt 19A, New York, NY 10128
Allen MISS Constance Churchyard—Tulsa'48
☎ (918) 786-7165 . . Meghan Coves 9, 31990 S 624 Place, Grove,
OK 74344
Allen REV David C . . . . Died at
Jupiter, FL in Feb 1995
Allen MRS De Leslie (Loma Moyer) Wh'lck'33
☎ (716) 271-6835 . . 1570 East Av, Apt 720, Rochester, NY 14610
Allen MR Douglas E—GeoW'69 . . of
☎ (908) 234-0194 . . "Corner House" 1641 Larger Cross Rd,
Far Hills, NJ 07931
☎ (515) 232-6661 . . 806—24 St, Ames, IA 50010
Allen MR & MRS Douglas F JR (Marie-Louise Fulweiler)
Rdc'71.Un.Ey.Ny.Cly.Dc.Dh.Ncd.Hb.H.'71
☎ (212) 427-8216 . . 8 E 96 St, New York, NY 10128
Allen MRS Edward Rudge (Nancy R Crow) Tex'58
5130 Green Tree Rd, Houston, TX 77056
Allen MISS Eleanor L (Bitner—Eleanor L Allen)
☎ (617) 643-7475 . . 9 Claremont Av, Arlington, MA 02174-5811
Allen MRS Francis O 4th (Priscilla Wright) V'44 . . . | ☎ (301) 774-7357
MISS Priscilla May—at Washington, DC . . . . . . | "Amersley"
MR David L H—at West Chesterfield, NH 03466 | Box 156,
MR Francis O 5th—at Jacksonville, FL . . . . | Sandy Spring, MD
| 20860

Allen MR & MRS Frank A 3d (Watson—Helen F Mills)
V'53.Cl'70.Cvc.Ne.Chr.Cly.Myf.USA'52 . . of
☎ (212) EN9-8845 . . 201 E 87 St, New York, NY *10128*
☎ (508) 992-7288 . . ''Quahog Farm'' Nonquitt, South Dartmouth,
MA *02748*

Allen MR & MRS Frederick H S (Annelyse M Fiaux)
Cl'70.H'62 . . . . ☎ (011-33-1)
MISS Emily M 47-53-70-14
MR Julian M C H—at Harvard . . . . 91 av de la
Bourdonnais,
75007 Paris, France

Allen MRS Frederick S (Barbara Rice)
☎ (415) 453-4095 . . 26 Sir Francis Drake Blvd, Box 1018, Ross,
CA *94957*

Allen MR & MRS George V JR (Josephine E | ☎ (202) 966-6646
Tetreault) V'59.Mt.Cvc.Sl.P'58 . . . . | 3100 Foxhall Rd
MR Theodore T—at U of Mich Grad . . . . | NW, Washington,
| DC *20016*

Allen MR Gordon M JR
☎ (410) 243-5320 . . 3534 Poole St, Baltimore, MD *21211*

Allen MRS Henry Freeman (Emily L Tuckerman) | ☎ (508) 356-4988
BMr'40.Chi. . . . . | 45 Heartbreak Rd,
MISS Emily T—at ☎ (352) 475-1996 | Ipswich, MA *01938*
7603 NE 221 St, Melrose, FL *32666* . . . . |
MISS Rosamond W—at ☎ (617) 259-1088 |
147 S Great Rd, Lincoln, MA *01773* . . . . |
MR Freeman T—at ☎ (516) 673-9789 |
175 Taft Crescent, Centerport, NY *11721* . . . . . |

Allen MR & MRS Howard Wheatley (Rosemary A | of ☎ (415)928-1002
Hexberg) CalArts'89.Bhm.Dth'63 . . . . | 2415 Larkin St,
MISS Daphne J . . . . | San Francisco, CA
| *94109*
| ☎ (707) 937-5401
| ''Mendocino''
| Box 632,
| Mendocino, CA
| *95460*

Allen MISS Jennifer S—Skd'95 . . see R U Jelinek

Allen MR & MRS John D (Louise C Mason) | ☎ (414) 679-0491
Wis'70.Wis'67.Wis'70 . . . . | W207 S6910 High
MR David D—at Lake Forest Coll . . . . | Bluff Dv, Muskego,
JUNIORS MR Matthew M . . . . | WI *53150*

Allen MRS John Herbert (Plummer—Dorothy R | ☎ (410) 221-0381
Vane) . . . . | 6208 Castle Haven
MR Robert S Plummer . . . . | Rd, Cambridge, MD
| *21613*

Allen MR John L . . see MRS J Lee

Allen MR & MRS Jonathan B (Jana Vaughan) . . . . . . | ☎ (415) 668-2098
MISS Alexandra . . . . | 116 Jordan Av,
MR Brooks V . . . . | San Francisco, CA
| *94118*

Allen MR Joshua C (late David C) . . . . | Married at Fargo, ND
Lempe MISS Kathleen (Joseph) . . . . | Jun 24'95

Allen MR & MRS Kenneth D (Rosanne W Tibbals) | ☎ (513) 848-2758
Mvh.Purd'57 . . . . | 2686 Lower
MR Kenneth J—at Jackson, MS . . . . | Bellbrook Rd,
| Spring Valley, OH
| *45370*

Allen MR Kevin S—Red'75
☎ (818) 760-0661 . . 10901 Whipple St, Toluca Lake, CA *91602*

Allen MR & MRS Langdon C (Alethea B Avery)
BMr'36.Me.Cw.Ac.Cda.P'38
☎ (610) MI2-7068 . . 443 Berkley Rd, Haverford, PA *19041*

Allen MISS Laura C—Skd'33
☎ (203) 966-9353 . . Laurel Rd, PO Box 415, New Canaan,
CT *06840-0415*

Allen MR & MRS Louis La B (Annette T Hadley) | ☎ (908) 277-0248
Hn.H'50 . . . . | 107 Bellevue Av,
MISS Hadley—at 1006 Garden St, Hoboken, NJ | Summit, NJ *07901*
07030 . . . . |
MISS Edith M—at 5F Avon Court, Chatham, NJ |
07928 . . . . |
MR Marston—at 120 W 78 St, New York, NY |
10024 . . . . |

Allen MRS M Bruns (Mary Ellen H Bruns) . . . . | ☎ (203) 966-3734
MISS Alexis S—at Prague-Charles U . . . . | 70 Rural Dv,
MISS Eliza C—PineM'93—at | New Canaan, CT
5802 Nicholson Av, Rockville, MD *20852* . . . . . | *06840*
MR George M H—at Yale . . . . |

Allen MR & MRS Nathan R JR (Mathilde E Thébaud) | ☎ (203) 869-5258
Nyc.Y'63 . . . . | 5 Dairy Rd,
MR Matthew T . . . . | Greenwich, CT
| *06830*

Allen, Philip 3d & Faris. Kathleen B—Pitt'74.Y'61
☎ (503) 224-3571 . . 3545 SW Dosch Court, Portland, OR *97221*

Allen MR & MRS Philip D (Elisabeth H Fell) | ☎ (908) 234-1861
Rcn.K.Eh.Shcc.Cly.AmU'61 . . . . | ''Brookfield Farm''
MISS Alexandra F—at ☎ (212) 355-4391 | 400 Long Lane,
475 Park Av, Apt 12A, New York, NY *10022* . . | Box 597, Far Hills,
MR Andrew D—at ☎ (212) 794-6533 | NJ *07931*
125 E 80 St, Apt 4A, New York, NY *10021* . . . |
MR Nicholas E . . . . |

Allen MR & MRS Radford R JR (Christine C Fisher) BostColl'76.Rr.AppSt'73
☎ (919) 783-5628 . . 3520 Williamsborough Court, Raleigh, NC *27609*

Allen MR & MRS Ralph W P 3d (Carol V Blagden) . . . . . . | ☎ (610) 272-3341
MISS Carol V—at ☎ (610) 584-1732 . . Box 505, | ''Winds Aloft''
Worcester, PA *19490* . . . . | Whitehall Rd,
MR R Stockton . . . . | RD 3, Norristown,
| PA *19403*

Allen MRS Richard D (Hamill—Janet F Brown) Sth'43.Cnt.
☎ (415) 461-5090 . . 641 Goodhill Rd, Kentfield, CA *94904*

Allen MR & MRS Robert H (Weber—N Karolyn Lacy) Valp'59.H'48
☎ (602) 258-7267 . . 2200 N Alvarado Rd, Phoenix, AZ *85004*

Allen MRS S Ker (Susanna W Ker)
☎ (212) 772-2691 . . 218 E 78 St, New York, NY *10021*

Allen MR & MRS Samuel W (Mary D Bowditch) Vt'81.ColC'79.ColM'87
☎ (303) 444-7578 . . 3380—4 St, Boulder, CO *80304*

Allen MRS Schuyler (Dalzell Schuyler)
☎ (408) 354-7737 . . 18400 Overlook Rd, Los Gatos, CA *95030*

Allen MR & MRS Thomas A (Theresa A Ohotnicky)
Conn'70.VillaN'75.Duke'78.Rc.H'71.Duke'75
☎ (610) 896-8129 . . 1433 Waverly Rd, Gladwyne, PA *19035*

Allen MRS W Cottingham (Smith—Alloo—Howell—Ethel D Sloan) DelB.Myf.Dar.Cda.
☎ (561) 272-3329 . . 1171 N Ocean Blvd, Apt 1AS, Gulf Stream, FL *33483*

Allen MRS Waldo M (Mary Penfield) Nw'26.On.
☎ (847) 234-0576 . . 250 Ahwahnee Lane, Lake Forest, IL *60045*

Allen MR & MRS William A 2d (Cynthia Gilbert) H.'50
☎ (508) 582-4220 . . 113 Kilburn St, Box 194, Lunenburg, MA *01462*

Allen DR & MRS Yorke 3d (C Lee Jones) Rdc'73.Nw'76.H'73.Cwr'78 . . . .
JUNIORS MR Yorke 4th . . . .
☎ (703) 893-4443
8424 Holly Leaf Dv, McLean, VA *22102*

Allen MR Zachariah 3d—Nrr.Y'60.H'67
☎ (011-48-22) 277137 . . Al Jerozolimskie 42 m 109, 00-024 Warsaw, Poland

Allenburger MR & MRS Christian A 3d (Susan F White) Miss'67.Miss'66 . . . .
MISS Catherine McK . . . .
MISS Emily S
☎ (601) 982-5302
14 Eastbrooke St, Jackson, MS *39216-4714*

Aller MR & MRS Harris Coles JR (Gouldner—Carolyn L Richardson) Pe.M.Ll.Wt.Cspa.Rv.Cw.Ac. Temp'50 . . . .
MR Harris C 3d—at 1124 Perkiomenville Rd, Perkiomenville, PA *18074* . . . .
of ☎ (610)527-4207
1459 County Line Rd, Rosemont, PA *19010*
☎ (207) 967-3644
PO Box 528, Kennebunkport, ME *04046*

Alley MRS James B (Lowe—Esther Hall) . . . . Died at Albuquerque, NM May 8'96

Allin RT REV & MRS John M SR (Frances A Kelly) Ark'48.C.So'43
☎ (601) 982-3856 . . 2015 Douglas Dv, Jackson, MS *39211*

Alling MR & MRS Charles B JR (Abigail P McMaster) Ws'50.Myf.Cda.Yn.Y'47
☎ (207) 985-2822 . . Box 2, Parsons Beach, Kennebunk, ME *04043*

Allinson MRS Edward P JR (Louise E Rothermel) Me.
☎ (610) 525-2495 . . 74 Pasture Lane, Bryn Mawr, PA *19010*

Allinson MISS Jeanne P . . . .
MISS Anne S . . . .
☎ (610) 696-5064
425 W Barnard St, West Chester, PA *19382-2822*

Allis MR Bayard A . . . . Died at Newtown Square, PA Jun 28'96

Allis MRS Bayard A (Octavia Roberts)
☎ (610) 558-9764 . . White Horse Village V176, 535 Gradyville Rd, Newtown Square, PA *19073*

Allis MRS Frederick S JR (Hughes—Laura Reasor) Wash'59.Tv . . . .
MISS Frances M D'O Hughes . . . .
of ☎ (508)432-9121
340 Long Pond Rd, RD 1, Harwich, MA *02645*
☎ (617) 267-5775
30 Ipswich St, Boston, MA *02215*

Allis MR William P—Mit'23 . . of
☎ (617) 876-7535 . . 33 Reservoir St, Cambridge, MA *02138-3335*
☎ (603) 563-8691 . . "Yonder Farm" Page Rd, Dublin, NH *03444*

Allison MR & MRS C FitzSimons (Martha A Parker) SCar'47.SCar'49.Ox'56
1081 Indigo Av, Georgetown, SC *29440*

Allison MR & MRS Donald G (Janet L Wright) Ford'95.Un.Plg.Snc.StA.Pa'72.Nw'73 . . . .
JUNIORS MR Charles S—at Groton . . . .
of ☎ (212)410-4566
1735 York Av, New York, NY *10128*
☎ (516) 653-8959
"Allison Wonderland" Box 652, 12 Ogden Lane, Quogue, NY *11959*

Allison MR & MRS Peter (Barbara L Nowland) Wil.Del'52 . . of
☎ (302) 656-3476 . . Box 3758, Greenville, DE *19807*
☎ (304) 497-2037 . . Cave Creek Farm, Box 36, Frankford, WV *24938*

Allison MR & MRS T Ellwood (Mary Franklin Sharples) . . . .
MR Thomas E . . . .
☎ (610) LO6-2280
2651 N Providence Rd, Media, PA *19063*

Allison MR & MRS Walter R (Helen Teckemeyer) CtCol'54.Hob'51.Me'68 ⚓
☎ (954) 781-4779 . . 2443 NE 25 St, Lighthouse Point, FL *33064*

Allnatt MR & MRS Matthew J (Margaret Sculley) Cal'85.Ealing'84
☎ (310) 573-9250 . . 959 Fiske St, Pacific Palisades, CA *90272*

Alloo MRS M Bright (Griswold—Jane P Stevens) V'44
☎ (603) 823-8175 . . Sugar Hill, NH *03585*

Allport MR & MRS George N (Grania N M Beauregard) Bost'75.Cl'78.Eh.Cly.GeoW'76 . . .
JUNIORS MR Peter B—at St George's . . . .
☎ (908) 781-7416
86 Willow Av, PO Box 605, Peapack, NJ *07977*

Allport MR & MRS Walter F P (Ann E Snyder) Wells'58.Cr'57.H'61
655 Palmer Av, Winter Park, FL *32789*

Allyn MR & MRS Charles S (Priscilla R Morse) M.Bz.Y'41 . . of
☎ (513) 293-2237 . . 2230 S Patterson Blvd, Apt 48, Dayton, OH *45409*
☎ (619) 742-3811 . . PO Box 656, Pauma Valley, CA *92061*

Allyn DR Compton—Va'46
☎ (513) 621-4246 . . 900 Adams Crossing, Apt 7200, Cincinnati, OH *45202*

Almirall MRS Joseph J (Madeleine M Smith)
☎ (203) 661-9016 . . 64 Cliffdale Rd, Greenwich, CT *06831*

Almond DR & MRS Douglas V (A Merriol Baring-Gould) Rdc'59.Roch'65.Y'57.H'61 . . . .
MISS Catherine C—Kas'89 . . . .
MISS Elizabeth M—Sth'90.H'95 . . . .
MR Christopher S—W&M'92—at U of Conn Med . . . .
MR Douglas V JR—Carl'93—at U of Cal Berkeley . . . .
☎ (860) 561-2147
17 Hillsboro Dv, West Hartford, CT *06107*

Almond MR & MRS Richard W (Roxanne M Elmquist) Cl'67.Cl'93.Vca.StJ.Ncd.Cda.Dar. Y.'56.Rut'61 . . . .
MR Weston M F—Rv.Cw.—at NYU . . . .
336 E 95 St, New York, NY *10128*

Almy MR & MRS Charles (Katharine S Chisholm) Conv'77.Wis'68
☎ (804) 979-9222 . . Box 706, Charlottesville, VA *22902*

Almy MR & MRS David (Bergh—Barbara Hamilton) Ec.Myf.
☎ (508) 526-4255 . . 27 Proctor St, Smith's Point, Manchester, MA *01944*

Almy MR George Blair
☎ (617) 631-3302 . . 266 Pleasant St, Marblehead, MA *01945*

Almy MRS Marguerite C (Marguerite P B Cline)
☎ (508) 993-9520 . . Nonquitt, South Dartmouth, MA *02748*
Almy MR & MRS Thomas (Mary E Roy) RI'86.Mass'85
☎ (508) 992-2667 . . 413 County St, New Bedford, MA *02740*
Almy MRS William JR (Pettway—Letitia C Maxson) Cy.
☎ (508) 636-3800 . . 480 Rock O'Dundee Rd, South Dartmouth, MA *02748*
Almy MR William 3d—H'50
☎ (914) 337-5691 . . 133 Sagamore Rd, Tuckahoe, NY *10707*
Almy MR William 4th
☎ (617) 641-3389 . . 19 Church Hill Av, Arlington, MA *02174*
Alsdorf MRS James W (Markham—Marilynn Bruder) Nw'46.Cas.Cnt.Fy.
☎ (312) 664-0090 . . 180 E Pearson St, Apt 4504, Chicago, IL *60611*
Alsop MR & MRS Benjamin P JR (Em Bowles Locker) V'37.Cw.Rv.Cc.Cly.Va'32
☎ (804) 741-7255 . . ''New Place'' 9300 Cragmont Dv, Richmond, VA *23229*
Alsop MISS Carter Boardman
5908 Grove Av, Richmond, VA *23226*
Alsop MR & MRS John deK (Augusta McL Robinson) Yh.Yn.Y'37
☎ (860) 434-5547 . . 33 Neck Rd, Old Lyme, CT *06371*
Alsop MRS Peter S (Williams—Catherine M Banszky) GeoW'71.Pace'80
☎ (212) 517-6246 . . 230 E 79 St, New York, NY *10021*
Alsop MR Peter S—Un.P'58
☎ (212) 737-2685 . . 360 E 65 St, Apt 11H, New York, NY *10021*
Alsop DR & MRS Reese F (Elise Coates) | ☎ (516) 427-7438
Csh.C.H'36.Cl'44 . . . . | 33 Fort Hill Dv,
MR Reese P . . . . | Lloyd Neck,
| Huntington, NY
| *11743*
Alsop MR & MRS Robert C (H Suzette Morgan) C.Lx.H.'45
☎ (413) 243-1660 . . ''Sky Hill Farm'' Main Rd, Tyringham, MA *01264*
Alsop MRS Stewart J O (Patricia B Hankey)
☎ (202) 363-5389 . . 3520 Springland Lane NW, Washington, DC *20008*
Alsop MRS Susan M (Patten—Susan M Jay)
☎ (202) 338-5868 . . 1611—29 St NW, Washington, DC *20007*
Alspaugh MR Robert O—Rcn.Cy.Un.Ri.It.Cwr'34
☎ (216) 752-7055 . . 13705 Shaker Blvd, Apt 3B, Cleveland, OH *44120-1507*
Alt MR & MRS George D (McMillan—Lambert—Jane Wells) Nw'34
☎ (805) 969-7767 . . 909 Camino Viejo, Santa Barbara, CA *93108*
Altemus MR & MRS Edward L (Eleanor Harner Ward) ChHill'84.Pc.Pe.Fw.Wt.Ac.Sdg.Dar.Pa'39
☎ (610) 584-3866 . . Meadowood at Worcester, 10 Dogwood Knoll, Lansdale, PA *19446-5839*
Altemus MR Edward Lee JR—Pa'65
☎ (215) 628-2985 . . 34 E Butler Pike, Ambler, PA *19002-4527*
Altemus MR & MRS Nicholas W (Marie Sailer) | ☎ (610) 488-1699
Wt.Pa'70 . . . . | ''Whelawood''
MISS Marie E—at Roanoke Coll . . . . | RD 1, Box 139,
| Robesonia, PA
| *19551-9734*
Althaus MR & MRS Lauren B (Karen L Carpenter) Ariz'86.Redlands'86.Redlands'90
☎ (909) 945-3071 . . 9843 Coca St, Alta Loma, CA *91737*

Althouse MR & MRS Alfred K JR (Dorothy S Ristine) | ☎ (610) 644-2068
Me.Pe.Fw.Rv.Ncd.Dar.Tufts'48 . . . . | 378 Bear Hill Rd,
MISS Patricia R—Denis'78—at | Paoli, PA *19301*
☎ (213) 931-9222 . . 366 N Curson Av, Apt 6, Los Angeles, CA *90036* . . . .
Altschul MR Arthur G (late Frank) . . . . Married at New York, NY
Smith MRS Madelyn (Madelyn Dey) . . . . Apr 27'96
Altstatt MR & MRS (DR) Leslie B (Alice L Hackney) BMr'49.Van'52.Ariz'52
☎ (301) 593-1118 . . 1016 Chiswell Lane, Silver Spring, MD *20901*
Alvarez de Toledo MR & MRS Fernando (Margaret F | ☎ (508) 369-1397
Emmet) Y'57 . . . . | 229 Fairhaven Hill,
MR Frederic R . . . . | Concord, MA *01742*
Alvis MISS Millican Grace (g—W Lloyd Lancaster JR) . . . . Born at
Montgomery, AL Apr 7'95
Amark MR & MRS Edwin G (Lillian M Dillman) Fr.
☎ (415) 474-3472 . . 2030 Vallejo St, Apt 1101, San Francisco, CA *94123*
Amason DR & MRS Thomas G JR (Caroline Yates | ☎ (205) 871-9105
Middleton) Hlns'66.Cy.Aub'62.Ala'66 . . . . | 3224 Rockledge Rd,
MISS Caroline Y—at Wash'n & Lee . . . . | Birmingham, AL
MR Thomas G 3d—at 13 Russell Rd, Alexandria, | *35213*
VA *22301* . . . . |
Amato BRN Carlo C B & BRNSS (De Bergendal—Lorraine M Dresselhuys) K.URio'66
☎ (212) 481-0479 . . 176 E 71 St, New York, NY *10021*
Ambach MR & MRS Gordon M (Lucy D Emory) Rdc'61.Y'56
☎ (202) 338-4599 . . 2715—31 Place NW, Washington, DC *20008-3518*
Amberg MR & MRS Richard H JR (Virginia Beverley | ☎ (334) 263-1999
Sharp) Ncd.H'64 . . . . | 845 Felder Av,
MISS Elizabeth L—at Harvard . . . . | Montgomery, AL
JUNIORS MR Richard H 3d—at Harvard . . . . | *36106*
Ambler MR Christian D (Michael Nash) . . Married at Shaker Heights, OH
Phillips MISS Lorraine A (Daniel L) . . . . May 20'95
Ambler MR & MRS Christian D (Lorraine A Phillips) OWes'90.OWes'92.DePaul'95
☎ (630) 545-2608 . . 289 Elm St, Glen Ellyn, IL *60137*
Ambler MRS L Todd (Louise L Todd) BMr'56 . . . . | ☎ (617) 484-7164
MR William N—P'88.Lond'92—at | 30 Orchard St,
☎ (212) 722-0877 . . 131 E 93 St, Apt 9D, | Belmont, MA
New York, NY *10128* . . . . | *02178-3010*
Ambler MISS Mary Cary (Finley—Mary Cary | ☎ (914) 472-6029
Ambler) Swb'67.Cl'75.Ncd. . . . . | 282 Evandale Rd,
JUNIORS MISS Jaquelin Cary Finley . . . . | Scarsdale, NY
JUNIORS MR John T A Finley—at U of Va . . . | *10583-1506*
Ambler MR & MRS Michael Nash (Marsha W Dancy) Un.Plg.Cly.P'58.Cl'61 . . of
☎ (212) 861-8516 . . 655 Park Av, New York, NY *10021*
☎ (516) 653-4581 . . 8 Foster Rd, Box 692, Quogue, NY *11959*
Ambler MR & MRS Michael Nash JR (Deborah M Stalker) P'84.P'85
☎ (207) 892-2997 . . 88 Albion Rd, Windham, ME *04062*
Ambler MR & MRS Peter W (Combs—Lindsay M Miller) Ws'69.P'56.Bac'68
☎ (617) 547-1733 . . 984 Memorial Dv, Apt 604, Cambridge, MA *02138*

Ambrus DR & MRS (DR) Julian L (Clara M Bayer) ..... of ☎ (716)883-8382
Zürich'49.Jef'55.St.Cos.G.Zürich'49. Jef'54 ... | 143 Windsor Av,
DR Julian L JR—Y'75.Jef'79—at 4328 Laclede | Buffalo, NY
Av, St Louis, MO *63108* .... | *14209-1020*
MR Steven G—at Carrera 2, Torna 11-72, | ☎ (716) 941-3394
Apt 102, Bogatá, Columbia .... | "West Hill Farms"
MR Charles T G .... | 9943 Emerling Rd,
| Boston, NY *14025*

Ambrus MASTER Peter Julian (g—Julian L Ambrus) .... Born May 17'96

Ames MRS Alden JR (Jane H Campiglia) Tcy.Sfy.Cp.
☎ (415) 424-4341 .. 501 Portola Rd, Box 8024, Portola Valley,
CA *94028*

Ames MR & MRS Alden 3d (Jill A Ferroggiaro) | ☎ (415) 435-1602
Sfy.SanDiegoSt'73 ⛵ .... | 216 Jamaica St,
MISS Melissa M .... | Tiburon, CA *94920*
JUNIORS MR Kevin B

Ames MR Amyas (late Oakes) .... Married at Glen Cove, NY
Millham MRS Newton (Lucia Pink) .... Feb 3'95

Ames MR & MRS Amyas (Millham—Lucia Pink) StLaw'32.C.H'28
☎ (617) 674-1471 .. 1010 Waltham St, Apt 9F, Lexington, MA *02173*

Ames MRS Azel (Josephine E Church) Sth'31
☎ (513) 821-9155 .. 7508 Evergreen Ridge Dv, Cincinnati, OH *45215*

Ames MRS Catherine D (Lawrence C JR) . Married at San Francisco, CA
Abele MR Lawrence R (Lawrence G) .... Apr 17'96

Ames MR & MRS Charlton H (Eleanor P Goodfellow) | ☎ (207) 781-3659
Sm.Cyb.H'63 .... | "Greyhouse"
MISS Alexandra H—H'93 .... | 113 Foreside Rd,
MISS Isabel H .... | Cumberland
| Foreside, ME *04110*

Ames MRS Cortlandt F 3d (Watson—Doris Mansur) Ncd.
☎ (203) 655-3814 .. 3 Fairfield Av, Darien, CT *06820*

Ames MRS David (Elizabeth Motley) Cy.Chi.Yh.... | of ☎ (508)238-6500
MISS Nancy—at ☎ (617) 232-3452 | 35 Oliver St,
144 Coolidge St, Brookline, MA *02147* .... | PO Box 250,
| North Easton, MA
| *02356*
| ☎ (617) 262-1928
| 180 Beacon St,
| Boston, MA *02116*

Ames MR & MRS David JR (Sally A Bear) | ☎ (617) 492-8965
Vt'64.H'64 .... | 221 Mt Auburn St,
MISS Amelia E—at Trinity .... | Cambridge, MA
| *02138*

Ames MR & MRS Edward A (Noel—Sue Holtz) | ☎ (718) 548-8090
C.H'55 .... | 2 Spaulding Lane,
MR Benjamin B—at Colby .... | Bronx, NY *10471*
MR Zachary A—at Milton................. | .. MRS absent

Ames MR Frederick L—Sbc.Sm.Ub.Bost'86.Bab'92
☎ (508) 768-3222 .. 79 Western Av, Essex, MA *01929*

Ames MR & MRS George J (Annabell E Sweeney) | of ☎ (210)824-2713
A.Cda.Ty'64.................. | 424 Ivy Lane,
MR Edward S .... | San Antonio, TX
MR George S...................... | *78209*
| ☎ (210) 833-5870
| Crooked Tree
| Ranch, General
| Delivery, Blanco,
| TX *78606*

Ames MR & MRS James B (Parker—Suzannah C Ayer) H'32
☎ (617) 259-8729 .. 12 Browning Lane, Lincoln, MA *01773*

Ames MISS Jennifer D (Washburn—Rosalini—Jennifer D Ames) Y'83
☎ (312) 266-1110 .. 1409 N Dearborn P'kway, Chicago, IL *60610*

Ames MR & MRS John D (Simpson—Constance Hasler) Rc.On.Fy.
☎ (847) 234-1199 .. 600 N Washington Rd, Lake Forest, IL *60045*

Ames MR & MRS John D JR (Dorothy L | ☎ (847) 486-9118
de Vausney) P'52.H'56 .... | 1900 Chestnut Av,
MISS Elizabeth W—Wash'80 .... | Apt 308, Glenview,
| IL *60025-1658*

Ames MR & MRS John S 3d (Mary L Alford) | ☎ (207) 236-4413
Cyb.Sm.H'58 .... | Beauchamp Point,
MR John S 4th—Rens'86 .... | PO Box 540,
MR Gavin H—Syr'87 .... | Rockport, ME *04856*

Ames DR & MRS John Worthington (Lori Lee Street)
Md'77.Stan'77.GeoW'87
☎ (410) 720-4354 .. 8523 Woodstaff Way, Columbia, MD *21045*

Ames MISS Katrine W—V'69
☎ (212) 799-8611 .. 215 W 75 St, New York, NY *10023*

Ames MRS Lawrence C (Helen Rodolph)
☎ (510) 893-9879 .. 244 Lakeside Dv, Apt 19, Oakland, CA *94612*

Ames MR & MRS Lawrence C JR (Smith—Betty Mitchell)
Cal'47.Bhm.Stan'47
☎ (510) 652-2406 .. PO Box 11277, 221 El Cerrito Av, Piedmont,
CA *94611-0277*

Ames MISS Nathalie E—Vt'89 .. see L C Sudler JR

Ames MR & MRS Nicholas (Fitzpatrick—Sandra | ☎ (415) 921-5791
Steinthal) Bur.Menlo'68 .... | 3326 Jackson St,
MISS Alexandra K Fitzpatrick—Col'92 ..... | San Francisco, CA
MR Kenneth F Fitzpatrick 3d—Ore'91...... | *94118*

Ames MRS Oliver (Ellen P Moseley) Ncd.
PO Box 430, Hamilton, MA *01936*

Ames MR & MRS Oliver (Perry—Rebecca J Larsen) | ☎ (617) 235-6202
Bost'71.Sm.Cy.Bost'68 .... | 279 Oakland St,
MISS Kirsten McD—at Pine Manor .... | Wellesley, MA
MISS Chilton M...................... | *02181*

Ames MR & MRS Oliver F (Esther W Doolittle) | ☎ (508) 238-6800
Br'54.Sm.Cy.Chi.H'43 .... | 135 Elm St, Box
MISS Abby A D—HRdc'86—at 263 Beacon St, | 187, North Easton,
Boston, MA *02116* .... | MA *02356*
MISS Mary I—Br'93 .... |
MR Samuel T A—CtCol'93 .... |

Ames, Peter J & Endicott, Eve—Rdc'70.Y'73.H'67.H'71
☎ (617) 731-0512 .. 90 Ivy St, Brookline, MA *02146*

Ames MR & MRS Sanford S (Elizabeth Clarke) H'60
☎ (513) 221-1486 .. PO Box 20108, Cincinnati, OH *45220*

Ames MRS Van Meter (Betty C Breneman)
V'29.Nd. . . . . | ☎ (513) 861-1718
MISS Damaris—at Beaver Pond Rd, Beverly, MA | PO Box 20108,
01915 . . . . | Cincinnati, OH
| *45220*
Ames MR & MRS William S (Nancy W Hood)
Cho.P'55 . . . . | ☎ (617) 742-8899
MR Jeffrey S . . . . | PO Box 368,
MR Peter B . . . . | Topsfield, MA
| *01983-0568*
Ames MRS Winslow (Anna R Gerhard)
☎ (610) 896-2401 . . The Quadrangle 1314, 3300 Darby Rd, Haverford,
PA *19041*
Amesbury CDR & MRS Walter R JR (Cécile M Dudley)
USN.Plg.Cspa.Fw.Ofp.Cw.Myf.Sar.Rv.Wt.Hl.Cs.H.'36. H'38
☎ (215) 627-7610 . . 427 Spruce St, Philadelphia, PA *19106*
Amestoy MR & MRS Michel F 2d (Helen H Monnette) BMr'41.Myf.Loy'33
☎ (310) 838-8581 . . 3300 Club Dv, Los Angeles, CA *90064*
Amidon MRS Charles S (Caroline G Wolferth)
B'gton'53.Gm. . . . . | ☎ (610) 286-2109
MR Charles S JR—at ☎ (215) 233-5168 | 784 Nantmeal Rd,
8319 Childs Rd, Wyndmoor, PA *19038* . . . . | RD 1, Glenmoore,
| PA *19343*
Amman DR & MRS Frederic C JR (Dorothy L Turpin) Tul'40.Cda.Loy'40
☎ (318) 322-2441 . . 2109 Island Dv, Monroe, LA *71201*
Ammidon MR & MRS Hoyt JR (Ashley Moore) Un.Ln.Cs.Y.'59 . . of
☎ (609) 683-5968 . . 209 Winant Rd, Princeton, NJ *08540*
☎ (212) 535-5034 . . 333 E 68 St, New York, NY *10021*
Ammidon MR & MRS Hoyt 3d (Pamela J Lipscomb) Mid'83.VPI'84
☎ (609) 844-0847 . . 9 Toftrees Court, Princeton, NJ *08540*
Ammons MR & MRS Clifford Barnes (Patricia A | ☎ (601) 856-5410
Goodman) Mlsps'75.Mlsps'75 . . . . | 114 Covington
JUNIORS MISS Patricia M . . . . | Court, Ridgeland,
JUNIORS MR Clifford B JR . . . . | MS *39157*
Amory MRS Carolyn P (Geddes—Amory— | of ☎ (805)969-7346
Milbank—Haile—Carolyn M Pesnell) Ri.Cly. | ''Stratford''
Nyc.StJ. | 2085 Stratford Place,
MR Robyn G Geddes—T.LakeF'77—at | Montecito, CA
1377 Lexington Av, New York, NY *10128* . . | *93108*
MR Grant M Geddes . . . . | ☎ (508) 228-3993
| ''The East Brick''
| 93 Main St,
| Nantucket, MA
| *02554*
Amory MRS E Jackson (Elisabeth A Jackson) . . . . . | ☎ (803) 723-3827
MISS Caroline C—at ☎ (404) 875-1467 | 33 New St,
475 Rock Springs Rd NE, Atlanta, GA *30324* . . | Charleston, SC
MISS Gillian B—at ☎ (813) 930-6642 | *29401*
8413 N Armenia Av, Tampa, FL *33604* . . . . |
Amory MR & MRS Francis I JR (Edith A Beadleston) Sbc.My.
☎ (508) 922-5723 . . Prince St, Beverly, MA *01915*
Amory MR & MRS Harcourt JR (Trudeau—Jean D Moore) Ri.B.Cly.Hn.H'50
☎ (561) 234-5454 . . 5680 N A1A, Apt 107, Vero Beach, FL *32963*
Amory MR & MRS John S (Porter—Marcelle E | ☎ (602) 945-1928
Eason) H'55 . . . . | 5665 N Saguaro Rd,
MISS Wendy B . . . . | Scottsdale, AZ
| *85253*
Amory MRS Robert JR (Mary Armstrong) Cvc.Csn.
☎ (202) 338-0879 . . 2801 New Mexico Av NW, Apt 1001, Washington,
DC *20007*

Amory MR & MRS Thomas Carhart (Doris R Mack) Ri.Plg.Ll.H'56
☎ (805) 969-6783 . . 804 Rametto Lane, Santa Barbara, CA *93108*
Amory MR & MRS Walter (Shirley G Waterman) Cy.Myf.Ncd.H.'46
☎ (617) 934-2685 . . Box 65, 46 Beaverbrook Lane, Snug Harbor,
Duxbury, MA *02331*
Amos MRS George H JR (Barbara J Hicks)
☎ (520) 299-1171 . . 5330 Via Alcalde, Tucson, AZ *85718*
Amos MR & MRS George H 3d (Theresa M McCready) Ariz'87.Ariz'81
☎ (520) 325-6047 . . 3110 E 4 St, Tucson, AZ *85716*
Amos MR & MRS Philip R (Mimi Parker) Ariz'82.SCal'86
☎ (520) 577-7331 . . 4854 N Territory Loop, Tucson, AZ *85715*
Amos MR & MRS Robert C (Anne H Rhodes) Pa'85.Woos'79
☎ (540) 662-7130 . . 106 W North Av, Winchester, VA *22601-3933*
Anable MRS Anne C S (Henriques—Anne C Steinert)
☎ (516) 944-9107 . . 7 Flower Hill Place, Port Washington, NY *11050*
Anagnostopoulos DR & MRS Constantine E (Reese— | 7 The Courtyard,
Madelaine L Lynch) Ill'70.Loy'79.Pr.Cly. | Locust Valley, NY
Geo'59.Geo'63 . . . . | *11560*
MISS Anne-Marie—at Yale . . . . |
MISS Anne H Reese—at Stanford Med . . . . . |
MR Peter P Reese—at Johns Hopkins Med . . |
Anathan MR & MRS Thomas J (Patricia K Scott) | of ☎ (860)286-2856
Nyc.San.Dar.Wms'66.Pa'69.Pa'71 | 12 Schuyler Lane,
MISS Leah K—Wheat'95—at ☎ (508) 655-3172 | Bloomfield, CT
70A Eliot St, South Natick, MA *01760* . . . . | *06002*
MISS Elizabeth B—at Boston Coll . . . . | ☎ (508) 228-1840
| ''Hillside''
| 68 Monomoy Rd,
| Nantucket, MA
| *02554*

Andersen MRS Louise McM (Louise H McMurtry) Cly.
129 E 69 St, New York, NY *10021*
Anderson MR & MRS Alexander McG (Brenda L Abbot) Ck.Buck'71.Pa'73
☎ (310) 459-8343 . . 732 Chapala Dv, Pacific Palisades, CA *90272*
Anderson MR Bodhi M—USN . . . see T R Sharkey 6th
Anderson MR & MRS Carl T (Betsy Neville) | 3 Farmer Rd,
Stan'70.Stan'71 . . . . | Westport, CT *06880*
MISS Neville W . . . . |
JUNIORS MR Marquard J 2d . . . . |
Anderson MR Clinton R G—H'81
☎ (815) 758-4780 . . 1701 Judy Lane, De Kalb, IL *60115*
Anderson MR & MRS Crawford (Dianne M Crawford) D. . | ☎ (508) 785-1879
MISS Rebecca C . . . . | 4 Tower Dv, Dover,
JUNIORS MR William G 2d . . . . | MA *02030*
Anderson MR & MRS Daniel G (Miller—Margot S | ☎ (301) 986-9136
West) Cvc.Y'50 . . . . | 1 W Irving St,
MISS Jennifer West—at Colo Coll . . . . | Chevy Chase, MD
MR Robert J Miller 3d—at Princeton . . . . | *20815*
Anderson MR & MRS David C (A Elizabeth Long)
NCar'87.Campb'91.NCar'87
☎ (803) 748-1066 . . 120 S Shandon St, Columbia, SC *29205*
Anderson MR David K . . . . Married at Williamsville, NY
Robinson MISS Laurie G (Edward L) . . . . Jun 26'96
Anderson MR & MRS Derby F (Hoover—Margaret C C C Pomeroy)
Cal'65.Csn.Cw.Dar.W&J'65
☎ (203) 255-3095 . . Box 787, Southport, CT *06490*

Anderson MR & MRS E Forrest (Alice E Charleston) ☎ (415) 948-9363
Cal'54.Bhm.Fr.Cal'53 . . . . 26493 Weston Dv,
MISS Lisa—Dth'90 . . . . Los Altos Hills, CA
MR Timothy F. 94022
MR Peter E . . . .

Anderson MISS Elizabeth M—Dc.Ncd. . . . . ☎ (513) 321-7716
MISS Annie W (Oglevee—Annie W Anderson) 2444 Madison Rd,
Dc.Ncd.Myf. . . . . Apt 1610,
                                                        Cincinnati, OH
                                                        45208

Anderson MISS Elizabeth S—Ty'95 . . see E L Meinfelder 2d

Anderson MR & MRS Ellis B (Mueller—Andrews—Jermain D Johnson)
Tufts'45.Ind'49.Ind'52.H'70 . . of
☎ (609) 921-6697 . . 52 Elm Rd, Princeton, NJ 08540
☎ (908) 899-6573 . . 1084 Barnegat Lane, Mantoloking, NJ 08738

Anderson MR & MRS Evans K (Susan L McCeney) W&J'69.Pa'73
☎ (301) 871-9036 . . 4108 Beverly Rd, Rockville, MD 20853

Anderson MRS Francesca S (Francesca F W ☎ (617) 862-5075
Schager) PineM'70.GeoW'72.Sb.Chi.Cly. . . . . . 56 Adams St,
MISS Lili H . . . . Lexington, MA
                                                        02173

Anderson DR & MRS Frank H (Constance D Miller) ☎ (202) 686-0054
ChHill'67.Cvc.Nyc.H'66.H'70 . . . . 5233 Partridge Lane
MISS Christina H—Duke'94 . . . . NW, Washington,
MR Robert B—Bow'92 . . . . DC 20016
JUNIORS MR David P . . . .

Anderson MR & MRS Gerald A (Ely—Gouldy— ☎ (301) 320-2492
Anna Wharton Phillips) JHop'80.Cda.Wash'74 . 5820 Durbin Rd,
JUNIORS MR Joshua F P . . . . Bethesda, MD
                                                        20817

Anderson CAPT (RET) & MRS Glenn G (Marcella Fisher)
USCG.Sth'55.Un.Kt.It.P'53.H'57
☎ (216) 831-4268 . . 2877 Plymouth Rd, Pepper Pike, OH 44124

Anderson MR & MRS Glenn G JR (Eleanor H Hitchcock)
OWes'83.Bost'84.Kt.Tv.OWes'83.Cwr'92
☎ (216) 397-8779 . . 21276 Fairmount Blvd, Shaker Heights, OH 44118

Anderson MR & MRS Harry B JR (Claire H Matz) ☎ (516) 883-5775
Ri.Y'39 . . . . 40 Cornwall Lane,
MR Jeffrey M—Ithaca'76.Tul'82—at Sands Point,
139 Franklin St, Brooklyn, NY 11222 . . . . Port Washington,
                                                        NY 11050

Anderson MRS Harry B 3d (Joie Angermeier) Pa'71 ☎ (212) 988-4790
MISS Claire McG M—at Kenyon . . . . 345 E 77 St,
JUNIORS MISS Elizabeth A . . . . New York, NY
                                                        10021

Anderson MRS Henry A (Ann E Schroeder) Tc.
☎ (412) 776-8222 . . Sherwood Oaks, 100 Norman Dv,
Cranberry Township, PA 16066

Anderson MR Henry H JR—S.Ny.Y'43
☎ (401) 847-7546 . . 9A Corne St, Newport, RI 02840

Anderson MR & MRS (REV) James M (Marjorie H ☎ (513) 248-1339
Caldwell) Van'65.TySem'94.Qc.Yn.Y'63.Van'66 9605 Shawnee Run
MISS Marjorie C . . . . Rd, Cincinnati, OH
MR Joseph H—at Case Western Reserve Med . . 45243
MR Hilding F . . . .

Anderson MR & MRS John B (Phillips—Ruth E 1188 W Valley Rd,
Coppersmith) Penn'63.Rc. . . . . Wayne, PA
MR John 2d—at ☎ (970) 256-0692 19087-1440
3 Dubonnet Court, Grand Junction, CO 81503 . .

Anderson MRS John C (Margaret H Fitler)
701 Park Av, Riverton, NJ 08077

Anderson MR & MRS Joseph A (Riley—Martha J Hartman) Aht'44
Box 35, Lumber Lane, Bridgehampton, NY 11932

Anderson MRS Joseph C (Eugenie W Riley) Cvc.
☎ (301) 229-1536 . . 4907 Rockmere Court, Bethesda, MD 20816

Anderson MR Lee B—Ia'46.Cl'47
☎ (212) 254-7385 . . 35 Stuyvesant St, New York, NY 10003

Anderson MRS Lorna McC (Lorna McClenahan) Csn.
☎ (203) 622-4800 . . 37 Mianus View Terr, Cos Cob, CT 06807

Anderson MR & MRS Mark A (Cristiana D Hutchinson)
Ws'84.Mt.Cvc.Ty'80.INSEAD'86
☎ (713) 293-0151 . . 14759 River Forest Dv, Houston, TX 77079

Anderson DR & MRS Martin E JR (Mary Lee B Christal)
RSage'52.Ncd.Dar.Pn.P'35.Cl'39
☎ (303) 388-5206 . . 361 Race St, Denver, CO 80206

Anderson MR & MRS McCutchen B (Ellen H Few) Duke'69.Duke'68
☎ (919) 833-1076 . . 216 E Park Dv, Raleigh, NC 27605

Anderson MR & MRS Michael H (Barbara Robbins) 5301 Westbard
SUNY'87.Cl'59 . . . . Circle, Bethesda,
MR James H—Aht'85.Tufts'91.Tufts'94—at MD 20816
☎ (703) 683-8548 . . 2327 Duke St, Alexandria,
VA 22314 . . . .

Anderson MR Montgomery—Sa.Plg.Lm.Pa'41
☎ (914) 876-4894 . . Box 302, Rhinebeck, NY 12572

Anderson MR N Calhoun JR—Va'74
704 E 44 St, Savannah, GA 31405-2474

Anderson MR & MRS Nils JR (Jean D Ferris)
Plg.Pqt.Cw.Wt.Cly.Cda.Dh.Wms'37 . . of
☎ (203) 259-0807 . . 935 Harbor Rd, PO Box 529, Southport, CT 06490
☎ (561) 234-3363 . . The Moorings, 703 Spyglass Lane, Vero Beach,
FL 32963

Anderson MRS O Kelley (Alma U Weichel) Sm.My.Cy.
☎ (617) 227-5691 . . 68 Beacon St, Boston, MA 02108

Anderson MR & MRS O Kelley JR (Biggs—Brenda A ☎ (212) 288-4706
Bolton) Rc.K.Ng.Sm.H'59 . . . . 150 E 73 St,
MR Oscar Kelley 3d . . . . New York, NY
                                                        10021

Anderson MR & MRS Paul G (King—Curtis—Hilda R Ayer)
☎ (508) 281-4327 . . 33 Sleepy Hollow Rd, Gloucester, MA 01930

Anderson MRS Peter Stickney (Hedges—Cynthia A ☎ (610) 642-3527
Reid) MooreArt'66. 417 Berkley Rd,
JUNIORS MR Reid S B . . . . Haverford, PA
    MISS Stephanie K Hedges—Ham'96 19041

Anderson REV DR Philip A & MRS (REV) Mary ☎ (216) 371-4480
Sterrett (Mary F Sterrett) ColC'67.It.Cly.H'70. 2581 Norfolk Rd,
EpiscTheo'73.Cwr'78. . . . . Cleveland Heights,
JUNIORS MISS Anne C—at Hawken . . . . OH 44106
JUNIORS MR William D—at University Sch . . . . .

Anderson DR & MRS Proctor R (Dorothy M Brey)
Sth'73.Ch'79.Van'68.Nw'72
☎ (847) 446-2862 . . 460 Orchard Lane, Winnetka, IL 60093

Anderson MRS Richard K (Mary G White) Dar.Ncd.Dc.
☎ (803) 494-2705 . . The Borough House, 440 N Kings H'way, Sumter, SC *29154*

Anderson MR Robert . . . . Died at
Fairfax, VA Apr 5'96

Anderson MR & MRS Robert Alexander (Margaret C Hand) Skd'73.Y'68 . . . .
MISS Julianne H . . . .
☎ (617) 861-6131
17 Carley Rd,
Lexington, MA
02173

Anderson MR & MRS Robert E (Lorndale—Ann L Stafford) Wa.Nw'36 . . . .
MR Robert S—Box 469, Lake Forest, IL *60045* .
☎ (919) 542-5378
492 Fearrington
Post, Pittsboro, NC
27312

Anderson MR Robert E JR—Miami'49
☎ (215) 493-2462 . . 501 Yardley Commons, Yardley, PA *19067*

Anderson MR & MRS Robert E 3d (Pauline S Roberts) Va'55 . . . .
MISS Deirdre P . . . .
☎ (804) 883-6159
Green Bank Farm,
16411 Woodman
Hall Rd, Montpelier,
VA *23192*

Anderson MR Robert F—Hiram'85.O'88
☎ (216) 831-4268 . . 2877 Plymouth Rd, Pepper Pike, OH *44124*

Anderson MRS Robert Gardner (Doris Tansill) Cnt.Fy.Ncd.
☎ (312) 944-2290 . . 229 E Lake Shore Dv, Chicago, IL *60611-1307*

Anderson MR & MRS Robert Gardner JR (Catherine H Olian) Y'72.Y'74.Y'72.Cl'73
55 Tanglewylde Av, Bronxville, NY *10708*

Anderson MR & MRS Robert O (Barbara H Phelps) Cal'76.Ln.Ph.Ch'39
☎ (505) 625-8700 . . PO Box 1000, Roswell, NM *88202*

Anderson MISS Sara Jane—Sth'49
☎ (415) 331-0821 . . 100 South St, Apt 104, Sausalito, CA *94965*

Anderson MR Stanley D—Ty'51
☎ (916) 972-8278 . . 524 Woodside Oaks, Apt 4, Sacramento, CA *95825*

Anderson MR & MRS Thomas D (Helen L Sharp) Tex'37.A.Cly.Sl.W&L'34
☎ (713) 622-0315 . . 3925 Del Monte Dv, Houston, TX *77019*

Anderson DR & MRS Thomas McDowell JR (Gretchen Oppmann) Rdc'69.Pn.P'66.H'70 . . . .
MISS Brigitte C—at Tulane . . . .
MISS Ingrid M—at Harvard . . . .
JUNIORS MISS Margaret J . . . .
☎ (773) 643-1312
5807 S Harper Av,
Chicago, IL
60637-1842

Anderson MRS Varya V (Varya V Milne) Ncd. . . . .
MISS Barbara E—at ☎ (803) 856-0123
PO Box 1326, Mt Pleasant, SC *29465* . . . .
MISS Nadya V (Bessette—Nadya V Anderson)—
Box 17367, West Palm Beach, FL *33416* . . . . . .
☎ (561) 832-4850
400 N Flagler Dv,
Apt 1401,
West Palm Beach,
FL *33401*

Anderson MR & MRS W Mark 3d (Jean S Dearman) Aub'66.Ala'60.Ala'62 . . . .
MR Richard D . . . .
☎ (334) 264-6616
2068 Myrtlewood
Dv, Montgomery,
AL *36111*

Anderson MR W Nelson—Ste.Pa'54
☎ (941) 945-3685 . . 5027 Pelican Blvd, Cape Coral, FL *33914*

Anderson CAPT & MRS Ward R (Kathleen M McConnell) USN.Buck'70.Cw.Cda.Buck'68
☎ (757) 722-6645 . . 27 Ivy Home Rd, Hampton, VA *23669*

Anderson MR & MRS Warren H (Jacqueline Appel) BMr'52.Yh.Minn'51
☎ (609) 924-4103 . . 37 Olden Lane, Princeton, NJ *08540*

Anderson MRS William Disston (Laura C Pomeroy) Me. . . . .
MR William P—VillaN'75.BMr'79—Box 1137, Bryn Mawr, PA *19010* . . . .
MR John D—Eliz'tn'80—at Greenville, SC . . . .
☎ (610) 525-0795
PO Box 274,
Bryn Mawr, PA
19010-0274

Anderson MR & MRS William G (Bergland—Dorothy H Mower) Elk.Sm.Mv.Hn.H'39 ⚓ . . of
☎ (410) 825-2435 . . Blakehurst 309, 1055 W Joppa Rd, Towson, MD *21204*
☎ (508) 653-5513 . . 20 Lookout Farm Rd, South Natick, MA *01760*

Anderson MR & MRS William W 5th (Rosemary Wire) Wheat'62.Cc.Sl.Dar.NCar'60 . . of
☎ (301) 469-6133 . . 8024 Lilly Stone Dv, Bethesda, MD *20817*
''Wadefield'' Box 34, Washington, VA *22747*
☎ (210) 563-2515 . . Double R Ranch, RR 1908, Spofford, TX *78877*

Anderson-Bell MR Andrew—Ny.Sm.Edin'53 ⚓
☎ (617) 868-6435 . . 1010 Memorial Dv, Apt 15A, Cambridge, MA *02138*

Andrade MR & MRS José E (Malle Tarto) Ck.B.Cly. .
MR José . . . .
MR Eduardo . . . .
☎ (212) 988-0823
150 E 73 St,
New York, NY
10021

Andresen MRS John E (Alice Farnsworth) Chi.Myf.
☎ (305) 367-2382 . . Key Largo Anglers Club, Key Largo, FL *33037*

Andrew REV CANON John G B—Ri.Plg.StJ.Ox'54
☎ (011-44-1225) 422-783 . . 93 Sydney Place, Bath BA2 GNE, England

Andrew MR & MRS Lucius A D 3d (Kellogg—Phoebe L Haffner) Rcn.Rcch.B.Pa'62.Nu'65 . . .
MISS Ashley W . . . .
MR L A David 4th—at Seattle U . . . .
  MISS Louise M Kellogg—Mid'92 . . . .
  MR Gaylord M Kellogg—Pa'84.UWash'92—
  at 270 Lake Dell Av, Seattle, WA *98122* . . . .
  MR Matthew K Kellogg—Skd'87—at
  3710 E McGilvra St, Seattle, WA *98112* . . . .
of ☎ (206)364-0061
The Highlands,
Seattle, WA *98177*
☎ (604) 653-4328
Musgrave Farm,
Box 64,
Fulford Harbour, BC
V0S 1C0, Canada

Andrew MR & MRS Thomas G JR (Marilyn J Whiting) Buf'68.W&L'63 ⚓ . . . .
MISS Mary S—UWash'95 . . . .
MR Thomas W—at U of Oregon . . . .
☎ (206) 328-1715
1501 E Lynn St,
Seattle, WA *98112*

Andrews MR & MRS Adolphus JR (Emily P Taylor) Bur.Pcu.P'43
☎ (415) 567-2814 . . 2828 Vallejo St, San Francisco, CA *94123*

Andrews MR & MRS Adolphus 3d (Chickering—Susan H Hall) V'66.Pcu.Cp.Stan'71 . . . .
MR Christopher Chickering . . . .
☎ (415) 567-4091
2611 Divisadero St,
San Francisco, CA
94123

Andrews MR & MRS Alexander McA (Julie Ann Sugalski) LErie'81.Bost'78.Cwr'81
☎ (614) 666-1344 . . Felkner-Anderson House, 9716 Fontanelle Rd, Gabriel Corners, Ostrander, OH *43061*

Andrews JUNIORS MISS Alexandra D . . see R C Ducommun

Andrews MR Charles L 3d—Tufts'48
MISS Frances L—Duke'82—at ☎ (916) 796-3464
Full Belly Farm, Box 222, End of Rd 43, Guinda, CA *95637* . . . .
MR Charles L 4th—P'83.Cal'91—at
☎ (408) 227-5898 . . 5355 Wong Court, Apt 232, San Jose, CA *95125* . . . .
111 N Race St,
Statesville, NC
28677

Andrews MR & MRS Charles W H (Elizabeth A Faunce) Vt'81.Nf.Ariz'77
☎ (508) 392-1325 . . "Boulderdash" 87 West St, Westford, MA *01886*

Andrews MRS E Wyllys 4th (Joann MacManus) Bnd'51 . . . . | ☎ (011-52-992) 5-10-04
MISS Margaret D—Tul'87 . . . . | Calle 13, 203A,
MR Edmund—at 3703 Heather Court, Alexandria, VA *22310* . . . . | San Cosme, Mérida, Yucatán, Mexico
MR David D—at Tulane . . . . |

Andrews MR & MRS E Wyllys 5th (Patricia Antell) CtCol'65.H'64 . . . . | ☎ (504) 899-0079
MISS Ruth W—at U of Chicago . . . . | 937 Henry Clay Av, New Orleans, LA
MR E Wyllys 6th—at Vanderbilt . . . . | *70118*

Andrews MISS Ellen D (Straus—Ellen D Andrews) Les'77.Les'78 . . of
☎ (716) 885-8097 . . "Piscina Nascosta" 38 St George's Square, Buffalo, NY *14222*
☎ (207) 288-3768 . . "Aldersea" PO Box 174, Bar Harbor, ME *04609-0174*

Andrews MR & MRS George R (Helga von L Schröder) P'53 . . . . | ☎ (617) 329-5543
MISS Christina H—at ☎ (305) 361-1220 | 20 Wood's End Rd, Dedham, MA *02026*
"Bahama House" 204 Sunrise Dv, Key Biscayne, FL *33149* . . . . |
MISS Courtenay H . . . . |

Andrews MR & MRS Gordon P (Pamela W Bradford) Stan'81.Bur.Pcu.Cal'79
☎ (415) 435-0747 . . 137 Geldert Dv, Tiburon, CA *94920*

Andrews MR & MRS Henry P (Clifton Drury) P'27
☎ (513) 561-8745 . . 3939 Erie Av, Apt 412, Cincinnati, OH *45208*

Andrews MISS Isabel Chapman (Owen W) . . . . Born at Boston, MA Jun 20'96

Andrews MR & MRS Joseph B JR (Betty Burlingham) CinCons'34.Va'34
☎ (513) 831-3224 . . 5825 Given Rd, Indian Hill, Cincinnati, OH *45243*

Andrews MR & MRS Joseph B JR (Jean D Cronk) StL'49 . . . . | of ☎ (314)994-0333
MISS Caroline C . . . . | 13 Twin Springs Lane, St Louis, MO *63124*
| ☎ (517) 738-7632 "Thumb Cottage" 1910 Cliff Rd, Pointe-Aux-Barques, Port Austin, MI *48467*

Andrews JUNIORS MISS Lindsey L . . see R C Ducommun

Andrews MRS Mark E (Lavone L Dickensheets) Rice'33.Rice'34.Cly.
☎ (713) 522-8234 . . 2121 Kirby Dv, Apt 109, Houston, TX *77019*

Andrews MR & MRS Mark E 3d (Elizabeth M Quay) Wheat'73.B.Ri.Fic.Ln.K.Cly.H'72.H'75 . . . . | ☎ (713) 521-2909
JUNIORS MISS Elizabeth Q . . . . | 2909 Inwood Dv,
JUNIORS MR Mark E 4th . . . . | Houston, TX *77019*

Andrews MR & MRS Oakley VanderPoel (Mary J Maloney) Un.Cv.Y'62.Cwr'65 . . . . | ☎ (216) 991-5328
MISS Susan Barclay . . . . | 2894 Winthrop Rd,
MISS Catherine VanderPoel . . . . | Shaker Heights, OH *44120*

Andrews MR & MRS Owen W (Eleanor Tittmann) Br'79.H'79
☎ (617) 491-5107 . . 34—2 St, Cambridge, MA *02141*

Andrews MRS Perkins (Nancy R Perkins) Cr'54 . . . | ☎ (415) 924-7521
JUNIORS MR Robert A P—at U of Cal Santa Cruz | 21 Rocklyn Court, Corte Madera, CA *94925*

Andrews MR & MRS Peter F (Marjorie Key) Pl.Cda . . .of
☎ (914) 278-2184 . . "Sherwood House" Sherwood Hill Rd, Brewster, NY *10509*
Yacht Av, Cape May, NJ *08204*

Andrews MR & MRS Prescott R (Virginia Hawkins) Rm.Cda.
☎ (908) 842-1478 . . 158 Black Point Rd, PO Box 284, Rumson, NJ *07760*

Andrews MR & MRS Prescott R JR (Susan J Witte) MmtMhn'78.Y'58 . . . . | ☎ (717) 937-4072
MISS Sarah H . . . . | Deer Run Farm, RD 2, Box 2595, Waymart, PA *18472*

Andrews MR & MRS Schofield JR (Judith H Ogilvie) H'44 . . . . | ☎ (307) 733-8305
MISS Mary S—at ☎ (401) 521-2698 | 755 E Moulton Loop
8 Cady St, Providence, RI *02903* . . . . | Rd, Jackson, WY *83001*
MR Laurence F B—at ☎ (310) 396-6387 |
35 Breeze Av, Venice, CA *90291* . . . . |

Andrews MR & MRS Schofield 3d (Eleanor G Bowne) Wheat'74.Sm.H'76
☎ (508) 468-7751 . . Black Brook Rd, Hamilton, MA *01936*

Andrews MR & MRS Stockton A (Eleanor L Dunham) Nf.Bhy.Me. ⚓
☎ (207) 288-3768 . . "Aldersea" PO Box 174, Bar Harbor, ME *04609-0174*

Andrews MR & MRS Stuart B (G Devereux Hunter) Gm.Nf.Rb.Ac.Cda.H'46 . . of
☎ (610) 525-7687 . . 421 Great Springs Rd, Rosemont, PA *19010*
☎ (207) 276-5578 . . Tennis Club Rd, Northeast Harbor, ME *04662*

Andrews MR & MRS Thomas G (Holsberry—Milbrey W Waller) Van'62.Ala'56 . . . . | ☎ (615) 383-5270
MISS Susan W . . . . | 208 Jackson Blvd,
MR John W . . . . | Nashville, TN *37205*
MR Thomas G 3d . . . . |

Andrews MR & MRS William T (Suzanne W Evans) Pa'48 ⚓
☎ (610) 644-3093 . . 1700 Indian Run Rd, Malvern, PA *19355*

Andrews MRS Wolcott Erskine (Anne K Lord) BMr'31.Cs.Dh.Hb. . . . . | ☎ (212) 662-5994
MRS Penelope A Sprague (Penelope Andrews) | 520 W 110 St, Apt 3A, New York, NY *10025*

Andrulis MR John . . see MRS R E Barnes
Andrulis MR Michael . . see MRS R E Barnes

Andrus MR & MRS Gerald L (Lucile G Isacks) Ln.Tul'28
☎ (504) 897-3242 . . 1309 Nashville Av, New Orleans, LA *70115*

Andrus MR & MRS Vincent D (Caroline S Parker) Ws'76.B.Yn.Y'63
☎ (860) 542-6942 . . 25 North St, Norfolk, CT *06058*

Angell MR & MRS Christopher C (Margaret J Blettner) C.Cs.H'66 . . . . | ☎ (212) BU8-4884
MISS Elizabeth M . . . . | 156 E 66 St,
MISS Margaret B . . . . | New York, NY
JUNIORS MR Christopher E . . . . | *10021*

Angell MR & MRS I Jackson (A Lea Osborne) Swb'63.Mo.Ty'61 . . . . | ☎ (908) 234-2498
MISS Jessica N . . . . | 84 Roxiticus Rd,
MR I Jackson 3d . . . . | Far Hills, NJ *07931*
JUNIORS MISS Sarah O . . . . |

Angell MISS Jennifer L—StLaw'92
  ☎ (212) 988-1101 . . 444 E 78 St, Apt 3, New York, NY *10021*
Angelo MRS Marjorie G (Marjorie T Gold) | ☎ (908) 920-9668
  Dick'72.Ht. . . . . | 186 Cartagena Dv,
  MR Hunter B—Cw.Rv.Wt.Ht.StA.Fw. . . . . | Brick, NJ
  | *08723-7005*
Angevin MR Robert P B—Wms'85 . . of
  ☎ (312) 397-1401 . . 636 N Orleans St, Apt 3N, Chicago, IL *60610*
  ☎ (508) 627-8664 . . ''Starbuck's Neck'' Starbuck's Neck Rd,
  Edgartown, MA *02539*
Angevin MISS Susan F . . see G F Kenly
Angevine MRS George B (Collin—Margaret V Muse) BtP.Rr.Evg . . .of
  ☎ (412) 741-8264 . . 625 Pine Rd, Sewickley, PA *15143*
  ☎ (561) 832-3269 . . 315 S Lake Dv, Palm Beach, FL *33480*
Angle MR & MRS Richard W (Jean Hobbs) Bvl.Ny.U'38 🛆
  ☎ (941) 466-9383 . . 5807 Turban Rd, Ft Myers, FL *33908*
Angle MR & MRS Richard W JR (Barbara Buddington)
  Wells'64.Ny.H.'63 . . of
  ☎ (212) 724-9014 . . 110 Riverside Dv, New York, NY *10024*
  ☎ (203) 453-6065 . . 52 Uncas Circle, Guilford, CT *06437*
Anglès MR & MRS Jean Paul (Eugénie G Auerbach) . | ☎ (011-33-1)
  MISS Nathalie—Br'82 . . . . | 45-27-73-61
  MISS Daphne . . . . | 57 blvd Beausejour,
  MR Eric—Br'91 . . . . | 75016 Paris, France
Anglin MISS Mary K—Va'73
  ☎ (704) 765-4294 . . PO Box 7, Penland, NC *28765*
Angulo MR Manuel R . . . . Died May 21'96
Angulo MRS Manuel R (Rockwell—Diana de B Hutchins) Ac.
  ☎ (610) 525-3711 . . Tedwyn, 840 Montgomery Av, Bryn Mawr,
  PA *19010*
Anikeeff MR & MRS Nicholas M (Nancy B W | ☎ (703) 356-7587
  Hotchkiss) An.Mich'36 . . . . | 1175 Dolley
  MISS Alexandra M—PineM'83.BostColl'87 . . . . | Madison Blvd,
  | McLean, VA *22101*
Anker-Simmons MRS Ronald S (Ferguson—F Bay Echols) Pr.Cly . . .of
  ☎ (904) 273-4845 . . Vicar's Landing Box H108, 1000 Vicar's Landing
  Way, Ponte Vedra Beach, FL *32082-9979*
  ☎ (212) 754-9382 . . 188 E 64 St, New York, NY *10021*
Annan MR & MRS John W (Kent—Hope H | ☎ (561) 655-2997
  Parkhurst) Evg.BtP.Cly.Ac.Cda.Linc'52.Ch'56 . | 150 Barton Av,
  MR Peter A Kent . . . . | Palm Beach, FL
  | *33480*
Annan MRS M Barbara (Hanson—M Barbara | ☎ (907) 457-1222
  Annan) Bost'68.BostColl'87.Les'90.Evg.BtP. . . | 1071 Roosterfish Rd,
  MISS Phaedra A Hanson—at | PO Box 73063,
  34 Harbor Towers, 85 E India Row, Boston, | Fairbanks, AK
  MA *02110* . . . . | *99707*
Anness MR Frederick H . . see MRS B H Marvin
Anness MR Peyton R 3d . . see MRS B H Marvin
Annibali MR & MRS Philip A (Mary-Louise Richmond) On.Wms'55 . . of
  ☎ (847) 234-4923 . . 1388 N Green Bay Rd, Lake Forest, IL *60045*
  ☎ (561) 546-2356 . . Coquina, 112 N Beach Rd, Hobe Sound,
  FL *33455*
Annibali MR & MRS William W (Cynthia H Brennan) Ne'92
  ☎ (847) 295-5346 . . 595 Washington Rd, Lake Forest, IL *60045*
Anstey MR Christopher L . . see MISS J M Lamy

Anthon MR & MRS Donald W (Victoria L Samuel) | ☎ (314) 991-1270
  Bv. . . . . | 29 Clermont Lane,
  MR Andrew R—at Jacksonville State . . . . | St Louis, MO *63124*
Anthony MRS Bettina M (Bettina de B Moran) | ☎ (561) 655-7918
  BtP.Cda. . . . . | 211 Dunbar Rd,
  MISS Laura de B—Ty'88—at ☎ (212) 223-7419 | Palm Beach, FL
  825 Fifth Av, New York, NY *10021* . . . . | *33480*
Anthony MR & MRS Edward L 2d (Constance Foss) | ☎ (808) 879-6766
  Cyb.Hn.Hb.H'43 . . . . | 3300 Wailea Alanui,
  MR Richard G D—at Perkins Sch . . . . | Ekahi 2C, Wailea,
  | Maui, HI
  | *96753-9516*
Anthony MR & MRS R Tate 3d (Josephine E Herkness)
  LakeF'82.Pc.Fw.W.Rol'78
  ☎ (610) 696-2408 . . 191 Pheasant Run Rd, West Chester, PA *19380*
Anthony MR & MRS S Reed (Magdelaine R Salvage) Pr.Myf.Y.'34
  ☎ (516) 676-2097 . . 57 Simonson Rd, Old Brookville, NY *11545*
Anthony MR & MRS Silas R JR (Anne C Sampsell) | of ☎ (212)249-5068
  SL'65.Rc.Cly.Myf.Hob'63 🛆 | 444 E 82 St,
  MISS Wendy C—at 2235 Laguna St, Apt 204, | New York, NY
  San Francisco, CA *94115* . . . . | *10028-5981*
  MR Silas R 3d—at Denison . . . . | ☎ (561) 747-0054
  | Searise C, Jupiter,
  | FL *33458*
Antoli-Candela DR & MRS Francisco (Elizabeth W | Magnolias 1,
  Arndt) Valencia'69. | Monteclaro,
  MISS Stephanie . . . . | 28023 Madrid, Spain
  JUNIORS MISS Irene . . . . |
  JUNIORS MR Francisco . . . . |
Anwyl MISS Pandora H C . . see MRS A Sheffield
Apgar MISS Hallowell (Nancy Hallowell)
  ☎ (918) 743-4662 . . 3914 S Norfolk Av, Tulsa, OK *74105-3125*
Apgar MR & MRS Mahlon 4th (Anne D Nelson) | ☎ (410) 377-7337
  Ws'70.Lond'71.Mt.Plg.Elk.Hn.Dth'62.Ox'65. | 7321 Brightside Rd,
  H'68. . . . . | Baltimore, MD
  JUNIORS MISS Sarah E T . . . . | *21212*
  JUNIORS MR Frederick C D . . . . |
Apostol MR & MRS Michael Mouravieff (Schmidt— | of ☎ (914)677-6713
  Mary M Saxon) Man'vl'69.Md'70.Cit'62.H'67 . | PO Box 1316,
  JUNIORS MISS Alexandra M . . . . | Millbrook, NY
  | *12545*
  | ☎ (011-41-22)
  | 463688
  | 31 rue de l'Athenée,
  | 1206 Geneva,
  | Switzerland
Appel DR & MRS John W (Marian Kirk) BMr'40.Ph.Me.Gm.Cs.H'32.H'36
  ☎ (610) 688-5509 . . 518 Oak Grove Lane, Radnor, PA *19087*
Appel MR & MRS Kenneth G (Laura A Kerrigan) | ☎ (201) 762-3786
  Man'vl'72.Me.Hn.H'68 . . . . | 19 Roosevelt Rd,
  JUNIORS MR John K . . . . | Maplewood, NJ
  JUNIORS MR Peter G. . . . . | *07040*
  JUNIORS MR Charles E . . . . |
Appelbe MRS John M (Tookie Ryan) . . . . | ☎ (602) 943-7563
  MISS Therese . . . . | 8108 N Central Av,
  MISS Jane . . . . | Phoenix, AZ *85020*
  MISS Margaret . . . . |

Appell MR Frederick W .... Died at Hanover, NH Jan 20'96

Appell MRS Frederick W (Ella T Beaver)
☎ (603) 643-2171 .. Thanksgiving Hill, Box 5090, 12 Storrs Rd, Hanover, NH *03755*

Appell MR & MRS George N (Laura W Reynolds)
McG'55.Hb.H'48.H'52.AusNatU'66
☎ (207) 639-3636 .. Cottle Brook Farm, Phillips, ME *04966*

Apple MR & MRS Raymond Walter JR (Brown—Betsey G Pinckney)
BMr'65.C.An.Pn.Cl'61.Denis'89.Knox'93.Gettys'95 .. of
☎ (202) 333-6974 .. 1509—28 St NW, Washington, DC *20007*
☎ (717) 642-5034 .. ''Copper Top Farm'' Orrtanna, PA *17353*

Appleby MR & MRS Edgar O (Paula M Verstraeten)
Rc.Pr.K.S.Snc.Cw.Ne. .... | ☎ (516) 676-4357 Peacock Point, Locust Valley, NY *11560*
MISS F Sandra—at 153 Old Princeton Rd, Hubbardston, MA *01452* ....
MISS Anne B—at 2406 Delphi Rd SW, Olympia, WA *98512* ....

Applegate MR & MRS A Lowrie (Elizabeth A Eighmy) Rr.P'37.H'39
☎ (412) 741-5341 .. PO Box 6, Sewickley, PA *15143*

Applegate MR & MRS L Thomas 3d (Cathleen H Sullivan) Col'71.Eyc.Col'71.Ant'72 .... | ☎ (513) 891-7410 8650 Keller Rd, Cincinnati, OH *45243*
MISS Claire S ....
JUNIORS MR William T ....

Applegate MR & MRS Leslie T (Marjorie B Pease)
☎ (513) 831-0080 .. 9655 Shawnee Run Rd, Cincinnati, OH *45243*

Applegate MR & MRS Ralph W JR (Helen E Alonso). of ☎ (312)943-2340
JUNIORS MISS Elisa E................... | 1364 N State P'kway, Chicago, IL *60610*
JUNIORS MR Ralph W 3d ....
☎ (602) 488-1389 35037 N El Sendero Dv, PO Box 2658, Carefree, AZ *85377*

Applegate MR & MRS Robert D (Bryanne B Marvin) Myf.Wash'66.StL'71 .... | ☎ (301) 840-2142 12 Briardale Court, Rockville, MD *20855*
MR Bryan D ....

Appleton MRS Ariel B (Ariel Bryce)
☎ (520) 327-0457 .. PO Box 890, Sonoita, AZ *85637*

Appleton MRS Benjamin B (Betty A Schaefer) .... | ☎ (716) 886-3333 16 Park St, Buffalo, NY *14201*
MISS Wendy W—at ☎ (716) 886-1936 916 Delaware Av, Apt 1H, Buffalo, NY *14209* .

Appleton MR Benjamin B—Colg'58
4254 SW Washouga Av, Portland, OR *97201-1375*

Appleton MISS Elizabeth P .. see N B Durfee JR

Appleton MRS Phebe G (Phebe Grauer) Skd'57 .. of
☎ (716) 882-6445 .. 23 Norwood Av, Buffalo, NY *14222*
☎ (905) 468-2802 .. 292 Johnson St, Niagara-on-the-Lake, Ontario L0S 1J0, Canada

Aquino MISS Jeannette Cox
☎ (805) 965-1393 .. 424 E Figueroa St, Santa Barbara, CA *93101*

Arbon MR & MRS Paul (Joan M Alker) Unn.S.Cc.
☎ (011-44-171) 351-9558 .. 46 Limerston St, Chelsea, London SW10 0HH, England

Archambault MR & MRS Bennett (Margaret H Morgan) Cho.Rc.Sc.Wa. .... | ☎ (773) 549-7243 3240 N Lake Shore Dv, Chicago, IL *60657*
MISS Suzanne M ....
MR Steven B ....

Archbold MRS Phoebe W (van Beuren—Phoebe R Wildman) GwynM'70 .... | 168 Carrick Bend Lane, PO Box 1472, Boca Grande, FL *33921*
MISS Jennifer D.......................
MR Michael M van Beuren—at ☎ (410) 263-7417 .. 239 Hanover St, Annapolis, MD *21401* ....

Archer MRS Fred Coleman (Marguerite P Hagemans) .... | ☎ (415) 564-1358 1310—28 Av, San Francisco, CA *94122-1513*
MR Geoffrey R—Duke'94.Duke'95 ....

Archer DR & MRS (DR) John H JR (Joanne M Brumbaugh)
Ws'80.Stan'86.P'80.Stan'86
☎ (415) 321-3146 .. 1932 Waverley St, Palo Alto, CA *94301-3847*

Archer MR & MRS John P JR (Mary C Lyman) Sar... | ☎ (410) 836-3748 2253 Price Rd, Darlington, MD *21034*
MR John P 3d ....
MR William S ....

Archer MR & MRS Pierce (Cynthia R Hill) Witt'74.Me.Rc.Colby'78
☎ (610) 293-7655 .. 750 Harrison Rd, Villanova, PA *19085*

Archibald MR Fred J—An.USA'45 .. of
☎ (301) 865-5155 .. ''Armadale Farms'' PO Box 74, Frederick, MD *21705-0074*
☎ (202) 338-3974 .. 2500 Wisconsin Av NW, Washington, DC *20007*

Ardrey MR & MRS James B (Wendy L Richardson)
Stan'80.SantaC'84.Tcy.Yn.Dth'80.Ch'84
☎ (203) 629-1242 .. 48 Pheasant Lane, Greenwich, CT *06830*

Arenchild MRS H Pirie (Heather A Pirie)
☎ (408) 373-6315 .. 1035 Lost Barranca, Pebble Beach, CA *93953*

Arensberg MR & MRS Charles C (Gertrude H Hays) Pg.Ht.H'34
☎ (412) 683-5018 .. 5031 Castleman St, Pittsburgh, PA *15232*

Arensberg MR & MRS Charles S (Anne C Miller) Knox'74.Knox'70. .... | ☎ (502) 637-2801 1375 S 4 St, Louisville, KY *40208*
MR Charles C M ....
JUNIORS MR W Austin A M ....

Arensberg MR & MRS Conrad M (Vivian Garrison) Sb.C.H.'31 .... | ☎ (212) 740-5040 100 Haven Av, New York, NY *10032*
MR Cornelius W ....

Arensberg MR & MRS Walter W (Susan L MacMillan) Sth'69.H'61 .... | ☎ (202) 333-1434 2810—36 Place NW, Washington, DC *20007*
JUNIORS MISS Chloe L M ....

Argenti MR & MRS Tristan J M (Barbara Flynn) StCaterina'52.Nu'59.Nu'60 .... | ☎ (941) 349-7976 4840 Featherbed Lane, Sarasota, FL *34242*
MR John P—Un.Tul'85.Duke'92—at ☎ (212) 717-4077 .. 228 E 85 St, New York, NY *10028*. ....
MR Nicholas P A—StAndr'89—at U Coll of London ..
MR Andreas P—Tul'91—at ☎ (504) 866-0384 8203 Jeannette St, New Orleans, LA *70118* ....

Argento MRS Henry F (Brittenham—Zwack de Wahl—Iris G Rogers) Cl'53.Cl'67.Ri....... MISS Iris M Zwack de Wahl............. MR John R Zwack de Wahl—NH'89 ....
of ☎ (908)766-0555 Hub Hollow Farm, PO Box 188, Far Hills, NJ *07931*
☎ (212) 308-0639 125 E 63 St, New York, NY *10021*

Arguimbau MR & MRS Vincent C 3d (Hilarie B Ford) NCar'74
☎ (203) 655-1429 . . 202 Mansfield Av, Darien, CT *06820*

Armat MRS C Brooke (Newton—Mary L Trotter)
☎ (202) 362-4724 . . 4616 Albemarle St NW, Washington, DC *20016*

Armat MRS Thomas JR (Croft—Virginia L Newall) Syr'40
☎ (202) 244-8445 . . 4724 Alton Place NW, Washington, DC *20016*

Armentrout MR & MRS Alexander Van Dyke (Packard—Paula F Goodridge) Husson'69.S. P'63.H'65............................ MISS Victoria F—Pars'89—at 145 Attorney St, Apt 1A, New York, NY *10002*............. MR Nicholas R—WashColl'92....
☎ (207) 865-2280 PO Box 422, South Freeport, ME *04078-0422*
☎ (208) 788-2465 . . 109 Greenhorn Gulch Rd, PO Box 3307, Hailey, ID *83333*............

Armentrout MR & MRS J Michael (Janet J Doman) Pa'71.CarnM'70.Temp'86
☎ (215) 542-7682 . . 480 Morris Rd, Ambler, PA *19002*

Armentrout MRS James S (D Virginia Roosevelt) Ac.Cda.Pn.
☎ (215) MI6-1515 . . 480 Morris Rd, Ambler, PA *19002*

Armistead MR & MRS Henry T (Mary E Mallam) Pa'66.Temp'71.Pa'63.Drex'68.............. MISS Anne T—at Oberlin .... MISS Mary D—at Clark U................. MR George L ....
of ☎ (215)248-4120 523 E Durham St, Philadelphia, PA *19119*
☎ (410) 745-2764 ''Rigby's Folly'' 25124 W Ferry Neck Rd, Royal Oak, MD *21662*

Armistead MR Hunter JR—Smu'75
☎ (615) 297-4589 . . 3101 W End Av, Apt 300, Nashville, TN *37203*

Armistead MR & MRS Leonard H 3d (Jacquelyn K Page) Memp'85.Smu'73
☎ (615) 383-6925 . . 112 Bonaventure Place, Nashville, TN *37205*

Armistead MR & MRS Robert H F (Stephanie J Shockley) Van'75
☎ (615) 353-1858 . . 610 Enquirer Av, Nashville, TN *37205*

Armistead MR & MRS Thomas Boyd 3d (Katherine M Kelly) Aht'39...................... MR Thomas B 4th—at ☎ (818) 349-5044 20134 Leadwell St, Canoga Park, CA *91306* . . .
☎ (310) 271-0180 10373 Ashton Av, Los Angeles, CA *90024*

Armistead MR & MRS William D JR (Susan Bell Wright) SCal'65.Stan'56 .... MISS Lauren B .... MR William D 3d .... MR James W ....
☎ (310) 476-5069 11066 Cashmere St, Los Angeles, CA *90049*

Armitage MR & MRS Arthur L (Lucht—Catherine A Seyler) Knox'63.Ny.Y.'54
☎ (914) 868-1262 . . 434 Knight Rd, Clinton Corners, NY *12514*

Armitage MRS Meredyth R (Meredyth N Rubidge) Sth'54.Rm......................... MR Thomas A—at 175 Kealaloa St, Makawao, Maui, HI *96768* ....
☎ (908) 842-1840 115 Ridge Rd, Rumson, NJ *07760*

Armour MRS A Watson 3d (Addington—Sarah S Wood) Rc.On.Sr.Cas.Ri . . .of
☎ (847) 234-9111 . . 303 Bluffs Edge Dv, Lake Forest, IL *60045*
☎ (561) 546-4121 . . Box 396, Hobe Sound, FL *33475*

Armour MR & MRS A Watson 4th (Mary A Gooch) Bost'65.Ch'69 .... MISS Jean S—at U of Vt................. JUNIORS MISS Mary P ....
☎ (719) 475-9684 11 W Cheyenne Mountain Blvd, Colorado Springs, CO *80906*

Armour MISS Cynthia (Ward—Cynthia Armour) Nw'89.Kel'91.Rc............ JUNIORS MR James A Ward ....
☎ (312) 951-0178 1448 N Lake Shore Dv, Chicago, IL *60610*

Armour MR & MRS George P (Isabel Blondet) Vh.Temp'43.Temp'49
☎ (818) 793-9268 . . 1621 Orlando Rd, Pasadena, CA *91106*

Armour MISS Hilda L—Ham'74.Sim'78.Sim'87
☎ (303) 442-3293 . . 194 Nugget Hill, Jamestown, CO *80455*

Armour MR & MRS Laurance H JR (Kelly—Margot Boyd) Rcn.On.Cho.Sr.Cas.Cyc.Ny.Pn.P'45 .... MR Steven S—at ☎ (713) 528-2112 2205 Albans Rd, Houston, TX *77005*........
☎ (409) 532-0052 ''Live Oak House'' Pierce Ranch, Pierce, TX *77467*

Armour MRS Lester (Romanoff—Alexandra Galitzine)
☎ (847) 234-0988 . . 123 E Onwentsia Rd, Lake Forest, IL *60045-3005*

Armour MRS Norman JR (Paine—Cynthia B Howe) Ri.K.Cly.
☎ (212) TE8-0800 . . 825 Fifth Av, New York, NY *10021*

Armour MR & MRS Norman 3d (Isabelle Ferté)
☎ (415) 381-1888 . . 8 Laurel St, Mill Valley, CA *94941*

Armour MRS P Kelley (Pamela Kelley) On.Rc.Cas.Fy.
☎ (847) 234-0943 . . 630 E Spruce Av, Lake Forest, IL *60045*

Armour MR & MRS Peter H (Catherine G Magruder) Bost'69.OWes'71.Stan'77 .... MISS Larkin A .... JUNIORS MISS Julie G....................
☎ (757) 229-1838 315 Archers Mead, Williamsburg, VA *23185*

Armour MRS Philip D JR (Julia R B Henry)
☎ (305) 858-5774 . . Grove Isle Apt 502, 1 Grove Isle Dv, Coconut Grove, FL *33133*

Armour MR & MRS Philip D 3d (MacDonald—M Kerstin M Lindberg) NewC'78.SFrSt'83.P'65. Cal'69 .... MR Philip D 4th .... MR D A Maximillian .... JUNIORS MR Nicholas E A ....
☎ (415) 442-0399 171 S Park St, Apt 3, San Francisco, CA *94107-1808* . . MRS absent

Armour MR & MRS T Stanton (Jean Reddy) On.Sr.Cnt.Y'49
☎ (847) 234-1779 . . 1144 Hawkweed Lane, Lake Forest, IL *60045*

Armour MR Vernon—Rc.On.Cho.Sr.Y'50
☎ (847) 295-0304 . . 187 Winthrop Lane, Lake Forest, IL *60045*

Armstrong MR & MRS A Joseph 3d (Ann P Howell) RISD'62.Wms'61.Mit'65
☎ (610) 696-l930 . . 450 Lucky Hill Rd, West Chester, PA *19382*

Armstrong MR & MRS Alexander (Louise D Allen) BMr'42.P'37
☎ (410) 823-1630 . . 2019 Skyline Rd, Ruxton, MD *21204*

Armstrong MISS Ann E . . see J J Edson 4th

Armstrong MISS Anne C—Van'83.WashColl'92.Cvc . . .of
☎ (202) 667-8167 . . 3100 Connecticut Av NW, Apt 107, Washington, DC *20008*
☎ (603) 823-8059 . . ''Muldoon House'' 1261 Main St, Sugar Hill, NH *03585*

Armstrong MR & MRS Charles M (Marie S Bostwick)
BostColl'79.Srr.A.TexTech'69
9000 SW Kanner H'way, PO Box 1139, Indiantown, FL *34956*

Armstrong MRS Donald (Wilmot—Rachel D Buntin) BtP.Ncd.Cda . . . . | ☎ (561) 832-8906 Water View Towers
   MRS C Wilmot Gray (Carolyn Wilmot) . . . . . | Apt 2006,
   MISS Evangeline W Gray—at Kenyon . . . . . . | 400 N Flagler Dv, West Palm Beach, FL *33401*

Armstrong MRS Edward McP (Sheila H Starr) Chr.Cly. . . . . | ☎ BU8-3127 135 E 74 St,
   MR Edward McP JR—H'62.Mar'69—at Stuttgart University, Stuttgart, Germany . . . . | New York, NY *10021*

Armstrong MR & MRS George A (Jane Griffiths) Cvc.P'45
☎ (301) 656-6782 . . 5504 Center St, Chevy Chase, MD *20815*

Armstrong MR George W 3d—Va'59
☎ (601) 445-9600 . . 821 Main St, Natchez, MS *39120*

Armstrong MRS Hamilton Fish (Christa von Tippelskirch)
☎ (212) GR5-5327 . . 2 Fifth Av, Apt 20A, New York, NY *10011*

Armstrong MR & MRS Henry H (Frances McKay) Chath'85.Pg.Rr.Y'53
☎ (412) 681-7773 . . 5228 Westminster Place, Pittsburgh, PA *15232*

Armstrong MR & MRS J Sinclair (Faircloth—Charlotte P Horwood)
Rdc'49.Un.Err.C.Chr.Eyc.Ny.Cvc.Plg.Cw.Ht.Snc.
StA.StJ.Sl.Cly.Cs.Cda.Dh.H.'38 . . of
☎ (212) 737-7880 . . 501 E 79 St, New York, NY *10021*
☎ (860) 868-7500 . . ''Charlecote'' PO Box 1127, Washington, CT *06793*

Armstrong MR & MRS James M (Elizabeth M Hill) P'90.P'90
431 Briarhill Lane NE, Atlanta, GA *30324*

Armstrong MRS John JR (Jane Fraser Wilson)
☎ (610) 527-0723 . . 840 Montgomery Av, Apt 104, Bryn Mawr, PA *19010*

Armstrong MR & MRS John B (Naumer—Carolyn Palmer) A.Tex'41 . . of
☎ (512) 592-4991 . . PO Box 193, Kingsville, TX *78363*
☎ (210) 822-6424 . . PO Box 6109, San Antonio, TX *78209-0109*

Armstrong MR & MRS John C (Hurlimann—Mary H Post)
Cly.Cda.Wms'40.Nu'42
☎ (203) 869-8311 . . 8 Grahampton Lane, Greenwich, CT *06830*

Armstrong MR & MRS John K (A Maria E van Haersma Buma) HuisLande'60.Plg.Chr.Ht. Dh.Hav'56.Y'60 . . . . | of ☎ (914)337-7026 14 Carlton Rd, Bronxville, NY *10708*
   MISS Marca C van H—AGSIM'94 . . . . |
   MR Jeb S—Hav'95 . . . . | ☎ (860) 435-9792 ''Bird Peak'' Box 190, Lakeville, CT *06039*

Armstrong MR & MRS John M (Rebecca A Wilson) P'74.Cl'82.Pn.P'67.H'75 . . . . | ☎ (203) 637-8068 59 Lockwood Av,
   JUNIORS MR Ian A McP . . . . | Old Greenwich, CT *06870*

Armstrong MR & MRS John S 3d (Drake—M Blair Morton) Myf . . .of
☎ (602) 948-7184 . . 6246 Joshua Tree Lane, Scottsdale, AZ *85253*
☎ (619) 459-7463 . . 8009 Calle de la Plata, La Jolla, CA *92037*

Armstrong MISS Julia R (A Joseph 3d) . . . . . . Married at Paul Smiths, NY Cramer MR William E (late Corwith JR) . . . . Aug 26'95

Armstrong MISS Katherine StJ—Van'95 . . see J M Brown 3d

Armstrong MR & MRS Kevin J (Julia G Allen) Ox'81
☎ (011-44-1580) 212-334 . . Tattlebury Cottage, Tattlebury Lane, Goudhurst, Kent TN17 1BS, England

Armstrong MISS Leigh T—P'93 . . see J M Brown 3d

Armstrong MISS Louise S (Rodney) . . . . Married at Boston, MA Barton MR Randolph 3d (Randolph JR) . . . . Jun 15'96

Armstrong MISS Lucie Carr—Ty'64
☎ (210) 562-3553 . . Williams Creek Ranch, PO Box 74, Tarpley, TX *78883*

Armstrong MR P Livingstone—S. . . . . | ☎ (011-41-21) 808-55-35
   MISS Rosemary A—at 5 Kitsbury Court, Kitsbury Terr, Berkhampstead, Hertfordshire, England . . . | ''Les Cassivettes'' 1173 Féchy, Vaud, Switzerland

Armstrong MR & MRS Richard M (Katherine A Maynard) Pe.Ac.Ncd.Mit'33
☎ (610) 696-7213 . . ''Cope's Bridge'' PO Box 566, West Chester, PA *19381*

Armstrong MR & MRS Richard M JR (Susan T Dole) Ph.Pe.Me.StA.Ac.Ncd.Yn.Wes'60.Pa'62 . . . . . . | ☎ (610) 696-2797 Some Chance Farm,
   MISS Katrina A—Ws'93.Me.—at | PO Box 633,
☎ (303) 543-0166 . . 2750 Moorhead Av, Apt 208, Boulder, CO *80303* . . . . | West Chester, PA *19381-0633*
   MR Richard M 3d—Me.Colby'85—at |
☎ (303) 442-7160 . . 710—35 St, Boulder, CO *80303* . . . . |

Armstrong MR & MRS Richard W (Barbara Robbins) H'54.JHop'59 . . . . | ☎ (201) 822-1310 10 Pomeroy Rd,
   MR Richard W JR . . . . | Madison, NJ *07940*

Armstrong MR & MRS Robert S (Potter—Healy— Phoebe S Hemenway) Wh'lck'71.Brdgwtr'93. Nu'75.CalLuth'93 . . . . | ☎ (703) 242-2153 2139 Statute Lane, Vienna, VA *22181-3267*
   JUNIORS MR James S—at Fork Union Military Acad . . . . |
   JUNIORS MR Matthew T Healy . . . . |

Armstrong MR & MRS Robert W (Mary O Kneass) Dth'40 . . . . | ☎ (704) 366-8845 1916 Sharon Lane,
   MISS Anne W . . . . | Charlotte, NC *28211*

Armstrong MR & MRS Rodney (Katharine P Cortesi) Wheat'67.Sm.Tv.Un.C.Gr.Wms'48 . . . . | ☎ (617) 523-0606 101 Chestnut St,
   MR Robert K—at Wesleyan . . . . | Boston, MA *02108*

Armstrong MR & MRS Thomas N 3d (V Whitney Brewster) K.Ri.Fic.Cr'54 . . . . | ☎ (212) 734-2688 36 E 72 St,
   MISS Amory A—Hlns'92—at 666 Greenwich St, New York, NY *10014* . . . . | New York, NY *10021*
   MR Thomas N 4th—at 306 E 71 St, New York, NY *10021* . . . . |
   MR Whitney B—Y'87—at ☎ (215) 351-6312 336 Lombard St, Philadelphia, PA *19147* . . . . . . |

Armstrong MR & MRS Tobin (Anne A Legendre) V'49.A.
☎ (512) 595-5551 . . Armstrong Ranch, Armstrong, TX *78338*

Armstrong MR & MRS Tobin JR (Ardon B Brown) Van'78.Tex'79
6162 Inwood Dv, Houston, TX *77057*

Arndt MR & MRS Charles H 2d (Melinda M Martinez) Sar.Ty'59 . . . . | ☎ (860) 523-1875
  MR Charles H 3d—at Dickinson . . . . | 262 Kenyon St,
  MR Jamie L—at Skidmore . . . . | Hartford, CT *06105*

Arndt MRS Flora L (Flora B Lewis) . . . . | ☎ (203) 637-2941
  MR Thomas B—Conn'88 . . . . | 7 Park Av,
  | Old Greenwich, CT
  | *06870*

Arndt MR & MRS John F JR (Furlong—Nancy Sutch) | ☎ (610) 649-0507
Pitt'63.Rv.Dth'52.LaS'89 . . . . | 1226 Gladwyne Dv,
    MISS Sharon S Furlong—at ☎ (312) 587-1721 | Gladwyne, PA
    40 E Delaware Place, Apt 901, Chicago, IL | *19035*
    60611 . . . . |
    MISS Cynthia E Furlong—SFr'92 . . . . |

Arndt MISS Margaret S
☎ (617) 964-2951 . . 99 Crescent St, Newton, MA *02166*

Arndt MRS Stephanie F (Stephanie B Fuguet)
☎ (610) 688-7083 . . 14 Sugar Knoll Dv, Devon, PA *19333*

Arndt MR Willis C JR—Fic.Yn.Y'90 . . see W P Wodell

Arnold MR & MRS Anthony (Ruth E Lowry) | ☎ (415) 892-0238
V'51.Y'50 . . . . | 19 Hayes St,
  MR William S—EverSt'84 . . . . | Novato, CA *94947*

Arnold MR & MRS David B JR (Dorothy Q Warren)
Btn.Ub.Sm.Chi.Ncd.H'44 ⚓ . . of
☎ (617) 723-4546 . . 107 Chestnut St, Boston, MA *02108*
☎ (508) 281-1860 . . 966 Washington St, Gloucester, MA *01930*

Arnold MRS Edward W (Ann W Lowrie) Bur.Fr.
☎ (415) 340-8559 . . 108 Stonehedge Rd, Hillsborough, CA *94010*

Arnold MRS George C JR (Stark—Louise S Wolf)
Evg.BtP.Nyc.Cly.Chi.Myf.Cw.Dar.
☎ (561) 655-5181 . . 141 Gulfstream Rd, Palm Beach, FL *33480-4707*

Arnold MR & MRS George J JR (Isaacs—Olivia R Stone)
Hampshire'77.Bab'87
☎ (508) 785-1625 . . 97 Centre St, Dover, MA *02030*

Arnold MRS Horace L (Mary J Williams) Ncd.
☎ (508) 369-1523 . . 100 Newbury Court, Apt 401, Concord, MA *01742*

Arnold MR & MRS James H (Sandra P Bunting) Ty'78.Ty'77
☎ (610) 648-9273 . . 419 Green Hill Lane, Berwyn, PA *19312*

Arnold COL (RET) & MRS Joseph C (Mary B | ☎ (703) 356-3899
Sethness) Wa.USA'64 . . . . | 6500 Anna Maria
  MISS Mary S—LakeF'94 . . . . | Court, McLean, VA
  MR Joseph C JR . . . . | *22101*
  JUNIORS MISS Emily E—at Madeira . . . . |
  JUNIORS MR Michael B . . . . |

Arnold MRS Julie M (Willauer—Wight—Julie M | ☎ (540) 338-7284
Arnold) V'56 . . . . | 19223 Otley Rd,
  MR William A Willauer—at | Purcellville, VA
    ☎ (508) 228-1277 . . Box 1106, Nantucket, | *20132*
    MA *02554* . . . . |

Arnold MR & MRS William Potter (Morton—Margaret L Barrows)
Cvc.Cc.Sl.GeoW'33
☎ (202) 338-4332 . . 1601 Caton Place NW, Washington, DC *20007*

Arnone DR & MRS Andrea (Elise M Chapin) Stan'86.Flor'88
☎ (011-39-55) 234-1156 . . Lungarno della Zecca Vecchia 22, 50122 Firenze, Italy

Arnot MRS Nathaniel du B (Alice C Bowie) Mv.Cda.
☎ (410) 321-6618 . . Blakehurst 307, 1055 W Joppa Rd, Towson, MD *21204*

Arnot MR & MRS Nathaniel du B JR (Mary H Sands) | ☎ (410) 235-3225
LErie'65.Gv.Ny.Md.Mv.DU'66 . . . . | 209 Ridgemede Rd,
  MISS Mary E—at Bowdoin . . . . | Baltimore, MD
  MR Nathaniel du B III—Ken'91 . . . . | *21210*
  MR John S—at U of Ore . . . . |
  JUNIORS MISS Rachel B . . . . |

Aronson MR & MRS Robert A (Julia E Bassett) | ☎ (908) 879-7011
Hob'72 . . . . | 14 State Park Rd,
  JUNIORS MISS Jennifer L . . . . | Chester, NJ *07930*

Arrington MRS John H (Schoettle—Romilly—Alicia van Doorn)
☎ (202) 338-8981 . . 2246—49 St NW, Washington, DC *20007*

Arrington MR & MRS Richard H 3d (Dorothy B Lane) Ala'76.Ala'77
2406 Hermitage Dv, Montgomery, AL *36111-2111*

Arrison MR & MRS James M 2d (Butler—Gertrude E Laning) Rv.Ncd.
☎ (561) 778-0508 . . 2300 Indian Creek Blvd W, Apt C215, Vero Beach, FL *32966*

Arrison CAPT & MRS James M 3d (Susan C | ☎ (703) 519-7656
Sheppard) Pa'65.An.Rv.USN'64 . . . . | 118 Madison Place,
  MISS Anne D—at U of Va . . . . | Alexandria, VA
  LT James M 4th—USN'92—aboard | *22314*
  USS Ingersoll, DD-990, Pearl Harbor, Honolulu, |
  HI *96818* . . . . |

Arrott MR & MRS Anthony S (Patricia Graham) | ☎ (212) 581-9315
CTech'54.Myf.CTech'48.Pa'50 . . . . | 24 W 55 St,
  MISS Helen G . . . . | New York, NY
  | *10019*

Arrott MRS Charles R (Foster—Taylor—Margaret Davis) Ct.
☎ (505) 983-9235 . . 714 Bishops Lodge Rd, Santa Fe, NM *87501*

Arrott MISS Elizabeth (Anthony S) . . . . Married at Moscow, Russia
Ekimian MR Raphael A (late Alexie) . . . . Sep 16'95

Arthur MR & MRS D Richardson (Mathews— | ☎ (518) 463-5750
Barbara R Shultz) Cl'74 . . . . | 198 Van Wies Point,
  MISS Barbara R Mathews . . . . | Glenmont, NY
  | *12077*

Arthur MR & MRS James R (Kelton M Himsl) Pitzer'85.Pitzer'84.Cal'90
☎ (415) 342-0739 . . 482 Chatham Rd, Burlingame, CA *94010*

Arthur MISS R Lee—Conn'84 . . see W T Dean

Arthur MR & MRS Stuart G (Ellen L Tanenbaum) Pa'75.Cl'76
☎ (212) 772-2230 . . 301 E 78 St, Apt 11F, New York, NY *10021*

Artman MR James A . . see D W Hass

Arundel MR & MRS Arthur W (Margaret C McElroy) | ☎ (540) 347-7144
Mt.H'51 . . . . | Merry Oak Farm,
  MR Thomas B . . . . | 5700 Merry Oaks
  | Rd, The Plains, VA
  | *20198*

Ash MR Francis J—WVa'49
☎ (334) 277-9138 . . 2014 Rexford Rd, Montgomery, AL *36116*

Ashbey MR & MRS William N (Julia E S Lovett)
Bnd'53.Cl'56.Myf.Dc.Pa'55
☎ (505) 984-8144 . . 3 La Vereda Compound, 707 E Palace Av, Santa Fe, NM *87501*

Ashbridge MISS Hewett McA—WChesU'90
☎ (215) 232-5924 . . 875 N Taylor St, Philadelphia, PA *19130*

Ashbridge MR & MRS Stephen D (Amy L Phillips)
L&C'78.Nu'84.VillaN'89
☎ (215) 236-6020 . . 2418 Poplar St, Philadelphia, PA *19130*
Ashbridge MRS Whitney (Mary G Naile) An.Myf.Ncd.
☎ (505) 275-3848 . . 10500 Academy Blvd NE, Apt 333, Albuquerque,
NM *87111*
Ashbridge MRS William H JR (Peterson—Agnes B Hamill)
☎ (215) CH7-7572 . . 724 Wolcott Dv, Philadelphia, PA *19118*
Ashburn MR & MRS Frank D (Jean T Lang) Y'25
☎ (617) 326-5194 . . Fox Hill Village 229, 10 Longwood Dv, Westwood,
MA *02090*
Ashburner MR C Blakiston—Ct.LSU'69
☎ (202) 483-7553 . . 1724—18 St NW, Washington, DC *20009*
Ashburner MRS James Eyre (Suzanne B La Cour)
☎ (757) 220-1171 . . 5701 Williamsburg Landing Dv, Apt 2,
Williamsburg, VA *23185*
Ashby MRS Elizabeth S C (Elizabeth S Campbell)
☎ (212) 427-6472 . . 8 E 96 St, New York, NY *10128*
Ashcraft MRS Edwin M 3d (Mildred V Winslow)
☎ (202) 337-7126 . . 3900 Watson Place NW, Washington, DC *20016*

Ashdown MR & MRS Cecil Spanton JR (Gartman—
Suffel—Marie A Matranga) Chr.Mto.P'44.H'48
MR Cecil Spanton 3d . . . .
MR Charles C . . . .
   MISS Vivian M Gartman . . . .
   MR John S Gartman . . . .
	☎ (212) PL5-2963
	25 Sutton Place S,
	New York, NY
	10022

Ashey MR & MRS Brian D (Nika G Stephanoff) . . . . MISS Sara E. . . . . MR David S . . . . JUNIORS MR Jonathan J	☎ (401) 783-5259 15 Diane Rd, Narragansett, RI *02882-2608*
Ashford MRS Robert S (Janet M Michellod) Md'60 . MR Robert Dole . . . . MR Anthony Patrick	☎ (954) 753-5917 8197 NW 6 St, Coral Springs, FL *33071*

Ashforth MR Alden B—Ober'58.P'60.P'71
☎ (504) 895-4485 . . 1010 Napoleon Av, New Orleans, LA *70115*
Ashforth MRS George T (Betty T Overton) BMr'31
☎ (203) 531-9157 . . 105 W Lyon Farm Dv, Greenwich, CT *06831*
Ashforth MRS H Adams (Madden—Elsie R Little) Evg.
☎ (203) 869-0104 . . 1 Milbank Av, Greenwich, CT *06830*
Jan 1 . . ☎ (561) 833-4723 . . 389 S Lake Dv, Apt 3G, Palm Beach,
FL *33480*

Ashley MRS Constance B (Wick—Constance Bowman) . . . . MR Davis M . . . . MRS Deborah A Fesler (Deborah M Ashley) .	10411 N 43 St, Phoenix, AZ *85028*

Ashmead MR & MRS Duffield 3d (Aspinwall—Mary T Saunders)
Au.Pc.Ph.Sg.Rv.Cspa.Cw.Ac.Pa'48.Pa'58
☎ (215) 233-0512 . . 509 Auburn Av, Wyndmoor, PA *19038*
Ashmead DR Duffield 4th—Au.Pn.P'80.Cl'84
☎ (860) 674-1616 . . ''Lancet House'' Old Mountain Rd, Farmington,
CT *06032*
Ashton MR & MRS David A (Beall—Charlotte C Dent) Cda.W&M'62
☎ (717) 235-5631 . . ''Gentle Farm'' RD 4, Box 4395, Glen Rock,
PA *17327*

Ashton MR & MRS David G JR (Dorothy M Wilson)
Snc.Cw.Myf.Rv.Ncd.Pn.P'50.Cl'58
☎ (802) 867-4133 . . Box 737, West Rd, Dorset, VT *05251*
Ashton MR & MRS John McL (Joan deF Hornby) Cal'49
☎ (619) 276-8163 . . 2835 Clairemont Dv, Apt 11, San Diego, CA *92117*

Ashton MR & MRS Thomas G (Ann V Laháns) Pkg.Fw.Pa'56.Dick'62 . . . . MISS Rebecca H—at U of Ill Champaign . . . . . . MR Thomas G JR—Box 789, Castine, ME *04421*	☎ (610) 827-7856 ''Parker Hill'' 1935 Horseshoe Trail, Chester Springs, PA *19425*
Ashton MR & MRS William H JR (Brenda J Huber) Pa'72.Pa'71 . . . . JUNIORS MISS Marian W . . . . JUNIORS MR William H 3d—at Brooks	☎ (804) 725-0046 ''Heron Run'' PO Box 800, North, VA *23128*
Aspegren MR & MRS John B (Lois F Barstow) So.Cly.Cda.Dc. . . . . MR John B JR—Ri.	☎ (212) 288-5123 120 E 81 St, Apt 6H, New York, NY *10028*

Aspinwall MR David
☎ (408) 476-4030 . . 1840—41 Av, Apt 102-117, Capitola, CA *95010*

Aspinwall MR & MRS Peter (Susan V Storey) H'54 . . MR Samuel—Dick'95—at ☎ (212) 228-1995 640 E 11 St, Apt 1W, New York, NY *10009* . . .	☎ (612) 476-0499 18520 Fifth Av N, Plymouth, MN *55447*
Astigueta DR & MRS Fernando D (Pamela C Bush) BeauSoleil'61.BuenosAiresU'48 . . . . MR Diego F—at Dickinson	☎ (212) 249-4049 900 Park Av, Apt 3E, New York, NY *10021*

Astor MRS W Vincent (Kuser—Marshall—Brooke Russell)
Cly.Ny.K.Plg.C.StJ.
778 Park Av, New York, NY *10021*

Astrop MR & MRS William B (Jean A Trimmer) BaldW'57.Ht.Cly.Rich'50.H'53 . . . . MR William B JR. . . . . MR Douglas Du B	☎ (404) 237-6061 205 Blackland Rd NW, Atlanta, GA *30342*

Atalay MASTER Eren William (Selim) . . . . Born at
Istanbul, Turkey Jan 15'96
Atalay MR & MRS Selim (Elizabeth L Fish) JHop'92
☎ (516) 862-7234 . . PO Box 794, Stony Brook, NY *11790*
Athearn MRS Leigh (Hope I Glenn) Cal'31
32 Bretano Way, Greenbrae, CA *94904*

Atherton MR & MRS Henry F 3d (Anne-Douglas Burrage) H'67 . . . . MISS Hope E . . . . JUNIORS MISS Lily S	☎ (540) 364-2973 PO Box 295, Warrenton, VA *20188*

Athey MR John M—On.Fla'40
☎ (847) 234-0392 . . 949 Verda Lane, Lake Forest, IL *60045*

Athey MR & MRS Preston G (Nancy H Marshall) CtCol'72.Gv.Md.Y'71 . . . . MISS Margaret G . . . . JUNIORS MR Clifford M	☎ (410) 363-7581 2707 Greenspring Valley Rd, Owings Mills, MD *21117*

Atkeson MISS Lindsay Wells (Mark G) . . . . Born at
Hartford, CT Aug 22'95
Atkeson MR & MRS Mark G (A Shannon Wells) Br'84.Y'86
Chengdu, Sichuan, China

Atkins MR & MRS James H (Kathleen L Wright) Ark'65.Ark'54
  ☎ (501) 663-6075 . . 42 Edgehill Rd, Little Rock, AR *72207*
Atkins MR & MRS Robert G (Bruce Wasley) Tufts'80.H.'78
  472 Bedford St, Concord, MA *01742*
Atkins MR & MRS Ronald R (Mary-Elizabeth Empringham)
  OWes'55.Dar.Pa'54.Cl'59
  ☎ (914) 234-7254 . . ''Hobby Hill Farm'' Mianus River Rd, Bedford,
  NY *10506*
Atkinson DR & MRS Basil E JR (Frances L Hall)
  TCU'46.A.SAus'52.TexSW'56
  ☎ (210) 822-6241 . . 7 Paddington Way, San Antonio, TX *78209*

Atkinson MR & MRS George B JR (Martha Vaughan) Wis'57.Ih.Duke'57	of 1225 Southwinds Blvd, Vero Beach, FL *32963*
MISS Susan S	
MR George B 3d	☎ (414) 275-3154 433 N Lake Shore Dv, Fontana, WI *53125*

Atkinson MRS Matthew S 3d (Leipold—Atkinson—Cromwell—
  Martha S Egerton) Elk.Ncd.
  ☎ (410) 323-5653 . . 6004 Roland Av, Baltimore, MD *21210-1112*
Atkinson MRS Wallace G (MacMillan—Elizabeth L Hoyt) . . . . Died at
  Wilmette, IL Apr 7'96
Atkinson MR Wallace G . . . . Died at
  Winnetka, IL Oct 17'94
Atlas MR Jeffrey L—Aht'79
  ☎ (415) 441-1075 . . 1075 Lombard St, San Francisco, CA *94109*
Atlas MR & MRS Martin (Liane R Wiener) V'43.Cos.Mt.Nu'34.Cl'35.Geo'44
  ☎ (202) 342-0919 . . 2254—48 St NW, Washington, DC *20007*
Atlee MRS Edward D (Elizabeth L Black)
  ☎ (610) 527-7837 . . 404 Cheswick Place, C11, Rosemont, PA *19010*

Atlee DR & MRS John L 3d (Barbara J Sanford) F&M'63.Temp'67	☎ (414) 538-4430 N 71 W 29436 Tamron Lane, Hartland, WI *53029*
MISS Sarah S	
JUNIORS MR John L	
Attaway MRS John R (Marguerite A Picolet d'Hermillon) Pa'55.Sg.	☎ (803) 769-6165 ''Hawkhurst'' Middleton Place, Ashley River Rd, Charleston, SC *29414*
MR Nicholas C	
Atterbury MRS Agnes W (Agnes L Wang) Franklin'70.Cl'72.BtP.	☎ (561) 820-9714 PO Box 2212, Palm Beach, FL *33480*
MISS Emily B—at Skidmore	
JUNIORS MISS Elizabeth S—at Hotchkiss	

Atterbury MR & MRS Boudinot P (Katharine T Talcott)
  Sth'51.Csn.P'47.Y'52
  ☎ (301) 657-1933 . . 7309 Brookville Rd, Chevy Chase, MD *20815*
Atterbury MRS Carsten S (Carsten W Sierck) . . . . name changed to Sierck
Atterbury MR & MRS George R (Isakson—Moira Mahony)
  Gm.Cry.Sa.Y'35.H'37
  ☎ (610) MU8-8779 . . 615 Newtown Rd, Villanova, PA *19085*
Atterbury MR Joseph R (late William Wallace) . . . . Married at
  Delray Beach, FL
  McLeod MRS E Bird (Elizabeth Bird) . . . . May 4'96

Atterbury MR & MRS R Rennie 3d (Lynda D Smith) Pa'60.Pa'63	315 W Crestwood Dv, Peoria, IL *61614*
MISS Kendall C B—MtH'93—at U of Va Grad .	

Atterbury MR S Ward—Y'89.Va'92
  ☎ (212) 988-2698 . . 171 E 84 St, Apt 12G, New York, NY *10028*

Atterbury, William W 3d & Redfield, Elizabeth C (Cowles—Elizabeth C Redfield) RISD'79.BtP. NCar'69	☎ (561) 848-4861 300 Queens Lane, Palm Beach, FL *33480*
JUNIORS MR Story A Cowles	

Atterbury MRS William Wallace (Dempsey—Virginia Gates) Rol'48
  ☎ (561) 287-4152 . . 13184 Gilson Rd, Palm City, FL *34990*

Atterbury-Jenney MRS Judy (Jenney—Judy Atterbury) Ws'46.Csn.	☎ (203) 966-4109 941 Silvermine Rd, New Canaan, CT *06840*
MR C Powers Jenney—Y'80— ☎ (203) 966-4203	
MISS Lucinda K Jenney (Swanger—Lucinda K Jenney)—at ☎ (213) 466-0184 2232 N Beachwood Dv, Apt 8, Hollywood, CA *90068*	

Attfield MISS Gillian—V'57.Cs.Cly.
  ☎ (212) 861-0477 . . 79 E 79 St, New York, NY *10021*

Attride MR & MRS Roy R B JR (M Helen Hayes) MaryW'66.An.NCar'64.SUNY'74	☎ (919) 870-7168 1717 Hunting Ridge Rd, Raleigh, NC *27615*
MR Roy R B 3d	
MR Thomas J H	

Atwell MR & MRS Anthony (Susan Lay) Wms'57.H'60
  ☎ (214) 526-3213 . . 4303 University Blvd, Dallas, TX *75205*
Atwell DR & MRS Robert B (Eleanor L Wenning) Fcg.Rr.Cr'50 . . of
  ☎ (412) 782-3458 . . 147 North Dv, Pittsburgh, PA *15238*
  ☎ (561) 231-1567 . . 300 Ocean Rd, John's Island, Vero Beach,
  FL *32963*

Atwell MR & MRS Robert F (Katherine P Schoedinger) Wheat'73.Dth'74	☎ (203) 259-1924 428 Galloping Hill Rd, Fairfield, CT *06430*
JUNIORS MR Christopher W	

Atwood MISS Emeline Noelle (William C) . . . . Born at
  Boston, MA May 7'96
Atwood MRS George B (Rebecca M Rood) Mo'34
  ☎ (314) 725-2692 . . 7520 Oxford Dv, St Louis, MO *63105*

Atwood MR & MRS J Baird (Shaw—Mavis Skeats) Edg.P'50	☎ (412) 741-6945 270 Grant St, Sewickley, PA *15143*
MR John B JR—at ☎ (412) 481-1157 2318 Jane St, Pittsburgh, PA *15143*	

Atwood MR & MRS John C 3d (Mary E Sanford) Sfy.Miami'57
  ☎ (415) 343-5498 . . 40 Knightwood Lane, Hillsborough, CA *94010*

Atwood MRS Philip Trowbridge (June D Beebe) Wa.	☎ (847) 251-9262 626 Warwick Rd, Kenilworth, IL *60043-1150*
MR James T—Pa'63—at 1408 Strand St, Manhattan Beach, CA *90266*	

Atwood MR & MRS William C (Elizabeth R Baker)
  U'84.H'89.H'95.BostColl'84.Cl'90
  ☎ (617) 696-6674 . . 46 Brandon Rd, Milton, MA *02186*
Atwood DR William G—H.'54
  ☎ (212) PL5-9246 . . 555 Park Av, New York, NY *10021*

Aubry MR & MRS Jules W (Moon—Julia D Andrus) Sth'37.Cs . . .of
☎ (212) AT9-4667 . . 17 E 89 St, New York, NY *10128*
☎ (203) 488-9623 . . 88 Notch Hill Rd, Apt 219, North Branford, CT *06471*

Auchincloss MR & MRS Blake L (Lauren S Moores) Buck'85.Wms'82
589 Main St, Hingham, MA *02043*

Auchincloss MR Conrad McI . . see H D Sedgwick

Auchincloss MR & MRS Douglas (Kelly—Larkin—Winston—Catherine M Hannon) K.Cly.Y'36 . . of
☎ (561) 546-0222 . . Box 308, 26 Gomez Rd, Hobe Sound, FL *33455*
☎ (212) 838-0800 . . 825 Fifth Av, New York, NY *10021*

Auchincloss MR Edgar S—Y'32
☎ (561) 746-0557 . . 100 Terrapin Trail, Jupiter, FL *33458-7722*

Auchincloss MR & MRS Edgar S 4th (Penelope A Clingman) Mariet'60 . . . . | ☎ (203) 263-4506
MR Leonard M . . . . | 185 Good Hill Rd,
MR Gordon B . . . . | Woodbury, CT *06798*

Auchincloss MR & MRS Edgar S 5th (Susan J Zeiss) RICol'84.RICol'85.Conn'86
☎ (860) 283-1186 . . 75 Newton Hill Rd, Northfield, CT *06778*

Auchincloss MR & MRS Edward H (Justine A Eaton) Bnd'54.Pr.Ln.Cs.Y'51.Cl'54
☎ (212) 744-5155 . . 25 East End Av, New York, NY *10028*

Auchincloss MRS Ellie (Lewis—Ellen Auchincloss) . | ☎ (203) 966-8964
MISS Catherine T Lewis . . . . | 242 Jelliff Mill Rd,
MISS Emily A Lewis . . . . | New Canaan, CT
MR George P Lewis . . . . | *06840*

Auchincloss MR & MRS Gordon 2d (Davis—R Anne Seminara) Syr'68.C.Y'39
☎ (212) 866-1811 . . 250 W 94 St, Apt 4F, New York, NY *10025*

Auchincloss MISS Hilary M . . see H D Sedgwick

Auchincloss DR & MRS Hugh (Katharine Lawrence Bundy) C.Csn.Y'38.Cl'42
☎ (201) 445-6147 . . 618 Warren Av, Ho Ho Kus, NJ *07423*

Auchincloss MR Hugh D 3d—Nrr.K.Mt.Srb.Y'50. | of ☎ (212)688-2470
Beirut'53.SalveR'88 . . . . | 200 E 66 St,
MISS Maya L—☎ (212) 750-8593 . . . . | New York, NY
MR Cecil L—B'gton'81 . . . . | *10021*
| ☎ (401) 846-0307
| ''The Castle''
| Hammersmith Farm,
| 203 Harrison Av,
| Newport, RI *02840*

Auchincloss MRS J Sibley (Jane H Sibley)
☎ (914) 677-3353 . . Woodstock Rd, Rte 3, Box 465, Millbrook, NY *12545*

Auchincloss MRS John W (Audrey Maynard) Cvc.Cly.Sl.
☎ (202) 338-1126 . . 2918 P St NW, Washington, DC *20007*

Auchincloss MR Louis S—C.Va'41 . . . . | of ☎ (212)FI8-3723
MR Andrew S—Y'86.V'89 . . . . | 1111 Park Av,
| New York, NY
| *10128*
| ☎ (914) 985-7588
| Claryville, NY
| *12725*

Auchincloss MRS Mary L (Mary Lober) . . . . | ☎ (610) 687-3233
MR Charles C 3d—at ☎ (610) 495-7871 | ''Deepdale Mews''
10 Hollow Rd, Kimberton, PA *19442* . . . . | 77 Deepdale Rd,
| Strafford, PA *19087*

Auchincloss MRS Patty M (Tirana—Patty M | ☎ (203) 637-5078
Auchincloss) Ws'61 . . . . | 319 Riverside Av,
MISS Elizabeth E Tirana . . . . | Riverside, CT *06878*

Auchincloss MR & MRS Philip S (Victoria C | ☎ (910) 722-2435
Sprague) Pg.Pa'63.Ch'73 . . . . | 2934 Buena Vista
MR William T—at ☎ (301) 984-7853 | Rd, Winston-Salem,
10827 Hampton Mill Terr, Apt 140, Rockville, | NC *27106*
MD *20852* . . . . |
JUNIORS MR Colin McK—at Woodberry Forest . . |

Auchincloss MRS Reginald L G JR (Frances D'Arcy) | ☎ (212) 688-0259
T.Cly. . . . . | 201 E 62 St,
MR Reginald L G 3d . . . . | New York, NY
| *10021*

Auchincloss MRS Richard S (Mary K Wainwright) | ☎ (610) 933-2575
Gm. . . . . | Box 516, Paoli, PA
MR Thomas F D . . . . | *19301*

Auchincloss MR & MRS Richard S JR (Mary M | ☎ (610) 688-7962
Rogers) Pa'71.Temp'74.Gm.Cc.Ac.Y.'64 . . . . . . | 121 Cornwall Lane,
MR Richard S 3d . . . . | St Davids, PA
| *19087*

Auchincloss MRS Samuel S (Lydia K Garrison)
☎ (941) 923-6020 . . 7979 S Tamiami Trail, Apt A113, Sarasota, FL *34231*

Auclair MR & MRS Nicholas C (Alison C Virgin) | ☎ (301) 870-4549
OState'81.OState'80.Philip'88 . . . . | 9570 Ironsides Rd,
JUNIORS MR Austin W . . . . | Nanjemoy, MD
| *20662*

Audrain MR & MRS Cecil R (Léontine Marié Toy) Ri.Ports'56
☎ (941) 377-6696 . . The Meadows, 5275 Myrtle Wood, Sarasota, FL *34235*

Auerbach MR & MRS Philip H (Ralston—Darlene | ☎ (630) 887-0594
McLachlan) Un.Cly.H'61 . . . . | 420 S County Line
MR Jonathan—at Princeton . . . . | Rd, Hinsdale, IL
MRS Philippe Berard (Auerbach—Frederica | *60521*
Stevens) Cly. . . . . |

Auersperg PRC Alexander & PRCSS (Nancy L Weinberg) Swb'81.Srb.Nrr.Ri.Br'82 . . of
829 Park Av, New York, NY *10021*
''Windswept'' 267 Harrison Av, Newport, RI *02840*

Auersperg MISS Anna Sharp (Alexander) . . . . Born Nov 17'95

Augsbury MR & MRS Frank A JR (Howard-Smith—Foster—Imogen R Snowden) USMMA'45 . . of
☎ (315) 393-0434 . . 7713 State H'way 68, Ogdensburg, NY *13669*
☎ (941) 262-1484 . . ''Duck Cottage'' 360 Bald Eagle Dv, Naples, FL *34105*

Augur MR & MRS Christopher W (Angela Wallace) | ☎ (520) 299-2953
Ariz'72. . . . . | 4560 Cerco Del
MISS Laura E . . . . | Corazon, Tucson,
| AZ *85718*

Augur MR & MRS Harrison H (Julia A Childs)
Bnd'69.Rcn.K.Y'64.Cl'67 . . . . ☎ (970) 925-4072
MR Avery H . . . . PO Box 4389,
JUNIORS MR Wheaton . . . . 1071 Willoughby
Way, Aspen, CO *81612*

Augur MRS Newell A (L Trimble Hoblitzelle) Cy.
☎ (314) 721-1699 . . 710 S Hanley Rd, St Louis, MO *63105*

Augustine MR & MRS Marlyn (Marguerite Leininger) Drake'44
☎ (602) 996-4164 . . 4139 E Beryl Av, Phoenix, AZ *85028*

Augustus MR & MRS Albert A 2d (Elizabeth C Hurlock) Kt.Pk.Un.Cv.
☎ (216) 942-4216 . . "Cobble Court" 9401 Hobart Rd, Waite Hill, Willoughby, OH *44094*

Auler MR & MRS Hugo Edwin (Susan Teeple) Tex'67.Tex'67.Tex'69
☎ (512) 476-3783 . . 1612 Watchhill Rd, Austin, TX *78703*

Aulisi MR & MRS Joseph E (Jill M Polacek)
Un.Rby.Srr. . . . . ☎ (518) 882-9736
MISS Pamela M—Wheat'88—at . . . . "Mavournin"
☎ (212) 956-1609 . . 305 W 52 St, New York, Box 189, Galway,
NY *10019* . . . . NY *12074*
MR Andrew C—Unn.Buck'90.Syr'92—at
☎ (415) 922-4541 . . 1623 Vallejo St,
San Francisco, CA *94123* . . . .

Ault MRS Bromwell (Allie Burchenal)
☎ (212) 249-6457 . . 1 E 66 St, New York, NY *10021*

Ault MR & MRS J Burchenal (Monks—Florence Hunter) C.Cly.Y'47
☎ (505) 455-2567 . . Rte 5, Box 253, Santa Fe, NM *87501*

Ault MR Lee A . . . . Died at
Locust Valley, NY Apr 7'96

Ault MRS Lee A (Laura H Leonard) Pr . . .of
☎ (212) 744-2949 . . 200 E 82 St, New York, NY *10028*
☎ (516) 671-9424 . . Feeks Lane, Locust Valley, NY *11560*

Austen MR David . . see MRS W C Peet

Austin MRS A Fleming (Angeline E Fleming)
☎ (609) 924-5012 . . "Eastfield" 27 North Rd, Princeton, NJ *08540*

Austin MRS Alexander G (Hilda L Lyon) . . . . ☎ (212) RE7-3517
MISS Barbara G L—Bm.Ne.—☎ (212) 772-1959 | 50 E 72 St,
New York, NY *10021*

Austin MISS Alexandra—V'91 . . see T Cohen

Austin MR & MRS Ben R (Gentry—Priscilla E Moerdyke)
Stan'38.Sth'41.Vh.Van'40 . . of
☎ (818) 795-2170 . . 1215 St Albans Rd, San Marino, CA *91108*
44049 Oran Court, Palm Desert, CA *92260*

Austin MR & MRS C Lee JR (McEvoy—McGleughlin | ☎ (212) 348-7200
—Diane Pollitz) Sth'51.H'53 . . . . | 145 E 92 St,
MISS Julie P McGleughlin—Hampshire'82—at | New York, NY
180 Pearl St, Cambridge, MA *02139* . . . . | *10128*

Austin MRS Charles Lee (Louise B Wilson)
☎ (508) 362-6066 . . PO Box 275, 65 Scudder Lane, Barnstable, MA *02630*

Austin MR & MRS Charles R (Katharine W Kales) | ☎ (603) 679-8627
Skd'60.Myf.Dar.Rens'55 . . . . | 37 Scrabble Rd,
MISS Elizabeth R—Keene'85 . . . . | Exeter, NH
MISS Sharon P—Bates'87—at Ft Collins, CO . . . | *03833-6023*

Austin MR & MRS F Reed JR (M Gordon Wasley)
Bost'77.D.Rc.Mid'75
☎ (508) 528-7042 . . 53 Noon Hill Av, Norfolk, MA *02056*

Austin MRS Francis R (Barbara K Hall) D . . .of
☎ (508) 785-0581 . . 118 Claybrook Rd, Dover, MA *02030*
☎ (508) 992-2559 . . Salters Point, South Dartmouth, MA *02748*

Austin BRIG GEN (RET) & MRS Frederick Victor (Odette E M d'A Jung)
USA.Y'28
☎ (914) 234-3311 . . Box 45, Bayberry Lane, Bedford, RD 2, Mt Kisco, NY *10549*

Austin MRS H Philips (Janet L Hays) Pa'49
☎ (610) 688-1017 . . 260 Iven Av, Apt 3B, St Davids, PA *19087*

Austin MRS Howard A (Mary V Snow) Sth'40.Bm.Ncd.
☎ (212) 750-3851 . . 200 E 66 St, New York, NY *10021*

Austin MR & MRS James E (Victoria C Kahn) NH'86.Ne'88.NH'84
☎ (603) 642-4958 . . 78 South Rd, Brentwood, NH *03833*

Austin MR & MRS James P 3d (Britt—A Tudor | ☎ (207) 439-0593
McBride) Ill'74.Coe'71.NIa'73 . . . . | "Phyllis Cove"
JUNIORS MISS Amanda L Walther . . . . | Lawrence Lane,
Box 278,
Kittery Point, ME
03905

Austin MISS Jeremy V W—Ncd.
☎ (212) 593-3062 . . 200 E 66 St, New York, NY *10021*

Austin DR & MRS John D (Mary Frances Delaney)
CalSt'57.Ill'94.ArizSt'50.Ind'56
☎ (602) 948-5422 . . 5901 E Red Wing Rd, Paradise Valley, AZ *85253*

Austin MR John F JR . . of
☎ (508) 548-6174 . . "Cedar Crest" 10 Lummis Lane, PO Box 408, West Falmouth, MA *02574*
☎ (808) 926-9989 . . "Diamond Head Vista" 2600 Pualani Way, Honolulu, HI *96815*

Austin MR & MRS Josiah T (Gordon—A Valer | ☎ (520) 824-3566
Clark) Md.DU'70 . . . . | El Coronado Ranch,
MISS Valerie A Gordon—at Harvard . . . . | Star Rte, Box 395,
MR Albert H Gordon 2d—at Vanderbilt . . . . . | Pearce, AZ *85625*

Austin MR & MRS Lawrence M (Elizabeth H Harrison) P'52
☎ (912) 354-6685 . . 201 Johnston St, Savannah, GA *31405*

Austin MRS Oliver L JR (Rich—Edythe A Parsons) BMr'27.GeoW'64
☎ (202) 237-7048 . . 5420 Connecticut Av NW, Washington, DC *20015*

Austin MR & MRS Peter S (Cathleen H M Nimick) Pg.Rr.Ken'82.Pitt'91
☎ (412) 422-5657 . . 5700 Fair Oaks St, Pittsburgh, PA *15217*

Austin MR & MRS Stephen D W (Linda P Garvin) | ☎ (508) 428-0288
⛵ . . . . | 12 Quail Rd,
MISS Sarah R—at Wheaton . . . . | Osterville, MA
JUNIORS MISS Emily B P . . . . | *02655*
JUNIORS MR Stephen D—at Proctor Acad

Austin MRS William Mason (Mitchell—Ruth | ☎ (207) 374-2467
Kieser) D.H'25 . . . . | PO Box 415,
MISS Francesca Mitchell . . . . | Water St,
MR Henry B Mitchell 3d—at | Blue Hill, ME
20 Sunnyside Av, Apt A353, Mill Valley, CA | *04614*
94941-1928 . . . . |
MR Edward B Mitchell—at Istanbul, Turkey .

Austin MRS Wright (Frances P Wright) Ncd.
☎ (207) 439-3832 . . 4 Tenney Hill, Box 275, Kittery Point, ME *03905*

Auten MR & MRS David C (Suzanne C Plowman) Denis'64.Pe.Ph.R.Fst.Ac.Sdg.Pa'60.Pa'63 . . . . . ☎ (215) 627-2535 120 Delancey St, Philadelphia, PA *19106*
MISS Anne C—at 850 W Newport Av, Apt 3W, Chicago, IL *60657* . . . .
MISS Meredith S . . . .

Au Werter MRS Jay Pearce (Ida Armstrong) It.Kt.
☎ (216) 464-1111 . . 2767 Inverness Rd, Shaker Heights, OH *44122*

Avant MR & MRS Grady JR (Katherine Yancey) Hlns'61.K.Mt.P'54.H'60 . . . . ☎ (313) 886-6264 406 Lincoln Rd, Grosse Pointe, MI *48230*
MISS Mary W Y
MR Grady M—at 347 W 39 St, New York, NY *10018* . . . .

Avegno MRS Beauregard B (Jacqueline Provosty) . . ☎ (504) 899-6192 901 State St, New Orleans, LA *70118*
MISS Micheline P B . . . .

Avenali MR & MRS Peter (Joan Ehrman) Cal'39.H'41 ☎ (415) 771-7299 1100 Union St, San Francisco, CA *94109*
MR Peter J . . . .
MR Michael C . . . .

Averell MR John B . . see H Meigs

Averill MRS John B (A Louise Eggleston) Sth'42
☎ (610) 527-9098 . . Beaumont 123, 74 Pasture Lane, Bryn Mawr, PA *19010*

Avery MR David A—WOnt'51
☎ (519) 426-1413 . . RR 2, Simcoe, Ontario N3Y 4K1, Canada

Avery MR & MRS Frederick L (Mary L Williams) Rens'32 . . . . ☎ (716) 632-1015 64 Garrison Rd, Williamsville, NY *14221*
MISS Mary Ann . . . .

Avery MISS Jillian F (David A) . . . . Married at Boston, MA
Maver MR John J JR (John J) . . . . Sep 7'96

Avery MRS Victoria J (Victoria J Jelke) Nw'60.Srb.Il. ⚓ . . . . ☎ (617) 235-6340 37 Carisbrooke Rd, Wellesley Hills, MA *02181*
MISS Alexandra F—Bates'93—at
☎ (207) 871-8699 . . 113 Vaughan St, Apt 6, Portland, ME *04102* . . . .
MISS Elizabeth A—at Colgate . . . .
MR Christopher A—at New England Conservatory

Axton MRS Florence G (Florence M Gotthelf)
☎ (303) 722-2909 . . Polo Club 701, 3131 E Alameda Av, Denver, CO *80209-3411*

Aydelotte MRS William O (Myrtle E Kitchell) Minn'39.Minn'47.Minn'55.C . . .of
☎ (319) 338-1791 . . 308 Montclair Park, 201 N First Av, Iowa City, IA *52245*
☎ (860) 443-7123 . . 149 Oswegatchie Rd, Waterford, CT *06385*

Aye HON Lobsang N & LADY (Phillips—Jane B Werner) . . of
☎ (212) 989-1829 . . 61 Grove St, New York, NY *10014*
☎ (518) 239-4717 . . ''Kailash House'' Travis Hill Rd, Preston Hollow, NY *12469*

Ayer MR & MRS Anthony J (Larsson—Nancy Sumwalt) Fla'64.Cr'60
☎ (809) 772-1026 . . 4 Estate Mt Washington, Frederiksted, St Croix, VI *00840*

Ayer MISS Constance . . see MRS J W Harris

Ayer MRS Frederick JR (Anne Moody)
☎ (508) 468-2944 . . PO Box 2577, South Hamilton, MA *01982-2577*

Ayer MR Frederick B . . see MRS J W Harris

Ayer MRS Hilda R (King—Curtis—Hilda R Ayer) . . . . Married at Gloucester, MA
Anderson MR Paul G (late Gerard R) . . . . Mch 15'96

Ayer MR James C (Frederick 2d) . . Married at Frederiksted, St Croix, VI
Van Wyck MRS Elizabeth T (Elizabeth Tyler) . . . . Aug 18'96

Ayer MR & MRS James C (Van Wyck—Elizabeth Tyler) Ey.Y'59 ⚓
☎ (617) 639-8162 . . 6 Ballast Lane, Marblehead, MA *01945*

Ayer MR Peter E—Mid'84.Cl'89
☎ (617) 639-8655 . . 0 Mariners Lane, Marblehead, MA *01945*

Ayers MRS Aileen B (Van der Las—Aileen A Bruch) . . . . ☎ (954) 764-4124 333 Sunset Dv, Apt 103, Ft Lauderdale, FL *33301*
MR Joseph B 3d—at ☎ (216) 397-0706
2915 Fairfax Rd, Cleveland Heights, OH *44118* .

Ayers MR & MRS David W P (Elizabeth M Vessels) StMWds'60.NotreD'58 . . . . ☎ (303) 688-3487 ''Ayrshire'' PO Box 9, Franktown, CO *80116*
MISS E Victoria M—Denis'86—at
☎ (212) 721-5178 . . 210 W 89 St, New York, NY *10024* . . . .
MR David F P 2d—Ariz'89—at
☎ (970) 949-5033 . . PO Box 251, Beaver Creek, Avon, CO *81620*

Ayers MR & MRS Nathan M (Frazier—Florence F Hyde) Mo'48.BtP.Evg.Rr.Cly.Ncd.Cda.GaTech'29 . . of
☎ (561) 833-0613 . . 369 S Lake Dv, Palm Beach, FL *33480*
☎ (910) 545-0740 . . 4100 Well Spring Dv, Apt 1203, Greensboro, NC *27410*

Aylward MRS Theodore C (Hoodless—Hamilton—Jane Buckman) An.Me.Gm.Ny.Ac.W.Ncd.Dll.
☎ (610) 642-8617 . . 100 Grays Lane, Haverford, PA *19041*

Ayres MR H Fairfax 3d—Nw'88.Va'96 . . see MRS F L Johnson

Ayres MR Henry F JR—Ll.Cw.Rv.Wt.
☎ (203) 869-8310 . . 521 Riversville Rd, Greenwich, CT *06831*

Ayres MR & MRS Richard E (Symington—Merribel S Levis) BMr'72.Dub'73.P'64.Y'69 . . . . ☎ (202) 966-4668 3040 Foxhall Rd NW, Washington, DC *20016*
MISS Alice E H—P'95—at Peizheng School, 2 Peizheng Rd, Dongshan, Guangzhou 510080, China . . . .
JUNIORS MR Richard A—at Landon . . . .

Azoy MR & MRS Philip L (Elizabeth M Fowler) Sth'42.Nu'53.Mg.Ny.Lm.Cw.StA.Cda.P'45. Nu'57 . . . . ☎ (201) 539-5283 PO Box 1044, Morristown, NJ *07962-1044*
MISS Katrina de P . . . .

B

Babcock MR & MRS Charles D (Sara Haigler) Ala'58.Kas'51 . . . . ☎ (334) 265-5885 3240 Warrenton Rd, Montgomery, AL *36111*
MR Robert H . . . .

Babcock MR & MRS Fred C (Marion R Barnes) MtH'36.Fcg.Dth'36
☎ (412) 781-2431 . . 22 Edgewood Rd, Pittsburgh, PA *15215*

Babcock MR & MRS Henry D JR (James—Erica Hohner) Y'62.Cl'70 . . . . of ☎ (516)367-3268 48 Snake Hill Rd, Cold Spring Harbor, NY *11724*
MISS K Chauncey—Y'94—at ☎ (415) 282-7421 1140 Sanchez St, Apt 1, San Francisco, CA *94114* . . . . ☎ (307) 739-9230 755 N Bar Y Rd, Jackson, WY *83001*
MISS Laura S—at ☎ (303) 447-0353 4133 Sunrise Court, Boulder, CO *80304* . . . . . .

Babcock MR & MRS Hugh H (Marion Somerville) H'35
☎ (941) 676-2211 . . Mountain Lake, Lake Wales, FL *33859-0832*

Babcock MR & MRS John B (Mary L D Scheerer) Y.'50
RD 2, Box 79A, Stanfordville, NY *12581*

Babcock MR & MRS Orville Elias 3d (Judith I Jones) Col'60.On.LakeF'64 . . . . ☎ (860) 395-0137 19 Otter Brook Dv, Old Saybrook, CT *06475-4313*
MISS Alison Ely—StLaw'93 . . . .

Babcock MRS Richard F (Gibb—Martha C Pease) Pr.Cda.
☎ (516) 676-3595 . . Piping Rock Rd, Locust Valley, NY *11560*

Babcock MISS Susan C—Cly.
☎ (540) 675-3406 . . "Delamore" Box 88, Washington, VA *22747*

Babcock MR & MRS William G (Sheila Watson)
☎ (334) 264-0808 . . 1703 Gillespie Dv, Montgomery, AL *36106*

Babcock MR & MRS William N (Victoria M Plimpton) Ws'78.Pqt.Ncd.H'78.Cl'80 . . . . ☎ (603) 673-0100 80 Mack Hill Rd, Amherst, NH *03031*
JUNIORS MR Charles N . . . .

Babson MR & MRS Sanford G (Becky Merkel) Hlns'62.Col'62
☎ (602) 956-2856 . . 2511 E Luke Av, Phoenix, AZ *85016*

Baccile MR & MRS Peter E (Katherine M King) Dth'86.Fic.Cr'84.Duke'86
☎ (203) 869-5677 . . "Beaurivage" 73 Burning Tree Rd, Greenwich, CT *06830*

Bacharach MR & MRS Richard S (Marylee Matthews) . . . . ☎ (246) 423-2353 Byde Mill, St George, Barbados
MISS Hillary McC . . . .
MR W Nicoll . . . .

Bachman MR & MRS Roger A (Evelyn M MacVeagh) Y'45w
☎ (503) 223-9796 . . 4436 SW Warrens Way, Portland, OR *97221*

Backerman MR & MRS Millard M (Lurie—Renée C Murphy) Nd.Wash'60.Nu'62 . . . . ☎ (314) 721-6446 801 S Skinker Blvd, Apt 8A, St Louis, MO *63105*
MR Elliot L—Van'89 . . . .
MR Steven R—Mich'93 . . . .
MISS Renée C Lurie—StL'89 . . . .
MISS Katherine C Lurie—Bost'91 . . . .

Bacon MISS Amy G—Cal'95 . . see MRS L P Fullerton

Bacon MR & MRS Benjamin W (Marjorie S Mackey) Y'53 . . . . ☎ (203) 637-3327 58 Winthrop Dv, Riverside, CT *06878*
MR Benjamin S—at RD 3, Box 513, Red Hook, NY *12571* . . . .
MR David M—at 67 Old Rd, Westport, CT *06880*

Bacon MISS Charlotte M (James E) . . . . Married at Franconia, NH
Choyt MR Brad W . . . . Jun 22'96

Bacon MR Daniel C—Pa'68
☎ (508) 927-3106 . . 60 Rantoul St, Apt 615N, Beverly, MA *01915*

Bacon MR J Nicholas . . see H F Kean

Bacon MR & MRS Louis Moore (Cynthia I Pigott) Colby'79.Unn.Cly.Cda.Mid'79.Cl'81 . . of
"Fairholme" 44 Mayo Av, Greenwich, CT *06830*
"Point House" Lyford Cay, Nassau, Bahamas

Bacon MR & MRS Peter A (Evalyn B Lee) S.Ox'85
☎ (212) 255-6917 . . 455 W 24 St, New York, NY *10011*

Bacon MR & MRS Robert H JR (Moore—Juliette W Fentress) Ill'52 . . of
☎ (847) 446-0944 . . 44 Locust Rd, Winnetka, IL *60093*
☎ (011-44-171) 584-8350 . . "Locust House" 22 Montpelier Walk, London SW7, England

Bacon MR Russell N . . see MRS L P Fullerton

Bacon MRS Susan M (Susan Makrianes) Ariz'76
☎ (508) 927-5281 . . 5 Chubb's Brook Lane, Beverly Farms, MA *01915*

Bacon MR & MRS Varick McN (Mary J Lenihan) H'55
☎ (212) 879-6392 . . 333 E 69 St, TH-1, New York, NY *10021*

Bacon MRS William Benjamin (Katharine Weld) My.
☎ (508) 922-5330 . . 16 Bay View Av, Beverly, MA *01915*

Bacon MR & MRS William T JR (Margaret L Hoyt) Cho.On.Sr.Ih.Yn.Y'45 . . . . ☎ (847) 234-4441 184 E Winthrop Lane, Lake Forest, IL *60045*
MR Hoyt W—at ☎ (714) 497-1777 1514 Skyline Dv, Laguna Beach, CA *92651* . . .
MR Christopher S . . . .

Baddour MISS Cynthia A . . see C Ryan

Baddour MR & MRS Frederick R (Annette M Casuso-Dons) Syr'78.UMiami'83
8600 SW 86 Av, Miami, FL *33143*

Baddour MR & MRS Raymond F (Anne M Bridge) Sb.Dar.NotreD'45.Mit'50.Mit'51
☎ (617) 484-9591 . . 96 Fletcher Rd, Belmont, MA *02178*

Badenhausen MR & MRS Bayard (Cintra Morgan) Pa'42 . . . . ☎ (914) 835-4233 96 Glen Oaks Dv, Rye, NY *10580-1224*
MISS Cintra H . . . .
MR Morgan . . . .

Bader MR & MRS William B (Gretta M Lange) Pom'53.Cos.Pom'53.P'60.P'64
☎ (703) 836-1662 . . 217 Gibbon St, Alexandria, VA *22314*

Badger MR & MRS Daniel B (Mariette S Arguimbau) Y'37
☎ (203) 869-4623 . . 235 N Maple Av, Greenwich, CT *06830*

Badger REV & MRS Edwin Hunt JR (Virginia A Curtis) Kent'69.Ch'40.SeabTheo'50.Ind'69
☎ (614) 772-4398 . . Governor's Place, 263 Constitution Dv, Chillicothe, OH *45601-2120*

Badger MRS Frances (Reichmann—Schofield—Frances S Badger) ArtInst'49
☎ (312) 787-8051 . . Atrium Village Apt 421, 300 W Hill St, Chicago, IL *60610*

Badger MRS Helen W (Helen F Webster) . . . . ☎ (717) 564-9086 1309 Hamilton Circle, Harrisburg, PA *17111*
MR Mark C . . . .

Badger MR & MRS Samuel C JR (Brooke S Babcock)
☎ (919) 852-4156 . . 305 Palace Green, Cary, NC *27511*

Badger MRS Theodore L (Alice Wetherbee) Ncd.Myf.
The Arbors, 52 Harbor Rd, Shelburne, VT *05482*

Badger MR & MRS Vincent M (Jennifer Beard) LakeF'70.Y.'66.Ch'71
☎ (212) 737-3442 . . 210 E 73 St, New York, NY *10021*

Badman MR & MRS John 3d (Katherine Ballantine) Gchr'77.Md'81.Cw.Myf.Ne.Cly.Ncd.Yn.Y'66.Y'69.Y'71
☎ (203) 629-1158 . . 20 Mackenzie Glen, Greenwich, CT *06830*

Baehr MR & MRS M R E Theodore (Liliana Milani)
Rice'69.Rice'71.S.Dth'69.Nu'72 . . of
☎ (404) 364-9697 . . 2876 Mabry Rd NE, Atlanta, GA *30319*
☎ (706) 268-3558 . . "Intermezzo" 478A Chestnut Rise, Big Canoe,
GA *30143*
Baena MR Christopher C—Ty'93 . . see C C Hart
Baena MISS Elizabeth A—Col'95 . . see C C Hart
Baer MR & MRS Gordon R JR (Nancarrow—Elisabeth | ☎ (410) 820-8420
L Myers) Va'58.Sg.Leh'50 ⚓ . . . . | "Galleon's Lap"
   MISS Melissa A Nancarrow—PineM'91—at | 27013 Bunny Lane,
   ☎ (617) 271-9865 . . 90 North Rd, Bedford, | Easton, MD *21601*
   MA *01730* . . . . |
   MR John William Nancarrow—HWSth'85—at |
   9302 Glenville Rd, Silver Spring, MD *20901* . |
Baer MR Gregory H—Alleg'88
1758 First Av, Apt 8, New York, NY *10128-5915*
Baer MR & MRS Richard H (Silvia M Sager) | ☎ (716) 834-1164
Cy.G.Norw'39 . . . . | 58 Ruskin Rd,
   MISS Silvia M . . . . | Eggertsville, NY
   MR Richard H JR . . . . | *14226*
   MR Jay T 2d . . . . | Jan 1 . .
    | ☎ (561) 229-6078
    | 8800 S Ocean Dv,
    | Hutchinson Island,
    | FL *34957*
Baer MR & MRS Theodore C 3d (Laurie B Diekmann) OWes'83.OWes'84
☎ (201) 963-7807 . . 721 Garden St, Hoboken, NJ *07030*
Baer MR & MRS William G 2d (Sherrerd—Gay B | ☎ (610) 651-2924
Windisch) Gm.Me.H'46 . . . . | 146 Tannery Run
   MR William G 3d—at 453 Tuckerman Av, | Circle, Berwyn, PA
   Middletown, RI *02842* . . . . | *19312*
Baetjer MR George V H—JHop'76.Reed'78
☎ (503) 636-7726 . . 99 Berwick Rd, Lake Oswego, OR *97034*
Baetjer MR & MRS Harry N 3d (Caryl J Michenfelder) Gv.Ty'70
Spring House Way, Unionville, PA *19375*
Bafford MR & MRS Joseph E (Margaret A Brand) | ☎ (212) BU8-1953
Cly.Ncd.NCar'55.Pa'57 . . . . | 117 E 72 St,
   MISS M Angeline B . . . . | New York, NY
   MR J Edmonds JR . . . . | *10021*
Bagley MRS Henry W (Frelinghuysen—Carey—Anya Smolianinoff) . . of
☎ (561) 832-6212 . . 142 Casa Bendita, Palm Beach, FL *33480*
☎ (212) TE8-0800 . . 825 Fifth Av, New York, NY *10021*
☎ (011-33-1) 42-60-19-51 . . 6 rue de Mondovi, 75001 Paris, France
Bahlman MR & MRS Baker DeC (Patricia C Wagner) Hlns'85.Denis'82
☎ (513) 231-7915 . . 968 Eversole Rd, Cincinnati, OH *45230*
Bahlman MR & MRS William Thorne JR (Nancy W DeCamp) Y'41
☎ (513) 321-5796 . . 1211 Hidden Wood Place, Cincinnati, OH *45208*
Bahlman MR & MRS William Ward (Sarah N Allyn) Ty'81.W'minster'76
☎ (513) 871-9081 . . 1283 Michigan Av, Cincinnati, OH *45208*
Bailey MR & MRS Charles W (Katharine M Palmer) | ☎ (617) 251-9161
H'34 . . . . | 10 Longwood Dv,
   MISS Katharine P—at 1541 Cambridge St, | Apt 132, Westwood,
   Cambridge, MA *02139* . . . . | MA *02090*

Bailey MR & MRS Charles W JR (Ann H Taliaferro) | ☎ (540) 885-8406
Sth'76.Cl'69 . . . . | "Springfield"
   JUNIORS MR C Taliaferro . . . . | Rte 1, Box 251,
   JUNIORS MR George H F . . . . | Mt Sidney, VA
    | *24467*
Bailey MISS Elizabeth S (James P JR) . . . . Married at Manassas, VA
   Slack MR Kevin T . . . . Mch 23'96
Bailey MRS Frederick Randolph (Constance F Gibboney) V'31 . . of
☎ (860) 435-9651 . . "Coole Rise" Box 382, Salisbury, CT *06068*
☎ (212) 879-2864 . . 120 E 79 St, New York, NY *10021*
Bailey MR & MRS Glenn W (Cornelia L Tarrant)
Ws'51.Plg.Cly.Wis'46.H.'51 . . of
☎ (561) 546-0260 . . 14 Bassett Creek Trail N, Hobe Sound, FL *33455*
☎ (212) 688-2634 . . 200 E 66 St, New York, NY *10021*
Bailey MR & MRS H Louis 2d (Truesdale— | ☎ (617) 232-1747
Antoinette E Russell) Sim'77.Cy.H'66 . . . . | 14 Hawthorn Rd,
   JUNIORS MISS Sintra R . . . . | Brookline, MA
    | *02146*
Bailey MRS Harwood (Esther Hill)
☎ (617) 834-4017 . . 4 Damon's Point Dv, PO Box 95, Marshfield Hills,
MA *02051*
Bailey MR & MRS Henry R (Nancy S Snow) Cw.
☎ (617) 333-0190 . . 1374 Canton Av, Milton, MA *02186*
Bailey MRS Horace C (Gardner—Gerry—Harriet B Wells) Pr.Fic.Cly.H.
☎ (516) 676-8881 . . 88 Town Cocks Lane, Locust Valley, NY *11560*
Bailey MR Irving W 2d (late Harwood) . . Married at Pee Wee Valley, KY
   Receveur MRS C Todd (Catherine Todd) . . . . Dec 9'95
Bailey MR & MRS James P JR (Elizabeth F McKenzie) Penn'59.Miss'61
☎ (703) 250-8579 . . 11128 Clara Barton Dv, Fairfax Station, VA *22039*
Bailey MR & MRS Omar (Bertinia Hallowell)
MtH'49.Temp'69.Nova'88.Hav'49 . . of
☎ (610) 436-6763 . . 670 Heatheron Lane, West Chester, PA *19380*
"Beaver Camp" Covey Rd, Big Moose Lake, Eagle Bay, NY *13331*
Bailey MISS Rebecca F . . see I H Chase
Bailey MR & MRS Samuel JR (Janet E Gaw) | ☎ (860) 677-1115
NH'67.Ny.Nyc.Ty'62 ⚓ . . . . | 211 Mountain
   JUNIORS MR David P—at Salisbury . . . . | Spring Rd,
   JUNIORS MR John S W—at St Paul's . . . . | Farmington, CT
    | *06032*
Bailey MR & MRS Vincent R (Kelley—Jennifer de B Turner) H'40
☎ (561) 833-8155 . . 115 Edmor Rd, West Palm Beach, FL *33405*
Bailey MR & MRS William P D (Madeleine H Reilly) | ☎ (212) RE4-3716
C.H.'46 . . . . | 501 E 87 St,
   MR William P R . . . . | New York, NY
    | *10128*
Baillière MR & MRS Thomas H G JR (Anne J | ☎ (410) 435-8789
Dobbin) BMr'63.Md'88.Elk.Md.Mv.Wms'61 | 913 Poplar Hill Rd,
⚓ | Baltimore, MD
   MISS Elisabeth J—H'89.Nw'94—at | *21210*
   2755 Franklin St, Apt 11, San Francisco, CA |
   94123 . . . . |
   MISS Alexandra R—Duke'92—at 1660 Mason St, |
   Apt 1, San Francisco, CA *94115* . . . . |
Baily MR & MRS O Lippincott (Joan Petzhold) Sth'56.Y'51
☎ (513) 321-3573 . . 6 Grandin Lane, Cincinnati, OH *45208*

Baily MRS V Montgomery (Virginia L Montgomery) ☎ (610) 286-5168
Sfh. . . . . "Cumbrae" RD 2,
  MISS Carol L—at ☎ (610) 469-6763 Elverson, PA *19520*
  Carriage House, RD 2, Pottstown, PA *19464* . . .
  MR H Paul . . . .

Bain MR Donald K—Y'57.H'61
  1177 Race St, Denver, CO *80206*

Bainbridge MRS Anne M (Anne C Mountcastle) ☎ (410) 366-3789
JHop'72.Mv. . . . . 204 Ridgewood Rd,
  MR George P—at Hampden-Sydney . . . . Baltimore, MD
  JUNIORS MISS Julia V *21210*
  JUNIORS MR R Garrett—at U of Rochester . . . . . .
  JUNIORS MR Clayton M . . . .

Bainbridge MR & MRS Frank M (Philippa H McClellan) Gchr'60.Ala'54
  ☎ (205) 871-9360 . . 18 Club View Dv, Birmingham, AL *35223*

Bainbridge MR John S JR—Elk.Cl'72
  ☎ (410) 329-1914 . . 1914 Geist Rd, Glyndon, MD *21071*

Bainbridge MR & MRS John Seaman (Chu—Elizabeth Kung-Ji Liu)
BMr'52.Fw.Rv.Hn.H'38.Cl'41
  ☎ (610) 388-2530 . . 17 Ringfield Rd, Chadds Ford, PA *19317*

Bainbridge MR & MRS Robert P (Mary Hastings) Cy.San.Chi.Ty'37
  ☎ (617) 232-7930 . . 68 Fairgreen Place, Chestnut Hill, MA *02167*

Baines MR & MRS Robert A (Ann M Armstrong)
Colby'88.Duke'90.Rm'88.Duke'89
  ☎ (610) 273-2868 . . 235 Hill Rd, Honey Brook, PA *19344*

Bair MRS John C (Marjoribanks—A Elizabeth Morris) V'33.Ht.
  ☎ (212) 988-6765 . . 785 Park Av, New York, NY *10021*

Baird MISS Abi A . . of
  ☎ (908) 899-9296 . . PO Box 831, Mantoloking, NJ *08738*
  Belle Alto, El Capistrano Apdo 6, Nerja, 29780 Malaga, Spain

Baird MRS Charles 3d (Lynn—Evelyn A Adamson)
  "Laurel Hill" PO Box 992, Middleburg, VA *20118*

Baird MR Gordon A—Tr.Ub.Ht.Cw.Emory'90
  ☎ (617) 367-4599 . . 99½ Myrtle St, Apt 5, Boston, MA *02114*

Baird MR & MRS Gordon P (Sarah B Fay) SL'47.Sm.H.'46
  ☎ (617) 259-9114 . . 331 Hemlock Circle, Lincoln, MA *01773*

Baird MR Harrison—Va'51
  ☎ (540) 364-1008 . . 3370 Whiting Rd, Marshall, VA *20115*

Baird MRS Jackson T (Rose Castor)
  ☎ (415) 567-9424 . . 2190 Washington St, Apt 503, San Francisco,
  CA *94109*

Baird MR & MRS John A JR (Emmons—Mary Clare Austin)
Me.Pe.An.Fw.Cc.Cw.Ll.Rv.Cspa.Ac.P'40
  ☎ (610) 642-2729 . . 108 Sunset Lane, Haverford, PA *19041*

Baird MRS Linda W (Curry—Livingston—Linda W Baird)
Col'69.H'mannMed'87.W.Cda.
  ☎ (303) 443-8020 . . 2081 Evergreen Av, Boulder, CO *80304*

Baird MR & MRS Matthew 2d (Elizabeth A Butcher)
Pa'88.Me.Rv.P'87.Cl'92
  ☎ (212) 219-8549 . . 50 White St, New York, NY *10013*

Baird MR & MRS Richard L (Hildegarde Gerstberger) D.Cw.Ht.Hb.Yn.Y'48
  ☎ (802) 253-9207 . . Chiridon House, 169 Upper Baird Rd, Stowe,
  VT *05672*

Baird MRS Samuel B D (Marjorie Y Battles) V'49.Bost'74.Me.
  ☎ (610) 964-8395 . . 215 Atlee Rd, Wayne, PA *19087*

Baise MR & MRS Craig Callen (Cynthia Ann Hart) ☎ (310) 454-0743
Stan'67.Stan'67 548 Alma Real Dv,
  MR Brian C . . . . Pacific Palisades,
  MR Christopher C . . . . CA *90272*
  JUNIORS MISS Susan E . . . .

Baker MR & MRS Alan G JR (Diana E Harbage) Cl'50.Lm.Snc.Cl'47.Cl'51
  ☎ (203) 966-8556 . . 120 Old Stamford Rd, New Canaan, CT *06840*

Baker MISS Alice W—Colg'88
  ☎ (212) 570-4507 . . 231 E 76 St, New York, NY *10021*

Baker MR & MRS Anthony K (Carol V Oelsner)
Wheat'81.Ck.Pr.B.Ny.S.BtP.Cly.Ty'67 ⚓
  ☎ (561) 655-9292 . . 150 Clarke Av, Palm Beach, FL *33480*

Baker MR & MRS Ashton H (Helen-Lucy Nichols) . . ☎ (401) 783-3861
  MR Ashton H JR . . . . 33 Harvey Lane,
  MR Reginald D . . . . Whale Rock Point,
  MR Giles B . . . . Narragansett, RI
  02882

Baker DR & MRS Benjamin M (Julia S Clayton)
V'38.Va'44.GeoW'77.Md.Elk.Rr.Mv.Va'22.Ox'24. JHop'27
  ☎ (410) 377-9469 . . 7332 Brightside Rd, Baltimore, MD *21212*

Baker MR & MRS Benjamin M 3d (Laura L Kautz)
Briar'70.Pqt.Ny.H'72.Y'76 ⚓
  ☎ (203) 259-1123 . . 174 Old South Rd, Southport, CT *06490*

Baker MR Brinton E—Tufts'78.H'83
  ☎ (415) 345-9422 . . 1153 Foster City Blvd, Apt 4, Foster City,
  CA *94404*

Baker MISS Carmen M . . see MISS P Martinez

Baker MISS Casey E . . see MISS P Martinez

Baker MR & MRS (REV) Crowell (Edyth E Knapp) ☎ (516) 569-4347
Bnd'55.Gen'lTheo'89.Chr.Plg.StJ.P'52.H'57 . . . 73 Park Row,
  MR L Crowell . . . . Lawrence, NY
  11559

Baker MR & MRS Danford M (Margaret J Shearer) ☎ (818) 799-7505
Scripps'65.Vh.Clare'65 . . . . 744 Plymouth Rd,
  MISS Catherine C . . . . San Marino, CA
  MISS Melinda S *91108-1745*
  MISS Karolyn S . . . .

Baker MR & MRS Daniel (Patricia A Grotz) ☎ (410) 828-6557
Elk.Mv.P'52 . . . . 1012 Cloverlea Rd,
  MISS Helen E . . . . Ruxton, MD *21204*
  MR John Daniel . . . .

Baker MR David A . . see T C Swett

Baker MRS David S JR (Ethel Prosser)
  ☎ (203) TO9-5327 . . 32 French Rd, Greenwich, CT *06831*

Baker MR & MRS E Bloxom 3d (Nancy H Rogers) ☎ (609) 924-8577
P'68 . . . . 65 Elm Rd,
  MR Charles W . . . . Princeton, NJ
  MR Henry H *08540-2524*
  JUNIORS MR Peter S . . . . MR absent

Baker MISS Elizabeth V (Danford M) . . . . Married at Pasadena, CA
  Halden MR Daniel A (Frank) . . . . Aug 6'94

Baker DR & MRS Francis F (Ruth M Vallee) Ham'36.Roch'41
  438 NW 48 Blvd, Gainesville, FL *32607*

Baker MR George D—Pr.Pa'68 . . . . 921 Ripley Lane,
  JUNIORS MISS Jennifer M . . . . Oyster Bay, NY
  11771

Baker MR George F—Ri.Rc.B.Ny.H'61
245 E 63 St, New York, NY *10021*

Baker DR & MRS George P JR (Katharine H Elliott) Cy.Cc.H'53
☎ (617) 566-0714 . . 29 Edgehill Rd, Brookline, MA *02146*

Baker MRS Gordon McA (Gordon McAllen)
Colby'53 . . . . | ☎ (503) 295-2446
MISS Hannah W—at Altoona, PA . . . . | 2950 SW
MR Joshua H . . . . | Bennington Dv,
| Portland, OR *97201*

Baker MR & MRS Harold d'O (Little—Nancy Stevenson)
Rc.Nrr.Plg.Cly.H'42.Cl'45
☎ (212) 879-1044 . . 150 E 73 St, New York, NY *10021*

Baker MR Harold W 3d—Me.
☎ (610) 687-9822 . . 725 Newtown Rd, Villanova, PA *19085*

Baker MRS Harry L (Virginia J Boardman) Tcy.Ncd.
☎ (415) 567-0315 . . 1400 Geary Blvd, Apt 1609, San Francisco,
CA *94109*

Baker MRS Henry S (Frances I Robinson)
☎ (410) 377-4378 . . Roland Park Place, 830 W 40 St, Baltimore,
MD *21211*

Baker MR & MRS Hollis MacL (Betsy J Brown)
B.Ri.L.BtP.Evg.DelB.Ny.Sar.Cly.Va'39 ⚓
☎ (561) 835-0010 . . Kirkland House 2C, 101 Worth Av, Palm Beach,
FL *33480*

Baker MR & MRS James F (Higbie—Julie B Ketting) | ☎ (941) 495-7859
MR Adam . . . . | 24891 Goldcrest Dv,
| Bonita Springs, FL
| *33923*

Baker MR James M—H'90.Camb'93 . . see C F Damon JR

Baker MRS Jesse H (Elizabeth L George)
Sherwood Oaks, 100 Norman Dv, Cranberry Township, PA *16066*

Baker MRS John Ezra (Buchbinder—Dudley Winston)
Apdo 1021, San Miguel de Allende, GTO 37700, Mexico

Baker MR John M—Conn'89 . . see MRS M Barry

Baker MR & MRS John Milnes (Elizabeth J | ☎ (914) 232-8569
Morrison) V'63.Bgt.C.Co.Plg.Snc.Hl.Lm.Ne. | ''Rivendell''
Ofp.Cw.Myf.Ncd.Mid'55.Cl'60 ⚓ . . . . | 85 Girdle Ridge Rd,
MR Ian A—Snc.Mid'80.Mid'85—Box 1373, | Katonah, NY *10536*
Kathmandu, Nepal . . . . |
MR James M—Co.Snc.WashColl'95 . . . . |
JUNIORS MR Hayden S—Snc.—at Middlebury . . . |

Baker MRS K Ervin (Katharine M Ervin) V'46
☎ (215) 646-3193 . . 617 Montgomery Rd, Ambler, PA *19002*

Baker MR & MRS Kane K (Mary M Fletcher)
☎ (516) 922-5858 . . 533 Centre Island Rd, Oyster Bay, NY *11771*

Baker MRS M Amory (Mary Amory) . . . . | ☎ (508) 927-5460
MISS Cornelia L—at 47 Fair St, Norwalk, CT | 212 Hart St,
06850 . . . . | Beverly Farms, MA
| *01915*

Baker MRS Marianna J (Marianna Johnson) | ☎ (212) 288-4457
Sth'66.Ri. . . . . | 830 Park Av, Apt
MISS Joanna J . . . . | 6C, New York, NY
MR George F 2d . . . . | *10021*

Baker MRS (REV DR) Milton G (Josephine Louise Redenius)
AmU'62.StCSem'81.EBap'84.EBap'90.Ac.
☎ (610) 688-1460 . . ''Tower House'' 920 Eagle Rd, Wayne,
PA *19087-3413*

Baker MR & MRS Newcombe C 3d (Dena J Conti) P'74
☎ (215) 233-0823 . . 70 N College Av, Flourtown, PA *19031*

Baker MRS Newton D 3d (Allen—Phyllis Ingham) May.It.
☎ (216) 921-8660 . . 19333 Van Aken Blvd, Apt 504, Shaker Heights,
OH *44122-3571*

Baker MR R Cass—Vt'92
☎ (312) 654-0529 . . 1544 N La Salle St, Chicago, IL *60610*

Baker MR Richard B—C.Gr.Y.'35.Ox'38
☎ (212) 427-6996 . . 1185 Park Av, New York, NY *10128-1310*

Baker MR & MRS Robert I (Leslie A Ptak) ArizSt'78.SSMT'77
☎ (520) 638-2260 . . Box 40, Grand Canyon, AZ *86023*

Baker MR & MRS Sheridan (Sandwich—Sally E Baubie) Mich'43.Cal'39
☎ (313) 973-2693 . . 2866 Provincial Dv, Ann Arbor, MI *48104*

Baker MR & MRS Talbot (Polly N Beale) . . . . | ☎ (508) 376-4443
MR Talbot JR—Bvl.Ub.H.'57 ⚓—at | 161 Forest Rd,
☎ (508) 748-2145 . . Tabor Academy, Front St, | Millis, MA *02054*
Marion, MA *02738* . . . . |

Baker MR & MRS Thomas R (Elizabeth A Hughes)
ArizSt'87.ArizSt'80.ArizSt'87
☎ (602) 894-8626 . . 920 E Concordia Dv, Tempe, AZ *85282*

Baker MR & MRS Wilder Du Puy (McGlade—Vanda Francese)
CtCol'57.Yn.Y'53
☎ (203) 655-9924 . . ''Tuckaway'' 4 Pratt Island, Darien, CT *06820*

Baker MR & MRS William C (Roberts—Mayer W Martin)
Ga'80.Elk.Ayc.Ty'76 ⚓
☎ (410) 849-2435 . . 502A Epping Forest Rd, Annapolis, MD *21401*

Baker MR & MRS William R JR (Louise M Hollingsworth)
Sth'78.Aga.Ub.Cr'74.Ox'78
☎ (508) 651-3317 . . 7 N Main St, Sherborn, MA *01770*

Baker MR & MRS William T (Elizabeth Baird)
Chr.Un.Cw.Myf.Coa.Cly.Ac.Ncd.Wms'29
☎ (212) 838-7190 . . 200 E 66 St, New York, NY *10021*

Baker MR William T JR—Un.Y.'65.Va'68 . . . . | of ☎ (212)249-6727
MISS Heather T—at Kenyon . . . . | 401 E 80 St, Apt
| 33B, New York, NY
| *10021*
| ☎ (518) 873-6890
| ''The Crags'' Rte 9,
| Elizabethtown, NY
| *12932*

Baker-Dugaw MR Charles S—WashSt'94 . . see J E Dugaw JR

Bakewell MRS Alexander McN (Elizabeth Stevens) . | of ☎ (314)991-9338
MISS Jane A—Box 1338, Bolton Landing, NY | 12 Magnolia Dv,
12814 . . . . | St Louis, MO *63124*
MISS Claire McN—at ☎ (303) 546-0662 | ☎ (809) 496-0253
Box 18944, Boulder, CO *80308* . . . . | ''Over The Hill''
| PO Box 500,
| Long Look,
| Tortola, BVI

Bakewell REV Anderson—StL'37
☎ (505) 982-5166 . . Box 4010, Santa Fe, NM *87502-4010*

Bakewell MR & MRS Anderson D (Francine L Stone) ☎ (011-44-1491)
MISS Petra............................. 641-485
JUNIORS MR Lorenzo .... Grimsdyke Cottage,
Nuffield Lane,
Crowmarsh Gifford,
Oxfordshire
OX10 6QW,
England

Bakewell MR & MRS Charles Adams (Lucia R ☎ (703) 790-0280
Urban) Y'63.Cl'66 .... 1162 Wimbledon
MR Geoffrey W—Y'86.Br'94—at 420 N 48 St, Dv, McLean, VA
Apt 4, Omaha, NE 68132 22101

Bakewell MRS Dorothy Jennings (Strong—Kelly—Stent—
Dorothy J Bakewell)
☎ (415) 398-1670 . . 1725 Kearny St, San Francisco, CA 94133

Bakewell MR Edward L 3d—Cy.Geo'68
☎ (314) 569-1455 . . 13 Chatfield Place Rd, St Louis, MO 63141

Bakewell MRS Edward Lilburn JR (Pacheco—Hannaford—Barbara Battin)
Cysl.
☎ (805) 969-2415 . . Birnam Wood Club, 1997 Lemon Ranch Rd,
Montecito, CA 93108

Bakewell MR & MRS Henry P JR (Elsie Ives ☎ (860) 388-4823
Goodrich) Sth'58.Ncd.Y'59.Penn'66 ⚓ ..... 193 Ayers Point Rd,
MISS Lucy A—Bab'87 .... Old Saybrook, CT
06475

Bakewell MISS Hester L (Hasbach—Hester L Bakewell) Conn'69.GeoM'91
1533 Crowell Rd, Vienna, VA 22182

Bakewell MR & MRS Hughes R (Nancy J Nestor) ☎ (303) 771-2197
Vt'47.Col'47 .... 9197 E Tufts Place,
MISS Lisa A—at 5545 E Yale Av, Apt 5C, Greenwood Village,
Denver, CO 80222 .... CO 80111

Bakewell MISS Jenifer J . . see C Simmons

Bakewell MISS Sarah (Cannon—Sarah Bakewell) . . of
☎ (314) 993-0459 . . 9675 Ladue Rd, St Louis, MO 63124
☎ (809) 494-3502 . . ''Little Bay'' Tortola, BVI

Bakewell MISS Susan (Hughes R) .... Married at Beaver Creek, CO
Bettino MR Lorenzo A (Achille) .... Jun 22'96

Bakewell MR & MRS Thomas W (Polly Oakleaf) ☎ (603) 525-6679
P'43 .... ''Point of View''
MISS Elizabeth A—at Brown............... RR 2, Box 544,
Spring Hill Rd,
Hancock, NH 03449

Bakker MR & MRS Peter A (Quinlan—Katharine L of ☎ (415)459-4769
Murdock) Rotterdam'59 .... ''Tigre D'or''
MR Anton W........................... 33 Laurel Grove Av,
MISS Kimberley L Quinlan—at U of So Cal . Ross, CA 94957
☎ (209) 787-2366
Oak Shadows
Ranch, Piedra Rd,
Sanger, CA 93657

Balaguer MISS Katherine Evans (Roberto JR) .... Born Oct 31'95

Balaguer MR & MRS Roberto JR (Janet M Butterworth) Dth'83.Au.Dth'83
☎ (770) 246-0696 . . 5548 Fitzpatrick Trace, Norcross, GA 30092

Balbach MR & MRS Charles E (Margaret Crofton) Sth'62.St.G.H.'56.H'60
☎ (716) 854-0458 . . PO Box 423, Orchard Park, NY 14127

Balboni MRS Victor G (Marjorie C Fletcher) Sth'42.Cy.Chi.Ncd.
☎ (617) 566-1805 . . 13 Fairgreen Place, Chestnut Hill, MA 02167

Balch DR & MRS Henry H (Julester L Post) Unn.Mt.Ayc.Sl.Dub'38 ⚓
☎ (202) 333-5879 . . 1726 Hoban Rd NW, Washington, DC 20007

Baldi MR & MRS Paul L (Carol O Holbrook) Swth'53.Ny.Yn.Y'49.H'53
☎ (860) 567-9567 . . 221 North St, PO Box 180, Litchfield, CT 06759

Balding MR Bruce E—Ln.Pr.Ne.Hn.Hb.H'54
☎ (603) 436-2111 . . 439 Middle St, Portsmouth, NH 03801

Balding MR & MRS Ivor G (Baldwin—Sheffield—Polly Potter)
☎ (803) 432-8703 . . 512 Chestnut St, Camden, SC 29020

Balding MRS Whitney (Barbara Whitney) Rdc'53
☎ (516) 671-0499 . . 24 The Glen, Locust Valley, NY 11560

Baldini MR Daniel H—Tufts'80.Stan'85 . . of
☎ (202) 338-9045 . . 3306 R St NW, Washington, DC 20007
☎ (011-44-171) 722-4527 . . 12A Ormonde Terr, London NW8, England

Baldini MR Edward B (late Mario G) ...... Married at Brookline, MA
Healey MISS (DR) Elizabeth A (Stephen J) .... Nov 4'95

Baldini MR & MRS (DR) Edward B (Elizabeth A Healey) H'84.H'88.Occ'84
☎ (617) 266-9352 . . 810 High St, Denham, MA 02026

Baldini MRS Mario G (Dorothy L Hovey) Cy. ..... ☎ (617) 566-5876
MISS Julia C (Sierra—Julia C Baldini) 329 Goddard Av,
Br'82.Pa'91—at ☎ (011-44-171) 727-7541 Brookline, MA
11C Sheffield Terr, London W8 7NG, England . 02146

Baldridge MISS Brooke B (Pelizza—Brooke B Baldridge)
☎ (919) 870-6222 . . 7425 Ashbury Court, Raleigh, NC 27615

Baldridge MR D Bouton JR (Dickson B) ..... Married at Wilmington, NC
Smaltz MISS (DR) Stacy C (Rhinehart—Stacy C Smaltz) .... May 19'96

Baldridge MR & MRS Dickson B (Ede Landell Dunn) ☎ (910) 251-0704
USMMA'43 .... 1317 Hawthorne Rd,
MRS C Branson (Brown—Seeliger—Christina Wilmington, NC
Branson Baldridge)..................... 28403
MISS Rebekah Bayard Brown............
MR N Allen Brown JR ....

Baldridge REV & MRS Kempton D (Isabel S Curtis) Bridgept'73.Cit'78.Y'88
☎ (302) 292-3742 . . 214 Kells Av, Newark, DE 19711

Baldridge MR & MRS Milton C (Patricia A Beckett) Pom'45.H'46
☎ (541) 440-1454 . . 645 Topaz Loop Lane, Roseburg, OR 97470

Baldridge MR & MRS Robert C (Nancy E Bierwirth) Y.'45
☎ (516) 239-7529 . . 232 Causeway, Lawrence, NY 11559

Baldwin MR & MRS Alexander T JR (Joan Morgan) ☎ (914) 666-3118
H'50................................. 712 Croton Lake
MISS Brooke—at ☎ (914) 669-9405 Rd, Mt Kisco, NY
Baxter Rd, Box 18, North Salem, NY 10560 ... 10549
MR Alexander T 3d—at ☎ (212) 396-9828
410 E 65 St, New York, NY 10021 ....

Baldwin MR Alfred W—Un.Hn.H.'31.Cl'34
☎ (617) 566-3200 . . 20 Chapel St, Apt 701C, Brookline, MA 02146

Baldwin MR Blair F—Srb.Plg.LakeF'69.Nu'71 .... ☎ (401) 846-1117
JUNIORS MR Blair F JR—at St Paul's .... 32 Clarke St,
Newport, RI 02840

Baldwin MR Cedric B 3d . . see MISS L M Paine

Baldwin MRS Charles E (Susannah F Bowie)
☎ (410) 366-1295 . . 3601 Greenway, Apt 401, Baltimore, MD 21218

Baldwin MR Edward R 2d—Y'57.Y'61
☎ (416) 364-4521 . . on Board Kelana'' 167 Richmond St E, Toronto,
Ontario M5A 1N9, Canada

Baldwin MR & MRS Edwin S (Margaret Kirkham) P'54.H'57
☎ (314) 991-5155 . . 1 Dromara Rd, St Louis, MO 63124

Baldwin MISS Frances S—Tcy.
☎ (415) 673-7292 . . 2124 Hyde St, San Francisco, CA *94109*
Baldwin MRS G Storer (Jenckes—Mollie W Cromwell) Cy.Chi.Ncd.
☎ (617) 566-3042 . . 73 Fairmount St, Brookline, MA *02146*
Baldwin MR & MRS Gustave B JR (Marguerite Cammack Brenchley) Tul'37
☎ (504) 643-1337 . . 2100 Front St, Slidell, LA *70458*
Baldwin MR & MRS Ian (Rose Weld) H'33
☎ (508) 295-1844 . . ''Blueberry Cottage'' 8 Bourne Point, Wareham, MA *02571*
Baldwin DR & MRS J Gilbert JR (Constance A Montague)
Conv'70.Cit'72.Cw.Ncd.Va'68.Va'72 . . of
☎ (803) 577-3096 . . 29 Hasell St, Charleston, SC *29401*
☎ (803) 869-2958 . . ''Blue House'' Box 211, Edisto Island, SC *29438*
Baldwin MRS James B (Carolyn D Thomson)
☎ (803) 671-2633 . . 37 Baynard Cove Rd, Hilton Head Island, SC *29928*
Baldwin MRS James French (Moore—Eileen Narizzano) Pr.Evg.Cly.DelB.
☎ (561) 278-5460 . . Seagate Tower 1204, 220 MacFarlane Dv, Delray Beach, FL *33483*
Baldwin MR & MRS James McCall JR (Karen K Johnsen) Ncmb'75.Tul'85
☎ (504) 897-6827 . . 3020 Prytania St, New Orleans, LA *70115-3315*
Baldwin MR James Todd—Cy.Ey.H'24
☎ (617) 329-6258 . . 10 Longwood Dv, Apt 238, Westwood, MA *02090*
Baldwin MR Joseph C—H'50
☎ (860) 721-9870 . . 411 Hartford Av, Wethersfield, CT *06109*
Baldwin MR Joseph L—Hn.Duke'53.Va'56.H'80
280 Waverley St, Palo Alto, CA *94301*
Baldwin MRS L Hubbard (Laura A Hubbard) Bgt. . . | ☎ (914) 234-7463
MISS M Amory—at South Salem, NY *10590* . . . | Bedford Center
MR Joseph C JR—at San Diego, CA . . . . | Rd, Bedford, NY *10506*
Baldwin MRS Lisa Leonard (Lisa Leonard) | of ☎ (314)993-0804
Lind'64.Cy.Myf.Dar.Dc.Dcw. . . . . | 1 Ladue Lane,
MISS Almira S . . . . | St Louis, MO *63124*
MR Lawrence T. . . . . | ☎ (314) 281-1275
MR Townsend L—at Georgetown Sch of | Emar Farm, RR 3,
Foreign Service . . . . | O'Fallon, MO *63366*
| ☎ (616) 526-2421
| Marina Village 7,
| 524 E Bay St,
| Harbor Springs, MI *49740*
Baldwin MRS Mary B (Mary B Holmes) Sth'58.Csn. | ☎ (415) 327-1065
MISS Pamela H—Ws'86.BMr'95 . . . . | 1378 Johnson St,
MISS Kathryn A—Aht'88.Y'95 . . . . | Menlo Park, CA *94025*
MISS Elizabeth B—Ober'92—at U of So Cal Law |
Baldwin MR & MRS Michael (Margherita Bailey) | ☎ (508) 748-2080
Un.H'62 ⚓ . . . . | ''Bagatelle-sur-
MISS Helena-Margherita . . . . | Mer'' 72 Water St,
MR Taylor C . . . . | Marion, MA *02738*
JUNIORS MR Nathaniel K . . . . |
Baldwin MR & MRS Morgan H (Bowman—Nancy S Darrell) Md.USN'37
☎ (410) 825-8237 . . Blakehurst 310, 1055 W Joppa Rd, Towson, MD *21204*

Baldwin MR & MRS Murray H (Shirley A French) | ☎ (718) 522-2221
Ky'58.Ne.H'59 . . . . | 93 Joralemon St,
MR Summerfield M—JHop'89.Bklyn'92 . . . . | Brooklyn, NY *11201-4057*
Baldwin MRS O H Perry (Elizabeth St J Webb) Me.Ncd.
☎ (610) 353-1985 . . Dunwoody Village, Woodlea 105, 3500 West Chester Pike, Newtown Square, PA *19073*
Baldwin DR Richard JR—Cy.Myf.P'62.Cin'68
☎ (314) 569-4225 . . 9939 Coddington Way, St Louis, MO *63132*
Baldwin MR & MRS Richard 3d (Deborah B Johnson) Rv.P'90
☎ (314) 862-5554 . . 665 S Skinker Blvd, Apt 9T, St Louis, MO *63105*
Baldwin MR & MRS Roger P (Mary L Stewart) Y'42 | ☎ (617) 259-9239
MR Michael P . . . . | Box 136,
| Lincoln Center,
| MA *01773*
Baldwin MR & MRS Rosecrans (Sarah S Griffin) | ☎ (312) 787-5210
Cas.Y'35 . . . . | 70 E Cedar St,
MISS Elizabeth L—JHop'83—at 1400 N State | Chicago, IL *60611*
P'kway, Chicago, IL *60610* . . . . |
Baldwin MR & MRS Rosecrans JR (Ann C Behr) | ☎ (203) 967-2799
Ken'73 . . . . | 26 Middlesex Rd,
MISS Leslie H . . . . | Darien, CT *06820*
MR Rosecrans B . . . . |
Baldwin MRS Sally C (Sally C Crittendon) Wheat'70
☎ (513) 871-1003 . . 2374 Madison Rd, Cincinnati, OH *45208*
Baldwin MR V Thomas (Virginia S Thomas) LakeF'68.Srb.
☎ (401) 847-0430 . . ''Ledge Point'' Bellevue Av, Newport, RI *02840*
Baldwin MR W Barton 3d—Srb.LakeF'67
☎ (303) 581-0262 . . 7447 Spy Glass Court, Boulder, CO *80301*
Baldwin MRS William I (Krebs—Elizabeth N Cooper) Salem'43
☎ (513) 533-0555 . . 3646 Ashworth Dv, Cincinnati, OH *45208*
Balis MRS C Wanton JR (Johnston—Deborah Butler) Ph.Me.Gm.Ac.
☎ (610) 520-0895 . . 3 Pond Lane, Bryn Mawr, PA *19010*
Balis MR & MRS Mark E (Rose J Townsend) Cda.Y'27
☎ (803) 722-4657 . . 25 E Battery St, Charleston, SC *29401*
Ball MR & MRS Christopher R (Daphne B LeFeaver) Sfg.H'79.Geo'83
☎ (415) 921-6858 . . 2817 Bush St, San Francisco, CA *94115*
Ball DR & MRS Eugene R (Sarah J Ashmun) | ☎ (212) RE4-0826
Rc.Pl.T.Fw.Myf.Cly.Dar.Ncd.Pa'45 . . . . | 328 E 69 St,
DR Perry A—Cl'79.Dth'85—at Norwich, VT | New York, NY
05055 . . . . | *10021*
Ball MR & MRS Harold A 3d (Amy K Zimpfer) Col'80.Cr'76.Stan'83
☎ (415) 285-2841 . . 330 Moultrie St, San Francisco, CA *94110*
Ball MRS Kilbourn (Helen A Kilbourn)
☎ (212) 289-5892 . . 65 E 96 St, Apt 15A, New York, NY *10128*
Ball MR & MRS Stephen F W (Elaine P Boschen) | ☎ (603) 643-8227
Skd'62.Rv.P'58 . . . . | 2 Algonquin Trail,
MISS Sarah W—CtCol'93—at U of N Mex . . . . . | Etna, NH *03750*
JUNIORS MR Stephen F W JR—at St Andrew's . . . |

Ball MRS T Arthur (Myers—Frances B Le Pere) Chr.Mto.Cly.Plg.Ne.Dc.Cda.Ht. . . . .
MISS Barbara Q Myers . . . .
of ☎ (212)288-2055 1030 Fifth Av, New York, NY *10028*
☎ (804) 296-4771 1515 Virginia Av, Charlottesville, VA *22903*

Ball MR & MRS Thomas J (Turben—Catherine C Eppinger) V'59.Woos'75 . . of
☎ (216) 423-4578 . . Battles Rd, Gates Mills, OH *44040*
☎ (011-39-41) 522-4035 . . 1677F Dorsoduro, Venice, Italy

Ball MR & MRS William E (Inga J Woodwell) MtH'44.Rc.Str.Aht'44
☎ (314) 434-8758 . . 13446 Conway Rd, St Louis, MO *63141*

Ballantine MR & MRS Andrew Van B (McChristian—D Dené A Binnié) Cw.Col'70.Rut'78
☎ (201) 786-5274 . . Tor Moria Farm, 49 Ballantine Rd, Andover, NJ *07821*

Ballantine DR H Thomas JR . . . . Died Apr 14'96

Ballantine MRS H Thomas JR (Elizabeth E Mixter) Sb.Chi.Ncd.
☎ (617) 523-1701 . . 30 Embankment Rd, Boston, MA *02114*

Ballantine MR & MRS John H 2d (Alexandra Wickser) Reed'77.Cly.RISD'77
☎ (914) 279-5808 . . "Spy Hill Farm" Enoch Crosby Rd, RD 9, Brewster, NY *10509*

Ballantine MRS John Holme (Davis—Dorothy Bortz)
☎ (561) 278-1306 . . 86 MacFarlane Dv, Delray Beach, FL *33483*

Ballantine MR & MRS Mark T (Phyllis E Harrison) MtVern'81.Rut'84
☎ (410) 820-7506 . . 6110 Westland Rd, Easton, MD *21601*

Ballantine MR & MRS Martin D (Anne S MacGregor) Hood'60.Cw.Myf.Dar.Ncd.P'58 . . .
MISS Gabrielle M—at Randolph-Macon W'mns .
MR Robert H—at 140 Green Turtle Lane, Apt 4, Charlottesville, VA *22901* . . . .
MR Martin D JR—USN.—at Newport, RI *02840* .
☎ (804) 295-9476 1 Tennis Rd, Farmington, Charlottesville, VA *22901*

Ballantine DR & MRS Percy 2d (Sara M Craig) Cl'69.Myf.Cw.P'68 . . . .
MISS Sara G . . . .
MR Andrew B . . . .
☎ (603) 643-2842 181 Three Mile Rd, Hanover, NH *03755*

Ballantine MR & MRS Percy H (Anne B Van Blarcom) Myf.Cw.Cda.Cr'37 . . . .
MISS Grier P—Ws'82.Myf.Cda.—at
☎ (212) 439-6732 . . 231 E 76 St, Apt 5A, New York, NY *10021* . . . .
☎ (201) 786-5235 30 Ballantine Rd, Andover, NJ *07821*

Ballantine MRS Peter (Elizabeth Stevens)
☎ (914) 297-5181 . . Box 220, Hughsonville, NY *12537*

Ballantine MR & MRS Robert D (Helen H Price) Hood'60.Cw.W&L'57
☎ (908) 735-4146 . . "Edgebrook" 227 Hamden Rd, Annandale, NJ *08801*

Ballantine MRS Robert W (Fahey—Thomas—Virginia McB Garesché)
☎ (520) 647-7410 . . X9 Ranch, Vail, AZ *85641*

Ballantine MR & MRS William P (Maxine H Jones) .
MISS Deirdre . . . .
MR W Parke JR . . . .
☎ (919) 726-4517 PO Box 1321, Morehead City, NC *28557*

Ballard MR Alexander F R . . see L S Huntington

Ballard MR & MRS Augustus S (Nancy V Abbott) Ac.Pa'48
☎ (215) 568-1883 . . Rivers Edge Apt 6E, 2301 Cherry St, Philadelphia, PA *19103*

Ballard MISS Elizabeth F R—Y'85
☎ (212) 613-9181 . . 240 Central Park S, New York, NY *10019*

Ballard MR & MRS Frederic L (Ernesta Drinker) Pa'39
☎ (215) 247-3807 . . 9120 Crefeld St, Philadelphia, PA *19118*

Ballard MR & MRS Frederic L JR (Dunning—Marion C Scattergood) Sth'61.Ph.Sl.H'63 . . . .
MR Robert L Dunning—Cal'90 . . . .
☎ (301) 320-3931 4413 Chalfont Place, Bethesda, MD *20816*

Ballard DR & MRS Ian M (Hoffman—Helen Clothier) Rose'79.M.Me.Laf'58.Temp'62 . . . . .
MR Ian M JR—Me.Bow'90.Va'95—at
☎ (215) 627-1733 . . 622 S Hancock St, Apt 3, Philadelphia, PA *19147* . . . .
☎ (610) 688-2004 529 County Line Rd, Radnor, PA *19087*

Ballard MISS Jennifer E (Hyde—Jennifer E Ballard) Laf'82
6264 Occoquan Forest Dv, Manassas, VA *20112*

Ballard MISS Laura Catherine (Mark R) . . . . Born May 11'95

Ballard MR & MRS Mark R (Marian Minton) Austin'86 . . of
☎ (214) 349-1279 . . 9639 Covemeadow Dv, Dallas, TX *75238*
☎ (512) 261-5442 . . 381 Brooks Hollow Dv, Austin, TX *78734*

Ballard MR & MRS Martha M (Martha M Muzzey) . . . . . .
MRS Wendy F R (Swindell—Gourd—Wendy F R Ballard) Cly.—at ☎ (561) 234-3493
PO Box 3832, Vero Beach, FL *32964* . . . .
☎ (908) 974-9332 1912C Old Mill Rd, Spring Lake, NJ *07762*

Ballard MR & MRS Robert F R (Talbot—Lucinda M Constable) Cal'72.Rc.Nyc.Plg.Rv.Cly.H.'56
☎ (212) 874-7800 . . 29 W 85 St, New York, NY *10024*

Ballenger MR & MRS James M (Jo McIlhattan) Char'ton'47.M.Rc.Ph.Char'ton'46.W&L'48
☎ (610) LA5-2791 . . 711 Williamson Rd, Bryn Mawr, PA *19010*

Ballenger MR & MRS Bruce Garrison (Agnes C Lee) NCar'76.NCar'88.Dav'52 . . . .
MR David E—at ☎ (704) 843-5068 911 Chambwood Rd, Monroe, NC *28110* . . . . . .
☎ (704) 365-9211 6605 Gaywind Dv, Charlotte, NC *28226*

Ballenger DR & MRS Peter L (Barbara M Maury) MempSt'61.Tenn'62 . . . .
MISS F Maury . . . .
MISS Brooke B . . . .
of ☎ (901)458-9934 2796 Central Av, Memphis, TN *38111*
☎ (615) 924-2819 "Eagle's Loft" Monteagle Assembly, Monteagle, TN *37356*

Ballenger MR & MRS Steven C C (Dawn C Duhé) Van'85.Van'85
2212 E 8 St, Charlotte, NC *28204*

Ballentine MRS Michael (Stettinius—Reynolds— Mary Ballou Handy) Swb'59 . . . . ☎ (804) 288-1273 6317 Three Chopt Rd, Richmond, VA 23226
MISS Mary Stuart Stettinius—Va'89—at ☎ (212) 254-9047 . . 56 W 12 St, Apt 4, New York, NY 10011 . . . .
MR Joseph Stettinius JR—at ☎ (540) 364-3212 . . PO Box 1712, Middleburg, VA 20118 . . . .
MR Edward R Stettinius—Va'84—Box 278, Upperville, VA 20185 . . . .
MR R Roland Reynolds—P'93—at ☎ (212) 799-8307 . . 11 W 69 St, Apt 7A, New York, NY 10023 . . . .

Balliet MR & MRS Michael (Peggy A Gafford) Ala'59.Cy.GaTech'58
☎ (205) 871-5212 . . 2335 Chester Rd, Birmingham, AL 35223

Ballinger MRS Robert I JR (de Mohrenschildt—Denton— Wynne Sharples) Rdc'45.BtP.Cda.
☎ (561) 832-9077 . . 235 Banyan Rd, Palm Beach, FL 33480

Ballinger DR & MRS Walter F 2d (Mary Randolph G Dickson) Wash'71.Cy.Ncd.Cr'46.Pa'48 . . . . ☎ (314) 994-3172 800 Barnes Rd, St Louis, MO 63124
MR Walter F 3d . . . .
MR Christopher B . . . .
MR David G . . . .

Ballman MR & MRS B George (Frances L Hurst) Gv.AmU'54.Wash'57.Geo'61.Geo'80 . . . . ☎ (301) 299-6600 12002 River Rd, Potomac, MD 20854
MISS Lynda H . . . .
MISS Kimberly S . . . .

Ballou MR & MRS F Remington (Frothingham—Priscilla W West) Y'50 . . of
☎ (401) 272-4368 . . 25 John St, Providence, RI 02906
☎ (508) 993-1816 . . "High Tide" 112 Mattarest Lane, South Nonquitt, South Dartmouth, MA 02748

Baltazar-Campos MR J Rafael . . see MRS G S Regan

Baltzell MR E Digby . . . . Died at Boston, MA Aug 17'96

Baltzell MRS E Digby (Jocelyn Carlson) Ws'55 . . . . ☎ (215) 546-5431 1724 Delancey Place, Philadelphia, PA 19103
MISS Eve F . . . .
MISS Jan C—at ☎ (215) 336-0967 1211 Federal St, Philadelphia, PA 19147 . . . . . .

Baltzell MRS Edwards (Sarah H Edwards) BMr'55.Temp'84.Cs.Ac. . . . . ☎ (215) 545-0734 226 W Rittenhouse Square, Apt 406, Philadelphia, PA 19103
MISS Virginia S—Bost'79—at ☎ (215) 928-9767 1006 Kater St, Philadelphia, PA 19147 . . . .
MR W Hewson 5th—P.Pa'79.Pa'85—at ☎ (212) 996-7775 . . 1255 Fifth Av, Apt 2E, New York, NY 10029 . . . .

Baltzell MR Francis D—Rcp.Sap.Pa'80
☎ (207) 276-5292 . . "Digby Lodge" Northeast Harbor, ME 04662

Baltzell DR & MRS William H 4th (Biddle—Martha Pickman) Pa'75.Ph.Sa.Cc.Pa'42.Jef'46
☎ (215) 247-9412 . . 208 Rex Av, Philadelphia, PA 19118

Bamberger MR & MRS Alan S (Louise K Rush) NewC'73.Cl'80.Ken'72
☎ (415) 922-3580 . . 2510 Bush St, San Francisco, CA 94115

Bance MR & MRS Edgar J D (Mary F Wallace) Vt'83.HampSydney'77
☎ (804) 589-4126 . . Byrd Grove Farm, Rte 1, Box 205, Palmyra, VA 22963

Bancroft MR & MRS Alexander C (Margaret A Armstrong) Rdc'60.H'60 . . . . ☎ (212) 369-8467 15 E 91 St, New York, NY 10128
MISS (DR) Elizabeth A—Wms'89.Cr'93 . . . .

Bancroft MISS Elizabeth A—H'79.Hn.
☎ (703) 734-0420 . . 1418 Wolftrap Run Rd, Vienna, VA 22182-1736

Bancroft REV Francis S 3d—Wes'56 . . . . ☎ (201) 941-0422 528 Morse Av, Ridgefield, NJ 07657
MR Wayne A Currey . . . .

Bancroft MR & MRS Frederic M (Suzanne G Coleman) Hlns'84.Rc.Fic.V'85
☎ (914) 234-7668 . . 741 Guard Hill Rd, Bedford, NY 10506

Bancroft MR & MRS Gregory M (Decker—Ruth A Woodrow) Juniata'85.Cal'87
☎ (540) 678-1314 . . 529 Timberlakes Lane, Clearbrook, VA 22624

Bancroft MRS Harding F (Merrill—Edith C Hall) Sl.
☎ (202) 342-1472 . . 1632—32 St NW, Washington, DC 20007

Bancroft MR & MRS Harding F JR (Helen H Goodbody) Ty'64 . . . . 30 Loading Rock Rd, Riverside, CT 06878-1126
MISS Kelly G—at Colo Coll . . . .
JUNIORS MR Alexander P—at Proctor Acad . . . . .

Bancroft MRS M Godwin (Mae Godwin) . . . . ☎ (415) 326-7749 140 Garland Av, Menlo Park, CA 94025
MISS Kimberly M—at 1268 Fifth Av, San Francisco, CA 94122 . . . .
MR Bradford M—at 1831 Gramercy Place, Hollywood, CA 90028 . . . .

Bancroft MRS Mary Jane (Casey—Collins—Mary Jane Bancroft) SL'64 . . . . ☎ (770) 426-6481 2261 Brookmont Trace, Marietta, GA 30064
JUNIORS MR Christian J Collins . . . .

Bancroft MR Monty E . . see G D Gould

Bancroft MR & MRS Thomas M JR (Wiedemann— Barbara H Symmers) Briar'68.Pr.Ng.Cly.P.'51 . of ☎ (516)626-0230 "Harrow Hill" Rte 25A, Muttontown, NY 11732
JUNIORS MR Townsend W—at Middlesex . . . . . .
MISS Anne S Wiedemann . . . .
MR Christopher B Wiedemann—Ty'93—at ☎ (212) 249-0089 945 Fifth Av, New York, NY 10021
☎ (718) 694-9820 . . 289 Adelphi St, Brooklyn, NY 11205 . . . .

Bancroft MRS William M (Gertrude C Storey) Rdc'46
☎ (860) 456-8189 . . Box 236, Windham, CT 06280

Bancroft MR & MRS (DR) William M JR (Alice D Murphy) P'88.Tufts'94.Ub.Br'83.RISD'92
☎ (617) 227-8552 . . 65 Anderson St, Apt 3A, Boston, MA 02114

Bancroft MR & MRS William W (Sarah Sturges) B.Pr.S.Cly.P'53
☎ (516) 759-4141 . . Hoaglands Lane, Old Brookville, NY 11545

Bandler MISS Elise de Struvé
☎ (415) 381-1065 . . 435 E Blithdale Av, Mill Valley, CA 94941

Bandler MR & MRS Richard (Eleanor S Trenholm) . . | ☎ (305) 538-1669 5266 Fisher Island Dv, Fisher Island, FL 33109
MISS Tatiana S—at ☎ (305) 868-9230 9133 Collins Av, Surfside, FL 33154 . . . .

Bane MR & MRS Charles A (Eileen Blackwell) Evg.BtP.Ch'35.Ox'37.H'38
☎ (561) 655-2953 . . 434 Chilean Av, Apt 3B, Palm Beach, FL 33480

Bane MR & MRS David M (McIlvain—Patricia H Miller) Duke'38.Pa'41
☎ (561) 793-8831 . . 2835 Polo Island Dv, Apt 103H, West Palm Beach, FL *33414*

Bangs MR & MRS Nathaniel S (Jean E Gridley) SL'49.Y'49 . . . . | ☎ (803) 768-9228 1068 Sparrow Pond, Kiawah Island, SC *29455*
MISS Elizabeth R—at ☎ (612) 646-6261 1979 Laurel Av, St Paul, MN *55104* . . . .

Banker MR & MRS Alexander C (Skipwith C W Redmon) Ty'87.Ty'83.H'91
☎ (617) 576-8698 . . 439 Huron Av, Cambridge, MA *02138*

Banker MR & MRS David L (Pamela G Sullivan) K.Ri.Pr.Y'54 . . . . | ☎ (212) 628-7080 150 E 73 St, New York, NY *10021*
MISS Leslie G—Denis'92 . . . .

Banker MR & MRS Douglas H (Sarah McL Griffin) C.Ri.Y'59.H'63 . . . . | ☎ (914) 424-3008 "North River Lodge" Castle Rock Rd, Garrison-on-Hudson, NY *10524*
MISS Abigail H—Ober'89—at ☎ (718) 622-3743 590 Carroll St, Brooklyn, NY *11215* . . . .

Banker MISS Jean G (Douglas H) . . . . Married at Garrison, NY
Miottel MR Ward J 3d (Ward J JR) . . . . Aug 10'96

Banker MR Peter A . . . . Died at Greenwich, CT Apr 8'96

Banker MR & MRS Vincent C (Day—Beverly Vander Poel) Rc.B.Lic.Ng.Pr.Cly.Y'54 . . . . | ☎ (516) 671-3356 15 The Glen, Locust Valley, NY *11560*
MISS Ashley V P . . . .
 MISS Kingsley V Day—Ty'93—at ☎ (212) 355-9199 . . 309 E 49 St, New York, NY *10017* . . . .
 MR Richard W Day JR—Nu'87—at ☎ (212) 929-1759 . . 448 W 19 St, Apt 4E, New York, NY *10011* . . . .

Banks MR & MRS Andrew (Horine—Jane R Moore) Swb'59.JHop'52 . . . . | ☎ (410) 825-3994 1414 Locust Av, Ruxton, MD *21204*
MISS Anne S . . . .

Banks MR & MRS J A Davis (Jean P Flanagan) P'42.Nu'52
☎ (203) 853-4404 . . 10 Indian Spring Rd, Rowayton, CT *06853*

Banks MR & MRS J Eugene (Vietor—Barbara Hall) Chr.Plg.Cly.Ncd.Wash'30 . . of
☎ (516) 584-7123 . . PO Box 125, St James, NY *11780*
☎ (609) 426-6038 . . Meadow Lakes 48-L10, Hightstown, NJ *08520-3317*

Bannerman DR & MRS Robin M (Franca A E Vescia) CathU'50.G.Ox'50 . . of
☎ (310) 377-5251 . . 28127 Lobrook Dv, Rancho Palos Verdes, CA *90274*
☎ (716) 886-2572 . . 657 Auburn Av, Buffalo, NY *14222*

Banning MR & MRS Derrick C (Gloria P Tripi) Ts.St.G.Y'39.Y'42
☎ (716) 886-1606 . . 193 Summer St, Buffalo, NY *14222*

Banta MRS Bruce F (Ethel B Green) Swb'55
☎ (601) 445-4848 . . "Hope Farm" 147 Homochitto St, Natchez, MS *39120*

Banta MR & MRS Charles U (Melissa P Wickser) Cy.Ts.St.G.Y.'39.H'41
☎ (716) 876-4735 . . 39 Hallam Rd, Buffalo, NY *14216*

Banta MR & MRS Charles W (Wyckoff—Jane P Schoellkopf) Bf.Ts.Y'70.H'72 . . . . | ☎ (716) 873-5103 133 Middlesex Rd, Buffalo, NY *14216*
MR Charles L . . . .
 MR Andrew P Wyckoff . . . .

Banta MASTER Maximilian Alexander (Philip L) . . . . Born at San Francisco, CA Apr 29'96

Banta MR & MRS Philip L (Pei—Susan G Johnson) GeoW'76.S.H'72
☎ (415) 460-0965 . . Sleepy Hollow, 15 Crane Dv, San Anselmo, CA *94960*

Barba DR & MRS William P 2d (Marjorie C Taylor) P'44.Pa'46 . . . . | ☎ (215) TU7-5331 326 Summit Av, Jenkintown, PA *19046*
MISS Katharine W—NH'79—at ☎ (301) 229-3817 . . 5135 Wissioming Rd, Bethesda, MD *20816* . . . .
DR William P 3d—Duke'77.Temp'81 . . . .
MR Philip S 2d—Blooms'84 . . . .

Barber MRS Anthony V (Hoge—Virginia McClamroch) Hlns'29.Cly.Ncd.
☎ (212) 534-6827 . . 1080 Fifth Av, New York, NY *10128*

Barber MR & MRS Charles P (Emilie H McIlvain) Ripon'65 . . . . | ☎ (610) 696-2105 1030 Little Shiloh Rd, Westtown, PA *19395*
MR Charles J . . . .

Barber MR & MRS David H (Jean L Bartell) UWash'75.Pa'81.Duke'72.Pa'81
☎ (206) 361-4631 . . 13237 Seventh Av NW, Seattle, WA *98177*

Barber MR & MRS Elliot H (Gail Watson) Grin'64.Y'69.H'75 . . . . | ☎ (617) 899-4344 526 North Av, Weston, MA *02193-1806*
MR Robert H C—at Curry . . . .
MR William T S—at Trinity . . . .
JUNIORS MR Andrew T—at St Mark's . . . .

Barber MRS Hughes (Eleanor Hughes)
☎ (704) 859-9203 . . 106 Broadway, Tryon, NC *28782*

Barber MR John T . . . . | ☎ (307) 332-5384 PO Drawer 1210, Lander, WY *82520*
 MISS Emily S Torrey—at Newmarket, England
 MR Owen C Torrey 3d—at 2311 Fountain View Dv, Houston, TX *77057* . . . .

Barber MR & MRS John T (Felicity I Forbes) Ws'71.Ec.Sm.Bab'71 . . . . | ☎ (508) 526-4373 Crooked Lane, Manchester, MA *01944*
MISS Isabel F . . . .

Barbey MRS Henry I (Lillian J Manger) Cly.So.Dar.Cda.Ht. . . . . | ☎ (212) 355-5210 570 Park Av, New York, NY *10021*
MISS Florence F—BtP.Cly.Cda. . . . .
MR Henry I 3d—Rv.—at 420 E 72 St, New York, NY *10021* . . . .

Barbieri MR & MRS Albert J (Elizabeth M Boland) StL'71.NMex'53 . . . . | 7606 Maryland Av, Clayton, MO *63105*
MISS Cecilia C . . . .
MISS Mariquita de L . . . .

Barbieri MR & MRS Ferruccio R (Alicia K Eimicke) H.'81
☎ (212) 734-8289 . . 524 E 72 St, Apt 29A, New York, NY *10021*

Barbier-Mueller MR & MRS Jean Gabriel (Mary Ann Smith) Tex'78
5941 Averill Way, Dallas, TX *75225*

Barbour MR Warren—Myf.Y.'50
☎ (914) 337-2011 . . 30 Forest Lane, Bronxville, NY *10708*

Barbour MRS William E JR (Fallon—Dunn—Marian S King) Stan'52
☎ (508) 369-9488 . . Box 460, Concord, MA *01742*

Barca-Hall MISS Annalisa Kristin (g—Stephen Galatti) . . . . Born at Los Gatos, CA Jly 2'96

Barclay MRS Albert H (Catharine P Hooker) V'40.Ncd.
☎ (203) 483-6835 . . 88 Notch Hill Rd, Apt 273, North Branford, CT *06471*

Barclay MR & MRS Brewster F (Julie H Webster) Dick'80.Ox'79.Font'81
☎ (011-32-10) 86-74-55 . . rue de Bossut 60, 1390 Nethen, Belgium

Barclay MR & MRS Charles M (Nancy J Pannebaker) | ☎ (215) 723-4440
Sa.Cry.Sg.Ph.Pa'58 . . . . | 118 Maron Rd,
MISS Jane M—at Drexel . . . . | Hatfield, PA *19440*
MISS Jean W—at Penn State . . . . |
MR Charles P—Box 12091, Honolulu, HI *96828* |

Barclay MRS George C (Elizabeth W Moore) V'25.Csn.
☎ (609) 448-5592 . . Meadow Lakes 47-02U, Hightstown, NJ *08520*

Barclay MR & MRS George C JR (Laura B Bilkey)
Ws'54.Dar.Hn.H'51.Mit'53 . . of
☎ (011-44-1626) 832280 . . "Whitstone House" Bovey Tracey, Devon TQ13 9NA, England
☎ (802) 492-3794 . . "Pengwerne" PO Box 332, Cuttingsville, VT *05738*

Barclay MR & MRS J Randell (Dianne E Richoz)
K'zoo'79.Nu'90.Lond'78.Nu'86 . . of
☎ (212) 475-9347 . . 149 E 19 St, New York, NY *10003*
☎ (802) 492-3794 . . "Pengwerne" PO Box 332, Cuttingsville, VT *05738*

Barclay MR & MRS Rutgers (di Carpegna—Leslie | ☎ (505) 982-1000
Boocock) K.Y'57 . . . . | "Rabbit Junction"
  MISS Allegra di Carpegna—at London, | Rte 9, Box 66,
  England . . . . | Santa Fe, NM *87505*
  MR Guelfo di Carpegna—at |
  ☎ (212) 541-5319 . . 35 W 54 St, New York, |
  NY *10019* . . . . |
  MR Rufo di Carpegna—at |
  ☎ (505) 982-8337 . . 616 Washington Av, |
  Santa Fe, NM *87501* . . . . |

Barclay MR William K 3d—Me.Ty'60
☎ (561) 234-3744 . . "Sea Oaks" 1538 Sabal Court, Vero Beach, FL *32963*

Bard DR & MRS Henry H (Meyer—Lucie C Taft) V'45.Pr.Cly.P'45.Cl'48
☎ (516) 676-6471 . . 205 Bayville Rd, Locust Valley, NY *11560*

Bard MISS Holly H—Duke'78
☎ (404) 872-5171 . . 1212 University Dv NE, Atlanta, GA *30306*

Bardenheier MRS Joan Marie Rose (Gorman— | ☎ (314) 567-4380
Harrison—Joan Marie Rose Bardenheier) | 8955 Ladue Rd,
Mar'vilSacredH'59.StJ. . . . . | St Louis, MO *63124*
  MR Jerome L Harrison—at 1103 Louisville |
  Av, Apt 2, St Louis, MO *63139* . . . . |
  MR Joseph B Harrison—at 89 Brookview, |
  Dana Point, CA *92629* . . . . |
  MR Christopher P Harrison—at 27670 US |
  H'way 98, Apt 9, Daphne, AL *36526* . . . . |

Bardenheier MR Joseph A JR . . . . Died at Chesterfield, MO Jun 9'96

Bardin DR & MRS C Wayne (MacDonald—Beatrice | ☎ (212) 737-4582
Clement) Grenoble'65.Bay'62 . . . . | 910 Park Av,
  MISS Cybille A MacDonald . . . . | New York, NY
 | *10021*

Barfield MR & MRS Edward D (Alice D Guthrie) NEng'86
☎ (617) 631-1132 . . 10 Redstone Lane, Marblehead, MA *01945*

Baring-Gould MRS Sabine L (Kellogg—Mary Elizabeth Sears) Chi.
☎ (617) 523-3492 . . 34½ Beacon St, Boston, MA *02108*

Bark MR & MRS Dennis L (Cochran—France M | ☎ (415) 326-0828
de Sugny) Pcu.Stan'64 . . . . | 692 Mirada Av,
  MR Dwight M Cochran 3d . . . . | Stanford, CA *94305*
  MR Matthew J Cochran . . . . |
  MR Samuel A Cochran . . . . |

Barkan MR & MRS Adolph William (Joan M Robbins)
Sfy.Pcu.Bur.Ncd.Stan'39.Stan'42
☎ (415) 375-8256 . . 25 Laureldale Rd, Hillsborough, CA *94010*

Barkan DR & MRS Thomas A (Victoria Morones | ☎ (415) 931-5910
Dosamantes) Pcu.Fr.Stan'48.Stan'53 . . . . | 3435 Pacific Av,
  MISS Caroline S . . . . | San Francisco, CA
 | *94118-2029*

Barker MR & MRS B Devereux 3d (Jilda K Breed)
NH'76.Myc.Ny.Rby.Ec.Cw.H.'60
☎ (508) 526-1026 . . "Tidewood" Box 752, Manchester, MA *01944*

Barker MISS Bridget Lauren (John JR) . . . . Born Feb 2'95

Barker MRS George S (Helen C Pennington) . . . . Died at Devon, PA Feb 10'96

Barker MR & MRS James R (Kaye E Schumacher) | of ☎ (203)655-0126
Mich'57.Ny.Uncl.Ln.Cl'57 ⚓ . . . . | 180 Long Neck
  MR Mark W . . . . | Point Rd, Darien,
 | CT *06820*
 | ☎ (802) 297-2558
 | "Shattarack"
 | Stratton, VT *05360*

Barker MRS John (Mary Cleave) Cy.Chi.
☎ (617) 566-7455 . . 79 Randolph Rd, Chestnut Hill, MA *02167*

Barker MR & MRS John JR (Maureen E Kelly) Sth'78.ColC'80
☎ (303) 388-4614 . . 440 Eudora St, Denver, CO *80220*

Barker MR & MRS John C (Anna M Staeble) Cal'89.Wms'78
☎ (510) 525-6030 . . 958 Neilson St, Albany, CA *94706*

Barker MR & MRS John Franklin (Louisa P Brandon) Swth'65.StJ.Hn.H'63
☎ (301) 652-3311 . . 5005 Westport Rd, Chevy Chase, MD *20815*

Barker MR Jonathan C . . see MRS W J A Veitch

Barker MRS Lisa S (Lisa B Sherrerd) Rich'81.Me.Ncd.
☎ (610) 688-4642 . . 452 W Valley Rd, Strafford, PA *19010*

Barker MR & MRS Michael (Rosina O Bateson) HRdc'79.Reed'75
☎ (202) 965-3618 . . 3320 N St NW, Washington, DC *20007*

Barker JUNIORS MISS Morgan A . . see C J Case

Barker MR & MRS Morgan R (Carol Munro) Cr'56.Cry.Ac.Cr'55 ⚓
☎ (610) 520-1090 . . 804 Potts Lane, Bryn Mawr, PA *19010*

Barker MR & MRS Peter K (Robin A Bailey) | 655 Hillside Terr,
SCal'69.Clare'70.Ch'71 . . . . | Pasadena, CA *91105*
  MISS Kelley . . . . |
  JUNIORS MR Todd . . . . |
  JUNIORS MR Ryan . . . . |

Barker MR Robert P—Cry.M.Me.Dick'81
☎ (610) 525-3619 . . 901 Rock Creek Rd, Bryn Mawr, PA *19010*

Barker MR & MRS Robert R (Elizabeth Van D Shelly) B.C.Hn.H'36
☎ (203) 966-2500 . . 809 Oenoke Rd, New Canaan, CT *06840*

Barker MRS Theodore R (Nancy Edwards)
☎ (314) 241-8021 . . 300 Mansion House Center, Apt 2211, St Louis, MO *63102*

Barkhorn MR & MRS Henry C (Jean D Cook) Mds.P.'36
☎ (212) LE5-5707 . . 36 E 72 St, New York, NY *10021*

Barkus MR & MRS Paul R (Christine G Wilmer)
Wells'77.Fic.Pg.Van'76 . . of
☎ (212) 879-7176 . . 123 E 75 St, New York, NY *10021*
☎ (914) 677-0014 . . Deep Hollow Rd, Millbrook, NY *12545*
Barlerin MISS Caroline P—V'95 . . see MRS P M Patterson
Barloga MISS Cindy Cay (Hall—Cindy Cay Barloga) WCar'82
☎ (904) 768-3114 . . 3820 Bessent Rd, Jacksonville, FL *32218*
Barloga MR & MRS Fred R (Sara H Stafford) VaPoly'59.Cl'60
☎ (904) 926-1499 . . 71 Oyster Bay Dv, Crawfordville, FL *32327*
Barloga MISS Kerrie Lee—VaPoly'82.Fla'84
☎ (904) 878-0053 . . 2367 May Apple Court, Tallahassee,
FL *32308-6247*
Barloga MR & MRS Scott Brian (Laura C E Bowland) FlaSt'90.FlaSt'90
PO Box 427, Highlands, NC *28741*
Barlow MR & MRS Brian B (Marie A Robbins) | 48 Bluff Rd,
Sg.Pa'56 . . . . | Yarmouth, ME
MR Alec C . . . . | *04096*
Barlow MR & MRS Joel (Eleanor Livingston Poe) | ☎ (561) 272-8211
Cvc.Mt.Ds.Ncd.Alma'29.GeoW'35 . . . . | Harbour's Edge 369,
MISS Eleanor Poe—Sth'61 . . . . | 401 E Linton Blvd,
☎ (207) 823-2259 . . "Lands Away" HC 68, | Delray Beach, FL
Box 418, Friendship, ME *04547* . . . . | *33483*
Barlow MR & MRS Malcolm B (Mary S Lloyd) Sg.Sa.Cts.Msq.Ty'60
☎ (215) 836-4527 . . 1799 E Willow Grove Av, Laverock, PA *19038*
Barnard MISS Anne . . see J Timpson
Barnard MR & MRS George B (Frances F Fleming) Gm.Wms'38
☎ (610) 645-8691 . . 1400 Waverly Rd, Villa 42, Gladwyne, PA *19035*
Barnard MR & MRS Henry W (Susan L Rogers)
Ty'73.Pa'76.Cy.Me.Roan'69.Pa'76
☎ (617) 326-2266 . . 72 School St, Dedham, MA *02026*
Barnard MISS Phoebe . . see J Timpson
Barnes MR Alexander Stewart—P'49
34 Gordon Way, Princeton, NJ *08540*
Barnes MISS Amanda K . . see MRS T B Knapp
Barnes MR & MRS C Scott (Kimberly M Rabenberg)
W&M'84.Mo'84.CentMoSt'86
☎ (314) 822-2554 . . 547 Oak Valley Dv, St Louis, MO *63131*
Barnes MR Chaplin Bradford (late Irston R) . . . Married at Stonington, CT
Reid MRS B Trowbridge (Sheriff—White—Barbara W Trowbridge) . . .
Apr 13'96
Barnes MR & MRS Chaplin Bradford (Sheriff—White | ☎ (860) 535-4135
—Reid—Barbara W Trowbridge) Va'63.Msq. | 75 Main St,
Why.Myf.Yn.Y'62.Y'65.Ox'67 . . . . | PO Box 227,
MISS Sarah C—at Wheaton . . . . | Stonington, CT
MISS Nathalie H Sheriff—at 7 Lewis St, | *06378*
Portland, OR *04101* . . . . |
Barnes MR & MRS Charles Le F (Laura T Danforth)
StLaw'85.Cy.Rc.Vt'83
☎ (314) 997-2290 . . 41 Fair Oaks, St Louis, MO *63124*
Barnes MR Charles McC—Smu'78.Wash'80
☎ (314) 962-8452 . . 9127 Wrenwood Lane, St Louis, MO *63144*
Barnes MRS D Kennedy (Dolores M Kennedy) Dc.Dh.Ncd.Lm.
☎ (904) 384-4065 . . 3803 Bettes Circle, Jacksonville, FL *32210*
Barnes MISS Diana B . . see MISS L D Cummings
Barnes MRS Eakins (King—Margaret Virginia Eakins)
☎ (207) 866-3906 . . Orono, ME *04473*

Barnes MR & MRS Kenneth E (Ann C Yelverton) ECar'69.NCar'69
☎ (919) 836-9081 . . 318 E Park Dv, Raleigh, NC *27605*
Barnes MRS Lila Cummings (Lila Cummings) . . . . name changed to
Cummings
Barnes MR Richard K—Hav'52
☎ (203) 438-9444 . . 13 Conant Rd, Ridgefield, CT *06877*
Barnes MR & MRS Robert E (Ervin—Ogden—Katherine | ☎ (609) 924-5307
Waller) Ht.Ncd.Dc. . . . . | 34 Gordon Way,
MR Michael Andrulis . . . . | Princeton, NJ *08540*
MR John Andrulis . . . . |
Barnes MR & MRS Robert G (Branch—Stimson—R | ☎ (860) 435-0339
Allyne Gade) Cly.Cl'37 . . . . | 235 Indian Mountain
MISS Faith A Stimson—at ☎ (617) 864-0743 | Rd, Lakeville, CT
31 Granville Rd, Apt 2, Cambridge, MA *02138* | *06039*
MR David G Stimson—at ☎ (415) 552-4698 |
1323 Masonic Av, San Francisco, CA *94117* . |
Barnes DR & MRS Robert H (Bettina E Muelling) Ncmb'50.LSU'73.Tul'49
☎ (601) 442-4334 . . 705 Washington St, Natchez, MS *39120*
Barnes MRS T Ellis 2d (Alice J Henry)
☎ (314) 994-9076 . . 11 McKnight Lane, St Louis, MO *63124*
Barnes MR & MRS T Ellis 3d (G Cristen Bunce) | ☎ (314) 993-0234
Sth'77.Cy.Rc.Nd.Cw.Rv.StL'70.StL'73 . . . . | 6 Pebble Creek Rd,
JUNIORS MISS Sarah E . . . . | St Louis, MO *63124*
JUNIORS MR T Ellis 4th . . . . |
Barnes MRS William 3d (Julia Terry) Cy.
☎ (314) 993-8722 . . 9032 Haverford Terrace Lane, St Louis, MO *63117*
Barnes MR & MRS William S (Mary West) Sm.Tv.Y'40.H'47
☎ (508) 369-5731 . . 47 Sandy Pond Rd, Concord, MA *01742*
Barnes MR & MRS Wilson K JR (Katharine R | ☎ (410) 377-7399
Longridge) Md'65.Gi.Wt.Sar.Dar.Balt'69 . . . . . | 4 St Michael's Way,
MR Wilson K 3d—Gi.Sar. . . . . | Baltimore, MD
MR David L—Gi.Sar. . . . . | *21212*
Barneson MR & MRS Lee H (Valerie J Halloran) | ☎ (310) 451-1819
Cal'71.Vh.Cal'69 ⚐ . . . . | 214 S Bristol Av,
MISS Laura Lee—at Santa Catalina Sch . . . . | Los Angeles, CA
| *90049*
Barnett MISS Alexis A (Joseph W JR) . . . . Married at
Cold Spring Harbor, NY
Myles MR George F (John L) . . . . Jun 29'96
Barnett MR & MRS Benjamin H (Catharine W Thacher) Me.Ac.Ncd.Pa'31
☎ (610) 642-3738 . . 1404 Knox Rd, Wynnewood, PA *19096*
Barnett MR & MRS Benjamin H JR (Anne E Mize) | ☎ (610) 642-2057
RMWmn'57.Me.Ac. . . . . | 700 Panmure Rd,
MISS Catharine Alexandra—RMWmn'92.Ac.— | Haverford, PA
at ☎ (202) 546-7405 . . 619 Massachusetts Av | *19041-1218*
NE, Washington, DC *20002* . . . . |
Barnett MR & MRS Benjamin H 3d (Elise B Miller) Me.Denis'85
☎ (609) 397-3830 . . 115 N Union St, Lambertville, NJ *08530*
Barnett MRS Elizabeth N (Elizabeth N | ☎ (610) 644-7166
Le Boutillier) Ncd. . . . . | 102 Biddle Rd,
MISS Elizabeth L—at Wash'n & Lee . . . . | Paoli, PA *19301*
Barnett MR James A—Pn.P'31
☎ (503) 220-0652 . . 706 NW Westover Terr, Portland, OR *97210*

Barnett MR & MRS James H (Faith Richardson) Rich'42.H'48 .... ☎ (401) 272-7718 57 Stimson Av, Providence, RI 02906
  MISS Mary R—at 24 Wildwood Av, Madison, CT 06443 ....
  MISS Faith H—at 42 Mt Vernon St, Brookline, MA 02146 ....
  MR James H JR—at 4708 Philco Dv, Austin, TX 78745 ....

Barnett MR Joseph W 3d . . see N Doubleday

Barnett MR & MRS Samuel T 3d (Miriam S Taylor) Temp'76.Wes'69.Temp'75
  ☎ (610) 566-7394 . . "New Moon" 230 S Ridley Creek Rd, Rose Valley, PA 19065

Barnett MR William H—Cal'51
  ☎ (619) 294-6748 . . 3043 State St, San Diego, CA 92103

Barney MR Alexander V N . . see L P Yandell

Barney MISS Frederica S—Geo'74
  ☎ (415) 992-2097 . . 1551 Southgate Av, Apt 328, Daly City, CA 94015

Barney MR & MRS Robert W (Claire C Paquot) Y'47
  ☎ (860) 434-2082 . . Sterling City Rd, Lyme, CT 06371

Barney MR & MRS William Hadwen (Katherine L Kennedy) Ws'41.Nyc.Ncd.Bow'43
  ☎ (941) 964-2757 . . 162 Carrick Bend Lane, PO Box 1002, Boca Grande, FL 33921

Barney MR & MRS William R JR (Newcomer—Caroline F Grund) Cv.May.Un.Wms'49
  ☎ (216) 423-4436 . . 7650 Deerfield Rd, Gates Mills, OH 44040

Barney MR William R 3d—Tvcl.Hills'75 .... ☎ (404) 351-0781 3135 Ridgewood Rd NW, Atlanta, GA 30327-1935
  JUNIORS MISS Kathleen McC ....
  JUNIORS MR William R 4th ....

Barngrove MRS H Grant (La Porte—Virginia I See) Box I204, 1000 Vicar's Landing Way, Ponte Vedra Beach, FL 32082

Barngrove MR & MRS James L JR (Ruth Hardcastle) Wash'29.Y'32
  ☎ (802) 484-7898 . . Bailey's Mill Rd, RR 1, Box 99, Reading, VT 05062

Barngrove MRS Sally Ann (McQuilkin—Sally Ann Barngrove) CtCol'64 .... of ☎ (818)793-7733 250 S Arroyo Blvd, Pasadena, CA 91105
  MISS Hilary B McQuilkin—at Bowdoin ..... ☎ (818) 793-4538 310 S San Rafael Av, Pasadena, CA 91105

Barnhart MR & MRS Gilbert R (DiPietro—Idelle M Stuckey) Syr'38.H'47
  ☎ (301) 656-9195 . . 7108 Brennon Lane, Chevy Chase, MD 20815

Barnhill MR & MRS Gregory H (Lisa P Angelozzi) Dick'77.Gv.Md.Nrr.Sar.Br'75
  ☎ (410) 484-2553 . . "St Anthony's Delight" 10801 Stevenson Rd, Stevenson, MD 21153

Barnum MRS A Savage (Anne L Savage) Pa'52 ... ☎ (203) 869-0114 8 Baldwin Farms N, Greenwich, CT 06831
  MISS Catherine H—at Rockport, ME 04856 ....
  MR Nathaniel P........................

Barnum MISS Harriet
  ☎ (215) 968-0159 . . Pennswood Village B101, Newtown, PA 18940

Barnum MR & MRS John W (Nancy R Grinnell) Sth'54.Mt.Cvc.Ny.Y'49.Y'57 ⚓ .... ☎ (202) 244-2530 5175 Tilden St NW, Washington, DC 20016
  MISS Sarah K ....
  MR Alexander S ....
  MR Cameron L ....

Barnwell MR & MRS John P (Alida D Sinkler) Hlns'80.Yh.Va'79
  ☎ (803) 577-9924 . . 7 Stolls Alley, Charleston, SC 29401

Barr MRS Dudley R (Laura P Hays) Chi . . .of
  ☎ (207) 363-3936 . . "TiLaRi" Box 464, Orchard Lane, York Harbor, ME 03911
  "Sea Skye" 4436 Waters Edge Lane, Sanibel, FL 33957

Barr MISS (DR) Elizabeth H (MacBride—Elizabeth H Barr) SL'77.Cl'82.Temp'87.Temp'95
  ☎ (215) 629-1596 . . 738 S Mildred St, Philadelphia, PA 19147

Barr MRS Nancy T (Nancy T Townsend) Qns'75.NCar'89
  ☎ (704) 896-2130 . . 17100 Grenache Court, Huntersville, NC 28078

Barr MR & MRS William A (Scarlett—Virginia B Penfield) SL'40.Gi.Elk.Mv.StJColl'42.Va'48.VPI'51 . . of
  ☎ (410) 323-3864 . . 38 Bouton Green Court, Baltimore, MD 21210
  ☎ (410) 255-1244 . . Gibson Island, MD 21056

Barratt MR Norris S 3d—Srr.Wt.Cw.Cspa.
  ☎ (610) 527-2529 . . Box 1022, Paoli, PA 19301-0940

Barratt MR Peter Levering
  ☎ (610) 436-9227 . . 317 Hannum Av, West Chester, PA 19380-2858

Barre MR & MRS Tyrus D (MacIntosh—Appel—Raimonda Bartol) Cal'41
  ☎ (202) 338-4459 . . 2811 Foxhall Rd NW, Washington, DC 20007

Barrell MR & MRS Michael A (Robin K Baker) Caz'70.St.Buf'65 .... ☎ (716) 874-0463 314 Lincoln P'kway, Buffalo, NY 14216
  JUNIORS MISS Jessica B ....

Barrell MRS Nathaniel A (I G Brigitte Steffan) St.G. | ☎ (716) 883-1145 65 Oakland Place, Buffalo, NY 14222
  MISS Brigitte A—WmSth'79.G. ....

Barrell MR & MRS Thomas F (Stephanie A Laws) Ind'81.Cl'86.Eisen'75
  ☎ (415) 386-3710 . . 759 Fourteenth Av, San Francisco, CA 94118

Barrett MR & MRS (DR) Beatrice H (Ribback—van Buren—Beatrice H Barrett) Ariz'50.Ky'52.Purd'57 ⚓ . . of
  Rte 5, Box 236A, Winter St, Lincoln, MA 01773
  33 Champlain Rd, Chatham, MA 02633-2511

Barrett MR C Francis—Qc. .... 3136 Victoria Av, Cincinnati, OH 45208
  JUNIORS MISS Elisabeth C ....
  JUNIORS MR Peter S ....

Barrett DR & MRS C Redington JR (Elizabeth E Biddle) V'58.Y'55.Cl'59 .... ☎ (201) 569-0336 40 Beech Rd, Englewood, NJ 07631
  MR R Morris—P'87—at ☎ (718) 624-6362 70 Clark St, Apt 2H, Brooklyn, NY 11201......

Barrett MISS (DR) Cynthia T—V'59.H'62 . . of
  ☎ (310) 457-2471 . . 6778 S Shearwater Lane, Malibu, CA 90265
  ☎ (805) 969-5226 . . 1350 E Valley Rd, Santa Barbara, CA 93108

Barrett MR & MRS David A (Laurie C Pile) Bost'75.U'74.Pa'80 .... ☎ (508) 748-1108 68 Pleasant St, Box 418, Marion, MA 02738
  JUNIORS MISS Elizabeth C ....
  JUNIORS MISS Jennifer P ....

Barrett MRS Edward W (Mason Daniel) Ncd. ..... ☎ (203) 531-3224 107 W Lyon Farm Dv, Greenwich, CT 06831
  MISS Margo M—at ☎ (212) AT9-3952 161 E 88 St, New York, NY 10128 ....

Barrett MR & MRS Harold E (Strubing—Louisa Condon)
Hlns'68.So'49.EpiscTheo'51
☎ (804) 295-8526 . . 932 Rosser Lane, Charlottesville, VA *22903*

Barrett MRS Harvey N JR (Taplin—Constance W Huntington) V'35
☎ (203) 481-5453 . . Evergreen Woods 143, 88 Notch Hill Rd,
North Branford, CT *06471*

Barrett MR & MRS John D 2d (Lucy A McClellan)   ☎ (203) 869-3769
V'57.Rcn.Y'57 . . . . 1 Rockwood Lane
MISS Amy R—Stan'88 . . . . Spur, Greenwich,
MR James W—P'83 . . . . CT *06830*

Barrett MR & MRS John F (Eileen M Ward)   ☎ (513) 561-4278
Wheat'73.Rcn.Qc.Cin'71 . . . . 9300 Shawnee Run
JUNIORS MISS Christine B . . . . Rd, Cincinnati, OH
                           45243

Barrett MR & MRS Lee (Eleanor D Haselton) Cy.Dth'41
☎ (617) 235-6070 . . 30 Ravine Rd, Wellesley Hills, MA *02181*

Barrett MRS Pratt (Register—Dorothy D Pratt) Bur.
☎ (415) 343-7445 . . 940 Parrott Dv, Hillsborough, CA *94010*

Barrett MR & MRS Robert J 3d (Tankoos—Catherine B Moore)
LeFleurou'66.Un.Evg.Dar.Geo'66.Cl'69.H'71 . . of
☎ (561) 833-7860 . . 608 Island Dv, Palm Beach, FL *33480*
☎ (212) 628-6464 . . 770 Park Av, New York, NY *10021*

Barrett MRS Susan V P (Susan H Vander Poel)   ☎ (203) 661-9116
Pa'72 . . . . 23 N Porchuck Rd,
MR Robert J 4th—at Georgetown . . . . Greenwich, CT
JUNIORS MR Graham H—at Lawrenceville *06831*

Barrett MRS Thurman JR (Magruder—Carolyn M   ☎ (210) 828-4335
Murray) A. . . . . 7731 Broadway St,
  MR Roy M Magruder—Tex'87 . . . . Apt 341,
                                  San Antonio, TX
                                  78209

Barrie MRS George 4th (Carolina M Winston)   of ☎ (310)478-7206
Cal'49 . . . . 1707 San Vicente
MISS Christine M . . . . Blvd, Santa Monica,
MR Winston A . . . . CA *90402*
MR Matthew C P . . . . ☎ (619) 755-4474
JUNIORS MR Riley A . . . . 2508 Ocean Front
                                  St, Del Mar, CA
                                  92014
                                  ☎ (208) 788-3933
                                  399 Broadford Rd,
                                  PO Box 793,
                                  Bellevue, ID *83313*

Barriger MISS Catherine B (John W 4th) . . . . . . Married at Winnetka, IL
Dunsby MR Adam W (Walter E) . . . . Jun 8'96

Barriger MR & MRS John W 4th (Evelyn Dobson) Mit'49.Y'50
☎ (847) 256-3335 . . 155 Melrose Av, Kenilworth, IL *60043*

Barriger MR & MRS John W 5th (Marianne C Fox)
☎ (847) 256-0450 . . 2246 Lake Av, Wilmette, IL *60091*

Barringer MRS Brandon (Richardson—Diana V R Johnson)
☎ (610) 687-4267 . . 550 Maplewood Rd, Wayne, PA *19087*

Barringer MR & MRS C Minor (Mary M Pratt) V'42.P'42
☎ (610) 388-6616 . . 146 Center Mill Rd, Chadds Ford, PA *19317*

Barringer MR John Paul . . . . Died Aug 15'96

Barringer MRS John Paul (Dunn—Dorothy A Pray) Ph.An.Pn.
☎ (609) 924-1566 . . 218 Hun Rd, Princeton, NJ *08540*

Barringer MR & MRS (DR) Lewin B (Lydia V Rigor)   ☎ (610) 896-0110
StThos'64.O'64 . . . . 201 S Buck Lane,
MISS Elizabeth A . . . . Haverford, PA
MR Lewin B 3d *19041*

Barringer MR & MRS Philip E (Bettyanne Rusen) Cos.P'38.Pa'48
☎ (202) 244-3492 . . 4609—38 St NW, Washington, DC *20016*

Barrington MR & MRS Felix M (Linda V Batten)   ☎ (941) 475-6848
Ariz'67 . . . . 970 Bayshore Dv,
MISS Felicity V . . . . Englewood, FL
MR Anton B *34223*

Barroll MR & MRS David O V (Ann C Athey) MaryB'59.Md.Wash'58
☎ (410) 778-0642 . . 202 David Dv, Chestertown, MD *21620*

Barroll MR & MRS F Lewis (Wendy van Hoorebeke)   ☎ (313) 882-1031
Cc.Va'52 . . . . 103 Merriweather
MISS Tessa—Vt'88—at ☎ (415) 921-3770   Rd, Grosse Pointe
2335 Washington St, San Francisco, CA *94115* .   Farms, MI *48236*

Barroll MR & MRS Lawrence L (Margery L Hitch)   ☎ (912) 233-2759
Rv.Cw.Ncd.Va'52 . . . . 331 E 44 St,
MR Lawrence L JR—at 331 S Smedley St,   Savannah, GA
Philadelphia, PA *19103* *31405*
MR John D B . . . .
MR Mark H . . . .

Barroll MISS Letitia H (Frederick—Letitia H Barroll) Ty'85.JHop'89.Ncd.
☎ (212) 983-6240 . . 25 Tudor City Place, Apt 719, New York,
NY *10017*

Barroll MISS Margaret C—Roan'86
☎ (203) 629-5930 . . 42 Alexander St, Greenwich, CT *06830*

Barroll MR & MRS Richard S W (Page K Roe) Gi.Cw.Mv.Ncd.
☎ (410) 252-2336 . . 734 Chapel Ridge Rd, Timonium, MD *21093*

Barroll MRS William L M (Sara D Gray) Syr'47
☎ (860) 726-2224 . . Duncaster T618, 20 Loeffler Rd, Bloomfield,
CT *06002*

Barron MRS Frederick M (Catherine K Linthicum)
☎ (954) 943-7264 . . 301 N Ocean Blvd, Apt 503, Pompano Beach,
FL *33062*

Barron MR & MRS Hugh D (Sarah M Moore) Cal'88.Vt'86
☎ (707) 769-8682 . . 960 Chileno Valley Rd, Petaluma, CA *94952*

Barron MISS Josephine D—BostColl'85
☎ (508) 945-4705 . . 90 Seaview St, Chatham, MA *02633*

Barron MR & MRS Timothy R (Leslie Lauck)   ☎ (209) 447-9737
KHam'tn'72.Dth'71.H'77 . . . . 6707 N Woodson
JUNIORS MISS Nicole L . . . . Av, Fresno, CA
JUNIORS MISS Brittany E *93711*

Barron MR & MRS William A 3d (Mary D Robertson) Cyb.H'45
RR 1, Box 325, Sea Meadows Lane, Yarmouth, ME *04096*

Barrow MRS Donald F (Constance L J Bruen) Csh.Cly.Lm.Ht.Cda.Dh.
☎ (516) 423-5981 . . ''Strathlea'' Box 276, Cold Spring Harbor,
NY *11724*

Barrow MR & MRS Kenneth P JR (Betty L Harris)   ☎ (610) 565-4340
Temp'73 ⛵ . . . . 733 Hemlock Rd,
MR Peter D . . . . Media, PA
JUNIORS MISS Margaret R *19063-1709*

Barrow MR Richard D—Wid'77.DelLaw'81
☎ (610) 604-0973 . . 117 S Chester Rd, Apt 504, Swarthmore, PA *19081*

Barrows MRS David Nye (Frances L Scoville)..... ☎ (212) 288-5053
MISS Lila H—Cs.Ncd..................... 120 E 81 St,
New York, NY
10028

Barrows MRS Elliot A (Amabel K Eshleman) Dc.
☎ (203) 762-9054 . . 372 Ridgefield Rd, Wilton, CT *06897*

Barrows MR & MRS Mercer B (Connolly—Joy T ☎ (610) 353-1530
Price) Pa'63.Gm.Me.Rc.Ac.Pa'51 .... 825 Briarwood Rd,
MISS L Nichols .... Newtown Square,
MR William K—at 1402 E Orange St, Tempe, AZ | PA *19073*
85281.................................
MR Joseph C Connolly—Dick'95—at
☎ (717) 241-5142 . . 140 W Louther St, Apt 3,
Carlisle, PA *17013* ....

Barrows MR & MRS Thomas S (Abigail S Liggett) Cry.Hb.H'59
☎ (609) 359-8868 . . 1129 Canal Rd, Princeton, NJ *08540*

Barrows MR & MRS William D (Laurie A Sinko)
Mass'81.Les'91.WashColl'79
☎ (508) 463-4394 . . 16 Washington St, Newburyport, MA *01950*

Barry MRS A Shelnutt (L Ann Shelnutt) BMr'69
☎ (212) 755-4267 . . 57 W 58 St, New York, NY *10019*

Barry DR & MRS David S 3d (Jane M McCall) ☎ (608) 244-2438
Sth'68.P'62.H'67.Wis'76 .... 124 W Gilman St,
MR Neville M 3d—at Smith .... Madison, WI *53703*
JUNIORS MISS Lydia S ....
JUNIORS MISS Margaret J ....

Barry MR John L 3d—Duke'53 .... ☎ (802) 824-6371
MISS Alison S .... ''Checkerberry
Hill'' South
Londonderry, VT
05155

Barry REV & MRS Kevin A (Caroline F Perera)
Mid'86.Ham'76.Van'81.Y.'87
☎ (516) 261-1281 . . 23 Schooner Rd, Northport, NY *11768*

Barry MRS Manning (Lucy Manning Brown) ☎ (617) 566-7314
Cy.Cly......................... 5 Perrin Rd,
DR Herbert 3d—H'52—at 552 N Neville St, Brookline, MA
Pittsburgh, PA *15213* *02146-7514*
MR John M Baker—Conn'89—at Columbia
Business ....

Barry MR & MRS Marten (Katherine Ann Fay)
☎ (415) 342-0375 . . 415 W Santa Inez Av, Hillsborough, CA *94010*

Barry MR & MRS Robert A JR (Tam Benoist) ☎ (314) VO3-3792
NotreD'47 .... 31 Aberdeen Place,
MR François Benoist—Mo'85—at Clayton, MO *63105*
1528 Thrush Terr, St Louis, MO *63144* ....

Barry DR & MRS Robert A 3d (Elizabeth M Lottes)
Tufts'81.Wash'76.Wash'80.StL'95
☎ (314) 984-0863 . . 1520 Andrew Dv, St Louis, MO *63122*

Barry COL & MRS Robert B (Bradner—Lydia Seltzer)
USA.Sth'39.OState'39
☎ (719) 635-0814 . . 1660 Mesa Av, Colorado Springs, CO *80906*

Barry MRS Robert R (Hermann—Anne R Benjamin) Bnd'48.Cly.
☎ (619) 328-2022 . . 71065 Clubview Dv, Box 5005, Rancho Mirage,
CA *92270*

Barstow MR & MRS Burrows JR (Moorhouse— ☎ (813) 823-2645
Katharine B Cooper) Dth'43 .... 751 Cordova Blvd
MISS Sarah G .... NE, St Petersburg,
MR Richard T Moorhouse .... | FL *33704*

Barth MISS Christina E—HRdc'83.Pa'90
☎ (011-44-171) 722-6441 . . 1 Elsworthy Terr, London NW3 3DR,
England

Barth MR Dominic G—Cal'85.Brooks'93
224 E 74 St, Apt 5C, New York, NY *10021-3666*

Barth MR & MRS Gilbert R (M Christine Giesler)
Ariz'87.Ala'89.Col'87.Col'91
☎ (303) 499-8210 . . 3165 Endicott Dv, Boulder, CO *80303*

Barth MR & MRS Gunther P (Ellen R Wood) ☎ (510) 527-0367
Rdc'58.Ore'55.H'62 .... 642 Santa Rosa Av,
MISS Giselle M—at U of Cal Los Angeles Law . Berkeley, CA *94707*

Bartholet MRS Elizabeth (Du Bois—Elizabeth Bartholet) Rdc'62.Hn.
☎ (617) 864-4593 . . 10 Farwell Place, Cambridge, MA *02138*

Bartholomay MR William C—Cho.On.Rc.Rcn.Sr.Sc.B.Ln.LakeF'55 . . of
☎ (312) 642-5634 . . 180 E Pearson St, Apt 3307, Chicago, IL *60611*
☎ (561) 659-7966 . . 433 Brazilian Court, Palm Beach, FL *33480*

Bartholomay MR William T—Sr.Rc.On.Cas.LakeF'76.Ch'79 . . of
☎ (773) 472-4155 . . 1960 N Fremont St, Chicago, IL *60614*
☎ (307) 537-5452 . . Boulder, WY *82923*

Bartholomew MR & MRS George L (Dorsaneo—Penelope L Churchman)
Alf'56
☎ (610) 688-2483 . . 553 W Wayne Av, Wayne, PA *19087*

Bartholomew MR & MRS James R (Elizabeth ☎ (609) 466-0852
Oberndorfer)......................... 223 Pennington-
MISS Elizabeth S—Duke'88—at Princeton Theo . Rocky Hill Rd,
MISS Sarah D—RISD'92 .... Pennington, NJ
JUNIORS MR William B *08534-0812*

Bartholomew MR & MRS Robert Le R (Barbara Page)
☎ (610) 353-3880 . . ''The Cottage'' 938 Plumsock Rd,
Newtown Square, PA *19073*

Bartle DR & MRS Stuart H (Barbara S Bishop)
Rdc'49.Va'68.Lx.C.Hn.H'50.Nu'54
☎ (413) 243-3389 . . ''February Hill Farm'' PO Box 692, West Rd, Lee,
MA *01238*

Bartle MR Thomas P 3d . . see F L Buddenhagen

Bartlett MR & MRS Arthur L (Matthew—Zoë Tibbetts) Sbc.H'41
☎ (508) 927-0073 . . 9 Grove St, Beverly Farms, MA *01915*

Bartlett MR & MRS Charles L (Josephine M Buck) Y'43
☎ (202) 338-0646 . . 4615 W St NW, Washington, DC *20007*

Bartlett MR & MRS David F (Stéfane ☎ (212) 744-0597
Abeille-Demay) Rc.Bcs.Cly.Y'49 .... 36 E 72 St,
MISS Stéfane F—Rich'92.Cly.—at New York, NY
☎ (011-33-1) 45-49-38-16 . . 8 rue Coëtlogon, *10021*
75006 Paris, France ....

Bartlett MR & MRS David M (Flora J Smith) Myf.USMMA'44
☎ (914) 255-5486 . . ''Walnut Grove'' 181 Libertyville Rd, New Paltz,
NY *12561*

Bartlett MR & MRS Edmund (Fairchild—Crews—Margery P Abbett)
Pr.Yh.Plg.Cly.P'33
☎ (516) 676-5522 . . 15 Locust Lane, Upper Brookville, Glen Head,
NY *11545*

Bartlett MR & MRS Edmund 3d (Mary T Richards)
Wheat'73.Suff'78.Md.Mt.Cvc.Sl.Y'69.H'73
☎ (301) 718-7288 . . 4 W Melrose St, Chevy Chase, MD *20815*
Bartlett MR & MRS Edwin P (Margaret J Cortellini) Dth'40
☎ (716) 282-1389 . . 5054 Forest Rd, Lewiston, NY *14092*
Bartlett MISS Elizabeth M (Warnock—Elizabeth M Bartlett)
☎ (410) 822-3660 . . 514 S Aurora St, Easton, MD *21601*
Bartlett MRS Evans E (Baldauf—Dorothy B Burnham) Buf.
33 Gates Circle, Buffalo, NY *14209*
Bartlett MRS Francis G JR (Sara T Hundley)
☎ (410) 476-3715 . . 2658 Ocean Gateway, Trappe, MD *21673*
Bartlett MR Francis G JR
☎ (410) 822-0269 . . Box 481, Easton, MD *21601*
Bartlett DR & MRS Frederick H 3d (Melanie W Roden)
MtH'79.Wms'77.Jef'81
2200 Inverness Lane, Huntingdon Valley, PA *19006*
Bartlett MR Harry G—Cvc.Cr'36
☎ (202) 451-0429 . . 6200 Oregon Av NW, Washington, DC *20015*
Bartlett MR & MRS Henry P (Natalie B Perkins) Ty'87.RISD'84
☎ (617) 923-8499 . . 117 W Boylston St, Watertown, MA *02172*
Bartlett MR & MRS Joseph W (Holt—Barbara T | ☎ (212) 996-5386
Bemis) Sm.C.H'55 . . . . | 1158 Fifth Av,
MISS Hilary E Holt . . . . | New York, NY
MR Andrew J Holt JR . . . . | *10029*
JUNIORS MR Bradley B Holt . . . . |
Bartlett MRS L Dortch (Louisa Bethune Dortch) Briar'69.Del'71.Wil.Ncd.
☎ (410) 472-0998 . . PO Box 534, Sparks, MD *21152*
Bartlett DR & MRS Marshall K (Barbara F Hume) | ☎ (617) 326-2246
V'34.Chi.H.Y'24 . . . . | 10 Longwood Dv,
MISS Barbara H—at ☎ (617) 227-5719 | Apt 345, Westwood,
2 Hawthorne Place, Boston, MA *02114* . . . . | MA *02090-1143*
Bartlett MR & MRS Marshall P (Margaret Van D | ☎ (201) 993-5974
Wilmer) Mg.P'65.H'69 . . . . | Box 489, Young's
MR John P . . . . | Rd, New Vernon, NJ
MR Stephen W—at Conn Coll . . . . | *07976*
Bartlett MRS May P (May A Parish) . . . . | ☎ (617) 236-4113
MR Charles W . . . . | 301 Berkeley St,
| Boston, MA *02116*
Bartlett MRS Philip Golden (Lysbet W Lefferts) Cly.Ncd.Dh.Lm.
☎ (212) SA2-7149 . . 1158 Fifth Av, New York, NY *10029*
Bartlett MISS Phyllis—RISD'60.Cs.Lm.
☎ (212) 289-8093 . . 152 E 94 St, New York, NY *10128-2575*
Bartlett MR & MRS Robert D 3d (Susan D Stevens) Hlns'76.Va'70
☎ (804) 741-9637 . . 8901 Allendale Rd, Richmond, VA *23229*
Bartlett MR & MRS Samuel B (Joan M Harding) | ☎ (508) 746-0751
Dth'57.H'61 . . . . | 226 Warren Av,
MR Thomas H . . . . | Plymouth, MA
| *02360*

Bartol MISS Anne Farr—Occ'82
☎ (303) 449-8982 . . 700—36 St, Boulder, CO *80303*
Bartol MISS Elisabeth W—Colg'92.Pqt.
☎ (212) 743-0116 . . 538 E 85 St, Apt 4B, New York, NY *10028*
Bartol MRS John G (Caroline C Schiller) R.Rcp.Ac.Ste.Myf.
☎ (602) 488-9897 . . ''Los Techos'' Box 1209, Carefree, AZ *85377*

Bartol CDR & MRS John H JR (Cynthia J Smith) | ☎ (703) 370-3555
USN.Tufts'63.An.Aub'62 . . . . | 3709 Ft Worth Av,
MISS Melanie A—Br'93.An. . . . . | Alexandria, VA
| *22304*
Bartol MR & MRS John Hone (Walker—Norma W Magnus)
Rcn.Fic.Fiy.H'36 . . of
☎ (203) 869-4106 . . 408 Riversville Rd, Greenwich, CT *06831*
☎ (561) 546-4915 . . 28 N Beach Rd, Hobe Sound, FL *33455*
Bartolec MR & MRS Thomas A (Corinne DeL Morris) Md'61.Md'64
☎ (561) 694-3044 . . 8164 Quail Meadow Trace, West Palm Beach,
FL *33412*
Barton MR & MRS Alexander K (Koontz—Collins—Cary L Keen)
Md.Ayc.Rv.Y'45 ⛵
☎ (410) 841-6162 . . ''Treetops'' Sherwood Forest, MD *21405*
Barton MRS Brooks (Cantini—Brooks Barton) Vt'85
☎ (212) 410-6645 . . 17 E 96 St, New York, NY *10128*
Barton MRS C Marshall JR (Louise Tunstall Barroll) Gv.Mv.
☎ (410) 363-1775 . . 325 Garrison Forest Rd, Owings Mills, MD *21117*
Barton MR & MRS David W JR (Cherry—Carol H | of ☎ (410)532-9509
Urban) Gchr'60.Elk.Evg.NCar'47 . . . . | 1101 Harriton Rd,
MR John M Cherry . . . . | Baltimore, MD
MR Henry A Cherry . . . . | *21210*
| ☎ (561) 848-3905
| 216 Jamaica Lane,
| Palm Beach, FL
| *33480*
Barton DR Evan M—Wms'24.JHop'29 | ☎ (773) 288-1984
MR Eric McM—Roch'64.Ill'75 . . . . | 5817 S Blackstone
| Av, Chicago, IL
| *60637*
Barton MR & MRS Francis L (Simpson—Phyllis M | ☎ (617) 934-5571
Saunders) Conn'38.H.'26 . . . . | 16 Bay Ridge Lane,
MR Davis Simpson JR—at Arlington St, | Box 251, Duxbury,
Newburyport, MA *01950* . . . . | MA *02331*
MR George W Simpson |
Barton MR & MRS H Hudson 4th (Jane P Meigs) Rc.Pc.Ph.Fw.Ac.Pa'39
☎ (215) CH7-4880 . . 444 W Chestnut Hill Av, Philadelphia, PA *19118*
Barton MR & MRS H Hudson 5th (Elisa D Menocal) | ☎ (610) 660-9419
Pa'77.Rc.Pa'76 . . . . | 744 Clarendon Rd,
JUNIORS MISS Zoë E . . . . | Penn Valley, PA
JUNIORS MISS Ashley J . . . . | *19072-1519*
Barton MRS Meta Packard (Meta M Packard) | ☎ (410) 377-6622
V'50.Loy'77.Mv.Elk. . . . . | 6507 Montrose Av,
MISS Blair Lee—Mid'77 . . . . | Baltimore, MD
| *21212*
Barton MR Randolph 3d (Randolph JR) . . . . Married at Boston, MA
Armstrong MISS Louise S (Rodney) . . . . Jun 15'96
Barton MR & MRS Randolph 3d (Louise S Armstrong)
Wms'93.Wh'lck'94.Ty'93
☎ (302) 656-7727 . . 1517 Tower Rd, Wilmington, DE *19806*
Barton MR Reginald McCarroll JR—David'73.NCar'77
☎ (910) 484-0771 . . 119 Hillside Av, Fayetteville, NC *28301*
Barton MRS Robert B M (Sally Parker) Ey.Mt.Myf.Ncd.Hn.H.
☎ (617) 631-2597 . . 329 Ocean Av, Marblehead, MA *01945*
Barton MR & MRS Robert O (Harriett R Thomas) Syr'44.Cy.G.Canis'41
☎ (716) 837-4430 . . 40 Brantwood Rd, Snyder, NY *14226*

Barton MR & MRS Thomas C JR (Harriette M Earle) Cry.Y'46
☎ (908) 899-8679 . . 1336 Bay Av, Mantoloking, NJ *08738*
Barton MR & MRS Thomas H (Jo Jeanne Millon)
V'48.Un.Cw.Snc.Cly.Dar.Nw'45.H.'48
☎ (212) TR6-6582 . . 1192 Park Av, New York, NY *10128-1314*
Bartow MRS Clarence W (Woolston—Elizabeth V Ingersoll) T.Fic.
☎ (941) 964-0117 . . Box 63, Boca Grande, FL *33921*
Bartow MRS Philip K (Mott—Johnson—Mary Neuman) Ri.Eh.Shcc.
☎ (908) 234-0384 . . Box 579, Far Hills, NJ *07931*

Bartow MR & MRS Philip K JR (Madeleine R Cresap) Csh.Wms'70. . . . . MISS Madeleine C—at Williams . . . . JUNIORS MR Philip K 3d—at Westminster	☎ (516) 271-4762 101 Woodchuck Hollow Rd, Cold Spring Harbor, NY *11724*

Bartow MR Samuel
☎ (603) 788-3345 . . Grange Rd, Box 232, Lancaster, NH *03584*
Bartram MR & MRS Brent E (Glenny L Dunlop) . . of
☎ (606) 441-5208 . . 32 Brigadier Court, Wilder, KY *41076*
☎ (502) 451-3795 . . 206 Flander's Court, Apt 5, Louisville, KY *40218*
Bartram MISS Elizabeth M (Henckels—Elizabeth M Bartram)
☎ (561) 833-1135 . . 200 Phipps Plaza, Palm Beach, FL *33480*
Bartram MRS J Burr (Mary S Sheppard) Ny.Cly . . .of
☎ (561) 546-5243 . . 276 S Beach Rd, Box 6, Hobe Sound, FL *33475*
☎ (203) 869-3115 . . 680 Steamboat Rd, Apt 3, Greenwich, CT *06830*
Bartram MR J Burr JR—Ny.
☎ (401) 846-6355 . . 675 Indian Av, Middletown, RI *02842-5717*
Bartram MR & MRS Stephen M (Ann W Cox) On.Rc.Cly.Mont'80
☎ (847) 234-3020 . . 320 Mayflower Rd, Lake Forest, IL *60045*

Baruch MR & MRS Ann R (Ann McD Ritchey) M.Me. . . . . MISS Mary C . . . . MR Richard F JR . . . . JUNIORS MR David G	☎ (610) MI9-9860 230 Laurel Lane, Haverford, PA *19041*

Baruch MR & MRS Earle E (Macy M Dewey) M.Ncd.Pn.P'54
☎ (803) 527-3148 . . "The Nest" DeBordieu Colony,
184 Bonnyneck Dv, Georgetown, SC *29440*

Baruch MR & MRS Fernand (Margery G Wyckoff) P'44 . . . . MISS Lucy D—at ☎ (908) 819-4935 17 S Tenth Av, Highland Park, NJ *08904*	☎ (941) 966-4325 3708 Sandspur Lane, Casey Key, Nokomis, FL *34275*

Baruch MR & MRS Fernand JR (Noeline Hargrave) Ithaca'76.Rm'73
☎ (804) 741-6679 . . 1205 Yellow Gate Rd, Manakin-Sabot, VA *23103*
Baruch MR & MRS Philip K (Cheryl V Flynn) Rol'86
☎ (904) 642-5085 . . 11356 Canvasback Court, Jacksonville, FL *32225*
Barzun MR Charles . . see MRS S Winthrop
Barzun MR Jacques—C.Cl'27
☎ (212) 289-4070 . . 1170 Fifth Av, New York, NY *10029-6527*

Barzun DR & MRS (DR) James L (Kathleen B Agayoff) Bnd'63.SUNY'67.H'61.Cl'66 . . . . MISS Alice L—at Columbia . . . . MISS H Kathleen—at Trinity	☎ (508) 456-8380 79 Prospect Hill, Harvard, MA *01451*

Barzun MISS Lucy . . see MRS S Winthrop
Barzun MISS Mariana . . see MRS S Winthrop
Barzun MR Matthew . . see MRS S Winthrop

Baskett MR & MRS Charles E (von Raab—Mary R Lambert) Un. . . . . MISS Alexandra L von Raab—Denis'95—at ☎ (415) 474-5989 . . 2733 Bush St, San Francisco, CA *94115*	of ☎ (212)755-2783 300 E 57 St, New York, NY *10022* ☎ (860) 434-8261 66 Hedlund Rd, East Haddam, CT *06423*

Bass MR & MRS Alexander (Gwendolyn Brooks) Dth'63 . . . . MR Matthew P—at U of NH . . . . MR Marshall P—at Dartmouth	☎ (603) 924-6472 81 Elm Hill Rd, Peterborough, NH *03458*

Bass MRS Anne H (Anne H Hendricks) V'63 . . . . . . MISS Hyatt A—P'91 . . . . MISS Samantha S—V'94	of ☎ (817)738-8812 1801 Deepdale Dv, Ft Worth, TX *76107* ☎ (212) 628-1820 960 Fifth Av, New York, NY *10021* ☎ (970) 925-6135 0071 Salvation Circle, Aspen, CO *81611*

Bass MRS Edith McB (Edith McBride) V'54 . . . . . . MISS Claire McB—Ken'79—at ☎ (818) 980-5222 10741 Camarillo St, Apt 111, North Hollywood, CA *91602* . . . . MR Jack M 3d—Tul'93—at ☎ (615) 385-5606 714 Clearview Av, Nashville, TN *37205*	☎ (615) 383-7555 202 Moultrie Park, Nashville, TN *37205-4717*

Bass MR Edward P—Y'68
☎ (817) 390-8400 . . 201 Main St, Ft Worth, TX *76102*

Bass MR George S—Cy.Y'53.Pa'58 . . . . MR Steedman L—Cy.Ham'91	of ☎ (617)739-6092 274 Chestnut Hill Rd, Chestnut Hill, MA *02167* ☎ (207) 276-3782 "Reef Point" Northeast Harbor, ME *04662*

Bass MRS Jane L (Jane B Liddell) Rdc'63.Cly.Dc.Cda.Ncd.Dh. . . . . MISS Margot S—P'93 . . . . MISS Catherine H—☎ (212) 876-3717	☎ (212) 369-7280 17 E 89 St, New York, NY *10128*

Bass MR & MRS Perkins (Riley—Rosaly Swann) Dth'34.H'38
☎ (603) 924-6412 . . Elm Hill Rd, Box 210, Peterborough, NH *03458*

Bass MR & MRS Robert M (Anne C Thaxton) Sth'70.Y'71.Stan'74 . . . . MISS Anne Chandler . . . . MR Christopher M . . . . MR Timothy R . . . . JUNIORS MISS Margaret L	☎ (817) 390-8500 6221 Westover Dv, Ft Worth, TX *76107*

Bass MR & MRS Shannon M (Pamela C Borthwick) Cr'84.Cal'86.Nu'89
☎ (415) 331-2624 . . 508 Johnson St, Sausalito, CA *94965*

Bassert LT COL & MRS David E JR (Linda F Hilgartner) USAR.Dick'74.Cc.Rv.Dick'74. Web'85 . . . . | ☎ (508) 478-5482 / 5 Bandy Lane, Milford, MA 01757-2343
 MISS Jessica F Basset . . . .
 JUNIORS MR Daniel E Basset . . . .
Basset JUNIORS MR Daniel E . . see D E Bassert JR
Basset MISS Jessica F . . see D E Bassert JR
Bassett MR & MRS Charles C 3d (Katharine R McCoy) Hn.H'50
 ☎ (207) 985-4425 . . RD 1, Kennebunkport, ME 04046
Bassett, George P 4th & Wilson, Nancy H—Wells'68.P'67
 ☎ (609) 530-0530 . . 118 Ardsley Av, Ewing, NJ 08638
Bassett MRS James V (Marilyn J Nelson) Elm'55 . . | ☎ (716) 634-4211 / 22 Morningstar Court, Buffalo, NY 14221
 MISS Susan L—Cr'83—at ☎ (561) 241-0951
 17732 Holly Brook Way, Boca Raton, FL 33487
Bassett MR & MRS John W (Lillian McC Friend) Sth'78.Stan'77.Hast'80
 ☎ (510) 655-0422 . . 148 Ronada Av, Piedmont, CA 94611
Bassett MISS Phebe L . . . . | ☎ (607) 847-8576 / 35 S Main St, Box 157, New Berlin, NY 13411
 MR James M S . . . .
Bassett MR Ralph P—Y'35
 ☎ (847) 251-1547 . . 434 Highcrest Dv, Wilmette, IL 60091
Bassett MRS Richard (Janet F Knight) . . . . | ☎ (617) 965-8315 / 20 Eden Av, West Newton, MA 02165
 MISS Susan P—at ☎ (520) 526-8313
 5961 Camden Rd, Flagstaff, AZ 86004 . . . .
Bassett MRS William B K (Constance Colt) Cc . . . . . | ☎ (803) 432-4424 / "Quarter Creek" 1805 John G Richards Rd, Camden, SC 29020
 MISS Nancy L—at ☎ (908) 832-2982 . . RD 4, Box 192, Califon, NJ 07830 . . . .
Bast MR & MRS Robert L (Beatrice Weeks) Sth'49.Fst.Sg.Ac.Y'48.H'51
 ☎ (215) 646-2072 . . 110 Spruce Lane, Ambler, PA 19002
Bast MR & MRS William L (Alice-Ann Salomon) Pa'83.Sg.Pa'82
 2112 Church Rd, Flourtown, PA 19031
Bastedo MR & MRS P Russell (Linda Bullard) | ☎ (860) 434-3386 / "Stone's Throw" 179 Grassy Hill Rd, Lyme, CT 06371
 Denis'72.C.ColC'62 . . . .
 MR Nils P—H'95 . . . .
 JUNIORS MISS Kip S . . . .
 JUNIORS MR Spencer C . . . .
Bastedo MRS Philip (Helen C Wilmerding) Csn. . . . | ☎ (603) 924-2112 / 144 River Mead, Peterborough, NH 03458
 MISS Cecily—at ☎ (603) 563-7036
 PO Box 1051, Dublin, NH 03444 . . . .
 MR Christopher K—at ☎ (212) 722-3202
 1641 Third Av, Apt 15JE, New York, NY 10128
Bastedo MRS Walter A (Julia G Post) Cly.Dc.Cda.
 ☎ (203) 966-9684 . . 7 Bank St, New Canaan, CT 06840
Bastick MR & MRS William F (Sarah McKinney) | ☎ (802) 483-9477 / PO Box 35, Pittsford, VT 05763
 Rdc'59 . . . .
 MISS Karen A . . . .
 MISS Lisa M . . . .
 MISS Julia P . . . .
 MISS Alison A . . . .
 MR Timothy J S . . . .

Batchelar MR & MRS Eugene C JR (Colleen Gutterson) Cr'39
 5710 Lynn Haven Rd, Pittsburgh, PA 15217
Batchelar MR John P—Cr'35
 ☎ (412) 784-8276 . . 904 River Oaks Dv, Pittsburgh, PA 15215
Batchelder MR & MRS Clifton B (Anne Stuart) Myf.Ncd.Norw'32
 ☎ (402) 571-7270 . . 6875 State St, Omaha, NE 68152-1633
Batchelder MRS Hannah W (Mills—Hannah A Weaver) Sth'56
 ☎ (802) 254-2073 . . Quarry Rd, Dummerston, VT 05301
Batchelder MR & MRS Robert F (Quillman—Park—Gail A Durnell) Wcc.Pc.Sa.Dar.Pa'53 . . . . | ☎ (610) 688-2373 / 426 Inveraray Rd, Villanova, PA 19085
 MISS Anne S—Rol'87—at ☎ (610) 527-7617
 19 Rodney Rd, Rosemont, PA 19010 . . . .
 MR David D Park . . . .
Batchelder MR Robert R—Mit'57
 207 Ashmont Court, Lynchburg, VA 24503
Bateman MRS Lawrence F (Charlotte E Hughes) . . . | ☎ (847) 382-5813 / 740 Orchard Dv, Barrington, IL 60010
 MR Peter L—Lakeland'68 . . . .
Bates MISS Barclay P . . see P C Leach
Bates MR & MRS Chapin C (Kathryn Shook) DeP'82.Hob'81
 ☎ (847) 853-0956 . . 718 Laurel Av, Wilmette, IL 60091
Bates MR & MRS Daniel M (Husted—Christine R Pabst)
 ☎ (520) 299-0605 . . 5240 N Campbell Av, Tucson, AZ 85718
Bates MR & MRS David T (Sharon Wilson) Cal'69.Pcu.P'68.Stan'76 . . . . | ☎ (408) 373-5795 / "Wingfields" 527 Loma Alta Rd, Carmel, CA 93923
 MISS Talcott N—at Princeton . . . .
 JUNIORS MR Roderick S . . . .
Bates MR & MRS John B (Nancy Witter) Cal'45.Pcu.Sfg.Tcy.Stan'40
 ☎ (510) 547-4429 . . 20 Bellevue Av, Piedmont, CA 94611
Bates MR & MRS Nicholas L (Susan P Muirhead) Wes'78.Sfy.Nrr.Tcy.Cp.Myf.Ariz'72
 ☎ (510) 547-7684 . . 109 Monte Av, Piedmont, CA 94611
Bates MRS Paul M (Helen E Girvin) Stan'38 . . . . . . | PO Box 4565, Kaneohe, Oahu, HI 96744-8565
 MR Paul M 3d—at ☎ (808) 988-5601
 2886 Komaia Place, Honolulu, HI 96821 . . . . . .
 MR Christopher D . . . .
Bates MR Richard J . . . . Died at Belvedere, CA Jly 20'96
Bates MRS Richard J (Reinecke—Gretchen Bush) Stph'57.Okla'59.Fr. . . . . | ☎ (415) 435-0676 / 17 Tamalpais Av, Box 42, Belvedere, CA 94920
 MR Lesley A . . . .
 MR Robert M Reinecke . . . .
Bates MR & MRS Robert E (Ann S Liggett) Str.Wash'43
 ☎ (314) 532-5540 . . 1453 Blue Roan Court, Chesterfield, MO 63005
Bates MRS Robert L (Mary L Moore) . . . . | ☎ (520) 299-1046 / 2820 E Cerrada Los Palitos, Tucson, AZ 85718
 MISS Mary L . . . .
Bates MISS Susan Hastings—Stan'78.Myf.
 ☎ (212) 879-2313 . . 360 E 72 St, Apt B505, New York, NY 10021
Bates MRS Talcott (Margaret S Pardee) Bnd'40.UWash'41.Ncd.
 ☎ (408) 375-4845 . . "Valenzuela Springs" 575 Viejo Rd, Carmel, CA 93923
Bates MRS Victoria F (Victoria Frelinghuysen) Dar.
 ☎ (941) 472-2257 . . PO Box 143, Sanibel Island, FL 33957

Bates MR & MRS William Maffitt JR (Werner—Anne K F Desloge)
V'49.Cy.Cly.StL'39.H'41
☎ (314) 837-3373 . . ''Beau Rivage'' 2709 Shackleford Rd, Florissant, MO *63031*

Bateson MR & MRS Douglas F (Marcia B Johnson) V'79.Un.H'74
10 Gracie Square, New York, NY *10028*

Bateson MR William M—W&M'87 . . see A H Nickerson

Baton MR & MRS Charles B (Wright—Frances Norton)
Hood'29.Rr.Ncd.P'30
☎ (910) 998-6664 . . 3106 Bermuda Village, Advance, NC *27006*

Bator MISS Alexa S—Stan'94 . . see MRS M S King

Bator MR Timothy C . . see MRS M S King

Batt MR & MRS Robert R (Mona Nystroem) Me.Rc.Cts.Ph.H.'41
☎ (610) 642-5875 . . 1345 Waverly Rd, Gladwyne, PA *19035*

Battams MR & MRS E DeWitt (Slagle—Anne Bayly Lloyd) Md.Mv.Ncd.
☎ (410) 366-0289 . . 12 St Martin's Rd, Baltimore, MD *21218*

Batten MR & MRS Michael E (Gloria E Strickland) V'63.Wa.Yn.Y'64.H'70 . . . . | ☎ (414) 639-6939
MISS Elizabeth S . . . . | 3419 Michigan
MISS Louise V . . . . | Blvd, Racine, WI
MR John H | *53402*

Battey MR Thomas B . . see W F Toole

Battey MR & MRS William R JR (Nancy R Hoversten)
ColC'80.Unn.Msq.Wms'75.Cl'78
☎ (203) 655-6962 . . 17 Tory Hole Rd, Darien, CT *06820*

Battin MR & MRS Francis S (Martha J Suppes) | ☎ (860) 364-0275
Sth'41.It.Penn'39 . . . . | 194 Low Rd,
MR Peter S | Sharon, CT *06069*

Battle MRS Elizabeth L (Roberts—Elizabeth L Battle)
Rdc'59.Bklyn'82.Mto.Cly.
☎ (212) 988-7962 . . 30 E 72 St, New York, NY *10021*

Battle MR T Westray . . see R M Scaife

Battles MRS Winthrop H (Marjorie Y Gibbon) Ac.
☎ (610) 645-6640 . . 1400 Waverly Rd, Rm 240, Gladwyne, PA *19035*

Battram MR & MRS Richard L (Patricia L Stone) StJ.But'59
☎ (314) 822-4995 . . 723 Haverford Rd, St Louis, MO *63124*

Batzer MRS Russel W (Veronica M Starr) Cwr'27
☎ (904) 285-1711 . . 2023 Palmetto Point Dv, Ponte Vedra Beach, FL *32082*

Bauch MR & MRS John Oliver (Michelle A Louis) Wis'88.Wis'77
☎ (608) 828-9423 . . 7693 Westman Way, Middleton, WI *53562*

Bauch MR & MRS Robert O (Alma O Moore) Wis'40 | ☎ (414) 261-0923
MISS Barbara B . . . . | 1014 Charles St,
Watertown, WI
53094

Bauer MR & MRS Charles A (Comparato—E Bowen | ☎ (415) 922-7790
Gerry) Cl'71.Myf.Loy'65.Pa'72 . . . . | 2311 Webster St,
JUNIORS MISS Elizabeth S H . . . . | San Francisco, CA
94115

Bauer MR & MRS Gregory W (Anne V Henderson)
Va'75.Cl'84.Y.Rut'77.Cl'84 . . of
☎ (212) 595-1665 . . 230 West End Av, New York, NY *10023*
☎ (908) 223-5821 . . ''T.L.H.'' 615 Cherokee Lane, Brielle, NJ *08730*

Bauer MRS Herbert F (Milford—Doris E Walker) Cal'36
☎ (415) 885-2255 . . 1200 California St, Apt 8D, San Francisco, CA *94109*

Bauer MR & MRS Joseph A JR (Parlee—Mary E | ☎ (617) 244-4969
Brown) Rdc'65.Hn.Wis'58 . . . . | 430 Quinobequin
MISS Elizabeth J Parlee—V'93 . . . . | Rd, Waban, MA
02168

Baugh MISS Carol A
☎ (212) 439-9554 . . 215 E 80 St, Apt 4M, New York, NY *10021*

Baugh MR & MRS Pierce A R (Margaret A Cavanaugh) Ty'53.Va'53
☎ (201) 337-7978 . . 883 Briarwoods Rd, Franklin Lakes, NJ *07417*

Baugh MRS William S (Pauline S Brown)
☎ (610) 889-9383 . . 3 Painters Lane, Wayne, PA *19087*

Baum MR & MRS Chester E (Cann—Smith—Phebe | ☎ (941) 637-7441
A Jacobs) Hav'40.H'46 | 524 Marlin Dv,
MR Price A—Towson'85—at ☎ (410) 226-5619 | Punta Gorda, FL
Oxford, MD *21654* . . . . | *33950*
MR William B Smith . . . . |

Bauman MR & MRS Robert P (Lewis—Patricia A Jones)
OWes'50.H'53 . . of
☎ (011-44-171) 589-6841 . . 10 Alexander Square, London SW3 2AY, England
☎ (561) 225-0403 . . 6720 SE Harbor Circle, Stuart, FL *34996*

Baumann MR & MRS Harald R (Hattery—Solange de Ridder)
Paris'45.Ch'42
☎ (508) 283-2983 . . ''Soborg'' 145 Atlantic Rd, Gloucester, MA *01930*

Baumann MR & MRS Marcus T (Rachel N Eide)
Wis'44.ArizSt'64.ConcC'50
☎ (602) 946-8220 . . 5919 E Thomas Rd, Scottsdale, AZ *85251*

Baumann MR & MRS Richard M (Katharine C Kinsolving) V'82.P'81
7A Courtfield Gardens, London SW5 0PA, England

Baumberger DR & MRS Peter F M (Dorrance—Mary Alice Bennett)
Okla'42.Bcs.Ac.Dar.Basel'40 . . of
☎ (011-41-22) 759-17-37 . . Chemin des Turaines 20, 1251 Gy, Geneva, Switzerland
☎ (516) 283-0954 . . 140 Meadow Lane, PO Box 5014, Southampton, NY *11969*
6043 N Hummingbird Lane, Paradise Valley, AZ *85253*

Baumgarten MRS Kimball (Nancy B Kimball) . . . . | ☎ (414) 868-3386
MR Charles S—RISD'75 . . . . | ''Wild Goose Nest''
MR Frederic K . . . . | W3503 County F,
Fish Creek, WI
54212

Baumgartner MR J Peter—Pcu.Bhm.Stan'51.SantaC'73 . . of
☎ (415) 664-2185 . . 124 Clarendon Av, San Francisco, CA *94114*
☎ (702) 832-7380 . . ''Winter Palace'' 24 Somers Loop, Crystal Bay, NV *89402*

Baurmeister MR Eric J (Hans U) . . . . Married at Nantucket, MA
Tevebaugh MISS Anne C (C Richard) . . . . Jun 29'96

Baurmeister MR & MRS Hans U (Jordan—Mary A Fox) Sg.Munich'58
☎ (203) 230-8951 . . 30 Meadowbrook Rd, Hamden, CT *06517*

Baxter MISS Anne W—Stan'70
☎ (415) 322-2235 . . 541C Cowper St, Palo Alto, CA *94301*

Baxter MRS C McGhee JR (Baxter—Ellie Wood Keith) Cda.
☎ (804) 295-5964 . . 1063 Barracks Farm Rd, Charlottesville, VA *22901*

Baxter MASTER Charles McGhee 4th (g—MRS C McGhee Baxter JR) . . . . .
Born at Orlando, FL Feb 21'96

Baxter MRS Cornelia B (Cornelia L Baker) Cnt.Fy.
☎ (207) 563-1166 . . Boulder Rd, Box 876, Damariscotta, ME *04543*

Baxter MR & MRS Daniel H (Carol B Neiley) Pa'82.Pars'87
☎ (914) 758-0909 . . RR 3, Box 159, Feller Newmark Rd, Red Hook, NY *12571*

Baxter MISS Edith P (Cope—Edith P Baxter)
Wheat'65.Ch'66 . . . . | ☎ (617) 271-1571
  MR Jonathan B Cope—at Princeton . . . . | 7 Hawthorne Lane, Bedford, MA *01730*

Baxter MR & MRS George Jaffray (N Peace Whitman) Bhm.Ny.Ty'58 . . . . | ☎ (215) 295-1294
  MISS Melinda R—at Evergreen State . . . . | 103 Warwick Rd, Yardley, PA *19067*

Baxter MR & MRS George W (Ruth Reynolds) Evg.BtP.Penn'40
☎ (561) 655-4328 . . 2 N Breakers Row, NPH-1, Palm Beach, FL *33480*

Baxter MR James A . . see MISS M A McAfee

Baxter MR & MRS James F (Emily M Nelson)
4317 Esteswood Dv, Nashville, TN *37215-3110*

Baxter MR & MRS John H (Virginia J Callan)
Un.Pr.Eyc.Cl'74 . . . . | ☎ (516) 676-1710
  JUNIORS MISS Diana L G—at Deerfield . . . . | 16 Watersedge, Locust Valley, NY
  JUNIORS MISS Theodora M . . . . | *11560*
  JUNIORS MR J Hanley JR—at Deerfield . . . . |

Baxter MR & MRS Justin M (Nancy L Dunning) Penn'70.Pc.StA.Myf.Dll.Cda.Penn'70 . . . . | ☎ (215) 836-7702
  JUNIORS MISS Elizabeth D . . . . | 523 Wyndmoor Av, Wyndmoor, PA
  JUNIORS MR J Morgan . . . . | *19038*

Baxter MRS Kate D (Baxter—Reid—Kate D Putnam) Sth'65.Nu'85 . . . . | ☎ (203) 869-7401
  MISS Eliza W—Mid'94—at ☎ (415) 929-7349 | 27 Mooreland Rd, Greenwich, CT
1146 Taylor St, San Francisco, CA *94108* . . . . . | *06831*

Baxter MRS Matthew A (Page—Barbara Jacobs) Tvcl.Uncl.
☎ (619) 773-0041 . . 258 Castellana S, Palm Desert, CA *92260*

Baxter MR Matthew A 3d . . . . Died at Yosemite Valley, CA Apr 1'96

Baxter MR & MRS Richard S (Katherine D Irving) So.H.'34
☎ (516) 283-1454 . . 467 First Neck Lane, PO Box 1292, Southampton, NY *11969*

Baxter MR & MRS Stephen B (Laura R Hopkins) Smu'83.Smu'84 . . of
☎ (916) 489-5600 . . 5700 North Av, Carmichael, CA *95608-3722*
☎ (916) 426-0727 . . "Snowy Pines" 8206 Muir Court, Serene Lakes, CA *95728*

Bayard MRS James A (Nancy W F Lennig) MooreArt'42.Ac.Ncd . . .of
☎ (302) 658-1147 . . "Tredinnock" Box 3884, Greenville, DE *19807*
☎ (410) 885-5525 . . "Bohemia Manor" Chesapeake City, MD *21915*

Bayard MR & MRS James A JR (Frances H Gibson)
LakeF'67.Tufts'68.LakeF'67.StMarys'73 . . . . . . | ☎ (302) 655-2789
  MISS Noël G . . . . | 122 School Rd, Wilmington, DE
  JUNIORS MISS Elise B . . . . | *19803*

Bayard MR & MRS Louis P (Ethel M Mooney)
USA'49.AmU'76 . . . . | ☎ (703) 560-0309
  DR Paul J—H'81.Cal'86.Cal'90 . . . . | 7984 Foxmoor Dv, Dunn Loring, VA
  MR Christopher S—Va'84.Nw'90 . . . . | *22027*
  MR Louis P JR—P'85.Nw'87 . . . . |

Bayard MR Nicholas H—Rr.Y'56 . . . . | ☎ (207) 443-4294
  MISS Elizabeth S—at St Lawrence U . . . . | 969 Washington St, Bath, ME *04530*
  JUNIORS MR Samuel M . . . . |

Bayles MR Charles D . . see A W Mattmiller 3d

Bayley MRS James C (Janet C Carr) . . . . | ☎ (617) 581-1786
  MR Richard B—at ☎ (617) 598-8813 | 1000 Paradise Rd,
61 Phillips Beach Av, Swampscott, MA *01907* . | PH-DS, Swampscott,
  MR Robert L—at ☎ (407) 351-4569 | MA *01907*
5232 Eaglesmere Dv, Orlando, FL *32805* . . . . . . |

Baylor MR John R—Neb'43 . . . . | ☎ (402) 435-0214
  MR Charles C—Neb'92 . . . . | 2736 Van Dorn St, Lincoln, NE *68502*
  MR John R JR—Stan'88 . . . . |
  MR James . . . . |

Bayne MRS Carroll S (Katherine M Smith)
☎ (212) 644-6438 . . 30 Sutton Place, New York, NY *10022*

Bayne MR & MRS David F (Carolyn J Golden)
StLaw'82.Nu'90.StLaw'83.Cl'88
☎ (203) 348-7185 . . 129 Holmes Av, Darien, CT *06820*

Bayne MISS Elizabeth L—Pars'87.Shcc.
☎ (303) 777-5631 . . 1059 S York St, Denver, CO *80209*

Bayne MR & MRS James E (Mary Lee C Skinner) | of ☎ (214)522-3529
Y'62.Cl'67 . . . . | 3204 St Johns Dv, Dallas, TX *75205*
  MISS Laura Lee P . . . . |
  MR James E JR—at ☎ (520) 776-7832 | ☎ (207) 244-3571
603 Campbell Av, Apt 3, Prescott, AZ *86301* . . | "Hio Hill"
  | Box 152, Manset, ME *04656*

Bayne MR & MRS James E 3d (Annette C Uihlein) | ☎ (516) 722-5618
Nu'55 . . . . | Beach Rd,
  MISS Lara . . . . | Box 2296, Aquebogue, NY *11931*

Bayne MRS Martha G (Martha C Gibb)
☎ (303) 741-0466 . . 7266 S Tamarac St, Englewood, CO *80112-1835*

Bayne MR & MRS William (Elizabeth B Shellabarger)
☎ (505) 298-7369 . . "B-Hive" 4404 Kellia Lane NE, Albuquerque, NM *87111*

Beach MRS George R (Tams—Mary V Finney) Sr.
☎ (954) 527-4107 . . 1710 S Ocean Lane, Ft Lauderdale, FL *33316*

Beach MRS Samuel F (Elizabeth B Kemp) Sl.Cda.
☎ (202) 337-5725 . . 4000 Cathedral Av NW, Apt 352B, Washington, DC *20016*

Beach MR & MRS Samuel F JR (Thompson—Kate P Todd) Mt.Cvc.Sl.Geo'60
☎ (202) 333-0035 . . 2810—35 St NW, Washington, DC *20007*

Beach MR Theodore T (Thomas E) . . . . Married at Bryn Mawr, PA
  Ayel MISS Neylan (Ruhan) . . . . Aug 21'96

Beacham MRS E Brand JR (Bessie Keith)
☎ (561) 231-1643 . . 181 Clarkson Lane, John's Island, Vero Beach, FL *32960*

Beacham MR & MRS Harold R (Schuetz—Cecile T Wood) Nh.Bow'56
☎ (508) 651-3136 . . "Watershed Farm" 127 Mill St, Box 203, Sherborn, MA *01770*

Beachboard MRS Walter W (Dunn—Cynthia Reed) Me.Ac.
☎ (610) 527-1064 . . 1064 Broadmoor Rd, Bryn Mawr, PA *19010*

Beadle MR & MRS J Grant 3d (Nancy Lee Oliver) V'55.Cm.Y'54 . . of
☎ (561) 231-3564 . . 550 Riomar Dv, Apt 39, Vero Beach, FL *32963*
☎ (616) 335-9027 . . "The Beams" 4503 S Audubon Dv, Holland, MI *49423*

Beadleston MISS Alexandra (William L) . . . . Married at Aspen, CO
Blake MR Peter D M (late Everngham) . . . . Jly 27'96

Beadleston MR & MRS Alfred N (Waud—Isabel P Morrell) Rm.Stc.Y'34 . . . . | ☎ (908) 747-1115
"Rivermarsh"
14 Edwards Point
Rd, Rumson, NJ
07760
MISS Helen H—Box 88, Woody Creek, CO 81656
MR Alfred N 4th—Box 88, Woody Creek, CO 81656 . . . .

Beadleston MR & MRS William L (PRCSS Marina Romanov) Rc.Nf.Y'60 ⚓ . . . . | of ☎ (970)920-2260
Box 88,
Woody Creek, CO
81656
☎ (212) 348-7234
60 E 91 St,
New York, NY
10128
MISS Tatiana . . . .
JUNIORS MISS Natasha . . . .
JUNIORS MR Nicolai . . . .

Beal MR & MRS Albert R (Ann Milburn) H'56 . . . . . | ☎ (215) CH2-0790
95 W Hampton Rd,
Philadelphia, PA
19118
MISS Nell van D . . . .
MISS Hélène F M . . . .
MR Albert R 3d . . . .
MR Bryan M . . . .

Beal MR Alexander M—P.'89
☎ (212) 598-9721 . . 220 E 18 St, Apt 4, New York, NY 10003

Beal MR George P
☎ (617) 734-0981 . . 15 Lee Rd, Chestnut Hill, MA 02167

Beal MR Louis M S—Rc.Chr.K.Cyb.Un.Sm.Plg.StJ.Cw.Rv.H.Rid'52
☎ (212) BU8-8233 . . 105 E 64 St, New York, NY 10021

Beal MR & MRS Robert L (Polly R Walker) Bost'63.Va'58 . . . . | ☎ (414) 351-0180
1080 W Dean Rd,
Milwaukee, WI
53217
MISS Daphne G . . . .
MISS Cecily W . . . .
JUNIORS MR Jonathan L . . . .

Beal MR & MRS Thomas Prince JR (Barbara P Beals) ColbyS'56.Bost'58.Chi.Wms'51 . . . . | of ☎ (617)259-9436
26 Baker Bridge Rd,
Lincoln, MA 01773
☎ (603) 253-4958
High Haith Rd,
Squam Lake,
Center Harbor, NH
03226
MR Thomas P 3d . . . .

Beale MR & MRS Benjamin (Marie L King) H'34
☎ (617) 326-5458 . . 430 Sandy Valley Rd, Westwood, MA 02090

Beale MR & MRS John S JR (Louise L Ritchie) Col'64.Cvc.Mt.Nyc.Sl.Md'64 . . . . | ☎ (301) 951-3913
3106 Cummings
Lane, Chevy Chase,
MD 20815
MISS Holly C—at 6514 Fifth Av NE, Seattle, WA 98115 . . . .
MISS Sarah C—at Bucknell . . . .
JUNIORS MISS Katharine S—at Holton-Arms . . . .
JUNIORS MISS Christina C—at Holton-Arms . . . .

Beale MR & MRS N Ridgely (Carmel A Philson) Pr.Rv.Va'72
☎ (516) 676-0842 . . Red Spring Colony, Glen Cove, NY 11542

Beales MR & MRS James A G 3d (Margaret E Haskins) Pc.Rv.Dar.Pa'48
☎ (803) 537-4245 . . "Wits End" 103 Patterson St, Cheraw, SC 29520

Beales MR & MRS Jonathan T (Louise H Jordan) Sg.Syr'75
see Dilatory Domiciles

Bealke MR & MRS Linn H (Jean L Wells) Rc.Bv.Ark'66.Wash'69 . . . . | ☎ (314) 997-8702
305 Carlyle Lake
Dv, St Louis, MO
63141
MISS Emily R . . . .
MR David Q W . . . .
JUNIORS MR Linn H JR . . . .

Beall MISS Charlotte Ashley—Vt'83
☎ (206) 782-3970 . . 6011—2 St NW, Seattle, WA 98107

Beall MISS Margaret Colhoun—Vt'86
☎ (415) 776-1182 . . 2847 Washington St, San Francisco, CA 94115

Beals MR & MRS Beauveau Borie (Beatrice Irving) H'30
☎ (215) 233-2550 . . 551 E Evergreen Av, Apt A309, Wyndmoor, PA 19038

Beals MRS E Mauran (Julia O Blake)
☎ (617) 566-5013 . . 29 Colchester St, Brookline, MA 02146

Bean MR & MRS Edwin T JR (Susan Roberts) ColbyS'45.Buf.Ts.G.Mit'46.Geo'50
☎ (716) 662-9864 . . 70 Henning Dv, Orchard Park, NY 14127

Bean MISS Michèle . . see MRS J de Sibour

Beane MR & MRS Arthur E (Mary Elizabeth L Clarke) Br'42
☎ (617) 585-2211 . . The Village at Duxbury, Apt 227, 290 King's Town Way, Duxbury, MA 02332

Bear MR & MRS Joe F JR (Mallory Gallion) MaryB'67.W&L'65
☎ (334) 834-2861 . . 2442 Midfield Dv, Montgomery, AL 36111

Beard MR & MRS Alexander R (Margaret A Over) StLaw'52.Va'50 . . . . | ☎ (610) 688-7319
427 Conestoga Rd,
St Davids, PA
19087-4811
MISS Mary Stuart—SCar'81.SCar'87—at
☎ (404) 365-8729 . . 55 Pharr Rd NW, Apt 104B, Atlanta, GA 30305 . . . .
MR Alexander R JR—Penn'81.Penn'83—at
☎ (303) 442-6099 . . 6148 Red Hill Rd, Boulder, CO 80302 . . . .

Beard MR Anson McC—Rc.Pr.Y'32
☎ (516) 759-2623 . . 111 High Farms Rd, Glen Head, NY 11545

Beard MRS Patricia D (Patricia Dranow) Cly. . . . . . | ☎ (212) 517-6984
151 E 83 St,
New York, NY
10028
MISS Hillary R—Mid'95 . . . .
MR Alexander—Tufts'93 . . . .

Beard MISS Sarah Katherine (gg—MRS George Willard Somers) . . . . . Born at Winchester, MA Nov 30'94

Beard MR Timothy Field—Chr.Snc.StA.Rv.Cw.Lm.Cc.Coa.Wms'53.Cl'62
☎ (860) 355-2100 . . "Closeburn" North St, PO Box 269, Roxbury, CT 06783

Beardsley MR & MRS Henry W (Trimble—Diana L Neill) P'33
☎ (561) 272-4214 . . 2727 N Ocean Blvd, Gulf Stream, FL 33483

Beardsley MR & MRS Mitchell W (Sheeler—Mildred Asbury) Me.Pa'49
☎ (610) 648-0981 . . 986 N Valley Rd, Paoli, PA 19301-1038

Bearns MRS Wendy H (Wendy M Hobson) NCar'61.Cl'67.Va'90 . . . . | ☎ (804) 979-4252
17 University Circle,
Charlottesville, VA
22903
MISS Melissa H—Bnd'95 . . . .
MISS Gillian K—V'96 . . . .

Beaton MRS Eleanor W (Eleanor M Walters) Ws'84
☎ (415) 749-5636 . . 1379 Vallejo St, San Francisco, CA 94109

Beattie MR & MRS James H (Olivia von S Cover)
☎ (941) 966-3365 . . 3204 Casey Key Rd, Nokomis, FL 34275

Beatty MRS John R A (Anne Kidder) Csn.Ncd.
☎ (910) 762-7267 . . 1840 S Live Oak P'kway, Wilmington, NC 28403

Beatty MR & MRS John T JR (Marila M Miller) Cho.Y'58.Ch'66 . . . . | ☎ (847) 446-6212
590 Thornwood
Lane, Northfield, IL
60093
MISS Emily F . . . .
MR John T 3d . . . .
MR W Oeric . . . .

Beatty MR & MRS Richard S (Barbara Boyd) | of ☎ (301)657-3392
Duke'56.Mt.Cvc.Wms'55.Geo'61 . . . . | 7001 Glenbrook Rd,
MR Charles T B—at 5302 Iroquois Rd, Bethesda, | Bethesda, MD
MD 20816 . . . . | 20814
MR Nicholas P . . . . | ☎ (941) 434-6538
 | 2600 Gulf Shore
 | Blvd N, Naples, FL
 | 34103

Beatty MR & MRS Ross J (Janet Ayer) Cho.On.Cnt.Ncd.P'29
☎ (847) CE4-2749 . . 111 E Onwentsia Rd, Lake Forest, IL 60045

Beaty MRS Julia C (Julia Corscaden) . . . . | ☎ (301) 216-5159
MISS (DR) Janet K—Bastyr'88—at Harvard, MA | 415 Russell Av, Apt
01451 . . . . | 701, Gaithersburg,
MR Jeffrey P—at Bracey, VA 23919 . . . . | MD 20877-2839

Beaty MISS Nancy W
☎ (011-44-1367) 860297 . . Upper Meadow Cottage, Kencot,
nr Lechlade, Gloucestershire GL7 3QX, England

Beaumont MR John E—Hn.H'33 . . of
☎ (504) 861-7925 . . 1718 Palmer Av, New Orleans, LA 70118
☎ (504) 643-2793 . . 254 Fenner Rd, Slidell, LA 70460

Beauregard MRS Pierre G T 3d (Huidekoper—Mary C Gruman) Cvc.
☎ (301) 656-7059 . . 15 Oxford St, Chevy Chase, MD 20815

Beaver MR & MRS Bentley H (Marilyn R Phelan) | ☎ (617) 235-5153
Skd'62.Colby'64.H'70 . . . . | 21 Manor Av,
MR John M—Colby'92 . . . . | Wellesley, MA
MR David H—at U of Vt . . . . | 02181

Beaver MR & MRS Martin J (Cutting—Mortimer—Katharine D Van Pelt)
BtP.Evg.Srb.Cly.Ox'56
☎ (011-44-171) 589-9824 . . 17 Ennismore Gardens, London
SW7 1AA, England

Bechtle MR & MRS Joachim (Parish—Nancy | ☎ (415) 931-6117
Hellman) . . . . | 3560 Washington St,
    MISS Jessica Parish . . . . | San Francisco, CA
 | 94118

Beck MRS Bernard (Antoinette V du P Irving) . . . . . | ☎ (516) 283-9048
MISS Antoinette D—Godd'77 . . . . | 99 Leland Lane,
 | Southampton, NY
 | 11968

Beck MR Edward R C—K.Nrr.Srb.
☎ (401) 847-3436 . . "Plaisance" Ledge Rd, Newport, RI 02840

Beck MISS Elizabeth R F—Ox'93.Ox'95 . . see R Hynson

Beck MR & MRS Gordon M (Lilian F B Andrews) Br'77.H'73
☎ (914) 834-0742 . . 9 Beach Av, Larchmont, NY 10538

Beck MRS H Brooks (Emily M Morison) Rdc'37 . . . | of ☎ (617)828-2802
MR Cameron W—NCar'69 . . . . | 4 Homans Lane,
 | Canton, MA 02021
 | ☎ (207) 276-5575
 | Good Hope,
 | Northeast Harbor,
 | ME 04662

Beck MR James M III—Srb.Pn.P'52
☎ (609) 683-1377 . . 6 Mercer St, Princeton, NJ 08540

Beck MR & MRS Jeffrey F (Anita B Brooke) LakeF'85.Pc.Penn'87
☎ (215) 628-2817 . . 579 Bolton Place, Blue Bell, PA 19422

Beck MR Robert L—Buda'95 . . see R Hynson

Beck MISS Virginia C
☎ (215) 545-7185 . . 1228 Spruce St, Apt 709, Philadelphia, PA 19107

Becker MR & MRS Charles J (Matheson—Katrina B Hickox)
☎ (803) 642-2859 . . "Oakmeade" 627 Magnolia Lane SE, Aiken,
SC 29801

Becker MRS E Lovell (Gernerd—Pontius—M Eleanor Holden) Ri.Bcs.
☎ (617) 326-6144 . . 10 Longwood Dv, Apt 448, Westwood,
MA 02090-1123

Becker MR & MRS Edward W (Ann W Day) Mlsps'84.Van'85
☎ (601) 981-0685 . . 3911 Hawthorne Dv, Jackson, MS 39206

Becker MR & MRS James A JR (Cheryl A Presley) Miss'54.Miss'58
☎ (601) 362-1185 . . 225 Glenway Dv, Jackson, MS 39216

Becker MRS John A (Martha E Thompson)
☎ (518) 463-5424 . . 498 Loudonville Rd, Loudonville, NY 12211

Becker MR & MRS John C (Georgiana E Hill) RISD'71.H.'75
☎ (617) 894-4756 . . 21 Hidden Rd, Weston, MA 02193

Becker MISS Margaret W—MmtMhn'79.Pace'81. | ☎ (212) 535-6169
Cly. . . . . | 133 E 64 St,
MR Frank L—Rv. | New York, NY
 | 10021

Becker MR & MRS Max JR (Cora H Dickinson) Cy.St.G.Aht'50
☎ (716) 885-9405 . . 80 Highland Av, Buffalo, NY 14222

Becker MR Robert L 3d—Pg.CUNY'81
☎ (212) 966-2474 . . 496 Broadway, New York, NY 10012

Becker MRS Sherburn M 3d (Becker—Clough— | ☎ (908) 842-2323
Marion E Pitts) Rm. . . . . | 630 Seven Bridges
MISS Sarah M—MtH'92 . . . . | Rd, Little Silver, NJ
MISS Anne S . . . . | 07739
MISS Elizabeth V—at Mt Holyoke . . . . |

Becker DR & MRS Terrence C (Daphne E de Marneffe)
HRdc'81.Cal'88.Cal'93.Stan'78.Cal'82
1240 Jackson St, San Francisco, CA 94109

Becket MRS G Campbell (Elise B Granbery) Ncd.
☎ (860) 435-9157 . . Noble Horizons, 17 Cobble Rd, Salisbury,
CT 06068

Beckett MR & MRS John C (Margot L Wrenn) An.Dar.Stan'38
☎ (415) 321-8844 . . 260 Coleridge Av, Palo Alto, CA 94301

Beckett MR & MRS Paul T (Ann R Keenan) | ☎ (408) 385-4518
Wyo'65.Wyo'86.Wyo'67 . . . . | PO Box 43,
MISS Margot W—Wyo'92 . . . . | Lockwood, CA
MISS Kathleen M . . . . | 93932
JUNIORS MISS Helena D . . . . |
JUNIORS MISS Sophie L . . . . |

Beckett MR & MRS William J (Juliet M Thomas) | ☎ (415) 494-6922
SFr'92 . . . . | 4189 Baker Av,
MISS Heather E—at Lawrence . . . . | Palo Alto, CA
 | 94306

Beckner MR Bruce A—Ayc.GeoW'48.Md'64 ⛵
☎ (410) 268-2166 . . 38 Southgate Av, Annapolis, MD 21401

Beckner MR & MRS R Bruce (Sallie R Low) | ☎ (301) 469-9161
Tex'74.P'71.JHop'72 . . . . | 9121 Burning Tree
JUNIORS MISS Laura E—at Nat'l Cath Sch . . . . . | Rd, Bethesda, MD
JUNIORS MISS Amanda F—at Nat'l Cath Sch . . . . | 20817
 | Feb 1 . .
 | 3225 Highland Place
 | NW, Washington,
 | DC 20008

Beck von Peccoz MR & MRS Charles M (Marian W Larkin) Cr'60.Cr'59 . . . . ☎ (513) 729-0184
MISS Shellie M—Van'89—at 609 Doepke Lane,
5807 Westchester Court, Worthington, OH *43085* Cincinnati, OH *45231*
Beck von Peccoz MISS Martha M—Munich'56.Wa.
☎ (847) 501-4692 . . 16 The Landmark, Northfield, IL *60093*
Beckwith MRS Dorothy S (Knoop—Dorothy Sweeney) Tcy.
☎ (415) 851-2726 . . 501 Portola Rd, Portola Valley, CA *94025*
Beckwith MRS George N (Virginia A Porter) Rr.Fcg.Tc.
☎ (412) 621-3351 . . Park Mansions, 5023 Frew St, Pittsburgh,
PA *15213*
Beckwith MR & MRS James S 3d (Alice W Snodgrass) Fcg.Rr.Pg.Y'53 . . of
☎ (412) 963-9198 . . 111 Greenwood Rd, Pittsburgh, PA *15238*
☎ (561) 234-4323 . . 291 Sabal Palm Lane, John's Island, Vero Beach,
FL *32963*
Becton MR & MRS Henry P JR (Jean C Redpath) ☎ (617) 891-8876
Tufts'68.Cy.Sm.Y'65.H'68 . . . . 338 Boston Post Rd,
MISS Sara C—at Conn Coll . . . . Weston, MA *02193*
JUNIORS MR Wilson P—at Concord Acad . . . . . .
Bédard MRS Pierre (Winter—Gertrude E King) Cly.Srb.K.Cda.Dar.
☎ (212) 753-1571 . . 200 E 66 St, New York, NY *10021-6728*
Bedford MR & MRS Erskine L (Benitz—Nancy L ☎ (540) 253-5080
Gerry) Cr'55 . . . . ''Old Whitewood''
MISS Cynthia L Benitz—Box 640, Upperville, 3760 Whitewood
VA *20185* . . . . Rd, The Plains, VA
MR Bryan M Benitz—at 2 Sloan Court E, *20198*
London SW3 4TF, England . . . .
Bedford MR & MRS Frederick T 3d (Jane S Waterman) MtH'60.Aht'59 . . of
☎ (603) 643-2524 . . ''Partridge Crest'' 23 Partridge Rd, Etna,
NH *03750*
☎ (561) 830-1510 . . ''Holiday Home'' 345 Brazilian Av, Palm Beach,
FL *33480*
Beebe MR & MRS John H JR (Caroline N Short) ☎ (847) 446-9135
Ih.Cw.Cda.P'54 . . . . 1294 Asbury Av,
MISS Anne M—at 6723 Stuart Av, Richmond, VA Winnetka, IL *60093*
23226 . . . .
MR John H 3d . . . .
MR William H—at 6415 Kensington Av,
Richmond, VA *23226* . . . .
Beebe MR & MRS Spencer B (Jane C Magavern) ☎ (503) 294-0147
Bost'68.Yn.Wms'68.Y'73 . . . . 1807 NW 32 Av,
MISS Lydia L . . . . Portland, OR *97210*
MR Silas S . . . .
MR Samuel M . . . .
Beebe MRS Tod H (Marguerite A Vermilye)
☎ (410) 822-6248 . . 305 Spring Dv, Easton, MD *21601-3841*
Beech MRS Joseph JR (Janet Maher)
☎ (513) 871-8057 . . 3939 Erie Av, Apt 204, Cincinnati, OH *45208*
Beech MR & MRS Joseph 3d (Carol L Schutte) ☎ (513) 561-3331
Sth'68.Aht'67 . . . . 5125 Ivyfarm Rd,
MR Scott E—at Amherst . . . . Cincinnati, OH
JUNIORS MISS Adrienne L *45243*
JUNIORS MISS Claire M . . . .
Beecheno MRS Peter M (Mary C Montgomery)
☎ (410) 235-7920 . . 116 W University P'kway, Baltimore, MD *21210*
Beecher MR Henry G—Ds . . see A L Perrin
Beecher JUNIORS MISS Katherine P . . see A L Perrin

Beecher JUNIORS MISS Lucile G . . see A L Perrin
Beecher MISS Olivia S . . see A L Perrin
Beegle MRS Frederick N 2d (Corley—Beegle— ☎ (215) 654-0982
Murdoch—Harriet K Royer) Roch'61 . . . . 932 Hedgerow
MISS Mary G—Gettys'94—at ☎ (215) 654-0769 Court, Blue Bell, PA
426A Ft Washington Av, Ft Washington, PA *19422*
19034 . . . .
Beehler MRS Cary B (E Cary Baxter)
☎ (410) 433-5080 . . 702 W St Georges Rd, Baltimore, MD *21210*
Beekman MRS Gerardus (France A Brouwier)
☎ (908) 277-3046 . . 29 DeBary Place, Summit, NJ *07901*
Beekman MR & MRS Stephen F R (Daniéle M ☎ (011-41-22)
Maury) Grin'68 755-41-77
MR Gerard J—at RI Sch of Design . . . . Les Débités 3,
JUNIORS MR Philippe M—at Drew . . . . 1295 Mies, Vaud,
Switzerland
Beekman MR & MRS William B (Helen P Hinckley)
Mls'71.C.K.Lm.H'71.Y'80
☎ (212) 431-3061 . . 284 Lafayette St, New York, NY *10012*
Beeler MR & MRS John H (Elizabeth S Wharton) Gm.Cda.JHop'38
☎ (610) 353-7645 . . Dunwoody Village C213, 3500 West Chester Pike,
Newtown Square, PA *19073*
Beemer MR Gordon G—Cas.DelB.Sc.Purd'30.Ind'48
☎ (561) 734-8604 . . Inlet Plaza B303, 6885 N Ocean Blvd,
Ocean Ridge, FL *33435*
Beer MR & MRS Claude André (Barbara Adams Augustus) Dar.Pa'60 . . of
☎ (561) 585-2455 . . Tower Vallencay, 2155 Ibis Isle Rd E,
Palm Beach, FL *33480*
☎ (401) 847-3767 . . ''Belair'' Old Beach Rd, Newport, RI *02840*
Beer MR & MRS John W (Rosemary S Tyson) V'55.Ln.Au.H'54
☎ (860) 677-0111 . . 12 Colton St, Farmington, CT *06032*
Beese MR & MRS J Carter JR (Natalie T Wilson)
VJ'76.Rcn.B.Md.Mt.Gv.StJ.Rol'78
☎ (410) 363-3367 . . 2 Golf Course Rd, Owings Mills, MD *21117*
Begg MR & MRS Charles B JR (Mary L McIlvain) ☎ (313) 881-5445
W&L'63 . . . . 279 Grosse Pointe
MISS Mary L—at U of Mich . . . . Blvd, Grosse Pointe
MISS Carolyn D—at Colo State . . . . Farms, MI *48236*
Begien MRS Julien F (Susan Spencer) Sm.Yn. . . . . . ☎ (617) 367-8664
MR Julien F JR . . . . 1 Devonshire Place,
MR William C—at ☎ (508) 526-4874 Apt 3515, Boston,
4 North St, Manchester, MA *01944* . . . . MA *02109-3517*
Begley MR & MRS Louis (Dujarric de la Rivière— ☎ (212) 628-4201
Anne Muhlstein) Paris'53.C.H'54 925 Park Av,
MR Peter H—at via degli Ausoni 3, New York, NY
00185 Rome, Italy *10028*
MR Robert Dujarric de la Rivière . . . .
Begley MR & MRS William E JR (Patricia J Kennedy) StM'76
☎ (713) 965-9531 . . 5405 Huckleberry Lane, Houston, TX *77056*
Béguelin MASTER Aaron Ogden Dayton (Robert D) . . . . Born at
Los Angeles, CA Feb 6'96
Béguelin MRS Dayton (Smith—Natalie Pickering) Rm.Ncd.
☎ (908) 291-2856 . . 531 Locust Point Rd, Locust, NJ *07760*
Béguelin MR & MRS Robert D (Susanna A Jones) P'81.Cl'87.Ny.Snc.Cda.
☎ (213) 936-4240 . . 201 S Arden Blvd, Los Angeles, CA *90004*
Béguelin MR & MRS W Drury (Sarah S Pierce) Sim'85.Stc.
☎ (508) 369-8013 . . 87 Ash St, Concord, MA *01742*

Beha MR & MRS James A 2d (Nancy Ryan) .... of ☎ (212)427-7459
Man'vl'73.Cl'90.Csh.Cly.P'71.H'75......... 50 E 91 St,
  MISS Mary A......................... New York, NY
  JUNIORS MR Christopher R.................. *10128*
  JUNIORS MR James J .... ☎ (518) 734-9738
    Brooksburg Rd,
    Windham, NY
    12496
Beha MR & MRS James J (Macy Ann Reilly) Cly.Wms'37.H'40
  ☎ (914) 967-1309 . . 43 Island Dv, Rye, NY *10580*
Behn MRS Sosthènes 2d (Beatrix Nogueira)
  Av Getulio Vargas 3163, Apt 1202, Curitiba, 80240-041 Paraná, Brazil
Behn MR William C....................... ☎ (305) 661-6946
  MR William S......................... 746 Benevento Av,
  MRS Aphra (Lesoeur—Aphra Behn)......... Coral Gables, FL
    MR & MRS Franck Le Pelletier (Monica *33146*
    Behn) . . MR absent ....
Behnke MR & MRS Thomas G (Kelly A McMahon) Col'81.Col'80
  ☎ (303) 670-8048 . . 1551 Prouty Dv, Evergreen, CO *80439*
Behr MR & MRS John L (Coleman—Barbara Stanley) On.Y'40.Y'47
  ☎ (847) 234-1103 . . 314 E Foster Place, Lake Forest, IL *60045*
Behr MR & MRS Karl H (Howard—Elaine L Oakley) Mds.Y'37
  ☎ (941) 676-6584 . . Mountain Lake, PO Box 832, Lake Wales,
  FL *33859*
Behr MR Richard P—ColC'71
  ☎ (804) 971-1757 . . 231 Turkey Ridge Rd, Charlottesville, VA *22903*
Beidler MRS Francis 2d (Eleanor S Chapman) BMr'33.BtP.Wa.Ncd.
  ☎ (847) 234-0502 . . 1050 E Walden Rd, Lake Forest, IL *60045*
Beidler MR & MRS Francis 3d (Prudence L ☎ (847) 234-3277
  Richardson) Ws'67.Ch'68.Rc.On.H'67.Nw'70 . . 20 S Stonegate Rd,
  MISS Prudence E....................... Lake Forest, IL
  MR Francis 4th *60045*
Beinecke MR & MRS Frederick W (Candace L of ☎ (212)737-0177
  Krugman) Nu'67.Ri.Y.'66 .... 998 Fifth Av,
  JUNIORS MR Jacob S .... New York, NY
  JUNIORS MR Benjamin B *10028*
    ☎ (413) 528-3636
    ''Wheelbarrow Hill
    Farm''
    Egremont Rd,
    Rte 23, Box 122,
    Great Barrington,
    MA *01230-0122*
Beir MR & MRS Howard F (Amy N Ward)
  Plg.An.Fw.StJ.Cly.Ncd.Myf.Pa'38
  ☎ (860) 435-9185 . . 89 Belgo Rd, Lakeville, CT *06039*
Beir MR & MRS John A (Diane E Rapalus) Ty'83.Ty'80
  ☎ (860) 561-5484 . . 155 Ridgewood Rd, West Hartford, CT *06107*
Beisswanger MR & MRS William J (Caroline T Short) Va'96.Va'96
  ☎ (201) 760-0955 . . 186 Mallinson St, Allendale, NJ *07401*
Belak MR & MRS Edmund R JR (Cynthia E Pierce) Man'vl'78.Cr'69.Wis'71
  ☎ (203) 966-0135 . . 2 Hidden Meadow Lane, New Canaan, CT *06840*
Belden MR & MRS William A (Mary M Cluett) BMr'51.Cly.Yn.Y'50.Ariz'54
  575 Hull's Farm Rd, Southport, CT *06490*
Belin MR & MRS G d'Andelot (Harriet L Bundy) Au.Ec.Cy.Tv.Y'39
  ☎ (617) 491-6145 . . 4 Willard St, Cambridge, MA *02138*

Belknap MRS D Callaway (Dorothy Callaway) .... ☎ (413) 698-2738
  MISS Jenny W—at Walker .... Cone Hill Rd,
  JUNIORS MR Matthew G—at Berkshire .... Richmond, MA
    01284
Belknap MISS Mary C (Robert E 3d) .... Married at Brooklyn, NY
  McKee MR Michael G (David) .... May 18'96
Belknap MR Michael H P—H'63.Camb'65
  ☎ (518) 781-4292 . . Warner Crossing Rd, Box 94, Canaan, NY *12029*
Belknap MR & MRS Robert E 3d (Mary J Sloan) of ☎ (718)625-1088
  StFran'95.Chr.Rby.Ne.Y.Va'61 ...... 128 Willow St,
  MISS Elizabeth T—F&M'91—at 202 Quarry Rd, Brooklyn, NY *11201*
  Stamford, CT *06903*.................... ☎ (441) 292-3119
  MISS Berkeley S—Y'92—at 60 E 8 St, Apt 5F, 6 Robin Hood Dv,
  New York, NY *10003* .... Pembroke HM 13,
    Bermuda
Belknap MR & MRS Thomas H (Alice N Bean) ☎ (508) 468-2851
  SIll'61.Myc.H.Yn.Y'62.Van'65 ⚓ 15 Morgan St,
  MISS Susan E—at Lesley .... Wenham, MA *01984*
  MR Thomas H JR—at Emory...............
Belknap MRS William E 2d (Byrne—Emmet— ☎ (516) 329-2691
  M Virginia Foster) Se'76.LaV'82.Myf.Cda.Ht. PO Box 807,
  Hb.H................................. East Hampton, NY
    MRS H Dunscombe Emmet (Castets—Helen D *11937*
    Emmet)..............................
Bell MR & MRS A Henry (Jane W Houser) Ncd.Tex'37 . . of
  ☎ (214) 528-3470 . . 3506 Harvard Av, Dallas, TX *75205*
  Valley Dv, Macatawa, MI *49434*
Bell MR & MRS Alexander C (Catharine R Johnson) P'34
  ☎ (518) 274-3143 . . 20 Lillian Lane, Troy, NY *12180*
Bell MRS Alfred D JR (Marjorie R Blyth) Bur.
  ☎ (415) 343-4185 . . 933 W Santa Inez Av, Hillsborough, CA *94010*
Bell JUNIORS MISS Barbara L . . see MRS B T Lincoln
Bell MISS Barrie R
  ☎ (520) 455-5201 . . Hope Springs Ranch, Papago Springs Rd,
  Box 290, Sonoita, AZ *85637*
Bell MR Bertrand F III—Hav'54
  see Dilatory Domiciles
Bell MR & MRS Bryan (Rubie S Crosby) ☎ (504) 895-0877
  V'47.Tul'50.Ncd.P'41.Tul'63............... 1331 Third St,
  MISS Helen E—at 2100 Connecticut Av NW, New Orleans, LA
  Washington, DC *20008* *70130*
  MISS Beverly S ....
  MR Bryan JR—at 1001 N 2 St, Harrisburg, PA
  17102 ....
Bell JUNIORS MR C Branson 3d . . see MRS B T Lincoln
Bell MR C Derek . . see A W McBain
Bell MR Christopher A . . see A W McBain
Bell MR David Paine—H'68.NMex'81
  ☎ (415) 221-4196 . . 1926 Fell St, San Francisco, CA *94117*
Bell MISS Elizabeth (John S) .... Married at Bloomfield Hills, MI
  Townsend MR Michael T (Terry M) .... Jun 15'96
Bell MRS Frank S (Mennel—Margery W Todd) V'37.BtP.Cda.
  ☎ (561) 844-1561 . . 231 Nightingale Trail, Palm Beach, FL *33480*
Bell MRS G Graham (Helen Stevens)
  ☎ (908) 449-5543 . . 217 Boston Blvd, Sea Girt, NJ *08750*
Bell MRS George de B (Roberta H McVey) Gm.Me.
  ☎ (610) MI2-8597 . . 1226 Rock Creek Rd, Gladwyne, PA *19035*

Bell MR & MRS George de B JR (Caroline M Minot) H'77.Pr.Rc.H'80
  ☎ (516) 671-0338 . . Crescent Beach Rd, Glen Cove, NY *11542*

Bell MR Gordon Knox—Rcn.Snc.Cw.Hn.H'25.Cl'30
  ☎ (919) 787-8009 . . 934 Wimbleton Dv, Raleigh, NC *27609*

Bell MRS James A (Mary Louise Succop)
  ☎ (412) 681-1588 . . 5023 Frew St, Pittsburgh, PA *15213*

Bell MR & MRS James B (Miriam S Reay) | ☎ (609) 924-2125
Minn'57.Minn'55.Ox'64 . . . . | 689 Mercer Rd,
MISS Vanessa M S—at 165 Griggs Dv, Princeton, | Princeton, NJ *08540*
NJ *08540* |
MR James B JR . . . . |
MR Elliott M . . . . |

Bell MR & MRS James E (Constance H Lavino) Rcp.Wil.Ac.Pa'40
  ☎ (561) 546-3441 . . ''Folie du Bois'' 166 S Beach Rd, Hobe Sound,
FL *33455*

Bell MR James T (late George de B) . . . . Married at Gladwyne, PA
  Story MRS S Baker (Susannah Baker) . . . . May 25'96

Bell MR Jeffrey M . . see A W McBain

Bell MRS John C JR (Sarah A Baker) Me.
  ☎ (610) 525-1797 . . 707 Pennstone Rd, Bryn Mawr, PA *19010*

Bell MRS John C 3d (Bell—Goodyear—C Le Vaun Pendergast) Cts.Gm.Me.
  ☎ (610) 525-5862 . . 962 Locust Grove Terr, Rosemont, PA *19010*

Bell MR & MRS John C 4th (M Ramsay Gross)
  Ty'77.Md'80.P'75.Va'81 . . of
  ☎ (203) 655-6471 . . 473 Hollow Tree Ridge Rd, Darien, CT *06820*
  ☎ (207) 883-5638 . . ''Bellhaven'' 8 Ferry Rd, Prouts Neck, ME *04074*

Bell MR & MRS John H (Edith W Muetze)
  ☎ (314) WO2-8152 . . 1335 Monier Dv, Glendale, MO *63122*

Bell MR & MRS Kelly (Ruth Stuart) Bnd'71 . . . . | ☎ (915) 682-1311
MISS M Bayard—at ☎ (713) 799-2549 | 206 Club Dv,
7777 Greenbriar St, Apt 1023, Houston, TX | Midland, TX *79701*
77030 . . . . |
MR Arch L—at Furman U . . . . |

Bell MISS Lauren Hunter (g—James E Bell) . . . . Born Feb 22'96

Bell MRS M Morian (Hopper—Mary J Morian) Ncd.
  ☎ (610) 584-3886 . . Meadowood at Worcester, 35 Hickory Heights
Place, Lansdale, PA *19446*

Bell MRS Marcus L (Landin—Alison Grubb) . . of
  ☎ (202) 362-2058 . . 4000 Massachusetts Av NW, Washington,
DC *20016*
  ☎ (540) 347-2770 . . Fauquier White Sulphur Springs, Box 194,
RR 2, Warrenton, VA *20188-8517*

Bell MISS Marion Dewar—Duke'88
  ☎ (210) 822-1171 . . 200 Patterson Av, Apt 1006, San Antonio,
TX *78209*

Bell MISS Mary-Knight T . . see MRS B T Lincoln

Bell MRS Phyllis K (Phillips—Phyllis K Bell) . . . . . | ☎ (212) 752-7142
MISS Deborah C Phillips . . . . | 340 E 57 St,
MISS Susan C Phillips . . . . | New York, NY
| *10022*

Bell MR Robert M—Daven'82.DU'85
  ☎ (561) 335-5155 . . 12240 SE Florida Av, Stuart, FL *34994*

Bell MR & MRS Stephen G (Lucy K Kennard) | 303 E Greenwood
Wash'66.Ncd.Cr'66 . . . . | Av, Lake Forest, IL
JUNIORS MR Randolph A G . . . . | *60045*

Bell MRS Stephen P (Meagher—Gibson—Ann H | 22 Lake Julia Dv N,
Brown) . . . . | Ponte Vedra Beach,
MR Christopher L Gibson . . . . | FL *32082*

Bell MR & MRS Stuart M (Carolyn J Maher) OWes'84
  ☎ (717) 868-8169 . . 225 Country Club Rd, Mountain Top, PA *18707*

Bell MR & MRS W Kirk (Helen W Spofford) Y'85.Fic.Ala'85
  ☎ (910) 692-0692 . . ''The Nuggett'' 260 E Pennsylvania Av,
Southern Pines, NC *28387*

Bell MRS William P (Sophie H Buckner)
  ☎ (513) 542-6077 . . 5300 Hamilton Av, Cincinnati, OH *45224*

Bellas MR & MRS Michael C (Helen A Eggleston) | ☎ (212) 427-4370
Un.Mds.Cly.Y'64.Mich'66.Cl'68 . . . . | 1095 Park Av,
MISS Belinda M . . . . | New York, NY
| *10128*

Beller MR & MRS Alan L (Leslie J Langworthy) | 867 President St,
Nu'73.Pa'76.Y'71.Pa'76 . . . . | Brooklyn, NY *11215*
JUNIORS MISS Elizabeth C . . . . |

Bellinger MRS Dunn (Adrian J Dunn) NCar'52.Cvc.
  ☎ (301) 652-1380 . . 3515 Hamlet Place, Chevy Chase, MD *20815*

Bellinger COL (RET) & MRS John B JR (Anne T Tynes)
  Stph'53.AmU'79.CathU'81.USA'48.Geo'63.Geo'77
  ☎ (703) 536-8954 . . 4001 N Ridgeview Rd, Arlington, VA *22207*

Bellinger MR & MRS John B 3d (Caroline D Renzy)
  Swb'84.Cc.P'82.H'86.Va'91
  ☎ (703) 841-4979 . . 4026 N 25 St, Arlington, VA *22207*

Bellingrath MR & MRS Ferdinand McM (Frances H Martin)
  Hendrix'51.Ark'50
  ☎ (501) 534-8817 . . 30 Longmeadow St, Pine Bluff, AR *71603*

Bellis MR & MRS James L (Blair Butler) Mo.Wes'46 . . of
  ☎ (561) 231-4801 . . 995 Painted Bunting Lane, Vero Beach, FL *32963*
  ☎ (908) 781-0073 . . PO Box 443, Bedminster, NJ *07921*

Bellis MR & MRS James L JR (Patricia A Taggart)
  NH'84.Eh.Mo.Shcc.LakeF'76
  ☎ (908) 234-2908 . . 1681 Lamington Rd, Bedminster, NJ *07921*

Belman MISS Anneka Erin (g—Murray J Belman) . . . . . Born Mch 29'96

Belman MR & MRS Murray J (Laura T Haines)
  Rdc'61.Sl.Ds.Cda.Cr'57.H'60
  ☎ (202) 362-2552 . . 3711 Fordham Rd NW, Washington, DC *20016*

Belson MR & MRS James A (Rosemary P Greenslade) | of ☎ (202)333-5569
TyDC'54.Cvc.Cos.Geo'53 . . . . | 2220—46 St NW,
MISS Elizabeth A—Geo'92 . . . . | Washington, DC
MR Stephen G—WVaWes'95 . . . . | *20007-1054*
| ☎ (410) 757-1747
| 12 W Severn Ridge
| Rd, Annapolis, MD
| *21401*

Belsterling MISS Jean I—Pa'74.Drex'76 . . see MRS J B Bowman

Belt MR & MRS Charles Banks JR (Louise H | ☎ (314) 432-4214
McKeon) Man'vl'57.StL'83.Wms'53.Cl'55.Cl'59 | 2559 Oak Spring
MISS Marguerite H—at ☎ (517) 355-7992 | Lane, St Louis, MO
919A Cherry Lane, East Lansing, MI *48823* . . . | *63131*
MR Aelred D . . . . |

Belt MR & MRS Edward S (Emily H Macsherry)   ☎ (413) 256-8203
NotreD'55.Wms'55.H'57.Y'63 . . . . | 116 Alpine Dv,
MISS Anne B—Woos'85—at Columbia Grad . . . | Amherst, MA 01002
MISS Agnes K—Woos'87—at ☎ (508) 481-6744
St Mark's School, 25 Marlborough Rd,
Southborough, MA 01772 . . . .

Belt MISS Emily H—Skd'85
☎ (413) 582-7938 . . 165 Crescent St, Northampton, MA 01060

Belt MR & MRS John H K (Mary Jane McCabe)   ☎ (516) 676-5592
MaryMt'62.Ck.JHop'61 . . . . | 43 Town Path,
JUNIORS MISS Amanda C . . . . | Glen Cove, NY
JUNIORS MISS Laura K . . . . | 11542

Belz DR & MRS John F (Helene Fulton)   ☎ (415) 322-5941
Stan'39.Stan'35.Nev'38 . . . . | 239 Felton Dv,
MISS Caroline (Mitchell—Caroline Belz) Stan'65 | Menlo Park, CA
  | 94025

Beman MR & MRS John B JR (Deborah J Dawson) Stan'38.Stan'38
☎ (714) 492-5404 . . 306 Av De Las Palmeras, San Clemente,
CA 92672

Bemberg MRS Edward P (Georgia B Hatch) B.Cly.
1 Sutton Place S, New York, NY 10022

Bement MR & MRS Russell (Viola M J Black)
Me.Ll.Rv.Wt.Cw.W.Cspa.Ofp.Sdg.Dar.Dll.Ncd.Pa'42
☎ (610) 527-9387 . . 138 Montrose Av, 43, Rosemont, PA 19010

Bemis MR Hal L . . . . Died at
Haverford, PA Mch 9'96

Bemis MRS Hal L (Mackintosh—Jeanne W Chatham) Me.
☎ (610) 896-7694 . . 101 Cheswold Lane, Haverford, PA 19041

Bemis MRS James R (Burke—Jane Simpson)
☎ (501) 887-6103 . . 711 E Main St, Prescott, AR 71857

Bemis MR & MRS Norman S (Dorothy S Wagner)   ☎ (610) 558-4916
Wheat'44.Y'44 . . . . | 535 Gradyville Rd,
MR Richard A—at ☎ (610) 525-1710 | Newtown Square,
426 Barclay Rd, Rosemont, PA 19010 . . . . | PA 19073

Benacerraf MR Ari—F&M'85.Cr'88
☎ (212) 987-4726 . . 360 E 88 St, Apt 5B, New York, NY 10128

Benasuli MR & MRS Alan (Nancy E Cooley)   ☎ (212) 744-9545
Cal'76.EcoleCom'64.H'66 . . . . | 39 E 79 St, Apt 7B,
MISS Marina I . . . . | New York, NY
MR Alexandre J . . . . | 10021

Bender MRS Hugh W (Maria E Bickham) Miami'27.Wis'46
☎ (513) 299-4448 . . 336 Ridgewood Av, Dayton, OH 45409

Bender MR & MRS Michael A (Martin—Belinda S Gilmer)
UWash'52.JHop'56 . . of
☎ (516) 744-9746 . . PO Box 666, Shoreham, NY 11786
☎ (941) 964-2359 . . PO Box 666, Boca Grande, FL 22901

Bender MR & MRS Richard J (Inez H Garesché)   ☎ (314) 994-9117
Cy.Ncd.P'44 . . . . | 6 Wendover Dv,
MR Richard J JR . . . . | St Louis, MO 63124

Bender MR & MRS Robert G (Carolyn B Jensen) Smu'81.Smu'81 ⚓
☎ (214) 369-7251 . . 3300 Southwestern Blvd, Dallas, TX 75225

Benedict MRS Edward B (Smith—Patricia Hatfield)
☎ (617) 932-3124 . . Country Club Heights 410, 3 Rehabilitation Way,
Woburn, MA 01801

Benedict MRS John P (Anne J Lewis) ColbyS'54
☎ (201) 226-7942 . . 12 Dorset Circle, Caldwell, NJ 07006

Benedict MR & MRS John T (Marjorie C Etienne)   ☎ (904) 285-1161
NotreD'39 . . . . | 532 Le Master Dv,
MISS Joan L—at 9791 E Sawgrass Dv, | Ponte Vedra Beach,
Ponte Vedra Beach, FL 32082 . . . . | FL 32082

Benedict MR & MRS John T JR (Kathryn R Elliott)   ☎ (604) 758-0816
LakeF'71 . . . . | 3014 King Richard
JUNIORS MISS Stephanie E . . . . | Dv, Nanaimo, BC
JUNIORS MISS John T 3d . . . . | V9T 1J8, Canada

Benedict MRS Julia B (Julia S Barber)
☎ (314) 727-6051 . . 6 Brighton Way, St Louis, MO 63105

Benedict MR & MRS Neil P (Nancy K Brenizer) V'72.Rc.Pr.Ri.Nyc.Cly.
☎ (212) 288-8240 . . 925 Park Av, New York, NY 10028

Benedict MR & MRS Peter B (Nancy T Huffman)   ☎ (561) 231-4111
V'60.Cda.Cly.Rol'59.Ariz'63 . . . . | 607 Lantana Lane,
MISS Anne A—at ☎ (303) 449-8988 | Vero Beach, FL
4463 Eldorado Springs Dv, Boulder, CO 80303 . | 32963

Benedict MR Peter B 2d (Peter B) . . . . Married at Melbourne, FL
Milligan MISS Melissa D . . . . Jun 29'96

Benedict MR & MRS Rodman W (Susan H Stanton) V'76.Au.Cly.Cl'74.Cl'77
☎ (212) 427-4125 . . 1165 Fifth Av, Apt 8D, New York, NY 10029

Benedict MRS Samuel (Elizabeth B Carruthers) . . . . Died at
Cincinnati, OH Apr 3'96

Benedict MR Samuel . . . . Died at
Cincinnati, OH Jly 14'94

Benedict MR & MRS William J (Helen Stiassni) Ri.Cly . . .of
☎ (212) 832-3164 . . 530 Park Av, New York, NY 10021
☎ (802) 824-5285 . . 83 Landgrove Rd, Weston, VT 05161

Benedict MR & MRS William J JR (Catherine G Roberts)
AmU'78.Rcn.A.Cly.DU'74
☎ (203) 869-7057 . . 135 Park Av, Greenwich, CT 06830

Benedict MR & MRS Williston R (Rosalind Candlin)   ☎ (860) 868-7224
Gr.Myf.Snc.P'51.H'54.Cl'73 . . . . | New Preston Hill
MISS Francesca . . . . | Rd, New Preston,
JUNIORS MISS Julia . . . . | CT 06777

Benenson MR & MRS Marcius K (Letizia Pitigliani)   of ☎ (212)799-7862
CUNY'51.Cl'56 . . . . | 585 West End Av,
MISS Daniela—at ☎ (212) 787-8439 | New York, NY
160 West End Av, New York, NY 10023 . . . . . | 10024
MR Alexander—at ☎ (503) 693-8975 | ☎ (011-39-6)
1223 NE Thomas St, Hillsboro, OR 97124 . . . . | 322-7406
  | via Antonio Allegri
  | 13, 00196 Rome,
  | Italy

Benét MR Thomas C—C.Y'49
☎ (415) 346-1772 . . 2637 Union St, San Francisco, CA 94123

Benham MR & MRS David B (Margaret M Wise)   ☎ (516) 676-3451
Pr.Lic.Evg. . . . . | "Rosegate"
MR Tyler M—NEng'94 . . . . | Piping Rock Rd,
MR Clifton E—at Lehigh . . . . | Box 529,
  | Locust Valley, NY
  | 11560

Benington MRS Arthur (Mathilde M Johnston)   ☎ (561) 546-2331
Ri.Cda. . . . . | PO Box 837,
MISS Mathilde S—at ☎ (212) 780-9519 | Hobe Sound, FL
30 E 9 St, New York, NY 10003 . . . . | 33475
MR George A—LakeF'88—at 31 Reservoir Dv,
Stamford, CT 06903 . . . .

Benitz MR Bryan M . . see E L Bedford

Benitz MISS Cynthia L . . see E L Bedford

Benjamin MRS Anne L (Redfield—Anne A Lockwood)
☎ (561) 835-8251 . . 400 S Olive Av, West Palm Beach, FL *33401*

Benjamin MR & MRS Edward B JR (Adelaide Wisdom)
Ncmb'54.Tul'56.Y'44.Tul'52 ⚓
☎ (504) 861-1381 . . 1837 Palmer Av, New Orleans, LA *70118-6215*

Benjamin MR & MRS Edward W (Helaine J Higgins) Duke'81.Tul'86
1823 Palmer Av, New Orleans, LA *70118*

Benjamin MR & MRS Henry Rogers (Diana M F | ☎ (516) 283-4243
Bennett) Syc.P'43 ⚓ . . . . | PO Box 731,
MR Gregory P—at 7710 Norcanyon Way, | 95 Down East Lane,
San Diego, CA *92126* . . . . | Southampton, NY
MR Douglas S—at 18 Spring View Dv, | *11969*
Crawfordville, FL *32327* . . . . |
MR Theodore C . . . . |

Benjamin MR & MRS Park 3d (Candice L Jennings) | ☎ (516) 922-2880
Ny.S.Ty'65.Nu'73 . . . . | ''Mill Pond House''
MR Park—Bost'93—at ☎ (617) 739-0274 | 1065 W Shore Rd,
17 Osborne St, Brookline, MA *02146* . . . . | Oyster Bay, NY
MR John J . . . . | *11771*

Benjamin MR & MRS Samuel N (Joan S Oakey)
Sa.Snc.Lm.Ll.Cly.Cda.Ty'38
☎ (212) OR5-6393 . . 10 St Luke's Place, New York, NY *10014*

Benjamin MR & MRS Stephen D (Helen M Ziegler) Bost'84.S.Y'78
☎ (203) 866-3655 . . 40 Quintard Av, South Norwalk, CT *06854*

Benjamin MR Stuart M—Y'87.Y'91
☎ (202) 332-8589 . . 1739 Corcoran St NW, Washington, DC *20009*

Benjamin MR & MRS W Hoffman (Joan Ellett) Sa.Snc.Cc.Cs.Ty'34 . . of
☎ (212) YU8-4617 . . 137 E 66 St, New York, NY *10021*
☎ (914) 424-3340 . . ''Lower Hayfields'' Avery Rd, Garrison, NY *10524*

Benkard MR & MRS James W B (Margaret W | ☎ (212) 427-4247
Spofford) K.Ri.Cc.H'59.Cl'63 . . . . | 1192 Park Av,
MR James R—at 351 N St SW, Washington, DC | New York, NY
20024 . . . . | *10128*

Benkard MISS Margaret M (James W B) . . Married at Fishers Island, NY
Chaves MR John M (Arthur A) . . . . Jun 22'96

Benkert MR Edward R—Rc.Ty'84
☎ (212) 995-0523 . . 40 Fifth Av, New York, NY *10011*

Benkert MRS L Woods (Levenson—Louise H Woods) Nw'58.Cs.
☎ (212) 861-2513 . . 970 Park Av, New York, NY *10028*

Benkhart MRS Bruce S (Carlyne R Rosati) RISD'75.Wes'79
☎ (401) 847-8104 . . ''Daybreak'' Atlantic Av, Newport, RI *02840*

Benkhart MR Bruce S—Cal'77
☎ (401) 849-1773 . . 455 Tuckerman Av, Middletown, RI *02842*

Benkhart MRS Donald R (Nancy S Howe)
☎ (516) CE9-3036 . . ''Windward'' Oxford Place, Lawrence, NY *11559*

Benkwith DR & MRS Sanders M (Linda A Mordecai) | ☎ (334) 263-1166
Htdon'71.So'69.Ala'73 . . . . | 2424 Rosemont
JUNIORS MISS Bonnie E . . . . | Place, Montgomery,
 | AL *36106*

Benner MR & MRS Robert V A JR (Rebecca M Boyd) Vt'81.Pa'81.Dth'87
☎ (508) 369-3270 . . 147 Independence Rd, Concord, MA *01742*

Bennet-Alder MR & MRS Grant (Ellen G Harwood)
MtH'77.Ofp.Myf.Dcw.Dar.Mass'75
☎ (508) 653-6243 . . 121 Walnut St, Natick, MA *01760-2028*

Bennett MR A Jeffrey Rives—Vt'91 . . of
☎ (212) 794-1153 . . 219 E 69 St, Apt 10M, New York, NY *10021*
☎ (802) 297-2490 . . 515 Styles Brook, Stratton, VT *05155*

Bennett MR & MRS Charles P (Catharine DeW | ☎ (703) 978-5953
Cabell) GeoW'61.Minn'54 . . . . | 8230 Toll House Rd,
MR Charles C—MaryW'86 . . . . | Annandale, VA
MR Benjamin P—WVa'87 . . . . | *22003*

Bennett MISS Christina deT . . see MRS J F Bruno JR

Bennett MRS Edward H JR (Phillips—Katharine Falley) Cho.On.Cas.
☎ (847) 234-0404 . . 530 N Green Bay Rd, Lake Forest, IL *60045*

Bennett MR & MRS Edward H 3d (Sekera—Marcia C | ☎ (847) 234-1275
Oonk) Barat'77.LakeF'71 . . . . | 966 W Deerpath Rd,
MR Christopher E—LakeF'92—at | Lake Forest, IL
☎ (312) 903-4326 . . 605 W Madison St, | *60045*
Apt 3307, Chicago, IL *60661-2443* . . . . |
MR Timothy R—at U of Detroit . . . . |
 MISS Katherine H Sekera—Loy'94—at |
☎ (773) 271-7274 . . 1428 W Balmoral Av, |
Chicago, IL *60641* . . . . |
 MR Jeffrey O Sekera—Tufts'92—at |
☎ (011-31-70) 354-9607 . . Berkenbosch |
Blockstraat 5, 2586 HD The Hague, |
The Netherlands . . . . |

Bennett MRS Elizabeth C (Elizabeth O Chew)
☎ (610) 688-2977 . . Box 8097, 207 Radnor-Chester Rd, Radnor,
PA *19087*

Bennett MR & MRS John C JR (Clements—D Hope | ☎ (215) 643-9727
Latta) Swth'61.Pc.Ph.Ll.P'61.H'64 . . . . | 801 Quinard Court,
MR J Hunter—at Temple Law . . . . | Ambler, PA *19002*
 MISS Leslie H Clements . . . . |

Bennett MRS John Connable (Eugenia Coleman) Sg.Ac.
☎ (215) 248-4392 . . 215 Lynnebrook Lane, Philadelphia, PA *19118*

Bennett MR John H JR—Yh.Cc.Cw.Ht.Wt.GeoW'68.SCar'71 . . of
☎ (803) 577-7810 . . 95 Rutledge Av, Charleston, SC *29401*
☎ (704) 749-1134 . . ''The Roost'' Crescent Rd, Saluda, NC *28776*

Bennett MR John P—P.'47
☎ (212) 288-3788 . . 116 E 66 St, New York, NY *10021*

Bennett MR & MRS John T JR (Ellen F Dunnell) | ☎ (603) 279-5117
Hn.Hb.H'50 . . . . | RD 3, Box 700,
MR John T 3d . . . . | College Rd,
MR David C . . . . | Meredith, NH *03253*
MR George M . . . . |

Bennett MR & MRS Joseph B JR (Bigham—Anabelle L Pennybaker) Neb'37
☎ (561) 439-0868 . . 527 Pine Tree Court, Atlantis, FL *33462*

Bennett DR & MRS Joseph S IV (Letty P Knight) | of ☎ (610)644-4822
Wcc.Sa.Ty'50.Pa'54 . . . . | PO Box 189, Paoli,
 MISS Amy Jo—Ty'83—at ☎ (610) 296-0104 | PA *19301-0189*
18 Algonquin Court, Wayne, PA *19087* . . . . . . | ☎ (609) 967-8216
 MR Wade K—Ty'85—at ☎ (610) 647-8497 | 45 E 13 St, Avalon,
1230 Brentford Rd, Malvern, PA *19355* . . . . . . | NJ *08202*
 MR Matthew MacGeorge—P'93—at |
☎ (610) 687-5749 . . 1027 Valley Forge Rd, |
Apt 176, Devon, PA *19333-1162* . . . . |

Bennett MR & MRS Matthew G (Jessica V R Warren) HWSth'84.HWSth'84
☎ (914) 232-7435 . . 26 Glen Ridge Rd, Katonah, NY *10536*

Bennett MR & MRS Paul H (Sally I Neff) Mto.Cspa.Ofp.Ht.Dar.OWes'38
☎ (561) 533-0060 . . Sutton Place S, Apt S305, 2778 S Ocean Blvd,
Palm Beach, FL *33480*

Bennett MR & MRS Philip O (Joyce Wimpenny) Sar.Rv.Wt.Ne.Dar.
☎ (201) 744-2127 . . 131 Lorraine Av, Upper Montclair, NJ *07043*

Bennett MR & MRS Richard Holland (Leslie A | ☎ (210) 824-3305
Wilson) Tex'67.A.Tex'66 . . . . | 615 Ciruela St,
MISS Lucia H . . . . | San Antonio, TX
MISS Leslie B . . . . | *78209*
JUNIORS MISS Megan K . . . . |

Bennett MR & MRS (DR) Robert E (Julia Wallace) P'83.Tufts'88.D.P'82.H'86
☎ (617) 749-9576 . . 6 Longmeadow Rd, Hingham, MA *02043*

Bennett MRS W Tapley JR (Margaret R White) | ☎ (202) 337-3415
Mt.Cvc.Csn.Sl. | 2500 Virginia Av
MISS Anne B—Gchr'72.Ch'74.H'89 . . . . | NW, Apt 1205,
MISS Victoria R—Tufts'75 . . . . | Washington, DC
 | *20037-1901*

Bennett MR & MRS Walter V (Joy A R Post) Wes'38 | ☎ (502) 228-1758
MISS Grace R—NCarArt'84 . . . . | "Stone House"
MISS Julester J (Ribeiro—Julester J Bennett) | 11715 Covered
Ky'86 . . . . | Bridge Rd, Prospect,
 | KY *40059*

Benney MR & MRS J B Neil JR (Cynthia H West)
MaryW'58.Co.Ey.W&L'59 ⚓ . . of
☎ (617) 631-8033 . . 3 Peabody Av, Marblehead, MA *01945*
☎ (603) 526-6128 . . "Ballad Ridge" 210 Little Sunapee Rd, Box 826,
New London, NH *03257*

Benning MR & MRS John A (Carole E Lund) Cr'60.Ey.Mt.Aht'57.Mich'82
☎ (617) 631-3929 . . 60 Lee St, Marblehead, MA *01945*

Benoist MRS Courtney M (Courtney Murphy) | ☎ (415) 923-0559
Man'vl'49 . . . . | 1400 Jones St, Apt
MISS Condé Lee M . . . . | 101, San Francisco,
 | CA *94109*

Benoist MRS G Grace (Geraldine C Grace) Fr.Bur.
☎ (415) 921-0827 . . 2298 Pacific Av, San Francisco, CA *94115*

Benoist MR & MRS Howard 3d (Patricia L Reigle) | ☎ (210) 490-4130
IncW'79.Wash'64.Pa'68 . . . . | 2003 Oak Mist Rd,
MISS Sara R . . . . | San Antonio, TX
MR Ian E . . . . | *78232*

Benoist DR & MRS Walter F (Claude V Fouke) | of ☎ (314)997-6633
Cy.Pa'68.Wash'72 . . . . | 850 Kent Rd,
JUNIORS MISS Claude C . . . . | St Louis, MO *63124*
 | ☎ (414) 868-3495
 | "Beechwood"
 | Fish Creek, WI
 | *54212*

Benoist MR & MRS William F JR (Irving R Simpson) Dth'44
☎ (847) 446-5766 . . 370 Berkeley Av, Winnetka, IL *60093*

Bensinger MR & MRS (DR) Peter B (Judith A | ☎ (847) 295-8555
Schneebeck) Nw'63.Nw'68.Sr.Y'59 . . . . | 5 E Laurel Av,
MISS Jennifer A—at St Lawrence U . . . . | Lake Forest, IL
MISS Elizabeth Brooke—at Millbrook . . . . . . | *60045*
MISS V Brette . . . . |

Benson MR Perry JR—Cc.Ursinus'69.Pa'73
☎ (215) 732-3628 . . 2135 Naudain St, Philadelphia, PA *19146-1218*

Bent MR & MRS Edward S (Lambert—Rebecca J Fotouhi)
Sim'69.H'83.Ri.Nyc.P'66
☎ (860) 868-0577 . . 69 Painter Ridge Rd, Washington Depot, CT *06794*

Bent MR & MRS George Payne 2d (Alice E Babst) | ☎ (203) 869-0146
Cly. . . . . | 707 Lake Av,
MISS Pamela B—at ☎ (303) 759-3201 | Greenwich, CT
2350 S Monroe St, Denver, CO *80210* . . . . | *06830*

Bent MR & MRS Gordon (Betts—Joan Oven) | ☎ (847) 234-0010
Cho.On.Sr.P'42 . . . . | 681 N Mayflower
MISS Elizabeth N Betts—at ☎ (312) 266-1087 | Rd, Lake Forest, IL
641 W Willow St, Chicago, IL *60614* . . . . . . | *60045*

Bentley MR & MRS Chester A (Dunham—Angelica | of ☎ (203)481-2406
Van R Fales) Au.Dc.Ht.Dh.Stv'41 . . . . | 54 Linden Av,
MISS Angelica Van R Dunham—at | Branford, CT *06405*
☎ (860) 669-3052 . . 79 N High St, Clinton, | ☎ (518) 576-9715
CT *06413* . . . . | "Heboma" PO Box
 | 584, St Huberts, NY
 | *12943*

Bentley MR & MRS James A (Crowe—Cecily F Teague) Me.Va'46 . . of
☎ (561) 231-0984 . . 290 Pelican Way, John's Island, Vero Beach,
FL *32963*
☎ (603) 569-3607 . . "Brick House" Mirror Lake, NH *03853*
☎ (610) 687-5118 . . 1017 Fletcher Rd, Wayne, PA *19087*

Bentley MR & MRS Leon F (Hickox—Catherine | ☎ (602) 949-9392
Childs) Mo'48 . . . . | 5202 N Casa
MISS Catherine V—at Colo State . . . . | Blanca, Paradise
MR Frederick D—at Vanderbilt . . . . | Valley, AZ *85253*

Bentley MRS Robert A L (Charlotte M Fowler)
Sth'30.Plg.StA.Snc.Dar.Ne.StJ.
☎ (212) 254-4199 . . 390 First Av, New York, NY *10010*

Bentley MR & MRS William A (Barbara Finn) | ☎ (415) 921-4040
Pcu.Sfg.Tcy.SFr'43.Cal'49 . . . . | 1080 Chestnut St,
MR William H . . . . | Apt 16B,
MR Howard A . . . . | San Francisco, CA
 | *94109*

Benton DR John J—Fla'42.JHop'45 . . . . | ☎ (904) 785-4756
MISS Rebecca G—at 831 Grace Av, | 809 Foster Av,
Panama City, FL *32401* . . . . | Panama City, FL
MISS Diana M—at ☎ (404) 633-9094 | *32401*
2445 Woodridge Rd, Decatur, GA *30033* . . . . . . |
DR Christopher B—StGeo'90—at |
☎ (423) 928-4756 . . 320 Lamont St, Apt B, |
Johnson City, TN *37604-6114* . . . . |

Benton MR & MRS Nicholas (Kate Bigelow) FIT'93.Co.Cw.Cs.H.'51
☎ (212) 249-8063 . . 129 E 82 St, New York, NY *10028*

Benvenuto DR & MRS John A (M Dominique | 812 W Galer St,
de Give) H'77.Cl'81.Geo'63.NYMed'68.Cl'81 . | Seattle, WA *98119*
MISS Kecia—at Stanford . . . . |

Benziger MRS Adrian F (Eleanor S Williams)
☎ (540) 825-4490 . . "Folly-Away Farm" RD 2, Box 106, Culpeper,
VA *22701*

Benziger MRS Peter H (Joan P Kelly) Rose'57.Mt.Cvc.
☎ (301) 229-4908 . . 5207 Westbard Av, Bethesda, MD *20816*

Berard MRS Philippe (Auerbach—Frederica Stevens) Cly.
see P H Auerbach

Berdell MRS Charles P 3d (Elizabeth E Farley)
☎ (212) 288-4893 . . 125 E 84 St, New York, NY *10028*

Berdell MR John F (late Charles P 3d) .. Married at Mexico City, Mexico
Barquin MISS Nora P (Manuel) .... Dec 2'95
Berens MRS Conrad (Baehr—Frances P Cookman) S.Ncd.
☎ (516) 626-9326 .. PO Box 532, Oyster Bay, NY *11771*
Berens MR Lawrence P—NDak'68.Ch'71 .... | ☎ (216) 932-6565
MISS Hope B .... | 2759 Hampshire Rd,
MISS Amy L .... | Cleveland Heights,
MISS Brooke Van A .... | OH *44106*
MISS Emily W .... |
Berens MR & MRS Rodney B (Elizabeth D Carmody) | ☎ (516) 626-1103
Mb.Pr.B.Ng.Pa'68.Pa'72 .... | 939 Ripley Lane,
MR Nicholas M .... | Oyster Bay, NY
JUNIORS MISS Eleanor C .... | *11771*
JUNIORS MR Michael C ....
JUNIORS MR Robert C ....
Beresford MR & MRS Peter G (Carrie L Peterson) NCar'79
see Dilatory Domiciles
Berg, H George JR & Love, Kathryn S—MtH'83.Nw'87.Nw'88
☎ (518) 426-7023 .. 3 Chestnut Hill S, Loudonville, NY *12211*
Berg MR & MRS John R (Hope Semler) Rby.Rut'63 . | ☎ (441) 236-4368
MISS Sacha H—Bost'89.Bost'93—at | ''Overboard''
☎ (617) 624-9696 .. 34 Irving St, Boston, MA | 2 Salt Kettle Lane,
02114 .... | Paget PG 01,
MR John R—Bab'87.RISD'94—at | Bermuda
☎ (617) 742-2396 .. 44 Prince St, Apt 7, Boston, |
MA *02113* ....
Berg MR & MRS Richard T (Elizabeth J Hehr) Leh'43
☎ (804) 979-3141 .. 30 Ednam Village, Charlottesville, VA *22903*
Bergen MR & MRS John R (Webb—Hannah Schoentgen)
CtCol'58.Y'52.Cl'53
☎ (818) 796-4559 .. 1471 Arroyo View Dv, Pasadena, CA *91103*
Bergen MR William B JR—Ayc.JHop'77
☎ (410) 321-0409 .. 226 Stanmore Rd, Baltimore, MD *21212*
Berger MISS Ann H (Blundon—Ann H Berger) V'71.Cvc.Rr.Pg.
☎ (202) 244-0455 .. 6110 Broad Branch Rd NW, Washington,
DC *20015*
Berger MISS Anna Isabella (Paul M) .... Born at
Baltimore, MD Feb 22'94
Berger MRS George R B (Mary M Wurts) V'44-5.Pg.
☎ (412) 421-9892 .. 5463 Kipling Rd, Pittsburgh, PA *15217-1037*
Berger MR & MRS Ira S (Deborah S Brown) Col'75.Col'74
544 Mariah Bay Dv, Heath, TX *75087*
Berger MR & MRS John Torrey JR (H Lee | ☎ (314) 579-9227
Thompson) Wash'61.Nd.Wash'63 .... | 1257 Takara Court,
MISS Helen E—Swb'88.................. | Town & Country,
DR John T 3d—Va'85.Wash'89 | MO *63131*
Berger DR & MRS Paul M (Juliana B Howard) Md'90
☎ (717) 533-6380 .. 1033 Hillview Lane, Hershey, PA *17033*
Berger MR William M B .... Married at Prouts Neck, ME
Johnson MISS Bernadette J (Nanovich—Bernadette J Johnson) ....
May 24'96
Berger MR & MRS William M B (Nanovich— | ☎ (303) 329-8767
Bernadette J Johnson) L.Yn.Y'48 ⚓ | 2450 E Alameda
MISS Katherine M B .... | Av, Denver, CO
MR George B .... | *80209*

Berggren CDR (RET) & MRS P Dow (Deborah M | ☎ (301) 530-4622
Kneedler) USN.NIa'54.................. | 9619 Bellevue Dv,
MR D Hunt—Towson'87—at 11903 Selfridge Rd, | Bethesda, MD
Silver Spring, MD *20906* .... | *20814*
Bergh MR & MRS R Throop (Constance L Miller)
Briar'68.Bost'70.Ec.My.Ty'60.Mit'67
☎ (508) 922-4787 .. 216 Hart St, Beverly Farms, MA *01915*
Bergin MR & MRS Robert (Hale—Stratford—Ursula Williamson)
Cal'33.Fr.Utah'34
☎ (415) 461-5088 .. 501 Via Casitas, Greenbrae, CA *94904*
Bergland MRS John McF (Julia Whitridge) Mv.
☎ (410) 243-4397 .. Roland Park Place, Apt 403, 830 W 40 St,
Baltimore, MD *21211*
Bergland MISS M Christy—Pa'70.H'mannMed'79
☎ (410) 235-4553 .. 4204 Wickford Rd, Baltimore, MD *21210*
Berglund MR & MRS Robert E (Barbara M Quintal) | ☎ (609) 737-1170
Sth'69.Aht'69.Pa'77 .... | 7 Park Av,
JUNIORS MISS Katherine H .... | Pennington, NJ
JUNIORS MR Theodore M .... | *08534*
Bergmann MR & MRS Michael R (Suzanne E Wells) Swb'87.H'87.Va'92
☎ (703) 237-2272 .. 3060 Cedarwood Lane, Falls Church, VA *22042*
Bergner CAPT & MRS Robert B (Elinore J Hubbard) USN.Rv.Dar.AmU'56
☎ (804) 282-5605 .. 101 Kanawha Rd, Richmond, VA *23226*
Bergsma MR & MRS Daniel B (Annette T Walsh) Duke'78.Cr'77.GaTech'85
☎ (847) 428-9041 .. 723 Jamestowne Rd, Sleepy Hollow,
IL *60118-1852*
Bering MRS Edgar A JR (Harriet C Aldrich) Cvc. ⚓
☎ (410) 226-5312 .. 4211 Windrush Rd, Oxford, MD *21654*
Bering MR & MRS Edgar A 3d (Barbara A Clark) Ws'74.Tex'79.H'67.Cal'74
☎ (713) 984-2979 .. 119 Warrenton Dv, Houston, TX *77024-6223*
Berkeley MR & MRS Alfred R 3d (Muriel L | ☎ (410) 243-7859
Van Dusen) B.Elk.Md.Ph.Va'66.Pa'68 .... | 301 Northfield
MISS Cary B—at Trinity Coll Cambridge ...... | Place, Baltimore,
MISS Helen E—at Wheaton .... | MD *21210-2817*
JUNIORS MISS Muriel Van D—at Phillips Exeter .
Berkeley MR Francis L JR—C.Va'34
☎ (804) 293-6408 .. 2600 Barracks Rd, Apt 248, Charlottesville,
VA *22901-2192*
Berkey MR & MRS Andrew DeGraff 2d (Jacquelyn R Lowry) Nw'51
☎ (310) 472-7732 .. 230 N Rockingham Av, Los Angeles, CA *90049*
Berkey MR Charles P .. see MRS F G McNally
Berkey MR & MRS J Addison 3d (Osborn—Marietta | ☎ (518) 398-1665
H Whittlesey) NewSchSR'75.Mt.Pars'70 ...... | ''The Brick House''
MISS Perrin R .... | 1218 Hunns Lake
MR John A 4th .... | Rd, Pine Plains, NY
| *12567*
Berkey MR & MRS John L (Kendall A De Matteo) Rol'89.WestStU'94
☎ (619) 341-8279 .. 72-616 Hedgehog St, Palm Desert, CA *92260*
Berkheimer DR & MRS George A (Margaret P Yates)
SL'37.Cl'43.Un.B.Rr.Nyc.Cly.Ncd.P.'34.JHop'38 .. of
☎ (212) 755-0313 .. 14 Sutton Place S, New York, NY *10022*
☎ (508) 228-0403 .. 8 Pine St, Nantucket, MA *02554*
Berkley MRS Brown (Constance Brown)
☎ (301) 530-4487 .. 5609 Madison St, Bethesda, MD *20817*
Berkowitz MR & MRS Mortimer 3d (Amelia F Manice)
Bnd'79.Rc.K.Srb.Fic.Fiy.Cly.H'76
☎ (212) 737-0190 .. 150 E 73 St, New York, NY *10021*

Berl MR Charles S W . . see P B Brainard
Berl MR Christopher N . . see P B Brainard
Berl MR E Ennalls 4th . . see P B Brainard
Berl MISS Rita S . . see P B Brainard
Berler MR & MRS Jeffrey H (Harriet Landsman) A. . | ☎ (210) 826-8320
JUNIORS MISS Elizabeth R . . . . | 121 Geneseo Rd,
      | San Antonio, TX
      | *78209*
Berlind MR & MRS Roger S (Brook R Wheeler) | ☎ (212) 734-1576
C.Ri.Cly.Ncd.P.'52 . . . . | 120 East End Av,
MR William P—P'95 . . . . | New York, NY
      | *10028*
Bermingham, David C & Searle, Marion S | ☎ (847) 295-9245
(Chandler—Marion S Searle) ColC'77.On. | 209 N Green Bay
Ithaca'77 . . . . | Rd, Lake Forest, IL
     JUNIORS MR William K Chandler . . . . | *60045*
Bermingham MR John R—Y'45.Cl'49 . . . . | ☎ (303) 322-8290
MISS Katherine D . . . . | 601 Franklin St,
MR John R JR . . . . | Denver, CO *80218*
MR Andrew W . . . . |
Bern DR & MRS Irving I (Helen Rosen) Troy'78.Ala'52.Ala'55 . . of
    ☎ (334) 264-0070 . . 2304 Midfield Dv, Montgomery, AL *36111*
    ☎ (904) 267-2326 . . ''Bern Beach House'' 5567 Scenic H'way 30A,
    Santa Rosa Beach, FL *32459*
Bernann MR Bruce K—Colg'61
    ☎ (203) 869-3774 . . 20 Church St, Apt B23, Greenwich, CT *06830-5648*
Bernard MR & MRS André P (Jennie F McGregor) Nw'80.Mvh.F&M'79
    ☎ (914) 478-4955 . . 77 Euclid Av, Hastings-on-Hudson, NY *10706*
Bernard MISS Elizabeth Eustis (André P) . . . . Born at
                    New York, NY Jun 8'96
Bernard MRS J Pierre (Sibyl M Darlington) . . . . Died at
                   Annapolis, MD Jun 15'96
Bernard MR & MRS Matthew L (Hilary M Lea) Ws'82.Cl'88.CtCol'83.Cl'88
    ☎ (203) 869-2260 . . Belle Haven, 83 Meadow Wood Dv, Greenwich,
    CT *06830*
Bernard MR & MRS Thomas N (Adelaide N Phillips) | ☎ (504) 899-1862
Ncmb'48.Tul'43 . . . . | 1328 Harmony St,
MISS Eleanor W . . . . | New Orleans, LA
      | *70115*
Bernbach MR & MRS Paul (Thérèse A Dorn) | ☎ (718) 875-0433
Dunb'67.Cl'67.Pa'70 . . . . | 1 Pierrepont St,
MISS Elizabeth . . . . | Brooklyn, NY *11201*
MISS Sarah . . . . |
JUNIORS MR Matthew . . . . |
Berne MR & MRS Chester H (Beaver—Mary Fogarty) Rol'74
    ☎ (414) 743-4161 . . 1443 S Lake Michigan Dv, Sturgeon Bay,
    WI *54235*
Bernet MISS Kebbie (Howard C JR) . . . . . Married at Vashon Island, WA
    Bedard MR Duane . . . . Aug 19'95
Bernet MISS Martha L—Wash'40
    PO Box 2127, Saratoga, CA *95070-0127*
Bernhard MR & MRS Jason Ruggles (Ashley C Briggs)
    Pa'88.Rc.Pa'88.Pa'93
    ☎ (718) 596-9486 . . 1 Pierrepont St, Brooklyn, NY *11201*
Berresford MISS Nancy C
    ☎ (215) 413-0188 . . PO Box 54278, Philadelphia, PA *19105-4278*

Berrien MR & MRS Price (Dupee—Constance Turner) Chi.My.Myf.H'35
    ☎ (508) 927-0260 . . 1-45 West St, Beverly Farms, MA *01915*
Berry MR & MRS Charles G (Kathryn McGraw) Cal'74.Ri.Cly.Y'72 . . of
    ☎ (212) 807-1499 . . 143 W 20 St, New York, NY *10011*
    ☎ (518) 537-5488 . . ''The White House'' Lasher Av, Germantown,
    NY *12526*
Berry MR & MRS Henry C (Nancy Van D Cooper) Myf.Dar.Ncd.Ga'39
    ☎ (706) 291-1598 . . 93 Featherston Court SW, Rome, GA *30165-8512*
Berry MR & MRS James R (Elizabeth W Gillett) | ☎ (818) 795-5524
Stan'66.Vh.Stan'65 . . . . | 932 S Oakland Av,
MISS Allison W . . . . | Pasadena, CA *91106*
Berry MR & MRS Loren C (Florence H Bateson)
    B'gton'38.Chr.Un.Pr.Csh.Plg.Cly.Y.'34.Cl'38 . . of
    ☎ (516) 692-7015 . . Box 146, Cold Spring Harbor, NY *11724*
    ☎ (941) 475-6681 . . Box 247, Englewood, FL *34295*
Berry MASTER Matthew Erik (Ronald A) . . . . Born at
                    Norwalk, CT May 31'96
Berry MR & MRS Ronald A (Georganna A Hoag) Towson'90.Myf.Hartw'89
    ☎ (203) 938-8852 . . 360 Black Rock Rd, Redding, CT *06896*
Berry MR & MRS Rynn (Nancy Lee Ward) Bnd'44.Ri.Pr.Cly.Y'37 . . of
    ☎ (212) 288-8398 . . 103 E 75 St, New York, NY *10021*
    ☎ (516) 922-7338 . . 151 Cove Neck Rd, Oyster Bay, NY *11771*
Berry MR Rynn JR—Pa'68
    ☎ (718) 622-8002 . . 159 Eastern P'kway, Brooklyn, NY *11238*
Berry MR & MRS William W (Buntin—Virginia Neely) Van'38.Van'40
    ☎ (615) 352-5110 . . 5110 Boxcroft Place, Nashville, TN *37205*
Bertish MISS Jane M . . see MRS W T Stewart JR
Bertish MISS Suzanne C . . see MRS W T Stewart JR
Bertozzi MRS Sheila K (Sheila Kenefick) V'53.St.G.
    ☎ (716) 842-0439 . . 240 Rivermist Dv, Buffalo, NY *14202*
Berwind DR & MRS John M (Catherine E Henderson) | ☎ (360) 423-5092
PugetS'70.Cwr'72.Wash'69.Cwr'73 . . . . | 2355 E Lynnwood
MISS Melissa A . . . . | Dv, Longview, WA
JUNIORS MR Nathaniel M . . . . | *98632*
Berwind MRS Morse (Jean F Morse)
    ☎ (360) 423-5735 . . 1332 Kessler Blvd, Longview, WA *98632*
Besse MR & MRS Ralph M (Augusta W Mitchell)
    OState'31.Un.Sar.HeidC'26.Mich'29
    ☎ (216) 371-4555 . . 2701 Ashley Rd, Shaker Heights, OH *44122*
Bestani MR & MRS Robert M (Marion W Raymond) | ☎ (704) 365-9539
GeoW'74.Nu'79.Cda.Rut'73.Ch'75 . . . . | 2126 Cortelyou Rd,
JUNIORS MISS Elizabeth D—at Phillips Exeter . . . | Charlotte, NC *28211*
JUNIORS MR William E—at Yale . . . . |
Besuden MRS D Lewis (Dorothy B Lewis) V'51 . . . | ☎ (703) 821-8739
MISS Emily L—Elon'85 . . . . | 1703 Westwind
      | Way, McLean, VA
      | *22102*
Betancourt MRS Raul (Charlotte M Cheston) | ☎ (215) 242-3411
Ph.Rb.Sg. . . . . | 608 W Hartwell
MISS Helen C . . . . | Lane, Philadelphia,
MR Ashton . . . . | PA *19118*
MR Charles B . . . . |
JUNIORS MISS Frances M . . . . |
Betekhtin MR & MRS Sergei O (Sara H Fischer) HRdc'81.H.
    ☎ (212) 307-1152 . . 30 Lincoln Plaza, Apt 26J, New York, NY *10023*
Bethea MR & MRS Edward P (Anne P Carr)
    4204 Mountaindale Rd, Birmingham, AL *35213*

Bethea MRS Osborne JR (Martha H Mann) CtCol'64 — ☎ (919) 408-8025
MISS Martha A . . . . 35 Bloomsbury Court, Chapel Hill, NC 27514

Bethea MR Osborne JR—David'63 . . . . — ☎ (704) 896-2863
MISS Laura E . . . . PO Box 1391, Davidson, NC 28036

Bethell MR Ralph A—PhilaArt'77
☎ (415) 346-2587 . . 2702 California St, San Francisco, CA 94115

Betner MRS Thomas E (Harriet C De Mott) Me.Myf.Ncd.
☎ (610) 642-1999 . . 3300 Darby Rd, 5210 Walnut, Haverford, PA 19041

Bettle MR & MRS Griscom III (Patricia Gros) — ☎ (941) 371-5038
Cr'65.Cr'65 . . . . 1660 Stone Ridge
MISS Sarah (Best—Sarah Bettle) . . . . Terr, Sarasota, FL 34232

Bettle MR Griscom IV (Griscom III) . . . . . . Married at Longboat Key, FL
Hinson MISS Kara E (Bruce) . . . . Jun 24'95

Betts REV & MRS Darby W (Elaine J Wiswall) — of ☎ (207)326-4332
Sth'47.C.W&L'34.VaTheo'38 . . . . Box 247, Perkins St, Castine, ME 04221
MR Darby W JR. . . . . ☎ (707) 579-6660 5555 Montgomery Dv, Santa Rosa, CA 95470

Betts MISS Elizabeth N . . see G Bent

Betts DR & MRS Henry Brognard (Monika C Paul) — of ☎ (312)664-0784
Rc.Fy.P'50 . . . . 1727 N Orleans St, Chicago, IL 60614
MISS Amanda M E—at N'western . . . . ☎ (305) 448-5412 3584 Main H'way, Coconut Grove, FL 33133

Beuerlein MISS Pamela—Les'90 . . see A V Leness
Beuerlein MR Robert—BostColl'92 . . see A V Leness
Beuerlein MISS Sandra—MtVern'91 . . see A V Leness

Beuf DR & MRS Francesco G (Crossland—Goss—Penni L Pearson)
TexTech'71.CalTech'55.Temp'76
1062 Utica Circle, Boulder, CO 80304

Beuttell MRS Richard C (Isabelle P Manger)
☎ (561) 567-0586 . . PO Box 2367, Vero Beach, FL 32961

Bevan MR D R Chandler . . see S A Dunn JR

Bevan MR David C—M.Ln.Hav'29.H'31 . . of
971 Idlewild Rd, Gladwyne, PA 19035
2000 N Ocean Blvd, Apt 506, Boca Raton, FL 33432

Bevan MRS David C JR (Page—Victoria M Tilney) — ☎ (212) 348-0441
Ty'75.Ri.Ln.Y. . . . . 1088 Park Av,
JUNIORS MR William C . . . . New York, NY 10128

Bevan MRS Marcy R (C Marcy Rymer) — ☎ (610) 896-8589
Mls'63.Pa'91.Me. . . . . 1117 Maplecrest
MR J Thomas—Colg'89.Pa'92 . . . . Circle, Gladwyne,
MR Mark L—Denis'90 . . . . PA 19035
MR Michael J—Denis'93 . . . .

Bever DR & MRS Christopher T (Josephine J Morton) Ws'42.H'40 . . of
☎ (301) 925-7204 . . 10450 Lottsford Rd, Apt 1004, Mitchellville, MD 20721-2734
☎ (207) 422-9077 . . Bay Av, Hancock Point, ME 04640

Beyea MRS Henry D (Marion A Christman) — ☎ (610) 647-5462
Dar.Ncd. . . . . 401 Millhouse Pond,
MRS Marianne B Ellis (Marianne M Beyea) — Wayne, PA
Dar. 19087-5518

Beyea MRS James S SR (Emily Norris)
☎ (610) 296-0855 . . 15 Leopard Rd, Apt 3D, Berwyn, PA 19312-1878

Beyer MRS Charlotte B (Weitman—Thomas— — ☎ (212) 929-1902
Charlotte B Beyer) Cs.Y. . . . . 69 Fifth Av, Apt 9J,
MISS Catherine S Weitman—at Vassar. . . . . . New York, NY
JUNIORS MR Michael B Weitman—at — 10003
Boston U . . . .

Beyer MR & MRS E Charles (Cochand—Cynthia S — ☎ (202) 333-6767
Darlington) Mt.Sl.W&M'69 . . . . 2802 N St NW,
MISS Ariane A. . . . . Washington, DC
MR Charles G 20007

Bianchi MR & MRS Adam 2d (Hamilton—McCormick—
Penelope L Whyte) SCal'69.Vh.Stan'61
☎ (213) 682-1487 . . 400 S San Rafael Av, Pasadena, CA 91105

Bianchi MR & MRS David W (Cherry J Carter) Vh.P'55
☎ (818) 793-2723 . . 477 W California Blvd, Pasadena, CA 91105

Biays MR & MRS W Tuckerman (Alice de P Todd) ⚓
☎ (305) 451-1300 . . ''Island House'' 633 Island Dv, Key Largo, FL 33037

Bickel MR & MRS William Croft (Minnette C Duffy) Pg.Fcg.Ncd.P'39
☎ (412) 681-6420 . . 816 St James St, Pittsburgh, PA 15232

Bicket MR & MRS Henry B (Katharine M Young) — ☎ (011-44-151)
Cly. 427-3449
MR Henry A C . . . . 3 The Orchard, N Sudley Rd, Liverpool L17 6BT, Merseyside, England

Bicket MR & MRS Robert M (Katherine P Hedger) ⚓
☎ (011-44-1983) 281-388 . . 1 Union Rd, Cowes, Isle of Wight PO34 7TW, England

Bickford MR Albert C—H'24.H'27
☎ (914) 591-7327 . . 33 Ardsley Av W, Ardsley-on-Hudson, NY 10503

Bickford MR & MRS Edward W (Katherine H May) — ☎ (617) 326-5455
Wells'70.D.Bab'71 . . . . 7 Dexter St,
MR Edward W JR—Denis'95—at 128 Hawthorne — Dedham, MA 02026
Court, Rockaway, NJ 07866 . . . .
MR William T—at Trinity . . . .
JUNIORS MISS Anne H . . . .
JUNIORS MR David G—at St Lawrence U . . . . . .

Bickford MR & MRS Nathaniel J (Jewelle A Wooten) — ☎ (212) 737-4051
SL'77.K.C.Ri.Plg.Ncd.H'61.Cl'64 . . . . 969 Fifth Av,
MISS Laura C—SL'84—at ☎ (213) 650-2390 — New York, NY
1601 Marlay Dv, Los Angeles, CA 90069 10021

Bickford MR & MRS Robert C (Margaretta H | of ☎ (914)265-2263
Murphy) Va'75.C.Cly.H. . . . . | RR 2, Box 366A,
MISS Elisabeth C—L&C'92—at | Cold Spring, NY
☎ (212) 932-1491 . . 420 Riverside Dv, | 10516
New York, NY 10025 . . . . | ☎ (212) 628-8554
MR Louis N—Vt'88—at ☎ (413) 585-0710 | 993 Park Av,
32 Bedford Terr, Apt 11, Northampton, MA | New York, NY
01060 . . . . | 10028

Bickham MR & MRS Abraham S (Margaret R Standish) P'32
☎ (513) 293-7393 . . 936 E Schantz Av, Dayton, OH 45419

Bicknell MR & MRS Warren 3d (Elizabeth A Heaton) | Sinkola Plantation,
Kt.Tenn'68.Van'73 . . . . | PO Box 1248,
MISS Sarah E . . . . | Thomasville, GA
MISS Constance H . . . . | 31799

Biddle MR & MRS A J Drexel 3d (Karen M Erskine)
Cr'71.Rc.Ph.Cr'70.Pa'75
☎ (215) 627-4954 . . 638 Panama St, Philadelphia, PA 19106

Biddle MRS Alexander W (Leimert—Virginia Hedrick) BtP.
☎ (561) 659-6622 . . 3800 Washington Rd, West Palm Beach, FL 33405

Biddle MRS Anna M (Anna Lodge Minot) Ac.
☎ (802) 388-7786 . . ''High Venture'' Ripton, VT 05766

Biddle MRS Anne G (Biddle—Mikhalapov—Anne G Biddle) BMr'47
☎ (610) EL6-7397 . . ''Crum Creek Farm'' 2900 Wayland Rd, Berwyn,
PA 19312

Biddle MRS Barbara K (Schoenbrod—Barbara P | ☎ (617) 547-7027
Kerstein) SL'55.Rdc'58 . . . . | 353 Harvard St,
MISS Olivia P . . . . | Cambridge, MA
MISS Claudia de H . . . . | 02138

Biddle MISS Brooke E . . see T M Havens

Biddle MR & MRS Charles (Phoebe E Taylor) W.P'47.H'51 . . of
☎ (609) 924-4457 . . 360 Rosedale Rd, Princeton, NJ 08540
☎ (011-590) 27-62-68 . . Cedex 3, Marigot, 97133 St Barthélemy,
Guadeloupe

Biddle MR & MRS Charles M 3d (Morrison—Phyllis | ☎ (215) 283-7377
Jenkins) Wells'43.Pc.Guil'35 . . . . | 1501 Foulkeways,
MISS Joan Van D Morrison—NH'76—at | Apt R1,
☎ (603) 642-4680 . . 47 Willow Rd, | Sumneytown Pike,
East Kingston, NH 03827 . . . . | Gwynedd, PA 19436

Biddle MISS Charlotte Hopkins (D'Amanda—Charlotte H Biddle) Me.
☎ (215) 247-0837 . . 8222 Ardleigh St, Chestnut Hill, PA 19118

Biddle MRS Constance (Constance M Biddle)
☎ (610) EL6-1685 . . 520 N Newtown Street Rd, Newtown Square,
PA 19073

Biddle MR & MRS David A T (Diane E Lishon) Cr'57
☎ (610) 293-1817 . . 16 Ringneck Lane, Radnor, PA 19087

Biddle MR & MRS Edmund R (Frances E Disner) Pa'50.Hn.H.Pa'65
☎ (610) 520-0343 . . Beaumont, 84 Middle Rd, Bryn Mawr, PA 19010

Biddle CAPT (RET) & MRS Edward (Janet M Stringfield)
Bvr'43.Gm.USN'44.Pa'75
☎ (610) 688-7221 . . 615 Crestlink Rd, Wayne, PA 19087-2314

Biddle MR & MRS Edward E (P Ridgely Horsey)
Bost'84.Y.Dth'84.Pa'89 . . of
☎ (914) 232-5106 . . ''Arcadia'' 30 Bedford Rd, Katonah, NY 10536
☎ (302) 227-7907 . . ''Ridgely Cottage'' 1 Stockley St, Rehoboth Beach,
DE 19971

Biddle MR & MRS Edward L (Noelie J Imbert) | ☎ (617) 547-0861
MassArt'76 . . . . | 428 Franklin St,
MISS Nathalie P A . . . . | Cambridge, MA
| 02139

Biddle MR & MRS Ernest L JR (Ana C Borgersen)
Nw'66.Rdc'67.Me.Rd.Pe.Sdg.Ac.Pa'65
☎ (610) 527-7802 . . 1028 Great Springs Rd, Rosemont, PA 19010

Biddle MRS Ernest Law (Biddle—Miller—Miller—Peggy Anne Huber)
☎ (610) 649-3962 . . 124 Haverford Village, Ardmore, PA 19003

Biddle MR & MRS Gardiner S (Margaret J McDevitt) | ☎ (610) 649-9061
Ph.Rv. . . . . | 422 Owen Rd,
MR Alexander H . . . . | Wynnewood, PA
JUNIORS MISS Virginia H . . . . | 19096

Biddle MR James—Ph.C.Ln.P'51
☎ (215) 639-2077 . . Box 158, Andalusia, PA 19020

Biddle MR & MRS James C (Kristin A Cater) Pa'88.Pa'89
☎ (215) 546-9189 . . 1520 Spruce St, Apt 301, Philadelphia, PA 19102

Biddle MR & MRS John S (Van Roden—Amy | ☎ (401) 423-0495
McKay) Ty'50 . . . . | 201 Beavertail Rd,
MISS Sophie M—Denis'86—see | Box 385,
Dilatory Domiciles . . . . | Jamestown, RI
MR J Scott JR—Buck'88 . . . . | 02835

Biddle MR & MRS Jonathan W (Emily R Boyle) Cal'77.Sw'80.Col'69.Sw'75
☎ (213) 462-8339 . . 2001 N Gramercy Place, Los Angeles, CA 90068

Biddle MRS Livingston L 2d (Neville—Suzanne H Burke)
Cly.Evg.Me.BtP.Ac.StJ.Cda.Dc.
☎ (561) 655-2955 . . 100 Worth Av, Box 2913, Palm Beach, FL 33480

Biddle MR & MRS Livingston L 4th (Joan K Seelye) Ty'75.P'72.Pa'86
☎ (215) 233-0253 . . ''The Knoll'' 6261 Henry Lane, Flourtown,
PA 19031

Biddle MISS Lydia S (Richard C D) . . . . Married at Philadelphia, PA
Cotter MR Joseph W (Joseph P) . . . . May 18'96

Biddle MISS Margaret G A . . see E L Robbins

Biddle MR & MRS Mark H (Melinda A Clothier) Denis'80.Me.Y'72.Pa'78
☎ (610) 642-2482 . . 468 Montgomery Av, Haverford, PA 19041

Biddle MRS Nancy H (Preston—Nancy U Harris)
☎ (212) 734-0663 . . 784 Park Av, New York, NY 10021

Biddle MRS Nicholas (Hunter—Virginia L Carpenter) . . . . Died at
Havre de Grace, MD Dec 17'93

Biddle MR & MRS Nicholas JR (Mary Hopkins) Gm.Cts.Fw.Cc.Ac.P'40
☎ (610) 664-8040 . . 838 Summit Rd, Penn Valley, PA 19072-1323

Biddle MR & MRS Nicholas JR (Joan A Moore) | ☎ (804) 979-1117
Swb'64.Csh.H'63 . . . . | Ivy Farm,
MISS Virginia M—Nu'91—at ☎ (213) 938-2119 | 2040 Foal Lane,
339 S Detroit St, Apt 3, Los Angeles, CA 90036 | Charlottesville, VA
MISS Barbara MacL—H'93—at | 22901
☎ (212) 633-9640 . . 394 West St, Apt 4,
New York, NY 10014 . . . .
MISS Katharine M—H'93—at ☎ (212) 734-4096
193 Bleecker St, Apt 10, New York, NY 10012 .

Biddle MR & MRS Nicholas D (Elena Thiebaut) Rcn.B.Ri.H'44
350 S Ocean Blvd, Palm Beach, FL 33480

Biddle MR & MRS Oliver C (Anthony—Mary | ☎ (215) CH2-2045
Van Sciver) Ph.Pc.W.H'43.Cl'51 . . . . | 422 W Moreland
MISS Vanessa S—H'92.W.—at ☎ (212) 431-8570 | Av, Philadelphia,
195 Spring St, Apt 24, New York, NY 10012 . . | PA 19118

Biddle MR Packard—Pershing'69 . . . . | ☎ (908) 224-0328
  MR John Packard . . . . | 98 Woodbine Av,
                                           Little Silver, NJ
                                           07739

Biddle MR & MRS Ralph E JR (Kathryn A Sullivan) Winth'72.Pa'69
  ☎ (215) 233-2507 . . 7815 Froebel Rd, Laverock, PA *19038*

Biddle MR & MRS Richard C D (Warfield—Crewe— | ☎ (561) 265-1044
  Jean W Miller) DelB.Pa'54.SCal'83 . . . . | 200 MacFarlane Dv,
  MISS Nina A—at ☎ (212) 662-7637 | Apt 201,
  323 W 100 St, Apt 8, New York, NY *10025* . . . | Delray Beach, FL
                                           33483

Biddle MR & MRS Robert 3d (Sally H Macleod) Ncd.
  ☎ (603) 253-6492 . . "Squam House" Box 302, Center Sandwich,
  NH *03227*

Biddle MISS Sheila
  ☎ (212) LE5-6065 . . 125 E 72 St, New York, NY *10021*

Biddle MR & MRS Stephen A (E McC Story Kirkland)
  Pa'83.VillaN'73.BMr'80
  ☎ (215) 357-0215 . . 235 Waverly Rd, Southampton, PA *18966*

Biddle JUNIORS MISS Susan S . . see T M Havens

Biddle MRS Tania G (Tania P Gopcevic) Pc. . . . . . . | ☎ (215) 233-3427
  MISS Tania A—at ☎ (202) 342-1609 | 8811 Duveen Dv,
  3837 Beecher St NW, Washington, DC *20007* . . | Wyndmoor, PA
  MR Christopher L . . . . | *19038*

Biddle MISS (DR) Virginia—Cl'65
  ☎ (207) 374-2216 . . Parker Point Rd, PO Box 1059, Blue Hill,
  ME *04614*

Biddle MR Wharton
  ☎ (401) 423-2834 . . 3H Bayview, 53 Conanicus Av, Jamestown,
  RI *02835*

Biddle MR & MRS William B (Anne C Peach) | ☎ (410) 798-6719
  Hlns'69.VaTech'73.W&L'70.Hlns'82 . . . . | 3287 Patuxent River
  MR Compton M—W&L'95 . . . . | Rd, Davidsonville,
  JUNIORS MR Peyton R . . . . | MD *21035*

Biddle MR & MRS Willing L (Catherine C Urstadt) Colby'85.Ken'83
  ☎ (914) 234-7585 . . 816 S Bedford Rd, Bedford, NY *10506*

Bidwell MISS Courtney E—Br'92.Br'93 . . see P J Moloney

Bidwell MRS Cynthia B (Cynthia H Barry) . . . Married at Washington, DC
  Shea MR Lewis A . . . . Apr 27'96

Bidwell MR & MRS J Truman JR (O'Neil—Katharine T Thomas)
  SL'59.Rc.Chr.Fic.Plg.Ri.Hb.Y'56.H.'59
  ☎ (212) 753-6014 . . 455 E 57 St, New York, NY *10022*

Bidwell MISS Kimberley W—Les'90 . . see P J Moloney

Bidwell MR & MRS Miles O JR (Lisa K Grimmelmann)
  NewSchSR'82.NewSchSR'88.Ihy.Ny.Dar.Cl'66.Cl'68. Cl'72 ⚓
  ☎ (203) 629-8969 . . 6 River Landing, 115 River Rd, Cos Cob,
  CT *06807*

Bidwill MISS Marina Nicole (William V JR) . . . . Born at
                                     Phoenix, AZ Jly 12'96

Bidwill MISS Nicole L (Powers—Nicole L Bidwill) MmtVa'88
  ☎ (602) 379-0101 . . 4037 E Palo Verde Dv, Phoenix, AZ *85018*

Bidwill MR & MRS Patrick C (Enelia del C Carrizo Escudero)
  ☎ (602) 431-8415 . . PO Box 888, Phoenix, AZ *85001-0888*

Bidwill MR & MRS William V (Nancy J Lavezzorio) | PO Box 888,
  Barat'55.Rcsl.Geo'53 . . . . | Phoenix, AZ
  MR Michael J . . . . | *85001-0888*
  MR Timothy F . . . . |

Bidwill MR & MRS William V JR (Nicole G Kugler) Smu'85.Geo'85
  ☎ (602) 379-0101 . . Box 25107, Phoenix, AZ *85002*

Biegler MR & MRS John C (Greer—A Carol Newman) Tenn'49.Ill'43 . . of
  ☎ (561) 626-7148 . . 11708 Lake House Dv, North Palm Beach,
  FL *33408*
  ☎ (540) 466-2510 . . 820 Long Crescent Rd, Bristol, VA *24201*

Bielenstein MR & MRS Hans (Gabrielle C Maupin) | ☎ (212) 663-3479
  Un.StA.Lm.Ncd.Dc.Ds.Ht.Stock'54 . . . . | 21 Claremont Av,
  MISS Danielle E M—at ☎ (703) 845-1963 | New York, NY
  2425 S Walter Reed Dv, Arlington, VA *22206* . | *10027*
  MISS Andrea J G—at ☎ (718) 802-1180 |
  70 Remsen St, Brooklyn, NY *11201* . . . . |

Bieler MR Louis H JR—P'63.Stan'65
  ☎ (415) 333-7876 . . 230 Miguel St, San Francisco, CA *94131*

Bierbaum JUNIORS MR Richard L . . see H T Mortimer JR
Bierbaum JUNIORS MISS S Caroline . . see H T Mortimer JR

Bierbower MR & MRS Mark B (Eleanor D Deane) Va'79.Mt.Nw'74
  8101 Merrick Rd, Bethesda, MD *20817*

Bierman MR & MRS Stephen K (Elizabeth | of ☎ (212)249-4594
  Carrington) Br'58 . . . . | 108 E 82 St,
  MR Frederick C—at Kenyon . . . . | New York, NY
                                           10028-0826
                                           ☎ (203) 435-9780
                                           "The Schoolhouse"
                                           552 Twin Lakes Rd,
                                           Salisbury, CT *06068*
                                           ☎ (246) 423-5061
                                           Carrington Cottage,
                                           Sam Lord's Castle,
                                           St Philip's Parish,
                                           Barbados

Bierwirth MR & MRS John C (Marion G Moise) Cly.Y.'45w.Cl'50
  ☎ (516) 569-4229 . . 300 Albro Lane, Lawrence, NY *11559*

Bieser MR & MRS Irvin G JR (Tracy A Hegamaster) O'71.Mvh.Bz.H'63.H'66
  ☎ (513) 299-4115 . . 790 E Schantz Av, Dayton, OH *45419*

Bigbie MR & MRS J Taylor (Nadine de Coninck) Rv.Cw.P'44.Va'48
  see Dilatory Domiciles

Bigelow MR & MRS Alden G (Dorita H Tuck) Nyc.Va'41
  ☎ (804) 973-6309 . . Rte 7, Box 221, Charlottesville, VA *22901*

Bigelow DR & MRS Bradley (Michelle Cousturier) | 447 E 84 St,
  H'44 . . . . | New York,
  MISS Claire E—at ☎ (212) 243-0630 | NY *10028*
  77 Christopher St, New York, NY *10014* . . . . . |

Bigelow MRS Charles W JR (Anne M Dolan) | ☎ (508) 758-2358
  Mis'dia'43 . . . . | 31 Ned's Point Rd,
  MISS Mary Ruth—at ☎ (508) 443-8569 | Mattapoisett, MA
  16 Curry Lane, Sudbury, MA *01776* . . . . | *02739*

Bigelow MR Edwin R—B.Pr.Rcn.Ny.Cw.Snc.Yn. | ☎ (303) 321-4336
  Y'50 . . . . | 1 Cheesman Place,
  MISS Bettina A—at ☎ (818) 766-0060 | 1201 Williams St,
  4308A Laurel Canyon Blvd, Studio City, CA | Denver, CO *80218*
  91604 . . . . |

Bigelow MR & MRS Ernest A (Marion G Howe) | ☎ (860) 535-3102
  Cl'49 . . . . | 13 Elm St,
  MR Ernest A JR—at 601 Lafayette Av, Buffalo, | Stonington, CT
  NY *14222* . . . . | *06378*

Bigelow MR & MRS George Folsom (Dorothy H Lydon) Cw.H.'38
☎ (508) 945-2829 . . 404 Old Queen Anne Rd, Chatham, MA *02633*
Bigelow MRS J Turnburke (Joan E Turnburke)
☎ (813) 446-1744 . . 625A Grand Central St, Clearwater, FL *34616*
Bigelow MR John E—Rv.Y'50 . . . . | ☎ (617) 237-9721
MISS Yvette E—Pa'84.Bost'87 . . . . | 81 Whittier Rd,
Wellesley Hills, MA
02181
Bigelow MR & MRS Joseph S 3d (Mary E Brown) Srb.H'43
☎ (617) 876-4469 . . 30 Elmwood Av, Cambridge, MA *02138*
Bigelow MR & MRS Wheelock JR (Barbara D Hammett) H'45
☎ (352) 245-9736 . . 17677 SE 102 Circle, Summerfield, FL *34491*
Biggs MISS Anna M—RISD'87
☎ (212) 233-1091 . . 265 Water St, New York, NY *10038-1718*
Biggs MRS Herron (Lillian E Herron)
☎ (314) 822-0968 . . 1008 N Taylor Av, Kirkwood, MO *63122-2844*
Biggs MR & MRS John 3d (Ann B Atwood) | ☎ (302) 996-0932
Wil.P'51.H'56 . . . . | 3 Foxhill Lane,
MR John A—at ☎ (213) 484-2330 | Wilmington, DE
1612 Lobdell Place, Los Angeles, CA *90026* . . . | *19807*
Biggs MISS (DR) Robin B (Jeremy H) . . . . Married at New York, NY
Noble DR Cyrus B (John) . . . . Apr 27'96
Biggs MR Thomas H
☎ (314) 966-0989 . . 1206 S Glenwood Lane, St Louis, MO *63122*
Bigham MR & MRS Michael F (Suzannah P Forbes)
Roan'87.K.Va'79.Stan'83
☎ (415) 326-6455 . . 750 Forest Av, Palo Alto, CA *94301*
Bigham MR & MRS T James (Judith C O'Connor) RISD'83.Ham'83 . . of
☎ (541) 298-1999 . . 6125 Rowena River Rd, The Dallas, OR *97058*
☎ (413) 229-8485 . . ''The Farm House'' Star Rte 70, Box 123,
Great Barrington, MA *01230*
Biglow MISS Anne S—Wis'84.Bost'91.Cda.
☎ (206) 842-6432 . . 12265 Arrow Point Dv, Bainbridge Island,
WA *98110*
Biglow MR & MRS Lucius H JR (Nancy Wheatland) | ☎ (206) 455-4571
Ncd.Y'45.H'52 . . . . | 2425 Evergreen
DR John R—Y'80.Dth'89—at ☎ (617) 661-7387 | Point Rd, Bellevue,
84 Henry St, Cambridge, MA *02139* . . . . | WA *98004*
Bilger MR & MRS Brent R (Cameron Crone)
Dth'80.Cit'81.LondEc'82.LondEc'90.Sfy. Dth'80.Dth'81.Cr'82
25901 Vinedo Lane, Los Altos Hills, CA *94022*
Billings MR Charles A JR (Charles A) . . . . Married at Orford, NH
MacDonald MISS Karen (Paul) . . . . May 26'96
Billings MISS Elise J . . see P T Richardson
Billings MR & MRS Jonathan L (Elizabeth P Gillespie) Swb'84.Cvc.Bow'77
☎ (301) 656-1636 . . 6200 Kennedy Dv, Chevy Chase, MD *20815*
Billings MR Kenney—Stan'57.Smu'79
5602 Greenbrier Dv, Dallas, TX *75209-3420*
Billings MASTER Matthew Monahan (Jonathan L) . . . . . . Born Feb 26'95
Billings MR & MRS Richard W (Martha Burdett) | ☎ (610) 296-3646
Wcc.Yh.Ac.Ncd.Y'50 . . . . | 549 Morris Lane,
MR Scott B . . . . | Berwyn, PA *19312*
MR David H . . . . |
Billingslea DR & MRS Christopher M (Alessandra Bertozzi)
Col'84.Col'84.Col'91
☎ (573) 336-3394 . . 16915 Lemming Lane, Waynesville, MO *65583*

Billington MRS Nelson (Gaunt—Billington—Chandor—Dorothy Lalor)
Me.Ac.Ncd.
☎ (610) 642-5480 . . 264 Montgomery Av, Haverford, PA *19041*
Billups BRIG GEN & MRS James S JR (Frances Heard) Ncmb'50.Rr.USA'39
☎ (210) 494-1313 . . 12522 Maltsberger Lane, San Antonio, TX *78216*
Billups MISS Marcella (James S JR) . . . . Married at San Antonio, TX
Symington MR J Fife IV (J Fife III) . . . . Mch 16'96
Bilodeau MR & MRS Harrison McC (C Arria D Chase) Pa'66
☎ (401) 751-2711 . . 137 Power St, Providence, RI *02906*
Bilodeau MR & MRS Harrison Otis C (Alessia Ortolani)
Hampshire'90.Hampshire'91
1843 Biltmore St NW, Washington, DC *20009*
Bingenheimer MR & MRS Thomas E (Kirkland—E | ☎ (610) 527-1396
Stokes Meade) V'68.Ant'70 . . . . | 9 Barley Cone Lane,
JUNIORS MISS Elise Story . . . . | Rosemont, PA
19010
Binger MR & MRS Andrew G (Shelby L Wyckoff) Col'86.Col'85
☎ (307) 733-0853 . . Box 935, Wilson, WY *83014*
Binger MR & MRS David G (Jane A Wilmerding) BMr'54.H'49
☎ (603) 298-8266 . . Box 83A, RFD 2, Old County Rd, West Lebanon,
NH *03784*
Binger MRS S Storck (Susan Storck) Rdc'53.Cs.
☎ (212) 348-3858 . . 25 E 94 St, New York, NY *10128*
Bingham MR & MRS A Walker 3d (Nicolette S | ☎ (212) 628-5358
Pathy) Un.Chr.StA.Cs.H.'51 . . . . | 19 E 72 St,
MISS Nicole P—at ☎ (212) 982-7037 | New York, NY
72 E 3 St, New York, NY *10002* . . . . | *10021*
MR Alexander D—at ☎ (415) 923-0829 |
1529A Golden Gate Av, San Francisco, CA |
94115 . . . . |
Bingham MRS Arthur W (Mary S Dunwody) Cs.
☎ (212) BU8-6568 . . 117 E 72 St, New York, NY *10021-4249*
Bingham MR & MRS Barry JR (Franchini—Edith W | ☎ (502) 893-3165
Stenhouse) Sth'85.H'56 . . . . | Glenview, KY
MISS Mary C—H'90 . . . . | *40025*
Bingham MR & MRS C Tiffany JR (Ann S Dickey) Tenn'71.Y'56
☎ (901) 452-7800 . . 239 Windover Grove Dv, Memphis, TN *38111*
Bingham MR Charles T 3d—OWes'66 . . see K A Gorman
Bingham DR & MRS David B (Anne B Waterman) | 50 White Birch Rd,
Wheat'61.Y'62 . . . . | Salem, CT *06420*
MISS (DR) Tiffany M—Y'89.Pa'94. |
DR David B 2d—Y'87.ClP&S'92—at |
Stanford University Hospital, Palo Alto, CA |
94305 . . . . |
Bingham MRS Elisabeth P B (Elisabeth P Brawner) | ☎ (561) 732-9996
Swb'51 . . . . | 1 E Ocean Av,
MR William H—at ☎ (919) 848-3769 | Ocean Ridge, FL
6316 Lakeland Av, Raleigh, NC *27612* . . . . . . | *33435*
MR Peirce S—at ☎ (407) 876-1365 |
PO Box 275, Windemere, FL *34786-0275* . . . . . |
Bingham MR & MRS Harry Payne JR (de Bustamante—Helen Ramsdell)
Rcn.Srr.Ln.An.Evg . . .of
☎ (561) 546-5174 . . 473 S Beach Rd, Hobe Sound, FL *33455*
☎ (802) 375-6669 . . Stone Gate Farm, Rte 1, Box 226, Shaftsbury,
VT *05262*
Bingham MRS Hiram (Rose L Morrison) . . . . Died at
Salem, CT May 20'96

Bingham MR & MRS Hiram A (Anne E Buswell)
K.Yn.Y'57.Cl'63 . . . . | ☎ (203) 531-6839
MISS Olivia T—Ty'90—at New York, NY . . . . . | 149 Weaver St,
MR Hiram E B—Col'88—at New York, NY . . . | Greenwich, CT
MR Matthew R A—Col'92—at New York, NY . | *06831*

Bingham MRS Holleman (Judith M Holleman)
☎ (011-33-1) 47-23-07-29 . . 20 rue de Bessano, 75116 Paris, France

Bingham MISS Isabel Putney (g—A Walker Bingham 3d) . . . . . . Born at
New York, NY Jan 31'96

Bingham MR J Reid—Mlsps'67 . . . . | ☎ (305) 444-8141
MR Joseph R JR . . . . | 915 Palermo Av,
JUNIORS MR Robert L . . . . | Apt 207,
| Coral Gables, FL
| *33134*

Bingham MISS Marian (Hubbell—Marian Bingham) | ☎ (860) 859-1169
CtCol'91 . . . . | Woodbridge Farm,
MISS Drika B Hubbell—Col'84—at | 30 Woodbridge Rd,
20 Church St, Greenwich, CT *06830* . . . . | Salem, CT *06420*
MR J Bradford Hubbell—Tul'88.UWash'95— |
at ☎ (415) 857-1261 . . 555 Bryant St, |
Apt 391, Palo Alto, CA *94301* . . . . |

Bingham MISS Penelope I—Ws'65.Ch'75
☎ (312) 951-0202 . . 850 N Dewitt Place, Apt 3A, Chicago,
IL *60611-2350*

Bingham MR & MRS Robert K (Anne Fairfax Carr) | ☎ (860) 889-4381
Hb.Y'65.Bost'68 . . . . | 42 Round Hill Rd,
MR Robert K JR—Wes'93—at ☎ (212) 529-7837 | Salem, CT *06420*
89 E 4 St, Apt 10, New York, NY *10003* . . . . . |

Bingham MRS Sally Grover (Davies—Davis—Sarah | ☎ (415) 929-1589
L Grover) SFr'89 . . . . | 7 Laurel St,
JUNIORS MR Wheelock R JR . . . . | San Francisco, CA
MISS Sarah M Davies . . . . | *94118*
MR Stephen T Davies . . . . |

Bingham MR Thomas A—Y'59
Salem, CT *06415*

Bingham MR W Richard—Pcu.Bur.Ri.Pr.Ln.Fic.Stan'57.H'61
☎ (415) 923-5246 . . 2350 Broadway St, San Francisco, CA *94115*

Bingham LT COL & MRS William L (H Virginia Potter) USAF.Ncd.USA'44
9009 Sawyer Brown Rd, Nashville, TN *37221*

Binkerd MRS Alfred A C (Joan Dunbar) SL'73
☎ (203) 661-9071 . . 183 Putnam Park, Greenwich, CT *06830-5782*

Binkerd MISS Julia Stedman—DU'71.Bab'84
☎ (212) 362-1892 . . 145 W 71 St, Apt 9G, New York, NY *10023*

Binney MISS Caroline Thorn (Dougherty—Caroline Thorn Binney) . . of
☎ (212) 307-5251 . . 314 W 58 St, Apt 3B, New York,
NY *10019-1811*
"Oakleigh" Rumstick Rd, Barrington, RI *02806*

Binney MR & MRS Robert H (Martha B Billings) Cy.Myf.
☎ (617) 566-2036 . . 77 Codman Rd, Brookline, MA *02146*

Binnian MR & MRS William (Jacqueline C Bolling)
Cs.Cda.Dc.Myf.H.'43 . . of
☎ (516) HA3-5316 . . Lloyd Lane, Lloyd Neck, Huntington, NY *11743*
☎ (207) 348-2391 . . "Binnacle" Box 1, Sunset, ME *04683*

Binstock MR & MRS Julian G (Elisabetta Pellegrini-Quarantotti) Ncd.H'51
☎ (916) 873-6125 . . 14915 Humbug Rd, Magalia, CA *95954*

Binz MR & MRS Urban G (June H Pynchon) So.Rby . . .of
☎ (011-41-21) 691-6084 . . Chemin du Bochet 76, 1025 St Sulpice,
Switzerland
☎ (516) 283-0703 . . 293 Little Plains Rd, PO Box 671, Southampton,
NY *11969*

Biondi MR & MRS Frank J JR (Carol Oughton) | of ☎ (718)601-8180
Eyc.Cs.P.'66.H'68 . . . . | 4551 Livingston Av,
MISS Anne O . . . . | Bronx, NY *10471*
MISS Jane O . . . . | ☎ (602) 948-2100
| John Gardiner's
| Tennis Ranch,
| Scottsdale, AZ
| *85253*

Birckhead MR & MRS Taylor A (Sylvia S Sigmond) | ☎ (410) 377-9216
M'vian'42.Leh'43 . . . . | 6 Farview Rd,
MISS Mary B—MaryW'83—at ☎ (410) 377-5254 | Baltimore, MD
324 Murdock Rd, Baltimore, MD *21212* . . . . . . | *21212*
MR Taylor A JR—Leh'73—at ☎ (610) 868-6445 |
1301 Gasper Dv, Bethlehem, PA *18017* . . . . . . |

Bird MR & MRS Collins (Andorfer—Mary E Mendle) Dar.
☎ (202) 234-0313 . . 2230 California St NW, Washington, DC *20008*

Bird MRS Goodwin (Mathilde Goodwin) Geo'47 . . | ☎ (505) 982-6662
MISS Kristina H M—at 67 Beech Glen St, Boston, | "El Convento del
MA *02118* . . . . | Arroyo"
MISS Zvia N—at York U Toronto . . . . | 529 Armijo St,
| Santa Fe, NM *87501*

Bird MR & MRS Howard JR (Shirley Hasler) Yn.Y'39
☎ (203) 966-5429 . . 121 Pocconock Trail, New Canaan, CT *06840*

Bird MR & MRS J Michael A (Adeline P Herrick) | ☎ (914) WO7-3656
Ox'43 . . . . | 75 Drake Smith
MR William M—Rens'78.Nu'81 . . . . | Lane, Rye, NY
| *10580*

Bird MRS Jackson (Audrey L Campbell) Ncd.Dar.
☎ (860) 767-1262 . . 5 New City St, Essex, CT *06426*

Bird MRS John R (Mary Emery)
☎ (703) 759-2502 . . 840 Leigh Mill Rd, Great Falls, VA *22066*

Bird MRS Junius B (Margaret McKelvy) BMr'31.Cs.
☎ (212) 744-2228 . . 10 E 85 St, New York, NY *10028*

Bird MRS Philip S (Margaret Kincaid)
☎ (216) 321-1274 . . 2275 Tudor Dv, Cleveland, OH *44106*

Birdsall MR & MRS Gregg C (Sturgill—Natalie | ☎ (207) 288-9387
Audibert) . . . . | 49 Mt Desert St,
MISS Marie—at ☎ (617) 327-5244 | Box 643,
43 Waterman Rd, Roslindale, MA *02131* . . . . . . | Bar Harbor, ME
| *04609*

Birgbauer MR & MRS Bruce D (Margaret A Wood) | ☎ (313) 882-3998
Conn'66.Wms'64.H'67 . . . . | 269 Cloverly Rd,
MISS Karen L . . . . | Grosse Pointe
JUNIORS MR Peter H . . . . | Farms, MI *48236*

Birgbauer MR John W (Bruce D) . . . . Married at Grosse Pointe, MI
Ruggles MISS Holli (Gerald) . . . . Oct 5'95

Birge MRS Armstrong (Biggs—Mildred Armstrong) Buf'60
8700 Jones Mill Rd, Chevy Chase, MD *20815*

Birge DR & MRS Clifford A (Carolyn J Byerly)   ☎ (314) 997-2529
Wash'58.Web'82.Aht'56.Wash'61 . . . .   12 Ridgetop Dv,
MR Clifford A JR . . . .   St Louis, MO *63117*
MR Andrew B . . . .
JUNIORS MR William R . . . .

Birmingham MR & MRS John M (Littell—Mary Lee   ☎ (520) 527-0369
Monroe) Roch'50.FlaAtl'66.Rv.Sar.Ht.Ofp.Dar.   5025 E Hawthorne
Dc.Cda.Dcw.Temp'49 . . . .   Dv, Flagstaff, AZ
MISS Georgia A—Ht.Dar.Dcw.—at N Ariz U . . .   *86004-7376*
MR John Monroe—Ht.Sar.Rv.—at
☎ (303) 202-1802 . . 5242 W Ninth Av,
Lakewood, CO *80214* . . . .

Birney MR & MRS Arthur A (Alison Bean) V'51.Cvc.Mt.Sl.W&L'50
☎ (202) 244-6782 . . 4846 Van Ness St NW, Washington, DC *20016*

Birney THE REV & MRS James G (Acton—Cantrell—Barbara A Sullivan)
Conn'55.Dth'50.VaTheo'53 . . of
☎ (610) 696-3753 . . 1142 Merrifield Dv, Hershey's Mill, West Chester,
PA *19380*
☎ (413) 269-6227 . . "Cove's End" PO Box 4042, East Otis, MA *01029*

Bisbee MISS Dorothy W—Br'86.Va'94 . . see F B Porter JR

Bisbee MR & MRS E Arnold (Ruth Borden) Wms'28
☎ (847) 584-3333 . . PO Box 707, Wayne, IL *60184*

Bisbee MR John B—Alf'90 . . see F B Porter JR

Bisbee MR Samuel M—Cl'90 . . see F B Porter JR

Bischof MR George P—P'58.Mich'62 . . . .   ☎ (619) 551-0360
MR George H—at San Francisco, CA . . . .   2420 Torrey Pines
MR Christopher C—at Stanford. . . . .   Rd, La Jolla, CA
  92037

Bischof MR & MRS Harrington (Constance Graham)   ☎ (847) 304-8710
Sth'64.Cho.Cw.P'57 . . . .   480 Park Barrington
MISS Elizabeth . . . .   Dv, Barrington, IL
  60010

Bischof MRS Jacob H (Sophia W Harrington) Cnt.On.
☎ (847) 234-0646 . . 501 N Oakwood Av, Apt 2B, Lake Forest,
IL *60045*

Bishop MR Andre S—C.H'70
☎ (212) 473-0699 . . 35 W 9 St, Apt 8B, New York, NY *10011*

Bishop MR Brooks O
see Dilatory Domiciles

Bishop MR C Timothy—V'77
☎ (904) 285-3387 . . 505-4 Villa Del Mar Dv, Ponte Vedra Beach,
FL *32082*

Bishop DR & MRS Don L (Joan K Draper) Cal'59 . .   of ☎ (406)449-7298
MISS Sara S . . . .   724 Monroe Av,
MR Colin D. . . . .   Helena, MT *59601*
MR Matthew K . . . .   ☎ (406) 677-2786
  "Larch Ridge"
  Placid Lake, MT
  59868

Bishop DR & MRS Harry C (Newbold—Deborah   ☎ (610) 658-0350
Dilworth) Co.Me.Dth'43.H'45 ⚓ . . . .   18 Thacher Court,
MISS Daisy D Newbold . . . .   251 W Montgomery
MISS Noel T Newbold . . . .   Av, Haverford, PA
  19041

Bishop MRS James D P (Doris J Zintek) Marq'52 . .   ☎ (941) 964-0473
MR Francis C—in California . . . .   221 West St, Box
  947, Boca Grande,
  FL *33921-0947*

Bishop MR & MRS John 6th (Daisy Le Boutillier) Ph.Gm.Ac.Ncd.P.'33 . . of
☎ (609) 298-0640 . . "Ogston" 26360 Mt Pleasant Rd, Columbus,
NJ *08022*
☎ (610) 645-8687 . . Waverly Heights Villa 38, 1400 Waverly Rd,
Gladwyne, PA *19035-1254*

Bishop MRS John Harding (Mixter—Lewis Watson) . . . . Died at
Boston, MA Jan 8'96

Bishop MRS Laura M (Harriss—Hunter—Laura McEldowney)
904 State St, Natchez, MS *39120-3575*

Bishop MRS Louis Faugères 3d (Alexandra Griggs) Cly.Dll.Dh . . .of
☎ (212) EL5-4157 . . 415 E 52 St, New York, NY *10022-6424*
☎ (914) OR7-5433 . . "Igloo" Rte 44, Millbrook, NY *12545*

Bishop MR & MRS Thomas B JR (Martha C Smith)   ☎ (804) 295-6568
Va'69 . . . .   The Barracks,
MISS Maria R—at Hollins . . . .   518 Barracks Farm
MISS Marianna R . . . .   Rd, Charlottesville,
  VA *22901*

Bishop MRS Thomas Benton (Dorothea Roeding) Tcy.
☎ (408) 626-4879 . . Carmel Valley Manor, 8545 Carmel Valley Rd,
Carmel, CA *93923*

Bishop MR & MRS Thomas L (Dorothy E Lyon) Ac.Pa'33
☎ (941) 485-5101 . . Inlets, 12 Inlets Blvd, Nokomis, FL *34275*

Bishop MR & MRS Warner B (Landy—Susan B Howard)
Sim'70.Unn.Un.Kt.Tv.Cv.BtP.Evg.It.Dth'41 . . of
☎ (561) 832-7872 . . 300 S Ocean Blvd, Palm Beach, FL *33480*
☎ (216) 423-1728 . . "Windgate" Brigham Rd, Gates Mills, OH *44040*

Bishopric MR Allison—Dyc.Sa.Y.'23
PO Box BQ, Amagansett, NY *11930*

Bispham MR & MRS Thomas P (Barbara C Shea)
Man'vl'68.Geo'70.Ford'81.Nyc.Myf.Vca.Cly.Cda.Dar. Laf'72
☎ (011-852) 2849-8533 . . Sky Court 6, 2 Barker Rd, The Peak,
Hong Kong

Bissell MRS Arthur D (Bissell—Caldwell—Laura H Smith)
☎ (805) 682-8642 . . 1976 Las Canoas Rd, Santa Barbara, CA *93105*

Bissell MRS Charles S Wurts (Jane Grubb Morris) . .   ☎ (802) 635-2213
MR Charles S W JR—P'65—at ☎ (610) 687-5073   RD 2, Box 1595,
38 Homestead Rd, Strafford, PA *19087* . . . . . .   Johnson, VT *05656*
MR John M 2d

Bissell MRS E Perot JR (Ann Packard) . . . .   ☎ (610) 353-3902
MR Francis R P . . . .   Dunwoody Village
  A320, 3500 West
  Chester Pike,
  Newtown Square,
  PA *19073*

Bissell MR & MRS E Perot 3d (Edith M Roach)   ☎ (201) 538-0151
Mg.M.H'57 . . . .   Fossil Hill Farm,
MISS Ann P—at ☎ (617) 241-0330   Red Gate Rd,
94 Baldwin St, Apt 2, Charlestown, MA *02129* .   Morristown, NJ
  07960

Bissell MR & MRS E Perot 4th (Melissa D Lighthill) Bnd'79.Cl'84.San.Cl'84
☎ (203) 698-2343 . . 33 Willowmere Circle, Riverside, CT *06878*

Bissell MR & MRS Frank S (Eleanor R Merrick) Ny. ⚓
☎ (410) 822-6132 . . 5989 Canterbury Dv, Easton, MD *21601*

Bissell MR & MRS G William (Childs—Kay M Ebbert) Pg.Wms'60.Pa'64 .... ☎ (412) 661-9166 6847 Reynolds St, Pittsburgh, PA 15208-2615
   MISS Louise K Childs—at 1535 Honey Grove Dv, Apt J, Richmond, VA 23229 ....

Bissell MR George P JR (Georgina T Miller) Wil.Cw.Ncd.
☎ (302) 655-5152 .. PO Box 3731, 3801 Centerville Rd, Greenville, DE 19807

Bissell MR & MRS James R 3d (Carol L Myers) Col'62.Col'58.H'69 .... ☎ (970) 586-4574 1884 Devil's Gulch Rd, Estes Park, CO 80517-9513
   MR Daniel M—at Middlebury ....

Bissell MRS John J (Margaret N Sachs) Pg.Rr.
☎ (412) 622-9229 .. Canterbury Place 506, 310 Fisk St, Pittsburgh, PA 15201-1708

Bissell MR & MRS Rolin P (Avery C Boling) Va'82.Va'86.Ph.Sa.Cl'82.Va'85
☎ (215) 248-1761 .. 8714 Prospect Av, Philadelphia, PA 19118

Bissell MR Tallman—P.'41.H'48
☎ (212) 688-6686 .. 301 E 48 St, New York, NY 10017

Bissinger MR & MRS Frederick L JR (Smith—Nancy Lois F Drexel) Rd.Y'65 .... ☎ (610) 525-6438 1502 Old Gulph Rd, Villanova, PA 19085
   MISS Alexandra D Smith ....
   MR Burchell P Smith ....

Bistrian DR & MRS Bruce R (Eleanor A Dix) Pars'65.Myf.Dc.Ncd.Nu'61.Cr'65.JHop'71. Mit'76 .... ☎ (508) 356-2458 229 Argilla Rd, Ipswich, MA 01938
   MISS Tennille R D ....
   MISS Jordan B D ....
   MISS Britton P D ....

Bitner MISS Barbara N
☎ (202) 667-0496 .. 1820 T St NW, Washington, DC 20009

Bitner MR & MRS John W (Martha L Connor) SL'38.Nyc.Pn.P'38
☎ (203) 869-5749 .. 146 Putnam Park, Greenwich, CT 06830

Bitner MR John W JR—P'67
☎ (617) 266-7154 .. 113 Commonwealth Av, Boston, MA 02116

Bittel MR & MRS Steven D (Diana N Howard) Ty'72.ClarkTech'67
☎ (610) MI9-7889 .. 625 Sussex Rd, Wynnewood, PA 19096

Bitting MRS Clarence R 3d (Ozanne—Betty M Bergasse) Pa'44
☎ (941) 383-6818 .. 607 Bayport Way, Longboat Key, FL 34228

Bitting MR & MRS George C (Davis—Frances Baldwin) Wash'67.StL'89.Br'57 .... ☎ (314) 721-0313 139 N Central Av, Apt K, St Louis, MO 63105
   MR Andrew O Davis ....
   JUNIORS MR Christopher B Davis ....
   JUNIORS MR John W Davis ....

Bitting MR & MRS Jonathan K (Elizabeth S Safe) Sim'78.Unn.Bost'77
☎ (203) 972-6644 .. 1051 Weed St, New Canaan, CT 06840

Bivins MRS Lee T (Betty Teel) O'41.StJ.
☎ (806) 372-1622 .. 2311 W Sixteenth Av, Amarillo, TX 79102

Bixby MRS William H JR (Lewis—M Helen Hamilton) Cy.
☎ (314) 993-6952 .. 4 Chatfield Place Rd, St Louis, MO 63141

Bixler MR Joseph O
☎ (213) 465-9390 .. 637 N Wilcox Av, Apt 1A, Los Angeles, CA 90004

Bjorlie MR & MRS (DR) John B (Harrison—Cynthia P Choate) Mass'80.StOlaf'70
☎ (508) 281-5261 .. 46 Mussel Point Rd, Gloucester, MA 01930

Black MR Alexander G—Bard'82 .. see MRS R E Clapp

Black MR Andrew A .. see A W Perry

Black MR & MRS Charles F (Hesterly Fearing) Vt'52 .... ☎ (802) 253-4141 Upper Pucker St, Stowe, VT 05672
   MR Benjamin F—at U of Vt ....

Black MRS Clinton R 3d (Woolman—Gene L O'Brien) Nw'47
701 Shady Lake Lane, Vero Beach, FL 32963

Black MR & MRS Dwight P (Ann-Elisa Wetherald) Sth'55.H'53 .... ☎ (561) 231-6265 1395 Shorelands Dv N, Vero Beach, FL 32963
   MISS Elizabeth D—at ☎ (914) 921-3630 79 Hix Av, Rye, NY 10580 ....

Black MR & MRS E Newbold IV (E Susan Crowley) MtH'67.Tr.Cw.Rv.Pa'51 .... ☎ (617) 266-3016 172 Beacon St, Boston, MA 02116
   JUNIORS MISS K Alexandra N ....

Black MRS Gary (Adams—Verina Borwick) Gv .. .of
☎ (410) 833-0377 .. Mantua Cottage, 13939 Mantua Mill Rd, Glyndon, MD 21071
☎ (011-44-1488) 648220 .. Shefford Woodlands House, Shefford Woodlands, Hungerford, Berkshire RG17 7AG, England

Black DR & MRS Harrison (Gertrude Diefenbach) Sm.Chi.P'40.H'43
☎ (508) 785-0040 .. 45 Willow St, Dover, MA 02030

Black MISS Heather S .. see A W Perry

Black MR James Gordon—Rc.Dyc.Ne.Fw.
☎ (212) 734-6492 .. 215 E 66 St, New York, NY 10021

Black MR Jeremiah W—H'84 .. see MRS R E Clapp

Black MR & MRS John L (Mary R Timanus) Fw.Cspa.P'35
☎ (215) 646-1630 .. 2D The Meadows, Box 271, Spring House, PA 19477

Black MR Morford L—Cl'36
☎ (212) 628-0095 .. 220 E 67 St, New York, NY 10021

Black MR & MRS Peter (Caroline S Warren) Ny.H'42 ♿
☎ (410) 822-2534 .. 27018 Rigbylot Rd, PO Box 100, Royal Oak, MD 21662

Black MRS Robert A (Jane H Jordan) Str.Rc.Ncd.Dar.
☎ (314) 727-8443 .. 816 S Hanley Rd, Apt 3D, St Louis, MO 63105

Black MR & MRS Robert L JR (Helen H Chatfield) Qc.Y'39
☎ (513) 561-8705 .. 5900 Drake Rd, Cincinnati, OH 45243

Black MISS Sophie C—Marlboro'80.Cl'84 .. see MRS R E Clapp

Black MISS Sylvia (Ripley—Sylvia Black)
☎ (206) 323-8854 .. 1129—22 Av E, Seattle, WA 98112

Black MR & MRS Van-Lear 3d (Green—Marion M Bischoff) Cent'y'55.Cy.Mo'53
☎ (314) 997-0022 .. 2030 S Warson Rd, St Louis, MO 63124

Black MR & MRS Van-Lear 4th (Tamara K Garrett) WakeF'80.Tul'79.Duke'89
2130 Hickory Dv, Chesterfield, MO 63005

Black MISS Virginia B
☎ (212) SA2-4042 .. 1111 Park Av, New York, NY 10128

Black DR & MRS William M (Mary E Hubbard) Sth'80.NH'75.StGeo'81.NH'94
☎ (603) 547-6453 .. PO Box M, Greenfield, NH 03047

Black MR & MRS William T JR (Seward—Susan M Souder) Br'59.P.'53 .... of ☎ (610)695-0895 2560 White Horse Rd, Berwyn, PA 19312
   MISS Laura A—Colg'88 ....
   MR John T—Hob'91 ....
   ☎ (609) 298-5574 ''The Locusts'' Wrightstown, NJ 08562

Black MRS Witherbee (Tucker—Ethel French)
☎ (212) PL5-2959 . . 470 Park Av, New York, NY *10022*
Black MR Witherbee JR
☎ (561) 231-0146 . . 183 Silver Moss Dv, John's Island, Vero Beach, FL *32963*
Blackburn MISS Susan E
☎ (860) 522-0340 . . 31 Woodland Rd, Hartford, CT *06105*
Blackburn MR & MRS William W (Buechner—Barbara W Satterlee) Y'41
☎ (212) BU8-4352 . . 174 E 74 St, New York, NY *10021*
Blacker LT & MRS William L (H Elizabeth Allison) USN.J'ville'87.SanJ'90
☎ (904) 886-9954 . . 5424 Pergran Court, Jacksonville, FL *32257*
Blackett MR & MRS Arthur B (Nancy Richmond) D.
☎ (508) 376-8680 . . 106 Forest Rd, Millis, MA *02054*
Blackford MR & MRS Staige D JR (F Bettina Balding) V'57.Va'52.Ox'54
☎ (804) 977-9713 . . 1857 Westview Rd, Charlottesville, VA *22903*
Blackiston MR Alexander H . . see R H Stone
Blackiston MR H Schuyler . . see R H Stone
Blackiston MR Henry C—P'32.H'35
☎ (804) 977-7793 . . "Boxley" 1570 Old Ballard Rd, Charlottesville, VA *22901*
Blackiston MR & MRS Henry C 3d (Sarah R Lathrop) ECar'72.Pn.P'65
☎ (203) 622-1271 . . 379 Round Hill Rd, Greenwich, CT *06831*

Blackman REV & MRS George L (Marian E S Hardie) H'41	☎ (603) 798-5934
	"Red Hall"
MR Henry D S	31 Blackman Rd,
MR Anthony G L	Chichester, NH
MR Hamish F H—at Brookline, MA	*03234*

Blackmon MR & MRS Stephen E JR (Evelyn H Byrd) MtH'77.SCar'75
☎ (615) 356-7454 . . 108 S Bellevue Dv, Nashville, TN *37205*

Blackmore MISS Patricia (Ziegler—Patricia Blackmore) BMr'61.Cly.	☎ (212) 879-2194
	68 E 86 St,
MR Timothy O Ziegler—at	New York, NY
5378 Locksley Av, Oakland, CA *94618*	*10028*

Blackmun MR JUSTICE & MRS Harry A (Dorothy E Clark)
1—1 St NE, Washington, DC *20543*

Blackwell MRS Constance W T (Constance W Taylor) Sth'56.Cl'77	☎ (011-44-171)
	267-6401
MISS Anne W—Minn'86	28 Gloucester
JUNIORS MR Theodore W—at Wadham Coll Oxford	Crescent, London NW1 7DL, England

Blackwell MRS James H (Gorman—Margaret Melville)
☎ (516) 689-7668 . . "Culross" Drawer 1574, Stony Brook, NY *11790-0875*

Blackwell MR & MRS James M 4th (Anne H Stires) SL'92.Hn.H'52	☎ (203) 438-8124
	20 Old S Salem Rd,
MISS Hillary Van C	Ridgefield, CT
MISS Carolyn T—Wheat'92	*06877*

Blackwell MR Nigel S—Ox'69
☎ (011-44-1367) 870-659 . . "Low Dow" Lake House, Pusey, nr Faringdon, Oxfordshire SN7 8QB, England
Blackwell MR & MRS Stephen H (Aleka Akoyunoglou) Nw'89.CtCol'87
☎ (423) 531-2882 . . 8422 Carl Valentine Circle, Knoxville, TN *37931*
Blackwood MR & MRS Terence R (Oot—Elizabeth V Dawson) V'50
☎ (410) 758-0433 . . "Fairview Farm" 220 Fairview Farm Lane, Centreville, MD *21617*

Blacque MR & MRS Richard E (Cushman—Elizabeth J Kamp) GeoW'68.Me.Rc.Rd.H'59.Cl'63
☎ (610) 527-6489 . . 800 Old Gulph Rd, Bryn Mawr, PA *19010*
Blacutt MR & MRS Sergio X (Gail L Sawyer) Ariz'87.SEMoSt'85
Camino del Pregonero 2799, Lo Barnechea, Santiago, Chile
Blagden MR Crawford—T.Rcn.Yh . . .of
☎ (803) 744-6880 . . Yeamans Hall Club, Box 9455, Charleston, SC *29410*
☎ (508) 540-3614 . . Box 667, Chapoquoit Island, West Falmouth, MA *02574*
Blagden MR & MRS George (Josephine C S Swan) V'53.Myc.Ncd.Myf.H'53 ⚓
☎ (508) 526-4846 . . 130 School St, Manchester, MA *01944*
Blagden MR & MRS Joseph W JR (Katherine J Remke) Col'77.NewC'75
☎ (505) 988-2224 . . 625 Camino Rancheros, Santa Fe, NM *87501*
Blagden MISS Julia W—V'82.AGSIM'86.Cda.
☎ (415) 282-7448 . . 1080 Church St, San Francisco, CA *94114-3413*
Blagden MR & MRS Timothy S (Beverly A Brine) Tufts'80.Syr'82.Myc.Ne'84
☎ (508) 526-7889 . . 18 Forest Lane, Manchester, MA *01944*
Blain MRS Deirdre G (Murray—Deirdre D Greenwell) WashColl'69.Ac.Rd.Dar.
☎ (610) 688-4159 . . 777 Harrison Rd, Villanova, PA *19085*
Blaine MRS Gloria B (Gloria Beckwith) G.
☎ (716) 883-3881 . . 751 W Ferry St, Buffalo, NY *14222*
Blaine DR & MRS Graham B JR (Lovell—Sandra A H Green) BMr'56.H'40
☎ (617) 547-4554 . . 7 Walnut Av, Cambridge, MA *02140*

Blaine MRS Richard G (Biddle—Shields—Katharine Mortimer)	☎ (212) 628-7283
	150 E 73 St,
MR Walker	New York, NY
MISS Katharine Shields	*10021*
MR William X Shields	

Blaine MR & MRS William M (Charlee Breneman) V'36.Qc.
☎ (513) 321-2899 . . 2345 Bedford Av, Cincinnati, OH *45208*
Blair MR & MRS Bowen (Joan H Smith) BtP.On.Cho.Cas.Sr.Y'40 . . of
☎ (847) 234-0715 . . 3 S Green Bay Rd, Lake Forest, IL *60045*
☎ (561) 835-3619 . . 417 Peruvian Av, 1, Palm Beach, FL *33480*
Blair MR & MRS Duncan W (Susan F Schneider) Skd'76.HampSydney'74
☎ (703) 548-3572 . . 222 Green St, Alexandria, VA *22314*
Blair MR & MRS Edward McC (Elizabeth G Iglehart) Cho.Sr.Cas.Y'38.H'40
☎ (847) 234-4077 . . Box 186, Sheridan Rd, Lake Bluff, IL *60044*

Blair MR & MRS Edward McC JR (Frances de Bretteville) Stan'69.Rc.Sc.R.Cho.Cas.Cly.Stan'65. H'71	☎ (312) 664-6314
	636 W Willow St,
	Chicago, IL *60614*
MISS Helen B—ColC'93	
MISS Jane—at Stanford	
MR Edward McC 3d—at Carleton Coll	

Blair MR & MRS Edwin James (Jean F du Pont) Y'59	☎ (504) 529-4200
MISS Alice Kane	2322 Camp St,
MR Edwin Foster 2d	New Orleans, LA
MR James Maxwell du Pont	*70130*

Blair MR & MRS Francis I (Margaret L Hooper) Stan'68.Rc.Y'66.H'73
☎ (312) 642-3861 . . 1236 N State P'kway, Chicago, IL *60610*
Blair MR & MRS George A (JoAnne White)
1065 Park Av, New York, NY *10128*

Blair MR & MRS George McK (McCullough—
Elizabeth V Foster) Rr.DelB.Cal'47 . . . .
   MR George F McCullough—Rr.Rol'82—at
   ☎ (307) 734-0137 . . Box 453, 4 Lazy F
Ranch, Jackson Hole, WY *83001* . . . .
   ☎ (412) 741-8005 Blackburn Rd, Sewickley Heights, PA *15143*

Blair MRS John B (Todes—Betty Watkins)
   ☎ (305) 294-9204 . . 516 Bahama St, Key West, FL *33040*

Blair MR & MRS Lawrence D (Sarah M Robinson) V'52.P'47
   ☎ (415) 567-5788 . . 2460 Broadway St, San Francisco, CA *94115*

Blair MRS Marie Bryan (Marie L B Bryan)
   ☎ (314) 361-4027 . . 4611 Maryland Av, St Louis, MO *63108-1912*

Blair MR & MRS Michael W (Edith B Moore) Y'77.Cly.Ncd.Y.'77 . . of
   ☎ (212) 427-7923 . . 1133 Park Av, New York, NY *10128*
   ☎ (203) 259-6343 . . 60 Brett Rd, Fairfield, CT *06430*

Blair MRS Oliver (Lewis—Barbara McDonnell) Fcg.Pg.Rr.
   ☎ (412) 622-9000 . . Canterbury Place, 310 Fisk St, Pittsburgh, PA *15201*

Blair MR & MRS Watson B (Jane L Golberg) Mls'81.Y'77.Cal'82
   ☎ (206) 329-7654 . . 1608 Federal Av E, Seattle, WA *98102*

Blair MR & MRS Watson K (Wallace—Ford—Valerie M Hollmann) Rcn.K.Cysl.Y'49
   ☎ (561) 546-1241 . . PO Box 218, Hobe Sound, FL *33475*

Blair MR & MRS William D JR (Jane F Coleman) Cvc.Mt.P'48.AmU'74 . . of
   ☎ (202) 362-5966 . . 5006 Warren St NW, Washington, DC *20016*
   ☎ (207) 863-2014 . . "Quarry Point" Box 822, Vinalhaven, ME *04863*

Blair MR & MRS William McC JR (Jelke—Catherine Gerlach) Ri.Stan'40.Va'47
   ☎ (202) 333-0433 . . 2510 Foxhall Rd NW, Washington, DC *20007*

Blair MR William W 3d—Y'54
   ☎ (412) 683-1604 . . 245 Melwood Av, Pittsburgh, PA *15213*

Blair MR Wolcott R—Cy.Ne'79 . . . .
   MISS Aloyse M . . . .
   ☎ (314) 991-8755 9119 Clayton Rd, St Louis, MO *63124*

Blaisdell MR & MRS Bruce F (Ann E Morris) Briar'70.Stc.Rm.Pa'70
   MISS Elizabeth—at Hollins . . . .
   MISS Taylor—at Elon . . . .
   MISS Courtney—at U of Colo . . . .
   of ☎ (908)747-6653 160 Blackpoint Rd, Rumson, NJ *07760* ☎ (242) 333-2717 "Half and Half" Harbour Island, Bahamas

Blaisdell MISS Susan C (Wharton—Coe—Susan C Blaisdell) Rm.Stc.Ncd.
   ☎ (908) 741-5365 . . 15 Rivers Edge Dv, Little Silver, NJ *07739*

Blake SIR Alfred L & LADY (Dick—Alison T Kelsey) SL'49.Lond'38
   ☎ (802) 867-2245 . . "Deerland" Foote Rd, PO Box 547, Dorset, VT *05251-0547*

Blake MR & MRS Benjamin S (Wood—Sarah B Ross) Ty'39
   ☎ (617) 383-1309 . . 143 Atlantic Av, Cohasset, MA *02025*

Blake MR & MRS Bradford E JR (Elizabeth C Buckley) Md'51 . . . .
   MISS Elizabeth C—at ☎ (914) 271-8332
97 Grand St, Croton, NY *10520* . . . .
   MR Bradford E 3d . . . .
   MR James E—at ☎ (410) 377-6466
1208 Fairfield Av, Baltimore, MD *21209* . . . . . .
   ☎ (410) 323-3984 16 Elmwood Rd, Baltimore, MD *21210*

Blake MR & MRS Brian P T (Gretchen Groat) Unn.Snc.Ofp.Cw.Ne.H'62 . . . .
   JUNIORS MR Brian A—at St Mark's . . . .
   ☎ (203) 881-1288 43 Peach Farm Rd, Oxford, CT *06478*

Blake MRS Brooke (McLean—Elizabeth M Brooke) Srb.
   ☎ (214) 521-0732 . . 3601 Turtle Creek, Apt 806, Dallas, TX *75219*

Blake MRS E Valentine (Ethel P Valentine)
   ☎ (212) 734-0720 . . 340 E 80 St, New York, NY *10021-0928*

Blake MRS Edith G (Edith S Graham) Eyc.
   ☎ (508) 627-8729 . . "Green Feathers" Edgartown, MA *02539*

Blake MISS Elinor L . . see H W English

Blake MRS Francis (Caroline A Hunnewell) Rdc'38.Cy.Sm.
   ☎ (508) 785-0013 . . Strawberry Hill St, Dover, MA *02030*

Blake MR & MRS Francis JR (Sandra A Davis) Pa'64.Hn.H'61 . . . .
   MR Peter S—USMC.H'93 . . . .
   MR Alexander W—H'96 . . . .
   MR Amory B—at Harvard . . . .
   ☎ (406) 932-4195 Keewaydin Ranch, Otter Creek Rd, HC 87, Box 2240, Big Timber, MT *59011*

Blake MR & MRS Francis S (Anne McChristian) Cl'76.Cl'80.H'71.Cl'76 . . . .
   JUNIORS MISS Margaret D . . . .
   JUNIORS MR Francis S JR . . . .
   ☎ (518) 433-1695 402 Loudonville Rd, Loudonville, NY *12211*

Blake MRS George Baty (Rosemary Shaw) Cy.
   ☎ (617) 277-0250 . . 61 Heath St, Brookline, MA *02146*

Blake MR & MRS Igor Robert (Elizabeth Denton) Cal'46.Cp.Ncd.Bow'51.Stan'53 . . . .
   MISS Laura . . . .
   ☎ (510) 254-4790 4165 Canyon Rd, Lafayette, CA *94549*

Blake MR & MRS James R (Cornelia A Cummins) K.
   MR Andrew C C—at Vanderbilt . . . .
   of ☎ (817)738-9450 19 Westover Rd, Ft Worth, TX *76107* ☎ (970) 879-0419 30550 Elk Lane, Box 881989, Steamboat Springs, CO *80488*

Blake MR & MRS John W (Jennifer J Jack) Aht'82.Sm.LakeF'75
   ☎ (508) 785-1265 . . 19 Strawberry Hill St, Dover, MA *02030*

Blake MR & MRS Richard R (Mary C Anderson) Wheat'52.Cw.Dar.Ncd.Y.'45w . . . .
   MR Nicholas C—Vt'79 . . . .
   MR Samuel W—Tufts'85—at Portsmouth, NH . .
   ☎ (215) CH7-8261 18 Summit St, Philadelphia, PA *19118*

Blake MR & MRS Robert M (Delia D Carrington) . . of
   ☎ (561) 546-3826 . . 258 S Beach Rd, Hobe Sound, FL *33455*
   ☎ (802) 867-4037 . . PO Box 735, Dorset, VT *05251*

Blake MR & MRS Robert O (Sylvia Whitehouse) Bnd'51.Ri.Mt.Cvc.Srb.Stan'43
   ☎ (202) 333-1290 . . 2211 King Place NW, Washington, DC *20007*

Blake MR & MRS Robert W (Martha L Dawson) Cal'79.Geo'81.Cp.Dar.Cal'79.SUNY'81
   ☎ (713) 578-0373 . . 1662 Kelliwood Oaks Dv, Katy, TX *77450*

Blakeley MRS G Bogart (Leonard—Stuber—Hope Sands) Rby.Srb. . . . .
   MR Bogart—at ☎ (207) 827-2970 . . Box 383, Bradley, ME *04411* . . . .
   ☎ (401) 847-8247 385 Green End Av, Middletown, RI *02842*

Blakeslee MR Peter R
2420 Alvord Lane, Redondo Beach, CA *90278*

Blanc MRS Jose M (Elizabeth Hunt) Hlns'83
   ☎ (011-44-171) 221-3777 . . 45 Matlock Court, Kensington Park Rd, London W11 3BS, England

Blanc MR Jose M—Hn.Madrid'78.Madrid'79.H'85
☎ (011-44-171) 371-1937 . . 72 Elsham Rd, Apt 1, London W14, England

Blanchard MR & MRS Alan F (Ann S Elliott) | of ☎ (212)860-3276
V'64.Rc.Ln.Un.Chr.Plg.Y.'61.Mit'66 . . . . | 1088 Park Av,
MISS Deborah G . . . . | New York, NY
MR A Elliott—at Yale . . . . | 10128
    ☎ (860) 535-2164
    21 Wall St,
    Stonington, CT
    06378

Blanchard MR & MRS Frederick C JR (Lesley H Finnell)
PineM'75.Bost'70.FairD'74
☎ (508) 785-2489 . . 1 Southfield Dv, Dover, MA 02030

Blanchard MR & MRS Gilduin M (Jennifer R Sulger) Pace'82
☎ (011-33) 94-08-19-14 . . Clos San Peyre, 229 rue Colonel Coudert, 83220 Pradet, France

Blanchard MR & MRS Hartman E (Eleanor L | ☎ (212) 249-0614
Lukens) H'63 . . . . | 112 E 74 St,
MR Clay W—at ☎ (212) 426-1474 | New York, NY
400 E 89 St, Apt 3N, New York, NY 10128 . . . | 10021
MR Wells M—at ☎ (603) 528-6640
2413 Messer St, Laconia, NH 03246 . . . .

Blanchard MR & MRS James A 2d (June Peterson)
Myf.Cw.Ofp.Rv.Pa'33 . . of
Ocean View Tower 4C, 7601 N Ocean Blvd, Myrtle Beach, SC 29572
☎ (207) 288-3262 . . ''Reverie Cove'' 7 Harbor Lane, Bar Harbor, ME 04609-1107

Blanchard MR James A 3d—Cw.Myf.LakeF'69.W&L'72
Box 1471, Charlottesville, VA 22902

Blanchard MRS John A (Ellis—Elizabeth D Watson)
☎ (617) 444-7555 . . 166 South St, Needham, MA 02192

Blanchard MRS Mercer C (Elizabeth D Pagon)
☎ (706) 323-4652 . . 908 Blandford Av, Columbus, GA 31906

Blanchard MR Peter Parrott JR—Rcn.Evg.BtP. | ☎ (201) 376-4696
P'35.Y'39 . . . . | 274 Old Short Hills
MR Peter Parrott 3d . . . . | Rd, Short Hills, NJ
    07078

Blanchard MR Robert M—BtP.Wms'48
☎ (212) 737-5312 . . 223 E 66 St, Apt 4C, New York, NY 10021-6486

Blanchard MR & MRS W Scott (Wanda M White) | ☎ (516) 569-0122
H'59 . . . . | 562 Atlantic Av,
MISS Tracy E—Cal'91 . . . . | Lawrence, NY
MR W Scott JR—Susq'94—at | 11559
1941 Freemont Av S, Apt 4, Minneapolis, MN
55403 . . . .

Bland MR & MRS D Gerald JR (Immacolata B | ☎ (212) 722-8329
Corsini) Wheat'76.NCar'73 . . . . | 12 E 88 St,
JUNIORS MISS Georgiana G . . . . | New York, NY
    10128

Bland MRS Edward M (Augusta W Howell)
☎ (215) PE5-6890 . . 1621 Spruce St, Philadelphia, PA 19103

Bland MISS Emily Bingham (g—Rufus S Frost 3d) . . . . Born Mch 15'96

Bland MISS Mary Brereton (g—Rufus S Frost 3d) . . . . . Born Mch 15'96

Bland MR & MRS Michael G (Laura S Miller) Hlns'87.Pc.Va'87
☎ (804) 784-5804 . . 302 Hill Point Rd, Richmond, VA 23233

Bland MASTER Nicholas Frost (g—Rufus S Frost 3d) . . . . Born Jan 17'95

Blanke MRS Albert G (Humphreys—Ruth Palmer) Cy.Nd.Ncd.
☎ (314) 997-2527 . . 20 Log Cabin Dv, St Louis, MO 63124

Blankin MR & MRS Grant L (Rosa T Hutson) MaryB'49.Pc.Va'45
☎ (215) 247-1012 . . 3 Tohopeka Court, Philadelphia, PA 19118

Blau MISS Amanda Sylvia Carafiol (Richard N) . . . . Born Nov 24'94

Blau MR & MRS Andrew McD (Leslie F Hodges)
Denis'85.Rc.Pr.M.Cly.Denis'85
☎ (212) 644-9501 . . 417 Park Av, Apt 10E, New York, NY 10022

Blau MR & MRS Richard N (Jane D Bradley) HRdc'81.My.H.Wash'75
☎ (508) 468-1870 . . 10 Miles River Rd, Hamilton, MA 01982

Blaxter MR & MRS G Harold (Barbara R Appleton) | ☎ (603) 772-1205
H'44.Pitt'49 . . . . | Franconia Village
MISS Jennifer D—at ☎ (408) 267-4755 | 216, 7 River Woods
934 Franquette Av, San Jose, CA 95125 . . . . . . | Dv, Exeter, NH
MR George H JR—at ☎ (508) 475-3756 | 03833
128 Andover St, Andover, MA 01810 . . . .

Blaxter MRS Henry Vaughan JR (E Sherley Tunnell) Fcg.Pg.
Fox Chapel Mews II, Apt 604, 302 Fox Chapel Rd, Pittsburgh, PA 15238

Bleakie MRS John M (Eleanor Gleason) Sth'41.Sm. . | of ☎ (617)367-6512
MR Michael S—Bost'83 . . . . | 28 Temple St,
    Boston, MA 02114
    ☎ (617) 545-1637
    Lion's Head Farm,
    Box 262, Cohasset,
    MA 02025

Bleakley MR & MRS William Jay JR (Gring—Gwendolyn Smith) Ey.Bab'48
☎ (617) 631-3707 . . 39 Wharf Path, Marblehead, MA 01945

Blenk MR & MRS Peter C (Natalie W Wilmer) | ☎ (011-44-171)
Wheat'70.Ham'68 . . . . | 731-7484
MISS Elisabeth F . . . . | 65 Perrymead St,
    London SW6 3SN,
    England

Blevins MRS (DR) Pengwynne Potter (Pengwynne E C Potter) BMr'64
☎ (847) 864-2466 . . 1320 Mulford St, Evanston, IL 60202

Blewer MRS Sondra G (Sondra Gerdau) | of ☎ (212)876-2446
Sth'53.Cly.Ne. . . . . | 1185 Park Av,
MISS Evelyn M—Y'79—at 133 rue Raymond | New York, NY
Losserand, 75014 Paris, France . . . . | 10128-1308
    ☎ (603) 823-7798
    Box 541,
    Sugar Hill, NH
    03585

Blind MR & MRS William C (Peggy A Kauffman)
Ny.Cly.Ncd.NotreD'32.H'35 . . of
☎ (201) 568-7991 . . 224 Cedar St, Englewood, NJ 07631
☎ (803) 524-1000 . . 5C Marsh Harbor, Beaufort, SC 29902
☎ (717) 390-1002 . . 1865 Villa Court, Lancaster, PA 17603

Blind MR & MRS William C JR (Rebecca D McCoy) | ☎ (212) 289-7104
Ny.Chr.Rby.Cly. . . . . | 1150 Fifth Av,
MISS Rebecca C—Del'92 . . . . | New York, NY
JUNIORS MR Burroughs C L W—at Pomfret . . . . | 10128

Bliss MR Cornelius N . . . . Died at
    Kennett Square, PA May 8'96

Bliss MR & MRS Donald A (Roxanne Waldhauser) Minn'63
☎ (602) 451-1234 . . 10892 E Fanfol Lane, Scottsdale, AZ 85259

Bliss MR & MRS Edward P (Anne D Osborn) Cy.Chi.Ncd.H'55
☎ (508) 651-0100 . . 38 Bullard St, Box 729, Sherborn, MA *01770*
Bliss MISS Mary P—Swb'85.Ey.
see Dilatory Domiciles
Bliss MR & MRS Richard M (West—Alicia Guerrero-Vallejo) Ri.Cs.Y'51
☎ (212) 535-7052 . . 10 Henderson Place, New York, NY *10028*

Bliss DR & MRS Thomas F JR (Josselyn Hallowell)
Bost'66.Br'75.Br'65.Geo'69 . . . . | ☎ (508) 252-6438
MISS Mary J . . . . | 84 Summer St,
MISS Anna H . . . . | Rehoboth, MA
MR Thomas F 3d . . . . | *02769*
JUNIORS MR James M . . . . |
JUNIORS MR Ned H . . . . |

Bliss MR & MRS William L (Lee Nichols) D.H'52 . . . | ☎ (617) 326-1062
MISS Jane H . . . . | 586 Bridge St,
MR William L JR . . . . | Dedham, MA *02026*

Bliss MR William W—Bhm.Pcu.Sfg.Cal'47 . . . . | ☎ (702) 749-5207
MR William T . . . . | Box 5, Glenbrook,
                                                          | NV *89413*

Blitzer DR & MRS Seth M (Letitia C Biddle) Vt'83.Vt'83.Pa'88
☎ (610) 667-0947 . . 380 N Highland Av, Merion, PA *19066*
Block MISS Elizabeth W—Ty'80
☎ (202) 785-7729 . . 4114 Davis Place NW, Apt 213, Washington,
DC *20007*
Block MR & MRS Huntington M (Eleanora Carroll Morgan)
LondArts'81.H'76
☎ (310) 573-4343 . . PO Box 674, Pacific Palisades, CA *90272-0674*

Block MR & MRS Huntington T (Amie Willard) | ☎ (202) 338-1308
Mt.Cvc.Sl.P'48 . . . . | 1312—30 St NW,
MR William B W—V'80—at 131 Entrada Dv, | Washington, DC
Apt 13, Santa Monica, CA *90402* . . . . | *20007*

Block MR Jonathan C—Syr'84
☎ (212) 941-1484 . . 175 Franklin St, New York, NY *10013*
Block MR & MRS Roger W (Miriam Fulton) Mt.Sl.StJ.Geo'60
☎ (202) 363-3348 . . 3308 Maud St NW, Washington, DC *20016*
Block MRS Theodore L (Faith F Jones) Sth'42.Ncd.
4000 Cathedral Av NW, Apt 335B, Washington, DC *20016-5249*
Blodget MR & MRS Alden S JR (Louise R French)
☎ (609) 921-8356 . . 10 Lambert Dv, Princeton, NJ *08540*
Blodget MISS Alexandra K—Colby'94 . . see T P Briney
Blodgett MASTER Cosimo Watson (Mark W) . . . . Born at
Florence, Italy Feb 21'96
Blodgett MRS Delos A 2d (Ryan—Foley—Carlisle Sullivan) Cly.Sl.
☎ (202) 966-6783 . . 4501 Connecticut Av NW, Apt 917, Washington,
DC *20008*

Blodgett MRS Emmons W (Helen C Boswell) . . . . . | ☎ (203) 348-1090
MISS Victoria F—at ☎ (603) 284-6823 | 253 Dolphin Cove
North Sandwich, NH *03259* . . . . | Quay, Stamford, CT
                                                      | *06902*

Blodgett MRS Henry W (Hearst—Ola M Hatfield)
☎ (314) 227-4434 . . 14443 Bantry Lane, Chesterfield, MO *63017*
Blodgett MR John W (Ferris—Edith Irwin) Ri.
☎ (616) 940-0719 . . 2740 Littlefield Dv NE, Grand Rapids, MI *49506*
Blodgett MR & MRS Mark W (Helen M Watson) Pitzer'78.StAndr'79 . . of
37 Chestnut St, Salem, MA *01970*
☎ (914) 868-7626 . . ''Rocky Reef Farm'' Box 224, Rte 82,
Stanfordville, NY *12581*

Blodgett MR & MRS Thomas N (Anne W Blagden) | ☎ (212) 737-8268
Ri.H'61.Camb'63.H'65 . . . . | 829 Park Av, Apt
JUNIORS MR Thomas N—☎ (212) 737-3425 . . . . | 5D, New York, NY
                                              | *10021-2846*

Bloemers MISS Gardner Louise—Tufts'90.Erasmus'94
Apollinansstrasse 21, 40227 Düsseldorf, Germany
Blok MR & MRS Christiaan J (Heather L MacLean) BrooksInst'90
☎ (602) 874-9057 . . 4525 N 66 St, Apt 93, Scottsdale, AZ *85251*
Blomquist MR & MRS Edwin Renken (Carol Joan Powers) On.Cnt.Pn.Nw'42
☎ (847) 234-0766 . . 535 N Mayflower Rd, Lake Forest, IL *60045*
Blood MRS Alice F (Alice S Fisher)
☎ (406) 844-3779 . . Box 141, Lakeside, MT *59922*
Bloom MR Gregory—Cr'92 . . see W S Sheppard
Bloom MR J Derek—Cr'94 . . see W S Sheppard
Bloom MR & MRS Lawrence H (H Ann Young) Swb'59.Me.Ac.Denis'62
☎ (610) MI2-2924 . . 283 Hathaway Lane, Wynnewood, PA *19096*
Bloss MISS Caroline A—Ithaca'75 . . see A W Smith JR
Blossom JUNIORS MISS Anne R . . see P D Raymond
Blossom MR George W 3d—On.Sr.Cho.Rc.Cas.Ln . . .of
☎ (847) 234-0375 . . 242 N Ahwahnee Lane, Lake Forest,
IL *60045-2003*
☎ (312) 664-2939 . . 1340 N Astor St, Apt 2408, Chicago,
IL *60610-2171*
Blossom MR Jonathan . . see J M Large JR
Blossom MISS Virginia . . see J M Large JR
Blount MRS Allen T (Elaine S Tweeddale)
☎ (410) 795-7175 . . Fairhaven, Uplands Hall 205, 7200 Third Av,
Sykesville, MD *21784*
Blount MISS Madeleine D—BMr'51
☎ (212) 831-7975 . . 1111 Park Av, New York, NY *10128*

Blount MRS Mary Katherine (Mary Katherine | ☎ (334) 265-1893
Archibald) Jud'42.Ri . . . . | 2060 Myrtlewood
MR Thomas A—at Atlanta, GA . . . . | Dv, Montgomery,
MR Joseph W—at Atlanta, GA . . . . | AL *36111*

Blount MR & MRS Winton M JR (Varner—Carolyn H Self)
Aub'47.Htdon'68.Cvc.Pl.Ri.
☎ (334) 272-7920 . . 5801 Vaughn Rd, Montgomery, AL *36116*
Blount MR & MRS Winton M 3d (Lucy D Dunn) Ala'70.So'66.Pa'68
☎ (334) 265-5600 . . 1919 S Hull St, Montgomery, AL *36104*
Blount MR & MRS Winton M 4th (Diana Dockery) Ala'90.B'hamS'87
see Dilatory Domiciles
Blow MR & MRS George (Sarah W Kuhn) Mt.Cvc.Cc.Cw.Sl.H'50.Va'53
☎ (202) 332-1832 . . 2424 Kalorama Rd NW, Washington, DC *20008*
Blow MR John M—Hob'62
☎ (954) 491-1491 . . 3200 Port Royale Dv N, Apt 1506, Ft Lauderdale,
FL *33308-7806*
Blow MISS Katharine C (Michael) . . . . Married at Easton, CT
McGloon MR Kevin J (J Howard) . . . . May 4'96
Blow MR & MRS Michael (Norfleet—Ayres—Diane C Jones)
Cly.Cc.Cw.Cda.Ht.Yn.Y'52
☎ (203) 869-2244 . . 546 North St, Greenwich, CT *06830*
Blua MR & MRS Piero L (Wilmer—Elisabeth F Green) Cly.GregU'55
☎ (203) 869-3571 . . 55 Perkins Rd, Greenwich, CT *06830*

Blue MRS E Stuart (Jackson—Economakis—E Stuart Blue) Cvc.Dc.Ncd. . . . . | ☎ (202) 298-5942
 MISS Elizabeth L Jackson—RISD'90 . . . . | 2801 New Mexico
 MR Richard L Jackson JR—ColC'90 . . . . | Av NW,
| Washington, DC
| *20007*

Blue MR & MRS William F (Katherine G Broaddus) | ☎ (410) 363-0970
Gv.Elk.Mv.Va'56.Va'60. . . . . | "The Briars"
 MISS Katherine M—Va'89 . . . . | 311 Golf Course Rd,
 MR Robert G—Va'85.Va'89 . . . . | Garrison, MD *21117*

Blum MR & MRS Andrew M (Stebbins—Felicia S Herzog) B.Ri.Lic.Nyc.
 ☎ (212) 832-7484 . . 439 E 51 St, New York, NY *10022*

Blum MR & MRS John R H (Thompson—Jeanne E Cotten) K.Ny.Csn.Cly.Y'51
 ☎ (860) 435-0317 . . "Fairfield Farms" 406 Sharon Rd, Lakeville, CT *06039*

Blum MR & MRS Richard K (Ruth Maginnis) Loy'81.Tul'78
 ☎ (504) 866-4737 . . 285 Audubon Blvd, New Orleans, LA *70125*

Blum MR Robert E—C.Plg.Yn.Y'21
 ☎ (860) 435-2043 . . 87 Canaan Rd, Apt 4A, Salisbury, CT *06068*

Blumeyer MR & MRS Christopher J (Elizabeth H | ☎ (314) 434-7790
Gilbert). . . . . | 49 Brook Mill Lane,
 MISS Elizabeth-Anne L . . . . | Chesterfield, MO
 MR Christopher J JR . . . . | *63017*
 MR C Hunt . . . . |
 MR Peter M 2d . . . . |

Blundon MR & MRS Carroll M (Felicity H Sargent) Pa'75.Ny.Csn.Ariz'72
 ☎ (540) 672-0585 . . "Sunnybrook Farm" Box 54, Somerset, VA *22972*

Blundon MR & MRS Montague JR (Lucy M Marbury) NCar'44.Cvc.Ncd.P'42
 ☎ (703) 893-6327 . . 8024 Georgetown Pike, McLean, VA *22102*

Blundon DR & MRS Montague 3d (Dillon—Juanita Doody) Cvc.Cc.P'71
 ☎ (301) 652-5980 . . 9 Primrose St, Chevy Chase, MD *20815*

Blunt MR Alexander R . . see J W Larson

Blunt MR Christopher C . . see J W Larson

Blunt MRS Sara Conrad (Sara T Conrad) . . . . | ☎ (202) 333-3320
 MISS Dorsey C—at New Canaan, CT *06840* . . . . | 3051 N St NW,
 MR William Winthrop—at Georgetown . . . . | Washington, DC
| *20007*

Blunt MR & MRS William W JR (Warriner—A Blair | ☎ (214) 717-5796
Whitehead) Sth'62.Mt.Y'58.H'61 . . . . | 4501 N O'Connor
 MISS Blair Warriner—Stan'94 . . . . | Rd, Apt 2105,
| Irving, TX *75062*

Blynn MISS Alexandra P . . see G D Mackenzie

Blynn MR & MRS Bryce JR (Maffei—Gulliver—Mary Frances Maresca)
 ☎ (561) 234-5603 . . 2045 Las Ramblas, Vero Beach, FL *32963*

Blynn MISS Frances A . . see G D Mackenzie

Blynn MR & MRS Henry R (Van Alen—Sydney Purviance) Cts.Gm.P'49
 ☎ (610) 964-1069 . . 304 Orchard Way, St Davids, PA *19087*

Blynn MR & MRS L Clarke (Barbara deP Converse) | ☎ (610) 687-5048
Col'78.Cr'79 . . . . | 428 School House
 JUNIORS MISS Kelly M . . . . | Lane, Devon, PA
 JUNIORS MR Jason C . . . . | *19333*

Blyth MRS Annis L (Annis L Pechin) . . . . | ☎ (847) 698-6383
 MISS Victoria . . . . | 1856 Prairie Av,
| Park Ridge, IL
| *60068*

Blyth MR Henry A—Fla'59
 ☎ (847) 692-9838 . . 53 Park Lane, Park Ridge, IL *60068*

Boak MRS J Clark (Julia I Clark) Rdc'68.H. . . . . . . | ☎ (212) 580-9086
 MISS Alexandra H—Nu'93 . . . . | 574 West End Av,
| Apt 104, New York,
| NY *10024*

Boal MISS Ann A—DU'69
 ☎ (602) 246-2827 . . 811 W Ocotillo Rd, Phoenix, AZ *85013*

Boal MR & MRS Stewart (Susan R Ballard) V'37.H'29
 ☎ (616) 547-2077 . . "Stewart's Folie" 09300 Boyne City Rd, Box 234, Charlevoix, MI *49720*

Boalt MR J Anthony—B.Evg.BtP.Mds.Y'50
 ☎ (561) 655-8262 . . 234 El Brillo Way, Palm Beach, FL *33480*

Board MR & MRS James G (Tracy A Pagenstecher) | ☎ (713) 558-5272
GreenMt'75.Rens'75 . . . . | 14751 Kellywood
 MISS Jennifer A . . . . | Lane, Houston, TX
 JUNIORS MR James G JR . . . . | *77079*

Board MR & MRS James M (Jane E Glazier) . . . . . . | ☎ (614) 891-2119
 MISS Susan P . . . . | 4835 Smoketalk
| Lane, Westerville,
| OH *43081*

Boardman MISS Clarinda S—Cly.Dc.Ncd.Lm.Dh.
 ☎ (516) 423-2298 . . "Gulls Rest" 12 Wincoma Dv, Huntington Bay, NY *11743*

Boardman MR & MRS D Dixon (Pauline M Baker) | of ☎ (212)288-6309
Rc.B.Pr.Ck.BtP.Plg.Evg. . . . . | 19 E 72 St,
 MISS Serena . . . . | New York, NY
 MISS Samantha . . . . | *10021*
| ☎ (561) 659-7899
| 5 S Lake Trail,
| Palm Beach, FL
| *33480*

Boardman MRS Francis (Anne D Hooker) V'45.Sl.Ncd.
 ☎ (202) 338-5941 . . 4647 Kenmore Dv NW, Washington, DC *20007-1914*

Boardman MR & MRS John S (Ngoc Chât Nguyen) | Colombo,
Y'64 . . . . | Sri Lanka, Dept of
 JUNIORS MR Daniel S . . . . | State, Washington,
| DC *20521-6100*

Boardman MR Ronald P JR—Btc.Y'52
 ☎ (847) 615-0434 . . 1510 N Green Bay Rd, Box 204, Lake Forest, IL *60045*

Boardman MR Theodore R—On.Btc.DU'54 . . . . . . | Box 632,
 MISS Carolyn F—Box 1799, Avon, CO *81620* . . | Lake Forest, IL
 MR T Christopher—Box 1799, Avon, CO *81620* | *60045*
 MR Robert B—Box 1799, Avon, CO *81620* . . . . |

Boardman MRS William H (Jane Carrott) Cy.Sm.
 ☎ (617) 734-9450 . . 190 Warren St, Brookline, MA *02146*

Boardman MR & MRS William H JR (Alice Korff) | ☎ (617) 566-6775
GeoW'65.Au.Hn.NCar'65 . . . . | 521 Hammond St,
 MR William H 3d—at 1 Primus Av, Apt 3, | Chestnut Hill, MA
Boston, MA *02114* . . . . | *02167*

Boardman MRS William J 3d (Nancy C Jett)
 ☎ (330) 836-2124 . . 275 N Portage Path, Apt 7A, Akron, OH *44303*

Bockman DR & MRS Richard S (Darcy B Kelley) | of ☎ (212)249-9646
Bnd'70.Rock'75.Dyc.Ny.Cly.JHop'62.Y'67. | 180 E 79 St,
Rock'71 . . . . | New York, NY
MISS Danielle R—at Kenyon . . . . | 10021
MR Alexander C—at Yale . . . . | ☎ (516) 725-3578
| 22 Spring St, Box
| 568, Sag Harbor,
| NY 11963

Bockmann MISS Jill O—Bow'89 . . see R G Smith
Bockmann MR Nathaniel V . . see R G Smith
Bodan MISS Susan R . . see MISS H R Yerkes
Bodeen MR & MRS George H (Nancy J Lindberg)
Nw'52.Cho.Cm.Wa.Nw'48.Nw'70
☎ (847) 441-1008 . . 1180 Whitebridge Hill, Winnetka, IL 60093-1548
Bodel MRS John K (Mary B Gibney) V'43.Pa'48.Ncd.
☎ (860) 435-2420 . . 31 Robin Hill Lane, Lakeville, CT 06039
Bodel MISS Mary-Garrett—V'80.Les'81.DU'92
☎ (703) 998-5473 . . 3730 Ingalls Av, Alexandria, VA 22302
Bodell MR & MRS Joseph J JR (Bayne—Jane R Leigh)
Cent'y'48.Hb.H'41.H'48 . . of
☎ (401) 751-7069 . . 72 Manning St, Apt 1, Providence, RI 02906
☎ (561) 234-5793 . . 2205 N Southwinds Blvd, Vero Beach, FL 32963
Boden MR & MRS Constantin R (Katharine Colt) | ☎ (617) 734-1725
Sm.Cy.Chi.Dth'57.H'61 | 26 Codman Rd,
MR Hans U—NH'84—at Max Planck Institute, | Brookline, MA
Bonn, Germany . . . . | 02146
Boden MISS Kip Kelso du P (late Harry Clark 4th) . . . . Married at
Budapest, Hungary
Crist MR Leland D (Frederick B) . . . . Mch 16'96
Boden DR & MRS (DR) Rodney (Elizabeth P Carey)
Nw'74.Pa'83.Rm.Stc.Lond'65.Pa'83
☎ (908) 842-3942 . . 107 Oceanport Av, Little Silver, NJ 07739
Bodenstab DR & MRS Alex B (M Lynn Cornell)
Cent'y'73.Jef'75.U'73.Jef'77
391 Smithbridge Rd, Chadds Ford, PA 19317
Bodine MR & MRS James F (Jean G Guthrie) Sth'49.Cts.Cs.Y.'44
☎ (215) 627-8393 . . 401 Cypress St, Philadelphia, PA 19106
Bodine MR & MRS Lawrence D (Barbara C Carty) | of ☎ (215)646-6630
Vt'74.Vt'74 | 299 W Mt Pleasant
JUNIORS MISS Chase E . . . . | Av, Ambler, PA
| 19002
| ☎ (802) 362-3932
| Rte 7, Manchester,
| VT 05254
Bodine MR Murray G—Bab'78
☎ (415) 383-9705 . . 325 Molino Av, Mill Valley, CA 94941
Bodine MRS Samuel T (Pauline Parsons) Ac.Me. . . . | ☎ (610) 645-8654
MISS Penelope . . . . | 1400 Waverly Rd,
| Villa 5, Gladwyne,
| PA 19035
Bodine MRS William W JR (Louise R Dilworth) | ☎ (610) LA5-3127
Gm.Cs. | 1829 County Line
MISS Barbara B . . . . | Rd, Villanova, PA
| 19085
Bodine MR William W 3d—LakeF'72
☎ (207) 594-8151 . . 19 Traverse St, Rockland, ME 04841

Bodman MRS Calvert (Elizabeth B S Calvert) Cly.
☎ (212) 754-7256 . . 200 E 62 St, New York, NY 10021-8209
Bodman MR & MRS Herbert L JR (Ellen-Fairbanks D Diggs)
San.NCar'49.P'55
☎ (919) 942-2778 . . 510 Hawthorne Lane, Chapel Hill, NC 27514
Bodman MR & MRS Taylor S (April A Ward) Sm.P'83
☎ (617) 259-1823 . . 75 Todd Pond Rd, Lincoln, MA 01773-3836
Bodoia DR & MRS Rodger D (Jennifer S Rand) UWash'85
6928 Budd St NW, Olympia, WA 98502
Boeckman MR & MRS Duncan Eugene (Elizabeth A Mayer)
Sth'54.Tex'48.Tex'51
☎ (214) 357-6942 . . 5380 Nakoma Dv, Dallas, TX 75209
Boeger MR & MRS William A JR (Elise I van Siclen) | ☎ (561) 746-6665
Cda.Ty'32 . . . . | 14 Splitrail Circle,
MISS Elise I—at ☎ (212) 722-2634 | Tequesta, FL 33469
1060 Park Av, New York, NY 10028 . . . . |
Boenning MR Dickson G—Nrr.P'69 | ☎ (401) 423-2937
MISS Polly A—at 31A Hancock St, Somerville, | "Bungalow Point"
MA 02144 . . . . | 38 Marine Av,
| Jamestown, RI
| 02835
Boenning MR & MRS Evan F (Nancy A Joski) | ☎ (970) 925-1665
Wis'71.Vt'71 . . . . | PO Box 4825,
JUNIORS MISS Anne W . . . . | Aspen, CO 81611
Boenning MR & MRS H Dickson S (Anne Wister | ☎ (215) 836-2856
Garnett) Rc.Sg.Rv.Fw.Ac.Cda.P'42 | 3 Biddle Woods
MR David E—at ☎ (401) 847-2736 | Lane, Wyndmoor,
37 Catherine St, Newport, RI 02840 . . . . | PA 19038
Boenning MR & MRS Henry D (Perkins—Sara A Hunt)
Me.Pe.Rv.Fw.Ac.Pa'35
☎ (610) LA5-6488 . . 936 Rock Creek Rd, Bryn Mawr, PA 19010
Boericke MR & MRS Frederic S 2d (Lois J Schaeffer) | ☎ (603) 673-6190
Me.Cr'70 . . . . | 1 Carleton Rd,
MR Willard G . . . . | Mont Vernon, NH
JUNIORS MR Frederic S 3d . . . . | 03057
Boericke MRS Gideon (Cadwalader—Catherine S | ☎ (215) 248-0992
Chambers) G. . . . . | 80 W Hampton Rd,
MR Gideon F. . . . . | Philadelphia, PA
| 19118
Boericke MR & MRS James F (Saragene Glass) | 153 W Margaret
PhPharm'66.Me.Duke'64 . . . . | Lane, Hillsborough,
MISS Margaret E—at U of NCar Chapel Hill . . . | NC 27278
MR James F JR—Duke'89 . . . . |
Boericke DR & MRS Ralph R (Nancy V Lynch) | ☎ (518) 399-9009
Me.Cr'60.PolyNY'67 . . . . | 9 Lolik Lane,
MISS Margaret V—HWSth'88.Me.—at Boston, | Glenville, NY 12302
MA. . . . . |
Boerke MR & MRS Richard E (Fredricka L von Redlich) Ncd.Dar. ⚓
☎ (561) 627-0331 . . 1640 Twelve Oaks Way, North Palm Beach,
FL 33408
Boersma MRS Milford (Mary E Lister) . . . . Died at
Ann Arbor, MI Apr 23'96
Boersma MR Milford—StJ.Mich'37.Mich'39 ⚓ . . | ☎ (313) 971-5530
MR Frederick L—Sar.H'62.Mich'63.Mich'77 . . . | 1125 Arlington
| Blvd, Ann Arbor,
| MI 48104

Boesel MR & MRS Kenneth S (Louise D Marsh) Fcg.Ncd.Dar.OState'33
Longwood at Oakmont A328, 500 Rte 909, Verona, PA *15147*
Boesel MR & MRS Peter M (Minnette C Bickel) Briar'71.Cl'77.Sar.Cda.Vt'73
☎ (713) 781-5814 . . 7811 Meadowvale Dv, Houston, TX *77063*
Bogardus MR & MRS Sidney T (Sully R McCauley) Ws'59.Un.Y'54.H'59
☎ (212) 772-7616 . . 122 E 76 St, New York, NY *10021*
Bogardus DR & MRS Sidney T JR (Julia B Hunt) Y'86.Rcch.Y'85.ClP&S'89
☎ (203) 387-5037 . . 279 Rimmon Rd, Woodbridge, CT *06525*
Bogart MR & MRS Adrian T JR (Letizia A L Corigliano)
S.Hl.Sar.ClarkTech'51 ⚓ . . of
☎ (516) 759-0533 . . PO Box 420, Mill Neck, NY *11765*
''Thimble Hall'' Locust Valley, NY *11560*
Bogart MR & MRS Adrian T 3d (Susan M Alexander) Drex'82.Hl.Vmi'81
☎ (410) 838-2788 . . 413 Sunny View Rd, Bel Air, MD *21014-5578*
Bogart MR Clinton F—S.Hl.TexA&M'84
☎ (713) 682-0042 . . 359 N Post Oak Lane, Apt 119, Houston, TX *77024*
Bogart MR G Douglas—Fst.StJ.Hl.Lm.
☎ (202) 338-0424 . . 2700 Virginia Av NW, Apt 704, Washington,
DC *20037*
Bogdan MRS Norbert A (Wilkin—Barbara Cates) Lx.Cly.Dar.Myf.StJ.
☎ (212) 879-0016 . . 830 Park Av, New York, NY *10021*
Bogert MR & MRS Bruce P (Marcia L Mills) SL'47.Chi.Hl.Mit'45
☎ (508) 546-6657 . . 8 Penryn Way, Rockport, MA *01966*
Bogert MRS H Lawrence (Margaret Milbank) Ri.Fic.Fiy.Snc.Cly . . .of
☎ (212) TR9-3900 . . 1 E 66 St, New York, NY *10021*
☎ (561) 546-5625 . . Box 1184, Hobe Sound, FL *33475*

Bogert MR & MRS H Lawrence 3d (Palmer—Eleanor | of ☎ (212)249-7063
P Wheeler) Un.Y.'61 . . . . | 130 E 75 St, Apt
MISS Hilary L—Ham'89.Cl'90—at 101 W 86 St, | 2B, New York, NY
New York, NY *10024* . . . . | *10021*
  MISS Blair W Palmer—HWSth'95—at | ☎ (516) 726-6789
  156 Bristol St, Canandaigua, NY *14424* . . . . . | 104 Cobb Isle Rd,
  MR Lansing R Palmer JR—HWSth'90—at | PO Box 562,
  61 Clarendon St, Boston, MA *02116* . . . . | Water Mill, NY
  | *11976*

Bogert MRS Harry Howe JR (Virginia C Robinson)
☎ (561) 243-4176 . . 1070 SW 20 Terr, Delray Beach, FL *33445*
Bogert MR & MRS Jeremiah M (Margot B Campbell)
SL'75.Rc.Ln.Fic.Fiy.Bgt.Y'63
☎ (914) 234-7341 . . 54 David's Way, Bedford Hills, NY *10507*
Bogert MISS Joan L—Swb'78
☎ (508) 356-1668 . . 10 Lanes End, Ipswich, MA *01938*

Boggess MR & MRS William P 2d (Judith A Norton) | ☎ (847) 234-5042
Sth'56.On.Rc.Va'52.H'56 | 191 Westleigh Rd,
MR Boyd S—at 801 N Ocean Blvd, | Lake Forest, IL
Delray Beach, FL *33483* . . . . | *60045*
MR Spencer N—at 1716—21 St NW, |
Washington, DC *20009* . . . . |
MR Russell T . . . . |

Boggess MR & MRS William P 3d (Stephena A Romanoff)
Bost'85.Rc.LakeF'83
☎ (847) 295-0477 . . 253 W Sheridan Place, Lake Bluff, IL *60044*

Boggs MR & MRS George T (Emilie L von Thelen) | ☎ (703) 276-8311
Cvc.Wil.Mt.Gi.Sl.P'69.Va'74 ⚓ . . . . | 4501 N 26 St,
JUNIORS MISS Blair M . . . . | Arlington, VA
JUNIORS MR G Trenholm JR . . . . | *22207*
Boggs MR Robert B—F&M'82
☎ (703) 506-0500 . . 20575 Snowshoe Square, Apt C302, Ashburn,
VA *20147*
Boghossian MR & MRS David M (Elizabeth D Bartle) Vt'80.H'78
☎ (617) 547-0923 . . 25 Ellsworth Av, Cambridge, MA *02139*
Bograd MRS Martha (Lubowski—Martha Bograd) | ☎ (212) 876-3442
SL'82 . . . . | 1155 Park Av,
  MISS Alicia E Lubowski . . . . | New York, NY
  MR Rubén N Lubowski . . . . | *10128*
Bogue MISS Jennifer C (Robert W JR) . . . . Married at Baltimore, MD
Kenerson MR John B 2d (Edward H 2d) . . . . Jly 13'96
Bogue MR & MRS (DR) Robert W JR (Lauren Lauck) | ☎ (410) 366-5674
Ws'68.Md'86.Elk.Y'66.Cl'71 . . . . | 4311 Rugby Rd,
  MISS Kimberley W—at N'western . . . . | Baltimore, MD
  MR R Peter—at Yale . . . . | *21210*
Bohannon MR & MRS P Lindsay (M Alice Mathews) Hlns'80.Van'79
☎ (615) 269-9365 . . 201 Clarendon Av, Nashville, TN *37205*
Bohlen MRS Betty White (Haines—Brown—Betty J White) Pa'43.Me.
☎ (610) 642-9444 . . 3300 Darby Rd, Apt 4205, Haverford,
PA *19041-1071*
Bohlen MR & MRS Curtis C (Linda T Elkins) Mit'87.Stan'83.Cr'89
☎ (301) 373-4811 . . 3099 Friendship School Rd, Mechanicsville,
MD *20659-3811*
Bohlen MR & MRS E U Curtis (Janet S Trowbridge) | ☎ (202) 362-0094
Sth'50.Cvc.H'51 . . . . | 4710 Quebec St
MISS Nina S—Stan'84—at ☎ (415) 488-4516 | NW, Washington,
PO Box 1070, Woodacre, CA *94973* . . . . | DC *20016*
Bohlen MISS Elizabeth H
☎ (617) 491-2474 . . 111 Chestnut St, Cambridge, MA *02139*
Bohlen MR & MRS Francis H 3d (Sarah R Villeré) Tul'48
☎ (410) 822-0655 . . 27886 Peach Orchard Rd, Easton, MD *21601*
Bohlen MRS John W (Evans—Katherine B Horsley)
☎ (609) 654-5817 . . 136 Medford Leas, Medford, NJ *08055*
Bohlen MR William F—Gm.Me.P'45
☎ (610) 293-0223 . . 67 Lakeside Av, Devon, PA *19333*
Boice MR & MRS Fred T (Ann Kelley) Pom'53.Ariz'68.Occ'52
☎ (520) 299-0021 . . 4741 E Paseo Del Bac, Tucson, AZ *85718*
Boies MR & MRS David (Eugenia Clark) Y'39 . . of
☎ (603) 964-8312 . . ''Sunshine Farm'' Box 1015, North Hampton,
NH *03862*
PO Box 1256, Hobe Sound, FL *33475*
Boies MR & MRS David 3d (Susan Fowler) V'65 . . . . | ☎ (603) 964-6319
MISS Katherine—Wms'96 . . . . | 27 Atlantic Av,
MR David W—NH'95 . . . . | Box 343,
  | North Hampton, NH
  | *03862*

Boileau MR & MRS Nicholas P (Elizabeth H Watts) Ox'63.Chi.Cda.Ox'64 . . . . | of ☎ (011-44-171) 935-8813
MR Edward A—Durham'90 . . . . | 11 Winsford House, Luxborough St, London W1M 3LD, England
MR Samuel E—Bristol'93 . . . . | ☎ (011-44-1335) 342-436 Wyaston Grove, Wyaston, Ashbourne, Derbyshire DE6 2DR, England

Boiselle DR & MRS Phillip M (Ellen W Curtis) Y'90.Cl'92.NCar'86.Duke'90
☎ (215) 574-1091 . . 510 Delancey St, Philadelphia, PA *19106*

Boit MR Charles-Frederick D . . see CTSS C Grote

Boland MRS John J (Betty Lloyd Hutchison) Cvc.Mt.Sl.
☎ (908) 449-4064 . . 100 Jersey Av, Spring Lake, NJ *07762*

Boldrick MR & MRS Neill JR (Calvert—Margaret Corning) Tex'56.StMarys'84.A.Tex'52.Tex'56
☎ (210) 824-6617 . . 7731 Broadway St, Apt 26, San Antonio, TX *78209*

Bole MR & MRS Richard H (Mary C Wick) CtCol'70.K.Kt.Cv.Geo'67.JHop'73 . . . . | ☎ (216) 423-3578 Epping Rd, Box 8, Gates Mills, OH *44040*
JUNIORS MISS Allayne E . . . . |
JUNIORS MR Richard H JR . . . . |

Bole MRS William C (Ruth E Stary) BaldW'45 . . . . | ☎ (216) 651-3058 10315 Cliff Dv, Cleveland, OH *44102*
MISS Mary Jo K—Mich'79 . . . . |

Boles MR & MRS Edgar H 2d (Elizabeth J Young) It.Kt.Tv.OWes'69.Cwr'73 . . . . | ☎ (216) 247-5355 621 Falls Rd, Chagrin Falls, OH *44022*
JUNIORS MISS Mary H . . . . |
JUNIORS MISS Elizabeth A . . . . |
JUNIORS MR Edgar H 3d . . . . |

Boles MRS Laurence H (Blossom L Miller)
☎ (216) 371-2203 . . 2229 Woodmere Dv, Cleveland, OH *44106*

Boline MRS Flanders (Mary S Flanders) BMr'37.Csn.
☎ (860) 635-5511 . . Covenant Village, Missionary Rd, Cromwell, CT *06416*

Bolling MR & MRS Charles L (Josephine Lea Harrison) Cts.Gm.Ac.P'45 . . . . | ☎ (610) 525-0169 449 Boxwood Rd, Rosemont, PA *19010*
MISS Mary D—Vt'78—at ☎ (510) 654-2878 5344 James Av, Oakland, CA *94618* . . . |

Bolling MR & MRS Robert H JR (Joan Ross) Nyc.Wil.P'48
☎ (302) 654-3575 . . 115 Buck Rd, Box 3655, Wilmington, DE *19807*

Bolling MR & MRS Robert H 3d (Martha W Miller) Conn'83.P'79
☎ (610) 388-0765 . . PO Box 128, 390 Fairville Rd, Chadds Ford, PA *19317*

Bolling MR & MRS Sterling R (Jane Sharon)
☎ (803) 849-6288 . . 937 Bowman Rd, Apt 211, Mt Pleasant, SC *29464*

Bollman MR & MRS McWilliam V (Lucile A H Roesler) Wheat'54.P.Nu'60 . . of
☎ (212) 860-5775 . . 445 E 86 St, New York, NY *10028*
☎ (518) 499-2349 . . "Rivendell" Bluff Head Rd, Huletts Landing, NY *12841*

Bolman MRS Katherine G (Katherine B Gaines) Wis'69
1415 Victoria St, Apt 801, Honolulu, HI *96822*

Bolt MR Eugene A JR—Fi.Rc.Pe.Ll.Wt.Rv.Pa'88.Pa'92
☎ (215) 735-9414 . . 2008 Spruce St, Philadelphia, PA *19103*

Bolton MR & MRS Earle W 3d (Katharine G Dall) Mid'55 . . . . | ☎ (803) 838-4242 "Yard Farm" PO Box 2442, Beaufort, SC *29901*
MISS Susanna B . . . . |
MR Timothy W . . . . |
MR Samuel H . . . . |

Bolton MR & MRS John Wood (Nancy J Van Zandt) Hlns'61.Y'57 . . . . | ☎ (804) 979-4229 2267 Garth Rd, Charlottesville, VA *22901*
MISS Catherine C—Hlns'92 . . . . |
MR Richard K Van Z—Va'88.Madrid'89.DU'92 |

Bolton MR & MRS John Wood JR (Cynthia H Lockhart) Lynch'88.Ct.Cw.Rr.Pg.Lynch'88
☎ (703) 917-9228 . . 6325 Kellogg Dv, McLean, VA *22101*

Bolton MRS Kenyon C (Mary I Peters) BMr'37.Un.Cv.It.Cly.Sl.Ncd. . . . . | of ☎ (561)832-7375 30 Blossom Way, Palm Beach, FL *33480*
MR Kenyon C 3d—at ☎ (617) 491-3088 11 Gray Gardens W, Cambridge, MA *02138* . . . |
MR John B—at ☎ (703) 536-4891 4942 N Old Dominion Rd, Arlington, VA *22207* | ☎ (216) 247-4651 3060 Chagrin River Rd, Chagrin Falls, OH *44022*

Bolton MR & MRS Nelson M (C Leigh Crowe) Smu'75.Cw.Myf.Wt.Rv.Md.Cda.Dar.Loy'70 . . . | ☎ (410) 549-1007 "Raincliffe" 935 Raincliffe Rd, Sykesville, MD *21784*
JUNIORS MISS Tacy K L . . . . |

Bolton MR & MRS Thomas C (Elizabeth L Day) Sth'63.Ri.Cl'64
☎ (704) 274-1744 . . 430 Vanderbilt Rd, Asheville, NC *28803*

Bolton MR & MRS William B (Katherine J Howard) Br'83.Unn.Tv.Pa'74
☎ (216) 541-6622 . . 12717 Lakeshore Blvd, Bratenahl, OH *44108*

Bomeisler MR & MRS Douglass M JR (Anne O Kniffen) Rc.Y'48
☎ (212) YU8-5913 . . 785 Park Av, New York, NY *10021*

Bomeisler MR & MRS Douglass T (Susanne J Brink) FIU'94.FlaAtl'94
☎ (561) 225-1664 . . 1108 NE Quinn Place, Jensen Beach, FL *34957*

Bomeisler MASTER Dylan Armstrong (Stuart Brent) . . . . Born at Hyannis, MA Feb 11'96

Bomeisler MR & MRS Stuart Brent (Melissa K Forman) MaryB'90.Pep'89
☎ (508) 228-6608 . . 61 Wauwinet Rd, Nantucket, MA *02554*

Bomonti MR & MRS Ralph M (Nancy G Moreland) Cly.
☎ (212) 472-0689 . . 162 E 80 St, New York, NY *10021*

Boncella MR & MRS Gary A (Elizabeth E Walker) JCar'75
☎ (216) 321-0388 . . 2297 Lamberton Rd, Cleveland Heights, OH *44118*

Bond MR & MRS Arthur D JR (Molly Graham) Cy.Sm.Chi.P'55
☎ (617) 868-6507 . . 12 Lakeview Av, Cambridge, MA *02138*

Bond MISS Bonnie Lee—Cly.Chr.Ncd.
☎ (212) 744-6054 . . 1 East End Av, New York, NY *10021*

Bond MR & MRS Calhoun (Jane L Piper) NCar'52.Md.Cw.Mv.W&L'43.Md'49
☎ (410) 549-3123 . . Fairhaven C021, 7200 Third Av, Sykesville, MD *21784*

Bond MR & MRS Calhoun JR (Sherry B Hinnant) NCar'79.NCar'88.Cw.Aht'79.NCar'88 . . of
☎ (919) 304-4161 . . 307 S 7 St, Mebane, NC *27302*
☎ (919) 478-3826 . . "Edgefield" 1066 Pine Ridge Rd, Zebulon, NC *27597*

Bond MRS James (Lewis—Mary F W Porcher)
☎ (215) 248-2770 . . 201 W Evergreen Av, Apt 1110, Philadelphia, PA *19118*

Bond MR & MRS Langhorne McC (Enriqueta P Carter) Ws'61.Mt.Cvc.Cos.Va'59 . . . . | ☎ (919) 545-0125 1066 Fearrington
  MISS Prescott McC—at Wofford . . . . | Post, 27 E Madison,
  MR Langhorne C . . . . | Pittsboro, NC *27312*

Bond MR & MRS Nelson L JR (Burdette—Gwendolen N Gorman) Gv.Leh'57.H'66 . . . . | ☎ (410) 363-6182 3210 Caves Rd,
  MISS Marjorie A Burdette—Rm'95 . . . . | Owings Mills, MD
  MR Timothy W Burdette—JHop'94 . . . . | *21117*

Bond MRS Richard C (Barbara B Batt) Me.Ac.
☎ (610) 525-5286 . . 65 Pasture Lane, Bryn Mawr, PA *19010*

Bonds MR & MRS David C (Charlotte L Prime) Hlns'61.Ht.Ofp.Dar.Ncd.Cl'61 . . . . | ☎ (804) 823-4123 "Cardinal Crest"
  MR David P—Cl'90—at ☎ (212) 595-6875 | Rte 1, Box 511,
155 W 70 St, New York, NY *10023* . . . . | Crozet, VA *22932*
  MR William C—at ☎ (804) 295-9314
2021 Ivy Rd, Apt C3, Charlottesville, VA *22903* |

Bondurant MRS William W JR (Carr—Nina M Jenkins) V'30.Csn.A.
☎ (210) 826-4493 . . 200 Patterson Av, Apt 216, San Antonio, TX *78209*

Bonebrake MR & MRS Michael H (Helen F Michalis) Vt'83.Pr.Vt'82
☎ (212) 722-4914 . . 152 E 94 St, New York, NY *10128*

Bonelli MR & MRS Robert M (Barbara A Becker) ArizSt'70.Ariz'50.ArizSt'56
☎ (602) 945-1596 . . 5843 Calle Del Norte E, Phoenix, AZ *85018*

Bonesteel MR & MRS Michael John (Susan E Schaaf) Ariz'66.Stan'61.SCal'66
☎ (310) 454-8127 . . 13688 Sunset Blvd, Pacific Palisades, CA *90272*

Boney MR & MRS Leslie N JR (Lillian M Bellamy) NCarSt'40
☎ (910) 763-6013 . . 2305 Gillette Dv, Wilmington, NC *28403*

Bonistall MR & MRS Ernest R (Nathalie L Smith) Neb'63 . . . . | ☎ (770) 446-8144 4210 Flippen Trail,
  MISS Linnéa N—GaSo'95 . . . . | Norcross, GA *30092*
  MR Ernest C—GaSo'93—at ☎ (912) 964-8329
1115 Wyndmeile Place, Garden City, GA *31408* |

Bonmartini CT Francesco & CTSS (Charlotte Doelger) Ws'57.Cly.Ncd.Rome'52 . . . . | of ☎ (302)571-1696 900 du Pont Rd,
  MISS Gioia G—Ws'86.Cly. . . . . | Wilmington, DE
19807
☎ (202) 337-8280
3615 T St NW,
Washington, DC
20007

Bonmartini MR Giovanni W—P'85
Salita San Onafrio 21, 06165 Rome, Italy

Bonnell MR & MRS Robert O JR (Barbara G Johnson) Ws'52.JHop'54.Elk.Md.Mv.USN'47 . . . . | ☎ (410) 243-7237 5 Stratford Rd,
  MISS Lila J H—Aht'91 . . . . | Baltimore, MD
21218

Bonnell MRS William F (Jean Booth)
☎ (817) 737-7891 . . 1231 Roaring Springs Rd, Ft Worth, TX *76114*

Bonner MR Charles W 3d—Snc. . . . . | ☎ (203) 637-9152
  MISS Caroline C—at 5010 Palisades Av, | "Bonnerstone II"
West New York, NJ *07093* . . . . | 16 Old Wagon Rd,
  MR Ian F van der L—at Lebanon Valley Grad . . | Old Greenwich, CT
06870

Bonner MR & MRS Henry S (Ballweg—Irma Adams) H'45
☎ (301) 863-8121 . . "Beechwoods" Snow Hill Way, PO Box 257, St Marys City, MD *20686*

Bonner MISS Jennifer—StMarys'90
Bitter End Yacht Club, North Sound, Virgin Gorda, BVI

Bonner MRS Paul Hyde (O'Neill—McGowan—C Elizabeth Calvin)
☎ (803) 722-3498 . . 91 E Bay St, Charleston, SC *29401*

Bonnet MR & MRS E Scofield (Judith F Woodhead) Sdy. . . . . | ☎ (619) 756-2619 Box 2092,
  MISS Susan G . . . . | Rancho Santa Fe, CA *92067*

Bonney MR & MRS James K (Margaret S Helm) Bost'70.My.OWes'69 . . . . | ☎ (508) 468-3430 90 Larch Row,
  MISS Alexandra H . . . . | Wenham, MA *01984*
  MR Andrew W . . . . |
  JUNIORS MISS Margaret G . . . . |

Bonnie MR & MRS Edward S (Cornelia B Winthrop) Srr.Yn.Y'49 . . . . | ☎ (502) 241-4647 "Stonelea"
  MR Shelby W—K.Lic.Va'86.H.'90—at | 4701 S H'way 1694,
☎ (415) 885-5946 . . 2238 Hyde St, Apt 14, | Prospect, KY *40059*
San Francisco, CA *94109* . . . . |

Bonnie MR & MRS Robert F (Cynthia A Polk) Va'86.H'89 . . of
☎ (202) 364-4683 . . 4201 Fordham Rd NW, Washington, DC *20016*
☎ (540) 592-3402 . . PO Box 961, Middleburg, VA *20118*

Bonoff MR & MRS Burton L (Barbara J Wasserman) Bvr'47
☎ (602) 253-1565 . . 2201 N Central Av, Phoenix, AZ *85004*

Bonsack MR Bradford C—Smu'82
3811 Azure Lane, Addison, TX *75244*

Bonsack MRS Frederick C (Dorothy F Fite)
☎ (318) 433-3557 . . 1326 Tenth St, Lake Charles, LA *70601*

Bonsal MR & MRS Dudley B (Faithfull—Lucia Turner) V'26.C.Cs . . .of
☎ (914) 234-7117 . . 24 St Marys Church Rd, Bedford, NY *10506*
☎ (212) 861-6917 . . 150 E 73 St, New York, NY *10021*

Bonsal MR & MRS Frank A JR (Helen Baldwin) Mt.Md.Gv.B.Elk.Fic.Mv.P'59 . . . . | ☎ (410) 833-2699 14014 Mantua Mill
  MISS Adair B—HWSth'89 . . . . | Rd, Glyndon, MD
  MISS Polly P—at Hamilton . . . . | *21071*
  MR Frank A 3d—NH'91 . . . . |

Bonsal MRS Hubbard (Nathalie Hubbard) Rdc'63.Hn.
☎ (301) 657-3324 . . 5608 Montgomery St, Chevy Chase, MD *20815*

Bonsal MR & MRS Stephen (Elizabeth W Lord) C.Y'56 . . . . | ☎ (203) 637-1352 30 Hendrie Av,
  MISS Elizabeth L—at 161 Bedford Av, Brooklyn, | Riverside, CT *06878*
NY *11211* . . . . |
  MISS Virginia P . . . . |
  MR Dudley B 2d—at 341 Summer St, Somerville,
MA *02144* . . . . |

Bonsal MRS Warwick P (Frances M Canfield) . . . . . | ☎ (803) 722-4585
  MISS Frances M—Yh. . . . . | 5 Stolls Alley,
  MR Warwick P . . . . | Charleston, SC
29401

Bonsall MR & MRS Edward H III (Patricia Ziegler)
Pc.R.Cspa.Ncd.Bene'66 . . . .
MR Richard S—Tufts'90 . . . .
of ☎ (215)247-1185
7711 St Martin's
Lane, Philadelphia,
PA *19118*
☎ (809) 469-3070
''Blue Roof''
Gingerland, Nevis

Bontumasi MR & MRS David A (Natalie S Mills) Nw'86
☎ (773) 883-1161 . . 1709 W School St, Chicago, IL *60657*

Boocock MRS Kenyon (Glenn H Winnett) Fic.Cly.
☎ (212) 838-4297 . . 580 Park Av, New York, NY *10021*

Boocock MR & MRS Roger B (Helen G Kimbark)
Mid'56.P'56 . . . .
MISS Dana G—P'83—at Friends Academy,
Duck Pond Rd, Locust Valley, NY *11560* . . . . .
MISS Sarah J—Y'85—at Newark Academy,
91 S Orange Av, Livingston, NJ *07039-4989* . . .
☎ (718) 549-6530
5223 Fieldston Rd,
Bronx, NY *10471*

Boogaard MR Thomas C (late Tom) . . . . Married at Middletown, CT
Sewall MISS Margaret H R (Tingey H) . . . . May 18'96

Boogaard MR & MRS Thomas C (Margaret H R Sewall) Wes'94.Hav'91
☎ (617) 876-4112 . . 113 Museum St, Somerville, MA *02143*

Boogher MR John P 3d—Gv.Md.P'35
☎ (540) 828-8123 . . 413 Brightwood, 100 Brightwood Club Dv,
Lutherville, MD *21093*

Booher MRS Edward E (Whitaker—Agnes W Martin)
☎ (609) 426-6021 . . Meadow Lakes 13-01U, Hightstown, NJ *08520*

Booher MR & MRS L Dale (Lisa Stamm) Nu'67.TexTech'55.Cl'60 . . of
☎ (516) 749-2189 . . ''Homestead'' 67 N Menantic Rd, PO Box 90,
Shelter Island Heights, NY *11965*
☎ (212) PL1-9077 . . 405 E 54 St, New York, NY *10022*

Boom MR & MRS Willem E (Stratton—Helen M
Elting) Man'vl'77.Bridgept'79.Dar.Swth'39 . . . .
MISS Lucinda Stratton—Tufts'89.Cl'92—at
☎ (617) 492-1318 . . 26 Hurlbut St, Apt 5,
Cambridge, MA *02138* . . . .
☎ (203) 869-6301
10 Glen Court,
Greenwich, CT
06830

Boomer MR & MRS George du P (Palmer—Nola Schafer) Unn.Yn.Y'42
☎ (941) 992-5041 . . 20690 S Tamiami Trail, PO Box 123, Estero,
FL *33928*

Boomer MR & MRS Robert E (Anne E Knapp)
Ncd.Wayne'49 . . . .
MISS Ellen M . . . .
☎ (941) 964-0665
PO Box 424,
Boca Grande, FL
33921

Boone MASTER Charles Philip (Philip S JR) . . . . Born at
San Francisco, CA Jun 3'96

Boone MR & MRS Charles W JR (F Blair Riggs)
☎ (703) 521-6258 . . 1510 S Edgewood St, Apt 541, Arlington,
VA *22204*

Boone MR Hilary J JR—Ky'41
☎ (606) 272-0636 . . 1725 Walnut Hill Rd, Lexington, KY *40515*

Boone MR & MRS Hilary J 3d (Caroline M Huger) Ky'81.Ky'79
☎ (606) 273-1704 . . 1451 Walnut Hill Rd, Lexington, KY *40515*

Boone MR & MRS Jonathan O (Danielle M de Boisblanc) CalPoly'87.Cal'85
☎ (510) 939-8842 . . 109 Villa Court, Lafayette, CA *94549*

Boone MISS Katherine A (late Philip S) . . . . Married
Taylor MR Zack . . . . Sep 3'95

Boone MR & MRS Philip S JR (Carol L Newton)
Stan'80.SFrSt'89.Bhm.Cal'73.Cal'77
☎ (415) 752-1022 . . 2959 Lake St, San Francisco, CA *94121*

Boone MISS Whitney Marie (Jonathan O) . . . . Born Apr 11'94

Boone MR William H—S.Snc.Cw.Rv.Swth'58.Cl'62 . . of
☎ (516) 627-6789 . . 160 Kensett Rd, Manhasset, NY *11030*
☎ (304) 645-1059 . . Montescena, Greenbrier, Box 1146, Lewisburg,
WV *24901*
☎ (561) 225-3006 . . ''Sandpebble'' 2571 NE Ocean Blvd, Stuart,
FL *34996*

Boorman MRS P Garrison (Pierce—Patricia L
Garrison) . . . .
MISS Cynthia W Pierce—at 2939 Van Ness St
NW, Washington, DC *20008* . . . .
☎ (301) 652-4434
3615 Thornapple St,
Chevy Chase, MD
20815

Boote MR & MRS A Shepard (Heath Drury)
CUNY'69.Colg'51.Cl'53.Stan'57.Cl'74.Cl'75
☎ (860) 928-1830 . . Bull Hill Rd, Woodstock, CT *06281*

Booth MRS John L (Louise P Camper) Nat'lB'39.Evg.
☎ (561) 278-8373 . . 3333 N Ocean Blvd, Gulf Stream, FL *33483*

Booth MR & MRS John L II (Rebecca P Chapman)
Y'72.Mich'75 . . . .
JUNIORS MISS Charlotte-Louise B . . . .
JUNIORS MISS John L III—at Hotchkiss . . . .
☎ (313) 882-1547
980 Lake Shore Rd,
Grosse Pointe
Shores, MI *48236*

Booth MR & MRS John T (Anne C Mott)
Swth'53.Ln.Plg.Aht'51.H'57
MISS Alison M—at ☎ (212) 879-9654
45 E 82 St, New York, NY *10028* . . . .
MISS Roxanna E—at ☎ (860) 233-4293
814 Farmington Av, West Hartford, CT *06119* . .
☎ (860) 567-9577
182 Whites Woods
Rd, Box 25,
Litchfield, CT *06759*

Booth MISS Miven (John T) . . . . Married at Litchfield, CT
Trageser MR Eric D (Paul) . . . . Jun 1'96

Booth MR & MRS Ralph H 2d (Winifred R Myers) H'76
☎ (313) 884-0821 . . 274 Provencal Rd, Grosse Pointe Farms, MI *48236*

Booth MRS Robert H (Constance M Ralston) . . . . Died at
Wilmington, DE Jun 2'96

Booth MR & MRS William N (Mary A Davis)
Wheat'72.Cy.Sm.Ub.Unn.Chi.Ncd.Ty'71 . . . . . .
JUNIORS MISS Phoebe W . . . .
JUNIORS MR Samuel H . . . .
539 Hammond St,
Chestnut Hill, MA
02167

Booth MRS William W (Adelaide Lanz) Fcg.
☎ (412) 776-8193 . . Sherwood Oaks 394, 100 Norman Dv,
Cranberry Township, PA *16066-4229*

Boothby MR & MRS Richard C (Mary-Helen C Sheppard) Rc.Pc.Sg.Bost'74
☎ (215) 247-2309 . . 612 W Hartwell Lane, Philadelphia, PA *19118*

Boothby MR & MRS Willard E JR (Florence E Clifford)
Sg.Rc.Pc.Ph.Ln.Ri.Ac.Cr'44.Leh'46
☎ (215) CH7-4900 . . 600 E Gravers Lane, Wyndmoor, PA *19038*

Boothby MR & MRS Willard S 3d (Linda D Kent)
Y'71.H'73.Ln.Ri.Ck.Cly.P'69.H'72 . . . .
JUNIORS MISS Elizabeth K . . . .
☎ (212) 860-8311
47 E 88 St, Apt 2D,
New York, NY
10128

Booz MISS Michelle S
☎ (312) 644-9359 . . 1448 N Bell Av, Chicago, IL *60622*

Borda MR & MRS Charles A 3d (Florence D Hopkins)
Sa.Cts.Rb.Ac.NCar'52 . . of
☎ (610) 687-2758 . . 18 Orchard Lane, Villanova, PA *19085*
☎ (207) 276-5397 . . Northeast Harbor, ME *04662*

Borden MISS Anna C (Gail F) . . . . Married at Alexandria, VA
    Anderson MR Christopher J (Donald E) . . . . Jun 3'95
Borden MRS E Bulkeley (Elizabeth Bulkeley McGinley) Rdc'50
    ☎ (617) 547-8797 . . 26D Bradbury Court, Cambridge, MA *02138*
Borden MR Frank H—Me.R.Cw.Ty'47.Pa'50
    ☎ (610) 527-3720 . . 77 Middle Rd, Apt 167, Bryn Mawr, PA *19010*

Borden MR & MRS Gail F (Hildegard M Laturnus) | ☎ (703) 370-0334
Wash'63.H'63.H'71 . . . . | 3614 Tupelo Place,
MR Gail P—at Rice . . . . | Alexandria, VA
 | *22304*

Borden MR & MRS James P (Marguerite L MacCoy) | ☎ (908) 277-0542
San.Ty'64 . . . . | 77 Prospect St,
MISS Elizabeth E . . . . | Summit, NJ *07901*
MR William M . . . . |

Borden MR & MRS Richard (Sweney—Beatrice | of ☎ (805)969-9664
Brown) Stan'42.H'33 . . . . | Casa Dorinda,
    MR John E Sweney—Br'79—at Houston, TX | 300 Hot Springs Rd,
 | Santa Barbara, CA
 | *93108*
 | La Jolla de Los
 | Cabos, San José del
 | Cabo, Baja
 | California Sur,
 | Mexico

Borden MR & MRS Robert R 3d (Flanders—Daphne | ☎ (508) 768-6036
LeLand) My.So'65 . . . . | ''Paynter Farm''
MISS Katherine—at U of Colo Boulder . . . . | Essex, MA *01929*
JUNIORS MR Robert R 4th—at Middlesex . . . . . |

Borders MRS Barbara B (Barbara D Burkham)
    ☎ (207) 284-5838 . . Biddeford Pool, ME *04006*
Borders MR William A JR—Cysl.Y'60 . . . . | 227 E 57 St,
MR William A 3d . . . . | New York, NY
 | *10022*

Borges MR Bruce S—Myf.
    ☎ (315) 536-5642 . . 876 Davy Rd, Penn Yan, NY *14527*
Borghese MR & MRS Livio M (Susanna H Keyser) Ws'68.K.Ng.Bcs.Pa'61
    ☎ (212) 288-1339 . . 79 E 79 St, New York, NY *10021*

Borie MR & MRS A Clay (Frances D Dunning) | ☎ (215) 233-2388
Rb.Pc.Ll.Ac. . . . . | 710 E Hartwell
MISS Julia C—NEng'75—at ☎ (703) 820-3083 | Lane, Wyndmoor,
5824—5 St S, Arlington, VA *22204* . . . . | PA *19038*

Borie MRS Beauveau 3d (Frances D Ellison)
    ☎ (215) CH7-5013 . . 318 W Springfield Av, Philadelphia, PA *19118*
Borie MR & MRS David B (Mary W Stewart) Rr.B.Cw.Rv.Cly.Ncd.Y'51
    ☎ (203) 661-5686 . . 580 Lake Av, Greenwich, CT *06830*
Borie MR David B JR—Rv.Cal'78
    ☎ (303) 771-1277 . . 6154 S Lima Way, Englewood, CO *80111*

Borie MR & MRS H Peter JR (Evans—Josephine M | ☎ (610) 356-2165
Shober) Me.Cc.Ncd.Yn.Y'49 . . . . | 513 Waters Edge,
MR H Peter 3d . . . . | Newtown Square,
    MR Victor M Evans . . . . | PA *19073-2131*

Borie MR & MRS J R McAllister (Helder—Judith A Hallerman)
Cin'56.Loy'77.Pc.
    ☎ (215) 836-7247 . . 521 E Mill Rd, Flourtown, PA *19031*
Borie MR & MRS J Stewart (Greta Zuckerkandel)
Pa'78.Pa'82.Rcp.Sar.Pa'78.Pa'86
    ☎ (619) 755-4050 . . 14275 Half Moon Bay Dv, Del Mar, CA *92014*

Borie MRS M Stiles (Mary E Stiles)
    ☎ (541) 744-8163 . . 3716 Oregon St, Springfield, OR *97478-6458*
Borie MR Peter—Lx.Y'35.Cl'38 . . of
    ☎ (215) 592-7676 . . Hopkinson House Apt 1517,
    602 Washington Square S, Philadelphia, PA *19106*
    ☎ (413) 298-3289 . . 2 Yale Hill, Box 857, Stockbridge, MA *01262*
Borie MR & MRS William J S JR (Peacock—Joann L Hutton) Pa'53
    ☎ (610) 430-3934 . . 282 Devon Way, West Chester, PA *19380*
Boring MISS Brooke Noelle (Douglas D) . . . . Born Dec 19'95
Boring MASTER Cody Jonathan Douglas (Douglas D) . . . . . Born Feb 4'94
Boring MR & MRS Dix (Marilyn Moore) Cal'56.Bhm.Fr.Cal'56
    ☎ (415) 922-0582 . . 2519 Broadway St, San Francisco, CA *94115*
Boring MR & MRS Douglas D (Judy A Rogers) Cal'83
    ☎ (916) 791-5395 . . 5980 Reba Dv, Granite Bay, CA *95746*
Borland MISS Anne J—Cal'68.Cs.Fic.
    ☎ (212) 737-3572 . . 66 E 83 St, New York, NY *10028*

Borland MR & MRS Bruce D (Dorothy G Juergens) | ☎ (914) 921-2870
Col'65.On.H'65 . . . . | 600 Purchase St,
MISS Sarah D—at Palm Desert, CA . . . . | Rye, NY *10580*
MISS Aubrey H—P'93—at Princeton, NJ . . . . . . |
MR John J—at Stanford . . . . |

Borland MR & MRS John J JR (Suzanne R Sivage) | ☎ (847) 295-7542
Nw'85.Rc.On.Wa.H'67.Ch'73 . . . . | 650 N Burton Dv,
MISS Elizabeth B—LakeF'95 . . . . | Lake Forest, IL
MR Edward S—DU'93 . . . . | *60045*
JUNIORS MR Samuel H—at Denver U . . . . |

Borland MR & MRS Myles (Linda E Dougherty) | ☎ (508) 475-2721
V'74.W&M'61 . . . . | 41 Jenkins Rd,
JUNIORS MR Rives | Andover, MA *01810*

Borland MISS Susan M
    ☎ (757) 422-3928 . . 116—88 St, Virginia Beach, VA *23451*
Borland MRS Virginia S (Virginia A Stockfish) Wells'51.Chr.
    ☎ (212) 535-7263 . . 110 East End Av, PH-K, New York,
NY *10028-7416*
Borland MR & MRS William F (Hooker—Walker—Nancy Morse)
Sr.Ln.H'41
    ☎ (408) 625-1641 . . Box 34, Pebble Beach, CA *93953*
Borman MR & MRS Earle K 3d (Pamela S Snyder) Man'vl'81.Nu'86
    ☎ (203) 866-1052 . . 18 Pine Point Rd, Rowayton, CT *06853*
Borneman MISS Katherine L (Scardino—Katherine L Borneman) Cin'82
    ☎ (513) 228-9162 . . 168 Henry St, Dayton, OH *45403*
Borneman MR William C JR—Cin'87
312 Garrard St, Apt 1, Covington, KY *41011*

Borner MR & MRS Steven P (Nancy H Benkhart) | ☎ (914) 234-9381
Bgt.Bost'63.Bost'66 . . . . | 19 Tarleton Rd,
MR Andrew H—Dick'92 . . . . | Bedford, NY *10506*
MR Brooke S—at Dartmouth . . . . |

Borthwick MR & MRS Thomas C (Josephine C | ☎ (910) 295-0553
Chapman) M.Rcp.Cr'51 . . . . | 315 Lake Forest Dv
MR George H—Me'85—at ☎ (206) 252-1838 | SW, Pinehurst, NC
18202 Smokey Point Blvd, Arlington, WA *98223* | *28374*

Bortz MR Richard C—K.Nu'90 . . of
    ☎ (212) 665-2989 . . 336 Central Park W, Apt 5C, New York, NY *10025*
    ☎ (610) 779-1101 . . Spring Hill Farm, 520 Antietam Rd, Reading,
PA *19606*

Bos MR & MRS Gerard A (Harriet W Pierpoint)   ☎ (704) 442-9848
NCar'73.WashColl'73.Tul'76 . . . .   3051 Ferncliff Rd,
JUNIORS MISS Abigail S . . . .   Charlotte, NC *28211*
JUNIORS MR Gerard P . . . .

Bose MR Henry E—Pn.P'57.Nu'62
see Dilatory Domiciles

Bose MR & MRS Joan B (Joan D Buhse) Sth'59 . . .   ☎ (408) 867-9100
MISS Virginia D—Cal'87 . . . .   15571 Peach Hill
MR William A—Cal'88 . . . .   Rd, Saratoga, CA
MR Brian H—Cal'91. . . . .   *95070*
MR David McD—NotreD'92 . . . .

Bosland MR & MRS Paul C (Helen S Nelson) Bg.Mo.Br'55.Nu'63
  ☎ (904) 277-4584 . . 16 Sea Marsh Rd, Amelia Island, FL *32034*

Boss DR & MRS Jack F 3d (Grace P Hammond)
NH'74.PTheo'85.Hawaii'89.Cly.Cda.OState'79. OState'81.Y'91
''Evergreen Vista'' 2520 Hayes St, Eugene, OR *97405*

Bossange MRS Hector (Hélène A de Lorimier) . . . . .   ☎ (617) 237-9198
MR William D—Hiram'76.Bost'82 . . . .   67 Parker Rd,
   Wellesley, MA
   02181

Bossi MRS Quentin A (Lilian W Nicoll)
  ☎ (508) 385-9948 . . 61 Nobscusset Rd, Box Q, Dennis, MA *02638*

Bossidy MRS B Haig (Alice R Bohmfalk) Bnd'45.Evg.Bgt.BtP.
  ☎ (561) 655-8126 . . 153 Cocoanut Row, Palm Beach, FL *33480*

Bossidy MR & MRS Bruce H (Dorothy C Pickering)
PineM'73.Bgt.Ty'74 . . of
  ☎ (212) 772-1382 . . 1 Gracie Terr, New York, NY *10028*
  ☎ (203) 259-9514 . . 298 Harbor Rd, Southport, CT *06490*

Bostrom MR & MRS Robert E (Elizabeth M O Leys)   ☎ (609) 466-8336
H'79.So.Hb.Hn.F&M'74.Cl'76.Bost'80 . . . .   160 Province Line
JUNIORS MISS Leys M . . . .   Rd, Skillman, NJ
JUNIORS MISS Ashley E *08558*
JUNIORS MISS Allison F . . . .

Bostwick MRS Albert C (Sage—Eleanor Purviance) Pr.Cly.Mb . . .of
  ☎ (212) 628-9593 . . 778 Park Av, New York, NY *10021*
  ☎ (516) 334-0876 . . PO Box 440, 25 Hillside Av, Old Westbury,
NY *11568-0600*

Bostwick MR & MRS Albert C JR (Handal—Linda M Barrett) K . . .of
  ☎ (803) 648-0559 . . 531 Berrie Rd SW, Aiken, SC *29801*
  ☎ (315) 369-6180 . . Bisby Lake, Thendara, NY *13472*

Bostwick MR & MRS Dunbar W (Burden—Jeanne Wight) Rcn.Mb.Pr.Y'32
  ☎ (802) 985-2173 . . Box 39, Bostwick Rd, Shelburne, VT *05482*

Bostwick MR & MRS George H (Dolly F von Stade)   ☎ (803) 649-6566
Srr.Pr.Mb.Cly. . . . .   Box 0411,
MISS Dolly von S . . . .   Aiken, SC *29801*
MR Charles S . . . .
MR Richard S . . . .

Bostwick MR & MRS George H JR (Lilias J Knott)   ☎ (516) OR6-5405
Rc.Pr.Mid'58 . . . .   500 Chicken Valley
MISS Janet K . . . .   Rd, Locust Valley,
   NY *11560*

Bostwick MR & MRS James F C (Diana Gray) Rc.Pr.   ☎ (516) MA6-1135
MISS Lisa G—SFrArt'88 . . . .   Brookville Rd,
JUNIORS MR Thomas S . . . .   Glen Head, NY
   11545

Bostwick MR & MRS James F C JR (Susan R Wight) Buck'85.Bgt.LakeF'85
  ☎ (914) 763-3562 . . 253 Honey Hollow Rd, Pound Ridge, NY *10576*

Bostwick MRS Laura (Benson—Laura Bostwick) NCar'68
  ☎ (910) 473-5609 . . ''West Coast'' Wanchese, NC *27981*

Boswell MISS Caroline S—Elmira'71.StL'73
  ☎ (314) 991-1438 . . 7 White Gate Lane, St Louis, MO *63124*

Boswell MR & MRS Jackson C (Molin—Ann O B Castle) NCar'60.GeoW'74
  ☎ (703) 522-6977 . . 2805 N 7 St, Arlington, VA *22201*

Boswell MR & MRS James D (Pamela Scott) Tulsa'65.Vh.Tulsa'64.Tulsa'66
  ☎ (818) 795-6147 . . 341 Palmetto Dv, Pasadena, CA *91105*

Bosworth DR & MRS Robert G JR (Alice F Cook) P'46.Cl'48
  ☎ (303) 399-0113 . . 2115 E Fourth Av, Denver, CO *80206*

Botsford MR Blake—Rol'88 . . see MRS K Van Rensselaer

Botsford MRS Cynthia S (Straub—Cynthia M Schwartz)
  ☎ (301) 654-0012 . . 4601 N Park Av, Apt 1821, Chevy Chase,
MD *20815*

Botsford MRS Edward P (Katharine F Eddy)
  ☎ (415) 435-3281 . . 1300 Mar W, Tiburon, CA *94920*

Bottomley MR & MRS John T (Nina Laughlin)   ☎ (603) 964-9048
Cyb.Rol'67 . . . .   Box 461,
JUNIORS MISS Lisa F . . . .   Rye Beach, NH
   03871

Boucher MR & MRS Jerome H P JR (Gabrielle   ☎ (602) 991-4491
Lundy) StJos'71.StLeo'70 . . . .   5230 Via Buena
MISS Tara M . . . .   Vista,
JUNIORS MR Jerome H P 3d . . . .   Paradise Valley, AZ
   85253

Boudreau MR & MRS David L (Christine R Leness) H'84.Cly.Hn.Carl'85
  ☎ (203) 762-1731 . . 99 Chicken St, Wilton, CT *06897*

Boulos MR & MRS William M (Knapp—Towne—   ☎ (206) 285-5832
Vivian M Dennistoun) Y'47 . . . .   2205 Bigelow Av N,
MR C Evan Knapp—at 30286 Grande Vista,   Apt 6, Seattle, WA
Laguna Niguel, CA *92677* *98109*

Boulware MISS Patricia I—Skd'91
  ☎ (510) 841-0855 . . 2505 Virginia St, Apt 1, Berkeley, CA *94709*

Boulware MR & MRS Thomas M 3d (Mary E Camp)
Stph'58.Ala'60.Cy.Ala'60
  ☎ (205) 879-1126 . . 4247 Chickamauga Rd, Birmingham, AL *35213*

Bouras MR & MRS James C (Katharine W Adams)   ☎ (212) 289-0591
Finch'69.Ford'82.Ford'93.Cs.Cr'63.Nu'66 . . . . .   17 E 95 St,
MR Ian C . . . .   New York, NY
   10128

Bourbon del Monte di San Faustino PRC Montino   ☎ (805) 969-2130
& PRCSS (Rita R McIntyre) . . . .   825 Rockbridge Rd,
JUNIORS MISS Camilla . . . .   Santa Barbara, CA
JUNIORS MISS Alexandra *93108*

Bourdelais MR & MRS David A (Susan M Wadsworth)
Colby'77.Tufts'89.Syr'84.Bost'85
  ☎ (603) 899-3008 . . 10 Mountain Rd, Rindge, NH *03461*

Bourgeix MR & MRS Pierre (Frances T Thieriot)
Cal'84.LoyMmt'90.LoyMmt'90
  ☎ (310) 394-6474 . . 1024—12 St, 5, Santa Monica, CA *90403*

Bouriez MR & MRS Philippe G (Lynch—Edith W Scott) V'47.Cs . . .of
  ☎ (212) 861-1329 . . 211 E 70 St, New York, NY *10021*
  ☎ (011-33-1) 45-24-47-78 . . 10 rue de la Cure, 75016 Paris, France
  ☎ (011-33) 59-26-48-14 . . ''Oihanean'' rte d'Ascain,
64500 St-Jean-de-Luz, France

Bourne MRS Philip E (Luette R Close). . . . . | of ☎ (617)241-9494
MISS Luette S . . . . | 22 Elm St,
MR Philip E JR . . . . | Charlestown, MA
02129
☎ (603) 563-8325
''Dead End''
Box 56, Dublin, NH
03444

Bourne MRS Philip W (Mary E Nicholson) Cda.
☎ (617) 275-8339 . . Carleton-Willard Village, 100 Old Billerica Rd,
Bedford, MA *01730*

Bourne MR & MRS William N JR (Katherine E Day) | of ☎ (617)232-1062
KeeSt'60.Y'56.H'84 . . . . | 52 High St,
MISS Katherine L—Y'87 . . . . | Brookline, MA
MR William A—Ken'84 . . . . | *02146*
☎ (603) 585-6854
''Fitz'' RFD 62B,
Fitzwilliam, NH
03447

Bouscaren MR & MRS Henri V (Kathrine McNulty) Cyb.Y'36
☎ (513) 871-7741 . . 3315 Menlo Av, Cincinnati, OH *45208*

Bouscaren MR & MRS Michael F (Edith E Clark) | ☎ (617) 277-4174
Bost'75.BMr'79.Cy.Y'69.H'75 . . . . | 60 Fernwood Rd,
JUNIORS MISS Chloe L . . . . | Chestnut Hill, MA
02167

Bovaird MR & MRS James A 3d (Elaine Tobin) | of ☎ (847)446-9038
Col'57.Dth'51 . . . . | 521 Walnut St,
MISS Anne E—at Paris, France . . . . | Winnetka, IL *60093*
☎ (941) 597-2394
10851 Gulfshore Dv,
Naples, FL *34108*

Bovaird MR James O—Wil'65 . . . . | ☎ (803) 473-3469
MISS Amy E—J&W'87—at 40 Pearl Rd, | 663 Country Club
New London, CT *06302* . . . . | Circle, RR 3,
MISS M Kathleen . . . . | Box 663, Manning,
MR James E 2d—at Marsh Lane, Apt 1114, | SC *29102*
Dallas, TX *75287* . . . . |

Bovet DR Bernard . . . . Died

Bovet MISS Daria L
18 Gramercy Park S, New York, NY *10003*

Bovet MR Robert E . . of
Château de Vullierens, CH 1115 Vaud, Switzerland
8 E 83 St, New York, NY *10028*

Bovey MISS Hilary
☎ (508) 369-5056 . . 60 Thoreau St, Concord, MA *01742*

Bovey MR & MRS William K (Katherine R MacLean) | ☎ (508) 369-4389
Y'51 . . . . | 170 Russell St,
MISS Julia H—Bnd'91 . . . . | Carlisle, MA *01741*
MISS Alexandra K—at U of Vt . . . . |
MR Edward H 2d—Emory'93 . . . . |

Bowart MISS Nuria L . . see MISS M M Hitchcock
Bowart MISS Sophia J . . see MISS M M Hitchcock
Bowden MR Adrian H H . . . . Died at
London, England Oct 17'95

Bowden MRS Adrian H H (Marjorie W Gordan) | ☎ (011-44-171)
Bnd'64.K.Csn. . . . . | 499-8129
MISS Stephanie F H . . . . | 33 Grosvenor
MR Alexander G H . . . . | Square, London
JUNIORS MR Richard W B H . . . . | W1X 9LL, England

Bowden MISS Emily M—Man'vl'66.Cr'77
☎ (203) 966-0428 . . 205 Park St, New Canaan, CT *06840*

Bowden MR & MRS Francis J 3d (Virginia D Penniman)
Mich'88.Rv.Ac.Cda.UArts'90
☎ (610) 995-2454 . . 10 Doyle Rd, Wayne, PA *19087*

Bowden MR Garrett R—T.Bm.
☎ (212) 879-4240 . . 220 E 72 St, New York, NY *10021*

Bowden MR & MRS John J (Suzanne J Helme) WmSth'78.Rd.Denis'79
☎ (610) 647-7187 . . ''Four Star Farm'' Sugartown Rd, Malvern,
PA *19355*

Bowditch MR & MRS Charles F (H Grier Patch) NH'77.Snc.
☎ (203) 655-9652 . . 270 Noroton Av, Darien, CT *06820*

Bowditch MRS E Francis (Anna M Hale) Ws'34.Ncd.
☎ (941) 964-2071 . . Box 421, Boca Grande, FL *33921*

Bowditch MRS Frederic C (Constance Barbey) V'22.Cy.
☎ (617) 449-7044 . . North Hill E401, 865 Central Av, Needham,
MA *02192*

Bowditch MR & MRS James L (Felicity J Sexton) | ☎ (215) 247-3904
Tvb.Y'61 . . . . | 712 St Andrew's
MR Matthew S—at 200 South Av, Weston, MA | Rd, Philadelphia, PA
02193 . . . . | *19118*
MR Andrew R—at ☎ (617) 964-4789 |
75 Hunnewell Av, Newton Corner, MA *02158* . |

Bowditch MR & MRS Nathaniel R (Margaret S | ☎ (215) 248-0753
Parsons) V'56.Temp'78.Ph.Cs.Cr'55.Stan'59 . . . | 5 E Hampton Rd,
MR William P—Roch'89.Mich'93—at | Philadelphia, PA
1400 Worcester Rd, Apt 7204, Framingham, MA | *19118*
01701 . . . . |

Bowditch MR & MRS Patrick F (Ethel D Simonds) | ☎ (307) 733-5785
Ht.Cly.Ncd.H'48 . . . . | 3720 Holly Dv,
MISS Lucy L—Bow'77.Ch'81.Ch'94.Ncd—at | PO Box 96,
☎ (212) 473-3729 . . 16 E 10 St, New York, NY | Teton Village, WY
10003 . . . . | *83025*
MR Frederick S—Cal'80—at ☎ (307) 733-3003 |
PO Box 2180, 8815 S Henrys Rd, Jackson, WY |
83001 . . . . |

Bowditch MRS Phebe A (Phebe P Alexander) V'54.Cs.
☎ (212) 861-7764 . . 150 E 77 St, New York, NY *10021*

Bowditch MR & MRS Richard L 3d (Carol S Beam) Va'84.Stan'81
☎ (718) 499-0332 . . 282 Sixth Av, Brooklyn, NY *11215*

Bowditch MR & MRS Samuel I (Marian P Rogers) Sth'28.H'28
☎ (603) 526-2755 . . 10 Lyon Brook, 100 Lakeside Rd, New London,
NH *03257*

Bowditch MISS Sarah L—Guil'92
☎ (617) 926-6384 . . 140 Hillside Rd, Apt 2, Watertown, MA *02172*

Bowdoin MRS George Temple (Garat—Oates—Betty Rowe) Cly.
☎ (813) 581-2984 . . 1150 Eighth Av SW, Apt 102, Largo, FL *33770*

Bowdoin MISS Helen M—Wheat'60
Box 317, Lincoln, MA *01773*

Bowen MR & MRS Brooks J (Nancy B Rogers) Hlns'70.Ct.Y'71.Va'74
☎ (301) 299-2946 . . 8308 Bells Mill Rd, Potomac, MD *20854*

Bowen MR & MRS Charles C (Calvine S Burnett) V'54.On.Fy.Ty'54
☎ (847) 234-2850 . . 234 N Western Av, Lake Forest, IL *60045*

Bowen MRS Clymer S (Esther S Ely) Ws'23.On.Fy.
☎ (847) 234-1349 . . 105 E Laurel Av, Apt 306, Lake Forest, IL *60045*

Bowen MISS Heather J (John de K 3d) . . . . Married at Ivy, VA
Bolus MR Jay J (Joseph J) . . . . May 25'96

Bowen MR & MRS Howell L (Janice M Feller) Hlns'59
☎ (804) 296-3326 . . "Blueberry Hill" 2200 Owensville Rd,
Charlottesville, VA *22901*

Bowen MR John de K
☎ (804) 293-6400 . . "Clay Hill" 2225 Owensville Rd, Charlottesville,
VA *22901*

Bowen MR & MRS John de K 3d (Constance M Jennings) MichSt'60
☎ (804) 296-9436 . . "The Pocket" 2233 Owensville Rd, Charlottesville,
VA *22901*

Bowen MRS Marshall (Mary M Marshall) Hlns'56
☎ (301) 951-9049 . . 3535 Chevy Chase Lake Dv, Apt 202,
Chevy Chase, MD *20815*

Bowen MRS Morrow (Carolyn N Morrow)
Cal'65.Vh. . . . . | 320 California Terr,
MISS Brooke A . . . . | Pasadena, CA *91105*

Bowen MR & MRS Sidney R 3d (Judith M Hubbard) Ihy.Bost'71.Dth'73
☎ (203) 358-8330 . . 35 Rogers Rd, Stamford, CT *06902*

Bowen COL (RET) Stuart W—Cvc.USA'56.Ariz'63
10441 Englishman Dv, Rockville, MD *20852*

Bowen MR & MRS William R (Julie T Gilmour)
Y'78.WNMex'92 . . . . | ☎ (505) 388-1467
JUNIORS MISS Zoë R—at Stony Brook Sch . . . . . | 1310 Bennett St,
JUNIORS MISS Erica S . . . . | Silver City, NM
| *88061*

Bower MRS Robert T (Just—Jean C Ramsay) V'57 . | ☎ (202) 337-5276
MISS Julia B Just (Azerrad—Julia B Just)—at | 2500 Q St NW,
149 Sullivan St, New York, NY *10012* . . . . . | Washington, DC
| *20007*

Bowers MRS Ann Lind (Ann B Lind)
MaryMt'59.Shcc.Eh.Cly. . . . . | of ☎ (908)234-1334
MISS Hilary G . . . . | "Noway Farm"
| 561 Holland Rd,
| Far Hills, NJ *07931*
| ☎ (212) 759-3950
| 345 E 52 St,
| New York, NY
| *10022*

Bowers MRS Cynthia S-H (Sinclair—Place—
Cynthia Smith-Hutton) . . . . | ☎ (212) 288-2860
MISS Sabrina C Place—Skd'89—at | 145 E 74 St,
330 E 54 St, New York, NY *10022* . . . . | New York, NY
| *10021*

Bowers MRS Dione T L (Dione Todd Lilly) . . . . | ☎ (415) 221-8648
MISS Samantha Todd—at ☎ (415) 753-1974 | 3804 Clay St,
1230 Fifth Av, San Francisco, CA *94122* . . . . . . | San Francisco, CA
| *94118*

Bowers MISS Ellen—V'49.Cly.
☎ (212) 838-3496 . . 200 E 66 St, New York, NY *10021*

Bowers MRS Frances C (Grand-Jean—Frances C | ☎ (847) 234-3057
Bowers) . . . . | 211 Maple Court,
MISS Laura R Grand-Jean—at U of NCar | Lake Forest, IL
Raleigh . . . . | *60045*

Bowers MR & MRS J Ros JR (Deborah E Rogers) Wash'88.Va'87.NCar'93
9 Shaw Rd, Wellesley, MA *02181*

Bowers MRS Lloyd W (Frances R Clow) | ☎ (847) 234-3057
Fy.On.Ncd. . . . . | 211 Maple Court,
MISS Martha—at ☎ (718) 858-0841 | Lake Forest, IL
143 Bond St, Brooklyn, NY *11217* . . . . | *60045*
MR Lloyd W JR—Y'67.Cl'70—at |
☎ (212) TE2-9441 . . 200 E 66 St, New York, |
NY *10021* |

Bowers MISS Page Bostick (J Ros JR) . . . . Born at
Boston, MA Jly 6'96

Bowers MR & MRS Philip J 4th (Jill M Suppes) Shcc.NH'84
☎ (212) 535-2873 . . 402 E 78 St, New York, NY *10021*

Bowers MR Robert C—Hob'79
☎ (860) 646-8956 . . 105 Russell St, Manchester, CT *06040*

Bowers MISS Ruthann—NH'85
☎ (212) 717-4661 . . 211 E 70 St, Apt 7D, New York, NY *10021*

Bowers MR Sampson P
☎ (707) 963-5392 . . 1500 Voorhees Circle, St Helena, CA *94574*

Bowers MR Spotswood D 3d—Y'75 . . of
21 Sunnyside Lane, Lincoln, MA *01773*
☎ (603) 863-6629 . . 21 Wedgewood Dv, Box 929, Grantham,
NH *03753*

Bowes MR & MRS John Garland (Frances Fay) Pcu.Stan'50.H'52
☎ (415) 775-9800 . . 800 Francisco St, San Francisco, CA *94109*

Bowie MR & MRS C Keating (Alice T Forbes) | of ☎ (410)235-6863
V'45.Elk.Md.Mv.P'36.H'39 . . . . | 3900 N Charles St,
MR Walter W W . . . . | Baltimore, MD
| *21218*
| ☎ (410) 226-5371
| "Evergreen Farm"
| Oxford, MD *21654*

Bowie MR & MRS Robert R (Theodosia Chapman)
Wash'33.Mt.Rv.Cw.Mv.Hb.P'31.H'34 . . of
☎ (202) 333-6468 . . 2801 New Mexico Av NW, Apt 410, Washington,
DC *20007*
☎ (410) 822-5803 . . "Stirling" 6918 Traveler's Rest Circle, Easton,
MD *21601*

Bowie MRS Williams C (Gordon—Anne Gordon) . . . . . . Died May 21'96

Bowie MR Williams C—Ub.Eyc.
☎ (508) 627-5561 . . PO Box 961, Edgartown, MA *02539*

Bowles MISS Beatrice V (Michael—Beatrice V | ☎ (415) 776-3010
Bowles) V'65.Fr.Cda. . . . . | 1629 Taylor St,
MR Peter Cannon Michael—Cal'94—at | San Francisco, CA
☎ (404) 634-4975 . . 10301 Brixworth Place | *94133*
NE, Atlanta, GA *30319* . . . . |

Bowles MR & MRS Chester B JR (Outten—Mary S | of ☎ (415)397-4280
Phelan) Ch'47.Y'54 . . . . | 71 Castle St,
MR Nathaniel—at Boîte Postal 2, Olargues, | San Francisco,
France . . . . | CA *94133*
MR Michael T—at 974 Lovell Av, Mill Valley, | ☎ (707) 857-3729
CA *94941* . . . . | "Flower Farm"
| Box 482,
| Geyserville, CA
| *95441*

Bowles MR George McN—Bhm.Gr.Sfy.Cal'52 . . of
☎ (415) 981-4487 . . 285 Telegraph Hill Blvd, San Francisco, CA *94133*
☎ (408) 842-8154 . . "Faraway" 100 Summit Rd, Watsonville,
CA *95076*

Bowles DR & MRS Harry F (Hollis R Kim)
Cal'81.Cal'84.Cal'79.Cal'82.SCal'86
☎ (818) 799-4592 . . 281 Wigmore Dv, Pasadena, CA *91105-3336*

Bowles MR & MRS John L (Kay D Moore) | ☎ (301) 229-7183
Swb'57.Mid'58.Mt.Cvc.Sl.W&L'52 . . . . | 5336 Falmouth Rd,
MR C Houston F . . . . | Bethesda, MD
 | *20816*

Bowles MR & MRS Philip E 3d (Jamie E Nicol) Bard'73.Pcu.Y'73 . . of
☎ (415) 931-7150 . . 3323 Washington St, San Francisco, CA *94118*
☎ (209) 827-3086 . . "Cottonwood Ranch" 11609 S Hereford Rd,
Los Banos, CA *93635*

Bowles MRS Ray M (Smart—Dorothy D Byrnes)
☎ (805) 969-0600 . . 2110 Ten Acre Rd, Santa Barbara, CA *93108*

Bowles MR & MRS W Alexander L (Joanne M | ☎ (301) 986-0483
Algren) Cvc . . . . | 4304 Kentbury Dv,
JUNIORS MISS Christina M . . . . | Bethesda, MD
 | *20814*

Bowling MRS William Glasgow (Violet Whelen) | ☎ (314) 537-0658
BMr'30 . . . . | 15201 Olive Blvd,
DR Townsend W—Wash'61.Mid'68.Y'76—at | Apt 254,
☎ (210) 492-9803 . . 2919 Meadow Thrush St, | Chesterfield, MO
San Antonio, TX *78231* . . . . | *63017*

Bowman MRS A Smith (Mary W Lee) Cly.Sl.
☎ (703) 528-9091 . . 1260 Crest Lane, McLean, VA *22101*

Bowman MISS Alexandra Kip—Wit'88 . . see G A Buffum

Bowman MR Bradford L . . see R S Scott

Bowman MR & MRS Fielding L (Nancy H Ober) Va'48
☎ (203) 966-2402 . . 5 Canaan Close, New Canaan, CT *06840-4928*

Bowman MR J Hunt 3d—Nath'lH'75 . . see R S Scott

Bowman MRS John B (Belsterling—Lovatt—Mary | ☎ (610) 645-8852
T Innes) M.Me.Sdg.Ncd. . . . . | 1400 Waverly Rd,
  MISS Jean I Belsterling—Pa'74.Drex'76—at | Blair 123,
  ☎ (609) 983-1119 . . 214 Shady Lane, Marlton, | Gladwyne, PA
  NJ *08053* . . . . | *19035*

Bowman MR & MRS John S (Carolyn Lawley) | ☎ (334) 281-2251
Ala'57.Ala'58.Ala'60 . . . . | 2455 Cherokee Dv,
MISS Mildred L . . . . | Montgomery, AL
 | *36111*

Bowman MRS John Webster (Eleanor Noyes Hempstone) GeoW'79.Cvc.
☎ (301) 652-4251 . . 5206 Wilson Lane, Bethesda, MD *20814*

Bowman MR Lindsey C—Cal'79.Cal'79.Pac'87
see Dilatory Domiciles

Bowman MR & MRS Richard P (Donna-Lindsey Cochran)
Cal'51.Bur.Pcu.Fr.Cal'50
☎ (415) 344-4691 . . 820 Eucalyptus Av, Hillsborough, CA *94010*

Bowman MR & MRS Samuel A 3d (Fowler—Grace O Grasselli)
Rdc'55.Ri.Cv.K.P'59 . . of
☎ (212) 744-5332 . . 142 E 71 St, New York, NY *10021*
☎ (914) 677-8655 . . Maple Av, PO Box 459, Millbrook, NY *12545*

Bowman MR & MRS Scott (Sarah B Schade)
☎ (317) 284-2566 . . 1901 N Bob O Link Dv, Muncie, IN *47304*

Bowman MR Thomas Merritt—Nev'66 . . of
☎ (808) 261-7177 . . 177 Ohana St, Kailua, HI *96734*
☎ (808) 696-2166 . . "Sand Buster" 84-965 Farrington H'way, Makaha,
HI *96792*

Bowman MR Timothy W . . see R S Scott

Bowman MISS Tracey (Geczik—Tracey Bowman) Edin'79 . . see R S Scott

Bowring MASTER Boyd Oliver (Douglas B) . . . . Born at
St Louis, MO Feb 29'96

Bowring MRS Charles W 3d (Julie Webber) Van'54 | ☎ (561) 278-1076
MISS Victoria M—at ☎ (615) 292-0427 | 27 East Rd,
4124 Wallace Lane, Nashville, TN *37215* . . . . | Delray Beach, FL
MR Charles W—at 3400 S Eagle St, Apt 201, | *33483*
Aurora, CO *80014* . . . . |

Bowring MR & MRS Douglas B (Emily S Godfrey) SantaC'86.Ga'86
☎ (314) 993-5658 . . 54 Loren Woods, St Louis, MO *63124*

Bowring MRS E Bonner (Helen Hulbert) Eyc.Cly.
☎ (508) 627-8728 . . PO Box 778, Edgartown, MA *02539*

Bowron DR & MRS J Shelby JR (Melinda Carnathan) Ala'73
1120 Hancock Dv NE, Atlanta, GA *30306-2514*

Bowron MR Paul J JR
2139 Avenida De La Playa, La Jolla, CA *92037*

Boyce MRS E Gillet (Virginia Davis) Gchr'28.Cy.
☎ (410) 823-2581 . . 1018 Wagner Rd, Ruxton, MD *21204*

Boyce MRS Edith T (Edith H Townsend) Gv.
☎ (410) 823-5602 . . 375 Old Trail, Baltimore, MD *21212*

Boyce MR & MRS E Grayson (Dorothy E Cooper) | ☎ (410) 321-0945
RMWmn'65.Md.Elk.HampSydney'63 . . . . | 7919 Sherwood Av,
MR E Gillet 2d . . . . | Baltimore, MD
JUNIORS MR G Graham . . . . | *21204*

Boyce MRS John C G (Barbara A Cobb) Sth'39.Cy.
☎ (410) 366-4613 . . 4300 N Charles St, Apt 3F, Baltimore,
MD *21218-1046*

Boyce MR & MRS John C G JR (Ann F Hagerty) | ☎ (410) 472-9069
Gv.Va'67 . . . . | PO Box 65,
MISS L Reid—Va'93.Gv. | 15408 Duncan Hill
JUNIORS MR Collis H G . . . . | Rd, Butler, MD
JUNIORS MR Sandford C G . . . . | *21023*

Boyce MR & MRS Sandford C (Mary P Bisig) | ☎ (847) 295-2192
Regis'74.Va'71.Va'74 . . . . | 1216 Edgewood Rd,
JUNIORS MISS M Gwendolyn . . . . | Lake Forest, IL
 | *60045*

Boyd MR & MRS A Shapleigh 3d (Jennifer H Dodge) | ☎ (941) 485-7530
So'62 . . . . | 840 The Esplanade,
MISS Jennifer D—So'88 . . . . | Apt 602, Venice, FL
 | *34292*

Boyd MR & MRS A Shapleigh 4th (Elizabeth L Garcia)
So'85.So'85.MidTennSt'87
☎ (615) 598-2800 . . 735 University Av, Sewanee, TN *37383-1000*

Boyd MR Allen R—P'55.JHop'60
☎ (941) 779-2122 . . 2101 Bay Dv N, PO Box 117, Bradenton Beach,
FL *34217*

Boyd MR Andrew C—NH'91
☎ (617) 859-7257 . . 27 Bay State Rd, Apt 6, Boston, MA *02115*

Boyd MR & MRS Crosby N JR (Julia H Wallace) | ☎ (313) 882-0460
Cvc.P'59 . . . . | 460 Rivard Blvd,
MISS Barbara A . . . . | Grosse Pointe, MI
MISS Jennifer L . . . . | *48230*

Boyd MRS David M (Louise C Van Deventer) . . . . . | ☎ (205) 979-9366
MISS Barbara J—at ☎ (616) 471-1179 | 1517 Ashley Wood
4170 E Tudor Rd, Berrien Springs, MI *49103* . . | Circle,
 | Vestavia Hills, AL
 | *35216*

Boyd MR & MRS Edwin T JR (Valentine—Mary Pratt) Cly.Lynch'50 . . . . | of ☎ (561)231-1999 551 Indian Harbor Rd, Vero Beach, FL *32963*
MR M Pratt Valentine . . . . | ☎ (804) 282-6998 300 Ridge Rd, Apt 71, Richmond, VA *23229*

Boyd MR & MRS George 5th (Sandra M Barr) Snc.Cc.W.Cspa.Wash'60
☎ (215) VE6-4549 . . 8111 Eastern Av, Wyndmoor, PA *19038*

Boyd DR & MRS Herschell H (Marili Podliessnie) Van'52
☎ (206) 365-5720 . . The Highlands, Seattle, WA *98177*

Boyd MRS Ingram F JR (Adeline E Smith) V'32.Cy.Nd.Csn.
☎ (314) 727-3525 . . 6400 Ellenwood Av, Clayton, MO *63105*

Boyd MR & MRS J Hallam JR (Ann B Wilder) Y'56
☎ (901) 327-0582 . . 98 Goodwyn Place, Memphis, TN *38111*

Boyd MR & MRS J Hallam 3d (Elizabeth G Daughdrill) Rhodes'89.Miss'87
☎ (901) 458-9189 . . 278 Palisade St, Memphis, TN *38111*

Boyd MASTER John Bradley (Peter L B) . . . . Born at Boston, MA May 9'96

Boyd MR & MRS Lew F (A Cary Stratton) Rdc'67.H.'67 . . . . | ☎ (508) 462-2436 210 Middle Rd, Newbury, MA *01922*
JUNIORS MISS Caroline S . . . . |

Boyd MRS Linda K (Linda Keady) . . . . | ☎ (914) 939-7896 61 Greenway Circle, Rye Brook, NY *10573*
MR James W JR—Mid'85—at ☎ (617) 424-8210 249 W Newton St, Apt 2, Boston, MA *02116* . . |

Boyd MR Nicholas G K JR . . . . Died at San Francisco, CA Dec 17'95

Boyd MRS Nicholas G K JR (Margaret V Clifton) Sfy.Tcy. ⚓ . . . . | ☎ (415) 931-9277 2619 Baker St, San Francisco, CA *94123*
DR Nicholas G K 3d—Wy'94 . . . . |

Boyd MR & MRS Peter L B (Bettine S Bikle) Salem'85.Bost'86
☎ (617) 241-0278 . . Constitution Quarters, Apt 3107, 42—8 St, Charlestown, MA *02129-4219*

Boyd MR & MRS Robert S (Katherine D Royes) Wes'87.Mid'83
☎ (011-44-181) 747-3601 . . 146 Park Rd, Chiswick, London W4 3HP, England

Boyd MR & MRS Thomas M (Jane E Clayton) Ph.Ty'62.Hart'72.WNe'83
☎ (215) 922-2454 . . 245 Delancey St, Philadelphia, PA *19106*

Boyd MR & MRS William JR (H Ann Willets) S.Y'37 . . of
☎ (412) 741-6569 . . Woodland Rd, Sewickley, PA *15143*
☎ (011-39-55) 540969 . . ''La Casellina'' via Bosconi, Fiesole, Italy

Boyd DR & MRS William D 2d (Carmel H Onofrio) Md'68.Md'67.GeoW'71 . . . . | ☎ (301) 884-8100 PO Box 7, Chaptico, MD *20621*
MISS Amber M . . . . |
MR Michael T . . . . |
JUNIORS MISS Hannah L . . . . |

Boyd MR & MRS William S (Nicholas—Katherine F Elkins) Bur.Pcu.Stan'38 . . . . | ☎ (415) DI4-0926 130 Bridge Rd, Hillsborough, CA *94010*
MISS Marie L . . . . |
MR William E . . . . |
MR David S . . . . |

Boyden MR & MRS Thomas N (Susan B Dalton) On.Wms'63.Ch'68 . . . . | ☎ (847) 234-9438 104 E Westleigh Rd, Lake Forest, IL *60045*
MISS Amy D—at Wooster . . . . |
MR Johnston D—Denis'94 . . . . |

Boyden MR W Lincoln 3d—Tv.H'53 . . . . | ☎ (617) 484-4091 24 Oak St, Belmont, MA *02178*
MISS Ruth E—at ☎ (617) 893-5572 111 Woerd Av, Waltham, MA *02154* . . . . |
MR Geoffrey L—at 52 Foster St, Cambridge, MA *02138* . . . . |

Boyer MR & MRS David C (Lydia A Richards) CtCol'53.Wil.Cw.Ncd.P'52
☎ (302) 652-6852 . . 5701 Kennett Pike, Wilmington, DE *19807*

Boyer MR F Alger JR—Cal'92 . . see D H Carnahan JR

Boyer MISS G Alexandra—Denis'93 . . see D H Carnahan JR

Boyer MR & MRS Georges C (Marion Talmage) Col'77.Shcc.Eh.Cly.DU'74.DU'76 . . of
☎ (212) 752-6170 . . 200 E 66 St, Apt B1005, New York, NY *10021*
☎ (908) 781-6553 . . Box 567, Far Hills, NJ *07931*

Boyer MR & MRS John (Jane D Rouillion) BMr'58.Y'54.Cl'57 . . . . | ☎ (860) 868-2723 PO Box 1021, Washington, CT *06793*
MISS Laura L—at 70 Waverly Park Rd, Branford, CT *06405* . . . . |
MISS Carol R—*see Dilatory Domiciles* . . . . |
MR Bryan R—*see Dilatory Domiciles* . . . . |

Boyer MR & MRS John W JR (Barbara Hoyt) M.Va'50
☎ (610) 688-7182 . . 539 St Davids Av, St Davids, PA *19087*

Boyer MR & MRS Markley H JR (Lindsay Soutter) P'83.P'81
☎ (718) 858-4119 . . 222 Clinton St, Brooklyn, NY *11201*

Boyer MR & MRS Willis B JR (Wilson—Martha Wright) Ursul'68.Cwr'71.Tv.Rr.Y'62.Pa'71
☎ (216) 247-2910 . . 10 Farwood Dv, Moreland Hills, OH *44022*

Boykin MASTER Coulter Stone (Robert I M) . . . . Born Jun 12'95

Boykin MISS Rebecca E (Schwaner—Rebecca E Boykin) Wesley'75.Loy'81.Gi . . . . | ☎ (301) 271-2524 ''Bucks Horn'' 15 Mountain Rd, Thurmont, MD *21788*
JUNIORS MR Mark A Schwaner . . . . |

Boykin MR & MRS Robert I M (Marcia Fail) . . . . | ☎ (970) 925-3389 926 Willoughby Way, Aspen, CO *81612*
JUNIORS MR Robert I M JR . . . . |

Boykin MR Samuel M (late Samuel M) . . . . . . Married at Palm Beach, FL Pendergrast MISS Mary P (late Lawrence H) . . . . Apr 13'96

Boykin MR & MRS Samuel M (Mary P Pendergrast) Memp'61.BtP.Evg.Cybm.W&L'49
☎ (561) 863-9828 . . 285 Jamaica Lane, Palm Beach, FL *33480*

Boykin MR Samuel M III—Ala'84
☎ (404) 355-4354 . . 2265 Riada Dv NW, Atlanta, GA *30305*

Boykin MRS Sandra R (Williams—Cartier—Sandra J Rousseau)
☎ (561) 659-3224 . . 250 Kawama Lane, Palm Beach, FL *33480*

Boylan MR & MRS Russell B (Jennifer Hill) LSU'73
3578 Westbury Rd, Birmingham, AL *35223-1469*

Boyle MR & MRS Michael G (Valerie H Hertz) FIT'82
☎ (908) 530-6399 . . 79 Lake Av, Fair Haven, NJ *07704*

Boyle MRS Ursula G (Ursula M Gahan) . . . . | ☎ (617) 723-2980
MR Robert K JR—Mass'86.Bab'95 . . . . | 2 Hawthorne Place,
MR John M—Y.'85.Cl'91—at | Apt 12E, Boston,
☎ (212) 570-9540 . . 353 E 78 St, Apt 12D, | MA *02114*
New York, NY *10021* . . . . |
Boynton MISS Meghan B—Tufts'87
677 W Ferry St, Buffalo, NY *14222*
Boynton MR & MRS Oren K (Elizabeth M | ☎ (860) 567-0662
Van Winkle) Pa'62 ⛵ | 211 North St,
MR William M—Bard'86—at ☎ (415) 642-7968 | PO Box 924,
605 Texas St, San Francisco, CA *94107* . . . . . . | Litchfield, CT *06759*
JUNIORS MR Alden K . . . . |
Boynton MRS Perry S (Mary E Heiss) Ws'32.Cs.
☎ (212) 734-6367 . . 49 E 73 St, New York, NY *10021*
Boynton MR & MRS Perry S 3d (Pauline W Hotchkiss) DU'71.Col'73
☎ (908) 221-1338 . . 20 Olcott Av, Bernardsville, NJ *07924*
Boyse MR & MRS Matthew G (Eleanore H Kuhn)
Tul'79.JHop'85.Hav'79.Cl'85
☎ (011-48-2) 642-1990 . . American Embassy, Warsaw, Poland,
Dept of State, Washington, DC *20521-5010*
Bozarth MR & MRS Robert S (Marsha Ketcham) | ☎ (804) 288-3695
Swb'67.Va'67.Va'75 | 1103 E Durwood
MR Howard A—Va'93—at ☎ (703) 892-1689 | Crescent, Richmond,
1111 Army-Navy Dv, Arlington, VA *22202* . . . . | VA *23229*
JUNIORS MR Robert B . . . . |
Bozorth MR & MRS Squire N (Louise C Mathews) | ☎ (914) 723-2398
Bnd'65.C.Cs.Ore'58.Nu'61 . . . . | 36 Olmsted Rd,
MISS Caroline R . . . . | Scarsdale, NY
MR Squire M . . . . | *10583*
Bracken MRS Barbara R (Barbara J Rice) Ac. . . . . | ☎ (303) 449-6148
MISS Mary E R—at ☎ (303) 939-9068 | 2616 Crestridge
2220—16 St, Boulder, CO *80302* . . . . | Court, Boulder, CO
MR David L—Box 972, Kilauea, Kauai, HI *96754* | *80302*
MR Thomas J . . . . |
Brackenridge MRS Belinda A (Ward—Wiesen— | ☎ (212) 288-1530
Belinda A Brackenridge) Cly.Mds. . . . . | 850 Park Av,
MR Gavin B Wiesen. . . . . | New York, NY
| *10021*
Brackenridge MRS Caroline L (Caroline D Lynch) . | ☎ (212) 288-8864
MISS Anne K—at Skidmore . . . . | 225 E 73 St,
| New York, NY
| *10021*
Brackenridge MR & MRS Gavin (Mary Kathryn | 493 Valley Rd,
McDonnell) Mds.Ri.Pa'69 . . . . | New Canaan, CT
JUNIORS MISS Kathryn F . . . . | *06840*
Brackett MR & MRS Joshua (Barbara H Amberger) | ☎ (508) 546-7498
H'56. . . . . | Big Parker's Pit,
MISS Anna C—Bates'87—at 128 E 4 St, Apt 2, | Rowe Av, Box 706,
New York, NY *10003* . . . . | Rockport, MA
MR Nathan C—Wis'91 . . . . | *01966*
Bradbury MRS Charles R (Charlotte M Lyon)
☎ (606) 266-9141 . . 3625 Humphrey Lane, Lexington, KY *40502-3603*
Bradbury MR John Randolph JR—Eyc.Buck'92 . . see M S Brown
Bradbury MR & MRS Reginald Lyon (Karen F Doyle) SCar'91.Ky'79
☎ (502) 894-8127 . . 4014 Waterford Circle, Apt 4, Louisville,
KY *40207-5269*

Bradbury MR & MRS Samuel 3d (Sarah H Vanneman) Leh'38
☎ (215) 984-8789 . . Cathedral Village C205, 600 E Cathedral Rd,
Philadelphia, PA *19128*
Bradbury MISS Sarah Riddle—Cr'95 . . see M S Brown
Braden MR & MRS William (Lachlan M Porter) Cly.Ncd.Cl'41
☎ (516) 367-9730 . . 26 E Gate Rd, Lloyd Harbor, Huntington,
NY *11743*
Bradford MR & MRS Charles E (Susan J Connally) | ☎ (215) 836-7533
Rc.Pn.P'64.Pa'70 . . . . | 7909 Pine Rd,
MISS Amanda Crowninshield—at U of Pa. . . . . . | Chestnut Hill, PA
MISS Susan Kendall . . . . | *19038*
Bradford MR & MRS James C JR (Lillian F | ☎ (615) 383-2093
Robertson) Van'63.P'55 . . . . | 530 Belle Meade
MR James C 3d—Mid'94 . . . . | Blvd, Nashville, TN
MR Bryan R—at Princeton . . . . | *37205*
Bradford MRS Judith R (Sadler—Judith S Rübel) . . | ☎ (617) 229-9934
MISS Rebecca E . . . . | 49 Arborwood Dv,
| Burlington, MA
| *01803*
Bradford JUNIORS MR Luke . . see J B Hannum JR
Bradford MRS M Heun (Margaret C Heun) Sl.
☎ (301) 656-4631 . . 5506 Glenwood Rd, Bethesda, MD *20817*
Bradford MR & MRS Robert W (Jeanette L Jackson)
Sth'85.Mich'91.P'84.Dth'89
☎ (313) 665-2518 . . 1207 Gardner St, Ann Arbor, MI *48104-4320*
Bradford JUNIORS MR Seth . . see J B Hannum JR
Bradford MRS William S C (Barbara V V Bennett) Ncd.
Pickering Dam Rd, RD 2, Phoenixville, PA *19460*
Bradlee MR Frederic
☎ (212) UN1-0312 . . 161 E 75 St, New York, NY *10021*
Bradley MR Cameron
☎ (207) 963-2615 . . "Reverie" Rte 186, Gouldsboro, ME *04607*
Bradley MR & MRS Charles D (Mary P Morey) | ☎ (203) 777-2211
Br'60.Va'63 . . . . | 27 Laurel Rd,
MISS Natalie P—OWes'94 . . . . | Hamden, CT *06517*
MR Tyler B H—AmU'92—at ☎ (212) 410-1549 |
345 E 93 St, New York, NY *10128* . . . . |
Bradley MR & MRS E Michael (Judith A Thompson) | of ☎ (212)472-2494
Un.Ri.Lic.Ng.Plg.Cly.Y'61.Va'64 . . . . | 125 E 72 St,
MR Samuel A—☎ (212) 794-1663 . . . . | New York, NY
| *10021*
| ☎ (516) 653-6907
| 27 Beach Lane,
| Quogue, NY *11959*
Bradley MR & MRS E Tremain JR (Carol U Harris) | ☎ (614) 587-0698
RI'62.Ill'64 . . . . | 348 Cedar St,
MISS Julie H—at Allegheny Coll . . . . | Granville, OH *43023*
Bradley MR Frederick W—Cal'58.GoldG'66 . . . . . . | ☎ (415) 492-8369
MR Craig H. . . . . | "Casa Marinwood"
| 30 Grande Paseo,
| San Rafael, CA
| *94903-1545*
Bradley MR & MRS George C JR (L Spencer Boyd) Y'77.Y'75
☎ (860) 526-3900 . . 82 W Main St, Chester, CT *06412*
Bradley MR & MRS J Douglas (Elizabeth W Brown) Ty'89.Ty'89
☎ (703) 684-9243 . . 730 S 26 St, Arlington, VA *22202*

Bradley MR & MRS James P (Herman—Lynch—
  Barbara R McCoun) CtCol'64.Bridgept'64 . . . . . | ☎ (203) 259-6349
    MISS Alexandra D Lynch . . . . | 111 Cherry Lane,
    MISS Lindsay R Lynch . . . . | Fairfield, CT *06430*
    MISS Elizabeth T Lynch—at Skidmore . . . . . .
    JUNIORS MR Charles H Lynch—at St George's
Bradley MRS James W (Helen L Eldredge) Cr'53.Cr'55.Myf.
  ☎ (617) 899-8043 . . 32 Cart Path Rd, Weston, MA *02193*
Bradley MRS John Freeman (Junia T Mason) Ncd.
  ☎ (603) 778-8850 . . 17 Hampton Rd, Apt 121, Exeter, NH *03833*
Bradley MR John L . . . . Died Jun 1'96
Bradley MRS John L (Gabrielle Wright) Bur.Cly.
  ☎ (415) DI3-1909 . . 711 Hayne Rd, Hillsborough, CA *94010*
Bradley MR & MRS John M (Jane D Carpenter) Rdc'49.Sbc.Ec.Chi.Mit'47
  ☎ (508) 526-1889 . . 9 Eagle Head Rd, Manchester, MA *01944*
Bradley MR & MRS Michael T (Melissa E Biggs)
  Y'89.Cl'93.Un.Ng.Bcs.Va'88.Va'94.Cl'96
  ☎ (212) 628-3790 . . 200 E 71 St, New York, NY *10021*
Bradley MR & MRS Montgomery S (Joanne Freytag)
  L&C'55.Mt.Sl.Hn.H'40 . . of
  ☎ (301) 229-5161 . . 4974 Sentinel Dv, Bethesda, MD *20816*
  1919 Gulf Shore Blvd N, Naples, FL *34102*
Bradley DR & MRS Robert H JR (Patricia B Pray) | ☎ (215) 283-7371
  Pc.Ncd.Wms'36.H'40 . . . . | 1403 Foulkeways,
  DR Peter P—Wms'70.H'74—at | Sumneytown Pike,
  ☎ (215) 242-9735 . . 201 W Evergreen Av, | Gwynedd, PA *19436*
  Philadelphia, PA *19118* . . . . |
Bradley MR & MRS Robert H 3d (Nancy H Alesbury) | ☎ (617) 237-4370
  Gchr'69.Cy.Wms'66.Tufts'71 . . . . | 61 Fox Hill Rd,
  MISS Katharine H—at Dartmouth . . . . | Wellesley, MA
  MISS Susan P—at Williams . . . . | *02181*
  JUNIORS MR Robert H 4th . . . . |
Bradley MR & MRS Robert L (Virginia H Whitney) | ☎ (617) 749-2139
  Curry'70 . . . . | "Beechwood"
  MISS Christina H . . . . | 89 Fearing Rd,
  MR Alexander R . . . . | Hingham, MA
  JUNIORS MR Robert L JR . . . . | *02043*
Bradley MR & MRS Robert M (Edna L Gilfillan) | ☎ (714) 549-0978
  SCal'56.Cal'58 . . . . | 2030 Goldeneye
  MR Brian Carter—at U of Nebraska . . . . | Place, Costa Mesa,
    | CA *92626*
Bradley MR Stephen T—Dth'84
  9 Mead Ridge Rd, Ridgefield, CT *06877-4824*
Bradley MR & MRS Thomas A JR (Elise F | ☎ (516) 922-5890
  Cavanagh) Pr.Ford'39 . . . . | 27 Mill River Rd,
  MISS Belle C . . . . | Oyster Bay, NY
    | *11771*
Bradley MR & MRS W Waldo (Jenny L Morse) Ga'64.Ga'56
  ☎ (912) 354-3260 . . Sylvan Island, Savannah, GA *31404*
Bradley MR & MRS Wilson JR (Ramsay—Barbara J Boid)
  UWash'58.Vh.CalTech'50
  ☎ (805) 684-1343 . . PO Box 480, Carpinteria, CA *93013*
Bradshaw MRS Charles B (Sarah F Robbins) V'45.Ncd.
  ☎ (617) 277-8789 . . 1550 Beacon St, Apt 6J, Brookline, MA *02146*
Bradshaw MRS John H (Laura F Ottis)
  ☎ (215) 794-8439 . . "Partridge Hall Farm" Lahaska, PA *18931*

Bradshaw MRS Thornton F (West—Patricia J Salter) K.Ri.Mt.Cs.Vh.
  ☎ (212) 980-1063 . . 435 E 52 St, New York, NY *10022*
Bradway MR & MRS Bruce M (Eleanore M Zeiss) | of ☎ (610)649-5952
  Cal'43.Ncd.P.'43 . . . . | 1643 Monk Rd,
  MR Jonathan C . . . . | Box 1, Gladwyne,
  MR Eric A . . . . | PA *19035*
    | Camp Wipigaki,
    | Lac du Flambeau,
    | WI *54538*
Brady MR & MRS Anthony N (Page B Merrill) WmSth'81.Pc.Shcc.Mid'79
  ☎ (215) 233-5646 . . 6016 Cricket Rd, Flourtown, PA *19031*
Brady MR & MRS Christopher D (Janet V Stickley) Mid'77.Mid'77
  Far Hills, NJ *07931*
Brady MR D Norman (Dunlop—L Courtney Stanley)
  ☎ (508) 627-4355 . . 40 S Summer St, PO Box 5075, Edgartown,
  MA *02539-5075*
Brady MR & MRS George T (Hope C V Tarpey) Pcu.Cp.Fr.Ncd.Dar.SFr'32
  ☎ (415) 346-3334 . . 1200 California St, Apt 7B, San Francisco,
  CA *94109*
Brady MR & MRS James C JR (Joan Babcock) | ☎ (908) 234-0228
  Srr.R.Eh.Y'57 . . . . | "Mill House"
  MISS Nonie—at ☎ (303) 444-2624 | Far Hills, NJ *07931*
  1110 Poplar Av, Boulder, CO *80304* . . . .
Brady MR & MRS James H (Julia L Trotman) H'89.Ayc.Ny.
  ☎ (617) 876-3668 . . 205 Mt Auburn St, Apt 2B, Cambridge, MA *02138*
Brady MR John—Buf'52 . . . . | ☎ (716) 636-1370
  MISS Marion M—at 10—7 St, Buffalo, NY *14201* | 2330 Maple Rd, Apt
    | 183, Williamsville,
    | NY *14221*
Brady MR & MRS Nicholas F (Katherine L Douglas)
  Srr.Rcn.Eh.Ln.Y'52.H'54
  ☎ (410) 476-3230 . . PO Box 156, Trappe, MD *21673*
Brady MISS Patricia J
  ☎ (415) 388-5531 . . 5 Park Terr, Mill Valley, CA *94941*
Brady MISS Robin E (late John A) . . . . Married at Southport, CT
  Mead DR Lawrence M 3d (Lawrence M JR) . . . . May 11'96
Brady MRS S Stansbury (Francisca Fargas) . . . . | ☎ (408) 267-0415
  MR Matthew J . . . . | 4070 Luneta Dv,
  MRS Muriel P Townzen (Muriel P Brady) . . . | San Jose, CA *95136*
Brady MR & MRS William J JR (Lois S Barrett) Rc.Pc.H'48
  108 W Moreland Av, Philadelphia, PA *19118*
Brady MR William J B 3d—Pc.P'87
  ☎ (415) 674-9779 . . 2438 Clay St, San Francisco, CA *94115*
Braff MR & MRS Douglas P (Margaret E Williams)
  Van'90.Pr.Rc.Myf.Van'82
  ☎ (212) 628-5504 . . 511 E 80 St, New York, NY *10021*
Braga MRS B Rionda (Mary S Booker) K.Cly.Cda.
  ☎ (540) 687-6241 . . Oakendale Farm, PO Box 389, Middleburg,
  VA *20118*
Braga MR & MRS David J (Marcia L Zimrin) | ☎ (212) 737-3511
  Pratt'74.Fic.H'67 . . . . | 40 E 83 St,
  MISS Caroline L S . . . . | New York, NY
    | *10028*
Braga MRS George A (Gioia I Marconi) . . . . Died at
  Englewood, NJ Jly 15'96
Bragdon MR Brooks J—Wms'68
  ☎ (315) 654-2671 . . "Stone House" Cape Vincent, NY *13618*

Bragdon MR David L—H'82
2566 NW Marshall St, Portland, OR *97210*

Bragdon MR & MRS Paul E (Nancy E Horton) Minn'51.C.Aht'50.Y'53
☎ (503) 774-7054 . . 7535 SE 31 Av, Portland, OR *97202*

Bragdon MR & MRS Peter J (Lois E Andrews) NCar'88.Aht'84.Y'91.Stan'93
7921 SE 31 Av, Portland, OR *97202*

Braham MR & MRS W Walter JR (I Ann Haines) | ☎ (412) 963-9856
Gchr'58.Fcg.P'51.H'56 ⛵ . . . . | 151 North Dv,
MISS Nancy S . . . . | Pittsburgh, PA
MR Robert B . . . . | *15238*

Braid MR & MRS Niels H (Margaret C W Larned)
☎ (410) 343-1086 . . 20315 Middletown Rd, Freeland, MD *21053*

Brainard MRS Harold J (Ruth H Bickford) . . . . | of ☎ (716)885-1275
MISS Joan B—Box 10001, Stanford, CA *93409* . | 32 Highland Av,
| Buffalo, NY *14222*
| ☎ (905) 834-4269
| RR 1, Lorraine,
| House 1145,
| Port Colborne,
| Ontario L3K 5V3,
| Canada

Brainard MR & MRS Peter B (Berl—Rosalie D | ☎ (860) 242-0874
Sellar) Hart'65 . . . . | 23 Duncaster Rd,
MISS Pamela H—at 68 Otter Cove Rd, | Bloomfield, CT
Old Saybrook, CT *06475* . . . . | *06002*
MR Peter B JR—*see Dilatory Domiciles* . . . .
MR Newton C—*see Dilatory Domiciles* . . . .
MISS Rita S Berl—Box 5025, Larkspur, CA
94977 . . . .
MR E Ennalls Berl 4th—at New York, NY . .
MR Charles S W Berl—Box 691, Newport, RI
02840 . . . .
MR Christopher N Berl—Box 691, Newport,
RI *02840* . . . .

Brainard MRS Walter M (Elizabeth Laufman) Pg.
☎ (412) 681-1213 . . 3955 Bigelow Blvd, Pittsburgh, PA *15213*

Brainerd MRS Anne E (Anne Eddison) V'51.H'55 . .
☎ (617) 576-1473 . . 169 Upland Rd, Cambridge, MA *02140*
☎ (802) 333-4208 . . ''Juniper Patch'' RR 1, Box 265, Fairlee, VT *05045*

Brainerd MISS Elizabeth B—Y'82.Cs.
☎ (212) 580-6628 . . 164 W 79 St, New York, NY *10024*

Brainerd MR & MRS Stanford H (Hart—Wendy | ☎ (212) 348-3559
Morgan Smith) SL'60.Rc.Cs.Cda.Y'53.H'56 . . . | 1192 Park Av,
MR Brooks R—V'84 ☎ (206) 526-5227 | New York, NY
1900 NE 68 St, Seattle, WA *98115* . . . . | *10128*
MISS Hilary B Hart—Y'86 . . . .
MR Howard S Hart—Mass'88 . . . .

Brakeley MR & MRS George A JR (Roxana Byerly) Rcp.Mt.Myf.Pa'38 . . of
☎ (203) 966-6906 . . 26 Hathaway Common, 185 South Av,
New Canaan, CT *06840*
☎ (941) 992-1053 . . 253 Lely Beach Blvd, Bonita Springs, FL *33923*

Brakenridge MRS John W (Brooke Hollister) . . . . . | ☎ (803) 768-2348
MISS Wendy H—at 828 Centennial Av, Apt 3, | 3311 The Lookout,
Sewickley, PA *15143* . . . . | Johns Island, SC
MISS Bonnie S—at 407 Timber Lane, Sewickley, | *29455*
PA *15143* . . . . |

Bramhall MRS Curtis (Ivison—Caroline C Curtis) Vh.
☎ (818) 799-0011 . . 955 S Pasadena Av, Pasadena, CA *91105*

Bramwell MR & MRS William M JR (Thyra | ☎ (212) 289-2453
Elizabeth Reed) BMr'62.Cl'67.Un.Bm.Ne.Plg. | 1225 Park Av,
Pl.Cs.Cda.Ncd.Y.'54.H'57 . . . . | New York, NY
MISS Hilary F—at Princeton . . . . | *10128*
JUNIORS MR Austin W—at Yale . . . . |

Branch MRS Benjamin C (Joan Swan) Bgt.Cly.Dar.
☎ (914) 234-3103 . . 180 Baldwin Rd, Mt Kisco, NY *10549*

Branch MISS Suzanne
☎ (212) 628-9677 . . 435 E 79 St, New York, NY *10021*

Brander MR & MRS Douglas K (Susan B Grandis) Mass'79.Va'82.Cw.
20 Summit Av, Hull, MA *02045*

Brander MR Thomas W JR
☎ (713) 781-6379 . . 2277 Winrock Blvd, Bldg 2, Apt 216, Houston,
TX *77057*

Brandi MR & MRS James H (Linda O Beard) | ☎ (212) BU8-1212
Dyc.Cly.Mds.Y'70.H'75 . . . . | 215 E 72 St,
MISS Katharine H—at Yale . . . . | New York, NY
JUNIORS MR Peter B—at Riverdale Sch . . . . | *10021*

Brandon MRS B Douglas JR (Elizabeth L Riggs) Ark'55
☎ (501) 666-6313 . . 5000 Country Club Blvd, Little Rock, AR *72207*

Brandt MRS C Patteson (Joan M Walsh)
☎ (212) 473-7874 . . 15 Gramercy Park S, New York, NY *10003*

Brandt MR & MRS Frederick A (Margaret Delafield) | ☎ (518) 785-9553
Stan'64.Stan'63.LIU'71.ArizSt'76.SUNY'86 . . . | 11 Vandenburgh
MR Matthew A—at 1750 Swann St NW, | Lane, Latham, NY
Washington, DC *20009* . . . . | *12110*
CAPT Edward R—USAF. . . . . |

Brandt MISS Jessamine
☎ (610) 664-4696 . . 76 Raynham Rd, Merion Station, PA *19066*

Brandt MR Kenneth C—AmU'77
☎ (410) 837-4593 . . 440 Grindall St, Baltimore, MD *21230*

Brandt MR & MRS Peter C (Laura S Burwick) Bnd'83.Nu'87
11 Hickory Dv, Stamford, CT *06902*

Brannan MISS Deborah C . . see MRS J H Heroy

Branscomb MR & MRS Lewis McA (Anne Wells)
NCar'49.H'51.GeoW'62.C.Duke'45.H'49
☎ (508) 369-1878 . . 155 Mildred Circle, Concord, MA *01742*

Bransome DR & MRS Edwin D JR (Janet L Williams) | ☎ (803) 649-5150
Y'54.Cl'58 . . . . | 621 Magnolia Lane,
MISS April G . . . . | Aiken, SC *29801*
MR Edwin D 3d—at 26160 Laguna Court, |
Apt 221, Laguna Hills, CA *92656* . . . . . . |

Branson MRS J Holmes (Phoebe W Fuller) Ncd.
☎ (804) 462-5441 . . PO Box 126, Lancaster, VA *22503*

Brant MR & MRS John R JR (Wendella L Kelsey) . . see MRS C C Kelsey

Braselman MR & MRS Shirley B (Lin Emery) | ☎ (504) 866-7775
Paris'49.Va'39 . . . . | 7520 Dominican St,
MR Brooks E . . . . | New Orleans, LA
| *70118*

Brasfield MR & MRS George F JR (Graham—Ann F | ☎ (202) 342-1108
Mitchell) Cv.Mt.Va'52 . . . . | 4634 Kenmore Dv
MISS Melanie M . . . . | NW, Washington,
| DC *20007*

Brash MRS Douglas Reid (Nancy Ludington)
Sth'48.Csn.Ncd. . . . . | ☎ (609) 921-3950
  MISS Diana R—SL'77.Sth'82—at | 45 Pine St,
☎ (215) 732-7861 . . 1326 Spruce St, | Princeton, NJ 08542
Philadelphia, PA 19107 . . . . |

Braswell MR & MRS Philip P (Marina S Utgoff) | ☎ (202) 338-3670
Duke'75.MichSt'71.NCar'75 . . . . | 3404 Fulton St NW,
  JUNIORS MISS Rebekah P . . . . | Washington, DC
 | 20007

Bratenahl DR & MRS Alexander (Roberta H Robb) | see
Rdc'42.Cal'49.W&L'41 . . . . | Dilatory Domiciles
  MR A Carl . . . . |

Brauer MR & MRS Henry G (Carolyn C Madeira)
WmSth'78.Me.Ey.Tufts'79
☎ (617) 631-2249 . . 30 Phillips St, Marblehead, MA 01945

Brauer MR & MRS Stephen F (Camilla C Thompson) | ☎ (314) 994-0038
Cy.Lc.W'minster'67 . . . . | 9630 Ladue Rd,
  MISS Rebecca R . . . . | St Louis, MO 63124
  MR Blackford F—at Princeton . . . . |
  JUNIORS MR Stephen F JR . . . . |

Braun MR & MRS Andrew G (Helen F Osborn) CtCol'62.Fiy.Mit'61
☎ (617) 734-9392 . . 464 Heath St, Chestnut Hill, MA 02167

Braun MR Fred JR
☎ (415) 776-8391 . . 1170 Sacramento St, Apt 17A, San Francisco,
CA 94108

Braun MRS James B (Salsbury—Evelyn Colucci)
☎ (212) 879-2040 . . 75 East End Av, New York, NY 10028

Braun DR & MRS John T (Frances V Keleher)
Mid'91.Ant'94.Ncd.Tex'85.Cr'89
☎ (210) 499-4122 . . 2103 Mollys Way Dv, San Antonio, TX 78232

Brauns MRS Robert A W (Benton—Sandra P Neave)
☎ (941) 957-3567 . . 770 S Palm Av, Sarasota, FL 33577

Brawley MRS Robert V (Emeline L Thorne) Cly.
☎ (910) 722-4374 . . 134 Cascade Av, Winston-Salem, NC 27127-2027

Brawner MRS H Peirce (Grace M Poe)
☎ (561) 732-9996 . . 1 E Ocean Blvd, Ocean Ridge, FL 33435

Braxton MRS Carter M (Frances D Clark) V'31.Cly.Ncd.Myf.
☎ (914) 723-6226 . . 1 Duck Pond Rd, Scarsdale, NY 10583

Bray MR & MRS Michael D (Karen Hanks)
FlaSt'63.Un.Plg.Myf.Fla'61.Fla'64
☎ (212) 988-2859 . . 3 E 75 St, New York, NY 10021

Brazer MR & MRS Wilson M (Mohn—Anne M M | PO Box 2507,
Wickham) Sth'47.Rv.W.Y'37 . . . . | New London, NH
  MISS Susan W Mohn . . . . | 03257

Breakwell MR & MRS Phillip J (Marye-Lahéns P Jones) FlaAtl'89
☎ (561) 279-9828 . . 102 NE 18 St, Delray Beach, FL 33444

Breasted MISS Isabella
 see Dilatory Domiciles

Breck MRS Manley du P (McClenahan—Speiden—Rachel Hammond)
☎ (860) 364-1238 . . 29 S Main St, Sharon, CT 06069

Breck MR & MRS William Rogers (Lydia C Maxam) | ☎ (609) 921-3506
Pa'50.Leh'50 . . . . | 292 Russell Rd,
  MISS Lydia C—Bnd'92—at U of Pa Wharton . . . | Princeton, NJ 08540
  MR William W . . . . |

Breckenfeld MR William G . . see MRS P W Travell

Breckenridge MRS Esther D (Esther C Dupuy)
☎ (504) 891-3020 . . 1584 Jefferson Av, Apt 7, New Orleans, LA 70115

Breckinridge MRS Isabella G (Dubow—Isabella G | ☎ (202) 298-7209
Breckinridge) SL'60.Sl. . . . . | 1413—35 St NW,
  MISS Alexandra B Dubow—H'87 . . . . | Washington, DC
 | 20007

Breckinridge MR & MRS Scott D JR (Helen V Babbitt) Cc.Ncd.Ky'41
☎ (606) 272-6087 . . 395 Redding Rd, Apt 13, Lexington, KY 40517

Breckner MR Kenneth D . . . . Married at St Louis, MO
  Rogers MRS Paul D (Frances L Clarkson) . . . . Mch 23'96

Breckner MR & MRS Kenneth D (Rogers—Frances L Clarkson)
Macalester'38
☎ (314) 963-9006 . . 98 Whitehall Court, St Louis, MO 63144-1027

Bredin MR & MRS J Bruce (Octavia M du Pont) Wil.Evg.Mt.
☎ (302) 654-4178 . . PO Box 3598, Greenville, DE 19807

Breed MR & MRS George (Harris—Martha A Garrett)
FlaSt'55.KasSt'57.Geo'80.Ayc.Ny.Ct.Cc.Y'41
☎ (410) 268-4433 . . 415 Monterey Av, Annapolis, MD 21401

Breed MR & MRS James H (Alice F Gerster) | 8199 Hunting Hill
Wheat'68.Bost'73.Colg'65.Cl'68.Cl'69 . . . . | Lane, McLean, VA
  JUNIORS MISS Vail R . . . . | 22102

Breed MISS Nancy R—SL'96.Pr.Ri.
☎ (516) 626-0404 . . 85 Piping Rock Rd, Glen Head, NY 11545

Breed DR & MRS R Huntington 2d (Lucy B Fowlkes)
Ford'76.Cl'78.Cly.Y'66.H'70
☎ (603) 746-3835 . . 308 Main St, Hopkinton, NH 03229

Breed MR William B JR—H'55.H'60
☎ (801) 655-3144 . . 1978 Picabo St, Park City, UT 84098

Breed MR & MRS William B 3d (Stephanie C Smith) Tul'84.Van'86
☎ (802) 867-2531 . . 1226 Danby Mountain Rd, Dorset, VT 05251

Breed MRS William C (Phillips—Croll—Helen S | ☎ (212) 472-8261
Schroeder) Cs.Cda.Dc. . . . . | 211 E 70 St,
  MISS Janet S Croll—at ☎ (619) 468-3279 | New York, NY
22477 H'way 94, Dulzura, CA 91917 . . . . . . | 10021

Breeden MR & MRS John R (Jane E Jackson) Tcy.Cal'39
☎ (808) 325-7966 . . PO Box 390580, Kailua Kona, HI 96739-0580

Breeding MR & MRS Edwin C JR (Paula de B | ☎ (860) 434-8599
Thébaud) Dar.U'46 . . . . | 81 Neck Rd,
  MISS Caroline G—at 40 Channing Rd, Dedham, | Box 1053,
MA 02026 . . . . | Old Lyme, CT
  MISS Robin T . . . . | 06371

Brégy MRS Philip A (Emilie M Rivinus) Ph.
☎ (215) 646-4061 . . Blue Bell Woods, 145 Orchard Court, Blue Bell,
PA 19422

Brégy MR Robert S—Br'60 . . . . | ☎ (704) 253-8044
  MISS Michelle L—Duke'92—at 2067B Walter | 108 Forsythe St,
Reed Dv, Arlington, VA 22206 . . . . | Asheville, NC 28801
  MISS Lauren E—at Gettysburg Coll . . . . |

Brehm MR & MRS Thomas J (Freda Rutherfurd) | ☎ (561) 967-6871
Cl'58 . . . . | 333 Emerson Circle,
  MISS Sharon . . . . | Palm Springs, FL
 | 33461

Breit MRS Ann L (Ann B Lane) B'gton'64.Ncd.Ne . . .C E Lane JR

Brenard MR & MRS Kris Thomas (Barbara B Powers) Ken'75
☎ (818) 914-2011 . . 1133 Hidden Springs, Glendora, CA 91740

Brendsel MR & MRS Jon C (Mary Lee Adelizzi) SCal'87.CalTech'86.Nw'91
☎ (310) 439-3771 . . 288 Glendora Av, Long Beach, CA 90803

Brengle MR & MRS George M (Anne B Blum) Nu'74.Csn.DU'72
☎ (508) 999-4786 . . 27 Maple St, New Bedford, MA 02740

Brengle MRS Laurence J (Natalie Munson) Gv.My.
 ☎ (410) 833-3632 . . 3717 Butler Rd, Glyndon, MD *21071-4913*
Brengle MR & MRS William C (Agnes C Crocker) Chi.Hn.H'46.Bost'62
 ☎ (508) 369-7419 . . 102 Musterfield Rd, Concord, MA *01742*
Brenizer MR & MRS William S (M Margaret Loughead)
 MtH'76.Rc.Pr.Nyc.Cly.NCar'74
 ☎ (212) 369-3808 . . 1035 Park Av, New York, NY *10028*
Brennan MR James T JR—Pa'75
 Colon 190, Cafayate, 4427 Salta, Argentina
Brennan MISS Martha Ellen—NECons'69.Pl.
 ☎ (310) 459-5394 . . 17869 Tramonto Dv, Pacific Palisades, CA *90272*

Brennan MRS William J JR (Lucy Curley Joyce)	☎ (212) 988-9084
Ng.Cly.Ne.Ncd.Dh.Dc.	129 E 69 St,
MISS Joyce L—Hlns'87.Cly.Ncd.	New York, NY
MISS Lindsley A—Tul'88.Cly.	*10021*

Brent MRS Helene K (Boothe—O'Brien—Helene	☎ (212) 753-6932
G Klotz)	166 E 61 St,
MR Stanford F JR—Hob'75	New York, NY
	10021

Brentlinger MR Christopher—Cal'82 . . see B M Gordon
Brentlinger MR Peter Perkins—RISD'84 . . see B M Gordon
Brereton DR Hugh G—Cal'35
 ☎ (707) 963-2471 . . 1897 Howell Mountain Rd, St Helena,
 CA *94574*
Breslin MRS Louis R JR (Vars—Nancy Kincaid) . . of
 ☎ (212) BU8-5485 . . 925 Park Av, New York, NY *10028*
 ☎ (315) 482-9721 . . Box 335E, 45496 Landon Rd, Wellesley Island,
 NY *13640*
Brett MRS Bruce Y (Jacqueline Dewey) Cr'45.Lm.Myf.
 ☎ (561) 746-3808 . . 40 Yacht Club Place, Tequesta, FL *33469*
Brett MRS Philip M JR (Pool—Mary B Schwab) Sth'47.Mds.Cly.Cda.
 ☎ (516) 324-1958 . . PO Box 957, 4 Lockwood Lane, East Hampton,
 NY *11937*

Brett MR & MRS Philip M 3d (Anne L Alexandre)	of ☎ (203)259-4991
Unn.Y'59	271 Westway Rd,
MR Peter M—Woff'94—at ☎ (864) 241-0859	Southport, CT *06490*
21 Century Circle, Apt 150F, Greenville, SC	☎ (802) 867-5595
29607	Box 92, Dorset, VT
JUNIORS MR James L	*05251*

Brett MRS William H (Mudge—Poe—Morgan—	☎ (410) 832-5420
Mary Lynn H Marburg) Towson'73.Elk.	''Les Arbres''
MR E Allan Poe 4th—at ☎ (305) 666-5622	PO Box 508,
5735 SW 61 St, South Miami, FL *33143*	2006 W Joppa Rd,
	Riderwood, MD
	21139

Brewer MRS Ann W (Ann A Wickes) Chi.Myc.Ny.	☎ (508) 526-1746
⚓	Nortons Point,
MISS Gale A—at New York, NY	Manchester, MA
	01944

Brewer MR & MRS Charles H (Cornelia H Haden) Cl'64.Y'49.Cl'68 ⛵
 ☎ (802) 875-3146 . . PO Box 338, Chester, VT *05143*
Brewer MRS George E (Ann Fraser) BMr'23.Csn.
 ☎ (301) 925-7338 . . 10450 Lottsford Rd, Apt 4006, Mitchellville,
 MD *20721*
Brewer MR George E 3d—Mex'55
 ☎ (305) 852-3023 . . 97652 Overseas H'way, Apt S4, Key Largo,
 FL *33037*

Brewer MR & MRS Lee R (Elizabeth A Spear)	☎ (908) 671-6396
But'67.Dar.Miami'62.Wis'71	78 Crawford Rd,
MISS Elizabeth A—at O'Daniel Av, Apt 8D,	Middletown, NJ
Newark, DE *19711*	*07748*
MR Lee R JR	

Brewer MR & MRS Michael F (Janet H Brown)
 Wms'73.H'78.Cvc.Hn.Hb.Wms'65.H'69
 ☎ (202) 965-1993 . . 2700 Virginia Av NW, Washington, DC *20037*
Brewer MR & MRS Robert C (Elizabeth B Johnson) Bow'90.Bow'92
 ☎ (617) 484-0441 . . 227 Trapelo Rd, Belmont, MA *02178*

Brewer MR & MRS Stephen E (Elizabeth G Wigton)	☎ (317) 497-3669
Stan'70.Purd'70.Nw'72	613 Ridgewood Dv,
JUNIORS MISS Cecily G	West Lafayette, IN
JUNIORS MR Benjamin W	*47906*

Brewer MRS Wilbert S (Champ—Hornbeck—Jeannette W Watson)
 Un.May.It . . .of
 ☎ (561) 278-9384 . . 401 E Linton Blvd, Apt 419, Delray Beach,
 FL *33483*
 ☎ (216) 991-2341 . . Moreland Courts, 13705 Shaker Blvd,
 Shaker Heights, OH *44120*
Brewer MR William C—Mt.Wms'43 ⚓
 ☎ (410) 867-3140 . . 4862 Church Lane, Galesville, MD *20765*
Brewster MR & MRS Benjamin (Antoinette L Roberts) Unn.Ln.So'70
 ☎ (804) 979-1493 . . ''Lanark'' 2877 Lanark Farm, Charlottesville,
 VA *22902*
Brewster MR & MRS Benjamin H (Davis—Harriet K Dodson)
 Elk.P'47 ⚓
 ☎ (602) 991-5202 . . 10779 N 75 Place, Scottsdale, AZ *85260*
Brewster MRS Carroll W (Ursula Mary Orange) . . . . Died at
              Ridgefield, CT Apr 23'96
Brewster MR Carroll W—C.Y'57
 ☎ (203) 438-2407 . . 126 Lounsbury Rd, Ridgefield, CT *06877*

Brewster MR David K—Sar.Myf.Yn.Del'65.Pa'70 .	☎ (561) 231-3205
MISS Rachel D—at U of Va	601 Honeysuckle
MISS Mary Elizabeth	Lane, Vero Beach,
MR William M—at Auburn	FL *32963*

Brewster MR & MRS Galen (Hathaway Tew) H'65 . .	☎ (410) 486-7400
MISS Paget	St Timothy's
MR Ivan	School, Stevenson,
	MD *21153*

Brewster MR & MRS J Leland 2d (Hazeleen Pace) Ky'56.Cm.Ky'50.Ky'57
 ☎ (513) 561-7203 . . 5155 Ivyfarm Rd, Cincinnati, OH *45243*
Brewster MRS K Peabody (Katharine Peabody) Cy.
 ☎ (617) 320-8289 . . 10 Longwood Dv, Apt 512, Westwood, MA *02090*
Brewster MRS Walter Rice (Stout—Dorothy W Gatins) C.Cly.Ncd.
 ☎ (212) EL5-7477 . . 200 E 66 St, New York, NY *10021*
Brewster MRS Warren D (Marion M Darrah) Cly.Ncd.
 ☎ (212) 427-1409 . . 15 E 91 St, New York, NY *10128*
Brewster MR & MRS William S (Brodeur—Hornblower—
 Malabar Schleiter) Rdc'53.Sm.Tv.Mit'39 . . of
 ☎ (617) 354-0812 . . 1010 Memorial Dv, Cambridge, MA *02138*
 ☎ (508) 255-1956 . . ''Beachy Head'' 371 Tonset Rd, Orleans,
 MA *02653*
Brey MR & MRS Robert N JR (Katharine M Burch)
 Cry.Pc.Rc.W.Fw.Cspa.Sdg.Pa'43
 ☎ (215) CH7-9092 . . 107 W Moreland Av, Philadelphia, PA *19118*

Breyer MRS Henry W (Margaret McKee) Me.
☎ (610) 896-6761 . . 101 Cheswold Lane, Haverford, PA *19041*

Breyer MR & MRS Henry W 3d (Joanne Braatz)
Ny.B.Mds.Evg.BtP.Cly.Va'53 . . . .
MISS Laura L—at 470 Park Av, New York, NY
10022 . . . .
MR Henry W 4th . . . .

of ☎ (561)655-2205
15 Golfview Rd,
PO Box 3308,
Palm Beach, FL
33480
☎ (516) 324-6855
40 Lee Av,
PO Box 5030,
East Hampton, NY
11937

Brice MRS C Carroll III (Charlotte A Duer) Ncd.
☎ (410) 889-2135 . . 100 W University P'kway, Baltimore, MD *21210*

Brick MR James E 2d . . of
☎ (561) 627-9570 . . ''Steeplechase'' 5771 Dixie Belle Rd,
Palm Beach Gardens, FL *33418*
☎ (305) 674-1809 . . Bell Isle 10F, 3 Island Av, Miami Beach,
FL *33139*

Brick COL & MRS Samuel T JR (Adams—Mary
Milling) USA.Md.Pa'64.Md'67 . . . .
MR Morgan J . . . .
JUNIORS MR Alexander R . . . .

☎ (703) 780-9495
2510 Cavendish Dv,
Alexandria, VA
22308

Bricken MR & MRS Jonathan M (Madeleine D Seaman)
Cl'82.Mds.Cly.Denis'77
8 Bayberry Hill Rd, Ridgefield, CT *06877*

Bricker MR Frederick J JR—Geo'52.Cl'59
☎ (212) 570-1059 . . 929 Park Av, New York, NY *10028*

Bricker MR Frederick J 3d—Unn.Rich'85.Ford'91
☎ (713) 789-8831 . . 301 Wilcrest Av, Apt 6012, Houston, TX *77042*

Bricker MRS Tracy (Anne M Tracy) Bm.Cs.Ne.
☎ (212) 838-8176 . . 30 Sutton Place, New York, NY *10022*

Brickley MR & MRS Richard L (Field—J Lynne
Templeton) SL'62.K.Sm.Km.Hn.U'41 . . . .
MR James P—at ☎ (617) 723-1874
103 Revere St, Boston, MA *02114* . . . .
MISS Corinne T Field—Stan'87—at
107 W 86 St, New York, NY *10024* . . . .

☎ (860) 567-0444
158 North St,
PO Box 744,
Litchfield, CT *06759*

Brickley MR & MRS Richard L JR (Nancy P Stanley)
Ws'75.Bost'86.Tr.Srb.Ofp.U'69.Suff'73 . . . . . .
MISS Katherine Hickox—at Occidental . . . .

☎ (617) 262-4534
4 W Cedar St,
Boston, MA *02108*

Bridewell MR & MRS David A (Mary Frances
Badger) So'30.P'32.Wash'38 . . . .
MR Alexander A . . . .

☎ (847) 446-4108
789 Burr Av,
Winnetka, IL *60093*

Bridge MR & MRS F Gardiner F (Patricia E Hansen)
Dth'42 . . . .
MR Gerald H—at 337 W Main St, Madison, WI
53703 . . . .
MR Jonathan E—Denis'82—at
516 W Broadway, Granville, OH *43023* . . . . . .

☎ (508) 255-9024
134 Barley Neck
Rd, PO Box 1107,
East Orleans, MA
02643-1107

Bridge MR & MRS G Flint (Davis—Elisabeth G Townsend)
Purd'78.Neb'81.Wis'73
☎ (414) 964-4499 . . 2511 E Newton Av, Shorewood, WI *53211*

Bridger MRS Neilson C (Mary A W Mechling) Sg.Ac.Ncd.
☎ (215) 984-8383 . . Cathedral Village WL104, 600 E Cathedral Rd,
Philadelphia, PA *19128*

Bridges MR Digby C—Arch'61
☎ (561) 278-1388 . . 124 NE Fifth Av, Delray Beach, FL *33483*

Bridges MRS Linda M (Linda P Morgan)
☎ (770) 955-6017 . . 906 Riverview Dv, Marietta, GA *30067*

Bridges MR & MRS Robert S JR (Kelly L Miller) Ken'88.Ken'86
☎ (203) 637-8792 . . 22 Hoover Rd, Riverside, CT *06878*

Bridgman MR & MRS Victor H 3d (Susan E Oliver)
MaryW'60.AmU'61.Md'66
☎ (302) 652-1869 . . 2302 Foster Place, Wilmington, DE *19806*

Brien MASTER Ethan Benjamin (Ronald F JR) . . . . Born at
Philadelphia, PA Feb 23'96

Brien MR & MRS Ronald F JR (Elizabeth S McKinney)
Pa'78.Pa'88.Penn'78.Pa'80.Vt'84
☎ (215) 483-8616 . . 497 Ripka St, Philadelphia, PA *19128-3331*

Briger MR & MRS Paul H (Keyes—Pauline Gray)
Un.Cs.Ty'61.Y'64 . . . .
MISS Annabel G . . . .
MR Samuel A O . . . .
MR Austin D Keyes . . . .

of ☎ (212)861-2640
167 E 65 St,
New York, NY
10021
☎ (860) 739-3650
209 Old Black Point
Rd, Niantic, CT
06357

Brigg MRS Derek G R (Elvira W Hughes)
☎ (561) 286-3949 . . 2218 SW Heronwood Rd, Palm City, FL *34990*

Briggs MR Basil M—B.Hills'58.H'61 . . . .
MR Basil M JR—at Oak Knoll Village,
29 Meadowview, Annandale, NJ *08801* . . . .

500 N Woodward
Av, Apt 100,
Bloomfield, MI
48304

Briggs MR J Alden JR—Wms'66
☎ (561) 833-1392 . . 225 Chilean Av, Apt 3, Palm Beach, FL *33480*

Briggs MR & MRS James B (Virginia C Moore) L.Ny.Mds.Cry.Dyc.
1615 E Boot Rd, Apt L307, East Goshen, West Chester, PA *19380*

Briggs MR Jason R—Cl'94 . . see E M Urbahn

Briggs MRS Joy H (Parkinson—D Joy Hirshon)
Pa'67.Pr. . . . .
MISS Dana R Parkinson—at
☎ (212) 988-2618 . . 308 E 79 St, Apt 15F,
New York, NY *10021* . . . .
JUNIORS MR A Troup Parkinson—at
St Lawrence U . . . .

☎ (212) 472-6440
2 E 70 St, Apt 3A,
New York, NY
10021

Briggs MR & MRS Taylor R (Jane A Genske) Skd'56.Rc.Wms'54.Cl'57 . . of
☎ (212) 664-7909 . . 27 W 55 St, New York, NY *10019*
☎ (413) 458-2723 . . 1425 Main St, Williamstown, MA *01267*

Brigham MR & MRS Charles A (Martha McEnerney)
Sfg.Cal'58.Hast'65 . . . .
MR Andrew C . . . .

☎ (415) 752-3084
39 Nineteenth Av,
San Francisco, CA
94121

Brigham MISS Eleanor C (Howell—Eleanor C Brigham) . . . . . Married at
St Moritz, Switzerland
Wehlen MR Thomas . . . . Mch 22'96

Brigham MR & MRS F Gorham JR (H Amy Bull)
Cy.Cc.Myf.Ofp.H.'37 . . . .
MR F Gorham 3d . . . .
MR Dana S . . . .

☎ (617) 332-9306
37 Perkins St,
West Newton, MA
02165-2302

Brigham MRS Frank H (Vera G Blenheim) T.
☎ (914) 351-2203 . . PO Box 593, Tuxedo Park, NY *10987*

Brigham MR & MRS Timothy G (Amy F Stackpole) CtCol'84.CtCol'84
☎ (914) 961-7332 . . 11 Kraft Av, Bronxville, NY *10708*
Brigham MR William A—Un.Ty'65.Pa'67
☎ (212) 535-0897 . . 110 East End Av, New York, NY *10028*
Bright MR & MRS J Clayton (M Starr Cummin) Y'78.Wil.Ac.
☎ (610) 347-9712 . . 1399 Doe Run Rd, Coatesville, PA *19320*
Bright MR & MRS J Reeve (Mellon—Anne S Stokes) | ☎ (561) 278-1851
Hob'70.UMiami'81 . . . . | ''Waves End''
JUNIORS MR Nicholas R . . . . | 700 Seasage Dv,
MR Matthew T Mellon . . . . | Delray Beach, FL
| *33483*
Bright MR & MRS Joseph C (Paluck—Mary Beth | ☎ (610) 525-2046
Brady) Mund'69.Pa'82.Rc.M.Me.H'64.Pa'70 . . . | 401 Colebrook Lane,
MISS Elizabeth A Paluck—at Trinity . . . . | Bryn Mawr, PA
JUNIORS MR Ronald T Paluck . . . . | *19010*
Bright JUNIORS MISS Laura S K . . see H Coonley 2d
Bright MR & MRS Lawrence L (Schroeder—Deborah F McKinley)
Pa'64.Au.PhilaArt'76
☎ (610) 286-5441 . . Joanna Plantation, RD 2, Box 267, Morgantown,
PA *19543*
Bright MISS Mary F—Me.
☎ (610) 688-3343 . . 229 Bloomingdale Av, Apt 10, Wayne, PA *19087*
Bright MISS Mary S W . . see H Coonley 2d
Bright MRS Nicholas (Eleanor F Hoey) Vt'78.Bost'86
☎ (508) 785-0666 . . 21 Springdale Av, Dover, MA *02030*
Bright MRS Stanley (Elizabeth N Reeve) B.
☎ (207) 276-5315 . . PO Box 158, Peabody Dv, Northeast Harbor,
ME *04662*
Brightwell MR & MRS Charles Pope 3d (Ruth P | ☎ (334) 262-1298
Collier) Aub'69.Aub'71 . . . . | 3057 Highfield Dv,
MISS Ruth M . . . . | Montgomery, AL
JUNIORS MR Charles P 4th . . . . | *36111*
JUNIORS MR James D . . . . |
Brightwell MISS Roxanna
☎ (212) 580-2531 . . 590 West End Av, New York, NY *10024*
Brimelow MR & MRS John (Ruth C Streeter) H'76.Un.Cly.Sussex'70
☎ (212) 348-2108 . . 1133 Fifth Av, Apt 3, New York, NY *10128*
Brinckerhoff MRS D Beard (Deborah Beard) Sth'59.Nu'85.Eyc . . .of
☎ (914) 472-8592 . . 187 Garth Rd, Scarsdale, NY *10583*
☎ (508) 627-8862 . . Star Rte 79, Edgartown, MA *02539*
Brinckerhoff MR & MRS Starr E (Mawicke—A | of 5 Tokeneke
Sandra Kolseth) V'63.Ty'64 . . . . | Beach Dv, Darien,
MISS Laura D . . . . | CT *06820*
MR Starr E JR . . . . | ☎ (802) 375-2704
MISS Adele R Mawicke—at 320 W 84 St, | Sandgate, Arlington,
New York, NY *10024* . . . . | VT *05250*
MR Andrew D Mawicke—Mich'89—in |
Singapore . . . . |
MR Frederick H Mawicke—at U of Ill . . . . . . |
Brinckerhoff MR & MRS (DR) William B (Theresa T H Nguyen)
JHop'90.Nu'94.JHop'90.OState'95
☎ (410) 560-5619 . . 800 Roundtop Court, Apt 2D, Lutherville,
MD *21093*
Brinckerhoff MR & MRS William H (Dejoux—Natalie R L Grace)
Sth'60.H'68.BtP.Chr.Pr.Dyc.Mds.Hl.Cly.Hn.P'51. JHop'53
☎ (561) 655-4798 . . 381 S Lake Dv, Palm Beach, FL *33480*

Briney MR & MRS Timothy P (Blodget—A Dallas | ☎ (518) 794-9089
Collingwood) Y.'69 . . . . | PO Box 129,
MISS Alexandra K Blodget—Colby'94—at | Old Chatham, NY
128 E 85 St, New York, NY *10028* . . . . . . | *12136*
Brinker MR & MRS Norman E (Leitstein—Nancy L | of ☎ (561)478-8095
Goodman) Ill'68 . . . . | 674 Island Dv,
MISS Christina . . . . | Palm Beach, FL
MR Eric B . . . . | *33480*
MR Mark . . . . | ☎ (214) 363-6038
| 9410 Alva Court,
| Dallas, TX
| *75220-2203*
Brinkley MR & MRS Amiel W JR (Katherine H Hamilton) At.Mit'50
☎ (334) 344-2440 . . 34 Buerger Rd, Mobile, AL *36608*
Brinkley MRS Lemmon (Elizabeth Minor Lemmon) | ☎ (901) 320-7924
Pars'60.At.Cda.Ncd. . . . . | 3004 Garden's Way,
MR Brandon Lemmon—at Jacksonville U . . . . . | Memphis, TN *38111*
MR Minor Dunbar . . . . |
Brinkley MR & MRS Sterling B JR (Clare P Botta) BostColl'79.Mb.Pr.Y'74
☎ (516) 759-2381 . . ''View Point'' 155 Factory Pond Rd,
Locust Valley, NY *11560*
Brinley MR & MRS Charles E 2d (M Nicoll | ''Windrift''
Cadwalader) Y'63 . . . . | PO Box 1816,
MR Charles E 3d—Ken'92 . . . . | Gloucester, VA
| *23061*
Brinton MR & MRS Charles M P (M Dixon Doughten) Me.P'42
☎ (610) 688-4513 . . 217 Sinkler Dv, Radnor, PA *19087*
Brinton MR & MRS Fullerton (Noel L Chambers) . . . | ☎ (703) 379-7662
MISS Heather A—Swb'92—at U of Ore Law . . . | 3405 Nevius St,
MISS Elizabeth F—at U of Pa . . . . | Falls Church, VA
| *22041*
Brisbane MR & MRS Charles A (Tate—Deborah H Merrick)
Wheat'73.Pr.LIU'77
☎ (516) 676-8051 . . Valley Rd, Locust Valley, NY *11560*
Briscoe MRS Arthur F L (Dorothy Wilson)
☎ (301) 475-8430 . . ''Glasgow Farm'' Compton, MD *20627*
Briscoe MR & MRS Dolph JR (Janey Slaughter) Tex'44.A.Tex'43
☎ (210) 278-9171 . . PO Box 389, Uvalde, TX *78802*
Bristow MR & MRS James D (Anne T Babcock) | ☎ (215) 794-5453
Hof'59.TrentSt'67.Md'58 . . . . | 33B Star Rte,
MISS Karin M . . . . | New Hope, PA
| *18938*
Britt MR Christopher D . . . . Married at Chestnut Hill, PA
Barth MISS Catherine A (late Howard) . . . . May 18'96
Brittain MR & MRS John S (Bromley—Anne Brewster)
Err.Gm.Rr.Eyc.Ac.Y.'44.Cl'49
☎ (215) 247-5950 . . 8400 Prospect Av, Philadelphia, PA *19118*
Brittain MR & MRS John S JR (Leslie A Jones) Eyc.Err.Tufts'81
77 Baltusrol Way, Short Hills, NJ *07078*
Brittingham JUNIORS MISS Colleen Taylor . . see D L Hall
Brittingham MR & MRS Scott C (Ella L McCormick) SCal'92.Wms'84
☎ (310) 454-4189 . . 15500 Sunset Blvd, Pacific Palisades, CA *90272*
Britton MR & MRS J Boyd (Pillsbury—Frances C | ☎ (561) 569-0958
Garvin) D.Ncd.Wash'29 . . . . | 2400 Indian Creek
MR Charles S B Pillsbury—at | Blvd, Apt E218,
☎ (603) 563-8420 . . Dublin, NH *03444* . . . . | Vero Beach, FL
| *32966*

Britton MR John D 2d—Dth'89.Cl'93
☎ (212) 724-8692 . . 310 West End Av, Apt 10D, New York, NY *10023*
Britton MRS Kathryn S L (Kathryn S Lines) Ws'63.StJos'87.StJos'90
☎ (860) 232-1884 . . 29 Timberwood Rd, West Hartford, CT *06117*
Britton MR & MRS Roy (Cushman—Sarah A | ☎ (914) 234-7237
Dinkins) Bnd'58 . . . . | PO Box 421,
  MR Allerton Cushman 3d—Ober'87 . . . . . . | 36 Aspetong Rd,
  MR Philip P Cushman—Col'92 . . . . | Bedford, NY *10506*
Britton MR & MRS Samuel S (Susan N Georgantas) Y'91.Cl'96.Y.'91
510 Cathedral P'kway, Apt 10B, New York, NY *10025*
Broadbent DR & MRS B Holly JR (Jacqueline Owen) | of ☎ (216)428-0669
Okla'52.Tv.It.Wr'52 . . . . | "Gull Cottage"
  MISS Elizabeth P—at 40 Willow Av, Somerville, | 7119 Whitesands
MA *02144* . . . . | Dv, Madison, OH
 | *44057*
 | "Laughing Loon
 | Cottage"
 | Livingstone Lake,
 | Dorset, Ontario,
 | Canada
Broadhurst MRS Anne T (Wood—Anne R Truesdale)
☎ (203) 762-2305 . . 100 River Rd, Wilton, CT *06897*
Broadhurst MRS William Juhring (McConnell—Guggenheim—
Gerhard—Mary E Newell) Dar.Cda.Ht.
☎ (212) 288-5935 . . 880 Fifth Av, New York, NY *10021*
Broadwater MR Bowden—H'42
☎ (212) 369-7349 . . 17 E 89 St, New York, NY *10128*
Broberg MR Richard H—Bost'90.Bost'92 . . see R H Crawford
Broberg MR Stephen M—Minn'92 . . see R H Crawford
Brock MISS Alexandra B
☎ (215) CH8-0194 . . 738 Wolcott Dv, Apt B2, Philadelphia, PA *19118*
Brock MR & MRS Charles Lawrence (Mary Jane | of ☎ (212)517-5170
Hipp) Swb'70.Un.Ny.Pr.Mds.Plg.Nw'64.H.'67. | 765 Park Av,
H'79 . . . . | New York, NY
  JUNIORS MISS Susanna L—at Chapin . . . . | *10021*
  JUNIORS MR W Walker—at Phillips Exeter . . . . . | ☎ (516) 324-7733
 | 173 Main St,
 | East Hampton, NY
 | *11937*
Brock MR & MRS Glen P JR (Shirley A Forbes) At.Aub'59.Ala'63.Nu'64
☎ (334) 344-8941 . . 737 Westmoreland Dv W, Mobile, AL *36609*
Brock MR & MRS Harry B JR (N Jane Hollock) Cy.Rm'48.Ala'49
☎ (205) 991-6509 . . 1 Yamasee Rd, Shoal Creek, AL *35242*
Brock MR Horace W—K.H'67.H'70.H'71.P'73.P'75
☎ (415) 854-1814 . . 905 Sherman Av, Menlo Park, CA *94025*
Brock MR & MRS Hugh (Maureen E MacRae) | ☎ (610) 286-0602
Sth'88.Pa'92.Sa.Pa'59 . . . . | RD 2, Box 457,
  MR Charles A—at 28 W Goshen Park, | Elverson, PA *19520*
West Chester, PA *19380* . . . . |
Brock MR & MRS Mitchell (Gioia F C Connell) V'51.Cda.P'49.Pa'53
PO Box 452, Boca Grande, FL *33921*
Brock MR Paul W . . . . Died at
 Mobile, AL Apr 14'96
Brock MRS Paul W (Louise M Shearer)
4768 Bexley Lane, Mobile, AL *36608-2482*

Brock MRS Robb (Thompson—Cornelia T Robb) . . | ☎ (215) 247-7643
  MISS Beatrix H Thompson—at | Hill Tower Apt 16K,
☎ (503) 697-0964 . . 4685C Galewood St, | 7600 Stenton Av,
Galewood Commons, Lake Oswego, OR *97035* | Philadelphia, PA
 | *19118*
Brockett DR & MRS Sheldon I (Helen E Eastman) Cal'39.Cal'37
☎ (619) 296-2658 . . 4522 Trias St, San Diego, CA *92103*
Brockway MR & MRS Douglas W (Genevieve M Houdry)
Hart'77.Msq.Wms'76
☎ (508) 263-1390 . . 12 Putnam Rd, Acton, MA *01720*
Brockway MR & MRS Ralph L (Ann C Lawler) | ☎ (410) 745-2559
IaState'48 . . . . | PO Box 1155,
  MISS Mary-Porter S—at ☎ (617) 492-6873 | St Michaels, MD
85 Prescott St, Cambridge, MA *02138* . . . . | *21663*
  MR Julian S—at ☎ (215) 248-9293 |
618 W Hartwell Lane, Philadelphia, PA *19118* . |
Broderick MR & MRS Brian T (H Louise Kennard)
V'61.Ne'80.Ne'86.Rby.Bab'63
☎ (617) 522-0030 . . 30 Allandale St, Jamaica Plain, MA *02130*
Broderick MR & MRS Shaun P (Jennifer T Jordan)
Bost'83.Rut'81.Seton'84.Nu'87
4 Evergreen Dv, Rumson, NJ *07760*
Brodeur MR Stephen B—Ty'86
☎ (617) 576-1943 . . 950 Massachusetts Av, Cambridge, MA *02139*
Brodhead MISS Heather—Skd'62
☎ (412) 683-1205 . . 144 N Dithridge St, PH-4, Pittsburgh, PA *15213*
Brodhead MR & MRS John JR (J Josephine Carr) | ☎ (314) 863-7665
Cy.Lc.Rr.Aht'40 . . . . | 710 S Hanley Rd,
  MISS Frances . . . . | Apt 9A, St Louis,
 | MO *63105*
Brodhead MRS Marie W B (Marie W Berl)
☎ (610) MU8-1820 . . 211 Atlee Rd, Wayne, PA *19087*
Brodhead MRS Robert Stafford (Alice Kinsman) Pa'33
☎ (302) 655-9534 . . 162 Stonegates, 4031 Kennett Pike, Greenville,
DE *19807*
Brodie MRS A Malcolm SR (Virginia R Colton) . . . . | ☎ (704) 884-2407
  MR W Phillips Colton—at Kingston, Ontario, | 256 Maple St,
Canada . . . . | Brevard, NC *28712*
Brodie MR & MRS Donald G (Gail Robison) | ☎ (802) 362-4265
L.Lic.Ck.Pa'60.Nu'69 . . . . | White Tree Farm,
  MISS Lesley T—Sth'92.Vt'95—at 59 N Shore Dv, | West Rd,
Burlington, VT *05401* . . . . | Manchester, VT
  MISS Alexandra P—MtH'91—at Paris, France . . | *05254-0425*
  MR Ian R—Mid'96—at ☎ (802) 443-5896 |
1 Franklin St, Middlebury, VT *05753* . . . . |
Brodie MR & MRS R Kirkwood 3d (Mary J Fry) Rc.Cin'65 . . of
☎ (773) 975-9511 . . 2130 N Lincoln Park W, Chicago, IL *60614*
☎ (616) 469-0369 . . "Ground Zero" Box 113, RR 1, New Buffalo,
MI *49117*
Brodsky MR & MRS Daniel J (Estrellita Bograd) | of 895 Park Av,
SL'73.Ri.Pa'66 . . . . | New York, NY
  MISS Katherine A . . . . | *10021*
  JUNIORS MR Alexander T . . . . | ☎ (516) 324-5855
 | Lily Pond Lane,
 | East Hampton, NY
 | *11937*

Broeksmit MR John C—Nw'93
☎ (773) 973-3877 . . 7510 N Eastlake Terr, Apt 1B, Chicago, IL *60626*
Broeksmit REV & MRS John S JR (Jane D Murray) V'49.Y'42 . . of
☎ (815) 584-1261 . . Rte 1, Box 173, Dwight, IL *60420-9635*
☎ (312) 335-3750 . . 1350 N Lake Shore Dv, Apt 601, Chicago, IL *60610*
Broeksmit MR Robert D (John S JR) . . . . . . Married at Charlottesville, VA
Bollendorf MISS Susan G (John) . . . . Oct 7'95
Broeksmit MR Samuel B—Wms'85
☎ (215) 546-2168 . . 1530 Locust St, Philadelphia, PA *19102*
Brokaw MRS Augustus Van Liew (Elizabeth C Gray) Wash'29.Ncd.
☎ (314) 862-6245 . . 665 S Skinker Blvd, Apt 5G, St Louis, MO *63105*
Brokaw MISS Christina V . . see G G Herrick
Brokaw MR & MRS Clifford V 3d (Elizabeth S Rogers) BMr'60.Un.Bcs.StJ.Fw.Ht.Chr.Plg.Cly. Myf.Cda.Y'50.Va'56 . . . .
MR George R—Un.Ht.Myf.Y'90.Va'94 . . . . | ☎ (516) 283-2233 "Spindrift" 78 Jule Pond Dv, PO Box 5002, Southampton, NY *11969-5002*
Brokaw MR John H Inman JR . . see G G Herrick
Brokaw MR & MRS Roberts Wyckoff 3d (Allison Huntting Egbert) Denis'78.Snc.Cw.Yn.Y'72.Y'72.H'74
☎ (908) 273-7708 . . 257 Oak Ridge Av, Summit, NJ *07901*
Bromberg MR & MRS Eugene Alexander (L Joyce Keenon) Ala'53.Cy.Ala'54
☎ (205) 879-9775 . . 25 Ridge Dv, Birmingham, AL *35213*
Bromberg MR & MRS Frank H JR (Lella H Clayton) Ala'55.Cy.Ala'54 . . . .
MISS Lella H . . . .
MR & MRS Charles C (Christy E Vlahos) . . . .
MR & MRS Frederick W (Nancy C Beaird) . . . . . . | ☎ (205) 967-0884 2801 Pump House Rd, Birmingham, AL *35243-1732*
Bromfield MR Innis S—Yn.Y'34
☎ (805) 969-8180 . . Casa Dorinda 177, 300 Hot Springs Rd, Santa Barbara, CA *93108*
Bromley MRS Charles S JR (Marjorie Reilly) Ac.Cts.
☎ (610) 642-4168 . . 851 Merion Square Rd, Gladwyne, PA *19035*
Bromley MISS Cynthia P—Tufts'79
☎ (508) 283-8638 . . 509 Washington St, Gloucester, MA *01930*
Bromley MR & MRS Edward P (Ruth B Hancock) Me.Gm.Ac.Mit'34 . . of
☎ (610) 525-7666 . . 81 Pasture Lane, Bryn Mawr, PA *19010*
☎ (941) 262-3888 . . 2171 Gulf Shore Blvd N, Naples, FL *34102*
Bromley MR & MRS Edward P JR (Barbara V Broomhead) Me.Cw.Pn.P'58.H'61 . . . .
MR Brinton O . . . . | ☎ (609) 446-0122 90 Province Line Rd, Skillman, NJ *08558*
Bromley MRS Henry S JR (Leake—Dorothy P Southworth) Ac. . . . .
MR Peter N—Mid'79.Pa'84—at 227 Avon Rd, Narberth, PA *19072* . . . . | ☎ (610) MI2-5570 219 State Rd, Gladwyne, PA *19035*
Bromley MR & MRS John JR (Tilghman—Marion T Pepper) Sg.Gm.
☎ (215) CH7-8375 . . 319 W Moreland Av, Philadelphia, PA *19118*
Bromley MR & MRS Richard N (Lois L Thompson) Me.Ac.Yn.Y.'37 . . of
☎ (610) 525-1712 . . 408 S Ithan Av, Villanova, PA *19085*
☎ (561) 276-3389 . . 1226 South Way, Delray Beach, FL *33483*

Bromley-Davenport MR & MRS William A (Elizabeth B Watts) . . . .
MISS Liberty C . . . .
MR Nicholas W . . . . | ☎ (011-44-1625) 861221 Capesthorne Hall, Macclesfield, Cheshire SK11 9JY, England
Bronkie MISS Dona B
☎ (716) 632-5537 . . 33 Milton St, Williamsville, NY *14221*
Bronkie MR & MRS Robert T JR (Susan W Jones) Norw'77
☎ (716) 655-0473 . . 12946 Williston Rd, East Aurora, NY *14052*
Bronner MR & MRS Frederick V (Judith S Batzer) Sar.U'46.
MR Geoffrey S V—Dth'91—at Hanover, NH *03755* . . . . | of ☎ (561)743-4004 Heritage Oaks, 18165 SE Laurel Leaf Lane, Tequesta, FL *33469* ☎ (860) 672-0118 "The Wick" Great Hollow Rd, Cornwall, CT *06753*
Bronson MRS H Dick (Cook—Helen Dick) On.
☎ (847) 234-0622 . . 461 E Westminster Rd, Lake Forest, IL *60045*
Bronson DR & MRS Nathaniel R 2d (Cornelia V R Goebel) Yn.Y'53.JHop'57
☎ (203) 259-5166 . . 101 Field Point Dv, Fairfield, CT *06430*
Brooke MISS Anna M—Sl.
☎ (202) 363-1451 . . 3379 Stephenson Place NW, Washington, DC *20015*
Brooke MR & MRS Brian W (Ann R Hammond) Roan'78.Md.Cc.Mv.W&L'79
☎ (410) 339-7270 . . 8206 Tally Ho Rd, Lutherville, MD *21093*
Brooke MR & MRS Dandridge (Isolde F Kluge) Wt. .
MISS Lynette . . . .
MISS Jessica L W . . . .
JUNIORS MR Jonathan R D . . . . | ☎ (410) 828-8459 206 E Seminary Av, Timonium, MD *21093*
Brooke MR Dandridge William—Wt.Loy'75.Balt'81
JUNIORS MISS Claire E F . . . . | ☎ (410) 377-7306 6117 Haddon Hall Rd, Baltimore, MD *21212*
Brooke MR & MRS George C 3d (Susan C Kennedy) Vt'84.Gm.P'83
☎ (610) 251-2274 . . 244 Dogwood Lane, Berwyn, PA *19312*
Brooke MR & MRS James B (Elizabeth A Heilman) Ws'81.Y'77
☎ (303) 620-9200 . . 32520 Woodland Dv, Evergreen, CO *80439*
Brooke MRS John L B (Louisa G Ludlow) Lx.
☎ (413) 637-0926 . . "Ludlow Cottage" 73 Main St, Lenox, MA *01240-1743*
Brooke MR & MRS Peter F (Dorothy J Swanson) Me.Cspa.Rv.NCar'59 . . . .
MISS Marion C—P'92—at 1 Fifth Av, New York, NY *10003* . . . . | ☎ (718) 834-9595 1 Pierrepont St, Brooklyn, NY *11201*
Brooke MAJ Randall W—USA. (Dandridge) . . . Married at Baltimore, MD
Deering MRS A R Ashton (A Russell Ashton) . . . . Jly 26'96
Brooke MAJ & MRS Randall W (Deering—A Russell Ashton) USA.Hlns'85.Wt.Loy'83
☎ (410) 821-1847 . . 829 Loyola Dv, Towson, MD *21204*

Brooke MRS Robert Clymer (Miriam R Clymer) . . of
☎ (610) 378-5584 . . 1801 Cambridge Av, C17, Wyomissing, PA *19610*
☎ (941) 598-4936 . . The Grosvenor 1204, 6001 Pelican Bay Blvd, Naples, FL *34108*

Brooke MR & MRS Robert Z (Helen Chase Kimball)
Mass'70.Paris'76.INSEAD'84.Camb'79.INSEAD'84
☎ (011-44-181) 998-1204 . . 35 Castlebar Rd, Ealing, London W5 2DJ, England

Brooke MRS Sallie C (Sallie B Carpenter) V'58.Pc. . | ☎ (215) 233-2651
MR Anthony C—Laf'94—at ☎ (415) 334-2344 | 504 Wyndmoor Av,
238 Evelyn Way, San Francisco, CA *94127* . . . . | Wyndmoor, PA *19038*

Brooke MRS Sarah M (Sarah A McDougal)
2857 Westwood Lane, Apt 4, Carmichael, CA *95608-4141*

Brooke MR & MRS Thomas R (Beverley A Cassidy)
Hlns'86.Lm.Ncd.Dc.Va'81
☎ (904) 384-4065 . . 3803 Bettes Circle, Jacksonville, FL *32210*

Brookfield MR & MRS Christopher M (Lynne | ☎ (804) 282-8420
Robinson) P'58.Cl'63.UnTheo'68 . . . . | 6406 Roselawn Rd,
MR Christopher L—Duke'86 . . . . | Richmond, VA *23226*

Brookfield MRS Gayle Evans (Gayle F Evans) | ☎ (914) 244-3494
Sth'66. . . . . | PO Box 351,
MR Jonathan L—Y'92.Camb'93—in Taiwan . . . | Bedford, NY *10506*
MR Christopher M—Wms'94—at
☎ (206) 325-1726 . . 1605—41 Av E, Seattle,
WA *98112* . . . .

Brookfield MRS Henry M JR (Elizabeth S Bradley) Sth'36.Myf.Cw.StJ.
☎ (914) 358-2760 . . 519 N Midland Av, Upper Nyack, NY *10960*

Brookfield MRS Samuel L (Alyce Pressprich) StJ.
☎ (203) 531-7034 . . 621 W Lyon Farm Dv, Greenwich, CT *06831*

Brookfield MR & MRS William Lord (Gillett—Jean N | of ☎ (941)466-5271
McGraw) Sth'37.Myf.Cw.Hn.H'29 . . . . | 4903 Lucina Court,
MISS Marian N Gillett . . . . | Ft Myers, FL *33908*
| ☎ (860) 542-5402
| "Brooktrout"
| Box 572, Doolittle
| Dv, Norfolk, CT
| *06058*

Brooks MRS A Lerch (Alberta L Lerch)
☎ (610) 373-3424 . . 1174 Garfield Av, Wyomissing, PA *19610*

Brooks MISS Abigail
623 Baltic Av SE, Rio Rancho, NM *87124-3189*

Brooks MR Alfred Pope—Unn.Yn.Y'35.Y'39
☎ (412) 481-2106 . . 1700 Grandview Av, Pittsburgh, PA *15211*

Brooks MR & MRS Amsbry M JR (Elisabeth O Hunter) Sar.Ht.Va'50
☎ (757) 428-8633 . . 1008 Brandon Rd, Virginia Beach, VA *23451*

Brooks MRS Arthur H JR (Jean Halladay) . . . . Died at
Cambridge, MA Mch 8'96

Brooks MR Arthur H JR—Sm.Cy.H'39 . . . . | ☎ (617) 547-0081
MR Arthur H 3d—at ☎ (212) 749-6880 | 115 Brattle St,
175 W 93 St, New York, NY *10025* . . . . | Cambridge, MA *02138*

Brooks MR & MRS Clinton C (Anne B Peters)
NCar'61.Gv.Ncd.Myf.Y'60.Y'62.Y'68
☎ (410) 484-5157 . . 10625 Park Heights Av, Owings Mills, MD *21117*

Brooks MR & MRS Clinton C JR (Cecilia D Laveran-Stiebar) Nu'91.Gv.Vt'90
☎ (610) 526-9640 . . 143 Fairfax Rd, Rosemont, PA *19010*

Brooks MISS Cynthia L . . see C W Cullen

Brooks MR & MRS Douglas A (Leslie M Chanler) Colby'79
☎ (908) 291-2447 . . 8 Browns Dock Rd, Locust, NJ *07760*

Brooks MRS Frances S (Frances S Seaver) D.
☎ (617) 326-0214 . . 163 Highland St, Dedham, MA *02026*

Brooks MR & MRS Francis A JR (Isabel van S | ☎ (214) 239-1469
Henderson) Wheat'58.W.Ncd.Dh.Br'55.Ox'65 . | 6246 Lafayette
MISS Jennifer . . . . | Way, Dallas, TX
MR Francis A 3d . . . . | *75230*

Brooks MR & MRS Francis H (Pamela Richards) | ☎ (617) 893-3390
H.'37 . . . . | 15 Farm Rd,
MISS Laura R . . . . | Weston, MA *02193*
MISS Holly H . . . . |

Brooks MR George R—Wms'51
☎ (314) FO1-5389 . . 11 Westmoreland Place, St Louis, MO *63108*

Brooks MR & MRS Gordon Vail (Anne G Clark) Mid'41
☎ (941) 365-6554 . . 1884 Hyde Park St, Sarasota, FL *34239*

Brooks MR Harold R—Edg . . .see MRS M B Woodbridge

Brooks MR & MRS Harry A (Lowell—Helen W Moffett)
Rc.B.Pr.Cly.P'35 . . of
☎ (516) 676-2583 . . "Turtle Walk" 41 Valentine Lane, Glen Head, NY *11545*
☎ (212) 838-6843 . . 200 E 66 St, New York, NY *10021*

Brooks MR & MRS Harvey S JR (Bray—Kelly F Gavin)
☎ (410) 823-6532 . . 1604 Jeffers Rd, Towson, MD *21204*

Brooks MR Henry G—Sm.H'44 . . . . | ☎ (207) 363-4698
MISS Alice S—Sth'77—at 4 Longfellow Place, | 23 Milbury Lane,
Boston, MA *02114* . . . . | PO Box 113,
MISS Sarah W—Ty'89—at 5123—44 St NW, | York Harbor, ME
Washington, DC *20016* . . . . | *03911*

Brooks MR J Judson JR
700 New Hampshire Av NW, Washington, DC *20037*

Brooks MR James B JR . . see R A Tilghman JR

Brooks MRS Jerrold L (Gladys L Rogers) Ncmb'61 . | ☎ (704) 669-7661
MISS Elizabeth R—David'85—at 4410 N 4 Rd, | PO Box 10, 113
Apt 6, Arlington, VA *22203* . . . . | Mecklenburg Circle,
MR Philip J H—David'90 . . . . | Montreat, NC *28757*

Brooks MR John I—Me.M.Pa'94
☎ (610) 251-0109 . . 483 School House Lane, Devon, PA *19333*

Brooks DR & MRS John R (Dorothy Kalbfleisch) Sth'41.Tv.H'40
Fox Hill Village 138, 10 Longwood Dv, Westwood, MA *02090*

Brooks MRS Kyle C (Anne C Boyd)
☎ (513) 321-5565 . . 3533 Holly Lane, Cincinnati, OH *45208*

Brooks MRS Kyle F (Bullock—Eleine E Hoffman)
☎ (513) 321-4500 . . 12 Garden Place, Cincinnati, OH *45208*

Brooks MR & MRS Philip (Eleonora Eaton) H'39 . . . | 73 Essex Court,
MISS Shana—at 1700 Chesapeake St, | Bedford, MA *01730*
Charlottesville, VA *22901* . . . . |
MR Tyler—at 1700 Chesapeake St, |
Charlottesville, VA *22901* . . . . |

Brooks MR & MRS Scott A (Laura Y Eiman) StLaw'75.Rcn.P'62
Bald Peak, Wilson Point, South Norwalk, CT *06854*

Brooks MR & MRS Shelton A (Mary Hope Lupfer) Cs.H.'49
☎ (212) 722-6445 . . 1170 Fifth Av, New York, NY *10029*

Brooks MR & MRS Shepherd (Esmée de Menocal) Rdc'49.Hn.H'36
24 Berkeley St, Cambridge, MA *02138*
Brooks MR W Denison . . . . Died at
Dedham, MA Mch 25'96
Brooks MRS W Denison (Reece—Elizabeth B Eshleman) D. ⚓
☎ (617) 329-0633 . . 159 Lowder St, Dedham, MA *02026*
Brooks MRS Walter B 3d (Sheedy—Tanya L Widrin) . . of
☎ (561) 659-6260 . . PO Box 3161, Palm Beach, FL *33480*
☎ (212) 249-4211 . . 207 E 74 St, New York, NY *10021*
☎ (516) 283-0494 . . PO Box 1484, Southampton, NY *11969*

Brooks MR & MRS William L (Margaret A Dortch) | ☎ (615) 665-2323
Swb'67.Van'63.Va'66 . . . . | 4406 Harding Place,
MISS Virginia A . . . . | Nashville, TN *37205*
JUNIORS MR William H—at U of Ga . . . . |

Brooks MASTER William Tucker Stuyvesant (Douglas A) . . . . Born
Jan 28'94

Brooks-Baker MR & MRS Harold Brooks (Irène | of ☎ (011-44-1722)
du Luart de Montsaulnin) Cvc.Mt.Gi.Ty'57 . . . . | 782-635
MISS Nadia E . . . . | 3 Dv Great Durnford
MISS Natasha Y D . . . . | Manor, Great
| Durnford, Salisbury,
| Wiltshire, England
| ☎ (011-44-171)
| 730-2342
| 23A Holland Villas
| Rd, London W14,
| England
| . . MRS absent

Brophy MR & MRS David H (Powers—Irene F Sippel) Pa'32
☎ (803) 524-3198 . . 404 New St, Beaufort, SC *29902*
Brophy MR & MRS Rex L (Virginia C Ward) MichSt'45.Denis'43 . . of
☎ (313) 884-0154 . . 175 Vendome Rd, Grosse Pointe Farms, MI *48236*
☎ (561) 231-0850 . . 90 Cowry Lane, John's Island, Vero Beach,
FL *32963*

Bross MR & MRS John A (Louise deM Smith) | ☎ (312) 642-9495
Sth'61.Ch'77.Ch'94.On.Rc.Fy.H'61.H'65 . . . . . | 1827 N Orleans St,
MISS Louise J deM—Nw'93—at | Chicago, IL *60614*
4328 N Hermitage Av, Apt 2W, Chicago, IL |
60613 . . . . |
MISS Medora deM—at Harvard . . . . |
MR Jonathan M—Rc.Br'91 . . . . |

Bross MISS Marie Suzette deM—Nw'90.Cly.
☎ (773) 395-6993 . . 1231 N Wolcott Av, Apt 3, Chicago, IL *60622*
Brossard JUNIORS MISS Genève Vallé . . see MRS M E Huffman

Brouder MR & MRS Bernard P (H Penelope Merrill) | ☎ (914) 234-3386
Sth'58.Buff'62 . . . . | 469 Cantitoe St,
MR Daniel M—Skd'85—at 1109 Ditmas Av, | Bedford, NY *10506*
Brooklyn, NY *11218* . . . . |

Brough MR & MRS John A JR (Adrienne P Benedict) | ☎ (203) 966-5811
AScott'67.Eyc.Err.Hob'65 . . . . | 5 Woodway Ridge
MISS Elizabeth P . . . . | Lane, New Canaan,
MR Alexander 3d—at U of Vt . . . . | CT *06840*

Broughton MR & MRS Donald A (Erle T Lionberger)
Hlns'81.Ncd.SEMoSt'87
☎ (314) 994-9880 . . 1033 Coddington Way, St Louis, MO *63132*

Brower MRS Edgar J (Caroline W Fraser) Cvc.Ncd.
☎ (610) 325-0538 . . Dunwoody Village, 3500 West Chester Pike,
Newtown Square, PA *19073*
Brower MR & MRS Prentice W (Mary P Francis) Nu'41.Nu'46
☎ (803) 689-6680 . . 55 Outerbridge Circle, Hilton Head Island,
SC *29926*
Brown MRS Abbott H (Louisa S McCoy)
☎ (860) 767-1883 . . 12 Curiosity Lane, Essex, CT *06426*
Brown MR Adam H—Denis'86
☎ (410) 472-2772 . . Loveton Farms, Windmill Chase, Apt 4D, Sparks,
MD *21152*

Brown MR & MRS Alan L (Suzanne R S Kirschner) . | PO Box 2047,
MISS Brynly L . . . . | Kamuela, HI *96743*
JUNIORS MISS Nanea Ii . . . . |

Brown MR & MRS Alexander C JR (Janet D Garfield) SL'37.Y'35
☎ (617) 326-1526 . . Fox Hill Village 532, 10 Longwood Dv, Westwood,
MA *02090*
Brown MISS Alice C—Sth'51.Cs.
☎ (212) 988-7472 . . 955 Lexington Av, New York, NY *10021*
Brown MR Alling C—Aht'55.Mich'61 . . of
☎ (847) 234-0734 . . 410 Washington Rd, Lake Forest, IL *60045*
☎ (202) 333-4387 . . 821—25 St NW, Washington, DC *20037*
Brown MISS Ann C—Nw'56.Mich'58
☎ (912) 638-4422 . . Cottage 291, Sea Island, GA *31561*

Brown MR & MRS Anthony C (Winifred Lee d'Olier) | ☎ (212) RE4-3280
B.Mds.Plg. . . . . | 301 E 78 St,
MISS Leelee d'O—Col'88 . . . . | New York, NY
| *10021*

Brown MR & MRS Anthony J (Sarah A Fergusson) | ☎ (610) 527-1852
Wheat'76.Ssk.Me.Au.Wms'75 . . . . | 107 Ashwood Rd,
JUNIORS MISS Anne J . . . . | Villanova, PA *19085*
JUNIORS MR Samuel F . . . . |

Brown MR & MRS Archibald M JR (Laura H Webb) | ☎ (520) 298-7770
Bost'65.Ariz'68 . . . . | 6161 E Miramar Dv,
MISS Hope E—at 740 E Kiowa St, | Tucson, AZ *85715*
Colorado Springs, CO *80903* . . . . |
MR Brewster J—CtCol'92 . . . . |
MR Alexander M . . . . |

Brown MRS Barrett B (Sylvia R Van Anda)
☎ (203) 762-9738 . . 27 Telva Rd, Wilton, CT *06897*
Brown DR Barrett B JR—Md'81.GeoW'87
☎ (703) 765-3804 . . 1221 Shenandoah Rd, Alexandria, VA *22308*
Brown MRS Brooks JR (Fuller—Marion R Thompson) Sth'38.Chi.
☎ (207) 363-5289 . . Ram's Head Farm, 251 Southside Rd, PO Box 6,
York, ME *03909*
Brown MR & MRS Bruce M (Elaine Eldredge)
InterDes'80.Me.Ac.Lawr'69.Ky'73
☎ (610) 688-5154 . . 350 Pond View Rd, Devon, PA *19333*
Brown MR & MRS Bruce W (Marian E Neall) Wcc.P'49
☎ (610) 644-5899 . . 319 Abbey Rd, Berwyn, PA *19312*
Brown MR & MRS Cabot (Mollie A Ward) Cal'83.H'83.H'87
☎ (415) 567-3002 . . 2744 Steiner St, San Francisco, CA *94123*
Brown MR & MRS Cameron (Werlein—Dymond—Jean McGrew)
Cho.Sr.On.Cas.Fy.Cnt.Ncd.Ill'37 . . of
☎ (847) 234-3033 . . 1400 N Green Bay Rd, Lake Forest, IL *60045*
☎ (805) 969-6063 . . 2004 Sandy Place, Santa Barbara, CA *93108*

Brown MR & MRS Charles H JR (Rosamond A Ferguson) Aht'58.H'62 . . . . ☎ (011-852) 2849-6181
MR Benjamin H D . . . . ''Hilden'' 5 Pollock's Path, The Peak, Hong Kong

Brown MISS Christie Gardner
☎ (212) 207-4587 . . 160 E 48 St, Apt 14P, New York, NY *10017*

Brown MR & MRS Clifford C (Hannelore Soltau) Kassel'63.P'53 . . . . ☎ (011-49-491) 3845
MISS Esther . . . . Moerkenstrasse 21,
MISS Isabella . . . . 26789 Leer, Germany

Brown MRS Clinton B D (Nona P Baldwin) V'39.Cl'40.Sl.Snc.StA.Ll.
☎ (202) 363-2066 . . 3801 Kanawha St NW, Washington, DC *20015*

Brown MR & MRS Clinton S (Jane K Egbert) . . . . . . ☎ (410) 820-7435
MISS Alison R . . . . 4718 Sailors Lane, Oxford, MD *21654*

Brown JUNIORS MR Clinton S . . see MISS E B Stewart

Brown MR Courtney W—Chap'94
see Dilatory Domiciles

Brown MISS Cynthia D—Pratt'84
☎ (970) 927-0282 . . 405 Park Av, Basalt, CO *81621*

Brown MRS Cyrus Winthrop 2d (Carol D Williams) Ws'62. . . . . ☎ (212) 787-0536 315 W 86 St, Apt
JUNIORS MISS Laura L D . . . . 15A, New York, NY *10024-3178*

Brown MR Cyrus Winthrop 2d—H.'60
☎ (212) 362-2798 . . 266 West End Av, New York, NY *10023*

Brown MR & MRS Daniel P JR (Nannie W Talbot) Wms'65.Y'68 . . . . ☎ (860) 653-7557 16 Broad Hill Rd,
MISS Allison P—Wms'92 . . . . West Granby, CT *06090*

Brown MR & MRS Darrell (Register—Lendy S Firestone)
☎ (606) 987-7020 . . Stonereath Farms, PO Box 610, Paris, KY *40361*

Brown MR David S—Va'73
☎ (212) 861-0930 . . 147 E 82 St, New York, NY *10028*

Brown MRS Dickerman (Honour R Dickerman) Cly . . .of
☎ (203) 264-9655 . . 207 Pomperaug Woods, Southbury, CT *06488*
☎ (860) 868-2970 . . ''Pengilly III'' 41 Buffum Rd, Washington Depot, CT *06794*

Brown MRS Donald A K (Mary McB Ryerson) Pqt.BtP.
☎ (561) 533-5258 . . 70 Spoonbill Rd, Point Manalapan, FL *33462*

Brown MISS Dorothy A—V'45-4.Chi.
☎ (508) 283-3247 . . 45 Fort Hill Av, Eastern Point, Gloucester, MA *01930*

Brown MRS Dudley B W (Jane S Acheson)
10856 Greentrail Dv S, Boynton Beach, FL *33436*

Brown MR & MRS Duncan F (Olivia Ramsey) H'42 . 801 Wake Robin
MISS Melissa—at 1801 Calafia St, Apt C, Dv, Shelburne, VT
Glendale, CA *91208* *05482*

Brown MR & MRS Edward G (Marjorie E Schmidt) Bg.Cs.Dar.
☎ (914) 677-5464 . . Box AD, Millbrook, NY *12545*

Brown MR & MRS Edward M (Catherine C Bellis) Cal'88.Mid'85
☎ (415) 921-7776 . . 3365 Clay St, San Francisco, CA *94118*

Brown DR & MRS Edward O (Stegall—Gail Ahlberg) H'52.ClP&S'56
☎ (607) 962-7270 . . 201 Pine St, Corning, NY *14830*

Brown MR & MRS Edward W (Gwendolyn G Cochran) Elk.Mv.Yh.P'23
☎ (410) 377-7043 . . 15 Woodbrook Lane, Baltimore, MD *21212*

Brown MRS F Gordon (Graham—Mulford—Gaines—Burton—Eleanor B Degener) Un.Cly.
☎ (212) RE7-6761 . . 1 E 66 St, New York, NY *10021*

Brown MR & MRS F Reese (Lois A Degener) Cs.Wash'39 . . . . ☎ (212) 737-5193 333 E 68 St,
MISS Eliza B—at 305 E 72 St, New York, NY New York, NY
10021 . . . . *10021*
MR Reese D—at 19—2 St, Newport, RI *02840* . .

Brown MR & MRS Fitzhugh L (Mary F M Kern) BMr'54.Pg.Sl.Hn.H'54
☎ (412) 741-6621 . . Persimmon Rd, Sewickley, PA *15143*

Brown MRS Francis (E Hope MacPherson)
☎ (207) 326-9022 . . Green St, Box 503, Castine, ME *04421*

Brown MR & MRS Francis C JR (Nancy A Leitzow) Myf.P'58.H'61 . . . . of ☎ (212)249-9657 520 E 86 St,
MISS Jennifer N—at Georgetown . . . . New York, NY
MR James H L—at 11970 Iowa Av, Los Angeles, *10028*
CA *90025* . . . . ☎ (203) 245-9034 28 Grove Av, Madison, CT *06443*

Brown MR & MRS Francis Shunk 3d (Sarah Hopkins) Pe.Cw.Myf.Rv.Wt.Laf'40.Pa'47
☎ (215) 242-5692 . . 219 W Gravers Lane, Philadelphia, PA *19118*

Brown MR & MRS Fred E (Hewetson—Darlington—Enid B Sillcox) Un.Cly.Okla'34.H'36
☎ (212) 755-4603 . . 580 Park Av, New York, NY *10021-7313*

Brown MRS Gae Maloney (Gae E Maloney) LIU'83 ☎ (516) 922-2624
MR Michael S—Wis'91—at ☎ (715) 425-2760 4 Anchorage Lane,
1119 S State St, Apt 262, River Falls, WI *54022* Apt 7B, Oyster Bay, NY *11771*

Brown MR & MRS George Edwin JR (Marian R Morton) V'47.Mt.H'45 . . . . of ☎ (203)966-9692 62 Country Club Rd,
MISS Lucy S—at ☎ (617) 864-5468 New Canaan, CT
1 Bailey Place, Cambridge, MA *02139* *06840*
MR George Edwin 3d—at ☎ (303) 778-7278 ☎ (802) 824-6517
855 S Medea Way, Denver, CO *80209* . . . . Peru, VT *05152*

Brown MRS George Estabrook JR (Lela H Cook) Mds.Snc.Ncd . . .of
☎ (513) 561-3904 . . 9375 Shawnee Run Rd, Cincinnati, OH *45243*
☎ (941) 262-2073 . . 3131 Ft Charles Dv, Naples, FL *34102*

Brown MRS George S (Alice N W Colhoun) Cda.
611 Queen St, Alexandria, VA *22314*

Brown MR & MRS George T (Mary E Donahue) Loy'40
☎ (706) 322-3223 . . 6400 Green Island Dv, Apt 28, Columbus, GA *31904*

Brown MR & MRS Georges P (Ann Louise H Hamilton)
☎ (617) 837-7916 . . 321 Congress St, Duxbury, MA *02332*

Brown MR & MRS H Tatnall JR (Mackinney—T Marjorie Disney) Me.
☎ (215) 893-9436 . . 226 W Rittenhouse Square, Apt 1412, Philadelphia, PA *19103-5746*

Brown MR & MRS H Templeton JR (Suzanne C Olsen) Y'52
14 Birch Mill Rd, Lyme, CT *06371*

Brown MISS Helen S . . see G R Wright

Brown MR & MRS Henry S (Caroline T Lowe) Snc.Cw.Cs.Ncd.Dc.P'51 . . . . ☎ (212) 923-8402 116 Pinehurst Av,
MISS Alice W—Dc.Ncd. . . . . New York, NY
MISS Caroline L *10033*

Brown MRS Hobson (Macfarlane—Kathryn Horwath) . . . .
MR A Carson—at 202 Baltic St, Brooklyn, NY *11201*. . . . .
MISS Jean P Macfarlane—at 102 Grayling Av, Narberth, PA *19072* . . . .
☎ (441) 236-3384
"BourHope"
8 Inglewood Lane, Paget PG 06, Bermuda

Brown MRS Hobson JR (Erwin W Parrott) Ln.Un.Wk.Cly.NCar'64.Pa'69 . . . .
MISS E Carter . . . .
MR Hobson 3d—at U of NCar . . . .
of ☎ (212)876-9649
70 E 96 St, New York, NY *10128*
☎ (717) 775-7371
Blooming Grove Hunt & Fish Club, Hawley, PA *18428*

Brown MRS Hope N (Hope C Nesbit) V'46
☎ (610) 993-9797 . . 419 Chandlee Dv, Berwyn, PA *19312*

Brown MR & MRS Howard H JR (Nancy A Houghton) BMr'55.Rdc'58.Cl'78.Rv.Mit'56. Mit'61 . . . .
MISS Lowrey R—at Stanford . . . .
MR Howland H—Wes'93 . . . .
172 River Rd, Grandview-on-Hudson, NY *10960*

Brown MR & MRS Irving J (Ann C Catterton) Tex'57.Pom'56. . . . .
MISS Ann B—at 24 Hawk Lane, Levittown, NY *11756* . . . .
☎ (915) 584-9584
6501 La Cadena Dv, El Paso, TX *79912*

Brown MRS J Crosby (M Locke P Kennedy) Sth'51.BMr'67.Cts.Ac.Ncd.
☎ (610) 293-9266 . . 463 Belrose Lane, Radnor, PA *19087*

Brown MR & MRS J Crosby IV (Louisa L Robinson) Denis'80.Wes'87
☎ (215) 699-6579 . . 320 W Montgomery Av, North Wales, PA *19454*

Brown MRS J Dorsey JR (Sibyl K Jackson) Gv. . . . .
MISS Sandra C—at 210 Tyrone Rd, Baltimore, MD *21212* . . . .
313 Brightwood Club Dv, Lutherville, MD *21093*

Brown MR & MRS J Stuart 3d (Carroll—Jones—Ann C Reber) Ph.Y'51 . . of
PO Box 831, York Harbor, ME *03911*
☎ (207) 363-6770 . . "Moonfleet" 131 Cider Hill Rd, York, ME *03909*

Brown DR & MRS J Warren (Louise A Williams) Cs.H'57.Cr'61 . . . .
MR Thomas Warren—Ty'86.Cl'91—at
☎ (603) 224-7896 . . 90 School St, Apt 3, Concord, NH *03301* . . . .
MR Peter Schuyler—Pars'91—at
☎ (212) 677-1875 . . 31 E 12 St, New York, NY *10003* . . . .
☎ (212) 831-7853
55 E 86 St, New York, NY *10028*

Brown MR & MRS James B JR (Sidney A Peard) Yn.Y'56
☎ (203) 972-7371 . . 42 Prides Crossing, New Canaan, CT *06840*

Brown MRS James Barrett (Phillips—Brown—Cunliff—Bertha Jane Phillips) Chath'32.Cy.Rr.Ncd.
☎ (314) 862-1035 . . 816 S Hanley Rd, St Louis, MO *63105*

Brown DR & MRS James C (Elliot—Mary Anna Portner) CathU'77.CathU'81.Cal'71.OState'83
☎ (301) 951-5249 . . 5302 Wakefield Rd, Bethesda, MD *20816*

Brown MRS James Elwyn (Caroline G Johnson) Cvc.Sl.
☎ (607) 783-2300 . . "Stonyledge" 13 Marion Av, Gilbertsville, NY *13776*

Brown MR & MRS James Fearon 2d (Cordula E A Drossel) Van'92.Van'91
☎ (206) 649-3749 . . 2224—173 Av NE, Redmond, WA *98052*

Brown MRS James M JR (Jean H Davis) Skd'28
☎ (203) 655-0174 . . 38 Pembroke Rd, Darien, CT *06820*

Brown MR & MRS James M 3d (Armstrong—Sarah C Webb) Y'56 ⚓ . . . .
MISS Leigh T Armstrong—P'93 . . . .
MISS Katherine StJ Armstrong—Van'95 . . . .
☎ (561) 283-2469
7964 SE Double Tree Dv, Hobe Sound, FL *33455*

Brown MR & MRS James M 4th (Eyvonne K Melemai) Hawaii'84.Y'81
☎ (808) 373-7117 . . 5018 Poola St, Honolulu, HI *96821*

Brown MR & MRS James Oliver JR (Lawrence—Joanne E Ralston) Y'75.H'77.Unn.H'70.Cal'79
☎ (617) 354-5419 . . 32 Avon Hill St, Cambridge, MA *02140*

Brown MISS Jane D
☎ (314) 997-4052 . . 13 Arbor Rd, St Louis, MO *63132*

Brown MR Jeremy P . . see MRS J Q Hunsicker 3d

Brown MRS John A (Helen Thacher) Cry.Ac. ⚓
☎ (610) MU8-3590 . . 599 Valley Forge Rd, Wayne, PA *19087*

Brown MR & MRS John K (Wendy E Buck) CtCol'83.Emory'80
☎ (804) 971-2044 . . 1505 Dairy Rd, Charlottesville, VA *22903*

Brown MR John M G (Joan Scull) Me.Ac.Ncd.
PO Box 220, Hainesport, NJ *08036*

Brown MR John N 3d—Ny.Cc.Hn.H'86
☎ (617) 864-6181 . . 20 Beech St, Cambridge, MA *02140*

Brown MR John R JR—Va'90 ⚓
☎ (540) 586-6807 . . Roaring Run Farm, Rte 1, Box 273, Goode, VA *24556*

Brown CAPT (RET) & MRS John Willoughby (M Betty Butzer) USN.Sth'48.GeoW'62 . . . .
MISS Elizabeth Otis—Ty'83—at
☎ (310) 392-3151 . . 2441—3 St, Apt 4, Santa Monica, CA *90405-3614*. . . . .
☎ (603) 643-5986
17 Downing Rd, Hanover, NH *03755*

Brown MR & MRS Joseph C (Susan B Judd) Rice'43.Tex'48 . . of
☎ (713) 621-1541 . . 274 Pine Hollow Lane, Houston, TX *77056*
☎ (915) 762-2412 . . Lambshead Ranch, Albany, TX *76430*

Brown MRS Katharine C (Jeffers—Katharine C Brown) Duke'75.NFla'82.NFla'83
☎ (904) 824-3769 . . 32 Marine St, Old St Augustine, FL *32084*

Brown MISS Katharine L—Ac.Me.Ncd.
☎ (610) 642-1420 . . 1347 Waverly Rd, Gladwyne, PA *19035*

Brown MRS Kay W (Kay A Wieland) Conn'59 . . . .
MR Carter L—Br'90—at 316 Independence Av SE, Washington, DC *20003* . . . .
☎ (714) 722-6946
1731 Skylark Lane, Newport Beach, CA *92660*

Brown MISS Laurie S—Vt'81.Pa'86
☎ (307) 734-0188 . . 400 Sagebrush Dv, Jackson, WY *83001*

Brown MRS Lawrance A (Morton—Coates—Esther V Larzelere) Me.
☎ (610) 642-1749 . . The Quadrangle 2215, 3300 Darby Rd, Haverford, PA *19041*

Brown MR & MRS Lawrance A JR (Elizabeth M Appel) SanJ'75.BMr'78.Cts.Pa'50
☎ (415) 321-8429 . . 1921 Middlefield Rd, Palo Alto, CA *94301*

Brown MR & MRS Lawrence J (Bonita A Baker) Colg'66 . . . .
MISS Leslie H—Hlns'93—at 6688 Wild Ridge Circle, Apt 2, Memphis, TN *38120* . . . .
MISS Lindsey P—Hartw'96 . . . .
☎ (901) 324-4835
238 Lombardy Rd, Memphis, TN *38111*

Brown MR & MRS Leland S (Mary M Mahony) StJ.Nw'30
☎ (914) 234-7338 . . ''Deer Run'' 196 Baldwin Rd, Mt Kisco, NY *10549*

Brown DR & MRS Lloyd (Laura W Dodge) H'34.H'38 ⚓
Parker Ridge H64, Box 270-260, Blue Hill, ME *04617*

Brown MR & MRS Lowell H JR (Ann M Towson) FlaSt'40.Ncd.P'41
☎ (352) 332-2756 . . 1125 NW 109 Dv, Gainesville, FL *32606*

Brown MISS M Patricia—Va'79
☎ (501) 664-0402 . . 5321 Hawthorne Rd, Little Rock, AR *72207*

Brown MRS Macauley (Barbara Macauley)
☎ (510) 944-7048 . . 896 Snyder Lane, Walnut Creek, CA *94598*

Brown DR & MRS Malcolm McD (Patricia M Athey) | ☎ (910) 761-8056
Sth'72.Y'69.Cl'73 . . . . | 1110 Arbor Rd,
MR Preston G . . . . | Winston-Salem, NC
MR Kenton R . . . . | *27104*

Brown MR & MRS Mason B (Karen A Kesmodel) Duke'88.Duke'89.Cal'92
☎ (310) 828-5013 . . 2601 Washington Av, Santa Monica, CA *90403*

Brown MR & MRS Matthews (Christy Ann Cowden) NMex'77.TexTech'77
☎ (915) 853-2496 . . Rte 1, Eldorado, TX *76936*

Brown MR & MRS Medford J (Master—Kneass—M Clarissa White)
Me.Sa.Ac.Wms'33.H'36 . . of
☎ (941) 261-4462 . . 3750 Rum Row, Naples, FL *34102*
☎ (610) 525-3286 . . 52 Pasture Lane, Bryn Mawr, PA *19010*

Brown MR & MRS Meredith M (Sylvia L Barnard) C.H'61.H'65
☎ (212) 360-6911 . . 1021 Park Av, New York, NY *10028*

Brown MR & MRS Michael M (Renée M Mullen) SUNY'83.Ore'84 . . of
☎ (011-852) 2577-7875 . . 11B Parkvale Dv, Discovery Bay, Hong Kong
☎ (808) 923-3155 . . PO Box 88047, Honolulu, HI *96830-8047*

Brown MR & MRS Michael T (Elizabeth A Nolte) LakeF'77.Ec.LakeF'77
☎ (508) 526-7985 . . 6 Old Neck Rd, Manchester, MA *01944*

Brown MRS Moreau D JR (Clark—Cynthia W Manchee) Sth'49.Unn.Dar.
☎ (203) 655-7322 . . ''Pond House'' 95 Half Mile Rd, Darien, CT *06820*

Brown MR & MRS Morgan Scott (Bradbury— | of ☎ (502)897-7911
Suzanne P C Robinett) Eyc.Y'62.Wes'73 . . . . . . | 434 Country Lane,
  MISS Sarah Riddle Bradbury—Cr'95—at | Louisville, KY
  50 Lexington Av, Apt 23D, New York, NY | *40207*
  10010 . . . . | ☎ (207) 935-2229
  MR John Randolph Bradbury JR—Eyc. | 152 Main St,
  Buck'92—at ☎ (202) 338-6328 | Fryeburg, ME *04037*
  1533 Foxhall Rd NW, Washington, DC *20007* |

Brown MRS Murray C (Merritt—Armstrong—Claresa F Meyer)
SCal'39.Cyc.Cas.
☎ (312) SU7-8285 . . 1301 N Astor St, Chicago, IL *60610*

Brown MR & MRS Myron D (Gay Correll) | ☎ (915) 584-5590
Tex'68.Tex'67 . . . . | 820 Rosinante Rd,
  MISS Courtney Gay—Stan'94—at U of Tex | El Paso, TX *79922*
  S'western Med . . . . |
  JUNIORS MR S Joshua . . . . |
  JUNIORS MR Micah A . . . . |

Brown MR N Allen JR . . see D B Baldridge

Brown MR & MRS Neilson (Ferguson—Jean Card) Ariz'35
☎ (602) 252-1226 . . 111 E Palm Lane, Phoenix, AZ *85004*

Brown CAPT (RET) & MRS Nicholas (Diane Vernes)
Ayc.Gv.Il.Ny.Cc.USN'56 ⚓
☎ (703) 276-9668 . . Weslie 602, 1401 N Oak St, Arlington, VA *22209*

Brown MISS Nina (Sprecher—Nina Brown) | ☎ (610) 896-6239
BMr'90.Cs. . . . . | ''The Village''
  MISS Alexandra Sprecher—LakeF'91—at | 1029 Black Rock
  ☎ (617) 497-8703 . . 18 Rice St, Apt 3, | Rd, Gladwyne, PA
  Cambridge, MA *02140* . . . . | *19035*
  DR Armand Grant Sprecher 3d— |
  Br'89.TJeff'94—at ☎ (816) 561-8772 |
  4317 Oak St, Kansas City, MO *64111* . . . . . . |
  MR Alexander Sprecher—Vt'94—at |
  ☎ (617) 497-8703 . . 18 Rice St, Apt 3, |
  Cambridge, MA *02140* . . . . |

Brown MR & MRS Owsley 2d (Christina S Lee) | of ☎ (502)895-8242
Cw.Ncd.Y'64.Stan'66 . . . . | 6501 Longview
  MISS Brooke L—at 2632 Hyde St, | Lane, Louisville,
  San Francisco, CA *94109* . . . . | KY *40222*
  MISS Augusta W—at U of Va . . . . | ☎ (502) 222-9786
  MR Owsley 3d—Va'93—at 2631 Clay St, | ''Breeze Hill Farm''
  San Francisco, CA *94115* . . . . | 6900 Shrader Lane,
   | Box 168C,
   | La Grange, KY
   | *40031*

Brown REV & MRS P Schuyler (Margaret E Meredith)
WOnt'67.Norw'93.Hn.H'52.Muenster'69
☎ (416) 241-5002 . . 85 Emmett Av, Apt 2002, Toronto, Ontario M6M 5A2, Canada

Brown MR & MRS Paul C (Claire Hilgedick)
☎ (717) 854-9372 . . 156 Scarboro Dv, York, PA *17403*

Brown MRS Pauline P (Schwerin—Pauline D Pratt) . | ☎ (617) 631-4631
  MISS Christina P Schwerin—Vt'90—at | 15 Circle St,
  ☎ (201) 653-0205 . . 420 Jefferson St, Apt 2B, | Marblehead, MA
  Hoboken, NJ *07030* . . . . | *01945*

Brown JUNIORS MR Peter H . . see MISS E B Stewart

Brown MR & MRS Peter Megaree (Stoddard— | of ☎ (212)427-6434
Alexandra Johns) Un.Chr.Plg.Snc.Rv.Ne.StJ. | 1125 Park Av,
Cly.Y'44 . . . . | New York, NY
  MISS Alexandra B Stoddard . . . . | *10128*
  MISS Brooke G Stoddard . . . . | ☎ (860) 535-1924
   | ''Rev John
   | Rathbone House''
   | 87 Water St,
   | Stonington, CT
   | *06378*

Brown MR & MRS Phillip F (T Elizabeth Via) | ☎ (334) 271-0606
TroySt'70.Htdon'70 . . . . | 1739 Croom Dv,
  JUNIORS MR Hunter M . . . . | Montgomery, AL
   | *36106*

Brown MR Preston 3d—K.Cc.H'58.H'61 . . . . | ☎ (202) 337-2083
  MISS Catherine St G—H'91—at Jakarta, | 2231—48 St NW,
  Indonesia . . . . | Washington, DC
  LT John P—USMC.H'95—at Quantico, VA | *20007*
  22134 . . . . |

Brown MISS Rebekah Bayard . . see D B Baldridge

Brown MR & MRS Richard P JR (Curtin—Virginia M Hanavan)
Sg.Ph.P.'42.Pa'48 . . of
☎ (215) 242-1053 . . 8800 Towanda St, Philadelphia, PA *19118*
☎ (246) 422-2182 . . ''High Trees'' Gibbs, St Peter, Barbados

Brown COL (RET) Robert C—USAF.Cal'37 . . . . ☎ (603) 924-3601
MISS Luise . . . . off Middle Hancock
MISS Elizabeth . . . . Rd, Peterborough, NH 03458

Brown MR & MRS Robert Dana (Hubbard—E Ann Kennedy) Ind'49.On.Rcch.BtP.Cho.Dth'46
☎ (561) 791-1451 . . Palm Beach Polo Club, 11874 Tilden Place, Wellington, FL 33414

Brown MRS Robert Gillespie (MacDougall—Major—Gloria S Boyd) Ri.StA.
☎ (203) 966-4209 . . 392 Brushy Ridge Rd, New Canaan, CT 06840

Brown MR & MRS Robert L (Charlotte A Banks) of ☎ (501)225-0060
So'63.Cl'65.Va'68 . . . . 10314 Cantrell Rd,
MR Stuart L—at U of South . . . . Little Rock, AR 72227
☎ (704) 743-2721 "High Mitre" Chatooga Woods Rd, Cashiers, NC 28717

Brown MRS Robert P (Mary C Clothier)
☎ (610) 933-2183 . . "Fox Spring Farm" Box 82, Paoli, PA 19301

Brown MR Robert U—Bhm.Nyc.Dth'34 . . of
☎ (212) 755-8072 . . 4 Sutton Place, New York, NY 10022
☎ (203) 869-3526 . . Creamer Hill Rd, Greenwich, CT 06830

Brown MRS Rodney W JR (Joanna O Palfrey)
☎ (617) 828-1238 . . 50 Green St, Canton, MA 02021

Brown MRS Russell SR (Parker—Dorothy Ferguson) MichSt'48.Myf.Ncd.Dar.
see Dilatory Domiciles

Brown MRS Sally P (Sally P Cook) Cent'y'50
☎ (904) 736-0500 . . Box 2942, De Land, FL 32723

Brown MISS Sandra B—Blooms'77
☎ (610) 527-7551 . . 1043 Conestoga Rd, Rosemont, PA 19010

Brown MR & MRS Shepard (Jane L Weld) *see*
Ws'54.Ec.Chi.H.'50 . . . . *Dilatory Domiciles*
MISS Elizabeth W . . . .

Brown MR & MRS Stanley N JR (Mary Duer) ☎ (301) 229-2191
BMuseum'87.K.Cly.Sl.H.'50 . . . . 4804 Ft Sumner Dv,
MISS Starr de Forest—Corc'89.Cly.—at Bethesda, MD 20816
☎ (202) 338-3636 . . 3267 N St NW, Apt 2, Washington, DC 20007-2839 . . . .
MR Henry A de F—Md'90.Pratt'92—at
☎ (212) 995-8680 . . 131 E 23 St, New York, NY 10010 . . . .

Brown MR & MRS Stephen Babcock (Elizabeth C of ☎ (212)535-6529
McGrath) Un.Cly.Pa'62 . . . . 1065 Lexington Av,
MISS Flemming H . . . . New York, NY 10021
JUNIORS MR D Winchester 3d . . . .
☎ (860) 672-4377 "Birch Cottage" 91 Pierce Lane, Cornwall, CT 06753

Brown MRS Stephen Cabot (Claudine Montgomery) ☎ (415) 579-5966
Sth'59.Bur. . . . . 1727 Forest View
MISS Amy C . . . . Av, Hillsborough, CA 94010

Brown MR & MRS Stephen M (Martha H Nichols) V'60.Ky'60
☎ (606) 255-5341 . . "Dunroven Stud" Box 13280, Lexington, KY 40583

Brown MISS Susan Coe (Davidson—Susan Coe Brown) Ty'78
☎ (310) 399-3459 . . 2441—3 St, Apt 4, Santa Monica, CA 90405-3614

Brown MRS Sylvia Battle (Sylvia M Battle) Pc.
☎ (215) CH2-3324 . . 409 E Evergreen Av, Philadelphia, PA 19118-2826

Brown MR & MRS T Wistar 4th (Blabon—Margaret P ☎ (610) 525-2139
Leonard) Me.Ac. . . . . 532 Maison Place,
MR Nicholas W—Me.—at ☎ (412) 343-8508 Bryn Mawr, PA 19010
514 Bellaire Av, Pittsburgh, PA 15210 . . . .

Brown DR & MRS T Wistar 5th (Emma Atkyns ☎ (215) 257-7332
Crowder) Rdc'66.VillaN'78.Me.Ac.P'63. 625 Hillcrest Dv,
Temp'67. . . . . Perkasie, PA 18944
MISS Katherine I . . . .
MISS Alice H . . . .

Brown MR & MRS Thatcher M 3d (Sarah L Brown) ☎ (212) 724-6482
Sth'61.Plg.Cs.Y.'58.Nu'65 . . . . 115 Central Park W,
MISS Eliza E . . . . New York, NY 10023

Brown MRS Thomas B Hynson JR (E Gillette Mingea) Ncd.Dc.
☎ (212) 831-2454 . . 425 E 86 St, New York, NY 10028

Brown MR Townsend 2d—Stan'51.Stan'52.H'55 . . of
☎ (212) 832-6591 . . 200 E 66 St, Apt 1101A, New York, NY 10021
☎ (516) 537-0131 . . "Green Ridge Cottage" Box 294, Sagaponack, NY 11962

Brown MISS Tracy J—Geo'86 . . see D C Thompson

Brown MR & MRS Travis Taylor (Ann du P Huidekoper) Cvc.NCar'30.NCar'32
☎ (202) 338-4222 . . 4848 Dexter St NW, Washington, DC 20007

Brown MR & MRS Vernon H JR (Ransom—Annette ☎ (203) 869-8757
H Bowles) Unn.DelB.Y'50. . . . . 28 Delwood Lane,
MISS Ashley B Ransom—Mid'88 . . . . Greenwich, CT 06830

Brown MR & MRS (REV) W Averell (Esther G Pierce) Hn.H'50
☎ (619) 326-4498 . . Box 817, Needles, CA 92363

Brown MR & MRS W Harman JR (Eleanor D ☎ (201) 335-1534
Winslow) . . . . 25 Larchdell Way,
MR William H 3d . . . . Mountain Lakes, NJ 07046

Brown MR & MRS W L Lyons JR (Alice Cary Farmer) Swb'59.K.Fic.Cly.Ncd.Va'58 . . of
☎ (502) 228-8143 . . "Fincastle" 7501 Wolf Pen Branch Rd, Prospect, KY 40059
☎ (212) 744-1600 . . 35 E 76 St, New York, NY 10021

Brown MR & MRS W Thacher (Lloyd A Hall) ☎ (610) 687-2688
NCar'68.Cry.Me.P'69.Pa'72. . . . . 360 Beaumont Rd,
MISS Quincy A . . . . Devon, PA 19333
MISS L Lee . . . .

Brown MR & MRS Walston S (Cook—Ellen F Regan) T.Ri.Rv.Stan'30
☎ (914) 351-2409 . . Box 772, Mountain Farm Rd, Tuxedo Park, NY 10987

Brown MR & MRS Walter F (Lenora Peace) Tex'55.A.Tex'56
☎ (210) 342-5400 . . 213 Sir Arthur Court, San Antonio, TX 78209

Brown MR & MRS Wesley H (Lucinda Siegler)
Sth'74.Emory'71 ....
JUNIORS MR Jeremy P 2d .... | of ☎ (413)773-3866
Box 167, Deerfield,
MA *01342*
☎ (413) 634-2151
523 Stage Rd,
Cummington, MA
01026

Brown MRS Willard R (Dann—Mary S Jacoby) Bnd'38.Chr.
☎ (305) 448-9928 . . 3720 Harlano St, Coral Gables, FL *33134-7195*

Brown MR & MRS William F L (Mary Ellen Hulsey) Hlns'82.W&L'82
☎ (908) 221-1352 . . 4 Fieldview Dv, Basking Ridge, NJ *07920-1117*

Brown MR & MRS William G (Solange M F Pezon)
Poitiers'66.On.P'64.H'67 ....
MISS Solange S P—at 1 Emerson Place, Apt 12A,
Boston, MA *02114* ....
MISS Sophie S P—at Princeton .... | of ☎ (561)546-1970
207 S Beach Rd,
Hobe Sound, FL
33455
☎ (847) 234-5018
1275 N Green Bay
Rd, Lake Forest, IL
60045

Brown MR & MRS William J W (Eliza F Smith)
MtH'77.S'Hall'60.CathU'63.Y'68 ⛵
☎ (412) 621-1011 . . 5367 Fair Oaks St, Pittsburgh, PA *15217*

Brown DR & MRS William Knox (Eleanor Brooks) Rice'43.Va'47
4025 Piping Rock Lane, Houston, TX *77027*

Brown MR & MRS Zadoc W (H Virginia Lowrey)
Bhm.Pcu.Cyb.P'41 ....
MR David T—at ☎ (808) 734-3595
3533 Alohea Av, Honolulu, HI *96816* .... | ☎ (808) 923-4238
3115 Noela Dv,
Honolulu, HI *96815*

Brownback MR & MRS John M (Elizabeth L Heppe) Cent'y'75.Elmira'76
☎ (610) 429-3994 . . 1409 Mill Creek Dv, West Chester, PA *19380*

Browne CAPT (RET) & MRS Aldis J JR (Bertha Erminger)
USN.Cho.On.An.Cw.Ofp.Ll.Cnt.Ncd.Y'35
☎ (305) 296-2943 . . 1600 Whalton St, Key West, FL *33040*

Browne MR & MRS Aldis J 3d (Reynolds—Maria C
Munroe) AmU'71.K.Cw.
MR Aldis J 4th—at 24 Thirtieth Av, Venice, CA
90291 ....
MR Ross S .... | of ☎ (310)301-6976
1614 Crescent Place,
Venice, CA *90291*
☎ (212) 744-8189
18 E 65 St,
New York, NY
10021

Browne MR & MRS Cecil (Jessie H Ehrenclou)
Myf.Cda.P'48.Cl'52 ....
MISS Sarah H .... | ☎ (410) 476-3796
Chancellor Point
Farm, PO Box 173,
Trappe, MD *21673*

Browne DR & MRS David A (Marilyn F Hudlin)
H'50.Va'55 ....
MISS Sarah R ....
MISS Amy H .... | ☎ (617) 585-6752
Box 177, Plympton,
MA *02367*

Browne MR & MRS F Sedgwick (Szigeti—Gloria Meneghini)
Trentino'72.Pr.Y'64
☎ (516) 367-3583 . . 1586 Laurel Hollow Rd, Syosset, NY *11791*

Browne MR & MRS Howell E (C Bliss Williams)
Y'71.H'74.Nw'78.Cw.H'68.Ch'76 ....
JUNIORS MISS Caroline B ....
JUNIORS MR Justin S .... | ☎ (773) 878-8834
910 Castlewood
Terr, Chicago, IL
60640

Browne MRS Junius H (Veirs C Allnutt) Cc.Ncd.....
MR Junius H JR—at 8831 Appian Way,
Los Angeles, CA *90046* .... | ☎ (415) 365-3622
601 Laurel Av, Apt
304, San Mateo, CA
94401

Browne MISS Lucy O (Watson—Lucy O Browne) CalArts'85
☎ (415) 386-6421 . . 539 Fourteenth Av, Apt 2, San Francisco,
CA *94118*

Browne MR & MRS Luis F V (Nathalie P Kuhn)
Ox'51.H'58 ....
MSRS Luis F V JR & Jeremy—at
☎ (561) 743-4108 . . 240 Eagle Dv, Jupiter, FL
33477 .... | ☎ (011-56-2)
208-3347
Clasificador 15,
Correo 10, Santiago,
Chile

Browne MR & MRS Merrick (Kathleen M Morrissey)
Cal'54.Bhm.SFr'50 ....
MISS Yvonne M ....
MISS Michele A ....
MR Merrick JR ....
MR Putnam H .... | of ☎ (510)522-5777
814 Ironwood Rd,
Alameda, CA *94501*
36690 Palm Court,
Rancho Mirage, CA
92270

Browne MRS Michael L (Marguerite B Mayer) Me. .
MISS Marguerite B—at ☎ (610) 293-9552
406 Bellevue Av, Wayne, PA *19087* .... | ☎ (610) MI9-5323
234 Booth Lane,
Haverford, PA
19041

Browne MR & MRS Stanhope S (Elizabeth W
Sturges) Ws'62.B.Rc.Ph.Ac.P.'53.H'56 ....
MISS Katrina C—P'89—at Berkeley, CA ......
MR Whitney R—Ty'91.Bost'94—at
☎ (212) 673-9716 . . 320 E 6 St, New York, NY
10003 .... | ☎ (215) 925-1372
306 S 2 St,
Philadelphia, PA
19106

Browne MR & MRS Timothy O (Denyse A Parsons)
Sth'65.Bhm.Ofp.Fr.Cly.Pa'64...............
MISS Natalie P ....
MISS Jennifer P .... | ☎ (415) 579-5886
2120 Parkside Av,
Hillsborough, CA
94010

Brownell MRS Frederic H (Hust—Nora Mead) Sg. .
MISS Samantha B—Sg....................
MISS Alexa B—at U of Va ....
MR Peter M—Sg. .... | ☎ (215) 646-3670
''Woodbridge
Meadow''
4 Timberfare Place,
Spring House, PA
19477

Brownell MR Frederic H—Sg.DU'67
see Dilatory Domiciles

Brownell MR Herbert .... Died at
New York, NY May 1'96

Brownell MR & MRS Kenneth Hyde (Esther M
McAlpin) Cly.Yn.Y'50.Stan'55 ....
MR Kenneth C—StLaw'81.Y'84 .... | ☎ (207) 829-6988
21 Sweetser Rd,
North Yarmouth,
ME *04097*

Brownell MR & MRS Lawrence D (Sarah M Whitin)
H'54...............................
MR Lawrence D JR—at ☎ (610) 630-9446
2119 Weber Lane, Norristown, PA *19403* .....
MR Stephen D—Drew'85 .... | ☎ (508) 992-0980
322 Smith Neck Rd,
South Dartmouth,
MA *02748*

Brownell MR Morris R—Sg.Rb.H.'30
☎ (610) 645-8809 . . 1400 Waverly Rd, Blair 040, Gladwyne, PA *19035*
Brownell MR & MRS Thomas H (Conchessa M Moran)
Wheat'85.Bab'90.Bow'83.Bab'89
☎ (802) 253-6958 . . PO Box 791, 356 W Shaw Hill Rd, Stowe,
VT *05672*

Brownell MR & MRS Timothy W (Margaret M Schneidman) Bnd'79.Tufts'83
☎ (313) 485-2609 . . 302 Oak St, Ypsilanti, MI *48198*

Browning MR & MRS George W (Ellen E Buck) | ☎ (617) 729-7456
Ne'65 . . . . | 2 Cabot St,
MISS Rebecca B . . . . | Winchester, MA
MR Carter W . . . . | *01890-3502*

Browning MRS Hays R (Green—Katherine | ☎ (202) 667-5151
Murchison) Cvc.Mt. | 2101 Connecticut
MR Hays R JR . . . . | Av NW, Apt 24,
| Washington, DC
| *20008-1754*

Browning MRS Jordice G (Jordice H Gigstad)
☎ (203) 762-7880 . . ''The Willows'' 457 Newtown Tpke, Wilton, CT *06897*

Browning MISS Kim—Humb'74
☎ (408) 375-3670 . . Box 222243, Carmel, CA *93922*

Browning MISS Margaretta W . . see D W Wood

Browning MR & MRS Robert M (Javoronok—Borie—Jeanne M Smith) Swth'34.LebVal'65
☎ (802) 457-3253 . . RR 2, 447 Church Hill, Woodstock, VT *05091*

Browning MRS Ward (Nancy Newsom)
821 I St, Eureka, CA *95501*

Browse MASTER Collin MacDonald (Timothy T) . . . . Born at
Concord, MA Jly 26'94

Browse MRS Robert H (Cintra Jones)
☎ (215) 345-8120 . . 519 Portsmouth Court, Doylestown, PA *18901*

Browse MR & MRS Timothy T (Susan B MacKinnon) StLaw'84.Bost'90.StLaw'81.Bost'90
☎ (508) 371-7130 . . 23 Saw Mill Rd, Concord, MA *01742*

Bruce MR David C—Md'93
3132 W Lambright St, Apt 208, Tampa, FL *33614*

Bruce MRS John G JR (Cora Edith Stafford) Nw'52 . | ☎ (508) 548-4329
MISS Amy E . . . . | 14 School St, Box
| 482, Woods Hole,
| MA *02543*

Bruce MR John G JR—VaPoly'51.Nw'52
☎ (601) 467-7144 . . 307 Gordon St, Waveland, MS *39576*

Bruce MISS Louise
☎ (212) 838-0800 . . 825 Fifth Av, New York, NY *10021-7268*

Bruce MR Thomas Allen—StJ.LaGrange'81.Aub'90
☎ (770) 941-6122 . . PO Box 408, Austell, GA *30001-0408*

Bruch MR & MRS John L 3d (Anne B L Carroll) Towson'83.Elk.Md.Myf.Sar.W&L'78
☎ (410) 377-5266 . . 122 Hopkins Rd, Baltimore, MD *21212*

Bruch MR & MRS Karl F JR (Virginia Chiles) Dth'40
☎ (216) 321-0831 . . 2284 N St James P'kway, Cleveland, OH *44106*

Brucker MRS Wallace H (Anne W Bradley) Cal'37 . | ☎ (915) 564-4512
LT COL & MRS Wallace M (Ella W Wolff) | 5000 Alabama St,
USA.NMex'66.SCal'75 . . . . | Apt 21, El Paso, TX
MISS Anne W—Tex'87 . . . . | *79930*

Bruechert MR & MRS Robert W P (Nancy C Siedlarz) Swb'81.Me.Rc.W.Dar.Ncd.Wis'77
☎ (610) 964-8184 . . 268 Berwind Rd, Radnor, PA *19087*

Bruel MR & MRS John C (Sybil E Schuyler) | ☎ (212) 877-6372
Ws'61.Ford'49 | 285 Central Park W,
MR John S—Geo'92 . . . . | New York, NY
MR Stephen W—Ty'94 . . . . | *10024*

Bruen MR Alexander H—Ty'74
☎ (703) 329-0725 . . Box 384, Alexandria, VA *22313*

Bruen MRS Alexander J (Lorna C Harrah) Cly.Dc.
☎ (401) 783-4098 . . ''Over Yonder'' 75 Robinson St, Box 571, Narragansett, RI *02882*

Bruen MR & MRS Edward F L (Marian S Gray) | ☎ (516) WA2-3546
Un.Pr.Plg.Lm.Snc.Hl.Fw.Cw.Ht.Ll.Vca.Ne.Coa. | 69 Mill River Rd,
Cly.Cl'36 | Oyster Bay, NY
MR Nicholas L—K.Plg.Ht.Lm.Pa'69—at | *11771*
☎ (212) CH2-3720 . . 14 Grove St, New York,
NY *10014* . . . .

Brumberger MR & MRS Neil A (Jacqueline H | ☎ (510) 376-9386
Heyward) Rob'tM'66.Br'69 . . . . | 121 Fiesta Circle,
JUNIORS MISS Heather A . . . . | Orinda, CA *94563*
JUNIORS MISS Leah H . . . . |

Brumder MR & MRS Robert C (Barbara Blakney) Stan'42
see Dilatory Domiciles

Brune MISS Constance T . . see G A Nordmann

Brune MRS J T Terry (Anne C Tilney) Cl'81.Cly.
☎ (804) 295-0981 . . 1706 Rugby Circle, Charlottesville, VA *22903*

Brune MR J T Terry—Unn.Hob'63 ⚓
☎ (804) 438-5168 . . PO Box 207, The Green, Irvington, VA *22480*

Brune MR Timothy H N . . see G A Nordmann

Brune MRS William H N (Josephine T Terry) Csn.
☎ (941) 966-8573 . . Bay Village, 8400 Vamo Rd, Sarasota, FL *34231*

Brune MR William H N 2d—StLaw'91 . . see G A Nordmann

Bruner MR & MRS Clark E (Pauline J Schrenk) Kt.It.Wes'36
☎ (216) 751-0535 . . 13515 Shaker Blvd, Cleveland, OH *44120*

Bruner DR & MRS William E 2d (Susan L Fraser) | ☎ (216) 921-3614
Kt.Tv.Wes'71 . . . . | 2906 Weybridge Rd,
JUNIORS MISS Amanda L . . . . | Shaker Heights, OH
JUNIORS MR Andrew E . . . . | *44120*

Brunet MR & MRS Stuart (Helen S Tower) Shcc.Mo.Hn.H'52.Va'58
☎ (201) 543-2456 . . ''Treetops'' 24 Corey Lane, Mendham, NJ *07945*

Brunet MR & MRS Stuart R (Carla J G de Módolo Sacon) HWSth'84
☎ (415) 459-8687 . . 94 Biscayne Dv, San Rafael, CA *94901*

Brunker MR & MRS Robert H (Beverly R Buck) Pa'51.Myf.Pa'50
☎ (209) 881-3375 . . 13278 Schell Rd, Oakdale, CA *95361*

Brunner MR & MRS Gordon F (Nadine M Slosar) | ☎ (513) 561-0013
Cm.Qc.Wis'61.Xav'65 . . . . | 7300 Sanderson
MISS Meggan T . . . . | Place, Cincinnati,
| OH *45243*

Brunner MR & MRS Kevin (Bronwyn P Mohun) Col'87.Cal'87
☎ (415) 885-5501 . . 2706 Laguna St, San Francisco, CA *94123*

Bruno MRS James Francis JR (Bennett—Sandra | ☎ (802) 867-4476
Isabella Skinker) Skd'63 . . . . | PO Box 753,
MISS Christina deT Bennett—at | West Rd, Dorset,
☎ (212) 831-7676 . . 171 E 88 St, Apt 2B, | VT *05251*
New York, NY *10128* |

Bruno MR James Francis JR—Pa'61 . . . . | PO Box 980,
MISS Michelle E—Bost'90 . . . . | Manchester, VT
MISS Jennifer L—Vt'93 . . . . | *05254*

Brunson MR & MRS Daniel P (Jennifer S Graham) Mich'86.NCarArts'89
☎ (212) 734-6663 . . 336 E 86 St, Apt 4H, New York, NY *10028*

Brush DR & MRS Charles F 3d (Ellen K Sparry) Sth'55.Cl'58.Cl'68.Un.C.Snc.Ne.Cs.Y.'47.Y'48.Cl'69
☎ (212) 831-5711 . . 1050 Fifth Av, Apt 5D, New York, NY *10128*

Brush MR Charles F 4th—Wit'86
☎ (212) 586-9272 . . 301 W 57 St, Apt 4AA, New York, NY *10019*
Brush MR & MRS Graham M (Katharine Van R Ulman)
V'51.Ds.Lm.Cly.Dth'46
☎ (860) 868-2703 . . PO Box 2546-0546, New Preston,
CT *06777-0546*
Brush MISS (DR) Karen Alexandra—Y'82.Cl'86.Camb'88.Camb'94 . . of
20 E 74 St, New York, NY *10021*
☎ (516) 749-1197 . . 42 Ram Island Rd, PO Box 2013, Shelter Island,
NY *11964*

Brush MR & MRS Peter W (Patricia E Cauffman)	☎ (914) 632-6767
Mariet'74.Mariet'74	63 Chester Place,
JUNIORS MISS Elizabeth E	Larchmont, NY
JUNIORS MR Peter W JR	*10538*

Bruton, Alastair M O & Eberstadt, Fernanda—Ox'82.Bristol'79 . . of
☎ (011-44-171) 581-2672 . . 48 Thurloe Square, London SW7, England
☎ (212) 861-8866 . . 791 Park Av, New York, NY *10021*
Brutschy MR & MRS Frederick J (Virginia L Skiff) Ariz'44.Dth'42.H'46
☎ (415) 948-3215 . . 11291 Magdalena Rd, Los Altos Hills,
CA *94024-5108*
Bryan MRS Ezra K (Marion B Shallenberger) May.
☎ (216) 247-6109 . . 250 Pheasant Run Dv, Chagrin Falls, OH *44022*
Bryan MRS Frederick van P (Denise F F Farquharson) Cs.
☎ (914) 832-9277 . . Deuel Hollow, Wingdale, NY *12594*

Bryan MR & MRS Gray MacW (Helen W Kincaid)	☎ (508) 627-8045
Eyc.	26 Shurtleff's Way,
MISS Anne G.	Box 351,
	Edgartown, MA
	02539

Bryan MR Hamilton V 2d
440A Lombard St, San Francisco, CA *94133*

Bryan MR & MRS Henry C JR (Sarah A McCarthy)	☎ (314) 994-1161
Wash'52.Wash'56	41 Ladue Terr,
MR Thomas C—Cal'84—at 146 Grand View,	Ladue, MO *63124*
Leucadia, CA *92024*	

Bryan MR & MRS John M (Florence A Eyre)	☎ (510) 547-4811
Bhm.Pcu.Tcy.Stan'47	10 Requa Place,
MISS Suzanne E	Piedmont, CA *94611*
MISS Amanda A	
MISS Anne de L	

Bryan MR & MRS Marsh A (Helen B Martin) Rm.P'55
☎ (908) 842-3462 . . 66 Buena Vista Av, Rumson, NJ *07760*
Bryan MR Michael A—NH'90
☎ (603) 431-3751 . . 51 Wentworth Rd, Rye, NH *03870*
Bryan MISS Nannette E
7 Attleboro Court, Shadow Lake Village, Red Bank, NJ *07701*

Bryan MR & MRS Richard D S (Betty Quirk) Rm.Ln.	☎ (908) 842-3730
MISS Martha M	10 Buttonwood Lane
	E, Rumson, NJ
	07760

Bryan VENERABLE & MRS Robert A (Faith B Lamb) Y.'54
☎ (508) 356-3509 . . 265 Argilla Rd, Ipswich, MA *01938*

Bryan MRS Sheldon M (Caroline E Barnett) Cs. . . .	of ☎ (212)988-6176
MISS Olive M—at ☎ (908) 549-3943	108 E 81 St,
45 Eggert Av, Metuchen, NJ *08840*	New York, NY
	10028
	☎ (860) 567-9240
	''Elephant Rock''
	49 Old Mt Tom Rd,
	Bantam, CT *06750*

Bryan MR Thomas M (Marsh A) . . . . Married at Jackson Hole, WY
Sharbrough MISS Amanda R (Frank) . . . . Sep 23'95
Bryan MR & MRS Thomas M (Amanda R Sharbrough) Colby'89.Denis'90
☎ (307) 733-0921 . . PO Box 61, Teton Village, WY *83025*
Bryan MRS W Wright (Ellen H Newell) Swb'26.Dar.Cda . . .of
☎ (404) 262-4516 . . Lenbrook Square 516, 3747 Peachtree Rd NE,
Atlanta, GA *30319-1361*
☎ (912) 638-3611 . . ''High Tide'' PO Box 644, Sea Island,
GA *31561*
Bryant MRS A Parker (C Elizabeth Dixon) V'32.Rcch.Evg.BtP.StJ.
☎ (561) 655-2727 . . 159 Australian Av, Palm Beach, FL *33480*
Bryant MISS Jennifer R—Les'92 . . see J N Byers 3d

Bryant MR & MRS John W (Anne C Phillips)	☎ (508) 526-9857
Sm.H'36	124 School St,
MISS Alida L	Manchester, MA
	01944

Bryant MRS S Beard (Hoffman—Suzan B Beard)	☎ (805) 969-6433
V'55	196 Santa Elena
MISS Suzan K—at ☎ (212) 982-8546	Lane,
205 Third Av, Apt 4L, New York, NY *10003* . .	Santa Barbara, CA
MR Robinson Thayer—at 9307 NE 118 Lane,	*93108*
Apt 202, Kirkland, WA *98034*	

Bryant MR Stearns J 3d—Denis'93 . . see J N Byers 3d
Bryce MRS Sylvie (Potter—Roop—Roop—Sylvie Bryce) Cly.
☎ (805) 969-5950 . . 1525 Monte Vista Rd, Santa Barbara, CA *93108*
Brydon MRS John C (Welthyan Harmon) Dar.
☎ (309) 647-2082 . . 1750 N Fourth Av, Apt 7, Canton, IL *61520*

Bubendey MR & MRS Paul F (Orrick—Holbrook—	☎ (561) 231-5799
Minor—Shirley K Smith) Plg.Cl'33	912 Seagrape Lane,
MR Paul F JR—at ☎ (415) 431-7745	Vero Beach, FL
406 Sanchez St, San Francisco, CA *94114*	*32963*

Buchanan MR & MRS Brooks R (Holly F Holman) Miss'83.Bay'83
☎ (601) 978-1995 . . 5362 Carolwood Dv, Jackson, MS *39211*
Buchanan MR & MRS Calumb J (Mary B Turner) Alf'93.Va'85.GeoM'90
4910 W Franklin St, Richmond, VA *23226*
Buchanan RR ADM (RET) Charles Allen—An.Cvc.Ny.Nrr.Cw.USN'26
2110 River Crescent Dv, Annapolis, MD *21401*

Buchanan MRS Charles M (Julia C Watts)	☎ (410) 435-8305
Swb'59.Elk.Mv.	104 W Melrose Av,
MISS Julia C	Baltimore, MD
MR William McM	*21210*
MR John S.	

Buchanan MRS De Witt W JR (Katherine L Hamilton) Sr.On.Cnt.Cas.Ncd.
☎ (847) 234-1587 . . 541 E Woodland Rd, Lake Forest, IL *60045*

Buchanan MR & MRS Eustace W (Joan S Gardner) ☎ (508) 922-1650
Ec.Un.Myc.Cw.Chi.Pn.P'50.H'56. . . . . 151 West St,
  MISS Emily S—at ☎ (212) 486-2864   Beverly Farms, MA
  141 E 62 St, New York, NY *10021* *01915*
  MR David H W—P'88—at ☎ (617) 723-5740
  20 Stillman St, Boston, MA *02113*. . . . .
  MR John L—Bates'93—at ☎ (212) 988-7137
  427 E 84 St, New York, NY *10028* . . . .

Buchanan DR & MRS J Robert (Susan T Carver) ☎ (860) 663-1211
Swth'52.Cl'56.Unn.Sm.Csn.Aht'50.Cr'54 . . . . . 5 Chestnut Hill Rd,
  MISS Allyn H—Col'90—at ☎ (303) 393-1769   PO Box 669,
  1628 Detroit St, Denver, CO *80206* . . . . Killingworth, CT
  06419

Buchanan MR & MRS James J (Joanne H Cherrington) Pn.P'46.H'48
4609 Bayard St, Apt 81, Pittsburgh, PA *15213*

Buchanan MR & MRS John Ewing (Ann E Wailes) Ncd.MissSt'49
☎ (601) 856-0699 . . 10 Whisper Ridge Dv, Madison, MS *39110*

Buchanan MR & MRS John G (McDougall—Olive E Johnson)
106 Old Billerica Rd, Apt 232, Bedford, MA *01730-1278*

Buchanan MR & MRS John G 3d (Denise E Chamberlain)
Wheat'72.Bost'78.Cvc.P'72.Ox'74.H'78
☎ (202) 966-5991 . . 3307 Newark St NW, Washington, DC *20008*

Buchanan MRS John Ripley (Howell—Jane Archer)
☎ (702) 735-7058 . . 350 Desert Inn Rd, Apt A101, Las Vegas,
NV *89109*

Buchanan MRS Kenneth H (Van Natta—Jennifer S ☎ (203) 221-7679
Harcourt) . . . . 24 Whitney St,
  MR Jason Van Natta. . . . . Westport, CT *06880*

Buchanan MR Kenneth H . . of
☎ (212) 929-0857 . . 30 W 15 St, New York, NY *10011*
☎ (516) 537-7942 . . 4 Five Rod H'way, PO Box 98, Sagaponack,
NY *11962*

Buchanan MRS Mary G (Hockenbury—Matthai—Mary G Buchanan)
MaryW'56.Gv.Gi.Ncd.
☎ (410) 269-6969 . . 11B2 President Point Dv, Annapolis, MD *21403*

Buchanan MR & MRS Ross T (Sharon M Flanagan)
Dth'87.Nw'92.Aht'87 . . of
☎ (612) 922-9226 . . 5328 Zenith Av S, Minneapolis, MN *55410*
☎ (860) 663-1211 . . 5 Chestnut Hill Rd, PO Box 744, Killingworth, CT
06419

Buchanan MR & MRS Stephen A (Louise Farnham) Dept of State,
Md'68 . . . . N'Djamena,
  MISS Sandra L—Evang'90—at 4112F Providence   Washington, DC
  Rd, Charlotte, NC *28211* *20521*
  MR Christopher D . . . .

Buchanan MRS Wiley T JR (Ruth E Hale) Cvc. . . . . ☎ (202) 362-1982
  MR Wiley T 3d—Mt.Cvc.Rol'69—at   4220 Nebraska Av
  ☎ (505) 986-6056 . . 125 Lincoln Av, Apt 400,   NW, Washington,
  Santa Fe, NM *87501* . . . . DC *20016*

Buchanan MR & MRS William H JR (Eleanor A ☎ (203) 966-5797
Lincoln) StA.Myf.Ncd.Pn.P'59.H'63 . . . . 151 Weeburn Dv,
  MISS Diana A—Ham'92.P.—at   New Canaan, CT
  ☎ (212) 580-9651 . . 201 W 77 St, New York,   *06840*
  NY *10024*. . . . .
  MISS Jessica R—Ham'94.P.—at
  ☎ (212) 580-9651 . . 201 W 77 St, New York,
  NY *10024*. . . . .

Buchen MR & MRS Walther H (Ellen D Smith) H'49
☎ (415) 435-1745 . . 42 Bayview Av, Belvedere, CA *94920*

Buchet MR Michael M X—Conn'85.Loy'90
☎ (301) 587-8079 . . 9900 Georgia Av, Apt 617, Silver Spring,
MD *20902*

Buchet MR Robert F—Lm.Snc . . . see MRS W G Marden

Buchtel MRS Hooker (McDonald—Andrews—Alice ☎ (615) 373-9367
K Hooker) Cda. . . . . 360 Vaughn Rd,
  MR John J H—at 245 E 58 St, New York, NY   Nashville, TN *37221*
  10022 . . . .

Buck MR & MRS Alexander K (Sara H Long) M.
☎ (609) 924-3261 . . 4535 Province Line Rd, Princeton, NJ *08540*

Buck MR & MRS C Austin (Marguerite A Doubleday)
Mo.Sm.L.Va'51.Leh'52
161 Clarkson Lane, Vero Beach, FL *32963*

Buck MRS Frank H JR (Corinne Hellier) Cal'33
☎ (916) 432-1429 . . 18564 Siesta Dv, Penn Valley, CA *95946*

Buck MRS Gladys R (Gladys A Rogers) ☎ (215) 238-9124
Pa'72.Dick'76 . . . . 602 Pine St,
  JUNIORS MR Frederick S 3d . . . . Philadelphia, PA
  19106

Buck MRS Gurdon (Elizabeth Jackson)
☎ (508) 997-0944 . . 8 Winter St, South Dartmouth, MA *02748*

Buck MR Harold P . . . . ☎ (516) 826-6337
  MR Harold P JR . . . . 82 Twin Lane N,
  MR Stephen L—Del'90 . . . . Wantagh, NY *11793*

Buck MRS J Mahlon (Grace I Knapp) Me.
☎ (610) 525-1458 . . 409 Garden Lane, Bryn Mawr, PA *19010-3625*

Buck MR & MRS J Mahlon JR (Elia G Durr) Me.M.Cs.P'46 . . of
☎ (610) 649-6247 . . 121 Rose Lane, Haverford, PA *19041-1724*
☎ (441) 236-7292 . . 48 Mizzentop, Warwick WK 06, Bermuda

Buck MR J Orton JR—Rv.Sar.Cw.Ofp.Snc.Ne.Cc.Coa.
☎ (541) 882-5677 . . 1842 Esplanade Av, Apt 4, Klamath Falls,
OR *97601-2267*

Buck MR & MRS Leonard J (Elizabeth C Gray) Va'85.Cl'89.Va'86
☎ (919) 967-0461 . . 713 Greenwood Rd, Chapel Hill, NC *27514*

Buck MR & MRS N Harrison (Nancy C P Brown) Va'83.Hob'81
☎ (609) 924-7781 . . 37 Pheasant Hill Rd, Princeton, NJ *08540*

Buck MR & MRS Robert B (Leslie L Patterson) ☎ (408) 624-5233
Dth'67.Hast'70 . . . . Box 710,
  MR Jeremiah E . . . . Pebble Beach, CA
  JUNIORS MISS Lindsay M *93953*
  JUNIORS MR Alexander R . . . .

Buck MR Roswell S—Bf.Buf.Y'26 ⚓
☎ (716) 881-4926 . . PO Box 1150, Buffalo, NY *14205*

Buck MR & MRS Walter H (Mary B Mulvey) Cal'65 . ☎ (203) 255-4403
  MISS Heather L—at Yale Grad . . . . 134 Center St,
  MR Stephen M—at U of Mich Grad . . . . PO Box 1127,
  JUNIORS MR Michael P—at N'western . . . . Southport, CT *06490*

Buck MR & MRS William C (Laura E Thomas)
Brad'51.Me.M.Gm.Ac.Laf'50 . . of
☎ (610) MU8-8593 . . 274 Hothorpe Lane, Villanova, PA *19085*
☎ (561) 234-5055 . . 560 Coconut Palm Rd, John's Island, Vero Beach,
FL *32963*

Buck MR & MRS William P (Carol C Pinger) ☎ (503) 227-7676
Mls'69.Duke'67 . . . . 1046 SW King St,
MR Peter R . . . . Portland, OR *97205*
JUNIORS MR Spencer McG . . . .

Buckingham MRS Fisher A (Helen Merrill) Cal'21.Dar.
☎ (510) 428-1062 . . 110—41 St, Oakland, CA *94611*

Buckingham MR & MRS Henry P (Janice of ☎ (805)642-5248
Van Duren) StMarys'48.Cal'51 . . . . 4720 Rockford
MISS Jennie A—SonSt'77.SonSt'81.Mass'84 . . . Court, Ventura, CA
MR Charles S *93003*
MR Mark V—Cal'82.SCal'88 . . . . ☎ (415) 669-7154
MR Andrew A—StMarys'84 . . . . ''Aldersea''
350 Aberdeen Way,
Inverness, CA *94947*

Buckley MR C Fitzgerald 3d
☎ (603) 237-8977 . . Fish Pond Rd, Box 166, Colebrook, NH *03576*

Buckley MR & MRS Christopher T (Lucy S Gregg) Wms'77.C.Yn.Y'76 ⚓
☎ (202) 244-1927 . . 3516 Newark St NW, Washington, DC *20016*

Buckley MR & MRS David G (Amelia P Blomquist) B'gton'83.Vt'72
☎ (802) 442-8601 . . 21 Main St, North Bennington, VT *05257*

Buckley MR & MRS Douglas E (Cooke—Judith M ☎ (011-64-6)
Mackesy) 874-7799
JUNIORS MR Sean F . . . . ''Hapua'' RD 14,
1668 Kahuranaki
Rd, Havelock North,
New Zealand

Buckley MR & MRS Geoffrey L (Alexandra MacColl)
CtCol'89.Ore'93.CtCol'87.Ore'92
☎ (301) 913-9546 . . 4826 Bradley Blvd, Chevy Chase, MD *20815*

Buckley MRS Howell (Elizabeth H Howell)
☎ (954) 523-2739 . . 100 SW Eighteenth Av, Ft Lauderdale, FL *33312*

Buckley MR & MRS James E (Frances E McMahon) ☎ (914) 967-7163
StEliz'70.Kt.P.'70.JCar'80 . . . . 9 Manursing Way,
MISS Ellen Claire—at Miami U. . . . . Rye, NY *10580*
MISS Kathryn Anne—at Princeton . . . .
MISS Mary Frances . . . .

Buckley MR & MRS John S (Elizabeth R Grimm) ☎ (207) 883-6815
Stv'46.Pa'50 . . . . 6 Bird's Nest Lane,
MISS Elizabeth M R . . . . Prouts Neck,
MR John S JR—Col'72—at 3333 E Bayaud Av, Scarborough, ME
Denver, CO *80209* *04074*

Buckley MR & MRS Julian G (Christina W 34 Goose Hill Rd,
Boardman) Bnd'38.Dc.H'28.Nu'37.Nu'52 . . . . . Box 156, Cold
MR James Lawrence—LIU'70 . . . . Spring Harbor, NY
11724

Buckley MR & MRS Martin B (Lucy M Knowles) Ws'71.SCar'64
☎ (803) 649-4422 . . 1141 Two Notch Rd SE, Aiken, SC *29803*

Buckley MRS Thomas C T (Elizabeth S Cheney)
☎ (716) 243-1206 . . 48 Westview Crescent, Geneseo, NY *14454*

Buckley MR & MRS William F JR (Patricia A Taylor) Bhm.Ny.C.Km.Y'50
Wallacks Dv, Stamford, CT *06902*

Bucklin MRS Charles M (Martha S Jackson) of ☎ (603)526-6675
Wheat'60 . . . . ''Meadow House''
MISS Caroline M—*see Dilatory Domiciles* . . . . . PO Box 183,
New London, NH
03257
☎ (941) 262-2452
3420 Gulf Shore
Blvd N, Apt 36,
Naples, FL *34103*

Bucklin MR & MRS William N 3d (McIntosh—Linda ☎ (415) 567-6281
Hale) Pcu.Cal'52 . . . . 2623 Divisadero St,
JUNIORS MR John H . . . . San Francisco, CA
MR Christian C McIntosh *94123*

Buckminster MR & MRS W Bradley (Charis B Box 4443,
Johns) Bhm.P'51 . . . . Carmel, CA *93921*
MISS Diana . . . .
MISS Marcia . . . .
MR W Bradley 3d . . . .

Bucknall MR & MRS G Stafford (M Bridget Burns) Bost'80.Vt'79
☎ (203) 622-3026 . . 12 Frontier Rd, Greenwich, CT *06807*

Bucknall MR & MRS William S (Ann M Hamilton) ☎ (203) 661-6727
Snc.Cly.Ncd.H'45 . . . . Mead Point,
MR William H—at ☎ (406) 222-3620 Greenwich, CT
Trail Creek S, Emigrant, MT *59027* *06830*

Bucknell MR Nathaniel S
☎ (212) 481-3120 . . 140 E 28 St, Apt 5E, New York, NY *10016*

Bucove DR & MRS Arnold D (Mayhew—Gladys H L Lloyd)
Cl'65.Cl'56.Nu'61 . . of
☎ (914) 677-8093 . . ''Deep Hollow Farm'' RR 1, Box 104, Deep
Hollow Rd, Millbrook, NY *12545*
☎ (607) 547-8773 . . ''Seven Maples'' RR 3, Box 240A, Greenough Rd,
Cooperstown, NY *13326*

Buddenhagen MR & MRS Frederick L (Bartle— ☎ (212) 288-5387
Kathleen I Burns) Mds.Cly.Y'65.Mit'67 . . . . . . 211 E 70 St,
MR Thomas P Bartle 3d . . . . New York, NY
10021

Buddenhagen MR & MRS Paul S (Patricia R Grafmueller) H'68
☎ (617) 277-9418 . . 137 Clinton Rd, Brookline, MA *02146*

Buell MR Charles C—Denis'61

Buell MR & MRS Charles C—Denis'61
☎ (504) 895-3586 . . 42426 Meadow Wood Dv, Ponchatoula, LA *70454*

Buell MISS Martha J . . see W B Fleming JR

Buell MRS Mary I (Mary L Igert) Ncmb'62
☎ (504) 866-2544 . . 2701 Palmer Av, New Orleans, LA *70118-6323*

Buell MISS N Catherine . . see C A Volmert

Buell MR & MRS William A (O'Shaughnessy—Mary W Cutler)
Il.Srb.P'46
☎ (401) 847-7751 . . 468 Purgatory Rd, Middletown, RI *02842*

Buff MRS Anderson (Marguerite S Anderson)
☎ (908) 291-3009 . . 60 Bay Av, Highlands, NJ *07732*

Buffinton MRS John M (Biddle—Kate H McCreary) Ncd.
☎ (401) 423-1109 . . 31 Bay View Dv, Jamestown, RI *02835*

Buffum MR & MRS Charles G 3d (Suzanne K Agnew) W&L'60
☎ (816) 333-6324 . . 645 Westover Rd, Kansas City, MO *64113*

Buffum MR Edwin C . . see MRS H P Krogstad

Buffum MR & MRS Fenwick N (Mildred C Streeter) Mid'33
☎ (540) 436-3299 . . ''Mil-Fen Farm'' Rte 1, Box 569, Maurertown,
VA *22644*

Buffum MR & MRS G Allen (Hepburn—Bowman— | ☎ (610) 645-0977
Kathleen Droescher) PAFA'59.Me.Fw.Y'44 ... | 200 N Wynnewood
  MISS Alexandra Kip Bowman—Wit'88 ..... | Av, Wynnewood,
| PA *19096*
Buffum MR & MRS Robert C (Sydney F Hinkle) Sth'51.Ty'52
  ☎ (941) 474-6693 . . 7660 Manasota Key Rd, Englewood, FL *34223*
Buffum MR & MRS Robert C JR (Linda A DePatie) | ☎ (617) 235-9340
BostColl'76.Ty'77 .... | 19 Aberdeen Rd,
  JUNIORS MISS Alexa C .... | Wellesley, MA
| *02181*
Buford MR & MRS A Sidney 3d (Lucy A Flippin) Vmi'34.Va'37
  ☎ (540) 463-7766 . . Old Manse, Rte 1, Box 234, Lexington, VA *24450*
Buford MR & MRS Anthony A JR (Carolyn W | ☎ (561) 231-3581
McCluney) Rcp.Me.M.Gm.Pa'62 .... | 131 Stingaree Point,
  MISS Elisabeth M—at ☎ (415) 928-0407 | Vero Beach, FL
1812 Green St, San Francisco, CA *94123* ..... | *32963*
  MR Anthony A 3d—at ☎ (610) 823-9479 |
308 Overlook Lane, Conshohocken, PA *19428* . |
  JUNIORS MR Nicolaus L .... |
Buice MR & MRS William T 3d (M Stuart Upchurch) | ☎ (212) 674-4039
Duke'64.Gr.Cs.W&L'61 .... | 32 Washington
  MISS Merrill S—Duke'88 .... | Square W,
  MR Charles U—Y'94 .... | New York, NY
| *10011*
Bulazel MR & MRS Alexander (Amanda A Snowden) Ham'87
78 John St, Greenwich, CT *06830*
Bulger MISS Jane—Ih.
  ☎ (847) 446-2071 . . 680 Green Bay Rd, Apt 106, Winnetka, IL *60093*
Bulkeley MR Christopher Z (John Z) .... Married at Sacramento, CA
Suzuki MISS Jo Anne (Stimson) .... Apr 29'95
Bulkeley MR & MRS John Z (Caroline H Spalding) | ☎ (415) 851-0949
Pcu.Aht'60.Cl'62 .... | 25 Woodview Lane,
  MR Geoffrey S—at 1743 Golden Gate Av, | Woodside, CA
Apt 12, San Francisco, CA *94115* .... | *94062*
Bulkeley MISS Virginia C (John Z) .... Married at Portola Valley, CA
Hull MR Robert S (Robert J) .... May 18'96
Bulkley MR Jonathan D—IIT'57 .... | ☎ (415) 668-2248
  MISS Adrienne..................... | 147 Tenth Av,
  MR Derick M—Cal'90 .... | San Francisco, CA
| *94118*
Bulkley MRS Robert J JR (Lorraine Warner)
see Dilatory Domiciles
Bull MR & MRS Donald (Susan J Spalding) | ☎ (415) 457-0444
Bhm.Cal'59 .... | 25 Quisisana Dv,
  MR Douglas E—Sfg.Cal'86—at | Kentfield, CA *94904*
  ☎ (415) 386-8845 . . 2539 Lake St, Apt 3, |
San Francisco, CA *94121* .... |
Bull MR Frederick K 2d .... | ☎ (207) 865-6198
  MR Michael C .... | Harraseeket Rd,
  MR Thomas D..................... | Box 62,
| South Freeport, ME
| *04078*
Bull MRS Henry H (Janice E Roche)
  ☎ (415) 323-2023 . . 1235 Santa Cruz Av, Menlo Park, CA *94025*

Bull MR & MRS R Alden (Rachel L Bacon) | 223 Kirk Rd,
Godd'66.Temp'72.Godd'65.Temp'72 .... | Boothwyn, PA
  MISS Tabitha B .... | *19061*
  JUNIORS MR Benjamin B .... |
  JUNIORS MR George E .... |
Bull MRS Richard C (Josephine B Rothermel) Fi.
  ☎ (610) 525-0348 . . 11 Pond Lane, Bryn Mawr, PA *19010*
Bull MR & MRS Richard C (Katherine L Stark) | of ☎ (202)625-6839
V'56.Sl.Ncd.P'54 .... | 3026 P St NW,
  MR Winston S T—at ☎ (314) 367-4848 | Washington, DC
4930 Washington Av, Apt 1W, St Louis, MO | *20007*
63108 .... | ☎ (540) 675-1544
| "Killermont House"
| 133 Rush River,
| Washington, VA
| *22747*
Bull MR & MRS Richard S 3d (Leslie McK Bass) Memp'81.Kas'77
  ☎ (847) 295-6218 . . 1256 N Edgewood Rd, Lake Forest, IL *60045*
Bull MR & MRS Stephen B (Quinlan—Jeanne Fugazzi)
Cin'69.StLaw'63 . . of
  ☎ (202) 462-1698 . . 2101 Connecticut Av NW, Washington, DC *20008*
  ☎ (410) 745-3102 . . "Tide Mill Cove" Box 2, Yacht Club Rd,
St Michaels, MD *21663*
Bullard MR Brian B . . see M McVickar
Bullard MR & MRS Edward D (Sharon C Smith) | ☎ (606) 266-2404
Cal'72.Pcu.Bhm.Cp.Cal'71.H'75 .... | 320 Ridgeway Rd,
  JUNIORS MISS Victoria K—at Groton .... | Lexington, KY
  JUNIORS MR Edward W—at Stanford .... | *40502*
Bullard MR Henry S—H'36
  ☎ (203) 259-0173 . . 449 Mill Plain Rd, Fairfield, CT *06430*
Bullard DR & MRS John C (Katharine Kilburn) H.'43
  ☎ (508) 994-2895 . . PO Box 61P, South Dartmouth, MA *02748*
Bullard MR & MRS Lyman G (Sarah A Bell) H.'44
  ☎ (508) 475-2813 . . 107 Highland Rd, Andover, MA *01810*
Bullen MR & MRS George H (Joyce A Graham) | of ☎ (561)546-9953
Ck.Mds.Lic.Ny.Nu'68 .... | 414 S Beach Rd,
  MISS Alicia G—at Rollins................. | Hobe Sound, FL
| *33455*
| ☎ (516) 676-7090
| Matinecock Farms,
| PO Box 357,
| Locust Valley, NY
| *11560*
Bullen MISS Melissa M (George H) .... Married at Hobe Sound, FL
Johnson MR Sargent S (Harry A JR) .... Apr 13'96
Bullen MR & MRS Richard H (de Leur—Anne-Marie Bloch)
Cly.UtahSt'41.H'43
  ☎ (212) FI8-4417 . . 1050 Fifth Av, Apt 14D, New York, NY *10028*
Bullerjahn MR & MRS Eduard H (Grant—Julianna Sweetser) Sm.Mit'43
  ☎ (401) 635-2651 . . "Stove House" 706 W Main Rd, Little Compton,
RI *02837*
Bullerjahn MR John te S
  ☎ (617) 255-0512 . . 15 Indian Lane, Marlborough, MA *01752*
Bullitt MRS Harrison (Louise H Harrison)
  ☎ (610) MU8-1723 . . 500 E Lancaster Av, Apt 121D, St Davids,
PA *19087*

Bullitt MRS L Ralston (Alleen Towle)
☎ (619) 472-6690 . . Mt Miguel Village 1054, 325 Kempton St,
Spring Valley, CA *91977*

Bullitt MR & MRS Logan McK 3d (Mary B Hirst) Pc.Pa'49
☎ (215) VE6-5649 . . 111 College Av, Flourtown, PA *19031-1931*

Bullitt MR & MRS Orville H JR (Thompson—Laura W Lee) Gm.Ac.Ph.Pa'41.Ill'44 . . . . | ☎ (610) 254-8284
MR A Scott—at ☎ (610) 889-9759 . . Box 357, | 402 Inveraray Rd,
Devon, PA *19333* . . . . | Villanova, PA *19085*
   MISS Laura Lee Thompson—at 507B Calais
   Rd, Worcester, VT *05682* . . . . |

Bullitt MR & MRS R Thayer (Judith H Renner) | ☎ (215) 242-9269
Hood'67.Pitt'67.Temp'78 . . . . | 8718 Prospect Av,
MR John S C—at U of Pa . . . . | Philadelphia, PA
JUNIORS MISS Shelby I—at Brooks . . . . | *19118*

Bullitt MR & MRS Thomas W (Judith A Bachelder)
Me'76.VaCmth'80.Cy.Ken'77
☎ (617) 734-8841 . . 423 Walnut St, Brookline, MA *02146*

Bullitt Thomas Walker (Menzies—Katharine Esther Stammers)
☎ (502) 426-2126 . . "Oxmoor" 7500 Shelbyville Rd, Louisville,
KY *40222*

Bullitt MR & MRS William C (Fay M Patterson) | ☎ (215) 242-5690
Tufts'68.Ph.Pc.H'68.Pa'71 . . . . | 103 W Moreland
MISS Susan Brooke—at Skidmore . . . . | Av, Philadelphia,
MR W Christian JR—at Trinity . . . . | PA *19118*

Bullock MR & MRS A George 2d (Carter—Gertrude | ☎ (617) 329-6449
B Ely) H'31 . . . . | 296 Stoney Lea Rd,
MR A George JR—at Princeton, MA *01541* . . . . | Dedham, MA *02026*

Bullock MR & MRS Charles S JR (Susanne Barbour) | ☎ (516) 324-1221
Sth'55.K.B.BtP.Mds.Y'54 . . . . | Lily Pond Lane,
MR Charles S 3d—at ☎ (512) 836-2242 | Box 1032,
9215 Great Hills Trail, Austin, TX *78759* . . . . . | East Hampton, NY
    | *11937*

Bullock MR & MRS David D R (Christine D Finch) Ny.Colby'87
☎ (212) 249-9051 . . 525 E 72 St, New York, NY *10021*

Bullock MRS Horace Ridgely (Mary J King) M.Me.
☎ (610) MI2-0797 . . 210 Elbow Lane, Haverford, PA *19041*

Bullock MR Hugh—Err.Rc.Ri.C.Un.Ny.Mt.Cvc.
Chr.Plg.Fw.Ne.StJ.Wms'21
☎ (212) TR9-5858 . . 1030 Fifth Av, New York, NY *10028*

Bullock Leslie Kitchell (de Braux—Leslie H | ☎ (203) 629-2558
Kitchell) Ny. | 470 N Maple Av,
MISS Sabrina C—at 246 SW 15 St, Apt 4A, Bend, | Greenwich, CT
OR *97702* . . . . | *06830*
MISS Karena R . . . . |

Bullock MRS Rufus (Mary K Colgate) Au.Cly. . . . . | ☎ (203) 661-9797
MISS Rachel D—at ☎ (212) 925-1728 | 50 Upland Dv,
89 Franklin St, New York, NY *10013* . . . . | Greenwich, CT
    | *06831*

Bullock MR & MRS Thomas F (Lucy S L Amerman) | ☎ (609) 795-3817
Rcp.LaS'73 . . . . | 101 Chews Landing
JUNIORS MR Ethan H T . . . . | Rd, Haddonfield, NJ
    | *08033*

Bultman MRS Richard P (Jane E Hoke)
☎ (201) 948-5734 . . 35 Kent Rd, Newton, NJ *07860*

Bump MRS Milan R (Betty B La Fean) . . . . | ☎ (203) 972-8606
MISS Josephine R—at Wellesley, MA *02181* . . . | Graystone 12,
    | 56 Lakeview Av,
    | New Canaan, CT
    | *06840*

Bundy MRS Frederick McG (Wheeler—Dodge—Elisabeth J Shrigley)
Ec.Cy.Chi.Ncd.
☎ (508) 526-1921 . . 102 Bridge St, Manchester, MA *01944-1414*

Bundy MR & MRS Graham L (Margaret Primm Anthon) NCar'91.NCar'91
☎ (314) 963-9192 . . 8671 Rosalie Av, St Louis, MO *63144*

Bundy MR & MRS Harvey H 3d (Blakely Fetridge) | ☎ (847) 446-4849
Wheat'66.Nat'lLouis'85.Cho.Ih.Y'66.Dth'68 . . . | 740 Ardsley Rd,
MISS Elizabeth Lowell . . . . | Winnetka, IL *60093*
JUNIORS MR Reed F—at Colby . . . . |

Bundy MRS Judith C (Judith A Cox) Neb'63.Ncd. . . | ☎ (203) 869-9654
MR Carter A—Va'90.Cal'95 . . . . | 9 River Rd,
    | Cos Cob, CT *06807*

Bundy MR & MRS McGeorge (Mary B Lothrop) Rdc'46.Y'40
170 E 79 St, New York, NY *10021-0436*

Bundy MR & MRS Thomas F JR (Royce—Marilyn J | of ☎ (203)869-3480
Maczko) V'64.Nu'83.K.Ty'62 . . . . | 120 Dingletown Rd,
MISS Jennifer H Royce—at Columbia . . . . . . | Greenwich, CT
MISS Amanda B Royce—at Trinity . . . . | *06830*
MR Charles M Royce JR—at Brown . . . . | ☎ (518) 589-5920
    | "The Whim"
    | Onteora Club,
    | Tannersville, NY
    | *12485*

Bunker MRS Ellen M (Gentil—Ellen M Bunker)
☎ (520) 575-8062 . . 2509 N Campbell Av, Apt 17, Tucson, AZ *85719*

Bunker MRS Garrett (Elizabeth F Bunker) | ☎ (860) 633-7671
Mls'42.Dar.Myf.Yn. | 46 Slater Rd,
MISSES Anne F & Eleanor V . . . . | Glastonbury, CT
MSRS John H & George | *06033*
MISS Elizabeth G (Kelley—Elizabeth G Bunker)
StJos'72—at ☎ (860) 657-3877
51 Forest Lane, Glastonbury, CT *06033* . . . . . . |
JUNIORS MISS Elizabeth A Kelley . . . . |

Bunker MR & MRS John B (Emma L Cadwalader) | ☎ (307) 322-4768
BMr'53.Nu'62.B.Yn.Y'50 . . . . | 1451 Cottonwood
MISS Jeanie C—at ☎ (510) 256-8809 | Av, Wheatland, WY
1370 Juanita Dv, Walnut Creek, CA *94595* . . . . | *82201*
MISS Harriet C—at ☎ (303) 444-1538
3313—11 St, Boulder, CO *80304* . . . . |
MISS Emma C (Newton—Emma C Bunker) . . . . |

Bunker MRS Mavis (Mavis McGuire)
☎ (212) 876-5693 . . 15 E 91 St, New York, NY *10128*

Bunker MR Sheffield—Rv.Y'63.Cl'69
☎ (516) 674-4427 . . 130 Pershing Av, Locust Valley, NY *11560*

Bunn MR & MRS George R JR (Jane G Adams) | ☎ (212) 650-0897
Un.Bcs.P'63.Y'68 . . . . | 126 E 56 St,
MISS Palmer H . . . . | New York, NY
MR G Regan 3d . . . . | *10022*
JUNIORS MISS Camilla A . . . . |

Bunn MR & MRS Thomas McC JR (Ruth H Woolfe) . | 2412 Burritt Av,
MR Austin McC . . . . | Redondo Beach, CA
MR Brian K . . . . | *90278*

Bunnell MRS C Sterling (Crimmins—Naneen Burnap) Sth'30.Csn.K.
☎ (860) 672-6118 . . 25 Town St S, Cornwall, CT *06753*
Bunten MR & MRS William H 2d (Elizabeth Wells) Pa'87.Pa'86
☎ (619) 298-6648 . . 2509 Madison Av, San Diego, CA *92116*
Bunting MRS John B (Miller—Margaret G Logue)
☎ (610) 649-5244 . . 34 W Montgomery Av, Apt 105, Ardmore, PA *19003*

Bunting DR & MRS Josiah 3d (Diana M	☎ (609) 896-0042
Cunningham) Hlns'66.Srb.B.Vmi'63.Ox'66	Foundation House,
MISS Elizabeth H	Lawrenceville
MR Josiah 4th	School,
	Lawrenceville, NJ
	08648

Bunting MRS Sydney S (Vivian Martin) Ny.	☎ (011-44-171)
CDR Geoffrey C—USNR.Me.An.Geo'66	930-9162
	97 Whitehall Court,
	London SW1A 2EL,
	England

Burbage MASTER Larkin Williams (g—Fred C Larkin) . . . . Born at
Denver, CO Aug 8'95
Burbank MR Robert Du B—Y'34
☎ (803) 432-9888 . . 1820 Fair St, Camden, SC *29020*
Burbank MR & MRS Walter W (Laura L Swift) Skd'41.Br'37
☎ (423) 821-0147 . . 122 Fairy Trail, Lookout Mountain, TN *37350*
Burch MISS Anne N (John W) . . . . Married at Radnor, PA
Hayes DR Timothy J (late Joseph) . . . . Sep 9'95

Burch MR & MRS Francis B JR (Mary Ann Podesta)	of ☎ (410)467-4523
Md.Cy.Geo'70.Md'74	4212 Greenway,
MISS Sara E.	Baltimore, MD
JUNIORS MR Francis B 3d	*21218*
JUNIORS MR Michael F	☎ (410) 820-9291
	"River House"
	26134 Bruffs Island
	Rd, Easton, MD
	21601

Burch MR & MRS John W (Robin N Sinkler) Me.M.Va'51
☎ (610) MU8-1727 . . 412 Conestoga Rd, Wayne, PA *19087*

Burch MR & MRS Robert L 3d (Dale Carter Jones)	of ☎ (212)744-5898
Rc.C.Ri.Mds.Cs.P'56.H'64	1040 Fifth Av,
MISS Catherine C W	New York, NY
MR Robert L 4th	*10028*
	☎ (516) 324-7077
	Terbell Lane,
	Box 1331,
	East Hampton, NY
	11937

Burchenal DR & MRS (DR) David H (Kathryn T Nason)
Drew'78.CathU'92.Dth'80.GeoW'88 . . of
☎ (203) 869-5197 . . 139 Lake Av, Greenwich, CT *06830*
☎ (212) 861-9395 . . 17 E 84 St, Apt 1A, New York, NY *10028*
Burchenal MR & MRS John J (Susan Starr) CtCol'49.Ncd.P'45
☎ (302) 655-6813 . . 712 Princeton Rd, Wilmington, DE *19807*
Burchenal MR & MRS John J JR (Ellen S McCurdy) StLaw'81.Ty'80
☎ (908) 277-0257 . . 128 Prospect St, Summit, NJ *07901*
Burchenal DR & MRS Joseph Holland (Joan B Riley)
V'46.Y'71.Au.C.Csn.P'34.Pa'37
☎ (203) 655-4114 . . Juniper Rd, Noroton, CT *06820*

Burchenal MISS Margaret K—P'74
☎ (617) 969-3294 . . 10 Read Court, Newton Center, MA *02159*
Burchfield MR & MRS William W (Cornelia G McLane) Ty'79.Bur.Mid'78
☎ (415) 347-1220 . . 1230 Vancouver Av, Burlingame, CA *94010*
Burden MR & MRS Childs F (Elaine C Siker) Mt.Va'73
☎ (540) 687-6940 . . Seven Springs Farm, 22857 Carters Farm Lane, Middleburg, VA *20117*
Burden MR & MRS D Frick (Tammy J McMillan) DU'80.Ri.DU'81
267 E Gregor St, Telluride, CO *81435*

Burden MRS Frances D (O'Malley—Frances D	☎ (617) 868-4249
Burden) Det'68.Ri.	121A Brattle St,
MISS Justine B O'Malley—at N'western	Cambridge, MA
MISS Alixine F O'Malley—at Denison	*02138*

Burden MR & MRS Henry S (Elizabeth B Weekes)	of ☎ (360)378-4590
ColC'71.ColC'71	"Westland"
MISS Elizabeth T	PO Box 684,
JUNIORS MISS Alice F	Friday Harbor, WA
JUNIORS MR Henry S JR	*98250*
	☎ (206) 283-3085
	1400 Second Av N,
	Seattle, WA *98109*

Burden MR & MRS I Townsend 3d (Valerie H	☎ (202) 337-3021
Knauer) Pa'67.Pa'72.Mt.Cvc.Ct.Sl.Pa'67.Pa'70 . .	3021 N St NW,
MISS Frances F	Washington, DC
MISS Virginia K—at U of Pa	*20007*

Burden MRS James A (Walker—Elizabeth H Leake) Cly.Ri . . .of
☎ (212) 888-2340 . . 1 Sutton Place S, New York, NY *10022*
☎ (246) 432-2007 . . "Chummery" St James, Barbados

Burden MR & MRS Ordway P (Lynch—Jean E Poor)	☎ (212) 534-8396
Bost'68.Mt.Sar.Ofp.Cw.Snc.Rv.Vca.Wt.Cc.	250 E 87 St, Apt
H'66.H'68 ⚓	31G, New York, NY
MISS Phoebe R Lynch—at Sarah Lawrence . .	*10128*

Burden MRS William A M (Margaret L Partridge) . . . . Died at
New York, NY Apr 25'96
Burdette MISS Marjorie A—Rm'95 . . see N L Bond JR
Burdette MR Timothy W—JHop'94 . . see N L Bond JR
Burdick MRS C Lalor (Alison Ward) Wil.Ncd.
☎ (302) 658-8899 . . 4031 Kennett Pike, Apt 79, Wilmington, DE *19807*
Burdick MR John R—Cal'58.Cal'69
☎ (202) 745-1415 . . 1401—17 St NW, Apt 803, Washington, DC *20036*

Burdick MR & MRS Lalor (Patricia M Norris)	☎ (617) 969-0414
Cy.Wil.Del'65.H'67	180 Dudley Rd,
MR Christopher L	Newton Center, MA
JUNIORS MR William W	*02159-2827*

Burdick MR & MRS W Newton (Dorothy R MacArthur) Ih.Cnt.Y'39
☎ (941) 649-4452 . . 2901 Gulf Shore Blvd N, Apt 703, Naples, FL *34103*

Burdick MR & MRS W Newton 3d (Krislov—	☎ (312) 944-3014
Kimberly Laidlaw) Skd'72.Cho.NCar'71.Ch'73 . .	401 E Ontario St,
JUNIORS MISS Jennifer L	Apt 3302, Chicago,
	IL *60611*

Burgard MRS Anika van K (Anika van Kooy) Ne. .	☎ (203) 622-0405
MR Clark van K—Ihy.—☎ (203) 869-4468	256 Riversville Rd,
	Greenwich, CT
	06831

Burger MRS Elizabeth G (Elizabeth L Godshalk) SCal'50.Pa'58.Me.Cda.
☎ (610) 964-0292 . . 266-1C Iven Av, St Davids, PA *19087*

Burger MR & MRS F Gregg (Koeniger—Kirkland—Martha G Weimar) Nw'45.W&L'42 ⚓ . . of
☎ (941) 966-5529 . . ''Oaks Preserve'' 151 Bishopscourt Rd, Osprey, FL *34229*
☎ (908) 892-4548 . . ''Bayvue'' 16 Bay Point Harbour, Point Pleasant, NJ *08742*

Burger MR Van Vechten—Ln.Plg.Snc.Y'26
☎ (516) 569-0072 . . 241 Polo Lane, Lawrence, NY *11559*

Burger MR & MRS (DR) Van Vechten JR (Mina Farhad) H'65.Un.Au.Rc.Ln.Y'62.H'67 . . . . | ☎ (212) 534-2619
MISS Leila E . . . . | 1088 Park Av, Apt
MISS Katrina I . . . . | 10D, New York, NY
MR Nicholas F . . . . | *10128*

Burgess MRS Isabel A (Ramus—Isabel Andrews) Mls'34
☎ (602) 947-5426 . . Scottsdale House Apt 275, 4800 N 68 St, Scottsdale, AZ *85251*

Burgess MR & MRS Richard B (Diane M Letchworth) | ☎ (414) 332-9882
Wa.W&M'68.ArizSt'70 . . . . | 3319 N Lake Dv,
JUNIORS MR R Reid—at St George's . . . . | Milwaukee, WI
JUNIORS MR Brice H—at Eaglebrook . . . . | *53211*

Burgevin MRS John (Clarissa Crawford Weekes) CtCol'40
☎ (513) 421-2888 . . 1071 Celestial St, Apt 2003, Cincinnati, OH *45202*

Burgin MRS C Rodgers (Helen Swain) Cy.
20 Longwood Dv, Apt 175, Westwood, MA *02090*

Burgin MR William T—Cy.Myc.Ln.Sm.Hn.H.'65 . . | ☎ (508) 785-1107
MISS Hillary W—H'94 . . . . | ''River Bend''
MR Nicholas F—P'96 . . . . | Box 580, Dover,
JUNIORS MR Angus R—at St Paul's . . . . | MA *02030-0580*

Burgwin MRS George C 3d (Lela C Hill) V'49.Rr.Pg . . . of
☎ (412) 687-9903 . . 5048 Fifth Av, Pittsburgh, PA *15232*
☎ (412) 593-7954 . . ''White Flag Farm'' Box 375, Star Rte, Rector, PA *15677*

Burke MR & MRS C S Taylor 3d (Henrietta V McCormick-Goodhart) Y'72
☎ (703) 768-0523 . . ''Beaurivage'' 837 Herbert Springs Rd, Alexandria, VA *22308*

Burke MISS Catherine M C—Me'93
☎ (203) 656-2070 . . 84 Rings End Rd, Darien, CT *06820*

Burke MR & MRS Duncan G (Fitzgerald—Nancy B | of ☎ (203)661-7849
Brookfield) V'69.Unn.Ihy.Dth'65.Cl'67 ⚓ . . . | 4 Perkins Rd,
MISS Marion M—at ☎ (415) 863-3924 | PO Box 628,
270 Dolores St, San Francisco, CA *94103* . . . . . | Greenwich, CT
MISS Alexandra J—at ☎ (617) 267-1937 | *06836*
215 W Newton St, Apt 3, Boston, MA *02116* . . | ☎ (561) 732-3170
MISS Adrian R—at ☎ (206) 548-0522 | 6849 N Ocean Blvd,
103 NE 44 St, Seattle, WA *98105* . . . . | Ocean Ridge, FL
MR Sean C—at ☎ (508) 540-7569 | *33435*
PO Box 669, Woods Hole, MA *02543* . . . . |
JUNIORS MISS Brooke A Fitzgerald—at |
Greenwich Country Sch . . . . |

Burke MR Edwin M 3d—Geo'95 . . see H L Clark JR

Burke MR & MRS Edwin Marston (Hutton—Virginia C Smith)
ColbyS'51.Rc.Pr.Evg.Cly.P'40 . . of
☎ (561) 848-3499 . . 1127 N Lake Way, Palm Beach, FL *33480*
☎ (212) 628-1614 . . 19 E 72 St, New York, NY *10021*

Burke MRS G Anderton (Polly Norment) . . . . | ☎ (703) 836-5098
MR Julian T 2d—Rich'81—at | 109 Prince St,
☎ (703) 836-7355 . . 624 S Columbus St, | Alexandria, VA
Alexandria, VA *22314* . . . . | *22314*
MR Clarence N—Va'78—at ☎ (703) 960-9532 |
5945 Monticello Rd, Alexandria, VA *22303* . . . |

Burke MR Geoffrey K—Cr'61 . . . . | ☎ (203) 254-8183
MISS Eleanor K L—Conn'92—at | 245 Unquowa Rd,
☎ (202) 333-3614 . . 1010—25 St NW, | Apt 27, Fairfield, CT
Washington, DC *20037* . . . . | *06430*
MR Malcolm A McM—W&L'96—at |
7532 Ambergate Place, Apt 3, McLean, VA |
22102 . . . . |
MR Edward H S—W&L'96 . . . . |

Burke MRS Gregory T (Jean F Robinson)
☎ (203) 655-1643 . . PO Box 3072, Noroton, CT *06820*

Burke MRS Jackson (Mary L Griggs) SL'38.Cl'44.Cs.Pr.S . . .of
☎ (212) 744-0057 . . 3 E 77 St, Apt 6A, New York, NY *10021*
☎ (516) 922-4763 . . 145 Centre Island Rd, Oyster Bay, NY *11771*

Burke MR James Van V . . see H L Clark JR

Burke MRS John W (Agnes A Spencer) Swb'40.Cvc.Mt.Ncd.
☎ (202) 362-7997 . . 5014 Glenbrook Rd NW, Washington, DC *20016*

Burke MR & MRS John W 3d (Judith E Ayres) | ☎ (415) 388-9234
Miami'66.H'80.Cvc.P'66.GeoW'73 . . . . | 5 Wildomar,
JUNIORS MISS Elizabeth C A . . . . | Mill Valley, CA
| *94941*

Burke MR & MRS M G Ashmead (Ruth Sansoucie) K.Va'65.Pa'68 . . of
☎ (601) 786-8742 . . Richland Plantation, Box 2026, Natchez, MS *39121*
☎ (011-44-171) 371-6945 . . 60 St Mary Abbot's Court, Warwick Gardens, London W14 8RA, England

Burke MISS Mary Lee—Rdc'55
☎ (504) 891-3824 . . 329 State St, New Orleans, LA *70118*

Burke MRS N Van Vleck (Nancy J Van Vleck)
☎ (908) 234-1154 . . PO Box 123, Bernardsville, NJ *07924*

Burke MR & MRS Nicholas R (Supplee—Claire J G | ☎ (202) 363-1941
Gardiner) Rb.Chi.H'68 . . . . | 4701 Woodway
JUNIORS MR James R . . . . | Lane NW,
| Washington, DC
| *20016*

Burke MR P Gibbons JR—So'85 . . of
10300 Jollyville Rd, Apt 814, Austin, TX *78759*
St John Plantation, St Martinville, LA *70582*

Burke MR & MRS Peter G (Virginia G Friedrichs) | of ☎ (504)482-8694
RMWmn'59.Syc.Ncd.Tul'56.Tul'60 ⚓ . . . . . . | 59 Maryland Dv,
MISS Mary-Shea . . . . | New Orleans, LA
MISS Eleanor S—So'94 . . . . | *70124*
| ''Ballingrobe''
| Covington, LA
| *70433*

Burke MR Quentin R
☎ (941) 923-7525 . . 3435 Fox Run Rd, Apt 360, Sarasota, FL *34231-7386*

Burke MRS Seija Nordling (Seija K Nordling) Hawaii'96
☎ (808) 875-2131 . . PO Box 483, Pu'unene, Maui, HI *96784-0483*

Burke MRS Thomas A (Martha H Wheeler)
Bnd'59.Cs.Dh. . . . . | ☎ (212) FI8-9230
  MISS Martha H—Woos'86 . . . . | 126 E 93 St,
  MISS Jennifer A—V'88 . . . . | New York, NY
  MR Thomas M—Vt'87 . . . . | 10128

Burkett MISS Elizabeth Locke (William C) . . . . Born at
Washington, DC Jly 11'94

Burkett MR & MRS William A (Lofton—Morrow—
Nancy Schallert) NCar'38.Cp.Neb'36.Neb'38 . . | ☎ (408) 624-1733
  MISS Melissa Lofton—at ☎ (408) 625-2358 | ''Fairview''
  PO Box 223634, Carmel, CA 93922 . . . . | 1548 Viscaino Rd,
   | Pebble Beach, CA
   | 93953

Burkett MR & MRS William C (Wynn E McClenahan)
Stan'81.Y'87.Cp.Yn.Stan'78.Y'83
☎ (415) 921-6700 . . 101 Laurel St, San Francisco, CA 94118

Burkham MRS Elzey G JR (Nancy Floyd) . . . . Died Jun 30'96

Burkham MR Elzey G JR—P'50
☎ (603) 964-5415 . . 42 Straws Point, PO Box 247, Rye Beach,
NH 03871

Burkham MRS James C (Barbara Wear) Cysl.
☎ (207) 283-3788 . . Box 181, Biddeford Pool, ME 04006

Burkhart MISS Catherine M C . . see P E Shipley

Burkhart DR & MRS Charles B (Linda L Allen) Yn.Y'53.Cl'57
☎ (406) 862-4844 . . 304 Fairway Dv, Whitefish, MT 59937

Burkhart MISS Clarissa A . . see P E Shipley

Burks MR & MRS D Parker (Marilyn Z Dixon)
Ind'59.Wes'58.Wms'62 . . . . | ☎ (603) 595-7061
  MISS Sarah L . . . . | 32 Dunbarton Dv,
   | Nashua, NH 03063

Burleigh MR William C—Ph.H'42
☎ (610) 644-5618 . . ''Crum Rapid'' 767 White Horse Rd, Berwyn,
PA 19312

Burley MRS Clarence A JR (Freeberg—Shirley B Albertson)
☎ (805) 872-3172 . . 6121 College Av, Bakersfield, CA 93306

Burley MR & MRS Dexter L (Pantaleoni—Hope L | of ☎ (617)267-3495
Baker) Bost'68.Cy.Sm.Btn.Cc.Chi.Ncd.Marl'68. | 146 Beacon St,
NH'71.NH'75 . . . . | Boston, MA 02116
  MISS Jane W . . . . | ☎ (603) 763-9153
  MR Benjamin T—at Reed . . . . | High Mowing Farm,
   | Between the
   | Mountains Rd,
   | Newbury, NH 03255

Burling MR & MRS Edward JR (Winslow—Frida Frazer) Mt.Ct.Sl.Y'29.H'32
☎ (202) 337-1339 . . 1339—29 St NW, Washington, DC 20007

Burling MRS Poe (Cotton—Ella K Poe) Ct.Mt.
☎ (202) 337-7650 . . 3308 R St NW, Washington, DC 20007

Burlingame MRS Anson (Elizabeth H Hussey) Hn.
☎ (203) 966-1265 . . 68 Brooks Rd, New Canaan, CT 06840

Burlingame MR & MRS Edward L (Perdita R T | ☎ (914) 232-5178
Plowden) C.H'57 . . . . | Nash Rd, Purdys,
  MISS Remony E—Ws'86 . . . . | NY 10578
  MISS Phyllida A—H'88 . . . . |
  MR Roger A—Wis'92 . . . . |

Burlingame MR & MRS John H (Baird—Dorcas G Hodges)
StMarys'62.Pk.Un.Wis'60.Wis'63
☎ (216) 371-9511 . . 2324 Roxboro Rd, Cleveland Heights, OH 44106

Burlingham MRS Morris B (Mary Titford)
☎ (513) 321-9416 . . 2820 Griffiths Av, Apt I, Cincinnati, OH 45208

Burnam MRS Frances M (Frances H Michael) | ☎ (301) 774-3783
Radford'65.Radford'68 . . . . | 9 Heritage Hills
  JUNIORS MISS Hadley A . . . . | Court, Brookeville,
   | MD 20833

Burnap MR Wilder Luke—Col'49
☎ (011-33-1) 39-37-20-39 . . 118 av Aristide Briand, 60230 Chambly,
France

Burnett MRS Andrew H (Helen Purvine) . . . . | ☎ (805) 965-2608
  MISS Alison H . . . . | 909 Arbolado Rd,
   | Santa Barbara, CA
   | 93103

Burnett MRS Dunn (H Hildreth Dunn) BMr'44.Chi.
☎ (617) 547-2287 . . 85 Brattle St, Cambridge, MA 02138

Burnett LT COL George P—BA . . . . | ☎ (011-44-1962)
  MR Audley G P . . . . | 860086
   | 3 Mason's Yard,
   | St Thomas St,
   | Winchester,
   | Hampshire
   | SO23 9JT, England

Burnett MR & MRS Harold K (Susan L Claska) Col'84.ColSt'84
☎ (207) 377-3969 . . RR 2, Box 5270, Winthrop, ME 04364

Burnett DR & MRS Joseph W (Kathleen B D | ☎ (410) 377-8510
Scarlett) Wheat'54.Elk.Mv.Y'54.H'58 . . . . | 7317 Bellona Av,
  MR P Jefferson—Rich'88.WakeF'90 . . . . | Baltimore, MD
  MR Mark G—Y'93 . . . . | 21212

Burnett MR & MRS Michael A (Alexandra M Tucker)
OWes'74.Me.M.Syd'59
☎ (011-61-3) 9827-7670 . . 22 Montalto Av, Toorak, Victoria 3142,
Australia

Burnett MR & MRS Robert R (Elizabeth A Bole) | ☎ (540) 347-4921
Y'59 . . . . | 5114 Laurel Lane,
  MR Alexander P—J&W'89—at | Broad Run, VA
  ☎ (540) 347-3882 . . 8464 Elway Lane, | 20137
  Warrenton, VA 20188 . . . . |
  MR Anthony C—Cl'89—at ☎ (415) 346-3664
  1369A Greenwich St, San Francisco, CA 94109

Burnett MRS W Griffin (Burnett—Lobdell—K | ☎ (908) 872-1660
Marka ReQua) Stc. . . . . | 5 Coquette Lane,
  MISS K Ryland—HWSth'83 . . . . | Monmouth Hills,
  MISS M Suzanne—LakeF'86 . . . . | Highlands, NJ 07732
  MISS M Eugenia—Vt'88 . . . . |
  MR W Griffin JR . . . . |

Burnham MR & MRS David H (Frances M Parry) | ☎ (617) 383-1339
Ne'64.Sm.Myf.Ne'64.H.'69 . . . . | 30 Atlantic Av,
  MISS Amery A—at ☎ (617) 354-5936 | Cohasset, MA 02025
  1 Newport Rd, Apt 6, Cambridge, MA 02140 . . |
  MR Hugh T R—Tufts'96 . . . . |

Burnham MRS De Witt K (Elizabeth L Stenborg) Tcy.
☎ (415) 567-1174 . . 2222 Lyon St, San Francisco, CA 94115

Burnham MR & MRS De Witt K JR (Peggy Marie Conroy) Cal'82.Cal'79
☎ (415) 668-7309 . . 2222 Lyon St, San Francisco, CA 94115

Burnham MR & MRS Douglass L (Jean M Bentz)   ☎ (203) 263-3618
Buck'51.Buck'54 . . . .   27 Ridgewood Rd,
  MISS Janet R . . . .   Woodbury, CT
  MR Jonathan M   06798
  MR David W . . . .
  MR Charles D . . . .
Burnham MISS Kim N—Gchr'80 . . see H M Robertson JR
Burnham MRS Rebecca L (Gardner—Rebecca L Mahoney)
ArizSt'77.Cal'80
see Dilatory Domiciles
Burnham MR Richard B—GeoW'74.Nw'77
  ☎ (602) 483-8863 . . 7701 N Moonlight Lane, Paradise Valley,
AZ 85253
Burnham MR & MRS Richard I (Fanchon M   ☎ (202) 338-3776
Watkins) V'66.Geo'83.Mt.Srb.Aht'58.H'61 . . . .   3554 Edmunds St
  MISS Helen M—Dth'96 . . . .   NW, Washington,
  MR John S—at Princeton . . . .   DC 20007
Burnham MRS Robert B (Leber—M Elaine Maxon)   ☎ (617) 259-9149
Bost'59 . . . .   Oak Knoll,
  MISS Louisa A—H'87—at ☎ (847) 733-8325   Lincoln, MA 01773
904 Hinman Av, Apt 4F, Evanston, IL 60202 . .
Burnham MR Robert Bailey—Bost'70
  ☎ (414) 425-7306 . . 10212 Parklane Court, Hales Corners, WI 53130
Burnham MRS Schroeder (Virginia G Schroeder) Cly.Cda.
  ☎ (203) 531-8011 . . ''Pygmalia'' 41 Duncan Dv, Greenwich, CT 06831
Burnham MRS William A (Sylvia C Winslow) Rdc'40.H.
  ☎ (617) 585-0854 . . 290 Kings Town Way, Apt 350, Duxbury,
MA 02332
Burns MISS Blandina E . . see M T Ijams
Burns MR & MRS Edward E JR (Winthrop Reid)   ☎ (203) 656-1011
Rm.Cly.Dth'58.Dth'59 ⚓ . . . .   36 Crooked Mile
  MR Christopher W—ColC'90 . . . .   Rd, Darien, CT
     06820
Burns MR & MRS Findley JR (Martha A Lobeck) Mt.Pn.P'39
  ☎ (910) 692-8500 . . 4 Village in the Woods, Southern Pines, NC 28387
Burns MISS Frances P—NCar'80 . . see MRS G C Fox
Burns MR & MRS Mark Allen (Lisa J Benson)
Duke'83.Duke'86.Cal'83.Cl'86
  ☎ (415) 917-9816 . . 386 Yerba Buena Av, Los Altos, CA 94022
Burns MISS Susan P—Sth'41
  ☎ (302) 654-4186 . . 1 Crawford Circle, Wilmington, DE 19805
Burns MRS Thomas R (Ingrid L Frohlich) Mds.Evg.BtP.Cly.
  ☎ (561) 655-5714 . . 100 Worth Av, Palm Beach, FL 33480
Burns MR & MRS Ward (Cynthia A Butterworth)   ☎ (203) 661-4742
BMr'59.Eyc.Ln.Plg.StA.Aht'50.H'52 . . . .   19 Angus Lane,
  MISS H Abby . . . .   Greenwich, CT
  MR David W   06831
  MR Walton L . . . .
Burpee MR & MRS George B (Callanan—Hughes—Jane A Porter)
Temp'72.Pc.Dar.Rens'46.Cr'48
  ☎ (610) 584-8563 . . PO Box 1, Lafayette Hill, PA 19444
Burr MR & MRS Benjamin M (Virginia Monks)   ☎ (561) 283-5710
Hn.Hb.H'45 . . . .   5630 SE Miles
  MISS Sarah M—at ☎ (718) 875-2963   Grant Rd, Stuart, FL
45 Grace Court, Apt 4C, Brooklyn, NY 11201 . .   34997
  MR Benjamin M JR . . . .
  MR John E . . . .

Burr MR & MRS Carleton (Gertrude Trumbull) V'45.H'43
  ☎ (508) 758-2478 . . 27 Ned's Point Rd, Mattapoisett, MA 02739-2198
Burr MR & MRS Francis H (Devens—Aldrich—Lucy T Aldrich)
Sm.Tv.Hn.H'35
  ☎ (508) 927-5474 . . 44 Prince St, Beverly, MA 01915
Burr MR George L 2d
see Dilatory Domiciles
Burr DR & MRS I Tucker 3d (Estelle T Eggins)   ☎ (603) 756-4228
H'39.Cr'51 . . . .   ''Brittany''
  MR Stephen V R—at 108 NE 56 St, Seattle,   Walpole, NH 03608
WA 98105 . . . .
  MR Duncan F T . . . .
Burr MR & MRS John T (Joan Ames) H'42
  ☎ (904) 934-9729 . . 604 Fairpoint Dv, Gulf Breeze, FL 32561-4112
Burr MRS R Peters (Mary Strong) . . . . Died at
                                North Haven, ME Apr 3'96
Burr DR & MRS (DR) Richard M (Patricia A LeMay)   of ☎ (210)829-3182
NTexSt'66.TexWmnU'68.NTexSt'73.A.Ala'72 .   119 Park Dv,
  MISS Ashley LeMay . . . .   San Antonio, TX
     78212
     ''Four Seasons''
     Crescent Beach,
     St Augustine, FL
     32084
Burr MR & MRS Robert Page (Elizabeth J Long) Bnd'49.Cr'44 ⚓
  ☎ (207) 366-3870 . . Matinicus, ME 04851
Burr MR Walter T—Bvl.H'84
27 Ned's Point Rd, Mattapoisett, MA 02739-2198
Burrage MR & MRS Walter S JR (Helen D Dupee)   of ☎ (617)731-5859
Cy.Ec.Myc.Cl'68 ⚓ . . . .   29 Hawthorn Rd,
  MISS Alyssa A . . . .   Brookline, MA
  JUNIORS MISS Katharine S   02146
  JUNIORS MISS Amanda B . . . .   ☎ (508) 526-4472
     ''Kettledrum''
     Coolidge Point,
     Manchester, MA
     01944
Burrill MR & MRS Douglas L (Nancy M Mulford)
Elmira'69.Kent'70.Md'76.Cr'67.Wash'69
  ☎ (415) 751-8919 . . 119—26 Av, San Francisco, CA 94121
Burrill MISS Helena Van Cortlandt
  ☎ (212) 722-0652 . . 11 E 92 St, New York, NY 10128
Burroughs MR & MRS Davis C JR (Weidlein—Margaret M Donahoe)
Okla'50.Pg.Rr.Ny.P'41.H'49
  ☎ (412) 621-6025 . . 5339 Northumberland St, Pittsburgh, PA 15217
Burroughs MR & MRS Vincent DeP (Deuel—Marta   ☎ (716) 243-3394
D Nagel) SUNY'73 . . . .   2605 Genesee St,
  MISS Maggie D Deuel—at Niagara U . . . . . .   Piffard, NY 14533
  JUNIORS MISS Sarah G Deuel . . . .
Burrows MR & MRS David D (Mary E Grant)   ☎ (203) 625-9445
B.Cc.Cl'69 . . . .   29 Hillside Dv,
  JUNIORS MISS Jennifer J . . . .   Greenwich, CT
  JUNIORS MISS Elisabeth W   06830
Burrows MR & MRS Frederick P (Jennifer L Cook) Cal'85.Cal'81
  ☎ (805) 969-2485 . . 151 Santa Elena Lane, Santa Barbara, CA 93108
Burrows MRS George S (Marjory Schlotzhauer) Fy.On.
  ☎ (847) 234-1156 . . 1416 N Lake Rd, Lake Forest, IL 60045

Burrows MRS Robert H (Nancy N Dennis) Cly.
☎ (805) 969-1680 . . 2755 Bella Vista Dv, Santa Barbara, CA *93108*
Burrows MR & MRS William David (Nancy B Rhodes) Stan'59.Vh.Y'47 . . . . | ☎ (818) 792-6629 1000 S Madison Av, Pasadena, CA *91106*
MR William D JR . . . . |
MR Robert G . . . . |
Burrows MRS William M (Linda Jo McCain) . . . . . | ☎ (215) 848-4561 3407 W Queens Lane, Philadelphia, PA *19129*
MISS Leah L—NCar'91.NCar'95 . . . . |
MR William M 3d . . . . |
Burrus MRS Jefferson D JR (Woodville—Mary C Curtis) Cvc.Cyb.Srb.
☎ (202) 244-1855 . . 3001 Veazey Terr NW, Apt 1101, Washington, DC *20008*
Burry MRS William B (Mary E Morgan)
☎ (216) 442-2369 . . 2559 Som Center Rd, Chagrin Falls, OH *44022*
Burt MR Christopher K . . see R T Riker
Burt MR & MRS James M 3d (Raggio—Olive Y Rousseau) K.BtP.Evg.Myf.Y'54 . . of
☎ (561) 832-2176 . . 7 Via Vizcaya, Palm Beach, FL *33480*
☎ (011-44-171) 730-3572 . . 43 Boscobel Place, London SW1, England
Burt MR & MRS Nathaniel (Margaret K Clinton) C.R.Cly.Cda.P'36
☎ (609) 924-4387 . . 13 Campbelton Circle, Princeton, NJ *08540*
Burt MR Russell B . . see R T Riker
Burton MR & MRS Bruce R (Dively—Charlotte D Lyeth) P'cpia'65.BtP.Cly.Conn'67
☎ (203) 853-3703 . . 21 Indian Spring Rd, Rowayton, CT *06853*
Burton MR & MRS C Thomas JR (Elizabeth Rulon-Miller) Hlns'71.W&L'66.Va'72 . . . . | ☎ (702) 832-7241 PO Box 3450, Incline Village, NV *89450*
MISS Virginia T—at Brown . . . . |
JUNIORS MR Calvin T 3d—at St Paul's . . . . |
Burton MRS David C (Dixon—Amanda C Cadwalader) Ac.Gm.Me.
☎ (610) 688-1710 . . 114 Quail Lane, Radnor, PA *19087*
Burton MISS Elizabeth A—SL'41.Cvc.Sl.Srb.
☎ (202) 232-4455 . . 2339 Massachusetts Av NW, Washington, DC *20008*
Burton MRS Ernest B (Sarah F Harris)
☎ (203) 972-0378 . . 50 Chichester Rd, New Canaan, CT *06840*
Burton MISS Jenepher S—Skd'88.MeArt'92
☎ (207) 761-0917 . . 113 Vaughan St, Apt 5, Portland, ME *04102*
Burton MR & MRS John H 2d (Lucy G Williams) Hob'53.Wis'58 . . . . | ☎ (508) 468-3646 188 Sagamore St, South Hamilton, MA *01982*
MISS Sarah D—Hartw'85.Mass'91—at . . |
☎ (509) 946-4554 . . 800 Winslow Av, Richland, WA *99352* . . . . |
Burton MR & MRS John R (Evangela D Sandys) Plg.Ne.Cly.Mit'35.H'37
☎ (212) 348-7707 . . 1185 Park Av, New York, NY *10128*
Burton MR & MRS John R 3d (Geraldine Deutsch) Unn.Cw.Snc.Ne.NH'70 . . . . | ☎ (603) 225-3413 34 Rocky Point Dv, Bow, NH *03304-4112*
MISS Pamela S—at New England Coll . . . . . . |
JUNIORS MR John R 4th . . . . |
Burwell MR John T 3d—H'72 . . see MRS A Page
Burwell MISS Lesslie B . . see MRS A Page
Busby MRS Archibald H (Kate P Shepard)
☎ (561) 286-1134 . . 6041 SE Landing Way, Apt 5, Stuart, FL *34997*
Busch MRS Niven (de Sanz—Suzanne Te Roller)
☎ (415) 921-6611 . . 1200 Gough St, San Francisco, CA *94109*

Bush MR Alfred L—Gr.Cp.BrigY'57
☎ (609) 924-9021 . . 64 Valley Rd, Princeton, NJ *08540*
Bush MR & MRS George (Barbara Pierce) Bhm.Y'48
☎ (713) 686-1188 . . 10000 Memorial Dv, 900, Houston, TX *77024*
Bush MR & MRS Jonathan J (Josephine C Bradley) V'61.Ri.Y'53 . . of
☎ (860) 663-1771 . . 128 Chestnut Hill Rd, Killingworth, CT *06419*
☎ (212) 751-1191 . . 2 Sutton Place S, New York, NY *10022*
Bush MR & MRS Marc W (Anne B Taussig) Ws'73.Rc.
☎ (314) 367-8372 . . 5142 Westminster Place, St Louis, MO *63108*
Bush JUNIORS MR Peter D . . see B W Drew JR
Bush MR & MRS Robert M (Carolyn L Jorgensen) Van'64.GaTech'67 . . of
☎ (404) 874-8619 . . 120 Peachtree Circle NE, Atlanta, GA *30309*
☎ (912) 233-2654 . . 114 W Bolton St, Savannah, GA *31401*
Bush-Brown MRS Albert (Frances Wesselhoeft) C.Cly.
☎ (508) 362-3053 . . "Barrel Hill" 138 Pine Lane, PO Box 975, Barnstable, MA *02630*
Bush-Brown MR & MRS David F (Mary C Livingston) Skd'73.Bost'73.Bost'78
☎ (617) 329-1485 . . 927 High St, Dedham, MA *02026*
Bushing MR & MRS F William 3d (Sarah A Braun) SUNY'77.Hob'79
☎ (203) 655-0451 . . 7 Rocaton Rd, Darien, CT *06820*
Bushing MR & MRS Farrell W JR (Pamela M Moore) Ox'55.P'51.Cl'58
☎ (860) 824-0409 . . "Tree Tops" 415 Twin Lakes Rd, Taconic, CT *06079*
Bushnell MR & MRS Daniel (Bushnell—Isabelle K Marckwald) V'35.Cy.Cw.Chi.
☎ (617) 323-6604 . . PO Box 67251, Chestnut Hill, MA *02167*
Bushnell MR & MRS Nathan 3d (Margaret M Forsyth) Va'42 . . . . | ☎ (804) 288-0691 1002 Ridge Top Rd, Richmond, VA *23229*
MISS M Dorsey . . . . |
Bushnell MR Robert G JR—Ne.P'59
☎ (802) 325-3179 . . Box 265, Pawlet, VT *05761-0265*
Busk MR & MRS Joseph R JR (Tilt—Grace S Chambers) Ihy. . . . . | ☎ (561) 231-2745 600 Riomar Dv, Apt 13-East, Vero Beach, FL *32963*
MR Albert Tilt 4th—at ☎ (208) 456-2894 |
PO Box 766, Driggs, ID *83544* . . . . |
Busselle MISS Katherine Scott (Boyd—Katherine Scott Busselle) . . . .
name changed to Scott
Butash MR & MRS Adrian M (Susannah E Rake) Cl'77.Cly.Ford'58
☎ (805) 969-2763 . . "Boo's Nest" 435 Sea View Rd, Montecito, CA *93108*
Butcher MR Arthur C—Me.Pa'92
☎ (212) 595-9499 . . 292 W 92 St, Apt 6B, New York, NY *10025*
Butcher MRS Howard 3d (Taulane—Elizabeth S Shryock) BMr'34.Me.M.
71 Pasture Lane, Bryn Mawr, PA *19010*
Butcher MR & MRS McBee (Anne Currie) Me.M.Ac.Cs.Pa'61
☎ (610) LA5-0296 . . 594 Black Rock Rd, Bryn Mawr, PA *19010*
Butcher MR McBee JR—Ph.Rc.M.Me.Pa'89
☎ (215) 790-1803 . . 1919 Waverly St, Philadelphia, PA *19146*
Butcher MR & MRS W W Keen (Pagon—Madeleine A Kilvert) Nyc.Pc.Ph.Wms'38
☎ (215) CH2-8811 . . 8811 Towanda St, Philadelphia, PA *19118*

Butler MRS Charles M (Margaret H Lowry)
SL'31.Me.Ac.Ncd. . . . . | ☎ (610) 525-5469
MR C Howard—at ☎ (406) 843-5529 | 74 Pasture Lane,
502 E Idaho St, Box 175, Virginia City, MT | Apt 336,
59755 . . . . | Bryn Mawr, PA
 | 19010

Butler MR Desmond O . . see J F Mele

Butler MR & MRS Edwin F A (Patricia E Whitney)
Md'57 . . . . | ☎ (410) 377-5284
MISS Jennifer W—NotreD'93—at | 106 Thicket Rd,
616 Woodbine Av, Towson, MD 21204 . . . . | Baltimore, MD
 | 21212

Butler MR Frank Osgood 2d—BtP.Cas.K.Sar.
☎ (561) 833-9999 . . "Villa Tour Carrée" Golfview Rd 16, Palm Beach,
FL 33480-4608

Butler MR & MRS Frederick J C (Marie-Claude
Gervais) K.Cly.H'63 . . . . | ☎ (212) 534-8529
MISS Julia . . . . | 1050 Park Av,
JUNIORS MISS Daphne . . . . | New York, NY
 | 10028

Butler MRS Gilbert (Mary Kernan) . . . . | ☎ (315) 733-3605
MISS Martha G—Man'vl'60—at 3 Arden Dv, | 2809 Genesee St,
Amawalk, NY 10501 . . . . | Utica, NY 13501

Butler MRS Hugh H (Barbara Adams)
☎ (716) 473-4807 . . 165 Shoreham Dv, Rochester, NY 14618

Butler MR & MRS James (Margaret W Herbruck)
SL'67.Mvh.Cly.Yn.Y'65.Cl'67 . . . . | ☎ (203) 629-1810
MISS Shelley H . . . . | 12 Park Av,
MR James JR—Y.Ham'91—at ☎ (716) 442-7682 | Greenwich, CT
379 Barrington St, Rochester, NY 14607 . . . . . . | 06830
MR Michael T—Yn.Ham'93 . . . . |

Butler MR & MRS John F (Donovan—Marion
O'Brien) Y'58.Un.Cly.Geo'30 . . . . | ☎ (212) 879-8237
MISS Christine P Donovan—at 229 E 79 St, | 850 Park Av,
New York, NY 10021 . . . . | New York, NY
 | 10021

Butler CDR & MRS John L JR (Shepard—Helene Bosworth) USN.Y'40
☎ (717) 646-9082 . . "The Cottage" Stoddartsville, HC 1, Box 1134,
Blakeslee, PA 18610

Butler MR & MRS Jonathan P (Deborah D Rogers)
Bnd'66.Un.P.'62.P'65.Cl'66 . . . . | ☎ (212) BU8-4142
MISS Pauline W—H'94 . . . . | 1642 York Av,
MR Benjamin P—at Vassar . . . . | New York, NY
JUNIORS MISS Cynthia D—at Chapin . . . . | 10028

Butler MR Jonathan R—P'92
☎ (212) 673-7266 . . 145 E 17 St, Apt A1, New York, NY 10003

Butler MRS Marianna Moore (Marianna Moore) Tcy . . .of
☎ (510) 547-2472 . . 5301 Broadway Terr, Apt 3, Oakland, CA 94618
☎ (510) 656-1868 . . AA Moore Ranch, Box 3068, Fremont, CA 94539

Butler MISS Mary M
☎ (212) 838-3509 . . 116 E 63 St, New York, NY 10021

Butler MR & MRS Michael J (Karen L Schwefel) Sth'76.S.HolyC'71
☎ (773) 549-3465 . . 3240 N Lake Shore Dv, Chicago, IL 60657

Butler MR Percy C M JR . . see C W Dawson

Butler HON & MRS Piers J R (Laura B Gary) Cl'80.Rcch.
☎ (011-44-171) 924-6900 . . 44 Stanmer St, London SW11 3EG,
England

Butler MR Shane Lloyd—Cp.Loy'41 . . . . | 2201 Laguna St, Apt
MR S Michael—SFr'72 . . . . | 302, San Francisco,
 | CA 94115

Butler MR & MRS Sidney M G (Aileen S Taylor)
Plg. . . . . | ☎ (802) 387-2683
MISS Laura S—at ☎ (011-81-98) 956-9658 | "Hewitt House"
Dodds PSC 79, Box 20979, APO AP, | PO Box 213,
96364-0979 . . . . | Main St, Putney, VT
 | 05346

Butler MR & MRS Smedley D 3d (Susan S Leroux)
Pa'74.Me.R.Temp'67.Temp'70 . . . . | ☎ (804) 973-6255
JUNIORS MISS Amelia E . . . . | Mad Hatter Farm,
 | RD 3, Box 67A,
 | Earlysville, VA
 | 22936

Butler MAJ & MRS T Desmond (Dorothy West) BA.
☎ (603) 968-3591 . . "True Farm Cottage" Box 32, Holderness,
NH 03245

Butler MR Thomas R—Ph.Pe.R.Cspa.Rv.W.Cw.Fw.Wt.Swth'35.Pa'39
☎ (610) EL6-0369 . . 3501 Goshen Rd, Newtown Square, PA 19073

Butler MR & MRS Thomas S K (Bernadette Schepens) Sm.H'62
26 Sea Breeze Lane, Nahant, MA 01908

Butler MR & MRS Thorne G (Kelly A Allin)
Ala'74.H'79.Dth'70.H'79 . . . . | ☎ (601) 948-6288
MISS Cicely B—at Conn Coll . . . . | 1424 Pinehurst
MISS Rebecca S—at U of NH . . . . | Place, Jackson, MS
 | 39202

Butler MR Tyssen W . . see J F Mele

Butler MR Vincent K JR—Mit'45.Stan'48
☎ (415) 751-2314 . . 17 Wood St, Apt 101, San Francisco, CA 94118

Butler MR & MRS Vincent K 3d (Susan N Holloway) Cal'86.Cal'85
☎ (415) 474-8535 . . 1349 Francisco St, San Francisco, CA 94123

Butner MR & MRS Russell E (Alyce H Schloss)
Ws'79.Van'85.Ala'81.Van'85
☎ (770) 368-4075 . . 4810 Haydens Walk Dv, Alpharetta, GA 30202

Butsch MISS Janet F
☎ (303) 750-4191 . . 2429D S Xanadu Way, Aurora, CO 80014

Butsch DR & MRS John L (Lucy J Butt)
Wheat'62.Ts.G.P.'56.McG'60 . . . . | ☎ (716) 886-1210
MISS Mary C . . . . | 174 Soldiers Place,
MR John L O'B . . . . | Buffalo, NY 14222
MR Winfield S . . . . |

Butt MR Charles C—A.Nf.Ny.Nyc. ⚓
☎ (210) 271-0014 . . "River Place" 335 King William, San Antonio,
TX 78204

Butt MR Clement van B—CtCol'87
☎ (212) 987-9504 . . 1349 Lexington Av, New York, NY 10128

Butt MR & MRS Richard van Beuren (Pamela A
Clement) P'62.Nu'68 . . . . | ☎ (860) 434-9108
MISS Amédée V—RISD'90.RISD'91 . . . . | "Bayberry Farm"
 | 83 Joshuatown Rd,
 | Lyme, CT 06371

Buttenheim MR & MRS Donald V (Kathleen Howell Coursen)
Sth'38.Wms'37.H'56
☎ (413) 637-4267 . . Kimball Farms, 235 Walker St, Lenox, MA 01240

Buttenheim MR & MRS Richard M (Meta C Boykin)
Wms'63 . . . . | ☎ (518) 794-7328
MISS Melissa H—at Brown . . . . | PO Box 179,
JUNIORS MISS Paulette B . . . . | Old Chatham, NY
 | 12136

Butterfield LORD John & LADY (Isabel A Kennedy)
Rdc'47.Hn.Ox'45 . . . . | ☎ (011-44-1223)
MR Toby—at New York, NY . . . . | 328854
 | 39 Clarendon St,
 | Cambridge
 | CB1 1JX, England

Butterworth MISS Brooke Anne (G Forrest 4th) . . . . Born Dec 28'95
Butterworth MR & MRS David G (Susan V Cauffman)
Denis'80.Ph.Au.CtCol'80.VillaN'89
☎ (610) 688-3131 . . 235 Sugartown Rd, Devon, PA *19333*
Butterworth MR & MRS G Forrest 4th (Melody M Schallon) Cal'72
☎ (415) 692-9992 . . 3083 Arguello Dv, Burlingame, CA *94010*
Butterworth MR & MRS J Warner 2d (Diana B | ☎ (212) TR6-1823
Townsend) Au.Cly.Cda.H.P'59 . . . . | 1170 Fifth Av,
JUNIORS MISS Diana B T . . . . | New York, NY
JUNIORS MR James T—at Kent . . . . | *10029*
Butterworth MR & MRS James E JR (Nona M Angel) Au.Pp.P'50
☎ (704) 375-1187 . . 2041 Nolen Park Lane, Charlotte, NC *28209*
Butterworth MR & MRS James E 3d (Shawn L Gray) NCar'83.NCar'83
☎ (704) 366-4847 . . 5823 Doncaster Dv, Charlotte, NC *28211*
Butterworth MR & MRS John (Elsie W Large) Rose'78.Au.Fst.P'49.Pa'53
☎ (610) 688-1518 . . 260 Berwind Rd, Radnor, PA *19087-3702*
Butterworth MR & MRS John JR (Joan E Lada)
Ne'76.Purd'77.Bow'77.Peab'yColl'78.Conn'90
☎ (508) 832-5331 . . 3 Loring St, Auburn, MA *01501*
Butterworth MISS Julia Marley (James E 3d) . . . . Born May 12'95
Butterworth MR & MRS S Hughes JR (Espersen—Sharon C Swift) Tex'54
☎ (915) 584-7496 . . 6223 Pinehurst Dv, El Paso, TX *79912*
Button MR & MRS Edward N (Daphne E S Purry) | of ☎ (941)495-7429
Cv.Cycl.Pk.Camb'51 . . . . | 26850 Wedgewood
MR Graham R—Nw'80—at ☎ (212) 353-2628 | Dv, 101, Bonita
70 E 7 St, New York, NY *10003* . . . . | Bay, Bonita Springs,
| FL *33923*
| ☎ (011-44)
| 1399-7651
| 11 Lockesley
| Square, Lovelace
| Gardens, Surbiton,
| Surrey, England
Button MRS William H (Montane—Margarita von Hoffmann) Cly . . .of
☎ (212) 879-7096 . . 45 E 72 St, New York, NY *10021*
☎ (802) 372-8219 . . ''Over Lake'' Rte 1, Box 48, North Hero,
VT *05474*
Buttrick MRS Duncan (Charlotte E Magruder) Ncd.
☎ (401) 423-0078 . . 24 Prudence Rd, PO Box 546, Jamestown,
RI *02835*
Buttrick MISS Kathryn L—Va'84.Pa'86
☎ (617) 965-2825 . . 27 Faxon St, Apt 1, Newton, MA *02195*
Buttrick MR & MRS Samuel C (Lucinda B Moncrieff) Stan'80.Ch'85
☎ (914) 764-9252 . . 23 High Cliff Terr, Pound Ridge, NY *10576*
Buttrick MR & MRS Stedman (Anne T Riker) MtH'55.Nrr.Sm.Cw.H'51
☎ (508) 369-5619 . . 30 Oak Rd, Concord, MA *01742*
Butz MISS Claire DeHaven (David A) . . . . Born at
Ann Arbor, MI Jan 19'96
Butz MR & MRS David A (Harriet DeH Cuddihy)
Nw'85.Wash'81.Nw'83.Nw'86
☎ (313) 998-0128 . . 1615 Wells St, Ann Arbor, MI *48104*
Buxton MR & MRS George N (Catherine A Triant) Bnd'86.Bcs.Y'78
☎ (212) 472-7108 . . 140 E 72 St, New York, NY *10021*
Buxton DR & MRS Jorge N (Amalia Gonzalez)
Bcs.Cly.StGeo'40.BuenosA'47 . . of
☎ (212) 861-1866 . . 857 Fifth Av, New York, NY *10021*
☎ (518) 734-9749 . . 4 Clarence Lane, Windham, NY *12496*

Buzby MR George H—GeoW'88
☎ (703) 528-7650 . . 248 N Columbus St, Arlington, VA *22203*
Byard MRS D Spencer (Margaret L Mather) Sth'33.Cl'62.Cs.
☎ (212) 289-2107 . . 140 E 92 St, Apt 7S, New York, NY *10128*
Byczkowski MISS Anne—V'79 . . see MRS K M Dibble
Byers MR Buckley M (Herndon—Mary H Powell) Tenn'68.Emory'80.Rr.
2216 Cherokee Blvd, Knoxville, TN *37919*
Byers MR David Richmond 3d—Va'45
☎ (404) 875-4618 . . 25 W 26 St NW, Atlanta, GA *30309*
Byers MR & MRS (REV DR) James N 3d (Bryant— | ☎ (941) 794-5307
Finley—Katrina Rauch) Hart'65.Bost'82. | 3920 Mariner's
Bost'96.Au.Br'38 . . . . | Way, 322, Cortez,
MISS Jennifer R Bryant—Les'92 . . . . | FL *34215*
MR Stearns J Bryant 3d—Denis'93—at |
☎ (617) 730-9741 . . 114 Riverway, Apt 4, |
Boston, MA *02215* . . . . |
Byers MR & MRS John C (Victoria R Kelly) | *see*
Sth'60.Wms'61 . . . . | *Dilatory Domiciles*
MISS Adair R . . . . |
MR John C 3d—at U of Vt . . . . |
Byers MR & MRS Randolph K JR (Eleanor B Atwater) Ncd. ⚓ . . of
☎ (203) 762-3824 . . 111 Branch Brook Rd, Wilton, CT *06897*
☎ (401) 635-8984 . . 696K W Main Rd, Little Compton, RI *02837*
Byers MR & MRS W Russell G (Laurada Beacham) Y'64
8200 St Martins Lane, Philadelphia, PA *19118*
Byers MR & MRS W Russell G JR (W Russell G) . . . Married at Garden City, NY
Bennett MISS Anne D (James D) . . . . May 20'95
Byford-Brown MRS William E (H Adèle Taylor) Dar.
☎ (914) 337-8926 . . 69 Park Av, Bronxville, NY *10708*
Byington MR Charles H
821 Park Av, Baltimore, MD *21201*
Byram MISS Elizabeth Nye
☎ (212) 755-1143 . . 200 E 58 St, New York, NY *10022*
Byram MR & MRS Elizabeth W (Elizabeth E Wing) Cly . . . | ☎ (212) 860-1122
MR Samuel W—Denis'94—at ☎ (202) 543-7509 | 70 E 96 St,
319—10 St NE, Apt 3, Washington, DC *20003* . | New York, NY
| *10128*
Byram MR & MRS James A JR (Virginia E Nicholas)
Ala'77.Ala'79.Ala'76.Ala'79
☎ (334) 279-7852 . . 1749 Pineneedle Rd, Montgomery, AL *36106*
Byram MR Josiah Nye—Au.Y'63
''Salad Days'' Keene Valley, NY *12943*
Byrd MR & MRS Ames (Eleanor S Clarke) Cyb.H'75
☎ (802) 649-1597 . . RR 1, Box 296, Norwich, VT *05055*
Byrd MR & MRS Andrew W (Marianne Menefee) | ☎ (615) 665-1934
Van'76 . . . . | 4419 Harding Place,
MISS Marianne A . . . . | Nashville, TN *37205*
MISS Valere C . . . . |
JUNIORS MR Andrew W JR . . . . |
Byrd MR Damon W—StAndr'77
☎ (615) 297-2146 . . 432 Westview Av, Nashville, TN *37205*
Byrd MRS Emily S (Emily B Saltonstall) . . . . | ☎ (617) 232-0032
MR Harry F 2d—Vt'77—*see Dilatory Domiciles* | 240 Chestnut Hill
| Rd, Chestnut Hill,
| MA *02167-1333*

Byrd MR & MRS William (Scullin—Nesmith— Archer—Roberts—Joan Jacoby) H'26 . . . . ☎ (609) 924-0381 21 Castle Howard Court, Princeton, NJ *08540*
   MISS Lucy C Roberts—at ☎ (919) 250-0993
   3243 Calumet Dv, Apt F, Raleigh, NC *27610*

Byrholdt MISS Alden J—StLaw'88
   ☎ (202) 338-8508 . . 1657—31 St NW, Washington, DC *20007*

Byrholdt MR & MRS Alfred J (Bennett—I Alden Johnson)
   ☎ (301) 656-6225 . . 4701 Willard Av, Apt 705, Chevy Chase, MD *20815*

Byrne MRS H Sheridan (J Virginia McCauley)
   ☎ (215) 345-6974 . . Heritage Towers 202, 200 Veterans Lane, Doylestown, PA *18901*

Byron DR & MRS H Thomas JR (E Lee Kimball) Sth'67.MontI'72.Stone'65.Fla'73.Aub'77 . . . . . . ☎ (941) 371-2549 653 Sinclair Dv, Sarasota, FL *34240*
   MISS Lee Hayes—at Stanford . . . .
   MR Chase K—at ☎ (941) 349-4588
   129 Edmondson Av, Sarasota, FL *34242* . . . . . .

Byron-Patrikiades MR & MRS Charles A (Tarsaidze—Elizabeth Sverbeyeff) Paris'46.K.EcoleSciPol'39.H'47 . . of
   ☎ (212) 249-0088 . . 25 E 83 St, New York, NY *10028*
   ☎ (516) 726-7680 . . PO Box 1595, Southampton, NY *11969*

C

Cabaniss DR J Allen—Ht.Cw.Sar.Rhodes'32.Ch'39
   17 N Woods Dv, Grenada, MS *38901*

Cabanne MR & MRS Xavier (Isabel H Schaff) Duke'82
   ☎ (847) 317-7764 . . 1050 Tower Rd, Winnetka, IL *60093*

Cabeen MISS M Lea (Hussey—M Lea Cabeen) Les'87.Mass'93 . . . . . . 38 Broad St, Newburyport, MA *01950*
   MISS Alison E Hussey—Mass'96 . . . .
   JUNIORS MISS Alicia P Hussey . . . .

Cabell MR Benjamin 5th . . see D N Garrett

Cabell MR & MRS William D (Ellen E Rolston) K.Va'30
   ☎ (804) 457-4836 . . "Rock Castle" 700 Rock Castle Rd, Goochland, VA *23014*

Cabot MR & MRS Andrew L (Maud Henrichs) PineM'91.Ne'93
   ☎ (617) 266-3345 . . 1 Marlborough St, Boston, MA *02116*

Cabot MISS Camilla Pepperell (Christopher S) . . . . Born at Newton, MA Jly 25'96

Cabot MR & MRS Charles C JR (Dale D Pirie) D.Tv.H.'52.H'57 . . . . ☎ (508) 785-0834 225 Dedham St, Dover, MA *02030*
   MR Charles C 3d—H'79—at Wayland, MA *01778*

Cabot MR & MRS Chilton L (Victoria L J Thaler) Wheat'87.Myf.Pa'86
   ☎ (401) 884-1186 . . 183 Cedar Av, East Greenwich, RI *02818*

Cabot MR & MRS Christopher (Judith McD Kinnard) Ws'66.H'71 . . . . ☎ (508) 927-0388 6 Hart St, Beverly Farms, MA *01915*
   MISS Heath . . . .

Cabot JUNIORS MR Christopher C . . see E P Saltonstall JR

Cabot MR & MRS Christopher S (Brooke C Wight) Duke'88.BostColl'93.Ham'88
   ☎ (617) 461-8796 . . 83 Chestnut St, Dedham, MA *02026*

Cabot MR Edward O—Cl'87
   25 Central Park W, Apt 12C, New York, NY *10023*

Cabot MISS Elizabeth L—BMr'83.Chi.
   ☎ (212) 879-4924 . . 169 E 78 St, Apt 3C, New York, NY *10021*

Cabot MR & MRS Francis H (Anne Perkins) K.Cly.H'49 . . of
   ☎ (914) 265-3533 . . "Stonecrop" RR 2, Box 371, Cold Spring, NY *10516*
   ☎ (418) 665-2474 . . "Les Quatre Vents" 345 rue Fraser, La Malbaie, Quebec G5A 1A2, Canada

Cabot MR & MRS John G L (Carroll Lloyd Trimble) BMr'60.Sm.Ec.Mt.H'56
   ☎ (508) 526-1102 . . "Watch House" 1 Tuck's Point Rd, Manchester, MA *01944*

Cabot MR & MRS John R (Kathleen R Ballard) Cal'85.Cal'86
   206 Middle Rd, Newbury, MA *01922*

Cabot MR & MRS Lewis P (Susan C Knight) Sm.Ny.Mt.Chi.H'61 . . of
   ☎ (207) 833-6382 . . 530 Basin Point Rd, South Harpswell, ME *04079*
   ☎ (011-44-1734) 713-620 . . Chapel Row Cottage, Bucklebury, Reading, Berkshire RG7 6PB, England

Cabot MRS Lynne O (Lynne M O'Berry) Stan'60
   ☎ (617) 326-9462 . . 838 High St, Dedham, MA *02026*

Cabot JUNIORS MR Matthew P . . see E P Saltonstall JR

Cabot MR & MRS Mitchell W (Margaret N Freeman) Wheat'73.CambC'92
   ☎ (617) 329-3736 . . 108 Highland St, Dedham, MA *02026*

Cabot MR & MRS Paul C JR (Saltonstall—Jennifer B Felton) Chi.H.'53 . . . . ☎ (617) 329-4066 151 Grove St, Westwood, MA *02090*
   MISS Cornelia C . . . .
   MISS Jennifer F . . . .

Cabot MRS Ropes (Harriet Ropes) BMr'30.Chi.Ncd.
   ☎ (508) 428-6353 . . Box 266, Cotuit, MA *02635*

Cabot MR & MRS Samuel 3d (Rosa S Gallardo) Ec.Dth'63 . . . . ☎ (508) 526-7636 9 Ashland Av, Manchester, MA *01944*
   MR Samuel G—Dth'91 . . . .
   MR David G—Dth'93 . . . .

Cabot MRS Thomas D (Virginia Wellington) Cy.Sm.Chi.
   ☎ (617) 893-0605 . . "Hidden Hearth" 31 Farm Rd, Weston, MA *02193*

Cabot MR & MRS Thomas D JR (Mary P McGrath) H'44 . . . . 10 Copper Beech Rd, Greenwich, CT *06830*
   MR Robert M . . . .
   MR James W . . . .

Cabot MR & MRS Timothy P (Sara R E Snow) ClCol'89
   ☎ (011-44-1244) 346-546 . . 4D Kings Bldg, Kings St, Chester CH1 2HA, England

Cabot MISS Victoria Sears (Chilton L) . . . . Born Jun 26'95

Cabot MR & MRS Walter M (Dorothy Scullin) H'84.D.H'55 . . . . ☎ (508) 785-0512 74 Center St, Dover, MA *02030*
   MISS Linda N—at 352 Harvard St, Apt 1D, Cambridge, MA *02138* . . . .

Cabral MR & MRS Douglas A (Lafue—Margaret M Meigs) CarnM'78.BostColl'67
   ☎ (508) 645-2421 . . RR 1, Box 282, Middle Rd, Chilmark, MA *02535*

Caddis MR & MRS Charles Owings (Trent Douglass) Ala'65.Ala'65
   ☎ (205) 870-0110 . . 3235 Rockledge Rd, Birmingham, AL *35213*

Cadwalader MRS Cynthia W (Cynthia Saunders White) Wheat'78.Ncd.
   ☎ (207) 374-2953 . . "Millstream" PO Box 1174, Blue Hill, ME *04614*

Cadwalader MR & MRS Gardner A (Kathryn L Kaercher) Pa'74.Pa'70.Pa'76 . . . .
JUNIORS MISS Genevieve A . . . .
☎ (215) 248-2228 90 W Mermaid Lane, Philadelphia, PA *19118-4024*

Cadwalader MR & MRS Gouverneur JR (McNichol—Joan L Hayden) Ph.B.Ssk. . . . .
MR Anthony J D—LakeF'86 . . . .
☎ (610) 347-2337 PO Box 717, Unionville, PA *19375*

Cadwalader MRS Henry (Caroline R Seelye) V'44.Ac. . . . .
MR Henry JR—Nasson'82.SMaineTech'94 . . . . .
MRS Caroline C Leland (Caroline C Cadwalader)—at 7818 Flourtown Av, Wyndmoor, PA *19038* . . . .
☎ (207) 363-3937 Box 656, 10 Seabury Rd, York Harbor, ME *03911*

Cadwalader CAPT (RET) & MRS John (Lea T Aspinwall) USN.V'44.Ph.Cda.Pa'32
☎ (215) 643-4639 . . 120 Norristown Rd, Blue Bell, PA *19422-2803*

Cadwalader MISS Mary Helen
☎ (410) 877-7606 . . "The Mound" 2008 Old Joppa Rd, Joppa, MD *21085*

Cadwalader MR & MRS R Kent (Susan H Curry) Y'78.Ssk.Ph.Rd.Ac.
☎ (610) 687-2592 . . "Homewood" 710 Newtown Rd, Villanova, PA *19085*

Cadwalader MR & MRS Stephen (Karen A Hoopes) Roan'74
2925 Rising Sun Rd, Ardmore, PA *19003*

Cadwalader MR & MRS Thomas F JR (Norrie—Phyllis J Clegg) Ste.Pa'34
☎ (410) 323-4043 . . 733 Colorado Av, Baltimore, MD *21210*

Cady MRS K McCarthy (Karen A McCarthy) Skd'68 . . . .
JUNIORS MR Colin L . . . .
1507 Williston Rd, South Burlington, VT *05403*

Caesar MR & MRS Henry A 2d (Allison Garver) Rv.P'37.Y'40 . . . .
MR John G—Elmira'79 . . . .
☎ (203) 966-1470 50 Hemlock Hill Rd, New Canaan, CT *06840*

Cagle MR & MRS J Stanford 3d (Catherine Crowell) Tex'83.Tex'86
☎ (915) 584-4854 . . 5038 Ocotillo St, El Paso, TX *79932*

Caglieri MR Guido E
Box 2151, San Francisco, CA *94126*

Cahill MR & MRS Anthony T (Whitney O Kellett) Skd'88
☎ (916) 758-7338 . . 1225 F St, Davis, CA *95616*

Cahill MR & MRS J Peter (Carroll T Kales) Cal'47.Bhm.Pcu.Tcy.Cal'46 . . . .
MISS Sarah A—at 156 Walter Hayes Dv, Palo Alto, CA *94301* . . . .
MISS Susan M—Box 947, Ross, CA *94957* . . . . .
☎ (415) 851-7617 280 Whiskey Hill Rd, Woodside, CA *94062*

Cahill MR & MRS John E (Helen W Kennedy) Cal'38.Sfg.Pcu.Tcy.Stan'36
☎ (415) 492-2505 . . 100 Thorndale Dv, Apt 405, San Rafael, CA *94903-4581*

Cahill MR & MRS John E JR (Patricia A Leahy) Sth'65.Mid'66.Bhm.Pcu.Stan'66.H'68 . . . .
JUNIORS MISS Kathryn L . . . .
JUNIORS MR John C . . . .
☎ (415) 457-0232 245 Laurel Grove Av, Kentfield, CA *94904*

Cahill MR & MRS William R (Jeanne L Jamison) Miami'72.Pcu.Stan'73.Cal'78
☎ (415) 485-5354 . . 120 Lagunitas Rd, PO Box 440, Ross, CA *94957*

Cain DR & MRS Marvin J (Parnell—Julia D Thieriot) Cly.OState'55
☎ (540) 554-8183 . . "Molehill" 20465 Unison Rd, Round Hill, VA *20142*

Cain MR & MRS Thomas H (Emily J M Smith) Rdc'57.Y'61.Y'62.Tor'53.Tor'56.Wis'59 . . . . . .
MR Patrick E M—Tor'91 . . . .
☎ (416) 648-1070 Walnut Hill Farmhouse, RR 1, Jerseyville, Ontario L0R 1R0, Canada

Calawa DR Steven P—Nw'78
☎ (603) 880-6604 . . 168 Charles Bancroft Rd, Litchfield, NH *03052*

Calder MR & MRS Donald G (Ann E Martin) Rc.Un.Lic.L.So.Cly.Myf.Ht.Ncd.P'59.H'65 . . . .
MISS Cornelia M—Bow'94 . . . .
MISS Isabella S—at Brown . . . .
MR Donald G JR—AmUParis'92 . . . .
of ☎ (212)744-2623 164 E 72 St, New York, NY *10021*
☎ (516) 283-7337 "Pheasants' Field" First Neck Lane, Southampton, NY *11968*

Calder MRS Joan N (Woolverton—Joan L Newton) S . . .of
☎ (214) 871-2773 . . Terrace House 12G, 3131 Maple Av, Dallas, TX *75201*
☎ (011-52-376) 60939 . . "Las Bodegas" Privada Libertad 38, Ajijic, 45920 Jalisco, Mexico

Caldwell DR & MRS David W (Lisa Lillard) B'gton'76.StlCity'88.Dth'74.Dth'77 . . . .
JUNIORS MISS Catharine L . . . .
JUNIORS MISS Clarissa D . . . .
☎ (505) 986-9665 1841 Sun Mountain Dv, Santa Fe, NM *87505*

Caldwell MR & MRS Edward E (Katharine C Nash) Myf.Ncd.NCar'38
☎ (919) 918-3647 . . Carol Woods Apt 192, 750 Weaver Dairy Rd, Chapel Hill, NC *27514-1466*

Caldwell MR & MRS J Alexander IV (Gutierrez—Maria Teresa Ortiz de Barron Ituarte) Aht'65 . . .
MR Alejandro Gutierrez . . . .
MR Christian A Gutierrez . . . .
JUNIORS MR David Gutierrez . . . .
1717 E Mendocino St, Altadena, CA *91001*

Caldwell MR J Emott
☎ (415) 851-0342 . . 225 Whiskey Hill Rd, Woodside, CA *94062*

Caldwell MR & MRS James E JR (Philipa A Redlich) Stan'66.Bhm.Wms'64.Y'69 . . . .
MISS Rebecca S—at Occidental . . . .
JUNIORS MR James E 3d—at RI Sch of Design . .
☎ (415) 851-7312 121 Fox Hollow Rd, Woodside, CA *94062*

Caldwell MR & MRS Josef (Louise S Phinney) Swb'60.Myf.Tex'55.PTheo'65.Tex'69 . . . .
MISS Jane B . . . .
MR Josef JR . . . .
MR Charles P . . . .
☎ (214) 521-5508 3621 Cornell Av, Dallas, TX *75205*

Caldwell MR & MRS Joseph I (Eleanor Platt) H'45
☎ (805) 684-4065 . . 6659 Arozena Lane, Carpinteria, CA *93013*

Caldwell MR & MRS Kenneth S (Alice E Featherstone) Keuka'43.Cr'50.May.Cal'47
☎ (910) 949-2006 . . 46A N Lakeview Dv, Whispering Pines, NC *28327*

Caldwell MR & MRS Kenneth S 3d (Dixon—Teresa L Major) SanDiego'80.SanDiego'83.Sdy.Tex'81
☎ (805) 482-6810 . . 5235 Mission Oaks Blvd, Apt 673, Camarillo, CA *93012*

Caldwell MR & MRS Robert H (Sharon H Stevenson) P'45
  ☎ (423) 821-1538 . . 1002 Scenic H'way, Lookout Mountain, TN *37350*
Caldwell MR & MRS Wentworth JR (Barry Mitchiner) | ☎ (615) 352-2554
So'63.Conv'64 . . . . | "Cliff Lawn"
MISS Ashley M—So'91. . . . . | 103 Hillwood Dv,
MISS Barry M—Miss'92 . . . . | Nashville, TN *37205*
MISS May E
MISS Wentworth . . . .
Caldwell MRS Wiley N (Jean M Clarke) Elm'21 . . of
  ☎ (310) 454-2840 . . 341 Alma Real Dv, Pacific Palisades, CA *90272*
  ☎ (619) 782-3383 . . "Despacio" Camino Ortega, Warner Springs,
  CA *92086*
Cale MR & MRS Charles G (Jessie L Rawn) | ☎ (310) 472-6014
SCal'74.P'cpia'61.Stan'64.SCal'66 . . . . | 449 N Rockingham
JUNIORS MISS Whitney R . . . . | Av, Los Angeles,
                                             | CA *90049*
Cale MR & MRS Dutro C 2d (Maryett K Finney) P'37
  ☎ (203) 949-0640 . . 3302 Ashlar Village, Wallingford, CT *06492*
Calfee MR & MRS John B (Nancy E Leighton) Sth'41.Un.May.Pk.Y'35
  ☎ (216) 381-2423 . . 4892 Clubside Rd, Cleveland, OH *44124-2539*
Calfee MR & MRS Peter H (Gift—Janice O'Connell)
OWes'72.May.Stan'73.Ch'76
  ☎ (216) 247-0262 . . 102 Champion Lane, Chagrin Falls, OH *44022*
Calhoun MR & MRS G Clay (Bennett—Lucy V McClintock)
SMColl'85.Emory'71
  ☎ (770) 786-6703 . . 516 H'way 81 SW, Covington, GA *30209*
Calhoun MRS John C 3d (Lorraine H Swanson)
8106 Highwood Dv, Bloomington, MN *55438-3101*
Califano MR & MRS Joseph A JR (Byers—Hilary Paley) Mt.HolyC'52.H'55
  ☎ (860) 354-8473 . . 11 Raven Rock Rd, Roxbury, CT *06783*
Calil MRS Frances C (Frances B Condon)
  ☎ (901) 454-4898 . . Chickasaw Gardens, 2979 Gardens Way, Memphis,
  TN *38111*
Calkins MRS C Delevan (Sullivan—Frances G Caskey) Lind'32
  ☎ (561) 272-0249 . . 1717 Homewood Blvd, Apt 271, Delray Beach,
  FL *33445*
Calkins MR John T—Bhm.Mt.Sar.Syr'49.Geo'57 . . of
  ☎ (202) 364-2797 . . Metropolitan Club, Box 39, 1700 H St NW,
  Washington, DC *20006*
  ☎ (941) 263-4512 . . 2011 Gulf Shore Blvd N, Naples, FL *34102*
Callaghan MISS Elisabeth P . . see A K Weymouth JR
Callaghan MISS Sara G . . see A K Weymouth JR
Callahan MR Alfred J JR—Bcs.Geo'67
  ☎ (516) 283-1625 . . 40 Barnhart St, Southampton, NY *11968*
Callahan MRS Philip E (Deborah Oughton)
  ☎ (217) 546-5912 . . 1404 S Grand Av W, Springfield, IL *62704*
Callahan MR Robert F—Ri.H.'45 . . . . | of ☎ (212)980-0168
MISS M Carroll Kiernan—Geo'79.Y'85—at | 1 Beekman Place,
  ☎ (703) 532-6638 . . 1618 N Lexington St, | New York, NY
Arlington, VA *22205* . . . . | *10022*
DR Michael J Kiernan—Wms'81.Cl'85—at | ☎ (561) 546-5509
  ☎ (802) 863-8079 . . 11 S Union St, | 222 S Beach Rd,
Burlington, VT *05401* . . . . | Hobe Sound, FL
                                        | *33455*
Callan MR Edwin C—Bhm.Sfg.Sfy.Pcu.Cal'42
  ☎ (415) 433-7335 . . 1441 Montgomery St, Apt 4, San Francisco,
  CA *94133*

Callan MR & MRS John C (Eugenia M Riordan) | of ☎ (415)386-3734
Cal'50.Pcu.Bhm.Sfg.Fr.Cal'50 . . . . | 150—24 Av,
MISS Leslie M—at ☎ (415) 563-6098 | San Francisco, CA
975 Union St, San Francisco, CA *94133* . . . . . . | *94121*
                                        | ☎ (707) 935-1136
                                        | Sonoma, CA *95476*
Callan MR & MRS John C JR (A Penland Kaisel)
Cal'82.SFr'87.Bhm.Cal'78.SFr'82
  ☎ (415) 751-8650 . . 155—27 Av, San Francisco, CA *94121*
Callander DR & MRS John N (Barbara J Kendrick) | ☎ (415) 931-5514
Bhm.Pcu.Sfg.Fr.Stan'45.JHop'47.Cal'49 . . . . . . | 2540 Filbert St,
DR Peter W—Stan'87.StL'95 . . . . | San Francisco, CA
                                        | *94123*
Callard MR & MRS David J (Strawbridge—Morgan | ☎ (212) 876-6266
—Mary C Rockefeller) V'60.Cl'90.Un.K.Elk. | 1120 Fifth Av,
P'59.Nu'69 . . . . | New York, NY
MISSES Anne L & Elizabeth H—at 5706 Visitation | *10128*
Way, Baltimore, MD *21210* . . . .
MSRS Francis J & Samuel P—at 5706 Visitation
Way, Baltimore, MD *21210* . . . .
Callard MR & MRS George D (Tracy L Taylor)
Geo'86.Cwr'91.U'85.Cwr'92 . . of
  ☎ (773) 871-7546 . . 665 W Irving Park Rd, Apt 3410, Chicago,
  IL *60613*
  ☎ (561) 738-1229 . . 6059 Old Ocean Blvd, Ocean Ridge, FL *33435*
Callard DR & MRS George M (Linda S Siple) | ☎ (513) 871-9452
Qc.P'56.JHop'60 . . . . | 3021 Erie Av,
MISS Susan K . . . . | Cincinnati, OH
MR Henry P—Bost'86 . . . . | *45208*
MR David M—P'88 . . . .
MR William S . . . .
Callaway MR & MRS L David 3d (Essex—Brenda L | of ☎ (561)833-2628
Teagle) Rc.BtP.Evg.Mb.Pr.Ri.W&L'62 | 200 Algoma Rd,
MR Christopher W | Palm Beach, FL
MR D Andrew—at U of Utah . . . . | *33480*
  MISS Brenda L Essex . . . . | ☎ (516) 671-0678
  MISS Amanda T Essex . . . . | "Duck Hook"
  MR Winfield S Essex 3d. . . . . | 24 Wellington Rd,
                                        | Locust Valley, NY
                                        | *11560*
                                        | ☎ (212) 744-4206
                                        | 164 E 72 St,
                                        | New York, NY
                                        | *10021*
Callaway MR & MRS Norman T (Hare—Barbara B | ☎ (609) 924-2185
Rose) ColbyS'66.Dar. | 149 Hodge Rd,
MISS Elizabeth B Hare . . . . | Princeton, NJ *08540*
MISS Katherine W Hare . . . .
MR Hobart N Hare . . . .
Callaway MR & MRS Samuel R (Dorothy Harding) H'32
  ☎ (203) 264-9564 . . 332 Pomperaug Woods, Southbury, CT *06488*
Callaway MR & MRS Trowbridge JR (Diana Stokes) Hn.
  ☎ (561) 243-0176 . . 400 Seasage Dv, Delray Beach, FL *33483*

Callaway MR & MRS Trowbridge 3d (Phyllis J Anderson) Cho.On.Br'60 . . . . ☎ (561) 369-0028 / 67 Spanish River Dv, Ocean Ridge, FL 33435
   MISS Leslie A—at ☎ (614) 799-0639 4728F Heathstead Dv, Dublin, OH 43017 . . . . .
   MR William T—at 208 S 3 St, Philadelphia, PA 19106 . . . .

Callaway MR & MRS Tyler S (Melinda G Fisher) ☎ (619) 459-0251 . . 652 Westbourne St, La Jolla, CA 92037

Callen MR & MRS Andrew B (Dicksie A Hoyt) Skd'68.Neb'67 . . . . ☎ (508) 369-0145 / 205 Fairhaven Hill, Concord, MA 01742
   MISS Jennifer H—Va'94 . . . .
   MR Andrew B JR—StLaw'93 . . . .

Callen MR & MRS John H JR (Carolyn P Coleman) Rm.Stc.Ty'55 . . . . ☎ (802) 325-3039 / "Mettowee Valley Farm" Box 55, Rupert Mountain Rd, Pawlet, VT 05761
   MR John H 3d—at ☎ (617) 928-0844 75 Brookside Av, Newtonville, MA 02160 . . . .
   MR J Hunter . . . .

Callery MR & MRS James (Holly S Simonds) B.P'60 ☎ (802) 425-2754 / RR 2, Box 2750, Charlotte, VT 05445
   MISS Virginia R . . . .
   MISS Sprague E . . . .

Calmer MRS Edgar (Gloria F Hercik) Pl . . .of
   ☎ (212) 582-7534 . . 333 W 57 St, New York, NY 10019
   ☎ (516) 239-1321 . . 125 Ocean Av, Lawrence, NY 11559

Calvert MR Charles B—Rm'65 . . . . ☎ (410) 377-4117 / 208 Murdock Rd, Baltimore, MD 21212
   MR Charles B 4th—Rut'92 . . . .
   JUNIORS MR Robert N . . . .

Cálves MRS Herbert E (Eleanor H Spear) Pc.
   ☎ (215) 233-0303 . . Penn's Wood J38, 20 Haws Lane, Flourtown, PA 19031

Cálves MR Herbert E JR—Pc.Mit'58 . . . . ☎ (704) 332-1664 / 232-43 Queens Rd, Charlotte, NC 28204
   MISS Alexandra V P—at U of NCar Chapel Hill.
   MISS Stephanie H—at Ithaca Coll . . . .

Calvocoressi MR & MRS John L (Frances S Whitall) Dc.Ncd.H'38
   ☎ (860) 267-4010 . . Shipyard Rd, Middle Haddam, CT 06456

Calvocoressi MR & MRS Thomas J (Lisa C Petti) V'76.Conn'82.Hart'74.Conn'82 . . . . ☎ (860) 828-0516 / 718 Beckley Rd, Berlin, CT 06037
   MISS Gabrielle J—at Sarah Lawrence . . . .

Camden MR & MRS Andrew L (Gayle P Shaw) Dar.MichSt'63.Det'71
   ☎ (313) 885-1234 . . 552 Rivard Blvd, Grosse Pointe, MI 48230

Cameron MRS Brodnax (Julia D Sprigg) Mv. . . . . ☎ (410) 838-5980 / 300 N Toll Gate Rd, Bel Air, MD 21014
   MR George—Ken'51.H'53—at ☎ (612) 488-1460 2116—23 Av S, Minneapolis, MN 55404 . . . . .

Cameron MR & MRS Brodnax JR (Mignon A Bell) P'43
   ☎ (410) 879-1049 . . "Point of Woods" 310 N Toll Gate Rd, Bel Air, MD 21014-4208

Cameron MR & MRS C Lindsley (Butler—C Lindsley Cameron) B'gton'69
   ☎ (212) 989-3992 . . 108 Fifth Av, Apt 5A, New York, NY 10011

Cameron MISS Carrington H
   835 Guinda St, Palo Alto, CA 94301

Cameron MR Daniel D JR—NCar'73
   ☎ (919) 942-5554 . . 1003 Lamond Av, Durham, NC 27701

Cameron MR & MRS Donald Churchill (Fowle—Eleanor Cranston) Stan'33
   ☎ (415) 948-4893 . . 27060 Old Trace Rd, Los Altos, CA 94022

Cameron DR & MRS Donald J (Alison S Wright) StA.Aht'51.Cr'55
   ☎ (914) 779-3098 . . 15 Woodland Av, Bronxville, NY 10708

Cameron MR & MRS Douglas W (Tara L Warrick) NCar'94.Rol'88.AmU'93
   ☎ (212) 447-1624 . . 151 E 31 St, Apt 7F, New York, NY 10016

Cameron MR & MRS Gerard G 2d (Wendy W Mairs) Fic.Yn.Y'70 . . . . ☎ (203) 655-8027 / 15 Beach Dv, Darien, CT 06820
   MISS Elizabeth W . . . .
   MR David M—at Yale . . . .

Cameron DR & MRS J Price JR (Louisa Huger Pringle) Hlns'75.David'68 . . . . of ☎ (803)722-1801 / 19 Archdale St, Charleston, SC 29401
   JUNIORS MR J Price 3d—at Asheville Sch . . . . . .
   ☎ (704) 698-8418 / "Clunes" PO Box 34, Zirconia, NC 28790

Cameron MR & MRS John J G (Manley—Sheila M Hickey) . . . . ☎ (914) 738-4552 / 169 Hudson St, Pelham Manor, NY 10803
   MISS Jennifer A Manley—at 20 Division St, Greenwich, CT 06830. . . . .
   MISS Alexandra C Manley—at 109 Bartlett St, Apt 2, Charlestown, MA 02129 . . . .

Cameron MR & MRS John W (Elizabeth Fairbank) Fy.Ariz'70 . . . . ☎ (312) 988-9348 / 119 W Delaware Place, Chicago, IL 60610
   JUNIORS MISS Anne F . . . .
   JUNIORS MR John P . . . .

Cameron MR & MRS Juan M (Nora Leake) Rdc'64.Ny.H'46.H'56 . . . . ☎ (202) 338-8772 / 2823 N St NW, Washington, DC 20007
   MISS Nora C S . . . .
   JUNIORS MR Roderick L—at Westminster . . . . . .

Cameron MISS Laura H—Denis'91.Sim'94
   ☎ (203) 661-8297 . . 20 Fairfield Rd, Greenwich, CT 06830

Cameron MR & MRS Nicholas A (Wilson—Leslie Wood) Mg.Ste.Yn.Y'60 . . of
   ☎ (201) 822-2596 . . 5 Noe Av, Madison, NJ 07940
   ☎ (802) 824-6333 . . "Cam-Run" Bromley Village, Peru, VT 05152

Cameron MR & MRS Thomas W L (Carol L Soliday) Rc.Wcc.H'49 . . of
   ☎ (803) 768-1963 . . 332 Catbrier Court, Kiawah Island, Johns Island, SC 29455
   ☎ (610) 687-5533 . . 15 Sugar Knoll Dv, Devon, PA 19333

Cameron MR & MRS William A (Forkner—Katharine Torrey) Ford'82.Nu'88.Un.Dyc.Mds.Plg.Cly.P'49.H'53
   ☎ (212) 421-8607 . . 200 E 66 St, New York, NY 10021

Cammann MR & MRS Frederic G (Nora F Francke) Bnd'54.H.'51
   ☎ (516) 537-0993 . . Box 1072, Ocean Rd, Bridgehampton, NY 11932

Cammann MR Hamilton F . . . . ☎ (508) 693-1512 / PO Box 150, West Tisbury, MA 02575
   JUNIORS MR Nicholas F . . . .

Cammann MR & MRS Robert L (Priscilla Cranstoun) Lm.Hn. . . . . of ☎ (860)435-2476 / 105 Interlaken Rd, Lakeville, CT 06039
   MISS Carola C—Capital'73.Ncd.—at
   ☎ (203) 325-0383 . . 71 Strawberry Hill Av, Stamford, CT 06902
   ☎ (803) 723-8161 / 164½ Queen St, Charleston, SC 29401

Cammann MRS Schuyler van R (Muir—Mary Lyman Cox) BMr'45.Cda.Dc.
   ☎ (503) 786-6270 . . 15115 SE Rupert Dv, Milwaukie, OR 97267

Cammann MR William Bayard—Pars'88
☎ (609) 494-6944 . . PO Box 432, Brant Beach, NJ *08008*

Camp MRS Ehney A JR (Mildred F Tillman) B'hamS'30.Cy.
☎ (205) 967-5200 . . 3605 Ratliff Rd, Birmingham, AL *35210*

Camp MR & MRS Ehney A 3d (Patricia J Hough) | ☎ (205) 967-0140
Ala'66.Cy.Dth'64 . . . . | 3510 Victoria Rd,
MISS Margaret S . . . . | Birmingham, AL
MR Ehney A 4th . . . . | *35223*

Camp MRS Frederic E (Alida D Milliken) Sth'30.Csn.Ey. ⚓
☎ (207) 374-2824 . . ''Blueberry Hill'' East Blue Hill, ME *04629*

Camp MISS Juliet A . . see R B Dickson

Camp MR Mark E—SanDiegoSt'84 . . see R B Dickson

Campagna MR & MRS David W (Maria E Garcés-Echavarria)
CathU'76.Cl'78.Rc.Cly.P'63
☎ (212) 737-7549 . . 50 E 77 St, Apt 15C, New York, NY *10021*

Campbell LADY (Moore—Shelagh J Morrison-Bell)
☎ (011-44-1252) 615-364 . . 12 Frere Av, Fleet, Hampshire
GU13 8AP, England

Campbell MR Alfred M JR . . . . Died at
Bryn Mawr, PA Feb 12'96

Campbell MRS Alfred M JR (Dearden—Alice V Fox) Me.
☎ (610) 527-4004 . . 74 Pasture Lane, Apt 202, Bryn Mawr, PA *19010*

Campbell MRS Alfred M 3d (Vidinghoff—Watt— | ☎ (610) 527-9555
Pamela S Kogge) Me.Pe.Ste.Ac.StA. . . . . | Orchard Way,
MISS Alison C Vidinghoff . . . . | PO Box 1306,
MISS Ashley M Watt . . . . | Bryn Mawr, PA
MR J David Vidinghoff . . . . | *19010-7306*
JUNIORS MR John H Watt |

Campbell MRS Anne M (Anne L Meigs) | ☎ (603) 643-9410
MtH'63.Hb. . . . . | PO Box 287,
MISS Camilla K—MtH'91 . . . . | Etna, NH *03750*
MISS Meriweather W—at Colo Coll . . . . |
MR Andrew R—at U of Cal Berkeley . . . . |

Campbell MR Archibald—Nu'79.Nu'80.Cl'85
☎ (914) CO5-3693 . . ''Timbercove'' PO Box 32, Cold Spring,
NY *10516*

Campbell MR & MRS Benjamin K (Gough—Karyn R Webb) Ws'80.Fic.Tr.
☎ (617) 235-4660 . . 42 Hundreds Circle, Wellesley, MA *02181*

Campbell MR & MRS Christopher S (von | ☎ (207) 866-3276
Moschzisker—Margaret Eakins King) | 16 Spencer St,
H'68.Me'75.H'80 . . . . | Orono, ME *04473*
JUNIORS MISS C Camilla P . . . . |

Campbell MRS Daniel S (Harriet C Woods) BMr'43
☎ (513) 871-1404 . . 6 Forest Hill Dv, Cincinnati, OH *45208*

Campbell MR & MRS David M (Victoria M Hurd) Nu'82.Conn'76
☎ (941) 953-7793 . . 1631 Spring Creek Dv, Sarasota, FL *34239*

Campbell MR & MRS Dix McD (Elizabeth H Miller) | ☎ (617) 484-8826
MtH'60.Sb.H'60.Pa'63 . . . . | 150 Prospect St,
MISS Jessica E . . . . | Belmont, MA *02178*
MR Benjamin D . . . . |

Campbell MR & MRS Donald B (Lucy D Harrison) | ☎ (510) 848-0534
Bhm.Ncd.Cal'47 . . . . | 1 Atlas Place,
MISS Martha S . . . . | Berkeley, CA *94708*

Campbell MR & MRS Douglas JR (Elizabeth C MacColl) Sim'44.Y'42
☎ (313) 881-9431 . . 33 Lakecrest Lane, Grosse Pointe Farms, MI *48236*

Campbell MR & MRS Douglas 3d (Gwynne MacColl) Ty'77.NH'75.Va'80
☎ (203) 325-3373 . . 7 Alpine Lane, Darien, CT *06820*

Campbell MR Douglas K—Knox'74
☎ (312) 664-8729 . . 1310 N Ritchie Court, Apt 19B, Chicago, IL *60610*

Campbell MR & MRS Douglass (Strachan—Marion Danielson)
Cho.Chr.Rcch.St.Cv.Ri.StA.Plg.StJ.Cw.Ne.Cs.Chi.Sl. Y'41
☎ (212) 734-7676 . . 3 E 71 St, New York, NY *10021*

Campbell MR Duncan H (Lee—Canaday—Mary Flagg)
☎ (617) 326-6730 . . 10 Longwood Dv, Apt 164, Westwood, MA *02090*

Campbell MR & MRS Duncan MacColl (Maura L Reardon)
Hills'82.StJ.Col'82.MichSt'94
☎ (517) 332-7735 . . 2692 Linden St, East Lansing, MI *48823*

Campbell MR & MRS Dwight Douglas (Wendelyn A Ward)
☎ (818) 957-5250 . . 5201 Castle Rd, La Cañada, CA *91011*

Campbell MR Edward L—Edg.Bow'36
☎ (412) 741-5361 . . 516 Irwin Dv, Sewickley, PA *15143*

Campbell MRS Eunice G (Montoya—Eunice G Campbell) Pr.
☎ (516) 922-3432 . . 533 Centre Island Rd, Oyster Bay, NY *11771*

Campbell MR & MRS George L (Helen Hughes) | ☎ (860) 536-7896
SL'50.Hn.Hb.H'44 . . . . | ''Tidesflow''
MR G Stuart—Ken'82 . . . . | 88 Cove Rd,
MR Robert L—Denis'83 . . . . | Stonington, CT
| *06378*

Campbell MR & MRS Gordon C (Judith A Brewer) Pc.Fw.Wms'52.Pa'56
☎ (215) AD3-4858 . . 8102 Ardmore Av, Wyndmoor, PA *19038*

Campbell MISS Harriet T
☎ (561) 545-9464 . . 11779 SE Plandome Dv, Hobe Sound, FL *33455*

Campbell MRS Hatfield (Helen Hatfield) Cda.
☎ (805) 969-0508 . . Casa Dorinda B42, 300 Hot Springs Rd, Montecito, CA *93108*

Campbell MR & MRS Hazard K (Virginia E Klopp)
☎ (716) 874-0144 . . 85 Meadow Rd, Buffalo, NY *14216*

Campbell MRS Howard D 2d (Harriet D Turner) . . of
☎ (561) 747-3891 . . 19670 Beach Rd, Jupiter Island, FL *33469*
☎ (717) 848-2455 . . 1032 Smallbrook Lane, York, PA *17403*

Campbell MR & MRS J Melfort (Barbara K Hubbard) On.Ox'48
☎ (847) 234-4454 . . 40 Greenwich Court, Lake Bluff, IL *60044*

Campbell MR & MRS James A (Linda J Wise) Dar.Knox'67
☎ (415) 775-0321 . . 1177 California St, Apt 1431, San Francisco, CA *94108*

Campbell MRS John B S (Angela Mitchell)
☎ (513) 561-7344 . . 8675 Camargo Club Dv, Cincinnati, OH *45243*

Campbell MR John C E (Valerie T Parry) | ☎ (610) 358-4813
Temp'76.VillaN'81 . . . . | 220 Wawa Rd,
JUNIORS MR Angus C . . . . | Wawa, PA *19063*
JUNIORS MR Shane P . . . . |

Campbell MR John C E—Ph.Rc.Ll.Syr'67
☎ (215) 928-5581 . . Residences at Pier Five, 7 N Christopher Columbus Blvd, Philadelphia, PA *19106-1422*

Campbell MR & MRS John P (Eleanor M Seggerman) | ☎ (207) 363-3390
H'46.Cl'49 . . . . | Western Point,
MR Frederick B—H'73—at ☎ (212) 866-4820 | PO Box 561,
895 West End Av, New York, NY *10025* . . . . . | York, ME *03909*

Campbell MR & MRS John P III (Lisa H Hooker) V'82.H'82.Tul'87
☎ (615) 665-2288 . . 4432 Tyne Blvd, Nashville, TN *37215*

Campbell MR Jules D—Wash'32.Wash'33
☎ (314) 993-4381 . . 1 McKnight Place, Apt 150, St Louis, MO *63124-1981*

Campbell MR & MRS Levin H (Eleanor S Lewis) Sth'50.Cy.Un.Chi.H'48 . . . . | ☎ (617) 876-3096
MR Levin H JR . . . . | 17 Bates St, Cambridge, MA *02140*

Campbell MRS M Schuyler (McPherson—Mary Schuyler Campbell) Dar.Lm. . . . . | ☎ (864) 233-1160
MISS E Schuyler—at ☎ (803) 577-0451 | 420 Belmont Av, Greenville, SC
200 Grove St, Charleston, SC *29403* . . . . | *29601-4306*

Campbell MR Morrow G—Ds.Fw.StA. . . . . | ☎ (610) 436-8993
MR E Graham—at ☎ (310) 547-3530 | 449 Eaton Way,
2733 Gaffey St, San Pedro, CA *90731* . . . . | Hershey's Mill,
MR G Ross—at ☎ (714) 496-7855 | West Chester, PA
33781 Alcazar Dv, Dana Point, CA *92629* . . . . . | *19380*
MRS Katherine C (Millard—Teisan—Katherine C Campbell)—at ☎ (310) 305-1611
520 Washington Blvd, Apt 590, Marina Del Rey, CA *90292* . . . . |

Campbell DR & MRS Robert B (Kerry Ann McChesney) Miami'73.Mit'80 . . . . | ☎ (409) 321-3666
JUNIORS MISS Jennifer B . . . . | 63 Deerfern Place, The Woodlands, TX *77381*

Campbell DR & MRS Robert E (Nancy M Johnson) Me.Ph.H.'53.Pa'57 . . . . | ☎ (610) 896-5074
MR Robert E JR—Me.StA.Buck'87—at | 121 Orchard Lane,
☎ (206) 281-1646 . . 37 W Dravus St, Apt 3, | Haverford, PA
Seattle, WA *98119* . . . . | *19041-1709*
MR Frederick McK 2d—Me.M.StA.Ty'91—at
☎ (610) 520-0339 . . 113 Debaran Lane, Rosemont, PA *19010* . . . .
MR Colin A—Me.M.StA.H'92—at
☎ (201) 653-7198 . . 645 Garden St, Hoboken, NJ *07030* . . . .

Campbell DR & MRS Rolla D JR (Baker—Stevens—Kim Kendall) Ck.Evg.BtP.Fic.H'41.Cl'45 . . of
☎ (561) 835-1028 . . ''Dunbar Mead'' 257 Dunbar Rd, Palm Beach, FL *33480*
☎ (516) 788-7803 . . ''Life Saving House'' Box 261, East Harbor, Fishers Island, NY *06390*

Campbell MR & MRS Ross L (J Marcia Weaver) Fst.Sg.Rc.Pa'60 . . . . | ☎ (215) MI6-9176
MR Ross L JR—at ☎ (617) 738-9668 | 675 Lewis Lane,
54 Marshall St, Apt 3, Brookline, MA *02146* . . . | Ambler, PA *19002*
MR Ian W . . . . |

Campbell MRS S James (Mary Jo Thomas) Cy.Md.Ncd. . . . . | ☎ (410) 825-2704
MR A Thomas—at 6 Strathmere Club, Amesbury, | 1904 Indian Head
MA *01913* . . . . | Rd, Ruxton, MD *21204*

Campbell MR & MRS Samuel R (Camille C Rogers) Sth'58.Bcs.H.'47 . . . . | ☎ (516) 283-1498
MR Peter B—Wis'89 . . . . | ''Soupçon''
143 Meadowmere Lane, PO Box 904, Southampton, NY *11969*

Campbell MR & MRS Samuel R (Ames—Rebecca B Gardner) HRdc'76.Bost'86.Ub.My.H.Hn.H'73
☎ (508) 526-7887 . . 9 Old Neck Rd, Manchester, MA *01944*

Campbell MR & MRS Thomas Norton (M Nicole Lee) Sim'84.SCal'76
☎ (818) 458-9936 . . 919 Roxbury Rd, San Marino, CA *91108*

Campbell MR & MRS Thomas R B (Barbara H Hunt) Ws'63.Cl'95.Au.P'61 . . . . | ☎ (518) 392-2490
MISS Elizabeth H—Ober'92 . . . . | Box 232,
MR Thomas E H—P'91 . . . . | Ghent, NY *12075*
MR John R B—Ober'90 . . . . |

Campbell MR & MRS Ward C (Sarah W Loomis) BMr'49.Csh.Ny.StA.Cr'45 . . . . | ☎ (516) 692-6227
MISS Priscilla L . . . . | Middle Hollow Rd,
MR Michael T . . . . | Box 121, Cold Spring Harbor, NY *11724-0121*

Campbell MR & MRS William W JR (Douglas—Kelly—Marjorie K Campbell) L.St.G.SCal'52
☎ (203) 661-9122 . . 9 Bayberry Lane, Greenwich, CT *06831*

Campodonico MR & MRS A Anthony (Anne M Wyler) . . . . | ☎ (415) 456-7205
JUNIORS MISS Laura M . . . . | 255 Poplar Dv,
JUNIORS MR Corey A . . . . | Kentfield, CA *94904*

Campodonico MR A Hampton—Sar. . . . . | ☎ (702) 266-4135
MISS Elena—at ☎ (408) 554-1599 | PO Box 1180,
3778 Flora Vista Av, Santa Clara, CA *95051* . . . | Gardnerville, NV *89410*

Campodonico MR & MRS John R (Joan M Johnson) Minn'66.Pcu.Sar . . .of
☎ (415) 921-2219 . . 2780 Vallejo St, San Francisco, CA *94123*
☎ (916) 525-1236 . . 4000 W Lake Blvd, Tahoe Pines, CA *96141*

Canavan MRS James McG (Minerva C Nichols) . . . | ☎ (314) 961-2287
MISS Minerva C—at 3508 Kirkwood Place, | 344 Bristol Rd,
Boulder, CO *80304* . . . . | St Louis, MO *63119*

Canby MR & MRS Peter G (Anne E Putnam) Rdc'73.Bgt.H.Swth'72
☎ (914) 234-6487 . . PO Box 189, Bedford, NY *10506*

Canda MISS Catherine B—Dh.
☎ (212) RE4-7769 . . 71 E 77 St, New York, NY *10021-1834*

Candler MR Peter F B—Wms'49
☎ (941) 922-6430 . . 6947 Antigua Place, Sarasota, FL *34231-8125*

Caner MR & MRS George C JR (Judith A Brentlinger) Sth'51.Ec.Cy.H.'46 . . . . | ☎ (617) 734-2536
MR Daniel F—P'86—at ☎ (510) 524-9193 | 355 Hammond St,
880 Regal Rd, Berkeley, CA *94708* . . . . | Chestnut Hill, MA *02167*

Caner DR & MRS John E Z (Phoebe Barnes) H'52 . . | ☎ (206) EA5-2603
MISS Phoebe—Cr'80—at 5225—12 St NE, | 520—36 Av E,
Seattle, WA *98105* . . . . | Seattle, WA *98112*
MISS Harriet Z—WmSth'77.PugetS'81—at
1711 E Republican St, Seattle, WA *98112* . . . . .
MR John E Z JR—H'80—at U of Cal Business Los Angeles . . . .

Canfield MRS Befani (Gabriella Befani) Nu'72 . . . . | ☎ (212) 533-1511
MR Temple Emmet—Colg'91— | 129 W 22 St,
☎ (212) 777-0453 . . . . | New York, NY
MR Lewis Cass—Wes'91 . . . . | *10011*

Canfield MR & MRS Franklin O (Hope Brown) Bcs.C.So.Cly.H'32.Cl'36 . . of
☎ (212) 755-3890 . . 14 Sutton Place S, New York, NY *10022*
☎ (516) 283-4431 . . PO Box 1225, Southampton, NY *11969*

Cann MR & MRS William F JR (Bohling—Susan C Clark) Mo'68.Purd'68.Wash'75 . . . . | ☎ (314) 994-9408
MISS Kelly W—W&M'92 . . . . | 18 Warson Terr, St Louis, MO *63124*

Cannaday MR Richard L
☎ (212) 289-4299 . . 1158 Fifth Av, New York, NY *10029*
Cannaday MRS Royall G (Ramelle B Smith) . . . . Died Aug 9'96
Cannell MR & MRS J Carlo (Jennifer T Bradley)
Tufts'87.Sfy.Unn.Pn.P'85.Ox'88
☎ (415) 221-0496 . . 46 Kittredge Terr, San Francisco, CA *94118*
Cannell MR & MRS James C (Joanella R Gibbons) Bvl.
3 Water St, Box 53, Mattapoisett, MA *02739*
Cannell MR & MRS Michael T (Elisabeth W Hartman)
P'85.H'90.Rc.P'82.Cl'86
☎ (212) 799-4854 . . 101 W 81 St, New York, NY *10024*
Cannell MR & MRS Peter B (Ann Van A Eberstadt) BMr'49.Pr.Cly.P.'49
☎ (516) 759-7770 . . Peacock Point, 16 Pomeroy Lane, Locust Valley,
NY *11560*
Cannell MR & MRS Peter F (Amanda J Henderson) Bow'77.Bow'76
☎ (301) 229-8658 . . 5901 Cranston Rd, Bethesda, MD *20816*
Cannell MR & MRS William B (Alexandria M Hughes) Ny.
☎ (207) 236-4592 . . Outer Bayview, Camden, ME *04843*
Cannon MR & MRS Alexander P (Kathleen A Bishop)
Ws'47.Mds.Plg.Snc.Cw.Coa.Ht.Dll . . .of
☎ (561) 231-2474 . . 1255 Winding Road Circle E, Apt 604,
Vero Beach, FL *32963*
☎ (516) 324-2710 . . 29 The Mews, PO Box 415, East Hampton,
NY *11937*
Cannon MR Beekman C—C.Y.'34 . . of
☎ (203) 777-0193 . . 178 Bishop St, New Haven, CT *06511*
☎ (607) 264-8171 . . ''Londonderry Farm'' Cherry Valley, NY *13320*

Cannon MR & MRS Henry B JR (Kathleen D	916 Dayton Dv,
Johnsen) Mich'65.Y'60	Scottsboro, AL
MR Henry B 4th	*35768*
JUNIORS MR John A	

Cannon MRS Henry Brevoort (Anne D Sibley)
☎ (607) 264-8063 . . ''Glensfoot'' Box 484, Cherry Valley, NY *13320*
Cannon MR & MRS Howard W (Dorothy Pace) Ariz'37 . . of
☎ (703) 448-0655 . . 1213 Encore of McLean, 1808 Old Meadow Rd,
McLean, VA *22102*
☎ (702) 458-6226 . . 3079 Monte Rosa Av, Las Vegas, NV *89120*

Cannon MR & MRS J Dormer (Grauer—Jane E	of ☎ (246)432-1635
Egeressy) Unn.Cvc.Y'44.Va'48	''Jotari''
MISS Amanda J Grauer—Box 36, Verbank,	Sandy Lane Estates,
NY *12585*	St James, Barbados
	☎ (860) 435-2629
	''The Farmhouse''
	266 Farnham Rd,
	Lakeville, CT *06039*

Cannon MR & MRS Maurice L (Nancy L Bayard) MooreArt'71.Wil.P'71
☎ (302) 656-9464 . . 1105 N du Pont Rd, Westover Hills, Wilmington,
DE *19807*

Cantey MR & MRS Samuel Benton 4th (Sara J	☎ (817) 735-8772
Lunsford) W&L'64	4024 Shadow Dv,
MISS Samantha J	Ft Worth, TX *76116*
JUNIORS MR Samuel B 5th	

Cantini MRS B Barton (Brooks Barton) . . . . name changed to Barton
Cantlay MR & MRS D Davison (Patricia J King) Briar'77.HampSydney'79
Lawrenceville School, PO Box 6008, Lawrenceville, NJ *08648*

Cantlin MR & MRS Richard A (Maureen Laflin)	☎ (503) 228-0481
Ws'68.Ws'71.Geo'68	2675 SW Grenwolde
MR Alan R—at Princeton	Place, Portland, OR
JUNIORS MISS Elizabeth L	*97201*

Canton MR & MRS Anthony M (Candace K Thorne) .	☎ (214) 404-0082
MR A Boughton—at ☎ (202) 237-5644	6706 Northcreek
4139 Harrison St NW, Washington, DC *20015* .	Place, Dallas, TX
	75240

Canty MR & MRS Richard J (Hope B Woodhouse) Geo'78.H.Bost'69
☎ (212) 838-3316 . . 136 E 64 St, New York, NY *10021*

Capen MR & MRS Marshall D (Mary M McGrail) . . .	☎ (508) 587-9475
MR Christopher E	969 Court St,
	Brockton, MA
	02402

Capers MR & MRS Rushton T (Christine S Shumate) Me.So'67
☎ (610) 793-2315 . . 1004 General Stevens Dv, West Chester, PA *19382*
Caperton MR & MRS Charles Barrington (Wolfe—English—
Alice M Cattell) Md'27.GaTech'25
☎ (714) 650-8653 . . 1221 West Coast H'way, Apt 207, Newport Beach,
CA *92663* . . MR absent
Caplow MISS Dorothy D (Theodore) . . . . Married at Seattle, WA
Munro MR Edwin (Winthrop) . . . . Jun 20'96
Caplow MR Theodore JR (Theodore) . . . . Married at Lenox, MA
van Kipnis MISS Pascale (Gregory) . . . . Aug 4'96

Capomazza di Campolattaro MR & MRS Carlo	☎ (504) 861-8337
(Rosemonde Kuntz) Ncd.MontSwitz'64	1614 State St,
MR Carlo E—Pep'94	New Orleans, LA
MR Stefano D R	*70118*

Cappel MR & MRS Charles Ward (Patricia Aileen	300 Santa Rosa
Pauley) NotreD'66	Lane, Santa Barbara,
JUNIORS MR Carter P	CA *93108*

Caracciolo di Forino CT François & CTSS (Shirley	☎ (011-39-75)
Howell) SL'53.Rome'49	8947483
MR Riccardo—Mid'89	''Monte Calvo''
	Quadro, Todi,
	Perugia, Italy

Carchidi MR & MRS (DR) Bruce G (Victoria S E Kirkland)
Pa'80.Pa'84.Pa'87.Pa'77
''Possom Hollow'' 20 Anderson St, Palmerston North, New Zealand

Carden MRS Constance P (Adams—Constance P	☎ (212) 860-2459
Carden) Rdc'66.C.	115 E 90 St,
MISS Elizabeth C Adams	New York, NY
	10128

Carden DR G Alexander—Y'62.Cl'72
see Dilatory Domiciles
Carden MRS George A (Constance S Sullivan) . . . . Died at
New York, NY May 23'96
Carden DR George A . . . . Died at
New York, NY Aug 10'96
Carden MR William V
☎ (212) 864-6492 . . 175 W 93 St, New York, NY *10025*
Cardew MRS J Ziegler (Jessica M Ziegler) . . . . . name changed to Ziegler
Cardew MR Piers A—Camb'78.H.'84
☎ (212) 721-3864 . . 30 W 70 St, New York, NY *10023*

Cardon MR & MRS Patrick D (Carol B Moon) Sth'68.Nu'77.Woos'69.Nu'76 . . . . ☎ (011-33-54) 32-58-98
MISS Stéphanie A . . . . "Chantelune"
JUNIORS MISS Alexandra M . . . . 30 rue Marcel
JUNIORS MISS Caroline C . . . . Thénot, 41400 Pontlevoy, France

Carega MR & MRS Paolo F (Patricia Ladd) Sl.H'67 . ☎ (305) 661-5681
MISS Francesca—at Georgetown . . . . 225 Vistalmar St,
MISS Alessia—at Georgetown . . . . Coral Gables, FL
JUNIORS MR Marco 33143

Carell MR & MRS Walter S JR (Alexandra R Davis) Penn'61.Mich'62 . . . . ☎ (908) 647-5499
"1731 House"
MISS Caroline F—Wit'89—at ☎ (908) 598-0199 47 Old Mill Rd,
61 DeForest Av, Summit, NJ 07901 . . . . Millington, NJ
MR Walter S 3d 07946

Carew MR G Stephen—Cysl.Va'39 . . . . ☎ (561) 969-6655
MR G Stephen JR . . . . 7130 Clarke Rd,
MR Timothy L—Cysl.NCar'69 . . . . West Palm Beach,
MR Lawrence R . . . . FL 33406

Carew MRS J Stewart (Marian G Thompson) . . . . . . ☎ (813) 584-0363
MR Gordon S . . . . 316 Ponce de Leon Blvd, Belleair, FL 34616

Carey MR & MRS Christopher W (Lucinda H Gray) Conn'79.Pa'79
☎ (203) 966-6453 . . 330 White Oak Shade Rd, New Canaan, CT 06840

Carey MRS Churchill G (Juliet G McAdams) V'39.Mv.
☎ (410) 828-1363 . . 510 Brightwood Club Dv, Lutherville, MD 21093

Carey MR & MRS Francis J (Emily N Large) of ☎ (215)646-4050
Rc.Ri.Sa.Fst.Sg.Myf.Pa'45.Pa'49 . . . . 485 Lewis Lane,
MISS Emily N—Conn'80.Myf.— Ambler, PA 19002
☎ (215) 646-6395 . . . . ☎ (212) 492-1101 50 Rockefeller Plaza, New York, NY 10020

Carey MR & MRS Francis J III (Gretchen R Frank) Skd'70.Stan'76.Ste.Sg.Pa'73
☎ (215) 643-4664 . . "Dawesfield" 525 Lewis Lane, Ambler, PA 19002

Carey MRS G Cheston JR (Le Boutillier—Carroll—Clelia Delafield) Bnd'51.Elk.Cda.
☎ (410) 435-1445 . . 5710 Stony Run Dv, Baltimore, MD 21210

Carey MR & MRS George G 4th (Anna K Steck) Cin'75.Cw.Pn.P'55 . . . . ☎ (513) 474-3292
4150 Mt Carmel Rd,
MISS Eugenia M . . . . Cincinnati, OH
MR Frederick R 45244

Carey MR & MRS George G 5th (H Hampton R Daniel) Va'85.Cl'95.W&L'82
☎ (203) 932-0366 . . 21 Sanfordtown Rd, Redding, CT 06896

Carey MR & MRS H Augustus (Jennifer R Dodge) S'Hmptn'81.Ox'82.Fst.Sg.Myf.Aht'79.Ox'84
☎ (215) 321-4542 . . 1470 Greenmeadows Rd, Yardley, PA 19067

Carey MRS James (Laura J Hanson) Mv.Cly.Ncd.Ht. ☎ (201) 325-3640
REV CANON Benedict H Hanson—Rv.Cc.Ht. Llewellyn Park,
Cw.JHop'36 . . . . West Orange, NJ 07052

Carey MRS James (Coonley—Livingston—Deborah P Locke) . . . . ☎ (919) 493-9255
2701 Pickett Rd,
MISS Carol L Coonley—at 5703 Three Oaks Apt 2028, Durham,
Dv, Raleigh, NC 27612 . . . . NC 27705-5610

Carey MR James Bayard . . of
☎ (505) 983-6524 . . 3233 El Trebol Court, Santa Fe, NM 87505
☎ (310) 471-0255 . . Bel Air House, Bel Air, CA 90024
☎ (518) 797-3390 . . "The Thwait" Pond Hill Rd, Rensselaerville, NY 12147

Carey MR & MRS W Ward JR (Heidi S Kirkland) Bnd'86.Mds.Cly.Cl'88
☎ (415) 752-4545 . . 530 Tenth Av, San Francisco, CA 94118

Carey MR William Polk—B.Rc.Plg.Ste.Myf.P'52.Pa'53 . . of
☎ (212) 371-2738 . . 525 Park Av, New York, NY 10021
☎ (518) 797-3600 . . "Fullerlea" Rensselaerville, NY 12147

Carhart MR Amory S—Nf.Bcs.
☎ (516) 283-2784 . . "Beau Tems" PO Box 5020, 616 Ox Pasture Rd, Southampton, NY 11969

Carhart MR & MRS Amory S JR (Karen S Ekberg) Stph'76.Colg'73
☎ (011-41-1) 201-41-91 . . Richard Wagner Strasse 30, CH 8002 Zürich, Switzerland

Carhart MR & MRS Thomas (Edith B Moore) 1158 Fifth Av, New York, NY 10029

Carhart MISS Wendy H—Bcs.
☎ (212) 472-2873 . . 137 E 66 St, New York, NY 10021

Carhartt MR & MRS Michael S (Brooke Byrd Phillips) Chap'79.CalPoly'77
☎ (805) 688-0685 . . "Rancho Santa Ynez" 1691 Alamo Pintado Rd, Solvang, CA 93463

Carleton MRS Bukk G (M Elizabeth Tucker) Rdc'33.Ncd.Hn.
☎ (203) 966-4480 . . 61 Parade Hill Lane, New Canaan, CT 06840

Carleton MR Bukk G 3d—Rcp.Me.Hb.H'61.Stan'64 ☎ (802) 649-1463
Beaver Meadow Rd,
MISS Samantha L—at ☎ (617) 267-5666 Norwich, VT 05055
427 Marlborough St, Boston, MA 02115 . . . . . .
MISS Heather T—at U of Mont . . . .

Carleton MR Peter F . . . . Died at Seattle, WA Jan 13'96

Carleton MRS Peter F (Catherine M Stinson) Ws'59
☎ (603) 563-8396 . . "Road's End" PO Box 146, Dublin, NH 03444

Carleton MISS Sara B (late Peter F) . . . . . . Married at Charlottesville, VA
McGhee MR Craig T (Donald) . . . . Aug 31'96

Carlisle MRS Edith H (Edith M Hall) Ne.
☎ (516) 549-8562 . . 9 Anthony Court, Huntington, NY 11743

Carlisle MR F Lewis—An.Ne.Rv.Yn.Va'64
☎ (410) 819-8130 . . 213 S Harrison St, Easton, MD 21601

Carlisle MR & MRS Henry C (Olga Andreyev) C.Stan'50
☎ (415) 776-4128 . . 1100 Union St, San Francisco, CA 94109

Carlisle MR & MRS Miles (Margo Duer Black) ☎ (202) 965-5324
Cvc.Mt.Nyc.Stan'54.Pa'57 . . . . 3221 Garfield St
MR Tristram C . . . . NW, Washington, DC 20008

Carlson MR & MRS David G (Margaret S L Deering) Denis'85.Gv.Tr.Dth'84.Dth'89
☎ (617) 237-1636 . . 9 Earle Rd, Wellesley, MA 02181

Carlson MR & MRS Richard W (Hunt—Patricia C Swanson) Mt.Plg. . . . . | of ☎ (703)734-7718 "Tulip Hill"
MR Buckley S P—at 420 Burges Dv, Nashville, TN *37209* . . . . | 7718 Georgetown Pike, McLean, VA *22102*
☎ (410) 643-0041 "Swan Haven" 111 Carlson Lane, Kent Island, MD *21666*

Carlson MR & MRS Robert F (Badger—Elizabeth B Borden) H'75.Cal'83.Cal'88.Cal'43.H'48
☎ (805) 569-0443 . . 502 Plaza Rubio, Santa Barbara, CA *93103*

Carlson MR & MRS Tucker S McN (Susan T Andrews) StLaw'91.Ty'91
☎ (703) 329-6420 . . 6042 Edgewood Terr, Alexandria, VA *22307*

Carlton MRS Winslow (Margaret M Gillies) C.Csn.Hn.H. . . . . | ☎ (508) 548-0625 80 Church St, Woods Hole, MA *02543*
MISS Ann W—Sth'62—at 304 W 88 St, New York, NY *10024* . . . . |

Carlton-Foss MR & MRS John A (Rhona N Carlton) Cl'73.H'77.Mit'67.Mit'69.H'73.Sayb'81
☎ (617) 899-8313 . . 338 Conant Rd, Weston, MA *02193*

Carmack MRS Coleman (Woolworth—Carmack—E Ann Coleman)
see Dilatory Domiciles

Carmalt MR & MRS Samuel W (Lindy S Richards) Tulsa'80.Hb.Yn.Y'66 . . . . | ☎ (011-41-22) 758-1031 1 Chemin du Jura, 1292 Chambésy, Switzerland
MISS Jean M—at Vassar . . . . |

Carmalt MR & MRS Woolsey (Sarah L Robbins) Cos.Sl.Y'37
☎ (202) 337-1773 . . 2475 Virginia Av NW, Apt 630, Washington, DC *20037*

Carman MISS Deborah D
☎ (908) 832-5846 . . RR 5, Box 2, 6 Farmersville Rd, Califon, NJ *07830*

Carmany MR & MRS George W 3d (Judith J Lawrence) V'66.Rc.Ny.Sm.Chi.Aht'62 . . . . | of ☎ (617)720-2824 4 Lime St, Boston, MA *02108-1103*
MISS Elizabeth M J—at Brown . . . . |
MR G William W . . . . | ☎ (516) 653-6802 12 Shinnecock Rd, Box 1371, Quogue, NY *11959*

Carmichael MISS Caroline Grace (g—J Donald Carmichael) . . . . Born at Poway, CA Oct 27'94

Carmichael MR & MRS Charles E (Sarah D Wakefield) Ga'46.ChArt'47
☎ (601) 366-7494 . . 4730 Old Canton Rd, Jackson, MS *39211*

Carmichael MR & MRS Donald S (Mary G Dickinson) Ri.Cv.Bf.Hn.H'35.Mich'42
☎ (603) 795-4009 . . Hardscrabble Rd, Lyme, NH *03768*

Carmichael MISS Elizabeth Ashley (g—J Donald Carmichael) . . . Born at Pleasanton, CA Aug 14'94

Carmichael MR & MRS Frederick H (Marjorie Shelburne) Purd'45.Van'42 . . of
☎ (561) 622-8639 . . Lost Tree Village, Church Lane, North Palm Beach, FL *33408*
☎ (704) 274-0787 . . 1617 Hendersonville Rd, Asheville, NC *28803*

Carmichael MR & MRS Hubert McR (Charlotte S Loftis) Rich'34.Mlsps'36
☎ (601) 981-4740 . . 4217 Oakridge Dv, Jackson, MS *39216*

Carmichael DR & MRS J Donald (Mary Alice Beatty) HowC'60.Cy.Myf.Cda.Dar.Ala'54.JHop'58 . . of
☎ (205) 879-7849 . . 2857 Canterbury Rd, Birmingham, AL *35223*
☎ (334) 346-2252 . . "Dellmont" County Rd 7, Forest Home, AL *36030*
☎ (205) 245-7859 . . "Carmichael Place" 4310 E Mill Rd, Goodwater, AL *35072*
"Loch Haven" County Rd 7, Forest Home, AL *36030*

Carmichael MASTER James Faulkner Crenshaw (g—J Donald Carmichael) .
Born at Birmingham, AL Aug 11'95

Carmichael MRS Jere M (Emma P Crowell)
☎ (508) 693-1674 . . East Chop, PO Box 1007, Oak Bluffs, MA *02557*

Carmody MR & MRS Christopher G (Carol A Lovell) Denis'77.Y'84.Geo'61 . . . . | 11 Blueberry Lane, Lincoln, MA *01773*
MR Christopher B . . . . |
JUNIORS MISS Meagan L . . . . |
JUNIORS MR Francis W . . . . |

Carnahan MR & MRS David H JR (Boyer—Gay M Hedlund) Cly.Pa'62 . . . . | ☎ (212) 734-2173 40 E 66 St, New York, NY *10021*
MISS G Alexandra Boyer—Denis'93 . . . . . . |
MR F Alger Boyer JR—Cal'92 . . . . |

Carnahan MR & MRS George (Alison T Bruère) Csn.H'37 . . . . | ☎ (617) 491-4452 9 Wyman Rd, Cambridge, MA *02138*
MISSES Lucinda M & Jane B—at 201 E 66 St, New York, NY *10021* . . . . |

Carne MRS Rew P (Rew Price) Swb'59.Wa. . . . . . . | ☎ (619) 259-9220 803 Cofair Court, Solana Beach, CA *92075*
MISS Elinor P—Whitt'85 . . . . |

Carnett MR & MRS J Berton 3d (Margaret A Coleman) Rose'62 . . . . | ☎ (610) 964-1827 14 Radnor Way, Radnor, PA *19087*
MISS Alicia S . . . . |
MR John B 4th . . . . |

Carney MR & MRS James H 2d (Laurie W Gordon) Rol'66.Rcn.Ct.Sb.Fic.Au.Rol'65.Wes'75 . . . . . . | ☎ (617) 326-9886 31 Chestnut St, Dedham, MA *02026*
MISS Winston H . . . . |

Carney MRS Robert B JR (Natalie Sutherland)
☎ (703) 684-9146 . . 2631 S Ives St, Arlington, VA *22202*

Carney MR & MRS William J (Kyle Adams) Cho.On.Sr.Cnt.Fy.P'41
☎ (847) 234-3877 . . 1230 N Western Av, Apt 306-7, Lake Forest, IL *60045*

Caroe MISS Catherine Stewart (Timothy R) . . . . Born at
New Milford, CT Apr 13'96

Caroe MR Michael R—Ox'46 . . . . | ☎ (860) 868-7788 18 Parsonage Lane, Washington, CT *06793-0087*
MISS Shelley H . . . . |

Caroe MR & MRS Timothy R (M Katherine Schrader) EmbRid'81
☎ (203) 263-2997 . . PO Box 623, 47 Judson Av, Woodbury, CT *06798-0623*

Caron MRS D Welwood (Diana N Welwood)
☎ (561) 225-2720 . . 524 NE Plantation Rd, Apt 4504, Stuart, FL *34996*

Caron MR & MRS Peter E (Ragna Mellander) H'45. . | ☎ (208) 622-7234 PO Box 2134, Ketchum, ID *83340*
JUNIORS MR Robert M . . . . |
JUNIORS MR James E . . . . |

Carothers DR & MRS Charles O (Stern—Lucille Klau) CtCol'45.Cw.Wms'44.H'46 . . of
☎ (513) 821-8488 . . 2727 Walsh Place, Cincinnati, OH *45208*
☎ (305) 367-3041 . . Ocean Reef Club, 12 Bay Ridge Rd, Key Largo, FL *33037*

Carothers MR & MRS Neil 3d (Herrick—Katryna R Brett) Mt.Cvc.Sl.Pn.P'41.Ox'50 . . . .
MR Neil 4th . . . .
MR Andre S . . . .
   MR Jason N R Herrick—at Balliol Coll Oxford
   MR Adam G F Herrick—at W Va Weslyan . .
   JUNIORS MR Timothy B G Herrick—at Denison
☎ (202) 965-1318 1318—28 St NW, Washington, DC *20007-3121*

Carpender MISS Catharine C
☎ (910) 763-1659 . . 1519 Princess St, Wilmington, NC *28401*

Carpenter MRS Allen (Gott—Patricia Allen)
☎ (203) 655-7182 . . 7 Concord Lane, Darien, CT *06820*

Carpenter MRS Anne R (L Anne Rafferty) Wheat'57
☎ (908) 747-9177 . . 25 Doughty Lane, Fair Haven, NJ *07704*

Carpenter MR & MRS Arthur G (Alexandra K Wettlaufer) P'82.P'83
☎ (512) 323-6695 . . 4111 Av C, Austin, TX *78751*

Carpenter MISS Carol A—Gchr'61
☎ (414) 352-9526 . . 656 Evergreen Court, Milwaukee, WI *53217*

Carpenter MRS Carol V V (Carol Van Vlissingen) Ws'49 . . . .
MISS Frances B—Br'84.Sth'90—at Yale . . . .
☎ (203) 221-7047 120 Kettle Creek Rd, Weston, CT *06883-2223*

Carpenter DR & MRS Charles C J JR (Sally R Fisher) P'52.JHop'56
☎ (401) 245-1904 . . 12 Half Mile Rd, Barrington, RI *02806*

Carpenter MR & MRS Clarkson 3d (Mary T Holmes) Wash'80.Lind'82.Cy.Cw.StL'70.Wash'72
☎ (314) 361-3545 . . 4646 Pershing Place, St Louis, MO *63108*

Carpenter REV David G—P'91
☎ (805) 379-1837 . . 895 St Charles Dv, Apt 1, Thousand Oaks, CA *91360*

Carpenter MISS Dorothy M . . of
☎ (212) 475-5358 . . 36 Gramercy Park E, New York, NY *10003*
☎ (314) 725-5358 . . 515 Westgate Av, St Louis, MO *63130*

Carpenter MR & MRS Dorr B (Elizabeth G Strachan) StLaw'51 . . . .
MISS Diana B . . . .
MR Strachan D . . . .
MR T Ethan . . . .
☎ (804) 985-6188 "Hilldale" Rte 1, Box 137C, Stanardsville, VA *22973*

Carpenter MR & MRS Edmund N 2d (Gates—Frances C B Morgan) Rcn.Wil.BtP.Fic.Fiy.P'43. H'48 . . . .
MISS E Lea . . . .
   MISS Ashley du Pont Gates . . . .
of ☎ (302)654-7558 600 Center Mill Rd, Wilmington, DE *19807*
☎ (561) 655-6149 748 Island Dv, Palm Beach, FL *33480*

Carpenter MR & MRS Edward N (Van Rensselaer—Margaret A Owen) V'56.Cly.Y'42
☎ (516) 239-1421 . . 275 Barrett Rd, Lawrence, NY *11559*

Carpenter MRS Edward R (Patricia M Edwards) Ws'54.Swth'60 . . . .
MISS Jennipher S—at 486—36 St, Apt 4, Oakland, CA *94609* . . . .
☎ (310) 221-0322 South Pointe 110, 2235 W 25 St, San Pedro, CA *90732*

Carpenter MRS Francis F (Ellsworth—McClelland—Bickel—Dorothea F Wirth) ⚓ . . of
☎ (412) 963-9740 . . 5 Salem Circle, Pittsburgh, PA *15238*
☎ (561) 687-3237 . . 23 Waltham Av, West Palm Beach, FL *33417*

Carpenter MR & MRS Francis N (Prindle—Barbara Hayward) Va'34 . . . .
MISS B Hilary—LakeF'89 . . . .
☎ (561) 272-1398 333 Palm Trail, Delray Beach, FL *33483*

Carpenter MR & MRS Frank H (Margaret R Steck) Sth'60.H'61.P'58.Stan'62 . . . .
MISS Elizabeth R—P'90—at Case Western Reserve . . . .
MR Frank H JR—Wms'92—at U of Colo Boulder
☎ (216) 321-4053 2307 N St James P'kway, Cleveland Heights, OH *44106*

Carpenter MISS Frederica L
☎ (508) 627-9232 . . "Garden House" 8 High St, PO Box 1213, Edgartown, MA *02539*

Carpenter MRS Henry G (Hedwig T Haiges) . . . . . .
MR Henry G JR—Rich'92 . . . .
☎ (610) LA5-9817 429 Hollybush Rd, Rosemont, PA *19010*

Carpenter REV DR & MRS James A (Mary L Dunbar) V'51.G.Duke'51
☎ (706) 736-9169 . . 2529 Tupelo Dv, Augusta, GA *30909-3787*

Carpenter MR & MRS John S JR (Emilie D Wierman) Au.Ncd.
☎ (609) 935-4537 . . 550 Kings H'way, Salem, NJ *08079*

Carpenter DR & MRS John T (McKenna—Calleran—Joan M Gorman) End'60.Me.M.Sa.Pa'48. Pa'52 . . . .
   MR John J McKenna III—Col'90—at
☎ (215) 844-4073 . . 5500 Wissahickon Av, Apt 809, Philadelphia, PA *19144* . . . .
   MR Trevor C McKenna—WVa'93—at
☎ (610) 486-0965 . . 1470 Fairview Rd, Coatesville, PA *19380* . . . .
   MR Todd A McKenna—WVa'93—at
☎ (610) 857-0405 . . Unionville, PA *19375* . .
☎ (610) 896-9290 18 Haverford Station Rd, Haverford, PA *19041*

Carpenter MISS Margaret M (Fantaci—Margaret M Carpenter) . . . . Married at Lawrence, NY
Jones MR Jeffrey R (Ralph) . . . . Mch 16'96

Carpenter MR & MRS Mark D (Amy C Edmondson) H'81.Duke'82
☎ (505) 466-4162 . . 85 Apache Ridge Rd, Santa Fe, NM *87505-8919*

Carpenter MR & MRS Peter R (Janet R Buck) Penn'62.ArizSt'93.Sar.Penn'62
☎ (602) 860-9370 . . 13076 N 101 St, Scottsdale, AZ *85260*

Carpenter MR & MRS Robert H (Vest—Janice L Ogden) Stan'52 . . . .
   MR Michael E Vest . . . .
☎ (213) 936-6740 164 S Las Palmas Av, Los Angeles, CA *90004*

Carpenter MISS Sophie E C
☎ (314) 725-6173 . . 215 N Central Av, St Louis, MO *63105*

Carpi MR Colin C JR—Cr'84
☎ (610) MO4-0779 . . 221 Ardleigh Rd, Penn Valley, Narberth, PA *19072*

Carr MR Alvan S—Ey.Bab'64 . . . . | ☎ (617) 631-2854
MR Alvan S JR . . . . | 63 Bubier Rd,
MR Matthew P . . . . | Marblehead, MA
MR William N. . . . . | *01945*
Carr MISS Carolyn K—Louvre'68.Mo'70.Mo'71.CentMoSt'88
  ☎ (314) 994-0456 . . 93 Pebblebrook Lane, Creve Coeur, MO *63146*
Carr MR D Phillips—Ala'61
  ☎ (334) 265-7945 . . 2041 Hazel Hedge Lane, Montgomery, AL *36106*
Carr MR Dayton T—Ny.Ri.Srb.Br'63.H'65 ⚓
  ☎ (212) 935-0806 . . 424 E 52 St, New York, NY *10022*
Carr MISS Ellen K—Hlns'86.Ct.Cvc . . .of
  ☎ (540) 882-3840 . . Glenn Owen Farm, Rte 1, Box 679, Waterford,
VA *20197*
  ☎ (202) 338-6602 . . PO Box 3773, Washington, DC *20007*
Carr MR F William—B.Ng.So.BtP.Evg.Pa'35 . . . . . | ☎ (561) 881-8662
MISS Frances R—at Manor Downs, TX . . . . | 254 Plantation Rd,
MR F William JR—at Austin, TX . . . . | Palm Beach, FL
                      | *33480*
Carr MR & MRS John F JR (Sheelagh G T Stevens) | ☎ (414) 377-6872
NotreD'62 . . . . | N57 W 6470 Center
MISSES Mary M & C Mercy—at 222—3 St SE, | St, Cedarburg, WI
Apt 3, Washington, DC *20003* . . . . | *53012*
MISS Kathleen A . . . . |
Carr MR John F 3d (John F JR) . . . . Married at Milwaukee, WI
  Wilbourne MISS Amy E (Preston) . . . . Aug 17'96
Carr MR John N—WakeF'88.SantaC'92 . . see MRS J Y Stick
Carr MR & MRS Keith Armistead (Kathleen A Walsh)
Ct.Cvc.Mt.W&L'63.Md'65 . . of
  ☎ (301) 654-8006 . . 3702 Curtis Court, Chevy Chase, MD *20815*
  ''Nancy's Fancey'' Cumberland Island, GA *31558*
Carr MISS Margaret T—L&C'93.Ct . . .of
  ☎ (404) 367-9871 . . 1 Biscayne Dv NW, Apt 712, Atlanta, GA *30309*
  ☎ (508) 432-0077 . . 54 Harbor Rd, Harwich Port, MA *02646*
Carr MR Michael—Brist'87 . . see G L Smith
Carr MR Richard F JR—Md'82 . . see MRS J Y Stick
Carr MR & MRS Richard R (Elise N Wallace) | ☎ (610) 896-7206
GeoW'66.Me.Cry.Ac.Ncd. . . . . | 1125 Rose Glen Rd,
MR Edward W . . . . | Gladwyne, PA
MR Ian N . . . . | *19035*
MR Richard R JR—at Hobart . . . . |
Carr MRS Robert Adams (Margaret M Wiley) SL'32.Cyc.Cnt.Cas.Fy.Ncd.
  ☎ (312) 787-2899 . . 1440 N Lake Shore Dv, Apt 35M, Chicago,
IL *60610*
Carr MRS Robert F (Margaret E Rich)
  ☎ (561) 231-1035 . . 251 Island Creek Dv, John's Island, Vero Beach,
FL *32963-3304*
Carr MR & MRS Robert F III (Whitney—Barbara | ☎ (847) 234-1152
Thiele) Denis'64.Rc.On.Sr.Bab'62 . . . . | 549 King Muir Dv,
MISS Mary D—at 30 E Elm St, Chicago, IL | Lake Forest, IL
60611 . . . . | *60045*
MR Robert F IV . . . . |
Carr MRS Robert N (Harriet K Simonds) Kt.
  ☎ (216) 729-0559 . . 12989 W Chester Trail, Chesterland, OH *44026*

Carr MR & MRS Sabin W JR (Deborah D Maserang) | ☎ (214) 691-8716
Mo'70.SanJ'67 . . . . | 3523 Rosedale Av,
MISS Cynthia—at 59 W 8 St, Apt 3A, New York, | Dallas, TX *75205*
NY *10011* . . . . |
MISS Laura E . . . . |
JUNIORS MISS Serena N . . . . |
Carr MR & MRS Samuel B (Rosamond Whitney) | ☎ (617) 333-0539
Cc.Cw.H'44 . . . . | 676 Brush Hill Rd,
MISS Christina—MtH'74—at St Louis, MO . . . . | Milton, MA *02186*
MISS Deborah—H'87 . . . . |
MR Henry W—NH'80 . . . . |
Carr MISS Sarah C (William Plack JR) . . . . Married at Dallas, TX
  Roberts MR Thomas H 3d (Thomas H JR) . . . . Jun 14'96
Carr MR & MRS Stephen H (Virginia W McMillan) | ☎ (847) 491-1362
Cwr'62.Cwr'66.Nw'76.Cin'65.Cwr'67.Cwr'70 . | 2704 Harrison St,
JUNIORS MISS Rosamond E . . . . | Evanston, IL *60201*
JUNIORS MISS Louisa R . . . . |
Carr MRS Susanne Earls (Susanne Earls) Ncd.
  ☎ (212) 772-7292 . . 223 E 66 St, New York, NY *10021*
Carr MR Thomas W—Cyc.Cw.LakeF'64
  6171 Sheridan Rd, Apt 2606, Chicago, IL *60660*
Carr MR & MRS Walter S (Mary F Baine) Gchr'69.Cw.Pa'67.Ch'70
  ☎ (773) 528-5454 . . 507 W Briar Place, Chicago, IL *60657*
Carr MRS William D (Margaret A Tackett)
  Westminster-Canterbury, 250 Pantops Mountain Rd, Charlottesville,
VA *22901*
Carr MR & MRS William Plack JR (Lyde H Wall) Tex'62.Nyc.
  ☎ (214) 528-1569 . . 3832 Turtle Creek Dv, Dallas, TX *75219*
Carr MR & MRS Wilson Murray JR (Catherine Stoneham) Va'32
  ☎ (814) 237-3472 . . 500 E Marylyn Av, Apt B17, State College,
PA *16801-6269*
Carrère MR & MRS Frederic (Leslie R Dingle) Cr'77
  ☎ (607) 272-4675 . . 1067 Taughannock Blvd, Ithaca, NY *14850*
Carrick MRS Alan W (Elizabeth M Bates) BMr'36.Lm.Ncd.
  ☎ (609) 426-6047 . . Meadow Lakes 7-01L, Hightstown, NJ *08520-3336*
Carrier MR & MRS Russell N JR (Joy L Slater)
  ☎ (610) 383-7587 . . ''Fat Chance Farm'' Unionville, PA *19375*
Carrillo de Albornoz MR & MRS René (Patton—Evelyn E Denison)
Pn.P'31 . . of
  ☎ (609) 924-0040 . . 35 Olden Lane, Princeton, NJ *08540*
  ☎ (802) 362-1583 . . PO Box 933, Manchester Village, VT *05254*
Carrington MR & MRS E Claiborne (Alice K | ☎ (210) 826-5200
Clement) Tex'77.A.Tex'69 . . . . | 101 Claiborne Way,
MISS Alisa A . . . . | San Antonio, TX
MR Claiborne A . . . . | *78209*
Carrington COL & MRS George W (Mann—Else L Jorgensen)
USMC.SCal'46.Y'42.AmU'63.Ox'73 . . of
  ☎ (310) 859-0721 . . 9560 Hidden Valley Rd, Beverly Hills, CA *90210*
  ☎ (508) 748-0696 . . 11 Rose Cottage Lane, Marion, MA *02738*
Carroll MR & MRS Barry J (Barbara A Pehrson) | ☎ (847) 234-1627
ColC'65.On.BtP.Mt.Cho.Cw.Wa.Hb. | ''Wyldwoode''
Shimer'66.H'69.Shimer'95 ⚓ | 55 Mayflower Rd,
MISS Deirdre H . . . . | Lake Forest, IL
MISS Colleen P—at Boston Coll . . . . | *60045*
MR Sean P . . . . |
JUNIORS MISS Oona K—at Phillips Andover . . . . |

Carroll MR Brewster B—NCarSt'81
☎ (212) 721-8151 . . 201 W 70 St, Apt 20H, New York, NY *10023*

Carroll MR & MRS Charles 3d (Anne B Johnson) | ☎ (410) 821-1717
JHop'79.Elk.Mv.P'54 . . . . | 7804 Ruxwood Rd,
MR George D—WashColl'89 . . . . | Baltimore, MD
| *21204*

Carroll DR & MRS Charles 4th (Geraldine B | ☎ (847) 501-2814
Thomas) JHop'80.Elk.Wms'76.Md'82 . . . . | 1046 Vine St,
JUNIORS MISS Constance B . . . . | Winnetka, IL *60093*

Carroll MR Christopher A—Emory'92
☎ (615) 320-0110 . . 710 Fatherland St, Nashville, TN *37206*

Carroll MR & MRS H Taylor (Charlotte R Casler) . . . | PO Box 1508,
MR Taylor B . . . . | Cashiers, NC *28717*
MR Brooks A . . . . |

Carroll MR & MRS J B Randol JR (E Anne Lampman) Gchr'61.P'57
☎ (610) 430-6855 . . 1022 Dogwood Lane, West Chester, PA *19382*

Carroll MR & MRS J Otis (Ruth E Ogden) Y'49 . . . . | ☎ (203) 966-5346
MR J Otis JR—Dth'90 . . . . | 113 Logan Rd,
MR Ogden—Leh'93 . . . . | New Canaan, CT
| *06840*

Carroll MRS James A JR (Cordelia E B | ☎ (441) 236-4630
MacPherson) Sth'50.Rby.Cyb.Chi. . . . . | "Hestia"
MISS Elizabeth H—Vt'85—at ☎ (970) 482-4437 | 7 Bellevue Dv,
510 E Mulberry St, Ft Collins, CO *80524* . . . . . | Paget PG 06,
| Bermuda

Carroll MR & MRS James B M (Stewart—Damon—Anne Louise H Baker)
Ncd.Yn.Y'50
☎ (904) 285-3725 . . 318 Ponte Vedra Blvd, Ponte Vedra Beach,
FL *32082*

Carroll MR James R T H—Denis'84.SFr'95 . . see MRS F T H Manning

Carroll MR & MRS John L (Cornelia A Thomas) | ☎ (212) 988-9367
BMr'58.Rc.K.H'49 . . . . | 215 E 72 St,
MISS Genevieve A . . . . | New York, NY
MR John L JR . . . . | *10021*
MR Thomas T . . . . |

Carroll MR & MRS Lee Wingate (Madeline St George)
Upsala'49.Mit'22.Nu'63 . . of
☎ (561) 736-9986 . . 10671 Quail Covey Rd, Boynton Beach, FL *33436*
☎ (201) 543-9132 . . 21 Wexford Dv, Mendham, NJ *07945*

Carroll MR & MRS Lucius W 2d (Cullet—Lucie L | ☎ (615) 297-7907
Miller) NCar'71.Van'63 ⚓ . . . . | "Sugartree"
JUNIORS MISS Catherine B . . . . | 139 Prospect Hill,
| Nashville, TN *37205*

Carroll MR Philip—K.H'46
Doughoregan Manor, 3500 Manor Lane, Ellicott City, MD *21042*

Carroll MRS Ralph C (Vetterlein—Edith McWilliams) Yn.
☎ (610) 645-8653 . . Waverly Heights B039, 1400 Waverly Rd,
Gladwyne, PA *19035*

Carroll MR & MRS Robert B (R Lindsay Green) Rich'81.Denis'79
☎ (410) 823-0189 . . 123 Brandon Rd, Baltimore, MD *21212*

Carroll DR & MRS Robert E (Clay—Jane C Chace) Sth'53.Cly.Y'38 . . of
☎ (212) 879-9625 . . 131 E 69 St, New York, NY *10021*
☎ (508) 771-1354 . . Great Island, Box 516, West Yarmouth, MA *02673*

Carroll MISS Sarah A—HWSth'93
☎ (615) 292-7178 . . PO Box 50765, Nashville, TN *37205*

Carruthers MRS Barbara A (Barbara A Anderson) Carr'78
☎ (614) 431-0755 . . 119 W Riverglen Dv, Worthington, OH *43085*

Carruthers MR & MRS John D (Letah H Hickman) Smu'82.LakeF'78
☎ (314) 997-2239 . . 923 N Lay Rd, St Louis, MO *63124*

Carruthers MR & MRS Ralph R (Donna J Young) Miami'56
☎ (513) 863-3138 . . 601 Glenway Dv, Hamilton, OH *45013*

Carruthers MISS Sara Procter—Miami'84
☎ (513) 863-6291 . . 601 Glenway Dv, Hamilton, OH *45013*

Carruthers MR & MRS Thomas H 4th (Patricia M Dennis) Cin'50 ⚓
☎ (513) 771-6090 . . 400 Oak Rd, Glendale, OH *45246*

Carruthers MR Thomas H 5th—Carr'77
☎ (614) 228-8821 . . 385 Jackson St, Columbus, OH *43206*

Carse MR & MRS Donald R JR (Wickes—Barbara | of ☎ (011-44-181)
Bain Schwab) Unn.Ac.Dar.Cda.Pn.Cl'67.Cl'69 . | 673-2032
JUNIORS MISS Alexandra R—at Benenden . . . . . . | 70 Endlessham Rd,
MR Nicholas du P Wickes . . . . | London SW12 8JL,
| England
| ☎ (802) 867-4174
| PO Box 573, Dorset,
| VT *05251*

Carse MRS Isabelle W (Isabelle D Wedemeyer) GeoW'65.H.'75.Dyc.
☎ (212) 245-2094 . . 415 W 55 St, New York, NY *10019*

Carson MR Chris
☎ (210) 226-1246 . . 1408 Wiltshire Av, San Antonio, TX *78209*

Carson MISS Georgia Chapin—Sth'81.Cly.
☎ (212) 362-0239 . . 250 W 85 St, Apt 12G, New York, NY *10024*

Carson MR James G—Ken'74.Ch'75.Ill'84
☎ (847) 491-1743 . . 1408 Elmwood Av, Apt 1N, Evanston, IL *60201*

Carson MR & MRS James Tyson (Forbes—Patricia A S Noble)
Ph.Rv.Ac.Pa'50
☎ (610) 356-0260 . . "Tyca Farm" Gradyville Rd, Box 274,
Newtown Square, PA *19073*

Carson MR & MRS Joseph (Hornor—Marian Sadtler)
☎ (215) WA5-1110 . . 706 S Washington Square, Philadelphia,
PA *19106*

Carson MISS Katherine S (Robert R JR) . . . . Married at Newport, RI
Miller MR Gerald C (Arnold) . . . . May 10'96

Carson MRS Ralph Moore (Naugle—Cécile Bellé) Evg.Csn.
☎ (561) 842-4761 . . 240 Mockingbird Trail, Palm Beach, FL *33480*

Carson MR Robert James JR (Elizabeth L Brown) Ncd.
☎ (804) 979-3266 . . 2600 Barracks Rd, Apt 323, Charlottesville,
VA *22901-2100*

Carson MR & MRS Robert R JR (K Serena Evans) | ☎ (201) 568-1722
Ham'66 . . . . | 46 Hillside Av,
MR Robert R 3d—Ham'91 . . . . | Englewood, NJ
MR Peter R . . . . | *07631*

Carson MR & MRS Rory McL (Nancy Riley) | ☎ (610) 388-1826
Wheat'68.GeoW'72 . . . . | 600 Willow Glen
MISS Alison S—at Johns Hopkins . . . . | Rd, Kennett Square,
MISS Margaret McL—at Colgate . . . . | PA *19348-2119*
MISS Lindsay R . . . . |

Carson MR & MRS William C (Georgia A Sims) V'52.P'50.Stan'56
☎ (505) 982-9147 . . 978 Indian Ridge Rd, Santa Fe, NM *87501*

Carstensen MR & MRS Hans L JR (Toland—Jane B Van Pelt)
Ph.Gm.Rb.Yh.Ac.H'38
☎ (610) 649-1504 . . 334 Aubrey Rd, Wynnewood, PA *19096*

Carstensen MR & MRS Hans L 3d (Mary W Starr) ☎ (206) 236-2133
Stan'72.Stan'70.Stan'74 . . . . 5320 W Mercer
MISS Elizabeth N . . . . Way, Mercer Island,
JUNIORS MR Edward S . . . . WA *98040*

Carter MR Adam Augustine—Rr.Mt.Geo'87.Geo'91
☎ (202) 265-8722 . . 2015 Q St NW, Washington, DC *20009-1009*

Carter MISS Alantha C (David L) . . . . Married at Hopewell, NJ
Mehltretter MR Peter G . . . . Jly 2'95

Carter MISS Amy (Jimmy) . . . . Married at Plains, GA
Wentzel MR James (Jim) . . . . Sep 1'96

Carter MISS Amy L (Clulow—Amy L Carter) Wheat'80
☎ (203) 846-0882 . . 134½ Main St, Norwalk, CT *06851*

Carter MR & MRS Burnham JR (Sue H McLeod) Pg.Pn.P'44
☎ (617) 329-0856 . . 43 School St, Dedham, MA *02026*

Carter MR & MRS C Carroll JR (F P Lia Alesci) Nu'85.Geo'83
☎ (212) 772-2318 . . 85 East End Av, New York, NY *10028*

Carter MR & MRS Charles Carroll (Rosemary C Casey)
Rose'56.Rr.Km.Mt.Cvc.NotreD'49.AmU'59
☎ (202) 686-0999 . . 5016 Lowell St NW, Washington, DC *20016*

Carter MR & MRS Charles H 3d (Robinson—Elizabeth L Lindhardt) Va'33
☎ (407) 644-3242 . . 403 N Interlachen Av, Winter Park,
FL *32789-3202*

Carter MRS Christopher S (Helen T Deuell) Br'54 . | Cloud Nine,
MR David S—Loy'85—at 132 E 19 St, | 6075 Pelican Bay
New York, NY *10003* . . . . | Blvd, Naples, FL
| *34108*

Carter MISS Cintra E . . see MRS J T Sundlun

Carter MR & MRS David G (Louise Belknap) BMr'49.Gr.Cly.P'45.H'49
☎ (203) 787-4343 . . 100 Edgehill Rd, New Haven, CT *06511*

Carter MR & MRS David L (Hope C Hemphill) Sth'50.P'49
☎ (609) 466-0302 . . 32 Stony Brook Rd, Hopewell, NJ *08525*

Carter MR & MRS David R (Pauline de Leusse) | of ☎ (011-33-1)
H'50.H'52 | 45-04-17-56
MISS Sylvia—at ☎ (011-33-3) 44-53-54-48 | 6 av Raphaël,
5 rue des Veterans, 60300 Senlis, France . . . . . . | 75016 Paris, France
| ☎ (011-33-3)
| 44-53-17-47
| 24 Place Gérard de
| Nerval, 60300
| Senlis, France

Carter MRS Diana D (Diana J Duff) . . . . | ☎ (415) 388-1476
MR Christopher D—LoyMmt'93—at | 1027 Erica Rd,
☎ (310) 574-3089 . . 8161 Manitoba Av, Apt 10, | Mill Valley, CA
Playa Del Rey, CA *90293* . . . . | *94941*

Carter MRS Donaldson (Holden—Virginia Donaldson) Dar.
☎ (512) 451-3202 . . 4100 Jackson Av, Apt 221, Austin, TX *78731*

Carter REV & MRS E Lawrence (Murray—Katrina B Ely) ImmacH'80
☎ (818) 355-3889 . . 535 W Highland Av, Sierra Madre, CA *91024*

Carter MR Edward G L
☎ (415) 441-7825 . . 1210 Lombard St, San Francisco, CA *94109*

Carter MRS Edward P (Margaret S Leonard) . . . . Died at
San Francisco, CA Aug 4'96

Carter MR Edward W . . . . Died at
Los Angeles, CA Apr 25'96

Carter MRS Edward W (Caldwell—Hannah H Locke) Bur.Tcy . . .of
☎ (213) 879-6000 . . 626 Siena Way, Los Angeles, CA *90077*
☎ (415) 347-1000 . . 1721 Manor Dv, Hillsborough, CA *94010*

Carter MR & MRS Francis M (Susan J Bower) | ☎ (703) 370-2871
RMWmn'59.Okla'63.Mt.Cw.Geo'55 . . . . | 3618 Trinity Dv,
MR Francis M JR—Marq'91—at | Alexandria, VA
☎ (414) 481-3867 . . 3234A S Pine Av, | *22304*
Milwaukee, WI *53207* . . . . |

Carter MR & MRS Frederic D JR (Susan B Morris) | ☎ (914) 677-5901
Bgt.Y'45w.H'49 . . . . | N Tower Hill Rd,
MISS Alice S—at Stamford, CT *06905* . . . . | PO Box 1410,
| Millbrook, NY
| *12545*

Carter MRS Georgina Woolworth (Niman—Georgina B Woolworth)
☎ (707) 935-7758 . . 111 Anthony Court, Sonoma, CA *95476*

Carter MRS H Adams (Ann H Brooks)
☎ (617) 698-9074 . . 361 Centre St, Milton, MA *02186*

Carter MRS H LeRoy JR (Alice B Tunstall)
☎ (410) 377-5272 . . 6111 Bellinham Court, Apt 1221, Baltimore,
MD *21210*

Carter DR & MRS Hill (Devereux Stokely) | ☎ (804) 537-5743
Cvc.Rv.Cc.Sl.Ncd.Va'26 . . . . | South Wales Farm,
MISS M Devereux—at 6865 Melrose Dv, McLean, | Box 102, Ashland,
VA *22101*. . . . . | VA *23005*

Carter MRS Hodding (Betty Werlein) Ncmb'31
123 E Oakridge Park, Metairie, LA *70005-4018*

Carter MR & MRS Hugh D (Marie J Dempsey) Sth'76.Va'74 . . of
☎ (804) 288-7709 . . 6102 St Andrews Lane, Richmond, VA *23226*
☎ (418) 665-4613 . . "Ciel sur Mer" Murray Bay, La Malbaie,
Quebec G5A 1S5, Canada

Carter MR & MRS J Newman (McMeekin—Charlie | ☎ (703) 356-8108
L Townes) Gchr'47.MdArt'63.Gi.Cvc.Mv. | 909 Turkey Run Rd,
Geo'52 ⚓ . . . . | McLean, VA *22101*
MR Braxton P—FtLew'88 . . . . |

Carter MR & MRS Jimmy (Rosalynn Smith)
Plains, GA *31780*

Carter MRS John B (Hope Elliot) . . . . | ☎ (203) 966-5816
MISSES Hope E & Helen E . . . . | 492 Mariomi Rd,
MISSES Ann E & Katherine E . . . . | New Canaan, CT
MISS Elizabeth E . . . . | *06840*
MSRS Charles E, Henry & George E . . . . |

Carter MR & MRS John B JR (Bayless—Elizabeth L Langston)
Tex'50.B.Tex'46
5422 John Dreaper Dv, Houston, TX *77056*

Carter MRS Lawson A (Tompkins—Louise G White) Dar.
☎ (860) 435-2616 . . 54 Main St, PO Box 423, Salisbury, CT *06068*

Carter MRS Levis (Earnshaw—Nolte—Jane Levis Carter) W.
☎ (610) 558-1725 . . White Horse Village A221, 535 Gradyville Rd,
Newtown Square, PA *19073*

Carter MR & MRS Lewis A JR (Gilman—Beverly A | ☎ (617) 259-0917
Sechler) PhilaArt'71.D.Pa'63 . . . . | 212 Old County Rd,
MISS Eliza E—CtCol'94—at ☎ (212) 245-0901 | Lincoln, MA *01773*
62 W 62 St, New York, NY *10023* . . . . |
MISS Amanda H . . . . |
JUNIORS MR Matthew E Gilman . . . . |

Carter MR & MRS M Hill (Judy E Temple) Millers'85.GeoW'91.Cvc.Md'86
☎ (301) 593-1938 . . 10111 Portland Rd, Silver Spring, MD *20901*

Carter MRS Mai Garesché (Geffinger—Mai G Pitts) ☎ (813) 789-9118
RMWmn'62.Dar.Cda. | PO Box 588,
MISS Caroline N G . . . . | Crystal Beach, FL
MR L H Sullivan . . . . | *34681*

Carter MISS Mary M (Francis M) . . . . Married at Sea Girt, NJ
LaMountain MR Joseph S JR (Joseph S) . . . . Oct 14'95

Carter MR & MRS Michael C (Lillian H Russell) ☎ (603) 827-3437
Ncd.Wms'50 . . . . | ''Brookhill''
MR James O—Pa'87—at ☎ (011-39-6) 589-6887 | 9 Brown Rd,
via Lucciano Manaraio Scala A, Int 6, 0153 | Marlborough, NH
Rome, Italy. . . . . | *03455-4209*

Carter MR Michael R E . . see MRS J T Sundlun

Carter MR Nicholas S F (D M June Allan) ☎ (617) 698-5307
B'gton'59.Wms'60 . . . . | 115 Randolph Av,
MISS Elizabeth S—York'93—at 246 Montrose | Milton, MA *02187*
Av, Toronto, Ontario M6G 3G7, Canada . . . . . . |

Carter MISS Nina Casey (C Carroll JR) . . . . Born at
New York, NY Sep 5'94

Carter MR & MRS Peyton F 2d (Elizabeth A Scott) ☎ (860) 572-2911
Unn.Va'50 . . . . | Bishop's Cove,
MR Peyton F 3d—NEng'94—at Boston, MA . . . | 10 Kensington
| Court, Mystic, CT
| *06335*

Carter MRS Raymond H (Harwood—Nancy W Snow) Cyb.Pn.
☎ (207) 236-4280 . . 19 Calderwood Lane, Rockport, ME *04856*

Carter MR & MRS Richard J (Jane C Douglass) . . . . ☎ (508) 563-5383
MISS Susan J—H'90 . . . . | 25 Glen Av,
| PO Box 22,
| North Falmouth,
| MA *02556*

Carter MR & MRS Robert L JR (Karen M Kouvel)
MtStMary'87.Mt.MtStMary'87.CathU'90
☎ (703) 356-2093 . . 1358 Macbeth St, McLean, VA *22102*

Carter MR & MRS Robert L JR (Joan M Laughlin) ☎ (703) 356-6724
Mt.Cvc.Geo'53.Miami'61 . . . . | 6151 Kellogg Dv,
MISS Mary Ella—Ty'88.Geo'93—at | McLean, VA *22101*
☎ (202) 333-4795 . . 4884 MacArthur Blvd NW,
Washington, DC *20007* . . . . |
MISS Mercedes—MtStMary'91 . . . . |
MISS Kathryn M—MtStMary'93.Tenn'96 . . . . . . |
MISS Anna Carroll—MtStMary'93.VaTech'96 . . |
MISS Deborah T—MtStMary'95—at |
☎ (703) 525-4688 . . 906 N Garfield St,
Arlington, VA *22201* . . . . |
MISS Elizabeth Lee—at Mt St Mary's . . . . |
MR John Laughlin—VaTech'89.CathU'92—at |
☎ (202) 686-6870 . . 5510 Sherrier Place NW,
Washington, DC *20016* . . . . |

Carter MRS Rudulph Ellis (Reed—Mead—Mary M McLain)
Ph.Sa.Srb.Nrr.Cly.Cc.
☎ (212) 472-0414 . . 30 E 65 St, New York, NY *10021*

Carter MR Samuel C (Charles Carroll) . . . . . . Married at Washington, DC
Stamos MISS Suzanne K (James T) . . . . Dec 9'95

Carter MR & MRS Samuel C (Suzanne K Stamos)
Conn'90.Hart'93.Cc.StJColl'88.Ox'92.CathU'96
☎ (202) 237-8030 . . 4530 Connecticut Av NW, Apt 400, Washington,
DC *20008*

Carter MR & MRS Shane P (Courtney A Llewellyn)
☎ (207) 288-8203 . . 7 Shannon Way, Bar Harbor, ME *04609*

Carter MR Stephen W—Qns'85
☎ (718) 728-1435 . . 21-22 Ditmars Blvd, Astoria, NY *11105*

Carter MR & MRS Thomas L JR (Eugenia F Graves) Tex'73
3614 Piping Rock Lane, Houston, TX *77027*

Carter Trimble (Runnells—Winifred Trimble) BMr'54
☎ (713) 626-9444 . . 3435 Westheimer Rd, Apt 1414, Houston,
TX *77027*

Carter MISS Virginia B
☎ (520) 296-3832 . . 7101 E Sabino Vista Circle, Tucson, AZ *85715*

Carter MR & MRS Warwick M SR (Louise M Cahill) of ☎ (202)966-8867
Cvc.Mt.BtP.San.Cw.Cc.Sl.Pa'49 . . . . | 4810 Glenbrook Rd
MISS Lee C—Denis'89.Ch'93.Cda.—at | NW, Washington,
☎ (301) 652-6894 . . 6752 Kenwood Forest Lane, | DC *20016*
Chevy Chase, MD *20815* . . . . | ☎ (561) 659-8351
MR Prescott C—Denis'88—at | Dorset House,
☎ (718) 625-3692 . . 7—1 Place, Brooklyn, NY | 190 Bradley Place,
11231 . . . . | Palm Beach, FL
| *33480*

Carter MR Warwick M JR (Warwick M SR) . . Married at Washington, DC
Stillman MISS Lyle D . . . . Jun 22'96

Carter MR & MRS Warwick M JR (Lyle D Stillman)
Cr'86.Mt.Cvc.Cw.Cc.Denis'86.Cin'88.CathU'91.Geo'94
☎ (212) 753-4542 . . 136 E 55 St, Apt 3A, New York, NY *10022*

Carter MR & MRS William G (Susan T Parrish) ☎ (207) 846-6283
NH'72.Earl'69.IaState'83 . . . . | RR 2, Box 500F,
MR Henry J . . . . | Yarmouth, ME
JUNIORS MR Charles N . . . . | *04096*
JUNIORS MR Samuel M . . . . |

Carter MR & MRS William Phelps (Lloyd—M Elizabeth Wiedersheim)
Pn.Y'38
☎ (203) 966-2191 . . Woods End Rd, New Canaan, CT *06840*

Carter MR & MRS George T (Constance C Lowry) ☎ (207) 781-3813
Hav'49 . . . . | 311 Middle Rd,
MR George T 3d . . . . | Falmouth, ME
| *04105*

Cartier MR & MRS John G (Salisbury—Suzanne Jackson) Mds.Cly.P'60 . . of
☎ (212) 988-0860 . . 103 E 84 St, New York, NY *10028*
☎ (516) 324-5731 . . 105 Main St, East Hampton, NY *11937*

Carton MISS Barbara S . . see P B Hemp

Carton DR & MRS Robert W (Jean A Keating) Ih.Cnt.Fy.Ncd.P'42.Nw'45
☎ (847) 446-2347 . . 674 Hill Rd, Winnetka, IL *60093*

Carton MRS Sybil B (Sybil K K Baker) S. . . . . ☎ (516) 628-3447
MISS Alexandra Noël—at U of NH . . . . | 54 Beechwood
MISS Caroline Dana—at Widener . . . . | Court, Glen Cove,
| NY *11542*

Cartwright MR & MRS Carroll L (Dillon—Constance of ☎ (212)750-9216
A Bauerdorf) Ri.Cs.Wash'39 . . . . | 435 E 52 St,
MR Carroll L 3d—B'gton'80 . . . . | New York, NY
| *10022*
| 32 rue Mazarine,
| 75006 Paris, France

Cartwright MRS John W P (Joan Baldwin)
☎ (941) 472-0328 . . 1026 Bird Watch Way, Sanibel, FL *33957*

Cartwright MR & MRS Paul Colby (Wendy C Davis)
SoMiss'87.SoMiss'88.Dar.Hendrix'86.SoMiss'88
☎ (601) 894-1099 . . PO Box 485, Hazlehurst, MS *39083*

Carty MR & MRS Robert C JR (Christianne E Engs) Cal'79.SCal'81
☎ (310) 657-2630 . . 814 N La Cienega Blvd, Los Angeles, CA *90069*

Carty MR & MRS Winthrop P (M Lee Anderson) . . . | ☎ (202) 338-2566
MISS Elizabeth R—at ☎ (510) 524-4243 | 3900 Watson Place
625 Euclid Av, Berkeley, CA *94708* . . . . | NW, Apt 4D-A,
| Washington, DC
| *20016*

Caruso MR & MRS Jake A (Elena F Miller)
Geo'89.SantaC'92.Bur.SantaC'89.SantaC'92
☎ (415) 344-2315 . . 25 Denham Court, Hillsborough, CA *94010-6109*

Carvell MR & MRS Frank R (Ann Tracy) ColbyS'37.Cwr'36
☎ (502) 443-7455 . . 164 Kennedy Rd, Paducah, KY *42001*

Carver MRS Clifford M (Madeline M Smith) . . . . . . | ☎ (516) 676-5886
MR Douglas G . . . . | 89 Duck Pond Rd,
| Glen Cove, NY
| *11542*

Carver MR & MRS Ian B (Wendy French) StLaw'80.StLaw'80.Duke'82
☎ (617) 237-8860 . . 35 Sterling Rd, Wellesley, MA *02181*

Carver MR & MRS John A H (Cécile Parker) Bnd'46.Ne.Cw.P'43
☎ (207) 883-2379 . . ''Hubbards Rocks'' Marion Jordan Rd,
Scarborough, ME *04074*

Carver MR Peter M—P'72
Jakarta, Indonesia

Carver MR Richard M (Charlotte P Benjamin)
☎ (914) 266-5527 . . RD 1, Box 501, Malone Rd, Salt Point, NY *12578*

Carver MRS Richard P (Gordon—Mary L | ☎ (203) 869-2025
Hathaway) . . . . | ''Whitecroft''
MISS Kathryn A—P'83.Minn'86—at | 54 Old Mill Rd,
☎ (612) 825-2509 . . 3136 Irving Av S, | Greenwich, CT
Minneapolis, MN *55408* . . . . | *06831*
MR Blake H—at ☎ (312) 951-0270 |
1730 N Clark St, Apt 2112, Chicago, IL *60614* . |

Cary MISS Catherine—Cly.Chr.Ncd.Dh.Dc.StJ.
☎ (212) BU8-1951 . . 340 E 72 St, New York, NY *10021*

Cary MRS Charles (Rhoda G Coogan) Cyb.G.
☎ (561) 278-3909 . . 4475 N Ocean Blvd, Delray Beach, FL *33483*

Cary MR Guy F—K.Srb.H'46
☎ (212) 861-5314 . . 150 E 73 St, New York, NY *10021*

Cary MRS William L (Katherine L F Cooper) Cs.Fy. | ☎ (212) AT9-0175
MISS Katherine F C—Y'81.Cs.—at | 1120 Fifth Av,
☎ (212) 724-2175 . . 6 W 77 St, New York, NY | New York, NY
10024 . . . . | *10128-0144*

Case MR & MRS Colin J (Barker—Ann E Ricks) | ☎ (415) 386-4191
Ny.UWash'72 . . . . | 166 Arguello Blvd,
JUNIORS MISS Morgan A Barker . . . . | San Francisco, CA
| *94118-1405*

Case MR & MRS George S (Mary Bell De Long) | ☎ (203) 661-0028
Sth'65.Cly.Bost'65.Conn'76 . . . . | 116 Pecksland Rd,
MISS Amanda D . . . . | Greenwich, CT
MR G Sumner JR . . . . | *06831*
MR Charles De L . . . . |

Case DR Paul H—GeoW'34
☎ (602) 340-9238 . . 2201 N Central Av, Phoenix, AZ *85004*

Casey MR & MRS A Michael (Jean Kirkwood) | ☎ (415) 662-2002
Cal'66.Pcu.Cp.Tcy.Cal'64.Hast'67 . . . . | PO Box 526,
MISS Shannon B . . . . | Nicasio, CA *94946*
MISS Kimberly K . . . . |
MISS Katherine A . . . . |

Casey MR & MRS Alexander M (Harvey—Meta M Stauder) Pcu.
☎ (619) 568-0816 . . 47-483 Tangier Dv, Palm Desert, CA *92260*

Casey MR C Alexander (late Craig W) . . . . . Married at Woods Hole, MA
O'Herron MISS Sarah (Jonathan) . . . . Aug 10'96

Casey MRS Celia V (Celia Vassos)
☎ (212) 369-0293 . . 1150 Park Av, New York, NY *10128-1244*

Casey MR & MRS Coleman H (Jo Champlin) V'70.JHop'72.Aht'69.Y'73
☎ (860) 233-6675 . . 31 Woodside Circle, Hartford, CT *06105*

Casey MRS Craig W (Margaret Williams) Sth'60 . . . | ☎ (203) 661-0664
MISS Ellen W—Skd'95—at ☎ (212) 595-9329 | 39 Brookridge Dv,
11 W 89 St, Apt 4B, New York, NY *10024* . . . . | Greenwich, CT
| *06830*

Casey MRS Donna M (Donna E Miller) Stan'71 . . . | ☎ (415) 921-2119
MR Lyman Robert . . . . | 310 Walnut St,
MR Charles Ranieri . . . . | San Francisco, CA
| *94118-2015*

Casey MRS E Geyelin (Sims—Eleanor Geyelin)
☎ (860) 535-1714 . . 190 Water St, PO Box 20, Stonington, CT *06378*

Casey MR & MRS James J (Claudia Prout) | of ☎ (908)234-0531
Rc.B.Nrr.Ny.Shcc.Srb.Cly.Cl'37 . . . . | ''Dower Farm''
MISS Edith B—at ☎ (212) 874-7751 | PO Box 18,
15 W 81 St, New York, NY *10024* . . . . | 25 Highland Av,
| Peapack, NJ *07977*
| ☎ (212) 713-0925
| 17 W 54 St,
| New York, NY
| *10019*

Casey MR & MRS John L JR (Marilyn Anne Fuller) | ☎ (516) 653-5794
Cly.H.'44 . . . . | ''Inquogneeto''
MR Edward C—Duke'91—at 2015 Laguna St, | 5 Shinnecock Rd,
San Francisco, CA *94115* . . . . | PO Box 999,
| Quogue, NY
| *11959-0999*

Casey MR Lyman H—Bhm.Pcu.Bur.GoldenG'71
☎ (415) 931-1463 . . 2511 Pierce St, San Francisco, CA *94115*

Casey MR & MRS Samuel B JR (Dobbins—Helen A | ☎ (941) 566-8703
Mikkelson) Cho.Sc.Ln.Rr.Rcch.Cas.Penn'50 . . . | ''El Nido''
MISS Ann M—at ☎ (413) 664-8586 | 507 Bay Villas
71 River St, North Adams, MA *01247* . . . . | Lane, Naples, FL
MISS Margaret C—at ☎ (703) 818-0789 | *34108-2867*
14844 Maidstone Court, Centreville, VA *20120* . |

Casey DR & MRS William J 2d (Alexandra McEwen) | ☎ (707) 963-2410
Cal'75.StJ.Fr.JHop'58.JHop'62 . . . . | PO Box 224,
MISS Gillian L . . . . | St Helena, CA
MISS Brooke L . . . . | *94574*

Casey MRS William W (Helen B Mix) Cwr'26
Gateway Health Center, 3 Gateway Dv, Euclid, OH *44119*

Cash MR & MRS Harvey Berryman (Tripplehorn—Dianne E Cecil)
Smu'66.TexA&M'61.Mich'64
☎ (214) 521-4125 . . 3701 Crescent Av, Dallas, TX *75205*

Cashman MRS E Miller (Estelle Miller) V'64.D. . . . | ☎ (617) 444-6074
MISS Amanda G . . . . | 768 Chestnut St,
MISS Josephine I—at Barnard . . . . | Needham, MA
 | 02192

Cashman MR Eugene R JR—LaS'60
 ☎ (617) 235-2863 . . 19 Audubon Rd, Wellesley, MA 02181

Cashman MR & MRS W Timothy 2d (Diana C | ☎ (302) 652-4296
Plumb) Wil.Bab'57 . . . . | 1101 Nottingham
MISS Alison P . . . . | Rd, Wilmington, DE
MR John A . . . . | 19805

Casini MR & MRS Nicolò (Joan S Coburn) | ☎ (011-39-577)
H'84.Flor'88 . . . . | 309309
MISS Elisa G—at U of Florence . . . . | "I Colli"
MISS Rebecca—at LUISS Rome . . . . | Monteriggioni,
MISS Alessandra S—at U of Florence . . . . | 53035 Siena, Italy
JUNIORS MR Clemente C . . . . |

Caskey MRS John L (Clark—Reese—Miriam Ervin) BMr'52
 ☎ (011-30-1) 72-35-424 . . 43 Ypsilantou St, GR 10676 Athens, Greece

Caskin MRS Francis H (Susan McKnew) Sth'48.Cvc.
 ☎ (202) 966-4716 . . 4716—48 St NW, Washington, DC 20016

Casner MR & MRS Andrew J JR (Potter—Gaynor | ☎ (617) 899-0219
Davol) Rdc'62.H'81.H.'53.H'59 . . . . | 75 Cart Path Rd,
MR Jeffrey D Potter—Ham'89 . . . . | Weston, MA 02193
MR James M Potter—Ham'92 . . . . |

Casner MR & MRS Edward Hunter SR (Irene M Drummond) Tex'47.Tex'46
 ☎ (915) 581-8835 . . 1102 Los Jardines Circle, El Paso, TX 79912

Caspari MRS Charles E JR (S Elizabeth Wyman)
 ☎ (314) 997-6744 . . Gatesworth, 1 McKnight Place, St Louis,
MO 63124

Caspersen MR & MRS Erik M W (Anna R Coquillette)
Bnd'92.LondEc'93.BostColl'96.K.P'92.LondEc'93. H.'96
 ☎ (212) 860-6616 . . 1150 Park Av, Apt 8C, New York, NY 10128

Caspersen MR & MRS Finn M W (Barbara W | of ☎ (201)786-5068
Morris) Ws'67.Drew'90.K.Shcc.Cly.Br'63.H'66 | "Crows Nest"
MR Finn M W JR—at 93 Mt Vernon St, | PO Box 800,
Apt 2, Boston, MA 02108 . . . . | Andover, NJ 07821
MR Samuel M W—at 9 Washington Av, | ☎ (401) 322-7189
Cambridge, MA 02140 . . . . | "Ranvik"
MR Andrew W W—at Princeton . . . . | 105 Donizetti Rd,
 | Shelter Harbor,
 | Westerly, RI 02891

Cass MR & MRS Edward H (Susanne Balkwill) H'51. | ☎ (216) 921-4889
MR James P—at Boulder, CO . . . . | 21262 Byron Rd,
 | Shaker Heights, OH
 | 44122

Cassard MRS David (Olga J Hajek)
 ☎ (616) 949-4236 . . 2445 Oakwood Dv SE, East Grand Rapids,
MI 49506

Cassatt MRS Anne G (Bussey—Anne E Gaunt) Roan'65
 ☎ (207) 326-9376 . . PO Box 211, Brooksville, ME 04617

Cassatt MR Robert K—H'51
 ☎ (207) 326-8636 . . Box 234, Wharf Rd, Brooksville, ME 04617

Casscells MRS S Ward (S Oleda Dyson) Va'49.Evg . . .of
 ☎ (561) 848-9874 . . 756 N Lake Way, Palm Beach, FL 33480
Tuscawilla Ranch, Winter Springs, Casselberry, FL 32708

Casscells DR & MRS S Ward 3d (Roxanne F Bell)
Wyo'82.Cvc.Ct.Ub.Y'74.H'79
 ☎ (713) 520-6026 . . 1110 Milford St, Houston, TX 77006

Cassetti MR & MRS Robert K (Elizabeth Q Eddy) CarnM'79.CarnM'79
 ☎ (607) 936-9327 . . 142 E 3 St, Corning, NY 14830

Cassidy MR & MRS Arch W (Dolores K Barnes) Lm.Dc.Ncd.Fla'55
 ☎ (904) 384-4065 . . 3803 Bettes Circle, Jacksonville, FL 32210

Cassidy MR & MRS Robert T (Mary H Warrington) Lawr'80.JMad'74
 ☎ (513) 561-7035 . . 7350 Cayuga Dv, Cincinnati, OH 45243

Cassinerio MR Ambrogio—On.
 ☎ (847) 234-3341 . . 105 E Laurel Av, Lake Forest, IL 60045

Castellini MR & MRS Robert H (Susan S Fox) Bnd'63.Qc.Geo'63
 ☎ (513) 533-0984 . . 2180 Grandin Rd, Cincinnati, OH 45208

Castle MR Alfred L 2d—Cl'80
 ☎ (619) 945-0322 . . 206 Alta Mesa Dv, Vista, CA 92084

Castle MISS Alison—Cal'58
 ☎ (510) 845-5500 . . 2856 Webster St, Berkeley, CA 94705

Castle MRS J Manderson JR (Markle—Jean | ☎ (302) 239-6312
Schwartzenberg) Ill'32 . . . . | Cokesbury Village,
MISS Louisa J—at 1505 W 11 St, Wilmington, DE | Box 302,
19806 . . . . | 726 Loveville Rd,
MR James M 3d—at 106 Robert Lane, | Hockessin, DE
Wilmington, DE 19807 . . . . | 19707

Castle MR John W—P'55.Ch'60 . . . . | ☎ (815) 756-9239
MISS Amy W . . . . | 208 Miller Av,
MSRS John L, Harry D & David B . . . . | De Kalb, IL 60115

Castleton MRS Edward L JR (Webber—Rosalia M | ☎ (415) 775-7261
Siska) . . . . | 1921 Jackson St,
MR Edward L 3d—Ch'95.IEPParis'96 . . . . | San Francisco, CA
 | 94109

Casto MR & MRS Don Monroe 3d (Ann Harrison) | ☎ (614) 253-7600
Stan'68.Stan'71.Stan'66.Stan'69 . . . . | 10 Sessions Dv,
MISS Katherine A . . . . | Columbus, OH
 | 43209

Castroviejo MR Christopher R—Rc.Pr.H'71 . of
 ☎ (212) 734-1364 . . 157 E 82 St, New York, NY 10028
 ☎ (516) 726-6883 . . 199 Water Mill Towd Rd, Water Mill, NY 11976

Caswell MR & MRS John R (Carolyn F Bradley) H'53.Cal'54
 ☎ (617) 259-0830 . . 2 Beaver Pond Rd, Box 6098, Lincoln Center,
MA 01773

Caswell MR William W 3d—H'49
 ☎ (011-506) 289-9958 . . Mirador Pico Blanco, PO Box 900,
San Antonio de Escazu, Costa Rica

Catáo MR & MRS Alvaro L B (Tara C Mitton) Rcch.H'72
 ☎ (561) 997-0031 . . 2877 NW Banyan Blvd Circle, Boca Raton,
FL 33431

Cate MR William C . . . . | ☎ (617) 547-1425
MISS Aroline U . . . . | 17 Highland St,
MR Delavan B D . . . . | Cambridge, MA
 | 02138

Cates MRS Dudley F (Barbara O Damgard) SL'59.Bcs. .... of ☎ (212)355-2549 200 E 66 St, Apt 1101C, New York, NY *10021*
MR Dudley F JR .... ☎ (516) 287-3596 471 Hill St, Southampton, NY *11968*

Cates MR Dudley F—Pr.H.
☎ (212) 288-0823 . . 233 E 69 St, New York, NY *10021*

Cates MRS John M JR (Morales—Lopez—Nelia F Barletta) C.Mt.Plg.StJ.Snc.Yn.
☎ (242) 362-4969 . . "La Sfida" Box N7776, Lyford Cay, Nassau, Bahamas

Cates MRS Willard (Danenhower—Ethel C Mitchell) Ncd.Yn. .... ☎ (860) 434-9393 "Widsbrook"
  MR & MRS Sloan M Danenhower (Overdurff— Judith A Read) SConn'73 .... Ben Franklin Rd, PO Box 813,
  MISS Megan Overdurff—at Colby .... Old Lyme, CT *06371-0813*

Cates MR & MRS William C (de Saint-Remy—M A Guyonne de Fontaine de Logeres) K.Ch'46.Cl'48
☎ (011-33-90) 36-04-78 . . 7 Quai Paul Gontard, 84110 Vaison-la-Romaine, France

Cathcart MRS James A (Margaret S Strawn) On.Ncd.
☎ (847) 234-0453 . . 501 N Oakwood St, Apt 2C, Lake Forest, IL *60045*

Cathcart MR & MRS Silas S (Corlene A Hobbs) On.Cho.Ln.Fy.P'47 .... 1000 Walden Rd, Lake Forest, IL
  MISS Corlene A *60045*

Cather MR & MRS Edward W 2d (Grant—Indie S G Thomasson) USN'58.Va'66 .... ☎ (703) 548-1662 421 Wilkes St,
  MR Thomas A Grant 3d .... Alexandria, VA *22314*

Catherwood MRS Cummins (Ault—Littler—Dorothy Smith) Cly . . .of
☎ (954) 923-1090 . . 2131 Hollywood Blvd, Apt 507, Hollywood, FL *33020*
☎ (011-52-731) 26050 . . Netzahualcoytl 127, Cuernavaca, Morelos, Mexico

Catherwood MR & MRS Cummins JR (Susan D Williams) Stan'65.Gm.Rc.Me.Ac.Stan'65.Va'67 ... ☎ (610) 527-3455 622 Rose Lane,
  MR Morgan D—Me. .... Bryn Mawr, PA *19010*

Catledge MRS Turner (Izard—Abby Ray) Cly.
☎ (504) 522-2429 . . 2316 Prytania St, New Orleans, LA *70130*

Catlin MR & MRS Avery (Edith J Reed) Eyc.Va'47 ⚓ .... ☎ (804) 293-2905 "Thimble Farm"
  MISS Beverly L—Hlns'74—at ☎ (804) 293-9683 202 Riverside Av, Charlottesville, VA *22902* ... 2325 Owensville Rd, Charlottesville, VA *22901*

Catlin DR & MRS Brian (Rosalie Hornblower) Rdc'68.H'61 .... ☎ (203) 869-4112 85 Round Hill Rd,
  MISS Doris—at U of NH .... Greenwich, CT
  MISS Laine—at Middlebury *06831*
  JUNIORS MISS Amy ....
  JUNIORS MISS Tracy ....

Catlin DR Daniel—Cc.Y'32.H'36
☎ (203) 975-9494 . . 77—3 St, Apt J2, Stamford, CT *06905*

Catlin MR & MRS Daniel JR (Dundeen Bostwick) Ln.Yn.Y'60 .... ☎ (508) 369-0167 88 Walden St,
  MR Dan W .... Concord, MA *01742*
  MR Blake H ....
  MR Todd B ....

Catlin MRS Ephron (Priscilla Saltonstall) My.
☎ (508) 468-1647 . . 27 Boardman Lane, South Hamilton, MA *01982*

Catlin MR & MRS Loring (Susan C Johnson) Cc.H'62.H'65 .... of ☎ (561)234-8121 400 Ocean Rd, John's Island, Vero Beach, FL *32963*
  MISS Elizabeth J—H'89 .... ☎ (603) 563-8885 "Redtop" W Lake Rd, Dublin, NH *03444*

Catlin DR & MRS Randolph (Marian Woolston) K.H.Va'52 .... ☎ (508) 359-8044 314 North St,
  MISS Laura L .... Medfield, MA *02052-1204*

Catlin MR Randolph 3d (Randolph) .... Married at Camden, ME
Perry MISS Laura A (Thomas E) .... Sep 25'93

Catron MISS Barbara W . . see P B Hemp

Catterfeld MR & MRS James A (Bertrude B White) Ariz'80.MichTech'77
☎ (206) 842-8575 . . 7089 NE Bay Hill Rd, Bainbridge Island, WA *98110*

Cattier MRS Jean (Marianne P Vowels) Cin'49.Pr.Cly. .... ☎ (516) 676-0806 384 Oyster Bay Rd,
  MR Alan R .... Locust Valley, NY
  MR Henri R *11560*
  MR Jacques E ....

Cauffman MRS Cynthia I (Cynthia L Ives) WakeF'79 28 Medbury Rd, Wallingford, PA *19086*

Cauffman MR & MRS D Hughes (Heyward—Josephine M Vincent) Ph.Fw.Ac.Ncd.Pa'40
☎ (610) MU8-9073 . . 340 Harbison Rd, Wayne, PA *19087*

Cauffman MR & MRS George (Barbara A Conrad) Rose'82.Ac.Ph.Ncd.
☎ (610) 644-1213 . . 764 Conestoga Rd, Berwyn, PA *19312*

Cauffman MR & MRS George 3d (Jan G De Riemer) Syr'82.Pa'86.Laf'75.IMD'80
☎ (610) 408-9124 . . 8 Greenstone Way, Malvern, PA *19355*

Cauffman MR Philip P
☎ (610) 286-8961 . . Hidden Hollow Farm, 347 N Manor Rd, Elverson, PA *19520*

Caulfield MR & MRS Jerome J (Rosita N Murray) Dll.Geo'71 .... ☎ (203) 869-7780 35 Stanwich Rd,
  JUNIORS MR Andrew McC .... Greenwich, CT *06830-4842*

Caulk MR & MRS John R III (Elizabeth C Schneider) Temp'62.Ph.Ac.P'60.Pa'62
☎ (215) 735-2273 . . 2322 Spruce St, Philadelphia, PA *19103*

Caulkins MRS Dan Platt (Collier—Carhart—Dixie Thompson) Cly.StJ.
☎ (561) 546-8691 . . 350 S Beach Rd, Hobe Sound, FL *33455*

Cauro MR & MRS Olivier A (Lee L Estin) DU'74.Paris'76.Mit'82 . . of
☎ (011-33) 62-47-10-50 . . 76 av Jean Rieux, 31500 Toulouse, France
☎ (011-33) 53-20-78-82 . . "Terrefort" Fargues-sur-Ourbise, 47700 Casteljaloux, France

Cavaglieri MR Alberto—Rome'41
☎ (011-39-6) 855-8210 . . via Panama 52, 00198 Rome, Italy
Cavalla, David & McCutcheon, Corwen—Cal'79.Camb'82.Cl'83. Camb'78.Camb'82
☎ (011-44-1223) 565634 . . 6 Tenison Av, Cambridge CB1 2DX, England
Cavallero MR & MRS Robert C (Lenore E Seymour) Pcu.Bur.Ncd.
☎ (415) 344-0114 . . 980 Baileyana Rd, Hillsborough, CA *94010*
Cavanagh MRS Carroll (Mona A Schmid) Man'vl'38 . . . .
MR Christopher W . . . . ☎ (203) 866-7401 89 Old Saugatuck Rd, East Norwalk, CT *06855*
Cavanagh JUNIORS MR Carroll J 3d . . see G O Dove 3d
Cavanagh MISS Deirdre B—Man'vl'68.Cly.
☎ (201) 746-3311 . . 51 Beverly Rd, Upper Montclair, NJ *07043*
Cavanagh MISS Dorothy M . . see G O Dove 3d
Cavanagh MRS Edward F JR (Nancy M Miller) Srb.Cly.
☎ (401) 847-5003 . . "Inchiquin" 719 Bellevue Av, Newport, RI *02840*
Cavanagh MR & MRS Harry J (Geri L Gale) ArizSt'83
☎ (602) 948-1692 . . 7570 N Silvercrest Way, Paradise Valley, AZ *85253*
Cavanagh MR & MRS James B (Cavanagh—Santora—Davenport—Caroline Pratt) Cly.Yn.Y'42.Temp'50 . . of
☎ (561) 231-2556 . . 5554 N A1A, Apt 105, Vero Beach, FL *32963*
☎ (302) 655-6099 . . 4031 Kennett Pike, 43, Greenville, DE *19807*
Cavanagh MR Lawrence D—Y'33
☎ (203) 866-9879 . . 83 Old Saugatuck Rd, East Norwalk, CT *06855*
Cavanagh MRS Michael G (Jan Sherwood) . . . .
MR Andrew S
JUNIORS MISS Brooke G . . . .
JUNIORS MR John G . . . . ☎ (203) 222-9311 223 Weston Rd, Weston, CT *06883*
Cavanagh MR & MRS Roderick A (Carol J Andrus) Rcn.Nrr.Pr.Srb.LIU'68.LIU'70
☎ (401) 846-0746 . . 47 Oak Forest Dv, Middletown, RI *02842*
Cave MRS Edwin F (Spalding—Lincoln—Joan Tozzer) Cy.Chi.H.
☎ (617) 566-5754 . . 15 Kingsbury Rd, Chestnut Hill, MA *02167*
Cavender MR & MRS William Byrd (Betty A Menefee) Tex'52.A.Tex'52
☎ (210) 826-8707 . . 324 Paseo Encinal St, San Antonio, TX *78212*
Cawley MRS Eric H (Mary D Wigglesworth) Rdc'57.Chi.
☎ (617) 862-3558 . . 18 Belfry Terr, Lexington, MA *02173*
Cay MR & MRS John E 3d (Mary H Daniel) NCar'68
MISS Catherine P . . . .
MR John E 4th . . . .
MR Christopher W . . . . ☎ (912) 897-1225 "Camellia Cottage" Turners Rock, Rte 6, Savannah, GA *31410*
Cayzer MAJ & MRS H Stanley (de Holguin—Beatrice F Murray-Jacoby) BA.Bnd'47.BtP.Dar.Cda . . .of
☎ (561) 659-1193 . . "Southcôte" 190 S County Rd, Palm Beach, FL *33480-4250*
☎ (011-44-171) 636-4847 . . 105 Hallam St, London W1, England Cundy Street Flats, London SW1, England
Cecconi MR & MRS Giuseppe E (Erharter—Sarah J Coleman) Cly . . .of
☎ (011-44-171) 235-1590 . . 30 Eaton Mews N, London SW1X 8AS, England
☎ (408) 624-0152 . . PO Box 303, Pebble Beach, CA *93953*

Cecil MR & MRS Charles G (Hilary Halpern) Ws'65.Cl'80.Pr.Cl'78.Cl'79 . . . .
JUNIORS MISS Francesca C . . . . ☎ (212) 888-0765 525 Park Av, New York, NY *10021* . . MR absent
Cecil MR & MRS Russell C (Nancy C Ake) Y'48.C.Y'47.Y'49
☎ (914) 967-1395 . . 56 Lynden St, Rye, NY *10580*
Cecil DR & MRS (DR) Russell N A (Marion M Preston) Y'74.Y'74
☎ (518) 829-7280 . . Kayaderosseros Creek Farm, Ft Johnson, NY *12070*
Chabrier MRS Gwendolyn S (Gwendolyn Simpson) Nu'70.Nu'72.Paris'88.Ri.Pr.C . . .of
☎ (212) 879-1270 . . 47 E 67 St, New York, NY *10021* 10 rue Guenegaud, 75006 Paris, France
Chabrier MRS Jacques R (Vasquez—Marie A Smith) BMr'43.K.Ncd. . . . .
MISS Yvonne V (Sheldon—Yvonne V Chabrier) BMr'65—at ☎ (508) 462-1016 . . 17 Charter St, Newburyport, MA *01950* . . . . ☎ (860) 567-0729 11 Emerson Court, Westleigh, Litchfield, CT *06759*
Chabris MR Peter D—Cl'39
MR John P . . . . ☎ (201) 783-4488 101 Gates Av, Apt J11, Montclair, NJ *07042*
Chabris MR Peter D JR—Geo'96 . . see MRS M S Richardson
Chace MRS Arnold B (Ledyard—Evelyn Thayer)
☎ (803) 589-7111 . . "Twickenham Plantation" Yemassee, SC *29945*
Chace MISS Barbara B . . see H G Kemp JR
Chace MISS Diana Kortlyn—V'72
☎ (415) 383-3944 . . 106 Barbaree Way, Tiburon, CA *94920*
Chace MR Malcolm G JR . . . . Died at West Yarmouth, MA Aug 11'96
Chace MR & MRS Minturn de S V (Helen C Symington) Rdc'63.Ri.Nf.Ny.StJ.H'63.H'69
☎ (914) 234-3984 . . 20 Bayberry Lane, RD 2, Mt Kisco, NY *10549*
Chadbourne MR Richard M—H'39
☎ (212) TE8-7638 . . 550 Park Av, New York, NY *10021*
Chadsey MRS Murrell R (Bowden—Patrick—F Murrell Rickards) Swb'44.Cly.Ncd . . .of
☎ (757) 640-1338 . . 512 Mowbray Arch, Norfolk, VA *23507*
☎ (802) 765-4072 . . "Sweetwood" Beacon Hill, Box 260, RR 1, Strafford, VT *05072*
Chadwick MISS Constance W—MtH'52
☎ (508) 548-0496 . . 23 Millfield, Woods Hole, MA *02543*
Chadwick MISS Elizabeth A . . see W A Lashley
Chadwick MRS Rosamond A (Rosamond Adams) V'63 . . . .
MISS R Macy—Wash'94—at 1810 NW Everett St, Apt 302, Portland, OR *97209* . . . .
MR Thomas A—WorPoly'92.WorPoly'94—at 3302K Forest Edge Court, Richmond, VA *23294* ☎ (561) 234-4110 2609 Ocean Dv, Vero Beach, FL *32963*
Chadwick MRS Thomas M (Wilkinson—Hannah B Willis) Rdc'46
☎ (207) 725-5046 . . 72 Matthew Dv, Brunswick, ME *04011*
Chadwick-Collins MR & MRS Richard D (Marianne Condoleon) B.Pn.P'36.Pa'39
☎ (011-58-2) 265-7790 . . Apdo 68-316 Altamira, Carácas, Venezuela

Chaffe MR & MRS David B H 3d (Nancy R McIver) of ☎ (504)895-5157
Ncmb'55.Rv.Cw.Tul'55 . . . . 1546 Jefferson Av,
MISS Anne M . . . . New Orleans, LA
70115
☎ (601) 255-1161
"Halcyon Days"
25510 Marchetich
Lane, DeLisle,
Pass Christian, MS
39571

Chaffe MRS John C (Ann E Lukens) . . . . ☎ (610) 644-7685
MISS A Pamela . . . . 1535 Ashby Rd,
MISS Catharine L—Box 80142, San Diego, CA Paoli, PA *19301*
92138 . . . .

Chalfant MR & MRS Holland F JR (Susan O Carr) Sth'54.W'minster'47
☎ (314) 991-1265 . . 19 Ladue Manor, St Louis, MO *63124*

Chalfant MR & MRS John W (Jessie M Lilly) BowlG'37
☎ (304) 487-2144 . . 34 Quail Valley Manor, Princeton, WV *24740*

Chalker MR Dwight E—W'minster'68
☎ (808) 945-3923 . . PO Box 75196, Honolulu, HI *96836*

Chalmers MR & MRS E Laurence JR (Van De Riet—Hani Kamp)
FlaSt'59.FlaSt'63.A.P'48.P'50.P'51
208 Deer Trail Rd, Durango, CO *81301-8590*

Chamberlain MRS George N JR (Gaither—Elizabeth Hamlin) Cy.Ncd.
☎ (617) 326-1885 . . 9 Rocky Ridge, Dedham, MA *02026*

Chamberlain MRS J Maxwell (Marileeds Heard) My.
☎ (508) 927-0051 . . 950 Hale St, Beverly Farms, MA *01915*

Chamberlain MR & MRS Lemoyne R (Marcella H Maxwell) Col'50
☎ (513) 825-3087 . . 11840 Fairsprings Court, Cincinnati,
OH *45246-2101*

Chamberlain MRS Melissa H (Melissa A Hickey)
☎ (314) 727-7887 . . 710 S Hanley Rd, Apt 12B, St Louis, MO *63105*

Chamberlain MR & MRS Philip G (Elizabeth I Smit)
WmW'ds'82.W'minster'83
☎ (314) 966-3643 . . 245 Elm Av, St Louis, MO *63122*

Chamberlain MRS Thomas G (Gertrude Geoghegan) BtP.Evg . . .of
☎ (212) 734-1358 . . 870 Fifth Av, New York, NY *10021*
Everglades Club, 356 Worth Av, Palm Beach, FL *33480*

Chamberlin MR & MRS Alexander R (Mary E Stowe)
☎ (717) 384-4128 . . RR 3, Box 333, Mountain Grove, Bloomsburg,
PA *17815-9213*

Chamberlin MR & MRS Larry L (Wendy T Wardell) ☎ (941) 594-0885
NCar'65.Csh.Ck.Van'64.Cl'67 . . . . 830 Bentwood Dv,
MR Hunter H—Ham'95—at ☎ (516) 692-7371 Naples, FL *34108*
15 Woodcutters Lane, Cold Spring Harbor, NY
11724 . . . .

Chamberlin MR & MRS W Lawson (Warren—Ann Carpenter) SL'44.Y'38
☎ (717) 587-2325 . . 3 Orchard Lane, Clarks Summit, PA *18411*

Chamberlin MR & MRS W Macy (Irma Morell) Unn.San.StJ.
Hillsboro Club, Pompano Beach, FL *33062*

Chambers MR & MRS Edward B (Aimée L MacLea) L&C'80.Alleg'67
☎ (410) 523-0836 . . 1411 Bolton St, Baltimore, MD *21217*

Chambers DR & MRS Ewan B (Laurette W Debnam) Elk.JHop'39
☎ (410) 377-8698 . . 7206 Bellona Av, Baltimore, MD *21212*

Chambers MR & MRS Francis T (Roselle L Toland) Cc.P'47
☎ (011-353-94) 23290 . . Bracklagh, Newport, Co Mayo, Ireland

Chambers MR & MRS Frank G (Rosekrans—Jean ☎ (415) 456-9923
Snodgrass) Bhm.Fr.Utah'37.H'39 . . . . "Triple C Ranch"
MISS Allison . . . . San Anselmo, CA
MISS Leslie *94960*
MISS Cordelia Rosekrans . . . .

Chambers MR H Wick—Yn.Y'31 . . . . ☎ (203) 776-8747
MISS Elizabeth L—at 281 Augur St, Hamden, CT 272 Edgehill Rd,
06517 . . . . Hamden, CT
06517-4015

Chambers MR & MRS Michael T E (Margaret M ☎ (215) KI5-6063
Barclay) V'56.Gc.H'55 . . . . 2036 Waverly St,
MR Charles M B . . . . Philadelphia, PA
19146

Chambers MR & MRS Richard H (Eileen A Engett) Pcu.Ariz'29.Stan'32
☎ (520) 325-8311 . . 3204 E 3 St, Tucson, AZ *85716*

Chamness MR & MRS James T JR (Cynthia L ☎ (314) 997-7546
Powers) Cy.Nd.W&L'71 . . . . 4 Woodcliffe Rd,
MISS Helen M . . . . St Louis, MO *63124*
JUNIORS MR John P . . . .
JUNIORS MR J Hunter . . . .

Champe MRS Carlton G (Mary Folsom) Sth'31.Cs.Myf . . .of
☎ (207) 364-4300 . . Star Rte Box 75, Rumford Center, ME *04278*
☎ (212) RE7-3455 . . 444 E 86 St, New York, NY *10028*

Champlin MR & MRS Ryland L (Martha M Muckerman) MtStMary'77
☎ (302) 645-7732 . . 39 Sussex Dv, Lewes, DE *19958*

Chance MR Britton—Cry.Sa.Pa'35.Camb'43 ⚓
☎ (215) 222-1888 . . 4014 Pine St, Philadelphia, PA *19104*

Chance MR & MRS Edwin M (Janet F Wrigley) Rd.Pe.Pa'61.Lond'65 ⚓
☎ (011-44-1420) 87896 . . 3 Malthouse Cottages, Chawton, Alton,
Hampshire GU34 1SH, England . . MRS absent

Chance MR & MRS Henry M 2d (Elisabeth Reese) Rd.Pa'34
☎ (610) 388-7216 . . 30 Lonsdale Lane, Kennett Square, PA *19348*

Chance MRS Lilian S L (Lucas—Lilian C Streeter) ☎ (610) 644-4085
BMr'57.Au.Ac.Ncd. . . . . "Troutbeck Farm"
MISS Margaret M . . . . 730 Monument Rd,
MR Benjamin P . . . . Malvern, PA *19355*

Chance MRS Nancy Laird (Mooney—Nancy L Loomis)
☎ (518) 392-5641 . . PO Box 96, Austerlitz, NY *12017*

Chance MR & MRS Steven K (Colleen B Meyle) ☎ (610) 687-0776
Cry.Wes'67.Lond'68.Pa'73 . . . . 1212 Weybridge
MISS Anna Benson . . . . Lane, Radnor, PA
19087-4635

Chandlee MR Edward E JR—Me.Rv.
☎ (610) 642-1329 . . 100 Llanalew Rd, Apt 12, Haverford,
PA *19041-1564*

Chandlee MRS W Blakeley (Frances L Jopson) ☎ (610) 642-2579
Cry.Me. . . . . 366 Youngsford
MISS Ann Heath—at ☎ (407) 658-0935 Place, Gladwyne,
6633 Breezeway, Orlando, FL *32807* . . . . PA *19035*

Chandlee MR & MRS William B JR (Nancy Loomis ☎ (610) 527-1720
Bell) Me.Rb.Ssk.NH'64 . . . . 739 Woodleave Rd,
MR Michener B—Roan'91—at Barcelona, Spain Bryn Mawr, PA
19010

Chandler MR Allan E—Van'93 . . see MRS F H Chatfield

Chandler MISS Blake . . see J B Sibley

Chandler MR & MRS Bruce (MacKenzie—Jenny M Stewart) On.Y'50
☎ (847) 234-8178 . . 178 N Western Av, Lake Forest, IL *60045*

Chandler DR Charles F—Cc.Y'36.H'40 . . . .
MR Nicholas . . . .
MR & MRS Charles F JR (Nancy V Borstelmann)
Duke'73—☎ (207) 389-1565 . . . .
  | ☎ (207) 389-1567
"Ons Huis"
Box 253,
Small Point Rd,
Sebasco Estates, ME
04565

Chandler MR Charles L JR—Ph.H.'45.H'52
☎ (610) 274-8694 . . PO Box 181, Mendenhall, PA *19357*

Chandler DR & MRS (DR) Christopher L (Elisabeth M Higgins)
Camb'82.NewCas'82.W'minster'86
☎ (011-44-171) 720-0551 . . 11 Mackay Rd, London SW4, England

Chandler MR & MRS David (Katharine L Reynolds)
Bost'71 . . . .
MISS Elinor B . . . .
MR Philip R . . . .
JUNIORS MR David JR . . . .
  | ☎ (508) 365-7149
206 Chace Hill Rd,
Sterling, MA *01564*

Chandler MR & MRS Henry T (Clarissa G Haffner)
V'48.On.Glc.Fy.Cnt.Y'45w ⚓
☎ (847) 234-1747 . . 902 N Green Bay Rd, Lake Forest, IL *60045*

Chandler MISS Hilary K . . see C Adamson

Chandler MR & MRS John R (Tania Thurlow) Y'68 .
MISS Abigail B—Colby '96 . . . .
MISS Hannah R—at U of Chicago . . . .
MISS Katherine H B . . . .
  | ☎ (011-90-216)
304-1044
The Koç School,
PO Box 38, Pendik,
Istanbul 81481,
Turkey

Chandler MR & MRS Kent JR (Frances Robertson) On.Cnt.Fy.Y'42
☎ (847) CE4-3241 . . 921 E Westminster, Lake Forest, IL *60045*

Chandler MR Logan M—Pa'82.Nw'86.Pa'93 . . see C Adamson

Chandler MR & MRS Malcolm A (Claudia P Old) Btc.H'47
☎ (847) 234-1231 . . 172 W Laurel Av, Lake Forest, IL *60045*

Chandler MR & MRS Nathan (Phyllis A Russell) Yn.Y'44
☎ (207) 666-5595 . . RR 3, Box 3120, Bowdoinham, ME *04008*

Chandler MISS Nora F—V'50.Fy.
☎ (847) 234-0279 . . 180 Winthrop Lane, Lake Forest, IL *60045*

Chandler MR & MRS Peter C (S Blair Nichols) CtCol'83.Bgt.Cly.Bow'83
☎ (303) 442-0403 . . 740 S 41 St, Boulder, CO *80303*

Chandler MR & MRS Stuart B (Faith S Thomson) Hlns'85.Tr.NH'86.Bost'93
☎ (617) 267-2295 . . 14 Medfield St, Boston, MA *02215*

Chandler JUNIORS MR William K . . see D C Bermingham

Chandor MR & MRS Christopher B (E Whitney
Rorer) W&L'68.VillaN'72 . . . .
MISS Kathryn C—Swb'93 . . . .
  | ☎ (215) 598-0313
"Hickory Hill"
2895 Windy Bush
Rd, Pineville, PA
18946

Chandor MR Christopher B JR—Tul'91
☎ (215) 348-8872 . . 815 Hayfield Court, Doylestown, PA *18901*

Chandor MR & MRS Craig D (Grant—Carol S Johnson)
NCol'74.Bab'70.Bab'72
☎ (508) 785-0703 . . 23 Saddle Ridge Rd, Dover, MA *02030*

Chandor MR Harold A JR—Bg.
☎ (215) 345-4588 . . PO Box 28, Doylestown, PA *18901*

Chandor MR & MRS Jeffrey F (Mary R McDonald)
Syr'63.Shcc.Ty'64 ⚓ . . . .
MISS Heather J—at Syracuse U Grad . . . .
MR Jeffrey M—at Wooster . . . .
  | ☎ (908) 766-7372
127 Old Army Rd,
Basking Ridge, NJ
07920

Chandor MRS Keith F (Jean F Troxell)
☎ (908) 766-1668 . . 2D Claremont Court, Bernardsville, NJ *07924*

Chanler MR & MRS Bronson W (Evelyn W Rogers) K.Tvb.H'45 ⚓
☎ (914) 876-3809 . . "Orlot" 140 River Rd, Rhinebeck, NY *12572*

Chanler MRS Hubert W (Gertrude Laughlin) Cly. . .
MR Oliver H—at 5706 Bradley Blvd, Bethesda,
MD *20814* . . . .
  | "Fall Brook House"
PO Box 248,
Geneseo, NY *14454*

Chanler MR & MRS William A 3d (Rosalie G Maury)
ColbyS'73.Rcn.Lm.Ncd.Dc.Nasson'73
☎ (203) 656-0395 . . 2 Knollwood Lane, Darien, CT *06820*

Chanler MR & MRS William Astor JR (Innes G
James) Cw.Lm.Cda. . . . .
MR Bayard S—Lm. . . . .
  | ☎ (207) 236-8213
12 Penobscot Av,
Camden, ME *04843*

Chanler MRS William C (Rogers—F Randall Williams) K.Cly.
☎ (914) CE2-4368 . . Nash Rd, Goldens Bridge, NY *10526*

Channing MISS A Kathleen
☎ (860) 535-1113 . . 45 Water St, Stonington, CT *06378*

Channing MRS William E (Enid C A Mellor) B.Plg.
☎ (011-44-171) 370-7838 . . 47 Coleherne Court, The Little Boltons,
London SW5 0DN, England

Chapin MR & MRS Aldus H (Gove—Dolly Langdon)
Mt.Cvc.C.Sl.Hn.H'52
MISS Elizabeth R—Tufts'79—at
1848 Wyoming Av NW, Washington, DC *20009*
MR Aldus N—Denis'83—at ☎ (212) 362-1578
58 W 72 St, Apt 6D, New York, NY *10023* . . . .
  MR Alexander B Gove—H'87—at
3327 Clay St, San Francisco, CA *94118* . . . . .
  | of ☎ (202)337-3999
1628—29 St NW,
Washington, DC
20007
☎ (207) 883-6686
Prouts Neck,
Scarborough, ME
04074

Chapin MR Bayard S (Edward W) . . . . Married at Hillsborough, NH
Gibson MISS Lauren K (Raymond) . . . . Jun 29'96

Chapin MR & MRS Bedford (Anne L Allen) Elk.Cy.Mv.
☎ (410) 823-2102 . . 1720 Circle Rd, Ruxton, MD *21204*

Chapin MR & MRS Charles A (Helen Gillette) Sdy.Dar.Ch'34 ⚓
☎ (619) 756-1143 . . PO Box 734, Rancho Santa Fe, CA *92067-0734*

Chapin MR & MRS Charles M 3d (Jean T Marckwald)
Sth'60.Rcn.Eh.Shcc.Pn.P'58
☎ (908) 439-3445 . . "Cold Brook Farm" Box 56, Oldwick, NJ *08858*

Chapin MR & MRS Christopher K (Carroll H Thornton)
Miss'69.H'82.Mt.Cvc.Sl.Yn.Y'67.Pa'72
☎ (202) 387-7830 . . 2136 Leroy Place NW, Washington, DC *20008*

Chapin MRS Dorothy B (Chambers—Dorothy H Babcock) Au.
☎ (203) 966-9933 . . 227 South Av, New Canaan, CT *06840-5813*

Chapin MR & MRS E Dexter (Ruth K Brooks) P'43 .
MR & MRS Peter B (Mary-Ruth A Yannuzzi) . . . .
  | ☎ (410) 823-2060
1316 Berwick Rd,
Ruxton, MD *21204*

Chapin MR & MRS Edward W (Ethel D Stout)
V'56.Stc.Y'54.Va'57 . . . .
MR E Whiting JR—Stc.—at ☎ (212) 346-9818
105 Duane St, New York, NY *10007* . . . .
MR Bruce B . . . .
  | ☎ (212) 831-2313
1088 Park Av,
New York, NY
10128

Chapin MRS Henry De F (Margaret E Crowley)
ImW'52
MISS Hannah De F—KeeSt'89 . . . .
  | ☎ (617) 383-1149
76 Beach St,
Cohasset, MA *02025*

Chapin MR & MRS Melville (Elizabeth A Parker)
Err.Eyc.Cy.Un.Chi.Yn.Y'40.H'43 . . of
☎ (617) 354-7038 . . 15 Traill St, Cambridge, MA *02138*
☎ (508) 627-5901 . . "Cup House" 70 N Summer St, Edgartown, MA *02539*

Chapin MR Neil JR—Nich'49
☎ (941) 349-2299 . . 6157 Midnight Pass Rd, Sarasota, FL *34242*

Chapin MR & MRS Newton JR (Mariana Lippincott)
☎ (412) 741-5862 . . 441 Woodland Rd, Sewickley, PA *15143*

Chapin MR & MRS Richard (Maryan G Fox)
V'54.Ny.Tv.Chi.H'46 . . . .
MISS Margery R . . . .
MISS Marya M . . . .
MR Richard D . . . .
☎ (617) 864-2522
13 Kennedy Rd,
Cambridge, MA
02138

Chapin MR & MRS Robert W (Amy P Martin) H'33
☎ (610) 793-2139 . . 12 Coniston Dv, West Chester, PA *19382*

Chapin MR & MRS Schuyler G (Mortimer—Catia S Zoullas) Ws'60.C.Mto.Cly. . . . .
MISS Liza Mortimer—at ☎ (212) 446-9043
245 E 62 St, New York, NY *10021* . . . .
MR E Nicholas Mortimer—at
☎ (212) 388-7405 . . 151 First Av, Apt 49,
New York, NY *10003* . . . .
of ☎ (212)734-5553
655 Park Av,
New York, NY
10021
☎ (516) 283-0332
S Main St,
PO Box 557,
Southampton, NY
11969

Chaplin COL & MRS Duncan D III (Ann H Theopold)
USMC.Stph'49.An.Ofp.Sar.Cw.Myf.Dar.Va'51
☎ (603) 269-4371 . . RFD 2, Box 668, Wingate Rd, Center Barnstead, NH *03225*

Chaplin DR & MRS Hugh JR (Alice E Dougherty)
C.P'44.Cl'47 . . . .
MISS Monique H . . . .
MR John H . . . .
☎ (314) 721-6846
159 Linden Av,
St Louis, MO *63105*

Chaplin MISS Susan
☎ (603) 266-2010 . . PO Box 966, Concord, NH *03302*

Chapman MRS C Brewster (Luce—Botond—Patricia L L Potter)
☎ (202) 342-9272 . . 700 New Hampshire Av NW, Apt 1019, Washington, DC *20037*

Chapman MRS Daniel K (Carroll H Ferguson)
☎ (914) MO6-4911 . . "Petersville Farm" 12 Petersville Rd, Mt Kisco, NY *10549-9628*

Chapman MR E Blackwell JR . . . . Died at Villanova, PA Mch 22'96

Chapman MRS E Blackwell JR (Lynne N Wildman)
Me.Ph. . . . .
MISS Ashley L—Colg'94 . . . .
MR Mills M—at Hamilton . . . .
☎ (610) 527-8699
1324 Old Gulph Rd,
Villanova, PA
19085-1920

Chapman MR Eustace B . . . . Died at Charlottesville, VA Mch 6'96

Chapman MRS F Burnham (Eschauzier—Susannah S Osborn) My. . . . .
MISS Philippa deV Eschauzier . . . .
MISS Isabelle C Eschauzier . . . .
"Thissel House"
PO Box 157,
Prides Crossing, MA
01965

Chapman MR & MRS Gilbert W JR (Judith R Coste) SL'56.Rc.Pr.Cly.Y'56
☎ (516) 676-3128 . . 121 Factory Pond Rd, Locust Valley, NY *11560*

Chapman MR & MRS Gilbert W 3d (Emily K Bruce) Rc.Pr.OWes'83
☎ (212) 348-4684 . . 115 E 86 St, Apt 154, New York, NY *10028*

Chapman MR & MRS Henry O JR (Judith S Mann) Cr'55
☎ (540) 687-6566 . . "Rockaway" 23378 Sally Mill Rd, Middleburg, VA *20117*

Chapman MR & MRS Henry O 3d (Martha R Amburn) NCar'80.OWes'79
☎ (540) 253-7726 . . Cotland Farm, The Plains, VA *20198*

Chapman MR & MRS James A B (M Mayela Rivera) Tex'89.Laf'86
☎ (860) 674-8590 . . 102 Songbird Lane, Farmington, CT *06032-3427*

Chapman MR & MRS James P (Lillian Anne Dinning) Wesley'94
☎ (410) 836-3595 . . "October Mist" 3405 Mill Green Rd, Street, MD *21154*

Chapman MR & MRS John D 2d (Sally Putnam) Myf.Rv.Wms'56
☎ (561) 460-1595 . . 8431 Immokolee Rd, Ft Pierce, FL *34951*

Chapman MR & MRS John S (Aldys Squire) Cly.Chi.Dc.Cda.Dar.
☎ (508) 228-1295 . . 16 Cliff Rd, Nantucket, MA *02554*

Chapman MR John S—Mit'65
☎ (201) 379-2856 . . 33 Bruce Path, Short Hills, NJ *07078*

Chapman MR & MRS John S JR (Edith K Hine)
Rv.Myf. . . . .
MISS Peyton S . . . .
MISS Kathryn D . . . .
MR John S 3d . . . .
☎ (216) 243-7067
308 Oakdale Rd,
Berea, OH *44017*

Chapman DR & MRS Lewis Peyton JR (Rachel M Hamilton) Ala'65.Cda.B'hamS'64.Ala'70.Pa'73
MR Lewis P 3d . . . .
MR William H . . . .
JUNIORS MR Bain B . . . .
☎ (334) 277-3495
1726 Hillwood Dv,
Montgomery, AL
36106

Chapman MR & MRS Peter H (Diane C Clark) Rc.Ln.Pr.Sa.Cly.Ncd.Cl'77
☎ (212) 860-7880 . . 200 E 87 St, Apt 8J, New York, NY *10128*

Chapman MR & MRS Richard P JR (Cynthia S Miltimore) Ws'59.Un.Sm.Cw.H'57 . . . .
MISS Elizabeth M . . . .
MR Richard P 3d—H'89 . . . .
of ☎ (617)734-9462
107 Upland Rd,
Brookline, MA
02146
☎ (802) 649-3486
"Idle Hours"
PO Box 615,
Norwich, VT *05055*

Chapman MR & MRS Robert D (Fisher Dixon) Sa.Pa'62
☎ (610) 644-2220 . . 750 Bair Rd, Berwyn, PA *19312-1416*

Chapman MR Robert W . . see F J R Mullin JR

Chapman MISS Sarah Elizabeth (James A B) . . . . Born at Hartford, CT May 30'96

Chapman MR Scott W . . see F J R Mullin JR

Chapman MR & MRS T Taggart JR (Ann D Driver). .
MISS Baylor F . . . .
MISS Suzanne P . . . .
☎ (815) 777-0087
5495 Rte 20 W,
Galena, IL *61036*

Chapman MR & MRS Theodore A (Renate Wagner) Y'55.H'62
☎ (540) 675-3502 . . Greenfield Farm, 30 September Song Lane, Washington, VA *22747-9801*

Chapman MR William J—Dth'35
10 Overbrook Dv, St Louis, MO *63124*

Chapoton MR & MRS John Edgar (Sarah M Eastham)
Sth'62.Cvc.Sl.Ncd.Tex'58.Tex'60 . . . .
MISS Clare E . . . .
MR John Edgar JR . . . .
☎ (202) 966-1826
4910 Indian Lane
NW, Washington,
DC *20016*

Chapoton MR & MRS O Donaldson (Mary Jo Kelley)
Tex'68.Fic.Cvc.Cly.Tex'60 . . . . | ☎ (202) 338-0711
MISS Kelley W—at Wash'n & Lee . . . . | 4744 Foxhall
JUNIORS MR Hunt D. . . . . | Crescent NW,
Washington, DC
20007
Chappell MRS George S JR (Caroline B Smith) On.Cnt.Wa.Myf.Ncd.
☎ (847) 234-2365 . . 390 N Mayflower Rd, Lake Forest, IL 60045
Chappell MR & MRS Hayward H (Thomas—Olivia L | of ☎ (609)924-8354
Kloman) Cvc.P'51 . . . . | 34 Cameron Court,
MISS Hilleary T Thomas—at 15 Lenape Lane, | Princeton, NJ 08540
Skillman, NJ 08558 . . . . | ☎ (207) 372-8550
MR Stephen L Thomas JR—at 15 Lenape Lane, | ''The Barn''
Skillman, NJ 08558 . . . . | Harts Neck Rd,
Box 533,
Tenants Harbor, ME
04860
Chappell MR & MRS John Wade (Coujard de Laplanche—
Catherine A Mussat) Chr.Plg.Va'61
☎ (757) 545-6202 . . 2900 Bainbridge Blvd, Chesapeake,
VA 23324-1752
Chappell MR & MRS Richard L (Alice C Merckens) | ☎ (212) 472-8586
V'64.Cl'73.P'62.JHop'70 . . . . | 103 E 75 St,
MISS Carol L—at Amherst . . . . | New York, NY
MISS P Dreux—at Amherst . . | 10021
Chappell MRS Tobey J (Lason—Tobey J Greene) . . | ☎ (503) 231-1949
MR Brett S—at 39 Quai de Valmy, 75010 Paris, | 1605 SE 42 Av,
France . . . . | Portland, OR 97215
Chappell MR & MRS Walter F 3d (Jean Zachry) P'48
☎ (504) 865-1304 . . 7038 Prytania St, New Orleans, LA 70118-4924
Chappell MR & MRS William B JR (Percilla A Lincoln)
Un.Cly.Colby'57 . . of
☎ (212) 410-7061 . . 1088 Park Av, New York, NY 10128-1132
☎ (914) 855-3250 . . ''Wind Meadows Farm'' 37 N Quaker Hill Rd,
Pawling, NY 12564-1710
Chapple MR & MRS William D (Wendy D Wood) | ☎ (860) 455-9779
V'62.H'58.Syr'60.Stan'64 . . . . | 604 Phoenixville Rd,
MR Samuel E 2d . . . . | Chaplin, CT 06235
Charles MR Allan E—Bhm.Pcu.Stan'25
☎ (415) 885-3169 . . 850 Francisco St, San Francisco, CA 94109
Charles MISS (REV) Ann S—Sth'69
☎ (860) 243-0489 . . 2 Knollwood Rd, Bloomfield, CT 06002
Charles MR & MRS Robert H (Leiter—Marion S Oates) Sl.Y'35
☎ (202) 333-3259 . . 3259 R St NW, Washington, DC 20007-2941
Charleston MRS Ernest E (Elizabeth Forderer) Pcu.Sfg.
☎ (415) 492-2562 . . 100 Thorndale Dv, Apt 462, San Rafael, CA 94903
Charlton MR Edward J—Drex'31
☎ (609) 654-3194 . . 194 Medford Leas, Medford, NJ 08055
Charman MRS Walter M JR (Virginia McG Osborne) Kt.Uncl.
☎ (941) 964-2539 . . PO Box 565, Boca Grande, FL 33921
Charman MR & MRS William O (Patricia S Floyd) Skd'85.Y'84
☎ (011-44-171) 727-0069 . . 44 Chepstow Villas, Apt A, London
W11 2QY, England
Charpentier MR & MRS Jean C (Margaret P | ☎ (011-44-171)
Robbins) Bnd'67 . . . . | 937-6459
MISS Alix . . . . | 4 Victoria Rd,
MISS Camilla. . . . . | London W8,
England

Charrington MR & MRS Arthur M R 3d (Ardis C Borden)
FlaSt'78.Me.AmU'71
☎ (610) MI2-0417 . . 121 Cheswold Lane, Haverford, PA 19041
Charrington MR & MRS Peter R (Anna M Hulse)
Pa'69.VillaN'74.Vmi'66.VillaN'76
126 Trianon Lane, Villanova, PA 19085
Chase MR & MRS A Mabis (Mathers—Jane Van Hoven) Evg.
☎ (561) 626-1058 . . Lost Tree Village, 1042 Palm Way,
North Palm Beach, FL 33408
Chase MR Anthony C—Y'58
☎ (415) 821-0863 . . 19 Miguel St, San Francisco, CA 94131
Chase MRS Barbara S (Barbara Stone) Chi.Cyb.Ncd.
☎ (407) 647-6475 . . 106 S Interlachen Av, Apt 519, Winter Park,
FL 32789
Chase MISS Caroline P—Cly.
☎ (212) 535-0082 . . 45 East End Av, New York, NY 10028
Chase MISS Christine D . . see H C Robbins
Chase MR & MRS Edward T (Ethelyn Atha)
C.Ri.Dyc.Mds.Plg.StJ.Cly.Cs.P'41
☎ (212) 879-2229 . . 840 Park Av, New York, NY 10021
Chase MR Eric H . . see H C Robbins
Chase MR & MRS Irving H (Bailey—Rebecca C | ☎ (617) 259-8877
Bradford) Sth'49.Csn.Chi.Ncd.H.'39 . . . . | Wayside Farm,
MISS Rebecca F Bailey—at ☎ (415) 488-9230 | 80 Trapelo Rd,
Box 828, Woodacre, CA 94473 . . . . | Box 322,
Lincoln Center, MA
01773
Chase MR & MRS John H (Barbara M Philen) V'56.Sfy.Mid'56
☎ (707) 963-7407 . . 2000 Sage Canyon Rd, St Helena, CA 94574
Chase MR & MRS Martin S (McAllister—Diana Winsor)
Cal'59.Pcu.Tcy.P'57
☎ (415) 461-2618 . . 8 Upper Toyon Dv, Kentfield, CA 94904
Chase MISS Mary R—Nu'68.Nu'73 . . . . | ☎ (413) 229-8412
MR George B—at ☎ (907) 248-4962 | ''Bow Wow Farm''
7341 Clairborne Dv, Anchorage, AK 99502 . . . . | 1096 Limekiln Rd,
Great Barrington,
MA 01230
Chase MR & MRS Paul J (Doubleday—Florence F McKim)
B.Ln.Pr.Mb.Y.'39.Va'42
☎ (516) 922-9368 . . 149 Heather Lane, Mill Neck, NY 11765
Chase MRS Ryland E D (Alison A Ferrara) Cly.Ne.
☎ (212) 249-5594 . . 25 E 83 St, New York, NY 10028
Chase MRS Sally L (Daniel—Sally L Chase) Sth'60 | ☎ (202) 333-4788
MISS Nell L Daniel . . . . | 1546—34 St NW,
Washington, DC
20007
Chase MR W Rowell—Qc.Cm.H'26.H'28
☎ (513) 321-5575 . . 3424 Paxton Av, Cincinnati, OH 45208
Chatard MRS Ferdinand E (Constance B Lyon) . . . . | ☎ (410) 363-0473
MISS Katherine D B—at 402 Hess Rd, Monkton, | 12237 Garrison
MD 21111 . . . . | Forest Rd,
Owings Mills, MD
21117-1105

Chatfield MR & MRS Charles W (Post—Mary C Putnam) Newt'50.Tv.K.H'48 . . . . | of ☎ (617)484-2293 16 Hay Rd, Belmont, MA *02178*
MISS Sarah H—at 130 County St, Seekonk, MA *02771* . . . . | ☎ (207) 236-2269 Rockport, ME *04856*
MR C Hubert—at 335 Forest Av, Apt 411, Portland, ME *04101* . . . . |
   MISS Barbara St C Post—at 42 Crescent St, Cambridge, MA *02138* . . . . |
   MISS Caroline C Post—at Houston, TX . . . . . |

Chatfield MR Charlton H—Dyc.DU'69.DU'70
  ☎ (203) 661-0429 . . 12 Corrigan Lane, Greenwich, CT *06831*

Chatfield MR Christopher R—NCar'73 . . see MRS T Gardiner

Chatfield MRS Frederick H (Fisher—Chandler—M Carter MacRae) Qc. . . . . | ☎ (513) 271-0303 4305 Drake Rd, Cincinnati, OH *45243*
  MR Allan E Chandler—Van'93—at
  ☎ (212) 439-9827 . . 200 E 75 St, New York, NY *10021* . . . . |

Chatfield MR Frederick H—Qc.H'42
  ☎ (513) 561-7742 . . 8375 Camargo Club Dv, Cincinnati, OH *45243*

Chatfield MR Frederick H JR—H'70 . . see MRS T Gardiner

Chatfield MISS Helen H—Ariz'68
  ☎ (303) 758-6582 . . 4060 S Clermont St, Englewood, CO *80110*

Chatfield MRS Henry H (Margaret A Rowe) Qc.Dyc.
  4400 Willow Hills Lane, Cincinnati, OH *45243*

Chatfield MR & MRS William H (Anne B Whitney) Cin'80.NCar'69 . . of
  ☎ (513) 321-1066 . . 10 Peasenhall Lane, Cincinnati, OH *45208*
  ☎ (502) 484-5087 . . "Blue Wing Landing" Gratz, KY *40327*

Chatwin MRS C Bruce (Elizabeth Chanler) Rdc'60
  Homer End, Ipsden, Oxfordshire OX10 6QS, England

Chauncey MRS Raymond (Shedd—Eliza S Parish) Cly.Ncd.
  ☎ (516) 239-1546 . . 281 Edward Bentley Rd, Lawrence, NY *11559*

Chauncey MR & MRS Tom W 2d (Mary K LaCroix) Nw'70.ArizSt'73
  ☎ (602) 254-7457 . . 66 N Country Club Dv, Phoenix, AZ *85014*

Cheek MR & MRS James H 3d (Sigourney Woods) Man'vl'67.Duke'64.Van'67.H'68 . . . . | ☎ (615) 292-4576 4404 Honeywood Dv, Nashville, TN *37205*
MR James H 4th . . . . |
MR Daniel W . . . . |
MR Matthew H . . . . |

Cheesewright MR & MRS Robert W (Gwendolyn L Milner) Vh.Y'36
  ☎ (213) 681-7911 . . 905 Hillcrest Place, Pasadena, CA *91106*

Cheever MR & MRS David (Marian L Minot) Sm.Chi.Ncd.H'31
  ☎ (617) 329-4996 . . 10 Longwood Dv, Apt 111, Westwood, MA *02090*

Cheever DR & MRS F Sargent (Cheever—Jane Garfield) Sm.Tv.Pg.Hn.H'32 . . . . | ☎ (617) 235-0077 30 Pond Rd, Wellesley, MA *02181-5706*
MR Charles E JR—Box 544, East Sandwich, MA *02537* . . . . |

Chéhab MRS C Riker (Cornelia Riker) Stc. . . . . . | ☎ (908) 842-8066 18 Lennox Av, Rumson, NJ *07760*
MISS Randa . . . . |
MISS Carina . . . . |
MR Eric L—H'91 . . . . |

Chellas MR & MRS Brian F (Merry E Morehouse) FlaSt'62.Stan'69 . . . . | ☎ (403) 282-4923 2755 Cannon Rd NW, Calgary, Alberta T2L 1C5, Canada
MISS Anne Morehouse—at 700 Bathhurst St, Toronto, Ontario M5S 2R3, Canada . . . . |

Chellis MR Bradford A . . see MRS W G Kay JR

Chen MRS Christopher C Y (Maie-Lee Ng) Tex'46.K.Cly.Csn.
  ☎ (908) 234-1062 . . "Merry Brook Farm" PO Box 839, Far Hills, NJ *07931-0839*

Chen MR & MRS Kimball C (Grazioli-Venier—Patrizia Grill) K.Sm.Shcc.Cly.H'73.H'78 . . . . . | ☎ (212) 289-6301 1192 Park Av, Apt 8B, New York, NY *10128*
JUNIORS MISS Assia Grazioli-Venier . . . . |
JUNIORS MR Saverio E Grazioli-Venier . . . . . . |

Cheney MRS Middleton (Kleeman—Ruth Middleton) V'42 . . of
  ☎ (011-33-90) 66-13-27 . . "Le Belvédère" Impasse du Belvédère, 84210 Venasque, France
  ☎ (860) 567-5454 . . "White Oak Farm" 199 E Litchfield Rd, PO Box 1436, Litchfield, CT *06759*

Chenoweth DR & MRS Beach M JR (Barbara S Dow) Duke'42.Dar.Ala'35.JHop'39
  ☎ (205) 879-4501 . . 4156 Glenbrook Dv, Birmingham, AL *35213*

Cherbonnier MISS Adelaide
  ☎ (314) 367-1220 . . 16 Kingsbury Place, St Louis, MO *63112*

Cherbonnier REV DR & MRS Edmond La B (Phyllis White) BMr'43.StJ.H'39
  ☎ (860) 233-7460 . . 843 Prospect Av, West Hartford, CT *06105*

Cherouny MRS Arthur S (Janet R Little)
  20 Devonwood Lane, Apt 333S, Farmington, CT *06032*

Cherry MR Henry A . . see D W Barton JR

Cherry MR John M . . see D W Barton JR

Cherry MR & MRS Thomas C (Nancy L Herron) Sth'43.H'37
  ☎ (803) 681-3529 . . 99 Birdsong Way, Apt D305, Hilton Head Island, SC *29926*

Cheshire MR & MRS William P (Lucile Geoghegan) MaryW'58.Cc.NCar'58
  "Riverside" Rte 5, Box 51, Washington, NC *27889*

Chesney MRS A Hasler (Audrey Hasler)
  ☎ (561) 793-3624 . . 281 Wood Dale Dv, Wellington, West Palm Beach, FL *33414*

Chesser MR & MRS Don F (Angela T Supplee) O'66.CentMich'77
  ☎ (614) 451-8141 . . 750 Carruthers Dv, Columbus, OH *43235*

Chester MR & MRS Colby M (Jane P Robinson) Rv.Ll.Y'35
  ☎ (561) 546-6097 . . 159 Gomez Rd, Hobe Sound, FL *33455*

Chester MR & MRS Hawley T JR (Helen Cronkhite) Rcn.Pn.P'41
  ☎ (203) 869-4488 . . 450 Lake Av, Greenwich, CT *06830*

Chester MR & MRS Hawley T 3d (Langman—Penny S Warren) Pr.DU'69
  955 Buckhorn Dv E, Dunwoody, GA *30350*

Chester MR J Chapman—Cvc.Mt.Ct.Pn.P'52
  2101 Connecticut Av NW, Apt 83, Washington, DC *20008*

Cheston MR & MRS Charles S JR (V Lois Powell) H.'56 . . . . | ☎ (508) 887-6048 "Lothian Spring Farm" Topsfield, MA *01983*
MR John Papps . . . . |

Cheston MISS Courtney C (Eugene M JR) . . . . Married at Darien, CT
Lee MR Christopher J (Stephen E) . . . . Jun 1'96

Cheston MR & MRS E Calvert (Nancy Meyer) Sg.Fst.P'32.Pa'35
  ☎ (215) 643-5824 . . 432 Militia Hill Rd, Ft Washington, PA *19034*

Cheston MR & MRS Eugene M JR (Gregory—Elsie B Lovering) Pa'56 . . of
  ☎ (203) 966-9275 . . Leefair, 27 Bank St, New Canaan, CT *06840*
  ☎ (561) 546-1602 . . Loblolly Pines, 6399 Mourning Dove Way, Hobe Sound, FL *33455*

Cheston MR & MRS G Frazier (G Lois Jordan) Pa'43
  ☎ (610) 869-3437 . . "Lothian Farm" Street Rd, Chatham, PA *19318*

Cheston MR & MRS George M (McIlvain—de Bragança—
Winifred D Seyburn) Ph.Gm.Ssk.B.Ac.H'39
☎ (215) 925-3356 . . 229 Spruce St, Philadelphia, PA *19106*

Cheston MR George M—Srr.
☎ (630) 983-5572 . . 319 Camarie Court, Naperville, IL *60540*

Cheston MISS Martha—DU'72
☎ (215) 233-9448 . . 705 Linden Rd, Wyndmoor, PA *19038*

Cheston MR & MRS Morris JR (Cynthia W Mitchell) | ☎ (215) MI6-4008
Rb.Sg.Ph.P'59 . . . . | 560 Lewis Lane,
MISS Melinda K—Colby'89 . . . . | Ambler, PA *19002*
MR Morris 3d—P'92 . . . . |
MR James 2d—at Colby |

Cheston MR & MRS Robert M (Clagett—Christine J Tjarda
van Starkenborgh-Stachouwer) Md.Elk.Ct.Cw.Va'44
☎ (410) 235-1783 . . 312 Overhill Rd, Baltimore, MD *21210-2906*

Chew MR & MRS Beverly C (Constance M | ☎ (804) 977-8928
De Wilde) K.Snc.Cc.Cw.Cly.Ty'53 . . . . | "Holly Crest"
MISS Cory L—SCal'95—at ☎ (213) 932-6352 | 606 Flordon Dv,
5763 W 6 St, Los Angeles, CA *90036* . . . . . . | Charlottesville, VA
MR Alexander B—Col'91—at ☎ (303) 413-8637 | *22901*
2830—17 St, Boulder, CO *80304* . . . . |
MR Frederick D—Ithaca'91—at |
☎ (303) 938-8622 . . 3250 Oneal, Boulder, CO |
80301 . . . . |

Chew MR David G
☎ (206) 842-7750 . . 323 Wyatt Way NE, Bainbridge Island,
WA *98110-1841*

Chew MR & MRS H Richard (Judith Brown)
Geo'68.GeoW'79.Mt.Rby.Va'50.GeoW'57 ⚓
☎ (703) 241-2250 . . 1610 N Greenbrier St, Arlington, VA *22205-3628*

Chew MR John T JR—Ssk. . . . . | ☎ (610) 688-9431
JUNIORS MR John T 3d . . . . | PO Box 382,
| Wayne, PA *19087*

Chew MR & MRS Peter T (Virginia T Gaillard) | ☎ (202) 363-7898
V'52.Cvc.P'46 . . . . | 4664 Garfield St
MR Peter T JR . . . . | NW, Washington,
MR Benjamin G . . . . | DC *20007*

Chew MR & MRS Richard S JR (Gresh—Margaret | ☎ (610) 667-2740
Downey) Pa'54 . . . . | 440 Haverford Av,
MISS Alyce C—Buck'94 . . . . | Narberth, PA *19072*
MR Richard S 3d—Buck'91.W&M'92—at |
Wm & Mary |

Chew MR & MRS Samuel JR (Albertson—Carolyn | ☎ (805) 969-9612
Roblin) Cal'65.Gm.Temp'65 . . . . | 346 Hot Springs Rd,
MR Andrew B . . . . | Santa Barbara, CA
| *93108*

Chew MR & MRS William D M (J Kendall | ☎ (610) 525-5164
Eisenbrey) Pa'59.Me.Pa'58.Pa'61 . . . . | 312 N Ithan Av,
MISS Carol H—at 24 Garrett Av, Rosemont, PA | Rosemont, PA
19010 . . . . | *19010*
MR William D M JR—at 300 W 23 St, |
New York, NY *10011* . . . . |

Chewning MR & MRS E Taylor JR (Hernstadt— | ☎ (561) 388-0178
Prince—Jonna R Leonard) K.Ny.Srb.Mt.Cas. | 10645 Fife Av,
Y'45 . . . . | Vero Beach, FL
MR Scott C Wood Prince—at | *32963*
☎ (773) 871-8551 . . 4135 N Greenview Av, |
Chicago, IL *60613* . . . . |
MR Patrick B Wood Prince—at |
☎ (773) 486-3609 . . 1621 N Paulina St, |
Chicago, IL *60622* . . . . |

Cheyney MR & MRS H Stanton (Rita P Weinig) St.G.Buf'52
☎ (716) 885-6803 . . 707 Potomac Av, Buffalo, NY *14222*

Chick MRS Elizabeth L (Elizabeth L Perry) . . . . | ☎ (617) 941-2296
MISS Alice A—Ty'93 . . . . | 9 Jane Dv,
MISS Elizabeth A—Ty'96 . . . . | Saugus, MA *01906*
MR Stephen C—Bab'92—at ☎ (617) 744-7634 |
195 Cyprus St, Newton, MA *02159* . . . . |
MR Timothy C—Ty'96 |

Chick MR Peter C—Cy.Ty'69.Bab'71
☎ (617) 329-1153 . . 553 Common St, Dedham, MA *02026*

Chickering MR Allen L . . . . Died at
Carmel, CA Aug 15'96

Chickering MRS Allen L (Moore—Margaret Roeding) Bur . . . of
☎ (408) 625-0359 . . 8545 Carmel Valley Rd, Carmel, CA *93923*
☎ (510) 656-1868 . . Box 3068, Fremont, CA *94539*

Chickering MR Christopher . . see A Andrews 3d

Chickering MR & MRS Howard A (Elizabeth D | ☎ (203) 661-4091
Dalton) Sth'68.Rcn.Ny.Ncd.Pa'66.Stan'71 . . . . . | 80 Otter Rock Dv,
MISS Caroline H—at Middlebury . . . . | Greenwich, CT
MR Philip D . . . . | *06830*

Chickering MR Nicholas R—Stan'64
☎ (916) 265-5774 . . PO Box 238, Nevada City, CA *95959*

Chickering MRS Sherman (Jean Rawlings) Pcu.Tcy.
☎ (415) 771-2709 . . 864 Francisco St, San Francisco, CA *94109*

Chidsey DR & MRS Charles A 3d (Muriel-Anne Walker)
Sth'53.Ty'50.ClP&S'54
☎ (307) 537-5449 . . Cross Temple Ranch, PO Box 38, Boulder,
WY *82923*

Chilcote MRS Lee A (White—Virginia Horn) | ☎ (941) 472-7335
Ws'41.DelB.Cv.Uncl.Cycl.May . . . . | Sanibel Moorings,
MR John T White JR . . . . | 845 Gulf Dv,
| Sanibel Island, FL
| *33957*

Chilcott MRS James C (Ruth Hackney)
☎ (201) 538-1717 . . Village Rd, PO Box 128, New Vernon, NJ *07976*

Child MR & MRS Josiah H JR (Susan Furlow) | ☎ (617) 523-7881
V'50.H'81.Sm.Tv.Ub.Cy.K.H'48 . . . . | 81 Beacon St,
MR Josiah H 3d—Ub.Pa'88—at Mt Sinai | Boston, MA *02108*
Sch of Med . . . . |

Childress MRS Clifford C (Butler—Noble—Bickford—Mathias—
Dunaway—Marjorie von Stresenreuter) BtP.Evg.Cas.
☎ (561) 832-8900 . . 16 Golf View Rd, Palm Beach, FL *33480*

Childress MRS Fielding T (Ruth B E McElroy) Cy.
☎ (314) 367-3517 . . 1 McKnight Place, St Louis, MO *63124*

Childress MR & MRS William C (M Sandra Zaring) | ☎ (517) 669-5448
ColC'57.Va'58 . . . . | 3856 Tumbleweed
MR William C JR—MichSt'88 . . . . | Lane, De Witt, MI
MR Douglas R . . . . | *48820*

Childs MISS Ariel—Cr'93
☎ (212) 787-8591 . . 328 W 76 St, New York, NY *10023*

Childs MRS Blair (Virginia Fiske) Mt.Pg.
☎ (202) 333-3321 . . 3321 Dent Place NW, Washington, DC *20007*

Childs MR & MRS Charles O (Barbara J McGill) Cin'50
☎ (205) 592-3398 . . 720—43 St S, Birmingham, AL *35222*

Childs MR & MRS Clinton L JR (Margaret B Orr) Pg.Edg.Yn.Y'38
☎ (412) 741-6896 . . 650 Grove St, Sewickley, PA *15143*

Childs MRS Cole (Mary H Cole) Csn.
☎ (202) 338-9510 . . 700 New Hampshire Av NW, Washington, DC *20037*

Childs MR & MRS David M (Anne W Reeve)
Mt.C.B.Y'63.Y'67 . . . .
MISS Jocelyn R . . . .
MR Joshua H—at Boston, MA . . . . | of ☎ (212)427-9022 49 E 86 St, New York, NY *10028*
☎ (518) 576-4777 ''Red Oak'' Box 73, Keene Valley, NY *12943*

Childs MRS Edward P (Lucinda E Corcoran)
see Dilatory Domiciles

Childs MRS Eleanor (Eleanor vom Rath) Pr . . .of
☎ (603) 823-5687 . . ''Mittersill'' Sunset Ridge Rd, Franconia, NH *03580*
☎ (516) 676-2197 . . 29 Valentine Lane, PO Box 168, Old Brookville, NY *11545*

Childs MRS Eleanor M (M Eleanor Metcalf) . . . . . .
MR G Tucker . . . .
MR Andrew L . . . .
MR W Barton . . . . | ☎ (802) 843-2631 PO Box 14, Grafton, VT *05146*

Childs MRS F Newell (Doss—Barbara M Moore) DelB.On . . .of
PO Box 831, Lake Forest, IL *60045*
☎ (561) 368-1311 . . 4545 N Ocean Blvd, Apt 10A, Boca Raton, FL *33431*

Childs MRS Frederick Robbins (M Alixandra Hitchcock) Mls'31.Cly.
☎ (203) 655-1159 . . ''Three Trees'' 173 Long Neck Point Rd, PO Box 3035, Noroton, CT *06820*

Childs MR & MRS Harvey JR (Barbara E Leech) Pg.Rr.Y'45w
☎ (412) 593-6108 . . Indian Rock Farm, PO Box 167, Stahlstown, PA *15687*

Childs MR & MRS J Mabon (Sally F Hillman) SL'49.Pg.Rr.Fcg.Ln.Y'44
☎ (412) 621-3436 . . 5453 Albemarle Av, Pittsburgh, PA *15217*

Childs MRS James H JR (Elizabeth D Littell) Chi . . .of
☎ (561) 276-3283 . . 4475 N Ocean Blvd, Delray Beach, FL *33483*
☎ (207) 363-4632 . . ''Short Sands'' 5 Stage Neck Rd, PO Box 267, York Harbor, ME *03911*

Childs MISS Louise K . . see G W Bissell

Childs MRS Marquis W (McBaine—Jane F Neylan) Cos.Ri.
☎ (415) 397-3282 . . 1000 Mason St, San Francisco, CA *94108*

Childs MR & MRS Richard H L (Lora G Barzin) Y'52
☎ (803) 525-1370 . . Spring Island, Rte 6, Box 284R, Okatie, SC *29910*

Childs MR & MRS Thomas S JR (Susan Knott) Y'62 .
MR Benjamin P—at Burlington, VT . . . . | of ☎ (860)434-3561 76 Joshuatown Rd, Lyme, CT *06371*
☎ (212) 734-1715 140 E 81 St, New York, NY *10028-3120*

Childs MR Thomas W—P'28.Ox'31.Y'32 . . of
☎ (441) 236-0212 . . Stancombe Glade, 42 Harbour Rd, Paget PG 02, Bermuda
☎ (860) 868-2392 . . Painter Ridge Rd, Washington, CT *06793*

Childs MR Thomas W 4th—Rcn.Cr'60 . . . .
MISS Jenika L—at ☎ (202) 639-8958
425—8 St NW, Apt 849, Washington, DC *20004* | of 1489 Marine Dv, West Vancouver, BC V7T 1B8, Canada
☎ (330) 478-8942 4587 Morgate Circle, Canton, OH *44708*

Childs DR & MRS Timothy W (Hope S Kane)
C.Mt.Cvc.Yh.Cc.Sl.Yn.Y'57.JHop'61.Geo'82 . . of
☎ (202) 363-4423 . . 3520 Tilden St NW, Washington, DC *20008*
☎ (860) 542-5726 . . ''Spitehouse'' 300 West Side Rd, Norfolk, CT *06058*

Childs MR & MRS Walton (Gray—Lee Butvay) Edg..
JUNIORS MISS Elizabeth W—at Choate Rosemary
JUNIORS MR J Brentley—at Trinity-Pawling . . . .
MR John V Gray—at 2143 E 10 St, Tempe, AZ *85281* . . . . | ☎ (516) 367-2231 38 Turkey Lane, Cold Spring Harbor, NY *11724-1702*

Childs MR & MRS William A P (Elisabeth G D E Rogalla von Bieberstein) Münster'64.P'64 . . . . .
MISS Christiane G I—Cr'89 . . . .
MR Thomas C C—at Yale . . . . | ☎ (609) 921-1229 90 Carter Rd, Princeton, NJ *08540*

Chinn MR & MRS Garretson W (Nancy Deering) OState'62.Y'62.Mit'68
☎ (212) 472-1315 . . 34 E 75 St, New York, NY *10021*

Chisholm MR Corning—Tv.Y'37
☎ (216) 541-5411 . . 1 Bratenahl Place, Cleveland, OH *44108*

Chisholm MR & MRS Frank A (Katherine Crutcher) Ga'51.Cc.Y'32
☎ (912) 925-8631 . . 24 Rockwell Av S, Savannah, GA *31419*

Chisholm MR Henry L—Ll.Yn. . . . .
MISS Anne E—at ☎ (617) 327-7154
18 Hackensack Circle, Chestnut Hill, MA *02167* | ☎ (954) 792-1990 3511 W Commercial Blvd, Ft Lauderdale, FL *33309*

Chisholm MR & MRS William H (Edith E Griffiths) Pa'45.Pa'46.Wk.Yn.Y'40
☎ (203) 869-5428 . . 45 Lismore Lane, Greenwich, CT *06831*

Chisholm MR & MRS William W JR (Sue McQ Grantham) Ga'71.Ga'71 . . . .
JUNIORS MISS Katherine McQ . . . . | ☎ (912) 897-3337 10 Commodore Court, Savannah, GA *31410*

Chisolm MR & MRS Guy M JR (Elise P Townsend) TexA&M'46
☎ (410) 744-0780 . . 2300 Whitby Court, Baltimore, MD *21228*

Chisolm DR & MRS J Julian JR (Sylvia R Larsen)
P'44.JHop'46 . . . .
MR Edward L—Hob'76 . . . . | ☎ (410) 771-4304 2007 Stringtown Rd, Sparks, MD *21152*

Chisolm MR William A—Un.P'45 . . . . | ☎ (212) 348-3100
MISS Elizabeth W—at ☎ (773) 288-4511 | 47 E 88 St,
1454 E 54 St, Chicago, IL *60615* . . . . | New York, NY
| *10128-1152*

Chittenden MR & MRS George H (Parker—Sarah M Price)
B'gton'46.Y.'39 . . of
☎ (914) 967-4636 . . 37 Water's Edge, Rye, NY *10580*
☎ (203) 245-2984 . . 155 Buffalo Bay, Neck Rd, Madison, CT *06443*

Chitty MR Frederick J P
☎ (804) 293-9397 . . "Spero House" 3 Tennis Rd, Farmington,
Charlottesville, VA *22901*

Choa MR & MRS Christopher J (Nina T Train) SL'85.Lond'92.Y'80.H'87
☎ (212) 243-1755 . . 112 W 18 St, New York, NY *10011*

Choate MRS Arthur O JR (Elkins—Fleming—Eloise R Weld)
☎ (610) 869-2860 . . 535 W Street Rd, RD 1, Kennett Square, PA *19348*

Choate MRS Charles F (Jhan C English) . . . . | ☎ (508) 526-8209
MISS J Edith—at ☎ (508) 283-5847 | PO Box 359,
28A Rocky Neck Rd, Gloucester, MA *01930* . . . | Manchester, MA
| *01944*

Choate MRS Joseph H (Kellogg—Sarita S Blagden)
☎ (508) 448-6684 . . 46 Long Hill Rd, Box 602, Groton, MA *01450*

Choate MR & MRS Roger N (Lisa W Wendelius) | ☎ (011-46-8)
Uppsala'57.Pom'62.Cl'65 . . . . | 754-0521
MISS Abigail L . . . . | Allévägen 8G,
| 19177 Sollentuna,
| Sweden

Choate MR & MRS Thomas H (Jane Harte) Rc.Mb.Pr.Ln.Cly.H'37
☎ (516) 626-0318 . . 50 Wheatley Rd, Brookville, NY *11545*

Cholmeley-Jones MR & MRS Richard G 2d (Grainger—Marion Goldsmith)
Rv.Ht.Cw.Wms'45
☎ (203) 847-1017 . . 6 Tod Rd, Norwalk, CT *06851-1536*

Choremi MR & MRS Alec M (Aglaia Coumantaros) | ☎ (516) 676-7170
Ck.Cly. . . . . | PO Box 413,
MR Philip N—at ☎ (516) 423-6347 | Locust Valley, NY
43 Hildreth Av, Huntington, NY *11743* . . . . . . | *11560-0413*

Chorley MRS Edward C (Marcia T Blankarn)
☎ (561) 743-7744 . . 16575 Traders Crossing S, Apt 140, Jupiter,
FL *33477*

Chorley MR Edward C
20 Hawthorne St, White Plains, NY *10603*

Choumenkovitch MR Iliya A M—Roch'85
☎ (612) 542-8280 . . 12700 Sherwood Place, Apt 200, Wayzata,
MN *55305*

Choumenkovitch MR & MRS Nicolas M (Silvina M Furlong)
BuenosA'90.Occ'86.Va'92
☎ (617) 441-5170 . . 29 Concord Av, Apt 411, Cambridge, MA *02138*

Chouteau MRS Auguste (Joan Bakewell) Rc.Cy. . . | ☎ (314) 993-3634
MISS Eugenie—at ☎ (314) 994-7366 | 36 Magnolia Dv,
887 Berick Dv, St Louis, MO *63132* . . . . | St Louis, MO *63124*

Chouteau MR & MRS Pierre P (Agnes F Potter) | ☎ (314) PA1-3434
Ncd.Wash'47 . . . . | 4 Tuscany Park,
MISS Marie T . . . . | St Louis, MO *63105*
MR Pierre . . . . |

Chrapkiewicz MR Covington A . . see MRS L C Davies

Chrapkiewicz MR William A A . . see MRS L C Davies

Chrisman MR & MRS William H (Craig—Margaret M Baker)
Nw'52.H'58.H'55
☎ (602) 948-3666 . . 6235 E Catesby Rd, Paradise Valley, AZ *85253*

Chrismen MR & MRS James J (Leslie S Miller) . . see MRS R N Miller 3d

Christ MR & MRS Donald C (Van Ingen—Paine—Russell—Iris V Smith)
Evg.B.Pr.Mb.Cly.Y . . .of
☎ (516) 922-0077 . . "Llama Woods" Cleft Rd, Mill Neck, NY *11765*
☎ (541) 382-7799 . . "Llama Woods Farm" 65500 Gerking Market Rd,
Bend, OR *97701*

Christ MR & MRS M Hallsted (Ann C Gilbert) | ☎ (410) 476-5050
Colg'53.Nu'55 . . . . | "Mallard Point
MISS Marian G—Col'90 . . . . | Farm" 32123
MR John R—Guil'90 . . . . | Clark's Wharf Rd,
| Trappe, MD *21673*

Christensen MR & MRS Paul W JR (Sarah Ellen Ernst) Qc.Cm.Cr'42 . . of
☎ (513) 561-4242 . . 4660 Drake Rd, Cincinnati, OH *45243*
☎ (305) 367-4244 . . Ocean Reef Club, 30 Dilly Tree Park, Key Largo,
FL *33037*

Christhilf MR Bryson G . . . . Died at
Ruxton, MD Feb 12'96

Christhilf MRS Bryson G (Elizabeth B Myers) | ☎ (410) 821-8806
Md.Cy.Cw. . . . . | 602 Brightwood
MR Bryson G JR—Md.Cy.—at | Lane, Lutherville,
111 Versailles Circle, Baltimore, MD *21204* . . . | MD *21093*
MR James M—Cy.—at 1418 Broadway, |
Lutherville, MD *21093* . . . . |

Christian MR & MRS Robert G JR (Ellen A Kremer) Ober'86.Stan'85
see Dilatory Domiciles

Christiansen MR & MRS Stephen B (Nina L Neilson) | of ☎ (610)286-7337
Au.W.Ncd.Mon'74 . . . . | "Hearthstone Farm"
JUNIORS MISS Brita N . . . . | Elverson, PA *19520*
JUNIORS MR Kjell I . . . . | ☎ (518) 576-4226
| "Icy Brook"
| Ausable Club,
| St Huberts, NY
| *12943*

Christman MR & MRS Raymond R (Clark—Eileen S | ☎ (412) 422-1015
Hoffman) Pitt'84.FlaSt'71.Pitt'74 . . . . | 1877 Shaw Av,
MISS Margot S Clark—Van'95—at | Pittsburgh, PA
☎ (615) 298-5729 . . 805 S Wilson Blvd, | *15217*
Nashville, TN *37215* . . . . |

Christmas MRS B Frank (Mary E Grason)
☎ (410) 252-1363 . . 600 Boxmere Court, Timonium, MD *21093*

Christy MR & MRS Arthur H (Osborne—Gloria Garvin) C.Y.'45.Cl'49
☎ (212) 308-3346 . . 430 E 57 St, New York, NY *10022*

Christy MR & MRS Duncan H (Jayne Wardwell) H'74
☎ (914) 833-2574 . . 28 Edgewood Av, Larchmont, NY *10538-2336*

Christy MRS Muriel H (Muriel A Horgan)
☎ (914) 833-2574 . . 28 Edgewood Av, Larchmont, NY *10538-2336*

Chronis MR & MRS Gregory G (Jean E Carpenter)
Ariz'88.ArizSt'93.Colby'88.ArizSt'91
☎ (602) 451-3776 . . 9019 E Corrine Dv, Scottsdale, AZ *85260*

Chrystie MISS Adden B—StLaw'83
☎ (212) 472-2066 . . 315 E 68 St, Apt 12J, New York, NY *10021*

Chrystie MR James McD—Skd'88
☎ (406) 585-2985 . . 407 W Koch, Bozeman, MT *59715*

Chrystie MR & MRS Thomas L (Eliza S Balis) Cc.Csn.Cl'55.Nu'60
☎ (307) 733-4940 . . ''Moose Bluff'' PO Box 640, Wilson, WY *83014*
Chubb MR & MRS Charles F JR (Mary T Sedlak) Ford'54.P'41
☎ (516) 626-1202 . . 25 Meadowood Lane, Brookville, Glen Head, NY *11545*
Chubb MRS Percy (Corinne R Alsop) Ny.Cly.
☎ (908) 234-1314 . . 100 Pottersville Rd, PO Box 419, Chester, NJ *07930*

Chubb MR & MRS Percy 3d (Sally G Gilady) Ny.Eh.Shcc.Cly.Y'56 . . . .
MISS Lucy A—H'86 . . . .
MR Percy L—Y'81 . . . .
☎ (908) 221-0713 431 Claremont Rd, Bernardsville, NJ *07924*

Chubb MRS R Walston (Louise Langenohl)
☎ (314) 993-6554 . . 43 Godwin Lane, St Louis, MO *63124*

Chubb MR Talbot A—P'45.NCar'51 . . . .
MISS Constance L . . . .
☎ (703) 536-4427 5023—38 St N, Arlington, VA *22207*

Churbuck MR & MRS David C (Daphne M Fullerton) Ty'80.Ub.Y'80
☎ (508) 428-6948 . . 854 Main St, Box 720, Cotuit, MA *02635*
Church MRS Caroline W (Gunnell—Caroline W Church) AmU'91
☎ (540) 347-7973 . . PO Box 297, Warrenton, VA *20188*
Church MRS Dimitra T (Dimitra T Asimakopoulos)
320 E 58 St, PH-B, New York, NY *10021*
Church MISS Emily W (Gerald B) . . . . Married at Boston, MA
Hatch MR Seamus J P (Desmond) . . . . May 18'96
Church MRS Frank (Bethine Clark) Mich'45
☎ (208) 389-1064 . . 480 N Walnut St, Boise, ID *83712*
Church MRS Frederic C (Agnes D Boardman) Sm.Ec.
☎ (508) 927-0075 . . 425 Hale St, Prides Crossing, MA *01965*

Church MR & MRS Frederic C JR (Katharine L Mahony) Cy.H.'55 . . . .
MISS Elise P—at ☎ (212) 254-9515
173 Bleecker St, New York, NY *10012* . . . .
MISS Courtney—at ☎ (617) 241-9083
13 Eden St, Charlestown, MA *02119* . . . .
MISS Lindsay C . . . .
☎ (617) 731-6173 327 Heath St, Chestnut Hill, MA *02167*

Church MR & MRS Gerald B (Maria Bright) Cy.Tr.Ub.H.'58 . . . .
MISS Alison C—at 109 Museum St, Cambridge, MA *02138* . . . .
MISS Laura B—at 201 E 75 St, New York, NY *10021* . . . .
☎ (617) 566-0852 78 Randolph Rd, Chestnut Hill, MA *02167*

Church MR & MRS Herbert JR (Gerber—Gail L Graham) RI'45.Y'48.H'44.Pa'52
☎ (603) 225-2472 . . 1 Pleasant View Av, Concord, NH *03301*
Church MR & MRS John F JR (Edwards—Catherine Neth) Mvh.Qc.Colby'59.CTech'61 . . of
☎ (513) 772-1850 . . 116 Oak St, Glendale, OH *45246*
☎ (616) 526-7119 . . ''Heather Highlands'' 242 Camelot St, Harbor Springs, MI *49740*
☎ (941) 594-1143 . . Bay Colony, Contessa 203, 8111 Bay Colony Dv, Naples, FL *34108*

Church MISS Mary N . . see T C Jenkins

Church COL Richard B—USMC.USN'38.H'49 . . . .
MR Barry H . . . .
see Dilatory Domiciles

Church MISS Susan M . . see T C Jenkins

Churchill MRS Albert G (Tayloe Hannaford) . . . . . .
MR Creighton H . . . .
☎ (510) 547-4605 455 Wildwood Av, Piedmont, CA *94611*

Churchill MR & MRS Colin W (Jane B Athey) Dth'39 . . . .
MISS Wendall S—Mid'86.Va'91—at
☎ (410) 235-2178 . . 5007 Roland Av, Baltimore, MD *21210* . . . .
☎ (803) 671-6754 10 Liberty Place, Hilton Head Island, SC *29928-4130*

Churchill MR Colin W JR—OWes'84.Bost'89
☎ (617) 720-2947 . . 18 Garden St, Boston, MA *02114*
Churchill MR & MRS Delos B (Eleanor E Blackwell) S.Mit'40.BklynPoly'55
☎ (860) 434-8549 . . PO Box 94, Old Lyme, CT *06371*

Churchill MRS Edward D JR (Ellen Buntzie Ellis) Pa'61 . . . .
MISS Eva L . . . .
MR Eric C . . . .
☎ (609) 795-7019 119 Mountwell Av, Haddonfield, NJ *08033*

Churchill MR & MRS Frederic E JR (Virginia D Byers) Wms'90.Wms'88
see Dilatory Domiciles
Churchill MR & MRS W Philip (Tarbox—Mary L Powell) Me'30.Geo'35 . . of
☎ (912) 638-7209 . . 110 Palm Dv, St Simons Island, GA *31522*
☎ (501) 741-3990 . . 2 Hickory Acres, Harrison, AR *72601*
Churchman MRS Anne W (Anne W Myers) VillaN'74
☎ (610) 688-2542 . . 658 Knox Rd, Wayne, PA *19087*

Churchman MR & MRS Joseph S (Linda M Murphy) Case'68.Case'67.Stan'74 . . . .
MISS Anne C . . . .
MR Joseph S JR . . . .
MR James L . . . .
JUNIORS MR Montgomery D . . . .
☎ (508) 376-8721 6 Myrtle St, Millis, MA *02054-1715*

Churchman MRS Lee M (Donaldson—K Lee McIlvaine) NFla'75.Me.Ncd. . . . .
MISS Lee Stirling—at Cornell . . . .
JUNIORS MISS Leidy McI—at Brewster . . . .
☎ (610) 525-5660 719 Cedar Lane, Villanova, PA *19085*

Churchman MR & MRS W Morgan 3d (Dechert—Deborah S Payson) M.Me.Cry.Roan'65 . . . .
MR J Alexander—at ☎ (610) 594-8716
221 Lindenwood Dv, Exton, PA *19341* . . . .
MISS Martha P Dechert—Br'92.Me.—at
☎ (610) 617-7261 . . . .
of ☎ (610)525-2889 344 Thornbrook Av, Rosemont, PA *19010*
☎ (561) 588-5657 La Coquille Villas 102D, 550 S Ocean Blvd, Manalapan, FL *33462*

Churchman MR & MRS William B 3d (Forman—Betty Beeler) Rc.Sg.
☎ (610) 642-7970 . . 360 Youngsford Place, Gladwyne, PA *19035*
Chute MRS Judith Chandler (Caruso—Judith C Chute) Bnd'60
☎ (617) 383-1752 . . 46 Beach St, Cohasset, MA *02025*

Cisneros MR & MRS Gustavo A (Patricia P Phelps)
Wheat'69.Ri.K.Bab'68 . . . .
MISS Carolina P . . . .
MISS Adriana M . . . .
MR Guillermo A . . . .
of ☎ (212)717-5880
960 Fifth Av,
New York, NY
10021
La Cañada, Caracas
Country Club,
Caracas, Venezuela
"Casa Bonita"
Punta Mini Tas 1,
La Romana,
Dominican Republic

Cist MRS Franklin M (Clara L Giese)
☎ (602) 840-8412 . . 6707 N 48 St, Scottsdale, AZ *85253*

Cist MR & MRS J David (Mary H N Schaefer)
Cw.Ncd.P'42.Mit'48 . . . .
MISS Dorothea B . . . .
MISS Mary Harding L . . . .
MR David B . . . .
☎ (302) 656-7237
1102 Brandon Lane,
Wilmington, DE
19807-3007

Claflin MR John A—Fic.H'90
☎ (310) 478-9770 . . 2337 S Bentley Av, Los Angeles, CA *90064*

Claflin MR & MRS R Morton (Jane E Darrah) Tul'38.Cy.Sm.Chi.H'36
☎ (617) 723-9459 . . 10 Byron St, Boston, MA *02108*

Claflin MR Richard M 2d—H'92
☎ (213) 650-0802 . . 1246 N Harper Av, Los Angeles, CA *90046*

Claflin MR & MRS Robert D (Kyri Watson) Bost'77.H'68.Cl'72
☎ (603) 526-6974 . . 46 Shaker Rd, New London, NH *03257*

Claflin MR & MRS Thomas M 2d (Perry—Rachel A
Cale) Cy.Sm.Ub.H.'63 . . . .
MISS Julia W Perry . . . .
☎ (617) 523-7471
160 Mt Vernon St,
Boston, MA *02108*

Clagett MR & MRS Brice McAdoo (Knop—Diana W
Sinkler) GeoW'66.Ct.Rd.Mt.Cvc.Cc.Ac.Hn.
P'54.H'58 . . . .
MISS Ann C B—at Tulane Law . . . .
MR John B de T . . . .
of ☎ (301)855-6999
"Holly Hill"
PO Box 86,
Friendship, MD
20758
☎ (202) 337-5097
3331 O St NW,
Washington, DC
20007
☎ (610) 644-2415
"Milfern" Malvern,
PA *19355*

Clagett MR C Thomas JR—Mt.Cvc.Nrr.Ayc.Il.Ny.S.Sar.Cc.StJ'39 ⚓
☎ (202) 965-6455 . . 2700 Virginia Av NW, Washington,
DC *20037-1908*

Clagett MISS Christine F—Mid'77
☎ (410) 867-2052 . . 4029 Solomon Island Rd, Harwood, MD *20776*

Clagett MR & MRS Henry C B JR (Begg—Jeanne F van den Bosch)
Mt.Md.Cvc.Sl.P'38 . . of
☎ (301) 261-4016 . . "Roedown" 3856 Wayson Rd, Davidsonville,
MD *21035*
☎ (809) 774-0003 . . "Peacock Hill" 13 Water Island, St Thomas,
VI *00802*

Clagett MR & MRS Page B (Dorothy Q Tirrell) Cvc.Sl.Ncd.Va'38
☎ (202) 332-2317 . . 2314 Wyoming Av NW, Washington,
DC *20008-1641*

Clagett MR & MRS Tjarda van S (Lillian W Hill)
V'71.GeoW'74.Ri.StJ.P'71.H'76 . . . .
JUNIOR MISS Alidia T van S . . . .
of ☎ (212)860-0693
40 E 94 St,
New York, NY
10128
"Sasscers Green"
7108 Crain H'way,
Upper Marlboro,
MD *20772*

Claggett CAPT (RET) & MRS B Dulany (Rhea A Robinson)
Hood'36.Cvc.Ny.Sl.USN'35
☎ (301) 564-9255 . . Maplewood Park Place, Bethesda, MD *20814*

Claggett MR Charles E—Cy.Lc.Nd.P'31 . . . .
MR Daniel E—at ☎ (314) 968-1653
16 Hillard Rd, St Louis, MO *63122* . . . .
of ☎ (561)231-2975
2636 Ocean Dv,
Vero Beach, FL
32963
☎ (314) 993-0201
201 S Warson Rd,
St Louis, MO *63124*

Claggett MR & MRS William M (Rogers—Barbara J
Clark) Hlns'64.BtP.Evg.Cysl.Rcsl.B.Va'51.
OState'53 . . . .
MISS Susan E . . . .
☎ (561) 655-6972
235B Chilean Av,
Palm Beach, FL
33480

Claghorn MR & MRS Edward T (Katrina Van Buren)
NCar'75.Ofp.Rv.Dh.NCar'74 . . . .
JUNIORS MR Edward T JR . . . .
457 Weadley Rd,
Wayne, PA *19087*

Claghorn MR & MRS Frederic S JR (Mary H Scott)
Pc.Rv.Ofp.Laf'73 . . . .
MISS Mary K . . . .
MISS Tara T . . . .
JUNIORS MISS Anne S . . . .
JUNIORS MR Frederic S 3d . . . .
☎ (215) 699-3110
"New Tisbury"
908 Surrey Dv,
Gwynedd Valley,
PA *19437*

Claghorn MR & MRS Frederic Strawbridge (Katharine Taws)
Sg.Rv.Ofp.Sdg.Ncd.
☎ (215) 248-1855 . . "Kathorn" 9401 Meadowbrook Lane, Philadelphia,
PA *19118*

Claghorn MR & MRS John W JR (Margery E Richardson) Ofp.
☎ (609) 921-6813 . . 43 Vandeventer Av, Princeton, NJ *08542*

Claghorn MR & MRS John W 3d (Margaret E Jump)
Md'71.Rc.Bost'77 . . . .
JUNIORS MISS Lila S . . . .
JUNIORS MR John W 4th . . . .
☎ (212) 410-6060
1148 Fifth Av,
New York, NY
10128

Claiborne MRS John H (Patricia Alexandre) . . . . . .
MR William C C . . . .
☎ (803) 525-1437
Box 1173, Beaufort,
SC *29901*

Claiborne MR John H 3d . . . . Died at
Barrington, IL May 22'96

Claiborne MRS John H 3d (Harriet A Witt)
Ariz'67.Ariz'69.Unn.Cw. . . . .
MISS Elizabeth L . . . .
MR John H 4th—at Ind U . . . .
☎ (203) 775-1365
34 Junction Rd,
Brookfield, CT
06804

Claiborne MRS John T 3d (Cox—Cornelia D Sharp)
☎ (561) 753-6083 . . 11679 Wimbledon Circle, West Palm Beach,
FL *33414*

Clancy MR & MRS Andrew O (Denyse R Finn) Y'89.Cl'92.Aht'88.Nw'94
☎ (214) 827-2184 . . 5201 Goodwin Av, Dallas, TX *75206*

Clancy MR & MRS John A (Godwin—Joan M Frederick)
Cal'53.Wab'41.Nw'44
☎ (408) 624-8064 . . 25525 Shafter Way, Carmel, CA *93923*

Clancy MR & MRS John Franklin (Paula Jean | ☎ (214) 385-7518
Johnson) Nw'59.Nw'59 . . . . | 12519 Degas Lane,
MISS Allison Holmes—Miss'93 . . . . | Dallas, TX *75230*

Clapham MR & MRS John B (Mary Hacker) Pc.Sar.Ncd.Pa'38
Meadowood at Worcester, 25 Hickory Heights, Lansdale, PA *19446*

Clapham MR & MRS John H (Dorothy S Hallowell) | ☎ (610) 647-0379
Sar.Susq'66 . . . . | 1052 Signal Hill
MISS Wendy S—VillaN'95 . . . . | Lane, Berwyn, PA
MISS Holly R—at Ithaca . . . . | *19312*
MR Andrew H—Bost'93 . . . . |

Clapp MR & MRS David D (Linda R Beam) Br'61 . | ☎ (603) 778-1516
MISS Rachel O—at Bowdoin . . . . | 141 Exeter Rd,
| Box 367, Newfields,
| NH *03856*

Clapp MRS Harvey R JR (Wyckoff—Jackson—Jane S Edson) Elk.
Bishop White Lodge, 600 E Cathedral St, Philadelphia, PA *19128*

Clapp MR & MRS Harvey R 3d (Ann S Kinczel) | ☎ (410) 235-1806
Pa'63.Elk.Mv.P'65.H'68.Loy'76 . . . . | 4207 Greenway,
MR David S . . . . | Baltimore, MD
| *21218-1135*

Clapp MRS Nathaniel D (Mary B Loring)
☎ (617) 275-9882 . . 49 Concord Court, Bedford, MA *01730*

Clapp MRS Roger E (Black—Linda Cabot) Rdc'51 . | of ☎ (617)354-0451
MR Alexander J—Y'83—at 202 Rusholme Rd, | 5 Hilliard Place,
Toronto M6H 2Y7, Canada . . . . | Cambridge, MA
  MISS Sophie C Black—Marlboro'80.Cl'84—at | *02138*
  New York, NY . . . . | ☎ (207) 526-4414
  MR Alexander G Black—Bard'82—at | "Garden Cove
  26 Wavecrest Av, Venice, CA *90291* . . . . . . | House"
  MR Jeremiah W Black—H'84—at | Swans Island, ME
  ☎ (212) 255-4718 . . 22 Perry St, New York, | *04685*
  NY *10014* . . . . |

Clare MRS N Holmes (Barbara A Kepler) | ☎ (212) 988-8771
Un.Cda.Myf. . . . . | 135 E 83 St,
MR N Holmes JR . . . . | New York, NY
| *10028*

Clarey MR John E—Wms'52
☎ (561) 835-3651 . . 1200 S Flagler Dv, Apt 1705, West Palm Beach,
FL *33401-6707*

Clark MISS A Kiersted C . . see W T Woodhull JR

Clark MRS Alfred R (Simone Newcomb)
☎ (860) 434-9222 . . 2 Whippletree Lane, Old Lyme, CT *06371-1434*

Clark MISS Amy
☎ (610) KI4-2510 . . 356 Lynn Rd, Springfield, PA *19064*

Clark MISS Anna Holbrook—Cs.
☎ (212) 772-8335 . . 217 E 66 St, Apt 5A, New York, NY *10021*

Clark MRS Anne C (Anne B Crichton) Ty'73.Me.
☎ (610) 649-2233 . . 418 N Rose Lane, Haverford, PA *19041*

Clark MR & MRS Anthony E (Christine Semenenko) B.Srb.Col'72
☎ (212) 750-8462 . . 215 E 68 St, New York, NY *10021*

Clark MRS Avery B (Patricia Hughes) Ac.Me.
☎ (610) LA5-4364 . . 921 Field Lane, Villanova, PA *19085*

Clark MRS Benjamin S (Charlotte C Lyman) | ☎ (914) 764-5171
C.Sm.Cly.Snc. . . . . | 336 Stone Hill Rd,
MISS Elizabeth Van C—at Deerfield Rd, | Pound Ridge, NY
Pound Ridge, NY *10576* . . . . | *10576-1422*

Clark MISS Carnzu A—V'36
☎ (805) 964-5535 . . 4850 Via Los Santos, Santa Barbara, CA *93111*

Clark MRS Caulkins (Bliss Caulkins) Mich'66.Mich'90
☎ (313) 886-5007 . . 40 Tonnancour Place, Grosse Pointe Farms,
MI *48236-3033*

Clark MRS Charles Martin JR (Helen Lonergan) Cly.
☎ (212) 753-1307 . . 200 E 66 St, New York, NY *10021*

Clark MR Christopher B JR . . see T E Donnelley 2d

Clark MR Christopher N
66 Main St, Hingham, MA *02043*

Clark MR Christopher S . . see A G Clarke

Clark MR & MRS Christopher T (Eloise D Morris) | ☎ (914) 967-2122
Sth'63.K.H'62 . . . . | 10 Manursing Way,
MISS Diana F—H'95 . . . . | Rye, NY
MR Christopher T JR—CtCol'91—at Duke . . . . . | *10580-4312*

Clark MR & MRS Clarence H 5th (Kathleen E Corby) Leh'78.Leh'82
4 Appletree Circle, Wrightsville, PA *17368*

Clark MR & MRS David C (Elizabeth H Ives) H'49
☎ (516) 922-5445 . . 91 Cove Rd, Oyster Bay, NY *11771-2417*

Clark MR & MRS David C JR (Peri M Frost) B'gton'75
☎ (212) 831-4535 . . 65 E 96 St, New York, NY *10128*

Clark MR & MRS David W (Anne T Newbold) | ☎ (610) 647-8159
BMr'50.Cts.Ph.Rb.H'42 . . . . | 2305 White Horse
MISS Emily R . . . . | Rd, Berwyn, PA
| *19312*

Clark MR & MRS E McMichael JR (Linda E Wiesmann)
Buck'78.Temp'82.Ck.Buck'76
☎ (516) 627-8786 . . 21 Durand Place, Manhasset, NY *11030*

Clark MRS E Roe (Eleanor B Roe) SL'46
☎ (415) 349-3298 . . 1132 Shoreline Dv, San Mateo, CA *94404*

Clark MR & MRS Edward F JR (Rosemary Reddick) Pl.H.'28
☎ (914) 265-3366 . . 3 Grandview Terr, Cold Spring, NY *10516*

Clark MR Edward H (Mora Brennan)
☎ (415) 931-8832 . . 2265 Broadway St, San Francisco, CA *94115*

Clark MISS Elise C—Colg'93
☎ (415) 775-7019 . . 1181 Green St, San Francisco, CA *94109*

Clark MISS Elizabeth Ashley (g—George M Wood JR) . . . . Born at
Tulsa, OK Jan 22'96

Clark MR & MRS Ernest C JR (Mary C Fahnestock) D.Pa'42
☎ (603) 772-1782 . . 7 River Woods Dv, Exeter, NH *03833-4373*

Clark MRS F Douglas (Louise F Henry) Cly.Dc.Dh.Cda.Lm.Ht.
☎ (203) 966-0801 . . 344 Wahackme Rd, New Canaan, CT *06840*

Clark MRS Florence W (George—Altemus—Florence B Whitney) Bgt.Msq.
☎ (914) 234-3945 . . Aspetong Rd, Bedford, NY *10506*

Clark MR & MRS Forrester A JR (Radsch—Jennifer C | ☎ (508) 468-3077
Johnston) Curry'75.My.Ub.Un.H.'58 . . . . | 308 Sagamore St,
MR Forrester A 3d . . . . | South Hamilton, MA
MR Cameron B . . . . | *01982*
JUNIORS MR Matthew R . . . . |

Clark MRS Frances K (Frances H Kingsford) Chi.
45 West St, Beverly Farms, MA *01915*

Clark MR & MRS Francis A (Margaret J Hanlon) Un. ☎ (607) 547-2000
MISS Claudia G—at ☎ (617) 437-9147 "Ravenna Hill"
12 Stoneholm St, Apt 416, Boston, MA *02115* . Box 643,
MR Francis A JR . . . . Cooperstown, NY
MISS Robin J (Stryker—Robin J Clark)—at *13326*
☎ (203) 972-7423 . . 476 Silvermine Rd,
New Canaan, CT *06840* . . . .

Clark MR & MRS Frederic W (Virginia C Bradley) ☎ (610) 964-0227
Ws'65.Ph.H'61.Pa'68. . . . . 878 Parkes Run
MISS Allison B—H'92 . . . . Lane, Villanova, PA
JUNIORS MR Edward C. *19085-1136*

Clark MR & MRS Frederick W (Rosalie L Smith)
AmCM'47.AmCM'48.Plg.Cw.Sar.Myf.Dar.H'42.Neb'58
1625 Normandy Way, Leesburg, FL *34748-6733*

Clark MR & MRS Garnett Y JR (Thacher—Mary J Hansen)
Ayc.Gm.Me.StJColl'36 . . of
☎ (410) 266-1108 . . 6105 River Crescent Dv, Annapolis, MD *21401*
☎ (610) 642-6642 . . 370 Youngsford Place, Gladwyne, PA *19035*

Clark DR & MRS Geoffrey E (Selz—Martha M Fuller)
Mls'64.Bost'77.Sb.Myf.H'60.Nu'68
☎ (603) 431-6626 . . Langeley Boardman House, 152 Middle St,
Portsmouth, NH *03801*

Clark MR & MRS George R (May D Howe) Ph.Rb.Ac.H'32.H'34
☎ (610) 520-9558 . . 14 Pond Lane, Bryn Mawr, PA *19010-1772*

Clark MR Gordon T—Y'62 . . . . | ☎ (212) 206-7913
MISS Alexandra C—at St Margaret's School, 55 W 11 St, Apt 6G,
PO Box 158, Tappahannock, VA *22560*. . . . . . . New York, NY
MR Timothy B—at 470 Argyle Av, PO Box 187, *10011*
Garrett Park, MD *20896* . . . . |

Clark MRS Grenville JR (Barnum—Hansen—Elizabeth Lamb)
Ws'87.Bost'90.Sm.My.Myc.Cy.K . . .of
☎ (617) 237-0092 . . 85 Grove St, Wellesley, MA *02181*
☎ (212) 799-4890 . . 35 W 90 St, Apt 7J, New York, NY *10024*

Clark MR & MRS H Nichols B (Trinkett Clark)
Conn'73.GeoW'76.H'69.Del'75.Del'82
☎ (757) 423-1729 . . 1650 Longwood Rd, Norfolk, VA *23508*

Clark MRS H Remsen (Efthymiadis—Helen R Clark)
☎ (011-30-1) 82-31-167 . . 7 Saripolou St, 106-82 Athens, Greece

Clark MR & MRS Henry C (Jennifer B Jordan)
P'78.Va'82.Nu'88.Cly.Ncd.Cr'81
☎ (212) 744-1345 . . 150 E 73 St, Apt 8A, New York, NY *10021-4362*

Clark MR & MRS Hervey Parke (Isabel A Pringle) Tcy.
☎ (415) 424-4428 . . 501 Portola Rd, Portola Valley, CA *94028*

Clark MR & MRS Howard L JR (Burke—Karen M | of ☎ (203)869-3508
Kaess) Rcn.Ri.Ln.Bost'67.Cl'68. . . . . 404 Round Hill Rd,
MR Howard L 3d—at Tulane . . . . Greenwich, CT
MR Edwin M Burke 3d—Geo'95—at *06831*
515 E 72 St, Apt 16D, New York, NY *10021* ☎ (561) 546-0385
MR James Van V Burke—at Georgetown . . . "Seaview"
9 N Beach Rd,
Hobe Sound, FL
33475

Clark MRS Huguette M (Gower—Huguette M Clark)
907 Fifth Av, New York, NY *10021*

Clark MRS J Dudley JR (Elizabeth C Grant) Hn . . .of
☎ (609) 924-2840 . . 42 Elm Rd, Princeton, NJ *08540*
"Believe It or Not" Harbour Island, Bahamas

Clark MR J Dudley 3d—Ty'63
☎ (603) 523-7776 . . Cardigan Mountain School, Canaan, NH *03741*

Clark MR & MRS J H Cullum (Nita C Prothro) Mls'91.Y'89
☎ (212) 860-5570 . . 1160 Fifth Av, Apt 610, New York, NY *10029*

Clark MR J T Jarod
☎ (415) 474-5663 . . 2200 Franklin St, San Francisco, CA *94109*

Clark MR & MRS James H JR (Tobian—Carolyn Levy) ⛵
☎ (214) 358-4706 . . 5381 Nakoma Dv, Dallas, TX *75209*

Clark MR & MRS James R (Caroline T Mitchell) Y'80.Cl'84.Y'80
☎ (011-44-171) 243-8717 . . 48 Bedford Gardens, London W8 7EH,
England

Clark MRS Jean Q (Eddy—Boas—Jean Q Clark) Btn.Cy.
☎ (617) 566-7261 . . 39 Rangeley Rd, Chestnut Hill, MA *02167-3017*

Clark MISS Jennifer U
☎ (914) 687-4011 . . 349 County Rte 2, Accord, NY *12404*

Clark MRS John Bigelow (Heath—Eves—Johanna V Smith)
☎ (860) 526-5098 . . Chester Village W, Apt 2203, 317 W Main St,
Chester, CT *06412*

Clark MRS John D (Betty J Webb)
☎ (314) 432-4653 . . 11928 Conway Rd, St Louis, MO *63131*

Clark MR & MRS John R (Cecily Geyelin) Ph.Me.H'38
☎ (610) 687-1119 . . 264 Abrahams Lane, Villanova, PA *19085*

Clark MR & MRS John Sheldon (Marguerite M Jenkins) Un.Lic.Pr.S.Pa'69
☎ (516) 922-9409 . . 317 Yacht Club Dv, Centre Island, Oyster Bay,
NY *11771*

Clark MRS John T JR (Elizabeth M Williams)
☎ (860) 688-1142 . . Delamere Woods Apt 317, 625 Palisado Av,
Windsor, CT *06095*

Clark DR & MRS Jonathan C D (Katherine Redwood Penovich)
Duke'81.JHop'89.Camb'72.Camb'76.Camb'82
☎ (913) 843-8803 . . 823 Broadview Dv, Lawrence, KS *66044*

Clark MRS Joseph Sill (Richey—Iris Cole) Ac.Pc.
☎ (215) CH7-8173 . . 440 Rex Av, Philadelphia, PA *19118*

Clark MRS Kerbey Williams (Kerbey Williams) Tex'55
☎ (214) 350-0535 . . 4624 Southern Av, Dallas, TX *75209*

Clark MR & MRS Laurance R (Anne H Dyrud) Lawr'83.Lawr'83 ⛵
☎ (617) 631-0002 . . 79 Pleasant St, Marblehead, MA *01945*

Clark MR & MRS Lewis H (Barbara H Hale) Cy.Chi.Ncd.H'47
☎ (617) 731-6818 . . 66 Fairgreen Place, Chestnut Hill, MA *02167*

Clark MR & MRS Lewis Hamilton JR (Caroline C Addison) Br'75.Edg.Ty'72
☎ (412) 741-0119 . . 211 Academy Av, Sewickley, PA *15143*

Clark DR Lowell F—Emory'74.RCollSurg'80 . . . . . | 1100 Mission Lane,
JUNIORS MISS Christina L. . . . . | Howey-In-The-Hills,
| FL *34737*

Clark MRS Margaret R (MacElree—Margaret A Robertson)
25 Buena Vista Rd, Asheville, NC *28803*

Clark MISS Margot S—Van'95 . . see R R Christman

Clark MR & MRS Marshall (Shepard—Vallory Willis) Rcn.Dth'43
☎ (203) 531-5504 . . 4 E Lyon Farm Dv, Greenwich, CT *06831*

Clark MRS Martha S (Martha Hilton Sulzby) Srb. . . | ☎ (205) 879-3242
MISS Melissa W—at ☎ (415) 921-2466 "Le Petit Relais"
1340 Lombard St, Apt 205, San Francisco, CA 3242 Country Club
94109 . . . . Rd, Birmingham,
AL *35213*

Clark MR & MRS Merrell E JR (V Hollister Logan) Wells'44.Ri.Y'44
☎ (212) PL5-4889 . . 45 Sutton Place S, New York, NY *10022*

Clark MRS Monika F (Grassman—Monika Fetzer) .
JUNIORS MISS Antonia H . . . . ☎ (415) 474-5533
1033 Green St,
San Francisco, CA
94133

Clark MISS (DR) Nina S—Cal'84.CalPsych'90
☎ (415) 563-0737 . . 308 Presidio Av, Apt 5, San Francisco, CA *94115*

Clark MR & MRS P Hamilton 3d (P Gail Jackson)
Ga'74.Me.Gm.Ct.Myf.H'71.Pa'76
☎ (716) 381-5861 . . "Hampton Court" 3565 Elmwood Av, Rochester, NY *14610*

Clark MRS Percy H JR (Edith Earle) Pa'43.Gm.Myf.
☎ (610) 526-0151 . . 41 Pond Lane, Bryn Mawr, PA *19010*

Clark MR & MRS Peter S I (Leah H Haggerty)
☎ (914) 763-9242 . . Box 80, Mead St, Waccabuc, NY *10597*

Clark MR Ralph E JR—Y'36.Cin'39 . . . . ☎ (303) 722-5893
MR William L—at ☎ (310) 459-2570 Porter House Apt
1547 Michael Lane, Pacific Palisades, CA *90272* 502, 1001 E Yale
Av, Denver, CO
80210-5828

Clark MR & MRS Raymond S (Gorman—Marjorie A A Pendleton)
B.Md.H'36.Y'39 . . of
☎ (410) 323-8079 . . 124 E Melrose Av, Apt B, Baltimore, MD *21212*
☎ (207) 284-5813 . . PO Box 216, Biddeford Pool, ME *04006-0216*

Clark MR & MRS Reed (Audrey A Iselin) Pr.Ri.Lic.An.USN'42 . . of
☎ (561) 546-4957 . . 4 Isle Ridge W, Hobe Sound, FL *33455*
☎ (516) 621-9376 . . 198 Valentine Lane, Glen Head, NY *11545*

Clark MRS Reuben B 3d (Arabella Huber) Me. ⚓
☎ (610) MI2-3816 . . 119 Llanfair Rd, Ardmore, PA *19003*

Clark MR & MRS Reuben B 4th (Linda H Child) Me.
☎ (610) 296-7878 . . 280 Winthrop Rd, Berwyn, PA *19312*

Clark MR & MRS Richard H (Hilary J Wickersham)
Stan'75.Vh.Dth'75.Stan'79
☎ (818) 799-6248 . . 876 S Grand Av, Pasadena, CA *91105*

Clark MR & MRS Robert G (Rebecca L Heckman)
Me.Thiel'70 . . . . ☎ (610) MI9-5063
MISS Catherine H—Rich'92.Me.— 233 St George's Rd,
☎ (610) 642-2374 Ardmore, PA *19003*
MR Robert G JR—Gm.Me.F&M'94. . . . .

Clark MR & MRS Robert Ober (Bennett—Virginia Allison) Y'26
☎ (801) 532-1091 . . 1217 Chandler Circle, Salt Lake City, UT *84103*

Clark MR & MRS Roosevelt L (Norma Taylor) Pa'48
☎ (609) 494-1689 . . "Heartsease" 16 Cedar Dv, Loveladies, NJ *08008*

Clark MR & MRS Russell B (Romalda B Whiton)
My.H'61. . . . . ☎ (508) 468-2366
MISS Laura H—at U of NH. . . . . 278 Cutler Rd,
MR Russell B JR . . . . PO Box 370,
Hamilton, MA
01936

Clark MR & MRS Samuel Adams (Roy—Hughes—Meredith M Dunlap)
Stan'49.Rcn.
☎ (209) 383-5668 . . 1085 Vermont Dv, Merced, CA *95340*

Clark MRS Stephen C JR (McGusty—Leib—Kathryn James)
☎ (540) 687-5928 . . PO Box 1180, Middleburg, VA *20118*

Clark MR & MRS Sydney P JR (Elizabeth S Frey)
Rby.H'51 . . . . of ☎ (203)288-5355
MISS Christina L—Sth'91 . . . . 78 N Lake Dv,
Hamden, CT *06517*
☎ (441) 238-0461
"Kailua"
22 Church Rd,
Southampton
SN 01, Bermuda

Clark MR & MRS Thomas C 3d (Elizabeth C Bartlett) Syr'76
☎ (510) 524-8050 . . 175 Ardmore Rd, Kensington, CA *94707*

Clark MR Thomas Hart—Me.R.Cry.Rc.Ph.Ty'72.Pa'76
☎ (610) 254-8581 . . 686 Glenmary Rd, Radnor, PA *19087*

Clark REV & MRS Walter D JR (Sarah A W Locke)
RMWmn'64.TexA&M'81.Va'61.VaTheo'67 . . . ☎ (540) 436-3797
MR Stephen S—Ty'92—at ☎ (210) 737-8338 "Locke Farm"
225 Laurel Heights Place, San Antonio, TX 532 Zion Church
78212 . . . . Rd, Maurertown,
MR Benjamin L—Ty'95—at ☎ (210) 737-8338 VA *22644*
225 Laurel Heights Place, San Antonio, TX
78212 . . . .

Clark MR & MRS Warren JR (Spiro—Elizabeth A Petersen)
Rdc'58.Mt.Wms'58.JHop'69.H'74.Geo'76
☎ (202) 537-1279 . . 2929 Macomb St NW, Washington, DC *20008*

Clark MR & MRS Warren H (Wiles—Claire C Barth)
Munich'50.Bur.Pcu.H'52
☎ (415) 775-3535 . . 1055 California St, San Francisco, CA *94108*

Clark MRS William H (Rosemary Dudley) . . . . Died at
Bennington, VT May 26'96

Clark MR William K—A.Tex'42.Stan'48
☎ (210) 826-0237 . . 4001 N New Braunfels Av, Apt 1404, San Antonio, TX *78209*

Clark MR & MRS William S (Polly R Luchsinger) Cal'43.Tcy.Dth'42.Dth'47
☎ (415) 931-2486 . . 2580 Vallejo St, San Francisco, CA *94123*

Clarke MRS Alexandra G (Alexandra Grinnell) . . . . ☎ (508) 636-8278
MR Christopher S Clark—at U of So Cal . . . . 409 Horseneck Rd,
Westport, MA
02790-1322

Clarke MR Amory Y . . see P B Fisher JR

Clarke MR & MRS Arthur M (Virginia B Brown)
Sbc.H'50 . . . . ☎ (508) 768-7008
MISS Virginia B—at ☎ (617) 524-7880 84 Choate St, Essex,
27 Kingsboro Park, Jamaica Plains, MA *02130* . MA *01929*
MR Thomas H—at ☎ (617) 236-4470
6 Gloucester St, Apt 6, Boston, MA *02115* . . . .
MR William G—at ☎ (415) 731-8332
864 Ashbury St, San Francisco, CA *94117*. . . . .

Clarke MR & MRS Arthur R H (Rosanna Schimenz)
Y'51.Loy'66 . . . . of ☎ (607)547-2148
MISS Elizabeth A—Nu'79—at "Houghton House"
☎ (011-39-743) 45948 . . Bazzano Sup 29, Box 182,
06049 Spoleto, PG, Italy . . . . Springfield Center,
NY *13468*
☎ (212) 986-8240
320 E 42 St,
New York, NY
10017

Clarke MRS Bolling B (E Bolling Byrd) Swth'49
807 Ridley Creek Dv, Media, PA *19063*

Clarke MR & MRS Charles F (Nelson—Katherine H Duffy) TexWmn'48.TexWmn'49.Un.Tv. W&L'38.Mich'40 . . . . ☎ (216) 321-0223 2262 Tudor Dv, Cleveland Heights, OH *44106*
 MISS Margaret—Box 3314, Boston, MA *02101* .

Clarke MR & MRS Charles F JR (Eleanor M O'Connor) On.Br'51 . . . . ☎ (847) 234-5288 234 W Westminster Rd, Lake Forest, IL *60045*
 MISS Jennifer A . . . .
 MR Timothy S . . . .

Clarke MR Charles F JR—Tv.Mich'81.H'86
 ☎ (216) 464-3139 . . 3046 Edgewood Rd, Pepper Pike, OH *44124*

Clarke MR Dumont—Myf.P'34
 Highland Farms, Apt D57, 200 Tabernacle Rd, Black Mountain, NC *28711*

Clarke MR & MRS Eliot C (Susanne M Low) K.Plg.Cc.Cly.H'51 . . . . ☎ (914) 677-9305 "Lithgow" Box 110, RD 1, Millbrook, NY *12545*
 JUNIORS MR Eliot C L . . . .

Clarke MR & MRS George M 3d (Sally K Larson) AmU'68.GaSt'72 . . . . 984 Springdale Rd NE, Atlanta, GA *30306*
 MISS Elizabeth L . . . .
 MR G Marshall—at Presby Coll . . . .

Clarke MRS Jeremiah (Virginia Béguelin) Ncd.Ht.Dc. . . . . ☎ (401) 846-1177 78 Church St, Newport, RI *02840*
 MR Jeremiah JR—RISD'58 . . . .
 MR John W—Ht.Rv.BaldW'68 . . . .

Clarke MR Laughlin H . . see P B Fisher JR

Clarke MR & MRS Laurence W JR (Ricketts—Helen Payne) Yn.Y'45w
 ☎ (561) 369-5407 . . 5311 Osprey Dv, Ocean Ridge, FL *33435*

Clarke MRS Lewis A (Doris B White) Pn.
 12 Pinecroft Rd, Greenwich, CT *06830*

Clarke MISS Margot . . see C A Wright

Clarke MRS Mary Louise (Mary Louise Foulk) WVa'41 . . . . ☎ (404) 231-0991 3770 Peachtree Rd NE, Apt 2, Atlanta, GA *30319*
 MR Campbell P—Merc'84—at
 ☎ (404) 351-7666 . . 1907 Claremont St NW, Atlanta, GA *30318* . . . .

Clarke MISS Penelope . . see MRS E B Gardner

Clarke MRS Phillips H (Suzanne C Hill) Cda. . . . . . ☎ (202) 363-6765 4000 Massachusetts Av NW, Apt 231, Washington, DC *20016*
 MISS Suzanne C . . . .
 MR John P H—Cc.Woff'70 . . . .

Clarke MR & MRS Phillips H 3d (Yazmet Gerena Colón-Nevares) Loy'80.Ct.Mt.Cc.Wms'68.Pa'74
 ☎ (212) 570-9614 . . 125 E 81 St, New York, NY *10028*

Clarke MR & MRS R Semmes (Constance M Kilbourn) Plg.Cl'41 . . . . ☎ (201) 744-5059 15 Chester Rd, Upper Montclair, NJ *07043*
 MISS Catherine K . . . .

Clarke MR & MRS Richard S (Statter—Amy C Plant) Cl'33
 ☎ (206) 441-4666 . . 2100 Third Av, Seattle, WA *98121*

Clarke MR & MRS Thomas C (Tullis—Schurz— Robin S Rowan) V'60.H'53.H'59 . . . . ☎ (410) 819-0304 "The Reach" 8850 Marengo Farm Rd, Easton, MD *21601*
 MISS Tracy Tullis—Br'86—at
 148 Sterling Place, Brooklyn, NY *11217* . . . .
 MR Paul R Tullis—Cal'92—at 1641—18 St, San Francisco, CA *94107* . . . .

Clarke MR & MRS Thurston B (Antonia R Bullard) Ox'76.Y.'68.Lond'69
 ☎ (518) 963-7403 . . 406 Point Rd, Willsboro, NY *12996*

Clarke MISS Victoria A L . . see P B Fisher JR

Clarke MRS William N (Andrée de L Marconnet) Nancy'42.Unn.
 ☎ (207) 633-2213 . . West Side Dv, Box 75A, Boothbay, Trevett Island, ME *04571*

Clarkson MR & MRS Andrew M (Carole F Grant) Ox'60.H'66 . . . . ☎ (203) 966-4138 328 Greenley St, New Canaan, CT *06840*
 MISS Jennifer M . . . .
 JUNIORS MR William M . . . .

Clarkson DR & MRS Bayard D (Virginia L Clark) LIU'70.Pr.S.Ri.Lm.Ds.Cly.Y'48.Cl'52 . . of
 ☎ (516) 676-2779 . . 223 Piping Rock Rd, Glen Head, NY *11545*
 ☎ (212) 753-9565 . . 45 Sutton Place S, New York, NY *10022*

Clarkson MR & MRS Christopher (Hitt—Emmet—Kubie—Knox— Evelyn B Clark) Lx.Srb.
 ☎ (860) 526-2033 . . PO Box 743, Old Lyme, CT *06371*

Clarkson MISS Courtney S—Cal'73.Sfy.
 ☎ (415) 921-3610 . . 2416 Bush St, San Francisco, CA *94115*

Clarkson MR & MRS Geoffrey L (Huffard—Sylvia M Bullock) Colby'78.NCar'68 . . . . ☎ (203) 869-6304 53 Old Mill Rd, Greenwich, CT *06831*
 MR Geoffrey L JR—at Salem, OR . . . .

Clarkson MRS John L (Hinchman—Warner—Julia Polk)
 ☎ (941) 261-7036 . . 1930 Gulf Shore Blvd N, Apt 203C, Naples, FL *34102-4640*

Clarkson MRS Robert L JR (Murphy—Joan M Le Roy) Pr.S.Cly.Cda.
 ☎ (516) 922-3446 . . 344 Centre Island Rd, Centre Island, Oyster Bay, NY *11771*

Clarkson MR & MRS Robert L 3d (Teresa M Curran)
 ☎ (603) 363-8212 . . N Shore Rd, Spofford, NH *03462*

Clarkson MRS William F (Mary A Robinson) Ht.Ncd. . . . . ☎ (919) 542-3785 584 Fearrington Post, Fearrington Village, NC *27312-8570*
 MISS Margaret F—Sim'87—at ☎ (212) 725-8818 207 E 30 St, Apt 8C, New York, NY *10016* . . .
 MISS Catherine F—WConn'91—at
 ☎ (415) 923-1415 . . 1246 Bush St, San Francisco, CA *94109* . . . .

Clarkson MR & MRS William M E (Elisabeth A Hudnut) Wils'47.Ts.Bf.G.Tor'47 . . of
 ☎ (716) 885-5283 . . 156 Bryant St, Buffalo, NY *14222*
 ☎ (518) 251-2362 . . "Log House" Windover, North Creek, NY *12853*

Clary MR & MRS Everett B (Mary De Friest) Stan'44.Vh.Stan'43.Stan'49 . . of
 ☎ (818) 799-3407 . . 1127 S Orange Grove Blvd, Pasadena, CA *91105*
 ☎ (619) 765-1230 . . "Indian Hill" 3220 Pine Hills Rd, Julian, CA *92036*
 ☎ (619) 346-5270 . . Marrakesh Country Club, 47-458 Medina Dv E, Palm Desert, CA *92260*

Classen DR & MRS Charles H (Jeanne C Crook) Me.Gm.P'34.JHop'38
 ☎ (610) 525-2898 . . 310 Countryview Dv, Bryn Mawr, PA *19010*

Classen DR David C—Me.Myf.Va'78.Va'82
☎ (801) 532-3633 . . 561 E Northmont Way, Salt Lake City, UT *84103*
Classen MR & MRS H Ward (Sibley Gillis)
Ty'81.Pa'87.Elk.Md.Ty'82.CathU'85.Pa'90
☎ (410) 337-2273 . . 7822 Chelsea St, Ruxton, MD *21204*
Classen MR & MRS John N (Margaret T Speer) | ☎ (410) 377-8899
Elk.Rr.P'38.JHop'42 . . . . | 6517 Montrose Av,
DR J Barthelow—Elk.Md'83.Md'88 . . . . | Baltimore, MD
MR Taylor S—Elk.Md.NCar'86 . . . . | *21212*
Clattenburg MISS Julie A—Av'tt'66
☎ (603) 924-7411 . . 20 Old Jaffrey Rd, Peterborough, NH *03458*
Clattenburg MR & MRS Richard N (Henrietta R Battle) H'35.Pa'38
☎ (603) 924-7338 . . 243 River Mead Rd, Peterborough, NH *03458*
Clattenburg MR Theodore—Pe.Pc.Me.Sar.Rv.Pa'31
☎ (610) 527-1393 . . 74 Pasture Lane, Apt 225, Bryn Mawr,
PA *19010-1766*
Clattenburg MR & MRS Theodore JR (Anita G Martinez)
Pc.Rv.Cw.H'63.Stan'66
505 Cresheim Valley Rd, Wyndmoor, PA *19038*
Claude MR & MRS Abram J (Thorson—C Elizabeth | ☎ (914) 232-6602
James) NCar'57.Bgt.Y.'52 . . . . | 9 Bedford Rd,
MR Robert D Thorson JR—Bgt.Vt'88 . . . . | Katonah, NY *10536*
Claude MRS Dee (Harding—Mary H Dee) . . . . | ☎ (212) 734-9686
MR Andrews . . . . | 28 E 73 St,
| New York, NY
| *10021*
Clawson MR & MRS Harry Q M (Mary Louise Kirkland) Rdc'50.Ht.Ncd.
☎ (803) 723-4988 . . 2½ Legare St, Charleston, SC *29401*
Clawson MR William W
☎ (408) 270-5179 . . 2758 Gumdrop Dv, San Jose, CA *95148*
Claxton MRS Oliver H P (Dorothy B Fiske)
☎ (802) 824-5203 . . Box 3, South Londonderry, VT *05155*
Clay MR & MRS Edward B JR (Julia J Myers) RMWmn'47.Ph.Sg.Ac.P'47
☎ (215) AD3-0566 . . 513 Auburn Av, Wyndmoor, PA *19038*
Clay MRS George R (Ann C Robinson) V'47 . . . . . . | ☎ (802) 362-1656
MISS Abigail H . . . . | ''Wild Farm''
MR W Clement . . . . | RD 2, Arlington, VT
| *05250*
Clay MR George R—Hn.H'43 . . of
☎ (802) 362-1758 . . Prospect St, Box 992, Manchester, VT *05254*
☎ (617) 661-8167 . . 863 Massachusetts Av, Apt 23, Cambridge,
MA *02139*
Clay MR Henry J—Un.B.Pr.Lic.Plg.U'39.Va'42 . . of
☎ (212) 753-4957 . . 200 E 66 St, New York, NY *10021*
☎ (516) 676-6320 . . 1 Fox Ridge Rd, Locust Valley, NY *11560*
Clay MR & MRS John W JR (Anne J Campbell) | ☎ (615) 292-6080
Van'65.Van'63 . . . . | 418 Ellendale Dv,
MISS Eleanor S . . . . | Nashville, TN *37205*
MR Stewart C
Clay MR & MRS Jonathan C (Whitney A Fite) Sth'86.H'84
267 W 89 St, New York, NY *10024*
Clay MR & MRS Peter E (M Kathleen Yuscavage)
Ws'78.Bost'81.Mit'78.H'82
☎ (410) 992-8916 . . 10315 Tower Hill Court, Ellicott City, MD *21042*
Clay MR & MRS Peter M (Julie F Miller) Tufts'81.Sbc.Tufts'79
☎ (508) 468-5160 . . 14 Arbor St, Wenham, MA *01984*

Clay MR & MRS Philip G (H Lydia Kenworthy) | ☎ (203) 966-5653
LakeF'75.DU'74 . . . . | 38 Carriage Lane,
JUNIORS MISS Elizabeth S . . . . | New Canaan, CT
| *06840*
Clay MR & MRS William D (Mary J Rogers) On.Fy.
☎ (847) 234-5466 . . 146 E Woodland Rd, Lake Bluff, IL *60044*
Clay MR & MRS William L JR (Helen LeR Smith) | ☎ (516) 862-9030
Cc.Cly.Cda.Va'30 . . . . | PO Box 325,
MR William L 3d—Cc.W&L'66—at | St James, NY *11780*
☎ (718) 273-5467 . . 1126 Richmond Terr,
Staten Island, NY *10310* . . . . |
Clayman MR & MRS John M (Lalande L Keeshan) Bost'75.Ny.Nyc.Dth'75
☎ (508) 921-1659 . . 804 Hale St, Beverly Farms, MA *01915*
Claypoole MRS Julie G (Julia K Gaines) | ☎ (510) 944-1906
Penn'68.Ncd. . . . . | 3012 Peachwillow
MISS Katherine C K . . . . | Lane, Walnut Creek,
| CA *94598*
Clayton MR & MRS Charles Trueheart JR (Louise H Bradford)
Ala'62.Cy.Ala'61
☎ (205) 871-4271 . . 2950 Canterbury Rd, Birmingham, AL *35223*
Clayton MR & MRS J O'Neal JR (Marguerite V Huggins) Ala'82.Ala'82
☎ (615) 352-1484 . . 120 Windsor Dv, Nashville, TN *37205*
Clayton MISS Martha A . . see R E Noble
Clayton MR & MRS Theodore M (Howell—Anne R Thomas) O'More'75
☎ (615) 298-1027 . . 1201 Nichol Lane, Nashville, TN *37205*
Claytor MRS Norris Vaux (Lynda K Leonard) PhilaArt'69.Mt.
☎ (610) 525-6735 . . 1800 Montgomery Av, Villanova, PA *19085*
Claytor MR Norris Vaux—Ssk.Urs'64 | ☎ (610) 687-2435
MISS Cassandra Nierncée—at ☎ (610) 354-9771 | ''Roconante Farm''
200 Prince Frederick Blvd, Apt H3, | Brower Rd,
King of Prussia, PA *19406* . . . . | Radnor, PA *19087*
MR Thomas Ash—Colby'85 . . . . |
MR Warren Ingersoll—Colby'92 ⚓—at |
U of Pa Grad . . . . |
Claytor DR & MRS R Brannon (Sarah A Hefford)
StM'85.P'93.Colby'88.Jef'96
☎ (508) 852-2602 . . 176 Parker Av, Holden, MA *01520*
Cleavenger MR & MRS Timothy Q (Margaret R Anderson)
MtH'78.Sc.Wa.SFrArt'75
☎ (630) 377-7387 . . ''Broadmead'' Fletcher Rd, Wayne, IL *60184*
Cleeve MR Henry J . . . . | ☎ (011-353-56)
MISS Thalia O . . . . | 26102
| ''The Old Rectory''
| Gowran,
| Co Kilkenny, Ireland
Clegg MRS Charles B (Jeannette L Huffman)
☎ (941) 481-6076 . . Shell Point Village, 512 Periwinkle Court,
Ft Myers, FL *33908*
Clein MR & MRS Mark P (Nancy E Lemann)
210 W 101 St, Apt 10G, New York, NY *10025*
Clelland MR & MRS Richard C (Snipes—Anne C | ☎ (610) 687-1497
Buel) Swth'52.Pa'66.Csn.Ham'44.Pa'56 . . . . . . | 530 Hilaire Rd,
MISS Susan E—at 210 W 78 St, New York, NY | St Davids, PA
10024 . . . . | *19087*
Clement MRS Allen T JR (E Stephanie Jones) Ws'44
☎ (301) 972-3931 . . ''Lynwood Farm'' 25400 Frederick Rd, Clarksburg,
MD *20871*

Clement MR & MRS C Francis (André—Lucienne Van Muysen)
Me.Gm.Wt.Rv.Fw.Cw.Cspa.
☎ (610) 642-5099 . . 100 Grays Lane, Haverford, PA *19041*

Clement MISS Celeste
☎ (610) 293-0498 . . "Three Falls" 615 King of Prussia Rd, Radnor, PA *19087*

Clement MR & MRS Charles F 3d (Sadtler—Barbara A Koltes)
Minn'61.Me.Wt.Rv.P'65.Cl'67
☎ (610) 408-0522 . . 655 Augusta Court, Berwyn, PA *19312*

Clement MISS Constance—Hlns'70
☎ (203) 624-2157 . . 123 York St, Apt 17B, New Haven, CT *06511*

Clement MISS Damaris D—Rol'72.Pep'93.Dar.
☎ (213) 654-4606 . . 950 N Kings Rd, Apt 338, Los Angeles, CA *90069*

Clement MR & MRS Danforth (Patricia Harshman) GeoW'48.Nev'74
☎ (602) 961-9630 . . 4502 E Chuckwalla Canyon, Phoenix, AZ *85044*

Clement MRS David H (Constance Chambers) Cly.Ncd.
☎ (203) 787-3736 . . 237 E Rock Rd, New Haven, CT *06511*

Clement MR Edward S—Bab'71
☎ (860) 923-2899 . . 47 Chase Rd, PO Box 423, Thompson, CT *06277*

Clement MR Franklin G—On.Mit'23
☎ (561) 276-7051 . . 3951 N Ocean Blvd, Apt 402, Delray Beach, FL *33483*

Clement MR Frederick T J . . . . Died at Bryn Mawr, PA Jan 5'96

Clement MRS Frederick T J (McComas—Cordelia Ettl)
☎ (610) MI2-0758 . . 1407 Monk Rd, Gladwyne, PA *19035*

Clement MR & MRS Frederick T J JR (Despina Soppas) P'75.Me.Myf.P'72
☎ (610) 525-0826 . . 112 Browning Lane, Rosemont, PA *19010-1008*

Clement MRS Harold T JR (Sylvia I Wheeler) G.
☎ (716) 882-2631 . . 29 Oakland Place, Buffalo, NY *14222*

Clement MR & MRS (DR) Henry R (Elizabeth M Shea) Ty'75.Mass'85.Ty'74
☎ (413) 467-3162 . . "The Ledges" 54 Porter St, Granby, MA *01033*

Clement MRS James H (Ida L Larkin) A.
☎ (512) 592-6733 . . King Ranch, Kingsville, TX *78363*

Clement MRS Jill (Stephenie G Bughman) . . . . | ☎ (401) 348-2172
MR Edward S JR—Vt'91 . . . . | 199 Watch Hill Rd,
MR Taylor W—Mont'95 . . . . | Watch Hill, RI
| *02891-5030*

Clement MR John K 3d—Me.Rc.Wt.Ty'66 . . . . | ☎ (610) 647-8575
JUNIORS MR Timothy R . . . . | Leopard Lake,
| Berwyn, PA *19312*

Clement MISS Lisa T—Me.Myf.
☎ (610) 525-3304 . . Bryn Mawr Terrace, Rm 75, Haverford & Rugby Rds, Bryn Mawr, PA *19010*

Clement MISS Louise Y . . see MRS W S Sobel

Clement MRS Mary D (Mary M Duncan) | ☎ (212) 628-7143
Swb'65.CUNY'92 . . . . | 130 E 75 St,
MR James M—P.'96—☎ (212) 861-1926 . . . . . . | New York, NY
| *10021*

Clement MR Norman—Vh.Yn.Y'42.H'48
☎ (818) 799-9597 . . 645 S San Rafael Av, Pasadena, CA *91105*

Clement MR & MRS Peter W (Soffer—Stephanie L Doering)
Rc.Me.Wt.Rit'72
☎ (610) 642-0515 . . Leitrim Cottage, 519 Rose Lane, Haverford, PA *19041* . . MRS absent

Clement MR & MRS Peter Wickham (Victoria A Chave)
DU'71.RISD'84.Y'68.Pa'74
☎ (203) 776-0110 . . 230 Everit St, New Haven, CT *06511*

Clement MR Philip W (Charles F 3d) . . . . . Married at Salt Lake City, UT
Allen MISS Cheryl (Earl) . . . . Oct 22'94

Clement MR & MRS Richard M (Karen A Bryan) | ☎ (011-52-415)
MooreArt'71.FlaSt'69 . . . . | 25260
JUNIORS MR Max . . . . | Apdo 742,
JUNIORS MR Ian T . . . . | San Miguel de
| Allende, GTO
| 37700, Mexico

Clement MR Samuel B—Me.Laf'80
☎ (610) 526-6248 . . 105 Fairfax Rd, Rosemont, PA *19010*

Clement MRS Stephen M 2d (Barbara Pierce) St.
☎ (704) 859-5242 . . Hunting Wood, Box 1539, Tryon, NC *28782*

Clement MR & MRS Stephen M 3d (Sally B Dayton)
V'71.Sim'75.Nu'85.C.Cs.Y.'66.UTheo'70.H'77
☎ (212) 628-3365 . . 950 Park Av, New York, NY *10028*

Clement MR & MRS Thomas S (Marjorie F McCourt) RI'80.Wash'75
☎ (610) 527-4075 . . 718 Sproul Rd, Bryn Mawr, PA *19010*

Clément-Bayard MISS Allegra—Ken'95 . . see W F Kiefer JR

Clément-Bayard MISS Aurelie . . see W F Kiefer JR

Clements MRS Carter (Barbara G Carter) Sth'49
☎ (216) 292-4941 . . 34112 Chagrin Blvd, Apt 7108, Moreland Hills, OH *44022*

Clements MISS Leslie H . . see J C Bennett JR

Clements MISS Ninive M . . see B P Dohrmann

Clements MR R Caird . . see W H Hay

Clements DR & MRS Rex S JR (Anne L Whitney) | ☎ (215) 598-3597
ColbyS'61.Aht'60.Pa'64 . . . . | "Buttonwood
MR George W—at 54 Old South St, Northampton, | Bend"
MA *01060* . . . . | 1036 Durham Rd,
MR Nicholas S . . . . | PO Box 343,
| Pineville, PA *18946*

Clements MR & MRS Richard F (Charlotte Beard)
36 Stilehall Gardens, Chiswick, London W4, England

Clements MRS Robert M (Helen Teagle) Sth'30.It.Kt.
☎ (216) 991-4545 . . 3119 Kingsley Rd, Cleveland, OH *44122*

Clements MR & MRS Robert M (Anne D Borie) | ☎ (216) 338-8194
MooreArt'75.Pc.Va'72 . . . . | 116 Southwyck Dv,
JUNIORS MR MacMillan II . . . . | Chagrin Falls, OH
JUNIORS MR Jay R B . . . . | *44022*

Clements MR & MRS Robert M JR (Gutcheon—Beth | ☎ (415) 346-3530
M Richardson) Rdc'67.Fr.Ncd.P'65 . . . . | 3530 Washington St,
MISS Alice B—at 177 Ludlow St, Apt 2C, | San Francisco, CA
New York, NY *10002* . . . . | *94118-1849*
MR John B—at Princeton . . . . |
MR David S Gutcheon—at 173 Sullivan St, |
New York, NY *10012* . . . . |

Clements MR & MRS William M (Virginia L Krikorian) UWash'58
☎ (520) 881-6699 . . 40 N Plaza Del Encanto, Tucson, AZ *85716*

Clements MR William W—Uncl.P'48
☎ (415) 922-1433 . . 2068 Vallejo St, San Francisco, CA *94123*

Clements MR & MRS William W (J Karen Johnson) | ☎ (602) 258-1089
Vt'60.Stan'58.H'61 . . . . | 2224 Encanto Dv
MISS Kristin E—at ☎ (415) 771-3402 | NE, Phoenix, AZ
1188 Pacific Av, San Francisco, CA *94133* . . . . | *85007*

Clements DR & MRS William W JR (Nancy B Muth)
Ws'56.Me.Wes'53.Jef'58
☎ (610) 687-1947 . . 517 Tory Hill Rd, Devon, PA *19333*

Clementson MRS Merrill K (Manning—Pierce—Florence T Heaton)
☎ (415) 854-4225 . . 1240 Sharon Park Dv, Menlo Park, CA *94025*

Clemm DR & MRS F Michael von (Louisa B Hunnewell) B.H'56.Ox'62
☎ (011-44-171) 727-7723 . . 58 Bedford Gardens, London W8, England

Clemmer MR & MRS Calvin L (C Jean P Walton) Dar.
☎ (941) 263-1722 . . 275 Bahia Point, Naples, FL *34103*

Clemmer DR & MRS Richard I JR (Virginia S Brodhead) BMr'66.Jef'71.Wes'67.Jef'71 . . . . . .
MISS Kathryn A . . . .
JUNIORS MISS Charity E . . . .
JUNIORS MR Andrew B . . . .
☎ (302) 655-9630
108 Alapocas Dv,
Wilmington, DE
19803

Clemo MR & MRS Robert W (Deborah M Paul)
SCal'70.Vh.SCal'69 . . . .
MR Christopher P . . . .
MR Matthew L . . . .
☎ (818) 790-2885
533 Georgian Rd,
Flintridge, CA
91011

Clemson MR G Scott—H'77 . . see D H Mackenzie

Clemson MASTER Gray Alan (g—Duncan H Mackenzie) . . . . . . Born at Baltimore, MD Oct 13'95

Clephane MRS Arthur H (Hamilton—Anne C Laird) Me.
☎ (610) 642-5539 . . 421 Berkley Rd, Haverford, PA *19041*

Clephane MRS Caroline Chapin (Caroline Chapin)
Ny.Cda. . . . .
MR David Chapin—Snc.—at Trinity . . . .
☎ (212) 988-1818
785 Park Av,
New York, NY
10021

Cleveland MR & MRS Blair (Alward—Geraldine Bartlett) Wms'38
☎ (508) 369-7819 . . 29 Indian Hill Rd, Carlisle, MA *01741*

Cleveland MR & MRS Clement 4th (Pershing—Shirley H Gay) Menlo'69
☎ (970) 920-1333 . . 1445 Red Butte Dv, Aspen, CO *81611*

Cleveland MR & MRS Donald L (Caroline Coley)
NCar'37.Fic.Cly. . . . .
MR Donald L JR . . . .
☎ (203) 869-0221
24 Wooddale Rd,
Greenwich, CT
06830

Cleveland MR & MRS Douglas B (Sara C Ross) CtCol'77.Cc.CtCol'77
☎ (703) 556-8231 . . The Laurels, 8328 Georgetown Pike, McLean, VA *22102*

Cleveland MR & MRS Robert G (Mary A Manning)
Rdc'42.Cvc.Mt.Sl.Rol'32
☎ (202) 332-1217 . . 2911 Garfield St NW, Washington, DC *20008*

Clevenger MR & MRS William M (Mary W Thomas)
Sth'62.H'66.P'53.Ox'66 . . . .
MISS Caroline Murrie—Stan'91—at U of Pa Grad
MR James Thomas—HWSth'90—at
☎ (410) 268-9385 . . 1611 Cedar Park Rd,
Annapolis, MD *21401* . . . .
MR Andrew Whitall—Hav'93—at
☎ (212) 353-3327 . . 526 E 11 St, Apt 2,
New York, NY *10009* . . . .
☎ (301) 855-8352
Patuxent Manor,
3820 Lower
Marlboro Rd,
Owings, MD *20736*

Clewe DR Thomas H—Stan'49 . . . .
MISS Jane E—P'77—at 1032 Junipero Av,
Long Beach, CA *90804* . . . .
MR Craig T—Tul'81—at ☎ (415) 571-9858
1232 S Norfolk St, San Mateo, CA *94403* . . . . .
☎ (415) 328-1918
1450 Oak Creek Dv,
Apt 308,
Palo Alto, CA
94304

Clews MRS Henrietta T (Henrietta B Thompson)
Pa'67.Y'82 . . . .
MISS Margaret T—Presc'93 . . . .
MISS Leta H—at Earlham Coll . . . .
MISS Charlotte L—at Cornell . . . .
MR Henry A—StJ'93 . . . .
☎ (207) 374-2473
''Tall Trees''
Blue Hill, ME
04614

Clews MR & MRS M Madison (Margaret Strawbridge) Srb.Camb'38.Pa'49 . . . .
MISS Sylvia . . . .
☎ (603) 643-1957
Kendal at Hanover
212, 80 Lyme Rd,
Hanover, NH *03755*

Clifford MR & MRS Andrew H (Caroline C Shields)
Va'87.HampSydney'84.WakeF'90
6609 Van Buren Av, Richmond, VA *23226-3423*

Clifford MR & MRS H Pier (Judith H Adams)
V'53.Ph.Hn.H'51.Cl'52 . . . .
MISS Katherine H—at ☎ (718) 624-6641
344 Sackett St, Apt 2, Brooklyn, NY *11231* . . . .
MR Christopher R . . . .
MR Anthony S—at ☎ (215) 482-3773
4444 Main St, Apt B, Philadelphia, PA *19127* . .
☎ (610) 688-3902
446 Huston Rd,
Radnor, PA *19087*

Clifford MRS Henry H (Lucetta R Andrews) MtH'30
☎ (818) 792-4096 . . Villa Gardens Apt 421, 842 E Villa St, Pasadena, CA *91101-1259*

Clifford MR & MRS John C (Katherine O'N Lumaghi) NH'65.Tufts'69 . . . .
MISS Katherine D . . . .
MISS Elizabeth L . . . .
MR John JR . . . .
☎ (603) 964-8928
PO Box 287,
Rye Beach, NH
03871

Clifford MISS Mary F
☎ (314) 862-1756 . . 7708 Shirley Dv, Apt 1E, St Louis, MO *63105-2045*

Clifford DR & MRS Milton Henry (Lydia Höst)
Cy.Hn.H'27 . . . .
MISS Vera E . . . .
☎ (617) 275-5670
204 Badger Terr,
Bedford, MA
01730-1285

Clifford MR & MRS Nicholas R (Deborah Pickman)
Rdc'57.P'52 . . . .
MISS Rebecca H—at 88 Lexington Av, Apt 12F,
New York, NY *10016* . . . .
☎ (802) 453-4092
70 East St,
New Haven, VT
05742

Clifford MR & MRS O Morton (Judith R Kinsella)
Wash'46 . . . .
MR Peter Z—Van'83.Wash'87—at
☎ (773) 871-6404 . . 636 W Arlington Place,
Apt 40, Chicago, IL *60614* . . . .
☎ (314) 725-0768
8148 Kingsbury
Blvd, St Louis, MO
63105

Clifford MRS Susan L Burr (Susan L Burr) Ncd. . . . .
JUNIORS MR Henry F S—at U of Md College Park
JUNIORS MR George W B . . . .
☎ (410) 820-8946
''Kingston House''
30595 Kingston Rd,
Easton, MD *21601*

Clifford MRS Thomas C (Blake—Wynanda Bulkley)
☎ (802) 484-5562 . . ''Craggle Ridge Farm'' Reading, VT *05062*

Clinch MRS N Bayard (Virginia L Campbell)
4405 Larchmont Av, Dallas, TX *75205*

Cline MR & MRS Guernsey C (Whittemore—Florence A Hoskins)
☎ (561) 276-5082 . . 2950 Polo Dv, Gulf Stream, FL *33483*

Clinnin MR John W—Elk.Gi.Md.Md'76 ⚓
☎ (410) 435-4555 . . 5712 Roland Av, Baltimore, MD *21210*

Clinton THE PRESIDENT & MRS William J B (Hillary Rodham) Ws'69.Y'73.Geo'68.Ox'70.Y'73 . . . . . ☎ (202) 456-1414 The White House, Washington, DC *20500*
MISS Chelsea V—at Sidwell Friends . . . .

Close MR David P—Cvc.Plg.StJ.Wms'38.Cl'42 . . . . ☎ (540) 937-5567 ''Hungry Run Farm'' 40 Hungry Run Farm Lane, Amissville, VA *20106*
MISS Barbara E—Wms'84 . . . .

Close MR & MRS Edward B (Anne Merryweather) Sth'50.Ln.Y'49 . . . . of ☎ (303)771-0216 4875 S Fairfax Lane, Littleton, CO *80121*
MR Montgomery B—at 2172 Pacific Av, Apt 2, San Francisco, CA *94115* . . . . ☎ (970) 926-2017 0028 Eagle Crest Rd, Edwards, CO *81632*

Close DR & MRS William T (Bettine Moore) Cl'51
☎ (307) 276-5454 . . Box 158, Big Piney, WY *83113*

Closson MR & MRS A Burton JR (Reynolds—Susan A Mehnert) Wells'53.Unn.Cw.Y'52
☎ (513) 831-4745 . . 9665 Shawnee Run Rd, Cincinnati, OH *45243*

Closson MISS Fabia B . . see W W Windle

Closson MR Lawrence F . . see W W Windle

Clothier MRS Ann H (Lenssen—Ogden—Ann H Clothier) Pa'56
☎ (610) 688-0186 . . 428 West Av, Wayne, PA *19087-3208*

Clothier MR & MRS Isaac H 4th (Barbara K Massey) Rose'81.VillaN'90.Ph.Rc.Me.P'54.Pa'57
☎ (610) 525-8995 . . 611 Winsford Rd, Bryn Mawr, PA *19010*

Clothier MR & MRS Robert C JR (Maree T Horgan) Pa'53.Me.P.
☎ (610) MI2-9976 . . 24 Buck Lane, Haverford, PA *19041*

Clothier MR & MRS Robert C 3d (Anne C Freeman) Y'86.Pa'91.Me.P.'83.Ch'89
☎ (215) 247-3706 . . 108 W Springfield Av, Philadelphia, PA *19118*

Clothier MR & MRS William J (Goldstein—Evelyn Baram) PCPS'61.VillaN'80.Rc.Me.Nrr.Rb.Stc. T.Rv.Cw.Wt.Ac.H.'38 . . . . of ☎ (610)933-4580 ''Valley Hill Farm'' PO Box 8, Valley Forge, PA *19481*
MISS Steffanie E—at 1057 Emerson St, Denver, CO *80218* . . . . ☎ (212) 308-8787 200 E 66 St, New York, NY *10021*
MR Morris—at 200 E 61 St, Apt 40F, New York, NY *10021* . . . .

Clotworthy MR & MRS C Baker JR (Frances D Slinghuff) Mv.Cda.JHop'35
1308 Los Arboles NW, Albuquerque, NM *87107*

Clough MR & MRS Anson M (Siebert—Margaret M Anderson)
☎ (860) 232-5086 . . 275 Steele Rd, West Hartford, CT *06117*

Clough MR & MRS Anson W (Nancy A Peterson) Upsala'62 . . . . ☎ (508) 255-3111 ''Solbaken'' PO Box 1076, 11 Baxter Lane, East Orleans, MA *02643-1076*
MISS Alice J—Vt'88 . . . .

Clough MR & MRS Peter A (Lisa J Grant) Mid'86
☎ (215) 545-8164 . . 2210 Mt Vernon St, Philadelphia, PA *19130*

Clough MR Walter J—L.Ste.Cr'63 ⛵ . . . . ☎ (908) 219-8769 16 Holly St, Rumson, NJ *07760*
MR William McN—Hob'90 . . . .
MR Anson C—Bates'92—at ☎ (617) 738-8433 37 Dwight St, Brookline, MA *02146* . . . .
MR Walter J JR—at Middlebury . . . .

Clover MR & MRS C Chandler (Lois Smith) La'47.La'47
☎ (601) 366-7996 . . 15 The Barrington, 1200 Meadowbrook Rd, Jackson, MS *39206*

Clow MR & MRS Christopher B (Annette W Morriss) Stan'69.Y'76.Stan'72.Ch'83
☎ (914) 855-9693 . . 5 Quaker Lake Rd, Pawling, NY *12564*

Clow MR & MRS Gerald C (Frazier—Barbara G Hand) Mund'83.Y'70 . . . . 228 Farnam Rd, Lakeville, CT *06039*
JUNIORS MISS Elizabeth McN—at Hotchkiss . . . .
JUNIORS MR Christopher C—at U of Vt . . . .

Clow MR Harry B—On.Sr.Cho.Cas.Y'23 . . of
☎ (847) 234-0243 . . ''Out of Bounds'' Shoreacres Rd, Lake Bluff, IL *60044*
☎ (619) 346-6591 . . 73-543 Juniper St, Palm Desert, CA *92260*

Clow MISS Lenore B—LoyMmt'76
203 Halton Lane, Watsonville, CA *95076*

Clowes MR Allen W—Hn.H'39
☎ (317) 925-1113 . . ''Westerley'' 3744 Spring Hollow Rd, Golden Hill, Indianapolis, IN *46208*

Clowes MRS George H A (Margaret G Jackson) BMr'37
☎ (508) 785-0039 . . 19 Pegan Lane, Box 337, Dover, MA *02030-0337*

Clowney MR & MRS Frank S JR (Eleanor P Atwood) P'45
☎ (203) 637-9967 . . 40 Willowmere Circle, Riverside, CT *06878*

Clucas MISS Catherine de G . . see C J Kittredge

Clucas MRS Margaret M (Sherwood—Margaret G Moore)
☎ (860) 434-5146 . . 132 Brush Hill Rd, Lyme, CT *06371*

Cluett MRS E Harold (Johnson—Catharine H ReQua)
PO Box 152, Troy, NY *12181*

Cluett MR & MRS G Alfred JR (Smith—Virginia Ashcraft) ☎ (617) 326-1451 10 Longwood Dv, Apt D541, Westwood, MA *02090*
MR A Tucker—at Blue Hill, ME *04614* . . . .
MISS Ann A Smith—at 1180 Midland Av, Bronxville, NY *10708* . . . .
MR Ralph O Smith—at Portland, OR . . . .

Cluett MR & MRS John S (de Peyster—Maria-Luisa B Duke)
☎ (408) 667-2661 . . Marble Peak Ranch, Box 33, Big Sur, CA *93920*

Cluett MR & MRS Mark S (Elizabeth A Gummey) Hlns'61.Pcu.Fr.Wms'55.Va'61 ⛵ . . . . ☎ (912) 598-7043 13 Magnolia Crossing, Savannah, GA *31411-1417*
MISS Julia S . . . .

Cluett MRS W Scott (I Eustis Lowry)
☎ (912) 638-4727 . . ''Still Marsh'' PO Box 30123, Sea Island, GA *31561*

Cluett MRS William G (Briggs—Helen M Stedman) Cly.Evg.BtP.Ncd.StJ.
☎ (561) 832-2209 . . 217 Emerald Lane, Palm Beach, FL *33480*

Clulow MRS Margaretta M (Margaretta Mason Maganini) Cly.Dc.Dh.Ht.Ncd.Myf. . . . . ☎ (203) 852-8102 102 Shorefront Park, Norwalk, CT *06854*
MISS Evelyn K—Dc.Dh. . . . .

Clulow MR Quentin F D—Cw.
☎ (203) 853-0007 . . 24 Naromake Av, Norwalk, CT *06854*

Clute MR & MRS Peter R (Pamela T Isham) Col'72.Laf'71
☎ (303) 220-9914 . . 4300 S Dahlia St, Englewood, CO *80110*

Cluxton MR Harley E 3d—Cw.Tul'69.Tul'71 . . . . . ☎ (602) 998-0500
MISS Fallon P—at SMU . . . . 5509 E Alan Lane,
JUNIORS MR Harley E 4th . . . . Scottsdale, AZ
85253

Cluxton MRS Marcia M (Marcia G Mortensen) Tul'71
☎ (214) 520-0313 . . 3813 Miramar Av, Dallas, TX *75205*

Clyde MR & MRS J Edward (Brown—Ruth McCauley) Swth'27.Cry.
☎ (610) 353-9840 . . Dunwoody Village E203, 3500 West Chester Pike,
Newtown Square, PA *19073*

Clyde MR & MRS Thomas M (Christine S MacIver) ☎ (617) 227-8964
V'61.Sm.Tr.Myf.P'58.H.'61 . . . . 23 Chestnut St,
MISS Alexandra T . . . . Boston, MA *02108*
MR Thomas MacI . . . .
MR William C . . . .

Clyde MR & MRS William M (Sara A Bye) NCar'69 . | 217 Beatty Rd,
MISS Cynda M . . . . | Media, PA *19063*
MR John R . . . . |

Clymer MISS Emily E
103 Kendal Dv, Kennett Square, PA *19348-2328*

Clyne MR & MRS V Shannon (Pamela I Taylor) ☎ (213) 933-6890
Bur.Stan'65.Stan'68 . . . . 532 S Lorraine
MR A Taylor—Col'93—at ☎ (310) 312-1871 Blvd, Los Angeles,
1441 Butler Av, Apt 7, Los Angeles, CA *90025* CA *90020*
MR Andrew McC—at U of Mont . . . .

Coad MR W James 3d . . see J L Riley

Coakley MISS Lisa F (Tippitt—Lisa F Coakley)
21149 Colby Rd, Shaker Heights, OH *44122*

Coates MR & MRS Benjamin (Nancy Sloane)
K.B.Ri.Cly.Ac.Cda.P'39.Pa'46 ⚓ . . of
☎ (011-41-30) 4-27-90 . . Chalet Bijou des Alpes Unterbort,
3792 Saanen, Switzerland
☎ (011-33-1) 43-26-82-36 . . 24 quai de Bethune, 75004 Paris, France

Coates MR & MRS George G H (Eleanor B Henry) ☎ (610) 642-3091
BMr'87.Rc. . . . . 1103 Rose Glen Rd,
MR Alexander H—at Boston U . . . . Gladwyne, PA
19035

Coates MR George G H JR—Pe.Vca.Rv.Cspa.Fw.
☎ (215) 242-0919 . . 7512 McCallum St, Philadelphia, PA *19118*

Coates MRS H Fox (Hope Alden Fox)
☎ (215) 643-1071 . . ''Wild Field'' 908 Woodbridge Rd, Spring House,
PA *19477*

Coates MR & MRS Lloyd M JR (Jerilyn J Decker) ☎ (610) 668-8117
MooreArt'65.Me.Mid'58 . . . . ''Beauglen''
MR Lloyd M 3d . . . . 243 N Wynnewood
Av, Narberth, PA
19072

Coates MR & MRS W Shelby JR (White—Frana L ☎ (516) OR1-3380
Ward) Pr.Y.'52.Va'59 . . . . ''Encore''
MISS Susan F White—at Myrtle Beach, SC Piping Rock Rd,
29577 . . . . Locust Valley, NY
11560

Cobb MRS Ahira 2d (Neville—Hope Fay) Rdc'47.Hn.
☎ (609) 924-3297 . . 142 Mercer St, Princeton, NJ *08540*

Cobb MISS Alison Gallatin (Oliver E) . . . . Married at Seattle, WA
Herber MR Paul F (John A) . . . . May 27'95

Cobb MR & MRS Brodie L (Frances S Daniels) Tul'84.Tul'84.Tex'85
275 Mallorca Way, San Francisco, CA *94123*

Cobb MR & MRS Calvin H JR (Olive L Watson)
V'47.Cvc.Mt.Gi.Sl.Ncd.USN'45.Geo'49 . . of
☎ (941) 649-4352 . . 650 Jacana Circle, Naples, FL *34105*
☎ (301) 656-3664 . . 3571 Hamlet Place, Chevy Chase, MD *20815*

Cobb MR & MRS Calvin H 3d (Charlotte D Young)
Va'81.GeoW'86.Cvc.Mt.P'80.Geo'84
☎ (301) 320-2564 . . 4604 Tournay Rd, Bethesda, MD *20816*

Cobb MR & MRS Carl B (Susan A Bitner) Cwr'49 . . | 8 Weeping Willow
MR Jeffrey B . . . . | Lane, Asheville, NC
28804-1900

Cobb MISS Emily M
Old Pickard Farm, Littleton, MA *01460*

Cobb MRS Gallatin (Margaret H Gallatin) Cs.
☎ (212) 288-2495 . . 164 E 72 St, New York, NY *10021-4363*

Cobb MR & MRS Henry Ives (Parkinson—Elizabeth A Bliss) Csn.H'29
☎ (609) 426-6203 . . Meadow Lakes 44-07, Hightstown, NJ *08520*

Cobb MR & MRS Henry N (Joan S Spaulding) ☎ (212) RE7-5035
K.C.H'47 . . . . 969 Fifth Av,
MISS Sara Q—at 116 Pinehurst Av, New York, New York, NY
NY *10033* *10021*
MISS Emma T . . . .
MISS Pamela C . . . .

Cobb MR & MRS Howard L (Dewing—Wright— ☎ (561) 265-2289
Nancy Goodwin) Hart'62.StJ.Csn.Ncd.Dc.Y'31 . 500 Seasage Dv,
MISS Martha F Dewing—at ☎ (718) 935-0600 Delray Beach, FL
405 Clinton St, Brooklyn, NY *11231* *33483*
MR Harold A Dewing 3d—at
☎ (303) 722-8714 . . 1995 S Washington St,
Denver, CO *80210* . . . .

Cobb MR & MRS John W (H Bayard Hooper) ☎ (303) 440-0424
H'66.Cl'69 . . . . 254 Pine Tree Lane,
MR Joshua H—Mid'95 . . . . Boulder, CO
80304-4228

Cobb DR & MRS Oliver E (Gidlund—Pamela J ☎ (206) 546-1110
Frieze) UWash'62.Wms'52.Cl'56. 642 NW 163 St,
MISS (DR) Pamela P—Occ'88.GeoW'93—at Seattle, WA *98177*
1904 Uhle St, Arlington, VA *22201* . . . .
MR Henry E . . . .

Cobb CAPT (RET) & MRS Richard (Marian Van V Colwell)
USN.Ws'49.Nf.Ofp.Sar.Sl.Dar.Myf.Ncd.H'36
☎ (703) 768-6896 . . 1220 Tudor Place, Alexandria, VA *22307-2008*

Cobbs MR & MRS James W JR (Jill Stauffer)
Duke'79.Cl'83.Ihy.Pn.Ty'76.CUNY'84 ⚓
1 Maher Court, Greenwich, CT *06830*

Cobian MRS Rafael R (de Jong—Juliette Coronel) T.Cly . . .of
☎ (212) 535-1078 . . 625 Park Av, New York, NY *10021*
☎ (914) 351-5246 . . ''Crossview'' Cliff Rd, PO Box 133, Tuxedo Park,
NY *10987*

Coble MR & MRS Neely B JR (Claire S Kelton) Van'49
☎ (615) 298-1415 . . 118 Bonaventure Place, Nashville, TN *37205*

Coblentz MR & MRS Madison R (Carol Gillig) Stan'49
☎ (916) 546-3220 . . 7806 Tiger Av, Box 399, Kings Beach,
Lake Tahoe, CA *96143*

Coburn MR David MacG—Emer'72
☎ (206) 282-4531 . . 1418 Willard Av W, Seattle, WA *98119*

Coburn MR George M—H'46.H'49 . . of
☎ (202) 234-2054 . . 1661 Crescent Place NW, Apt 208, Washington, DC 20009-4047
☎ (305) 294-7172 . . 522 Louisa St, Key West, FL 33040

Coburn MR & MRS John (Joan S Shaw) D.H'39
☎ (617) 329-3252 . . 10 Longwood Dv, Apt 563, Westwood, MA 02090-1148

Coburn MRS John JR (Renwick—Elizabeth F Bishop) . . . . | ☎ (203) 966-5852
JUNIORS MR Timothy G . . . . | 62 Hoyt St, New Canaan, CT 06840

Coburn MR John JR—H'63 . . . . | ☎ (203) 324-3070
MR Tristram C—Skd'92—at ☎ (410) 685-6564 | 66 Glenbrook Rd, 713 Dover St, Baltimore, MD 21230 . . . . | Apt 4227, Stamford, CT 06902

Coburn MR John 3d—Skd'90
☎ (212) 628-2129 . . 1520 York Av, Apt 21F, New York, NY 10028

Coburn MRS Lawrence H (Alexandra Taylor) . . . . Died at Boston, MA Jun 2'96

Coburn MR Lawrence H—Au.H'56 . . . . | ☎ (617) 235-5954
MISS Priscilla S—at 2727—29 St NW, | 102 Old Colony Rd, Washington, DC 20008 . . . . | Wellesley Hills, MA 02181

Coburn MR & MRS Ralph G (Devens—Martha A Means) Hn.H'33
☎ (508) 668-2876 . . New Pond Village, Apt 220, 180 Main St, Walpole, MA 02081

Cochran MRS Alexander S (Caroline Sizer) Md.C.Cos.Csn.
☎ (410) 527-0821 . . 13801 York Rd, Apt B16, Cockeysville, MD 21030

Cochran MR & MRS Bradford (Elizabeth W Cornell) Shcc.P'37
☎ (908) 766-1356 . . "Wood Pile" Mt Harmony Rd, Bernardsville, NJ 07924

Cochran MR & MRS Carlyle Van D (Sheila M Smith) Cvc.Mt.H'43
☎ (301) OL6-4670 . . 8205 Kerry Rd, Chevy Chase, MD 20815

Cochran MISS Catherine . . see W H Frost

Cochran MRS Donald R (Josephine Gemberling) Ne.Ncd.Dar. . . . . | ☎ (610) 664-0740
MR Donald R JR—Cspa.W.Ken'57 . . . . | 340 Llandrillo Rd, Bala-Cynwyd, PA 19004

Cochran MRS Dwight M (Newstedt—Gregory—Stella C Adams) . . of
☎ (415) 343-8487 . . 601 Laurel Av, San Mateo, CA 94401
☎ (619) 346-4109 . . 47-483 Marrakesh Dv, Palm Desert, CA 92260

Cochran MR Dwight M 3d . . see D L Bark

Cochran MRS Edward W (Dunbar—Susan S Prentice)
☎ (757) 930-3866 . . 2 Willard Place, Newport News, VA 23606

Cochran MR & MRS George N (Barbara K Doepke) P'cpia'75.Rc.Cho.Wa.P'cpia'76.Nw'81
☎ (847) 256-6907 . . 320 Raleigh Rd, Kenilworth, IL 60043

Cochran DR & MRS George Van B (Caroline J Winston) Dth'53.Col'56 . . . . | ☎ (914) 762-6632
MISS Linsay R—at Colby . . . . | "Green Pools" 716 Kitchawan Rd, JUNIORS MR Alexander V B . . . . | Ossining, NY 10562

Cochran MR & MRS John (Emlen—Nina Cooke) . . . . | ☎ (207) 288-4678
MR Thomas F Emlen . . . . | "Fairfax" Hulls Cove, ME 04644

Cochran MR & MRS John C (Priscilla B Pierce)
1417 SW 143 St, Seattle, WA 98166

Cochran MR & MRS Joseph W 3d (Joan G Ralston) Wms'42
☎ (408) 624-5579 . . "Great Point" Box 476, Pebble Beach, CA 93953

Cochran MR Matthew J . . see D L Bark

Cochran MR & MRS Philip L (Grace C Newcomb) | ☎ (616) 334-3183
MtH'50.Wa.Wms'38 . . . . | "Jiggity Jog"
MISS Corinne—P'cpia'81—at 1660 N La Salle St, | 6538 Dunn's Farm Chicago, IL 60614 . . . . | Rd, Maple City, MI 49664

Cochran MR & MRS Philip L JR (Eileen E Laferty) | ☎ (616) 941-7926
StThos'81.MichSt'75 . . . . | 4161 Pintail Dv,
JUNIORS MISS Courtney—at 621 Park Av, | Traverse City, MI
Wilmette, IL 60091 . . . . | 49686
JUNIORS MR Philip L 3d . . . . |

Cochran MRS Samuel (Grace S Wallace) Bgt.
☎ (914) 276-2466 . . Heritage Hills, Somers, NY 10589

Cochran MR & MRS Samuel 3d (Jessica B Robinson) | ☎ (201) 635-7286
P'64 . . . . | 42 Edgewood Rd,
MISS Caroline W . . . . | Chatham, NJ 07928
JUNIORS MISS Allison M . . . . |

Cochran MR Samuel A . . see D L Bark

Cochran MR & MRS Thomas N (Dorcas O | ☎ (908) 766-1459
Cummings) Shcc.StA.Cly.P'59.H'61 . . . . | PO Box 356,
MISS Oakley D—Box 85071, Fairbanks, AK | Lake Rd,
99708 . . . . | Far Hills, NJ 07931
MR Philip N—at 5319 Ninth Av NE, Seattle, WA |
98105 . . . . |

Cochrane MR Alexander L 3d—Miss'85 . . see J R Coulter

Cochrane MISS Elizabeth P—LakeF'87 . . see J R Coulter

Cochrane MR & MRS James A 4th (Biddle—Sarah Gamwell) Pkg.Dth'56
☎ (610) 363-7033 . . 651 Nantmeal Rd, Glenmoore, PA 19343

Cochrane MR & MRS William H (Shepard—Deborah Collyer) Pn.P'35
☎ (561) 231-5829 . . 2320 Club Dv, Vero Beach, FL 32963

Cochrane MR & MRS William J (Annemarie G Lukacs) StLaw'86
☎ (610) 286-2113 . . Box 369A, RD 2, Nantmeal Rd, Elverson, PA 19520

Cockcroft MRS John Van V (Cynthia Mary Spencer) Wells'35.Va'51.Dar.Ncd.
☎ (804) 973-1240 . . 137 Georgetown Green, Charlottesville, VA 22901

Cockcroft MR & MRS John Van V JR (Martha J | ☎ (914) 962-6552
Henning) Sth'64.Va'60 . . . . | 6-2 Woodlands Dv,
MR Tristan H . . . . | Yorktown Heights,
JUNIORS MR John Van V 4th . . . . | NY 10598

Cockman MR & MRS Eric W (Lydia S Dougherty) Cry.Pa'87
☎ (610) 640-4417 . . 317 Brigade Court, Wayne, PA 19087

Cocroft MR & MRS Duncan H (Christina L Miller) | of ☎ (941)964-0588
ChHill'67.GeoW'71.Rcp.Md.Cw.Mv.Pa'65 . . . . | "Heron House"
MISS Constance G—at Williams . . . . | 1301—13 St W,
MISS Elizabeth S—at Trinity . . . . | PO Box 195, Boca Grande, FL 33921-0195
☎ (612) 359-9524
1117 Marquette Av, Minneapolis, MN 55403

Coddington MRS Stewart G (Jane A Bell) . . . . ☎ (309) 662-6446
MISS Kimberly A . . . . 4 Bedford Court,
MR James S—at ☎ (011-671) 477-4276 Bloomington, IL
PO Box 6890, Tamuning, Guam *96931-6890* . . . *61704-6270*
Coddington MR Stewart G—Ariz'62.IllSt'72
☎ (516) 487-0105 . . 1 Overlook Av, Great Neck, NY *11021-3750*
Coddington MRS W Gould (Winifred Dana Gould)
☎ (516) 487-2192 . . 1 Overlook Av, Apt 1-O, Great Neck, NY *11021*
Codman Laura D—Chi.Cly.
☎ (212) 988-9667 . . 301 E 64 St, New York, NY *10021*
Codman MRS Russell S JR (Jane D Ferguson) Sbc. . | of ☎ (617)266-2277
MISS Jane R—Chi. . . . . | 59 Marlborough St,
MISS June F. . . . . | Boston, MA *02116*
| ☎ (508) 526-1220
| "Namdoc"
| 30 Proctor St, Box
| 1558, Manchester-
| By-The-Sea, MA
| *01944*
Codman MR Samuel E—Ec.H'31
☎ (508) 927-0041 . . "Pompey's Garden" Prides Crossing, MA *01965*
Cody MR & MRS Coleman F (Hobbs—Sarah P Meigs) Sth'46.H.'45
☎ (508) 540-6787 . . 21 Rydal Mount Dv, Falmouth, MA *02540*
Coe MRS Diana D (Diana Dunn) V'59
☎ (970) 487-3501 . . "La Loba" Box 124, RD 1, Collbran, CO *81624*
Coe MR George V 3d—L.Rcn. . . . . | ☎ (908) 842-2393
MISS Elizabeth H . . . . | 89 Sleepy Hollow
MISS Holly R . . . . | Rd, Red Bank, NJ
| *07701*
Coe MR & MRS Henry E 3d (Nancy B Wesson) | ☎ (516) 239-5546
Wk.Un.Rr.Cc.Cly.Y'46 | 200 Sage Av,
MISS Elice J—at 444 S Euclid St, Pasadena, CA | Lawrence, NY
91101 . . . . | *11559*
MISS Alexandra C—Ken'83—at 1679 Laurel Av,
St Paul, MN *55104* . . . . |
Coe MRS Henry H R (Margaret L Shaw) Stph'37.Wyo'39
☎ (307) 587-4655 . . 1400—11 St, Cody, WY *82414*
Coe MR & MRS Henry H R JR (Martha Strannigan) | ☎ (307) 587-5221
Wyo'72 . . . . | Box 1088, Cody,
JUNIORS MISS Carey A . . . . | WY *82414*
JUNIORS MR Henry H R 3d . . . . |
Coe MR & MRS John T J (Gay K Larkin) Ariz'82.Ariz'82.Nu'87
384 Mendon Center Rd, Pittsford, NY *14534*
Coe MISS Nancy-Bell (Hebbe—Oakland—Nancy-Bell Coe) Ws'70
☎ (216) 321-1288 . . 2929 Washington Blvd, Cleveland Heights,
OH *44118-2449*
Coe MR & MRS Robert L (Mariella R Cartwright) Rens'31
☎ (314) 863-3408 . . 900 S Hanley Rd, Clayton, MO *63105*
Coe MR Robert S—T.H'56 . . . . | ☎ (970) 487-3055
MISS Cassandra H—H'85.Cal'89—at | "Rocking Lazy R
☎ (415) 366-2984 . . 439 Woodside Dv, | Ranch" PO Box
Woodside, CA *94062* . . . . | 137C, RD 1,
| Collbran, CO *81624*
Coerper MR & MRS Milo G (Lois Hicks) | ☎ (301) 652-8635
Col'52.An.Cvc.Mt.Sl.USN'47 . . . . | 7315 Brookville Rd,
MISS Allison L . . . . | Chevy Chase, MD
| *20815*

Coffin JUNIORS MISS Allison R . . see MISS (DR) M L Gallagher
Coffin MR & MRS David D (Rosemary H Baldwin) Au.Y'43
☎ (603) 772-2421 . . 7 Riverwoods Dv, Apt F211, Exeter, NH *03833*
Coffin MR & MRS Edmund (Price—Violet Bodman) Y'43
☎ (802) 765-4358 . . Box 61, Strafford, VT *05072*
Coffin MISS Elizabeth W . . see MISS (DR) M L Gallagher
Coffin MR & MRS G Jarvis (Barbara E Jerauld) Hob'53
☎ (315) 655-9723 . . 4050 Chenango St, Cazenovia, NY *13035*
Coffin DR & MRS Lewis A 3d (Angeline J W Glass) | ☎ (706) 579-1364
Va'52.Duke'56 . . . . | 800 Big Canoe,
MISS Jennifer N . . . . | Big Canoe, GA
MR Jared S . . . . | *30143*
Coffin MR & MRS Peter B (Ann B Rhame) Ham'81.Ham'82
255 Woodland Rd, Chestnut Hill, MA *02167*
Coffin LT CDR & MRS Peter D (Eleanore M Reed) USNR.
☎ (603) 642-7792 . . 11 Newton Junction Rd, Kingston, NH *03848*
Coffin MR & MRS Ralston H JR (Phyllis C Verkamp) | 4301 Torchlight
Yn.Y'56 . . . . | Circle, Bethesda,
MISS Claire R—at ☎ (212) 534-2453 | MD *20816*
1185 Park Av, New York, NY *10128* . . . . |
MR Jared R . . . . |
Coffin MR & MRS Robert Parker (Emily Elizabeth | ☎ (847) 634-3217
Magie) Y'39 . . . . | Box 4316 RFD,
MISS Barbara A . . . . | Long Grove, IL
| *60047*
Coffin MRS Susanne M (Susanne C Madeira) | ☎ (610) 975-0222
WmSth'79.Nf.Gm.Me.Cda. . . . . | 398 Colket Lane,
JUNIORS MISS Sarah N . . . . | Wayne, PA *19087*
Cogan REV & MRS Timothy B (Ruth W Mitchell) | ☎ (508) 689-3927
Eyc.H'56.VaTheo'59 . . . . | Brooks School,
MR John M—at 1374 First Av, New York, NY | 1160 Great Pond
10021 . . . . | Rd, North Andover,
MR Milo S—at 28 Montgomery St, Boston, MA | MA *01845*
02116 . . . . |
Coggeshall MR & MRS Clarke (Ethel B Ducey) | ☎ (617) 326-5195
Hn.H'52 . . . . | 11 Sandy Valley Rd,
MISS Katharine D . . . . | Dedham, MA *02026*
MISS Natalie M . . . . |
JUNIORS MR David C—at Colgate . . . . |
Coggill MRS George (Elizabeth M Harris) Chr.Myf.Dar.Dll.Ht.Y.
☎ (212) 682-4526 . . 321 E 43 St, New York, NY *10017*
Cogswell MR & MRS Arnold (Jessie Batcheller) V'49.Y.'50
☎ (518) 785-7849 . . 95 Old Niskayuna Rd, Loudonville, NY *12211*
Cogswell MRS C Cannon (Cynthia Cannon) Cly.
☎ (914) 677-6088 . . "Closeburn" Box 90A, RD 1, Millbrook,
NY *12545*
Cogswell MR & MRS James Kelsey 4th (Alexandra-Louise Emerson Sack)
Emory'83.NCar'84
☎ (404) 724-0481 . . 1750 Doncaster Dv NE, Atlanta, GA *30309*
Cohen MR & MRS Ted (Austin—Ann R Collier) | ☎ (773) 288-4694
V'57.Ch'62.H'65.H'72 . . . . | 4950 S Chicago
MISS Alexandra Austin—V'91—at | Beach Dv, Chicago,
☎ (773) 752-7573 . . 5550 S Dorchester Av, | IL *60615*
Chicago, IL *60637* . . . . |
Cohû MRS Henry W (Snowden—Dwight—Adelaide Farr) Cly.Cda.
☎ (610) 645-8906 . . 1400 Waverly Rd, Blair 312, Gladwyne, PA *19035*

Coit MR & MRS Chapin (Bell—Barbara J Wheeler) Buf'47
☎ (415) 751-4741 . . 65 Rossi Av, San Francisco, CA *94118-4217*

Coit MR Michael W—Mo'85
☎ (818) 592-6109 . . 22240 Victory Blvd, Apt E118, Woodland Hills, CA *91367*

Coker MR & MRS Priestley C 3d (Cynthia Kempson) SCar'67.SCar'64 . . . . | ☎ (803) 577-9485
MISS Rachel L . . . . | Box 176,
MISS Caroline G . . . . | Charleston, SC
JUNIORS MR P Cooper 4th . . . . | *29402*

Colas MR & MRS Josselin C (Elisa J Cosnard des Closets) Geo'89.Rennes'89
☎ (011-33-1) 34-69-48-06 . . Bagatelle I, Residence du Bois de Boulogne, 95290 L'Isle-Adam, France

Colas MR & MRS Pierre H (Ludington—Maryanne Cantrell) Caen'50 . . . . | ☎ (212) RE7-8503
MISS Marie-Noelle—Nu'90.Nu'94—at | 229 E 79 St,
☎ (212) 874-0572 . . 58 W 84 St, New York, NY | New York, NY
10024 . . . . | *10021*
MISS Valerie C—Bnd'94—at Brown . . . . |

Colbert MISS Madeleine Carlise (g—Joseph H McGee) . . . . Born at Chicago, IL Sep 24'95

Colburn MRS Irving W (Frances A Haffner) BMr'58.Sbc.Sm.Ec.Chi.Fy . . .of
☎ (508) 526-1627 . . "Sea Rock" 185 Summer St, Manchester, MA *01944*
☎ (617) 523-4152 . . 54 Beacon St, Boston, MA *02108*

Colburn MR & MRS Kenneth H (Crye—Virginia M Ventura) Conn'74.InterAmUPR'76.D.Why.Myf.Yn.Br'75.Y'78 ⚓
☎ (508) 785-0878 . . 20 Pegan Lane, Dover, MA *02030*

Colburn MR & MRS Oliver C (Cecily C Birmingham) Denis'85.Tr.Ec.H.'84.Bost'87
☎ (617) 227-3666 . . 1 W Hill Place, Boston, MA *02114*

Colby MR & MRS George H (Susan S Harding) NH'65.NH'67 . . . . | ☎ (703) 255-2848
MISS Rebecca G . . . . | 2040 Adams Hill
| Rd, Vienna, VA
| *22182*

Colby MR & MRS Robert L (Gretchen H Rogers) Cy.McG'67 . . . . | ☎ (617) 320-9424
MISS Jessie H—at Dickinson . . . . | 66 Lowder St,
MR Robert G—at Oberlin . . . . | Dedham, MA *02026*
JUNIORS MR Anthony L . . . . |

Colcord MR & MRS Bradford P (Helen B Johnson) B'gton'59.Y.'52.H'55 . . . . | ☎ (212) 996-0618
MISS Hilary P—Geo'89.Cl'94—at 1 Seymour Rd, | 1088 Park Av,
Fairview Heights, Midlevels, Hong Kong . . . . . . | New York, NY
MR Avery J—Y'87.H'93—at 914 Lincoln Av, | *10128*
Minneapolis, MN *55403* . . . . |

Coldren MISS Lindsay . . see J A Morgan

Cole MISS Bonnie L—Dar.Wt.
☎ (601) 734-2482 . . 2418 H'way 583 SE, Bogue Chitto, MS *39629*

Cole MR & MRS Charles J (Margery Manning) Sth'45.Y'40
☎ (860) 678-7317 . . 184 Garden St, Farmington, CT *06032*

Cole MRS Chisholm (Scott—Barbara Chisholm) Cly.
☎ (415) 441-3184 . . 2000A Washington St, San Francisco, CA *94109*

Cole MR & MRS F Crunden (Ardath Starkloff) Cy.Ncd.
☎ (314) 993-1874 . . 911 S Warson Rd, St Louis, MO *63124*

Cole MISS Helen C—Ws'40
☎ (216) 321-8275 . . 2701 Scarboro Rd, Cleveland, OH *44106*

Cole DR Henry P JR—Wms'59.MichSt'63.Alaska'78
☎ (907) 488-3493 . . Box 71490, Fairbanks, AK *99707*

Cole MR & MRS James E (Susan T Hill) Ws'67.Yn.Y'72
☎ (203) 966-9762 . . 130 Comstock Hill Rd, New Canaan, CT *06840*

Cole MR John Y JR—Stan'58 . . . . | ☎ (817) 921-3006
MISS Valerie S—TCU'86 . . . . | 2521 Rogers Av,
MR John Y 3d—Miss'89 . . . . | Ft Worth, TX *76109*

Cole CAPT (RET) & MRS L Fletcher (Anne M Magruder) An.Cvc.BtP.Cw.Cda.USA'31.Fla'49 . . of
☎ (561) 223-9212 . . "Sandhill Cove" 1499 SW Shoreline Dv, Palm City, FL *34990*
☎ (704) 743-2051 . . "Harmony Hall" PO Box 324, Cashiers Valley, NC *28717*

Cole MR & MRS Morton (Elizabeth S Harrington) Ofp.Myf.Dar.H'29
☎ (617) 749-3970 . . 7 Meadow View Rd, Hingham, MA *02043*

Cole MR & MRS Nathaniel P 3d (Stewart—Hartness—Leonie B Weeks) Bur.Ncd.
☎ (415) 851-3024 . . 1075 Godetia Dv, Woodside, CA *94062*

Cole MR Newcomb D
☎ (413) 637-4021 . . Kimball Farms 154, 235 Walker St, Lenox, MA *01240*

Cole MRS Robert E (Fuller—Christine G Rothe)
☎ (607) 569-2240 . . 1 E Lake Rd, Hammondsport, NY *14840*

Cole MRS Sheila D (Sheila R Dauphinot)
☎ (817) 293-8522 . . 13 York Dv, Ft Worth, TX *76134*

Cole MRS Susan H (Sabet—Susan Heyniger) Pars'76.VPI'79 . . . . | ☎ (914) 833-5055
JUNIORS MR Amman H Sabet . . . . | 1 Elm Av,
| Larchmont, NY
| *10538*

Cole MR & MRS Todd G (Pamela Wilds) V'75.Rcn.Rr.Ihy.Cly.LSU'39
☎ (305) 444-2804 . . 1400 Coral Way, Coral Gables, FL *33134*

Cole MRS Vaughan (Virginia Vaughan)
☎ (617) 749-2243 . . 9 Burditt Av, Hingham, MA *02043*

Cole MR & MRS Wallace H JR (Caroline P Bush) V'55.Cda.Minn'46 . . . . | ☎ (305) 446-6232
MISS Shelley C—at 17734 NW Elkcrest Court, | 3501 St Gaudens
Portland, OR 97229 . . . . | Rd, Miami, FL
| *33133*

Cole MR & MRS Wallace H 3d (Alice M Ehrenclou) Occ'80.Clare'79
☎ (305) 661-5383 . . 6545 SW 131 St, Miami, FL *33156*

Cole MRS Walter F JR (Elsa Hurlbut) V'49 . . . . | ☎ (860) 535-1368
MR Randy G—Bost'82 . . . . | 30 Orchard St,
| Stonington, CT
| *06378*

Cole MR & MRS William K (Duncan—Ula H Tenney) Cly.Yn.Y'36.Y'39 . . . . | ☎ (203) 264-2726
MR Peter S Duncan—Nasson'73 ⚓—at | 795B Heritage
☎ (860) 868-0374 . . 15 New Preston Hill Rd, | Village, Southbury,
New Preston, CT *06777* . . . . | CT *06488*

Cole MRS Wilton D (Howell—Gloria Hernandez) . . | ☎ (520) 742-5858
MR Steven R—at ☎ (520) 749-4024 | 7500 N Calle Sin
9898 Mt Pleasant Dv, Tucson, AZ *85749* . . . . . | Envidia, Tucson, AZ
| *85718*

Coleman MISS Alexandra K—Pa'67
☎ (610) 827-1577 . . "Glomar Farm" 85 Green Lane Rd, Malvern, PA *19355*

Coleman MR & MRS C Payson JR (Catharine L Conway) Pr.Ln.BtP.Wms'72 . . . . — of ☎ (516)621-2223 55 Valentines Lane, Old Brookville, NY *11545*
MISS Avery W—at Princeton . . . .
MR Charles P 3d—at Williams . . . .
JUNIORS MR Reed P—at Greenvale . . . . — ☎ (561) 655-5322 100 Royal Palm Way, Palm Beach, FL *33480*

Coleman MISS Cathleen R . . see MRS F B Finkenstaedt

Coleman MR & MRS Daniel T Le V (Irene H Conway) Man'vl'82.Rv.Myf.Pa'81.Cl'86
☎ (914) 779-4224 . . 341 Crestwood Av, Crestwood, NY *10707*

Coleman MR & MRS F Daniel Le V (Ingeborg T Pfaff) Vca.Rv.Cw.P.Colog'52 . . . . — ☎ (914) 961-5845 415 Hollywood Av, Crestwood, NY *10707*
MISS Eliza A—Geo'85.Nu'95.Dar.—
☎ (914) 337-3998 . . . .

Coleman MR & MRS Francis I G (Seymour—Julia G Montgomery) SL'44.Mt.Cvc.Sl.P'45 . . . . — of ☎ (202)234-8868 1807 Kalorama Square NW, Washington, DC *20008*
MISS Anne M—Mont'85—at ☎ (207) 829-3328 40 Sligo Rd Ext, North Yarmouth, ME *04097* . .
MR Bruce D—Duke'82—at ☎ (716) 264-0315 Box 10608, Rochester, NY *14610* . . . . — ☎ (717) 626-6472 "Elizabeth Farms" 2121B Furnace Hill Pike, Lititz, PA *17543*

Coleman MR Fraser D—Snc.Hob'91
☎ (510) 654-0206 . . 1531 Grand Av, Piedmont, CA *94611*

Coleman MR & MRS George L (Soles—Dawn Loomis) B.BtP.
☎ (561) 546-1426 . . 106 Bassett Creek Trail, Hobe Sound, FL *33455*

Coleman MR & MRS Jack H (C Louise Baton) Rr.West'59 . . . . — ☎ (412) 963-8715 1626 Powers Run Rd, Pittsburgh, PA *15238*
MISS Caroline B . . . .
MR Timothy A . . . .

Coleman MR James S . . see MRS F B Finkenstaedt

Coleman MR & MRS John JR (Constance A MacBride) On.Cly.P'40 . . . . — ☎ (847) 234-0979 60 Western Av, Lake Forest, IL *60045*
MISS Constance M—P'82.Cly.—at
☎ (212) 879-9487 . . 969 Park Av, New York, NY *10028* . . . .

Coleman MR John C—Pcu.Hb.Hn.H'34
☎ (415) 474-2171 . . 1201 California St, Apt 402, San Francisco, CA *94109*

Coleman MR John H JR—Snc.Cw.Rv.StA.Fla'49.Paris'57
☎ (954) 428-0396 . . 1423 E Hillsboro Blvd, Apt 222, Deerfield Beach, FL *33441*

Coleman MR Joseph E 3d
☎ (202) 686-5419 . . 3701 Connecticut Av NW, Washington, DC *20008*

Coleman DR & MRS Jules L (Mary P Griesedieck) Mo'64.Wis'77.CUNY'63.Rock'flr'72.Y'76
☎ (203) 287-0312 . . 57 Swarthmore St, Hamden, CT *06517*

Coleman MISS Laura—Stan'78 . . see G P Foley

Coleman MR & MRS Lawrence W JR (Harriett D Shanahan) Aub'92.Aub'92
☎ (334) 286-6054 . . 3317 Albans Lane, Montgomery, AL *36106*

Coleman MR Leighton H JR—B.Y'53 . . of
☎ (904) 261-0817 . . 3047 Sea Marsh Rd, Amelia Island Plantation, Amelia Island, FL *32034*
☎ (516) 751-0033 . . "East Farm" PO Box 226, Stony Brook, NY *11790*

Coleman MR Leighton H 3d—Snc.SUNY'87.Pars'91
☎ (516) 751-7402 . . PO Box 403, St James, NY *11780*

Coleman MISS Lindsay D—W&L'95 . . see R B Jewell

Coleman MR & MRS Loring W (Katinka Podmaniczky) . . . . — ☎ (508) 456-8055 39 Poor Farm Rd, Harvard, MA *01451*
MR Andrew G—at 47 Poor Farm Rd, Harvard, MA *01451* . . . .

Coleman MISS Martha J—MaryW'49.Dar.
☎ (904) 246-0987 . . 1542 Park Terr W, Atlantic Beach, FL *32233*

Coleman MRS N Tenney (Lloyd—Nancy C Tenney) Cly. . . . . — ☎ (203) 531-0061 625 W Lyon Farm Dv, Greenwich, CT *06831*
MISS Bertrande C—at ☎ (212) 288-3152 404 E 66 St, New York, NY *10021* . . . .
MISS Gwendolyn G—at ☎ (212) 722-4332 200 E 94 St, New York, NY *10128* . . . .
MR Robert S JR—☎ (203) 532-1347 . . . .

Coleman MR & MRS R Jackson (Judith L Hargrave) Dth'52 . . . . — ☎ (805) 434-1424 1280 Deerfield Rd, Templeton, CA *93465*
MR William T—SFrSt'84—at 1245 W Byron St, Chicago, IL *60613* . . . .

Coleman MR Randall C . . . . Died at Baltimore, MD Feb 20'96

Coleman MRS Randall C (Ellis—Caroline S Abell) Elk.Ncd.
☎ (410) 323-3075 . . 116 W Melrose Av, Baltimore, MD *21210*

Coleman DR Richard W—Cal'45.Cal'51 PO Box 540919, Orlando, FL *32854-0919*

Coleman MR & MRS Sheldon T (Katharine H Nicholson)
☎ (203) 869-8335 . . 8 Annjim Dv, Greenwich, CT *06830*

Coleman MR & MRS T Samuel (Cynthia B Balmer) Vh.ColC'63
☎ (818) 792-0561 . . 100 Club Rd, Pasadena, CA *91105*

Coleman MR & MRS Timothy C (Wenninger—Margaret E Huston) Wis'69.Wis'71.On.P'74. Nw'76 . . . . — 211 Sylvan Rd, Lake Bluff, IL *60044*
MISS Margaret E Wenninger—at Colo Coll . .
MR Theodore B Wenninger—StLaw'95 . . . . .

Coleman MR & MRS Wilfrid W (Diehl—Carolyn R Arend) Md'63.Rv.Thiel'68 ⚓
☎ (610) 431-7774 . . "Lucky Little Place" 500 Lucky Hill Rd, West Chester, PA *19382-1724*

Coleman MR & MRS William D (Mary M Fisher) Gm.Pc.Pa'76 . . . . — of ☎ (215)247-2775 8863 Norwood Av, Philadelphia, PA *19118*
JUNIORS MISS Lindsay A . . . . — ☎ (717) 626-7878 "Elizabeth Farms" 2121B Furnace Hill Pike, Lititz, PA *17543*

Colen MR & MRS Joseph E JR (Leach—Mary G Duer) Swb'64.Pa'68.Me.Rc.Ty'61 . . . . | of ☎ (610)527-4933
MISS Jennifer C—Ty'87 . . . . | 1520 Spring Mill
MR Joseph E 3d—J'ville'86 | Rd, Gladwyne, PA
   MISS Jennifer M Leach—Ty'92 . . . . | *19035*
   MISS Ambler P Leach—UMiami'94 . . . . | ☎ (301) 639-7908
                             | 4302 Piney Neck
                             | Rd, Rock Hall, MD
                             | *21661*

Coles MR & MRS Walter L (Frances M Sadtler) Va'33
  ☎ (610) 891-9711 . . Riddle Village, 118 Williamsburg, Media, PA *19063-6031*

Coles MR William A—Sb.StJ.Hn.H'51
  ☎ (602) 502-1357 . . 24350 N Whispering Ridge Way, 10, Scottsdale, AZ *85255*

Colesberry MRS Robert F (Jean Kelly)
  ☎ (215) 886-6564 . . 1061 Easton Rd, Apt C12, Roslyn, PA *19001-4417*

Colesberry MR & MRS Robert F JR (Hallowell—Karen L Thorson) Pa'72.Nu'74 . . of
  ☎ (212) 962-0438 . . 165 Duane St, Apt 6C, New York, NY *10013*
  ☎ (203) 661-3181 . . 10 Frost Rd, Greenwich, CT *06830*
  ☎ (208) 622-3168 . . ''Juniper Road'' PO Box 2210, Sun Valley, ID *83353*

Coletti-Perucca MR & MRS Sonio E (Astor—Gertrude R Gretsch) Ny.Pr.Rv.Cly.Rome'45
  ☎ (516) 626-3235 . . 8 Woodacres Rd, Brookville, NY *11545*

Coley MRS Jennifer B (Wright—Jennifer C Brady) SUNY'76
  ☎ (212) 744-4469 . . 230 E 73 St, New York, NY *10021*

Colfelt MR Andrew B W—Col'92 . . see MISS K P Taylor

Colfelt MISS E Avery—Col'92 . . see MISS K P Taylor

Colgan MRS John A JR (Anne T Brown)
  ☎ (610) LA5-1111 . . 221 S Spring Mill Rd, Villanova, PA *19085*

Colgate MRS Craig (Barbara Hobart) Sth'37.Mt.Sl.
2730 Chain Bridge Rd NW, Washington, DC *20016*

Colgate MRS John K (Florence Manuel) Au.Pr.Cly.
  ☎ (516) 674-3145 . . 40 Horse Hollow Court, Locust Valley, NY *11560*

Colgate MR & MRS John K JR (Creel—Diana M Forman) Au.Pr.Cly.Colg'57 . . . . | of ☎ (516)922-3111
MR John K 3d—Vt'96—at ☎ (212) 754-9040 | Mill Hill Rd,
340 E 57 St, New York, NY *10022* . . . . | Mill Neck, NY
                             | *11765*
                             | ☎ (914) 373-8003
                             | ''Heathcote Farm''
                             | Amenia, NY *12501*

Colhoun MISS Julia F—Colg'87 . . of
  ☎ (212) 598-0722 . . 2 Fifth Av, Apt 11K, New York, NY *10011-8838*
  ☎ (415) 703-0952 . . 230 Castro St, Apt 2, San Francisco, CA *94114*

Colhoun MR & MRS Michael Deere (Mary T Peterson) LakeF'75.Ncd.LakeF'74
3700 Montecito Av, Santa Rosa, CA *95404*

Colhoun MRS Stephen D (Horne—Kiser—Mary Bushnell) Msq.
  ☎ (860) 395-0409 . . 171 Ingham Hill Rd, Old Saybrook, CT *06475*

Colket MR Christopher G
  ☎ (610) 525-3419 . . 1615 Lark Lane, Villanova, PA *19085*

Colket MR & MRS Meredith B 3d (Kathleen S Gorman) Ws'73.Cr'70.P'74.P'76 . . . . | ☎ (860) 658-9502
JUNIORS MISS Laura K . . . . | 15 Buttonwood Dv,
JUNIORS MR J Alexander . . . . | Simsbury, CT *06070*

Colket MRS Patricia F (Patricia Finnell) Me.Sfh.
  ☎ (610) 527-1373 . . Andover House, B203 Summit Dv, Bryn Mawr, PA *19010*

Colket MR & MRS Tristram C (Thomson—Mary H Fletcher) Ac.Gm.Me.Cts.
  ☎ (610) 649-0663 . . ''Castle Hill'' Box 132, 415 Williamson Rd, Gladwyne, PA *19035*

Colket MR & MRS Tristram C JR (Ruth M Mueller) Rc.Me.Bhy.Cry.M.Wcc.Rd.Ac.Ty'61 . . . . | ''Rock Hill Farm''
MISS Carolyn M . . . . | PO Box 245,
MR Tristram C 3d—*see Dilatory Domiciles* . . . . | 2320 S Valley Rd,
MR Bryan D . . . . | Paoli, PA *19301*

Colket MR & MRS Tristram C 4th (Kathleen Redman) Rol'70 . . . . | ☎ (561) 778-8566
JUNIORS MISS R Elizabeth . . . . | 2020 Cordova Av,
JUNIORS MR Tristram C 5th . . . . | Vero Beach, FL
                             | *32960*

Colladay COL & MRS Edgar B JR (Virginia Lee Weir) USA'42
  ☎ (707) 538-2805 . . 248 Silver Creek Circle, Santa Rosa, CA *95409*

Collamore MRS Wallace R (Weedon—Joan M Kirkland) . . . . . Married at Ivy, VA
Keyser MR Campbell Dirck (late Richard L) . . . . Dec 16'95

Collard LT CDR (RET) & MRS Edward A J (Ruth Auchincloss) RN.T.Cda.
  ☎ (011-44-1624) 861-359 . . ''The Crofts'' Baldrine, Isle of Man IM4 6DG, UK

Collens MR & MRS William L (Mary J Poffenberger) Wms'38
  ☎ (717) 761-6317 . . 120 Winfield Dv, Camp Hill, PA *17011*

Colley MR & MRS Bryan O (Sarah L Gates) Duke'79.On.Cly.Ncd.Ithaca'77.Suff'79 . . of
  ☎ (914) 763-8006 . . ''Pine Hollow'' 83 N Salem Rd, Cross River, NY *10518*
  ☎ (212) 983-0497 . . 140 E 40 St, New York, NY *10004*

Collie MR & MRS Alastair MacR (Virginia Gwyer) Cy.Camb'48
  ☎ (410) 435-1805 . . 118 Taplow Rd, Baltimore, MD *21212*

Collie MR & MRS Hugh A (Gayle E Cooper) Cy.
  ☎ (410) 296-2030 . . 118 Stevenson Lane, Baltimore, MD *21212*

Collie MR & MRS Michael MacR (Bettina J O'Neill) Cy.
  ☎ (410) 592-9004 . . 13019 Dulaney Valley Rd, Glen Arm, MD *21057*

Collier MR & MRS Barron G 2d (Tami McGinty) FlaSo'81.Unn.BtP.Okla'74
  ☎ (307) 587-6275 . . 100 Valley Ranch Rd, Cody, WY *82414*

Collier MISS Dorothy B—NH'41.Cwr'49.Dar.
  ☎ (301) 879-0987 . . 101 Carlisle Dv, Silver Spring, MD *20904*

Collier MR Inglis U . . see W A Read JR

Collier MISS (DR) Mary B—Cal'75.Paris'90.Dar.
  ☎ (805) 966-3577 . . 1521 Dover Rd, Santa Barbara, CA *93103*

Collier MRS Sargent (Elizabeth H Moore) Madrid'68.Sm.My. . . . . | ☎ (508) 768-7575
MISS Leandra M—at Holderness . . . . | PO Box 927,
JUNIORS MISS Eliza D . . . . | Essex, MA *01929*
JUNIORS MR Sargent M McC . . . . |

Collier MR Sargent—Sm.My.Bow'64
  ☎ (508) 282-4394 . . PO Box 549, Essex, MA *01929*

Collier MRS Sargent F (Eleanor M McCormick) Cas.Bhy.On.Fy.Ncd . . . of
  ☎ (847) 234-6784 . . 115 Moffett Rd, Lake Bluff, IL *60044*
  ☎ (207) 288-3816 . . ''Gingerbread House'' 8 Barberry Lane, Bar Harbor, ME *04609*

Collin MR & MRS William E (Nona K Murphy) CtCol'87.Bcs.Rr.Duke'81.H'86
  ☎ (212) 838-9432 . . 300 E 56 St, Apt 28G, New York, NY *10022*

Collings MR & MRS Clifford C JR (Helen C Pennock)
Me.Gm.Fw.Sdg.Ncd.Pa'40
☎ (610) 896-7341 . . 35 Evans Lane, Haverford, PA *19041*
Jan 1 . . ☎ (561) 569-3932 . . 5225 E Harbor Village Dv, Apt 302,
Vero Beach, FL *32967*

Collins MRS Alan C (Stewart—Catherine L | ☎ (503) 636-1352
Pomeroy) Csn. | "The Silk Ear"
MISS C Jade—at U of London . . . . | 658—1 St,
MR Ewan J—at Sch of Mosaicist Italy . . . . | Lake Oswego, OR *97034*

Collins MR & MRS Albert E JR (Margaret L Blood) | ☎ (914) 967-2757
Dth'52 . . . . | 40 Highland Rd,
MISS (DR) Constance A—Denis'80.BMr'82. | Rye, NY *10580*
Nu'86—at ☎ (617) 734-1074 . . 61 Greenough
St, Brookline, MA *02146* . . . .
MR Stephen A—Denis'86—at ☎ (415) 292-6969
3350 Octavia St, San Francisco, CA *94123* . . . .
MR Michael H—Pa'90 . . . .

Collins MRS Alice L (Alice M Lascelles)
☎ (716) 885-3562 . . 35 Cleveland Av, Buffalo, NY *14222*

Collins MR & MRS Atwood 2d (Gilbert—Rosemary Worth)
Cc.Cw.Ncd.Y'39.Y'42 . . of
☎ (860) 242-8817 . . 6 Chambord Park, Bloomfield, CT *06002*
☎ (508) 992-7408 . . 25 Buzzard's Bay Av, South Dartmouth,
MA *02748*

Collins MR & MRS Atwood 3d (Cynthia M Williams) | of ☎ (203)655-1501
Fic.Fiy.Cc.Cw.Y'69 . . . . | 21 Fox Hill Lane,
MR A Porter . . . . | Darien, CT *06820*
JUNIORS MR Dwight M . . . . | ☎ (516) 788-7188
 | "Beach Cottage"
 | Fishers Island, NY *06390*

Collins MR Bradley I . . . . Died at
Palm Beach, FL Jly 18'96

Collins MRS Bradley I (M Carol Ohmer) | ☎ (561) 832-6699
V'47.Pr.Evg.BtP.Cly. . . . . | 300 S Ocean Blvd,
MISS Lee C—Y'80—at ☎ (704) 452-1271 | Palm Beach, FL *33480*
Box 1488, Waynesville, NC *28796* . . . .

Collins MR & MRS Bradley I JR (Amy M Fine) Swth'78.Cly.H'78
☎ (212) 996-7513 . . 1021 Park Av, Apt 4C, New York, NY *10028*

Collins JUNIORS MR Christian J . . see MRS M J Bancroft

Collins MR & MRS Daniel G (Crawford—Anne F | of ☎ (516)537-1228
Weld) Cly.Hof'51.Nu'54 . . . . | Mitchell Lane,
 MISS Serena W Crawford—Mid'92 . . . . | PO Box 32,
 MISS Evelyn F Crawford—at U of Vt . . . . . . | Bridgehampton, NY *11932*
 MR W Blake Crawford—Ty'91 . . . . | ☎ (212) 888-2044
 | 125 E 63 St,
 | New York, NY *10021*

Collins MR Daniel Wills—Myf.H'54
☎ (609) 235-0066 . . 633 E Main St, Apt B2, Moorestown, NJ *08057*

Collins MR & MRS David H (S Wendell Wood) NCar'83.Mid'83 . . of
☎ (609) 683-1690 . . 20 Academy St, Princeton, NJ *08540*
☎ (716) 753-3546 . . Collinswood Villa 13, Shore Dv, Box 146,
Point Chatauqua, Mayville, NY *14757*

Collins MRS Edward R (Elizabeth D Conklin) Hood'58.Gi.Ht.Cda.
☎ (410) 255-1250 . . Box 34, Broadwater Way, Gibson Island,
MD *21056-0034*

Collins MR & MRS Farnham F (E Anne Archbold) Gchr'60.Un.P'57
☎ (914) 677-3822 . . "Skyward" RR 1, Box 64, Millbrook, NY *12545*

Collins MR & MRS Henry L 3d (E Suzanne Kline) | of ☎ (212)486-4846
Bethany'71.Y.'75.Rc.Rd.Geo'64 . . . . | 14 Sutton Place S,
MR Henry L 4th—Vt'89—at Pratt Inst . . . . | New York, NY *10022*
MR Alexander C—Vt'90—at Whittier Coll Law . | ☎ (914) 677-5892
 | "Knockers Farm"
 | 311 N Smith Rd,
 | LaGrangeville, NY *12540*

Collins MR & MRS Hugh G (Frances O Fisher) Y'29
☎ (860) 726-2166 . . Duncaster T312, 40 Loeffler Rd, Bloomfield,
CT *06002*

Collins MR J Rawson—Qc.H'32
☎ (513) 871-7243 . . 3580 Shaw Av, Apt 627, Cincinnati, OH *45208*

Collins MR & MRS James C (Robin L Page) | ☎ (908) 439-3742
Eh.Shcc.NCar'52 . . . . | Homestead Rd,
MR James C JR . . . . | PO Box 167,
 | Pottersville, NJ *07979*

Collins MR & MRS James C (Virginia D Donelson) Hlns'76.Pr.H'80.Cl'86
☎ (212) 360-1179 . . 1641 Third Av, Apt 2AE, New York, NY *10128*

Collins MR James S JR—Myf.Laf'62.Temp'68
☎ (610) 520-1532 . . Radcliff House Apt C256, 1000 Conestoga Rd,
Bryn Mawr, PA *19010*

Collins MR & MRS John S (Linda G McKain) | Box 361,
WestSt'64 . . . . | New London, NH *03257*
MR John S JR . . . . |

Collins MR Mark McC—B.H'53 . . . . | ☎ (914) 677-8249
MISS Emily V—at Bard . . . . | "East Farm"
 | PO Box 1402,
 | Millbrook, NY *12545*

Collins MRS Patrick A (Schroeder—Charlotte D Church) Myf.
☎ (212) 744-1965 . . 333 E 68 St, New York, NY *10021*

Collins MRS Phyllis D (Huber—Phyllis E Dillon) Pqt.Cly.Ny.Ln.
☎ (203) 255-2066 . . 1760 Hillside Rd, Fairfield, CT *06430*

Collins DR & MRS R Deaver JR (Rebecca C Hiatt) | ☎ (601) 981-9118
Miss'74.NCar'76.Aht'74.Van'77.Y'80 . . . . | 219 Glenway Dv,
JUNIORS MR Deaver H . . . . | Jackson, MS *39216*

Collins MRS Richard (Cooley—Sheila McDonnell) . | ☎ (408) 624-2757
MISS Leslie A Cooley . . . . | Alva Lane,
MISS Sheila Cooley . . . . | Box 273,
MR R Pierce Cooley JR . . . . | Pebble Beach, CA *93953*
MR Sean Cooley . . . . |
MR Mark Cooley . . . . |

Collins MRS Richard G (Winifred E Burden)
☎ (011-44-181) 788-6316 . . 4 Dryburgh Mansions, Putney,
London SW15 1AJ, England

Collins MR & MRS Richard J JR (E Lee Garesché) | ☎ (314) 993-0434
Nd.Cy.Tufts'47.Va'50 . . . . | 69 Briarcliff St,
MISS Grace T (Fisher—Grace T Collins) . . . . . . | St Louis, MO *63124*

Collins MR & MRS Stephen G (Thomasene McC Clayton)
  ☎ (205) 871-9823 . . 1011 Melrose Place, Birmingham, AL *35209*
Collins MR & MRS Steven F (Patti L Marshall)
  AmU'86.Smu'89.Wis'84.TexA&M'91
  ☎ (214) 985-8936 . . 3529 Diamondhead Dv, Plano, TX *75075*
Collins MRS Susan B (Susan J Burt) WashColl'63 . . | ☎ (410) 778-4603
MISS Elizabeth B—Red'94 . . . . | ''Riverside''
MR James S 3d . . . . | 25857 Collins Av,
  | Chestertown, MD
  | *21620*
Collins MR & MRS Terence Winslow (Elizabeth K | ☎ (202) 338-0202
Rhein) Cvc.Mt.Sl.Wis'65.Nu'75 . . . . | 2722 N St NW,
JUNIORS MISS Sarah Winslow . . . . | Washington, DC
  | *20007*
Collins MR & MRS Thomas R (Margaret E Payne) Cy.Rc.Aht'42
  ☎ (314) 993-1679 . . 16 Willow Hill Rd, St Louis, MO *63124*
Collins MRS William Howes (Dorothy J Walker) Mls'32.Dar.
  ☎ (860) 767-0560 . . 26 Grove St, Essex, CT *06426-1006*
Collins MRS William M JR (Louise A Neff) On.Cas.Fy.
  ☎ (847) 615-1487 . . 105 E Laurel Av, Apt 307, Lake Forest, IL *60045*
Colloredo-Mansfeld MR & MRS Ferdinand (Susanna Lawrence)
  My.Ln.H.'61
  ☎ (508) 468-3310 . . Winthrop St, South Hamilton, MA *01982*
Colmery MR & MRS Harry W JR (Sallie E Morphy) Vh.Bhm.Dth'49 . . of
  ☎ (818) 796-1827 . . 1420 Park Place, San Marino, CA *91108*
  ☎ (619) 433-7093 . . 42 St Malo Beach, Oceanside, CA *92054*
Colmore MRS Charles B JR (Davis—Margareta B Erikson) Mv.
  ☎ (410) 243-5509 . . 818 W 40 St, Apt F, Baltimore, MD *21211*
Colmore MRS Henry P (Mary V N Thomas)
  ☎ (914) 234-7301 . . ''Frog Hollow'' 88 David's Hill Rd, Bedford Hills, NY *10507*
Colsman-Freyberger MR & MRS Ulrich (Susan B | ☎ (860) 542-5029
Painter) Cly.Munich'64.Bonn'67.Cl'72 . . . . | ''Out O'Bounds''
MR Charles McKee . . . . | Norfolk, CT *06058*
Colt MRS C Learned (Hope C Learned) Sth'58.Au. . | ☎ (609) 924-3117
MR Alexander D—at 14 Av A, New York, NY | 59 Wilson Rd,
10003 . . . . | Princeton, NJ *08540*
MR Ward S . . . . |
Colt MR & MRS Edward W D (Nelson—Suzanne | ☎ (212) 722-5654
Knickerbocker) Rdc'63.YeshivaU'80.Lond'62 . . | 12 E 88 St,
MISS Angela . . . . | New York, NY
  | *10128*
Colt MRS H Dunscombe (Walsh—Armida M T Bologna) Cly.Sl.
  ☎ (202) 338-7987 . . 3030 P St NW, Washington, DC *20007*
Colt MR & MRS James D (Elizabeth S Reynolds) | ☎ (508) 468-7160
Wheat'61.Un.Tv.H.'54.Va'59 . . . . | 18 Larch Row,
MISS Alexandra R . . . . | Larches View,
MISS Sarah F . . . . | Wenham, MA *01984*
Colt MRS Richard (Cynthia de Bottari) . . . . | of ☎ (713)626-1526
MR Richard T—at ☎ (713) 529-1603 | 4002 Meadow Lake
1717 Bissonnet St, Houston, TX *77005* . . . . | Lane, Houston, TX
  | *77027*
  | ☎ (409) 992-3820
  | Los Potrillos Ranch,
  | Cat Spring, TX
  | *78933*

Colt MR & MRS Rutger B (Patricia L Peterson) . . . . . | of ☎ (410)561-3382
MR Michael T—Loy'88 . . . . | 2214 Midridge Rd,
  | Timonium, MD
  | *21093*
  | ☎ (770) 936-9510
  | 3734F Ashford-
  | Dunwoody Rd NE,
  | Atlanta, GA *30319*
Colt MR Rutger B 3d—Del'85 . . of
  47 Murdock Rd, Baltimore, MD *21212*
  ☎ (770) 936-9510 . . 3734F Ashford-Dunwoody Rd NE, Atlanta, GA *30319*
Colt MR & MRS S Barclay (Hewitt—Julie G George) | ☎ (908) 352-8786
Bg. . . . . | 50 Georgian Court,
MR Edward Cooper Hewitt JR . . . . | Elizabeth, NJ *07208*
Colt MR & MRS S Sloan 2d (Mary F Rowley)
  ☎ (713) 932-1713 . . 13515 Tosca Lane, Houston, TX *77079*
Colt MASTER Samuel Crane (Zenas M C) . . . . Born at
  Atlanta, GA Jun 2'94
Colt MR & MRS William W (Melody K Schultz) NCar'82.Va'69
  ☎ (704) 283-8061 . . 404 S Church St, Monroe, NC *28112-5611*
Colt MR Zenas M C—Va'71 . . . . | ☎ (401) 783-2557
JUNIORS MISS Susannah . . . . | 697 Post Rd,
JUNIORS MR Zenas C 2d . . . . | Wakefield, RI *02879*
Colton MR & MRS Sabin W 5th (Graeme de L Grosvenor) Pa'46
  ☎ (610) LA5-4859 . . ''Dragontor'' Marlbridge Rd, Rosemont, PA *19010*
Colvin MR & MRS James S (Monica Van D Ball) Brist'68
  ☎ (011-44-171) 223-5761 . . 9 Hillier Rd, London SW11 6AX, England
Colwell MR & MRS David H (Katherine M Wood) Scripps'92.Pac'91
  ☎ (415) 456-2110 . . 318 C St, Apt B, San Rafael, CA *94901*
Colwell MR & MRS Kent L (Margaret C Hayes) | ☎ (415) 461-9729
Cal'62.Stan'51.H'57 . . . . | 15 Wolfe Glen Way,
MISS Hilary H—Cal'89.Cal'94 . . . . | Kentfield, CA *94904*
MISS Stacy A—V'91.BankSt'93 . . . . |
Colwill MR Stiles Tuttle—Md.Louis'74
  ☎ (410) 828-0885 . . Halcyon Farm, 11245 Greenspring Av, Lutherville, MD *21093*
Colyer MR & MRS Ralph C (Townsend—Virginia T Bottomley) V'45.Cs.
  ☎ (516) 692-7095 . . 55 Harbor Rd, Oyster Bay, NY *11771*
Combes MR & MRS Abbott C 4th (Constance W | of ☎ (914)666-8578
Wardrop) V'71.Dth'66 . . . . | 277 Haines Rd,
JUNIORS MISS M L deRaismes . . . . | Bedford Hills, NY
JUNIORS MISS Ada Barker . . . . | *10507*
  | Frigate Rd,
  | George Town,
  | Great Exuma,
  | Bahamas
Combs MR & MRS Christopher W (Charlotte F Hughes)
  HRdc'84.H'84.Stan'90
  ☎ (310) 278-5530 . . 1128 Cardiff Av, Apt 202, Los Angeles, CA *90035*
Combs MRS P Craig (Anne Morss) Rdc'58.Chi.Ncd.
  ☎ (213) 935-0064 . . 425 S Plymouth Blvd, Los Angeles, CA *90020-4706*

Comfort MR & MRS William T (Nathalie Pierrepont) Rc.Pr.Cly.Okla'59.Okla'61.Nu'64 . . . . of ☎ (516)676-7737 336 Duck Pond Rd, Box 507, Locust Valley, NY 11560
MR James T—at 1725 N Broadway, Shawnee, OK 74801 . . . .
MR Stuyvesant P—at ☎ (206) 322-3394 1629—43 Av E, Seattle, WA 98112 . . . .
200 E 69 St, New York, NY 10021
☎ (561) 546-2199 63 S Beach Rd, Box 503, Hobe Sound, FL 33475

Comfort MR & MRS William T 3d (Laura L Blodgett)
☎ (011-44-171) 235-6903 . . 155 Pavilion Rd, London SW1 X0BJ, England

Commons REV DR Harold T—Pc.Wms'27 . . of
☎ (215) 438-1096 . . 3119 Midvale Av, Philadelphia, PA 19129
☎ (518) 543-6553 . . "The Pines" Hague, NY 12836

Commons MR & MRS Harold T JR (Carolyn A Damours) Wheat'62.Gc.Pc.Wheat'62.Cr'68 . . . .
MR Richard B . . . .
JUNIORS MR Peter T . . . .
☎ (215) VI9-2241 3119 Midvale Av, Philadelphia, PA 19129

Compton MRS Beverley C (Wagner—Moss L Love)
☎ (410) 527-1878 . . Broadmead K4, 13801 York Rd, Cockeysville, MD 21030

Compton MR & MRS Douglass M (Marie Eugenie Thébaud) Y'32
☎ (203) 245-1859 . . 23 Aylesburg Circle, Madison, CT 06443

Compton MR & MRS Douglass M JR (Katherine H Borda) Vt'80.Hob'76
☎ (860) 521-3705 . . 15 Ten Acre Lane, West Hartford, CT 06107

Compton MR Lathrop . . . . Died at Terrace Park, OH Sep 17'94

Compton MRS Lathrop (Mary M Cope)
☎ (513) 831-7289 . . 1 Lexington Circle, Terrace Park, OH 45174

Comstock MRS Clyde N (Adelaide H Mason) Gchr'40
☎ (561) 732-2820 . . 5 Acacia Dv, Boynton Beach, FL 33436

Comstock MR & MRS John B 2d (Hill—Williams—Joan Morrison)
☎ (860) 399-6010 . . 41 Captains Dv, Pilots Point, Westbrook, CT 06498-1812

Comstock MISS Mary B
☎ (617) 277-8298 . . 54 Dudley St, Brookline, MA 02146

Conant MRS Donald B (Dean—Melville—Betty Jane Goss) Cy.Nh. . . . .
MISS Susan E Dean—Nh. . . . .
☎ (617) 235-8265 18 Columbine Rd, Weston, MA 02193

Conant MR & MRS George K JR (Ellen L Ryerson) Cy.Fic.Nd.
☎ (314) 725-9944 . . 123 N Bemiston St, St Louis, MO 63105

Conant MR & MRS (DR) Jonathan B (Emily R Fox) Vt'81.Pa'84.Rc.LakeF'70.H'80
☎ (215) 247-5413 . . 115 W Moreland Av, Philadelphia, PA 19118

Conaway MRS Howard H (Mary E Mitchell) Cy. . . .
MISS Anne W—Md'79—at ☎ (410) 363-3898 205 Inchcape Circle, Apt 1C, Owings Mills, MD 21117 . . . .
☎ (410) 467-5332 3908 N Charles St, Apt 303, Baltimore, MD 21218

Conaway MR Howard H JR—FP'74
☎ (410) 243-3906 . . 112 Hawthorne Rd, Baltimore, MD 21210

Conderman MRS Theodore H (Bridge—Penelope Gray) Rr.
☎ (619) 756-2792 . . PO Box 173, Rancho Santa Fe, CA 92067

Condie MRS Churchill C (Louise M McCormack)
☎ (314) 966-4038 . . 1001 Bernice Av, Kirkwood, MO 63122

Condie MR & MRS Parker B JR (Margaret A Mayer) Duke'85.Cy.Rr.Br'85.Pa'89
☎ (314) 991-9663 . . 36 Colonial Hills Dv, St Louis, MO 63141

Condie MASTER Peter Mayer (Parker B JR) . . . . Born May 23'95

Condo MRS Emily C (Emily D Clow) LakeF'74 . . .
JUNIORS MISS Elizabeth D . . . .
JUNIORS MISS Allison B . . . .
☎ (203) 655-6827 19 Revere Rd, Darien, CT 06820

Condon MR Martin J 4th . . see MRS R L Hoguet

Cone MR & MRS Loui P 3d (Nancy L Fuller) Aub'72.Aub'72
☎ (334) 834-4906 . . 2160 Rosemont Dv, Montgomery, AL 36111

Coney MR & MRS Aims C JR (Rita N Platt) Pitt'79.Pg.Y'51.Pa'54 . . of
☎ (412) 362-5160 . . 516 Glen Arden Dv, Pittsburgh, PA 15208
☎ (518) 352-7364 . . "Towahloondah" Box 242, Blue Mountain Lake, NY 12812

Congdon MR & MRS James B (Ballard—Annette N Griffitts) Sg.Y'45
☎ (215) 247-0488 . . 7205 Charlton St, Philadelphia, PA 19119

Congdon DR & MRS James B (Sarah-Braeme Bird) Pa'89.Ncd.Pa'72.Camb'75.Pa'77 . . . .
JUNIORS MR A Edward . . . .
☎ (610) 688-1030 39 Northwoods Rd, Radnor, PA 19087

Congdon MR & MRS Jeffrey H (Katherine C Burkett) Briar'70.Bhm.Tcy.Dar.Cal'64 . . . .
MISS Elisabeth B—at U of Cal Berkeley . . . .
JUNIORS MISS Katherine C . . . .
JUNIORS MR Chester A 3d . . . .
☎ (415) 921-1145 3675 Washington St, San Francisco, CA 94118

Conger MR & MRS Clement E (Lianne B Hopkins) Evg.Mt.Cvc.Sl.GeoW'44 . . . .
MR William R . . . .
MISS Shelley Louise (Dabrowski—Shelley Louise Conger) CtCol'76—at 3054 Donna Marta Dv, Studio City, CA 91604-4324 . . . .
of ☎ (703)276-3131 Jefferson Apt 2112, 900 N Taylor St, Arlington, VA 22203
☎ (561) 274-3444 Seagate Towers S, Apt 505S, 220 Macfarlane Dv, Delray Beach, FL 33483

Conger MISS Elizabeth B—Sth'76
☎ (202) 745-5901 . . 3133 Connecticut Av NW, Washington, DC 20008

Conger MR Frederic de P
☎ (212) 249-8942 . . 163 E 81 St, New York, NY 10028

Conger REV & MRS George M (Jane O'Hare) Sth'64.H'56 . . . .
JUNIORS MISS Anne V . . . .
☎ (914) 255-7626 9 Angel Rd, New Paltz, NY 12561

Conger MR & MRS Stephen McC (Mary M Calvert) Cvc.Sl.Ncd.P'44 . . . .
MISS Ann D . . . .
☎ (540) 882-3669 40489 Featherbed Lane, Lovettsville, VA 20180

Conkey MRS C Snowden (Jordan—Aileen H Harris) Dar.
☎ (301) 925-7295 . . 10450 Lottsford Rd, Apt 2215, Mitchellville, MD 20716

Conklin MR & MRS Charles C (Kathleen M Evans) Loy'64 . . . .
MISS Elizabeth E . . . .
MISS Emily T . . . .
JUNIORS MR James C . . . .
☎ (630) 858-2175 21 W 621 Kensington, Glen Ellyn, IL 60137

Conklin MR & MRS George W (Anne P Thomas) Dth'31.Pa'34
☎ (203) 387-6247 . . 10 Hickory Rd, Woodbridge, CT *06525-1442* ⚓
Conklin MR & MRS Louis H (Stone—Gretchen B Knowles) OState'50 ⚓
☎ (207) 529-5921 . . HC 60, Box 86C, Spruce Point, Medomak, ME *04551-9703*
Conklin MRS Reginald (Laura E Foshay) Ht.Cda.
☎ (212) RH4-7121 . . 333 E 68 St, New York, NY *10021*
Conklin MR & MRS Samuel E Egerton (Margaret B Gray)
☎ (602) 265-8282 . . 1656 W Whitton Av, Phoenix, AZ *85015*
Conklin MR & MRS Theodore B (Natalie H O'Brien)
Ny.Sa.Snc.Rv. ⚓ . . of
☎ (941) 964-0453 . . 8 Park Place, Box 1556, Boca Grande, FL *33921*
☎ (516) 288-1975 . . 14 Griffing Av, Westhampton Beach, NY *11978*
Conklin MR & MRS William T 3d (Lillian A Nellen) | ☎ (410) 321-1444
Hav'51 . . . . | 1906 Indian Head
MISS Kathleen—Ws'73—at 825 William St, | Rd, Ruxton, MD
Baltimore, MD *21230* . . . . | *21204*
Conkling MRS William H (Vassar M Townsend) Mv.Cda.
☎ (410) 467-8676 . . 230 Stony Run Lane, Apt 5B, Baltimore, MD *21210*
Conlan MRS Walter A JR (Wilkins—Ellen W Meirs) | ☎ (610) MI9-0475
Me.Ac.Sdg.W.Cda. . . . . | 225 Rose Lane,
MR William M—Me.W.Rich'88.AmU'91—at | Haverford, PA
☎ (610) 527-3529 . . 116 Radnor Av, Villanova, | *19041*
PA *19085* . . . . |
Conlan DR & MRS Walter A 3d (Kristin L Marcin)
Rol'89.Me.W.Ac.Emory'86.Jef'92
☎ (407) 645-4292 . . 1760 Via Contessa, Winter Park, FL *32789*
Conley MRS Charles H JR (Alice P Walker)
199 Baughman's Lane, Frederick, MD *21702*
Conlin MR & MRS Kelly P (Elizabeth A Gilmor) HRdc'82.Carl'82.H'87
☎ (617) 864-2233 . . 48 Buckingham St, Cambridge, MA *02138*
Connard MR & MRS Carroll S (Fraker—Anna S Hayes)
StFran'75.Wms'63 . . of
249 E 48 St, Apt 5C, New York, NY *10017*
''Needufeu Farm'' Wardwell Point Rd, RR 1, Box 65, Penobscot, ME *04476*
Connard MR & MRS David McK (Susan L | ☎ (603) 547-8814
Klingensmith) Temp'69.NCar'74 . . . . | Innholder Farm,
MISS Paula C—at Gettysburg Coll . . . . | 761-2 New
MR Christopher B—at Bates . . . . | Hampshire Tpke S,
JUNIORS MISS Alison K . . . . | Francestown, NH
JUNIORS MR Benjamin D . . . . | *03043*
Connard MR & MRS Frank L JR (Suzette H Waters) | ☎ (716) 248-8992
Pa'65.Pa'66.Dth'71 . . . . | 10 Little Spring
MISS Leila H . . . . | Run, Fairport, NY
| *14450*
Connard MR & MRS Frank L 3d (Rebecca D Martin) Mid'88.Pa'88
☎ (810) 540-2761 . . 390 S Adams Rd, Birmingham, MI *48009*
Connell MR George W—Sa.Me.Sg.Gm.Msq.Pa'58 . | ☎ (610) LA5-4106
MR James S . . . . | 621 Pembroke Rd,
JUNIORS MR Alexander M . . . . | Bryn Mawr, PA
| *19010*
Connell MR & MRS George W JR (Mary A Denison)
Denis'82.Gm.Me.Denis'83
☎ (610) 687-9740 . . 903 Hollow Rd, Radnor, PA *19087*

Connell MRS Henrietta L (Vastine—Gardner— | ☎ (011-44-171)
Henrietta Underwood Lizars) Evg.BtP. . . . . | 581-2273
MISS Frances Gardner—DU'77—at | 10 Trevor Place,
☎ (303) 756-3636 . . 1310 S Monaco P'kway, | London SW7 1LB,
Denver, CO *80224* . . . . | England
Connell MR & MRS James R (Ohmer—Louise Cantwell) Cly.
☎ (212) BU8-4662 . . 108 E 82 St, New York, NY *10028*
Connell MR John B—Pa'73.Y'78
Box 344, Brook Rd, Warren, VT *05674*
Connell MR & MRS Michael J (Karen G Perkins) . . . | 101 Rainbow Dv,
MR K Garett . . . . | Apt 2804,
| Livingston, TX
| *77351*
Connell MR & MRS Michael John (Susan L | ☎ (818) 799-7798
Hazeltine) ColC'63.Clare'65.H'61.H'64 . . . . | 535 Madeline Dv,
MISS Leith B . . . . | Pasadena, CA *91105*
MR Christopher J . . . . |
Connell MR & MRS Robert H (Elisabeth E Armstrong) Mid'86.Me.FlaSt'87
☎ (610) 347-0589 . . PO Box 765, Doe Run Rd, Unionville, PA *19375*
Connell MRS Robert J (Adams—Jeanne L Colket) | ''Cubbyhole Farm''
Ac. . . . . | 548 Knauss Rd,
MR Andrew McI C—Juniata'93 . . . . | Nazareth, PA *18064*
Connelly MR & MRS Albert R (Eleanor Milburn) Un.Mt.Cly.Y.'29
☎ (212) RH4-1711 . . 36 E 72 St, New York, NY *10021*
Connelly MISS Elizabeth M—Miami'89 . . see MRS J V Cracknell
Connelly MR & MRS George M (Sandra L Frazier) | ☎ (215) 836-9434
Ty'82.Pc.Duke'80 . . . . | 222 Glendalough
JUNIORS MISS Katherine F . . . . | Rd, Erdenheim, PA
| *19038*
Conner MR & MRS Edward J (Nancy S Rowe) | ☎ (415) 346-5702
Ws'64.Stan'66.Bur.Pcu.Cp.Cal'59 . . . . | 2698 Vallejo St,
MR Arthur R—Dth'91 . . . . | San Francisco, CA
MR George W—Ken'92 . . . . | *94123*
MR Edward R—Duke'95 . . . . |
Conner MR & MRS John T (Elizabeth B P Colhoun) P'86.Aht'77.Wis'81
☎ (508) 448-3363 . . Groton School, Box 991, Groton, MA *01450*
Conner JUDGE & MRS Lewis H JR (M Ashley | ☎ (615) 252-2383
Whitsitt) Van'60.Van'60.Van'63 . . . . | 163 Charleston Park,
MISS Holland A . . . . | Nashville, TN *37205*
MR Lewis F . . . . |
Conner MR & MRS Stephen P (Mary F Gilbert) StL'79.SWMo'75
☎ (214) 618-0937 . . 2229 Chadbourne Dv, Plano, TX *75023-1627*
Conner MR Thomas D JR
☎ (334) 262-4152 . . 2562 College St, Montgomery, AL *36106*
Connett MR & MRS William C IV (Josephine D Fusz) Wash'33
☎ (561) 369-7651 . . 6861 N Ocean Blvd, Ocean Ridge, FL *33435*
Connick MR & MRS Andrew J (Alice M Lamm) Mds.Ri.Y'52
☎ (212) 534-7433 . . 1060 Fifth Av, New York, NY *10128*
Connolly MR & MRS Christopher C (S Brooke Edelen)
see Dilatory Domiciles
Connolly MR & MRS G Peter 3d (Alice Roberts) V'49.My.
☎ (508) 526-1218 . . 18 Union St, Manchester, MA *01944*
Connolly MISS Helen R
☎ (770) 438-1351 . . 1720 Cedar Cliff Dv, Smyrna, GA *30080*
Connolly MR Joseph C—Dick'95 . . see M B Barrows

Connolly MR & MRS Joseph G J (Patricia A Quinn) | ☎ (610) 642-3517
BMr'91.Pa'93.Ph.R.Gm.Cry.Ac.Pa'62.Pa'65 . . . | 1609 Waverly Rd,
MR James J—Me.Pa'88—at Columbia Grad . . . . | Gladwyne, PA
| *19035*

Connor MR & MRS F Hayden JR (Louise M Bailey) Stan'67.P'59.H'65
☎ (303) 322-7063 . . 444 Grape St, Denver, CO *80220*

Connor MRS J Nothhelfer (Janet Nothhelfer) . . . . Married at Chicago, IL
Holabird MR John A JR (late John A) . . . . May 7'96

Connor MR & MRS John T (Mary O'Boyle) Ln.Cvc.Mt.Cly.Hn.Syr'36.H'39
☎ (561) 626-2147 . . 11854 Turtle Beach Rd, North Palm Beach,
FL *33408*

Connor MISS Sarah L . . see J A Holabird JR

Connor MR Walter F . . . . Died at
Darien, CT Jan 5'96

Connor MRS Walter F (Kathleen Kindred) | ☎ (203) 655-4312
Nw'63.Ch'68.Dar.Ncd.Pn. . . . . | 42 Contentment
JUNIORS MISS Amy—at Groton | Island Rd, Darien,
JUNIORS MISS Caroline . . . . | CT *06820*
JUNIORS MR Keith F—at Groton . . . . |

Connors MR Andrew L—Y'84
☎ (202) 234-3951 . . 1766 Lanier Place NW, Washington, DC *20009*

Connors MR & MRS Crandall S (Leslie R Megear) | ''Meadowspring''
Rc.Pr.B.Cly.Bab'69 | Duck Pond Rd,
MISS Brooke R—at Lynchburg . . . . | Glen Cove, NY
JUNIORS MISS Alexandra A—at Taft . . . . | *11542*

Connors MR & MRS Edward P (D Hope Stout) Y'58
☎ (303) 771-5842 . . 4 Cantitoe Lane, Englewood, CO *80110*

Connors MASTER Hamilton Phillips (Timothy P) . . . . Born at
Denver, CO Jly 14'94

Connors MISS Hope B—Vt'86.ArizSt'89
☎ (505) 982-0470 . . 708 Franklin Av, Santa Fe, NM *87501*

Connors MASTER Lachlan Cryder (Timothy P) . . . . Born at
Denver, CO Jly 24'96

Connors MR & MRS Timothy P (Elsie C Hamilton) Clare'82.Vt'83
☎ (303) 698-2655 . . 1015 S Gilpin St, Denver, CO *80209*

Conrad MR & MRS Barnaby (Slater—Mary Nobles) | ☎ (805) 684-2250
Bhm.Y'44 . . . . | 8132 Puesta del Sol,
MISS Kendall—at ☎ (310) 821-1009 | Carpinteria, CA
746 Marco Place, Venice, CA *90291* . . . . | *93013*

Conrad MR Barnaby 3d—Bhm.Yn.Y'75
☎ (415) 563-7418 . . 2101 Pacific Av, San Francisco, CA *94115*

Conrad CAPT (RET) MR & MRS Charles JR (Crane—Nancy E Fortner)
USN.Col'64.Col'66.P'53
☎ (714) 960-5323 . . 19411 Merion Circle, Huntington Beach, CA *92648*

Conrad MR David C—Br'90.Juilliard'95
☎ (212) 473-8074 . . 29 Av B, Apt 5E, New York, NY *10009*

Conrad MR & MRS Elbert A (Louisa L Vaughan) Chi.
☎ (508) 927-0091 . . 454 Hale St, Box 245, Prides Crossing, MA *01965*
Jan 1 . . ☎ (758) 450-8525 . . Manteca, Box 400, Castries, St Lucia

Conrad MR & MRS James W (Margaret F Clement) | ☎ (412) 242-4750
Me.Rc.P.StJ'48 . . . . | 129 Lloyd Av,
MR Philip T B—Dick'85.Duke'96—at | Apt 2, Pittsburgh,
Rte 9, Box 467, Chapel Hill, NC *27514* . . . . . . | PA *15218*

Conrad MR & MRS Jonathan M (Mary E Beers) Wheat'70.Csh.Cly.W&J'73
☎ (212) 722-2451 . . 1088 Park Av, New York, NY *10128*

Conrad MRS Melinda Parks (Melinda B Parks) . . . . | ☎ (203) 762-7242
MISS Melinda B—*see Dilatory Domiciles* . . . . . . | 29 Crofoot Rd,
MISS Amelia R—at ☎ (212) 255-7124 | Wilton, CT *06897*
96 Perry St, New York, NY *10014* . . . . |
MR John C JR—at ☎ (707) 939-7675 |
18702 White Oak Dv, Sonoma, CA *95476* . . . . . |

Conrad MR & MRS Thomas V (Katherine L Conlon)
Miami'86.Ty'80.StMarys'82
☎ (310) 541-7735 . . 6032 Flambeau Rd, Rancho Palos Verdes,
CA *90274*

Conrad MR & MRS William L (Joanne S Hodges) | ☎ (610) 642-3424
Pa'79.Me.Gi.Geo'80 . . . . | 303 Brentford Rd,
JUNIORS MR Morgan C . . . . | Haverford, PA
| *19041*

Conrad MR & MRS Winthrop B JR (Ellen B Rouse) | of ☎ (212)722-4848
Rdc'72.Lond'76.Cl'77.Bgt.Ri.Y.'67.H'71 . . . . . | 1120 Fifth Av,
JUNIORS MISS Louisa K | New York, NY
JUNIORS MR Parker R . . . . | *10128*
| ☎ (914) 234-3861
| 856 Old Post Rd,
| Rte 121, Bedford,
| NY *10506*

Conroy MISS Kimberley A (Tyrer—Kimberley A Conroy)
Dth'76.Cl'92.Y . . .of
☎ (212) 877-8390 . . 220 W 93 St, Apt 4A, New York, NY *10025-7412*
☎ (603) 448-1065 . . ''Slayton Hill'' RR 1, Slayton Hill Rd,
West Lebanon, NH *03784*

Conroy MR & MRS Robert G (Ann B Omara) | of ☎ (212)535-1247
Barat'48.Y.Dth'44.Dth'46 | 329 E 65 St,
MR Curtis H—Dth'78.Cl'85—at | New York, NY
☎ (415) 325-7226 . . 483 Willow Rd, | *10021*
Menlo Park, CA *94025* . . . . | ☎ (603) 448-1065
| ''Slayton Hill''
| RR 1, Slayton Hill
| Rd, West Lebanon,
| NH *03784*

Conroy MRS Sheila C (Sheila O S Catling) . . see MRS C A R Crosland

Consagra MR & MRS George D (Louisa J Moore) Cal'86.CtCol'84
☎ (415) 292-4689 . . 1580 Filbert St, Apt 16, San Francisco, CA *94123*

Constable MR & MRS George Webb (Elizabeth M | 16131 Old York Rd,
Whedbee) Md.Mv.Cda.P'33.Y'36 . . . . | Monkton, MD
MR Robert A . . . . | *21111*

Constable MR & MRS J Cheston (Priscilla B McCaffrey) Cly.Br'39
☎ (860) 767-8070 . . 53 Foxboro Point, Essex, CT *06426*

Constable MR & MRS James W (Chamberlin—Lott—Katherine M McLean)
Paris'66.Md.Nyc.Va'65.Md'68
☎ (410) 771-4568 . . ''Brerewood'' 2300 Shepperd Rd, Monkton,
MD *21111*

Constable MASTER Peter Oliver (g—Anthony D Jerauld) . . . . . . Born at
Boston, MA Jly 5'96

Constable MR & MRS Philip S (Melinda Oliver Kahle)
StLaw'87.Ub.H.Ham'82
☎ (617) 262-6772 . . 29 Fairfield St, Boston, MA *02116*

Constable MR & MRS Richard D J (Anne P Arnold) | ☎ (310) 541-6121
Snc. . . . . | 85 Yacht Harbor
MISS Ashley A . . . . | Dv, Rancho Palos
| Verdes, CA *90275*

Constable MR & MRS Timothy C (Ann-Louise Hittle) Syr'79
☎ (617) 491-4818 . . 15 Corporal Burns Rd, Cambridge, MA *02138*

Constantine MR & MRS Richard W (Mallory B Merriman) Cda.P'64.Purd'66 . . . . | ☎ (301) 460-5409
MR Wells W 3d—NH'92—at 1239 Union St, | 14801 Westbury Rd,
San Francisco, CA *94109* . . . . | Rockville, MD
MR Thaddeus B—at U of Richmond . . . . | *20853*
JUNIORS MISS Caroline H—at Hall . . . . |

Contomichalos MR & MRS Gerassimo (Sarah H Kinney) Y'85.Cly.Pa'80.Pa'85.Temp'87
☎ (212) 734-3320 . . 116 E 66 St, Apt 8B, New York, NY *10021*

Converse MRS Bernard T JR (Shirley G Smith) . . . . Died at
Bryn Mawr, PA Apr 1'94

Converse MR Bernard T JR—Me.Y.'38
☎ (610) 525-3852 . . 57 Pasture Lane, Bryn Mawr, PA *19010-1763*

Converse MR & MRS Chandler B (Jean A McElroy) Sth'55.BtP.Ri.Evg.Plg.Cw.Y'54.Stan'59
☎ (561) 655-3052 . . 400 N Flagler Dv, Apt 501, West Palm Beach, FL *33401*

Converse MR & MRS Chandler B JR (Karen D De Marco) Denis'83.Kt.Denis'81
☎ (216) 591-9791 . . 31005 Edgewood Rd, Pepper Pike, OH *44124*

Converse MR & MRS Costello C (Funsten—M | of ☎ (561)655-3203
deLancey Moser) Nrr.BtP.Cw. . . . . | 401 Brazilian Av,
MR Peter deL—at ☎ (520) 327-5420 | Palm Beach, FL
1441 E Blacklidge Dv, Tucson, AZ *85719* . . . . . | *33480*
| ☎ (787) 741-1553
| Bo Lujan, PO Box
| 1482, Vieques,
| Puerto Rico *00765*

Converse MR David A (Bernard T JR) . . . . . . Married at Bryn Mawr, PA
Reed MISS Cheryl R . . . . Oct 21'95

Converse MR & MRS Floyd McE (Caroline E Slusser) Duke'82.StLaw'82.Nw'87
☎ (212) 996-2995 . . 1170 Fifth Av, Apt 13D, New York, NY *10029*

Converse MR John H (Ruth M G Bolt) Rc.Gm.Me.Cc.P'42
☎ (610) 254-0344 . . "Inveraray" 502 Heather Circle, Villanova, PA *19085*

Conway MR & MRS Gerald A (Martine Vilas) | ☎ (216) 595-9665
Yn.Y'53 . . . . | 2840 Lander Rd,
MISS Martine . . . . | Pepper Pike, OH
MR Gerald A JR—at ☎ (614) 268-6682 | *44124*
533 Brevoort Rd, Columbus, OH *43214* . . . . |
MR Neil P—at ☎ (216) 442-1409 |
1569 Woodrow Rd, Mayfield Heights, OH *44124* |

Conway MR & MRS Hewitt A (Jeanne L O'Brien) | of ☎ (212)628-5614
Mto.K.Evg.BtP.Snc.Km.Myf.Cw.Vca.Cly.Y.'43. | 200 E 66 St,
Cr'49 . . . . | New York, NY
MISS Louise G—☎ (212) 888-1350 . . . . | *10021*
| ☎ (561) 659-3459
| 321 S Lake Dv,
| Apt 1, Palm Beach,
| FL *33480*

Conway MR & MRS John 4th (Sheridan L Putman) Wis'79.Wis'79
☎ (313) 882-8489 . . 33 Briarwood Place, Grosse Pointe Farms, MI *48236*

Conway MR & MRS Richard J (Ottilie A Wight) | ☎ (610) 642-7334
M.Pa'68.Pa'77 . . . . | 36 Crosby Brown
MISS Tenley M—at Cornell . . . . | Rd, Gladwyne, PA
JUNIORS MISS Lindsay G . . . . | *19035*

Conze MR & MRS Peter H (Elizabeth B Powers) Ny.Myf.P'42
☎ (203) 869-2834 . . 61 Dingletown Rd, Greenwich, CT *06830*

Conzelman MRS Clare S (Clare F Shepley) Cysl. . . | 158 Shoreham
MISS Shelley C . . . . | Village Dv,
MR James G 3d . . . . | Fairfield, CT *06430*

Conzelman MR James G JR—B.Bhm.Cysl.Br'60
☎ (203) 925-0026 . . 11 L'Hermitage Dv, Huntington, CT *06484*

Coogan MR & MRS David F (Margaret W Richards) NEng'85.NEng'85
☎ (617) 383-2512 . . 324 N Main St, Cohasset, MA *02025*

Coogan MR Fairfield G (Edith Park) H'49
PO Box 68, York, ME *03909*

Cook MRS A Werk (Steele—Jane Bancroft)
☎ (941) 955-5255 . . 1253 Hillview Dv, Sarasota, FL *34239*

Cook MR & MRS Arthur B 2d (Nevada L Brooks) SCal'73.Sw'77.Stan'71.SCal'75
☎ (310) 459-8604 . . 13701 Sunset Blvd, Pacific Palisades, CA *90272*

Cook MR & MRS Arthur F JR (Cornelia McL | of ☎(508)428-0257
Lombard) CtCol'58.D.Sm.Chi.Ford'55 . . . . | 42 Bates St,
MISS Nina . . . . | Osterville, MA
MR Laurence L—at 1935 Steamboat Blvd, | *02655*
Steamboat Springs, CO *80477* . . . . | ☎ (941) 493-0113
| 747 N Manasota
| Key Rd, Englewood,
| FL *34223*

Cook MR Averill H . . see MRS W H Vanderbilt

Cook MR & MRS Bruce Stewart (DeLancey K Hollos) Br'77.Unn.Msq.Cly.Dc.Myf.Ht.Ncd.Syr'74 . . of
☎ (203) 869-0614 . . 102 Parsonage Rd, Greenwich, CT *06830*
☎ (401) 348-8223 . . "Ridgecrest" Ridge Rd, Watch Hill, RI *02891*

Cook MRS Camilla W (Camilla S Wright) Ala'44.Ala'47.Cda.
☎ (205) 345-6720 . . 32 Ridgeland, Tuscaloosa, AL *35406*

Cook MR & MRS Charles B JR (Campbell—Barbara | of ☎ (603)253-4542
G Welch) Y'52 . . . . | Kent Island,
MR Charles B 3d—at Burlington, VT . . . . | Squam Lake,
MR Andrew W—at Boston Coll . . . . | Center Harbor, NH
| *03226*
| 118 Valley Rd,
| New Canaan, CT
| *06840*
| ☎ (242) 359-7055
| Cotton Bay,
| Eleuthera, Bahamas

Cook MR & MRS Daniel C (Katharine S Warner) | ☎ (203) 661-7178
Cly.Yn.Y'31 . . . . | 1 Mead Point Dv,
MISS Katharine S—Paris'75—at | Greenwich, CT
☎ (202) 265-8147 . . 1723 Euclid St NW, Apt 1, | *06830*
Washington, DC *20009* . . . . |

Cook MR & MRS Douglas G (J Blake Gardner) Col'81.Nu'85.Cly.Col'79.Ch'82
Pleasantville Rd, New Vernon, NJ *07976*

Cook MRS Earnshaw (Elizabeth H Keyes) Elk.Mv.
☎ (410) 243-5807 . . 830 W 40 St, Apt 858, Baltimore, MD *21211*

Cook MRS Edmund G (Susanna Wright) Sth'33.Ncd.
☎ (610) 642-8680 . . Elm 3310, 3300 Darby Rd, Haverford, PA *19041*

Cook MR & MRS George B (Jean H Kelly) NEng'80.LakeF'80
☎ (610) 971-2179 . . 115 Calvarese Lane, Wayne, PA *19087*

Cook MR & MRS H Clayton JR (Kelsey—Judith A Tabler) Briar'68.Va'71.Rcp.Cos.Cvc.Fic.Myf. P'56.Va'60 . . . .
MISS Rebecca L Kelsey—at Dickinson Law .
JUNIORS MR Parker B Kelsey—at U of Va . . .
☎ (703) 821-2468 1011 Langley Hill Dv, McLean, VA *22101*

Cook MRS Harold J (Nester—Harriet G Phinney) Buf'36
☎ (505) 291-3272 . . 10501 Lagrima De Oro Rd NE, Apt 272, Albuquerque, NM *87111-3742*

Cook MRS Hobart A H (Minot—Molly Cummings) V'40.Eyc . . .of
☎ (203) 869-1067 . . 215 W Old Mill Rd, Greenwich, CT *06831*
☎ (970) 923-1889 . . Snowmass Club TH-38, Harlston Green, Snowmass Center, CO *81615*

Cook MR Jerrold K—H'38
☎ (410) 377-9042 . . 204 Rodgers Forge Rd, Baltimore, MD *21212*

Cook MISS Joan M . . . .
MR Forbes Cleaveland Durey—StLaw'90 . . .
MR Peter Huntting Durey—Vt'94 . . . .
☎ (508) 356-2102 38 Candlewood Rd, Box 401, Ipswich, MA *01938*

Cook MRS John Ransom (Driver—Susan Carlyon-Evans) Ri . . .of
2909 S Ocean Blvd, Highland Beach, FL *33487*
☎ (954) 941-2220 . . Hillsboro Club, 901 Hillsboro Mile, Hillsboro Beach, FL *33062*

Cook MR & MRS John Ransom JR (Pope—Brooke H Chamberlain) Bost'71.H'83.Cy.StLaw'70 . . . . .
MISS Sarah A Pope . . . .
☎ (617) 232-9448 44 Allerton Rd, Brookline, MA *02146*

Cook MR & MRS Kevit R (Gail B Fairman) Cy.Ncd.Br'58 . . . .
MISS Cecily D—Br'85.NCar'89—at
☎ (212) 539-1003 . . 1 Fifth Av, New York, NY *10003* . . . .
☎ (508) 653-8057 102 Washington St, Sherborn, MA *01770*

Cook MR & MRS Langdon P (Lyn C Gillmore) Ln.P'60 . . . .
MISS Corey W—at Kenyon . . . .
MR Langdon C
MR Whitney A—at Hobart-Wm Smith . . . .
JUNIORS MR Frederick H
☎ (203) 869-9036 195 W Old Mill Rd, Greenwich, CT *06831*

Cook MRS Laura A (Laura S Armour) .
MISS Heather S—at 1141A June Creek Rd, Edwards, CO *81632* . . . .
MISS Jennifer C . . . .
MISS Jamie E . . . .
☎ (202) 244-1240 4808 Rockwood P'kway NW, Washington, DC *20016*

Cook MRS Peter G (Joan B Folinsbee) C.
☎ (609) 924-4835 . . "Heathcote Farm" Kingston, NJ *08528*

Cook MR & MRS Peter Trowbridge (Hutton—Anne C Blind) Cl'73.Rcn.Fic.Fiy.Cly.Y'65.H'68 . . . . . .
JUNIORS MR Cutler C T—at Eton Coll . . . .
☎ (202) 588-1450 2206 Kalorama Rd NW, Washington, DC *20008*

Cook MRS Philip (R Patricia Gillespie)
☎ (610) 696-8738 . . 950 N Hill Dv, West Chester, PA *19380*

Cook MR & MRS Ransom S (McGinn—Nan Hemphill) Tcy.Pcu.Stan'55.Stan'59 . . of
☎ (415) 391-4161 . . 1000 Mason St, San Francisco, CA *94108*
☎ (707) 795-5066 . . "The Ranch" 5307 Lichau Rd, Penngrove, CA *94951*

Cook MR & MRS Rodney W (Mary H Tobey) Vt'69 .
MISS Kelly H—at U of Ark . . . .
MR Charles S—at Furman U . . . .
☎ (404) 355-6617 309 Camden Rd NE, Atlanta, GA *30309*

Cook MR & MRS Stephen A (Cynthia A Parker) NCar'69.Ln.Ny.Fic.Fiy.Cly.Ncd.Pa'68.H'76 ⚓ . . of
☎ (212) 289-1222 . . 4 E 95 St, New York, NY *10128*
☎ (516) 788-7384 . . Box 52, Fishers Island, NY *06390*

Cook MR & MRS Thomas McK 3d (Genevieve M Huff) Sar.Myf.Dar.
☎ (410) 823-0840 . . 1405 Carrollton Av, Ruxton, MD *21204*

Cook MR & MRS Thomas P (Mildred D Benedict) Csn.P'32.Va'36
☎ (609) 924-3578 . . 7 Random Rd, Princeton, NJ *08540*

Cook MRS (DR) W Leigh JR (Anne H Rush) V'38.GeoW'46.Rr.
☎ (941) 261-8052 . . 263 Ninth Av S, Naples, FL *34102*

Cook MR Willard P . . see MRS W H Vanderbilt

Cook DR & MRS William Jesse JR (Judy M Wallace) JackSt'60.JackSt'60.Aub'68
☎ (334) 272-9088 . . 123 Foxhall Rd, Pike Road, AL *36064*

Cooke MR & MRS Bradford (Marion P Mundy) Vt'80.Ham'72
☎ (914) 738-7879 . . 421 Stellar Av, Pelham Manor, NY *10803*

Cooke MRS Carlton P (Norma Morgan)
☎ (609) 219-9189 . . Morris Hall M116, PO Box 6498, Lawrenceville, NJ *08648*

Cooke MR & MRS Caswell (Bittel—Marjorie P Adams) Stph'71.Msq.Rv.Dc.
JUNIORS MR Caswell JR—at Boston U . . . .
☎ (401) 348-8381 47 Spruce St, Westerly, RI *02891*

Cooke MR Charles B III—Rv.
☎ (203) 857-4447 . . PO Box 2373, Darien, CT *06820*

Cooke MR Charles B IV—Roch'84
☎ (212) 989-7026 . . 240 W 10 St, Apt 31, New York, NY *10014-2999*

Cooke MR & MRS Dudley P (Deborah B Crowther) Why.Cry.RI'55 ⚓
☎ (610) 527-3789 . . 1142 Calaway Lane, Bryn Mawr, PA *19010*

Cooke MR & MRS Edward S JR (Carol R Warner) Col'75.GeoW'78.Y'77.Del'79.Bost'84
☎ (617) 965-7154 . . 26 Lowell Av, Newtonville, MA *02160*

Cooke MISS F Elizabeth (Peter F) . . . . Married at Sydney, Australia
Haskins MR Craig O (T Richard) . . . . Mch 30'96

Cooke MR & MRS H Emerson (Elaine A Russell) VisArt'82.Bridgept'87
☎ (203) 854-9230 . . 118 W Norwalk Rd, Norwalk, CT *06850*

Cooke MR & MRS Henry E JR (Deborah Wilder) . . . .
MISS Martha H . . . .
☎ (847) 426-2776 Helm Rd, PO Box 36, Barrington, IL *60010*

Cooke MR & MRS James W 3d (Kimberley A Shryock) ArizSt'80
☎ (301) 776-3802 . . "Russett" 8613 Indian Springs Rd, Laurel, MD *20724-1901*

Cooke MRS Jay (Nancy Ellis)
☎ (508) 283-1934 . . "Killybracken" Eastern Point, Gloucester, MA *01930*

Cooke MR & MRS M Todd (Margaret S Groome) Rdc'58.Ph.Rb.Pn.P'42
☎ (610) 356-5461 . . "Greenlands" 620 S Newtown Street Rd, Media, PA *19063*

Cooke MR & MRS Merritt T JR (Grace E Sharples) Cr'80.P'76.Cal'85
US Embassy, Berlin, Germany, PSC 120 FCS, APO AE, *09265*

Cooke MRS Nancy P (Dwight—Nancy L Perry)
☎ (410) 323-5713 . . 119 Cross Keys Rd, Apt D, Baltimore, MD *21210*

Cooke MR & MRS Oakley W (Bibbero—Scott—Rita Bernard) Ne.Leh'42
☎ (212) MU8-2877 . . 20 Sutton Place S, New York, NY *10022*

Cooke MR & MRS Peter F JR (Hilary W Barclay) Pc.Rv.Me.Denis'87
☎ (215) 836-9604 . . 8118 Eastern Av, Wyndmoor, PA *19038*

Cooke MR & MRS R Caswell JR (Mary G Davis) | ☎ (609) 883-1989
Conn'62.Rv.Va'62.Y'67 . . . . | 831 Lawrenceville
MISS Mary G H . . . . | Rd, Lawrenceville,
MR Frederick P H—at Rutgers . . . . | NJ *08648*

Cooke MISS Rebecca C—PAFA'69
☎ (610) 896-0445 . . 429 Montgomery Av, Apt C1, Haverford, PA *19041*

Cooke MR & MRS Robert A (Altair Z Machado) | ☎ (908) 542-0653
Rm.Stc.Cly.Yn.Y'41 . . . . | ''Hockhockson
MISS (DR) Claudia M—SL'80.Tul'87 . . . . | Farm'' 228 Rte
| 537E, Colts Neck,
| NJ *07722*

Cooke MISS Rosena M
☎ (203) 866-6842 . . 11 Old Rock Lane, Norwalk, CT *06850*

Cooke MRS S Graff (Sara M Graff) Pc.Ncd . . . . | of ☎ (215)843-5964
MISS Laina K—Penn'92—at ☎ (215) 925-4136 | ''English Tudor III''
511 Pine St, Philadelphia, PA *19106* . . . . | 3421 Warden Dv,
MISS Sara R—Wells'93—at ☎ (215) 925-4136 | Philadelphia, PA
511 Pine St, Philadelphia, PA *19106* . . . . | *19129*
| ☎ (610) 584-3874
| 22 Hickory Heights,
| Lansdale, PA *19446*

Cooke MRS Susan E (Susan H Emerson) CentCtSt'57
☎ (203) 655-1223 . . 16 Pine Brook Lane, Darien, CT *06820*

Cooley MR & MRS A Crawford (Jess Porter) Bhm.Stan'49
☎ (415) 892-1535 . . ''Casa Mia'' Box 1146, Novato, CA *94948*

Cooley MR & MRS Charles P 3d (Lucy Grosvenor Robinson)
Y'79.Yn.Y'78.Dth'83
☎ (818) 798-1411 . . 1405 N Chester Av, Pasadena, CA *91104*

Cooley MR & MRS John B JR (Joan P Ferguson) | ☎ (970) 923-3369
Col'66.Cal'64 . . . . | 0346 Woods Rd,
MISS Kate P . . . . | Box Q, Aspen, CO
MR John B 3d . . . . | *81612*

Cooley MISS Leslie A . . see MRS R Collins

Cooley MR Mark . . see MRS R Collins

Cooley MR R Pierce JR . . see MRS R Collins

Cooley MR Sean . . see MRS R Collins

Cooley MISS Sheila . . see MRS R Collins

Coolidge MR & MRS A William (Smith—Morgan— | ☎ (207) 363-2934
Elizabeth W Winsor) . . . . | 9 Scotland Bridge
MISS Natalie B Smith (Hines—Natalie B | Rd, York, ME
Smith) . . . . | *03909*

Coolidge MR & MRS Francis L (Marylouise E Redmond)
Bost'69.Sm.Tv.Ub.Cy.K.Nrr.H'68.Bost'71 . . of
☎ (617) 723-4697 . . 62 Beacon St, Boston, MA *02108*
☎ (508) 636-2836 . . 1103 Horseneck Rd, South Westport, MA *02790*

Coolidge MRS Harold J (Martha T Henderson) Rdc'46.Rdc'56.Cos.Sm.
☎ (617) 547-4196 . . 19 Brewster St, Cambridge, MA *02138*

Coolidge MR J Randolph—C.H'38
☎ (603) 284-6449 . . ''Mull'' Rte 1, Box 23, Center Sandwich, NH *03227*

Coolidge MRS John P R (Mary Elizabeth Welch) H.
☎ (617) 354-4279 . . 24 Gray Gardens W, Cambridge, MA *02138*

Coolidge MR & MRS John W JR (Helen B Stillman) | ☎ (617) 631-6270
Skd'59.Ey.H'56.Va'64 . . . . | 247 Ocean Av,
MISS Jennifer W—CtCol'91 . . . . | Marblehead, MA
| *01945*

Coolidge MISS Julia—MtH'37
☎ (603) 284-6211 . . ''Coolidge Farm'' RR 1, Box 38, Center Sandwich, NH *03227*

Coolidge MR & MRS Lawrence (Myers—Nancy H Goldsmith)
Ws'58.Sm.Ub.H'58
☎ (617) 227-3230 . . 85 Mt Vernon St, Boston, MA *02108*

Coolidge MR & MRS Nicholas J (Eliska Hasek) | of ☎ (202)338-9415
Geo'63.Cvc.K.B.Sm.Mt.Sl.H'54.H'59 . . . . | 3200 Scott Place
MISS Alexandra R . . . . | NW, Washington,
| DC *20007*
| ☎ (212) 355-0450
| 800 Fifth Av,
| New York, NY
| *10021*

Coolidge MR Peter J—K.Sm.H'92
☎ (212) 517-3401 . . 10 Gracie Square, New York, NY *10028*

Coolidge MR Robert T—H'55.Cal'57.Ox'66 . . . . . . | ☎ (514) 932-3706
MR Miles C—at ☎ (213) 482-1805 | Box 4070,
1422 Ridge Way, Los Angeles, CA *90026* . . . . . | Westmount,
MR Matthew P—at ☎ (510) 268-3748 | Quebec H3Z 2X3,
499 Embarcadero, Oakland, CA *94606* . . . . | Canada

Coolidge MR & MRS Thomas R (Susan L Freiberg) | ☎ (860) 824-0373
Rdc'62.B.Ri.Plg.Cly.H'55.H'60 . . . . | ''Red Fox Farm''
MISS Laura J—P'89.H'93.Cly.—at | Falls Village, CT
☎ (011-44-171) 706-8856 . . 16 Hyde Park | *06031*
Square, London W2 2JR, England . . . . |
MISS Anne R—H.'91.Cly.—at ☎ (212) 753-4203 |
325 E 57 St, New York, NY *10022* . . . . |
MR Thomas L—at Georgetown Sch of |
Foreign Service . . . . |

Coolidge MRS William H (Eleanor Cole)
☎ (860) 346-7147 . . Lutheran Home, 628 Congdon St, Middletown, CT *06457*

Coolidge MRS Winthrop K (Cook—Catherine J Beresford-Owen) Sc.
☎ (520) 529-6361 . . 4532 N Via Entrada, Tucson, AZ *85718*

Coombe MR & MRS Michael A (Martha Tucker Jones)
Mid'83.Va'86.Y'82.Cl'86
☎ (513) 321-5348 . . 3526 Mooney Av, Cincinnati, OH *45208*

Coombe MR & MRS V Anderson (Eva Jane Romaine) | ☎ (513) 871-1266
BMr'52.Qc.Cm.Y'48 . . . . | 6 Corbin Dv,
MR Peter R—Y'83.H'88—at ☎ (212) 274-8256 | Cincinnati, OH
97 Kenmare St, New York, NY *10012* . . . . | *45208-3302*

Coombs MRS Francis P (Pierce—Amelia E Mason) Pa'49.Ck.
☎ (561) 659-2487 . . 196 Belmont Rd, West Palm Beach, FL *33405*

Coombs MR James L—H'38
☎ (304) 758-4838 . . Long Creek Farm, RD 2, Box 34, Sistersville, WV *26175*

Coonan MRS James F (Lurline Roth) Bur.
  ☎ (415) 366-5875 . . 176 Harcross Rd, Woodside, CA *94062-2316*
Cooney MISS Beatrice Ruth (Philip A) . . . . Born Apr 1'96
Cooney MR & MRS Philip A (Marney A Burke)
  RMWmn'81.Rich'81.VillaN'84
  ☎ (703) 960-7435 . . 1808 Edgehill Dv, Alexandria, VA *22307*
Coonley MISS Carol L . . see MRS J Carey
Coonley MISS Deborah B . . see F R S Sellers JR
Coonley MR & MRS Howard 2d (Bright—Martha K S   ☎ (215) 238-9947
  Walton) Swb'70.Me.Pa'66 . . . .   251 Pine St,
    MISS Mary S W Bright . . . .   Philadelphia, PA
    JUNIORS MISS Laura S K Bright *19106*
Coonley MR Howard 3d . . see F R S Sellers JR
Coons MRS Dorothy J (Dorothy H Johns)
  ☎ (805) 969-5772 . . 919 Alston Rd, Santa Barbara, CA *93108*
Coope MR & MRS Robert L (Beverly V Ray)   ☎ (602) 264-2453
  Roch'52.Stan'56.H'50.H'54 . . . .   42 W Marlette Av,
    MISS Katharine L—Duke'92 . . . .   Phoenix, AZ *85013*
    MR Robert R—Pa'84 . . . .
    MR Gordon R—H'85 . . . .
Cooper MR Alan A—McG'84 . . see R H Soule
Cooper MRS Alexandra M (Alexandra M Miller)   ☎ (617) 631-7320
  Ey. . . . .   15 Sevinor Rd,
    JUNIORS MR Grant D . . . .   Marblehead, MA
       01945
Cooper MR Angus R 2d—At.Ala'64 . . . .   of ☎ (334)928-8012
    MISS Ashley K Wadick—at ☎ (512) 467-7032   17475 Scenic H'way
  1517 Madison Av, Austin, TX *78757* . . . .   98, Point Clear, AL
       36564
       ☎ (504) 861-9324
       123 Walnut St, Apt
       801, New Orleans,
       LA *70118*
Cooper MR & MRS Bruce D F (Bonaventura Kenny)   ☎ (908) 277-6542
  Marq'70.Cw.Myf.W'ham'69 . . . .   39 Druid Hill Rd,
    MISS Melissa K . . . .   Summit, NJ *07901*
    MISS M Courtenay . . . .
    MISS Christine D . . . .
    JUNIORS MISS Caroline K . . . .
    JUNIORS MR Andrew C . . . .
Cooper MR & MRS Charles T (Nancy S Hovey)   ☎ (508) 768-6969
  Nf.Ny.My.Hob'72 . . . .   "Lilac Hill"
    JUNIORS MR Chandler H . . . .   8 John Wise Av,
    JUNIORS MR Charles L . . . .   Essex, MA *01929*
Cooper MR & MRS David J (Joanne Knowles) SAla'69.At.Ala'67
  ☎ (334) 476-6264 . . 102 Ryan Av, Mobile, AL *36607*
Cooper DR & MRS David Y (Cynthia Laughlin) Pa'48
  ☎ (610) 525-3665 . . 424 Colebrook Lane, Bryn Mawr, PA *19010*
Cooper MR Douglas C . . see R H Soule
Cooper MRS Elizabeth Fuller (Elizabeth Wiley Fuller) Myf.Cda.
  ☎ (212) AT9-6559 . . 55 E 87 St, New York, NY *10128*
Cooper MR & MRS Fowler F JR (Sanda C Leach) SL'70.So'63.Pa'67
  ☎ (704) 264-7385 . . Rte 4, Box 503M, Boone, NC *28607*
Cooper MR & MRS Harold B 3d (Geraldine P Christ) NEng'82.Cly.Wit'76
  ☎ (203) 894-8867 . . 42 Rolling Hill Rd, Ridgefield, CT *06877*
Cooper MR & MRS Henry E 3d (Terrell Porter) Rdc'44.Co.Ey.Chi.Ncd.P'44
  ☎ (617) 631-8642 . . 103 Beacon St, Marblehead, MA *01945-2620*

Cooper MR & MRS Henry Spotswood Fenimore   ☎ (212) AT9-4829
  (Mary L Langben) C.Gr.Y.'56 . . . .   1165 Fifth Av,
    MISS Hannah L F . . . .   New York, NY
    MISS Mary M F *10029*
Cooper MR & MRS James H (Cendy M Smith)   ☎ (334) 277-0184
  Aub'79.J'ville'71 . . . .   3550 Center Hill Rd,
    JUNIORS MR Jon C . . . .   Montgomery, AL
       36106
Cooper MR & MRS John L (Marie T McCook) D.Nh.K.Sm.Chi.Yn.Y'35 . . of
  ☎ (508) 785-0447 . . 36 Wilsondale St, Dover, MA *02030*
  ☎ (401) 635-2609 . . 113 Quicksand Pond Rd, Box 576,
  Little Compton, RI *02837-0576*
Cooper MR & MRS John L JR (Elizabeth Baptiste) Vh.LakeF'66
  ☎ (213) 258-5694 . . 1565 Poppy Peak Dv, Pasadena, CA *91105*
Cooper MR John N P—Hn.H'78 . . of
  ☎ (615) 684-3621 . . 413 E Lane St, Shelbyville, TN *37160*
  1790 Broadway, Apt 402, San Francisco, CA *94109*
Cooper MR John W W—Un.Plg.Cw.Myf.Va'71
  ☎ (212) 348-6009 . . 201 E 87 St, New York, NY *10128*
Cooper MR & MRS Joseph W J JR (Dorothea-Louise   of ☎ (212)517-6522
  Phelps) P'53.Va'58 . . . .   1035 Fifth Av, Apt
    MISS Dorothea Grier—at 2665 Pine St, Apt 1,   3B, New York, NY
  San Francisco, CA *94115* *10028*
    MR Joseph W J 3d . . . .   ☎ (802) 297-9363
    MR James H—at N'eastern . . . .   "Coopershaven"
    MR Brendon P . . . .   High Meadow Rd,
       Box 428, Stratton,
       VT *05155*
Cooper MRS Kiessling (Fay—Muriel Gurdon   ☎ (203) 966-0408
  Kiessling) . . . .   Box 567,
    MR W Bayard—at Phoenix, AZ . . . .   New Canaan, CT
       06840
Cooper MRS Leslie T (Struthers Joyce) . . . .   ☎ (610) MI9-1178
  DR Leslie T JR—Cc.Pa'85.Pa'90—at   211 Winsor Lane,
  ☎ (415) 497-0333 . . 1150 Welch Rd, Apt 525,   Haverford, PA
  Palo Alto, CA *94304* *19041*
Cooper MRS Morrill (Trott—Nancy E Morrill) . . . .   ☎ (441) 29-61226
  MISS Nancy W L—at 46 Lansdowne Rd,   "Greendale"
  London W11, England . . . .   Paget PG 02,
       Bermuda
Cooper MR & MRS N Lee (C Joy Clark) Ala'62.Cy.Ala'62.Ala'64
  ☎ (205) 879-8805 . . 2831 Southwood Rd, Birmingham, AL *35223*
Cooper LT COL & MRS Richmond J (Janet G Felton)   ☎ (703) 549-3041
  Mt.My.Cc.USA'48 . . . .   222 Jefferson St,
    MISS Hope G—Va'86.Va'89 . . . .   Alexandria, VA
    MR Phineas C—Rich'93 . . . .   *22314*
Cooper MR & MRS Robert E (Eunice A Hurst)   ☎ (205) 870-4262
  Ala'75.Ala'77.Ala'74.Ala'77 . . . .   118 Overbrook Rd,
    JUNIORS MISS Barbara E . . . .   Birmingham, AL
       35213
Cooper MR & MRS Thomas C JR (Elizabeth A   ☎ (860) 485-1417
  Waters) SL'83.Ihy.Yn.Y'51 . . . .   "Homewood"
    MISS Alice H . . . .   222 Woodchuck
    MR William O W . . . .   Lane, Harwinton,
       CT *06791*

Cooper MR & MRS Tom R JR (Alison Beach) SFrSt'65 . . . . / MISS Christina deF . . . . / MR Scott T . . . . ☎ (415) 327-5408 / 251 Greenoaks Dv, / Atherton, CA *94027*

Cooper MRS Virginia F (Batchelder—Virginia F Cooper) Pa'55.Ncd. / ☎ (954) 943-5049 . . 2961 NE 27 Av, Lighthouse Point, / Pompano Beach, FL *33064*

Cooper MR & MRS William B (Susan H Gates) Cal'78 / ☎ (510) 376-9067 . . 32 La Salle Dv, Moraga, CA *94556*

Cooper MR & MRS William S 3d (A Glyde / Greenfield) Cal'61.Tcy.Mit'58.Cal'63 . . . . / MR John S—Hn.H'93—at ☎ (202) 667-3022 / 2401 Calvert St NW, Apt 211, Washington, DC / *20008* . . . . / MR William B—H'93—at ☎ (212) 535-7832 / 161 E 81 St, Apt 1E, New York, NY *10028* . . . . ☎ (510) 526-3526 / 85 Southampton Av, / Berkeley, CA *94707*

Coords MRS Deane M (Priscilla S Todd) Lm.Dar. . . / MISS Barbara S—Lm.Dar.—at ☎ (860) 364-1130 / 144 East St, Sharon, CT *06069* . . . . ☎ (904) 423-4314 / 3501 S Atlantic Av, / New Smyrna Beach, / FL *32169*

Coorssen MRS Eugenia B (Eugenia Boies) . . . . / MISS Eugenia—at U of Fla . . . . / MR George G . . . . ☎ (941) 351-1924 / 5910 Middle Av, / Sarasota, FL *34243*

Cope MR Jonathan B . . see MISS E P Baxter

Cope MR & MRS Newton A (Derby—Marion R Moore) / Bur.Pcu.Sfg.Tcy . . .of / ☎ (415) 391-2120 . . 1000 Mason St, San Francisco, CA *94108* / ☎ (408) 626-1561 . . ''Casa Ladera'' 1658 Crespi Lane, Pebble Beach, / CA *93953*

Cope MR & MRS Paul M JR (Lowry—Mary L McKinney) Ac.Hav'47.Pa'50 / ☎ (215) 247-8148 . . 191 E Evergreen Av, Philadelphia, PA *19118*

Cope MR & MRS Walter E (Louise W Bergner) / ☎ (610) 353-3490 . . 720 Malin Rd, Newtown Square, PA *19073*

Copeland MRS Ann Bellah (Ann P Bellah) Cly.Pr.BtP.Cda.Dc.Ht . . .of / ☎ (212) 831-1240 . . 17 E 89 St, Apt 7B, New York, NY *10128* / ☎ (561) 842-0642 . . 232 Mockingbird Trail, Palm Beach, FL *33480*

Copeland DR & MRS Clyde X JR (Elizabeth A Wise) Rm'60.Cda.Mlsps'55 / ☎ (601) 982-3208 . . 1426 Roxbury Place, Jackson, MS *39211*

Copeland MR & MRS Gerret van S (Tatiana Brandt) Cal'66.Pr.Wil.Ht. / ☎ (302) 656-1675 . . 175 Brecks Lane, Box 4060, Greenville, DE *19807*

Copeland MRS Lammot du P (Pamela Cunningham) Cly.Ac.Ncd. / ☎ (302) 239-5236 . . Box 3570, Greenville, DE *19807*

Copeland MR & MRS Randall E (Jane B Muskat) / Ph.M.Myf.Ac.Ncd.Wis'31 . . . . / MISS Jane B—at 22 W Willow Grove Av, / Philadelphia, PA *19118* . . . . ☎ (610) 642-3355 / 1400 Waverly Rd, / Villa 30, Gladwyne, / PA *19035-1273*

Copp MR & MRS Daniel N (McFadden—Nancy C S Rockefeller) / Ws'49.Y'43 / ☎ (901) 754-7220 . . 2788 Germantown Rd, Germantown, TN *38138*

Coppins MR & MRS J Burge (Stephanie A Feola) ArizSt'82.ArizSt'74 / ☎ (602) 947-9354 . . 5747 E Camelback Rd, Phoenix, AZ *85018*

Corballis MR & MRS Edward A B (Kenworthy— / Inger Överland) StMartin'75.PugetS'78.Rol'64 . / MISS Kecia E Kenworthy—Sth'91 . . . . ☎ (203) 255-9117 / 121 Regents Park, / Westport, CT / *06880-5552*

Corbett MR Andrew J JR—Rc.B.Ec.Geo'64 . . of / ☎ (212) 535-8428 . . 1365 York Av, Apt 20F, New York, / NY *10021-4045* / ☎ (508) 768-7820 . . 76 Eastern Av, Essex, MA *01929*

Corbett MRS Victoria Phillips (Victoria A Phillips) / Cly . . . . / MISS Christina D . . . . / MR Andrew J 3d—at Holy Cross . . . . / JUNIORS MR William P—at Berkshire . . . . ☎ (212) 861-3747 / 150 E 69 St, Apt 3T, / New York, NY / *10021*

Corbin MRS Horace K JR (Edith D Milbank) V'37.Bg. / Meadow Lakes 19-08, Hightstown, NJ *08520*

Corbin MR & MRS Horace K 3d (Emilie M Wood) / San.Ty'63.Pa'72 . . . . / MISS Gretchen S . . . . / JUNIORS MISS Emilie O . . . . / JUNIORS MR Horace K 4th . . . . ☎ (201) 425-2228 / Peachcroft Rd, / Morristown, NJ / *07960*

Corbin MRS Justine M (Justine B Montgomery) . . . / MR R Beverley 3d—Vt'83—at ☎ (212) 688-5706 / 200 E 66 St, Apt D1503, New York, NY *10021* / MR C Suydam Cutting—at ☎ (970) 920-6870 / PO Box 12046, Aspen, CO *81612* . . . . of ☎ (516)283-5532 / ''Potpourri'' / PO Box 1276, / 224 Great Plains Rd, / Southampton, NY / *11969* / ☎ (212) 688-3793 / 200 E 66 St, / New York, NY / *10021* / ☎ (809) 494-2730 / Wyndcliffe, Havers, / Tortola, BVI

Corbin MR & MRS Peter S (Lillian S Pyne) Wes'68 . / JUNIORS MISS Lindsey P . . . . / JUNIORS MR Parker S . . . . ☎ (914) 677-9539 / ''Shooters Hill'' / RD 1, Box 128B, / Fraleigh Hill Rd, / Millbrook, NY / *12545*

Corbin MR & MRS R Beverley JR (Green—Patricia Peerson) / Tex'50.Rcn.Ri.Srb.Cly.H'47 / ☎ (401) 847-7900 . . ''Crow's Nest'' Price's Neck, Ocean Av, Newport, / RI *02840*

Corbyn MR & MRS Richard C (Wright—Helen L Troudner) Myf.Rv. / ☎ (806) 359-4966 . . 3801 Lewis Lane, Amarillo, TX *79109*

Corcoran MRS Charles De B (Jane L Roesler) . . . . . / MR Andrew P—StLaw'88 . . . . ☎ (516) 922-0402 / 41 Vernon Av, / East Norwich, NY / *11732*

Corcoran MR John B—Ck.Rc.Mid'86 / ☎ (212) 427-9264 . . 182 E 95 St, Apt 20A, New York, NY *10128*

Corcoran MR & MRS Thomas A (Fogg—Daphne K / Andresen) Dth'54.H'59 ⚑ / MISSES Christine E & Kathleen A—at / Town Square, Waterville Valley, NH *03215* . . . / MISS Kerry P—at 2320 Butch Cassidy Dv, / Bozeman, MT *59715* . . . . / MR Michael P—at W Branch Rd, / Waterville Valley, NH *03215* . . . . / MISS Daphne M Fogg—at 20 Chapel St, / Apt 611C, Brookline, MA *02146* . . . . ☎ (603) 236-4741 / Greeley Hill Rd, / Waterville Valley, / NH *03215*

Cordova MR Robert A JR . . see MRS C T McCormick
Corey MR & MRS Alan L JR (Patricia Grace) Rc.Mb.Pr.Y'40
☎ (516) 334-0102 . . Box 465, 6 Windsor Dv, Old Westbury, NY *11568*
Corey MR & MRS Alan L 3d (Raezer—Wetzel—Patricia Ellis)
Sim'63.YeshivaU'83.Unn.Pr.Y'65
☎ (803) 649-2075 . . 129 Easy St, Aiken, SC *29801*
Corey MR Alan L 4th . . see P J Pell
Corey MISS Christine M . . see P J Pell
Corey MISS Cynthia E . . see P J Pell
Corey MR R William . . see P J Pell
Corey MR & MRS W Russell G (Elizabeth S O'Brien) Rcn.Pr.Pa'69 . . . . | ☎ (561) 274-6436
1125 Waterway
JUNIOR MISS Elizabeth C . . . . | Lane, Delray Beach,
FL *33483*
Corley MRS Francis C (Barbara Barton) Bv.Ncd.
☎ (314) 991-5680 . . 51 Magnolia Dv, St Louis, MO *63124*
Corley MR & MRS Robert C JR (Judith A Voellinger) StL'62.StL'73.StL'63 . . . . | ☎ (314) 726-3245
15 E Brentmoor
MISS Mary S—at Columbia . . . . | Park, St Louis, MO
MR Robert C—at Notre Dame . . . . | *63105*
Cormier MR Clayton P—Rc.Rby.Mich'54.Mich'57
☎ (212) 360-6799 . . 246 E 94 St, New York, NY *10128*
Cormier MRS Judy C (Nicholls—Judy Carter) . . . . . | ☎ (212) 517-3993
164 E 72 St,
MISS Jamie C Nicholls—Aht'88.H'92—at | New York, NY
☎ (212) 717-4656 . . 211 E 70 St, Apt 28D, | *10021*
New York, NY *10021* . . . . |
Cornelius DR & MRS Chalmers E 3d (Sandra C | ☎ (610) 649-2056
Sidford) Pa'65.BMr'75.P'60.Pa'64 . . . . | "Four Winds"
MISS Grace S—at Princeton . . . . | 1 Andover Rd,
MISS Sara J—at Muhlenburg . . . . | Haverford, PA
19041
Cornell MR & MRS Allen D JR (A Joanne Norberg) Pa'51
☎ (610) 525-5064 . . 702 Hamilton Rd, Bryn Mawr, PA *19010*
Cornell MR & MRS James K (Shields—E Sara Rowbotham)
Lawr'85.Cy.NCar'85
☎ (617) 424-9373 . . 416 Commonwealth Av, Apt 103, Boston,
MA *02215*
Cornell MRS Jeanne S (Hoffman—Jeanne R | ☎ (610) 688-1413
Spoerer) NCar'64 . . . . | 229 Bloomingdale
MISS Lauren E Hoffman—Y'91.Me. . . . . . . | Av, Apt 5, Wayne,
MR Edward J Hoffman 3d—Cal'95 . . . . . . | PA *19087*
Cornell MRS Katharine F (M Keen) . . . . . . | Married at Sopron, Hungary
Gorka MR Sebestyén (Paul) . . . . | Jly 6'96
Cornell MR & MRS Owen M JR (Sally A Osborne) | ☎ (301) 983-1071
Miami'51.Cwr'54 . . . . | 11133 Hurdle Hill
MISS Martha O—Rm'83—at Phila Med Coll . . . | Dv, Potomac, MD
MISS Amy T—Del'85—at ☎ (703) 698-8027 | *20854*
7800 Willow Point Dv, Falls Church, VA *22042* |
MR Owen M 3d—JMad'82—at |
☎ (617) 247-7638 . . 186 W Brookline St, Apt 2, |
Boston, MA *02118* . . . . |
MR Cuyler J—Md'85—at ☎ (301) 365-5033 |
7505 Democracy Blvd, Bethesda, MD *20852* . . . |
Cornell MRS Pamela K (Sawyer—Pamela A Kent) Bur.
☎ (415) 851-0675 . . 3110 Woodside Rd, Woodside, CA *94062*
Cornell MISS Schuyler Van Rensselaer (James K) . . . . Born Oct 7'94

Cornell MR T H Maher—Me.Y'54 . . . . | ☎ (813) 734-3332
2138 Gulf View
MISS Hilary S—Del'83—at Philadelphia, PA . . . | Blvd, Dunedin, FL
MISS Elizabeth A—*see Dilatory Domiciles* . . . . . | *34698*
MISS Amy B—at Philadelphia, PA . . . . |
Corning MISS Ursula—Csn.
☎ (011-39-75) 932135 . . Civitella Ranieri, Umbertide,
06019 Perugia, Italy
Cornish MR & MRS John G (Alice P Smith) Cy.Ncd.H.'33
☎ (617) 734-5975 . . 106 Clyde St, Chestnut Hill, MA *02167*
Cornman DR & MRS Henry D 3d (Nancy L | ☎ (610) MI2-7736
Knowlton) Pe.Rv.Hav'41.Pa'44 . . . . | 229 Conshohocken
MR Henry D 4th . . . . | State Rd, Gladwyne,
MR Randell F . . . . | PA *19035*
Cornwell MR & MRS Alexander M JR (Mary G Seibel) Cy.Y'50
☎ (314) 991-2111 . . 63 Clermont Lane, St Louis, MO *63124*
Corrigan MR & MRS Hugh IV (Ann B Goddard) | ☎ (214) 520-0833
Smu'71.Smu'71 . . . . | 3809 Shenandoah St,
JUNIORS MR Bryan H . . . . | Dallas, TX *75205*
Corrigan MR & MRS James N (Carolyn L Martin) | ☎ (202) 966-0271
Gv.Mt.Cvc.Br'57 . . . . | 5054 Sedgwick St
MISS Nancy B . . . . | NW, Washington,
MR James N JR . . . . | DC *20016*
MR John M . . . . |
MR Peter B . . . . |
MR Michael F . . . . |
Corroon MRS Robert F (Helen V Maitland) Csn. . . . | ☎ (203) 869-0771
MISS Andrée B—at ☎ (212) 308-5077 | 27 Greenbriar Lane,
20 Beekman Place, New York, NY *10022* . . . . . | Greenwich, CT
MR Richard F 2d—at ☎ (212) 369-6807 | *06831*
110 E 87 St, New York, NY *10128* . . . . |
MSRS Peter M & Christopher L—at |
☎ (801) 654-4874 . . 743 S Southfield Dv, |
Heber City, UT *84032* . . . . |
Corroon MR & MRS Robert F JR (Elizabeth R Love)
Vt'81.Pratt'89.SantaFe'81.Nu'86.Nu'91
☎ (203) 255-8688 . . 1480 Cross H'way, Fairfield, CT *06430*
Corse MR & MRS Dean McN C (Bell—Roberta A Patrick)
Cc.Ll.Fw.Cw.Rv.Sar.Ne'70.Emer'78
☎ (603) 430-1055 . . 42 Beechstone St, Apt 1, Portsmouth, NH *03801*
Corser MR & MRS Dallas L (Blackman—Elizabeth S Bell)
Stph'56.Bgt.H.'54.H'58
☎ (914) 232-8619 . . 112 Cantitoe Rd, Katonah, NY *10536*
Corsini MR & MRS Russell V JR (Althea T Harty) | ☎ (617) 237-1322
Geo'65.Bab'67 . . . . | 19 Lincoln Rd,
MISS Lisa H . . . . | Wellesley Hills, MA
MR Russell V 3d—Leh'95 . . . . | *02181*
Corsini di Laiatico MR & MRS Alessandro (Michelle M de Kwiatkowski)
Ty'84.B.Bost'80
☎ (212) 888-2868 . . 570 Park Av, New York, NY *10021*
Corsini di Laiatico MCHSE Cino & MCHSA (Aimée G | ☎ (011-39-564)
Russell) B. . . . . | 832368
MISS Desideria—at ☎ (212) 888-0071 | 58018 Porto Ercole,
320 E 57 St, New York, NY *10022* . . . . | Grosseto, Italy
Corson MRS Alan JR (Law—Florence Sigafoos) Dll.
☎ (215) 928-1012 . . 708 Hopkinson House, 604 Washington Square S,
Philadelphia, PA *19106*

Corson MRS Bolton L (Carolyn R Davis) Pc.
see Dilatory Domiciles
Corson MR Edward F—P'76
☎ (201) 539-4170 . . 26 Speedwell Place, Morristown, NJ *07960*
Corson DR & MRS Joseph K (Charlton L Barnes)
Wells'45.Pa'72.W.Ll.Ac.Ncd.Colg'43.Pa'47 . . of
☎ (610) 828-0960 . . "Maple Hill" 3047 Spring Mill Rd,
Plymouth Meeting, PA *19462*
☎ (307) 455-2511 . . "Three Owls" E Fork Rd, Dubois, WY *82513*

Corson MR & MRS Walter H 2d (Kuhns—Ann S	☎ (703) 683-5030
Dusel) Cal'64.Ofp.P'54.H'71	1399 Orchard St,
MR Trevor C—at Princeton	Alexandria, VA
MR Ashley P—at Conn Coll	*22302-4215*
MISS Jennifer D Kuhns	
MISS Pamela G Kuhns—at Stanford	

Corson MR & MRS William C (Lauran A Fulton) Mich'78.Colg'82
☎ (908) 903-0700 . . 120 Governor Dv, Basking Ridge, NJ *07920*
Cort MR & MRS John (Doris I Meyer) Rv.Sar.
☎ (212) 777-6728 . . 18 Stuyvesant Oval, New York, NY *10009*
Cortelyou MRS George B JR (Irwin Fearn) Rm.
☎ (908) 842-1591 . . 76 W River Rd, Box 294, Rumson, NJ *07760*
Cortesi MRS Roger (Mary Hathaway Williams) Csn.
☎ (860) 535-0611 . . 76 Water St, Stonington, CT *06378*
Cortesi MISS Vanessa L . . see W D Priester
Corts DR & MRS Thomas E (Marla R Haas) H'ton'63.Cy.Geo'63
☎ (205) 969-0350 . . 2829 Overton Rd, Birmingham, AL *35223*
Coryell MR & MRS Lawrence V (Elder—Mary P Schueler) UWash'65
☎ (914) 677-8922 . . PO Box 1038, Millbrook, NY *12545*
Cosden MRS Joshua S (Foley—Barbara Ball) Myf.Dar.
☎ (212) 249-5764 . . 430 E 77 St, New York, NY *10021*
Cosnard des Closets MR & MRS Jean Pierre (Mary J McKeon) Sth'60.Dij'48
☎ (203) 269-8355 . . The Choate School, 333 Christian Rd, PO Box 788, Wallingford, CT *06492*

Cossé Brissac CT Charles L de—Cc.	☎ (011-33)
MISS Diane M de	37-26-81-25
	"Château de
	Blanville" 28190
	St Luperce, France

Cost MISS Catherine A . . see MRS M A Price

Coste MR & MRS Nicholas (Anne F Hord) Pc.An.	☎ (215) 836-7961
MISS Suzanne L	853 Grove Av,
MISS Sarah P	Flourtown, PA
	19031

Costello MRS E Dallett (Estelina L Dallett) . . . . . name changed to Dallett
Costello DR & MRS Joseph P JR (Ellen Denvir)
15145 Baxton Court, Chesterfield, MO *63017*

Costello MRS Mark H JR (Ruth T Clarkson) Swb'51	of ☎ (707)865-2274
MR Mark H 3d—Wash'76	21920 Russian River
	Av, Villa Grande,
	CA *95486*
	☎ (415) 332-7917
	B15 Waldo Point
	Harbor, Sausalito,
	CA *94965*

Coster CAPT (RET) Gerard H JR—USN.Unn.Plg.H'43
☎ (904) 247-5574 . . 1202 Fleet Landing Blvd, Atlantic Beach, FL *32233*
Costikyan MR Kent R 3d . . see A L Register 3d
Costikyan MR Timothy W . . see A L Register 3d
Costikyan MR Warren K . . see A L Register 3d
Costin MR & MRS W Gilmor 3d (Anne C King) NCar'72.H'84.Pa'67.Nu'81
☎ (310) 459-0044 . . 1146 N Amalfi Dv, Pacific Palisades, CA *90272*
Côté MR & MRS Edward T (Elizabeth J Wolff) Rr.Y'58
☎ (412) 238-9300 . . "Stones Throw" PO Box 750, Ligonier, PA *15658*
Côté MR & MRS Edward T JR (Storrs H Lamb) Vt'86.Rc.Bgt.Rr.Vt'83
☎ (914) 234-6615 . . 29 Long Ridge Rd, Bedford, NY *10506*
Côté MISS Jane W—LakeF'85.Rr.
☎ (203) 438-6662 . . 10 Kiwi Corner, Ridgefield, CT *06877*

Côté MRS Marcel O (Kate F McNally)	☎ (212) 369-6661
MISS Kate F F—Mid'92.W&M'95—at	21 E 90 St,
☎ (757) 221-0610 . . 4064 Midlands Rd,	New York, NY
Williamsburg, VA *23188*	*10128*

Côté MR & MRS Mark C (Katharine V Davis)	☎ (508) 428-9091
Mid'70.BostColl'72	1745 S County Rd,
JUNIORS MISS Jesse E	Box 373, Osterville,
JUNIORS MR Nathanael V	MA *02655*

Cothran MR & MRS Perrin G (Sarah F Boynton)	☎ (413) 567-6665
Rcn.Hob'65	37 Chatham Rd,
MISS Perrin A—at U of NH	Longmeadow, MA
MISS Anne G	*01106*

Cottafavi MR Francesco L—Pr.Rome'69	of ☎ (516)922-9010
MR Vittorio E—at Georgetown	127 Cove Rd,
	Oyster Bay, NY
	11771
	☎ (011-39-6)
	333-8219
	via Guido Banti 33,
	00191 Rome, Italy

Cotter MR & MRS George E (Ruth M E O'Hare)	☎ (310) 476-2072
Wes'41.Cr'46	1033 Chantilly Rd,
MISS Carol H	Los Angeles, CA
	90077

Cottingham MR & MRS William S (Sarah S Fay)
Cal'79.Ln.Bgt.Cly.McG'78.Clark'83
☎ (617) 491-6020 . . 110 Coolidge Hill, Cambridge, MA *02138*
Cotton MR Jefferson C—SFrArt'72
☎ (207) 529-5330 . . "Cotscove" Keene Neck Rd, Medomak, ME *04551*
Cotton MRS John Page JR (Sylvia B Newton) Chi.
☎ (207) 761-4787 . . 1 Edgecomb Court, Portland, ME *04103*
Coty MASTER Nicolas François (g—MRS Barbara B Uzielli) . . . . . Born at New York, NY Feb 14'96
Coudert MISS Anne M (Victor R JR) . . . . Married at New York, NY
Schreckinger MR Peter D (late Neil J) . . . . Apr 13'96
Coudert MR & MRS Charles O (Barbara A Sullivan) Y'53
☎ (508) 651-3067 . . 35 Stoney Brook Rd, Sherborn, MA *01770*
Coudert MISS Cynthia (Frederic R 3d) . . . . . . Married at Oyster Bay, NY
Morris MR Brian E (Robert F) . . . . Jun 29'96

Coudert MRS Dale (Hokin—Dale Manowitz) Nw'63.Fic. . . . . of ☎ (212)888-1611 485 Park Av, New York, NY *10022*
    MISS Dana Hokin—at ☎ (312) 654-0891 222 E Chestnut St, Chicago, IL *60611* . . . . . . Fishers Island, NY *06390*
    MISS Alexandra Hokin . . . . ☎ (561) 832-6610 Villa dei Fiori, 163 Seminole, Palm Beach, FL *33480*

Coudert MR Ferdinand W—C.Cw.H'30.Cl'37
    ☎ (305) 294-0495 . . 425 Caroline St, Key West, FL *33040*

Coudert MR & MRS Frederic R 3d (Margaret R McInnis) Rc.Pr.S.P.'53.Cl'56 . . . . of ☎ (212)860-0758 1150 Fifth Av, New York, NY *10128*
    MISS Sandra—H'90.Nu'94 . . . . ☎ (516) 922-3940 ''La Chaumiere'' 67 Cove Neck Rd, Oyster Bay, NY *11771*

Coudert MR & MRS Victor R JR (Virginia L Beach) Ny.Km.Yn.Y'46.H'50 . . . . ☎ (203) 869-6437 55 Indian Field Rd, Greenwich, CT *06830*
    MISS Catherine B—BostColl'84—at
    ☎ (203) 531-1389 . . 11G Putnam Green, Greenwich, CT *06830*
    MISS Lucy A—StLaw'93—at ☎ (212) 861-2866 354 E 66 St, New York, NY *10021* . . . .
    MR Matthew J—W&L'86—at ☎ (212) 599-2296 305 E 40 St, New York, NY *10016* . . . .
    MR Paul A—HampSydney'91 . . . .

Coues MR Benjamin P—Col'91
    ☎ (617) 523-4868 . . 73 Pinckney St, Apt 3, Boston, MA *02114*

Coues MR & MRS W Pearce 3d (Phoebe A Dewing) Ec.Bost'61
    ☎ (508) 526-1292 . . Maple Av, Manchester, MA *01944*

Coues MR & MRS William Pearce (Mildred C Davidson) Btn.Sm.Cc.Cw . . .of
    ☎ (207) 883-9499 . . ''Cammock Cottage'' 2 Bird's Nest Lane, Prouts Neck, ME *04074-9406*
    ☎ (617) 426-8127 . . 1 Bay St, Boston, MA *02116*

Coughlin MR & MRS Barring (Harriet S Curtiss) Un.Cv.P'35.H'38
    ☎ (216) 229-5880 . . 2290 Ardleigh Dv, Cleveland, OH *44106*

Coulson MR & MRS Robert (Cynthia B Cunningham) Sth'54.Ny.Y'49.H'53 . . . . ☎ (203) 637-1015 9 Reginald Rd, Riverside, CT *06878*
    MR Crocker—at 307 S La Peer Dv, Los Angeles, CA *90048*
    MR Christopher . . . .

Coulson MR Robert Cromwell—Rc.Ny.Smu'89
    ☎ (516) 749-1852 . . 15 Hudson Av, PO Box 832, Shelter Island Heights, NY *11965*

Coulter MISS Cheryl S . . see D F Cutler JR

Coulter MR & MRS James R (Cochrane—Virginia Lunding) Sth'58.Va'55 . . . . ☎ (847) 234-4266 Longmeadow Farm, 275 Saunders Rd, Lake Forest, IL *60045*
    MISS Jean N—Cl'94 . . . .
        MISS Elizabeth P Cochrane—LakeF'87—at
        ☎ (415) 931-9292 . . 38 Miley St, San Francisco, CA *94123*
        MR Alexander L Cochrane 3d—Miss'85—at
        ☎ (312) 943-7955 . . 1629 N Burling St, Chicago, IL *60614* . . . .

Countiss MR & MRS Frederick D (Katherine G Luxem)
    ☎ (773) 327-3612 . . 2440 N Lakeview Av, Chicago, IL *60614*

Coursen MR & MRS R Dennison (Alford—Carolyn H Yeaw) Cvc.Sl.Y'40 900 Riomar Dv, Vero Beach, FL *32963*

Courtemanche MR & MRS Robert H (Mary W Van Ingen) WmSth'80.Hob'80
    ☎ (201) 292-2563 . . PO Box 271, Hunter Dv, New Vernon, NJ *07976*

Courts MR & MRS Frank J (Elizabeth Tayloe) Va'72.VaMed'86.Ncd.Cda.Tex'75.Va'76.Va'79 . . . . ☎ (540) 592-3745 22035 Quaker Lane, Middleburg, VA *20117*
    JUNIORS MISS Elizabeth T . . . .
    JUNIORS MISS Anne B . . . .

Cousins MRS Ivan R (Dorothy McWilliams) B'gton'39
    ☎ (415) 332-1384 . . 139 Currey Av, Sausalito, CA *94965*

Cousins MR & MRS Robert E (Ellen C Cummin) Sth'78.Myf.Sar.
    ☎ (408) 867-4237 . . 20332 Miljevich Dv, Saratoga, CA *95070*

Cover MR & MRS Nelson (Sneeringer—Isabel M Tunstall)
    ☎ (410) 377-6364 . . Elkridge Estates, Apt 522, 6112 Bellinham Court, Baltimore, MD *21210*

Cover MR & MRS Richard L (Nice—Mary Anne P Lohmeyer) Gchr'62.Gv.Mv.P'51 . . . . ☎ (410) 363-1496 401 Chattolanee Hill, Owings Mills, MD *21117*
    MISS Catherine R—at RR 1, Box 1805, Hinesburg, VT *05461* . . . .
    MISS Sidney P Nice . . . .

Cover MRS S Detert (Stiling—Sandra L Detert) Stan'66.Stan'74 . . . . ☎ (415) 325-6499 1133 Harker Av, Palo Alto, CA *94301*
    JUNIORS MR William D . . . .

Coverley LT COL (RET) & MRS Edwin D (Golden—Marjorie Jane Hatch) USAF
    ☎ (619) 749-0065 . . ''Mostly Hall'' 29290 Lawrence Welk Lane, Escondido, CA *92026*

Covert MISS Hannah H—Mid'92
    ☎ (770) 437-8130 . . 608 Lakes Dv NW, Atlanta, GA *30339*

Covert MR & MRS Roger A (Frances O Holt) V'56.Purd'51.Mit'57
    ☎ (908) 671-6601 . . 94 Deepdale Dv, Middletown, NJ *07748*

Covington MR George M—Sr.Y'64.Ch'67 . . . . ☎ (847) 234-8046 Box 126, Shoreacres Rd, Lake Bluff, IL *60044*
    MISS Karen M . . . .
    MISS Jean T . . . .
    JUNIORS MISS Sarah I . . . .

Covington MR Treadwell D—NCar'50
    ☎ (212) RE4-1268 . . 150 E 72 St, New York, NY *10021*

Covington MR William S—Cr'51.Cr'53 . . . .
   MISS S Amy—Nu'86—at 213 E 10 St, New York,
NY *10003* . . . .
   MISS Emily I—RISD'87—at Hilltop Farm,
Colora, MD *21917* . . . .
   MR Bentley M—at 604 Blue Ridge St, McKinney,
TX *75070* . . . .
☎ (561) 689-3697
500 Executive
Center Dv, Apt 5N,
West Palm Beach,
FL *33401*

Cowan JUNIORS MR Miles B . . see P B Humphrey

Coward MISS Claire Frances—Bnd'89 . . see C A Wood

Coward MR & MRS Samuel H (Donaldson—Wadsworth—Mary Alphin)
KasCAI'48
   ☎ (941) 378-1449 . . 5575 Bountiful Dv, Sarasota, FL *34233*

Cowell MR & MRS Richard C (Sullivan—Jacqueline
McKissick) FlaSo'52.Rcn.Ri.Evg.BtP.H'52 . . . .
   MR Richard C JR—at ☎ (212) 628-9928
177 E 75 St, Apt 4A, New York, NY *10021* . . .
   MR Christopher—at Fla State . . . .
☎ (561) 655-4911
240 El Vedado Way,
Palm Beach, FL
33480

Cowell MRS Thaddeus G (Mary C Monks)
   ☎ (203) 227-4365 . . "Great Tew" 6 Cedar Lane, Weston, CT *06883*

Cowenhoven MISS Margaretta R—Ws'34
442 Heron Point, Chestertown, MD *21620*

Cowenhoven MR & MRS Nicholas R (Frances M
Sawtell) V'43.Rut'47 . . . .
   MISS Margaret S—at 700 Lexington St, Waltham,
MA *02154* . . . .
☎ (207) 729-3150
36 Matthew Dv,
Brunswick, ME
04011

Cowles MISS Charlotte Ainsley Winnifred (James C) . . . . Born at
New York, NY Jan 28'95

Cowles MR & MRS Chauncey D (Janet C Crowley) St.Ham'33
   ☎ (716) 885-6646 . . 1088 Delaware Av, Apt 4A, Buffalo,
NY *14209-1628*

Cowles MR & MRS James C (Kathryn C Maney)
VPI'77.Cl'82.So.Denis'77.Pa'79
   ☎ (212) 794-0711 . . 8 E 83 St, Apt 2B, New York, NY *10028*

Cowles MRS M L Beakes (Mary L Beakes) Ws'34 . .
   MR C Deming 4th—Laf'68.Va'71—at
   ☎ (202) 328-7422 . . 1652D Beekman Place NW,
Washington, DC *20009* . . . .
☎ (941) 638-1189
Oak St,
Hillcrest Heights,
Babson Park, FL
33827

Cowles JUNIORS MR Story A . . see W W Atterbury 3d

Cowles MR & MRS William S JR (Virginia F Lloyd-Smith) Y'45.Mit'49
   ☎ (505) 757-2334 . . Los Trigos Ranch, Rowe, NM *87562*

Cowley MR & MRS Brian J (Alexandra W Barney) Nu'83.Bryant'81
   ☎ (415) 457-6274 . . 172 Barber Av, San Anselmo, CA *94960*

Cowley MISS Gillian Catherine Ayres (Nicholas P T) . . . . Born at
New York, NY Mch 13'96

Cowley MR & MRS Nicholas P T (Page K Ayres)
Nu'75.OxPoly'76.Cl'79.Rc.Cs.
   ☎ (212) 877-0124 . . 169 W 88 St, New York, NY *10024*

Cowley MR & MRS Robert W (Edith P Lorillard)
Srb.H'56 . . . .
   JUNIORS MISS Olivia L—at Phillips Exeter . . . . . .
   JUNIORS MISS Savannah C L . . . .
of ☎ (212)535-6454
333 E 79 St,
New York, NY
10021-0960
☎ (860) 354-6636
"Sunnyfields"
5 Church Rd,
Sherman, CT
06784-1134

Cowperthwait MISS Sarah M
   ☎ (714) 661-2030 . . 34771 Camino Capistrano, Capistrano Beach,
CA *92624*

Cox MR & MRS Archibald (Phyllis Ames) Sth'35.Sm.C.H'34
   ☎ (508) 358-2346 . . "Brookway Farm" Box 393, Wayland, MA *01778*

Cox MR Archibald 3d—Drew'91
   ☎ (213) 651-3817 . . 740 N Alfred St, Apt 202, West Hollywood,
CA *90069*

Cox MR & MRS Basil M (Jayne A Edwards)
Wheat'70.Purd'73.Pg.Yn.Y'63.H'65 . . . .
   MISS Kiara M—at 1 Astor Place, Apt 11K,
New York, NY *10003* . . . .
   JUNIORS MISS Nell A F . . . .
☎ (412) 422-9592
1235 Wightman St,
Pittsburgh, PA
15217

Cox MRS Beryl H B (Beryl H Brigham) Ws'63 . . . .
   MR Duncan B 3d—Whit'91—at
   ☎ (509) 522-1034 . . Rte 2, Box 221A,
Walla Walla, WA *99362* . . . .
☎ (508) 526-7110
15 Ocean St,
Manchester, MA
01944-1532

Cox MR & MRS C Paul 2d (McCall—Joan C
Williams) V'51.Cl'56.Fiy.Y'44 . . . .
   MR John P McCall—B'gton'79—at
   ☎ (212) 847-4740 . . 253 W 72 St, New York,
NY *10023* . . . .
   MR Thomas C McCall—Ore'91 . . . .
☎ (410) 822-1669
28210 Old Country
Club Rd, Easton,
MD *21601*

Cox MR & MRS Charles H (Rachel B Tatnall) . . . . . .
   MR Andrew J O'Brien 3d . . . .
☎ (610) NI4-3811
1811 Yellow
Springs Rd,
Box 266, Paoli, PA
19301-0266

Cox MR & MRS Charles H 3d (Katherine S Wadhams) Temp'74.Del'79
   ☎ (610) 449-9994 . . 214 Paddock Rd, Havertown, PA *19083*

Cox MR & MRS David M (Julie Gibbons-Neff)
Md'74 . . . .
   JUNIORS MISS Sewall C—at Pomfret . . . .
   JUNIORS MR Jeffrey D—at Pomfret . . . .
☎ (410) 822-6019
Box 1835, Easton,
MD *21601*

Cox DR Denton Sayer—Ny.C.Rv.Snc.StJ.Cw.Sar.Coa.Y'48.Cl'52
   ☎ (212) 879-4003 . . 530 E 72 St, New York, NY *10021*

Cox MR Duncan B JR—Y'59.Y'64 . . . .
   MR E Brigham—Mid'93 . . . .
☎ (508) 281-8748
40 Fort Hill Av,
Gloucester, MA
01930-4436

Cox MR & MRS Edward F (Patricia Nixon) Un.Cw.P'68.H'72
10 E 70 St, New York, NY *10021*

Cox MR & MRS Edward V JR (Reinhardt—Mary R
Mather) Cal'48.Y'35 . . . .
   MISS Sandra S—at 21 Clubhouse Dv, Woodbury,
CT *06798* . . . .
☎ (203) 264-2904
295B Heritage
Village, Southbury,
CT *06488*

Cox DR & MRS Edward V 3d (Ila M Schmidt)
Sim'61.Cl'64.Y'65.Cl'69 . . . .
   JUNIORS MR Peter B—at St Paul's . . . .
☎ (508) 475-2870
56 Central St,
Andover, MA *01810*

Cox MR Edwin Lochridge—Smu'40.Tex'42.H'46
   ☎ (214) 522-3360 . . 4101 Beverly Dv, Dallas, TX *75205*

Cox MR Edwin T—Me.
   ☎ (609) 492-4230 . . 215 Belvoir Av, Beach Haven, NJ *08008*

Cox MISS Eirin Alexandra (g—MRS Knud B Muenter) . . . . Born at
Colorado Springs, CO Apr 7'95

Cox MISS Frances B
   ☎ (941) 346-1034 . . 1208 S View Dv, Sarasota, FL *34242*

Cox MRS Frederick K (Pomeroy—Betty W Pickles) Mid'47.Un.Dar.Myf.Ncd.Cda. . . . . | 3254 Belvoir Blvd, Beachwood, OH
MISS Elizabeth A—Mich'89.Myf. . . . . | *44122-3831*
Cox MRS Gardner (Phyllis M Byrne) Sb.Cy.Cly.Hn. | ☎ (617) 547-1323
MR James B—H'65 . . . . | 88 Garden St, Cambridge, MA *02138*
Cox MRS Gerard H (Edith C Martin)
☎ (619) 673-9212 . . 16450 Caminito Vecinos Dv, Apt 99, San Diego, CA *92128*
Cox MR & MRS H Bartholomew (Hoge—Hannah M S Caffery)
Cvc.Sl.Cc.Dc.Ncd.P'59.GeoW'62.GeoW'67.GeoW'76
☎ (301) 292-1333 . . ''Potomac Valley Farm'' 11305 Riverview Rd, Ft Washington, MD *20744*
Cox MRS Howard E (Anne C Delafield Finch)
Lic.Evg.Un.BtP.Cly.Cda.Dc.Dh.Ds.StJ . . .of
☎ (212) 355-0999 . . 200 E 66 St, Apt E1007, New York, NY *10021*
☎ (561) 655-7810 . . Everglades Club, Apt A2, 356 Worth Av, Palm Beach, FL *33480*
Cox MR & MRS Howard E JR (Julia B Dempsey)
Ws'68.Unn.Cy.Sm.Chi.P'64.Cl'67.H'69
☎ (617) 277-3780 . . 225 Sargent Rd, Brookline, MA *02146*
Cox MR & MRS James S (Ruth S Frick) Cw.Cc.Pa'39
☎ (610) 866-4268 . . 58 Wall St, Bethlehem, PA *18018*
Cox MR & MRS John C (Emily Van O Ford) Hlns'75.Cly.Mo'74 . . . . | ☎ (203) 869-1978
JUNIORS MISS Elizabeth F . . . . | 58 Doubling Rd, Greenwich, CT *06830*
Cox MR & MRS John Edward (Mollie C Walker) Cy.Loy'56.Nu'58 . . . . | ☎ (205) 871-3987
MISS Shelby C—Ala'92 . . . . | 4146 Appomatox Lane, Mountain Brook, AL *35213*
Cox MRS John L 2d (O'Brien—Mary Louise Mahoney)
LakeF'64.Man'vl'75
☎ (914) 277-8073 . . 125B Heritage Hills, Somers, NY *10589*
Cox MR & MRS John M (Leslie W Carr)
5537 Emerson Av, Dallas, TX *75209-5105*
Cox MR & MRS Louis A (Frances McK Dunn) Cvc.Sl.H'49
☎ (304) 274-2515 . . ''Hollow Hill'' RR 3, 109D, Martinsburg, WV *25401*
Cox MR & MRS Louis A JR (Christine A Lambert) Ws'79.Hb.H'78.Mit'86
☎ (303) 388-1778 . . 503 Franklin St, Denver, CO *80218*
Cox MISS Mazie L . . see B S Thorne
Cox MR & MRS Millard 3d (Norton—Peabody— Mina Jones) Wms'63.Va'70 . . . . | of ☎ (502)222-5670
MISS Mina B Peabody . . . . | 4600 Tingle Lane, Westport, KY *40077*
☎ (616) 526-6880 ''The Pines'' 51 Beach Dv, Wequetonsing, MI *49740*
☎ (406) 328-6497 Trout Creek Ranch, Absarokee, MT *59001*
Cox MISS Myrna Heulwen (g—MRS Sondra G Blewer) . . . . Born at Beverly, MA Jun 25'96

Cox MRS Paul V (Robsion—Betty Bartholomew) Cvc.Sl.Dc.Cda.
2700 Calvert St NW, Washington, DC *20008*
Cox MR & MRS Peter B (Stanley—Lucy S Patterson) Csn.
☎ (203) 375-8068 . . 963 Wells Place, Stratford, CT *06497*
Cox MR & MRS Roderick H (Mary Rutledge Burnet) Mich'33.H'41.H'68
☎ (301) 652-3374 . . 7100 Clarden Rd, Bethesda, MD *20814*
Cox MR & MRS Thomas R JR (Walker—Joan Buckley) Snc.Cw.Chi.Wms'40
☎ (941) 676-5381 . . Mountain Lake, Lake Wales, FL *33859*
Cox MR & MRS William C JR (Martha A Whiting) . . | 190 S Beach Rd,
MISS Heidi—at 390 Commonwealth Av, Boston, | Hobe Sound, FL
MA *02215* . . . . | *33455*
Cox MRS William D (Faulk—Edwina Hancock) Rcch.Sc.
☎ (912) 226-2470 . . 1015 Gordon Av, Thomasville, GA *31792*
Cox MR & MRS William D JR (Janet K Rasmussen) | of ☎ (630)654-2104
Nw'57 . . . . | 406 E 3 St,
MISS Christina L . . . . | Hinsdale, IL *60521*
MR David D . . . . | ☎ (715) 467-2716 Rasmussen Dv, Scandinavia, WI *54977*
Cox DR William H JR—Y'44
☎ (212) MU9-3445 . . 300 E 33 St, New York, NY *10016*
Cox MR & MRS William P JR (Caroline M Delafield) Woos'86.Ky'83
☎ (513) 871-8783 . . 4848 Le Blond Av, Cincinnati, OH *45208*
Coxe MR & MRS Brinton (Amy P Deisroth) Skd'62 . . . . . . | ☎ (214) 522-3443
MR B Tench . . . . | 4356 Livingston Av,
MR Cullen . . . . | Dallas, TX *75205*
Coxe MR & MRS Henry B 3d (Isabel M Allan) . . . . . | ☎ (215) 242-2462
MISS Caroline T—at ☎ (617) 738-3391 | 25 E Springfield Av,
31 York Terr, Brookline, MA *02146* . . . . | Philadelphia, PA
MISS Helen P—Hart'90—at 170 W 89 St, | *19118*
New York, NY *10024* . . . . |
Coxe MR & MRS Henry B 4th (Katrina Brunovskis) Ill'83.NEng'81
☎ (908) 889-7058 . . 197 Marion Av, Fanwood, NJ *07023*
Coxe MR Weld—Rcp.Hp. 🖴 . . . . | ☎ (401) 466-2865
MISS Sally M—Lin'76.Ore'85—at | ''Block Island
☎ (541) 345-1272 . . 991 Polk St, Eugene, OR | Studio''
97402 . . . . | PO Box 515,
MR Philip A Hayden—Conn'84.Del'89—at | Block Island, RI
☎ (609) 921-8259 . . 38 Washington St, | *02807*
Rocky Hill, NJ *08553* . . . . |
Coxhead MR & MRS Peter C (Sara A Whiting) | ☎ (561) 395-0381
BtP.LSU'58 . . . . | 324 Key Palm Rd,
MR Stephen F—Fla'90.Stet'95—at | Boca Raton, FL
☎ (305) 672-7815 . . 1200 West Av, Apt 1403, | *33432*
Miami Beach, FL *33139* . . . . |
Coy MR & MRS Peter McA (Mary K Anderson) | ☎ (804) 263-8802
MtH'82.Va'69.Va'71 . . . . | Rte 1, Box 384,
MISS Oona M . . . . | Faber, VA *22938*
JUNIORS MR Morgan M . . . . |
Coy MR & MRS Peter Meldrim (Sally McAdoo) Va'42 . . of
☎ (912) 234-8699 . . 218 E Taylor St, Savannah, GA *31401*
☎ (508) 693-0791 . . ''Elmholm'' Box 2345, Vineyard Haven, MA *02568*
Coy MR & MRS Timothy E (Delores M Tuten) Y'71
☎ (912) 232-2961 . . 315 E Huntingdon St, Savannah, GA *31401*

Coyle MR & MRS Elliott R (Carolyn H Loeffler) CarnM'37.Edg.DelB.StA.P'30 . . . . ☎ (561) 265-0793
MR Elliott R JR . . . . 1223 Sandoway Lane, Delray Beach, FL *33483*

Coyle MR & MRS Norton Van V JR (Lydia H Shelby) Pitt'65 . . . . ☎ (561) 278-1963
JUNIORS MISS Caroline H . . . . 1301 N Swinton Av, Delray Beach, FL
JUNIORS MR Peter E *33444*

Coyle DR & MRS William R 3d (Annamary P Monahan) Pn.P'55.Nu'60 . . . . ☎ (301) 292-9561
MISS M Kathleen R—at Bryn Mawr . . . . 12607 Tartan Lane, Tantallon, MD
MR William R 4th *20744*
MR James C—at Boston, MA . . . .

Coyne MR & MRS Charles C (Paula J Latta) Finch'73.Rc.StA.Pa'70.Temp'73 . . . . ☎ (610) 486-0485
JUNIORS MISS Anna E—at Madeira . . . . ''Sycamore Run Farm'' PO Box 155, Unionville, PA *19375*

Coyne MR & MRS James M (Sumner—Susan R Walthour) NEng'81.Rr.MeMarit'79
☎ (410) 692-2635 . . 3319 Charles St, Fallston, MD *21047*

Coyne MR & MRS John E 3d (Cecelia B Maas) Wis'74.Wis'74
☎ (608) 238-6298 . . 2209 Chadbourne Av, Madison, WI *53705*

Coyne MASTER Joseph Darby (James M) . . . . Born at Baltimore, MD Jan 2'96

Coyne MISS Susan O'Neil (James M) . . . . Born at Baltimore, MD Jly 27'94

Cozad MR Bryan S . . see R W Harrison

Cozens MRS Lee E (Deborah L Duffus) M.Ncd.
☎ (610) 525-0331 . . 117 Locust Grove Rd, Rosemont, PA *19010*

Crabb MR & MRS David L (Dorothy Fay Mixter) Ncd.Ham'60.Ch'63 . . . . ☎ (773) 241-7460
MISS Laura E—Mon'93—at Wheelock . . . . 5619 S Dorchester Av, Chicago, IL *60637*

Crabbe MR & MRS Charles Otto (Carole D Frech) Aub'66.Cy.Ala'65 . . . . ☎ (205) 967-0630
MISS C Collins . . . . 3319 E Briarcliff Rd, Birmingham, AL *35223*
JUNIORS MR Charles O JR . . . .

Crabtree MRS L Frost (Laura G Frost) . . . . ☎ (404) 355-0745
MISS Laura H . . . . 8 Nacoochee Place NW, Atlanta, GA *30305*

Cracknell MRS John V (Connelly—Fanny A Martin) Bnd'54 . . . . ☎ (704) 365-9795
MISS Elizabeth M Connelly—Miami'89—at 2347 Hayloft Circle, Charlotte, NC *28226*
☎ (617) 731-8006 . . 1161 Beacon St, Apt 4, Brookline, MA *02146* . . . .

Crafts MR & MRS Frederic A 3d (Sybille U Neidhart) Heid'77.Un.Cw.Myf.Denis'81
☎ (508) 746-9675 . . Sunset Hill Farm, 71 Warren Av, Plymouth, MA *02360*

Cragin MR Geoffrey S (Stuart W JR) . . . . . Married at East Hampton, NY Szot MISS Andrea (Robert J) . . . . Jun 29'96

Cragin MR & MRS Stuart W JR (Margaret R Mackall) V'58.Cl'77.Myf.Y'55.H'59 . . . . ☎ (203) 622-0888
MISS Grace S—Ty'93—at ☎ (212) 475-4764 108 Valley Rd, Cos Cob, CT *06807*
145 Fourth Av, Apt 148, New York, NY *10003* .
MR Reginald W—Col'91 . . . .
MR Benjamin M . . . .

Craig MR & MRS Berton A (Denton—Elizabeth C Russel) Cin'63.Ncd.Ken'52 . . . . ☎ (561) 335-4583
MR Michael S—Hob'93—at ☎ (212) 501-8924 2867 SE Wiltshire Terr, Port St Lucie, FL *34952-5734*
313 W 75 St, Apt 4B, New York, NY *10023* . . .
MISS Elizabeth C Denton—SL'90.Cin'94—at
☎ (614) 299-6153 . . 65 Clark Place, Columbus, OH *43201* . . . .
MR E Castner Denton 3d—BowlG'92—at
☎ (513) 961-7670 . . 410 Ludlow Av, Apt 52, Cincinnati, OH *45220* . . . .

Craig MR & MRS Howard R JR (Elena Socorro Revilla) H'48.H'50.Cin'63 . . . . ☎ (860) 364-5059
MISS Patricia C—RISD'87 . . . . 53 Fairchild Rd, Sharon, CT *06069*

Craig MR James B JR—Ste.P'45.Pa'53.Penn'64
☎ (860) 364-1257 . . PO Box 1032, 24 Rhynus Rd, Sharon, CT *06069*

Craig MRS Peggie Louise (Peggie Louise Lee) JHop'51
☎ (603) 837-2098 . . ''Ledgeview'' Mountain View Rd, Whitefield, NH *03598*

Craig MR & MRS Robert L (Elizabeth H Lamphere) NH'80.AmU'83.GeoW'94
☎ (301) 564-9427 . . 10318 Summit Av, Kensington, MD *20895*

Craig MISS Sally K—Hlns'65.Md'69
☎ (410) 269-0597 . . 141 Archwood Av, Annapolis, MD *21401*

Craigmyle MISS Lydia S—JHop'79.LIU'92
☎ (212) 912-0937 . . 375 South End Av, Apt 25N, New York, NY *10280*

Craigmyle MRS M Martin (Mary F Martin) Cly . . .of
☎ (212) 750-8694 . . 40 E 62 St, New York, NY *10021*
☎ (516) 653-6755 . . ''Merriehaven'' 5 Quogue St, Quogue, NY *11959*

Craigmyle MR & MRS Robert de R (McCarter—Nancy K Alker) Cl'74.Ri.Y'55.Cl'61
☎ (408) 353-4841 . . 21105 Brush Rd, Los Gatos, CA *95030*

Craigmyle MR Robert de R JR—Rcn.Ithaca'85
☎ (803) 345-3457 . . 2000 Amicks Ferry Rd, Chapin, SC *29036*

Cram MR Henry Sergeant—K.Md.Evg.Sar.Lm.Cw.Ofp.Ll.
☎ (803) 757-3306 . . Devil's Elbow Island, PO Box 185, Bluffton, SC *29910*

Cramer MRS Ambrose C (Mary Meeker) Chi.
☎ (602) 451-2285 . . 12000 N 90 St, Scottsdale, AZ *85260*

Cramer MRS Corwith (Risdon—Wolford—Margot C Smith)
☎ (410) 224-2183 . . 1308 River Crescent Dv, Annapolis, MD *21401*

Cramer MR George B . . . . Died Jly 12'95

Cramer MRS George B (Elizabeth Crooks) BtP.Evg.An.Myf.Hn. ☎ (704) 332-6657
MR George B JR . . . . 2733 Country Club Lane, Charlotte, NC *28205-3128*
MR Richard W . . . .

Cramer MR & MRS John E III (Gladys A Mangus) Geo'64 . . . . ☎ (314) 968-3418
MISS Katharine Anne . . . . 5 Willow Oak Lane, St Louis, MO *63122*
MR John E IV . . . .

Cramer LT William E—USN. (late Corwith JR) . . . . Married at
Paul Smiths, NY
Armstrong MISS Julia R (A Joseph 3d) . . . . Aug 26'95
Cramer LT & MRS William E (Julia R Armstrong) USN.Ham'90.Tul'86
☎ (301) 585-7371 . . 1706 White Oak Dv, Silver Spring, MD *20910*
Crampton MRS Richard S (Eleanor S Wistar)
☎ (215) 438-2976 . . 6300 Greene St, Apt W403, Philadelphia,
PA *19144*
Crandall MR & MRS F William (Cynara Boit) Y'50 . | ☎ (212) 988-7039
MISS Frith C . . . . | 161 E 79 St,
MR Timothy J . . . . | New York, NY
MR Stephen S . . . . | *10021*
Crandon MR & MRS A Seabury JR (Mary A Turner) MtH'50.Y'45w
☎ (412) 782-2329 . . 115 Westchester Dv, Pittsburgh, PA *15215*
Crane MR & MRS Edward M JR (Ijams—Jean | ☎ (609) 921-2535
Drummond) Snc.Mt.Fic.P'45 | 647 Rosedale Rd,
MISS Katharine P Ijams—Conn'86—at | Princeton, NJ *08540*
☎ (212) 875-0362 . . 201 W 74 St, Apt 11C,
New York, NY *10023* . . . .
Crane MASTER Henry Thompson (R Thompson 3d) . . . . Born at
Bryn Mawr, PA May 12'96
Crane MR & MRS James M (Peters—Jean M Coulter) Bhm.Y'44
☎ (561) 231-5901 . . 531 Sea Oak Dv, John's Island, Vero Beach,
FL *32963*
Crane MISS Kate C . . . . | ☎ (860) 535-1067
MR Charles T—Reed'37 . . . . | 7 Temple St,
| Stonington, CT
| *06378*
Crane MR Matlack C—So'47
☎ (860) 535-1067 . . 7 Temple St, Stonington, CT *06378*
Crane MR & MRS R Thompson 3d (Bright—Anne L Detweiler)
Del'89.GeoW'64
☎ (610) 527-9445 . . 113 Cumberland Place, Bryn Mawr, PA *19010*
Crane MRS Robert B (Kathleen E Ball)
☎ (847) 441-8223 . . 1709 Northfield Square, Northfield, IL *60093*
Crane MRS Robert T JR (Virginia M Ladd) . . . . | ☎ (610) MI9-3837
MISS Maria L . . . . | 416 Berkley Rd,
| Haverford, PA
| *19041*
Crane MRS Warren C (Wanda M Constable) Dar. . . | ☎ (207) 622-0444
MISS Carol E—at ☎ (207) 582-2951 | Box 212,
41 Winter St, Gardiner, ME *04345* . . . . | Manchester, ME
| *04351*
Crane MR & MRS William A (Margaret A Kerwin) | ☎ (847) 234-4805
Ws'53.On.Cas.Wa.Ch'48 . . . . | 480 N Green Bay
MISS Sarah Q—Geo'87.Loy'92 . . . . | Rd, Lake Forest, IL
| *60045*
Crane MR Winthrop M—Un.Plg.
☎ (413) 684-0136 . . ''Chilton House'' Dalton, MA *01226*
Cranmer MR & MRS Forrest (Elizabeth Comer) P'38
☎ (011-44-171) 352-3511 . . 27 Ormonde Gate, London SW3 4EX,
England

Crans MR & MRS Robert R (Doris L Beckwith) | of ☎ (301)469-7228
Sl. ⚓ . . . . | 8911 Burdette Rd,
MR Robert R JR—at ☎ (301) 320-7840 | Bethesda, MD
5920 Bradley Blvd, Bethesda, MD *20815* . . . . . | *20817*
| ☎ (941) 262-5325
| 3601 Gin Lane,
| Port Royal, Naples,
| FL *34102-7817*
Crater MR & MRS Douglas E (Susan A Bartlett) Bnd'83.Ham'81
☎ (914) 763-8327 . . 197 Spring St, South Salem, NY *10590*
Cravens MR & MRS Malcolm (Martha Hurley) | ☎ (415) WE1-4445
Bhm.Pcu.Bur.Sfg.Fr.P'30 . . . . | 2660 Scott St,
MISS Carol C—at ☎ (415) 776-7032 | San Francisco, CA
2545 Vallejo St, San Francisco, CA *94123* . . . . . | *94123-4635*
Cravens MR & MRS Rutherford R 2d (Anne B Baker) Tex'39.So'39 . . of
☎ (713) 621-0824 . . Inwood Manor, 3711 San Felipe St, Houston,
TX *77027*
☎ (409) 836-9197 . . ''Bois d'Arc Farm'' Skull Creek Rd, Shelby,
Round Top, TX *78954*
Crawford MR & MRS Alan JR (Barbara Townsend) | ☎ (610) 644-1151
BMr'52.Rc.Gm.Ph.Rb.Cts.Fst. . . . . | White Horse Rd,
MISS Elizabeth T—P'79—at 2225 White Horse | Box 795, Devon, PA
Rd, Berwyn, PA *19312* . . . . | *19333*
Crawford MR & MRS Alexander I (Deborah C Bandanza) Ws'88.H'88
☎ (617) 237-8643 . . 84 Overbrook Dv, Wellesley, MA *02181*
Crawford MISS Betty—Ala'36.Cda.
☎ (205) 967-6784 . . 2911 N Woodridge Rd, Birmingham, AL *35223*
Crawford MR & MRS Douglas James (Gillian A Moore) Skd'85.Msq.Why.
☎ (401) 596-8583 . . ''Watersedge'' 17 Misquamicut Rd, Watch Hill,
RI *02891*
Crawford MR & MRS Duncan (Stephanie W Pogue) | ☎ (203) 977-9243
Snc. . . . . | 92 Riverford Rd,
MISS Samantha H . . . . | Brookfield, CT
MR Adam B . . . . | *06804*
Crawford MISS Evelyn F . . see D G Collins
Crawford MR & MRS George (von Mueffling— | of ☎ (212)249-8036
Marsha Millard) NYSID'66.Rc.Bcs.Cly.H.'60 . . | 770 Park Av,
MR William A von Mueffling—Cl'90 . . . . . . | New York, NY
MR Charles F von Mueffling—Duke'92 . . . . . | *10021*
| ☎ (516) 283-9343
| Ox Pasture Rd,
| PO Box 525,
| Southampton, NY
| *11969*
Crawford MR & MRS George L (Margaret L Kendrick)
☎ (813) 785-3960 . . Box 576, Ozona, FL *34660*
Crawford MR & MRS Harden L 3d (Ailsa Moseley)
B.Ny.Rv.Ll.StA.Myc.Eh.Cly.Ncd.Cl'56 ⚓
☎ (908) 234-0126 . . ''Longrun'' PO Box 365, Far Hills, NJ *07931*
Crawford MR & MRS Harden L 4th (Kersti E Magi) UWash'86.Bost'85
☎ (203) 259-2239 . . ''Summerfield'' 195 Greens Farms Rd,
Greens Farms, CT *06436*
Crawford DR & MRS J Brooks (Christine M Mayne) | ☎ (415) 752-8619
Cal'55.Bhm.Tcy.Y'55.Cal'60 . . . . | 17 Jordan Av,
MISS Catherine H—Mid'87 . . . . | San Francisco, CA
MR Peter B—Y'90 . . . . | *94118*

Crawford MR & MRS J Hamilton (Van Ingen—Zella G Kunhardt) Pr.StA.P.'51.Cl'57 . . . . ☎ (516) 671-9276 Factory Pond Rd,
MISS Paige T . . . . Locust Valley, NY *11560*

Crawford MR & MRS J Hamilton 3d (Patricia B Johnson) 53 E 66 St, New York, NY *10021*

Crawford MR & MRS (REV) James E 3d (Alicia L Lydon) SeaWTheo'86.On.Rc.Cysl.Cas.P'68. ☎ (847) 234-9171
Ox'69 . . . . 7 N Green Bay Rd, Lake Forest, IL
MISS Lacy C DeM—at Princeton *60045*
JUNIORS MR James E 4th—at Groton . . . .

Crawford MR & MRS James W (Marian D Bradley) P'27
☎ (412) 241-1414 . . Sherwood Oaks, 100 Norman Dv, Cranberry Township, PA *16066*

Crawford MR & MRS John R (Howard—Eleanor G Spooner) So'28
☎ (207) 775-0634 . . 33 Bayview Dv, Portland, ME *04103*

Crawford MR & MRS Oliver Iselin (Margaret C Weaver) So'73 . . . . ☎ (803) 254-1822 1527 Devonshire
JUNIORS MISS Ruth W . . . . Dv, Columbia, SC *29204*

Crawford MR & MRS (DR) Rollin H (Broberg— Susan H Woodard) Skd'60.Minn'65.Minn'79. ☎ (612) 451-9400
Macalester'61.Minn'65 . . . . 1640 Atwater Path, Inver Grove Heights,
MR Stephen M Broberg—Minn'92 . . . . MN *55077*
MR Richard H Broberg—Bost'90.Bost'92 . . .

Crawford MR & MRS Roy J (Beverly A Ready) Ala'78.Ala'77.Nu'80
☎ (205) 870-3781 . . 1721 Somerset Circle, Birmingham, AL *35213*

Crawford MR & MRS Russell H (Lana L Holladay) Me.Cts.Ac.
☎ (610) LA5-7374 . . 566 Ferndale Lane, Haverford, PA *19041*

Crawford MRS S Coleman (Sally Coleman) Mor. . . ☎ (561) 697-2788
MR Matthew G—at ☎ (513) 223-2491 578 Green Springs
63 Brandt Pike, Dayton, OH *45404* . . . . Place, West Palm Beach, FL *33409*

Crawford MISS Serena W—Mid'92 . . see D G Collins

Crawford MR & MRS Seth T (Sterling—Aileen O'D Baltazzi) H'45
☎ (540) 364-2064 . . Box 172, Markham, VA *22643*

Crawford MR & MRS Steven C (Pesquera—Danielle P André) Spgfd'76.NH'77
☎ (703) 352-2036 . . 11912 Appling Valley Rd, Fairfax, VA *22030*

Crawford MR Thomas C—RI'88
☎ (617) 641-2622 . . 27 Cleveland St, Arlington, MA *02174*

Crawford MR W Blake—Ty'91 . . see D G Collins

Crawford MR & MRS W Michael (Cynthia H Gowen) Va'83.Mds.Br'81.Cl'85
☎ (212) 988-0706 . . 192 E 75 St, Apt 9B, New York, NY *10021*

Crawford MR & MRS Warren W (Vera B Martin) Wheat'52 "Meadow Pond" Box 506, Dorset, VT *05251*

Creekmore MR & MRS Wade H JR (Betsy A Salisbury) Mlsps'59.Miss'56.Miss'68
☎ (601) 366-5513 . . 2137 Heritage Hill Dv, Jackson, MS *39211*

Creel MR James R 4th—Ct.Gchr'96
☎ (202) 332-5890 . . 1834 Vernon St NW, Washington, DC *20009*

Creel MR & MRS Lawrence G (Jennifer M Coleman) PineM'86.Mb.Rc.Fic.LakeF'85
☎ (212) 327-4263 . . 155 E 72 St, Apt 7A, New York, NY *10021*

Creelman MRS Brenton W (Elizabeth Rollins) Pars'48.Cs.Ncd . . .of
☎ (212) 308-5498 . . 200 E 66 St, New York, NY *10021* Three Rivers Farm, Dover, NH *03820*

Creep MR & MRS Parker B JR (Conger—Anne Coles Brick) Ncd.Penn'42
☎ (561) 747-8093 . . Jupiter Inlet Colony, 206 Colony Rd, Jupiter, FL *33469*

Creese MRS James (Margaret V Morton) BMr'21
☎ (609) 448-4100 . . Meadow Lakes 15-08, Hightstown, NJ *08520*

Creighton MR & MRS Albert M JR (Hilary Holcomb) Sth'55.Sbc.Ec.Myc.Chi.H'41 . . . . ☎ (508) 526-1901 17 Old Neck Rd,
MR Peter H—Bates'87—at ☎ (617) 876-7240 Manchester, MA
456 Putnam St, Cambridge, MA *02139* *01944*

Creighton MR & MRS (DR) Thomas E JR (Lucy W Loomis) Y'74.Cwr'79.Y'76
☎ (303) 321-6401 . . 1759 Hudson St, Denver, CO *80220-1452*

Cremin MISS Susan E—V'69.Fy.Cho.Cas.Sc.Wa.
☎ (312) 558-5805 . . 12 E Scott St, Apt 4, Chicago, IL *60610*

Cresap MR Mark W 3d—Wms'74 . . see MRS S Mac R Wyeth

Cresswell MR & MRS Donaldson (Coxe—Helen E Piper) Ph.Rb.Gm.Ac.P'24.Pa'27
☎ (610) 525-2768 . . 400 Caversham Rd, Bryn Mawr, PA *19010*

Crew MR & MRS William W (Jean M Crossett) Purd'66 🏅 . . . . ☎ (805) 642-1881 2876 Sailor Av,
MISS Deborah J . . . . Ventura, CA *93001*
MR William W JR—at Yale . . . .
MR R John . . . .

Crews MISS Vicki J (Behr—Vicki J Crews) WakeF'74.WakeF'80.Va'84 506 Wellington Place, Charlottesville, VA *22903*

Crichton MR & MRS John H (Atherton—Flora Cameron) Bur.Evg.BtP.A.Mto.Ncd.LSU'49 315 Westover Rd, San Antonio, TX *78209*

Crider MRS Karen Koch (Karen Koch) Ws'67.Bost'73
☎ (617) 247-2032 . . 770 Boylston St, Apt 23H, Boston, MA *02199*

Crimmins MRS (DR) Jennifer M (d'Andrea—Jennifer M Crimmins) Bnd'55.Rome'69
☎ (011-33) 94-04-68-30 . . "Saluki House" Le Bouillidou, 83570 Cotignac, France

Crimmins MR & MRS Kevin B (Cynthia B Crump) Y'59 . . . . ☎ (203) 655-2035 165 Long Neck
MISS Lilly—HWSth'91—at 138 E 38 St, Apt 10F, Point Rd, Darien,
New York, NY *10016* . . . . CT *06820*

Crimmins MR & MRS Martin Lalor 3d (House—Martha P Thomson) V'53.Cly.Ncd.Cda.Cal'51 . . of
☎ (212) 472-1571 . . 125 E 72 St, New York, NY *10021*
☎ (914) 677-6122 . . "Deep Hollow Hill" Deep Hollow Rd, Millbrook, NY *12545*

Crimmins MR & MRS Patrick J (Sydney A Maxwell) Pitt'62
☎ (215) CH8-5224 . . 1 W Chestnut Hill Av, Philadelphia, PA *19118*

Crimmins MR & MRS Robert (Violet H Rothwell) Hn. . . . ☎ (203) 655-1683 176 Long Neck
MISS Susan H—Ty'75 . . . . Point Rd, Darien,
MISS Anne Van W (Rockwood—Anne Van W CT *06820*
Crimmins) DU'72 . . . .
MISS Allison C Rockwood—at U of Colo Boulder . . . .
JUNIORS MR John A Rockwood . . . .

Crisler MR & MRS Edgar Theodore JR (Emma Flautt)
Miss'61.Sar.Wt.Rhodes'56
☎ (601) 437-4410 . . 1108 Church St, PO Box 1002, Port Gibson,
MS *39150-1002*

Crisler MRS Richard C (Howard—Lucy Hagin) L.Yn . . .of
☎ (513) 321-3942 . . 2444 Madison Rd, Apt 505, Cincinnati, OH *45208*
☎ (606) 689-7228 . . ''Neboshon Farm'' 8368 River Rd, Hebron,
KY *41048*

Crisp JUNIORS MR John E . . see CTSS C Grote

Crisp MAJ (RET) John S—BA.
☎ (011-44-1986) 050845-477 . . Green Farm, Kirby Cane, Bungay,
Suffolk NR35 2HW, England

Crisp MR & MRS Peter O (Emily S Ridgway)
V'63.Ln.Pr.Fic.Fiy.Y'55.H'60 . . . . | ☎ (516) 922-4056
MISS Tina O—at ☎ (212) 996-4602 | 103 Horseshoe Rd,
201 E 87 St, Apt 22M, New York, NY *10128* . . | Mill Neck, NY
| *11765-1005*

Crispin MR & MRS Frederick E (Kochs—Snyder—Mildred M Swift)
Sc.Evg.Cw.Rv.Sar.Wa.Dar. ⚓
☎ (941) 966-4331 . . 560 N Casey Key Rd, Box 1098, Osprey, FL *34229*

Crissman MR & MRS James H (Louisa G Murray) | of ☎ (617)923-2036
Sth'59.H'63.Sb.Tv.CTech'60.H.'66 . . . . | 3 Brigham St,
MISS Sarah W de C—Ty'90.Les'93—at | Watertown, MA
☎ (216) 321-4247 . . 2265 Tudor Dv, | *02172*
Cleveland Heights, OH *44106* . . . . | ☎ (207) 549-7178
MR Charles W McM—Ty'91—at | ''Gaeloft''
☎ (406) 582-1460 . . 322 S Church Rd, | 149 Head Tide Rd,
Bozeman, MT *59715* . . . . | King's Mills,
MR William G—at Bowdoin . . . . | Whitefield, ME
| *04353*

Crittenden MR & MRS G Lamar (Gertrude B Shaw) Cy.D.P'41
☎ (508) 785-0289 . . 80 Strawberry Hill St, Dover, MA *02030*

Crittenden MR & MRS G Lamar JR (Abigail O | ☎ (617) 828-4012
Brown) Les'92.D.P'65.Y'70 . . . . | ''The Pigeon
MISS Sarah M . . . . | House''
| 34 Green St, Canton,
| MA *02021*

Crivelli MRS Gioconda M K (Colapinto—Rippel—
Gioconda M K Crivelli) . . of
☎ (212) 988-7872 . . 117 E 71 St, New York, NY *10021*
☎ (011-39-55) 47-42-17 . . ''I Colombi'' Vicolo San Marco Vecchio 34,
La Pietra, 50139 Firenze, Italy

Crocker MRS Alvah (Nancy Ladd)
☎ (203) 966-0759 . . 20 Prides Crossing, New Canaan, CT *06840*

Crocker MR & MRS Arthur M (Putnam—Barbara J Stout)
Unn.Pr.Csn.P'31.H'33
☎ (941) 261-2580 . . 126 Moorings Park Dv, Apt I204, Naples,
FL *34105*

Crocker DR & MRS (DR) Augustus T (Julie Schoepf)
V'48.Cl'49.Cl'53.H'39.Tufts'44
☎ (603) 563-8074 . . ''Crockern Tor'' Lake Rd, Box 500, Dublin,
NH *03444*

Crocker MR & MRS Charles (Whittemore—Lucinda J | ☎ (415) 921-8605
Campbell) Bhm.Pcu.Stan'60 . . . . | 3120 Jackson St,
MISS Sarah C—at 101 Ridge Rd, San Anselmo, | San Francisco, CA
CA *94960* . . . . | *94115*

Crocker MR & MRS Courtenay (Littler—Everett—Helen Cunningham)
Ey.Chi.Ch'40.Mit'42
☎ (508) 228-0182 . . ''Westward'' Madaket Harbor, 27 N Cambridge St,
Nantucket, MA *02554*

Crocker MR & MRS Davenport B (Jane B Richmond) | of ☎ (617)383-1098
Co.Myf.Cw.Ofp.Chi.Pa'60.Suff'72 ⚓ . . . . | 100 Pond St,
MISS Susan B . . . . | PO Box 276,
MR Davenport B JR . . . . | Cohasset, MA
MR Collamore R—Dth'93 . . . . | *02025-0276*
| ☎ (561) 575-0693
| 16878 Bay St,
| Jupiter, FL *33477*

Crocker MRS (DR) Diane W (Diane H Winston) | ☎ (312) 951-9015
Ws'47.Br'48.Bost'52 . . . . | 1440 N Lake Shore
MISS Deborah B . . . . | Dv, Apt 4H,
MISS Kimberly B—at ☎ (415) 965-3477 | Chicago, IL *60610*
456 Mountain Laurel Court, Mountain View, CA
94043 . . . . |

Crocker MRS Frank L (Jean Gallatin Cobb)
☎ (212) 348-9217 . . 1105 Park Av, New York, NY *10128*

Crocker MR & MRS John Howe (Jacquelyn D Elliott) | ☎ (516) 283-0468
Rc.Bcs.So.Wms'56 . . . . | PO Box 5075,
JUNIORS MISS Amanda E . . . . | Southampton, NY
| *11969*

Crocker MR & MRS Julian (Edith P Cunningham) | ☎ (603) 823-8400
Cyb.D.Chi.Ncd.H'44 . . . . | PO Box 41,
MISS Sarah H—at ☎ (802) 862-4387 | 1094 Forest Hill Rd,
885 S Prospect St, Burlington, VT *05401* . . . . | Franconia, NH
MR Samuel C—at ☎ (508) 468-2850 | *03580*
5 Northedge Rd, Hamilton, MA *01936* . . . . . . |

Crocker MR & MRS Robert G (Ruth E Cox) | ☎ (617) 235-4396
Sth'64.Cy.Myc.Chi.Ncd. . . . . | 90 Seaward Rd,
MISS R Sayre . . . . | PO Box 81195,
MR Andrew G . . . . | Wellesley Hills, MA
MR Peter B . . . . | *02181-0002*

Crocker MRS U Haskell (Eleanor Batchelder) Myc.Cy.Chi.Ncd. ⚓
☎ (508) 526-1917 . . 50 Proctor St, Manchester, MA *01944*

Crocker MRS Wethered T (Martha Rice) . . . . | ☎ (401) 421-2542
MISS Evelyn T—at ☎ (617) 262-5181 | 47 Manning St,
280 Beacon St, Boston, MA *02116* . . . . | Providence, RI
MISS Hope W—at ☎ (718) 261-5816 | *02906*
76-35—113 St, Forest Hills, NY *11375* . . . . . |

Crocker MR & MRS William H (Thomas—Jean E Galloway)
Stan'60.Bhm.Cos.Y'50.Wis'62
☎ (202) 333-1308 . . 3254 O St NW, Washington, DC *20007*

Crofoot MR & MRS David L (P Pepperrell Merrill) FineA'60
☎ (914) 666-5250 . . 133 Buxton Rd, Bedford Hills, NY *10507*

Crofts MR & MRS George D JR (Elizabeth P Walker)
Idaho'43.G.Cr'43.H'46.Cr'49
☎ (716) 834-2842 . . 95 Ruskin Rd, Buffalo, NY *14226*

Crofut MRS Burton L (Doris I Andrews) T.
☎ (914) 351-4314 . . Continental Rd, Box 413, Tuxedo Park, NY *10987*

Croghan MISS Maeve P—Reed'80
☎ (906) 847-6297 . . 10 W Bluff Av, Mackinac Island, MI *49757*

Crolius MR & MRS Thomas Potter (Patricia L Mosser) Hav'49
☎ (203) 227-6379 . . 25 Cavalry Rd, Westport, CT *06880*

Croll MISS Janet S . . see MRS W C Breed

Croll MRS Joseph D (Emily C Davis) Cly.Sl.
☎ (202) 265-4114 . . 2540 Massachusetts Av NW, Washington, DC *20008*
Cromelin MRS John S (Katherine L Young) Cas.
☎ (312) 787-9761 . . 1500 N Lake Shore Dv, Chicago, IL *60610*
Cromie DR & MRS William J (Cynthia P P Skinner) Ford'64.StL'86 . . . . | ☎ (773) 684-8486
MISS Clare F . . . . | 5811 S Dorchester
MR Daniel E . . . . | Av, Apt Top-G,
MR John C . . . . | Chicago, IL *60637*
JUNIORS MISS Virginia S . . . . |
JUNIORS MR William J JR . . . . |
Crompton MRS George 3d (Anna R Sultana)
☎ (508) 548-1321 . . Box 531, 73 Associates Rd, West Falmouth, MA *02574-0531*
Crompton MR John S . . see W R Wister JR
Crompton MR & MRS Robert H 3d (Georgia R Rose) B.Ny.Co.Cry.Cly.Leh'60.Pa'64
☎ (717) 529-2052 . . Colerain Farm, 36 Maple Shade Rd, Christiana, PA *17509*
Crompton DR Thomas F—Va'68
☎ (609) 327-8602 . . "Woodland Shores" 1227 Starling Dv, Millville, NJ *08332*
Cromwell MISS Christina C (M Jenkins JR) . . . . Married at Baltimore, MD
Borden MR Scott C . . . . Oct 14'95
Cromwell DR & MRS David McE (Patrice C C McConnell) P'84.Y'84.Y'89
☎ (410) 825-2882 . . 1932 Old Court Rd, Baltimore, MD *21204*
Cromwell MR & MRS Jarvis 2d (Shelby P Tison) OWes'80.Chr.Tufts'81
☎ (203) 966-4348 . . 1012 Silvermine Rd, New Canaan, CT *06840*
Cromwell MR Josias J 2d—Ty'67.Cr'72
☎ (410) 472-2883 . . 1360 Glencoe Rd, Sparks Glencoe, MD *21152*
Cromwell MR & MRS M Jenkins JR (Mary M Menadier) AMagnus'55.Cc.Rv.Mv.Y'52.Md'57 . | ☎ (410) 472-9054
MISS Mary M—StLaw'80.Mich'89 . . . . | 14910 Tanyard Rd,
MR Walter F 2d—Ty'79—at 3860 Adams Rd, | Sparks, MD *21152*
Oakland, MI *48363* . . . . |
Cromwell MISS Mae Carroll (David McE) . . . . Born at
Baltimore, MD Nov 2'95
Cromwell MR & MRS O Eaton JR (Mary P Twaddell) Me.Sa.Pa'39
☎ (610) 527-1886 . . 74 Pasture Lane, Apt 337, Bryn Mawr, PA *19010*
Cromwell MR W Kennedy (Margaret O Dunn)
☎ (410) 527-8884 . . 13801 York Rd, Apt C4, Cockeysville, MD *21030*
Cromwell MR W Kennedy 3d—Elk.P'46.Grin'48. JHop'49 . . . . | ☎ (410) 269-1274
MR William K 4th . . . . | 1513 Gordon Cove
MR Francis M—Grin'84 . . . . | Dv, Annapolis, MD
| *21403*
Crone MR & MRS Walter S (Prudence Wilson) V'52.St.Cw.G.Dar.Cr'50 . . . . | ☎ (803) 722-9023
MISS Elizabeth T—at Brown . . . . | 41 Church St,
| Charleston, SC
| *29401*
Crone MR & MRS Walter S JR (Graham—Marcia A Cain) Tex'73.Houst'78.Aht'78.Nu'80
☎ (713) 250-5850 . . PO Box 610070, Houston, TX *77208*

Cronin MR & MRS Ambrose M 3d (Helm—Anne Wangenheim) Ore'67 . . . . | ☎ (503) 223-8351
MISS Kathryn L—at 2720 SW Summit Dv, | 4400 SW Fairview
Portland, OR *97201* . . . . | Blvd, Portland, OR
MR Ambrose M 4th—at 4215 SW Strathfell Lane, | *97221*
Portland, OR *97221* . . . . |
MR Christopher A—at 7400 SW Barns Rd, |
Portland, OR *97225* . . . . |
MISS Molly M Helm . . . . |
MISS Charie J Helm . . . . |
Cronin MR & MRS Casey M (Elizabeth F Pearce) WmSth'80.ColC'79
☎ (317) 283-4862 . . 4335 N Pennsylvania St, Indianapolis, IN *46205*
Cronin MR & MRS Paul D (E Ann Swift) Rdc'62.Cr'81.Nyc.An.Stone'60.Pitt'67 . . . . | ☎ (804) 381-5966
MR Peter F—Denis'91—at ☎ (415) 781-0630 | "The Farmhouse"
350 Union St, Apt 609, San Francisco, CA *94133* | Farmhouse Rd,
MR David R—Ken'93—at ☎ (703) 379-8351 | Sweet Briar, VA
4884 S 28 St, Arlington, VA *22206* . . . . | *24595*
Cronin MR & MRS Robert N (Emily Carey) Sth'75.Wms'69.Sth'73 . . . . | ☎ (610) 664-3848
JUNIORS MR Jonathan Foster . . . . | 1294 Montgomery
| Av, Narberth, PA
| *19072*
Cronson MRS Mary Sharp (Mary Sharp) Ri.Cly.
☎ (212) 535-8245 . . 50 E 77 St, New York, NY *10021*
Cronson MR & MRS Paul (Caroline Milnes) Ox'84.Cl'89.Eyc.Cly.Cl'83
☎ (212) 737-2019 . . 111 E 80 St, New York, NY *10021*
Crook MR & MRS George W (Emily Keeble) Van'67 | ☎ (615) 297-9031
MISS Katherine K . . . . | 580 Jackson Blvd,
JUNIORS MR George W JR . . . . | Nashville, TN *37205*
Crooker MR & MRS Robert M JR (Susanne Thamm) Tufts'93.P'83
☎ (617) 489-2611 . . 49 Winslow Rd, Belmont, MA *02178*
Crooks MR & MRS William C (Karin B Johnson) Sth'71.Bost'75.L.Cw.Sar.Ncd.Yn.Pa'71.Pa'74.Pa'75
☎ (203) 869-4014 . . 132 Zaccheus Mead Lane, Greenwich, CT *06831*
Cropsey MR & MRS Henry C G (Melinda M Moore) Ty'81.Ty'82
☎ (413) 567-8019 . . 862 Longmeadow St, Longmeadow, MA *01106*
Cropsey MRS James H (Joyce Mackenzie) Mid'39.Dar.
☎ (860) 567-8326 . . "White Oak" 116 Blue Swamp Rd, Litchfield, CT *06759-2003*
Cropsey MR & MRS James M G (Roberta L Baker) Y'79.Cl'87.Dar.Ty'79.Bab'85
☎ (603) 286-4051 . . Drumlin Farm, 376 Sanborn Rd, Tilton, NH *03276*
Crosby MR & MRS (DR) B Taylor F (Elise G Werner) Stan'72.Y'85.Stan'71.Cal'77.Y'79
☎ (307) 674-4542 . . PO Box 7190, Sheridan, WY *82801*
Crosby DR & MRS Everett U (Candace Carter) Va'76.Nyc.Y'54.JHop'59
☎ (804) 973-7345 . . "Clover Hill" PO Box 7212, Charlottesville, VA *22906*
Crosby MR George de F—Unn.NH'80
☎ (011-352) 22-82-831 . . 7-11 av Pasteur, Banco Itau, Europa SA, L-2311 Luxembourg
Crosby COL & MRS H Ashton (Letitia E Jones) USA.Unn.Cvc.Mt.Chi.
☎ (603) 823-5679 . . "Latrobe Farm" Coal Hill Rd, Franconia, NH *03580*

Crosby MR H Ashton JR—Wms'62.Nu'64
☎ (914) 234-0331 . . 164 Old Post Rd, Bedford, NY *10506*
Crosby MR John O—C.Mto.Y'50
☎ (212) 832-8757 . . 48 E 63 St, New York, NY *10021*
Crosby MR & MRS Sheldon B (Virginia C Wier)
Wash'78.Mt.Ty'71.Wash'78.Dth'86
☎ (860) 561-3636 . . 157 Hunter Dv, West Hartford, CT *06107*
Crosby MR & MRS Thomas M JR (Eleanor G Rauch) | ☎ (612) 473-1141
Y'60 . . . . | 1612 Willow Dv,
MISS Brooke S . . . . | Long Lake, MN
MR Grant P . . . . | *55356*
Crosby MRS Virginia D (Virginia W Duel) . . . . | ☎ (212) 666-1256
MISS Heather de F—HWSth'89—at | 523 W 112 St,
☎ (212) 496-9753 . . 116 W 72 St, New York, | New York, NY
NY *10023* | *10025*
Crosier MR Louis M—Dth'87 . . see R N Pyle
Crosland MRS C Anthony R (Catling—Susan B | of ☎ (011-44-171)
Watson) . . . . | 937-7876
   MRS Sheila C Conroy (Sheila O S Catling) . . | 16 Stanford Court,
| Cornwall Gardens,
| London SW7 4AB,
| England
| ☎ (011-44-1295)
| 810340
| ''Old Mill''
| Adderbury,
| Oxfordshire,
| England
Cross MISS Cynthia P—Rol'83
☎ (203) 966-1029 . . 59 Hillside Av, New Canaan, CT *06840*
Cross MR & MRS E George 3d (Clare McLean) Pc.Sg.Ac.Pa'68
☎ (215) 654-7515 . . 7247 Beech Rd, Ambler, PA *19002*
Cross MRS Elizabeth E (Elizabeth Eager) Sim'74 . . | ☎ (617) 449-5079
JUNIORS MISS Elizabeth . . . . | 47 Charles River St,
| Needham, MA
| *02192*
Cross MR & MRS Jackson (Anne Meyer) Pqt.Dar.So'30
☎ (561) 231-2437 . . 122 Island Creek Dv, Vero Beach, FL *32963*
Cross MRS Jeannette W (Gillies—Jeannette W Gillies)
☎ (561) 243-3865 . . 821 NW 32 Av, Delray Beach, FL *33445*
Cross MR John W 3d—Ihy.Ln.Cw.Yn.Y'53
☎ (203) 869-4095 . . 30 Lismore Lane, Greenwich, CT *06831*
Cross MRS Mildred H (Schoeller—Mildred B Hayes) Ncd.
☎ (561) 279-9892 . . 800 Andrews Av, Delray Beach, FL *33483*
Cross MR & MRS Robert A (Jean M Worthington) Duke'89.Duke'89
☎ (401) 294-4755 . . 7 Bromley Court, North Kingstown, RI *02852*
Cross MR & MRS William R JR (Sally C Smith) V'51.Rc.Cs.Y.'41 . . of
☎ (914) 763-8967 . . 26 Hunt Farm, Waccabuc, NY *10597*
☎ (508) 645-2642 . . Abel's Hill, RD 1, Box 450, Chilmark, MA *02535*
Cross MR & MRS William R 3d (Ellen P Healy)
Ws'82.Nw'91.Yn.Y'81.H'86
☎ (508) 526-9002 . . 1 Coolidge Point, Manchester, MA *01944*
Crossan MR H James JR—Sm.My.Cal'42.H'48 . . . . | ☎ (508) 927-0576
MISS Constance W—Wheat'81—at 15 Apple Rd, | 15-45 West St,
Apt 24, Beverly, MA *01915* . . . . | Beverly Farms, MA
MR Peter J 2d—My. | *01915*

Crossan MR H James 3d—Roch'76
☎ (508) 468-2279 . . 347 Bridge St, South Hamilton, MA *01982*
Crossman MR & MRS John G (Nancy A Royse) | ☎ (602) 852-0884
Van'61.Ford'76.Yn.Y'58.Stan'60 . . . . | 4731 E Marston Dv,
MISS Claire R—RMWmn'87—at New York, NY | Paradise Valley, AZ
MR James B—ArizSt'93 . . . . | *85253*
Crossman MR & MRS Patrick F (Elizabeth F Davis) Y.'54.Va'60 . . of
☎ (212) 662-8344 . . 448 Riverside Dv, New York, NY *10027*
☎ (860) 542-5955 . . Beckley Bog Rd, Norfolk, CT *06058*
Crossman MR & MRS William L (Alison L Vietor) LakeF'79.Shcc.LakeF'78
Spring Island, Rte 6, Box 284, Okatie, SC *29910*
Crout MR & MRS Stephen A (Julia S Elliman) MtVern'86.Rol'86
☎ (703) 534-8483 . . 3848 N Dittmar Rd, Arlington, VA *22207*
Crouter MRS Gordon (Emily D Pierce) Sg.Ac.
see Dilatory Domiciles
Crouter MR & MRS Henry E (Agathe M Keliher)
Sth'56.Cl'64.Fst.Ph.Rb.Csn.Ac.P.'53.H'57
☎ (215) CH7-2495 . . 201 W Evergreen Av, Philadelphia, PA *19118*
Crowe MR Edward R
☎ (516) 821-7739 . . 414B Weymouth Court, Ridge, NY *11961*
Crowell MR & MRS Donald E (Mary Gannett) Ithaca'80
258 Edgewater Dv, Gilford, NH *03246*
Crowell MR Eldon H—Mt.Cvc.P'46.Va'51 . . of
☎ (202) 483-8709 . . 2101 Connecticut Av NW, Washington, DC *20008*
☎ (540) 635-7635 . . ''Laurel Ridge'' Box 456, Flint Hill, VA *22627*
Crowell MR & MRS G Alvin JR (Dettmer—Penny A Lattarulo)
CUNY'65.H.Yn.Y'55
☎ (617) 934-6480 . . PO Box 2146, 45 Grandview Av, Duxbury,
MA *02331*
Crowell MR & MRS James L (Sullivan—Elizabeth A Reichmann)
ChHill'64.Pa'66.Me.Rv.RISD'64
☎ (610) 527-5070 . . ''Rebel Hill Barn'' 127 Upper Gulph Rd, Radnor,
PA *19087*
Crowley MISS Rahel O'F . . see B S Wright JR
Crozer MRS Betsy Carlyle (Hagen—Jones—Betsy Carlyle Crozer)
Stockton'87.Minn'92.Ac.Ayc.Ncd. ⚓
☎ (410) 266-7945 . . 609 Admiral Dv, Apt 208, Annapolis, MD *21401*
Crozer MRS Charles Harper (Mary T Gillen) Me.Ac.Dll.Pn.
☎ (561) 659-5581 . . 300 S Ocean Blvd, Palm Beach, FL *33480*
Crozer MR & MRS John Price (Bowen—Edith W Gay) Me.Sfh.Ll.
☎ (610) 642-3275 . . 1362 Youngsford Rd, Gladwyne, PA *19035*
Crozer MR & MRS Robert P (T Taliaferro Flowers) | ☎ (912) 226-5418
Va'74.Me.Rr.Va'69.Va'72 . . . . | ''Netherleigh''
JUNIORS MR Robert P JR . . . . | 1011 Gordon Av,
| Thomasville, GA
| *31792*
Crudge MRS Vernon G (Anne de la M Chambers) V'57.Cs . . .of
☎ (212) 861-3249 . . 129 E 69 St, New York, NY *10021*
☎ (860) 379-3079 . . ''Hoppen Place'' New Hartford, CT *06057*
Crudgington MISS Olivia P B—Tufts'81.LondEc'83
☎ (011-33-1) 47-55-06-04 . . 84 rue Lauriston, 75016 Paris, France
Cruger MRS Bertram de N (Mary E Sales) T.
☎ (914) 351-4458 . . Clubhouse Rd, Tuxedo Park, NY *10987*

Cruice MR & MRS Charles S (Kathryn J Wilmarth) Del'81.Wil.DU'73 . . of
☎ (302) 654-6285 . . PO Box 3707, 4001 Centerville Rd, Greenville, DE *19807*
☎ (208) 726-8938 . . "Points West" 3009 Warm Springs Rd, Ketchum, ID *83340*

Cruice MR & MRS J Seth H (Barbara A Stine) SL'46.Wil.Ncd.Pa'43 . . of
☎ (561) 546-4219 . . "Soupçon" 177 Gomez Rd, Hobe Sound, FL *33455*
☎ (302) 658-9507 . . PO Box 3974, Greenville, DE *19807*

Cruice MR & MRS J Seth H JR (Valerie A Sarantos) Wheat'78.Va'81.Pa'75.Va'81 . . . . |
JUNIORS MISS Kinsey L . . . . |
☎ (203) 655-6682
68 Bumpalong Rd, Darien, CT *06820*

Cruice MRS John M (Mathilde E Fielding) Rose'53
☎ (610) 649-1293 . . 123 Harrogate Rd, Wynnewood, PA *19096*

Cruickshank MISS Blair F (Zack—Blair F Cruickshank) Ws'94
☎ (617) 489-4424 . . 39 Harrington St, Watertown, MA *02172*

Cruickshank MR & MRS William H (Dorinda T Pell) Lm.Dc.Ncd.Bab'49 . . of
☎ (617) 235-8282 . . 67 Lincoln Rd, Wellesley Hills, MA *02181*
☎ (941) 472-4479 . . "River's Edge" 1063 Blue Heron Dv, Sanibel, FL *33957*

Crumpacker MR & MRS James F (Elizabeth A Finkbeiner) Scripps'68.Ore'69 . . . . |
MISS Catherine E—at Colo Coll . . . . |
JUNIORS MR James F—at St Paul's . . . . |
of ☎ (503)636-2122 02107 SW Greenwood Rd, Portland, OR *97219*
☎ (208) 622-8000 "Sun Valley" 119 Picabo St, Ketchum, ID *83340*
☎ (541) 382-1208 "Tweed Mountain Farm" Tweed Rd, Tumalo, OR *97701*

Crunden MRS Warren C (Eleanor R Wheelwright) Sth'52. . . . . |
MR Warren C JR—at 555 Shore Rd, Apt 61, Somers Point, NJ *08244* . . . . |
MR John W—Box 122, South Seaville, NJ *08246-0122* . . . . |
MR Arthur C—at 7115 Cottonwood Circle, Sachse, TX *75048* . . . . |
☎ (704) 464-4185 1754 Fairway Dv, Newton, NC *28658*

Cryan MR Bruce McA (late Eugene W) . . . . Married at Minneapolis, MN
Simundson MISS Susan E (Daniel) . . . . Sep 17'94

Cryan MRS Eugene W (Alice McAlpin) Me.Gm.
☎ (610) 527-9464 . . 49 Parkridge Dv, Bryn Mawr, PA *19010*

Cryer MRS Caryl O (Caryl S Osborn) AmU'62
☎ (410) 267-7315 . . 1035 Norman Dv, Apt T2, Annapolis, MD *21403*

Cudahy MR & MRS J Michael (Carol H Whitney) Wheat'74.Bvl.Rol'75.Bost'94
☎ (508) 748-0583 . . 15 Allen St, Marion, MA *02738*

Cudahy MR & MRS William B (Hudson—Evelyn M Wilkinson) Evg.BtP.H'34
☎ (561) 842-6560 . . 742 Slope Trail, Palm Beach, FL *33480*

Cudlip MR & MRS Charles T (Page—Brittain Bardes) GeoW'69.Cvc.Mt.Srb.BtP.Va'63 . . . . |
MISS Charlotte L . . . . |
JUNIORS MISS Mary B . . . . |
MISS Olivia M Page—at Stanford . . . . |
MR Blakely C Page—Smu'96 . . . . |
☎ (540) 687-5774 "Merryvale" 39881 Snickersville Pike, Middleburg, VA *20117*

Culbert MISS Laura A—Cl'87
☎ (011-44-171) 792-9754 . . 20 Ossington St, London W2 4LY, England

Culbert MR & MRS William L 3d (Sandra F Pray) Rv.Ncd.Ken'56
☎ (203) 661-3906 . . 16 Deer Lane, Greenwich, CT *06830*

Cullen MISS Betty S . . see MRS B G Rafferty

Cullen MR & MRS Craig W (Brooks—Alice Y Baker) Me.Cry.Ty'61 ⚓ . . . . |
MISS Cynthia L Brooks . . . . |
☎ (610) 293-1376 483 School House Lane, Devon, PA *19333*

Cullen MR Craig W JR—Cry.Me.HWSth'86
255 Price Av, Berwyn, PA *19312*

Cullen MR & MRS Denis D (Elizabeth W Casey) Newt'75.Denis'76
70 White Hill Rd, Cold Spring Harbor, NY *11724*

Cullen MR E Geoffrey—Y'66.Va'69 . . . . |
JUNIORS MR Torrance S—at ☎ (314) 993-5984 9 The Orchards, St Louis, MO *63132* . . . . |
☎ (415) 574-8507 1919 Alameda de las Pulgas, Apt 8, San Mateo, CA *94403*

Cullen MRS Edward E 3d (Godshalk—Frances S Emlen) Gm.Ac.
☎ (610) 645-8693 . . 1400 Waverly Rd, Villa 44, Gladwyne, PA *19035*

Cullen MR & MRS George L (Marie E Le Fort) Me.Aht'38
☎ (561) 286-0343 . . 16 High Point Rd E, Stuart, FL *34996*

Cullen MRS J Cox (June O Cox)
☎ (516) 676-2312 . . PO Box 294, Locust Valley, NY *11560*

Cullen MRS Karon N (Karon Nunnally) MaryB'68
31 Muscogee Av NW, Apt 15, Atlanta, GA *30305*

Cullen MISS Lindsay S (Craig W) . . . . Married at Wayne, PA
Scott MR Sean D (William) . . . . Jun 8'96

Cullen MR & MRS Robert Le F (Mary L Gaffney) Pa'66 . . . . |
MISS Emily D—at Clemson . . . . |
MR Robert Le F JR—at Santa Barbara, CA . . . . . |
☎ (206) 236-0391 6229 Island Crest Way, Mercer Island, WA *98040*

Culley MRS Natalie C (Natalie H Cook) . . . . |
MISS Anne B—at ☎ (202) 965-4289 1339—27 St NW, Washington, DC *20007* . . . . . |
MR John A—at ☎ (773) 248-1125 2738 N Pine Grove Av, Apt 15B, Chicago, IL *60614* . . . . |
☎ (630) 232-1428 310 Hawley Dv, Geneva, IL *60134*

Culley MR & MRS Peter M (Elizabeth E Hohmann) Ariz'51
☎ (602) 945-4841 . . 5102 N Casa Blanca Rd, Paradise Valley, AZ *85253*

Cullum MRS Lee B (Clark—Lee B Cullum) Smu'61
☎ (214) 521-3667 . . 2718 Turtle Creek Circle, Dallas, TX *75219*

Cullumbine MRS Harry (Sullivan—Mary K Fox) Me.
☎ (610) 525-7974 . . 74 Pasture Lane, Apt 227, Bryn Mawr, PA *19010*

Cully MRS John J JR (S Joy Hall)
☎ (610) 347-0482 . . PO Box 523, Rte 82, Unionville, PA *19375*

Culman MR John K—Unn.Mt.Y'47.Cl'59 . . of
☎ (202) 625-6195 . . 1349—28 St NW, Washington, DC *20007*
☎ (540) 592-3177 . . "Raspberry Hall" Upperville, VA *20185-0272*

Culman MR & MRS Peter W (Anne S La Farge)
V'60.Wms'59 . . . . | ☎ (410) 366-6567
MR John La F—Wms'89 . . . . | 2 Merryman Court,
MR P William S—Hartw'92 . . . . | Baltimore, MD
| 21210

Culp MRS Thomas C (Margaret R Roberts) Ac.Ncd.
☎ (215) 493-3168 . . ''Tannamar'' 88 N Main St, Yardley, PA 19067
Culp MR & MRS Thomas C JR (Reid—Dorinda M
Kauffman) P'77.Ph.Pc.Pn.P'69.Pa'74 . . . . | ☎ (215) 247-2075
MISS Emily S . . . . | 8838 Crefeld St,
MISS Sarah R . . . . | Philadelphia, PA
| 19118

Culver MRS Bertram B JR (Jane Metcalfe) Cy . . . . . . | ☎ (314) 993-1197
MR Bertram B 3d—at ☎ (314) 997-1926 | 330 N Warson Rd,
22 Covington Meadows, St Louis, MO 63132 . . | St Louis, MO 63132

Culver MR & MRS Edward H (Mary Lee Oliver)
Al.D.Ht.Ncd.Dar.Yn.Y'40 | ☎ (617) 326-5651
MISS Anne A F—Ht.—at ☎ (703) 525-5358 | PO Box 189,
4626 N Carlin Springs Rd, Arlington, VA 22203 | Dedham, MA 02026

Culver MR & MRS Edward H JR (Susan A Chase) Cy.Cc.Yn.Y'69
☎ (508) 358-2009 . . 18 Draper Rd, Wayland, MA 01778

Culver MR H Harrison—Cy.Myf.Wms'39 . . . . | ☎ (314) 993-1937
MISS Elizabeth—at 26 S Spoede Rd, St Louis, | 41 Glen Eagles Dv,
MO 63141 . . . . | St Louis, MO 63124

Cumings MRS J Bradley 3d (Joyce A Rankin)
Tor'49 . . . . | ☎ (416) 921-4839
| 150 St Clair Av W,
MISS Susan G—BMr'90.Glasgow'94 . . . . | Apt 302, Toronto,
| Ontario M4V 1P6,
| Canada

Cumings MR John B 4th . . see R C Fenton
Cummin MR & MRS A Bevan (Alexandra M Davis) CtCol'89.Me.Rv.Pa'88
☎ (610) 783-7784 . . 901 Parkview Dv, Apt A102, King of Prussia,
PA 19406

Cummin MRS Arch W (Diane Kidman Young) Me. | ☎ (212) 289-3225
JUNIORS MISS Chandra K F . . . . | 1120 Fifth Av,
| New York, NY
| 10128

Cummin MR Arch W—Rc.B.Me.H'66.Pa'70
☎ (516) 537-3328 . . 41 Quimby Lane, Box 253, Bridgehampton,
NY 11932

Cummin MR & MRS G Jeremy (E Hutchinson Dawes)
Cry.Me.Ph.Fw.Rv.Cw.Cspa.W.Ncd.Pa'60
☎ (610) MU8-9251 . . 223 Radnor Street Rd, Wayne, PA 19087

Cummin MRS Graham F (Elizabeth S McIlwain) Ac.Me.Cs.Cda . . .of
☎ (215) 925-6824 . . 225 Spruce St, Philadelphia, PA 19106
☎ (011-33-1) 45-48-89-19 . . 16 rue du Pré aux Clercs, 75007 Paris,
France

Cummin MRS Pearson C JR (Mary N Crawford) V'45-4.Pa'49.Ac.Me.
☎ (610) 525-3621 . . 125 Ashwood Rd, Villanova, PA 19085

Cumming MR & MRS Edward G (Fagan—Paulson— | of ☎ (011-33-1)
Patricia McMillan) Snc.Ht.H'52 . . . . | 47-34-25-05
MR Charles K Fagan . . . . | 71 quai Branley,
MR John F Paulson . . . . | 75007 Paris, France
| ☎ (910) 777-1484
| 1257 Kent Place
| Lane,
| Winston-Salem, NC
| 27104

Cumming MRS Peter H B (Dorothy Classen) Rm. . . | ☎ (908) 842-0610
MISS Diane C—at 200 E 71 St, New York, NY | 19 Mitchell Place,
10021 . . . . | Little Silver, NJ
| 07739

Cummings MR & MRS Edward McL (Hélène | ☎ (202) 667-9056
de Marcellus) Rcch.Y'42 | 2700 Calvert St
MISS Rose | NW, Washington,
MR Amory—On.Rc.Y'74.Mich'77—at | DC 20008
☎ (312) 573-0407 . . 1730 N Clark St, Chicago,
IL 60614 . . . .
MR Alexander B—Van'85.Y.'93—at
☎ (212) 289-4689 . . 315 E 86 St, Apt 5B-E,
New York, NY 10028
MR McLean—H'87—at ☎ (410) 833-1696
PO Box 3672, Glyndon, MD 21071 . . . .

Cummings MR F Ramsdell—Bhm.Ofp.Cw.Cal'34
☎ (602) 234-1575 . . 236 W Berridge Lane, Phoenix, AZ 85013-1514

Cummings MRS Francis H (Chenoweth—Evelyn Lancaster) . . . . Died
Mch 4'95

Cummings MR Francis P—Myf.UMiami'57 . . of
☎ (561) 276-4098 . . 535 Banyan Rd, Gulf Stream, FL 33483-7403
☎ (718) 588-7262 . . 790 Concourse Village W, Apt 24F, Bronx,
NY 10451-3862

Cummings DR & MRS Harlan G (Robinson— | of ☎ (802)296-5087
Virginia De B Hinman) Eyc.Plg.Cly.Mid'58. | PO Box 892,
Tufts'61 . . . . | Norwich, VT
MR Sanger P Robinson II—at | 05055-0892
☎ (213) 467-7133 . . 5710 Waring Av, | ☎ (508) 627-8316
Los Angeles, CA 90038 . . . . | PO Box 1163,
| Edgartown, MA
| 02539

Cummings MRS Hollyday (Jensen—Hollyday Cummings) Nw'57
☎ (206) 778-0899 . . 8615—187 Place SW, Edmonds, WA 98020

Cummings MR & MRS (DR) Keith M (M Purita Tavares) Stan'73 . . of
☎ (011-351-2) 617-8330 . . Avenida Brasil 364, Apt 1E, 4100 Porto,
Portugal
☎ (011-55-474) 22-9886 . . Rua Ministro Calogeras 612, Janville,
Santa Catarina, Brazil

Cummings MR Lawrence B—K.Hn.H'76.H'80
☎ (561) 844-4764 . . 107 Indian Rd, Palm Beach, FL 33480

Cummings MISS Lila Douw (Barnes—Lila Douw | ☎ (914) 779-9185
Cummings) Ncd. | 15 Cranston Place
MISS Diana B Barnes—at Bowdoin . . . . | Bronxville, NY
| 10708

Cummings MR Milton C JR—Cos.Sth'54.Ox'56.H'60
☎ (202) 965-2692 . . 2811—35 St NW, Washington, DC 20007

Cummings MRS Minnette H (Minnette L Hunsiker) B'gton'40
☎ (207) 774-5152 . . 94 Neal St, Portland, ME 04102

Cummings MRS (DR) Nancy B (Nancy G Boucot) | ☎ (202) 362-8589
Ober'47.Pa'51.Cos. | 3900 Connecticut
MISS Susan S—P'87.GeoW'93—at ul Bagatela | Av NW, Apt 501F,
14V, 00585 Warsaw, Poland . . . . | Washington, DC
MR Christopher R—Y'83.H'87—at | 20008
1360 Lombard St, San Francisco, CA 94109 . . .

Cummings MISS Nina M—LakeF'78
☎ (773) 472-4741 . . 2238 N Lincoln Park W, Chicago, IL 60614

Cummings MR & MRS Robert C (Georgia A Donaldson) Hob'59
☎ (716) 886-1709 . . 14 Saybrook Place, Buffalo, NY *14209*
Cummings MR & MRS Robert L (Maxwell—Marie E Powers) Pr.H.'35
☎ (516) 671-2110 . . High Farms Rd, Glen Head, NY *11545*
Cummings MR & MRS Robert L 3d (Frances C Walsh) V'72.Pa'74
☎ (914) 234-3908 . . Millers Mill Rd, Bedford, NY *10506*

Cummings MR & MRS Sean H (Suzanne P Swift)	☎ (617) 749-4833
USA'59	9 Patriots Way,
MISS Elizabeth R	Hingham, MA
MISS Caroline H	*02043*

Cummings JUDGE Walter J—Rc.Sc.Mt.Km.Yn.	☎ (312) 787-3231
Y'37.H'40	229 E Lake Shore
MR Mark F—Sc.Stan'76—at ☎ (773) 338-2804	Dv, Chicago, IL
6123 N Francisco Av, Chicago, IL *60659*	*60611*

Cummings MR & MRS Walter J 3d (Pauline Field) Bur.Y'69.Stan'74
☎ (617) 278-9719 . . 219 Buckminster Rd, Brookline, MA *02146-5805*

Cunneen MR & MRS William E (Betsy G Burry)	☎ (630) 790-0078
Denis'71	779 Riford Rd,
JUNIORS MR William E JR	Glen Ellyn, IL
	60137

Cunningham MR & MRS C Baker (Georganne R	☎ (314) 727-8418
Rose) Bost'69.Wash'64.GaTech'66.H'70	6424 Cecil Av,
MISS Margaret B—David'93	St Louis, MO *63105*
MR Charles B 4th	

Cunningham MR & MRS C Seth (Sarah P Gardner)
P.'79.UnTheo'89.UnTheo'91.UnTheo'94.H.'79
☎ (212) 687-0455 . . 305 E 40 St, New York, NY *10016*
Cunningham MR & MRS Colin McA (Evelyn M Soule) D.Nh.
☎ (508) 785-0670 . . 43 Strawberry Hill St, Dover, MA *02030*

Cunningham MR & MRS David H (Mary C Burns)	☎ (202) 362-5195
Swb'71.Cvc.Va'72	4816 Quebec St
JUNIORS MISS Mary S S	NW, Washington,
	DC *20016*

Cunningham MR & MRS Jeffrey M (Elizabeth Moir)
Wheat'78.K.Ln.SUNY'74
☎ (203) 622-4370 . . 589 North St, Greenwich, CT *06830*
Cunningham MRS John H JR (Jill P Storey) Bvl.Chi.
☎ (912) 638-6594 . . River Club 1202, Sea Island, GA *31561*
Cunningham MR & MRS John J (Miller—Gordon—Karen R Kreidler)
WChesU'82.Me.Leh'60.Pa'65
☎ (610) 520-1250 . . ''Wrenfield'' 1335 Wrenfield Way, Villanova,
PA *19085*

Cunningham MR & MRS Michael J (Marla J	☎ (303) 674-3429
Armstrong) DU'70.DU'69	29885 Monterey
JUNIORS MISS Elizabeth A	Lane, Evergreen,
	CO *80439*

Cunningham MR Peter H—Me.Leh'87
☎ (201) 659-3657 . . 1029 Washington St, Apt 1, Hoboken, NJ *07030*
Cunningham MRS Robert Newton (Johnson—Long—Louisa B Carter)
Cos.Elk.
☎ (804) 971-9675 . . 2401 Old Ivy Rd, Apt 1210, Charlottesville,
VA *22903*

Cunningham MR & MRS Stephen S (Anne T Starr)	☎ (408) 866-2259
Pa'68.Cal'67.P'71	106 Casa Grande,
MISS Anne	Los Gatos, CA
JUNIORS MR John P	*95030*

Cunningham MR & MRS Thomas D JR (A Louise	☎ (914) 234-7328
Mills) V'45.Bgt.Chr.Ne.Plg.Cly.H'44	101 Hook Rd,
MR Dudley H—Br'75—at ☎ (302) 425-4984	Bedford, NY *10506*
1401 Pennsylvania Av, Wilmington, DE *19806* .	

Cunningham MR & MRS Thomas D 3d (Pamela H	☎ (203) 866-8336
Jones) H'71.Cl'73	8 Nearwater Rd,
JUNIORS MR T John	Rowayton, CT
	06853

Cunningham MR & MRS William W (Mary-Ellen	☎ (313) 885-1076
Lavin) MtH'56.H'57.Yn.Y'52.H'56	62 Cloverly Rd,
MISS Amy A—Y'84	Grosse Pointe
MISS Caroline McF—H'93	Farms, MI *48236*
MR William W 2d—Ty'87	
MR Courtland B—P'90	

Cunynghame SIR Andrew D F & LADY (Isabella K	☎ (011-44-171)
Watts) Cda.	792-1933
JUNIORS MISS AnnMarie A	12 Vicarage
	Gardens, London
	W8 4AH, England

Cupit REV James H JR—Me.Bow'41
PO Box 270, Bryn Mawr, PA *19010*
Curley MR & MRS Walter J (Mary T Walton) K.Ln.Y'44.H'48
☎ (212) 879-0465 . . 3 E 77 St, New York, NY *10021*

Curran MRS Ann Pew (Holton—Ann S Pew)	☎ (610) 525-2149
Gm.Me.	1632 Old Gulph Rd,
MR William T	Villanova, PA *19085*
MR Charles C—at Ohio Wesleyan	
MISS Alexandra C Holton—at St Croix, VI . .	
MR John M Holton 3d—at Concord, NH	

Curran MR D Edward—Gm.Me.Rc.Ste.Fst.Eyc.Pa'55
☎ (610) 525-2149 . . 1632 Old Gulph Rd, Villanova, PA *19085*
Curran MR Donald E 3d (D Edward) . . . . Married at Greenwich, CT
Hughes MISS Alexandra W (Edward R) . . . . Jly 30'94
Curran MR & MRS Donald E 3d (Alexandra W Hughes)
☎ (203) 327-6372 . . 80 Lawn Av, Apt 14, Stamford, CT *06902*

Curran MR & MRS Maurice J 3d (Kate Ewing	☎ (617) 566-7823
Walker) Cy.Ncd.Br'56	242 Woodland Rd,
ENS Maurice J 4th—Srb.USN'95	Chestnut Hill, MA
MR Coalter Cabell—Rc.—at U of Pa	*02167*

Curran MR & MRS William E (Anita Le R Bright)	☎ (914) 967-0250
Wheat'69.Pa'75.Rens'70.Pa'74	28 Jean St, Rye, NY
JUNIORS MISS Anna P	*10580*

Curran MR & MRS William G JR (Richards—Paula	of ☎ (011-44-171)
D Haworth) Lond'82.Y'51	235-1556
MISS Paola V—Y'90	65 Eaton Square,
MISS Melissa S—Leeds'91	London SW1W
	9BQ, England
	☎ (011-353-21)
	334-149
	''Dereen House''
	Coachford,
	Co Cork, Ireland

Currey MR & MRS Brownlee O JR (Agneta Akerlund)
Rc.Bcs.Ri.B.Van'49 . . of
☎ (615) 373-8591 . . River Circle Farm, 1115 Sneed Rd, Franklin,
TN *37069*
☎ (212) 371-1618 . . 1 Sutton Place S, Apt 6B, New York, NY *10022*
☎ (561) 798-2740 . . Palm Beach Polo & Country Club,
11906 Maidstone Dv, West Palm Beach, FL *33414*
Currey MASTER Brownlee Owen 2d (Christian B) . . . . . . Born Jun 24'96
Currey MR & MRS Christian B (Ashley A Trapp) NCarSt'84.Bcs.Van'84
☎ (615) 371-8896 . . 1041 Sneed Rd W, Franklin, TN *37064*
Currey MISS Stephanie C (Brownlee O JR) . . . . . Married at Nashville, TN
Ingram MR John R (late E Bronson) . . . . Apr 12'96
Currey MR Wayne A . . see F S Bancroft 3d
Currie MRS C George (Valentine—Phoebe Drayton) . . . . Died at
Philadelphia, PA May 15'96
Currie MR C George—R.Pe.Sg.Pc.Sa.Pa'49
☎ (215) 242-8615 . . 8410 St Martins Lane, Philadelphia, PA *19118*
Currie MISS E Jane
☎ (610) 429-1904 . . 429 Eaton Way, Hershey's Mill, West Chester,
PA *19380*
Currie MRS Francis (CTSS Teresita Sparre) | ☎ (860) 434-1345
BMr'43.Cl'84 . . . . | ''Ram's Horn
MISS Julie G—at ☎ (206) 325-8663 | Creek'' Joshuatown
325 Harvard Av E, Apt 101, Seattle, WA *98102* | Rd, Box 271,
 | Old Lyme, CT
 | *06371*
Currie MR Frederick M H—R.Me.Pe.Rv.
☎ (610) 645-8835 . . 1400 Waverly Rd, Blair 130, Gladwyne, PA *19035*
Currie MR & MRS Frederick M H JR (O'Donnell— | ☎ (201) 729-7059
Gail A Crooks) Pe.R.Rv.Laf'63.Pa'65 . . . . | 12 N Shore Terr,
MR Frederick M H 3d—Rut'93.Roch'95—at | Sparta, NJ *07871*
☎ (201) 963-3043 . . 130 Garden St, Hoboken, |
NJ *07030* . . . . |
MR John T C—at Rutgers . . . . |
Currie MR & MRS Patrick R (Carol W Hedblom) | ☎ (011-44-171)
Mass'75.Hampshire'75.Nw'78 . . . . | 823-5101
JUNIORS MISS Emily H . . . . | 4 Cheltenham Terr,
 | London SW3 4RD,
 | England
Currie MR & MRS Peter L S (Elizabeth D Mize)
Wms'78.Nu'80.Wms'78.Stan'82
☎ (206) 725-8462 . . 3233 Cascadia Av S, Seattle, WA *98144*
Currier MR C Bertram . . . . Died at
Cambridge, MA Jun 26'96
Currier MRS C Bertram (M Catharine Blake) Ncd.H . . .of
☎ (941) 261-7281 . . 292 Springline Dv, Naples, FL *34102*
☎ (617) 547-3193 . . 23 Cambridge Terr, Cambridge, MA *02140*
Currier DR & MRS Charles B JR (Lucille A Anstine) | ☎ (202) 244-8373
GeoW'56.GeoW'60.H'58.Bost'63 . . . . | 3751 Northampton
MISS Anna L—at 1901 S Queen St, York, PA | St NW, Washington,
17403 . . . . | DC *20015*
MISS Elizabeth A . . . . |
MR Charles B 3d . . . . |
MR William C . . . . |
Currier MR & MRS Charles G (Berry—Carol Joyce Underwood)
Aub'65.An.Rv.Cl'71
☎ (423) 584-7344 . . 6801 Stone Mill Dv, Knoxville, TN *37919*

Currier MR & MRS E Gray (Mary J Pfile) Rv.Bel'72 | ☎ (970) 223-7277
JUNIORS MISS Katharine E . . . . | 1426 Red Oak
 | Court, Ft Collins,
 | CO *80525*
Currier MRS Gilman S (Katharine N Gray) Cly.
☎ (212) SA2-8073 . . 17 E 89 St, New York, NY *10128*
Currier MR & MRS Jefferson D (Gwendolyn L | ☎ (805) 969-3537
Bowen) On.Vh. . . . . | 2117 Ten Acre Rd,
MISS Gwendolyn L—at 91 Arlington Dv, Apt 2, | Santa Barbara, CA
Pasadena, CA *91105* . . . . | *93108*
Currier MR & MRS Robert B (Elizabeth C Brooks) . . | ☎ (617) 826-6436
MISS Elizabeth C . . . . | 361 Water St,
MISS Nancy B . . . . | Hanover, MA *02339*
MR James B . . . . |
Curry MRS Albert JR (Joyce L Curd) Rr . . .of
PO Box 893, Ligonier, PA *15658*
Sutton Place NW, Washington, DC *20016*
Curry DR & MRS Charles M JR (Susanne T McGuire) | ☎ (908) 234-1285
B.L.Wk.HolyC'65.Pa'85 . . . . | PO Box 17,
MR C MacNeil 3d—at U of Pa . . . . | Oldwick, NJ *08858*
MR Fraser MacL 2d—at U of Pa . . . . |
Curry MR Henry M 3d—Y'39
☎ (412) 741-4393 . . 539 Boundary St, Sewickley, PA *15143*
Curry MRS John T JR (Marie Coudert) | ☎ (203) 531-8904
Man'vl'51.Ihy. . . . . | 22 Maher Av,
MISS Sheila M—at ☎ (212) 496-0394 | Greenwich, CT
25 W 54 St, Apt 3E, New York, NY *10024* . . . . | *06830*
Curry MR Michael O
☎ (203) 531-8904 . . 79 N Water St, Greenwich, CT *06830*
Curry MR & MRS Patrick D (Laura Cushing Riegel) Rol'80
☎ (970) 927-0788 . . 214 Lewis Lane, Basalt, CO *81621*
Curry MR & MRS Robert V K (Helen S Post) | ☎ (203) 966-5121
Cly.Cl'70.Cl'76 . . . . | 64 Ludlowe Rd,
MISS Ann S . . . . | New Canaan, CT
JUNIORS MISS Emily S . . . . | *06840*
Curry MR & MRS Robert W (Catharine H Hays)
☎ (520) 297-0698 . . 8202 N Placita Catavinos, Tucson, AZ *85704*
Curry MISS Sarah L (late John T JR) . . . . Married at Greenwich, CT
Larsen MR James G JR (James G) . . . . Apr 27'96
Curtis MR & MRS Charles B (Ellen M Whitaker) Sth'54.Y'51 . . of
☎ (203) 259-2076 . . 537 Verna Hill Rd, Fairfield, CT *06430*
☎ (802) 824-6771 . . ''Mountain Meadow Farm'' 3 Morgan Hill Rd,
Weston, VT *05161*
Curtis MR & MRS Charles F JR (Corinne W Collins) StLaw'84.NEng'83
☎ (508) 468-2322 . . 185 Woodbury St, Hamilton, MA *01982*
Curtis MR Charles P JR—WashColl'81
☎ (617) 262-5521 . . 50 Commonwealth Av, Apt 805, Boston,
MA *02116*
Curtis MR Daniel S—Sbc.Btn.Cw.Myf.Ofp.Sar.Rv.W.Cp.Bost'88.Sim'95
☎ (508) 526-4140 . . ''The Pavilion'' 10 Masconomo St, Manchester,
MA *01944*
Curtis MISS Diane—Sc.Cnt.Ncd.
☎ (312) SU7-9350 . . 1350 N Astor St, Chicago, IL *60610*
Curtis DR & MRS Earnest M JR (Anne D McShane) | ☎ (404) 351-5266
Ala'49 . . . . | 705 Woodward Way
MR Richard L . . . . | NW, Atlanta, GA
 | *30327*

Curtis MRS Harry J (Penelope M Trask) . . . . | PO Box 825,
MISS Catherine M . . . . | Sanbornville, NH
MISS Cassandra T . . . . | *03872*
Curtis MR Harry L JR (late Harry L) . . . . Married at Beverly, MA
Cyr MRS Elbridge (Edith Way) . . . . May 25'96
Curtis MR & MRS Harry L JR (Cyr—Edith Way) USN'47.Pa'51
☎ (508) 927-7863 . . 54 Hart St, Beverly Farms, MA *01915*
Curtis MR & MRS Harry L 3d (Alice L Ober) Wheat'78.Laf'76
☎ (609) 466-4189 . . 200 Rocky Hill Rd, Pennington, NJ *08534*
Curtis MR & MRS James F 3d (Field—Marion T | of ☎ (212)517-2552
Dana) Rc.Shcc.Pr.Eh.Ri . . . . | 800 Park Av,
MISS Devon Dana Field . . . . | New York, NY
MR Richard Field JR . . . . | *10021*
| ☎ (908) 766-9069
| Lake Road,
| Far Hills, NJ *07931*
Curtis MR & MRS John N (Helen Akeroyd) Pa'32 . . . | ☎ (561) 231-6870
MISS Judith A—at ☎ (561) 231-7738 | 961 Greenway Lane,
1322 Coral Park Lane, Vero Beach, FL *32963* . . | Vero Beach, FL
| *32963*
Curtis MR & MRS John N JR (Alison von Clemm) | ☎ (011-41-33)
Y'58.Pa'64 . . . . | 733-31403
MISS Jennifer . . . . | ''The Winter Term''
| Chalet Hohliebi,
| 3775 Lenk,
| Switzerland
Curtis DR & MRS John P (Ellen D Chinn) | RD 2, Box 354,
V'64.Y'60.YeshivaU'64 . . . . | Sharon Station Rd,
MR Jeptha P—Y'93—at Columbia Phys & Surg . | Millerton, NY *12546*
Curtis MR & MRS John R JR (Christine W | ☎ (203) 264-4675
von Goeben) Sth'51.GeoW'50.JHop'51 . . . . | 353A Heritage
MR Allen R—Box 1129, South Bend, WA *98586* | Village, Southbury,
MR Robert F—at 4040 Synott Rd, Apt 209, | CT *06488-1710*
Houston, TX *77082* . . . .
Curtis MR & MRS John R JR (Julia R Blodgett) V'62.Cly.H'62
176 Dennis Dv, PO Box KP, Williamsburg, VA *23187*
Curtis MRS Laura (Bostwick—Neville—Laura E Curtis) Pr.
☎ (516) 333-1148 . . ''Curtishill'' 137 Bacon Rd, Box 308,
Old Westbury, NY *11568*
Curtis MRS Laurence (Marie L Schryver) Sm.Ub.Cy.
20 Pleasant Place, Williamstown, MA *01267*
Curtis REV DR & MRS Lawrence R (Helen L Dickey) Mid'57.Mid'58
☎ (802) 878-0240 . . 139 Metcalf Dv, Williston, VT *05495*
Curtis MRS McCall (Ward—Beachboard—Anne L Curtis)
Tex'57.Me.Ac.Dar.Ncd . . .of
Cuadrante 8A, San Miguel de Allende, GTO 37700, Mexico
☎ (915) 597-2616 . . Z-Bar Ranch, Brady, TX *76825*
Curtis MR Ralston—Cal'55
☎ (415) 968-6864 . . 1683 Nilda Av, Mountain View, CA *94040*
Curtis MRS Robert M (Stark—A Hadley Lammert) Sth'53
5 Malvern Manor, Apt 2, Richmond, VA *23221*
Curtis MR T Knickerbacker JR—Wind'68
☎ (214) 358-2882 . . 8403 Midway Rd, Dallas, TX *75209*
Curtis MR & MRS Thomas G (Margaret H Eustis) | *see*
Al.Hn.Hb.H'36 . . . . | *Dilatory Domiciles*
MISS Margaret E . . . . |
DR T Gray JR—Mit'67 . . . . |

Curtis MR Thomas K
☎ (610) 793-1268 . . 275 S Creek Rd, West Chester, PA *19382*
Curtis MR William G 5th . . . . | ☎ (508) 356-5887
MR Truman M—at ☎ (212) 534-7433 | Turner Hill Farm,
1060 Fifth Av, New York, NY *10128* . . . . | 198 Topsfield St,
| Ipswich, MA *01938*
Curtiss MR & MRS Ward S (Essig—Adair H Miller) | of ☎ (610)431-1917
StJas'36.Pe.Rv.Cspa.Ofp.Cw.Ncd.Pa'58 . . . . . . | 427 Eaton Way,
MISS Erica L Essig . . . . | Hershey's Mill,
| West Chester, PA
| *19380-6931*
| ☎ (803) 785-2040
| ''Alia Vita''
| Ketch Court, Box
| 3137, Hilton Head
| Island, SC *29928*
Cushing MR & MRS Edward B (Philio E | ☎ (508) 526-9934
Wigglesworth) SL'80.Sim'91.My.Myc. . . . . | 44 Masconomo St,
MISS Amelia C—at Northfield-Mt Hermon . . . . | Manchester-By-The-
JUNIORS MISS Mae L | Sea, MA *01944*
Cushing MR & MRS Howard G JR (Griscom—Nora G | ☎ (212) 988-1019
Knott) Rc.B.Nrr.Srb.H'55 . . . . | 180 E 79 St,
JUNIORS MR Howard G 3d . . . . | New York, NY
| *10021*
Cushing MRS John C (Patricia M Freer) Pn.
☎ (630) 323-7511 . . 902 Chanticleer Lane, Hinsdale, IL *60521*
Cushing MISS Justine B—Rdc'62.Pr.
☎ (212) 288-4354 . . 186 E 75 St, New York, NY *10021*
Cushing MRS Justine C (Justine B Cutting) Mb.Pr.So . . .of
☎ (212) 861-1221 . . 159 E 82 St, New York, NY *10028*
☎ (516) 626-1589 . . 154 Wheatley Rd, Glen Head, NY *11545*
Cushing MISS Margaret C—Bost'78.Ncd.
☎ (212) 879-7066 . . 315 E 70 St, Apt 11Q, New York, NY *10021-5527*
Cushing MR & MRS R Dunbar (Sherwood—Cushing— | ☎ (203) 531-5115
Flood—Ruth S Dunbar) SL'54.Ri. . . . . | 12 Bailiwick Rd,
MISS Margaret Flood . . . . | Greenwich, CT
| *06831*
Cushman MR Allerton—H'29
☎ (602) 948-1635 . . 5029 Roadrunner Rd, Paradise Valley, AZ *85253*
Cushman MR & MRS Allerton JR (Gottschalk— | of ☎ (212)737-0474
Carole M D von T Janowski) Un.Chr.Cly.H'58 | 135 E 74 St, Apt
⚓ | 9B, New York, NY
MR Adam W H Gottschalk . . . . | *10021*
| ☎ (207) 326-4438
| Box 92, Rte 175,
| North Brooksville,
| ME *04617*
Cushman MR Allerton 3d—Ober'87 . . see R Britton
Cushman MR & MRS Andrew L (Kramer—Robin L | ☎ (516) 364-0707
Davis) Bvr'75.Pr.Va'75 . . . . | 179 Split Rock Rd,
JUNIORS MISS Katherine A Kramer . . . . | Syosset, NY
| *11791-2636*
Cushman JUNIORS MR Blinn L . . see A G McCall
Cushman MISS Catherine C—Smu'91 . . see S R Weltz JR
Cushman MISS Christina M—Tul'92.SCal'96
9167 W 3 St, Beverly Hills, CA *90210*

Cushman MR & MRS Curtis (A Dorothy Barta) Cly.Mid'50 . . . . ☎ (904) 641-6538 10141 Leisure Lane S, Jacksonville, FL 32256
MISS Susan—Wis'84.Marq'88.S.—Box 113, Syosset, NY 11791 . . . .
MR Jonathan C—UWash'86.OState'93—at ☎ (970) 407-9605 . . PO Box 1951, Ft Collins, CO 80522 . . . .

Cushman MR John M—Pa'59 . . . . ☎ (520) 529-1284 2725 E Avenida De Posada, Tucson, AZ 85718
MISS Elizabeth S . . . .
MISS Natalie S—at 150 W 76 St, New York, NY 10023 . . . .

Cushman DR & MRS Paul JR (Paulette Bessire) Un.C.Snc.Chr.Cly.Y'51.Cl'55 . . of
☎ (212) 427-4626 . . 1170 Fifth Av, New York, NY 10029
☎ (516) 367-7516 . . 1348 Ridge Rd, Laurel Hollow, NY 11791

Cushman MR Paul 3d . . . . Died near Dubrovnik, Croatia Apr 3'96

Cushman MR Philip P—Col'92 . . see R Britton

Cushman MR & MRS Roderick H (Verena von Flotow) Pr.Cly.Va'53.Cl'55 . . ☎ (307) 733-9730 PO Box 592, Jackson, WY 83001
MR Stefan H—at Glendale, AZ . . . .
MR Christoph v F—at Hamburg, Germany . . . . .

Cushny MR & MRS Theodorus V W (Cora Cavanagh) Snc.Y'54.Cl'57 . . of ☎ (212)912-1536 355 South End Av, New York, NY 10280
MISS Lillian B—Adelphi'79.Adelphi'81—at ☎ (606) 252-1799 . . 342 E High St, Apt 4, Lexington, KY 40507 . . . .
MISS Coralie C—Okla'88—at ☎ (814) 238-5489 840 Cricklewood Dv, Apt 309, State College, PA 16803 . . . . ☎ (410) 639-2441 PO Box 600, Rock Hall, MD 21661

Custard MR & MRS William Allen (Linda Pitts) Mls'60.Smu'57 . . of ☎ (214)526-2486 3703 Crescent Av, Dallas, TX 75205
MISS Martha E . . . . Bellwether Farm,
MISS Laura L . . . . PO Box 944,
MR W Allen 3d . . . . Van Alstyne, TX 75095

Custer RR ADM & MRS Ben Scott (Elizabeth Hawkins) Stan'33.Ny.Cvc.Dar.USN'26. Geo'49 . . . . ☎ (914) 967-3589 8 Holly Lane, Loudon Woods, Rye, NY 10580
MISS Penelope F—at 205 E 77 St, New York, NY 10021 . . . .

Cuthbert MR & MRS Richard I (Caroline W Brower) Me.Cvc.Ncd.Pa'60 . . . . ☎ (610) MI2-9295 251 Hathaway Lane, Wynnewood, PA 19096
MISS Caroline V—Aht'90.H'95 . . . .
MR Alexander J—Dth'87—at U of Cal . . . .

Cutler MRS Anne H (Anne W Hoffman) BtP.Dar.StJ. ☎ (561) 655-2629 . . 111 Dunbar Rd, Palm Beach, FL 33480

Cutler MASTER Benjamin Bontecou (Timothy G) . . . . Born at Morristown, NJ Aug 30'95

Cutler MR & MRS Donald F JR (Coulter—J Lloyd Ilsley) Cy.H.'36 . . . . of ☎ (617)232-6615 284 Woodland Rd, Chestnut Hill, MA 02167
MR Christopher G . . . .
MR Gregory T . . . .
MISS Cheryl S Coulter . . . . ☎ (910) 692-7381 ''Broadhearth'' 155 Highland Rd, Southern Pines, NC 28387

Cutler MR Donald F 4th . . see E N Vestner

Cutler MR E Newton JR (Beverly Waring) Err.Eyc.Ln.Mo.P'37 ☎ (201) 538-4439 . . Lindsley Rd, New Vernon, NJ 07976

Cutler MR & MRS E Newton 3d (Pell—Alexandra C Moulton) Ln.Err.Eyc.Bgt.Ty'62 . . . . ☎ (401) 245-3787 5 Mathewson Lane, Barrington, RI 02806
MISS Allison M Pell . . . .
JUNIORS MR Peter J Pell JR . . . .

Cutler MR Earle N 4th—LakeF'90 . . see R D Field

Cutler MR & MRS Eric (Nancy Ware) D.H.'40 ☎ (617) 326-1404 . . 255 West St, Dedham, MA 02026

Cutler MRS George C (Phyllis Tuckerman) Sbc.My.Yh.Chi. . . . . ☎ (508) 468-2030 Box 2008, 159 Asbury St, South Hamilton, MA 01982
MISS Phyllis—at 67 Cunningham Dv, South Hamilton, MA 01982 . . . .
MR George C JR—at 1 Emerson Place, Boston, MA 02114 . . . .
MISS Phyllis
JUNIORS MR Daniel

Cutler MR & MRS John W (Davisson—Marietta Howe) Cy.D. ☎ (617) 449-0558 . . 708 South St, Box 217, Needham, MA 02192

Cutler MISS Katharine S—LakeF'94 . . see R D Field

Cutler MR & MRS L Bradley 2d (Ebner—Linda A Beech) Miami'75.Cyb.H'71 4010 Wycombe Dv, Sacramento, CA 95864

Cutler MR & MRS Michael W (K Haven Filley) Colby'66 . . . . ☎ (508) 693-5792 PO Box 517, Christiantown Rd, West Tisbury, MA 02575
MR Michael W JR—at ☎ (207) 846-0966 10 Pleasant St, Yarmouth, ME 04096 . . . .
MR E Russell—Denis'93 . . . .

Cutler MR & MRS Nicholas B (Katherine C Brady) P'89.Vt'82 ☎ (202) 364-3374 . . 4915 Sedgwick St NW, Washington, DC 20016

Cutler MR Peter K—Skd'93 . . see R D Field

Cutler MR & MRS Philip (Rose P Gardner) Chi.H'41 ☎ (508) 748-0053 560A Point Rd, Marion, MA 02738
MR A David—H'75 . . . .

Cutler MR Q A Shaw . . see E N Vestner

Cutler MR Ralph H JR (Elizabeth Lee) BMr'52.Cda. ☎ (201) 538-0151 . . ''Fossil Hill'' Red Gate Rd, Morristown, NJ 07960

Cutler MR & MRS Richard M (Mary R Cecil) Char'ton'49.Sbc.Ub.My.Yh.H'43 . . . . ☎ (803) 722-1887 53 Legare St, Charleston, SC 29401
MR John R S—at ☎ (617) 720-4120 48 Beacon St, Apt 11F, Boston, MA 02108 . . . .

Cutler MR & MRS Robert B (Claire Demmer) Ec.H'35 ☎ (508) 927-0064 . . 675 Hale St, Box 5492, Beverly Farms, MA 01915

Cutler MR Robert B JR—Ln.H'63 . . . . ☎ (212) 534-1545 1435 Lexington Av, New York, NY 10128
MISS Vanessa—Col'91 . . . .
MR Adam A—Col'91 . . . .

Cutler MRS Robert W (Morene Parten)
☎ (817) 947-5467 . . ''Ridgeway'' PO Box 26, Salado, TX *76571*
Cutler MRS S Stubbs (Sue G Stubbs) Ncd.Myf.
☎ (860) 767-0408 . . 238 River Rd, Deep River, CT *06417*
Cutler MR & MRS Stewart L (Anne W Fox) Va'81.Nu'88.Fiy.H.'79.Dth'83
☎ (212) 534-2089 . . 1192 Park Av, Apt 2C, New York, NY *10128*
Cutler MRS Tarrant (Laura G Curtis) Ec.Myc.Sm.H'50
☎ (508) 526-4676 . . 5 Masconomo St, Manchester, MA *01944*
Cutler MR & MRS Thomas P (Sara B Brereton) Cyb.USN'44
☎ (401) 635-4840 . . 40 W Main Rd, Little Compton, RI *02837*
Cutler MR & MRS Thomas P JR (Caryn Sherwood) Okla'84.Cy.Chi.Rol'70
☎ (617) 329-3610 . . 250 Weatherbee Dv, Westwood, MA *02090*
Cutler MR & MRS Timothy G (Alice B Darlington)
Wheat'81.Mg.Cw.Chr.Cly.Ht.Pn.Van'77
☎ (201) 538-5672 . . 31 Headley Rd, Morristown, NJ *07960*
Cutler MR & MRS William B (Peckham—McGovern—McAdams—
Elizabeth L Winslow) Wms'47
☎ (860) 572-9669 . . 4 Pondside Court, Mystic, CT *06355*
Cutter MISS Amanda H . . see W A W Stewart 3d
Cutter MR & MRS Bruce A (Claudia M Steers) Stone'79.Conn'72
☎ (203) 461-8173 . . 34 Ethan Allen Rd, North Stamford, CT *06903*
Cutter MISS Kimberly E . . see W A W Stewart 3d
Cutter MR & MRS Louis A (Ann Hornor) H'48 . . . . . | ☎ (412) 361-8138
MR Henry A . . . . | 111 Yorkshire Rd,
| Pittsburgh, PA
| *15208*
Cutting MR & MRS George W JR (Lucy Pulling) Pr.Y'55
☎ (516) 922-7057 . . 33 Yellowcote Rd, Oyster Bay, NY *11771*
Cutting MR & MRS Heyward (Randell—Joan | ☎ (508) 369-3774
Faulkner) Ws'58.Tv.H'43.IIT'53 | 377 Main St,
MR Thomas W Randell—at 1843 San Ramon | Concord, MA *01742*
Av, Berkeley, CA *94707* . . . . |
Cutts DR & MRS Morgan (Cornell—Suzanne J Herrick)
SL'46.Cly.P'27.JHop'31
☎ (401) 751-4772 . . 229 Medway St, Providence, RI *02906*
Cutts MRS Richard Malcolm (Dorothea Lane) An.Mt.Sl.Cda.
☎ (540) 364-1781 . . ''Dondoric'' PO Box 504, The Plains,
VA *20198*
Cuvelier MR & MRS Guillaume (Andrea N Rizzo) Geo'89.Va'91
☎ (011-33-1) 42-88-95-79 . . 65 rue de Passy, 75016 Paris, France
Cuyler DR G Grenville—P'60.SL'73.Birm'ham'85
☎ (617) 241-9571 . . 19 Monument Square, Boston, MA *02129*
Czoernig von Czernhausen MRS Carl E (E Adele Moore)
☎ (610) 584-3772 . . Meadowood at Worcester, Robin Ridge 244,
Lansdale, PA *19446-5847*
Czoernig von Czernhausen MR & MRS Carl E JR (Martha F Yeaw)
Gettys'60
☎ (561) 274-9336 . . 900 Dogwood Dv, Apt 239, Delray Beach,
FL *33483*

D

Daane MR & MRS J Dewey (Barbara W McMann)
Av'tt'58.Duke'39.H'46.H'49
☎ (615) 385-2403 . . 102 Westhampton Place, Nashville, TN *37205*

Dabney MISS Fay—Btn.H.
☎ (617) 262-9073 . . 301 Berkeley St, Boston, MA *02116*
Dabney MRS Frederick L (Adie—Mary L Almy) Chi.
☎ (508) 636-2011 . . 794 Horseneck Rd, South Dartmouth, MA *02748*
Dabney MR & MRS Lucius B JR (Allene Hallberg) Miss'49
☎ (601) 636-3887 . . PO Box 947, 1 Old Warrenton Rd, Vicksburg,
MS *39181*
Dabney MR & MRS Watson B (Bluck—Lucy C Mercer) B.P.'46
☎ (502) 896-6666 . . 399 Mockingbird Valley, Louisville, KY *40207*
Da Costa MR & MRS Peter M (Shirley J Huggler) Rc.R.
☎ (610) 689-5198 . . PO Box 77, Limekiln, PA *19535*
Dagenhart MR & MRS Larry J (Sarah K Petty) AScott'55.David'53.Nu'58
☎ (704) 376-6652 . . 1601 Biltmore Dv, Charlotte, NC *28207*
Dague MR & MRS Arthur D (Starr—Emilie K Banks) | ☎ (904) 273-0595
Bnd'49.Cal'45 . . . . | 337 Pablo Rd,
MISS A Susan—MtH'81 . . . . | Ponte Vedra Beach,
| FL *32082*
Dahar MR & MRS William J (Donabeth Jensen) SUNY'81.SUNY'80
4034 Fay Hollow Rd, Hinsdale, NY *14743*
Dahlgren MRS J A Bernard (Coleman—Marjorie B
Munthe de Morgenstierne)
''Meadowbrook'' 107 S Madison St, Middleburg, VA *20117*
Dailey MR & MRS Richard R (Cameron—Corinne C Cardoff)
Csn.Yn.Y'50.Mich'56
☎ (860) 434-8622 . . ''Woodwinds'' 86 Cove Rd, Lyme, CT *06371*
Daine MRS Robert A (Barbara H Hoge) Nu'56.Ncd. | ☎ (203) 637-9243
MISS Virginia F—Duke'81—at | 12 Pierce Rd,
☎ (703) 641-8805 . . 2857 Coors Park Court, | Riverside, CT *06878*
Falls Church, VA *22043*— at |
MR James H—at Columbia . . . . |
Daingerfield MR McKim—P'37
☎ (516) JU4-5423 . . 34 Harbor Hill Rd, St James, NY *11780*
Dakin MR A Hazard—C.Cw.Ht.Snc.Pn.P'28.Ox'33
☎ (413) 253-2135 . . 355 S Pleasant St, Amherst, MA *01002-2541*
Dakin MISS Alicia . . see J P Lowney JR
Dakin MISS Cary . . see J P Lowney JR
Dakin MR & MRS Henry S (Vergilia I Paasche) H'58
☎ (415) 346-0666 . . 3456 Jackson St, San Francisco, CA *94118*
Dakin MISS Karla . . see J P Lowney JR
Dale MRS Chalmers (Nancy E Wilson) Ne.Cw.Fw.
☎ (203) 869-8108 . . 130 Havemeyer Place, Greenwich, CT *06830-6332*
Dale MR & MRS Dennis J (Sarah S Kreger) Ws'76.Conn'79.H'84
☎ (617) 729-3541 . . 147 Cambridge St, Winchester, MA *01890*
Dale MR & MRS Edwin L JR (Haythorne—Cross—Homet—
Meredith A Morgan) AmU'69.AmU'71.Cos.Y'45 . . of
☎ (561) 272-2474 . . 414 Andrews Av, Delray Beach, FL *33483*
☎ (202) 363-1726 . . 3050 University Terr NW, Washington, DC *20016*
Dale MRS Fanny C W (Fanny Cox Worrall) . . . . | ☎ (603) 431-4090
MISS Deborah W—NH'79—at ☎ (207) 361-1562 | PO Box 102,
19 Bayberry Lane, Cape Neddick, ME *03902* . . | New Castle, NH
| *03854*
Dale MRS John D (Madeline H McWhinney) | ☎ (908) 747-1184
Sth'43.Nu'47.Rm.Plg.Snc.Myf.Cw.Ncd . . . . | ''Birdwood''
MR Thomas D—Rcn.Rv.Myf.Ht.Fw.Va'85. | PO Box 458,
Pa'90 . . . . | 24 Blossom Cove
| Rd, Red Bank, NJ
| *07701*

Dale MR Neal W—Fla'37 . . of
  ☎ (305) 367-2829 . . FL 50A Lakeside Lane, Key Largo, FL *33037*
  ☎ (207) 644-8313 . . ''Bayledge'' HC 64, Box 211, Eastside Rd,
  South Bristol, ME *04568*
Dale MISS Patricia B—CtCol'66
  ☎ (212) 877-5715 . . 599 West End Av, New York, NY *10024*
Dale MR & MRS Robert V (Linda H Williams) Van'60.Cda.Vmi'59
  ☎ (615) 297-1716 . . 1414 Chickering Rd, Nashville, TN *37215*
Daley REV DR Alexander S—Cw.H'57.EpiscTheo'71.PittTheo'84
  ☎ (508) 686-6858 . . 390 Main St, North Andover, MA *01845*
Daley MISS Eliza D—B'gton'88 . . see MRS S E Everett

Daley MRS Robert L (J Lee Bradford) Hlns'48.Chi. .	☎ (617) 696-6762
MR R Bradford—H'86.Pa'93—at	46 Brook Hill Rd,
☎ (202) 319-7844 . . 1718—17 St NW, Apt 2,	Milton, MA *02186*
Washington, DC *20009*	

Daley MR William A 2d—Ty'92 . . see MRS S E Everett

Daley MR & MRS William C JR (Margit A Knerly)	☎ (216) 256-4777
Mid'69.Kt.Un.It.Ty'64	9215 Baldwin Rd,
JUNIORS MISS Daneen R	Kirtland Hills, OH *44060*

Dall MRS Curtis B (Katharine M Leas) Cda.Dar.
  ☎ (803) 525-8437 . . 6 Bajala Lane, PO Box 2331, Beaufort, SC *29901*

Dall MR Henry A—⚓	☎ (802) 222-9297
MISS Margaret H	Underwood Rd,
MISS Barbara	Box 868, Bradford,
MR Charles H A	VT *05033*

Dall MR & MRS Mark H (Pauline T Kingsland) Hn.H'37
  ☎ (408) 624-3346 . . PO Box 453, Pebble Beach, CA *93953*
Dall MR & MRS Stewart M (Margaret Meyerkort) H'38
  ☎ (603) 353-9451 . . Brick Hill Rd, Lyme, NH *03768*

Dallas MR & MRS George M (Sarah A Kraetzer)	☎ (508) 369-2143
Myf.H.'56.Pa'64	53 Middle St,
MISS Sarah H	Concord, MA *01742*
MISS Elisabeth W	

Dallett MISS C Athenaide H . . see J R Hinman JR
Dallett MRS Estelina L (Costello—Estelina L Dallett) H'87.H'93
  ☎ (202) 232-3173 . . 1956 Calvert St NW, Apt 1, Washington,
  DC *20009*
Dallett MR & MRS Francis James (Charlotte Houston Brown)
  Cw.Ac.Cda.Hav'50.Pa'55
  ☎ (860) 824-5874 . . PO Box 6, Taconic, CT *06079-0006*
Dallett MR & MRS Matthew C (Mary E Pritchard) L&C'78.P'78.Ne'84
  ☎ (508) 681-9981 . . 399 River Rd, Andover, MA *01810*
Dallett MR & MRS Richard S S (C Lloyd Gunther) Pa'81
  ☎ (212) 473-1226 . . 3 Great Jones St, New York, NY *10012*
Dalley MR & MRS Lawrence C (Agnes L Dunn) Cvc.Mt.Y'48 . . of
  ☎ (301) 654-1993 . . 3545 Hamlet Place, Chevy Chase, MD *20815*
  ☎ (410) 745-9109 . . Deep Neck Rd, Royal Oak, MD *21662*

Dallman COL & MRS James H (Elizabeth W Arnold)	☎ (616) 940-2748
On.Ncd.USA'45	2776 Hickorywood
MISS Janet C—at ☎ (616) 451-2818	Lane SE,
145 Auburn Av SE, Apt 2, Grand Rapids, MI	Grand Rapids, MI
49506	*49546*

Dalton MRS Diana (Hill—Diana L Heller) Cal'51
  ☎ (415) 749-1065 . . 2801 Jackson St, Apt 203, San Francisco,
  CA *94115*

Dalton MRS Eliot W (Marie L Hulburd) Chi.Gm.Ncd.Myf.
  ☎ (610) 388-3997 . . 101 Crosslands Dv, Kennett Square,
  PA *19348-2014*

Dalton MR & MRS Eliot W JR (Letitia R Baer)	of ☎ (518)966-8754
JUNIORS MISS Anne Marie	Greenville Arms, Greenville, NY *12083*
	☎ (518) 966-5219 ''The Carriage House'' South St, Greenville, NY *12083*

Dalton CAPT & MRS George Francis (M Harriett	☎ (610) 527-1617
Brown) R.Me.Ph.StA.Fw.StJ.Ac.Ncd.USN'38 . .	322 N Ithan Av,
DR John Shaw 2d—H'71.NCar'75—at	Rosemont, PA *19010*
☎ (410) 747-8144 . . 1201B Martin Court,	
Baltimore, MD *21223*	

Dalva COL & MRS David L II (Margaret Gelinas)	☎ (212) 861-1876
USAR.L.An.Mto.Vca.StJ.Ll.VillaN'56	320 E 72 St,
MISS Jean A—at ☎ (303) 831-4926	New York, NY *10016*
789 Clarkson St, Denver, CO *80218*	
MR David L III—at ☎ (212) 956-4701	
344 W 49 St, New York, NY *10019*	

Daly MR Daniel—K.Sa.
  ☎ (518) 398-5151 . . PO Box 308, Pine Plains, NY *12567*
Daly MR & MRS Donald F (Sandra R Godfrey) Ford'87.Un.Chr.Plg.StJ.Y.'50
  ☎ (212) 996-5897 . . 1361 Madison Av, New York, NY *10128*
Daly MR J Holmes (Bliss—Katharine Boston)
  ☎ (619) 551-8378 . . The Cloisters, 7160 Fay Av, La Jolla, CA *92037*
Daly MR & MRS Joseph A (Barbara K Mittnacht)
  Ty'82.VillaN'86.Pc.Temp'79.Temp'82
  ☎ (610) 642-2148 . . 272 Hathaway Lane, Wynnewood, PA *19096*
Daly MR & MRS Lee E (Rosemarie Heavey)
  ☎ (302) 227-6811 . . 109 Spring Lake, Rehoboth Beach, DE *19971*
Daly MR & MRS Rodney O (Martha S Stevens) LakeF'44.Cnt.Nw'38
  ☎ (941) 364-8700 . . 988 Blvd of the Arts, Apt 109, Sarasota, FL *34236*

Daly MR T F Gilroy	Died at Roxbury, CT Jly 11'96

Daly MRS T F Gilroy (G Stuart Stetson)	☎ (860) 350-5050
MISS K Loan	30 Tophet Rd,
MISS Anna L	Roxbury, CT *06783*
MR Timothy F G	
MR Matthew W	

Daly MAJ & MRS Thomas B (Lewis—Patricia H	☎ (802) 878-0438
Mueller) USA.	10 Chestnut Lane,
MISS Jennifer I	Essex Junction, VT *05452*
MR Michael J	
JUNIORS MR Timothy M	

Daly MR & MRS Thomas M (Post—Elizabeth B Thompson)
  Fairf'81.Ny.Bf.G.USN'68
  ☎ (716) 875-1042 . . 101 Meadow Rd, Buffalo, NY *14216*
Daly MRS Winston (Ehrenclou—Mary Winston)
  ☎ (908) 234-1450 . . PO Box 906, Far Hills, NJ *07931*
Dalzell MR & MRS K Whitney JR (Frances G Ill) Myf.P'39
  ☎ (813) 441-3941 . . 8 Belleview Blvd, Apt 703, Belleair, FL *34616*

Dalzell MR & MRS Robert F JR (Lee Baldwin) Sth'60.Aht'59 . . . . | of ☎ (413)458-9038 148 South St, Williamstown, MA 01267
MR Adams A . . . . | ☎ (207) 647-2667 Sweden, Harrison, ME 04040

d'Ambly MR & MRS A Ernest JR (Ruth M Thibault) Pa'40
☎ (803) 886-8590 . . 20 Lake Village Lane, Isle of Palms, SC 29451

Dame MR & MRS Thomas J (Alexandra Jensen) Nw'68 . . . . | 16 Stonegate Dv, Hurricane, WV 25526
MISS Laura . . . . |

Dame MR W Page 3d—Cc.Cw.Va'63 . . . . | ☎ (202) 463-7961 1308—21 St NW, Apt 201, Washington, DC 20036
MISS L Alexandra . . . . |
MR W Page 4th . . . . |

Dame MRS William Page (Harriet C Brent) Elk.Mv.Ncd.
☎ (410) 823-5695 . . ''Pagebrook'' 7529 Club Rd, Baltimore, MD 21204-6419

Damgard MR John M 2d—Bcs.
☎ (202) 483-0817 . . 2439 Tracy Place NW, Washington, DC 20008

Damgard MISS Julie M—Y'93 . . see R P E Leeds

Damgard MR & MRS Michael T (Lucy G Siewers) Va'89.Va'90
see Dilatory Domiciles

Damon MR & MRS Allen F (Delphine M Sloan) Ws'89.Cly.Y'82.H'87
☎ (415) 668-6774 . . 2034 Lake St, San Francisco, CA 94121

Damon MR & MRS Cyril F JR (Baker—Katharine C Kane) HawaiiLoa'84.Y'50 . . . . | of ☎ (808)734-4444 841 Pueo St, Honolulu, HI 96816
MR James M Baker—H'90.Camb'93 . . . . | ☎ (970) 476-0882 710 W Lionshead Circle, Vail, CO 81657

Damon MRS Deborah C (Damon—Hakkonsen—Childs—Deborah Allen Coward) . . . . | ☎ (808) 734-2791 3921 Lanipili Place, Honolulu, HI 96816
MR Andrew M—at ☎ (212) 979-9029 115 Fourth Av, Apt 5E, New York, NY 10003 .

Damon MRS H Gilroy (Virginia E Price) Cry.
☎ (610) 566-1503 . . 103 Blackthorn Rd, Wallingford, PA 19086

Damon MR & MRS Lawrence B (Elisabeth T Wheeler) Un.Cy.Cw.Cda.H'24
☎ (617) 326-7218 . . Fox Hill Village 255, 10 Longwood Dv, Westwood, MA 02090

D'Amore DR & MRS (DR) John J (Kimberly Jensen) StLaw'81.Roch'86.Vt'82
☎ (801) 295-3891 . . 3032 S 950 E, Bountiful, UT 84010

Dana MR & MRS Arnold G (Jean T Cammann) Cc.Ds.Cda.Yn.Y'47.H'50
☎ (941) 921-4960 . . 1503 N Lake Shore Dv, Sarasota, FL 34231

Dana MR David T . . . . Died at Westwood, MA Dec 19'95

Dana MRS David T (Swasey—Potter—Gladys Crocker) Lx.Cy.Chi . . .of
☎ (617) 320-0359 . . 10 Longwood Dv, Apt 257, Westwood, MA 02090
☎ (508) 748-2972 . . 10 South St, Box 585, Marion, MA 02738

Dana MRS Howard H (Brady—Rand—Eileen R McNulty) Sth'39.Pr.Cly.
☎ (516) 676-3483 . . Box 126, High Farms Rd, Glen Head, NY 11545

Dana MR & MRS Jacob (Dolores E Ryan) Bur.Cc.H'42
☎ (415) 347-6253 . . 20 Country Club Dv, Hillsborough, CA 94010

Dana MR & MRS John P (Priscilla H Shafer) P'83.ColC'88.Dth'96
☎ (315) 682-8949 . . 4734 Hadley Lane, Manlius, NY 13104

Dana MASTER Nathan Philip (John P) . . . . Born at Hanover, NH Aug 18'94

Danaher REV & MRS William J JR (Claire B Dober) Br'86.Y'96.Br'88.VaTheo'94
☎ (203) 776-9798 . . 146D Everit St, New Haven, CT 06511

Dancy MRS Marshall F (Camp—Mary V Wooten) Cly.
☎ (212) 734-6373 . . 177 E 75 St, New York, NY 10021

Dandy MR & MRS Walter E 3d (Jennifer P Keller) Sth'80.Md.H'73
☎ (970) 949-4533 . . 2121 N Frontage Rd, Apt 160, Vail, CO 81657

Dane MISS Barbara H—Pa'86
☎ (803) 685-5485 . . 331 Easter Branch Rd, Ridge Spring, SC 29129

Dane MRS Edward (Barker—Jean-Lamont Proctor) Cy.Chi.Ncd . . .of
☎ (561) 231-4073 . . 900 Beach Rd, John's Island, Vero Beach, FL 32963
☎ (603) 253-4583 . . ''Hearthstone'' RR 1, Box 108, Center Harbor, NH 03226
☎ (617) 326-3596 . . Fox Hill Village D535, 10 Longwood Dv, Westwood, MA 02090

Dane MR & MRS Edward H (Heather R Harmon) NH'88.NH'88
☎ (508) 526-7862 . . 9 Peele House Square, Manchester, MA 01944

Dane MR & MRS Edward Nathan (Arabella H Symington) Sm.Chi.H'57 . . . . | ☎ (603) 253-4641 Hillcrest Farm, Box 711, Rte 25B, Center Harbor, NH 03226
MISS Natalie S . . . . |
MR Charles E . . . . |

Dane MISS Eleanor H . . see MRS T C Sturtevant

Dane MR & MRS Herbert P (Sally J Johnson) Cy.Sm.Chi.H'65 . . . . | ☎ (617) 734-4484 47 Suffolk Rd, Chestnut Hill, MA 02167
MISS Harriet P . . . . |
MISS Lucy B . . . . |
JUNIORS MR Daniel S . . . . |

Dane MR & MRS Roger (Lydia H Stout) Brand'83.Mit'85.H'56
☎ (803) 685-7878 . . ''Edisto Farm'' 437 Easter Branch Rd, Ridge Spring, SC 29129

Danenhower MR & MRS Sloan M (Overdurff—Judith A Read) SConn'73
see MRS W Cates

Danforth MR & MRS A Edwards (Mary E Wagley) Rol'55.Nyc.Yn.Y'48
☎ (561) 747-1511 . . 1664 SE Colony Dv, Jupiter, FL 33478

Danforth MR & MRS Donald JR (Carolyn G Borders) Cy.Nd.Lc.Wash'54 . . . . | ☎ (314) 997-1114 26 Braeburn Dv, St Louis, MO 63124
MISS Carolyn B . . . . |
JUNIORS MR Christopher B . . . . |

Danforth MR & MRS John H (Antoinette V Kling) Cwr'37
22364 Douglas Rd, Shaker Heights, OH 44122

Danforth MR & MRS Murray S 3d (Judith C Pollard) Br'77.Br'77 . . . . | ☎ (401) 751-4036 17 Halsey St, Providence, RI 02906
JUNIORS MISS Merebea M . . . . |

Danforth MR & MRS Theodore N (Laura B Walker) CUNY'68.Rc.Pr.Aht'49 . . . . | ☎ (516) 676-2707 4 Old Lane Rd, Box 508, Locust Valley, NY 11560
MISS Alexandra S . . . . |
MR Theodore N JR . . . . |
MR Bryan N . . . . |
JUNIORS MISS Laura . . . . |

Danforth MR & MRS Thomas H (Rachel G Weaver) Cr'45.St.G.Cr'43
☎ (716) 626-4968 . . 193 Oakgrove Dv, Buffalo, NY *14221*

D'Angelo MR & MRS Christopher Scott (Betsy Hart Josephs) Sth'73.Me.Pe.Fst.Ac.Va'75.Va'78 . . . . | ☎ (610) 896-5863 212 Rose Lane,
JUNIORS MISS Caroline C . . . . | Haverford, PA
JUNIORS MR J Robert . . . . | *19041*
JUNIORS MR Christopher H . . . . |

d'Anglejan-Chatillon BRN Bernard & BRNSS (Abreu—Mary Sargent Ladd) see MRS R W Davenport

Dangler MR David W—Y'37
☎ (312) 664-1328 . . 1320 N State P'kway, Chicago, IL *60610*

Dangremond MR & MRS David W (Mary Plant Spivy) Sth'76.Wms'79.C.K.Gr.Nrr.Cw.Csn.Ncd.Yn. Aht'74.Del'76.Y'87
☎ (860) 434-1494 . . "Johnnycake Hill" PO Box 910, Old Lyme, CT *06371*

Daniel MRS Lewis B (Marjorie L Gibson)
☎ (513) 791-6384 . . 8480 Fox Cub Lane, Cincinnati, OH *45243*

Daniel MRS Margaret Carr (Margaret N Carr) Sth'59
☎ (212) 877-0145 . . 522 West End Av, New York, NY *10024*

Daniel MISS Nell L . . see MRS S L Chase

Daniel MRS Polly Reed (Polly G Reed)
☎ (713) 522-4565 . . 2722 Ferndale St, Houston, TX *77098*

Daniel MR & MRS Robert W JR (Pollard—Witt—Linda S Hearne) Ny.Mt.Fic.Cc.StJ.Va'58.Cl'61
☎ (757) 866-8486 . . Brandon Plantation, 23500 Brandon Rd, Spring Grove, VA *23881*

Daniel-Dreyfus MR & MRS Marc A (Faerber—Susan B Russe) Sb.Ncd.H.Y'62.Y'63 . . . . | ☎ (617) 731-0284 120 Middlesex Rd,
JUNIORS MISS E Cable D . . . . | Chestnut Hill, MA
| *02167*

Daniels MR Edwin A JR—Md.Colg'49
☎ (410) 583-8169 . . 8 Hiddenwood Court, Baltimore, MD *21208*

Daniels MR & MRS Frank A 3d (Teresa A Davidson) Kas'78.Duke'78
☎ (919) 836-1231 . . 2342 Churchill Rd, Raleigh, NC *27608*

Daniels MR Richard C—Evg.Clark'49.Col'51
☎ (561) 659-3920 . . 424 Brazilian Av, Palm Beach, FL *33480*

Daniels MR & MRS William G (Martha B Sharples) Conn'80.Cc.Pa'87
☎ (610) 527-4407 . . 32 Tenmore Rd, Haverford, PA *19041*

Danielson MR & MRS Lee (Barbara Norris) UAmericas'73.UMiami'71 . . . . | ☎ (804) 977-5758 "Tally Ho"
MISS Audrey M . . . . | Box 6, Rte 22,
JUNIORS MISS Molly E . . . . | Keswick, VA *22947*

Danielson MRS Richard E JR (Molly O'Daniel) . . . . Died at Santa Barbara, CA Aug 26'96

Dann MR E Webster—Leh'52 ⚓
Gratwick Manor, 25 Marjann Terr, Buffalo, NY *14223*

Dann MRS Joan H (Joan B Harriman) G. . . . . | ☎ (716) 836-7876
MISS Helen G—at Rte 8, Box 1000, Blairsville, | 161 Summit Av,
GA *30512* . . . . | Buffalo, NY *14214*
MR Christopher H . . . . |

D'Anneo MR John F P . . see A N Gansa

D'Anneo MR Paul A . . see A N Gansa

Dantzler DR & MRS William H (Barbara L Poag) Wells'57.Cl'58.P'57.Cl'61.Duke'64
☎ (520) 299-6692 . . 1601 Entrada Octava E, Tucson, AZ *85718*

Daras MR & MRS Dimitri J (Wendy H A Brewer) Y'80.GeoW'75
☎ (212) 876-4061 . . 108 E 96 St, Apt 10D, New York, NY *10128*

Darby MR Bruce R B (D Weston JR) . . . . Married at Key West, FL
Egan MISS Kerry C (Michael T) . . . . May 4'96

Darby MR & MRS Bruce R B (Kerry C Egan) Ind'91.Me.Guil'90
☎ (305) 294-3311 . . on board Water Bear'' PO Box 4411, Key West, FL *33041*

Darby MR & MRS D Weston JR (Margarette A Kortina) Ph.Rc.Pe.Me.Nyc.Sdg.Ac.Y'53
☎ (610) 942-3418 . . "Herminie Hill Farm" Honey Brook, PA *19344*

Darby MRS Donald W (Barclay—G Maxine Westervelt)
☎ (410) 778-4701 . . 103 Heron Point, Chestertown, MD *21620*

Darcy MR & MRS Cornelius P (Eleanor H Starr) Sth'54.Bow'50.H'51.Cl'70 . . . . | ☎ (410) 848-9424 21 Smith Av,
MR Cornelius H—Mariet'81—at | Westminster, MD
☎ (314) 963-9139 . . 222 Jefferson Rd, | *21157*
Webster Groves, MO *63119* . . . . |
MR Andrew J—Bow'84 |
MR D Alexander—Ham'87—at |
☎ (314) 963-9139 . . 222 Jefferson Rd, |
Webster Groves, MO *63119* . . . . |

D'Arcy MR & MRS William C JR (Lillyblad—June Berkey) Cysl.P'39 . . of
☎ (561) 546-5349 . . PO Box 847, Hobe Sound, FL *33475*
☎ (507) 280-0086 . . 1710 Lakeview Dv SW, Rochester, MN *55902*

Dargan MR & MRS R Alan (Kyle A Conroy) Ck.Ln.Ty'74 . . of
☎ (011-44-171) 938-3287 . . 2 Phillimore Place, London W8 7BU, England
☎ (011-353-45) 41257 . . Eyrefield House Stud, The Curragh, Co Kildare, Ireland

Darling MASTER Evan Scott (F C Darling JR & J R Just) . . . Born Sep 2'94

Darling F Corey JR & Just, Jennifer R—Br'81.Alf'81
☎ (860) 276-1004 . . 62 Academy St, Southington, CT *06489*

Darling COL (RET) & MRS Joseph W McNab (Egbert —Cynthia A Hearne) USA.W&M'59.Pc.Pe. Cvc.Rv.Fw.Cw.Ll.Cspa.Hb.H'30.Pa'34. GeoW'54 . . . . | ☎ (703) 339-0749 Raceway Farm,
JUNIORS MR Joseph H McNab—at St James . . . . | 6823 Silver Ann Dv,
MISS Vena H (Temple—Vena H Darling) | Lorton, VA *22079*
Pa'65.GeoW'75.Sth'80.Cvc.Sl. |
MR Garth L Egbert . . . . |

Darlington MRS Charles A JR (Virginia W Glenn) Sth'46.Pc.Dar.
☎ (215) 233-0993 . . 201 Heatherwood Rd, Erdenheim, PA *19038*

Darlington MR & MRS Christopher N (Muriel A Zunz) H'65.Cl'67 . . . . | 8905 Old Dominion
JUNIORS MISS Noelle C . . . . | Dv, McLean, VA
JUNIORS MR Christopher H . . . . | *22102*

Darlington MRS Dorothea F (Page—Dorothea Fiske) Cly.T. . . . . | ☎ (212) 772-9517 875 Fifth Av,
MISS Susan M Page—at 1300 Upper Canyon | New York, NY
Rd, Santa Fe, NM *87501* . . . . | *10021-4952*
MR F Le Moyne Page—T. |
☎ (212) 233-2227 . . 68 Thomas St, |
New York, NY *10013* . . . . |
MR Peter F Page—at ☎ (505) 471-5793 |
69 Rainbows End, Cerrillos, NM *87010* . . . . . |

Darlington MR & MRS Harry (Jennie Russell) BtP.Nf. ⚓ . . . . | ☎ (540) 364-1290 Chilly Bleak Farm,
MR Harry 4th . . . . | PO Box 945,
| Marshall, VA *20115*

Darlington MR & MRS Henry JR (Barratt-Brown—Carla Paterno)
Un.Chr.Pr.Plg.Evg.Ri.Rv.StA.StJ.Fw.Snc.Cw.Ht.Sar. Coa.Wt.Cl'49 . . of
☎ (212) 935-3553 . . 30 E 62 St, New York, NY *10021*
☎ (212) 889-1909 . . 1115 Fifth Av, New York, NY *10128*
☎ (561) 832-5965 . . Park Place, 369 S Lake Dv, Palm Beach,
FL *33480*
Darlington MR & MRS Henry 3d (Curry C Meredith) Snc.Rv.Ht.Dar.W&J'73
☎ (803) 671-3159 . . 8 Acorn Lane, Hilton Head Island, SC *29928*
Darlington MRS Joseph H (Scarlett—Kathleen S Davis) Mv.Cda.
☎ (410) 821-5048 . . 504 Brightwood Club Dv, Lutherville, MD *21093*
Darlington MRS McCullough (Edith F Pearson) Cvc.Mt.Sl . . .of
☎ (202) 332-4264 . . 2456 Tracy Place NW, Washington, DC *20008*
☎ (540) 364-2192 . . ''Grouse House'' The Plains, VA *20198*
Darlington MR & MRS Paul G (Susan H Welsh) Drex'83.Pa'75
☎ (215) 886-6817 . . 736 Argyle Rd, Glenside, PA *19038*
Darlington MISS Rebecca P—Cvc.
☎ (202) 244-6464 . . 4830 Butterworth Place NW, Washington,
DC *20016*
Darlington MR & MRS Richard S B (Joan Thomas) StJos'51
☎ (610) 647-9250 . . 304 Penns Lane, Malvern, PA *19355*
Darlington MR & MRS Thomas (Marcia W McMichael)
Bnd'49.Cl'51.San.Rv.Snc.StA.Cw.Cl'51 . . of
☎ (201) 379-2179 . . 55 Lakeview Av, Short Hills, NJ *07078*
☎ (407) 724-9175 . . 443 Sandy Key, Melbourne Beach, FL *32951*
Darman MR & MRS Richard G (Kathleen Emmet) | ☎ (703) 528-6023
Rdc'64.Mt.H'64.H'67 . . . . | 1137 Crest Lane,
MR William T E—at Harvard . . . . | McLean, VA *22101*
JUNIORS MR Jonathan W E . . . . |
Darneille MRS Hopewell H (Virginia Clark) Cvc . . .of
☎ (301) 229-7131 . . 5304 Boxwood Court, Bethesda, MD *20816*
☎ (207) 647-5524 . . ''Nawandyn'' RR 3, Box 1074, Bridgton,
ME *04009*
Darneille MR & MRS Hopewell H 3d (Diane D Davenny)
Wash'71.GeoW'73.GeoW'77.Mt.Cvc.Y'68.Geo'74
☎ (301) 229-6030 . . 7104 Loch Lomond Dv, Bethesda, MD *20817*
d'Arnoux CTE Edouard & CTSSE (Mary A | ☎ (011-33-1)
Alexander) Myf.Dar. . . . . | 42-22-41-10
MISS Alexandra J—☎ (011-33-1) 45-44-32-98 . . | 133 blvd Raspail,
| 75006 Paris, France
Darovskikh MR & MRS Vitaly A (Jane C Haux) SUNY'88.UPerm'90
☎ (315) 253-9151 . . 44 Havens Av, Auburn, NY *13021*
Darrell MR Andrew H—Ri.Eyc.Csh.Geo'85.Tufts'88.Va'91
127 W 79 St, Apt 11D, New York, NY *10024*
Darrell MR Francis S (Ethel T Hix) Ncd.
☎ (410) 823-8533 . . 25 Ruxview Court, Apt 302, Baltimore, MD *21204*
Darrell MRS George H (Marjorie S Hamill)
☎ (617) 326-4974 . . 10 Longwood Dv, Apt 208, Westwood, MA *02090*
Darrell MR & MRS John Stewart (Irene D Gibson) | ☎ (804) 979-5814
San.Va'64 . . . . | 1 Oak Circle,
MISS Parthenia R . . . . | Charlottesville, VA
MISS Nora L . . . . | *22901*
MR Stewart . . . . |
Darrell MISS Marian W (John Stewart) . . . . . . Married at Greenwood, VA
Fife MR David E (Eugene V) . . . . Jun 15'96
Darrell MRS Norris (Churchill—Mary D Hand) BMr'27.Plg.
☎ (212) 369-7285 . . 1107 Fifth Av, New York, NY *10128*

Darrell MR & MRS Norris JR (Henriette M Haid) Ri.Eyc.Csh.Plg.H.'51.H'54
☎ (516) 692-9654 . . 44 Walnut Tree Lane, Cold Spring Harbor,
NY *11724*
Darrell DR & MRS Richard W (Constance C | ☎ (908) 530-0875
Jackson) H'55.H'59.Cl'65 . . . . | 129 Tower Hill Dv,
MR Trevor J—Pa'88—at MIT . . . . | Red Bank, NJ *07701*
Darrow MR & MRS William H 2d (Linda McDaniel). | ☎ (513) 372-0132
JUNIORS MR Bryan P . . . . | 2345 Monterey Dv,
JUNIORS MR Kevin M . . . . | Xenia, OH *45385*
Darwin MR & MRS George P (Angela M B Huxley) | ☎ (011-44-171)
Bnd'61.Camb'51 . . . . | 937-2750
MISS Lucy W—Edin'89—Box 720, Kiambu, | 2 Campden Hill
Kenya . . . . | Court, Observatory
MISS Clare B—Manch'92 . . . . | Gardens, London
JUNIORS MR William H—at Manchester U . . . . . | W8 7HX, England
Daspit MR & MRS Richard W (Barbara L Drake) | ☎ (410) 476-3744
Nw'44.Ch'63 . . . . | 29994 Bolingbroke
MISS Elizabeth P—at ☎ (410) 476-3549 | Lane, Trappe, MD
29996 Bolingbroke Lane, Trappe, MD *21673* . . | *21673*
MISS Amy D . . . . |
Dassonville MR Donald Perry
☎ (501) 925-3974 . . 8643 Lakeshore Dv, Rte 6, Rogers, AR *72756-8777*
Date MR Sydney S—P'37
☎ (847) 492-2972 . . 41 Knox Circle, Evanston, IL *60201-1912*
Daub MR & MRS William J 3d (Edith T West) Va'61
☎ (610) 253-3494 . . 525 Klein Rd, Easton, PA *18042*
Dauch MRS Alan D (Heezen—Wilmot—E Christine de Schirding) Rr.
☎ (412) 683-6305 . . 3955 Bigelow Blvd, Pittsburgh, PA *15213*
Daudon MR & MRS Marc D JR (Maud W Smith) Hampshire'78.Bow'77
☎ (206) 324-4007 . . 1128—38 Av, Seattle, WA *98122*
Daudon MR & MRS Marc Daniel (Ann Rebmann) Wil.Hav'49
☎ (302) 652-7304 . . 10 Haslet Way, Wilmington, DE *19807*
Daughaday MR Thomas L
☎ (847) 869-5336 . . 930 Washington St, Apt 4B, Evanston, IL *60202*
Daughdrill MR & MRS James H JR (Elizabeth A Gay) Emory'56
☎ (901) 323-9570 . . 91 Morningside Park, Memphis, TN *38104*
Daughdrill MR & MRS James H 3d (Vicki G Hall) Tex'74.Van'77
☎ (601) 362-9895 . . 139 Lower Windrush, Jackson, MS *39208*
Daugherty MISS Lisa (Wilson—Lisa Daugherty) SanDiegoSt'89
☎ (619) 437-8909 . . 314 Glorietta Blvd, Coronado, CA *92118*
Dautel MRS Charles P (Seville J Pickands) . . . . | 5824 Masters Court,
MAJ REV Terrence P—USA.Cwr'68.Cwr'73. | Charlotte, NC *28226*
Cwr'75.Bexley'78—at ☎ (216) 442-6198 |
Box 62, Gates Mills, OH *44040* . . . . |
Dautel MR & MRS Timothy P (Diane M Flament) | ☎ (704) 542-1460
BowlG'67.Denis'67 . . . . | 3146 Ingelow Lane,
MISS Sharon E. . . . . | Charlotte, NC *28226*
MR Michael P . . . . |
MR Brian P . . . . |
JUNIORS MISS Jacqueline M . . . . |
Davalos MR & MRS Gerald C (Sallyanne O'Brien) | ☎ (415) 661-2480
Stan'62.Bhm.Cp.Utah'65 . . . . | 140 San Fernando
MISS Linda A—at Boston U . . . . | Way, San Francisco,
MISS Leslie L—at U of Cal Berkeley . . . . | CA *94127*
MR Stephen O'B—at U of Cal Berkeley . . . . |

Davant MR & MRS James W (Mary E Westlake)
Ariz'43.Unn.Ln.B.Evg.Pr.Ck.DelB.Plg.Va'39
☎ (561) 278-2859 . . 4333 N Ocean Blvd, Apt CN2, Delray Beach, FL 33483

Davant MISS Mary D
☎ (516) 671-4569 . . 23 Cedar Lane N, Glen Head, NY 11545

Davenport MISS Carolyn W (Dumas—Carolyn W Davenport)
Denis'74.Cwr'80
☎ (203) 637-7803 . . 86 Havemeyer Lane, Old Greenwich, CT 06870

Davenport MR & MRS David W (Carol J Babcock) Dth'40
☎ (941) 966-5084 . . 415 Oak Point Rd, Osprey, FL 34229

Davenport MISS Glorianna W—MtH'66.CUNY'70
☎ (617) 267-7420 . . 3 Exeter St, Boston, MA 02116

Davenport MRS John A (Marie Van V Hayes) Cda . .
MR John . . . .
☎ (908) 671-0271
''Bayberry Spinney'' 127 Red Hill Rd, PO Box 397, Middletown, NJ 07748

Davenport MRS Russell W (Ladd—Natalie Potter) .
BRN Bernard & BRNSS d'Anglejan-Chatillon (Abreu—Mary Sargent Ladd) . . . .
MR Miguel Abreu . . . .
of ☎ (561)231-4422 21 Dove Shell Lane, John's Island, Vero Beach, FL 32963
☎ (212) 355-3322 2 Sutton Place S, New York, NY 10022-3070

David MR & MRS George A L (Barbara D Osborn)
Wells'64.Unn.Ny.Ihy.Cly.H'65.Va'67 . . . .
MISS Eliza P . . . .
MISS Hannah L . . . .
JUNIORS MR Henry G . . . .
☎ (860) 236-6626 62 Westwood Rd, West Hartford, CT 06117-2252

Davidge MISS Dorsey (late John W JR) . . . . Married at Madison, CT
Chapin MR David D (John C) . . . . Jun 1'96

Davidge MR & MRS John W 3d (Engel—Deborah M Lott)
Cr'81.Cvc.Mt.Mto.Cc.Godd'75.Cl'81 . . of
☎ (212) 749-1637 . . 865 West End Av, New York, NY 10025
☎ (914) 677-8439 . . RR 1, Box 194, Chestnut Ridge Rd, Millbrook, NY 12522

Davidge MR & MRS Nicholas A (Jill Rabon) Char'ton'82.Mt.Mid'77
☎ (203) 245-9361 . . 7 Fence Creek Dv, Madison, CT 06443-3113

Davidson MR & MRS Alexander J (Ellen P Breslin) Mass'86.Bost'86
☎ (301) 699-9413 . . 4615 College Av, Apt 1, College Park, MD 20740

Davidson MRS Eugene A (Hamill—Zurcher—Suzette Morton) . . . . Died at
Santa Barbara, CA May 18'96

Davidson MR Eugene A—Y'27
☎ (805) 969-6988 . . 780 Riven Rock Rd, Santa Barbara, CA 93108

Davidson DR & MRS L Stacy JR (Fay Spruill) Miss'58.Miss'57
☎ (601) 843-5262 . . 530 Hillcrest Circle, Cleveland, MS 38732

Davidson MR & MRS Malcolm (Barbara A Herrmann) Wheat'56.Mid'55 . . . .
MR Malcolm C—at Los Angeles, CA . . . .
53 Lowell Rd, Wellesley Hills, MA 02181

Davidson MRS Marian J (Marian Q Jackson)
Fic.Pr.Cly. . . . .
MISS Helen A—Mid'89—at ☎ (919) 929-9219 6418 Gold Mine Loop, Chapel Hill, NC 27516 .
MISS Marian L—at Trinity
MR Matthew H—at ☎ (904) 398-5509 838 LaSalle St, Jacksonville, FL 32207 . . . . . .
☎ (516) 671-0087 66 Bayville Rd, Locust Valley, NY 11560

Davidson MISS Mary B—V'71
☎ (914) 277-4105 . . 346C Heritage Hills, Somers, NY 10589

Davidson MRS Murat H JR (Jean Russert) Pr.
☎ (516) 671-8777 . . 40 Matinecock Farms Rd, Glen Cove, NY 11542

Davidson MR Murat H JR—Pr.Van'67.
Nw'72 . . . .
MISS Katherine H . . . .
JUNIORS MR Christopher H—at Kent . . . .
☎ (516) 759-2637 420 Duck Pond Rd, Locust Valley, NY 11560

Davidson MRS Norman L (Frank—Dorothy H Pagenstecher)
☎ (941) 351-6223 . . 5711 Timber Lake Dv, Sarasota, FL 34243

Davidson MR P Marqués . . . . Died at
Mt Kisco, NY Jly 3'96

Davidson MRS P Marqués (Elizabeth P Frost)
Doug'66.Me.Ste. . . . .
MISS Brooke L—at SUNY Binghamton . . . .
JUNIORS MR Langford F . . . .
JUNIORS MR Eric M . . . .
☎ (914) 277-6908 8 Livery Lane, North Salem, NY 10560-3642

Davidson MR & MRS Philip J (Ward—Gordon—Campbell—Campbell—Winifred E Miller)
Fcg.Rr. . . . .
MISS Katharine G Gordon . . . .
of ☎ (602)991-7715 6259 N 73 Way, Scottsdale, AZ 85250
☎ (412) 963-6969 207 Kensington Court, Fox Hall, Pittsburgh, PA 15238

Davidson MR Robert L—Mass'79
☎ (512) 327-3665 . . 2800 Barton's Bluff Lane, Apt 602, Austin, TX 78746

Davidson MISS Sarah MacT—V'83.S.
☎ (212) 421-5813 . . 30 E 37 St, Apt M5, New York, NY 10016

Davidson MR & MRS Sidney W JR (Grace Moffat)
V'41.Unn.Ht.Csn.Yn.Y'44
☎ (860) 434-2468 . . 7 Joshua Lane, Lyme, CT 06371

Davidson MR Sidney W 3d—Y'75
☎ (212) 420-0451 . . 143 Av B, New York, NY 10009

Davidson MR & MRS Stuart C (Sally L Foulis)
An.Mt.Cvc.Cc.Sl.Hn.H'45 . . of
☎ (202) 333-7691 . . 3415 Volta Place NW, Washington, DC 20007
☎ (970) 925-7952 . . North of Nell, Apt 3K, 555 E Durant Av, Aspen, CO 81611

Davidson MISS Susan M—Wheat'68
☎ (603) 643-6109 . . 23 Maple St, Hanover, NH 03755

Davidson MRS Thomas E (Caroline E Hogg)
☎ (513) 871-2920 . . 1001 Rookwood Dv, Cincinnati, OH 45208

Davidson MR William A—Pr.Y'58.Stan'62
☎ (203) 262-1773 . . PO Box 142, Waterbury, CT 06720

David-Weill MR & MRS Michel A (Hélène Lehideux) K.B.Ck.InstSciPol'53
820 Fifth Av, New York, NY 10021

Davie MR & MRS E T Bedford (Williams—Chandor—Mitchell—Diana M Wing) Evg.So.Y'36
☎ (561) 844-1022 . . 2 Windsor Court, Palm Beach, FL *33480*

Davies MR & MRS Dwight R (Jennifer T Jackson) Buck'78.Me.Drew'69
☎ (201) 543-9623 . . 17 Glenbrook Dv, Mendham, NJ *07945*

Davies DR & MRS Edward A (Suzanne E Thompson) Ri.Cs.H'53
☎ (212) 369-5312 . . 1158 Fifth Av, New York, NY *10029*

Davies MR Hugh M—P'70
☎ (619) 454-3541 . . 3141 Curlew St, San Diego, CA *92103*

Davies DR & MRS John A K (Alice G Ingraham) Rdc'65.H'65 . . . . . . 75 Woodchester Dv, Weston, MA *02193*
MISS Laura H—H'93 . . .
MISS Katharine I—at Harvard . . .
MR John H—at Harvard . . .

Davies MR & MRS John H (Nagy—Frances P Roberts) Ws'66.Ill'62.Ill'65.H'68 . . . . . 1916 Pine St, Philadelphia, PA *19103*
☎ (215) 732-0586
MISS Sarah M—at Conn Coll . . .
MR Daniel B—at Rutgers . . .

Davies MRS L Covington (Chrapkiewicz—Lynn Covington) V'54.Ncd. . . . of ☎ (561)832-3979 400 N Flagler Dv, Apt 601, West Palm Beach, FL *33401*
MR William A A Chrapkiewicz—at ☎ (619) 231-7711 . . 557 Fourth Av, San Diego, CA *92101* . . .
MR Covington A Chrapkiewicz—at ☎ (505) 291-9294 . . 12899 Central Av NE, Apt 450, Albuquerque, NM *87123* . . .
☎ (801) 649-1199 ''Bessie'' 2225 Little Bessie Av, Park City, UT *84060*

Davies MRS Mary M (Mary W Murphy) SCal'83.Loy'86.Loy'88.Wa.
☎ (847) 835-2619 . . 575 Sheridan Rd, Glencoe, IL *60022*

Davies MR & MRS Peter E (Alison M More) Y'84.Nu'91
☎ (203) 861-7185 . . 15 Ridgeview Av, Greenwich, CT *06830*

Davies MRS Ralph K (Louise Stivers) Fr.
☎ (415) UL1-1401 . . 122 Lakeview Dv, Woodside, CA *94062*

Davies MR Richard L—P'42
☎ (954) 360-9045 . . 1147 Hillsboro Mile, Apt 115, Hillsboro Beach, FL *33062-1715*

Davies MISS Sarah M . . see MRS S G Bingham
Davies MR Stephen T . . see MRS S G Bingham

Davis MR & MRS Albert H II (Hubbard—Suzanne Arguimbau) Ncd.P'30 . . . of ☎ (561)231-0034 467 Silver Moss Dv, John's Island, Vero Beach, FL *32963*
MISS Carolynne M—at 5300 Keystone Place N, Seattle, WA *98103* . . .
☎ (203) 655-0920 16 Raiders Lane, Darien, CT *06820*

Davis MISS Alexandra L . . see A A Houghton 3d
Davis MR Andrew O . . see G C Bitting
Davis MR & MRS Asa B 3d (Deborah Carson) Cly.Yn.Y'56 . . . ☎ (912) 236-2500 ''Little Oak House'' 7 W Charlton St, Savannah, GA *31401*
MISS Katharine C—at ☎ (404) 252-0865 6101 Chastain Dv NE, Atlanta, GA *30342* . . .

Davis MRS Atkinson (Marguerite P Atkinson) Ws'44 . . . ☎ (561) 229-0647 8750 S Ocean Dv, Jensen Beach, FL *34957*
MISS Deborah A—at Santa Barbara, CA . . .
MISS L Whitney—at 26 Mead St, Somerville, MA *02144* . . .

Davis MISS Betsey W (Hopkinson—Betsey W Davis) Pa'88 . . . ☎ (610) 527-3777 ''Indian Springs'' 1509 Lafayette Rd, Gladwyne, PA *19035*
MR Edward Hopkinson . . .

Davis MR & MRS Charles H (Suzanne S Mitchell) Man'vl'62.Ph.Me.Ste.Ssk.Pa'56.Pa'62 . . . ☎ (610) 688-9085 150 Biddulph Rd, Radnor, PA *19087*
MR Charles H C—Temp'93 . . .

Davis MR & MRS Charles S (Kate E Ball) Cr'38 . . . ☎ (508) 255-7169 Box 463, Freeman Lane, Orleans, MA *02653*
MR Charles S JR . . .

Davis MR & MRS Chester R JR (Anne Meserve) Rdc'58.Pn.P'51.H'58 . . . ☎ (847) 446-8636 670 Blackthorn Rd, Winnetka, IL *60093*
MISS Julia S—P'86.Ch'91—at ☎ (914) 238-8187 161 Birchwood Close, Chappaqua, NY *10514* . . .
MISS Elizabeth M—Ws'89—at U of Ill Grad . . .

Davis JUNIORS MR Christopher B . . see G C Bitting
Davis MR Christopher L—St.NCar'71.Buf'75 . . . 11134 Bowen Av, Great Falls, VA *22066*
JUNIORS MR George P . . .

Davis MR & MRS Christopher W (Susanne Albertsson) Tufts'81.Mid'81
☎ (802) 425-6515 . . PO Box 309, Charlotte, VT *05445*

Davis MR & MRS Craig M (Lucy Ann Christensen) Milt'75.V'75 748 Watch Point, Cincinnati, OH *45230*

Davis MR David O—HawaiiLoa'75 ⛵
☎ (808) 235-5329 . . PO Box 967, Kailua, Oahu, HI *96734*

Davis MR De Forest P—H'34 . . . ☎ (312) 787-2197 70 E Cedar St, Apt 1101, Chicago, IL *60611*
MISS Diane—at ☎ (212) 737-1191 . . 176 E 77 St, New York, NY *10021*

Davis MR & MRS De Forest P JR (Dorothy L Monek) Cho.Rc.On.Cas.Wa.LakeF'65 . . . ☎ (312) 337-6271 1530 N State P'kway, Chicago, IL *60610*
MISS Valerie L . . .
MISS Daphne D . . .
JUNIORS MISS Christina A . . .

Davis MR & MRS Duncan S (Hoffmann—Lenore Fleschler) SFrSt'48.Nu'50 . . . ☎ (916) 481-7666 5424 Tree Side Dv, Carmichael, CA *95608*
MR Duncan C—CalSt'94 . . .

Davis MR & MRS Dwight F 3d (Anne Marie L Cassinari) Paris'61.Rc.B.H'57 . . . of ☎ (203)637-8990 333 Palmer Hill Rd, Riverside, CT *06878*
MR Christopher P—at Harvard . . .
☎ (212) 737-1667 164 E 72 St, New York, NY *10021*

Davis MR & MRS E Morris 4th (M Birgitta Warnhammar) Lund'64.Me.Rc.Sa.Rv.Cc.Cw.Cspa.Temp'67 . . . ☎ (610) 687-0970 1024 Hedgerow Circle, Wayne, PA *19087-2218*
MISS Christina W . . .
MR Edward M 5th—Me.Cc.Rv.—at Tufts . . .

Davis DR E William JR—Un.C.Ln.Pr.Wes'47.Cr'51
☎ (212) 737-2868 . . 168 E 73 St, New York, NY *10021*

Davis MR & MRS Edward L JR (Juliet P Gill) Sl.Pa'49
☎ (202) 625-0614 . . 2237—48 St NW, Washington, DC *20007*

Davis MR & MRS Edward S (Mueenuddin—Barbara J Thompson) Ws'55.C.H.'54.H'59 . . of
☎ (212) 581-5448 . . 205 W 57 St, New York, NY *10019*
☎ (516) 324-3808 . . 21 Old Stone H'way, East Hampton, NY *11937*

Davis MISS Eleanor V—StMarys'92 . . see A A Houghton 3d

Davis MRS Elizabeth C (Elizabeth J Cochrane) Myf.
☎ (813) 866-0059 . . 1101—54 Av S, St Petersburg, FL *33705*

Davis MR & MRS Fellowes (Alice M Plummer) My.Hn.H'42
☎ (508) 468-4938 . . 560 Bay Rd, Box 217, Hamilton, MA *01936*

Davis MRS Ferdinand H (Hudson—Jane Rule) Cs.
☎ (212) 861-6627 . . 30 E 72 St, New York, NY *10021*

Davis DR & MRS Frank W JR (Mary McMenamy) Gv.Duke'44
☎ (410) 363-0750 . . 438 Garrison Forest Rd, Owings Mills, MD *21117*

Davis MR & MRS Frederick L (Ann M Blackinton) JHop'39
☎ (314) 963-2150 . . 21 N Old Orchard Av, Apt 219, St Louis, MO *63119*

Davis MR & MRS Frederick T (Mary V McGowan) Ws'67.C.H'67 . . . .
JUNIORS MR Samuel S—at Milton . . . .
of ☎ (212)799-8244
285 Central Park W,
New York, NY
10024
☎ (518) 392-4981
Old Chatham, NY
12136

Davis MR G Vietor JR
☎ (757) 229-1344 . . 2721 Jockey's Neck Trail, Williamsburg, VA *23185*

Davis MR & MRS George H (Irene W Curtis) Cl'58.Van'57
☎ (501) 663-5678 . . 7 Sunset Dv, Little Rock, AR *72207*

Davis MRS Geraldine Hempel (Geraldine A Hempel)
MR Clinton H T—ODom'95 . . . .
☎ (757) 623-2411
310 Botetourt St,
Norfolk, VA *23510*

Davis MR & MRS Glenn E (Martha L Russell) Wheat'80.DeP'76
☎ (508) 369-7225 . . 89 Ripley Hill Rd, Concord, MA *01742*

Davis MISS Helen H—Pars'89
☎ (303) 477-3441 . . 1529 Spruce St, Apt 8, Boulder, CO *80302*

Davis MR Henry A—Pn.P'65.Va'69
☎ (202) 328-7074 . . 3133 Connecticut Av NW, Apt 624, Washington, DC *20008*

Davis MR Henry Patterson—Cr'88.Y'93
☎ (212) 219-2556 . . 36-38 White St, New York, NY *10013*

Davis MR & MRS Holbrook R (Sarah deF Maynard) V'45.Chi.H'43 . . . .
MISS Sarah H—at 226 Myers Rd, Lansing, NY *14882* . . .
☎ (508) 428-6084
249 Seapuit Rd,
Box 572, Osterville,
MA *02655*

Davis MR & MRS Howland (Frances Fabyan) Snc.Ds.Cs.H'39 . . . .
MISS F Dennie—Bost'74—at Tivoli, NY *12583* .
☎ (212) 734-6713
333 E 68 St,
New York, NY
10021

Davis MR Ian . . see P Rulon-Miller

Davis MR & MRS J Hornor 4th (Frederica M Miller) Ty'76.Msq.Va'75
☎ (304) 345-8432 . . "Plumnearly" 1201 Johnson Rd, Charleston, WV *25314*

Davis MRS J Phillips (Jean S Miller)
☎ (412) 622-9000 . . 310 Fisk St, Pittsburgh, PA *15201*

Davis MR & MRS J Staige 3d (Martha A Wolcott) Vt'82.Vt'76
☎ (802) 685-0397 . . 153 Summit St, Burlington, VT *05401*

Davis MRS J Stanley (Cox—Nomina Twining) Myf.Dar.
☎ (813) 633-1621 . . 1010 American Eagle Blvd, Apt 617, Sun City Center, FL *33573*

Davis MR & MRS James H (Margaret T Porter) Ny.Rm.
☎ (508) 945-5618 . . 21 Elizabeth's Way, Chatham, MA *02633*

Davis MRS John (Catherine H Lazenby) Cy.Gi.
☎ (410) 243-8202 . . 105 Wendover Rd, Baltimore, MD *21218*

Davis MR & MRS John C (Anne T Lucius) Wis'86.Mid'85.Bost'89.Bost'91
☎ (414) 962-9502 . . 2102 E Jarvis St, Shorewood, WI *53211*

Davis MR & MRS John E (Maude R Bouvier) Cly.Dc.Dll. .
MISS Maude S—Cly.Dc.—at ☎ (212) 628-5250
315 E 70 St, New York, NY *10021* . . . .
☎ (212) SA2-6321
1165 Park Av,
New York, NY
10128

Davis MR John G—Rcn.H'58
☎ (803) 722-7212 . . 16 Orange St, Charleston, SC *29401*

Davis MR & MRS John M Kelso (Mignon E Foerderer) An.Ac.Ll.Dar.Ncd.Y'29
☎ (860) 726-2105 . . Duncaster 220G, 80 Loeffler Rd, Bloomfield, CT *06002*

Davis MR & MRS John P JR (Mary McC Oates) Fcg.H'47 . . . .
MISS Mary O . . . .
☎ (412) 963-6339
144 North Dv,
Pittsburgh, PA
15238

Davis JUNIORS MR John W . . see G C Bitting

Davis MISS Julianne—PCTS'84
☎ (616) 975-3832 . . 4474 Braeburn Dv SE, Grand Rapids, MI *49546*

Davis MISS Kirsten M . . see W P Jones

Davis MR & MRS Lincoln 3d (Susan B Daigle) Me'73
☎ (207) 529-5176 . . Box 61D, HC 60, Town Landing, Medomak, ME *04551*

Davis MRS Loraine B (Nicholas H) . . Married at Westhampton Beach, NY
von Moltke MR Albrecht (Heinrich) . . . . Sep 30'95

Davis MRS M Boss (Marguerite Y Boss) . . . .
MISS Marguerite T—at ☎ (405) 359-1679
Fox Lair Farm, Rte 2, Box 326, Guthrie, OK *73044* . . . .
☎ (617) 934-0626
PO Box 302,
Snug Harbor Station,
Duxbury, MA *02331*

Davis MR & MRS Mark A H (Michelle S Heydenreich) Va'90.Va'94.Va'90.W&M'92
☎ (804) 378-8007 . . 1900 Swamp Fox Rd, Midlothian, VA *23112*

Davis MR & MRS Michael Hamilton (Daphne D Barnard) Unn.K.Msq.Plg.Cly.Y'58.Nu'69 . . of
☎ (860) 535-0048 . . "Redbrook" 325 N Main St, Stonington, CT *06378*
☎ (860) 535-0420 . . "The Farmhouse" Stonington, CT *06378*

Davis MR & MRS Michael J (Laura W Lassen) Myf.
☎ (302) 324-9555 . . 34 Paxton Lane, Bear, DE *19701*

Davis MR & MRS Murdoch (Aldys B Chapman) Me.Myf.Dc.Ncd.Del'55.VillaN'88 . . . .
MR Christopher S . . . .
MR Hunter . . . .
MR Peter D—at Villanova . . . .
☎ (610) 525-6144
256 Broughton
Lane, Villanova, PA
19085

Davis MR & MRS Nathanael V (Lois H Thompson) Chi.Ncd.H'38.LondEc'39 . . of
☎ (508) 428-2109 . . 50 Fox Island Rd, Box 309, Osterville, MA *02655*
☎ (941) 964-0504 . . "High Hope" 204 Waterways Av, Box 1125, Boca Grande, FL *33921*

Davis MR & MRS Nathaniel (Elizabeth K Creese) ☎ (909) 624-5293
Ober'54.Cos.Br'44 . . . . | 1783 Longwood Av,
MR James C—at Brown Grad . . . . | Claremont, CA
MR Thomas R—at NYU Law . . . . | *91711*

Davis MRS Newlin F (Elizabeth T Sullivan) Me.Gm.Nyc.Ac.Ncd . . .of
☎ (610) 527-9089 . . 75 Pasture Lane, Bryn Mawr, PA *19010*
☎ (508) 228-9478 . . ''Broom Patch'' 1 Lincoln Av, Nantucket,
MA *02554*

Davis MR & MRS Orlin (Lisa J Mackintosh) Un.Rcp.Pe.Penn'60
☎ (718) 935-0712 . . 56 Willow St, Brooklyn, NY *11201*

Davis MR & MRS Paul B (Eunice C Lyth) St.
2330 Maple Rd, Apt 303W, Buffalo, NY *14221-4060*

Davis COL (RET) & MRS (COL) Paul B JR (Vlach—Nancy F Pusateri)
USAF.Neb'74.Aub'82.St.An.NCar'67.Okla'79
5108 Heritage Lane, Alexandria, VA *22311*

Davis MR & MRS Peter W (F Jayne Cobbs) Rdc'60.Tcy.Ncd.Ore'65
☎ (510) 655-1052 . . 6160 Acacia Av, Oakland, CA *94618*

Davis MR R Neville
☎ (203) 438-7621 . . Box 342, 160 Nod Rd, Ridgefield, CT *06877*

Davis MR & MRS Richard G (Marlene F Suran) Chath'58.Bow'57
☎ (303) 770-7416 . . 7086 S Cook Way, Littleton, CO *80122*

Davis MR Robert E—Gettys'96 . . see MRS K E Jackson

Davis MR Robert F
☎ (617) 492-7556 . . 48 Fresh Pond Lane, Cambridge, MA *02138*

Davis JUNIORS MR Robert K 3d . . see J M Simons

Davis MR & MRS Robert L (Susan E Baenziger) . . . . | ☎ (914) 757-4250
JUNIORS MISS Elizabeth F . . . . | Woods Rd, Tivoli,
| NY *12583*

Davis MR & MRS Robert L (Sally C Paxson) | ☎ (610) 688-8611
Me.Ste.Ac.Ncd.Pa'60 | 152 Biddulph Rd,
MISS Caroline H . . . . | Radnor, PA *19087*
MR Douglas K—Me.Gettys'92 . . . . |

Davis MR & MRS Robert W (Williams—Patricia G Murdock) Cl'65
☎ (914) 265-4512 . . ''Willowshade'' Lane Gate Rd, Box 190,
Cold Spring, NY *10516*

Davis MR & MRS Robert W (Alice L R Sadtler) | ☎ (770) 971-7807
Aub'66 . . . . | 4871 River Farm
MISS Julie S . . . . | Rd, Marietta, GA
MISS Paige W . . . . | *30068*
MR Gavin H II . . . . |

Davis MR Rodman Townsend—Pa'58.Pa'59
49 Hyatt Av, Norwalk, CT *06850*

Davis MR Rodman Townsend JR . . see L H Sackett

Davis MISS Ruth Gardner . . see L H Sackett

Davis MR & MRS S Boyer (Janet Wesbrook) P'36.H'41
☎ (805) 969-0433 . . PO Box 525, Summerland, CA *93067*

Davis MR Samuel C JR—Rc.Cy.Nd.Fic.Wms'59
575 Barnes Rd, St Louis, MO *63124*

Davis MR & MRS Samuel R (Warren—Dorothy Harvey) V'45.H'45
☎ (508) 224-7455 . . 794 Long Pond Rd, Plymouth, MA *02360*

Davis MR & MRS Scott L (Martin—Christina | ☎ (509) 747-6724
Williams) LIU'68.Dar.Cal'61.Cl'68 . . . . | 1224 W Riverside
MR Scott L JR—at 30272 Rainbow Hill Rd, | Av, Apt 906,
Golden, CO *80401* . . . . | Spokane, WA *99201*

Davis MRS Shelby Cullom (Kathryn E Waterman) K.Cs.P . . .of
☎ (914) ME1-8787 . . ''Broad Oak'' 193 Wilson Park, Tarrytown,
NY *10591*
14 Riverview Rd, Hobe Sound, FL *33455*

Davis DR & MRS Thorp J (R Fraser Gibson) Aht'90.Va'86.Va'90
5916 N Evanston Av, Indianapolis, IN *46220*

Davis MR W Bowdoin (Trimper—Savage—Carol Bradley) Elk.
☎ (410) 377-8974 . . 2 Over Ridge Court, Baltimore, MD *21210*

Davis MR W Bowdoin JR—Br'59.Ind'63 . . . . | ☎ (410) 235-7357
MISS A Staige—Duke'88—☎ (410) 235-4891 . . | 2111 Lake
| Montebello Terr,
| Baltimore,
| MD *21218*

Davis MR W Curtis Carroll—Cy.Cos.Cc.Cw.Wt.Rv.Snc.Yn.
Y'38.Col'39.Duke'47
☎ (410) 889-4488 . . 10 Overhill Rd, Baltimore, MD *21210*

Davis MR & MRS W Lipscomb JR (Florence P Stumb) | ☎ (615) 298-3120
Van'53 . . . . | 929 Tyne Blvd,
MISS Virginia A . . . . | Nashville, TN *37220*

Davis MR & MRS Wendell JR (Penelope Case) | of ☎ (914)834-1168
Chr.Cs.H.'54 | 28 Huguenot Dv,
MISS Jennifer C—Dth'92—at Princeton . . . . . . | Larchmont, NY
MISS Virginia W—StLaw'94 . . . . | *10538*
MR Peter T—at Haverford . . . . | ☎ (518) 781-4887
| ''Sunnycrest''
| Upper Queechy Rd,
| Canaan, NY *12029*

Davis REV & MRS William M (Louise McC Eddy) | ☎ (412) 362-2845
Bow'49.PhilaDiv'53 . . . . | 209 S Evaline St,
MISS Laura D—V'79 . . . . | Pittsburgh, PA
MISS Helen T—Chat'80 . . . . | *15224*

Davis MR & MRS William P 3d (Phoebe Harding) Gm.P'31
☎ (610) 645-8888 . . 1400 Waverly Rd, Blair 247, Gladwyne, PA *19035*

Davis MR & MRS William R Q (Carey E Anderson-Talmage)
Mont'92.NCar'92
☎ (413) 774-7411 . . Eaglebrook School, Deerfield, MA *01342-0701*

Davison MR Andrew B—Ken'87
☎ (505) 244-3441 . . 2026 Alhambra Av SW, Albuquerque, NM *87104*

Davison MR & MRS C Hamilton JR (Dorothy D Schneeberger)
Van'83.StL'87.Van'82.Tex'85
☎ (401) 331-0461 . . 33 Hazard Av, Providence, RI *02906*

Davison MR & MRS Charles H (Lessie H L Busbee)
FlaSt'51.FlaSt'52.Rcn.Ih.Cho.Cas.Wa.Dth'50.Nu'54
☎ (561) 231-0452 . . 551 Indian Harbor Dv, John's Island, Vero Beach,
FL *32963*

Davison MR & MRS Daniel P (Catherine Cheremeteff)
BMr'52.Un.Ny.S.Pr.Cly.P.Y'49.H'52 ⚓ . . of
☎ (212) 755-8134 . . 200 E 66 St, New York, NY *10021*
☎ (912) 769-3622 . . ''Peacock Plantation'' 905 Jr Suber Rd,
Norman Park, GA *31771*

Davison MR & MRS Daniel P JR (Kathryn C Pinson) NCar'80.Wms'77
☎ (214) 824-8036 . . 6738 Avalon St, Dallas, TX *75214*

Davison MR & MRS George P (Judith F Rivkin) Y'79.Y'79.Cl'84
☎ (212) 877-7979 . . 255 W 90 St, Apt 5A, New York, NY *10024*

Davison MR & MRS Henry P 2d (Kristina T Perkin)
H.'89.Cl'93.Cl'94.Un.S.Y'84 .. of
☎ (212) 535-7633 .. 315 E 68 St, New York, NY *10021*
☎ (516) 674-5129 .. "Shaque d'Amour" 76 Peacock Lane,
Locust Valley, NY *11560*

Davison MR J Lang—Dth'83.Cl'87.Cl'94
☎ (212) 864-1148 .. 312 W 107 St, Apt 2A, New York, NY *10025*

Davison MR & MRS John E JR (Christina G Cox) | ☎ (610) 687-5485
Del'65.Rc.Me.Gm.Ty'67 . . . . | 5 Canterbury Lane,
MISS Christina E . . . . | St Davids, PA
MISS Lindsey C. . . . . | *19087*
MISS Amanda H . . . . |

Davison MRS William M 3d (Louise Wigton) Cry.Cspa.
☎ (610) 687-0470 .. 219 Steeplechase Rd, Devon, PA *19333*

Davison-Ackley MR George W—Rc.Ri.Wes'68.Y.'70.Cl'74.Cl'80 .. of
☎ (914) 677-8405 .. "Overlook Farm" RD 3, Box 201, Millbrook,
NY *12545*
☎ (011-33-1) 47-63-54-55 .. 9 bis rue Georges Berger, 75017 Paris,
France

Davlin MR H Dalton . . see E M de Windt

Davlin MISS Virginia-Marie . . see E M de Windt

Davlin MR & MRS William E B (F Tracy Wenzell) Laf'88.Ford'94
☎ (212) 327-2990 .. 167 E 67 St, Apt 8A, New York, NY *10021*

Davol DR & MRS (DR) Peter B (Anna Y C Lo) | 89 Crescent Rd,
BMr'64.Cl'68.H'64.Cl'69 . . . . | Concord, MA
MR Samuel B—at 124 Thompson St, | *01742-2207*
Apt 21, New York, NY *10012-3132*. . . . . |
MR Angus P—at Brown . . . . |

Davol DR & MRS Rector T (Evers—Anne Gruen)
Nu'48.Ihy.Myf.Yn.Y'37.Cl'41
☎ (809) 773-9197 .. PO Box 758, Kingshill, St Croix, VI *00851*

Davol MR Ward M—Ny.Myf.
☎ (203) 869-4650 .. 51 Mooreland Rd, Greenwich, CT *06831*

Dawes MRS Charles C (Ellis—Ione Judson) . . . . Died Apr 27'96

Dawson MR & MRS Alec B (Nancy M Morton) H'59 | ☎ (508) 636-2119
MR Bruce S. . . . . | Box 3084,
| 58 Cornell Rd,
| Westport, MA
| *02790*

Dawson MR & MRS Benjamin G (Cornelia A Barrett) P'82.P'82.Dth'88 .. of
☎ (508) 785-1710 .. 45 Farm St, Dover, MA *02030*
"Wunnegin" 551 W Main Rd, Little Compton, RI *02837*
Cold Springs Farm, RR 1, PO Box 106-5, Airport Rd, Warren,
VT *05674*

Dawson MRS John A (Annie Joe Howel) Dar.
☎ (847) 750-3472 .. 3201 Simpson St, Apt 204, Evanston,
IL *60201-1916*

Dawson MRS John E (Elizabeth Brayton) Wh'lck'51.D.Chi.
☎ (401) 635-8609 .. "Wunnegin" 551 W Main Rd, Little Compton,
RI *02837-1131*

Dawson MR John S W—Un.Sa.Cl'82 .. of
☎ (212) 860-2764 .. 155 E 91 St, New York, NY *10128*
Gipsy Trail Club, Carmel, NY *10512*

Dawson MR & MRS Louis Y 3d (Elizabeth N Verner) Yh.GaTech'52
☎ (803) 577-6794 .. 33 Church St, Charleston, SC *29401*

Dawson MR & MRS Matthew B (Pamela Webb) Vt'84.Vt'84
☎ (802) 425-4102 .. RR 1, Box 1292, North Ferrisburg, VT *05472*

Dawson MRS Ralph B (Nancy Scott Causey) Cl'51.Cl'57.Cly.
☎ (212) 861-7692 .. 164 E 72 St, New York, NY *10021*

Day MISS Allison P—Y'90.NCar'96
☎ (773) 878-8763 .. 4705 N Talman Av, Chicago, IL *60625*

Day MR Andrew—Temp'84
☎ (215) 546-8641 .. 331 S Smedley St, Apt 10, Philadelphia, PA *19103*

Day MRS Antoinette Peters (Antoinette Peters) | ☎ (508) 263-4485
Mass'72 . . . . | 14 Ticonderoga Rd,
MISS Monica P . . . . | Acton, MA *01720*
MR Robert P . . . . |

Day MR & MRS Arden Lapham JR (Dinsmore—Nancy Reynolds) Va'43
☎ (310) 276-8149 .. 875 Comstock Av, Apt 4E, Los Angeles, CA *90024*

Day CDR (RET) Charles Pope JR—USN.An.Fw.P'54.Van'59
☎ (201) 376-4473 .. 93 Highland Av, Short Hills, NJ *07078*

Day MR & MRS Charles W (Carla L Dean) | ☎ (703) 406-4112
Wils'63.Y'54.Cl'57.Ch'58 . . . . | 101 Sinegar Place,
MR Charles W JR—Y'87.Ch'93—at Geo Wash'n | Great Falls, VA
Law . . . . | *22066*
MR Spencer D—NDak'91—at
100 S Martin Luther King Blvd, Apt 1082,
Las Vegas, NV *89106* . . . . |

Day, Christopher A & Lukens, Elizabeth B—P'79.Pa'86.Hav'81.Temp'89
☎ (215) 247-3196 .. 330 Wellesley Rd, Philadelphia, PA *19119*

Day MR & MRS Clifford JR (Esther D Hoppe) W&L'43
☎ (314) 962-5278 .. 9384 White Av, Brentwood, MO *63144*

Day MRS Conway W (Lacagnina—E Conway McLean) .. of
☎ (203) 966-3787 .. 35 Canaan Close, New Canaan, CT *06840*
☎ (805) 565-3820 .. 1650 Moore Rd, Montecito, CA *93108*

Day MR & MRS Ethan S (Teresa M Tapia) NMexSt'89
☎ (505) 820-7617 .. 1660 Old Pecos Trail, Apt A308, Santa Fe,
NM *87505*

Day MR & MRS Fairfield P JR (Smith—Susan C | of ☎ (803)853-7483
Zurn) Ws'62.Fic.Yh.Cw.Snc.Rv.Ht.Dar.H'61 . . . | 36 N Adgers Wharf,
MISS Amy H—at 2800 Kalmia Av, Apt C206, | Charleston, SC
Boulder, CO *80301* . . . . | *29401*
MR Fairfield P III—at 6201B Chesterfield Av, | ☎ (803) 529-1856
Austin, TX *78752* . . . . | "The Marshes"
MISS Bailey H Smith . . . . | Yeamans Hall,
| 900 Yeamans Hall
| Rd, Charleston, SC
| *29406*

Day MRS Gail E (Toner—Gail C Engler) | ☎ (970) 845-8704
StL'73.StL'80. . . . . | PO Box 2466,
MISS Christy K . . . . | Avon, CO *81620*

Day MR & MRS H Corbin (Dorothy S Jemison) | 2986 Cherokee Rd,
Br'59.Pa'63 . . . . | Birmingham, AL
MR H Corbin JR . . . . | *35223*

Day MR & MRS H Mason (M Germana D Fabbri) Vt'85.Stan'83
☎ (415) 563-7480 .. 2627 Broderick St, San Francisco, CA *94123*

Day MISS Hélène C (Seward—Kilby—Hélène C Day)
PO Box 302, Virginia City, NV *89440*

Day MRS Henry B (Clementine S Corbin) Cly .. of
☎ (609) 426-6602 .. Meadows Lakes 46-08, Hightstown, NJ *08520*
☎ (908) 892-1452 .. 962 S Lagoon Lane, Mantoloking, NJ *08738*

Day MR Jeffrey F . . see C B Drake JR

Day MR & MRS Jerome C (Julie Sage) Laf'59 . . . . . .
  MISS Cindy S—at NYU . . . .
  JUNIORS MR Nicholas S—at Eagle Hill Sch . . . . .
  ☎ (201) 736-4490 Llewellyn Park, 55 Mountain Av S, West Orange, NJ *07052*

Day MRS Joan G (Joan E Goodin) . . . .
  MISS (DR) Deborah—Cal'73.GeoW'78.GeoW'83. Cal'90—at ☎ (818) 906-8066 3801 Ventura Canyon Av, Sherman Oaks, CA *91423* . . . .
  ☎ (540) 687-5533 ''Innisfree'' PO Box 132, Middleburg, VA *20118*

Day MR & MRS John Anthony (Slater—Joanna Sadtler) Pa'66.Temp'72.Pc.H'37.Va'48 . . . .
  MR John G T Slater JR—Ham'83.Cl'92—at ☎ (203) 226-9645 . . 18 St John Place, Westport, CT *06880* . . . .
  ☎ (610) 825-3689 3004 Park Av, Lafayette Hill, PA *19444*

Day MR & MRS John C (M Alixe Utgoff) McG'74.Qnsland'67.Qnsland'71.McG'76
  ☎ (508) 475-4126 . . 26 Bellevue Rd, Andover, MA *01810-4418*

Day MR & MRS John F (Linda C Long) ArizSt'69.ArizSt'73 . . . .
  MISS Diana
  JUNIORS MR John F 2d . . . .
  ☎ (602) 443-3813 7000 E Doubletree Ranch Rd, Paradise Valley, AZ *85253*

Day MR & MRS John MacL (Janet B Brinkman) Wash'57.Stan'62 . . . .
  MISS Elizabeth B—at ☎ (608) 255-3421 811 Spaight St, Madison, WI *53703* . . . .
  ☎ (616) 780-3863 1485 Forest Park Rd, Muskegon, MI *49441*

Day MISS Kathleen Sayles (H Mason) . . . . Born at San Francisco, CA Jun 30'96

Day MISS Kingsley V—Ty'93 . . see V C Banker

Day MR Laurence C—Rc.Pn.P'55 . . . .
  MR Stephen L—Bost'84 . . . .
  ☎ (314) 997-3226 1 Watch Hill Rd, Ladue, MO *63124*

Day MR Lincoln W (Stanley R) . . . . Married at Chicago, IL
  Thompson MISS Stephanie M (Edward R) . . . . Sep 30'95

Day MISS Mary B—ColbyS'72
  ☎ (215) 722-2141 . . 7700 Castor Av, Philadelphia, PA *19152*

Day MR & MRS Peter A (Eileen E Igoe) StLaw'87.Les'89.OWes'85
  ☎ (215) 540-8022 . . 301 Militia Hill Rd, Ft Washington, PA *19034*

Day MISS Rebecca B—SWMo'80
  23 Ross Av, Chestnut Ridge, NY *10977*

Day MR Richard W JR—Nu'87 . . see V C Banker

Day MR & MRS Rodney D 3d (Evelyn M Scattergood) V'62.L.Cts.Ln.Rb.Me.M.Ri.Gm.Ac.Ty'62 . . of
  ☎ (212) 644-8646 . . 12 Beekman Place, New York, NY *10022*
  ☎ (610) 525-2831 . . 630 Carisbrooke Rd, Bryn Mawr, PA *19010*

Day MRS Rufus S JR (Elizabeth G Crofut) Sth'34.Un.It.
  ☎ (216) 751-1337 . . 13710 Shaker Blvd, Apt 1005, Cleveland, OH *44120*

Day MR & MRS Stanley R (Lynn O Weyerhaeuser) V'53.Ken'48 . . . .
  MR Frederick K W—at 1920 N Clark St, Chicago, IL *60614* . . . .
  ☎ (313) 881-1151 3 Woodland Place, Grosse Pointe, MI *48230*

Day MR Stanley R JR—Tul'80.Nw'84
  ☎ (312) 664-5880 . . 1920 N Clark St, Chicago, IL *60614*

Day MISS Sylvia C . . see C B Drake JR

Dayton MRS Alice S (Strickland—Alice S Dayton) Ws'66
  ☎ (212) 769-4874 . . 130 W 67 St, Apt 15G, New York, NY *10023*

Dayton MR & MRS S Grey JR (Slaymaker—Margaret A Munro) Cry.Me.R.Ph.Gi.Ll.Cw.Ac.Pn.P.'43 ⚓
  ☎ (610) 353-6221 . . 613 Glendale Rd, Newtown Square, PA *19073*

Dayton MR & MRS William B 3d (Ruth E MacLaren) Cc.
  ☎ (207) 367-2698 . . ''Companionway'' RR 1, Box 2944, Stonington, ME *04681*

Dazet MR & MRS Michael E (Heather W Swartwood) Ala'95
  ☎ (504) 828-4386 . . 111 Aris Av, Metairie, LA *70005*

Deacon MRS B Barrett (Beatrice A Barrett) Br'48.Ncd.
  ☎ (610) 688-5054 . . 30 Wingstone Lane, Devon, PA *19333-1651*

Dean MR Arthur H (Mary T Marden) Pr.Cly.
  ☎ (516) 922-4735 . . ''Homewood'' 57 Mill River Rd, Oyster Bay, NY *11771*

Dean MR & MRS Bruce C (Pamela M Prator) SoMiss'79.StLaw'80.Tul'84
  ☎ (504) 866-8851 . . 508 Hillary St, New Orleans, LA *70118-3834*

Dean MR & MRS Charles W (Patricia C Dean) DU'65
  ☎ (617) 383-0439 . . 207 Jerusalem Rd, Cohasset, MA *02025*

Dean DR & MRS David C (Jean L Butler) Sth'54.Bf.Bow'52.Hop'56 . . . .
  MISS Laurie S—StLaw'83.Mit'92—at 80 Margaret St, Arlington, MA *02174* . . . .
  ☎ (716) 839-3085 65 Huxley Dv, Buffalo, NY *14226*

Dean COL (RET) & MRS Guy K 3d (Victoria Norris) USA.Skd'62.Rc.Rv.Sar.Cw.Ofp.Fw.Snc.StA.Pn. Rut'62.Nw'74.Rider'81 . . . .
  MISS Anne T W—at Hobart-Wm Smith . . . .
  JUNIORS MR Andrew B N . . . .
  of ☎ (609)921-6356 11 Lemore Circle, Rocky Hill, NJ *08553*
  ☎ (717) 595-2058 ''Todburn'' C408, Buck Hill Falls, PA *18323*

Dean MR & MRS Howard B (Andrée B Maitland) Cl'74.Un.Mds.Plg.Y'42
  ☎ (212) 876-4433 . . 1035 Park Av, New York, NY *10028*

Dean MR & MRS J Simpson JR (McConnell—Margaret A Mahler) Wil.BtP.Evg.Rv.Cw.Bab'49 . . of
  ☎ (561) 832-8888 . . 291 El Vedado Way, Palm Beach, FL *33480*
  ☎ (302) 655-7777 . . ''Redley'' PO Box 4039, Greenville, DE *19807*

Dean MR & MRS James H (Winn Phillips) Clare'77.Vh.Purd'40.H'42
  ☎ (818) 795-6451 . . 1321 W Haven Rd, San Marino, CA *91108*

Dean MR & MRS James H (Virginia D Lynch) ColC'77.Unn.Cly.Bost'77
  ☎ (203) 255-5353 . . ''Floradean'' 215 Fair Oak Dv, Fairfield, CT *06430*

Dean MR & MRS John H (H Elizabeth Webster) Wheat'34.Hn.H'34
  ☎ (617) 383-0936 . . 42 Atlantic Av, Box 102, Cohasset, MA *02025*

Dean MR & MRS John S (Mia Youngquist) DU'69.DU'71 . . . .
  MISS Alida A . . . .
  MR Benjamin Y—at U of Denver . . . .
  JUNIORS MISS Erica S . . . .
  JUNIORS MR Carl C . . . .
  ☎ (617) 383-6416 Meadow Lane, Cohasset, MA *02025*

Dean MISS Mary H
  ☎ (510) 528-5347 . . 682 Ensenada Av, Berkeley, CA *94707*

Dean MISS Susan E—Nh . . . see MRS D B Conant

Dean MRS Walter E 2d (Lenoir McNamara) Fr.
  ☎ (707) 996-6945 . . 7600 Sonoma Mountain Rd, Glen Ellen, CA *95442*

Dean MR & MRS William Tucker (Arthur—
Rosamond G Roberts) Sth'44.Cs.H'37.Ch'40.
H'47 . . . . ☎ (516) 367-4512
    MISS R Lee Arthur—Conn'84—at
    ☎ (212) 475-0412 . . 7 Bond St, Apt 3B,
    New York, NY *10012* . . . .
116 White Hill Rd,
PO Box 21,
Cold Spring Harbor,
NY *11724*

Deane MR & MRS Daniel Thomas (Mary K
McMurry) Pa'51 . . . . ☎ (215) 884-7263
MISS Ann P—Mercy'86 . . . .
143 Woodland Rd,
Wyncote, PA *19095*

Deans MR & MRS Robert B JR (May—Elisabeth De B Prickett)
Rc.Ck.S.Cly.Y'47.Nu'51
  ☎ (516) 922-4051 . . "Turbillon" Frost Mill Rd, Mill Neck, NY *11765*

Dearborn MRS Angelica G (Angelica L Gerry) Fic. . ☎ (203) 972-6613
MISS Ashley L . . . .
MISS Lindsay H . . . .
80 Turtleback Lane
E, New Canaan, CT
06840

Dearborn MR Philip N—Ln.Pr.H'66
  ☎ (617) 451-5589 . . 71A Chandler St, Boston, MA *02116*

Dearden MR & MRS Edward C 3d (Anne F Carrigan) Me.Pa'53
  ☎ (610) LA5-7513 . . 774 Mt Moro Rd, Villanova, PA *19085*

Dearie MR & MRS Christopher F (Direxa V Dick)
Plg.Geo'64 . . . . of ☎ (212)369-5723
MISS Direxa V . . . .
MISS Honora A . . . .
MR Christopher F JR . . . .
JUNIORS MR William D . . . .
JUNIORS MR John C . . . .
17 E 89 St,
New York, NY
10128
☎ (516) 626-9773
"Panda's Ledge"
Clock Tower Lane,
Old Westbury, NY
11568

Dearth MISS Deborah H—Syr'75.STex'80
  ☎ (212) 213-0313 . . 235 E 22 St, Apt 10J, New York, NY *10010*

Dearth MISS Margaret D (Linley—Margaret D Dearth) SacredH'92
  ☎ (203) 226-8465 . . 2 Marvin Place, Westport, CT *06880*

DeBardeleben MR & MRS Newton H JR (Clemmons ☎ (205) 871-6431
—Pamela D Allen) Rens'66.Purd'67 . . . .
MISS Virginia S—at Auburn . . . .
MR Newton H 3d—at Tex Christian . . . .
JUNIORS MISS Pamela A . . . .
776 Montgomery
Dv, Birmingham,
AL *35213*

DeBardeleben MR & MRS Prince JR (Anne W Welch) Cy.Evg.Y'45
  ☎ (205) 969-0222 . . 4222 Old Leeds Rd, Birmingham, AL *35213*

de Bary MR & MRS Marquette (Du Vivier—Gary— of ☎ (212)752-4046
Patricia E Murrill) Rc.Bcs.Cly . . . .
    MISS E Tracy Du V Gary—at
    ☎ (415) 461-5535 . . PO Box 428, Ross, CA
94957 . . . .
1 Sutton Place S,
New York, NY
10022
☎ (011-33-1)
43-59-54-64
7 av Matignon,
75008 Paris, France

DeBevoise MR Charles R . . . . Died at
Basking Ridge, NJ May 28'96

DeBevoise MRS Charles R (Lillie B Ryan) Me.Hl.
  ☎ (201) 538-6665 . . Young's Rd, RD 1, Basking Ridge, NJ *07920*

Debevoise MR & MRS Eli Whitney 2d (Heidi B ☎ (301) 229-3610
Herrington) Denis'74.Dick'77.C.Cvc.Sl.Yn.
Y'74.H'77 . . . .
JUNIORS MISS Hadley H . . . .
5207 Falmouth Rd,
Bethesda, MD
20816

Debevoise MRS Thomas (Ruth G Macfarlane) Edg.
  ☎ (412) 741-7494 . . 1204 Colonial Place, Sewickley, PA *15143*

Debevoise MRS Thomas M 2d (Ann Taylor) Swth'47.C.Ct.Csn.Yn . . . of
  ☎ (802) 457-3000 . . PO Box 568, 2 Pleasant St, Woodstock, VT *05091*
  ☎ (802) 457-1186 . . "Pinnacle Farm" RR 2, Box 787, Cox Rd,
  Woodstock, VT *05091*

de Blank MR & MRS Paul M B (Laura T Kennedy) ☎ (602) 266-7160
Stan'67.Stan'67 . . . .
MISS J Gabriel B—at Milton . . . .
MR M J Bastiaan—at Ithaca, NY . . . .
MR Peter M K—at Stanford . . . .
317 W Montebello
Av, Phoenix, AZ
85013

de Bragança MISS Michele—CalArts'89
  ☎ (415) 641-8488 . . 4234—22 St, San Francisco, CA *94114*

de Bragança MR & MRS Miguel (Scholz—Ann Hughson) Bgt.Evg.Cly.H'37
  ☎ (561) 844-0850 . . 596 N County Rd, Palm Beach, FL *33480*

de Bragança MR & MRS Miguel (Barbara H Fales)
Wheat'76.B.Eyc.Sm.Cy.Yn.Pa'72.Y'78
  ☎ (617) 267-9009 . . 301 Berkeley St, Boston, MA *02116*

de Braux MISS Ariane (Peter) . . . . Married at New York, NY
  Lacy MR Thomas W (William H) . . . . May 18'96

de Bretteville MRS Charles (Frances W Mein) B.Bur.Tcy.
  ☎ (408) 624-8954 . . PO Box 1246, Pebble Beach, CA *93953*

de Bretteville MISS Leslie (Hall—Leslie ☎ (415) 921-1128
de Bretteville) Tcy . . . .
MR Ian de Bretteville Hall . . . .
MR Cameron Hall . . . .
886 Chestnut St,
San Francisco, CA
94133-2206

de Broglie PRC François & PRCSS (Marie Blanche de Bagneux) Paris'50
  ☎ (011-33-1) 45-51-36-34 . . 18 av de la Motte Picquet, 75007 Paris,
France

de Brossard MR & MRS Boyd P (Harrison—Pauline L du Pont)
Pr.Cos.Cly . . .of
  ☎ (212) 734-4617 . . 730 Park Av, New York, NY *10021*
  ☎ (212) 734-4739 . . 35 E 76 St, New York, NY *10021*

de Bruyne MRS Leila P (Leila H Pile) Wheat'71
  ☎ (203) 698-1082 . . 5 MacArthur Dv, Old Greenwich, CT *06870*

de Bullet MR & MRS Eugene G JR (Sharon A ☎ (817) 236-4200
Johnson) TexC'67.StM'70 ⚓ . . . .
JUNIORS MISS Courtney R . . . .
"Shell Rock"
7916 Summit Cove,
Eagle Mountain
Lake, Ft Worth, TX
76179

de Butts MRS Daniel D (Josephine P Dame) Mv . . . . ☎ (410) 467-2249
MISS Josephine D . . . .
1 Beechdale Rd,
Baltimore, MD
21210

de Buys MRS Harry D (Elizabeth P Handy) . . . . ☎ (205) 967-5439
MR Harry D JR—at 1201 S Courthouse Rd,
Arlington, VA *22204* . . . .
3337 Cherokee Rd,
Birmingham, AL
35213

De Buys MR & MRS John F JR (Dewey—Martha E Rast) Ala'70.Cy.Van'65
  ☎ (205) 870-3226 . . 504 Pine Ridge Trail, Birmingham, AL *35213*

De Buys MR & MRS John F 3d (Katherine A Kent)
Van'90.Cy.HampSydney'88
  ☎ (205) 870-5368 . . 6 Pine Crest Rd, Birmingham, AL *35223*

DeCamp MRS Johnson (Diane P Johnson) Swb'55
  ☎ (513) 831-0644 . . 1 Stoney Creek Dv, Terrace Park, OH *45174*

De Camp MR & MRS Richard S (Boyce—Patricia Storey) Br'55
☎ (606) 266-8590 . . 644 Montclair Dv, Lexington, KY *40502*

de Castro MR & MRS J Edmund JR (Melissa P | ☎ (716) 886-1174
Sullivan) RosH'75.Daemen'79.Buf.St.Cw.Myf. | 132 Lexington Av,
Rv.Sar.Dar.Canis'52.Buf'53 ⚓ . . . . | Buffalo, NY
MISS Alicia P—SUNY'89.SUNY'91.Dar.—at | *14222-1810*
☎ (716) 885-2822 . . 574 Bird Av, Apt 1,
Buffalo, NY *14222* . . . .
MR Julian E 3d—Rv.—at State Coll Buffalo . . .
MR Samuel F—at Deerfield . . . .

de Chabert-Ostland MR & MRS Michel L F (Muriel V Hutton) Y'64
☎ (561) 835-9563 . . 133 Greenwood Dv, West Palm Beach, FL *33405*

De Chard MR & MRS Richard J (Carol J Goddard) WorPoly'56
99 Gates St, Portsmouth, NH *03801*

Dechert MISS Martha P—Br'92.Me . . .see W M Churchman 3d

Dechert MR & MRS Peter (Phoebe J Booth)
Rdc'49.Pa'51.Rv.Pa'48.Pa'50.Pa'55
☎ (505) 983-2148 . . PO Box 636, Santa Fe, NM *87504-0636*

Dechert MRS Philip (Anne L Ross)
☎ (508) 996-8108 . . Box 271P, Nonquitt, South Darmouth, MA *02748*

Decker MRS Arnold F A (Kate Delano Condax) Swb'68.Ac.StA.Myf.Ncd.
☎ (609) 231-1245 . . 314 E Central Av, Moorestown, NJ *08057*

de Clairville MR & MRS Raymond (Gwendolyn K Gwynne) D.Pr.Cw.Cly.
☎ (941) 474-2240 . . 7660 Manasota Key Rd, Englewood, FL *34223*

de Coppet MISS Laura—Bnd'68
☎ (212) 475-3267 . . 50 E 10 St, New York, NY *10003*

de Cordova MR & MRS Eustace JR (Biddle—Peniston | ☎ (212) 628-1454
—Aimée H Crossan) Cal'61.Rc.Cly. . . . . | 215 E 68 St,
MR & MRS E Winchester Peniston (S Lyerly | New York, NY
Spöngberg) . . . . | *10021*

de Dominicis MR & MRS Danilo M (Averyl S | ☎ (610) 353-0533
Phipps) ColbyS'64.CollComm'54.CalSt'71 . . . . | 22 Old Covered
MISS Daphne P—at Trinity . . . . | Bridge Rd,
| Newtown Square,
| PA *19073*

Deeds JUNIORS MR Blake . . see D R Taylor

Deehan MR & MRS Alan C (Sara W Hill) BostColl'83.P'81.Nu'88
☎ (201) 746-0840 . . 23 Park Terr, Upper Montclair, NJ *07043*

Deely MR & MRS James S (Patricia S Johnson)
Adelphi'77.CUNY'79.Lx.C.Yh.Cs.Wms'43.H'48
☎ (212) 737-6908 . . 320 E 72 St, New York, NY *10021*

Deely MR & MRS Philip S (Hilary L Somers) | ☎ (413) 243-4263
SimR'71.Lx.Hob'69.Ch'71 . . . . | ''Normal Corners''
MISS Mary S—at Hall . . . . | Main Rd,
| Tyringham, MA
| *01264*

Deering MRS A R Ashton (A Russell Ashton) . . Married at Baltimore, MD
Brooke MAJ Randall W—USA. (Dandridge) . . . . Jly 26'96

Deering MR C Randall—Cy.Gv.Loy'78
☎ (410) 321-1333 . . 605 Baltimore Av, Towson, MD *21204*

Deering MR & MRS L Patrick (Mildred L H Foley) Cy.Gv.Cl'48
1001 Malvern Av, Ruxton, MD *21204*

Deering MR & MRS Mark M (Deborah H Crocker) JMad'76.Denis'76
☎ (410) 323-9237 . . 114 Castlewood Rd, Baltimore, MD *21210*

Dees MR & MRS Bowen C (Sarah Sanders) Cos.Ac.Miss'37.Nu'42
140 N Camino Miramonte, Tucson, AZ *85716*

de Fontnouvelle MR & MRS Patrick Y de F (Nathalie
Nespoulous-Neuville) P'87
☎ (515) 292-7746 . . 211 Hughes Av, Ames, IA *50014*

de Fontnouvelle CT Pierre de F & CTSS (Anne S Burke) Gi.Paris'39
☎ (301) 657-2415 . . 7109 Oakridge Av, Chevy Chase, MD *20815*

de Forest MRS Taber (Marion Archbald)
☎ (941) 594-1536 . . 100 Glenview Place, Naples, FL *34108*

de France HRH PRCSS Chantal . . see F X de Sambucy

de Fremery MRS Peter W (Green—Mary B Shand)
☎ (541) 382-1848 . . 2115 Merritt Court, Bend, OR *97702*

de Frise MRS A Campbell (Clark—Alison | ☎ (312) 664-3188
Campbell) Ws'54.Cas.Fy. . . . . | 1209 N Astor St,
MISS Victoria L—at 3258 N Racine Av, Chicago, | Chicago, IL *60610*
IL *60657* . . . .
MR Alexander P—at 3258 N Racine Av, Chicago,
IL *60657* . . . .

Defty MRS S Bixby (Sarah T Bixby) V'53 . . . . | ☎ (011-49-30)
MR Matthew B—V'82.Rice'88 . . . . | 324-0357
| Schiller Strasse 73,
| 10627 Berlin,
| Germany

Defty MR Stephen C—Tufts'80
☎ (011-49-30) 342-5725 . . Kaiser Friedrichstrasse 16, 10585 Berlin 10,
Germany

de Ganay CT Thierry S & CTSS (Frances A Spence) Mls'74 . . of
☎ (011-33-1) 42-25-76-13 . . 53 av Montaigne, 75008 Paris, France
☎ (212) 744-8637 . . 765 Park Av, New York, NY *10021*

de Garbolewski MR & MRS C Edward T S | ☎ (410) 275-8841
(Johnson—Brenda Phillips) Drex'58 . . . . | 479 Stoney Battery
MR Mark E . . . . | Rd, Battery Point
| Farms, Earleville,
| MD *21919*

Degener MRS Edens (Ann Edens) Tex'49 . . . . | ☎ (210) 655-5441
MISS Sophie C—at ☎ (773) 506-8355 | 3803 Barrington St,
2442 W Sunnyside Av, Chicago, IL *60625* . . . . | Apt 8A,
| San Antonio, TX
| *78217*

Degener MR & MRS J Michael (Korfmann—Helen | of ☎ (212)737-3910
MacD Zottoli) LErie'63.Cly.Wms'56.Nu'72 . . . | 151 E 83 St,
MISS Carol M—Bnd'83.Cl'84.H'87.Cly.—at | New York, NY
☎ (212) 249-0860 . . 155 E 73 St, New York, NY | *10028*
10021 . . . . | ☎ (860) EN4-0593
MR J Michael JR—Bost'81—at | ''Nid d'Alcyon''
☎ (413) 584-3892 . . 6 Ahwaga St, Northampton, | 130 Sharon
MA *01060* . . . . | Mountain Rd,
MISS Joan Hall—at ☎ (207) 372-8908 | Sharon, CT *06069*
Box 815, HCR 35, Tenants Harbor, ME *04860*

de Give MR & MRS David de B (Josephine C Fisher) Rdc'65.H'64.Nu'71
☎ (540) 592-3889 . . ''Belle Grove'' 1402 Winchester Rd, Delaplane,
VA *20144*

de Give MISS Ghislaine (Weber—Poulden—Ghislaine de Give)
H'69.Bost'77.Bost'86
☎ (011-44-171) 924-6687 . . 69 Bramfield Rd, London SW11 6PZ,
England

de Give MR & MRS Paul de B (Eleanor Hoguet) So.H'34
☎ (516) 283-0987 . . 119 Breese Lane, Southampton, NY *11968*

DeGraw MR & MRS Austin R (Melissa H Huffman) Sth'68.Cda.
☎ (818) 991-8753 . . 28241 Driver Av, Agoura, CA *91301*

de Grazia MR & MRS Sebastian (Ballantine—Lucia
B Heffelfinger) C.Cos.Csn.Pn.Ch'39 . . . . | ☎ (609) 924-4947
MR Tancredi . . . . | 914 Great Rd,
Princeton, NJ *08540*

De Groff MR & MRS Ralph L JR (Sinwell—Marion S | of ☎ (410)494-9149
Parsons) Gchr'61.Elk.Md.Cc.Cw.Hl.Mv.P'58. | 1002 Rolandvue Rd,
Va'60 . . . . | Baltimore, MD
MR Andrew E Sinwell—Elk.P'87 . . . . | *21204*
☎ (212) 737-6439
7 Gracie Square,
New York, NY
10028

de Grosse MRS Aristid V (Irina Lieven)
☎ (714) 951-7309 . . 25301 Mackenzie St, Laguna Hills, CA *92653*

de Guigné MR & MRS Charles—B.Cl'73 . . of
☎ (011-33-56) 70-20-11 . . Château de Sénéjac, Le Pian-Médoc,
33290 Gironde, France
☎ (408) 624-7300 . . ''Sunset Point'' Box 122, Pebble Beach, CA *93953*

de Guigné MR & MRS Christian 4th (Vaughn A Hills) Bhm.B.Bur.Pcu.Cp.
☎ (415) 342-9222 . . PO Box 1739, San Mateo, CA *94401*

de Gunzburg BRN & BRNSS Dimitri (Brokaw—Ingham—
Shawn McWeeney) Cly.P'56 . . of
☎ (011-44-171) 589-9232 . . 22 Thurloe Square, London SW7 2SD,
England
☎ (011-33) 90-72-29-39 . . ''Le Mas de Pierredon'' rte de Bonnieux D3,
Menerbe, France

de Haven MR & MRS William T (F Jane Bruford) | ☎ (412) 741-2131
Edg.Ham.'61 . . . . | 22 Linden Place,
MISS Rebecca—Duke'89—at Arlington, VA. . . . | Sewickley, PA
JUNIORS MR Peter J—at Princeton . . . . | *15143*

de Heeren MRS Rodman A (Lopes—Aimée de Sa Sottomaior) . . of
☎ (212) 289-0621 . . 17 E 90 St, New York, NY *10128*
☎ (561) 848-5060 . . 473 N County Rd, Palm Beach, FL *33480*
☎ (011-33-1) 45-51-88-98 . . 73 rue de Varenne, 75007 Paris, France
☎ (011-33) 59-24-07-29 . . ''Villa La Roseraie'' 12 rue Martias,
64200 Biarritz, France

de Hellebranth MRS Roland T (Emilie S Busch) Ac.Csp.Myf.W.Ncd.
111 S Frankfort Av, Ventnor City, NJ *08406*

de Hemricourt de Grunne CT Bernard & CTSS (Deming P Beyer)
LoyMmt'87.Pratt'94.Louvain'80.Y.'87
☎ (212) 628-6806 . . 3 E 75 St, New York, NY *10021*

DeJarnette MR & MRS Edmund T JR (Katia L Escartin)
Va'59.Va'63.GeoW'78
☎ (804) 798-7253 . . 400 S James St, Ashland, VA *23005-1927*

de Jong MR & MRS James M JR (Melanie H Cabot) T.Cly.Geo'83
☎ (914) 351-5311 . . ''Hemlock Gate'' E Lake Stable Rd, Tuxedo Park,
NY *10987*

de Jong DR John H—Tr.Tufts'78.Tufts'85
☎ (617) 424-8488 . . 50 Commonwealth Av, Boston, MA *02116*

Dejonge MRS Louis (Alice Graves) H.
☎ (508) 342-1811 . . 103 Prospect St, Fitchburg, MA *01420*

Dejoux MR & MRS Edouard H G (Blair C Hopkins) Ty'90.Pr.Dyc.CtCol'90
☎ (516) 624-7646 . . PO Box 184, Oyster Bay, NY *11771*

Dejoux MR Jacques H L—Dyc.Pr.Bab'69 . . . . | of ☎ (516)671-0728
MR Morgan A G—Vt'94—at ☎ (212) 421-6958 | 1 Ayer Rd,
360 E 57 St, Apt 4A, New York, NY *10022* . . . | PO Box 73,
Locust Valley, NY
11560
☎ (011-33-78)
38-36-47
6 Place des
Jacobins, 69002
Lyon, France

de Kay REV & MRS Eckford J (Laughlin—Roberta A | ☎ (408) 978-3470
Gill) Cw.Hl.Snc.Rv.Cr'49 . . . . | 1670 White Creek
MR Kenneth L—at U of Cal Chico . . . . | Lane, San Jose, CA
MR Timothy A—StMarys'95—at | *95125*
☎ (408) 445-5278 . . 1930 Almaden Rd, Apt 74,
San Jose, CA *95125* . . . .

de Kay MR & MRS George C (Booke—Miranda | of ☎ (212)PL5-9735
Knickerbocker) Bnd'59.C.Tufts'46 . . . . | 400 E 52 St,
MISS Sarah H—Swth'78 . . . . | New York, NY
MR Colman D—Colg'77 . . . . | *10022-6042*
MR Charles A . . . . | ☎ (860) 535-1094
''The Hill''
Grand St,
Stonington, CT
06378

de Kay DR Joseph R D—SUNY'74.SUNY'75.Kirkvl'79
☎ (207) 625-4730 . . Hampshire St, East Hiram, ME *04041*

de Kay MR & MRS Ormonde (Roosevelt—Barbara E | ☎ (212) 369-6030
Scott) C.Hl.H.'45 . . . . | 1225 Park Av,
MR Thomas S—Wes'90 . . . . | New York, NY
10128

de Kay MRS Timpson (Joan H Timpson) . . . . | ☎ (516) 671-7461
MR George G T | 110 Feeks Lane,
Lattingtown, NY
11560

de Kertanguy CTE Loic & CTSSE (Rebecca D | of 1040 Fifth Av,
Williams) Briar'71.Mds.Ri.Dyc.Mich'67 . . . . . . | New York, NY
MISS Valerie . . . . | *10028*
☎ (516) 324-8794
PO Box 1205,
East Hampton, NY

de Labar MRS Margot (Grill—Margot Adams Hoagland de Labar)
Paris'79.Ht.Hl.
☎ (909) 679-7742 . . 27526 Calle Ganado, Sun City, CA *92586*

De La Cour MR & MRS Willis S (Eleanore L Piper) Gm.Ph.Ac.Y'31
☎ (610) 525-4410 . . 825 Colony Rd, Bryn Mawr, PA *19010*

Delafield MRS B Reed (Barbara de S Reed) | ☎ (609) 466-3043
Wheat'58 . . . . | 4 Cotswold Lane,
MR M Livingston JR—at 1515 Montecito Rd, | Princeton, NJ *08540*
Ramona, CA *92065* . . . .

Delafield MISS Cecily—Csn.
☎ (561) 231-2782 . . 576 Banyan Rd, Vero Beach, FL *32963*

Delafield MR Charles B—Err.Pr.Un.H.'27
☎ (516) 921-1778 . . PO Box 305, Rte 106, East Norwich,
NY *11732-0305*

Delafield MR & MRS J Dennis (Jo Ann M Sawyer) Au.Plg.Snc.Cw.Cs.P'57
☎ (212) 831-6341 . . 1105 Park Av, New York, NY *10128*

Delafield MR John Dennis JR (J Dennis) . . . . Married at Seattle, WA
Roach MISS Cecile H (J Thurston 2d) . . . . Aug 17'96
Delafield MR & MRS John Dennis JR (Cecile H Roach) P'90.H'96.P'89.H'95
see Dilatory Domiciles
Delafield MRS Joseph L (Anna S Howe)
☎ (617) 862-0836 . . Brookhaven C357, 1010 Waltham St, Lexington,
MA *02173*
Delafield MR Stephen S—H.'54.CUNY'93
☎ (212) 725-8457 . . 326 E 35 St, New York, NY *10016*
Delafield MR & MRS Walter B (Jean L Tanburn) Un.Cly.
☎ (212) 371-0272 . . 200 E 66 St, New York, NY *10021*
Delafield MRS William F (Brengle—Helen W Fox) Sg.
☎ (215) 984-8377 . . 600 E Cathedral Rd, Apt K004, Philadelphia,
PA *19128*

de Laire MRS Antoine R (Mohl—Maria-Hélène Manville) K.Cly. . . . . | of ☎ (603)643-6647
MR Georges F—StLaw'88—at St John's | 3 Balch Hill Lane,
Seminary . . . . | Hanover, NH
MISS Catherine M Mohl—V'81—at | *03755-1623*
☎ (011-33) 66-80-42-89 . . La Source, | ☎ (011-33)
rue des Pouzes, 30250 Junas, France . . . . | 31-65-22-77
| ''Le Petit
| Bonneville''
| 14800
| Englesqueville-en-
| Auge, France

de la Morandière MISS Anne J Potier—NCar'68.H'79.Myf.
☎ (212) 535-2442 . . 340 E 72 St, New York, NY *10021*

Deland MRS F Stanton JR (Susan R Reeves) V'37.Cy.Chi.Ncd.
☎ (617) 239-7473 . . 10 Longwood Dv, Apt E171, Westwood,
MA *02090*

Delaney MR & MRS Timothy G (Farr—Katherine E | ☎ (914) 234-3737
Putnam) MtH'73.Nu'79.Bgt.Eyc.Ford'70.Cal'79 | 243 Pound Ridge
MISS Eleanor L Putnam-Farr . . . . | Rd, Bedford, NY
| *10506*

Delano MR & MRS Frederic A (Thalia Holmes)
☎ (904) 388-8966 . . 2970 St John's Av, Jacksonville, FL *32205*
Delano MR & MRS Lyman (Diana B Pool) | ☎ (203) 869-2679
OWes'77.Cly.Ht.Dc.Lm.Ncd.Ty'75 . . . . | 143 Old Church Rd,
JUNIORS MISS Laura F . . . . | Greenwich, CT
| *06830*
Delano MRS Warren (Elizabeth Washburn)
☎ (207) 439-2121 . . PO Box 218, Kittery Point, ME *03905*
Delanoy MR & MRS Douglas JR (Carolyn Brokaw) | ☎ (954) 566-4663
P'50 . . . . | 3021 NE 40 St,
MR Craig C—FlaAtl'87 . . . . | Ft Lauderdale, FL
| *33308*

Delapalme MRS Alexandra M (Alexandra D | of ☎ (011-33)
McConihe) . . . . | 38-58-03-93
JUNIORS MISS Pauline M D . . . . | ''Le Gué du
| Ruisseau'' 45510
| Vannes-sur-Cosson,
| France
| ☎ (011-33)
| 93-76-13-79
| La Ferme St Jean,
| Apt 14D, 15 av de la
| Liberation, 06230
| St-Jean-Cap-Ferrat,
| France
Delapalme MR David P N M—Geo'71 . . . . | ☎ (011-33-1)
JUNIORS MR Alexander McD . . . . | 47-04-80-02
| 12 av Paul Doumer,
| 75116 Paris, France

de Lara MISS Angela D (Wallia—Angela D de Lara) Alleg'70.Cl'78
71 Gate Ridge Rd, Fairfield, CT *06432*
de Lara MRS Juan J (Jonne E S C Low) Cl'59.Cly.Ncd.Myf.Dc.
☎ (203) 966-2823 . . 43 Bank St, New Canaan, CT *06840*
de la Renta MR & MRS Oscar (Reed—Anne F | ☎ (212) 517-7190
Engelhard) Cly. . . . . | 660 Park Av,
MISS P J Eliza Reed—Br'92—at 302 W 12 St, | New York, NY
Apt 5C, New York, NY *10014* . . . . | *10021*
MR Charles V Reed—at 12 Ash Place, |
Cambridge, MA *02138* . . . . |
de Lasa MR Jose Maria 3d—Geo'42.Hav'43
☎ (212) 355-4360 . . 400 E 55 St, Apt 18D, New York, NY *10022*
Deleplanque MR & MRS Christian R (Jennifer B | ☎ (011-33)
Gilmour) EcoleArt'95. . . . . | 50-41-16-43
JUNIORS MISS Shanti J . . . . | 14 Bois Chatton,
| 01210 Versonnex,
| France
de Lesseps MRS Tauni (Downs—Fougner—Harjes—Schoales—
Tauni de Lesseps) Ri.Evg.Ihy . . .of
☎ (561) 832-3993 . . ''Poseidon'' 452 Worth Av, Palm Beach, FL *33480*
☎ (203) 661-1717 . . ''Sauzir'' 80 Oneida Dv, Greenwich, CT *06830*
de Liagre MRS Alfred JR (Mary Howard) | of ☎ (212)759-3572
Ri.Mds.Plg. . . . . | 322 E 57 St,
MISS Christina—SL'70—at | New York, NY
☎ (011-33-1) 48-87-30-21 . . 9 Place des Vosges, | *10022*
75004 Paris, France . . . . | ☎ (516) 324-1144
| ''The Pelican''
| H'way-Behind-the-
| Pond,
| East Hampton, NY
| *11937*
de Liagre MR & MRS Nicholas (Virginia O'Neil) StLaw'80.NCar'70
☎ (212) 688-4931 . . 429 E 52 St, New York, NY *10022*

de Limur MR & MRS Charles (Eleanor S Walsh) Bhm.Bur.Pcu.Sfg. . . . . of ☎ (415)474-7628 945 Green St, San Francisco, CA 94133
MISS A Christine—at ☎ (415) 776-6512 3699 Clay St, San Francisco, CA 94118 . . . .
MR Philip A—at ☎ (415) 922-7864 1200 Gough St, San Francisco, CA 94109 . . . . .
☎ (707) 963-3726 "Limur Winery" 771 Sage Canyon Rd, St Helena, CA 94574

Dellenback MR & MRS Robert J (Geraldine McA Webster) Cal'50 . . . . ☎ (307) 733-8409 PO Box 8610, 250 E Cottonwood Dv, Jackson, WY 83002
MISS Geraldine McA—ColbyS'90—at ☎ (307) 739-3069 . . 3355 Ten Sleep Dv, Apt 29, Jackson, WY 83001 . . . .
MISS Martha McA—Bryant'92—at ☎ (617) 254-4391 . . 36 Arlington St, Brighton, MA 02135-2164 . . . .
MR Ian McA—at ☎ (802) 864-1561 47 Adams St, Burlington, VT 05401 . . . .

Dellenbaugh MR & MRS Geoffrey G (Joanna L Campbell) Chath'69.Csn.P'65.Stan'66.Pitt'71. Ch'74 . . . . ☎ (201) 514-5979 41 Prospect St, Madison, NJ 07940
MISS Virginia L—at Vanderbilt. . . . .
MR Samuel—P'96. . . . .
JUNIORS MISS Mary H . . . .

de Lone MR & MRS H Francis (Madeline Heckscher) Rc.Me.H'37.Pa'40 ☎ (610) NI4-5518 . . 444 Chandlee Dv, Berwyn, PA 19312-2062

De Long MR & MRS Thomas A 2d (Katharine R Clark) Rcn.Pqt.BtP.Snc.Rv.Ll.Vca.Lm.Coa.Cly. Cda.Ht.Dh.Wms'57.Cl'59.Nu'69 . . . . ☎ (203) 255-4768 "Beechcrest" 51 Mill Hill Lane, Southport, CT 06490
MISS Sarah R—FP'94.Cda. . . . .
MISS Elizabeth C—at Hobart-Wm Smith . . . . . .

Delori MRS Philippe P (Claire Schepens) Ws'60 . . . ☎ (011-32-2) 346-5979 51 av de Floréal, 1180 Brussels, Belgium
MISS Henrietta. . . . .
MISS Caroline . . . .

DeLoskey DR & MRS Albert F (Anne L Deering) JHop'74.Fla'78.JHop'73.Fla'78 . . . . ☎ (410) 366-7629 212 Woodlawn Rd, Baltimore, MD 21210
JUNIORS MISS Alexandra . . . .
JUNIORS MISS Clare . . . .

de Luca MR & MRS Robert N (Henry—Elizabeth K Swain) BMr'69.Hav'62.Pa'65 . . . . ☎ (610) LA5-7972 617 Woodleave Rd, Bryn Mawr, PA 19010
MISS Elizabeth H—at Yale . . . .
JUNIORS MR Robert F. . . . .

de Lyrot CTE Alain & CTSSE (Mary E Allen) B. . . . . of ☎ (011-33-1) 42-22-13-46 23 rue du Cherche Midi, 75006 Paris, France
MR Antoine. . . . .
☎ (011-33-2) 97-57-31-80 "Ile Renaud" Locmariaquer, 56740 Morbihan, France

de Lyrot MR & MRS Hervé J (Katy M Goffre) Nice'77.Paris'88 ☎ (011-33-1) 45-79-41-74 . . 4 rue Robert De Flers, 75015 Paris, France

de Maigret CTE Hervé & CTSSE (Pamela Painter) Cal'61.Csn.Paris'53 . . . . ☎ (310) 476-4550 427 N Bundy Dv, Los Angeles, CA 90049
MR Clarke—Cal'93 . . . .

de Mailly MISS Diane B—BMr'76 ☎ (310) 821-0920 . . 14000 Tahiti Way, Apt 312, Marina Del Rey, CA 90292

de Marcellus MR & MRS Robert (Mildred C Flournoy) AScott'50.GaTech'51 . . . . ☎ (561) 848-3833 280 Orange Grove Rd, Palm Beach, FL 33480
MISS Sarah T—Sth'88—at ☎ (202) 546-3632 616 E Capitol St NE, Washington, DC 20003 . .
MISS Mary L—at Princeton . . . .
MR Roland F—Pa'84.P'90—at ☎ (202) 546-3632 . . 616 E Capitol St NE, Washington, DC 20003 . . . .
MR R Cabell—Duke'90—at ☎ (011-33-1) 43-26-13-06 . . 17 rue Mongue, 75005 Paris, France . . . .
ENS Paul C—USN.Cr'94—at ☎ (904) 969-1393 4845 Peacock Dv, Pensacola, FL 32503 . . . .

Demarest MR Daniel A—K.Hl.H'48 ☎ (212) 988-6345 . . 510 E 85 St, New York, NY 10028

Demarest MISS Rosemary R—SL'34 ☎ (212) RE4-8493 . . 430 E 86 St, New York, NY 10028

Demarest MR & MRS William (Millar—Eluned A McLaren) V'44.Cas.P'40 ☎ (803) 524-0973 . . PO Box 2086, Beaufort, SC 29901

de Margitay MR & MRS Gedeon (Harris—Virginia V Martin) StJ.Cly.Ncd.Dh. ☎ (212) 722-3325 . . 65 E 96 St, New York, NY 10128

de Marneffe DR & MRS Francis (Hopkins—Barbara C Rowe) Va'52.Cy.Sm.Chi.Ncd.H.Lond'50 . . . . ☎ (617) 354-6300 126 Coolidge Hill, Cambridge, MA 02138-5522
MR Peter L—at ☎ (602) 922-1436 5877 N Granite Reef Rd, Scottsdale, AZ 85250 .

Demas DR & MRS Christopher P (Anne Eckardt) Skd'79.P'77 ☎ (520) 529-0770 . . 5732 E Territory Dv, Tucson, AZ 85715

de Matteo MR & MRS Ross A 2d (Alwilda J Ferris) Dar.Br'35 ☎ (941) 755-0878 . . "Wild Oak Bay" 6408 Wood Owl Circle, Bradenton, FL 34210

de Meaux VCTE & VCTSSE Marc (Katherine D M Tuck) Gen'82.Strasbourg'86 ☎ (011-33-1) 43-06-15-18 . . 13 bis rue Carrier Belleuse, 75015 Paris, France

de Mello MR & MRS Michael E S S (Deborah Fiuza) Rcn.Cl'79.Cl'81 ☎ (011-351-1) 467-2966 . . Avenida de Inglaterra 30, 2765 Estoril, Portugal

de Menil MRS Jean (Dominique Schlumberger) Sorb'25 . . of ☎ (713) 622-8724 . . 3363 San Felipe Rd, Houston, TX 77019 ☎ (212) 744-2649 . . 111 E 73 St, New York, NY 10021

de Menocal MR & MRS Daniel C (Grace W Niedringhaus) Nyc.Ds.Y'50 ☎ (914) 967-4394 . . 27 Grace Church St, Rye, NY 10580

de Menocal MR & MRS Daniel C JR (Linda K Simons) Kas'78.Ds.Rol'75.Ford'81 ☎ (914) 234-0084 . . Court Rd, Bedford, NY 10506

de Menocal MR & MRS George W (Sarah S Lyon) Nyc.Ds.Hartw'78 ☎ (203) 966-8117 . . 57 Laurel Rd, New Canaan, CT 06840

de Menocal DR Peter B—Ds.StLaw'82.RI'86.Cl'91
☎ (212) 580-2387 . . 53 W 87 St, Apt 1A, New York, NY *10024*
DeMent MR & MRS Ira (Ruth L Posey) AScott'55.An.Ala'53.Ala'58
☎ (334) 834-5300 . . 3437 Warrenton Rd, Montgomery, AL *36111*
Deméré MR & MRS John B (Patricia B Hogan) Ga'72
201 Merrie Way Lane, Houston, TX *77024*
Deméré MR & MRS Raymond S (Martha M Teasley) Ga'82.Cw. ⚓
☎ (334) 288-6030 . . 3343 Southview Av, Montgomery, AL *36111*
DeMicheli MR & MRS Robert J (Judith R MacLean)
LondDsgn'75.Ant'86.Sfy.SFrSt'74.CenMich'80
☎ (415) 668-9978 . . 747 Twelfth Av, San Francisco, CA *94118-3620*
DeMichelis MR & MRS David R (Margaret E Carey)
F&M'80.Cin'80.NCol'86
☎ (303) 399-0370 . . 1688 Newport St, Denver, CO *80220*
de Milhau MRS John W (Dorothea M Harrison)
☎ (203) 637-1314 . . 94 Silo Circle, Riverside, CT *06878*
Deming MR & MRS David V (Jamie B Tilghman) | ☎ (516) 922-7305
Ty'75.Csh.Ln.S.Hob'75 ⚓ . . . . | 84 Cove Rd,
JUNIORS MISS Julia B . . . . | Oyster Bay, NY
JUNIORS MR Peter H. . . . . | *11771-2417*
Deming MR & MRS Donald L (Meleanor Lazo) Pr.Y'47.Y'50 . . of
☎ (516) 759-2713 . . 36 Matinecock Farms Rd, Glen Cove, NY *11542*
☎ (941) 395-2935 . . 4210 Old Banyan Way, Sanibel, FL *33957*
de Montebello MR & MRS Guy-Philippe Lannes | ☎ (212) 289-4475
(Edith B Myles) Rdc'61.K.Myf.H'58 . . . . | 1150 Fifth Av,
MISS Laure—at 1036 Park Av, New York, NY | New York, NY
10028 . . . . | *10128*
MR Charles—at ☎ (212) 534-0008
1199 Park Av, New York, NY *10128*. . . . . |
de Montebello MR & MRS Henry Lannes (Beatrice de Vigneral) Hn.H'74
see Dilatory Domiciles
DeMott MR & MRS Richard W (Mary B Scarlett) | ☎ (215) 646-2635
Bnd'51.Rc.Fw.Myf.Hl.Ht.Pa'42 . . . . | "Fox Hollow"
MISS Phoebe Van W . . . . | 612 Norristown Rd,
MR Richard W JR—at ☎ (415) 738-9995 | PO Box 283,
985 Regina Way, Pacifica, CA *94044*. . . . . | Spring House, PA
MR Bayard M . . . . | *19477*
de Mouchy DUKE & DCHSS (Moseley—Luxembourg—Joan D Dillon)
Cly . . .of
☎ (212) 288-8687 . . 175 E 74 St, New York, NY *10021*
☎ (011-33-1) 42-22-52-27 . . 54 rue de Varenne, 75007 Paris, France
DeMoville MISS Margaret Jock (Carnathan—Margaret Jock DeMoville)
MissSt'70.Dar.Dcw.
☎ (601) 842-7913 . . 2309 Parkway Dv, Tupelo, MS *38801-1113*
Dempsey MR & MRS Bourne P (Louise A Pomeroy) | ☎ (216) 451-6060
Un.Tv.Y'52.H'55 . . . . | 12821 Lake Shore
MR Lawrence P . . . . | Blvd, Cleveland, OH
| *44108*
Dempsey DR & MRS Cedric W (Beverly June Luke) Albion'54.Albion'54
☎ (913) 339-1906 . . 6201 College Blvd, Overland Park, KS *66211*
Dempsey MR & MRS James H JR (Julia C Bolton) Kt.Un.Tv.Pk.Cv.Y'38 . . of
☎ (216) 423-3350 . . "Second Wind" 2659 River Rd, Chagrin Falls,
OH *44022*
"Roundhead" Harbour Island, Bahamas
Dempsey MRS John B (Jeannette Johnson) Un.It.
☎ (216) 721-1541 . . Judson Manor 1105, 1890 E 107 St, Cleveland,
OH *44106*

Dempsey MR & MRS John B 2d (Marie T Gravel) | ☎ (561) 231-5286
Un.Tv.H'47 . . . . | "Seagrove"
MR James H 3d—Ken'83 . . . . | 1820 Ocean Way,
| Vero Beach, FL
| *32963*
| Apr 14 . .
| ☎ (216) 541-1600
| 1 Bratenahl Place,
| Apt 1107, Bratenahl,
| Cleveland, OH
| *44108-1155*
Dempsey MR & MRS William L JR (Barbara L Rice) MtH'52.Va'49.Pa'52
☎ (203) 637-2555 . . "Wild Hedges" 22 Cove Rd, Old Greenwich,
CT *06870*
de Mun MQS Philippe M A
10 av Foch, 75116 Paris, France
de Narvaez MRS Felix (Gimbel—Denney—Fern Tailer)
☎ (561) 848-3010 . . 250 El Dorado Lane, Palm Beach, FL *33480*
Denault MAJ (RET) & MRS Herbert M (Parker—Mary | ☎ (301) 229-8960
N S Whiteley) USA.Cvc.Myf.Ncd.Geo'66 . . . . . | 5313 Falmouth Rd,
MR Peyton Bradford Parker—PaArt'82 . . . . . | Bethesda, MD
| *20816*
Denby MR & MRS D Reed (Sally T Nimick)
☎ (215) 862-2654 . . 44 Old Windy Bush Rd, New Hope, PA *18938*
Denby MRS Peter (Peggy A O'Hearn) Sth'54.Rr . . .of
☎ (412) 741-9697 . . 518 Irwin Dv, Sewickley, PA *15143*
☎ (941) 964-1393 . . 245 Waterways Av, PO Box 761, Boca Grande,
FL *33921*
Denckla MRS C Paul (Mary F Leiper)
☎ (617) 271-9001 . . 74 Essex Court, Bedford, MA *01730*
Denckla MR & MRS C Paul JR (Catherine C Ham) | ☎ (847) 234-1424
MooreArt'67.On.Pa'64.H'69 . . . . | 506 N Washington
MISS Sarah T—Wheat'92—at ☎ (773) 244-1605 | Rd, Lake Forest, IL
2348 N Clark St, Chicago, IL *60614* . . . . | *60045*
MISS Catherine T—at 8511 Interlake Av N,
Seattle, WA *98103* . . . .
MISS Joan B—at Bowdoin . . . .
MR Christian P 3d—Colby'96 . . . .
Denckla MRS Rodgers (Ordway—Katherine N Rodgers) Cly.Ncd.
☎ (516) 283-0518 . . Great Plains Rd, PO Box 1336, Southampton,
NY *11969*
Denebeim MR & MRS Keith Webster (Marie L O'Dea) Cal'82.Sfy.SFrSt'85
☎ (415) 388-7271 . . 413 Maple St, Mill Valley, CA *94941*
Denègre MR & MRS George (Gayle Stocker) Ncmb'49.Mt.Y'44.Tul'48
☎ (504) 899-1033 . . 1525 Webster St, New Orleans, LA *70118*
de Nemethy MR & MRS Bertalan (Loomis—Emily Myles) Myf.
☎ (941) 349-9410 . . 7263 Plover's Way, Sarasota, FL *34242*
de Neufville MR David T—Cr'62
☎ (908) 231-0844 . . Box 5342, North Branch, NJ *08876*
de Neufville MR Hugo R . . . . Died Aug 3'96
de Neufville MRS Hugo R (Margaret W Thomas)
☎ (201) 543-4833 . . Box 326, Mendham, NJ *07945*
de Neufville MR John P (Suzanne Bayon) | ☎ (201) 543-7001
Y'61.H'70 . . . . | Indian Hollow Rd,
MR Peter B—Tul'91 . . . . | RD 1, Mendham, NJ
MR Thomas P—StAndr'95 . . . . | *07945*
JUNIORS MR John H . . . . |

de Neufville MR & MRS Lawrence E (Brown—Esther Bonter) Ht.Dar.Hn.Ox'34
☎ (860) 521-7549 . . 16 Hunter Dv, West Hartford, CT *06107-1014*
de Neufville MR & MRS Richard (Virginia D Lyons) MaryMt'70.Sim'90.Mit'60.Mit'65 . . of
☎ (617) 491-2921 . . 10 Acacia St, Cambridge, MA *02138*
☎ (508) 636-7266 . . 1101 Horseneck Rd, Westport, MA *02790*
de Neufville MR Robert E—Hn.H'92
☎ (510) 841-4058 . . 2821 Hillegass Av, Apt 8, Berkeley, CA *94705*

Denham MR & MRS Willard A S (Cynthia Fulenwider) Wil.Cw.Cda.Va'53 . . . . MISS Susanna S	☎ (302) 658-9026 3216 Swarthmore Rd, Wilmington, DE *19807*
Denham MR & MRS William B JR (Marvel—Margaret S Springer) Y'51 . . . . MISS Margaret S . . . . MR James M D Marvel	☎ (302) 654-8615 2305 Ridgeway Rd, Wilmington, DE *19805*

Deniau MR & MRS François X (Alexandra P Molden) Paris'81.EcolePoly'76.EcoleNat'81
"La Tardivière" Escrignelles, 45250 Briare, France
Denicke MRS Ernest W (Edith Louise Gunn)
☎ (415) 456-6144 . . 30 El Camino Bueno, PO Box 916, Ross, CA *94957*
Denison MISS Hope Lindsay (g—MRS Linda P Denison) . . . . Born at Boston, MA Sep 14'95
Denison MRS Julie H (Piper—Julie C Hoffer) SUNY'72.NELaw'77.Dar.
☎ (518) 432-9616 . . 188 Lancaster St, Albany, NY *12210*
Denison MRS Linda P (Linda Petrasch)
☎ (914) 666-3783 . . 9 Letitia Lane, Mt Kisco, NY *10549*

Denk MR & MRS Gregory P (Ann Kitchell) WmWds'74.KasSt'71 . . . . MISS Kari . . . . JUNIORS MR Clayton P	☎ (602) 970-5515 4 Casa Blanca Estates, Paradise Valley, AZ *85253*
Denkinger REV & MRS M Esty (Mary E Lockman) MtH'56.P.'56 . . . . MISS Mary F—P'79—at Mountain View, CA . . . MR Thomas L—Vt'86—at Blue Ridge School, Dyke, VA *22935* . . . . MR Eric Michael	☎ (704) 782-2023 3720 Winterberry Court, Concord, NC *28027*
Dennehy MR & MRS Charles (Daphne Bedford) On. . MISS Daphne L	☎ (847) 234-6662 51 Alden Lane, Lake Forest, IL *60045*

Dennehy MISS (DR) Virginia—Creigh'70.InstPsych'87.On.
☎ (415) 326-6115 . . 539 Lincoln Av, Palo Alto, CA *94301*
Dennett MRS Roger H (Barbara A Brown)
☎ (904) 284-5473 . . 222 Bay St, Green Cove Springs, FL *32043*
Dennis MRS Anne P (Anne T Pyle) Au.
☎ (518) 576-2212 . . "Pegasus" Airport Rd, Keene Valley, NY *12943-9707*

Dennis DR & MRS (DR) Daniel A 3d (Roxanna Stewart) TroySt'75.SAla'76 . . . . JUNIORS MR Daniel A 4th . . . . JUNIORS MR Joseph S	☎ (334) 343-1210 4105 Ridgelawn Dv, Mobile, AL *36608*

Dennis MR & MRS Landt (Elizabeth M Jones) Hn.H'59.Pa'63
☎ (505) 986-1106 . . "Tumbleweed" Leaping Powder Rd, Rte 9, Box 73LD, Santa Fe, NM *87505*

Dennis DR & MRS Michael T B (Phyllis D Harrison) BtP.Cda.H'64 . . . . MISS Melinda D—at 95 Orchard St, Apt 2, Somerville, MA *02144* . . . . MR Michael T B JR . . . . MR Phillip S—at 1920 Eleventh Av, Greeley, CO *80631*	of ☎ (805)969-6169 2030 E Valley Rd, Santa Barbara, CA *93108* ☎ (561) 842-9737 "Coconut Cottage" 1231 N Lake Way, Palm Beach, FL *33480*

Dennis MRS Richmond B (Barbara A Deasy)
☎ (818) 796-5550 . . 535 S Orange Grove Blvd, 8, Pasadena, CA *91105*

Dennis MR & MRS Robert W (Lucette Buell) Myf.Alb'52 . . . . MISS Jennifer V—at 136 E 55 St, New York, NY *10022* . . . . MR R Winslow JR—Hamp'87—at 136 E 55 St, New York, NY *10022*	☎ (904) 264-8210 Majorca 9, 2223 Astor St, Orange Park, FL *32073*

Dennis MR & MRS Samuel S 3d (Lillian E Williamson) Ws'34.Cy.H.'32 ⚓ . . of
☎ (617) 934-5505 . . 175 Washington St, Box 2565, Duxbury, MA *02331*
☎ (305) 367-2382 . . Key Largo Anglers Club, C42, 50 Clubhouse Rd, North Key Largo, FL *33037*
Dennis MR & MRS Thomas G (Makrianes—Diane J Milam) B'gton'47.Cl'55 . . of
☎ (212) 744-0498 . . 47 E 64 St, Apt 10A, New York, NY *10021*
☎ (904) 285-4098 . . "Barn on the Beach" 501 Ponte Vedra Blvd, Ponte Vedra Beach, FL *32082*
Dennis-Browne MR John F—Pr.Ox'61 ⚓
☎ (516) 671-6272 . . 115 Duck Pond Rd, Glen Cove, NY *11542*
Dennison DR & MRS (DR) Allen M (Jane Mackenzie) Br'76.Cl'80.H'75.Cl'80
☎ (401) 274-5353 . . 315 Angell St, Providence, RI *02906*
Dennison MR & MRS Charles E P (Wharton—Jane D Russell) Plg.Csn.P'39.H'49.Cl'53
☎ (609) 924-7122 . . 11 Haslet Av, Princeton, NJ *08540*
Dennison MR & MRS E Allen (Frances I Ferry) Nu'66.StJ.Cs.H'37.Y'40 ⚓
☎ (718) 543-5018 . . 715 W 246 St, Bronx, NY *10471-3501*
Denniston MRS George C (Martha M Averett) . . . . Died at Philadelphia, PA Mch 16'96
Denniston DR & MRS George C JR (Willing—Martha C Kent) BMr'41.Wash'65.Ncd.Hn.P'55.Pa'59.H'61
☎ (206) 367-8473 . . 13030 Twelfth Av NW, Seattle, WA *98177*
Denny MR & MRS Charles S (Ann M Hodges) Cos.H'34
☎ (603) 526-9263 . . 104 Hilltop Place, 50 Newport Rd, New London, NH *03257*

Denny MR & MRS John H (Margaret A McGuinness) RISD'58.Au.Mid'55 . . . . MR John H JR—Mid'85—at ☎ (212) 988-7426 488 E 74 St, Apt 7B, New York, NY *10021* . . .	☎ (609) 924-0571 "Goose Cove" 721 Prospect Av Ext, Princeton, NJ *08540*

Denny MR & MRS R Breck (Ninna T Fisher) Kt.Ln.Pr.Cly.Van'70 . . . . | of ☎ (216)397-0607 19616 Shelburne Rd, Shaker Heights, OH *44118*

MISS Elizabeth W . . . .

JUNIORS MISS Mary C . . . .

☎ (860) 927-3776 3 Cobble Heights Rd, Kent, CT *06757*

Denny MR & MRS Robert O (Kiser—Margot T Potter)
☎ (520) 886-9918 . . 6412 E Santa Elena, Tucson, AZ *85715*

DeNormandie MASTER Joseph Cornelius Rathborne (Philip Y) . . Born at Boston, MA Jun 27'94

DeNormandie MR & MRS Philip Y (Ernestine N Rathborne) H'73.Ri.Cly.H'71
☎ (617) 491-3351 . . 18 Craigie St, Cambridge, MA *02138*

de Noüe MR & MRS Jehan-Sébastien (Leslie L Castle) Pitzer'79.Ford'78
☎ (203) 431-9017 . . 45 Bayberry Hill Rd, Ridgefield, CT *06877*

Dent MR & MRS Daniel F (Mary F Decker) Md.P'63.Pa'68 . . . . | ☎ (410) 323-6532 16 Blythewood Rd, Baltimore, MD *21210*

MISS Melissa D—at Rollins . . . .

MR Michael A—Rm'94—at Vail, CO . . . .

MR Matthew F—at Brown . . . .

Dent MISS Deborah du V
☎ (603) 726-4362 . . PO Box 280, Campton, NH *03223*

Dent MR & MRS Frederick B (Mildred C Harrison) Yn.Y'44
☎ (864) 585-4992 . . 221 Montgomery Dv, Spartanburg, SC *29302*

Dent MR Harry M JR (Gloria J Gress) Buff'46.G.
☎ (561) 278-3247 . . 2150 S Ocean Blvd, Delray Beach, FL *33483*

Dent MR & MRS John Elliott (Sandra Slaughter) Fla'69.Ct.Cvc.GaTech'67.GeoW'75 . . . . | of ☎ (703)821-6993 1655 Hunting Ridge Court, McLean, VA *22101*

MISS Sarah-Rutledge S—at U of NCar Chapel Hill . . . .

JUNIORS MR Elliott Johnstone 3d—at Hampden-Sydney . . . .

☎ (803) 527-1490 Mt Hope Plantation, Rte 2, Georgetown, SC *29440*

Dent MRS Magruder JR (Rosemary Romeyn) Pa'43
☎ (804) 973-6026 . . Polaris Farm, Rte 5, Box 278, Hydraulic Rd, Charlottesville, VA *22901*

Dent MRS Maida W (Mitchell—Maida W Dent) Nat'lCollEd'87
238 Westside Dv, Iowa City, IA *53246-4342*

Dent MR Richard H . . . . Died at Greenwich, CT Aug 9'96

Dent MRS Richard H (Julie M Burk) Cw . . . . | ☎ (203) 966-5212 807 Smith Ridge Rd, New Canaan, CT *06840*

MISS Victorine du P—Bnd'81—at
☎ (212) 645-2490 . . 463 W 21 St, New York, NY *10011* . . . .

Dent MISS Susanna L . . see D P Ross JR

Dent MR & MRS Thomas A 3d (Geraldine K Tyner) Lm.Cr'44
41 Maple Av, Apt 2B, Hastings-on-Hudson, NY *10706*

Denton MR David S—BtP.
213 Sunset Rd, West Palm Beach, FL *33401*

Denton MR E Castner 3d—BowlG'92 . . see B A Craig

Denton MISS Elizabeth C—SL'90.Cin'94 . . see B A Craig

Denton MRS Sherwood E (Marjorie D Clifford) Mich'58
☎ (602) 840-1574 . . 5306 E Wonderview Rd, Phoenix, AZ *85018*

Denton MR & MRS Stuart P (Sylvia Klesse)
☎ (561) 287-1203 . . 6954 SW Wisteria Terr, Palm City, FL *34990*

Denton MRS Willard K (Faith D de Baubigny)
☎ (203) 266-4233 . . Woodbury Hill 18, Woodbury, CT *06798*

de Pedroso MR & MRS José L (Reece—Charlotte Worthen) Gm.Me.Fst.San.Ac.Myf.Cda.Pa'39
☎ (610) 527-4325 . . 447 Colebrook Lane, Bryn Mawr, PA *19010-2903*

de Peyster MR & MRS F Ashton 3d (Margo M Donahue) BtP.Va'67.Stan'71
☎ (561) 835-8126 . . 306 Worth Av, Palm Beach, FL *33480*

de Peyster MR & MRS F van Cortlandt (Karen D Kermode) Sfy.Miami'68
☎ (702) 747-4737 . . 4053 Waterhole, Caughlin Ranch, Washoe Co, NV *89509*

de Peyster MRS George L (Luckenbach—Maria W Wolkonsky)
☎ (805) 969-2918 . . 1506 Mimosa Lane, Santa Barbara, CA *93108*

de Peyster MR & MRS George L JR (Electra B Ducommun)
☎ (707) 544-1616 . . ''Redwood Hill'' 2000 Mark West Springs Rd, Santa Rosa, CA *95404*

de Peyster MR & MRS James A (Dorothy S Siems) BtP.Cw.Cda.
☎ (561) 655-8753 . . 227 Brazilian Av, Palm Beach, FL *33480*

de Peyster MR James A JR—Plg.P'61.Geo'66 . . . . . | ☎ (914) 478-0955 357 Warburton Av, Hastings-on-Hudson, NY *10706*

MR James A 3d—P'85—at 1940 Delaware St, Berkeley, CA *94709* . . . .

de Peyster MR Nicholas L M (James A JR) . . . . Married at Rye, NY Hicks MISS Julia R (Paul De F JR) . . . . May 25'96

de Peyster MR & MRS Nicholas L M (Julia R Hicks) P'86.P'88.Nu'95
☎ (212) 832-8802 . . 36 Sutton Place S, Apt 4E, New York, NY *10022*

de Peyster MISS Suzanne—West'69
☎ (802) 375-6005 . . ''Peyman Farm'' Sandgate, VT *05250*

DePree MR & MRS Julian F JR (Joan K Pillsbury) On.Ty'66 . . . . | ☎ (847) 234-4278 999 S Ringwood Rd, Lake Forest, IL *60045*

MISS Priscilla R . . . .

MR Edmund A . . . .

d'Eprémesnil MR & MRS Jacques (Susan Mayes) GeoW'55.W&L'53
☎ (301) 948-5198 . . ''Old Mill Farm'' 14000 Turkey Foot Rd, North Potomac, MD *20878*

d'Eprémesnil MISS Nadine Marie (Hesse—Nadine Marie d'Eprémesnil) Duke'88.NCar'93
☎ (910) 722-6080 . . 925 Oaklawn Av, Winston-Salem, NC *27104*

Derby MR & MRS John M (Leslie Van der Leur) Drew'74.Tex'73.AmInt'l'75
☎ (908) 842-5817 . . 19 Lafayette St, Rumson, NJ *07760*

Derby MISS Kayla Eliana (g—MRS Nicholas G K Boyd JR) . . . . Born Sep 21'93

Derby MRS Roger A JR (Nash—Corbett—Marie K Baird) Dc.Cda.Hn . . .of
☎ (561) 231-5524 . . 937 Sandpiper Lane, Vero Beach, FL *32963*
☎ (540) 349-2420 . . ''Derbyshire'' PO Box 3070, Warrenton, VA *20188*

de Rham MRS Anne McK (Farquhar—Anne McKnight)
☎ (603) 823-7152 . . ''White Wings'' PO Box 185, Franconia, NH *03580*

de Rham MR & MRS Casimir JR (Elizabeth M Evarts) Sb.Cy.H'46.H'49
☎ (617) 354-7415 . . 47 Lake View Av, Cambridge, MA *02138*

de Rham MR & MRS Charles (Shober—Chandlee—Ellen F Smith) Ac.Hn.H'51 . . . . | of ☎ (610)527-2004 1527 Montgomery Av, Rosemont, PA *19010-1659*
  MR Edward W Shober 3d . . . . | ☎ (603) 823-5267 "Mittersill" Box 958, Franconia, NH *03580*

de Rham MRS David P (Rachael K Thompson) Sth'54.Hn. . . . . | ☎ (860) 677-2292 31 Pinnacle Ridge Rd, Farmington, CT *06032*
  MR John M M—Colby'88 . . . . |

de Rham MISS Elizabeth M—Tufts'82
  ☎ (617) 576-2472 . . 25 Granville Rd, Cambridge, MA *02138*

de Rham MR J Christopher—McG'81
  ☎ (212) 534-1321 . . 345 E 93 St, Apt 20G, New York, NY *10128*

de Rham MR & MRS Jeremiah E (Amy Wang) P'79.Sb.Pa'78
  67 W Clay St, San Francisco, CA *94121*

de Rham MRS Richard D (Lee S McCabe) V'32 . . . | ☎ (914) 424-3160 "Watergrass Hill" Garrison, NY *10524*
  MR Pierre R . . . . |

de Rham MRS William (Foristall—Vera K Chapin) Srb.
  ☎ (212) 472-0198 . . 970 Park Av, Apt 11 South, New York, NY *10028-0324*

de Rham MR & MRS William (Glenna L Maduro) R.P'56 | ☎ (561) 278-4962 "Fox Haven" 134 Seabreeze Av, Delray Beach, FL *33483*
  MISS Lee L . . . . |
  MR Stephen L—at 1017 W Nickerson St, Seattle, WA *98119* . . . . |

de Rham MR & MRS William JR (Eugenie M B Potter) Geo'79
  ☎ (215) 546-2931 . . 1608 Addison St, Philadelphia, PA *19146*

de Ropp MR & MRS Harald S (Constance D Staudt) Chi.Cly.Yn.Del'59.Pa'61 | ☎ (508) 428-6358 Box 2025, Oyster Harbors, Osterville, MA *02655*
  MISS Eleanor D—BostColl'92.Cly.Y.—at
  ☎ (212) 861-5138 . . 215 E 66 St, New York, NY *10021* . . . . |
  MR Harald S JR—Bost'90 . . . . |

de Ropp MRS Zoé Van W (Weinman—Zoé Van W de Ropp) Cly.Cda. . . . . | ☎ (516) 653-5198 "Pine Neck" Josiah Foster's Path, East Quogue, NY *11942*
  MR Michael L de R Weinman—Adelphi'90 . . |

DeRosa MASTER Brian Gorman (Thomas J) . . . . Born at Baltimore, MD Jly 3'94

DeRosa MR & MRS Thomas J (Leslie R Gorman) Geo'82.Md.Geo'80.Cl'88
  ☎ (410) 467-7283 . . 7 Whitfield Rd, Baltimore, MD *21210*

de Roulet MRS Vincent (Lorinda Payson) Cly.Ny.Ln. ⚓ | ☎ (516) 627-4488 Powerhouse Rd, Manhasset, NY *11030*
  MISS Sandra—at ☎ (914) 677-3326 Oak Summit Rd, Millbrook, NY *12545* . . . . |

Derr JUNIORS MR Andrew L . . see MRS A W Clement

Derr MISS Helen D H . . see MRS A H Weir

Derrickson MR Edward M—Ithaca'80 . . see MRS M C Mellon

Derringer MR & MRS George W (Pamela M Hall) Pa'68.Nyack'70.BethSem'74
  ☎ (617) 631-5386 . . 107 W Shore Dv, Marblehead, MA *01945*

de Russow MRS Helmuth B (Audrey Thrasher)
  ☎ (516) 941-4145 . . 177 Old Field Rd, Box 2123, Setauket, NY *11733*

de Saint Phalle MRS Elene C (Isles—Elene Canrobert) Ri.T. . . . . | ☎ (212) 744-6969 765 Park Av, New York, NY *10021*
  MISS Diane . . . . |
  MR Marc—Duke'88 . . . . |

de Saint Phalle MR Jacques—Wis'83
  ☎ (212) 627-9204 . . 108 Fifth Av, Apt 4C, New York, NY *10011*

de St Phalle MR & MRS Pierre (M Virginia Wall) Pc.Ac.Y'40
  ☎ (215) 233-2628 . . 514 Cresheim Valley Rd, Wyndmoor, PA *19038*

de Saint Phalle MR & MRS Thibaut (Smith—Mariana V Mann) Mt.Sl.H'39.Cl'41 . .
  ☎ (202) 332-8898 . . 2231 Bancroft Place NW, Washington, DC *20008*
  ☎ (941) 643-4337 . . 280 Fourth Av N, Naples, FL *34102*

de Sambucy BRN François-Xavier & de France | 4 rue Denis Poisson, 75017 Paris, France
  HRH PRCSS Chantal . . . . |
  JUNIORS BRNSS Kildine . . . . |
  JUNIORS BRN Axel . . . . |
  JUNIORS BRN Alexandre . . . . |

de Sanctis MR & MRS Francesco M (Lydia E Andrade) Cly. . . . . | ☎ (011-39-6) 85351221 via Panama 26, 00198 Rome, Italy
  MISS Felicia M—Geo'90.Cly.—at 1 E 66 St, New York, NY *10021* . . . . |
  MR Pier F—Vt'95 . . . . |

de San Damián MQS Carlos Figueroa & MQSE (DeWilde—Harrison—Ross—Barbara Crass) Madrid'55 . .
  ☎ (561) 840-1494 . . 225 Tradewind Dv, Palm Beach, FL *33480*
  ☎ (011-34-15) 76-39-89 . . Nuñez de Balboa 79, 28006 Madrid, Spain
  ☎ (011-34-49) 26-01-50 . . Finca Miralcampo, Azuqueca de Henares, Guadalajara, Spain

De Santo MISS Denise . . see MRS J W Harris

de Schauensee MISS Maude T—Ws'58.Ac.
  ☎ (610) 687-2165 . . 101 S Devon Av, Devon, PA *19333*

Deshler MRS C Franklin (Nancy E Montgomery) Dar . . .of
  ☎ (904) 441-7372 . . "Pelican Watch" 1903 John Anderson Dv, Ormond Beach, FL *32176*
  ☎ (508) 283-4609 . . 14 Nashua Av, Gloucester, MA *01930*

de Sibour CTSSE (Newhouse—Graham—Markowski—Patricia Shewan) Cly.BtP.
  ☎ (561) 659-5942 . . 330 Cocoanut Row, Palm Beach, FL *33480*

de Sibour MRS Jacqueline (Burrows—Bean—Imbert—Jacqueline de Sibour) Cly. . . . . | ☎ (212) 838-0800 825 Fifth Av, Apt 10A, New York, NY *10021*
  MISS Michèle Bean . . . . |
  MR Marc Imbert . . . . |
  MR Christophe Imbert . . . . |

de Sibour MR Raoul L—Duke'82
  ☎ (561) 833-1829 . . 2800 N Flagler Dv, West Palm Beach, FL *33407*

de Sibour MISS Stephanie S (Stinchcomb—Stephanie S de Sibour) Geo'67
  see Dilatory Domiciles

De Silver MR & MRS Harrison (Collette Flynn) TrMonti'47.Y.'37.Cl'53 . . . . | ☎ (914) 591-5780 River House 3, Irvington-on-Hudson, NY *10533*
  MISS Margaret . . . . |
  MISS Serena . . . . |
  MR Albert—at Boulder, CO . . . . |

Desloge MR & MRS George B (Mary R O'Brien)   ☎ (314) HE2-4895
NotreD'47 . . . . 119 Frontenac
MISS Julie K . . . . Forest, St Louis,
MR Michael L—at ☎ (919) 876-1485   MO *63131*
5034B New Hope Rd, Raleigh, NC *27604* . . . . .
MR Edward O'B . . . .
MR Thomas B—at ☎ (615) 646-1729
210 Wynbrook Court, Nashville, TN *37221* . . . .
MR Patrick G—at ☎ (314) 567-3246
1151 Olive Lake Dv, Apt F, St Louis, MO *63132*

Desloge MR & MRS Joseph JR (Martha A Seredynski)   ☎ (314) 837-3269
MISS Martha M—at ☎ (314) 862-0301   2711 Shackelford
7029 Tulane Av, St Louis, MO *63130* . . . . Rd, Florissant, MO
MISS Cynthian McI—*see Dilatory Domiciles* . . .   *63031*
MR Joseph G—at ☎ (617) 491-1084
238 Columbia St, Cambridge, MA *02139* . . . . . .
JUNIORS MR Frank S . . . .

Desloge MR & MRS Stephen F (Ann H Drescher) StLaw'82.Cy.Mo'78
☎ (314) 993-6119 . . 29 Black Creek Lane, Ladue, MO *63124*

Desmond MR Christopher T . . see J P Miller JR

Desmond MISS Leslie F . . see J P Miller JR

Despard MR & MRS Clement L (Burchard—Lucy B Edwards) H'52 . . of
☎ (212) 369-2677 . . 1150 Fifth Av, New York, NY *10128*
☎ (860) 535-1410 . . 3 Main St, Stonington, CT *06378*

Despard MR Douglas C JR
☎ (408) 624-2080 . . 8545 Carmel Valley Rd, Carmel, CA *93923*

Despard MRS Severin (Marion Severin)
☎ (408) 761-9046 . . 88 Bright View Lane, Watsonville, CA *95076*

de Spoelberch MR & MRS Eric (Katharine K Stewart) Ac.Me.
☎ (610) 642-9372 . . The Quadrangle 2322, 3300 Darby Rd, Haverford,
PA *19041*

de Spoelberch MR & MRS Jacques A (M Elaine   ☎ (203) 852-1396
Gaskell) Cyb.P'58 . . . . 9 Shagbark Rd,
MR Christopher W—at Boston Coll . . . . Wilson Point,
JUNIORS MR Nicholas J . . . . South Norwalk, CT
JUNIORS MR Gregory S *06854*

Dest MR & MRS Leonard R (Beverly J Teel) JHop'72.Va'74.Leh'71.Leh'73
☎ (310) 553-9150 . . 1709 Club View Dv, Los Angeles, CA *90024*

de Surian MQSE (Mildred A Cowgill) Bur.
☎ (540) 775-0671 . . 5451 White Fox Lane, King George, VA *22485*

de Szinay MRS Andrew B (Barnes—Longaker—   ☎ (540) 832-3103
Isabel Farrar) . . . . ''Glen Oaks''
MISS Bettina Longaker . . . . 8258 Open Gate Rd,
                                     Gordonsville, VA
                                     22942

Detchon MRS Elliott R (Coleman—Patricia Disston) Gm.Me.Ac.Ncd.
☎ (610) 525-4408 . . 1054 Rock Creek Rd, Bryn Mawr, PA *19010*

Detchon MRS Susan L M (Susan L McGlothlin)   ☎ (203) 622-6689
Briar'68 . . . . 100 Cat Rock Rd,
MR Elliott B . . . . Cos Cob, CT *06807*
JUNIORS MR Christopher H . . . .
JUNIORS MR Peter T . . . .

Detert MRS Gunther R (Marie-Louise Whittell) . . of
☎ (415) 492-2488 . . 100 Thorndale Dv, Apt 103, San Rafael, CA *94903*
☎ (707) 944-2306 . . 1500 Walnut Dv, Oakville, CA *94562*

Dethlefs MR & MRS David G (Huidekoper—Elizabeth L Emerick)
Swb'43.D.H'46
☎ (617) 326-7273 . . 14 Franklin Square, Dedham, MA *02026*

Detmer MR & MRS Martin J (Jan-Ann L Turner)
Cda.Dar.Ofp.Wms'50.Ch'55
☎ (630) 469-4772 . . 578 Park Blvd, Glen Ellyn, IL *60137*

Detmer MR & MRS Martin J JR (Julia Evans) StMarys'81.NotreD'81.Loy'82
☎ (507) 289-0210 . . 908 Kaito Lane SW, Rochester, MN *55902*

de Tristan CTE Marc & CTSSE (Byington—Langdon—June Lee)
Pcu.Bur.Sorb'31
The Towers, 40 W Third Av, San Mateo, CA *94402* . . MR absent

Detweiler MR & MRS John C (Carole C Singer)   ☎ (011-966-2)
Pitt'66.Pc.Pn.P'65.Pitt'68 651-6000
MR John C JR—in Singapore . . . . PO Box 5335,
                                     21422 Jeddah,
                                     Saudi Arabia

Detweiler MRS Lynn L (Irene B McCune) Pc. . . . . . Cathedral Village,
MISS Anne L—at 28 Kittredge St, Boston, MA   129 Bishop White
02131 . . . . Lodge, 600 E
                                     Cathedral Rd,
                                     Philadelphia, PA
                                     19128

Deuel MISS Maggie D . . see V DeP Burroughs

Deuel JUNIORS MISS Sarah G . . see V DeP Burroughs

Deuel MISS Virginia—CtCol'37.G.
☎ (716) 652-0767 . . 234 Falls Rd, West Falls, NY *14170*

Deupree MRS Richard R JR (Hilda A Taylor) Qc . . .of
☎ (513) 651-5559 . . 550 E 4 St, Cincinnati, OH *45202*
☎ (602) 948-2520 . . 7850 San Carlos Rd, Scottsdale, AZ *85258*

Devaney MR & MRS John G (Sandra A MacDonald)   ☎ (617) 876-4046
Marl'69 . . . . 421 Broadway,
MISS Clover L . . . . Cambridge, MA
JUNIORS MISS Laurel MacD *02138*

Devaney MR & MRS Richard T (Mary G Crowell)   of ☎ (610)644-1611
⚓ . . . . 162 Kentsdale
MISS Susan P—Pa'94—at ☎ (212) 752-9742   Court, Malvern, PA
404 E 63 St, Apt 12, New York, NY *10021* *19355-2671*
MR Craig W—Buck'91—at ☎ (404) 816-7552   ☎ (561) 286-5057
215 Alberta Dv NE, Atlanta, GA *30305* . . . . Yacht & Country
                                     Club, 3302 SE
                                     Fairway W, Stuart,
                                     FL *34997*

de Vargas Machuca DUCA Diego . . . .   ☎ (011-39-2)
MISS Diana M 498-6017
MR Tomas A . . . . Piazza Amendola 3,
                                     20149 Milan, Italy

de Vargas Machuca MRS Stevens G (Stevens Greeff)
☎ (603) 563-7056 . . Pierce Rd, Dublin, NH *03444*

De Vault MR & MRS Walter D 3d (Catherine M Pickering) SFla'74.Hav'78
☎ (561) 655-2875 . . ''Villa Giardina'' 341 Peruvian Av, Palm Beach,
FL *33480*
MR at . . ☎ (813) 632-0862 . . 15350 Sherwood Forest Dv, Tampa,
FL *33647*

De Vecchi MR & MRS Robert P (Duke—Douglass—Wainwright—
Betsy S Trippe) C.Mt.Plg.Mds.StJ.Y.'52.H'56 . . of
☎ (212) 838-8285 . . 125 E 63 St, New York, NY *10021*
☎ (516) 324-0185 . . 12 W Dune Lane, PO Box 1398, East Hampton,
NY *11937*
de Vegh MR Pierre J—K.Eyc.H.'58
☎ (212) 249-9636 . . 8 E 83 St, New York, NY *10028*
Devens MRS A Lithgow (Leanice Martin)
☎ (617) 581-0617 . . 11 Valley Rd, Nahant, MA *01908*
Devens MR & MRS Charles (Edith P Wolcott) Cy.Sm.Ub.Ncd.H'32
☎ (617) 333-0603 . . 1702 Canton Av, Milton, MA *02186*

Devens MR Charles JR—Ub.Ec.H'59.H'64 . . . . MR Charles 3d—Vt'93—at ☎ (617) 738-9233 1284 Beacon St, Brookline, MA *02146* . . . . JUNIORS MR Samuel W—at Middlesex	☎ (508) 768-7514 89 Southern Av, Essex, MA *01929*

Devens MR & MRS Richard M JR (Rita C Sheehan)
BostColl'76.AmU'76.AmU'79.Cl'80
☎ (301) 585-8940 . . 9106 Bradford Rd, Silver Spring, MD *20901*

Devens MR & MRS Robert S (Eleanor W Covington) Rc.T.Sm.H'65 . . . . MR William L—David'92—at ☎ (617) 738-8433 37 Dwight St, Brookline, MA *02146* . . . . . MR Robert S JR—Stan'94—at ☎ (212) 662-8189 750 Columbus Av, Apt 10F, New York, NY *10025*	of ☎ (212)369-4220 1165 Fifth Av, New York, NY *10029* ☎ (914) 351-5585 Clubhouse Rd, Tuxedo Park, NY *10987*

Devereux MR Antelo—Gm.Ph.Rb.Ssk.H'36
☎ (610) 356-5001 . . Dunwoody Village CH128,
3500 West Chester Pike, Newtown Square, PA *19073*

Devereux MR & MRS Antelo JR (Copsey—Margaret S Bockius) H'65.Pa'71 . . . . JUNIORS MISS Georgeanna S	☎ (610) 869-3009 Friendfield Farm, 443 E London Grove Rd, West Grove, PA *19390*

Devereux MR & MRS John C (Winifred B Wheeler) Ssk.Bost'73 . . . . JUNIORS MISS Laura W	☎ (610) 293-0256 569 County Line Rd, Radnor, PA *19087*

Devereux MRS Lelia W (Lelia A Wagner) Snc. . . . . MISS Ramsey W—at Prescott	☎ (757) 422-9729 3946 Ocean Hills Court, Virginia Beach, VA *23451*

de Vienne CTE Arnaud G & CTSSE (Ariane V von Kleist) . . of
☎ (011-33-1) 45-63-62-40 . . 1 av Friedland, 75008 Paris, France
☎ (011-33) 37-96-74-15 . . "Osmoy" 27000 Dangeau, France
☎ (212) 794-0225 . . 150 E 73 St, New York, NY *10021*
Devine MRS C Robert (Lichine—Gisèle Edenbourgh) Ri.Plg.
☎ (212) 308-4152 . . 200 E 66 St, New York, NY *10021*
Devine MR & MRS Henry C (Alessandra A Hillman)
Swth'75.Cl'81.Un.Pa'73.Cl'79
☎ (212) 627-9249 . . 470 W 24 St, New York, NY *10011*
Devine MR & MRS Joseph E (Nina W Cave) BMr'50.Unn.Csn.
☎ (203) 762-3650 . . 145 Millstone Rd, Wilton, CT *06897*
Devine MR & MRS Kevin J (Cynthia W Coe) PineM'76.Stan'70 ⚓
☎ (916) 243-5012 . . 795 Lakeview Dv, Redding, CA *96001*

Devine MR & MRS Robert W JR (Mary K Boland) V'49.Un.Cly.Mit'47
☎ (212) 319-8897 . . 200 E 66 St, Apt A1907, New York, NY *10021*
Devine MR & MRS Rodney W (Eugenie Hoffmeyer)
Gchr'77.Cl'83.Unn.Plg.Ht.Dh.DU'71
☎ (860) 767-3462 . . 10 Little Point St, PO Box 536, Essex, CT *06426*
Devine MRS Williams (Louise C Williams)
☎ (561) 278-1089 . . 1153 Lowry St, Delray Beach, FL *33483*
Devitt MRS James E (Emmet—Judith B Morrell) . . of
☎ (941) 778-2176 . . 5400 Gulf Dv, PO Box 1874, Holmes Beach,
FL *34218*
☎ (011-33-1) 40-50-19-27 . . 1 rue des Bauches, 75016 Paris, France

Devlin MR & MRS Raymond J JR (Frances M Butler) Barat'63.Gv.Mv.Y'59.Conn'62 . . . . MISS Dorothy M . . . . MISS Celia M . . . . MISS Catherine B . . . . MR Raymond J 3d	☎ (860) 567-0690 Echo Farm, Rte 3, 43 E Litchfield Rd, Litchfield, CT *06759*

Devlin MR Robert T—Pcu.Bur.Cal'61 . . . . MISS Jane V . . . . MR Patrick A	☎ (415) 563-0393 3331 Jackson St, San Francisco, CA *94118*

De Voe MRS Natalie S (Natalie E Smissaert) Rdc'59.Ne. . . . . MR Lawrence H—Mid'89 . . . . MR Malcolm M	of ☎ (212)535-5763 170 E 77 St, New York, NY *10021* ☎ (203) 966-1773 "The Barn" 444 Oenoke Ridge Rd, New Canaan, CT *06840*

de Vries MR & MRS Peter J M (Adèle L Hallowell) Cly.Ariz'65 . . . . MISSES Priscilla A M & Caroline A—at ☎ (860) 535-3059 . . 1 Main St, PO Box 92, Stonington, CT *06378*	☎ (207) 348-9933 392 Reach Rd, PO Box 655, Deer Isle, ME *04627-0655*

Dew MR T Roderick—Ds.Y'63
1124 N Hancock Av, Colorado Springs, CO *80903*

de Wangen MRS Lorna Hyde (de Wangen—Hefner —Lorna Hyde) Ri. MISS Stephanie A—at Trinity	☎ (212) 734-4340 40 E 66 St, New York, NY *10021*

Dewar MR & MRS James M (Margaret L Cawley) Ty'77.Cos.Ty'66 . . . . MISS Leah Marie—at Gleneagles, Scotland	of ☎ (011-33-1) 45-55-16-30 6 Cité Martignac, 75007 Paris, France ☎ (011-33-16) 85-44-41-58 "Aux Trois Saisons" Le Prémoy BP6, Dracy-le-Fort, 71640 Givry, France

Dewar MR & MRS Porter King F (Jennifer Sullivan)
☎ (714) 493-5063 . . 9 Deer Run, Dove Canyon, CA *92679*
Dewar MR & MRS Roderick L (Grannis—Wiseman—Suzanne J Mack)
Stan'52.Stan'54
☎ (408) 624-6860 . . "Abalone Hill" 4058 Mora Lane, Pebble Beach,
CA *93953*

Dewart MR Alan—Bf.Mid'64.Cr'68 . . . . ☎ (716) 662-7671
MISS Carolyn L—at ☎ (716) 875-6915 | 3799 Baker Rd,
96 Elmhurst Place, Buffalo, NY *14216* . . . . | Orchard Park, NY
MR Stephen R—at Duke . . . . | *14127*
JUNIORS MR Andrew G . . . . |

Dewart MR Brian—Hob'64.Cr'67.SUNY'92 . . . . . . | 350 Ellis Hollow
MISS Elizabeth A—at SUNY Buffalo . . . . | Creek Rd, Ithaca,
| NY *14850*

Dewart MRS (DR) Dorothy B (Dorothy P Boardman) Temp'81.Pc.
☎ (215) 242-3933 . . 748 St Georges Rd, Philadelphia, PA *19119*

Dewart REV & MRS Russell (Ann de D Stevenson) H.'25
☎ (508) 740-0921 . . John Bertram House, 29 Washington Square N,
Salem, MA *01970*

Dewart MR & MRS Timothy R (Ann L Koval) Wayne'72.Rol'62.Wis'65
☎ (508) 922-9229 . . 83 Old Standley Rd, Beverly, MA *01915*

Dewey MR Albert B JR (Alice R Ross) P.Ct.
☎ (540) 364-3106 . . 6590 Rock Hill Mill Rd, The Plains, VA *20198*

Dewey MR & MRS Bradley 3d (Marietta B Pillsbury) | of ☎ (011-41-22)
ColbyS'63.Wh'lck'65.Ncd.Dth'65.Ch'67 . . . . . . | 51-1118
MR Bradley B . . . . | 243A rue de
MR Cameron H . . . . | Chevrens,
JUNIORS MR Jonathan C . . . . | Hermance, 1248
| Geneva, Switzerland
| Old Harrisville Rd,
| Dublin, NH *03444*

Dewey MRS Carpenter (Alexandra O'N Davies) BMr'55.Cly.
☎ (610) 688-1116 . . 43 Dunminning Rd, Newtown Square, PA *19073*

Dewey MR Carpenter—P'53
☎ (610) 688-7994 . . 44 Paper Mill Rd, Newtown Square, PA *19073*

Dewey MR & MRS Chauncey F (E Thayer Archer) Cvc.M.Srb.Nrr.Y'54
☎ (401) 846-1513 . . ''Felicity'' 604 Bellevue Av, Newport, RI *02840*

Dewey MR Frederick N D
☎ (303) 444-3134 . . 2165 S Walnut St, Apt 12, Boulder, CO *80302*

Dewey MR & MRS Gordon C (Frances B Dear) | ☎ (212) 535-2506
Un.Ny.Cs.H.'46 . . . . | 157 E 65 St,
MISS Frances W—StAndr'85 . . . . | New York, NY
MR Frederick R—Br'80—at ☎ (310) 392-6936 | *10021*
2825—2 St, Santa Monica, CA *90405* . . . . . |
MR John H D—Duke'88—at ☎ (718) 599-1560 |
75 Roebling St, Brooklyn, NY *11211* . . . . |

Dewey MR & MRS Paul C G JR (Alexandra P Sheerar)
Cal'91.Me.Duke'84.Cl'94
☎ (212) 678-1186 . . 600 W 111 St, Apt 2C, New York, NY *10025*

Dewey MR Talbot JR . . see A Houghton JR

Dewey MR & MRS Thomas E JR (Ann R Lawler) | ☎ (212) 988-3696
V'59.Cl'61.Cl'68.Un.Plg.Cs.P'54.H'58 . . . . | 79 E 79 St,
MISS Elizabeth D—Skd'91 . . . . | New York, NY
MR George R—Geo'94 . . . . | *10021*

Dewhurst MR & MRS Walter Albert (Virene A Munighan)
W'dbury'39.Sdy.Cal'38 ⚓
☎ (619) 454-7503 . . 5646 Rutgers Rd, La Jolla, CA *92037*

de Windt MR & MRS E Mandell (Davlin—Ennis— | of ☎ (561)546-4952
Mary D Scheffler) Cl'56 . . . . | 36 Riverview Rd,
MISS Virginia-Marie Davlin—at | Hobe Sound, FL
☎ (704) 527-5707 . . 3419 Selwyn Farms | *33455*
Lane, Charlotte, NC *28209* . . . . | ☎ (212) 988-2360
MR H Dalton Davlin . . . . | 179 E 70 St,
MR Thomas W Ennis . . . . | New York, NY
| *10021*

Dewing MRS Allen (Phoebe O Prentice) Ec.
☎ (508) 526-7035 . . 601 Summer St, Manchester, MA *01944-1625*

Dewing MISS Cythlen A . . see P L Maddock JR

Dewing MR Harold A 3d . . see H L Cobb

Dewing MISS Martha F . . see H L Cobb

DeWitt MR & MRS Anthony P (Faye Nikov)
Ober'73.Tufts'74.Tufts'75.San.Wms'68.Tufts'69. Tufts'70.Tufts'80
☎ (203) 655-7844 . . 109 Stephen Mather Rd, Darien, CT *06820*

de Witt MR & MRS Clinton J (Patricia L McLeod) | ☎ (916) 488-1072
Cal'63.Cal'66 . . . . | 610 Laurel Dv,
MISS Catherine H—Ore'83 . . . . | Sacramento, CA
| *95864*

De Witt MRS H Sanford (Annette M Kite) . . . . | ☎ (513) 782-6410
MISS Jessica S—Wells'79—at ☎ (718) 389-4220 | 643 Maple Trace,
182 Norman Av, Brooklyn, NY *11222* . . . . | Springdale, OH
| *45246*

DeWitt MR & MRS William O JR (Katharine C | ☎ (513) 271-6014
Cramer) Qc.Y'63.H'65 . . . . | 5695 Drake Rd,
MISS Katharine M . . . . | Cincinnati, OH
MISS Margaret H . . . . | *45243*
MR William O 3d . . . . |
MR Andrew E . . . . |

de Wolf MR & MRS Bradford C (Laylin—Gesine | ☎ (703) PL9-2247
Rott) Mt. . . . . | 1001 White
MR B Colt JR—Va'84 . . . . | Chimney Court,
MR Buckmaster—Mid'87 . . . . | Great Falls, VA
| *22066*

de Wolf MRS Francis Colt JR (PRCSS M Dorota Drucka Lubecka)
Mt.Cvc.Srb.
☎ (202) 342-1467 . . Watergate East, 2500 Virginia Av NW,
Washington, DC *20037*

de Wolf MR Francis Colt 3d (late Francis Colt JR) . . . . Married at
Washington, DC
Lagesse MISS Nathalie A B (Guy) . . . . Apr 27'96

DeWyngaert MR & MRS Richard A (Susan T Keon) Geo'82.Pa'92.Geo'81
☎ (215) 829-4496 . . 335 S 7 St, Philadelphia, PA *19106*

Dexter MR Charles E JR (Hildreth Lange) Edg. . . . . | *see*
MR Lowell E . . . . | *Dilatory Domiciles*
MR Charles E 3d . . . . |

Dexter MR Nathaniel T—Sb.Sm.Ub.H'50
☎ (617) 742-2143 . . 85B Mt Vernon St, Boston, MA *02108*

Dexter MR & MRS Philip (Opdycke—Susan Wolcott) Rdc'52.H'51
☎ (314) 994-0256 . . 6 Terry Lane, St Louis, MO *63124-1723*

Dexter MR & MRS William H JR (C Penelope Phillips) Cit'63
☎ (205) 871-5471 . . 128 Peachtree Rd, Mountain Brook, AL *35213*

De Young MR & MRS Andrew G (Geralyn K Kleypas) Tex'76.Houst'81
☎ (713) 538-1119 . . 133 Bayou Bend Dv, League City, TX *77573*

De Young MRS Guy O JR (Josephine W Bradley) Dar.
Air Force Village 1, Apt 1607, 4917 Ravenswood Dv, San Antonio,
TX 78227-4344
De Young MRS Herbert C (Virginia Winston) Ih.Cnt.
☎ (847) 251-5247 . . 336 Raleigh Rd, Kenilworth, IL 60043
De Young MR & MRS James W (Penelope Wick)
Ih.Rc.Cho.Cw.Wa.Cnt.W&L'65.Nw'68 . . . . | ☎ (847) 446-2113
  MR James W JR . . . . | 22 Indian Hill Rd,
  MR Peter D . . . . | Winnetka, IL 60093
  JUNIORS MR Wick C . . . . |
  JUNIORS MR Andrew M . . . . |
de Zalduondo MRS J Antonio (Barbara N Orvis)
Cly.Ht.Cda.Dc.Dar. . . . . | ☎ (508) 228-0572
  MISS Barbara O—Rdc'73.Dc.Dar.Ht.—at | 13 Cliff Rd,
  ☎ (202) 244-4745 . . 4710—49 St NW, | Nantucket, MA
  Washington, DC 20016 | 02554
Dhody MRS Dinesh C (Joanne M Santa Maria) . . . . | ☎ (215) 242-8132
  MISS Anna N . . . . | 20 W Bells Mill Rd,
  MISS Allia D . . . . | Philadelphia, PA
  | 19118
Dhody MR Dinesh C—Pa'66
430 W Moreland Av, Philadelphia, PA 19118
Diacre de Liancourt MR & MRS Piers L (Cynthia T | ☎ (011-44-181)
  Walker) | 870-6742
  JUNIORS MR Alexander—at Geo Wash'n . . . . . . | 17 Westover Rd,
  JUNIORS MR Nicholas—at Eton . . . . | London SW18 2RE,
  | England
Dial MISS Elizabeth M—Bnd'89
☎ (212) 877-4907 . . 35 W 85 St, Apt 2B, New York, NY 10024
Dial MR N Minter (N Victor) . . . . Married at Paris, France
Arazolla MISS Yendi . . . . Sep 2'95
Diana MR & MRS Ronald S (Alix Clark) | ☎ (201) 543-4190
  Eh.Colg'52.Cl'55 . . . . | 164 Talmage Rd,
  MISSES Alix & Kate B—at ☎ (617) 266-4047 | Mendham, NJ 07945
  100 Jersey St, Apt 406, Boston, MA 02215 . . . . |
  MR Alexander C—at ☎ (212) 721-2819 |
  156 W 86 St, Apt 6A, New York, NY 10024 . . . |
  MR Christopher B—at ☎ (212) 228-6261 |
  179 Prince St, New York, NY 10012 . . . . |
Dibble MRS Kathleen M (Byczkowski—Kathleen C | ☎ (415) 931-0575
  Moulder) Hlns'50 . . . . | 1000 Green St,
  MISS Anne Byczkowski—V'79—at | Apt 1101,
  105 Lake St, San Francisco, CA 94118 . . . . . | San Francisco, CA
  | 94133
Dibblee MRS Harrison (Katherine R Drury) | ☎ (415) 499-8711
  Sth'30.Tcy. . . . . | 100 Thornhill Dv,
  MR Thomas L . . . . | Apt 253, San Rafael,
  | CA 94903
Di Capua MR & MRS Peter A (Harriet T Herrick) | of ☎ (516)239-2383
  Skd'58.Adelphi'71.SUNY'72.Post'75 . . . . | 365 Barrett Rd,
  MR Anthony—SUNY'86 . . . . | Lawrence, NY
  MR Lawrence H—Rc.Ds.Snc.Vt'84—at | 11559
  ☎ (212) 628-0392 . . 412 E 65 St, New York, NY | ☎ (805) 646-5439
  10021 . . . . | ''Flor-de-Mar''
  MR Peter A JR . . . . | 4550 Grand Av,
  | Ojai, CA 93023

di Carpegna MISS Allegra . . see R Barclay
di Carpegna MR Guelfo . . see R Barclay
di Carpegna MR Rufo . . see R Barclay
Dick MRS Albert B III (Bent—Susan Drake) Cho.On.Sr.
☎ (847) 234-3330 . . 1510 Tara Lane, Lake Forest, IL 60045
Dick MR & MRS Anthony (Hilary Limbocker) Skd'88.Rc.Srb.Nrr.Ty'86
☎ (212) 861-7380 . . 162 E 80 St, New York, NY 10021
Dick MR & MRS C Mathews JR (Mary A Milholland)
Rcn.Mt.B.Ln.Srb.Nrr.Cho.H'46
☎ (202) 333-2904 . . 3006 P St NW, Washington, DC 20007
Dick MISS Diana H (Cave—Diana H Dick) Wheat'68.Geo'74
124 Oakley Rd, Belmont, MA 02178
Dick MRS Edison (Jane Warner) On.Cho.Sr.Cas.
☎ (847) 234-0427 . . Box 290, 612 Woodland Rd, Lake Forest, IL 60045
Dick MISS Genevieve du Pont (Anthony) . . . . Born at
New York, NY Mch 6'96
Dick DR & MRS H Lenox H (Helene Biddle) BMr'41.Pa'41.Jef'44
☎ (360) 892-2657 . . 3214 SE Biddle Rd, Vancouver, WA 98683
Dick DR & MRS Henry J B (Winifred A James) Sth'77.H'83.Pa'69.Y'75
☎ (508) 540-3290 . . 392 Boxberry Hill Rd, Hatchville, MA 02536
Dick MR & MRS John H (Brenda M Johnson) | ☎ (847) 234-6267
  On.Rc.Cho.Nasson'69.LakeF'75 . . . . | 900 Woodbine Lane,
  MISS Elisabeth G . . . . | Lake Forest, IL
  MISS Phoebe A . . . . | 60045
  JUNIORS MR John H JR . . . . |
Dick MR & MRS Ronald A (Louise S Ervin) Lond'48 | ☎ (416) 483-5393
  MR David L . . . . | 319 Inglewood Dv,
  MR Andrew R . . . . | Toronto, Ontario
  | M4T 1J4, Canada
Dick MR & MRS Ronald F (Gee—Lillian A Rothe) | ☎ (401) 847-3466
  Rcn.B.H'50 . . . . | ''Ocean View''
  MISS Annelisa A Gee—Tufts'91 . . . . | Bellevue Av,
  MISS Sarah D Gee—Ham'94 . . . . | Newport, RI 02840
  JUNIORS MISS Christina G Gee . . . . |
  JUNIORS MR Alexander R Gee . . . . |
Dick MR & MRS Spencer B (Mary E Reagan) Ore'71.Port'81
☎ (503) 227-5749 . . 1524 SW Spring St, Portland, OR 97201
Dick MR Stratford L M JR—Dth'89 . . see J W Hasler
Dick MR & MRS Will K (Sandra F Mueller) | ☎ (617) 734-4295
  Bost'71.Cy.Chi.H'71 . . . . | 81 Fairmount St,
  JUNIORS MISS Alexandra M . . . . | Brookline, MA
  JUNIORS MR William T . . . . | 02146
Dickason MR & MRS James Frank (Linda C Stewart) | ☎ (818) 792-3900
  Gchr'57.Clare'87.Bhm.Vh.Pcu.H'44.Stan'51 . . . | 930 Rosalind Rd,
  MR Bradford S—at 1617 Pasadena Glen Rd, | San Marino, CA
  Pasadena, CA 91107 . . . . | 91108
Dicke MR & MRS James F II (Janet E St Clair) | ☎ (419) 629-2424
  Ty'68.A.Ty'68 . . . . | 422 Easthaven Dv,
  MISS Jennifer St C . . . . | New Bremen, OH
  | 45869
Dicke MR James F III (James F II) . . . . Married at San Antonio, TX
Groen MISS Katherine L (Douglas) . . . . Sep 16'95

Dickenson MR & MRS Melville P JR (Virginia A Paul) Pn.P'49 . . . .
MISS Julia T—at Santa Fe, NM . . . .
of ☎ (609)627-7777 Pine Valley Golf Club, Pine Valley, NJ *08021*
☎ (802) 765-4428 "Pompey Pines" South Strafford, VT *05070*

Dickerman MR Watson B—Sm.H'69
☎ (617) 354-6100 . . 19 Chauncy St, Cambridge, MA *02138*

Dickerman MRS William C (Livingston—Marion La B Browne) K.Cly.Ncd.Cw.
☎ (212) LE4-5278 . . 1050 Fifth Av, New York, NY *10028*

Dickerson MRS John S (Engelina E Cuypers)
☎ (941) 395-1293 . . 1344 Tahiti Dv, Sanibel, FL *33957*

Dickerson MR & MRS Thomas P (Claire A Moore) Ws'71.Cl'74.Nu'81.H.'71.H'74.H'79
☎ (914) 967-8524 . . 76 Overlook Place, Rye, NY *10580*

Dickerson MRS W Mahlon (Whitman—Elizabeth D Brown) Ny.S.Cly.Dc.
☎ (212) 838-2895 . . 200 E 66 St, New York, NY *10021*

Dickey MR Alexander G—Aht'82
3207 Commonwealth Av, Alexandria, VA *22305*

Dickey MR & MRS B Gordon (Ladue—Joyce N Moyle) Ct.Wms'44.GeoW'48 . . . .
MISS Lelia S . . . .
MR Douglas G . . . .
☎ (703) 683-1021 109 Pommander Walk, Alexandria, VA *22314*

Dickey MR & MRS Charles D JR (Helen B Lynch) Y'40
☎ (610) 688-9285 . . 649 Dorset Rd, Devon, PA *19333-1812*

Dickey MR & MRS Charles D 3d (Sheila A Wyckoff) Pac'79.Ne'82.Pa'71.Pa'76
☎ (206) 322-2108 . . 144 Madrona Place E, Seattle, WA *98112*

Dickey MR & MRS Clyde E 4th (Eleanor P Washburne) Mich'80.Smu'80
☎ (214) 690-3050 . . 2011 Nantucket Dv, Richardson, TX *75080*

Dickey MRS Frank B (Jeanne Soulé) Stan'47
☎ (415) 851-7586 . . 430 Summit Springs Rd, Woodside, CA *94062*

Dickey MISS Kara D'A . . see MRS R W Fleming JR

Dickey MISS Kimberley A—Swb'90.AmU'91
☎ (303) 831-4770 . . 790 Washington St, Apt 602, Denver, CO *80203*

Dickey MRS Lucy Baker (Harfield—Lucy Baker) ⚓ . . of 406 Shelton Av, Alexandria, PA *16611*
☎ (011-599) 555-288 . . "Morning Glory" 6 Roberts Dv, Simpson Bay, St Maarten, Netherlands Antilles

Dickey MR & MRS Paul B JR (Lucile H Ingham) BtP.Ihy.Ty'51 ⚓ . . . .
MISS Laura H . . . .
MR William Y H—Char'ton'90 . . . .
☎ (203) 869-9324 20 Pine Ridge Rd, Greenwich, CT *06830*

Dickey MR & MRS Peter M (Janet R Gilchrist) . . . . .
MISS Eleanor G . . . .
MR Alexander G—Aht'82—at 3207 Commonwealth Av, Alexandria, VA *22305*
☎ (703) 471-0572 1670 Chimney House Rd, Reston, VA *20190*

Dickey MR & MRS Robert 3d (Elizabeth P Beckwith) Rr.Fcg.Pg.P'39
☎ (412) 621-5994 . . 5606 Dunmoyle St, Pittsburgh, PA *15217*

Dickey MR & MRS Robert 4th (Orbison—Cynthia C Bishop) Fcg.Pc.Rr.P'77.Pa'84
☎ (215) 248-0395 . . 301 W Springfield Av, Philadelphia, PA *19118*

Dickinson MISS Amy Thorp—BMr'68
28488 Ivy Lane, Libertyville, IL *60048*

Dickinson MR & MRS Haskell L 2d (Margaret M Nestrud) Ark'72.Ark'70 . . . .
MISS Eleanor L . . . .
MR Haskell L 3d . . . .
JUNIORS MR Thomas H . . . .
☎ (501) 664-7923 6 W Palisades Dv, Little Rock, AR *72207*

Dickinson MR Howard C JR—Sar.Myf.H'58.Y'66 . .
MR Alexander S—NH'90 . . . .
☎ (603) 447-2266 Baird Hill Rd, Center Conway, NH *03813*

Dickinson MRS James Alfred (Nancy Ann Ohmer)
☎ (412) 621-1890 . . 123 University Place, Pittsburgh, PA *15213*

Dickinson MR & MRS Thomas W (Rita M Harkins) NAriz'72.Cal'77 . . . .
JUNIORS MR Joseph H . . . .
☎ (602) 955-2772 2002 E Rancho Dv, Phoenix, AZ *85016-2702*

Dickinson MR & MRS W K Read (Elizabeth W Moore) Nich'60.Me'64 . . . .
MR Christian W—at Lake Forest Coll . . . .
☎ (207) 846-4021 35 Hillside St, Yarmouth, ME *04096*

Dickinson MRS William R JR (Anne L Knowles) On.Cas.Ncd.
☎ (847) 234-1985 . . 770 W Westleigh Rd, Lake Forest, IL *60045*

Dickison MR Matthew P . . see R P Paine

Dickison MISS Sara E . . see R P Paine

Dickson MRS Dennis C (Platt—Dennis Covel) Sth'58
☎ (203) 629-4370 . . 249 Milbank Av, Apt 326, Greenwich, CT *06830*

Dickson MR & MRS Edgar V (Mallinckrodt—Rosalie F Randolph) Cy . . . .
MISS Rosalie R Mallinckrodt . . . .
☎ (314) 994-0377 9936 Litzsinger Rd, St Louis, MO *63124*

Dickson MR & MRS Richard B (Camp—Culbert—Avery K Hallock) Leh'50 . . . .
MISS Lynne E—Mid'87.Rut'89—at
☎ (412) 441-0773 . . 5506 Harriet St, Pittsburgh, PA *15232* . . . .
MISS Juliet A Camp—at ☎ (801) 531-6577 PO Box 4041, Salt Lake City, UT *84110* . . . .
MR Mark E Camp—SanDiegoSt'84—at
☎ (310) 679-0900 . . 12512 Manor Dv, Hawthorne, CA *90250* . . . .
☎ (860) 434-5535 "Rockledge" 73 Neck Rd, PO Box 85, Old Lyme, CT *06371*

Dickson MR William D S—Wes'64
☎ (610) 935-9798 . . 474 Grant St, Phoenixville, PA *19460*

Dicus DR & MRS Paul E (Gay B Edelen) GeoW'70.Ariz'67.GeoW'79 . . . .
MISS Amy E—Box 883037, Steamboat Springs, CO *80488* . . . .
MISS Katherine F . . . .
MR Christopher W—at 827 S Gilpin St, Denver, CO *80209* . . . .
MR Kevin D—at 86 Grant St, Denver, CO *80203*
☎ (303) 758-7414 2543 S Kearney St, Denver, CO *80222*

Diebold MR A Richard . . . . Died Jun 18'96

Diebold MRS A Richard (Dorothy O Roosen) Chr.Cly.
☎ (941) 964-2818 . . PO Box 667, Boca Grande, FL *33921*

Diebold MR & MRS David K (Catherine D Stone) Mt.St.G.Cr'67
2910 Glover Driveway NW, Washington, DC *20016*

Diederichs MRS John K (Janet Wood) Ws'50.Cho.Tv.Ri.Cas.Wa.
☎ (312) 943-0504 . . 229 E Lake Shore Dv, Chicago, IL *60611*

Diedrick MRS Age Buer (Age Buer) . . . . | ☎ (212) 755-7311
MISS Samantha G—at ☎ (617) 254-3880 | 300 E 59 St, Apt
100 Tremont St, Apt 3, Newton, MA *02158* . . . | 1806, New York,
| NY *10022*

Diedrick MR & MRS Arthur H JR (Tara I Stacom) Leh'80.Rc.Ri.Y'59 . . of
☎ (212) 759-5577 . . 485 Park Av, New York, NY *10022*
☎ (860) 567-5087 . . ''Indian Hill'' PO Box 37, Litchfield, CT *06759*

Diefenbach MR & MRS Robert C (Mary-Stuart Montague Price) An.Ncd.Dar.
☎ (301) 652-1899 . . 3119 Rolling Rd, Chevy Chase, MD *20815*

Diefenbach DR & MRS William Paul (Geraldine M Musche)
York'68.Cl'72.Cl'79
☎ (520) 742-9240 . . 7401 Christie Dv, Tucson, AZ *85718*

Diesel MRS Jan M (R Jan Meyer) WmW'ds'47
1203 Berthea St, Houston, TX *77006*

Diesel MR & MRS John H 2d (M Brooks Armour) P'85.On.Rice'82
☎ (409) 532-4252 . . Pierce Ranch, Pierce, TX *77467*

Dietrich MR E Alexander JR—Cw.
☎ (410) 323-3957 . . 12 Elmwood Rd, Baltimore, MD *21210*

Dietrich MR H Richard JR—K.Pkg.R.Pe.Gr.Fiy. | ☎ (610) 827-7719
Srr.Rv.Wes'60 . . . . | ''Arkadia''
MISS Cordelia Biddle—SL'89—at 24 Fifth Av, | 1337 Art School Rd,
New York, NY *10011* . . . . | Chester Springs, PA
MR H Richard 3d—Wes'92—at Yale . . . . | *19425*
MR Christian Braun—at Princeton . . . . |

Dietz MRS (DR) J Herbert JR (Sarah E Flanders) BMr'35.Cr'39
☎ (860) 526-5912 . . 7205 Chester Village W, Chester, CT *06412*

Diffee MASTER Chandler Baylor (Craig W) . . . . Born at
Richmond, VA Apr 16'96

Diffee MR & MRS Craig W (Alexandra Baylor Sherrer) Longwood'84
☎ (804) 754-1197 . . 1603 Tobak Court, Richmond, VA *23233*

Diffenbach MRS John E (June G Douglas) . . . . | 445 Concord Rd,
MISS Molly G . . . . | Weston, MA *02193*
JUNIORS MISS Julie N . . . . |

Diffenderffer MR & MRS C Rich (McCoy—Thouron | ☎ (302) 654-0509
—Carol V Kitchell) Me.Ste.Cts.Rcp.Md.Wil. | PO Box 141,
Va'55 . . . . | 190 Rockland Rd,
MISS Anne W—at ☎ (011-44-1865) 242-550 | Montchanin, DE
Manor Farm, North Hinksey, Oxfordshire | *19710*
ONX2 0NA, England . . . . |
 MR George G Thouron 3d—at |
 Randolph-Macon . . . . |

Diffenderffer MR Michael K—Me.
☎ (011-44-1666) 822-518 . . Park House, Charlton Park, Malmesbury,
Wiltshire SN16 90J, England

Digges MR & MRS Edward W (Polly P Pintler) Ht.Sar.Dar.JHop'52
32460 Mill Ridge Rd, Cordova, MD *21625*

Digges MR & MRS John J M (Mary C Bush) Loy'56 . | ☎ (757) 229-5996
MISS Anne B—at 5407 Skalak Dv, Williamsburg, | 512 S Henry St,
VA *23188*. . . . . | Williamsburg, VA
MR Ralph E B—at 151 Ruth Lane, Williamsburg, | *23185*
VA *23188*. . . . . |
MR James A I—at 1103 Moore House Rd, |
Yorktown, VA *23690*. . . . . |

Diggs MRS James B JR (Sally P Strobel)
☎ (410) 323-5684 . . 5705 Stony Run Dv, Baltimore, MD *21210*

Dike MISS Deborah A
☎ (011-41-22) 781-14-60 . . 3 Place du Cirque, 1204 Geneva,
Switzerland

Dike MRS Norman S JR (Naef—Catherine M du B Pochon)
☎ (011-41-22) 321-8888 . . 4 rue de Hesse, 1204 Geneva, Switzerland

Dilks MR & MRS Charles D (Gene L Felix) | ☎ (215) CH2-9479
Rc.Pc.Rv.Wt.Y'63 . . . . | 215 W Willow
MISS Christina D . . . . | Grove Av,
MR Charles D JR . . . . | Philadelphia, PA
JUNIORS MR Mark P . . . . | *19118*

Dilks MRS John Hyland (Margaret D Day) Sg.Pc.Ac.Ncd.
☎ (215) CH7-3733 . . 641 St George's Rd, Philadelphia, PA *19119-3341*

Dilks MRS Peter D (Helene H Duncan) Pc.Rc.Ph. . . | ☎ (215) 848-0595
MISS Hollis T . . . . | 1009 Westview St,
MR Nicholas H . . . . | Philadelphia, PA
| *19119*

Dill DR & MRS James N JR (McCall—Jane M French) | of ☎ (412)421-0973
H'43.Fcg.Pg.Tc.Dar.W&M'40 . . . . | 5600 Aylesboro Av,
MISS Frances F McCall . . . . | Pittsburgh, PA
| *15217*
| ☎ (910) 692-4166
| ''Gypsy Stream
| Farm'' Box 1244,
| Southern Pines, NC
| *28388*

Dillard MRS Tyree (Mary B Beers) Sth'36.Mad'70 . | ☎ (213) 661-8668
DR James N—Cal'80.Rush'90—at | 1932 N Normandie
☎ (212) 929-4984 . . 201 W 16 St, New York, | Av, Los Angeles,
NY *10011* . . . . | CA *90027*

Dillard MR Tyree 3d
☎ (805) 649-4514 . . 280 Alto Dv, Oak View, CA *93022*

Dillard MR & MRS William T 2d (Bearden—Mary Amanda Boreing)
Ark'69.Dar.Ark'66.H'68
☎ (501) 664-3609 . . 6 Edgehill Rd, Little Rock, AR *72207*

Dillenbeck MRS Suzanne V (Suzanne G Voth) | ☎ (516) 671-5058
Ws'55.Pr.P. | 11 Ryefield Rd,
MISS Anne G. | Locust Valley, NY
| *11560*

Diller MRS Theodore C (Barbara Cox) V'31.Ncd.
☎ (703) 385-3355 . . 9229 Arlington Blvd, Apt 131, Fairfax,
VA *22031-2510*

Dillingham MRS Andrews (Frances Andrews)
☎ (415) 922-5586 . . 2500 Steiner St, Apt 3, San Francisco, CA *94115*

Dillingham MR Benjamin F 3d—H'67
☎ (619) 225-1181 . . 4494 Tivoli St, San Diego, CA *92107*

Dillon MR & MRS C Douglas (Bassett—Buchanan—Sage—Susan Slater)
Rc.Ln.K.C.Plg.Cw.Cc.Lm.Cly.H'31 . . of
☎ (212) 288-7255 . . 960 Fifth Av, New York, NY *10021*
☎ (561) 546-5054 . . ''Harlequin'' 169 S Beach Rd, Hobe Sound,
FL *33455*

Dillon MR C W Larue—Laf'56
☎ (610) MI2-8421 . . 454 Booth Circle, Haverford, PA *19041*

Dillon MR Charles H—Eh.Denis'81
☎ (908) 719-2877 . . 401A Fowler Rd, Far Hills, NJ *07931*

Dillon DR & MRS Edward V (Anne S Carpenter) Sth'52.M.Me.Sa.P'48.Pa'52 . . . . | 797 Darby-Paoli Rd, Bryn Mawr, PA *19010*
MR Eugene V—Ty'85—at 169 Madison St, Hartford, CT *06106* . . . .
DR Richard L—Ty'87.Jef'93 . . . .

Dillon MR & MRS George C (Joan A Kent) Sth'47.Csn.H'44 . . . . | ☎ (816) 531-2330 5049 Wornall Rd, Kansas City, MO
MR Kent C—at 690 Greenwich St, New York, NY *10014* . . . . | NY *64112*

Dillon MRS Hardenbergh (Elizabeth K Hardenbergh) Shcc.
☎ (908) 221-0110 . . 1127 Fellowship Rd, Basking Ridge, NJ *07970*

Dillon MRS Herbert L JR (Renée Danal) . . . . Died at Montecito, CA Mch 2'94

Dillon MR Herbert L JR (late Herbert L) . . . Married at Santa Barbara, CA Montgomery MRS Haddon B (Farrell—Montgomery—McAdam— Haddon F Bowen) . . . . May 27'96

Dillon MR & MRS Herbert L JR (Farrell—Montgomery—McAdam— Haddon F Bowen) P'47 . . of
☎ (805) 969-6708 . . 1666 E Valley Rd, Santa Barbara, CA *93108*
☎ (805) 969-4102 . . PO Box 50324, Santa Barbara, CA *93150*

Dillon MR & MRS John S (Astrid J Dickson) Ws'55.Rv.Ht.Cw.Ofp.Laf'51.Pa'55 . . . . | ☎ (941) 395-1136 201 Daniel Dv, Sanibel, FL *33957*
MISS Christina V—Van'89—at
☎ (215) 569-1338 . . 2400 Chestnut St, Apt 2904, Philadelphia, PA *19103* . . . .
MISS Julie D—Laf'91—at ☎ (206) 860-7346 603 Twelfth Av E, Apt 202, Seattle, WA *98102*
MR John S 2d—at Duke

Dillon MRS Milton S JR (Moyer—Virginia B Finlay) Cly.
☎ (908) 766-3103 . . ''Willow Pond House'' Box 14, Bernardsville, NJ *07924*

Dillon MR R Forrest—So'70 . . of
☎ (207) 729-1785 . . 299 Maine St, Brunswick, ME *04011*
☎ (207) 244-5087 . . ''Foothold'' PO Box 1, Dix Point Rd, West Tremont, ME *04690*

Dillon DR & MRS Richard S (Susan Holt) Me.P'55.Pa'59 . . . . | ☎ (610) 896-8986 150 Mill Creek Rd, Ardmore, PA *19003*
MISS Ella V—P'94.Me . . . .
MR Richard S JR—Me.Wit'90 . . . .
MR Thomas H—Me.P'91 . . . .

Dillon MR & MRS Sidney G (Dorothy D Hardin) V'45-4.Rut'72.Shcc.P'46.Va'51
☎ (908) 234-9510 . . PO Box 441, Gladstone, NJ *07934*

Dillon MR & MRS Thomas H (Patricia A Hurley) ColbyS'75.Shcc.Eh.Clark'75
☎ (908) 439-2362 . . PO Box 7, Oldwick, NJ *08858*

Dilworth MR Ernest Nevin—Ken'33
☎ (610) 868-5466 . . 1906 Main St Ext, Bethlehem, PA *18017*

Dilworth MR & MRS J Richardson (Elizabeth McK Cushing) C.K.Ln.Plg.Y'38
☎ (609) 924-2120 . . 141 Hodge Rd, Princeton, NJ *08540*

Dimond MR F Ronald—Yn.Y'58.Cl'60 . . . . | ☎ (203) 329-7440 789 Riverbank Rd, Stamford, CT *06903*
MISS Allison B—at Lindsley Rd, West Falmouth, MA *02574* . . . .
JUNIORS MR James L—at Lindsley Rd, West Falmouth, MA *02574* . . . .

Dimond MRS Pamela C (Pamela D Coues) . . . . | ☎ (203) 966-4113 14 White Oak Shade Rd, New Canaan, CT *06840*
MISS Ashley D—Ken'90 . . . . |

Dimond MR Renwick De G—Unn.Br'57.Pa'59 Breakers West, 1070 Lytham Court, West Palm Beach, FL *33411*

Dimond MR & MRS Renwick De G JR (Ellen B Doyle) Denis'91.Denis'89
☎ (804) 358-3558 . . 4517 W Franklin St, Richmond, VA *23221*

Dimsey MR & MRS Peter S P (Virginia Mitchell) Ny.Camb'59 ⚓ . . . . | of ☎ (212)734-7058 150 E 73 St, New York, NY *10021*
MR Christopher P M—at Tufts . . . . |
☎ (203) 838-5301 1 Woodland Rd, Wilson Point, South Norwalk, CT *06854*
☎ (302) 658-0202 104 Ponds Lane, Wilmington, DE *19807*

Dinan MRS Camilla C (Camilla M Cronin) . . . . | ☎ (516) 569-4950 1 Meadow Dv, Apt 3C, Woodmere, NY *11598*
MR John F JR—Denis'82 . . . . |

Dingle MR Christopher B—Cr'88.Cr'89
☎ (212) 929-1051 . . 181 Seventh Av, Apt 5C, New York, NY *10011*

Dingle MR & MRS Jeffrey L (Susan A Poor) Cr'79.Cr'79
☎ (617) 631-6341 . . 24 Gregory St, Marblehead, MA *01945*

Dingle MR Michael H—Cr'74 . . see MRS S L Warner

Dingledine MR & MRS William S JR (Dale C Woods) Hlns'73.Ds.Myf.Cda.Ncd.Va'73.JHop'84 . . . . . . | ☎ (864) 297-6155 15 Aldrich Dv, Greenville, SC *29607*
JUNIORS MISS Grace W . . . . |

Dingman MRS Martha T (Martha D Trainer) Elm'65 | ☎ (208) 336-6884 1431 Candleridge Dv, Boise, ID *83712*
MISS Kimberly G—at U of Colo . . . . |
JUNIORS MR Jeffrey R—at U of Wash'n . . . . |

Dingman MR Robert J—StLaw'63
☎ (208) 336-0474 . . 1376 E Braemere Rd, Boise, ID *83702*

DiNitto MISS Anita—Sim'94 . . see MRS N Gorham

DiNitto MR Tory—Syr'95 . . see MRS N Gorham

Dinkel MISS Sallie C F . . see R M Foster

Dinning MR E Lawrence 3d— ⚓
☎ (954) 565-9154 . . ''Fiddlers Green'' 2856 NE 27 St, Ft Lauderdale, FL *33306*

Dinning MR & MRS E Lawrence 4th (Carroll F Hopkins) ⚓ . . . . | ☎ (410) 676-0211 908 W Baker Av, Abingdon, MD *21009*
MR Ernest L . . . . |

Dinning MR & MRS John B (Jennings—Kathleen W Fitchett)
☎ (410) 472-4114 . . ''Prettyland Farm'' 16522 Pearce Rd, Monkton, MD *21111*

Dinning MISS Kathleen G
☎ (410) 472-2231 . . 15831 Carroll Rd, Monkton, MD *21111*

Dinning MRS Sarah D (Heuer—Spender—Sarah D Zantzinger) BMr'54
☎ (202) 625-1060 . . 1654—32 St NW, Washington, DC *20007*

Dinsmore MR & MRS Francis William (Sallie M Kite)
Pa'84.Gm.Ac.Ncd.P'35
☎ (215) CH8-2490 . . 8000 Seminole Av, Philadelphia, PA *19118*

Dinsmore MR & MRS Wiley (Hays—Schaefer—M Elizabeth Legg) Qc.H'56
☎ (513) 871-5411 . . 21 Weebetook Lane, Cincinnati, OH *45208*

di San Faustino PRCSS Ranieri (Casey—Geneviève B Lyman) Bur.
☎ (415) 346-0542 . . 2513 Pierce St, San Francisco, CA *94115*

Diserens MRS Robert C (Helen L Barnett) Mich'41
☎ (914) 666-8544 . . 111 Tripp St, Mt Kisco, NY *10549*

Disston MR & MRS Geoffrey W JR (Charlotte Cameron Reece)
Stet'78.Cda.Hob'81
☎ (203) 438-0705 . . 312 North St, Ridgefield, CT *06877*

Disston MR & MRS Henry (Worrell—Reed—Mary C Clay) Sg.Ac.P'47
☎ (215) 242-4084 . . 235 E Evergreen Av, Philadelphia, PA *19118*

Disston MR & MRS Henry JR (Ellen E Lea) Penn'71 . | ☎ (215) MI6-5364
MISS Lea C .... | Willow Lake Farm,
MR John H .... | Box 426, Ambler,
| PA *19002*

Disston MR & MRS Jacob S 3d (Collins—June M Adams) Sg.
☎ (242) 362-4447 . . "The Hitching Post" Box N7776, Nassau,
Bahamas

Disston MRS Kate (Kate von Moschzisker)
☎ (207) 781-3267 . . 8 Applegate Lane, Falmouth Foreside, Portland,
ME *04105*

Disston MR & MRS William L (Julia P Morris) Rb.Sg.
☎ (215) 643-4608 . . 6032 Sheaff Lane, Ft Washington, PA *19034*

Distad MR & MRS R Neall (Marcella C Anderson)
Sth'81.Sim'85.RogerW'82.BostArch'89
☎ (216) 491-8420 . . 3346 Ingleside Rd, Shaker Heights, OH *44122*

Ditmore MISS Brooke W . . see MRS R W Ghan

Ditmore MR Nathan C . . see MRS R W Ghan

Ditzen MRS Lowell R (Cheesborough—Tydings—Eleanor Davies)
V'25.Cvc.Sl.Ncd.
☎ (202) 462-5462 . . 2700 Calvert St NW, Washington, DC *20008*

Divine MR & MRS Edward F (Christy B Hoover) | ☎ (912) 352-4979
Hood'76.Va'73 | 1408 Bacon Park
JUNIORS MR Christopher B .... | Dv, Savannah, GA
JUNIORS MR Tasker A .... | *31406*

Divine MR & MRS William H (Elizabeth G Bliss) Ayc.USN'42
☎ (410) 268-8231 . . 205 Wardour Dv, Annapolis, MD *21401*

Dix MR George E—K.Mt.Y'34
Collington, 10450 Lottsford Rd, Mitchellville, MD *20721-2734*

Dix MRS Norman B (Eleanor Clemens) Cly.Ncd. . . . | ☎ (516) 288-1198
MISS G Brooke .... | "Niaway" Box 787,
| Westhampton
| Beach, NY *11978*

Dixon MRS Barbara D (Burck—Barbara B Douglas) | ☎ (319) 363-6368
MRS Borden B Stevens (M Borden Burck) . . . | 314 Nassau St SE,
MISS Joelle B Stevens .... | Cedar Rapids, IA
MR Scott B Stevens—Ia'90 .... | *52403*

Dixon MR Ben Franklin III—Ct.Cc.NCar'39
☎ (202) 333-4311 . . 3282 N St NW, Washington, DC *20007*

Dixon MR & MRS Bruce De W (Barbara Engel) Sth'55.Uncl.Tvcl.Ihy.H'55
☎ (203) 629-1043 . . 20 Greenbriar Lane, Greenwich, CT *06831*

Dixon MR & MRS Courtlandt P (Penelope A Harrison) MtH'39.Y'39
☎ (860) 434-9365 . . "Palmer's Court" 7 Mill Pond Lane, Old Lyme,
CT *06371*

Dixon MR & MRS Dennis C (Wendy F Cole) | ☎ (508) 526-4795
Sth'74.Err.Eyc.Pa'75.Va'79 .... | 295 Summer St,
JUNIORS MISS Caroline C .... | Manchester, MA
| *01944*

Dixon MR & MRS Fitz Eugene JR (Edith B Robb)
Srr.BtP.Rc.Evg.Ph.Sg.Cry.DelB.Ny.Cw.Ac.Ncd.
☎ (215) 836-7500 . . "Erdenheim" Box 178, Lafayette Hill, PA *19444*

Dixon MR & MRS Francis C (Constance Hoadley) Sth'42.Y'42
☎ (860) 535-0835 . . 286 N Main St, Stonington, CT *06378*

Dixon MR & MRS Gilbert W (Spence—Gretchen Woodall) P'27
☎ (410) 243-5677 . . 830 W 40 St, Apt 616, Baltimore, MD *21211*

Dixon MR Harold G—Va'61 .... | ☎ (804) 320-9161
MR H Andrew—at ☎ (804) 973-8359 | 2956 Hathaway Rd,
122 Georgetown Green, Charlottesville, VA | Apt 209, Richmond,
22901 .... | VA *23225*
MISS Meredith A (Teague—Meredith A Dixon)— |
at ☎ (804) 973-8359 . . 122 Georgetown Green, |
Charlottesville, VA *22901* .... |

Dixon MR & MRS John Shipley JR (M Elizabeth Boyd)
Me.Cw.Rv.W.Ac.Ncd.
☎ (610) 527-7271 . . 74 Pasture Lane, Apt 211, Bryn Mawr, PA *19010*

Dixon MR & MRS John W (Loren J Poole) StLaw'88.StLaw'88.JM'92
☎ (847) 295-0044 . . 123 E Woodland Av, Lake Bluff, IL *60044*

Dixon MASTER John Wilson JR (John W) .... Born at
Chicago, IL Apr 29'96

Dixon MR & MRS Peter T (Candida A Mabon) H'51 . | ☎ (212) 737-7804
MR Peter M—Bost'84 .... | 79 E 79 St,
MR John C—H'85 .... | New York, NY
MR Mark C M—H'90 .... | *10021*

Dixon MR & MRS Piers (Mavroleon—Ann Van V Davenport)
Bnd'64.Camb'52
☎ (011-44-171) 828-6226 . . 22 Ponsonby Terr, London SW1P 4QA,
England

Dixon MR & MRS (DR) Richard W (Rosina O Berry) | ☎ (908) 766-3558
Rdc'64.H'58 .... | 43 Old Wood Rd,
MISS Erica H—H'95 .... | Bernardsville, NJ
MR Douglas R—at Bucknell .... | *07924*
JUNIORS MR Andrew D—at Middlebury .... |

Dixon MR Stewart S—On.Rr.Cho.Y'52.Mich'55 . . . | ☎ (847) 234-6222
MISS Romayne W—StLaw'91 .... | 734 E Westminster
| Av, Lake Forest, IL
| *60045-2204*

Dixon MR & MRS Stewart S JR (Catherine A Miller) Nw'87.Ithaca'87
☎ (847) 295-0562 . . 55 E Witchwood Lane, Lake Bluff, IL *60044*

Dixon MR & MRS T Henry (Elizabeth P Thayer) Cts.Gm.Me.P'40
☎ (610) 688-1412 . . 333 Edgehill Rd, Wayne, PA *19087*

Dixon MR & MRS Terence A (Sydney F Cruice)
Penn'81.Drex'92.TyDub'87.Cl'93
☎ (212) 799-7040 . . 20 W 64 St, Apt 17N, New York, NY *10023*

Dixon MRS Wesley M (Kribben—Eleanor Cushman) | ☎ (847) CE4-0275
On.Cas.Fy. .... | 620 Mayflower Rd,
MR Delafield Kribben—at ☎ (808) 572-0131 | Lake Forest, IL
Box 1586, Makawao, Maui, HI *96768* ...... | *60045*

Dixon MRS William J 3d (Perot—Sally M Macon).. ☎ (610) 827-7127
MISS Jocelyn M Perot—Buck'94 .... "Fox Run Farm"
MR A Morris Perot JR—StLaw'90 .... 174 Hollow Rd,
RD 1, Malvern, PA
19355

D'Lauro MR Frank A JR—Pc.Rc.Rv.W&L'62.Pa'65
☎ (610) 584-1601 .. "Long Lane Farm" Box 674, Worcester, PA *19490*

Doak MR Kenelm W—P'49 .... ☎ (603) 225-6529
MISS Elizabeth C—at ☎ (505) 255-2024 53 Stickney Hill Rd,
1806 Silver Av SE, Albuquerque, NM *87107*... Concord, NH *03301*

Dober MR & MRS Richard P (Eleanor Lee Lyman) Bnd'49.Bklyn'53.H.'57
☎ (617) 876-0963 .. 8 Buena Vista Park, Cambridge, MA *02140*

Doble MRS Sheilah J (Sheilah L James) .... ☎ (201) 335-2687
MR Douglas P—WVa'96 .... 8 Farrand Dv,
Parsippany, NJ
07054

Doble MR William S .... Married
Rendeiro MISS Susanne N .... Nov 18'95

Dodd MR & MRS Robert E (Margaret L Wilson) Cy.St.G.
☎ (716) 833-5535 .. 127 Brantwood Rd, Buffalo, NY *14226*

Doddridge MR & MRS John Edwin (Elaine C Carpenter) Cin'50.Sdy.Ky'45
☎ (619) 756-2402 .. Box 1328, Rancho Santa Fe, CA *92067*

Dodds MRS Deborah D (Deborah N Detchon) ☎ (412) 391-2773
V'65.Fcg.Pg. .... 326 Third Av,
MR Zachary B .... Pittsburgh, PA
MR Seth D *15222*

Dodds MR & MRS Robert F (Andrea B Lawrence) ☎ (202) 625-0716
Yn.Y'61 .... 3403 P St NW,
MR Robert F .... Washington, DC
MR John E *20007*
MR Christopher W ....

Dodds MR & MRS Robert J JR (Enright—Virginia ☎ (941) 262-3760
Totten) Rr.Yn.Y'37.Pa'40 .... 100 Wilderness
MR Anthony J .... Way, Apt 247,
Naples, FL *34105*

Dodge MR & MRS Clarence JR (Lalla F Harrison)
Cvc.Mt.Sl.Ncd.P'36 .. of
☎ (202) 362-8496 .. 5146 Palisade Lane NW, Washington, DC *20016*
☎ (912) 638-4585 .. "Herons' Roost" Cottage 418, Sea Island,
GA *31561*

Dodge MR & MRS Cleveland E JR (Phyllis Boushall) Csn.P'43
☎ (802) 823-7355 .. "Quarry Hill Farm" Pownal, VT *05261*

Dodge MR & MRS Donald D JR (Ruth P Drayton) P'45
☎ (406) 586-1161 .. 3185 Bridger Canyon Rd, Bozeman, MT *59715*

Dodge MR & MRS Douglas S (Garfield—Christine Fuller Henriques) Y'43
☎ (203) 453-8588 .. 45 Long Hill Farm, Guilford, CT *06437*

Dodge MR & MRS Frederic P (Janet M Dest) ☎ (508) 526-7950
Wheat'76.Ec.O'73 .... 6 Running Ridge
JUNIORS MISS Alice R .... Row, Manchester,
JUNIORS MR Marshall J 2d .... MA *01944*

Dodge MR & MRS Geoffrey L (Zoë N Wood) RISD'86.SacredH'78
☎ (914) 533-2529 .. 207 Kitchawan Rd, South Salem, NY *10590*

Dodge MR & MRS Howard P (Marjorie Cave) H'58 .. ☎ (401) 254-2281
MR Laurence P 2d—Wes'81.Mit'85—at 144 Windward Lane,
101 Hillside Av, Melrose, MA *02176*........ Bristol, RI
02809-1551

Dodge MRS Karl JR (Marlene L Duhon) Rc....... of ☎ (610)647-1789
MISS Alison L .... 207 Vincent Rd,
MISS Virginia M—at La Jolla, CA .... Paoli, PA *19301*
MR Andrew M—at Newport Beach, CA .... ☎ (412) BE8-9128
"Pines" Ligonier,
PA *15658*

Dodge MR Marshall J JR—Fic.Fiy.Y'33
☎ (941) 377-2930 .. B417 Kobernick, 1955 N Honoré Av, Sarasota,
FL *34235*

Dodge MRS William L (Violetta T Brown) ☎ (617) 227-8334
Sth'51.Me. .... 72 Robbins St,
MR Charles L—Me.—at ☎ (860) 739-8645 Milton, MA *02186*
12 W Lane, Old Black Point, CT *06357*...

Dodson MR & MRS Robert H T (Gertrude T Robertson) Hn.H'47
☎ (202) 965-0373 .. 2734 P St NW, Washington, DC *20007*

Doebler MR Charles H 4th—Br'48
☎ (401) 421-2547 .. 86 Brown St, Providence, RI *02906*

Doehring MR & MRS Walter E (Jessica Story) SCar'86.FlaTech'86
☎ (601) 872-7192 .. 9121 Point Aux Chenes, Ocean Springs, MS *39564*

Doelger MISS Emily K .. see T H P Whitney JR

Doelger MR Matthew M .. see T H P Whitney JR

Doelger MR Peter W—Sm.Ub.Srb.Cyb.BtP.Mid'60
☎ (561) 832-4864 .. 134 Worth Court N, West Palm Beach, FL *33405*

Doelger MRS William P (Cole—Josephine Warren)
Evg.BtP.Ofp.Cda.Dc.Myf.
☎ (561) 655-6218 .. 2 Major Alley, Palm Beach, FL *33480*

D'Oench MR & MRS Russell G (Ellen D Gates) Lm.
☎ (860) 347-5969 .. 147 Phedon P'kway, Middletown, CT *06457*

Doepke MR & MRS Frederick W (Margaret L Lillard) Ken'38
☎ (203) 637-1480 .. 1 Tower Lane, Old Greenwich, CT *06870*

Doering MR Alfred C—H'69.Nw'93 .... ☎ (773) 489-6640
MISS Christen E .... 2035 W Charleston
MR Jonathan C .... St, Apt 404,
Chicago, IL *60647*

Doering MR & MRS Edmund J 2d (Wakeman—Sally of ☎ (847)234-0514
Crowder) Rc.On.Sr.Bvl.Chi.H'40 .... 485 Oakwood Av,
MISS W Snow Wakeman—at C2, Lake Forest, IL
☎ (802) 888-7365 .. Box 5, Greensboro, VT *60045-1961*
05841 .... ☎ (508) 748-0297
58 Register Rd,
Marion, MA *02738*

Doering MR & MRS Eugene C 2d (Wagner—Elizabeth B Barrow)
☎ (516) 922-4484 .. 112 Kellogg St, Oyster Bay, NY *11771*

Doering MR & MRS Peter E (Amy T Lewis) OWes'82.StLaw'78.H'87
☎ (203) 655-0550 .. 101 Brookside Rd, Darien, CT *06820*

Doering MASTER Peter Eckart JR (Peter E) .... Born Aug 15'96

Doermann MR & MRS Humphrey (Elisabeth A ☎ (612) 224-0921
Wakefield) V'53.H'52 .... 736 Goodrich Av,
MISS Julia L—Stan'83.Wis'90—at Salem, OR .. St Paul, MN *55105*

Dohan MRS F Curtis (Marie Postenrieder) Pa'38.BMr'64.BMr'69.Cs.
☎ (610) 664-1993 .. 80 E Princeton Rd, Bala-Cynwyd, PA *19004*

Dohan DR & MRS F Curtis JR (Jean Rittmueller)
StOlaf'69.Y'71.NatUIre'77.H'84.P'57.H'61
☎ (901) 682-4504 .. 109 Wallace Rd, Memphis, TN *38117*

Dohan MR Michael B—Vt'90
☎ (206) 517-5309 .. 6826 Sixteenth Av NE, Seattle, WA *98115*

Dohan MR & MRS Michael R (Blanche E Burpee) Hav'61.Mit'69 . . . . | ☎ (516) 549-1805 1 St Marks Place, Cold Spring Harbor, NY *11724*
  MR Douglas R—at ☎ (206) 517-5309 6826 Sixteenth Av NE, Seattle, WA *98115* . . . .

Dohan MR & MRS Thomas R (Jane C Allen) Geo'31
  ☎ (513) 771-7716 . . 846 van Nes Dv, Glendale, OH *45246*

Dohan MR & MRS Thomas R JR (Judith A Nelson) Miss'64
  8860 Cook Rd, Bailey, MS *39320*

Doherty MR & MRS D'Arcy R (Jane McL Kennedy) McG'64 . . . . | ☎ (416) 925-8222 56 Warren Rd, Toronto, Ontario M4V 2R5, Canada
  MR Manning L . . . .
  MR D'Arcy P . . . .

Dohrmann MR & MRS Bruce P (Clements—Ninive Tous) Motolinia'63.Bhm.Y'51.Cal'56 . . . . | of ☎ (415)921-5709 2448 Clay St, San Francisco, CA *94115* ☎ (011-34-71) 402829 Paseo Sagrera 9, Palma de Mallorca, Spain
  MISS Ninive M Clements . . . .

Dohrmann MRS Elizabeth O (Elizabeth Anne Otto)
  ☎ (415) 922-2930 . . 3203 Pacific Av, San Francisco, CA *94118*

Dohrmann MR Eric B—Bhm.Y'53.Cal'58
  ☎ (415) 921-0551 . . 2481 Vallejo St, San Francisco, CA *94123*

Dohrmann MRS Jane B (Jane C Bosworth) My. . . . | ☎ (505) 988-1996 RR 19, Box 90-JBD, Santa Fe, NM *87505-9812*
  MISS Natalie B . . . .
  MR William F 4th . . . .
  MR Ross G . . . .

Dohrmann MR & MRS Robert L (Phoebe Maltby) Stan'31
  ☎ (818) 796-8179 . . 453 S Orange Grove Blvd, Apt 1, Pasadena, CA *91105*

Dohrmann MR William F 3d—P'57
  45 Lawton Rd, Canton, CT *06019*

Dolan MR & MRS Brooke K (Costello—Lenora Dame) Dick'80.Cts.SFrArt'77
  ☎ (717) 795-0963 . . 40 Green Ridge Rd, Mechanicsburg, PA *17055*

Dolan MR & MRS H Hoffman JR (Leas—A Kingsley Houghton) Me.Cts.Gm. . . . . | of ☎ (610)525-0483 1201 Valley Rd, Villanova, PA *19085* ☎ (561) 231-5301 2607 Ocean Dv, Vero Beach, FL *32963*
  MISS Pauline T—Vt'89 . . . .

Dolan MR & MRS Thomas 4th (Kenworthy—H Elizabeth Gubb) Ph.Ac.Myf.Cr'48 . . of
  ☎ (215) CH2-3517 . . 721 Glengarry Rd, Philadelphia, PA *19118*
  ☎ (406) 222-2647 . . W Boulder Reserve, McLeod, MT *59052*

Dole MR Charles H JR—Ariz'65
  ☎ (541) 476-2453 . . 2451 W Jones Creek Rd, Grants Pass, OR *97526*

d'Olier MR Franklin JR—Ph.Ssk.Mds.Pn.P.'33
  ☎ (610) 525-3222 . . 59 Pasture Lane, Bryn Mawr, PA *19010-1763*

Dollard MR & MRS John D (Palance—Dollard—Joan C Ganis) Yn.Y'58
  ☎ (512) 327-2728 . . 1827 Westlake Dv, Austin, TX *78746*

Doman MR & MRS Nicholas R (Perrin—Judith A Nicely) BMr'50.Fy.Col'35.Buda'36 . . of
  ☎ (212) 628-2136 . . 1035 Fifth Av, New York, NY *10028*
  ☎ (516) 749-0006 . . PO Box 298, Shelter Island, NY *11964*

Domínguez MR & MRS Martín (Alexandra H Rush) Pa'69.Pa'72.Pa'67.Pa'69.Pa'71
  ☎ (011-34-91) 310-16-74 . . Calle General Arrando 34, 28010 Madrid, Spain

Dominick MR & MRS Gayer G 2d (Patricia Coggeshall) Y'65 . . . . | ☎ (360) 866-1638 5920 Athens Beach Dv NW, Olympia, WA *98502*
  MISS Wendy A—SanDiego'90—at 2518 Polk St, San Francisco, CA *94109* . . . .

Dominick MR Theodore W . . . . Died at Washington, DC Jly 27'96

Dominick MRS Theodore W (Howland—Elizabeth R Poole) Sth'25.Mt.Cvc.Sl.
  ☎ (202) 667-1731 . . 2500 Massachusetts Av NW, Apt 3, Washington, DC *20008-2821*

Dommerich MR & MRS Louis A (K Jane Morgan) BtP.Evg.Cly.Myf.Ht.Dar.Cda.H'52
  ☎ (561) 833-8147 . . 28 Middle Rd, Palm Beach, FL *33480*

Donaghy MR & MRS Edwin C JR (Sophie S Bell) Me.Gm.Cts.Rv.Ac.Y'45w
  ☎ (610) 525-1797 . . 707 Pennstone Rd, Bryn Mawr, PA *19010*

Donahoe MR & MRS Daniel J 3d (Anne Bradley) Sth'61.Bhm.Pcu.H'55 . . . . | ☎ (602) 948-8540 7618 Las Brisas Lane, Scottsdale, AZ *85253*
  MISS Brooke B—H'94—*see Dilatory Domiciles* .

Donahoe MR Daniel J 4th—Bost'92
  ☎ (415) 474-5852 . . 964 Central Av, San Francisco, CA *94115*

Donahoe MISS Gabrielle—Denis'86
  ☎ (415) 749-0788 . . 2701 Green St, Apt 12, San Francisco, CA *94123*

Donahue MR & MRS Frank R (Barbara A Cashen) GwynM'52.Rc.Pe.R.P'39.Pa'42 . . . . | ☎ (610) 649-6490 461 Glyn Wynne Rd, Haverford, PA *19041*
  MISS Allaire N—MaryMt'92 . . . .
  MR F Scott—P'92 . . . .

Donahue MR & MRS James A (Veale—Jane M C Purinton) Nu'72.HolyC'69.P'72.TheoUn'84 . . . . | ☎ (202) 337-8370 3315 P St NW, Washington, DC *20007*
  JUNIORS MR Lucius C Veale—at Georgetown .

Donald MR David L
  ☎ (212) 732-7749 . . 376 Broadway, Apt 4B, New York, NY *10013*

Donald MR & MRS Douglas D (Grace M Retz) Chr.Snc.Rv.Cs.Dar.P.'44.Cl'47 . . of
  ☎ (212) CA8-9576 . . 45 Gramercy Park, New York, NY *10010*
  ☎ (516) 653-8478 . . Deer Path & Pheasant Run, Quogue, NY *11959*

Donald MR & MRS Glenn H JR (M Kenneith Wilson) Aub'86.Cy.Aub'85
  ☎ (205) 879-7769 . . 7 Honeysuckle Lane, Mountain Brook, AL *35213*

Donald MRS Malcolm (Gertrude Hunnewell) Cy.Chi.
  ☎ (617) 277-5649 . . 54 Sargent Rd, Brookline, MA *02146*

Donald MR Malcolm—Pcu.H'62 . . . . | *see Dilatory Domiciles*
  MR Alexandre—at Oberlin . . . .
  JUNIORS MR Samuel . . . .

Donald MISS Marian S—Bost'83.Emer'95
  ☎ (508) 758-2286 . . 33 Ned's Point Rd, Mattapoisett, MA *02739*

Donald MRS Peter G (Miller—Elizabeth C Heard) GeoW'79
  ☎ (212) 360-7151 . . 245 E 93 St, Apt 10B, New York, NY *10128*

Donald MR Peter G—P.'80
  ☎ (212) 260-0166 . . 22 Irving Place, New York, NY *10003*
Donaldson MISS Beirne (Patton—Rusmisel—Beirne | ☎ (201) 543-2633
Donaldson) V'68 . . . . | 13 Roxiticus Rd,
  JUNIORS MISS Margo A Rusmisel . . . . | Mendham, NJ *07945*
Donaldson MRS Francis JR (Elizabeth Townsend)
  ☎ (508) 759-3696 . . 245 County Rd, RFD 1, Buzzards Bay, MA *02532*
Donaldson MR & MRS Joseph W (Mary E Lester) B'hamS'82.Lips'78
  ☎ (334) 286-4004 . . 106 Glynlakes Dv, Pike Road, AL *36064*
Donaldson MRS Robert Montgomery 2d (Adelaide R Chaqueneau)
Cly.Cda.Ht.Dh.Ncd . . .of
  ☎ (212) 593-7166 . . 200 E 66 St, Apt 506C, New York, NY *10021*
  ☎ (561) 833-2207 . . 354 Chilean Av, Palm Beach, FL *33480*
Donan MR & MRS Holland R (Nancy M Carroll) | ☎ (941) 455-8075
Pn.P'51 . . . . | 5918 Almaden Dv,
  MR Peter J . . . . | Naples, FL *34119*
Donery MRS Katharine A R (Katharine A Rust) . . . . | ☎ (510) 454-6305
  MR David P . . . . | 32 Savannah Av,
  MR Christopher B . . . . | San Anselmo, CA
  | *94960*
Donham MR & MRS Paul JR (Valerie F Lawrence) | ☎ (617) 868-3596
RISD'64.Va'69 ⚓ | 42 Winslow St,
  MISS Phoebe L—at Smith . . . . | Cambridge, MA
  JUNIORS MR Samuel L . . . . | *02138*
Donlon MR & MRS David D (Suzanne E Saunders) | of ☎ (415)921-2918
Mls'58.Pcu.Bhm.Cp.Cal'54 . . . . | 2298 Pacific Av,
  MISS Frances K . . . . | San Francisco, CA
  MISS Alexandra E . . . . | *94115*
  | ☎ (415) 669-7130
  | "Inver House"
  | 11 Woodhaven Rd,
  | Inverness, CA *94937*
Donnan MR & MRS David Hibbs (Elizabeth C Pauly)
NMex'60.Nf.Bab'49 ⚓
  ☎ (207) 276-5522 . . "Windover" Manchester Rd, Northeast Harbor, ME *04662*
Donnell MR Bruce B—Cp.Cl'67.Cl'70
  ☎ (505) 983-7511 . . 1 Casas de San Juan, Santa Fe, NM *87501*
Donnell MR & MRS Ellsworth (Susan B R Mentz) Cda.SCal'47
  ☎ (011-44-171) 584-3673 . . 12 Connaught Square, London W2 2HG, England
Donnell MR & MRS John R (Caraboolad—Maureen Nahas)
Ursul'54.BtP.Evg.Srb.Nrr.Cv.Cy.Un.Rr.Case'34.H'56 . . of
  ☎ (561) 655-2297 . . "Villa Contenta" 300 Parc Monceau, Palm Beach, FL *33480*
  ☎ (216) 851-2297 . . 1 Bratenahl Place, Apt 1401, Bratenahl, OH *44108*
Donnell MISS Susan W (Shepard—Susan W Donnell)
80 Overlook Rd, Morristown, NJ *07960*
Donnelley MISS Deborah E—SL'84
34 Dana Place, Amherst, MA *01002*
Donnelley MRS Gaylord (Dorothy W Ranney) On.Sr.Cho.Rc.Gr.Ln.Cas.Wa.
  ☎ (847) 362-4393 . . 31780 N Almond Rd, Libertyville, IL *60048-9998*
Donnelley MR & MRS James R (Nina Herrmann)
Nw'65.Ch'76.Cho.B.Gr.Ln.Ny.Cw.Cas.Dth'57.Ch'62
  ☎ (312) 642-0618 . . 1500 N Lake Shore Dv, Apt 11-12B, Chicago, IL *60610*

Donnelley MRS Margaret C (Margaret E Crook) . . . | ☎ (561) 686-8779
  MISS Shawn Margaret . . . . | PO Box 1470,
  MR Willard David . . . . | West Palm Beach,
  MR Angus Gaylord . . . . | FL *33402-1470*
Donnelley MR & MRS Robert G (Miranda C | ☎ (847) 234-4898
Sampsell) Cho.On.Rc.Cc.Ncd.Y'60.H'63. | 1050 W Melody Rd,
Kent'70 | Lake Forest, IL
  MR Marshall S—LakeF'92 . . . . | *60045*
Donnelley MR & MRS Thomas E 2d (Clark—Barbara | of ☎ (773)525-5660
Coleman) On.Cw.Cas.Y'55 | 2440 N Lakeview
  MR Christopher B Clark JR . . . . | Av, Apt 17F,
  | Chicago, IL
  | *60614-2714*
  | ☎ (406) 842-5891
  | Timber Creek
  | Ranch, PO Box 48,
  | Alder, MT *59710*
Donnelly MRS William M (Honoria A Murphy) Mds.
  ☎ (561) 844-0400 . . 33 Ocean Av, Apt 512, Palm Beach Shores, FL *33404*
Donnem MR & MRS Roland W (Sarah Brandon | ☎ (216) 751-1090
Lund) V'58.Unn.Un.T.Kt.Cvc.Mt.It.Cly.Ncd. | 2945 Fontenay Rd,
Y'52.H'57 . . . . | Shaker Heights, OH
  MISS Sarah Madison—JHop'88.CathU'92—at | *44120*
  ☎ (301) 294-3376 . . 104 Calvert Rd, Rockville, |
MD *20850* . . . . |
Donner MR & MRS Joseph W (Pamela Cushing) Rc.Bhm.Ht.P'49 . . of
  ☎ (305) 361-1667 . . 520 S Mashta Dv, Key Biscayne, FL *33149-1733*
  ☎ (212) 794-2607 . . 3 E 71 St, Apt 11A, New York, NY *10021-4151*
Donner MR & MRS Richard E (Martha A Wheeler) . . of
  ☎ (901) 285-3701 . . 1005 Troy Av, Dyersburg, TN *38024*
  ☎ (941) 966-4833 . . "The Oaks" 75 Osprey Point Dv, Osprey, FL *34229*
Donnon MR & MRS Edward D (Gwen F Bonsall) Syr'81.Pc.Syr'81
  ☎ (215) 540-9897 . . 1317 Biwood Rd, Ambler, PA *19002*
Donoghue MR Daniel C 3d
  ☎ (941) 966-3518 . . 3113 Casey Key Rd, Nokomis, FL *34275*
Donohoe MRS Edward (Dorsch—Evgeniya Nicolaievna)
  ☎ (415) 851-0302 . . 435 Whiskey Hill Rd, Woodside, CA *94062*
Donohoe MRS Joan R (Garceau—Joan Rolfe) . . . . . | ☎ (415) 321-2994
  MR William J JR . . . . | 150 Alma St, Apt
  | 116, Menlo Park,
  | CA *94025*
Donohoe MR & MRS Joseph A 4th (Yvonne Dibblee) Pcu.Cp.
  ☎ (415) 325-2675 . . 125 James Av, Atherton, CA *94025*
Donohoe MR Joseph A 5th—Pcu.Cp.Cal'67 . . of
  ☎ (415) 885-6398 . . 2160 Leavenworth St, San Francisco, CA *94133*
  ☎ (408) 842-3992 . . "Lion Oaks" PO Box 1085, Gilroy, CA *95021*
Donohoe MRS A James (Barbara Le R Sanford) | ☎ (914) 779-2563
Sth'64.Y. | 6 Northern Av,
  MISS Claire B . . . . | Bronxville, NY
  MR Benjamin F . . . . | *10708*
Donohue MRS Charles D (Frances L Rich)
  ☎ (518) 456-6928 . . 100 Heritage Rd, Guilderland, NY *12084*
Donohue MRS Francis M (Mary Marvel) Csn.Ncd.
  ☎ (302) 652-8896 . . 1105 Barley Mill Rd, Greenville, DE *19807*

Donovan MR & MRS Alfred L (Tucker—Melinda A | ☎ (617) 232-2235
Nichols) RMWmn'66.Cy.Km.H'57 . . . . | 4 Alwington Rd,
   MISS Diana R—Br'90 . . . . | Chestnut Hill, MA
   MISS Blair F—SFrSt'96 . . . . | *02167*
   MR Alfred L JR—Mass'93 . . . . |
      MISS Anne P Tucker—at Harvard . . . . |
      JUNIORS MR John M Tucker—at Bates . . . . . |

Donovan MISS Catharine-Mary—Man'vl'55.BMr'56. Sbc.Chi.Cly.Btn.Cy.
   ☎ (617) 266-2263 . . 117 Beacon St, Boston, MA *02116*

Donovan MISS Christine P . . see J F Butler

Donovan MR & MRS Doran W F (Susan D Gardner) | ☎ (617) 859-3802
Hlns'66.Ll.Dar.Geo'63.Cl'67 . . . . | 90 Commonwealth
   MISS Nina H—SanDiego'94 . . . . | Av, Boston, MA
   MR Doran L—Geo'91 . . . . | *02116-3034*

Donovan MR & MRS Henry L (Lucy Davis) Ub.H'60 | ☎ (207) 773-7725
   MR Alfred F—at Delaware, OH . . . . | 44 Bowdoin St,
   MR Lincoln D—at Arlington, VA . . . . | Portland, ME *04102*

Donovan MR & MRS Lee M (Catherine B McKee) | ☎ (410) 315-9075
Tufts'72.Ayc.Pa'63 ⛵ . . . . | 141 Drexel Dv,
   MISS Stacy M—at Va Comwth U . . . . | Millersville, MD
   MISS Kendall McK . . . . | *21108*
   JUNIORS MISS Megan C . . . . |

Donovan MRS Thomas Alton (Christiana S Wygant)
   ☎ (402) 467-0257 . . 225 N 56 St, Apt 317, Lincoln, NE *68504*

Doolittle MRS Roy W (Grauer—Harriet Richmond) . . . . Died at
      Niagara-on-the-Lake, Ontario, Canada Jly 7'96

Doolittle MR & MRS Roy W JR (Cynthia Keating).St.Ts.G . . of
   ☎ (716) 885-5655 . . 100 Chapin P'kway, Buffalo, NY *14209*
   ☎ (905) 834-9884 . . Lorraine, Port Colborne, Ontario L3K 5V7, Canada

Doolittle MR William M—Pn.P'28
   ☎ (860) 435-2631 . . Noble Horizons, Cottage M1, 17 Cobble Rd,
Salisbury, CT *06068*

Doran MR & MRS Andrew D (Alice Spivey) TroySt'67.TroySt'75
   ☎ (334) 260-0609 . . 3922 McCain Lane, Montgomery, AL *36106*

Doran MR & MRS Robert W (Evelyn Hollingsworth) | ☎ (617) 734-6359
Cy.Sm.Chi.Y'55 . . . . | 25 Jefferson Rd,
   MISS Eleanor H . . . . | Chestnut Hill, MA
   MR David L . . . . | *02167*

Dorland MR & MRS Dodge O (Bonita G Zeese)
Nu'76.Nu'78.Snc.Hl.Cw.Rv.Vca.Y.Colg'70
   ☎ (212) 628-6067 . . 755 Park Av, New York, NY *10021*

Dorn MR Carl S (Sally C Hayes)
   ☎ (703) 506-1983 . . 8340 Greensboro Dv, Apt 1014, McLean,
VA *22102*

Dorn MR Christopher H—Cl'86
   ☎ (212) 348-1088 . . 305 E 86 St, Apt 5BW, New York, NY *10028*

Dorn DR Gregory H—Cl'90.Cl'96
   ☎ (310) 207-8904 . . 1415 S Bundy Dv, Apt 8, Los Angeles, CA *90025*

Dorn MR John Z—Cl'78
   ☎ (212) 695-7413 . . 529 W 42 St, 6R, New York, NY *10036*

Dorr MR & MRS Glenn Bert III (Eleanor M Waud)
Mid'88.Suff'93.On.Woos'88 . . of
   ☎ (847) 234-7240 . . 635 Green Briar Lane, Lake Forest, IL *60045*
   ☎ (603) 744-6003 . . ''Tappalot'' Pike's Point, Newfound Lake, Bristol,
NH *03222*

Dorr MR & MRS Williams P (Tully—Sally Mitchell) | ☎ (312) 787-3607
Ariz'65.Sc.Hav'66.Nu'69 . . . . | 1335 N Astor St,
   MISS Alison . . . . | Chicago, IL *60610*
   MISS Lisa . . . . |
   MISS Hilary . . . . |

Dorrance MR & MRS Bennett (Jacquelynn B Williams) Ariz'69.Bcs.Ariz'69
   ☎ (602) 596-5000 . . 7400 N Shadow Mountain Rd, Paradise Valley,
AZ *85253-3381*

Dorrough MR & MRS Richard H (Shirley Crawford) | ☎ (334) 272-4225
V'68.Ala'71.Wash'67.Ala'70 . . . . | 1701 Croom Dv,
   MISS Carolyn E . . . . | Montgomery, AL
   | *36106*

Dorsel MR & MRS A Clifford (Vivian Packard) Wms'80.Mass'84
   ☎ (413) 698-2282 . . 205 Summit Rd, Richmond, MA *01254*

Dorsey MISS Elise W—Y'87 . . of
   ☎ (415) 563-3674 . . 1592 Union St, Apt 435, San Francisco, CA *94123*
   ☎ (707) 938-5860 . . 1221 Sobre Vista Dv, Sonoma, CA *94576*

Dorsey MISS Elizabeth C—Gonzaga'96 . . see A D Terry

Dorsey DR & MRS J Henderson (Matilda H Woodward) H'54.JHop'58 ⛵
   3737 Millender Mill Rd, Butler, MD *21023*

Dorsey REV CANON James C—Md.Cc.Loy'54.PhilaDiv'58
   ☎ (215) 548-8959 . . St Alban's Rectory, 257 W Somerville Av,
Philadelphia, PA *19120-3220*

Dorsey MRS Joshua W 3d (Leslie A B Smith) Md'51.Sl.Cc.Cda.
   ☎ (301) 695-9366 . . ''Marlborough House'' 101 Record St, Frederick,
MD *21701*

Dorsey MRS Stephen P (Carolyn Du B Cosby) Sl.
   ☎ (202) 966-3006 . . 4101 Cathedral Av NW, Apt 717, Washington,
DC *20016-3585*

Dorsey MR & MRS William H JR (Vicki L Keller) Cal'64.H'66.Y'64 . . of
   ☎ (011-44-1692) 631000 . . Beeston Hall, Beeston St Lawrence,
Norfolk NR12 8YS, England
   ☎ (410) 323-2959 . . Cross Keys, 38 Olmsted Green Court, Baltimore,
MD *21210*

Dorson MR & MRS William S (Mercedes de G | 52 E 91 St,
Littlejohn) Pa'74.Ny.Pr.Pa'72.Ch'76 . . . . . . | New York, NY
   JUNIORS MISS Carolina de G . . . . | *10128*

Dortch MRS Madalyn B (Madalyn T Breitzke)
   ☎ (501) 961-1555 . . ''Little Gate'' 2807 Bearskin Lake Rd, Scott,
AR *72142*

Dossett MR & MRS William K (Mary C Goodyear) Tul'86.Tul'83.Miss'89
   ☎ (601) 846-0567 . . 301 S Fifth Av, Cleveland, MS *38732*

Doswell MR & MRS Joseph W (Kelsh—Diana K | ☎ (410) 257-6577
Brewster) VaWes'74.Va'75.USN'73 . . . . | 12128 Palisades Dv,
   JUNIORS MR James B . . . . | Dunkirk, MD *20754*

Doty MR & MRS James J (Paula P Newell) Cy.Cw.Myf.H.'59
   ☎ (617) 326-8975 . . 1020 High St, Dedham, MA *02026*

Doty MRS Lockwood R 2d (Mary A Brayer) . . . . . . | ☎ (703) 751-1373
   MISS M Louise B . . . . | 5300 Holmes Run
   | P'kway, Apt 902,
   | Alexandria, VA
   | *22304*

Doty MRS Sharon H S (Sharon H Staub) DU'72 . . . | ☎ (860) 567-3366
   MISS Brownson S—at U of Vt . . . . | 19 Wolcott St,
   | PO Box 655,
   | Litchfield, CT *06759*

Doub MR & MRS George C JR (Mary W Tyler) Gv.Mv.H'62 .. of
☎ (410) 363-1260 .. 2700 Caves Rd, Owings Mills, MD 21117
☎ (809) 946-4413 .. Forbes Rd, Providenciales, Turks & Caicos Islands
Doub MR & MRS George C 3d (Rebecca S Fenger)
Cal'84.SanDiego'89.Gv.Mt.UMiami'86
☎ (310) 377-4967 .. 6726 Kings Harbor Dv, Rancho Palos Verdes,
CA 90274

Doub MR & MRS William O (Mary G Boggs) Gchr'53.Ct.Mt.Ncd.W&J'53.Md'56	☎ (301) 469-6263 6 Warde Court,
MR J Peyton—at 19520 Shepherdstown Pike, Keedysville, MD 21756	Potomac, MD 20854
MR Albert A 2d—at 6500—36 St, Arlington, VA 22213	

Doubleday DR & MRS Charles W (Verlinde V Hill)
Pitzer'76.SwTex'78.Tex'76.Tex'81
☎ (713) 961-1575 .. 5302 Fieldwood Dv, Houston, TX 77056
Doubleday MR G Chester—Rcn.Me.Rv.P'28
☎ (610) 645-8698 .. 1400 Waverly Rd, B211, Gladwyne,
PA 19035-1254

Doubleday MR & MRS George 2d (Lucinda Burling) Cly.Y'61	☎ (415) 929-1808 2684 Green St,
MISS Jennifer—Vt'88—at ☎ (415) 775-3195 499 Marina Blvd, San Francisco, CA 94123 ...	San Francisco, CA 94123
MR Stephen T—Col'91—at ☎ (503) 335-0436 2430 NE Stanton St, Portland, OR 97212	
Doubleday MR & MRS Nelson (Barnett—Sandra Pine) Rcn.Pr.Mb.Ln.P'55	☎ (561) 546-5406 Box 605,
MR Joseph W Barnett 3d	Hobe Sound, FL 33475

Doucette MR Donald F JR .. see MRS C E Kinkade

Dougherty MR & MRS A Webster JR (Janet I Spencer) Me.Rc.Ac.	☎ (610) 688-3824 775 Mancill Rd,
MISS Jennifer W—Skd'89	Wayne, PA
MISS Cynthia S—Eastern'95	19087-2004
MISS Andrea G—Rich'92	

Dougherty MISS Ann S .. see MRS M T Jenney

Dougherty MRS Charles G (Mary Holland)	☎ (757) 496-1393 3100 Shore Dv, Apt
MR Charles W—at 1018 Angler Lane, Virginia Beach, VA 23451	702, Virginia Beach, VA 23451

Dougherty MR & MRS David J 4th (Julie J Rowe)...	☎ (716) 634-6811 299 Sagewood Terr,
MR David J 5th	Williamsville, NY
MR James P	14221
MR Peter L	

Dougherty MR & MRS Francis S (Julia V Ravenel)
Char'ton'43.Cw.Dar.USN'45
☎ (803) 723-7380 .. 50 Legare St, Charleston, SC 29401

Dougherty MR & MRS Geoffrey B (Nancy M Taylor) Rc.Cry.Sa.Pa'55 ⚓	☎ (610) 783-0180 1789 Hamilton Dv,
MR Edward W—at ☎ (610) 519-9106 122 Garrett Av, Rosemont, PA 19010	PO Box 554, Valley Forge, PA
MR G Bromley JR	19481

Dougherty MR Graham 3d .. see MRS C Everett

Dougherty MR & MRS Howard W (Laureys—Maria V van Ronzelen
de Villarreal) SacredH'39.Bhm.Vh.Cp.Stan'38 .. of
☎ (305) 446-6241 .. 610 Valencia Av, 301, Coral Gables, FL 33134
☎ (504) 897-6591 .. 2434 St Charles Av, Apt 204, New Orleans,
LA 70130
Dougherty MR & MRS J Chrysostom 3d (Randle—Sara M Blair)
Tex'34.Tex'66.A.Tex'37.H'40
☎ (512) 472-4092 .. 6 Green Lanes, Austin, TX 78703
Dougherty MRS John K (Helen Batcheller)
☎ (802) 253-4596 .. 5615 Mountain Rd, Stowe, VT 05672

Dougherty MR & MRS Kenneth W (Katharine N Sutro) Mg.Chr.Ph.Mo.Sap.Cly.Pa'48	☎ (201) 539-6677 Spring Valley &
MISS Sarah B—Wes'85.H'90—at	Van Beuren Rds,
☎ (617) 863-8317 .. 11 N Hancock St, Lexington, MA 02173	Morristown, NJ 07960

Dougherty MISS Marian H
7607 N Arbory Way, Laurel, MD 20707

Doughten MRS Barbara P (Barbara D Payne)......	☎ (847) 205-0777 1871 Mission Hills
MISS Lisa M—NCar'89.LondEc'92—at	Lane, Northbrook,
☎ (011-385-41) 551-228 .. OFDA-DART, US Embassy, Zagreb, Croatia..............	IL 60062

Doughten MISS Kimberley D—NCar'86
☎ (770) 986-9040 .. 2870 Dresden Square Dv, Atlanta, GA 30341
Doughten MR William S—P'36
☎ (212) RI9-4419 .. 230 Riverside Dv, Apt 14-O, New York, NY 10025
Doughty MR & MRS J Sanford (Fairbank—Cynthia Cleveland) Wms'32.H'34
☎ (540) 463-7774 .. 804 Bowyer Lane, Box 743, Lexington, VA 24450
Douglas MR & MRS Archibald 3d (Wayne V Goss) V'56.Y'52
☎ (609) 924-8556 .. 4370 Province Line Rd, Princeton, NJ 08540
Douglas MRS Archibald G (BRNSS Margareta C H Lagerfelt) Sl.
☎ (804) 978-2002 .. Rivanna Farm, 2973 Stony Point Rd,
Charlottesville, VA 22911-9140
Douglas MR Barclay JR (late Barclay) .... Married at Newport, RI
Barrett MISS Diana M (James) .... Oct 21'95
Douglas MISS Deirdre H (Archibald 3d) ..... Married at Narragansett, RI
Carey MR Daniel W (Charles J) .... Jly 20'96
Douglas DR Donald B JR—P'44
☎ (212) OR9-0457 .. 222 E 35 St, New York, NY 10016

Douglas MRS Eleanor Dick (Eleanor S Dick) Ncd...	☎ (617) 242-8260 197—8 St, 11,
MISS Dorothy H	Charlestown, MA
MISS Emilie D	02129

Douglas MRS Isabelle Z (Isabelle F Zimmerman) Dar.
☎ (860) 767-8447 .. 31 Riversedge, Ivoryton, CT 06442
Douglas MRS J Gordon (Kruming—Mary W Lummus) Nrr.Cly.
☎ (803) 723-0223 .. 22 Elliott St, Charleston, SC 29401

Douglas MR & MRS John W JR (Lucy S Simpson) Rr.Dick'63	of ☎ (412)681-6375 1436 Inverness Av,
MR John W 3d	Pittsburgh, PA
MR Alexander S	15217
	☎ (412) 238-3324 "Bantry Hill" PO Box 61, Rector, PA 15677

Douglas MR & MRS Lewis W JR (Melinda F Stanley) ☎ (303) 744-0005
Wells'66.Y'45w . . . . 2525 E Exposition
JUNIORS MR Justin S . . . . Av, Denver, CO
80209

Douglas MRS Percy L (Katherine S Douglas) Cly . . of
☎ (212) 838-8425 . . 550 Park Av, New York, NY *10021*
☎ (914) 693-2271 . . "Glenalla" Winding Road Farm, Ardsley,
NY *10502*

Douglas MR & MRS Peter R (Camille M Jensen)
Sth'73.H'77.K.Ri.H'72.H'75 . . of
☎ (212) 753-8366 . . 328 E 51 St, New York, NY *10022*
☎ (518) 239-6227 . . "North Farm" Box 55, Medusa, NY *12120*

Douglas MR & MRS Roderick McI (Margaret L Miller) Pg.Rr.Fcg.WOnt'66
☎ (905) 335-7093 . . 2483-1 Side Rd, RR 1, Burlington,
Ontario L7R 3X4, Canada

Douglas MR & MRS Stuart T (Lane—Dorothy Dew) ☎ (713) 626-5686
Cw. . . . . 3656 Wickersham
MR Andrew G . . . . Lane, Houston, TX
77027

Douglas MR & MRS Timothy J (J Alison Schmidlapp) Tul'79.Tul'77
☎ (615) 665-2838 . . 818 Lynnwood Blvd, Nashville, TN *37205*

Douglas MR & MRS William C (McIlvaine—Manker—
Adele E Arrowsmith) V'50.Fy.Ncd.P'45 . . of
☎ (847) 295-1511 . . 1393 N Western Av, Lake Forest, IL *60045*
☎ (970) 926-5525 . . PO Box 1458, Edwards, CO *81632*

Douglas-Hamilton LADY Malcolm (Winslow—Latham—Paine—
Natalie S Wales) Dar.
☎ (212) 988-4468 . . 174 E 74 St, New York, NY *10021*

Douglass MRS Earl S (Horn—Dorothy M Griggs)
☎ (209) 532-9541 . . 73 W Jackson St, Apt 1, Sonora, CA *95370*

Douglass MRS Louise S (Crim—Ferguson—Louise J Douglass) DU'72
☎ (303) 761-6988 . . 2450 Cherryridge Rd, Englewood, CO *80110*

Douglass MR & MRS Robert D (Lucy Wyer) Macalester'81.On.Macalester'79
☎ (847) 295-0491 . . 550 Stable Lane, Lake Forest, IL *60045*

Douglass MR & MRS Thomas Edward (Elizabeth S ☎ (314) 432-1712
Jones) Br'66.Wash'72.Br'66.Wash'73 . . . . 41 Briarcliff,
MISS Katherine E . . . . St Louis, MO *63124*
JUNIORS MR Richard T . . . .
JUNIORS MR Stephen J . . . .

Douglass MR & MRS Wade A (Claudia E Lipscomb) ☎ (615) 451-3390
NCar'60.Tenn'76.Van'55.Nu'62 . . . . "Oak Haven Farm"
MR Cullen E—Aub'88—at 1512 Compton Av, 558 Douglass Lane,
Nashville, TN *37212* . . . . Gallatin, TN *37066*

Douglass MR & MRS William A (Stephanie Howell) ☎ (011-44-1892)
Yn.Y'51 511785
MISS Victoria H—Ken'92—at ☎ (203) 972-3244 41 Madeira Park,
96D East Av, New Canaan, CT *06840* . . . . Tunbridge Wells,
MISS Fiona E—Manch'93—at ☎ (011-44-171) Kent TN2 5SY,
582-4515 . . 50 West Square, London SE11 4SP, England
England . . . .

Douthit MR & MRS Philip S (Elizabeth Osborne)
Shmptn'72.Msq.Why.Webb'72
☎ (203) 622-0737 . . 290 Riversville Rd, Greenwich, CT *06830*

Dove MR & MRS Guy O 3d (Cavanagh—Valerie of ☎ (540)364-4453
Mixter) Unn.Cvc.Md.Mt.Ty'61 . . . . "Ballantrae"
MISS Dorothy M Cavanagh . . . . PO Box 796,
JUNIORS MR Carroll J Cavanagh 3d . . . . Middleburg, VA
20118
☎ (202) 244-3331
4448 Westover
Place NW,
Washington, DC
20016

Dow MR & MRS James P (Cynthia Lee) Cr'91.Cr'91
☎ (214) 956-8903 . . 7640 W Greenway Blvd, Apt 8K, Dallas, TX *75209*

Dow MR & MRS Peter A (Jane Ottaway) W&M'55.Mich'55 ⚓ . . of
☎ (313) 886-1424 . . 191 Ridge Rd, Grosse Pointe Farms, MI *48236*
Tarpon Flats, PO Box 254, Islamorada, FL *33036*

Dow MRS Richard A (Bertolet—Phoebe P Crosby) ☎ (207) 734-8826
Chi.Ncd. . . . . Hewes Point,
MR Richard A JR—at ☎ (201) 867-3705 Box 187, Islesboro,
833 Boulevard E, Weehawken, NJ *07087* . . . . . . ME *04848*

Dowd MR & MRS Edward L JR (Jill P Lowrey) Pa'73.StL'71
☎ (314) 997-6432 . . 805 S Warson Rd, St Louis, MO *63124*

Dowdall MRS Richard J (Banister—Catron—Rodney M Davis) . . of
☎ (520) 299-9777 . . 4220 E Pontatoc Canyon Dv, Tucson, AZ *85718*
☎ (805) 969-3662 . . Montecito Shores, 70 Seaview Dv, Santa Barbara,
CA *93108*

Dowler MR & MRS Moulton Shreve JR (Pamela A ☎ (210) 826-8267
Morton) MaryB'72.A.W&L'68.Tex'72 . . . . 110 Ridgemont Av,
MISS Emily M . . . . San Antonio, TX
JUNIORS MISS Claire G *78209*

Dowley MISS Elise P . . . . ☎ (215) CH7-4434
MISS Ruth S—Pa'43.Pa'45 400 E Evergreen
MR Dwight Van R—P'34.H'37 . . . . Av, Philadelphia,
MR F Hotham—P'36.Ch'53—at PA *19118*
☎ (773) 955-0705 . . 5550 S Dorchester Av,
Chicago, IL *60637* . . . .

Dowling MR & MRS John L (Hebe Sanders) of ☎ (212)744-2242
Hlns'64.Pqt.Ln.Rv.Km.Cly.Tufts'59 . . . . 120 East End Av,
MISS Meaghan H—P.'91.Cly.—at New York, NY
☎ (212) 362-9314 . . 46 W 69 St, New York, NY *10028*
10023 . . . . ☎ (203) 259-0444
MR John W—H.'94—at 5 MacDougal Alley, 110 Beachside Av,
New York, NY *10011* . . . . Greens Farms, CT
JUNIORS MR Peter S—at Groton *06436*

Dowling MR & MRS Joseph J JR (Karen M Obes) Bost'72.LIU'78.Nu'91
☎ (914) 764-9436 . . 29 Upper Shad Rd, Pound Ridge, NY *10576-2107*

Dowling MRS Walter C (Alice Jernigan)
☎ (912) 234-8238 . . 321 Abercorn St, Savannah, GA *31401*

Downe MRS Susan C (Susan Campbell)
☎ (212) 759-5235 . . 430 E 57 St, New York, NY *10022*

Downer MR Charles W JR—AmUParis'92
☎ (011-242) 832291 . . Nouabalé-Nkodi Project, Brazzaville, Congo,
US Dept of State, Washington, DC *20521-2090*

Downer MRS H Draper (Harriette C Draper) ☎ (011-33-1)
Ws'80.Chi. 45-51-39-21
MISS Elizabeth B—Geo'90—at NYU Grad . . . . . "Paros"
Port de Suffren,
75015 Paris, France

Downer MRS Jannett T (Jannett L Tucker) Cly. . . . . | ☎ (212) 288-3818
   MR William T. . . . . | 875 Park Av,
                              | New York, NY
                              | *10021-0341*

Downer MR & MRS Joseph P (Mahoney—Louise W Swenson)
   Pr.Cs.H'43.H'48 . . of
   ☎ (516) 759-4277 . . 16 Rabbit Run, Matinecock Farms, Glen Cove,
   NY *11542*
   ☎ (561) 546-5003 . . 7900 SE Little Harbor Dv, Loblolly Bay,
   Hobe Sound, FL *33455*

Downes MR John—Br'60
   303 Walnut St, Englewood, NJ *07631*

Downes MRS Katherine Y (Katherine W Young) | ☎ (201) 567-7891
   CtCol'60. . . . . | 212 Davison Place,
   MISS Anne W—Br'91—at 119 College Av, | Englewood, NJ
   West Somerville, MA *02144* . . . . | *07631*

Downey MR & MRS Bruce J 3d (Victoria A Stewart) | ☎ (334) 281-1612
   NCar'65 . . . . | 3363 Southview Av,
   MISS Victoria Tyler. . . . . | Montgomery, AL
   JUNIORS MR Bruce J 4th . . . . | *36111*
   JUNIORS MR John S

Downey MR & MRS Dixon P (Virginia O Robinson) | of ☎ (561)231-6441
   Yn.Y'41 ⚓ | 806 Painted Bunting
   MR Dixon P 3d—at Fairfield U . . . . | Lane, Vero Beach,
                          | FL *32963*
                          | Cornish Cay, Marsh
                          | Harbour, Box 411,
                          | Abaco, Bahamas

Downey MRS Fairfax D (Mildred Adams) . . . . Died at
                West Springfield, NH Aug 19'96

Downey MR & MRS Robert N (Nancy J Adams) | of ☎ (212)861-5675
   Un.Bm.Cly.Dth'58 . . . . | 755 Park Av,
   JUNIORS MISS Elizabeth L—at Spence . . . . | New York, NY
   JUNIORS MR Daniel J—at Taft . . . . | *10021-4255*
                          | ☎ (914) 225-4913
                          | Gipsy Trail Club,
                          | Carmel, NY *10512*
                          | ☎ (970) 262-1374
                          | Keystone, CO *80435*

Downing MR & MRS James B JR (Patricia A | ☎ (561) 286-3697
   Del Piano) Gv.P'53 . . . . | 47 S Sewalls Point
   MISS Katherine M . . . . | Rd, Stuart, FL
   MISS Megan E . . . . | *34996*

Downing MR & MRS James B 3d (Elizabeth C Armstrong)
   Bow'77.Msq.Yn.Rens'76.Y'82
   ☎ (011-44-171) 937-2706 . . 2 Inkerman Terr, Allen St,
   London W8 6QX, England

Downing MR & MRS John O (Frances S von Stade)
   Van'78.B.Eh.Van'78.Va'82
   ☎ (201) 966-0987 . . Blue Mill Rd, Morristown, NJ *07960*

Downing MR & MRS Raymond G (Amanda D | ☎ (516) 288-1681
   Howard) Cr'48 . . . . | 12 Woodland Av,
   MISS Fernanda H—at Oberlin . . . . | Westhampton
   MR Thomas R . . . . | Beach, NY *11978*
   MR William B—Alf'86 . . . . |
   JUNIORS MISS Elizabeth G—at Dalton . . . . |

Downing MR & MRS Thurman (Ritzenthaler—Terry | ☎ (216) 921-1818
   Scully) Cy.Un.It.W&L'53 . . . . | 18600 S Park Blvd,
   MISS Mary V. . . . . | Shaker Heights, OH
                          | *44122*

Downs MRS Fox (Diane B C Fox)
   ☎ (212) 288-1883 . . 500 E 85 St, New York, NY *10028*

Downs MRS Robert N 3d (Alletta d'A Laird) Ac.Ds.
   ☎ (302) 998-3925 . . 933 Center Rd, Wilmington, DE *19807-2823*

Doxford MR & MRS Robert D (Hiscox—Lucy Mills) | ☎ (011-44-171)
   MR Renshaw Hiscox . . . . | 589-5471
   MR Frederick Hiscox . . . . | 58 Cadogan Square,
                          | London SW1X 0JW,
                          | England

Doyle MR & MRS David S (Eda W Darneille) . . . . . . | Rte 3, Box 273A-13,
   JUNIORS MR Charles S II . . . . | Berkeley Springs,
                          | WV *25411*

Doyle MR & MRS Geoffrey C JR (Gabriela A Lombardi)
   Myf.Sar.UMiami'80.Syr'82
   ☎ (305) 864-6554 . . 620 S Shore Dv, Miami Beach, FL *33141*

Doyle MR & MRS J Carol (Louise duP Rhinelander) | ☎ (407) 855-2156
   Bnd'60.NotreD'57.Cl'60 . . . . | 5012 St Denis
   MR Christopher H H . . . . | Court, Orlando, FL
   MR Andrew C R—at ☎ (404) 888-0628 | *32812*
   1207 Renaissance Way NE, Atlanta, GA *30308* .

Doyle MR & MRS John Timothy (Sharon A Smith) | ☎ (415) 566-1822
   Man'vl'69.Fmy.HolyC'69.SantaC'72 . . . . | 1345 Fifth Av,
   MISS Elizabeth A . . . . | San Francisco, CA
   MISS Shannon M . . . . | *94122*
   JUNIORS MISS Courtney P. . . . . |
   JUNIORS MR Morgan R . . . . |

Doyle MR & MRS L F Boker (Susanna A Stone) | of ☎ (212)866-2703
   Rdc'55.C.Y'53 . . . . | 315 W 106 St,
   MISS Victoria J B . . . . | New York, NY
   MISS Jessica D B. . . . . | *10025*
                          | ☎ (914) 962-4891
                          | Box 842, Katonah,
                          | NY *10536*

Doyle MRS M Dorland (Coonley—Morgan—Sarah B Jackson)
   see Dilatory Domiciles

Doyle MR & MRS Mark J (Elizabeth A Garvy) SanDiego'85.DeP'83.Loy'94
   ☎ (708) 246-5257 . . 4122 Lawn Av, Western Springs, IL *60558*

Doyle MR & MRS Morris McK (Kirkwood—Kuhn—Jean H Gerlinger)
   Cal'32.Pcu.Bhm.StJ.Tcy.Stan'29.H'32
   ☎ (415) 921-3002 . . 3098 Pacific Av, San Francisco, CA *94115*

Doyle MR & MRS Thomas J (Linda M Markus) | ☎ (314) 821-6165
   Mo'75.SantaC'74 . . . . | 511 E Jefferson Av,
   JUNIORS MISS Erin E . . . . | Kirkwood, MO
   JUNIORS MR Patrick T . . . . | *63122*

Doyle MR & MRS William K (Cheryl L Secrest) | ☎ (818) 799-5205
   Stan'68.SCal'80.Vh.Stan'68.H'72 . . . . | 501 Arroyo Square,
   MISS Joanne P . . . . | South Pasadena, CA
   JUNIORS MR William K JR . . . . | *91030*

Doyle MRS William T (Ruth M Sartorius)
   ☎ (415) 664-3873 . . 135 San Buenaventura Way, San Francisco,
   CA *94127*

Dozier MR & MRS John O JR (Margaret S Baldwin) P'81.DU'74
   ☎ (314) 991-5299 . . 1 Warson Terr, St Louis, MO *63124*

Draesel REV & MRS Herbert G JR (Ada D Morey) | of ☎ (212)289-6427
CtCol'64.Pa'66.Ty'61.Gen'lTheo'64 . . . . | 332 E 88 St,
MISS Margaret B—at ☎ (212) 889-1854 | New York, NY
240 E 27 St, New York, NY *10016* . . . . | *10128*
MISS Irene R—at ☎ (212) 987-1640 | ☎ (908) 899-1723
345 E 93 St, New York, NY *10128* . . . . | 411 East Av,
| Bay Head, NJ *08742*

Drain MISS Caroline E M
☎ (314) 353-8759 . . 6337A Sutherland Av, St Louis, MO *63109*

Drain MRS Charles M (Marie M Kilgen) . . . . | ☎ (314) PA1-4811
MISS Catherine Von P . . . . | 6826 Kingsbury
DR Charles Michael—Tufts'88—at 695 Park Av, | Blvd, St Louis, MO
New York, NY *10021* . . . . | *63130*
MR Christopher O'S . . . . |
MR Kevin R . . . . |

Drain MR & MRS Frederick J JR (Celeste N Michel) . | ☎ (314) 863-6838
MR James N—at ☎ (314) 721-5529 | 7530 Cornell Av,
1060 Roth Av, St Louis, MO *63130* . . . . | St Louis, MO *63130*

Drake MR & MRS Carl B JR (Day—Charlotte S | ☎ (612) 454-4607
Hannaford) Y'41 . . . . | 1695 Delaware Av,
  MISS Sylvia C Day—at 36956 SW Laurelwood | St Paul, MN *55118*
Rd, Hillsboro, OR *97123* . . . . |
  MR Jeffrey F Day—at 1211 Ordway St, |
Berkeley, CA *94706* . . . . |

Drake MRS Carlos C (Tanton—Winifred M Dennis)
☎ (011-351) 281501 . . rua da Bela Vista 91A, 2750 Cascais, Portugal

Drake MR & MRS Carlos C JR (Cheryl O Paul) | ☎ (717) 843-8275
Ch'55.Cl'67 . . . . | 1601 Randow Rd,
MR Nathaniel C—at ☎ (212) 505-9712 | York, PA *17403*
543 E 5 St, New York, NY *10009* . . . . |
JUNIORS MISS Megan C |

Drake MR & MRS Clifford JR (Kathleen M L Sladen) Stv'47 . . of
☎ (941) 349-0339 . . 7333 Turnstone Rd, Sanderling, Sarasota,
FL *34242*
☎ (802) 295-1085 . . 3 Angell Trail, Quechee, VT *05059*

Drake MISS Daphne J
☎ (803) 449-7701 . . 311—71 Av N, Myrtle Beach, SC *29572*

Drake REV & MRS Francis A (Shows—Louise M | ☎ (802) 545-2126
Higgins) Sth'45.Y'29 . . . . | New Forest Lodge,
MISS Katherine L—MtH'85 . . . . | Box 582,
MR Michael D S—Vt'80 . . . . | Middlebury, VT
MR John M S—at 2 Home Place E, Apt 4, | *05753*
Oakland, CA *94610* . . . . |

Drake MR & MRS Franklin G (Harriet Y Bouvy) V'52.Mich'48
☎ (503) 292-3208 . . 4004 SW Scholls Ferry Rd, Portland, OR *97221*

Drake MRS Harry La B (Alice Bremner) Cas.On.Wa.
☎ (312) 787-5235 . . 209 E Lake Shore Dv, Chicago, IL *60611*

Drake MR & MRS J William 3d (Anne B Lewis) Br'79.StLaw'77.H'81
☎ (203) 637-3217 . . 50 Breezemont Av, Riverside, CT *06878*

Drake MR & MRS Lawrence (Morris—Cassandra S Franklin)
V'47.Pkg.Me.P'41.Pa'52
☎ (610) 645-8681 . . 1400 Waverly Rd, Villa 32, Gladwyne, PA *19035*

Drake MR & MRS Matthew B (Amanda M Mullally)
1890 SW Hawthorne Terr, Portland, OR *97201*

Drake DR & MRS Peter F (Charenton H Zelov) Wells'76.Me.On.Bow'76
255 Mayflower Rd, Lake Forest, IL *60045*

Drake MRS Rockwell (Louise Howland) BMr'31.Myf.
☎ (404) 233-3000 . . Lenbrook Square 213, 3747 Peachtree Rd NE,
Atlanta, GA *30319*

Drake MR Thomas E—Fi.Stan'28.Mich'30.Y'33 . . of
☎ (212) 355-6969 . . 2 Sutton Place S, New York, NY *10022*
☎ (809) 954-3515 . . "Fountain Hill" Good Hope, Falmouth, Jamaica

Drake DR & MRS Thomas F (Laurie A Humphrey) | ☎ (507) 388-6085
H'64.Cwr'68 . . . . | 23 Sumner Hill Rd,
MISS Mary R—StOlaf'95 . . . . | Mankato, MN *56001*
MR Matthew T—H'93 |
MR Mark H . . . . |

Drake MR William McC JR—Rc.Cho.H'54.H'61 . . . | of ☎ (773)276-5500
MISS Ascha K—Skd'95—at Cranbrook Art Grad | 2141 W North Av,
MR Mason H—H'87.Nw'93—at | Chicago, IL *60647*
☎ (212) 628-8871 . . 192 E 75 St, New York, NY | ☎ (217) 947-2337
10021 . . . . | "Old Gillett Farm"
| Elkhart, IL *62634*

Draper MR & MRS Alexander Y (Melinda F Duryea) Va'91.Va'88
☎ (310) 316-6376 . . 208½ N Prospect Av, Redondo Beach, CA *90277*

Draper MR & MRS Arthur F (Sarah H Hayward) | ☎ (860) 535-0230
Ny.Y'32 . . . . | 8 Front St,
MISS Sarah H—UWash'79.UWash'81—at | Stonington, CT
☎ (206) 322-1859 . . 2004—31 Av S, Seattle, | *06378*
WA *98144* . . . . |

Draper MISS Elizabeth P—Bvr'54.T.Myf.Cda.
☎ (914) 351-2825 . . Box 771, Tuxedo Park, NY *10987*

Draper MRS Ford B (Katharine R Reeve) Ac.Ncd.
☎ (610) 388-6044 . . 88 Rocky Hill Rd, Chadds Ford, PA *19317*

Draper MR & MRS Ford B JR (Brian B Dougherty) | of ☎ (302)654-3272
Wil.Nf.Cw.Ac.Ncd.Y'65.Cl'67 . . . . | 909 Nottingham Rd,
MR Ford B 3d—Lynch'90 . . . . | Wilmington, DE
MR Avery L—at Coll of Charleston . . . . | *19805*
| 89 Rocky Hill Rd,
| Chadds Ford, PA
| *19317*

Draper MRS George (Sophie C Whitin) Chi.
☎ (617) 266-6123 . . 50 Commonwealth Av, Boston, MA *02116*

Draper MR & MRS J Sumner 2d (Jean Hunter | ☎ (561) 832-1103
Hallowell) . . . . | 140 Monroe Dv,
MISS Pamela A—at ☎ (617) 241-2260 | West Palm Beach,
7 Arizona Terr, Apt 5, Arlington, MA *02174* . . . | FL *33405*
MISS Dabney A—at ☎ (212) 753-0620 |
531 Main St, Apt 1413, New York, NY *10044* . |
MR James S 3d . . . . |

Draper MISS Lavinia H (J Sumner 2d) . . . . Married at Zamora, Spain
González López MR Isidro (Lazaro) . . . . Feb 18'96

Draper MR & MRS Lawrence A (Lori Heatley) | ☎ (406) 961-5580
Cal'63.Sfg.Bur.Pcu.SanJ'65 . . . . | 711 Fred Burr Rd,
MISS Katherine K . . . . | Victor, MT *59875*
MR Stuart L . . . . |

Draper MISS Nancy-Carroll
☎ (307) 587-4077 . . "Slide Mountain Ranch" 2 Slide Mountain Lane,
Cody, WY *82414*

Draper MR Thayer P JR—Wag'66.StJ'73 . . . . | ☎ (914) 478-1389
MISS Meredith L—Bates'94 . . . . | 58 Main St,
JUNIORS MR John W . . . . | Hastings-on-Hudson,
| NY *10706*

Draper MR William F—C.K.H.'35
☎(212) 737-2735 . . 160 E 83 St, New York, NY *10028*
Drayton MISS Cynthia A—DU'75
☎(212) 737-3797 . . 301 E 69 St, New York, NY *10021*
Drayton MR Frederick R 3d . . see S V Gardner
Drayton MR & MRS Geoffrey W (Cynthia D McKinney)
MtH'81.Nu'83.Rc.Au.NCar'82
☎(610) 933-5565 . . ''Agile Rabbit Farm'' Box 147, Country Club Rd,
Valley Forge, PA *19481*
Drayton MR & MRS James D (M Josephine Millspaugh)
Mmt'75.Gv.Cda.Rich'78
☎(410) 252-8274 . . 11806 Green Spring Av, Owings Mills, MD *21117*
Drayton MASTER James Verplanck (John W JR) . . . . Born at
New York, NY Feb 24'95
Drayton MR & MRS John W (Cynthia Whitney) Rb.Cts.P'43.Pa'48
☎(610) 296-2096 . . 220 Darby Rd, Paoli, PA *19301*
Drayton MR & MRS John W JR (Alexandra M Woodhouse)
Bow'83.Syr'79.GeoW'86
☎(212) 724-2069 . . 35 W 90 St, New York, NY *10024*
Drayton MR & MRS Richard (Fytie Ludington) BMr'53.Au.P'53 . . of
☎(610) 688-3016 . . 857 Lesley Rd, Villanova, PA *19085*
☎(518) 576-4345 . . ''Breezeknoll'' Keene Valley, NY *12943*
Drayton MR & MRS Whitney (Catherine J Mactier) Syd'84.ColC'80
☎(203) 637-8492 . . 16 Shore Acre Dv, Old Greenwich, CT *06870*
Dreher MRS Karen C (O'Brien—Karen D Cassard)
BMr'50.Chr.Cly.Cs.Dyc . . .of
☎(212) 697-8624 . . 310 E 46 St, Apt 8A, New York, NY *10017*
☎(516) 324-8259 . . 4 Sunset Lane, East Hampton, NY *11937*
Drescher MR & MRS John M JR (Katherine A White)
V'48.Mich'50.Nd.Cy.P'49.Wash'53
☎(314) 993-9222 . . 29 Foreway Dv, St Louis, MO *63124-1618*

Drew MR & MRS Ben W JR (Wilson—Bush—Emily | of ☎(802)649-5717
Walker) Wheat'60.Sim'81.Dth'93.Dth'59.Dth'60 | ''This Is It''
  MISS Amy Wilson—at 154 Union Av, | PO Box 1308,
  Framingham, MA *01701* . . . . | Turnpike Rd,
  MR Philip D Wilson—at 218½ Market St, | Norwich, VT *05055*
  Venice, CA *90291* . . . . | ☎(802) 333-4094
  MR Charles S Wilson—at 544 Brookfield Way, | ''Snowfields Farm''
  Jonesboro, GA *30236* . . . . | Vershire, VT *05079*
  MR Scott C Wilson—at 942 Venezia Av, |
  Venice, CA *90291* . . . . |
  JUNIORS MR Peter D Bush . . . . |
Drew MISS Catherine L—Cl'79
☎(212) 431-5787 . . 67 Vestry St, New York, NY *10013*
Drew REV & MRS Charles D (Jean S Sinnott) | ☎(516) 689-9619
Rdc'74.H'72 . . . . | 6 Penelope Dv,
  JUNIORS MISS Sarah W . . . . | Setauket, NY *11733*
  JUNIORS MR Edward A 2d . . . . |
Drew MR & MRS John F (Leslie A Moran) Dth'80.Mass'72
☎(617) 566-7473 . . 232 Woodland Rd, Chestnut Hill, MA *02167*

Drew MRS Thayer Hoffstot (Unterman—Thayer | of ☎(540)832-7284
Drew Hoffstot) Cly . . . . | Old Blue Ridge
  JUNIORS MISS Megan D Unterman—at Kent . . | Tpke, Gordonsville,
  JUNIORS MR Ian H Unterman—at Kent . . . . . . | VA *22942*
   | ☎(561) 585-4089
   | 2100 S Ocean Blvd,
   | Palm Beach, FL
   | *33480*
Drew MR & MRS Thomas E 3d (Susan L Wearn) Rdc'53
☎(803) 928-3666 . . 590 Pointing Brittany Lane, Awendaw, SC *29429*
Drewes MRS Robert J (Caroline Clifton) Tcy.
☎(415) WA1-6413 . . 3367 Washington St, San Francisco, CA *94118*
Drewes MR Stephen R—Cal'70.Cal'73.Brand'76
☎(415) 221-8338 . . 2267 Hayes St, San Francisco, CA *94117*
Drewsen MRS Edmond T JR (Eunice L Hull) V'56.StA.
☎(561) 225-0575 . . 6831 SE Harbor Circle, Sailfish Point, FL *34996*
Drexel MR & MRS John R 3d (HON M S Noreen Stonor)
Unn.K.Nrr.Ri.Ny.Evg.BtP.Srb.Plg.StJ.Cly.Cda.
☎(561) 655-2333 . . ''Canterbury House'' 250 Sanford Av, Palm Beach,
FL *33480*
Drexel MR & MRS John R 4th (M Jacqueline Astor)
Nu'72.K.Ln.Srb.Plg.StJ.Cly.
☎(212) 410-0272 . . 40 E 94 St, New York, NY *10128*
Drexel MR & MRS Victor L (Godfrey—Patricia A Geyelin) Cry.Gm . . .of
☎(207) 276-3235 . . ''Southwind'' S Shore Rd, Northeast Harbor,
ME *04662*
☎(610) 889-0522 . . 440 Chandlee Dv, Berwyn, PA *19312*
Dreyer MR & MRS Frank A (Mary D Rudd)
☎(907) 248-3840 . . 3840 Runestad Circle, Anchorage, AK *99515*
Driggs MRS Laurence La T (Ethel H Sewell)
☎(410) 822-0162 . . 8038 Lee Haven Lane, Easton, MD *21601*

Driggs MR & MRS Laurence La T 3d (Margaret F | ☎(410) 822-2889
Barton) AScott'64.San.Sap.Pa'60 . . . . | ''Hove To''
  MISS Carol E . . . . | 27040 Rigby's Lot
  MISS Katherine A . . . . | Rd, Easton, MD
   | *21601*
Driscoll MR & MRS Bernard E 2d (Elizabeth R Parker) Dick'76.Dick'77
☎(610) 692-0145 . . 1238 Upton Circle, West Chester, PA *19380*
Driscoll MR & MRS David A (Rider—Mary McGary)
☎(912) 638-4742 . . PO Box 30322, Cottage 142, 8 St, Sea Island,
GA *31561-0322*

Driscoll MR & MRS Edward C (Nancy Bell) | ☎(215) 242-8980
Ph.Pc.Sg.Ac.Pa'51 . . . . | 615 St Andrews Rd,
  MISS Susan H . . . . | Philadelphia, PA
   | *19118*
Driscoll MR & MRS George T JR (Jane Monahan) Ty'46.St.Geo'47
☎(716) 874-2710 . . 84 Middlesex Rd, Buffalo, NY *14216*
Driscoll MRS Lee F (Hanson—Maquita E Santa Maria) Pc.
☎(215) 984-8828 . . Cathedral Village D213, 600 E Cathedral Rd,
Philadelphia, PA *19128-1933*

Driscoll MR & MRS Lee F JR (Phoebe P Albert) | ☎(215) 699-9648
BMr'54.Pa'49.Pa'53 . . . . | 720 Swedesford Rd,
  MISS Helen L—Br'89—at Jefferson Med . . . . . . | Ambler, PA *19002*
  MR Lee F 3d—Pa'84.Ox'86.Va'89 . . . . |
  MR Patrick McG—Denis'86.Stan'93 . . . . |

Driscoll MR & MRS Peter E (Farnum—Melissa L Hunsiker)
Col'73.Cvc.Pg.Bow'69.GeoW'77
☎ (301) 229-9167 . . 5320 Albemarle St, Westmoreland Hills,
MD *20816*

Driscoll MR & MRS Robert M (Crawford—Elizabeth McK Camp)
RI'87.Msq.Why.Y'60
☎ (401) 348-8492 . . 13 Wapan Rd, Watch Hill, RI *02891*

Driscoll DR & MRS Robert W (Sonya E Dehon) | ☎ (610) 275-2950
Man'vl'59.Pc.Pa'55 . . . . | 551 Plymouth Rd,
MISS Sonya Elizabeth—WashColl'91.Pa'95 . . . . | Plymouth Meeting,
MR Robert W JR—Vt'88.Pa'95 . . . . | PA *19462*

Driver MR & MRS Richard A (Mary A Winter) Barat'77.NCar'69
☎ (847) 295-2128 . . 135 Oak Terr, Lake Bluff, IL *60044*

Driver MR & MRS William R JR (Barnes—Phoebe Washburn)
Sm.Cy.Chi.Hn.H'29
☎ (617) 320-0702 . . Fox Hill Village 462, 10 Longwood Dv, Westwood,
MA *02090*

Drowne MR Bradley C—Myf.Rv.P'53 . . . . | 27 Slayton Dv,
MR Bradley C JR—VillaN'83—at 125 Orchard | Short Hills, NJ
Lane, Haverford, PA *19041* | *07078*

Drowne MR & MRS Rhodes F (Lisa A Dinallo) AmU'91.AmU'85
☎ (610) 525-1229 . . 917 Old Gulph Rd, Bryn Mawr, PA *19010*

Druckenmiller MR & MRS Stanley F (Beker—Fiona K Biggs)
Bnd'84.Ng.Bow'75 . . of
☎ (212) 628-1205 . . 117 E 72 St, New York, NY *10021*
☎ (516) 287-0065 . . 233 S Main St, Southampton, NY *11968*

Drum COL & MRS J Hunter (Kenney—Elizabeth A Burke) Cvc.Sl.USA'37
☎ (860) 767-2433 . . 311 Essex Meadows, Essex Meadows, CT *06426*

Drum MR John JR—Pcu.
☎ (415) 346-9442 . . 2113 Bush St, San Francisco, CA *94115*

Drummond MRS Kenneth (Rachel L Cuendet)
☎ (609) 219-0115 . . Morris Hall, Apt M208, 1 Bishops Dv,
PO Box 6498, Lawrenceville, NJ *08648-0498*

Drumwright MR & MRS James R (Elenita Milbank) | ☎ (610) 649-5518
V'59.Stan'61.Cly.H'51.H'55 . . . . | 328 Grays Lane,
MISS Elizabeth . . . . | Haverford, PA
MR Eliot . . . . | *19041*

Drury MR & MRS Andrew S JR (Margaret M Reeves)
Yh.Cc.Ne.Cw.GeoW'77.Cit'82
☎ (307) 684-7000 . . PO Box 157, Buffalo, WY *82834*

Drury MR & MRS David L (Deborah A Herman)
Mich'64.St.Ts.G.Mich'61.Mich'63
☎ (716) 689-4766 . . 166 Brandywine Dv, Williamsville, NY *14221*

Drury MRS July G (July C Glogau) . . . . | ☎ (561) 287-9548
MISS Anne K—at ☎ (301) 854-3099 | 1800 SE St Lucie
6721 Montell Court, Highland, MD *20777* . . . . . | Blvd, Apt 6-107,
MR William C—at ☎ (808) 575-2040 | Stuart, FL *34996*
2003 W Lelehuna, Haiku, Maui, HI *96708* . . . . . |

Drury MR & MRS Peter A 3d (Millen—Leila M | ☎ (803) 577-5305
Dryden) Yh. . . . . | 184½ Tradd St,
MR Frederic Millen—Pa'67—at | Charleston, SC
☎ (415) 775-5445 . . 1840 Green St, Apt 4, | *29401*
San Francisco, CA *94123* . . . . |

Drury MRS Samuel S (E Tracy Keppel)
☎ (802) 229-2259 . . HCR 34, Box 285, Montpelier, VT *05602-9806*

Drymalski MR & MRS Raymond H (Sarah E Fickes) | ☎ (312) 943-9848
Man'vl'62.Geo'58.Mich'61 . . . . | 443 W Eugenie St,
MISS Paige—Wis'90—at ☎ (773) 975-1676 | Chicago, IL *60614*
530 W Arlington St, Apt 304, Chicago, IL *60614* |
MR Robert—Wis'91 |

Duane MRS Richard B JR (Carolyn W Philbin) Stc.
☎ (908) 291-0884 . . Box 397, Locust, NJ *07760*

DuBarry MRS Joseph N 4th (Elizabeth Gardner)
MtH'38.Nyc.Me.Gm.Ac.Ncd.
☎ (610) 525-0884 . . Beaumont 355, 77 Middle Rd, Bryn Mawr,
PA *19010*

DuBarry MR & MRS Joseph N 5th (Lindsay W | ☎ (610) 971-0456
McCown) Rose'71.Me.Wt.Myf.Ncd.Wid'73 . . . | 11 Paper Mill Rd,
MISS Meredith S—at Middlebury . . . . | Newtown Square,
MISS Sandra C—at Colby . . . . | PA *19073*

Dubell MR & MRS Owen B (Shirley C Wood) Fw. . . | ☎ (707) 545-4608
MISS Ann W . . . . | 1712 Norte Way,
MISS Leslie W . . . . | Santa Rosa, CA
MR Edward G . . . . | *95404*

Duble MRS Nancy S (Nancy S Stead)
☎ (203) 248-7508 . . 165 Tokeneke Dv, North Haven, CT *06473-4367*

Du Bois MRS Adrienne A (Adrienne B Allen) Tor'60.Csn.
☎ (203) 629-2566 . . 15 Lafayette Court, Greenwich, CT *06830*

Du Bois MRS Allen C (Quayle—Margaret E McCann)
☎ (561) 278-4269 . . 2665 N Ocean Blvd, Gulf Stream, FL *33483*

Du Bois DR & MRS Arthur B (Roberdeau Callery) | ☎ (203) 777-8135
Cos.Cly.Ac.Cda.Hp.Hn.Cr'46 . . . . | 370 Livingston St,
MISS Anne R—Cly.Chi. . . . . | New Haven, CT
MR James E F . . . . | *06511*

Dubois MRS Christina (Christina Nawojchik) NH'72
☎ (802) 645-0913 . . Rte 153, West Pawlet, VT *05775*

Du Bois MRS Eugene (Carol J Mali) . . . . | ☎ (516) 922-7345
MISS Caroline S . . . . | 156 Cove Rd,
MISS Abigail . . . . | Oyster Bay, NY
| *11771*

Du Bois MRS Frederic M (Katherine Wiener) Drake'58.W.Ncd.
☎ (215) 283-7237 . . 510 Foulkeways, Sumneytown Pike, Gwynedd,
PA *19436-1022*

Du Bois MRS J Delafield (Elizabeth McC Gibson) | ☎ (203) 869-0332
BMr'27 . . . . | Mead Point,
MISS Serena D—BMr'70 . . . . | Greenwich, CT
| *06830*

Dubois MR Laurence R—CastleSt'71
☎ (904) 456-6213 . . 813 Esconditas Place, Pensacola, FL *32506*

Du Bois MR & MRS Peter C (Helen R Wardwell) | ☎ (212) 431-9770
Wheat'58.Snc.Cs.P'56 . . . . | 105 Hudson St,
MISS Laura M—at Oakland, CA . . . . | New York, NY
MR Christopher M. | *10013*

Du Bois MR Peter J . . . . Married at Portland, OR
Dankmeyer MISS Ingrid . . . . Jun 22'96

DuBois MR & MRS Raymond F JR (Helen R Runnells)
Y'78.Cvc.An.P'72 . . of
☎ (202) 342-1974 . . 1545—35 St NW, Washington, DC *20007*
☎ (540) 987-9212 . . ''Lone Oak'' 50 Manahoac Lane, Sperryville,
VA *22740*

Du Bois MR & MRS Samuel S M (Saranne Borda)
Hlns'55.Rb.Sg.Pn.W&L'53
☎ (215) 247-6390 . . 526 Telner St, Philadelphia, PA *19118*
Du Bois RR ADM (RET) Thomas H—USN'34
☎ (619) 435-5833 . . 1124 Glorietta Blvd, Coronado, CA *92118*
Du Bose MR & MRS Charles F (Sarah R Peters) Va'81.DU'82.Cc.NCar'80
☎ (804) 971-7261 . . ''Ruddington'' 4042 Ivy Rd, Charlottesville,
VA *22903*

DuBose MR & MRS Charles W (Diana B Easter) . . . . | ☎ (803) 432-3414
MISS Edith W—So'93—at 3850 Pony Lane, | 1906 N Mill St,
Jackson, WY *83002* | Box 729, Camden,
MR Brooks E—at Hampden-Sydney . . . . | SC *29020*

Du Bose MISS Elizabeth Porcher (Charles F) . . . . Born at
Charlottesville, VA Aug 23'95
DuBose MRS Robert E M (Walz—Deirdre E Drew) Cc.
☎ (803) 524-3540 . . ''Dolphin Point'' 24 Indigo Loop, Beaufort,
SC *29902*
Du Bose MISS Sarah Robinson (Charles F) . . . . Born at
Charlottesville, VA Feb 2'94
Dubow MISS Alexandra B—H'87 . . see MRS I G Breckinridge
Dubow MR Charles S (Arthur M) . . . . Married at New York, NY
Ely MISS Melinda (C Geist) . . . . Jun 1'96
Dubow MR & MRS Charles S (Melinda Ely) Bost'87.Nu'87
☎ (212) 688-9185 . . 350 E 57 St, New York, NY *10022*
Dubow MR & MRS Martin (Anne C Dillard) Bnd'73
☎ (818) 956-1103 . . 1536 Fairfield St, Glendale, CA *91201*
Dubow MRS Tatyana Y (Tatyana Yassukovich) . . see S M Yassukovich

Du Brul MRS Antonia P (Antonia Paepcke) | ☎ (212) 988-9240
Rdc'57.Mds. . . . . | 950 Park Av,
MISS Jennifer E—H'94 . . . . | New York, NY
MR Nicholas P—Mid'88.Cl'94 . . . . | *10028*

Ducar MR & MRS Michael P (Deborah McK Baggs) | ☎ (612) 920-4551
Sth'63.Hn.Geo'59.H'62 | 4616 Wooddale Av,
MISS Jennifer Anne—Ty'89—at | Edina, MN *55424*
☎ (508) 927-9938 . . 6 Judson St, Beverly, MA |
01915 . . . . |
MISS Sandra E—Ithaca'94—at ☎ (617) 268-3245 |
483 E Broadway, Boston, MA *02127* . . . . |
MR Christopher McK—HolyC'91—at |
☎ (617) 566-8234 . . 50A Amory St, Brookline, |
MA *02146* . . . . |

Ducas MRS Robert (Meyer—Georgiana de Ropp) | of ☎ (212)486-7157
Cly. | 110 E 57 St, Apt
MR Christopher H Meyer . . . . | 20B, New York, NY
| *10022*
| ☎ (518) 584-0975
| ''Zareba Farm''
| 150 Meadowbrook
| Rd, Saratoga
| Springs, NY *12866*

Ducas MR & MRS Robert I (Chinn—Louise S Lins) Srr.Ncd.Dc.Yn . . .of
☎ (212) 751-8857 . . 360 E 55 St, New York, NY *10022*
☎ (860) 542-5733 . . 244 Westside Rd, Norfolk, CT *06058*
Ducey MR & MRS John F JR (Hoopes—Marion C Schmidt) Nf.Hn.H'36
☎ (561) 546-5990 . . 6 Bassett Creek Trail N, Hobe Sound, FL *33455*

Ducommun MR & MRS Robert C (Andrews—Lynn E | ☎ (212) 348-8780
Laporte) SL'75.Bhm.Cly.Stan'73.H'78 . . . . | 1155 Park Av,
JUNIORS MISS Lindsey L Andrews . . . . | New York, NY
JUNIORS MISS Alexandra D Andrews . . . . | *10128*

Dudley MR & MRS Ambrose F JR (Margaret M O'Neill) NotreD'43
☎ (901) 683-0763 . . 4636 Hemlock Lane, Memphis, TN *38117-3916*
Dudley MR & MRS Bernard F (Strong—Anne W Rudderow) . . of
☎ (941) 597-1146 . . 7032 Oakmont P'kway, Pelican Bay, Naples,
FL *34108*
☎ (802) 763-7848 . . High Lake, Sharon, VT *05065*

Dudley MR & MRS David D—Mit'49 . . . . | ☎ (404) 325-5816
MISS Beth D . . . . | 2996 Briarlake Rd,
MR B David . . . . | Decatur, GA *30033*
MR Peter A . . . . |

Dudley MR & MRS E Alexander JR (Elizabeth D Peters) Va'78.Va'72
☎ (804) 979-7878 . . 1101 W Leigh Dv, Charlottesville, VA *22901*
Dudley MR & MRS Guilford JR (Jane G Anderson) B.Ri.So.Evg.BtP.Van'29
☎ (561) 655-7810 . . Everglades Club, 356 Worth Av, Palm Beach,
FL *33480*
Dudley MR Michael W S
High Lake-Hilltop, RR 1, Box 292, Sharon, VT *05065*
Dudley MRS Robert W (Cunningham—Hirshhorn—
Olga M Zatorsky) Cvc.
☎ (941) 262-2407 . . 600 Admiralty Parade W, Naples,
FL *34102-7803*
Dudley MR & MRS Wesley C (Lucinda V Nash) Bf.Y'55 🏛
☎ (757) 253-0651 . . 10 Bray Wood, Williamsburg, VA *23185*
Duemling MR & MRS Robert W (Biddle—Louisa d'A duP Copeland)
Cvc.C.Mt.Cly.Sl.Y'50.Y'53 . . of
☎ (202) 364-4690 . . 2950 University Terr NW, Washington, DC *20016*
☎ (410) 778-3568 . . 11966 Andelot Farm Lane, Worton, MD *21678*

Duer MR & MRS A Adgate (Morgan—Molesworth— | ☎ (410) 363-0895
MacKay—Katherine Bancroft Poe) Cc.Gv. | 452 Garrison Forest
P'39.Va'42 . . . . | Rd, PO Box 187,
MR John M Morgan JR—at ☎ (910) 392-9054 | Owings Mills, MD
294 Military Cutoff Rd, 24, Wilmington, NC | *21117*
28405 . . . . |

Duer MR & MRS Beverley C (Helen J M Crandell) | of ☎ (212)988-4189
Un.Chr.Snc.Cw.Cly.ColM'53.Cal'62 . . . . | 340 E 72 St,
MISS Alexandra de F—Pars'91.AmUParis'95.Cly. | New York, NY
MR John B—Un.Cw.Dth'85.Bost'89.UMiami'93 | *10021-4768*
—☎ (212) 570-9455 . . . . | ☎ (401) 635-8644
| ''The Cottage''
| 86 Warrens Point
| Rd, Little Compton,
| RI *02837*

Duer MRS Edward L JR (Susan W Roach) Peab'yCons'76
☎ (302) 888-1043 . . 1710 N Scott St, Wilmington, DE *19806*
Duer MR John L L—P'51.Nu'58
☎ (212) 421-0580 . . 357 E 57 St, New York, NY *10022*
Duerr MR Dana M . . see MRS N Newland
Duff MR Daniel S R—Geo'65
☎ (202) 667-7139 . . 1757 Q St NW, Apt D, Washington,
DC *20009-2487*

Duff MRS John M (Anne Roberts).. of
☎ (412) 661-1232.. 1174 Murray Hill Av, Pittsburgh, PA *15217*
☎ (412) 627-8894.. "Sunny Brook Farm" RD 4, Waynesburg, PA *15370*

Duff MR & MRS Louis D (Alice W Baker)
Sth'65.Kas'50 . . . . ☎ (203) 869-1918
MISS Elizabeth G—Ty'89—at N'western . . . . . . 63 Midwood Rd,
MR Louis D 3d—Rc.Ty'92—at Deer Park,
☎ (212) 534-5616.. 100 E 87 St, New York, NY Greenwich, CT
10128 . . . . *06830*
MR Alexander W—Duke'95 . . . .

Duff MR & MRS Richard M JR (Julie S Schieren). . . . ☎ (415) 461-4620
MR Richard M 3d—Cal'91—at U of San Fran .. Box 156, Kentfield,
MR Brendan S—at Ariz State U . . . . CA *94914*

Duffee MRS Deborah H (Deborah M Hall) ☎ (508) 745-8446
Wheat'66.Bost'95 . . . . 18 Beach Av,
MISS Gabrielle—Bost'90 . . . . Salem, MA *01970*
MR Alexander M—Bost'94 . . . .

Duffy MR & MRS John P (Anne Kinney) ☎ (201) 540-9520
Mg.Km.Pn.P'63 . . . . Box 116 AA, RD 1,
MISS Hilary—Hartw'91 . . . . Young's Rd,
MR Kevin—Hartw'95 . . . . Basking Ridge, NJ
07920

Duffy MISS Julia B . . . . *see*
MISS Jennifer W . . . . *Dilatory Domiciles*

Duffy MR Robert C—Laf'51.Geo'55
see Dilatory Domiciles

Dugan MRS F Markoe JR (Melissa M Cunningham)
☎ (714) 361-6976.. 415 Bolivia, San Clemente, CA *92672*

Dugan DR & MRS Francis Markoe (Elizabeth J ☎ (410) 825-0717
Mitchell) Mv.Geo'39.JHop'51 . . . . 1807 Circle Rd,
MISS Mary L—Wheat'73.Adelphi'78 . . . . Ruxton, MD *21204*
MR G W Mitchell—NH'83—at Babson . . . .

Dugan MRS Hammond J JR (Octavia W Chatard) Mv.
☎ (410) 252-4836.. St Elizabeth Hall, 2300 Dulaney Valley Rd, Towson, MD *21204*

Dugan DR & MRS Hammond J 3d (Hildagarde M of ☎ (410)377-5515
Petit) Gv.Mv.HolyC'58.Md'62 . . . . 3 Devon Hill Rd,
MR Hammond J 4th—Md.Gv.Denis'86—at Apt 3D, Baltimore,
☎ (410) 820-3113.. 712 Western Run Rd, MD *21210*
Hunt Valley, MD *21030* . . . . ☎ (410) 822-4088
"Holly House"
9338 Bantry Rd,
Easton, MD *21601*

Dugan MRS Madeleine B (Madeleine Bronson) On.. ☎ (847) 234-4667
JUNIORS MR Thomas A . . . . 910 N Sheridan Rd,
Lake Forest, IL
60045-1436

Dugaw DR & MRS John E JR (Baker—E Virginia ☎ (360) 855-1711
Ingram) ODom'73.Port'67.Creighton'71 . . . . . . 1327 Railroad Av,
MR Charles S Baker-Dugaw—WashSt'94 . . . Sedro Woolley, WA
98284

Dugdale MR & MRS William Matthew S (Fisk—Paige S Perkins) SL'83
☎ (011-44-1827) 711-653.. "Merevale Hall" Atherstone, Warwickshire CV9 2HG, England

Duggan MR Stephen P—H'31.. of
☎ (212) 861-0848.. 10 E 78 St, New York, NY *10021*
☎ (914) 534-4330.. "Remote" 69 Deer Hill Rd, Cornwall-on-Hudson, NY *12520*

Duggar DR & MRS Roger S (Judy C Layton) ☎ (334) 279-9739
Ala'70.Ala'70 . . . . 2642 Aimee Dv,
MISS Cameron C . . . . Montgomery, AL
MR Christopher R *36106*
JUNIORS MR William L . . . .

Duhme MR & MRS H Richard JR (Ware—Carol L McCarthy)
V'39.Cy.Wash'53
☎ (314) 993-5488.. 8 Edgewood Rd, St Louis, MO *63124*

Dujardin MR & MRS Yves (Rosalind M Cross) Vt'82.Shcc.Eh.Paris'74
☎ (201) 538-2120.. Pleasantville Rd, New Vernon, NJ *07976*

Dujarric de la Rivière MR Robert.. see L Begley

Duke MRS A Biddle (Lynn—Robin C Tippett)
Bcs.B.Ri.So.Cly.StJ.Cw.Fw . . . of
☎ (212) 759-9145.. 435 E 52 St, New York, NY *10022*
☎ (516) 283-2799.. "Wyndecote Barn" 45 Gin Lane, PO Box 5072, Southampton, NY *11969*

Duke MR & MRS A Biddle JR (Idoline A Scheerer) Vt'83.Duke'85.Nu'88
☎ (011-54-1) 393-8506.. Arenales 896, 3 Piso, 1061 Buenos Aires, Argentina

Duke MR & MRS Anthony Drexel (Longaray—Maria ☎ (516) 324-1596
L Alcebo) LIU'89.Rc.Ri.Pr.Mds.P'41 . . . . "Harbor House"
MISS Lulita C—Duke'96 . . . . PO Box 177,
JUNIORS MR Washington A—at Duke . . . . East Hampton, NY
JUNIORS MR James B—at Vermont Acad *11937*

Duke MR & MRS Frank M (Susan P Barry) M'saps'64.Van'52
☎ (601) 362-4313.. 2228 Bellingrath Rd, Jackson, MS *39211*

Duke MR George StG B—Duke'82.. of
☎ (406) 962-3454.. PO Box 21, Edgar, MT *59026*
☎ (406) 328-6494.. Trout Creek Ranch, PO Box 610, Absarokee, MT *59001*

Duke MR & MRS H Benjamin JR (Maud B Banks) V'44.Wms'43
☎ (303) 771-1555.. "Highline Farm" 5550 S Steele St, Littleton, CO *80121*

Duke MR & MRS H Benjamin 3d (Laurette W Chambers) Bates'78.Wms'75
☎ (303) 646-4699.. 32300 County Rd 15, Elizabeth, CO *80107*

Duke MR & MRS John F JR (Mary I Taylor) NotreD'49.Gi.JHop'49
☎ (410) 435-7002.. 205 Upnor Rd, Baltimore, MD *21212*

Duke MR Nicholas R—Van'69
☎ (804) 971-3763.. 1419 Old Ballard Rd, Charlottesville, VA *22901*

Duke MR & MRS William T (Ellen M Foxen) P'77.Ln.Y.Dth'76
☎ (212) 777-5660.. 318 Second Av, New York, NY *10003*

Duke MR & MRS Winslow H (Sears—Pauline R ☎ (508) 433-6802
Thayer) Tufts'53 . . . . "Coontree Farm"
MR John W . . . . 84 Jewett St,
Pepperell, MA
01463

Dukehart MRS Edward C (Miller—Sybil K Williams) Mv.
☎ (410) 557-7163.. "Shoulderbone Farm" 4246 Madonna Rd, Jarrettsville, MD *21084*

Dulles LT (RET) Allen M—USMC.P'51.Stan'83
☎ (505) 988-3321.. 409 E Coronado Rd, 1, Santa Fe, NM *87501*

Dulles MR & MRS John W F (Eleanor F Ritter) | ☎ (210) 657-2765
Sth'39.P'35.H'37.Ariz'43 . . . . | 9306 Village Dv,
  MR R Avery—at ☎ (210) 696-5750 | San Antonio, TX
  6123 Sunset Haven St, San Antonio, TX 78249 . | 78217

Dumaine MR & MRS Brian H (Caroline M Sutton) Wes'75.Aht'75
4 Kitching Place, Dobbs Ferry, NY 10522

Dumaine MR & MRS Dudley B (Susan B Emery) | ☎ (617) 899-1098
Sth'56.Bost'60 . . . . | 8 Hidden Rd,
  MR Frederic C 4th . . . . | Weston, MA 02193
  MR C Andrew . . . . |

Dumaine MRS Frederic C (Margaret K Williams) . . . . Died at
Weston, MA Jly 6'96

Dumaine MR Frederic C—Un.Cy.Cw.
☎ (617) 899-2346 . . ''Dogwood'' 201 Newton St, Weston, MA 02193

Dumke MRS Glenn (Dorothy D Robison) . . . Married at Los Angeles, CA
Elliott MR Bruce C (late Harry W) . . . . Nov 17'95

Dunaway MR & MRS Carlyle M JR (Susan G Fordyce) Pr.Stan'66.Va'69
☎ (212) TR9-8177 . . 124 E 84 St, New York, NY 10028-0915

Dunaway MRS Gwendolyn F (Streuber— | ☎ (505) 983-1200
de Figueiredo—Waterman—Gwendolyn F | 369 Montezuma,
Dunaway) . . . . | Box 131,
  MISS Jorie M Waterman—H'95 . . . . | Santa Fe, NM 87501

Dunbar MR & MRS Davis T (Stanton—Charlotte Shafer) Hn.H'40
☎ (610) 691-0776 . . 438 High St, Bethlehem, PA 18018

Duncan MR & MRS Andrew P (Laurel W Horne) Macalester'85.Mich'91
☎ (313) 665-1514 . . 1422 Broadway St, Ann Arbor, MI 48105-1810

Duncan MR & MRS Charles W JR (Anne Smith) | ☎ (713) 623-4105
Cvc.Rice'47 . . . . | 9 Briarwood Court,
  MR Charles W 3d—at 5744 Shady River Dv, | Houston, TX 77019
Houston, TX 77057 . . . . |

Duncan MISS Charlotte D
☎ (215) 848-1760 . . 3547 Sunnyside St, East Falls, PA 19129

Duncan DR & MRS Donn G (Hiller—Pamela Humphrey) Ariz'76.Kas'56
47 Circle Dv, Compound, Santa Fe, NM 87501-9593

Duncan MRS Dyson (Mildred P S Hooker) Cly.
☎ (914) 241-2042 . . ''Windyridge'' 340 Armonk Rd, Mt Kisco,
NY 10549

Duncan MR & MRS James A (Laura G Miller) Bvr'75.Yn.Y'75.H'79
☎ (011-44-171) 585-0647 . . 74 Clapham Common Westside,
London SW4 9AX, England

Duncan MISS Jean W
☎ (212) 477-5964 . . 55 E 9 St, New York, NY 10003

Duncan MRS Louis C (Miers—Ada E Hastings) Wash'57.An.Myf.Ncd.
☎ (630) 325-7230 . . Ruth Lake Woods, 775 Ruth Lake Court, Hinsdale,
IL 60521-8123

Duncan MR Peter S—Nas'73 . . see W K Cole

Duncan MR & MRS Ransom H (Judith S Fenn) . . . . . | ☎ (518) 327-3378
  MISS Barbara S—at Rte 3, Box 90, Alachua, | PO Box 295,
FL 32615 . . . . | Lake Clear, NY
  MISS Judith L—at 73 Hawley St, Northampton, | 12945-0295
MA 01060 . . . . |
  MR Ransom E—at 83 McCormack, Apt 2, |
Malden, MA 02148 . . . . |

Duncan MR & MRS William M (Susan E Richardson) | ☎ (860) 658-1648
Ws'66.Cl'69.Pn.P'66.Cl'69 . . . . | 4 Dogwood Lane,
  MISS Karen M—at Wellesley . . . . | Simsbury, CT 06070
  LT David R—P'94—USA.—in Germany . . . . . . |

Duncanson MR & MRS Thomas JR (Arabella Peyton Adams) Myf.StA.
☎ (561) 336-1268 . . 12778 Mariner Court, Palm City, FL 34990

Dunckel MR & MRS Peter B (Jeanette Maddux) | ☎ (415) 387-8566
Pcu.Fr.Y'53 . . . . | 52 Seventh Av,
  MR Jackson M . . . . | San Francisco, CA
   | 94118

Dunham MISS Angelica Van R . . see C A Bentley

Dunham MRS C Dary (Margaret Todd)
☎ (914) 276-2203 . . 46B E Hill Dv, Somers, NY 10589

Dunham MR Carroll 4th . . . . Died at
Essex, CT Aug 17'95

Dunham MRS Carroll 4th (Carol M Reynolds) MtH'37.Y'41.Hn.
☎ (860) 434-1991 . . ''Lord Hill'' Lyme, CT 06371

Dunham DR Edward K—Hb.H'55.Cl'68 . . | ☎ (207) 276-3753
  MISS Clara—SL'88 . . . . | ''Wayside''
  MISS Edith—at Reed . . . . | Seal Harbor, ME
   | 04675

Dunham MRS Hustead D (Sharon J Corbet) . . . . . . | ☎ (415) 648-2051
  JUNIORS MISS Marion J . . . . | 311 Duncan St,
   | San Francisco, CA
   | 94131

Dunham MISS Josephine
☎ (508) 369-5313 . . 80 Deaconess Rd, Apt D21, Concord, MA 01742

Dunham MR & MRS Lawrence B 3d (Margaret E Magie)
☎ (612) 642-9197 . . 921 Bayless Av, St Paul, MN 55114

Dunham MRS Lawrence D (Woodson—Millicent R | ☎ (415) 931-6772
Maas) Pcu.Fr. . . . . | 2835 Divisadero St,
  MISS Mila M . . . . | San Francisco, CA
   | 94123

Dunham MRS Mary D (Mary B Dall) . . . . | ☎ (401) 846-6415
  MR Christopher D . . . . | PO Box 324,
  MR Nicholas T . . . . | Newport, RI
   | 02840-0003

Dunham MR & MRS Peter (M Patricia Hopkinson) Au.H'43
☎ (203) 264-7694 . . 908A Heritage Village, Southbury, CT 06488

Dunham MR & MRS Samuel G (Nancy C P Mayo) Vh.Pa'51
☎ (818) 796-7019 . . 1484 Arroyo View Dv, Pasadena, CA 91103

Dunham MR & MRS William P (Nearing—Edith Williams) Au.San.
☎ (941) 566-9163 . . 716 Bentley Dv, Naples, FL 34110

Dunham DR & MRS Wolcott B (Isabel C Bosworth) Hn.Cl'24
☎ (410) 494-6156 . . Blakehurst, 1055 W Joppa Rd, Towson, MD 21204

Dunham MR & MRS (DR) Wolcott B JR (Joan S | of ☎ (212)534-1829
Findlay) Cl'72.Nu'74.Cl'79.Cl'95.Un.Nf.H.'65. | 1148 Fifth Av,
H'68 . . . . | New York, NY
  JUNIORS MISS Mary F . . . . | 10128
   | ☎ (518) 398-1539
   | Brookhill Farm,
   | 371 Bean River Rd,
   | Pine Plains, NY
   | 12567

Dunlaevy MR Edgar P—Pr.Mit'24
☎ (516) 922-4928 . . Box 120, Oyster Bay, NY 11771

Dunlaevy MR Erik N—Ty'61 . . . . | ☎ (516) 922-2803
  MR Henrik P . . . . | 141 Centre Island
   | Rd, Oyster Bay, NY
   | 11771

Dunlaevy MR & MRS Michael A (Joanne M Randall) S.StLaw'68.AGSIM'72
☎ (011-44-171) 736-9406 . . 44 Ellerby St, London SW6 6EZ, England

Dunlap MR & MRS J Gaff (Laura E Keys) of ☎ (513)771-7366
Cin'40.Cw.Myf.Ncd.Cr'36 . . . . 965 Laurel Av,
MR John G JR . . . . Glendale, OH 45246
MR William O . . . . ☎ (616) 238-7393
"Pinestead"
Columbus Beach,
Indian River, MI
49749

Dunlap MR & MRS John M JR (Sherlock—Mareon L Fulle) Pemb'47.Bow'48
☎ (207) 833-5500 . . Menikoe Haven, RD 1, South Harpswell,
ME 04079

Dunlap MR & MRS Robert B (Fitzpatrick—Heather A Furlong)
CalSt'81.Sierra'93.Vh.Clare'51
☎ (818) 287-2215 . . 8518 E Roanoke Rd, San Gabriel, CA 91775

Dunlop MR G Thomas—Br'84.Juilliard'88
☎ (212) 874-0473 . . 134 W 81 St, New York, NY 10024

Dunlop MR & MRS James N JR (Rosemary Royce) ☎ (407) 644-5253
Cw.Ht.Myf.P'42 . . . . 1807 Via Amalfi,
MR Paul C . . . . Winter Park, FL
32789

Dunn MR & MRS C Wesley JR (Olivia Endicott ☎ (203) 255-0070
Hutchins) Unn.Rcn.Pqt.Ny.Cly.Mid'53 . . . . 580 Sasco Hill Rd,
MR Charles W 3d—ColC'87.LondEc'90 . . . . . . Fairfield, CT 06430
MR John E—Col'96 . . . .

Dunn MR & MRS Edward D JR (Frances Le B Stoddard) Myf.Dc.Dar.Ncd.
☎ (912) 792-6464 . . Greenfield Plantation, Rte 1, Box 122, Morgan,
GA 31766

Dunn MRS Edward K (Anne Butler) Mv.Elk . . . . . . of ☎ (410)243-5396
MISS Anneen . . . . Roland Park Place,
Apt 665, 830 W 40
St, Baltimore, MD
21211
☎ (410) 489-7369
"Waterford Farm"
Jennings Chapel Rd,
Woodbine, MD
21797

Dunn MR & MRS Edward K JR (Janet Evans) Gchr'81.Elk.Md.Mv.P'57.H'60
☎ (410) 377-5641 . . "Vesper Hill" 7315 W Bellona Av, Baltimore,
MD 21212

Dunn MR & MRS George J (Rebecca D Fisher) RMWmn'59.Un.Y'57.H'60
☎ (216) 371-3594 . . 2374 Roxboro Rd, Cleveland Heights, OH 44106

Dunn MISS Helen C
☎ (908) 280-7917 . . 201 Second Av, Apt 2C, Belmar, NJ 07719

Dunn MRS Kempton (Susan B Gill) Ncd.
☎ (203) 966-2230 . . Box 1344, 114 Bridle Path Lane, New Canaan,
CT 06840

Dunn MISS Linda F (Tarulis—Linda F Dunn) Nw'89.Bost'91.Cly.Pr.
☎ (212) 831-2131 . . 166 E 96 St, Apt 5C, New York, NY 10128

Dunn MISS Margaret H
☎ (203) 777-0825 . . 25 Clark St, New Haven, CT 06511

Dunn MRS Maryann W (Prescott—Maryann W Dunn)
☎ (510) 945-0243 . . 1165 Elmwood Dv, Walnut Creek, CA 94596

Dunn MR & MRS Noel L (Mauney—Mignon Durham) Duke'73.NCar'64
☎ (910) 945-9522 . . "Brookfield" 7590 Brookfield Dv, Lewisville,
NC 27023

Dunn MRS Paxton T (Louise H Meière) Csn.Pn.
☎ (203) 322-7018 . . 82 Erskine Rd, Stamford, CT 06903

Dunn MRS Peyton Hawes (Peyton E Hawes) . . . . Died Jly 18'96

Dunn MR & MRS Richard P (Sturtevant—Elizabeth P Wheeler) Cvc.Sl . . .of
☎ (410) 810-0860 . . 108 N Water St, Chestertown, MD 21620
☎ (207) 359-8571 . . Box 158, Brooklin, ME 04616

Dunn MR & MRS Steven M (Mary B Ede) Beloit'84.Syr'84.Bab'93
34 Mayflower Lane, Duxbury, MA 02332

Dunn MR & MRS Stewart A JR (Bevan— ☎ (201) 467-5670
Anne S McIver) Wheat'63.Ncd.McKinne'65 151 Hobart Av,
MISS Anne Renwick McKinne—at Colgate . . . . Short Hills, NJ
MR D R Chandler Bevan—at Morrisville, VT 07078
05661 . . . .

Dunn MR & MRS Sydney B JR (Nelson—Mary M of ☎ (610)688-5623
Knox) ColbyS'57.WChesU'86.Me.Wt.Rv.Ac. 204 Hermitage Dv,
Ncd.Cr'40 . . . . Radnor, PA 19087
MISS E Pegge Nelson—PugetS'90.Pitt'96. ☎ (803) 671-6957
Me.—at ☎ (412) 687-7650 . . 5437 Ellsworth "Dunn Inn"
Av, Pittsburgh, PA 15232-1851 . . . . 1913 S Beach Rd,
Hilton Head Island,
SC 29928

Dunn MRS T Evans JR (Jackson—Alice D Benedict) R.Fw.Y.
☎ (610) 356-4115 . . Dunwoody Village W117, 3500 West Chester Pike,
Newtown Square, PA 19073

Dunn MR & MRS Thomas L (Stevenson—Mary ☎ (610) 827-7111
Louise Fowler) . . . . 1541 Art School Rd,
MR Thomas L JR . . . . Chester Springs, PA
MR Jonathan W 19425

Dunn MR & MRS William T JR (Laura M Franklin) Pr.Cly.Cr'43
☎ (561) 546-8448 . . 101 Palmetto Trail, Hobe Sound, FL 33455

Dunne MR & MRS Maurice F JR (Eleanor D Isham) ☎ (847) 234-3369
On.Nw'49.H'52.Nw'80 728 Rosemary Rd,
MISS Tara G—Bnd'88—at ☎ (773) 296-4135 Lake Forest, IL
2615 N Halsted St, Chicago, IL 60614 60045
MR Ralph I—at ☎ (813) 595-9427
173 Marina Del Ray, Clearwater, FL 34630 . . . .
CAPT Maurice F 3d—USA'84.Geo'96 . . . .

Dunne MR & MRS Peter F 3d (Kay Van Vliet) ☎ (415) 344-5663
Stan'52.Bur.Sfg.Cal'52 . . . . 175 Pepper Av,
MISS Elizabeth L . . . . Burlingame, CA
MISS Samantha 94010
MR Peter F 4th . . . .

Dunnell MRS William W JR (Ellen Frothingham) . . . ☎ (508) 358-2982
MR Jacob—H'57—Box 34, Holderness, NH 204 Old Connecticut
03245 . . . . Path, Wayland, MA
01778

Dunnell MR & MRS William W 3d (Patricia L ☎ (603) 284-7384
Ceresole) H'55 . . . . "The Hovel"
MISS Caroline C—at ☎ (617) 523-7624 PO Box 359,
86 Myrtle St, Boston, MA 02114 . . . . Center Sandwich,
MR Jacob 2d . . . . NH 03227

Dunning MR & MRS George A 2d (Yvonne Neely) Ll.Myf.Dll.
☎ (215) 836-1609 . . 1609 Church Rd, Oreland, PA 19075

Dunning MR Robert L—Cal'90 . . see F L Ballard JR

Dunning MR & MRS William S (Catherine P Biddle) Ty'88.Duke'95
☎ (212) 734-1354 . . 42 E 73 St, Apt 3A, New York, NY *10021*

Dunnington MRS (DR) Miller (Jacqueline d'Oggier Miller) Paris'55.Nu'70.Cl'75.Cly. . . . . "Mandala"
MISS India M L—NMex'85.Cl'91 . . . . | Box 1393, Santa Fe, NM *87504-1393*

Dunnington MR & MRS Walter G JR (Patricia MacPhee) Rcn.Ng.B.So.Va'48
☎ (540) 672-3464 . . "Montebello" PO Box 149, Orange, VA *22960*

Dunnington MR Walter G 3d (Walter G JR) . . . Married at New York, NY
Liff MISS Janet (late Julius) . . . . Sep 9'95

du Pont MR A Felix JR—Wil.Pn.P'29
☎ (302) 652-2645 . . "Elton" 3120 Kennett Pike, Wilmington, DE *19807*

du Pont MRS A Felix 4th (Livesay—Ewell B Stewart) MooreArt'70.Cl . . . . | 3700 Pelican's Nest
MISS Ewell B—at Geo Wash'n . . . . | Dv, Bonita Springs,
JUNIORS MR A Felix 5th . . . . | FL *34134*

du Pont MISS Alexandra Katherine (Alfred B) . . . . Born at
Wilmington, DE Nov 20'95

du Pont MR & MRS Alexis I (Anne E Smith) Del'51 . | ☎ (904) 760-7759
MISS Irene S . . . . | 2891 Borman Court,
MR Thomas M—at 122 W Hillendale Rd, | Daytona Beach, FL
Kennett Square, PA *19348* . . . . | *32124*

du Pont MR & MRS Alfred B (Katherine A Baker) Drake'93.Wil.
☎ (610) 444-8166 . . 820 Merrybell Lane, Kennett Square, PA *19348*

du Pont MISS Allaire . . see W Prickett

du Pont MR & MRS Anthony A (Schnier— Hambuechen—Carol L Williams) Y'55 . . . . . . | ☎ (619) 454-7584
MISS Blair E Hambuechen—Bost'90 . . . . . | 2180 Calle Frescota,
| La Jolla, CA *92037*

du Pont MR Benjamin Franklin—Ny.Wil.Tufts'86
☎ (302) 654-3999 . . 504 Rockland Rd, PO Box 4, Rockland, DE *19732*

du Pont MR & MRS Charles F (Ransom—Clark—Nedinia T Schutt) Wil.Cw.Ncd.Pn.IIT'73
☎ (610) 388-6987 . . Spar Hill Farm, PO Box 4158, Greenville, DE *19807*

du Pont MRS Constable (Gertrude J Constable) . . . | ☎ (310) 544-4994
MISS Mary M A—Biola'88 . . . . | 3 Clipper Rd,
MR Anthony C—SCal'74 . . . . | Rancho Palos
| Verdes, CA *90275*

du Pont MR & MRS David B (Barbara L Freeman) Pa'68.Pa'72.Pa'67.Pa'72
☎ (914) 793-2383 . . 101 Warwick Rd, Bronxville, NY *10708*

du Pont MR David W . . see H C Frick 2d

du Pont MR & MRS E Paul 3d (Helen H Platt) Bard'74.Cry.Un.Ny.P'64
☎ (212) 650-0104 . . Box 20280, Cherokee Station, New York, NY *10028*

du Pont MR & MRS Edmond A R (Nancy B Carlson) Cal'80.SantaC'84.Cal'82
☎ (714) 722-6176 . . 1506 Irvine Av, Newport Beach, CA *92660*

du Pont MR & MRS Edward B (Ruth A Vallett) Sullins'56.Del'61.Wil.Ny.Cly.Y'56.H'59 . . of
☎ (302) 658-2715 . . 1000 Snuff Mill Rd, Wilmington, DE *19807*
☎ (561) 234-8493 . . 158 Anchor Dv, Vero Beach, FL *32963*

du Pont MR & MRS Edward Bradford JR (Priscilla H Altmaier) Ty'86.Wil.Wms'86
☎ (610) 388-2420 . . PO Box 1155, Chadds Ford, PA *19317*

du Pont MRS F George (A Beatrice Churchman) Cry. . . . . | ☎ (203) 259-1808
MR William C—Marl'76—at ☎ (410) 589-6372 | 235 Mine Hill Rd,
Box 4642, Annapolis, MD *21403* . . . . | Fairfield, CT *06430*

du Pont MR & MRS F George JR (Patricia Sweney) Yn.Y'63.Pa'70 . . . . | ☎ (203) 866-2272
JUNIORS MISS Alexandra B . . . . | 18 Rocky Point Rd,
JUNIORS MR George F . . . . | Rowayton, CT
| *06853*

du Pont MRS Henry B 3d (Joan Wheeler) DelB.Pqt . . .of
☎ (561) 272-2923 . . Somerset, 2613 N Ocean Blvd, Gulf Stream, FL *33483*
☎ (203) 259-6589 . . "Havenfield" 303 Hulls Farm Rd, Southport, CT *06490*

du Pont MR Henry B 4th—Wil.Ny.Cry.Pqt.U'90 ⛵
☎ (302) 239-5250 . . PO Box 3568, 2270 Creek Rd, Wilmington, DE *19807*

du Pont MR & MRS Henry E I (Schneider—Martha A | "Montmorency"
C Verge) . . . . | PO Box 4000,
MISS Sophie M . . . . | Greenville, DE
MR Henri V—at 576 Capital Trail, Newark, DE | *19807*
19711 . . . . |
MR Henry E I II . . . . |

du Pont MR & MRS Irénée JR (Barbara Batchelder) | ☎ (302) 656-9626
Cry.Wil.Ncd.Mit'43 . . . . | Box 38,
MISS Sally C . . . . | Montchanin, DE
MISS Grace . . . . | *19710-0038*

du Pont MASTER Laine Belin (Alfred B) . . . . Born at Rehoboth Beach, DE Apr 24'94

du Pont MRS Nicholas R (Genevieve L Estes) Cly . . .of
☎ (302) 654-3114 . . "Ridgely" PO Box 3704, Greenville, DE *19807*
☎ (561) 848-0784 . . "Casuarina" Palm Beach, FL *33480*

du Pont MR & MRS Pierre S (Elise Ravenel Wood) Temp'76.Pa'79.Wil.Ny.Cly.Ac.P'56.H'63
☎ (302) 654-9075 . . "Patterns" Rockland, DE *19732*

du Pont MRS Richard C (H Allaire Crozer) Srr.
☎ (410) 885-5805 . . "Woodstock Farm" PO Box 179, Chesapeake City, MD *21915*

du Pont MR Richard S JR . . see H C Frick 2d

DuPre MR & MRS Charles W (Aimee E Brown) Cda.
☎ (601) 442-6988 . . 1 Elm St, Natchez, MS *39120*

Dupree MR & MRS Frederick F JR (Sunny A Seiler) | ☎ (617) 868-0088
Wash'65.GeoW'68.Nf.Cy.Sm.Ri.Chi.Tenn'55 . . | 88 Appleton St,
JUNIORS MISS Lila L S . . . . | Cambridge, MA
JUNIORS MR F Aubin S . . . . | *02138*

Dupuy MR Arnold C—GeoM'88.GeoM'94
☎ (703) 280-5383 . . 7342 Lee H'way, Apt 201, Falls Church, VA *22046*

Dupuy MRS Christine G (Christine Geissbühler)
☎ (508) 385-6144 . . Scargo Pines, PO Box 487, Dennis, MA *02638*

Dupuy MR & MRS David Davis (Smith—L Dabney Heald) Tul'38
☎ (318) 369-3768 . . "Dabney Hall" 2404 Blue Haven Dv, New Iberia, LA *70560*

Dupuy MR & MRS Fielding D (Constance L Hunter) Nu'89.Cl'94.StJ'88
☎ (212) 627-0814 . . 145 W 10 St, Apt 5D, New York, NY *10014*

Dupuy MISS Mirande E—Mass'81.Cl'89
see Dilatory Domiciles

Durand MR & MRS Harry S (Eldredge—M Killeen Swartz) Rc.Plg.Snc.Rv.Cw.Ht. . . . .
  MR Thomas H—at ☎ (617) 522-7206
  5 Pond St, Jamaica Plain, MA *02130* . . . .
    MISS Margaret M Eldredge—at
    ☎ (303) 258-7239 . . 641 Coughlin Meadow
    Rd, Boulder, CO *80302* . . . .
of ☎ (212)427-6254
401 E 88 St,
New York, NY
10128
☎ (303) 938-9466
3850 N 26 St,
Boulder, CO *80304*

Durant MR & MRS Frederick C 3d (Carolyn G Jones) Cos.Leh'39
  ☎ (301) 654-1613 . . 109 Grafton St, Chevy Chase Village, MD *20815*

Durbin MR Winfield T—Rcch.Wms'34.H'37
  ☎ (619) 459-8249 . . 7755 Sierra Mar Dv, La Jolla, CA *92037*

Dure MR & MRS Leon S 3d (Verner—Ann P Hammond) Swb'61 . . . .
  MR Beau K . . . .
☎ (706) 548-2886
820 Riverbend
P'kway, Athens, GA
30605

Durey MR Forbes Cleaveland—StLaw'90 . . see MISS J M Cook

Durey MR Peter Huntting—Vt'94 . . see MISS J M Cook

Durfee MR & MRS Allison B (Virginia G Nyvall) Skd'63.D.Chi.Yn.Y'60 . . . .
  MISS Susan B—Hlns'93 . . . .
☎ (617) 329-9384
25 Allindale Way,
Dedham, MA *02026*

Durfee MR & MRS N Barry JR (Appleton—Florence R Wyckoff) Yn.Y'55 . . . .
  MR N Barry 3d . . . .
    MISS Elizabeth P Appleton . . . .
☎ (561) 234-1749
100 Oyster Cut,
John's Island,
Vero Beach, FL
32963

Durfee MR & MRS S Brayton JR (Katherine A Prezzano) F&M'89.Ham'88
  ☎ (914) 234-0476 . . 33 Clinton Rd, Bedford Hills, NY *10507*

Durfee MR & MRS Sherman B (Beulah J Woolston) Bgt.Fic.Y'58 . . . .
  MISS Elizabeth V—at ☎ (212) 737-9513
  200 E 75 St, Apt 3A, New York, NY *10021* . . .
  MR Christopher S . . . .
☎ (914) 234-3044
55 Long Meadow
Rd, Bedford, NY
10506

Durgin MR & MRS Don (Colin—Catherine V Meacham) Nu'78.Ck.Ng.Pr.Cc.Cly.Dar.Ncd. P'45.Nu'54 . . . .
  MR William R—at Museum Sch of Fine Arts . . .
of ☎ (516)676-7173
Box 264, Feeks
Lane, Mill Neck,
NY *11765*
☎ (212) 861-5321
155 E 72 St,
New York, NY
10021

Durham MR & MRS John A D B (Amalia C Osborne) Cly.Cda.
  ☎ (011-44-171) 828-1101 . . 13 Victoria Square, London SW1W 0RA, England

Durland MR & MRS John S (Ann E Verplanck)
  ☎ (203) 655-4379 . . 27 Edgerton St, Darien, CT *06820*

Durling MR & MRS C Correll (Eleanor H White) Bg.Bryant'75 . . . .
  JUNIORS MR C Chapin . . . .
of ☎ (908)534-4646
Box 692, Oldwick,
NJ *08858*
''Millrace''
Whitehouse, NJ
08888

Durocher DR & MRS John R (Louise D Bowman) Wms'63.Pa'67
  ☎ (410) 639-7315 . . Tavern Creek Farm, 6631 Swan Creek Rd, Rock Hill, MD *21661*

Durrance MR & MRS John R JR (Kinzel—Amy M Davenport) Stan'69
  ☎ (802) 229-0612 . . 38 Liberty St, Montpelier, VT *05602*

Duryea MR & MRS George R JR (Marita B Halloran) St.Mit'51 . . . .
  MISS Ellen V . . . .
  MISS Katharine H . . . .
☎ (716) 875-2889
71 Nottingham Terr,
Buffalo, NY *14216*

Duryea MR & MRS James M (Linda F Vander Poel) Bnd'69.B.Pr.Fic.Cly. . . . .
  MISS Megan M—Geo'94—at ☎ (212) 717-0936
  201 E 69 St, New York, NY *10021* . . . .
  JUNIORS MR Oakley V P—at Georgetown . . . . . .
☎ (516) 676-2721
35 Overlook Rd,
Locust Valley, NY
11560

Duryea MR & MRS William M JR (E Lovejoy Reeves) L.Csh.Wk.Snc.Vca.StJ'67 . . . .
  JUNIORS MR Robert A . . . .
  JUNIORS MR David McS . . . .
☎ (212) 737-3721
173 E 80 St,
New York, NY
10021

Duryea MR William M 3d—Wes'85
  ☎ (813) 251-1330 . . 209 S Westland Av, Apt 3, Tampa, FL *33606*

Duryee MISS Cynthia A G—Ncd.
  40 S Russell St, Boston, MA *02114*

Duryee MR William R—Cos.Y'27
  ☎ (703) 538-4335 . . 3241 N Woodrow St, Arlington, VA *22207*

Duschatko MRS Rebecca F (Rebecca D Fulweiler) Sth'67.Ec. . . . .
  JUNIORS MISS Beth C . . . .
  JUNIORS MR W Baird . . . .
☎ (508) 526-1872
13 Jersey Lane,
Manchester, MA
01944

Dusenbury MR & MRS Donald S (Angela M Cuno) GaSt'81.USA'63 . . . .
  MISS Annette C . . . .
  MR Nicholas C . . . .
☎ (703) 821-0764
2003 Miracle Lane,
Falls Church, VA
22043

Dush MR & MRS Michael W (Susan D Myers) HWSth'83.Msq.Why.Prov'69.AlbLaw'73
  ☎ (203) 622-5146 . . 75 Fairfield Rd, Greenwich, CT *06830*

Dutterer MRS Downing Huber (Ruth Downing Huber) AmU'69 . . . .
  MR Daniel W—at 5 Harmony Lane,
  Hobe Sound, FL *33455* . . . .
☎ (941) 921-1798
3322 Thornwood
Rd, Sarasota, FL
34231

Duty MRS Spencer C (G Allene Beaumont) Cwr'35.It.May . . .of
  ☎ (216) 991-3431 . . 19425 Van Aken Blvd, Apt 510, Cleveland, OH *44122*
  ☎ (941) 349-1391 . . 6154 Midnight Pass Rd, Sarasota, FL *34242*

Duval MRS Barbara (Kieffer—Barbara Duval) Ncd. . .
  MISS Jenifer W Kieffer—JMad'88.AGSIM'92
  —at ☎ (602) 922-3218 . . 6349 N 78 St,
  Scottsdale, AZ *85250* . . . .
  MISS Phebe W Kieffer—MmtVa'91.CentFla'95
  MR A Christopher Kieffer . . . .
☎ (407) 366-4046
Country Club
Village,
1302 Augusta
National Blvd,
Winter Springs, FL
32708

Duval MR Bradford B—L&C'95 . . see R P Rose

Du Val MR & MRS Clive L 2d (Susan H Bontecou) V'40.Mt.Y'35
  ☎ (703) 356-3011 . . 1214 Buchanan St, McLean, VA *22101*

Du Val MR & MRS Daniel H (Karen L Keys) Va'76.Mt.H'76
  ☎ (703) 847-9498 . . 1221 Merchant Lane, McLean, VA *22101*

Du Val MR & MRS Philip L R (Emmons—Janis L Lee) Plg.StA.Yn.Y'43 . . . .
  MR David W Emmons . . . .
☎ (203) 966-0695
193 Park St,
New Canaan, CT
06840

Du Vivier MRS David (Hall—Freedman—Georgine Fleming) Wil'46.Cl'67.H'mann'87
  ☎ (609) 924-2186 . . 18 Wheatsheaf Lane, Princeton, NJ *08540*

Du Vivier MR & MRS Paul F (Margaret E de Ropp) Mt.Csn.Sl.Cda.P'38.Geo'40.Geo'77 . . . . | ☎ (410) 785-0369 13801 York Rd, Apt L10, Hunt Valley, MD *21030*
  MR & MRS Edwin B Green III (Anne K Du Vivier) Mid'74.Va'77—at
  ☎ (202) 462-1406 . . 3013 Cleveland Av NW, Washington, DC 20008 . . . .

Duxbury MRS Pauline C (Pauline E Carver) Mls'70.Bur. . . . . | ☎ (011-44-171) 352-7827 76 Chelsea Park Gardens, London SW3 6AE, England
  MISS Alison . . . .
  MISS Sarah C—at Penang, Malaysia . . . .
  MISS Lindsay H—at Kenyon . . . .
  JUNIORS MISS Katherine—at Westminster . . . . .

Duytschaever MR & MRS George E (Helen A Shelton) 10226 Olympia Dv, Houston, TX *77042*

Dwight MISS Anne V . . see MISS K Long

Dwight MR & MRS George H P (Gardiner—Eleanor M Collier) SL'60.Cl'64.Nu'84.Cly.H'50.Cl'52 . | ☎ (212) 724-9432 315 Central Park W, New York, NY *10025*
  MR Sargent C Gardiner—Cr'91—at U of Pa Grad . . . .

Dwight MRS Georgie P (Georgie F Potts) ☎ (212) 838-4598 . . 150 E 61 St, New York, NY *10021*

Dwight MR James E T . . see MRS J Stewart

Dwight JUNIORS MR John K JR . . see MISS K Long

Dwight DR Richard W—Cy.H.'25 Fox Hill Village 272, 10 Longwood Dv, Westwood, MA *02090*

Dwinell MR & MRS John (Collins—Ruth D Stone) Unb.Hb.H'38 ☎ (941) 922-3346 . . 7979 S Tamiami Trail, Apt 256, Sarasota, FL *34231*

Dwinell MR & MRS John A (Linda O Lawrence) D.Quin'70 . . . . | ☎ (508) 785-1706 170 Claybrook Rd, Dover, MA *0203*
  MISS Susanna D—at 160 Sea Breeze Av, Palm Beach, FL 33480 . . . .
  MR John L—Rich'95—at Mardoqueo Fernandez, Apt 403, Santiago, Chile . . . .

Dworkin DR & MRS Ronald W (Alexandra Roosevelt) Stan'67.Mv.Swth'81.Cal'85.JHop'95 . . of ☎ (410) 433-2127 . . 103 Goodale Rd, Baltimore, MD *21212* ☎ (212) 986-3144 . . 2 Tudor City Place, Apt 12DN, New York, NY *10017*

Dwyer MRS Page W (Dwyer—Secor—P Page Williams) . . . . | ☎ (302) 529-7437 2301 Lorelei Lane, Ardentown, DE *19810*
  MISS Claudia P—Del'95—at ☎ (302) 798-1097 3 Devon Rd, Wilmington, DE *19809* . . . .

Dwyer MR Thomas R (Guittard—Susie J Quealy) Sfg.Bur. ☎ (415) 751-0307 . . 3871 Jackson St, San Francisco, CA *94118*

Dye MR & MRS Alexander M (Louise B Young) Sth'81.Br'78.Mich'81 ☎ (212) 645-0342 . . 59 W 12 St, Apt 2C, New York, NY *10011*

Dye MRS Anna-Marie (Jones—Anna-Marie Zoller) Gv.Mv. ☎ (410) 833-5222 . . 13941 Mantua Mill Rd, Glyndon, MD *21071*

Dyer MR Alexander H—P'95 . . see MRS J de R Heyward

Dyer MRS Elisha (Katharine R Whitaker) Pr.Cly.Cda. ☎ (516) 671-8027 . . Piping Rock Rd, Box 541, Locust Valley, NY *11560*

Dyer MR & MRS Elisha JR (Natalie D Hubbard) Cc.Cly.Br'58 . . . . | ☎ (860) 868-7254 16 Buffum Rd, Washington Depot, CT *06794*
  MISS Natalie S—Mid'87 . . . .
  MISS Diana G—Skd'90 . . . .
  MISS Elizabeth D . . . .

Dyer MISS Elizabeth S—Ham'91 . . see MRS J de R Heyward

Dyer MRS Randolph H (Elizabeth Huntington) . . of ☎ (215) 968-6197 . . Pennswood Village K113, Newtown, PA *18940* ☎ (413) 337-4928 . . Heath, MA *01346*

Dyett MR E Granger 3d—WorPoly'73 ☎ (508) 760-2838 . . 24 Longview Rd, Yarmouth Port, MA *02675*

Dyett MRS Edmond G (E Marion Smith) Cr'24 ☎ (802) 375-2744 . . Sugar Bush Farm, Arlington, VT *05250*

Dyett MR & MRS Edmond G JR (Adrienne I Murray) Mit'47.Va'48 ☎ (617) 527-7923 . . 59 Prince St, West Newton, MA *02165*

Dyett MR & MRS H Thomas 2d (Eleanor Gillespie) Un.Hob'65 . . . . | ☎ (914) 967-2941 15 Cayuga St, Rye, NY *10580*
  MISS Julia S . . . .
  JUNIORS MISS Charlotte C . . . .

Dyett MRS John H (Marston—Sally B Russell) Msq. ☎ (561) 546-5354 . . 102 Grassy Trail, Hobe Sound, FL *33455*

Dyett MR & MRS Michael Van V (Harrison—Hildegard Richardson) Cal'75.H'68 . . of ☎ (415) 389-6342 . . 82 Walnut Av, Mill Valley, CA *94941* ☎ (707) 963-3185 . . ''Sage Cottage Farm'' 1515 Sage Canyon Rd, St Helena, CA *94574*

E

Eager MR & MRS Bainbridge (Ellen B Watson) . . . . . | ☎ (202) 363-6066 3111 Macomb St NW, Washington, DC *20008*
  MISS Susan B . . . .

Eager MR & MRS William G 3d (Carolyn A Hall) Ark'67.Emory'65 . . . . | ☎ (912) 242-1280 902 Mossway, Valdosta, GA *31602*
  MR W Grant . . . .
  JUNIORS MR Allen H . . . .

Eagle MR & MRS J Frederick 3d (Sarah T Vaughan) Colby'66.Bost'71 ☎ (805) 684-5631 . . Cate School, 1960 Cate Mesa Rd, PO Box 5005, Carpinteria, CA *93013-5005*

Eagleton MRS Mark D JR (Elaine O'Reilly) . . . . | ☎ (314) 863-4334 8121 Westmoreland Dv, St Louis, MO *63105*
  MISS Mimi . . . .
  MISS Libby . . . .
  MR David . . . .
  MR Stephen . . . .

Eakins MRS William S (Jean Pickup) Ck. ☎ (516) 676-0765 . . 36 Weir Lane, Locust Valley, NY *11560*

Eamer MR & MRS Richard K (Eileen T Laughlin) SCal'51.SCal'56.SCal'59 ☎ (310) 476-3316 . . 1619 San Remo Dv, Pacific Palisades, CA *90272*

Earl MRS Kathleen R (Kathleen C Reardon) ☎ (314) 997-2091 . . 6 Cricklewood Place, St Louis, MO *63131*

Earl MRS Philip (Anita R Farrington) ☎ (310) 377-1683 . . 2640 Palos Verdes Dv W, Palos Verdes Estates, CA *90274*

Earle MR & MRS David P 3d (Alexandra Cromelin)
Ch'66.Ch'79.Rc.Fy.Wms'59.Ch'62.Ch'64 . . . . . | ☎ (312) 944-0361
MISS Elizabeth A . . . . | 6 E Scott St,
MR David P 4th—at 151 Columbia Heights, | Chicago, IL 60610
Brooklyn, NY 11201 . . . . |

Earle MRS Eleanor F O (Eleanor F Owens) H'87.Me.Dc . . .of
☎ (401) 783-8920 . . ''Twin Gables'' 352 Ocean Rd, Narragansett,
RI 02882-1390
☎ (714) 673-5585 . . 300 Dahlia Av, Corona Del Mar, CA 92625-2817

Earle MR & MRS Francis 3d (Gillian C Fenwick) Dar.Myf.Col'64 ⛵
☎ (360) 384-6136 . . 4000 Mayne Lane, Sandy Point, Ferndale,
WA 98248

Earle MRS George H 3d (Jacqueline M G Sacré)
☎ (315) 386-2004 . . 17 State St, Canton, NY 13617

Earle MR & MRS George H 5th (Pearson—Ann E
Lindley) Hood'70.Me.Tufts'68 . . . . | ☎ (610) 527-0868
MISS Amy R P . . . . | 455 Boxwood Rd,
| Rosemont, PA
| 19010

Earle MRS Hubert P (Elizabeth M Wright) Me.Ac.Ncd.
☎ (610) 525-2309 . . 51 Pasture Lane, Bryn Mawr, PA 19010

Earle MR & MRS Hubert P JR (Bonica Banks)
Bost'68.Me.Eyc.Tufts'69.Bost'73 . . . . | ☎ (203) 655-1078
MISS Witney D—at Wheaton | 93 Raymond St,
| Darien, CT 06820

Earle MR M B Kenly (Miriam B Kenly) . . . . | ☎ (508) 927-6955
MR Frank T 3d—at N'eastern Law . . . . | 5 Beverly Commons
MR Michael K—at Suffolk Law . . . . | Dv, Beverly, MA
| 01915

Earle MR & MRS Ralph 2d (Collins—Julie von Sternberg)
Ph.Mt.B.H'50.H'55
☎ (202) 298-6528 . . 1411—29 St NW, Washington, DC 20007

Earle MR Richard (Frances Clement)
322 Crescent Rd, Waco, TX 76710

Early MISS Elizabeth—Dar.
☎ (206) 527-0464 . . 6008 Oberlin Av NE, Seattle, WA 98115

Early MR John C—Pn.P'40.H'47
34 Whiffletree Lane, New Canaan, CT 06840

Easby MR George G Meade—Ll.Art'41
☎ (215) 247-4876 . . ''Baleroy'' 111 W Mermaid Lane, Philadelphia,
PA 19118

Easter MR Donald Woodward
☎ (804) 295-5432 . . Springhaven Farm Cottage, 2679 Free Union Rd,
Charlottesville, VA 22901

Easter MR Douglas F (Peter) . . . . Married at Greenwood, VA
Laughlin MISS Page L (Edward H) . . . . Nov 11'95

Easter MR & MRS Douglas F (Page L Laughlin) Col'85.Col'86
☎ (303) 871-8979 . . 500 S Corona St, Denver, CO 80209

Easter MR & MRS James M 2d (Theodosia H Currier)
V'40.Gv.Md.Mv.Cr'41
☎ (410) 557-7177 . . 3300 Jarrettsville Pike, Monkton, MD 21111

Easter MR & MRS Peter (Carol Osborne) Dth'60 . . . . | ☎ (804) 984-1212
MISS Deborah A—at ☎ (804) 293-6658 | ''Springhaven
2731 Free Union Rd, Charlottesville, VA 22901 | Farm'' 2679 Free
| Union Rd,
| Charlottesville, VA
| 22901

Easterby LT & MRS David E (Rebecca P Webb) USN.Ws'89.Mit'87
☎ (713) 852-0269 . . 20810 Lake Park Trail, Kingwood, TX 77345

Easterby MR Edwin A (Stewart D 3d) . . . . Married at Houston, TX
Derryberry MISS Brandy K . . . . Apr 13'96

Easterby MR & MRS Stewart D 3d (Judith G Abbot) | ☎ (713) 358-7595
Miss'62.Mo'64 . . . . | 2907 Woods Estate
LT Stewart D 4th—USN.Pa'90 . . . . | Dv, Kingwood, TX
| 77339

Eastman MR & MRS John L (Josephine L Merrill) | ☎ (212) 772-0014
Cl'62.Rc.Mds.Cly.Stan'61.Nu'64 . . . . | 120 East End Av,
MR John L JR . . . . | New York, NY
MR Lee V 2d . . . . | 10028

Eastwood MR & MRS Stuart A (Margaret O Howard) Clark'75.Lanc'77
☎ (011-44-1524) 42-5310 . . 196 Lancaster Rd, Morecambe,
Lancashire LA4 5TL, England

Eaton MRS Frederick A (Louisa N Griffin) . . . . | ☎ (914) 967-7740
MISS Elizabeth M . . . . | 172 Highland Rd,
MR Frederick M . . . . | Rye, NY 10580
MR Thomas H . . . . |
MR Griffin A . . . . |

Eaton MR Frederick A—Ln.H'57
☎ (212) 472-8043 . . 350 E 77 St, New York, NY 10021

Eaton MRS Fredrick McC (Justine C Allen) Cly . . .of
☎ (212) 980-1853 . . 570 Park Av, New York, NY 10021
☎ (603) 563-8630 . . Box 128, Dublin, NH 03444

Eaton MR & MRS James H 4th (Elizabeth T Meyer)
LakeF'78.Msq.LyndSt'84
☎ (508) 475-5055 . . 3 Cattle Crossing Circle, Andover, MA 01810-4736

Eaton MR & MRS John M (Marie C Gooding) Ncd.H'40
☎ (508) 369-9255 . . 280 Estabrook Rd, Concord, MA 01742

Eaton DR & MRS John M (Mary E Beale) | ☎ (916) 587-1492
Sim'60.Stan'56.H'60 . . . . | Box 808, Truckee,
MISS Michelle L—at 1775 Marco Polo Way, | CA 95734
Burlingame, CA 94010 . . . . |
MR John M JR—Cal'84—at 144 Idora Av, |
San Francisco, CA 94127 . . . . |

Eaton MRS Monroe D (Laura Mitchell) Stan'27 . . . . | Webster House Apt
MISS Lydia . . . . | 406, 401 Webster St,
| Palo Alto, CA
| 94301

Eaton MR & MRS V Amory (Loomis—La Farge—Violet Amory)
☎ (508) 748-3183 . . 12 Vine St, Marion, MA 02738

Eaton MR & MRS William F (Froebe—Louise W Cropley) Sl.Ncd.Y'57
☎ (202) 337-0958 . . 4000 Cathedral Av NW, Washington, DC 20016

Eaton MRS William Mellon (Elizabeth W Witsell) | ☎ (212) 289-5639
V'49.Cs. . . . . | 17 E 89 St,
MISS Sarah E—Br'87.H'91 . . . . | New York, NY
DR Alexander Mellon—Duke'83.Duke'87—at | 10128
☎ (941) 332-5512 . . 1301 Poinciana Av, |
Ft Myers, FL 33901 . . . . |

Ebbert MRS George S JR (Lowrie C Wurts) Pg.Rr.
☎ (412) 521-0281 . . 6630 Kinsman Rd, Pittsburgh, PA 15217

Ebbert MR & MRS James Kay (Elizabeth B Coolidge) Pg.Rr.
☎ (412) 682-6444 . . 5023 Frew St, Pittsburgh, PA 15213

Eberhart MR & MRS Frank 3d (Delphine S Espy)
Pa'77.Rc.Ny.Cly.Cr'62 ⛵
☎ (212) 288-8227 . . 310 E 82 St, New York, NY 10028

Eberhart MRS Walter M (Elizabeth S Berger) Chr.Cly.
☎ (212) 832-7250 . . 200 E 66 St, New York, NY 10021

Eberhart MRS Walter M JR (Relyea—Pamela D Shearer) Wells'67 . . . . | ☎ (203) 661-6380 30 Old Mill Rd, Greenwich, CT 06831
MISS Caroline McG—StLaw'94—at 419 E 78 St, New York, NY 10021 . . . .
MISS Julie E—at Colgate . . . .

Ebersole MR & MRS R Bruce (Annabel F Ripley) AmU'78.Catawba'68 . . . . | American Embassy, PSC 801, Box 35, FPO AE, 09498-4035
JUNIORS MISS Clara H . . . .
JUNIORS MISS Elizabeth M . . . .

Eberstadt MISS Fernanda . . see A M O Bruton

Eberstadt MR & MRS Frederick (Isabel J Nash) Au.K.Nu'91 . . of
☎ (212) RE7-8232 . . 791 Park Av, New York, NY 10021
☎ (603) 962-5414 . . 9 Atlantic Av, North Hampton, NH 03862

Eberstadt MR & MRS Nicholas N (Mary C Tedeschi) Cr'82.Hn.H'76
☎ (202) 966-4857 . . 3511 Lowell St NW, Washington, DC 20016

Eberts MR & MRS Frederick W (Frazer—Evelyn S Allen) DelB.Dar.Myf. . . . . | ☎ (561) 276-5743 1007 Harbor Dv, Delray Beach, FL 33483
MR Dustin W—at U of Fla . . . .

Ebling MR & MRS R Hilliard (Best—Catharine M Brown) Denis'75.Ore'73
☎ (508) 468-7298 . . 155 Cherry St, Wenham, MA 01984

Ebright MR & MRS Harold R JR (Katherine A Fairlie) Cal'42.Cal'44 . . . . | ☎ (415) 892-3216 500 Indian Springs Rd, Novato, CA 94947
MR Harold R 3d—at ☎ (916) 541-5040 Box 7034, South Lake Tahoe, CA 96158 . . . . . .

Eccles VCT & VCTSS (Hyde—Mary Morley Crapo) K.Gr.Cly.Chi.C.
☎ (908) 725-0966 . . "Four Oaks Farm" 350 Burnt Mill Rd, Somerville, NJ 08876

Eckelberry MR & MRS John E (Houghton—Mollie McM Stark) B.Mb.Pr.Y'55
☎ (516) WA1-2229 . . 1936 Midlane, Syosset, NY 11791

Eckelberry MRS Renée D (Renée Duke) Rdc'48 . . . | ☎ (213) 469-8068 1803½ N Van Ness Av, Los Angeles, CA 90028
MR Stephen R—at 24100 Killion St, Los Angeles, CA 91367 . . . .

Eckerberg MR & MRS C Lennart (Willia F Fales) Swb'61.Cvc.Sl.Stock'53 . . . . | ☎ (202) 966-0594 3812 Klingle Place NW, Washington, DC 20016
MISS Alice R D . . . .
MR John F . . . .
MR Christopher F . . . .

Eckfeldt MRS Theodore E (Mildred O Ross) Sg.Ac.
☎ (215) 984-8405 . . Cathedral Village L110, 600 E Cathedral Rd, Philadelphia, PA 19128

Eckman MRS John W (Ziesing—Jane Haussman) Nyc. . . . . | ☎ (610) 469-6648 "Heatherlea Farm" 101 Iron Bridge Rd, Glenmoore, PA 19343
MISS Jane D Ziesing . . . .
MISS Heather W Ziesing . . . .

Econn MR & MRS James W (Christine Kockos) SCal'47
☎ (310) 203-9944 . . 2347 Century Hill, Los Angeles, CA 90067

Ecton MR & MRS Stephen M (Catharine de R Hollister) Mls'66.Smu'61 . . . . | 7725 Tomlinson Av, Cabin John, MD 20818
MR Thomas L—at U of Va . . . .

Eddison MRS (DR) Grace G (Dunne—Grace B Gere) Ws'49.Cl'60
☎ (803) 237-2679 . . PO Box 507, 202 Wyndham Rd, Pawleys Island, SC 29585-0507

Eddy MISS Dale Johnson (Thomas P) . . . . Born at Boston, MA May 17'96

Eddy MR & MRS David C (Laura G D Hersloff) Mt.Myf.Cda.Wes'75
☎ (410) 822-3814 . . "Cross Cove Cottage" 26398 Presquisle Rd N, Easton, MD 21601

Eddy MASTER Eben Jackson (John R) . . . . Born at Rock Hill, SC Apr 8'96

Eddy MR & MRS Ernest A JR (Williams—Marjorie A Cizek) Nd.Cy.Cw.Aht'41
☎ (314) 993-3512 . . 20 Brae Burn Dv, St Louis, MO 63124-1608

Eddy MR & MRS John P B (F Kathryn King) Rcn.Nrr.Ny.Tufts'81
☎ (201) 669-0980 . . Ramble Oak Farm, Glen Av, Llewellyn Park, West Orange, NJ 07052

Eddy MR & MRS John R (Robin M More) SUNY'80.Man'vl'82
☎ (803) 548-1733 . . 4085 Alana Court, Tega Cay, SC 29715-9217

Eddy MR & MRS John S (Ellen B Stover) Sth'61.Wash'53
☎ (201) 379-7932 . . 16 Beechcroft Rd, Short Hills, NJ 07078

Eddy MRS Morris R 2d (Kean—Joan E Jessup) Ih.Cly.Cda . . .of
☎ (847) 256-4773 . . 1630 Sheridan Rd, Wilmette, IL 60091
☎ (561) 546-6641 . . "Cardinal House" 97 S Beach Rd, Hobe Sound, FL 33455

Eddy MR Morris R 3d—Brad'73
☎ (847) 441-5791 . . 861 Spruce St, Winnetka, IL 60093

Eddy MISS Nathalie K . . see MRS S L H Phillips

Eddy MR & MRS Paul C (Connor—Nancy C Culbertson) Srb.Cy.Ny.Nrr.Curry'70 . . . . | of ☎ (617)326-4551 79 Martin Bates St, Dedham, MA 02026 ☎ (401) 849-0707 "The Gardener's Cottage" 30 Hammersmith Rd, Newport, RI 02840
MSRS C Clark & Charles F—at ☎ (213) 934-3364 502 Altavista Blvd, Hollywood, CA 90036 . . . .

Eddy MR Philip S . . see MRS S L H Phillips

Eddy MR & MRS R Post (Jeane B Saxer) S.Ny.Cyb.Cly.Hb.H'44 . . of
☎ (212) 734-0043 . . 169 E 71 St, New York, NY 10021
☎ (941) 964-0274 . . PO Box 756, Boca Grande, FL 33921

Eddy MR & MRS Randolph P JR (Susan A Fletcher) Bost'72.Ck.Edg.Curry'70 . . . . | ☎ (412) 741-9170 130 Centennial Av, Sewickley, PA 15143
MISS Elizabeth—at Vanderbilt . . . .
MR Randolph P 3d—at Brown . . . .
JUNIORS MISS Christen . . . .

Eddy MR & MRS Selwyn 2d (Frances E Budd) Rcn.Sfg.Pcu.Fr.Y'27 ⚓ . . of
☎ (415) 324-4614 . . 49 Heather Dv, Atherton, CA 94027
20802 Soneto Dv, Boca Raton, FL 33433

Eddy MASTER Thomas Gibbs (Thomas P) . . . . Born at Boston, MA Feb 4'95

Eddy MRS Thomas P (Ethelind A Giltinan) Sth'51.Pg.
☎ (412) 661-7393 . . 130 Yorkshire Rd, Pittsburgh, PA 15208-1045

Eddy MR & MRS Thomas P (Jennifer M Johnson) StLaw'82.Pg.Ey.Va'81.Duq'86.H'88
☎ (617) 631-3646 . . 6 Ft Sewall Terr, Marblehead, MA 01945

Ede MR & MRS Jared C (Baldwin—Carol R Duncan) Ore'59
☎ (415) 567-2381 . . 2215 Pacific Av, San Francisco, CA 94115

Edelen MR & MRS John W (Frances A Fenwick) Md.
☎ (410) 778-6917 . . 2 Byford Court, Chestertown, MD 21620

Edelen MR & MRS William B (Marian E Harvey) | ☎ (410) 377-3382
Elk.Md. . . . . | 6436 Cloister Gate
MISS Wendy N—at Boston, MA . . . . | Dv, Baltimore, MD
       21212

Edens MR & MRS Gary D (Hannah S Walter) | ☎ (602) 952-0333
M'dith'64.NCar'64. . . . . | 6239 N 47 St,
MISS Ashley F. . . . . | Paradise Valley, AZ
MISS Emily B . . . . | *85253*

Edey MRS Maitland A (Helen W Kellogg) . . . . | of ☎ (212)831-0331
MR Winthrop K—at ☎ (212) TR3-9753 | 1199 Park Av,
14 W 83 St, New York, NY *10024* . . . . | New York, NY
       10128
       ☎ (508) 693-2386
       ''Seven Gates
       Farm'' Vineyard
       Haven, MA *02568*

Edgar MR & MRS Antony (Beatrice W Hallowell) | ☎ (312) 266-1645
Bost'64.D.Ph.Ac.Okla'60 . . . . | 641 W Willow St,
MR Ian H—Dick'91—in Hong Kong . . . . | 118, Chicago, IL
       60614

Edgar MR & MRS (REV) David L R (Bull—Barbara A Look) H'87.H'47
☎ (508) 240-0657 . . 56 Clayton Circle, Orleans, MA *02653*

Edgar REV & MRS George B (Anne B Lukens) | ☎ (407) 682-4665
BMr'35.Hav'31.P'34 . . . . | 540 Village Place,
MISS Mary F—Swth'72.Geo'81—at | Apt 206, Longwood,
☎ (301) 649-3923 . . 123 Kinsman View Circle, | FL *32779*
Silver Spring, MD *20901* . . . . |

Edgar MR & MRS George L (Anne B Harlan) | ☎ (703) 536-4244
Dth'63.GeoW'70 . . . . | 3200 N Albemarle
MISS Gillian L—P'94 . . . . | St, Arlington, VA
MR Jonathan H—at Princeton . . . . | *22207*

Edgar MR & MRS James A JR (Mary D Saunders) | of ☎ (914)724-3557
Wms'56.Cl'60 . . . . | ''Blueberry Hill''
MR David S . . . . | 100 Deer Hollow
MR Christopher W . . . . | Rd, Poughquag, NY
       12570
       ''Allamanda''
       Windermere Island,
       Eleuthera, Bahamas

Edgar MR & MRS Robert F JR (Patricia H Pitcairn) Ws'51.Tc.Mit'50
☎ (412) 963-9297 . . 712 Robinhood Rd, Pittsburgh, PA *15215*

Edgar MR Robert G—Dth'53
☎ (313) 886-6010 . . 114 Kercheval Av, Grosse Pointe Farms, MI *48236*

Edgar MR & MRS Robert V (Sarah S Osborne) | 1215 Fifth Av,
Tufts'78.H.'69 . . . . | New York, NY
JUNIORS MISS Valentine B—at Groton . . . . | *10029*

Edgar MR & MRS William 3d (Barbara S Smyth) | ☎ (215) 884-6334
Ht.Hn.H'66. . . . . | 501 Twickenham
MISS Deborah B—H'95 . . . . | Rd, Glenside, PA
MR William K—H'91—*see Dilatory Domiciles* . | *19038*

Edgell MRS Henry W (M Elizabeth Spangler)
☎ (603) 627-2958 . . 411 Lucas Rd, Manchester, NH *03109-5120*

Edgell MISS Stephanie—V'43.Cl'62.Cs . . .of
☎ (212) PL3-8989 . . 1 Beekman Place, New York, NY *10022*
☎ (203) 661-8655 . . 23 Cliffdale Rd, Greenwich, CT *06831-2901*

Edgell MRS Stephen M (Claudia M Kelty) . . . . | ☎ (617) 729-2153
MR Stephen M 3d . . . . | 8 Sheffield W,
       Winchester, MA
       01890

Edgerly MR Peter DeF
☎ (617) 769-7766 . . PO Box 152, Norwood, MA *02062*

Edgerly MRS Susan R (Susan R Chapin)
☎ (617) 383-1861 . . 41 Hobart Lane, Cohasset, MA *02025*

Edgerton MR & MRS Albert S (Diana Hunt) | ☎ (510) 547-4514
Fr.Nw'49 . . . . | 199 Indian Rd,
MISS Kimberly—at ☎ (415) 929-1263 | Piedmont, CA *94610*
2240 Bay St, San Francisco, CA *94213* . . . . . . |
MR Edward J—CollId'90 . . . . |

Edgerton DR & MRS Bradford W (Lynne H Todd)
Van'69.Van'72.Y'79.Ri.Van'69.Van'73
☎ (213) 937-0947 . . 400 S Plymouth Blvd, Los Angeles, CA *90020*

Edgerton MR & MRS Malcolm J JR (Arnold—Jackson—Jane Lowe)
Ny.Au.Yn.Y'42.Nu'48
☎ (203) 357-7371 . . 130 Wallacks Point, Stamford, CT *06902*

Edgerton MR & MRS Philip (Elizabeth Hubbard) | ☎ (215) 699-4770
V'57.Hav'51 . . . . | Box 306,
MR Charles H . . . . | Gwynedd Valley,
MR James P—at U of NH . . . . | PA *19437*

Edgeworth MR & MRS Arthur B JR (Elizabeth D Walker)
Cvc.Mt.Ncd.Wms'51.Va'54.Geo'57
☎ (301) 907-9111 . . 3907 Thornapple St, Chevy Chase, MD *20815-5039*

Edinger MR John S—Sar.Aht'51.H'53 . . of
☎ (302) 654-5791 . . 1002 Kensington Lane, Greenville, DE *19807-2540*
☎ (561) 274-0827 . . 1209 Crestwood Dv, PO Box 1806, Delray Beach,
FL *33447*

Edinger MR & MRS John S JR (Laurie Mather) WestMd'82.WestMd'82
☎ (302) 888-2202 . . 105 Dickinson Lane, Wilmington, DE *19807*

Edington MR & MRS Robert Sherard (Patricia A | of ☎ (334)433-1750
Gentry) Aub'60.At.Rhodes'50.Ala'56 . . . . | 1220 Selma St,
MISS Virginia E. . . . . | Mobile, AL *36604*
MR Sherard C . . . . | ☎ (334) 626-9224
       ''Mossy View''
       325 Whiting Court,
       Daphne, AL *36526*

Edlin MRS Frank W (Katherine B Chadwick) Cr'50.Cl'62
☎ (203) 869-2638 . . 50 Lafayette Place, Greenwich, CT *06830*

Edmeades MR & MRS Michael D (Fabienne H B Mander)
Lond'79.Plg.Y.Ox'77 . . of
☎ (813) 677-8107 . . 10218 Elbow Bend Rd, Riverview, FL *33569*
☎ (914) 373-8674 . . ''Brigand Hill'' RR 1, Box 413, Smithfield,
Amenia, NY *12501*

Edmonds MRS Catharine L (Catharine van B | 185 Bedford Rd,
Livingston) V'72 . . . . | Pleasantville, NY
MISS Olivia L . . . . | *10570*
MISS Eugenia F . . . . |

Edmonds MR & MRS Dean Stockett JR (Adams—Wendy A Nickerson)
Wheat'60.Cos.Ec.Sb.Plg.Myf.Mit'50.P'52.Mit'58
☎ (941) 649-8341 . . ''Seventh Heaven'' 1019 Spyglass Lane, Naples,
FL *34102*

Edmonds MRS Field (Worth—Dorothy S Field)
☎ (413) 256-3466 . . 150 University Dv, Amherst, MA *01002*

Edmonds MR & MRS George P JR (Sally L Reeves) Cy.Ny.Chi.Mit'55 . . . . ☎ (617) UN4-8942
MISS Helen M . . . . 48 Fayerweather St, Cambridge, MA 02138

Edmonds MR Robert C—Rv.Snc.Bard'68.NYLaw'71
☎ (914) 244-3136 . . 33 Winthrop Rd, Chappaqua, NY 10514

Edmonds MRS Thomas S (Noble—Helene O Edmonds)
☎ (941) 489-0262 . . 1499 Brandywine Circle, Apt 207, Ft Myers, FL 33919

Edmonston MR & MRS Charles E (Lyn P Tiffany) Beloit'73.Wash'70
☎ (914) 234-9067 . . Box 550, Washington Av, Bedford, NY 10506

Edmonston MR & MRS Charles H (Elmina R Tilden)
Bgt.Cly.Ncd.Myf.P.'35.H'37
☎ (914) 234-7332 . . PO Box 236, 39 Long Meadow Rd, Bedford, NY 10506

Edmonston MR & MRS William E (Rosemary Finney)
☎ (520) 743-0305 . . 4805 W Jojoba Dv, Tucson, AZ 85745

Edmunds MRS Elizabeth P W (Perkins—Jenks— Elizabeth P Wallace) Cts.Ac. . . . . ☎ (802) 785-2132
MISS Anne R Perkins—B'gton'78—at 131 Chrystie St, New York, NY 10002 . . . . . RR 1, Box 9A, Thetford Center, VT 05075
MR William S Perkins—at 1219—12 St NW, Washington, DC 20009 . . . .

Edson MR Henry JR—Gc.Y'43
☎ (610) MI2-0137 . . 833 Buck Lane, Haverford, PA 19041

Edson MR John Joy IV—Pitt'53 . . . . ☎ (803) 776-1383
MISS Ann E Armstrong—at London, England 501 Pelham Dv, Apt D203, Columbia, SC 29209

Edson MR & MRS John Joy 5th (Eileen M Farrell) Denis'82.Tufts'83.Duq'89
☎ (412) 741-2449 . . 214 Centennial Av, Sewickley, PA 15143

Edson MISS Mary Trinity (Green—Mary Trinity Edson) Ariz'87
3135 Octavia St, San Francisco, CA 94123

Edwards MRS Alison I (Alison A Ives) . . . . Married at Lake Forest, IL
Hodges MR John L (Charles H 3d) . . . . Aug 17'96

Edwards MR & MRS Archibald C (Sarah S Gordon) ☎ (405) 427-7620
H'28 . . . . 5631 N Kelley Av, Oklahoma City, OK 73111
MISS Mary D—Cl'66.Cl'69.Cl'75.Cl'86—at
☎ (212) 923-2260 . . 601 W 115 St, New York, NY 10025 . . . .
MR Archibald C JR—H'68.H'71—at
☎ (617) 926-4643 . . 45 Coolidge Hill Rd, Watertown, MA 02172 . . . .

Edwards MISS Christiana (g—John Munroe) . . . . Born at
Alexandria, VA Mch 9'96

Edwards MRS Ellen T (Ellen R Turnbull) Ws'63 . . . ☎ (415) 668-9141
MISS Daphne H—at Washington, DC . . . . 3 Atalaya Terr,
JUNIORS MR Nicholas H . . . . San Francisco, CA 94117

Edwards MRS George W (Helen M Horan) Me.
☎ (610) 525-6507 . . 27 Pond Lane, Bryn Mawr, PA 19010

Edwards MR Hilary G—K.H'58
☎ (011-33-1) 45-44-70-58 . . 195 blvd St Germain, 75007 Paris, France

Edwards MR & MRS J Jeffrey (Elizabeth Greer) Mid'84.Y'88.CalPoly'81
☎ (206) 271-0674 . . 11503 SE 173 St, Renton, WA 98055

Edwards DR & MRS James B (Ann N Darlington)
Cl'48.Cda.Char'ton'50.Louis'55.Pa'58
☎ (803) 884-3493 . . 100 Venning St, Mt Pleasant, SC 29464

Edwards MR James C . . . . Died at
East Hampton, NY Aug 4'96

Edwards MRS James C (Sally A Matson) Un.Mds.Cly.Y.
☎ (212) 879-2349 . . 115 E 67 St, New York, NY 10021

Edwards MR & MRS James C JR (Barbara H Lord)
BufSt'76.Unn.Mds.Wms'74.Cl'77
93 Rockwood Lane, Greenwich, CT 06830-3814

Edwards MR & MRS Leo M (Elizabeth L Ames) Cal'69.NotreD'68
☎ (011-32-65) 2278-67 . . 37 rue du Grand Jour, 7050 Masnuy, St Jean, Belgium

Edwards MR Louis Ward . . . . Died at
Kalamazoo, MI May 5'96

Edwards MR M Beach C . . see R R Odén

Edwards MISS Melinda C
☎ (203) 966-0555 . . 584 Frogtown Rd, New Canaan, CT 06840

Edwards MR & MRS Oliver (Anita M Schubeler) of ☎ (212)861-1247
Y'68.Ford'75 . . . . 108 E 82 St,
JUNIORS MISS Margaret K . . . . New York, NY 10028
☎ (516) 862-8715
25 Harbor Rd, St James, NY 11780

Edwards MR & MRS Stephen A (Mary S Hallock)
Minn'78.Ph.Rv.Cw.Ht.Ncd.Mich'75.Mich'78
Estoril 06-02, 95 Holland Rd, Singapore 278539

Edwards MR W Neilson 2d—Pa'57
Hillside House, 4641 Roosevelt Blvd, Philadelphia, PA 19124

Edwards DR & MRS William H (Frances N McGaughy)
Van'53.Van'76.Van'49.Van'53
☎ (615) 383-9085 . . 50 Concord Park E, Nashville, TN 37205-4705

Edwards MR & MRS William H JR (Diane M ☎ (615) 665-0959
Peterson) Van'77.Van'77.Van'81 . . . . 915 Drew Place,
JUNIORS MISS Elizabeth H . . . . Nashville, TN 37205

Edwards DR & MRS Winston T (Marguerite Whitehead) B'hamS'66.Ala'63
☎ (334) 277-7619 . . 664 Horseshoe Curve, Pike Road, AL 36064

Eells MRS John S JR (Juliet G Oakes)
☎ (803) 328-6463 . . 623 Meadowbrook Lane, Rock Hill, SC 29730

Eells MR & MRS Jonathan W (Brenda L Grogg) Wit'92.OWes'89
☎ (970) 395-0491 . . 5133 W 11 St, Apt 712, Greeley, CO 80634

Eells MR & MRS Samuel JR (Elizabeth H McConnell) ☎ (216) 338-1084
Sth'60.Kt.Wms'57 . . . . 112 Manor Brook
MISS Catherine N . . . . Dv, Chagrin Falls,
MR Samuel 3d—at 156 Av 64, Pasadena, CA OH 44022
91105 . . . .

Eells DR William H—Fst.Un.Sar.Cc.Pn.OWes'46
☎ (614) 363-0331 . . ''Honeystone'' 54 Elmwood Dv, Delaware, OH 43015

Egan MRS Burgevin (Illiaschenko—Julia D Burgevin) Chr.Dar.Cda.Dc.
☎ (904) 280-0677 . . 1000 Vicar's Landing Way, Apt I206, Ponte Vedra Beach, FL 32082

Egan MR & MRS Gerald B (Boone—Edith P Gallatin) Ds.
☎ (908) 449-3697 . . 109 Madison Av, Spring Lake, NJ 07762

Egan MR & MRS Peter S (Neva E Dyer) Wis'71.Ch'74
☎ (847) 446-6896 . . 550 Ash St, Winnetka, IL 60093

Egan MR & MRS Sean J (Katherine Bailey Simons)
Myf.Ht.Cda.Ncd.Hn.SUNY'79.H.'81
☎ (610) 642-8812 . . 223 Winsor Lane, Haverford, PA *19041*

Egbert MR Garth L . . see J W McN Darling

Egbert MR & MRS George P JR (Judith E Barrett)
Ne.Cw.Y'51 . . . . | ☎ (203) 359-8818
MISS Melissa Mary-Barrett—Dar.—at | ''Windcroft''
Fairfield U | 83 Rogers Rd,
MR George P 3d—Cw.—at St Lawrence . . . . . . | Shippan Point,
| Stamford, CT *06902*

Egbert MR & MRS Richard Cook (Anne Merrill | ☎ (203) 629-5821
Becker) CtCol'53.Plg.Snc.Cw.Cly.Cda.Y'50 . . . | 250 Old Church Rd,
MR Richard Cook JR—Br'86.Pitt'91—at | Greenwich, CT
709 Fitzgerald St, Pittsburgh, PA *15213* . . . . . . | *06830*

Egerton MR & MRS Stuart 2d (Grotz—Franke— | 6437 Cloister Gate
Marr—Eleanor C Harvey) VJ'62.Md.Elk. | Dv, Baltimore, MD
HampSydney'62 . | *21212*
MISS Ann R—Gchr'86—at 3 Warren Lodge |
Court, Cockeysville, MD *21030* . . . . |
MR Stuart 3d—at 622 Charles Street Av, |
Baltimore, MD *21204* . . . . |
CAPT William A Grotz 3d—USA'88 . |

Egerton MRS Stuart W (Pegram—Elizabeth A Foster) Elk.Mv.Ncd.
☎ (410) 243-6567 . . 830 W 40 St, Apt 216, Baltimore, MD *21211*

Egge DR & MRS Ronald D (Marguerite B Tuck) | ☎ (334) 277-0990
Aub'68.Aub'67 . . . . | 1625 Wentworth Dv,
MISS Katherine M . . . . | Montgomery, AL
MR Ronald D JR . . . . | *36106*

Eggers MR & MRS L Christopher B (Gabriella A Finnell) Hart'71
☎ (609) 921-1954 . . 44 Knoll Dv, Princeton, NJ *08540*

Eggert MR & MRS James D (Cornelia L F Read) SL'87.Syr'84
☎ (303) 938-8956 . . 1913 Mapleton Av, Boulder, CO *80304*

Egginton MRS Hersey B (Mary F Twining) Sth'33
☎ (413) 584-8840 . . 71 Hawthorn Lane, Northampton, MA *01060*

Eggleston MR & MRS Richard H JR (Gretchen G Hatfield)
Pa'65.Sa.Ac.Pa'83.Geo'71 . . of
☎ (215) 438-3469 . . 308 Carpenter Lane, Philadelphia, PA *19119*
☎ (212) 861-8037 . . 229 E 80 St, New York, NY *10021*

Eggli MR & MRS John R (Jodi L Oliver) Cal'87
☎ (415) 364-6506 . . 1000 Wilmington Way, Redwood City, CA *94062*

Eglin MR T Wilson JR—Msq.Rv.CtCol'86
☎ (212) 496-5187 . . 235 West End Av, Apt 14H, New York, NY *10023*

Eglin MRS Thomas W (Edith H Baird) | ☎ (609) 896-1136
Wheat'57.BtP.Msq.Ac.Ncd. | 6 Edgewood Av,
MR Edward S—Rv.P'92—at 213 Beacon St, | Lawrenceville, NJ
Apt 3, Somerville, MA *02143* . . . . | *08648*

Ehrbar MRS A Kennedy (Anne F Kennedy) Nw'70. | 3 Top Sail Rd,
MR Eugene M . . . . | Norwalk, CT
JUNIORS MR John A . . . . | *06853-1518*
JUNIORS MR Edward R . . . . |

Ehrenclou MR & MRS Alfred M (Reilly—Wilson—B Natasha Simkus) P'49
☎ (561) 842-8886 . . 5200 N Ocean Dv, Singer Island, FL *33404*

Ehrenclou MISS Anne E . . see MRS D M Irwin

Ehrenclou MRS Elizabeth G (M Elizabeth Goeller) . . . . Married at
Camden, SC
Shaw DR James S . . . . May 11'96

Ehrenclou MR John O—P'51.H'56
292 Middlesex Rd, Columbia, SC *29210*

Ehret MISS Alexandra F
☎ (610) 642-4080 . . 414 Old Lancaster Rd, Haverford, PA *19041*

Ehrhard MR & MRS Louis E JR (Dorothy M | ☎ (847) 382-8624
Simmons) Colg'57 . . . . | 603 S Cook St,
MISS Catherine M—Colg'89 . . . . | Barrington, IL
| *60010*

Ehrhard MR & MRS Matthew H (Jennifer D McInnis) Rc.LakeF'87.Ill'91
☎ (773) 227-2222 . . 1250 W Augusta Blvd, Chicago, IL *60622*

Ehrhorn MRS George C A 2d (Alles—Mary Gray) Cda.
☎ (561) 287-3505 . . PO Box 1152, Palm City, FL *34991*

Ehrlich MRS Delia F (Delia Fleishhacker) . . . . | ☎ (415) 921-1106
MISS Joan D—at ☎ (213) 462-3456 | 2170 Jackson St,
2202 Holly Dv, Los Angeles, CA *90068* . . . . . . | San Francisco, CA
MISS Jill D—at ☎ (541) 955-8861 | *94115*
980 Crow Rd, Merlin, OR *97532* . . . . |
MR James S |

Ehrlich MR & MRS Paul R (Guggenhime—Emlen F | ☎ (415) 346-0705
Hall) Ws'64.Dth'57 . . . . | 2445 Buchanan St,
MISS Lisa J Guggenhime . . . . | San Francisco, CA
MISS Mia E Guggenhime—at 2101 California | *94115*
St, Apt 10, San Francisco, CA *94115* . . . . . . |
MR Andrew L Guggenhime—Mid'90—at |
New York, NY |

Eichorn MISS Jane deDoliete (Mark D) . . . . Born at
New York, NY May 27'95

Eichorn MR & MRS Mark D (Jane deD Kidd) Va'87.Rc.Fic.H'86
☎ (212) 876-7403 . . 1150 Fifth Av, Apt 11E, New York, NY *10128*

Eide MR & MRS Richard P (Patricia Tewksbury) Cv.Kt.
☎ (216) 975-1920 . . 6771 Waite Hill Rd, Willoughby, OH *44094*

Eide MR & MRS Richard P JR (Lulie S Pierpont) | ☎ (201) 564-6377
Bnd'71.D.Wms'68 . . . . | 36 Montview Av,
JUNIORS MISS Langley . . . . | Short Hills, NJ
JUNIORS MISS Christine . . . . | *07078*

Eidt MR & MRS Edward Duncan (Mary Bellan) NELa'79.Miss'50
☎ (601) 442-7719 . . 211 S Rankin St, Natchez, MS *39120*

Eifler MISS Elin C W . . see K S Fennebresque

Eiman DR & MRS John W (Daisy L Biddle) | ☎ (717) 646-3309
P'43.Pa'45 . . . . | North Shore, Pocono
MR John B—at 1407 Delores St, San Francisco, | Lake Preserve, PA
CA *94110* . . . . | *18348*

Eimicke MR & MRS Victor W (Thome—Maxine Howard) Mto.Nu'45
☎ (914) SP9-7694 . . 20 Hereford Rd, Bronxville, NY *10708*

Eiseman MISS Alice D (Richard D) . . . . Married at Cambridge, MA
Adelkind MR Alan (late Sam) . . . . Oct 24'94

Eiseman MRS James (Townsend—Mary E Lewis) Cs.Pc.
☎ (215) 233-5895 . . 524 E Evergreen Av, Wyndmoor, PA *19038-8304*

Eiseman MR & MRS Richard D (Louise Freedman) Tex'51.Nu'41
☎ (214) 361-0221 . . 10221 Waller Dv, Dallas, TX *75229-6614*

Eiseman MR & MRS Richard D JR (Elizabeth W Reed)
☎ (214) 528-7634 . . 3900 Shannon Lane, Dallas, TX *75205*

Eiseman MASTER Richard David 3d (Richard D JR) . . . . Born at
Dallas, TX Apr 5'96

Eisenbeis MISS Christina H (Zane—Christina H Eisenbeis)
see M E Pulitzer

Eisenbeis MR M Culver . . see M E Pulitzer

Eisenbeis MR William H S . . see M E Pulitzer

Eisenbeiss MR Christian Richard . . see D McI Kendall

Eisenbrey MRS J Kenton (Elizabeth N Hentz) Me.
   ☎ (610) 525-5652 . . 74 Pasture Lane, Apt 315, Bryn Mawr, PA *19010*
Eisenhart MR & MRS Edward C (Black—Sarah M Albert)
   Cvc.M.Ncd.Pn.P'42
   ☎ (804) 293-8882 . . 7 Ivy Lane, Farmington, Charlottesville, VA *22901*

Eitel MR & MRS Walter T (Berry Reavis)   of ☎ (212)879-5160
   Ck.Ri.Me'55 . . . . 176 E 77 St,
   MISS Alexandra N . . . . New York, NY
   MR Reavis H *10021*
                                      ''The Cabin''
                                      Mt Crescent Rd,
                                      Randolph, NH
                                      03570

El Bouhali MR & MRS Abdelouahab (Nancy F   ☎ (914) 241-2083
   Reeder) SL'67.Y'70.Cda. . . . . 22 Sarles St,
   JUNIORS MISS Leyla . . . . PO Box 667,
                                       Bedford Hills, NY
                                       10507

Elder MISS Alice L . . see MRS C F Vilter
Elder MRS Alicia O (Alicia F Oakes)
   ☎ (516) 283-1425 . . PO Box 2205, Southampton, NY *11969*
Elder MR & MRS R Duncan (Frances Noyes)   of ☎ (516)692-6936
   V'42.Csh.Au.Cs.Y.'39.Cl'46 . . . . 61 White Hill Rd,
   MISS Sarah M . . . . Cold Spring Harbor,
                                       NY *11724*
                                       ☎ (518) 576-9898
                                       Keene, NY *12942*

Elder MR William V 3d—P'54
   ☎ (410) 239-8181 . . 4101 Black Rock Rd, Upperco, MD *21155*
Eldredge MRS Arthur S (Roselle M Rice)   *see*
   Ws'51.Cc. . . . . *Dilatory Domiciles*
   MISS Joanna . . . .
   MISS Sarah—BMr'82.Mich'85 . . . .
Eldredge MR & MRS John McC (Arabella A James)
   RMWmn'76.GeoW'82.Dth'76.Dth'79
   ☎ (207) 829-4540 . . 620 Pleasant Valley Rd, Cumberland Center,
   ME *04021*
Eldredge MISS Margaret M . . see H S Durand
Eldredge MISS Melissa F (Ashton G JR) . . . . . . Married at Estes Park, CO
   Young MR James R . . . . Sep 6'96
Eldridge MRS Huntington (Barbara Buchanan)   ☎ (847) CE4-3132
   On.Ct.Wa.Un. . . . . 1201 N Elm Tree
   MR Peter B . . . . Rd, Lake Forest, IL
                                       60045
Eldridge MR & MRS Huntington JR (Deborah M West)
   Rcch.On.Rr.Wa.F&M'73
   ☎ (901) 683-1003 . . 4151 Walnut Grove, Memphis, TN *38117*
Eldridge MRS William A (Barbara F Jones) Cs . . .of
   ☎ (212) PL3-3650 . . 200 E 66 St, Apt D502, New York, NY *10021*
   ☎ (819) 843-1997 . . ''Greenbank'' Georgeville, Quebec J0B 1T0,
   Canada
Elebash MISS Alice Palmer . . see J M Rivers JR
Elebash MRS Baisley P (Marjean M Hoyt) T.
   ☎ (602) 948-5163 . . 5907 N Rocking Rd, Phoenix, AZ *85253*
Elek REV & MRS Henry Drinker (Sara F Barton)
   Ken'89.BankSt'90.H'87.Y'95
   ☎ (703) 931-4151 . . 4201 S 35 St, Arlington, VA *22206*

Elek MR & MRS Peter S (Mary E Drinker)   ☎ (610) 525-9558
   Rdc'49.VillaN'76.Me.Ac.Ncd.Bud'45.Camb'49 . 1035 Old Gulph Rd,
   MISS Susanna Middleton . . . . Bryn Mawr, PA
   MISS Daphne Drinker—StAndr'93 . . . . *19010*
Elias MR & MRS Archibald C JR (Susan W Homans)   ☎ (215) CH7-2527
   Pc.P'66.Y'73 . . . . 318 W Highland Av,
   MISS Abigail H . . . . Philadelphia, PA
   MISS Margaret W *19118*
   JUNIORS MISS Clara C . . . .
Eliot MR & MRS John (Sylvia A Hewitt)   ☎ (301) 949-4639
   BMr'57.H'56 . . . . 2705 Silverdale Dv,
   MISS Mary A . . . . Silver Spring, MD
                                        20906
Eliot MRS Thomas H (Lois Jameson) Cy.
   986 Memorial Dv, Cambridge, MA *02138*
Eliott DR Matthew S . . . . Married at North Salem, NY
   Finlay MISS (DR) Alexis E (Hunt—Alexis E Finlay) . . . . . . May 25'96
Eliott DR & MRS (DR) Matthew S (Hunt—Alexis E   ☎ (914) 669-5566
   Finlay) NewC'72.H'mannMed'81.Purd'79.   River Horse Farm,
   Purd'83 . . . . 260 Hunt Lane,
   JUNIORS MISS Allison B . . . . North Salem, NY
   JUNIORS MR Matthew E *10560*
Elkins MR & MRS George W 4th (Alethea S Hawley) Rich'93.Va'93
   1527 Spring Av, Rydal, PA *19046*
Elkins MR & MRS James A III (Mary V Arnold)
   Tex'80.Duke'82.P'74.Tex'76
   ☎ (713) 524-3335 . . 3335 Inwood Dv, Houston, TX *77019*
Elkins MRS Stephen B (Isabel A Devereux) Cvc.Mt.   ☎ (301) 654-5641
   MR Stephen B 4th . . . . 8305 Kerry Rd,
                                        Chevy Chase, MD
                                       20815
Elkins DR & MRS William L (Helen T MacLeod)   of ☎ (610)649-8922
   Sth'63.Wil.Cts.Ac.P'54.H'58 . . . . 130 Avon Rd,
   MISS Sheila M—P'90 . . . . Haverford, PA
   MR Jacob S—P'92—at Harvard Med *19041*
                                        ☎ (610) 486-0789
                                       Buck Run Farm,
                                       3575 Doe Run
                                       Church Rd,
                                       East Fallowfield, PA
                                       19320
Elkus MR & MRS Christopher J (Duryea—Gretchen   ☎ (212) 737-3507
   B Miller) Rc.Pr.Rr.Cly.Y'63.Nu'69 . . . . 155 E 72 St,
   MR James M—at Geo Wash'n . . . . New York, NY
                                        10021
Elledge MR & MRS Edman L (Molzen—Deborah A Day) V'55.Wis'53
   ☎ (203) 227-9252 . . 202 Harvest Commons, Westport, CT *06880*
Elledge MRS Michael S (Patricia L Chilcote) . . . . Died Aug 17'96
Elledge MR Michael S—V'77.Cl'81
   ☎ (810) 681-9356 . . 4105 Old Dominion Dv, Orchard Lake, MI *48323*
Ellicott MRS K Rodgers (McLaughlin—M Katharine   ☎ (410) 377-8685
   T Rodgers) Gchr'82.Ncd. . . . . 6029 Hunt Ridge
   MR Daniel J McLaughlin—Tufts'74 . . . . Rd, Baltimore, MD
   MR Robert T McLaughlin—Denis'77 . . . . *21210-1105*
Ellicott MRS Valcoulon LeM (Mary P Gould) Elk.Ncd . . .of
   ☎ (410) 527-0570 . . 13801 York Rd, Apt C16, Cockeysville, MD *21030*
   ☎ (717) 525-3331 . . ''Ellicott Cottage'' Box 33, Eagles Mere, PA *17731*

Elliman MR & MRS D Trowbridge (Claudia L Wright) Rcn.Cc.Yn.Y'50 .... ☎ (802) 253-4206 ''Nevermore''
MR William B—at ☎ (302) 651-9401
601 Way Rd, Hockessin, DE *19707* .... PO Box 609, Cottage Club Rd, Stowe, VT *05672*

Elliman MR & MRS D Trowbridge 3d (Leatrice L Dean) Hampshire'80
☎ (302) 654-9913 . . ''Nemours'' Box 35, Montchanin, DE *19710*

Elliman MR & MRS Edward S (Ann Rockefeller) Rcn.
☎ (203) 869-4824 . . 30 Bobolink Lane, Greenwich, CT *06830-3801*

Elliman MR Peter B—P'55.Va'57 .... ☎ (603) 229-4694
MR George T 2d—Mid'85.Va'90—at St Paul's School,
☎ (713) 523-1279 . . 2335 Wroxton Rd, Houston, 325 Pleasant St,
TX *77005* .... Concord, NH
MR Peter B JR—Va'91—at U of Va Business . . . *03301-2591*

Elliman MR & MRS Thomas T (Elizabeth M King) ☎ (313) 343-0060
Wheat'66.Cc.Wes'65 .... 244 Fisher Rd,
MISS Amy F—at ☎ (617) 666-6799 Grosse Pointe
24A Cherry St, Somerville, MA *02144* .... Farms, MI
MISS Samantha T—at Colo Coll *48230-1213*

Ellinwood MR & MRS George S (Jacqueline H ☎ (415) 931-5329
Isenbruck) Cal'44 .... 2424 Divisadero St,
MR George S JR—Cal'70 San Francisco, CA *94115*

Elliott MR Byron K—Cy.Sb.Plg.Cw.Rv.Ll.Ind'20.H'23
☎ (617) 267-5962 . . 780 Boylston St, Apt 23I, Boston, MA *02199*

Elliott MR & MRS C Douglas (Lynda A Mersereau) Van'76.Mt.Cvc.Fla'75.AmU'77
☎ (301) 652-2751 . . 5311 Oakland Rd, Chevy Chase, MD *20815*

Elliott MR David R—H'64
☎ (617) 247-1969 . . 231 Beacon St, Boston, MA *02116*

Elliott MR & MRS David R JR (Margaret Benoist Ravenel) Catawba'94.Catawba'94
522 Spencer St, Asheboro, NC *27203*

Elliott MR Forbes—Myf.Guil'62
648 Webster Av, New Rochelle, NY *10801*

Elliott DR & MRS Frank A (Whitney—Marvel—Gwladys C Hopkins) Ph.Ac.Cda.Cape'34
☎ (215) 842-9526 . . 3339 W School House Lane, Philadelphia, PA *19144*

Elliott MR & MRS Henry P JR (Diane Pingitore) ☎ (914) 967-0908
Man'vl'63.Ford'66.Ford'85.Lm.P'57 .... 370 Grace Church
MISS Amy C—P'94 .... St, Rye, NY *10580*
MR Henry P 3d—at Mary Wash'n ....

Elliott MRS Howard JR (Justine Prince) Hn.
☎ (203) 262-6663 . . East Hill Woods 22B, 611 E Hill Rd, Southbury, CT *06488*

Elliott MR & MRS Howard JR (Susan J Spoehrer) ☎ (314) 997-0589
Sth'58.Cy.Cvc.Nd.Br'56 .... 46 Clermont Lane,
MISS Elizabeth G—at 3926A Sacramento St, St Louis, MO *63124*
San Francisco, CA *94118* ....

Elliott MR & MRS John JR (Eleanor L Thomas) Bnd'48.Bgt.Gr.C.Rv.Cly.Ncd.H.'42
☎ (212) BU8-4774 . . 1035 Fifth Av, New York, NY *10028-0135*

Elliott MISS Kathryn S (Howard JR) .... Married at St Louis, MO
Love MR George F C (Jack W) .... Nov 5'94

Elliott MRS Mary Jane (Mary Jane Wagner) ☎ (302) 658-6046
Ky'68.Del'73.Wil. .... 1404 Greenhill Av,
MISS Julia W—at Harvard.................. Wilmington, DE
MR R Gibbons 3d—at U of Mont *19806*
MR T Scott—at Amherst ....

Elliott MR & MRS N Dodson 3d (Barbara E Johnston) ☎ (904) 264-7888
Denis'62.Pa'57 .... 2350 Egremont Dv,
MISS Susan J—Ken'92 .... Orange Park, FL
MR Gregory C—at Lynchburg Coll.......... *32073*

Elliott MRS Robert H E (Mary A Turnbull) Ncd.
☎ (609) 426-6298 . . Meadow Lakes 46-05U, Hightstown, NJ *08520*

Elliott MR & MRS Thomas A JR (Constance A ☎ (415) 386-2172
Kiesewetter) Sth'66.Bur.Fr.Ncd.GaTech'68. 32 Presidio Terr,
NCar'70 .... San Francisco, CA
MR Linton A—at 4041-16 Cornerwood Lane, *94118*
Charlotte, NC *28211* ....
MR Charles L—at U of Wisc ....
JUNIORS MR Jonathan B ....

Elliott MR Thomas R—Ala'83
☎ (212) 725-0304 . . 211 E 35 St, Apt 11B, New York, NY *10016*

Elliott MRS Virgil L (Helen M Cranfill) .... ☎ (415) 922-1267
MISS Ina Mary .... 3134 Jackson St, San Francisco, CA *94115*

Elliott MR & MRS William B (Turner—Elliott—Diane Keeves) P'35
☎ (719) 576-5766 . . 2755 Fawngrove Court, Colorado Springs, CO *80906*

Elliott MRS William C (Anita D Kurtz) Me.Ac.Ncd.
☎ (610) 645-8671 . . Waverly Heights, Villa 22, 1400 Waverly Rd, Gladwyne, PA *19035*

Elliott MR William C—Rcp.Me.Bab'75
☎ (617) 266-3050 . . 790 Boylston St, Apt 26G, Boston, MA *02199*

Ellis MRS A Leonard (Virginia Miller) Wils'40
☎ (603) 547-6821 . . 130 Cross Rd, Francestown, NH *03043*

Ellis MRS Anne K (Anne B Kneeland) BMr'63 .... ☎ (360) 468-3399
MISS Elizabeth T .... Rte 2, Box 3366,
MR Timothy K .... Lopez Island, WA *98261*

Ellis MR Arthur L JR
☎ (201) 428-0016 . . 83 Camelot Rd, Parsippany, NJ *07054*

Ellis MR & MRS D Rowland (Edith B Wetherill) Ncd. ⚓
☎ (954) 452-7774 . . ''Lily Pond House'' 470 SW Petersburg Terr, Plantation, FL *33325*

Ellis DR & MRS F Henry JR (Mary J Walsh) ☎ (617) 232-3252
Emman'78.Cy.H.Yn.Y'41.Cl'44.Minn'53 ..... 21 Fairmount St,
JUNIORS MR Michael G Walsh .... Brookline, MA *02146*

Ellis MR & MRS G Corson (Jewett—Constance C Comly)
V'56.Stc.Cs.Y.'51 . . of
☎ (212) 348-6698 . . 40 E 89 St, New York, NY *10128*
☎ (908) 291-3424 . . 746 Navesink River Rd, Red Bank, NJ *07701*

Ellis MR & MRS G Corson 3d (Marion F Freeman) P'73.Y'80.Stc.Yn.Aht'77.Cl'84
☎ (207) 865-0799 . . 10 Cushing Briggs Rd, Freeport, ME *04032*

Ellis MR Hedrick W—Br'85.H'93
☎ (617) 629-4938 . . 207 Lowell St, Apt 3, Somerville, MA *02144*

Ellis DR & MRS Herman (Amanda S Fahle) ChicoSt'79.SanDiegoSt'80.CalPenn'71.Duq'72. IaState'77 . . . . ☎ (916) 342-4488 53 Skymountain Circle, Chico, CA
  JUNIORS MISS Erica M *95928*

Ellis MR & MRS J Wiley (Marguerite C Duane) MaryB'66.Emory'62.Va'65.Va'66 . . . . ☎ (912) 925-3999 30 Rockwell Av S, Savannah, GA
  MISS Marguerite C . . . .
  MR Benjamin D *31419*
  MR Robb W

Ellis MR James Reed—StJ.Y'42.UWash'48.L&C'68.Seattle'81.Whit'92
  ☎ (206) 454-3705 . . 903 Shoreland Dv SE, Bellevue, WA *98004*

Ellis MRS Joan F (Joan Ferguson) V'51
  ☎ (908) 291-1422 . . 625 Cooper Rd, Atlantic Highlands, NJ *07716*

Ellis MR John A Fitler—Pars'55 . . of
  ☎ (415) 703-0911 . . 555 Buena Vista Av W, Apt 501, San Francisco, CA *94117-4142*
  ☎ (860) 824-1113 . . ''Eureka'' PO Box 313, Falls Village, CT *06031-0313*

Ellis MRS John C (Anne T Haskell) . . . . ☎ (908) 741-7276 ''Aulde House''
  MISS Isobel L—at F'klin & Marshall . . . . Box 134, Cooper
  MR John C . . . . Rd, Red Bank, NJ *07701*

Ellis MRS Marianne B (Marianne M Beyea) Dar . . .see MRS H D Beyea

Ellis MR & MRS Ralph E (Brewster—Nancy Dickinson Buell) Ste.Y'36
  ☎ (561) 278-7033 . . 3883 Gulf Stream Rd, Gulf Stream, FL *33483*

Ellis MR Scott H . . . . Married at Pearl Harbor, HI
  Barnett MISS Rebecca E (Allen F) . . . . Apr 26'96

Ellis MR Van Zandt (Sharvy—Victoria C Southwell) Nu'71
  ☎ (212) 650-2335 . . 110 Mercer St, New York, NY *10012*

Ellis MR & MRS William M (Beardsley—Elizabeth C Ellis) Ty'29
  ☎ (941) 966-5611 . . 8400 Vamo Rd, Sarasota, FL *34231*

Ellison MR & MRS David A (Alison J Fischer) LakeF'83.LakeF'83
  ☎ (908) 874-3720 . . 182 North St, Belle Meade, NJ *08502*

Ellsworth MR & MRS Robert A (Bastian—Alexandra McMicking) Col'66.Pcu.Fmy.Cal'58.Hast'62 . . of
  ☎ (415) 922-3040 . . 2928 Steiner St, San Francisco, CA *94123-3904*
  ☎ (707) 963-5884 . . ''Los Olivos'' 1640 Whitehall Lane, St Helena, CA *94574*

Ellzey MR & MRS Robert Theron JR (Virginia R Dumas) Ark'58 . . . . ☎ (501) 862-6217 716 N Madison, El Dorado, AR
  MISS Mary V *71730*
  MR Richard D . . . .

Elmer DR David B—Tufts'80.Tufts'84 . . . . ☎ (508) 362-1156 568 Shoot Flying Hill Rd, Centerville, MA *02632*
  JUNIORS MR Peter D—at Winchendon Sch . . . . .

Elmer MR & MRS Stephen B (Isabel Lincoln) Bnd'49.USA'46 . . . . ☎ (508) 255-4688 3 Uncle Ben's Way, Orleans, MA *02653*
  MISSES Isabel A & Lucy L—at ☎ (508) 255-1094 11 Bayview Dv, Orleans, MA *02653*

Elmlinger MR & MRS Paul J (Jennifer N Riegel) Duke'81.Dth'80.Geo'84
  ☎ (212) 517-5286 . . 108 E 82 St, New York, NY *10028*

Elmore MRS S Churchill (Betty R Buchanan) Cvc.Ncd.
  ☎ (202) 244-8994 . . 5142 Tilden St NW, Washington, DC *20016-1942*

Elmore MR Stancliff C JR—Cvc.Mt.Van'84.Y'90 . . of
  ☎ (202) 667-2724 . . 2829 Connecticut Av NW, Washington, DC *20008*
  ☎ (302) 539-6287 . . 7 Evans Rd, Bethany Beach, DE *19930*

Elsaesser MR & MRS Donald C (Petersen—Carol C Lucas) Denis'44 . . of
  ☎ (314) 966-2025 . . 1718 Warson Estates Dv, St Louis, MO *63124*
  ☎ (619) 568-0175 . . 47-171 El Agadir Circle, Palm Desert, CA *92260*

Elsberry REV & MRS Terence L (Sloan—Nancy Olds) Bgt.Drake'66.VaTheo'84 . . . . ☎ (914) 234-7836 PO Box 293, Bedford, NY *10506*
  MISS Margaret S Sloan—LakeF'91 . . . .
  MISS Holly M Sloan—LakeF'93 . . . .

Elsey DR & MRS Edward C (Isabella M Lee) Cin'33.Cin'31 . . . . 12050 Montgomery Rd, Apt 505, Cincinnati, OH *45249*
  MISS Elizabeth L—at ☎ (513) 281-8743 3731 Hyde Park Av, Cincinnati, OH *45209* . . . .

Elsey MR & MRS George McKee (Sally P Bradley) GeoW'50.Mt.Ct.StJ.Pn.P'39.H'40.AmInt'l'82
  ☎ (202) 966-6119 . . 5351 MacArthur Blvd NW, Washington, DC *20016-2539*

Elsom MRS Kendall A (Katharine G O'Shea) Wis'24.Pa'27.Cl'57.Cs. . . . . ☎ (610) 642-8146 32 E Old Gulph Rd, Box 222, Haverford, PA *19041*
  MRS Harriet Rothstein (Harriet Elsom) . . . . . .

Elting MR & MRS John W (Nancy A Johnston) Rcn.Cl'66 . . . . 1150 Park Av, New York, NY *10128*
  MISS Aleta A . . . .
  JUNIORS MISS Melissa H . . . .

Elting MRS Josephine F (Josephine F Fairman) On.
  ☎ (847) 816-6809 . . 26550 Longwood, Lake Forest, IL *60045*

Elting MRS Marjorie H (Heyworth—Marjorie M Horton) On.Rcch.Fy . . .of
  ☎ (860) 364-5930 . . Mudgetown Rd, Sharon, CT *06069*
  ☎ (941) 472-1320 . . ''Tee-Pee House'' Captiva Island, FL *33924*

Eltz CT Franz J—Vien'82
  52 Sagamore Rd, Bronxville, NY *10708*

Eltz CTSS Katharine (Katharine E O'Donoghue) Ken'73 . . . . ☎ (914) 337-4193 7 Midland Gardens, Apt 03, Bronxville, NY *10708*
  JUNIORS MISS Fiona F—at Indian Mtn Sch . . . . .
  JUNIORS MR Philipp J . . . .

Ely MR & MRS A Courtlandt 3d (Mary J McLaughlin) WChesU'65.Rv.Cw.Ofp.Sar.Wt.Vca.StJ.Snc.Coa. UMiami'58
  ☎ (201) 784-0288 . . Closter Dock Rd, Box 1139, Alpine, NJ *07620*

Ely MR & MRS Alfred (Virginia H Cliffe) P'41 . . . . . ☎ (520) 648-0989 1842 W Camino Urbano, Green Valley, AZ *85614*
  MISS Kathryn C (Hatle—Kathryn C Ely)—at ☎ (505) 281-0330 . . 44 Babalos Dv, Tijeras, NM *87059* . . . .

Ely MR & MRS B Danforth (Deborah A Bromberg) Utah'74.Utah'80.AGSIM'81.Va'56 . . . . ☎ (908) 781-0136 140 Mosle Rd, PO Box 732, Far Hills, NJ *07931*
  MISS Jane S—MtH'85 . . . .
  MR Timothy N—StLaw'86 . . . .

Ely MISS Barbara Revell—P'76
  18 Saratoga Av, Pleasantville, NY *10570*

Ely MR C Geist—Rc.P'54
  ☎ (212) 879-3900 . . 1 E 66 St, New York, NY *10021*

Ely MR & MRS Duncan Cairnes (Elizabeth C Wickenberg)
AScott'75.Cl'76.Gen'lTheo'89.Pe.Cc.Fw.Wt.Ll.Myf.
Ne.Rv.Sar.Snc.Ht.Dar.Ariz'74.Gen'lTheo'88 . . of
  ☎ (864) 585-1750 . . "Skidaway" 605 Crystal Dv, Spartanburg,
  SC 29302-2716
  ☎ (803) 838-7690 . . "Sea Urchins" 440 Tarpon Blvd, Fripp Island,
  SC 29920-9582

Ely MR & MRS George W (Bernice A MacKenzie) Bhm.Stan'49.Stan'51
  ☎ (510) 283-3918 . . 3711 Highland Court, Lafayette, CA 94549

Ely MRS John I (Harriet Jackson) . . . . Died Jun 27'95

Ely MR John I—Dyc.Cc.Ds.Y'35.Y'39
  ☎ (203) 865-1464 . . 221 Everit St, New Haven, CT 06511

Ely MISS Kimberly D (William Brewster) . . . . . . Married at Nashville, TN
Heim MR William G (William F) . . . . Mch 2'96

Ely MR & MRS Leonard W (Shirley N Rose) Bhm.Tcy.Stan'48.Stan'50
  ☎ (415) 321-8414 . . 2161 Bryant St, Palo Alto, CA 94301

Ely MISS Melinda (C Geist) . . . . Married at New York, NY
Dubow MR Charles S (Arthur M) . . . . Jun 1'96

Ely DR & MRS Parry H (Elizabeth S Magee) | of ☎ (916)265-6600
Stan'70.Rr.Stan'67.SCal'71 . . . . | 508 Broad St,
MR Sims . . . . | Nevada City, CA
JUNIORS MISS Rebecca J | 95959
| Scott Flat Lake,
| Casci Ranch Rd,
| Nevada City, CA
| 95959

Ely MR & MRS Stephen (Gaines—Susan Le F | ☎ (516) OR6-0379
Barclay) L.Mt.Pr.P'61 . . . . | "Nonameyet"
MISS Lyda Barclay—StLaw'87 . . . . | 251 Bayville Rd,
MISS Lynn Tompkins—StLaw'94 . . . . | Locust Valley, NY
MISS Sara Sterling—at Denison . . . . | 11560
JUNIORS MR Sterling Barclay—at Green Vale Sch

Ely MR & MRS William Brewster (Sandra M Skinner) | ☎ (505) 856-3566
Rv.Myf. . . . . | 50 Rock Ridge Dv
MR William Brewster JR—at U of NM . . . . | NE, Albuquerque,
| NM 87122

El-Yacoubi DR & MRS (DR) Hassan H S (Jane B | ☎ (215) 247-4831
Merritt) Col'73.Col'83.Col'73.Col'75 . . . . | 7830 Winston Rd,
JUNIORS MISS Fatima H . . . . | Philadelphia, PA
JUNIORS MR Salime H . . . . | 19118
JUNIORS MR Mohammed H . . . . |

Emberling MR & MRS David M (Stapley Wonham) Ty'79.Cal'74
  ☎ (203) 221-9219 . . 32 Silent Grove N, Westport, CT 06880

Emberling MISS Rachel Hayden (David M) . . . . Born Dec 9'94

Embler MR John W—Va'75
  ☎ (212) 316-3313 . . 305 W 98 St, New York, NY 10025

Embree MR & MRS Jeb N (Connelly—Dianne | ☎ (212) 744-2152
Thomson) Ny.Hob'63. . . . . | 155 E 72 St,
MISS Leslie P . . . . | New York, NY
| 10021

Embry MR & MRS Talton R (Marguerite Tenney) Ng.Cly.Rut'68
  ☎ (212) 996-5881 . . 17 E 89 St, New York, NY 10128

Emeny MRS Brooks (Barbara Cox) Cly.Rr.Yh.
  ☎ (609) 924-1060 . . 221 Elm Rd, Princeton, NJ 08540

Emeny MRS Frederick Latham (Caroline G Bush) | ☎ (216) 541-5541
Kt. . . . . | 2 Bratenahl Place,
MISS Ruth B . . . . | Apt 7FE, Bratenahl,
| OH 44108

Emerson MR & MRS Edward E JR (May Starr) | ☎ (802) 765-4049
Sth'67.Dth'63 . . . . | "Tamarack Hill
MR Edward E III . . . . | Farm" RR 1,
MR Benjamin T . . . . | Box 234, Strafford,
| VT 05072
| Jan 1 . .
| ☎ (910) 695-0895
| Youngs Rd,
| PO Box 2266,
| Southern Pines, NC
| 28388

Emerson MR & MRS H Truxtun JR (M L Tyler Lewis)
Qc.Cw.Ncd.Dc.Y'39.H'42
  ☎ (941) 261-0983 . . 1221 Gulf Shore Blvd N, Apt 502, Naples,
  FL 34102

Emerson MR & MRS Jonathan E (Jane A Colby) Cr'60 ⚓
  ☎ (860) 677-6900 . . 129 Tunxis Village, Farmington, CT 06032

Emerson MR & MRS Raymond 2d (Jennifer E Pennoyer) Sim'79.BostColl'90
  ☎ (508) 369-9747 . . 1061 Monument St, Concord, MA 01742

Emery MR & MRS Andrew C (Lea K Reams) MtH'88.Ty'85
  ☎ (513) 221-8067 . . 2145 St James Av, Cincinnati, OH 45206

Emery DR & MRS Edward S 3d (Ann Badger) | ☎ (802) 862-6246
Sth'59.P'57.Cl'61 . . . . | 1549 Hinesburg Rd,
MISS Margaret—P'90 . . . . | South Burlington,
MR Theodore A—Stan'94 . . . . | VT 05403

Emery MRS George I (Helen J Fitch) V'34.Rdc'37
  ☎ (617) 455-6626 . . North Hill D404, 865 Central Av, Needham,
  MA 02192

Emery MR & MRS James J (Allison B Rumsey) Mid'85.Reed'78
  ☎ (202) 244-7061 . . 5201—38 St NW, Washington, DC 20015

Emery MRS John J (Olyphant—Adele S Hammond) Ri.Cly.
  ☎ (201) 539-0027 . . "Still Pond Cottage" Box 125, New Vernon,
  NJ 07976

Emery MR & MRS John M 2d (Patricia C Monroe) | ☎ (516) 569-0432
Ln.P'53.H'58 . . . . | 231 Polo Lane,
DR John M 3d—P'79.Cl'85—at | Lawrence, NY
  ☎ (209) 571-5447 . . 210 Brook Way, Modesto, | 11559
CA 95354. . . . . |

Emery MRS Manning (Madeline Jackson)
  ☎ (207) 846-3814 . . 29 Blueberry Cove, Yarmouth, ME 04096

Emery MRS Rose B (Rose B Burks) Swb'61
  ☎ (804) 977-3767 . . 12 Oak Circle, Charlottesville, VA 22901

Emery MR Willard—H'59.Va'62 ⚓
  ☎ (941) 349-6924 . . 7220 Point of Rocks, Siesta Key, Sarasota,
  FL 34242

Emery MR & MRS William 3d (Shelley H Dwight) | ☎ (203) 966-3433
Sth'57.San.Y'56 . . . . | 677 Weed St,
MR Nicholas D—at ☎ (303) 258-7813 | PO Box 1222,
PO Box 927, Nederland, CO 80466 . . . . | New Canaan, CT
| 06840-1222

Emes MR Edward L JR (late Edward L) . . . . . . Married at Washington, DC
Dalton MISS Elizabeth A (late Horace M) . . . . Mch 16'96

Emes MR & MRS Edward L JR (Elizabeth A Dalton) | ☎ (202) 333-7879
Conv'71.Cvc.Ncd.Duke'52 . . . . | 322 N St NW,
  MISS Virginia Radley—at Mt Holyoke . . . . | Washington, DC
                                            | *20007*

Emig REV & MRS James A (Elodie S Ballantine) Drew'78
  ☎ (303) 477-9726 . . 3837 King St, Denver, CO *80211*

Emigholz MR & MRS Lawrence F (Nancy P Beaumont)
  ☎ (216) 338-5597 . . ''Woodpecker Hill'' 13634 Northwood Rd,
  Novelty, OH *44072-9796*

Emlen MRS Alan L (McLane—Claire Fuller) Cly.
  ☎ (212) SA2-8897 . . 1220 Park Av, New York, NY *10128*

Emlen MR & MRS Robert L (Cora W Peabody) Rcp.Csp.Dth'38
  ☎ (603) 643-3036 . . Kendal at Hanover 1032, 80 Lyme Rd, Hanover,
  NH *03755*

Emlen MR Thomas F . . see J Cochran

Emmerich MR & MRS Theodore H (Katherine Harmon)
  Cm.Qc.Cin'50.Cin'63 . . of
  ☎ (513) 751-4224 . . 1201 Edgecliff Place, 1052, Cincinnati, OH *45206*
  ☎ (954) 522-1582 . . Orleans Chateau Villa 303, 2000 S Ocean Lane,
  Ft Lauderdale, FL *33316*

Emmet MISS Caroline—Bnd'86
  ☎ (011-33-1) 48-74-43-04 . . 48 rue Notre Dame de Lorette, 75009 Paris,
  France

Emmet MR & MRS Edouard C (Linda L Berlin) H'53 | ☎ (011-33-1)
  MR Edouard—at ☎ (212) 260-7549 | 45-04-96-70
  145 E 2 St, New York, NY *10009* . . . . | 16 rue Desbordes
                                             | Valmore,
                                             | 75016 Paris, France

Emmet MRS Elizabeth Thigpen (Elizabeth L Thigpen) Ala'55.Cda.
  ☎ (334) 288-0817 . . 3444 Thomas Av, Montgomery, AL *36111*

Emmet MRS Grenville T (Gammack—Burden—Elizabeth Chace) Bgt.Hn.
  ☎ (561) 546-3858 . . Box 997, Hobe Sound, FL *33475*

Emmet MR & MRS Grenville T 3d (Beach—Beall— | of ☎ (202)328-3829
  Dita A Holloway) Fic.H.'60 . . . . | 2700 Calvert St
  MISS Samantha B—at Wash'n Coll . . . . | NW, Washington,
  MSRS Grenville T 4th & Bradford C—at | DC *20008*
  234 Pea Pond Rd, Katonah, NY *10536* . . . . | ☎ (212) 888-6551
                                             | 400 E 59 St,
                                             | New York, NY
                                             | *10022*

Emmet MRS H Dunscombe (Castets—Helen D Emmet)
  see MRS W E Belknap 2d

Emmet MR & MRS Henri W (M Louise Santry) H'48 | ☎ (212) 472-2562
  MISS Diana Louise—☎ (212) 988-7446 . . . . | 176 E 71 St,
                                             | New York, NY
                                             | *10021*

Emmet MR & MRS Herman Le R 3d (J Elaine Osborn)
  Nw'64.K.Geo'67.MdArt'74 . . of
  ☎ (516) 324-7638 . . PO Box 807, East Hampton, NY *11937*
  ☎ (212) 873-9094 . . 41 Central Park W, New York, NY *10023*

Emmet MISS Katharine Temple (True—Katharine | of ☎ (212)255-4553
  Temple Emmet) Cly. | 104 Bedford St, Apt
  MISS Gabriella M True—at ☎ (212) 966-5709 | 4C, New York, NY
  457 Broome St, New York, NY *10012* . . . . . . | *10014*
                                             | ☎ (802) 325-3098
                                             | Herrick Brook Rd,
                                             | Pawlet, VT *05761*

Emmet MR & MRS Robert (Gail Putnam) | ☎ (216) 338-5217
  Bost'68.Myf.Ncd.Y'67.H'73 . . . . | 50 Fairfax Dv,
  MR Richard S 2d—at Cornell . . . . | Chagrin Falls, OH
  JUNIORS MR Robert P . . . . | *44022*

Emmet MISS Sheila Dahlgren . . . . Died at
                                           Newport, RI Aug 5'96

Emmet DR & MRS William Le R 2d (Marja T | ☎ (207) 529-5779
  Pukkila) Pa'67.Cal'75.Tex'79 . . . . | ''Merituuli''
  MISS Katherine T—Man'vl'92 . . . . | PO Box 194,
  MISS Marja-Leena—Skd'95 . . . . | Medomak, ME
  JUNIORS MR William Le R 3d—at St Mark's . . . . | *04551*

Emmet MR & MRS Winthrop S (Laidlaw— | ☎ (413) 232-4359
  Mary-Jane McGuckin) V'58.Lx.H'33 . . . . | 46 W Center Rd,
  MISS Jane E . . . . | Box 327,
    MR William C Laidlaw . . . . | West Stockbridge,
                                             | MA *01266*

Emmons MISS Catherine D—Sth'80
  ☎ (617) 441-2571 . . 2 Ware St, Apt 206, Cambridge, MA *02138*

Emmons MR David W . . see P L R Du Val

Emmons MRS Diane Neal (Diane E D Neal) | ☎ (508) 526-1271
  Sth'55.H.'78.Chi. . . . . | 115 School St,
  MR Robert W 3d—Mass'82 . . . . | Manchester, MA
                                             | *01944*

Emmons MR & MRS Thomas P (Margaret T Hillsley) Duke'50.Pc.Fi.P.'48
  ☎ (215) 247-2201 . . 8233 Crittenden St, Philadelphia, PA *19118*

Emmons MRS William B JR (M Elizabeth Barlow) | ☎ (802) 457-1478
  Sm. . . . . | ''Cloudland Farm''
  MISS M Dana . . . . | RR 1, Box 38,
                                             | Woodstock, VT
                                             | *05091*

Emory MR Dennis S—P'70.Pa'72 ⚜ . . of
  ☎ (307) 733-3601 . . Box 190, Wilson, WY *83014*
  ☎ (207) 244-5066 . . Box 200, Bass Harbor, ME *04653*

Emory MRS German H H (Katherine E Riegel) Cly.Ncd . . .of
  ☎ (203) 259-0226 . . 1155 Sasco Hill Rd, Box 434, Southport, CT *06490*
  ☎ (212) 288-2576 . . 200 E 66 St, New York, NY *10021*

Emory MR Morris S—Me.Gm.P'38
  ☎ (610) 642-7196 . . 518 Thornbury Rd, Haverford, PA *19041*

Emory MR & MRS Morris S JR (Brigitte M Berthe) | ☎ (817) 354-6917
  Louis'75.Ky'77 . . . . | 4304 Pembrooke
  MISS Stephanie L . . . . | P'kway W,
                                             | Colleyville, TX
                                             | *76034*

Ems MR & MRS A Frederick (Sargent—Mary Jewett) | ☎ (303) 979-4432
  OState'50 . . . . | 7022 S Lamar St,
  MR Adolf F JR—WestSt'80—Box 1185, | Littleton, CO *80123*
  Crested Butte, CO *81224* . . . . |

Emsden MRS Katharine N (Katharine P T Nicely) Swth'61
  19 Brooks Rd, Lincoln, MA *01773-1308*

Endicott MR & MRS Charles M (Marianne R Trombley) MtH'53
  ☎ (313) 882-6483 . . 349 Notre Dame St, Grosse Pointe, MI *48230*

Endicott MISS Eve . . see P J Ames

Endicott MISS Katharine L—Wheat'81
  90 Park St, Apt 27, Brookline, MA *02146*

Engel MR & MRS Thomas E (Suzanne M Gallaudet)
RISD'68.K.H.'67 . . . . | of ☎ (212)794-5049
  MISS Phoebe D—at Haverford . . . . | 215 E 72 St,
  MR Montgomery E—at Wesleyan . . . . | New York, NY
  JUNIORS MISS Alice G . . . . | *10021*
  | ☎ (914) 439-5413
  | "Maple Farm"
  | Box 127,
  | Lew Beach, NY
  | *12753*

Engelbert MR & MRS Robert W (Georgia E Ganson) | ☎ (216) 333-8067
Cr'47.Cr'49 . . . . | 3809 E Surry Court,
  MISS Margaret H—IaState'81—at | Rocky River, OH
  ☎ (216) 331-7853 . . 19775 Henry Rd, | *44116*
  Fairview Park, OH *44126* . . . .
  MR David G—IaState'81—at ☎ (816) 746-4299
  7424 N Rhode Av, Kansas City, MO *64152* . . . .

Engelhard MRS Charles W (Mannheimer—Jane Brian) Eh.
  ☎ (908) 766-1504 . . "Cragwood" 221 Ravine Lake Rd, Far Hills,
NJ *07931*

Engelhardt DR & MRS M Bonner (Margaret V | ☎ (334) 265-6548
McCall) Tul'63.Tul'60 . . . . | 2622 Fernway Dv,
  MISS Margaret S . . . . | Montgomery, AL
  MR Miller B JR . . . . | *36111*
  JUNIORS MR Samuel McC . . . . |

Engelhardt MR & MRS Philip L (Keith—Helen E Paine)
  ☎ (415) 322-2590 . . 935 Menlo Oaks Dv, Menlo Park, CA *94025*

Engert MR & MRS Roderick M (Jane Soule) Y'50 . . . | ☎ (202) 363-0118
  MISS Jane M . . . . | 4509 Ellicott St
  MR William S . . . . | NW, Washington,
  MR James C . . . . | DC *20016*

England MR & MRS Sanford H (Jacquelin Potts) Pa'56.Pa'60
  ☎ (617) 375-9060 . . 370 Marlborough St, Boston, MA *02115*

Engler MR & MRS J Curtis (Rosalie McR Ewing) Cent'y'68.Rc.Cy.StL'70
  ☎ (314) 991-1039 . . 24 Lorenzo Lane, St Louis, MO *63124*

English MRS Charles Clement JR (Roberta A Cecil) . | ☎ (540) 943-1096
  MR Robert C—Box 4082, Chico, CA *95926* . . . . | 1311 Keesling Av,
  | Waynesboro, VA
  | *22980*

English MISS Edith C
  ☎ (610) 525-0775 . . 404 Cheswick Place, Apt 111, Rosemont,
PA *19010*

English MR Edwin H 3d—Pc.Ste.Pa'51 . . of
  ☎ (941) 723-1679 . . "Winterset" Box 92, 8515 US H'way 41 N,
Palmetto, FL *34221*
  ☎ (401) 783-5808 . . "Windswept" 137 Bonnet Shores Rd, Narragansett,
RI *02882*

English MR Henry W—Y'43 . . . . | ☎ (203) 777-8675
  MISS Elinor L Blake . . . . | 265 E Rock Rd,
  | New Haven, CT
  | *06511*

English MR & MRS Oscar B (Carroll Bever) Tex'48.Tex'39 . . of
  ☎ (214) 521-2561 . . Park Plaza 706, 4500 Roland Av, Dallas,
TX *75219*
  ☎ (011-44-171) 402-3784 . . St George's Fields, Hanover Steps 35,
Albion St, London W2 2YG, England
Laureles Apt 102, Tabachines 1, Acapulco GRO, Mexico

English MRS William D (Sherrill—May Gould) | ☎ (508) 927-0478
Sth'33.Chi. . . . . | 118 Valley St,
  MISS Sarah B Sherrill—at ☎ (212) 249-2497 | Beverly Farms, MA
  155 E 72 St, New York, NY *10021* . . . . | *01915*
  MISS Jane W Sherrill—at ☎ (508) 369-3682
  Box 1160, Concord, MA *01742* . . . .

Englund MRS Richard B (Gage Bush) Cly.Ncd . . . . | ☎ (334) 928-1625
  MISS Alixandra G—at Brown . . . . | "Alabama Waters"
  MISS Rachel R . . . . | 17367 Scenic H'way
  | 98, PO Box 469,
  | Point Clear, AL
  | *36564*

Engman MR & MRS William C (Marilyn Berger) | ☎ (314) 966-4348
Wash'56.Wash'55 . . . . | 410 Elm St,
  MR David T . . . . | Glendale, MO *63122*

Engs MR & MRS Edward W 3d (Joyce A Gableman) | ☎ (818) 799-3046
Pcu.Cal'52 . . . . | 430 Laguna Rd,
  MISS Francis H—at 1916 Pine St, Apt 2, | Pasadena, CA *91105*
  San Francisco, CA *94109* . . . . |

Engs MR & MRS Edward W 4th (Anita J Leahy)
PortSt'82.SCal'89.Ore'85.SCalInA'89
  ☎ (310) 478-5392 . . 10414 Troon Av, Los Angeles, CA *90064*

Enloe MR & MRS Robert Ted 3d (Bess A Fraser) | ☎ (214) 352-4772
Smu'60.LaTech'61 . . . . | 8823 Briarwood
  MISS Mary R . . . . | Lane, Dallas, TX
  MISS Sara E . . . . | *75209*

Ennis MR & MRS Bruce J JR (Newhall—Emily A Fowler)
Wheat'71.Dth'62 . . of
  ☎ (202) 966-3015 . . 4518 Klingle St NW, Washington, DC *20016*
  Sunset Lake Rd, Marlboro, VT *05344*

Ennis MRS George H (Bernice A Brinkema)
  ☎ (805) 987-5446 . . 41027 Village 41, Camarillo, CA *93012*

Ennis MR Thomas W . . see E M de Windt

Enos MR & MRS Alanson T 3d (Alice H Plimpton) H'39
  ☎ (203) 869-3366 . . 312 Taconic Rd, Greenwich, CT *06831*

Enos MR & MRS Alanson T 4th (June H Graves) | ☎ (908) 234-1321
Eh.San.NCar'66 . . . . | Box 315,
  MISS Sara N—at Gettysburg Coll . . . . | Bedminster, NJ
  MISS Laura G—at Bowdoin . . . . | *07921*
  JUNIORS MR Alanson T 5th—at Cornell . . . . |

Epstein DR & MRS Stephen E (Lee—A Cary Brown) Va'84.SL'81
  ☎ (804) 979-4622 . . "Tandem" Rte 10, Box 266, Charlottesville,
VA *22903*

Erdman MR & MRS Michael P (Scullin—Barbara | ☎ (610) LA5-5146
DuBarry) Err.Eyc.Me.Pn.P'57 . . . . | 206 Avon Rd,
  MISS Barbara B Scullin—Ty'87—at | Haverford, PA
  ☎ (703) 553-0535 . . 1949 Columbia Pike, | *19041-1613*
  Apt 43, Columbia Crossing, Arlington, VA
  22204 . . . .

Erdmann MR Gregory S—Vt'87
  ☎ (802) 482-8799 . . 33 Lakeview Terr, Burlington, VT *05401*

Erdmann MR & MRS John F 2d (Tanis Higgins) Rdc'59.Colg'54.Cl'59
  ☎ (203) 966-3411 . . 143 Rosebrook Rd, New Canaan, CT *06840*

Erdmann MR & MRS John F 3d (Barbara A Korfman) OWes'85
  ☎ (203) 855-1845 . . 3 Woodland Rd, Wilson Point, Norwalk,
CT *06854*

Erdmann MR Robert H—Colby'89
☎ (401) 841-5482 . . 182 Tuckerman Av, Middletown, RI *02842*
Erdreich MR & MRS Benjamin L (Ellen M Cooper) | 2706—36 St NW,
Ws'62.Y'60.Ala'63 . . . . | Washington, DC
MISS Anna B . . . . | *20007-1421*
MR Jeremy C . . . . |
Erdreich MISS M Elizabeth—Tul'85
☎ (617) 266-0644 . . 200 W Newton St, Apt 3, Boston, MA *02116*
Erdreich MR & MRS Stanley M JR (Beverly H Blumberg) Ncmb'61.W&L'57
☎ (205) 967-2357 . . 3560 River Bend Rd, Birmingham, AL *35243*
Erdreich MR Stanley M 3d
36 Gramercy Park E, Apt 9E, New York, NY *10003-1777*
Erensel MR & MRS Brent B (Nina Pearce) FIT'86.Lawr'78.Nu'82
60 East End Av, Apt 33B, New York, NY *10028*
Erhard MR & MRS John W (Joan F Williams) H'38 . | ☎ (508) 468-1040
MISS Nancy A . . . . | Box 1, Wenham,
MR John W JR . . . . | MA *01984*
MR Edward W . . . . |
Erhart MR & MRS Charles H JR (Sylvia M Montgomery)
Bnd'84.Rc.Chr.Ny.Y.'49
☎ (212) RE4-0171 . . 149 E 73 St, New York, NY *10021*
Erickson MR & MRS David O (Marcia W Haight) | ☎ (919) 846-7467
Nu'80.Hn.Pa'59 . . . . | 8220 Harps Mill Rd,
JUNIORS MR Ian A . . . . | Raleigh, NC *27615*
JUNIORS MR Jon W . . . . |
Erickson MISS Jessica (g—MRS Robert W Michell) . . . . Born Mch 15'94
Erisman MR & MRS Otis W (Eleanor W Platt)
Ws'46.Pa'79.Rc.Me.H'45.H'48
☎ (610) 649-0536 . . 1536 Monticello Dv, Gladwyne, PA *19035*
Eristoff . . **see Sidamon-Eristoff**
Erker MISS Marianna S—Cda.
☎ (404) 325-7617 . . 3100 Briarcliff Rd NE, Atlanta, GA *30329*
Erler MISS Elise L—Dth'76.Mit'87
☎ (801) 355-9325 . . 480 H St, Salt Lake City, UT *84103*
Ermini MISS Antonina M
☎ (818) 563-2453 . . 1930 Parish Place, Burbank, CA *91504*
Ernst MR & MRS Charles A 4th (Karen H Griffin)
Laf'87.StJos'92.Me.Wt.Eastern'90
☎ (610) 649-3509 . . 239 Crosshill Rd, Wynnewood, PA *19096*
Ernst MR & MRS Charles Augustus JR (Jacqueline E Walker)
Me.Nyc.Cry.Cts.M.Ac.Cr'35 . . of
☎ (610) 649-4825 . . 209 Ivy Lane, Haverford, PA *19041*
☎ (305) 367-2181 . . 205 Andros St, North Key Largo, FL *33037*
Ernst MR Charles Augustus 3d (Charles Augustus JR) . . . . Married at
Paoli, PA
Schottland MRS Mary B M (Mary B Mann) . . . . May 24'96
Ernst MR & MRS Charles Augustus 3d (Schottland— | ☎ (610) 964-8294
Mary B Mann) Me.Nyc.W.Wid'67.VillaN'91 . . | 284 Stonegate Dv,
MR Fletcher B Schottland—at St Joseph's U . | Devon, PA *19333*
JUNIORS MISS Katherine M Schottland . . . . . . |
JUNIORS MR Joshua S Schottland—at |
Valley Forge Military Acad . . . . |
JUNIORS MR David N Schottland . . . . |

Ernst MRS Elizabeth Du B (Elizabeth Du Barry) | ☎ (610) 658-2455
NYSID'63.Nyc.Me.Ac.Ncd. . . . . | 435 Berkley Rd,
MISS Alexandra C—PineM'93.Me.—at | Haverford, PA
☎ (617) 327-0113 . . 110 Knoll St, Apt 2, | *19041-1508*
Roslindale, MA *02131* . . . . |
MR Christopher G—Me.Wt.Hartw'89—at |
☎ (703) 448-8676 . . 7744 Marshall Heights |
Court, Falls Church, VA *22043* . . . . |
MR Timothy W—Me.Wt.—at Villanova . . . . . . |
Ernst MASTER Matthew Walker (Charles A 4th) . . . . Born at
Bryn Mawr, PA Aug 15'96
Ernst MR & MRS Robert A (Patricia S Church) | ☎ (301) 229-0274
K.Me.Cry.Nyc.Sl.Cr'70 . . . . | 4906 Scarsdale Rd,
MISS Leigh R—Br'93.Van'96 . . . . | Bethesda, MD
MR Peter A—Van'95 . . . . | *20816*
MISS Anna J . . . . |
MR Graham S—at Davidson . . . . |
Erskine MR J Drummond 3d—Fw.
☎ (516) 692-7721 . . Box 185, Cold Spring Harbor, NY *11724*
Erskine MR & MRS James S (Katharine M Hardy) Denis'84.Montclair'82
☎ (609) 840-0870 . . 702 Cornwallis Dv, Mt Laurel, NJ *08054*
Ertman MRS C Eric (Margaret C Behn)
☎ (011-47-371) 518-97 . . Solsiden 10, Risor 4950, Norway
Ertman MR C Eric
☎ (011-47-371) 519-75 . . Tangensgt 11, Risor 4950, Norway
Ervin MISS Adele Q
☎ (508) 526-1912 . . ''Cove Cottage'' 113 Ocean St,
Manchester-By-The-Sea, MA *01944*
Ervin MISS Elisabeth M—Dick'79
☎ (303) 278-1875 . . 1606 Utah Court, Golden, CO *80401*
Ervin MR & MRS Robert L (Elisabeth S Turman) Ws'54.Sg.
☎ (215) 643-0785 . . 285 W Mt Pleasant Av, Ambler, PA *19002*
Ervin MR & MRS Robert L JR (Linda M MacEachern) StJos'81
☎ (215) 643-2289 . . 550 Morris Rd, Blue Bell, PA *19422*
Ervin MR & MRS Spencer JR (Florence W Schroeder) | ☎ (207) 244-4195
Pa'62.Me.Ac.H'54 . . . . | PO Box 383,
MISS Miriam R—GeoW'93 . . . . | Bass Harbor, ME
MISS Helen S . . . . | *04653*
Erving MR Rowland—Fcg.P'30 . . . . | ☎ (412) 963-1770
MR Rowland JR . . . . | 137 Springhouse
| Lane, Pittsburgh, PA
| *15238*
Esbenshade DR & MRS John F (Sylvette Norré) Louvain'77.Stan'71
☎ (503) 623-4887 . . 2545 James Howe Rd, Dallas, OR *97338*
Esbenshade MRS John Howry (Clementine A Wyman) Occ'28.Vh.
☎ (805) 967-4103 . . 777 Via Hierba, Santa Barbara, CA *93110*
Esberg MR & MRS Milton H (Shaler—Prudence | ☎ (415) 922-2042
Talbot) Fmy.Cal'24 . . . . | 1960 Vallejo St,
MISS Prudence . . . . | San Francisco, CA
MR Milton G . . . . | *94123*
Eschauzier MISS Isabelle C . . see MRS F B Chapman
Eschauzier MISS Philippa deV . . see MRS F B Chapman

Escher MRS M Muirhead (C Marie Muirhead)
Mls'52 . . . . | ☎ (415) 340-8081
 MISS Sarah L—Mls'90—at ☎ (415) 347-5562 | 211 Elm St,
 1407 Floribunda Av, Burlingame, CA *94010* . . . | Apt 102,
 MR Robert H—SFrSt'86—at ☎ (415) 366-6944 | San Mateo, CA
 535 Lake Blvd, Redwood City, CA *94062* . . . . . | *94401*

Escher MR & MRS Thomas C (Paula Sullivan)
Bhm.Pcu.Menlo'65. . . . . | of ☎ (415)346-7766
 MISS Hilary S . . . . | 21 Presidio Av,
 MR Thomas C JR. . . . . | San Francisco, CA
 | *94115*
 | ☎ (707) 963-2255
 | 1901 St Helena
 | H'way, Rutherford,
 | CA *94573*

Eshleman MRS B Franklin 2d (Eshleman—Potts—Phoebe L Davis)
Bnd'37.Sg.
 ☎ (508) 693-4456 . . 78 Franklin St, Box 2037, Vineyard Haven,
MA *02568*

Eshleman MR & MRS Charles L JR (Helen E Turner)
Ncmb'46.Cw.Wt.Tul'45 ⚓ . . . . | ☎ (504) 866-0890
 MR & MRS W Parker Stewart (Eileen Eshleman) | 722 Lowerline St,
 —at ☎ (504) 865-9373 . . 7419 Hampson St, | New Orleans, LA
 New Orleans, LA *70118* . . . . | *70118*

Eskridge MR & MRS William I (Josephine P Haas) Ala'91.Ala'91
 ☎ (205) 870-8002 . . 129 Cherry St, Birmingham, AL *35213*

Espinosa de los Monteros MR & MRS Alvaro F | of ☎ (303)442-1151
(Eugenia C Carver) StL'57.Dy.StL'57 ⚓ . . . . | 3940 Sunshine
 MSRS John F & Edward P . . . . | Canyon Dv,
 MSRS James J & Martin A . . . . | Boulder, CO
 MSRS Michael L & Charles G . . . . | *80302-9722*
 | "Condo Sol"
 | 51 LaBonte St,
 | Dillon, CO *80435*

Espy DR & MRS John W (Mary B Fowlkes)
Un.Ri.Nyc.Plg.StJ.Cly.Ncd.F&M'53.Cr'56 . . . . | ☎ (212) RE4-7918
 JUNIORS MR Peter W—at Conn Coll . . . . | 765 Park Av,
 | New York, NY
 | *10021*

Espy MR & MRS Thomas P (Lisa T Hearst) CtCol'85.Ng.Bcs.StLaw'82 . . of
 ☎ (303) 377-8735 . . 124 Cherry St, Denver, CO *80220-5637*
 ☎ (516) 287-2344 . . 95 N Sea Mecox Rd, Southampton, NY *11968*

Essex MISS Amanda T . . see L D Callaway 3d
Essex MISS Brenda L . . see L D Callaway 3d
Essex MR Winfield S 3d . . see L D Callaway 3d

Essig MISS Erica L . . see W S Curtiss

Estabrook MRS James M (Martha Rogerson) . . . . . . | ☎ (516) 496-8752
 MISS Helen—at ☎ (713) 789-1446 | 18 Southwoods Rd,
 1956 Winrock Blvd, Apt 341, Houston, TX | Syosset, NY *11791*
 77057 . . . . |

Estes MR & MRS Carl L 2d (Gay Gooch) | ☎ (713) 622-6012
Tex'59.Tex'57.Tex'60 . . . . | 5010 Longmont Dv,
 MISS Adrienne V—at 101 Broad Oaks Circle, | Houston, TX *77056*
 Houston, TX *77056* . . . . |
 MISS Margaret E—at 701 Bering Dv, Houston, |
 TX *77057* . . . . |

Estes REV & MRS James G (Virginia C Darneille) | ☎ (619) 740-1720
V'60.NEng'58.Y'61 . . . . | 1472 Rimrock Dv,
 MR Matthew J—Pom'88 . . . . | Escondido, CA
 | *92027*

Estes MR & MRS Paul W (Alison B Miller) NH'81.NH'81
 ☎ (602) 788-6256 . . 5514 E Kelton Lane, Scottsdale, AZ *85254*

Estey MASTER Ezra Harper Purinton (g—John S Estey) . . . Born Jan 6'95
Estey MASTER Harper Glenn (g—John S Estey) . . . . Born May 25'95
Estey MR & MRS John S (Dial—Alexandra | of ☎ (215)735-1056
Montgomery) Sth'60.Rc.Ph.Ac.Hav'47.Y'50 . . . | 1830 Delancey
 MISS Caroline E—Carl'86—see | Place, Philadelphia,
 Dilatory Domiciles . . . . | PA *19103*
 | ☎ (561) 778-1236
 | 5805 Magnolia
 | Lane, Vero Beach,
 | FL *32967*

Estill MRS Holland (Tweed—Barbara Banning) Sth'30.Cs . . .of
 ☎ (212) 288-0092 . . 10 Gracie Square, New York, NY *10028*
 ☎ (516) 688-2981 . . "Derby House" 139 DeForest Rd, Montauk,
NY *11954*

Esty MR & MRS Donald C (Mae Welfley) . . of
 ☎ (610) 293-0415 . . 21 Wingstone Lane, Devon, PA *19333*
 ☎ (207) 244-3417 . . "Nearby" Box 38, Greening Island,
Southwest Harbor, ME *04679*

Esty MRS Harold M (Rosemary Guile) G.St.Pl. . . . . | of ☎ (716)947-4736
 MR John A—at ☎ (716) 947-5551 | "Rosegarth"
 "Gablegarth" 6828 Lake Shore Rd, Derby, NY | 6828 Lake Shore
 14047 . . . . | Rd, Derby, NY
 | *14047*
 | ☎ (941) 964-2838
 | Box 232,
 | Boca Grande, FL
 | *33921*

Esty MR & MRS Robert W (Karen E Kennedy) | ☎ (610) 644-3509
W&J'73.DU'76 . . . . | 12 Oak Tree Lane,
 MISS Kristen E . . . . | Malvern, PA *19355*
 JUNIORS MISS Laura A . . . . |

Etheridge MR & MRS Tammy H (Nora Reagan) MissSt'55 . . of
 ☎ (601) 992-1515 . . 1 Little Creek Rd, Jackson, MS *39208*
 "Rockport" 4095 Sugar Farm Rd, Hazelhurst, MS *39083*

Etherington MR & MRS Burton H JR (Margaret P Lowe)
Err.M.Me.Cspa.Myf.Rv.P'33
 ☎ (610) 645-8962 . . Waverly Heights A210, 1400 Waverly Rd,
Gladwyne, PA *19035*

Etherington MR & MRS Frederick H (Frances M | ☎ (610) 525-0613
Grubbs) M.Cspa.Rv.Myf.P'35 . . . . | 16 Pond Lane,
 MISS A Lawrence—at ☎ (203) 327-1068 | Bryn Mawr, PA
 136 Woodside Green, Apt 1A, Stamford, CT | *19010*
 06905 . . . . |

Etherington MR & MRS Frederick H JR (Priscilla V | ☎ (573) 335-2396
Fox) Spgfd'67.Cda.Dick'65 . . . . | 158 Navajo Dv,
 MISS Christina V—at U of Mo Columbia . . . . . . | North Hills Estates,
 | Cape Girardeau, MO
 | *63701*

Ethridge MR Harrison Mosley—An.Rich'65.CathU'77 . . of
 ☎ (202) 829-8877 . . 6500—16 St NW, Washington, DC *20012*
 1829 Sherwood Rd, Petersburg, VA *23805*

Etting MRS Emlen Pope (Gloria Braggiotti) C.
 ☎ (561) 659-0324 . . 369 S Lake Trail, PH-D, Palm Beach, FL *33480*
Etz MISS Elizabeth S
 ☎ (912) 236-1626 . . 5 E Gordon St, Savannah, GA *31401*
Etzold MR & MRS David E (Mary Francis) Sar.Ncd.Dar.Cit'47
 ☎ (915) 533-0263 . . 1800 N Mesa St, Apt 801, El Paso, TX *79902*
Eustis MR & MRS David L (Lucy C Reardon) | ☎ (504) 891-4904
Ncmb'66.Rv.Tul'64 . . . . | 1727 Napoleon Av,
MR David L JR . . . . | New Orleans, LA
MR William R . . . . | *70115*
JUNIORS MR Robert T . . . . |
JUNIORS MR Stephen M . . . . |
Eustis MR Francis W . . . . Died at
               Cincinnati, OH Aug 2'96
Eustis MRS Francis W (Viola Y Stevens)
 ☎ (513) 561-6738 . . 8405 Eustis Farm Lane, Cincinnati, OH *45243*
Eustis MR & MRS Frederic G (Lisa Field) Les'72.H'71
 ☎ (508) 474-0726 . . 93 Spring Grove Rd, Andover, MA *01810*
Eustis MRS George (Herberta Stone)
 ☎ (513) 321-3747 . . 2341 Bedford Av, Cincinnati, OH *45208*
Eustis MRS George P (Lee Ann S King) V'57 . . . . . | ☎ (970) 963-3707
MR Evan David . . . . | PO Box 238,
              | Carbondale, CO
              | *81623*
Eustis MR Harold—So'37
 ☎ (601) 332-5368 . . 913 McAllister St, Greenville, MS *38701*
Eustis MR & MRS Richmond M (Catherine L Baños) | ☎ (504) 861-9310
Loy'71.Rv.Va'67 . . . . | 289 Audubon St,
MISS Julie B . . . . | New Orleans, LA
              | *70118*
Eustis MR & MRS Timothy W (Sarah E Rothstein) Sth'90
 ☎ (415) 255-1285 . . 4172—20 St, Apt A, San Francisco, CA *94114*
Eustis MR & MRS William E C (Mary H Armstrong) BMr'44.Hb.H'42 ⚓
 ☎ (603) 883-2052 . . 37 Sherri-Ann Av, Nashua, NH *03060*
Evans MRS Allyn Phelps (Jean Frazier)
 ☎ (617) 320-8565 . . Fox Hill Village 136, 10 Longwood Dv, Westwood,
MA *02090*
Evans MR & MRS Andrew W (Stephanie F Onstott) | 450 Palm Av,
Cal'69.Bhm.Sfg.Pars'67 . . . . | Kentfield, CA *94904*
JUNIORS MR Michael A . . . . |
JUNIORS MR Brooks F . . . . |
Evans MRS Benjamin C JR (Jan A King) Cvc.Sl . . .of
 ☎ (202) 234-6251 . . 3033 Woodland Dv NW, Washington, DC *20008*
 ☎ (813) 446-3770 . . 1140 Mandalay Point, Clearwater Beach, FL *34630*
Evans MR & MRS Berne Holbrook III (Linda C Houghton) Vh.
 ☎ (818) 793-6364 . . 1400 Park Place, San Marino, CA *91108*
Evans MR & MRS C Anthony (Stephanie V Smith) OWes'86.OWes'85
 ☎ (630) 986-0614 . . 267 Churchill Place, Clarendon Hills, IL *60514*
Evans MR & MRS C Frazier (Elisabeth J V | ☎ (617) 232-3777
Schuschny) Cy.Y'62 . . . . | 20 Circuit Rd,
MISS Lisa P—Tufts'95 . . . . | Chestnut Hill, MA
MR Russell B—at AGSIM Thunderbird . . . . | *02167*
Evans MR & MRS Craig C (Lucy Lee C Grimes) | ☎ (203) 972-1096
Rdc'67.Roch'77.Cl'81 . . . . | 160 Old Kings
JUNIORS MISS Natalie D . . . . | H'way,
JUNIORS MR James I—at Pomfret . . . . | New Canaan, CT
              | *06840*

Evans MR David C—Pg.Fcg.Pa'67
 ☎ (412) 238-5208 . . Orchard House, Laughlintown, PA *15655*
Evans DR & MRS David D (Jennifer A Vietor) Colg'79.Unn.Cw.H'76
 ☎ (203) 661-7560 . . 35 Sawmill Lane, Greenwich, CT *06830*
Evans MR & MRS David M (Clark—Gail L Roberts) | ☎ (202) 363-2226
Tufts'88.An.Cos.Srb.Ll.Rv.H'58.H'61 . . . . | 5153 Yuma St NW,
MISS Meredith S B—Nu'91 . . . . | Washington, DC
              | *20016*
Evans MRS Dwight D (Armstrong—Joan Estelle Carroll) Rdc'46.Cy.Csn.
 ☎ (617) 696-4581 . . 40 Canton Av, Milton, MA *02186-3408*
Evans MR Edward P—Srr.Rr.Y'65.H'67 . . of
960 Fifth Av, New York, NY *10022*
''Spring Hill Farm'' Casanova, VA *20139*
Evans MR Emlen H—Fi.
 ☎ (802) 229-1422 . . RD 3, Box 2745, Montpelier, VT *05602*
Evans MR Eric B . . . . Died at
              Miami, FL Apr 26'96
Evans MR & MRS Evan C 3d (Joan Macdonough) | ☎ (415) 457-0661
Cal'45 . . . . | 2 Arroyo Dv,
MR Barnaby M—Br'75—at ☎ (401) 331-7203 | Kentfield, CA *94904*
101 Regent Av, Providence, RI *02908* . . . . |
Evans MR & MRS Francis C (Rachel W Brooks) BMr'37.Hav'36.Ox'39
 ☎ (313) 761-3275 . . 1050 Wall St, Apt 5D, Ann Arbor, MI *48105*
Evans MR & MRS Gale Richard (Suter—Barbara K Schneider)
Tufts'74.B'hamS'73
3037 E Lostwood Dv, Sandy, UT *84092*
Evans MR & MRS George J JR (Nancy H Wendell) | ☎ (508) 358-4832
Ncd.Dth'64 . . . . | 75 Claypit Hill Rd,
MISS Nancy Tay—at Colby . . . . | Wayland, MA *01778*
MISS Priscilla W—at Dartmouth . . . . |
JUNIORS MISS Tamsen W . . . . |
Evans MR & MRS J Hart (Betty J Hebrank) | ☎ (203) 966-3685
NotreD'47.StL'50 . . . . | 81 Evergreen Rd,
MISS Susan H—Conn'83—at ☎ (619) 552-8473 | New Canaan, CT
7244 Shoreline Dv, Apt 146, San Diego, CA | *06840*
92122 . . . . |
Evans MRS James D JR (Margaret G Rhoads)
 ☎ (803) 671-9252 . . 21 Old Military Rd, Hilton Head Island, SC *29928*
Evans MR & MRS James F 3d (Mary Selden Metz) HRdc'78.H.'75
 ☎ (315) 655-9816 . . Pompey Hollow Rd, Cazenovia, NY *13035*
Evans MR & MRS James H (Clare Westerfield) Menlo'80.Pep'85
 ☎ (415) 342-7958 . . 1548 Barroilhet Av, Burlingame, CA *94010*
Evans MR Jeremy A M—StAndr'93 . . see D F Morley
Evans DR & MRS John A (Odell—King—Runyon— | of ☎ (212)355-4143
Anne A Wilson) Cs.Cr'35 . . . . | 200 E 66 St, Apt
MISS Suzanne W Odell . . . . | B404, New York,
MISS Alison W Odell . . . . | NY *10021*
              | ☎ (516) 749-1010
              | ''Wood Winds''
              | 3 Crescent Way,
              | PO Box 143,
              | Shelter Island
              | Heights, NY *11965*
Evans MR & MRS John D (Ernestine H Hutchins) | ☎ (707) 935-7761
Cal'52 . . . . | 453 France St,
MR W Barrett—at 4630 S Lakeshore Dv, | Sonoma, CA *95476*
Apt 170, Tempe, AZ *85282* . . . . |

Evans MR & MRS John F (Dorothy A Warner)
Caz'60.Colg'60.Ariz'63 . . . .
MISS Catherine R—OState'84—at
☎ (703) 448-0226 . . 2063 Pieris Court, Vienna,
VA 22182 . . . .
MISS Constance R—OState'84—at
☎ (302) 652-6895 . . 2307 Pennsylvania Av,
Wilmington, DE 19806 . . . .
MISS Elizabeth G—Rich'90—at
☎ (202) 362-6090 . . 5529—39 St NW,
Washington, DC 20015 . . . .
MR John F 3d—Drex'92 . . . .
| ☎ (609) 769-3262
14 Bowen Av,
Woodstown, NJ
08098

Evans REV John Miles—StJ.Ne.Yn.Y'61.Camb'64.Y'67
☎ (011-44-1631) 564-722 . . Bon Accord, Glenmore Rd, Oban,
Argyll PA34 4ND, Scotland

Evans MR & MRS Johnston L (Lisa N McGrath)
Rdc'70.Rc.Mb.Pr.Bost'70 . . . .
MISS Grace H C . . . .
MISS Justine B S . . . .
JUNIORS MISS Charlotte F S . . . .
JUNIORS MISS Lily L R . . . .
| ☎ (516) 626-5527
156 Wheatley Rd,
Brookville, NY
11545

Evans MISS Margaret MacColl (Thomas G JR) . . . . Born Dec 27'95
Evans CAPT (RET) & MRS Philip W (Josephine T Ullom)
USN.V'42.Cvc.So'40
☎ (860) 663-3350 . . 25 Bargate Trail, Killingworth, CT 06419-1372
Evans MR & MRS Raymond F (Elizabeth R Whitney) Kt.Tvcl.Pk.P'31
☎ (912) 435-8628 . . 6621 Tallassee Plantation Circle, Albany,
GA 31707

Evans MR & MRS Robert B (Jane C Preston)
Srb.BtP.Evg.Rr.Bhm.Cly. . . . .
MR Robert B JR—at 726 Front St, Lewisville, CO
80027 . . . .
| of ☎ (313)881-0458
984 Lake Shore Dv,
Grosse Pointe, MI
48236
☎ (561) 833-4872
1472 S Ocean Blvd,
Palm Beach, FL
33480

Evans MRS Roger K (Pauline P Marean) Wheat'63 .
MISS Emily W—Sth'94 . . . .
MR Stephen K . . . .
| ☎ (508) 744-3357
11 Church St, Apt
311, Salem, MA
01970

Evans MR & MRS Samuel M (Patricia M Hodder)
Va'63 . . . .
MISS Claire I . . . .
| ☎ (011-44-171)
824-8243
32 St Leonard's
Terr, London
SW3 4QG, England

Evans MR & MRS Samuel S (Anna E C Brady)
Pa'85.Rc.Pc.H.AmU'83.H.'87 . . of
☎ (212) 861-1053 . . 108 E 66 St, Apt 9A, New York, NY 10021
☎ (516) 725-7558 . . 11 E Harbor Dv, Sag Harbor, NY 11963
Evans MISS Sarah D—Rol'95.Cda.
☎ (561) 844-3382 . . 248½ Colonial Lane, Palm Beach, FL 33480
Evans MISS Susan D (late Dwight D) . . . . Married at Milton, MA
Bohan MR John C (Thomas L) . . . . Aug 3'96
Evans MR & MRS Thomas G JR (Emily W Eastlake) Hlns'92.W&L'91
☎ (413) 498-5459 . . 187 Main St, Apt 1, Northfield, MA 01360
Evans MRS Thomas Goodwin (Juliet I Merryweather)
☎ (215) 836-2546 . . 6 Haws Lane, Apt C2, Flourtown, PA 19031

Evans MR Thomas Goodwin—Pc.Bab'64 . . . .
MR Andrew M—WashColl'94—at New York,
NY . . . .
MR Charles H—at U of Pittsburgh . . . .
| ☎ (215) MI6-4013
''Merrywin''
335 Skippack Pike,
Ft Washington, PA
19034

Evans MR & MRS Thomas M JR (Gyurkey—Morgan
—Tania Goss) V'59.Rr.B.L.Cly.Ncd. . . . .
MR Mark J . . . .
| of ☎ (802)843-2241
RR 3, Box 283,
Chester Hill Rd,
Grafton, VT 05146
☎ (307) 733-1334
Box 259, 6805 W
Trail Creek County
Rd, Wilson, WY
83014

Evans MR & MRS Thomas Mellon (Ready—Loomis—Betty B Barton)
Srr.Mds.Pg.Edg.B.Ri.Ny.Csn.Cly.Yn.Y'31
☎ (203) 869-6462 . . 500 Round Hill Rd, Greenwich, CT 06831
Evans MR & MRS Tilghman B (Margaret T Red) Del'84.Y'54.H'57
☎ (206) 780-0188 . . PO Box 11281, Bainbridge Island, WA 98110
Evans MR Victor M . . see H P Borie JR

Evans MR & MRS William H (Bindley—Phyllis
Hoelzel) Rr.Uncl.Pk.It.P'33 . . . .
MR William H JR—Box 158, Idleyld Park, OR
97447 . . . .
| ☎ (561) 278-1986
1919 N Ocean Blvd,
Gulf Stream, FL
33483

Evans MR & MRS William J (Jones—Christina P
Clare) Rc.Ncd.Va'54 . . . .
JUNIORS MR Elliot S . . . .
MISS Palmer D Jones—at Trinity . . . .
JUNIORS MR Oliver H Jones . . . .
JUNIORS MR Frederick K Jones . . . .
| of ☎ (212)876-3030
17 E 89 St,
New York, NY
10128
☎ (518) 589-5360
''Swallow's Nest''
Onteora Club,
Tannersville, NY
12485

Evarts MISS Alice C (Schipper—Alice C Evarts) SL'80.Wms'85.Cl'90
☎ (212) 288-6466 . . 340 E 74 St, New York, NY 10021
Evarts MR & MRS Edwin D M (Caroleigh Ritz) Ken'84.Dar.H'80
☎ (203) 972-6850 . . 51 Scofield Lane, New Canaan, CT 06840
Evarts MR & MRS James M (Rebecca S Martin) Rdc'74.Rcn.H'74
☎ (617) 646-0916 . . 41 Academy St, Arlington, MA 02174-6433

Evarts MR & MRS Jasper M (Wendy Hammond)
Sb.H'56 . . . .
MR Nathaniel N—at ☎ (617) 254-5317
71 Oakland St, Apt 1, Brighton, MA 02135 . . . .
| of ☎ (802)824-5926
''Partridge Corner''
RR 1, Box 238,
Landgrove, VT
05148
☎ (617) 437-1703
50 Commonwealth
Av, Apt 902,
Boston, MA 02116

Evarts MRS Maxwell (Josephine C Harrison) Bgt.
☎ (914) 666-4040 . . PO Box 682, Mt Kisco, NY 10549-0682
Evarts MR & MRS William M JR (Helen R Coleman)
Ri.Cs.H.'49.H'52.Cl'70.Nu'73 . . of
☎ (212) 879-6674 . . 7 Gracie Square, New York, NY 10028
☎ (914) PE9-7844 . . Rte 1, Box 42, Diamond Hill Rd, Garrison,
NY 10524

Everdell MR & MRS Coburn D (M Elizabeth Earls)
Col'69.Eyc.Bur.Pa'68.H'72 . . . . | ☎ (415) 221-1124
JUNIORS MISS Eleanore E . . . . | 250 Cherry St,
JUNIORS MISS Abigail B . . . . | San Francisco, CA
JUNIORS MR Coburn D JR . . . . | *94118*

Everdell MR & MRS Preston (Sarah K Jayne)
WashColl'71.Col'74.Me'84 . . . . | ☎ (410) 758-2466
JUNIORS MISS Marian P . . . . | Gunston School,
JUNIORS MR Nicholas P . . . . | Box 200,
| Centreville, MD
| *21617*

Everdell MR & MRS William (Bellamy—Eleanore H Darling)
Ln.Pr.Eyc.Plg.Cly.Myf.Wms'37.Y'40 . . of
☎ (516) 674-3475 . . 273 Piping Rock Rd, Glen Head, NY *11545*
☎ (212) TR9-3900 . . 1 E 66 St, New York, NY *10021*

Everdell MR & MRS William R (Barbara L Scott)
CUNY'70.P'63.H'65.Nu'72 . . . . | ☎ (718) 596-9456
MR Christian R—at Princeton . . . . | 9 Garden Place,
| Brooklyn, NY *11201*

Everett MR & MRS Chandler H (Wiegand—Hoffman—
Marsha Crandall Brayton) Cent'y'59.Cv.Kt.Tv.Yn.Y'60.Cwr'70
☎ (216) 932-0363 . . 12546 Cedar Rd, Apt 2, Cleveland Heights,
OH *44106*

Everett MR & MRS Chandler P (Rebecca B Lytle) Skd'88.ClevSt'92.Bow'89
☎ (216) 269-1586 . . 2675 River Rd, Willoughby Hills, OH *44094*

Everett MRS Charles (Dougherty—Kelso Alsop)
Ncd. . . . . | ☎ (302) 655-2631
MR Graham Dougherty 3d . . . . | 1407 Clinton St,
| Wilmington, DE
| *19806*

Everett MISS Cordelia C—StAndr'80.Del'84
☎ (609) 921-8662 . . 115 Patton Av, Princeton, NJ *08540*

Everett MR & MRS Francis D (Eleanor Delafield) Snc.Coa.Cly.H'45.H'49
☎ (212) LE5-6714 . . 125 E 84 St, New York, NY *10028*

Everett MR & MRS Frank E JR (Margaret C Bryant) Miss'34.Ncd.Miss'34
☎ (601) 636-4617 . . 4 Glenwood Circle, Vicksburg, MS *39180*

Everett MR & MRS Hulbert H (Williams—Doris Ann Witter)
Cal'49.Vh.Stan'43
☎ (818) 449-8282 . . 230 S Arroyo Blvd, Pasadena, CA *91105*

Everett MRS Morris (Eleanor Egan) Sth'33.Kt.It.Cv.Yh.
☎ (216) 442-1250 . . 37350 Fairmount Blvd, Chagrin Falls, OH *44022*

Everett MR & MRS Morris JR (Ours—Diana
DiFranco) Wit'70.Va'71.Kt.Tv.Un.Va'63 . . . . . . | ☎ (216) 256-8396
MISS Elizabeth E . . . . | 8180 Monterey Dv,
MR Morris 3d—at ☎ (310) 822-0868 | Kirtland, OH *44094*
18 S Venice Blvd, Venice, CA *90291* . . . . |
MISS Alice C Ours—☎ (216) 256-6877 . . . . . |
MR John W Ours JR—☎ (216) 256-6877 . . . . |
JUNIORS MR Adam S Ours—☎ (216) 256-6877 |

Everett MR & MRS Nicholas S (Nancy H Reade)
Skd'73.H'73.H'77 . . . . | ☎ (914) 967-9418
JUNIORS MISS Clematis S . . . . | 19 Palisade Rd, Rye,
| NY *10580*

Everett MR & MRS Oliver S (Susan H Heath)
H'66.Wes'75 . . . . | ☎ (860) 274-6656
MISS Christy H—at ☎ (603) 744-3614 | Taft School,
New Hampton School, Main St, New Hampton, | 110 Woodbury Rd,
NH *03256* . . . . | Watertown, CT
MR Andrew B—at ☎ (203) 862-9866 | *06795*
79A Northfield St, Greenwich, CT *06830* . . . . . |

Everett MRS S Evers (Daley—Sally Evers)
Sth'64.Kt.Tc. . . . . | ☎ (216) 464-3307
MISS Eliza D Daley—B'gton'88—at | 3515 Leeds Rd,
Cleveland, OH . . . . | Pepper Pike, OH
MR William A Daley 2d—Ty'92—at | *44122-4261*
Boston, MA . . . . |

Everett MRS Virginia S (Virginia M Sauerbrun)
Woos'61.SeaPac'90 . . . . | ☎ (206) 454-0284
MR Alexander U—at 2501—148 Av SE, | 8408 NE 19 Place,
Bellevue, WA *98007* . . . . | Bellevue, WA *98004*

Evers MRS Walter F (Grosjean—Emlen K Davies) V'38
☎ (619) 435-8829 . . 1525 Ynez Place, Coronado, CA *92118-2928*

Eversole MR & MRS John B (Barbara B Miller)
☎ (904) 285-3332 . . 25 Lake Julia Dv S, Ponte Vedra Beach, FL *32082*

Ewald MR & MRS Charles R (D Chase Reynolds)
Y'85.Cal'90.H'79.Ox'81.Stan'83
☎ (415) 789-9108 . . 77 Mt Tiburon Rd, Tiburon, CA *94920*

Ewald MR & MRS Karl Raymond JR (Bethany Baker) Kas'43.Cr'42
☎ (601) 442-6776 . . Box 783, Natchez, MS *39120*

Ewald MRS William G (Rand—S Frances Moore) Cy.Ncd.Dar.
☎ (410) 243-2506 . . 4225 Wickford Rd, Baltimore, MD *21210*

Ewart MR & MRS Craig K (Anne H Dunham) Nf. . . . | 6981 Colonial Dv,
MISS Kimberly D . . . . | Fayetteville, NY
JUNIORS MR Scott K . . . . | *13066*

Ewart MRS James H M (Eleanor Whelan) Cly.
☎ (212) 759-2491 . . 200 E 66 St, New York, NY *10021*

Ewart MR & MRS Robert B (Musser—Carol L Reed) | of ☎ (814)275-3959
Cit'57.IndPa'62 . . . . | 217 Penn St,
MISS Lisa D Musser . . . . | New Bethlehem, PA
| *16242*
| ☎ (216) 777-9141
| 25151 Brookpark
| Rd, North Olmsted,
| OH *44070*

Ewell MRS John W (Nancy V Chapman) Bnd'42.Chi.
☎ (561) 283-3213 . . I69 Mariner Cay, 3901 SE St Lucie Blvd, Stuart,
FL *34997*

Ewer MISS Evangeline
☎ (215) 763-9922 . . 2434 Aspen St, Philadelphia, PA *19130*

Eweson MISS Frazer (Strutt—Aeriel Frazer)
☎ (401) 847-0078 . . 29 Green St, Newport, RI *02840*

Ewing MR & MRS George McC (Marie-Merrill Hubbard)
Va'49.Roch'72.Sl.P'44
☎ (716) 394-6573 . . 128 Thad Chapin St, Canandaigua, NY *14424-1618*

Ewing MR & MRS George McC JR (Margaret F La Douce) Sth'80.Ken'75
☎ (716) 394-5436 . . 79 Howell St, Canandaigua, NY *14424*

Ewing MR & MRS Gordon R (Joan Silver) JHop'55 . . | ☎ (410) 323-1628
MISS Carolyn S—Roan'91—at ☎ (703) 924-1763 | 6200 Mossway,
6014 Stoddard Court, Apt 301, Alexandria, VA | Baltimore, MD
22315 . . . . | *21212*

Ewing MRS J G Blaine JR (Glazebrook—M Suzanne | ☎ (914) 234-7815
Howard) Bgt. . . . . | PO Box 474,
MR Otis A Glazebrook 4th . . . . | Bedford, NY *10506*
MR Michael T Glazebrook . . . . |

Ewing MR & MRS J G Blaine 3d (Phyllis C Walker) | ☎ (803) 722-3149
Van'70.W&L'67.Nu'72 . . . . | 48 Laurens St,
JUNIORS MR James G B 4th . . . . | Charleston, SC
| *29401*

Ewing MR & MRS John H (Alison Pyne) Eh. . . . . . . | ☎ (908) 234-0763
MR John H JR—at ☎ (423) 499-9043 | Larger Cross Rd,
6220 Shallowford Rd, Chattanooga, TN *37421* . | Box 187, Peapack,
| NJ *07977*

Ewing MRS Joseph N (Anne Ashton) . . . . | ☎ (610) 458-0587
MR Samuel E 3d—Sfh.P.'52 . . . . | Eagle Farms,
| 2301 Eagle Farms
| Rd, Chester Springs,
| PA *19425-3727*

Ewing MR & MRS Joseph N JR (Margaret C Howe) V'51.Wcc.P.'47
☎ (610) 696-1076 . . 1109 Lincoln Dv, West Chester, PA *19380-5721*

Ewing MR & MRS L Rumsey (Rosalie McRee) Cy.Rc.Dth'42
☎ (314) 993-0332 . . 9035 Ladue Rd, St Louis, MO *63124*

Ewing MISS (DR) Madeleine Q—BMr'69.Pa'73.Ac. | ☎ (215) 569-8010
MR David Q 3d—at 114 E 21 St, Ship Bottom, | 2101 Locust St,
NJ *08008* . . . . | Philadelphia, PA
| *19103*

Ewing MR & MRS Richard C (Jeanne A Mercury) | ☎ (617) 235-0664
FineA'68.Myf.Syr'71 . . . . | 64 Beverly Rd,
MR Stephen C—at Colby . . . . | Wellesley, MA
JUNIORS MR David P . . . . | *02181*

Ewing MRS S Blaine (Eliza G Jackson) V'45-4
☎ (508) 255-3618 . . 20 Highland Rd, Box 785, Eastham, MA *02642*

Ewing MR & MRS S Finley JR (Gail B Orand) Tex'54.W&L'52
☎ (214) 368-4249 . . 5038 Brookview Dv, Dallas, TX *75209*

Ewing MR William . . . . Died at
Noroton, CT Jun 28'96

Ewing MRS William (Mary Challinor) Ln.Plg.
☎ (203) 655-1006 . . 203 Long Neck Point Rd, Noroton, CT *06820*

Ewing MR & MRS William H (Anne L Constant) | ☎ (215) CH7-8807
Rdc'60.Rdc'62.P'61.Pa'65 . . . . | 510 E Mt Pleasant
MISS Susannah C—at Hermann Ehlers-Haus | Av, Philadelphia,
Z107, Fibigerstrasse 163, 22419 Hamburg, | PA *19119*
Germany . . . . |
MISS Rebecca H—at ☎ (718) 237-1051 |
8 Pierrepont St, Apt 5, Brooklyn, NY *11201* . . . |

Ewing MR & MRS William Sanford (Sandra H Wickenden) Plg.
☎ (410) 876-5427 . . 2606 Jeffrey Lori Dv, Finksburg, MD *21048*

Exnicios MRS Marshall O (Lunke—Ursula E M Hofmann) An.Msq.Cvc.
☎ (401) 596-6439 . . 66 Elm St, Apt 12, Westerly, RI *02891*

Exum MRS Helen McDonald (Helen J McDonald) RMWmn'47.Ncd.
☎ (706) 820-2237 . . 1100 Lula Lake Rd, Lookout Mountain, GA *30750*

Eyer MR & MRS George A JR (Furlaud—Lisa Auchincloss) Cly.Y.'37 . . of
☎ (212) 879-9096 . . 620 Park Av, New York, NY *10021*
☎ (914) 855-5785 . . Box 630, N Quaker Hill, Pawling, NY *12564*

Eyre MR Edward E JR—Bhm.Pcu.Y'49
☎ (702) 782-7829 . . 183 Carson St, Genoa, NV *89411*

Eyre MRS Edward Engle (Suzanne de Lenclos) Tcy.
☎ (415) 343-3989 . . 601 Laurel Av, San Mateo, CA *94401*

Eyre MR Edward L—Stan'79
☎ (415) 325-4540 . . 208 Robin Way, Menlo Park, CA *94025*

Eyre MR & MRS F Beverley 2d (Jennifer L Tullos) Cal'94.Cal'95
☎ (310) 839-0203 . . 9053 3-4 Hubbard St, Culver City, CA *90232*

Eyre MR Henry N JR—Y'52 . . . . | ☎ (860) 673-5449
MISS T Leigh . . . . | 36 Mountain Spring
| Rd, Burlington, CT
| *06013*

Eyre MRS Janet H (Janet D Hartwell) Sth'48
☎ (415) 851-7838 . . 5 Quail, Portola Valley, CA *94028*

Eyre MISS Janet V S (Pierret—Janet V S Eyre) H'76.Tcy.
☎ (415) 221-4431 . . 49 Sixth Av, San Francisco, CA *94118*

Eyre MR & MRS John L (Cornelia Le Boutillier) | ☎ (514) 538-2591
Rdc'46.Yn.Y'40.Ford'50 . . . . | 110 Chemin des
MR Stephen L—at 33 Collingwood St, | Erables,
San Francisco, CA *94114* . . . . | Frelighsburg,
MR M Banning . . . . | Quebec J0J 1C0,
| Canada

Eyre MISS Riley Elizabeth (F Beverley 2d) . . . . Born at
Los Angeles, CA Jun 30'95

Eyre MR & MRS Stephen C (Jolene E Park) | ☎ (516) 676-4099
Un.Mb.Pr.Cly.Y'45w . . . . | 69 Dogwood Lane,
MISS Jolene Y—Cly. . . . . | Box 590,
| Locust Valley, NY
| *11560-0590*

Eyre MR & MRS William H (Margaret A Lerner)
Bnd'48.Snc.Rv.Wms'45 . . of
☎ (212) 737-0280 . . 150 E 72 St, New York, NY *10021*
☎ (860) 364-0433 . . "Singing Bird Farm" Gay St, Sharon, CT *06069*

Eyre MR & MRS William H JR (Ellen J Ackerman) | ☎ (610) 642-8326
Hampshire'77.Gm.Rc.Wms'73 . . . . | 444 College Av,
JUNIORS MISS Avery C . . . . | Haverford, PA
| *19041*

F

Fabbioli MR & MRS Joseph M (Anne W Combs) HRdc'86.Cda.Hn.H'85
☎ (847) 291-4831 . . 1709 Ferndale Av, Northbrook, IL *60062*

Faber MRS Albert H (Jeffery—Elizabeth P Meek) | ☎ (203) 661-7912
V'45.Man'vl'76 . . . . | 9 Andrews Rd,
MR Charles R Jeffery—at Santa Barbara, CA | Greenwich, CT
MR Patrick G Jeffery—Bost'87—at | *06830*
☎ (203) 629-2542 . . 521 E Putnam Av, |
Greenwich, CT *06830* . . . . |

Fabri MR Paul O O—Prag'31
☎ (212) 838-5084 . . 200 E 66 St, New York, NY *10021*

Faesy MR & MRS A Robert (Nancy Niles) C.Y'63
☎ (203) 762-8076 . . 957 Ridgefield Rd, Wilton, CT *06897*

Faesy MISS (DR) Lydia . . see C T Wanzer

Faesy MR & MRS Richard (Ann E Bove) Vt'84.Vt'86
Shaker Mountain Farm, RR 1, Box 2505, Starksboro, VT *05487*

Fagan MR Charles K . . see E G Cumming

Fagan MRS Warren (Mary E Warren) Bur . . .of
☎ (212) 472-7114 . . 3 E 77 St, New York, NY *10021*
☎ (516) 283-0353 . . 32 S Main St, Southampton, NY *11968*

Fahle MR Robert L—Ds.Myf.Wash'48 . . of
☎ (415) 285-0611 . . 611 York St, San Francisco, CA *94110*
☎ (707) 875-3218 . . 21121 Hummingbird Court, Bodega Harbour
Country Club, Box 872, Bodega Bay, CA *94923*

Fahnestock MRS Anthony E (Andrea Henderson) Sth'80.Cl'85.Ln.Lic.Stc.
☎ (908) 291-5131 . . 114 Browns Dock Rd, PO Box 381, Navesink, NJ *07752*

Fahnestock MRS Harris (Frances C Jeffery) Lx.Nh.Cy.Chi.Ncd. . . . . | ☎ (617) 227-9378
   MISS Deborah T—Chi. . . . . | 81 Beacon St,
                                                   Boston, MA *02108*

Fahnestock MRS Marion B (Marion F Beardsley) . . | ☎ (212) 369-2336
   MISS Lisa E—Ken'89—☎ (212) 348-9826 . . . . . | 115 E 90 St,
   MISS Jenny H . . . . | New York, NY *10128*

Fahnestock MRS Pamela R (Pamela A Robbins) . . . | ☎ (203) 322-6042
   MISS Margaret R—at ☎ (203) 461-9117 | 1 Mill Rd, Stamford,
221 Pepperidge Rd, Stamford, CT *06902* . . . . . . | CT *06903*
   MISS Fiona E—at ☎ (212) 249-3526
12 E 86 St, New York, NY *10028* . . . .
   MISS Samantha A . . . .

Fahnestock MR & MRS Sheridan Z (Joyce B | ☎ (360) 457-0678
Baldwin) H'61 . . . . | 681 Karpen Rd,
   JUNIORS MR Adam B . . . . | Port Angeles, WA *98363*

Fahs MRS Raymond Z (Mary E Nichols) | of ☎ (212)722-3274
Sth'58.Nu'87 | 49 E 96 St, Apt 7D,
   MR Thomas R—Drew'92 . . . . | New York, NY *10128*
                                                    ☎ (516) 692-4093
                                                    ''Applewyck'' Box 153, Syosset, NY *11791*

Fahy LT Christian Carter—USCG. (Richard H) . . . . Married at Chatham, MA
  McMullen MISS Elizabeth A (Edwin R JR) . . . . Jun 29'96

Fahy LT & MRS Christian Carter (Elizabeth A McMullen) Bost'90.USCG'87.Tufts'93
☎ (617) 266-0298 . . 8 Garrison St, Apt 406, Boston, MA *02116*

Fahy MISS Christina C—RI'88.UWash'95
☎ (206) 524-1386 . . 829 NE 56 St, Seattle, WA *98105*

Fahy MR & MRS Richard H (Anita C Burroughs) | ☎ (603) 539-7767
Va'61.Dth'85 . . . . | ''Change O'Winds''
   LT Nathaniel G—USMC.Va'89 . . . . | 86 Bayle Mountain Rd, Conner Pond, Center Ossipee, NH *03814*

Fahy LT CDR Richard H JR—USN.Tul'85.NH'96
☎ (603) 539-5566 . . 88 Bayle Mountain Rd, Center Ossipee, NH *03814*

Fain MR & MRS William Hart JR (Jennifer L Nelson) | ☎ (213) 857-0931
Ind'72.Cal'68.H'75 . . . . | 425 S Windsor
   JUNIORS MISS Elizabeth N . . . . | Blvd, Los Angeles, CA *90020*

Fair MRS Frederick M (Claire L Evans) Cly. . . . . . | ☎ (212) 755-9727
   MR Luke J—at Denver, CO . . . . | 440 E 57 St, New York, NY *10022*

Fair MR & MRS J Henry JR (Ravenel—Mary T | ☎ (803) 884-9181
Curtis) Sth'63.Ht.Ncd.GaTech'52 . . . . | 101 Mary St,
   MISS Tiphaine T Ravenel . . . . | Mt Pleasant, SC *29464*
   MR Curtis deSt Julien Ravenel—at
    ☎ (803) 883-9141 . . 2867 Brownell St,
Sullivan Island, SC *29482* . . . .
   MR Ramsay M Ravenel . . . .

Fairbank MR & MRS (DR) David E (Judith W Smith) P'79.Cl'83.USMMA'81.Nu'88 🛥️
☎ (011-254-2) 712271 . . PO Box 30134, Nairobi, Kenya

Fairbank MISS Elsa . . see MISS M Mahon

Fairbank MR & MRS Kellogg 3d (Hanneke Van Den | *see*
Eerenbeemt) Utrecht'71.Rcch.Fy.H'63.Ch'73 . . . | *Dilatory Domiciles*
   JUNIORS MR Kellogg N . . . .
   JUNIORS MR Andrew A . . . .

Fairbank MR Livingston—Y'48.Va'51
☎ (360) 598-3535 . . 17842 Division Av, Suquamish, WA *98392*

Fairbank MISS Nancy Ayer (David E) . . . . Born Feb 29'96

Fairbank MISS Wendy (Hatch—Wendy Fairbank) . . see MISS M Mahon

Fairbanks MRS Margarita L (Silvestri—Meeker— | ☎ (805) 684-0181
Margarita L Fairbanks) . . . . | 3375 Foothill Rd,
   JUNIORS MISS Jessica C Meeker . . . . | Apt 1114,
   JUNIORS MISS Alena M Meeker. . . . . | Carpinteria, CA *93013*

Fairbarns MR & MRS Timothy J D (Sarah E Gillespie)
☎ (360) 299-0370 . . 5610 Kingsway, Anacortes, WA *98221*

Fairburn MR & MRS David H (Barbara L | ☎ (203) 661-9313
Farnsworth) Ihy.Ny.H'59 🛥️ | 409 Round Hill Rd,
   MISS Hilary R—at 9 Swan Court, | Greenwich, CT
Chelsea Manor St, London SW3, England . . . . . | *06831*

Fairburn MR & MRS Gordon R (Phoebe G Pier) | ☎ (203) 966-1085
Yn.Y'62.Y'88 . . . . | 494 Weed St,
   MISS Ramsay P—Hav'86—at ☎ (301) 799-1788 | New Canaan, CT
4334 Clagget Rd, Hyattsville, MD *20782* . . . . . | *06840*
   MISS Phoebe E—StLaw'89—at
    ☎ (909) 625-4767 . . 431 W 7 St, Claremont, CA *91711* . . . .
   MR Arthur D—at ☎ (970) 353-9507
1602 Fourteenth Av, Greeley, CO *80631* . . . . . .
   MR James G—Dick'95 . . . .

Fairchild MRS Emily F (Rand—Emily S Franklin) Pr.
☎ (516) 674-0446 . . 26 Beechwood Court, Glen Cove, NY *11542*

Fairchild MR Julian Douglas—Unn.P'38
see Dilatory Domiciles

Fairchild MR Peter T—Snc. . . . . | ☎ (508) 699-6729
   MR Peter T JR—at ☎ (203) 977-7042 | 89 Circular St, Apt
11 Hoyt St, Darien, CT *06820* . . . . | 1, North Attleboro, MA *02760*

Fairley MRS James Vardaman (Eleanor R McWane) NCar'44.Cy.
☎ (205) 871-1163 . . 19 Cross Creek Dv, Birmingham, AL *35213*

Fairman MISS Brooke
see Dilatory Domiciles

Fairman MR & MRS Endsley P (Marie B Fraley) Wil.Cw.P'30
☎ (610) 388-2575 . . Box 866, Mendenhall, PA *19357*

Fales MR & MRS De Coursey JR (Scott—Iten Noa) Unn.H.'41 .. of
☎ (617) 354-0475 .. 11 Hilliard St, Cambridge, MA *02138*
☎ (617) 934-6867 .. "Solar House" 63 Upland Rd, Duxbury,
MA *02332*

Fales MR & MRS Haliburton 2d (Katharine Ladd) C.Unn.Cl'47
☎ (908) 234-1490 .. 560 Pottersville Rd, Gladstone, NJ *07934*

Fales MRS Samuel (Barbara Foote)
☎ (954) 941-3229 .. 3414 Beacon St, Pompano Beach, FL *33062*

Falla MR & MRS Francisco J (Bonnie L Smithers) HWSth'82 .. of
7907 NW 53 St, Apt 635, Miami, FL *33166*
☎ (011-502-9) 320-409 .. Antigua Guatemala, Guatemala

Fallon MR & MRS John T (Pauline A Mayer) Ny.Al.BostColl'46
☎ (617) 899-6776 .. 55 Hidden Rd, Weston, MA *02193-2404*

Fallow MRS John S JR (Elise P Holt) .... Died at
Marion, MA Jly 25'96

Fallow MR John S JR—Bow'48
☎ (508) 748-0271 .. Piney Point, Marion, MA *02738*

Fangboner MRS Harold D (Jean Hatton) Cvc.Mt.Sl.
☎ (301) 598-8770 .. 15115 Interlachen Dv, Apt 223, Silver Spring,
MD *20906*

Fanjul MR & MRS Alexander L (Leidy—Nicole Von G Redfield)
Evg.BtP.Miami'74 ⚓
☎ (561) 835-3882 .. 110 Chateaux Dv, Palm Beach, FL *33480*

Fanjul MR & MRS J Pepe (Emilia S May) Bnd'68.B.Evg.BtP.VillaN'66.Nu'68	of ☎ (561)655-1814 "Casa Alegre" 105 Jungle Rd, Palm Beach, FL *33480*
MISS Emilia H	
MR J Pepe JR	☎ (941) 763-4699 "Amistad" 13551 SE 34 St, Okeechobee, FL *33472*
	☎ (212) 472-6696 3 E 77 St, New York, NY *10021*
	☎ (809) 562-6594 "Casa Grande" Casa de Campo, La Romana, Dominican Republic

Fanning MR & MRS Philip F N (Slater—Joy B Landreth) Eh.P'51
☎ (610) 486-6012 .. "Foxbrook Farm" Unionville, PA *19375-0607*

Fant MR & MRS John F JR (Mary P McCrea) Ws'46.Kt.Un.Pa'48
☎ (216) 729-2258 .. 13271 Caves Rd, Chesterland, OH *44026*

Fantauzzi MISS Samantha F .. see H F Taylor 3d

| **Farber** MR & MRS Brent H JR (Bettie R Field) Me.Elk.W&L'40 | ☎ (610) 520-0958 74 Pasture Lane, Apt 327, Bryn Mawr, PA *19010* |
| MISS Bettie F—at ☎ (413) 584-0898 24 Grant Av, Northampton, MA *01060* ...... | |

| **Faris** MR Charles W—Al.Tex'57.Pa'60 .... | ☎ (603) 772-7366 10 Chestnut St, Apt 8F, Exeter, NH *03833* |
| MISS Nancy W .... | |

Faris MISS Kathleen B .. see P Allen 3d

Farley MR & MRS Alexander T (Nina E Swift) LakeF'76.Pr.Pc.Conn'75
☎ (215) 247-9321 .. 603 W Hartwell Lane, Philadelphia, PA *19118*

Farley MASTER Alexander Thomson JR (Alexander T) .... Born at
Philadelphia, PA Nov 18'95

Farley MR & MRS David L JR (Carol F Duncan) Pa'47.Pa'50
☎ (804) 795-1348 .. "Hardens" Box 97, Charles City, VA *23030*

Farley MR & MRS Edward I (Coleman—Peterkin—Helen D Minton)
V'48.Ck.Myf.H'38
☎ (516) 676-4434 .. 27 Le Britton St, Locust Valley, NY *11560*

Farley MR Frank C JR .... Died Jly 26'96

Farley MR & MRS Louis C 3d (Joann Silcox) Hartw'76
☎ (970) 259-2921 .. 10 Town Plaza, Apt 51, Durango, CO *81301*

| **Farley** MR & MRS Philip W (Peters—Phyllis Rothschild) SL'46.Y'42 | ☎ (212) 935-0053 580 Park Av, New York, NY *10021* |
| MISS Augusta P—at Santa Fe, NM .... | |

Farlow MR & MRS John S JR (Catherine H Tappan) D.Myf.Ncd.H'32
☎ (617) 449-5984 .. North Hill G111, 865 Central Av, Needham,
MA *02192*

Farlow MISS Susan W
☎ (617) 444-4573 .. 75 Lawton Rd, Needham, MA *02192*

Farman-Farmaian MR & MRS Alexander (Patricia P Barlerin)
Bnd'89.Cl'95.Ri.P.'87
☎ (212) 472-6711 .. 300 E 74 St, PH-A, New York, NY *10021*

| **Farmer** MR & MRS C Richard (Mary Suzanne Nissley) Ac.Cly.Hn.Aht'40.H'42 .... | ☎ (717) 394-3908 1400 Country Club Dv, Lancaster, PA *17601* |
| MR & MRS Daniel N (Marilyn J Corrigan) F'klin'72 .... | |

Farmer MR & MRS Richard T (Joyce Barnes) Miami'57.Cm.Miami'56 .. of
8525 Fox Cub Lane, Cincinnati, OH *45243*
Ocean Reef Club, 2 Sunrise Cay, Key Largo, FL *33037*

Farmer MISS Suzanne (Fryer—Suzanne Farmer) OWes'72	☎ (717) 394-5515 205 Heatherstone Way, Lancaster, PA *17601*
MISS Amanda Fryer	
JUNIORS MISS Abigail Fryer	

| **Farnam** MRS Henry W JR (Eleanor L Dow) .... | ☎ (203) 245-7633 10 Sandgate Circle, Madison, CT *06443* |
| MR William D—Y'66—at 2000 S 2 St, Arlington, VA *22204* .... | |

Farnum MRS Edward S W (McIlvaine—Louise W Bickley) Cda.
☎ (215) 247-0708 .. 724 Wolcott Dv, Chestnut Hill, PA *19118*

Farnum MRS Henry W (Edith C Sellers) Ac.
☎ (610) MI2-1838 .. 56 Righter's Mill Rd, Narberth, PA *19072*

Farnum MR & MRS Michael (Elizabeth J Kuntner) Luton'78.Cc.Tenn'69	☎ (703) 356-2555 1138 Swinks Mill Rd, McLean, VA *22102-2429*
JUNIORS MISS Melissa L	
JUNIORS MR Samuel E	

Farnum MR & MRS Peter R (Linda F Pamp) Pc.Rc.Cspa.Pa'71	☎ (215) CH2-9740 7940 Cherokee St, Philadelphia, PA *19118*
MR Peter R 2d	
JUNIORS MISS Elizabeth S W	

Farnum MRS Ralph (Elizabeth M Sharp) .... Died Sep 29'95

Farr MR & MRS C Sims (Byrnes—Muriel StJ Tobin)
Nu'64.Ln.C.Ri.Yh.Plg.StJ.P'42.Cl'48 .. of
☎ (212) 832-9474 .. 200 E 66 St, New York, NY *10021*
☎ (803) 723-6223 .. 81 King St, Charleston, SC *29401*

Farr MRS F Shelton (Register—Farr—Schacker—Elizabeth Heard) Ncd.Dc.
☎ (504) 524-1941 .. 920 Chartres St, Apt 5, New Orleans, LA *70116*

Farr MRS F W Elliott (Anne B Hinchman) PhilaArt'39.Cs.
☎ (610) 642-4636 . . 122 Righters Mill Rd, Gladwyne, PA *19035*

Farr MR & MRS Francis B (Susan Andrews) MaryMt'66.Rc.So.Ri.P'43 . . of
☎ (212) 753-6624 . . 800 Fifth Av, New York, NY *10021*
☎ (516) 283-3033 . . ''The Studio II'' 194 Sebonac Rd, Southampton, NY *11968*

Farr MR & MRS George 3d (Joan Williams)
Cs.Ken'57.H'61.
MISS Lucy—H'92—at Yale Law . . . .
MISS Elizabeth—at Duke . . . .
☎ (212) 744-4373
180 E 79 St,
New York, NY
10021

Farr MRS H Bartow (Rockefeller—Sloan—Florence Lincoln) Cly.Ncd.
☎ (212) TE2-8094 . . 535 Park Av, New York, NY *10021*

Farr MR & MRS H Bartow JR (de Bilderling—Mary E Roberts)
Rcn.Bgt.P'43.Cl'48
☎ (910) 724-2353 . . 1020 Kent Rd W, Winston-Salem, NC *27104*
Jan 1 . . ☎ (941) 597-7958 . . 10691 Gulfshore Dv, Naples, FL *34108*

Farr MR & MRS H Bartow 3d (Esham—Martha J
Wagner) P'66 . . . .
MISS Blair W—at Princeton . . . .
☎ (202) 338-9383
1602 Caton Place
NW, Washington,
DC *20007*

Farr MRS Hollon W (Anne V Mathews)
Bnd'46.C.Csn.
MR James W—Dowl'79.LIU'81.Ford'86—at
☎ (516) 447-6681 . . 77-405 Waverly Av,
Patchogue, NY *11772* . . . .
MR John M—GeoW'79.GeoW'81—at
☎ (617) 969-5718 . . 206 Sumner St,
Newton Center, MA *02159* . . . .
☎ (407) 647-4938
1005 S Lakemont
Circle, Winter Park,
FL *32792*

Farr MR & MRS Thomas A (Lawrence—M Terry
Livingston) P'54 . . . .
MR Kenneth H—at ☎ (505) 820-6054
601 W San Mateo Rd, Santa Fe, NM *87505* . . . .
MR Edward L—at ☎ (212) 879-5944
434 E 75 St, New York, NY *10021* . . . .
☎ (803) 524-9071
78 Dolphin Point
Dv, Beaufort, SC
29902

Farran MR & MRS William N 3d (Anne R R Culp)
Ursinus'71.VillaN'72.Pc.Ncd.Pa'72.Cwr'76 . . . .
JUNIORS MISS Katherine R . . . .
JUNIORS MR Bradley W . . . .
☎ (215) 579-9660
429 Brownsburg Rd,
Newtown, PA *18940*

Farrand MR & MRS A Brady (Jeffery—Katharine L McMillan)
Stan'69.Cal'72 . . of
☎ (510) 832-8566 . . 103 Oakmont Av, Piedmont, CA *94610*
☎ (707) 963-4266 . . ''Soda Valley Ranch'' 4000 H'way 128, St Helena, CA *94574*

Farrand MR & MRS John E (Fanny-Colette
Boudeville) Msq.Cly.Mich'42 . . . .
MISS Antoinette Le C . . . .
MR Christopher P . . . .
☎ (401) 348-8228
''To Windward''
10 Pautipaug Way,
Watch Hill, RI
02891

Farrar MRS Clayton A (Van Wyck—Patricia White)
Fi. . . . .
LT COL David S—USA.Rv.So'69—at
☎ (804) 359-2759 . . 2300 Floyd Av, Richmond,
VA *23220-4408* . . . .
☎ (501) 349-5562
Arrowhead Farms,
Box 805,
Tuckerman, AR
72473

Farrar MRS John F P (Isabel Greenlee) Cnt.Ncd.
☎ (504) 635-3911 . . ''Laurel Hill'' 11210 Harris Corner Rd,
St Francisville, LA *70775*

Farrar MRS Louis V (Hoyt—Alison R Erskine)
☎ (603) 795-4106 . . Lyme, NH *03768*

Farrar MRS Maud Ellen (Kirkpatrick—Maud Ellen Farrar) Ncmb'48.Tul'52
☎ (504) 899-9912 . . 2419 Chestnut St, New Orleans, LA *70130*

Farrell MR Bowen C (Charles F JR) . . . . Married at New York, NY
Goldman MISS Olexa Celine (Robert I) . . . . Apr 6'96

Farrell MR & MRS Bowen C (Olexa Celine Goldman)
Un.Pr.Cal'82.H.'88 . .
☎ (212) 744-1046 . . 784 Park Av, New York, NY *10021*
☎ (805) 969-4102 . . PO Box 50324, Santa Barbara, CA *93150*

Farrell MR & MRS J Michael (Kegg—Jennison—
Virginia K Macdonald) SL'76.Cr'52.Nu'56 . . . .
MR William B Kegg 3d—Cal'82—at
385 N Parkview Av, Columbus, OH *43209* . .
☎ (203) 966-4588
1134 Weed St,
New Canaan, CT
06840

Farrell MISS Kristin A—V'91 . . see T W Marshall

Farrell MR & MRS Michael J (Carolyn H Morris)
Temp'68 . . . .
JUNIORS MR John M . . . .
☎ (610) 527-1577
533 Oriole Lane,
Villanova, PA *19085*

Farrell MR & MRS Thomas V JR (Martha B Cox) Nyc.VPI'83
☎ (212) 988-9422 . . 131 E 69 St, New York, NY *10021*

Farrell MR & MRS W Mason (Julia L Pattison) Cal'86.NCarSt'85
☎ (805) 684-6460 . . 5412 Granada Way, Carpinteria, CA *93013*

Farrelly MR & MRS Louis C R (Dorothy M Fell)
Rcn.Au.Cly.Rol'64 . . . .
MISS Elisabeth W—Wash'94—at
☎ (617) 876-4219 . . 1257 Cambridge St, Apt 3,
Cambridge, MA *02139* . . . .
MR Stephen R R—Rol'92—at ☎ (212) 879-8530
517 E 82 St, Apt 4W, New York, NY *10028* . . .
☎ (201) 543-2255
PO Box 249,
Pleasant Valley Rd,
Mendham, NJ *07945*

Farrelly MR & MRS Peter R (Borders—Jean Cottrill) StL'54
9800 Countryshire Place, St Louis, MO *63141*

Farrelly MRS William L (Patricia B Kinsella) . . . . .
MISS Judith L . . . .
MR Robert R . . . .
☎ (314) 726-0533
7142 Lindell Blvd,
St Louis, MO *63130*

Farrimond MR & MRS Brent T (Katherine H Zbinden)
1604 Palma Plaza, Austin, TX *78703*

Farrington MISS Andrea H—Dth'84.Mid'86
☎ (212) 431-9488 . . 118 Forsyth, New York, NY *10002*

Farrington MR & MRS Douglas F (Veronica M
Pease) Cw.Myf.Bab'50 . . . .
MISS Lee F—Sth'84—at ☎ (617) 242-4969
37 School St, Charlestown, MA *02129* . . . .
MR Edward F . . . .
☎ (617) 326-4439
15 County St,
Dedham, MA *02026*

Farrington MRS Harold P (Isabelle Thompson) Bm.BtP.
125 Mill Plain Rd, Danbury, CT *06811*

Farrington MR & MRS Henry M (Antonia Madarang) GeoW'74 . . of
☎ (202) 337-9190 . . 3004 R St NW, Washington, DC *20007*
Keyes Ferry Acres, Harpers Ferry, WV *25425*

Farrington MRS Phillips (Mary J Hazzard) Rdc'50.Dth'88.Myf.
☎ (603) 643-9104 . . 14 Willow Spring Circle, Hanover, NH *03755*

Farrington MR Phillips T—Aht'81.Mich'85.Tufts'94
1750 Kilbourne Place NW, Washington, DC *20010*

Farrington MR & MRS Roger D (Colleen A Babson)
Mass'72.Les'88.Conn'75
☎ (617) 524-9244 . . 36 Cedarwood Rd, Jamaica Plain, MA *02130*

Farrington MRS William B (Gertrude E Eby) Myf.Dar.
☎ (714) 830-5975 . . 2405-2H Via Mariposa W, Laguna Hills, CA *92653*

Farris MRS Jack M (Rowan—Carolyn E Peck) V'53.Vh.
☎ (619) 454-2220 . . 7404 Hillside Dv, La Jolla, CA *92037*

Farwell MRS Arthur (Russell—Barbara Korff)
BMr'33.Ncd. . . . . | ☎ (864) 457-4689
  MISS Diana Russell—BMr'65.S.Ny.—at | ''Tall Pines''
  ☎ (516) 922-2655 . . 313 Centre Island Rd, | 308 Hearthstone
Oyster Bay, NY *11771* . . . . | Ridge, Landrum, SC *29356-9602*

Farwell MR Cameron W . . . . Died Apr 8'96

Farwell MRS Cameron W (Betsy C McAlvin) . . . . . | ☎ (847) 234-9118
  MISS (DR) Mary E—Vt'92—at 465 Buckland Hills | 810 E Illinois Rd,
Dv, Apt 22313, Manchester, CT *06040* . . . . | Lake Forest, IL *60045*
  MR Cameron W JR—at ☎ (508) 376-2237 |
1 Pleasant Park, Millis, MA *02054* . . . . |
  MR John C—at ☎ (617) 848-3304 |
728 Washington St, Braintree, MA *02184* . . . . . |

Farwell MRS F Evans (Lynne P Hecht) Ncmb'35
☎ (504) 899-2962 . . 5824 St Charles Av, New Orleans, LA *70115*

Farwell MR Fred W—Cl'31
☎ (203) 655-4449 . . 6 Pasture Lane, Darien, CT *06820*

Farwell MR & MRS James P (G F Gay LeBreton)
Ncmb'74.Tul'77.Tul'69.T11.Camb'72
☎ (504) 895-3280 . . 1542 Calhoun St, New Orleans, LA *70118*

Farwell MRS John V 3d (Margaret Willing) Sc.
☎ (312) 944-7339 . . 1260 N Astor St, Chicago, IL *60610*

Farwell MR & MRS John V 4th (Elisabeth A | ☎ (847) 367-7622
Oppmann) Rc.Cho.Y'52 . . . . | Box 767,
  MR Stephen F Janeck . . . . | Libertyville, IL
  MR Mark I Janeck . . . . | *60048*

Fates MR & MRS Harold L (Miller—Twining—Margery Gerdes)
V'43.Y'45.Csh.Pr.Plg.Cly.Cda.Y'32
☎ (516) 922-1680 . . 7 Fieldstone Lane, Oyster Bay, NY *11771*

Faulconer MR & MRS Thomas P (Lillian A Mathis) Sdy.Cal'40
☎ (619) 224-8051 . . 1354 Clove St, San Diego, CA *92106*

Faulkner MR & MRS Avery C (Alice B Watson)
SL'53.Cvc.Mt.Gi.Sl.Y'51.Y'54.Y'55
☎ (540) 364-3225 . . ''Tall Chimneys'' 9335 Blackpond Lane,
Delaplane, VA *20144*

Faunce MRS John H JR (Katherine S Chambers)
☎ (561) 231-4003 . . PO Box 3237, 607 Spyglass Lane, Beach Station,
Vero Beach, FL *32964*

FauntLeRoy MR & MRS Reid (Harriet Van B | ☎ (410) 239-8129
Shriver) Gchr'55 . . . . | ''Sunnyside''
  MR William R 2d—StMarys'90 . . . . | 3022 Groves Mill
  | Rd, Westminster, MD *21157*

Faurot MRS George S (Keturah MacArthur Reagan)
L210 Highland Farms, Black Mountain, NC *28711*

Faurot MR Henry 3d
☎ (561) 569-0316 . . PO Box 3176, Vero Beach, FL *32964*

Fava MRS Guido (Martha P Trasel)
☎ (207) 781-4864 . . 6 Sea Cove Rd, Cumberland Foreside, ME *04110*

Faville MR & MRS R William (Joan L Sims) Stan'52 | ☎ (540) 837-2324
  MR Jonathan N L . . . . | Locust Hill Farm,
  | PO Box 7, Millwood, VA *22646*

Fawcett MR & MRS Michael S (Dana—Polly V | ☎ (561) 833-1410
Osborn) My.BtP.Chi.Ham'66.Pitt'69 . . . . | ''La Loma''
  MR Courtney—Br'90 . . . . | 196 Banyan Rd,
  JUNIORS MISS Madeleine J . . . . | Palm Beach, FL *33480*

Fawcett MR & MRS Robert E JR (Ann B Ingrum) A.Tex'52
☎ (210) 822-1061 . . 200 Patterson Av, Apt 512, San Antonio,
TX *78209*

Faxon MRS Henry H (Campbell—Sophia D Doolittle) . . . . Died at
Chestnut Hill, MA Oct 23'95

Fay MRS Edward H (Pickford—Payne—Lucy W Hill)
☎ (508) 255-3256 . . 17 Blue Rock Rd, PO Box 844, East Orleans,
MA *02643*

Fay MR Edward H JR
Box 3511, Kailua-Kona, HI *96745*

Fay MRS Eliot (Mary A Eliot)
☎ (508) 295-7227 . . 21 Warren Point Rd, Wareham, MA *02571*

Fay MISS Elizabeth S
☎ (508) 548-7756 . . PO Box 63, Nobska Point, Woods Hole,
MA *02543*

Fay MRS Ernest B (Carolyn H Grant) V'36.Godd'77.A.S . . .of
☎ (713) 522-9118 . . 1111 Hermann Dv, Apt 29B, Houston, TX *77004*
☎ (713) 339-1055 . . ''Bay House'' Texas Corinthian Yacht Club,
Kemah, TX *77565*

Fay MR & MRS Paul B JR (Anita R Marquez) Bhm.Pcu.Cvc.Sfg.Stan'41 . . of
☎ (415) 752-9596 . . 3766 Clay St, San Francisco, CA *94118*
☎ (619) 862-2267 . . 74-641 Arroyo Dv, Indian Wells, CA *92210*

Fay MR & MRS Paul B 3d (Laura E Merriam) | ☎ (415) 221-2606
GeoW'72.B.Bhm.Rcn.Bur.Pcu.Stan'72 . . . . | 179—27 Av,
  JUNIORS MISS Alexandra R | San Francisco, CA
  JUNIORS MISS Francesca F . . . . | *94121*

Fay MR & MRS Richard Saltonstall (M Alison | ☎ (212) 752-2917
MacBain) Stan'60.Bgt. . . . . | 580 Park Av,
  MISS Lisa A . . . . | New York, NY
  MR Keith S . . . . | *10021*

Fearey MR & MRS Gordon (Jacqueline L Dwight) Yn.Y'36
☎ (203) 966-9607 . . 16 King's Grant, 377 Main St, New Canaan,
CT *06840*

Fearey MR John L—Sg.Y.'39
☎ (215) CH7-0674 . . 240 W Evergreen Av, Philadelphia, PA *19118*

Fearey MISS Mary K E (Dewar—Storie—Mary K E Fearey)
Ariz'86.ArizSt'89.A.
5931 N Placita Del Conde, Tucson, AZ *85718*

Fearey MRS Morton (Mary C Senior) V'37.Eyc.Cs.
☎ (212) 879-7259 . . 79 E 79 St, New York, NY *10021*

Fearey MR & MRS Morton JR (Beverly A | ☎ (203) 834-2085
McMonagle) Unn.Err.Eyc.Plg.Br'63.Cr'66 . . . . . | 300 Ridgefield Rd,
  MR Christopher L—StLaw'93—at | Wilton, CT *06897*
  ☎ (617) 732-0043 . . 501 Boylston St, Brookline, |
MA *02146* |

Fearey MR & MRS Peter S (Christine B Ball) Dth'92.Dth'91
☎ (508) 443-6229 . . 455 Peakham Rd, Sudbury, MA *01776*

Fearing MR & MRS George R JR (Barbara Bennett) | ☎ (508) 748-1890
Vt'58 . . . . | 110 Olde Knoll Rd,
  MISS Sarah H—Skd'89 . . . . | Marion, MA *02738*
  MR Russell B—Ty'87 . . . . |

Fearing MR Travers . . see MRS H S Kiaer

Featheringill MR & MRS William W (Carolyn Burgess) RMWmn'69.Van'64 .... JUNIORS MISS Elizabeth W .... of ☎ (205)871-8897 3211 Pine Ridge Rd, Birmingham, AL *35213* ☎ (205) 338-1924 ''Osprey Cove'' PO Box 330, Cropwell, AL *35054*

Feder MR & MRS Andrew M (Abigail L Jones) V'85.Co.Ny.S.Cda.V'85 ⛵ ☎ (516) 922-2804 . . 5 Mill River Rd, Upper Brookville, NY *11771*

Fedor MR & MRS David A (Katherine S Stone) Sth'93.Br'91 ☎ (408) 446-1416 . . 20749 Celeste Circle, Cupertino, CA *95014*

Fee MR & MRS Joseph M JR (Elizabeth J Crawford) Cal'45.Pcu.Tcy.Y'45w.H'51 ☎ (415) 567-1973 . . 1940 Vallejo St, Apt 8, San Francisco, CA *94123*

Feeley MR & MRS William L (Julia R Whittlesey) Penn'65.Ub.RI'64........................ MR Roger W—at U of Cal Santa Barbara ...... JUNIORS MR Christopher B .... ☎ (503) 292-2538 2375 SW 81 Av, Portland, OR *97225-3835*

Fegela MR & MRS John R (Elizabeth N Underhill) CalSt'64 ⛵ .... MRS Irving S Underhill (Elizabeth B King) . . ☎ (603) 431-7647 613 Union St, Portsmouth, NH *03801*

Fehlig MR & MRS Edward K (Sarah C Gatch) StL'59 MISS Delphine P .... MISS Helen K .... JUNIORS MR Edward K JR .... ☎ (314) 361-7318 16 Washington Terr, St Louis, MO *63112*

Feick MR & MRS William JR (Chisholm—Rosemary Fennell) Aht'46 ☎ (212) 319-1048 . . 641 Fifth Av, New York, NY *10022*

Feid MR & MRS Stephen B (Helen H Hummer) Skd'82.Rc.Bgt.Mds.Cly.Ty'78 413 Harris Rd, Bedford Hills, NY *10507*

Feigen MISS Philippa C—Bnd'88 ☎ (212) 794-2035 . . 210 E 68 St, New York, NY *10021*

Feigen MR Richard L—Cas.Y'52.H'54 .... MR Richard W B—at NYU................. of ☎ (914)232-8476 ''Cantitoe House'' 99 Cantitoe Rd, Katonah, NY *10536* ☎ (212) 288-1774 953 Fifth Av, New York, NY *10021* ☎ (312) 440-1290 950 N Michigan Av, Chicago, IL *60611*

Feinstein MR & MRS Martin (James—Marcia E Teller) V'61.C.Nc'42.Wayne'43............. MISS Katherine B James—at 6313 Riverview Way, Houston, TX *77057*.............. MR Arthur W James—at 15 BR East Main St, Brookside, NJ *07926* ☎ (703) 821-1421 6959 Duncraig Court, McLean, VA *22101*

Feiss MR & MRS Carl (Alleen Kelly) Sth'30.Cos.Pa'31.Mit'38 .... MISS Caroline L—at ☎ (206) 322-3758 1433—38 Av, Seattle, WA *98122* .... ☎ (352) 373-4821 2801 NW 83 St, Gainesville, FL *32606-6299*

Felch MR & MRS Robert D (Marianne D Hutton) Swb'79.Ithaca'75 .... JUNIORS MISS Sarah P .... ☎ (201) 635-1679 22 Peppermill Rd, Chatham, NJ *07928*

Felch DR & MRS William C (Nancy C Dean) SL'46.P'42.Cl'45 ☎ (408) 625-6593 . . 26337 Carmelo St, Carmel, CA *93923*

Felch MR & MRS William C JR (Clayton—Virginia Steele) P'71 .... MISS Kristin C—BMr'92—at Washington, DC . . MR Jason A—BostColl'95 .... of ☎ (415)868-2040 203 Dipsea, Box 457, Stinson Beach, CA *94970* ☎ (415) 474-7161 2659 Filbert St, San Francisco, CA *94123*

Feld MR & MRS Alan David (Anne Sanger) Ws'58.Smu'57.Smu'60 ☎ (214) 522-2128 . . 4235 Bordeaux Av, Dallas, TX *75205*

Feld MR & MRS David (Anne C Smith) NMex'78.NMex'77 .... JUNIORS MISS Katherine L .... JUNIORS MR Matthew D.................. ☎ (011-44-1932) 863-796 ''High Meadow'' 25 Eaton Park Rd, Cobham, Surrey KT11 2JJ, England

Felder MISS Bettina H ☎ (212) 879-2634 . . 155 E 73 St, New York, NY *10021*

Felder MRS Thomas B (Elizabeth Rice) Dyc. ☎ (516) 324-1065 . . Box 1103, East Hampton, NY *11937*

Felder MR & MRS Wilson N 2d (Laura L Stottlemyer) Emory'75.Va'78.An.Va'68.Va'78 . JUNIORS MISS Julia R .... JUNIORS MR William L .... ☎ (202) 686-1320 5327—29 St NW, Washington, DC *20015*

Felker MR & MRS David L (Edith G Hellyer) Conv'80.Wis'79.IaState'82.IaState'84 ☎ (502) 228-7725 . . 2921 Autumn Court, Prospect, KY *40059*

Fell MR Jeffrey L—Ty'90 ☎ (415) 386-1461 . . 10 Parker Av, Apt 2, San Francisco, CA *94118*

Fell MR John R .... Died Jun 6'96

Fell MR & MRS John R 3d (Evelyn McL Van Ingen) F&M'83.Me.Pr.Gm.StLaw'82 ☎ (610) 688-2732 . . 9 Northwoods Rd, Radnor, PA *19087*

Fell MR Michael B—Vt'84 ☎ (408) 263-5425 . . 142 N Milpitas Blvd, Apt 213, Milpitas, CA *95035*

Fell MR & MRS Ogden M (Nancy G Briggs) Rcn.S. 84 Carver Lane, Narragansett, RI *02882-5036*

Fell MRS Philip S P (Elisabeth J West) Pr.Cly. ☎ (516) 922-3950 . . ''Badgewood'' 198 Cove Rd, Oyster Bay, NY *11771*

Fell MR Philip S P JR—Rcn.L.Wk. ☎ (713) 367-3355 . . 506 Spring Pines Dv, Spring, TX *77386*

Feller DR John Quentin—Loy'62 ☎ (717) 341-9841 . . Oakmont Gardens, 21 Laurel Dv, Scranton, PA *18505-2213*

Fellowes-Gordon MRS Lisa McL (Lisa McLean) ... MR Timothy S .... ☎ (011-44-171) 821-7205 114 Belgrave Rd, London SW1, England

Felton MR & MRS Cornelius C (Stuart—Ruth B Storey)
Rdc'50.My.Sm.Chi.Ncd.Va'42
☎ (508) 927-0093 . . 407 Hale St, Prides Crossing, MA *01965*

Felton MR & MRS Samuel M (Erler—Elise L Jones) Ac.Hb.H'48.H'50
☎ (207) 244-9845 . . 73 Seawall Rd, PO Box 729, Southwest Harbor,
ME *04679*

Feltus MR & MRS William J 4th (Mary Louise Hobson) Ncmb'76.Cvc.Y'76
☎ (301) 654-6396 . . 4005 Underwood St, Chevy Chase,
MD *20815* . . MR absent

Fenn MR & MRS Henry A JR (Jeanne D Trudeau) ⎫ ☎ (413) 698-3373
McG'67.W&L'63 . . . . ⎪ 2131 Dublin Rd,
MISS Katharine H . . . . ⎬ Richmond, MA
MR Edward A—at SUNY Binghamton . . . . ⎪ *01254*
JUNIORS MR William T—at Rutgers . . . . ⎭

Fennebresque MRS John (Frances Campbell) Pr.
☎ (516) 759-1498 . . 56 Piping Rock Rd, Locust Valley, NY *11560*

Fennebresque MR & MRS Kim Samuel (Eifler— ⎫ of ☎ (212)570-5452
Deborah A Johnson) Y'71.Y'74.Rc.Ln.Pr.Sa. ⎪ 800 Park Av,
Ty'72.Van'75 . . . . ⎬ New York, NY
⎪ *10021*
MISS Elin C W Eifler . . . . ⎭ ☎ (516) 671-4994
140 Duck Pond Rd,
Glen Cove, NY
11542

Fenner MR & MRS Clarke J (Elizabeth de Coursey Scott-Paine)
☎ (603) 430-3031 . . 221 Washington St, Rye, NH *03870*

Fenner MR & MRS Darwin C (Mary Jane Carter) Ncmb'55.Tul'54.Tul'69
☎ (504) 895-6331 . . 1936 Jefferson Av, New Orleans, LA *70115*

Fenton MRS Eugénie H (Christenson—Eugénie H ⎫ ☎ (508) 759-4534
Cochrane) Sth'60.Ne'72 . . . . ⎬ Box 25,
MR Alexander C . . . . ⎭ 468 County Rd,
Monument Beach,
MA *02553-0025*

Fenton MR John L—C.Ht.Rv.Y.'36
☎ (212) 988-0907 . . 125 E 84 St, New York, NY *10028*

Fenton MRS Martin (Katharine E Douglas) Cly.
☎ (408) 624-0790 . . Box 1054, Pebble Beach, CA *93953*

Fenton MR & MRS Martin JR (Griffith—Majella K ⎫ ☎ (619) 456-1938
Clark) Y'56 . . . . ⎪ 8070 La Jolla
MISS Lauren W—at 5635 E Sixth Avenue ⎪ Shores, Apt 446,
P'kway, F, Denver, CO *80220* . . . . ⎬ La Jolla, CA *92037*
MR Walker—at 3519 South Court, Palo Alto, ⎪
CA *94306* . . . . ⎪
MISS Caroline C Griffith—at Middlebury . . . . ⎭

Fenton MR & MRS Richard C (Cumings—Gregg— ⎫ ☎ (970) 925-2834
Mary J Gardner) Camb'42 . . . . ⎪ Box 1565,
MR John B Cumings 4th . . . . ⎬ 0579S Starwood Dv,
MR Hamilton S Gregg 3d . . . . ⎭ Aspen, CO *81612*

Fenton MR & MRS Wendell (Jeannie H Woolston) ⎫ of PO Box 3954,
Wil.Yn.Y'61.H'65 . . . . ⎪ Greenville, DE
MR Joshua W—Y.'91—at ☎ (212) 223-7431 ⎪ *19807*
160 E 48 St, New York, NY *10017* . . . . ⎬ ☎ (610) 388-6861
MR Nicholas W—at U of Rochester . . . . ⎪ Hill Girt Farms,
MR Lewis D—at Vanderbilt . . . . ⎭ 4323 S Creek Rd,
Chadds Ford, PA
19317
☎ (307) 733-7240
PO Box 447,
Teton Village, WY
83025

Fenton MR & MRS William (Elizabeth M Griffin) Hb.Yn.Y'34
☎ (207) 288-4942 . . ''Chilmark'' 354 Main St, Bar Harbor, ME *04609*

Fentress MRS Calvin (Frances E Wood) . . . . Died at
Hobe Sound, FL Mch 19'96

Fentress MR David L—FlaSt'88 . . see MRS A F Kammer

Fentress MR Robert W
☎ (818) 763-6244 . . 12421 Mulholland Dv, Beverly Hills, CA *90210*

Fenwick MRS Ann S (Ann D Stewart) Gv.Md. . . . . . ⎫ ☎ (410) 472-9390
MISS M Elizabeth—Ty'95 . . . . ⎪ 2509 Butler Rd,
MISS Emily S . . . . ⎬ Butler, MD *21023*
MR Charles C 3d—at F'klin & Marshall . . . . . . ⎭

Fenwick MR & MRS Charles C (Elizabeth E White) ⎫ ☎ (410) 833-4188
Gv.Md. . . . . ⎬ 3302 Belmont Rd,
MR Peter R . . . . ⎭ Glyndon, MD *21071*

Fenwick MR Charles C JR—Md.Ty'70
☎ (410) 771-4106 . . Box 1, Butler Rd, Butler, MD *21023*

Fenwick MR Hugh H—Shcc . . .of
☎ (908) 766-0103 . . 400 Mendham Rd, Bernardsville, NJ *07924*
☎ (305) 296-9889 . . 102-2 Southard St, Key West, FL *33040*

Fenwick MR & MRS John A B (Mary G Addison) ⎫ ☎ (202) 363-1944
StM'71.Ct.Md'76 . . . . ⎪ 4925 Butterworth
MISS Elizabeth D . . . . ⎬ Place NW,
MISS Whitney Y . . . . ⎭ Washington, DC
20016

Fenwick MR John G
1111 Cockey's Mill Rd, Reisterstown, MD *21136*

Fenwick MRS Leigh E (Leigh E S Grubstein) ⎫ ☎ (908) 766-0098
GeoW'71.Eh.Cly. . . . . ⎪ 100 Peachcroft Rd,
MISS Sibyl S . . . . ⎬ Bernardsville, NJ
JUNIORS MISS Leigh H . . . . ⎪ *07924*
JUNIORS MR Bayard S . . . . ⎭

Fenzl MR & MRS Terry E (Barbara L Pool) ⎫ ☎ (602) 266-0071
Wis'67.Wis'66 . . . . ⎪ 6610 N Central Av,
MISS Allison A—at BP 226, Maradi, Niger. . . . . ⎬ Phoenix, AZ *85012*
MISS Ashley E. . . . . ⎪
MR Andrew B . . . . ⎭

Ferchill JUDGE & MRS Patrick W (M Cantey ⎫ of ☎ (817)732-6118
Hendricks) TCU'69.Smu'68.Tex'72 . . . . ⎪ 1408 Washington
MR Patrick B T—at Louisiana State U . . . . ⎬ Terr, Ft Worth, TX
JUNIORS MR Edward C . . . . ⎭ *76107*
☎ (817) 659-2312
''Cantey Ranch''
Palo Pinto, TX
76072

Fergus MR & MRS Gary S (Isabelle S Beekman) Sth'73.Stan'76 . . of
☎ (415) 567-3129 . . 3024 Washington St, San Francisco, CA *94115*
☎ (415) 669-1531 . . "House with the Red Door" PO Box 886,
193 Park Av, Inverness, CA *94937*

Ferguson MR & MRS Charles L (Barbara H Olson) | ☎ (303) 773-0560
Neb'56.Neb'56 . . . . | 5808 E Powers Av,
MR Craig C—at 1215 Mapleton Av, Boulder, CO | Greenwood Village,
80304 . . . . | CO *80111*

Ferguson MR & MRS David L (Katharine Crowninshield)
Srr.Cy.Chi.Ncd.H'56
☎ (617) 329-0771 . . 541 Gay St, Westwood, MA *02090*

Ferguson MISS Eliza F . . see J B Grace

Ferguson MR & MRS J Howard 3d (Johnson—Patricia L Zoch) A.Ri . . .of
☎ (210) 828-7080 . . 350 Argyle Av, San Antonio, TX *78209*
☎ (408) 624-1514 . . "Otter Echo" 3221 Whitman Place, Box 1495,
Pebble Beach, CA *93953*

Ferguson DR & MRS James J JR (Martha R Saunders) | ☎ (301) 652-5188
SL'51.Me.Sl.Roch'45 . . . . | 5600 Wisconsin Av,
MISS Katherine E—at ☎ (561) 398-3209 | Apt 1607,
2512 SE Anchorage Cove, Apt H3, Port St Lucie, | Chevy Chase, MD
FL *34952* . . . . | *20815*

Ferguson MISS Jane S—Col'74.Cal'76.Cal'92
☎ (310) 451-3092 . . 926—2 St, Apt 405, Santa Monica, CA *90403*

Ferguson MISS Jennifer F . . see J B Grace

Ferguson MR & MRS Mark E (Elizabeth B Yntema)
Va'80.Mich'84.Chi.Wa.Nw'90.Mich'83
☎ (847) 295-0871 . . 215 N Sheridan Rd, Lake Forest, IL *60045*

Ferguson MISS Nancy Gayle—J'ville'80.Me.
☎ (610) 645-6525 . . 1319 E Montgomery Av, Apt 1L, Wynnewood,
PA *19096*

Ferguson MRS Robert E (Frances Korbel) Mls'44.Pcu.Tcy.
☎ (209) 477-1550 . . 7436 Meadow Av, Stockton, CA *95207*

Ferguson MR & MRS Scott N (Kimberly A Brown) Tufts'83.Il.Mich'84
☎ (401) 423-1092 . . PO Box 265, Jamestown, RI *02835-0265*

Ferguson MR Shaun P . . see J B Grace

Ferguson DR & MRS Thomas B (Elizabeth Shanley)
Duke'47.Cy.Duke'45.Duke'47
☎ (314) 994-0369 . . 14 Hacienda Dv, St Louis, MO *63124*

Ferguson MRS Walton (Nancy T Pearman)
☎ (203) 655-1205 . . 3 Rabbit Lane, Darien, CT *06820*

Ferguson MR & MRS William C (Sheila N Milne)
☎ (215) 248-8106 . . 8106 Seminole Av, Philadelphia, PA *19118*

Fergusson MR & MRS A Carter (Ruth H Coe) Au.Me.Gm.Ac.Yn.Y'45w
☎ (610) 896-8950 . . "Glen Brae" 1029 Waverly Rd, Gladwyne,
PA *19035*

Fergusson MRS Ian L (Elisabeth Catlin) Me.Ac.
☎ (215) 794-8706 . . "Pinecrest Farm" 3055 Burnt House Hill Rd,
Doylestown, PA *18901*

Fergusson MR & MRS Jeremy L (Holly V Buenzle) | ☎ (610) 687-8036
Penn'72.Me.GeoW'68 . . . . | 223 Walnut Av,
JUNIORS MISS Alexandra A . . . . | Wayne, PA
| *19087-3422*

Fern MR & MRS George M (Alis H Lovering) Pa'51 . | 672 Sand Hill
MISS Mary H—at 2132 Via Camino Verde, Apt 3, | Circle, Menlo Park,
Oceanside, CA *92054* . . . . | CA *94025*
MR John P—at 356A Kaelepulu Dv, Kailua, HI
96734 . . . .

Fernald MR & MRS Mason (Helen Merriman) Sm.H'40
☎ (617) 354-0254 . . 18 Reservoir St, Cambridge, MA *02138*

Fernandez MR & MRS Rafael A (Margaret Dangler) | ☎ (413) 458-4009
Ws'52.UMiami'53 . . . . | 51 Cold Spring Rd,
MISS Laura M—at 509 W 112 St, Apt 2W, | Williamstown, MA
New York, NY *10025* . . . . | *01267*
MISS Elena I—Ithaca'93—at 75 Forest Av,
Fairfield, CT *06430* . . . .

Fernley MR David B—Sar.Me'85.Bvr'91 . . see MRS R S Hines

Fernley MR J Randolph—Sar.Pac'74 . . see MRS R S Hines

Fernley MR & MRS Robert C (Alice M Guerin) Penn'68.Sa.Rv.Pa'44
☎ (215) 641-0682 . . 60 Penllyn Pike, Blue Bell, PA *19422*

Fernley MR & MRS Thomas A 3d (Sarah J Ross) | ☎ (215) 643-1772
Pc.Sg.Ac.Ncd.Denis'63 . . . . | 7251 Beech Rd,
MISS Landis S—Vt'94 . . . . | Ambler, PA *19002*
MR T Adamson 4th—Col'93 . . . . |

Fernow MISS Carola B . . see MRS D B Moseley

Fernow MR Steven D—Y'74 . . see MRS D B Moseley

Ferrante di Ruffano MCHSE Antonio & MCHSA | ☎ (011-32-2)
(Sunshine H Allen) Cda.Flor'39 . . . . | 647-07-01
MISS Virginia S . . . . | 30 Square du
| Solbosch, 1050
| Brussels, Belgium

Ferrarini LT & MRS Brant G (Tawni Hunt)
USAF.SIll'85.Wash'88.Wash'93.UWash'88
15034 SW 91 Av, Tigard, OR *97224*

Ferrarini CAPT & MRS Richard L (Ann G Polhemus)
USN.SanJ'59.Menlo'54 ⚓
☎ (206) 392-3083 . . 1571 Hillside Dv SE, Issaquah, WA *98027*

Ferrarini MR & MRS Steven P (Jennifer A Callies) Seattle'90.UWash'89
☎ (503) 235-7155 . . 2444 SE Tibbetts St, Portland, OR *97202*

Ferrell MISS Merri McI—FlaAtl'74.VaCmth'81
202 Lighthouse Rd, Northport, NY *11768*

Ferrell MR R Anderson—NCarSt'72 . . of
☎ (212) 757-1366 . . 320 W 56 St, New York, NY *10019*
"Merriewold Park" 2674 Rte 42, Forestburgh, NY *12777*

Ferrer MRS C O'Hara (Catherine E O'Hara) | ☎ (216) 371-5177
Cal'65.Cwr'91 . . . . | 2303 Scholl Rd,
MR Hugh G—P'90 . . . . | University Heights,
| OH *44118*

Ferrer MISS Florence C
8476 New Salem St, 79, San Diego, CA *92126*

Ferrer MR & MRS James C (Jeanne K Franklin) . . . | ☎ (516) 922-0348
MR James C B . . . . | 4 E Woods Lane,
JUNIORS MR Andrew K . . . . | Oyster Bay, NY
| *11771*

Ferrer MRS José M (Mary Schumacher) Cly.
☎ (212) 744-0023 . . 177 E 75 St, New York, NY *10021*

Ferrer MISS (DR) M Irené—BMr'37.Cl'41.Cs.
☎ (212) RE7-5663 . . 200 E 66 St, New York, NY *10021*

Ferrer MAJ & MRS Robert N JR (Elizabeth Gravatt)
USMC.VaCmth'82.An.Rv.Cspa.Fw.Cit'82
☎ (804) 633-6862 . . "Chase's End Farm" 17237 Antioch Rd, Milford,
VA *22514*

Ferrer MISS Terry—BMr'40
☎ (804) 293-4974 . . 618 Kearsarge Circle, Charlottesville, VA *22903*

Ferrer MR Thomas H—Unn.Kt.P'64
☎ (216) 491-9371 . . 3208 Warrensville Center Rd, Apt 308, Shaker Heights, OH *44122*

Ferrin MR & MRS Allan H (Barbara L Weaver) Wis'73.NMex'75 . . . .
JUNIORS MISS Leigh E . . . .
| ☎ (206) 441-3066 6015 Crystal Springs Dv, Bainbridge Island, WA *98110*

Ferrin MR & MRS Allan W (Barbara A Hogate) Evg.BtP.Cw.Ll.Cly.Ncd.Cda.Pn.P'43
☎ (561) 832-5880 . . The Villas, 425 Worth Av, Palm Beach, FL *33480*

Ferris MRS George F (Ashforth—Barbara Evans)
☎ (602) 947-3259 . . 6015 Cameldale Way, Paradise Valley, AZ *85253*

Ferris MRS Morris Douw JR (Callen—Gloria I Batten) Cl'61
☎ (941) 361-7172 . . Plymouth Harbor N205, 700 John Ringling Blvd, Sarasota, FL *34236-1550*

Ferris MR & MRS Peter T (Diana P Davis) Va'80.OWes'79
☎ (202) 965-1770 . . 4610 Greene Place NW, Washington, DC *20007*

Ferris MR & MRS Robert C (Needham—Martha J Singleton) Nw'54.Sr.Ill'50
☎ (847) 432-7686 . . 125 Michigan Av, Highwood, IL *60040*

Ferriss MR & MRS David P (Schneider—Ruth F Knight) Sth'48.Qc.Yn.Y'40
☎ (513) 871-6610 . . 3649 Traskwood Circle, Cincinnati, OH *45208*

Ferriss MRS Ford (Marion H Ford) Ncd.
☎ (314) 727-2034 . . 900 S Hanley Rd, St Louis, MO *63105*

Ferriss MR & MRS Franklin (Lacey—Nancy L Atkins) Y'33
☎ (314) 862-7423 . . 8425 Colonial Lane, St Louis, MO *63124*

Ferry MR & MRS Herbert T (Rosalie L Hunter) OWes'86.LaS'95.Rc.Pc.Temp'90
☎ (215) 572-5669 . . 727 Willow Grove Av, Glenside, PA *19038*

Ferry MR & MRS John M (Elizabeth B Gibson) H'42.H'49
☎ (401) 789-3188 . . 619 Ministerial Rd, Wakefield, RI *02879*

Fesler MRS Deborah A (Deborah M Ashley) . . see MRS C B Ashley

Fessenden MRS Alexandra I (Meehan—Alexandra D Irving) So.Cly.
MR Michael J Meehan 3d . . . .
MR Alexander D Meehan . . . .
| of ☎ (516)283-8614 25 Ochre Lane, PO Box 2686, Southampton, NY *11969-2686* ☎ (212) 579-0004 1 Lincoln Plaza, New York, NY *10023*

Fessenden MR & MRS Edward E (Bannard—Marion H Sutphen) Pr.Y'35
☎ (813) 251-2054 . . 503 Suwanee Circle, Tampa, FL *33606*

Fessenden MR Jerald D—Un.Plg.Y'60.Pa'66
☎ (212) 348-5583 . . 1060 Fifth Av, New York, NY *10128*

Fessenden MR & MRS Samuel (Catherine Buck) V'35.Y'32.Pa'35
MISS Abbe—Bnd'62—at ☎ (301) 951-3809 3535 Chevy Chase Lake Dv, Chevy Chase, MD *20815* . . . .
| ☎ (215) 283-7249 609 Foulkeways, Sumneytown Pike, Gwynedd, PA *19436*

Fessenden MR Sewall H . . . . Died at Sherborn, MA Aug 6'96

Fetcher MR Frederick S
☎ (415) 453-3922 . . 92 Wimbledon Way, San Rafael, CA *94901*

Fetridge MR & MRS Clark W (Jean H Huebner) Cas.Rc.Sc.Cho.Cyc.Cw.LakeF'69.BostColl'71 . .
JUNIORS MR Clark W 2d . . . .
| ☎ (312) 664-1988 1310 N Ritchie Court, Chicago, IL *60610*

Fetridge MRS William Harrison (Bonnie-Jean Clark) Rc.Cas.Ncd.Dar.
☎ (773) 348-2255 . . 2430 N Lakeview Av, Chicago, IL *60614-2714*

Fetter MR & MRS Thompson (Jane S Trevor) Stan'58.Stan'56.Stan'58.Cal'67
☎ (619) 459-2857 . . 6820 Country Club Dv, La Jolla, CA *92037*

Fetter MR & MRS Trevor (Melissa Foster) Stan'82.Sdy.Hn.Stan'82.H'86 ⚎
☎ (310) 472-3926 . . 156 S Carmelina Av, Los Angeles, CA *90049*

Feulner MR & MRS George J (C Lynn Youngren) Ariz'70.StM'68.Ariz'71.Nu'72 . . . .
MISS Sara P . . . .
MISS Cory C . . . .
| ☎ (520) 298-3213 6230 E Calle Alta Vista, Tucson, AZ *85715*

Feurich MRS Werner M (A Suzanne ReQua) . . . . . .
MISS Kathryn J . . . .
MISS Alice M V . . . .
MR Werner H E . . . .
| ☎ (630) 469-2545 22 W 270 Rte 53, Glen Ellyn, IL *60137*

Few MR & MRS Benjamin F JR (Sarah A P McNeal) SL'60.Cly.Duke'57.Va'60
☎ (502) 425-0675 . . ''Lyndon Cottage'' PO Box 22086, Louisville, KY *40252*

Few MR & MRS Lyne S (Ellen Hale) V'38.Rdc'41.Duke'35.Duke'37.H'41 . . . .
MISS Mary R—at 12 Arnold Circle, Cambridge, MA *02139* . . . .
| of ☎ (703)534-2572 6731 Nicholson Rd, Falls Church, VA *22042* ☎ (518) 962-8689 ''Yellow House'' Lake Shore Rd, Westport, NY *12993*

Fewell DR & MRS J William U (Layne—Betty T Luck) P'46.Va'54
☎ (610) LA5-2696 . . 101 Hickory Lane, Rosemont, PA *19010*

Fichtel MRS Robert S (Sylvia C Dilworth)
☎ (412) 781-8295 . . 1108 River Oaks Dv, Pittsburgh, PA *15215*

Fick MR & MRS Harold A JR (Nancy R Alverson) Bur.Fr.Cp.Pac'61.SanJ'63
☎ (415) 342-9358 . . 1495 Tartan Trail, Hillsborough, CA *94010*

Fick MR & MRS Ronald G (Valerie L Peterson) Cp.SanJ'63 . . . .
MR David Bovet . . . .
MR Bradley Borel . . . .
| ☎ (415) 325-8773 96 Parkwood Dv, Atherton, CA *94027*

Fick MR & MRS Stephen Borel (Abbie D Halden) Syr'91.SacrSt'94.Bur.Cp.Pac'90
☎ (415) 917-9324 . . 79 Chester Circle, Los Altos, CA *94022*

Ficks MRS Gerald J (Katharine B Sutphin) Eyc. ⚎
2412 Ingleside Av, Apt 6D, Cincinnati, OH *45206*

Fiechter MR & MRS Bayard R (Sullivan—Stacy H Warth) Rol'85.Fst.Pc.Sg.Ph.Sa.Ty'72
☎ (215) 247-2622 . . 8009 Crefeld St, Philadelphia, PA *19118*

Fiedler MRS George (Agnes Amberg)
☎ (847) 446-4391 . . 711 Oak St, Apt 407, Winnetka, IL *60093*

Field MR & MRS Augustus B 3d (Susan E Rynne) H'55
☎ (803) 432-9356 . . 1819 Brevard Place, Camden, SC *29020*

Field MISS Cassandra A—Md'88
13120 Chestnut Oak Dv, North Potomac, MD *20878*

Field MR & MRS Charles D (Frances H King) Bur.Fr.
☎ (415) 441-3716 . . 1170 Sacramento St, San Francisco, CA *94108*

Field MISS Corinne T—Stan'87 . . see R L Brickley

Field MR & MRS Daniel (Harriet Beecher) Rdc'60.H'59.H'68 . . . . ☎ (802) 234-9890
MR Richard H—Y'85—at ☎ (718) 789-5923 ''The Red
36 Plaza St, Apt 12C, Brooklyn, NY *11238* . . . . Farmhouse''
MR Jonathan B—Wash'91—at ☎ (773) 278-2118 Barnard,
2026 W Iowa St, Chicago, IL *60622* . . . . RFD 2, Box 157,
South Royalton, VT
05068

Field MISS Devon Dana . . see J F Curtis 3d

Field MRS Earl (Margaret P Earl)
☎ (803) 671-4663 . . ''Sea Pines Plantation'' 15 Oyster Landing Lane, Hilton Head Island, SC *29928*

Field MRS Field (Deirdre D Field) Cly.
☎ (011-33-1) 43-26-85-41 . . 33 quai d'Anjou, 75004 Paris, France

Field MR & MRS Frederick C JR (A Meredith Holladay) P'38
☎ (302) 998-4219 . . 4923 Lancaster Pike, Wilmington, DE *19807*

Field MR & MRS H James JR (Janet M Isham) ☎ (401) 272-8742
Briar'70.LakeF'71 . . . . 120 Congdon St,
MISS Elisabeth I—at Cornell . . . . Providence, RI
JUNIORS MISS Jennifer D—at Groton *02906*

Field MRS Harold J (Hartog—Nancy Doering) . . . . . ☎ (401) 751-4105
MR Christopher C—at ☎ (303) 744-2826 9 Stimson Av,
15 Clarkson St, Apt 210, Denver, CO *80209* . . . Providence, RI
02906

Field MR & MRS Henry F (Ward—Simpson—Mary Jo Laflin)
IIT'78.Sc.H'62.Ch'65 ⚓
☎ (773) 929-1044 . . 2344 N Lincoln Park W, Chicago, IL *60614*

Field MR James A . . . . Died at
Newtown Square, PA Jun 24'96

Field MRS James A (Lila R Breckinridge) Ws'40
☎ (610) 356-1322 . . 3500 West Chester Pike, CH5, Newtown Square, PA *19073*

Field MR & MRS John E (Jane B Wilmot) ☎ (415) 342-7621
Ws'61.H'64.H'64 . . . . 2165 Carmelita Av,
MR John E JR—Stan'92 Hillsborough, CA
MR Christopher E—Aht'89—at Brown *94010*

Field MR Jonathan—Y'56.Cl'68
☎ (802) 365-4007 . . ''Far Afield'' Timson Hill Rd, PO Box 406, Newfane, VT *05345*

Field MRS Joseph N (Carroll—Irene M Peebles)
☎ (310) 476-2549 . . 10701 Bellagio Rd, Los Angeles, CA *90077*

Field MRS Malcolm G (Cornelia F Morris) . . . . Died at
Shelburne, VT Mch 26'96

Field MR & MRS Marshall 5th (Jamee B Jacobs)
Rc.B.Cho.Cas.Sc.On.Sr.Ri.H'63
☎ (847) 234-6007 . . 980 N Green Bay Rd, Lake Forest, IL *60045*

Field MR & MRS Marshall 6th (Louise C Wales) Tufts'84.SL'90
☎ (914) 266-3477 . . ''Hidden Brook Farm'' Hibernia Rd, Salt Point, NY *12578*

Field MISS Mary B—Ober'74
☎ (773) 465-4719 . . 1415 W Glenlake Av, Chicago, IL *60660*

Field MR & MRS R Henry (Hoover—Rennell—Dodge—Nancy A May)
Sm.Csn.Cda.Wms'29.H'31 . . of
☎ (561) 546-3881 . . 425 S Beach Rd, Hobe Sound, FL *33455*
615 W Lyon Farm Dv, Greenwich, CT *06831*

Field MR Richard JR . . see J F Curtis 3d

Field MR & MRS Richard D (Cutler—Schuyler V C ☎ (203) 966-8962
Wilson) Unn.B.Cly.Cda.Ty'63 . . . . 964 Smith Ridge
MISS Katharine S Cutler—LakeF'94—at Rd, New Canaan,
☎ (212) 717-6955 . . 231 E 81 St, New York, CT *06840*
NY *10028* . . . .
MR Earle N Cutler 4th—LakeF'90—at
☎ (212) 744-3670 . . 30 East End Av,
New York, NY *10028* . . . .
MR Peter K Cutler—Skd'93 . . . .

Field MR & MRS Robert B JR (Elizabeth C Hoopes) ☎ (603) 964-8763
Denis'67.Chi.Ncd.Dth'64.Bost'70 . . . . ''Pretty Penny''
MR Robert B 3d—at 225 E 95 St, Apt 31D, 123 Mill Rd,
New York, NY *10128* . . . . North Hampton, NH
MR Charles S—at Amherst *03862-2218*

Field MR & MRS Spencer (Frances Pierce) H'42
☎ (617) 696-2860 . . 378 Canton Av, Milton, MA *02186*

Field MR Thomas P—Y'28.H'30 . . . . ☎ (214) 361-5617
MR Thomas P JR . . . . 3608 Caruth Blvd,
Dallas, TX *75225*

Field MR & MRS Thornton S JR (Fiala—Katzenbach ☎ (609) 397-9254
—M Dolores Daley) Sar.Ht.Cw.Rm'55 . . . . 6 Waterford Court,
JUNIORS MR Timothy FitzRandolph—at Lambertville, NJ
Hobart-Wm Smith *08530*

Field MR & MRS Tylor 2d (Katherine C Alexander) ☎ (401) 846-7223
Pa'74.Ariz'78.Ny.Nrr.Srb.Cw.Cda.USN'59 . . . . ''Eastover''
MISS Deborah A—at Providence, RI . . . . 144 Wapping Rd,
Portsmouth, RI
02871

Field MR William Alexander . . . . Died at
Ft Lauderdale, FL Feb 20'96

Field MRS William Alexander (Rohde—Thanis G Alexander)
☎ (954) 941-9549 . . Seasons Apt 415, 1371 S Ocean Blvd, Pompano Beach, FL *33062*

Fielding MR & MRS Geoffrey W (Claudia B Rose) . . ☎ (410) 433-8118
MR Christopher P . . . . 104 St Johns Rd,
Baltimore, MD
21210

Fielding MR & MRS H Page (Judith A Janusz) F&M'61
☎ (609) 883-8043 . . 9 Randi Way, Titusville, NJ *08560*

Fielding MISS Margaret Fairfax
☎ (410) 539-0761 . . 1425 Haubert St, Baltimore, MD *21230*

Fielding MR & MRS Richard M (Ellen M Wright) F&M'56.Va'58
☎ (610) 687-3493 . . 216 Walnut Av, Wayne, PA *19087*

Fields MRS Stephen F (Mary P Hallock) Ncd. . . . . . ☎ (847) 256-1822
MISS Tracy H—Vt'95 . . . . 621 Maple Av,
MR Carter T—Cc.Leh'94 . . . . Wilmette, IL
JUNIORS MR Edward P *60091-3433*

Fieve DR & MRS Ronald R (Katia von Saxe) of ☎ (212)288-1595
So.BtP.H.'55 . . . . 930 Park Av,
MISS Lara . . . . New York, NY
MISS Vanessa *10028*
☎ (561) 832-9887
1540 S Ocean Blvd,
Palm Beach, FL
33480

Figg MRS James A 3d (Allegra Braga) MmtMhn'82.Cly.
see Dilatory Domiciles

Figg MR James A 3d—K.Lx.Fic.Au.LakeF'76
☎ (914) 358-2776 .. ''Rive Gauche'' 177 S Highland Av,
Grand View-on-Hudson, NY *10960-4118*
Filley MR & MRS Oliver D (Moira L Redmond) Lm.Hn.H'45
☎ (908) 234-1069 .. 440 Holland Rd, Far Hills, NJ *07931*
Filley MR & MRS Patrick O (Marion Robinson Duff) | ☎ (203) 762-0814
NCar'72 . . . . | 25 English Dv,
JUNIORS MISS Amanda D . . . . | Wilton, CT *06897*
JUNIORS MISS Vanessa L . . . . |
Filmer MR & MRS Christopher M (Lucie A L Buckley)
Bost'87.Tufts'86.INSEAD'93
2—13 St, Parkhurst 2193, Johannesburg, South Africa
Fina MISS Aidan Isabella (g—Burton J Kinerk) . . . . Born at
Tucson, AZ Aug 8'95
Finch MISS Anne W
☎ (908) 756-3853 .. 302 W 8 St, Plainfield, NJ *07060-2329*
Finch MR & MRS Charles A (Maxine D Christiansen) H'46.Ia'48
☎ (602) 840-5524 .. 4314 E San Miguel Av, Phoenix, AZ *85018*
Finch MR Charles B . . . . Died at
New York, NY Jly 15'96
Finch MRS Charles B (Angela C Havens) Cly.Dar. . | 4 Park Av,
MR William P—SL'78 . . . . | New York, NY
| *10016*
Finch MR Charles B JR—Y.'74
☎ (212) 673-5427 .. 310 E 12 St, New York, NY *10003*
Finch JUNIORS MISS Charles B 3d .. see J L Hill
Finch MR & MRS David Shrady (Barbara P Pettit) | ☎ (908) 872-1425
Rv.Snc.Cw.Dar.Rut'51 . . . . | ''Pour les Oiseaux''
MISS Anna Barbara Shrady . . . . | Monmouth Hills, NJ
MR Alexander Morison Shrady . . . . | *07732*
Finch MRS E C Kip (Ruth E Woodward) BMr'37.Cda.
☎ (203) 966-0777 .. 19 Four Winds Lane, New Canaan, CT *06840*
Finch MR Earle Kip—Fairf'84
19 Four Winds Lane, New Canaan, CT *06840*
Finch MR & MRS Rufus C JR (Madeira—Louisa W Coxe) Chr.Snc.Cda.P'51
☎ (561) 626-0472 .. 115 Lakeshore Dv, Apt T48, North Palm Beach,
FL *33408*
Finch MR & MRS Stephen B (Margaret R Whipple)
Srr.Un.Chr.Snc.StJ.Cly.Cda.Y'44
☎ (516) CE9-5977 .. 70 Causeway St, Lawrence, NY *11559*
Finch MR & MRS Stephen B JR (Jones—Pinero—Nancy A New) Snc.Y'69
☎ (703) 631-2793 .. 12509 Paradise Spring Rd, Clifton, VA *20124*
Findlay DR & MRS Charles W JR (Peggy Eagle) Y'39.Cl'43
☎ (508) 636-8426 .. 70 Brayton Point Rd, Westport Harbor, MA *02790*
Findlay MR & MRS Donald R (Glover—Katherine D Wiman)
Au.Cly.Ncd.Dar.
☎ (561) 546-2591 .. 185 S Beach Rd, Hobe Sound, FL *33455*
Findlay MR & MRS Joshua P (Lesley A Mentzer) Bost'91.Me.Bost'90
☎ (212) 744-8986 .. 311 E 72 St, Apt 3B, New York, NY *10021*
Findley MRS William D (Walker—Elizabeth A | ☎ (860) 364-1257
Mullins) . . . . | PO Box 1032,
DR Mark C Walker—FlaAtl'82.AmUC'90—at | Sharon, CT *06069*
☎ (212) 977-4547 .. 515 W 59 St, Apt 12H, |
New York, NY *10019* . . . . |
Finerty MRS John F (Mitchell—Catherine Palmer)
900 E Harrison Av, Apt B39, Pomona, CA *91767*

Finger MRS L Clement (Leslie L Clement) A. . . . . . | ☎ (512) 592-3963
MISS Henrietta C . . . . | Box 1120,
MR Perry C . . . . | Kingsville, TX
| *78364*
Finger MR Perry H—StM'67
4940 Broadway St, San Antonio, TX *78209-5732*
Fingleton MR & MRS Anthony J (Pamela Wolcott) | ☎ (212) 472-3304
H'67 . . . . | 168 E 74 St,
MISS Samantha—at ☎ (212) 873-6985 | New York, NY
115 W 82 St, New York, NY *10024* . . . . | *10021*
MISS Priscilla—at ☎ (210) 734-4475 |
818 E Magnolia Av, San Antonio, TX *78212* . . . |
Fink MR Bruce W . . . . Died at
Washington, DC May 25'93
Fink MRS Bruce W (Rodzianko—Patricia H Boyd)
☎ (202) 332-1932 .. 2370 Champlain St NW, Washington,
DC *20009-2634*
Finkenstaedt MRS Frederick B (Coleman—Cathleen | ☎ (441) 236-2013
Reardon) Ct. . . . . | ''Crow Lane
MISS Cathleen R Coleman—at | House''
☎ (202) 342-1015 .. PO Box 3699, | 17 Harbour Rd,
Washington, DC *20007* | Paget PG 02,
MR James S Coleman—at ☎ (212) 594-1466 | Bermuda
448 W 37 St, Apt 11B, New York, NY *10018* |
Finlay MRS Kirkman JR (Mary Fleming H Willis) | ☎ (803) 783-0659
Swb'66 . . . . | ''Millwood''
MR Kirkman 3d—Va'92 . . . . | 100 Hampton Place,
| Columbia, SC *29209*
Finlayson MR & MRS D Aylesbury (Thurgood—Gammon—
P June Brodie) P.'26
☎ (516) CE9-7068 .. 1 Albert Place, Lawrence, NY *11559*
Finletter MRS Thomas K (Geist—Eileen Wechsler) | ☎ (212) 772-1995
Sth'47.K.Cs. . . . . | 220 E 72 St,
MR Stephen Geist—at ☎ (212) 876-1442 | New York, NY
1435 Lexington Av, New York, NY *10128* .. | *10021*
Finley MR & MRS Charles B 3d (Eleanor L Reading) Pa'36
7305 River Crescent Dv, Annapolis, MD *21401*
Finley JUNIORS MISS Jaquelin Cary .. see MISS M C Ambler
Finley MR & MRS John H 3d (Margot M Gerrity) | ☎ (617) 566-2323
V'67.Tv.Cy.Aga.Chi.H'58 . . . . | 35 Spooner Rd,
MISS Charlotte D . . . . | Chestnut Hill, MA
MR John H 4th . . . . | *02167*
JUNIORS MR Samuel W . . . . |
Finley MR John J—Un.StA.H.'68.Va'71 .. of
☎ (212) 265-3266 .. 75 West End Av, Apt R37B, New York, NY *10023*
PO Box 151, Livingston, NY *12534*
Finley MR John M—Pc.Hav'39
☎ (215) CH2-3771 .. 730 St Andrews Rd, Philadelphia, PA *19118*
Finley JUNIORS MR John T A .. see MISS M C Ambler
Finley DR Knox H—Sfy.Pom'26.Y'30 .. of
☎ (415) 567-8951 .. 1400 Geary Blvd, Apt 2509, San Francisco,
CA *94109*
☎ (415) 868-1328 .. ''Monarch Halt'' Box 145, Stinson Beach,
CA *94970*

Finley MRS William T JR (Julie F Hamm)
Cvc.Mt.Sl. . . . . | ☎ (202) 338-2849
MR Benjamin E 2d . . . . | 3221 Woodland Dv
MR Abner M . . . . | NW, Washington,
| DC 20008
Finnell MRS Samuel C JR (Margaret A Larned) Sdg.Pc.Sfh.Ac.Ncd.
☎ (215) 247-3007 . . 7808 Lincoln Dv, Philadelphia, PA 19118
Finnerty MR & MRS Peter F JR (Caroline P Simons) Hlns'81.SUNY'80
☎ (203) 656-1097 . . 5 Driftway Lane, Darien, CT 06820
Finocchio MRS Sarah Elting (Sarah S Elting)
Bnd'69 . . . . | ☎ (310) 459-6045
MISS Amy W . . . . | 18453 Clifftop Way,
MISS Amanda C . . . . | Malibu, CA 90265
JUNIORS MR Leigh E . . . . |
Finucane MR & MRS Brendan E (Elizabeth S Buntin) Van'65.Van'65
☎ (615) 356-2363 . . 115 Westover Dv, Nashville, TN 37205
Fiorato MR & MRS Hugo (Pogue—Scott—Gilchrist | of ☎ (203)259-0888
—Joelyn S Littauer) Bnd'46.Pqt.Cly. . . . . | PO Box 886,
MISS Stephanie S Gilchrist—at | 459 Hull's H'way,
☎ (802) 253-2893 . . 43 Shawhill Rd, Stowe, | Southport, CT
VT 05672 . . . . | 06490-0886
| ☎ (508) 583-4915
| "Tower House"
| on Lamberts Cove,
| PO Box 757,
| West Tisbury, MA
| 02575
Fioratti MR & MRS Nereo (Helen E Costantino) | ☎ (212) 832-8411
Pars'50.Cly.Padova'36 . . . . | 555 Park Av,
MISS Arianna C—HRdc'89.P'92.Cly. . . . . | New York, NY
| 10021
Firestone MR & MRS A Brooks (Catherine Boulton) | ☎ (805) 688-3940
Cl'61 . . . . | Box 36,
JUNIORS MR Andrew B . . . . | Los Olivos, CA
| 93441
Firestone MR David M . . see C Runnells
Firestone MR & MRS Jeffrey B (Heather H Gow) MtVern'87.Tex'81
2917 Sunset Blvd, Houston, TX 77005
Firestone MR & MRS John D (Susan C Paul) | ☎ (202) 462-3955
Ct.Mt.Cvc.Fic.Sl.P'66.Pa'70 . . . . | 2320 Wyoming Av
MISS Mary C . . . . | NW, Washington,
JUNIORS MISS Lucy D . . . . | DC 20008
Firestone MR & MRS Leonard K (Lynch—Caroline Hudson)
Bhm.Ck.Pcu.BtP.Evg.StJ.Cly.Ncd.P'31 . . of
☎ (619) 324-3868 . . 69-844 H'way 111, Apt C, Rancho Mirage,
CA 92270
☎ (408) 624-1550 . . 1491 Bonifacio, Box 455, Pebble Beach, CA 93953
Firestone MRS Peter S (Julie Nelson) . . . . | ☎ (602) 948-5440
MISS Lisa S—P'90 . . . . | 6035 N Casa Blanca
| Rd, Scottsdale, AZ
| 85253
Firman MRS Pamela H (Hanna—Pamela Humphrey) Cv.It.Un.Kt.
☎ (216) 942-1450 . . "Fox Spring Farm" 9011 Booth Rd, Mentor,
OH 44060
Firth MR & MRS Douglas L (Rebecca M Hemphill) Pa'76.Pa'78.Pa'85
☎ (410) 822-7938 . . 6482 Fairway Lane, Easton, MD 21601

Firth MR & MRS Nicholas L D (Slocum—Neilson— | of ☎ (212)734-9284
Edmée C de Montmollin) Bost'69.Fic.Bgt.C. . . . | 152 E 78 St,
MISS Katherine V—at ☎ (212) 879-6070 | New York, NY
111 E 78 St, New York, NY 10021 . . . . | 10021-0406
MISS Marie-Louise C Slocum—at | ☎ (914) 234-6138
☎ (202) 333-6118 . . 3112 N St NW, | 55 Mianus River Rd,
Washington, DC 20007 . . . . | Bedford, NY 10506
MISS M Olivia J Slocum—at |
☎ (505) 984-0673 . . 114 Lugar De Oro St, |
Santa Fe, NM 87501 . . . . |
MR John J Slocum 3d—at ☎ (212) 979-6230 |
110 E 13 St, Apt 3B, New York, NY 10003 . . |
Firth MRS Rogers (Georgiana F Hooker) . . . . Died at
Trappe, MD Oct 24'95
Firth MR Rogers . . . . | ☎ (410) 476-3277
MISS Frances B . . . . | "Beauvoir"
MR Michael R . . . . | 27465 S Island
| Creek Rd, Trappe,
| MD 21673
Firth MISS Susan M (Rogers) . . . . Married at Easton, MD
Wood MR Earle B 3d (Earle B JR) . . . . Jun 9'95
Fischbach MRS Victor W (Sampson—Lee E Quinn) Qc.
☎ (513) 871-7109 . . 3201 Griest Av, Cincinnati, OH 45208
Fischelis MISS Mary L—Ken'90
see Dilatory Domiciles
Fischelis MR Robert L—Yn.H'49.H'57
☎ (203) 787-2472 . . 1268 Yale St, New Haven, CT 06520
Fischelis MR William Churchill—Lawr'87 . . of
☎ (206) 632-2153 . . 4529 Bagley Av N, Seattle, WA 98103
☎ (802) 333-9015 . . "Churchill Tree Farm" Strafford, VT 05072
Fischer MRS Ashton J (Elizabeth L Nicholson)
☎ (504) 834-2521 . . 3 Wavertree Court, Metairie, LA 70005
Fischer MR C Henry 3d—Me.Myf.Sar.
☎ (610) 642-3045 . . 296 River Rd, Gladwyne, PA 19035
Fischer DR & MRS Edwin G (Angela B Brown) | ☎ (401) 847-0211
Rdc'60.Il.Ny.Srb.Cyb.Sm.Ncd.Hn.H'59.Cl'63 | "Halidon House"
⚓ | Halidon Av,
MR Chad B—Br'90—at 8 Halidon Av, Newport, | Newport, RI 02840
RI 02840 . . . . |
Fischer MR & MRS F Wood (Constance Linington Froeb) Geo'71.Pa'62 . . of
☎ (516) 749-0878 . . PO Box 1025, Shelter Island Heights, NY 11965
☎ (561) 278-0869 . . 1000 Lowry St, Delray Beach, FL 33483
Fischer MR & MRS George W (Josephine S | of ☎ (603)544-3098
Hamilton) Pa'64.Gm.OWes'62 . . . . | Bald Peak Colony
MISS Katherine R—Mid'93—Box 6610, Jackson, | Club, PO Box 201,
WY 83002 . . . . | Melvin Village, NH
| 03850
| ☎ (941) 676-9139
| Mountain Lake,
| Lake Wales, FL
| 33859
Fischer MR & MRS George W (Suzannah C White) DeP'91.Wab'91
☎ (718) 834-8328 . . 53 Dean St, Apt 1, Brooklyn, NY 11201
Fischer MR & MRS Heinz G (Groesbeek—Burdet—Linda L Gray)
Cly.Konstanz'52
☎ (802) 626-5680 . . Box 128, Vail Hill, Lyndon Center, VT 05850

Fischer MR James B
☎ (606) 278-4805 . . 228 Zandale Dv, Lexington, KY *40503*

Fischer MR John W—Md'60
☎ (408) 655-3609 . . 230 Grove Acres, Apt 313, Pacific Grove,
CA *93950-2342*

Fischer MR & MRS Julian D (Tatiana C Pertzoff)
Chi.Bost'65 . . . . ☎ (207) 372-6760
MISS Anastasia I . . . . Horse Point Rd,
MISS Alexandra G—at NYU . . . . Port Clyde, ME
MISS Ariana S—at Boston U . . . . | *04855*

Fischer MR & MRS Lindsay E (Joanna Koehler) Rdc'55.H'56
☎ (719) 634-1787 . . 55 Marland Rd, Colorado Springs, CO *80906*

Fischer MR & MRS Lindsay K (Mandy-Jayne Richardson) . . of
76 Gibbon Rd, Kingston upon Thames KT2, England
233 Weteringschans, 1017 XH Amsterdam, The Netherlands

Fischer MR & MRS M Peter (Appell—Suzanne
Chichester) V'63.NCar'65.Duke'57.Wash'60.   of ☎ (314)965-9990
Nu'61 . . . . 9900 Old Warson
MISS Martha C—V'95—at 200 S Brentwood   Rd, St Louis, MO
Blvd, Apt 11B, St Louis, MO *63105* . . . . | *63124*
MR Matthew A —at Skidmore . . . . ☎ (508) 432-6627
MR Michael P—at Grinnell . . . . 80 Forest Beach Rd
                                                    Ext, South Chatham,
                                                    MA *02659*

Fischer MR P L Charles JR
☎ (606) 275-1634 . . 105 Shady Lane, Lexington, KY *40503*

Fischer MR & MRS Philip L C (Elizabeth A Willis)
☎ (606) 277-5998 . . 760 Albany Rd, Lexington, KY *40502*

Fischer MR & MRS Thomas C (Nancy Knight) Sth'50.H'46
☎ (719) 471-1498 . . 2801 Country Club Dv, Colorado Springs,
CO *80909*

Fischer MR & MRS W Gordon (A Diana Paterson)
Y'52.JHop'57 . . . . | ☎ (416) 322-9098
                                                    350 Lonsdale Rd,
MISS Astrid D—at McGill . . . . Apt 407, Toronto,
JUNIORS MR Tristan G A—at Cambridge . . . . . . Ontario M5P 1R6,
                                                    Canada

Fish MASTER Alexander William Joseph (Jason M) . . . . Born at
San Francisco, CA Feb 5'96

Fish MRS Frederick (Lucy T Lewis) Ncd.Hn . . . . . . | ☎ (201) DR9-3385
MISS Mary T—at 47 Encampment Dv,   12 Canoe Brook Rd,
Bedminster, NJ *07921* . . . . | Short Hills, NJ
                                                    07078

Fish MR Hamilton JR . . . . Died at
Washington, DC Jly 23'96

Fish MR & MRS Jason M (G G Courtney Benoist) Cal'81.P'80
☎ (415) 346-7572 . . 2301 Pacific Av, San Francisco, CA *94115*

Fish MRS Peter S (Florence W Voorhees) San.
1816 Millers Rd, Wilmington, DE *19810*

Fish MRS Richard R (Heckert—Callender—Margaret Gibbons)
Woos'44.SUNY'52
☎ (619) 744-8696 . . 1508 Circa Del Lago, Apt B111, San Marcos,
CA *92069*

Fish MRS Stuyvesant (Diana Turner) Pcu.
☎ (408) 624-7744 . . "Palo Corona Ranch" Box 222095, Carmel,
CA *93922*

Fish MRS William H (Colt—Virginia Fuller) Cs.
☎ (516) 862-7234 . . PO Box 794, Stony Brook, NY *11790*

Fisher MRS A Murray (Lucretia Billings) Elk. . . . . . | ☎ (410) 823-5730
MISS N Lark—at 415 Schwartz Av, Baltimore,   "Redwings"
MD *21212* . . . . | 1907 Ruxton Rd,
                                                    Baltimore, MD
                                                    21204

Fisher MR & MRS A Murray JR (Mary R Reed) | ☎ (804) 784-5117
VaCmth'67.Cl'66 . . . . Brookview Farm,
MISS Jane T . . . . Box 126,
JUNIORS MR Murray L . . . . | Manakin-Sabot, VA
                                                    23103

Fisher MR & MRS Aiken W (Jane I Marshall) Fcg.Rr.Pg.Y'29
☎ (520) 684-5254 . . "Quail Haven" 2165 S Mesa Dv, Wickenburg,
AZ *85390*

Fisher MR & MRS Alfred J 3d (Barbara L | ☎ (313) 885-6440
Muckerman) Geo'70 . . . . 273 Ridge Rd,
MISS Ashley M . . . . Grosse Pointe, MI
MR Alfred J 4th . . . . | *48236*

Fisher MRS Benjamin R (Lilian C Hall) Pg.Rr.
☎ (412) 621-8822 . . 5023 Frew Av, Pittsburgh, PA *15213*

Fisher MRS Bennett (Elsie H Lawson) Ihy.Cda.Yn. | ☎ (203) 869-5066
MISS Elsie M—at 228 Cottonwood Lane, Aspen,   9 Sabine Farm Rd,
CO *81611* . . . . Greenwich, CT
MISS Constance M . . . . | *06831*

Fisher MR & MRS Bennett L (Susan B Huntington) | ☎ (203) 322-4890
Bost'65.Iona'75.Ihy.Yn.Y'65 . . . . Barn Hill Rd,
MISS Louisa H—at New England Coll . . . . Greenwich, CT
JUNIORS MR James B—at Dartmouth . . . . | *06831*

Fisher MRS Caroline C (Caroline L Copeland)
☎ (412) 683-4281 . . 3955 Bigelow Blvd, Apt 401, Pittsburgh,
PA *15213-1235*

Fisher MISS Caroline T—Cda.
☎ (410) 823-4093 . . Blakehurst 709, 1055 W Joppa Rd, Towson,
MD *21204*

Fisher MR Charles N JR—Wms'54
☎ (412) 661-6826 . . 6315 Marchand St, Pittsburgh, PA *15206*

Fisher MR & MRS Chester G 3d (Laura E Smith)
Geo'77.Pitt'80.Rr.Pqt.Pa'74 . . of
☎ (412) 688-8595 . . 5540 Dunmoyle St, Pittsburgh, PA *15217-1015*
☎ (412) 238-2332 . . "Log Cabin Farm" Barron Rd, Ligonier, PA *15658*

Fisher MR & MRS David J A (Sarah McA Wheatland) Lond'83.Camb'72
☎ (011-44-171) 229-7853 . . 7 Artesian Rd, London W2 5DA, England

Fisher MRS George C (Jean K Sprague) Paris'30.Cwr'35.May.
☎ (216) 932-6053 . . 2639 S Belvoir Blvd, Cleveland, OH *44118*

Fisher MISS Helen E (Bergquist—Helen E Fisher) Nu'68.Col'75
☎ (212) 744-9870 . . 4 E 70 St, New York, NY *10021*

Fisher MR & MRS Henry (Ann M Yeager) | ☎ (412) 521-8992
Alleg'59.Pg.Pitt'60 . . . . 5473 Kipling Rd,
MR William B . . . . Pittsburgh, PA
                                                    | *15217*

Fisher MASTER Henry Aiken (Chester G 3d) . . . . Born at
Pittsburgh, PA Jun 18'96

Fisher MR & MRS Henry J II (Robin A Bodell) Ty'75.Ihy.Ny.Cyb.Cr'76 . . of
☎ (203) 622-0380 . . 552 Lake Av, Greenwich, CT *06830*
☎ (802) 583-2548 . . Intervale, Sugarbush Woods Rd, Warren,
VT *05674*

Fisher DR & MRS (DR) J Rush S JR (Phoebe P Driscoll) BMr'86.Pa'92.Dth'84.Pa'89
☎ (215) 482-8576 . . 4014 Lauriston St, Philadelphia, PA *19128*

Fisher MR & MRS Jack O'D (Sheila Williams)
☎ (410) 557-9764 . . 2511 Houcks Mill Rd, Monkton, MD *21111*

Fisher MR & MRS James A (Edith C Hall) Pg.Rr.Y'42
☎ (412) 683-2111 . . 5414 Kipling Rd, Pittsburgh, PA *15217*

Fisher DR & MRS John R S (Marianna S O'Donovan) Srr.Wil.Ac.Pa'61 . . . .
MISS Katharine S—at ☎ (202) 333-8099
3008 R St NW, Apt 2, Washington, DC *20007* .
☎ (610) 384-3902 | "Glenderro Farm" RD 3, Coatesville, PA *19320*

Fisher MR & MRS Julian P 2d (Fay S Roosevelt) S. "Bonnie Brae" 38 Horse Hollow Court, Locust Valley, NY *11560*

Fisher MR & MRS Kenneth W (Whipple—Mettie R Barton) Van'47.Ht.Dar.Lond'53 . . . .
MR Sean H—at Syracuse U . . . .
☎ (609) 921-2146 | 33 Stuart Close, Princeton, NJ *08540-7506*

Fisher MRS Peter R (Cary R Fox) Bnd'55 . . . .
MISS Elizabeth C—Va'88 . . . .
☎ (516) 922-6504 | "Cricket Cottage" 65 Sandy Hill Rd, Oyster Bay, NY *11771*

Fisher MR & MRS Philip B JR (Clarke—Diana Y Dillon) P'49.Pa'52 . . . .
MISS Emily L . . . .
MISS Katherine N . . . .
MR Philip B 3d . . . .
MR Nicholas T . . . .
  MISS Victoria A L Clarke . . . .
  MR Amory Y Clarke . . . .
  MR Laughlin H Clarke . . . .
of ☎ (212)831-5570 | 1150 Fifth Av, New York, NY *10128* ☎ (207) 963-4083 "Orchard Farm" Winter Harbor, ME *04693*

Fisher MRS Pieter A (M Helen Anderson) DeP'69.Wash'71.Mds.Ri.
☎ (707) 963-9633 . . 1103 Brittany Lane, St Helena, CA *94574*

Fisher MR & MRS Richard W (Nancy M Collins) Ws'72.Hn.H'71 . . . .
JUNIORS MISS Alison E . . . .
JUNIORS MR Anderson C . . . .
☎ (214) 720-1944 | 3644 Beverly Dv, Dallas, TX *75205*

Fisher MR & MRS Robert G (Gwendolyn L Harrington) Mo'66.Cl'59.Cl'63
☎ (816) 252-6413 . . 3114 Norton Av, Independence, MO *64052*

Fisher DR & MRS Robert M (Katharine S Morris) Sim'48.H.'35.Cl'39
447 Great Springs Rd, Bryn Mawr, PA *19010*

Fisher MRS Sheila A (Sheila R Atkinson) . . . .
MISS Alexandra K . . . .
MR Eric N . . . .
MR Richard Q . . . .
5850 Centre Av, Pittsburgh, PA *15206*

Fisher MR Sydney T—Ph.Pa'54.Cr'59
☎ (215) 836-4547 . . 151 Terminal Av, Erdenheim, PA *19038*

Fisher MRS Thomas (Martha A Burdick) Me.Ncd.
☎ (610) 645-8699 . . 1400 Waverly Rd, Villa 50, Gladwyne, PA *19035*

Fisher MR & MRS Thomas K (Sandra L Martin) Geo'70 . . . .
MISS Stephanie M . . . .
MISS Sarah K . . . .
☎ (313) 886-5428 | 1400 Blairmoor Court, Grosse Pointe Woods, MI *48236*

Fisher MR & MRS Timothy O (Audrey H Hillman) Fcg.Pg.Rr.DU'71.Va'76 . . . .
MISS Lilah H . . . .
MR J Brooks . . . .
JUNIORS MISS Nina . . . .
JUNIORS MR Matthew H . . . .
of ☎ (412)661-9555 | 5901 Braeburn Place, Pittsburgh, PA *15232* ☎ (603) 968-9221 PO Box 567, Holderness, NH *03245*

Fisher MRS W Yule (Genevieve W Marsh) Swb'38.Sl.Ncd.
☎ (301) OL6-1123 . . 5514 Center St, Chevy Chase, MD *20815*

Fisher MRS William A JR (Mary Le G Slingluff) Elk.Mv.Cda.Pn.
☎ (410) 323-3814 . . Cross Keys, 8 Olmstead Green Court, Baltimore, MD *21210*

Fisher MR & MRS William A 3d (Sarah H Morten) Hlns'73.Elk.Md.Cc.Cw.Mv.Ty'72.Va'77
☎ (410) 823-1108 . . 1708 Circle Rd, Baltimore, MD *21204*

Fisk MR Averell H—Rcn.DU'72.Cl'75
☎ (561) 845-2851 . . 1191 N Lake Way, Palm Beach, FL *33480*

Fisk MR & MRS Bernard C (Alice L Collins) Roch'67.Roch'69.Yn.Y'61.Y'63 . . . .
MISS Ridgely McL—P'95—at Harvard Med . . . .
MR B Carter JR—U of Cal Los Angeles . . . .
☎ (302) 656-1586 | "Beaubower" 807 Owl's Nest Rd, Greenville, DE *19807*

Fiske MISS Emily Hale (g—John N Fiske) . . . . Born at Boston, MA May 22'96

Fiske MRS Francis (Jane L Noble) . . . .
MR Francis JR—H'50 . . . .
☎ (603) 357-0014 | 3 Leahy Rd, Keene, NH *03431*

Fiske MR & MRS George F JR (Hoffman—Elaine Walker) Wheat'68.Bab'85.Nh.Sm.Bentley'72 . .
JUNIORS MISS Abigail W—at St Mark's . . . .
  MISS Kirke T Hoffman—Ham'93 . . . .
  MR Tyler P Hoffman—Bab'96 . . . .
☎ (508) 655-5150 | Box 190, 23 Hollis St, Sherborn, MA *01770*

Fiske MRS John (Rosalie A Cheney)
☎ (860) 677-5299 . . 20 Devonwood Dv, Farmington, CT *06032*

Fiske MR & MRS John C (Janet S Murray) H'30
☎ (208) 882-2087 . . 910 East B St, Moscow, ID *83843*

Fiske MR & MRS John N (Jean-Lamont Barker) Swb'59.Myf.Ncd.H'54 . . of
☎ (617) 899-1557 . . 41 Summer St, Weston, MA *02193*
☎ (603) 253-6277 . . "Needle Point" Center Harbor, NH *03226*

Fiske MRS John W (Ruth L Winckelmann)
☎ (717) 595-2624 . . Box 235, 731 Oak Hill Dv, Buck Hill Falls, PA *18323*

Fiske MR & MRS William E (Sarah R Pitney)
PO Box 398, Morristown, NJ *07963-0398*

Fiske MR & MRS William J (Diana P Furse) Ty'81.Ty'82
☎ (860) 658-5038 . . "Trug House" 36 Beldenwood Rd, Simsbury, CT *06070*

Fitch MR & MRS George Hopper (Bouché—Denise Lawson-Johnston) Unn.C.Sfy.Plg.Pcu.Snc.StJ.Y'32
☎ (415) 931-1112 . . 1960 Broadway, San Francisco, CA *94109*

Fitch MR Walter 3d—B.Sfg.Stan'39.H'41
☎ (619) 454-7565 . . 7904 Roseland Dv, La Jolla, CA *92037*

Fitler MR & MRS Ralston B JR (Mary J Schneider) .. | of ☎ (412)934-3739
MISS Tamsin L—Penn'86 .... | 2623 Fountain Hills
MISS Susanna R—Denis'91 .... | Dv, Wexford, PA
MR Ralston B 3d—W&L'88 .... | *15090*
  | ☎ (803) 686-4307
  | ''Sunny Daze''
  | Palmetto Dunes,
  | Hilton Head Island,
  | SC *29925*

Fitler MR William W 3d—Me.Ph.Rv.
   ☎ (610) 642-0442 .. 449 Montgomery Av, Haverford, PA *19041*

Fitts MR & MRS Alan C (Josephine P Chandlee) | ☎ (610) LA5-1011
Me.Laf'58.DU'71 .... | 119 Browning Lane,
MR Alan C JR .... | Rosemont, PA
JUNIORS MR Caleb P .... | *19010*

Fitzgerald JUNIORS MISS Brooke A .. see D G Burke

FitzGerald MR & MRS Gerald J (Katherine Jane | ☎ (415) 388-4171
Edgerton) GeoBr'68.Menlo'61 .... | 240 Perry St,
MR Scott T—at MIT Grad .... | Mill Valley, CA
  | *94941*

Fitz-Gerald MR & MRS Michael R (Pauline Bayless)
Ariz'71.ArizSt'78.Ariz'71
   ☎ (602) 943-1755 .. 7151 N 13 St, Phoenix, AZ *85020*

Fitzgerald MR & MRS Peter A (Suzanne M Daniel-Dreyfus)
Bnd'87.Melb'81.Cl'88
   ☎ (011-61-3) 416-3875 .. 409A Brunswick St, Fitzroy, Victoria 3065,
Australia

Fitz-Gerald MRS Taylor (Helen L Taylor) V'34.Ncd.
   ☎ (216) 851-8200 .. McGregor Home, 14900 Private Dv,
East Cleveland, OH *44112*

Fitzmorris JUNIORS MR Scott W .. see R B Wallace
Fitzmorris JUNIORS MR Tyson W .. see R B Wallace
Fitzpatrick MISS Alexandra K—Col'92 .. see N Ames
Fitzpatrick MR Kenneth F 3d—Ore'91 .. see N Ames
FitzSimmons MRS L Mack (Linda C Mack) ..... name changed to Mack

Flaccus MR & MRS Charles L III (Moe—Anne L | ☎ (610) 935-2723
Hall) Cent'61.Rcn.Ihy.WashColl'63 ⚓ ..... | PO Box 987,
MISS Lisa L .... | Valley Forge, PA
MR Charles L 4th .... | *19482*

Flaccus MRS Elmer W (Virginia L Roberts) Ariz'34.Dar.
   ☎ (520) 290-9790 .. 3450 N Winslow Rd, Tucson, AZ *85750*

Flaccus MISS Jane L—Fcg.Rr.
725 Dorseyville Rd, Pittsburgh, PA *15238-1121*

Flachbarth MR Charles T P—Cc.Hav'65.Van'68
   ☎ (703) 931-2161 .. 2601 Park Center Dv, Apt C402, Alexandria,
VA *22302*

Flacker MASTER Ryan Ede (Wesley F) .... Born at
                         Portland, OR Feb 28'96

Flacker MR & MRS Wesley J (Laurie D Ede) Ore'90.Ore'90
   ☎ (503) 297-6917 .. 8400 SW Woodside Dv, Portland, OR *97225*

Flagg MR W Allston—B.Ng.Pr.Rc.H'52 .. of
   ☎ (212) 724-8439 .. 27 W 72 St, New York, NY *10023*
Cove Rd, Oyster Bay, NY *11771*

Flagle MR & MRS Charles D (Dryden—Janet S | ☎ (410) 823-5649
Waters) Gi.JHop'40.JHop'53 .... | 1822 Circle Rd,
MR Douglas A .... | Ruxton, MD *21204*

Flaherty MR & MRS Francis E (Michelle B | ☎ (610) 664-3207
Patterson) Dll.Y'45 .... | 311 Berkeley Rd,
MR Christopher D—Penn'89—at | Merion Station, PA
   ☎ (415) 903-0868 .. 338 Higdon St, | *19066*
Mountain View, CA *94041* .... |
MR Geoffrey S—KutzU'90—at |
   ☎ (301) 495-0349 .. 8502—16 St, Apt 106, |
Silver Spring, MD *20910* .... |
MR Andrew S .... |

Flail MR & MRS Charles M (Phyllis F Brégy) | ☎ (602) 483-0851
Duq'64.Reed'68 .... | 6020 E Sapphire
MR David B .... | Lane,
  | Paradise Valley, AZ
  | *85253-2270*

Flake MR & MRS Andrew A (June B Richards) AmInt'l'76.Cy.Ne'73
   ☎ (508) 693-4656 .. RFD 191, Iroquois Av, Vineyard Haven,
MA *02568*

Flake MRS Carlyle G (Susan A Binney) Cy.
   ☎ (617) AS7-9005 .. 191 Fairway Rd, Chestnut Hill, MA *02167*

Flam MR & MRS Morris (Pamela Bowring) Pars'91.Cl'79
   ☎ (914) 687-4507 .. 15 Blueberry Hill Rd, Accord, NY *12404*

Flanagan MR & MRS Joseph F (Robinson—Alva Sergeant)
   ☎ (410) 557-7117 .. 2510 Pocock Rd, Monkton, MD *21111*

Flanagan MR & MRS Joseph P (Mary E Mayock) Ph.Rc.Pc.P.USN'47.Pa'52
   ☎ (215) AD3-2316 .. 401 E Mill Rd, Flourtown, PA *19031*

Flanagan MRS Laura M (Laura Melano) .... | ☎ (212) 348-9308
MR Michael S .... | 1601 Third Av,
JUNIORS MR Brian J .... | New York, NY
  | *10128*

Flanagan DR & MRS Thomas R (Elizabeth Jenny F Kreger)
Wes'83.Mass'79.Wes'82
   ☎ (401) 245-0204 .. 117 Highland Av, Barrington, RI *02806*

Flanagin MR & MRS Neil (Mary Mead) Ih.Y'53 .... | ☎ (847) 441-9128
MISS Margot .... | 1010 Mt Pleasant,
MISS Nancy .... | Winnetka, IL *60093*
MISS Jill .... |

Flanigan MR & MRS John P (Ann R Allen) | ☎ (314) 994-3311
Myf.StL'35 .... | 30 Rolling Rock
MISS Ann R—Wash'79 .... | Court, St Louis, MO
MR David W—Regis'83—at ☎ (314) 537-1231 | *63124*
2018 Claymills Dv, Chesterfield, MO *63017* ... |
MR Christopher A—Rkhst'84—at |
   ☎ (314) 991-1279 .. 10127 Fieldcrest Lane, |
St Louis, MO *63124* .... |

Flanigan MR & MRS Peter A (Elizabeth R Engelsman) Swb'82.Geo'72
16 Lorenzo Lane, St Louis, MO *63124*

Flannery MR & MRS Christopher (Kathleen | ☎ (909) 624-1437
Berwind) Pom'72.Clare'75.SCal'77.Cal'71. | 435 Blaisdell Dv,
Clare'75.Lond'76 .... | Claremont, CA
MISS Mary C .... | *91711*
JUNIORS MISS Jean M .... |

Flather MR & MRS William J (Nancy J Sweetser) Cvc.Mt.Sl.Ncd.P'39
   ☎ (202) 966-9007 .. 4100 Cathedral Av NW, Washington, DC *20016*

Flather-Morgan MISS (DR) Alexandra W—P'85.Y'89 .. see H S Morgan

Fleck MRS Francis E (Sweeney—Isabelle M Seltzer) BMr'37.Ny.Sl.Dar. . . . . ☎ (717) 762-1388 · 201 Clayton Av, Waynesboro, PA *17268*
   MISS Elaine C—at 4100 Cathedral Av NW, Washington, DC *20016* . . . .

Fleeman MR & MRS William J JR (Helen Zwick) Mo'35.Vh.Stan'38
   7450 Olivetas Av, Apt 316D, La Jolla, CA *92037-4929*

Flegenheimer MR & MRS Mark S (Anne de L Hepting) GeoW'85.DeP'83
   ☎ (517) 793-0283 . . 555 Foxboro Rd, Saginaw, MI *48603*

Fleischmann MR & MRS Charles 3d (Burd B Stevenson) Ny.Y'50 . . . . ☎ (513) 831-5553 · 9575 Cunningham Rd, Cincinnati, OH *45243*
   MISS Louisa B—at 3748 Sachem St, Cincinnati, OH *45226* . . . .

Fleischmann MR Charles F
   ☎ (203) 255-8908 . . 831 Hillside Rd, Fairfield, CT *06430*

Fleischmann MRS Dorette L (Bear—Ransohoff—Seignious—Dorette L Fleischmann) Sth'52.Ct.
   ☎ (540) 253-5129 . . Over the Grass Farm, PO Box 398, The Plains, VA *20198*

Fleishhacker MR & MRS David (Victoria J Escamilla) Stan'64.P'59.Cal'66 . . . . ☎ (415) 563-4887 · 3424 Jackson St, San Francisco, CA *94118*
   MISS Eleanor D—at ☎ (415) 387-9123 658 Tenth Av, San Francisco, CA *94118* . . . . . .
   JUNIORS MR Jeffrey D—at Columbia . . . .

Fleitas MR Albury N JR . . see J M Smartt

Fleitas MRS Allison F (Maddock—Ruth M Quigley) BtP.Evg.
   ☎ (561) 659-7371 . . 369 S Lake Dv, Apt 5G, Palm Beach, FL *33480*

Fleitas MR Allison F 2d—Pc.Del'69 . . . . ☎ (215) 248-3945 · 8212 St Martins Lane, Philadelphia, PA *19118*
   JUNIORS MR Bayard A . . . .

Fleitas MISS Garrett H . . see J M Smartt

Fleitas MR & MRS Gilbert (Lisa H Eaton) Duke'88.H'79.Stan'83
   ☎ (212) 327-2131 . . 175 E 79 St, Apt 3C, New York, NY *10021* . . MR absent

Fleitas MRS Haskell (Elizabeth D Haskell) Ac.
   ☎ (941) 964-2950 . . PO Box 53, 255 Gilchrist Av, Boca Grande, FL *33921*

Fleitas MR & MRS J Albury (Madeleine F Newbold) Sg.Cry.Fw.Ac.Cda.P.'35
   ☎ (215) 247-2133 . . "Linden Court" 111 W Willow Grove Av, Chestnut Hill, PA *19118-3953*

Flemer MR & MRS Stevenson (Leslie Fulton) Dth'50.H'55 . . . . ☎ (802) 496-3936 · PO Box 509, Waitsfield, VT *05673*
   MISS Wrenn W . . . .
   MR Stevenson JR . . . .
   MR Benjamin . . . .

Fleming MR Alexander M A—Rcn.K.Cw.Rv.Cp.
   ☎ (805) 688-6666 . . Zaca Ranch, Box 147, Los Olivos, CA *93441*

Fleming MISS Catherine Seymour (Porter Farrar) . . . . Born at New York, NY Aug 7'96

Fleming MRS Charles L (Katharine H Edgar) Sth'54.H'61.Chr.Cly.Ncd.Dc.Dh.Lm.
   ☎ (212) 688-1124 . . 200 E 66 St, Apt D1901, New York, NY *10021*

Fleming MR & MRS David W 2d (Devon T Porter) MtVern'84
   ☎ (203) 966-5425 . . 93 Thayer Dv, New Canaan, CT *06840*

Fleming MASTER David Wilson 3d (David W 2d) . . . . Born Jun 26'96

Fleming MR & MRS Edward S JR (Catharine P Hull)
   ☎ (703) 528-1470 . . 1155 Crest Lane, McLean, VA *22101*

Fleming MISS Francesca Fay—Pace'84.Smu'91.Cly.
   ☎ (214) 521-4361 . . 3675 Asbury St, Dallas, TX *75205*

Fleming MRS Joan H (Fleming—Aldridge—Joan T Hibbard) Bnd'51.Csn. . . . . ☎ (713) 622-4458 · 52 Raintree Place, 10 S Briar Hollow Lane, Houston, TX *77027*
   MR William C . . . .
   MR Alexander T . . . .

Fleming MRS Page (Anna McC Page) . . . . ☎ (301) 229-8854 · 5210 Falmouth Court, Bethesda, MD *20816*
   MR Richard B L—at 1247 N Crescent Heights, Los Angeles, CA *90046* . . . .

Fleming MR & MRS Peter E (Margaret V Wood) NEng'84.Rc.Br'80
   ☎ (215) 242-4263 . . 7911 Navajo St, Philadelphia, PA *19118*

Fleming MR & MRS Porter Farrar (Lilian W Manger) Hlns'88.Rc.Ri.Bcs.Cw.Rv.Cp.Snc.Cly.Myf.Ncd. ColM'82.FP'85 . . of
   ☎ (212) 288-2708 . . 215 E 72 St, Apt 7W, New York, NY *10021*
   ☎ (805) 688-6666 . . Zaca Ranch, PO Box 147, Los Olivos, CA *93441*

Fleming LT COL R Walton JR—USA. . . . . Died at Middleburg, VA May 10'96

Fleming MRS R Walton JR (Dickey—Joan M Dambrie) . . . . ☎ (540) 687-3019 · 23470 Dover Rd, Middleburg, VA *20117*
   MISS Kara D'A Dickey—at Sweet Briar . . . .

Fleming MR Robert W—Mt.Cvc.GeoW'41
   ☎ (301) 229-8127 . . 5106 Cammack Dv, Bethesda, MD *20816*

Fleming MR & MRS Samuel W 3d (Beverly Cochran) Fst.Yh.Gm.Bow'49. . . . . ☎ (803) 744-4019 · Yeamans Hall Club, PO Box 9455, Charleston, SC *29410*
   MISS Nancy C—at Conway Rd, Williamsburg, MA *01096* . . . .

Fleming MR & MRS Steven B (Anne P Dennison) StLaw'81.Ey.U'75
   ☎ (617) 631-1796 . . 8 Calumet Lane, Marblehead, MA *01945*

Fleming DR & MRS T Corwin (Cynthia C L Dunn) Ws'55.Chi.Ncd.H'52.H'56
   ☎ (617) 267-0030 . . 208 Beacon St, Boston, MA *02116*

Fleming MR Thomas J
   ☎ (619) 488-7668 . . 5329 La Jolla Hermosa Av, La Jolla, CA *92037*

Fleming MR & MRS Thomas T (Phyllys C Betts) Rc.Ln.Hav'49
   ☎ (215) CH2-6288 . . 500 W Chestnut Hill Av, Philadelphia, PA *19118*

Fleming MRS William T (Esther Haney) WVa'40.Ac. . . . . ☎ (352) 750-1582 · 434 Hildalgo Dv, Lady Lake, FL *32159*
   MR Gerry L . . . .

Fleming, Wilson B JR & Buell, Martha J—Van'85.Tul'89.NCar'96.Van'84
   ☎ (302) 266-9296 . . 319 Wyoming Rd, Newark, DE *19716*

Flershem MRS Taussig (Elizabeth B Taussig) . . . . . ☎ (609) 884-0387 · "Parsley Hall" 110 York Av, West Cape May, NJ *08204*
   MR Gerald B . . . .

Fletcher MR & MRS Andrew JR (Vincel—Frank—Ann S Burford) Un.So.B.Srb.Chr.Snc.StJ.Ne. . . . ☎ (516) 283-2975 · "Caramar IV" 420 Hill St, Southampton, NY *11968*
   MISS Carolyn A Vincel . . . .

Fletcher MR & MRS Dugald A (Sarah P Huntington) — ☎ (516) 671-0897
Rdc'56.Rc.Pr.H'52.H'56 . . . . | 28 Shelter Lane,
MISS Sarah P—H.'80.Pr.—at ☎ (212) 570-4630 | Locust Valley, NY
510 E 82 St, Apt 1D, New York, NY *10028* . . . | *11560*

Fletcher MRS F Livingston (Katharine M Alexander)
74 Pasture Lane, Apt 106, Bryn Mawr, PA *19010*

Fletcher MRS Henry M (Anne V Beers) . . . . Died May 22'96

Fletcher MRS Jane G (Jane G Coxe) Cda.
☎ (610) 644-2002 . . ''Willisbrook Farm'' 266 Boot Rd, Malvern,
PA *19355*

Fletcher MR John M W—FlaSo'49 . . . . | ☎ (215) 257-2794
MISS Susan W . . . . | Green Hill Rd,
| Box 533, Lahaska,
| PA *18931-0533*

Fletcher MISS Mary L—Br'51
☎ (212) 758-8973 . . 12 Beekman Place, New York, NY *10022*

Fletcher MRS Paul F (Margaret E Mudd) Ncd.Dc.
☎ (314) 862-2141 . . 816 S Hanley Rd, St Louis, MO *63105*

Fletcher MR & MRS Willis H (Jane Cotton)
SanDiegoSt'33.Lind'81.Sdy.Ore'29
☎ (619) 224-5695 . . 575 San Gorgonio St, San Diego, CA *92106*

Flicker MR & MRS Richard H (Jane M Mason) | of ☎ (561)744-0769
Dth'46.Rut'48.Nu'57 . . . . | 3860 Shearwater Dv,
MISS Meredith A—*see Dilatory Domiciles* . . . . . | Jupiter, FL *33477*
MR John M—at ☎ (212) 534-5616 | ☎ (516) 653-5912
100 E 87 St, New York, NY *10128* . . . . | ''The Cottage''
| Quogo Neck Lane,
| Quogue, NY *11959*

Flickinger MRS (DR) Bonnie G (Bonnie G Gordon)
SUNY'64.SUNY'68.SUNY'85.SUNY'94.Buf.Ts.Ne.
☎ (716) 875-8335 . . 31 Nottingham Terr, Buffalo, NY *14216-3619*

Flickinger MR & MRS Geoffrey R (Michelle A Ferrall)
LakeF'84.Bgt.Fic.Denis'81
☎ (914) 763-5352 . . ''Catalpa Farm'' 218 Spring St, South Salem,
NY *10590*

Flickinger MRS Glenn W (B Awdry Griffith) | ☎ (716) 873-4111
Bf.G.St. . . . . | 144 Middlesex Rd,
MR William S—Cy.St.—at 45 Red Wing Court, | Buffalo, NY *14216*
Amherst, NY *14226* . . . . |

Flickinger MASTER Henry Ferrall (Geoffrey R) . . . . Born at
South Salem, NY Jun 21'96

Flickinger MR & MRS Peter B (King—Genevieve Roe) St.G.Mid'52
☎ (716) 876-8500 . . 39 Nottingham Terr, Buffalo, NY *14216*

Flickinger MR & MRS Thomas R (Phoebe A Raymond)
Cy.St.Ts.G.H'54 . . of
☎ (716) 885-1960 . . 75 Penhurst Park, Buffalo, NY *14222*
☎ (905) 834-7994 . . RR 1, Lorraine, Port Colborne, Ontario L3K 5V3,
Canada

Flickinger MR & MRS Thomas R (Margaret E McCoy)
NCar'83.Nw'87.Cr'82.Cl'87
780 Rosewood Av, Winnetka, IL *60093*

Flight MR & MRS Curtis C (Barbara F Russell)
P'81.Bost'89.D.Dth'80.Dth'81.Bost'89 . . of
☎ (508) 785-1887 . . 22 Main St, Dover, MA *02030*
☎ (603) 763-4664 . . ''Granitehead'' 48 Fisher's Bay, Sunapee,
NH *03782*

Flinn MR C Maurice—Md.Cc.StJ.Va'46
☎ (804) 977-2778 . . 34 Ednam Village, Charlottesville, VA *22901*

Flinn MR & MRS David G (Mary A Quick) Cr'60
☎ (607) 533-4797 . . 866 Ridge Rd, Lansing, NY *14882*

Flinn MR & MRS Lawrence JR (Stephanie H Strubing) | of ☎ (203)869-7958
Mds.Y'57.Cl'60 . . . . | 209 Taconic Rd,
MISS Marion de V—at 400 E 71 St, New York, | Greenwich, CT
NY *10021* . . . . | *06831*
MISS Adriane S—Col'95 . . . . | ☎ (561) 546-2881
MR Lawrence 3d—Col'91 . . . . | 160 Gomez Av,
| Hobe Sound, FL
| *34955*

Flinn MR & MRS Michael de V (Hanes—Ann D | ☎ (203) 869-0271
Gulliver) Rcn.Mds.Fic.Plg.Rr.Ri.Ln.Cvc.Sar. | 295 Round Hill Rd,
Y'62.H'65 . . . . | Greenwich, CT
MISS Randall E—Pitzer'96 . . . . | *06831*
MR Michael de V JR—Cr'90 . . . . |
MR T Rex—Col'91 . . . . |
MISS Allison P Hanes—at ☎ (212) 245-0901
62 W 62 St, Apt 4B, New York, NY *10023* . .
MR Jonathan Y Hanes—CtCol'96

Flint MRS John Gardiner (Laura M Hancock)
☎ (309) 694-7016 . . Riverview 315, 500 Centennial Dv, East Peoria,
IL *61611-6767*

Flint MR & MRS Peter H (Karen R Gebhart) | ☎ (302) 652-7642
Ober'64.Wil.Y'64 . . . . | 205 Center Meeting
MR Peter H JR . . . . | Rd, Box 3971,
| Greenville, DE
| *19807*

Flint MRS Robert B (Lucile E du Pont) Wil.
☎ (302) 652-4172 . . PO Box 3763, Greenville, DE *19807*

Flood MR & MRS David B (Georgia A Clark) Pa'82.Del'78.Pitt'79
☎ (508) 356-3602 . . 141 County Rd, Ipswich, MA *01938*

Flood MR & MRS E Thomas 2d (Margaret E Bulas)
☎ (610) 869-7585 . . ''Paw Pad Farm'' 608 Coatesville Rd, West Grove,
PA *19390*

Flood MRS James (Elizabeth Dresser) Bur.Ny.
☎ (415) 851-7321 . . 331 Greer Rd, Woodside, CA *94062*

Flood MR & MRS James C (Astrid E Sommer) | ☎ (415) 751-5365
Bhm.Pcu.Ln.Bur.Stan'61 . . . . | 3742 Washington St,
MISS Elizabeth—Geo'89 . . . . | San Francisco, CA
MISS Karin—Geo'90 . . . . | *94118*
MISS Christina—Duke'93 . . . . |

Flood MISS Margaret . . see MRS R D Cushing

Flood MR & MRS Robert N (Josephine G Peyton) | ☎ (804) 295-9843
Sar.Va'36.Va'39 . . . . | 1701 Burnley Av,
MISS Mary E G—☎ (804) 979-2375 . . . . | Charlottesville, VA
| *22903*

Flood MR & MRS Terence C (Tribuno—Joan L Elmendorf) Cda.McG'47
☎ (970) 949-1782 . . PO Box 5750, Beaver Creek, CO *81620*

Florance MR Andrew C—Pn.P'86
☎ (301) 320-4948 . . 4948 Western Av, Chevy Chase, MD *20815*

Florance MR & MRS Colden L'H R (French—Wendy | ☎ (301) 733-2091
Nelson) Cvc.Mt.P'52.P'55 . . . . | Over the Mountain
MISS Ashley N French—Bost'92—at | Farm, 20032 Toms
435 E 65 St, New York, NY *10021* . . . . | Rd, Boonsboro, MD
| *21713*

Florian MR & MRS Paul A 3d (Marianna Bolognesi) ☎ (847) 256-7342
Cho.Ih.Cas.Cnt.Fr.Fy.Ch'42 . . . . 1630 Sheridan Rd,
MR Paul G—at Chicago, IL . . . . Apt 10M, Wilmette,
IL *60091*

Flöttl MR & MRS Wolfgang K (Echavarria—Flöttl—B Anne Eisenhower)
Cly.Vien'78.H.'81 . . of
☎ (441) 295-1590 . . 52 Tucker's Town Rd, St George HS 02, Bermuda
☎ (212) 879-3900 . . 1 E 66 St, New York, NY *10021*

Flour MR & MRS Jean-Michel (Alexandra S Berl) Srb . . .of
''Seaweed'' 740 Bellevue Av, PO Box 402, Newport, RI *02840*
☎ (011-33) 93-62-53-96 . . 17 rue Benoît Bunico, 06300 Nice, France

Flower MR & MRS Walter C 3d (Ella S Montgomery) of ☎ (504)899-5106
Ncmb'67.Tul'60.H'64 ⚓ . . . . 1604 Fourth St,
MISS Lindsey Montgomery—P'92—at Oxford New Orleans, LA
Grad *70130*
☎ (504) 892-0675
''Wildwood''
Wildwood Lane,
Covington, LA
70433

Flowers MR & MRS James P (Simon—Helen Kenny) H.Ga'49.Cl'52
☎ (212) 737-6136 . . 158 E 74 St, New York, NY *10021-3542*

Flowers MR John Baxton 3d—StJ.Cc.Cw.Wt.Rv. ☎ (706) 738-3228
Ht.ECar'71.NCar'73 . . . . ''Summerville''
MR John B K—Cc . . . . 1209-6 Monte Sano
Av, Augusta, GA
30904

Flowers MR & MRS Samuel R (Mildred K Coffman) ☎ (205) 879-9190
Ala'62.Ala'61 . . . . 4224 Harpers Ferry
JUNIORS MR Samuel R JR . . . . Rd, Birmingham,
AL *35213*

Floyd MR & MRS George R (Alicia L Iverson) ☎ (410) 465-5283
Mv.VPI'52 . . . . 10250 Burleigh
MISS Eleanor I—at ☎ (410) 785-4833 Cottage Lane,
PO Box 154, Butler, MD *21023* . . . . Ellicott City, MD
21043

Floyd MR & MRS J P Chadwick (Brenda C Huffman)
Cin'75.Y'80.Exy.Cc.Cw.Fw.Yn.Y'66.Y'73
☎ (860) 767-8412 . . 1 Teal Lane, Essex, CT *06426-1046*

Floyd MRS John Paul (Floyd—Kingsland—Maryan F Chadwick)
An.BtP.Ct.Evg.Hn . . .of
☎ (561) 655-2738 . . 3800 Washington Rd, Apt 404, West Palm Beach,
FL *33405*
☎ (202) 244-0574 . . 4201 Cathedral Av NW, Apt 23W, Washington,
DC *20016-4903*

Floyd-Jones MR & MRS William JR (Margaret A Herz)
SUNY'78.StJ'85.Pr.Bost'77.GeoW'81
☎ (516) 624-7415 . . PO Box 261, East Norwich, NY *11732-0261*

Fluegge MR H Henning von—Cl'56 . . . . RD 2, Box 1902,
MISS Isabel L von—Br'86—at 304 Mulberry St, Middlebury, VT
New York, NY *10012* *05753*
MISS Caroline S von—Tufts'88—at
1035 Penny Lane, Marietta, GA *30067* . . . .

Fluegge MRS Sigrid von (Sigrid von Hammerstein-Retzow)
RD 3, Box 3306, Goshen, VT *05733*

Flues MR & MRS A Gilmore (Anne L Jamieson) Cvc.Sl.P'26.H'29
☎ (301) 654-5388 . . 3519 Chevy Chase Lake Dv, Chevy Chase,
MD *20815*

Flurry MR & MRS R Luther 3d (Jarmila T Packard) Y'83.Y.'82
☎ (718) 768-3466 . . 527—9 St, Brooklyn, NY *11215*

Flynn MISS Abigail W . . see J Pulitzer 4th

Flynn MR & MRS Allan A A (Carlson—Judith L Lee)
Rc.Ck.Y.'53.Cl'59 ⚓
☎ (516) 365-8042 . . ''Willets Farmhouse'' 33 Willets Lane, Plandome,
NY *11030*

Flynn MR & MRS Charles W 3d (Joan D Burgher) V'42.StJ.P'41
☎ (214) 368-7609 . . 3939 Lovers Lane, Dallas, TX *75225*

Flynn MRS Patricia C (Patricia A Clarke) . . . . | ☎ (847) 234-1374
MISS Helen C . . . . | 319 E Woodland
MISS Robin V . . . . | Rd, Lake Forest, IL
MR Edward J . . . . | *60045*

Foerderer MISS Florence de R
☎ (717) 946-5113 . . ''Fly-Away'' Box 275, Rte 42, Laporte,
PA *18626-0275*

Fog MR & MRS Stephen C (Wendy M Dixon) | ☎ (203) 966-6002
Skd'75.Col'75 . . . . | 30 Siwanoy Lane,
JUNIORS MISS Merritt L—☎ (203) 966-6797 . . . . | New Canaan, CT
JUNIORS MISS Courtney A—☎ (203) 966-6797 . . | *06840*

Fogarty MR & MRS Edward T (Johnson—Mary S | ☎ (212) 472-5055
Elliott) H'57 . . . . | 137 E 66 St,
MISS Anne C . . . . | New York, NY
MR Edward A—Mid'95 . . . . |

Fogarty MR & MRS Gerald J JR (Sarah J Faile) CtCol'63.HolyC'63
☎ (401) 245-6676 . . 600 Middle H'way, Barrington, RI *02806*

Fogg MISS Daphne M . . see T A Corcoran

Fogg MRS George P JR (Frances C Knight) Cy.Chi.Ncd.
☎ (617) 566-2582 . . 61 Spooner Rd, Chestnut Hill, MA *02167*

Fogg MR & MRS George P 3d (Jane T Nichols) | ☎ (617) 566-3435
Sth'54.Cy.Chi . . . . | 91 Spooner Rd,
MISS (DR) Jane F—HRdc'87.Cl'93 . . . . | Chestnut Hill, MA
02167

Fogg MR & MRS Joseph G 3d (Leslie K Solbert) | of ☎ (516)626-1890
SL'69.H'71.Un.Csh.Mb.Ng.Pr.B.Nf.Ny.Y'68. | ''Four Winds''
H'70 . . . . | 1888 Muttontown
MISS Elizabeth P—at Yale . . . . | Rd, Muttontown,
MR Nathaniel T G—at Yale . . . . | NY *11791*
☎ (941) 434-7880
4295 Cutlass Lane,
Naples, FL
34102-7960

Folds MR & MRS Charles W (Beaton—Suzanne Lord) Ih.Cho.Cnt.Y'32
☎ (847) 446-0377 . . 1200 Whitebridge Hill, Winnetka, IL *60093*

Foley MISS Carolyn B—Dar . . . . | ☎ (212) 744-4091
MISS Lucy L—Dar.—at ☎ (212) 734-8692 | 130 East End Av,
120 East End Av, New York, NY *10028* . . . . . . | New York, NY
MISS Claire E—Dar.—at ☎ (212) 734-8692 | *10028*
120 East End Av, New York, NY *10028* . . . . . . |

Foley MR & MRS Gifford P (Harper—Ellen J Coale) | ☎ (561) 231-5374
Ih.Hav'32 . . . . | 715 Riomar Dv,
MISS Laura Coleman—Stan'78—at | Vero Beach, FL
2331 Hanover St, Palo Alto, CA *94306* . . . . . | *32963*

Foley MRS Gifford T (April J Hoxie)
Sth'69.H.'75.Y. . . . . ☎ (914) 533-6161
JUNIORS MISS Catherine L . . . . 45 Smith Ridge Rd,
JUNIORS MR Gifford T JR . . . . South Salem, NY
    10590
Foley MRS James E 3d (Jennifer A Seymour) Stan'84.Srb.Ncd.
    ☎ (415) 986-6267 . . 840 Powell St, Apt 501, San Francisco, CA *94108*
Foley MR James E 3d—Wk.Pcu.Srb.L.Me'75
    ☎ (401) 848-9709 . . ''Brenton Cottage'' 125 Brenton Rd, Newport,
RI *02840-4207*
Foley MRS Regula (Regula von Muralt) Ny.S.Cs . . .of
    ☎ (212) 570-2063 . . 525 E 80 St, New York, NY *10021*
    ☎ (516) 922-8108 . . Box 313, Seawanhaka Rd, Centre Island,
Oyster Bay, NY *11771*
    ☎ (011-41-22) 786-38-18 . . 24 rte de Malagnou, 1208 Geneva,
Switzerland
Foley MR Thomas C—Rcn.Ln.K.Ny.Hn.H'75.H'79 ⚓
    ☎ (203) 622-6250 . . 62 Khakum Wood Rd, Greenwich, CT *06831*
Folger MISS Elizabeth J—Pom'83.SFr'90
14 Rossi Av, San Francisco, CA *94118*
Folger MRS John Clifford (Kathrine Dulin)
Evg.BtP.Sl.Mt.Cvc.Cly. . . . . of ☎ (202)667-2991
MR John D—Cvc.Mt.B.H'53 . . . . 80 Kalorama Circle
    NW, Washington,
    DC *20008*
    ☎ (561) 655-5804
    400 S Ocean Blvd,
    Palm Beach, FL
    33480
Folger MR & MRS Lee M (Birmingham—Juliet Campbell)
Sbc.Bhm.Cvc.Mt.B.Ec.Sl.H'56
    ☎ (202) 332-8080 . . 725—15 St NW, Washington, DC *20005*
Folger MRS Peter (Beverly Mater)
405 El Camino Rd, Apt 221, Menlo Park, CA *94025*
Folger MR & MRS Peter M (Barbara B Waterman)
Bur.Pcu.Myf.Stan'67 . . . . ☎ (415) 386-5006
MISS Katharine B—Tufts'90.SFr'96 . . . . 3755 Jackson St,
MISS Sarah S—at Conn Coll . . . . San Francisco, CA
MISS Abiah A—at Trinity *94118-1608*
JUNIORS MR Peter . . . .
JUNIORS MR James A . . . .
Follansbee MRS N Walton (Nancy McM Walton)
Fcg. . . . . ☎ (412) 781-8929
MISS Nancy W . . . . 109 Buckingham
MISS Brooks W . . . . Rd, Pittsburgh, PA
    15215
Follett MRS (DR) Nancy E (Nancy P Ennis) Nw'62 . . of ☎ (011-44-1734)
MISS Daena L—at 1 Chemin du Nugent, 320-949
78610 St-Leger-en-Yvelines, France . . . . Hinton House,
MR Saul H . . . . Hurst, Berkshire
JUNIORS MISS Morgane M T . . . . RG10 0BP, England
    ☎ (011-44-1258)
    454-016
    ''Paddenswick''
    Old Dorchester Rd,
    Blandford Forum,
    Dorset DT11 0LX,
    England

Follett MR & MRS William R (Barbara D Wickersham)
Sim'83.Snc.Sar.Ofp.Dar.GreenMt'83
    ☎ (203) 978-0644 . . 30 Birchwood Rd, Stamford, CT *06907*
Follis MRS R Gwin (O Ann Young) StJ . . . . ☎ (415) 931-1313
MR James G—Pcu.P'55—at ☎ (707) 895-3665 3690 Washington St,
PO Box 346, Philo, CA *95466* . . . . San Francisco, CA
    94118
Foltz MR & MRS Charles R (Pullman—Elinor C Notz)
On.H'60.Paris'61.H'64
    ☎ (847) 234-2330 . . 1380 N Elm Tree Rd, Lake Forest, IL *60045*
Fondaras MR & MRS Anastassios (Miller—Weicker—
Elizabeth T Robertson) Ri.Mds.Cly.H'53 . . of
    ☎ (212) 988-0839 . . 2 E 70 St, New York, NY *10021*
    ☎ (011-33-1) 43-25-16-18 . . 18 quai d'Orleans, 75004 Paris, France
Foote MR Douglass G—Cr'43
    ☎ (615) 352-3764 . . 105 Lincoln Court, Nashville, TN *37205*
Foote MR & MRS Douglass G JR (Lisa C Bass) LakeF'82
    ☎ (615) 352-0972 . . 6201 Robin Hill Rd, Nashville, TN *37205*
Foote MR & MRS Edward T 2d (Roberta W
Fulbright) Cal'60.Y'59 . . . . ☎ (305) 666-7715
MR Edward T 3d . . . . 8565 Old Cutler Rd,
    Coral Gables, FL
    33143
Foote MRS Hastings 2d (Cottier—Felicity Wottrich)
Snc.Eyc. . . . . ☎ (203) 869-9373
MR H E Jochi—at ☎ (304) 258-5304 339 Round Hill Rd,
RR 1, Box 456L, Berkeley Springs, WV *25411* . Greenwich, CT
    06831
Foote MR & MRS Richard L (Woods—M Daniele of ☎ (860)434-2660
Hampton) ShenCons'58.WConn'85.Ey.Cl'50 . . . ''Three Chimneys''
MISS Elizabeth R—Emer'92 . . . . PO Box 335,
MR Richard L JR . . . . 172 Brush Hill Rd,
    Lyme, CT *06371*
    ☎ (203) 434-2660
    ''Hampton Heights''
    12 Hillcrest Court,
    Ridgefield, CT
    06877
Foote MR & MRS Robert L (Barbara K Austin) ☎ (847) 835-1480
V'40.Csn.Y'38.H'41 . . . . 587 Longwood Av,
MISS Marion R—at ☎ (312) 664-2691 Glencoe, IL *60022*
1209 N Astor St, Chicago, IL *60610* . . . .
Foote MR William F R
    ☎ (516) 325-1014 . . Box 322, 146 S Country Rd, Remsenburg,
NY *11960*
Foraker MISS Julia B
    ☎ (202) 234-8841 . . 3133 Connecticut Av NW, Apt 825, Washington,
DC *20008*
Forbes MR & MRS Alexander C (I Helen Robbins) Sbc.Sm.My.H'32 . . of
    ☎ (561) 622-9132 . . 11772 Lake House Dv, North Palm Beach,
FL *33408*
    ☎ (508) 526-4904 . . 4 Blossom Lane, Manchester, MA *01944*
Forbes MR Charles B W (late Charles W) . . . Married at Sydney, Australia
Welsh MISS Tara-Jane (Christopher) . . . . Oct 21'94
Forbes MR & MRS Charles Stewart (Dorothy Lockwood) Cy.H.'61 . . of
    ☎ (617) 522-5753 . . 18 Slocum Rd, Jamaica Plain, MA *02130*
    ☎ (508) 994-1544 . . ''Birchfield Farm'' 4 South Lane,
South Dartmouth, MA *02748*

Forbes MR & MRS Christopher C (BRNSS Astrid M
von Heyl) K.C.Eh.Gr.Plg.StJ.P'72 . . . .
  MISS Charlotte A M . . . .
☎ (908) 234-9483
"Timberfield"
95 Old Dutch Rd,
Far Hills, NJ *07931*

Forbes MISS Diana (Lloyd—Closson—Diana Forbes) BMr'54.Ec.
  ☎ (508) 356-4109 . . 7 Juniper St, Box 328, Ipswich, MA *01938*

Forbes MR Douglas B (H A Crosby) . . . . Married at Boston, MA
  Spiro MISS Laura M (Lionel) . . . . Jun 15'96

Forbes MR & MRS Douglas B (Laura M Spiro) Cl'96
  ☎ (212) 579-0905 . . 127 W 79 St, Apt 5A, New York, NY *10024*

Forbes MR & MRS Edward K (Martha C Phemister)
Br'62 . . . .
  MR Scott R—at Portland, ME . . . .
  MR Christopher K—Colby'88—at Boulder, CO .
of ☎ (617)237-6464
62 Leighton Rd,
Wellesley Hills, MA
02181
☎ (207) 967-4648
"Instead"
Goose Rocks Beach,
Kennebunkport, ME
04046

Forbes MR & MRS Elliot (Kathleen B Allen) V'38.Hn.H'40
  ☎ (617) 864-6787 . . 975 Memorial Dv, Apt 210, Cambridge, MA *02138*

Forbes MR F Murray—Tv.Sm.Ub.Camb'27
  ☎ (508) 526-1238 . . 15 Old Neck Rd, Manchester, MA *01944*

Forbes MR & MRS Francis C (Eleanor Ainsworth)
Sth'39.Rb.Sa.Ll.Fw.Cspa.Cw.Rv.Wt.Pa'41 . . . . .
  MR Tench C—Ll.Cc.Cw.Duke'80—at
  ☎ (617) 643-4117 . . Box 1464, West Concord,
MA *01742* . . . .
☎ (610) 296-3997
1303 Weatherstone
Dv, Paoli, PA *19301*

Forbes MR Gordon D
see Dilatory Domiciles

Forbes MR & MRS Griswold (Martha Moffett) P'41.Cl'49
  ☎ (203) 438-8197 . . "Oak Knoll" 154 Barry Av, Ridgefield, CT *06877*

Forbes MR & MRS H A Crosby (Grace W Pierce) Rdc'49.H'50.H'62
  ☎ (617) 864-9833 . . 38 Arlington St, Cambridge, MA *02140*

Forbes MRS Howard M (Celeste S Terry) Sth'23
  ☎ (617) 275-0451 . . Carleton-Willard Village, Llewsac Lodge 211,
Bedford, MA *01730*

Forbes DR & MRS John Douglas (Mary E Lewis)
CarnM'75.Pcu.Cp.Cal'31.Stan'32.H'37 ⛵ . . .
  JUNIORS MR Michael . . . .
☎ (804) 295-9410
PO Box 3607,
Charlottesville, VA
22903

Forbes MR & MRS Malcolm S JR (Sabina C
Beekman) Gr.Plg.P'70 . . . .
  MISS Roberta A . . . .
  MISS Sabina B . . . .
  MISS Catherine I . . . .
  MISS Moira S . . . .
☎ (908) 234-2175
"Southdown"
Burnt Mills Rd,
Bedminster, NJ
07921

Forbes MRS Natalie S (Natalie Saltonstall) Br'62 . . .
  MISS Heidi C—Col'95—at 811—9 St, Boulder,
CO *80302* . . . .
☎ (508) 369-5456
67 Bow St, Concord,
MA *01742*

Forbes MISS P Seton—GeoW'74.BritCl'88
  ☎ (604) 733-7594 . . 925 Lameys Mill Rd, Vancouver, BC V6H 3P4,
Canada

Forbes MRS Pamela (Johnson—McLane—Pamela
Forbes) Rdc'60.Tcy. . . . .
  MISS Sophia F McLane—Occ'94 . . . .
☎ (415) 927-0737
PO Box 564,
Corte Madera, CA
94976

Forbes MR & MRS Peter (Erica L de Berry)
Mid'90.Rcn.Nrr.C.Mich'66.Y'67 . . . .
  MISS Anne de M . . . .
  MR Alexander J . . . .
☎ (617) 227-9140
65 E India Row,
Boston, MA *02110*

Forbes MR & MRS Robert L (Raurell-Soto—Lydia S
Appel) Cl'95.Rc.Shcc.Eh.NCar'71 . . . .
  MR A Miguel Raurell-Soto . . . .
of ☎ (212)620-2460
211 Central Park W,
New York, NY
10024
"Timberfield"
95 Old Dutch Rd,
Far Hills, NJ *07931*

Forbes MISS Siena Seton (g—James Tyson Carson) . . . . Born at
Sydney, Australia Aug 25'95

Forbes MR & MRS Timothy C (Anne S Harrison) Br'76
  ☎ (212) 228-4160 . . 60 W 11 St, New York, NY *10011*

Forbes MRS Wallace F (Betty A Goldsmith) Sth'53
  ☎ (212) 628-0185 . . 174 E 74 St, New York, NY *10021*

Forbes MR Wallace F—P.'49 . . . .
  MISS Alexandra E—at 30 W 86 St, New York,
NY *10024* . . . .
  MR Bruce C . . . .
☎ (914) 941-8341
609 Sleepy Hollow
Rd, Briarcliff
Manor, NY *10510*

Forbes DR & MRS William I 3d (Barbara L
Frederick) P'64.ThosJef'72.ThosJef'73 . . . .
  MSRS David S & William F—at Colonial Towers
H6, 27 E Central Av, Paoli, PA *19301* . . . .
☎ (315) 629-5754
27815 Call Rd,
PO Box 309,
Evans Mills, NY
13637

Forbes MR & MRS William Innes (Catharine H Patterson)
Me.Gm.Rb.Cc . . .of
  ☎ (610) 527-2227 . . 1205 Denbigh Lane, Radnor, PA *19087*
  ☎ (561) 278-2788 . . The Landings, 790 Andrews Av, Apt 104A,
Delray Beach, FL *33483*

Forcier MRS Guy S (Nancy Marshall) Sth'49.Nd.Bv.Rr.
  ☎ (314) 994-0089 . . 3 Cricklewood Place, St Louis, MO *63131*

Ford MR & MRS A James (Ruth A Jenkins) Menlo'37
  ☎ (916) 929-5020 . . 907 Commons Dv, Sacramento, CA *95825*

Ford MR & MRS Alfred W (Catharina Skjöldebrand)
Cal'58 . . . .
  MISS Christina W—at HCR 01, Box 11,
Lake Placid, NY *12946* . . . .
  MR Thomas W . . . .
of ☎ (301)229-2983
5435 Mohican Rd,
Bethesda, MD
20816
☎ (207) 633-6857
"Pine Cliff"
HCR 66, Box 473,
Pine Cliff Rd,
West Southport, ME
04576

Ford MR & MRS Brin R (Joy Winder) H'64 . . . .
  MISS Brinley S—at ☎ (203) 966-9982
6 Ledge Av, New Canaan, CT *06840* . . . .
  MISS Jennifer M—at ☎ (505) 820-2495
836A E Palace Av, Santa Fe, NM *87501* . . . . . .
☎ (203) 776-9532
411 Temple St,
New Haven, CT
06511

Ford MR & MRS Bruce G (A Laurie Garner) WakeF'84.StA.WakeF'85
  ☎ (757) 238-2448 . . 8020 Clubhouse Dv, Suffolk, VA *23433*

Ford MR & MRS Christopher P (Laura A Noonan) Va'85 . . of
320 E 57 St, New York, NY *10022*
  ☎ (203) 869-4588 . . "Meadowbrook" 72 Doubling Rd, Greenwich,
CT *06830*

Ford MR & MRS Daniel B JR (Cornelia A Manuel) Y'55 . . . . ☎ (508) 255-4135 50 Defiance Lane, Orleans, MA *02653*
  MISS Elise M—at Bayview Dv, Orleans, MA *02653*
  MR Daniel B 3d

Ford MRS Espy (S Carlotta Espy) Sth'33.Ncd.
  ☎ (912) 238-4741 . . 535 E 52 St, Savannah, GA *31405*

Ford MRS Eugene E (Vera E McNamara) May.Un.It. . . . . ☎ (216) 752-2993 2948 Courtland Blvd, Shaker Heights, OH *44122*
  MR Anthony M—at 10676 Weymouth St, Bethesda, MD *20814*

Ford MR & MRS F Richards 3d (Pray—Natasha Boissevain) Man'vl'77.B.P'50.Va'53 . . . . ☎ (203) 869-4975 16 Doverton Dv, Greenwich, CT *06831*
  MISS Melanie B Pray

Ford MR F Richards 4th—Ithaca'79 . . see MRS M H Lewis

Ford MR Frank Richards—Unn.Ny.Pqt.Evg.P'26
  ☎ (203) 259-1573 . . "Driftway" 307 Willow St, Box 307, Southport, CT *06490*

Ford MR & MRS Gerald R (Warren—Elizabeth Bloomer) Bhm.Mich'35.Y'41
  ☎ (619) 324-1763 . . Rancho Mirage, CA *92270*

Ford MR & MRS Gerard F (Martin—Margaret W Howe) . . . . ☎ (516) 751-4244 19 Hopewell Dv, Stony Brook, NY *11790*
  MISS Katharine W Martin—at 1517 Crete St, New Orleans, LA *70119*
  MR John T Martin—at 4506 Speedway St, Austin, TX *78751*

Ford MR & MRS H Ross (Louisa C Gurney) Shcc.StA.Leh'55
  ☎ (908) 766-2333 . . "Clarkspur" 80 Clark Rd, Bernardsville, NJ *07924*

Ford MR H Ross 3d—FairD'89
  ☎ (214) 241-5326 . . 14608 Tanglewood Dv, Farmers Branch, TX *75234*

Ford MR & MRS James A (Elizabeth L Brooks) Hn.H'37 . . . . ☎ (704) 684-7062 155 Carrie Lane, Fletcher, NC *28732*
  MISS (DR) Mary E—SCar'81—at Tupelo Rd, Elgin, SC *29405*
  MR James A JR—at 285 Acton St, Carlisle, MA *01741*
  MR William T

Ford MR & MRS Jeremiah 3d (Stewardson— Elizabeth M Dana) MtH'58.P'54.P'59 . . . . ☎ (609) 921-2412 820 Pretty Brook Rd, Princeton, NJ *08540*
  MISS Caroline C Stewardson—Bost'87—at ☎ (508) 228-9161 . . Nantucket, MA *02554* . .

Ford MR & MRS Joe T (Jo Ellen Wilbourn) Ark'59.Pk.Ark'59
  ☎ (501) 664-1363 . . 2100 Country Club Lane, Little Rock, AR *72207*

Ford MR & MRS John B (Low—Mary Holland) Cly.Ncd.
  ☎ (313) 885-2377 . . 35 Winthrop Place, Grosse Pointe Farms, MI *48236*
  Jan 1 . . ☎ (561) 546-2581 . . PO Box 353, Hobe Sound, FL *33475*

Ford MR John H—Rc.Mich'47
  ☎ (314) 534-1146 . . 4440 Lindell Blvd, St Louis, MO *63108*

Ford MR & MRS Jonathan (Barbara M Hotaling) Cv.W&L'38
  ☎ (216) 693-4126 . . "Boxwood House" 7767 Parkman Mespo Rd, RD 2, Middlefield, OH *44062*

Ford MRS Lucile (Novi—Lucile Ford Schoettle)
  ☎ (212) 838-8761 . . 200 E 66 St, Apt 1806B, New York, NY *10021*

Ford MISS Mariah Hope—Champ'88 . . see MRS M H Lewis

Ford MR & MRS Mills H (M Elise Mallon) CtCol'74.Canis'82.DU'68.DU'72 . . of
  ☎ (303) 798-9629 . . 1894 E Orchard Rd, Littleton, CO *80121*
  ☎ (941) 964-0494 . . 1140—11 St, PO Box 606, Boca Grande, FL *33921*

Ford MISS Naneen E—Cly.
  ☎ (212) 570-6552 . . 169 E 69 St, New York, NY *10021*

Ford MR & MRS Norbert M (Ludlow C Boyd)
  ☎ (011-353-1) 280-1461 . . "Mornington House" Sandycove Point, Co Dublin, Ireland

Ford MR & MRS Peter B (Amanda C Millspaugh) Bost'78 ⚓ . . . . ☎ (561) 234-4749 1789 Coral Way S, Vero Beach, FL *32963*
  MISS Jessica B

Ford MR & MRS Quintin U (Wheeler—Barbara A Burdick) Rcn.Pa'42
  ☎ (203) 655-1066 . . 660 Hollow Tree Ridge Rd, Darien, CT *06820*

Ford MR & MRS Robert D (Barbara Johnston) Bhm.Bur.Pcu.Sfy.Tcy.Stan'36
  ☎ (415) 454-1984 . . PO Box 235, Ross, CA *94957*

Ford MRS Sydney B (Enid Sharp) . . . . | 77 Harrison Av, Sausalito, CA *94965*
  MR Glenn T—at Los Angeles, CA . . . .
  MR Robert C

Ford MR & MRS Thomas P (Dolph—Mary L McGovern) MaryMt'53.Ri.Evg.NotreD'40.H'43
  MR William McG . . . . of ☎ (561) 845-1510 315 Tangier Av, Palm Beach, FL *33480*
  ☎ (203) 245-7723 154 Middle Beach Rd, Madison, CT *06443*

Ford MRS William D (Robinson—Helen Pidgeon). H.
  ☎ (212) 752-7824 . . 30 Sutton Place, New York, NY *10022*

Fordyce MRS Dorothy M (Dorothy W MacElree) Cl'47.Gm.
  ☎ (610) 527-0211 . . 74 Pasture Lane, Bryn Mawr, PA *19010*

Fordyce MR S Wesley 5th—Geo'78.Pa'84
  ☎ (314) 831-2223 . . "Beaux Eaux" 2701 Shackelford Rd, Florissant, MO *63031*

Fordyce MRS William C (Kluckhohn—Elizabeth D Russe) Sth'34.Nd.Cw.Ncd . . .of
  ☎ (314) 725-7458 . . 709 S Skinker Blvd, St Louis, MO *63105*
  ☎ (314) 482-4007 . . Fordyce Farm, 550 Crow Creek Lane, Augusta, MO *63332*

Foreman MISS Nell—Sth'80.Cl'88.Ck.Me.Ht.H.
  ☎ (212) 972-8914 . . 330 E 39 St, New York, NY *10016*

Foreman MR Winfield A 3d—Me.Rcp.Ste.Ht.Rv.Pa'80.Pa'83
  ☎ (310) 453-1259 . . 1164 Berkeley St, Apt C, Santa Monica, CA *90403*

Forgan MR J Russell—Rc.B.BtP.Plg.P'52 . . of
  ☎ (561) 659-0421 . . 353 Seaspray Av, Palm Beach, FL *33480*
  ☎ (212) 980-6576 . . 200 E 66 St, New York, NY *10021*

Forker MRS David M (Elizabeth Nichols) . . . . | ☎ (513) 321-3630 2243 Grandin Rd, Cincinnati, OH *45208*
  MR David M 3d—at 1610 Crest Dv, Columbus, GA *31906*

Forman MR & MRS Edward J (Lesley B Schwab) Conv'65.Cl'65 . . . . | 24 Westwood Rd, West Hartford, CT *06117*
  MR Peter B—at St Lawrence U
  JUNIORS MR James B—at St Paul's
  JUNIORS MR Edward M—at St Paul's

Forney MR G David JR—P'61 . . . . ☎ (617) 868-4855
MR Mark H—P'88—at ☎ (510) 548-9625 | 6 Coolidge Hill Rd,
1614 Edith St, Berkeley, CA *94703* . . . . | Cambridge, MA
MR William McD—P'93 . . . . | *02138*
Forrestal MRS Peter O (Katherine N Callahan) Bard'65.Srb.
☎ (212) PL2-5779 . . 435 E 52 St, New York, NY *10022*
Forrestel MR & MRS Richard E JR (Annabelle V Irey)
P'80.VillaN'84.Cy.Ac.Pp.P'80.Mich'82
☎ (716) 839-2317 . . 171 Darwin Dv, Snyder, NY *14226*
Forrester MR & MRS Peter C (Edith W Brooks) | ☎ (617) 536-0225
D.Un.Bost'66 | 136 Beacon St,
MISS Melinda B—LakeF'90—at | Boston, MA *02116*
☎ (617) 536-4120 . . 233 Beacon St, Boston, MA
02116 . . . .
Forrester MR & MRS Robert R JR (Lilley—Elena Musto)
Evg.Mds.Cly.H.'30 . . of
☎ (561) 278-2497 . . 3550 Gulfstream Rd, Gulf Stream, FL *33483*
☎ (516) 324-1967 . . PO Box 1397, East Hampton, NY *11937*
Forsberg MRS Torsten P (Beatrice V Moore) Cda.Dar.
☎ (203) 637-2787 . . 11 Quintard Av, Old Greenwich, CT *06870*
Forsch MRS Peter D (Barbara W Booth) Dar . . .of
☎ (203) 869-3628 . . 12 Will Mary Lane, Greenwich, CT *06831*
☎ (441) 238-1346 . . ''Wynk Beyond'' 20 Riddell's Bay Rd,
Warwick WK 06, Bermuda
Forster MR Bayard S—Rcn.Rv.Plg.H.'44
☎ (561) 820-8875 . . 1701 S Flagler Dv, Apt 501, West Palm Beach,
FL *33401*
Forster MR & MRS Christopher A (Elizabeth M | ☎ (212) AT9-2193
Cheston) Sth'56.Y.'54 . . . . | 1105 Park Av,
MISS Emily C—Colg'90—at ☎ (206) 729-0651 | New York, NY
6522 Fourth Av NE, Seattle, WA *98115* . . . . . . | *10128*
MR David A—Y'86—at ☎ (011-44-171)
373-1172 . . 58 Lexham Gardens, London W8 JA,
England . . . .
Forster MR Gerald M—StL'72 . . . . | 12922 Huntercreek
MISS Christine . . . . | Rd, St Louis, MO
MISS Jean M . . . . | *63131*
JUNIORS MR G Mark JR
Forster MR & MRS Hamilton F (Elizabeth Hartz) | ☎ (212) 534-4452
Shcc.H.'54 . . . . | 1158 Fifth Av,
MISS Elisabeth E . . . . | New York, NY
MISS Laura L—Col'92 . . . . | *10029*
Forster DR & MRS Robert E 2d (Elizabeth H Day) | ☎ (610) 649-9348
BMr'47.Sim'49.Ph.Me.Y.'41.Pa'43 . . . . | 501 Oakley Rd,
MISS Julia B—Syr'74—at 136 Highland Av, | Haverford, PA
Somerville, MA *02143* . . . . | *19041-1212*
Forsthoff MR & MRS Mark A (Marylee W Littell) Barat'87.Ht.Dar.
☎ (847) 398-7240 . . 1221 W Clarendon Rd, Arlington Heights,
IL *60004*
Forsyth MR William H—C.P'30
☎ (609) 426-6277 . . Meadow Lakes 44-08, Etra Rd, Hightstown,
NJ *08520-3349*
Fort MISS Betty Carter—Sth'44.Cvc.An.
☎ (202) 333-4789 . . 3537 Edmunds St NW, Washington, DC *20007*
Fort MISS Chloe F (Lenderman—Chloe F Fort) Swb'62.Cda.
☎ (615) 292-4314 . . 430 Sunnyside Dv, Nashville, TN *37205*

Fort MRS William L (Preston—Doris Alford) Cly.
☎ (212) 832-9023 . . 139 E 63 St, New York, NY *10021*
Forté MR & MRS Donald (Mason—Joan Jackson) Chi.Ncd.H.'43
☎ (941) 261-3085 . . 3291 Green Dolphin Lane, Naples, FL *34102*
Forte MR & MRS Earl M JR (Emilie H Thornton) Rc.Me.Ncd.Pa'50
☎ (610) 688-6008 . . 230 Steeplechase Rd, Devon, PA *19333-1231*
Forte MR Earl M 3d—Rc.Pa'79.SanDiego'85
☎ (610) 254-0467 . . 485 Red Fox Rd, Strafford, PA *19087*
Fortenbaugh MR & MRS Michael W (Sharon L Phair) P'85
☎ (908) 362-6343 . . 31 Gaisler Rd, Blairstown, NJ *07825-9665*
Fortune MRS George C (Helen Hind) . . . . Died at
Carmel, CA Jly 13'96
Fosbroke MRS (DR) Gerald E (Spencer—L Lindley Powers)
Sth'48.Wis'63.Wis'68
☎ (508) 540-4043 . . 70 Carey Lane, Quissett Harbor, Falmouth,
MA *02540*
Fosbroke MR Gerald E—Md'37.Md'38.H'41
PO Box 844, Wrentham, MA *02093*
Fosburgh MRS Helen E (Helen B Edwards)
☎ (212) LE5-6670 . . 108 E 82 St, New York, NY *10028*
Fosburgh MR & MRS James H E (E Blair Wardenburg) H'86.Y'86.Y'91
21 Chester St, Winchester, MA *01890*
Fosburgh MR & MRS P Whitney JR (Abbie B Littlejohn)
Stan'83.Tufts'88.Geo'84.Y'88
☎ (202) 338-4060 . . 4887 MacArthur Blvd NW, Washington, DC *20007*
Fosburgh MRS Pieter W (Cunningham—M Elizabeth Edmondson) MtH'51
☎ (518) 658-2502 . . PO Box 29, Cherry Plain, NY *12040*
Foshay MR & MRS William W JR (Adrianne P L | ☎ (540) 854-4923
Dormer) Rcn.Br'61 . . . . | ''Analoch Farm''
MISS Thomasin A—Swb'93 . . . . | 21060 Monrovia Rd,
MR William W 3d—H'93 . . . . | Orange, VA *22960*
JUNIORS MR Alexander P R
Foss MRS Eugene N 2d (M Winifred Brown) Chi.Ncd.
☎ (617) 329-1452 . . Fox Hill Village 505A, 10 Longwood Dv,
Westwood, MA *02090*
Foss MR & MRS George E 3d (Bonnet—Sara S | ☎ (603) 823-5571
Crane) Br'62.Ne'67 . . . . | ''Brayton Cottage''
JUNIORS MISS Eleanor D . . . . | Sunset Rd, Box 751,
Franconia, NH
03580
Foss MR Lyman S—Col'73 . . . . | ☎ (802) 867-4492
JUNIORS MISS Charlotte M . . . . | Manchester, VT
05255-1111
Foss MR & MRS Paul W (Karen A McGlinchey)
NH'70.Cl'81.NH'70.INSEAD'71
☎ (603) 823-7194 . . 13 Carriage House, Dow Academy St, Franconia,
NH *03580*
Foss MRS Virginia V (Virginia L Vincent)
RR 1, Box 145, Dorset, VT *05251*
Foss MRS Wilson P (Mae K Chandlee) Bgt . . .of
440 Bowline Dv, Naples, FL *34103*
Holly Hill Lane, Katonah, NY *10536*
Fossel MR & MRS Scott G (Petria M Horner)
Rdc'73.Cl'80.Au.Yn.LakeF'75.Dth'77
☎ (203) 629-4720 . . 5 Winterset Rd, Greenwich, CT *06830*
Foster MR Allen S . . . . Died at
Saratoga, CA Mch 22'96

Foster MR Benjamin B JR
☎ (415) 883-1482 . . 111 Panorama Dv, Novato, CA *94949*

Foster MR & MRS Benjamin R (Karen J Polinger) | ☎ (203) 284-9258
MtH'71.Y'76.P'68.Y'75 . . . . | 40 Jones Rd,
JUNIORS MISS Constance . . . . | Wallingford, CT
JUNIORS MISS Ruth . . . . | *06492*

Foster MR & MRS Charles H W (Barbara Duchaine)
Ant'53.D.H.'51.Mich'53.Mich'56.JHop'69
☎ (617) 444-6266 . . 484 Charles River St, Needham, MA *02192*

Foster MR Christopher P (Nancy H Pomeroy) Bost'86
☎ (860) 342-1352 . . 399 Main St, Portland, CT *06480*

Foster MISS Cornelia A—Cal'73
2560 Polk St, Apt 12, San Francisco, CA *94109*

Foster MR Daniel W—R.Me.Fst.Hav'69
☎ (610) 296-0945 . . 419 Littlebrook Rd, Berwyn, PA *19312*

Foster MR & MRS David V (Judith N Kurz) | of ☎ (212)873-5723
K.Fic.C.H'68 . . . . | 215 W 91 St, Apt
JUNIORS MISS Julia K . . . . | 32, New York, NY
JUNIORS MISS Lily A . . . . | *10024*
| ☎ (914) 424-4240
| PO Box 277,
| Travis Corners Rd,
| Garrison, NY *10524*

Foster MISS Frances H (Simons—Frances H Foster) P'77.Y'81.Stan'87.Pn.
☎ (314) 726-3443 . . 750 S Hanley Rd, Apt 430, Clayton, MO *63105*

Foster MISS Gail M—Cr'82.Geo'95
☎ (703) 558-0448 . . 2100 Lee H'way, Apt 119, Arlington, VA *22201*

Foster DR & MRS Giraud Vernam (Carolyn E | of ☎ (410)323-1275
Lindquist) Me'51.Ht.Cly.Mv.Ty'52.Md'56. | 917 Poplar Hill Rd,
Lond'66 . . . . | Baltimore, MD
MISS Nicola B—Ws'90 . . . . | *21210*
| ☎ (803) 768-2307
| 2247 Catesby's
| Bluff, Seabrook
| Island, Johns Island,
| SC *29455*

Foster MR Glen S—Ny.S.Br'52
☎ (212) 486-0969 . . 1 Beekman Place, New York, NY *10022*

Foster MRS Gray S (Charlot R Childress) BtP.Ncd. . | ☎ (561) 655-5263
MR Eugene Hegeman—Rol'57.Mainz'61—at | 227 Brazilian Av,
☎ (212) 935-3936 . . 348 E 58 St, Apt 6A, | Palm Beach, FL
New York, NY *10022* . . . . | *33480*

Foster MR & MRS H Crosby 2d (Sally D Harrison) | ☎ (970) 926-5466
Eyc.Ihy.Pa'61 . . . . | 61 Foal Circle,
MR H Crosby 3d—Leh'92—at 394 Marlborough | PO Box 1371,
St, Boston, MA *02115* . . . . | Edwards, CO
| *81632-1371*

Foster MR & MRS Herbert H 3d (Christine T | ☎ (914) 241-0570
Paddock) Bgt.Bost'69 . . . . | 81 Springhurst Rd,
MR Franklin H—at Middlebury . . . . | Bedford Hills, NY
JUNIORS MR Charles W . . . . | *10507*

Foster MR Howard C—Cal'69.Ore'75.Cal'93
☎ (510) 848-1241 . . 14 Panoramic Way, Berkeley, CA *94704*

Foster MRS Howard H (Dorothy J Ernst)
☎ (908) 224-7670 . . 40 Riverside Av, Apt 6B, Red Bank, NJ *07701*

Foster MRS Hugh K (Barbara Hunter) Cal'55.A.Sl. . | ☎ (805) 566-9300
MISS Adelaide E—H'88—at 15870 Bridger | 3293 Padaro Lane,
Canyon Rd, Bozeman, MT *59715* . . . . | Carpinteria, CA
MISS Jennifer B F—at 1026 Gold Brook Rd, | *93013*
Stowe, VT *05672* . . . . |
MR Hugh K JR—at 398 Columbus Av, Box 291, |
Boston, MA *02116* . . . . |

Foster MR & MRS Hugh W (Frances E Dillingham) | ☎ (415) 923-1213
Bur.Pcu.Cc.Colg'65.Stan'69 . . . . | 2712 Broadway St,
MISS Edwina—Stan'93 . . . . | San Francisco, CA
MISS Tamsin E—Tul'96—at ☎ (504) 588-9021 | *94115*
410 Dauphine St, Apt 23, New Orleans, LA |
70112 . . . . |
LT Charles A 3d—USN.—at ☎ (415) 391-4456 |
2130 Stockton St, Apt 109, San Francisco, CA |
94133 . . . . |
JUNIORS MISS H Skye—at Thacher Sch . . . . |
JUNIORS MR Hugh W JR—at Thacher Sch . . . . . . |

Foster MISS Jane de M (Lorber—Reece—Jane de M | of ☎ (561)659-1139
Foster) Finch'70.Nf.Cly.BtP. . . . . | 17 Middle Rd,
JUNIORS MISS Augusta H B Lorber—at | Palm Beach, FL
St Mark's . . . . | *33480*
JUNIORS MR Giraud van N F Lorber . . . . | ☎ (212) 988-0328
| 71 E 71 St,
| New York, NY
| *10021*

Foster MRS Lucy C S (Lucy C Sprague) SL'51.Mv . . .of
☎ (410) 833-0360 . . 12700 Bonita Av, Glyndon, MD *21071*
☎ (904) 635-0127 . . ''Chimney's'' Drawer B, Cumberland Island,
Fernandina Beach, FL *34035*

Foster MRS M Reed (Marion Reed Keator)
☎ (203) 259-4789 . . 952 Old Post Rd, Fairfield, CT *06430*

Foster MR & MRS Malcolm C (Marie du P Ryburn) | ☎ (410) 757-3092
Tufts'77.Colby'75.Wes'77 . . . . | 1155 Willow Lane,
JUNIORS MISS Merrill H . . . . | Beacon Hill,
JUNIORS MISS Lindsay R . . . . | Annapolis, MD
| *21401*

Foster MR & MRS Mark E (Cornelia M Adams)
BMr'78.Tex'82.Cly.TexTech'79.Tex'82
☎ (512) 453-2723 . . 5204 Ridge Oak Dv, Austin, TX *78731*

Foster MR & MRS Patrick A (Jane C Rogers) . . . . . | 693 Lobelia Court,
MISS Lynne R—at 17 W 67 St, New York, NY | Sonoma, CA *95476*
10023 . . . . |

Foster MR Paul S JR . . . . Died at
San Francisco, CA Dec 26'95

Foster MRS Paul S JR (Lowe—Barbara Keast) Fr. . . | ☎ (415) 921-0926
MISS Barbara Lowe—at 2252 Bronson Hill Dv, | 3610 Washington St,
Los Angeles, CA *90068* . . . . | San Francisco, CA
| *94118*

Foster MR & MRS Paul S 3d (Jane E McLaughlin) | ☎ (415) 383-6817
Bhm.Cal'66 . . . . | 305 Hillside Av,
MR Scott M . . . . | Mill Valley, CA
JUNIORS MR Brian A . . . . | *94941*

Foster MR & MRS Reginald 3d (Mary G Warren) BMr'54.Ec.Myc.Yn.Y'53
☎ (508) 526-4454 . . 19 Highland Av, Manchester, MA *01944*

Foster MRS Reuben (Eleanor Whiteley) . . . . | ☎ (410) 323-4499
MISS Sally L . . . . | 213 Edgevale Rd,
| Baltimore, MD
| *21210*
Foster MR & MRS Richard W (Elizabeth Read)
V'33.Cl'34.Y'38.Ph.R.Fi.Fst.Me.Pa'31
☎ (610) 688-1673 . . 205 Strafford Av, Wayne, PA *19087*
Foster MR & MRS Ridgely M (Dinkel—Leta F | ☎ (561) 655-5489
Austin) Hlns'62.BtP.Nf.Cda.Cly. . . . . | ''The Grey House''
MR Varick P . . . . | 345 Pendleton Lane,
JUNIORS MISS India R—at Groton . . . . | Palm Beach, FL
MISS Sallie C F Dinkel—at ☎ (212) 421-5918 | *33480*
424 E 52 St, New York, NY *10022* . . . .
Foster MRS Robert N (Mary C Kuhl) Nw'48
☎ (520) 325-3107 . . 4201 E Cooper St, Tucson, AZ *85711*
Foster MR & MRS Rockwood H (Marguerite Peet) | of ☎ (202)965-3951
Sth'47.Mt.Cvc.Ct.Sl.H'45 . . . . | 3047 W Lane Keys
MR Adam R—at ☎ (310) 396-2523 | NW, Washington,
2102—5 St, Santa Monica, CA *90405* . . . . | DC *20007-3057*
| ☎ (540) 554-8377
| Rockwood Ridge
| Farm, Rte 1,
| Bluemont, VA
| *20135*
Foster MR & MRS Timothy (Dorothy Colotte) Me.R.. | ☎ (610) 687-5653
MISS Elizabeth A—at Harvard . . . . | 331 Radnor-Chester
| Rd, Villanova, PA
| *19085*
Foster MRS Vincent W JR (Elizabeth Braden) | ☎ (501) 663-0141
Swb'67 . . . . | 5414 Stonewall Rd,
MISS Laura B . . . . | Little Rock, AR
MR Vincent W 3d . . . . | *72207*
JUNIORS MR John B . . . .
Foster MR & MRS Volney W (Ellen Adair Orr) Sr.On.H'38
☎ (847) 234-0436 . . 45 Pembroke Dv, Lake Forest, IL *60045*
Foth MR & MRS Robert F (Elizabeth C Hodges) Rut'67
☎ (201) 299-7878 . . 16 Midvale Rd, Mountain Lakes, NJ *07046*
Fotterall MR & MRS W W Law 3d (Kathleen A Pannepacker) Temp'72
☎ (215) 643-6446 . . Cornerstone Farm, 1525 Limekiln Pike, Jarrettown,
PA *19025*
Fotterall MRS Walter W L JR (Suzanne Park Eakins)
☎ (610) 469-0526 . . ''Mt Pleasant School House'' RD 2, Pottstown,
PA *19464*
Fouke MR & MRS Lucien R JR (Becky W Jones) | ☎ (314) 997-4042
Cy.Y'63.Wash'70 . . . . | 66 Briarcliff,
MR Lucien R III—at ☎ (314) 725-3290 | St Louis, MO *63124*
6253 Northwood Av, St Louis, MO *63105* . . . . .
MR Edward W—at ☎ (212) 889-7236
200 E 33 St, Apt 3I, New York, NY *10016* . . . .
Foulke MR & MRS Walter L (Wendy S Taylor) | ☎ (215) CH2-8991
Wheat'65.Pc.Rc.Ph.H'65 . . . . | 25 Summit St,
MISS Laura T—Bow'91.H'95 . . . . | Philadelphia, PA
☎ (415) 292-4793 . . 1545 California St, | *19118*
San Francisco, CA *94109* . . . .
MR David P—Dth'89.Pa'95—at
☎ (212) 598-4219 . . 141 E 3 St, Apt 12E,
New York, NY *10009* . . . .

Foulke MR & MRS William G (Louisa L Wood)
Ph.Rc.Sg.Ac.Cda.Pn.P.'34 ⚓
☎ (215) 247-4176 . . ''Rose Grange'' 321 E Evergreen Av, Philadelphia,
PA *19118-2824*
Foulke MR & MRS William G JR (Wendy H Robbins) | ☎ (914) 234-6658
Rc.P'64.Cl'69 . . . . | ''River Hills''
MISS Jennifer R . . . . | 14 Mianus River Rd,
MISS Louisa L . . . . | Bedford, NY *10506*
MR Adam . . . .
Fountain MR & MRS Rex Edward (Barbara L Michel) SCal'63.SCal'59
☎ (310) 375-8613 . . 4 El Portal, Palos Verdes Estates, CA *90274*
Fournier DR & MRS Donald F (Nancy C Hamm) | of ☎ (602)264-3350
ArizSt'76.Stan'52.SCal'53.Neb'58 . . . . | 86 E Country Club
JUNIORS MISS Catharine J . . . . | Dv, Phoenix, AZ
JUNIORS MR Jacques E . . . . | *85014*
| ☎ (520) 333-4450
| ''South Point''
| Eager, AZ *85925*
Fournier MR & MRS Donald F JR (Kristen M Dingman) ArizSt'83.ArizSt'86
☎ (602) 252-6532 . . 501 W Palm Lane, Phoenix, AZ *85003*
Fournier MR & MRS John R (McLarty—Rhonda R Bennett) Ariz'83
☎ (602) 257-9291 . . 1625 N Eleventh Av, Phoenix, AZ *85007*
Fowkes MR & MRS William I (Jane G Clarke) Y.'72.Nw'73.Nw'77
☎ (914) 793-2283 . . 119 Pondfield Rd W, Bronxville, NY *10708*
Fowle MR & MRS Wilson F (Audrey L Smith) Va'48
☎ (912) 598-1015 . . 14 Cotton Crossing, Skidaway Island, Savannah,
GA *31411*
Fowler MRS Alberto C (Paulette Van der Schueren) | ☎ (561) 659-1965
Louvain'52 . . . . | 215 Coral Lane,
MISS Lillian M . . . . | Palm Beach, FL
MR Paul F . . . . | *33480*
Fowler MR & MRS Anderson (Pitney—Elaine Darlington) Srr.Rcn.Eh.P'35
☎ (908) 234-0030 . . 50 Fowler Rd, Gladstone, NJ *07934*
Fowler MISS Angela W—Franklin'75.Bost'78.Va'88.Cly.
☎ (212) 722-1561 . . 49 E 96 St, Apt 7A, New York, NY *10128*
Fowler LT COL & MRS C Worthington 2d (Lucy A Barr)
USAF.Penn'53.Pa'56.Sar.Cc.Dar.Myf.Pitt'52 ⚓
☎ (757) 431-2576 . . 2532 Torrey Place, Virginia Beach, VA *23454*
Fowler MISS Catherine Anne (Donoway—Catherine Anne Fowler)
Pa'84.Me.
☎ (610) 783-7071 . . 1051 Penn Circle, B-G, Apt 114, King of Prussia,
PA *19406*
Fowler MR & MRS Conrad Murphree JR (Rachel | ☎ (205) 669-6887
Brown) Ala'69.Ala'91.Ala'69.Ala'72 . . . . | 121 Bolton Lane,
MISS Catherine L . . . . | Columbiana, AL
MISS Elizabeth B . . . . | *35051*
Fowler MR & MRS Cruger D G JR (Nancy A | ☎ (212) 427-7684
Thompson) Un.Plg.Ds.Cly.Ncd.Ne. . . . . | 1155 Park Av,
MR Cruger D G 3d—Bost'91—at | New York, NY
☎ (212) 752-5742 . . 400 E 58 St, New York, | *10128*
NY *10022* . . . .
MR Scudder T—Cl'95 . . . .
Fowler MR Douglas B—Syr'87
☎ (914) 454-5236 . . 82 Beechwood Av, Poughkeepsie, NY *12603*
Fowler MRS Earle B (Barbara Blatchford) V'16.Myf.Ncd.
☎ (847) 381-1530 . . 229 Donlea Rd, Barrington, IL *60010*

Fowler MRS F Hunter (Frances A Hunter) Me...... ☎ (610) 356-6881
MR E Anderson JR—Ty'77—at 505 Waters Edge,
☎ (610) 622-4075 . . 7236 Glenthorne Rd, Newtown Square,
Upper Darby, PA *19082* . . . . PA *19073*

Fowler MR & MRS George A JR (Scholastica K A ☎ (011-65)
Auyong) Tor'75 738-8935
JUNIORS MR George A 7th . . . . 2A Balmoral
JUNIORS MR Hilary A . . . . Crescent, Singapore
  1025

Fowler MR & MRS Gordon B (Mary Rulon-Miller) Sth'57.Ncd.P'57.Cl'58
☎ (860) 561-0502 . . 21 Cliffmore Rd, West Hartford, CT *06107*

Fowler MR & MRS Gordon B JR (Patricia L Ralph)
Br'81.Conn'89.Br'81.Nu'85
☎ (203) 972-1846 . . 46 Turtle Back Lane E, New Canaan, CT *06840*

Fowler MRS Grace M (Grace Montgomery) Cly.
☎ (212) 754-2375 . . 350 E 54 St, New York, NY *10022*

Fowler MR & MRS H S Winthrop JR (Gigi A Collins) Franklin'74.Pace'82
☎ (907) 345-7432 . . 5100 Woodridge Dv, Anchorage, AK *99516*

Fowler MRS Harry S W (Tucker—Emily G O'Connor) K.Bgt.Fic.Cly.
☎ (914) 234-4491 . . 50 Pound Ridge Rd, Bedford, NY *10506*

Fowler MR & MRS Howland A (Shirley J Boers) ☎ (301) 320-4820
P'51.Br'57 . . . . 4924 Sentinel Dv,
MISS Amy A—P'90.Mich'95—at Apt 203, Bethesda,
☎ (617) 876-1330 . . 27 Garfield St, Apt 3, MD *20816*
Cambridge, MA *02138* . . . .

Fowler MR Hunter A—Ty'78.Rens'79
☎ (410) 385-2323 . . PO Box 20509, Baltimore, MD *21223*

Fowler MR & MRS Larned B (Biggs—Jennifer L Branson) Rcn.P'76
☎ (714) 493-9774 . . 24402 Timothy Dv, Dana Point, CA *92629*

Fowler MR Lindsay Anderson—Wms'75
PO Box 23592, Pleasant Hills, CA *94523*

Fowler MR & MRS Lucius L (Rhonda K Nelson) Wells'83.K.Ln.Cly.Tufts'78
☎ (612) 443-3312 . . 8825 Victoria Dv, Chaska, MN *55318*

Fowler MR & MRS Paul D (Christy B Latham) ☎ (203) 966-3163
Rut'68 . . . . 609 Weed St,
MISS Hillary B—at Covenant Theo . . . . New Canaan, CT
MR David I—at Bucknell *06840*

Fowler MR & MRS Philip F (Helen Gilbert) Pom'44
☎ (310) 858-8108 . . 9744 Wilshire Blvd, PH, Beverly Hills, CA *90212*

Fowler MR & MRS Robert A (Berman—Monica E Hedén)
K.Ri.Cv.P'50.H'55
☎ (713) 871-8907 . . 1205 Park Square One, 49 Briar Hollow Lane,
Houston, TX *77027*

Fowler MR & MRS Thomas G (Holder—Elizabeth A Traynor)
H'84.Cv.It.Denis'80
☎ (216) 491-9748 . . 13805 Shaker Blvd, Shaker Heights, OH *44120*

Fowler MR & MRS William H 2d (Deborah A Branciforte)
Bnd'77.Cl'80.P'79
☎ (713) 785-9070 . . 2514A Nantucket Dv, Houston, TX *77057*

Fowlkes MISS Daphne B (George A) . . . . Married at Nantucket, MA
Mitchell MR Leslie C JR (late Leslie C) . . . . Aug 10'96

Fowlkes MR & MRS George A (Jeannette C Sanford)
Un.Plg.B.Nyc.StJ.Cly.P'57.H'61
☎ (212) 288-1519 . . 755 Park Av, New York, NY *10021*

Fowlkes MR & MRS J Winston 3d (Isabel ☎ (212) 734-3228
Lenkiewicz) K.StJ.P'55 765 Park Av,
MISS Isabel Blair—at Princeton . . . . New York, NY
MR Gregory G—Stan'91 . . . . *10021*
MR Stephan W—B'gton'93 . . . .

Fownes MR & MRS Henry G (Godfrey—Harrison—Paulette Bragg)
Ri.Cly.Y.'45 . . of
439 E 51 St, New York, NY *10022*
Calumet Av, La Jolla, CA *92037*

Fox MR & MRS Alexander P JR (Jeanne-Cerre C ☎ (314) 227-8296
Murphy) SpgH'57 . . . . 236 Cedar Trail,
MR George A . . . . Ballwin, MO *63011*

Fox MR B Wilmsen 2d—CtCol'92 . . see S C Graves JR

Fox MR & MRS Barry M B (Maxine M Green) ☎ (504) 523-7559
Ncmb'66.Tul'63 . . . . 1539 Philip St,
MISS Elizabeth M . . . . New Orleans, LA
MR Barry M B JR—at 305 E 86 St, Apt 9PW, *70130*
New York, NY *10028* . . . .

Fox MR & MRS Bernhard W (Hope Alden Meade) Fst.Sg.
☎ (215) 646-0256 . . 1301 Dogwood Lane, Gwynedd Valley, PA *19437*

Fox MRS C Keely (Florence H Wells)
☎ (804) 264-6323 . . 1600 Westbrook Av, Apt 649, Richmond,
VA *23227*

Fox MR & MRS Caleb F 4th (Patricia N Wheeler) Sg.Rc.Fst.Ty'68.Pa'70
☎ (215) CH7-1199 . . 423 W Mermaid Lane, Philadelphia, PA *19118*

Fox MISS Cecilia Rose (John MacRae) . . . . Born at
Norfolk, VA Apr 17'96

Fox MR Charles Clayton
☎ (814) 237-9862 . . 1909 Norwood Lane, State College, PA *16803*

Fox MR E Tunnicliff JR (Julia E Hildebrandt) ☎ (804) 359-7714
Ncd.Dar. . . . . 13 Hampton
MR Ralph C—at 1631 Princeton Rd, Richmond, Commons Terr,
VA *23227* . . . . Richmond, VA
  23226-2167

Fox MISS Elizabeth M (Zimmerman—Elizabeth M Fox) Ws'74
☎ (617) 492-3708 . . 2 Sparks Place, Cambridge, MA *02138*

Fox MR George Chandler (Burns—Frances D ☎ (410) 453-9165
Gould) Cy.Ncd. 941 W Padonia Rd,
MISS Frances P Burns—NCar'80 . . . . Cockeysville, MD
  21030

Fox MRS George F 3d (Virginia H Campbell) Pa'39.Pe.Dar.Ncd.
☎ (908) 273-4465 . . 21 Essex Rd, Summit, NJ *07901*

Fox MRS Heywood (Elizabeth Wells) Chi.Ncd.
☎ (203) 966-0405 . . 73 Oenoke Ridge, New Canaan, CT *06840-4100*

Fox MR & MRS Jarvis P (Elke U Smith) ☎ (610) 827-7255
MtStMary'62.Mid'64.Wis'66 . . . . 1425 Yellow
MISS Lisa J—at Penn State . . . . Springs Rd,
  Chester Springs, PA
  19425

Fox MR & MRS John B (Julia Garrett) ☎ (617) 527-0295
Ws'69.H'59.Ox'61 125 Prince St,
MISS Sarah C—P'93 . . . . West Newton, MA
MR Thomas B—H'95 . . . . *02165-2603*

Fox MR & MRS John MacRae (Maria T Wagner) StCath'82.Hav'75.Y'79
☎ (757) 424-4877 . . 5392 Hargrove Blvd, Virginia Beach, VA *23464*

Fox MR & MRS John MacRae (Maria T Wagner) StCath'82.Hav'75.Y'79
☎ (757) 424-4877 . . 5392 Hargrove Blvd, Virginia Beach, VA *23464*
Fox MR & MRS Joseph Carrère (MacLean—Alison Barbour)
BMr'47.B.Mt.Nf.Cw.Cs.Y.'38.Nu'51 . . of
☎ (718) 549-7147 . . 5475 Palisade Av, Bronx, NY *10471*
☎ (860) 542-5170 . . ''Woodcreek Farm'' Norfolk, CT *06058*
Fox MR Lawrence W 3d
☎ (212) 348-8545 . . 18 E 93 St, New York, NY *10128*
Fox MRS Louise L (Houser—Louise Lameyer) RISD'49
☎ (610) 696-4770 . . 1131 Paoli Pike, West Chester, PA *19380*
Fox MR & MRS Malcolm (Griswold—Patricia M
Henry) . . . . | ☎ (916) 583-3901
MISS Pauline F—at U of Nev Sch of Mines . . . . | PO Box 2135,
| Olympic Valley, CA
| *96146*
Fox MISS Marie-Etienne C
☎ (314) 227-8296 . . 236 Cedar Trail, St Louis, MO *63001*
Fox MRS N Kilborne (Nancy T Kilborne)
☎ (203) 438-5266 . . 33 Deer Hill Dv, Ridgefield, CT *06877*
Fox MISS Nell C . . see S C Graves JR
Fox MR Porter T—Mid'94 . . see S C Graves JR
Fox MR & MRS Reeder R (Marion C Laffey) | ☎ (610) MI9-1475
Pa'61.Me.M.Cs.Y'56.H'59 . . . . | ''Fox Hollow''
MISS Vanessa S—at St Lawrence U . . . . | 124 St George's Rd,
MR Drew D—at U of Va . . . . | Ardmore, PA *19003*
Fox MR & MRS Richard L 2d (Ashton F W Lilly) NCar'68.MethCol'68
☎ (910) 868-1498 . . 240 Summertime Rd, Fayetteville, NC *28303*
Fox MR & MRS Richard Ottley Beaufort (Jane H Shober)
Tul'50 ⚓
☎ (504) 833-2971 . . 301 Northline, Metairie, LA *70005*
Fox MR S Crozer—Pa'64
7 East St, Newport, RI *02840*
Fox DR & MRS (DR) Samuel M 3d (Mary A Vann)
NCar'44.Pa'48.Hav'44.Pa'47
☎ (207) 244-5301 . . 6 Pretty Marsh Rd, Mt Desert, ME *04660*
Fox MR & MRS Samuel M 4th (Andrea L Boissevain)
V'83.Y'86.An.USN'77.Dth'89
317 Sturges Rd, Fairfield, CT *06430*
Fox MR Shawhan L—Juniata'90
see Dilatory Domiciles
Foxworth MR & MRS Walter Lenoir 2d (Carolyn G Burns) Tex'57.Tex'59
☎ (214) 239-2093 . . 7047 Elmridge Dv, Dallas, TX *75240*
Foy MRS Fred C (Elizabeth J Hamilton) Pg.Rr.
☎ (412) 238-6982 . . ''L'Escalier'' Rector, PA *15677*
Foy MR & MRS Louis A (Katharine B Schaefer) Cs. . | ☎ (212) 988-2456
MR Louis E—Cl'78.Cl'86 . . . . | 333 E 68 St,
| New York, NY
| *10021*
Fraker MR & MRS Harrison S (Richardson—Riehle—Rulon-Miller—
Barbara A Anderson) Nyc.Pn.P'39 ⚓
☎ (910) 295-3232 . . ''Nassau Cottage'' Box 1525, Pinehurst, NC *28374*
Fraley MRS Pierre C (Cornelia H Dodge) | ☎ (610) 827-7453
Mls'44.Pkg.Pc.Cs.Hn. . . . . | PO Box 87,
MR Cresson D . . . . | Kimberton Rd,
| Chester Springs, PA
| *19425*
Frame MRS Howard A (Tootell—Brady—Anne Parsons) Mls'24.Ncd.
☎ (206) 624-3700 . . 900 University St, Apt 2WX, Seattle, WA *98101*

Franchot MR & MRS Nicholas V V 3d (Anne M | ☎ (314) PA5-6326
Christy) Rc.Nd.Cw.Ncd.Y'41 . . . . | 6325 Alexander Dv,
MISS Lida W . . . . | St Louis, MO *63105*
Francine MRS Jacques L (Narrow—Delores | ☎ (207) 793-8441
Stanton) SMaine'84 . . . . | ''French Brook''
MISS Emilie E (Ward—Emilie E Francine) | RD 2, Box 894,
SMaine'94.CalSt'96 . . . . | Limerick, ME *04048*
Francis MR & MRS Bernard A JR (Katharine L | ☎ (610) 525-2660
Hancock) Roan'72.Rc.Gm.Fst.Temp'79 . . . . | 334 Strathmore Rd,
MISS Christina Lea—at Mt Vernon Coll | Rosemont, PA
MISS Caroline Elizabeth—at Shippensburg . . . . . | *19010*
Francis MR & MRS Carleton S 3d (D Susan | ☎ (508) 432-0766
Tattersall) Cl'60 . . . . | 20 Chase St,
MISS M Anne—Rol'94—at Longspur Crossing, | Box 515,
Apt 111, 701 W Longspur Blvd, Austin, TX | West Harwich, MA
78753 . . . . | *02671*
MR Lawrence A . . . . |
Francis MR & MRS Charles A (Kathryn W Cruice) MaryW'75.OWes'74
☎ (610) 695-9265 . . 48 Manchester Court, Berwyn, PA *19312*
Francis MRS Edward L (Margaret T Ford) Rdc'32.Chi.Ncd.
☎ (617) 320-0998 . . 10 Longwood Dv, Apt 576, Westwood, MA *02090*
Francis MRS Felice H (Hobson—Smolianinoff—Felice H Rosen) Cly.Chr.
☎ (212) 838-4636 . . 200 E 66 St, New York, NY *10021*
Francis MR & MRS George T JR (Francis—Cayley—Elinor Ward)
Swb'37.Me.Gm.Ac . . .of
☎ (610) 527-3355 . . 409 Caversham Rd, Bryn Mawr, PA *19010*
☎ (561) 276-4259 . . 582 Palm Way, Gulf Stream, FL *33483*
Francis MRS I Hathaway (Anne McP Treat) . . . . | ☎ (610) LA5-2368
MR I Hathaway 4th—at ☎ (703) 435-1595 | Bryn Mawr Av,
White Stone, VA *22578* . . . . | Bryn Mawr, PA
| *19010*
Francis MR & MRS James A (Michele C Murphy) | ☎ (314) 997-7306
Bv.Rc. . . . . | 10609 Greywyck
JUNIORS MISS Michele C C . . . . | Lane, Creve Coeur,
| MO *63141*
Francis MR & MRS James B JR (Sally M Gowen) WmSth'80.Me.Alb'77
☎ (610) 688-6953 . . 31 Paper Mill Rd, Newtown Square, PA *19073*
Francis MR John M—Me.H'64.Pa'70 | ☎ (617) 964-6904
JUNIORS MR Garret M—at U of Colo Boulder . . . | 1839 Washington St,
JUNIORS MR Damon W . . . . | Auburndale, MA
| *02166*
Francis MR & MRS Peter T (Susan L Stanton) | 12529 N Lake
Mntcello'68.Hill'70 . . . . | Court, Fairfax, VA
MR Cameron S . . . . | *22033*
JUNIORS MR Peter T JR |
Francis MRS Samuel A (Margaret Edwards) . . . . . . | ☎ (508) 748-0056
MISS Christina A . . . . | ''Gate House''
| Converse Point,
| Marion, MA *02738*
Francis MR Samuel A—Sb.Bvl.Bow'50.H'90
☎ (508) 748-0243 . . 18 Pitcher St, Box 26, Marion, MA *02738*
Francis MR & MRS Sidney R JR (Mary M Westberg) ColbyS'41.Y'39
☎ (201) 543-4556 . . 1 Pembroke Dv, Mendham, NJ *07945-2005*
Franciscus MISS Alexandra
☎ (203) 458-0822 . . 704 Mulberry Point Rd, Guilford, CT *06437*
Franciscus MISS Monica—SL'85
☎ (212) 688-4869 . . 348 E 58 St, Apt 5A, New York, NY *10022*

Franck MISS Mary Louise—Cal'54.Fr.
☎ (415) 346-1808 . . 2298 Pacific Av, San Francisco, CA *94115*

Franck DR & MRS Peter T (Fay M Martin) | ☎ (916) 246-8955
MtH'59.H'58.H'63 . . . . | 2141 Olive Av,
MISS Valerie M . . . . | Redding, CA *96001*
MISS Cynthia S . . . . |

Francke MR & MRS Albert 3d (Gould—Sargent— | ☎ (011-44-171)
Renée Vollen) Wis'56.SCal'69.Cal'78.Rcn.Nf. | 727-3781
Y'56.Stan'61 . . . . | 16 Norland Square,
MISS Caitlin B . . . . | London W11 4PX,
MISS Tapp F . . . . | England

Francklyn MR & MRS Reginald E (Phyllis De Veau) V'51.Y'50.Va'55
☎ (803) 432-1631 . . ''Phoenix Farm'' 768 Red Fox Rd, Camden,
SC *29020*

Franco MR & MRS Christopher P (Lauren S Piper) Geo'81.Geo'81
☎ (203) 637-0306 . . 37 Lockwood Lane, Riverside, CT *06878*

Frangopoulos MR & MRS Zissimos A (Ruth Snowdon Hoopes)
Swb'69.Cl'80.Ln.Cly.Ncd.Y.'67.Cl'69 . . of
☎ (212) 860-0789 . . 17 E 96 St, New York, NY *10128*
☎ (610) 388-0733 . . 141 Center Mill Rd, Chadds Ford, PA *19317*

Frank MR & MRS A Carlyle (H Ashley Smith) ChHill'86.Pc.Y'72
☎ (610) 941-6746 . . 5130 Militia Hill Rd, Plymouth Meeting,
PA *19462*

Frank MR Alan I W—H'54.Cl'60 . . . . | ☎ (412) 441-7800
MISS Darcy M—H'89 . . . . | 96 E Woodland Rd,
MISS Kimberly deV—H'91 . . . . | Pittsburgh, PA
 | *15232*

Frank MR & MRS Armin C (Suzanne White)
CtCol'46.Cry.Sg.Pc.Ac.Y'45.H'47 . . of
☎ (215) 836-1015 . . 8725 Montgomery Av, Wyndmoor, PA *19038*
☎ (802) 253-8298 . . ''High Meadow'' 3296 Week's Hill Rd, Stowe,
VT *05672*

Frank MR & MRS Charles A 3d (Elizabeth J Taylor) | of ☎ (215)732-3524
V'64.Me.Y'63.Nu'67 . . . . | 1520 Spruce St,
MR Garrett T—Y'92—at ☎ (212) 979-1222 | Philadelphia, PA
60 Second Av, New York, NY *10003* . . . . | *19102*
MR Reade A—Y'94 . . . . | ☎ (860) 364-2223
 | PO Box 85, Sharon,
 | CT *06069*

Frank MR Gerald W—Camb'50
☎ (503) 585-8411 . . PO Box 2225, Salem, OR *97308*

Frank MR & MRS Jonathan W (Sarah J Greve) | ☎ (215) 233-9215
Ty'75.Pc.Ty'74.Pa'76 . . . . | 508 Auburn Av,
MISS Katherine W . . . . | Wyndmoor, PA
JUNIORS MISS Sarah Elizabeth . . . . | *19038*
JUNIORS MR Andrew J . . . . |

Frank MR & MRS Lionel Seaton (M Jane Spangler) V'38
☎ (561) 744-6590 . . Jonathan's Landing, Apt 254, 16050 W Bay Dv,
Jupiter, FL *33477*

Frank MR & MRS Stephen H (Jane F Reny) Duke'85.Duke'85.Cl'87
☎ (203) 629-0349 . . 18 Flower Lane, Greenwich, CT *06831*

Frank MR & MRS Terrence D (Mary E O'Brien) Loy'83.Loy'83
☎ (314) 993-6811 . . 10357 Capitol Place, St Louis, MO *63131*

Frank MRS Walter N JR (Oesch—Margaret G | of ☎ (516)671-8020
Douglas) Pr.Cly. . . . . | 99 Factory Pond Rd,
MISS Melinda M—at Duke Law . . . . | Locust Valley, NY
MISS Stephanie E Oesch—at U of Ore . . . . . . | *11560*
MR Peter I Oesch . . . . | ☎ (212) 734-3503
 | 3 E 77 St,
 | New York, NY
 | *10021*

Frank MR & MRS William A (Cornelia H Dooley) Wash'42.H'43 . . of
☎ (314) 567-5938 . . 7 Chatfield Place, St Louis, MO *63141*
☎ (941) 261-4559 . . 958 Spyglass Lane, Naples, FL *34102*

Franke MRS Edward P JR (Elizabeth B Garth) Elk.Mv.
☎ (410) 435-7156 . . 705 W St Georges Rd, Baltimore, MD *21210*

Frankenhoff MR & MRS William P (Jill T Hyland) | ☎ (212) 249-6908
Ln.Ri.Y'45w . . . . | 19 E 72 St,
MISS Christine H—Dth'95—at ☎ (212) 861-0906 | New York, NY
200 E 72 St, New York, NY *10021* . . . . | *10021*
MR William P JR—ColC'92—at |
☎ (212) 876-3851 . . 200 E 89 St, New York, NY |
10128 . . . . |

Frankenthal MR & MRS Charles P A (Ann P Krugler) Y'55 . . of
☎ (561) 575-6146 . . 129 Lighthouse Dv, Jupiter, FL *33469*
☎ (715) 545-2088 . . 1406 Bear Tail Point, Phelps, WI *54554*

Franklin MRS A Kerr (Ann Kerr) Cly.Pr.
☎ (516) 676-1448 . . ''Old Trees'' Duck Pond Rd, PO Box 636,
Locust Valley, NY *11560*

Franklin MR Benjamin 3d—P'39.Y'42
☎ (415) 567-1432 . . Cathedral Hill D202, 1215 Ellis St, San Francisco,
CA *94109*

Franklin MR George S . . . . Died at
New York, NY Mch 5'96

Franklin MRS George S (Helena Edgell) C.Ri.Csh.S.Cs.
☎ (212) 876-9516 . . 1220 Park Av, New York, NY *10128*

Franklin MR & MRS Hugh H (Madeleine L'Engle Camp)
Sth'41.C.StJ.Nw'38
☎ (212) 316-7495 . . 924 West End Av, Apt 95, New York, NY *10025*

Franklin MR & MRS John H JR (Elizabeth A Way) | 338 Simon Dv,
NotreD'72.Sar.Rob'tM'72 . . . . | Hudson, OH *44236*
JUNIORS MR William H . . . . |

Franklin MR & MRS John O (M Claudia Shortman)
Ariz'61.Ariz'85.Ariz'61.Ariz'64
☎ (520) 298-6445 . . 6501 E Santa Elena, Tucson, AZ *85715*

Franklin MR & MRS Jonathan M (Mary E Laidlaw) Sth'81.Bgt.Camb'79
☎ (914) 234-3127 . . 356 Cantitoe St, Bedford Hills, NY *10507*

Franks MR & MRS Henry T (Barbara R Frazer) Ken'81.Rr.FlaTech'78
☎ (804) 330-5531 . . 4412 Waumsetta Rd, Richmond, VA *23235*

Fransioli MR Thomas A SR—Pa'30
☎ (508) 468-7243 . . 55 Dodges Row, Wenham, MA *01984*

Frantz DR Andrew G—Un.C.H'51.Cl'55
☎ (212) AT9-0369 . . 1185 Park Av, New York, NY *10128*

Frantz MR & MRS Angus M JR (Mary A Graeve) Y'51
☎ (609) 924-9381 . . 22 Edgehill St, Princeton, NJ *08540*

Frantz MR & MRS L Scott (Allison C Hanley) Ln.Pn.Pn.P'82 ⚓
☎ (203) 637-9104 . . 123 Meadow Rd, Riverside, CT *06878*

Frantz MR & MRS Leroy JR (Sheila T Garrity) Ny.Why.P'51 ⚓ . . . . | of ☎ (203)661-4709 15 Wyckham Hill Lane, Greenwich, CT 06831
MISS Stephanie H . . . . |
MISS Joan H . . . . |
MISS Heather C . . . . | ☎ (011-590) 27-80-99 ''Villa Lee'' Camarouche, St Barthélemy

Frantz MRS Robert L (Suzanne H Allen) Ky'49.Pg.Ncd.Dar.
☎ (412) 441-3030 . . 1049 Highmont Rd, Pittsburgh, PA 15232

Fraser MRS Duncan (Dorothy Sollers)
615 Chestnut Av, Apt 1311, Towson, MD 21204

Fraser MR Geith St John . . see MRS V M Ludgate-Fraser

Fraser MR Ian H—Hampshire'87 . . . . | ☎ (413) 586-2031
MR Hugh C—Conn'87 . . . . | 44 Harlow Av, Northampton, MA 01060

Fraser MR & MRS John M JR (Clare C Lundbeck)
☎ (212) 737-3479 . . 133 E 64 St, New York, NY 10021

Fraser DR & MRS Richard A R (Sara A Rasmussen) Dth'75.BritCl'61
☎ (914) 967-6867 . . 97 Apawamis Av, Rye, NY 10580

Fraser MR & MRS Ronald G (Patricia Dodd) Pn.P'54.H'58 . . . . | ☎ (561) 844-1534 205 Colonial Lane, Palm Beach, FL 33480
MISS Alison M . . . . |
MR Ian M . . . . |

Frazer DR & MRS D Hugh JR (Johnnie B Swetenburg) Conv'63.Emory'64.Tul'58.Tul'61 . | 70 Cherry Hill Place, Montgomery, AL 36117-2606
MISS Bowie S . . . . |
MR David H . . . . |

Frazer MISS Jean Riley (John R) . . . . Born at Atlanta, GA Feb 8'96

Frazer MR John JR—Sap.Cw.Ht.Cc.Pa'47.JHop'49
☎ (410) 267-7160 . . 220 Claude St, Annapolis, MD 21401

Frazer MR & MRS John G JR (Barbara Bitting) Pg.Rr.P'37.H'40
☎ (412) 741-3042 . . Box 372, Blackburn Rd, Sewickley, PA 15143

Frazer MR & MRS John R (Connie Jones) Ala'86.Cit'86 . . of
☎ (404) 350-9259 . . 3028 Rhodenhaven Dv NW, Atlanta, GA 30327
Sarah Martin Lodge, Streety Rd, Lowndesboro, AL 36752

Frazer MR & MRS Nimrod T (Patricia L Martin) Htdon'54.H'56 . . of
☎ (334) 265-5224 . . 663 Cloverdale Rd, Montgomery, AL 36106
☎ (334) 278-4429 . . ''Lighting Rod'' Germany Rd, Lowndesboro, AL 36752

Frazier MR & MRS B Graeme 3d (Barbara A Peake) Pc.Sa.Ty'57
☎ (215) 836-5682 . . 7950 Pleasant Av, Wyndmoor, PA 19038

Frazier MR & MRS B Graeme 4th (Elizabeth D Spahr) Mid'86.Pc.Ty'84
☎ (610) 825-8757 . . 2176 Harts Lane, Conshohocken, PA 19428

Frazier MR & MRS Benjamin W (H I Michalina Openchowska) Sth'49 . . . . | ☎ (914) 424-3649 ''Hennett Hill'' Rte 2, Box 68, Philipse Brook Rd, Garrison, NY 10524
MISS Julia R—Sth'90 . . . . |

Frazier MRS Benjamin West (Leila Canby)
☎ (215) CH7-7460 . . 118 W Abington Av, Philadelphia, PA 19118

Frazier MR Christopher S JR—Sg . . . see MRS C W Welsh 2d

Frazier MR Gibson—Me.Cal'92
☎ (213) 851-9277 . . 6853 Alta Loma Terr, Los Angeles, CA 90068

Frazier MRS J Rollins (Joan P Rollins) Ant'80.Me.Gm. . . . . | 218 Strafford Av, Wayne, PA 19087
MISS Ramsey R—at Cornell . . . . |

Frazier MRS John W 3d (Marjorie M Starr)
☎ (610) MU8-1249 . . 244 Steeplechase Rd, Devon, PA 19333

Frazier MISS Moffat Canby . . see MRS C W Welsh 2d

Frazier MR Stephen C . . see J T Jackson 3d

Frazier DR Thomas G—Me.Gm.W&J'64.Pa'68
☎ (610) 525-1155 . . 607 Winsford Rd, Bryn Mawr, PA 19010

Frazier MR & MRS W West 4th (Lois Thayer) Ac.
☎ (207) 288-4260 . . PO Box 97, Hulls Cove, ME 04644

Frech MR & MRS Hans A (Patricia H Powers) Cly.Ht.Cda.Dh.Lm.
☎ (212) 996-1019 . . 1105 Park Av, New York, NY 10128

Frech MR & MRS Harry E JR (Peggy W O'Reilly) Wash'40
☎ (941) 497-2358 . . 1619 Del Monte Court, Venice, FL 34293

Frederick MISS Alexandra C M (Baker—Alexandra C M Frederick) CambColl'83
☎ (212) 879-3253 . . 1045 Lexington Av, Apt 5P, New York, NY 10021

Frederick MR & MRS Halsey A (Downton—Warder— Elisabeth C Crosman) Me.Fw.Rv.Sdg.Dll.Myf.Colby'40
☎ (610) LA5-3245 . . ''Timber Town'' 530 Fishers Rd, Bryn Mawr, PA 19010

Frederick REV & MRS John B M (Procter—P Jean Norman) Pn.P'51.Birm'ham'73
☎ (609) 924-7590 . . 32 Chestnut St, Princeton, NJ 08542-3806

Frederick MISS Sarah A T (Thompson—Sarah A T Frederick)
☎ (718) 855-8969 . . 200 Clinton Av, Apt 1B, Brooklyn, NY 11201

Frederick MR Walter S—Fmy.Cal'28
☎ (408) 624-0224 . . 270 Del Mesa Carmel, Carmel, CA 93923

Frederick MR & MRS William H JR (Nancy C Greenewalt) BMr'50.Wil.Swth'48.Dick'51
☎ (302) 656-6075 . . 1472 Ashland-Clinton School Rd, Hockessin, DE 19707

Freed MR & MRS Christopher J (Alice F Mauran) Pitzer'78.RI'78.IdahoSt'94
☎ (513) 848-9093 . . 4395 Knob Hill Dv, Bellbrook, OH 45305

Freeman MR & MRS Daniel A 3d (Sybilla G Flatau) H.Y'57
☎ (617) 659-4811 . . 638 Main St, Norwell, MA 02061

Freeman MR & MRS David F (Hazel S Farr) P'40.Y'43 . . . . | ☎ (908) 872-0899 ''Tall Trees'' 6 Clay Court, Locust, NJ 07760
MISS H Sims (Turner—H Sims Freeman) Cr'71 . |

Freeman MR & MRS David N (Ellen S Wood) Sth'57.BMr'76.Y'55.Cr'63
☎ (610) 353-2567 . . 817 Loudan Lane, Newtown Square, PA 19073

Freeman MRS E Lavalle (Elaine Lavalle) Bcs.Cly. . | ☎ (212) 362-0050 119 W 77 St, New York, NY 10024
MISS Ellen C—Box 983, Ben Lomond, CA 95005 |

Freeman MR & MRS Eldridge J (Mary E Arey) M.Me.Fw.Myf.P.'32 . . of
☎ (610) 525-0717 . . 31 Pond Lane, Bryn Mawr, PA 19010
☎ (561) 231-4882 . . 550 Beach Rd, Vero Beach, FL 32963

Freeman MRS Felix J JR (Land—Phoebe Ann Davis)
☎ (401) 789-3838 . . Box 399, 5 Old Boston Neck Rd, Narragansett, RI 02882

Freeman MRS H Dodge (Ann Rutledge) V'43
see Dilatory Domiciles

Freeman MR & MRS (DR) Harry B 3d (Susan H Johnston)
Nu'79.CUNY'87.Rm.StJ.Cly.Pa'73
☎ (212) 861-5398 . . 200 E 74 St, New York, NY *10021*

Freeman DR & MRS (DR) Jonathan K (Katharine E O'Donnell)
Scran'84.Y'84
50 Manchester Rd, Brookline, MA *02146*

Freeman MR & MRS Joseph S (Thorndike—Cynthia F Lyman)
Ws'76.Ub.Cy.Sm.Ncd.Yn.Y'66.H'72.H'79
☎ (617) 566-4806 . . 346 Lee St, Brookline, MA *02146*

Freeman MR & MRS Louis M JR (Courtney A de la Houssaye)
Ncmb'87.Tul'86 ⚓
☎ (504) 837-0179 . . 33 Nassau Dv, Metairie, LA *70005*

Freeman MR & MRS Louis McDaniel (Judith Waite) Ncmb'63.B.Ny.Cw.Myf.Dar.Ncd.Tul'62 . . . . . . MISS (DR) Laura Louise—Mid'85.LSU'91—at 206 Henri St, Folsom, LA *70437*	of ☎ (504)861-0429 3 La Salle Place, New Orleans, LA *70118* ☎ (601) 452-9249 ''Boisdore'' 300 Havana Dv, Pass Christian, MS *39571*
Freeman MR & MRS Murray F (A Aileen Sallom) Pn.Hav'48.P'49 . . . . MR Richard M S—Drawer 404, Paupack, PA *18451*	☎ (717) 857-0658 ''High Piers'' PO Box 411, Paupack, PA *18451*

Freeman MR & MRS Peter Lawrence (Catherine T Gornto) Swb'92.W&L'91
☎ (504) 861-7700 . . 2516 Palmer Av, New Orleans, LA *70118*

Freeman MR & MRS Richard W (Freeman—Sandra Draughn)
Ncmb'60.Tul'80.Tul'60 . of
☎ (504) 891-5334 . . 1234 Henry Clay Av, New Orleans, LA *70118*
☎ (504) 796-9126 . . Oak Hill Ranch, PO Box 957, Folsom, LA *70437*

Freeman MR & MRS Richard W 3d (Angela Bradford)
PO Box 51299, New Orleans, LA *70151-1299*

Freeman MRS Richard West (Montine McDaniel) Ncmb'36.Cda.Ncd.
☎ (504) 861-2142 . . 295 Walnut St, New Orleans, LA *70118*

Freeman MR & MRS Robert S (Dorothy C Macfarlan) Ac.Ncd.Aht'44 . . . . MISS Lisa H	☎ (610) 644-6869 1530 Morstein Rd, Frazer, PA *19355*
Freeman MR & MRS Samuel M 2d (Margaret O Davison) Col'66.Pc.Wes'58 . . . . MR William H—at Cornell . . . . MR Jonathan C—at Trinity	☎ (215) 247-8886 8408 Navajo St, Philadelphia, PA *19118*
Freeman MR & MRS William G JR (Ruth I Mitchell) SL'75.Yn.Y'52 . . . . MISS Ruth I—Ober'77 . . . . MISS Carol F—Ws'83	☎ (203) 966-4831 270 Frogtown Rd, New Canaan, CT *06840*

Freemon MR & MRS Richard D (Merces S de Quevedo Pessanha)
Gen'60.Bhm.Stan'57 . . of
☎ (415) 921-2322 . . 3659 Washington St, San Francisco, CA *94118*
☎ (011-41-30) 44632 . . ''Chalet Sunnegg'' 3780 Gstaad, Switzerland

Freer MR & MRS Robert E JR (Roberta S Renchard) Col'70.Mt.Cvc.Cc.Sl.P'63.Va'66 . . . . MISS Kimberly D . . . . MISS Ashleigh H . . . . MR R Elliott 3d . . . . JUNIORS MR Daniel R	☎ (301) 656-6206 ''Greenacre'' 1 W Melrose St, Chevy Chase, MD *20815-4243*

Freiberg MR & MRS Randolph L (Sonia L Soares) NCar'77
Rua Antilhas 88, São Paulo 01438, Brazil

Freisenbruch MR & MRS Michael D (Rebecca L S Allan) Rby.York'74
☎ (441) 295-2520 . . Westbrook Cottage, 8 Shaw Wood Rd,
Spanish Point, Pembroke, Bermuda

Frelinghuysen MR & MRS Denis de V (Susan W Alden) WmSth'80.Hob'81
☎ (203) 655-2781 . . 50 Talmadge Hill Rd, Darien, CT *06820*

Frelinghuysen MR & MRS Frederick (Mary E Voyatzis)
Pa'78.Lond'85.Pn.P'75.Y'79
☎ (520) 577-1102 . . 2200 E Calle Lustre, Tucson, AZ *85718*

Frelinghuysen MR George G—Cw.
☎ (561) 585-8619 . . 4901 S Flagler Dv, West Palm Beach, FL *33405*

Frelinghuysen MR & MRS George L K (Alice K B Cooney)
P'76.Del'78.Un.P.'73.Cl'75
☎ (212) 249-8692 . . 940 Park Av, New York, NY *10028*

Frelinghuysen MRS Henry O H (Seherr-Thoss—Marian C Kingsland)
BtP.Evg.Lx.
☎ (908) 439-2058 . . ''Primrose House'' 11 King St, Oldwick, NJ *08858*

Frelinghuysen MR & MRS Joseph S (Emily Lawrance) Cly.P'34
☎ (908) 766-0131 . . 50 Hidden Valley Rd, Far Hills, NJ *07931*

Frelinghuysen MR & MRS Joseph S JR (Sylvia M Stiassni) Eh.Shcc.P'63 . . . . MISS Joy . . . . MR Nicholas	☎ (908) 766-4562 Post Rd, Bernardsville, NJ *07924*
Frelinghuysen MR & MRS Peter (Barrett Brady) V'64.Ln.P'63.Y'68 . . . . MISS Elizabeth B—V'92—☎ (212) 727-3324 . . MR Cyrus T—P'96 . . . . JUNIORS MR Anson B—at Middlesex	☎ (212) 794-1303 941 Park Av, New York, NY *10028*

Frelinghuysen MRS Peter H B (Beatrice S Proctor) . . . . Died at
Morristown, NJ Jun 3'96

Frelinghuysen MR Peter H B—Mo.Mg.Eh.Cvc.Lx.Cw.P'38.Y'41
☎ (201) 538-3267 . . Sand Spring Lane, Morristown, NJ *07960*

Frelinghuysen MR & MRS Rodney P (Virginia T Robinson)
SL'76.Unn.Sm.Mo.Hob'69
☎ (201) 538-6147 . . Wexford Farm, James St, Morristown, NJ *07960*

Frelinghuysen MR & MRS T Kinney R (Linda K Kast) Ds.
☎ (413) 698-2632 . . 155 Orchard Circle, Richmond, MA *01254*

Frelinghuysen MRS Thomas T K (Roselyne de Viry) Ds. . . . . JUNIORS MISS Jessica R	☎ (609) 924-5643 170 Prospect Av, Princeton, NJ *08540*

Fremantle MR & MRS Hugh D (Susan F Stevens) Ore'72.Geo'66 . . of
☎ (212) 410-1082 . . 1082 Park Av, Apt 3, New York, NY *10128*
☎ (415) 928-7707 . . 2525 Union St, San Francisco, CA *94123*

Fremont-Smith MR Matthew T—Unn.Ham'84.Dth'89
☎ (011-852-5) 525-6708 . . 9 Old Peak Rd, Apt 601, Hong Kong

Fremont-Smith MR & MRS Maurice JR (Harriet G Bateman) Ty'52 . . . . MISS Amy . . . . MR Gregory . . . . MR Michael . . . . MR John Xavier	☎ (617) 736-0231 258 Bishops Forest Dv, Waltham, MA *02154*
Fremont-Smith MR & MRS Paul JR (H Carol Stokes) Hb. . . . . MR Thomas P—at West State Coll	☎ (207) 276-3642 ''The Tides'' Seal Harbor, ME *04675*

Fremont-Smith CAPT (RET) Richard—USCG.Ll.H'58.Cl'69.GeoW'72
☎ (954) 832-0888 . . 2401 E Las Olas Blvd, Ft Lauderdale, FL *33301*
Fremont-Smith MR & MRS Thayer (Anne R Jeffery) | 15 Bellevue Av,
Rdc'54.H.'53 . . . . | Melrose, MA *02176*
MR James J . . . . |
MR Phillip H . . . . |
French REV & MRS Alan C (Mary R Parkman)
Denis'80.Cl'85.Ncd.Duke'75.Gen'lTheo'79
☎ (908) 322-7459 . . 15 Old Forge Lane, Berkeley Heights, NJ *07922*
French MRS Anne H (Anne W Hubbell) Ws'63 . . . . | ☎ (914) 234-7729
MISS Susanna H . . . . | Mianus River Rd,
MR Daniel J . . . . | Bedford, NY *10506*
French MRS Arthur E (Pauline P Day) Dar.
☎ (201) 379-4704 . . Short Hills Village, 24B Forest Dv, Springfield,
NJ *07081-1124*
French MISS Ashley N—Bost'92 . . see C L'H R Florance
French MR Charles Stacy—H'30
☎ (415) 948-8318 . . 11970 Rhus Ridge Rd, Los Altos Hills, CA *94022*
French MRS Cynthia R (Cynthia W Renchard) . . . . | ☎ (303) 604-2411
MISS Cynthia W—Gettys'92—at | 1220 Warrior Way,
☎ (202) 362-5804 . . 3620 Macomb St NW, | Lafayette, CO *80026*
Washington, DC *20016* . . . . |
MISS Alison H—at U of Colo Boulder . . . . |
MR Seth B 4th—Bost'90—at ☎ (410) 730-0564 |
5411 Columbia Rd, Columbia, MD *21044* . . . . . |
French MRS Dorothy F (Gorman—Dorothy S Fleming)
☎ (609) 924-7050 . . 45 Constitution Hill W, Princeton, NJ *08540*
French MR & MRS Edward D (Carpenter—Lois A Waterbury)
☎ (804) 435-6885 . . PO Box 607, White Stone, VA *22578*
French MR & MRS G Remick (Marianne Sysak) Conn'84.WorPoly'82
☎ (207) 767-2703 . . 6 Roundabout Lane, Cape Elizabeth, ME *04107*
French MR & MRS G Ross (Katharine C Iglehart) Gv.Elk.Mv.Pa'43 . . of
☎ (410) 337-6959 . . 608 Brightwood Club Dv, Lutherville, MD *21093*
☎ (561) 276-8232 . . 4475 N Ocean Blvd, Apt 44C, Delray Beach,
FL *33483*
French MR & MRS Harry B (Phyllis P McLean) | of ☎ (610)642-1600
Me.W.Br'47.H'52 . . . . | "Heatherfield"
MISS (DR) Pamela P—Swb'80.PaMed'86.Me. | 1510 Monk Rd,
W.—at ☎ (610) 254-9529 . . 11 Harford Lane, | Gladwyne, PA
Radnor, PA *19087* . . . . | *19035*
MR William McL—Me.W.HampSydney'83. | ☎ (941) 964-1046
Va'85—at ☎ (610) 254-9529 . . 11 Harford Lane, | Boca Grande Club,
Radnor, PA *19087* . . . . | Gasparilla Island,
MR Clayton G—Me.W.Dick'86.VillaN'88— | Boca Grande, FL
☎ (610) 896-6486 . . . . | *33921*
French MR & MRS Hollis 3d (Rosemary Spier) Ty'81.Ec.H'83
191 Main St, Wenham, MA *01984*
French MR & MRS Hollis S (Kellogg—Juliet Richardson) Tv.Ncd.H'26
☎ (508) 283-5541 . . 3 Chester Square, Annisquam, MA *01930*

French MR & MRS John 3d (Gundlach—Marina | of ☎ (212)879-2617
Kellen) Lausanne'62.Ri.K.C.Mto.Cs.Dth'55. | 33 E 70 St,
H.'58 . . . . | New York, NY
MISS Annabelle K Gundlach—at | *10021*
☎ (212) 535-7348 . . 784 Park Av, New York, | ☎ (203) 438-3014
NY *10021* . . . . | "Log House"
MR Andrew S Gundlach—at 115 E 86 St, | 178 Ned's Mountain
New York, NY *10028* . . . . | Rd, Ridgefield, CT
| *06877*
French MRS John H 2d (Leonard—Sally W Rial) Ws'62.Srb.Rr.
☎ (212) 734-8483 . . 1365 York Av, Apt 23M, New York, NY *10021*
French MR John H 2d—Un.B.Srb.Nrr.Y'52.H'55 . . of
☎ (212) 734-4172 . . 300 E 75 St, New York, NY *10021*
☎ (401) 849-2940 . . "Oakwood" PO Box 368, Newport, RI *02840*
French MR & MRS John R (Quasha—Leigh Catlin) | of ☎ (203)661-8440
H'62.H'66 . . . . | 39 Birch Lane,
MISS Jennifer C Quasha . . . . | Greenwich, CT
| *06830*
| ☎ (516) 537-3129
| "Windswept"
| Matthews Lane,
| PO Box 817,
| Bridgehampton, NY
| *11932*
French MR & MRS John S (Alexandra B Pagon) Wms'81.Nyc.Wms'79
☎ (215) 679-4278 . . Box 39A, RD 1, Palm, PA *18070*
French MR & MRS Joseph W (Janet C Rice) Buf'38 . . . . . | ☎ (716) 631-0231
MISS Patricia S . . . . | 39 Tee Court,
MISS Barbara R (Pace—Barbara R French) . . . . . | Williamsville, NY
| *14221*
French MR & MRS L Robert JR (Marcia M Fuller) | of ☎ (915)683-5661
Tex'46 . . . . | 1010 W Wall St,
MR Richard West . . . . | Midland, TX
MR Powhatan E K . . . . | *79701-5116*
| ☎ (619) 346-8081
| 47-475 E Eldorado
| Dv, Indian Wells,
| CA *92210*
French MR & MRS Peter S (Katherine P Ryan) AmU'63
☎ (603) 887-3812 . . "Dexter House" 124 Chester St, Chester,
NH *03036*
French MR & MRS Raymond A (Joan C Foy) Pr.Dar.Yn.USMMA'46
☎ (561) 546-2464 . . 299 S Beach Rd, Hobe Sound, FL *33455*
French MR & MRS Robert A (Nancy H Woods) | ☎ (609) 466-0365
Bhy.Rv.Ht.Cw.Hav'68 . . . . | 374 Bedens Brook
JUNIORS MR Grayson P . . . . | Rd, Skillman, NJ
| *08558-9740*
French DR & MRS Ronald J (Flora S Fenner) Gchr'60.Tul'63
☎ (504) 866-3290 . . 1705 Calhoun St, New Orleans, LA *70118*

French MR & MRS Seth B JR (Frederica P Ripley) Unn.B.Pr.Y'41 . . . . | ☎ (804) 923-0938 525 Kellogg Dv, Ednam, Charlottesville, VA *22903* Jan 1 . .
MISS Elizabeth D—Va'89—at ☎ (804) 973-2342 1018 Fray's Mountain Rd, Earlysville, VA *22936*
☎ (561) 753-6131 13224 Polo Club Rd, Apt 103A, West Palm Beach, FL *33414*

French MR & MRS Steven B (Debra J Fischer) Hartw'80.Hartw'80
☎ (508) 688-2694 . . 1092 Great Pond Rd, North Andover, MA *01845*

French MRS Theodore (Katharine L Dunlop) Ws'38.Sl.Ncd . . .of
☎ (301) 493-6149 . . 10500 Rockville Pike, Apt 521, Rockville, MD *20852-3339*
☎ (516) 583-5997 . . Cottage 81, Point O'Woods, NY *11706*

French MISS Virginia D—Wis'70.Md'75
☎ (410) 628-2559 . . 15044 Jarrettsville Pike, Monkton, MD *21111*

Frenning MRS Alfred B (Blanche B Borden) . . . . Died at Little Compton, RI Jly 4'96

Frenning MR Alfred B
☎ (716) 881-5534 . . 849 Delaware Av, Buffalo, NY *14209*

Frenning MISS Ann C—Bates'89.Geo'90.Myf.
17 Durham St, Apt 3R, Boston, MA *02115-5302*

Frenning MR & MRS John W (Mary Wotton) Bost'53.Bost'75.Myf.H'44
☎ (207) 338-3167 . . "Dwelling Place" PO Box 184, Belfast, ME *04915*

Frenning MR & MRS Peter B (M Norita Armesto) D'Youville'50.H'52.Pa'58 . . . . | ☎ (716) 839-3031 77 Bentham P'kway, Snyder, NY *14226*
MISS Ellen S . . . .

Frentzel MR & MRS David G (Kari A Urbowicz) Cr'82.Cr'83.Stan'82.Cr'83.Ch'90
☎ (508) 651-1091 . . 13 Pleasant St, Sherborn, MA *01770*

Frentzel MASTER George William (David G) . . . . Born at Newton, MA Jan 11'96

Frentzel MR H Christian—Geo'80.Pa'89
☎ (212) 535-9059 . . 235 E 73 St, Apt 5G, New York, NY *10021*

Frentzel MR Herman E—Y'52.Stan'53
☎ (415) 332-0635 . . 424 Bee St, Sausalito, CA *94965*

Frentzel MRS J Titzell (Joan W Titzell) Stan'53
☎ (415) 435-5627 . . 39 Lagoon Vista, Tiburon, CA *94920*

Frenzel MR & MRS Michael A (Julia D Pinckney) Char'ton'92.Dc.WakeF'87
☎ (423) 588-8199 . . 703 Forest Heights Dv, Knoxville, TN *37919*

Frère MR & MRS Christian M J (Edith Dunn) Stan'65.GénM'63 . . . . | 436 S Las Palmas Av, Los Angeles, CA *90020*
JUNIORS MISS Marie L . . . .

Freston MISS Katherine F
☎ (914) 225-9334 . . RFD 2, Logger's Row, Carmel, NY *10512*

Freund MR & MRS Gerald (Peregrine W Whittlesey) Scripps'66.Cl'69.C.Cs.Hav'52.Ox'55 . . of
☎ (212) 737-3105 . . 345 E 80 St, New York, NY *10021*
☎ (203) 762-3097 . . 29 Chicken St, Wilton, CT *06897*
☎ (802) 457-2118 . . General Delivery, North Pomfret, VT *05053*

Frey MRS Charles Daniel (Caldwell—Charlotte Goodlett) Cnt.Cas.Fy.Tv.
☎ (312) 787-5600 . . 232 E Walton Place, Chicago, IL *60611*

Frey MR & MRS Frank G 3d (Madeline P Becker) Pa'64.Sg.Pa'67 . . . . | 5 Joining Brook, Spring House, PA *19477*
MISS Cleaves M . . . .
MISS Sydney B—at Skidmore . . . .

Frick DR & MRS H Clay 2d (du Pont—Emily G Troth) Rcn.Au.S.Pr.B.C.Ny.P'42 . . . . | ☎ (201) 768-2293 Box 178, Closter Dock Rd, Alpine, NJ *07620*
MR Richard S du Pont JR—at 480 Canal St, Apt 805, New York, NY *10013*
MR David W du Pont—at 88 Lexington Av, New York, NY *10016* . . . .

Frick MR & MRS Richard T JR (Katherine B Reid) B. | ☎ (802) 824-4095 68 Old Tavern Rd, Weston, VT *05161*
MISS Katherine B . . . .
MISS Virginia R . . . .

Frick-Humes MISS Julia E
☎ (011-32-2) 275-8343 . . 76 rue Henri Van Zuylen, 1180 Brussels, Belgium

Fridy MR & MRS John H (McKenna—Sally McCawley) R'velt'85.H'mannMed'73 . . . . | 451 Darby-Paoli Rd, Paoli, PA *19301*
MR William R McKenna—at Killington, VT *05751* . . . .
MR Andrew S McKenna—at Vail, CO *81657*

Friedel MAJ & MRS Steven P (Alison C Riker) Rol'87.An.USA'85
☎ (703) 690-6116 . . 7906 Hollington Place, Fairfax Station, VA *22039*

Friedeman MR & MRS William B (Laurie L Schmitt) Skd'74.Rc.On.Sc.Wa.Hills'69 . . . . | ☎ (847) 234-2214 281 W Laurel Av, Lake Forest, IL *60045*
JUNIORS MISS Blair F . . . .

Friedeman MRS William S (Lillian Lampert) Cas . . .of
☎ (312) 787-3920 . . 1310 N Ritchie Court, Apt 14C, Chicago, IL *60610*
PO Box 156, Wickenburg, AZ *85358*

Friend MRS Charles W (Karin E Kretschmer) . . . . . | ☎ (941) 377-8371 1411 Cedar Bay Lane, Sarasota, FL *34231*
MISS Andrea V—at 930 Sherman St, Denver, CO *80203* . . . .

Friend MISS Elizabeth R—Wms'90
770 Filbert St, Apt 4, San Francisco, CA *94133*

Friend MR John E—Pa'42 . . . . | ☎ (212) PL5-3387 242 E 50 St, New York, NY *10022*
MISS Ann G—at 1 Colville House, Talbot Rd, London W11, England . . . .
MISS Lovel—at 122 Dolphin Cove Quay, Stamford, CT *06902* . . . .

Friend MR Pierson—Wms'88
38 Leroy St, New York, NY *10014*

Friend MR Theodore P—H'85
245 W 75 St, Apt 6B, New York, NY *10023*

Friend MR & MRS Theodore W 3d (Elizabeth Pierson) McG'55.Y'57.Ph.Wms'53.Y'58
☎ (610) 964-1873 . . 264 Radnor-Chester Rd, Villanova, PA *19085*

Fries MR & MRS H H Hugo (Warden—Charlotte A Hubbard)
☎ (302) 654-7188 . . 908 Greenhill Av, Wilmington, DE *19805*

Fries COL & MRS Stuart G (Helen S Haynes) An.Sar.Ncd.Dar.USA'35.SCal'49
☎ (205) 883-2046 . . 409 Zandale Dv, Huntsville, AL *35801*

Fries MR William 2d—Cp.Cal'43 . . of
☎ (415) 567-7673 . . 1908 Broadway St, San Francisco, CA *94109*
"Sagewood" 2093 Sandalwood Dv, Palm Springs, CA *92260*

Frisbie MR & MRS Robert N (Kristine Bast) Sth'75.Pe.H'75
☎ (215) 628-0444 . . ''Harner Farm'' 6101 Sheaff Lane, Ft Washington,
PA *19034*
Fritts MR & MRS Guy A (Phyllis Van B Richard)
Sth'64.Csh.Pr.Va'64 . . . .
MR James A—Ham'91 . . . .
MR Garretson V—at U of Ariz . . . .
| ☎ (516) 673-0591
| 16 Abbington Dv,
| Lloyd Harbor,
| Huntington, NY
| *11743*
Fritz MR & MRS Arthur Joseph JR (Barbara F Carr)
Pcu.Sfy.Fr.Dth'62.Stan'65 . . . .
MISS Jenner Lee . . . .
MR Arthur J 3d . . . .
MR Clayton B . . . .
| ☎ (415) 922-2741
| 2006 Washington St,
| San Francisco, CA
| *94109*
Fritz DR & MRS William F (Susan E Baker)
V'49.Elk.Md.Mv.Cda.Muhl'45.JHop'49 . . of
☎ (410) 825-3940 . . 4 Riderwood Station, Towson, MD *21204*
☎ (603) 532-7655 . . ''Still Pond'' 25 Gilson Rd, Jaffrey, NH *03452*
Fritz MR William F B (William F) . . . . Married at St Michaels, MD
Monkman MISS Susan E (late Wesley G) . . . . Jun 1'96
Fritze MR & MRS Gunther E A (Anita W Murphy)
Rdc'64.Cy.H'58.H'62 . . . .
MISS Liese A . . . .
MR Johannes P—P'93.Camb'95—at
☎ (011-44-171) 937-6516 . . 16 Duchess of
Bedford House, Duchess of Bedford Walk,
London W8 7QL, England . . . .
| ☎ (617) 566-6747
| 84 Spooner Rd,
| Chestnut Hill, MA
| *02167*
Frobes MR & MRS David Bruce (Carole E Battey) DeP'62.DeP'62
☎ (602) 998-4037 . . 7520 E McLellan Lane, Scottsdale, AZ *85250*
Froeb MR & MRS Cornelius F (Hill—Catherine J Richards) BMr'39.P'40
☎ (410) 778-6687 . . 202 Mt Vernon Av, Chestertown, MD *21620*
Froelich MR & MRS Robert L (Denise McNamara)
Sth'60.Eh.Eyc.Shcc.Cly.P'60 . . . .
MISS Cecilia C—at ☎ (212) 873-7955
30 W 70 St, New York, NY *10024* . . . .
MISS Emma E B—at Brown . . . .
MISS Helen McN—at Middlebury . . . .
| of ☎ (212)737-7967
| 875 Park Av,
| New York, NY
| *10021*
| ☎ (908) 439-2960
| ''Hollybourne
| Farm'' Oldwick, NJ
| *08858*
Froelicher MRS Hans JR (Frances H Morton) Sth'34.Cl'38
☎ (410) 523-2213 . . 1402 Bolton St, Baltimore, MD *21217*
Fröhlich MRS H L Van Liew (Helen Louise Van Liew) Cda.
☎ (864) 457-2413 . . Box 112, Landrum, SC *29356*
Froment MR Frank L—Mo.Pn.P'31
Emmaus Court, 3112 Fellowship Rd, Basking Ridge, NJ *07920*
Fromson MR & MRS Brett D (Carmel S Wilson) BostColl'75.Stan'76
☎ (202) 338-1052 . . 3532 Edmunds St NW, Washington, DC *20007*
Fronk MISS Katherine C . . see MRS R L Stevenson
Frost MR & MRS Christian McK (Sarah D Richards)
Fla'79.AmU'86.Oakland'79
☎ (908) 522-1165 . . 5 Rose Lane, Summit, NJ *07901*
Frost MRS Floyd D (Henrietta Q Brockenbrough) Dar.
☎ (410) 549-6772 . . 7200 Third Av, Apt C013, Sykesville, MD *21784*
Frost MISS Marie B—Csn.Myf.
☎ (203) 259-2200 . . 140 Lansdowne, Westport, CT *06880*
Frost MR & MRS Marvin H JR (Elizabeth B Quinsler) Ariz'43.Ariz'44
☎ (209) 439-0138 . . 2499 W Celeste Av, Fresno, CA *93711-2216*
Frost MISS Natalie Ann (g—Rufus S Frost 3d) . . . . Born Aug 12'95

Frost MR & MRS Reginald R (Evelyn Comey)
Sth'51.Ncd.Aht'51 . . . .
MR Michael L—NewColl'75 . . . .
| ☎ (603) 778-0216
| 1 Jady Hill Av,
| Apt J9, Exeter, NH
| *03833*
Frost MR & MRS Rufus S 3d (Mary Brereton) Sar.Myf.Ncd.Nichols'64
☎ (508) 829-7070 . . 602 Torrey Lane Ext, Holden, MA *01520-1792*
Frost MRS Thomas B (M Evelyn Kuhn) Cyb.Sm.Hn.
MR Nicholas S—SL'90 . . . .
| ☎ (505) 982-0665
| 808 E Zia Rd,
| Santa Fe, NM
| *87505-4938*
Frost MR & MRS Winston H (Cochran—Margaret L
Lawrance) Rc.Bcs.So.Ng.H'36.Va'40 . . . .
MISS Dorothy W . . . .
MISS Catherine Cochran . . . .
| ☎ (516) 283-3601
| 285 Hill St,
| PO Box 572,
| Southampton, NY
| *11969*
Frothingham MR & MRS A Michael (Sara Struthers)
SL'44.Dth'43.Y'48 . . . .
MISS Victoria S . . . .
MR Eric . . . .
| ☎ (561) 234-4381
| 1901 Bay Rd,
| Vero Beach, FL
| *32963*
Frothingham MR Andrew (A Michael) . . . . Married at Rye, NY
Decker MISS Lynn K (Lawrence) . . . . Dec 30'95
Frothingham MR & MRS Diana S (Diana L Smith) . . . . . .
MR Charles E . . . .
MR Peter M . . . .
| 2 Fox Chase Lane,
| Weston, MA *02193*
Frothingham MASTER Evan Decker (g—A Michael Frothingham) . . . Born
at New York, NY Jun 23'96
Frothingham MRS H Hoyt (Martha Binding)
☎ (803) 831-7674 . . River Hills Plantation, 1 Fairway Ridge,
Lake Wylie, SC *29710*
Frothingham MR & MRS Nathaniel (Mary King) H'50
☎ (508) 539-2120 . . 34 Nobska Rd, PO Box 2422, Mashpee, MA *02649*
Frothingham MR & MRS William B JR (Pollie A P Thompson)
Sbc.Ec.Chi.Cda.H'52
☎ (508) 526-7727 . . 117 School St, Manchester, MA *01944*
Frye DR & MRS Frederick A (Joy E Brunner) Sdy.Stan'56
☎ (619) 223-8800 . . 666 San Elijo St, San Diego, CA *92106*
Frye MR & MRS Roland M (Jean E Steiner) R.Cos.Myf.Cc.Cs.Pn.P'43
☎ (610) 687-3195 . . 226 W Valley Rd, Wayne, PA *19087*
Fryer JUNIORS MISS Abigail . . see MISS S Farmer
Fryer MISS Amanda . . see MISS S Farmer
Fryer MR & MRS Appleton (Angeline D Kenefick)
Buf.St.Rv.Cw.Hl.Lm.Myf.G.P.'50
☎ (716) 884-2376 . . 85 Windsor Av, Buffalo, NY *14209*
Fryer DR & MRS Minot P (Whiting—Luise Brunell) Br'36.JHop'40.Br'71
☎ (812) 424-4650 . . 408 SE Riverside Dv, Evansville, IN *47713*
Fuchs MRS Barrington K (D Barrington King) . . . . .
MISS Holly A—Md'81 . . . .
MISS Kimberley C—Eckerd'84—at
☎ (714) 673-9358 . . 207 Opal Av,
Balboa Island, CA *92662* . . . .
| ☎ (203) 531-5380
| Putnam Green,
| Apt 1E, Greenwich,
| CT *06830*
Fuchs MR & MRS David C (Stout—Elizabeth G
Pierce) Tufts'65.Csh.Myf.Ne.Ncd.Y'50.Roch'51
MR Joseph S Stout 3d . . . .
MR William C Stout . . . .
| ☎ (516) 271-5254
| 28 Middle Hollow
| Rd, Lloyd Harbor,
| Huntington, NY
| *11743*
Fuguet MR & MRS Stephen G (Myra P Morris) W.Cspa.
''Rough Water'' PO Box 412, Trappe, MD *21673*

Fuhrmann MR & MRS Charles J 2d (Martha M Harris) Cal'77.A.Ri.Hn.H'67.H'69 . . . . ☎ (210) 822-3737
MISS Katherine R—at New York, NY . . . . 550 Ivy Lane,
MISS Alexandra L—at New York, NY . . . . San Antonio, TX
78209-2825

Fuiks MR & MRS Lewis J (Calder—Elizabeth Dodge) Colg'41
2415 Club Dv, Vero Beach, FL 32963

Fulenwider MR & MRS L Calvin JR (Elizabeth M James) Col'33
☎ (303) 733-3817 . . 2552 E Alameda Av, Apt 59, Denver, CO 80209

Fulenwider MR & MRS Michael C (Constance C ☎ (617) 891-1145
Morrow) Cy.Y'62.Mit'65 . . . . 633 Boston Post Rd,
MISS Anne M—at Harvard . . . . Weston, MA 02193
MISS Wendy M P—at Duke . . . .

Fuller MISS Abigail J (Peter D) . . . . Married at Rye Beach, NH
Catalano MR Michael JR . . . . Sep 24'94

Fuller MRS Andrew P (Spreckels—Geraldine Spreckels) K.So.Evg.Cly.
☎ (561) 655-6786 . . 100 El Vedado Way, Palm Beach, FL 33480

Fuller MR & MRS Benjamin A G (Roberta L Taylee) Cda.Dar.P'40.H'52
☎ (508) 688-1364 . . New Pond Village, Apt B112, 180 Main St,
Walpole, MA 02081

Fuller MR & MRS Benjamin A G JR (Leslie R Swem) Pa'69.P'67.Pa'75
HCR 68, Box 196C, Cushing, ME 04563

Fuller MR Cary C—Rol'65
☎ (914) 934-8129 . . 1 Landmark Square, Apt 402, Port Chester,
NY 10573

Fuller MR & MRS D Craig (Linda A Graham) ☎ (610) 525-3102
Cspa.Cw.Rv.Dll.Bab'67.Cl'69 . . . . 1218 Old Gulph Rd,
JUNIORS MISS Ann P . . . . Rosemont, PA
JUNIORS MISS Graham C 19010

Fuller MRS Donald F C (Jane M Grove) Vic'68.Ind'70
74 Chaytor St, Karori, Wellington 5, New Zealand

Fuller MR Donald F C—Vic'72
☎ (011-64-4) 764876 . . 21 Homewood Av, Karori, Wellington 5,
New Zealand

Fuller MISS Elizabeth H—Cly.
☎ (212) 289-2738 . . 1120 Fifth Av, New York, NY 10128-0144

Fuller MR & MRS Ernest M (Dorothy J Barrett) ☎ (203) 966-2394
Hn.H'39 . . . . 67 Orchard Dv,
MISS Faith B . . . . New Canaan, CT
MISS Elizabeth D—at ☎ (212) 535-4691 06840
330 E 83 St, New York, NY 10028 . . . .
MR Samuel A—SUNY'80—at RR 1,
PO Box 4872, Camden, ME 04843 . . . .

Fuller MR & MRS Frank L 3d (Martha R Ely) San.Va'40.Va'48
☎ (802) 325-3549 . . "Indian Pipe" Box 828, Wells, VT 05774

Fuller MR Frederic J—Un.B.T.Mds.Plg.Fw.Km.Geo'39
☎ (212) 289-2738 . . 1120 Fifth Av, New York, NY 10128

Fuller MR G Garry . . see C A Gillespie

Fuller MR Gilbert E—H.'34
☎ (617) 864-1621 . . 364 Rindge Av, Apt 21G, Cambridge, MA 02140

Fuller MR & MRS Hugh (Georgia E Whippo) ☎ (703) 524-1267
AmU'67.AmU'66 . . . . 605 N Florida St,
MR H Robinson—at Wm & Mary . . . . Arlington, VA
22203

Fuller MR & MRS J Kemp G JR (Barbara A Ciullo)
AMagnus'66.Rr.Rv.Cw.Ken'59 . . of
☎ (914) 337-1097 . . 47 Langdon Terr, Bronxville, NY 10708-5910
☎ (516) 537-3730 . . PO Box 91, Bridgehampton, NY 11932

Fuller MR & MRS John M (Virginia E Gadsby) ☎ (415) 342-1608
Bhm.Bur.Cp.Stan'41.Stan'47 . . . . 425 Pinehill Rd,
MRS Catherine W (Steele—Catherine W Fuller) Hillsborough, CA
Stan'70 94010

Fuller MISS Kit . . see C A Gillespie

Fuller MRS M Lea R (Marilyn Lea Ridgley) Purd'58 ☎ (770) 452-7505
MISS Jennifer Lea—GaSt'92—at 2960 Appling Circle,
☎ (770) 642-7980 . . 119 Thrush Dv, Roswell, Chamblee, GA
GA 30075 30341

Fuller MISS Marilynn J
☎ (202) 966-4046 . . 5415 Connecticut Av NW, Apt 541, Washington,
DC 20015

Fuller MR Peirce—H'35
☎ (617) 659-2653 . . Box 323, 110 Chittenden Lane, Norwell,
MA 02061

Fuller MR & MRS Peter D (Joan B Marcotte) 10 Stone Av,
Al.Myf.H.'48 . . . . Chestnut Hill, MA
MISS Jessica L—at ☎ (954) 474-4076 02167-3953
9656 NW 7 Circle, Apt 18-22, Plantation, FL
33324 . . . .
MISS Michelle N M—at ☎ (617) 969-2423
57 Jasset St, Newton, MA 02158 . . . .

Fuller MR & MRS Robert Gorham (Constance W ☎ (617) 461-8326
Bader) Aga.Sm.Cw.Myf.Chi.Ncd.Dar. ⚓ . . . . 10 Longwood Dv,
MR Randolph J—Cw.Myf.Pa'64—at Apt 265, Westwood,
43 Commonwealth Av, Boston, MA 02116 . . . . MA 02090

Fuller MR & MRS Stephen D (Emily Clarkson Hurry)
Pr.Plg.Cc.Cw.Myf.Ds.Cly.Dc.Ncd.Dh.H'30
☎ (516) 922-6560 . . "Harewood" 45 Moores Hill Rd, Oyster Bay,
NY 11771

Fuller MR & MRS Stephen W (Margaret L Cooper)
Va'76.Myf.Cc.NCar'70.Cl'79
☎ (417) 782-4549 . . 3822 Chelsea Dv, Webb City, MO 64870

Fuller MR & MRS Walter G (Erica G Sullivan) Ore'68 . . of
☎ (415) 345-6959 . . 906 Aruba Lane, Foster City, CA 94404
☎ (707) 963-2255 . . 1901 St Helena H'way, Rutherford, CA 94573

Fuller MR & MRS William C JR (Sarah F Wilder) ☎ (617) 326-6433
D.H'73 . . . . 610 High St,
JUNIORS MR Charles L . . . . Westwood, MA
02090

Fullerton MR & MRS E Dwight (Ardelle S Moseley) Myf.H'37
☎ (508) 785-0174 . . 100 Centre St, Dover, MA 02030

Fullerton MR George L—Yn.Md'55
☎ (415) 375-0543 . . 212 Eaton Rd, 32, San Mateo, CA 94402

Fullerton MRS Lindsay P (Bacon—Lindsay F Pettit) ☎ (415) 347-8119
Bur. . . . . 519 Iowa Dv,
MISS Amy G Bacon—Cal'95 San Mateo, CA
MR Russell N Bacon—at Vanderbilt 94402

Fullerton MRS Mallan (Dorothy H Mallan) . . . . ☎ (415) 861-1630
MR Nicholas R—at ☎ (415) 621-3465 145 Connecticut St,
118 Texas St, San Francisco, CA 94107 . . . . . . San Francisco, CA
94107

Fullerton MRS Mary W (Pickett—Mary W ☎ (508) 785-1654
Fullerton) Myf. 3 Meeting House
MR Sean L . . . . Hill Rd, Dover, MA
JUNIORS MR Adam B 02030

Fullerton MR & MRS Reginald H JR (Kathleen G
Knudson) Ln.Why.K.Msq.Y'57 . . . . ☎ (401) 348-8158
 MISS Kimberly G—at ☎ (610) 565-7976 | "The Dormers"
5 Arbor Lane, Rose Valley, PA *19065* . . . . | 3 Everett Av,
 MISS Kirsten K—at Roanoke Coll . . . . | Watch Hill, RI
| *02891*
Fullerton MR & MRS Stuart L (Shelby L Haverson)
Wes'82.Geo'87.Cal'83.Geo'87
 ☎ (610) 667-9265 . . 358 Valley Rd, Merion, PA *19066*
Fulmer MR & MRS Stephen T (Whitney L McGoodwin) Woos'92.Woos'93
 ☎ (207) 865-1216 . . 18 Wardtown Rd, Freeport, ME *04032*
Fulrath MISS Irene—Wheat'67
 ☎ (212) 421-6413 . . 150 E 56 St, New York, NY *10022*
Fulstone MISS H Annette—Col'83
PO Box 747, Silt, CO *81652*
Fulstone MR & MRS Richard N (Georgia M Ames) Bhm.Pcu.Fr.Nev'50
 ☎ (702) 465-2341 . . PO Box 61, Smith Valley, NV *89430*
Fulton MRS James M (Anne H O'Connor) . . . . ☎ (508) 693-1960
 MR James M JR—Cal'79—at | PO Box 79,
13908 Piccadilly Place, Sylmar, CA *91345* . . . . | Mink Meadows,
| Vineyard Haven,
| MA *02568*
Fulton MR & MRS James R (Hayden B O'Rear)
2105 Rexford Rd, Montgomery, AL *36116*
Fulton MISS Leasha C . . see MISS I J Abell
Fultz MRS J Morton JR (Mary L Barrows) Dar.Ncd.
 ☎ (610) 645-5604 . . 3300 Darby Rd, Apt 7309, Haverford,
PA *19041-1075*
Fulweiler MR Hull P—Cc.Snc.Lm.Ht.Va'77
 see Dilatory Domiciles
Fulweiler MISS Pamela S—BMr'73.Cly.Ht.Dc.Dh.Ncd.
 ☎ (212) 534-6158 . . 108 E 91 St, New York, NY *10128*
Fulweiler MRS Spencer B (Patricia L Platt)
BMr'45.Cl'50.Chr.Cly.Ncd.Dc.Cda.Ht. ⚓ . . of
 ☎ (203) 866-6709 . . 3 Hilltop Rd, Wilson Point, South Norwalk,
CT *06854*
 ☎ (212) 744-5395 . . 158 E 83 St, New York, NY *10028*
Fulweiler MR & MRS Spencer B JR (Rena M Zurn)
Conn'82.Y'84.Y'89.Ny.Sfy.Bhy.San.StA.Lm.Snc.Cly. Pa'80
 ☎ (510) 735-3719 . . 357 S Overlook Dv, San Ramon, CA *94583*
Fulweiler MR Thomas B—Sa.Me.Pa'36
 ☎ (610) 525-5860 . . 77 Middle Rd, Apt 156, Bryn Mawr, PA *19010*
Funk DR & MRS Elmer Hendricks JR (Martha J | ☎ (610) 649-9898
Snader) Me.Cs.Hav'44.Jef'47 . . . . | The Quadrangle
 MISS Ellen H—Gord'77.Pa'80.Me.—at | C904, 3300 Darby
 ☎ (610) 649-9474 . . 2945 Berkley Rd, Ardmore, | Rd, Haverford, PA
PA *19003* . . . . | *19041-1065*
Funk MR & MRS W John (Mary Reath) | ☎ (603) 224-7204
ColbyS'68.P'67 | 16 Rockland Rd,
 JUNIORS MISS Lisa A . . . . | Concord, NH *03301*
 JUNIORS MR James T . . . . |
Funkhouser MR & MRS A Paul (Eleanor R Gamble) B.Pn.P'45.Va'50
 ☎ (804) 359-5497 . . 214 Berkshire Rd, Richmond, VA *23221*

Funkhouser DR & MRS John J (M Avery Thompson) | ☎ (508) 548-1394
Wh'lck'61.Y.'59.Va'63 . . . . | "Sandy Rock"
 MISS Margaret A—Wes'94 . . . . | 32 Chapoquoit Rd,
 MR Christopher T—Va'86.Va'88—at | Box 394,
 ☎ (518) 435-0450 . . 8 Caldwell Av, Albany, NY | West Falmouth, MA
12208 . . . . | *02574*
 MR Stewart M—W&L'88—at ☎ (401) 885-1507 |
16 Herbert St, Warwick, RI *02878* . . . . |
Funnell MR & MRS E Stephen (Stern—Susan A Guernsey)
Stph'72.Pitt'76.Camb'69
 ☎ (011-44-181) 767-8600 . . 15 Hendham Rd, London SW17 7DH,
England
Funsten MISS de Lancey—Col'80.Wes'90
 ☎ (203) 662-0737 . . 82 Pear Tree Point, Darien, CT *06820*
Funsten MR & MRS Edward S JR (Cook—Marilyn N Hitchcock)
Cal'47.Cysl.Yn.Y'44
 ☎ (860) 767-8145 . . 9 Primrose Ledge Rd, PO Box 401, Essex,
CT *06426*
Funston MRS G Keith (Elizabeth Kennedy) Rr.Ln.C.Plg.StJ . . .of
 ☎ (203) 869-5524 . . 74 Vineyard Lane, Greenwich, CT *06831*
 ☎ (941) 472-1115 . . 911 Strangler Fig Lane, Sanibel Island, FL *33957*
Furlaud MRS Banks (Elspeth H Banks) Ri.
 ☎ (212) 831-0358 . . 124 E 92 St, New York, NY *10128*
Furlaud MR & MRS Maxime Jay (Alice E Nelson) Rdc'51.P'47
 ☎ (508) 349-2132 . . Box 965, Holsbery Rd, Truro, MA *02666*
Furlaud MR & MRS Richard M (Allen—Philbin—Isabel G T Phelps)
Ln.Ri.Mds.BtP.Evg.Cly.P'44.H'47 . . of
 ☎ (561) 848-2267 . . 745 High Mount Rd, Palm Beach, FL *33480*
 ☎ (212) 355-5419 . . 435 E 52 St, New York, NY *10022*
Furlong MISS Cynthia E—SFr'92 . . see J F Arndt JR
Furlong MISS Sharon S . . see J F Arndt JR
Furness MISS Anne W—Bost'50.Sim'51.Ncd.
 ☎ (617) 864-2639 . . 4 Channing Circle, Cambridge, MA *02138-4716*
Furniss MR & MRS Richard A JR (Reventlow— | ☎ (860) 672-0034
Rosalie W Ripley) Benn'70.Pa'60.Pa'62 . . . . . . | 163 Cornwall
 JUNIORS MR R Vanneman—at Skidmore . . . . | Hollow Rd,
| West Cornwall, CT
| *06796*
Furrh MR & MRS James B JR (Mary L Hendee) NCar'54.Tex'50
 ☎ (601) 982-9177 . . 4015 Boxwood Circle, Jackson, MS *39211*
Furse MRS G Ronald (McKim—C Pamela Fowler) . . . . Died at
West Hoathly, Sussex, England May 2'96
Furse MR G Ronald—K.Fic. | ☎ (011-44-1342)
 MISS Elizabeth W—Wheat'79—at | 715-219
186 Stony Hill Rd, Hampden, MA *01036* . . . . . | Old House,
 MR William R—Box 712, Claverack, NY *12513* | West Hoathly,
 MISS Charlotte W McKim—at | Sussex RH19 4RA,
 ☎ (201) 746-7559 . . 24 Edgecliff Rd, | England
Upper Montclair, NJ *07043* . . . . |
Fusz MR Daniel D
 ☎ (314) 469-1969 . . 12 Woods Hill Dv, St Louis, MO *63011*
Fusz MR & MRS Louis J (Martha L Downard) Ursul'45.Evg.Geo'41 . . of
 ☎ (314) 994-1640 . . 925 N Lindbergh Blvd, St Louis, MO *63141*
 ☎ (561) 655-4842 . . 1617 N Flagler Dv, West Palm Beach, FL *33407*

Fusz MR & MRS Louis J JR (Corinne E Whitelaw) | ☎ (314) 994-1770
Cy.Geo'69 . . . . | 750 Kent Rd,
MISS Corinne O'D. . . . . | St Louis, MO *63124*
JUNIORS MR Louis J 3d . . . .
JUNIORS MR Randolph W. . . . .
JUNIORS MR Peter D. . . . .
Fusz MR Philip R (Louis J) . . . . Married at St Louis, MO
Wiegman MISS Marla (Marvin) . . . . Apr 13'96
Futcher DR Palmer H—Ph.H'32.JHop'36 . . . | 13801 York Rd, Apt
MISS Marjorie R . . . . | D11, Cockeysville,
MISS Jane P—at ☎ (415) 382-8048 | MD *21030*
235 Shevelin Rd, Novato, CA *94947* . . . . |

G

Gable MISS Elizabeth B—Van'83
☎ (202) 333-6055 . . 3339 Dent Place NW, Washington, DC *20007*
Gable MR James S (Robert E) . . . . Married at Washington, DC
Guillermin MISS Lisa V A (A Pierre) . . . . Apr 13'96
Gable MR John S—Van'87.Duke'93
2250 NW Kearney St, Apt 409, Portland, OR *97210*
Gable MR & MRS Robert E (Emily B Thompson) Swb'55.Stan'56
☎ (502) 695-1674 . . 1715 Stonehaven Dv, Frankfort, KY *40601*
Gabriel MR & MRS K Georg (Margaret De Vecchi) | ☎ (202) 232-2401
Bnd'51.Mt.Sl.H'56 . . . . | 2401 Tracy Place
MISS Wendy—Bnd'90. . . . . | NW, Washington,
| DC *20008-1628*
Gabriel MR & MRS Robert P (M Megan Roberts)
MmtVa'87.Mt.V'85.Geo'96
☎ (202) 338-3412 . . 3412 Q St NW, Washington, DC *20007*
Gadsden MR & MRS Charles C (Marie E Dittmann) | of ☎ (914)738-3999
Sth'46.Ny.Aht'45 . . . . | Pelham Manor
MISS Pamela D—AmU'85—at 4105 Wisconsin | Gardens, Apt 2B,
Av NW, Washington, DC *20016* . . . . | 4810 Boston Post
MR Charles C JR . . . . | Rd, Pelham Manor,
| NY *10803*
| ☎ (401) 635-8638
| 66 Bailey's Ledge,
| Little Compton, RI
| *02837*
Gadsden MR & MRS Christopher H (Eleanore R B | ☎ (215) 242-8265
Hoeffel) Ws'69.Ph.Pc.Y'68.Y'73 . . . . | 140 W Chestnut Hill
MISS Eleanore P—at Yale . . . . | Av, Philadelphia,
MR William C—Y'94 . . . . | PA *19118*
JUNIORS MISS Patricia C. . . . . |
Gadsden MRS Henry W (Patricia Parker)
☎ (610) 645-8661 . . 1400 Waverly Rd, V12, Gladwyne, PA *19035*
Gaffney MR & MRS Frank J (Klopfer—Virginia B | ☎ (412) 963-6298
Reed) BMr'44.Fcg.Tc.StJos'42 . . . . | 320 Ft Duquesne
MISS Rachel R—at ☎ (617) 354-4219 | Blvd, Apt 6D,
6 Linnaean St, Cambridge, MA *02138* . . . . | Pittsburgh, PA
| *15222-1107*
Gagarin MR & MRS Andrew (Jamie Porter) B'gton'39.Ri.Y'37
☎ (860) 567-5237 . . 108 Gallows Lane, Litchfield, CT *06759*

Gagarin MR & MRS Peter S (Nancy E Tyner) Yn.Y'45w
☎ (203) 869-7885 . . 11 Round Hill Club Rd, Greenwich, CT *06831*
Gagarin MR & MRS Serge S (Frances W Moore) | ☎ (203) 259-7332
Y'40. . . . . | ''Banks House''
MR Charles P—Y'72. . . . . | 975 Banks North
| Rd, Fairfield, CT
| *06430*
Gage MR Alan K—Y.'39
☎ (212) 535-3774 . . 30 E 71 St, New York, NY *10021-4956*
Gagel MR & MRS J Frederic (L Jane Earnshaw) Mvh.Mor.Y'35
☎ (513) 298-4422 . . 56 Briar Hill Rd, Dayton, OH *45419-3429*
Gagné MR & MRS Philip B (Doreen F Gunnett) Penn'84.Hob'79 . . of
☎ (410) 544-3104 . . 21 Windward Dv, Severna Park, MD *21146*
☎ (609) 368-6953 . . 2090 Sixth Av, Avalon, NJ *08202*
Gagné MR & MRS W Roderick (Pamela J Bashore)
Van'77.Dick'80.Pc.R.Rc.Ds.Ac.Dar.Ithaca'76. Dick'80.Geo'83
☎ (215) 233-5737 . . 515 Cresheim Valley Rd, Wyndmoor, PA *19038*
Gahagan MR & MRS William G (Katharine H du Pont) Wil.Y'52
☎ (302) 655-9183 . . 601 Smiths Bridge Rd, Wilmington, DE *19807*
Gaier MR & MRS Mark J (Kathryn P Beckwith) Fcg.Pg.Rr.AmU'84
☎ (412) 963-1463 . . 192 Woodland Farms Rd, Pittsburgh, PA *15238*
Gaillard MR & MRS E Davis (Allen Van Tine) | ☎ (518) 439-2080
Duke'43 . . . . | 21 Ridge Rd,
MISS Mary B—Wheat'72—at ☎ (212) 691-7031 | Delmar, NY *12054*
29 Jones St, New York, NY *10014* . . . . |
Gaillard MRS Elizabeth H (Love—Elizabeth F Hitchcock) Cs.
☎ (212) 249-1030 . . 325 E 72 St, New York, NY *10021*
Gaillard MR Stephen L—Duke'46.H'47
☎ (212) MO1-3273 . . 325 E 41 St, New York, NY *10017*
Gaillard MR & MRS William D (Katharine J Freie) | ☎ (203) 661-4716
Ws'56.Nu'68.Pn.P'53.H'56 . . . . | 17 Meeting House
MR David L—Wms'89 . . . . | Rd, Greenwich, CT
MR Jeffrey S—Dth'92. . . . . | *06831*
Gaillard DR & MRS (DR) William D (Adelaide S Robb)
Sth'83.JHop'87.Y'80.Y'85
☎ (301) 657-9019 . . 3700 Kenilworth Dv Way, Chevy Chase,
MD *20815*
Gaines MRS Frances P (Frances M Poor) Skd'66
☎ (203) 853-4450 . . 15 Pennoyer St, Rowayton, CT *06853*
Gaines MR L Ebersole—Cvc.Rr.P'51
☎ (202) 362-1104 . . 4369 Westover Place NW, Washington, DC *20016*
Gaither MRS John D (Maxine West)
☎ (602) 933-0632 . . 18170 N 91 Av, Apt 1122, Peoria, AZ *85382*
Gaither MR & MRS John S (Shirley A Anderson) | ☎ (919) 471-2202
WmW'ds'72.Cw.Pa'67.EuroInst'72 . . . . | Fox View Farm,
JUNIORS MISS Christina E. . . . . | 1220 Hopkins Rd,
| Bahama, NC *27503*
Galacar MR & MRS Frederic L (Kathleen Wick) Tufts'69
☎ (508) 526-1749 . . ''Image Hill'' 27 Old Neck Rd, Manchester,
MA *01944*
Galatti MR & MRS Stephen (Hall—Correll Clancy) H'52.Va'56
☎ (914) 677-5000 . . PO Box 1433, Millbrook, NY *12545*
Galban MR & MRS Leandro S JR (Beverley C Mountain)
B'gton'60.H.'57 . . of
☎ (212) 674-5674 . . 1 Fifth Av, New York, NY *10003*
☎ (516) 537-0089 . . 453 Hedges Lane, Box 453, Sagaponack, NY *11962*

Galban MR Leandro S 3d (Leandro S JR) . . . . . Married at Lewiston, ME
Voisine MISS Carol-Ann (late Milferd) . . . . Jun 4'93
Galbraith MR & MRS Evan G (Marie H Rockwell) ☎ (212) 772-0944
V'52.Cly.Y.'50.H'53 . . . . 133 E 64 St,
MISS Christina M . . . . New York, NY
MR Evan G 3d *10021*
MR John H . . . .
Galbraith MRS George S R (Helen N Boyle) Bnd'38
☎ (914) 722-4811 . . 120 E Hartsdale Av, Apt 4G, Hartsdale, NY *10530*
Gale MR & MRS Daniel B 2d (Nancy S Miller) Pcu.Fr.Wash'57
☎ (415) 435-1185 . . 280 Belvedere Av, Belvedere, CA *94920*
Gale MR Daniel Bailey III—Humb'90
☎ (707) 443-1783 . . PO Box 4656, Arcata, CA *95518-4656*
Gale MR & MRS Gordon E (Chesson—Angela G ☎ (803) 784-6461
Sigmon) NCar'67.Cc.Va'73 . . . . Red Bluff
JUNIORS MR Elbridge StJ—at 1618 Oxford Rd, Plantation, Rte 1,
Charlottesville, VA *22903* . . . . Box 169,
  Hardeeville, SC
  29927
Gale MISS Jane—RSage'48
☎ (518) 283-7636 . . 32 McKinley Way, Apt E4, Wynantskill, NY *12198*
Gale MR Oliver Marble—Cm.Qc.H'31.H'37
☎ (513) 321-3920 . . 3798 Ashworth Av, Cincinnati, OH *45208*
Gale MRS Robert A (Karen M Buell) Dll. . . . . ☎ (203) 972-7895
JUNIORS MR John R . . . . 33 Old Stamford Rd,
  Apt 1, New Canaan,
  CT *06840*
Gale MRS Robert I JR (Frances E White) Un.It.Kt.
☎ (216) 946-0173 . . 8020 S Center St, Mentor, OH *44060*
Gales MRS Seaton (Marguerite Decroix) Cly.Bgt . . .of
☎ (212) RH4-4966 . . 149 E 73 St, New York, NY *10021-3555*
☎ (914) 234-3348 . . "Carefree Cottage" Guard Hill Rd, Bedford,
NY *10506*
Gallagher MRS Charles T (Sarah C Woodworth) ☎ (603) 225-5203
Ncd. . . . . 34 Little Pond Rd,
MR T Parker—H'83—at ☎ (617) 864-3924 Concord, NH *03301*
929 Massachusetts Av, Apt 3G, Cambridge, MA
02139 . . . .
Gallagher MR & MRS Charles W (Patricia C Shattuck)
Wis'82.NH'91.Wis'82.VtLaw'86
HCR 69, Box 10, Sanbornton, NH *03269*
Gallagher MR & MRS James R L (Aroline F Stone)
Colby'70.Col'78.NCar'71.ColM'79
☎ (207) 846-3418 . . 18 Cumberland St, Yarmouth, ME *04096*
Gallagher MISS Joan Killian (Warden—Joan K Gallagher) AmU'71 . . of
☎ (212) 779-2532 . . 155 E 34 St, New York, NY *10016*
☎ (203) 966-8839 . . "Pink Gables" 196 Main St, New Canaan,
CT *06840*
Gallagher MR John M JR—Ph.Va'49
☎ (506) 752-2317 . . "Tir-na-N'og" Campobello Island, NB E0G 3H0,
Canada
Gallagher MISS (DR) Marilee Lucas (Coffin— ☎ (216) 831-8334
Marilee Lucas Gallagher) MtH'71.Kt. . . . . . . 2685 Cranlyn Rd,
MISS Elizabeth W Coffin . . . . Shaker Heights, OH
JUNIORS MISS Allison R Coffin *44122*

Gallagher MR & MRS Michael H (Theo T Schwabacher)
Occ'78.Fmy.Tcy.Nu'77 . . of
☎ (415) 921-1144 . . 3050 Pacific Av, San Francisco, CA *94115-1014*
"Casa Albert" 2265 Bear Creek Rd, Alpine Meadows, CA *95730*
Gallagher MRS Peter R (Marion L Everett) . . . . . . ☎ (415) 969-3829
MISS M Elizabeth . . . . 23500 Cristo Rey
  Dv, Apt 201C,
  Cupertino, CA
  95014
Gallagher DR & MRS Rollin McC 3d (Brush— ☎ (516) 689-2271
Virginia A Rauh) Mid'69.H'65 . . . . 28 Conscience
MISS Krysia M Lowell—1422 E Eighth Av, Circle, Strong's
Denver, CO *80218* . . . . Neck, Setauket, NY
MISS Anne Burnett—Box 1162, Ketchum, ID *11733*
83340 . . . .
MR Rollins McC 4th—at Pitzer Coll . . . .
Gallagher MRS Thomas A (Eleanor S Donahue)
Cathedral Village A316, 600 E Cathedral Rd, Philadelphia, PA *19128*
Gallatin MRS James P (Sarah G Heyburn) of ☎ (212)831-2267
V'46.Yh.Pr.Cly.Chr.Plg.StJ.Snc.Ncd. . . . . . . 1165 Fifth Av,
MR Andrew H—at 200 W 70 St, New York, New York, NY
NY *10023* *10029*
  ☎ (516) 692-7008
  34 Middle Hollow
  Rd, Huntington, NY
  11743
Gallatin MR & MRS Thomas G JR (Patricia A McSweeney)
P'72.Pa'77.Ny.Snc.P.'73.Syr'77 ⛵ . . of
☎ (516) 484-9484 . . 16 Addison Lane, Greenvale, NY *11548*
☎ (561) 225-2605 . . Little Ocean Club, 1457 NE Ocean Blvd,
Hutchison Island, FL *34957*
Gallavan MR & MRS Richard A (McKown—Evans—Suzanne L Whiting)
SL'68.An.Mv.Cw.Cda.
☎ (561) 844-3382 . . 248 Colonial Lane, Palm Beach, FL *33480*
Gallaway MR & MRS John M (Grace Bremer) 12938 Coles Cove,
Cr'60.Cl'61 . . . . Gulfport, MS *39503*
MR William D—at 5757 Westheimer Rd,
Apt 3-276, Houston, TX *77057*
MR Steven M—BostColl'96 . . . .
Gallaway MRS Robert W (Charlot—Grace E Draper) . . . . Died Mch 5'96
Galleher DR & MRS Earl P JR (Martha H ☎ (410) 377-9078
Wheelwright) JHop'79.Elk.Md.Mv.Pn.P'49. 17 Meadow Rd,
JHop'53 . . . . Baltimore, MD
MR Earl P 3d *21212*
MR Henry C—Elk.Denis'85 . . . .
Galliher MR John—Leh'35
☎ (212) 355-7712 . . 125 E 63 St, New York, NY *10021*
Gallison MR & MRS H Bailey (Sharilyn L Lemkuil) IaState'66.Mo'70.Mo'48
☎ (619) 457-3834 . . 2874 Torrey Pines Rd, La Jolla, CA *92037*
Galloway DR & MRS Jackson R (Elizabeth Eugenia of ☎ (318)445-3549
Condray) TexTech'66.Tul'70.Sar.Dar.Ncd. 2049 Thornton
Smu'53.LSU'55.Minn'66 . . . . Court, Alexandria,
JUNIORS MISS Claire C . . . . LA *71301*
JUNIORS MR Jackson R JR . . . . ☎ (601) 442-2053
  604 State St,
  Natchez, MS *39120*

Gallún MRS Marjorie M (Marjorie Corcoran McMahon)
☎ (415) 435-8525 . . 14B Beach Rd, Belvedere, CA *94920*

Galpin MR & MRS Stephen K (Ruth B Schwab) Pqt.Yn.Y'43 ⚓
☎ (203) 255-1383 . . 350 Harbor Rd, Southport, CT *06490*

Galston MR & MRS Clarence E (Shields—Nina Moore)
V'35.Cl'38.Au.Pr.Csn.Hn.H'30.H'33
☎ (617) 326-2267 . . 10 Longwood Dv, Apt 330, Westwood, MA *02090*

Galston MR & MRS John W (Mary Lou A Dennin) | ☎ (516) 692-5549
Rc.Au.Csh.Pr.Ny.Mt.Tufts'62.Y.'65 ⚓ . . . . . . | 1580 Laurel Hollow
MISS Alexandra M | Rd, Laurel Hollow,
MR John W JR—at Georgetown . . . . | NY *11791*
JUNIORS MR Matthew D—at Phillips Exeter . . . . |

Galt MISS Judith B—Wash'40
☎ (314) 821-9973 . . 123 E Washington Av, St Louis, MO *63122*

Galt MR & MRS Martin E 3d (Marianne Schultz) | ☎ (314) 991-5010
Cy.Lc.Nd.W&L'64.Wash'67 . . . . | 48 Glen Eagles Dv,
MISS Margaret Farrell . . . . | St Louis, MO *63124*
MR Frederick Scott . . . . |

Galt MR William C . . . . | ☎ (312) WH4-5668
MISS Inez A . . . . | 56 E Division St,
MISS Mary. . . . . | Chicago, IL *60610*

Galt MRS William M 3d (Huston—Nancy E Gardner) . . of
☎ (610) 527-4370 . . ''The Hermitage'' 1218 Round Hill Rd,
Bryn Mawr, PA *19010*
☎ (561) 276-6390 . . 4333 N Ocean Blvd, Apt CN3, Delray Beach,
FL *33483*

Galvis MR & MRS Sergio J (Mary Lee White)
P'87.Cl'92.Ln.Mto.W&M'80.H.'83
☎ (212) 517-3898 . . 1000 Park Av, Apt 4A, New York, NY *10028*

Gambee MISS Fay—V'62.Cs.Nyc.Ncd.
☎ (212) 734-4744 . . 130 East End Av, New York, NY *10028*

Gambee MR & MRS Robert R (Elizabeth G Heard)
Ws'74.Nyc.Cs.P.'64.H'66 . . of
☎ (212) AT9-9393 . . 1230 Park Av, New York, NY *10128*
☎ (914) 967-2424 . . 120 Wendover Rd, Rye, NY *10580*

Gamble MRS Addison (Josephine B Addison) Sl.Mv.Cda.
☎ (202) 362-6493 . . 5040 Glenbrook Terr NW, Washington, DC *20016*

Gamble MRS David S (Frederica V Webb) | ☎ (617) 461-4588
MISS Frederica G—at ☎ (212) 260-6036 | 10 Longwood Dv,
242 E 19 St, New York, NY *10003* . . . . | Apt 511, Westwood,
                                                         | MA *02090*

Gamble MRS Joseph N (Ruth S Baker)
☎ (941) 262-2375 . . 2244 Gulf Shore Blvd N, Naples, FL *34102*

Gamble MR & MRS Launce E (Joan Law) | ☎ (415) 776-6394
Bhm.Pcu.Bur.Stan'58.Cal'60 . . . . | 809 Francisco St,
MISS Sydney . . . . | San Francisco, CA
MR Mark D . . . . | *94109*

Gamble MR & MRS Launce L (Amanda B Michael)
1625—20 St, San Francisco, CA *94107*

Gamble MR & MRS Robert B (Christine Dellard)
Purd'74.Nw'75.Rv.Myf.Hob'73.Bost'74.Emory'76
☎ (414) 832-8360 . . 4013 Windcross Dv, Appleton, WI *54915*

Gamble MRS Robert McD (Brown—Prudence Bredt) B'gton'36
☎ (610) 687-3163 . . 330 Devon State Rd, Devon, PA *19333*

Gamble MR & MRS Theodore R JR (Susan L Stupin)
P'75.H.'79.Rc.B.Ln.Ri.K.Mto.StJ.Cly.Hb.P.'75. H.'77.H'79
860 United Nations Plaza, New York, NY *10017*

Gambrell MRS Charles G (Sarah W Belk) | ☎ (704) 375-3205
Swb'39.Cly.Csn.Ncd.Dar. . . . . | 300 Cherokee Rd,
MISS Sarah B . . . . | Charlotte, NC *28207*

Games MR & MRS Edmund B JR (Elizabeth LeB | ☎ (617) 326-2465
Marshall) Ws'59.Sim'89.D.H.'59 . . . . | 315 Westfield St,
MISS Alison F—H'85.P'92—at ☎ (202) 547-7852 | Dedham, MA *02026*
606 Independence Av SE, Washington, DC *20003* . |

Gammill MR & MRS Lee M JR (Jane Houchin) | ☎ (212) 759-3273
Okla'58.Bhm.Ln.Pcu.Cly.Dth'56 . . . . | 200 E 66 St, Apt
MISS Sarah L—at ☎ (415) 456-3055 | C2103, New York,
PO Box 1148, Ross, CA *94957* . . . . | NY *10021*
MR Christopher M—at ☎ (212) 758-6408 |
200 E 66 St, Apt B1002, New York, NY *10021*. . |

Gammon MRS Audrey Z (von Clemm—Hobson— | ☎ (215) 247-4827
Audrey Zimmermann) . . . . | Hill House Apt 618,
MR John Lea 2d—USN. . . . . | 201 W Evergreen
    MR Jeffrey F Scott—Cr'91. . . . . | Av, Philadelphia,
                                                         | PA *19118*

Gammon MR Blair C—Unn.NCar'47. . . . . | ☎ (804) 984-0393
MISS Cecily C—at ☎ (212) 860-9741 | 323 Harvest Dv,
1060 Park Av, New York, NY *10128*. . . . . | Charlottesville, VA
                                                         | *22903-4852*

Gammon DR & MRS G Davis (Patricia G | ☎ (203) 777-1772
MacLaughlin) Pa'71.Pa'70.Pa'72.Temp'76 . . . . | 33 Edgehill Terr,
JUNIORS MISS Amanda F . . . . | Hamden, CT *06517*

Ganier MR Albert F 3d . . . . | ☎ (615) 352-0458
MISS Patricia P . . . . | 7011 River Road
MISS Alice A. . . . . | Pike, Nashville, TN
JUNIORS MISS Katheryn K . . . . | *37209*

Gannaway MR & MRS Bryan W (C Leigh Flowers) RMWmn'93
☎ (205) 879-7011 . . 2650 Beverly Dv, Birmingham, AL *35223*

Gannett MR & MRS William B (Nancy Y Farnam) | ☎ (508) 473-2516
V'49.Chi. . . . . | 144 Freedom St,
MR W Bristow JR—Lawr'72—at | Hopedale, MA
☎ (713) 438-0738 . . 2931 Robinson Rd, | *01747-1613*
Missouri City, TX *77459* . . . . |

Gannon MISS Elizabeth M (Cook—Morrill—Elizabeth M Gannon)
Md'71.Md'75
☎ (410) 252-9018 . . 46 Tudor Court, Lutherville, MD *21093*

Gano CDR Paul—USN.
☎ (415) 461-3869 . . 223 Evergreen Dv, Kentfield, CA *94904*

Ganoe MR & MRS Charles S (Frances Sue Williams) | ☎ (609) 924-3745
Au.Me.Ds.Pn.Pp.P'51.Pa'52. . . . . | 23 Constitution Hill
MISS Alice N—Ham'86—at ☎ (212) 874-4995 | W, Princeton, NJ
50 W 77 St, New York, NY *10024* . . . . | *08540*

Ganoe MISS F Hemsley (Charles S) . . . . Married at Princeton, NJ
Hughes MR James M (Francis J) . . . . Jun 29'96

Gansa DR & MRS Alexander N (D'Anneo—Jean Charles) Stan'52.Pcu.Tcy.CalTech'54 .... of ☎ (415)922-1201 212 Spruce St, San Francisco, CA *94118*
MR Alexander W von S—P'84—at
☎ (310) 396-7193 . . 2637—4 St, Santa Monica, CA *90405* . . . . 779 Las Olas Dv, Aptos, CA *95003*
MR Andrew N von S—Stan'86 . . . .
MR Charles R von S—Nu'93—at
☎ (212) 334-4171 . . 252 Mott St, Apt 5R, New York, NY *10012* . . . .
MR John F P D'Anneo . . . .
MR Paul A D'Anneo . . . .

Gant MR & MRS William Eugene (Ann L Hammett) Ala'54.B'hamS'56 . . . . ☎ (334) 272-4877 6424 Wynwood Place, Montgomery, AL *36117*
MR William Eugene 3d—SpgH'90.Aub'92 . . . . .
MR Brooks Hammett . . . .

Gantner MR Anthony F . . see MRS S H Sinton JR

Gantner MR John O—Bhm.Cp.Stan'31 . . of
☎ (415) 441-7866 . . 1101 Green St, Apt 601, San Francisco, CA *94109*
☎ (707) 963-4240 . . Schoolhouse Vineyards, Spring Mountain Rd, St Helena, CA *94574*

Gantner MR Stephen E . . see MRS S H Sinton JR

Garcia MR & MRS Luis A (Leslie A Schlumberger) Tex'88.Tex'90
☎ (210) 737-9530 . . 117 W Elsmere Place, San Antonio, TX *78212*

Garcia-Mansilla MR & MRS Lucio S (Jane C Riggs) Pa'67.Rc.B.Pr.Pa'66 . . . . ☎ (516) 922-0556 154 Horseshoe Rd, Mill Neck, NY *11765*
MISS Alexandra R—H'95 . . . .
MR L Riggs—at U of Colo Boulder . . . .

Garde MRS John F JR (Dixon—Harriet P Merritt) Pr.
☎ (516) 671-2695 . . 139 Skunk's Misery Rd, Locust Valley, NY *11560*

Gardiner MR & MRS A Denny (Dervorgilla Kavanagh) Rcn.Pa'70
☎ (203) 661-9512 . . 291 Lake Av, Greenwich, CT *06830*

Gardiner MRS Arthur D (Mary E Courtney)
☎ (413) 532-7322 . . 23 Worthington Dv, South Hadley, MA *01075*

Gardiner MRS Asa B (Harriet C Gibbs) V'41.Ncd.
☎ (904) 388-4270 . . 1660 Pershing Rd, Jacksonville, FL *32205*

Gardiner MR & MRS Charles W (Jane T Lothrop) V'53.Tv.Ec.H'50 . . . . ☎ (508) JA6-1557 52 Bridge St, Manchester, MA *01944*
MISS Elizabeth L—H'87 . . . .
MR Charles L—NCar'82 . . . .

Gardiner MR & MRS E Nicholas P (Bron—Sigrid Becker) Rc.B.Cc.Y.'61 . . of
☎ (212) 628-0037 . . 23 E 74 St, New York, NY *10021*
☎ (914) 351-5386 . . Westlake Stable Rd, Tuxedo Park, NY *10987*

Gardiner MR & MRS Gordon A (Nina C Smith) P'80.CUNY'83.SCalArch'91.H'79
☎ (510) 658-6868 . . 129 Bonita Av, Piedmont, CA *94611-3901*

Gardiner MR & MRS Henry (Bramwell—Katharine H Emmet) Unn.Au.C.Pn.P'38
7 Meadow Lakes, 04-06U, Hightstown, NJ *08520-0070*

Gardiner MR & MRS Henry G (Ward—Haymes—Eunice Schirrman) H'50
☎ (561) 697-2867 . . 2885 Eagle Lane, West Palm Beach, FL *33409*

Gardiner MR & MRS Ian H (Joanne Gardella) Col'69.Sm.Ec.H'68.H'74 . . . . ☎ (508) 922-8512 38 Paine Av, Prides Crossing, MA *01965*
MISS Abigail H—Ham'95 . . . .
MR Ian H JR—at Middlebury . . . .

Gardiner MR & MRS J Brooke (Beth Lloyd) San.Hav'51.NCar'57 . . . . ☎ (908) AD3-5270 1364 Stony Brook Lane, Mountainside, NJ *07092*
MR Allen B—JHop'92 . . . .
MR Blair L

Gardiner MR & MRS J Matthew (Rebekah L Lord) PhilaArt'87.Pa'88
☎ (617) 893-4082 . . 16 Warren Place, Weston, MA *02193*

Gardiner MR & MRS James B 2d (Gaines—Haddock—Alice May) Snc.Cc.Cw.Ht.Rv.Ofp.Sar.Coa. Y'28 . . . . ☎ (212)982-6815 5 Stuyvesant Oval, New York, NY *10009*
MR James B 3d—Box 8671, Moscow, ID *83843*
1250 S Washington St, Alexandria, VA *22314*

Gardiner MR John J 3d—Bhm.Bost'70
☎ (415) 441-6383 . . 999 Green St, Apt 1105, San Francisco, CA *94133*

Gardiner MR & MRS Philip D (Dominique S M Demonchaux) NewHaven'79
☎ (610) 917-9275 . . 96 S Forge Manor Dv, Phoenixville, PA *19460* . . MRS absent

Gardiner MR & MRS Richard E (Malgorzata Jozwik) U'73
☎ (703) 569-6782 . . 7404 Estaban Place, Springfield, VA *22151*

Gardiner MR & MRS Robert D L (Oakes—Eunice J Bailey) Rcn.Ny.Chr.Dyc.Evg.Snc.Cw.Cc.Rw.Fw.Ht.Cl'34. LIU'70
☎ (561) 655-6028 . . 165 Atlantic Av, Palm Beach, FL *33480*

Gardiner MR & MRS Robert M (Margaret L Johnston) NCar'37
☎ (804) 793-1739 . . 118 Lady Astor St, Danville, VA *24541*

Gardiner MR & MRS Robert M (Valentine—Elizabeth G Walker) Man'vl'59.Shcc.Ln.Err.Eh. Eyc.DelB.Cly.P'44 . . . . ☎ (908) 766-0269 "Mayfields" Box 265, Lake Rd, Far Hills, NJ *07931*
MISS Glynn Valentine—Vt'88.Shcc. . . . .

Gardiner MR Sargent C—Cr'91 . . see G H P Dwight

Gardiner MRS Thomas (Chatfield—L Lansdale Daley) Sm.Chi.Ncd. ☎ (207) 443-4300 Box 801, RR 3, Phips Point, Woolwich, ME *04579*
MR Frederick H Chatfield JR—H'70—at 85 Fowler Rd, Far Hills, NJ *07931* . . . .
MR Christopher R Chatfield—NCar'73—at "Hunts End Farm" Lincolnville, ME *04849* .

Gardiner MR Timothy M . . see B P Webb

Gardner MRS Ainslie A (Farley—Mary Ainslie Anderson) Rdc'45.Sm.Chi.Srb.
☎ (401) 846-2165 . . "Roselawn" 701 Bellevue Av, Newport, RI *02840*

Gardner MR & MRS Arthur W (Joan A Landor) Mt.Cvc.B.Sl.
☎ (202) 337-5577 . . 3010 Woodland Dv NW, Washington, DC *20008*

Gardner MR & MRS David T (Dana L Mericle) ClmbusC'95.Stan'84
☎ (706) 569-8869 . . 5508 Southlea Lane, Columbus, GA *31909*

Gardner MRS Edward P (Clapp—Ruby N Smith) . . ☎ (203) 966-3778 131 Mariomi Rd, New Canaan, CT *06840*
MR Edward P JR—at ☎ (203) 375-6437 103 Lordship Rd, Stratford, CT *06497* . . . .

Gardner MRS Edward T JR (Elizabeth Paxton)
☎ (561) 734-1089 . . 6830 N Ocean Blvd, Maisonettes South, Apt 2, Ocean Ridge, FL *33435*

Gardner MISS Elinor Mericle (David T) . . . . Born at Traverse City, MI Jly 14'95

Gardner MR Esmond B . . . . Died at New York, NY Jun 6'96

Gardner MRS Esmond B (Merryweather—Clarke—Nancy Bruff) Cs.Ht.Cda. . . . . ☎ (212) 752-8774 200 E 66 St, Apt D803, New York, NY *10021*
  MISS Penelope Clarke—at Lasqueti Island, BC, Canada

Gardner MISS Eva—H'81
  ☎ (212) 431-6164 . . 140 Grand St, New York, NY *10013*

Gardner MISS Frances—DU'77 . . see MRS H L Connell

Gardner MR & MRS Frederick (Gael Williams) Y'55.Camb'57 . . . . ☎ (609) 466-9472 ''Weathertop Farm'' 46 North Hill Rd, Ringoes, NJ *08551*
  MISS Clare W
  MR Frederick P

Gardner MR & MRS Frederick D (Martha J Pranger) NotreD'57 . . . . 8126 Gannon Av, St Louis, MO *63130*
  MISS Martha C—at 6329 N Rosebury Av, Clayton, MO *63105* . . . .

Gardner MR & MRS George P (Tatiana Stepanova) Tv.Cy.Ln.Chi.H'39 . . of
  ☎ (617) 232-3781 . . Greenhill, 135 Warren St, Brookline, MA *02146*
  160 Seaview Av, Palm Beach, FL *33480*

Gardner MRS Henry Alfred (Bland—Mary Briscoe Shepherd) Cvc.
  ☎ (603) 436-5957 . . 290 Pleasant St, Portsmouth, NH *03801*

Gardner MR & MRS Henry K (Barbara W Crawford) Sr.Cho.Cnt.Fy.Y'45 . . of
  ☎ (847) 234-3381 . . 693 E Spruce Av, Lake Forest, IL *60045*
  ☎ (941) 262-3874 . . 1065 Gulf Shore Blvd N, Apt 408, Naples, FL *34102*

Gardner MR & MRS John L (Susan B Kobusch) Sbc.Tv.Sm.My.H.'45 . . . . ☎ (508) 468-1200 ''Stormfield'' 375 Bridge St, South Hamilton, MA *01982*
  MR John L JR

Gardner MR & MRS John R (McPherron—Dorothy S Hannon) Cas.Cho.Ih.Wa.Y'65.Ch'67 . . . . of ☎ (847)251-3758 94 Indian Hill Rd, Winnetka, IL *60093*
  MISS Elizabeth F—StLaw'86.Mid'88—at
  ☎ (312) 226-5458 . . 835 N Wood St, Apt 305, Chicago, IL *60622* . . . . ☎ (970) 926-2786 Box 1318, Edwards, CO *81632*
  MISS Dorcas W—Cl'90—at 147 Broadway, Brooklyn, NY *11211* . . . .
  MISS Melissa D—NEng'93—at 500 E-Ku-Sumee Dv, Candor, NC *27229*
  MR William A H—at New England Coll . . . . . .

Gardner MR & MRS John W (Aida Marroquin) Stan'35 836 Lathrop Dv, Stanford, CA *94305*

Gardner MRS Ledyard D (F Barbara Legg)
  ☎ (561) 775-9037 . . Prosperity Oaks Apt 524, 11381 Prosperity Farms Rd, Palm Beach Gardens, FL *33410*

Gardner MR & MRS M Dozier (Margaret S Butler) Cy.Sm.H.P'55 . . . . ☎ (617) 734-5725 100 Upland Rd, Brookline, MA *02146*
  MISS Diana S

Gardner CDR & MRS Richmond (Helen M Lovejoy) Ny.USN'51.Mit'57 . . . . ☎ (617) 729-3526 15 Edgehill Rd, Winchester, MA *01890-3915*
  MISS Amy E—Box 2742, Decatur, AL *35602* . . .
  MR Richmond L—BostColl'90—aboard USS L Y Spear, AS 36, FPO AE, *09547-2600* . .
  MR David F—Wag'88—at ☎ (212) 627-0835 351 W 14 St, New York, NY *10014* . . . .

Gardner MRS Robert H JR (Wilma A Murphy) Clar'52
  ☎ (704) 859-6529 . . 212 Glenwalden Circle, Tryon, NC *28782*

Gardner MR & MRS Robert H 3d (Meredith V Martin) NFla'92.Woff'77 . . . . ☎ (904) 645-5628 8144 Pine Lake Rd, Jacksonville, FL *32256*
  JUNIORS MISS Caroline F . . . .

Gardner MR Stephen V (late Colin) . . . . . . Married at Little Compton, RI Thayer MRS Sydney 3d (Drayton—Edith M Bettle) . . . . Jun 15'96

Gardner MR & MRS Stephen V (Drayton—Thayer—Edith M Bettle) Mvh.Me.Y'52 . . . . of ☎ (912)638-4505 309 Bowler Av, PO Box 30204, Sea Island, GA *31561*
  MR Frederick R Drayton 3d—at
  ☎ (617) 965-3907 . . 1110 Chestnut St, Upper Newton Falls, MA *02164* . . . . ☎ (941) 964-2560 1935—19 St, PO Box 1526, Boca Grande, FL *33921*

Gardner MR & MRS Wilfred E (Elizabeth E Ballantine) V'62.Br'65.Ncd.F&M'60.H.'63 . . . . ☎ (617) 235-7707 76 Garden Rd, Wellesley Hills, MA *02181*
  MR James E—Rens'95 . . . .

Gardner MRS William E (Gloria Hohnke) Mv.Mor.
  ☎ (513) 293-9032 . . 3780 Ridgeleigh Rd, Ridgeleigh Woods, Dayton, OH *45429*

Gardner MR William K . . . . Died Feb 13'96

Gardner MRS Wray R (Pitcairn—Florence P Humphrey)
  ☎ (412) 622-9804 . . Independence Court, 4700 Fifth Av, Pittsburgh, PA *15213*

Garesché MR & MRS Edmond A B 3d (C Diane Raith) Rcsl.P'52
  ☎ (941) 594-5431 . . 748 St George's Court, Naples, FL *34110*

Garesché MRS Gladys M (Finnegan—Gladys M Bonney)
  ☎ (407) 831-0589 . . 439 Orange Dv, Altamonte Springs, FL *32701*

Garesché MR & MRS Thomas K (Margaret I Labourdette) Wh'lck'55.Ford'55 . . . . ☎ (914) 238-4830 45 Commodore Rd, Chappaqua, NY *10514*
  MR Edmond L—CathU'89 . . . .
  MR Alfred V Z—AmU'91 . . . .
  MR John M—Bates'93 . . . .

Garesché MR & MRS Thomas M (Donna L Doherty) StAnselm'88.StAnselm'88
  ☎ (617) 784-5543 . . 157 East St, Sharon, MA *02067*

Garesché MRS William McB (Bertha R Arsenault)
  ☎ (314) 965-1640 . . 435 N Harrison Av, St Louis, MO *63122*

Garfield MISS Eleanor—Cy.Chi.Ncd.
  ☎ (617) 731-5255 . . 10 Longwood Dv, Westwood, MA *02090*

Garfield MR & MRS Michael R (Mary C Seymour) H'63.Bost'66 . . . . ☎ (508) 358-7686 142 Pelham Island Rd, Wayland, MA *01778*
  MR Michael R JR—StLaw'88 . . . .

Garland MRS Charles S (Aurelia Stoner) Mv.Cda.
  ☎ (410) 243-5321 . . 830 W 40 St, Apt 653, Baltimore, MD *21211-2134*

Garlich MR & MRS Greg A (Elizabeth B Smyth) UMiami'79.UMiami'77.Wash'86 . . of
  ☎ (314) 569-1445 . . 12 Crosswinds Dv, Olivette, MO *63132-4300*
  ☎ (417) 779-5127 . . 1000 Paradise Landing, Kimberling City, MO *65686*

Garmey MR & MRS Ronald (Diana O Bangs) | of ☎ (617)424-9039
Cy.Ub.Chi.H.'60.H'63 . . . . | 242 Beacon St,
MISS Amory—at 130B Loomis St, Burlington, VT | Boston, MA *02116*
05401 . . . . | ☎ (413) 298-4974
JUNIORS MR James O—at Hobart-Wm Smith . . . . | Box 1200,
| Train Hill Rd,
| Stockbridge, MA
| *01262*

Garnant MRS Jack W (Gertrude Jewett) Myf. . . . . . | ☎ (914) 359-1932
MR Gregory B—Myf.Rv.Nu'78.Nu'83 . . . . | "Watercrest"
| 66 Andre Av,
| Tappan, NY *10983*

Garnett MR & MRS Anthony T (Lucie C Palmer) | ☎ (314) 367-8080
Y'68.Ox'54 . . . . | 5399 Lindell Blvd,
MISS Lucie C—Bow'94 . . . . | St Louis, MO *63112*
MR William J—at Bates . . . . |

Garnett MR & MRS Bradford L (Melanie H Fleischmann)
Pa'77.Pl.Cly.W'ham'70
☎ (914) 669-5283 . . "Jumpstart Hill" 698 Titicus Rd, North Salem,
NY *10560*

Garnett MRS James H P (Maria D M Deyo) Cvc.
☎ (207) 439-3916 . . PO Box 191 "Hookes Cove" Kittery Point,
ME *03905*

Garnett MRS Muscoe R H (Helene D Wallace) Ncd.Dc.
☎ (804) 443-2051 . . "Elmwood" Loretto, VA *22509*

Garretson MR & MRS James 2d (Sara C Panks) MtH'63.Pratt'67 . . of
370 Central Park W, New York, NY *10025*
☎ (518) 794-7716 . . "Fox Hollow" Hunt Club Rd, Old Chatham,
NY *12136*

Garrett MR & MRS Darryl N (Cabell—Janet M | ☎ (202) 333-6967
West) Swb'65.Cvc.TexTech'72.NMexSt'74.H'85 | 3327 Cleveland Av
MR Benjamin Cabell 5th—at Worcester | NW, Washington,
Polytech . . . . | DC *20008*

Garrett MR David T—Y'88.H'91.Cl'94
☎ (718) 624-3877 . . 100 Remsen St, Apt 4G, Brooklyn, NY *11201*

Garrett REV & MRS Edwin A 3d (Margaret E | ☎ (207) 288-5362
Whitaker) Cw.H'46 . . . . | "Otter Cove Farm"
MR Edwin A 4th—W.Cw.Rv.Ht.Me'82.Me'91 . . | Otter Cliffs Rd,
| PO Box 355,
| Bar Harbor, ME
| *04609*

Garrett MR & MRS George P (Susan P Jackson) Pn.P'52
☎ (804) 979-5366 . . 1845 Wayside Place, Charlottesville, VA *22903*

Garrett MR & MRS Richard G (Sylvia B Houghton) | ☎ (410) 822-4378
Cly.Cda.Ncd.P'47.Y'54 . . . . | 27873 Le Gates
MR Michael H . . . . | Cove Rd, Easton,
MR David R . . . . | MD *21601*
MR Stephen B . . . . |

Garrett MR & MRS Robert (Jacqueline E Marlas) | ☎ (212) 570-0791
Ri.K.Plg.StJ.Nyc.Cs.Cly.P'59.H'65 . . . . | 941 Park Av,
MR Robert JR—P'90—at ☎ (212) 873-6536 | New York, NY
115 W 74 St, Apt 4B, New York, NY *10023* . . . | *10028*
MR Johnson—P'91 . . . . |

Garrett MRS Thomas Cresson (Adelaide McC Jefferys)
☎ (941) 349-7346 . . 8436 Midnight Pass Rd, Sarasota, FL *34242*

Garrett DR & MRS Thomas H (Marie-Louise K | ☎ (707) 542-8170
Detert) P'61.JHop'66 . . . . | 1104 McDonald Av,
MR Thomas H JR—Mid'93 . . . . | Santa Rosa, CA
MR John W—Cal'95 . . . . | *95404*

Garrett MRS William Calvert (Harris P Kramer) Sth'48
☎ (214) 692-5803 . . 5805 Farquhar Dv, Dallas, TX *75205*

Garrett DR & MRS William S JR (Ann Lucas)
Skd'53.Cwr'57.Tc.Leh'51.H'55
☎ (412) 781-6123 . . 405 E Waldheim Rd, Pittsburgh, PA *15215*

Garrigue MISS Anne M
see Dilatory Domiciles

Garrigue MR & MRS Paul (Sheila K Hogg) H'54 . . . | ☎ (914) 666-9322
MISS Elizabeth K M—H'87 . . . . | 17 Ludlow Dv,
MR Matthew D—H'82.H'87 . . . . | Chappaqua, NY
MR Andrew H—H'86 . . . . | *10514*

Garrison MRS John D (Edith Hooe) Yn.
☎ (860) 767-2419 . . 247 Essex Meadows, Essex, CT *06426*

Garrison MR & MRS Maynard (Mary E Spalding) | ☎ (415) 752-5050
Sfg.Ds.P'50.Stan'53 . . . . | 50 Arguello Blvd,
MISS Elizabeth S—StAndr'92—at | San Francisco, CA
☎ (415) 386-8660 . . 12 Commonwealth Av, | *94118*
San Francisco, CA *94118* . . . . |

Garrison MR & MRS William B JR (Newbold—Mary | ☎ (703) 548-1030
W Day) Cvc.Duke'70 . . . . | 608 Cameron St,
MR Thomas D Newbold | Alexandria, VA
MR James F Newbold . . . . | *22314*

Garside MR & MRS Grenville (Barbara W Lawrence) Sth'56.P'52.Va'59
☎ (860) 542-5622 . . 289 Grantville Rd, Norfolk, CT *06058*

Garstin MRS Geoffrey S (Ann Nields) Pa'36.Ncd.
☎ (302) 655-2319 . . 5603 Kennett Pike, Wilmington, DE *19807*

Gartman MR John S . . see C S Ashdown JR

Gartman MISS Vivian M . . see C S Ashdown JR

Garvan MRS Anthony N B (Lippincott—Beatrice W Bronson) Rc.Cs.
☎ (215) MI6-3310 . . "Llan-Gwydden" PO Box 304, Spring House,
PA *19477*

Garvan MRS Jackson (Hope Jackson) Cly.
☎ (212) 249-3740 . . 47 E 64 St, New York, NY *10021*

Garver MR & MRS John A (Humes—Suzanne Lanctot)
Pr.K.Csh.Y.'67.Ford'70
☎ (516) OB4-8959 . . 201 Sunset Rd, Oyster Bay, NY *11771*

Garvey DR & MRS James McB JR (Mary Blair Buggie) V'50.P'50.Cl'54
☎ (513) 871-4063 . . 1 Nita Lane, Cincinnati, OH *45208*

Garvey MR John P—Y'52
☎ (212) 675-8658 . . 10 Morton St, New York, NY *10014*

Garvin MR & MRS B Russell W (Margaret G Perry) | ☎ (415) 661-6100
LakeF'63.Tufts'67.FlaSt'64.FlaSt'66 . . . . | 235 Grattan St,
JUNIORS MR Perry R . . . . | San Francisco, CA
| *94117*

Garvy MR & MRS Eugene J (Adeline M Harrington) | ☎ (630) 887-8473
Rc.Y'41.H'43 . . . . | 801 The Pines,
MR Anthony J—LoyCh'90—at | Hinsdale, IL *60521*
☎ (312) 335-9726 . . 1560 N Sandburg Terr, |
Chicago, IL *60610* . . . . |

Garwood MR & MRS Calvin B 3d (Tarlton—Sally M Howe) Tex'84
4006 Piping Rock Lane, Houston, TX *77207*

Garwood MR John M . . see C Runnells

Gary MR Arthur J—Plg.Bcs.Chr.Nu'36.Cl'38
☎ (212) 876-6503 . . 1212 Fifth Av, New York, NY *10029-5210*
Gary MISS E Tracy Du V . . see M de Bary
Gary MRS Wyndham L (Hatch—Shirley D Spaulding) Rm.Cly . . .of
☎ (908) 747-3578 . . 39 Cheshire Square, Little Silver, NJ *07739*
☎ (619) 321-1853 . . 351 Westlake Terr, Palm Springs, CA *92264*
Garza-Laguera MR & MRS David (Yolanda Santos de Garza)
795 Fifth Av, Apt 400, New York, NY *10021*

Garzon MR & MRS George A (Marjorie V von Gal) | ☎ (334) 279-8688
Htdon'55 . . . . | 2506 Leonidas Dv,
MISS Marjorie V . . . . | Montgomery, AL
MISS Frances J . . . . | *36106*
MISS Georganne V . . . . |
JUNIORS MR George H . . . . |

Gasch MRS (DR) Alice T (Alice W True) Mid'72.Cvc.Ncd.
PO Box 9711, Washington, DC *20016*
Gaskill MR & MRS Scott C (Isabel McN Hatfield) Buck'84.Drex'85
☎ (610) 251-2327 . . 1552 Maple Av, Paoli, PA *19301*

Gast MR & MRS William R (Vivian A A Wagner) | ☎ (215) 628-3101
PhilaArt'63.PhilaArt'68 . . . . | 1411 E Butler Pike,
JUNIORS MISS Victoria A . . . . | Ambler, PA *19002*

Gaston MR Alexander—Fic.
☎ (808) 941-3865 . . 1860 Ala Moana Blvd, Apt 1810, Honolulu,
HI *96815*
Gaston MR & MRS Benjamin McT (Evans—Hegarty—Betty D Cooke)
Ch'39.Me.Tenn'31.Pa'32
☎ (610) 688-8509 . . 139 Kynlyn Rd, Radnor, PA *19087*
Gaston MR & MRS Benjamin McT JR (Dawn S Bates) Va'55.Pa'60 ⚓
☎ (305) 289-7313 . . 1466 Overseas H'way, Marathon, FL *33050*
Gaston MR & MRS Frederick K 3d (Julia Y Yawkey) Yn.Y'57 . . of
☎ (203) 762-8140 . . 19 Deacon's Lane, Wilton, CT *06897*
☎ (802) 824-6276 . . ''Brightmeadows'' Dale Rd, Weston, VT *05161*
Gaston MISS G Kemper . . see G F Morris
Gaston DR & MRS James P (Gail Chandler) Sth'74.Cly.Bow'54
☎ (212) 744-0070 . . 202 E 75 St, New York, NY *10021*

Gaston MR John JR—Fic.Cl'70 . . . . | ☎ (305) 294-1731
MISS Deven D—at ☎ (804) 293-3450 | Truman Annex,
327 Campbell Rd, Keswick, VA *22947* . . . . . . | 520 Emma St,
| Key West, FL *33040*

Gaston MRS Lynch (Getty—Louise T D Lynch) | ☎ (310) 394-2216
Hn. . . . . | PO Box 1799,
MISS Louise Christina T . . . . | Santa Monica, CA
| *90406*

Gaston MR Robert F . . see A H Moss
Gaston MR Talbot L . . see G F Morris
Gaston MR & MRS Thomas Y (Jill E Marchant) Bates'83.Bates'85
☎ (508) 435-4841 . . 7 Pond St, Hopkinton, MA *01748*
Gatch MRS Calvin F (M Delphine Polk)
☎ (314) 991-1680 . . 19 Magnolia Dv, St Louis, MO *63124*

Gatch MR & MRS Hayward H (Olive C Colfelt) Y'52 | ☎ (805) 969-7214
MISS Georgia A. | 1863 San Leandro
| Lane, Santa Barbara,
| CA *93108*

Gatchell MRS G Gordon (Elizabeth K M Emory) Cda.
Blakehurst 431, 1055 W Joppa Rd, Towson, MD *21204*

Gatchell MR & MRS G Gordon JR (Esther A MacLea) | ☎ (617) 259-8988
Cc.Bab'57 . . . . | 127 Bedford Rd,
MISS Catharine A . . . . | Lincoln, MA *01773*
MR William H . . . . |

Gatchell MISS Margaret P . . see C L Stout
Gatchell MR Richard Emory—Md.Elk.JHop'56
☎ (410) 494-9404 . . 1411 Walnut Hill Lane, Baltimore, MD *21204*
Gatchell MR Richard Emory JR (Richard Emory) . . . . Married at
Baltimore, MD
Nes MISS Catherine M (Charles M 3d) . . . . Jun 3'95
Gatchell MR & MRS Richard Emory JR (Catherine M Nes)
Rm'91.Loy'93.Elk.Mv.Del'87
☎ (410) 323-6095 . . 117 Fireside Circle, Baltimore, MD *21212*

Gatchell MR & MRS Robert T (Dale—Amy Bell) . . . | ☎ (609) 921-6469
MISS Lucretia B . . . . | Box 6282,
| Lawrenceville, NJ
| *08648*

Gately DR & MRS Hugh L (Elizabeth D Lamberton) Linf'85.Wis'74.Wis'78
☎ (503) 697-4845 . . 12550 SW Edgecliff Rd, Portland, OR *97219*
Gates MISS Ashley du Pont . . see E N Carpenter 2d
Gates MR & MRS Courtlandt D (Natalie S Bigelow) H'81.Cr'85.H'81.H'86
☎ (415) 461-5524 . . PO Box 1524, Ross, CA *94957*
Gates MRS Edward L SR (J Jane Powning)
☎ (941) 263-1873 . . 4760 West Blvd, Apt F102, Naples, FL *34103*

Gates MR & MRS Geoffrey (Wende E Devlin) | ☎ (908) 233-0081
Syr'66.Rcn.Bcs.Pn.P'54 . . . . | 100 W Dudley Av,
JUNIORS MR Christopher D . . . . | Westfield, NJ *07090*

Gates MASTER Jackson Brush (John Davis JR) . . . . Born at
Charlottesville, VA Apr 18'96
Gates MR & MRS John Davis JR (Priscilla J Forney) P'90.H'88
3520 Red Hill Rd, Charlottesville, VA *22903*

Gates MRS John M (Bliss—Evelyn B Dows) K . . . . . | of ☎ (716)468-3847
MR Jonathan—at ☎ (412) 361-8066 | PO Box 565, Nunda,
1119 N St Clair St, Pittsburgh, PA *15206* . . . . . | NY *14517*
| ☎ (212) 737-5412
| 220 E 72 St, Apt 7F,
| New York, NY
| *10021*

Gates MR & MRS John M JR (Letitia Ambrose) Lm.Cc.H'50
☎ (561) 833-3091 . . 141 Atlantic Av, Palm Beach, FL *33480*
Gates MR & MRS John S (Christine L Schaefer) On.Cho.Fy.Ncd.Mont'40
☎ (847) 234-0743 . . 246 W Laurel Av, Lake Forest, IL *60045*
Gates MR & MRS John S JR (Eloise R Henkel)
PineM'79.Cas.Rc.Tv.Sap.Sc.Ty'76 . . of
☎ (773) 883-1998 . . 2151 N Cleveland Av, Chicago, IL *60614*
☎ (219) 787-8234 . . ''Dune Acres'' 14 Shore Dv, Chesterton, IN *46304*

Gates MR & MRS Peter P McN (Joan Bryan) | ☎ (212) 628-7119
Sth'54.Plg.Lm.Cc.H'56.Cl'63 . . . . | 163 E 65 St,
MISS Katharine L . . . . | New York, NY
MR Peter McN . . . . | *10021*

Gates MR & MRS Peter R (Deborah P Marshall) Sth'73.Cy.P'73
155 Summer St, Weston, MA *02193*
Gates MRS Robert F (Peet—Sarita Weekes)
☎ (202) 965-1594 . . 2620 Dumbarton Av NW, Washington, DC *20007*
Gates MRS Samuel E (Philomène Asher) FlaSt'38.GeoW'42.Cs.StJ.
☎ (212) 876-6080 . . 1112 Park Av, New York, NY *10128*

Gates MRS Thomas S (Millicent A Brengle) Cly.
☎ (610) MU8-0453 . . ''Mill Race Farm'' 435 Beaumont Rd, Devon, PA *19333*

Gates MR & MRS Timothy G (Katerina Salteri) H'56.Mich'63 . . . . | ☎ (508) 526-4979
JUNIORS MR Michael G . . . . | 2 Desmond Av,
JUNIORS MR Christopher M . . . . | PO Box 1521, Manchester-By-The-Sea, MA *01944*

Gates MRS William N (Elizabeth Berenson)
☎ (508) 636-8935 . . 787 Pine Hill Rd, Westport, MA *02790*

Gathings MR Wilson Randolph—Chr.Cc.Cw.Ht.Rv.Snc.Ne.Cl'57.Paris'59
☎ (512) 474-2160 . . 807 W Lynn St, Apt 118, Austin, TX *78703*

Gatje MRS Barbara W (Ball—Barbara M Wright) LSU'54.Cs. . . . . | ☎ (212) 749-1928
MISS Alexandra L—Skd'82—at | 382 Central Park W,
☎ (212) 532-4616 . . 221 E 33 St, New York, NY | New York, NY
10016 . . . . | *10025*
MISS Margot K—at ☎ (212) 486-5303
141 E 55 St, Apt 6D, New York, NY *10022* . . .

Gatje MR Robert F—C.Cr'51
☎ (212) 861-7906 . . 1040 Fifth Av, New York, NY *10028*

Gaud MR & MRS Henry T JR (Susan Mabrey) Conn'68.Nw'73.StAndr'72.Col'77 . . . . | ☎ (847) 864-6469
JUNIORS MISS Emily D . . . . | 2809 Lincoln St, Evanston, IL *60201*

Gaudieri MR & MRS Alexander V J (Millicent E Hall) Ri.Paris'63 . . . . | ☎ (914) 298-2244
JUNIORS MR Alexandre B E—at St Mark's . . . . . | ''Locust Grove'' 370 South Rd, PO Box 1649, Poughkeepsie, NY *12601-5234*

Gaudreau MR & MRS Thomas L (Cooper—Allen—M Anne Spencer) Gchr'51.JHop'50
☎ (410) 827-6999 . . ''Wye Cottage'' 1128 Cheston Lane, Queenstown, MD *21658-1355*

Gault MR & MRS Matthew (Rosemary Ford) P'42 . . . | ☎ (609) 466-3160
MISS Rosette F . . . . | 130 Cleveland Rd, Princeton, NJ *08540*

Gaunt MR & MRS William L (Wendy A Hilles) Me.Cry.W&J'68.Cwr'71
☎ (610) 688-4813 . . 6 Canterbury Lane, St Davids, PA *19087*

Gauvreau MR & MRS Douglas K (Andrea L Woods) Vt'69
☎ (207) 781-4183 . . 12 Waites Landing Rd, Falmouth, ME *04105*

Gavales MRS Manuel (Helen T Welwood) Ds. . . . . | ☎ (212) 734-4296
MISS Diana H . . . . | 306 E 84 St, New York, NY *10028*

Gavales MR Manuel
☎ (212) 645-1514 . . 470 W 24 St, Apt 9J, New York, NY *10011-1233*

Gaver MR James M—B.Ct.P'64
☎ (803) 649-2345 . . 902 S Boundary, Aiken, SC *29801*

Gavin MRS J Louis (Julia B Pierson)
☎ (410) 825-1994 . . 7701 Rider Hill Rd, Baltimore, MD *21204*

Gavin MR & MRS Kevin P (Deborah L Bazzell) Loy'85
☎ (410) 828-4060 . . 621 Chestnut Av, Baltimore, MD *21204*

Gawthrop MR & MRS Alfred JR (Murray—Daphne N Wood) Col'61.Cal'64 . . . . | ☎ (916) 482-3401
MISS Daphne C Murray—at ☎ (312) 943-9236 | 475 Bret Harte Rd,
''The Coach House'' 3925 N Janssen Rd, | Sacramento, CA
Chicago, IL *60613* | *95864*
MR R Nelson Murray JR—Va'86—at
☎ (713) 963-0679 . 3133 Buffalo Speedway, Apt 8311, Houston, TX *77098* . . . . |

Gawthrop MRS Kathleen (Kathleen Tansey) Col'61 | ☎ (415) 789-0066
MISS Blair—at 3002 Pacific Av, Apt 2, Venice, | 25 Corinthian Court,
CA *90291* . . . . | 31, Tiburon, CA
MR Alfred 3d—at 2116 S Humbolt St, Denver, | *94920*
CO *80210* . . . . |

Gawthrop MR & MRS Robert S JR (Borden—Janet D Pinckney) P.
☎ (610) 696-2158 . . 253 Chatham Way, West Chester, PA *19380*

Gay MR & MRS Edgar L T (Karatassos—Kim Hampton) Emory'68
PO Box 8375, Savannah, GA *31412-8375*

Gay MRS H Burton (Adeline A Ferguson) Me.M.
☎ (610) 525-5865 . . 35 Pond Lane, Bryn Mawr, PA *19010*

Gay MR John . . . . Died at West Palm Beach, FL Jly 15'96

Gay MRS John (Cynthia Tuckerman) Bcs.
☎ (516) 283-8492 . . 19 Cooper St, PO Box 339, Southampton, NY *11969*

Gay MR & MRS John JR (Woodard—Gallagher—Deborah Hearst) BtP.My.So.UMiami'70
☎ (561) 655-9620 . . 227 Australian Av, Palm Beach, FL *33480*

Gay MR & MRS Paul G (Caroline F Williams) Dick'67.H'69 . . . . | ☎ (617) 326-2761
JUNIORS MISS Louisa R . . . . | 235 Westfield St,
JUNIORS MR Bradford F—at Middlebury . . . . | Westwood, Needham, MA
JUNIORS MR Andrew W . . . . | *02192*

Gay MR & MRS Peter A (Evelyn Spencer) Va'54 . . . . | ☎ (561) 336-2416
MISS Virginia—at 839 Marigny St, New Orleans, | 2520 Seagrass Dv,
LA *70117* . . . . | Palm City, FL *34990*

Gay MR & MRS S Tucker 3d (Mary J Brenner) Mo'51.West'51
☎ (941) 924-8302 . . 1435 Kimlira Lane, Sarasota, FL *34231*

Gay MR & MRS Thomas S JR (Stuckert—Henrietta Scott) Ds.
☎ (215) 283-7280 . . 903 Foulkeways, Sumneytown Pike, Gwynedd, PA *19436*

Gaylord MRS Harvey (Ann D Flershem) Csn.
☎ (860) 739-5313 . . 273 Old Black Point Rd, Niantic, CT *06357*

Geare MR John E—Gi.Pn.Ty'36
☎ (410) 255-4878 . . Broadwater Way, Box 47, Gibson Island, MD *21056*

Geary MRS John W 2d (Hilary S Roche) B.Bcs.Ng.. | of ☎ (212)980-8881
MR Alfred H 2d . . . . | 580 Park Av,
JUNIORS MR John W 3d . . . . | New York, NY
| *10021*
| ☎ (516) 283-4444
| ''Fairfield''
| Great Plains Rd,
| Southampton, NY
| *11968*

Gebhardt MR & MRS Ronald E (Cora A St John) MtH'55.Cr'52 . . . . ☎ (412) 741-8102 / 214 Creek Dv, Sewickley, PA 15143
MISS Joy D . . . .
MR Ronald E JR—at ☎ (011-852) 2813-9848 The Manhattan 42H, 33 Tai Tam Rd, Tai Tam, Hong Kong . . . .

Geddes MR & MRS E Maxwell JR (Aileen T Turnbull) V'60.Rc.Pr.Ln.Cly. . . . . ☎ (516) 624-7732 / 85 Shutter Lane, Oyster Bay, NY 11771
MISS Lydia L—at ☎ (773) 549-2253 1338 W Waveland Av, Chicago, IL 60614 . . . . .
MR William G—at ☎ (212) 799-4464 215 W 78 St, Apt 8D, New York, NY 10024 . . .

Geddes MR & MRS Gerald K (Knechtel—Annette L Longnon) Ws'67.Plg.So.Syc.Dyc.Cs.Myf.Cda. . . of ☎ (212)517-4740 / 130 East End Av, New York, NY 10028
JUNIORS MR Adam L . . . .
☎ (561) 585-7407 3300 S Ocean Blvd, Palm Beach, FL 33480

Geddes MR Grant M . . see MRS C P Amory

Geddes MR & MRS Robert A (Anne R Hildt) Rc.Pr.Mb.Ln.StLaw'62 . . . . ☎ (516) MA6-3102 / Rte 25A, Upper Brookville, East Norwich, NY 11732
MISS Lauren F—Van'95—at ☎ (212) 980-7037 220 E 60 St, New York, NY 10022 . . . .
JUNIORS MISS Eliza B—at Taft

Geddes MR Robyn G—T.LakeF'77 . . see MRS C P Amory

Gede MR & MRS Thomas F (Juliet G Messimer) Pac'71.SCal'74.Stan'70.Hast'81
☎ (916) 756-2113 . . 1210 Rosario St, Davis, CA 95616

Gedman MR & MRS Albert E (Lacagnina—Arian L Johnson) Fr.ClarkTech'50 . . of
☎ (707) 987-0350 . . ''Oat Hill Meadow'' 24950 Oat Hill Rd, PO Box 953, Middletown, CA 95461
☎ (415) 776-2251 . . 2230 Leavenworth St, San Francisco, CA 94133

Gee JUNIORS MR Alexander R . . see R F Dick

Gee MISS Annelisa A—Tufts'91 . . see R F Dick

Gee MR Charles MacQ JR
☎ (706) 789-2402 . . RR 2, Danielsville, GA 30633

Gee JUNIORS MISS Christina G . . see R F Dick

Gee, Geoffrey K & LaMothe, Kimerer L—Wms'85.H'89.Berklee'92
☎ (617) 646-8327 . . 32 Edmund Rd, Arlington, MA 02174

Gee MISS Sarah D—Ham'94 . . see R F Dick

Geer MR Benjamin O JR—Yh.Va'57 . . . . ☎ (803) 853-3296 / 1 King St, Apt 308, Charleston, SC 29401
MISS Eleanor H . . . .
MISS Sarah F . . . .
MISS Louisa E . . . .
JUNIORS MR Benjamin O 3d . . . .

Geer MR Charles L—Hn.H'67.H'69 . . . . ☎ (617) 259-0301 / PO Box 2, Lincoln, MA 01773-0002
MISSES Tara W & Eliza B—at 213 Brattle St, Cambridge, MA 02138 . . . .

Geer DR & MRS E Throop (Viola T Culbertson) Wms'41.Temp'44 85 Silo Circle, Riverside, CT 06878

Geer DR & MRS Francis G (Miriam F Lewis) Un.Rm.Chr.Snc.StJ.Cly.Y'38.Cl'42 . . of
☎ (212) 753-6186 . . 200 E 66 St, Apt E207, New York, NY 10021
☎ (908) 842-0970 . . 284 Clearbrook Court, PO Box 236, Little Silver, NJ 07739

Geer REV & MRS Francis H (Sarah W Davis) H'71.Rut'70 . . . . ☎ (914) 424-3653 / The Rectory, St Philip's in the Highlands, PO Box 158, Rte 9D, Garrison, NY 10524
JUNIORS MISS Phoebe T . . . .
JUNIORS MR Samuel L . . . .

Geer MR Garrow T—Bcs.
☎ (516) 759-5439 . . ''Wing House'' West Island, Glen Cove, NY 11542

Geer MR & MRS John F (Carolyn V Boston) P.'52 . . ☎ (212) 724-9986 / 151 Central Park W, New York, NY 10023
MISS Evelyn R—at ☎ (212) 772-7662 301 E 75 St, New York, NY 10021 . . . .

Geer MR Lewis F—Y'70
☎ (505) 988-3704 . . 1041 Governor Dempsey Dv, Santa Fe, NM 87501

Geer MRS Mariana Griswold (Mariana Van R Griswold) CtCol'70.NMex'83.Ht. . . . . ☎ (505) 989-7477 / 911 Old Pecos Trail, Santa Fe, NM 87501
MISS Elizabeth L . . . .

Geer MR & MRS R Taggart (Juliana Ernst) Pkg.Sfh.Nyc.P'61.Va'65 . . . . ☎ (610) 827-7267 / 1944 Conestoga Rd, Chester Springs, PA 19425
MISS Jacqueline E—Mid'90—at 26 Linwood St, Arlington, MA 02174-6622 . . . .
MISS Emily B—at U of Richmond . . . .
MR Ralph T JR—Ken'93—at 328 W 88 St, New York, NY 10024 . . . .

Geer MR R Winslow (Rose O'N Winslow)
☎ (914) 351-2862 . . Tower Hill Rd, Tuxedo Park, NY 10987

Geer MR & MRS Walter H (M Ann Davenport) RMWmn'43.Cw.Wes'47.H.'49
☎ (610) KI3-6011 . . 617 Academy Rd, Swarthmore, PA 19081

Geier MR Eugene L—Wms'49
☎ (513) 321-0508 . . 33 Weebetook Lane, Cincinnati, OH 45208

Geier DR & MRS Philip O (Susanne Ernst) Cin'45.Cm.Qc.Wms'37.H'39 . . of
☎ (513) 561-9639 . . 6000 Redbird Hollow Lane, Cincinnati, OH 45243
☎ (941) 262-2277 . . 777 Gulf Shore Blvd N, Naples, FL 34102

Geier DR & MRS Philip O 3d (Amy M Yeager) Skd'74.Syr'76.Wms'70.Syr'76.Syr'80 . . . . ☎ (505) 425-1926 / PO Box 277, Montezuma, NM 87731
MISS Katherine D . . . .
JUNIORS MISS Elizabeth S . . . .
JUNIORS MR Christopher E . . . .

Geiger RR ADM & MRS Robert K (Sibyl V Godfrey) An.Ayc.USN'48.Mit'56 . . of
3273 Charles McDonald Dv, Sarasota, FL 34240
☎ (540) 338-4914 . . ''Fernside'' PO Box 163, Philmont, VA 20131

Geisel MR & MRS C Meade JR (Hessler—Saskia Lahann) M.Me.Rc.Ph.Buck'60.H'85 . . . . of ☎ (610)658-2750 "Wood Hill" 1411 Youngs Ford Rd, Gladwyne, PA *19035*
MR G Stuart—at ☎ (801) 649-5819
4661 Quail Meadows Rd, Park City, UT *84060* .
JUNIORS MISS Martha B—at Shipley . . . .
JUNIORS MR Andrew F—at Shipley . . . .
☎ (561) 545-1120
7176 SE Greenview Place, Hobe Sound, FL *33455*

Geisler REV CANON & MRS William F (Barbara A Reichmuth) Tcy.H'57 . . . . ☎ (415) 258-0567 40 Woodruff Rd, San Anselmo, CA *94960*
MISS Elizabeth M G—at Bethany . . . .

Geissbühler MRS Arnold (Elisabeth Chase) . . of
☎ (212) CH2-7932 . . 4 Grove Court, New York, NY *10014*
☎ (508) 385-3879 . . Scargo Pines, PO Box 202, Dennis, MA *02638*

Geissler DR Edwin N—Br'76.Pa'81 . . of
☎ (617) 437-1752 . . 118 Commonwealth Av, Apt 1, Boston, MA *02116*
☎ (617) 826-0361 . . 368 Pleasant St, Pembroke, MA *02359*

Geist MR Bradley B—Rc.Dick'66
☎ (212) 433-1200 . . 1025 Park Av, New York, NY *10028*

Geist MRS Nancy S (Nancy L Sands) . . . . 101 W 81 St, New York, NY *10024-7237*
MISS Tyler L—at 210 E 73 St, New York, NY *10021* . . . .
MR Bradley B JR—Rcn.Dick'89—at 218 E 79 St, New York, NY *10021* . . . .
MR Nicholas Van V—at U of Vt . . . .

Geist MR Stephen . . see MRS T K Finletter

Gelette MR & MRS Grantland W (Nina A Beal) Bost'62 ⚓
☎ (508) 991-4801 . . 14 Salt Creek Rd, South Dartmouth, MA *02748-1541*

Gelpi-Toro MR & MRS William R (Elise P Patterson) Pa'66.Ac.Cda.PuertoR'62
41 Dellwood Circle, Bronxville, NY *10708*

Gemes MR & MRS Kenneth E (Marian B Thayer) MaryW'84.Ga'78
☎ (914) 395-1497 . . 4 Sunnybrae Place, Bronxville, NY *10708*

Gemmill MISS Helen J . . see MISS J C Manternach

Genrich MR & MRS Timothy W (Constance A Perry) NCol'81.NAriz'88.NCol'80
☎ (602) 265-8824 . . 135 E Ocotillo Rd, Phoenix, AZ *85012*

Genth MRS Jane W (Jane C Wylie) V'58.Cs.
☎ (718) KI9-3163 . . 4601 Henry Hudson P'kway, Bronx, NY *10471*

Gentry MR & MRS Frank L (Sarah E Kildea) LErie'66.Clem'64.CarnM'66 . . . . ☎ (704) 552-0674 3028 Brookmont Place, Charlotte, NC *28210*
MR David Y—at Wingate . . . .

Gentry MRS William Richard (Elizabeth F Estes) . . . . Died at St Louis, MO Sep 7'93

Geoffroy MR & MRS Charles H (Alida B McClenahan) BMr'52.Hav'49 . . . . ☎ (503) 635-4222 11511 SW Military Lane, Portland, OR *97219-8430*
MR Evan L—at ☎ (503) 331-0782
6116 NE Skidmore St, Portland, OR *97218* . . . .
MR Douglas B—Whit'83—at ☎ (503) 620-3283
9325 Edgewood Rd, Tigard, OR *97223* . . . .

Geoffroy MR & MRS Mark L (Kate H Lind) Y'80.BostColl'88.Hav'79.BostColl'89
☎ (207) 772-7036 . . 77 Rackleff St, Portland, ME *04103-3040*

Geoghegan MRS M Gilbert (Madeleine M Gilbert) . 7924 Camino Circle, Miami, FL *33143*
MR Howard F . . . .

George MR & MRS Michael M (Clara E Balfour) Un.H'60 . . . . ☎ (212) 288-6944 125 E 72 St, New York, NY *10021-4250*
MISS Regina E. . . . .
MISS Vivian B . . . .
MISS Monica R . . . .

George MR & MRS Robert J (Pamela J Jones) Sm.Tr.K.Sb.Mo'67.H.'86 . . . . ☎ (508) 653-8868 Nishkenon Farm, 138 Farm Rd, Sherborn, MA *01770*
MISS Kristen E . . . .
JUNIORS MISS Lindsay K . . . .

George MRS Samuel K 3d (Kail—Margaret E Rastetter)
☎ (803) 342-2870 . . 11 Birdsong Way, Apt 103E, Hilton Head Island, SC *29926*

George MR & MRS William D 3d (Wright—Sonja J Krusee) Pn.P'56 . . of
☎ (412) 741-7731 . . 911 Centennial Av, Sewickley, PA *15143*
☎ (011-52-415) 2-2299 . . "Solana" 65 Salida à Queataro, San Miguel de Allende, GTO, Mexico

Gephart MR & MRS George W JR (Elizabeth N Starr) Pa'79.Me.Gm.Y.'75.Pa'79
☎ (610) 356-7550 . . 653 Andover Rd, Newtown Square, PA *19073*

Gerard MR & MRS Anthony R H (Kathleen A Ryan) Geo'69.Mds.Ri.H'71 . . . . ☎ (212) 570-2091 120 E 79 St, New York, NY *10021*
JUNIORS MR Rupert B C . . . .

Gerard MR & MRS C H Coster (Alison Daly) Man'vl'54.Rc.T.K.Snc.Myf.Y'46 . . . . of ☎ (212)288-1528 27 E 73 St, New York, NY *10021*
MISS Emily M—NMex'91 . . . .
MR Charles H C JR—H'82.Cl'86 . . . .
MR Daniel B—Conn'84 . . . . ☎ (201) 764-4652 41 Meadowburn Rd, Vernon, NJ *07462*

Gerard MRS Frank H (Marie L Swartz)
☎ (610) 527-4283 . . Tedwyn 704, 840 Montgomery Av, Bryn Mawr, PA *19010*

Gerard MISS Harriet C—SL'84
☎ (212) 242-3124 . . 405 W 21 St, New York, NY *10011*

Gerard MRS James W (Jean B Shevlin) . . . . Died at Paris, France Aug 5'96

Gerard MR James W 5th—Ln.Un.T.Snc.Rv.Ht.Myf.GeoW'83
☎ (212) 982-3556 . . 63 E 9 St, Apt 12L, New York, NY *10003*

Gerard MR Julian M—Y'40
☎ (203) 938-2039 . . "Brookstone" Box 71, West Redding, CT *06896*
Jan 1 . . ☎ (561) 844-6717 . . 226 List Rd, Palm Beach, FL *33480*

Gerard MR & MRS Peter H (Elizabeth W Browning) Bgt.Nich'71
☎ (914) 764-8599 . . 11 Pound Ridge Rd, Pound Ridge, NY *10576*

Gerard MR & MRS Robert A (Johnston—Philippa C W Groves) Bcs.Ln.Cly.H'66 . . . . of 1401 Crocker St, Sarasota, FL *34231*
MISS Celia C—at ☎ (212) 628-0831
116 E 66 St, New York, NY *10021* . . . . ☎ (011-44-171) 823-9760 33 Sumner Place, London SW7 3NT, England
MR Robert G—at Eugene, OR . . . .
JUNIORS MR William A . . . .

Gerard MR & MRS Sumner (Teresa Dabrowska) Rc.K.Ny.Camb'37
☎ (212) 517-8497 . . 320 E 72 St, New York, NY *10021*

Gerber MR & MRS George C (Betty J W T Johnson)
GeoW'58.Cvc.Sl.Snc.Myf.Ncd.Dc.Duke'54
☎ (703) 442-0309 . . 1309 Ballantrae Court, McLean, VA *22101*

Gerber MR John D T—B.Cvc.Plg.Snc.Rv.P.'84.H.'87
☎ (212) 831-6358 . . 49 E 92 St, Apt 5A, New York, NY *10128*

Gerbner MR & MRS John C (Anne R Jarvis) | ☎ (215) 247-6809
Pa'75.Pa'76.Pa'73.Pa'76 . . . . | 230 E Gravers Lane,
JUNIORS MISS Katharine R . . . . | Philadelphia, PA
 | *19118*

Gerdau REV Carlson—Unn.Hn.H'55
☎ (773) 363-6647 . . 1321 E 56 St, Chicago, IL *60637*

Gerdine DR & MRS Leigh (Meyer—Alice C Strauch)
Cy.Nd.NDak'38.Ox'40.Ia'41
☎ (314) 725-7025 . . 801 S Skinker Blvd, Apt 14B, St Louis, MO *63105*

Gerdsen MR & MRS James N (Cynthia C Clegg) | of ☎ (513)871-5349
Cin'68.Cin'68. . . . . | 3666 Grandin Rd,
MISS Margot S—Syr'93 . . . . | Cincinnati, OH
MR James T—at U of Miami . . . . | *45226*
 | Black Island,
 | Rice Lake, Ontario,
 | Canada

Gerez MRS Cassandra Webb (Cassandra Webb) . . . . | ☎ (011-52-415)
MISS Cristina—SL'92 . . . . | 2-2514
MR Juan—at Tex A & M . . . . | Montitlan 20,
 | Apdo Postal 199,
 | San Miguel de
 | Allende, GTO
 | 37700, Mexico

Gerhard MRS William G (Wight—Ann L Weisenbach) M.
☎ (610) 688-6313 . . ''Holly Brook House'' 607 King of Prussia Rd,
Radnor, PA *19087*

Gerli MR & MRS David C (Gram—Anne W Harvey) Ri.Mds.
☎ (212) 752-6236 . . 201 E 62 St, New York, NY *10021*

Germic MISS Eloise Ravenel (Stephen A) . . . . Born at
Grosse Pointe, MI Sep 5'95

Germic MR & MRS Stephen A (Catherine R Boomer) Alb'90.Alb'89
☎ (313) 885-6674 . . 482 Neff Rd, Grosse Pointe, MI *48230*

Gernerd MR & MRS Frederick H (P Brooks Bishop)
H'84.Hn.RISD'72.BostArch'83
☎ (508) 785-1456 . . 17 Old Meadow Rd, Dover, MA *02030*

Gerrish MR & MRS Campbell T (Janet McN Hester) | ☎ (914) 967-9026
Nu'76.P.'73 . . . . | 2 Windcrest Rd,
JUNIORS MR Campbell McN . . . . | Rye, NY *10580*

Gerrity MR & MRS Daniel W (Maria M Farley) | ☎ (617) 730-9940
V'72.Unn.Cy.Chi.Plg.Va'70 . . . . | 54 Fairmount St,
MISS Jeanne S . . . . | Brookline, MA
JUNIORS MISS Vera V B . . . . | *02146*

Gerrity MR & MRS Edward M (Joe Ann C Thatcher) | ☎ (303) 773-0164
Memphis'67.Ncd.StL'66 . . . . | 6550 S Heritage
MISS Corrigan T—Col'94 . . . . | Place W,
MISS Ryan K . . . . | Englewood, CO
MR E Michael 4th—Pa'92—at Moscow, Russia . | *80111*

Gerrity MR & MRS J Frank 2d (Ruth Mathes) Cy.Chi.Ncd.H'39.H'43 . . of
☎ (617) 232-3500 . . 59 Cramond Rd, Chestnut Hill, MA *02167*
☎ (207) 363-5200 . . ''Mainescape'' Box 77, York Harbor, ME *03911*

Gerrity MR & MRS James Francis 3d (Melissa H | ☎ (617) 891-1592
Dempsey) Y'71.H'75.Cy.Chi.H'69.H'74 . . . . . | 247 Meadowbrook
JUNIORS MISS Melissa C . . . . | Rd, Weston, MA
JUNIORS MR James F 4th . . . . | *02193*

Gerrity MR Joseph W JR—Srr.Tf.Myf.H.'38
☎ (518) 472-9550 . . 40 Turner Lane, Loudonville, NY *12211*

Gerrity MR & MRS Robert T (Judith Van Daam) | ☎ (518) 392-4420
ColC'70.LaTrobe'76.DU'69.LaTrobe'75-. . . . . | PO Box 15,
MISS Alexa Van D . . . . | Chatham, NY *12037*
JUNIORS MISS Gretchen Van D . . . . |

Gerry MISS Alison R (Elbridge T JR) . . . . . Married at Locust Valley, NY
Rodney Kevin J (Dennis) . . . . Aug 24'95

Gerry MR & MRS Edward H (Martha B Farish) Mb.Pr.Ln.Cly.H'36 . . of
☎ (516) OR1-0540 . . Box 374, Factory Pond Rd, Mill Neck, NY *11765*
☎ (561) 546-9830 . . 157 Gomez Rd, Hobe Sound, FL *33455*
☎ (904) 997-3367 . . Pinckney Hill Plantation, Rte 1, Monticello,
FL *32344*

Gerry MR & MRS Elbridge T (Marjorie Y Kane) R.Pr.Mb.Ln.Cly.H'31
☎ (607) 832-4250 . . Lake Delaware Farm, Delhi, NY *13753*

Gerry MR & MRS Elbridge T JR (Carolyn Almy) | ☎ (516) 759-1496
Rc.Pr.Mb.Ln.H'55 . . . . | 4 Laurel Lane,
MISS Louisa L . . . . | Locust Valley, NY
MISS Amy . . . . | *11560*

Gerry MR & MRS Henry A (Nancy Whitney) Pr.Ln.Ri.Fic.H'36.Cl'39 . . of
☎ (516) 671-2727 . . 5 Cherry Wood Rd, Locust Valley, NY *11560*
☎ (941) 964-2604 . . PO Box 870, Boca Grande, FL *33921*

Gerry MR & MRS (DR) Peter G (Tuten—Alexandra | ☎ (609) 466-3275
Wetherill) Pa'68.Pa'80.Rcn.Ln.H'68.H'73 . . . . | ''Linlithgow''
JUNIORS MISS Alexandra . . . . | 126 Moores Mill
JUNIORS MR Christopher . . . . | Rd, Hopewell,NJ
JUNIORS MR Peter . . . . | *08525*

Gerry MR & MRS William F (G Caroline Vincent) SL'77.Pr.H'78 . . of
☎ (212) 860-5630 . . 25 E 86 St, New York, NY *10028*
☎ (516) 726-5952 . . Cobb Isle Rd, PO Box 482, Water Mill, NY *11976*

Gerstell MRS Marguerite F (Washburn—Marguerite F Gerstell)
Rdc'66.H'91.CalTech'95
☎ (818) 792-1082 . . 2845 E California Blvd, Pasadena, CA *91107*

Gerster MR & MRS John A (Mary E Brennan) | of ☎ (914)967-2374
Wis'67.Ny.LakeF'70 . . . . | 82 Halsted Place,
MISS Eileen McM—Bost'94—at . . . . | Rye, NY *10580*
☎ (212) 737-1811 . . 433 E 75 St, Apt 21, | ☎ (802) 362-5812
New York, NY *10021* | Windhill Farm,
MR J Brennan—at Boston U . . . . | Windhill Rd,
 | Manchester Center,
 | VT *05255*

Gerster DR & MRS John W (Joan McCreery) C.Y'41.Cl'44
☎ (203) 869-7136 . . 51 Cherry Valley Rd, Greenwich, CT *06831*

Gerster MR & MRS Peter W (Sandra L Lewis) | ☎ (203) 531-6581
O'74.O'73 . . . . | 11 East By Way,
JUNIORS MR Philip W . . . . | Greenwich, CT
 | *06831*

Gerstle MR Mark L
☎ (702) 363-6532 . . 9044 Villa Ridge Dv, Las Vegas, NV *89134*

Getchell MR & MRS Charles W JR (Angela Winthrop) | ☎ (508) 468-2728
Rdc'58.Tv.Stan'51 . . . . | PO Box 291,
MISS Katharine C . . . . | Ipswich, MA *01938*
MISS Sarah F . . . . |

Getty MR & MRS Gordon P (Ann Gilbert)
☎ (415) 921-5150 . . 2880 Broadway St, San Francisco, CA *94115*

Getz MRS James R (Betsy Needham) On.Cho.
☎ (847) 234-0464 . . PO Box 847, Lake Forest, IL *60045*

Getze MRS E Bioren (Josephine Fraley) . . . . | ☎ (610) 356-1364
  MISS Susan M—at ☎ (610) 525-1154 | Dunwoody Village
Radwyn Apts L31, 275 Bryn Mawr Av, | CH18, 3500 West
Bryn Mawr, PA *19010* . . . . | Chester Pike,
  MR Frederick B—Duke'73.Drex'78—at | Newtown Square,
☎ (302) 731-0680 . . 807 Chrysler Av, Newark, | PA *19073*
DE *19711* . . . . |

Geupel MRS John C (Hamilton—Ann H Mulville) | ☎ (561) 546-1276
Ty'58 . . . . | 53 S Beach Rd,
  MISS Sarah Hamilton—Box 23662, Flagstaff, | Hobe Sound, FL
AZ *86002* . . . . | *33455*
  MR William C Hamilton 3d—at 444 Arden Rd, |
Columbus, OH *43214* . . . . |

Gevalt MRS Frederick C JR (Sally W Young) SL'42
☎ (860) 435-2020 . . "Crossroads" 300 Wells Hill Rd, Lakeville,
CT *06039*

Gevalt MR & MRS Peter Y (Lorene C Stefan) Nu'69.Rc.Ln.Nyc.Cly.NCar'70
☎ (212) 737-5296 . . 215 E 72 St, New York, NY *10021*

Gevers MR Maximilian E . . . . Died at
                  Monte-Carlo, Monaco Jly 28'96

Gevers MRS Maximilian E (Bagley—Wainwright—Rosalie de F Crosby)
So.B.Cly.StJ.
☎ (011-33) 93-30-92-09 . . "Le Mirabeau" 2 Av des Citronniers,
98000 Monte-Carlo, Monaco

Geyelin MR Anthony A—Me.Va'68.VillaN'74
☎ (610) 935-8500 . . 526 Egypt Rd, Phoenixville, PA *19460*

Geyelin MRS Antony L (Mary Virginia Allen)
☎ (610) MU8-5074 . . 622 Brookside Av, Ithan, Villanova, PA *19085*

Geyelin MRS Emile C (Cecily W Barnes)
☎ (610) 526-7038 . . 601 N Ithan Av, Apt 202, Bryn Mawr, PA *19010*

Geyelin MR Henry R—Un.Y'39
☎ (212) 737-3171 . . 151 E 79 St, New York, NY *10021*

Geyelin MRS Susan H (Susan H Hilles) Me. . . . . . . | ☎ (610) 688-1549
  MISS Elise H—at U of Va. . . . . | 323 St Davids Rd,
  JUNIORS MR Antony L 3d—at U of Va . . . . | St Davids, PA
                                     | *19087*

Geyer MRS John R (Carlota Herkness) Gchr'46.BankSt'78.Ihy.
☎ (203) 348-1593 . . 40 Flying Cloud Rd, Stamford, CT *06902*

Gezelschap MRS Carl G (Endicott—Elizabeth T Appleby) Cly.Ncd.Dh.
☎ (561) 278-9202 . . 3211 Polo Dv, Gulf Stream, FL *33483*

Ghan MRS Ronald W (Ditmore—B Gray Nugent) | ☎ (805) 543-5318
ColC'66 . . . . | 2036 Skylark Lane,
  MISS Brooke W Ditmore . . . . | San Luis Obispo,
  MR Nathan C Ditmore . . . . | CA *93401*

Gherardi MRS Walter R (Lilia Tuckerman) Cly.
☎ (508) 668-5842 . . 180 Main St, Apt 226, Walpole, MA *02081*

Ghiselli MR & MRS Stephen G (Grace L Fick) Pac'85.Bur.Cal'78
☎ (415) 341-3762 . . 195 Spuraway Dv, San Mateo, CA *94403*

Gholson MR & MRS Hunter M (Hortense A Jones) Lond'61.Miss'55
☎ (601) 328-5331 . . 110 N 6 St, Columbus, MS *39701*

Ghriskey MR & MRS H Williamson (Flora Roberts)
Rcn.Plg.Cly.Pn.P'34.H'36
☎ (203) 869-8994 . . 26 Grahampton Lane, Greenwich, CT *06830*

Ghriskey MR & MRS H Williamson JR (Elizabeth M | ☎ (203) TO9-8278
Jack) Rcn.NCar'66.Rut'68 . . . . | Buckfield Lane,
  MISS Lindsey E . . . . | Greenwich, CT
  MR H Williamson 3d . . . . | *06831*
  MR Benjamin M . . . . |

Giacomuzzi-Moore MR & MRS Lorenzo (Giovanna | ☎ (011-39-432)
Coccitto) Venice'78.MilanPoly'60 . . . . | 511180
  MISS Carolina . . . . | via Brenari 29E,
  MR Marco . . . . | 33100 Udine, Italy

Giard MR & MRS George P JR (Thomas—Wendell Adams) Evg.BtP.
☎ (561) 655-3889 . . 312 Worth Av, Apt C, Box 453, Palm Beach,
FL *33480*

Gibb MR John B—H'71
PO Box 222, Oldwick, NJ *08858*

Gibbons MRS Anne T (Anne M Thomas) V'48.Cs.Pqt . . .of
☎ (203) 259-3858 . . PO Box 145, Greens Farms, CT *06436*
☎ (212) 288-4482 . . 111 E 75 St, New York, NY *10021*

Gibbons MR & MRS James C (Judith H Williams) | ☎ (516) 367-7645
Csh.Aht'69.Nu'75 . . . . | 49 Titus Lane,
  MISS Marjorie M—at Kenyon . . . . | Cold Spring Harbor,
  MISS Wendy C—at Whitman . . . . | NY *11724*
  MR David W—HWSth'94—at ☎ (617) 789-5418 |
72 Gardner St, Boston, MA *02134* . . . . |

Gibbons CAPT & MRS John D (Vera Converse) | ☎ (508) 758-2669
Sth'55.Bvl.BtP.Chi.Ncd.MMA'44 . . . . | 1 Water St, Box 55,
  MISS Vera B . . . . | Mattapoisett, MA
  MR John D JR . . . . | *02739*
  MR Roger C . . . . |

Gibbons MR & MRS Maxfield S (Raynor—Sally E | ☎ (203) 869-4614
Knott) MtH'48.Dar.Yn.Y'45w . . . . | 60 Midwood Rd,
  MR George R 2d—Nw'82.Cr'92 . . . . | Deer Park,
    MISS Sarah M Raynor—Boca'87 . . . . | Greenwich, CT
                                      | *06830*

Gibbons DR & MRS William E (McElroy—Linda Harris) Smu'58.Smu'49
☎ (214) 528-1512 . . 3906 Normandy Av, Dallas, TX *75205*

Gibbons-Neff MR & MRS Grellet (Phyllis Barba)
☎ (610) MU8-4105 . . 225 Old Lancaster Rd, Devon, PA *19333*

Gibbs MR David K—W'minster'73
☎ (314) 862-6083 . . 7330 Pershing Av, Apt 2E, St Louis,
MO *63130-4218*

Gibbs MISS Emilie M—FlaSt'83
☎ (407) 423-4430 . . 525 Greeley St, College Park, FL *32804*

Gibbs MR & MRS G Alva 3d (Hallie W Trimmier) Ala'96.Aub'93
☎ (205) 879-4945 . . 118 Fairmont Dv, Birmingham, AL *35213*

Gibbs MR & MRS Harry C (Jean Fisher) Wash'41
☎ (314) 962-5257 . . 55 S Gore Av, Apt 1C, Webster Groves,
MO *63119*

Gibbs MRS T Harrison (Maurine W Montgomery) . . | ☎ (309) 685-5090
  MISS Ramona H . . . . | 3905 Lynnwood
                                      | Place, Peoria, IL
                                      | *61614*

Gibbs MR & MRS W H Holden (Ellen B Bordley)
Elk.Mv.Cda.F&M'55.Va'57
☎ (410) 472-4772 . . Thistle Downs Farm, 115 Quaker Bottom Rd,
Sparks, MD *21152*

Gibian MR & MRS Paul P (Schneider—Martha H Parke) MaryB'56.Ford'93.Pqt.Cos.CarnM'47. Mit'48 . . . .
   MR Andrew B—DU'81—at ☎ (303) 722-0757
   2105 Buchtel Blvd, Apt 110, Denver, CO *80210*
   of ☎ (203)255-2063
   715 Pequot Rd,
   Southport, CT
   06490-1416
   ☎ (508) 257-9867
   ''Star Hill''
   47 Chuck Hollow
   Rd, Siasconset, MA
   02564
   ☎ (011-42-2)
   24-24-70-46
   Halstalske NAM 3,
   11000 Prague,
   Czech Republic
   ☎ (011-42-7)
   316-930
   U Dolna 2, 81102
   Bratislava, Slovakia

Gibson MRS Carlos (Florence C Anderson) Cal'44.Cvc.Sl.
   ☎ (202) 363-3429 . . 4626 Garfield St NW, Washington, DC *20007*

Gibson MR Christopher L . . see MRS S P Bell

Gibson MR & MRS Christopher M (Reynolds—Carol C Myer) Hood'78.Rv.
   ☎ (717) 548-2233 . . 1032 Osceola Dv, Drumore, PA *17518-9771*

Gibson MR David—Y'42 . . . .
   MISS Serena—at 135 Marlborough St, Boston, MA *02116* . . . .
   MISS Victoria . . . .
   MR Eric . . . .
   ☎ (202) 965-0896
   1080 Wisconsin Av
   NW, Apt 407,
   Washington, DC
   20007

Gibson MRS David C (Lloyd—Helen H McPherson) V'25.Ncd.
   13801 York Rd, Apt C23, Cockeysville, MD *21030*

Gibson MR & MRS George B L (Lynn D Updegrave) Godd'81.F&M'80
   ☎ (610) 689-5124 . . 1520 Schoffers Rd, Birdsboro, PA *19508*

Gibson MR & MRS George W (Diana Marvin) B'gton'42.H'31 . . . .
   MISS Ellen V—at ☎ (617) 323-3074
   55 Stella Rd, Roslindale, MA *02131* . . . .
   MR David H—H'79—at ☎ (518) 877-8678
   Longkill Rd, Box 406, Ballston Lake, NY *12019*
   of ☎ (207)622-9831
   ''The Vaughan
   Homestead''
   1 Litchfield Rd,
   Hallowell, ME
   04347
   ☎ (212) 879-4939
   135 E 71 St,
   New York, NY
   10021

Gibson MR & MRS Gregory L (Priscilla H Cook) Hv.Laf'52 . . . .
   MR Christopher C—at ☎ (215) 542-8130
   135 Macklenburg Dv, Penllyn, PA *19422* . . . . .
   ☎ (215) WI7-1860
   2286 Deer Path Rd,
   Huntingdon Valley,
   PA *19006*

Gibson MR & MRS Henry C JR (Dugan—Phillips—Paula M Hober) BtP.Cc.Sar.P'44 . . . .
   MISS Adeline W—at Stuart, FL *33495* . . . .
   of PO Drawer 1329,
   Roseland, FL
   32957-1329
   ☎ (561) 589-7030
   ''Erewhon''
   13790 Ruffner Lane,
   Sebastian, FL *32958*

Gibson MRS Herbert D (Constance D Lewis) BMr'24.Cl'30
   ☎ (212) 475-7469 . . 22 Gramercy Park S, New York, NY *10003*

Gibson MR & MRS J Chester 3d (Elizabeth A Knipmeyer) Ws'81.Cry.Rv.Ac.Ncd.Rm'77.W&M'79
   ☎ (717) 560-5935 . . 253 Buckfield Dv, Lititz, PA *17543*

Gibson MR & MRS John McCullough (Sally D Mather) Cl'45.Ny.Cry.StJ.Rv.Wt.Cly.Ac.Ncd. Wms'42.Nu'48 ⚓ . . . .
   MR Jonathan McC—Rv. . . . .
   MR Anthony W . . . .
   MR Douglas W—Rv. . . . .
   ☎ (717) 548-2309
   ''Downpatrick''
   1719 Fern Glen Dv,
   Drumore, PA
   17518-9711

Gibson MRS Joseph R (Barnett—Frances Southgate) Ll.P.
   ☎ (610) MI2-7703 . . 622 Walnut Lane, Haverford, PA *19041*

Gibson MRS Langhorne (Parthenia B Ross)
   ☎ (540) 456-6860 . . ''Ramsay'' PO Box 98, Greenwood, VA *22943*

Gibson MR & MRS Langhorne 3d (Elizabeth de V Roberson) Va'90.Van'93.Unn.Plg.Va'90.Nu'95
   ☎ (203) 661-6395 . . 7 River Rd, Apt 302, Cos Cob, CT *06807*

Gibson MR & MRS Mark De W (Roberta Buchan O'Connell) Hlns'67.Va'61 . . . .
   MR Charles D—at 1820 Clydesdale Place NW, Apt 203, Washington, DC *20009* . . . .
   ☎ (804) 286-3533
   ''Mount Walla''
   PO Box 549,
   Scottsville, VA
   24590

Gibson MISS Meredith Wylie (J Chester 3d) . . . . Born at Lancaster, PA Jun 20'96

Gibson MR & MRS Nicholas J (Luke—Anne S Roosevelt) OState'86.OState'88.Tul'75.OState'86.OState'88
   X9 Ranch, Vail, AZ *85641*

Gibson MR & MRS R Dana (Leslie F Larned) Eh.Cly.H'37
   ☎ (860) 868-7546 . . PO Box 1068, Washington, CT *06793*

Gibson MR Robert M 2d—Me.V'90
   ☎ (415) 921-7608 . . 228 Anzavista Av, San Francisco, CA *94115*

Gibson MRS (DR) Sarah S (Sarah D Satterthwaite) V'68.Y'69.Tor'81.Lm.Cda.Ds.Dc. . . . .
   JUNIORS MISS Margaret F Y . . . .
   JUNIORS MISS Katherine H M . . . .
   ☎ (416) 925-7736
   384 Sackville St,
   Toronto, Ontario
   M4X 1S5, Canada

Gibson MRS Susan P
   ☎ (714) 759-0523 . . 2900 Park Newport, Apt 226, Newport Beach, CA *92660*

Gibson MR & MRS William L (Lorraine W Besch) Col'70.DU'73.Buck'72.Nu'87
   ☎ (908) 766-3966 . . 8 Lone Oak Rd, Basking Ridge, NJ *07920*

Gibson MR William T—Me.Va'50
   ☎ (610) 353-5205 . . Dunwoody Village CH7, 3500 West Chester Pike, Newtown Square, PA *19073*

Giddens MR & MRS James W (Virginia B Means) Sth'66.Dth'59.Y.'66 . . of
   ☎ (212) 308-6410 . . 2 Sutton Place S, Apt 14A, New York, NY *10022*
   ☎ (413) 298-3418 . . ''Dartmoor'' PO Box 2181, Lenox, MA *01240*

Gifford MRS A Winsor (Adelaide Winsor)
   ☎ (401) 635-4407 . . Quicksand Pond Rd, PO Box 911, Little Compton, RI *02837-0911*

Gifford MR & MRS Stephen N (Lee C Peck) Cy.Cw.Ncd.Bow'74
   22 Chestnut St, Dedham, MA *02026*

Gifford MR & MRS Stephen W (Enid Fessenden) V'45.D.Cw.H'44
   ☎ (617) 326-4806 . . 78 Village Av, Dedham, MA *02026*

Gignoux MRS Adrienne (Adrienne Morton-Smith) . .
MISS Consuela S . . . .
MISS Camilla E . . . .
MR P Alan . . . .
☎ (011-44-171) 730-8081
101 Eaton Terr, London SW1W 8TW, England

Gignoux MR & MRS Frederick E 3d (H Struthers
Harrower) Ty'59.Va'62 . . . .
MISS Noël M—at ☎ (212) 744-8640
116 E 66 St, New York, NY *10021* . . . .
☎ (804) 984-2770
1500 Rugby Rd, Charlottesville, VA *22903*

Gignoux MR & MRS Reginald (Newberry—Joan F
Landon) Wheat'67.Mich'68.Cly. . . . .
JUNIORS MR Christopher C—at Brooks . . . .
MR Gardner C Newberry—Bates'96 . . . . . .
JUNIORS MR James W Newberry—at Skidmore
☎ (802) 985-3889
170 Harbor Rd, Shelburne, VT *05482*

Gignoux MR & MRS Regis (Cross—Sheilah B Ross) V'50.Bgt.Nyc.Cly.Y'49
☎ (914) 234-7943 . . Greenwich Rd, Bedford, NY *10506*

Gilbert MISS A Mary
☎ (212) 628-5138 . . 860 Fifth Av, New York, NY *10021*

Gilbert MRS Alice K (Alice M Kobbé) Dc. . . . .
MISS Helen K—PineM'84 . . . .
☎ (203) 762-8221
65 Village Walk, Wilton, CT *06897-4044*

Gilbert MR & MRS Allan A (Gwendolyn M Moore)
Cw.P'46 . . . .
MISS Elizabeth M—Sth'73—at ☎ (617) 489-9953
72 Maple St, Belmont, MA *02178* . . . .
☎ (314) 993-8483
35 Dromara Rd, St Louis, MO *63124*

Gilbert REV & MRS Cass 3d (Grace G Cholmeley-Jones)
Tufts'52.Cc.Y'47.Bost'73
☎ (802) 867-2217 . . "Brook House" Dorset Hollow Rd, Dorset, VT *05251*

Gilbert MR & MRS Clinton JR (Paton—Jane S
Treman) Rc.Pr.Cly.P'51 . . . .
MISS Ann M—at 54 Mill Rd, Rhinebeck, NY
12572 . . . .
MISS Nina B—at ☎ (970) 927-3375
6B Riversedge Court, Basalt, CO *81621* . . . . . .
☎ (802) 867-4147
Box 247, Dorset Orchard, Dorset, VT *05251*

Gilbert MISS Cornelia D (Harris—Cornelia D Gilbert) . . . . Married at Providence, RI
Harris MR J Gary (James) . . . . Jly 23'94

Gilbert MR & MRS Dudley A (Johnson—Katharine McK Olyphant)
☎ (860) 739-6015 . . 46 Heritage Rd, East Lyme, CT *06333*

Gilbert MR E Morgan JR—H'54.Cl'59 . . . .
MISS Diana T—V'90 . . . .
☎ (703) 556-8760
6661 McLean Dv, McLean, VA *22101*

Gilbert MRS Emily P (Emily P Tracy) Cly.
☎ (860) 444-2428 . . 225 Great Neck Rd, Waterford, CT *06385*

Gilbert MR Francis B JR—S.Br'59
☎ (970) 879-5048 . . PO Box 770028, Steamboat Springs, CO *80477*

Gilbert MR Francis H . . see G Rublee 2d

Gilbert MR & MRS Frank E (Elizabeth A Lucas)
StL'40 . . . .
MR Christopher L . . . .
☎ (314) 227-0899
15049 Claymoor Court, Chesterfield, MO *63017*

Gilbert MR Geoffrey N (Clinton JR) . . . . Married at Austin, TX
Stovall MISS Helen (George) . . . . Nov 12'94

Gilbert MRS Gloria M (Gloria J Metzger) Gm. . . . .
MR John—Sa.Ty'84.Temp'87 . . . .
☎ (610) 688-8692
102 Cambria Court, St Davids, PA *19087*

Gilbert MR & MRS Jackson B (Maria M
Diez y Ponce de Léon) Madrid'56.Unn.Pr.Cvc.
Ri.Mt.Cly.Va'53.Va'56 . . . .
MISS Victoria E—Va'87—at ☎ (212) 427-3956
12 E 89 St, New York, NY *10128* . . . .
of ☎ (305)448-0863
2843 S Bayshore Dv, Apt 16D, Coconut Grove, FL *33133*
☎ (202) 462-1203
1823 Kalorama Square, Phelps Place NW, Washington, DC *20008*

Gilbert MR & MRS Richard C (Dorothy F Perkins) MassArt'74.DU'70
☎ (610) 964-9404 . . 10 Welwyn Rd, Wayne, PA *19087*

Gilbert MR & MRS Theodore V JR (Susan H Murdoch) Bow'79
☎ (215) 836-9457 . . 710 Glendalough Rd, Erdenheim, PA *19038*

Gilbert MR & MRS Thomas S (Shelley S Rea)
Hlns'69.Dyc.Ri.T.P'66.H'68 . . of
☎ (212) 876-2345 . . 1100 Park Av, New York, NY *10128*
☎ (516) 537-7862 . . 8 Georgica Association, PO Box 1028, Wainscott, NY *11975*

Gilbreath MR & MRS Cabanné de Mun (Mary P Silberberg)
FIT'81.Unn.Tex'81.Tex'88
☎ (713) 526-3148 . . 2819 Colquitt St, Houston, TX *77098*

Gilchrist MISS Stephanie S . . see H Fiorato

Gilder MR & MRS George F (Cornelia E Brooke)
V'71.C.H'61 . . . .
MISS Louisa L—at Dartmouth . . . .
JUNIORS MISS Mary Ellen T . . . .
☎ (413) 243-0161
"Red House" Tyringham, MA *01264*

Gildersleeve MR & MRS Oliver De P JR (Kirsten M
Hansen) Pa'65.Pa'76 . . . .
MISS Kristine M . . . .
MR Oliver De P 3d . . . .
MR Christian N . . . .
☎ (415) 328-6087
893 Sharon Court, Palo Alto, CA *94301*

Gildersleeve MR & MRS Stephen R (Susan S Cole)
SanJ'85.Mass'71 . . . .
MR Paul M—at U of NH . . . .
JUNIORS MR Adam S . . . .
☎ (603) 938-2505
RFD 1, Box 292A, West Rd, Bradford, NH *03221*

Gildersleeve MR & MRS William L F (Huestis—Taylor—
Anita Richardson) Wms'35
5 Flower Hill Rd, New Milford, CT *06776*

Gildred MR & MRS George Lewis (Alison J Frost)
Stan'64.Sdy.Stan'55 ⚐ . . . .
MISS Julie F . . . .
JUNIORS MR G Lewis JR . . . .
☎ (619) 232-6361
667 San Elijo St, San Diego, CA *92106*

Gile MRS Clement D (June H Tyner)
☎ (508) 945-4168 . . Hill House, North Chatham, MA *02650*

Gilfillan MR & MRS Graeme A (Constance Elizabeth
Lewis) Cal'77.Vh.Cal'75 . . . .
JUNIORS MISS Sarah E . . . .
☎ (818) 585-0022
1290 Hillcrest Av, Pasadena, CA *91106*

Gilfoy MR & MRS Peter G (Margaret F Wiehl)
Colby'71.Colby'70 . . . .
JUNIORS MR Nathan . . . .
☎ (508) 655-6822
50 Oldfield Dv, Sherborn, MA *01770*

Gilhuley MR & MRS Stephen E (Anna D Skacel) Wis'68.Pr.Cly.Y'66.Van'69
☎ (516) 922-7365 . . 112 Blair Rd, Oyster Bay, NY *11771*

Gilkyson MR & MRS Hamilton H 3d (Chandlee—Josephine P Duer) Sap.Pa'40 . . . .
MR Hamilton H 4th—at 1732 Maltman Av, Los Angeles, CA *90026* . . . . | ☎ (505) 982-1716 PO Box 2474, Santa Fe, NM *87501*

Gill MR & MRS Bruce Cooper (Clement—Jill Berguido) Swb'67.Temp'75.Me.Mor'72.GeoW'76
☎ (610) 649-2313 . . 515 Old Lancaster Rd, Haverford, PA *19041*

Gill MR Paul H JR—Al.Bost'66
7 Kessler Farm Dv, Apt 189, Nashua, NH *03063*

Gill MR & MRS Peter T (Barbara E Butt) Un.
☎ (914) 961-2623 . . 36 Tanglewylde Av, Bronxville, NY *10708*

Gill MRS Robert Lee (Buckingham—Hamilton—Eileen W Chamberland)
48 N 300 E, Alpine, UT *84004*

Gill MR & MRS Robert Lee (Melanie Snyder) Rc.
☎ (212) 628-3388 . . 66 E 79 St, New York, NY *10021*

Gill MR & MRS Robert M (Joan Tucker) Chi.Y'42
☎ (561) 231-9168 . . 1180 Reef Rd, Apt 23A, Vero Beach, FL *32963*

Gillespie MR & MRS Bruce A (M Gale Sanson) Pe.Me.R.W.Sar.Rv.Cs.Sdg.Clem'70 . . . .
JUNIORS MR Benson B . . . . | ☎ (610) LA5-2233 ''Tuckaway'' 1530 Montgomery Av, Villanova, PA *19085-1917*

Gillespie MRS C Waring (Jane Baldwin) Mds.
☎ (912) 927-8257 . . John-Wesley Villas, 231 W Montgomery Crossroads, Savannah, GA *31406*

Gillespie CAPT DR & MRS Cameron A (Tomoko Usami) USN.Keio'70.Va'70 . . of
☎ (804) 476-6996 . . Mayfield Farm, 1148 Swain Rd, Halifax, VA *24558*
☎ (804) 792-0131 . . ''Danville Ordinary'' 34 Baldwin St, Danville, VA *24541*
☎ (919) 490-5989 . . 1001 Norwood Av, Durham, NC *27707*
☎ (804) 476-8106 . . ''Taro's Lodge'' Halifax, VA *24558*

Gillespie MR & MRS Chandler (Elizabeth B Acher) Me.Pe.R.Rv.Cspa.Sar.Fw.W.Sdg.Pa'40
☎ (610) 896-6160 . . 533 Avonwood Rd, Haverford, PA *19041*

Gillespie MR & MRS Charles A (Fuller—Osgood—Jane Hewlett) Stan'38.Bur.Stan'34 . . . .
MISS Kit Fuller—at ☎ (310) 474-1456 1670 Malcolm Av, Apt 101, Los Angeles, CA *90024* . . . .
MR G Gary Fuller—at ☎ (517) 828-5593 7732 S Mission St, Mt Pleasant, MI *48859* . . | of ☎ (415)434-0131 290 Lombard St, San Francisco, CA *94133* ☎ (415) 851-0894 160 Greer Rd, Woodside, CA *94062*

Gillespie MR David H . . see N S Lamont

Gillespie MR Duncan M
☎ (617) 242-2926 . . 103—9 St, Apt 133, Charlestown, MA *02129*

Gillespie MR & MRS Edward A (Marie E Turro) Nu'48.Evg.Coa.StA.Myf.Sar.Cw.Rv.Snc.Vca.Ne.Ht.Wt. . . of
☎ (516) 742-8171 . . 94—3 St, Garden City, NY *11530*
☎ (561) 833-2884 . . 389 S Lake Dv, Palm Beach, FL *33480*

Gillespie MRS Harold E (Mary M Kress)
☎ (804) 264-6669 . . Westminster-Canterbury 548, 1600 Westbrook Av, Richmond, VA *23227*

Gillespie MR & MRS John L (Sandra H Barnes) Dth'54.Cr'62 . . . .
MR John L JR—Colg'90—at U of Va . . . . | ☎ (603) 643-8406 4 Montview Dv, Hanover, NH *03755*

Gillespie MRS Julian E JR (Joan G O'Neill) Ty'56.Cvc.Sl. . . . .
MR Julian E 3d—Cvc.Cc.W&L'91—at 2070 Pacific Av, Apt 305, San Francisco, CA *94109* . . . . | ☎ (301) 656-5206 3 E Lenox St, Chevy Chase, MD *20815*

Gillespie MRS Lee D (Nancy Lee Day) Ws'49.Cly.Chi. . . . .
MISS Abigail D—StJ'79—at Rome, Italy . . . . . .
MR Thaddeus R—Bow'78—at ☎ (617) 547-7358 1010 Memorial Dv, Apt 19A, Cambridge, MA *02138* . . . . | ☎ (617) 492-0076 1010 Memorial Dv, Apt 3A, Cambridge, MA *02138-4853*

Gillespie MRS R Reed (Ruth Reed) Cs.
☎ (212) 988-1385 . . 163 E 81 St, New York, NY *10028*

Gillespie MR & MRS Richard R (Johnson—Patrice E Phillips) Tufts'71.Pn.P'52
☎ (203) 834-1491 . . 258 Silver Spring Rd, Wilton, CT *06897*

Gillespie MR & MRS Stuart P SR (Helen C Macpherson) 🚲
☎ (207) 677-2400 . . 23 Old Harrington Rd, Pemaquid, ME *04558*

Gillespie MR Timothy A . . see N S Lamont

Gillet MR & MRS F Warrington JR (Boykin—Elesabeth Ridgely Ingalls) Evg.Gv.Ny.Rr.Srb.BtP.JHop'52
☎ (561) 655-6789 . . Pelican Hall, 159 Via Del Lago, Palm Beach, FL *33480*

Gillet MR Nairn' Bowland . . see MRS W P C Muñoz

Gillett MISS Marian N . . see W L Brookfield

Gillette MR & MRS Edwin (Jean H Fremont) Cal'50.Stan'33.SCal'53 🚲
☎ (310) 472-5604 . . 480 N Bundy Dv, Brentwood, Los Angeles, CA *90049*

Gillette MR & MRS Howard F (Mary S Hale) Cy.Chi.Fy.H'35 . . . .
MISS Mary D—Tufts'73—at ☎ (508) 627-7416 PO Box 2742, Vineyard Haven, MA *02568* . . . . | ☎ (617) 734-1644 55 Fairgreen Place, Chestnut Hill, MA *02167*

Gillette MR Hyde—Cvc.Mt.Cw.Myf.P'28.H'30
☎ (617) 320-9008 . . 10 Longwood Dv, Apt 404, Westwood, MA *02090-1144*

Gillette MR & MRS Richard C (Debra P Jennings) SFr'78.Col'77. . . . .
JUNIORS MISS Kate J . . . . | ☎ (803) 363-5131 12 Marsh View Rd, Hilton Head Island, SC *29928*

Gillette MR & MRS Richard P (Marion R Cochran) Stan'51.Evg.Ri.Y'50
☎ (561) 832-4935 . . 1200 S Flagler Dv, Apt 1202, West Palm Beach, FL *33401*

Gillette MR William S—Tufts'79
347 E 53 St, New York, NY *10022*

Gilliam MRS Sara B (Sara W Brown) . . . .
MISS Sara C—Va'90.Van'94—at ☎ (714) 833-2263 . . 10 Via Ricasol, Apt A418, Irvine, CA *92612* . . . . | ☎ (804) 971-7243 1629 Inglewood Dv, Charlottesville, VA *22901*

Gillie MR Robert C—StA.Wms'60
☎ (603) 795-2615 . . 129 Franklin Hill Rd, PO Box 268, Lyme, NH *03768*

Gillies MR & MRS Archibald L (Linda L Boyer) | ☎ (212) 496-1757
SL'61.C.P'56 . . . . | 275 Central Park W,
MISS Isabel B . . . . | New York, NY
MR Andrew T—at Middlebury Paris . . . . | *10024*

Gillies MRS George J (Lazo—Mary M Hepburn) . . . . Died Jun 4'96

Gilligan MRS Francis S (Fernanda M Kellogg) | of ☎ (212)362-4972
Nu'66.Ri. . . . . | 88 Central Park W,
MISS Fernanda K . . . . | New York, NY
| *10023*
| ☎ (914) 677-3271
| ''Fitch's Corner''
| 154 N Mabbettsville
| Rd, Millbrook, NY
| *12545*

Gilligan MR Francis S—Ri.WorC'59
☎ (617) 536-4619 . . 770 Boylston St, Boston, MA *02199*

Gillis MISS Anne C
☎ (914) 677-0036 . . RR 1, Box 93, Millbrook, NY *12545*

Gillmore MR & MRS Frederick H JR (Dolores N Airey)
Cal'79.K.Rv.Cly.Y.'70.H'74 . . of
☎ (212) 628-3346 . . 131 E 69 St, New York, NY *10021*
☎ (518) 589-5210 . . Onteora Club, Tannersville, NY *12485*

Gillock MR & MRS John T 2d (MacCornack—Louise B Whipple) Kas'76
☎ (502) 586-7592 . . .2610 Rapids Rd, Franklin, KY *42134*

Gillotti MR & MRS Albert F (Susan S McCabe) V'60.Plg.H.Y'60.NCar'64
☎ (508) 696-6072 . . RR 2, Box 201L, Vineyard Haven, MA *02568*

Gilman JUNIORS MR Matthew E . . see L A Carter JR

Gilman MR & MRS Stewart B N (Mary Ann | ☎ (310) 277-7677
Marchant) Barton'62.Y'60 . . . . | 10365 Holman Av,
MISS Margaret E . . . . | Los Angeles, CA
MR Gregory A . . . . | *90024*

Gilmor MR Christopher C . . see F A Irwin

Gilmor MR Mark C . . see F A Irwin

Gilmor MASTER Michael Samuel (Robert 3d) . . . . Born Sep 8'95

Gilmor MR Robert—Pr.H'31
☎ (610) 325-5653 . . Dunwoody Village CH18, 3500 West Chester Pike,
Newtown Square, PA *19073*

Gilmor MR & MRS Robert 3d (Janet L Charzuk) SUNY'86.Csh.Woos'87
☎ (516) 266-2203 . . 303 Cuba Hill Rd, Huntington, NY *11743*

Gilmor MR & MRS William Gavin (Sandra L Plant) | ☎ (516) OR1-3331
Pr.Ht.H'63.Cl'69 . . . . | Meadow Spring
MISS A Hetherington . . . . | Lane, Glen Cove,
MISS Ashley L . . . . | NY *11542*

Gilmore MR & MRS John S (Charlotte Geary) Cal'58.Hast'61
1061—45 St, Sacramento, CA *95819*

Gilmore MRS William E (Marjorie E Young) Gv.Pn.
200 Wyndemere Way, Apt 201B, Naples, FL *34105*

Gilmour MR & MRS Andrew S (Carol R Hansen)
Aug'75.JHop'77.H'85.H'83.JHop'85
☎ (301) 972-7833 . . 14921 Sugarland Rd, Poolesville, MD *20837*

Gilmour MR & MRS (DR) David L (Anula K Jayasuriya)
H'80.Camb'82.H'89.H'91.H'93.H'80.H'82.H'84
☎ (415) 949-2248 . . 26010 Torello Lane, Los Altos Hills,
CA *94022-2041*

Gilmour MRS Joan T (Stehli—Joan P Thompson)
☎ (603) 323-7413 . . Box 31, South Tamworth, NH *03883*

Gilpatric MR Roswell L . . . . Died at
New York, NY Mch 15'96

Gilpatric MRS Roswell L (Cahners—Thorne—Miriam A Rose)
Ri.C.Evg.Pr.Plg.
☎ (212) 758-2425 . . 435 E 52 St, New York, NY *10022-6445*

Gilpin MASTER Alexander Vincent (David V) . . . . Born at
Christiana, DE Jun 20'95

Gilpin MR & MRS David V (Sharon V Guthrie)
Towson'82.Duke'86.Ty'81.Duke'86
☎ (610) 430-1205 . . 1906 New Market Court, West Chester, PA *19382*

Gilpin MR & MRS Edward U (Caroline Crosson)
CtCol'82.Temp'86.StLaw'83.Cl'91
☎ (914) 723-0207 . . 171 Lyons Rd, Scarsdale, NY *10583*

Gilpin MRS John W (Phoebe S Barkan) Cal'46.Tcy.Bur.Ncd.
☎ (415) 342-0349 . . 1275 San Raymundo Rd, Hillsborough, CA *94010*

Gilpin MR Kenneth N JR . . . . Died at
Boyce, VA Apr 29'96

Gilpin MR & MRS McGhee Tyson (Heard—Maria Hortencia Mesa) P'42
☎ (540) 837-1031 . . Lakeville Farm, PO Box 207, Boyce, VA *22620*

Gilpin MISS Megan Crosson (Edward U) . . . . Born at
White Plains, NY Oct 25'95

Gilpin MR & MRS Thomas T (Jean E Rose) | ☎ (540) 955-4216
P'75.Rr.P'75. . . . . | 101 Smith St,
JUNIORS MR Thomas T JR—at Duke . . . . | Berryville, VA
JUNIORS MR William M—at Hotchkiss . . . . | *22611*

Gilpin MR & MRS Vincent JR (Elizabeth Udall) Wils'53.Rd.Hav'52
☎ (610) 644-6960 . . 13 Colonial Way, Malvern, PA *19355-3512*

Gimbel MR S Stinor—Bcs.IaState'54
☎ (212) 570-9124 . . 157 E 78 St, New York, NY *10021-0405*

Gimbel MR & MRS Thomas S T (Lesley Bush-Brown)
Bow'76.Pr.B.Rv.Cly.Bow'76.Cl'78 . . of
☎ (516) 759-6467 . . 22 Duck Pond Rd, Glen Cove, NY *11542*
☎ (212) 249-7376 . . 205 E 77 St, New York, NY *10021*

Ginn MR & MRS Alexander (Helen M Vilas) Cv.May.It.P'34.Y'38
☎ (216) 464-2819 . . 3911-1 Lander Rd, Chagrin Falls, OH *44022-1328*

Gioia MR & MRS Anthony H (Donna M Hornung)
Bf.Ts.Cy.G.SUNY'64.SCal'65
☎ (716) 876-1744 . . 55 Meadow Rd, Buffalo, NY *14216*

Giordano MR & MRS John C 3d (Errol C Train) Ty'81.Rcn.Vt'80
☎ (908) 236-2213 . . Cokesbury Hill Farm, 33 Cokesbury-Califon Rd,
Lebanon, NJ *08833*

Girard MR & MRS Peter Francis (Leslie V Gehres) Cal'40
8001 Vista Dv, La Mesa, CA *91941*

Giroux MR & MRS Paul A (Margaret R Hester) Nu'79.Rc.Ln.Pr.Cs.Bost'80
☎ (516) 676-2052 . . 19 Rabbit Run, Glen Cove, NY *11542*

Girvin MR & MRS Robert (Hester St C Northrop) Ncd.H.'52
☎ (508) 248-5495 . . 93 Partridge Hill Rd, Charlton, MA *01507*

Girvin MRS William Harper (Bonnie M Smith)
Forest Park, 700 Walnut Bottom Rd, Carlisle, PA *17013*

Githens MR W French—Fw.Cl'27
☎ (703) 237-7583 . . Vinson Hall, 6251 Old Dominion Dv, McLean,
VA *22101-4818*

Gitlin MR & MRS Louis J (Edith L Dixon) | ☎ (610) 647-5034
DU'69.Wcc.DU'68 . . . . | 12 Indian Way,
MISS Marian D . . . . | Malvern, PA *19355*
MR Timothy P . . . . |

Glaccum MR & MRS Denis M (Anne H Ellis)
Stc.FairD'67 . . . . ☎ (610) 347-2024
MISS Anne E . . . . 1420 Doe Run Rd,
MR John-Amory . . . . PO Box 82,
Unionville, PA
19375

Glancy MR & MRS Richard D JR (H Keyser Harris) Hlns'89.W&M'89
☎ (804) 360-7639 . . 6001 Melcroft Court, Glen Allen, VA *23060*

Glanville MRS James W (Nancy E Hart)
Scripps'49.B. . . . . of ☎ (713)840-0206
MR Charles D—Ty'78.Smu'86—at 1912 Larchmont Rd,
521 Caledonian Rd, Islington, London N7 9RH, Houston, TX *77019*
England . . . . ☎ (203) 655-3652
MR Robert E—P'88—at Moscow, Russia . . . . . . ''Blue Haven''
11 Contentment
Island Rd, Darien,
CT *06820*

Glanville MR John H—Leh'78.Tex'85
627 S Marengo Av, Pasadena, CA *91106*

Glanville MR & MRS Thomas S (Laurie K Novak)
TexA&M'82.B.Va'80.ColM'84
2415 Morrison St SW, Calgary, Alberta T2T 3J4, Canada

Glanz MR & MRS Christopher K (Mary W Runnells) Nw'77.Wis'73.Wis'76
☎ (847) 492-1543 . . 1827 Grant St, Evanston, IL *60201*

Glascock MRS Elizabeth W (Boyer—Elizabeth B White) Sl.Mv.
☎ (505) 986-9096 . . ''La Tierra Nueva'' 1049 Buckman Dv, Santa Fe,
NM *87501-9481*

Glascock MR & MRS George F (Lilian Weiland) Ariz'81.AGSIM'82
☎ (415) 323-4465 . . 175 Greenoaks Dv, Atherton, CA *94027*

Glascock MR & MRS John W (Amy L Sellers) P'cpia'82.DU'82
☎ (314) 391-2045 . . 14624 Summer Blossom Lane, Chesterfield,
MO *63017*

Glasgow MR & MRS W Merrill (Elizabeth P
Fauntleroy) Cry.H'50.H'52 . . . . of ☎ (713)626-4290
MISS Virginia S . . . . 3620 Meadow Lake
MISS Julia M M . . . . Lane, Houston, TX
77027
Gaylord Farm,
Gay Hill, TX *77833*

Glass MR & MRS Charles F (Susan B Grace) of ☎ (313)393-5380
Mich'67.MichSt'65 . . . . 300 Riverfront Dv,
MR Charles F JR . . . . Apt 511, Detroit, MI
MR D Carter *48226-4517*
JUNIORS MR William J . . . . ☎ (616) 526-9563
''Pineyrie''
3445 N Lake Shore
Dv, Harbor Springs,
MI *49740*

Glass MR & MRS Edgar T (Elizabeth de Vaulogé) Y'42
☎ (860) 677-0902 . . 33 Reservoir Rd, Farmington, CT *06032*

Glass MRS Frederick M (Marcia J Hubbard) Mass'60.Mt.
☎ (212) 838-6097 . . 201 E 62 St, New York, NY *10021*

Glass MRS J Hall (Joannah C Hall) Rd.W.Ncd.
☎ (610) 869-3993 . . ''Bryn Lea'' Hood Rd, Box 39, Chatham,
PA *19318*
Nov 1 . . ☎ (803) 648-0100 . . ''Bryn Lea Farm'' 3549 Charleston
H'way, Aiken, SC *29801*

Glass MR & MRS John B JR (Martha K Vietor)
Un.Err.Eyc.Ri.Plg.StJ.Cly.Cda.Ncd.Dc.Dh.So'74
☎ (212) 996-2309 . . 1158 Fifth Av, New York, NY *10029*

Glass MR Laurence d'A M—P'58.P'59 . . see MRS D B Sherman

Glass MR & MRS Peter J P (Elisabeth A C Flynn) Hlns'78
☎ (303) 841-2383 . . 6872 N Trailway Circle, Parker, CO *80134*

Glasser MR & MRS James J (Louise D Rosenthal) of ☎ (847)234-6009
CtCol'62.Rc.On.Sr.Cho.Cas.Fy.Y'55.H'58 . . . . . 464 N Mayflower
MISS Mary C—at ☎ (617) 576-3080 Rd, Lake Forest, IL
56 Concord Av, Apt 1, Cambridge, MA *02138* . *60045*
MR Daniel R . . . . ☎ (520) 749-9439
13262 E Saddlerock
Rd, Tucson, AZ
85749

Glaze DR & MRS Robert Pinckney (Barbara C ☎ (205) 970-0683
Malloy) Roch'59.So'55.Roch'61 . . . . 3610 Dunbarton Dv,
MISS Jennifer D . . . . Birmingham, AL
MR David W *35223-2888*

Glazebrook MR & MRS James G (Joan M Dobson)
Cl'90.Wh'lck'73.Mid'77.Cwr'80
☎ (407) 629-4722 . . 1624 Barcelona Way, Winter Park, FL *32789*

Glazebrook MRS James R (Rebeckah DuBois) V'41
☎ (941) 966-3519 . . 442 N Casey Key Rd, Osprey, FL *34229-9775*

Glazebrook MR Michael T . . see MRS J G B Ewing JR

Glazebrook MR Otis A 4th . . see MRS J G B Ewing JR

Gleason MR & MRS Aleta M (Aleta N Murphy) H'82
☎ (860) 691-1652 . . 24 Cottage Lane, Niantic, CT *06357*

Gleason DR & MRS Donald M (Margaret E Garvie) H'53
☎ (520) 298-1193 . . 6001 E San Cristobal Dv, Tucson, AZ *85715*

Gleason MR Edward S—Bost'84.Lond'85 . . see R I Johnson

Gleiber MR John Sward—Ct.P'cpia'49
☎ (202) 462-1901 . . 1901 Wyoming Av NW, Washington, DC *20009*

Glen MRS Alixe R (Alixe C Reed) Hlns'79
5810 Madaket Rd, Bethesda, MD *20816*

Glen DR & MRS Dulaney (Wendy Walker)
Y'55.Cl'67 . . . . ☎ (910) 924-0400
MISS Melissa W . . . . ''Pfolly Pfarm''
MISS Julie M . . . . 4691 Vienna-Dozier
MR Michael W—at ☎ (212) 534-2498 Rd, Pfafftown, NC
328 E 89 St, Apt 3W, New York, NY *10128* . . . *27040*

Glen MR Mark D (Dulaney) . . . . Married at Swarthmore, PA
Urban MISS Ann C (Percy L) . . . . Apr 13'96

Glen MR Robert M—Ln.Mt.NCar'78.JHop'87
67 E 11 St, Apt 518, New York, NY *10003*

Glendinning MR & MRS David P (Nina S Hacker) Franklin'89.Bvr'92 . . of
☎ (610) 825-2954 . . 141 W Tenth Av, Conshohocken, PA *19428*
High Island, Upper St Regis Lake, Lake Clear, NY *12945*

Glendinning MRS Henry P (Elizabeth Parrish) Sth'51
☎ (215) 646-2364 . . 7128 Sheaff Lane, Ft Washington, PA *19034*

Glendinning MR & MRS R Bruce (Heather Q McKenna) Lynch'88.J'ville'82
☎ (215) 542-8232 . . 6132 Butler Pike, Blue Bell, PA *19422*

Glendinning MR & MRS Robert 2d (Sandra E Dufort) ☎ (215) 248-9658
StA.Fst.Pc.Sg.Ac. . . . . 604 W Mermaid
MISS Gray R—StL'89 . . . . Lane, Philadelphia,
PA *19118*

Glenn MR & MRS J Wooderson 3d (Glenny L ☎ (516) 922-0895
Oelsner) S.Hof'60 . . . . ''Creek House''
MISS Hope R—Vt'94 . . . . 332 Centre Island,
MR James W . . . . Oyster Bay, NY
MR Edward L *11771*

Glenn MRS Joan W (Joan L Woolman) . . . . see H N Woolman JR
MISS Holly T . . . .
MR George S JR . . . .
Glenn MR & MRS Lawrence R (Anne D Dunlaevy) ☎ (516) 676-5339
S.Ny.Pa'60.GeoW'65 . . . . "Robin Hill"
MISS D'Arcy A—Rm'90—at ☎ (212) 932-8539 Town Cocks Lane,
230 Riverside Dv, New York, NY *10025* . . . . . . Locust Valley, NY
MISS Allison L—at Bowdoin *11560*
MR Lawrence R JR—Bow'89—at 259 W 10 St,
New York, NY *10014* . . . .
Glennon MR & MRS Harrison R (Dickie G Bailey)
Char'ton'39.Sar.Ncd.USN'37
☎ (203) 637-2232 . . 30 Dawn Harbor Lane, Riverside, CT *06878*
Glidden MR & MRS Philip Schuyler (Elena Marti-Ventosa Lieta)
Barcelona'86.LakeF'83
☎ (508) 526-7522 . . 164 Summer St, Manchester-By-The-Sea,
MA *01944*
Glidden MRS William Townsend (Jane J Walsh) V'50.Ec.Ncd.
☎ (561) 225-6565 . . 221 NE Plantation Rd, Apt 202, Stuart, FL *34996*
Glines MRS E Stanley (Parke—Catherine Van A Stevenson)
☎ (902) 485-6261 . . Poplar Hill, Scotsburn, Nova Scotia B0K 1R0,
Canada
Gloeckner MRS Frederick H (Mudd—Emily B Hartshorne)
Pa'36.Pa'50.Pc.Me.Cs.Cos.
☎ (610) 642-3372 . . 734 Millbrook Lane, Haverford, PA *19041*
Glore MRS Charles F JR (Fairbank—Foley—Barbara R Estelle) Sc.
☎ (312) 266-2898 . . 1555 N Astor St, Chicago, IL *60610*
Glore MR & MRS Robert Hixon (Elizabeth Dilworth Brundred)
Scripps'43.On.Cas.Fy.Chi.Pa'48
☎ (847) 234-1580 . . 59 Warrington Court, Lake Bluff, IL *60044*
MRS at . . Wealshire, 150 Jamestown Rd, Lincolnshire, IL *60069*
Glos MRS Stanislav M (Margaret Taft Beach) ☎ (212) 722-9294
Sth'58.Cs. . . . . 129 E 94 St,
MISS Maya C—Colby'92 New York, NY
MR Alexander B—at Dr Wintrich Strasse 8A, *10128*
8017 Ebersberg, Germany . . . .
MR Andrew B . . . .
Glover MRS Charles C 3d (Virginia Dougherty) Sth'43.Sl.
☎ (410) 822-7870 . . 28111 S Island Creek Rd, Trappe, MD *21673*
Glover MR James G
☎ (011-44-1349) 63529 . . Meikle Ussie House, Maryboro, Ross,
Scotland
Glover MR & MRS Price P (Isobel C Hinckley) . . . . . ☎ (212) 722-8952
MISS Julie M—at 19365 Lake Av, Deephaven, 1111 Park Av,
MN *55391* . . . . New York, NY
MR Jonathan L *10128*
Glynn MRS Thomas A JR (Julia A Devereux) ☎ (011-52-98)
Wh'lck'67.Wh'lck'70.Dar.Ncd. 851491
MR T Anthony 3d—at Colo Coll . . . . 2401 Cancun Plaza,
20.5 Km Av
Kulkulcan, Zona
Hotelera, Cancun,
Q Roo 77500,
Mexico
Glynn MR Thomas A JR—SheltonAby'61
☎ (410) 377-0111 . . 6114 Buckingham Manor Dv, Baltimore,
MD *21210*

Gnichtel MR William Van O (late William S) . . Married at New York, NY
Gayley MISS Mary B (Strater—Mary B Gayley) . . . . Jun 7'96
Gnichtel MR & MRS William Van O (Strater—Mary of ☎ (617)259-3457
B Gayley) Sth'58.K.Un.Snc.Cs.Ty'56 . . . . PO Box 431,
MR Edwin M—at ☎ (201) 377-4468 Lincoln, MA *01773*
Chatham Hill Apt C19, 25 Hickory Place, ☎ (201) 377-7568
Chatham, NJ *07928* . . . . "Loosebox"
32 Barnsdale Rd,
Madison, NJ *07940*
☎ (518) 589-6333
"The Briars"
Onteora Club,
Tannersville, NY
12485
Gnichtel MR & MRS William Van O JR (Debra A Flocco)
☎ (914) 357-2928 . . 556 Haverstraw Rd, Montebello, NY *10901*
Gober MR & MRS Glenn D (Margaret W Parke) LaS'93
☎ (610) 543-0807 . . 27 President Av, Rutledge, PA *19070*
Gober MISS Margaret W—Rut'90
☎ (610) 873-8954 . . P Patch Farm, 1206 E Lancaster Av, Downingtown,
PA *19335*
Gober MR Robert D
740 W Lincoln H'way, Downingtown, PA *19335*
Goddard MR & MRS C Convers (Katherine Van I Downey) Bhm.Y'44
☎ (707) 942-9412 . . PO Box 1008, Calistoga, CA *94515*
Goddard MR & MRS Edward Q (Nancy J Poerstel) Cal'83.Col'81
☎ (301) 229-1388 . . 6622 Broad St, Bethesda, MD *20816-2604*
Goddard MR & MRS George A (Margaret G Henkle) . . at
☎ (314) WY4-7679 . . 5 Layton Terr, St Louis, MO *63124*
☎ (561) 234-4416 . . 2075 Porpoise Point Lane S, Vero Beach,
FL *32963*
Goddard MISS Jennifer (Scott—Jennifer Goddard) Va'88
☎ (804) 823-5109 . . PO Box 162, Free Union, VA *22940*
Goddard MR & MRS Livingston (A Elizabeth 13819 Crown Point,
Flothow) Yn.Y'32.H'35 . . . . Sun City, AZ *85351*
MR William L
Goddard MR & MRS Preston L (Ashley W King) Rich'83.LakeF'79
☎ (203) 857-4818 . . 8 Stephen Mather Rd, West Norwalk, CT *06850*
Goddard MR & MRS Robert H I (Hope L Drury) ☎ (401) 272-4713
Yn.Y'32.H'34 . . . . 64 Angell St,
MR Robert H I 3d—H'63—at 1709—34 St NW, Providence, RI
Washington, DC *20007* *02906*
Goddard MR & MRS Stanhope S (Jean C Lane) V'49.B.Ne.Y'42
☎ (203) 869-1972 . . 18 Georgetown N, Greenwich, CT *06831*
Goddard MR & MRS William H D (Katharine W of ☎ (401)751-8146
Ferris) Nu'68.Bost'69 . . . . 66 Power St,
MISS Charlotte I—at Skidmore . . . . Providence, RI
02906
☎ (508) 283-9989
45 Dollivers Neck
Lane, Gloucester,
MA *01930*
☎ (619) 977-1857
"China Ranch"
Santa Ysabel, CA
92070
Godfrey JUNIORS MISS Cori T . . see E StC Purdon

Godfrey MR Cyrus Vincent—Cal'71
☎ (310) 278-5753 . . 1534 N Doheny Dv, Los Angeles, CA *90069*

Godfrey MRS Ellwood W (Sophia Moore) Sth'36 . . of
☎ (561) 234-1799 . . 2814 Cardinal Dv, Vero Beach, FL *32963*
☎ (207) 374-5697 . . HC 64, Box 242, Blue Hill, ME *04614*

Godfrey JUNIORS MISS Kristin D . . see E StC Purdon

Godfrey MR Lincoln 3d . . . . | of ☎ (610)388-2194
JUNIORS MISS Emily . . . . | 403 Ring Rd,
JUNIORS MR Lincoln 5th . . . . | Chadds Ford, PA
| *19317*
| "Cricket Hill"
| Blowing Point,
| Anguilla

Godfrey MR & MRS Loren (Cynthia K Burbank) | ☎ (860) 677-7358
Mg.Mit'60.Rens'65.Rut'72 . . . . | 386 Old Mountain
MISS Helen S—Box 2174, Truckee, CA *95734* . . | Rd, Farmington, CT
MR Loren JR—at 284 Park Place, Brooklyn, NY | *06032*
11238 . . . . |
MR Nathaniel F . . . . |

Godfrey MISS Marian A—Rdc'70.Y'75.Hn.
☎ (215) 551-7046 . . 1169 S 13 St, Philadelphia, PA *19147*

Godfrey JUNIORS MR Mark A . . see E StC Purdon

Godfrey MISS Paula D . . . . | ☎ (970) 925-7075
MR Andrew H . . . . | 505 N 8 St, Aspen,
| CO *81611*

Godfrey MR & MRS Peter (Margaret K Meister) Gm.Ph.Nf.Rb.H.'48
☎ (610) 525-1634 . . "Faunamede" Villanova, PA *19085*

Godfrey MR & MRS Peter JR (Lisa W Clark) Y'82.H'86.Pa'89.Ariz'85.Pa'92
☎ (215) 248-1340 . . 8 Tohopeka Lane, Philadelphia, PA *19118*

Godfrey MR & MRS Peter S (J Nancy Thompson) | ☎ (203) 629-2748
Sth'66.Ihy.Ny.Yn.Y'63.Camb'65 . . . . | 31 Guinea Rd,
MISS Alexandra E T—GeoW'93 . . . . | Greenwich, CT
MR Thompson C—Wis'95 . . . . | *06830*

Godfrey MR & MRS Raymond H JR (Susan J Schoch) Wheat'65.P.Y'67.H'69
☎ (212) 876-3043 . . 9 E 93 St, New York, NY *10128*

Godfrey MR Robert D JR—Pa'49 | ☎ (610) 827-9634
MISS Sarah C—V'73.Cr'75.Ac.—at | 42 Valley Hill,
☎ (213) 462-5633 . . 591 N Windsor Blvd, | RD 1, Malvern, PA
Los Angeles, CA *90004* . . . . | *19355*
MISS Constance W . . . . |

Godfrey MRS Robert H (Rachel A Ogilvie) | ☎ (914) 232-6229
SL'90.SL'92 . . . . | 21-16 Croton Lake
MISS Nicola H—NCar'89—at 707 Van Buren St, | Rd, Katonah, NY
Raleigh, NC *27604* . . . . | *10536*
MISS Emma E—NCar'87—at 614 Polk St, |
Raleigh, NC *27604* . . . . |

Godfrey MR Robert H—Ty'57
☎ (914) 764-5401 . . 41 Cradle Rock Rd, Pound Ridge, NY *10576*

Godfrey MR & MRS Thomas B A (Susan S Strong) | ☎ (207) 863-2254
Hn.H'42 . . . . | Coombs Neck,
MR Thomas B A JR—at East Side Rd, Box 35, | Vinalhaven, ME
Addison, ME *04606* . . . . | *04863*

Godwin MRS Richard (M Sayre Noble)
☎ (334) 264-8661 . . 2244 Rosemont Dv, Montgomery, AL *36111*

Goehring MR & MRS J Brown (Ouida L Reaves) | ☎ (540) 463-4898
ECar'58.David'56.NCar'62 . . . . | 700 Sunset Dv,
MISS Patricia R—NCar'91 . . . . | PO Box 1410,
MR Alexander B—at Bethany . . . . | Lexington, VA
| *24450*

Goehring MR & MRS Westlake L (Karen M Brower) | ☎ (970) 353-1275
Ober'60 . . . . | 4070 W 11 St,
MISS Elizabeth L . . . . | Apt 14, Greeley, CO
| *80634*

Goelet MR Francis—K.Rcn.B.Ln.Sm.Mto.Snc.Hl.H'47
☎ (203) 637-2568 . . 52 Dawn Harbor Lane, Riverside, CT *06878*

Goelet MR & MRS Robert G (Tufo—Alexandra G Creel)
Bnd'74.Y'76.Rc.B.Ln.Dyc.Srb.Mds.Mt.Cly.Hl.Ncd.H'45
☎ (212) MU8-3865 . . 7 Sutton Place, New York, NY *10022*

Goessling MR & MRS John G (Lowrey—Margaret F Ziegler) P'50
☎ (314) 961-0940 . . 41 Deerfield Rd, St Louis, MO *63124*

Goessling MR & MRS John G JR (Alisa A Bowen) Va'83.Vt'83
☎ (314) 991-1401 . . "Dogwood Hollow" 12 McKnight Lane, St Louis,
MO *63124*

Goetchius REV DR & MRS Eugene V N (Ann O | ☎ (508) 362-3041
Kirkpatrick) Va'41 . . . . | "Prince Gorham
MSRS Charles L T & N Kirkpatrick . . . . | House" 4260 Main
MSRS Edward Van N & John M . . . . | St, PO Box 262,
| Cummaquid, MA
| *02637-0262*

Goetz MR Alexander F H—CalTech'67
☎ (303) 449-5654 . . 4861 Curie Court, Boulder, CO *80301*

Goff MR & MRS Frederick Harris (Anne L Williams)
Ws'46.Ofp.Myf.Sar.Dar.Cwr'50
☎ (216) 932-0182 . . 2724 Coventry Rd, Shaker Heights, OH *44120*

Goff MRS James M (del Val—Jennifer J Anderson) Chi.
☎ (910) 295-3214 . . Box 1781, Pinehurst, NC *28374*

Goff MASTER Samuel Wrangham (g—MRS Josefa M Wrangham) . . . . . Born
at San Francisco, CA May 24'95

Goff MR William H—Myf.Sar.Ofp.Denis'77
☎ (216) 451-5623 . . 10024 Lake Shore Blvd, Bratenahl, OH *44108*

Goffinet MR François M P J—K.
☎ (804) 979-9495 . . PO Box 4381, Charlottesville, VA *22905*

Goggin MRS Lilla D (Mason—Leonard—Lilla D Goggin) Tex'72.Ncd.
☎ (915) 533-1073 . . 1223 Rim Rd, El Paso, TX *79902*

Gogolak MR & MRS Charles P (Marion Madeira) | ☎ (617) 326-0794
Pa'72.D.P'66.GeoW'69 . . . . | 35 Jackson Pond Rd,
MR Charles A—P'95 . . . . | Dedham, MA *02026*
JUNIORS MR Stephen S . . . . |

Goheen MR & MRS Edward B (Virginia N VanderBuecken) Dick'37.Dick'38
☎ (215) 233-1463 . . 8307 Flourtown Av, Wyndmoor, PA *19038*

Going MR & MRS Michael P (Joanna E Johnson) NH'83.Pc.Va'84.WakeF'87
☎ (215) 248-1748 . . 316 Wellesley Rd, Philadelphia, PA *19119*

Goings MR & MRS Harold H (Jane Powell) | ☎ (205) 879-7479
RMWmn'70.Cy.Ala'68.Cumb'71 . . . . | 2812 Surrey Rd,
MISS Elizabeth P . . . . | Birmingham, AL
JUNIORS MR Harold H JR . . . . | *35223*

Goiran MR Philip de la H—Br'64.Pa'73
☎ (203) 966-4699 . . 134 Main St, New Canaan, CT *06840*

Goiran MR Roger—Paris'30 . . . . | ☎ (813) 734-8269
MISS (DR) Anne F—FtWr'74.Col'79.Col'83—at | 634 Edgewater Dv,
8147 W Virginia Av, Lakewood, CO *80226* . . . | Dunedin, FL
MISS Jo Lucie—Nu'75—at 9 Monroe Lane, | *34697-1044*
Topsham, ME *04086* . . . . |

Gold MR & MRS William B (Marjorie F Tonner)
Pc.R.Pe.Fi.An.Plg.Cw.Wt.Rv.StA.Ht.Ne.Vca.Ll.
Coa.Cspa.Sar.Fw.Snc.Ac.Sdg.Dll.Pn.P'35.H'38
☎ (609) 753-2358 . . .Harvest Village D102, 114 Hayes Mill Rd, Atco,
NJ *08004*

Goldberg MR & MRS Tom J (Katherine M Briggs)
Mich'78.Mich'74.Wayne'77
☎ (810) 646-8387 . . 340 Barden Rd, Bloomfield Hills, MI *48013*

Golden MR & MRS Kenneth Hughes (Fuller—Frances Hoodenpyle)
SanDiegoSt'64.Sdy.SanDiegoSt'47.Cal'60
☎ (619) 224-2228 . . 3011 Rogers St, San Diego, CA *92106*

Golden MR William T—C.Cos.An.Pa'30 . . . . | of ☎ (212)737-3227
MISS Sibyl R—H'75 . . . . | 730 Park Av,
MISS (DR) Pamela P—H'80.NCar'85—at | New York, NY
Tucson, AZ . . . . | *10021*
| ☎ (914) 657-8983
| ''Rock Ledge''
| Olivebridge, NY
| *12461*

Golding MR & MRS Colin F M (Laura B Wheeler)
☎ (610) 296-5545 . . RD 3, Box 126, Swedesford Rd, Malvern,
PA *19355*

Golding MASTER Harrison Stell (g—Michael E Pulitzer) . . . . Born at
San Francisco, CA Mch 1'96

Goldman DR & MRS Allen S (Kise—Rachel Bok)
Pa'77.Rcp.Csp.Br'51.Br'53.SUNY'58 ⚓
☎ (312) 751-1411 . . 1411 N State P'kway, Chicago, IL *60610*

Goldsborough MR & MRS Leslie E JR (Dorothy B Snodgrass)
Cw.Rv.Cc.Mv.Ncd.
☎ (410) 377-7945 . . 6009 Overlook Place, Baltimore, MD *21210*

Goldsborough MR & MRS Nicholas (Spring— | ☎ (410) 626-7103
Kathleen C Martin) DU'59.Ayc.Va'59.GeoW'64 | 825 Holly Dv E,
⚓ . . . . | Annapolis, MD
MR Nicholas JR—at ☎ (704) 566-8626 | *21401*
1644 Chippendale Rd, Charlotte, NC *28205* . . . . |

Goldsborough MR Nicholas Tilghman—Hn.Hob'67
☎ (213) 463-9692 . . 514 N Cahuenga Blvd, Los Angeles, CA *90004*

Goldsmith MR & MRS John M JR (Ann S Mulgrew) | ☎ (540) 342-3576
Vmi'62.Cl'70 . . . . | 3314 Somerset St
MISS Sarah L—David'94—at U of Miss Grad . . | SW, Roanoke, VA
MR John M 3d . . . . | *24014*
JUNIORS MISS Frances A—at Asheville Sch . . . . . |

Goldsmith MR & MRS Robert H (Kathryn R Boyl) | ☎ (415) 924-0282
Mls'66.Bhm.Pcu.Sfy.Cp.Cal'66 . . . . | 40 Blue Ridge Rd,
MISS Leigh J—at 247 Newbury St, Boston, MA | Kentfield, CA *94904*
02116 . . . . |

Goldthwait MRS Joel A (Henrietta Atwater) Nh.Chi.
☎ (508) 359-6271 . . ''Longacre Farm'' Medfield, MA *02052*

Goldwater MISS Carolyn (Sexson—Thompson—Erskine—
Carolyn Goldwater) Cal'34
4705 E Porter Dv, Phoenix, AZ *85018*

Goltra MR & MRS O Renard (Smith—Alice B | ☎ (847) 234-0043
Cotsworth) Rc.On. . . . . | 195 E Onwentsia
JUNIORS MISS Carolyn S—at Deerfield. . . . . | Rd, Lake Forest, IL
JUNIORS MR Andrew R—at Deerfield . . . . | *60045*

Goltra MR & MRS Peter S (Gail A Wright) | of ☎ (540)687-6976
Br'64.Un.Ny.StJ.Cly.Cs.P.IIT'69 . . . . | ''Newmary''
MR Edward S—Cl'90—at N'western Kellogg | Goltra Lane,
Grad . . . . | Middleburg, VA
MR Alexis O—H'92.Camb'94.Va'95—at | *20117*
U of Va Law . . . . | ☎ (212) RE7-8182
| 25 East End Av,
| New York, NY
| *10028*

Gomila MR & MRS Moylan F JR (C Gwathmey H Finlay) Va'95.Va'91
☎ (504) 891-9088 . . 1311 Octavia St, New Orleans, LA *70115*

Gonzalez MR & MRS Alfred G (Elizabeth Wilson) MooreArt'74.Rc.Duke'57
☎ (610) 942-4504 . . Glenmoore Farms, PO Box 397, Glenmoore,
PA *19343*

González MR Eugene R—B.Ri.Rc.Ct.Pcu.Mt.Y'51
☎ (212) 744-5685 . . 165 E 66 St, Apt 6B, New York, NY *10021*

Gonzalez MR & MRS Peter W (Diana M Preston) | ☎ (212) 369-0907
Ny.Cly.NCar'66 . . . . | 1021 Park Av,
MR Peter W JR—at Georgetown . . . . | New York, NY
JUNIORS MISS Brooke E—at Deerfield . . . . | *10028*

Gonzalez MR & MRS Richard I (Mary C Miller) Bur . . .of
☎ (415) 851-1436 . . 389 Manuela Rd, Woodside, CA *94062*
☎ (011-34-7) 276-9329 . . ''Mas Rajoleriá'' Foixá, 17132 Gerona, Spain

Good MR & MRS William F (Linette De Roeck) Pc.Sg.Ac.
☎ (215) CH8-3475 . . 9253 Germantown Av, Philadelphia, PA *19118*

Goodale MRS Benjamin A (Dewey—Patricia Byford) Evg.
☎ (561) 655-5853 . . 330 Cocoanut Row, Palm Beach, FL *33480*

Goodale MRS Emery (Irene Emery) . . . . | ☎ (404) 261-6908
MISS Kate D—at ☎ (617) 354-8629 | 490 Broadland Rd
34 Bowdoin St, Cambridge, MA *02138* . . . . | NW, Atlanta, GA
| *30342*

Goodale DR & MRS Fairfield JR (Mary M Lyman) H'45.Wr'50
☎ (207) 359-2503 . . Black Hawk 100, Rte 175, Box 2090,
North Brooklin, ME *04661*

Goodale MR & MRS Fairfield 3d (E Lindsay Hitch) VaCmth'73
RR 1, Box 177, Penobscot, ME *04476*

Goodale MR & MRS John B (Martha H Lowe) Va'77.Bost'75
☎ (508) 448-2277 . . 30 Drumlin Hill Rd, Groton, MA *01450*

Goodale JUNIORS MR M Wing . . see A T Oppersdorff

Goodale MR & MRS Nathaniel B E (Elizabeth S Leonard) Hav'76
☎ (207) 548-0147 . . 93 E Main St, Searsport, ME *04974*

Goodall MR & MRS Herbert W 3d (Susan E | ☎ (904) 285-4553
Gallagher) Nyc.Bost'71 ⚓ . . . . | 109 Teal Nest Court,
MISS Eliza H S—at U of South . . . . | Ponte Vedra Beach,
MR Robert D 2d . . . . | FL *32082-1944*

Goodall MISS Mary E
☎ (410) 472-4544 . . ''Outfoxed Farm'' 1930 Western Run Rd, Butler,
MD *21023*

Goodall MR & MRS (DR) McChesney 3d (Anne H Horst) Va'86.Va'96
920 Rosser Lane, Charlottesville, VA *22903-1623*

Goodan MRS William (Mary E Phleger) Vh.
☎ (213) 681-8020 . . 895 Hillcrest Place, Pasadena, CA *91106*

Goodby MR & MRS Richard L (Elizabeth P Snyder) Cda.GroveCity'65.Pa'67 . . . . | ☎ (610) 296-0626 1040 Beaumont Rd, Berwyn, PA *19312*
MISS Virginia L . . . . |
MISS Rebecca W . . . . |
JUNIORS MR John L . . . . |

Goodenough MR & MRS Oliver R (Alison H Clarkson) H'77.Mto.H.'75.Pa'78 . . of
☎ (802) 457-4627 . . 18 Golf Av, Woodstock, VT *05091-1307*
☎ (518) 251-4073 . . "Hill House" Windover, North Creek, NY *12853*

Gooder MR & MRS Grenville MacD JR (Linda G Clark) Br'61 . . . . | ☎ (609) 921-7095 385 Cherry Valley Rd, Princeton, NJ *08540*
MR Grenville MacD 3d—Br'94—at 311 E 73 St, Apt 4B, New York, NY *10021* |
JUNIORS MR Grant C—at Brown . . . . |

Goodfellow MRS Emily C (Yeoman—Emily C Goodfellow) P'76
☎ (609) 860-6642 . . 6 Westminster Place, Cranbury, NJ *08512*

Goodfellow MR & MRS Thorp Van D (Joan Caner) Gm.Me.Rb.P.'41
☎ (610) 649-8555 . . 243 Glenmoor Rd, Gladwyne, PA *19035*

Goodhew MR & MRS Dixon A (Frances D Scott) Samford'70.Samford'77 . . . . | ☎ (205) 871-2478 316 Mountain Av, Birmingham, AL *35213*
MR Dixon S . . . . |
JUNIORS MR Franklin W . . . . |

Goodhue MRS Albert (Pulitzer—S Helen Dempwolf) BMr'50.Ey.BtP.Chi.Cda.Ncd.
☎ (561) 655-4130 . . 333 Pendleton Lane, Palm Beach, FL *33480*

Goodhue MR & MRS Albert 3d (Sherrie L Hovey) Bost'81.Myc.Ey.Myf. ⚓
☎ (508) 745-1205 . . 6 S Pine St, Salem, MA *01970*

Goodhue MR Edmund M—H'68.H'70.Cal'80 3326 N Green Rd, Oak Harbor, WA *98277*

Goodhue MRS Francis A JR (Mary E Brier) V'42.Mich'44.Bgt.Cly.
☎ (914) 666-8291 . . Box 450, Mt Kisco, NY *10549*

Goodhue MR & MRS H Shippen (Lydia R Davis) V'39.Cw.H'38
☎ (617) 235-5370 . . 90 Dover Rd, Wellesley, MA *02181*

Goodhue MR & MRS Henry S JR (Lucy C Chase) Bost'82.H'73 . . . . | ☎ (617) 749-8336 8 Chestnut Place, Hingham, MA *02043*
MISS Eliza W . . . . |
JUNIORS MISS Abigail C . . . . |

Goodhue MRS Hugh G B (Fanny Bright) . . . . | ☎ (818) 799-4918 310 Arlington Dv, Pasadena, CA *91105*
MR Nicholas B—Wms'64—at ☎ (310) 453-4321 1025—17 St, Santa Monica, CA *90403* . . . . . . |

Gooding MR & MRS Frederic JR (Mary T Latta) Pa'64.H'54
☎ (803) 664-1139 . . 305 Timrod Park Dv, Florence, SC *29501*

Gooding MR & MRS Judson (Françoise T Ridoux) C.Rv.Yn.Y'48 . . of
☎ (011-33-1) 45-53-36-32 . . 16 rue Spontini, 75116 Paris, France
☎ (603) 756-4162 . . N Main St, Box 745, Walpole, NH *03608*

Goodlett MRS George L (Patricia O O'Neill) . . . . . . | ☎ (415) 928-7708 1101 Green St, San Francisco, CA *94109*
MRS Virginia O'N (Covino—Swain—Virginia O'N Goodlett) . . . . |

Goodman MR David P—Bur.Y'58 . . . . | ☎ (208) 726-5023 Box 3144, Ketchum, ID *83340*
MR Nicholas D—HawaiiLoa'91 . . . . |

Goodman MR & MRS Edward T (Carolyn V Cutler) Eyc.Ph.Err.Gm.Sa.Me.Rb.Cts.Ty'62 . . . . | ☎ (610) 687-1424 840 Lesley Rd, Villanova, PA *19085*
MISS Samantha W . . . . |
MISS Beverly P . . . . |
MISS Allison C . . . . |

Goodman MR & MRS James C (Lilah T Toland) Sth'73.SFrArt'72.LoneMt'75
☎ (415) 868-0304 . . PO Box 725, 10 Av Olema, Stinson Beach, CA *94970*

Goodman MISS Mary B—Stan'87.Geo'91
☎ (202) 546-5346 . . 152—11 St SE, Washington, DC *20003*

Goodman MR & MRS Maurice JR (Georgine L Rake) Wis'46.Ri.Cly.Y.'43 . . . . | of ☎ (212)288-1329 177 E 80 St, New York, NY *10021*
MR John R—Hob'79—at ☎ (509) 493-1896 Box 734, Bingen, WA *98605* . . . . |
☎ (860) 435-2014 "Dragonfly" 526 Undermountain Rd, Salisbury, CT *06068*

Goodman MRS Stanley J (Lapin—Levy—Alice Rudolph) Nd.Hn.
☎ (314) 432-2144 . . 21 Spoede Lane, St Louis, MO *63141*

Goodman MR & MRS William E 4th (Manette L Carpenter) Wheat'57.Y'55
☎ (561) 231-5617 . . 371 Sabal Palm Lane, John's Island, Vero Beach, FL *32963*

Goodman MR & MRS William E 5th (Bridgette S Gibson) SanDiegoSt'89.Col'85
☎ (310) 798-3641 . . 532—1 St, Manhattan Beach, CA *90266-6533*

Goodman MR & MRS William F JR (Edwina A McDuffie) Beth'51.Mlsps'49
☎ (601) 366-2724 . . 4166 Dogwood Dv, Jackson, MS *39211*

Goodrich MISS Catherine D—Duke'96 . . see J W Mettler III

Goodrich MR Dennett W . . see J C Jay

Goodrich MR & MRS John Alden (H R Valaer van Roijen) K.Rc.Cly.Pa'61 . . . . | of ☎ (212)734-5962 155 E 72 St, New York, NY *10021*
JUNIORS MISS Lauren V . . . . |
☎ (203) 972-1618 720 West Rd, PO Box 1714, New Canaan, CT *06840*

Goodrich MRS John W (Rapalyea—Florence B Ruthrauff) Cy.Ec.
☎ (617) 329-6455 . . 10 Longwood Dv, Apt 170, Westwood, MA *02090*

Goodrich MR Ramsey W . . see J C Jay

Goodrich MRS Wendy (Wendy Coulter) . . . . | ☎ (617) 327-4669 146 Beverly Rd, Chestnut Hill, MA *02167*
JUNIORS MISS Melissa H—at Noble & Greenough |

Goodsell MR Percy Hamilton JR—Plg.Snc.Myf.Cw.Rv. Ht.Ll.Cc.Ds.Wt.Lm.Y'34
☎ (203) 272-8326 . . "Pandemonium" Tress Rd, Box 192, Cheshire, CT *06410-0192*

Goodspeed MR & MRS Norwick B H (Mary F Detmer) Miami'77.Y'72.Stan'77
☎ (714) 640-2151 . . 2006 Kewamee Dv, Corona Del Mar, CA *92625*

Goodwin MRS B Benjamin (Beverley C Benjamin) . | ☎ (212) 472-0303
MISS Alexandra C—Mich'88—at | 315 E 72 St,
☎ (213) 655-5424 . . 6436 Lindenhurst Av, | New York, NY
Los Angeles, CA 90048 . . . . | 10021
MISS Leslie T—CtCol'90—at ☎ (212) 758-4979
200 E 66 St, New York, NY 10021 . . . .
Goodwin MR & MRS Charles (Lord—Charlotte M Ober)
Elk.Chi.Mv.Br'47.H'59
☎ (410) 467-9075 . . 4204 Underwood Rd, Baltimore, MD 21218
Goodwin DR & MRS Charles B (Anne Cuningham)
Paris'79.Paris'81.Paris'82.Nu'83.Rc.Mb.H'72.Cin'76 . . of
☎ (212) 472-6135 . . 129 E 69 St, Apt 8A, New York, NY 10021
☎ (516) 624-9174 . . 367 Split Rock Rd, Syosset, NY 11791
Goodwin MR & MRS E Howard (Alice Cocke) Ln.Va'42
☎ (804) 979-2858 . . 2033 Hessian Rd, Charlottesville, VA 22903
Goodwin MRS Elliot H (M Hope Talcott) Pr.
☎ (516) 674-9328 . . 19 Matinecock Farms Rd, Glen Cove,
NY 11542-3343
Goodwin MR H Sage—Y'27
☎ (860) 677-0157 . . 24 Ciderbrook Rd, Avon, CT 06001
Goodwin MR & MRS J Baeton (Elizabeth L Fentress) | ☎ (203) 625-2627
Hlns'69.T.W&L'69 . . . . | 29 Fairway Lane,
MISS Carson H . . . . | Greenwich, CT
JUNIORS MR Eliot W . . . . | 06830
Goodwin MISS Jane-Fenwick—Ncd . . .of
☎ (404) 355-4212 . . 2492 Alton Rd NW, Atlanta, GA 30305
☎ (305) 294-6082 . . 522 Margaret St, Key West, FL 33040
Goodwin MRS Macdonald (Hope Erwin) V'47.Ncd.. | ☎ (941) 638-1696
MR Macdonald E . . . . | PO Box 133,
MR Bruce N . . . . | Babson Park, FL
MR Norton—Hn.H'38 . . . . | 33827
Goodwin MRS Marguerite H (Marguerite S | ☎ (508) 777-5099
Hopkins) Skd'74 . . . . | 67 Burley St,
MISS Lori A . . . . | Danvers, MA 01923
MR W Hooper 3d . . . .
Goodwin DR & MRS Melvin H 3d (Sandra E Taylor) U'74.Ariz'68
☎ (803) 577-5697 . . 38 Wentworth St, Charleston, SC 29401
Goodwin MR & MRS Richard H (Esther Bemis) V'33.Cyb.Ncd.H'33
☎ (860) 873-8514 . . PO Box 2040, Salem, CT 06420
Goodwin MR & MRS W H Baldwin (Boyce—Katherine Kauffman)
☎ (410) 377-6144 . . 3 Knoll Ridge Court, Baltimore, MD 21210
Goodwyn MR Scott M . . see M Wallop
Goodwyn MR & MRS William B JR (Jean Fleming) Aub'53
☎ (334) 265-3763 . . 3119 Pinehurst Dv, Montgomery, AL 36111
Goodyear MR & MRS (DR) Austin (Sara Suleri)
Kinn'74.Punjab'76.Ind'83.Y'92 ⚓
☎ (207) 359-8949 . . HCR 64, Box 474, Reach Rd, Brooklin, ME 04616
Goodyear MR & MRS David L (Sally L Chapman) | ☎ (504) 892-1767
Ncmb'63.Y'58 . . . . | 624 S Massachusetts
MISS Ella C—Tul'89.Tul'94 . . . . | St, Covington, LA
623 Nashville Av, New Orleans, LA 70115 . . . . | 70433
MISS Julianna R—Van'93—at
3510 Woodmont Blvd, Nashville, TN 37215 . . .
Goodyear MR & MRS Frank H (Chew—Margaret Kerr) Rb.Gm.Ac.Y'41
☎ (610) 526-2655 . . 77 Middle Rd, Apt 365, Bryn Mawr, PA 19010

Goodyear MR & MRS Frank H JR (Elizabeth W | ☎ (307) 527-5239
Balis) K.Sg.Ssk.Y'66 . . . . | 1323 Sunset Blvd N,
MISS Grace W—at ☎ (703) 671-8995 | Box 2048, Cody,
4666 S 34 St, Apt 2B, Arlington, VA 22206 . . . | WY 82414
MR Frank H 3d—at ☎ (512) 482-0581
809B E 30 St, Austin, TX 78705 . . . .
Goodyear MR & MRS George F (Gurney—Marion Spaulding)
St.Ts.Y'27.H'31
☎ (716) 886-5891 . . 925 Delaware Av, Apt 5C, Buffalo,
NY 14209-1843
Goodyear MR & MRS Richard (Constance Martin) | ☎ (415) 362-1155
Y'64 . . . . | 940 Green St,
MR Charles . . . . | San Francisco, CA
MR James . . . . | 94133
JUNIORS MR Sam . . . .
Goozée MR & MRS Stevan K (Christine P Brown) Stet'82.Stet'81
☎ (205) 823-3959 . . 2460 Regent Lane, Birmingham, AL 35226
Gordan MR C McIntosh—Va'38
☎ (410) 242-4815 . . 719 Maiden Choice Lane, Apt BR622, Baltimore,
MD 21228
Gordan MR & MRS John D 3d (Catherine H | ☎ (212) 369-2607
Morot-Sir) Rdc'68.C.Cs.H'66 . . . . | 1133 Park Av,
MISS Elizabeth LeS—at Harvard . . . . | New York, NY
JUNIORS MR John D . . . . | 10128
Gordan MRS Judith P (Randol—Judith Paterson) | ☎ (410) 235-4731
Mv. . . . . | 230 Stony Run
MISS Eliza P Randol . . . . | Lane, Apt 3B,
MISS Lucinda L Randol . . . . | Baltimore, MD
| 21210
Gordon MR Albert H—Rc.Ri.Ln.Pr.Fic.Fiy.Sm.H'23
☎ (212) BU8-2251 . . 10 Gracie Square, New York, NY 10028
Gordon MR Albert H 2d . . see J T Austin
Gordon MRS Bailey (Edith S Sharpe) . . . . Died in Jun 1995
Gordon DR & MRS Bertram M (Brentlinger— | ☎ (510) 549-1144
Suzanne Perkins) Ch'57.Sth'66.Cal'80. | 1612 Walnut St,
Bklyn'63.Rut'64.Rut'69 . . . . | Berkeley, CA 94709
MR Christopher Brentlinger—Cal'82—at
1532 Ramita Court, San Jose, CA 95128 . . . .
MR Peter Perkins Brentlinger—RISD'84 . . . .
Gordon MR Crawford—Sm.Ri.H'39
☎ (307) 738-2345 . . ''Gordon Ranch'' 1742 Mayoworth Rd, Kaycee,
WY 82639
Gordon MRS David C (Nanetta Head) . . . . Died Apr 11'96
Gordon MR & MRS David C JR (Margaret Russell) Mid'67
see Dilatory Domiciles
Gordon MISS Frances
☎ (914) 831-8877 . . Fishkill Health Center, Dogwood Lane, Beacon,
NY 12508
Gordon MR & MRS George A (Elsa P Bartlett) | ☎ (912) 238-1213
Yn.Y'34.Ox'36 . . . . | 34 E 48 St,
MR Arthur McG—at 19 Wallace St, Durham, NC | Savannah, GA
27707 . . . . | 31405
Gordon MR & MRS John R (Alice L Brady) Ty'64 . . | ☎ (914) 738-0720
MISS Amanda R—at Middlebury . . . . | 1323 Roosevelt Av,
JUNIORS MR Nicholas R . . . . | Pelham Manor, NY
| 10803

Gordon MR & MRS Joseph K (Ray McLean)   ☎ (610) 642-5675
Ws'53.Rc.Me.Ph.Cts.Gm.Ac.P'48.Pa'51 ...... 441 Glyn Wynne
MISS Sarah W—Hawaii'86 .... Rd, Haverford, PA
     19041

Gordon MISS Katharine G . . see P J Davidson

Gordon MR & MRS Kilbourn JR (Mary E S Butler) Fw.Leh'42
☎ (803) 522-0344 . . 98 James F Byrnes Rd, Beaufort, SC *29902*

Gordon MR & MRS Lewis H (Enyart—Kate P Dickerman)
☎ (203) 483-8436 . . Evergreen Woods 157, 88 Notch Hill Rd,
North Branford, CT *06471*

Gordon MR & MRS Lewis H JR (Nadel—Elizabeth E Dunham) H'54
☎ (011-44-1403) 265016 . . Warnham Place, Warnham, Horsham,
West Sussex RH12 3QQ, England

Gordon MR & MRS Maitland A (Lacey—Betty J   ☎ (610) 399-1595
Nafzger) F&M'61.OState'61 .... Box 159,
   MR Brent P Lacey .... Chadds Ford, PA
     19317

Gordon MR Nicholas T JR—Pars'67
☎ (609) 263-5510 . . 31 Tecumseh Av, Strathmere, NJ *08248*

Gordon MRS Patricia P (Patricia B Powell)
☎ (212) RE4-5519 . . 530 E 86 St, New York, NY *10028*

Gordon MRS Peter A (N Bayard Howard)   ☎ (212) 289-3284
Lx.Ri.Cly................................ 49 E 86 St, Apt 2C,
   MR J Kingman—Rc.Mid'93 .... New York, NY
     10028

Gordon MR Peter A—Ri.GeoWms'61
655 Park Av, New York, NY *10021*

Gordon MR Raymond C—Nh.Ill'40.H.'46
☎ (508) 655-6623 . . 165 Forest St, Sherborn, MA *01770*

Gordon MR & MRS Richard H IV (Frances R di Lustro) Va'86.Va'86
60 Gramercy Park N, Apt 3J, New York, NY *10010*

Gordon DR & MRS Spencer JR (Fouquet—   ☎ (301) 652-4739
Mary-Truxtun Hill) Cvc.Cc.P'52.H'56 .... 5600 Wisconsin Av,
   MR Spencer 3d—Bost'84—in Massachusetts ... Apt 608,
   MR Thomas T—Hampshire'89—at SUNY Chevy Chase, MD
Stony Brook *20815-4410*

Gordon MISS Valerie A . . see J T Austin

Gordon MRS W Richard (Mary A Wagner) MtH'48. | ☎ (610) 644-3314
   MR Douglas A—Pa'81.Pa'94 .... 109 Arlington Rd,
     Paoli, PA *19301*

Gordon MR William A—Rr.Hn.H'24
☎ (412) 741-4033 . . Box 375, Sewickley, PA *15143*

Gordon MR William D (Herrick—Gibbons—Denny—Lee Coney) Pg.Fcg.
☎ (412) 621-1322 . . 5351 Northumberland St, Pittsburgh, PA *15217*

Gordon MRS William H (Amelia Cheek) SL'35.Mv.Ncd.
☎ (410) 823-4782 . . 1217 Berwick Rd, Ruxton, MD *21204*

Gordon MR & MRS William S (Helen G Tilghman) | ☎ (804) 295-4727
Ncd.Rut'70........................... "Quiet Entry"
   MISS Mary D T .... Keene, VA *22946*
   JUNIORS MR William S JR ....

Gore THE VICE PRESIDENT & MRS Albert A JR (Mary | ☎ (202) 456-7022
E Aitcheson) H'69 .... Vice President's
   MISS Karenna .... House, Washington,
   MISS Kristin .... DC *20501*
   MISS Sarah ....
   JUNIORS MR Albert A 3d ....

Gore MAJ & MRS Humphry G N (Leslie M Peabody) | ☎ (011-44-1732)
BA................................. 453265
   MR Mark S—at ☎ (203) 366-3877 "Red Cottage"
Park Royal Apts, 2600 Park Av, Bridgeport, CT South Park,
06604............................ Sevenoaks, Kent
     TN13 1EL, England

Gore MR Philip Larner—Cvc.Mt.P'31.GeoW'34 ... | ☎ (202) 333-3341
   MR Michael—Mt.Cvc.Ct.P'63.Grenoble'64—at 1506 Dumbarton
☎ (540) 869-5270 . . Belle Grove Plantation, Rock Court NW,
Middletown, VA *22645* .... Washington, DC
     20007

Gores MR & MRS Guido J (Mary I Callaway) V'42.Ncd.P'38.H'41
☎ (513) 321-8304 . . 2 Grandin Riverview St, Cincinnati, OH *45208*

Gores DR & MRS Guido J JR (Adriana H Schwartz)
Cal'83.Pom'79.Wright'86
☎ (415) 668-8004 . . 295—31 Av, San Francisco, CA *94121*

Gores MRS Landis (Pamela Whitmarsh)
☎ (203) 966-9627 . . Cross Ridge Rd, New Canaan, CT *06840*

Gorham DR & MRS George W (Ann F Willens) | ☎ (212) 371-5270
Cly.Y'50.JHop'54 .... 200 E 66 St,
   MISS Sarah C—Y'91.Nu'95 .... New York, NY
   MR John W—Y'95—at 43 Wiggins St, Princeton, *10021*
NJ *08408* ....

Gorham MRS Nathaniel (Mary L Budik) .... | ☎ (716) 662-4053
   MISS (DR) Grace—NYMed'74—at 526 W 111 St, S4303 Freeman Rd,
New York, NY *10025* .... Orchard Park, NY
     MISS Anita DiNitto—Sim'94 .... *14127*
     MR Tory DiNitto—Syr'95 ....

Gorham MR & MRS Nathaniel 8th (Janalin M Shuler) Cr'70
☎ (415) 856-0500 . . 15829 Stonebrook Rd, Los Altos Hills, CA *94022*

Goriansky MR Alexander Yale—Nf.
☎ (617) 227-8127 . . 77 Mt Vernon St, Boston, MA *02108*

Goriansky MR Michael E—Ken'56
☎ (508) 686-2218 . . 95 Millpond, Pleasant St, North Andover,
MA *01845*

Gorka MR & MRS Sebestyén (Katharine F Cornell)
see Dilatory Domiciles

Gorman MISS Frances P—Pa'70
☎ (415) 441-8620 . . 2655 Franklin St, Apt 4, San Francisco, CA *94123*

Gorman MR & MRS K Aubrey (Bingham—Alice B | ☎ (207) 236-1031
Condon) Pn.P'46 .... "Two Ponds"
   MR Charles T Bingham 3d—OWes'66—at 4470 Howe Hill Rd,
☎ (901) 766-4600 . . 889 Ridge Lake Blvd, Camden, ME *04843*
Memphis, TN *38119* ....

Gorman MR & MRS Kernan F (Mardie Madden) | ☎ (011-44-171)
Unn.Mds.Cl'50.H'54 584-6935
   MISS Annabel C .... 31 Trevor Square,
     London SW7,
     England

Gorman MISS Kristen S . . see MISS J Sargent

Gorman MRS Paul A (Richards—Althea D Robinson) Bg.Rr . . .of
☎ (561) 278-3782 . . 4333 N Ocean Blvd, Apt BN1, Delray Beach,
FL *33483*
☎ (412) 741-4521 . . Merriman Rd, Box 33, Sewickley, PA *15143*

Gorman MRS Rita R (Rita K Reiss) Cly.Ne. . . . . . . ☎ (212) 744-1748
MISS Ruth A—at ☎ (908) 531-2454
514½ Page Av, Allenhurst, NJ *07711* . . . . | 3 E 84 St,
New York, NY
10028

Gorman MR Robert E—Vca.
☎ (212) 753-0927 . . 21 W 58 St, Apt 4C, New York, NY *10019*

Gorog MR & MRS William Christopher (Ellen MacMillan)
SanDiegoSt'78.SanDiegoSt'77
1416 Havenhurst Dv, Apt 2C, Los Angeles, CA *90046-3885*

Gorog MR & MRS William F (Gretchen E Meister) Mor.Dar.USA'49 . . of
☎ (703) 821-1135 . . 1307 Daviswood Dv, McLean, VA *22102*
☎ (970) 925-9232 . . PO Box 1273, Aspen, CO *81612*
☎ (941) 566-6046 . . Marquesa Apts, 8990 Bay Colony Dv, Naples,
FL *34108*

Gosling MR Bernard T JR . . . . | ☎ (441) 295-6232
MISS Joanne B Williams—at Kenilworth Apts, | ''Old Homestead''
2979 W School House Lane, Germantown, PA | Pembroke HM 05,
19144 . . . . | Bermuda

Goss MR & MRS Edward C (Jane T Hotchkiss) Clark'51
☎ (561) 231-5946 . . 905 Reef Lane, Vero Beach, FL *32963*

Goss MR & MRS Richard W 2d (Michele W | ☎ (415) 567-1719
du Pont) Pcu.Bur.Sfg.Fic.StJ.Fr.Yn.Y'55 . . . . . . | 2545 Divisadero St,
MISS Holland H—Geo'91 | San Francisco, CA
MR Jared du P—at 28 E 73 St, New York, NY | *94115*
10021 . . . . |

Gottschalk MR Adam W H . . see A Cushman JR

Gottschalk DR & MRS (DR) P Christopher H (Katherine A Schneider)
Sth'86.Cl'92.ClP&S'95.JHop'84.ClP&S'90
☎ (203) 315-5024 . . 593 Towner Swamp Rd, Guilford, CT *06437*

Gottsegen, Daniel A & Jackson, Margaret—Ober'82.Br'80 . . of
☎ (415) 388-0857 . . 703 Cabin Dv, Mill Valley, CA *94941*
☎ (508) 893-2273 . . Nonquitt, South Dartmouth, MA *02748*

Gotwald MR & MRS Stephen McC (M Mercedes Rudkin) BtP.Leh'77 . . of
☎ (607) 547-5654 . . PO Box 447, Cooperstown, NY *13326*
''The Farmhouse'' Fly Creek, NY *13337*
☎ (561) 798-6613 . . 2449 Vista Del Prado Dv, West Palm Beach,
FL *33414*

Gouge MRS F Hamilton (Cyrena K Sneath) Gm.
☎ (561) 231-6927 . . 8745 Lakeside Blvd, Apt 101, Vero Beach,
FL *32963*

Gould MR Albert P. | ☎ (508) 448-6692
MRS Anna E Lenos (Anna E Gould) . . . . | 101 Longley Rd,
MISS Heidi Lenos . . . . | Groton, MA *01450*
MR Daniel E Lenos . . . . |
MRS Elizabeth L Reeves (Elizabeth L Gould) |
MISS Elizabeth L Reeves . . . . |

Gould MR & MRS Alexander Whitman (Anne Marie Melloy)
☎ (804) 974-7540 . . Locust Grove Farm, HCR 1, Box 54,
Charlottesville, VA *22901*

Gould MR & MRS Curtis E L (O'Brien—Jean H Kirkpatrick) Ll.
☎ (803) 838-7134 . . 724 N Reeve Rd, Dataw Island, SC *29920*

Gould MRS Edward Wanton (Cavedo—Earline Mann) Cy.Chi . . .of
☎ (508) 362-2434 . . 115 Rendezvous Lane, Box 636, Barnstable,
MA *02630*
☎ (804) 320-6140 . . 1211 Hathaway Tower, 2956 Hathaway Rd,
Richmond, VA *23225*

Gould CDR (RET) Franklin P—USN.Md.Cybl.JHop'30
☎ (202) 541-0400 . . 6200 Oregon Av NW, Washington, DC *20015*

Gould MR & MRS George D (Jane C Mack) | ☎ (212) 755-4578
Duke'60.Bcs.B.R.Ln.Cs.Y'51.H'55 . . . . | 1 Sutton Place S,
MR George W—Tufts'85.Cal'93—at | New York, NY
☎ (415) 567-8003 . . 19 Retiro Way, | *10022*
San Francisco, CA *94123* . . . . |
MR Monty E Bancroft—at ☎ (914) 764-1554 |
RR 5, Box 99, Pound Ridge, NY *10576* . . . . . |

Gould MR & MRS George M L (Rachael W Kilbourne) Conn'52.Y'52
☎ (864) 457-3073 . . 9 Jackson Grove, Landrum, SC *29356*

Gould MR Gordon R—Pitzer'93 . . see S S Shuman

Gould MR Howard B . . see S S Shuman

Gould MR Lyttleton B P JR—Cw.Yn.Y'43
☎ (860) 434-1407 . . 151 Brush Hill Rd, PO Box 99, Hadlyme,
CT *06439*

Gould MRS Martha T (Martha A Thorson)
☎ (441) 293-0248 . . ''Dolphin Terrace'' Harbour Rd, Warwick WK,
Bermuda

Gould MR & MRS Robert R (Sarah C Copeman) Camb'80.Unn.Ln.Y'81
☎ (908) 766-7931 . . 30 Peachcroft Dv, Bernardsville, NJ *07924*

Gould MR & MRS William S 3d (Jean G Rose) | ☎ (914) 357-2699
Ws'55.T.Y.'54.H'56 . . . . | 638 Haverstraw Rd,
MISS Carol H—*see Dilatory Domiciles* . . . . | Suffern, NY *10901*
MR Richard G—at 109 Beacon St, Somerville, |
MA *02143* . . . . |

Gourd MR & MRS Henri N (Erica S Lindberg) Ken'80.Ken'78 . . of
69 Tanglewylde Av, Bronxville, NY *10708*
☎ (860) 535-3778 . . ''Minnow'' 90 Water St, Stonington, CT *06378*

Gourd MRS Stanley (Josephine Stanley)
☎ (203) 431-0913 . . 27 Ritch Dv, Ridgefield, CT *06877*

Gourdin MISS Virginia B—Winth'41.Cl'42.SCar'51.Ncd.Ht.Dar.
☎ (803) 723-7341 . . 14 Tradd St, Charleston, SC *29401*

Gourlay MR & MRS Lawrence (Harris—M Elizabeth | ☎ (941) 927-1942
Parkinson) CarnM'63.Wms'49 . . . . | 1728 Kestral P'kway
MISS Diana H—at Washington, DC . . . . | S, Sarasota, FL
MISS Brooke J Harris—at New York, NY . . . | *34231*

Gove MR Alexander B—H'87 . . see A H Chapin

Gow MR & MRS Robert H (Barbara L Lord) Sth'48.Y'55
☎ (713) 467-4751 . . 11911 McLeod's Lane, Houston, TX *77024*

Gowen MR & MRS Francis I (Olive M Massie) Rb.P'51
☎ (610) LA5-0555 . . 307 Fishers Rd, Bryn Mawr, PA *19010*

Gowen DR & MRS George F (E Page Roberts) | ☎ (610) 323-1506
Ph.Ac.Pa'48.Jef'52 . . . . | River Bend Farm,
MISS Marguerite H—Tufts'89—at | RD 1, Pottstown, PA
137 Clifford Terr, San Francisco, CA *94117* . . . | *19465*

Gowen MR & MRS George F JR (Karen L Jordan) HWSth'86.Rc.
☎ (610) 388-0136 . . 391 Spring Mill Rd, Chadds Ford, PA *19317*

Gowen MR & MRS George W 2d (Marcia A Fennelly)
Ri.Mds.Rc.Rv.Mt.Plg.P.'52.Va'57
☎ (212) UN1-2539 . . 122 E 76 St, New York, NY *10021*

Gowen MR & MRS James E 2d (Eliza Mellon)
☎ (610) 408-9706 . . 427 Littlebrook Rd, Berwyn, PA *19312*

Gowenlock MRS Fisher (Zarada Fisher) Cas.
☎ (312) 337-3337 . . 680 N Lake Shore Dv, Apt 1204, Chicago,
IL *60611*

Gowing MRS Charles D (Pratt—Elizabeth Stuart) Ncd.
☎ (207) 354-6581 . . ''Seafields'' Box 155, HCR 68, Cushing, ME *04563*

Grace MISS Catherine Kelley (g—Charles M Grace) . . . Born Mch 12'95

Grace MR Charles B JR—Gm.Me.Rc.K.Ph.P'56.Pa'62
☎ (610) 827-9242 . . ''Bryn Coed Farm'' 1272 St Matthews Rd, Chester Springs, PA *19425*

Grace MR & MRS Charles M (Margaret M VanDerpool) Unn.Gr.StA.Cly.Dar.Km.Cl'60 . . . | 11340 W Olympic Blvd, Apt 185,
MR James V . . . . | Los Angeles, CA
MR Joseph R—at 1703—172 Court NE, Bellevue, WA *98008* . . . . | *90064*

Grace MR Charles M JR (Charles M) . . . . Married at Virginia Beach, VA
Kelley MISS Elizabeth J (Verne) . . . . Jly 17'93

Grace MR & MRS D Richard (Barry M Stewart) Pr.S.Pa'72 | ☎ (516) 549-4626
MISS Corey H . . . . | 36 Harbor Hill Dv,
JUNIORS MISS Kelly E . . . . | Lloyd Harbor, NY
JUNIORS MR Stewart R . . . . | *11743*

Grace MR Eric W . . see MRS W P Wood

Grace MR Eugene . . see B R Neilson

Grace MR & MRS Eugene G (Shattuck—Baugh—Barsha Powers) Gm.Ph.Ac.P'37
☎ (610) 527-6035 . . 816 Pennstone Rd, Bryn Mawr, PA *19010*

Grace MRS Gerd Morris (Gerd K Morris) SL'82 . . . | ☎ (212) 288-5330
MISS Melissa de W—Col'88—at 283 W 12 St, New York, NY *10014* . . . . | 161 E 79 St, New York, NY
MISS Gerd M—at 1566 Grove St, Apt 3, San Francisco, CA *94117* . . . . | *10021*
MR Charles B 3d—Bates'87—at 1819 Q St NW, Washington, DC *20009* . . . . |

Grace MR & MRS J Brewster (Ferguson—Anne Fusz) | 1617 N Flagler
MISS Eliza F Ferguson—at Colo Coll . . . . . . | Blvd, Apt 2,
MISS Jennifer F Ferguson—at Ben'gton . . . . . | West Palm Beach,
MR Shaun P Ferguson—at Regis . . . . | FL *33407*
| Chemin Petoliere,
| 1261 Lemuids,
| Switzerland

Grace MR Jeremy B . . see MRS W P Wood

Grace MR & MRS John Philip (Ruthann Kent) Ariz'65.MexCC'57.Ariz'66
☎ (602) 948-0322 . . 5334 E Paradise Canyon Rd, Paradise Valley, AZ *85253*

Grace MR & MRS John S (Lola A Nashashibi) Stan'79.Stan'83.Unn.Pr.BtP.Cly.Geo'79
1940 S Ocean Blvd, Manalapan, FL *33462*

Grace MR & MRS M Stephen (Maureen Miller) NotreD'68.Ariz'67 . . . . | ☎ (908) 234-1403
MISS Christina M . . . . | 34 Liberty Corner
MR Jeffrey M . . . . | Rd, Far Hills, NJ
| *07931*

Grace MISS Maureen
☎ (617) 266-6954 . . 20 Commonwealth Av, Apt 5, Boston, MA *02116*

Grace MRS Morgan H (Natalie O Watts) Mds.
☎ (516) HU7-3491 . . 9 Robin Hill Rd, Great Neck, NY *11024-1410*

Grace MR & MRS Morgan H JR (Robin W Rutherfurd)
Duke'79.Lond'81.Bcs.Dyc.Cw.Y.'67.Pa'78 . . of
☎ (516) 287-4740 . . ''High Hedges'' 292 Ox Pasture Rd, Southampton, NY *11968*
☎ (516) 487-5768 . . 9 Robin Hill Rd, Great Neck, NY *11024-1410*

Grace MRS Nancy B (Nancy B Dougherty)
☎ (215) 627-3030 . . 400 Cypress St, Philadelphia, PA *19106*

Grace MRS Oliver R (Carroll—Lorraine Graves) S.Pr.BtP.Cly.Cs.Ncd . . .of
☎ (516) 922-6078 . . ''Yellow Banks'' 49 Cove Neck Rd, Oyster Bay, NY *11771*
14 E 90 St, New York, NY *10128*

Grace MR & MRS Oliver R JR (Carolyn O Meyer)
Van'76.BtP.Ck.Pr.Un.Van'76
☎ (516) 671-9667 . . 32 Wellington Rd, Locust Valley, NY *11560*

Grace MR & MRS Patrick P (Margaret P McMenamin) NotreD'79.Cl'86
see Dilatory Domiciles

Grady MISS Carolyn Adelaide (Tyler del Valle) . . . . Born at Winter Park, FL Apr 16'95

Grady MR & MRS Hugh A (Myers—Jean H Longnecker) Br'42
☎ (610) NI4-7856 . . 2133 Buttonwood Rd, Berwyn, PA *19312*

Grady MRS Michael (Cary S Igleheart)
see Dilatory Domiciles

Grady MR & MRS Reginald del Valle (Maclean—Betty Kline)
Bhm.Pcu.Bur.Cp.Ncd.Dar.Cal'40 . . of
☎ (415) 344-7420 . . 601 Laurel Av, Apt 1003, San Mateo, CA *94401*
☎ (408) 625-9476 . . ''Tol Tac'' 26399 Rio Av, Carmel, CA *93923*

Grady MR & MRS Reginald del Valle JR (Susan C Moore) Bur.Cp.Cal'76
☎ (415) 344-8396 . . 230 Chesterton Place, San Mateo, CA *94401*

Grady MR & MRS Stafford Robert (Roberta Patterson) Vh.GeoW'47
☎ (818) 790-3202 . . 555 Meadow Grove St, Flintridge, CA *91011*

Grady MR & MRS Tyler del Valle (Anne S Calkins) WakeF'79.Cp.Ore'81
☎ (407) 645-3859 . . 1302 Alberta Dv, Winter Park, FL *32789*

Graebner MR & MRS Clark E JR (Kendall L Losee) MtVern'90
☎ (202) 244-7089 . . 4395 Embassy Park Dv NW, Washington, DC *20016*

Graeber MR & MRS Conrad R 3d (Susan M Diggs) MdArt'80.OWes'77
☎ (410) 526-3771 . . 4709 Butler Rd, Glyndon, MD *21071*

Graeber MR & MRS George K (Elizabeth V Beale) Cvc.Nu'41
☎ (202) 232-3525 . . 2926 Garfield St NW, Washington, DC *20008*

Graff MR & MRS Austin B (Evans—Kathleen A Horne) Sth'54.Mt.Me.Sl.Yn.Y'52.Pa'59
☎ (202) 333-3435 . . 1319—28 St NW, Washington, DC *20007*

Graff MR & MRS F Malcolm JR (Love—Yveta Synek) Mto.Plg.P'52.H'54 . . . . | ☎ (212) 289-0332
MR Steven S Love—at ☎ (213) 655-6038 | 1120 Park Av,
657 N Harper Av, Los Angeles, CA *90048* . . | New York, NY
MR Brett J Love—at ☎ (310) 470-6765 | *10128*
2035 Selby Av, Los Angeles, CA *90025* . . . . |

Graff MR & MRS Robert T (Frances R Kennedy)
PO Box 3245, Hilton Head Island, SC *29928*

Graff MR & MRS William E (Murray—Eddy—Pakenham—Fairly—Mary M Connelly) Cly . . .of
☎ (804) 758-2812 . . PO Box 969, Urbanna, VA *23175*
☎ (518) 873-2219 . . Underwood Club, New Russia, NY *12964*

Grafmueller MRS Albert M (Clark—Diana M Brodie)
see Dilatory Domiciles

Graham MR & MRS Albert H (Mary B Dunham)
Wms'32 . . . . | ☎ (803) 671-2499
MISS Mary B—at 260 Valley Rd, Rochester, | 10 Spanish Moss
NY *14618* . . . . | Rd, Hilton Head
| Island, SC *29928*
Graham MRS Barbara P (Barbara Putnam) Sbc. . . . . | ☎ (508) 921-5722
MISS Katharine—Bost'65—at ☎ (508) 526-1922 | 847 Hale St,
58 Masconomo St, Manchester, MA *01944* . . . . | Beverly Farms, MA
| *01915*
Graham MISS Dorothy Jane Washington (John R) . . . . . Born May 28'95
Graham MRS E Thom (Elizabeth K Thom) Cal'57.Mv.Cda.
☎ (310) 276-9024 . . 1260 Angelo Dv, Beverly Hills, CA *90210*
Graham MISS Elisabeth W—Nu'69.Cda.
see Dilatory Domiciles
Graham MRS Frederic W W (Bertha F Smythe) . . . | ☎ (215) 984-8728
MR Frederic W W JR—Leh'59—at | Cathedral Village
☎ (610) 688-4092 . . 315 Old Eagle School Rd, | A315, 600 E
Wayne, PA *19087* . . . . | Cathedral Rd,
| Philadelphia, PA
| *19128*
Graham MR & MRS Gordon (Phillips—Kirby E Smith)
Ne.StA.Cs.Y.'47 . . of
☎ (212) 988-5215 . . 129 E 69 St, New York, NY *10021*
☎ (718) 885-0861 . . 5 Deepwater Way, Bronx, NY *10464*
☎ (561) 231-4818 . . Riomar Sands 103, 2636 Ocean Dv, Vero Beach,
FL *32963*
Graham MR & MRS Gordon JR (Cathleen A Colella)
BostColl'91.StA.Myf.Dar.Emers'91
☎ (516) 676-8736 . . 540 Chicken Valley Rd, Locust Valley, NY *11560*
Graham MRS Hoffstot (Marion G Hoffstot) . . . . | ☎ (561) 395-5118
MR Peter M . . . . | 100 NE Spanish
| Trail, Boca Raton,
| FL *33432*
Graham MRS James Staples (Sarah J Sillcocks) V'35.Ncd.
☎ (609) 924-6285 . . 1 Markham Rd, Apt 2B, Princeton, NJ *08540*
Graham MR & MRS John (Ripley—Alexandra E Braid)
V'55.Geo'49.H'54.JHop'60
☎ (804) 295-9900 . . "Lafayette Hill" Rte 1, Box 380, Keswick,
VA *22947*
Graham MR John C—Bgt.Y'36
☎ (914) 234-6436 . . 179 Greenwich Rd, Bedford, NY *10506*
Graham MRS John MacD (Janet Welldon) Cs. . . . . . | ☎ (914) 876-4254
MR Samuel W—Ty'73—at ☎ (213) 667-2671 | 107 Mill St,
2232 Echo Park Av, Los Angeles, CA *90026* . . . | Rhinebeck, NY
| *12572*
Graham MR & MRS John R (Margaret M Fetter)
Stan'84.Sdy.Wms'83.Stan'87
☎ (310) 445-5491 . . 2234 Greenfield Av, Los Angeles, CA *90064*
Graham MR & MRS Philip L (Barraclough—Anne L Baker)
Camb'73.Lond'76
☎ (011-44-181) 715-7999 . . 51 Cliveden Rd, Wimbledon,
London SW19 3RD, England
Graham MRS R Hilles (Conkling—Claire L Wentworth Rump)
☎ (202) 364-4992 . . 4956 Eskridge Terr NW, Washington, DC *20016*
Graham MR R Hilles—Elk.Ct.AmU'66
☎ (202) 333-5124 . . 2801 New Mexico Av NW, Apt 207, Washington,
DC *20007*

Graham MR & MRS Walter E (Cleone G Tiffany) | ☎ (617) 527-0976
Ub.Wms'62.H'66 . . . . | 36 Magnolia Av,
MISS Aïsha F T—at 511 E 73 St, New York, NY | Newton, MA *02158*
10021 . . . . |
JUNIORS MISS Sabra-Jenks E—at Proctor Acad . . |
JUNIORS MR Lyman K T . . . . |
Grainger MR Isaac B—Ln.Plg.Cw.Pn.P'17
☎ (910) 762-1434 . . 1226A Columbus Circle, Wilmington, NC *28403*
Grambs MRS Paul L (Mary E Carroll)
☎ (212) 666-7455 . . 720 West End Av, New York, NY *10025*
Granbery MR & MRS E Carleton JR (Diana Allyn) | ☎ (203) 453-2449
B'gton'41.Yn.Y'35.Y'38 | 111 Old Quarry Rd,
MISS Pamela (Foley—Pamela Granbery) | Leetes Island,
B'gton'70.CUNY'82.Srb.—at ☎ (401) 331-9249 | Guilford, CT *06437*
362 Lloyd Av, Providence, RI *02906* . . . . |
Granbery MR John—Y'34
☎ (860) 435-0261 . . "Trackside" Salisbury, CT *06068*
Granbery MR & MRS W Preston (Ann R Hoffman) | ☎ (201) 539-0494
Gchr'68.RISD'71.RISD'72.P'69.VillaN'76 . . . . | Box 117, Millbrook
JUNIORS MR J Hastings—at Conn Coll . . . . | Rd, New Vernon, NJ
JUNIORS MR C Weld—at Middlesex . . . . | *07976*
Grand MRS Gordon (Ruth Young) . . . . | ☎ (203) 972-8083
MR Timothy W—Y'85 . . . . | Leefair East,
| 21 Bank St,
| New Canaan, CT
| *06840*
Grand MR & MRS Gordon 3d (Cecily W Fowler) | ☎ (914) 669-8270
Gv.H'70.Va'75 . . . . | 424 Hawley Rd,
MISS Angela W . . . . | North Salem, NY
JUNIORS MR Harry S . . . . | *10560*
JUNIORS MR Jake W . . . . |
Grandin MR & MRS John L (Susanne P Wilson) BMr'39.Cy.Chi.Ncd.H'32
☎ (617) 277-8305 . . 169 Chestnut Hill Rd, Chestnut Hill, MA *02167*
Grand-Jean MISS Laura R . . see MRS F C Bowers
Grandy MR Jeffrey McK—Rens'87 . . . . | ☎ (510) 443-1150
MR Edward B—at ☎ (801) 364-4937 | 1192 Portola
15 S 300 E, Apt 5, Salt Lake City, UT *84111* . . | Meadows, Apt 172,
MR A Stuart—at Evergreen State . . . . | Livermore, CA
| *94550*
Granelli JUNIORS MISS Alexis . . see MISS E P Seybolt
Grange MRS Herman K (Strawbridge—E Ann Schwarz) Me.Ncd.
☎ (610) 525-1008 . . 77 Middle Rd, Apt 164, Bryn Mawr, PA *19010*
Grange MR & MRS John W (Rulon-Miller—Shirley G Putnam) Gm.P'27
☎ (610) 527-0246 . . 737 Waverly Rd, Bryn Mawr, PA *19010*
Granger MR Blair H—Pa'86.VillaN'89
☎ (610) 489-2118 . . 112 Magnolia Court, Collegeville, PA *19426*
Granger MR & MRS David (Clyde—M Lee Mason)
Un.K.Bcs.Chr.C.So.Plg.StJ.Cs.Ncd.Myf.Y.'24
☎ (212) 744-5558 . . 640 Park Av, New York, NY *10021*
Granger MR & MRS Harold C (Alison A De Laney) Mid'80.Ty'78
☎ (860) 677-5285 . . 199 Mountain Spring Rd, Farmington, CT *06032*
Grannis MRS Adrienne E (Adrienne H Ely) . . . . | ☎ (608) 249-4009
MR Anthony E—at ☎ (305) 295-0506 | 51 Golf P'kway,
1611 Venetian Dv, Key West, FL *33040* . . . . . . | Madison, WI
| *53704-7024*

Grannis MR & MRS Alexander B (Snellings—A Ainslie Dinwiddie) Rut'64.Va'67
☎ (212) 794-2165 . . 501 E 87 St, New York, NY *10128*

Grannis MRS Arthur E 3d (Jerri J Ziegenhein)
Nw'60.Chi.Eyc.Err.D.Nh.Cw.Myf. . . . . | ☎ (508) 785-1192
MISS Lindsey W | 7 Pleasant St,
MISS Hilary E (Wendland—Hilary E Grannis) . . | Dover, MA *02030*

Grannis MRS Dustin (Mary A Mahone) On.
☎ (847) 234-8540 . . 1301 N Western Av, Apt 319, Lake Forest, IL *60045*

Grannis MRS Jane G (Arvystas—Jane G Grannis) LakeF'66.Kean'79
☎ (201) 434-1817 . . 11 Vroom St, Jersey City, NJ *07306*

Grannis MR & MRS Jonathan G (Kendra J Pfisterer) | ☎ (847) 446-3723
Cyc.Fy. . . . . | 368 Ridge Av,
JUNIORS MR Charles D . . . . | Winnetka, IL *60093*

Grannis MR & MRS Uri B JR (Marjory A Banks) On.Fy.Ncd.P'35
☎ (847) 234-5695 . . 404 Sunrise Av, Lake Bluff, IL *60044*

Grant MR & MRS Arthur Joe JR (Lucille Leatherbury) | ☎ (334) 265-4354
Ala'57.Ncd.Aub'57 . . . . | 1845 S Hull St,
MISS Carolyn E | Montgomery, AL
MR Thomas L . . . . | *36104*

Grant DR & MRS Austin R (Helen M Linehan) Dth'39.McG'41
☎ (602) 277-0529 . . 229 W Berridge Lane, Phoenix, AZ *85013*

Grant MR & MRS Christopher (Anne Gilmour) D.Cw.H'51
☎ (617) 326-2851 . . 1076 High St, Dedham, MA *02026*

Grant MR & MRS David A (Deborah P Jordan) Rc.Ty'62 . . of
☎ (212) 581-9735 . . 27 W 55 St, New York, NY *10019*
☎ (413) 458-2693 . . 214 Gale Rd, Williamstown, MA *01267*

Grant MR & MRS Francis C 3d (Sands—Jean B | of ☎ (212)486-6783
Minskoff) Nu'76.Nu'79.Nf.Pe.Ph.Pa'71.Pa'72 . . | 500 Park Av,
MR Francis C 4th—at Coll of Charleston . . . . . . | New York, NY
| *10022*
| ☎ (914) 967-4554
| 55 Stratford Rd,
| Harrison, NY *10528*

Grant MRS Frederic D (Madeleine J Batten) MtH'51.Ncd.
☎ (617) 235-4760 . . 84 Washburn Av, Wellesley Hills, MA *02181*

Grant MR & MRS Galt (Susan B Copeland) | ☎ (617) 383-0854
Cw.Va'55. . . . . | 388 King St,
MR John G . . . . | Cohasset, MA *02025*

Grant MR & MRS Halcott G (Cornelia Paine) Cw.H.'48
☎ (617) 899-4693 . . 227 Ash St, Weston, MA *02193*

Grant MRS Hugh J (Rollinson—Lucie R Mackey) Sth'31.Cly . . .of
☎ (212) 288-2617 . . 141 E 72 St, New York, NY *10021*
☎ (561) 272-1274 . . St Andrews Club, Apt 43H, 4475 N Ocean Blvd, Delray Beach, FL *33483*

Grant MR Ian M (William C JR) . . . . Married at Westport, NY
Gauntlett MISS Juliet B (Roger) . . . . Jun 3'95

Grant MRS J Barrett (E Swan McLean)
☎ (203) 869-6281 . . 44 Burying Hill Rd, Greenwich, CT *06831*

Grant MR & MRS J Gordon (Lynne H Summerell) | ☎ (912) 233-1057
Ga'64. . . . . | 1530 E 51 St,
JUNIORS MISS Elizabeth K . . . . | Savannah, GA
| *31404-4040*

Grant MRS James B (Irina A Kisseleff) Ihy.Ny. . . . . | ☎ (203) 869-2854
MR James B JR . . . . | 19 Meadow Rd,
| Deer Park,
| Greenwich, CT
| *06830*

Grant MISS Jill C—Colg'87
☎ (212) 308-1710 . . 245 E 54 St, New York, NY *10022*

Grant DR & MRS Joseph L (Mary Drayton) | ☎ (802) 649-1273
Nf.H'43.Pa'46 ⚓ . . . . | Box 285, Norwich,
MISS (REV) Priscilla R—Swb'83.VaTheo'92—at | VT *05055*
☎ (703) 912-3913 . . 8120 Kingsway Court,
Springfield, VA *22152* . . . . |

Grant MR & MRS Richard de G (Nickerson—Mellick—Priscilla Howes) Y'40
☎ (802) 462-2104 . . Sampson Rd, RD 2, Middlebury, VT *05753*

Grant MR & MRS Richard R H 3d (Mary E Brainard)
☎ (513) 426-7102 . . ''Little Fox Farm'' 4600 Brown Rd, Dayton, OH *45440*

Grant MRS S Kerlin (Du Pont—Sarah Kerlin Astley) Pa'73.Sim'89
☎ (617) 631-3816 . . 47C Independence Way, Marblehead, MA *01945*

Grant MR Thomas A 3d . . see E W Cather 2d

Grant MR & MRS Thomas W (Mary F Ingram) | ☎ (516) 626-1055
Rc.Pr.Cly.Cda.NCar'63 . . . . | PO Box 93,
MISS Mary F—Roan'92—at ☎ (212) 593-1508 | Locust Valley, NY
357 E 57 St, New York, NY *10022* . . . . | *11560*
MR Thomas W JR—HWSth'96 |

Grant MR William C JR—Dth'49.Y'53
☎ (413) 458-8625 . . Sweetbrook Croft Farm, Williamstown, MA *01267*

Grant MR & MRS William R (Carol E McGregor) | ☎ (847) 251-9114
Ih.Duke'65 . . . . | 1018 Pawnee St,
MISS Elizabeth M | Wilmette, IL *60091*

Grantham MR & MRS Jesse 3d (Katharine K | ☎ (916) 973-0427
Barnett) Denis'66.Y'71.WChesU'70 . . . . | 3241 Morse Av,
JUNIORS MISS Mary S | Sacramento, CA
JUNIORS MR Christopher W . . . . | *95821*

Grape MR & MRS Thomas Hamilton (Anne M Egbert) Sth'81.Ithaca'80
☎ (617) 965-4433 . . 25 Prospect St, West Newton, MA *02165*

Grassi MR & MRS Edward A (Judith H Le Sage) LakeF'78.Elk.P'76
☎ (410) 557-9084 . . 4282 Madonna Rd, Jarrettsville, MD *21084*

Grassi MR & MRS Marco (Cristina Sanpaolesi) | of ☎ (212)879-0255
K.C.Cly.P'56 . . . . | 158 E 71 St,
MISS Irene—at Conn Coll . . . . | New York, NY
MR Matteo—at NYU . . . . | *10021*
| ☎ (914) 424-8339
| ''Hayfields''
| Avery Rd,
| Garrison-on-Hudson,
| NY *10524*

Grassi MR & MRS Temple (Eleuthèra B Smith) | ☎ (301) 654-0064
Rcn.Mt.Cvc.Gv.Sl.NCar'69 . . . . | 5900 Connecticut
JUNIORS MISS Melissa S . . . . | Av, Chevy Chase,
JUNIORS MISS Charlotte McC . . . . | MD *20815*

Grasty MRS Catherine L (Catherine Lewis) Va'31
☎ (540) 672-4781 . . 213 Red Hill Rd, Orange, VA *22960*

Gratry MR & MRS Jerome R (Barbara Bolton) K.Cv.   ☎ (216) 247-2211
MR Oliver C—at Yale . . . .   3050 Chagrin River
JUNIORS MISS Adrienne B—at Deerfield . . . . . .   Rd, Chagrin Falls,
JUNIORS MR Julian P . . . .   OH *44022*

Gratwick MISS Katharine . . see MRS L McDill
Gratwick MISS Laura B—Wes'95 . . see MRS L McDill
Gratz MR Clifford B—Curry'74
  ☎ (508) 526-7182 . . 3 School St, Apt 1, Manchester, MA *01944*

Grau MR & MRS Fritz H (McCormick—Susan V   ☎ (415) 342-9699
Locklin) Bur.Stan'47 . . . .   556 W Santa Inez
MR Fritz I . . . .   Av, Hillsborough,
  MISS Laura L McCormick—Cal'91—at   CA *94010*
  ☎ (415) 771-3130 . . 3060 Scott St, Apt 204,
San Francisco, CA *94123* . . . .

Grauer MISS Amanda J . . see J D Cannon
Grauer MR & MRS Frederick M (Frances Thacher)
  ☎ (561) 231-5726 . . 522 Bay Dv, Vero Beach, FL *32963*

Graupner MRS Adolphus E JR (Cobb—Margaret Stuart) Mls'37.Tcy.Ncd.
  ☎ (510) 843-4460 . . 21 Tanglewood Rd, Berkeley, CA *94705-1420*

Graves MR & MRS Eugene F JR (Barbara R Frey) SL'39.Tex'29
  ☎ (505) 988-4551 . . Rte 9, Box 66AA, Santa Fe, NM *87505*

Graves MR & MRS Harry Hammond (Lynne E Reichart) Mid'78.Ty'78
''Belcaro'' PO Box 54433, Cincinnati, OH *45254-0433*

Graves MR & MRS John H (Kathleen G Carskadon) Rdc'60.H'57
  ☎ (617) 899-8297 . . ''Trapelo Farm'' 470 Forest St, Waltham,
MA *02154-5725*

Graves MRS Jonathan K (Sara Grey Terry)   ☎ (207) 443-4918
Wheat'60 . . . .   PO Box 235,
MISS Laura M . . . .   Phippsburg, ME
  04562

Graves MISS Marilyn P—Dc.Ncd.
  ☎ (212) 744-3281 . . 655 Park Av, New York, NY *10021*

Graves MR & MRS Sidney C (Harris—Alice D Brown) Sth'28.Cy.
  ☎ (617) 449-7359 . . North Hill A302, 865 Central Av, Needham,
MA *02192*

Graves MR & MRS Sidney C JR (Fox—Robin Reath)   ☎ (617) 326-6565
Nf.H'58.RISD'65 . . . .   20 Woods End Rd,
MISS Monica W—Vt'87.Un.—at   Dedham, MA *02026*
  ☎ (617) 731-1082 . . 55 Boylston St, Brookline,
MA *02146* . . . .
  MR Sidney C 3d—at 710 E Harbor Circle,
Grand Junction, CO *81506* . . . .
  MR Martin F—Ne'94—at ☎ (617) 661-5387
79 Hampshire St, Cambridge, MA *02138* . . . . . .
    MISS Nell C Fox—at Middlebury . . . .
    MR B Wilmsen Fox 2d—CtCol'92—at
  ☎ (617) 864-0268 . . 86 Kirkland St,
Cambridge, MA *02138* . . . .
    MR Porter T Fox—Mid'94—at
  ☎ (307) 734-8048 . . Box 1286, Jackson Hole,
WY *83001* . . . .

Graves MR & MRS William M JR (Beverly M   *see*
Vaughn) Rol'77.Rol'78.Rol'77.Rol'78 . . . .   *Dilatory Domiciles*
JUNIORS MR William M 3d . . . .
JUNIORS MR Reid N . . . .

Gray MR & MRS Alexander L (Elizabeth M Wagg) NCar'91.StLaw'90
PO Box 532, Canaan, NH *03741*

Gray MR & MRS Allan J (Elizabeth T Arndt) Cent'y'84.Niagara'70.FairD'90
  ☎ (908) 758-0673 . . 204 Riveredge Rd, Tinton Falls, NJ *07724*

Gray MRS Anne Badger (C Anne Badger)   ☎ (410) 823-3360
Sth'48.Mv. . . . .   1200 Copper Hill
MISS Theodora R . . . .   Rd, Baltimore, MD
MR Edward A—at 120 Beacon St, Boston, MA   *21209*
02116 . . . .
MR Philip L—at 235 Park Dv, Boston, MA *02215*

Gray MR & MRS Austen T (Beatrice Milo Gray) Rc.Plg.Pr.H'30
  ☎ (516) 621-2330 . . 720 Motts Cove Rd, Roslyn Harbor, NY *11576*

Gray MR & MRS Austen T JR (Lynn Merrill)   ☎ (516) 671-3267
Rc.Pr.Cc.H'68.Idaho'77 . . . .   ''Cherrywood''
JUNIORS MISS Lily Merrill . . . .   111 Piping Rock Rd,
JUNIORS MR Austen T 3d . . . .   Locust Valley, NY
  11560

Gray MRS Bowman 3d (Kimberly—Josephine   of ☎ (212)752-2635
Whitman) Cl'59.Ln.B.Mt.Fic. . . . .   345 E 57 St,
MR Oliver A Kimberly 3d . . . .   New York, NY
  10022
  ☎ (203) 966-2756
  139 Oenoke Ridge,
  New Canaan, CT
  06840

Gray MR Bowman 4th . . see T O Moore JR
Gray MRS Burton C (Dorothy C Stephens) Cvc.Nf . . .of
  ☎ (202) 686-8833 . . 4200 Massachusetts Av NW, Apt 808, Washington,
DC *20016*
  ☎ (703) 821-8733 . . 710 Bulls Neck Rd, McLean, VA *22102*

Gray MRS C Wilmot (Carolyn Wilmot) . . . .   see
MISS Evangeline W . . . .   MRS D Armstrong

Gray MRS Carl A (Kenan—Harriet Du Bose) Cly.Ncd.
see Dilatory Domiciles

Gray MR & MRS Colby S (Cynthia M D Prideaux-Brune) Ty'80.SCal'83
  ☎ (510) 631-1640 . . 882 Camino Ricardo, Moraga, CA *94556*

Gray MRS Cynthia Hunt (Cynthia A Hunt) . . . .   ☎ (610) 793-1645
MISS Lisa L . . . .   960 Brinton's
  Bridge Rd,
  West Chester, PA
  19382

Gray MR & MRS David A (Alexandra L James)
''Cedar Ledge'' 4 Sachuest Dv, Middletown, RI *02842*

Gray MR Francis C JR—H'46
  ☎ (508) 994-3351 . . Birchfield Farm, South Dartmouth, MA *02748-1534*

Gray MR & MRS Harvey L (Margaret C Bartlett)   ☎ (203) 259-7379
Rcn.Mid'61.Cl'66 . . . .   Box 436, Southport,
MR Elliot W—StLaw'93 . . . .   CT *06490*

Gray MR & MRS John B (Virginia H Tripp) V'49.D.H'49
  ☎ (508) 785-0261 . . 175 Dedham St, Dover, MA *02030*

Gray MRS John D (Mary D Washburn) Rdc'37
  ☎ (212) 980-7858 . . 166 E 63 St, Apt 16A, New York, NY *10021-7640*

Gray MR & MRS John L 3d (Hennes—Frances W Pratt) H'52.Y'53
  ☎ (914) 967-0360 . . 110 Apawamis Av, Rye, NY *10580*

Gray MR John V . . see W Childs
Gray MR & MRS Julian C M (Helen I Sanders) Y'87.Camb'89.Camb'89
  ☎ (011-44-181) 767-2100 . . 138 Mantilla Rd, Tooting Bec, London
SW17 8DU, England

Gray MISS Kristina S .... Married at Philadelphia, PA
  Horvath MR John M (John) .... Apr 20'96
Gray MRS Mark F (Curtin—Ellen W Manganaro) Br'73.W.Ds.
  ☎ (713) 896-0104 . . 13507 Hampton Falls Dv, Houston, TX *77041*
Gray MR & MRS Morris (Keturah G Irwin) D.Sb.Cw.Cc.Chi.H'43
  ☎ (617) 326-6444 . . 223 Highland St, Dedham, MA *02026*

Gray MR & MRS Peyton Randolph (Jane C Webster) | ☎ (215) 247-3451
StLaw'75.Fic.Pc.Sg.Ac.NCar'73 .... | 38 Summit St,
  JUNIORS MISS Elizabeth S .... | Philadelphia, PA
  JUNIORS MR Peyton Randolph JR .... | *19118*

Gray MR & MRS Robert B (Elizabeth C Lord) Ty'73.B.Pr.Cly.Camb'72
  ☎ (011-44-181) 789-5424 . . 9 St Simon's Av, London SW15 6DU,
England

Gray MR & MRS Robert D (Carol G Crow) | ☎ (203) 661-2553
Ln.Fic.NCar'64 .... | 751 Lake Av,
MR Robert D JR .... | Greenwich, CT
MR Clifton L .... | *06830*
  JUNIORS MR Adrian G .... |

Gray MR & MRS Robert G JR (Louise Torrey) Va'66 | ☎ (215) 887-4482
MR Robert M .... | 510 Oreland Mill
  JUNIORS MR Andrew D .... | Rd, Oreland, PA
  | *19075*

Gray MR & MRS Robert L 3d (Elizabeth D Elkins) | of ☎ (610)520-1724
Sth'59.Rc.Y.'59.Pa'63 .... | 1229 Denbigh Lane,
MR James E—at ☎ (617) 557-9221 | Radnor, PA *19087*
56 S Russell St, Boston, MA *02114* .... | ☎ (603) 544-7339
  | Bald Peak Colony
  | Club, Colony
  | Cottage, Melvin
  | Village, NH *03850*

Gray MRS Roland 3d (Jean B Hawkes)
2001 Headwater Lane, Austin, TX *78746*
Gray MR Roland 3d—Ub.Cw.Myf.Stan'66.Bost'69
594 Green St, Cambridge, MA *02139-3121*

Gray MR & MRS Samuel P M (Margaret G Zink) | ☎ (617) 329-3438
RMWmn'62.Bvl.Cy.Chi.H'59 ⚓ .... | 1041 High St,
MISS Alicia L—in Bolivia .... | Dedham, MA *02026*
MISS Caroline G—at Wooster .... |

Gray MR & MRS Sherman (Barbara C Bintz) Stan'41.H'41
  ☎ (516) 676-6507 . . 32 Cedar Lane N, Glen Head, NY *11545*

Gray MR & MRS Stephen V (Patricia Donahue) | ☎ (617) 259-1426
BostColl'69.P'64.H'70 .... | 3 Goose Pond Rd,
MISS Melissa O .... | Box 6193, Lincoln,
  JUNIORS MR Jesse V .... | MA *01773*

Gray MR & MRS Taylor C (Virginia Selden) Hlns'84.Cly.Br'84 . . of
  ☎ (203) 698-0590 . . 60 Binney Lane, Old Greenwich, CT *06870*
Onteora Club, Tannersville, NY *12485*
Gray MR & MRS W Ashley JR (Anne E Sullivan) Cysl.Rcsl.Nd.
  ☎ (561) 231-3297 . . 431 N Peppertree Dv, Vero Beach, FL *32963*

Gray MR & MRS W Latimer JR (Judith C White) | ☎ (508) 295-1355
Bvl.Chi.H'55 ⚓ .... | 48 Bourne Point Rd,
MISS Melinda G—H'88—at ☎ (617) 876-1534 | Wareham, MA
2 Ware St, Apt 104, Cambridge, MA *02138* ... | *02571*

Gray MR & MRS Wallace H (Helen T Frederick) | ☎ (860) 868-7649
StCol'51 .... | Box 1031,
MISS Carla F—Ty'87—at ☎ (617) 524-3754 | Washington Depot,
384 Arbor Way, Apt 3, Jamaica Plain, MA *02130* | CT *06793*

Gray MR & MRS Walter F (Susan A Mair) Nw'54.Cysl.Elk.Nw'51
  ☎ (602) 488-4567 . . ''The Boulders'' 7544 Club Villa Circle, Scottsdale,
AZ *85262*

Gray MRS William A (Hulick—Smith—Elizabeth F | of ☎ (561)272-3162
Lewis) MdArt'28.Ncd. .... | 2220 S Ocean Blvd,
MISS Elizabeth C Hulick—-V'58—at | PH-1203,
  ☎ (212) 744-3456 . . 501 E 85 St, New York, | Delray Beach, FL
NY *10028* .... | *33483*
  | ☎ (201) 736-1855
  | 20 Tulip Rd,
  | Llewellyn Park,
  | West Orange, NJ
  | *07052*

Gray MR & MRS William S (Cynthia F Chace) Loy'77.Au.Cly.Hob'77
  ☎ (203) 322-5859 . . 295 Erskine Rd, Stamford, CT *06903*
Grayson MR & MRS Eric D (Natasha Justina Pray)
Hartw'86.Ihy.StLaw'79.Tul'82
  ☎ (203) 869-5535 . . 65 Buckfield Lane, Greenwich, CT *06831*
Grayson MR George—Srr.Mt.Van'82 . . of
  ☎ (202) 387-0355 . . 2540 Massachusetts Av NW, Washington,
DC *20008*
  ☎ (540) 592-3608 . . ''Blue Ridge'' Upperville, VA *20185*

Grayson MR & MRS J Gordon (Rohrbach—Laura M | ☎ (540) 687-3767
Norris) GeoW'45.Mt.Cvc.Cda.Y'40 .... | PO Box 213,
MR Brison C Rohrbach—Mt.Ariz'86—at | Upperville, VA
  ☎ (703) 836-3435 . . 801 N Pitt St, Alexandria, | *20185*
VA *22314* .... |

Grayson MR & MRS Mark W (Sarah R Houghton) Vt'79.H'79.Cl'87
  ☎ (203) 866-5857 . . 141 W Norwalk Rd, Norwalk, CT *06850*
Grayson MISS Maud M P—MtH'63
  ☎ (516) 944-8752 . . 85 Park Av, Port Washington, NY *11050*

Graziano MR & MRS Anthony W JR (Robin L | ☎ (317) 966-5480
Ryckman) HolyC'63.Bg.Va'66. .... | 3913 Backmeyer Rd,
MISS Robin Virginia—Buck'96—at | Richmond, IN *47374*
  ☎ (201) 377-4472 . . 17 Waverly Place, Madison, |
NJ *07940* .... |

Graziano MR Anthony W 3d—Buck'92
  ☎ (804) 295-9834 . . 1214 Swan Lake Dv, Apt 401, Charlottesville,
VA *22902*
Graziano JUNIORS MISS Jessica D . . see D L Larson JR
Grazioli-Venier JUNIORS MISS Assia . . see K C Chen
Grazioli-Venier JUNIORS MR Saverio E . . see K C Chen

Grchich von Cvetkovacz MR & MRS Alexander | of ☎ (011-33-1)
(Molden—Mary C Platt) Ws'48.Cda.Buda'46. | 45-56-04-62
Paris'51.Paris'52 .... | 51 rue de
MR Pierre G .... | Bellechasse, 75007
  | Paris, France
  | ☎ (011-33)
  | 53-94-11-58
  | ''Trevey''
  | 47410 Lauzun,
  | Lot et Garonne,
  | France

Greaves MR & MRS Harry B JR (Kathryn A Finley)
Okla'58.Dar.Cda.Okla'56
  ☎ (915) 584-2061 . . 733 Rinconada Lane, El Paso, TX *79922*

Grebe MRS Frank (Sylvia Thresher)
☎ (203) 230-8987 . . 200 Leeder Hill Dv, Apt 636, Hamden, CT *06517*

Greeff MR & MRS Edward R (Gilbert—Elizabeth F Dean) Rby.S.Pr.Lic.Ny.
☎ (516) 922-3371 . . 151 Horseshoe Rd, Mill Neck, NY *11765*

Greeff MR & MRS Pieter (Lucas—Patricia G Edgar) LErie'62.H'58
☎ (540) 465-4404 . . Box 151, Strasburg, VA *22657*

Greeff MRS Theodore (Hurd—Catherine M Stevens) . . of
☎ (561) 546-3367 . . 127 Gomez Rd, Hobe Sound, FL *33455*
☎ (802) 867-5522 . . PO Box 544, Dorset, VT *05251*

Greely MRS John A (Mary Ives)
☎ (508) 627-5018 . . PO Box 1635, Edgartown, MA *02539*

Greely MR & MRS John C (Jane C Grimball) Cvc.Geo'48 | of ☎ (803)577-4790 35 Tradd St, Charleston, SC *29401*
MISS Rose N—Ken'88—Box 11272, Portland, ME *04104* . . . . | ☎ (603) 447-2290 ''Hidden Harbor'' Box 16, Center Conway, NH *03813*

Green MR & MRS Alan JR (Joan Irwin) Mt.Sl.Stan'49 . . of
☎ (503) 223-0159 . . 1707 SW Hawthorne Terr, Portland, OR *97201*
☎ (619) 325-7134 . . Smoke Tree Ranch, 1800 S Sunrise Way, Palm Springs, CA *92264*

Green MASTER Alexander Colgate (g—John K Colgate JR) . . . . . . Born at New York, NY Apr 5 '95

Green MR Ashbel—Cl'50 . . . . | ☎ (212) SA2-8560 70 E 96 St, New York, NY *10128*
MISS Alison McK—P'90 . . . . |

Green MR & MRS Ashbel S (Shara Alexander) Bel'89.Wes'86
see Dilatory Domiciles

Green MRS Bernard (Marshall—Judith Carrington) Nu'62 . . . . | ☎ (212) 289-6393 1136 Fifth Av, New York, NY *10128*
JUNIORS MR Tyler K
MISS Blair C Marshall . . . . |

Green CAPT & MRS David H (Nancy A Rutter) USN'42
☎ (919) 426-7634 . . Rte 1, Box 840, Hertford, NC *27944*

Green MR & MRS David W (Wilhelm—Barbara L Booth) MaryW'63.SWTex'70
☎ (713) 286-9752 . . 15711 El Dorado Oaks Dv, Houston, TX *77059*

Green MR Edmund M F
☎ (540) 672-5702 . . 281 Belleview Av, Orange, VA *22960*

Green MR & MRS Edwin B III (Anne K Du Vivier) Mid'74.Va'77
see P F Du Vivier

Green MISS Frances S
☎ (410) 823-5180 . . 33 Southland Court, Towson, MD *21204*

Green MR & MRS George Gardiner JR (Nelson—Bobbie L Shelby) Miss'61.Dar.P'63
☎ (601) 428-8843 . . 1304 Homewood Dv, Laurel, MS *39440*

Green MR & MRS Gregory H (Whitaker—Elise Hillman) Vt'85.Cl'94.Wt.GeoW'85 . . of
☎ (212) 628-7189 . . 155 E 72 St, Apt 4D, New York, NY *10021*
☎ (508) 645-2573 . . ''Waterwheel Farm'' Box 297, Chilmark, MA *02535*

Green MRS Helen A (Helen Allen) Hlns'69.Dar. . . . | ☎ (703) 860-4243 2514 Penny Royal Lane, Reston, VA *20191*
JUNIORS MISS Kathleen A . . . . |
JUNIORS MR Carter C . . . . |

Green MR & MRS Jon A (Niver—Judson S Carstensen) HoustBap'67.Juilliard'75
☎ (212) 860-3794 . . 1623 Third Av, New York, NY *10128*

Green MRS Joseph C (Gertrude H Norris)
☎ (301) 652-9163 . . 3610 Raymond St, Chevy Chase, MD *20815*

Green MR & MRS Joshua 3d (Pamela K Pemberton) H'58 . . . . | ☎ (206) 324-1155 1932 Blenheim Dv E, Seattle, WA *98112*
MISS Paige C . . . . |

Green MR & MRS Marshall (Lispenard S Crocker) Mt.Cvc.Ncd.Y'39 . . of
☎ (202) 244-5474 . . 5063 Millwood Lane NW, Washington, DC *20016-2619*
☎ (207) 439-3745 . . ''Bayberry Rocks'' 44 Pocahontas Rd, Kittery Point, ME *03905*
☎ (207) 439-2953 . . 28 Goose Point Rd, Kittery Point, ME *03905*

Green MRS Martha T (Martha F Tilford)
2105 Howell Branch Rd, Apt 47B, Maitland, FL *32751*

Green MISS Mary S—Rdc'43 . . . . | Harrison House Apt 412, 300 Strode Av, Coatesville, PA *19320*
MR N Bleecker—Box 304, Royse City, TX *75089* |

Green MR & MRS Michael P (Karen C Andretta) UWash'65.Y'63
☎ (602) 956-0536 . . 6544 N 36 St, Phoenix, AZ *85018*

Green MRS Seymour L (Frances E Hunter) Ne.Dar.
☎ (610) 526-7039 . . Beaumont, Liseter Hall 203, 601 N Ithan Av, Bryn Mawr, PA *19010*

Green MR & MRS Seymour L JR (Ludwick—Andrea Wilson) Tex'84.Syr'68
☎ (817) 444-2024 . . 1020 Oak Ridge Dv, Azle, TX *76020*

Green MR & MRS Thomas M 3d (du Pont—Dulcinea H Lee) Sth'55.P'48
☎ (912) 598-8150 . . 6 Captain Kirk Lane, Savannah, GA *31411*

Greenan MISS Eleanor J—Pr.Chr.Ne.
☎ (212) RH4-1757 . . 2 E 70 St, New York, NY *10021*

Greenaway MR John H 3d . . . . | ☎ (603) 465-7696 Box 546, Hollis, NH *03049*
MISS N Holly—at 56 Coaning St, Beverly, MA *01915* . . . . |

Greene MRS Franklin I (Bassett—Elizabeth B Thomas) V'25
☎ (207) 644-8421 . . SR 64, Box 686, South Bristol, ME *04568*

Greene MR & MRS George S (Elinor C Robinson) Ph.Pc.Fw.Y.'43 | ☎ (215) 247-7249 415 Gate Lane, Philadelphia, PA *19119*
MISS Anne T . . . . |
MISS Elinor R . . . . |
MISS Eliza T . . . . |

Greene MR & MRS James C (Elizabeth Rollins) Sth'38.Y'36.Y'39
☎ (818) 796-3056 . . 1085 Glen Oaks Blvd, Pasadena, CA *91105-1107*

Greene MRS John A (Jett—Miriam Horn) MtH'35.It.Dar.
☎ (216) 464-1385 . . 21876 Shelburne Rd, Shaker Heights, OH *44122*

Greene MR & MRS John B (Williams—Anne J Sawyer) Bhm.M.Mv.Bz.Dc.Y'34
☎ (513) 299-3519 . . 4365 Delco Dell Rd, Dayton, OH *45429-1210*

Greene MR & MRS Jon R (Moffitt—Peggy J Booth) Rv.Wash'61
☎ (314) 965-5844 . . 12330 Borcherding Lane, St Louis, MO *63131*

Greene MRS M Thompson (Marion McL Thompson)
☎ (212) PL3-3921 . . 200 E 66 St, New York, NY *10021*

Greene MR Nathanael B JR—Y'63 . . of
☎ (617) 235-0040 . . 37 Pond Rd, Wellesley, MA *02181*
☎ (603) 924-3725 . . Windy Row, Peterborough, NH *03458*

Greene MRS Philip E N (Barbara Baker) Rm.Pn.
☎ (908) 842-0563 . . 238 Kemp Av, Fair Haven, NJ *07704*

Greene MRS Philip G (Gail J McNealy)
Stan'59.Tcy.Ncd. . . . . | ☎ (415) 668-9199
MISS Caroline W . . . . | 3750 Clay St,
MR Nathanael M . . . . | San Francisco, CA
  | *94118*

Greene MRS Stephen (Janet C Gould) Stan'41.Csn.Ncd.
☎ (802) 464-5584 . . "Cloudlands" Greene Rd, PO Box 368,
West Dover, VT *05356*

Greene MISS Stuart T
☎ (202) 965-3736 . . 3331 N St NW, Washington, DC *20007*

Greene MR & MRS Thomas Gordon (Elizabeth M Patchin) Ncd.Cal'30
☎ (408) 624-9483 . . Box 5923, Carmel, CA *93921*

Greene MR & MRS Thurston (Davies—Norris—Marta Brodie)
Chr.Cs.Wms'29.H'32
☎ (914) 677-5545 . . "Vercolline" RR 1, Box 63, Crescent Rd,
Millbrook, NY *12545*

Greene MR & MRS Timothy W (Jane Gates Le Roy) PlymSt'90.NEng'90
☎ (617) 335-0895 . . 56 Manatee Rd, Hingham, MA *02043*

Greeney MR & MRS Robert A (Allyn M Wolcott) | ☎ (610) 827-9482
Bost'74.Minn'71 . . . . | RD 1, Box 225A,
MISS Heather N . . . . | Bodine Rd,
JUNIORS MR Sean M . . . . | Chester Springs, PA
  | *19425*

Greenfield MR & MRS John E (Cynthia M Kehl) Col'90
☎ (303) 665-2281 . . 153 S Cleveland Av, Louisville, CO *80027*

Greenfield DR & MRS Paul S (Pratt—Sandra C Steele)
Bost'69.Bost'77.Cy.Ub.Pa'70.GeoW'74
☎ (617) 227-0217 . . 60 W Cedar St, Boston, MA *02114*

Greenleaf MRS Ellen W (Ellen H Worrall) . . . . | ☎ (215) 233-4541
MISS Sara W . . . . | 402 Longfield Rd,
MISS Allison McC—Geo'95—at | Glenside, PA *19038*
☎ (703) 448-8559 . . 1831 Dalmation Dv,
McLean, VA *22101* . . . . |

Greenleaf MISS Victoria S—Hampshire'83.Pr.Cly . . .of
☎ (212) 369-6278 . . 1225 Park Av, PH-B, New York, NY *10128*
☎ (516) 922-7565 . . 37 Frost Mill Rd, Mill Neck, NY *11765*

Greenlee MR & MRS G Richard (Victoria A Love) | ☎ (601) 981-7334
Miss'64.Miss'59 . . . . | 6 E Hill Dv,
MISS Victoria L—Miss'94 . . . . | Jackson, MS *39216*
MR George R JR—Miss'93 . . . . |

Greenlee MR Randall Hagner—Md.Sar.JHop'48
☎ (410) 235-9687 . . Broadview 1310, 116 W University P'kway,
Baltimore, MD *21210*

Greenlee MRS Robert E (Julia S Hanrahan) Cda. . . . | ☎ (803) 796-2034
MISS Evelyn B H . . . . | 100—7 St Ext,
  | Box 105,
  | West Columbia, SC
  | *29169*

Greenough MRS Hamilton P (Helen M Jensen) Myf. | ☎ (805) 969-6271
MR George H P . . . . | 935 Mariposa Lane,
  | Santa Barbara, CA
  | *93108*

Greenough MR & MRS Malcolm W (Catherine R | ☎ (508) 927-0044
MacKenna) Ec.Ub.Sm.H'48 . . . . | 23 Thoreau Circle,
MR Charles W—at Gettysburg Coll . . . . | Beverly, MA
MR Andrew S . . . . | *01915-1345*
JUNIORS MR George P—at Vermont Acad . . . . . |

Greenough MR & MRS Peter B (Beverly Sills) | ☎ (212) 873-8585
H'75.Cc.H'39 . . . . | 211 Central Park W,
MISS Meredith H . . . . | New York, NY
MR Peter B JR . . . . | *10024-6020*

Greenough MRS William 2d (West—Patricia M | ☎ (202) 333-1595
Rosicki) Mt.Cvc. . . . . | 3900 Watson Place
MISS Geraldine W West . . . . | NW, Washington,
  | DC *20016*

Greenway MR & MRS Hugh D S (Joy B Brooks)
Bnd'59.Cy.C.Sm.Tv.Yn.Y'58 ⚓
☎ (617) 235-0353 . . "Homewood" 634 Charles River St, Needham,
MA *02192*

Greenwood MR Daniel B . . . . | ☎ (610) 430-0610
MISS Mary L . . . . | 255 E Chestnut St,
MISS Caroline A . . . . | West Chester, PA
JUNIORS MR Daniel B JR . . . . | *19380*

Greenwood MRS Daniel R (Dorothy L Ogden)
☎ (610) 642-7949 . . 100 Llanalew Rd, Apt 1A, Haverford, PA *19041*

Greenwood MR & MRS Douglas (Phebe A Prescott)
Stan'79.H'85.Stan'79.Stan'89
☎ (804) 741-7863 . . 504 Gaslight Dv, Richmond, VA *23229*

Greenwood MR & MRS Douglas C W (Susan N Coleman)
Wms'75.Ln.L.Cly.P'73
☎ (203) 972-3129 . . 172 Dan's H'way, New Canaan, CT *06840*

Greenwood MRS Edith R (Edith F Rantoul) York'70.Cs.
☎ (212) 628-0025 . . 333 E 68 St, Apt 9E, New York, NY *10021*

Greenwood MR & MRS John E D (Charlotte E Sabey)
QU'43.McG'48.Rc.T.Ln.Cly.McG'48.Y'51
☎ (914) 986-2490 . . 19 Park Av, Warwick, NY *10990*

Greenwood MR & MRS Richard H (Jean E MacPhee) | ☎ (508) 632-1224
MISS Jennifer . . . . | 78 Fairlawn Av,
MR Richard N 2d . . . . | Gardner, MA *01440*

Greenwood MRS Richard N (Crowell—Marjorie Groce) V'28
☎ (508) 747-4367 . . 251 Sandwich St, Plymouth, MA *02360*

Greenwood MR & MRS Richardson C (Lee P | ☎ (610) 328-9688
Broadley) Temp'71 . . . . | 114 Cornell Av,
MISS Heather Emily—Bost'92—at New York, NY | Swarthmore, PA
MISS Josephine H—at NCar State . . . . | *19081*

Greenwood MR & MRS Robert S (Patricia A Griffin)
Ore'47.Pcu.Tcy.Cal'48 . . of
☎ (510) 547-4818 . . 220 Mountain Av, Piedmont, CA *94611*
☎ (702) 749-5233 . . 165 The Back Rd, PO Box 46, Glenbrook,
NV *89413*

Greenwood MR & MRS Thomas S (Rosalind H McMeekin) Pc.Sg.Ncd . . .of
☎ (215) 542-4345 . . 256 Tulip Tree Court, Blue Bell, PA *19422*
☎ (941) 261-7938 . . Indies W, T2, 2210 Gulf Shore Blvd N, Naples,
FL *34102*

Greenwood MR & MRS Thomas S JR (Sandra L | ☎ (215) 233-9262
Storm) DU'74.Ph.Pc.StA.DU'74 . . . . | 511 Auburn Av,
JUNIORS MISS Sarah S . . . . | Wyndmoor, PA
  | *19038*

Greer DR & MRS Alexander P (Dorothy Latimer) Y'50.Pa'55
☎ (509) 448-9256 . . 7415 S Regal St, Spokane, WA *99223*

Greer MASTER Henry James Perot (Timothy P) . . . . Born at
New York, NY May 17'96

Greer MR & MRS John T (Sara C Gotcher) Cal'79.Bur.Wms'77
☎ (415) 342-0321 . . 1035 Vista Rd, Hillsborough, CA *94010*

Greer MRS Robson L (E Florianne Traub) | ☎ (610) 688-2826
Pars'19.Me. . . . . | 502 St Davids Av,
MR Robson L JR—Denis'50 . . . . | Box 7162,
| St Davids, PA
| *19087*

Greer MR & MRS Timothy P (Kathryn I Matthews)
NotreD'81.Unn.Yn.Y'79.H'82
☎ (203) 966-8547 . . 193B Park St, New Canaan, CT *06840*

Greer DR & MRS William R (Tracy J Ball) Y'81.Y'81.Pa'93
☎ (610) 296-2393 . . 230 Leopard Rd, Berwyn, PA *19312*

Greeson MR Howard B—Pc.Pa'47
☎ (215) 735-1811 . . 1810 S Rittenhouse Square, Apt 205, Philadelphia,
PA *19103*

Gregg MR & MRS Arthur W (Sally P Cook) | ☎ (919) 932-5050
NCar'63.Ty'61.Ty'67 . . . . | 222 Stagecoach Rd,
MR Timothy W—NCar'92—at Vanderbilt Law . | Chapel Hill, NC
MR Stephen S—at Trinity . . . . | *27514*

Gregg MRS Hamilton S 2d (Carolyn H | ☎ (212) 786-0589
Breckenridge) Mid'65 . . . . | 225 Rector Place,
MISS Kimberley B—at U of Cal Berkeley . . . . . . | Apt 16B,
| New York, NY
| *10280*

Gregg MR Hamilton S 3d . . see R C Fenton

Gregg MR & MRS James G (Martha H Bellis) Ty'78
☎ (415) 752-4280 . . 234 Sixteenth Av, San Francisco, CA *94118-1018*

Gregg MRS John M (Darsie Hamilton)
☎ (810) 685-7904 . . 710—1 St, Milford, MI *48381*

Gregg MRS Robert E (Taylor—Phebe Russell) . . . . . | ☎ (617) 444-4395
MR Benjamin R Taylor—at ☎ (415) 435-2067 | North Hill B304,
PO Box 1004, Tiburon, CA *94920* . . . . | 865 Central Av,
| Needham, MA
| *02192*

Gregg MR & MRS Robert E JR (Mary W Williams) . . | ☎ (603) 428-7550
MISS Robina K—Hartw'88.Spgfd'94—at | 26 Bear Hill Rd,
801 Mamaroneck Av, Box 24, White Plains, NY | Henniker, NH *03242*
10605 . . . . |
MR Walter H—NH'93 . . . . |

Gregg MR & MRS Robert E 3d (Katherine E Dorr) NH'93.NH'90
☎ (413) 527-1520 . . Williston Northampton School, 19 Payson Av,
Easthampton, MA *01027*

Gregory MISS Ann C . . see W W Perry

Gregory MR C Stuart
☎ (212) 875-0109 . . 235 W 71 St, Apt 51, New York, NY *10023*

Gregory MISS Carol L
153 Pine St, Byram, CT *06830*

Gregory MR & MRS Daniel P (Mary C Lowrey) | ☎ (415) 752-3190
P'75.Y'73.Cal'82 . . . . | 233 Third Av,
JUNIORS MISS Eliza N . . . . | San Francisco, CA
| *94118*

Gregory MR Donald M JR—Bhm.Pcu.Y'50.Pa'56
☎ (415) 931-3169 . . 3248 Washington St, San Francisco, CA *94115*

Gregory MR & MRS John D (Helen C Powell) Y'45
☎ (410) 472-3014 . . 2400 Monkton Rd, Monkton, MD *21111*

Gregory MRS John H (Evelyn Q Clark)
☎ (408) 438-1207 . . 701 Canham Rd, Scotts Valley, CA *95066*

Gregory MR & MRS Quintard (Patricia W Hunter) | of ☎ (415)324-0629
Nw'68.Bhm.Cal'66.Cal'70 . . . . | 98 University Dv,
MISS Diana H—at 15 Westview Place, Riverside, | Menlo Park, CA
CT *06878* . . . . | *94025*
MR William W—at Colgate . . . . | ☎ (408) 628-3219
JUNIORS MISS Lilla B . . . . | "Rancho Cienega
| del Gabilan"
| 1636 Thomas Rd,
| Hollister, CA *95023*

Gregory MR Robert W . . see W W Perry

Gregory MRS Tyler G JR (Simpson—Sarah Morgan Strater) Sth'55.Vh.
☎ (310) 552-9357 . . 262 S Spalding Dv, Beverly Hills, CA *90212*

Gregory MRS William H 3d (Gregory—Elizabeth C Finlayson) Pr.
☎ (207) 798-4660 . . 49 Wildwood Dv, Brunswick, ME *04011*

Gregory MR & MRS William H 4th (Miller—Catherine S Aquino)
see Dilatory Domiciles

Greif DR & MRS Roger L (Alice J Falvey) | ☎ (212) 794-2992
Gchr'51.Cs.Hav'37.JHop'41 . . . . | 534 E 87 St,
DR Peter C—Cr'81—at National Inst of Health, | New York, NY
Bethesda, MD *20814* . . . . | *10128*
MR Matthew P—at 106 Sewall Av, Brookline, |
MA *02146* . . . . |

Greig MR Pickett M—Cw.Va'45
☎ (401) 423-0111 . . 21 Bay View Dv, Jamestown, RI *02835*

Greiner MR & MRS Peter H (Nancy B Sharp) Mariet'81.O'81
☎ (216) 921-8481 . . 16619 Aldersyde Dv, Shaker Heights, OH *44120*

Grenata COL (RET) & MRS Michael C (Bauman—Elisebeth Taylor)
Ch'29.An.Dar.USA'18
☎ (703) 777-1161 . . 201 Cornwall St NW, Leesburg, VA *20176*

Grenfell DR & MRS Raymond F (Maude B Chisholm) SCar'41.Pitt'41
☎ (601) 366-6395 . . 190 Ridge Dv, Jackson, MS *39216*

Grenier MR & MRS G Thomas (Vieva F Christy) | ☎ (908) 832-5345
Eh.Shcc.Rut'61 . . . . | 4 Longview Rd,
MISS Emilie F—at Dickinson . . . . | Lebanon, NJ *08833*

Grenier MISS Jennifer B (G Thomas) . . Married at Gladstone, NJ
Kandel MR Laurence J JR . . . . May 13'95

Greppin MR & MRS Ernest H JR (Barbara Dana) | ☎ (617) 326-4949
V'63.D.Chi.Hob'60 . . . . | 490 Gay St,
MISS B Ripley—Conn'87 . . . . | Westwood, MA
| *02090*

Gresh MR Andrew K (W Perry) . . . . Married at Salt Lake City, UT
Pendleton MISS Jean M (Brian) . . . . Jun 15'96

Gresh MR & MRS Perry C (Lisa P Skillern) Alb'82.Me.Rv.Skd'85
☎ (610) 964-9327 . . 893 Hollow Rd, Wayne, PA *19087*

Gresh MR & MRS W Perry (V Tucker Catherwood) Dth'56
☎ (610) 647-9979 . . 2416 Grubbs Mill Rd, Berwyn, PA *19312*

Grew MR Christopher A—Unn.Plg.Mich'84.Camb'86
☎ (011-44-171) 704-8238 . . 15 Noel Rd, London N1 8HQ, England

Grew MR & MRS Edward S (Dudley—Priscilla C Perkins)
BMr'62.Cal'67.Cos.Myf.Dar.Dth'65.H'71
☎ (402) 421-3785 . . 16 Bishop Square, Lincoln, NE *68502*

Grew MR Henry S—Sm.Nrr.B.Srb.
☎ (401) 846-7372 . . 72 Spring St, Newport, RI *02840*

Grew RT REV & MRS J Clark (Jones—Sarah W Loomis) Tvb.Nf.On.Csn.H'62 . . . . ☎ (216) 295-5620 13705 Shaker Blvd, Apt 6A, Cleveland, OH *44120*
MISS Sarah W . . . .

Grew MRS James H (Alma Clayburgh) Chi. . . . . . . ☎ (617) 329-6997 10 Longwood Dv, Apt 466, Westwood, MA *02090*
MISS Alma—at ☎ (860) 232-7672 . . 140 Kane St, West Hartford, CT *06119* . . . .
MR James H JR—at ☎ (941) 324-3011 310 Overlook Dv, Winter Haven, FL *33880* . . . .

Grew MR Raymond E—Plg.Mich'48 28124 Hamden Lane, Escondido, CA *92026*

Grew MR & MRS Robert R (Anne G Bailey) Mich'54.Un.Plg.Cs.Mich'53 ☎ (212) 688-0994 . . 139 E 63 St, New York, NY *10021*

Grey MR & MRS Schuyler E (Georgia Hendrix) Dth'54 ☎ (303) 757-4020 . . 2115 S St Paul St, Denver, CO *80210*

Grey MR & MRS Schuyler E 3d (Sarah A Carter) Col'82.ColC'82 333 Clermont St, Denver, CO *80220*

Gribble MR & MRS James L 2d (Mary E Mullen) Me'76.Nyc.Bost'77.Me'80 ☎ (207) 865-4771 . . "Weatherwood" 5 Balsam Lane, Spar Cove, South Freeport, ME *04032*

Gribbel MR & MRS John 2d (Pearson—Eleanore M Hershey) Pe.Fw.Y'38 ☎ (603) 544-2335 . . Bald Peak Colony Club, Box 411, Melvin Village, NH *03850*

Gribbel MR & MRS Theodore G (Susie N Logan) Ws'74.Stan'79.RI'79 ☎ (207) 865-4257 . . 6 Roos Hill Dv, Box 4405D, Freeport, ME *04032*

Grice MR & MRS Theodore N JR (Gretchen N Carr) Dav'56.Rut'59 ☎ (910) 760-1658 Cold Spring Rd, Winston-Salem, NC *27106*
MR Carter N—at Santa Fe, NM . . . .
MR Spencer D—at Washington, DC . . . .

Griebel MR Evan W . . see MRS L T Walker

Griebel MR Webster A—Del'96 . . see MRS L T Walker

Gries MR & MRS David D (Cordes—Thomas—Susan G Dawson) Ws'59.Cal'75.Cos.Y'54 . . . . ☎ (202) 965-2844 4855 Reservoir Rd NW, Washington, DC *20007*
MISS Susan G Thomas—Cl'91—at ☎ (718) 788-7559 . . 142 Seventh Av, Apt 4, Brooklyn, NY *11215* . . . .
MR Colin M Thomas—Skd'94 . . . .

Grieves MR & MRS James R JR (Katherine F Deering) Elk.Towson'82 ☎ (410) 821-7572 . . 332 Old Trail, Baltimore, MD *21212*

Griff MR & MRS Gary J (M Laurie Macdonald) SCal'69.SCal'69 . . . . 1316 SW Mitchell Lane, Portland, OR *97201-2826*
MISS Kimberly K . . . .
MISS May B . . . .

Griffen MR & MRS J Pennypacker (Louise J Small) StLaw'82.Va'83 ☎ (803) 723-9190 . . 21 Elliott St, Charleston, SC *29401*

Griffen MR Thomas K—Buck'80 ☎ (504) 362-6222 . . 3312 Timberlane Way, Apt 149, Harvey, LA *70058*

Griffen MR & MRS William W (Nancy K Luke) Yh.R.Wcc.Ste.Ac.Va'51 ☎ (610) 647-4712 . . 1287 Argyle Rd, Berwyn, PA *19312*

Griffen MAJ William W JR—USMC.H'77 ☎ (803) 559-2997 . . New Cut Rd, Wadmalaw Island, SC *29487*

Griffin MR & MRS Andrew (Wyman—Sharon Crary) Cal'59.Sfg.Pcu.Cal'58 . . . . ☎ (415) SK1-2227 151 Commonwealth Av, San Francisco, CA *94118*
MR Sherman G—at 2875 Greenwich St, San Francisco, CA *94123* . . . . . .
MR Mark C—at 107 Queensbury St, Apt 10, Boston, MA *02215* . . . .

Griffin MR & MRS Anthony (Jennifer Barnes) Bhm.Pcu.Cal'58.Cal'61 ☎ (415) 921-5245 . . 4 Miley St, San Francisco, CA *94123*

Griffin MR & MRS Christopher A F (M Calvert C Saunders) Va'90.Un.Pr.Ck.Cly.Y.Va'91 ☎ (212) 861-3853 . . 200 E 71 St, Apt 16B, New York, NY *10021*

Griffin MR Dustin H—Cw.Dth'28 ☎ (314) 394-7841 . . 1039 Cy Ann Dv, Town & Country, MO *63017*

Griffin MR & MRS F Hastings JR (Mary D Mifflin) Me.Rc.Rd.Ac.Ncd.P'43.H'48 . . . . ☎ (610) 353-7923 7037 Goshen Rd, Newtown Square, PA *19073*
MISS M Lloyd . . . .

Griffin MR & MRS J Tyler (Sonia M Worrell) Cts.Gm.P'45 ☎ (610) MU8-4656 . . 624 Dorset Rd, Devon, PA *19333*

Griffin MR & MRS J Tyler JR (Mary C Barili) Me.Wms'72 ☎ (610) 431-3662 . . 192 Pheasant Run Rd, West Chester, PA *19380*

Griffin MR & MRS Michael G (Colley Rhodes) Ala'70.Ala'70 . . . . ☎ (334) 277-1000 1661 Gilmer Av, Montgomery, AL *36104*
MISS Rebecca C . . . .
JUNIORS MR Michael S . . . .

Griffin MR & MRS Nathaniel M (Jane E Boudreau) TexA&I'68.W&L'64.OState'67 . . . . ☎ (601) 982-2468 4320 Roswell Court, Jackson, MS *39211*
MISS Natalie B . . . .
MR Andrew W . . . .
JUNIORS MR James H . . . .

Griffin MISS Rebecca Carter Saunders (Christopher A F) . . . . Born at New York, NY Jun 11'96

Griffin MR & MRS Samuel W M (Holly Hughes) Elmira'76.Me.Rd.Ac.VillaN'76 ☎ (610) 692-9035 . . 451 King Rd, West Chester, PA *19380*

Griffin MR & MRS T McLean (M Hope Wiswall) Rdc'46.Ey.H'43.H'49 . . . . ☎ (508) 744-7899 14 Beckford St, Salem, MA *01970*
MR David C—Mass'89—at Brown . . . .

Griffin MR & MRS W L Hadley (Phoebe M Perry) Cy.Bgy.Wms'40 ☎ (314) 434-4009 . . 1294 Mason Rd, St Louis, MO *63131*

Griffin MR & MRS William J 4th (Geraldine M Nager) Sth'81.Msq.Why.Va'77 . . of ☎ (212) 534-6232 . . 1601 Third Av, Apt 17A, New York, NY *10128* ☎ (401) 596-4129 . . 22 E Hills Rd, Watch Hill, RI *02891*

Griffis MISS Andrea E—Duke'79 *see Dilatory Domiciles*

Griffis MR & MRS Hughes (Sharon A F Tripp) Y'67.Cr'72 . . . . ☎ (860) 443-0740 605 Pequot Av, New London, CT *06320*
MISS Jennifer D—Sim'96 . . . .
MR Buckley—Syr'93 . . . .
MR Nicholas R—at Suffolk U . . . .

Griffis MRS Thomas J (Carol J G Steffan) SUNY'49 ☎ (212) 582-4048 . . 27 W 55 St, New York, NY *10019*

Griffith MISS Caroline C . . see M Fenton JR

Griffith MR & MRS Edward A (C Joyce Tomlin) Hlns'51.An.Mv.Pn.P'49 . . . . ☎ (410) 825-2319 1913 Old Court Rd, Ruxton, MD *21204*
MR Edward A 4th . . . .
MR William T . . . .

Griffith MR & MRS Edward McC (Helen E Atkinson) Bur.Pcu.Cp.Cal'39 ☎ (415) 771-2123 . . 945 Green St, Apt 4, San Francisco, CA *94133*

Griffith MR & MRS Edwin Lord (Esther Bullard) Bhm.Tcy.Cp.Ncd. ☎ (415) 491-1408 . . 600 Deer Valley Rd, Apt 3F, San Rafael, CA *94903*

Griffith MRS Hoyt S (Williams—Frances B Toulmin)
☎ (941) 639-8128 . . 540 Via Cintia, Punta Gorda, FL *33950*

Griffith MR & MRS Stephen E (Louise Cavanaugh) Stan'57.Stan'58
☎ (213) 939-9581 . . 439 N June St, Los Angeles, CA *90004*

Griffith MR & MRS Thomas G (Susan A Hackett) | ☎ (415) 342-9993
Bhm.Bur.Sfy.Cp.Fr.Cal'64 . . . . | 532 Maple St,
MR Charles L III—at U of Pacific . . . . | San Mateo, CA
MR Millen VI—at Salisbury . . . . | *94402*

Griffith MR & MRS William L (Joan R Sanger) | ☎ (410) 889-0187
Sth'61.P'51 . . . . | 524 Woodlawn Rd,
MISS Elizabeth W—Loy'95—at | Baltimore, MD
☎ (970) 870-1748 . . Box 5703, | *21210*
Steamboat Springs, CO *80477* . . . .
MR William J L—Ken'93 . . . .

Grigg MR & MRS William T M (Martha W Livdahl) Hlns'56.W&L'56
☎ (301) 652-1864 . . 4607 Merivale Rd, Chevy Chase, MD *20815*

Griggs MR & MRS Northam L JR (Moseley—Davis—Miles—
Nina J Miller) V'54.Va'56.Yn.Y'51 . . of
☎ (203) 661-0141 . . "Point Option" 380 Stanwich Rd, Greenwich,
CT *06830*
☎ (508) 775-1675 . . "Fairlea" 689 Scudder Av, Hyannis Port,
MA *02647*

Grigsby MR & MRS Ronald Philip (Catharine C Evans)
NCar'84.CNewman'80
2123 Reaney Rd, Lakeland, FL *33803*

Grill MASTER Michael Christopher (g—Charles F Morgan) . . . . . . Born
Feb 14'96

Grimball MR & MRS Richard B (B Adele Crawford) | of ☎ (803)577-3337
Y'50.H'54 . . . . | 64 Tradd St,
MR Richard B JR—at Charleston Coll . . . . | Charleston, SC
| *29401*
| ☎ (803) 869-3340
| "Gone Away"
| Edisto Island, SC
| *29438*

Grimball MR & MRS William H JR (Frieda S | ☎ (904) 434-7203
Benson) Cc.So'68 . . . . | 111 W Gonzalez St,
MISS Marian S . . . . | Pensacola, FL *32501*
JUNIORS MR William H . . . .

Grimes MRS Melanie G (Melanie W Gordon) | ☎ (860) 434-8079
Ws'73 . . . . | 27 Lyme St,
JUNIORS MISS Ashley T . . . . | Box 752,
JUNIORS MR Spencer B—at Trinity . . . . | Old Lyme, CT
JUNIORS MR Terence H . . . . | *06371*

Grimes MR & MRS Thomas J (Anne B Bouscaren) Man'vl'45.NotreD'42
☎ (703) 860-8596 . . 11502 Running Cedar Rd, Reston, VA *20191*

Grimm MRS Sara H (Mahone—Villalba—Griffin— | 55 Peables Cove Rd,
Sara H Grimm) . . . . | Cape Elizabeth, ME
MISS Sonia M Villalba—at ☎ (505) 699-5601 | *04107*
1111 Buckman Rd, Santa Fe, NM *87501* . . . .

Grimstad MR & MRS Charles M (Julia M Howard) | ☎ (412) 361-3640
Wheat'61.Pg.Aht'54.H'57 . . . . | 134 Yorkshire Dv,
MISS Ann Lee—Va'92—at ☎ (413) 498-5561 | Pittsburgh, PA
Northfield-Mt Hermon School, Box 4891, | *15208*
206 Main St, Northfield, MA *01360-1089* . . . . .
MISS Elizabeth W—at ☎ (212) 327-0453
324 E 77 St, Apt 5A, New York, NY *10021* . . .

Grindinger MR & MRS Kent J (Sharon E Nichols) Stan'79.Cr'82
☎ (214) 713-7209 . . 6630 Duffield Dv, Dallas, TX *75248*

Grinnan MR Lewis Porter JR . . . . Married at Dallas, TX
Clark MRS Dick H JR (Susanna Saville) . . . . Nov 10'95

Grinnan MR & MRS Lewis Porter JR (Clark—Susanna Saville) Rcn.Pcu.
☎ (214) 521-4408 . . 4408 Lakeside Dv, Dallas, TX *75205*

Grinnell MR & MRS Alexander (Bodman—Helen K Dunn) C.Cs.Y'57.Y'60
☎ (212) 369-6933 . . 25 E 86 St, New York, NY *10028*

Grinnell MR Lawrence I 2d—H'59.H'61.Cl'68
☎ (802) 496-3054 . . Box 216, Waitsfield, VT *05673*

Griscom MRS Clement A (Priscilla A Husted) | ☎ (401) 596-0476
StJ'55.RI'74.NewHaven'85.Msq. . . . . | 3 Shore Rd,
MISS Eliza U—Tufts'91 . . . . | Westerly, RI *02891*
MR Andrew H—Y'82.Jef'89 . . . .
MR Ellery S—Skd'92 . . . .

Griscom MR Lloyd P SR . . . . Died Sep 24'95

Griscom MRS Lloyd P SR (Abby A K T Van Pelt)
BMr'52.B.K.Evg.BtP.Cc.Cda.
PO Box 4414, Tequesta, FL *33469*

Griscom MR Lloyd P JR—Rcn.Pa'65.Cl'67
☎ (970) 927-9395 . . 36 Holland Hills Rd, Basalt, CO *81621*

Griscom MISS Nonie K
☎ (212) 772-2506 . . 225 E 73 St, New York, NY *10021*

Griscom MRS Rodman E (Peet—Watts—Elizabeth A Snowden)
☎ (619) 459-2578 . . 6623 Avenida Mañana, La Jolla, CA *92037-6229*

Griswold MRS A Whitney (Mary M Brooks) Sth'28.Csn.Ncd.
☎ (617) 326-8503 . . 10 Longwood Dv, Westwood, MA *02090*

Griswold MR & MRS Benjamin H 3d (A Leith Symington)
Md.Elk.Gv.L.P'33
☎ (410) 771-4422 . . "Fancy Hill" 3615 Hess Rd, Monkton, MD *21111*

Griswold MR & MRS Brehon S (N Kathryn Stanley) Bost'79.My.Bost'78
☎ (508) 356-4301 . . 23 Labor In Vain Rd, Ipswich, MA *01938*

Griswold REV & MRS Brendan (Heyniger—Adelaide Cole)
St.Ts.Bf.Cly.G.Pom'40.Y'50 ⚓
☎ (561) 231-6627 . . 300 Harbour Dv, Apt 401A, Vero Beach,
FL *32963-2869*

Griswold MISS Eliza T (Frank T 3d) . . . . . . Married at Chestnut Hill, PA
Allen MR Christopher D (Philip D) . . . . Jun 8'96

Griswold RT REV & MRS Frank T 3d (Phoebe | ☎ (312) 944-4480
Wetzel) Sth'62.H'59.Ox'62 . . . . | 70 E Cedar St,
MISS Hannah E . . . . | Chicago, IL *60611*

Griswold MR H Bridgman—Ny.
☎ (561) 234-0086 . . 100 Cowry Lane, John's Island, Vero Beach,
FL *32963*

Griswold MR & MRS Hector W JR (Barbara Swatling)
Skd'75.W&M'79.Mid'71.Bost'76
☎ (609) 466-3967 . . 109 Lambertville-Hopewell Tpke, Hopewell,
NJ *08525*

Griswold MR & MRS John A 2d (Zdenka Seiner)
Br'78.CUNY'82.Ford'92.Wms'75
☎ (718) 638-9103 . . 110 Park Place, Brooklyn, NY *11217*

Griswold MRS John W (Susan B Somervell) B.Yh.
☎ (508) 768-7676 . . 18 Apple St, Essex, MA *01929*

Griswold REV DR & MRS Lincoln T (Jean S Coghlan)
Doug'52.Rut'56.Woos'52.P'55.Temp'57.P'75
☎ (215) 233-5355 . . 707 Bethlehem Pike, Erdenheim, PA *19038*

Griswold MRS Mac Keith (Mac Johnston Keith) McG'64 . . . .
MISSES Belinda J & Anna B—at 5337 College Av, Apt 736, Oakland, CA *94618*.
☎ (212) 580-8816
251 W 92 St, New York, NY *10025*

Griswold MR & MRS Roger P (Stephanie Anne Hankey) Hn.H'54 . . . .
MISS Jean C . . . .
☎ (508) 636-4251
PO Box 218N, Westport, MA *02790*

Griswold MR & MRS Roger P JR (Stephanie B Fairchild)
☎ (212) 289-2721 . . 1100 Park Av, New York, NY *10128*

Griswold MR & MRS Stephen W (Sandra C Smith) Tcy.Cal'61
☎ (415) 775-4272 . . 2150 Hyde St, San Francisco, CA *94109*

Griswold MRS Tracy H (F Tracy Haight) Cly.Cda.Ncd.Ht.StJ.
☎ (860) 567-8051 . . ''Barkhamsted House'' PO Box 732, 44 Chestnut Hill, Litchfield, CT *06759*

Groat MRS Robert A (Smith—Jane D Durston) Hl.Myf . . .of
☎ (860) 739-0109 . . 10 Francis Lane, Old Black Point, Niantic, CT *06357*
☎ (805) 969-9911 . . PO Box 5337, Santa Barbara, CA *93150*

Groesbeck MISS Gretchen A (Bowes—Gretchen A Groesbeck) WChesU'86 . . . .
MISS Genevieve de B—BMr'86—at U of Pa Grad
☎ (215) 417-7534
3817 Spruce St, Box 315, Philadelphia, PA *19104-6101*

Groff MR & MRS William D 3d (Mary C M Jarratt) Gv.Cc.Cw.Mv.Ncd.Rm'69 . . . .
MISS Courtenay J . . . .
☎ (410) 363-1880
PO Box 8, Owings Mills, MD *21117*

Groman MRS Henry N (Florence M Richardson) . . .
MISS Elizabeth L . . . .
MR Henry N JR—at Perth, Australia . . . .
☎ (207) 967-5517
''The Tamaracks'' Kennebunkport, ME *04046*

Groman MR & MRS (DR) Phillip S (Sarah R Newell-Price) StBart'79.Gettys'71 . . . .
JUNIORS MR Christopher H . . . .
☎ (011-263-19) 41663
Pvt Bag AC162, Ascot, Bulawayo, Zimbabwe

Groome MR & MRS Harry C 3d (Evelyn S Richardson) Pa'68.Pa'74.VillaN'81.Ph.Cts.Me. Au.Pa'63 . . . .
MISS Evelyn S—H'88—at U of So Cal . . . .
MR Harry C—Ham'86—at 1539 Shradee St, San Francisco, CA *94111* . . . .
MR Peter Z—Ham'90—at 18 W 95 St, Apt 1B, New York, NY *10025* . . . .
☎ (610) 525-2763
964 Conestoga Rd, Rosemont, PA *19010*

Grose MRS Pickering (Marie-Louise Pickering) Swb'61
☎ (212) TE1-8161 . . 1435 Lexington Av, New York, NY *10128*

Grose MR & MRS Thomas Pierpont (Herlin—Eleanor F Evans) Bost'65.Hof'62 ⚓ . . . .
MISS Signe P . . . .
MISS Vanessa P . . . .
MISS Heather B . . . .
JUNIORS MR William F P . . . .
of ☎ (011-44-171) 603-7046
7 St Mary Abbot's Place, London W8 6LS, England
☎ (207) 644-8150
''Seascape'' Christmas Cove, ME *04568*

Grose MR William R 2d—K.Hav'61 . . of
☎ (212) 879-2216 . . 929 Park Av, New York, NY *10028*
☎ (860) 868-9648 . . ''Owls'' 128 Blackville Rd, Washington, CT *06794*

Grosjean MRS Diane D (Bergfeld—Diane D Grosjean)
☎ (212) 722-3103 . . 40 E 94 St, New York, NY *10128*

Grosjean MISS Maria Emlen—Cs.
☎ (516) 725-2292 . . ''Watch Case House'' PO Box 1482, 67 Suffolk St, Sag Harbor, NY *11963-0056*

Gross MR Charles Edward
☎ (334) 821-7508 . . 433 N College St, Auburn, AL *36830*

Gross MR & MRS Charles T (Mary E Williamson) Ala'69.ETex'71.Smu'79 . . . .
JUNIORS MISS Mary W . . . .
☎ (334) 265-9368
2056 Myrtlewood Dv, Montgomery, AL *36111*

Gross MR & MRS Courtlandt D (Shirley B Davis) Nyc.Sfy.S.H'70 . . of
☎ (805) 969-1978 . . 818 Hot Springs Rd, Santa Barbara, CA *93108*
☎ (415) 332-4808 . . 52 Prospect St, Sausalito, CA *94965*

Gross MRS George Mason (Hanley—McAlpin—McDevitt—Jean I J Brown) Drake'40.Dar . . .of
☎ (561) 278-6878 . . 790 Andrews Av, Apt G101, Delray Beach, FL *33483*
☎ (401) 635-8509 . . 100 Sakonnet Point Rd, Little Compton, RI *02837*

Gross MRS Henry McC (Mallinson—Catherine M Elliott) Ct.
☎ (011-44-171) 235-4629 . . 64 Cadogan Place, London SW1X 9RS, England

Gross MR & MRS Rainer (Cynthia Cannell) Bnd'81
☎ (212) 249-7307 . . 108 E 82 St, New York, NY *10028*

Gross MR & MRS William A O (Abby M Minot) Sth'46.Hn.Bow'37 . . . .
MR Bayard M . . . .
of ☎ (203)869-8144
20 Hill Rd, Greenwich, CT *06830*
☎ (207) 725-6025
3089 Mere Point Rd, Brunswick, ME *04011*

Grosvenor MR & MRS Charles B (Louise B Wheeler) Bnd'53.Un.Srb.Ne.Cly.H'50 . . of
☎ (212) 879-9342 . . 300 E 75 St, Apt 11N, New York, NY *10021*
☎ (401) 847-4817 . . ''Windswept'' 208 Ocean Av, Newport, RI *02840*

Grosvenor MR & MRS Charles B JR (Cordelia O Brunson) Srb.Nrr.Vt'83
☎ (512) 478-9451 . . 1406A Mohle Dv, Austin, TX *78703*

Grosvenor MRS Melville Bell (Anne E Revis) Cvc. .
MISS Sara A . . . .
☎ (301) 530-1442
5510 Grosvenor Lane, Bethesda, MD *20814*

Grosvenor MR & MRS Richard (Margot K K Sullivan) Hb.H'51
☎ (401) 846-3052 . . ''Sunstone'' 126 Carroll Av, Newport, RI *02840*

Grote CTSS Christine (Lombard—Boit—Crisp—CTSS Christine Grote) . . . . of ☎ (011-44-171) 798-8650
MR Charles-Frederick D Boit . . . . 04 Hood House, Dolphin Square, London SW1V 3NQ, England
JUNIORS MR John E Crisp . . . . ☎ (011-44-1508) 518-477 Green Farmhouse, Honeypot Lane, Kirby Cane, Bungay, Suffolk NR35 2HW, England

Grote MR & MRS G Peter (Mary S Robinson) Ws'60.Chi.H'62 . . . . of ☎ (603)832-8444 "Ghorapani" 1437 Easton Rd, Franconia, NH *03580*
MISS Ann B. . . . .
MR William A. . . . . ☎ (011-49-69) 773733 Hans-Sachs Strasse 12, 60487 Frankfurt am Main, Germany

Grote MR Otto F—Ri.H'53.H'57
☎ (603) 427-2022 . . PO Box 640, New Castle, NH *03854*

Groton MR & MRS Nathanael B JR (Juanita H Brown) H'37 . . . . ☎ (215) 242-1554 235 Rex Av, Philadelphia, PA *19118*
MISS Anne H—at ☎ (507) 645-7356 815 W 2 St, Northfield, MN *55057* . . . .

Grotz CAPT William A 3d—USA'88 . . see S Egerton 2d

Grout MRS H McIntyre (Carlson—L Louise Allen) Ws'29
☎ (609) 654-3454 . . 454 Medford Leas, Medford, NJ *08055-2212*

Grove MISS Alexandra Lawton (David D) . . . . Born at Warminster, PA Feb 19'96

Grove MR & MRS Brandon Hambright JR (Parsons—Fleming—Mariana C Moran) Sth'55.Sl. Bard'50.P'52 . . . . ☎ (202) 232-2365 2029 Connecticut Av NW, Washington, DC *20008*
MISS Michele Parsons—Sth'85 . . . .

Grove MR & MRS David D (Holly E Lawton) Blooms'94.Pc.Buck'86
☎ (215) 643-3846 . . 108 Davis Dv, North Wales, PA *19454*

Grove MR & MRS Henry S 3d (Joan Hemmerly) Pc.Dar.P.'55 ⚓ . . . . 1 Joining Brook, Spring House, PA *19477*
MR Donald H—Penn'79 . . . .

Grove MR & MRS Lloyd B (Diana V Morgan) JHop'80.Cvc.Y'76
☎ (301) 656-6364 . . 4308 Rosemary St, Chevy Chase, MD *20815*

Grove COL & MRS Robert N (Rachel M Cox) USA.Cin'36.Ind'37.Victoria'80.Victoria'85
☎ (011-64-4) 476-6285 . . 33 Duthie St, Wellington 6005, New Zealand

Grover MRS L Chace (Esther L Turner) Ogontz'30.Sfg.Fr.
☎ (415) 441-8026 . . 1000 Chestnut St, San Francisco, CA *94109*

Grover MR & MRS Robinson A (Percy—Nancy F Dow) V'62.K.Ncd.Y'58.Br'69 . . of
☎ (860) 233-2021 . . 777 Prospect Av, West Hartford, CT *06105*
☎ (516) 324-1256 . . "The Carriage House" 132 Apaquogue Rd, East Hampton, NY *11937*

Groves MR & MRS Benjamin A (Karlson—Elizabeth P Scott) Sth'53.Rby.Cly.Cda.Ht. . . . . ☎ (508) 430-1323 10 Pleasant St, Harwich Port, MA *02646*
MR Christopher S Karlson . . . .

Grubb MRS (LT COL) Drusilla B (Drusilla Brown) USA.NEng'75
6333 La Jolla Blvd, Apt 171, La Jolla, CA *92037*

Grubb MR & MRS Joseph Spenser (Ellen S Sexton) Me.Pa'51
☎ (610) 642-5405 . . 116 Bleddyn Rd, Ardmore, PA *19003*

Gruber MR & MRS Alan S (Treffer—Elizabeth L Divine) Del'70.JHop'89.Temp'78 . . . . ☎ (410) 268-3740 502 Tayman Dv, Annapolis, MD *21403*
JUNIORS MSRS Scott F & Jonathan E S—at 148 Sycamore Av, Bridgewater, NJ *08807* . . . . .
MISS Christine E Treffer . . . .
JUNIORS MISS Kimberly A Treffer. . . . .

Gruber MR Matthew J (Donald J) . . . . Married at Southampton, Bermuda Snyder MISS Karen M (Frederick) . . . . Mch 15'96

Grubstein MRS Joseph F (Sibyl J S Herzog) Bnd'44.Mo.Eh.Y . . .of
☎ (908) 766-7171 . . 70 Dryden Rd, Bernardsville, NJ *07924*
☎ (212) 758-9133 . . 30 E 62 St, New York, NY *10021*

Grubstein MR & MRS Peter S H (Valeska A Watters) SCal'80.Eh.Yn.Y'77
☎ (805) 565-4762 . . 1705 E Valley Rd, Santa Barbara, CA *93108*

Gruen MR & MRS Peter J (Anne L Elliott) SL'66.Rr.Rut'65.Cl'76 . . . . ☎ (609) 924-1911 7 Cleveland Lane, Princeton, NJ *08540*
JUNIORS MISS Skye E . . . .

Gruener MR & MRS Edward L (Terry A Poulin) Sth'61.Stan'62.Cw.Myf.Bost'60.Bost'61 . . . . . . ☎ (207) 236-3726 "Mountain Greenery Farm" Camden, ME *04843*
MR James E—at ☎ (508) 740-0332 126 Federal St, Salem, MA *01970* . . . .

Grummon MR & MRS John H (Klaussmann—Elizabeth M Chapin) Sth'66.Chi.P'60 . . . . . . ☎ (617) 354-5685 45 Walker St, Cambridge, MA *02138*
MISS Elizabeth M Klaussmann—at Barnard . .
MR Eric K Klaussmann—Bost'94 . . . .

Grund MR & MRS David L (E Graham Latimer) It.Cv.
☎ (216) 231-7178 . . 2560 N Moreland Blvd, Cleveland, OH *44120*

Gruner MR & MRS Otto Harry III (Nancy V Evans) V'51.Pg.Rr.Fcg.Fic.Y'50
☎ (412) 963-9883 . . 584 Squaw Run Rd E, Pittsburgh, PA *15238-1922*

Grunwald MR & MRS Henry (Savitt—Melhado—Louise Liberman)
☎ (212) 879-0881 . . 720 Park Av, New York, NY *10021*

Grymes MR & MRS A Johnson 3d (Joanne S Day) Ny.Eh.Fw.
☎ (561) 234-4155 . . 845 Painted Bunting Lane, Vero Beach, FL *32963*

Gryska MR & MRS Peter H (Mary C Cole) Sth'81.Wes'81
☎ (704) 328-8530 . . 1045 Eighteenth Av NW, Hickory, NC *28601*

Guarino DR & MRS Christopher A (Gloria J Robins) MtStV'48.ClP&S'47
☎ (520) 298-7016 . . 6710 E Opatas St, Tucson, AZ *85715*

Gubelmann MR & MRS James B (Kate C Crichton) Ny.So'70 . . . . ☎ (908) 766-5767 "Antenna Farm" 136 Mt Harmony Rd, Bernardsville, NJ *07924*
MISS Tantivy A . . . .
MISS Phoebe G . . . .
JUNIORS MR James G . . . .

Gubelmann MISS Marjorie Barton—NEng'91.Srb.Cda.
☎ (212) 758-0508 . . 188 E 64 St, Apt 702, New York, NY *10021*

Gubelmann MRS Susan McC (Susan McCammon) . ☎ (970) 920-1998 900 E Durant, Apt 180, Aspen, CO *81611*
MR Wyeth S McC—at ☎ (970) 728-5202 Box 492, 309 E Columbia Av, Telluride, CO *81435* . . . .

Gubelmann MRS Walter S (Barton Green) Ny.Srb.Evg.BtP.Myf.Cda.
☎ (561) 659-1300 . . ''Due East'' 700 S Ocean Blvd, Palm Beach,
FL *33480*

Gubelmann MR & MRS William S (Shelley Page) Rcn.S.BtP.
☎ (561) 659-1303 . . 670 Island Dv, Palm Beach, FL *33480*

Guenther MR J Jarden—Hav'42
☎ (516) 584-5411 . . ''East Hill'' PO Box 57, St James, NY *11780*

Guenther MR & MRS Jack Egon (Valerie Urschel) | ☎ (210) 826-1649
Stan'61.Stan'63.A.Tex'56.StMarys'59.Nu'60 . . . | 1 Ironwood Rd,
MISS Abigail C—*see Dilatory Domiciles* . . . . . . | San Antonio, TX
MR Jack Egon JR—at 47 Haverhill Way, San | *78212*
Antonio, TX *78209* . . . . |

Guenther MR & MRS William H (Deirdre G Loew) Y'78.Sbc.H'72.Nu'75
☎ (508) 741-4821 . . 365 Essex St, Salem, MA *01970*

Guernsey MR & MRS David T (Jacqueline A Chapman) Err.Ny.Y'49
☎ (860) 567-9157 . . ''Teaticket'' 15 Webster Rd, Litchfield,
CT *06759-1228*

Guernsey MR & MRS David T JR (Susan J Craig) | ☎ (757) 489-5234
OWes'76.Err.OWes'76 . . . . | 1219 Larchmont
JUNIORS MISS Margaret A . . . . | Crescent, Norfolk,
JUNIORS MISS Elizabeth H . . . . | VA *23508*

Guernsey MR & MRS George T 4th (Carol A Miller) Mo'70.Yn.Y'71 . . of
☎ (011-44-171) 221-4462 . . 81 Palace Court, London W2 4JE, England
☎ (011-44-1386) 841530 . . ''Rose Cottage'' Broad Campden,
Gloucestershire GL55 6US, England

Guernsey MR & MRS Kent C (Laura S A Lovelace)
Char'ton'81.Eyc.Md.Buck'80
☎ (410) 280-0349 . . 3124 Portway, Annapolis, MD *21403*

Guernsey MR & MRS Peter E (Barbara Thurston) Rc.Err.Pr.Cly.Y'44 . . of
☎ (212) BU8-1531 . . 45 E 72 St, New York, NY *10021*
☎ (508) 627-4342 . . Kent Harbor, RFD 149, Edgartown, MA *02539*

Guest MR & MRS John S C (Margaret H Houck)
BMr'37.Rcn.Csn.Fic.Fiy.Camb'34.H'37
☎ (203) 966-9840 . . 839 Weed St, New Canaan, CT *06840*

Guest MR & MRS Richard L (Cynthia R Vaiden) | ☎ (203) 849-0534
Rcn.Fic.Pa'77.Cl'84 . . . . | 5 James St,
JUNIORS MISS Sarah F V . . . . | Norwalk, CT *06850*

Guggenhime MR Andrew L—Mid'90 . . see P R Ehrlich

Guggenhime MISS Lisa J . . see P R Ehrlich

Guggenhime MISS Mia E . . see P R Ehrlich

Guida MR & MRS James F (Alice E Warden) NCar'73
☎ (860) 828-9913 . . 86 Barker Lane, Kensington, CT *06037*

Guild MR & MRS Bayard S (Kay T Dunlap) Rol'55
☎ (508) 785-0191 . . 11 Main St, Dover, MA *02030*

Guild MR & MRS David D (M Gretchen Schwartz) HolyC'86.Ty'83
☎ (603) 887-2987 . . 93 Chester St, Chester, NH *03036*

Guild MR & MRS Edward M JR (Alexandra D Evans)
V'76.Lond'80.LakeF'69.Suff'80
☎ (617) 383-9300 . . Box 501, Cohasset, MA *02025*

Guild MISS Eliza Bayard (David D) . . . . Born Apr 24'96

Guild MR & MRS Henry R JR (Gale A Robb) Btn.Cy.Tv.Ec.Chi.Sm.H'50
☎ (508) 785-0525 . . 36 Farm St, Dover, MA *02030*

Guild MR & MRS William H (Barbara L Connolly) Rdc'46.H'46 . . of
☎ (603) 383-9334 . . ''The Inside Edge'' Jackson, NH *03846*
☎ (617) 925-3221 . . Spinnaker Island, Allerton, MA *02045*

Guilfoil MR & MRS Rodney (Betty Jacobsen) Sfy.Cp.Cal'41
☎ (408) 626-4862 . . 8545 Carmel Valley Rd, Carmel, CA *93923*

Guimont MR Charles E—NewSchSR'91
☎ (718) 388-1393 . . 100 Metropolitan Av, Brooklyn, NY *11211*

Guimont MR & MRS Maurice S (Juliet S Welton) McG'61.McG'62 ⚓
☎ (804) 693-5543 . . PO Box 756, Lewis Av, Gloucester, VA *23061*

Guinan MR & MRS James L (Anne E Ward)
V'86.Smu'89.Me.Dar.Creigh'86.Smu'89 . . of
☎ (214) 239-6578 . . 4425 Twin Post Rd, Dallas, TX *75244*
Z Ranch, H'way 377, Brady, TX *76825*

Guinan MR & MRS Thomas F (Sharon M Behn) Mid'81.UMiami'82.H'94
☎ (202) 467-3333 . . 2001 M St NW, Washington, DC *20036*

Gulden MR & MRS Charles JR (Trulsson—von Schnitzler—Vernon—
Leonetta Nunes) Ihy . . .of
☎ (203) 324-4226 . . 25 Brightside Dv, Stamford, CT *06902*
☎ (561) 231-5200 . . 8830 Sea Oaks Way S, Apt 105, Vero Beach,
FL *32963*

Gulden MR & MRS Charles F (Jennifer L Wentzel) Denis'85.Denis'83
☎ (561) 997-9969 . . 3360 NW 53 Circle, Boca Raton, FL *33496*

Gulden MRS Katherine K (Katherine A Keogh)
☎ (904) 285-0117 . . 78 Fishermans Cove, Ponte Vedra Beach,
FL *32082*

Gulden MR & MRS Michael I (Mary Jean Summers) | ☎ (561) 659-2088
Pr.BtP.Evg.Cly.Y'61 . . . . | 437 Primavera Way,
MR Christopher A—Pr.OWes'92—at | Palm Beach, FL
U of San Fran Business . . . . | *33480*
MR David G—Roan'95 . . . . |

Gulick DR & MRS C Richard (Nancy J Susman) Mo'66.Cy.W'minster'66
☎ (314) 991-1915 . . 22 Upper Ladue Rd, St Louis, MO *63124*

Gullen DR & MRS David J (Mary E Dawson) | ☎ (602) 947-0929
V'69.P'70 . . . . | 6040 E Calle Rosa,
MISS Amy E . . . . | Scottsdale, AZ
MR Matthew D . . . . | *85251*

Gummere MR & MRS F Barton (McWilliam—Claire Miller)
Tcy.Yh.Hav'32 . . of
☎ (803) 722-0536 . . 61 1-4 S Battery Place, Charleston, SC *29401*
☎ (803) 837-3955 . . Moss Creek Plantation, Cottage III,
Devils Elbow Lane, Hilton Head Island, SC *29926*

Gummere MR & MRS Francis B JR (Judith M Beebe) Sth'60.Ty'61
☎ (847) 234-3100 . . 213 Ascot Court, Lake Bluff, IL *60044*

Gummere MR & MRS Richard M (Janet B Kelly) | ☎ (301) 934-1633
AmU'77.Geo'71 . . . . | Neglect Farm,
JUNIORS MISS Margaret B—at Episcopal Sch . . . . | PO Box 2215,
JUNIORS MR George W K . . . . | La Plata, MD *20646*

Gummere MR & MRS William 3d (Jane E Priory) | ☎ (201) 891-6477
StJos'63 . . . . | 467 Blue Hill Terr,
MISS Elizabeth A—at 41 Surrey St, Brighton, | Franklin Lakes, NJ
MA *02135* . . . . | *07417*
MISS Megan . . . . |
MR William 4th . . . . |
MR Joseph P . . . . |

Gummey MR & MRS Charles F (Joan D Fairman) | ☎ (610) 388-6781
Wil. . . . . | Hickory Hill Rd,
MR Michael F—Getty'94 . . . . | Box 324,
 | Mendenhall, PA
 | *19357*

Gummey MISS Lea C (Charles F) . . . . Married at Wilmington, DE
Quimby MR Steven H (late Harry A) . . . . Jun 22'96

Gumprecht MRS Nicholas W (Potter—Pamela Howard) SL'63 . . . . 　☎ (516) 922-7784
　MR Ian N H—at N'eastern . . . . 　"Centre Court"
　JUNIORS MR Christopher B—at Pomfret. . . . . 　510 Centre Island
　MR Jack R H Potter—at Union Coll. . . . . 　Rd, Oyster Bay, NY
　　　　　　　　　　　　　　　　　　　　　　　11771
Gumprecht MR Nicholas W—Ny.S.
　327 Centre Island Rd, Oyster Bay, NY *11771*
Gund MR & MRS Graham de Conde (Ann S Landreth)
　Wheat'68.Sm.Cy.Ken'63.H.'68.H'69
　☎ (617) 491-8080 . . 25 Craigie St, Cambridge, MA *02138*
Gundlach MR Andrew S . . see J French 3d
Gundlach MISS Annabelle K . . see J French 3d
Gunn MR & MRS Robert G (Carrie G Newton) A.Rr.Sar.Dar.U'39 . . of
　☎ (210) 824-8701 . . 225 Westover Rd, San Antonio, TX *78209*
　☎ (210) 238-4044 . . "Windy Hill" FM 1340, Hunt, TX *78024*
Gunnell MR & MRS Bruce C (Virginia A Burt)
　Banbury Cross Farm, PO Box 875, Middleburg, VA *20118*
Gunnell MRS Jane R (Benoit—Amory—Jane R 　☎ (540) 687-6864
　Gunnell) . . . . 　Banbury Cross
　MISS J Page . . . . 　Farm,
　　　　　　　　　　　　　　　　　　　　　　　PO Box 271,
　　　　　　　　　　　　　　　　　　　　　　　Middleburg, VA
　　　　　　　　　　　　　　　　　　　　　　　20118
Gunnell MR T Nelson
　☎ (540) 687-4168 . . Covington Farm, PO Box 2061, Middleburg, VA *20118*
Gunness MR & MRS Robert Charles (Beverly Osterberger)
　LSU'36.Bhm.Mass'32.Mit'34.Mit'36
　☎ (619) 756-3577 . . 16721 La Gracia, Box 538, Rancho Santa Fe, CA *92067*
Gunnin MISS Lisa C . . see MISS S E Kernan
Gunson MR & MRS Leo J JR (Rose E Carnevali) 　☎ (415) 322-4652
　Rcp.Pa'50 . . . . 　35 Greenoaks St,
　MISS Jane V . . . . 　Atherton, CA *94027*
　MISS Elizabeth F . . . .
　MISS Mary R . . . .
　MR Leo J 3d . . . .
　MR John C . . . .
Gunter MRS Davis (Alice R Davis)
　3219 Audubon Rd, Montgomery, AL *36106*
Gunter MRS W Davis (Wightman—Taylor—Margaret Cabell) Cy.
　☎ (314) 994-0231 . . 14 Upper Price Rd, St Louis, MO *63132*
Gunter MR William A 4th—Ala'80
　☎ (334) 264-2778 . . 1110 Westmoreland Av, Montgomery, AL *36106*
Guntharp MR Alfred E JR . . see MRS E Van R Stires
Gunther MR & MRS Charles F (Patricia E Darrell) 　☎ (415) 563-5242
　L.Stan'50 . . . . 　2739 Broderick St,
　MR Harrison D . . . . 　San Francisco, CA
　　　　　　　　　　　　　　　　　　　　　　　94123
Gunther MR Jack D JR—Ln.Rc.Plg.P'63.Cl'66
　☎ (212) 831-2020 . . 1225 Park Av, New York, NY *10128-1758*
Gurin MR & MRS Richard S (Susan P Swartz) Ham'62 ⚓
　☎ (610) 346-8913 . . 2146 California Rd, Richlandtown, PA *18955*
Gurnee MRS Walter S (Virginia L Flanders)
　☎ (516) 329-3506 . . 55 Mill Hill Lane, East Hampton, NY *11937*

Gurney MR William H JR—St . . .of
　☎ (561) 655-0976 . . 6 Via Vizcaya, Palm Beach, FL *33480*
　☎ (803) 723-0045 . . "Fern Court" 16 Atlantic St, Charleston, SC *29401*
Gustavson MR & MRS Richard E (Dyer—Eliza Ann 　☎ (617) 237-2216
　Tompkins) Wheat'64.Cy.Chi.Myf.Ncd.Dc. 　14 Sawyer Rd,
　Mich'62.Stan'63 . . . . 　Wellesley Hills, MA
　MISS Jennifer D—Ncd. . . . . 　*02181*
　MR Richard T—P'94—at Georgetown . . . .
Gutcheon MR David S . . see R M Clements JR
Guth MR & MRS John H J (Davidson—Polly Wheeler) Cly.Chi.H'48 . . of
　☎ (212) 570-6890 . . 1 E 66 St, New York, NY *10021*
　☎ (607) 962-2017 . . "Kalimera" 37 Spencer Hill Rd, Corning, NY *14830*
Guthans MR & MRS Robert A (Barbara A Taylor) Ala'54.At.Vmi'51
　☎ (334) 342-2248 . . 14 Kingsway, Mobile, AL *36608*
Guthans MR & MRS Robert A JR (Patricia L Turner) Ala'83.At.Van'81
　☎ (334) 344-7094 . . 113 Claridge Rd E, Mobile, AL *36608*
Guthans MASTER Robert Anthony 3d (Robert A JR) . . . . Born at Mobile, AL May 22'96
Guthrie MR & MRS Alexander D (Elizabeth J Ashcroft) Ariz'76
　☎ (203) 255-9404 . . 3022 Burr St, Fairfield, CT *06430*
Guthrie MR & MRS Henry B (Elizabeth C Archer) Sth'29.P'24.H'27
　☎ (914) 234-7346 . . 50 E Middle Patent Rd, Bedford, NY *10506*
Guthrie MRS Jo Carol (Blattner—Jurgensen—Jo Carol Guthrie) Nw'60.H'61
　☎ (212) 734-2527 . . 14 E 75 St, New York, NY *10021*
Guthrie MISS Jo Welton—Colby'88
　☎ (617) 566-2825 . . 144 Middlesex Rd, Apt 1, Chestnut Hill, MA *02167*
Guthrie MR & MRS Lucien S Yokana (Caroline E Wood) Ox'87.Un.Drew'78
　☎ (212) 289-2373 . . 1160 Fifth Av, Apt 506, New York, NY *10029*
Guthrie MR & MRS Nicholas D (Carol C Jones) 　☎ (203) 655-6231
　Sth'72.Cl'81.Y'65.H'69 . . . . 　2 Mystic Lane,
　JUNIORS MR Edward C—at Dartmouth . . . . 　Darien, CT *06820*
Guthrie DR & MRS Randolph H JR (Beatrice M 　of ☎ (307)733-0997
　Holden) K.Un.P'57.H'61 . . . . 　Box 25006, Jackson,
　MR Randolph H 3d . . . . 　WY *83001*
　MR Michael P . . . . 　☎ (212) 249-0420
　JUNIORS MR Philip H . . . . 　15 E 74 St,
　　　　　　　　　　　　　　　　　　　　　　　New York, NY
　　　　　　　　　　　　　　　　　　　　　　　10021
　　　　　　　　　　　　　　　　　　　　　　　☎ (011-39-41)
　　　　　　　　　　　　　　　　　　　　　　　52-38-302
　　　　　　　　　　　　　　　　　　　　　　　"La Casetta Rossa"
　　　　　　　　　　　　　　　　　　　　　　　2887 San Marco,
　　　　　　　　　　　　　　　　　　　　　　　30124 Venice, Italy
Guthrie MR & MRS Robert D (Rogers—Tremaine—Beatrice R Brown) Cly.Mich'36
　☎ (305) 367-3205 . . 100 Anchor Dv, Box 49, Key Largo, FL *33037*
Gutierrez MR Alejandro . . see J A Caldwell IV
Gutierrez MR Christian A . . see J A Caldwell IV
Gutierrez JUNIORS MR David . . see J A Caldwell IV
Gutterson MR & MRS Herbert L (Johnson—Dora D 　☎ (508) 257-6338
　P Becker) Wms'37 . . . . 　"Eastward"
　MISS Dorrit C—Rol'76 . . . . 　93 Baxter Rd,
　　　　　　　　　　　　　　　　　　　　　　　Box 106, Siasconset,
　　　　　　　　　　　　　　　　　　　　　　　MA *02564*

Guy MRS Benjamin W 2d (Arnold—Julia T Matheson) Cvc.Gi.Sl.
☎ (202) 338-0677 . . 4808 Dexter St NW, Washington, DC 20007
Guy MR & MRS Benjamin W 3d (Martha R Baldwin) Sth'73.Cvc.Wms'69
☎ (508) 636-8963 . . 7 Charles St, PO Box 0092, Westport Point,
MA 02791-0092
Guy MISS Valerie M—Me. . . . . | ☎ (610) LA5-1074
MISS Althea S . . . . | 1128 Ashbridge Rd,
| Rosemont, PA
| 19010-2807
Guy MR & MRS William B JR (Klinefelter—Mary B Forman)
Cy.Md.Cw.Cc.Wt.Va'41
☎ (410) 235-7877 . . 4300 Rugby Rd, Baltimore, MD 21210
Guyer DR Grant P—Wms'77.Ox'85
1009 NW Hoyt St, Apt 201, Portland, OR 97209
Gwathmey MR & MRS Archibald L (Anne L McNiff) Pars'81.H'74
☎ (314) 432-7247 . . 26 Briarcliff, St Louis, MO 63124
Gwathmey MRS Gaines JR (McGrail—Anne L | ☎ (516) 626-0373
Jones) Pr. | 160 Hegeman's
MISS Anne L McGrail—at ☎ (561) 624-1723 | Lane, Glen Head,
707 St Giles Court, Palm Beach Gardens, FL | NY 11545
33418 . . . . |
MR Thomas H McGrail—at |
☎ (212) 628-5838 . . 52 E 78 St, New York, |
NY 10021 . . . . |
Gwathmey MRS Rachel P (Rachel M Parker) . . . . Died May 8'96
Gwinn MR David M—Rd.R.Pe.Me.Rc.Fi.
☎ (610) 645-8860 . . 1400 Waverly Rd, Blair 210, Gladwyne, PA 19035
Gwinn MR & MRS Richard H (Lickdyke—Brita | ☎ (610) 688-4878
Patten) Me.Rc.Cry.Gm.Y.'60 . . . . | 288 Hares Lane,
MR David J P . . . . | Radnor, PA 19087
Gwinn DR Ryder P (Richard H) . . . . Married
Barron MISS Eileen . . . . Dec 30'95
Gwynn MRS Charles G (Ribbel—Mary H Fitzpatrick) Cal'30.Ncd.
☎ (415) 885-1332 . . 1400 Geary Blvd, Apt 1401, San Francisco,
CA 94109

H

Haack MR & MRS Frederick L (Hobson—Ann Kendall) Ri.Cly.Wyo'48
☎ (504) 522-6622 . . 1224 Jackson Av, New Orleans, LA 70130
Haack MR & MRS Frederick L 3d (Mary Lita Kean)
LakeF'77.Ph.Gm.Shcc.LakeF'79
☎ (610) 964-9464 . . 865 Box Hill Lane, Radnor, PA 19087
Haas MRS Edward T (Haas—Dean—Syida Griggs) Sfy.
☎ (415) 673-2562 . . 2120 Steiner Blvd, San Francisco, CA 94115
Haas MR Edward T—Cp.SantaB'70.SantaB'71 ⚓
☎ (805) 968-7534 . . 6882 Trigo Rd, Goleta, CA 93117
Haas MR & MRS George C (Dorothy Marston) Myf.Yn.Y'42
☎ (561) 967-1923 . . Windswept Farm, 4301 Polo Rd, Lake Worth,
FL 33467
Haas MRS Henry P (Dora P Smith) Ala'51.Dar.Ncd.
☎ (334) 277-3111 . . 1615 Pineneedle Rd, Montgomery, AL 36106
Haas MR & MRS J Sanders (Betty K Hardeman)
Okla'45.Cw.Myf.Ncd.Wms'45
☎ (904) 668-6825 . . 8999 Winged Foot Dv, Tallahassee, FL 32312

Haas MRS Josephine Baum (Josephine Baum) W'burn'36
☎ (415) 897-4021 . . 568 McClay Rd, Novato, CA 94947
Haas DR & MRS Robert G (Sheila N Young) Montevallo'90.Ala'85
☎ (205) 871-3110 . . 2728 Cherokee Rd, Mountain Brook, AL 35216
Haas MRS Walter A (Evelyn Danzig) Wheat'39.Fmy.Pcu.
☎ (415) 921-2024 . . 2666 Broadway St, San Francisco, CA 94115
Haas MR & MRS William W (Suzanne K Grau) . . . . . | ☎ (415) 424-4442
MR James W—Stan'64.Cl'69—at | 501 Portola Rd,
☎ (415) 285-5048 . . 163 Prospect St, | Box 8019,
San Francisco, CA 94110 . . . . | Portola Valley, CA
| 94025
Haase MISS Debra L . . see E J Parker 3d
Habenicht MR & MRS Frederick K JR (Rebecca A | ☎ (847) 864-0166
Sample) MtH'58.Wes'52 | 2529 Orrington Av,
MISS Helen H | Evanston, IL 60201
MISS Gratia M . . . . |
MR Fritz |
MR William L |
Haberstock MR & MRS R Alan (Mary-Emory | ☎ (203) 762-7991
Eysmans) Cr'55 | ''Laurel Hill''
MR Alan E—StLaw'85.Y'90 . . . . | 207 Old Boston Rd,
| Wilton, CT 06897
Hachman MR & MRS Timothy J (Judith K Musto) | ☎ (209) 465-2270
Cal'65.Bhm.Fr.Cal'63.Hast'66 . . . . | 3621 Country Club
MISS Carter K—Cal'91—at ☎ (415) 563-6562 | Blvd, Stockton, CA
1245 California St, Apt 402, San Francisco, CA | 95204
94109 . . . . |
MR Timothy D M—Cp.Cal'95—at |
☎ (415) 386-7471 . . 3010 Turk St, |
San Francisco, CA 94118 . . . . |
Hacker MR & MRS A Heathcote 3d (Hazel Nettell) | ☎ (610) 527-4592
Syr'62 | 145 Morlyn Av,
MISS Emily P | Bryn Mawr, PA
MISS Theodora S . . . . | 19010
MR Arthur H 4th . . . . |
Hacker MRS William (Florence L Wood) Ncd.
☎ (610) 645-8854 . . 1400 Waverly Rd, Blair 127, Gladwyne,
PA 19035-1254
Hackett MR & MRS B Peterson (Barbara J Peterson) Wells'68
☎ (212) 838-0875 . . 570 Park Av, New York, NY 10021
Hackett MR & MRS George H (Maynard—Emily McL Merryman) D.H'43
☎ (617) 326-0488 . . 15 School St, Dedham, MA 02026
Hackett MRS Montague H (Flavia A Riggio)
☎ (212) 737-6140 . . 19 E 72 St, New York, NY 10021-4145
Hackett MR Montague H JR—Rc.Bcs.Ng.So.P'54.H'59
☎ (212) 838-0875 . . 550 Park Av, New York, NY 10021
Hackett MR & MRS Randall W (McLean—Eleanor G Cumings)
Rc.Ri.Cly.H'57.Cl'59
☎ (212) 734-1089 . . 150 E 73 St, New York, NY 10021
Hackett MR & MRS Robert J (E Anita Carlile) | ☎ (602) 254-8038
Cl'65.Cl'67.Rut'64.Duke'67 . . . . | 1834 Palmcroft Dv
MR Robert J JR . . . . | NE, Phoenix, AZ
JUNIORS MISS Kathryn M . . . . | 85007
JUNIORS MR John P 3d . . . . |

Hackl MR & MRS George C S (Ann S Whitman) Sth'58.P'55 . . . . | "Tristram Copp Farm" Ledge Hill Rd, Box 143, Center Tuftonboro, NH *03816*
MISS Diane S—at 585 Pika Rd, Boulder, CO *80302* . . . .
MISSES Yvonne E & Katherine D—at
☎ (609) 397-0684 . . "Cricket Hill" 118 Sandy Ridge, Mt Airy Rd, Stockton, NJ *08559* . . . . . .

Hackley MRS Helena J (May—Helena Johnson) Pr.
☎ (212) 737-8614 . . 784 Park Av, New York, NY *10021*

Hackman DR & MRS John E (Jeanne F Leighton) StTer'62.Cin'63.Ky'70 . . . . | of ☎ (334)834-2482 3230 Thomas Av, Montgomery, AL *36106*
MISS Jennifer J—at Birmingham, AL . . . .
MR Jonathan L—at San Francisco, CA . . . . | Hickory Grove, Ramer, AL *36069*

Haddad MR & MRS Robert M (Helen C Rogerson) Pitt'52.Mich'54.H'64 . . . . | 240 E 47 St, Apt 36B, New York, NY *10017*
MISS Leila H—H'88—at 34 Spring St, Apt 3, Somerville, MA *02143* . . . .
MISS Josette H—Cr'90 . . . .
MR George R . . . .

Hadden DR & MRS David Rodney (Margaret H Ledford) Cal'27.H'31
☎ (916) 333-1988 . . 8260A H'way 193, Garden Valley, CA *95633*

Hadden MR & MRS Hamilton (Sarah M Russell) Rc.Pr.Mb.StA.Cly.H'37
☎ (516) 921-4764 . . 210 Brookville Rd, Muttontown, Glen Head, NY *11545*

Hadden MRS John A JR (Elaine Grasselli) V'53.Un.Cv.It.
☎ (216) 371-3082 . . 2507 Stratford Rd, Cleveland Heights, OH *44118*

Hadden DR & MRS John W (Elba L Más) Y'61 . . . . | of ☎ (813)253-5350 824 S Orleans Av, Tampa, FL *33606-2939*
MR Paul J . . . .
☎ (516) 367-3502 428 Harbor Rd, Cold Spring Harbor, NY *11724*

Hadden MR & MRS John W 2d (Victoria S Hillebrand) Pars'95.Tul'91 . . of
☎ (617) 661-0608 . . 6 Soldiers Field Park, Apt 603, Boston, MA *02163*
☎ (516) 692-6319 . . "Laurel Brake" 428 Harbor Rd, Cold Spring Harbor, NY *11724*

Haddow MR & MRS Robert S (Virginia M Dillingham) StA.Ncd.Stan'45 . . . . | 61 Sherwood Av, Greenwich, CT *06831*
MISS Susan H . . . .

Hadley MRS Willis D (Jacqueline B Jones) Cy.Nd . . .of
☎ (314) 843-4541 . . Box 22028, 12255 Hadley Hill Rd, St Louis, MO *63127*
☎ (561) 243-0523 . . "Jamaica Square" 1111 N Ocean Blvd, Delray Beach, FL *33483*

Haebler MR Theodore—Rm.
PO Box 444, Rumson, NJ *07760*

Haff MR C Barse . . . . Died May 5'96

Haff MRS C Barse (Elizabeth W Ely)
☎ (860) 434-2482 . . 2 Littlefield Lane, Old Lyme, CT *06371*

Haffenreffer MR & MRS John D (Laura H Garesché) Roan'76.Cy.Dth'76
☎ (314) 993-9234 . . 12 Cricklewood Place, St Louis, MO *63131*

Haffenreffer MR Theodore C 3d—Wash'72
☎ (207) 767-0072 . . 44 Cottage Farms Rd, Cape Elizabeth, ME *04107*

Haffner MR & MRS Charles C 3d (Anne P Clark) Rc.Cho.Sc.Cas.Wa.Y'50 . . . . | ☎ (312) 664-2703 1524 N Astor St, Chicago, IL *60610*
MR Edward C . . . .
MR William C . . . .

Haffner MR & MRS David M (Stephens—Mary Jane Samuel) Colg'65 . . . . | ☎ (314) 993-4917 4 Black Creek Lane, St Louis, MO *63124*
JUNIORS MISS Lindsay M . . . .
JUNIORS MISS Alexandra P . . . .
MISS Laura L Stephens . . . .

Hafkenschiel DR & MRS Joseph H (Rush—Carol MacD Smith) Gm.M.Sfg.Swth'37.JHop'41
☎ (610) 688-1241 . . 870 Lesley Rd, Villanova, PA *19085-1118*

Hafter MR & MRS Jerome C (Jo Cille Dawkins) Belh'68.Rice'67.Ox'69.Y'72 . . . . | ☎ (601) 335-1806 316 S Broadway St, Greenville, MS *38701-4011*
JUNIORS MR Jerome B . . . .

Hagan MR & MRS John W (Alice N Neel) . . . . | ☎ (919) 688-5359 1023 Demerius St, Durham, NC *27701*
MR Brooks W—at U of NCar Chapel Hill . . . . .

Hagar MR & MRS George L (Kari Hanto) Buck'60.Wcc.Buck'59 . . . . | ☎ (610) 647-0582 459 Bair Rd, Berwyn, PA *19312*
MR G Gregory—Buck'90 . . . .

Hagen MR & MRS Lee R (Mary G Mead) Va'86.MontSt'75.Cl'95
☎ (609) 497-2943 . . 27 Armour Rd, Princeton, NJ *08540*

Hagen MR & MRS R Peter JR (Katharine Winthrop) Wh'lck'78.Les'84.Chi.USA'67.Stan'74
☎ (212) 472-9581 . . 25 East End Av, New York, NY *10028*

Hagenbuch MR John J—Bur.Pcu.P'74.Stan'78
☎ (415) 752-3673 . . 3673 Jackson St, San Francisco, CA *94118*

Hager MR & MRS August W 3d (Carolyn Naunheim) Mo'71.Cy.Mo'71 . . . . | ☎ (314) 994-3060 551 Barnes Rd, St Louis, MO *63124*
MISS Margaret D—at Rollins . . . .

Hager DR & MRS Edward B (Jane P Eastin) Swb'67.Hb.Aht'52.Wash'55 . . . . | Pinnacle Mountain Farms, South Lyndeborough, NH *03082*
MISS Katrina M . . . .
MR Edward C . . . .
JUNIORS MISS Jennifer P . . . .
JUNIORS MISS Jane W . . . .

Hager MR & MRS John H (Margaret D Chase) Wheat'63.Purd'58.H'60 . . . . | ☎ (804) 355-6210 4600 Sulgrave Rd, Richmond, VA *23221*
MR John V—at Hampden-Sydney . . . .
JUNIORS MR Henry C—at St Christopher's . . . . .

Haggie MR Michael R—Cr'78
3214 McGinnes Rd, Millington, MD *21651*

Haggin MR Ben Ali—Rc.Ng.So.T.Plg.ColC'56 . . . . | ☎ (212) 988-0871 200 E 78 St, New York, NY *10021*
MISS Leslie B—at ☎ (914) 351-4401 . . Box 568, Tuxedo Park, NY *10987* . . . .
MISS Terah W—at 1812 Delaware St, Berkeley, CA *94705* . . . .

Haggin MRS John Ben Ali (Norris—Naoma Donnelley) Ri.BtP.Evg.
☎ (561) 655-4005 . . 757 Island Dv, Palm Beach, FL *33480*

Hagin MR & MRS Robert L (M Lynn McCune) Cal'70.Gm.M.Ac.Cal'58.Cal'61.Cal'66 . . . . . . | ☎ (610) 896-8051 9 Tunbridge Circle, Haverford, PA *19041*
JUNIORS MISS Katherine C—at Agnes Irwin . . . .

Hagner MRS Alexander B (Salmon—Virginia T Peters)
☎ (202) 244-7121 . . 4307 Westover Place NW, Washington, DC *20016*

Hagner MRS Randall H JR (Sargent—Adlumia D Sterrett) Sl.Cvc.Mt.Ncd.
☎ (202) 966-0032 . . 3530 Springland Lane NW, Washington, DC *20008*

Hague REV & MRS William (Jane P Milliken) Geo'77.Ct.VaTheo'80
☎ (301) 949-2467 . . 3902 Everett St, Kensington, MD *20895*

Hahn MR & MRS Charles J (Anne H Davey) Sth'48.St.Ts.G.Buf.P'49.H'60
☎ (716) 885-4931 . . 70 Windsor Av, Buffalo, NY *14209*

Hahn DR & MRS Davis M (Anne R Peter)
Dunb'69.Md'71.Md'87.Cy.JHop'67.Va'71
☎ (410) 321-4573 . . 30 Woodward Lane, Lutherville, MD *21093*

Hahn MRS Frederic H JR (Ann P Deely) Lx.
PO Box 541, Lee, MA *01238*

Haig GEN (RET) & MRS Alexander M JR (Patricia Fox) | ☎ (202) 429-9788
Km.USA'47.Geo'61 . . . . | 6041 Crimson Court,
MISS Barbara E . . . . | McLean, VA *22101*

Haight MR & MRS Charles S JR (Mary Jane Peightal) V'53.Chr.Y'52.Y'55
500 Pearl St, New York, NY *10007*

Haight MR Daniel L . . see C G Jameson

Haight MR David C . . see N H Miller

Haight MR Edward A SR—Wis'31.H'34
☎ (847) 432-4034 . . 364 Central Av, Highland Park, IL *60035*

Haight MRS G Winthrop (Mary L Uppercu) Cly.
☎ (212) UN1-6292 . . 155 E 82 St, New York, NY *10028*

Haight MR & MRS George I 2d (Eleanor G Stubbs) | ☎ (619) 758-1455
Stph'60.Ch'62 . . . . | 1417 Foothill Dv,
MISS Elizabeth A—Ariz'92—at | Vista, CA *92084*
☎ (415) 647-4966 . . 3945—20 St, Apt 2,
San Francisco, CA *94114* . . . .

Haight MR & MRS John McV JR (Deborah D Smith) V'45.Pn.P'40.Nw'53
☎ (610) 865-1466 . . 55 E Church St, Bethlehem, PA *18018*

Haight MR Jonathon O . . see C G Jameson

Haight MR & MRS Sherman P JR (Margaret E Grahame)
☎ (540) 338-3640 . . ''Thunder Run'' PO Box 286, Hamilton, VA *20159*

Haigler MR & MRS Charles Brightman JR (Susan | of ☎ (334)227-8886
McC Foster) Ala'61.Dar.Ala'57 . . . . | 1221 Old Fort Rd,
MR Charles B 3d . . . . | Ft Deposit, AL
36032
☎ (334) 961-7557
''Blue Bayou''
30498 Magnolia St,
Perdido Beach, AL
30650

Haigney MR & MRS Dayton P 3d (Alexandra K Deering)
Scripps'85.FIT'88.StLaw'84.W&L'87
☎ (212) 535-6742 . . 501 E 87 St, Apt 1B, New York, NY *10128*

Hailand MR & MRS Arthur G JR (Mildred Bunn) | ☎ (847) 234-2578
Cho.On.Sr.Cas.Ny. | 10 S Green Bay Rd,
MR Jeffress B—at 38 Willow Hill, St Louis, MO | Lake Forest, IL
63124 . . . . | *60045*

Hailand MR & MRS Arthur G 3d (Rebecca C Howe) Rol'78.Cy.Ny.LakeF'74
☎ (314) 993-6919 . . 22 Gouvenor Lane, St Louis, MO *63124*

Haines MRS Charles H (Margery Speakman) . . . . Died at
Philadelphia, PA Feb 7'96

Haines MR Charles H . . . . Died at
Philadelphia, PA Mch 20'96

Haines MR & MRS George R (Barbara Williamson) Pa'39
☎ (215) OL9-3799 . . 1747 Edgehill Rd, Abington, PA *19001*

Haines MRS Harold A JR (Emily L Richards) Me.Ac.Ncd.
PO Box 747, Buckingham, PA *18912*

Haines MRS J Barr (Isobel Y Sheppard)
☎ (412) 741-4433 . . 33 Woodland Rd, Sewickley, PA *15143*

Haines DR & MRS James B (Martha M Scull) | ☎ (412) 761-9221
Sth'62.Br'65.Dth'62.Br'64.Pitt'75 ⚓ . . . . | 6820 Prospect Av,
MR Thomas W—Dth'90.Cal'94—at | Pittsburgh, PA
☎ (206) 726-0499 . . 1547 Seventeenth Av E, | *15202-2016*
Seattle, WA *98112* . . . . |

Haines MR R Montgomery—P'36 . . . . | ☎ (215) 242-0873
REV Stephen D—Camb'71—at 3 Lyndhurst | 7703 McCallum St,
Square, London SE15, England . . . . | Philadelphia, PA
19118

Haines MR T F Davies—Y'24
☎ (212) 751-5393 . . 139 E 63 St, New York, NY *10021*

Haines MR & MRS Thomas D (Stephany Warick) | ☎ (718) UL5-6987
V'61.Chr.Snc.Y'59 . . . . | 77 State St,
MR Samuel H—StAndr'95 . . . . | Brooklyn, NY *11201*
MR Thomas D JR—at Princeton . . . . |

Haines MR & MRS William W (Frances S Tuckerman)
☎ (714) 450-5392 . . The White Sands, 7450 Olivetas Av, La Jolla,
CA *92037-4902*

Hains MISS Mary J
☎ (202) 541-0419 . . 6200 Oregon Av NW, Apt 419, Washington,
DC *20015*

Halaby MRS Margaret A (Margaret E Adam)
☎ (520) 881-2861 . . 207 Camino Del Norte, Tucson, AZ *85716*

Haladey MR & MRS Edward G (Marguerite E | ☎ (914) 723-8725
Palmer) Ws'52.Cl'61.Bklyn'53.Y'56.Cl'64 . . . . | 4 Southwoods Lane,
MISS Diana M—Dth'89 . . . . | Scarsdale, NY
MR Thomas P—Ala'90 . . . . | *10583*

Halberstadt MR & MRS Robert LeC (Eda C Nelson)
Okla'34.Cspa.Cw.Rv.Wt.Ll.Fw.Ncd.Dll.Dar.Hav'30
☎ (215) 575-9583 . . Logan Square E, Apt 1403, 2 Franklin Town Blvd,
Philadelphia, PA *19103*

Halbkat MRS James E (Ballinger—Dorothy A Coon)
☎ (704) 697-1994 . . 108 Balsam Rd, Hendersonville, NC *28792*

Halbreich MR & MRS Jeremy Lynn (Nancy D Strauss) Tex'71.H'74
☎ (214) 373-9779 . . 9700 Inwood Rd, Dallas, TX *75220*

Hale MR & MRS Bradley H (Mary E Henderson) Miss'85.Cy.LakeF'75
☎ (617) 237-2650 . . 8 Sumner Rd, Wellesley Hills, MA *02181*

Hale MISS Elizabeth—Wheat'64.Cl'70 . . . . | ☎ (202) 337-9721
MISS Abigail G—Vt'76—at ☎ (802) 658-6047 | 4020 Beecher St
73 Pitkin St, Burlington, VT *05401* . . . . | NW, Washington,
MR Matthew JR—H'66—at ☎ (703) 998-6149 | DC *20007*
4906—29 Rd, Apt A2, Alexandria, VA *22206* . . |

Hale MR & MRS F Sheffield (Elizabeth W Medlin)
David'81.Cc.Cw.Ncd.Ga'82.Va'85 . . at
☎ (404) 350-0847 . . 47 Brighton Rd NE, Atlanta, GA *30309*
☎ (334) 628-6096 . . Paulling Place, Thomaston, AL *36783*

Hale MR & MRS George N JR (Ann A Thoron) Yn.Ch'44.Y'48
☎ (415) 673-5405 . . 1800 Gough St, San Francisco, CA *94109*

Hale MR & MRS Hamilton (Hale—Anne L Pattee)
see Dilatory Domiciles

Hale MISS Joanna M
☎ (508) 369-1070 . . 167 Monument St, Concord, MA *01742*

Hale MR & MRS Nathan (Barbara A Skluth) | ☎ (212) 924-2578
BMr'71.Un.Ln.Plg.H'52.................. | 175 W 13 St,
JUNIORS MR Nathan—at Phillips Andover ..... | New York, NY
| *10011*

Hale MRS Newton J (Beatrice Caughey) Stan'22.Bur.
☎ (415) 342-3297 . . 45 Downey Way, Hillsborough, CA *94010*

Hale MRS Prentis Cobb (Gigante—Minnelli—Denise Radosavljevic)
Pcu.Bur.
☎ (415) 441-8295 . . 945 Green St, San Francisco, CA *94133*

Hale MR R Walter 3d—Plg.P'66.Pa'70 .... | ☎ (615) 297-1176
MISS Virginia P—Smu'92—at SMU Grad ..... | 426 Ellendale Av,
MR Patrick S—at SMU .... | Nashville, TN *37205*

Hale MR & MRS Richard T JR (Eleanor A Gibson) | ☎ (410) 377-4240
V'70.Pa'74.Md.B.Elk.Mv.Y'68.Pa'71 .... | 205 Woodbrook
MISS Delia T .... | Lane, Baltimore,
JUNIORS MR Richard T 3d .... | MD *21212*

Hale MR Stephen F—Ken'83
☎ (314) 231-0877 . . 1925 S 9 St, St Louis, MO *63104*

Hale MR & MRS Thomas H (Nancy Brooks) | of ☎ (303)839-5530
Card'60.Minn'68 .... | 930 Humboldt St,
MR Mark C—at Wittenberg .... | Apt 4, Denver, CO
JUNIORS MR Christopher R F—at Pomfret ...... | *80218-3518*
| ☎ (719) 539-4253
| ''Can Doo''
| 604 Crestone Av,
| Salida, CO *81201*

Hale VERY REV & MRS William M (Helen H Frost)
Sth'57.Ncd.Br'49.Gen'lTheo'54
☎ (603) 876-4407 . . ''Hillside'' PO Box 368, 59 Frost Hill Rd,
Marlborough, NH *03455*

Hale MR William Manning JR—J&W'82
☎ (207) 892-7486 . . PO Box 1403, Portland, ME *04104*

Hall DR Arthur P—H'47.Cl'52
☎ (617) 332-2064 . . 133 Dudley Rd, Newton Center, MA *02159*

Hall MRS Barbara G (Barbara K Granbery) FairD'86 | ☎ (415) 941-5954
MISS Elizabeth W—HWSth'90—at Wash'n U | 12864 Viscaino Rd,
Sch of Arch .... | Los Altos Hills, CA
MR J Douglass—Cal'93 .... | *94022*

Hall MASTER Benjamin Gregory (g—Stephen Galatti) .... Born at
Northampton, MA Jan 27'94

Hall MR Bradford JR—Cal'79
☎ (818) 795-0850 . . 773 S Oakland Av, Pasadena, CA *91106*

Hall MR & MRS Brooks JR (Carole Butler) DU'76.DU'76
☎ (405) 840-5300 . . 6917 NW Grand Blvd, Oklahoma City, OK *73116*

Hall MR & MRS C Barrows (Eleanor L Crosby) | The Cliff,
Ty'73.Unn.Pa'69.P'76 .... | 11 Carmichael Rd,
JUNIORS MISS Letitia L—at Groton .... | Bombay 400 026,
JUNIORS MR C Barrows JR—at Groton .... | India

Hall MR Cameron . . see MISS L de Bretteville

Hall MASTER Carson Charles Donnell (g—Stephen Galatti) ..... Born at
Lexington, MA Sep 25'94

Hall MISS Catherine E—Dar.Lm.
☎ (201) 731-9052 . . 242 Clarken Dv, West Orange, NJ *07052*

Hall MR & MRS Charles S (Elsie P French) Br'77.Cyb.DU'72
☎ (207) 775-6727 . . 256 W Concord St, Portland, ME *04103*

Hall MISS (DR) Christiana E Penn-Gaskell— | ☎ (505) 292-3281
SCar'84.AugCol'88.GaMed'95 | 14108 Marquette Dv
MR Peter T—Rich'88—at ☎ (610) 458-8420 | NE, Albuquerque,
191C Conestoga Rd, Glenmoore, PA *19343* .... | NM *87123*

Hall MR & MRS Christopher S (Lisa M Vasconcellos)
☎ (919) 481-9180 . . 210 Tapestry Terr, Cary, NC *27511*

Hall MRS Craig M (Alice G Carnett) Skd'65.Pe.Ac.. | ☎ (610) 828-4583
MISS Diana L—at ☎ (215) 545-3670 | 1008 Trinity Lane,
1924 Waverly St, Philadelphia, PA *19146* ..... | Gulph Mills, PA
| *19428*

Hall MR David W—Bhm.Cp.Cal'47
☎ (415) 435-4201 . . 8 Cliff Rd, PO Box 92, Belvedere, CA *94920*

Hall MRS de Léon (Irma de Léon y Zayas)
☎ (508) 748-1226 . . 46 Piney Point Rd, Marion, MA *02738*

Hall MR & MRS Donald L (Brittingham—Susan C | ☎ (803) 266-7791
Burr) GreenMt'77.AugCol'67 .... | 716 Springfield Rd,
JUNIORS MISS Colleen T Brittingham .... | Williston, SC
| *29853-1248*

Hall MR & MRS Eben C (Jane E Terhune) V'43.Pn.P'39 . . of
☎ (561) 234-4386 . . 300 Harbour Dv, Apt 204A, Vero Beach, FL *32963*
☎ (401) 635-8918 . . ''Red Rock'' 102 Round Pond Rd, Little Compton,
RI *02837*

Hall DR & MRS Edward C 4th (Francine S Cigole) | ☎ (513) 321-9837
Miami'70.OState'73 .... | 4 Handasyde Lane,
MISS Susan van N—at 1401 Broadview, | Cincinnati, OH
Columbus, OH *43212* .... | *45208*
MISS Sarah C ....
JUNIORS MISS Betsy F ....

Hall MISS Elizabeth B—SL'88 . . see B G Waters 3d

Hall MISS Eloise Holly (Metzger—Eloise Holly Hall) Loy'86
☎ (410) 472-9155 . . ''Dogwood Cottage'' 15132 Wheeler Lane, Sparks,
MD *21152*

Hall MRS Eloise Joy S (Todd—Eloise Joy Sheaffer)
☎ (910) 295-5306 . . ''Maythorn Cottage'' Box 1222, Pinehurst,
NC *28374*

Hall MR & MRS Elton W (Jennifer S McCormick) | ☎ (508) 993-4198
RSage'69.Ty'66.Del'68 .... | 167 Bakerville Rd,
MR Chandler W—at Cornell .... | South Dartmouth,
| MA *02748*

Hall MRS F Bailey (Josephine B Dawes) SL'39.Cly.Ncd . . .of
☎ (201) 569-1362 . . 275 Engle St, Englewood, NJ *07631*
☎ (860) 542-5883 . . Golf Dv, Norfolk, CT *06058*

Hall MR & MRS Frederick G 2d (Priscilla A Bohlin)
☎ (617) 631-7495 . . 9 Goodwins Court, Marblehead, MA *01945*

Hall MRS Garrison K (Betty A Jensen) Bost'51.Ey.
☎ (617) 631-4277 . . Dock Ledge, Marblehead, MA *01945*

Hall MR & MRS George G (Betty L Rohde) Cal'45.Bhm.Tcy.Cal'49
☎ (510) 254-5393 . . 121 Van Ripper Lane, Orinda, CA *94563*

Hall MR & MRS George H (Smith—Dunn—Nancy M Houser)
Cy.Wash'32.Cl'33
☎ (314) 862-0856 . . 625 S Skinker Blvd, St Louis, MO *63105*

Hall MR & MRS Gordon B 3d (Laura C Weyher) NCar'82.Cly.Rol'81
☎ (212) 360-6336 . . 175 E 96 St, Apt 28G, New York, NY *10128*

Hall MR Gregory J
☎ (212) 674-7481 . . 345 E 18 St, New York, NY *10003*

Hall MR H Seymour JR—Unn.
☎ (540) 253-9888 . . September House Farm, Middleburg, VA *20118*

Hall MR Ian de Bretteville . . see MISS L de Bretteville
Hall MRS J Cruickshank (Joy Cruickshank)
  ☎ (011-52-642) 80052 . . C Juarez 34, 85760 Alamos, Sonora, Mexico
Hall MR & MRS James L JR (Barbara M Bates) | ☎ (415) 751-6369
Sfg.Pcu.Fr.Stan'42.Stan'45 . . . . | 218—28 Av,
  MISS Susan B . . . . | San Francisco, CA
    | 94121
Hall MR & MRS James M JR (Louise S Hall) Ty'72 . . | ☎ (513) 745-0087
  MISS Katherine C . . . . | 10043 Wimbledon
  JUNIORS MR James M 3d . . . . | Court, Cincinnati,
  JUNIORS MR Alexander G . . . . | OH 45242
Hall MISS Joan . . see J M Degener
Hall MR & MRS John H (Erika E M Pick) Unn.Chr.Mt.Snc.Cw.Wms'49
  ☎ (203) 661-9655 . . 182 Otter Rock Dv, Greenwich, CT 06830
Hall DR John H JR—HampSydney'37.Temp'41 . . . . | ☎ (610) MU8-4453
  MISS Cynthia M . . . . | 604 General Scott
    | Rd, Wayne, PA
    | 19087
Hall MR & MRS John L 2d (Ann S Tuckerman) | ☎ (617) 277-5950
ColbyS'68.Ec.Cy.Myc.Sm.Bost'65 . . . . | 85 Sears Rd,
  MISS Emily B—Mid'89 . . . . | Brookline, MA
  MISS Daphne—Vt'91 . . . . | 02146
  MISS Sarah—at Middlebury . . . . |
  JUNIORS MISS Ashley—at Middlesex . . . . |
  JUNIORS MR Jake . . . . |
Hall MR & MRS John M (Jane B Shiverick) Sbc.Sm.Cy.My.Y'32.H'35
  ☎ (617) 277-7693 . . 157 Clyde St, Chestnut Hill, MA 02167
Hall MRS John M (Katherine H James) Cy . . .of
  ☎ (314) 997-6996 . . 31 Enfield Rd, St Louis, MO 63132
  ☎ (561) 231-2144 . . 251 Silver Moss Dv, John's Island, Vero Beach,
FL 32963
Hall MR & MRS Joseph L 5th (Frances J Kreger) | ☎ (513) 772-5812
Miami'70 . . . . | 885 Congress Av,
  MISS Page E . . . . | Glendale, OH 45246
  MISS Barbara M . . . . |
  JUNIORS MR Joseph L 6th . . . . |
Hall MR Julia T (Julia T McLane) Cly.
  ☎ (914) 677-9555 . . ''Schoonhoven'' RR 1, Box 133, Kennels Rd,
Millbrook, NY 12545
Hall MISS Margaret S—Briar'72.Dar.
see Dilatory Domiciles
Hall MRS Melville W (Jaffe—Evelyn Annenberg) B.BtP.K.Chr.Srb.Plg.Snc.
  ☎ (212) 838-8228 . . 640 Park Av, New York, NY 10021
Jan 1 . . ☎ (561) 844-1304 . . 241 El Dorado Lane, Palm Beach,
FL 33480
Hall MRS Nathaniel Ross (Mary E Taylor) SUNY'54.SUNY'62.Dar.
  ☎ (716) 756-5518 . . 9 Lamont Circle, Cortland, NY 13045
Hall MR & MRS Newell N (Jane N Gallagher) TyU'77.Bow'77.H'89
  ☎ (617) 698-1564 . . 215 Canton Av, Milton, MA 02186
Hall MR & MRS Nicholas H J (Mary Lou Mullen)
Geo'79.K.Cly.Ox'79.Ox'85
  ☎ (212) 249-7031 . . 21 E 67 St, New York, NY 10021
Hall MR & MRS Peter D (Alice A Fioramonti) Stan'70
12617 Lake Normandy Lane, Fairfax, VA 22030

Hall MR & MRS Philip von P (V Jane Price) . . . . | ☎ (314) 367-0064
  MISS Jane T—at ☎ (314) 721-6760 | 5101 Westminster
152 N Brentwood St, Clayton, MO 63105 . . . . . | Place, St Louis, MO
    | 63108
Hall MRS R Clifford (Elizabeth W de Bullet)
  ☎ (703) 549-4375 . . 316 Mansion Dv, Alexandria, VA 22302
Hall MR & MRS R Tucker (Dorothy C Hilbert) | *see*
V'55.VillaN'80.Hav'52 ⚓ . . . . | *Dilatory Domiciles*
  MR Philip H . . . . |
  MR Andrew W . . . . |
  MR Mark R . . . . |
Hall MRS Randolph F (Barclay—Lyda M Womelsdorf)
  ☎ (516) 283-0204 . . 66 Huntting St, Southampton, NY 11968
Hall MR & MRS Richard Loomer (Coles—Ethel S Febiger) Sm.Y'49
  ☎ (508) 526-1564 . . PO Box 144, Manchester, MA 01944-0144
Hall MRS Ridgway M (Lucy E Wayland) Ncd.
  ☎ (203) 488-4481 . . Evergreen Woods 364, 88 Notch Hill Rd,
North Branford, CT 06471-1853
Hall MR & MRS Ridgway M JR (Anne L Harken) | ☎ (202) 363-4229
V'65.Y'63.H'66 . . . . | 5025 Lowell St NW,
  MISS Anne M—at Oberlin . . . . | Washington, DC
  MR Ridgway H—at Santiago, Chile . . . . | 20016
  MR Alden W—at Minneapolis, MN . . . . |
Hall REV & MRS Robert C JR (Lenore B Patterson) Rv.JHop'51.Berk'68
  ☎ (804) 435-3536 . . ''Somerset'' Box 4865, White Stone, VA 22578
Hall MRS Robert Charles (Marian Gilmor Howard) Ncd.
  ☎ (410) 795-4535 . . Fairhaven A112, 7200 Third Av, Sykesville,
MD 21784
Hall MR & MRS Robert Townsend (Margaret Warner Kellogg)
DU'70.My.Msq.Pa'72
  ☎ (508) 526-7996 . . 22 Proctor St, Manchester, MA 01944
Hall MRS Rodney D (Carol Benedict) V'43
  ☎ (561) 231-0096 . . 300 Harbour Dv, Apt 305B, Vero Beach, FL 32963
Hall MR & MRS Roger B (Elizabeth C Nott) Swb'86.Denis'86
  ☎ (310) 271-4512 . . 456 S Doheny Dv, Beverly Hills, CA 90211
Hall MR & MRS Roger G (Katherine S Knight) | ☎ (215) 242-8224
Colby'58.Pc.R.NCar'47 . . . . | 224 W Willow
  MISS Mary Stockton . . . . | Grove Av,
  MR Alexander S . . . . | Philadelphia, PA
    | 19118
Hall MISS Rosalys Haskell
  ☎ (401) 846-7566 . . 6 Coddington St, Newport, RI 02840
Hall MASTER Ryan Tyler (g—Stephen Galatti) . . . . Born at
    Glen Cove, NY Aug 18'96
Hall MRS Stella E (Stella E Reeves) . . . . | ☎ (609) 466-1517
  MISS Lynne D . . . . | ''Justa Caixinha''
    | 225 Amwell Rd,
    | Hopewell, NJ 08525
Hall MR & MRS Stephen J (Humphrey—Susan L | ☎ (314) 991-5916
Rouse) V'65.Cy.CulverStock'72 . . . . | 30 Oakleigh Lane,
  MR Stephen S Humphrey . . . . | St Louis, MO 63124
  MR Brian C Humphrey . . . . |
  JUNIORS MR Edward D Humphrey . . . . |
Hall MR & MRS Thomas Cartwright (Garber—Louise C Simrall)
  ☎ (513) 771-9425 . . 850 van Nes Dv, Glendale, OH 45246
Hall MR & MRS Thomas Cartwright JR (Sally D Clarke) O'76.O'76
  ☎ (513) 681-7280 . . 4225 Florida Av, Cincinnati, OH 45223

Hall MR & MRS Thomas J (Ada McI Huffman) Dth'33
☎ (414) 725-3060 . . 131 E North Water St, Apt 104, Neenah, WI *54956*

Hall MRS Thomas S (Tompkins—Mary B Taussig) BMr'33.Wash'38.Csn.
☎ (314) 361-4744 . . 4969 Pershing Place, St Louis, MO *63108*

Hall MR Virginius C—P'54 . . . . | 1071 Celestial St,
MISS Maria A—at 161 Gilbert St, Apt 16, | Apt 2004,
San Francisco, CA *94103* . . . . | Cincinnati, OH
MISS Susannah M—at 2400—41 St NW, Apt 309, | *45202*
Washington, DC *20007* . . . . |

Hall MRS Warren S JR (Rita W Eichhorn). Eh.
☎ (908) 781-9127 . . 8 Hurlingham Club Rd, Far Hills, NJ *07931*

Hall MR Winthrop T—Emer'92 . . see B G Waters 3d

Hallahan MR & MRS Donald G (Cynthia K | ☎ (412) 781-3430
Harkness) V'57.Fcg.Tc.Ill'52.Nw'57 . . . . | 715 Delafield Rd,
MISS Melissa H—at ☎ (617) 723-8478 | Pittsburgh, PA
145 Charles St, Apt 145, Boston, MA *02114* . . . | *15215*
MR G William 2d—at ☎ (610) 687-5656 |
1027 Valley Forge Rd, Devon, PA *19333* . . . . . |

Hallanan MR Paul K—SFr'75
2702 California St, San Francisco, CA *94115*

Hallanan MR & MRS W Simms (Doris L Mehlinger) | of ☎ (415)567-7788
WVa'47 . . . . | 2686 Green St,
MISS D Blake—Stan'76.Cl'83—at | San Francisco, CA
☎ (415) 666-0567 . . 118 Eighth Av, | *94123*
San Francisco, CA *94118* . . . . | ☎ (011-353-27)
| 67184
| Rosskerrig,
| Ahakista, Durrus,
| Co Cork, Ireland

Hallberg MR Garth R—Y.Cl'64
☎ (914) 763-3754 . . E Ridge Rd, Waccabuc, NY *10597*

Halle MR & MRS Andrew P (Elizabeth S Dougherty) Colg'78.Ox'77
☎ (214) 696-5219 . . 9711 Hollow Way Rd, Dallas, TX *75220*

Halle MRS Chisholm (Cynthia A White) Kt.
☎ (954) 764-5888 . . 1922 S Ocean Lane, Ft Lauderdale, FL *33316*

Hallen MR & MRS John R (Laurie E P Grenley) | of ☎ (212)722-0887
V'67.Cl'68.Pr.Un.Cly.WakeF'65.Pa'69 . . . . | 1088 Park Av,
MISS D Alexandra—at Yale . . . . | New York, NY
JUNIORS MR John R JR . . . . | *10128*
| ☎ (516) 653-6013
| "Boxwood"
| PO Box 288,
| Quogue, NY *11959*

Hallenborg MRS Charles E (Hopkins—Dorothy R | ☎ (212) 288-7937
Peck) Cly. . . . . | 1 E 66 St,
MISS Leslie R Klotz—at ☎ (212) 319-3279 | New York, NY
111 E 60 St, New York, NY *10022* . . . . | *10021*

Halleran MRS Thomas A (Marsh—Gwendolyn Fisk)
☎ (212) 753-3978 . . 139 E 63 St, New York, NY *10021*
Dec 1 . . ☎ (809) 465-8876 . . Lemon Grove Villa 12,
Golden Lemon Hotel, Dieppe Bay, St Kitts

Hallett MR & MRS E Archer (Elizabeth Hoblitzelle)
☎ (941) 474-4938 . . 10 Bermuda Circle, Englewood, FL *34223*

Hallock MRS Lettys E (Jackson—Lettys E Curtis) Cly.Ncd.
☎ (215) 860-0506 . . Pennswood Village L106, Newtown, PA *18940*

Hallowell MRS Alfred B (Priest—Francine N Bull) Ncd.
☎ (314) 962-4733 . . 9743 Litzsinger Rd, St Louis, MO *63124*

Hallowell MR & MRS Andrew W (Leslie Pomeroy Eustis) Cl'90.Cal'88
18 Fernald Dv, Apt 21, Cambridge, MA *02138*

Hallowell MR Edward R—Ken'67.Camb'71
☎ (610) 323-3643 . . "Longmeadow" 438 Ellis Woods Rd, Pottstown,
PA *19464*

Hallowell MRS Francis J (Priscilla A Allen)
☎ (860) 535-1396 . . 1 Main St, PO Box 387, Stonington, CT *06378*

Hallowell MR & MRS Frederick C JR (Anna B | ☎ (610) EL6-0998
McCormick) Mit'48 | 622 Newtown Street
MISS Susan F—Col'85.Pa'87.Pa'93 . . . . | Rd, Newtown
| Square, PA *19073*

Hallowell MR & MRS Frederick C 3d (Nancy L Kepler) Del'80
☎ (610) 431-0346 . . 765 Old Westtown Rd, West Chester, PA *19382*

Hallowell MR & MRS Frederick H (Maureen A | ☎ (770) 594-1016
Slowik) W'ham'69.Ofp.Myf.W'ham'69 . . . . | 1180 Oakhaven Dv,
MISS Marion H . . . . | Roswell, GA *30075*
MR Christian H . . . . |

Hallowell MRS Henry R (Dorothy Saylor) . . . . Died at
Philadelphia, PA Feb 17'96

Hallowell MRS James M (Mary F McKey) . . . . | ☎ (401) 751-4684
MR James M 3d—H'69—at ☎ (617) 547-0550 | 355 Blackstone
17 Gray St, Cambridge, MA *02138* . . . . | Blvd, Apt 110,
| Providence, RI
| *02906*

Hallowell MR & MRS John G (Quay—Constance H B | ☎ (561) 732-4935
Case) . . . . | 111 SW 9 St,
MR John G 3d . . . . | Boynton Beach, FL
| *33426*

Hallowell MR & MRS Lee Hunter (Daphne Emmet) | ☎ (518) 962-4594
SL'58.Chi.H'54 . . . . | "Headlands"
MR Christopher E—at Champlain . . . . | Westport, NY
| *12993-0409*

Hallowell MR & MRS Morris L 4th (Yung—Ann S Ballard) Bard'67.Colg'71
☎ (203) 869-2190 . . 340 W Putnam Av, Greenwich, CT *06830*

Hallowell MRS N Penrose JR (Priscilla Choate)
☎ (508) 356-2679 . . 92 Argilla Rd, Ipswich, MA *01938*

Hallowell MR & MRS Roger H (Noble—Barbara E Warner) Ec.Myc.Ncd.
☎ (508) 526-4416 . . 10 Bridge St, Manchester-By-The-Sea, MA *01944*

Hallowell MR & MRS Roger H JR (Anderson-Bell— | of ☎ (520)323-8909
Elinor B Lamont) Bnd'58.Chi.Csn.H'61 . . . . . . | 115 N Calle
JUNIORS MR Nicholas L—at 27 Kenwood P'kway, | Resplendor, Tucson,
St Paul, MN *55105* . . . . | AZ *85716*
| ☎ (207) 867-4463
| "The Lookout"
| North Haven, ME
| *04853*

Hallowell MR & MRS Samuel H JR (Elizabeth M | ☎ (401) 751-4558
Stuart) Bost'70 . . . . | 231 George St,
MISS Sarah H—at Bates | Providence, RI
JUNIORS MR Samuel H 3d—at Conn Coll . . . . . . | *02906*

Halpern MR & MRS Barry D (Cynthia A Zedler) | ☎ (602) 943-3384
Kas'72.Kas'71.Kas'73 | 116 W Orangewood
MISS Amanda M . . . . | Av, Phoenix, AZ
JUNIORS MR Trevor H . . . . | *85021*

Halperson MR Michael A—Sb.U'68.Mass'70 . . of
  ☎ (508) 543-0361 . . 78 Cannon Forge Dv, Foxborough, MA *02035*
  ☎ (941) 377-1367 . . "The Knolls" 4267 Carriage Dv, Sarasota,
FL *34241*

Halpin MR William C—Dth'51
  ☎ (305) 294-6192 . . 1616 Atlantic Blvd, Apt 9, Key West, FL *33040*

Halsey MR & MRS Alexander Van R (Martha T Blankarn)
BMr'51.Stc.Rm.Plg.P'51
  ☎ (908) 291-1022 . . "Briarfield" Locust Point Rd, Locust, NJ *07760*

Halsey MRS Bates (Bettyjane Ruwe) Wells'40 . . . . . | ☎ (203) 869-8246
MISS Sally J—at 67 Halsey Dv, Old Greenwich, | 471 Lake Av,
CT *06870* . . . . | Greenwich, CT
                                         | *06830*

Halsey MRS Charles D (Helen L Pendergast) Cly.
  ☎ (212) RH4-1884 . . 125 E 72 St, New York, NY *10021*

Halsey MR & MRS Charles D JR (Elizabeth H MacRae) P.'50
  ☎ (212) 753-7422 . . 200 E 66 St, New York, NY *10021*

Halsey MR & MRS Charles W (Christy—Vieva F Banks) Shcc . . .of
  ☎ (908) 236-2525 . . 76 Bissell Rd, Lebanon, NJ *08833*
  ☎ (904) 285-4302 . . Vicar's Landing Way, Apt C305,
Ponte Vedra Beach, FL *32082*

Halsey MR Donald H—P'32
  ☎ (504) 561-8083 . . 1441 Jackson Av, Apt 5B, New Orleans, LA *70130*

Halsey MR & MRS Hugh J (Diana E Humphrey) Bnd'79.So.NCar'79
  ☎ (617) 444-6289 . . 50 Maple St, Needham, MA *02192*

Halsey MR & MRS Stephen S (Louise E R Elliot) K.Plg.Pn.P'50 . . of
  ☎ (908) 842-0325 . . 9 Linden Lane, Buena Vista Av, Rumson,
NJ *07760*
  19B Headland, Shek O, Hong Kong

Halstead MR & MRS Clark P (Carol L Pope) | of ☎ (212)288-6089
Buck'63.Un.Cr'63.Cl'70 . . . . | 329 E 82 St,
MISS Heather L—Dth'96 . . . . | New York, NY
JUNIORS MISS Hilary P—at Brearley . . . . | *10028*
                                           | Gipsy Trail Club,
                                           | Carmel, NY *10512*

Halsted MR & MRS David C (June Pearson) | ☎ (011-27-21)
GeoW'68.Dth'63.GeoW'68 . . . . | 797-5959
MISS Sarah T—at Kenyon . . . . | American Consulate
MR Edward O—at 533—8 St, Apt 2L, Brooklyn, | General, Capetown,
NY *11215* . . . . | Dept of State,
JUNIORS MR David C JR . . . . | Washington, DC
                                           | *20521-2480*

Halsted MRS Osborne (Katharine Patterson) V'30
  ☎ (617) 449-6574 . . 865 Central Av, Apt 406A, Needham, MA *02192*

Halsted MR & MRS Scott S (M Elizabeth Lorillard) Ty'81.Sfy.Dth'81
  ☎ (415) 383-4950 . . 76 Ethel Av, Mill Valley, CA *94941*

Halton MR & MRS Denis A (C Anita Kernan) | ☎ (714) 494-6750
Sth'65.Ox'64 . . . . | 559 Alta Vista Way,
MISS Anita L . . . . | Laguna Beach, CA
                                           | *92651*

Ham MRS Richard C (Charlotte Russell) Cp.
  ☎ (415) 928-2166 . . 2222 Hyde St, San Francisco, CA *94109*

Hamachek MR & MRS Tod R (Barbara Callister) | ☎ (206) 462-6000
Ore'68.Wms'68.H'70 . . . . | 720 Overlake Dv E,
MISS Elizabeth M . . . . | Medina, WA
MR Mark R . . . . | *98004-4817*

Hamann MR & MRS Charles M (Ethel L B | ☎ (617) 484-5553
McFarlan) Wheat'62.Un.Chi.Ncd.Y'61.H'64 . . . | 28 Temple St,
MR Charles F—Ham'88—at 542 Yorkshire Dv, | Belmont, MA *02178*
Apt 83, Rochester Hills, MI *48307* . . . . |

Hamberger MR & MRS Edward R (Susan J Armstrong)
GeoW'74.Cvc.Geo'72
  ☎ (301) 320-2798 . . 4908 Jamestown Rd, Bethesda, MD *20816*

Hambleton MR & MRS Chalkley Jay JR (Genevieve A Cremin)
Ih.Cas.Fy.LakeF'78
  ☎ (847) 446-3904 . . 160 Woodley Rd, Winnetka, IL *60093*

Hambleton MR George B E—Nf.Md.Gv.B.Eh.Mt. | ☎ (908) 832-2046
Pn.P'52 ⚓ | "Stone Valley
MISS Anne C—at 3022½ R St NW, Washington, | Farm" 163 Burrell
DC *20007* . . . . | Rd, Lebanon, NJ
MSRS Charles M & James E—at 1085—14 St, | *08833*
Apt 1098, Boulder, CO *80302* . . . . |

Hambleton MR & MRS T Edward (Merrell Hopkins)
B'gton'43.Sth'45.C.Pl.Md.Mv.Csn.Y'34
  ☎ (410) 252-2233 . . Box 25, Timonium, MD *21093*

Hambley MISS Catherine Rutsen
  ☎ (914) 876-6419 . . "Wilder Fox" PO Box 421, 110 S Mill Rd,
Rhinebeck, NY *12572-0421*

Hambuechen MISS Blair E—Bost'90 . . see A A du Pont

Hamel MR & MRS John Jacob 3d (Baynham— | ☎ (609) 466-2532
Eleanor P Evans) Cda.Yn.Miami'47 . . . . | PO Box 63,
MISS Gwyneth E . . . . | The Great Rd,
MR J Eric—Cl'86 . . . . | Blawenburg, NJ
                                           | *08504*

Hamersley MR & MRS L Gordon JR (Mihok—Madeline H Hellum)
Bcs.H.'50
  ☎ (516) 283-0070 . . 3 Turtle Pond Rd, Southampton, NY *11968*

Hamill MR & MRS Hunt (Jean M Hume) H'40
  ☎ (561) 234-8074 . . 1941 Club Dv, Vero Beach, FL *32963*

Hamill MR & MRS Jonathan Corwith (Nancy R | ☎ (847) 381-8381
Hibbeler) Cho.Cw.Y'60.Nw'62 . . . . | 545 Oak Knoll Rd,
MISS Susan Corwith—Mid'89.Dth'96—at | Barrington Hills, IL
  ☎ (212) 787-1954 . . 160 W 71 St, Apt 4N, | *60010*
New York, NY *10023* . . . . |
MISS Kimberly Corwith—StLaw'93—at |
  ☎ (773) 248-6507 . . 2453 N Halsted St, |
Chicago, IL *60614* . . . . |

Hamill MISS Mary A—Sth'53
  ☎ (513) 321-6780 . . 488 Sheffield Av, Cincinnati, OH *45208*

Hamill MR & MRS Robert B (Tracey E McGan)
Br'84.H'88.Bgt.Myf.Hn.Ham'84.H'88
  ☎ (203) 972-7454 . . 72 Apple Tree Lane, New Canaan, CT *06840*

Hamill MRS Samuel M (Margaret La Farge) Cly.
  ☎ (609) 896-0237 . . 45 Carter Rd, Princeton, NJ *08540*

Hamill MR & MRS Samuel M JR (Mary R Townsend) | ☎ (609) 921-1031
Rdc'63.Temp'73.Cl'61.Pa'74 . . . . | 146 Carter Rd,
MR Samuel—at Coll of Atlantic . . . . | Princeton, NJ *08540*
JUNIORS MISS Natalie—at Princeton Day Sch . . . |

Hamill MR William D—NH'54 . . . . | ☎ (207) 846-4639
MISS Susan K—Sim'79—at ☎ (207) 846-6341 | PO Box 480,
14 Willow St, Yarmouth, ME *04096* . . . . | Yarmouth, ME
MISS Elizabeth R—at ☎ (561) 691-0106 | *04096*
6086 Kendrick St, Palm Beach Gardens, FL
33418 . . . .
MISS Anne F—Utah'87—at ☎ (801) 583-2331
1871 Harvard Av, Salt Lake City, UT *84108* . . .
MR Sherwood N—at ☎ (207) 761-0552
2 Atlantic St, Portland, ME *04101* . . . .
MR William D 3d—Col'87—at
☎ (801) 655-0858 . . 4993 W Ponderosa Dv,
Park City, UT *84060* . . . .

Hamilton MISS Anne—V'38
☎ (203) 637-5123 . . 14 Clark St, Old Greenwich, CT *06870*
Hamilton MRS Charles D P 3d (Jean McWilliams) Cy.Nd.Rc.
☎ (314) 862-5656 . . 200 S Brentwood Blvd, Clayton, MO *63105*
Hamilton MR & MRS Christopher B (Mary D Carlisle) Duke'84.Cvc.Md'87
☎ (301) 530-4929 . . 5510 Hoover St, Bethesda, MD *20817*
Hamilton MR & MRS Daniel H (Nicholson—Jane S | ☎ (803) 577-5209
Evans) Ht.Myf.Cc.Cw.Ds.Dc.Dcw.Dar. . . . . | 19 Lamboll St,
MR T Heyward M . . . . | Charleston, SC
| *29401*

Hamilton MR David B
☎ (520) 775-5179 . . PO Box 27030, Prescott Valley, AZ *86312-7030*
Hamilton MR & MRS David R (H Catharine Cline) | ☎ (312) 951-8911
Finch'69.Rc.Rcn.Sc.Cas.Cly.Wa.Rice'61.H'66 . . | 1500 N Lake Shore
MISS Catharine E . . . . | Dv, Chicago, IL
JUNIORS MISS Tennessee A . . . . | *60610*

Hamilton MISS Deborah B
☎ (203) 656-3898 . . Box 74, 31 Contentment Island Rd, Darien,
CT *06820*
Hamilton MRS Edward Morse (Belcher—Lillian Harriet Holbrook)
☎ (415) 321-2116 . . 94 Faxon Lane, Atherton, CA *94025*
Hamilton MRS Ferris F (Mary Ann Stevens) . . . . . . | ☎ (303) 741-0362
MISS Elizabeth—at ☎ (508) 468-1453 | 5060 E Quincy Av,
PO Box 561, 24 Sagamore Farm Rd, Hamilton, | Englewood, CO
MA *01936* . . . . | *80110*

Hamilton MR & MRS Frederic C (Jane Murchison)
CtCol'52.B.Ln.Fic.Ri.Cly.
☎ (303) 778-6788 . . 5 Polo Club Rd, Denver, CO *80209*
Hamilton MR & MRS Frederic C JR (Emory Graham Alexander) Pa'74
☎ (210) 821-6216 . . 303 E Mandalay Dv, San Antonio, TX *78212*
Hamilton MRS Frederick J (Olivia K Walker) Bm.BtP.
☎ (561) 585-2636 . . "Pelican Palace" 2185 Ibis Isle Rd, Palm Beach,
FL *33480*
Hamilton MR & MRS George H (Polly B Wiggin) BMr'39.C.Ncd.Y'32
☎ (413) 458-8626 . . 121 Gale Rd, Williamstown, MA *01267*
Hamilton MASTER George Nickerson (Thomas M) . . . . . . Born May 3'96
Hamilton MRS H Marim Pew (H Marim Pew) | ☎ (610) 525-5022
Me.Ac.Ncd. | "Belerion"
MISS Hannah M—Ober'88.Me.—at | 1010 Spring Mill
☎ (212) 399-2506 . . 124 W 60 St, Apt 19H, | Rd, Villanova, PA
New York, NY *10023* . . . . | *19085*

Hamilton MR Henry D—Rc.Ty'57
☎ (212) 369-2404 . . 12 E 87 St, Apt 2C, New York, NY *10128-0524*

Hamilton MR Henry W—Ty'89 . . see R L Wood JR
Hamilton MR & MRS J Andrew JR (Eliza E | ☎ (202) 537-3536
Rathbone) H'59 . . . . | 3430—34 Place
MISS M Saskia . . . . | NW, Washington,
MR John A . . . . | DC *20016*
JUNIORS MISS Claudia . . . . |

Hamilton DR & MRS James A (Marjorie Angell) Cal'34.Fmy.Cal'34.Stan'41
☎ (415) 922-8833 . . 2643 Union St, San Francisco, CA *94123*
Hamilton MR & MRS John Craig (Monica C MacNamara) Cvc.Mt.F&M'71
☎ (301) 654-3232 . . 6671 Hillandale Rd, Chevy Chase, MD *20815*
Hamilton MRS John de Z (Angeline Mary Bray)
☎ (215) 234-8789 . . "Needlebrook" 512 Green St, Green Lane,
PA *18054*
Hamilton MRS John Louis (Patricia Eleanor Paine) Cvc.Mt.
☎ (202) 338-0888 . . 4635 Dexter St NW, Washington, DC *20007*
Hamilton MR & MRS John T 2d (Kerrigan—Ordway—Kelley—
Gloria Staniford) B.Evg.BtP.Cly.P'34
☎ (561) 832-3932 . . 525 S Flagler Dv, Apt 24C, West Palm Beach,
FL *33401*
Hamilton MISS Julie—Dar.
☎ (203) 661-5481 . . 1 Putnam Hill, Apt 2E, Greenwich, CT *06830*
Hamilton MISS Kelly Hayford (g—MRS G Denmead Le Viness) . . . . . Born
Jan 30'96
Hamilton MISS (DR) Lanier M—Conn'79.WashSt'91
☎ (307) 332-5856 . . PO Box 944, Lander, WY *82520*
Hamilton DR & MRS Lewis L (Townsend—Hager— | of ☎ (607)547-9710
Lucy Battel) Au.Ri.Srr.Y'60.Cl'64 . . . . | "Pomeroy Place"
MISS Heidi B—at Bryn Mawr . . . . | 11 Main St,
| Cooperstown, NY
| *13326*
| ☎ (607) 547-5475
| Deerfoot Farm,
| RD 3, Box 160,
| Richfield Springs,
| NY *13439*

Hamilton MR Lewis Thorne . . see J M Marrin
Hamilton MR & MRS Palmer C (Amy R St John) So'78.At.Ala'70.Duke'73
☎ (334) 432-0502 . . 1159 Palmetto St, Mobile, AL *36604*
Hamilton MR & MRS Perrin C (Bette J Shadle)
O'43.Sdg.Me.Cspa.Rv.Ac.Dick'43
☎ (610) MI9-2728 . . 210 Glenn Rd, North Ardmore, PA *19003*
Hamilton MR & MRS Richard 2d (Lucinda M | ☎ (610) 527-0103
Pantaleoni) Rdc'64.Me.Ac.H'65 . . . . | 708 Pennstone Rd,
MISS Ellen E—at Harvard . . . . | Bryn Mawr, PA
| *19010*

Hamilton JUNIORS MR Rylan . . see T G Stemberg
Hamilton MR & MRS S Matthews V JR (Anne H | ☎ (610) 525-3050
Fritchman) Bost'78.Gm.Me.Nrr.Srb.Rd.Ac. | "Hazy Hill"
AmU'78 . . . . | 1001 Rock Creek
JUNIORS MISS Dorrance H . . . . | Rd, Bryn Mawr, PA
| *19010*

Hamilton MR & MRS Samuel M V (Dorrance Hill)
Me.Ph.Gm.Nrr.San.Srb.Ac.Cly.Ncd.Pa'49 . . of
☎ (610) 688-4171 . . 218 Strafford Av, Wayne, PA *19087*
☎ (941) 403-0360 . . 4444 Gordon Dv, Naples, FL *34102-7901*
Hamilton MISS Sarah . . see MRS J C Geupel

Hamilton MR & MRS Thomas J (Sadtler—Frances Gurney Thomas) Pkg.Cda.
☎ (610) 431-3768 . . 103 Ashton Way, Hershey's Mill, West Chester, PA *19380*

Hamilton MR & MRS Thomas M (Eugenie Nickerson) Durham'88.Y'84
☎ (203) 629-5239 . . 270 Greenwich Av, Greenwich, CT *06830*

Hamilton MR & MRS Thomas W (Karen J Nastase) Ind'70.Pitt'72.Hills'69.Duq'74 . . . . | ☎ (203) 268-6225
JUNIORS MR Jason P . . . . | 3 Robin Lane, Monroe, CT *06468*

Hamilton MR & MRS Wilbur H 3d (Jill E Ballard) Buck'83.Pc.GeoW'84
☎ (610) 449-6130 . . 9 Yale Rd, Havertown, PA *19083*

Hamilton MR & MRS William (Eden Collinsworth) B'gton'76.Y'62 . . . . | ☎ (212) 369-7166
MISS Alexandra M V—at ☎ (212) 674-8285 | 115 E 89 St,
221 E 17 St, New York, NY *10003* . . . . | New York, NY *10128*

Hamilton MR William C 3d . . see MRS J C Geupel

Hamilton MR & MRS William G 3d (Nan W Whitridge) MtH'62.P'58.H'63
☎ (215) 572-0779 . . 1612 Amity Rd, Rydal, PA *19046*

Hamlen MR & MRS Devens H (Margery L MacMillan) B.Tr.Cy.Sm.Bow'64
☎ (508) 358-2979 . . ''Mainstone Farm'' 87 Old Connecticut Path, Wayland, MA *01778*

Hamlen MRS Frederick R (Patricia A Williams) V'45.H'57 . . . . | ☎ (508) 785-0651
MISS Pamela F . . . . | 21 Whiting Rd,
MISS Ames | Dover, MA *02030*
MR R Cushing—at ☎ (612) 631-3662
2610 Snelling Curve, Apt 19, Roseville, MN *55113* . . . .

Hamlen MR James M—Cy.
☎ (508) 358-4948 . . 242 Rice Rd, Wayland, MA *01778*

Hamlen MRS Joseph R (Cyrilla Page)
☎ (212) AT9-2821 . . 17 E 97 St, New York, NY *10029*

Hamlen MR & MRS William T (Lynn Northwood) Miami'68.Cyb.Tvb.Hn.H'45.H'47 . . . . | ☎ (203) 655-8522
MISS Anna N—at Colby . . . . | 7 Davis Lane,
JUNIORS MR William T JR—at Salisbury . . . . | Darien, CT *06820*

Hamlin MR Jerome F—Y'66 ⚓
☎ (212) 751-7414 . . 126 E 64 St, New York, NY *10021*

Hamlin MRS John F (Dorothy Jaeckel) Mds.Cly.
☎ (805) 371-9414 . . 2105 Portola Lane, West Lake Village, CA *91361*

Hamlin MISS Lucile—SL'62 . . see PRCSS K Scherbatow

Hamlin MR & MRS Robert T JR (Sandra L Killion) V'66.Cy.Sm.H'66.Pa'71
☎ (617) 739-0460 . . 60 Codman Rd, Brookline, MA *02146*

Hamm MR & MRS William H 3d (J Candace Sinclair) Bur.Pcu.Fr.Y'57 . . . . | ☎ (415) 922-3281
MR William C—Duke'91 . . . . | 3281 Jackson St, San Francisco, CA *94118*

Hammann MRS Mary C (Mary E Conklin) . . . . | ☎ (410) 296-6972
MISS Christine E . . . . | 114 Stanmore Rd,
MISS Julie T . . . . | Baltimore, MD
MR C Gordon 3d . . . . | *21212*

Hammer MR & MRS James S (Joan B Moore) Sa.NCar'67 . . . . | of ☎ (847)615-0491
MISS Bess W—Denis'95 . . . . | Lake Forest
MR James G—at Denison . . . . | Academy, 1500 W
| Kennedy Rd, Lake Forest, IL *60045*
| ☎ (607) 547-8405
| Box 68, Fly Creek, NY *13337*

Hammer MRS John L JR (Josephine L Wilson) R.Sap.San . . .of
☎ (305) 745-1930 . . 23090 Wahoo Lane, Summerland Key, FL *33042*
☎ (609) 921-2074 . . 103 Mercer St, Princeton, NJ *08540*

Hammer CAPT (RET) & MRS John L 3d (Dorrice J Griffith) Penn'62.USN'62.GeoW'85 . . . . | ☎ (802) 425-4065
MISS Erica S . . . . | PO Box 101, Charlotte, VT *05445*

Hammer MR John L 4th—Bentley'91
☎ (213) 650-1661 . . 2415 Laurel Pass, Los Angeles, CA *90046*

Hammer MR & MRS Joseph W (Katherine L Carton) Ln.Sm.Cy.Srb.H'64 . . . . | ☎ (617) 734-8582
JUNIORS MISS Alexandra C . . . . | 173 Woodland Rd, Chestnut Hill, MA *02167*

Hammer MISS Judith A (Ladd—Judith A Hammer) . . of
☎ (305) 745-1930 . . 23090 Wahoo Lane, Summerland Key, FL *33042*
☎ (609) 921-2074 . . 103 Mercer St, Princeton, NJ *08540*

Hammett MR & MRS Philip M (Palmer—Mary Jane Dowd) Man'vl'48.Rc.H'42.Pa'48 . . . . | ☎ (215) 790-0014
MISS Ann W—Gchr'84—at ☎ (206) 782-5044 | 1914 Spruce St,
518 Fourteenth Av E, Seattle, WA *98117* . . . . . | Philadelphia, PA
MR Christopher D Palmer—Colg'86.Nu'88— | *19103*
at ☎ (011-44-171) 460-2518
8A Marloes Rd, Kensington, London W8 5LJ, England . . . .

Hammett MR William Henry—Rc.
☎ (215) 836-5209 . . 9425 Stenton Av, Erdenheim, PA *19038*

Hammond MR & MRS Christopher C FitzS 3d (Marcia O Davis) Aub'62.Cc . . . . | ☎ (912) 925-9184
MR Sean C D . . . . | 502 Old Mill Rd, Savannah, GA *31419*

Hammond MR Frank H—H'43.Cl'48 . . . . | ☎ (202) 363-2219
MISS Helen M—at ☎ (617) 354-6524 | 4851 Tilden St NW,
173 Hancock St, Cambridge, MA *02139-1736* . . | Washington, DC
MR F Eldridge—Emory'77—Box 13014, | *20016*
San Luis Obispo, CA *93406-3014* . . . .

Hammond MR & MRS Harry S JR (Constance P Johnston) Wheat'43.Nyc.Ne.Cda.Dar.Ncd. H'41.Cl'50 . . . . | of ☎ (203)488-5378
MISS Jane W—Mid'80.W'minsterTheo'96.Cly. | 23 Pawson Rd,
Co.Cda. . . . . | Branford, CT *06405*
MISS Helen J—Mid'83.Co.Cda.Dar. . . . . | ☎ (508) 228-5123
| ''Mistover'' Monomoy, Nantucket, MA *02554*

Hammond MRS Hull (Diane D Hull) Cda.
☎ (011-506) 234-7485 . . Residencia de la Alhambra, Casa 27B, Sabanilla, San Pedro de Montes de Oca, Costa Rica

Hammond REV & MRS James A (Gina B Bronkie)
V'70.Md'68 . . . .
MISS Carolyn E—at 401 Westshire Rd, Baltimore,
MD *21229* . . . .
☎ (703) 754-0259
4240 Berry Rd,
Gainesville, VA
20155

Hammond MR & MRS James R JR (Isabel Dávila)
K.H.'59 . . . .
MR Peter A—Tul'87—at ☎ (617) 566-5295
80 Harvard Av, Brookline, MA *02146* . . . .
MR Nicholas—RISD'93—at ☎ (401) 331-1972
51 E George St, Providence, RI *02906* . . . .
☎ (212) 517-2369
785 Park Av, Apt
9B, New York, NY
10021

Hammond MR James R 3d—Ub.Cl'87
☎ (617) 264-7986 . . 80 Harvard Av, Brookline, MA *02146*

Hammond MR & MRS John Phelps (Cynthia W
Rainold) Ncmb'54.Tul'49.Tul'51 . . . .
MISS Hilda P . . . .
MR John Phelps JR . . . .
MR Peirce A 2d . . . .
see
Dilatory Domiciles

Hammond MRS Livingston (McVickar—M Jacqueline Livingston)
Pinard Cottages, Apt T, Annandale Rd, Newport, RI *02840-6954*

Hammond MR & MRS Mason (Florence H Pierson) Sm.H'25.Ox'28
☎ (617) 864-7978 . . 153 Brattle St, Cambridge, MA *02138*

Hammond MRS Ogden H (Montgomerie—Marsyl
Stokes) . . . .
MR Robert S Montgomerie—K.Nrr. . . . .
☎ (540) 937-3091
''Liberty Hall''
PO Box 399,
Rixeyville, VA
22737

Hammond DR & MRS Ogden H (Ingrid A Heenan)
K.San.Mit'69.Mit'73 . . . .
MR Ogden H JR—at Johns Hopkins . . . .
JUNIORS MISS Ingrid C H . . . .
☎ (508) 759-8400
PO Box 324,
Monument Beach,
MA *02553*

Hammond MR & MRS P Theodore (Karen
Marculescu) SCal'69.SCal'69 . . . .
MISS Courtney A . . . .
MR Robert E . . . .
JUNIORS MR James McP . . . .
☎ (818) 281-3260
2021 Sherwood Rd,
San Marino, CA
91108

Hammond MR Samuel . . . . Died at
Princeton, NJ Apr 28'96

Hammond MRS Samuel (Overman—Johnson—Marion French) Hn.
☎ (609) 426-6208 . . Meadow Lakes 43-04, Hightstown, NJ *08520-3348*

Hammond MRS William C JR (Gertrude Green) V'36 . . of
☎ (207) 422-3205 . . ''Hammondwood'' Hancock Point, ME *04640*
☎ (305) 664-4180 . . Box 549, Coral Cove, Islamorada, FL *33036*

Hammond MR & MRS William C 3d (Victoria C Karel) KasCAI'73.NCar'70
☎ (617) 749-0810 . . 33 Lafayette Av, Hingham, MA *02043*

Hammonds MRS Katherine F (Katherine F Fay) Bur.
☎ (415) 931-3236 . . 3236 Pacific Av, San Francisco, CA *94118*

Hammonds MR William E—Sfg.Bhm.Bur.Pcu.Reed'72.SFr'76.H'91
☎ (209) 364-6156 . . 47375 W Dakota Av, Firebaugh, CA *93622*

Hamon MRS Jake Louis (Taylor—Nancy L Blackburn) A.
☎ (214) 352-5419 . . 4738 Shadywood Lane, Dallas, TX *75209*

Hampson MR & MRS Alfred A (Elizabeth Griffin)
Stan'43.Bhm.Tcy.Ncd.Stan'43.H'46
☎ (415) 435-2405 . . 1902 Mar West, Tiburon, CA *94920*

Hampton MR & MRS Gregory J (Kathryn M Bryan)
Bhm.Bur.Pcu.Cal'71.SantaC'80
☎ (415) 344-4116 . . 1805 Elmwood Rd, Hillsborough, CA *94010*

Hampton MISS Larimore—Cly.Ri.
☎ (212) 688-4417 . . 444 E 52 St, New York, NY *10022*

Hampton MR & MRS Wesley G (Mary V Phelps)
Stan'75.SCal'84.Vh.Stan'74.SCal'79
☎ (818) 285-9406 . . 2605 Lorain Rd, San Marino, CA *91108*

Hamren MR & MRS Jonathan M (Virginia D Thomson)
HRdc'79.H'85.Ant'77.Stan'80
☎ (415) 346-8150 . . 2030 Lyon St, San Francisco, CA *94115*

Hamric MRS Darrell H (Shelton—M Janen
Denman) . . . .
MISS Eleanor S—at 1310 W Palmaire Dv,
Phoenix, AZ *85021* . . . .
MR Darrell H JR—at ☎ (512) 441-9647
3100 Dolphin Dv, Austin, TX *78704* . . . .
☎ (214) 351-4530
5570 Nakoma Dv,
Dallas, TX *75209*

Hamrick MR & MRS Charles F (Marguerite J Darnell) Cly.David'36 . . of
☎ (561) 276-6648 . . 2000 S Ocean Blvd, Apt 704, Delray Beach,
FL *33483*
☎ (704) 274-2017 . . 7 Bourne Lane, Asheville, NC *28803*

Hanahan MRS Roger P (Efird—Mary E Simpson) Cw.Ht.
☎ (803) 577-9072 . . 58 S Battery St, Charleston, SC *29401*

Hanchett MR Corbet—Cal'40
☎ (415) 567-6445 . . 1580 Beach St, San Francisco, CA *94123*

Hanchett MRS Lewis E (Stout—Gwynn Corbet) Cal'40.Tcy.
☎ (408) 688-3968 . . 755 Oakhill Rd, Aptos, CA *95003*

Hanckel MRS William H (Glass—Marianna R du Pont)
☎ (803) 723-1960 . . 6 Tradd St, Charleston, SC *29401*

Hancock MRS Charles Wagandt (Lamblé—Anne C Bradley) Cy.Dar.
☎ (410) 675-1285 . . Church Home 416, 101 N Bond St, Baltimore,
MD *21231-1535*

Hancock MR & MRS F Woodson 3d (Poll—Leslie B Tompkins)
Un.Ph.Me.Ac.Cly.JHop'71.H'81
☎ (212) 288-3118 . . 351 E 84 St, New York, NY *10028*

Hancock MR & MRS Morris C (Linda Peyton)
SL'76.EpiscDiv'80.Pa'74.Cr'81
☎ (207) 865-4067 . . 42 Flying Point Rd, Freeport, ME *04032*

Hancock MR Walker—Sb.C.
☎ (508) 283-6921 . . ''Quarry Woods'' Box 7133, Lanesville,
Gloucester, MA *01930*

Hancock MR & MRS William P W (Patricia Clay) Me.Rb.Ac.Pa'53
☎ (802) 824-6851 . . RR 1, Box 35, Brook Rd, South Londonderry,
VT *05155*

Hand MRS Alfred (Elizabeth A Grant) Sl.
☎ (202) 966-3031 . . 4101 Cathedral Av NW, Apt 1017, Washington,
DC *20016*

Hand MRS Barbara M (Barbara Mumford) Tufts'73.
JUNIORS MISS Julie—at Deerfield . . . .
JUNIORS MISS Jennifer—at Holderness . . . .
☎ (802) 867-0105
Meadow Lane,
Box 869, Dorset, VT
05251

Hand MR & MRS J M Colton (Margaret Fullbrook
Tait) Mt.Laf'35.Cl'40 . . . .
MISS Victoria B C—Cal'80.Pep'83 . . . .
DR J M Colton 2d—Va'87.Dth'88—at Dartmouth
☎ (703) 356-3964
''Fullbrook''
1344 Ballantrae
Lane, McLean, VA
22101

Hand MR James B—Conn'74
☎ (617) 262-2644 . . 167 Beacon St, Apt 6, Boston, MA *02116*

Hand MR & MRS W Brevard (Allison Denby) RMWmn'46.Ala'47.Ala'49
1855 Dauphin St, Mobile, AL *36606*

Hand MR & MRS William J (Nancy A Dubé) Y.'58. . | ☎ (914) 337-5304
MISS Caroline D—Y'95—at 455 Park Av S, | 233 Pondfield Rd,
Apt 504, New York, NY *10016* . . . . | Bronxville, NY
MR William A—at Middlebury . . . . | *10708*

Handler MR & MRS Steven B (Elizabeth C Pyle) Sth'87.RStockt'84
☎ (617) 449-5247 . . 317 Great Plain Av, Needham, MA *02192-4130*

Handy MR & MRS Albert M (Nancy H Lynch) | ☎ (603) 563-8014
Sth'50.Yn.Y'52 . . . . | Box 447, Dublin,
MISS Susan F—Ham'85 . . . . | NH *03444*
MISS Kate M—at U of NH . . . . |
MR Peter—SL'93 . . . . |

Handy MRS Chalmers (Elkinton—Elizabeth McNeill) Unb.Ncd.
☎ (401) 635-2086 . . 86 South of Commons Rd, Little Compton,
RI *02837*

Handy MISS Judith P—Cl'65
☎ (212) 838-3262 . . 200 E 66 St, New York, NY *10021*

Handy MR & MRS Parker D (Sally Woodbury) ColbyS'49.Br'51
☎ (860) 434-9317 . . Joshua Lane, Lyme, CT *06371*

Haneman MRS Elizabeth B (M Elizabeth Breed)
☎ (203) 264-4962 . . 598A Heritage Village, Southbury, CT *06488*

Haneman MR & MRS William F JR (Nancy P Jacobs) | ☎ (914) 967-0547
Sth'68.Ds. . . . . | 70 Fairway Av, Rye,
MISS Patricia S—Ty'95 . . . . | NY *10580*
MISS Nicolle P—at Dartmouth . . . . |

Hanes MISS Allison P . . see M de V Flinn

Hanes MR & MRS John W JR (Hoagland—Elizabeth C Millard) Mt.Y'50
☎ (406) 587-4819 . . PO Box 8010, Bozeman, MT *59773-8010*

Hanes MR Jonathan Y—CtCol'96 . . see M de V Flinn

Hanes MR & MRS R Philip JR (M Charlotte Metz)
ECar'76.C.Mt.Bhm.Yn.Y'49 . . of
☎ (910) 722-9952 . . 2721 Robinhood Rd, Winston-Salem, NC *27106*
☎ (910) 363-2440 . . Roaring Gap, NC *28668*

Hanford MR & MRS John M JR (Marilyn T Fisher) Swb'50.P'46
☎ (303) 771-4057 . . 8725 E Roundtree Av, Greenwood Village,
CO *80111*

Hanhausen MR & MRS William J (Andrea W Pinson)
Rice'87.Dar.Anahuac'87
☎ (011-52-5) 545-5335 . . Campos Eliseos 49-2, Col Polanco,
Mexico DF 11560, Mexico

Hanke MISS Christine Flagler . . see MRS M V Martin

Hanke MR & MRS G F Robert (Lynn S Washburn) | 875 Fifth Av,
Rc.An.Un.Ri.Mds.StJ.Fw.Cly.Y'60.Geo'70 . | New York, NY
JUNIORS MISS Leigh F . . . . | *10021*

Hanke MR G F Robert JR . . see MRS M V Martin

Hanke MR John Vincent . . see MRS M V Martin

Hankey MR & MRS Charles W (Leslie O Gardner) Ga'79.Van'78.Ga'82
☎ (770) 977-0704 . . 571 Ridgewater Dv, Marietta, GA *30068*

Hanks CAPT & MRS E Ralph (Frances E Herrick) USN.
☎ (505) 387-5126 . . ''Christmas Tree Canyon'' Box 239, Mora,
NM *87732*

Hanley MISS Brooke F (William Lee JR) . . Married at Buck Hill Falls, PA
Bell MR Halsey (James) . . . . Jun 29'96

Hanley MR John J—SUNY'74.Cal'81.Cal'82
☎ (510) 841-2171 . . 65 Roble Rd, Berkeley, CA *94705*

Hanley MR & MRS Walter A JR (Priscilla S Matthews) Cal'78
☎ (213) 654-1316 . . 2056 Stanley Hills Place, Los Angeles, CA *90046*

Hanley MRS William Lee (Elizabeth W Niles) Evg.BtP.Cly.
☎ (561) 655-0725 . . 155 Hammon Av, Palm Beach, FL *33480*

Hanley MR & MRS William Lee JR (Alice A | ☎ (203) 661-8254
Hoffman) Skd'65.B.Fic.BtP.Cly.Y'64 . . . . | 81 Butternut Hollow
MISS Nicole . . . . | Rd, Greenwich, CT
JUNIORS MISS Merrill—at St Paul's . . . . | *06830*

Hanna MR & MRS Colin A (Anne P Hemphill) | ☎ (610) 793-2085
Pa'68.Pa'69 . . . . | Radley Run Country
MISS Jean P—at U of Pa . . . . | Club, 603 Fairway
JUNIORS MR Colin Alexander . . . . | Dv, West Chester,
| PA *19382*

Hanna MR & MRS John R (A Rebecca Sponsler) Ncd.Dar.
☎ (301) 695-4895 . . Fairfield Suites 14-3, 104 Mercer Court, Frederick,
MD *21701*

Hanna MRS Richard R (Sherman—Patricia Wilson) | of ☎ (415)348-1945
Bur. . . . . | 2250 Forest View
MR Wilson R Sherman—at ☎ (619) 458-5960 | Rd, Hillsborough,
8528 Via Mallorca, Apt G6, La Jolla, CA | CA *94010*
92037 . . . . | ☎ (415) 892-1745
| ''Montecito del
| Roblas''
| Hanna Ranch Rd,
| Novato, CA *94948*

Hannafin MRS Frances H (Frances S Heberton) | ☎ (215) 247-3278
ColbyS'53 . . . . | 8305 Crittenden St,
MR Mark S—HWSth'90 . . . . | Philadelphia, PA
| *19118*

Hannan REV & MRS Donald J 3d (Katherine P Wise)
Duke'82.B.Wil.Cly.Yn.Ariz'73.Y'84
☎ (860) 688-4570 . . 301 Broad St, Windsor, CT *06095*

Hanneken MR & MRS Christopher L (Heléne B Olds)
☎ (510) 455-4934 . . 1441 Calvery Lane, Livermore, CA *94550*

Hannum MR & MRS John B JR (Menocal—Bradford | ☎ (610) 268-2340
—Anne Stroud) Pa'66.Dick'73 . . . . | ''Hollowtree''
MISS Christianna P . . . . | 245 Stroud Lane,
MISS Curtiss P S . . . . | West Grove, PA
MR George D . . . . | *19390*
JUNIORS MR Seth Bradford . . . . |
JUNIORS MR Luke Bradford. . . . . |

Hanratty MR Michael W . . see MRS J Lee

Hansel MR & MRS J Parker JR (Sarah E Hall) | ☎ (603) 357-5133
Ws'71.Pa'70. . . . . | Hurricane Rd,
MR John P 3d . . . . | Keene, NH *03431*
JUNIORS MISS Sarah D . . . . |
JUNIORS MR Eben C. . . . . |

Hanselman MISS Margaret J—OreSt'69
☎ (415) 340-1619 . . 1115 Southdown Rd, Hillsborough, CA *94010*

Hansen MR & MRS Carl L (Norma L Warren) Fr.Ncd.Whit'40
☎ (415) 885-1105 . . 1310 Jones St, San Francisco, CA *94109*

Hansen MR & MRS Eric R (Susan M Kelsey)
☎ (203) 655-0720 . . 31 Arrowhead Way, Darien, CT *06820*

Hansen MR & MRS Frederick F (Huebing—Annelore J Schaefer)
Kreis'57.BtP.B.Evg.Hn.Wis'48.H'50 . . of
☎ (414) 351-2006 . . 8990 N Range Line Rd, Milwaukee, WI *53217*
☎ (561) 655-7810 . . Everglades Club, 356 Worth Av, Palm Beach,
FL *33480*

Hansen MR & MRS H Baird (Sarah P Hart) U'78.Cda.Va'76.Syr'80
☎ (315) 478-6049 . . 170 Chatham Rd, Syracuse, NY *13210*
Hansen MRS H Leighton (Katharine D Baird) Cda . . .of
☎ (315) 655-8373 . . ''Westerlea'' 4502 Syracuse Rd, Cazenovia, NY *13035*
☎ (561) 231-3787 . . 240 Sabal Palm Lane, Vero Beach, FL *32963*
Hansen MR & MRS Herbert W (Develin—Susan E | ☎ (603) 863-1542
Lockwood) WmSth'55.Dth'57 . . . . | Burpee Lane,
MISS Kathryn I—at Atlanta, GA . . . . | PO Box 917,
| Grantham, NH
| *03753*
Hansen MR Lee C—Fcg.Buck'89.Nw'93
☎ (212) 799-1832 . . 146 W 74 St, Apt 2, New York, NY *10023*
Hansen MRS Norbert C (Harriet Cox) Sm.Cly.Ncd . . .of
☎ (212) 288-3564 . . 830 Park Av, New York, NY *10021*
☎ (908) 832-2161 . . ''Sky Line Farm'' 157 Mt Grove Rd, Califon, NJ *07830*
Hansen MR & MRS Samuel C (Applegate—Julia K Patterson) Sc.DelB.Cry.Wa.Cal'49 . . of
☎ (312) 787-0505 . . 1300 N Lake Shore Dv, Apt 28A, Chicago, IL *60610*
☎ (602) 488-4805 . . PO Box 3555, Carefree, AZ *85377*
Hansen MR & MRS Stephen C (Ethel H Olmsted) P'62.Va'66
☎ (412) 963-8150 . . 106 Ridgedale Lane, Pittsburgh, PA *15238*
Hansen MR W Van Adrian—H'34
☎ (847) 438-7087 . . 1 Robin Crest Rd, Hawthorn Woods, IL *60047*
Hanser MR & MRS Frederick O (Katharine R | ☎ (314) 994-1620
Thompson) Sth'64.Cy.Y'63 . . . . | 5 Rio Vista Dv,
MISS Katharine R—Y'91—at Columbia Med . . . | St Louis, MO *63124*
Hanser MR Timothy F—Y'89
☎ (202) 333-8966 . . 2917 O St NW, Washington, DC *20007*
Hanson MISS Adelaide Berry—AScott'65.GaSt'83.GaSt'89
☎ (770) 270-8999 . . 4324 Darwen Court, Tucker, GA *30084-7911*
Hanson MISS Ashley C . . see R L Reese
Hanson REV CANON Benedict H—Rv.Cc.Ht.Cw.JHop'36
see MRS J Carey
Hanson MR Bradley N—Cal'83
2644 San Pasqual St, Pasadena, CA *91107*
Hanson MR Brewster B 3d . . see R L Reese
Hanson MRS Clarence B JR (Sara E F Fletcher) Cy.Cly.
☎ (205) 967-4923 . . 4055 Old Leeds Rd, Birmingham, AL *35213*
Hanson MR & MRS Fridolf A (Polly C Stone) Col'89.Ny.Col'91.WakeF'95
☎ (212) 628-1451 . . 137 E 66 St, Apt 8C, New York, NY *10021*
Hanson MR Gilman—Rc.RISD'77
☎ (215) 483-1158 . . 4153 Apple St, Philadelphia, PA *19127*
Hanson MR & MRS Harry A (E Terry Ponvert) Cal'52
☎ (415) 342-2679 . . 1830 Brookvale Rd, Hillsborough, CA *94010*
Hanson MR & MRS Harry A 3d (Ann Hollingsworth) Cal'82.Ub.Un.Cal'79
☎ (508) 358-0148 . . 8 Concord Rd, Wayland, MA *01778*
Hanson MR J Stillman—WakeF'94 . . see D F Ogilvy
Hanson MR & MRS John H JR (Marian K Melcher) Mid'78.Rol'71
☎ (860) 675-4131 . . 1 Maple Lane, Avon, CT *06001*
Hanson MR & MRS Maurice F (Margaret E Hixon) Y'30
☎ (941) 594-8275 . . 405 Arbor Lake Dv, Naples, FL *34110*

Hanson MISS Phaedra A . . see MRS M B Annan
Hanson CAPT (RET) & MRS Robert McD (Susan | ☎ (619) 423-8767
Somers) USN.SCal'66.NPS'80.SalveR'90 . . . . . | 80 Trinidad Bend,
MISS Katrina . . . . | Coronado, CA
MR Robert M . . . . | *92118*
Hanson MRS Susan G (Susan Gilman) Me.Dc.Cda.
☎ (610) 687-9869 . . 206 Grouse Lane, Radnor, PA *19087*
Harbison MR & MRS James W JR (Margaret G | of ☎ (212)988-1779
Morgan) Sth'59.Ncd.Duke'56.Y.'59 . . . . | 30 East End Av,
MR James W 3d . . . . | New York, NY
| *10028*
| ☎ (914) 534-9884
| Box 225, Deer Hill
| Rd, Cornwall-on-
| Hudson, NY *12520*
Harbison MR & MRS Samuel P 3d (Diana L Drew) Roch'75.Pitt'77.PTheo'82.Rr.P'74.CarnM'80
☎ (412) 681-8275 . . 840 Canterbury Lane, Pittsburgh, PA *15232*
Harcum MRS Jacqueline G (Knox—Jacqueline E | ☎ (610) 296-5337
Green) . . . . | ''Fairwater Falls''
MISS Cynthia B Knox—SL'83 . . . . | 133 Grubb Rd,
| Malvern, PA *19355*
Hard MR & MRS Frederick G B (Hildegarde | ☎ (203) 329-0245
Stevenson) Rcn.Ny.Err.Cly. . . . . | 462 Old Long Ridge
MR David F—at ☎ (303) 499-8777 | Rd, Stamford, CT
335 S 39 St, Boulder, CO *80303* . . . . | *06903-1113*
Hard MR & MRS Michael W (Kathryn L Lockett) | of ☎ (520)299-2071
Y'59 . . . . | 2037 E Miraval
MISS Jennifer S—at U of Ariz . . . . | Quinto, Tucson, AZ
MR Christopher L—Ariz'87—at | *85718*
☎ (520) 325-3222 . . 2926 E Exeter St, Tucson, | ☎ (520) 774-1018
AZ *85716* . . . . | Rte 4, Box 985,
| Flagstaff, AZ *86002*
Harde MRS Dudley Brown (Frances M Barker) Yn.
☎ (203) 259-0464 . . 637 Round Hill Rd, Fairfield, CT *06430*
Harder MRS George A JR (Sally Knight) Skd'56
☎ (201) 890-1178 . . 1147 Stephanie Dv, North Caldwell, NJ *07006*
Harder MR & MRS Henry U (Calista Lincoln) V'51.Bg.Ln.Cly.Y'45 . . of
☎ (207) 846-4059 . . 18 Royal Point Rd, Yarmouth, ME *04096*
☎ (518) 891-1304 . . ''Red Pine Point'' Box 259, Lake Clear, NY *12945*
Harder MR & MRS Lewis B (Dorothy D Butler) B.Bgt.Cly.H'41
☎ (914) 232-7119 . . 120 Mt Holly Rd, Katonah, NY *10536*
Hardie MISS Delia Lane
☎ (504) 899-8501 . . 4206 Danneel St, New Orleans, LA *70115*
Hardie DR Edward T L—Y'85.Stan'89.Stan'92 . . see P C Robinson
Hardie MR & MRS Thomas G 2d (Ruth C Dion) Skd'48.Md.P'43
☎ (410) 472-4773 . . ''Thornhill Farm'' PO Box 34, 2620 Butler Rd, Butler, MD *21023*
Hardie MR & MRS William H JR (Harris—C Alix | ☎ (334) 344-5231
Winter) Y'59.Va'63 . . . . | 3267 Stein St,
JUNIORS MR Frank W . . . . | Mobile, AL *36608*
Hardie MR & MRS William H 3d (Jean M Stallard) Duke'84.Van'87.Dar.Ala'84.Van'87
☎ (504) 895-1744 . . 2850 Coliseum St, New Orleans, LA *70115*

Hardigg MR & MRS James S (Alice L Hendrick) Dth'44.Mit'45 . . . . | ☎ (413) 369-4628 / 36 Upper Baptist Hill Rd, Box 625, Conway, MA *01341*
MISS Thea Catharine B . . . .
MISS Genevieve P . . . .
MISS Elinor L—at 10528 Cross Fox Lane, Columbia, MD *21044* . . . .
MR James McC . . . .

Hardiman MR & MRS Joseph R (Katherine McCampbell) Gchr'63.Ln.Mt.Md.Elk.Rr.Md'59.Md'62
☎ (410) 377-6428 . . 8 Bowen Mill Rd, Baltimore, MD *21212*

Hardin MRS B Lauriston JR (Dorcas F Hull)
☎ (202) 333-0535 . . 3028 P St NW, Washington, DC *20007*

Hardin MISS E Virginia—Swb'37
☎ (847) 272-3056 . . 701 Lee Rd, Northbrook, IL *60062*

Hardin MRS Louis S (Shirley Garnett) Rc.
☎ (630) 552-8091 . . Rock Creek Farm, 2970 Rock Creek Rd, Plano, IL *60545*

Harding MISS Brenda B . . see G W Patterson 3d

Harding MR Charles L JR—H'26
☎ (207) 363-4386 . . PO Box 460, York Harbor, ME *03911*

Harding MRS Deborah S (Deborah S Schust) Ford'74.Nu'76.NewSchSR'82 . . of
☎ (914) 838-2844 . . 52B Colonial Rd, Beacon, NY *12508*
☎ (207) 865-1896 . . 11 Flying Point Way, Freeport, ME *04032*

Harding MR & MRS Edward P (Margaret M Bright) H'58
☎ (203) 322-9160 . . Barn Hill Rd, Greenwich, CT *06831*

Harding MRS Francis Appleton (Caroline G Read)
☎ (617) 326-0881 . . 10 Longwood Dv, Apt 110, Westwood, MA *02090*

Harding MR & MRS George J (Howard—Phebe McK Sargent) Gm.Ph.Rc.Me.Y'40 . . . . | ☎ (610) LA5-2039 / 921 Mt Pleasant Rd, Bryn Mawr, PA *19010*
MISS Phebe A . . . .
MR George McK—at 1235 Wendover Rd, Rosemont, PA *19010* . . .

Harding MR George M JR—Pa'44.Cl'48
☎ (610) MI2-1399 . . "Boxwood" 1231 Montgomery Av, Wynnewood, PA *19096*

Harding MR & MRS George R JR (Thérése M Adrian) Bnd'52.H'43 . . of
☎ (401) 521-0544 . . 200 Grotto Av, Providence, RI *02906*
☎ (561) 265-1143 . . 525 Middle Rd, Gulf Stream, FL *33483*

Harding MR & MRS John L (Steere—Nancy L Young) RI'72.D.H'52
☎ (617) 326-5439 . . 121 Cedar Lane, Westwood, MA *02090*

Harding MR & MRS John Mason (Margaret Riker) V'54.Lx.Cly.H'51.H'54
430 W 116 St, New York, NY *10027*

Harding MR L Branch 4th—H.'74
☎ (617) 738-0716 . . 145 Woodland Rd, Chestnut Hill, MA *02167*

Harding MISS Margaret C—Ken'85
☎ (508) 369-2777 . . 61 Hubbard St, Concord, MA *01742*

Harding MISS Marie (Allen—Marie Harding) SL'64 | ☎ (505) 438-9873 / Synergia Ranch, RR 2, Box 271, Santa Fe, NM *87505*
MISS Eden A . . . .

Harding MRS Nancy J (Nancy J Dickey) . . . . | of ☎ (703)442-0491 / 1803 Westwind Way, McLean, VA *22102* / ☎ (352) 403-0411 "Querencia" 13530 SW Airport Rd, Cedar Key, FL *32625*
MISS Michelle H—Box 2150, Dillon, CO *80435*.

Harding MR & MRS Robert S O (Diana Pike) Sth'58.H'52.Cal'73 . . . . | ☎ (610) LA5-6692 / 738 S Roberts Rd, Bryn Mawr, PA *19010*
MISS Alexandra . . . .
MISS Eliza . . . .

Harding REV Stephen R—Colby'80.UnTheo'93.Gen'lTheo'95
☎ (718) 596-2698 . . 1 Clark St, Brooklyn, NY *11201*

Harding MR Thomas H—Aht'84
☎ (703) 525-6728 . . 1818 N Stafford St, Arlington, VA *22207*

Hardwick MRS Elizabeth T (Johnson—Elizabeth I Townsend) V'46.Chi . . .of
☎ (561) 231-4121 . . 1001 Bay Rd, Apt 105B, Vero Beach, FL *32963*
☎ (207) 363-6269 . . PO Box 451, York Harbor, ME *03911*

Hardy MISS Anita C—Bard'88
☎ (914) 271-1327 . . 30 Palmer Av, Croton-on-Hudson, NY *10520*

Hardy MISS Ann R—Cly.Ncd.
☎ (908) 850-9040 . . "Titmouse Haven" PO Box 72, Allamuchy, NJ *07820-0072*

Hardy MR Brook J
121 Lansdowne, Westport, CT *06880-5650*

Hardy MRS Charles L (Donnelley—Ann Steinwedell) Cas.On.Cnt.Ncd.
☎ (847) 234-1012 . . 1121 Ringwood Rd, Lake Forest, IL *60045*

Hardy MR & MRS David R (Anne T Davidson) Y.'77.Reed'71.Geo'75.Nu'79
☎ (914) 763-9312 . . 73 Mead St, Waccabuc, NY *10597*

Hardy MISS Elizabeth H—Minn'86
☎ (617) 244-1921 . . 65 Ashmont Av, Newton, MA *02158*

Hardy MR & MRS G Ridgely (Leila T Penniman) Va'86.Gv.Cda.Va'87
☎ (410) 654-0554 . . "Melindas Choice" 12330 Garrison Forest Rd, Owings Mills, MD *21117*

Hardy MISS Johanna D (Rodney D) . . . . Married at Minneapolis, MN
Willegalle MR Michael A (Henry) . . . . Aug 31'96

Hardy MR & MRS John A JR (June Dorflinger) Bm.Unn.Chr.Cly.Del'52.McG'55.Nu'77
☎ (941) 514-0488 . . Marquesa Apt 401, 8990 Bay Colony Dv, Naples, FL *34108*

Hardy MISS Kate Talbot (G Ridgely) . . . . Born at Baltimore, MD May 25'96

Hardy MRS Norman B JR (Audrey H Swanson) MichSt'49 . . . . | ☎ (609) 368-5332 / 18—91 St, Stone Harbor, NJ *08247*
MISS Lisa M . . . .
MISS Amy S—at 2—91 St, Stone Harbor, NJ *08247* . . . .

Hardy MR & MRS Randolph Willson (Eleanor W Merryman) SCar'66.Mv.SCar'65 . . . . | ☎ (717) 843-0400 / 136 E Springettsbury Av, York, PA *17403*
MR N Benjamin Merryman . . . .
JUNIORS MR Randolph Willson JR

Hardy MR & MRS Rodney D (Katharine T Ducey) H'60.Pa'63
☎ (612) 926-7156 . . 5300 Oaklawn Av, Edina, MN *55424*

Hardy MR & MRS William R (Barbro A Medin) | ☎ (513) 321-1970
Cw.P'56.H'63 . . . . | 1339 Michigan Av,
MR William R JR—U'91.U'93 . . . . | Cincinnati, OH
| *45208*

Hare MRS E Waln (Jean S Gibbs)
☎ (609) 730-1499 . . 107 Treymore Court, Trenton, NJ *08638*
Hare MISS Elizabeth B . . see N T Callaway
Hare MR & MRS Emlen G (Evelyne J van der | ☎ (902) 543-9400
Linden) Ds.P'59 . . . . | 81 Alexandra Av,
MISS Astrid van der L—at King's Coll . . . . | Bridgewater,
MR Alexander E—at Dalhousie. . . . . | Nova Scotia
| B4V 1H3, Canada
Hare MR & MRS Harry T (Edda Drescher) | ☎ (610) MI2-2318
Me.Rc.Y'60.Pa'66 . . . . | 201 Old Gulph Rd,
MISS Kristina W—Tufts'87—at 1114—14 St, | Wynnewood, PA
Apt G, Santa Monica, CA *90403* . . . . | *19096*
MISS Alexandra D—Bost'90 . . . . |
MISS Margaret W—at U of Colo . . . . |
Hare MR Hobart N . . see N T Callaway
Hare MISS Katherine W . . see N T Callaway
Hare MRS Martha M (Martha M Michalis) Cly.
☎ (212) 628-5318 . . 10 E 70 St, New York, NY *10021*
Hare MR & MRS Nicholas Stallworth (Clements—Mary A Crabtree) Ala'35
☎ (334) 743-3486 . . 252 Pineville Rd, Monroeville, AL *36460*
Hare MR & MRS Nixon W (Caroline B Erdman) Hob'79.Rcn.Eyc.ColC'67
☎ (609) 466-4012 . . 23 Planters Row, Skillman, NJ *08558*
Hare MR & MRS T Truxtun JR (Winifred Thorndike) Ph.Rb.Ac.Y'31
☎ (610) 459-3366 . . "Piper's Hill" Box 675, Edgemont, PA *19028*
Hare MR & MRS T Truxtun 3d (Beth G Clouser) | ☎ (610) 975-9852
Buck'81.Rc.Y'61 . . . . | 850 Tall Oaks Rd,
MISS Abigail C . . . . | Radnor, PA *19087*
MISS Katharine S . . . . |
Harfield MR & MRS Henry (Marion G Bussang)
Sth'32.Cl'35.C.Cs.Y.'34.Cl'37
☎ (212) TR9-4746 . . 520 E 86 St, New York, NY *10028*
Hargrave MR & MRS Alexander MacK (Louisa V | ☎ (516) 734-5158
Thomas) P'68.H'69 . . . . | "Alvah's Cottage"
JUNIORS MISS Anne MacK—at Porter . . . . | Private Rd,
JUNIORS MR Alexander S—at Phillips Exeter. . . . | Cutchogue, NY
| *11935*
Hargrave MR Homer P JR—Cho.Rcch.Cant'48
☎ (812) 988-9355 . . 762 Helmsburg Rd, Nashville, IN *47448*
Hargrave MR William A . . see W W Wirtz
Hargraves MISS Elizabeth L (Gordon Sellers) . . . . Married at
Cold Spring Harbor, NY
Macía Urrea MR Felipé (Joaquin) . . . . May 18'96
Hargraves MR & MRS Gordon Sellers (Margaret E | ☎ (516) 549-4296
Magavern) P'53.H'57 . . . . | 423 W Neck Rd,
MISS Anna B—at 476 S Logan St, Denver, CO | Huntington, NY
80209 . . . . | *11743*
MR Gordon S JR—at 325 Elliot St, Newton, MA |
02164 . . . . |
MR Samuel M . . . . |
Harjes MRS A Whitehouse (Alice V Whitehouse)
☎ (203) 655-3675 . . "La Mouette" Brush Island Rd, Box 3068,
Noroton, CT *06820*

Harjes MR & MRS Henry H JR (Judith A Ibey) | ☎ (603) 643-1278
VPI'67 . . . . | 384 Dogford Rd,
MR Henry H 3d—at 9336 Windbell Way, | Etna, NH *03750*
Columbia, MD *21045* . . . . |
Harkins MR & MRS John G JR (Beatrice G McIlvain) Rd.Me.Ac.Ncd.Pa'53
☎ (610) MU8-5453 . . "Lowbrook" Box 813, Devon, PA *19333*
Harkness MR & MRS Kenneth K (Antoinette Murphey)
Ws'57.Wms'56.H'62 . . of
☎ (847) 441-8802 . . 805 Heather Lane, Winnetka, IL *60093*
☎ (414) 275-2665 . . 443 N Lake Shore Dv, Fontana, WI *53125*
Harloff MISS Veda W (Walthuis—Veda W Harloff)
☎ (212) 252-4621 . . 2 Lexington Av, New York, NY *10010*
Harlow MRS P Maddux (Polly A Maddux) CtCol'54 | ☎ (703) 698-7498
MR Evan F—Bost'84 . . . . | 3315 Dauphine Dv,
| Falls Church, VA
| *22042*

Harmar MISS Alice L
☎ (617) 227-7321 . . 112 Pinckney St, Boston, MA *02114*
Harmar MR & MRS Charles K (Emily A Franklin) P'88.Pc.P.'71
☎ (215) 884-7691 . . 524 Fox Rd, Glenside, PA *19038*
Harmar MR & MRS William 3d (Anna P Hults) | ☎ (215) 248-2266
Pc.Cc. . . . . | 301 W Hartwell
MR William K . . . . | Lane, Philadelphia,
| PA *19118*

Harmeier DR Charles A JR—Pitt'30.Pitt'31
☎ (412) 826-5787 . . Longwood at Oakmont A331, 500 Rte 909,
Verona, PA *15147-3853*
Harmon MR & MRS Barrie H 3d (Laura Lowe) Wes'72.Ala'72 . . of
☎ (334) 834-7724 . . 3400 Bankhead Av, Montgomery, AL *36111*
☎ (904) 267-2321 . . "Beach Manor" Tops'l Racquet Club, Destin,
FL *32541*
Harmsworth HON Esmond V—Br'90.H'95 . . of
☎ (617) 247-2098 . . 359 Beacon St, Apt 4, Boston, MA *02116*
46 Rutland Gate, Apt 1, London SW1, England
Harnes DR & MRS Jack R (Joan F Tomick) Cl'45 . . . | of ☎ (212)535-2126
MISS Anne E . . . . | 730 Park Av,
| New York, NY
| *10021*
| ☎ (914) 855-1204
| 64 S Quaker Hill
| Rd, Pawling, NY
| *12564*

Harney MR John M—P'46.H'48
☎ (314) 367-5920 . . 4628 Maryland Av, St Louis, MO *63108*
Harp DR & MRS Vernon C JR (Mary M Casey)
Cal'39.Bhm.Sar.Cal'41.Cal'43
☎ (415) 771-7522 . . 1020 Union St, San Francisco, CA *94133*
Harper MR D A Campbell—Ll.
☎ (610) LA5-4595 . . "Eastdene" Mt Moro Rd, Villanova, PA *19085*
Harper MR & MRS Daniel R (Ruth T Butler) SimR'74.CrawfNaut'70
☎ (207) 963-7476 . . RR 1, Box 485, Gouldsboro, ME *04607*
Harper MR Douglass B—Duke'86
☎ (773) 384-4111 . . 1631 N Oakley Av, Chicago, IL *60647*
Harper MR Duncan T . . see M F O'Reilly

Harper MR Emery W—Un.Plg.Snc.Aht'58.Y'61 . . of
☎ (212) 355-5114 . . 200 E 57 St, Apt 18N, New York, NY *10022*
☎ (860) 927-4221 . . ''Selective Cutting'' 122 Treasure Hill Rd,
South Kent, CT *06785*

Harper MRS Fletcher M (Prudence Oliver) Cs. . . . . | ☎ (212) RH4-3536
MR Peter O—Ken'88 . . . . | 45 E 85 St,
| New York, NY
| *10028*

Harper MR Francis A—Va'40
☎ (805) 969-3752 . . 120 Hixon Rd, Santa Barbara, CA *93108*

Harper MR Harry H JR (Mary H Jopling) ⚓
☎ (215) 643-1488 . . 1705 Foulkeways, Sumneytown Pike, Gwynedd,
PA *19436*

Harper MISS Helen Leale—Bm.Dar.Dll.Dc.
☎ (914) 738-0418 . . 66 Harmon Av, Pelham, NY *10803-1708*

Harper MR & MRS James A (Mai Duane) Bnd'48.Chr.Ds.Ncd.Dc.H.'46
☎ (212) 744-1956 . . 163 E 81 St, New York, NY *10028*

Harper MR James G—Rc.Pe.Sa.Rv.Ty'87
☎ (011-39-6) 575-0456 . . Clivo dei Publicii 2, 00153 Rome, Italy

Harper MR & MRS James R (Annette E Fogo) | ☎ (610) 353-0277
Cr'58.Cts.Wcc.Cr'58 . . . . | 617 Golf Club Rd,
MISS Hadley R—Cr'87 . . . . | Newtown Square,
MR Alexander W—Dth'92 . . . . | PA *19073*

Harper REV DR & MRS John C (Barbara J Quarles) Sth'51.Mt.Fic.H.'46
☎ (202) 244-1571 . . 4436 Westover Place NW, Washington, DC *20016*

Harper MR & MRS Jonathan M (Jane S Sheppard) | ☎ (215) 628-3372
Pa'63.Pa'63.Pa'67 . . . . | 1320 Dogwood
MISS Heather M—Ham'92 . . . . | Lane, Gwynedd
MISS Margaret S—Vt'94 . . . . | Valley, PA *19437*

Harper MRS Judith H (Judith Van N Hover) | ☎ (212) BU8-7681
Sth'59.Dar. . . . . | 161 E 79 St,
MISS Caroline C . . . . | New York, NY
| *10021*

Harper MR & MRS Nelson V JR (Gloria M Barnes) | ☎ (212) 535-5683
Un.Coa.Myf.Ht.Cw.Snc.Rv.Ofp.Ac.Ncd.Dar.Cda. | 45 E 82 St, Apt
Dll.Dc.W&L'55 . . . . | 11W, New York,
MISS Christine R—Nw'91.Dc.Cda. . . . . | NY *10028-0326*
MR James V—Rv.Dth'92 . . . . |

Harper MR & MRS Owen W (Kathleen C McEnerney) Pcu.Bur.Ln.W&L'59
☎ (415) 854-8370 . . 30 Belbrook Way, Atherton, CA *94027*

Harper MR Stuart L (late Richard M H) . . . . . . Married at Hamburg, NY
Piontek MISS Laura A (Richard J) . . . . Apr 13'96

Harrah MR Eric—H'50
☎ (401) 783-5672 . . 14 Dobson St, Wakefield, RI *02879*

Harrell MR & MRS Paul H JR (Margaret P Thouron) | ☎ (302) 429-0709
NCar'63 . . . . | 201 Adams Dam
MISS Piper B . . . . | Rd, Greenville, DE
MR Michael P . . . . | *19807*

Harriman MRS W Averell (Churchill—Hayward—Pamela Digby) . . of
☎ (540) 687-5446 . . ''Willow Oaks'' Rte 626, Middleburg, VA *20117*
US Embassy, Paris, France, Unit 21551, Box A128, APO AE, *09777*

Harrington MR & MRS Charles J (Hoopes—Dewart—Elinore I Hoelzel)
Wil.Fic.Cly.Pn.P'33.Mit'38 . . of
Box 3756, 3705 Kennett Pike, Greenville, DE *19807*
☎ (561) 278-6946 . . 721 Seasage Dv, Delray Beach, FL *33483*

Harrington MR Dennis L—NCol'80
☎ (207) 866-5854 . . 24 Crosby St, Orono, ME *04473*

Harrington MR & MRS Edward A (Ashley P Riegel)
LakeF'82.Fic.Bgt.Wil.Guil'76 ⚓
☎ (914) 232-0335 . . 119 Beaver Dam Rd, PO Box 511, Bedford,
NY *10506*

Harrington MR & MRS Francis X B (Lelia D Gwathmey)
Vt'84.Ck.Prov'78.Wes'91
☎ (516) 671-3114 . . 66 Midway Av, Locust Valley, NY *11560-2032*

Harrington MR & MRS John T (Deborah Reynolds) Ncd.H'42
☎ (414) 962-4052 . . 2023 E Glendale Av, Whitefish Bay, WI *53211*

Harrington MRS Margaret A (Margaret A Lukens) . . . . . name changed to
Lukens

Harrington MRS Mary B (Snitzler—Mary B Harrington) Sc.
Whitehall, 1901 N Lincoln Park W, Chicago, IL *60614*

Harrington MR & MRS Matthew J (Elizabeth A Abell) Denis'85.Denis'84
☎ (510) 601-1685 . . 3 Greenbank Av, Piedmont, CA *94611*

Harris MRS (DR) Alexandra M (Alexandra E Marvin) FlaSt'90.Myf.
☎ (954) 421-0449 . . 757 Siesta Key Trail, Apt 1116, Deerfield Beach,
FL *33441*

Harris MISS Ann B . . . . | ☎ (908) 295-0083
MR Percival van R—Pa'48—at | Box 17, Bay Head,
☎ (212) FI8-6386 . . 1199 Park Av, New York, | NJ *08742*
NY *10128* . . . . |
MR Lawrence C—Pa'47—at ☎ (415) 332-2232 |
553 Sausalito Blvd, Sausalito, CA *94965* . . . . . . |

Harris MISS Annie C
☎ (508) 744-6996 . . 28 Chestnut St, Salem, MA *01970*

Harris MRS Benjamin H (Mary C Aldridge) At.
☎ (334) 928-8667 . . Box 416, Point Clear, AL *36564*

Harris MISS Brooke J . . see L Gourlay

Harris MISS Charles D (Janet B Jeffery) Gchr'30.Elk . . of
☎ (410) 296-4882 . . Blakehurst 311, 1055 W Joppa Rd, Towson,
MD *21204-3732*
☎ (302) 227-4442 . . 75 Tidewaters, Henlopen Acres, Rehoboth Beach,
DE *19971*

Harris MR & MRS Charles S (Carroll D Randall)
Hampshire'84.Hampshire'84
☎ (203) 845-0046 . . 16 Dry Hill Rd, Norwalk, CT *06851*

Harris CDR (RET) & MRS Christopher B (Kay L | ☎ (601) 769-7541
Hubel) USN.Duke'64.MichSt'73 . . . . | 805 Warren St,
MR Eric P . . . . | Pascagoula, MS
| *39567*

Harris MR & MRS Christopher H (Talbot Chamberlin) Ham'92.Hob'92
☎ (203) 637-6768 . . 24 Irvine Rd, Old Greenwich, CT *06870*

Harris MR David W—Au.Pa'67
☎ (203) 622-4160 . . 20 Dingletown Rd, Greenwich, CT *06830*

Harris MR David W JR—Fairf'96
☎ (212) 787-9232 . . 48 W 68 St, Apt 7F, New York, NY *10023*

Harris MRS E Spenker (Elizabeth A Spenker) | ☎ (203) 661-3649
Briar'68.Au.Cly. . . . . | 29 Pecksland Rd,
MISS Julia de P—at ☎ (212) 312-1707 | Greenwich, CT
41 Park Av, Apt 11A, New York, NY *10016* . . . | *06831*
MISS Margaret R—at 25 Cypress St, Brookline, |
MA *02146* . . . . |
JUNIORS MISS Emily D—at St Mark's . . . . |

Harris MRS Francis M (Barbara L Sharpe). . of
☎ (408) 423-6833 . . "Empress Ranch" 2500 Empire Grade Rd,
Santa Cruz, CA *95060*
☎ (619) 323-2295 . . 2582 Calle Palo Fiero, Palm Springs, CA *92264*

Harris MR & MRS George B (Florence Butcher) V'39.Co.Me.Va'32 ⛵
☎ (610) 642-8940 . . 1014 Merion Square Rd, Gladwyne, PA *19035*

Harris MR & MRS George I E (Kate B Webb) | ☎ (212) 772-9030
Hlns'70.Mto.Cly.Ty'65 . . . . | 79 E 79 St,
JUNIORS MISS Amanda H . . . . | New York, NY
JUNIORS MR Jonathan J . . . . | *10021*

Harris MR Gregory S—⛵
☎ (508) 927-4188 . . 111 Water St, Apt 12, Beverly, MA *01915*

Harris MRS Gwathmey (Nancy Gwathmey) Gm.Ac.
☎ (610) 527-5426 . . 412 S Ithan Av, Villanova, PA *19085*

Harris DR & MRS H Patterson (Josephine Emery) Y'32.Duke'36.Y'65
☎ (203) 259-4344 . . 472 Mill Hill Dv, Southport, CT *06490-1223*

Harris MR & MRS Henry F (A J Penelope Parsons) | ☎ (215) 836-4383
Sg.Ph.Nf.Rb.Ssk.Unn.Ac. . . . . | 575 E Evergreen
MISS Elizabeth H . . . . | Av, Wyndmoor, PA
MR Henry F JR . . . . | *19038*

Harris MR & MRS Henry P U JR (Mary Jeanne Johnston)
Pr.Ri.Cly.Stan'51 . . of
☎ (516) 626-0055 . . 37 Brookville Rd, Glen Head, NY *11545*
☎ (603) 968-3635 . . "Loon Rock" PO Box 193, Holderness,
NH *03245*

Harris MR & MRS Henry P U 3d (Eleanor M | ☎ (757) 423-8939
Magruder) Swb'74.Nh.Ln.Ncd.Va'74.Va'76 ⛵ | 1503 N Shore Rd,
JUNIORS MR Gregory M . . . . | Norfolk, VA *23505*

Harris MR & MRS Holton E (Jeanne C Deming) | 5 Newtown Tpke,
Ncd.Mit'47.Duke'49. . . . . | Westport, CT *06880*
MISS Dorothy S—Mariet'90 . . . . |
MR Walter D—Mit'86.Mit'87 . . . . |

Harris MR & MRS J Andrews 5th (Marlis Heckelmann) Oldenburg'86
☎ (415) 648-7344 . . 3770—21 St, San Francisco, CA *94114*

Harris MR & MRS J Gary (Harris—Cornelia D Gilbert)
☎ (401) 331-5082 . . 45 Boylston Av, Providence, RI *02906*

Harris MRS James C (Caroline C Gower)
☎ (864) 233-6980 . . 2 Woodland Way Circle, Greenville, SC *29601*

Harris MR & MRS James Hoban (Anne Reuther) | of ☎ (212)421-1917
Sth'57.Rc.Plg.Cly.P'46 . . . . | 200 E 66 St,
MR Gordon W—at 300 Flax Hill Rd, | New York, NY
South Norwalk, CT *06854* . . . . | *10021*
| ☎ (203) 866-2017
| "Bois Joli"
| 10 Woodland Rd,
| Wilson Point,
| South Norwalk, CT
| *06854*

Harris MASTER James Walker (J Gary) . . . . Born May 26'96

Harris MR & MRS John A 4th (Annie L Ryerson) Ac.Pn.P'51.Pa'67
☎ (610) 296-5914 . . 2035 Twinbrook Rd, Berwyn, PA *19312*

Harris MR & MRS John S (Clarinda S Muhlhofer) Cin'86.Cin'85
☎ (513) 232-8669 . . 2130 Flaxen Court, Cincinnati, OH *45244*

Harris MRS John W (Ayer—Eleanore M Potter) | ☎ (516) 324-5785
Ck.Mds. . . . . | "Pound Foolish"
MISS Denise De Santo . . . . | 76 Woods Lane,
MISS Constance Ayer . . . . | East Hampton, NY
MR Frederick B Ayer . . . . | *11937*

Harris MR & MRS Jonathan M (Cynthia A Bidart)
Ida'81.Pa'87.H'76.Wes'84
☎ (610) 642-7304 . . 104 Mansion Lane, Wynnewood, PA *19096*

Harris MR & MRS Joseph M JR (Barbara P Dane) | ☎ (407) 773-6584
Sth'60.Aht'59 . . . . | 10 Windjammer
MR Stephen C—Tul'87—at 3700 Carlyle Close, | Point, South Merrit
Mobile, AL *36609* . . . . | Island, FL *32952*
MR Thomas C—at Clemson . . . . |

Harris MR & MRS Kristof D (Janae Roberts) LSU'93
451 Constellation, Apt 412, League City, TX *77573*

Harris MRS Lawrence J (Constance Binney) . . . . . . | ☎ (401) 246-2713
MISS Marilyn—Ne'80 . . . . | 1 Carriage Trail,
MR David L—Ne'82 . . . . | Barrington, RI
| *02806*

Harris MR Leon A JR—C.Hn.H'47
☎ (214) 526-0565 . . 4300 St Johns Dv, Dallas, TX *75205*

Harris MRS Marjorie Knight (Marjorie C Knight) | ☎ (561) 283-0333
Myf. . . . . | 500 Flamingo Av,
MISS Jennifer W . . . . | Stuart, FL *34996*
MISS Christina W . . . . |

Harris MISS Mary Virginia—Ch'38.Cs.Me.
☎ (610) KI3-7157 . . Swarthmore Apts, Swarthmore, PA *19081*

Harris MR & MRS Montgomery (Rosanna Chanler) Ph.Rv.Ac.
☎ (410) 820-8554 . . 8662 Marengo Farm Rd, Easton, MD *21601-5160*

Harris MR Montgomery 3d (Montgomery) . . . Married at Tunis Mills, MD
Bowden MISS Nancy F (Francis J JR) . . . . Jun 22'96

Harris MR & MRS Montgomery 3d (Nancy F Bowden) Pc.Ph.Rv.Bost'76
☎ (610) 687-9717 . . 204 Gulph Creek Rd, Radnor, PA *19087*

Harris MASTER Nicolas Henry Upham (Jonathan M) . . . . Born at
Wynnewood, PA Mch 6'96

Harris DR & MRS P Randolph (Susan Carter) V'54.H.'52.Cl'58
☎ (508) 475-8063 . . 11 Dorset Circle, Andover, MA *01810*

Harris MR & MRS Peter W (Harriet B Reed) | ☎ (508) 785-2475
Nu'77.D.Srb.An.USN'76.Geo'82 . . . . | 10 Pleasant St,
JUNIORS MISS Alexandra . . . . | Dover, MA *02030*

Harris MR & MRS R Macy 3d (Louise B Ward) Md'81.Hartw'79
☎ (716) 586-6493 . . 1066 Allens Creek Rd, Rochester, NY *14618*

Harris MRS Rebecca P (Rebecca R Paul) F&M'82.Pc.
☎ (215) 836-5327 . . 7908 Pine Rd, Wyndmoor, PA *19038*

Harris MR & MRS Robert H (Jo Ann Harris) Ala'69.USAF'69.Cumber'76
☎ (334) 277-9311 . . 2147 Vaughn Lane, Montgomery, AL *36106*

Harris MR & MRS Shawn A (Carolyn A Scott) HWSth'86.Cda.Alaska'95
☎ (518) 851-3188 . . 82 Scott Rd, Hudson, NY *12534*

Harris MR & MRS Shepard (Melissa L Smallidge) Temp'83.PhilaArt'83
☎ (207) 829-4446 . . 135 Tuttle Rd, Cumberland, ME *04021*

Harris MRS Victor B (Sprengnether—Roberta C | ☎ (314) 664-6363
Lucas) StL'55.StL'64 . . . . | 3137 Longfellow
MR Ronald J Sprengnether—StL'67.Mo'84 . . | Blvd, St Louis, MO
| *63104*

Harris MRS Victor S (Phyllis Voysey) Swth'54 . . . . | ☎ (212) 722-0862
MISS Elise C—P'92 . . . . | 56 E 91 St,
 | New York, NY
 | *10128*

Harris MR & MRS W Gibson 2d (Pamela L Dixon) | of ☎ (203)637-8290
Rol'68.Yn.Y'66.Va'68 . . . . | 69 Cedar Cliff Rd,
MISS Barbara Dixon—at Vanderbilt . . . . | Riverside, CT *06878*
JUNIORS MR W Gibson 3d—at Bucknell . . . . . . | ☎ (561) 776-0754
 | Lost Tree Village,
 | 11310 Golf View
 | Lane, North Palm
 | Beach, FL *33408*

Harris MRS W Hall 3d (Sarah Louise Fairfax) Mv.Cda.
 ☎ (410) 467-1446 . . 523 W 40 St, Baltimore, MD *21211-2217*
Harris MR W Marks—Ala'81
 ☎ (334) 265-9445 . . 3127 Woodley Terr, Montgomery, AL *36106*
Harris MR & MRS William R JR (Adelaide M Herkert) Ham'79.Cly.
 ☎ (860) 435-2021 . . PO Box 1628, Reservoir Rd, Lakeville, CT *06039*
Harris MISS Zoe Elizabeth (Charles S) . . . . Born Feb 25'94
Harrison MISS (DR) Anne—RochMed'57
 14 Oatka Place, Scottsville, NY *14546*
Harrison MR & MRS Berkeley G (Kristen E Techentin)
 SanDiego'91.Vh.Duke'90.SCal'95
 ☎ (818) 578-0024 . . 625 Magnolia Av, Pasadena, CA *91106*
Harrison MRS C Fenton (Chesley Fenton Requardt)
 ☎ (410) 337-6868 . . 3 Ruxview Court, Apt 201, Ruxton, MD *21204*
Harrison MRS Charles C 4th (Gibson—Hubbard—Mary E Wickham) Me.
 ☎ (610) 688-9116 . . 505 E Lancaster Av, Apt 109, St Davids, PA *19087*
Harrison MR & MRS Charles C 5th (J Leanne Prillaman) Roan'88.Roan'82
 8315 Saddle Ridge Terr, Ellicott City, MD *21043-7927*
Harrison MR & MRS Charles M (Porter—Linda K Rawson) H'76.Hn.H'71
 ☎ (505) 989-1381 . . 3212 Calle Celestial, Santa Fe, NM *87501-9612*
Harrison MR Christopher P . . see MRS J M R Bardenheier
Harrison MRS Dorothy O (Dorothy G Osgood) | ☎ (603) 472-8394
Ws'58.Ncd. . . . . | 25 Smith Rd,
MISS Sarah M—Ws'89—at 4 Anthony Lane, | Bedford, NH *03102*
Billerica, MA *01821* |

Harrison MRS Edward T (Carkener—Gallowhur—Mary L Gary)
V'31.Bur.Tcy.Fr.StJ . . .of
 ☎ (415) 348-1823 . . 1 Baldwin Av, Apt 823, San Mateo, CA *94401*
 ☎ (415) 459-7016 . . 2 Madrone Av, Kentfield, CA *94904*
Harrison MRS H Stuart (Suzanne Brookhart) V'41.It.
 ☎ (216) 991-5695 . . 22770 Canterbury Lane, Shaker Heights,
 OH *44122*
Harrison MISS Holly N—Denis'93 . . see B Murdoch
Harrison MR & MRS Horace W (Wilson—Catherine | ☎ (410) 828-5341
H France) Gv.Ncd.P'43 . . . . | 1802 Indian Head
 MISS Susan P Wilson—at 965 Hyde St, | Rd, Ruxton, MD
 Apt 10, San Francisco, CA *94109* . . . . | *21204*

Harrison MR J Randolph—H'27
 ☎ (609) 426-6608 . . Meadow Lakes 48-04L, Hightstown,
 NJ *08520-3342*
Harrison MR & MRS James B (Holderness—Jane R Munson) Ri.
 ☎ (212) 860-4559 . . 27 E 95 St, New York, NY *10128*

Harrison MRS James G (Maria W Sheerin) Ncd. . . . . | ☎ (804) 458-5479
MISS Catherine B—Va'83—at 1204 Rothesay Rd, | 1100 Coggins Point
Richmond, VA *23221* . . . . | Rd, Hopewell, VA
 | *23860*

Harrison MRS James S 3d (Free—Medlen—Mary A | ☎ (561) 659-6015
T T Phillips) BtP.Evg.Cly.Cda. . . . . | 161 Clarke Av,
MISS Lucy Gurnee—Rol'89 . . . . | PO Box 3325,
 | Palm Beach, FL
 | *33480*

Harrison MR Jerome L . . see MRS J M R Bardenheier
Harrison MRS John L (Anne Gray)
 ☎ (717) 393-3758 . . 1319 Clayton Rd, Lancaster, PA *17603*
Harrison MR & MRS John L JR (Alice M Wieland) | ☎ (215) 483-1438
Sth'59.Ph.Y'57.Pa'63 . . . . | 8520 Hagys Mill
MR J Sergeant—Y'87 . . . . | Rd, Philadelphia, PA
MR David A—Dth'92 . . . . | *19128*

Harrison MR & MRS John T (Patricia Wood) | of ☎ (860)767-2347
Rcn.Unn.Plg.Csn.Y'35 . . . . | 263 Essex Meadows,
MR Frederick W—at Kolburne School, | Essex, CT *06426*
New Marlborough, MA *01230* . . . . | ☎ (802) 442-4292
MR Daniel H—Y'78—at ☎ (860) 526-1244 | "Four Corners"
488 Joshuatown Rd, Lyme, CT *06371* . . . . | RR 2, Box 72,
 | Shaftsbury, VT
 | *05262*

Harrison MR Joseph B . . see MRS J M R Bardenheier
Harrison MR & MRS Joseph H (Louise Lynah)
 501 E 44 St, Savannah, GA *31405*
Harrison MR & MRS Joseph H JR (Gloria L Horton) Peab'yColl'70.Ga'66
 ☎ (912) 234-6474 . . 220 E 45 St, Savannah, GA *31405*
Harrison MRS June A (Wells—June F Auslander)
 ☎ (212) 935-0070 . . 565 Park Av, New York, NY *10021*
Harrison MRS Melissa T (Gray—Melissa A Travis) . . . . Married
Mohlman MR Don T . . . . Jun 2'95
Harrison MR & MRS Peter D'A (Alexandra C | ☎ (505) 856-3424
Madeira) Tor'59.Pa'70 . . . . | 1003 Tramway Lane
MR Andreas R . . . . | NE, Albuquerque,
 | NM *87122*

Harrison MR & MRS Philip D (Catherine C Griffiths) Dth'90.Pc.Dth'89
 ☎ (215) 247-7418 . . 8833 Norwood Av, Philadelphia, PA *19118*
Harrison MR & MRS R Brandon JR (Agnes W Smith) | ☎ (513) 831-9666
Err.Eyc.Ny.Cw.H'61 . . . . | 815 Miami Av,
MISS Sarah C . . . . | Terrace Park, OH
MISS Emily D . . . . | *45174*
MISS Catherine W . . . . |

Harrison MR & MRS Randolph (Amey Mackinney) | ☎ (516) WA2-5288
Rdc'56.Rc.Pr.Mb.B.Lic.H'55 . . . . | Frost Mill Rd,
MR Alexander McF—BostColl'81—at | Mill Neck, NY
 ☎ (212) 995-8181 . . 45 First Av, New York, NY | *11765*
10003 . . . . |

Harrison MR & MRS Randolph JR (M Whitney Wright)
Bost'79.Pars'81.Sa.Pa'78
 ☎ (215) 646-7226 . . Box 86, Gwynedd Valley, PA *19437*

Harrison MR & MRS Ridgely W (Cozad—Johnson—
Josephine E Streeter) Rc.Evg.Ng.BtP. . . . . | of ☎ (561)833-3471
  MR Bryan S Cozad. . . . . | 101 Jungle Rd,
Palm Beach, FL
33480
☎ (212) 772-9611
30 E 72 St,
New York, NY
10021

Harrison MRS Robert B (A Elizabeth Fontaine) W&M'63
9100 Belvoir Woods P'kway, Apt 108, Ft Belvoir, VA *22060*

Harrison MR & MRS (DR) Robert B 3d (Katharine D | ☎ (410) 235-3546
Santos) Gchr'69.Md'86.Elk.JHop'64.Md'67 . . . | 308 Northfield
  MISS Anne F . . . . | Place, Baltimore,
  MR R Barker 4th . . . . | MD *21210*

Harrison MR & MRS Robert C (F Diane Cox) | 307 Golden Wings
StMarys'65.NCarSt'65.Riv'80 . . . . | Way, Greer, SC
  MR R Scot—at Kill Devil Hills, NC *27948* . . . . . | *29650*
  JUNIORS MR Randolph C . . . . |

Harrison MR & MRS Robert Carter (Ilona de Rosty-Forgach) H'59
☎ (212) 535-3624 . . 39 E 79 St, New York, NY *10021*

Harrison MRS William Henry 3d (Evelyn | ☎ (561) 665-0619
Prebensen) BtP. . . . . | 1200 S Flagler Dv,
  MISS Alexandra E—Geo'89—at 1200 S Flagler | Apt 1605,
Dv, Apt 302, West Palm Beach, FL *33401* . . . . . | West Palm Beach,
FL *33401*

Harrison MR & MRS William R (Karen C Graham) | ☎ (860) 561-3335
MaryB'67.Va'67 . . . . | "Sunset Farm"
  MR William R JR . . . . | 8 Greenridge Lane,
  MR Christopher W . . . . | West Hartford, CT
  MR Kenneth G . . . . | *06107*

Harrity MRS Colleen S (Schwartz—Colleen I | ☎ (610) MU8-1189
Spicer) . . . . | 214 Dorset Rd,
  MR Mark C—Me. . . . . | Devon, PA *19333*

Harrity MR & MRS R Johnstone (Louise B Hoopes)
Me.Gm.Myf.Ncd.Wms'46
☎ (610) 525-4614 . . 326 N Ithan Av, Rosemont, PA *19010*

Harrity MR & MRS (DR) Robert J JR (Janet A Madigan)
MtH'74.NYMed'77.Y'81.Me.Ty'70.Va'72 . . of
☎ (203) 772-7917 . . 307 Lawrence St, New Haven, CT *06511*
☎ (603) 253-9921 . . Squam Lake, Old Harvard Rd, Box 177K,
Center Harbor, NH *03226*

Harrity MR & MRS William F JR (Wood—Virginia A | of ☎ (610)527-4532
Weis) M.Me. . . . . | 456 Colebrook Lane,
  MISS Alden R Wood . . . . | Bryn Mawr, PA
19010
☎ (941) 955-9392
246 Robin Dv,
Bird Key, Sarasota,
FL *34236*

Harrold MRS Paulette D (Paulette M Devinck)
☎ (312) 751-0868 . . 1335 N Astor St, Chicago, IL *60610*

Harrower MRS Lyle (Léontine Lyle)
☎ (619) 759-5610 . . PO Box 7213, 3805 Avenida Feliz,
Rancho Santa Fe, CA *92067-7213*

Harrower MR Ronald L—EverSt'84 . . . . | 7 Clinton St,
  MR Gordon 3d—Hob'83 . . . . | Saratoga Springs,
NY *12866*

Harsch MR & MRS Joseph C (Anne E Wood)
Sb.C.Mt.Cos.Wms'27.Camb'29 ⚓
☎ (401) 423-0690 . . "Windswept" 275 Highland Dv, PO Box 457,
Jamestown, RI *02835*

Harsch MR & MRS Paul A 3d (Merry Anderson) | ☎ (802) 823-5411
Godd'69.Wms'69 . . . . | "High Meadow"
  MISS Sarah W . . . . | RD 2, Box 23,
  MR Caleb C . . . . | Pownal, VT *05261*
  JUNIORS MISS Katherine A . . . . |
  JUNIORS MISS Jessica L . . . . |

Harsch MRS Rae H (Rae E Hanewald) B'gton'61 . . | ☎ (912) 236-7799
  MISS Christiana W . . . . | 206 E Gaston St,
Savannah, GA
31401

Hart MRS Albert Edward JR (Jean MacColl)
☎ (803) 648-9455 . . "Edencroft" 517 Sumter St SE, Box 2788, Aiken,
SC *29801*

Hart MR & MRS Allison B (Joy Van Tine) | ☎ (908) 766-4777
Chr.Myf.Sar.Pa'32 . . . . | PO Box 326,
  MISS Melissa Van T . . . . | 200 Mendham Rd,
  MR Andrew R Van T . . . . | Bernardsville, NJ
07924

Hart MR & MRS Augustin S (Margaret Stuart) Fy.P'37
☎ (847) 234-1272 . . 1272 N Green Bay Rd, Lake Forest, IL *60045*

Hart DR & MRS Brandon B (Katrina V N O Bogert) | ☎ (508) 468-2342
P'54.McG'59.Pa'60 . . . . | 893 Highland St,
  MISS Eliza W—Pa'92 . . . . | Box 211, Hamilton,
MA *01936*

Hart MR & MRS Bruce W (Anne Elizabeth Jones) Cal'78.Bhm.Cp.Stan'73
☎ (415) 459-7522 . . PO Box 1620, Ross, CA *94957*

Hart MR C Caldwell JR (Charles C) . . . . Married at Bryn Mawr, PA
  Wysocki MISS Sylvia A (Carl E) . . . . May 4'96

Hart MR & MRS Charles C (Baena—Marilyn McC | ☎ (610) 527-5775
Converse) Me.Rc.W&L'63 . . . . | 227 Trianon Lane,
  MISS Elizabeth A Baena—Col'95 . . . . | Villanova, PA *19085*
  MR Christopher C Baena—Ty'93 . . . . |

Hart MR Christopher P—Ty'93 . . see J W Sinwell

Hart MR & MRS David E (Caroline H Gold) Ht.Dar.Dll.
☎ (908) 974-0439 . . 311 Jersey Av, Spring Lake, NJ *07762*

Hart MR & MRS Douglas E (Lydia Melville Day) | ☎ (617) 326-2376
Cy.Ub.Bhm.Bost'76 . . . . | 215 Village Av,
  JUNIORS MISS Caroline B . . . . | Dedham, MA
  JUNIORS MR Andrew E . . . . | *02026-4230*

Hart DR & MRS Francis F (Marie H Newbold) | ☎ (215) 646-2485
Sg.Ac.P'32.Pa'36 . . . . | PO Box 477,
  MR Joshua F—Tufts'79 . . . . | Ambler, PA *19002*

Hart MR & MRS George D (Jessica W Ely) Bhm.Tcy.Ncd.Stan'31
☎ (415) 454-2070 . . PO Box 156, Ross, CA *94957*

Hart MR & MRS George D JR (Sarah Coonan) | ☎ (970) 923-5048
Stan'73.Bhm.Tcy.Bost'71 . . . . | 126 Meadow Rd,
  MISS Derith H . . . . | Snowmass Village,
  JUNIORS MR Ross W . . . . | CO *81615*

Hart MR H Rodes JR—Van'83
118 Westover Dv, Nashville, TN *37205*

Hart MISS Hilary B—Y'86 . . see S H Brainerd

Hart MR Howard S—Mass'88 . . see S H Brainerd

Hart MR John A . . . . Died at
St Augustine, FL Feb 26'96
Hart MRS John A (M Malotte Houser)
☎ (904) 829-8410 . . 57 Water St, St Augustine, FL *32084*
Hart MR & MRS John H (Sarah R Miller) . . of
☎ (610) 838-6516 . . 1919 Pine Court, Hellertown, PA *18055*
☎ (516) 569-7090 . . "Haywood" 2 Village Way, Lawrence, NY *11559*
Hart Lewis J (Margaret L Lowery)
☎ (610) LA5-3855 . . 1429 Orchard Way, Rosemont, PA *19010*
Hart MR & MRS Lewis J JR (Julia R Mullen) | ☎ (914) 666-3494
Hlns'77.Pa'69.Pa'77 . . . . | 136 Seven Bridges
JUNIORS MR Lewis J 3d . . . . | Rd, Chappaqua, NY
| *10514*
Hart MRS M Webb (Margaret O Webb) Sth'71
2517 Winterbury Court, Raleigh, NC *27607*
Hart MR & MRS Robert J K (Marian Hodges) | ☎ (516) 569-3308
Ny.P.'40 ⚓ | 190 Briarwood
MISS Marian H—at 74 Charles St, New York, NY | Crossing, Lawrence,
10014 . . . . | NY *11559*
MR Robert J K JR . . . . |
MR Charles K—at 101 E Liberty St, Savannah, |
GA *31401* . . . . |
Hart MRS Sarah P (Sarah B Pardue) Belm'84
☎ (615) 352-1364 . . 403 Hillwood Blvd, Nashville, TN *37205*
Hart MRS Thomas (Harrison—Virginia Dilkes)
250 S 18 St, Philadelphia, PA *19103*
Hart MR & MRS Thomas Van Tine (Hannon— | ☎ (919) 783-8767
Martha C Horton) NCar'76.FairD'73 . . . . | 3316 Churchill Rd,
JUNIORS MR Thomas W—at Hargrave Mil Acad . | Raleigh, NC *27607*
Hart MR & MRS Thornley A (Barbara P Ingram) Rcn.Gv.Md.Cly.NCar'70
☎ (410) 581-8118 . . 3126 Golf Course Rd W, Owings Mills, MD *21117*
Hart MRS Thornley W (Joan F Johnson)
☎ (212) YU8-2069 . . 114 E 72 St, New York, NY *10021*
Hart MR & MRS Todd C (Zoë de Ropp-Weinman) Cl'87.H'93.Cly.Cda . . .of
☎ (212) 875-0991 . . 100 W 80 St, Apt 2B, New York, NY *10024*
☎ (516) 653-5198 . . "Pine Neck" Box 63, East Quogue, NY *11942*
Hart MR & MRS William D JR (Swan—Jeanne A | ☎ (203) 966-1521
Dewey) Sth'50.Y'40.H'43 . . . . | Deer Park Rd,
MISS Catharine R Swan—Hartw'82—at | New Canaan, CT
☎ (202) 298-865 . . 2200—40 Place NW, | *06840*
Apt 4, Washington, DC *20007* . . . . |
Hartenstein MRS Pliney E (Dorothy A Bray)
713 Reed's Landing, Springfield, MA *01109-2054*
Hartigan MRS Charles C (Frances P Morgan) | ☎ (301) 657-2384
Skd'45.Cvc.Sl. . . . . | 3709 Underwood St,
MISS Cynthia M . . . . | Chevy Chase, MD
MISS Margaret T . . . . | *20815*
MR Christopher C . . . . |
Hartigan MRS Dudley K (Miller—W Dudley Klinck)
☎ (914) 331-6918 . . 188 Marcott Rd, Kingston, NY *12401*
Hartley MRS Elizabeth Fletcher (Eager—Elizabeth Fletcher Hartley)
☎ (410) 377-9650 . . 6673 Walnutwood Circle, Baltimore, MD *21212*
Hartley MR & MRS James R (Hillyard—Barbara Johnson) . . of
☎ (303) 830-1400 . . 14 Cheesman Gardens, 1510 E Tenth Av, Denver,
CO *80218*
☎ (303) 674-4257 . . 160 County Rd 480, Evergreen, CO *80439*

Hartley MR & MRS Louis A 2d (Kate S Heroy) | ☎ (423) 584-3248
Cwr'67.Cr'69 . . . . | 2324 Craig Cove
MR Garrett A . . . . | Rd, Knoxville, TN
MR Richard P . . . . | *37919*
JUNIORS MR Stuart H . . . . |
Hartman MR & MRS William G (Hilary W Curtis) Nw'85.Drake'83
☎ (847) 729-2412 . . 2446 Bel Air Dv, Glenview, IL *60025-4860*
Hartman MR & MRS William R JR (Barbara C Cauffman)
Ken'86.Pa'91.Ken'86.Pa'91
☎ (610) 647-4376 . . 57 Knox Av, Berwyn, PA *19312*
Hartmann MR & MRS Rolf D (Carlotta M Hellier) | ☎ (516) 367-9371
H.'55 . . . . | Box 201,
MR Christian P . . . . | Cold Spring Harbor,
MR Alexander D . . . . | NY *11724*
Hartmeyer MR & MRS Stuart H (Mimi T French) Un.Ck.Pr.P.'84
☎ (516) 922-9008 . . 765 Remsens Lane, Oyster Bay, NY *11771*
Hartnett MR Lawrence K
349 Hemlock St, Vacaville, CA *95688*
Hartnett MR & MRS Leonard J (Margaret E Watson) Ncd.Cal'75
☎ (707) 448-3027 . . 491 Deodara St, Vacaville, CA *95688*
Harts MRS William W (Murdock—Catherine Hulbert)
☎ (540) 687-5499 . . Box 1276, Middleburg, VA *20118*
Hartshorne MR Harold—Cho.P'40
☎ (803) 449-8459 . . Gator Gap Apt 614, 100 Lands End Blvd,
Myrtle Beach, SC *29572*
Hartt MR & MRS Dudley N (Anne Barbey) | of ☎ (315)655-3846
Sth'46.H'37 . . . . | PO Box 90,
MISS S Madeleine J—Ham'82 . . . . | Cazenovia, NY
MR Edmund A M—Ken'79—at | *13035*
☎ (207) 763-3466 . . RR 1, Box 4838, | ☎ (011-353-28)
Lincolnville, ME *04849* . . . . | 36296
| Castletownshend,
| Co Cork, Ireland
Hartwell MR & MRS Mortimer H (Susan M Bishop) OreSt'60.Y'50.Mich'53
☎ (503) 635-4279 . . 12231 SW Tryon Hill Rd, Portland, OR *97219*
Hartwell DR & MRS Shattuck W JR (Mary Jane Davis)
Ws'50.Cv.Tv.It.Aht'50.Mich'54 . . of
☎ (216) 247-3191 . . 35845 Old Kinsman Rd, Hunting Valley, OH *44022*
☎ (208) 622-4730 . . 4336 Fairway Nine, PO Box 1695, Sun Valley,
ID *83353*
Hartwick MR & MRS Ronald S (Kathleen A Jones) Cal'81.Y'65
☎ (310) 476-1232 . . 2012 Mandeville Canyon Rd, Los Angeles,
CA *90049*
Harty MISS Hilary P—DU'65.Sim'69
☎ (617) 566-0648 . . 8 Kilsyth Terr, Brookline, MA *02146*
Harty MR & MRS R Philip (Anne Piper) St.Ts.G.Dth'38
☎ (716) 882-1898 . . 86 Rumsey Rd, Buffalo, NY *14209*
Harvey MRS A Charlotte (Rienhoff—A Charlotte Harvey)
see MRS A O'D Wilson
Harvey MR Bennet B—Cw.Myf.P'25
☎ (773) 561-2900 . . 909 W Foster Av, Apt 234, Chicago, IL *60640*
Harvey MR & MRS Bennet B JR (Karen L Guttormsen)
Wis'65.JM'83.P'56.H'59
☎ (773) 472-4496 . . 2119 N Bissell St, Chicago, IL *60614*
Harvey MR Bruce F E—Chr.Plg.StJ.Cw.Ox'29
☎ (203) 869-5835 . . 478 North St, Greenwich, CT *06830*

Harvey MR & MRS C Randolph (Rouvina—Elizabeth Raney) Rv.Hav'48.Pa'51 . . . . | ☎ (610) 644-4479
  MISS Julia E Rouvina—Mich'83—at | 314 N Fairfield Rd,
  ☎ (610) 983-0367 . . 32 Sheffield Court, | Devon, PA *19333*
  Collegeville, PA *19426* . . . . |

Harvey MRS Catherine M (Harvey—von Helms—Catherine F McElvain)
  ☎ (505) 988-4541 . . PO Box 2148, Santa Fe, NM *87504*

Harvey MRS Charles Daggett (Wood—Jane Wood) Cas . . .of
  ☎ (773) DI8-0232 . . 2430 N Lakeview Av, Chicago, IL *60614*
  ☎ (011-41-30) 4-41-26 . . ''Chalet Matteli'' 3780 Gstaad, Switzerland

Harvey MR & MRS Curran W JR (Marjorie J Simons) V'52.Elk.Y'51
  ☎ (941) 434-2521 . . 3780 Ft Charles Dv, Naples, FL *34102*

Harvey MR & MRS Cyrus I JR (Rebecca P Miller) | ☎ (860) 928-0092
  Hb.H'47 . . . . | PO Box 50,
  MISS Natasha—Pa'92.Ste.—at ☎ (202) 338-1029 | Woodstock, CT
  1657—31 St NW, Apt B5, Washington, DC | *06281*
  20007 . . . . |

Harvey MISS Dereke Jay
  ☎ (802) 948-2892 . . ''Hauxhurst'' PO Box 268, Brandon,
  VT *05733-0268*

Harvey MR & MRS Edward F JR (E Anne Rodgers) | ☎ (757) 258-0203
  Pa'49 . . . . | ''Rabbit Race''
  MISS Pamela A—at ☎ (703) 931-9557 | 7 Whitaker Court,
  4207 S 35 St, Arlington, VA *22206* . . . . | Ford's Colony,
  | Williamsburg, VA
  | *23185*

Harvey MRS Eldon JR (Eleanor M Ashforth) V'46.Rby.Dc . . .of
  ☎ (860) 535-2060 . . ''Pond House'' PO Box 447, Stonington, CT *06378*
  ☎ (941) 475-6126 . . ''Heron Cove'' 7485 Manasota Key Rd,
  Englewood, FL *34223*

Harvey MR & MRS F Barton JR (Grace W Locke) | ☎ (410) DR7-8144
  V'44.Elk.B.Fic.Mv.H'42 . . . . | 2 Lindsay Lane,
  MR F Barton 3d . . . . | Baltimore, MD
  | *21212*

Harvey MR & MRS George W (Elizabeth Drake) Ch'25
  ☎ (813) 253-3972 . . 3501 Bayshore Blvd, Apt 1202, Tampa, FL *33629*

Harvey MR & MRS H Darrell (Robin A Bailey) | of ☎ (203)655-7888
  Ws'72.K.H'71 . . . . | 18 Peach Hill Rd,
  JUNIORS MISS Anne D . . . . | Darien, CT *06820*
  JUNIORS MISS Katharine B . . . . | ☎ (603) 464-3973
  JUNIORS MR John B . . . . | ''The Homestead''
  | Rte 1, Box 200,
  | Reservoir Rd,
  | Deering, NH *03244*

Harvey MR Henry C—Tv.Rr.It.Kt.Y'36
  ☎ (216) 951-1284 . . 39393 Kirtland Rd, Willoughby, OH *44094*

Harvey MR & MRS John S C 3d (Fitler—Joan Kellett) Me.Hav'54.H'57
  ☎ (610) 642-3496 . . 414 Rose Lane, Haverford, PA *19041*

Harvey MR & MRS Julian W (Katherine E Abler) Rc.Cas.Fy.Y'65.Nw'68
  ☎ (312) 649-0414 . . 1209 N Astor St, Chicago, IL *60610*

Harvey JUNIORS MR Nathan A . . see MISS A C Toogood

Harvey MR & MRS Robert D H (Nancy C Gross)
  Nu'46.Md.Elk.Mt.Mv.Pn.P'42.JHop'53
  ☎ (410) 377-5984 . . 1 Lindsay Lane, Baltimore, MD *21212*

Harvey MR & MRS Robert E (Karen N Simpson) | of ☎ (203)655-9865
  Denis'70.Les'74.Rcn.Bow'76.Va'80 . . . . | 4 Kona Rd, Darien,
  JUNIORS MISS Jennifer S . . . . | CT *06820*
  JUNIORS MR James R S—at Milton . . . . | ☎ (603) 529-4304
  | ''Newstead''
  | Homestead Farm,
  | Deering, NH *03244*

Harvey MR & MRS Thomas B JR (Archer St Clair) | ☎ (609) 655-3104
  BMr'64.W.Ncd.Hav'57 . . . . | 40 Cranbury Neck
  MR Thomas B 3d . . . . | Rd, Cranbury, NJ
  | *08512*

Harvey MR & MRS W F Atlee (Mary Ellen McKeon) | ☎ (610) MO4-4559
  Newt'56.VillaN'59.Rv.Hav'52 . . . . | 459 Rockland Rd,
  MR Terence A—SCar'94—at ☎ (404) 636-5582 | Merion, PA *19066*
  1332 Weatherstone Way NE, Atlanta, GA *30324* |

Harvey MR William P—TriSt'28
  ☎ (770) 992-2619 . . Chambrel 233, 1000 Applewood Dv, Roswell,
  GA *30077*

Harvie MR & MRS J Beverly (Faith G Hall) | ☎ (914) 358-2571
  V'45.Cly.Y.'30 . . . . | 4 Salisbury Point,
  MR Scott C—RI'75—at 120 Washington St, | South Nyack, NY
  Camden, ME *04843* . . . . | *10960*

Harvie-Watt MR Euan . . of
  ☎ (212) 758-1291 . . 333 E 56 St, Apt 16E, New York, NY *10022*
  ☎ (011-44-1333) 330-747 . . ''Yarborough'' Elie, Fife, Scotland

Harvie-Watt MISS Jennifer—Pitzer'91 . . see D M Leale

Harwell MR & MRS Robert E JR (Elizabeth L Creighton) Van'59.Van'57
  ☎ (615) 269-6402 . . 4416 Sheppard Place, Nashville, TN *37205*

Harwood MR & MRS Donald E (Joan W Powers) | ☎ (912) 897-3661
  Minn'58 . . . . | 109 Dombey Court,
  MR William B . . . . | Savannah, GA
  | *31410*

Hascoe MR & MRS Lloyd A (Abbe M Schneider) Syr'78.Syr'81
  ☎ (212) 996-7703 . . 1095 Park Av, New York, NY *10128*

Hasell MRS Samuel M (Annie B Simons) Ncd.Ht. . . | of ☎ (203)655-7888
  MISS Ann Simons—Char'ton'38.Ncd. . . . . | Charleston, SC
  | *29401*
  | ☎ (704) 693-4809
  | ''Prospect Hill''
  | 540 Fairway Dv,
  | Hendersonville, NC
  | *28739*

Haselton MR & MRS Philip H (Shirley Brown) Cr'49
  ☎ (201) 376-4964 . . 25 Jefferson Av, Short Hills, NJ *07078*

Hasen MR & MRS George M (Charlotte H Binger) | of ☎ (212)369-6773
  BMr'45.Cs.Dh.Ncd.Cal'43.H'49 . . . . | 1185 Park Av,
  MISS (REV) Elizabeth S—Aht'77.VaTheo'91—at | New York, NY
  2435 Saratoga Dv, Louisville, KY *40205* . . . . . | *10128*
  | ☎ (802) 533-2277
  | Greensboro, VT
  | *05841*

Hasen MR & MRS John H (Anne E Janson) Hart'83.Aht'73
  ☎ (802) 985-2953 . . 16 Harbor Rd, Shelburne, VT *05482*

Haskell MRS Eileen N (Eileen Nicoll) . . . . ☎ (303) 777-4886
MISS Ione N—at 79 St Boat Basin, New York, 90 Corona St,
NY *10024* . . . . Denver, CO *80218*
MISS Pamela C—at 633 King St, Santa Rosa,
CA *95404* . . . .
Haskell DR & MRS Eric T (Danielle A M Floquet) ☎ (909) 607-2766
Pom'73.Cal'79 . . . . 761 W 11 St,
MISS Olivia H . . . . Claremont, CA
JUNIORS MR Jean-Christophe *91711*
Haskell MRS Francis W (M Noelle Delafield Finch) An.Snc.Lm.Cda.
☎ (703) 356-3645 . . 1107 Harvey Rd, McLean, VA *22101*
Haskell MR & MRS John H F JR (Francine G of ☎ (212)744-1823
Le Roux) Bhm.Ln.Mb.USA'53.H'58 . . . . 120 East End Av,
MISS Diana F T—Cr'87.Cl'92 . . . . New York, NY
10028
☎ (518) 734-3362
Clarence D Lane
Rd, Windham, NY
12496
Haskell MRS M Howard (Dewey—Ball—Margaret Howard) Rdc'48.Ncd.H.
☎ (617) 631-7528 . . 9 Risley Rd, Marblehead, MA *01945*
Haskell MR Macdonald T—Rm.Stc.Hob'80
☎ (212) 362-4314 . . 2166 Broadway, Apt 21A, New York, NY *10024*
Haskell MR Michael J—Skd'79.AGSIM'82
☎ (602) 443-3089 . . 8043 N Via Palma, Scottsdale, AZ *85258*
Haskell MR P Thomson 3d (Paul T JR) . . . . Married at Providence, RI
Griswold MISS Anna S (William E) . . . . Aug 31'96
Haskell MR & MRS Paul T JR (B Burrill Watson) ☎ (914) 234-9509
Mls'67.Va'68.Bgt.Ty'63 . . . . 20 Turtle Pond
MR E Livingston B—Va'94 . . . . Lane, Bedford, NY
10506
Haskell MR & MRS Preston H 3d (Joan E Smith) ☎ (904) 384-6288
Ln.Cc.Ncd.P'60.H'62 . . . . 4971 Morven Rd,
MR Preston H 4th—at 5 Novinsky Blvd, Moscow Jacksonville, FL
121099, Russia *32210*
Haskell REV & MRS Robert F (Margaret W Joggerst)
SUNY'72.Snc.Cr'65.Nu'71.EpiscTheo'73
☎ (215) 357-2414 . . 1495 Stephen Way, Southampton, PA *18966*
Haskell DR & MRS Samuel D (Anne E Smotherman)
Tenn'72.Sar.Snc.Cr'68.Tenn'74.Tenn'77.GaTech'84
☎ (770) 920-2810 . . 8606 Creekview Court, Douglasville, GA *30135*
Haskell MR & MRS William P (Helen B Park) ☎ (203) 869-5255
Ws'39.Mit'41.H'36 . . . . 54 Butternut Hollow
MR William B—at 85 Summer St, Oakland, ME Rd, Greenwich, CT
04963 . . . . *06830*
Haskins MISS Catherine B—H'86
510 S Mills St, Madison, WI *53715*
Haskins MRS Charles Allen (Seiler—Janet Weakley) Sth'44.Ct.
☎ (202) 965-5028 . . 1515—33 St NW, Washington, DC *20007*
Haskins MR & MRS Craig O (F Elizabeth Cooke) Denis'88
☎ (011-61-2) 9922-4885 . . 12-28 Bent St, Neutral Bay, NSW 2089,
Australia
Haskins MRS George Lee (Gertrude E Lounder)
C.Sm.Mt.Plg.Myf.Cw.Wt.Cspa.
PO Box 97, Hancock, ME *04640*

Haskins MRS Stanley G (Minturn—Mary Y McCawley)
☎ (508) 468-4993 . . 32 Boardman Lane, Box 477, Hamilton,
MA *01936*
Haskins MR & MRS Thomas E (Saralee O Patch) Wyo'57.H'57 . . of
☎ (508) 653-2831 . . 13 Park Av, Natick, MA *01760*
☎ (860) 739-8655 . . 239 Old Black Point Rd, Niantic, CT *06357*
Haskins MR & MRS William Chandler (Elizabeth Ivins) Chi.Ncd.Hn.H'37
☎ (508) 369-5642 . . 62 Coolidge Rd, Concord, MA *01742*
Hasler MR & MRS John W (Dick—Faith M Kelley) ☎ (847) 234-4607
Ariz'65.On.Loy'65 . . . . 315 W Washington
MR Stratford L M Dick JR—Dth'89 . . . . Rd, Lake Bluff, IL
60044
Haslett MR & MRS John J 2d (Alida B McIlvain)
Conv'73.Me.Rc.Ph.Wms'62
☎ (610) 896-7057 . . 701 Panmure Rd, Haverford, PA *19041*
Hasley MR & MRS Michael S (Elizabeth L Fisher) ☎ (510) 891-9529
Ken'76.Nw'80 . . . . 752 Longridge Rd,
JUNIORS MISS Margaret B . . . . Oakland, CA *94610*
JUNIORS MISS Phoebe M . . . .
Haspel MR & MRS Peter (Allen—Naugle—M Lynn Yarbrough)
Miss'64.Pa'61
☎ (504) 837-8681 . . 122 Wood Av, Metairie, LA *70005*
Hass MRS Anthony (Patricia C Cecil) Mt. . . . . of ☎ (212)288-0948
MISS Elizabeth C . . . . 830 Park Av,
New York, NY
10021
☎ (202) 333-4858
1815—45 St NW,
Washington, DC
20007
Hass MR & MRS D Winthrop (Artman—Mary K ☎ (414) 964-1406
Roozen) Ill'66.Rcch.Lawr'65.Wis'68 . . . . 2534 N Terrace Av,
MISS Anne E—at U of Wisc Milwaukee . . . . . . Milwaukee, WI
MR James A Artman *53211*
Hass MR & MRS John R (Ellen R Nalle) Ty'81.P'83
☎ (215) 242-4484 . . 9509 Wheelpump Lane, Philadelphia, PA *19118*
Hastie MR & MRS J Drayton (Fernanda deMohrenschildt) NCar'38
☎ (803) 556-7657 . . Magnolia Plantation, Rte 4, Charleston, SC *29414*
Hastings MR & MRS Caryl C B (Katherine L ☎ (617) 891-9456
Sherman) Skd'67.Cc.H'62.H'66 . . . . 50 Colchester Rd,
JUNIORS MR Craig C B . . . . Weston, MA *02193*
JUNIORS MR Richard O M . . . .
Hastings MR & MRS David B (Ann L Boyd) Me.Ncd.Ham'53
☎ (610) MI2-8628 . . 101 Marple Rd, Haverford, PA *19041*
Hastings MR & MRS David B JR (Mary H Cauffman) OWes'78.Denis'78
☎ (610) 647-4088 . . 236 Leopard Rd, Berwyn, PA *19312*
Hastings MR & MRS Edward Earnshaw (Barbara N ☎ (610) LA5-7785
Shore) Me.Ncd.P'51 . . . . 28 Wistar Rd,
MISS Anne C . . . . Villanova, PA
MISS Gabriela M Martinez *19085*
Hastings MRS Ellison (Mary Ellison)
9 Judkins Av, Apt 15, Bath, ME *04530*
Hastings MRS Hubbard (Roberta J Hubbard)
☎ (617) 227-0075 . . 63 Mt Vernon St, Boston, MA *02108*
Hastings MR & MRS John O JR (Sara G Neuhaus)
☎ (713) 666-8170 . . 4128 Oberlin St, Houston, TX *77005*

Hastings MR & MRS John V 3d (Christie Weatherby) | ☎ (610) 649-1261
Cs.Cr'45 . . . . | 220 Glenn Rd,
MISS Kim C . . . . | Ardmore, PA *19003*
MR Mark W . . . . |
Hastings MR & MRS Matthew T (Linda F Steele)
Rdc'72.Va'75.Sfh.Cw.Ne.Ncd.Ht.H.Pots'74.Penn'78 . . of
☎ (540) 338-7667 . . ''Maple Hill'' Philomont, VA *20131*
115 E 90 St, New York, NY *10128*
Hastings DR & MRS Peter L (Rosina M de Barros Gomes)
Rio'84.Berklee'83.H'85.Stan'88.P'92.Mit'95 . . of
2590 Dearborn Dv, Hollywood, CA *90068*
''Vente Du Fromage'' rue des Cheveux, Céret, France
Hastings MRS T Mitchell JR (Thacher—Margot L Campbell) . . . . . Died at
Edgartown, MA Apr 12'96
Hatab MR & MRS John O (Sara T Carothers) | ☎ (201) 467-9263
Leh'65.Seton'70 . . . . | 130 Hobart Av,
MISS Elisabeth S—Leh'88 . . . . | Short Hills, NJ
  | *07078*
Hatch MRS Alden R (Allene P Gaty) Cs.Cda.
☎ (212) 832-2703 . . 200 E 66 St, New York, NY *10021*
Hatch MR Charles L—SCal'93
☎ (816) 753-2549 . . 4801 Jarboe St, Kansas City, MO *64112*
Hatch MRS Eric S (E Constance De Boer) Nw'41.Dar.
☎ (773) 493-8514 . . 1700 E 56 St, Apt 2410, Chicago, IL *60637*
Hatch MR James S . . . . | ☎ (413) 637-0426
MR Duncan S—ColC'95 . . . . | Buck Lane, Lenox,
  | MA *01240*
Hatch MRS Jeanne G (Jeanne Gignoux) V'65
☎ (303) 543-7798 . . 2500 Yarrow Court, Boulder, CO *80303*
Hatch MR John Davis—Gr.Cos.StJColl'93
☎ (505) 984-9985 . . 640 Camino Lejo, Santa Fe, NM *87505*
Hatch MR & MRS John M (Amy B Beltz) | ☎ (313) 343-0349
AmU'62.Ripon'60 . . . . | 527 University
MISS Amy E—Mich'95 . . . . | Place,
JUNIORS MR David A—at U of Mich . . . . | Grosse Pointe, MI
  | *48230*
Hatch MRS L Robertson (Laura Lea Robertson) Cly.Ncd.
☎ (516) 584-8940 . . 28 Moriches Rd, PO Box 135, St James,
NY *11780*
Hatch MR & MRS Robert M (Catalina I Shin) Mich'87.Mich'86
☎ (312) 939-4617 . . 1143 S Plymouth Court, Apt 303, Chicago,
IL *60605*
Hatch MR & MRS Thomas F (Susan E Shink) Mich'89.Mich'87.Wayne'91
464 Cloverly Rd, Grosse Pointe Farms, MI *48236*
Hatch MR & MRS W Ross (Susan W Schweizer) | ☎ (860) 232-3333
Ham'62 . . . . | 219 Kenyon St,
MISS Katherine R—at SMU . . . . | Hartford, CT *06105*
JUNIORS MISS Victoria D |
Hatcher MR James B—Wis'27
136 Berkeley Lane, Williamsburg, VA *23185*
Hatcher MRS Lloyd B (Barbara Holdsworth) Cly.Ncd.
☎ (212) 355-6034 . . 201 E 62 St, New York, NY *10021-7627*
Hatchette DR & MRS James B 3d (Mary Farrar) | ☎ (210) 644-2438
Ncmb'64.Tul'71.Tul'60.LSU'64 . . . . | Rte 1, Box 173,
MISS Constance McC . . . . | Fredericksburg, TX
MR Charles V 2d . . . . | *78624*
Hately MISS Jennifer W . . see F F Seidler

Hately MR Peter W
☎ (011-34-72) 31-83-71 . . 1 Cala Corbs, Apdo de Correos 103,
17200 Palafrugell, Gerona, Spain
Hatfield MISS Avery Ann (g—Edward R Hatfield) . . . . Born at
Summit, NJ Nov 2'95
Hatfield MR & MRS Charles J 2d (Nancy Nicholas)
☎ (011-44-171) 225-1754 . . 20 Coulson St, London SW3 3NA, England
☎ (011-44-1264) 781-660 . . ''Roumain Cottage'' Over Wallop,
Hampshire SO20 8HZ, England
Hatfield MR Charles J 3d—Col'86
☎ (908) 874-5705 . . 1105 Canal Rd, Princeton, NJ *08540*
Hatfield MR & MRS Edward R (Isabel L McNaugher) Cent'y'57.Leh'55
☎ (410) 778-4328 . . PO Box 177, Chestertown, MD *21620*
Hatfield MR George W—Snc.Myf.Ofp.Hl.Cw.Cl'33
☎ (860) 434-2412 . . PO Box 58, Hadlyme, CT *06439*
Hathaway MR & MRS E Phillips (Barbara S Mallory)
Unn.Eyc.Elk.Md.Gv.Mv.Va'42
☎ (410) 363-0753 . . 11008 Baronet Rd, Owings Mills, MD *21117*
Hathaway MISS Mallory (Tone—Gravière—Mallory Hathaway)
☎ (212) 734-7723 . . 945 Fifth Av, New York, NY *10021*
Hattersley MRS Robert C (Tew—Virginia Luke) | ☎ (941) 921-7460
Pr.Cly. . . . . | 7979 S Tamiami
MR John G—at ☎ (213) 650-5233 | Trail, Apt 316,
7732 W Norton Av, Los Angeles, CA *90046* . . . | Sarasota, FL *34231*
Hauer MR & MRS William S (Kay Foley) Cin'51.Cin'54
14 Garfield Place, Cincinnati, OH *45202*
Haueter MR & MRS Eric S (Cynthia A Willoughby)
Wms'80.Bur.Fr.Wms'75.Cl'79.Cl'80
☎ (415) 344-0206 . . 555 El Arroyo Rd, Hillsborough, CA *94010*
Hauhart CDR (RET) & MRS James N (Bayanne L | ☎ (703) 684-7190
Herrick) USN.Fr.Dc.Ncd.Cr'62 . . . . | 500 Malcolm Place,
JUNIORS MR Dutton R . . . . | Alexandria, VA
  | *22302*
Hauslohner MRS Robert A (Lorna U McAlpin) Me.Ac.Ncd.
☎ (610) 525-7210 . . 618 Woodleave Rd, Bryn Mawr, PA *19010*
Haussermann MRS Whitney (Mary B Whitney)
☎ (561) 278-2249 . . 326 SW First Av, Delray Beach, FL *33444*
Hausslein MR & MRS Robert W (Evelyn B Bullitt) | ☎ (617) 861-0378
Ws'60.Mit'58 . . . . | 20 Slocum Rd,
MISS Evelyn B—Ws'95 . . . . | Lexington, MA
MR Thomas B . . . . | *02173*
Haux MR & MRS George E (Ann E Curry) | ☎ (315) 685-6222
Chath'60.Fairf'59 . . . . | 39 W Elizabeth St,
MISS Suzanne E . . . . | Skaneateles, NY
MISS Heather V . . . . | *13152*
Havemeyer MR Christian—Drew'70
☎ (410) 778-1389 . . ''The Reward'' 24031 Walnut Point Rd,
Chestertown, MD *21620*
Havemeyer MR & MRS Frederick C 3d (S Cecile Hoge) Rv.Nu'69 . . of
PO Box 550, Southampton, NY *11969*
☎ (516) 537-0119 . . ''Overlook Farm'' Montauk H'way,
Bridgehampton, NY *11932*
Havemeyer MR & MRS Harry W (Eugénie Aiguier) V'51.Rv.Cs.Cda.Y'52
☎ (212) 535-1836 . . 35 E 75 St, Apt 4A, New York, NY *10021*
Havemeyer MRS Horace JR (Rosalind Everdell) Cly.
☎ (212) 249-4918 . . 1 E 66 St, New York, NY *10021*

Havemeyer MR & MRS Horace 3d (Eugenie C Cowan) Rv.Exy.Cs.Hob'64
☎ (212) 288-2862 . . 10 Gracie Square, New York, NY *10028*

Havemeyer MR & MRS William E (Jane Litzenberg) | of ☎ (212)628-5725
Ny.Snc.Rut'66.Cl'76 . . . . | 925 Park Av,
MR William MacG—Bow'96 . . . . | New York, NY
                 | *10028*
  | ☎ (860) 350-0404
  | PO Box 68,
  | Roxbury, CT *06783*

Havens MR & MRS Collier (Joan Carson) Ncd.P'44
☎ (610) EL6-7515 . . Box 291, Newtown Square, PA *19073*

Havens MR & MRS John Paul (Cushny—Wendy B Doubleday)
Nw'81.Rc.Un.Ln.Lic.Pr.B.H.'79
21 Hoaglands Lane, Old Brookville, NY *11545*

Havens MRS Margaret S (Margaret J Stockdale) | ☎ (610) 520-9687
Pitt'65.Me. . . . . | 1210 Denbigh Lane,
MR Paul M—at 160 W 95 St, Apt 1B, New York, | Radnor, PA *19087*
NY *10025*. . . . . |
MR David S . . . . |

Havens MRS Michael C (Mary Wallace Talbot) | PO Box 1327,
Me.Md. . . . . | Bryn Mawr, PA
MISS Elizabeth R . . . . | *19010*
MISS Lesley H . . . . |

Havens MR & MRS Peter H (Louise A Van Zanten) | ☎ (610) 525-8843
VillaN'78.Md.Me.H.'76.Cl'81 . . . . | 250 N Ithan Av,
JUNIORS MISS Victoria L . . . . | Villanova, PA *19085*

Havens MR & MRS R Wick (Nancy V Bergstrom) | ☎ (215) 732-8991
Rc.Col'67 . . . . | 2216 Rittenhouse
MISS Robin . . . . | Square, Philadelphia,
  | PA *19103-5505*

Havens MR & MRS Richard W (Bettle—Sally A Atwater)
Rcp.Me.R.Ac.Pa'42
☎ (401) 635-2515 . . 509 W Main Rd, Little Compton, RI *02837-1043*

Havens MR & MRS Timothy M (Biddle—Pamela A | ☎ (210) 668-0446
Bentsen) Smu'73.Rcp.Me.Pitt'69 . . . . | 1101 S Peking St,
MISS Brooke E Biddle . . . . | McAllen, TX *78501*
JUNIORS MISS Susan B Biddle . . . . |

Havens MRS W Paul (Ida M Hessenbruch) Rc.Me.Ac.
☎ (610) MI2-4712 . . 117 Cheswold Lane, Haverford, PA *19041*

Haverstick MRS Iola S (Iola W Stetson) Bnd'46.Gr.Cly.Cs.StJ.Ncd . . .of
☎ (212) 744-0108 . . 179 E 70 St, New York, NY *10021*
☎ (860) 567-5626 . . 195 South St, Litchfield, CT *06759*

Haverstick MR John M—Aht'41
☎ (609) 924-0094 . . 164 Griggs Dv, Princeton, NJ *08540*

Haverstick MR & MRS S Alexander 2d (Jessica S | ☎ (201) 376-4615
Whalen) MtH'75.Bg.Y'74.Cl'77 . . . . | 25 Madison Terr,
MISS Emily W . . . . | Short Hills, NJ
JUNIORS MR Samuel A 3d . . . . | *07078*

Havighurst MRS Bruce J (Barbara J Corell) | ☎ (216) 752-0218
Stph'59.O'62 . . . . | 20861 Byron Rd,
MISS Lauren C . . . . | Shaker Heights, OH
  | *44122*

Havighurst MR Bryan J (late Bruce J) . . . . Married at
                                      Cleveland Heights, OH
Segbers MISS Diane M (David) . . . . Jun 22'96

Havighurst MR & MRS Bryan J (Diane M Segbers)
☎ (216) 691-3932 . . 2496 Milton Rd, University Heights, OH *44118*

Havill MR & MRS Jessen T (Elizabeth M Vincent)
Buck'93.Buck'92.W&M'94
☎ (757) 220-2376 . . 1340G S Mt Vernon Av, Williamsburg, VA *23185*

Havre MR Jay P . . see J E Pierce

Hawes MRS Alexander B (Breed—Rosilla M Hornblower) Mt.Ct.Cvc.Csn.
☎ (202) 338-0853 . . 2512 Q St NW, Washington, DC *20007*

Hawes MR & MRS Frederick L (Florence L Weld) | ☎ (314) 993-1959
Cy.P'49 . . . . | 801 Kent Rd,
MR Frederick L JR—at 1140 Lay Rd, St Louis, | St Louis, MO *63124*
MO *63124* . . . . |

Hawes MRS Louis (Diana W Mallory) | ☎ (812) 336-4695
Bnd'68.Ind'84 . . . . | 1329 S High St,
MR Christopher M . . . . | Bloomington, IN
MR Daniel . . . . | *47401*

Hawes MR & MRS Richard B (Kelly A Wardlaw) Mo'79.Cy.Wms'75
☎ (314) 993-0173 . . 4 Huntleigh Downs, St Louis, MO *63131*

Hawes MR Robert G—Ct.Y'59 . . . . | of ☎ (805)684-4662
MISS Jeannette S . . . . | PO Box 5668,
MISS Katherine V . . . . | Santa Barbara, CA
  | *93150*
  | ☎ (805) 688-6673
  | "Loma de
  | Venados" 3160 Box
  | Canyon Rd,
  | Santa Ynez, CA
  | *93460*

Hawkes MR Andrew F (late Dudley F) . . . . Married at Eureka, MT
Reilly MISS Janet M (Richard J JR) . . . . Aug 31'96

Hawkes MRS (REV) Dudley F (Daphne W Parker) | ☎ (609) 921-2404
Penn'60.PTheo'75.Ds.Ncd . . . . | 50 Patton Av,
MISS Jennifer D—at 4454 Reservoir Rd NW, | Princeton, NJ *08540*
Washington, DC *20007* . . . . |
MR Timothy W . . . . |

Hawkey MR & MRS Harold W (Joan Harris) | ☎ (516) 626-3264
Sth'50.Au.Pr.Cly.Va'50 . . . . | 33 Brookville Rd,
MISS Elizabeth H—Mid'85—at | Glen Head, NY
1762 Commonwealth Av, Boston, MA | *11545*
02135-5530 . . . . |

Hawkings MR & MRS D Mark (Manville—Susan D Smith)
☎ (908) 899-4338 . . 936 Barnegat Lane, Mantoloking, NJ *08738*

Hawkings MR & MRS David M JR (Elisabeth J Wright) Wms'86.Buck'82
☎ (202) 363-2133 . . 4332 Albemarle St NW, Washington,
DC *20016-2012*

Hawkings MISS Parish H (Bogliaccini—Parish H Hawkings)
Br'86.Rut'94 . . of
☎ (703) 931-9643 . . 2701 Park Center Dv, Apt B409, Alexandria,
VA *22302*
☎ (908) 899-4338 . . 936 Barnegat Lane, Mantoloking, NJ *08738*

Hawkins MRS Arthur H (Wybro—Nancy L Pilson)
☎ (201) 944-7632 . . 396 Allaire Av, Leonia, NJ *07605*

Hawkins MR Ashton—K.C.H'59.H'62
☎ (212) 362-2607 . . 151 Central Park W, New York, NY *10023*

Hawkins DR & MRS David A (Katherine L Somers) NCar'90.Cal'90
25107 Central Way, Davis, CA *95616*

Hawkins MRS David R (Wadsworth—Weston—Phoebe A Helmer) . . . Died
                                    at Hightstown, NJ Feb 20'96

Hawkins MRS Dexter Clarkson (Evelyn B Eliot) Cly.
☎ (212) PL1-0285 . . 24 Central Park S, New York, NY *10019*
Hawkins MR & MRS Howard R JR (Linda L Whitmarsh) Plg.Cly.H'72
☎ (212) 254-2866 . . 40 Fifth Av, New York, NY *10011*
Hawkins MR Ira 3d—Wms'51
221 W Canton St, Boston, MA *02116*
Hawkins MRS Lisa (May—Elisabeth Hawkins) . . . . | ☎ (207) 338-3145
  MR Andrew May—Ken'81 . . . . | Box 536A,
  MR Brian May—SimR'83 . . . . | Jesse Robbins Rd,
  MR Laurence May . . . . | Belfast, ME *04915*
Hawkins MRS Richard H JR (Christina Ekengren) Cvc.Csp.Sl.
☎ (202) 244-1768 . . 4100 Cathedral Av NW, PH-4, Washington, DC *20016*
Hawkins MISS Susan H—Myf.Ds.
☎ (314) 531-1675 . . 4483 Lindell Blvd, Apt 512, St Louis, MO *63108-2410*
Hawley MRS Clifford B (Sarah A Clark)
☎ (704) 859-9547 . . 217 Chestnut St, Tryon, NC *28782*
Hawley MR & MRS John F (Barbara J Hale) SCal'77.SCal'77
☎ (213) 463-5888 . . 238 S Lorraine Blvd, Los Angeles, CA *90004*
Hawley MR & MRS Philip M (Mary Catherine Follen)
Cal'49.Bhm.Ln.Pcu.Cal'48
☎ (213) 239-6511 . . 336 S Hudson Av, Los Angeles, CA *90020*
Hawtin MRS Raymond F (Ware—Elise H Fay) Rdc'42.Csn.
☎ (207) 276-3648 . . ''Pedders Corner'' Northeast Harbor, ME *04662*
Haxall MRS Bolling W (Rainsford—Elizabeth | ☎ (413) 733-5937
Dodge) Hn. . . . . | 30 Colony Rd,
  MR D Barton—at ☎ (315) 628-4601 | Longmeadow, MA
23569 Hax Rd, La Fargeville, NY *13656* . . . . . . | *01106*
Haxall MR & MRS John D (Leticia F Scott) | ☎ (619) 966-1102
Penn'74.Va'48 . . . . | 1405 Crestridge Dv,
  MISS E Lee—SCal'81.SCal'82—at | Oceanside, CA
☎ (213) 954-1169 . . 912 Alandele Av, | *92054*
Los Angeles, CA *90036* . . . . |
  MR Thomas McC—at ☎ (717) 975-2339
3 S 40 St, Camp Hill, PA *17011* . . . .
  MR Douglas G . . . . |
Hay MR & MRS Andrew W (Troster—Nina E Riggio)
Cl'94.Rc.Au.Colg'83.Cl'88
☎ (212) 737-0629 . . 241 E 76 St, New York, NY *10021*
Hay MR & MRS Jess T (Betty Jo Peacock) Smu'52.Smu'53.Smu'55
☎ (214) 368-4059 . . 7236 Lupton Circle, Dallas, TX *75225*
Hay MISS Laura Stanhope
☎ (310) 204-1904 . . 10021 Farragut Dv, Culver City, CA *90230*
Hay MR & MRS Richard J (Lucinda A Smith) Ws'78.Tor'77
Cranley Grange, Cranley Rd, Burwood Park, Walton-on-Thames, Surrey KT12 5BP, England
Hay MR & MRS William H (Clements—Helen L | ☎ (608) 233-0953
Card) Hav'38.Br'39 . . . . | 39 Bagley Court,
  MISS Miranda P—at 14 Wedge Pond Rd, | Madison, WI *53705*
Winchester, MA *01890* . . . . |
    MR R Caird Clements—at 100 Grant St,
    Lexington, MA *02173* . . . . |
Hayden MRS Curtiss JR (Alice B Dollar) . . . . | ☎ (415) 453-3526
  MISS Alice D. . . . . | 15 Morrison Rd,
  MISS Mara Lisa . . . . | Box 487, Ross, CA
                                         | *94957*

Hayden MR Philip A—Conn'84.Del'89 . . see W Coxe
Haydock MR & MRS Charles E (Kugel—Marianna Ward) Myf.P'34
☎ (203) 762-0549 . . 18 W Meadow Rd, Wilton, CT *06897*
Haydock MR & MRS Charles T (Candace A | ☎ (617) 734-6268
Spielberger) V'76.Cy.Sm.Un.H.'74.Dth'76 . . . . | 59 Reservoir Av,
  JUNIORS MISS Emily L . . . . | Chestnut Hill, MA
                                          | *02167*
Haydock MR & MRS Francis B (Sarah E Thorndike) | ☎ (508) 356-2040
My.Chi.Ncd.H'46 . . . . | 160 Argilla Rd,
  MR Roger—at ☎ (802) 257-4819 . . Box 1052, | Box 196, Ipswich,
Brattleboro, VT *05301* . . . . | MA *01938*
Haydock DR George G—H'41 . . . . | ☎ (508) 993-6907
  MISS Rebecca H—at 60 Crescent St, Apt 1, | PO Box P26,
Cambridge, MA *02138* . . . . | Nonquitt,
                                          | South Dartmouth,
                                          | MA *02748*
Haydock MR & MRS Samuel (Susan R Maynard) | ☎ (617) 326-2132
Cy.H'44 . . . . | Wampatuck Rd,
  MISS Augusta K . . . . | Dedham, MA *02026*
Haydock DR & MRS Timothy G (Averil P Meyer) | *see*
H'71 . . . . | *Dilatory Domiciles*
  JUNIORS MISS Zoe M . . . . |
Haydon MR & MRS R Winston (Anne H Clothier)
P'80.Rcn.Me.Ht.Pn.JHop'79
☎ (203) 972-9181 . . 20 Summer St, New Canaan, CT *06840*
Hayes MR & MRS C Kirtland JR (Winifred H Date)
Sth'73.Wa.Myf.MichTech'75
☎ (847) 234-0433 . . PO Box 650, Lake Forest, IL *60045-0650*
Hayes DR & MRS David (Carolyn H Judd) H'47.H'51
☎ (860) 443-8122 . . 740 Ocean Av, New London, CT *06320*
Hayes DR & MRS David P (Robin Duncanson)
CalPoly'71.CalSt'78.CalPoly'72.Cal'82
☎ (208) 888-2244 . . 7100 N Pollard Lane, Meridian, ID *83642*
Hayes MR & MRS Geoffrey N (Cox—Rosane B | ☎ (505) 822-7967
André) NMex'82.Myf.NMex'83 . . . . | 7404 Vivian Dv NE,
  MISS Jocelyn J . . . . | Albuquerque, NM
                                          | *87109*
Hayes MRS Guy S (Dorothy H Barbour) Tvb.
☎ (207) 359-8373 . . HC 64, Box 1015, Brooklin, ME *04616*
Hayes MRS Henry G (Katharine H Collins) BMr'29
☎ (415) 461-9729 . . 15 Wolfe Glen Way, Kentfield, CA *94904*
Hayes MR & MRS Henry G IV (Marjorie R Oliver) Cal'61.CalSt'75.Stan'56
☎ (916) 422-0344 . . 28 Lakeshore Circle, Sacramento, CA *95831*
Hayes MR Horace O—Cp.Duke'57
☎ (415) 917-9411 . . PO Box 422728, San Francisco, CA *94142*
Hayes MR & MRS J Stoddard JR (Sophia F | ☎ (610) 696-0675
Cadwalader) Pa'71.VillaN'82.Wil.Pa'70.NCar'74 | 507 N High St,
  MR James S 3d—Emory'95 . . . . | West Chester, PA
  JUNIORS MR Joshua F—at U of NCar Chapel Hill | *19380*
Hayes MR John A 3d—Geo'58
☎ (540) 253-5015 . . ''Cottage at Glenville'' PO Box 370, The Plains, VA *20198*
Hayes MR Miles V—Y'32.Mit'34.H'47.H'50.Dth'68
☎ (610) 525-6475 . . 27 Pond Lane, Bryn Mawr, PA *19010*
Hayes MR Nicholas—Unn.Ct.Ty'69
PO Box 240, Rectortown, VA *20140*

Hayes MR & MRS Patrick H JR (Mary K Sheridan)
Wheat'88.OklaCity'93.Cam'88.OklaCity'94
☎ (719) 852-3552 . . 592 Spruce St, Monte Vista, CO *81144*

Hayes MR & MRS Richard C (Hilary C Downe) Nw'81.Durham'79
☎ (011-44-1865) 391-076 . . Ford House, Ford Lane, Frilford Heath,
Oxfordshire OX13 5NT, England

Hayes MR & MRS Sadler (Agnes MacArthur) Cly. . . . | ☎ (212) BU8-3357
MISS Alice MacA—Tufts'75—at | 325 E 79 St,
☎ (704) 554-8312 . . 3215C Heathstead Place, | New York, NY
Charlotte, NC *28210* . . . . | *10021*

Hayes MR Stephen O—Univ'lTech'84
☎ (916) 387-5551 . . 7040 Forman Way, Sacramento, CA *95828*

Haygood MR & MRS Paul M (Charlotte S Smither) | of ☎ (504)895-1980
Ncmb'68.LSU'64.H'67 . . . . | 1240 Harmony St,
JUNIORS MISS Charlotte H . . . . | New Orleans, LA
JUNIORS MISS Katherine S . . . . | *70115*
| ☎ (504) 635-4208
| Hazelwood
| Plantation, Old
| Laurel Hill Rd,
| St Francisville, LA
| *70775*

Hayhurst MR & MRS L Nelson (Marjorie R Peppin) | ☎ (209) 222-1400
Stan'29. . . . . | 806 E Buckingham
MISS Nancy J—at ☎ (415) 693-9686 | Way, Fresno, CA
155 Jackson St, Apt 1702, San Francisco, CA | *93704*
94111 . . . . |

Hayne MR & MRS Elliot A (Gail C Field) Pcu. . . . . | ☎ (415) 898-9651
MR Mark C—at Princeton . . . . | 20 Tamarin Lane,
| Novato, CA *94945*

Hayne MR & MRS W Alston (Elisabeth Church) | ☎ (707) 963-5180
Cal'45.Stan'49.Tufts'60 . . . . | 1832 Sulphur
MR & MRS William A 4th (Adrian Rae Kopjanski) | Springs Av,
MtH'76.Pa'80.P'75.Pa'80—at | St Helena, CA
☎ (707) 963-0129 . . 1562 Grayson Av, | *94574*
St Helena, CA *94574* . . . . |

Haynes MISS Elizabeth—Sth'44.Cs.Ht.
☎ (212) SA2-1026 . . 1040 Park Av, New York, NY *10028*

Haynes MR & MRS Elwood M (Kuechler—Suzanne J Lake)
Cal'60.Pcu.Sfg.Fr.Stan'51
☎ (415) 775-2274 . . 945 Green St, San Francisco, CA *94133*

Haynes MR & MRS James M JR (Dietrich—Nancy C Bennett)
SCal'70.Cvc.Ty'59
☎ (703) 777-3244 . . 602 Lasswell Court SW, Leesburg, VA *20175*

Haynes MRS Justin O'Brien (Hamm—Evelyn M Green)
☎ (212) MU8-7186 . . 580 Park Av, New York, NY *10021*

Haynes MR & MRS Patrick R JR (Letitia E Crosby) | ☎ (540) 839-5291
P'75.P'74 . . . . | Barn Hill, Bacova,
JUNIORS MISS Crosby de F . . . . | VA *24412*

Haynes MR Robert B—K.Plg.Bcs.Ht.H'50.Y'54
☎ (212) 246-2518 . . 45 W 55 St, Apt 4F, New York, NY *10019*

Haynes MRS Sophy P-Q (Soutter—Sophy | of ☎ (212)666-1707
Pellegrini-Quarantotti) Bnd'49.Cl'52.Cly.Ncd. . . | 801 West End Av,
MR Schuyler B . . . . | New York, NY
MR Robert Van R . . . . | *10025*
| ☎ (516) 283-6552
| ''Hopeland 3d''
| 134 Herrick Rd,
| Southampton, NY
| *11968*

Haynes-Dale MRS Amanda H (Dale—Amanda H Haynes) Ri.Mds.
☎ (212) 688-7381 . . 117 E 57 St, New York, NY *10022*

Hays MR & MRS Donald Osborne (Oliver—Mary Katherine Jackson)
Mt.Sar.Col'29.Cl'37.AmU'51
☎ (601) 856-0592 . . 200 Dominican Dv, Apt 3212, Madison,
MS *39110-8630*

Hays DR & MRS F Whiting (Helen D Hibbard) | ☎ (508) 369-7073
CtCol'58.Chi.Cda.Y'56.NYMed'60 . . . . | 70 Lexington Rd,
MISS Daphne D—CtCol'85—at | Concord, MA *01742*
☎ (617) 730-9792 . . 103R Fuller St, Brookline, |
MA *02146* . . . . |
MR Frederick W JR—Hartw'88 . . . . |
MR William S—CtCol'90—at ☎ (212) 473-6135 |
651 E 14 St, New York, NY *10009* . . . . |

Hays MR & MRS Thomas A (Julia P Kinloch) | ☎ (410) 823-2127
JHop'43 . . . . | 203 Ridgefield Rd,
MR Thomas A 3d . . . . | Lutherville, MD
| *21093*

Hays DR & MRS Thomas R (Edith D Haight) | ☎ (817) 387-0732
Smu'65.TexWmn'88.Dar.Smu'66.Smu'71 . . . . . | 2120 Crestwood St,
MISS Victoria C—SCal'94—at 8360 Via Sonoma, | Denton, TX
Apt C, La Jolla, CA *92037*. . . . . | *76201-2106*
MR Geoffrey E S—at U of NTex . . . . |

Hays MR & MRS William Henry JR (Elizabeth St J Whiting) Dc.Dar.
☎ (203) 869-0301 . . 1 Putnam Hill, Greenwich, CT *06830-5701*

Hays MR & MRS William Henry 3d (Lucile T Walker)
Nyc.Chi.Cly.Y'51.H'58
☎ (508) 228-1272 . . Box 1108, Nantucket, MA *02554*

Haythe MR & MRS Madison H (Hersloff—Frances D | ☎ (203) 869-9007
Penrose) Sth'49.Chr.Ny.B.Plg.StJ.Cly.Myf. | 441 Round Hill Rd,
Cda.P'33 . . . . | Greenwich, CT
MISS Lydia B Hersloff—Myf.Cda.—at | *06831*
☎ (303) 938-0687 . . 3150 Repplier St, |
Boulder, CO *80304*. . . . . |

Haythe MR & MRS Thomas M (Sabine Cailliau-de | ☎ (203) 869-5251
Gaulle) Ny.Ln.Ihy.Chr.H'61 . . . . | 21 Mayfair Lane,
MISS Pamela F—at 210 E 75 St, Apt 4A, | Greenwich, CT
New York, NY *10021* . . . . | *06831*
MISS Jennifer H—at Columbia Phys & Surg . . . . |

Hayward MISS Barbara A—Duke'81 . . of
☎ (919) 620-0133 . . 5000A Old Oxford H'way, Durham, NC *27712*
☎ (610) 525-4507 . . 104 Orchard Way, Rosemont, PA *19010-1609*

Hayward MR & MRS Frank E (Edwards—Diana M Blake)
Pcu.ColM'32.Stan'34
☎ (415) 507-1868 . . 200 Deer Valley Rd, San Rafael, CA *94903*

Hayward MRS Johnston (Patricia M Johnston) Me.Ac.Ncd . . .of
☎ (610) 525-4507 . . 104 Orchard Way, Rosemont, PA *19010-1609*
☎ (518) 523-9339 . . Camp Gordon, Lake Placid, NY *12946*

Hayward MISS Nancy L (Burian—Nancy L Hayward)
  ☎ (212) 860-7443 . . 47 E 87 St, Apt 3A, New York, NY *10128-1005*
Hayward MR & MRS Robert B JR (Barbara G Duling)
  Buck'76.Me.Dar.Laf'75
  ☎ (717) 299-0158 . . 1322 Clayton Rd, Lancaster, PA *17603*

Hayward MR & MRS Thomas Z JR (Sally A Madden)	☎ (847) 381-0025
Cho.Wa.Nw'62.Nw'65.Ch'70.	Rte 2, Box 8,
MR Thomas Z 3d	W County Line Rd,
JUNIORS MR Robert M	Barrington Hills, IL
	60010

Hayward MISS Wilhelmina
  RR 1, Box 433A, Bonners Ferry, ID *83805-9744*
Haywood MR & MRS Edward Gregory (Debra Bergman)
  ☎ (410) 836-0721 . . 202 Charter Oak Place, Bel Air, MD *21014*
Haywood MR & MRS T Holt JR (Nancy A Ahern) So.Cc.Cw.Cly.H.
  ☎ (212) 838-7774 . . 136 E 64 St, New York, NY *10021*
Haywood MISS Tami Samantha—EcoleSuper'88.Cly.
  ☎ (212) 888-9651 . . 220 E 60 St, Apt 4C, New York, NY *10022*
Hazard MR & MRS Jeffrey (Grace M Turner)
  ☎ (410) 337-9728 . . 1813 Circle Rd, Baltimore, MD *21204*
Hazard MR & MRS Oliver C (Pell—Sarah E Halsey) Bgt.L.Nyc.Y.'54 ⚓
  ☎ (914) 234-3969 . . 594 Old Post Rd, PO Box 124, Bedford, NY *10506*
Hazard MRS Vincent H (Mary C Coburn) Sth'29
  ☎ (617) 862-7808 . . Brookhaven D534, 1010 Waltham St, Lexington, MA *02173*
Hazlett MR & MRS James V JR (Helen S Greer) Pc.Rm.Stv'47
  ☎ (908) 747-8458 . . 118 Hillcrest Rd, Fair Haven, NJ *07704*
Hazlett MRS William H (Catherine Patrick) Ncd.
  ☎ (312) 787-1152 . . 1242 N Lake Shore Dv, Chicago, IL *60610*
Head MR & MRS Beverly P JR (Jane M Hill) Cy.Ala'35
  ☎ (205) 879-5552 . . 3528 Victoria Rd, Birmingham, AL *35223*
Head MRS Edward Nugent (Robinson—Mary Jane Cassidy) . . . . . . Died at Marbella, Spain Mch 15'96
Heald MRS William E (Anne S Haydock) . . of
  ☎ (513) 321-5583 . . 3828 Broadview Dv, Cincinnati, OH *45208*
  ☎ (616) 223-4454 . . ''The Maples'' 14540 Prospect, Traverse City, MI *49684*
Healy MR H Harris 3d—Ham'78.Drew'80
  ☎ (212) 696-0709 . . 35 Park Av, New York, NY *10016*
Healy MR & MRS Harold H JR (Elizabeth A Debevoise)
  Mt.C.Plg.Cly.Cda.Y'43.Y'49
  ☎ (212) 876-0140 . . 1170 Fifth Av, New York, NY *10029*

Healy MRS Jane O (Jane Olt) Dar.	1 bis rue de Friant,
MISS Hope G—at ☎ (773) 665-0958	75014 Paris, France
2124 N Hudson Av, Chicago, IL *60614*	
MR Thomas A—at 3636 Ashworth Av, Seattle,	
WA *98103*	

Healy JUNIORS MR Matthew T . . see R S Armstrong

Healy MR & MRS William T (Gail F Hull)	☎ (520) 296-3616
Skd'55.Col'54 ⚓	6171 E Miramar Dv,
MR William T JR	Tucson, AZ *85715*
MR Sean P	

Heaney MR & MRS James S (M Victoria Mora)	☎ (610) 525-9828
Cl'59.Cry.Me.Ac.Pa'49	916 Field Lane,
MR James J—Me.Roch'91	Villanova, PA *19085*
MR Hunter M—Me.Cry.Pa'91.H'96	

Heap MISS Angela D—HWSth'93 . . see MRS H C Wilmerding

Heap MISS Jane A—Skd'93.LondEc'95 . . see MRS H C Wilmerding

Heaphy MRS Edward T JR (Candace Wilder)	☎ (413) 567-4462
Gchr'66.San.	47 Concord Rd,
MISS Emily D	Longmeadow, MA
MISS Christina M	*01106*

Heaphy MR Edward T JR—San.Cl'62
  ☎ (413) 736-8805 . . PO Box 1529, Springfield, MA *01101-1529*

Heard MR & MRS Charles W (Corina S Higginson)	☎ (603) 569-9510
Unb.Hb.Y'53	8 Mill St,
MISS Sarah	PO Box 1210,
MR Drayton.	Wolfeboro, NH
	03894-1210

Heard MR & MRS Drayton JR (Helen H Owsley)	☎ (203) 562-0550
Msq.Yn.Y'40	596 Prospect St,
MR John O—NCar'68	New Haven, CT
	06511

Heard MR & MRS Edwin Anthony JR (Phyllis M Gregory) Plg.Cly.P'48
  ☎ (615) 269-6363 . . 3901 Harding Rd, Box 68, Nashville, TN *37205-1837*
Heard MR & MRS Hamilton (Virginia T Scott) H.'56
  ☎ (508) 228-0340 . . 10 Fulling Mill Rd, Box 448, Nantucket, MA *02554*
Heard MISS Susan E—Bost'81
  ☎ (516) 624-7632 . . 105 Mill River Rd, Oyster Bay, NY *11771*
Hearfield MR David 4th
  ☎ (415) 922-6060 . . 2090 Broadway St, San Francisco, CA *94115*
Hearin MISS Ann B—Swb'59
  ☎ (334) 928-3552 . . Box 505, Scenic H'way 98, Point Clear, AL *36564*
Hearin MR & MRS William J (Shearer—Van Antwerp—Emily H Staples) At.
  ☎ (334) 473-1512 . . 301 E Delwood Dv, Mobile, AL *36606*
Hearst MR John Augustine C
  875 Fifth Av, New York, NY *10021*
Heath MRS Ola W (Frazier—Ola Warren)
  ☎ (813) 251-1537 . . 2611 Bayshore Blvd, Tampa, FL *33629*
Heath MR & MRS Richard B (Nancy Foss) Cw.H'34
  ☎ (617) 698-0308 . . 334 Adams St, Milton, MA *02186*

Heatwole MR & MRS Mark M (Sarah A Collier)	☎ (847) 234-1348
RMWmn'70.Sr.Rc.W&L'69.W&L'72	1220 Elm Tree Rd,
MISS Mary P—at Wash'n & Lee	Lake Forest, IL
JUNIORS MISS Elizabeth C	*60045*

Hebard MR & MRS Morgan JR (Wells—Jean T Ballard) Ph.Sg.Y'43
  ☎ (215) CH7-3186 . . ''Vanilla Villa'' 8864 Towanda St, Philadelphia, PA *19118*

Hebb MR & MRS Donald B JR (Sybil K Miller)	☎ (410) 771-4049
Br'66.Md.Ken'64.H'67.H'70	''Chapter Eleven''
MISS Sybil K.	2616 Butler Rd,
MISS Piper J	Glyndon, MD *21071*

Heberling MR & MRS Peter D W (Elizabeth M Trent)
  Gchr'72.Unn.JHop'72.Cl'76
  ☎ (910) 274-2545 . . 1000 Country Club Dv, Greensboro, NC *27408*
Hebert MR & MRS Richard T (Frances L Hood) Ken'82.Ken'80
  ☎ (410) 453-9493 . . 11533 Falls Rd, Lutherville, MD *21093*
Heberton MR & MRS Craig 3d (Ellen G Buchanan) Hav'51
  ☎ (216) 831-8733 . . 30947 Edgewood Rd, Pepper Pike, OH *44124*
Heberton MR & MRS Robert M JR (Kathryn R Perris) MtH'51.Pc.
  235 Lancaster Av, Devon, PA *19333*

Hebrank MR & MRS Roger A (Suzanne Bartell) Wash'55.Str.Wash'54
☎ (314) 997-2699 . . 18 Maryhill Dv, Ladue, MO *63124*

Heck MR & MRS George C 3d (Ann F Russell)
Quinn'78.S.Pace'72 . . . .
MISS Brooke T . . . .
| ☎ (860) 669-0519
| 32 Pleasant Valley
| Rd, Clinton, CT
| *06413*

Hecking MR & MRS Dirck J II (Marguerite Van Dyke Dohan) Miss'96
☎ (770) 451-5576 . . 5167 Tilly Mill Rd, Dunwoody, GA *30338*

Heckman MR & MRS Guy C (Margaret I Jenks)
Pa'78.Eh.Nf.Ln.Nd.Cysl.Shcc.Ty'73 . . . .
JUNIORS MR William A M . . . .
| ☎ (908) 439-3015
| Black River Rd,
| PO Box 609,
| Far Hills, NJ *07931*

Heckman MRS William Guy (Moulton—Margaret L Carter)
Nd.Cy.Ln.Lc . . .of
☎ (314) 991-1992 . . 7 Upper Price Rd, St Louis, MO *63132*
238 S Beach Rd, Hobe Sound, FL *33455*

Heckscher MR & MRS August (Claude Chevreux) C.Y'36.H'39
☎ (212) 517-4830 . . 333 E 68 St, Apt 8A, New York, NY *10021*

Heckscher MR & MRS Benjamin H (Pratt—Nancy B
Turner) Hood'62.Me.H'57 . . . .
MR Benjamin H JR—U'84 . . . .
☎ (203) 637-7596 . . The Common, Apt 625,
1465 E Putnam Av, Old Greenwich, CT *06870* .
MR David M—WashColl'89—at
☎ (406) 682-7551 . . General Delivery,
MacAllister, MT *59740* . . . .
MR Christopher D—Rol'90—at
☎ (504) 899-0996 . . 320 Webster St,
New Orleans, LA *70118* . . . .
| ☎ (610) 543-8398
| 5 Guernsey Rd,
| Swarthmore, PA
| *19081*

Heckscher MRS Charles H (Marjorie M Newhall)
☎ (610) 649-3288 . . 429 Montgomery Av, Apt A401, Haverford,
PA *19041*

Heckscher MR & MRS Gustave A 2d (Anna S Harris) Fw.Cw.Cspa.Rv.Ac.
☎ (610) 645-8865 . . 1400 Waverly Rd, Apt 215, Gladwyne, PA *19035*

Heckscher MRS J G Richard (Anna D Hallowell) . . . . Died at
Devon, PA Feb 18'96

Heckscher MR Martin A—Sg.H'56.H'59
☎ (215) 848-4439 . . 1014 W Hortter St, Philadelphia, PA *19119*

Heckscher MR & MRS Maurice (Constance A Butcher) Ph.Sg.H.'28
☎ (215) 984-8907 . . Cathedral Village G318, 600 E Cathedral Rd,
Philadelphia, PA *19128*

Heckscher MR & MRS Morrison H (M A Fenella Greig)
Ox'64.C.Wes'62.Del'64.Cl'86
☎ (212) 873-4220 . . 176 W 87 St, New York, NY *10024*

Heckscher MRS Sarah S (Sarah W Stevens)
Rdc'57.VillaN'75.Pc. . . . .
MISS Elizabeth W—H'83.Cl'94—at
☎ (213) 667-1093 . . 3400 Ben Lomond Place,
Apt 126, Los Feliz, CA *90027* . . . .
MR Stevens 2d—ColC'82—at ☎ (303) 667-4642
3300 S Tamarac Dv, Apt C117, Denver, CO
80231 . . . .
MR Christopher A—H'87.Dth'94—at
☎ (617) 482-9319 . . 5 St Charles St, Apt 2,
Boston, MA *02116* . . . .
| ☎ (215) 247-8321
| 8018 Navajo St,
| Philadelphia, PA
| *19118*

Hector MR & MRS Louis J (White—Hilles—Nancy Bean)
Swb'43.C.K.Mt.Csn.Wms'38.Y'42
☎ (305) 446-2353 . . 3507 St Gaudens Rd, Coconut Grove, FL *33133*

Hedberg MR & MRS Gregory S (Margaret J Stewart)
Rc.StJ.P'68.Nu'70.Nu'80 . . . .
JUNIORS MR Stewart T . . . .
| ☎ (212) 861-5911
| 336 E 69 St,
| New York, NY
| *10021*

Heddens MRS Cornelia D (McCain—Cornelia V
Davis) Cw.Sar. . . . .
MISS Claudia V McCain—Box 1456,
Ketchum, ID *83340* . . . .
MR Charles S McCain 3d—at
1454 E 140 Place, Glenpool, OK *74033* . . . . .
| ☎ (208) 726-5749
| PO Box 491,
| Ketchum, ID
| *83340-0491*

Hederman MR & MRS H Henry JR (Sara K Holloman) Miss'68.Miss'68
☎ (601) 982-4830 . . 4115 Sandridge Dv, Jackson, MS *39211*

Hedges MR & MRS Donald W (Diane Scheid)
Nw'63.Me.Pa'43.Pa'47 . . . .
MISS Hillary C—P'93.Me.—at
☎ (212) 727-3086 . . 300 W 10 St, New York,
NY *10014* . . . .
MR Scott A—Me'90—at ☎ (512) 884-2634
101 N Shoreline Blvd, Apt 325, Corpus Christi,
TX *78401* . . . .
| ☎ (610) 649-8161
| 1401 Waverly Rd,
| Gladwyne, PA
| *19035*

Hedges MISS Stephanie K—Ham'96 . . see MRS P S Anderson

Heed MRS Charles H (Emma F Klapp)
Ac.Me.Sdg.Pkg.Ncd. . . . .
MR Wilbur P Klapp 2d—Me.Rv.Ll. . . . .
| ☎ (610) 688-7005
| 150 Kynlyn Rd,
| Radnor, PA *19087*

Heed MR Charles H—Me.
☎ (610) 688-7756 . . Regency Apt 54, 313 Creek Rd, St Davids,
PA *19087*

Heekin MR & MRS Kenneth P (Barbara A Barrett) Mid'54.Wms'52.Cin'54
53 Worcester Rd, Box 61, Princeton, MA *01541*

Heersema DR & MRS Philip (Doyle—Kathleen Cassidy) Stan'33.Pa'33
☎ (415) 563-5766 . . 2052 Green St, Apt 3, San Francisco, CA *94123*

Hees MRS William Rathbun 3d (Berta C Stinchfield) Vh.
☎ (408) 462-4891 . . 7311 Viewpoint Dv, Aptos, CA *95003*

Hefter MISS Allison Claire (J Scott) . . . . Born at
Greenwich, CT Dec 23'94

Hefter MR & MRS J Scott (Anne H Crocker) Br'88.Pa'93.CtCol'81
☎ (203) 622-0792 . . 11 Birch Lane, Greenwich, CT *06830*

Heidelberg MR & MRS R Webster 3d (Michelle St C
Favrot) Ncmb'70.Tul'74.Miss'67.Tul'73 . . . . . .
JUNIORS MISS Hollis St C . . . .
JUNIORS MR Joseph W . . . .
| ☎ (601) 544-7306
| 905 Adeline St,
| Hattiesburg, MS
| *39401*

Heilman MR & MRS W Strickland (C Fay Smith)
LHgts'75.DU'75. . . . .
MISS Tarin S—at Hollins . . . .
JUNIORS MR Colin S—at Bucknell . . . .
| ☎ (540) 338-5320
| 35361 Paxson Rd,
| Round Hill, VA
| *20142*

Heimbecker DR & MRS Raymond O (Kathleen H H
Jensen) BMr'47.Tor'43.Tor'45 ⚓ . . . .
MISS Dorothy A T—QU'79 . . . .
MISS Constance M H—QU'81.QU'83—at
U of Toronto . . . .
MR Harry O 2d—QU'77 . . . .
| of ☎ (705)445-9649
| ''Brooklet Farm''
| RR 1, Collingwood,
| Ontario L9Y 3Y9,
| Canada
| ''Toad Hall''
| Hope Town, Abaco,
| Bahamas

Heine DR & MRS M Wayne (Millie J Phillips) ETenn'57.Duke'58
☎ (520) 529-0948 . . 7257 N Cathedral Rock Rd, Tucson, AZ *85718*
Heiner MR & MRS David A (Anne T Crandon) MtH'76.Fcg.Pa'76.CarnM'78
☎ (412) 826-0176 . . 314 Cornwall Dv, Pittsburgh, PA *15238*
Heiner MRS William G JR (Frances C Lyne) Fcg.Ncd.
☎ (412) 963-8887 . . 302 Fox Chapel Rd, Apt 210, Pittsburgh, PA *15238*

Heintz MR & MRS Paul C A (Jane Develin) | ☎ (610) 896-6419
Pa'61.Me.Ste.Pe.Ken'62.Pa'65 . . . . | 269 Booth Lane,
MISS Helen C—at ☎ (212) 877-9765 | Haverford, PA
100 W 73 St, New York, NY *10023* . . . . | *19041*
MISS Sandra DeH—at ☎ (617) 244-9287 |
72 Pearl St, Newton, MA *02158*. . . . . |
MR Robert B D—at ☎ (508) 228-0312 |
1 Salros Rd, Nantucket, MA *02554* . . . . |
MR Edward S A . . . . |

Heinz MRS Henry J II (Mackenzie Robertson—Maher—Drue M English)
Rr.Ri.StJ . . .of
☎ (412) 741-5757 . . ''Goodwood'' Sewickley, PA *15143*
1 Sutton Place, New York, NY *10022*

Heise MR E Dixon—Pcu.Cp.Sar.Cal'38
☎ (415) 346-5414 . . 2298 Pacific Av, San Francisco, CA *94115-1452*

Heiserman MRS Hewitt (Mary Cooper Cox) . . . . . . | 8 Wingstone Lane,
MISS Margaretta H . . . . | Devon, PA *19333*
MR David S . . . . |

Heiserman MR Hewitt JR—Ken'82
☎ (508) 229-0668 . . 10 Central St, Southborough, MA *01772*
Heiserman MR Robert B 3d . . see J B Sibley
Heisinger MR & MRS Scott David (Lisbeth A Lorenzen) Whit'91.Whit'91
see Dilatory Domiciles
Heitner MR & MRS Norman E (Georgia R Morse) Bv.Nd.Ncd.Wash'36
☎ (314) 993-2552 . . 3 Twin Springs Lane, St Louis, MO *63124*
Helfenstein MR J Gouverneur M—Lm.Snc.
☎ (212) 744-0026 . . 222 E 71 St, New York, NY *10021*
Helfet MR & MRS Anthony B (Marjorie H McMahon) Fic.Pcu.Cl'66
☎ (415) 457-0667 . . 109 Oak Av, Kentfield, CA *94904*

Helie MRS Diana S (Morgan—Diana M Sweeney) | ☎ (203) 966-5775
Myf.Ht.Dar.Ne. . . . . | 11 Wahackme Lane,
MISS Alexandra W Morgan . . . . | New Canaan, CT
| *06840*

Hellauer MR & MRS Joseph F 3d (Katrine S Otto) StLaw'83.Assumption'82
☎ (314) 963-9883 . . 238 Park Rd, St Louis, MO *63119*
Heller MR Anthony K—Me'71 ⛵
☎ (207) 374-5308 . . PO Box 144, Blue Hill, ME *04614*

Heller MR & MRS Charles R (Nancy B Crane) | ☎ (201) 635-6614
DeP'60.Rdc'61.Hn.H'50.H'55 . . . . | 60 Hall Rd,
MISS Anne B—DeP'90 | Chatham, NJ *07928*
MR Charles O—Ken'89 . . . . |

Heller MRS Homer K (Frances McC Kennedy)
1718 Brook Dv, Camden, SC *29020*

Helling MR & MRS Robert E (Clare Hudson) | ☎ (941) 923-7681
NCar'48.ArtDes'46 | 4893 Kestral P'kway
MISS Elizabeth S—at 245 Sunny Ridge Av, | N, Sarasota, FL
Fairfield, CT *06430* . . . . | *34231*
MISS Roberta H—at New York, NY . . . . |
MR Alan B—at 95 Soundview Av, Norwalk, CT |
06854 . . . . |

Hellman MRS Marco F (Coppoletta—Dorry Ellis) Cal'59.Cal'62
☎ (510) 654-3300 . . 121 Hillside Av, Piedmont, CA *94611*
Hellmann MRS Richard H (Winton—Merwin—Janette Main) Cly.
☎ (805) 969-0761 . . 1931 Boundary Dv, Santa Barbara, CA *93108*

Hellmuth MR & MRS George F (Mildred L Henning) | of ☎ (314)994-9194
Km.Wash'28 . . . . | 5 Conway Lane,
DR Nicholas M—H'66 . . . . | St Louis, MO *63124*
| ☎ (573) 858-3385
| ''Timber Farms''
| HCR 62, Box 460,
| Salem, MO *65560*

Hellmuth MR & MRS Joseph A (Katherine B Gatch) | of ☎ (508)655-4216
SL'46 . . . . | 25 Fairway Circle,
MISS Harriet—Mid'85 . . . . | Natick, MA *01760*
| ☎ (508) 432-4947
| 456 Long Pond Dv,
| East Harwich, MA
| *02645*

Hellmuth MR & MRS Theodore N JR (Elizabeth S | ☎ (216) 247-8447
Biggar) Swb'74.Hills'74. . . . . | 180 Mill Creek
MISS Katherine J—at Coll of Charleston . . . . . . | Lane, Chagrin Falls,
JUNIORS MISS Kimberly K | OH *44022*
JUNIORS MR Theodore N 3d . . . . |

Hellmuth MR & MRS William K (Nancy R Le Sage) Msq.Va'75.P'77
☎ (202) 966-1678 . . 5220 Watson St NW, Washington, DC *20016*
Hellyer MR & MRS Arthur T (Cynthia R Martin) Ariz'77
☎ (864) 579-4484 . . 518 Gaston Dv, Spartanburg, SC *29307-2502*

Hellyer MRS Eloise Le G (Mollaioli—Eloise Le G | ☎ (011-39-75)
Hellyer) . . . . | 394299
MISS Lucia C Mollaioli | Strada di Collestrada
MISS Diana Le G Mollaioli . . . . | 4A, 06080
| Collestrada, Perugia,
| Italy

Hellyer MR John T
☎ (520) 642-3520 . . 8393 Mescalero Place, McNeal, AZ *85617*
Hellyer MRS Philip W (Marguerite Beach)
☎ (708) 447-0442 . . 180 Scottswood Rd, Riverside, IL *60546*
Hellyer MR & MRS Walter 2d (Jeanne A Vidal) Nw'57.Nw'56
☎ (414) 868-2213 . . PO Box 190, Fish Creek, WI *54212*
Helm MISS Charie J . . see A M Cronin 3d
Helm MISS Molly M . . see A M Cronin 3d

Helm MR & MRS William L JR (Eleanor Lloyd) | of ☎ (215)233-2143
Pc.Sg.Ac.P'46.Stan'72 . . . . | 521 E Moreland Av,
MR Peter L—at 69 Fifth Av, Apt 5M, | Wyndmoor, PA
New York, NY *10003* . . . . | *19038*
MR William L 3d—Box 26, Chocorua, NH *03817* | ☎ (603) 323-8647
| ''The Deck House''
| Fowlers Mill Rd,
| Box 26, Chocorua,
| NH *03817*

Helme MISS Elizabeth S E—P'75.Ny.Pn.
☎ (401) 842-0969 . . 12 Dennison St, Newport, RI *02840*
Helme MR George W 4th—Wil.Hav'72.Cr'75
Park Plaza Apt 202, 1100 Lovering Av, Wilmington, DE *19806*
Helme MR & MRS Jay E (Mary E S Bonnage) Ny.P.'54
☎ (516) 749-3398 . . ''Harbor Lights'' 8 Clinton Av,
Shelter Island Heights, NY *11965*

Helme MR & MRS Jay E JR (Nancy M Gleske) Il.Hob'82
☎ (401) 846-6711 . . 1256 Wapping Rd, Middletown, RI *02842*

Helme MRS Karen R (Karen J Rundell) WmSth'78
☎ (302) 655-1383 . . 6 Willing Way, Wilmington, DE *19807-3130*

Helms MR & MRS J Michael (Alison C Pell) EverSt'82.EverSt'82
☎ (360) 794-9381 . . 11715 Ingraham Rd, Snohomish, WA *98290*

Helmsing MR & MRS Frederick G (Margaret S Oswalt) Ala'67.At.SpgH'63.Ala'65.Nu'67 . . . . . | ☎ (334) 342-6943
MISS Margaret S . . . . | 240 E Ridgelawn
MR Frederick G JR . . . . | Dv, Mobile, AL
MR Joseph G . . . . | *36608*

Hemenway MR & MRS Brewster R (Elizabeth G Stidger) Alleg'51.St.G.Y'50.Cl'65
☎ (716) 837-1058 . . 229 Beard Av, Buffalo, NY *14214*

Hemenway MR & MRS Henry J (Harriet C Rawle) RSage'49.RSage'53.Colg'50.Y'56
☎ (207) 367-2632 . . Old Quarry Rd, PO Box 122, Stonington, ME *04681*

Hemenway MR & MRS John T (Phoebe S McCreary) Btn.H.'46 . . . . | of ☎ (617)828-1654
MR Nathaniel T . . . . | 12 Hemenway Dv,
MR John F—Pa'78 . . . . | Canton, MA *02021*
| ☎ (802) 765-4324
| Strafford, VT *05072*

Hemenway MR & MRS Thomas S JR (Jacqueline La Motte) Y'45w
☎ (860) 434-7313 . . 24 Saunders Hollow Rd, Old Lyme, CT *06371*

Hemingway MR David S—P'36 . . . . | ☎ (203) 637-9855
MISS Margaret—at ☎ (202) 966-5589 | 1465 E Putnam Av,
5752 MacArthur Blvd NW, Washington, DC | Apt 606,
20016 . . . . | Old Greenwich, CT
MISS Barbara—Hlns'70.H'83—at | *06870-1337*
☎ (011-54-1) 785-6390 . . American Embassy,
Buenos Aires, Argentina, APO AA, *34034* . . . . .
MR D Stuart JR—at ☎ (203) 637-1830
21 Summit Rd, Riverside, CT *06878* . . . .
MR Samuel S—Cr'74—at 1 W 54 St, New York,
NY *10019* . . . .

Hemingway MR & MRS Patrick (Carol Thompson) Swth'52.Y'55.CarnM'72.Yn.H'51
☎ (406) 586-3233 . . 2890 Springhill Rd, Bozeman, MT *59715*

Heminway MRS John H (Semenenko—Virginia Boyd) Why.K.B.Ln.Msq.
☎ (212) 838-8000 . . 795 Fifth Av, New York, NY *10021*

Heminway MR John H JR—B.Rc.K.Why.Msq.P'66 . . of
☎ (212) UN1-8038 . . 36 E 70 St, New York, NY *10021*
☎ (518) 392-2580 . . "Wind's Eye" RR 2, Box 2006, S Cross Rd, Chatham, NY *12037*

Hemp, Paul B & Carton, Barbara W—Pa'72.Bost'74.Whit'75.H'82
☎ (617) 720-2802 . . 12 Chestnut St, Apt 5, Boston, MA *02108*

Hemphill MRS Alexander (Jean C Cálves) . . of
☎ (215) 242-9174 . . 8014 Crefeld St, Philadelphia, PA *19118*
☎ (410) 226-5480 . . "Connemara" 4570 Bringman Farm Rd, Oxford, MD *21654*

Hemphill MR & MRS David Van S (Caroline L McMullen) Sth'76.Cs.Y.'62.Pa'65
☎ (914) 738-8152 . . 34 The Hamlet, Wynnewood Rd, Pelham Manor, NY *10803*

Hemphill MR & MRS David W (Ann S Matthews) Hob'66.Cr'73 . . . . | ☎ (904) 384-3709
JUNIORS MR James T . . . . | 4717 Avon Lane,
| Jacksonville, FL
| *32210*

Hemphill MASTER Garret DeWitt (William R JR) . . . . Born at
Austin, TX Aug 9'95

Hemphill MR & MRS John JR (Wenche Smith) P'47
☎ (604) 592-2344 . . 152-2345 Cedar Hill Crossroad, Victoria, BC V8P 5M8, Canada

Hemphill MR & MRS Joseph K (Jacobs—Robin Fowler) Duke'73.Stc.Pars'70
☎ (908) 842-6722 . . 5 Buena Vista Av, Rumson, NJ *07760*

Hemphill MRS Julian (Anne E Kelly) Rm. . . . . | ☎ (908) 842-1475
MR J Alexander—Laf'71—at ☎ (801) 466-6648 | "Shady Oaks"
1236 Roosevelt Av, Salt Lake City, UT *84105* . . | 80 Privet Place,
| Red Bank, NJ *07701*

Hemphill MR Julian JR—Bost'68 . . . . | ☎ (415) 681-0534
MISS Kelly M . . . . | 1419 Cole St,
MISS Kristin A . . . . | San Francisco, CA
| *94117*

Hemphill MR & MRS William R JR (Abigail Lounsbery) Hlns'86.W&L'86.Smu'91
☎ (512) 452-5092 . . 3504 Lakeland Dv, Austin, TX *78731*

Henagan MR & MRS William F (Barbara L Mills) P.'81.Un.Van'80
☎ (212) 724-1196 . . 222 W 83 St, Apt 11C, New York, NY *10024*

Henchey MR & MRS C Bickford (Squires—Ruth Black) Nf.Ny.Sa.Sar.Pa'52
☎ (914) 934-0223 . . 98 Brush Hollow Close, Rye Brook, NY *10573*

Henchey MISS Winifred W—Conn'86
☎ (617) 625-4337 . . 74 Craigie St, Apt 6, Somerville, MA *02143*

Henckels MR Kirk—Un.Cw.Stan'74.H'76 . . of
☎ (212) 628-8020 . . 210 E 73 St, New York, NY *10021*
325 Worth Av, Palm Beach, FL *33480*
☎ (914) 868-1543 . . "Pondfields Farm" Box 628, Bangall, NY *12506*

Hencken MRS Hugh O'Neill (M Thalassa A Cruso) Lond'32.Chi.
☎ (508) 748-0500 . . 70 Water St, Marion, MA *02738*

Henderlite MR & MRS Hunter F (Mary E Higgins) Penn'79.Penn'84
☎ (713) 292-2075 . . 18 White Fawn Dv, The Woodlands, TX *77381*

Henderlite MR Robert L—Penn'87 . . see J H Rowland JR

Henderson MRS (DR) Anne Atkinson (Anne Atkinson) Rhodes'62
☎ (601) 833-1377 . . 421 Perkins Dv, Brookhaven, MS *39601*

Henderson MR & MRS Branton H JR (Donna J Helsing) Sim'55.Me.Wcc.Cw.Cc.Rv.P.'47.H'53
☎ (610) 647-3316 . . 1048 Derwydd Lane, Berwyn, PA *19312*

Henderson MR & MRS Charles C (Kirsten E Dufficy) Cal'84 . . . . | ☎ (415) 344-4028
JUNIORS MISS Michelle A . . . . | 100 Chateau Dv,
| Hillsborough, CA
| *94010*

Henderson MR & MRS Charles F (Pamela T Fenton) Witt'65.Dth'64
☎ (847) 256-3133 . . 133 Lawndale Av, Wilmette, IL *60091*

Henderson MR & MRS Dan F (Carol D Hardin) Nw'55.UWash'82.Ncd.Whit'44.Mich'45.H'49
☎ (206) 325-1321 . . 632—36 Av E, Seattle, WA *98112*

Henderson MR & MRS David R (Cassandra F | of ☎ (617)247-9330
Hyland) H'77.Cy.Sm.Pom'73 . . . . | 120 Beacon St,
MISS Consuelo C—at Georgetown . . . . | Boston, MA *02116*
JUNIORS MR G L Cabot—at Harvard . . . . | ☎ (508) 228-8771
| 6 Winter St,
| Nantucket, MA
| *02554*

Henderson MR & MRS E Carlisle A (Emily M Smith)
Emory'91.SoMiss'94.SoMiss'95.SoMiss'94
Chapel Towers Apt 2E, 1315 Morreene Rd, Durham, NC *27705*

Henderson MR & MRS Edward T (Wendy P Crisp)
StLaw'87.Rcn.Fic.Rm.Stc.Geo'84
☎ (908) 842-2441 . . 4 Markwood Lane, Rumson, NJ *07760*

Henderson MISS Elena D—Cal'91.Bur.
see Dilatory Domiciles

Henderson MR & MRS Ernest F 3d (Mary L | ☎ (617) 235-1835
Campbell) H'46 . . . . | 171 Edmunds Rd,
MISS Roberta C . . . . | Wellesley Hills, MA
| *02181*

Henderson MR & MRS G L Cabot (Elliott—Sarah G | 76 West St,
Bever) Mass'84.Mid'73 . . . . | Beverly Farms, MA
MISS Davina M—at Occidental . . . . | *01915*

Henderson MR & MRS Gerald van S (Joan A Bristol)
Me.Cw.W.Wt.Cc.H.'53
☎ (610) MU8-7347 . . 419 Glenwyth Rd, Strafford, PA *19087*

Henderson MR & MRS Gerald van S JR (Susan L Emerich)
Duke'82.Me.Cc.StLaw'83.Leh'85.Temp'91
☎ (704) 845-0460 . . 1334 Sea Mist Dv, Matthews, NC *28105*

Henderson MRS Harold G (Mary A Benjamin) Bnd'25
☎ (518) 263-4730 . . PO Box 255, 658 Scribner Hollow Rd, Hunter,
NY *12442*

Henderson MR & MRS J Welles (Hannah L Bradley) | of ☎ (610)642-7171
Rdc'49.Me.Ph.Cts.Ec.Chi.Ncd.P'43.H'49 . . . . . . | 101 Cheswold Lane,
MRS Peter B Hoagland (Elizabeth M | Apt 5H, Haverford,
Henderson) B'gton'77 . . . . | PA *19041-1866*
| ☎ (508) 526-7900
| "Whimsey"
| 19 Old Neck Rd,
| Manchester, MA
| *01944*

Henderson MR & MRS James A (Melinda E Fenton) Cal'88.Bhm.SFrSt'87
☎ (415) 567-4360 . . 2837 Baker St, San Francisco, CA *94123*

Henderson MR & MRS James R (Carol B Brinckerhoff)
Vt'87.Nu'90.Rc.Stc.Rm.Geo'86
☎ (212) 772-9076 . . 205 E 78 St, Apt 5L, New York, NY *10021*

Henderson MR & MRS Jeffrey S (Mary C Landon)
Kas'82.Wcc.P'80.VillaN'88
☎ (610) 688-5872 . . 43 Briar Rd, Wayne, PA *19087-2602*

Henderson MRS John D (Meghan—Helen E Barnhart) JHop'34.Cy.
☎ (410) 889-3312 . . 4206 Roland Av, Apt B1, Baltimore, MD *21210*

Henderson MR & MRS John T (Trevania D Dudley) Duke'80.Nw'82.Dth'87
☎ (617) 266-2424 . . 100 Pembroke St, Boston, MA *02118*

Henderson MR & MRS Joseph W 3d (M Lucia | ☎ (202) 483-2885
Bosqui) V'69.K.Mt.Fic.Fiy.Cvc.Sl.H'67 . . . . | 3067 Whitehaven St
MISS Lucia R—at Hotchkiss . . . . | NW, Washington,
JUNIORS MR J Welles 4th—at Harvard . . . . | DC *20008*

Henderson DR & MRS Julian C (Merle F Masters) SELa'59.NAla'57
☎ (601) 982-5383 . . 2153 Eastover Dv, Jackson, MS *39211*

Henderson MR Mark W . . see J S Morshead

Henderson MR & MRS Peter JR (Anne Vinton) Y'42 . | ☎ (908) 295-2212
MISS Aline J—Van'72—at ☎ (202) 265-1621 | 78 Bay Point
2828 Connecticut Av NW, Washington, DC | Harbour,
20008 . . . . | Point Pleasant, NJ
MR Peter 3d—at ☎ (201) 656-6022 | *08742*
174 Ogden St, Jersey City, NJ *07202* . . . . |

Henderson MR & MRS Ronald H (Mary Anne Stefik)
Rol'79.Cw.Cc.Hb.H'53.H'58
☎ (941) 927-2703 . . 7263 Regina Royale Blvd, Sarasota, FL *34238*

Henderson MRS W Peter (Elizabeth T E Reynolds) | ☎ (516) 676-6498
Pr.Cly. . . . . | Duck Pond Rd,
MISS Melissa M—Va'92—at ☎ (804) 295-1935 | Locust Valley, NY
105 Minor Rd, Charlottesville, VA *22903* . . . . . . | *11560*

Henderson MRS Wellington S (Harriet E Walker)
Bur.Pcu.Sfg.Tcy.Cda . . . of
☎ (415) 343-1545 . . 77 New Place Rd, Hillsborough, CA *94010*
☎ (916) 525-7726 . . Lone Pine Point, Tahoma, CA *96142*

Henderson MR Wellington S—Bhm.Pcu.Bur.P'53
☎ (415) 343-1545 . . 77 New Place Rd, Hillsborough, CA *94010*

Henderson MR & MRS William B JR (Rebecca L Sizemore)
☎ (404) 892-4657 . . 1460 E Rock Springs Rd NE, Apt 4, Atlanta,
GA *30306*

Hendrick MR Robert E P—Pl.Y'55.Del'60 . . of
☎ (410) 732-6637 . . 2901 Boston St, Baltimore, MD *21224*
☎ (516) 537-3889 . . "Kildobbin" Georgica Association, Wainscott,
NY *11975*

Hendrickson MISS Katherine Ayres . . see MRS H A Moore

Hendrickson MISS Rebecca Clark . . see MRS H A Moore

Hendrickson MRS Reiland (V Reiland Cobb) . . . . . | ☎ (212) 288-7589
MR Robert A 3d . . . . | 28 E 73 St,
| New York, NY
| *10021*

Hendrix MR & MRS Clifford R JR (Alicia R | ☎ (415) 567-1522
Magnuson) V'58.Mid'45 | 2800 Vallejo St,
MISS Karen T—at Pacific U . . . . | San Francisco, CA
MR Peter C—at ☎ (847) 615-0853 | *94123*
26 E Washington St, Apt 1, Lake Bluff, IL *60044* |

Henkels MISS Jody Sothern (g—MRS Nancy B Henkels) . . . . Born at
Boston, MA Dec 5'95

Henkels MRS Nancy B (Nancy L Bullock) . . . . | ☎ (610) 687-2519
MR Scott L—Cl'74—at 14 Radnor Way, Radnor, | 1027 N Valley
PA *19087* . . . . | Forge Rd, PO Box
| 143, Devon, PA
| *19333*

Henneman MR & MRS Edward O (Penelope J Case) Sth'59.Y'59.H'62
☎ (540) 463-3091 . . PO Box 702, Shepherd Dv, Lexington, VA *24450*

Henneman MRS John B (Esther G Ogden) Sth'30
☎ (804) 983-2735 . . "Indian Gap" RD 2, Box 226, Dillwyn, VA *23936*

Henneman MR & MRS John B JR (Margery M | ☎ (609) 921-0757
Clifford) Ws'59.Pn.P'57 . . . . | 78 Shady Brook
MISS Margery L—P'90 . . . . | Lane, Princeton, NJ
| *08540*

Henneman MISS Neeltje Van B—Aht'85
☎ (718) 596-2816 . . 45 Pineapple St, Apt 7B, Brooklyn, NY *11201*

Henneman MRS Nuncia Digges (M Nuncia Digges) MmtVa'86
☎ (757) 220-1991 . . 308 S Boundary St, Williamsburg, VA *23185*

Hennessy MRS B Rial (Doherty—Kelley—Bruce Rial) . . . . | of ☎ (212)734-8739
   MR John E T Kelley—Rc.GeoW'89—at | 215 E 68 St,
   ☎ (212) 369-1202 . . 177 E 93 St, New York, | New York, NY
   NY *10128* . . . . | *10021*
   | ☎ (516) 283-4644
   | 56 Linden Lane,
   | Southampton, NY
   | *11968*

Henney LT COL & MRS Frederic A (Carolee J Wells)
USAF.MaryB'51.W&M'73.USA'51.NCar'57.W&M'73
☎ (757) 898-6083 . . Marlbank Farms, 407 Wormley Creek Dv,
Yorktown, VA *23692*

Henning MRS Basil D (Alison C Peake) Cly.Ncd.
☎ (203) 777-0123 . . 223 Bradley St, New Haven, CT *06511*

Henning MR Cameron H—UWash'77
☎ (203) 782-2277 . . 32 High St, Apt 611, New Haven, CT *06510*

Henning MR Geoffrey B . . see J G Leonard

Henning MISS Kimberly V . . J G Leonard

Henning MR & MRS William P (Sandra Sorensen) | ☎ (908) 741-8466
Stc.StA.Y'69 . . . . | 45 Lafayette St,
   JUNIORS MISS Alicia P . . . . | Rumson, NJ *07760*

Hennings MRS Thomas C (Setz—Elizabeth Stallcup) Mo'31.Dar.
☎ (412) 563-5267 . . 62 Hoodridge Dv, Pittsburgh, PA *15228-1802*

Henningsen MR & MRS Victor W JR (Mary F B Ludington)
Swb'48.Ln.Ihy.Rby.Y.'50 . . of
☎ (914) 738-2141 . . 1045 Esplanade, Pelham Manor, NY *10803*
☎ (441) 236-2136 . . 7 Mizzentop, 14 Harbour Rd, Warwick WK 06,
Bermuda

Henny MR & MRS David C 3d (Marion B Fay) Ncd. . | ☎ (360) 321-5225
   MISS Julia F . . . . | 6290 S Bayview Rd,
   MR Mark P . . . . | Clinton, WA *98236*

Henriques MRS Claire W (Claire A Werner) V'52. . | ☎ (203) 869-6153
   MISS Alice D—Ty'78—at ☎ (212) 860-0403 | 3 Hekma Rd,
   425 E 86 St, Apt 16D, New York, NY *10028* . . | Greenwich, CT
   MISS Elizabeth W—H'82—at ☎ (212) 627-8483 | *06831*
   322 W 20 St, New York, NY *10011* . . . . |

Henriques MR Horace F JR—Wk.Y'51
☎ (218) 343-2301 . . 5312 Wolf Knoll, Orr, MN *55771-9504*

Henriques DR & MRS Horace F 3d (Kathleen V Rosenauer) H'77.Cin'82
☎ (603) 795-2524 . . Storrs Hill Lane, Lyme, NH *03768*

Henriques MR & MRS Peter G (Jeanne M O'Neil) Sim'79.Syr'80.Cl'84
☎ (203) 661-3390 . . 4 Maher Av, Greenwich, CT *06830*

Henry MISS Alexandra Schlumberger (Edward J) . . . . Born at
Dallas, TX Aug 3'94

Henry MR C Wolcott 3d—On.Denis'79.Nw'83 . . of
3220 Volta Place NW, Washington, DC *20007*
Box 35, Hobe Sound, FL *33475*

Henry MISS Carolina Marie (Edward J) . . . . Born at
Dallas, TX Mch 15'96

Henry MR & MRS Clement M (Elizabeth N Bouri) | ☎ (512) 328-2395
Cc.H'57 . . . . | 1509 Westlake Dv,
   MISS Jehanne E . . . . | Austin, TX *78746*
   MR J Ryder . . . . |

Henry MR & MRS Edward J (J Claire Schlumberger) Smu'89.Smu'88
☎ (214) 528-8690 . . 4316 Shenandoah Av, Dallas, TX *75205*

Henry MR & MRS Guido Rombauer JR (Phillips— | of ☎ (802)362-7217
Aileen F Anthony) Drex'63.Vh.Cr'57 . . . . | Wind Hill Rd,
   MR Derek A Phillips—Cal'89.Pac'93—at | RR 1, Box 2632,
   ☎ (818) 796-1747 . . 787 S Euclid Av, | Manchester, VT
   Pasadena, CA *91106* . . . . | *05255*
   | PO Box 797, Dorset,
   | VT *05251*

Henry MR & MRS H Blakeney (Schott—Dorothy F Steiner) P'47
☎ (212) 586-2630 . . 60 W 57 St, PH-A, New York, NY *10019*

Henry MR & MRS Howard G (Getman—Judith B Ogden) V'41.Rv.Pa'39
☎ (410) 287-6121 . . 500 Piney Creek Lane, North East, MD *21901*

Henry MR Howard G JR—Me.R.PaMil'64
☎ (907) 455-6539 . . ''Goldstream House'' Box 71651, Fairbanks,
AK *99707-1651*

Henry MR Hoyt C (Nancy Hoyt Cummings) V'54 . | ☎ (561) 546-5051
   MR H Alexander . . . . | PO Box 35,
   | 180 Gomez Rd,
   | Hobe Sound, FL
   | *33475*

Henry MR & MRS J Gordon (Sudler—Carol J | ☎ (941) 394-0749
Seaman) W&J'38.Ch'41 . . . . | 540 Alameda Court,
   MISS Elizabeth E Sudler—at | Marco Island, FL
   ☎ (718) 230-0493 . . 20 Plaza St, Brooklyn, | *33937*
   NY *11238* . . . . |
   MR Carroll H Sudler 4th—at |
   ☎ (813) 254-0200 . . 2117 Dekle Av, Apt G2, |
   Tampa, FL *33606* . . . . |

Henry MR John R 2d—ColC'67.Y'71
☎ (203) 758-1595 . . PO Box 1, Middlebury, CT *06762*

Henry MISS Josephine de N—Ac.
☎ (610) 525-5555 . . 802 Stony Lane, Gladwyne, PA *19035*

Henry MRS L Lennig (Louise G Lennig) Sl.Ac.Me.Cda.Ne.
☎ (610) 896-5806 . . Mansard House 401, 264 Montgomery Av,
Haverford, PA *19041*

Henry MR & MRS Richard H (Paulette Daumen) Me.Cc.Cw.Va'38
☎ (301) 229-8570 . . 5905 Onondaga Rd, Bethesda, MD *20816*

Henry MR & MRS Richard L (Anne E Marshall) | of ☎ (609)896-3574
Sth'66.Pn.P'64.H'67 . . . . | Box 6763,
   MISS Margaret E—P'91 . . . . | Lawrenceville, NJ
   MISS Marion C—P'95—at U of Pa . . . . | *08648*
   JUNIORS MR John K M—at Wm & Mary . . . . . . | ☎ (803) 768-2305
   | 425 Snowy Egret,
   | Kiawah, SC *29455*

Henry MRS S Morgan (Pool—Olivia A Peters) Cly.Ht.Myf.Cda.
☎ (212) TR9-9653 . . 7 Gracie Square, New York, NY *10028*

Henry MRS Samuel J JR (Anne G Turner) V'40
☎ (602) 956-1861 . . 6305 N 30 Court, Phoenix, AZ *85016*

Henry de Tessan MRS Joan C T (Joan | ☎ (415) 921-5431
Chatfield-Taylor) Sth'62 . . . . | 2066 Green St,
   MISS Christina . . . . | San Francisco, CA
   JUNIORS MR Matthew—at Hamilton . . . . | *94123*

Hensel MR & MRS Carl N (Margery W Franks) Sth'52.Minn'38
1513 Hollybrook Rd, Wayzata, MN *55391-1379*

Henshaw MR & MRS Guy R (Susan K Siegel)
Ripon'68.Pcu.Ripon'68.Pa'70 . . . . | ☎ (510) 939-6321
   MISS Christine E—Bates'90.SCal'95—at | 149 Arlene Dv,
12035 Washington Place, Apt 102, Los Angeles, | Walnut Creek, CA
CA *90066* . . . . | *94595*
   MISS Victoria K—ExeterU'94 . . . . |

Henshaw MR John H—H'31 . . . . | ☎ (207) 729-9330
   MR John H JR—H'56—at ☎ (207) 725-7476 | ''The Chase''
351 Bunganuc Rd, Brunswick, ME *04011* . . . . . | 380 Bunganuc Rd,
    | Brunswick, ME
    | *04011*

Henshaw MR John H 3d—Mass'83.Tufts'85 . . see G R McCullough

Henshaw MRS Richard T JR (Elizabeth D Vought)
Rye, NY *10580*

Henshaw MR & MRS Richard T 3d (Helen F
Huggins) Rv.Lm.P.'61 . . . . | ☎ (914) 763-3348
   MR D Ross—JHop'91—at Columbia Phys & Surg | PO Box 189,
    | Waccabuc, NY
    | *10597*

Henshaw MR & MRS William G 3d (Patricia A Madigan)
Cal'49.Pcu.Fr.Cal'46
   ☎ (510) 547-5417 . . 1 Indian Gulch Rd, Piedmont, CA *94611*

Hensley MR & MRS Robert T JR (Mower—Frances Newhard) Cy.Wash'54
   ☎ (314) 997-6919 . . 1717 S McKnight Rd, St Louis, MO *63124*

Henson MR & MRS Garry V (Anne S Perry) Miss'83.Ncd.Miss'77
   ☎ (601) 853-5074 . . 493 Bellechase Place, Madison, MS *39110*

Hentic MR & MRS Yves F M (Irving—N Pandora | ☎ (516) 283-3315
Duke Biddle) Bcs.Ri.Coa.Snc.Cw.Rv.Geo'70. | ''The Box''
H'75 ⚓ . . . . | 77 Great Plains Rd,
   JUNIORS MR Frank H W—at Buckley . . . . | Southampton, NY
    | *11968*

Henward MR & MRS DeBanks M 3d (Barbara J Hayes) Syr'59
   ☎ (602) 951-8945 . . 5225 Paradise Canyon Rd, Paradise Valley,
AZ *85253*

Henze MR & MRS Raymond F 3d (Susanne M | of ☎ (203)661-5537
Bucklin) Stan'75.Vh.Wms'74 . . . . | 71 Otter Rock Dv,
   JUNIORS MISS Megan W . . . . | Greenwich, CT
    | *06830-7027*
    | ☎ (619) 757-3701
    | 113 Eaton St,
    | St Malo Beach,
    | Oceanside, CA
    | *92054*

Hepburn MR & MRS Austin B (Taylor—Huber—Adele Hunter)
Sfh.Pa'51 . . of
   ☎ (610) 642-3529 . . 208 St George's Rd, Ardmore, PA *19003*
   ☎ (941) 945-4067 . . 215 SE 45 St, Cape Coral, FL *33904*

Hepburn MR & MRS Austin Barry JR (Hannah C Wood) AppSt'82.SCar'80
   ☎ (610) 688-4335 . . 253 Upper Gulph Rd, Radnor, PA *19087*

Hepburn DR & MRS Charles McG (Moran— | ☎ (215) 233-4060
Priscilla Ann Biddle) Br'57.Pc.Stan'50.Stan'57. | 1524 E Willow
Stan'66 . . . . | Grove Av,
   MR J Douglas Moran JR . . . . | Wyndmoor, PA
   MR James B Moran—Pa'87 . . . . | *19038-7654*

Hepburn MRS Marion S (Switz—Marion K Sellers) | ☎ (610) HI6-4290
   MISS Susan K Switz . . . . | 3029 Robin Lane,
    | Havertown, PA
    | *19083*

Hepburn MR Philip R—Sa.R.H'25.Pa'28
   ☎ (610) 649-8178 . . 1534 Monticello Dv, Gladwyne, PA *19035*

Hepburn MR W Horace—Cc.Pa'45
   ☎ (610) 642-2231 . . Elm Gardens Apt 1-3, 1301 Montgomery Av,
Wynnewood, PA *19096*

Hepp MR & MRS William S (Upson—Kay | ☎ (941) 793-1535
Wallingford) Cin'56 . . . . | 2437 Kings Lake
   MISS Marianne L . . . . | Blvd, Naples, FL
    | *34112*

Heppe MR Christopher W—Rv.Cw.Cc.Ht.W.StAndr'70
   ☎ (202) 966-9088 . . 4927 Butterworth Place NW, Washington,
DC *20016*

Heppe MR & MRS John E (Patricia M Austin) | ☎ (610) LA5-3184
Me.Ste.Gm.Ac.Ncd.Pa'43 . . . . | 607 Woodleave Rd,
   MR John E JR—Me.M.Rc.Ty'72—at | Bryn Mawr, PA
   ☎ (610) 649-1554 . . 237 W Montgomery Av, | *19010*
Apt 1B, Haverford, PA *19041* . . . . |

Heppe MR & MRS Marcellus J McD (Bettie J Casey) M.Me.
   ☎ (610) 688-3373 . . 511 Brookside Av, Wayne, PA *19087*

Heppenheimer MR & MRS William S (Martha J Ball)
Denis'77.Mds.Ncd.FlaSt'77
   ☎ (516) 324-6279 . . PO Box 144, Amagansett, NY *11930*

Heppner LT COL (DR) & MRS D Gray JR (Mary V Leach)
USA.Va'83.An.Sar.Va'78.Va'83
   ☎ (011-66-2) 591-0688 . . USAMC, AFRIMS, APO AP, *96546-5000*

Hepting MR Dyson D (G Carleton) . . . . Married at Bedford, NY
Mele MISS Samantha A (Alfonse) . . . . Jun 15'96

Hepting MR & MRS Dyson D (Samantha A Mele) GeoW'90
40 Borica St, San Francisco, CA *94127*

Hepting MR & MRS G Carleton (Diana Duncan) | ☎ (401) 849-3217
Srb.Cly.NCar'60 . . . . | 25 Bridge St,
   MISS Caroline S—Curry'88 . . . . | Newport, RI *02840*

Herber MR & MRS Paul F (Alison Gallatin Cobb) Scripps'86.UWash'84
   ☎ (303) 526-9879 . . 24100 Genesee Village Rd, Golden, CO *80401*

Herbert MRS Campbell (Jennette H Campbell) | ☎ (919) 571-9616
CtCol'64.Va'67 . . . . | 1311 Westfield Av,
   MISS C Deming—Va'90.JMad'94—in | Raleigh, NC *27607*
US Peace Corps, Madagascar . . . . |
   MISS S Carlyle—Sth'94—at ☎ (912) 750-9245 |
331 College St, Macon, GA *31201* . . . . |

Hereford MR Brice H—Pn.P'31
   ☎ (609) 924-3869 . . Mountain Av, Box 5, Princeton, NJ *08542*

Hereford MR Robert O—P'27
   ☎ (904) 626-9997 . . 6228 Robin Hood Rd, Milton, FL *32570*

Herff DR & MRS August F JR (Cornelia Dumas) A.Tex'49.Jef'53
   ☎ (210) 826-5073 . . 7 Garden Square, San Antonio, TX *78209*

Hering MR & MRS J Clayton (Susan D Boyd) | ☎ (503) 223-5201
Sim'62.H'63.Dth'63 . . . . | 1708 SW Highland
   MISS Lisa A . . . . | Rd, Portland, OR
   MISS Molly McG . . . . | *97221*
   MISS Kristin B . . . . |

Hering MRS J Gamble (Joan M Gamble) Sth'53
   ☎ (503) 222-4051 . . 4310 SW Warrens Way, Portland, OR *97221*

Herkert MR C John—Y'48
   ☎ (914) 241-2559 . . Box 384, Bedford, NY *10506*

Herkert MRS Henrietta V (Henrietta A Voorhees) | ☎ (914) 764-5483
V'45.Bgt. . . . . | 56A West Lane,
MR C John JR—at ☎ (914) 234-0703 | Pound Ridge, NY
504 Bedford Center Rd, Bedford, NY *10506* . . . | *10576-1622*

Herkness MR & MRS Joseph E (Irmgard Schlimmer)
Heidel'44.Rc.Fw.Rv.Cspa.
☎ (610) TU4-6511 . . 1205 Barrowdale Rd, Rydal, PA *19046*

Herkness MR & MRS Lindsay C (Brock—Elizabeth Disston)
Sg.Rb.Ny.Fw.Rv.Ncd.USA'39
☎ (215) 984-8363 . . Cathedral Village J302, 600 E Cathedral Rd,
Philadelphia, PA *19128*

Herkness MR Lindsay C III—Un.Pr.BtP.Lic.Ty'65
☎ (212) 628-4058 . . 160 E 65 St, New York, NY *10021*

Herkness MR & MRS Wayne 2d (Eleanor O Wallis) USN'39
☎ (304) 645-1338 . . 25 Mary's Lane, Lewisburg, WV *24901*

Herman MISS Theresa D—Ws'72
☎ (301) 774-6545 . . 17221 Old Baltimore Rd, Olney, MD *20832*

Hermann MR & MRS Robert R JR (Signa V Merrill) | ☎ (314) 997-6828
StLaw'83.Cy.Rc.P'75 | 30 Foreway Dv,
JUNIORS MISS Elizabeth L B . . . . | St Louis, MO *63124*

Herndon MR Edward T JR—Smu'61
☎ (202) 554-0384 . . 301 G St SW, Washington, DC *20024*

Hero MR & MRS Andrew W (Jeanne Bell) | ☎ (713) 432-0500
Col'70.Wms'62.H'66 . . . . | 2724 Glen Haven
MISS Eleanor R—at Williams . . . . | Blvd, Houston, TX
 | *77025*

Heroy MRS James H (Brannan—Anne G Seibels) | ☎ (205) 879-8028
Yn. . . . . | 20 Pinecrest Rd,
MISS Deborah C Brannan . . . . | Mountain Brook,
 | Birmingham, AL
 | *35223*

Herpin MR & MRS Allen J (Nancy V Stimmel) . . . . . | ☎ (817) 244-0756
MR Timothy A | 3025 Conejos Dv,
JUNIORS MR Christopher W . . . . | Ft Worth, TX *76116*

Herrera MR & MRS Roberto (Carol Cole) Dth'43.Cl'45
Apartado Postal 1510, 01901 Guatemala City, Guatemala

Herrick MR Adam G F . . see N Carothers 3d

Herrick MRS Anita G (Kearns—Anita G Herrick) | ☎ (202) 337-6699
SL'67 . . . . | 3104 Dumbarton Av
MISS Jessica G Kearns . . . . | NW, Washington,
MR J Nicholas Kearns—at Princeton . . . . . . | DC *20007*

Herrick MR & MRS B Brooks JR (Leslie A Davis) SFrSt'82.Sfy.Cp.Cal'74
☎ (415) 457-8235 . . PO Box 3004, San Rafael, CA *94912*

Herrick MRS Bayard B (Suzanne Hiller) | ☎ (415) 453-4872
Sfy.Cc.Ncd. . . . . | San Pedro Cove,
MR H Crowell 2d—Cp.Humb'81—Box 3004, | 587 Point San Pedro
San Rafael, CA *94912* . . . . | Rd, San Rafael, CA
 | *94901*

Herrick MRS Caroline C (Glauber—Caroline C Herrick) Mls'68.Cl'91 . . of
☎ (212) 831-4751 . . 46 E 92 St, New York, NY *10128*
☎ (860) 364-5400 . . Herrick Rd, Sharon, CT *06069*

Herrick MR & MRS George Gardner (Brokaw— | ☎ (202) 337-1799
Kreizel—Nannette C Cavanagh) Cos.K.Srb. | 2720 Dumbarton Av
Cly.H'60.Ox'62 . . . . | NW, Washington,
MISS Christina V Brokaw . . . . | DC *20007*
MR John H Inman Brokaw JR . . . .
JUNIORS MR Justin A Kreizel—at Taft . . . . . .

Herrick MRS Harold E JR (Mary H Williams)
☎ (315) 654-3820 . . 1042 E Joseph St, Cape Vincent, NY *13618*

Herrick MR Jason N R . . see N Carothers 3d

Herrick MR & MRS John D (Elizabeth S Greene) | ☎ (207) 780-6021
Bost'70 . . . . | 100 Park St,
MR Peter B—at Skidmore . . . . | Portland, ME *04101*
MR Samuel O—at Syracuse U . . . . |

Herrick MR & MRS Peter (Beatricia Bierau) | of ☎ (914)779-6521
Plg.Wms'50 ⚓ . . . . | 42 Sunnybrook Rd,
MR David S—at ☎ (516) 878-1677 . . Main St, | Bronxville, NY
East Moriches, NY *11940* . . . . | *10708*
 | ☎ (561) 575-2186
 | 3464 Southern Cay
 | Dv, Jupiter, FL
 | *33477*

Herrick MISS Robin F . . see J D Phyfe

Herrick MR & MRS Sherlock A JR (Joy T Field) Cw.Rv.Myf.Cr'50
☎ (716) 652-5382 . . 395 Girdle Rd, East Aurora, NY *14052*

Herrick MISS Suzanne W . . of
☎ (401) 847-7103 . . 245 Eustis Av, PO Box 357, Newport, RI *02840*
☎ (860) 364-5400 . . Herrick Rd, Sharon, CT *06069*

Herrick MR & MRS Thomas G (Dorothy I Rhoades) | ☎ (216) 729-1520
Sar.Myf.Cwr'48 . . . . | ''Beaumanor
MR William T P—Sar.Myf.L'land'84—at | Farms''
☎ (216) 834-2787 . . 15707 Ravenna Rd, Burton, | 9578 Mulberry Rd,
OH *44021* . . . . | Chesterland, OH
 | *44026*

Herrick JUNIORS MR Timothy B G . . see N Carothers 3d

Herrick MR Trevor S—Occ'93 . . see J D Phyfe

Herring MR & MRS James M JR (Louise F Munson) | 1329 Dutton Rd,
BMr'62.Mit'58 . . . . | Rochester Hills, MI
MISS Suzannah W—Duke'86—at | *48306*
US Peace Corps, ul Bukowinska 24, 02-703
Warsaw, Poland . . . .
MISS Charlotte B—Laf'90—at Block Island, RI
02807 . . . .
MR James M 3d . . . .

Herring MR & MRS Paul L (Purdon—Mary Benjamin)
☎ (410) 867-0355 . . ''Arden'' 449 Harwood Rd, Harwood, MD *20776*

Herring MR & MRS Skyler B (Elizabeth B Wight) Wash'82.CalPoly'51 . . of
☎ (573) 485-7966 . . Rockford Farms, RR 4, Box 76, Eolia, MO *63344*
☎ (314) 725-0485 . . 8120 Whitburn Dv, St Louis, MO *63105*

Herrlinger MR Berton H—CtCol'92
☎ (513) 321-4873 . . 2713 Erie Av, Apt 27, Cincinnati, OH *45208*

Herrlinger MR & MRS Edward F 2d (Herrlinger— | of ☎ (513)871-8809
Gail A Hathaway) Eyc.Ny.Srb.Yn.Y'50 ⚓ . . . | 8 Corbin Dv,
MR David H . . . . | Cincinnati, OH
 | *45208*
 | ☎ (809) 952-1488
 | ''Windsong''
 | Hopewell, Hanover,
 | Jamaica

Herrlinger MR & MRS Harry W (Sally Shepherd) | ☎ (513) 561-9741
Cin'62.Ill'64 . . . . | 6802 Miami Bluff
MR Christopher P—*see Dilatory Domiciles* . . . | Dv, Cincinnati, OH
MR Andrew S . . . . | *45227*

Herrlinger MR Mark H
☎ (307) 332-2009 . . 915 Amoretti, Lander, WY *82520*

Herrlinger MR & MRS Roth F JR (Sarah K Hogle) | ☎ (513) 831-4031
MtH'56.Cl'58.Xav'53.Stan'57 . . . . | 8088 Ashley View
  MISS Sarah K—DeP'94 . . . . | Dv, Cincinnati, OH
  MR Roth F III—Dth'90.Stan'96 . . . . | *45227*

Herrmann MR John K . . of
☎ (203) 245-2500 . . ''Windfall'' 76 Island Av, Box 13, Madison,
CT *06443*
☎ (803) 671-6212 . . 21 Calibogue Cay Rd, Hilton Head Island,
SC *29928*

Herrmann MR & MRS R Leith (Susan A Speers) | ☎ (410) 692-6704
Sth'70.Rm'69 . . . . | 2404 Lady Margaret
  JUNIORS MISS Virginia G . . . . | Dv, Monkton, MD
  JUNIORS MR William deW . . . . | *21111*

Herrmann MR Robert H—Cr'41
☎ (410) 433-5779 . . 18 Palmer Green Court, Baltimore, MD *21210*

Herron MR John—Denis'41.Y'49
☎ (508) 752-6196 . . 80 William St, Worcester, MA *01609*

Herron MR John JR—Hampshire'74.Ch'78 . . of
☎ (212) 243-7262 . . 37 W 12 St, New York, NY *10011*
☎ (860) 928-4363 . . 550 Rte 169, Woodstock Hill, Woodstock,
CT *06281*

Herron MR & MRS Lewis 2d (Sybil E Adams) Cl'55 | ☎ (216) 247-6603
  MR Peter W . . . . | 45 W Summit St,
    | Chagrin Falls, OH
    | *44022*

Herron MISS Liza G—Schil'78
☎ (212) 831-2905 . . 345 E 93 St, Apt 18D, New York, NY *10128*

Herron MISS Mary D (John) . . . . Married
  Richardson MR Seth F C . . . . Jly 2'95

Herron MRS Polly P (Polly A Presnell) . . . . | 14623 NE 174 St,
  MR S Davidson 3d—Cal'86.Mich'93—at | Woodinville, WA
☎ (415) 346-7270 . . 2755 Laguna St, Apt 3, | *98072*
San Francisco, CA *94123* . . . . |

Herschede MRS Mark P (Huffman—Joan Roth) Glc. | ☎ (513) 321-3161
  MR Lawrence B 2d—at Devon, PA . . . . | 1144 Edwards Rd,
  MISS Deborah L Huffman . . . . | Cincinnati, OH
    | *45208*

Hersloff MISS Lydia B—Myf.Cda . . . see M H Haythe

Herter MRS Cable (Senior—Susan Cable)
☎ (505) 455-2539 . . PO Box 3409, Santa Fe, NM *87501*

Herter MR & MRS Christian A JR (Cameron—Catherine E Hooker)
Cvc.Cos.Mt.Sl.H'41
☎ (202) 333-1440 . . 1525—28 St NW, Washington, DC *20007*

Hertz MR & MRS Daniel L JR (Hurd—Isabel P | ☎ (908) 872-1800
  Waud) Chr.Stc.Rm. | 734 Navesink River
  MR Benjamin N Hurd—at 2103 N Patrick | Rd, Red Bank, NJ
  Henry Dv, Arlington, VA *22205* . . . . | *07701*

Hertz MISS Suzanne E—Col'82
☎ (212) 633-8610 . . 229 W 20 St, Apt 4B, New York, NY *10011*

Hesse MR George E 2d—Denis'85
☎ (910) 395-6635 . . 2046 Albert Circle, Wilmington, NC *28403*

Hesse MR & MRS George L (Arleen McLean) An.Dar.Cl'42.Nu'57
☎ (202) 234-1498 . . 2325 Tracy Place NW, Washington, DC *20008*

Hesser MR & MRS Terry A (Helene H Hartenstein) . . of
☎ (413) 566-8926 . . ''Rocky Hill'' 20 Old Coach Circle, Hampden,
MA *01036*
☎ (941) 422-1233 . . 55 Aspen Dv, Grenelefe, Haines City, FL *33844*

Hessler MR & MRS Robert B (Elizabeth B Wright) | ☎ (302) 656-6726
USInt'l'70.Ac.GeoW'69 | 104 Oxford Place,
  JUNIORS MISS Margaret B B . . . . | Wilmington, DE
    | *19803*

Hester MR & MRS James McN (Janet Rodes) C.Cs.Ncd.P'46.Ox'49 . . of
☎ (212) 289-1673 . . 45 E 89 St, Apt 39C, New York, NY *10128*
☎ (609) 921-6727 . . 25 Cleveland Lane, Princeton, NJ *08540*

Hester MR & MRS Montgomery Raymond (Diane Walter) Vh.Y'50
☎ (805) 969-4492 . . 612 Cowles Rd, Santa Barbara, CA *93108*

Hetfield MR & MRS Lee M (Sarah M Curtis) Hampshire'91.Mass'91
☎ (212) 533-1213 . . 32 Gramercy Park, Apt 18D, New York, NY *10003*

Hetherington MR & MRS Arthur F JR (Betty A Smith) V'38.Edg.Yn.Y'37
316 Beaver St, Apt 401, Sewickley, PA *15143*

Hetherington DR & MRS Arthur F 3d (Gertrude I | ☎ (503) 223-4584
  Oliver) Rr.Y'65 . . . . | 3435 SW Heather
  MISS Ann P H . . . . | Lane, Portland, OR
  MISS Elizabeth I H . . . . | *97201*
  JUNIORS MR James O . . . . |

Hetherington MR & MRS Edwin S (Helen H Heard) | ☎ (011-44-171)
Sth'72.Msq.Pn.P'71.Cr'75 . . . . | 792-8564
  JUNIORS MISS Holly H . . . . | 10 Vicarage
  JUNIORS MR Thomas S . . . . | Gardens, London
    | W8 4AH, England

Hetherington MRS James A 2d (Mary W Dallas)
☎ (908) 234-0445 . . ''Dalhethe'' Box 60, Gladstone, NJ *07934*

Hetherington MR & MRS John W (Hope S Luke) | ☎ (203) 966-9355
Skd'74.Rv.Y'60.Y'63 . . . . | 697 Valley Rd,
  JUNIORS MISS Jane S . . . . | New Canaan, CT
  JUNIORS MR Kells L—at Hotchkiss . . . . | *06840*

Hettler MR & MRS Sangston JR (Malmquist—Joanne M Lichter)
☎ (847) 446-6693 . . 2311 Birchwood Lane, Northfield, IL *60093*

Hettrick MR John L . . . . Died at
Buffalo, NY Mch 18'96

Hettrick MR & MRS John L JR (Jane A Cox) Geo'82.Cy.St.LakeF'78
☎ (716) 876-1323 . . 115 Meadow Rd, Buffalo, NY *14216*

Heuer MRS Scott JR (Spender—Ann F Lynch) . . . . . | of ☎ (202)965-4705
  MISS Catherine A . . . . | 4705 Foxhall
    | Crescent NW,
    | Washington, DC
    | *20007*
    | ☎ (504) 486-5196
    | 6550 Oakland Dv,
    | New Orleans, LA
    | *70118*

Heuer MR Scott C—Mid'77.CathU'90
☎ (202) 244-5737 . . 4924 Albemarle St NW, Washington, DC *20016*

Heuermann MR William W—Colg'55
☎ (207) 785-6173 . . 386 Searsmont Rd, Appleton, ME *04862*

Heurtley MRS Pervan (Ames—Jasna Pervan) Cl'55
☎ (212) 348-2792 . . 16 E 98 St, New York, NY *10029*

Heussler MR & MRS Davis R (Nancy J Gunner) Ty'78.U'73
☎ (716) 655-4218 . . 478 Linden Av, East Aurora, NY *14052*

Heussler MR Donald A—St.Cy.Mds.
☎ (716) 885-1771 . . 977 Delaware Av, Buffalo, NY *14209-1805*

Hewes MR & MRS Henry F (Jane Fowle) H'39 . . . . . | ☎ (212) AT9-5679
MR Tucker F—Conn'73 . . . . | 1326 Madison Av,
MR Havelock—SUNY'80 . . . . | New York, NY
                                          | *10128*

Hewes MR & MRS Laurence I 3d (Mary C Darling) | ☎ (202) 829-1821
BMr'56.Cos.Csn.Yn.Y'56.Y'59 . . . . | 1821 Randolph St
MISS Mary C D . . . . | NW, Washington,
MR Laurence I 4th . . . . | DC *20011*
MR H Patrick D . . . . |

Hewes MR & MRS Robert M 3d (Janet M Johnson) Cry.
☎ (410) 778-2033 . . ''Bachelor's Hope Farm'' 4849 Cliffs City Rd,
Chestertown, MD *21620*

Hewitt MRS Anderson F (Lomasney—Ellen D Fales) Pr.Cly.
☎ (941) 954-1981 . . 1762 Bay St, Apt 302, Sarasota, FL *34236*

Hewitt JUNIORS MISS Anna G . . see J P Kipp JR

Hewitt MR & MRS C F Lindsay (Elizabeth T | ☎ (516) MY2-4798
Dempsey) . . . . | 17 Ridge Rd,
MISS Elizabeth T—Hartw'89 . . . . | Harbor Ridge,
MISS Cassandra A—at Parsons Sch of Design . . . | Cold Spring Harbor,
                                          | NY *11724*

Hewitt JUNIORS MISS Caroline A . . see J P Kipp JR

Hewitt MRS Charles L (Dorothy M Lyman) Csh. . . . | ☎ (516) 692-6861
MR Edward L—P'68 . . . . | 1240 Moores Hill
                                          | Rd, Laurel Hollow,
                                          | Syosset, NY *11791*

Hewitt MR Edward Cooper JR . . see S B Colt

Hewitt MR William A—Bhm.Pcu.Plg.Cal'37 . . of
☎ (707) 963-7810 . . ''La Villette'' 1877 St Helena H'way, PO Box 240,
Rutherford, CA *94573*
☎ (415) 563-2866 . . 2690 Broadway St, San Francisco, CA *94115*

Hewitt MR & MRS William D (Eastman—Rives G Dalley) Van'72.Ga'75
☎ (404) 231-0334 . . 3311 Wood Valley Rd NW, Atlanta, GA *30327*

Hewlett MRS Roger S (Grew—Selina R Wood) Cly.Cda.
☎ (860) 434-9796 . . 14 Library Lane, Old Lyme, CT *06371*

Hewson MRS Charlotte W (Charlotte M Wolf)
☎ (212) 685-6323 . . 77 Park Av, Apt 7G, New York, NY *10016*

Hewson DR & MRS James Stokes (Nancy E Pool) | ☎ (508) 927-3120
Ec.Chi.Y'50.Temp'56 . . . . | 800 Hale St,
MISS Polly S—at Amsterdam, The Netherlands . | Beverly Farms, MA
MR William H—at Philadelphia, PA . . . . | *01915*

Hewson MR & MRS Thomas A (Elizabeth R Gurley) Swb'46.Mit'45
☎ (407) 454-3375 . . 125 Crispin St, Merritt Island, FL *32952*

Hewson MR W Newlin—Gc.Gettys'49
☎ (202) 484-6090 . . 1301 Delaware Av SW, Washington, DC *20024*

Hewson MR & MRS William B JR (Tunnell—Helen J | ☎ (203) 655-9982
Lockwood) Penn'63.P'57 . . . . | 8 Hanson Rd,
MISS Elizabeth S—Colg'93 . . . . | Darien, CT *06820*
MR Andrew L—StLaw'90 . . . . |
JUNIORS MR Charles W . . . . |
   MISS Tory L Tunnell—at Johns Hopkins . . . . |
   MR Bertram A Tunnell 3d—Ken'95 . . . . |

Heydt JUNIORS MR Charles E . . see MISS B E Metcalf

Heydt MRS Herman A (Marion Stebbins) Cly.Pr.
☎ (212) 759-4066 . . 200 E 66 St, Apt 1505C, New York, NY *10021*

Heyer DR & MRS Robert A (Caroline Washburne) | ☎ (704) 375-3591
So'69 . . . . | 2001 Queens Rd W,
MISS Ashley E—at Barnard . . . . | Charlotte, NC *28207*
MR Robert H—at Wash'n & Lee . . . . |

Heyes MRS Fred L (Catharine G O'Neill) Pr.Cly . . .of
☎ (516) 676-0077 . . 20 Overlook Rd, Matinecock Farms, Glen Cove,
NY *11542*
☎ (561) 234-0210 . . 2711 Ocean Dv, Vero Beach, FL *32963*

Heyl MR & MRS John L (Mary J Moore) | ☎ (301) 424-9583
Tufts'74.Hn.Ty'66 . . . . | 12308 Over Pond
JUNIORS MISS Katherine W—at Nat'l Cath Sch . . | Way, Potomac, MD
                                          | *20854*

Heyl JUNIORS MISS Nancy H . . see E W Stetson 3d

Heyl MRS Wolcott McM (Alice Morris)
☎ (215) CH8-2745 . . 147 W Gravers Lane, Philadelphia, PA *19118*

Heyward MR & MRS Allan McA (Marianna C | ☎ (804) 740-8352
Marshall) Ds.Sar.Dc.Cit'44 . . . . | 202 N Mooreland
MISS Virginia R . . . . | Rd, Richmond, VA
MR Wayne M—Cit'86—at 5211 Monument Av, | *23229-7102*
Apt 3, Richmond, VA *23226* . . . . |

Heyward MR George C—VillaN'71
☎ (803) 757-3144 . . 1 Water St, Bluffton, SC *29910*

Heyward MRS Josephine de R (Dyer—Josephine | ☎ (610) 688-2497
de R Heyward) Swb'67.M.Ac.Ncd. . . . . | 767 Newtown Rd,
MISS Elizabeth S Dyer—Ham'91—at | Villanova, PA *19085*
☎ (212) 744-1663 . . 440 E 79 St, Apt 8H, |
New York, NY *10021* . . . . |
MR Alexander H Dyer—P'95—at |
☎ (561) 747-5573 . . 9929 SE Buttonwood |
Way, Jupiter, FL *33469-1607* . . . . |

Heyward MR & MRS Robert B (Jacqueline McCormick) Cr'39
☎ (912) 638-2162 . . 2233 Bruce Dv, St Simons Island, GA *31522*

Hiam MR & MRS Edwin W (Katharine C Watson) D.Cy.Chi.Mit'48
☎ (617) 739-0335 . . 17 Glenoe Rd, Chestnut Hill, MA *02167*

Hiatt DR & MRS Warren A JR (Meredith M Golden) Miss'73.Van'69
☎ (601) 896-1975 . . 18 Keyser Lane, Gulfport, MS *39507*

Hibbard MR & MRS Dwight H (Gerry L Bishop) FlaSo'43.Qc.Aht'45.Mit'49
☎ (513) 871-5522 . . 2121 Alpine Place, Apt 902, Cincinnati, OH *45206*

Hibbard MRS William M (Kathleen H Gilman)
☎ (603) 224-5944 . . 59 Knox Rd, Bow, NH *03304*

Hickenlooper MR John W—Wes'74.Wes'80
☎ (303) 455-1211 . . 1792 Wynkoop St, Apt 304, Denver,
CO *80202-1042*

Hickey MR & MRS Peter A (Carolyn C Baruch)
☎ (303) 740-8661 . . 7918 S Pontiac Way, Englewood, CO *80112*

Hickman MRS Benjamin F 3d (Joan A Harms) . . . . Died Jun 28'96

Hickman MR Benjamin F 3d—Cy.
☎ (314) 997-1636 . . 1 Robin Hill Lane, St Louis, MO *63124*

Hickman MRS Norman Gilbert (James—D'Oench—Wood—Donovan—
Minnie Fell Cassatt) BMr'53.B.Ri.So.Plg.
☎ (561) 655-3838 . . 135 Chilean Av, Palm Beach, FL *33480*

Hickman MR & MRS Patrick N (Gail M St Aubyn) . . of
☎ (011-44-171) 244-9555 . . 65 Onslow Gardens, London SW7 3QD,
England
☎ (011-44-1725) 22217 . . Hale Park, nr Fordingbridge, Hampshire
SP6 2RF, England

Hickok MRS Daniel H (Mary Isabel Voorhees)
☎ (717) 599-5108 . . 211 Hidden Valley Lane, Harrisburg, PA *17112*

Hickox MRS Charles (Perkins—Martha Eaton) BMr'39
☎ (216) 831-9935 . . 10 Pepper Ridge Rd, Cleveland, OH *44124*

Hickox MR & MRS Charles C (Moulton—Linda L Janien)
Pr.S.Mto.L.BtP.Cly.Cl'61 . . of
☎ (212) 794-2055 . . 730 Park Av, New York, NY *10021*
☎ (203) 629-4346 . . 79 Harbor Dv, Greenwich, CT *06830*
☎ (561) 659-2425 . . 528 Island Dv, Palm Beach, FL *33480*

Hickox MR & MRS Charles R (Walker—Edith L Porter)
Sth'42.Ne.StJ.Ncd.Y'43
☎ (214) 357-7839 . . 5431 Surrey Circle, Dallas, TX *75209*

Hickox MRS Charles V (Hawkins—Kyra Schutt) Pr.
☎ (516) 921-0427 . . 1873 Muttontown Rd, Syosset, NY *11791-9655*

Hickox JUNIORS MR James A B . . see MISS (DR) D S Shaw

Hickox MRS James P (Barbara J Raymond) Me. . . . | ☎ (561) 231-1866
MISS Polly C—at ☎ (212) 534-6359 | 1776 Mooringline
170 E 87 St, Apt W-16B, New York, NY *10128* | Dv, Apt 202,
MR James P JR . . . . | Vero Beach, FL
| *32963*

Hickox MRS Louise F (Louise C Fitzhugh) . . . . | ☎ (502) 228-1567
MR George F. . . . . | 6411 Wolf Pen
| Branch Rd,
| Harrods Creek, KY
| *40027*

Hicks MASTER Benjamin Taylor (Stephen W) . . . . Born at
New York, NY Feb 28'96

Hicks MR & MRS Edward L 3d (Elizabeth S Kean) Cly.Yn.Y'42.Cl'61 ⚓
☎ (203) 869-5918 . . 55 Round Hill Rd, Greenwich, CT *06831*

Hicks MRS Graham H (Sarah G Turner) MissStW'26.Dar.
☎ (541) 963-6087 . . 900 Main Av, La Grande, OR *97850*

Hicks MR & MRS Harry C (Mary A Rhodes) Mg.Ll. . | of ☎ (201)838-1598
MR James P . . . . | 309 Cherry Tree
| Lane, Smoke Rise,
| Kinnelon, NJ *07405*
| ☎ (561) 231-3558
| 100 Ocean Rd,
| John's Island,
| Vero Beach, FL
| *32960*

Hicks MISS Julia R (Paul De F JR) . . . . Married at Rye, NY
de Peyster MR Nicholas L M (James A JR) . . . . May 25'96

Hicks MR & MRS Matthew B (Audrey M Grabfield) Sth'80.Wes'86.U'80
☎ (518) 642-9027 . . 9 Pine St, Granville, NY *12832*

Hicks MR & MRS Paul De F JR (Barbara H Edwards) Rdc'61.P'58.H'61
☎ (914) 967-0799 . . 637 North St, Rye, NY *10580*

Hicks MR & MRS Stephen W (Elizabeth Hazan) BMr'86.ColC'77.Cl'84.Y'95
☎ (212) 255-5863 . . 16 W 11 St, New York, NY *10011*

Hicks MISS Vanessa H (Paul De F JR) . . . . Married at Rye, NY
Voorham MR Markus A B (Anthonius J) . . . . Sep 24'94

Hidalgo MR & MRS Alfonso (Elizabeth S Hall) LosAndes'85.Drex'87
☎ (011-57-1) 235-8435 . . Carrera 1A, 76A-72, Apt 301, Bogotá,
Colombia

Hields MR & MRS Paul W R (Margo C Muckerman) Col'84.Leeds'82
PO Box 1941, Avon, CO *81620*

Hiemenz MR & MRS Christopher B (Susan L Hollocher)
SpgH'84.StL'87.Cy.Regis'83
☎ (314) 821-2292 . . 1101 North Dv, St Louis, MO *63122*

Hiemenz MR & MRS W M Donovan (Melanie L McClellan)
Fontb'78.Cy.StL'78.StL'79
☎ (314) 434-1001 . . 12755 Conway Lake, St Louis, MO *63141*

Hiestand MR & MRS Harry K (Nancy M Price) | ☎ (610) 527-0690
B'gton'53.Gm.Ph.Pa'50 . . . . | 40 Aldwyn Lane,
MR Philip M . . . . | Villanova, PA *19085*

Higbie MR & MRS Hugo S (Marian Chapin) | ☎ (313) 886-1954
Cda.Wms'48 . . . . | 17 Preston Place,
MISS Faye T . . . . | Grosse Pointe
MISS Hope C . . . . | Farms, MI *48236*
MR Mark S . . . . |

Higdon MR Robert M JR—Y'77.Y'78
☎ (202) 223-5691 . . 1280—21 St NW, Apt 606, Washington, DC *20036*

Higgerson MR & MRS Richard McI (Phyllis R G Trevor)
MtVern'92.Srb.Cly.Vt'89
☎ (802) 457-4383 . . "Hill House" Box 87, South Pomfret, VT *05067*

Higgins MR & MRS Austin D (Ellen E Monks) | ☎ (207) 799-0023
Chi.Y'43 . . . . | Ram Island Farm,
MR Nicholas H S . . . . | Cape Elizabeth, ME
| *04107*

Higgins MR Daniel P
295 E Boot Rd, Malvern, PA *19355*

Higgins MRS Decatur S (Elise M Farley) Pr.
☎ (516) 676-1534 . . 20 Midway Av, Locust Valley, NY *11560*

Higgins MR & MRS James C 2d (Kathryn S Krause)
Colg'81.Eh.Shcc.Bost'75
☎ (908) 234-9396 . . 14 Ski Hill Dv, Bedminster, NJ *07921*

Higgins MR & MRS James H (Elysabeth C Barbour)
SL'44.Edg.Rr.Ln.Cly.Myf.Yn.Y'39
☎ (412) 741-7756 . . 608 Maple Lane, Sewickley, PA *15143-1026*

Higgins MR & MRS James H 3d (Martha M Robinson)
Bow'78.Unn.Eh.Shcc.NCar'71.Dth'74
☎ (201) 539-8488 . . "Peacemeal" 140 Washington Valley Rd,
Morristown, NJ *07960*

Higgins MRS John F (Jane G Fletcher) Eastern'69.Ac.Cda.
☎ (610) MU8-6522 . . 532 W Wayne Av, Wayne, PA *19087*

Higgins MRS Lawrence (Roberts—Angela G Honan)
☎ (011-52) 280-1155 . . Av Cicerón 608, Los Morales,
Mexico 5, DF 11510, Mexico

Higgins MISS Maura E . . see MISS L L Uihlein

Higgins MR & MRS Michael J 3d (Beaty—Bowers—Quartier—
Helen Wolcott Corscaden) Wash'43
☎ (561) 844-4348 . . 324 Southwind Dv N, Palm Beach, FL *33408*

Higgins MR & MRS R Scott (Molly L Osborn) | ☎ (617) 444-3567
Cy.Chi.Ncd.H'62 . . . . | 40 Edgewater Lane,
MISS K Page—at ☎ (212) 722-6036 | Needham, MA
1716 Second Av, Apt 5C, New York, NY *10128* | *02192*
MR John B O—at 20 Hubbard St, Apt 4, |
Cambridge, MA *02140* . . . . |
MR R Scott JR . . . . |

Higgins MRS Raymond M (Joan S Griess) . . . . Died Mch 13'96

Higgins MR & MRS William M (Jane W Thiele) — ☎ (513) 561-3200 / 5360 Miami Rd, Cincinnati, OH 45243
Denis'66.Mvh.Dth'66 . . . .
MISS Molly C—Dth'91—at Harvard Business . .
MR William M JR—Ind'93—at 64 Green St, Dayton, OH 45402 . . . .
JUNIORS MR John A—at Dartmouth . . . .

Higginson MR & MRS Charles (Genevra A Osborn) Ws'56.Cvc.Sl.H'54 . . of
☎ (202) 338-0973 . . 2222 King Place NW, Washington, DC 20007
☎ (617) 383-9427 . . ''Cedar Ledges'' 159 Atlantic Av, Cohasset, MA 02025

Higginson MR James J—B.Pr.Rc.H'44
☎ (212) 838-1248 . . 800 Fifth Av, New York, NY 10021

Higginson MRS John M (Isabella R B Lukens) Ws'31
☎ (303) 839-7526 . . Park Manor Apt 526, 1801 E Nineteenth Av, Denver, CO 80218-1232

Higginson MR & MRS Thomas L JR (Feroline P Burrage) Va'74.K.Pr.Cvc.Mt.Srb.Nrr.H'72.Va'76
☎ (540) 364-2787 . . ''Claybrook'' PO Box 109, Rectortown, VA 20140

High MRS Kenneth G (Christine S Miller)
☎ (415) WA1-1910 . . 2309 Broderick St, San Francisco, CA 94115

High MR Leslie C—Me.Fw.StA.
☎ (610) 525-7640 . . 74 Pasture Lane, Apt 221, Bryn Mawr, PA 19010

High MISS Margaret P—Sth'59.Cly.
☎ (212) 980-8012 . . 200 E 66 St, New York, NY 10021

Highet MR & MRS Ian D (Lea W Paine) H'88.Rc.Shcc.Hb.H'88
☎ (212) 517-6608 . . 125 E 84 St, Apt 6C, New York, NY 10028

Highmore MR & MRS Wilson L JR (Mary E Moest) — ☎ (860) 443-7002 / 25 Westomere Terr, New London, CT 06320
WmSth'56.Hob'53 . . . .
MISS Sarajane E—at ☎ (805) 963-0333
110 Camino Alto, Santa Barbara, CA 93103 . . .

Higholt DR Howard W—Minn'61 . . . . — ☎ (310) 541-8855 / 4 Possum Ridge Rd, Rolling Hills, CA 90274-5015
JUNIORS MR Jonathan C . . . .

Higinbotham MR & MRS Harlow N (Susan E Spika) Minn'74.Wa.H'68.Ch'76 . . of
☎ (312) 266-0661 . . 1500 N Lake Shore Dv, Apt 13C, Chicago, IL 60610
☎ (815) 727-7200 . . ''Harlowarden'' RD 2, Joliet, IL 60432

Higley DR Stephen R—Drake'71.Ill'75.Ill'92
☎ (205) 322-8699 . . 3350 Altamont Rd S, Apt D8, Birmingham, AL 35205

Hiland MR & MRS Christopher P (Cassandra L Taliaferro) Wms'90.Mid'89
126 Maywood Lane, Charlottesville, VA 22903

Hiland MR & MRS R Bruce (M Virginia Callender) Pemb'64.Y'83.Br'61.Pa'66
☎ (802) 462-3550 . . ''Aurora Farm'' RD 2, Box 544, Middlebury, VT 05753

Hilbert MR & MRS Samuel R (Anita L Smith) Nu'52 — ☎ (804) 744-8066 / 13912 McTyre's Cove Lane, Midlothian, VA 23112
MISS Corinne W—at ☎ (212) 996-4129
26 E 91 St, Apt 4B, Box 1, New York, NY 10128
MISS Elspeth R—at ☎ (505) 424-0181
4301 Calle Andrew, Apt A, Santa Fe, NM 87505

Hildebrandt MR & MRS David D (Mary Maguire) — ☎ (602) 483-7006 / 9150 N 70 St, Paradise Valley, AZ 85253
ArizSt'73.Cal'75 . . . .
JUNIORS MISS Lauren E . . . .

Hildebrandt MRS Donald H (Mary Helen Detrick) . . of
☎ (602) 998-1844 . . 7400 E Gainey Club Dv, Apt 147, Scottsdale, AZ 85258
☎ (520) 527-4087 . . 6081 E Laurel Loop Rd, Flagstaff, AZ 86004

Hildesley REV & MRS C Hugh (Constance C Palmer) — ☎ (212) 772-3239 / 570 Park Av, New York, NY 10021
Rc.Pr.StJ.StJTheo'76 . . . .
MISS Melissa M . . . .
MR Mark A . . . .

Hildreth DR & MRS Eugene A (Dorothy A Myers) — ☎ (610) 775-3421 / Echo Hollow Farm, RD 3, Box 3960, Mohnton, PA 19540
W&J'43.Va'46 . . . .
MISS Anne S—at ☎ (802) 785-4127
PO Box 25, East Thetford, VT 05043 . . . .

Hildt MR & MRS John (Barney—Wick—Dorothy C Tremaine) Sth'49.Cv.Kt . . .of
☎ (216) 423-3279 . . 1653 Berkshire Rd, Gates Mills, OH 44040
☎ (619) 324-8608 . . 30 Churchill Lane, Rancho Mirage, CA 92270

Hilgartner MRS Haynes (Frances G Haynes) GeoW'51.Sl.Ncd.
☎ (703) 978-0034 . . 4513 Overcup Court, Fairfax, VA 22032

Hilgenberg MR & MRS C Edward (Carlisle—Alexandre—F Gilbert Tucker) Md.Dc.Va'32
☎ (410) 822-3065 . . 20 Lynnebrook Terr, Easton, MD 21601

Hilgenberg MR & MRS Carl R (Elizabeth L Rianhard) — ☎ (410) 628-0483 / Broadmead A11, 13801 York Rd, Cockeysville, MD 21030
V'29.Md.Elk. . . . .
MR Carl G—Godd'61—at Franconia, NH 03580

Hilgenberg MR & MRS John C (Twells—Evelyn B Handy) Elk.Md.Y'63.Va'65 . . . . — ☎ (410) 235-4593 / 810 Drohomer Place, Baltimore, MD 21210
MISS Elizabeth Crady . . . .

Hilken MR & MRS Keith D (Eleanor Engs) — ☎ (209) 478-7381 / 3876 Fourteen Mile Dv, Stockton, CA 95219
Cal'54.Bhm.Fr. . . . .
MISS Jean—Cal'82 . . . .
MR Keith D JR—Box 947, Tahoe City, CA 96145

Hill MR Andrew B . . see MRS W Minot

Hill MISS Ann . . see L E MacElree

Hill MR & MRS Charles B 3d (Sheila J Brewster) — of ☎ (941)927-1401 / 4762 Antler Trail, Sarasota, FL 34238
LakeF'61 . . . .
MR Charles B 4th . . . .
☎ (414) 245-1080 / 1229 Terrace Court, Lake Geneva, WI 53147

Hill MRS Charles C (Rosemary D Kernan) . . . . — ☎ (914) 358-3914 / 110 Rockland Garden Apts, Nyack, NY 10960
MRS Linda (Burck—Linda Hill) Tor'64 . . . .
MISS Rosemary C Yiameos . . . .

Hill MISS Charlotte . . see L E MacElree

Hill MR Christopher C—A.Tex'78 . . of
☎ (210) 736-4488 . . 757 Grandview Place, San Antonio, TX 78209
☎ (505) 983-0777 . . 1005 Canyon Rd, Santa Fe, NM 87501

Hill MR David H . . see MRS W Minot

Hill MR & MRS Dean E (Kate van D Sanson) BMr'75.Me.P'73
☎ (847) 446-1807 . . 610 Spruce St, Winnetka, IL 60093

Hill MR & MRS Edward D (Caroline A Walker) | ☎ (912) 234-2923
StMarys'63.SCar'62 — | 2 E Taylor St,
MISS Elsie T—at RI Sch of Design . . . . | Savannah, GA
| *31401*

Hill MRS Freeman W (Hankey—Dangan—Elizabeth A Papillon)
☎ (508) 636-6718 . . PO Box 119, Westport Point, MA *02791*

Hill MR Freeman W JR—Rol'65
☎ (212) 371-4000 . . 36 Central Park S, New York, NY *10019*

Hill MR George E B (Leslie Eustis)
☎ (415) 461-5648 . . 107 Diablo Dv, Kentfield, CA *94904*

Hill DR & MRS (DR) George J (Helene Zimmermann) | of ☎ (201)736-0738
Sth'50.Brand'64.An.Myf.Hn.Hb.Y'53.H'57 . . . . | 3 Silver Spring Rd,
MISS Sarah—Ken'84 . . . . | West Orange, NJ
MISS Helena R—Sterling'85 . . . . | *07052-4317*
MR James W—Rut'85.Rut'92 . . . . | ☎ (603) 447-4214
| Paul Hill Rd, Eaton,
| NH *03832*

Hill MRS Henry B (Esther McGuire) Hb.
☎ (941) 349-8887 . . ''Hill & High Water'' 1372 Point Crisp Rd,
Sarasota, FL *34242*

Hill MRS Hope H (Cook—Choate—Hope P Henry)
☎ (209) 533-2452 . . PO Box 3906, Sonora, CA *95370*

Hill MR & MRS J Bennett JR (Patricia T Gardiner) | ☎ (610) 688-4455
Wh'lck'75.Me.Myf.Swth'52 . . . . | 29 Briar Rd,
JUNIORS MISS Elizabeth M . . . . | Strafford, PA *19087*

Hill MRS J Edgar (Harrison—Jeanne A Edgar) Me.
☎ (610) 525-4498 . . 9 Pond Lane, Bryn Mawr, PA *19010*

Hill MR & MRS J Tomilson 3d (Janine A Wolf) | of ☎ (212)734-9015
Paris'71.H'74.Ln.Pr.Ri.Mb.Cly.H'70.H'73 . . . . . | 4 E 72 St,
JUNIORS MISS Margot . . . . | New York, NY
JUNIORS MISS Astrid . . . . | *10021*
| ☎ (516) 759-9169
| 248 Piping Rock Rd,
| Locust Valley, NY
| *11560*

Hill MRS James T JR (Dorothy H Kutcher) Cs.
☎ (212) 752-2594 . . 200 E 66 St, New York, NY *10021*

Hill MR & MRS Jefferson B (Gabrielle M Tourville) | of ☎ (202)544-4387
Cal'63.Mt.H'63 . . . . | 639 E Capitol St SE,
MISS Corinna B . . . . | Washington, DC
JUNIORS MISS Lydia R . . . . | *20003*
| ☎ (508) 693-9426
| Barnard's Inn Farm,
| Vineyard Haven,
| MA *02568*

Hill MR & MRS Jeffrey D (Diana M Price) Unn.Yn.Y'66
☎ (415) 389-6703 . . 10 Overhill Rd, Mill Valley, CA *94941*

Hill DR & MRS John B (Elaine T Mackenzie) Wis'44.Cl'52
☎ (919) 942-2962 . . 800 Houston Rd, Chapel Hill, NC *27514*

Hill COL (RET) & MRS John F P (Jeffress—Elizabeth R Hume)
USA.An.Ct.Mv.Dc.Ncd.Hb.H'38
☎ (410) 366-8236 . . 204 St Martins Rd, Baltimore, MD *21218*

Hill MR John H—Fcg.Rr.Y'62.Y'65
☎ (412) 687-7299 . . 4722 Bayard St, Pittsburgh, PA *15213-1708*

Hill MRS John J 3d (Crew—Mary Marsh) Rd.
☎ (610) 469-6778 . . ''Nantmeal Hunt Farm'' 3111 Horseshoe Trail,
Glenmoore, PA *19343*

Hill MR John J 5th—Syr'90 . . see P W Jacobs

Hill MR & MRS John L (Finch—Mary McC Truitt) | 418 Duvall Lane,
SL'81.Cl'86.Mass'85.W&M'91 . . . . | Annapolis, MD
JUNIORS MR Charles B Finch 3d—at | *21403*
Phillips Andover . . . . |

Hill MR & MRS John P (A Leith Benjamin) H'88
☎ (516) 751-7551 . . 40 Cedar St, Stony Brook, NY *11790-1758*

Hill MR & MRS Jonathan J (Julie A Kelly)
108 Gaskarth Rd, London SW12 9NW, England

Hill MR & MRS Joseph J (Elizabeth Van H Bartlett) | ☎ (610) 527-0997
Rc.Me.Pa'61 ⚓ . . . . | 726 Cedar Lane,
MISS Susannah B . . . . | Villanova, PA *19085*
MR Alexander McC . . . . |
MR Michael H . . . . |

Hill MR & MRS Louis G (Young—Marilyn J Ashton)
Ant'55.Temp'82.H'46.Pa'49
☎ (215) CH2-5843 . . 615 St George's Rd, Philadelphia, PA *19119*

Hill MR & MRS Melville C JR (Mary Johnson) Nw'54.Ih.Aht'47.H'49
☎ (847) 446-5794 . . 271 Linden St, Winnetka, IL *60093*

Hill MR Melville Coulter III (Melville C JR) . . . . Married at
| Highland Park, IL
Ronan MISS Catherine M (late Thomas A) . . . . May 4'96

Hill MR Michael C—HWSth'84
☎ (617) 332-9236 . . 34 Hartford St, Newton, MA *02161*

Hill MRS Ray R (Jessie H Leonard) Cly . . .of
☎ (212) 988-3666 . . 215 E 72 St, New York, NY *10021*
☎ (207) 734-6785 . . PO Box 236, Islesboro, ME *04848*

Hill MR & MRS Raymond M (Jerauld Lollar) Dar.Cda.Houst'51
☎ (713) 468-4304 . . 1307 Potomac Dv, Houston, TX *77057*

Hill MR & MRS Robert B (Harriet A Chandler) Cw.Dth'42
☎ (617) 235-6896 . . 27 Crown Ridge Rd, Wellesley, MA *02181*

Hill MR & MRS Robert Carey (Beth Fennimore) Cal'43.Cal'43
☎ (213) 933-2148 . . 464 N June St, Los Angeles, CA *90004*

Hill MR Robert F—Un.Hob'68
☎ (212) 535-6719 . . 179 E 79 St, New York, NY *10021*

Hill MR & MRS Robert W JR (Lopez—Joanne M | ☎ (802) 453-3728
Schneider) Va'74.Md'76.Wil.H'56 . . . . | RR 1, Box 143B,
MR Robert W 3d—Mid'83—at | Quaker Village Rd,
☎ (860) 651-9777 . . Westminster School, | Middlebury, VT
995 Hopmeadow St, Simsbury, CT *06070* . . . . . | *05753*
JUNIORS MISS Catherine E . . . . |
JUNIORS MISS Laura V Lopez . . . . |

Hill DR & MRS S Richardson JR (Janet Redman) V'49.Duke'43.WakeF'46
☎ (205) 969-3446 . . 3337 E Briarcliff Rd, Birmingham, AL *35223*

Hill MR Samuel R 2d—Rc.Ham'69
☎ (212) 628-4768 . . 151 E 83 St, New York, NY *10028*

Hill MR & MRS Serge J (Priscilla F Baker) Rcn.Bg.
☎ (201) 467-2923 . . 6 Knollwood Rd, Short Hills, NJ *07078*

Hill MR & MRS T Bowen 3d (Maria C Paschall) | ☎ (334) 272-7881
Ala'51.Ala'53 ⚓ . . . . | 3721 Vaughn Rd,
MR Chappell H . . . . | Montgomery, AL
| *36106*

Hill MR & MRS Thomas J (H Kemp Passano) Va'80.Va'79 . . of
☎ (804) 977-3481 . . 1204 Rugby Rd, Charlottesville, VA *22903*
Dagwood Farms, Ware Neck, VA *23178*

Hill MRS Vianda Hale (Vianda P Hale) Van'70 . . . .
MISS Nicki P—at Georgetown. . . . .
JUNIORS MISS Christiane L. . . . .
☎ (615) 292-1911
203 Lynwood Blvd,
Nashville, TN *37205*

Hill MRS William E (Jane E Herrmann) Ln.Cho.Plg.
MISS Sarah K . . . .
☎ (212) 744-8551
125 E 74 St,
New York, NY
10021

Hill MR & MRS William I 2d (Sarah F Hightower)
Tul'61.Ala'62. . . . .
MISS Martha E I . . . .
☎ (334) 262-0819
3201 Southview Av,
Montgomery, AL
36106

Hillard MR George O JR . . . . Died Jly 23'96

Hillard MRS George O JR (W Jane Tupper)
☎ (520) 648-8367 . . 501 S La Posada Circle, Apt 242, Green Valley,
AZ *85614*

Hilles MRS Frederick W (Susan T Morse) Csn.
301 Berkeley St, Boston, MA *02116*

Hilles MRS R Webster JR (Margaret H P Fenn) Me.Pn.
☎ (610) 645-8656 . . 1400 Waverly Rd, Villa 7, Gladwyne, PA *19035*

Hilliard MR Charles L
☎ (212) EL5-4824 . . 447 E 57 St, New York, NY *10022*

Hilliard MR & MRS David S (Helen D Matheson)
Va'86.Rcn.Cly.WashColl'87
☎ (415) 457-1982 . . PO Box 272, 88 Shady Lane, Ross, CA *94957*

Hilliard MR & MRS Henry R JR (Anne F Rose)
Rdc'44.P'43 . . . .
MISS Christina F—at 343 South Av, Weston, MA
02193 . . . .
MR Henry R 3d—at Boston, MA
17 Lanewood,
Cumberland
Foreside, ME
04110-1409

Hilliard MISS Larkin A L—UWash'80.Cal'88
☎ (805) 683-5855 . . 1411 Holiday Hill Rd, Santa Barbara, CA *93117*

Hillman MR & MRS David 5th (Susan L Whitesell)
Ky'66.Cc.Cw.Myf.Bost'66. . . . .
MISS Phoebe C . . . .
MISS Elizabeth L. . . . .
☎ (609) 453-0273
"Dragonfly Farm"
Box 276, Fairton, NJ
08320

Hillman MR Ernest JR—Mto.Yn.Y'33
☎ (203) 259-2994 . . 3236 Congress St, Fairfield, CT *06430*

Hillman MR & MRS Gilbert R (Rachel B Read)
Wis'64.SConn'69.Houst'82.H'65.Y'69 . . . .
MISS Laura R—at 2346 N Limestone St, Apt 3,
Springfield, OH *45503* . . . .
☎ (713) 486-7713
1827 Barleton Way,
Houston, TX *77058*

Hillman MR & MRS Henry L (Elsie M Hilliard)
Pg.Fcg.Rr.P'41 . . . .
MR William T—at 1 W 64 St, New York, NY
10023 . . . .
☎ (412) 681-2078
Morewood Heights,
Pittsburgh, PA
15213

Hillman MRS Howard B (Sandra Fales) . . . .
MR Howard B JR—Buck'84 . . . .
☎ (203) 661-3698
"Stoneybrook"
29 Taconic Rd,
Greenwich, CT
06830

Hillman MR Howard B—P'56.H'60
☎ (203) 966-7700 . . 158 Main St, New Canaan, CT *06840*

Hillman MR & MRS Robert S (Sandra L Schwartz) Penn'62.JHop'60.H'63
☎ (410) 664-1654 . . 5514 S Bend Rd, Baltimore, MD *21209*

Hills MR & MRS Austin E (Erika M Brunar)
Vien'64.Bhm.Pcu.Stan'57 . . . .
JUNIORS MR Austin . . . .
JUNIORS MR Justin . . . .
of ☎ (415)922-7111
2546 Jackson St,
San Francisco,
94115
☎ (707) 963-4577
PO Box 139,
Rutherford, CA
94573

Hills MR & MRS Carter H (Joan B Luke)
Cal'59.SFr'65.Fr.Cl'48.P'50. . . . .
MISS Jennifer L—CtCol'90—at Johns Hopkins. .
MISS Alison C—Cl'96 . . . .
☎ (202) 462-9190
2132 Leroy Place
NW, Washington,
DC *20008*

Hills MR & MRS Edwin A (Margaret S Brydon) H'37
☎ (617) 749-0046 . . 22 Martin's Lane, Hingham, MA *02043*

Hills MR & MRS Reuben W 3d (Ingrid von Mangoldt)
Camb'63.Pcu.Bur.Stan'44
☎ (415) 346-9297 . . 2920 Broadway St, San Francisco, CA *94115*

Hillsmith MRS Fannie L (Welchman—Fannie L Hillsmith). . of
☎ (212) 753-3817 . . 166 E 63 St, Apt 7B, New York, NY *10021*
☎ (603) 532-7132 . . "Wedgwood" Jaffrey, NH *03452*

Hillyer MRS Stanley H (Laura Venini)
☎ (508) 922-2137 . . 7 Curtis Point, Beverly, MA *01915*

Hilton MR & MRS John A JR (Julia L Hansen)
Nyc.Rc.On.Vt'68 . . . .
MISS Julia H—at St Lawrence U . . . .
MISS Katharine B . . . .
JUNIORS MISS Ashley S . . . .
☎ (847) 234-3839
1310 N Green Bay
Rd, Lake Forest, IL
60045

Hilton MR & MRS Robert W JR (Mathilde M Biddle) Cin'42.W&L'38.H'41
☎ (513) 321-3040 . . 3277 Hardisty Av, Cincinnati, OH *45208*

Hinchman MRS Denise H (Denise H Harmon)
☎ (847) 501-2823 . . 1725 Northfield Square, Northfield, IL *60093*

Hinckley MR Albert P JR—B.Rcn.Pn.P'55.Mit'59
☎ (540) 364-1771 . . "Hawthorne" PO Box 27, Orlean, VA *20128-0027*

Hinckley MR & MRS David M (Wood—Francis M
McCarthy) Drew'70 . . . .
MISS F Parnell Wood—CtCol'89 . . . .
MR Frederic D Wood . . . .
☎ (201) 543-2737
174 Days Hill Rd,
Mendham, NJ *07945*

Hinckley MR G F Steedman . . . . Died at
New York, NY Aug 27'96

Hinckley MRS G F Steedman (Ingrid A Mjornell)
B.Cly. . . . .
MISS Katherine S P—at Princeton . . . .
☎ (540) 364-2333
"Henchman's Lea"
PO Box 37, Orlean,
VA *20128*

Hinckley MRS Helen P (Helen Pettit) Mich'75
☎ (415) 903-0554 . . 23500 Cristo Rey Dv, Cupertino, CA *95014*

Hinckley MRS Low (Marli Low)
☎ (212) 877-8778 . . 251 W 71 St, New York, NY *10023*

Hinckley MRS Nancy F (Nancy A Frohan) Ill'79
☎ (415) 331-5813 . . 117 Caledonia St, Apt 1, Sausalito, CA *94965*

Hinckley CAPT & MRS Robert M (Bernice M Smith)
Ny.USN'35 ⚓ . . . .
MISS Marion . . . .
☎ (011-34-965)
84-8082
"Casa Redonda"
Sierra de Altea 69,
Altea, Alicante,
Spain

Hinckley MR Samuel H—Lm.Cal'79.SFrSt'92 ⚓
☎ (415) 927-3157 . . 9 Pepper Av, Corte Madera, CA *94925*

Hinckley MR Samuel N—Pcu.Snc.Lm.Hn.H'39
☎ (415) 492-2561 . . Villa Marin Apt 459, 100 Thorndale Dv, San Rafael, CA *94903*

Hind MR James M . . of
☎ (702) 782-2754 . . Box 276, Minden, NV *89423*
☎ (702) 749-5262 . . 18 Golf Links Rd, Glenbrook, NV *89413*

Hindman DR & MRS Stephen H (Madalyn Cunningham) Belh'70.Miss'69 . . . .
MISS Tracy C . . . .
JUNIORS MR Douglas H . . . .
☎ (601) 992-1337
157 Dogwood Place, Jackson, MS *39208*

Hine MR Edwin W 2d—Sg.Leh'42
☎ (215) CH7-8616 . . 8000 Seminole Av, Philadelphia, PA *19118*

Hine MRS Francis L (Helen L McChristie)
☎ (609) 451-7337 . . PO Box 36, Greenwich, NJ *08323*

Hines MR & MRS Edward M W (Caroline M Knapp) Cs.H.'61.Y'64 . . . .
MISS Alexandra E—Ty'93 . . . .
JUNIORS MISS Laura L . . . .
☎ (212) 486-0403
116 E 63 St, New York, NY *10021*

Hines MR & MRS Edwin Y (Elizabeth M Cay) Vmi'66 . . . .
MISS Elizabeth H—at Wash'n & Lee . . . .
MISS Anne W—at Hollins . . . .
of ☎ (404)355-4487
2839 Dover Rd NW, Atlanta, GA *30327*
☎ (803) 784-3231
''Summer Duck Farm'' Rte 1, Box 93H, Hardeeville, SC *29927*

Hines MR & MRS Marion E (Julie W Viele) CalTech'40
☎ (617) 248-0346 . . 44 W Cedar St, Boston, MA *02114*

Hines MR & MRS Richard K (Cornelia E Yarbrough) Duke'31.Ncd.
☎ (803) 853-9448 . . 3 Ford Court, Charleston, SC *29401-2512*

Hines MR & MRS Richard K 5th (Annette G Jones) Vmi'66.Van'72 . . . .
MISS Paget B L . . . .
JUNIORS MR Bolling F . . . .
4073 Conway Valley Rd NW, Atlanta, GA *30327*

Hines MRS Robert S (Fernley—Ann C Taylor) NCar'44.Pc.Ac.Fw.
MR J Randolph Fernley—Sar.Pac'74—at 98-110 Moanalua Aiea, Honolulu, HI *96701* .
MR David B Fernley—Sar.Me'85.Bvr'91—at 325 Rosemary Av, Ambler, PA *19002* . . . . . .
☎ (215) 646-5646
Whitpain Farm, 12 Fetlock Lane, Blue Bell, PA *19422*

Hines MRS Roy H JR (Joanne Barbour) Myf.
☎ (561) 692-9359 . . PO Box 1122, Stuart, FL *34995*

Hinken DR & MRS Michael Van D (Joan L Otis) Ill'52.Loy'55 . . . .
REV Michael Van D JR—NotreD'78 . . . .
☎ (501) 922-5603
12 Antigua Lane, Hot Springs Village, AR *71909*

Hinkson MRS J H Ward (McMichael—Eileen Hart)
☎ (415) 492-2620 . . Villa Marin Apt 262, 100 Thorndale Dv, San Rafael, CA *94903*

Hinman MR George L—Ln.C.Plg.P'27.H.'30
☎ (607) 724-3134 . . 1645 Pennsylvania Av, Binghamton, NY *13903*

Hinman, John R JR & Dallett, C Athenaide H—H'83.AmU'90.H'92. Cda.Rut'86.Va'92
☎ (860) 927-1723 . . Kent School, PO Box 2006, Kent, CT *06757*

Hinson MR Harry Lee—W&M'63
☎ (212) 737-3656 . . 30 E 68 St, New York, NY *10021*

Hinton MRS Longstreet (Odette O'Higgins) Ck.Plg. .
MISS Marianne—Cly.—at 34 Cornwall Gardens, London SW7, England . . . .
MR Charles-Patrick—at Lucca, Italy . . . .
☎ (516) 676-5810
161 Linden Farm Rd, Locust Valley, NY *11560*

Hird MR & MRS Samuel Ainsworth JR (Drogoul—Benacerraf—Webb—Diane C Meentemeier) Dth'39 ⚓ . . of
☎ (201) 444-6389 . . 82 Fairmount Rd, Ridgewood, NJ *07450*
☎ (516) 749-0037 . . PO Box 254, 8 Shore Rd, Dering Harbor, Shelter Island Heights, NY *11965*

Hires MR & MRS William L (Perrott—Karen E Reynolds) Buck'58.BMr'82.Rb.Ph.Me.Pe.Cc.Cw. Snc.Hav'49.Pa'72 . . . .
MISS Jennifer L—at U of Vt . . . .
☎ (610) 642-4373
106 Righters Mill Rd, Penn Valley, PA *19072*

Hirons MR & MRS Frederic C (Marianna C Cox) Qc.Cc.Cw.Ncd.Y'39 . . . .
MR Frederic C 3d—at ☎ (206) 282-0913 17 Valley St, Apt 202, Seattle, WA *98109* . . . . .
☎ (513) 561-4532
5824 Mohican Rd, Cincinnati, OH *45243*

Hirsh MISS Margaretta H . . see MRS M Thayer

Hirsh MISS Paget T (Malcolm McC) . . . . Married at Unionville, PA
Bennett MR Wesley R (late Geoffrey) . . . . Jun 3'95

Hirsh MRS Willard (Sarah F Cole) Ws'38.Cwr'45.Yn . . .of
☎ (216) 932-1819 . . 2507 Fairmount Blvd, Cleveland, OH *44106*
☎ (216) 286-7268 . . ''Vengreen Farm'' 12987 GAR H'way, Chardon, OH *44024*

Hirst MRS Anthony A (Loulie G Donalson) Ncd.Dar.
☎ (912) 246-3078 . . PO Box 1015, Bainbridge, GA *31717-1015*

Hirst MR John C 3d—Pa'44
☎ (610) 688-8570 . . 621 Arlyn Circle, Wayne, PA *19087*

Hirst MRS Sydney (Stevens—Sydney Hirst)
☎ (904) 763-2065 . . 1236 Beck Av, Lot 9, Panama City, FL *32401*

Hiscox MR Frederick . . see R D Doxford

Hiscox MR Renshaw . . see R D Doxford

Hitchcock MR & MRS David I (R Lee Williamson) SL'49.Cos.Dth'50
☎ (301) 229-2944 . . 4990 Sentinel Dv, Bethesda, MD *20816*

Hitchcock MR & MRS Ethan A (Watts—Mari Boies) C.Yn.Y'31.H'34 . . . .
MISS Constance—at 84 rue Michel-Ange, 70016 Paris, France . . . .
☎ (908) 439-2319
''Upper Farm'' Box 143, Oldwick, NJ *08858*

Hitchcock MR & MRS Henry (Eleanor Hoblitzelle) Cysl.Y'28
☎ (520) 885-8300 . . 6315 E Miramar Dv, Tucson, AZ *85715*

Hitchcock MR John JR—Ey . . . .
MR Crosby—Ey.H'46 . . . .
☎ (508) 887-2729
230 Middleton Rd, Boxford, MA *01921*

Hitchcock MR & MRS John E (Marilyn W Morgan) Wor'67 . . . .
MR William L . . . .
JUNIORS MR Andrew M . . . .
☎ (216) 338-1495
953 Bell Rd, Chagrin Falls, OH *44022*

Hitchcock MISS Margaret Mellon (Scarrone—Bowart—Margaret Mellon Hitchcock) . . . .
MISS Sophia J Bowart . . . .
MISS Nuria L Bowart . . . .
☎ (520) 722-1956
3705 Old Sabino Canyon Rd, Tucson, AZ *85715*

Hitchcock MR & MRS Meacham (Jean R Hyde) Kt.Un.Tv.Y'50
☎ (216) 681-2299 . . 10501 Lake Shore Blvd, Apt 2, Cleveland, OH *44108*
Jan 1 . . ☎ (941) 474-0185 . . 7515 Manasota Key Rd, Englewood, FL *34223*

Hitchcock MR Nelson B—FairD'92
☎ (212) 889-3433 . . 151 Lexington Av, Apt 5F, New York, NY *10016*
Hitchcock MRS Peter S (Elizabeth P Gaddis) Skd'41.Kt.Tv.Cv.
☎ (216) 255-8698 . . "The Homestead" Berkshire Farm,
8853 King Memorial Rd, Mentor, OH *44060*

Hitchcock MR & MRS Peter T (Cecily G Kohlsaat)
Pn.P'53.Cl'59 . . . . | ☎ (713) 493-9198
MISS Courtney A . . . . | 11418 Pecan Creek
| Dv, Sherwood Oaks,
| Houston, TX *77043*

Hitchcock MRS Thomas (Laughlin—Margaret Mellon) Cly.Ri.Rr.BtP . . .of
☎ (561) 655-7768 . . 265 Emerald Lane, Palm Beach, FL *33480*
☎ (212) 744-3062 . . 10 Gracie Square, Apt 5B, New York, NY *10028*
Hitchcock MR & MRS Thomas 3d (Suzanne A Kent) Rc.
☎ (212) 249-7748 . . 120 East End Av, New York, NY *10028*

Hitchings MR & MRS Sinclair H (Catherine H
Farlow) Gchr'63.Sb.Gr.Dth'54 . . . . | ☎ (617) 646-7048
MR S Hamilton JR—Roch'88 . . . . | 120 Jason St,
| Arlington, MA
| *02174*

Hitschler MRS Diana T (Diana Timmerman) Me. . . . | ☎ (610) 527-8336
MISS W Rehn—at ☎ (215) 731-1592 | 730 Woodleave Rd,
2028 Delancey Place, Philadelphia, PA *19103* . . | Bryn Mawr, PA
MISS Pamela B . . . . | *19010*

Hixon MR & MRS Robert B (Sara S Armstrong) | ☎ (713) 622-9024
Tex'75.Smu'78.Wms'70 . . . . | 3412 Meadowlake
JUNIORS MR Robert G . . . . | Lane, Houston, TX
JUNIORS MR Alexander J . . . . | *77027*

Hoag MRS Knowlton (Amey D Denny) Cly.Chr.Dc.Myf.Cda.
☎ (203) 438-6740 . . 21 Yankee Hill Rd, Ridgefield, CT *06877*

Hoag MR & MRS T Denny (Ann E Hummel) | ☎ (313) 886-9045
Rv.Ty'59 . . . . | 192 Lothrop Rd,
MR Thomas D—OWes'93 | Grosse Pointe
MR Andrew D—Denis'94 . . . . | Farms, MI *48236*

Hoag MR & MRS William K JR (Lillian A Sharp) | ☎ (203) 438-6740
Bates'60.Myf.Snc.Bates'59 . . . . | 21 Yankee Hill Rd,
MR William K 3d—RI'88 . . . . | Ridgefield, CT
| *06877*

Hoagland MR & MRS Amos N (Ruth L Mole) Hl.Ht.
☎ (909) 679-7742 . . 27526 Calle Ganado, Sun City, CA *92585*
Hoagland MR & MRS G Stewart (Cynthia Kimball) L.Ncd.
☎ (302) 654-2774 . . 13 Brandywine Falls, Wilmington, DE *19806*
Hoagland MRS Henry W JR (Biehl—A Ray Watkin)
Rice'36.Rice'44.Chi.Ncd . . .of
☎ (713) 840-9331 . . 4718 Hallmark Dv, Apt 1001, Houston, TX *77056*
☎ (713) 785-9826 . . 822 Augusta Dv, Houston, TX *77057*

Hoagland MRS Jackson (Sarah L Eells) Ncd. . . . . . | ☎ (402) 553-4901
MISS (DR) Sarah L—Cin'75—at | 801 S 52 St, Apt
2244 W Winona St, Chicago, IL *60625* . . . . | 409, Omaha, NE
| *68106*

Hoagland MRS La Bar P (Marys Bird) Hl.
☎ (401) 789-4838 . . 428 Bridgetown Rd, Saunderstown, RI *02874*
Hoagland MR & MRS Leigh W (Eleanor T Martin) Ws'73.P'72.H.'74
☎ (212) 737-0133 . . 7 Gracie Square, New York, NY *10028*
Hoagland MRS Peter B (Elizabeth M Henderson) B'gton'77
see J W Henderson
Hoagland MR & MRS Porter JR (Cornelia E Register) Hl.Y'50
☎ (860) 536-9537 . . 25 Main St, Noank, CT *06340*

Hoar MR & MRS Roger S 2d (Julia D Carter)
☎ (508) 563-7169 . . 67 Glen Av, North Falmouth, MA *02556*
Hoar MR & MRS William P H (Antoinette R Geyelin) Bnd'72.Un.StJ.H'71
☎ (212) 427-5316 . . 16 E 96 St, New York, NY *10128*

Hobart MR & MRS Aaron A (Swan—Selina Strong) Ny.Nich'39 ⚓
☎ (803) 838-5111 . . 643 S Reeve Rd, Dataw Island, SC *29920*

Hobart MR & MRS Edward P (Joy K Jones) Y'38 . . . | ☎ (508) 428-1014
MISS Carol P (Sansum—Carol P Hobart)—at | 218 Ice Valley Rd,
1517 Stanford Dv NE, Albuquerque, NM *87106* | Box 418, Osterville,
| MA *02655*

Hobart MR & MRS William H (Julia R De Camp) | ☎ (513) 335-2345
M.Mv.Y'49.Pa'50 . . . . | 250 Ridge Av, Troy,
MISS J N Surridge—Col'95—at Ohio State | OH *45373*
Vet Med . . . . |
MR William Harrison III—Y'88—at Ann Arbor, |
MI . . . . |

Hobbs MR & MRS David W (Mary E Boulware) Swb'86.HampSydney'86
906 Sheridan Dv, Birmingham, AL *35213*
Hobbs MASTER Edmund James MacDonald (James D JR) . . . . Born at
San Francisco, CA May 9'95
Hobbs MR & MRS Franklin W (Margery G Baird)
Sm.Cy.Chi.Ncd.H'46.M'52 . . of
☎ (617) 277-1060 . . 44 Fairgreen Place, Chestnut Hill, MA *02167*
☎ (508) 993-1060 . . "Eden Voe" Box P231, South Dartmouth,
MA *02748*

Hobbs MR & MRS Franklin W 4th (Linda B Read) | of ☎ (212)861-6538
Ln.Rc.Ng.H.'69.H'72 . . . . | 720 Park Av,
JUNIORS MISS Ashley R . . . . | New York, NY
JUNIORS MR Nicholas B . . . . | *10021*
| ☎ (516) 239-7620
| 279 Albert Place,
| Lawrence, NY
| *11559*

Hobbs MRS Frederick H JR (Elizabeth Parmely)
☎ (614) 481-9708 . . 1852A Riverside Dv, Columbus, OH *43212*
Hobbs MR & MRS James D JR (Helen T MacDonald) CtCol'83.Sfg.Cal'82
☎ (415) 221-6953 . . 465—36 Av, San Francisco, CA *94121-1611*
Hobbs JUDGE & MRS Truman McG (Joyce D Cummings)
V'49.NCar'42.Y'48
☎ (334) 263-0184 . . 2301 Fernway Dv, Montgomery, AL *36111*
Hoblitzell MR & MRS Alan P JR (Prentice—M Louise Perkins) Nu'71.P'53
☎ (410) 828-1906 . . 326 S Wind Rd, Baltimore, MD *21204*
Hoblitzelle MR & MRS George K (Katharine L Wells) P'43
☎ (314) 862-2250 . . 7801 Pershing Av, St Louis, MO *63105*
Hobson MR & MRS Anthony W (Mary P Grote)
Smu'78.Toledo'84.Col'78.Va'82
☎ (513) 871-0681 . . 3645 Kroger Av, Cincinnati, OH *45226*
Hobson REV DR & MRS George H JR (Dearborn—Victoria A Lewis)
SL'64.H'62.Ox'82.Ox'89 . . of
☎ (011-44-1865) 510960 . . 31A Norham Rd, Oxford OX2 6SQ, England
☎ (011-33-1) 47-20-64-44 . . 23 av George V, 75008 Paris, France
☎ (011-33-65) 33-66-81 . . Puy del Claux, Gintrac, 46130 Bretenoux,
France
Hobson MR & MRS Henry Wise JR (Elizabeth Balch)
Ws'44.Qc.Cm.Ncd.Y'43
☎ (513) 561-5520 . . 8545 Camargo Club Dv, Cincinnati, OH *45243*

Hobson MR & MRS J Kendall (Ketchum—Kathleen L Friel) Tul'73.Tul'87 . . . . | ☎ (504) 891-4571 5207 Chestnut St, New Orleans, LA 70115
JUNIORS MR John K JR . . . .

Hocker MR & MRS Lon (Esther W Sands) P'31
☎ (508) 540-0847 . . 177 Fay Rd, Woods Hole, MA 02543

Hodge MR & MRS Andrew W (Alexandra H Scott) GeoW'60.Va'56.Ariz'71 . . . . | ☎ (520) 647-7434 14750 E Rincon Creek Ranch, Rte 8, Tucson, AZ 85747
MISS A Hilary . . . .

Hodge DR & MRS Charles 5th (Mary McG Greaves) Kas'77.Ph.David'73.Temp'77
☎ (913) 384-4016 . . 5925 Sunrise Dv, Fairway, KS 66205

Hodge MRS Edward A (Prudence Hemenway) V'40
☎ (914) 277-4154 . . 19A Heritage Hills, Somers, NY 10589

Hodge MR & MRS Edward B JR (Judith F Schwartz) Stan'66.Me.Pn. . . . . | 236 Lambertville-Hopewell Rd, Hopewell, NJ 08525
JUNIORS MR Edward B 3d—at Kenyon . . . .
JUNIORS MR William P B . . . .

Hodge MR & MRS John H (Mary E Gindhart) Rid'71.Me.P'66 . . . . | ☎ (610) MU8-3246 246 Chester Rd, Devon, PA 19333
JUNIORS MR J Cortlandt—at Bowdoin . . . .

Hodges MR Alexander W (Arthur C) . . . . Married at Pittsburgh, PA Klug MISS M Elizabeth (William F 4th) . . . . Jun 1'96

Hodges MR & MRS Alexander W (M Elizabeth Klug) Tex'89.Pitt'92.Myf.NCar'90
☎ (011-52-5) 545-5782 . . Hans Christian Andersen 522, Col Polanco, Mexico DF CP11560, Mexico

Hodges MR & MRS Arthur C (Eloise Weld) Rdc'62.Ec.Tv.Ub.H'57
☎ (508) 768-6376 . . 93 Apple St, Essex, MA 01929

Hodges MR & MRS Arthur C JR (Sunhee Juhon) H'85.Cal'89.Myf.H'85
☎ (303) 722-6097 . . 1058 S High St, Denver, CO 80209

Hodges MISS Elizabeth J
☎ (617) 354-0759 . . 19 Lowell St, Cambridge, MA 02138

Hodges MISS Elizabeth W (Slattery—Elizabeth W Hodges)
700 Ardmore Av, 301, Ardmore, PA 19003

Hodges MR & MRS Fletcher III (Chantal Leroy) Bnd'56.H'57.Err.C.Eyc.Plg.Myf.Cw.Ne.Cs.Gr. H'56 . . . . | ☎ (212) 749-4196 755 West End Av, New York, NY 10025
MISS Rebecca . . . .

Hodges MR & MRS G Heyward 2d (Loicka Coisne) Paris'74.SCal'76 . . . . | ☎ (601) 981-3579 2450 Lake Circle, Jackson, MS 39211
MISS Elisa M . . . .
JUNIORS MISS Emily G . . . .
JUNIORS MR Marc T . . . .

Hodges MRS Jean G (Jean M Glover)
☎ (610) 642-2204 . . 700 Ardmore Av, 301, Ardmore, PA 19003

Hodges MRS John S B (Roma M Sullivan) . . . . | ☎ (619) 450-5141 7450 Olivetas Av, Apt 141, La Jolla, CA 92037
MISS A Jacqueline . . . .

Hodges MR & MRS Lorin C (Eleanor M Lyman) Cly.Ne. . . . . | ☎ (212) 249-2127 340 E 72 St, New York, NY 10021
MISS Orlanda C—at 7201 Chastain Dv NE, Atlanta, GA 30342 . . . .

Hodges MISS Olivia Ferris (Sewall F) . . . . Born at New York, NY Apr 30'96

Hodges MR Russell F—M.Fw.Mit'49 . . of
☎ (610) LA5-7484 . . 1529 County Line Rd, Rosemont, PA 19010
☎ (941) 434-5918 . . 261 Third Av N, Naples, FL 34102-8407

Hodges MR & MRS Sewall F (O'Shea—Kathryn E Needham) ColC'78.Pc.Rcp.Cr'78.Pa'82
☎ (718) 643-6814 . . 82 Pierrepont St, Brooklyn, NY 11201

Hodges MR & MRS Stuart T (June A Jenkins) Pa'84.Temp'95.Pc.Drex'82.Temp'93
☎ (609) 429-7239 . . 711 E Greenman Rd, Haddonfield, NJ 08033-2719

Hodges MR & MRS Thomas V (Elizabeth N Wilbur) BMr'50.Swth'49
☎ (610) 525-1230 . . 107 Ringwood Rd, Rosemont, PA 19010

Hodges MR & MRS William Van D (June Cantwell) Y'32.H'35
☎ (303) 698-2611 . . 2552 E Alameda Av, Denver, CO 80209

Hodges MR & MRS Winthrop M (Marjorie B Mooney) P'62 . . . . | ☎ (617) 749-7678 108 Main St, Hingham, MA 02043
MISS Cecil A . . . .
MISS Elizabeth D . . . .

Hodgkins MR & MRS Robert C (Allan—Noyes—Rosalind V Townsend) On.Cly.Y'55 . . . . | ☎ (847) 234-4053 435 King Muir Rd, Lake Forest, IL 60045
MISS Hilary E . . . .
MISS M Samantha A—Stan'90—at 1560 Jackson St, San Francisco, CA 94109 . . . .
MISS Rosalind C—at U of Ky . . . .
MR Robert C JR—Nw'83.Nw'84—at 24 Colonial Rd, Hingham, MA 02043 . . . .

Hodgkins MR & MRS Thomas D (Mary A BonDurant) Nw'58.On.Rc.Cnt.Br'58.Ch'62 . . . . | ☎ (847) 615-3232 1500 W Kennedy Rd, Lake Forest, IL 60045
MISS Katherine E—at 425 W Surf St, Apt 608, Chicago, IL 60657 . . . .
MR Thomas S . . . .

Hodgkins MRS W Press (Dennehy—Marion Warner) On.Fy.
☎ (847) 295-3000 . . 660 N Westmoreland Rd, Apt 207, Lake Forest, IL 60045

Hodgman MR & MRS Charles S (Bruce—Marjorie Stradella) . . . . | ☎ (860) 672-6991 "Wintergreen II" 64 Valley Rd, Cornwall, CT 06753
MR Peter G—EMich'84—at ☎ (810) 428-9445 11530 Pleasant Lake Rd, Manchester, MI 48158

Hodgson MR & MRS Howard B (Muriel P Hubbard) Sm.Chi.Ncd.H'45
☎ (506) 529-3007 . . "Bellenden" St Andrews, NB E0G 2X0, Canada

Hodgson MR & MRS Howard B JR (Wendy L LeStage) Skd'83.Ub.Sm.Ne'78
89 Argilla Rd, Ipswich, MA 01938

Hodgson MR & MRS William C (C Jan Hambrick) Aub'77.Aub'80.Aub'77 . . . . | ☎ (334) 277-2572 6712 Luxembourg Circle, Montgomery, AL 36117
JUNIORS MISS Margaret B . . . .

Hoecker MR & MRS Gary Wayne (Priscilla C Gillett) SCal'68.Vh.Cal'65.SFr'68 . . . . | ☎ (818) 578-0760 260 California Terr, Pasadena, CA 91105
MISS Anne E . . . .
MR Charles G . . . .

Hoeffel DR & MRS Joseph M JR (Eleanore Balderston) Me.Ac.Cda.W.Wis'39.Wis'43
☎ (610) 520-9569 . . 25 Pond Lane, Bryn Mawr, PA 19010

Hoeffner MR & MRS Jeff D (Marie T Belson) Gettys'87.MontSt'84
☎ (406) 458-5817 . . 1340 Ranch View Rd, Helena, MT 59601

Hoeffner MASTER Kenneth Griffin (Jeff D) . . . . Born at Helena, MT Apr 7'95

Hoeksma MR & MRS Gerben F (Jill P Goodhue) ☎ (310) 472-4242
Col'67.SCal'68.SCal'71 . . . . 449 Bonhill Rd,
JUNIORS MISS Nicole G . . . . Los Angeles, CA
JUNIORS MISS Anne B . . . . | 90049
Hoelscher MR & MRS S Shiels (Yvonne M Newell)
☎ (415) 369-6609 . . 1480 Crestview Dv, San Carlos, CA 94070
Hoerle MR & MRS Robert F (Sheila S Armstrong) ☎ (212) 517-4522
Un.Ny.Eyc.Plg.Y.'57.H'62 . . . . 155 E 72 St, Apt
MR Jeffrey—Y'90—at 108 E 91 St, New York, 13A, New York, NY
NY 10128 . . . . | 10021
MR W Scott—Ty'92 . . . . |
MR Alexander F—at Cornell . . . . |
Hoff MR Henry B—Snc.Lm.Y'67.Ford'74
☎ (212) 532-2962 . . 67 Park Av, New York, NY 10016
Hoff MR & MRS William B (Christina W Buckley) Pa'60
☎ (914) 693-0043 . . 21 Grandview Av, Dobbs Ferry, NY 10522
Hoffberger MR & MRS Michael S (Margaret S Allen) | ☎ (410) 377-6121
Md'74.Cy.Upsala'72.Balt'85 6527 Montrose Av,
JUNIORS MR T Christopher . . . . Baltimore, MD
21212
Hoffman MRS Albert L JR (Florence C Meyer) Ck.Nf. ⚓
☎ (516) 759-5279 . . 16 Peacock Pond Rd, Glen Cove, NY 11542
Hoffman MR & MRS David F (Gale Hayman) Skd'78.Wms'74
☎ (610) 527-4432 . . 511 Lynmere Rd, Bryn Mawr, PA 19010
Hoffman MRS Edward F 3d (Nadine Kalpaschnikoff)
☎ (610) 688-4279 . . 353 Oak Terr, Wayne, PA 19087
Hoffman MR Edward J 3d—Cal'95 . . see MRS J S Cornell
Hoffman MR & MRS Eric (Pope—Ronna C | ☎ (619) 773-1045
Hitchcock) Cl'57.Stan'48 47-000 E Eldorado
MR Guy W Pope—at ☎ (503) 248-9255 Dv, Indian Wells,
3304 NW Vaughn St, Portland, OR 97210 . . . CA 92210
MR Frederick C B Pope—at ☎ (970) 476-1956
4682 E Meadow Dv, Vail, CO 81657 . . . . |
Hoffman MR & MRS Harrison B W (Martin—Louise | ☎ (203) 869-8463
E Sinkler) Man'vl'76.Yn.Dth'42.Cl'66 . . . . 519 Stanwich Rd,
MR Nicholas O—Bard'83 . . . . Greenwich, CT
MR Crozer W Martin . . . . | 06831
Hoffman MRS J Gordon (Elizabeth J Gibson) . . of
☎ (941) 346-0236 . . 111 Whispering Sands Circle, Sarasota,
FL 34242-1624
☎ (203) 637-2770 . . 31 Lake Dv S, Riverside, CT 06878
Hoffman MR & MRS John H (Janetta C Dunlaevy) | of ☎ (203)661-6066
Ihy.Dar.Ncd.Cal'51 . . . . 16 Cornelia Dv,
MISS Cordelia P—Denis'90 . . . . Greenwich, CT
MR Andrew W—Emory'88 . . . . | 06830
☎ (561) 833-9307
3701 S Flagler Dv,
West Palm Beach,
FL 33405
Hoffman MR & MRS John N JR (Chapman—Elizabeth C Ultes)
Mercy'86.Ht.Dar.
☎ (914) 241-8476 . . 15 Robinhood Rd, Bedford Hills, NY 10507
Hoffman MISS Katharine McL—Gv.
☎ (410) 363-1648 . . 17 Cliffholme Rd, Owings Mills, MD 21117
Hoffman MISS Kirke T—Ham'93 . . see G F Fiske JR
Hoffman MISS Lauren E—Y'91.Me . . see MRS J S Cornell

Hoffman MR & MRS Lindley M F (Judy A C Wells) | of ☎ (561)844-2631
BtP.Snc.Va'55 . . . . 211 Bermuda Lane,
MR Nicholas M W—Va'90.Pa'94 . . . . Palm Beach, FL
33480
☎ (212) 724-5122
17 W 67 St,
New York, NY
10023
Hoffman MRS Martin C (Eileen M Lucey) Cr'34.Ford'40.Rr.
☎ (412) 238-9790 . . HCR 64, Box 41, Ligonier, PA 15658
Hoffman MR & MRS Martin C JR (Jane E Rubin) DU'75.Va'72
☎ (303) 796-7999 . . 6 Waring Lane, Littleton, CO 80121
Hoffman MISS Mary F
☎ (561) 272-5704 . . 716 N Lake Av, Delray Beach, FL 33483
Hoffman MR & MRS Peter B (Lucinda Taylor) PortSt'72
☎ (503) 227-2800 . . 445 NW Hilltop Rd, Portland, OR 97210
Hoffman MR & MRS Peter K (Lindsey A Murkland) Wheat'80.Nyc.LakeF'78
☎ (212) 758-0431 . . 455 E 57 St, Apt 8B, New York, NY 10022
Hoffman MISS Rebecca B—OState'83.LaTech'85.Cwr'93
☎ (216) 321-2992 . . 3414 Meadowbrook Blvd, Cleveland Heights,
OH 44118
Hoffman MR Redwood W—Sfh.
☎ (610) 644-8748 . . 619 Kromer Av, Berwyn, PA 19312
Hoffman MR & MRS Richard C (Michelle E Borisa)
☎ (703) 680-1558 . . 16017 Laconia Circle, Woodbridge, VA 22191
Hoffman MR Tyler P—Bab'96 . . see G F Fiske JR
Hoffmann MR & MRS Bernhard A (Deborah J Potter)
☎ (011-41-1) 980-1364 . . Höhenstrasse 6, 8127 Forch, Switzerland
Hoffmann MR & MRS Briggs A JR (Sadler—Mary Anne T Bryan) Cy.
☎ (314) 991-2028 . . 26 Oakleigh Lane, St Louis, MO 63124
Hoffmann MR & MRS James E (A Christine Henry) Cal'81.Ty'82
☎ (619) 756-3447 . . PO Box 307, Rancho Santa Fe, CA 92067
Hoffmann MR & MRS Thomas J (Janet Van W Stanley)
LakeF'63.Ih.Cnt.Ncd.Ken'62.Mich'63.GeoW'67
☎ (206) 286-8607 . . 341 W Olympic Place, Apt 3, Seattle,
WA 98119-3791
Hoffstot MR Henry P—Pg.BtP.Rr.H'39 . . of
☎ (412) 621-1159 . . 5057 Fifth Av, Pittsburgh, PA 15232-2128
☎ (561) 655-0894 . . 822 S County Rd, Palm Beach, FL 33480
Hoffstot MR & MRS Henry Phipps 3d (Daryln U T Brewer)
Skd'76.K.Pg.Rr.BtP.Cly.H'79.Cl'85 . . of
☎ (412) 593-2436 . . RD 4, Box 98, Ligonier, PA 15658
☎ (212) 744-6064 . . 125 E 74 St, New York, NY 10021
Hofheins MR Robert F—Colg'31 . . of
Marolar, Yabucoa, Puerto Rico 00767
Abbott Rd, North Boston, NY 14110
Hofmann MR & MRS John R JR (Mary Macdonough)
Cal'49.Bhm.Pcu.Tcy.Cal'43.H'49 . . of
☎ (415) 435-0092 . . 7 Britton Av, Belvedere, CA 94920
☎ (707) 279-4713 . . ''Windover'' 8272 Peninsula Dv, Kelseyville,
CA 95451
Hogan LT & MRS Michael Joseph (Alexandra Montague Price)
Va'91.Ct.USN'88
☎ (703) 548-0337 . . 1105 Portner Rd, Alexandria, VA 22314
Hoge MRS Francis H (Shafer—Helene S Gales)
☎ (212) 685-8839 . . 77 Park Av, New York, NY 10016

Hoge MR & MRS Warren M (von Bismark-Schonhausen—Olivia Larisch)
SacreC'64.Y'63
☎ (212) 319-6461 . . 139 E 63 St, New York, NY *10021*

Hogen MR Timothy L . . . . Married at Stonington, CT
Boone MISS Elizabeth W . . . . Nov 5'94

Hoguet MISS Diana L . . see G E Wantz

Hoguet MRS Elizabeth B (Elizabeth N Beers) Ri.
☎ (914) 232-0720 . . 314 Mt Holly Rd, Katonah, NY *10536*

Hoguet MR Geoffrey R—Rc.Ri.Sa.Pa'72	☎ (212) 517-6966
JUNIORS MR Max R	1 E 66 St, New York, NY *10021*

Hoguet MR J Peter—Ri.Pr.	☎ (212) 861-2365
MR Eric P—at 332 Wood Av, Montreal, Quebec H3Z 1Z2, Canada	125 E 74 St, New York, NY *10021*

Hoguet MR L Dudley
☎ (954) 476-1417 . . 7921 NW 3 Place, Plantation, FL *33324*

Hoguet MR & MRS Peter W (Sheila J Zehntner)	☎ (212) 832-8142
Plg.Fw.H'37.Nu'47	200 E 66 St,
MISS Denise M—Geo'81—at ☎ (212) 879-8445	New York, NY
209 E 66 St, New York, NY *10021*	*10021-6728*
MR Mark P—Y'90	

Hoguet MRS Robert L (Condon—Alice Berry)	☎ (941) 964-2167
SL'36.Cly.Ncd.	250 Gilchrist Av,
MR Martin J Condon 4th—at	Boca Grande, FL
☎ (423) 970-2661 . . 701 Cedar Lane,	*33921*
Knoxville, TN *37912*	

Hoguet MR & MRS Robert L 3d (Laura Banfield) Rdc'64.Dyc.Ri.H.'63
☎ (212) 628-5766 . . 139 E 79 St, New York, NY *10021*

Hoguet MRS Roland H (Billings—Aileen C Jackson) Cly.
☎ (561) 231-4471 . . 2615 Ocean Dv, Vero Beach, FL *32963-2054*

Hoit MR & MRS Roger W (B Gentry Ashmore) Geo'86.Cl'90.Aht'86
☎ (908) 273-8939 . . 83 Blackburn Rd, Summit, NJ *07901*

Hoke MR Martin R—Un.Aht'73.	☎ (216) 469-0679
JUNIORS MISS Elizabeth L	12700 Lake Av, Lakewood, OH *44107*

Hokin MISS Alexandra . . see MRS D Coudert

Hokin MISS Dana . . see MRS D Coudert

Holabird MR John A JR (late John A) . . . . Married at Chicago, IL
Connor MRS J Nothhelfer (Janet Nothhelfer) . . . . May 7'96

Holabird MR & MRS John A JR (Connor—Janet	☎ (312) 649-1771
Nothhelfer) Purd'48.H'42.	200 E Pearson St,
MISS Ann B—Syr'93	Apt 3W, Chicago,
MISS Lynn D	IL *60611*
MISS Sarah L Connor	

Holberton MR & MRS Terry Hamilton 3d (Valerie S Smith) Cal'66.Cal'66
☎ (310) 476-3459 . . 475 Tuallitan Rd, Los Angeles, CA *90049*

Holbrook MR & MRS Christopher C (Alice B Hager) Emer'86.Grin'86.Nu'91
☎ (203) 869-7023 . . 12 Mead Point Dv, Greenwich, CT *06830*

Holbrook MR & MRS David D (Holly C Gales) Bgt.Ln.Ri.Y'60 . . of
☎ (212) 759-1118 . . 2 Beekman Place, New York, NY *10022*
☎ (914) 232-3502 . . Katonah's Wood Rd, Katonah, NY *10536*

Holbrook MR & MRS Dean (Christina Flander) Sar.P'56.Y.'59.Nu'67 . . of
☎ (914) SC3-8595 . . 34 Edgewood Rd, Scarsdale, NY *10583*
☎ (518) 623-3567 . . ''Crane View'' Henry Wescott Rd, Thurman,
NY *12885*

Holbrook MR & MRS Donald R (Martha R Paterson)	☎ (415) 332-5483
West'60.Wash'55.Stan'58	654 Main St,
MR Christopher Paterson	Sausalito, CA *94965*

Holbrook DR & MRS John P (Weed—Hibner—Jane Wraith)
Ariz'51.Ariz'49.Bost'53
☎ (520) 299-1177 . . 6749 N Chapultepec Circle, Tucson, AZ *85750*

Holbrook MR & MRS Peter Moffitt (Stephanie H	☎ (415) 346-2600
Wharton) Pars'67.Bur.Pcu.Sfg.DU'70	2600 Broadway,
MISS Tania M—at U of Ariz	San Francisco, CA *94115*

Holbrook MR & MRS Robert K (Anne R Page)
☎ (310) 472-5400 . . 154 N Bowling Green Way, Los Angeles,
CA *90049*

Holbrook MISS Sandra M (Peter Moffitt) . . Married at San Francisco, CA
James MR Geoffrey L (James R JR) . . . . May 11'96

Holbrook MR & MRS William Sumner 3d (Sally A Davis)
Pom'54.Sl.H'52 ⚓
☎ (818) 792-4497 . . 1440 Vista Lane, Pasadena, CA *91103*

Holch MR & MRS Eric S (Elspeth M Royster)	☎ (508) 228-7654
Nyc.Ny.Hob'70	11 Wauwinet Rd,
MISS Serena B	Nantucket, MA
MR Sven C	*02554*

Holcomb MRS Franklin P (Suzanne Slingl900uff)	of ☎ (202)483-3613
Mt.Cvc.Ny.Sl.	2101 Connecticut
MR Franklin P JR	Av NW, Washington, DC *20008* ☎ (242) 366-0201 ''Joshua Barney House'' Hope Town, Abaco, Bahamas

Holcombe MR & MRS Shepherd M JR (Elizabeth S Cammann)
Hart'75.Hart'77.Conn'84.Lm.Cw.Myf.Ncd.Mid'69.Nu'90 . . of
☎ (860) 521-4238 . . 190 Walden St, West Hartford, CT *06107*
☎ (603) 823-5285 . . Grandview Rd, Sugar Hill, NH *03585*

Holden MISS Catharine C—Stan'67
☎ (415) 929-8291 . . 2510½ Bush St, San Francisco, CA *94115*

Holden MR & MRS Charles St G (Roberta A Cohen)
SFr'73.Bhm.Cal'71.Hast'75
☎ (415) 922-5343 . . 2547 Filbert St, San Francisco, CA *94123*

Holden MRS Elizabeth H (Elizabeth G Hattauer)	☎ (516) 627-2476
Bnd'57	90 Aldershot Lane,
MISS Cynthia G—at 144 Portola, Point Reyes, CA	Manhasset, NY
94956	*11030*

Holden MISS Ellen B—Pa'74.Cal'83
☎ (310) 477-0016 . . 10517 Rountree Rd, West Los Angeles, CA *90064*

Holden MR & MRS Michael H (Judith E Milliken)	☎ (203) 661-2111
Hlns'72.Unn.Rcn.Ihy.L.Va'67	224 W Old Mill Rd,
JUNIORS MR W Hale	Greenwich, CT
JUNIORS MR Bradley P	*06831*

Holden MR & MRS Richmond Y (Mary Jane S Muzzy) Al.
☎ (617) 899-0055 . . 63 Wellesley St, Weston, MA *02193*

Holden MR & MRS St George (Moira B Kennedy) Bhm.Fr.
  ☎ (415) 567-5343 . . 2555 Filbert St, San Francisco, CA *94123*

Holder MR & MRS Geoffrey L (Carmen P | ☎ (212) 873-9474
De Lavallade) QnsRoyal'50 . . . . | 565 Broadway,
MR Léo A L . . . . | New York, NY
  | *10012*

Holder MRS Jean H (Jean B Howard) . . . . | 215 E 80 St,
MISS Heidi . . . . | New York, NY
MR A Howard . . . . | *10021*

Holder DR Jonathan D—Colby'81.NYMed'90
  ☎ (617) 630-9228 . . 122 East Side P'kway, Newton, MA *02158*

Holder MR & MRS Nicholas P (Mary K Hilbert)
SantaC'81.Col'84.Cy.Sb.Al.Un.H'82.Bost'91
  ☎ (508) 650-4252 . . 102 N Main St, Sherborn, MA *01770-1511*

Holder MRS Richmond (Marcia S Black) B'gton'50.Cy.Chi.Ncd.Hn.
  ☎ (617) 734-4888 . . 130 Clyde St, Chestnut Hill, MA *02167*

Holdsworth MRS David Bethune (Lorraine G Bacon) Mt.Sl.Cda.
  ☎ (703) 356-3022 . . 1101 Chain Bridge Rd, McLean, VA *22101*

Holdsworth MR & MRS David G (Elizabeth L | ☎ (201) 377-8773
Whitesides) Cl'64.Cw.Myf.Ncd.P'54 . . . . | Village Rd,
MISS Katherine I—Wis'92 . . . . | Green Village, NJ
  | *07935*

Hole MR & MRS James W B (Heidi D Thiermann) Pa'88.Me.Cry.F&M'87
Valley Brooke Farm, PO Box 609, Wayne, PA *19087*

Hole MR & MRS Richard W (Tacey Belden) | ☎ (610) 688-4767
Me.Gm.Wms'45 . . . . | 125 Colket Lane,
MISS Marcia R—Pa'86—at ☎ (610) 964-1797 | Devon, PA *19333*
115 Pine Tree Rd, Radnor, PA *19087* . . . . |

Hole DR & MRS Richard W JR (Settle—Anita | ☎ (610) 649-1623
Venzara) V'71.Mo'75.Me.Wms'70.Pa'75 . . . . . | 128 Edgewood Rd,
JUNIORS MISS Elizabeth B . . . . | Ardmore, PA *19003*
JUNIORS MR Edward D . . . . |

Holladay MRS A Randolph (Lawrence—Elisabeth R Lieb)
  ☎ (619) 756-2146 . . Box 668, Rancho Santa Fe, CA *92067*

Holland MR & MRS E Morton (Dorothy P Mullins) | ☎ (508) 257-9692
Sth'36. . . . . | "Primrose Cottage"
MISS Dorothy P—at ☎ (508) 462-4193 | 4 Burnell St,
79 Pine Island Rd, Newbury, MA *01951* . . . . . | Box 611, Siasconset,
  | MA *02564*

Holland MISS Eugenia Calvert—Ncd.
  ☎ (410) 243-6637 . . Roland Park Place, Apt 263, 830 W 40 St,
Baltimore, MD *21211*

Holland MR & MRS Lawrence R (Anésia C de Araujo) Ala'81.Hp.H'52
  ☎ (205) 837-9612 . . 4605 Wilshire Cove, Huntsville, AL *35816*

Holland MRS William King (Dorothy Garesché) | ☎ (314) 863-7228
Mar'vil'26.Wash'50 . . . . | 7527 Oxford Dv,
MR Garesché W F . . . . | St Louis, MO *63105*

Hollenback MR & MRS William M JR (Worrall—Patterson—
Mae G Cadwalader) Ph.Ssk.Rc.Rb.B.Sg.Ac.Cry.P'40
  ☎ (215) 247-4177 . . 159 Bethlehem Pike, Philadelphia, PA *19118*

Holleran MR & MRS Romer (Deming Pratt) | ☎ (603) 643-6454
Rdc'65.Tr.H'65.Pa'68 . . . . | 27 Rope Ferry,
MISS Demer A—P'89—at ☎ (610) 658-0966 | Hanover, NH *03755*
100 E Wynnewood Rd, Apt 12F, Wynnewood, |
PA *19096* . . . . |
MISS Jennifer P—H'90—at ☎ (202) 237-8838 |
3872 Porter St NW, Apt C357, Washington, DC |
20016 . . . . |
MISS Lauren S—Dth'95—at ☎ (603) 744-7820 |
PO Box 483, New Hampton, NH *03256-0483* . . |
JUNIORS MISS Alexa R . . . . |

Holleran MR & MRS Charles JR (Murray—Pakula—Hope E Lange)
Rc.Plg.Wms'50
  ☎ (212) 355-6433 . . 435 E 57 St, Apt 14A, New York, NY *10022*

Hollerith MR Charles 3d—Bel'86
  ☎ (815) 623-2020 . . 10079 Tybow Trail, Roscoe, IL *61073*

Hollern MR & MRS Terrence L (Barbara A Jones) UWash'40.Vh.Dth'38
  ☎ (818) 793-7958 . . 481 S Orange Grove Blvd, 5, Pasadena,
CA *91105*

Holliday MRS Floyd N (Orr—Nancy G Willard)
  ☎ (802) 442-3271 . . Ledgely Dv, Shaftsbury, VT *05262*

Hollingshead MASTER Ryan Martin (Wickliffe Stewart 2d) . . . . Born
  Apr 12'96

Hollingshead MR & MRS Wickliffe (Mary Cloud | ☎ (609) 423-0172
Hamilton) Ncd.Dar.W&L'61 . . . . | 356 Kings H'way,
MRS W Stewart (Hannah L Snyder) . . . . | Clarksboro, NJ
  | *08020*

Hollingshead MR & MRS Wickliffe Stewart 2d (Janet M Kirton) Drew'88
  ☎ (610) 896-5186 . . 2950 Oakford Rd, Ardmore, PA *19003*

Hollingshead MR & MRS William Keith (Daphne L Peaslee)
  ☎ (609) 224-0218 . . 348 Kings H'way, Clarksboro, NJ *08020*

Hollingsworth MR & MRS Amor (Eleanor Gibson) Cy.Chi.Ncd.H'31 . . of
  ☎ (617) 326-2369 . . Fox Hill Village 245, 10 Longwood Dv, Westwood,
MA *02090*
  ☎ (941) 964-2618 . . PO Box 147, 1901 Shore Lane, Boca Grande,
FL *33921*

Hollingsworth MR Arthur W—Hn.H'85
  ☎ (214) 470-0375 . . 9914 Silver Creek Rd, Dallas, TX *75243*

Hollingsworth MRS Curtis (Pauline Curtis)
  ☎ (617) 354-0650 . . 23 Willard St, Cambridge, MA *02138*

Hollingsworth MRS Mark (Caroline Jeanes) . . . . | ☎ (207) 363-2721
MISS Caroline McC—at ☎ (617) 527-5787 | "Swanwicke"
29 Marlboro St, Newton, MA *02158* . . . . | Box 11,
MISS Jane P . . . . | Western Point Rd,
  | York Harbor, ME
  | *03911*

Hollingsworth MR & MRS Roger P (Shay—Isabelle Dodd) Pe.Sa.Fw.Pa'33
  ☎ (610) 388-6336 . . 47 Ulverston Dv, Kennett Square, PA *19348*

Hollingsworth MR & MRS Schuyler (Marshall—Anne D Grant) Cy.Cw.H.'40
  ☎ (617) 277-4144 . . 151 Middlesex Rd, Brookline, MA *02167*

Hollingsworth MRS Valentine (Thayer—Margaret C Thayer) Rdc'48
  ☎ (207) 967-2666 . . 32 Fairfield Hill Rd, Kennebunkport, ME *04046*

Hollingsworth MR & MRS William I 3d (Pickett—Marilyn D Seaman) Finch'62.B.Pr.Mb.Cly. Clare'63 . . . .
   MISS Jocelyn M Pickett—Ty'93—at
   245 E 72 St, New York, NY *10021* . . . .
of ☎ (212)737-3573 155 E 72 St, New York, NY *10021*
☎ (516) 922-7770 Box 572, Oyster Bay Rd, Locust Valley, NY *11560*

Hollins MRS Gerald V (Elizabeth Armour) On.
   ☎ (847) 234-0052 . . 501 Oakwood Av, Lake Forest, IL *60045*

Hollins MR Michael J—Humb'83
   ☎ (916) 246-9161 . . 3049 Sunglow Dv, Redding, CA *96001*

Hollis MR & MRS John E (Hollowell—Slocumb Davis) Kt.Dc.Ncd.USN'38.H'40
   ☎ (216) 321-0721 . . 2396 Demington Dv, Cleveland, OH *44106*

Hollister MR & MRS A Dunham JR (Edith M Lamb) Mariet'73.Mariet'73 . . . .
   MR James D—at Johnson & Wales . . . .
☎ (610) 458-8622 "Cedarcroft" 208 Greenridge Rd, Glenmoore, PA *19343*

Hollister MR & MRS Buell 3d (Elizabeth C Parker) Rol'72.Cc.Myf.Rol'66.Rol'73
   ☎ (802) 985-2242 . . 23 Pierson Dv, Shelburne, VT *05482*

Hollister MR & MRS Buell 4th (Margaret F Russell) Rby.Va'64 ⛵
   MR James B—at ☎ (617) 973-6635
   349 Hanover St, Boston, MA *02113* . . . .
   MR Matthew T—at ☎ (617) 739-0968
   239 Washington St, Brookline, MA *02146* . . . . .
☎ (617) 232-4978 44 Davis Av, Brookline, MA *02146*

Hollister MR & MRS Buell 4th (Megan L Thomas) Rol'88.Rol'89
   5135 Neal Ranch Rd, Colorado Springs, CO *80906*

Hollister MISS Callie Ames (Buell 4th) . . . . Born at Colorado Springs, CO Jan 31'96

Hollister MRS Dickerman (Juliet Garretson) Csn.
   ☎ (203) 661-0463 . . 661 Steamboat Rd, Greenwich, CT *06830*

Hollister MR & MRS G Clay 2d (Caroline H Krause) Duke'64.Duke'63
   ☎ (301) 654-6342 . . 7209 Delfield St, Chevy Chase, MD *20815*

Hollister MISS Gambrill H—Rice'92
   ☎ (919) 929-7428 . . 605 Jones Ferry Rd, Apt KK04, Carrboro, NC *27510*

Hollister MR Gerald A B—Ogle'68
   ☎ (561) 278-8073 . . 2150 S Ocean Blvd, Delray Beach, FL *33483*

Hollister MR & MRS John B JR (R Elizabeth Boyle) Cv.Kt.Un.Tv.Pk.Y'49
   ☎ (216) 423-3458 . . 36000 Cedar Rd, Gates Mills, OH *44040*

Hollister MR & MRS John B 3d (Cynthia L Treat) StLaw'74.Penn'79.Un.Tv.Aht'74.Penn'79 . . . . .
   JUNIORS MR William C . . . .
☎ (216) 338-3649 110 Dorset Dv, Chagrin Falls, OH *44022*

Hollister MR Louis H—Y'43
   ☎ (212) 988-0375 . . 333 E 68 St, New York, NY *10021-5693*

Hollister MISS Sarah S (G Clay 2d) . . . . Married at Millersville, MD Perkins CAPT L Parker 3d—USMC. (Lionel P JR) . . . . Jun 22'96

Hollister MR & MRS Thomas J (Diane M Dziama) Sth'77.Aht'77
   ☎ (617) 431-7767 . . 17 Cavanagh Rd, Wellesley, MA *02181*

Hollmeyer MR Harry W—Unn.H'40 . . . .
   JUNIORS MISS Serena N W . . . .
of ☎ (011-55-21) 274-3025 Rua Timóteo da Costa 805, Rio de Janeiro, RJ 22450, Brazil
☎ (011-43-5446) 2339 "Haus Albona" 6580 St Anton-am-Arlberg, Tirol, Austria

Holloman MR & MRS Leonidas C JR (McBain—Margaret Keith) Cnt.Sw'29
   ☎ (520) 648-8406 . . 750 S La Posada Circle, Apt 6, Green Valley, AZ *85614*

Hollos MR & MRS Paul A (Sherley Young) Sth'61.Pa'67.Ncd.Br'59.H'61 . . . .
   MISS Kate S—Roch'93—at ☎ (212) 737-7359
   504 E 88 St, New York, NY *10128-7790* . . . . .
   MISS Ann-Bevan—at Conn Coll
☎ (610) 688-8843 611 Maplewood Rd, Wayne, PA *19087-4720*

Hollos MRS Paul E (Hornor—Innes Kane Drury) Why.Msq.BtP.Ncd.Ht.Dc . . . of
   ☎ (401) 348-8223 . . "Ridgecrest" 9 Ridge Rd, Watch Hill, RI *02891*
   ☎ (561) 659-6157 . . 1200 S Flagler Dv, West Palm Beach, FL *33401*

Holloway MR Brett . . see MISS M A Tudor

Holloway MR & MRS Charles L (Sanford—Bell—Jane Cook) RISD'34
   ☎ (607) 532-4411 . . Lawara Farms, County Rd 153, Interlaken, NY *14847*

Holloway MR & MRS Edward JR (Kennedy—Gail Fiske) Cl'60.Snc.Cw.Dar.P.'40.Y'47 . . . .
   MISS Hope L—at Bucknell . . . .
☎ (212) 724-5648 205 W 89 St, New York, NY *10024*

Holloway MRS Jerome K (Mary G Unger)
   ☎ (314) 371-5487 . . 4400 Lindell Blvd, St Louis, MO *63108*

Holloway MR Jerome K JR . . . .
   MISS Karen M . . . .
   MR Jerome K 3d . . . .
   MR Nicholas H . . . .
☎ (401) 847-7155 72 Webster St, Newport, RI *02840*

Holloway MR John Ennis (Ann S Clegg) GeoW'50
   ☎ (202) 363-0548 . . 5431—30 Place NW, Washington, DC *20015*

Holloway MISS Mara . . see MISS M A Tudor

Holloway MR & MRS Phelps (Nancy Newell)
   ☎ (508) 428-9370 . . "Holly's Hostel" 247 Crystal Lake Rd, Wianno, MA *02655*

Holloway MR & MRS R Marcus (Leslie R Grosvenor) Duke'85.Cl'87.Nrr.Srb.Cly.Va'85.Cl'88
   ☎ (203) 972-7964 . . 372 Cedar Lane, New Canaan, CT *06840*

Hollstein COL (RET) & MRS Jean W (Kistler—Dell W Proctor) USA.NCar'47.OreSt'41
   ☎ (910) 484-6318 . . 323 Birnam Dv, Fayetteville, NC *28305*

Hollyday MISS Louise Este
   ☎ (410) 239-7305 . . 4615 Beckleysville Rd, Hampstead, MD *21074*

Hollyday MR & MRS Richard C JR (Jane B Perry) San.P'50.Cl'53 . . . .
   MISS Anne B . . . .
   MR Richard C 3d . . . .
   MR Thomas P . . . .
☎ (561) 231-4051 80 Passage Island, Vero Beach, FL *32963*

Hollyday MR & MRS Thomas J (Malloy—Janet C Symmons) BostColl'68.BostColl'86.Sb.Cw.Wt. JHop'64.JHop'69.Clark'73 . . . . | ☎ (617) 894-4361
55 Chestnut St, Weston, MA *02193*
MISS Jennie V . . . . |

Holman MR & MRS William H JR (Sandra L Sutherland) SoMiss'57.GaTech'52 . . . . | of ☎ (601)981-3311
114 Woodland Circle, Jackson, MS *39216*
MISS Sandra H—at 6295 Old Canton Rd, Jackson, MS *39211* . . . . | ☎ (904) 837-4221
506 Gulf Shore Dv, Destin, FL *32541*
MISS Jane E—at 7717 Walnut Hill Lane, Dallas, TX *75230* . . . . |

Holman MRS William M (Emily S Laighton) Ncd.
☎ (206) 454-8425 . . Box 332, Medina, WA *98039*

Holmes MRS Allen C (M E Louise Quirk) Un.Cv.Ln.Pk.Tv.Mt.
☎ (216) 851-2715 . . 2 Bratenahl Place, Apt 6BC, Bratenahl, OH *44108*

Holmes MRS Anne Tilney (Sage—Anne M Tilney) Cly.BtP. . . . . | ☎ (201) 736-0860
Llewellyn Park, 45 Mountain Av S, West Orange, NJ *07052*
MR Lanman T JR . . . . |

Holmes MR & MRS Douglas Q (Melinda B Palmer) Skd'77.Kt.Un.Fic.Cv.Tv.Ken'78.Dth'84
☎ (216) 851-2715 . . 2 Bratenahl Place, Bratenahl, OH *44108*

Holmes MRS E Williams (Evelyn O Hatch) Cly.Cda.
☎ (212) AT9-6016 . . 1112 Park Av, New York, NY *10128*

Holmes MR & MRS Fielding L (Lucie E Brennan) Cy.Rc.Mo'67
☎ (314) 997-4189 . . 43 Glen Eagles Dv, St Louis, MO *63124*

Holmes COL (RET) & MRS Frederick S JR (Elisabeth B Nicholson) Ncd.USA'56.Mit'62.GeoW'69.Mit'73
☎ (703) 560-5234 . . 7323 Masonville Dv, Annandale, VA *22003-1637*

Holmes MR & MRS George B (K Nancy Trowbridge) Sth'48.Mt.Cvc.Y'45w. . . . . | of ☎ (202)363-1508
3845 Macomb St NW, Washington, DC *20016*
MISS Sarah B—at ☎ (202) 338-2737
2600 Tunlaw Rd NW, Washington, DC *20007* . . | ☎ (207) 348-2479
Deer Isle, ME *04627*

Holmes MR & MRS Gordon (Willis—Nancy Hooe) D.
☎ (617) 326-5817 . . 31 Old Farm Rd, Dedham, MA *02026*

Holmes MRS Hilary (Joan Halsted) SL'40
☎ (718) 549-6687 . . 5445 Palisade Av, Bronx, NY *10471*

Holmes MR & MRS Hilary H (Anita R Heppenheimer) Pratt'80.Mds.DU'72
☎ (516) 324-1378 . . PO Box 632, Rolling Woods Court, Wainscott, NY *11975*

Holmes MR & MRS John A JR (Knight—Irene L Schock) Cy.Rc.
☎ (314) 991-0889 . . 200 N Warson Rd, St Louis, MO *63124*

Holmes MR & MRS John G (Lord—Ruth Ellen du Pont) V'43.Y'50.Cly.Cda.Y'34 . . . . | of ☎ (860)739-0311
White Gate Farm, Box 253, East Lyme, CT *06333*
MR Henry Lord—Mass'86—at ☎ (203) 782-2595 . . 313 Audubon Court, New Haven, CT *06510* . . . . | ☎ (203) 776-5491
190 St Ronan St, New Haven, CT *06511*

Holmes MRS John R (Jean Bullard) . . . . Died at Pasadena, CA Apr 23'96

Holmes MR John R—Bhm.Vh.Mich'38
☎ (818) 792-5616 . . 790 Huntington Garden Dv, Pasadena, CA *91108*

Holmes MR John R JR—SFrSt'67
☎ (415) 362-2772 . . 180 Montgomery St, Apt 1080, San Francisco, CA *94104-4230*

Holmes MRS Joseph H (Carolyn T E Miller) . . . . . . | ☎ (203) 966-2204
95 Colonial Rd, New Canaan, CT *06840*
MISS C Collinson—☎ (203) 972-1655 . . . . |

Holmes MRS K Barney (Katherine L Barney) Briar'68.Pa'69.Nyc.Ncd. . . . . | ☎ (202) 965-2924
1528—31 St NW, Washington, DC *20007*
MISS Lucinda A—at Miami U . . . . |

Holmes MRS Larry A (Bonnie L Tansill) . . . . | ☎ (817) 732-2521
1223 Belle Place, Ft Worth, TX *76107*
MR Kirby B . . . . |

Holmes MRS Martin J (Armstrong—Ann A Walbridge)
☎ (716) 655-1898 . . 382 Girard Av, East Aurora, NY *14052*

Holmes (REV) Olivia (Robinson—Olivia Holmes) H'91.Ny. ⚓
☎ (203) 378-9111 . . 96 Chapel St, Stratford, CT *06497*

Holmes MR & MRS Peter B (Klingenstein—Ann H Jones) . . . . | of ☎ (212)737-0912
315 E 70 St, New York, NY *10021*
MR Christopher Klingenstein—at Lake Forest Coll . . . . | ☎ (201) 379-6838
15 E Beechcroft Rd, Short Hills, NJ *07078*

Holmes MR Richard F—An.Ofp.Hb.Wms'46.Lond'69
☎ (011-27-21) 7882240 . . Cable Close, Marina da Gama, Cape Town 7945, South Africa

Holmes DR & MRS Robert R (Elizabeth H Harris) LErie'63.RI'67.Ncd.Aht'59.Ty'62.Br'68 . . . . . . | ☎ (804) 737-4987
708 Washington St, Highland Springs, VA *23075*
MISS Deborah A—Aht'91.W&M'94 . . . . |
MISS Rebecca A—W&M'92 . . . . |

Holmes MR Scott M (late Larry A) . . . . Married at Ft Worth, TX
Chapman MISS Sharon R (Herbert) . . . . Feb 10'96

Holmes MR & MRS Sidney S (Ruth S Elliott) Colby'67.Wis'67 . . . . | ☎ (810) 540-5976
2344 Hunt Club Dv, Bloomfield Hills, MI *48304*
MISS Sarah E—at Colby . . . . |
MR Nicholas S—Emory'95 . . . . |

Holmes MRS Stanley A (Blake—Mary A Blake)
☎ (617) 337-7427 . . 161 Ft Point Rd, North Weymouth, MA *02191*

Holmyard MR & MRS Harold R (Tanner—Alexandra Todd) Wms'44
☎ (203) 531-3232 . . 516 W Lyon Farm Dv, Greenwich, CT *06831*

Holt MR Andrew J JR . . see J W Bartlett

Holt JUNIORS MR Bradley N . . see J W Bartlett

Holt MR & MRS Charles C 3d (Diana M Blabon) Rol'63.Msq.Why.R.Evg.BtP.Ste.Ac.Pa'60 ⚓ . | ☎ (561) 655-2080
320 Island Rd, Palm Beach, FL *33480*
MISS Lily B M—MtVern'92—at ☎ (561) 655-0796 . . 310 Island Rd, Palm Beach, FL *33480* . . . . |
MISS Merrilee P B—Col'93—at ☎ (561) 655-6555 . . 310 Island Rd, Palm Beach, FL *33480* . . . . |

Holt MRS Charles Dudley (Eva L Taylor) Cly.
☎ (212) CI7-7143 . . 24 W 55 St, New York, NY *10019*

Holt MR & MRS Henry B (Mary E Dey) Lx.
☎ (413) 243-3184 . . PO Box 699, 125 Golden Hill, Lee, MA *01238*
Holt MR Henry M R—Col'84 . . see R H Lee JR
Holt MISS Hilary E . . see J W Bartlett
Holt MR & MRS Ivan L 3d (Judith Wright) Wash'70 . | ☎ (610) 444-5014
MISS Mary F . . . . | 125 Beverly Dv,
MR Ivan L 4th . . . . | Kennett Square, PA
| *19348*
Holt MR & MRS Ivan Lee JR (Rojena J Kabbaz) Sar.Ch'35
☎ (573) 754-6400 . . ''White Gate'' Rte 1, Box 165, Louisiana,
MO *63353*
Holt MRS Jane Wells (Jane Wells)
☎ (208) 345-2658 . . 2113 Division Av, Boise, ID *83706*
Holt MR John W P—Bow'79.Y'88 . . see R H Lee JR
Holt MR & MRS Philetus H 3d (Nancy de F Brownley) Bnd'49.P'50.P'52
☎ (609) 921-6024 . . 3472 Lawrenceville Rd, Princeton, NJ *08540*
Holt MR & MRS Robert d'A (Stavers—Elizabeth J Davis) Cda.
☎ (406) 777-3653 . . 743 S Sunset Bench Rd, Stevensville, MT *59870*
Holt MR & MRS William J JR (Gourd—Elizabeth B Garrett) USN'39
☎ (904) 247-1957 . . Fleet Landing, 5515 Rigel Court, Atlantic Beach,
FL *32233*
Holth MR & MRS Fredrik D (Constance C Quinn) | ☎ (860) 434-5243
Pa'66.Hart'73.Prov'62.Ford'67 . . . . | 159 Blood St,
MISS Christina L . . . . | Lyme, CT *06371*
JUNIORS MR Fredrik T . . . . |
Holton MISS Alexandra C . . see MRS A P Curran
Holton MR John M 3d . . see MRS A P Curran
Holton MR & MRS Richard C (Carlota C C Hermann) | ☎ (314) 993-0904
Cy.Rc.StL'70 . . . . | 3 Wendover Dv,
MISS Christy Busch—☎ (314) 993-3032 . . . . . | Ladue, MO *63124*
MR Richard C JR . . . . |
JUNIORS MR Robert H B . . . . |
Holzman MR & MRS Robert S (Muriel G Richards) | ☎ (513) 961-8518
Ncd.Cin'60.Cin'63 . . . . | 6 Annwood Lane,
JUNIORS MISS Perin P . . . . | Cincinnati, OH
JUNIORS MR R Langdon . . . . | *45206-1419*
Homans MRS George C (Nancy P Cooper) Tv.Cy . . . | ☎ (617) 547-4737
MISS Elizabeth C . . . . | 11 Francis Av,
| Cambridge, MA
| *02138*
Homans MRS Robert (Barnes—Mary Aldrich)
☎ (207) 734-8875 . . 79 Main St, Islesboro, ME *04848*
Homer MR Charles Le B 3d
PO Box 335, Villanova, PA *19085*
Honan MR & MRS William Holmes (Nancy L Burton)
Nu'71.Ober'52.Va'55 ⚓
147 Cross H'way, West Redding, CT *06896*
Honey MRS Marcus R (Vera E Ganelin) Hn.
☎ (802) 442-4888 . . 69 Monument Av, Old Bennington, VT *05201*
Honeyman MR & MRS R Stewart JR (Cochran—Barbara J Taylor)
Cal'75.H'79
☎ (803) 589-8000 . . Early Branch Plantation, Early Branch, SC *29916*
Hood MR & MRS Barry G (Tomlin—Eliza H Frazer) Ws'77.Rr.
☎ (406) 443-5719 . . PO Box 1282, Helena, MT *59624*
Hood MISS Christianna T—HWSth'84
☎ (212) 932-3615 . . 11 W 94 St, Apt 4B, New York, NY *10025*

Hood MR & MRS Clifford C R (Charlotte P Stevenson) Pc.Pa'51
☎ (215) 233-0964 . . 8319 Flourtown Av, Wyndmoor, PA *19038*
Hood MR & MRS Louis (Agnes M Birney) | ☎ (610) 687-3916
Me.Cvc.Aht'46 . . . . | 1169 Radnor Rd,
MR Peter C—at ☎ (215) 482-1495 | Wayne, PA *19087*
450 Domino Lane, Philadelphia, PA *19127* . . . . |
Hooe MR & MRS Nelson D JR (Susanne Shaw) | ☎ (617) 326-1899
D.Y'51 | 347 Westfield St,
MISS Elizabeth D—at ☎ (617) 787-8070 | Dedham, MA *02026*
89 Brayton Rd, Brighton, MA *02135* . . . . |
MR Nelson S . . . . |
Hooff MRS Charles R JR (Elizabeth T Dunn) Mt.Ct.San.Cw.
☎ (703) 370-3300 . . 502 N Quaker Lane, Alexandria, VA *22304*
Hook MR & MRS Thomas W (Miranda D Jackson) | ☎ (203) 849-9784
Nu'72.Colg'70 | Strawberry Woods
JUNIORS MR William J . . . . | Lane, Apt A6,
| Norwalk, CT *06851*
Hooker MRS Edward G (Marian Butler)
☎ (212) 758-6259 . . 200 E 66 St, New York, NY *10021*
Hooker MR & MRS Henry G (Janine A Roeth) | ☎ (408) 457-0332
Br'85.Stan'68.Cal'84 . . . . | 407 Ocean View
MISS Elizabeth R . . . . | Av, Santa Cruz, CA
| *95062*
Hooker MR & MRS Henry W (Alice L Ingram) V'55.Van'54.Tul'58 . . of
☎ (615) 373-9892 . . 370 Vaughn Rd, Nashville, TN *37221*
☎ (615) 293-2828 . . ''Hound's Ear'' Fox Ridge Rd, Cornersville,
TN *37047*
☎ (561) 790-6989 . . Equestrian Club Estates, 14239 Calypso Lane,
West Palm Beach, FL *33414*
Hooker MR & MRS Michael G (Constance L | ☎ (415) 221-2219
Colladay) SanJ'71.Bur.Pa'57.Fla'59 . . . . | 3838 Clay St,
JUNIORS MISS Anne A . . . . | San Francisco, CA
JUNIORS MR Samuel T—at Cate . . . . | *94118*
Hooker MR Philip O'D—Nw'31
4650—54 Av S, Apt 516, St Petersburg, FL *33711*
Hooker MRS Robert G JR (Jean G Harvey) . . . . . . | ☎ (011-44-171)
MISS Tanya M . . . . | 373-2510
MISS Dolly C S . . . . | 16A Cresswell
MISS Katherine G G . . . . | Gardens, London
MR Nicholas G—P'90—at ☎ (212) 505-9385 | SW5, England
172 E 4 St, Apt 3H, New York, NY *10009* . . . . |
Hooker MR Robert G JR—H'50
see Dilatory Domiciles
Hooker MR & MRS Rodman L JR (Juliet A Burkett) | ☎ (206) 325-5688
Mls'65.Pcu.Bur.Dar.SCal'65 . . . . | 2030 Parkside Dv E,
MISS Juliana M—at Mt Holyoke . . . . | Seattle, WA *98112*
MR Peter B—at 345 Lexington, Burlingame, CA |
94010 . . . . |
JUNIORS MR Rodman L 3d—at U of So Cal . . . . . |
Hooker MISS Simone Roeth (Henry G) . . . . Born Jly 29'95
Hooker MR & MRS Timothy I (Nancy E Prant) Rol'85.Drew'87
☎ (615) 370-0483 . . 1186 Sneed Rd, Franklin, TN *37064*
Hooper MR & MRS Adrian S (Elizabeth W Shober) | 222 Waterloo Rd,
Rc.Sa.Cry.Pa'50 . . . . | Devon, PA *19333*
MISS Elizabeth H . . . . |
Hooper MRS Carrington D (Harriet Carrington Dame)
☎ (410) 494-4570 . . 1810A York Rd, Apt 222, Lutherville, MD *21093*

Hooper MRS Charles (D Elizabeth Gundry) . . . .
   MISS Hilary L Maisey—at Roanoke Coll . . . .
☎ (302) 227-8553
50 Park Av,
Rehoboth Beach, DE
19971

Hooper MR & MRS James R (Helen M Lang) H.'37
  ☎ (617) 383-6840 . . 4 Jerusalem Lane, Cohasset, MA *02025*

Hooper MR & MRS John A (Patricia R Lowrey)
Pcu.Stan'38.H'41 . . . .
MR Lawrence D—at Balky Hill Rd, Box 98,
Twisp, WA *98856* . . . .
☎ (415) 851-0729
501 Portola Rd,
Portola Valley, CA
94028

Hooper MR & MRS John B (Joan Colt)
Tufts'51.Ey.Tufts'51 . . . .
MISS Sarah B—at 177 Federal St, Salem, MA
01970 . . . .
☎ (617) 631-7487
70 Beacon St,
Marblehead, MA
01945

Hooper MR & MRS John C (Mary P Bolton) H'72.H'68.Bost'71
  ☎ (415) 552-8144 . . 201 Buena Vista Av E, San Francisco, CA *94117*

Hooper MR & MRS Lawrence L (Oliver—Marion D Marshall)
Rdc'49.NCar'48
  ☎ (941) 966-5489 . . 3750 Casey Key Rd, Nokomis, FL *34275*

Hooper MR & MRS Robert C (Gulielma Tyler) Sm.H'41 . . of
  ☎ (617) 864-0664 . . 48 Brewster St, Cambridge, MA *02138*
  ☎ (508) 546-6295 . . "Haulabout House" Halibut Point, Pigeon Cove,
MA *01966*

Hooper MR & MRS Roger F (Patricia Bentley)
Tcy.H'39 . . . .
MR Roger F 3d—PugetS'76—at 32 Woodland
Av, San Francisco, CA *94117* . . . .
☎ (415) 454-0386
70 Ivy Dv, Box 746,
Ross, CA *94957*

Hoopes MISS B Holliday—Del'78
  ☎ (540) 338-2022 . . PO Box 411, Middleburg, VA *20118*

Hoopes MR David M—Cvc.Wil.Pn.P'62 . . . .
MISS Helen M—V'86—at Canaan Valley, WV . .
MISS Martha F—Wms'87—at Woodland, CA . . .
MISS Nancy M—Wes'90—at San Francisco, CA
MISS Wendy A—Nu'92—at New York, NY . . . .
MISS Rachel M—at Simons Rock Coll . . . .
☎ (202) 363-4079
4521 Garfield St
NW, Washington,
DC *20007*

Hoopes MR James E . . see M H Walrath 3d

Hoopes MRS Joseph C (Elizabeth R Snowdon) Wil.Rr.Ncd . . .of
  ☎ (302) 655-4330 . . 4031 Kennett Pike, Apt 31, Greenville, DE *19807*
  ☎ (941) 263-7604 . . 2210 Gulf Shore Blvd N, Apt T1, Naples,
FL *34102*

Hoopes MR & MRS Joseph C JR (Lesley W Bissell)
Swb'68.Un.Wil.Ny.Plg.Del'67 ⚓ . . . .
MISS Elliott T . . . .
MR Joseph C 3d . . . .
☎ (212) 628-2414
149 E 73 St,
New York, NY
10021

Hoopes MISS Pamela E . . see M H Walrath 3d

Hoopes MR & MRS Samuel P (Patricia Bixby) Dth'48
MISS Charnell—at Wells, ME *04090* . . . .
☎ (518) 644-9755
"Still Waters"
Fish Point,
Box 757,
Bolton Landing, NY
12814

Hooton MRS Bruce D (Higginson—Theodora Winthrop) Cly.Srb.Pr.C . . .of
  ☎ (516) 626-1345 . . 55 Wheatley Rd, Upper Brookville, Glen Head,
NY *11545*
  ☎ (212) 722-2621 . . 40 E 94 St, New York, NY *10128*

Hoover MR F Herbert—Sar.Mar'vil'52 . . . .
MR Cleveland P—at ☎ (704) 625-0078
Whispering Creek Farms, 2547 Laughter Rd,
Mill Spring, NC *28756* . . . .
of ☎ (415)771-3347
1629 Green St,
San Francisco, CA
94123
☎ (707) 996-3375
Meadow Gardens,
Apt 26,
225—2 St E,
Sonoma, CA *95476*

Hoover MRS Munroe (Charlotte Munroe)
  ☎ (602) 998-3089 . . 8260 E Arabian Trail, Apt 272, Scottsdale,
AZ *85258*

Hoover MR & MRS Vernon V (Ann C Roach)
Rcp.Susq'58 . . . .
MISS Alexandra R—CalSt'95 . . . .
MISS Aimée R—CalSt'93 . . . .
MISS Angela R . . . .
☎ (305) 461-4716
3699 Bougainvillea
Rd, Coconut Grove,
FL *33133*

Hope MR & MRS Frank L JR (Barbara L Pritchard) Cal'52.Sdy.Cal'53
  ☎ (619) 223-1010 . . 2726 Shelter Island Dv, San Diego, CA *92106*

Hope MRS Norman L (Hope Douglas) Cly.
  ☎ (212) BU8-4090 . . 103 E 75 St, New York, NY *10021*

Hopkins MRS Anthony C (Elise W Woodward)
  ☎ (609) 429-0877 . . 113 Redman Av, Haddonfield, NJ *08033-2309*

Hopkins MR & MRS Anthony P (Margarethe V Wolff) Pa'54
  ☎ (860) 523-5587 . . 1300 Boulevard, West Hartford, CT *06119*

Hopkins MRS B House (Bess A House) Chi.
  ☎ (617) 547-4871 . . 989 Memorial Dv, Cambridge, MA *02138*

Hopkins MRS Ben F JR (Josephine L Ryan)
Rol'44.Cy.Un. . . . .
MISS Kim L D . . . .
of ☎ (561)626-5962
Old Port Cove F-1R,
1140 Marine Way,
North Palm Beach,
FL *33408*
☎ (216) 561-8462
"The Oliver
House" 3715
Warrensville Center
Rd, Shaker Heights,
OH *44122*

Hopkins MR & MRS David L JR (Suzanne Bunker)
Ln.Cly.P'50 . . . .
MISS Suzanne B . . . .
☎ (410) 472-3312
15200 Old York Rd,
Monkton, MD
21111-2208

Hopkins DR & MRS Gordon Bruce (Edna K Taylor) Sdy.MedWis'66
  ☎ (619) 488-5738 . . 5336 Calle Vista, San Diego, CA *92109*

Hopkins MR & MRS Hammond Warfield (Marjorie L
Hightower) Smu'53.Tex'53 . . . .
MISS Cheryl L . . . .
☎ (214) 363-1147
7274 Lane Park Dv,
Dallas, TX *75225*

Hopkins MISS Jennifer . . see D E Mead

Hopkins DR & MRS John E (Mary K Bazemore) MtH'48.Y'44.Pa'47
  ☎ (803) 853-8123 . . 3 Meeting St, Charleston, SC *29401*

Hopkins MRS Kendal C (Nancy Pemberton)
  ☎ (215) 836-2875 . . 551 E Evergreen Av, Apt C311, Wyndmoor,
PA *19038*

Hopkins MRS Mark (Fenno—Virginia Chapman) Cy.Chi.Ncd.
  ☎ (617) 566-5001 . . 100 Old England Rd, Chestnut Hill, MA *02167*

Hopkins MR Peyton S
2200 NE 37 St, Ft Lauderdale, FL *33308*

Hopkins MR & MRS R Stockton B (Elizabeth W Drayton) Sa.Rb.Cts.Me.Pa'50. . . . .
MISS Mary G—Pa'82—at ☎ (201) 692-8463
1367 Academy Lane, Teaneck, NJ 07666. . . . . .
MISS Elizabeth D—Cent'y'88.Me.—at
☎ (610) 520-2140 . . 275 Bryn Mawr Av,
Apt G3, Bryn Mawr, PA 19010 . . . .
MR R Stockton B JR—at ☎ (610) 964-0349
121 Old Forge Crossing, 1027 Valley Forge Rd,
Devon, PA 19333 . . . .
| ☎ (610) 725-9944
| 53 Cabot Dv,
| Chesterbrook, PA
| 19087

Hopkins MR & MRS Robert D (Jean D Griffith)
Towson'82.Md.Gv.Ln.WashColl'83
☎ (410) 557-6445 . . ''Hog Manor'' 4426 Harford Creamery Rd,
Whitehall, MD 21161

Hopkins MRS Robert H (Margaret H Sims) V'27
☎ (802) 985-8551 . . 3315 Wake Robin Dv, Shelburne, VT 05482-7574

Hopkins MISS S Antoinette . . see D E Mead

Hopkins MR & MRS Samuel (Anne E Dankmeyer)
Gchr'50.Penn'52.Gi.Mv.JHop'34.Md'38
☎ (410) 467-0169 . . 45 Warrenton Rd, Baltimore, MD 21210

Hopkins MR & MRS Samuel B (Genya M Currens)
MtH'63.Mid'90.H'61.H'64.JHop'69 . . . .
MISS Helenka P—Bnd'90 . . . .
MR Holt E—CtCol'94 . . . .
| ☎ (410) 366-8540
| 4200 Wickford Rd,
| Baltimore, MD
| 21210

Hopkins MR Thayer—Bhm.StJ.Wms'39.Stan'46 . . .
MR Charles A . . . .
MR David P . . . .
| ☎ (415) 921-9070
| 2221 Divisadero St,
| San Francisco, CA
| 94115

Hopkins MR & MRS Timothy B (Amelia R Hamill) Denis'86.Ham'84.Cl'88
☎ (203) 348-8275 . . 18 Phillips Lane, Darien, CT 06820

Hopkins MR & MRS Wallace A JR (Louisa M R Young) GeoW'69.Loy'85.Md.JHop'67 . . . .
MISS Louisa M R—Colg'93 . . . .
MISS Elizabeth DeV—Emory'96 . . . .
JUNIORS MR Alexander McL—at Wooster . . . . .
| ☎ (410) 771-4811
| Box 158, 1317
| Western Run Rd,
| Butler, MD 21023

Hopkins MR & MRS Warren B (Lange—Joan C Fletcher) Ac.Cda.Syr'51 . . . .
MISS Ann Lange—Cda.—☎ (610) 644-6187 .
| ☎ (610) 647-1286
| ''Willisbrook Farm''
| Malvern, PA 19355

Hopkins MRS William G (Loeff—Nelletje A van Essen) . . . . Died Jun 2'96

Hopkins MR William G—Pa'47
☎ (011-31-45) 5421348 . . Oucle Molenweg 143, 6417 GX Heerlen,
The Netherlands

Hopkins MR & MRS William R (Pyle—Edith A Rose)
Y'49.Gi.Mit'44.Bost'50
☎ (410) 544-3071 . . 282 Oak Court, Severna Park, MD 21146

Hopkinson MR Edward . . see MISS B W Davis

Hopkinson MR & MRS Francis JR (McIntire—Jane Nace)
Ph.Cry.Ssk.Cc.Wt.Pa'65
☎ (610) 527-6531 . . 1145 Ginkgo Lane, Gladwyne, PA 19035

Hopkinson MR & MRS James P (Hopkinson—Rachel W Read)
Ph.Me.Cs.Ac.Pa'45
☎ (610) 525-6234 . . 1123 Ginkgo Lane, Gladwyne, PA 19035

Hopkinson MR & MRS Mark (Rodger—B Sealy Hathaway) Va'82.Ph.Pa'69
340 E 57 St, Apt 3B, New York, NY 10022

Hopkinson MR & MRS Peter (Natasha Radoonsoff)
Mls'66.Tv.P'54.P'60 . . . .
MR Ivan E . . . .
| of ☎ (617)723-9471
| 17 W Cedar St,
| Boston, MA 02108
| ☎ (401) 635-8753
| 24 Meadow Lane,
| Little Compton, RI
| 02837

Hopkinson MASTER Phillips (Mark) . . . . Born at
New York, NY Jly 24'96

Hopper MR & MRS Harry S 2d (Klevan—Ann Buccierelli)
2003 Covered Bridge Rd, Holland, PA 18966

Hopper MRS Rea E (Whittell—Mary H Patchin)
☎ (310) 395-4432 . . 334 S Cliffwood Av, Los Angeles, CA 90049

Hopper MR & MRS Walter E (Sudrow—Diana Kerensky)
An.Mt.Plg.Cc.Hl.Rv.Ll.Cw.Fw.Snc.Myf.Ht.Ofp.Vca. StJ.Dll.Cr'37
☎ (212) 737-4531 . . 715 Park Av, New York, NY 10021

Hoppin MR & MRS Charles S (Harrison—Nancy Dewey)
Csh.Nf.K.Cly.H'53.Cl'59
☎ (212) 877-0246 . . 262 Central Park W, New York, NY 10024

Hoppin MRS Frederic G (May W Swords) Cly.Cda.
☎ (617) 326-8847 . . 10 Longwood Dv, Apt 270, Westwood, MA 02090

Hoppin MRS Mariana F (Mariana Field). . . . .
MISS Ashley G—Pom'89—at ☎ (212) 751-1403
200 E 66 St, New York, NY 10021 . . . .
MR David F—Ham'87—at ☎ (703) 243-3121
1125 N Vernon St, Arlington, VA 22201 . . . . . .
| ☎ (212) 289-4665
| 1133 Park Av,
| New York, NY
| 10128

Hoppin MR Thomas B JR—Col'91
see Dilatory Domiciles

Horan MISS Honora—Sth'66.Cs . . .of
☎ (212) 662-3379 . . 777 West End Av, New York, NY 10025
☎ (860) 672-6056 . . 7 Hurlburt Place, Cornwall Hollow, RFD,
Falls Village, CT 06031

Horan MR & MRS John R (Damaris S S Smith)
C.Cs.Dth'59.Y'62 . . . .
MR Quincy—Pitzer'94 . . . .
MR Patrick—U'94 . . . .
| of ☎ (212)772-8345
| 122 E 65 St,
| New York, NY
| 10021
| ☎ (860) 672-0085
| Rexford Rd,
| West Cornwall, CT
| 06062

Horan JUNIORS MR T Bramwell Welch . . see MISS (DR) M G Welch

Horan MRS Woodward (Quita Woodward)
Pc.Sg.Ac. . . . .
MR Charles Woodward—at ☎ (215) 247-5150
700 W Mermaid Lane, Apt 204, Philadelphia,
PA 19118 . . . .
| ☎ (215) 247-4843
| 8008 Crefeld St,
| Philadelphia, PA
| 19118

Horchow MISS Regen (Pillsbury—Regen Horchow) Y'84.NTex'88.Nyc.
☎ (214) 890-3491 . . 5036 Seneca Dv, Dallas, TX 75209

Horchow MR & MRS S Roger (Carolyn Pfeifer)
CtCol'56.K.Nyc.Y.'50 . . . .
MISS Sally—Y'92—at 6063 Scenic Av,
Los Angeles, CA 90068 . . . .
| of ☎ (214)369-0612
| 5722 Chatham Hill
| Rd, Dallas, TX
| 75225
| ☎ (212) 879-3900
| 1 E 66 St,
| New York, NY
| 10021

Hord MR Stephen Y—Col'51
☎ (415) 781-1117 . . 50 Alta St, San Francisco, CA *94133*

Hord MR & MRS William T (Elizabeth Anne Edwards)
An.Pc.Rv.Cw.Fw.Cc.Ll.Ac.Ncd.Y.'34 . . of
☎ (215) 283-7302 . . 1011 Foulkeways, Sumneytown Pike, Gwynedd, PA *19436*
☎ (518) 647-8080 . . "Rappahannock Lodge" 71 N Shore Lane, Silver Lake, Au Sable Forks, NY *12912*

Horine MR & MRS John H (G Paige Rolfes) WashColl'85.Md.
☎ (410) 823-2830 . . 1512 Ruxton Rd, Baltimore, MD *21204*

Horkan MR & MRS George A JR (Lindgren—Ann M Lagergren)
Cvc.Sl.Mt.Pa'43.GeoW'48
☎ (540) 592-3519 . . Cleremont Farm, 20854 Trappe Rd, Upperville, VA *20185*

Horn MR Fraser M . . see R R Plum

Horn MR & MRS Garfield Henry (Alexandra Matz) C.K.H'40
☎ (516) 692-6761 . . 247 Jennings Rd, Cold Spring Harbor, NY *11724*

Horn MR Geoffrey M (John F) . . . . Married at Baltimore, MD
Tomlinson MISS Elizabeth S (Edward) . . . . Jun 1'96

Horn MR & MRS L Stoddard (Leslie A Sullivan) . . . . | ☎ (212) 794-6162
MR Anthony G—at ☎ (212) 734-2634 | 150 E 73 St,
203 E 72 St, New York, NY *10021* . . . . | New York, NY *10021*

Horn MR & MRS Richard A (Rothman—Hope H Miller) Br'76.Tex'74
☎ (404) 982-9414 . . 2240 Heritage Dv NE, Atlanta, GA *30345*

Horn MASTER Samuel Anderson (Richard A) . . . . Born Feb 15'94

Horn MR & MRS Stoddard A M (Ann M Keith) Franklin'82.Bgt.Bcs.
☎ (914) 533-2438 . . 17 Wakeman Rd, South Salem, NY *10590*

Hornblower MR Alexander W . . see D K Thorne

Hornblower MR & MRS Henry 3d (Patricia R | ☎ (617) 329-3226
Bandler) D.Cw. . . . . | 176 Court St,
JUNIORS MR Richard B—at Boston U . . . . | Dedham, MA *02026*
JUNIORS MR Henry S—at St Sebastian's . . . . . . |

Hornblower MR Josiah C . . see D K Thorne

Hornblower MR & MRS Marshall (Marne Lloyd-Smith) P'39.Y'42
☎ (202) 337-2229 . . 4800 U St NW, Washington, DC *20007*

Hornblower MRS Ralph JR (Phoebe M Blumer) . . . . | ☎ (203) 869-4118
MR James W—Ham'86 . . . . | 10 Pine Ridge Rd,
MISS Priscilla (Colt—Priscilla Hornblower) . . . . | Greenwich, CT *06830*

Hornblower MR & MRS Ralph 3d (Margot | ☎ (213) 937-1620
Roosevelt) Rdc'71.H'70.Va'74 . . . . | 315 S Lorraine
JUNIORS MR Samuel R . . . . | Blvd, Los Angeles,
JUNIORS MR Luke R . . . . | CA *90020*

Horne MR & MRS Benjamin (Jean L Yarian) | ☎ (617) 259-9753
Cw.P'58 . . . . | Todd Pond Rd,
MR Benjamin D—at 404 Tamamori Biru, 5-8 | Lincoln, MA *01773*
Enomachi, Naka-ku, Hiroshima 730, Japan . . . . |
MR Terence D—at U of Colo . . . . |

Horne MR & MRS Dwight A (Dorothy L Edwards) Plg.Sm.Pn.P'33.Nu'55
☎ (508) 775-0318 . . 90 Wachusett Av, Box 426, Hyannis Port, MA *02647*

Horne MRS Lee C (Lee C Ellis) BMr'58.Pa'88.Fi . . . | ☎ (215) 546-1636
MR Joseph S—at ☎ (610) 896-5338 | 2518 Panama St,
931 Youngsford Rd, Gladwyne, PA *19035* . . . . . | Philadelphia, PA *19103*

Horne MR & MRS Michael D (Kimberly A Ayers) Ithaca'87.Ithaca'87
4409 Black Stallion Rd, Roswell, GA *30075*

Horne MR & MRS Peter D (Patricia Collins) | ☎ (847) 446-6091
Sth'81.P'55 . . . . | 791 Bryant Av,
MISS Katherine C . . . . | Winnetka, IL *60093*

Horne MR & MRS Robert D (Kelly A Crowe) Miami'85.Bost'85
☎ (847) 446-4757 . . 162 Fuller Lane, Winnetka, IL *60093*

Horne MR S Hamill—R.Pa'56
☎ (610) 649-3548 . . 1436 Rose Glen Rd, Box 33, Gladwyne, PA *19035-0033*

Horne MR & MRS Theodore L (Kathleen E Roche) | ☎ (847) 381-4731
LakeF'65.Nw'65 . . . . | "Ponditch"
MISS Amanda F . . . . | 254 Otis Rd,
JUNIORS MR George Q . . . . | Barrington, IL *60010*

Horne MR & MRS William C (Mary E Lembo) Loy'79.Van'80
☎ (770) 740-9466 . . 10565 Centennial Dv, Alpharetta, GA *30202*

Horner MRS C Scudday (Roberts—Virginia Howard)
☎ (334) 264-1742 . . 2227 Rosemont Court, Montgomery, AL *36111*

Horner MISS D'Arcy McK—TexA&M'82 . . . . | of ☎ (307)742-3112
MISS Ellen G—at Chicago, IL . . . . | 4705 Sunset Dv, Laramie, WY *82070* ☎ (011-61-74) 646-828 "Pengana" 203 S Deebing Creek Rd, Yamanto, Queensland 4905, Australia

Horner MR & MRS J W Maitland (Tracey M Burde) Rut'82.OreSt'83
☎ (301) 571-0126 . . 5810 Wyngate Dv, Bethesda, MD *20817*

Horner MR & MRS Martin (Anne M C Orsoni)
UPParis'85.Rc.Vt'81.NYLaw'84
☎ (212) 427-6982 . . 139 E 94 St, Apt 2B, New York, NY *10128*

Horner REV DR Thomas M—Rv.Wt.Elon'46.Duke'49.Cl'55.ECar'90
☎ (601) 466-2704 . . 212 Ballentine, Bay St Louis, MS *39520*

Hornor MR & MRS DeWitt (Edith Sterrett)
Un.Srr.DelB.Ny.Plg.Cly.H'38 ⚓
☎ (212) 876-1619 . . 1220 Park Av, New York, NY *10128*

Hornor MR Gurdon W—AmInt'l'83
113 W Bluegill Lane, Suffield, CT *06078-1951*

Hornor MR John W—Ham'77.Pa'83
☎ (413) 584-5403 . . 46 Ladyslipper Lane, Northampton, MA *01060*

Hornor MRS Thomas R (Joy H B Young) Dar. . . . . | ☎ (904) 784-9260
MR Thomas R . . . . | "Lion's Watch"
MR Nicholas M . . . . | 4903 Highpoint Dv, Panama City, FL *32404*

Hornor MR & MRS Townsend (Elizabeth L Saunders) Sth'54.Ny.Chi.H.'52
☎ (508) 428-2142 . . 239 Eel River Rd, Osterville, MA *02655*

Hornsey MR & MRS John W 3d (Sewall | 1121 Seven Oaks
Gibbons-Neff) Cry.VillaN'62 . . . . | Rd, Chester Springs,
MISS Katherine H—at 168 Sutherland Av, Apt 7, | PA *19425*
London W9 1HR, England . . . . |
MR John W . . . . |

Hornung MRS Robert M (Gertrude Seymour) Un.Csn.
Jan 1 . . ☎ (808) 923-0324 . . 1102 Colony Surf, 2895 Kalakaua Av, Honolulu, HI *96815*
May 1 . . ☎ (216) 283-5636 . . 13801 Shaker Blvd, Apt 4B, Cleveland, OH *44120*

Horris JUNIORS MISS Alexa M J . . see MISS E M Trapnell

Horsey MRS Outerbridge (Mary H Lee) Cvc.Cda . . .of
☎ (202) 333-2451 . . 3305 Dent Place NW, Washington, DC *20007*
☎ (304) 897-6483 . . ''Squirrel Nest'' Lost River Valley, Lost River, WV *26810*

Horsey MR & MRS Outerbridge (Georgina O Owen) Bnd'81.Mt.Cc.Pa'75.Pa'80
☎ (202) 965-0506 . . 1249—31 St NW, Washington, DC *20007*

Horst MR & MRS Jesse B (Diane Tappan) At.MempSt'65.Ala'68
☎ (334) 342-7644 . . 60 Hillwood Rd, Mobile, AL *36608*

Horton MR & MRS George S JR (Shreve—Jane C Cowles) Ind'75.Tufts'73.Mich'77
☎ (011-44-171) 584-5417 . . 10 Sloane Av, London SW3 3JE, England

Horton MRS Nomina Cox (Fay—Jones—Rimes—Nomina N Cox) Chr.Myf.Dar.Ncd.
☎ (813) 633-1621 . . 1010 American Eagle Blvd, Apt 617, Sun City Center, FL *33573*

Horton MR Richard M—Me.CTech'57
☎ (617) 523-5413 . . 4 Longfellow Place, Apt 510, Boston, MA *02114*

Horton DR & MRS William P (Eleanor B Bessellieu) Reed'43.Ore'46
☎ (410) 377-9663 . . 6515 Montrose Av, Baltimore, MD *21212*

Horton MR & MRS Wilmot R (Hallie N Powell) Tex'78.Tex'74
☎ (512) 477-2662 . . 2507 El Greco Cove, Austin, TX *78703-1510*

Horwitz DR & MRS Orville (Nataline B Dulles) Ph.Gm.Ll.Ac.H'32.JHop'38
☎ (610) 688-6653 . . 2 Private Way, Strafford, PA *19087*

Hosbein MR & MRS Peter C (Allison A Willoughby) P'79.Marq'76
15050 Watertown Plank Rd, Elm Grove, WI *53122*

Hosch MR & MRS Burton B JR (Patricia M Ronan) MissStW'70.MissSt'71 . . . . | ☎ (601) 442-6989 / 104 Dana Rd,
MISS Ann C . . . . | Natchez, MS *39120*
JUNIORS MISS Patricia W . . . . |

Hoscheit MR & MRS Mark E (Diana M Hutz) Del'86.Wid'85.Wid'96
☎ (302) 529-1084 . . 2205 Arosa Lane, Wilmington, DE *19810*

Hosken MR & MRS James C (Worrall—Foster— Gwendolen W Fearing) Sb.Ox'30 . . . . | ☎ (617) 326-3761 / 329 Fox Hill St,
MR Andrew C—at ☎ (213) 851-7072 | Westwood, MA
2049 N Las Palmas Av, Los Angeles, CA *90068* | *02090*

Hoskinson MR J Henry—Mt.Ct.P'40
☎ (202) 232-2335 . . 2101 Connecticut Av NW, Washington, DC *20008*

Hoskinson MR John K—Cvc.Mt.GeoW'69
☎ (202) 462-4499 . . 2401 Calvert St NW, Washington, DC *20008*

Hosler MR & MRS Robert M (Dunn—Helen B Johnson) Un.Csn.
☎ (216) 451-8437 . . 2 Bratenahl Place, Apt 2EF, Cleveland, OH *44108*

Hosmer MISS Alicia Watts—Md'88.Wis'91
☎ (301) 365-2559 . . 7545 Spring Lake Dv, Bethesda, MD *20817*

Hosmer MR & MRS Stephen T (Lucretia W De Wolf) Sth'51.Mt.Sl.Y'53 . . . . | ☎ (301) 656-1159 / 5412 Edgemoor
MISS Laura B—OWes'92 . . . . | Lane, Bethesda, MD
MR Stephen D . . . . | *20814*

Host MR & MRS Stig (Jeanne Grinnell) Ihy.Ny.Hn.H'51 ⚓ . . of
☎ (203) 629-6257 . . 103 Oneida Dv, Greenwich, CT *06830*
☎ (603) 272-5876 . . ''The Pond'' Indian Pond Rd, Orford, NH *03777*

Hoster MR & MRS Thomas C (Joan L Zwiep) Stan'75.Y'77.Yn.P'72.Stan'76
☎ (415) 322-1246 . . 2345 Byron St, Palo Alto, CA *94301*

Hostetler MR & MRS Charles A (D Anne Gore) Duke'53.WakeF'49
☎ (910) 875-2745 . . 305 W Elwood Av, Raeford, NC *28376*

Hotchkiss MRS Henry (Robinson—Prudence Wagoner) . . . . | ☎ (508) 693-3122 / Mink Meadows,
MR Henry W—Sar.Myf.Bow'58—at | 7 Fuller Rd,
☎ (508) 996-2513 . . 80 Fort St, Fairhaven, MA | Vineyard Haven,
02719 . . . . | MA *02568*

Hotchkiss MR & MRS Horace L (Ann C Griswold) Ober'45.Ht.Myf.Y'43 . . . . | ☎ (302) 378-9415 / Box 158,
MISS Lucinda C—Ws'79.Roch'93—at | 203 High St,
☎ (212) 580-3677 . . 176 W 86 St, New York, | Odessa, DE *19730*
NY *10024* . . . . |
MR Benjamin G—at ☎ (302) 234-9836 |
1639 Braken Av, Bldg R, Wilmington, DE *19808* |

Hotchkiss MR & MRS John F (Potts—Mary W Eggert) Cly.Cda.Dh.CarnM'28
☎ (941) 466-2937 . . 2509 Harbor Court, Ft Myers, FL *33908-1652*

Hotchkiss MR & MRS Joseph W (H Eugenia L Whitney) V'44.Cw.Ty'42 . . . . | ☎ (203) 869-6958 / 9 Park Place,
MISS Anne W . . . . | Greenwich, CT
 | *06830*

Hotchkiss MR & MRS Winchester F (Jane H Ellsworth) Ri.Fic.Plg.Snc . . .of
☎ (561) 546-4104 . . 154 S Beach Rd, Hobe Sound, FL *33455*
☎ (516) 788-7853 . . ''Windex'' Box 702, Fishers Island, NY *06390*

Hotle MISS Mercedes E J . . see M H McNabb

Houdry MR & MRS Jacques H (Reese—Dorothée Ann Pass) B.Evg.Gm.Me.Pn.P'49
☎ (561) 835-0494 . . PO Box 3192, 421 Brazilian Av, Palm Beach, FL *33480*

Houdry MR & MRS Pierre D (Louise W Walker) BMr'45.Msq.
☎ (561) 546-5843 . . S Beach Rd, PO Box 612, Hobe Sound, FL *33475-0612*

Hough MISS Elizabeth B—Ncd.
☎ (617) 876-8879 . . 5 Craigie Circle, Cambridge, MA *02138*

Hough MISS (DR) Héloïse Beekman—Bnd'29.Ncd.
☎ (212) MO6-7999 . . 80 La Salle St, New York, NY *10027*

Hough MR & MRS William F (Joan F Erhard) End'73.Mariet'71 . . . . | ☎ (908) 647-2123 / 77 Addison Dv,
JUNIORS MR Jeremy F . . . . | Basking Ridge, NJ
 | *07920*

Houghton MRS Amory (Laura Richardson) Cly.
☎ (607) 962-1234 . . 12 South Rd, Corning, NY *14830*

Houghton MR & MRS Amory JR (Dewey—Priscilla Blackett) Ln.Ri.Rr.Cvc.Chi.Ncd.Hn.H'50 . . . . . . | of ☎ (202)333-5512 / 3512 P St NW,
MR Talbot Dewey JR—at ☎ (508) 655-4007 | Washington, DC
18 Everett St, Sherborn, MA *01770* . . . . | *20007*
 | ☎ (617) 383-0554 / 91 Atlantic Av,
 | Cohasset, MA *02025*

Houghton MR Andrew A—CarnM'92
☎ (412) 362-1099 . . 616 Hastings St, Pittsburgh, PA *15206*

Houghton MR Arthur A (Horstman—Nina Rodale) Gchr'59 . . of
☎ (410) 827-7163 . . PO Box 6, 154 Carmichael Farm Rd, Queenstown, MD *21658-0006*
PO Box 100, 341 Gilchrist Av, Boca Grande, FL *33921-0100*

Houghton MR & MRS Arthur A 3d (Davis—Linda B Livingston) SL'64.Mt.Fic.H'62.H'81 . . . . ☎ (202) 337-8859 3043 N St NW, Washington, DC 20007
 MISS Alexandra L Davis—Pitzer'86—at ☎ (303) 543-1250 . . 3087 Redstone Lane, Boulder, CO 80303 . . . .
 MISS Eleanor V Davis—StMarys'92—at ☎ (503) 231-0830 . . 2588 SE 35 Place, Portland, OR 97214 . . . .
Houghton MR Charles G 3d—Cysl.H'67 ☎ (914) 384-6148 . . ''Octagonal House'' Frog Hollow Farm, PO Box 111, Esopus, NY 12429-0111
Houghton MR & MRS David (Phoebe A Coues) Macalester'85.Vt'86 ☎ (401) 789-4672 . . 29 Smallpox Trail, West Kingston, RI 02892
Houghton MR & MRS H Arnold (Helen W Tiers) H'21 . . of ☎ (904) 285-3302 . . 1000 Vicar's Landing Way, Apt H308, Ponte Vedra Beach, FL 32082 ☎ (518) 963-7747 . . RR 1, Box 83, Essex, NY 12936
Houghton MR & MRS Henry O JR (Jeanette M Berry) Van'74.Btn.Yn.Wms'53 ☎ (508) 369-6188 . . 53 Garland Rd, Concord, MA 01742
Houghton MISS Hollister D (Haggard—Hollister D Houghton) Cly. PO Box 1699, Boca Grande, FL 33921
Houghton MRS Lindley S (Billie Jean Hiers) ☎ (508) 468-2136 . . 471 Bridge St, South Hamilton, MA 01982
Houghton MR & MRS Neil L (Mary W Tompkins) BMr'84.Cry.Me.W&L'66.Cr'68 . . . . ☎ (610) 688-8533 21 Orchard Lane, Villanova, PA 19085
 MISS Katherine T—at 2100 Walnut St, Apt 10L, Philadelphia, PA 19013 . . . .
 MR Neil L JR—at 82 Myrtle St, Apt 5, Boston, MA 02114 . . . .
Houghton MRS Ruth W (Ruth West) Ri.Cly. ☎ (212) 838-6699 . . 580 Park Av, New York, NY 10021
Houghton MRS Sherrill M (Sherrill Mulliken) Rdc'64.Myf. ☎ (202) 966-9192 . . 3729 Cumberland St NW, Washington, DC 20016
Houghton MRS William M (Elizabeth B Richards) ☎ (617) 275-6039 . . 303 Winthrop Terr, Bedford, MA 01730
Houglan MR Timothy E 2d . . see MISS D F Munroe
Houser MRS George C (Mary Ruby Hillman) Cy.Myf.Ht.Dar.Dcw.H. ☎ (617) 232-2358 . . 220 Clyde St, Chestnut Hill, MA 02167-2904
Houser MR & MRS James G (Sue Ann Slauson) Mo'54.Ore'60 . . . . ☎ (314) HE4-4896 13782 Clayton Rd, Manchester, MO 63011
 MISS Carole K . . . .
 MR Eric G . . . .
Houston MR & MRS Frederic K (Marie H Sturges) Newt'61.Ts.G.Sa.Cly.Ty'59.Pa'62 . . . . ☎ (716) 652-6922 1000 Willardshire Rd, East Aurora, NY 14052
 MR Thomas R . . . .
Houston MR & MRS Frederic P (HON Lisa C Fairbairne) Chr.Cly.Wms'31.H'34 ☎ (207) 563-3536 . . HC 61, Box 142, Bristol, ME 04539
Houston MR Howard E—Cvc.Cl'32 ☎ (860) 726-2191 . . Duncaster, 20 Loeffler Rd, Bloomfield, CT 06002-2275
Houston MR & MRS J Gorman JR (Martha Martin) Ala'56.Aub'54.Ala'56 ☎ (334) 834-4414 . . 7 Clayton St, PH-1, Montgomery, AL 36104
Houston MR & MRS James A (Alice D Watson) Sth'59.C. ☎ (860) 535-4199 . . 24 Main St, Stonington, CT 06378-1446

Houston MRS Lawrence R (Jean W Randolph) ☎ (202) 362-6057 . . 4101 Cathedral Av NW, Apt 711, Washington, DC 20016
Houston DR & MRS William R M (Marguerite La B Browne) Sth'54.Rv.Cly.Myf.Dar.Cwr'48 . . . . . . of ☎ (419)524-0381 456 W Park Av, Mansfield, OH 44906
 MISS M Elisabeth La B—Ken'93—at Case Western Reserve Law . . . .
 MR Selby C T V—at U of Ariz . . . . ☎ (520) CY7-4188 6950 Orange Grove Circle, Tucson, AZ 85704
Hover MRS John C 2d (Downie—Dorothy P Schneirla) Sth'65.StA. ☎ (215) 862-2631 . . ''Honey Hollow Falls'' PO Box 442, Solebury, PA 18963
Hover MR John C 2d—K.Cw.StA.StJ.Snc.Pa'65. Pa'67 . . . . of ☎ (212)861-2515 47 E 64 St, New York, NY 10021
 MISS Margaret B—Leh'95—at 422 E 89 St, Apt 7A, New York, NY 10128 . . . . ☎ (215) 794-2074 ''Glenloch'' 3039 Durham Rd, PO Box 676, Buckingham, PA 18912
Hoversten MR & MRS Moris T (Anne S Richardson) Rcn.Rc.On.Cho.So.Cnt.Ncd.Minn'40 . . . . ☎ (847) CE4-1596 697 N Washington Rd, Lake Forest, IL 60045
 MISS Barbara S—at ☎ (419) 661-1544 29235 Bates Rd, Perrysburg, OH 43551 . . . .
Hoversten MR & MRS Philip E (Alison A Hubby) Bnd'69.Rcn.Ng.ColC'70.Pa'72 . . . . ☎ (970) 479-0518 1183 Cabin Circle, Vail, CO 81657
 JUNIORS MISS Tiffany W . . . .
Hovey MR Chandler JR—Ny.S.Ey.H.'39 ☎ (617) 720-0861 . . Harbor Towers Apt 2F, 65 E India Row, Boston, MA 02110
Hovey MRS Charles F (Anita C Hinckley) Sm.Cy.Chi.Ncd. . . . . ☎ (617) 566-0795 334 Newton St, Apt C, Chestnut Hill, MA 02167-2715
 MR Benjamin C . . . .
Hovey MR & MRS Charles F JR (Nancy S Meyer) DU'71.Ec.Ny.Sm.DU'70 . . . . ☎ (508) 526-7464 0 Woodholm Rd, Manchester, MA 01944
 JUNIORS MISS Averill S—at Foxcroft . . . .
Hovey MR William C—Mid'91 . . see J H Walton JR
Howard HON Barnaby J—Plg.Camb'48 ☎ (904) 264-7335 . . 1224 River Rd, Orange Park, FL 32073
Howard MR & MRS C Alexander (Gregg—Barbara S Vitz) Y'54 . . of ☎ (513) 831-1081 . . 9546 Cunningham Rd, Cincinnati, OH 45243 ☎ (561) 231-5266 . . 381 Silver Moss Dv, John's Island, Vero Beach, FL 32963
Howard MISS Catherine Alger—Nu'81 ☎ (212) 427-8997 . . 110 E 87 St, Apt 9E, New York, NY 10128
Howard MR Charles N ☎ (610) 353-6145 . . Dunwoody Village, 3500 West Chester Pike, Newtown Square, PA 19073

Howard MR Duncan L—Bhm.Pcu.SFr'70 . . . . ☎ (415) 775-1234
MR Lent Duncan . . . . 1000 California St,
MR Lyman D . . . . San Francisco, CA
94108-2204

Howard MR & MRS George (Tarafa—Ilse Bay) Roan'67
☎ (802) 362-0638 . . PO Box 1522, Manchester Center, VT *05255*

Howard MR & MRS George H JR (Gloria B Hartmeyer) Rc.Pr.Dth'47
☎ (516) 676-1388 . . 15 Cherrywood Rd, Locust Valley, NY *11560*

Howard MR & MRS George H 3d (Alexandra C ☎ (516) 692-6689
Miller) Cda.Ty'69 . . . . 1438 Ridge Rd,
MR George H 4th . . . . Laurel Hollow,
JUNIORS MISS Heidi S . . . . Syosset, NY *11791*
JUNIORS MR Livingston G . . . .

Howard MR & MRS Henry S JR (Karen E Adams) . . . ☎ (619) 453-7899
MR Devon C . . . . 7125 Cather Court,
JUNIORS MR Bret S . . . . San Diego, CA
92122

Howard MR & MRS Herbert G (Margaretha ☎ (617) 631-3683
Vandaele) Ey.H'53 . . . . 21 Dennett Rd,
MISS Alexandra G—Cal'93 . . . . Marblehead Neck,
MA *01945*

Howard MRS J Tenney (Hofgren—Joan L Tenney) ☎ (212) 472-1255
Bcs. . . . . 242 E 72 St,
MR Charles T—Bost'89—at ☎ (212) 717-5054 New York, NY
203 E 72 St, New York, NY *10021* *10021*
MR Christopher T—Denis'92—at
☎ (415) 474-9759 . . 1949 Pine St,
San Francisco, CA *94109* . . . .

Howard MR & MRS Jack R (Eleanor S Harris) Bhm.Ri.S.Plg.Y.'32 . . of
☎ (212) 737-1157 . . 120 East End Av, New York, NY *10028*
☎ (516) 922-7524 . . "Bagamoyo" 214 Centre Island Rd, Centre Island,
Oyster Bay, NY *11771*

Howard MRS John E JR (Jean S Berry) . . . . "Triagain"
MISS Margaret C . . . . 9610 Labrador Lane,
Cockeysville, MD
21030

Howard MR & MRS John L (Susan W Hunsiker) Denis'79.Pg.Mass'77
9 School St, Dedham, MA *02026-4309*

Howard MR & MRS John S (Wainwright—Patsy of ☎ (203)622-4028
Gilchrist) Sth'66.Cl'68.Un.Mds.Cs.Y'55 . . . . . . 68 Patterson Av,
MISS Katherine P . . . . Greenwich, CT
MR John W *06830*
☎ (516) 324-4904
8 Cross H'way,
East Hampton, NY
11937

Howard MR & MRS Macauley (Mary C Sharp) An.
☎ (202) 362-2071 . . 3200 McKinley St NW, Washington, DC *20015*

Howard MR & MRS Morton (Susan McInnes) ☎ (610) 649-4226
Pa'60.Me.Y'56 . . . . 411 Fishers Rd,
MISS Anne B—Bow'87 . . . . Bryn Mawr, PA
MR Robert M—Bow'84 . . . . *19010*
MR Nicholas—Mid'85
MR Alexander McI—at Skidmore . . . .

Howard MRS Nancy Cave (Montgomery—Nancy Cave)
223 E 66 St, New York, NY *10021*

Howard MR & MRS Philip K (Alexandra C Cushing) ☎ (212) 982-6187
SL'70.Pr.Rc.Y'70 . . . . 24 Gramercy Park S,
MISS Charlotte I C . . . . New York, NY
JUNIORS MISS Olivia C *10003*

Howard MISS Priscilla D
☎ (703) 824-1021 . . 4800 Fillmore Av, Apt 321, Alexandria, VA *22311*

Howard MR & MRS Reese Evans (Graham—Jean L Hiscoe)
Srr.B.Nrr.Wk . . .of
☎ (203) 259-3998 . . PO Box 2, Southport, CT *06490*
☎ (203) 255-3956 . . 178 Taintor Dv, Southport, CT *06490*
☎ (941) 964-1472 . . Box 927, 731 Palm Av, Boca Grande, FL *33921*

Howard MR & MRS Reese Evans JR (Janet A Schierloh) Buck'83.Rut'86
☎ (908) 730-8283 . . 4 Fawn Dv, Lebanon, NJ *08833*

Howard MR & MRS Robert Pike (Carolyn B Schwing) Y'45
☎ (504) 895-8883 . . 2625 Chestnut St, New Orleans, LA *70130*

Howard MRS Suzette A (Suzette Alger) V'52
☎ (803) 649-5219 . . 242 Ray Lane, Aiken, SC *29801*

Howard MR & MRS Thomas B (Mary S S Stiles)
☎ (301) 872-4666 . . "Reflections on the Calvert" PO Box 54,
St Marys City, MD *20686*

Howard MISS Victoria B—Bost'75.Pr.
☎ (516) 676-9193 . . 85 Maple Av, Locust Valley, NY *11560*

Howard MR Walter K—Minn'36
☎ (610) 527-9616 . . 77 Pasture Lane, Bryn Mawr, PA *19010*

Howard DR & MRS (DR) William M (Eckelkamp—Linda M Klahs)
Web'90.ArizSt'94.Rcsl.Mo'56.Mo'58.ArizSt'95
☎ (954) 916-9416 . . 872 E Plantation Circle, PO Box 17900,
Ft Lauderdale, FL *33318-7900*

Howard MR & MRS William T (Evelyn W Gaskill) ☎ (610) 296-8559
Col'72.Pa'78.Rd.Gm.Col'68.Pa'72 . . . . 250 Line Rd,
MISS Erin W . . . . Malvern, PA *19355*
MR William T JR

Howard MR & MRS Willing (Ann F Waite)
☎ (610) 527-1582 . . 200 Avon Rd, Haverford, PA *19041-1613*

Howard-Smith MR Stuart S—Cal'77
☎ (561) 547-0101 . . 338 Valley Forge Rd, West Palm Beach, FL *33405*

Howat MR & MRS John K (Anne Hadley) Rdc'59.Un.C.Cs.H'59.H'62
☎ (212) 722-4821 . . 1100 Park Av, New York, NY *10128*

Howat MISS Karen L—Y'81
☎ (011-33) 80-30-34-19 . . 15 rue Verrerie, 21000 Dijon, France

Howat MISS Laura A—AmColLond'87
☎ (212) 831-4459 . . 49 E 96 St, Apt 11A, New York, NY *10128*

Howcott MR & MRS Harley B (Simpson—Peggy M Logan) Cw.Rv.
☎ (504) 891-0246 . . 1550 Second St, Apt 8E, New Orleans, LA *70130*

Howe MR Arthur K—Y'34 . . . . ☎ (704) 697-9750
MISS Danilie D—Box 332, Emigrant, MT *59027* 3159 Cheryl Dv,
Hendersonville, NC
28792

Howe MR & MRS Arthur W 3d (Asche—Jean F Craig) Sth'51.Ph.Wms'45
☎ (803) 768-0175 . . 213 Yellow Throat Lane, Kiawah, SC *29455*

Howe MR & MRS Barclay G (Judith D Du Lyn) ☎ (860) 658-9167
Man'vl'66.Y'63 . . . . 5 Highwood Rd,
JUNIORS MISS Margaret S—St Paul's . . . . Simsbury, CT *06070*
JUNIORS MR Barclay G JR—at Yale
JUNIORS MR Henry W—at St Paul's . . . .

Howe DR & MRS Calderon (Sarah A Drury) Srb.Mt.Y'38.H'42
☎ (401) 846-0580 . . 90 Annandale Rd, Newport, RI *02840*

Howe MR & MRS Edward R JR (Jocelyn Grace)
Col'72.Rd.Me.Cts.Gm.Fst.DU'70 . . . . ☎ (610) 325-7340
JUNIORS MISS Kingsley G . . . . 6035 Goshen Rd,
JUNIORS MISS Nicole P. . . . . Newtown Square, PA *19073*

Howe MR & MRS George E (Katherine B Susman)
CtCol'68.SUNY'71.Stan'68.Stan'69 . . . . ☎ (713) 461-4693
MISS Katherine B—at Columbia . . . . 12111 Broken Arrow St, Houston, TX *77024*

Howe MRS James C (Lockwood—Barbara Batchelder) Cyb.
☎ (904) 273-5583 . . 1000 Vicar's Landing Way, Apt F103, Ponte Vedra Beach, FL *32082*

Howe MR & MRS James H 3d (Elizabeth C Scudder)
Cy.Evg.BtP.Wash'43 . . of
☎ (314) 993-0500 . . 3 Upper Price Rd, St Louis, MO *63132*
☎ (561) 659-6591 . . 432 Seabreeze Av, Palm Beach, FL *33480*

Howe MR & MRS John S (Frances F Hovey)
Rdc'52.Sm.Ncd.H'36 . . . . of ☎ (617)232-9737
MISS Emily D—Y'78 . . . . 25 Bowker St, Brookline, MA *02146*
☎ (508) 922-0017 ''Beach House'' Box 238, Prides Crossing, MA *01965*

Howe MRS Julia (Peacock—Julia M Ridgely)
☎ (603) 837-9427 . . Highland House, Apt 114, Whitefield, NH *03598*

Howe MR & MRS Lawrence (Ellen G Vaughan)
Nw'73.Ih.Cho.Fy.H'42.Ch'47
☎ (847) 446-2691 . . 175 Chestnut St, Winnetka, IL *60093*

Howe MRS Margaret Hamilton (Luce—Cobb—Margaret E Hamilton)
Rdc'52.Csh.
☎ (516) 367-8215 . . 25 Snake Hill Rd, Cold Spring Harbor, NY *11724*

Howe MR & MRS Nathaniel S (Alison Gilman) Y'44.Mit'62
☎ (860) 677-7986 . . 92 Main St, Farmington, CT *06032*

Howe MR Ralph E—Rcn.Pr.Y'63 . . . . ☎ (813) 894-5911
MISS F Avery—at ☎ (212) 734-8121 1333 Monterey Blvd
11 E 68 St, New York, NY *10021* . . . . NE, St Petersburg,
MISS Clare C . . . . FL *33704*

Howe MR & MRS Richard O (Sadie R H Hall)
Ncd.H'37 . . . . ☎ (617) 484-4873
MR Reginald H 2d—H'62 . . . . 49 Tyler Rd,
MR Richard O JR—H'69 . . . . Belmont, MA *02178*

Howell MR Alfred H . . . . Died at Bronx, NY Apr 23'96

Howell MR & MRS Charles D (Sturtevant—Smith— ☎ (508) 653-5583
Margaret Gray) D.H'41.H'47 . . . . 4 Fieldstone Lane,
MISS Carla A . . . . South Natick, MA
MR Douglas H—at Washington, DC *01760*

Howell MR & MRS Hampton P (Katharine E Van Buren)
Sth'34.Ofp.Myf.Cw.Sar.Wt.Dar.Ncd.Dh.Y'27
☎ (804) 295-6525 . . The Colonnades A351, 2600 Barracks Rd, Charlottesville, VA *22901*

Howell MRS J Taylor (Truslow—Elizabeth A Jennings) V'35.Csn.
☎ (215) 321-0143 . . 8 Spring Court, Washington Crossing, PA *18977*

Howell MRS John A (Wigley—Crespi—Florence Patten)
B.Eh.Mo.Rr.Shcc.Myf.Dar.Ht.
☎ (214) 361-2625 . . ''Villa Fiorenza'' 5555 Walnut Hill Lane, Dallas, TX *75229*

Howell MR T T Anthony JR (Thomas T A) . . . . Married at New York, NY
Le Jacq MISS Sarah T (Louis F) . . . . May 18'96

Howell MR & MRS T T Anthony JR (Sarah T Le Jacq)
Stone'90.Nu'89.Rut'93
☎ (212) 772-7127 . . 444 E 82 St, Apt 29F, New York, NY *10028*

Howell MRS Thomas A (Alice Whitfield)
☎ (410) 228-6534 . . 2 Shawnee Rd, Cambridge, MD *21613*

Howell MRS Thomas Paull (Mary C Simmons) Ws'42.Cda.
☎ (561) 231-4889 . . 970 Beacon Lane, Vero Beach, FL *32963*

Howell MR & MRS Thomas T A (Margot Deubgen) Mo.Va'60
☎ (201) 538-1747 . . ''Woodside'' 47 Sherwood Dv, Morristown, NJ *07960*

Howells MR Edward S (William Dean) . . . . . . Married at Baltimore, MD
Healy MISS Patricia M (Thomas P) . . . . Feb 24'96

Howells MR & MRS Edward S (Patricia M Healy)
☎ (415) 431-1786 . . 4053—19 St, San Francisco, CA *94114*

Howells MRS Henry C (Fahnestock—Powel—Alice M Post)
Evg.Cvc.Msq.Cda.
see Dilatory Domiciles

Howells MR & MRS Horace W (Ivy E Symons) Bost'90
☎ (202) 244-4803 . . 3530—30 St NW, Washington, DC *20008*

Howells MR & MRS William Dean (Benitha C ☎ (202) 965-4337
Lindeman) Tvb.Mt.H'54.Cl'60 . . . . 2600—31 St NW,
MISS Rose Marie . . . . Washington, DC
MR John M—at ☎ (202) 686-3714 *20008*
3420—39 St NW, Washington, DC *20016* . . . . .

Howells MR & MRS William White (Muriel Gurdon Seabury)
Tv.Sm.Chi.Cly.Ncd.H'30 . . of
☎ (207) 439-1302 . . 11 Lawrence Lane, Kittery Point, ME *03905*
☎ (617) 267-2398 . . 274 Beacon St, Boston, MA *02116*

Hower MRS Edwin N (McIntosh—Grace E Wright) ☎ (410) 339-3469
Rr. . . . . 403 Brightwood Rd,
MISS Ann L McIntosh—at ☎ (410) 557-7594 Lutherville, MD
3810 Beatty Rd, Monkton, MD *21111* *21093*

Howland MR & MRS Abbett P (Mary A Hall)
Van'84.Ford'90.Un.JHop'84.Nu'92 . . of
☎ (212) 288-7249 . . 155 E 76 St, Apt 12D, New York, NY *10021*
☎ (914) 373-7019 . . ''Troutbeck'' Green Rd, Amenia, NY *12501*

Howland MRS Cornelius De F (Priscilla E Post) . . . ☎ (212) 260-3441
MISS Leila S—StLaw'86.Cly.—at 440 E 23 St,
☎ (212) 794-8697 . . 510 E 85 St, New York, NY New York, NY
10028 *10010*

Howland MR & MRS Cornelius De F 3d (Colleen F Gibbs)
Stph'82.Un.Chr.CUNY'92
☎ (212) 420-8505 . . 524 E 20 St, New York, NY *10009*

Howland MR & MRS David (Nancy Moller) Y'33 . . . ☎ (617) 275-3010
MR Charles P—Y'68—at ☎ (415) 824-4426 404 Winthrop Terr,
4182 Army St, San Francisco, CA *94131* . . . . Bedford, MA *01730*

Howland MR & MRS Edward M 2d (Marianna H Cooper) Nh.Sm.
☎ (508) 653-8499 . . 52 Brush Hill Rd, Sherborn, MA *01770*

Howland MRS George (Margaret C Clarke) Chi.
☎ (617) 523-7348 . . 101 Mt Vernon St, Apt 2, Boston, MA *02108*

Howland MR & MRS John R (Frances T Harrison) Ripon'56
☎ (205) 525-5890 . . 200 Lakeview Circle, Cropwell, AL *35054*
Howland MR & MRS John S (Ann P Richardson) Mit'60.Mit'62.Mit'66
☎ (603) 382-5781 . . Box 999, 207 Main St, Danville, NH *03819*
Howland MR & MRS Llewellyn (Sarah Ives)
☎ (508) 636-8909 . . 140 Fisherville Lane, South Westport, MA *02790*
Howland MR & MRS Llewellyn 3d (Jessie M | ☎ (617) 522-5281
Williams) Rdc'63.Tv.H'59 . . . . | 100 Rockwood St,
MR Cornelius—at 406 E 9 St, New York, NY | Jamaica Plain, MA
10009 . . . . | *02130*
Howland MISS Margaret G—Bnd'37
☎ (716) 839-1437 . . 467 Campus Dv, Snyder, NY *14226*
Howland MRS Murdoch (Jane R Murdoch)
☎ (212) RE7-3322 . . 196 E 75 St, New York, NY *10021*
Howland MR Richard Hubbard—K.C.Cos.Fst.Cc.StJ.Cw.Br'31
☎ (202) 337-2521 . . 3900 Cathedral Av NW, Apt 712A, Washington, DC *20016*
Hoyer-Ellefsen MR Richard M—Mass'95
☎ (301) 941-8865 . . 2950 Van Ness St, Apt 328, Washington, DC *20008*
Hoyer-Ellefsen MR Sigurd—Mit'56.Mit'57.Mit'62 . . of
☎ (561) 347-0488 . . 540 Kay Terr, Boca Raton, FL *33432*
Ski Mountain Acres, PO Box 1645, Blowing Rock, NC *28605*
Hoyt MR & MRS Coleman W JR (Amy Brauer) Bel'75.GeoW'78.Bel'74
☎ (508) 369-1377 . . 31 Indian Spring Rd, Concord, MA *01742*
Hoyt MRS Diana C (Diana L Chace) Au. . . . . | ☎ (508) 356-5146
MR Andrew L—H'88 . . . . | 42 Heartbreak Rd,
MR Eliot L—H'90 . . . . | Ipswich, MA *01938*
Hoyt MR Edward P—An.USA'90.Ox'92
☎ (415) 928-3302 . . 916 Union St, San Francisco, CA *94133*
Hoyt MRS Granbery (Joya Weld Granbery) V'66.CtCol'73.SalReg'77 . . of
☎ (401) 846-7212 . . ''Briarpatch'' 115 Ellery Av, Middletown, RI *02842*
''Briarpatch West'' Box 141, T-Anchor Dv, Borrego Springs, CA *92004*
Hoyt MR & MRS Henry M (Helen I Hall) Mo.H'36 . . | ☎ (201) 539-2305
MISS Frances I . . . . | 44 Colles Av,
MR Paul S . . . . | Morristown, NJ
MR Alexander D . . . . | *07960*
Hoyt MR & MRS N Landon 3d (Barbara J McAdams) Ih.
☎ (847) 446-8424 . . 1175 Hill Rd, Winnetka, IL *60093*
Hoyt MR & MRS W C Alexander (Blair T Brown) Coe'74.Rut'71
☎ (212) 865-7531 . . 314 W 100 St, New York, NY *10025*
Hoyt MR Walter MacN—Colg'92
☎ (617) 926-1119 . . 74 Prentiss St, Apt 3, Watertown, MA *02172*
Hoyt MR & MRS William H (Moira J McKinnie)
☎ (540) 720-1374 . . 101 Eaton Court, Stafford, VA *22554*
Hoyt MR & MRS William V (Nancy P Hale) Ws'63.Dc.Ncd.Hn.H'64 . . of
☎ (941) 676-3237 . . Mountain Lake, Lake Wales, FL *33859-0832*
☎ (540) 854-5333 . . Mill Run Farm, 9221 Zachary Taylor H'way, Unionville, VA *22567*

Hoyt MR & MRS William W (Julie L Smith) | of ☎ (508)468-7396
My.Yn.Y'62 . . . . | ''Ballachurry''
MISS Kimberly M . . . . | Box 90,
MISS Ashley S . . . . | 90 Moulton St,
MISS Allison L . . . . | Hamilton, MA
JUNIORS MR Winthrop S . . . . | *01936*
| ☎ (802) 824-5055
| ''Ballavitchel''
| Londonderry, VT
| *05148*
Hruska MR Roman L—Creigh'29
☎ (402) 345-1133 . . 2139 S 38 St, Omaha, NE *68105-3005*
Hubbard MR & MRS Bruce B (Webel—Proctor— | ☎ (915) 537-6507
Suzanne E Coles) Rv.Ncd.Tex'71 . . . . | 544 Springcrest Dv,
JUNIORS MISS Mary B . . . . | El Paso, TX *79912*
JUNIORS MR Bruce B . . . . |
Hubbard MR & MRS Charles C (Henrietta F Hill) Swb'50.Cda.W&L'48
☎ (334) 264-7990 . . 3346 Stratford Lane, Montgomery, AL *36111*
Hubbard MR & MRS Charles W 3d (Chapman—M Elizabeth Smith)
Cy.Sar.Chi.Ncd.H'37
☎ (617) 444-1109 . . North Hill A405, 865 Central Av, Needham, MA *02192*
Hubbard MR & MRS Cortlandt van D (Kampmann— | ☎ (215) 233-1817
Pepper—Lillian H Schwartz) Pc.Pe.Fw.Cw.Rv. | 8498 Flourtown Av,
Cspa.StA.Sg.Ac.H.'34 . . . . | Wyndmoor, PA
MISS Margaret D . . . . | *19038*
MISS Megan H Kampmann—at |
☎ (215) 233-3557 . . 808 Southampton Av, |
Wyndmoor, PA *19038* . . . . |
Hubbard MRS D Seeley (Michelle M Ryan) Ny. | ☎ (203) 655-3708
⚓ . . . . | 23 Raiders Lane,
MISS Stephanie A . . . . | Darien, CT *06820*
MISS Katherine K . . . . |
Hubbard MR D Seeley—Ny.Ty'67.Conn'70
16 Raiders Lane, Darien, CT *06820*
Hubbard MR & MRS David R (Margaret Ackerly) Ncd.Y'39.Cr'47
☎ (860) 726-2075 . . Duncaster P316, 60 Loeffler Rd, Bloomfield, CT *06002*
Hubbard MR & MRS Eliot 3d (Margaret Van Hook) | ☎ (617) 259-8087
Sm.H'41 . . . . | 24 Birchwood Lane,
MR Eliot 4th—at 67 Greene St, New York, NY | Lincoln, MA
10012 . . . . | *01773-4929*
Hubbard MR & MRS Ford JR (Patricia Peckinpaugh) Tex'51.Cry.Tex'51
☎ (713) 523-6281 . . 3015 Chevy Chase Dv, Houston, TX *77019*
Hubbard MR Hugh J—K.Y.'66
☎ (212) 534-2791 . . 115 E 90 St, New York, NY *10128*
Hubbard MR & MRS John F JR (Barbara E Rielly)
☎ (617) 862-4650 . . 6 School St, Lexington, MA *02173*
Hubbard MRS Otis L (Ethel DeF Johnston) On.
☎ (847) 234-2695 . . 555 E Woodland Rd, Lake Forest, IL *60045*
Hubbard MR & MRS Ralph H JR (Gibson—Mary Henry)
Rice'39.Coa.Cw.Snc.StA.Pn.P'34
☎ (409) 856-4371 . . 36 Winged Foot Dv, Conroe, TX *77304*
Hubbard MRS Thomas B (Keedick—Renner—Mary E Bourne)
☎ (212) 759-8188 . . 40 Central Park S, New York, NY *10019*
Hubbard MR & MRS Thomas R (Christina L Hohl) Web'71.Muhl'72
☎ (203) 579-2377 . . 124 Jeniford Rd, Fairfield, CT *06430*

Hubbard MR & MRS William N 3d (Whitney—Robin Davies)
Rc.Pqt.Cly.Wms'64.Va'67 . . of
☎ (212) 758-1560 . . 116 E 63 St, New York, NY *10021*
☎ (203) 259-7781 . . 534 Harbor Rd, Southport, CT *06490*
Hubbell MISS Drika B . . see MISS M Bingham
Hubbell MR J Bradford—Tul'88.UWash'95 . . see MISS M Bingham
Hubbell MRS William B (Dorothy W Twyeffort) V'30.Csn.Bgt.
☎ (207) 729-8033 . . Thornton Hall, 25 Thornton Way, Brunswick,
ME *04011*

Hubby MR & MRS David G (Sarah P Foote) | ☎ (919) 942-4465
Va'59.Geo'63 . . . . | 1252 Falmouth
MISS Elizabeth A—at 5010 Keokuk St, Bethesda, | Court, Chapel Hill,
MD *20816* | NC *27514*
MR Peter K—at S Beach Marina Apt 4-106, |
2 Townsend St, San Francisco, CA *94107* . . . . . |

Hubby MR & MRS Frank W 3d (Kingsley Kahler) Y'29.H'32
☎ (860) 739-8544 . . 249 Old Black Point Rd, Niantic, CT *06357-3732*

Hubby MR & MRS Robert N (Buzby—Kathryn B | ☎ (215) 836-2675
Pyles) Pc.Y'61 . . . . | 659 Church Rd,
MR Robert N JR . . . . | Flourtown, PA
| *19031*

Huber MRS Charles W JR (Dorothy M Manwaring) Rol'37
☎ (561) 546-6144 . . 5 Harmony Lane, Hobe Sound, FL *33455*

Huber MR & MRS Daniel (Pamela W Hamrick) Louis'75 ⛵
☎ (714) 496-0400 . . 24843 Del Prado, Apt 302, Dana Point, CA *92629*

Huber MR & MRS Horst W (Louisa G Fitzgerald) H'65.H'74.Munich'61
☎ (617) 354-6075 . . 20 Prescott St, Cambridge, MA *02138*

Huber MR & MRS Joel C 3d (Christine L Jones) | ☎ (919) 682-8910
Ws'69.P'67 . . . . | 1212 Hill St,
MISS Mary H . . . . | Durham, NC *27707*
JUNIORS MISS Amanda M . . . . |

Huber MRS John Y JR (Peterson—Jane H Chapman) Me.Ncd.
☎ (610) 688-3434 . . 319 S Wayne Av, Wayne, PA *19087*

Huber MR & MRS John Y 3d (Margaretta B Black) Fw.Y'42
☎ (912) 598-7607 . . 7 Oyster Reef Rd, Savannah, GA *31411-2213*

Huber MR & MRS John Y 4th (Mary Jo Helmer) ArizSt'76
☎ (602) 991-6219 . . 6740 E Camino De Los Ranchos, Scottsdale,
AZ *85254*

Huber MR & MRS Joseph F (Louise H Hine) | ☎ (847) 234-2445
Ny.Cry.M.Laf'68 . . . . | 361 N Ahwahnee
JUNIORS MISS Margot H . . . . | Rd, Lake Forest, IL
JUNIORS MR Stephen L . . . . | *60045*

Huber MRS Pehr C (Tabitha R Andrews) | ☎ (908) 842-7085
CtCol'55.Stc.Rm.Cda. . . . . | 12 Oyster Bay Dv,
MR Eric C . . . . | Rumson, NJ *07760*

Huber MR Richard M—Yn.P'45.Y'53
☎ (202) 362-9387 . . 2950 Van Ness St NW, Apt 926, Washington,
DC *20008*

Huber MR & MRS Richard M JR (Lucile B Olson)
MmtVa'87.Hampshire'76.Y'83
☎ (202) 625-0471 . . 1218 Bank St NW, Washington, DC *20007*

Huber MR & MRS Thomas W (Mary L Savage) . . . . | ☎ (410) 778-4932
MR Anthony S . . . . | 201 Water St,
MR Thomas W JR . . . . | Chestertown, MD
| *21620*

Huber MR & MRS Timothy B (Susan C Ware) | ☎ (617) 262-5563
Pa'67.H'69 . . . . | 191 Commonwealth
MISS Kathleen E . . . . | Av, Boston, MA
MR Timothy B JR . . . . | *02116*

Hubner MR & MRS Robert W (Katherine L Huick)
Wash'42.Err.B.Cos.Eyc.Ny.Plg.Wash'41 . . of
☎ (203) 655-9659 . . 9 Butler's Island, Darien, CT *06820*
☎ (508) 627-5604 . . "Windswept" 112 Tower Hill, Edgartown,
MA *02539*

Hucks MR & MRS Herbert deM 3d (Servais— | PO Box 119031,
Marjorie L Whitcomb) W&M'72.Clem'72 ⛵ . | Hialeah, FL *33011*
JUNIORS MR Herbert deM 4th . . . . |

Huddleston MR & MRS C Elsworth (Watson— | ☎ (410) 819-8771
Dorothy H Burnett) WmW'ds'35.Cr'29 . . . . . . | Easton Club,
MISS May C—GlasSt'75—at Atlantic City, NJ . . | 28525 Augusta
| Court, Easton, MD
| *21601*

Huddleston MR John R
☎ (510) 704-8728 . . 1621 Blake St, Apt 8, Berkeley, CA *94703*

Huddleston MISS Margaret M (Missel—Margaret M Huddleston)
CtCol'65.H'80.Ac.Me.
☎ (617) 497-9431 . . 205 Lake View Av, Cambridge, MA *02138*

Huddleston MR & MRS Thomas J (Mary E Duffey) | ☎ (410) 479-1037
Duke'70.NEng'69 . . . . | 7660 Harmony Rd,
MISS Jennifer D . . . . | Preston, MD *21655*
JUNIORS MISS Caitlin E . . . . |

Hudnut MRS William H (Elizabeth A Kilborne)
1570 East Av, Rochester, NY *14610*

Hudson MR & MRS E Randall 3d (Carolyn F Tarride) Tex'81.W&L'83
312 N Bailey St, Ft Worth, TX *76107*

Hudson MR & MRS Edward R JR (Ann Frasher)
Tex'58.A.K.Tex'55.H'58 . . of
☎ (817) 732-7795 . . 55 Westover Terr, Ft Worth, TX *76107*
☎ (970) 925-8269 . . 750 Castle Creek Dv, Aspen, CO *81611*

Hudson MR & MRS Joseph L JR (Jean B Wright) Y'53
180 Ridge Rd, Grosse Pointe Farms, MI *48236*

Hudson MISS Louise W—PineM'84.Cly.
☎ (212) 861-2154 . . 156 E 79 St, Apt 13C, New York, NY *10021*

Hudson MR & MRS Manley O JR (Olivia d'Ormesson) C.K.H'53
☎ (011-44-171) 584-2281 . . 11 Pelham Crescent, London SW7 2NP,
England

Hudson MR & MRS Thomas B JR (Caroline F | ☎ (207) 326-9564
Wadsworth) Fcg. | Box 604, Castine,
MISS Sarah F . . . . | ME *04421*
MISS Caroline C . . . . |

Hudson MR & MRS William H (Elizabeth E | ☎ (214) 351-6602
Van Upton) Rcn.Wms'50 . . . . | 4722 Shadywood
MR Andrew C . . . . | Lane, Dallas, TX
MR James C C—at ☎ (214) 369-0519 | *75209*
4741 Roxbury Lane, Dallas, TX *75229* . . . . . . |

Hudson MR & MRS William P C (Kolowitz—M | ☎ (210) 504-6650
Antonia R Ramirez) Tex'75 . . . . | "Casa Tonia"
JUNIORS MISS Vanessa L . . . . | 2300 Coffee Port
JUNIORS MR John H P . . . . | Rd, Brownsville, TX
JUNIORS MR Michael R H . . . . | *78521*
MISS Emma H Kolowitz . . . . |

Hudson MR & MRS William R (Powers—Grenville Dodson)
Rose'94.M.Me.Pa'49.H.'52.. of
☎ (610) LA5-1412.. 522 Fishers Rd, Bryn Mawr, PA *19010*
☎ (941) 263-0650.. ''Twin Palms'' 630 Banyan Circle, Naples,
FL *34102-5114*

Huebner MR & MRS J Stephen (Emily M Zug) | ☎ (301) 229-5367
Gchr'64.Gchr'65.Cos.P'62.JHop'67 ⛵ ...... | 6102 Cromwell Dv,
MR Jeffrey W .... | Bethesda, MD
| *20816*

Huebner MR John M—Me.Pa'31
61 Pasture Lane, Bryn Mawr, PA *19010-1763*

Huebsch MR & MRS Michael C (Suzanne d'H Hooper)
Denis'80.Cl'84.Ty'80.Pa'85
☎ (203) 655-2468.. 20 St Nicholas Rd, Darien, CT *06820*

Huey MR & MRS Charles M JR (Clementson—Cynthia Ladd) A.Okla'69
☎ (210) 824-1709.. 402 Alamo Heights Blvd, San Antonio, TX *78209*

Huey MR & MRS G H Harris (Edith C MacVeagh)
B'gton'48.Ny.Cly.Hn.Cal'39 ⛵
☎ (805) 969-5275.. 970 Lilac Dv, Santa Barbara, CA *93108*

Huff MR & MRS J Craig 3d (Janet C Wallace) KeeSt'78.Ken'80
☎ (508) 448-9661.. 358 Whiley Rd, Groton, MA *01450*

Huff MR & MRS John Craig JR (Ann E Millspaugh)
Sth'42.San.Chi.Ncd.Wms'42
☎ (401) 295-8165.. ''Stook Hill House'' 451 Gilbert Stuart Rd,
Saunderstown, RI *02874*

Huffard MR & MRS P Phillip 3d (Deborah W Battin) Col'73.Ihy.Ri.Br'62
☎ (203) 622-6799.. 107 Maple Av, Greenwich, CT *06830*

Huffman MR & MRS Byron K JR (Christine F | ☎ (703) 759-6219
Renchard) CtCol'63.Mt.Y'64.Y'67.......... | 117 Commonage
MISS Heather O'B—Ken'91 .... | Dv, Great Falls, VA
| *22066*

Huffman MISS Deborah L.. see MRS M P Herschede

Huffman MR Gerald M JR .... | ☎ (213) 484-0658
MISS Hurley M—Ore'92—at ☎ (310) 289-5114 | 831 N Benton Way,
841 Westmount Dv, West Hollywood, CA *90069* | Los Angeles, CA
| *90026*

Huffman MRS Huston (Augusta Jay)
☎ (405) 843-3645.. 1202 Huntington Av, Oklahoma City, OK *73116*

Huffman MRS Maria Ewing (Brossard—Maria | of ☎ (212)226-8771
Ewing Huffman) Cly.................. | 114 Spring St,
JUNIORS MISS Genève Vallé Brossard .... | New York, NY
| *10012*
| ☎ (516) 324-9375
| 12 Hawthorne Lane,
| East Hampton, NY
| *11937*

Huffman MRS Moore P (Grace V Ewing) Cly...... | ☎ (970) 923-2130
MISS Felicity—at ☎ (212) 947-2894 | PO Box 310,
529 W 42 St, Apt 7V, New York, NY *10036* ... | Woody Creek, CO
MR Moore P JR—Box 640, HIC 42, Kirby Rte, | *81656*
Busby, MT *59014* .... |

Huffman MR & MRS Paul B 3d (Taylor—Melissa Glavin) Mls'84.Cal'86
☎ (510) 284-7375.. 1076 Carol Lane, Lafayette,
CA *94549* .. MRS absent

Hufnagel MR & MRS Frederick B (Stefanie R Shattuck) Ws'65.H'64
☎ (508) 462-9247.. 6 Fulton St, Newburyport, MA *01950-3909*

Hufty MR & MRS Page (Frances Archbold) Cvc.Evg.BtP.Mt.B.Ri.Cly.
☎ (561) 655-6760.. 330 Island Rd, Palm Beach, FL *33480*

Hufty MRS Page L (Griswold—Page L Hufty) Stan'69.BtP.Evg.Cvc.
☎ (561) 655-6769.. 340 Island Rd, Palm Beach, FL *33480*

Huger MISS Barbara B.. of
☎ (213) 650-0163.. 2368 Sunset Plaza Dv, Los Angeles, CA *90069*
☎ (704) 274-2149.. 9 Cedarcliff Rd, Asheville, NC *28803*

Huger MRS Bernard J (Lucie A Furstenberg)
1623 View Woods Dv, St Louis, MO *63122-3522*

Huger MR Daniel E—NCar'75
☎ (704) 274-8899.. 9 Cedarcliff Rd, Asheville, NC *28803*

Huggins MR Charles N—Bhm.Ken'49
☎ (415) 851-8816.. 350 Family Farm Rd, Woodside, CA *94062*

Huggins MRS Gordon (White—Maria H von Mering) K.Csn.Chi.
☎ (508) 468-2087.. 17 Miles River Rd, South Hamilton, MA *01982*

Huggins MR & MRS John R (Nancy V Gwinn) | ☎ (508) 369-1262
Pa'64.Me.Pa'59 .... | 91 Coolidge Rd,
MISS Julia G .... | Concord, MA *01742*
MR Marshall G .... |

Huggins MRS Kenneth R (Barbara L Merrill) Sth'53 | of ☎ (212)580-7905
MISS Elise M—Pom'91—at ☎ (510) 644-3037 | 173 Riverside Dv,
2143 Woolsey St, Berkeley, CA *94705* .... | New York, NY
MISS Jennifer L—L&C'93—at ☎ (802) 496-9409 | *10024*
Box 1124, Waitsfield, VT *05673* .... | ☎ (802) 496-9409
MR Mark P—Rol'91—at ☎ (407) 679-2954 | E Warren Rd,
1120 Reflections Circle, Casselberry, FL *32707* . | Waitsfield, VT
| *05673*

Hughes MISS Alexandra W (Edward R) ...... Married at Greenwich, CT
Curran MR Donald E 3d (D Edward) .... Jly 30'94

Hughes MRS Arthur M R (Sarah L Jay) Exy.Ncd.
☎ (203) 458-3630.. 201 Granite Rd, Apt 207, Guilford, CT *06437*

Hughes MISS Frances M D'O.. see MRS F S Allis JR

Hughes MR & MRS George S JR (Allison L Peck) Bost'79.On.H'79
1111 Ashley Rd, Lake Forest, IL *60045*

Hughes DR & MRS Gordon B (Myra Madden) Pg.Dth'70.Cwr'74
☎ (216) 229-4741.. 2189 Harcourt Dv, Cleveland Heights, OH *44106*

Hughes MR & MRS J Lawrence (Rose M Pitman) Pqt.C.Plg.StJ.Cly.Y'48
☎ (203) 259-8957.. 1 Church St, Box 430, Southport, CT *06490*

Hughes MR & MRS John Brassington (Sally B | of ☎ (609)924-1964
Stevenson) W&M'46.Pn.P'47.P'53 | 160 Mercer St,
MISS Alison B—P'79—at ☎ (011-34-1) 265-0208 | Princeton, NJ *08540*
Mira el Rio Alta 6, Apt 4B, 5 Madrid, Spain ... | ☎ (011-34-1)
| 344-0449
| Juan Ramon
| Jimenez 2, 28036
| Madrid, Spain

Hughes MR John C—Ariz'50
☎ (602) 952-1272.. 6653 N Hillside Dv, Paradise Valley, AZ *85253*

Hughes REV DR John Jay—H'48
☎ (314) 721-8737.. 7316 Balson Av, St Louis, MO *63130-2901*

Hughes MR & MRS John W (Mary F Lavezzorio)
Cho.On.Sr.H'42.Va'48.. of
☎ (847) 234-1031.. 71 S Stonegate Rd, Lake Forest, IL *60045*
☎ (602) 922-0912.. 7357 E Tuckey Lane, Scottsdale, AZ *85250*

Hughes MRS Joseph D (Jane S Blackistone)
Pg.Mt.Cvc.Ncd. . . . . | 1331 Bennington
  MR Gerard B—Pg.Rr.Y'70.Va'74 . . . . | Av, Pittsburgh, PA
    15217

Hughes MISS Josephine
Walnut Spring Farm, 4331 Black Rock Rd, Upperco, MD *21155*

Hughes MR & MRS Ralph R (Walther—Coffey—Florence Hard)
☎ (561) 737-0402 . . 1318 Partridge Place N, Quail Ridge,
Boynton Beach, FL *33436-5408*

Hughes MR & MRS Robert A (Page A Chisolm) P'85.Nu'90
☎ (212) 980-2888 . . 58 W 58 St, Apt 16E, New York, NY *10019*

Hughes MR Robert D JR—Cr'42.H'43
☎ (616) 882-9501 . . 2179 Alden Dv, Beulah, MI *49617*

Hughes MR & MRS Robert David (Carlissa K Richards)
Nw'90.Nw'95.Nw'88.Loy'96
☎ (847) 864-3592 . . 3224 Otto Lane, Evanston, IL *60201*

Hughes MR & MRS Sidney (Annette S McMaster)
Un.K.Chr.B.Pl.Coa.Cw.StJ.Cly. . . . . | ☎ (212) 838-5632
  MISS Nancy M—BMr'78—at ☎ (212) 288-5765 | 200 E 66 St,
124 E 84 St, New York, NY *10028* . . . . | New York, NY
    10021-6728

Hughes MR & MRS Thomas L (Kuczynski—Jane D Casey)
Ws'60.Cos.Cvc.Carl'47.Ox'49.Y'51
☎ (301) 656-1420 . . 5636 Western Av, Chevy Chase, MD *20815*

Hughes MR Thomas M—Pg.Col'78
☎ (303) 258-3394 . . Box 780, Nederland, CO *80466*

Hughes MR & MRS Thomas M (Catherine McVay) P'82.Pa'86.Un.P'82
☎ (212) 732-9234 . . 176 Broadway, New York, NY *10038*

Hughes MR & MRS Thomas R JR (Hopkins—Janice L Peters) Md.Rm'71
☎ (410) 822-0454 . . ''Chenar'' 9284 Chenar Farm Rd, Easton,
MD *21601*

Hughes MR & MRS William L (Rebecca E Chase) Hlns'85.HampSydney'86
☎ (203) 698-3037 . . 321 Sound Beach Av, Old Greenwich, CT *06870*

Huguley MR & MRS Martin C (Suzanne V McCance) Fic.
☎ (201) 816-0548 . . 98 Surrey Lane, Tenafly, NJ *07670*

Huidekoper MR & MRS Henry S (Batchelor—Sheila K Smith) Cvc . .of
☎ (561) 231-0226 . . 341 Island Creek Dv, Vero Beach, FL *32963*
☎ (508) 994-6728 . . ''Huideway'' Nonquitt, South Dartmouth,
MA *02748*

Hulick MISS Elizabeth C—V'58 . . see MRS W A Gray

Hulick MR W Hayward—Ripon'72
☎ (410) 676-7371 . . 495 Winterberry Dv, Edgewood, MD *21040*

Hulitar MRS Philip (Mary P Gerstenberg) SL'48.Evg.BtP.Cda.
☎ (561) 844-4309 . . 980 N Ocean Blvd, Palm Beach, FL *33480*

Hull MR Edward L . . see MRS W T Skallerup JR

Hull MR & MRS Gordon F 3d (Barbara W Kelly)
Ws'63.Cnt.Ncd.Myf.Dth'63.H'64 . . . . | ☎ (847) 256-5430
  MISS Sarah K—Dth'93 . . . . | 726 Roger Av,
  MISS Jennifer C—at Colo Coll . . . . | Kenilworth, IL
    60043-9998

Hull RR ADM & MRS Harry (L Catherine A Clement)
BMr'43.Ny.Chi.Ncd.USN'32
☎ (508) 526-1809 . . ''Uplands'' Highland Av, Manchester, MA *01944*

Hull MR & MRS Jeffrey R (Bonnie J Lethbridge) Blooms'77.LeTourn'79
☎ (903) 759-0201 . . 1322 Chad St, Longview, TX *75604*

Hull MR & MRS John B (Blayney Anderson) An.USA'43
☎ (804) 977-3168 . . 500 Court Square, Apt 1004, Charlottesville,
VA *22902*

Hull MR Kenneth Duryee JR—Cvc.Stan'50
☎ (301) 986-8529 . . 3505 Hamlet Place, Chevy Chase, MD *20815*

Hull MR Kimball E C—U'70
☎ (617) 497-6177 . . 2 Cogswell Place, Cambridge, MA *02140*

Hull MR & MRS Philip G (Gretchen E Gaebelein)
BMr'50.Csh.Mid'49.Cl'52
☎ (516) 922-7193 . . 1120 Cove Edge Rd, Oyster Bay Cove,
Syosset, NY *11791*

Hulme MRS Alfred P (Alice B Davis) . . . . | ☎ (203) 245-7279
  MISS Elizabeth R—Box 411, Southport, CT *06490* | 17 Downing Way,
    Madison, CT *06443*

Hulting MRS Patricia L (B Patricia Landis)
Stan'57.Ncd. . . . . | ☎ (415) 221-3848
  MR Frederick L . . . . | 3855 Washington St,
  MR William F . . . . | San Francisco, CA
    94118

Humann MR & MRS Edgar (Faith Low)
K.Ny.Cly.Br'61.Va'64 . . . . | ☎ (441) 236-0853
  MR Christian—at ☎ (510) 843-5821 | ''Lockward House''
2508 Ridge Rd, Apt 7, Berkeley, CA *94709* . . . | 54 Harbour Rd,
    Paget PG 02,
    Bermuda

Hume MR Andrew . . . . Died at
Chicago, IL Nov 26'94

Hume MR & MRS Anthony (Judith D Hanson)
TexWmn'91.H'62.Mich'65 . . . . | ☎ (214) 661-9384
  MISS Alexandra S—at U of Chicago . . . . | 6936 Robin Willow
  MISS Katharine H . . . . | Dv, Dallas, TX
    75248

Hume MR & MRS George H (Leslie P Bryant)
Rdc'69.Stan'79.Bhm.BtP.Bur.Pcu.Fr.Y'69. . . . . . | ☎ (415) 922-2569
Stan'75 . . . . | 235 Locust St,
  JUNIORS MR Parker H—at Groton . . . . | San Francisco, CA
    94118

Hume MRS Jaquelin H (Caroline E Howard) Bur.Fr.
☎ (415) 929-1234 . . 3355 Pacific Av, San Francisco, CA *94118*

Hume MR & MRS Patrick H (Allen—Helen L G Minnigerode) Cda.GeoW'34
☎ (202) 244-2772 . . 3830 Macomb St NW, Washington, DC *20016*

Hume MR & MRS R Stuart JR (Elisabeth W Hull)
Skd'61.Myf.Bab'50 . . . . | ☎ (603) 433-9092
  MR Douglas A . . . . | 24 Ducks Head,
  MR David M—at 1138 Arcadian Av, Apt A, | PO Box 2005,
Chico, CA *95926* . . . . | New Castle, NH
    03854

Hume MRS Russell S (McDermott—Beatrice P Schmulling) Ford'50
☎ (912) 638-4364 . . PO Box 30771, Sea Island, GA *31561*

Hume MR & MRS William J (L Patricia
Balazs-Tagle) Bhm.Pcu.Fr.Y'61.H'67 . . . . | ☎ (415) 922-4230
  MISS C Lucy—Br'94—at Geo Wash'n Med . . . . | 3640 Washington St,
  JUNIORS MR J George—at Trinity . . . . | San Francisco, CA
    94118

Humes MRS David W (Marie R Maxwell) Trans'89
☎ (606) 846-5541 . . PO Box 3998, 419 Mill Rd, Midway, KY *40347*

Humes MR David W—Cent'76
☎ (606) 873-5555 . . PO Box 999, Versailles, KY *40383-0999*

Humes MR & MRS James C (Dianne Stuart)
Ws'54.B.Pc.Fi.Plg.Cspa.Snc.Cw.Wt.Rv.Ac. | ☎ (215) CH2-4711
GeoW'59.GeoW'62 . . . . | 203 W Chestnut Hill
  MISS Rachel B . . . . | Av, Philadelphia,
    PA *19118*

Humes MRS (DR) John P (Jean C Schmidlapp)
V'45.Cr'49 . . . . | of ☎ (516)676-2194
  MR Christopher L—at ☎ (561) 697-8256 | 345 Oyster Bay Rd,
1815 S Olive Av, Apt 2, West Palm Beach, FL | Locust Valley, NY
33401 . . . . | 11560
  MR F Cooper—at Frost Mill Rd, Mill Neck, NY | ☎ (212) TR9-8360
11765 . . . . | 960 Fifth Av,
                       | New York, NY
                       | 10021

Humes MR & MRS William O (Frick—Heidi E Bramwell) Au.
  ☎ (303) 670-0501 . . ''Pineridge'' 25614 Independence Trail, Evergreen,
CO 80439

Humm MR & MRS William W (Katherine R | 271 Walnut Lane,
Hempstead) Br'59.Ncd.Roch'58 . . . . | York, PA 17403
  MISS Kendall C . . . . |

Hummeler DR & MRS Klaus (Mary F P Billings) Gm.M.Ox'47.Hamb'48
  ☎ (610) 525-9996 . . 1745 Montgomery Av, Villanova, PA 19085

Hummer MR & MRS Philip W (Lynn Ryan) | ☎ (312) 944-6273
Cho.Rc.Cas.P'53 . . . . | 1430 N Lake Shore
  MISS Elizabeth W—Syr'88 . . . . | Dv, Chicago, IL
                       | 60610

Humphrey MR Brian C . . see S J Hall

Humphrey MRS Downey (Joan F Downey)
  ☎ (617) 329-3525 . . 10 Longwood Dv, Apt 465, Westwood, MA 02090

Humphrey JUNIORS MR Edward D . . see S J Hall

Humphrey MRS Frank J (C Frances Sise) . . . . | ☎ (941) 964-2944
  MISS Susan A . . . . | PO Box 892,
                       | 361 Lee Av,
                       | Boca Grande, FL
                       | 33921

Humphrey MR & MRS G Watts JR (Sally H Schriber) | Box 91, Scaife Rd,
Cysl.Rcsl.Srr. . . . . | Sewickley, PA
  MISS Victoria . . . . | 15143
  MR G Watts 3d . . . . |

Humphrey MR George L . . . . Died at
                              Provincetown, MA Apr 1'96

Humphrey MRS Gilbert W (Louise Ireland) Uncl.Cv.Cly.It.
  ☎ (904) 893-2808 . . Woodfield Springs Plantation, Miccosukee,
FL 32309-9102

Humphrey MR & MRS Joseph J H (Katherine N | ☎ (203) 637-3058
Reed) Mich'62.Y'63.Ford'58.Mich'61.Nu'66 . . . | 9 Dorchester Lane,
  MISS Abigail A . . . . | Riverside, CT 06878
  MR Pieter R . . . . |

Humphrey MRS Marguerite B (Marguerite R | ☎ (216) 423-4596
Burton) V'63.Kt.Cv.Rr.Cly.It. . . . . | 1199 W Hill Dv,
  MISS Mary O . . . . | Gates Mills, OH
                       | 44040

Humphrey MRS Nathan T (Helen S Lea)
  ☎ (215) 646-2315 . . 1 Pastern Lane, Blue Bell, PA 19422

Humphrey MR & MRS Peter B (Cowan—Barbara | ☎ (201) 429-9232
Baker) CtCol'72.UMiami'83.T.P'68.Cl'74 . . . . . | 30 Hillcrest Rd,
  JUNIORS MR Miles B Cowan . . . . | Glen Ridge, NJ
                       | 07028

Humphrey MR Stephen S . . see S J Hall

Humphrey MR William D—Dick'61
  ☎ (314) 825-2044 . . 1561 Autumn Leaf Dv, Ballwin, MO 63021

Humphreys MR & MRS A Stephenson 3d (Jennifer A Johnston)
Denis'90.Denis'90
  ☎ (803) 762-6790 . . 176 Clark Av, Charleston, SC 29412

Humphreys MR & MRS Alan S JR (Patricia Evans) Pitt'56
  ☎ (803) 768-4584 . . 172 Marsh Island Dv, Johns Island, SC 29455

Humphreys MR & MRS Benjamin D (Lisa K Hinds) H'91
  ☎ (216) 932-0340 . . 3101 Coleridge Rd, Cleveland Heights, OH 44118

Humphreys MR Charles E (Alan S JR) . . . . Married at Whiteville, NC
  Ogden MISS Kathryn C . . . . Mch 2'96

Humphreys MR & MRS David A (Lydia K Fox)
  ☎ (209) 951-7014 . . 8049 Thornton Rd, Stockton, CA 95209

Humphreys MR David H
  ☎ (508) 775-4372 . . 41 Mt Vernon Av, PO Box 172, Hyannis Port,
MA 02647

Humphreys MRS David M (Margaret A Cutler)
  ☎ (508) 775-0076 . . 17 Hawthorne Av, PO Box 427, Hyannis Port,
MA 02647

Humphreys DR George H 2d—C.H'25.H'29
  ☎ (802) 464-5520 . . ''Littlebrook'' HCR 63, Box 17, Handle Rd,
West Dover, VT 05356

Humphreys MASTER Ian Taney (gg—J Charles Taney 2d) . . . . . . Born at
                             Greenwich, CT Jly 7'95

Humphreys MISS Inness (Nielsen—Inness Humphreys) Colby'70
  ☎ (860) 927-4217 . . ''Menagerie Manor'' Bull's Bridge Rd, South Kent,
CT 06785

Humphreys DR & MRS Michael H (Sheila C Morrin) | ☎ (510) 654-2835
Sth'63.Pcu.Tcy.H'60.Cwr'66 . . . . | 2914 Forest Av,
  MISS Elizabeth H—Bow'93—at | Berkeley, CA 94705
  ☎ (415) 564-4213 . . 1260 Second Av,
San Francisco, CA 94122

Humphreys MRS Richard F (Mary M Campbell)
  ☎ (617) 923-2196 . . 19 Alden Rd, Watertown, MA 02172

Humphreys MR & MRS Robert F (Solange M C | ☎ (941) 923-3572
Assailly) W&L'61 . . . . | 3752 Prairie Dunes
  MISS Patricia E—at ☎ (757) 425-8650 | Dv, Sarasota, FL
1741 Chase Point Circle, Virginia Beach, VA | 34238
23454 . . . . |

Humphreys MR & MRS William Y 3d (Brooks—Suzanne E White)
Chi.Ncd.Mit'45
  ☎ (561) 231-9224 . . 1825 Cutlass Cove Dv, Vero Beach, FL 32963

Humpstone MRS John H (Maribel Cheney) Sl.
  ☎ (202) 333-9130 . . 3339 Reservoir Rd NW, Washington, DC 20007

Humpstone MR & MRS John H JR (Jane H Armstrong) V'49.Pr.Cda.
  ☎ (516) OR6-5510 . . PO Box 307, 9 Wood Lane, Locust Valley,
NY 11560

Humpstone MR John H 3d . . . . Died at
                             New York, NY Jun 22'96

Hundley MR J Douglas 2d . . see S L Mutart

Hundley MR & MRS James W JR (Virginia C Baird) | ☎ (410) 823-2937
Msq.Why.Mv.Cda.P'40 . . . . | 305 Greenwood Rd,
  MR James W 3d—P'72 . . . . | Baltimore, MD
                       | 21204-3613

Hundley MISS Laura L . . see S L Mutart

Hundt MR & MRS George S (Sheila M Wall) | ☎ (610) 644-9481
Rose'59.Rd.Pa'52 . . . . | ''Braeburn Farm''
  MISS Mary N—Ken'87 . . . . | RD 2, Malvern, PA
  MISS Ashley W . . . . | 19355

Hundt MR & MRS George S JR (Alexandria A Aiello) MtH'82.Geo'86.Nu'93
☎ (212) 593-3770 . . 400 E 52 St, Apt 6J, New York, NY *10022*

Hundt MR & MRS Lester T JR (Frances L Headley)
Ws'67.Va'76.Rd.Sa.Ll.Fw.Cspa.W.Cw.Ncd.Pa'51
☎ (610) 359-9995 . . "Rosereath" 7003 Goshen Rd, Newtown Square,
PA *19073-1120*

Hungerford MR Charles S JR—Cw.Wms'43
☎ (203) 966-2362 . . 153 East Av, New Canaan, CT *06840*

Hungerford MISS Katharine C (Fuessenich—Katharine C Hungerford)
☎ (860) 567-4368 . . 89 Old South Rd, Litchfield, CT *06759*

Hungerford MISS Sally-Byrd (Breeney—Sally-Byrd Hungerford) Bost'78
☎ (860) 567-2233 . . 3 Tapping Reeve Village, Litchfield, CT *06759*

Hunn MR & MRS David T (Florence deM Urban) BufSt'77.Ham'67
☎ (518) 271-7810 . . 115 Brunswick Rd, Troy, NY *12180*

Hunnewell MR & MRS Arnold W (Rosalind R | ☎ (508) 653-8633
Lawrence) Ws'63.Chi.H'50 . . . . | "Indian Farm"
MISS Amory P—Swth'87—at ☎ (617) 241-5278 | 155 Glen St,
43 Chestnut St, Apt 1, Charlestown, MA *02129* . | South Natick, MA
MISS Robin W—Bow'94 . . . . | *01760*
MR Arnold W JR—CtCol'91 . . . . |

Hunnewell MR & MRS Francis O (Elizabeth G | ☎ (617) 237-0278
Milton) Hlns'59.B.Rcn.Cy.Tr.Ds.Chi.Ncd.H'60 . | 863 Washington St,
MISS E B Lee—Mich'94 . . . . | Wellesley, MA
MR Francis O JR—Syr'92 . . . . | *02181*

Hunnewell MR & MRS H Hollis (Edith J Elliott) Chi.Ncd.H'51 . . of
☎ (617) 581-0559 . . "Nettlebed" 174 Willow Rd, Nahant, MA *01908*
☎ (603) 323-8022 . . "Stonewall Farm" Bunker Hill Rd,
South Tamworth, NH *03888*

Hunnewell MR & MRS James F (Eleanor W McClurg)
Cy.Sm.Chi.Csn.Ncd.H'37
☎ (617) 326-0770 . . 401 Sandy Valley Rd, Westwood, MA *02090*

Hunnewell MISS Jane P—Rdc'40
☎ (617) 235-0072 . . 848 Washington St, Wellesley, MA *02181*

Hunnewell MR John C—Col'84 . . of
☎ (516) 725-7797 . . "Haven" Laurel Lane, Sag Harbor, NY *11963*
PO Box 2349, East Hampton, NY *11937*

Hunnewell MR & MRS Ogden McC (Nina LeRoy) Mid'80.Ub.Cy.H.P'74
☎ (617) 277-3063 . . 105 Willard Av, Brookline, MA *02146*

Hunnewell MR Richard F—C.Srb.Chr.Ne.H.'44
☎ (212) 737-7988 . . 131 E 81 St, New York, NY *10028*

Hunnewell MISS Sarah F—Ty'75.Pa'84 ⚓ . . of
☎ (516) 726-4656 . . 99 Halsey Lane, PO Box 75, Water Mill,
NY *11976-0075*
☎ (212) 362-3264 . . 176 W 87 St, New York, NY *10024*

Hunnewell MR Thomas B—H.'40
☎ (617) 536-0204 . . 273 Clarendon St, Boston, MA *02116-1404*

Hunnewell MR & MRS Walter (M Luisa de la | ☎ (617) 235-0422
Borbolla) Cy.Chi.H'39 . . . . | 845 Washington St,
MISS Jane P—H'84—at 21 W 86 St, New York, | Wellesley, MA
NY *10024* . . . . | *02181*

Hunnewell MR & MRS Walter JR (Clarissa H Colburn)
P'83.H'87.Ec.Chi.H'79
☎ (617) 227-8818 . . 13 Chestnut St, Boston, MA *02108*

Hunnewell MR & MRS Willard P (Dorothea E Klemperer) Col'59.H'43 . . of
☎ (617) 235-0151 . . 855 Washington St, Wellesley, MA *02181*
☎ (505) 982-4755 . . 242 Loma Entrada, Santa Fe, NM *87501*

Hunnewell MR & MRS Willard P JR (Catherine M Schmoker)
Smu'87.Cda.LakeF'86
☎ (612) 933-7917 . . 5600 Highwood Dv, Edina, MN *55436*

Hunnicutt CAPT William R—Cvc.USN'38.Pa'48
☎ (717) 349-7416 . . Keystone Mill Farm, PO Box 195,
Willow Hill, PA *17271*

Hunsaker MRS J Peter (Frances B Lowell) Chi.Ncd.
☎ (508) 362-3564 . . "Nushka" 312 Commerce Rd, Barnstable,
MA *02630*

Hunsaker MR & MRS Jerome C III (Marcie Gunnell)
DU'72.Sbc.Au.Sm.My.DU'71
☎ (508) 468-3775 . . 16 Larch Row, Wenham, MA *01984*

Hunsicker MRS J Quincy 3d (Johnson—Brown— | ☎ (203) 966-7213
Janet B Pierce) . . . . | 30 Prides Crossing,
MR Jeremy P Brown—at ☎ (603) 588-2838 | New Canaan, CT
30 Eaton Av, Bennington, NH *03442* . . . . . . | *06840*

Hunsicker MISS Jackie Strawbridge—Nu'71
☎ (818) 506-0249 . . 3251 Coldwater Canyon Dv, Studio City,
CA *91604*

Hunsiker MR Harold W—Pg.Y'38 . . . . | ☎ (412) 521-7831
MISS Marguerite H B—at ☎ (202) 544-5233 | 5622
5705 Nevada Av NW, Washington, DC | Northumberland St,
20015-2545 . . . . | Pittsburgh, PA
MISS Mary B—at ☎ (703) 525-8690 | *15217*
1810 N Key Blvd, Arlington, VA *22201* . . . . . |

Hunt DR & MRS Andrew D (Lotta H Mayberry) | ☎ (912) 638-3160
Hav'37.Cr'41 . . . . | 201 Hermitage Way,
MISS (DR) Judith P—MichSt'81.MichSt'85—at | St Simons Island,
☎ (508) 388-4993 . . 45 Whitehall Rd, | GA *31522*
Amesbury, MA *01913* . . . . |

Hunt CDR & MRS C Lansdowne (Ethel A Klima) | ☎ (703) 503-3110
ClevSt'65.Cvc.USN'69 . . . . | 9101 MacMahon
MISS Jennifer R—Ind'93 . . . . | Dv, Burke, VA
MR Elliott L . . . . | *22015-1621*

Hunt MR & MRS David P (F Randall Chanler) | of ☎ (202)333-4035
Wheat'63.Mt.Cvc.Colby'63 . . . . | 3503 Fulton St NW,
MISS Elizabeth W—at ☎ (202) 686-1447 | Washington, DC
5012 Cathedral Av NW, Washington, DC *20016* | *20007*
MISS Frances R—at ☎ (202) 363-2182 | ☎ (410) 745-5248
4821—48 St NW, Washington, DC *20016* . . . . | Lowes Point Farm,
MISS Lucy St J . . . . | Sherwood, MD
| *21665*

Hunt MRS E Norton (Catharine E Montgomery) Ac.Cda.
☎ (610) 687-8551 . . 505 E Lancaster Av, Apt 301, St Davids, PA *19087*

Hunt VERY REV DR & MRS Ernest E 3d (Elsie Beard)
Tex'59.Mo'72.Unn.Csn.Stan'56.Stan'65.P'80
☎ (011-33-1) 47-23-67-26 . . "The Deanery" 23 av George 5th,
75008 Paris, France

Hunt MR Ernest E 4th—Un.Stan'81.H'85
☎ (212) 371-0520 . . 200 E 66 St, Apt 1502D, New York, NY *10021*

Hunt MR & MRS Frederick T Drum (Eleanor Conly)
Mt.Cc.Ll.Cda.Dc.GeoW'35
☎ (301) 229-8868 . . 5309 Carvel Rd, Westmoreland Hills, Bethesda,
MD *20816*

Hunt MRS George P (Anita C Eller) C.An . . .of
☎ (561) 546-4790 . . PO Box 1202, Hobe Sound, FL *33475*
☎ (207) 667-6169 . . Newbury Neck Rd, Surry, ME *04684*

Hunt MR Henry G—Y'29.Y'32
  ☎ (203) 483-3765 . . 88 Notch Hill Rd, North Branford, CT *06421*

Hunt CDR (RET) & MRS J Conway (Hunt—Margaret
Lansdowne) USN.Cvc.Ll.Sar.Rv.Se'41 . . . .
  MISS Julia H . . . .
| of ☎ (301)229-1535
| 5225 Westpath Way,
| Bethesda, MD
| *20816-2260*
| 4600 Duke St, Apt
| 815, Alexandria, VA
| *22304*

Hunt MR & MRS R Peter (Barbara K Borland)
Rcch.Cas.Y'58.Y'65 . . . .
  MISS Miranda B—SL'90—at ☎ (212) 721-3211
106 W 86 St, Apt 14G, New York, NY *10024* . .
| ☎ (804) 693-5337
| PO Box 100,
| Freewelcome Lane,
| Dutton, VA *23050*

Hunt MR & MRS Torrence M (Joan Kilner) Pg.Fcg.Rr.Wms'44 . of
  ☎ (412) 682-3449 . . 5050 Amberson Place, Pittsburgh, PA *15232-1404*
  ☎ (412) 238-9664 . . "Sporting Hill" Old Forbes Rd, Box 27,
Laughlintown, PA *15655*

Hunt MR & MRS Torrence M JR (Mary Caroline
Baker) Alleg'70.Fcg.Rr.Pg.NCar'70 . . . .
  MISS Cathryn J . . . .
  JUNIORS MISS Caroline H . . . .
| ☎ (412) 681-9346
| 5220 Pembroke
| Place, Pittsburgh,
| PA *15232*

Hunt MR & MRS William H G (Mary A H Scheetz) .
  MR William H G JR . . . .
  JUNIORS MR Thomas H . . . .
| ☎ (703) 771-1967
| "Morrisworth"
| 21000 Gulick Mill
| Rd, Leesburg, VA
| *20175*

Hunt MR William O JR—Cho.Rcch.Sc.Cas.Y'61
  ⚓
  MISS Hilary B . . . .
  MISS Fiona McC . . . .
  MR Ian C . . . .
  MR Christopher . . . .
| PO Box 7951,
| Aspen, CO *81612*

Hunter MR Andrew A—Hb.H'51
  ☎ (904) 649-5454 . . 143 Bayou Dv, HCR 1, Box 450-88, Satsuma,
FL *32189-9202*

Hunter MR & MRS Andrew McA (Ann E Merritt) Sa.Sg.Pa'58
  ☎ (215) 646-3263 . . 571 Bolton Place, Blue Bell, PA *19422*

Hunter MR & MRS Derek K (Fredericka Haswell) Ariz'58
  ☎ (415) 851-7735 . . 15 Blue Ridge Lane, Woodside, CA *94062*

Hunter MISS Elizabeth S . . see J M Stewart

Hunter MR & MRS Hale van B (Bonnie Hunter)
  ☎ (415) 472-5023 . . 400 Deer Valley Rd, Apt 2E, San Rafael,
CA *94903*

Hunter MR & MRS Harold James JR (Sally Logan)
Cal'56.Vh.Stan'55.Stan'60
  ☎ (818) 792-2432 . . 744 Sierra Madre Blvd, San Marino, CA *91108*

Hunter MRS James G (R Lindley Reed) Pg.Ncd.
  ☎ (412) 683-4880 . . 430 Coventry Rd, Pittsburgh, PA *15213*

Hunter MR & MRS John L (Brett Howes) SCal'81.Vh.Cal'81
  ☎ (818) 287-0387 . . 742 Kerns Av, San Gabriel, CA *91775*

Hunter MR Kent—Pa'53 . . . .
  JUNIORS MSRS Bradford L & Tyler C—at
525 Terrace Oaks Dv, Roswell, GA *30075* . . . . .
| ☎ (970) 595-3989
| PO Box 617,
| Winter Park, CO
| *80482*

Hunter MRS Lawrence M (Louise E Ettelt)
  ☎ (910) 692-3733 . . "Blink Bonnie" Country Club of NC, Box 1528,
Pinehurst, NC *28374*

Hunter MRS Madeline M (Madeline V Mix) . . . . . .
  MISS Alexandra M . . . .
  MR Nicholas S . . . .
  JUNIORS MR Timothy M . . . .
| ☎ (860) 364-5431
| "Woodwinds"
| Oblong Valley Rd,
| Sharon, CT *06069*

Hunter MRS Phelps Stokes (Chandler—
Bermingham—Ginevra F Mitchell) . . . .
  MISS Cynthia F . . . .
| ☎ (415) 851-0854
| 85 Roberta Dv,
| Woodside, CA
| *94062*

Hunter MR & MRS Robert D (Elizabeth I Valsam)
McG'67.Sb.Nh.Chi. . . . .
  JUNIORS MISS Catherine B . . . .
| ☎ (508) 668-6073
| 492 Lincoln Rd,
| Walpole, MA *02081*

Hunter MR & MRS Robert E JR (Smith—Ann Case)
UWash'48.Bhm.Pcu.StJ.Sfg.Y'45 . . of
  ☎ (415) 563-7270 . . 145 Laurel St, Apt 9, San Francisco, CA *94118*
  ☎ (707) 996-4527 . . 15655 Arnold Dv, Sonoma, CA *95476*

Hunter DR & MRS Robert L JR (Rebecca W
Ericsson) MtH'63.Myf.Dar.H'61.Ch'65 . . . .
  MISS Alice S—Ober'94 . . . .
  MR David E—Cr'91 . . . .
| ☎ (770) 939-5157
| 3640 Churchwell
| Court, Tucker, GA
| *30084*

Hunter MR & MRS W Whitney (Michelle F Chapin)
Denis'91.Sg.Me.Denis'88
  ☎ (610) 645-7533 . . 2908 Mapleshade Rd, Ardmore, PA *19003*

Huntington MR & MRS Anthony P (Smith—Ann J
Letchworth) G. . . . .
    MR David O Smith JR . . . .
    MR Andrew L Smith—at 56266 Old Lake
Shore Rd, Lake View, NY *14085* . . . .
| ☎ (011-44-1832)
| 733247
| The Old Rectory,
| Sudborough,
| nr Kettering,
| Northamptonshire
| NN14 3BX, England

Huntington MR & MRS Charles G (Correa—Elizabeth Winchester)
Scripps'41.Cly.Dc.Ncd.Myf.
  ☎ (619) 742-1202 . . PO Box 87, Pauma Valley, CA *92061*

Huntington REV MSGR Christopher—Hb.Hn.H'32.CathU'52
  ☎ (603) 643-1468 . . Kendal at Hanover 253, 80 Lyme Rd, Hanover,
NH *03755*

Huntington MR & MRS (DR) Francis C (Patricia F
Skinner) Sth'62.Cal'63.Rut'85.Cs.H.'53. . . . . . .
  MR David S—P'89.Tufts'95 . . . .
  MR Thomas P—at U of Chicago Business . . . . .
| ☎ (212) 222-0334
| 253 W 101 St,
| New York, NY
| *10025*

Huntington MRS Howard E (de Peyster—Kernick-Cole—
Shirley T Hull) Cly.
  ☎ (805) 969-7221 . . 2442 Shelby St, Box 1259, Summerland, CA *93067*

Huntington MR & MRS Lawrence S (Ballard—
Caroline C A Hankey) C.Ny.Ihy.H'57 . . . .
  MR Alexander F R Ballard . . . .
| ☎ (212) 288-0634
| 12 Henderson Place,
| New York, NY
| *10028*

Huntington MRS Prescott B (Sarah H Powell) . . . . Died at
St James, NY Jun 23'96

Huntington MRS William R (Lovell—Léonie
Pennock) . . . .
  MISS Katherine G Lovell . . . .
| ☎ (802) 649-5366
| Box 199A, RR 2,
| Bragg Hill Rd,
| Norwich, VT *05055*

Hunton MR & MRS Eppa 5th (Mary B Peters)
W&M'70.Rol'70.Va'80 . . . .
  MISS Eleanor B . . . .
  JUNIORS MR Eppa 6th . . . .
| 5904 Three Chopt
| Rd, Richmond, VA
| *23226*

Huntoon MR & MRS Christopher L (Louise H Wright) Ub.Sm.H.'71 . . . .
MISS Rosamond L L . . . .
JUNIORS MISS Anne C H . . . .
☎ (508) 468-3964
175 Main St,
Wenham, MA *01984*

Hupper MR & MRS David R (Marian N Faesy) Ty'90.Ty'90
☎ (508) 443-4828 . . 25 Concord Rd, Sudbury, MA *01776-2328*

Hupper MR Joel H—Bow'54
☎ (203) 762-8236 . . 25 Millstone Rd, Wilton, CT *06897*

Hupper MR & MRS John R (Joyce S McCoy) Un.Cs.Bow'49.H'52 . . . .
MISS Gail J—Wms'79.Cl'85 . . . .
☎ (212) RE7-8858
105 E 67 St,
New York, NY
10021

Hupper MRS Roscoe H (Dorothy W Healy) Cly.Csn. . . . .
MR Roger W—Bow'50.Cl'54—at
☎ (813) 831-1056 . . 3501 Bayshore Blvd,
Tampa, FL *33629* . . . .
☎ (207) 372-6365
"Spruce Coves"
Box 604,
Tenants Harbor, ME
04860

Huppman MISS Elizabeth R H . . see MRS K B Marty
Huppman MR George H . . see MRS K B Marty
Huppman MASTER Hugh Houghton Wolfe (L Reed) . . . . Born at Baltimore, MD Feb 15'96
Huppman MR & MRS L Reed (Susan T Wolfe) P'83.Bost'73.JHop'80
16120 Dark Hollow Rd, Upperco, MD *21155*

Hurd MR Benjamin N . . see D L Hertz JR
Hurd MR & MRS Bruce W (Lucille E Reich) Vt'84.Rcn.Vt'84
25 Five Mile River Rd, Darien, CT *06820*

Hurd MRS Christopher W (St John—Sammis—Joy I C Dickerman) . . Died at Cambridge, MA Mch 19'96

Hurd MR & MRS David P (Ann Hamilton Whitman)
☎ (011-56-2) 228-4597 . . Alcántara 669, Las Condes, Santiago, Chile

Hurd MR Edward A JR—Rc.Cw.
☎ (312) 337-6770 . . 1325 N State St, Chicago, IL *60610*

Hurd MRS Eliot P (Janet Heymann) Ayc.
☎ (410) 366-3166 . . Winthrop House 802, 4100 N Charles St, Baltimore, MD *21218*

Hurd MRS Frederick (Berresford—Katherine V Marsters) Cs.Ncd.
☎ (212) 838-5757 . . 200 E 66 St, New York, NY *10021*

Hurd JUDGE & MRS George N JR (Elizabeth B Cunningham) Tv.D.H'42.Bost'49 . . . .
MISS Nancy N—Box 52, Breckenridge, CO *80424*
MISS Elizabeth B—at 2957 E 17 St, Tucson, AZ *85716* . . . .
☎ (617) 698-2849
189 Canton Av,
Milton, MA *02186*

Hurd MR & MRS H Ward (Cox—Elizabeth Hertz) . .
MISS Claire L . . . .
MR Holcombe W JR . . . .
787 Jackson Valley
Rd, Oxford, NJ
07863

Hurd MR & MRS James Douglas (Nancy E Schwartz) Rcn.Mt.Cvc.Sl.Y'43 . . . .
MISS Madeleine M—at ☎ (301) 608-3481
607 Maplewood Av, Takoma Park, MD *20912* .
MR James Daniel—at 158 Laidley St,
San Francisco, CA *94131* . . . .
MR Christopher M . . . .
☎ (202) 337-8844
1612—28 St NW,
Washington, DC
20007

Hurd MR John—Wms'31
☎ (401) 683-0545 . . 54 Pheasant Dv, Portsmouth, RI *02871*

Hurley MR & MRS Geoffrey K (Collins—Anne M Faulconer) V'70.Ox'73.Un.Ri.Ln.Pr.Ct.Mt.Cly.Ncd.Hav'70.Van'73
☎ (212) 772-6940 . . 1 East End Av, Apt 13C, New York, NY *10021*

Hurley MR & MRS John D (Constance F Barrow) Ford'73.Pars'71 . . . .
MISS Elizabeth . . . .
JUNIORS MR Dennis . . . .
☎ (516) 673-6987
41 Dunlop Rd,
Huntington, NY
11743

Hurley MR & MRS John L (Maryann Haberl) Cy.Bf.G.Geo'48.Geo'51 . . . .
MISS Anne B—at 1301 N Court House Rd,
Arlington, VA *22201* . . . .
MISS Barbara B—at 31 Branch St, Boston, MA *02108* . . . .
MR Kevin B—at 130 E 94 St, New York, NY *10128* . . . .
of ☎ (716)886-5828
800 W Ferry St,
Buffalo, NY *14222*
2195 Ibis Isle Rd,
Palm Beach, FL
33480

Hurley MR & MRS Stephen Nash (Phyliss P Meaders) Hlns'79.Cy.Hn.Aht'66.H'72 . . . .
MISS Kimberly T—at 50 Hancock St, Boston, MA *02114* . . . .
MR Stephen Nash JR—Aht'96 . . . .
of ☎ (617)742-1688
52 River St, Boston,
MA *02108*
☎ (508) 645-2570
"Quitsa Mooring"
135 South Rd,
RFD 29, Chilmark,
MA *02535*

Hurlimann MISS Susan A (late Conrad G) . . . . Married at Greenwich, CT
Herz MR J Peter (late Herbert) . . . . May 4'96

Hurst MASTER Conley Karlovic (Howard C) . . . . Born at Little Rock, AR Jun 14'95

Hurst MR & MRS Howard C (Stacy L Johnson) Ark'84.Ark'80
☎ (501) 663-2791 . . 4608 Club Rd, Little Rock, AR *72207*

Hurst MR & MRS John E 4th (Letitia F Trimper) P'54 . . . .
MR Byron W . . . .
☎ (407) 839-0650
1401 Country Lane,
Orlando, FL *32804*

Hurt MISS Dorothy M—Tex'80
3½ E Wall St, Apt 2, Norwalk, CT *06851*

Hurt MR & MRS Robert H (Virginia C Armat) V'70.Merc'65.GeoW'77
☎ (202) 966-7223 . . 4811 Butterworth Place NW, Washington, DC *20016*

Hurt MR & MRS William R (Dana D Cumby) Houst'84.Va'76.Houst'86
☎ (713) 520-1666 . . 3314 Sackett St, Houston, TX *77098*

Husband MRS Margaret B (van Saun—Margaret H Bates) . . . .
MR Timothy B—at ☎ (212) 362-9248
323 W 83 St, New York, NY *10024* . . . .
☎ (941) 463-9633
5920 Estero Blvd,
Ft Myers Beach, FL
33931

Huser MR & MRS Thomas E (Clara J Pinkley) H'49
☎ (561) 848-3006 . . 528 Driftwood Rd, North Palm Beach, FL *33408*

Hussey JUNIORS MISS Alicia P . . see MISS M L Cabeen
Hussey MISS Alison E—Mass'96 . . see MISS M L Cabeen

Hustead MR & MRS Walter Bugh 3d (Mary P S McCormick) SFr'72 . . . .
MR Walter Bugh 4th . . . .
of 11019 N 75 St,
Scottsdale, AZ
85260
☎ (520) 527-3981
2665 Valley View
Dv, 10122,
Flagstaff, AZ *86001*

Husted MR James W JR—Y'55
☎ (561) 844-1973 . . 1510 N Lake Way, Palm Beach, FL *33480*

Husted MR & MRS John G W (Keeling—Elizabeth Hanbury-Williams) B.Nyc.Plg.Y'49 . . . .
   MR Patrick J Keeling—at
   27 Pembridge Square, London W2 4DS, England . . . .
☎ (508) 228-5511
2 Wannacomet Rd,
PO Box 896,
Nantucket, MA
02554

Husted MR & MRS John S (Elizabeth G Minich) Fla'80
☎ (617) 326-2876 . . 128 High Rock St, Westwood, MA 02090

Husted MR William A—Hob'59
☎ (914) 234-3981 . . 46 Greenwich Rd, Bedford, NY 10506

Husting MR & MRS Eugene E (Cooke—Betty Chapin) Pr.Nw'31
☎ (516) 676-6399 . . Frost Pond Rd, Locust Valley, NY 11560

Husting MR & MRS James C (Caroline Larsen) Kent'77.CalPoly'83
PO Box 1005, Woodbridge, CA 95258

Huston MR Andrew R—Hn.Hb.H'73
☎ (908) 832-6985 . . 37 Anthony Rd, Glen Gardner, NJ 08826

Huston MR & MRS Aubrey JR (Katharine W Myers) P'44
☎ (609) 924-1030 . . 8 Deer Run, Princeton, NJ 08540

Huston MR & MRS Harland W (Helen E Hoague) Wis'95.Mit'47.H'49
☎ (414) 367-6453 . . 31453 W Hill Rd, Hartland, WI 53029

Huston MR & MRS John J JR (Harriet B Staub) Occ'79.Yn.Y'76.H'79
2868 Main St, Lawrenceville, NJ 08648

Huston MR Morrison C—P'41
☎ (610) 458-8678 . . 909 Fellowship Rd, Chester Springs, PA 19425

Huston MR & MRS Morrison C JR (Elizabeth C Hillman) Pa'85.Me.Rc.Pe.Myf.Dc.Pa'68 . . . . . .
   MR M Coates 3d—Hob'94—at New York, NY .
   MR Churchill H—Nu'94—at Atlanta, GA . . . . . .
☎ (610) 649-3605
201 Cheswold Lane,
Haverford, PA
19041

Huston MRS P Havemeyer (Eldredge—Priscilla Havemeyer) Cly. . . . .
   MISS Priscilla H—at Camphill Village, Kimberton, PA 19442 . . . .
☎ (610) 688-6229
30 Sugar Knoll Dv,
Devon, PA 19333

Hutcheson MR & MRS Neale C (Millard—Anne G McChord) Trans'72.Rv.Sar.StA.San.Cda.Ncd.Duke'78
☎ (203) 966-0548 . . 379 South Av, New Canaan, CT 06840

Hutchings MR & MRS C H Ford (Elizabeth Preston) Cly . . .of
☎ (212) 751-9448 . . 150 E 61 St, New York, NY 10021
☎ (441) 293-0835 . . ''Roughill'' 6 Long Lane, Tucker's Town HS 02, Bermuda

Hutchings MR & MRS George F (Sandra C Peters) Minn'73.Duke'81.Pa'90
☎ (441) 232-0255 . . ''Egg's Nest'' 18 Turk's Heads Lane, Devonshire DV 07, Bermuda

Hutchings MR & MRS Nathaniel W (Walthew—Sarah E Willim) . . . .
   MISS Carroll P W—at ☎ (441) 238-8834 Southampton, Bermuda . . . .
☎ (441) 236-0602
''Llangollen''
38 Middle Rd,
Paget PG 03,
Bermuda

Hutchings MR & MRS Robert E (Christine H Hagen) S.Evg.UMiami'53 . . . .
   MISS Christine R—S.
   MR William H—Ore'90 . . . .
of ☎ (561)626-5057
500 Ocean Dv,
Juno Beach, FL
33408
☎ (516) OR6-1503
''Fox Brae''
Box 305,
Locust Valley, NY
11560

Hutchins MRS Chauncey Keep (Polly G Wardwell) On.Sr.Cas.Fy.Ofp.
☎ (847) 234-2374 . . 299 E Onwentsia Rd, Lake Forest, IL 60045

Hutchins MR & MRS John S (Anne S Bigham) KHam'tn'78.Ck.Ham'75
☎ (011-31-1751) 77078 . . Lange Kerkdam 5, 2242 BN Wassenaar, The Netherlands

Hutchins MR & MRS Waldo 3d (Devendorf—Carol P Fennelly) Ck.Myf.Y'51.Cl'57 . . . .
   MISS Anne R—Y'84.Va'88—at
☎ (212) 475-8056 . . 24 E 20 St, Apt 5, New York, NY 10003 . . . .
of ☎ (516)626-0880
3 Chapel Gate Lane,
Glen Head, NY
11545
☎ (212) 860-3824
141 E 88 St,
New York, NY
10128

Hutchinson MRS Anne (Noble—Anne Hutchinson) Ec. . . . .
   MR Robert W Noble . . . .
☎ (508) 526-1146
''Blynman House''
700 Summer St,
Manchester, MA
01944

Hutchinson MRS Charles B (Pauline Forbes)
☎ (610) 431-3689 . . 214 W Union St, West Chester, PA 19382

Hutchinson MR Charles B—P'43
☎ (609) 723-5931 . . ''Dublin'' Highland Rd, Jobstown, NJ 08041

Hutchinson MR Daniel L (late Mahlon JR) . . . Married at Bryn Mawr, PA Beach MRS K Taylor (Katherine Taylor) . . . . Feb 17'96

Hutchinson MR & MRS Daniel L (Beach—Katherine Taylor) Me.H.'59
☎ (610) 649-0307 . . 119 E Montgomery Av, Apt 2, Ardmore, PA 19003

Hutchinson MR & MRS (DR) Daniel L JR (Olivia H Zanft) H.'89.Cl'93.Me.H.'89
☎ (212) 535-2905 . . 401 E 74 St, Apt 20F, New York, NY 10021

Hutchinson MISS Eleanor Stiles (James H) . . . . Born at Englewood, NJ Apr 13'95

Hutchinson MISS Emily B—Wh'lck'76.BostSt'81
☎ (617) 335-5108 . . 158 Pleasant St, South Weymouth, MA 02190-2541

Hutchinson DR & MRS George F JR (Mary A W Meirs) Carl'58.Laf'53 . . . .
   MR Richard W—PugetS'92—at Tex A & M Vet Med . . . .
☎ (609) 924-3895
174 Springdale Rd,
Princeton, NJ 08540

Hutchinson MR & MRS George F 3d (Julia S Dittmer) Guil'85.Guil'86.Emory'89
1228 Lochshyre Court, Lawrenceville, GA 30243

Hutchinson MR & MRS James H (Tamara J Williams) Tul'88
☎ (201) 728-0295 . . 9 St Charles Av, Hewitt, NJ 07421

Hutchinson MR Mahlon 3d—Me . . .see MRS E Samuel

Hutchinson MR & MRS Pemberton (Elizabeth P Townsend) Ph.Sg.Rb.Va'54
☎ (215) 233-5178 . . 614 E Gravers Lane, Wyndmoor, PA 19038

Hutchinson MR & MRS Peter (Laura M McGraw) Ec.Colby'62 . . . .
   MISS Barbara T . . . .
   MISS Laura L . . . .
☎ (508) 263-9319
30 Simon Willard
Rd, Acton, MA
01720

Hutchinson MR & MRS William N L JR (Kathleen M Graham) Cal'64.Pcu.Sfg.Fr.Stan'46 . . . .
   MISS Isabella E . . . .
   MR William N L 3d . . . .
☎ (415) 441-1065
1000 Green St,
San Francisco, CA
94133

Hutchinson MASTER William Spencer (Daniel L JR) . . . . Born at New York, NY Apr 28'96

Hutner MR Nathaniel C—Plg.Ne.H'72 .. of
☎ (718) 403-0078 .. 205 Warren St, Apt 2A, Brooklyn, NY *11201*
☎ (802) 388-6543 .. ''Dragon Farm'' Box 48, East Middlebury,
VT *05740*

Hutter MR & MRS Charles G 3d (Collie S
Langworthy) CarnM'68.Pa'70.Rens'66 .... | ☎ (702) 882-8160
| 4110 County Line
JUNIORS MISS Katherine J | Rd, Carson City, NV
JUNIORS MR Karl G—at U of Pa .... | *89703*

Hutton MRS Caroline DuBois (Caroline D DuBois) | ☎ (203) 226-2587
Myf.Ne.Ncd. .... | 160 N Compo Rd,
MISS Virginia D—Sth'95 .... | Westport, CT *06880*

Hutton MISS Consuelo V (Seherr-Thoss—Consuelo V Hutton) Mds.
Snake Hollow Rd, Pound Ridge, NY *10576*

Hutton MISS Inez C (Coffin—Inez C Hutton)
☎ (508) 228-9295 .. 49 Polpis Rd, PO Box 1288, Nantucket, MA *02554*

Hutton MR & MRS Robert C (Alice A Fay) Rv.Dar.Pa'50
☎ (904) 246-4992 .. 1820 Sevilla Blvd, Apt 204, Atlantic Beach,
FL *32233-5631*

Hutton MR & MRS William E (Joan K Chapin) Ln.Mb.Pr.Plg.Cly.H'30
☎ (516) 676-2211 .. 680 Chicken Valley Rd, Locust Valley, NY *11560*

Hutton MR William E 3d—B.BtP.
☎ (561) 833-3503 .. 350 Cocoanut Row, Palm Beach, FL *33480*

Hutton-Miller MR & MRS William E (Wiklund—Lydia A Iversen) Stan'26
☎ (617) 331-1803 .. 40 Garey St, Weymouth, MA *02188*

Hutz MR & MRS R Eric (Debra J Ufberg) GeoW'87.Leh'85.GeoW'88
☎ (302) 421-9939 .. 1300 Chadwick Rd, Wilmington, DE *19803*

Hutz MR & MRS Rudolf E (Elizabeth M Hall) Sth'60.Pn.P'59.Geo'62
☎ (610) 444-3544 .. ''Hungry Hill'' 401 Chandler Mill Rd,
Kennett Square, PA *19348*

Huxley MRS Charles G (Frederica L Huxley) ...... | ☎ (011-44-181)
MR Josceline G—Brunel'94 .... | 296-0193
MR Hugh G G.......................... | 47 Wimbledon Hill
MR Alexander R G .... | Rd, London SW19
| 7PH, England

Huxley MR Charles G—Ox'65
☎ (011-44-171) 735-5105 .. 82 Claylands Rd, London SW8 1NJ,
England

Huxley MISS Virginia H—Hlns'74.Va'80
☎ (573) 442-6402 .. 128 Lindell Dv, Columbia, MO *65203*

Hyatt COL & MRS John K JR (Campbell—Jennie R Fowlkes)
USMC.Hlns'58.Ny.An.USN'53
☎ (410) 822-7677 .. ''Asagao'' 27168 Anchorage Rd, Easton,
MD *21601-5026*

Hyde MR & MRS Albert F 2d (Mary Anne Wall) .... | ☎ (203) 227-6206
MR Anthony—Colby'65.Bost'71—at | 35 Old Redding Rd,
248 Brookline St, Cambridge, MA *02139* ..... | Weston, CT *06883*

Hyde MR & MRS Alexis L (Helen A Stickel) | ☎ (011-41-22)
Geneva'79 . ..... | 349-61-61
JUNIORS MISS Sandrine L .... | 16F Chemin de
| Bédex, 1226
| Thonex, Switzerland

Hyde MR & MRS Benjamin D (Mildred H Brown) V'42.H'39
☎ (207) 729-6706 .. ''The Highlands'' 26 Elm St, Topsham, ME *04086*

Hyde MR Christopher W—Laf'83.NYLaw'87
☎ (201) 993-9199 .. 18-7A Max Dv, Morristown, NJ *07960*

Hyde MR & MRS Edward K 3d (Ana M L Almansa) Madrid'86.Cal'77
☎ (011-351-89) 413-603 .. Poco Geraldo 8100, Loulé, Algarue, Portugal

Hyde MR & MRS George H (Barbara A Cowan) | of ☎ (561)231-6861
Wms'45 .... | Oceangate 103,
MR George H JR .... | 5000 N A1A,
| Vero Beach, FL
| *32963*
| ☎ (520) 885-9411
| 7190 Onda Circle,
| Tucson, AZ *85715*

Hyde MR & MRS Henry B (Piper—Elizabeth Prokoff) Ri.Camb'36.H'39
☎ (212) PL2-3581 .. 565 Park Av, New York, NY *10021*

Hyde MRS Hugh M (E Condict Freeman) Eh.C.Shcc.
☎ (908) 234-0345 .. ''Spook Farm'' 280 Spook Hollow Rd, Far Hills,
NJ *07931*

Hyde MR & MRS J Hindon (Joan L Iselin) Y'49
☎ (860) 739-5286 .. 11 King Arthur Dv, Apt 1J, Niantic, CT *06357*

Hyde MR & MRS James F C JR (Enid A Griswold) Mt.Cvc.USA'42.Pa'49
☎ (301) 229-8192 .. 5402 Duvall Dv, Bethesda, MD *20816*

Hyde MRS Jennifer B (Jennifer E Ballard) ...... name changed to Ballard

Hyde MISS Jennifer T (Richard E JR) .... Married in Vatulele, Fiji
Sann MR Ronald N (late Murray) .... Mch 25'96

Hyde MR & MRS Laurence W (Elzbieta Wózniacka) MCurieS'79.Cal'67
☎ (916) 583-4043 .. 1024 Bayview Av, Napa, CA *94559*

Hyde MISS Leslie C—Ty'76
☎ (207) 879-0972 .. 90 Clinton St, Portland, ME *04103*

Hyde MRS Louis G V (Cross—Jacqueline D J Jaggi) ..... Died Apr 3'95

Hyde MR Louis G V—Unn.Hn.H'43 | ☎ (011-41-22)
MISS Caroline S—at ☎ (011-41-22) 735-76-28 | 735-20-74
38 rue des Vollandes, 1207 Geneva, Switzerland | 5 Av Th Flournoy,
| 1207 Geneva,
| Switzerland

Hyde MR & MRS Orra C 3d (Sharon C Little) | ☎ (510) 284-1955
Pcu.Fr.Cal'58 .... | 4090 Happy Valley
MISS Emily C—at ☎ (203) 855-0901 | Rd, Lafayette, CA
66 Rowayton Woods Dv, Norwalk, CT *06852* .. | *94549*
MISS Shelley M—at ☎ (415) 346-1950
66 Cervantes Blvd, San Francisco, CA *94123* ..
MR Crosby K—at ☎ (510) 474-4145
1490 Jefferson St, Apt 304, San Francisco, CA
94123 ....
MR Jeffery C—at ☎ (702) 588-0754
PO Box 14367, South Lake Tahoe, CA *96151* ..

Hyde MRS Richard E (Virginia Hudson) Bur.
☎ (415) 851-1541 .. 190 Greer Rd, Woodside, CA *94062*

Hyde MR & MRS Richard E JR (Karen B Krauskopf) | ☎ (415) 435-0813
Bhm.Pcu. .... | 10 Bayview Av,
MR Richard E .... | Belvedere, CA
| *94920*

Hyland MR & MRS Douglas K S (Alice R Merrill) | ☎ (210) 829-0630
Pa'69.Mich'81.A.Pa'71.Del'80 .... | 512 Elizabeth Rd,
MISS Octavia du P B .... | San Antonio, TX
MR Samuel I du P .... | *78209*
JUNIORS MISS Cassandra A .... |

Hyland MR & MRS William B (Janet F Brodhead) Cy.Geo'48
☎ (314) 994-0508 .. 1 Normton Dv, St Louis, MO *63124*

Hyland MR & MRS William S (Jean R Harrison) Me.Wms'62
☎ (610) 527-3890 .. 900 Potts Lane, Bryn Mawr, PA *19010*

Hynson MR Peter D—Elk.
☎ (410) 889-0470 . . 105 Elmhurst Rd, Baltimore, MD *21210*

Hynson MR & MRS Richard (Beck—Eloise R Fullerton) Bost'65.Elk.Mv.Ncd. . . . . | of ☎ (410)435-3555 30 Olmsted Green, Baltimore, MD *21210*
   MISS Elizabeth R F Beck—Ox'93.Ox'95—at London, England . . . .
   MR Robert L Beck—Buda'95—at Budapest, Hungary . . . . | ☎ (908) 899-1679 1053 Ocean Av, Mantoloking, NJ *08738*

Hyson DR & MRS Charles D (Winifred C Prince) Rdc'45.Au.H'43
☎ (301) 656-4582 . . 7407 Honeywell Lane, Bethesda, MD *20814*

I

Iaccaci MRS Paul T (Stevens—Richardson—Hope Norton) Cly.
☎ (805) 969-8155 . . Casa Dorinda 300, 300 Hot Springs Rd, Montecito, CA *93108*

Ide MRS John Jay (Dora B Donner) Sfg.Fr.
☎ (415) 922-1990 . . 1960 Broadway, San Francisco, CA *94109*

Idsal MR & MRS Warren B (Katharine A Armstrong) Leh'67.Cl'78
☎ (214) 522-6035 . . 4519 Westway Av, Dallas, TX *75205*

Iglehart MR & MRS Iredell W (Courtney Garland) V'52.Elk.Au.Mv.Cda.P.'49 . . of
☎ (410) 832-2779 . . 2 Tall Tree Court, Baltimore, MD *21208*
☎ (518) 576-4540 . . St Huberts, NY *12943*

Iglehart DR & MRS Iredell W 3d (Virginia Hollyday) P'80.Cl'82.Au.P'79.JHop'83
☎ (410) 323-8260 . . 7 Longwood Rd, Baltimore, MD *21210*

Iglehart MR & MRS Philip C (Susan Lonsdale) Rcn.B.Gv.Mb.Md.Nyc.Mt. . . . . | ☎ (410) 833-3530 3565 Butler Rd, Glyndon, MD *21071*
   MISS Laura C—at ☎ (617) 254-9169 39 Brooksdale Rd, Brighton, MA *02135* . . . . . .

Iglehart MR Philip L (Philip C) . . . . Married at Glyndon, MD
Ehrhardt MISS Jennifer G (Dyson P) . . . . Sep 7'96

Iglehart MR & MRS Edgar A (Shinkle—Marie Elizabeth Benoist) Pn.P'45 . . of
☎ (812) 426-1951 . . 4021 Fairfax Rd, Evansville, IN *47710*
☎ (502) 436-5397 . . "Isabella" 1040 Snipe Creek Rd, Murray, KY *42071*

Igoe MR & MRS Harold E JR (Ann B Boatwright) Coker'57.NCar'62 . . . . | ☎ (803) 723-0529 21 Legare St, Charleston, SC *29401*
   MR Harold E 3d . . . .

Igoe MR & MRS John R (Louise M Newhouse) StL'68.StL'70 . . . . | ☎ (573) 486-3996 233 W 2 St, Hermann, MO *65041*
   MISS Eleanor K . . . .
   MR John R JR . . . .

Ijams MRS Alexandra B (Alexandra A Bunn) . . . . . | ☎ (212) 427-6460 55 E 87 St, New York, NY *10128*
   MR Maitland T JR—at 129 S Main St, Scranton, PA *18503* . . . .

Ijams MR & MRS Henry W (Virginia C Corpening) Salem'86.Chr.Snc.Roch'85
☎ (203) 629-3389 . . 19 Kent Place, Cos Cob, CT *06807*

Ijams MR & MRS John H 2d (Sarah H Blatchford) Bow'79.Sim'83.Bow'79
☎ (203) 255-2343 . . 122 Pequot Av, Southport, CT *06490*

Ijams MISS Katharine P—Conn'86 . . see E M Crane JR

Ijams MR & MRS Maitland T (Burns—Blandina E Babcock) H'48 . . . . | ☎ (315) 724-4441 2646 Graffenburg Rd, New Hartford, NY *13413*
   MISS Blandina E Burns—at 2312 Apalachee P'kway, Tallahassee, FL *32301*

Ijams MR & MRS Porter (Cabot—Naneen S Cutler) Pr.Hn.H'53
☎ (561) 276-0495 . . 725 Palm Trail, Apt 15, Delray Beach, FL *33483*

Ijams MRS Seton (Nancy Mellen)
☎ (207) 443-4124 . . 55 Bedford St, Bath, ME *04530*

Ijams MR W Seton—Chr.Snc.W'minsterCC'81
☎ (212) BU8-8002 . . 311 E 71 St, New York, NY *10021*

Iler MR & MRS William M (Edith W Devens) Ub.P'51 . . . . | ☎ (508) 922-0010 17 Lake Shore Av, Beverly, MA *01915*
   MISS Edith D—Mid'87—Box 3845, Ketchum, ID *83340* . . . .
   MR W Matthew JR—Mid'88—at U of Vt Law . .
   MR Samuel B—at U of Cal Santa Cruz . . . .
   MR Alexander W—at U of NH . . . .

Iliff MRS Susan G (Susan G Rogers) . . . . | ☎ (619) 793-0478 4123 Sturgeon Court, San Diego, CA *92130*
   JUNIORS MR G Rogers . . . .
   JUNIORS MR Michael S . . . .

Iliff MR & MRS Warren J (Ghislaine de Brouchoven de Bergeyck) H'58
5630 N Delos Circle, Scottsdale, AZ *85253-7507*

Ill MR & MRS Charles L (Florence M Hessenbruch) Ny.Cry.Ac.Br'49 . . . . | ☎ (410) 758-1432 Cedar Brook Farm, 1325 Land's End Rd, Centreville, MD *21617*
   MISS Anna W . . . .

Ill MR & MRS Charles L 3d (Ellen M Manzo) Doug'78.Cry.Leh'76
☎ (203) 978-0710 . . 277 Stamford Av, Stamford, CT *06902*

Ill MISS Jeannette H—Del'77.GeoW'80
☎ (703) 698-8713 . . 2128 Haney Lane, Vienna, VA *22182*

Ill MR & MRS Peter M (Mary H Slingluff) Va'82.P'81
☎ (757) 428-7751 . . 1242 N Bay Shore Dv, Virginia Beach, VA *23451*

Illick MR & MRS Christopher D (S Selden Dunbar) BMr'81.Unn.Ln.Ty'61.Va'64 . . . . | of ☎ (609)924-2999 22 Mountain Av, Princeton, NJ *08540*
   MR Christopher D—Stan'89 . . . . | ☎ (603) 786-9301 Box 483A, RFD 1, Rumney, NH *03266*

Illoway MR & MRS L Stockton (Eleanor Morris) Pa'73.Pa'83.Rd.Rc.Sfh.Rv.H.'65
☎ (610) 935-0203 . . Cricket Hill Farm, RR Box 395, Merlin Rd, Phoenixville, PA *19460-2064*

Illoway MR Lawrence S (Peter S) . . . . Married at Pinedale, WY
Sedke MISS Laila (Sam) . . . . Aug 5'95

Illoway MR & MRS Peter S (Karen S Fosher) Utah'75.Rv.ColSt'64 . . . . | ☎ (307) 635-2973 9607 Carbine Trail, Cheyenne, WY *82009*
   MISS Lucinda K—at Pinedale, WY *82941* . . . . .

Ilyinsky MR & MRS Paul R (Angelica P Kauffmann) B.Qc.BtP.Va'53
☎ (561) 655-5764 . . 270 Algoma Rd, Palm Beach, FL *33480*

Imbert MR Christophe . . see MRS J de Sibour

Imbert MR Marc . . see MRS J de Sibour

Imbs MR & MRS R Christopher (Lisa L Parriott) Smu'86.Rc.SpgH'82
  ☎ (314) 991-0028 . . 4 Pebble Creek Rd, St Louis, MO *63124*

Inch MRS Arlene (Arlene Giesser) . . . . | ☎ (415) 956-7119
  MR Edgar G . . . . | 26 Walton Plaza,
  | 170 Pacific Av,
  | San Francisco, CA
  | *94111*

Inch MR & MRS Robert W (Oliver—Hester—Jennie R Thomas)
  Cal'58 ⚓
  ☎ (415) 593-2340 . . 7 Dickens Court, San Carlos, CA *94070*

Inch MR & MRS Robert W JR (Jane E Stanley) Cal'86.Cal'85
  ☎ (510) 547-1519 . . 165 Indian Rd, Piedmont, CA *94610*

Inches MRS Charles E (Mary N Luscia) Btn.
  ☎ (617) 267-8672 . . 180 Beacon St, Apt 11D, Boston, MA *02116*

Inches MR & MRS Henderson JR (M Joanna Ray) | of ☎ (617)235-5566
  Cy.Cw.Chi.H'46.Bab'51 . . . . | 8 Windsor Rd,
  MISS Alison A . . . . | Wellesley Hills, MA
  | *02181*
  | ☎ (508) 758-2016
  | "The Paddock"
  | 12 Ned's Point Rd,
  | Mattapoisett, MA
  | *02739*

Infante MRS T Gillette (Tatiana Gillette)
  ☎ (352) 472-3354 . . "Tiger's End" PO Box 1725, Newberry, FL *32669*

Ingalls MRS David S JR (Katherine S Stewart) Un.Tv.Cv.It.Kt.
  ☎ (216) 247-5080 . . "Oak Hill Farm" Chagrin Falls, OH *44022*

Ingalls MR John J . . see MRS G K Simonds JR

Ingalls MR & MRS Melville E JR (Barbara M Moore) | ☎ (305) 367-4444
  Rcn.H'55 . . . . | 36 Anchor Dv,
  MR Melville E—H'80—at ☎ (303) 871-8272 | Apt B, Key Largo,
  501 S Race St, Denver, CO *80209* . . . . | FL *33037*
  MR Bradley D—Bab'85—at ☎ (212) 645-0324
  211 W 10 St, Apt 4D, New York, NY *10014* . . .

Ingersoll MRS Archer (Harriet K Archer) . . . . Died at
  Philadelphia, PA Nov 25'95

Ingersoll MRS Charles E (Martin—Vivian Bebout) Ac.Sg.
  ☎ (215) 643-0431 . . 1413 Gypsy Hill Rd, PO Box 7417, Penllyn,
  PA *19422*

Ingersoll MR & MRS Charles J II (Patricia D Brock) | ☎ (215) 247-2829
  Ph.Cw.Pa'69 . . . . | 417 E Gowen Av,
  MR Andrew W—Vt'94 . . . . | Philadelphia, PA
  | *19119-1025*

Ingersoll MR & MRS Henry McK (Cullen—Elizabeth Quinlan)
  Mich'60.Ph.Rb.Me.Ssk.
  ☎ (610) 527-2425 . . 409 Colebrook Lane, Bryn Mawr, PA *19010*

Ingersoll MR & MRS Joseph R (Patricia S Royce) | ☎ (215) 646-6823
  Pc.W.Pa'63.Pa'65 . . . . | Box 841,
  MR J Reed JR—Rol'89—at ☎ (415) 759-5673 | 829 Penllyn Pike,
  2157—48 Av, San Francisco, CA *94116* . . . . . . | Spring House, PA
  MR Richard S . . . . | *19477*

Ingersoll MRS Marie-Louise G (Standish—Currie—
  Marie-Louise B Graham)
  ☎ (610) 688-5851 . . 79 Hunters Lane, Devon, PA *19333*

Ingersoll MR & MRS Paul M (Eleanor S Koehler) Me.Ssk.P.'50
  ☎ (610) 525-4997 . . 638 Morris Av, Bryn Mawr, PA *19010*

Ingersoll MRS Robert S JR (Fox—Marion A Galey) Temp'39.Rc.Fw.
  ☎ (215) 646-1006 . . "Maylling" Box 7097, Penllyn, PA *19422*

Ingham MISS Ames—Pitzer'92
  ☎ (213) 468-9177 . . 314 N Curson Av, Apt 103, Los Angeles,
  CA *90036*

Ingham MR & MRS William P (Ruth A Loker)
  Colby'66.Colby'66.UWash'72
  ☎ (206) 329-4173 . . 3956 E Olive, Seattle, WA *98122*

Inglis MR & MRS Richard (Anne B Edwards)
  FSM'48.Cwr'62.Cwr'71.H'33.H'40
  ☎ (617) 329-3216 . . 10 Longwood Dv, Apt 536, Westwood, MA *02090*

Ingold DR & MRS John Arthur (Sally L Woodruff) Mich'54.Mich'56
  ☎ (810) 642-8511 . . 601 Bennington Dv, Bloomfield Hills, MI *48304*

Ingraham MRS David (Laura H Jennings) | ☎ (603) 643-2233
  B'gton'39.Cr'40 . . . . | Kendal at Hanover,
  MR David JR—Bost'67.Cl'68—at | Apt 1029,
  ☎ (516) 692-6703 . . 428 Harbor Rd, | 80 Lyme Rd,
  Cold Spring Harbor, NY *11724* . . . . | Hanover, NH
  | *03755-1237*

Ingraham MR Frederic B—Bost'66.Ford'69
  ☎ (516) 922-6959 . . 3 Timber Ridge Dv, Laurel Hollow, Oyster Bay,
  NY *11771-4203*

Ingraham MRS Sally Smoot (Sarah M Smoot) | ☎ (516) 692-4822
  Van'70 . . . . | 1654 Moore's Hill
  JUNIORS MISS Sarah J . . . . | Rd, Laurel Hollow,
  JUNIORS MR David S . . . . | Syosset, NY *11791*

Ingram MR & MRS John R (Stephanie C Currey) Van'86.P'84.Van'86
  ☎ (615) 269-0707 . . 311 Jackson Blvd, Nashville, TN *37205*

Ingram MR & MRS Robert W JR (Coburn—Patricia A Nugent)
  Mo'56.Miami'55
  ☎ (919) 467-3345 . . 301 E Maynard Rd, Cary, NC *27511*

Ingram MR & MRS Walter E 3d (J Lee Erickson) | ☎ (360) 671-9776
  Bost'68.Br'66 . . . . | 421 S Clarkwood
  MISS Celise D—Br'94 . . . . | Dv, Bellingham,
  MR Stede W—Br'92 . . . . | WA *98225*

Inkley DR & MRS Scott R (Josephine Newcomer) | ☎ (216) 423-4790
  Cv.Un.Tv.It.Hn.H'43.Cwr'45 . . . . | 13500 County Line
  MISS Sabrina A—Skd'77 . . . . | Rd, Chagrin Falls,
  | OH *44022*

Inman MR & MRS William S (Mimi R Caroe)
  ☎ (803) 642-2899 . . 316C Laurens St SW, Aiken, SC *29801*

Innes MR & MRS Murray JR (Jean I Kennedy) Tcy.Stan'28.Cal'36
  ☎ (415) 324-2962 . . 93 Edwards Lane, Atherton, CA *94027*

Inscoe MR & MRS James T (Elmore B Bartlett) | ☎ (334) 265-7402
  Ala'60.Cda.NCar'62 . . . . | 2048 Allendale Rd,
  MISS Elmore B . . . . | Montgomery, AL
  MISS Allison W . . . . | *36111*
  JUNIORS MR James T . . . .

Into MR & MRS A Norman JR (Jane S Timberman) Y'52
  ☎ (216) 338-3635 . . 14620 Russell Lane, Novelty, OH *44072*

Iodice MR & MRS Scott C (C Blair Price) Va'87.Gv.Mv.Cda.Mid'85
  ☎ (410) 828-7622 . . 3 Laurel Circle, Lutherville, MD *21093*

Ippolito DR & MRS Thomas L (Peabody—Nina H Coogan)
  Nu'32.NYMed'36
  ☎ (203) 834-2273 . . "Coogan's Bluff" 98 Cedar Rd, Wilton, CT *06897*

Ireland MRS Catherine F (Catherine H Friend)
SUNY'79 . . . .
MISS Olivia—at Harvard . . . .
MISS Thalia E . . . .
☎ (609) 683-0229
189 S Harrison St,
Princeton, NJ 08540

Ireland MR & MRS George R (Elisabeth T Williams)
Sth'79.Pa'84.Rcn.Fic.Mich'80 . . of
☎ (303) 329-6510 . . 2025 E Fourth Av, Denver, CO 80206
☎ (970) 476-4254 . . ''The Potato Patch'' 950 Red Sandstone Rd, Vail,
CO 81657

Ireland MRS James D (Cornelia W Allen) Kt.Cv.Cly.Ncd.
☎ (216) 932-4821 . . 2513 Marlboro Rd, Cleveland, OH 44118

Ireland MR & MRS James D 3d (Anne F Hollis)
SL'76.Unn.Un.Tv.Kt.Pr.It.Cly.Dc.Ncd.Cl'72.Cl'75
☎ (216) 321-3244 . . 2711 Sherbrooke Rd, Shaker Heights, OH 44122

Ireland MRS Kate—It.Csn. ⛵
☎ (904) 893-2556 . . Foshalee Plantation, Rte 1, Box 530, Tallahassee,
FL 32312-9745

Ireland MRS R Livingston (Grimes—Louise D Ireland) Un.Cv.Csn.It.
1 Bratenahl Place, Apt 703, Cleveland, OH 44108

Ireland MR & MRS Robert L III (Gray—Anne C
Sweetser) Bhm.B.Ln.Unn.Mt.Lm.Cly.Y'42.Y'47
⛵
MR Robert L JR—HampSydney'89—at
☎ (212) 691-6106 . . 181 Seventh Av, Apt 12C,
New York, NY 10011 . . . .
☎ (912) 226-4600
347E Blackshear
Dv, Thomasville,
GA 31792

Ireland MR & MRS Thomas E (Nancy S Roosevelt)
V'74.Ln.Cly.Y'74 . . . .
JUNIORS MISS Kate M . . . .
☎ (203) 869-6167
45 Patterson Av,
Greenwich, CT
06830

Irey MRS I Grant JR (Todd—Annabelle V Pierson) Ac.Me.
☎ (610) MU8-8559 . . 310 Croton Rd, Strafford, PA 19087

Irish MR Charles F JR—Rc . . of
☎ (212) 570-9641 . . 210 E 68 St, New York, NY 10021
☎ (860) 364-0015 . . Herrick Rd, Sharon, CT 06069

Irish MR & MRS James L (Henchey—Winifred S Ward)
Cl'61.Wes'87.Wms'51
☎ (603) 586-4372 . . ''Bashaba'' Jefferson, NH 03583

Irish MR Thomas Weddell—Yn.Y'55.Cwr'62
☎ (407) 658-9198 . . 788 Eldridge St, Orlando, FL 32803

Irons MR G Chester—Pn.P'81
☎ (407) 876-2418 . . 5300 Isleworth Country Club Dv, Windermere,
FL 34786

Irons MR & MRS Henry C (Patricia Doubleday) Pn.P'51 . . of
☎ (561) 231-2246 . . 914 Seagrape Lane, Vero Beach, FL 32963
PO Box 2702, Vail, CO 81658

Irvin MR & MRS Lawrence L (Charlotte L Rockwood) Wms'85.So'84
133 Argo Av, San Antonio, TX 78209-5153

Irvine MISS Heather H—Skd'90
☎ (518) 587-1711 . . 19 Jaipur Lane, Saratoga Springs, NY 12866

Irvine MR & MRS John O (Harriette H Thaxter) . . . .
MR Roger T—NEng'95 . . . .
of ☎ (561)225-6513
6360 SE Harbor
Circle, Stuart, FL
34996
☎ (612) 429-4645
2503 Manitou
Island, White Bear
Lake, MN 55110

Irvine MR & MRS Kenneth A (Bettina S Brown)
Wis'65.Hn.Mich'63.H'66 . . . .
JUNIORS MR K Andrew JR . . . .
☎ (203) 869-5271
147 Cat Rock Rd,
Cos Cob, CT 06807

Irvine MR William B 3d—Sa.Rv.Cw.Wt.Cl'80
☎ (212) 860-0599 . . 1455 Lexington Av, New York, NY 10128

Irving MR & MRS Alan M M (Carlotta P Hutton)
Hob'67 . . . .
MISS Elizabeth R—at Penn State . . . .
MR Preston M—at New England Coll . . . .
of ☎ (610)687-2406
109 Gail Rd, Devon,
PA 19333
☎ (011-7-3272)
53-28-24
Samal 1, Apt 85,
Almaty, Kazakhstan

Irving MR & MRS Alexander D 2d (Colette D Gay) So.Snc.H'39
☎ (516) 283-1721 . . 320 Little Plains Rd, Southampton, NY 11968-4938

Irving MR & MRS Christopher C (Jeanne E Achorn) Srb.
☎ (561) 286-5240 . . 4363 SE Mulford Lane, Stuart, FL 34997

Irving COL & MRS Frederick F (Alice T G Blue)
Cvc.Myf.Ncd.Dc.USA'51.P'57
☎ (904) 388-5280 . . 4618 Apache Av, Jacksonville, FL 32210

Irving MRS James T (Janet M O'Conor)
☎ (508) 526-1458 . . 5 Peele House Square, Manchester, MA 01944

Irving MR & MRS John E duP (Louise R Russell)
Rcn.H.'42 . . . .
MISS Carol R . . . .
MR Douglas P . . . .
MR David D . . . .
☎ (610) 347-2159
Box 465, Unionville,
PA 19375

Irving MR & MRS Malcolm D W (Roberta R C Marshall) Ny.Plg.Csn.Dc.
☎ (203) 762-3273 . . ''Close Quarters'' 192 Belden Hill Rd, Wilton,
CT 06897

Irving MR & MRS Pierre duP (Katherine E Riess)
Srb.Il.NCar'72 ⛵ . . . .
JUNIORS MISS Elizabeth J . . . .
JUNIORS MISS Katherine F . . . .
☎ (401) 846-4390
223 Carroll Av,
Newport, RI 02840

Irving MR Washington—Srb.Nrr.Snc.UMiami'75
☎ (401) 849-2444 . . ''Drum Cottage'' 96 Glen Farm Rd, Portsmouth,
RI 02871

Irwin MR & MRS Charles D (Dona M Carter)
MmtVa'83.H'84.Un.Pr.Plg.Cly.Nu'82.Nu'84
☎ (212) 860-8743 . . 49 E 96 St, New York, NY 10128

Irwin MAJ & MRS Charles J (Jane R Darlington)
USMC.V'42.S.Ny.Un.An.Plg.StJ.Cly.Cda.Dc.
Ht.Dh.Dar.Smu'42 . . of
☎ (212) 288-4144 . . 139 E 79 St, New York, NY 10021
☎ (516) 922-4194 . . ''Seven Pillars'' 75 Cove Neck Rd, Oyster Bay,
NY 11771

Irwin MRS D King (Long—Barbara Ridder) Eyc.Sm.Pn.
☎ (201) 539-3513 . . Village Rd, Box 158, New Vernon, NJ 07976

Irwin MRS David M (Ehrenclou—Francisca W
Paine) . . . .
MISS Anne E Ehrenclou—see
Dilatory Domiciles . . . .
☎ (518) 963-7120
Rte 1, Box 80,
Essex, NY 12936

Irwin MR & MRS Fred A (Gilmor—Janet B Clarke) | ☎ (516) 757-1332
Rdc'57.SUNY'90.Csh.Wes'51.Nu'57 . . . . | 88 Laurel Hill Rd,
MISS Maria B . . . . | Northport, NY
MR C Russell—Bost'87—at ☎ (212) 861-7109 | *11768*
344 E 65 St, Apt 3C, New York, NY *10021* . . .
  MR Christopher C Gilmor . . . .
  MR Mark C Gilmor . . . .

Irwin MR & MRS Henry M (Cunningham—H Chauncy Lloyd) P'47.Pa'51
  ☎ (617) 251-9863 . . 960 High St, Dedham, MA *02026*

Irwin MR & MRS John N 2d (Reynolds—Reimers—Jane German)
Bhm.Ri.Ln.C.Cvc.Plg.Cly.Csn.P'37.Ox'39
  ☎ (203) 966-9775 . . 848 Weed St, New Canaan, CT *06840*

Irwin MR & MRS John N 3d (Jeanet E Hardigg)
  ☎ (212) 472-2825 . . 988 Fifth Av, New York, NY *10021*

Irwin MR & MRS Robert F 3d (Lucretia G Fleitas) Sg.
  ☎ (215) 242-1194 . . 48 W Willow Grove Av, Philadelphia, PA *19118*

Irwin MRS Robert F 4th (Knight—Gail B Davies) | ☎ (215) 233-5106
Pc.Ac.StA. . . . . | ''Dunover''
JUNIORS MISS Elizabeth W . . . . | 517 Spring Lane,
JUNIORS MISS Sybil F . . . . | Wyndmoor, PA
  | *19038*

Irwin MR Robert F 4th—Sa.Pc.StA.Pa'66
  ☎ (610) 825-6909 . . 6001 Joshua Rd, Ft Washington, PA *19034*

Irwin MR & MRS Robert J A JR (Donna V Henwood) | ☎ (716) 885-7960
St.Cw.G.Dh.Colg'49 ⚓ | 6 St Andrews Walk,
MR Ronald H—Ty'92—at 1 Highstead Flats, | Buffalo, NY *14222*
1 Highstead Rd, 7700 Rondebosch, Cape Town,
South Africa . . . .
MR Derrick M—Colg'93—at 91-97 Fitzroy St,
St Kilda, Victoria 3182, Australia . . . .

Irwin MRS Samuel B (Carter Hammett)
  ☎ (215) CH7-1263 . . 116 W Abington Av, Philadelphia, PA *19118*

Irwin MR & MRS Thomas B (Grant—Worrall—Elizabeth A Cooke) D.P'42
  ☎ (617) 326-5797 . . 26 Wampatuck Rd, Dedham, MA *02026*

Irwin MRS Yukiko (Hollie—Yukiko Irwin) TokyoWmn'46.Ind'55.Ds.Ncd.
  ☎ (212) 628-9158 . . 340 E 74 St, New York, NY *10021-3744*

Isaacs MRS Kenneth L (Helen C Adams) Sm.K.B.Nrr.Srb.Cly.Chi.Cda.Hn.
  ☎ (617) 742-2641 . . 68 Beacon St, Boston, MA *02108*

Iselin MR & MRS Frederick D (Sallie C B Drury) | ☎ (803) 432-1555
MtVern'73.Va'73 . . . . | 102 Greene St,
JUNIORS MR Charles O . . . . | Camden, SC *29020*

Iselin MR & MRS John J (J Lea Barnes) H'56 . . of
  ☎ (212) 989-3598 . . 153 W 12 St, New York, NY *10011*
  ☎ (518) 672-4534 . . Ghent, NY *12075*

Iselin MRS Lewis (Sarah C Curtis) Cly. ⚓ . . of
  ☎ (212) 734-1433 . . 11 E 73 St, New York, NY *10021*
  ☎ (011-33-1) 45-51-91-27 . . 8 Place du Palais Bourbon, 75007 Paris,
France

Iselin MR & MRS Peter (Margaretta S L Duane) Un.Rc.S.Plg.H'43 . . of
  ☎ (212) 288-7623 . . 953 Fifth Av, New York, NY *10021*
  ☎ (516) 922-5593 . . 514 Centre Island Rd, Oyster Bay, NY *11771*

Iselin MR & MRS William D (Charlotte H von Clemm) H'87.H'92.Hn.H'87
49 Kensington Court, Apt 3, London W8 5DB, England

Isham MR & MRS George S (Sally Ann O McPherson)
On.Cho.Sr.Fy.Y'44 . . of
  ☎ (561) 231-1366 . . 250 John's Island Dv, Vero Beach, FL *32963*
  ☎ (847) 234-3145 . . 1070 N Elm Tree Rd, Lake Forest, IL *60045*

Isham MR & MRS Heyward (Sheila B Eaton)
BMr'50.C.Mt.StJ.Y'47.Cl'50 . . of
  ☎ (212) 447-6596 . . 77 Park Av, New York, NY *10016*
  ☎ (516) 537-1222 . . ''Skyfields'' 872 Sagg Main St, Box 418,
Sagaponack, NY *11962-0418*

Isham MR & MRS Ralph H (Kneissl—Annie-Laurie von Auersperg)
Srb.Y'79.H.'83 . . of
  ☎ (212) 427-1426 . . 1215 Fifth Av, New York, NY *10029*
  ☎ (516) 537-7566 . . ''Hilltop'' Noyack Path, Bridgehampton, NY *11932*

Isham MR & MRS Robert T (Bleecker S Burnett) On.Sr.Fy.Y'43
  ☎ (805) 969-3535 . . 335 Hot Springs Rd, Santa Barbara, CA *93108*

Isham MR & MRS Robert T JR (Nancy W Thompson)
ODom'74.On.Rc.Y'76.Mont'82
  ☎ (847) 295-0419 . . 701 Park Place, Lake Bluff, IL *60044*

Isler MR & MRS Justus F (Perkins—Ritter—Margaret Straessley)
  ☎ (505) 856-0664 . . 7224 Laster Av NE, Albuquerque, NM *87109-6066*

Isler MR & MRS Peter Farnham (Jennifer A Fetter) Y'85.Sdy.Y'78
  ☎ (619) 454-7490 . . 6828 Country Club Dv, La Jolla, CA *92037-5605*

Isles MRS Alexandra M (Alexandra Moltke) Cly. . . . | 1133 Park Av,
MR Adam R—Y'91—at Harvard Law . . . . | New York, NY
  | *10128*

Isles MR & MRS Christopher (Elizabeth B Wood)
Hartw'85.Nu'89.T.SUNY'87.Nu'96
  ☎ (914) 238-6803 . . 711 Quaker Rd, Chappaqua, NY *10514*

Israel MR & MRS Thomas C (Barbara Frelinghuysen) | of ☎ (212)249-1377
Wheat'67.Ln.Eyc.Err.Cly.Y.'66 . . . . | 21 E 79 St,
MISS Emily F . . . . | New York, NY
MR Peter C . . . . | *10021*
JUNIORS MISS Wendy V R . . . . | ☎ (914) 232-4271
  | ''Steepway Farm''
  | 296 Mt Holly Rd,
  | Katonah, NY *10536*

Istel MR & MRS Jacques-Andre (Felicia J Lee) Rcn.Pn.P'49 . . of
''Northview'' Felicity, CA *92283*
  ☎ (011-33-1) 47-20-36-87 . . 10 rue Galilee, 75116 Paris, France

Itgen MR & MRS Frank A JR (Bancroft—Ione Allen) | ☎ (610) 525-8315
M.Fw.Penn'38 . . . . | 922 Montgomery
MR F Allen—HampSydney'76 . . . . | Av, Apt C2,
  | Bryn Mawr, PA
  | *19010*

Ittmann MR & MRS Robert W (Sarah J Barlow) . . . . | ☎ (011-44-171)
MISS Sarah McC . . . . | 792-2146
MR Daniel McL . . . . | 28 Ladbroke Square,
JUNIORS MR George W . . . . | London W11 3NB,
  | England

Ittner MR & MRS George D (Margaret G Goddard) | ☎ (203) 655-2372
Yn.Mo'69 . . . . | 71 Stony Brook Rd,
JUNIORS MR Charles D . . . . | Darien, CT *06820*

Ittner MR & MRS H Curtis (Doris W Dahlen) Nd.Bv.Wash'51
  ☎ (314) 432-4149 . . 124 Frontenac Forest, St Louis, MO *63131*

Ittner MR & MRS H Curtis JR (Susan W Shepherd) Duke'82.Nd.Rc.DeP'80
  ☎ (314) 993-8164 . . 14 Narragansett Dv, St Louis, MO *63124*

Ivanoff MR & MRS Ivan V (Thorn T Welden)
  ☎ (212) 427-5226 . . 1172 Park Av, Apt 6D, New York, NY *10128*
Apr 1 . . ☎ (011-44-171) 235-6964 . . 64 Eaton Place,
London SW1X 8AT, England

Ives MR & MRS Joseph S JR (Freer—Enid C Snow) Sl.
☎ (561) 368-2464 . . 2221 Acorn Palm Rd, Boca Raton, FL *33432*
Ives MR & MRS Kenneth A JR (Cornelia C Spencer) B.Chi.H.Y'55
☎ (603) 643-1299 . . "The Bough House" PO Box 5070, Hanover, NH *03755*
Ives MR & MRS Michael M (Nina A Kimberly) Wms'85.Y'80
☎ (203) 966-5641 . . 242 Silvermine Rd, New Canaan, CT *06840*
Ives MR & MRS Philip A (Carol E Cooley) Ty'55 . . . | ☎ (561) 842-4442
JUNIORS MR Alexander C . . . . | 237 Jamaica Lane, Palm Beach, FL *33480-3321*
Ives MR & MRS Timothy J S (Sonia F Votoras) RI'85.NEng'84
see Dilatory Domiciles
Ives MR & MRS Timothy R (Adrienne A Osborne) SL'54.Cc.
☎ (309) 663-1542 . . "Oak Hill" Rte 1, Box 104, Bloomington, IL *61704*
Ivey MR & MRS Ronald J (Cory—Laura P Williams) Wells'64.CalSt'75.DU'66.Va'81
☎ (202) 333-5836 . . 4620 Charleston Terr NW, Washington, DC *20007*
Ivison MRS Nancy K (Morton—Nancy M Kenna) . . | ☎ (203) 966-3019
MISS Catherine C . . . . | 33 Ferris Hill Rd, New Canaan, CT *06840*
MR Douglas T . . . . |
Ix MR & MRS Raymond E JR (Dorothy MacG Mather) Ham'85.Srr.Ph.Pe.Pc.Ac.StJos'86
☎ (215) 233-8029 . . 7807 Ardmore Av, Wyndmoor, PA *19038*

J

Jabaley DR & MRS Michael E (Mary A Galbreath) | ☎ (601) 982-4031
Van'58.Van'57 . . . . | 4709 Calnita Place, Jackson, MS *39211*
MISS Kate G . . . . |
MR John W . . . . |
Jackman MR & MRS George A (Lucinda U Ritter) Mid'86.Tr.Tor'82.Tex'87
☎ (508) 263-3345 . . 14 Minuteman Rd, Acton, MA *01720*
Jacks MISS Elizabeth B—Duke'91.Nw'96 . . see A L Scott
Jacks MR Robert LeRoy JR—Duke'94.Stan'95 . . see A L Scott
Jackson MR Alexander—Rc.Un.Mds.Plg.H'50
☎ (516) 324-2474 . . 62 Mill Hill Lane, East Hampton, NY *11937*
Jackson MR & MRS Charles A (Mary E | ☎ (508) 785-0231
Frothingham) Hn.H.'31 . . . . | 33 Farm St,
MISS Sarah R—at 290 West End Av, New York, | Dover, MA *02030*
NY *10023* . . . . |
MR Charles 3d—at North Pomfret, VT *05053* . . . |
Jackson MR & MRS D Eldredge JR (Mary J Hilliard) H'36 . . of
☎ (401) 751-0566 . . 72 Waterman St, Providence, RI *02906*
☎ (802) 457-1537 . . "High Time" South Woodstock, VT *05071*
Jackson MR & MRS D Eldredge 3d (Katharine K | ☎ (612) 473-6415
Keith) Sim'65.W&L'63 . . . . | 1055 Edgewood Hill
MISS Katharine K K . . . . | Rd, Wayzata, MN
MR D Eldredge 4th . . . . | *55391*
Jackson MRS Douglass G (Day—Melissa W Read)
☎ (334) 262-4291 . . 1443 Midlane Court, Montgomery, AL *36106*

Jackson MRS Edmund B (Willauer—Louise K Russell) Sl.
☎ (011-502) 320-307 . . 3A Avenida Sur, 10, Antigua Guatemala, Guatemala
Jackson MISS Elizabeth B—BMr'33
☎ (508) 785-0139 . . 40 Pegan Lane, Dover, MA *02030*
Jackson MISS Elizabeth L—RISD'90 . . see MRS E S Blue
Jackson MR & MRS F Gardner JR (Pamela G Hardee) | ☎ (617) 326-6039
Sim'85.Cy.Chi.H'65 . . . . | 978 High St,
MR Patrick G—H'91—at Columbia Phys & Surg | Dedham, MA *02026*
MR William C—H'91—at Columbia Law . . . . . . |
Jackson MR Frost B—S.W&L'63
☎ (516) 671-8339 . . "The Maples" Locust Valley, NY *11560*
Jackson MR & MRS Gilder D 3d (Truesdale— | of ☎ (313)886-3956
Suzanne C Havens) Dar.Y'45 . . . . | 600 Rivard Blvd,
MISS Elliot A—Mich'85—at ☎ (773) 334-0970 | Grosse Pointe, MI
5560 N Lakewood Av, Apt 1, Chicago, IL *60640* | *48230*
MR Gilder D 4th—Mich'86 . . . . | ☎ (207) 348-6868
MISS Suzanne C Truesdale—at | "Bronté" Bridge St,
5047 Greene St, Philadelphia, PA *19144* . . . . | Deer Isle, ME *04627*
Jackson MRS Henry B (Mary A Field) Cy.C.Yh.Chi.Hn.
☎ (617) 444-5644 . . 865 Central Av, Apt E404, Needham, MA *02192*
Jackson MR J Hamilton . . of
860 Park Av, New York, NY *10021*
☎ (516) 288-6365 . . 47 Sunswyck Lane, Westhampton Beach, NY *11978*
Jackson MR & MRS J Theodore JR (Angelina Barnes) Sam'66.Va'69
☎ (334) 277-1856 . . 211 Foxhall Rd, Pike Road, AL *36064*
Jackson DR & MRS James H (Susan G Miller) BMr'40.H.'38.H'43
☎ (617) 277-8447 . . 356 Walnut St, Brookline, MA *02146-7562*
Jackson MR & MRS John T (Suzanne H Bartley) | ☎ (561) 863-1634
Rc.Me.Gm.Ph.Evg.Myf.Cr'42 . . . . | 210 Ocean Terr,
MR John T JR—Me.Buck'81.Buck'89—at | Palm Beach, FL
☎ (908) 429-0420 . . 1002 Doolittle Dv, | *33480*
Bridgewater, NJ *08807* . . . . |
Jackson MR & MRS John T 3d (Frazier—Biddle—M | ☎ (520) 299-6766
Latimer Coleman) Ncd.Ky'43 . . . . | 5655 E Paseo De La
MR Stephen C Frazier . . . . | Tirada, Tucson, AZ *85715*
Jackson MRS Katharine E (Patty—Davis— | ☎ (914) 679-6094
Katharine F Evans) BMr'61.Rd. . . . . | "Acorn Hill"
MR William A Patty 4th—at 230 Central Park | PO Box 15,
W, Apt 7K, New York, NY *10024* . . . . | Bearsville, NY
MR Robert E Davis—Gettys'96 . . . . | *12409*
Jackson MR & MRS Lionel S (McAuliffe—Patricia H | ☎ (805) 969-7783
Johnstone) | 175 Olive Mill
MR E Timothy McAuliffe JR—Cr'95 . . . . | Lane, Montecito, CA *93108*
Jackson MRS M Mackenzie (Madeleine G | ☎ (203) 259-6464
Mackenzie) SL'60.Cnt.Ncd. . . . . | 89 Green Acre Lane,
MISS Aubrey A R—at Boston, MA . . . . | Fairfield, CT *06430*
MISS Jessica S N—at Boston U . . . . |
MR G Cameron Mackenzie—Tul'90—at |
☎ (212) 431-8569 . . 10 Hubert St, New York, NY *10013* . . . . |
Jackson MR & MRS M Roy (Gretchen L Schaefer) Pa'59.Pa'61
☎ (610) 647-4337 . . "Lael Farm" 546 Street Rd, West Grove, PA *19390*

Jackson MISS Margaret . . see D A Gottsegen
Jackson MRS Millard H JR (Ella B Sinkler) . . . . . . | ☎ (610) 688-4998
MISS Virginia R (Simpson—Virginia R Jackson) | 185 Steeplechase
at ☎ (803) 795-7678 . . 2151 Coker Av, | Rd, Devon, PA
Charleston, SC 29412 . . . . | 19333
Jackson MR & MRS Orton P (Butcher—Parker—Noël H Smyth)
V'40.Gm.Me.Ph.Ac.Hn.H'29 . . of
☎ (610) 525-0746 . . Beaumont, 66 Middle Rd, Bryn Mawr, PA 19010
☎ (207) 374-5602 . . ''Left Bank'' PO Box 809, Blue Hill, ME 04614
Jackson MR Orton P JR—Bost'74 | ☎ (207) 967-3753
JUNIORS MISSES Sarah T & Anna P—at | ''Sea River Oaks''
22 Scituate Rd, York, ME 03909 . . . . | PO Box 560A,
| Kennebunkport, ME
| 04046
Jackson MRS Patrick T (Helen E Stevens) Cyb . . .of
PO Box 244, Newcastle, ME 04553
☎ (207) 633-3949 . . ''The Farm'' Oak Point, Boothbay Harbor,
ME 04538
Jackson MR & MRS Patrick T JR (Christina C | ☎ (207) 846-5472
Converse) Sth'63.Chi.Bab'61 . . . . | PO Box 642,
MISS Mary E—at ☎ (617) 859-7944 | Brown's Point Rd,
696 Tremont St, Apt 1, Boston, MA 02116 . . . . | Yarmouth, ME
| 04096
Jackson MRS Peter A (Joan D Benkard) Adelphi'51 | ☎ (718) 796-3945
MISS Vivian L—at 303 E 94 St, New York, NY | 4525 Henry Hudson
10128 . . . . | P'kway, Bronx, NY
MISS Jeannie U—at 3900 Greystone Av, Bronx, | 10471
NY 10463 . . . . |
MR Peter A JR . . . . |
Jackson MR & MRS Philip C JR (Barbara E Ritch) Ala'51.Cvc.Mt.Ala'50
☎ (205) 967-0189 . . 3000 N Woodridge Rd, Birmingham, AL 35223
Jackson MR Raymond S JR—Wms'60.H'66
☎ (212) LE3-3417 . . 44 Gramercy Park N, New York, NY 10010
Jackson MR Richard L JR—ColC'90 . . see MRS E S Blue
Jackson MR & MRS Richard M (Martha E Turner) Pr.H'42
☎ (516) HA1-4045 . . 273 Southdown Rd, Huntington, NY 11743
Jackson MR & MRS Richard S (Mary F Mathes) V'40.Aga.Lx.Dth'39
☎ (413) 442-7154 . . 777 West St, Pittsfield, MA 01201
Jan 1 . . ☎ (561) 231-0061 . . 300 Harbour Dv, Apt 308D, Vero Beach,
FL 32963
Jackson MR & MRS Richard S JR (Linda J Wesselman)
Skd'70.Bost'80.Sm.StJ.C.Lx.Y'65
☎ (413) 637-1041 . . ''Lakeside'' Box 1782, Lenox, MA 01240
Jackson MR & MRS Robert H (Hope M Clark) | ☎ (617) 235-6081
Eyc.Cw.Br'48 . . . . | 9 Whiting Rd,
MISS Victoria H—at ☎ (207) 443-8916 | Wellesley Hills, MA
24 Washington St, Bath, ME 04530 . . . . | 02181
Jackson MR & MRS Roy D JR (Glasier—Frances T Hoard)
Tex'37.Tex'39 . . of
☎ (915) 581-1357 . . 916 Thunderbird Dv, El Paso, TX 79912
☎ (915) 986-2498 . . ''Jackson Ranch'' Box 357, Sierra Blanca,
TX 79851

Jackson MR & MRS Timothy (Susan J Olson) | ☎ (617) 326-6558
Cy.H'line'69 | 199 Lowder St,
MISS Sally M . . . . | Dedham, MA 02026
MR Nicholas C . . . . |
MR Samuel B . . . . |
JUNIORS MISS Susannah E . . . . |
Jackson MRS Wayne G (Richmond—Doris Foote)
☎ (202) 338-3675 . . 3324 Reservoir Rd NW, Washington, DC 20007
Jackson MR & MRS William E (Nancy D Roosevelt) | ☎ (212) 879-0113
Ri.C.Plg.Y'41.H'44 | 530 E 87 St,
MISS Marina Q—at 231 W 15 St, New York, NY | New York, NY
10011 . . . . | 10128
Jackson MR & MRS William S JR (Patricia M McLaughlin) H'42
☎ (303) 831-0059 . . 670 Emerson St, Denver, CO 80218
Jacob MR & MRS Leonard JR (Rita Simard) | ☎ (207) 967-4849
Wms'51.Cl'56 | 35 Great Hill Rd,
MR Leonard 3d—at 5320 Fifth Av, Pittsburgh, PA | Kennebunk, ME
15232 . . . . | 04043
MR Peter S . . . . |
Jacob MR & MRS William Le G (Rhonda McComas) Cl'53.RN'45
☎ (011-44-1394) 38-2948 . . Brook House, Cumberland St, Woodbridge,
Suffolk IP12 4AD, England
Jacobi MR & MRS Jan de G (Virginia P Newton) Ripon'77.Bv.Stan'67
☎ (314) 725-0859 . . 86 Aberdeen Place, St Louis, MO 63105
Jacobs MR & MRS Charles Clark JR (Alley—Rosemary Wilson)
Miss'42.Miss'47
☎ (601) 843-5719 . . 514 Robinson Dv, Cleveland, MS 38732
Jacobs MR & MRS Denholm M (Sanne—Margaret B Weed)
V'43.Sb.Cw.Y'45 . . of
☎ (207) 276-5394 . . ''Windfall'' Box 625, Northeast Harbor, ME 04662
☎ (011-33) 90-05-75-57 . . Les Bassals, 84490 St-Saturnin-d'Apt, France
Jacobs DR Francis—P'37.Pa'41
☎ (610) 696-4845 . . 200 E Biddle St, West Chester, PA 19380
Jacobs MR & MRS Francis B 2d (Patricia P Harrison) | ☎ (610) 647-9529
Bost'66.Sa.Ty'65 . . . . | 411 Lantern Lane,
MISS Mary C . . . . | Berwyn, PA 19312
MR Francis 3d—OWes'93—at ☎ (610) 525-3984 |
653 Dayton Rd, Bryn Mawr, PA 19010 . . . . |
MR Harrison P—OWes'95 . . . . |
MR C Stockton—at Trinity . . . . |
Jacobs MR & MRS George M (Jacqueline B Sperow) Salem'87.Srb.
☎ (910) 748-0936 . . PO Box 1133, Winston-Salem, NC 27102-1133
Jacobs MR & MRS James A (Olivia T Pierson)
StJColl'82.TexWmn'89.F&M'78.Tex'81
☎ (415) 381-6456 . . 707 View Point Rd, Mill Valley, CA 94941
Jacobs MR & MRS Peter W (Hill—Alix H Rockwell) | ''Register House''
Pa'63.Roan'68 | 28 Marlborough Rd,
JUNIORS MR Peter A R—at U of Colo Boulder . . | Newtown Square,
MR John J Hill 5th—Syr'90 . . . . | PA 19073
Jacobs MR & MRS Philip M (Eliot H Ammidon) P'85.P'82
☎ (203) 762-8168 . . 14 Pin Oak Lane, Wilton, CT 06897
Jacobs MR Richard S C—Nrr.Srb.GeoW'83
☎ (401) 847-6292 . . ''Rock Pasture'' PO Box 4251,
283 Third Beach Rd, Middletown, RI 02842
Jacobs MR & MRS Ted S (Romney—Janet S Adams) Mannes'48
☎ (212) 362-5702 . . 9 W 82 St, New York, NY 10024

Jacobson MR Edward—Carl'42.H'43.Ariz'46
☎ (602) 252-2511 . . 2201 N Central Av, Phoenix, AZ *85004-1424*
Jacquette MRS B Leech (Barbara F Leech) Cr'61.Adelphi'74.ArizSt'83
☎ (602) 504-9773 . . 731 W Grandview Rd, Phoenix, AZ *85023*
Jaffray MR & MRS James F (Lippincott—Helen H Zabriskie) Y'41
☎ (207) 374-5172 . . PO Box 937, Blue Hill, ME *04614*
Jahncke MRS Cornelia D (Cornelia R Dickerman) V'39
☎ (203) 531-4546 . . 125 W Lyon Farm Dv, Greenwich, CT *06831*

Jahncke MR & MRS Davis Lee JR (Alice Pickslay Pipes) LSU'71.Tul'67.Tul'73 . . . .
JUNIORS MR Davis Lee 3d . . . .
☎ (504) 897-2156
3303 Coliseum St,
New Orleans, LA
70115

Jaicks MR & MRS Wilson A JR (Reidy—Barbara G Tennant) Sr.Cnt. . . . .
MR David A . . . .
MR James T Reidy—at Los Angeles, CA . . . .
☎ (847) 446-5075
2081 Norfork Rd,
Northfield, IL *60093*

Jamali JUNIORS MISS Samar . . see R S Pfeil
James MR Arthur W . . see M Feinstein

James MRS Christy F (Christy L Franchot) Ncd. . . . .
MISS Constance F—Roch'93—at
☎ (503) 653-6626 . . 10500 SE 26 Av,
Milwaukie, OR *97222* . . . .
MISS Martha P. . . . .
MR T Frank 4th. . . . .
☎ (314) 725-8181
1113 Buck Av,
St Louis, MO *63117*

James MR & MRS Daniel (Marshall—Margaret W Fisher) Cal'34.StJ.Ind'27.Ind'29.H'31
☎ (860) 767-1110 . . Riversedge 1, 65 Main St, Ivoryton, CT *06442*
James MR & MRS David F (Robelyn R Schrade) Juilliard'77.Auckld'71.Peab'yCons'73 . . of
☎ (212) 861-7330 . . 505 E 79 St, New York, NY *10021*
☎ (413) 238-5854 . . Sevenars, Ireland St S, Worthington, MA *01098*
James MRS Denis N R (Miles—M Elizabeth Horner)
☎ (201) 569-9021 . . 74 Dana Place, Englewood, NJ *07631*
James MISS Elaine F—Wells'46.G.Myf.
☎ (716) 837-5707 . . 24 Coniston Rd, Buffalo, NY *14226*
James MR & MRS Geoffrey L (Sandra M Holbrook) DU'90.Menlo'87
☎ (415) 331-7696 . . 104 Spencer Av, Sausalito, CA *94965*
James MR & MRS George J (Lisa M Campodonico)
☎ (415) 363-5992 . . 977 Upland Rd, Redwood City, CA *94062*

James MR & MRS Hamilton E (Amabel G Boyce) Ws'74.Ri.Cly.H'73.H'75 . . . .
JUNIORS MISS Meredith E. . . . .
JUNIORS MISS Rebecca L . . . .
of ☎ (212)734-6629
1001 Park Av,
New York, NY
10028
☎ (203) 655-6462
51 Contentment
Island Rd, Darien,
CT *06820*

James MISS Katherine B . . .see M Feinstein
James MR & MRS Leland T (Creel—Marion D von Mayrhauser) Wheat'70.Va'60
☎ (804) 438-5335 . . PO Box 267, Irvington, VA *22480*
James MISS Margaret Alice (Guffey—Margaret Alice James) "Seneschal" RR 2, Box 142, Perryopolis, PA *15473-9109*
James MISS Mary C—Cal'78
☎ (415) 924-6233 . . 63 Olive Av, Larkspur, CA *94939*

James CAPT (RET) & MRS Nathaniel W 3d (Alexandra Austin) CtCol'48.USN'39.H'51 . . . .
MR Robert R . . . .
☎ (207) 863-4313
Box 547,
Vinalhaven, ME
04863

James DR Nathaniel W 4th—Loy'77.Md'83
☎ (207) 767-0724 . . 59 Pitt St, South Portland, ME *04106*
James MR & MRS Oliver B JR (Cassidy—Norma E McNeill) Sdy.Y'45w
☎ (808) 885-6595 . . 68-1399 Mauna Lani Dv, D101, Kamuela, HI *96743-9783*
Mch 1 . . ☎ (619) 454-4519 . . 1504 Buckingham Dv, La Jolla, CA *92037*
James MR & MRS Philip R (Colla—Mai Wood Zara) Cl'51
☎ (212) NA8-7682 . . 200 E 78 St, New York, NY *10021*
James MR R Campbell—K.Nrr.
☎ (401) 848-7663 . . 41 Mill St, Newport, RI *02840*
James MRS Warner Rutherford (McDonald—Katherine I Magner) Cly.
☎ (212) 879-3899 . . 930 Park Av, New York, NY *10028*

James DR & MRS William C (Helen B Anthony) Rdc'55.H'54.GeoW'61 . . . .
MR William C JR—Cal'84.Cal'93—at
☎ (310) 207-3983 . . 11771 Montana Av,
Los Angeles, CA *90049* . . . .
☎ (808) 572-6893
461 Aulii Dv,
Pukalani, Maui, HI
96788

James MR William D—Sg.LakeF'91 . . see R C Wallis

Jameson MR & MRS Colin G (Haight—Nancy Ordway) Sl.Wms'30.H'35 . . . .
MISS Adair—at Townshend, VT *05353*. . . . .
MR Jonathon O Haight—at
4811 Battery Lane, Bethesda, MD *20814* . . . .
MR Daniel L Haight—at 25 Cabrillo Place,
Oakland, CA *94611* . . . .
☎ (305) 294-1589
1501 Olivia St,
Key West, FL *33040*

Jameson MR Edwin C JR—Rcn.BtP.K.S.Srb.Snc.Cw.
☎ (561) 833-1179 . . 1801 S Flagler Dv, West Palm Beach, FL *33401*
Jameson MR Owen—Pcu.Wms'34.H'37 . . of
☎ (415) 346-3222 . . 2500 Steiner St, San Francisco, CA *94115*
☎ (415) 851-7449 . . "Oakleigh" 680 Mountain Home Rd, Woodside, CA *94062*
Janeck MR Mark I . . see J V Farwell 4th
Janeck MR Stephen F . . see J V Farwell 4th

Janes MR & MRS Michael V (Franziska Pawlenka) StL'68 . . . .
MISS Franziska M V . . . .
MR Thomas C V . . . .
JUNIORS MR David M V . . . .
☎ (314) 432-8195
8 Glenview Rd,
St Louis, MO *63124*

Janeway MRS Edward G (Elinor White) Au.Ln.Csn.
☎ (802) 824-6330 . . "Middletown Farm" South Londonderry, VT *05155*
Janin MR & MRS Blaine C (Susan J York) Stan'79.Stan'65 . . of
☎ (415) 931-5921 . . 3020 Scott St, San Francisco, CA *94123*
☎ (707) 865-1244 . . "The Kremlin" 21361 Monte Cristo Av, Monte Rio, CA *95462*
Jannetta DR & MRS Peter J (Davant—Rose—Diana L Risien) Duke'58.Pg.Rr.Pa'53.Pa'57
☎ (412) 682-1708 . . 214 Schenley Rd, Pittsburgh, PA *15217*

Janney MRS Jervis S JR (Macy B Putnam) Bz.Mvh. . | ☎ (513) 461-3977
MISS Allison B—Ken'82—at ☎ (212) 580-5567 | 40 Stonemill Rd,
148 W 76 St, Apt 3B, New York, NY *10023* . . . | Dayton, OH *45409*
MR Henry L—Ty'84—at ☎ (612) 224-5702
1043 Grand Av, Apt 356, St Paul, MN *55105* . .
Janney MR Jervis S JR—Bz.Mvh.P'56.H'60
31 Tecumseh St, Dayton, OH *45402*
Jansing MR Christopher C—Roan'90
☎ (212) 879-4323 . . 310 E 65 St, Apt 4A, New York, NY *10021*
Jansing MR & MRS John C (Flora S Bush) Ck.Ln.Ng.Dth'48
☎ (561) 546-5874 . . 162 S Beach Rd, Hobe Sound, FL *33455*
Janvier MRS Charles 2d (L Joy Bagnell)
☎ (504) 899-9719 . . 902 Nashville Av, New Orleans, LA *70115*
Janvier MR & MRS William P (Ann C Tilson) PineM'90.Rice'89.NCar'92
☎ (919) 783-1876 . . 3617 Dade St, Raleigh, NC *27612*
Janvrin MISS Mary . . see MRS G Wiggins
Jaques MISS Polly
☎ (508) 526-7037 . . 1 Sumac Lane, Manchester, MA *01944*
Jaques MR & MRS Willard K (Gertrude Matthews)
V'36.On.Cnt.Wms'34 . . of
☎ (847) 234-2242 . . 776 N Green Bay Rd, Lake Forest, IL *60045*
☎ (561) 278-6422 . . 1111 N Ocean Blvd, Gulf Stream, FL *33483*
Jaques MR William H B—Lx.H'45
☎ (011-33-1) 45-48-00-28 . . 98 bis rue du Cherche Midi, 75006 Paris, France
Jarratt MR & MRS James H 3d (Roslyn M Potter) | ☎ (011-61-2)
Pratt'70.Flor'71 . . . . | 446836
MISS Katrina J . . . . | 7 Boolarong Rd,
MR Timothy C . . . . | St Ives,
JUNIORS MISS Penelope K . . . . | NSW 2075,
JUNIORS MR Ross A . . . . | Australia
Jarrett MISS E Jean—Pa'56.Sfh.
☎ (610) 688-2358 . . 402 Homestead Rd, Strafford, PA *19087*
Jarrett MR & MRS John D (Morse—Ellenor Colgate Buzby) Gv.Mv.Va'57
☎ (410) 486-2247 . . "The Cottage" 10530 Burnside Farm Rd, Stevenson, MD *21153-9999*
Jarrett MR & MRS John D JR (Dowling—Marion W Forrester) Van'88
☎ (617) 523-3870 . . 112 Pinckney St, Apt 54, Boston, MA *02114*
Jarrett MRS Richard B (Sarah A Skillern) . . . . | ☎ (610) MU8-0198
MISS Sally C—at ☎ (914) 238-3403 | 1148 W Valley Rd,
129 Hamilton Rd, Chappaqua, NY *10514* . . . . . | Wayne, PA *19087*
Jarrott MR Emory L—Cw.Cc.Ht.Rv.StJ.
☎ (912) 238-4842 . . 418 E Charlton St, Savannah, GA *31401*
Jarvis MR & MRS J Andrew (Elizabeth J Farmer) Swb'76.Pc.Pa'74
☎ (215) CH8-9744 . . 129 Bethlehem Pike, Philadelphia, PA *19118*
Jarvis MR & MRS John A (Sarah P Melcher) Swb'49.Ncd.StAndr'48.Pa'53
☎ (717) 394-6671 . . 230 N Charlotte St, Lancaster, PA *17603*
Jarvis MISS Sarah P
☎ (215) 732-9942 . . 2052 Locust St, Philadelphia, PA *19103*
Jay MR & MRS John C (Goodrich—Emily Weller) | ☎ (508) 526-1745
Wms'66 . . . . | 18 Sea St,
MR Hunter G . . . . | Manchester, MA
MR Dennett W Goodrich . . . . | *01944*
MR Ramsey W Goodrich . . . .
Jay MRS Lois G (Lois T Goodnow) Cly.
☎ (413) 458-4053 . . "Windridge" Gale Rd, Williamstown, MA *01267*

Jay MR & MRS Robert D (Cynthia M White) Pars'48.Csh.H.'42
☎ (516) 421-0955 . . 8 Fort Hill Dv, Huntington, NY *11743-9767*
Jeanes MR & MRS Isaac W 2d (Frances W Parham) | ☎ (540) 672-3745
NCar'37 . . . . | Walnut Hills Farm,
MR Isaac W 3d—Dick'69—at 119 Spruce St, | Orange, VA *22960*
Pulaski, VA *24301* . . . .
MR Joseph Y . . . .
Jeanes MR Joseph Y JR . . . . Died at
Hockessin, DE Jan 11'96
Jeanes MR & MRS Marshall M (Scott—Pamela H | of ☎ (908)439-2026
Vandeveer) Ln.Eh.Shcc.Cly.H.'57 . . . . | "Windmill Farm"
MR Henry T . . . . | PO Box 750,
MR Christopher B . . . . | Long Lane,
MISS Wendy V Scott—at ☎ (212) 861-4311 | Far Hills, NJ *07931*
220 E 73 St, New York, NY *10021* . . . . | ☎ (212) 737-1620
MR M Simon Scott . . . . | 156 E 79 St,
MR Andrew F Scott . . . . | New York, NY
| *10021*
Jeanes MRS William W (Helen H Frazer) Ac.
☎ (410) 275-2282 . . "Dividing" 1000 Cherry Grove Rd, Earleville, MD *21919*
Jeanrenaud MR & MRS Pierre M (Rumsey—Patricia | ☎ (011-44-1843)
Binkerd) EAnglia'74 . . . . | 588401
MISS Tessa A S Rumsey—SL'92—at | 46 Ellington Rd,
94 Carl St, San Francisco, CA *94117* . . . . | Ramsgate, Kent
| CT11 9SR, England
Jeffers MRS William N (Lucy L Gordan) Swb'39.Cs.Ncd.
☎ (212) 369-7520 . . 40 E 88 St, New York, NY *10128*
Jefferson MR & MRS Harry D (Gay Lewis) Sth'59.Cal'60
☎ (808) 521-1890 . . 60 N Beretania St, Apt 3503, Honolulu, HI *96817*
Jefferson MR & MRS John A (Wright—Lenore M Voorhees)
Ac.Ncd.Buck'50
☎ (610) 296-0240 . . 433 Margo Lane, Berwyn, PA *19312*
Jefferson MRS Philip L (Jefferson—Read—Katherine R Morrow)
☎ (609) 235-4089 . . The Mews, 10 E Close, Moorestown, NJ *08057*
Jeffery MRS Ann Folliss (Ann V Folliss) Briar'73
☎ (212) 879-4372 . . 903 Park Av, New York, NY *10021*
Jeffery MR Charles R . . see MRS A H Faber
Jeffery MR Patrick G—Bost'87 . . see MRS A H Faber
Jeffery MRS Sarah P (Sarah D Penhallow) | ☎ (203) 926-8497
WmSth'53 . . . . | 109 Country Place,
MR David E 3d—at ☎ (817) 294-5949 | Shelton, CT *06484*
4315 Segura Court N, Ft Worth, TX *76132* . . . .
Jefferys REV William H . . . . Died at
Berlin, VT Mch 1'96
Jefferys MRS William H (Ena V Baur) Rdc'36.Me.
☎ (802) 496-3324 . . "Old Strong Farm" Carey-Strong Rd, Fayston, VT *05660*
Jeffords MRS Walter M (Kathleen McLaughlin) Ph. | ☎ (212) 249-7775
MR George McL . . . . | 4 E 66 St,
MR John D . . . . | New York, NY
| *10021*
Jeffress MRS Gardner N (Janet A Hollands) | ☎ (804) 784-6728
Camb'66 . . . . | 4 Buck Branch Dv,
MR Stanley G—W&M'94 . . . . | Richmond, VA
MR Alan S—at Auburn U . . . . | *23233*

Jeffress MR Gardner N—Rv.
10100B Palace Way, Richmond, VA *23233*

Jeffries DR & MRS (DR) Peter F (Jeanne F Arnold)   ☎ (617) 395-8660
Colby'57.Bost'61.H'56.Bost'60 . . . .   15 Mitchell Av,
  MISS (DR) Jennifer F—MtH'88.Bost'94 . . . .   Medford, MA
  MR John A—Cr'90 . . . .   *02155-1728*
  MR Charles F M—Rens'93 . . . .
  MR Arthur E . . . .

Jeffries MR & MRS Stephen B (Rogina L Haase)
MtH'82.Un.Sm.S.Ny.Ey.Cc.Sar.Rv.Cw.Ofp.Snc.Chi.Cda. Dar.Ch'83 . . of
☎ (617) 742-0494 . . 12 Brimmer St, Boston, MA *02108-1002*
340 E 93 St, New York, NY *10128*

Jelich MR & MRS John M 2d (Anne K Bartlett) WashColl'79.WashColl'79
☎ (410) 820-7643 . . 4425 Roslyn Farm, Trappe, MD *21673-1949*

Jelinek MR & MRS (REV DR) Richard U (Allen—   ☎ (617) 740-9055
Bonnie Scott) LakeF'67.Y'69.ANewton'83 . . . . .   124 South St,
Ncd.Dar.Wheat'69.Bost'71.P'77 . . . .   Hingham, MA
  MISS Jennifer S Allen—Skd'95 . . . .   *02143*

Jellinghaus MRS C Butler (Carol C Green) Cly . . . . .   ☎ (914) 591-9229
  MISS Catherine P . . . .   202 Hermits Rd,
    Irvington, NY *10533*

Jenkins MR & MRS A Diehl (Patricia A Hurlbut)   ☎ (617) 326-8130
Cy.Ey.Chi.Myf.Bost'65 . . . .   31 Wampatuck Rd,
  MISS Patricia D—at 99½ Myrtle St, Boston, MA   Dedham, MA
  02114-4300 . . . .   *02026-4222*
  MR Jonathan P—at Boston U . . . .
  JUNIORS MR David W—at Taft . . . .

Jenkins MRS Alan N (Barbara Hoffstot) Sl.Cda . . . .of
☎ (561) 231-4043 . . ''Melaleuca'' PO Box 1476, Vero Beach,
FL *32961*
☎ (540) 347-1529 . . ''Leeton Hill'' PO Box 191, Warrenton,
VA *20188-0191*

Jenkins MISS Alexandra . . see J W Wastcoat

Jenkins MR & MRS David N JR (Lailey H Roudebush)
ColC'81.Cwr'85.FlaTech'76.MassMarit'79
☎ (216) 286-1028 . . ''Kings Creek Farm'' 10075 Wilder Rd, Chardon,
OH *44024*

Jenkins MRS Farish A (Le Maire—Muriel Gerli)
☎ (561) 626-1803 . . 12125 Lost Tree Way, North Palm Beach,
FL *33408*

Jenkins MR & MRS George P (Marian E O'Brien)   ☎ (201) 744-0025
Ln.Bg.Plg.Dar.P'36.H'38 . . . .   485 Ridgewood Av,
  MR Richard G—David'81—at 200 E 78 St,   Glen Ridge, NJ
  New York, NY *10021* *07028*

Jenkins MRS Guy R (Jane H Guérin) Dar.
☎ (201) 543-4564 . . 13 Yardley Rd, Mendham, NJ *07945*

Jenkins MR & MRS Hyde Rust 2d (Beverly Phillips)   ☎ (601) 446-7842
Miss'74.Sar.Miss'71 . . . .   PO Box 1747,
  JUNIORS MR Lemuel P . . . .   Natchez, MS *39120*
  JUNIORS MR Hyde D . . . .

Jenkins MR Jonathan W . . see J W Wastcoat

Jenkins MISS Lora H—GeoW'75.Cly.Ct.Sl.Cda.
☎ (540) 364-1364 . . ''Willow Run'' PO Box 123, Orlean, VA *20128*

Jenkins MRS Louisa Bradbury (Martinelli—Louisa   ☎ (415) 461-3370
Bradbury Jenkins) Cal'48.SFr'83 . . . .   1005 S Eliseo Dv,
  MR Peter J Martinelli—Cal'86 . . . .   Apt 14, Greenbrae,
  CA *94904*

Jenkins MISS Marion W—Cal'84.Cal'91
☎ (916) 753-0106 . . 1806 Birch Lane, Davis, CA *95616*

Jenkins MR & MRS Richard (Anne Atlee)   ☎ (215) 572-0400
Pc.Rv.W.Sdg.Leh'46 . . . .   612 Bridle Rd,
  MISS (DR) Julia A—H'88.Pa'94.W. . . . .   Glenside, PA
  19038-2004

Jenkins MR & MRS Robert N (Heidi L Gage) Rc.ColC'73.Cl'80
☎ (212) 534-7761 . . 1185 Park Av, New York, NY *10128*

Jenkins MR & MRS T Christopher (Church—Jane   ☎ (540) 347-7973
Tull) NCar'61.Dar.Rol'65 . . . .   PO Box 297,
  MISS Eleanor E—at ☎ (904) 255-2693   Warrenton, VA
  PO Box 2341, Daytona Beach, FL *33115-2341* .   *20188*
  MISS Mary N Church—at 1603 Second Av,
  New York, NY *10028* . . . .
  MISS Susan M Church . . . .

Jenkins MR & MRS Thomas S (Virginia F Worrall) Rm'71
☎ (540) 687-6584 . . ''Hickory Hollow'' PO Box 1325, Middleburg,
VA *20118*

Jenkins MR William P JR . . see J W Wastcoat

Jenks MRS Ann K (Ann S Kelly) Cal'58 . . . .   ☎ (510) 254-7210
  MISSES Kathrine & Megan K . . . .   215 Village Gate,
  MSRS Livingston 3d & Douglas K . . . .   Orinda, CA *94563*

Jenks MR Anthony W—OWes'85
☎ (610) 388-2058 . . ''Chaddwynn Farm'' 1753 Brinton's Bridge Rd,
Chadds Ford, PA *19317*

Jenks MAJ & MRS John P (Kathryn M Bricker) USA.Radford'83.Radford'83
30 Sutton Place, New York, NY *10022*

Jenks DR & MRS John S (Elizabeth C Harrigan)
Char'ton'79.Pc.Ph.Nf.Ncd.Rol'70
☎ (804) 295-1948 . . 1 Boar's Head Place, Charlottesville, VA *22903*

Jenks MRS M Mathews (Thompson—Margaret D Mathews) Ac.Ncd.
''Quail Hollow'' 7 Sunningdale Dv, St Louis, MO *63124*

Jenks MR & MRS T Story JR (Claudia L Elliman)
Hampshire'79.Sap.Ph.Pa'83
☎ (802) 897-5155 . . ''Tottingham Farm'' RR 1, Box 215A, Shoreham,
VT *05770*

Jenne MR & MRS Arthur K (Linda L Morris)   2110 Hughes Shop
Towson'70.WestMd'73 . . . .   Rd, Westminster,
  MISS Karen L—WestMd'95 . . . .   MD *21158-2823*
  MR Arthur K 2d—at Western Md . . . .

Jenne MR & MRS Kirk Q (Margaret Keats)   612 Heather Lane,
Pa'67.Pa'71 . . . .   Lancaster, PA
  JUNIORS MR Thomas L *17603-2333*

Jenness MRS Francis W (Beal—Cecily D Livermore) . . . . Died at
Falmouth, ME May 18'96

Jenness MR Francis W—H'33 . . . .   ☎ (207) 781-2777
  MISS Anne L—at 20 Charlesgate W, Apt 209,   164 Foreside Rd,
  Boston, MA *02215* . . . .   Cumberland
  Foreside, ME *04110*

Jenney MR C Powers—Y'80 . . see MRS J Atterbury-Jenney

Jenney MRS Joan B (Joan Burnett) Cy.Chi.
☎ (617) 277-5013 . . 77 Fairway Rd, Chestnut Hill, MA *02167*

Jenney MR & MRS John L K (Wise—Mary C Mellon) Wil.Cw.Ncd.Pn.P'25
☎ (302) 652-4679 . . PO Box 123, Montchanin, DE *19710*

Jenney MR John L K JR—Pe.Ssk.Sap.Wil.Pa'65.Pa'67
☎ (302) 652-1149 . . ''Walls'' PO Box 306, Rockland,
DE *19732-0306*

Jenney MISS Lucinda K (Swanger—Lucinda K Jenney)
see MRS J Atterbury-Jenney
Jenney MR & MRS Marshall W (Scott—Bettina Lindsay) Srr.Wil.P'63
☎ (610) 869-8686 . . Derry Meeting Farm, Box 150, Cochranville,
PA *19330*
Jenney MR & MRS Meredith T (Dougherty—Meredith | ☎ (561) 655-1811
Townsend) Ac.Wil. . . . . | 220 Clarke Av,
  MISS Caroline K . . . . | Palm Beach, FL
  MR John L K 3d . . . . | *33480*
  JUNIORS MR Marshall T . . . . |
    MISS Ann S Dougherty. . . . . |
Jennings MRS A Gould (Grace V N Swackhamer). . of
☎ (212) 289-8185 . . 108 E 91 St, New York, NY *10128*
☎ (203) 655-4879 . . ''The Cottage'' Box 3034, Noroton, CT *06820*
Jennings MR & MRS Christopher R (Cordelia A | ☎ (717) 566-5560
Willis) WashColl'76.Rut'79.Ste.Myf.Pa'65. | 1051 Knoll Dv,
Pa'67.H'93. . . . . | Hummelstown, PA
  MISS Elise B—Denis'95—at ☎ (617) 536-2714 | *17036*
725 Boylston St, Apt 5, Boston, MA *02115* . . . . |
Jennings MR Christopher R JR
☎ (215) 628-9942 . . 3337 Walnut St, Philadelphia, PA *19104*
Jennings MR & MRS Evan D 2d (Van Ingen— | ☎ (412) 593-2814
Cynthia S Booth) V'55.Fcg.Rr.Pg. . . . . | HC 64, PO Box 349,
  MR Mark G—at Ft Collins, CO . . . . | Rector, PA *15677*
Jennings MR & MRS James W (Helen A Lippincott) | ☎ (610) 527-3376
Pa'66.Me.Gm.P'59.Pa'65 . . . . | 1401 Montgomery
  MISS Elizabeth Alder—Buck'92 . . . . | Av, Rosemont, PA
  MR James M—David'95 . . . . | *19010*
Jennings MR & MRS Keith S (Beverly A Bowers) | ☎ (610) 896-6050
Cyb.M.Me.Gm.Cs.P'66.Bost'69 . . . . | ''Tyn-Y-Coed''
  MISS Kimberly A—P'95—at 205 E 95 St, | 401 Mill Creek Rd,
New York, NY *10128* . . . . | Wynnewood, PA
  MISS Caroline L—at U of Ore. . . . . | *19096*
Jennings MRS Sara L (Sara E Lupton) Ant'59.Cwr'61.NewSchSR'81 . . of
☎ (804) 266-4496 . . 5618 Crenshaw Rd, Apt 822, Richmond,
VA *23227-2561*
☎ (212) 923-7802 . . 116 Pinehurst Av, New York, NY *10033*
Jennings MR & MRS W Croft JR (Ann Richmond) | ☎ (803) 776-4578
Sth'62.Ty'60 . . . . | 21 Granville Rd,
  MISS Gwendolyn C—at 1301—30 St, Boulder, | Columbia, SC *29209*
CO *80303* . . . . |
Jennings MRS William M (Elizabeth M Hite) Cly.
☎ (203) 531-8572 . . ''Clifton'' 157 Byram Shore Rd, Greenwich,
CT *06830*
Jennison MR & MRS David R (Joëlle M T N Husson) Parnasse'77.Hob'80
☎ (011-44-171) 937-9658 . . 26 Kelso Place, London W8 5QG, England
Jennison MASTER Nicolas Philip Roger (David R) . . . . Born at
London, England Mch 11'94
Jennison MR & MRS Peter H (Alexandra J Curran)
☎ (212) 831-7098 . . 201 E 87 St, PH-G, New York, NY *10128*
Jenrette MR Richard H—Ln.B.Mid.NCar'51.H.'57 . . of
☎ (212) 876-0669 . . 69 E 93 St, New York, NY *10128*
☎ (803) 723-6519 . . 9 E Battery St, Charleston, SC *29401*
Jens MR Stifel W . . . . Died at
Richmond Heights, MO Oct 26'95
Jens MRS Stifel W (Hale—Quinette Cowan) Cos.
1 McKnight Place, Apt 141, University City, MO *63124-1981*

Jensen MRS Frode (Hudson—Camille McL | ☎ (203) 966-8568
Anderson) Csn. . . . . | 7 Hatfield Mews,
  MR Peter—at ☎ (510) 235-2958 | New Canaan, CT
122 Martina St, Point Richmond, CA *94801* . . . | *06840*
Jensen MR & MRS Frode 3d (Catherine S Hall) | ☎ (203) 966-5184
Hlns'76.Ncd.Wms'72.Cl'76 . . . . | 528 Canoe Hill Rd,
  JUNIORS MR Christian McL . . . . | New Canaan, CT
| *06840*
Jensen MR & MRS Peter G (Jerri L Case) SUNY'88
☎ (315) 526-6878 . . 493 Voak Rd, Penn Yan, NY *14527*
Jensen MRS Philip J (M Anne McCarthy) Ant'77 . . | ☎ (410) 363-0143
  MR Philip J 3d . . . . | 16 St Thomas Lane,
| Owings Mills, MD
| *21117*
Jensen DR & MRS Robert O (Donabeth Shoop) | ☎ (315) 536-8711
Roch'50 . . . . | 136 South Av,
  MISS Kristen . . . . | Penn Yan, NY
| *14527*
Jensen MR & MRS (DR) Robert O JR (Julie R Donovan)
Wis'79.Roch'86.MeMarit'79
23 W 240, Hampton Circle, Naperville, IL *60540*
Jensen MR Rollin A—Cal'60 . . . . | ☎ (415) 671-0401
  MISS Margaret B—at 1420 Turk St, Apt 704, | 1419 Palou Av,
San Francisco, CA *94115* . . . . | San Francisco, CA
| *94124*
Jepson MR Edward B . . see R F Pew
Jerauld MR & MRS Anthony B (Kahle—Melinda A Smith) St.Ts.Tr.Pa'62
☎ (617) 262-1340 . . 250 Beacon St, Boston, MA *02116*
Jernigan MR & MRS Stephen A (Daugherty—Susan | ☎ (405) 840-3200
R Hicks) Col'75.Okla'70 . . . . | 6710 NW Grand
  JUNIORS MR Philip M. . . . . | Blvd, Oklahoma
| City, OK *73116*
Jerome MR & MRS C L Alexander (O'Grady—Susan M E Hines)
PO Box 2046, Manhattan Beach, CA *90266*
Jerome MR J J Ramsay—Cal'85
☎ (310) 798-1748 . . 1750—5 St, Manhattan Beach, CA *90266*
Jerome MISS S E Jane—Ariz'83
☎ (408) 995-0403 . . PO Box 612492, San Jose, CA *95161-2492*
Jerrems MISS Eleanor M
60 rue des Courcieux, 78570 Andrésy, France
Jessop MISS Heidi S R . . see P W Ness JR
Jessop MISS Stephanie E G . . see P W Ness JR
Jessup MR Henry S—Br'74.Cl'79 . . see MRS D B Kipp
Jessup MR & MRS Philip C JR (Cook—Helen Ibbitson)
Melb'56.Lond'73.Lond'88.C.Csn.Y'49.H'52 . . of
☎ (202) 342-2131 . . 3415 O St NW, Washington, DC *20007*
☎ (860) 542-5677 . . ''Pinefield'' 97 Gamefield Rd, Norfolk, CT *06058*
Jewell MISS Lucinda A—Mid'80.H'90
☎ (617) 497-8677 . . 7 Ellsworth Av, Cambridge, MA *02139-1009*
Jewell MR & MRS Pliny 3d (J Sue Shelly) Au.Chi.H'54
☎ (508) 369-4959 . . 108 Stearns St, Carlisle, MA *01741*
Jewell MR & MRS Raymond B (Coleman—Antoinette | ☎ (610) 286-2924
J Leroux) VaWes'72 . . . . | ''Pleasant Hill
  MISS Lindsay D Coleman—W&L'95 . . . . | Plantation''
| 151 Little Conestoga
| Rd, Glenmoore, PA
| *19343*

Jewell MR & MRS Samuel R (Sheila F Balding)   ☎ (803) 521-9630
H'59.H'62.Mass'65.ColSt'72.Col'82 . . . . | 18 Harborview
   MISS Flora—at ☎ (303) 477-8672 | Circle, Beaufort, SC
4467 King St, Denver, CO *80211* . . . . | *29902*

Jewett MISS Brooke E (Jonathan) . . . . Married at Lyme, CT
   Nadell MR Bernhardt M (Raymond) . . . . Jun 15'96

Jewett MR & MRS Charles W (Mary A Sheafe) Mich'34.Y'37
☎ (860) 434-8745 . . 121 Mt Archer Rd, Lyme, CT *06371*

Jewett MR & MRS Charles W JR (Martha J Stuart)   ☎ (202) 882-7490
WmSth'68.Cr'70.Hob'66.O'79 . . . . | 5318 Colorado Av
   JUNIORS MISS Caroline P—at Stone Ridge . . . . . . | NW, Washington,
   JUNIORS MR Andrew W—at St Anselm's . . . . . . | DC *20011*

Jewett MR & MRS Edgar B 3d (Frances B Appleton) Ny.St.Buf'50
☎ (716) 447-0476 . . 92 Middlesex Rd, Buffalo, NY *14216*

Jewett MR & MRS Freeborn G JR (Joan Sanford Lewis)
Au.Mt.Cvc.Gi.Sl.Cda.Y'50.Y'53 ⚓
☎ (703) 893-9075 . . 8700 Lewinsville Rd, McLean, VA *22102*

Jewett MR & MRS George F JR (Lucille W McIntyre)
PugetS'50.Bhm.Pcu.Bur.Srb.Sfy.Sdy.Ny.StJ.Dth'50 . . of
☎ (415) 981-3390 . . 2990 Broadway St, San Francisco, CA *94115*
☎ (808) 882-7796 . . ''Beachbound'' HC 01, Box 578,
Mauna Kea Beach, Kamuela, HI *96743*

Jewett MR George M—Mds.
☎ (702) 474-6927 . . 2021 Waldman Av, Las Vegas, NV *89102*

Jewett MR & MRS Jonathan (Nancy M Robertson)   of ☎ (212)369-7472
H'65.Pa'68 . . . . | 1261 Madison Av,
   MISS Lindsay S—H'92—at Columbia . . . . | New York, NY
   JUNIORS MR Ian S—at Salisbury . . . . | *10128*
| ☎ (860) 434-7787
| 100-1 Joshuatown
| Rd, Lyme, CT
| *06371*

Jewett MRS Margaret N (Margaret R Nichols)   of ☎ (702)878-1376
V'67.Cin'71.Ri.Cly.Mds.Dyc. . . . . | 2813 Cameo Circle,
   JUNIORS MR Lamon H . . . . | Las Vegas, NV
| *89107*
| ☎ (606) 255-3520
| ''Walnut Hall''
| 3719 Newtown Pike,
| Lexington, KY
| *40511*

Jhaveri MR & MRS Ajay (Jennifer S Farrington) Xav'79.Cl'83
☎ (805) 287-3208 . . 24035 W Mill Valley Rd, Valencia, CA *91355*

Jobson MR J Roger—Bhm.Vca.StA.Snc.Ll.Ht.Cp.Rv.
☎ (510) 865-3112 . . 348 Laguna Vista Dv, Alameda, CA *94501*

Jobson MR Mark deV—Cp.Ll.Cal'83
☎ (619) 299-9737 . . 1043 University Av, Apt 150, San Diego,
CA *92103*

Jodice MR & MRS Patrick G R (Laura L Williams)
Wms'85.Me'89.Me'83.Fla'90
☎ (541) 758-7554 . . 275 SE Villa Dv, Corvallis, OR *97333*

Johannsen MR & MRS Peter G (Marion S Myers)   ☎ (617) 237-9651
Ws'67.Wms'64.H'67 . . . . | 37 Glen Rd,
   MISS Marion P—at Dartmouth . . . . | Wellesley Hills, MA
   MR Peter V—Wms'92 . . . . | *02181*
   MR G Rem—Denis'96 . . . .
   JUNIORS MISS Elizabeth C—at Milton . . . .

Johansen MRS Mary L (Mary L Longcope) Rdc'44.Csn.
☎ (413) 243-3315 . . Box 62, Lee, MA *01238*

Johns MR & MRS F Winston (Anne W Churchman)   ☎ (540) 554-8300
Va'54 . . . . | Drawer F,
   MISS Sibley W—Va'86—at ☎ (804) 977-7009 | Bluemont, VA
1804 Chesapeake St, Charlottesville, VA *22901* . | *20135*

Johns MR & MRS Lionel S (Mariby Burrowes)   ☎ (703) 548-8092
Conn'59.Va'55 ⚓ . . . . | 410 S Pitt St,
   MISS Lindsay N—at 3201 Landover St, | Alexandria, VA
Apt 1718, Alexandria, VA *22305* . . . . | *22314*
   MR Lionel S JR—Box 645, Charlottesville, VA
22902 . . . .

Johns MR William Potter—B.K.Chr.Plg.Snc.Cw.Ht.Ne.Coa.P'57.H'59
☎ (212) 628-0211 . . 222 E 71 St, New York, NY *10021*

Johnsen MR & MRS Erik F (Parker—Dolly Ann Souchon)
☎ (504) 866-0869 . . Park VII, Apt 9H, 170 Walnut St, New Orleans,
LA *70118*

Johnson MR & MRS A Bryan 3d (Daphne S S   ☎ (206) 525-8230
Williams) Y'62 . . . . | 4830 NE 43 St,
   MISS Adrienne D—StLaw'92 . . . . | Seattle, WA *98105*

Johnson MRS A Reid (Judith M Colt) Ncd.
☎ (410) 785-0889 . . 13801 York Rd, Apt K17, Cockeysville,
MD *21030-1808*

Johnson MRS Alexander B (H Louise Huntting)   of ☎ (904)285-1658
Cly.Yn. . . . . | Vicar's Landing
   MR John A—DU'72 . . . . | Way, H306,
| Ponte Vedra Beach,
| FL *32082*
| ☎ (203) 966-4143
| 16 Mead St,
| New Canaan, CT
| *06840*

Johnson MR Allan M . . . . Died Aug 15'96

Johnson MRS Allan M (Jean M Anderson)
☎ (610) 525-8069 . . 404 Cheswick Place, C2, Rosemont, PA *19010*

Johnson MR Belton K—Rcn.Bhm.Au.Ri.Ln.Cr'52
200 Ridgemont Av, San Antonio, TX *78209*

Johnson MRS Billy F (Ann B Ilsley) Skd'53
☎ (203) 637-4047 . . 41 Miltiades Av, Riverside, CT *06878*

Johnson MR & MRS Brian D (Kortny S Darby) Hlns'86.Me.Ac.Drex'87
327 Koser Rd, Lititz, PA *17543*

Johnson MR & MRS Broaddus (Kate de F Chamberlin) Y'48
☎ (914) 234-7098 . . 63 Hook Rd, Box 355, Bedford, NY *10506*

Johnson MR & MRS Charles R JR (Barbara Lounsbery)
WmSth'78.Bgt.Hob'77
☎ (914) 764-0720 . . 45 Deerfield Rd, Pound Ridge, NY *10576*

Johnson JUNIORS MR Christopher E . . see J E Newlin 3d

Johnson MR & MRS Christopher W (Jane B Botsford)
B.Rc.Ri.Mds.Col'81.Nu'86 . . of
☎ (212) 593-5789 . . 435 E 52 St, Apt 11A, New York, NY *10022*
☎ (516) 324-8552 . . 75 Dunemere Lane, East Hampton, NY *11937*

Johnson MR & MRS Collister (Eleanor W Muir) Sm.Cly.Y'39
☎ (908) 234-0665 . . 65 Holland Rd, Far Hills, NJ *07931*

Johnson MR & MRS Craig N (Sally P Van Dusen) ☎ (215) VE6-7287
Pa'69.Rc.Sg.Pc.Pa'63 . . . . 515 Auburn Av,
MISS Maria P—Ham'96 . . . . Wyndmoor, PA
JUNIORS MISS Samantha B 19038

Johnson MR & MRS Crawford T 3d (Virginia J Goodall) RMWmn'47
☎ (205) 871-2049 . . 3829 Forest Glen Dv, Birmingham, AL 35213

Johnson MR & MRS David C (Ann F Snowden)
Ws'85.Nu'89.Why.Msq.MdArt'80
☎ (212) 861-6937 . . 500 E 77 St, Apt 901, New York, NY 10021

Johnson MR & MRS David C JR (Caroline H Davenport)
Colg'78.Ln.Stc.NCar'78.Va'82
☎ (212) 721-9296 . . 354 West End Av, New York, NY 10024

Johnson MR & MRS David L (A Landon Stonesifer) Duke'88.Cl'94.Y'83
☎ (416) 485-2260 . . 247 Forman Av, Toronto, Ontario M4S 2S4,
Canada

Johnson MR David L JR—Dth'35.H'38
☎ (508) 945-1654 . . PO Box 359, West Chatham, MA 02669

Johnson MRS Deane F (Ford—Anne McDonnell) . . . . Died at
New York, NY Mch 29'96

Johnson MR Deane F—Ln.Bcs.Ng.Stan'39.Stan'42
☎ (212) 249-2905 . . 834 Fifth Av, New York, NY 10021

Johnson MR & MRS Douglas S (Emily S Eckelberry)
Denis'86.Pr.Cly.StLaw'84
☎ (516) 671-6158 . . "The Hayloft" 45 Hawthorne Rd, Sea Cliff,
NY 11579

Johnson MR Dudley D—Un.Ny.Ht.Snc.Va'68 . . of
☎ (315) 655-8191 . . "Carriage Cove" 4709 E Lake Rd, Cazenovia,
NY 13035
☎ (212) 861-3945 . . 157 E 75 St, New York, NY 10021

Johnson JUNIORS MR E Reed . . see J E Newlin 3d

Johnson MR & MRS Edward C 3d (Elizabeth B Hodges)
Un.Btn.Myf.Chi.Ncd.H'54
☎ (617) 523-4069 . . 1 Charles River Square, Boston, MA 02114

Johnson MR Edward C 4th—Ub.Ne'93
☎ (617) 720-4610 . . 17 Union Wharf, Boston, MA 02109

Johnson MR & MRS Edward M (Elizabeth B Childs) Nu'84.Pom'67.Y.'71
☎ (212) 628-7852 . . 531 E 88 St, New York, NY 10128

Johnson MR & MRS Edward R (Kimberley W Graff) ☎ (860) 536-1589
Ste. ⚓ 87 Main St, Noank,
MISS Lacy K— ⚓ . . . . CT 06340

Johnson MISS Eliza Dooley (James Lee 3d) . . . . Born at
St Louis, MO Jun 10'96

Johnson MISS Elizabeth G (Lucius W JR) . . . . . Married at Woodside, CA
Lee MR Elgin H . . . . May 31'95

Johnson MISS Elizabeth L
☎ (617) 536-3337 . . 250 Beacon St, Boston, MA 02116

Johnson MRS Evelyn M (B Evelyn Murray) Dar.
☎ (813) 345-9651 . . 6450—28 Av N, St Petersburg, FL 33710

Johnson MR & MRS F Coit (Holly E Harrison) ☎ (212) 722-7288
Bnd'60.Rc.Pr.Cly.Myf.P.'52 . . . . 4 E 95 St, Apt 8C,
MISS Holly-Katharine C . . . . New York, NY
MR Christian A H 10128

Johnson MRS F Lincoln (Le Boutillier—Ayres— ☎ (203) 531-9406
Patterson—Deirdre G Jones) V'50.Cly. . . . . . . 512 W Lyon Farm
MR H Fairfax Ayres 3d—Nw'88.Va'96 . . . . . Dv, Greenwich, CT
06831

Johnson MR & MRS Francis E (Helena N Edey) Shcc.Eyc.Err.Hn.H'35
☎ (908) 234-0978 . . "Kirtleton" 66 Holland Rd, Far Hills, NJ 07931

Johnson MR & MRS Francis E 3d (Mary J Mason) ☎ (212) 535-1609
GeoW'73.Bm.Cly.Ncd.Rut'71.Mass'73 . . . . 103 E 84 St,
JUNIORS MISS Christina M—at Porter . . . . New York, NY
10028

Johnson MR & MRS Francis Mitchell JR (Felicia D McIntyre)
Char'ton'85.Yh.David'73
☎ (803) 577-9994 . . 55 Society St, Charleston, SC 29401

Johnson MR & MRS Franklin R (Compton—Mary La F Bechdolt)
Pa'51.Ne'39
☎ (508) 369-4143 . . 100 Keyes Rd, Apt 216, Concord, MA 01742

Johnson DR & MRS Garry A (Prine—Antoinette C ☎ (314) 821-7616
Murphy) Mar'vil'76.Cal'75.Cal'80 . . . . 1926 Firethorn Dv,
MR Stephen C Murphy . . . . St Louis, MO 63131
JUNIORS MR E Evan C Murphy . . . .

Johnson MRS George F B JR (Pile—Thérèse G ☎ (401) 849-6335
Tuckerman) Srb . . . . 94 Washington St,
MR Roger S Pile JR—at 200 Blood St, Lyme, Newport, RI 02840
CT 06371 . . . .

Johnson MR & MRS George Fenimore (V Dale ☎ (410) 778-0539
Lindsay) Me.Ayc.Cry.Ny.Ac.Ht.Myf.Dar.Ncd. "Shell Point"
Wyo'50 . . . . 5165 Deep Point
MR Bradford F—Cry.Wash'83—at Dv, Chestertown,
☎ (610) 687-3947 . . 49 Beaumont Rd, Devon, MD 21620-9803
PA 19333 . . . .

Johnson MRS Gerald J 2d (Lourié—Chaplin— ☎ (401) 348-8041
Campbell—Elizabeth W Taft) Cl'60.Msq.Why. . "Waveland
MISS Carolyn N—at 174 Seminole Dv, Marietta, Cottage"
GA 30060 . . . . 21 Misquamicut Rd,
MISS Elizabeth S Lourié—at 14519 Whitman Watch Hill, RI
Av N, Seattle, WA 98133 02891

Johnson MR Gordon L
☎ (808) 524-6969 . . 60 N Beretania St, Apt 402, Honolulu, HI 96817

Johnson MR & MRS Greene F (Caroline Lovell) Ncd.Ga'25.H'28.StJ'37
☎ (706) 549-9423 . . 21 S Stratford Dv, Athens, GA 30605

Johnson MR & MRS Hallett JR (Mary Ellen Cooke) Ws'52.P'46
☎ (609) 924-1514 . . 841 Pretty Brook Rd, Princeton, NJ 08540

Johnson MRS Hamilton S (Jean M Rooney)
☎ (207) 839-7054 . . 117 School St, Gorham, ME 04038

Johnson MR & MRS Harald (Lynn E Crawford) Day'81.Tex'70
4066 Watts Passage, Charlottesville, VA 22911

Johnson MRS Harold F H (Joan F Brinton) Ncd.
☎ (610) 399-0941 . . 220 W Street Rd, West Chester, PA 19382-8420

Johnson MRS Helen H (Helen C Hanford) Ncd.
☎ (716) 889-1096 . . Box 102, Scottsville, NY 14546

Johnson MR & MRS James Ford 3d (Elaine Oberwager) Un.Fw.Cly.Y.'40
☎ (914) 277-5540 . . 14 Heritage Hills Dv, Somers, NY 10589

Johnson MR & MRS James L JR (Bettie B Schroth) V'56.Cy.Lc.Nd.P'55
☎ (314) 991-1025 . . 8921 Moydalgan Rd, St Louis, MO 63124

Johnson MR & MRS James Lee 3d (Suzanne Lawless) StLaw'86.Cy.Van'86
☎ (314) 993-8416 . . 27 The Orchard, St Louis, MO 63132

Johnson MR & MRS Jeffrey S (Sarah R Arndt) Denis'86.Bab'81
☎ (207) 846-1037 . . 93 W Main St, Yarmouth, ME 04096

Johnson MISS Jesse K . . see F X Knott

Johnson MR & MRS John B (Margaret G Scott) Pa'40.Ny.Ds.Pa'39
☎ (203) 227-4916 . . 263 S Compo Rd, Westport, CT 06880

Johnson MR & MRS John D (Carol Davis) Dth'38
☎ (305) 279-2656 . . 8520 SW 74 Terr, Miami, FL *33143*
Johnson MR & MRS John G (Bahnson—de Bragança—Katharine King)
Evg.Cly . . .of
☎ (910) 722-8745 . . .2200 Brookfield Dv, Winston-Salem, NC *27106*
☎ (619) 756-5708 . . 7015 La Valle Plateada, Rancho Santa Fe,
CA *92067*
Johnson MISS Judith E—Cl'80
☎ (818) 242-7063 . . 1809 Verdugo Loma Dv, Glendale, CA *91208*
Johnson MISS Katherine Ann (David C) . . . . Born at
New York, NY Jan 18'96
Johnson MR & MRS Kiehner (Elizabeth S Sterner)
OState'50.Mich'50.Mich'52
☎ (614) 252-2705 . . 291 S Columbia Av, Columbus, OH *43209*

Johnson MR & MRS L Oakley (Frances B Wells) | of ☎ (301)926-9778
DU'70.Cvc.Mt.DU'70.JHop'72 . . . . | "Woodbyrne Farm"
MR Parker W . . . . | 14625 Seneca Rd,
JUNIORS MR O Tod . . . . | Darnestown, MD
20874
☎ (207) 422-9593
"Summersalt"
Sorrento, ME *04677*

Johnson MRS Laurence S (Van Nimwegen—Sarah Faxon) Col'61.Pr.Cs.
☎ (516) 626-1557 . . 843 Orchard Lane, Oyster Bay, NY *11771*

Johnson MR & MRS Lawrence JR (Esther Demas) | ☎ (215) 247-2026
GeoW'50.Pc. . . . . | 8018 Roanoke St,
MISS Caroline—PhilaArt'87.Cranbr'94 . . . . | Philadelphia, PA
19118

Johnson MR & MRS Lawrence 3d (Shelley K Andrews)
Gettys'90.Ph.Gettys'89.VillaN'96
☎ (610) 429-1009 . . 300 E Evans St, Apt L252, West Chester,
PA *19380*
Johnson MRS Lucius W JR (Frances D Pierson) . . . . Died at
Palo Alto, CA May 6'94

Johnson MR Lucius W JR—Cr'49 . . . . | ☎ (415) 494-1445
MISS Dorothy F . . . . | 439 San Antonio
Rd, Palo Alto, CA
94306

Johnson MRS Lyndon B (Claudia A Taylor)
"LBJ Ranch" Stonewall, TX *78671*
Johnson MR & MRS M Blake 2d (Cherry Hannan) Dth'36.H'41
PO Box 2546, Delray Beach, FL *33447*
Johnson MRS Margaret H (Doughty—Margaret Hill) EdinArt'43.Mass'83
☎ (617) 834-7279 . . off Summer St, Box 75, Marshfield Hills,
MA *02051*
Johnson JUNIORS MR Marshall B . . see F X Knott

Johnson MRS Melvin M JR (Virginia B Rice) | ☎ (203) 776-4735
Cyb.Ri.Myf. . . . . | 100 York St,
MRS Gail V (Cronin—Gail V Johnson)—at | Apt 10M,
☎ (203) 782-2763 . . 111 Park St, Apt 2B, | New Haven, CT
New Haven, CT *06511* . . . . | *06511*

Johnson MR & MRS Melvin T (Barbara W | ☎ (610) 687-3851
Zimmermann) Sth'48.Gm. | 520 Montgomery
MISS Alice T—Colby'92—at ☎ (703) 527-5856 | Lane, Radnor, PA
2611 N 18 St, Arlington, VA *22201* . . . . | *19087*

Johnson MR Michael T—Syr'68
☎ (516) 537-0645 . . 53 Hedges Lane, Box 103, Sagaponack, NY *11962*

Johnson MRS Mildred T (Mildred F Thornton) Btn. | ☎ (207) 244-3889
MISS Shannon E . . . . | Box 262, Mt Desert,
MR M Maynard 4th . . . . | ME *04660*
MR Lewis B . . . . |

Johnson MR & MRS Morse (Betty K Freyhof)
Ws'44.Hav'47.Csn.Cr'37.H'40 . . of
☎ (513) 871-0091 . . 9 Far Hills Dv, Cincinnati, OH *45208*
☎ (804) 325-2094 . . "Renvoi" Wintergreen, Rte 1, Box 567, Roseland,
VA *22967*
Johnson MR Murrey M—Cal'38.H'40
☎ (510) 932-2316 . . 2956 Tice Creek Dv, Walnut Creek, CA *94595*
Johnson MR & MRS N Platt (Nancy Hutchinson) Tampa'75.Ny.Tufts'77
☎ (401) 846-4421 . . 82 Aquidneck Av, Middletown, RI *02842*
Johnson MR & MRS Norman Dudley (Virginia H Couper)
Hlns'41.Un.Sa.Err.B.Chr.Ny.Eyc.Plg.Coa.
Ne.Snc.Cw.Ht.StJ.Cly.Cda.Dc.Wms'30 . . of
☎ (212) 744-4321 . . 38 E 70 St, New York, NY *10021-4928*
☎ (508) 627-4895 . . "Capt Morse House" 80 N Water St, PO Box 34,
Edgartown, MA *02539-0034*
Johnson MRS Pierrepont E (Snow—Lilias S S Moriarty) Srb.Chi.Ncd.
☎ (401) 847-0827 . . 29 Mary St, Newport, RI *02840*

Johnson MR & MRS R Kemp JR (Barbara Y | ☎ (215) 542-7649
Hamilton) Pc.Ds.Cr'40 . . . . | 1501 Clair Martin
MR Reeves K 3d . . . . | Place, Ambler, PA
19002

Johnson MR & MRS R Tenney (Marilyn B Meuth)
RMWmn'52.Ty'55.Cos.Roch'51.Ty'55.H'58
☎ (301) 365-2835 . . 8424 Magruder Mill Court, Bethesda, MD *20817*
Johnson MRS Raymond C (Alice H Willard) BtP.
☎ (561) 832-0763 . . 400 N Flagler Dv, Apt 2104, West Palm Beach,
FL *33401*

Johnson MR & MRS Richard I (Gleason—Marrian L | ☎ (617) 566-2801
Geer) Bost'71.Hn.H.'51 | 124 Chestnut Hill
MR Edward S Gleason—Bost'84.Lond'85 . . . | Rd, Chestnut Hill,
MA *02167-1310*

Johnson MR Richard M W—Hart'88
☎ (617) 749-0594 . . 302 North St, Hingham, MA *02043*
Johnson MR & MRS Ridgely C (Claudette M Fisher)
Col'81.Mit'88.Snc.Ht.Cw.P'80.Lond'92
☎ (011-44-1923) 828-497 . . 4 Penn House, Main Av, Moor Park,
Northwood, Middlesex HA6 2HH, England
Johnson MR & MRS Robert A (Linda B Bassett) V'56.It.Y'55.Y'61
☎ (216) 991-9294 . . 2980 Fontenay Rd, Shaker Heights, OH *44120*
Johnson MR Robert C JR—Htdon'51
☎ (334) 272-9617 . . 9431 Winfield Place, Montgomery, AL *36117*
Johnson MR & MRS Robert deL (Haines—Audrey P Oakley) Yn.Y'42
6123 Fellowship Rd, Basking Ridge, NJ *07920*
Johnson MR Robert L 3d—P'66.Tex'69
see Dilatory Domiciles

Johnson MR & MRS Roger L (Wendy Miller) | ☎ (503) 636-4241
GreenMt'70.PacNw'74.Gonz'65 . . . . | 02030 SW Military
MISS Cory L . . . . | Rd, Portland, OR
JUNIORS MISS Lesley . . . . | *97219*

Johnson DR & MRS Rollin M (Penelope L Delafield) Y'73.Y'79.Cos.H'60
☎ (413) 268-9310 . . 5 Hatfield St, Haydenville, MA *01039-9711*
Johnson MRS Sallie B (Sallie B Moore) SL'46.Cda.
☎ (212) 758-1362 . . 424 E 52 St, New York, NY *10022*

Johnson MISS Sally B
  ☎ (212) 758-1362 . . 424 E 52 St, Apt 10D, New York, NY *10022*
Johnson MRS Samuel S (Elizabeth A Hill) Miami'35.Ws'37.Fr.
  ☎ (541) 548-3186 . . 415 S Canyon Dv, Redmond, OR *97756*

Johnson MRS Sheryl B (Sheryl Z Bolton)	of ☎ (713)965-9836
Tul'67.Tex'70	3802 Del Monte Dv,
JUNIORS MISS Meredith	Houston, TX *77019*
JUNIORS MR Robert L 4th	☎ (409) 830-1214
	''Gopher Hill''
	Bleiblerville, TX
	78931

Johnson MR & MRS Sidney G 2d (Susan Scott)	☎ (415) 454-7285
Stph'62.Denis'64.W&L'63.Cr'66	11 Lagoon Place,
MISS Elizabeth B—Bay'91	San Rafael, CA
MR Scott E—Bay'94	*94901*

Johnson MR Stephen S 2d . . of
  ☎ (212) 744-9488 . . 370 E 76 St, New York, NY *10021*
  ☎ (860) 739-7170 . . 12 Great Wight Way, Old Black Point, Niantic,
  CT *06357*

Johnson MRS Steven B (Mautz—Sharel J Kaiser) . .	☎ (011-61-75)
MISS Elizabeth A Mautz—at Bryn Mawr	33-5310
MISS Jennifer N Mautz	''Eagle Crest''
	Springbrook Rd,
	Springbrook,
	Queensland 4213,
	Australia

Johnson MR Stuart C (Robert A) . . . . Married at Guilford, CT
  Del Mauro MISS Carol A (Gene) . . . . Apr 13'96
Johnson MR & MRS Stuart H 3d (Susan M O'Connell)
  Bnd'73.H'84.Mto.Pr.C.Cly.Y'76
  ☎ (212) 369-0841 . . 14 E 90 St, New York, NY *10128*
Johnson MISS Theodora L—GeoW'41
  Santa Cruz Av, Menlo Park, CA *94025*
Johnson MR & MRS Thomas W (Laura B Laughlin)
  Ty'81.Fic.Gv.Cly.Ty'79.H'86
  ☎ (410) 433-3161 . . 202 Upnor Rd, Baltimore, MD *21212*
Johnson MR Timothy C—Rcn.Mit'83
  ☎ (802) 948-2369 . . Burke Rd, Orwell, VT *05760*
Johnson MR Timothy Swaim—Col'64
  ☎ (802) 875-3770 . . ''Wishbone Lodge'' Box 698, Chester, VT *05143*
Johnson MR & MRS Victor H (Thornley—Ann D L Webster)
  Pa'50.Sfh.Luth'50.Wis'52
  ☎ (610) 631-0856 . . 820 Stonybrook Dv, Jeffersonville, PA *19403*
Johnson MR & MRS Ward L (Jean Taylor) San.Wms'43
  ☎ (860) 767-2222 . . PO Box 820, 56 N Main St, Essex, CT *06426*

Johnson MR & MRS Wayne JR (Mary Goodrich)	☎ (203) 661-8604
Cly.H'44	360 Cedar Hill,
MR Wayne 3d—Col'86—at ☎ (212) 410-4679	Greenwich, CT
301 E 94 St, New York, NY *10128*	*06830*

Johnson MRS Wentworth P (D Elizabeth Leahey)	☎ (610) 525-3613
Me.	714 Woodleave Rd,
MR W Paul 3d—Me.	Bryn Mawr, PA
	19010-1709

Johnson MISS Wilhelmina C—Roch'82.Sl . . . see MRS W D Vanderpool JR
Johnson MR & MRS William H 3d (Melanie E McLendon)
  Ala'80.Livingston'67
  ☎ (334) 284-5161 . . Rte 1, Box 287D, Montgomery, AL *36105*

Johnson MR & MRS William L (Marjory Bruce Hughes) V'51.P'50.Cl'55
  ☎ (410) 226-5085 . . 4397 World Farm Rd, Oxford, MD *21654*
Johnson MR & MRS William P (Rosemary H Wilson)
  see Dilatory Domiciles
Johnston MR & MRS Alan R (Eleanor C Smith)
  BMr'37.Ih.Cyc.P'37.Mich'41
  ☎ (561) 234-1541 . . 1855 Bay Rd, Vero Beach, FL *32963*

Johnston MR & MRS Alfred M (Eleanor C Tierney) .	☎ (610) 687-6619
MISS Amy J—at ☎ (610) 520-0369	250 Matsonford Rd,
Thornbrook Apt 3B, 819 Montgomery Av,	Radnor, PA *19087*
Bryn Mawr, PA *19010*	
MR P Mark—at ☎ (610) 896-7881	
107 Walnut Av, Ardmore, PA *19003*	
MR C Robin—at ☎ (610) 649-0503	
801 Biddle St, Ardmore, PA *19003*	

Johnston MR & MRS Allan L JR (Sandra J W Wood)	of ☎ (513)298-6850
Bz.Mvh.Witt'64	25 Ivanhoe Av,
MR Peirce W—Bz.Ken'89	Dayton, OH
	45419-3808
	☎ (407) 723-0805
	530 Hammock Rd,
	Melbourne Village,
	FL *32904*

Johnston MISS Azile Kelly
  2351 Washington St, Apt 304, San Francisco, CA *94115*
Johnston MR & MRS Douglas C (Cornelia N Perkins)
  Wash'83.Wash'84.Wash'83.H'87
  ☎ (508) 634-8737 . . 8 Park St, Hopedale, MA *01747*
Johnston MR & MRS Edward R 2d (D Sophia Ibrahim)
  Lond'85.Lond'87.Brussels'91.H'77
  Acadian Farm 3, Young's Mountain Rd, Bar Harbor, ME *04609*
Johnston MR & MRS Edwin M JR (Schoellkopf—Susan Fiske Surdam)
  St.G.Y'55
  ☎ (716) 874-3722 . . 161 Middlesex Rd, Buffalo, NY *14216*
Johnston MR & MRS Edwin McC 3d (Alexandra G Spofford)
  Y'82.D.Fic.Y'82
  see Dilatory Domiciles

Johnston MR & MRS G Sim 3d (Lisa Ferwerda) H'73	of ☎ (212)410-4254
JUNIORS MR George A	1105 Park Av,
	New York, NY
	10128
	☎ (516) 283-7850
	PO Box 41,
	Southampton, NY
	11969

Johnston MRS George S (Cynthia Cogswell) Ford'80.Cly.
  ☎ (212) 832-9153 . . 580 Park Av, New York, NY *10021*
Johnston MR & MRS Henry O (Sally F Curby) Cy.
  ☎ (314) 993-0860 . . 4 Town & Country Dv, St Louis, MO *63124*
Johnston MRS Hugh McB (Sheffield—Ellen J Wacker) Cly.StJ.
  ☎ (847) 735-0771 . . PO Box 826, Lake Forest, IL *60045*
Johnston MR & MRS Hugh McB 3d (Detweiler—Louise McI Roberts)
  Pc.Sg.Cts.Ham'60
  ☎ (215) 247-9355 . . 9 Norman Lane, Philadelphia, PA *19118*
Johnston MRS Hulburd (McLennan—McLennan—
  Margaretta F G Purves)
  ☎ (941) 472-1328 . . PO Box 429, Captiva, FL *33924*

Johnston MR & MRS J Buckhout (Emma D Smith)
Villa Marin Apt 354, 100 Thorndale Dv, San Rafael, CA *94903*
Johnston MRS J Clement (Smith—M Elizabeth Talbot) G.
☎ (561) 746-5527 . . 102 Golfview Dv, Tequesta, FL *33469*
Johnston MR & MRS J Murray (Nancy Gill Wylie) Shcc.
☎ (203) 483-1061 . . 88 Notch Hill Rd, Apt 325, North Branford,
CT *06471*

Johnston MR John W—Rcn.Cl'66 . . . . | ☎ (561) 731-2969
MISS Dana C—Vt'96 . . . . | 902 SW 34 Av,
MISS Alix V—at Trinity . . . . | Boynton Beach, FL
| *33435*

Johnston MRS Lisa A (Lisa A Oliver) . . . . | ☎ (360) 563-2400
JUNIORS MISS Rochelle R . . . . | 6011—157 Av SE,
| Snohomish, WA
| *98290*

Johnston MR & MRS Oswald L JR (Susan M | ☎ (301) 229-2840
Anderson) Gchr'65.H'55 . . . . | 4418 Boxwood Rd,
MISS Laura A . . . . | Bethesda, MD
| *20816*

Johnston MR & MRS Philip P (Marion C Ely) SL'34.Mit'35
☎ (610) 584-3746 . . Meadowood at Worcester, 203 Meadowlark Point,
Lansdale, PA *19446-5845*

Johnston MR & MRS Robert O (Margaret E M | ☎ (301) 320-2146
Portner) RMWmn'66.Cvc.W&M'68.W&M'75 . . | 6542—80 St,
MISS Laura E . . . . | Cabin John, MD
JUNIORS MR Robert O JR . . . . | *20818*
JUNIORS MR McCullough M . . . . |

Johnston DR & MRS Thomas S (Jettie L Bergman) | ☎ (912) 598-7488
Dick'58.Me.Rd.Ac.Buck'57.Temp'61 . . . . | 2 Pennystone
MISS Jettie L—PCTS'86.Me.—at | Retreat, Savannah,
☎ (610) 525-2516 . . Rosemont Apt 302, | GA *31411*
1062 Lancaster Av, Rosemont, PA *19010* . . . . . |
MR Thomas S JR—Me.Buck'93—at |
☎ (706) 560-0439 . . 1210 Huntington Dv, |
Augusta, GA *30909* . . . . |

Johnston MRS Toulson (Helen I Toulson) | of ☎ (410)377-7030
RSage'50.Cy.Mv.Dar. . . . . | 6621 Weymouth
MISS Elizabeth S—Gchr'84 . . . . | Court, Baltimore,
| MD *21212*
| ☎ (757) 678-5820
| "Oak Grove"
| Eastville, VA *23347*

Johnston MR & MRS Waldo C M (Weyburn—Chapman—Anschutz—
Renze Wilshire) V'41.C.Ny.Ct.Exy.Sl.Ncd.Y'37
☎ (860) 767-8107 . . 10 Hanna Lane, Essex, CT *06426*

Johnston MR & MRS Waldo C M JR (Caroline E | ☎ (919) 493-3801
Dern) V'68.Y'64.Cl'68 . . . . | 14 Surrey Lane,
MISS Caroline W—Y'93 . . . . | Durham, NC *27707*
MR W Cory M 3d—Y'95 . . . . |

Johnston MRS Watkins C (Edith E Rushton)
see Dilatory Domiciles
Johnston MR & MRS William C (Victoria Eidell)
Stan'74.H'78.Ln.Ng.Cly.Hn.H'75.Stan'77
701 Tavistock, 10 Tregunter Path, Hong Kong
Johnstone MR & MRS James W (Elisabeth S Baker) Me.Cw.Cr'46
☎ (610) 642-9917 . . 305 Hamilton Rd, Wynnewood, PA *19096-1701*

Johnstone MR & MRS Philip M (Elizabeth L McGovern)
Msq.Cly.Duke'83.Pa'86
☎ (860) 535-9094 . . 330 Al Harvey Rd, Stonington, CT *06378*
Jolas MR & MRS Philip G (Lucy G Bates) ColC'74.DU'77.Col'73.Col'77
☎ (303) 770-1589 . . 8622 E Grand Av, Denver, CO *80237*
Jonas MISS Eloise A
☎ (415) 221-5118 . . 1428 Lake St, San Francisco, CA *94118*
Jonas MRS Robert P JR (Peck—Louise D Irons) Ck.Laf'46
☎ (561) 545-0888 . . Loblolly Pines, 7139 SE Greenview Place,
Hobe Sound, FL *33455*
Jones MR A Townsend—Hob'40
751 Hillsdale Dv, Apt 135, Charlottesville, VA *22901-3301*
Jones MISS Adelaide Holdship (William McM JR) . . . . Born at
Pittsburgh, PA Jly 29'96

Jones MR & MRS Alfred H JR (Marye Y Fuller) | ☎ (401) 423-0695
Cw.Dar. . . . . | "Green Chimneys"
MISS Blair B . . . . | 185 Walcott Av,
MISS Victoria H—at Guilford . . . . | Jamestown, RI
| *02835*

Jones MRS Alfred Winslow (Mary Carter) Cs.StJ.
☎ (212) 517-5888 . . 116 E 66 St, New York, NY *10021*

Jones MRS Alison M (MacEwan—Alison M Jones) | 98 Rowayton Av,
GeoW'71 . . . . | Rowayton, CT
MISS Pamela T MacEwan—at Hampshire Coll | *06853*
MISS Elizabeth P MacEwan . . . . |

Jones MR & MRS Andrew B (Janet B Wallace) P'44.Y'52 . . of
☎ (505) 988-1812 . . 718 Bishops Lodge Rd, Santa Fe, NM *87501*
☎ (860) 434-9604 . . 302 Ferry Rd, Old Lyme, CT *06371*
Jones MR Andrew B—Rv.Cc.Cw.Snc.Geo'82.Y'85
☎ (212) 647-9878 . . 317 W 11 St, New York, NY *10014*

Jones MR & MRS Anthony W (Magda A Rydlo) | ☎ (212) 799-5123
Cs.H'63 . . . . | 101 Central Park W,
MISS Caroline A—at Conn Coll . . . . | New York, NY
MR Adrian W—at Occidental . . . . | *10023*

Jones MR & MRS Arthur E JR (Webber—Pansy B | ☎ (610) 688-3032
Ward) Ncd.WChesU'67 . . . . | 891 Tall Oaks Rd,
JUNIORS MR A Ward . . . . | Radnor, PA *19087*

Jones MRS Arthur M (Anstiss Dana) . . . . | ☎ (508) 526-1197
MISS A Derby—at ☎ (617) 965-8144 | 47 Forest St,
25 Harrington St, Newton, MA *02160* . . . . | Manchester, MA
| *01944*

Jones MR & MRS Benjamin C 3d (Anne W C Smith) | ☎ (703) 777-7856
Cc.Va'67.Tex'72 . . . . | 7 Wirt St NW,
MR Benjamin B C . . . . | Leesburg, VA *20176*

Jones MRS Benjamin F 4th (Norma A Pendergast) Cly.Fic.
☎ (860) 535-4340 . . 11 Main St, Stonington, CT *06378*
Jones, Bryan D & Packard, Elise B—Br'88.Br'89
☎ (703) 379-4613 . . 5708 S 4 St, Arlington, VA *22204*

Jones MR & MRS Carleton S (Dona B Van Arsdale) | ☎ (301) 652-3456
Denis'64.Y'67 . . . . | 6604 Kennedy Dv,
MISS Emily B . . . . | Chevy Chase, MD
JUNIORS MR Timothy D . . . . | *20815*

Jones MR & MRS Charles H JR (Hope Haskell) | ☎ (561) 881-7124
BMr'56.Rcn.Rm.Stc.BtP.Rv.Cc.Cda.Va'56 . . . . | 218 Via Linda,
MR Henry M T—HampSydney'94—at | Palm Beach, FL
☎ (212) 702-0847 . . 123 E 54 St, Apt 7D, | *33480*
New York, NY *10022* . . . . |

Jones MR Charles H 3d—Rm.Stc.P'90
☎ (703) 671-7641 . . 1200 N Quaker Lane, Alexandria, VA *22302-3000*

Jones MR & MRS Charles R (Julia S Moore) Tex'59.Tex'59
☎ (915) 584-1848 . . 5588 Westside Dv, El Paso, TX *79932*

Jones MR & MRS Charles W (Sally D Pickrell) | ☎ (212) 688-6290
Mls'45.Juilliard'39 . . . . | 311 E 58 St,
MR Cameron J . . . . | New York, NY
| *10022*

Jones MR & MRS Charles W (Lindsay A Pomeroy) Ken'74.Ken'74.Bost'83
2195 Middlefield Rd, Cleveland Heights, OH *44106*

Jones MR & MRS Christopher B (Kerry E O'Neill) MtH'87.Hob'85
☎ (508) 468-3734 . . "Lord's Lot" 180 Larch Row, Wenham,
MA *01984*

Jones MR & MRS Christopher W (Jennifer A Fenton)
Bost'90.Man'vl'93.Colby'90.Tufts'93
159 Elsinore St, Concord, MA *01742*

Jones MR & MRS Clarke F G (Whitney M Williams)
Van'87.Wash'90.Cy.Pk.Rcch.Van'87
☎ (216) 321-4225 . . 21180 Colby Rd, Shaker Heights, OH *44122*

Jones MISS Cynthia S (Sisk—Cynthia S Jones) Bvr'82.Dar.
☎ (619) 979-9953 . . 2833 N Arroyo Dv, San Diego, CA *92103*

Jones MRS David Humphreys (Ann E Read) . . . . . . | ☎ (540) 463-6560
MR Landon H—W&L'85.JMad'95 . . . . | 101 Rebel Ridge
| Dv, Lexington, VA
| *24450*

Jones MR & MRS David Lloyd (Flagg—Hattie—Hildegard Schneider)
Un.Plg.Ny.Co.Bm.L.So.Chr.Bcs.Ne.Snc.Cw.Rv.Myf. W&L'45.H.'46 . . of
☎ (561) 655-5566 . . 100 Worth Av, Palm Beach, FL *33480-4464*
☎ (212) 355-4321 . . 200 E 66 St, New York, NY *10021*
Mch 1 . . ☎ (970) 925-3069 . . PO Box 12049, Aspen, CO *81612*

Jones MR & MRS (DR) Dayton L (Debra K Grubb)
Carl'79.SCal'86.Carl'74.Cr'81
☎ (818) 952-7624 . . 224 Starlight Crest Dv, La Cañada, CA *91011*

Jones MRS De Lancey F J (Barbara C Parsons) . . . . Died at
Williamstown, MA May 5'96

Jones MR De Lancey F J—Ham'38.Cl'39
☎ (413) 458-8552 . . 416 Hemlock Brook Park, Williamstown,
MA *01267*

Jones MR Dryden—H'46
☎ (904) 824-6001 . . 3145 N Coastal H'way, 1136, Box 3575,
St Augustine, FL *32085*

Jones MR & MRS Dryden JR (Wendy V Collinson) | ☎ (513) 561-4407
Finch'71.Rol'70 . . . . | 6665 N Clippinger
MISS Millicent H . . . . | Dv, Cincinnati, OH
MISS Alison F . . . . | *45243*
JUNIORS MISS Christen C . . . . |

Jones MR & MRS E Powis (Anne Keating) Un.Gr.Cs.
☎ (212) 734-1160 . . 925 Park Av, New York, NY *10028*

Jones MISS Edith B—Pa'77.Pa'81.H'86
☎ (617) 241-5452 . . 8 Mystic St, Charlestown, MA *02129*

Jones MR & MRS Edward E JR (Helen Sawyer) | of ☎ (212)249-4202
Rc.Br'64 . . . . | 1065 Lexington Av,
MR Tyler L—at U of Vt . . . . | New York, NY
| *10021*
| ☎ (860) 434-9329
| Box 942, Old Lyme,
| CT *06371*

Jones MR & MRS Edward S (Patricia H Bleecker)
S.Cw.Snc.Ht.Dh.Ofp.Myf.Cda.P'50
☎ (212) 831-8184 . . 110 E 87 St, Apt 6C, New York, NY *10128-1119*

Jones MR & MRS Edwin S (Hope V DePew) | ☎ (314) WY1-0765
Cy.Lc.Rc.Nd. . . . . | 765 Cella Rd,
MR Douglas DeP—at ☎ (541) 343-4333 | St Louis, MO *63124*
2798 Norbert Lane, Eugene, OR *97401* . . . . |

Jones MISS Elizabeth W—Denis'89
☎ (617) 859-1848 . . 82 Carr Rd, Concord, MA *01742*

Jones MR & MRS Ellis B (Lisa S Taylor)
☎ (310) 275-8204 . . 1718 Angelo Dv, Beverly Hills, CA *90210*

Jones MR & MRS Ellwood F JR (Ethel M Henderson) | ☎ (610) 828-2817
Rv.Sar.Dar.Pa'53 . . . . | "Rabbitwood"
MR E Franklin 3d—JHop'79—at | Miquon Rd,
☎ (619) 223-2018 . . 3035 Kingsley St, | Conshohocken, PA
San Diego, CA *92106* | *19428*

Jones MR & MRS Evan Voorhees (Palmer—Sarah L Stevens) Sdy.Stan'39
☎ (619) 223-9994 . . 530 San Fernando St, San Diego, CA *92106*

Jones MR & MRS Frank Charles (Laura A Benedict) | ☎ (205) 967-7402
Aub'65.So'62.Mit'63 . . . . | 3301 Overcrest Rd,
MISS Laura B . . . . | Birmingham, AL
JUNIORS MR Caldwell C . . . . | *35223*

Jones MRS Frank J (Harriet S Neithercut) Sth'28
☎ (860) 434-5126 . . 7 Town Landing Rd, Box 525, Old Lyme,
CT *06371*

Jones MR Franklin D—Fic.Bost'85
☎ (617) 742-7181 . . 93 Pinckney St, Boston, MA *02114*

Jones JUNIORS MR Frederick K . . see W J Evans

Jones MR Gilbert E—H'38
☎ (561) 546-9861 . . 7142 SE Golf Ridge Way, Hobe Sound, FL *33455*

Jones MR & MRS Glenn D (Patricia J Van Andel) ArizSt'63.Stan'49
☎ (602) 678-5333 . . 7012 N 22 St, Phoenix, AZ *85020*

Jones MRS Henry W (Juska—Pauline E Ash) Pc. . . . | ☎ (215) CH2-1033
MISS Diane E—Scripps'63—at ☎ (619) 327-5639 | 233 W Allen's Lane,
2550 N Kitty Hawk Dv, Palm Springs, CA *92262* | Philadelphia, PA
MR Edward F Juska JR—at 108 Morris Av, | *19119*
Long Branch, NJ *07740* . . . . |

Jones MR & MRS Herbert N (Jane P Bond) Nd.Cy.Y'27
☎ (314) PA7-0343 . . 8010 Pershing Av, Clayton, MO *63105*

Jones MR & MRS Horace C (Helen M Allen) Ph.Sg.Ri.Ac.P.'38 . . of
☎ (215) 247-4765 . . Hill House Apt 610, 201 W Evergreen Av,
Philadelphia, PA *19118*
☎ (508) 994-0456 . . "Buzzards Nest" PO Box P153, Nonquitt,
South Dartmouth, MA *02748*

Jones MRS Horace G (Hardin—Betty Smith) . . . . . . | see
MR Richard H . . . . | *Dilatory Domiciles*

Jones MR & MRS Howard Lee JR (Cook—Sherry D Scarbrough)
Houst'75.Dar.LSU'60
☎ (601) 442-3091 . . Providence Plantation, 91 Providence Rd, Natchez,
MS *39120*

Jones MR & MRS Howland B JR (Elizabeth F Lyon) Chi.Stv'49 🚣
☎ (508) 432-0046 . . Harbor Rd, Harwich Port, MA *02646*

Jones MR & MRS Hoyle C (Elizabeth E A Burdick) Rc.Pr.W&L'60 . . of
☎ (212) 861-7243 . . 61 E 80 St, New York, NY *10021*
☎ (516) 922-6798 . . "Beaver Hollow" Frost Mill Rd, Mill Neck,
NY *11765*

Jones MRS J Stuart JR (Gladys C Whittle) Gchr'29
Roland Park Place, 830 W 40 St, Baltimore, MD *21211*

Jones MR J Turner—Ga'39.GaTech'40
☎ (954) 522-2629 . . 1586 S Ocean Lane, Ft Lauderdale, FL *33316*

Jones MR & MRS Jeremiah W (Louisa A Gebelein) Ripon'78.Hob'75.H'84
☎ (860) 928-1122 . . Pomfret School, Rte 44, Pomfret, CT *06258*

Jones DR & MRS John Allen 3d (Frances J Hardwich)	☎ (334) 269-6514
GaSt'68.Van'65.Emory'70	2138 Rosemont Dv,
MISS Laura K	Montgomery, AL
	36111

Jones MR & MRS John L (Charlotte Johnson) Cal'37.Bhm.StJ.Cal'37
☎ (415) 868-0133 . . 322 Seadrift Rd, PO Box 147, Stinson Beach, CA *94970*

Jones MR & MRS Kaye Harding (Anne M Churchill)
Wells'50.Pn.Utah'39.Cl'48
1801 Crayton Rd, Naples, FL *34102*

Jones MR & MRS Kenneth B (Sally B Montgomery) Denis'84.Nw'89
7313 N Hazel Av, Fresno, CA *93711-0223*

Jones MR & MRS Lee Richardson (Maud Dulany Barker) Mv.Cda.
☎ (410) 356-3807 . . ''Fair Warning'' 24 Old Tollgate Rd, Owings Mills, MD *21117*

Jones MRS Linda R (Grant—Linda C Ryan) Rd.Srb.	☎ (401) 751-2826
MISS Virginia R	63 Manning St,
JUNIORS MISS Alexandra D	Providence, RI
	02906

Jones MR & MRS Loren F (Mary A Larzelere) Pc.Myf.Wash'26.Stan'29
☎ (215) 984-8356 . . Cathedral Village I506, 600 E Cathedral Rd, Philadelphia, PA *19128*

Jones MR & MRS Louis W JR (Marie Cunningham) Scripps'52.Vh.Occ'49
☎ (818) 799-1800 . . 2030 Oak Knoll Av, San Marino, CA *91108*

Jones MRS M Troy (Boyer—Strawbridge—Mary B Holmes)
Ac.Me.Gm.Rd.Pkg.Cly.Ncd.
☎ (610) 933-2858 . . PO Box 337, White Horse Rd, Paoli, PA *19301-0337*

Jones MR Mark ap Catesby—Rcn.Plg.StJ.
☎ (817) 246-6677 . . 717 Verna Trail N, Ft Worth, TX *76108-4308*

Jones MR & MRS Maury A (Martha G Milam) W&L'34
☎ (314) 965-2324 . . 131 E Adams Av, Apt 1D, St Louis, MO *63122*

Jones MR Maury F
☎ (314) 966-6521 . . 519 N Taylor Av, Kirkwood, MO *63122-4458*

Jones MR & MRS Meredith C 3d (Corinne L Dennig) Vt'83.Cy.Nd.Vt'84
☎ (314) 721-8797 . . 212 Linden Av, St Louis, MO *63105*

Jones MISS Nancy Q—StLaw'83
☎ (202) 333-3763 . . 2132—37 St NW, Washington, DC *20007*

Jones JUNIORS MR Oliver H . . see W J Evans

Jones MISS Palmer D . . see W J Evans

Jones MR & MRS Parry von S (Tappan—Judith H	☎ (516) OR1-1955
Lockton) Pr.L.Br'58	Feeks Lane,
MISS Alexandra V	Mill Neck, NY
MR Nicholas P	*11765*
MISS Alice M Tappan	
MR Michael A Tappan JR	
MR David L Tappan	

Jones MR & MRS Patrick S JR (Katherine H Mellon)
StLaw'86.Shcc.Eh.Macalester'86
☎ (908) 439-9226 . . PO Box 310, 24 Hill & Dale Rd, Oldwick, NJ *08858*

Jones MR & MRS Peter C (Blum—Charlotte M Frieze)
Sth'74.Un.Gr.RISD'74
☎ (212) 628-6226 . . 125 E 84 St, New York, NY *10028*

Jones MR & MRS Peter D (Leslie R Murphy) Ithaca'85.K.Y'60.Cl'63
☎ (212) 876-4040 . . 1105 Park Av, New York, NY *10128*

Jones MR & MRS Peter R (Margot Potter Kiser)
DU'82.DU'84.Mds.Ox'81 . . of
☎ (011-255-57) 8547 . . Ndarakwai Game Reserve, PO Box 49, Arusha, Tanzania
☎ (406) 585-7865 . . 701 S 6 St, Bozeman, MT *59715*
☎ (406) 932-6212 . . ''Twisted Stick'' W Boulder River Rd, McLeod, MT *59052*

Jones MR & MRS Proctor P (Martha E Martin)	☎ (415) 922-1102
Bhm.Tcy.Uncl.Cwr'37.Cwr'48	2010 Jackson St,
MISS Jessica H	San Francisco, CA
	94109

Jones MRS Ralph JR (Marian Gresh) G.
☎ (561) 394-0984 . . 951 Holly Lane, Boca Raton, FL *33486*

Jones MRS Richard 3d (Reeder—Barbara Durston) Pn.
☎ (617) 326-9429 . . 10 Longwood Dv, Apt 515, Westwood, MA *02090*

Jones MR & MRS Richard W (Sarah S Bartlett)	☎ (201) 768-1832
Sth'61.Nu'66.Lm.Cl'63	124 La Roche Av,
MR Philip B—Woos'94	Harrington Park, NJ
	07640

Jones MR & MRS Richard W S (Grace J Ellicott)	of ☎ (717)546-6450
WashColl'54.Leh'54	223 S Main St,
MR Andrew E—Leh'84.Leh'85.Roch'87—at	Box 383, Muncy,
U of Rochester Grad	PA *17756*
MR Purnell M—at Penn State	''Ellicott Cottage''
	Eagles Mere, PA
	17731

Jones MR & MRS Richard Welton (Cynthia Gordon Cronkhite)
Bhm.B.Cal'46
☎ (818) 796-5274 . . 303 California Terr, Pasadena, CA *91105*

Jones MR & MRS Robert A (Harriet H White)
☎ (617) 846-6293 . . 640 Pleasant St, Winthrop, MA *02152*

Jones MRS Robert C (Chapman—Jille Romney)
☎ (242) 362-4080 . . Lyford Cay, Box N7776, Nassau, NP, Bahamas

Jones MR & MRS Robert D (Suzanne English)	☎ (847) 446-5345
Wells'80.Ih.Cnt.Ind'55	326 Woodland Av,
MR R Anthony—SCal'88	Winnetka, IL *60093*
MR Christopher E—SantaC'94	

Jones DR & MRS Robert E (Florence B V Vaught) Ariz'44.Nw'41.Tul'44
☎ (602) 265-9760 . . 130 E Missouri Av, Phoenix, AZ *85012*

Jones MR & MRS Robert Metcalf (Ynez C Broome) Pcu.Fr.Ia'34.SCal'38
☎ (415) 921-2230 . . 2612 Scott St, San Francisco, CA *94123*

Jones MR Robert Trent—Myf.Yn.Cr'30
3801 Bayview Dv, Ft Lauderdale, FL *33308*

Jones MR & MRS Robert Trent JR (A Claiborne	☎ (415) 367-1015
Smith) Swb'61.Bhm.Sfg.Y'61	198 Churchill Av,
MISS E Taliaferro	Woodside, CA
MR Robert Trent 3d	*94062*

Jones MR & MRS Robert W (Alice L S Cole) Lx.SUNY'48
☎ (518) 794-8944 . . ''The Century'' West Lebanon, NY *12195*

Jones MR & MRS Roger L (Christina Masters) Ty'82.Pc.Pa'81
☎ (215) 836-2075 . . 211 Heatherwood Rd, Erdenheim, PA *19038*

Jones MR & MRS Roger M (F Margaret Taylor) .... ☎ (242) 327-7986
MISS Margaret F—at ☎ (540) 547-2352 | Sulgrave Manor,
3100 N Merrimac Rd, Culpeper, VA *22701* .... | W Bay St,
MR Andrew G—at Boston, MA .... | Box N7790,
| Nassau, Bahamas

Jones MR & MRS Russell C (Mary A Nicol) NotreD'72
☎ (415) 323-7280 . . 402 Oak Grove Av, Menlo Park, CA *94025*

Jones MR & MRS Samuel B 4th (Patricia Starr) Exy. | of ☎ (203)966-1675
MR Samuel Bancroft—Mid'92 .... | 60 Old Rock Lane,
MR Christopher S—Denis'94 .... | New Canaan, CT
| *06840*
| ☎ (802) 824-3172
| Landgrove Rd,
| RR 1, Box 231,
| Landgrove, VT
| *05148*

Jones MR & MRS Stephen B (Elizabeth A Rowley) ChHill'66.Chr.Tufts'60
☎ (212) 289-2219 . . 1435 Lexington Av, New York, NY *10128*

Jones MR & MRS Stephen C (Jody L Clark) Wash'81.Cy.Nd.Y'70
☎ (314) 994-9628 . . 15 Cedar Crest, St Louis, MO *63132*

Jones MR Thomas Lee
☎ (212) 794-2499 . . 12 E 86 St, New York, NY *10028*

Jones MR & MRS W Boardman JR (Rebecca Wells) Cy.Nd.P'37
☎ (314) 993-2921 . . 19 Fordyce Lane, St Louis, MO *63124*

Jones MR & MRS Walter R (Nancy Rose) Cwr'49 ... | ☎ (216) 561-3899
MISS Barbara B—Miami'88 .... | 2906 Woodbury Rd,
| Shaker Heights, OH
| *44120*

Jones MR Whipple Van N—Cysl.H'32
335 Glen Eagles Dv, Aspen, CO *81611*

Jones MRS Whitson McL (Ogelsby—Isabel W Martin) Ncd.
☎ (619) 454-6773 . . PO Box 9001, La Jolla, CA *92038*

Jones MR & MRS William McM JR (Katharine H Jones)
Tufts'82.Pg.Unn.Rr.GeoW'80
☎ (412) 782-3809 . . "The Cottage" 711 W Waldheim Rd, Pittsburgh,
PA *15215*

Jones MR & MRS William P JR (M Elizabeth Higgins)
Qns'83.Pars'85.Hn.H'73
☎ (203) 656-2204 . . 14 Edgehill Dv, Darien, CT *06820*

Jones MRS William Pickering (Elizabeth Jarvis Beach) .... Died at
New York, NY Mch 25'96

Jones MR William Pickering .... Died at
Darien, CT Mch 29'96

Jones MRS William Powell (Marian R Ginn) Cv.
☎ (216) 423-4553 . . "Moxahela" Gates Mills, OH *44040*

Jones MR & MRS Winfield P (Davis—Miller— | ☎ (212) 371-8568
Madeleine D Burns) MmtMhn'84.B.Cly.H'63 .. | 14 Sutton Place S,
MISS Kirsten M Davis .... | New York, NY
JUNIORS MR Robert B Miller............. | *10022*

Jonklaas MR & MRS Anthony (Claire H Bolton) | ☎ (912) 228-0566
Sm.H'52................................. | "Melrose
MISS Claire Hanna—LakeF'88 .... | Plantation"
| 1368 Lower Cairo
| Rd, Thomasville,
| GA *31792*

Jonson MISS Dana A—Fairf'95 . . see H B Satterthwaite

Jonson MR Randolph S—HWSth'94 . . see H B Satterthwaite
Jopson MR Harry G M—Hav'32
☎ (540) 828-3115 . . 114 Broad St, Box 26, Bridgewater, VA *22812*

Jordan MR & MRS Daniel P JR (Lewellyn L | ☎ (804) 295-4384
Schmelzer) Miss'61.Miss'62.Miss'60.Miss'62. | "Monticello"
Va'70 .... | PO Box 316,
MISS Grace D—at 763 Washington St, Apt 11, | Charlottesville, VA
New York, NY *10014* .... | *22902*
MISS Katherine L .... |
MR Daniel P 3d—at 1517 St Ann St, Jackson, MS |
39202 .... |

Jordan MR & MRS David C (Anabella Guzmán) BuenosA'63.H'57
☎ (804) 295-4698 . . 1190 Owensville Rd, Charlottesville, VA *22901*

Jordan MR & MRS Eben (Ellen T Van Pelt) Wheat'81.Syr'80
☎ (610) 647-5575 . . 319 Monument Av, Malvern, PA *19355*

Jordan MRS F Peter (Beatrice L Renwick) Ac.
☎ (610) 933-8441 . . "Rolling Acres" Box 127, Valley Forge,
PA *19481-0127*

Jordan MR & MRS George E (Florence P Evans) Ala'61.Cda.Ala'57
☎ (334) 279-9554 . . 1606 Croom Dv, Montgomery, AL *36106*

Jordan DR & MRS Henry A (West—Barbara J | ☎ (610) 827-7351
McNeil) Ph.Rc.Ac.Ncd.H.'58.Pa'62 .... | 1465 Horseshoe
MISS Gretchen McN—Colg'93—at 220 E 24 St, | Trail,
Apt 1H, New York, NY *10010* .... | Chester Springs, PA
MR Michael H—Vt'92—at 137 N 22 St, | *19425*
Philadelphia, PA *19103* .... |
JUNIORS MR Douglas L .... |

Jordan MRS James C (Mittnacht—Keo England) Pc.
☎ (215) 542-8224 . . 201 Copper Beech Dv, Blue Bell, PA *19422*

Jordan MR & MRS John D (Paula J Kuebler) Hn.H'59
☎ (908) 842-1919 . . 10 Brookside Dv, Rumson, NJ *07760*

Jordan MR & MRS Philip H JR (Sheila A Gray) | of ☎ (614)427-2171
Ws'55.P'54.Y'56.Y'62 .... | 401 Gaskin Av,
MR Philip H 3d—Wms'89.H'93 .... | Gambier, OH *43022*
MR John G 2d—Colby'94.................. | ☎ (207) 846-5618
| "Stone Sloop"
| Chebeague Island,
| ME *04017*

Jordan MRS R Bennett (Ruth A Bennett) SL'46.NYLaw'81.Csh.Cly.Cda.
☎ (212) 832-3717 . . 200 E 66 St, New York, NY *10021-6728*

Jordan MISS Victoria V (David C) .... Married at Ivy, VA
Roberts MR John C .... Apr 20'96

Jordan MR & MRS William JR (Burton—Sheila A Garside)
Un.Rby.Plg.Cw.Snc.Wes'39.H'42 . .
☎ (212) 685-5645 . . 150 E 38 St, New York, NY *10016*
☎ (203) 438-8667 . . "Old Oaks" 31 Whipstick Rd, Ridgefield,
CT *06877*

Jordan MR & MRS William C (Grace R Vance) Briar'74.SCal'54
☎ (805) 379-0348 . . 4607 Club View Dv, Westlake Village, CA *91362*

Jordan MR William Norris JR—Rc.Sg.Vt'84
☎ (215) 731-9733 . . 1741 Addison St, Philadelphia, PA *19146*

Jordan MR William W—Hob'78
☎ (718) 832-1883 . . 103 Prospect Park W, Apt 1, Brooklyn, NY *11215*

Jorgensen MR Edvard—H'72.H'76 . . of
☎ (212) 686-8522 . . 16 Park Av, New York, NY *10016*
☎ (516) 423-1118 . . 3 St Mark's Place, Cold Spring Harbor, NY *11724*

Joseph MR & MRS L Anthony JR (Marguerite S Reeves) Conv'62.Un.Rc.K.Ri.Plg.Cly.StJ.Ncd. Tex'63.Tex'68 . . . . of ☎ (212)879-4541 149 E 73 St, New York, NY *10021*
MISS Marguerite S . . . .
MISS Courtney V—at Roanoke Coll . . . . ☎ (803) 722-4922 27 Meeting St, Charleston, SC *29401*
JUNIORS MISS E Reeves—at Deerfield . . . .
JUNIORS MR A Michael . . . .

Josephs MR & MRS Devereux C JR (Gray Wells) Hn.H'47
☎ (303) 698-2343 . . 3333 Belcaro Dv, Denver, CO *80209*

Josephson MR & MRS Wayne A (Margaret D Ijams) Emory'71.Pa'76
☎ (203) 761-8754 . . 15 Snowberry Lane, Wilton, CT *06897*

Josey MR & MRS Clinton Wiley JR (Betty Smith)
☎ (214) 521-3953 . . 4402 Westside Dv, Dallas, TX *75209*

Josey MR & MRS Jack Smyth (Neuhoff—Donna Jo Pearson) Swb'64.Tex'38 . . . . of ☎ (713)522-2116 1537 Kirby Dv, Houston, TX *77019*
MISS Donna A Neuhoff . . . .
MISS Emily P Neuhoff—at 4217 Allencrest Lane, Dallas, TX *75244* . . . . ☎ (409) 249-5645 PO Box 156, Round Top, TX *78954*
MISS Virginia F Neuhoff—at ☎ (212) 734-7942 . . 328 E 78 St, Apt 5, New York, NY *10021*
MR Joe O Neuhoff 3d—at 4217 Allencrest Lane, Dallas, TX *75244* . . . .

Joss MR & MRS Frederick A (Diana B Dickey) Cvc.Wms'54.Pitt'67
☎ (412) 441-7585 . . 433 Denniston Av, Pittsburgh, PA *15206*

Joy MRS Frederick van B (Edith L P Greacen) Mg.Mo.Cda.
☎ (904) 427-2753 . . 384 Gleneagles Dv, New Smyrna Beach, FL *32168*

Joyce MR & MRS Alexis J (Cumbest—M Cayce McAlister) Miss'79.Louis'80.Van'76.Mich'78.GaTech'85
☎ (615) 331-4607 . . 1105 Otter Creek Rd, Nashville, TN *37220*

Joyce MR & MRS Douglas Henry (Sue M Smythe) Woff'79
☎ (615) 373-2556 . . ''Trillium Pastures'' 1950 Chickering Rd, Nashville, TN *37215*

Joyce MR & MRS H Sherman (Eda A Martin) Sth'80.P'82.CathU'87
☎ (703) 548-8155 . . 505 E Braddock Rd, Apt 408, Alexandria, VA *22314*

Joyce MISS Margaret Sinclair (Douglas Henry) . . . . Born at Nashville, TN May 28'96

Joyce MISS Sue Atherton (Douglas Henry) . . . . Born at Nashville, TN May 28'96

Joyce MRS Thomas F JR (Schultz—Katharine Flint) PO Box S3256, Carmel, CA *93921-0589*

Joyce MR & MRS William R JR (Mary-Hoyt Sherman) Cvc.Mt.Sl.Loy'42 . . . . of ☎ (202)244-7648 4339 Garfield St NW, Washington, DC *20007-1141*
MISS Helen Floyd-Jones—Rich'85 . . . . ☎ (607) 547-5123 ''The Distillery'' 11 River St, Cooperstown, NY *13326-1051*

Jubitz MR & MRS M Albin (Nancy A Thompson) Ore'68.Y'66.Ore'68 . . . . ☎ (503) 292-0046 5505 SW Hewett Blvd, Portland, OR *97221*
MISS Katherine A—Skd'94 . . . .
MISS Sarah C—at Trinity . . . .

Judson MR & MRS Arthur 2d (Bright Miller) An.Pe.Fw.Sdg.Dth'52.H'56 . . . . ☎ (215) 836-7459 ''Andorra Corners'' 149 W Northwestern Av, Philadelphia, PA *19118*
MR Christopher B—Drexel'95 . . . .

Judson MRS Cyrus F (Virginia W Needham) Cr'23
☎ (703) 578-7552 . . 3440 S Jefferson St, Apt 901, Falls Church, VA *22041*

Judson MRS Francis E (Henrietta P Chapman) Ac.Ncd.
☎ (610) MU8-6622 . . 201 Windermere Av, Wayne, PA *19087*

Judson MR & MRS Gilbert H (Mohr—Blair B Bellis) LakeF'77
☎ (415) 507-9268 . . 25 Circle Rd, San Rafael, CA *94903*

Judson MISS Henrietta C (Elliott—Henrietta C Judson) OWes'90.Dar.
☎ (512) 860-3176 . . 2600 Lake Austin Blvd, Apt 6103, Austin, TX *78703*

Judson MISS Katherine Blair (Gilbert H) . . . . Born at San Francisco, CA Aug 13'96

Judson MR & MRS Robert D (Mary D Scribner) Ih.Ncd.P'47 . . . . of ☎ (847)446-1955 74 Locust Rd, Winnetka, IL *60093*
MR Douglass S . . . . ☎ (561) 546-7591 on board First Afloat'' PO Box 877, Hobe Sound, FL *33475*

Judson MR & MRS Robert D JR (Janice E Huckins) Sfg.Bur.SCal'71.Ariz'73
☎ (415) 342-6421 . . 230 Amherst Av, San Mateo, CA *94402*

Judson MRS William David (M Hooker Woodward) MR Stephen Y—at 8133 Elrita Dv, Los Angeles, CA *90046* . . . . ☎ (860) 434-0241 ''Edge Lea'' South Lyme, CT *06376*

Judy MR & MRS J Lawrence (Ann M Clary) Vh.Clare'67 . . . . of ☎ (818)304-9294 485 Maylin St, Pasadena, CA *91105*
MISS Margaret B . . . .
MR Carter E . . . . ☎ (415) 296-9068 1 Pine St, Apt 2204, San Francisco, CA *94111*

Julian MRS Morrow (Barbara Morrow) Cal'52 . . . . . of ☎ (202)337-1937 2475 Virginia Av NW, Washington, DC *20037*
MR Charles . . . . ☎ (602) 423-9950 ''My Cottage'' 4800 N 68 St, Scottsdale, AZ *85251*

Julien MR & MRS George W (R Therese Ryan) Miami'56.ClevSt'85.Y'50 . . . . ☎ (216) 721-0101 1950 Denton Dv, Cleveland Heights, OH *44106*
MISS Jennifer R—at ☎ (907) 272-3036 1435 W 25 Av, Anchorage, AK *99520* . . . .
MISS Jocelyn M . . . .
MR George W JR . . . .
MR Don H . . . .

Julien MR Richard E H JR—Mit'60.Cal'63 . . of
220 Montgomery St, Apt 710, San Francisco, CA *94104*
☎ (916) 436-2460 . . "Vineland Cottage" Julien Rd, Box 306, Grenada, CA *96038*

Junkin MRS Joseph de F (Lois Swan) . . . . Died at
Boca Grande, FL May 17'96

Junkin MR & MRS Joseph S (Sara A Caldwell) │ ☎ (617) 894-3576
V'76.Au.Sm.Chi.H.'61 . . . . │ 209 Meadowbrook
MR Joseph R . . . . │ Rd, Weston, MA
MR Angus H . . . . │ *02193*

Junod MRS Henri Pell (Gertrude M Busch) Tex'36.Cv.Kt . . .of
☎ (216) 321-0725 . . 20200 N Park Blvd, Shaker Heights, OH *44118-5003*
☎ (941) 262-1278 . . 1121 Gulf Shore Blvd N, Naples, FL *34102*

Junod MR Henri Pell JR—Kt.Cv.Lm.Ty'66.Cwr'69.Cwr'70
☎ (216) 321-0725 . . 20200 N Park Blvd, Shaker Heights, OH *44118-5003*

Juska MR Edward F JR . . see MRS H W Jones

Just MISS Jennifer R . . see F C Darling JR

Just MISS Julia B (Azerrad—Julia B Just) . . see MRS R T Bower

Justi MR & MRS Henry K (Helen B Milne)
Me.Ste.Cry.Rv.Myf.Ac.Pa'60 . . of
☎ (610) 525-1361 . . 1138 Red Rose Lane, Villanova, PA *19085*
☎ (242) 366-0365 . . "Surf Song" Hope Town, Abaco, Bahamas

Justi MR & MRS Henry M (Melinda S Mazaheri)
F&M'80.Dick'83.Me.WmSth'81.Dick'84
☎ (610) 527-8552 . . 1030 Old Gulph Rd, Bryn Mawr, PA *19010*

Justi MR & MRS Thomas R (Rebecca J Spratt) │ of ☎ (610)783-7122
Gm.Me. │ 507 Richards Rd,
MR David M—J'ville'84 . . . . │ Wayne, PA
│ *19087-1005*
│ ☎ (561) 336-2957
│ 2010 Laurel Oak
│ Lane, Palm City, FL
│ *34990*

K

Kadey MR & MRS Frederic L JR (Brenda Boocock) Rut'41.H'47
☎ (561) 795-1415 . . 14127 Aster Av, Wellington, FL *33414*

Kahle MR & MRS G Kent (Cynthia S Vietor) Colby'74.Br'74.Pa'82
☎ (713) 840-0443 . . 3460 Ella Lee Lane, Houston, TX *77027*

Kahle MR & MRS Jeffrey L (Elizabeth J Goulian) Y.'84
☎ (212) 875-1933 . . 100 W 80 St, Apt 3E, New York, NY *10024*

Kahn MR & MRS Leonard C (Courtney C Pyles) Va'80.Va'82
☎ (415) 771-6190 . . 2832 Octavia St, San Francisco, CA *94123*

Kaier MR & MRS Edward J (Annette B Thomas) │ ☎ (610) LA5-7494
Ph.Me.H.'67.Pa'70 . . . . │ 111 N Lowry's
JUNIORS MISS Elizabeth A . . . . │ Lane, Rosemont, PA
│ *19010*

Kaiser MR & MRS C Hayden JR (Barbara G Brandon)
Miss'62.Cda.Dar.LSU'52
☎ (601) 445-8646 . . 202 Dana Rd, Natchez, MS *39120*

Kaiser MISS Diana T—Franklin'76
☎ (202) 342-1178 . . 3901 Tunlaw Rd NW, Apt 205, Washington, DC *20007*

Kaiser MR & MRS Franck H (Beverly J Hurt)
☎ (314) 434-0021 . . 146 Babler Rd, St Louis, MO *63141-8002*

Kaiser MR Franck H JR │ ☎ (407) 768-2299
MISS Courtenay A—at ☎ (508) 993-7780 │ 605 Sheridan Woods
378 Cottage St, New Bedford, MA *02740* . . . . . │ Dv, West
│ Melbourne, FL
│ *32904-3303*

Kaiser MR Robert A JR—Bost'80
☎ (202) 667-7646 . . 2718 Devonshire Place NW, Washington, DC *20008*

Kaiser MR Stephen Hyatt . . . . │ ☎ (954) 561-1154
JUNIORS MR Stephen Hyatt JR . . . . │ 2633 NE 26 Av,
│ Ft Lauderdale, FL
│ *33306*

Kales MRS Davis (Betty Baxter)
☎ (203) 655-0558 . . 41 Hancock Lane, Darien, CT *06820*

Kales MR & MRS William R 2d (Nancy B Ely)
Sth'64.Sfy.Fr.Dc.Ds.Ncd.P'62.Cl'66
☎ (415) 922-3481 . . 2634 Broderick St, San Francisco, CA *94123-4605*

Kallio MRS Sylvia A (de Flogny—Sylvia Anderson)
☎ (202) 338-1364 . . 2632—44 St NW, Washington, DC *20007*

Kallop MR & MRS William M (Deborah B Farber) │ ☎ (212) 517-4488
Cr'68.Mds.Cly.P.'65.H'67 . . . . │ 1030 Fifth Av,
MR Brooks M . . . . │ New York, NY
JUNIORS MR Brent McK . . . . │ *10028*

Kalt MRS Pryor H (Mary Gayle Dowson)
☎ (212) BU8-4907 . . 850 Park Av, New York, NY *10021*

Kaltenbach MRS Henry J (Read—Waterworth—Laura Dean)
Me.Gm.Ac.Ncd.
☎ (610) 525-3647 . . 74 Pasture Lane, Apt 340, Bryn Mawr, PA *19010*

Kamihachi MR & MRS James D (Louise L Henry) │ of ☎ (703)836-8914
BaldW'71.Wms'71.H'73 . . . . │ 3317 Old Dominion
JUNIORS MISS Caroline H . . . . │ Blvd, Alexandria,
JUNIORS MISS Catherine G . . . . │ VA *22305*
│ ☎ (410) 287-2853
│ 700 Piney Creek
│ Lane, North East,
│ MD *21901*

Kamilli MR & MRS Robert J (Diana F Chapman) │ ☎ (520) 749-0302
V'63.Rut68.Myf.Rut'69.H'76 . . . . │ 5050 N Siesta Dv,
JUNIORS MISS Ann C . . . . │ Tucson, AZ *85750*

Kaminer MR Peter H—C.Mt.Basle'36.Y'39
☎ (212) 288-1824 . . 830 Park Av, New York, NY *10021*

Kaminer MR Stevenson S—Unn.Mt.Ayc.Aht'74.Y'79 ⚓
☎ (202) 797-1499 . . 2737 Devonshire Place NW, Washington, DC *20008*

Kamm MR & MRS Charles R (Alice Baldwin) │ ☎ (408) 636-9106
P'38.Stan'40 . . . . │ 50 Villa Pacheco
MR Charles M—at ☎ (415) 381-3272 │ Court, Hollister, CA
26 Catalpa Rd, Mill Valley, CA *94941* . . . . │ *95023*
MR Peter R . . . . │

Kammer MR A Frederick . . . . Died at
Hobe Sound, FL Feb 21'96

Kammer MRS A Frederick (Fentress—Barbara L Warner) Ac. . . . .
   MR David L Fentress—FlaSt'88—at
   ☎ (561) 288-2624 . . 4244 SE Centerboard Lane, Stuart, FL *34997* . . . . |
☎ (561) 546-5091
446 S Beach Rd, Hobe Sound, FL *33455*

Kampmann MR & MRS Eric M (Anne P Hilmer) Pc.Pl.Br'66
   ☎ (203) 637-0607 . . 93 Riverside Av, Riverside, CT *06878*

Kampmann MISS Megan H . . see C van D Hubbard

Kanaga MR & MRS Clinton R (Victoria H Elmer) Mass'84.Mass'86
   ☎ (508) 255-4017 . . 21 Anchor Dv, Orleans, MA *02653*

Kane MR Alexander F
   ☎ (719) 382-5100 . . "Kane Ranch" Box 219, Fountain, CO *80817*

Kane MR & MRS Charles F JR (Anne W Eldridge) Wms'78.Nf.Ub.Un.Bab'73
   ☎ (617) 934-0354 . . 251 Harrison St, Box 241, Duxbury, MA *02332*

Kane MR & MRS John Kent 2d (Nancy C Baumes) RMWmn'57.Cry.Ll.Rv.Snc.W&L'56.VaPoly'61
   MR John Kent 3d—VaPoly'81.Rens'84—at Mathews, VA . . . .
   MR Robert T—at Newport News, VA . . . .
   MR Evan Paul—at Orlando, FL. . . . . |
☎ (757) 898-6953
101 Sleepy Hollow Lane, Yorktown, VA *23692*

Kane MRS Larzelere (Elizabeth C Larzelere)
   ☎ (401) 423-2928 . . "Sand Point" 1243 N Main Rd, Jamestown, RI *02835*

Kane MR & MRS Louis I (Katharine F Daniels) Sth'56.Ub.Sm.Hn.H.'53
   ☎ (617) 523-7651 . . 10 Chestnut St, Boston, MA *02108*

Kane DR & MRS Peter B (Sandra M Bonney) Ll.Rv.H'60.Pa'64
   MISS Catherine H—at Vassar . . . .
   JUNIORS MR Thomas B . . . . |
☎ (315) 655-8720
4462 Lincklaen Rd, Cazenovia, NY *13035*

Kania MR & MRS Arthur J JR (Elizabeth B Young) Roan'85.Me.Buck'78
150 Tunbridge Circle, Haverford, PA *19041*

Kanovsky MR & MRS Stephen M (Mary C Wood) Skd'83.Pa'89.Ac.Pa'84.Temp'93
   ☎ (215) 862-1936 . . 88 Old York Rd, New Hope, PA *18938*

Kaplan MRS Sheldon Z (Megan Vondersmith) Ws'45.Cos. . . . .
   MR Eldon M—Rv.Sar.LakeF'74.Ty'81.CathU'87
   MR Daniel B . . . .
   MR Philip J—Sar.W&L'78.Ox'79.Tul'84—at
   ☎ (310) 394-1568 . . 1413 Palisades Beach Rd, Santa Monica, CA *90401* . . . . |
☎ (301) 652-4488
7810 Moorland Lane, Bethesda, MD *20814*

Karl MRS (DR) Helen W (Helen L Weist) Sth'70.Va'76 . . . .
   JUNIORS MISS Katherine L . . . . |
☎ (206) 527-4838
4303 NE 33 St, Seattle, WA *98105*

Karlinski MR & MRS Frank J 3d (Tamia J Patterson) Kirk'73.Rut'83.Ham'70 . . . .
   JUNIORS MISS Elizabeth T . . . .
   JUNIORS MR Frank J 4th. . . . . |
☎ (908) 747-0989
39 Church St, Fair Haven, NJ *07704*

Dec 1 . .
52 Browns Lane, Fair Haven, NJ *07704*

Karlson MR Christopher S . . see B A Groves

Karol MR & MRS John J JR (Portia L Fitzhugh) V'71.C.Tvb.Wms'58.Y'62 . . . .
   JUNIORS MR Fitzhugh B—at Deerfield . . . . |
☎ (603) 353-9067
Main St, Orford, NH *03777*

Károlyi MR & MRS Anthony (Lutz—Josette de G Daly) T.Cho.
Plaza de la Primavera 6, Buzén 62, La Virginia, 29600 Marbella, Malaga, Spain

Karpeles MR & MRS Leo M JR (Ruth A Long) Ala'68.Cy.Ala'62 . . . .
   MISS Margaret F—at Vanderbilt . . . .
   JUNIORS MR Leo M 3d . . . . |
☎ (205) 871-2308
4 Church St, Birmingham, AL *35213*

Karr MR & MRS George W JR (Barbara G Mulford) Gchr'59.Leh'59 . . . .
   MISS Tara L . . . .
   MR Jeffrey M . . . .
   MR David W . . . . |
☎ (215) TU4-4048
1425 Stockton Rd, Meadowbrook, PA *19046*

Karr MR Randolph—Bhm.Stan'26.Stan'29
   ☎ (213) 931-3144 . . 360 S Burnside Av, Los Angeles, CA *90036*

Karrick MR & MRS David B JR (Mary E McCann) AmU'83.Cvc.Mt.Rv.Y'65 . . . .
   MISS Emilie McC—Pitzer'96 . . . .
   MR James V—Bost'92 . . . . |
☎ (603) 456-2163
PO Box 328, 107 Old Pumpkin Hill Rd, Warner, NH *03278*

Karri-Davies MRS Walter T C (Anne Howard)
   ☎ (508) 526-4455 . . 32 Proctor St, Manchester, MA *01944*

Kase MR & MRS Charles M (Evans—Picking—Elizabeth J Parker) Cal'34.Y'33
300 Hot Springs Rd, Santa Barbara, CA *93108*

Kass, Douglas A & Welsh, Leah B—Occ'92.Wes'86.SCal'94
   ☎ (213) 651-1883 . . 756½ N Alfred St, Los Angeles, CA *90048*

Kassebaum MR & MRS John Philip (Sinkler—Llewellyn H Hood) Hlns'58.Un.Rc.Ri.Mt.Nyc.Mto.Cly.Kas'53.Mich'56
   MISS Linda J . . . .
   MR John P JR—Yh. . . . .
   MR Richard L . . . .
   MR William A . . . .
     MR G Dana Sinkler JR . . . .
     MR Huger Sinkler 2d . . . . |
of 430 N Crestway St, Witchita, KS *67208*
☎ (212) 486-0893
225 E 73 St, New York, NY *10021*

Kasten MR & MRS Walter 2d (Eileen Joan Farrell) Cho.Ih.Rc.Wms'58 . . . .
   MR Walter S . . . .
   MR Christopher M. . . . . |
☎ (847) 835-0499
117 Old Green Bay Rd, Winnetka, IL *60093*

Kastendike MR & MRS George H 4th (L Suzzanne Kooper) GaSt'72
   JUNIORS MR George H 5th . . . . |
☎ (610) 353-1743
5 Bradford Terr, Newtown Square, PA *19073*

Kastendike MR & MRS T Graham R (Deborah G Belury) OWes'74.Gi.OWes'74 ⚓
   ☎ (410) 561-3203 . . 8 Silver Stirrup Court, Timonium, MD *21093*

Kates MR & MRS Andrew K (Emily R Terry)
15A Northfield St, Greenwich, CT *06830*

Katzenbach MR & MRS E Thomas (H Brooke McLean) Sth'82.NAriz'75.Mid'87
   ☎ (011-65) 466-8293 . . 6 Mt Sinai Walk, Singapore 276783

Katzenbach MR Edward L 3d—P'66.H'71 . . . .
   MISS Allita M—Wheat'96 . . . . |
☎ (202) 338-4053
2222—48 St NW, Washington, DC *20007-1035*

Katzenbach MR & MRS L Emery (Marley Marseilles) | ☎ (914) 763-3085
Sth'50.Ln.Cly. . . . . | Box 250,
   MR Christian D—at RR 1, Box 151C, Irasburg, | Carriage House Rd,
VT 05845 . . . . | Waccabuc, NY
                                        | 10597

Katzenbach MRS M Thomas (Maude A Thomas) BMr'42
   ☎ (202) 338-4053 . . 2222—48 St NW, Washington, DC 20007-1035

Kauders MRS Erick (Wooldredge—Wheeler—Louise Sigourney) Ncd.
   ☎ (617) 275-3012 . . 307 Winthrop Terr, Bedford, MA 01730

Kauffmann MRS Godfrey W (Jane L Knapp) V'40.Cvc.
   ☎ (301) 656-1615 . . 4 Quincy St, Chevy Chase, MD 20815

Kauffmann MRS John H (Chamberlain—Patricia Bellinger) Cvc.
   505 E Washington St, Lewisburg, WV 24901

Kauffmann MR John M—Cvc.Cos.Mt.P'45 . . of
   ☎ (207) 244-3617 . . ''Oak Hill'' HCR 62, Box 47, Mt Desert,
ME 04660-9702
   ☎ (603) 636-1079 . . Waterside Lodge, Percy Summer Club, Groteton,
NH 03582

Kaufman MR & MRS Barry L (Ford—Judith F | ☎ (713) 827-0633
Snyder) Kas'67 . . . . | 34 Williamsburg
   MISS Laura F . . . . | Lane, Houston, TX
   JUNIORS MR Andrew H H . . . . | 77024

Kay MR & MRS James Murray JR (Helen C Ferguson) Me.R.Ll.Pa'55
   34 Central Dv, Plandome, NY 11030-1450

Kay MRS Sanford S (Sanford P Stallworth) Me. . . . . | ☎ (610) 642-7467
   MISS Caroline W . . . . | 4 Llanalew Rd,
                                       | Haverford, PA
                                       | 19041

Kay MRS William G JR (Chellis—Marcia Quale) | ☎ (561) 832-8320
Nw'61.H'79 . . . . | ''La Casita''
   MR Bradford A Chellis . . . . | 200 N Ocean Blvd,
                                        | Palm Beach, FL
                                        | 33480

Kayes MR & MRS Alan (Bruckner—Crawford—Cecily Elmes) Penn'32
   ☎ (212) 755-0428 . . 201 E 62 St, New York, NY 10021

Kayser MRS Victor P (Frances Matz)
   ☎ (630) 323-3265 . . ''The Woods'' 190 Pheasant Hollow Dv,
Burr Ridge, IL 60521

Keady MR & MRS Robert R (Kathryn M Updegraff) | of ☎ (408)338-6122
Cal'56.Me.Wash'60 . . . . | ''Quail Haven''
   MR Kevin I . . . . | PO Box 63,
   MR Michael G . . . . | Quail Haven Lane,
   MR Robert R JR . . . . | Boulder Creek, CA
                                        | 95006
                                        | ☎ (011-44-1)
                                        | 43-29-32-20
                                        | 13 rue Jacob,
                                        | 75006 Paris, France

Kean MR & MRS Hamilton F (Bacon—Edith M | of ☎ (212)535-5351
Williamson) V'58.C.K.Chr.Cs.P'47.Cl'54 . . . . . | 130 East End Av,
   MR J Nicholas Bacon . . . . | New York, NY
                                        | 10028
                                        | ☎ (914) 677-3961
                                        | PO Box 451,
                                        | Millbrook, NY
                                        | 12545

Kean MR & MRS John (Wojcicki—Pamela A Summers)
Fic.Shcc.S.Cw.Lm.Rv.H'53 ⛵ . . of
   ☎ (908) 766-6488 . . 251 Mt Harmony Rd, Bernardsville, NJ 07924
   ☎ (561) 231-2137 . . 176 N Shore Point, John's Island, Vero Beach,
FL 32963

Kean MR & MRS John JR (Abigail M Murphy)
BostColl'82.Cl'83.Shcc.Eh.LakeF'79.H'94
   ☎ (908) 221-0560 . . 40 Mountain Top Rd, Bernardsville, NJ 07924

Kean MRS Luz M (Luz M Silverio) . . . . | ☎ (212) 860-0489
   MR Christopher—at ☎ (212) 475-4805 | 1192 Park Av,
   295 Park Av S, New York, NY 10010 . . . . | New York, NY
                                        | 10128

Kean MR & MRS Robert W JR (Tobeason—Katherine Tchoukaleff)
Ri.BtP.Cly.P'44 . . of
   ☎ (212) 751-6295 . . 435 E 52 St, New York, NY 10022
   ☎ (908) 439-3134 . . PO Box 618, Oldwick, NJ 08858

Kean MRS Robert W 3d (Patricia C Patterson) Eh.
   ☎ (908) 234-1522 . . PO Box 822, Far Hills, NJ 07931

Kean MR Robert W 3d—Eh. . . . . | ☎ (908) 766-4428
   JUNIORS MR Robert W 4th . . . . | Pennbrook Farm,
                                        | 144 Lake Rd,
                                        | Far Hills, NJ 07931

Kean MR Stewart B—Unn.Lm.Rv.Va'57
   ☎ (702) 454-5387 . . 3258 Brookfield Dv, Las Vegas, NV 89120

Kean MR & MRS Thomas H (Deborah E Bye) | ☎ (908) 439-3203
K.Fic.Pn.P'57 . . . . | ''Long Last''
   MISS Alexandra D—at Colby . . . . | PO Box 332,
   MR Reed S . . . . | Bedminster, NJ
                                        | 07921

Keane MR Carter
   ☎ (415) 435-1087 . . 103 Beach Rd, Belvedere, CA 94920

Kearney MRS Richard J (Caroline H Archer) Cda.
   ☎ (813) 286-2110 . . 4510 Dale Av, Tampa, FL 33609

Kearns MR George E JR . . . . Died at
                                  Killaloe, Co Clare, Ireland Mch 8'95

Kearns MR J Nicholas . . see MRS A G Herrick

Kearns MISS Jessica G . . see MRS A G Herrick

Kearns MR Robert L—K.P'63
   ☎ (617) 227-9716 . . 94 Beacon St, Apt 3, Boston, MA 02108

Keasbey MRS Aertsen P JR (Lamb—Mary P McCormack) Sth'47.Bgt.
RD 2, Mt Kisco, NY 10549

Keast MRS W R Morton (Grace T Gemberling) Ac.Ncd.Dar.
   ☎ (610) MO4-0740 . . 340 Llandrillo Rd, Bala-Cynwyd, PA 19004

Keating MR & MRS Brian E (Anne C Ginther) | of ☎ (716)835-5634
Syr'69.Cy.St.Canis'68.Bab'70.LondEc'71 . . . . . | 210 Morris Av,
   JUNIORS MR Brennan E . . . . | Buffalo, NY 14214
   JUNIORS MR Ryan E . . . . | ☎ (905) 894-5674
                                        | Holloway Bay,
                                        | Humberstone,
                                        | Ontario L3K 5V3,
                                        | Canada

Keating MR & MRS Cletus JR (Martha L Frost) Rol'42.Geo'39
   ☎ (516) 671-7785 . . PO Box 416, Locust Valley, NY 11560

Keating MR & MRS Cletus 3d (Regina Qualey) Char'ton'64.Rut'69
   ☎ (303) 278-3706 . . 798 Cressman Court, Golden, CO 80403

Keating MRS John H JR (White—Margaret Lee Hurley) Man'vl'54.Rm.Stc.
   ☎ (609) 683-0864 . . 91 Riverside Dv, Princeton, NJ 08540

Keating MR & MRS Marshall P (Peggy B Eustis) Ri.P.'52.Cl'55
☎ (212) 737-9393 . . 935 Park Av, New York, NY *10028*

Keatley MR & MRS Robert L (Catharine D Williams) | ☎ (202) 333-7151
Wis'69.Nu'74.HongKong'88.Wash'56.Stan'59 . | 3109 Cathedral Av
JUNIORS MISS Heather E . . . . | NW, Washington,
JUNIORS MR Eric L . . . . | DC *20008*

Keech MR & MRS Gilbert W (Mary G L Murray) Cvc.Sl.Y'49 . . of
☎ (301) 654-6621 . . 5509 Grove St, Chevy Chase, MD *20815*
☎ (902) 295-2626 . . Baddeck, Nova Scotia B0E 1B0, Canada

Keech MR & MRS Gilbert W JR (Anne M Callahan) Swb'81.Cvc.Hob'75
☎ (301) 656-7756 . . 7004 Beechwood Dv, Chevy Chase, MD *20815*

Keech MISS Virginia W—Dick'77.Md'85.Cvc.Sl.
☎ (301) 530-8687 . . 5111 King Charles Way, Bethesda, MD *20814*

Keefe MR & MRS Christopher H (Anne Russenberger) GeoW'81.Geo'73
☎ (207) 667-6732 . . Laurel St, Ellsworth, ME *04605*

Keefe MR & MRS Harry V JR (de Lesseps—Anita H Lihme)
Ny.Aht'43 ⚓ . . of
☎ (203) 869-8339 . . 21 Aiken Rd, Greenwich, CT *06831*
☎ (561) 231-9273 . . 624 Ocean Rd, John's Island, Vero Beach, FL *32963*

Keefe MRS Roger M (Nancy Hunter) Pa'46.Csn. | ☎ (203) 866-4824
Cda.Yn. . . . . | 11 Nathan Hale Rd,
MISS Susan A—at 2920 Chapel Hill Rd, Apt 6C, | Wilson Point,
Durham, NC *27707* . . . . | South Norwalk, CT
| *06854*

Keefe MISS Victoria M—Ty'86
☎ (212) 223-3656 . . 245 E 62 St, Apt 20-24, New York, NY *10021*

Keefer MRS Chester S (Dorothy M Campbell) Cy.
☎ (617) 277-0118 . . 71 Upland Rd, Brookline, MA *02146*

Keefer MISS Jane Aderton (Lee M JR) . . . . Born Jun 26'96

Keefer MR & MRS Lee M JR (Victoria V Anthon) DavEl'86
☎ (314) 961-8273 . . 645 N Forest Av, St Louis, MO *63119*

Keeler MR Marston W JR . . see E W Roberts

Keeler MR & MRS Robert T (Mithoefer—Buxton—Margaret A Palmer)
Dth'36.Y'39
☎ (513) 871-3586 . . 3126 Ononta Av, Cincinnati, OH *45226*

Keeling MR Patrick J . . see J G W Husted

Keen MR & MRS George B (Margery Newbaker) | ☎ (410) 757-5662
Rv.Wt.Md'52 . . . . | 659 White Swan Dv,
MISS Barbara B . . . . | Arnold, MD *21012*
JUNIORS MISS Cary D . . . . |

Keen MISS Kristen W . . see G H Quist

Keenan MR & MRS Henry C (Lasker—McKeever—Doris Lachman)
Stan'38.Mont'41
☎ (415) 474-4777 . . 1330 Jones St, San Francisco, CA *94109*

Keenan MRS Kevin W (Barbara E Belfield) Pa'55
☎ (215) 947-4186 . . 1402 Grasshopper Rd, Huntingdon Valley, PA *19006*

Keenan MRS Martin G (Joan D Shepperd)
☎ (610) 525-5044 . . 930 Montgomery Av, Bryn Mawr, PA *19010*

Keene MR & MRS John C (Navarro—Ana Maria | ☎ (610) 642-1354
Delgado) Me.Ac.Y'53.H'59.Pa'66 . . . . | 212A Glenn Rd,
MR John E . . . . | Ardmore, PA *19003*
MR Peter F . . . . |
MR Carlos F Navarro—at 1801 Montgomery |
Av, Villanova, PA *19085* . . . . |
MR René R Navarro—Ky'78—at |
☎ (610) 251-2174 . . 902 Stoneham Dv, |
West Chester, PA *19382* . . . . |

Keene MISS Katharine—Bost'90
☎ (508) 696-7566 . . PO Box 1025, West Tisbury, MA *02575*

Keeney DR & MRS Edmund L (Penniman—Esther C L Wight)
Cda.Ind'30.JHop'34
338 Via Del Norte, La Jolla, CA *92037*

Keesee MR & MRS Thomas W JR (Patricia Hartford)
Rdc'50.Rc.Au.Bgt.K.Plg.Cos.Duke'35.H.'38
☎ (914) 666-4835 . . 140 Sarles St, RD 3, Mt Kisco, NY *10549*

Keesee MR & MRS Thomas W 3d (Carvalho—Angela O
Bandeira de Mello) Rc.Pe.Pa'76.Pa'79 . . of
☎ (212) 535-2358 . . 520 E 86 St, Apt 14C, New York, NY *10028*
☎ (914) 677-3672 . . Box 107C, RR 1, Deep Hollow Rd, Millbrook, NY *12545*

Keesling MR & MRS Francis V JR (Mary Heath) Pcu.Y'30.Stan'33
☎ (415) 673-2255 . . 930 Chestnut St, San Francisco, CA *94109*
MR at . . ☎ (415) 435-4385 . . 60 San Rafael Av, Belvedere, CA *94920*

Keeter MR & MRS Edward H (Wessell—Ellen W Manning)
StLaw'75.ECar'72.ECar'74.TexA&M'78
☎ (757) 491-1749 . . 905 Cardinal Rd, Virginia Beach, VA *23451*

Keevil MR & MRS Philip C (Augusta D McGrail) | of ☎ (212)369-5766
Rc.B.Ln.Pr.Lic.K.Cly.Ox'68.H'75 | 17 E 89 St,
MISS Augusta H—at U of Va . . . . | New York, NY
MR Adrian A C—at Yale . . . . | *10128*
| ☎ (516) 624-8268
| "Mill Brook"
| 155 Cove Rd,
| Oyster Bay, NY
| *11771*

Kegelman MR & MRS Brian J (Joan A Clark) StP'73
☎ (908) 273-1046 . . 7 Oaklawn Rd, Summit, NJ *07901*

Kegg MR William B 3d—Cal'82 . . see J M Farrell

Kehl MR & MRS David C (Jane C Everett) Dth'61 . . . | ☎ (415) 453-5775
MR Jonathan E—Dth'94 . . . . | 35 Culloden Park
| Rd, San Rafael, CA
| *94901*

Kehl MR & MRS David C JR (Leise Davis) Cal'90
☎ (415) 472-3022 . . 611 Tanbark Terr, San Rafael, CA *94903*

Kehoe MR & MRS Richard G (Zingg—Elizabeth C | of ☎ (860)526-5844
Foulk) V'44.Chr.Ne.Y'43 . . . . | "Merry Farm"
MR J Drew Zingg—V'81—☎ (212) 861-2583 | 332 Joshuatown Rd,
| Lyme, CT *06371*
| ☎ (212) 861-1915
| 116 E 66 St,
| New York, NY
| *10021*

Keidel MR & MRS Albert JR (Justine F Lewis) V'37.Md.Gv.Elk.Mv.Ncd.Pn.P'33 ⚓ . . . .
MISS Anne G—Bost'68.Van'69—at Goethestrasse 4, 8700 Würzburg, Germany . . . . |
of 404 Brightwood Club Dv, Lutherville, MD *21093*
☎ (305) 367-3190 Ocean Reef Club, 104 Andros Rd, North Key Largo, FL *33037*

Keidel REV & MRS Christian L (Frances Parkinson Keyes) Wheat'64.Pc.Pa'69.W'minsterTheo'73 . .
MISS Kimberly A . . . .
MISS Sarah F . . . .
JUNIORS MR Christian L JR . . . . |
☎ (610) 254-9222 455 Timber Lane, Devon, PA *19333*

Keil MR & MRS Bryant L (Shelia K Swift) StLaw'91.Geo'86 1320 N State P'kway, Chicago, IL *60610*

Keil DR & MRS Francis C (Eleanor Schalck) Occ'39.Mls'41.Pr.Csh.Cl'31.Cr'37
☎ (607) 257-4301 . . 312 Savage Farm Dv, Ithaca, NY *14850*

Keilty MR & MRS Robert A (Ruth Sloane Sharp) Van'86.Cly.WOnt'84
☎ (416) 231-8587 . . 45 Sunnylea Av W, Etobicoke, Ontario M8Y 2J8, Canada

Keiser MISS Anne B (Krumbhaar—Anne B Keiser) Mid'70.Csn.Sl.
☎ (202) 333-4938 . . 3104 Hawthorne St NW, Washington, DC *20008*

Keiser MRS David M (Sylvia S Kodjbanoff) Csn.
☎ (203) 762-7919 . . 105 Seeley Rd, Wilton, CT *06897*

Keith MR & MRS Alastair J (Jayne W Teagle) Wheat'70.B.Ri.Pr.BtP.Evg.H'69.H'71 . . . .
JUNIORS MISS Serena B . . . .
JUNIORS MR Alexander T . . . . |
of ☎ (212)772-3821 150 E 73 St, New York, NY *10021*
☎ (561) 655-7176 688 Island Dv, Palm Beach, FL *33480*

Keith MR & MRS Allan R (Winifred A Ward) Aht'59.H'61 . . . .
MISS Lesley P . . . .
MISS Coral D . . . . |
☎ (617) 934-4650 278 Standish St, Duxbury, MA *02332*

Keith MR & MRS Frederick W JR (Sidney P Meeker) Me.Y'42.Pa'51 . . of ☎ (610) 649-9015 . . The Quadrangle 5105, 3300 Darby Rd, Haverford, PA *19041*
☎ (941) 383-0572 . . 640 Longview Dv, Longboat Key, FL *34228*

Keith CDR (RET) & MRS James (Sue A Oakes) USN.Cvc.Cda.GeoW'58
☎ (703) 356-1863 . . 1105 Dogwood Dv, McLean, VA *22101*

Keith MR Norman C . . . . Died at Locust Valley, NY Mch 15'96

Keith MRS Norman C (Milholland—Kathleen Hanley) Mds.B.Mb.Pr.Lic.Mt.Cvc. . . . .
MISS Normandie C (Avery—Normandie C Keith) |
☎ (516) 759-0384 18 Cherrywood Rd, Locust Valley, NY *11560*

Keith MR & MRS Sidney (Susan G W Decker) Pa'61.Me.Pe.Pa'55 . . . .
MISS Emily G W—Gchr'92 . . . .
MISS Dorothy F P . . . . |
☎ (610) 642-8351 136 Buck Lane, Haverford, PA *19041*

Keleher MISS Heather B—StLaw'88
☎ (617) 242-9367 . . 31 Monument Square, Apt 2, Charlestown, MA *02129*

Keleher MR & MRS Walter D (Wendy K Webster) Ub.Chi.Dc.Ncd.Cl'66 . . . .
MR Christopher D—Alf'86—in Indonesia . . . . . |
☎ (617) 934-5867 7 Freeman Place, Box 262, Snug Harbor, Duxbury, MA *02331*

Kelham MR & MRS Rawson (Nicholsen—Susanna P B Rogers) Pcu.
MR Ronald C Nicholsen . . . .
MR Hamilton R Nicholsen . . . . |
of ☎ (707)944-8063 Kelham Vineyards, PO Box 2707, Yountville, CA *94599*
Seadrift, 269 Seadrift Rd, Stinson Beach, CA *94970*

Kell MR & MRS John R (Beautyman—Main— Kathleen A Vick) Wells'69.Drex'75.Cts.Pa'71. Temp'74. . . . .
MR Benjamin R—at 2111 Second Av W, Seattle, WA *98119* . . . . |
☎ (610) 459-5334 ''The Liberties'' 300 Wawa Rd, Wawa, PA *19063*

Kellar MR & MRS Lorrence T (Helgeson—Barbara A Weeks) Cin'60.Cin'64.Qc.Va'60
☎ (513) 321-8151 . . 2615 Grandin Rd, Cincinnati, OH *45208*

Kelleher MR & MRS Harry B (Nellie M Bartlett)
☎ (504) 866-5188 . . 2001 Palmer Av, New Orleans, LA *70118*

Kelleher MR & MRS Harry B JR (Claudia T Fitz-Hugh) Tul'63 . . . .
MISS Elizabeth F . . . .
MR Harry B 3d . . . . |
☎ (504) 866-1236 8018 Jeannette St, New Orleans, LA *70118*

Kelleher MISS Page E . . see R D Sears 3d

Kelleher MR & MRS Warren F (Hyrne—A Frances Haile) Bow'51
☎ (415) 369-0479 . . 158 Stockbridge Av, Atherton, CA *94027*

Keller MR & MRS Christopher S (Susan H Humphrey)
☎ (415) 771-4022 . . 2374 Vallejo St, San Francisco, CA *94123*

Keller MR & MRS David W (Sharon L Smith) Mls'64.B.Y'63 . . . .
MR Michael R . . . . |
of ☎ (310)459-2129 649 Amalfi Dv, Pacific Palisades, CA *90272*
☎ (307) 739-1724 ''Wise Acres'' PO Box 7420, Jackson, WY *83001*

Keller MR & MRS Henry R (Dorothy F Aschbacher) Buf'39.Cybf.G.Cr'39
☎ (941) 434-5539 . . 4401 Gulf Shore Blvd N, Apt 505, Naples, FL *34103*

Keller MR & MRS James G (Betsy A Holden) Tcy.SFr'57 . . . .
MISS Holly S . . . .
MR James G JR . . . .
JUNIORS MR Thomas H . . . . |
☎ (415) 346-3050 2524 Union St, San Francisco, CA *94123*

Keller MR & MRS John P (Judith A Klein) Ws'61.Kt.Uncl.Rc.Sr.Cas.Y'61.H'63 . . . .
MISS Susan A—at ☎ (312) 280-8020 1360 N Lake Shore Dv, Chicago, IL *60610* . . . . |
☎ (847) 446-4606 1095 Pine St, Winnetka, IL *60093*

Keller MR & MRS Peter J (Laura F Burrows)   ☎ (847) 234-1172
Ncd.Ty'69 . . . . | 520 Butler Dv,
MISS Laura D . . . . | Lake Forest, IL
JUNIORS MISS Sandra M . . . . | 60045
JUNIORS MR Thomas W . . . . |

Kellett MR & MRS Morris C (Anne O Bacon) Me.Ph.Cw.P'57.Pa'63
☎ (610) LA5-3129 . . 227 Broughton Lane, Villanova, PA 19085

Kellett MR & MRS Roderick C (Ann E Hedges) Rich'92.Lynch'91
☎ (703) 379-5398 . . 3049 A1 S Buchanan St, Arlington, VA 22206

Kellett MRS Roderick G (Dorothy Clothier) Ac.Me.Ncd.
☎ (610) 356-4703 . . Dunwoody Village D209, 3500 West Chester Pike,
Newtown Square, PA 19073

Kelley MR Augustus W III—Ihy.
☎ (561) 286-1128 . . 3933 SE Top Sail Court, Stuart, FL 34997

Kelley MRS Bayne (Morgan—Millicent C von Kienbusch) Cly.Yn.
☎ (203) 869-7967 . . 75 Doubling Rd, Greenwich, CT 06830

Kelley MR & MRS Edmund R T (Rollins—Maureen Sullivan) Gm.Me.P'44
☎ (941) 434-2829 . . 165 Edgemere Way S, Naples,
FL 34105-7108

Kelley MRS Edmund S JR (Elizabeth P Emery)
☎ (617) 329-5331 . . 10 Longwood Dv, Apt 108, Westwood, MA 02090

Kelley JUNIORS MISS Elizabeth A . . see MRS G Bunker

Kelley MRS H Kendall (Joan Ohlund)
13705 Shaker Blvd, Apt 4A, Cleveland, OH 44120

Kelley MR John E T—Rcn.GeoW'89 . . see MRS B R Hennessy

Kelley MR Marc W—Ihy.Aht'76.Cl'78
☎ (914) 297-1877 . . 113 New Hackensack Rd, Wappinger Falls,
NY 12590

Kelley MR Russell P—Rcch.Y'48
☎ (561) 659-3293 . . 340 Brazilian Av, Palm Beach, FL 33480

Kelley MR & MRS Russell P 3d (Lynn K Raisor)
Sth'71.Bost'75.Ty'71.Bost'74
☎ (011-33-1) 40-49-00-21 . . 207 blvd St Germain, 75007 Paris, France

Kelley MR & MRS Stephen M (Susan T Strong) SUNY'78.StJFisher'88
☎ (716) 243-2286 . . 14 Main St, Geneseo, NY 14454

Kellison MR & MRS J Bruce (Audrey S Cresswell)   ☎ (202) 338-6062
Mt.Cvc.Rich'43.GeoW'48 . . . . | 2801 New Mexico
MISS Elizabeth S—Wms'87—at Chapel Hill, NC | Av NW, Apt 1409,
MISS Julia C—Br'90—at Philadelphia, PA . . . . . | Washington, DC
                                 | 20007

Kellner MR & MRS George A (Martha Henry   of ☎ (212)535-2691
Bicknell) Cl'66.Cl'80.Rc.Un.Mds.Ty'64.Cl'67. | 117 E 78 St,
Nu'74. . . . . | New York, NY
MISS Catherine Sara—V'92.Nu'95 . . . . | 10021
MR Peter Bicknell—P'91 . . . . | ☎ (516) 329-0578
                                   | 80 Hither Lane,
                                   | East Hampton, NY
                                   | 11937

Kellogg MISS Consuelo M
☎ (303) 777-2599 . . 281 S Clarkson St, Denver, CO 80209

Kellogg MR & MRS David W (Dorothy Q Nelson) Br'81.Br'82
☎ (401) 273-7316 . . 162 Meeting St, Providence, RI 02906

Kellogg MR & MRS Edmund D (Carol A Kelso) Vt'79.Vt'80
☎ (617) 729-8407 . . 14 Webster St, Winchester, MA 01890

Kellogg MRS Edmund H (Celina Robbins) Sm.Chi.
Kendal at Hanover 1007, 80 Lyme Rd, Hanover, NH 03755

Kellogg MR Edward Blagden—H.'66
☎ (617) 492-3751 . . 992 Memorial Dv, Apt 106, Cambridge, MA 02138

Kellogg MR Francis L—Rc.Un.B.Bhy.Ny.Plg.Snc.StA.
Coa.StJ.Rv.Ofp.Sar.Cw.Fw.Ll.P'40
☎ (212) 734-2741 . . 775 Park Av, New York, NY 10021

Kellogg MR & MRS Frederic R (Mitchell—Molly Shulman)
Tex'63.Tvb.C.H'64.H'68.GeoW'78.GeoW'83
☎ (202) 234-4620 . . 2027 Q St NW, Washington, DC 20009-1009

Kellogg MR Gaylord M—Pa'84.UWash'92 . . see L A D Andrew 3d

Kellogg MR & MRS Howard (Frances S Perkins) Cs.H'37
☎ (215) 283-7380 . . 1504 Foulkeways, Sumneytown Pike, Gwynedd,
PA 19436

Kellogg MR & MRS James McN (Sally A Schlesinger) Cly.Cda.Duke'65
☎ (212) 410-9636 . . 1095 Park Av, New York, NY 10128

Kellogg MR & MRS John M JR (Ann L Willet)   ☎ (215) MI6-0269
Nyc.Rid'52 . . . . | PO Box 234,
MR Daniel C . . . . | Spring House,
                                   | PA 19477

Kellogg MR Justin . . . . Died at
                                   Devon, PA Sep 10'95

Kellogg MR Justin K (Stephen) . . . . Married at Buffalo, NY
Ringle MISS Leslie A (William) . . . . Jly 13'96

Kellogg MR & MRS Justin K (Leslie A Ringle)
Denis'90.SUNY'95.Rol'90.SUNY'93
☎ (716) 882-0025 . . 2 Oakland Place, Buffalo, NY 14222

Kellogg MASTER Lachlan Case (Stephen JR) . . . . Born Feb 6'94

Kellogg MISS Louise M—Mid'92 . . see L A D Andrew 3d

Kellogg MR Matthew K—Skd'87 . . see L A D Andrew 3d

Kellogg MR & MRS Spencer 2d (Mary L Webster) Pr.Cly.Cr'37
☎ (516) 676-0292 . . 25 Valentine Lane, Glen Head, NY 11545

Kellogg MR & MRS Stephen (Carolyn Karcher)   ☎ (716) 881-3519
SUNY'91.SUNY'93.Ts.G.Ty'61.SUNY'66 . . . . | 55 Windsor Av,
MISS Carolyn B—at San Diego State . . . . | Buffalo, NY 14209
MR Loren L—at U of Fla Grad . . . . |

Kellogg MR & MRS Stephen JR (Annette Estrada) ITT'86.Ariz'86
☎ (716) 881-4481 . . 16 Claremont Av, Buffalo, NY 14222

Kellogg MR & MRS Thomas R (Sheila Bromley)   ☎ (610) 644-6152
MooreArt'64.Sa.Myf.Rv.Ll.Wt.Ofp.Wms'58.H.'61 | 1745 Indian Run Rd,
MISS Laura C . . . . | Malvern, PA 19355
MR Edward R W . . . . |

Kelly MR A Stephen . . . . | ☎ (540) 592-3650
MISS Newell M . . . . | PO Box 234,
                                   | Upperville, VA
                                   | 20185

Kelly MISS Alexandra Williams (g—Arthur L Kelly) . . . . Born Jan 22'94

Kelly MISS Alison W (Gestri—Alison W Kelly) CalSt'88
☎ (916) 345-2595 . . 1066 Lupin Av, Chico, CA 95926

Kelly MR & MRS Arthur L (Cain—Diane J Rex)
Cho.B.Cas.Rc.Cm.Myf.Cnt.Yn.Y'59.Ch'64
☎ (312) 649-5964 . . 1260 N Astor St, Chicago, IL 60610

Kelly MR & MRS Bartow (Ann W Turner) Chi.H'40
☎ (508) 345-4528 . . ''Echo Hill'' High Rock Rd, Fitchburg, MA 01420

Kelly MR & MRS Charles J (Marguerite Stehli)
BMr'53.Rcn.Mt.Yn.Stan'51.Y'54 . . . . | ☎ (202) 625-7729
MISS Marguerite G—Y'89—at ☎ (202) 237-2917 | 3018 N St NW,
3825 Porter St NW, Washington, DC 20016 . . . | Washington, DC
MISS Lisa S—H'92—at ☎ (216) 421-2642 | 20007
2005 Chestnut Hills Dv, Cleveland Heights, OH
44106 . . . .
Kelly MASTER Charles James (John F JR) . . . . | Born Oct 10'94
Kelly MR Edward J JR—Sg.Urs'51 . . . . | of ☎ (561)790-6572
MR Michael McL—Sg.Fla'84 . . . . | Palm Beach Polo
| Club, 2828
| Hurlingham Dv,
| West Palm Beach,
| FL 33414
| ☎ (610) 581-0343
| ''Wrenfield''
| 1017 Canterbury
| Lane, Villanova, PA
| 19085
Kelly MISS Elizabeth J—Mich'81
400 W Deming Place, Chicago, IL 60614
Kelly MISS Emily Anderson (g—Arthur L Kelly) . . . . | Born Jan 22'94
Kelly MRS Flaminia O (Flaminia E Odescalchi) V'55
☎ (303) 321-8713 . . 475 Josephine St, Denver, CO 80206
Kelly MR & MRS Francis J 3d (Heather G Mayfield)
Dth'78.H'83.Ec.Aht'78.H'83
☎ (617) 893-3979 . . 8 Pine St, Weston, MA 02193
Kelly MISS Johanna E—V'81
500 Williams St, Denver, CO 80218
Kelly MR & MRS John A JR (Joyce S Judson) Mich'56.Mich'53.Mich'56
☎ (847) 446-6459 . . 645 Hill Rd, Winnetka, IL 60093
Kelly MR & MRS John F JR (Emilie P Barton) Br'83.StLaw'86
☎ (303) 697-0658 . . 215 S Park Av, Morrison, CO 80465
Kelly MR John Fleming—Y.'47.Y'50
☎ (212) 639-9094 . . 57 E 82 St, Apt 1F, New York, NY 10028
Kelly MR & MRS John W (Barrett—Jennifer Benson)
Mass'84.H'89.K.S.Bost'80
☎ (508) 468-1544 . . 14 Pleasant St, Hamilton, MA 01982
Kelly MISS Karen J—Colg'89.Cl'94
☎ (612) 377-9026 . . 2309 Irving Av S, Minneapolis, MN 55405
Kelly MR & MRS L Owen (M Ann C Robinson)
Ncmb'73.Cda.Dth'72.Van'74
☎ (615) 356-2873 . . 15 White Bridge Rd, Nashville, TN 37205
Kelly MASTER Logan Simms (John W) . . . . | Born at
| Boston, MA May 11'96
Kelly MISS M Mary
☎ (718) 789-6613 . . 130 Eighth Av, Brooklyn, NY 11215
Kelly MR & MRS Richard B (Jerilyn Tabbert) | ☎ (602) 945-3738
MichSt'69.H'67 . . . . | 5320 N Casa Blanca
MISS Colleen M . . . . | Dv, Paradise Valley,
JUNIORS MISS Kimberly S . . . . | AZ 85253
Kelly MR & MRS William Cody (Garrison—Karen L Brown) Fic.Y'44
☎ (305) 534-5893 . . 19224 Fisher Island Dv, Fisher Island,
FL 33109-1166
Kelman MISS Emily Boardman (g—MRS Francis Boardman) . . . . | Born at
| Boston, MA Mch 16'96

Kelsey MR & MRS Cadwallader W (Elise G Boyce) Elk.Wms'38 . . of
☎ (203) TO9-5595 . . 1016 Lake Av, Greenwich, CT 06830
☎ (561) 234-5749 . . 2120 Via Fuentes, Vero Beach, FL 32963
Kelsey MRS Charles C (Dorothy Bugbee) . . . . | ☎ (317) 769-6200
MR Charles C JR—at Houston, TX . . . . | 9240 E 350 South,
MR & MRS John R Brant JR (Wendella L | Zionsville, IN 46077
Kelsey) . . . . |
Kelsey MR Henry B—K.Rcn.
☎ (713) 621-0258 . . 1601 Hollyhurst Lane, Apt D17, Houston,
TX 77056
Kelsey MR & MRS Henry B JR (Deborah L Hightower) Ky'88.Cent'85
☎ (502) 327-9268 . . 2306 Donleigh Court, Louisville, KY 40222
Kelsey MRS John D (Swift—Rosamond Whitney) . . | ☎ (941) 474-5283
MISS Madeleine B Swift—at | 7250 Manasota Key
☎ (213) 665-4817 . . 2072½ N Commonwealth | Rd, Englewood, FL
Av, Los Angeles, CA 90027 . . . . | 34223
Kelsey DR & MRS Mavis P (Mary R Wilson)
V'32.GeoW'36.TexA&M'32.Tex'36.Minn'47
☎ (713) 686-3768 . . 2 Longbow Lane, Houston, TX 77024
Kelsey MR & MRS Mavis P JR (Winifred S Wallace) | ☎ (713) 529-1492
BMr'68.W&L'68 . . . . | 3111 Virginia St,
MISS Winifred W—at Princeton . . . . | Houston, TX 77098
JUNIORS MR Cooke W—at St Paul's . . . . |
Kelsey JUNIORS MR Parker B . . see H C Cook JR
Kelsey MISS Rebecca L . . see H C Cook JR
Kelsey MR & MRS Stephen T JR (Drum—Reed—Bushnell—Margaret Kipp)
Fic.Y'39
☎ (610) 647-8173 . . 360 Keller Rd, Berwyn, PA 19312
Kelsey MR & MRS Thomas R (Margaret A | ☎ (713) 965-9993
Heinzerling) Sth'66.W&L'66 . . . . | 5313 Bayou Glen,
MISS Margaret H—P'95 . . . . | Houston, TX 77056
MR William R—TexA&M'93 . . . . |
JUNIORS MR Mavis P 3d—at Kinkaid . . . . |
Kelso LT COL & MRS Robert Earl (Roberts—Betty Ann Stieren)
USA.Ty'80.A.Tulsa'54
☎ (210) 822-2870 . . 640 Ivy Lane, San Antonio, TX 78209
Kemble MISS Cecilia L . . see L A McMakin
Kemble MR Peter—Ty'61.H'67
☎ (617) 864-9182 . . 6½ Grant St, Cambridge, MA 02138
Kemble JUNIORS MISS Phoebe P . . see L A McMakin
Kemmerer MR & MRS John L JR (Mary E Halbach) Bg.P'33
☎ (908) 647-3525 . . 4111 Fellowship Rd, Basking Ridge, NJ 07920
Kemp MR & MRS Charles C D (R Elizabeth Moody) MtStMary'59
☎ (757) 484-4357 . . 4617 Kemp Dv, Portsmouth, VA 23703
Kemp DR & MRS Harvey G JR (Chace—Barbara J | ☎ (212) 734-2330
Burding) Wheat'58.Un.Cly.Okla'55.JHop'59 . . . | 150 E 69 St,
MISS Barbara B Chace—at Haddonfield, NJ | New York, NY
08033 . . . . | 10021-5153
| . . MR absent
Kemper MR & MRS A Claude (Gwendolyn | ☎ (212) 759-2794
de Clairville) Rc.Cly.Va'58 . . . . | 200 E 62 St,
MR Stephen G—Br'86.Dth'94 . . . . | New York, NY
MR Christopher S—Tampa'92—at | 10021
☎ (516) 427-6462 . . Box 460, Huntington, NY |
11743 . . . . |

Kemper MR & MRS A Claude JR (Tracy H Shiland)
StLaw'86.Nu'89.Pr.Ham'85
☎ (516) 922-2843 . . 300 Highwood Circle, Oyster Bay Cove,
Oyster Bay, NY *11771*

Kemper MRS Alfred R (Taylor—Mary D Plumb)
see Dilatory Domiciles

Kempton MR William B JR
375 W Parisian Way, Westminster, MD *21157*

Kenady MR & MRS Charles W (Williamson—Elizabeth Case)
Stan'46.Pcu.Sfg.Y'43.Y'48 . . of
☎ (415) 221-5813 . . 33 Fifth Av, San Francisco, CA *94118*
☎ (707) 965-2256 . . Dalraddy Vineyards, 3928 Chiles Valley Rd,
St Helena, CA *94574*

Kendall MRS Annie N (Ann New) MissStW'65
185 Westhaven Circle, Winston-Salem, NC *27104*

Kendall MR Charles H JR—Gc.W.Rv.Stan'63 . . see W L Sheppard JR

Kendall MR & MRS Donald McIntosh (Eisenbeiss—	☎ (203) 661-7040
BRNSS Sigrid I Ruedt von Collenberg) Ri.	18 Porchuck Rd,
MR Edward McDonnell	Greenwich, CT
MR Kent Collenberg	*06831*
MR Christian Richard Eisenbeiss	

Kendall MRS Donna Lee (Warren—Model—Donna Lee Kendall) Whit'70
☎ (803) 577-5378 . . 17 Meeting St, Charleston, SC *29401*

Kendall MRS Gloria G (Gloria A Gicker) Me.Gc . . .of
☎ (908) 806-3269 . . Hunter Hills G4, Flemington, NJ *08822*
☎ (215) 877-3000 . . ''Hilltop'' 5918 Drexel Rd, Philadelphia, PA *19131*

Kendall MR Henry W—Cy.Aht'51.Mit'55
☎ (617) 784-5648 . . 396 Moose Hill St, Sharon, MA *02067*

Kendall MR & MRS Jerry T (Charlotte A Webb)	☎ (813) 823-8924
AScott'65.GaTech'66.GaSt'67	520 Brightwaters
MISS Charlotte A	Blvd NE,
JUNIORS MISS Sara C	St Petersburg, FL
	33704

Kendall MR John Atterbury—W.Rv.USN'64.Pa'72
☎ (713) 467-7148 . . 734 Country Lane, Houston, TX *77024*

Kendall MR & MRS John P (Nancy N Feick)	☎ (520) 455-5310
Mls'51.Cyb.Chi.Aht'51.H'53	Lone Mountain
MR David F—at Summerhaven Dv,	Ranch, Patagonia,
East Syracuse, NY *13057*	AZ *85624*

Kendall MRS Pauline K (Fuller—Pauline H Kelly)
2352 Hyde St, San Francisco, CA *94109*

Kendrick MR & MRS Edmund H (Mayotta Southworth)
Sth'44.My.Cw.Ncd.D'43.H'48
☎ (508) 468-1943 . . Arbor St, Box 576, Wenham, MA *01984*

Kendrick DR & MRS M Hayne (Patricia P Ferrell)	☎ (703) TE6-0308
Ala'32.H'35	720 W Braddock
MISS Barbara B—at Waynesboro, VA *22980* . . .	Rd, Alexandria, VA
MISS Eleanor P—at Durham, NC	*22302*

Kendrick MRS Marron (Mary E Roth) Bur.Fr.
601 Laurel Av, Apt 201, San Mateo, CA *94401*

Kendrick DR & MRS Marvin H JR (Kathleen Snow)	☎ (617) 369-7752
StL'70.Bost'71.H'68.Tufts'72	''Willowvale''
JUNIORS MISS Julia B	21 Lincoln St,
JUNIORS MR Jeffrey	Weston, MA *02193*

Kendrick MR & MRS Robert C (Sylvia G Decker)	☎ (415) 668-1167
Mls'68.Cal'73.Fr.Myf.Ncd.Stan'68.SFr'73	3747 Jackson St,
MR Charles L—at Stanford	San Francisco, CA
	94118

Kendrick MR & MRS Stephen H (Katharine R Lewis)
Y'71.H'76.Pcu.Bhm.Hn.Wms'72.H'76
☎ (415) 928-0659 . . 1020 Broadway St, San Francisco, CA *94133*

Kendrick MR & MRS Stephen L 2d (Helenanne Page)
Ty'83.Ncd.Ne'77.Bentley'83
☎ (630) 904-4684 . . 3531 Eliot Lane, Naperville, IL *60564*

Kenefick MR & MRS John C (Ryan—Helen P Walker) Ln.W.Pn.P'43
☎ (402) 558-1991 . . 410 Fairacres Rd, Omaha, NE *68132*

Kenly MR F Corning JR—Ec.H'37
☎ (508) 526-1878 . . PO Box 400, Spy Rock Hill, Manchester,
MA *01944*

Kenly MR & MRS Granger F (Angevin—Stella W	☎ (847) 234-5478
Brown) Sth'51.On.Eyc.Cho.Fy.H'41	945 Beverly Place,
MISS Susan F Angevin	Lake Forest, IL
	60045

Kenly MRS Suzanne W (Suzanne Warner) SL'46.Cnt.Ih.
☎ (847) 446-2428 . . 1327 Hackberry Lane, Winnetka, IL *60093*

Kenna MR & MRS Timothy C (Laura A Moorhouse) RISD'90.V'88
17 McGregor Rd, Woods Hole, MA *02543*

Kennard MRS John H (Lydia M Lund)
☎ (603) 228-5330 . . 149 E Side Dv, Apt 211, Concord, NH *03301*

Kennard MR & MRS Samuel J (Blackman—Joanna E Mangan) Fla'36
☎ (904) 261-6007 . . 104 Sea Marsh Rd, Amelia Island, FL *32034*

Kennard MRS Samuel M 3d (Mildred K Hill) . . . . Died at
St Louis, MO Mch 8'96

Kennard MR Samuel M 3d—Cy.	of ☎ (314)361-7489
MISS Anne M	4970 Pershing Place,
	St Louis, MO *63108*
	☎ (561) 278-0075
	1040 Lewis Cove,
	Delray Beach, FL
	33483

Kennedy MR Alexander S—Nf.P'62.Pa'72	☎ (212) 996-1099
MISS Anna S	70 E 96 St, Apt 5C,
MR Thomas A	New York, NY
	10128

Kennedy MRS Andrew M JR (Ann F Stimson) Ny.
☎ (561) 272-9842 . . 401 E Linton Blvd, Apt 507, Delray Beach,
FL *33483*

Kennedy MISS Catharine C—Cwr'70
☎ (518) 392-5756 . . 1511 Rte 28, Chatham Center, NY *12184-4208*

Kennedy MR & MRS Frank J JR (Rebekah MacL G	☎ (410) 234-0749
Neal) Cl'78.Cl'53	20 E Mt Vernon
MR Donald MacL—at ☎ (410) 235-5357	Place, Baltimore,
3203 N Charles St, Baltimore, MD *21218*	MD *21202*

Kennedy MR & MRS Gilbert R (Elizabeth D Harris)	☎ (314) 721-3689
Hlns'28.Ncd.	7137 Maryland Av,
MISS Ellen D—Ncd.—at ☎ (713) 664-0606	St Louis, MO *63130*
6211 Royalton St, Apt D, Houston, TX *77081* . .	

Kennedy MR & MRS Gilbert R H (Caroline McDermott) Yn.Y'57.Y'64 .... ☎ (713) 522-8911 1800 Hazard St, Houston, TX *77019*
MISS Sarah B—Bost'88—at 415 S Livingston St, Madison, WI *53703* ....
MR Gilbert M—at 2325 Spruce St, Philadelphia, PA *19103* ....

Kennedy MRS Gordon JR (Joan E Burke) Ws'52.Cvc.Sl.
☎ (301) 229-1638 . . 5620 Wood Way, Bethesda, MD *20816-1915*

Kennedy MR & MRS Grafton S (G Avery Harder) SL'42.Sar.Dar.Y'47.Cin'56 ⚓ .... ☎ (603) 743-3442 Old Orchard Farm, 42 Nute Rd, Madbury, NH *03820*
MR David B—FlaIT'87 ....

Kennedy MR & MRS Gregory D (Victoria S Reese) V'90.Stan'88.Stan'92
☎ (212) 374-0456 . . 105 Duane St, Apt 22A, New York, NY *10007*

Kennedy MR & MRS James C 2d (Barbara A Shahin) Nw'81
☎ (503) 591-9818 . . 7774 SW 171 Place, Beaverton, OR *97007*

Kennedy MR & MRS John B (Nancy A Kleir) Tex'64.Tex'63 .... ☎ (314) 721-4806 7140 Westmoreland Dv, St Louis, MO *63130*
MISS Elizabeth L—at Boston, MA ....
MR John B JR—at Milwaukee, WI ....

Kennedy MR John F JR
see Dilatory Domiciles

Kennedy MRS Joseph W JR (Jane Harper) SL'32
☎ (501) 922-0082 . . 5 Cortez Rd, Apt 226, Hot Springs Village, AR *71909*

Kennedy MRS Kevin (Clara W Banta) Sth'45.Pn. . . ☎ (508) 693-9439 "Husselton Head" RR 2, Box 180, Vineyard Haven, MA *02568*
MR Alexander W ....

Kennedy MR & MRS (DR) Kevin W (Karen E Andresen) Man'vl'71.Cl'91.Ham'70.H'74 ..... ☎ (201) 447-6658 280 Greenway Rd, Ridgewood, NJ *07450*
MR Coleman W ....
JUNIORS MR William F ....

Kennedy MISS Lin
☎ (215) 732-8121 . . Lenox Apt 3E, Box 31, 250 S 13 St, Philadelphia, PA *19107-5615*

Kennedy MR & MRS Mark B (Cantrell—Heath Mirick) Rc.R.Me.Ac.Pa'70.Mich'73 .... ☎ (610) MI2-9975 101 Cherry Lane, Ardmore, PA *19003*
MISS Devon W ....
JUNIORS MISS Ashley L ....
JUNIORS MR Christopher R..................
JUNIORS MR Tyson C ....

Kennedy MRS Moorhead C (Anna D Scott) K.Plg.
☎ (212) 722-1923 . . 66 E 79 St, New York, NY *10021*

Kennedy MR & MRS Moorhead C JR (Louisa A Livingston) Mt.K.Chr.Cs.P'52.H'58 .... ☎ (212) 964-5292 55 Liberty St, Apt 7A, New York, NY *10005*
MR Andrew M—Mid'83—at ☎ (202) 797-9533 1622—19 St NW, Washington, DC *20009* .....
MR Duncan R—Wis'87—at 390 Arguello St, San Francisco, CA *94118* ....

Kennedy MR & MRS Philip L (Hillary T Simmers) Bost'85.Vt'82 . . of
☎ (914) 921-1914 . . 6 White Birch Dv, Rye, NY *10580*
☎ (508) 349-7395 . . "Ramble Roof House" Longnook Rd, Truro, MA *02666*

Kennedy MR Robert C—Snc.Wes'42.JHop'49
☎ (212) 861-4236 . . 162 E 80 St, New York, NY *10021*

Kennedy MRS Robert F (Ethel Skakel)
☎ (703) 734-9481 . . 1147 Chain Bridge Rd, McLean, VA *22101*

Kennedy MRS Sheila R (Sheila B Rauch) Wheat'71 ☎ (617) 492-7940 194 Lake View Av, Cambridge, MA *02138*
JUNIORS MR Matthew R ....
JUNIORS MR Joseph P 3d ....

Kennedy MRS Stuart R (Frances C Judson) .... of ☎ (212)995-9617 8 Peter Cooper Rd, Apt 12C, New York, NY *10010*
MISS Martha C ....
☎ (801) 647-3380 Aspen Hollow 11, PO Box 2603, Park City, UT *84060-0914*

Kennedy MRS Taylor L (Jane S Cloud) Sth'43.Sc.Wa.
☎ (312) 337-1540 . . 1040 N Lake Shore Dv, Chicago, IL *60611-1107*

Kennedy MR & MRS William P (Douglas—Thomas—Alice M Frost)
1460 Linda Ridge Rd, Pasadena, CA *91103*

Kennedy MR & MRS William T (Priscilla T Taylor) V'69.Bvl.H'69 .... ☎ (508) 748-1746 312 Delano Rd, Marion, MA *02738*
MISS Emily L—at Cornell ....
MISS Abigail T—at Kenyon ....

Kennelly MISS Ellen L (Brown—Ellen L Kennelly) H'85 . . of
☎ (617) 868-5294 . . 111 Lake View Av, Cambridge, MA *02138*
☎ (603) 563-8419 . . Charcoal Rd, PO Box 55, Dublin, NH *03444*

Kennelly MRS R Grice (Ellen Lee Bayard) Chi.Ncd.
448 Court Place, Santa Barbara, CA *93108*

Kennelly MR & MRS Richard B JR (Margery M Trimble) H.'87.H.'87
☎ (508) 526-9676 . . 46 Forster Rd, Manchester, MA *01944*

Kenney MR & MRS Charles C II (Judith A Braber) Stan'90.Red'80.DU'81 .... of ☎ (415)564-1772 226 Edgewood Av, San Francisco, CA *94117*
JUNIORS MISS Theresa A ....
☎ (707) 833-6802 "Redwood Springs Ranch" 7639 Sonoma H'way, Santa Rosa, CA *95409*

Kenney MR & MRS Horace S JR (Lindsley—Mary E Moore) Y'48
☎ (508) 748-2872 . . Box 203, 69 East Av, Planting Island, Marion, MA *02738*

Kenney MR Horace S 3d—UWash'83
☎ (303) 377-7114 . . 918 Race St, Denver, CO *80206*

Kenniston MR & MRS Salvador (Havens—Katharine Faulconer) .... ☎ (619) 561-4228 11367 High Ranch Rd, Lakeside, CA *92040*
MISS Heidi Ann.....................
MISS Angela ....

Kent MR & MRS A Atwater 3d (Williams—Pamela Gamage) Rd . . .of
☎ (610) 353-2090 . . PO Box 183, Newtown Square, PA *19073*
☎ (561) 833-8797 . . "Lemmon Tree Cottage" 410 Australian Av, Palm Beach, FL *33480*

Kent MR & MRS Donald W JR (Caroline Simons)
Wheat'49.Y.'48.Temp'60 . . . . | ☎ (610) 544-5781
  MISS Anna P—Y'81.H'86—at ☎ (215) 242-4717 | 510 Walnut Lane,
210 E Gravers Lane, Philadelphia, PA *19118* . . . | Swarthmore, PA
  MISS Laura K—Duke'90 . . . . | *19081*
Kent MR & MRS E Hewlett (Sheree L Ladove) Rol'88.BtP.Nf.DU'84
  ☎ (561) 276-7065 . . 520 Middle Rd, Gulf Stream, FL *33483*
Kent MRS Eleanor (Schermerhorn—Eleanor Kent) Rdc'53.SFrSt'65
  ☎ (415) 647-8503 . . 544 Hill St, San Francisco, CA *94114*
Kent MR & MRS Geoffrey J W (Shober—Kendall— | of ☎ (561)589-8080
Richardson—Jorie F Butler) B.BtP.Cly. . . . . | River Point,
  MR Hugo J A . . . . | 12505 N A1A,
 | Vero Beach, FL
 | *32963*
 | ☎ (011-254-2)
 | 891-320
 | Bahati,
 | PO Box 59749,
 | Nairobi, Kenya
Kent MRS (DR) Gerald T (Janet T Dingle) V'36.Cwr'40
  ☎ (941) 594-1231 . . 100 Glenview Place, Apt 613, Naples,
FL *34108-3130*
Kent MR & MRS Mark B (Martha A Hart) Salem'86.M.WakeF'85
  ☎ (864) 232-1102 . . 23 Riverside Dv, Greenville, SC *29605*
Kent MR Peter A . . see J W Annan
Kent DR & MRS Raleigh B JR (Lysbeth B Hawkins)
Aub'89.Cy.Ala'52.Aub'61
  ☎ (205) 871-8645 . . 2805 Cherokee Rd, Birmingham, AL *35223*
Kent MRS Richard JR (Nancy O L Jones)
  ☎ (520) 284-1701 . . 132 Piñon Woods Dv, Sedona, AZ *86336*
Kent MRS W Thompson (P Elaine Baruch) Me.
  ☎ (864) 277-5742 . . 128 Hidden Hills Dv, Greenville, SC *29605*
Kenworthy MRS J MacLeod (Janet MacLeod Jelke)
  ☎ (301) 320-2676 . . 5407 Goldsboro Rd, Bethesda, MD *20817-6314*
Kenworthy MISS Kecia E—Sth'91 . . see E A B Corballis
Kenyon MR & MRS Geoffrey R T (Sidney W Anderson)
Van'82.Cl'83.Sm.Nw'80.Cl'84 . . of
  ☎ (617) 696-9896 . . 150 School St, Milton, MA *02186*
  ☎ (802) 672-3047 . . ''Boxford Cottage'' Bridgewater, VT *05034*
Kenyon MRS W Houston JR (Hardy—Harriett Hickok) Cwr'31.Mt.
  ☎ (212) 744-0120 . . 340 E 72 St, New York, NY *10021*
Keogh MISS Adele C—Cly . . .of
  ☎ (212) 535-7565 . . 340 E 66 St, New York, NY *10021*
  ☎ (202) 363-0100 . . 4650 Garfield St NW, Washington, DC *20007*
Keogh MR George P . . see N N Solley
Keppel MRS Francis (Edith M Sawin) Cos.
  ☎ (617) 492-1121 . . 983 Memorial Dv, Cambridge, MA *02138*
Keppel MR & MRS John (Grace M Wood) | ☎ (860) 767-2006
Csn.Hn.H'40 . . . . | 22 N Main St,
  MR David—Ox'79—☎ (860) 767-2508 . . . . . . | Essex, CT *06426*
Ker MR & MRS David S I (Wettlaufer—Gail S Summerfield)
V'58.G.Tor'45 ⚓
  ☎ (905) 628-6264 . . 30 Victoria St, Dundas, Ontario L9H 2B8, Canada
Kerbaugh MISS Mary C—Pa'49.Me.
  ☎ (610) 525-0878 . . 183 S Spring Mill Rd, Villanova, PA *19085*

Kerekes de Kelecsény MR Tibor—Mto.Geo'48
  ☎ (203) 259-1909 . . ''Bel Campo'' 81 Sturges Rd, Fairfield,
CT *06430-4956*
Kerlin MR & MRS Gilbert (Sarah Morrison) | of ☎ (718)543-5551
Rdc'34.Cs.H'33 . . . . | 4690 Dodgewood
  MR Jonathan O—at ☎ (415) 664-7689 | Rd, Bronx, NY
1457 Tenth Av, San Francisco, CA *94122* . . . . . | *10471*
 | ☎ (802) 899-3602
 | Old Pump Rd,
 | Jericho, VT *05465*
Kernan MR Benjamin T—Au.K.Geo'64
  ☎ (802) 948-2484 . . Mt Independence Farm, RR 1, Box 85, Shoales Rd,
Orwell, VT *05760*
Kernan MISS Brigid D—Man'vl'69.SantaC'89
  ☎ (410) 323-1049 . . 8 Bouton Green Court, Baltimore, MD *21210*
Kernan MR & MRS Bruce S (van Maasdijk—Edna | ☎ (011-593-2)
Maria Iturralde) AmdeQ'67.Ham'77.Y'81 . . . . . | 551-809
  MISS Diana van Maasdijk . . . . | Floradorno de
  MR Eric van Maasdijk . . . . | Cusubamba, Box
  JUNIORS MR Willem van Maasdijk . . . . | 1025, SUC16 CEQ,
 | Quito, Ecuador
Kernan MRS Francis K (Maud T Tilton) Au.Fic.Cly.Cs.Km . . .of
  ☎ (212) 288-5572 . . 116 E 66 St, New York, NY *10021*
  ☎ (941) 964-2625 . . 420 Lee Av, Box 492, Boca Grande, FL *33921*
Kernan MR & MRS Francis K JR (Katherine S | ☎ (914) 241-0605
Sheffield) Cl'68.Fic.Bgt.Cr'58 . . . . | 340 McLain St,
  MISS Katherine P . . . . | Bedford Hills, NY
  MR Francis J—at Ohio Wesleyan . . . . | *10507*
  JUNIORS MR Michael S . . . . |
Kernan MR Henry S—H'38.Y'41 | ☎ (607) 397-8805
  MISS Patricia McC—Wis'85.RISD'88—at | 300B County Rte
  ☎ (518) 426-7537 . . 602 Madison Av, Albany, | 40, South Worcester,
NY *12208*. . . . . | NY *12197*
  MR Henry D—☎ (607) 397-9446 . . . . |
  MR Christopher N—Cr'77.Tex'92—at |
  ☎ (305) 661-0627 . . PO Box 560273, Miami, FL
38256 . . . .
Kernan MR & MRS John D (Una R Greene) Cc.Lm.H'34.Cl'37
  ☎ (203) 787-1933 . . 222 Blake Rd, Hamden, CT *06517*
Kernan MR & MRS John D JR (Karen Clemens) Ill'70.Pa'65
  ☎ (203) 481-4478 . . 576 Leete's Island Rd, Stony Creek, CT *06405*
Kernan MISS Maud T (Benjamin T) . . . . Married at Southport, CT
Lonergan MR Michael T (Hal) . . . . Aug 6'95
Kernan MRS Sheilah E (Gunnin—Macdonald— | ☎ (713) 558-3382
Sheilah E Kernan) . . . . | 778 Thornbranch
  MISS Lisa C Gunnin—at U of Houston . . . . . | Dv, Houston, TX
 | *77079*
Kernan MISS Sophia R (Benjamin T) . . . . Married at New York, NY
Kramer MR Andrew L (Frederic S) . . . . May 18'96
Kernan MR Thomas S—H.'29
  ☎ (315) 733-3605 . . 2809 Genesee St, Utica, NY *13501*
Kernan MRS Walter A (C Leslie Hadden) Cly. . . . . | ☎ (212) 722-7092
  MISS Beatrice L—at 150 E 93 St, New York, NY | 1105 Park Av,
10128 . . . . | New York, NY
  MR Charles P H—Conn'85—at 150 E 93 St, | *10128*
New York, NY *10128* . . . . |

Kerns MR & MRS John S JR (Stephanie E Culbertson) Md.Rv.Cw.Dar.Bab'57
☎ (410) 243-3141 . . 4300 N Charles St, Apt 6E, Baltimore, MD *21218-1049*
Kerns MR Robert A JR—Me.Pa'54
☎ (610) 296-3664 . . 201 Cohasset Lane, West Chester, PA *19380*
Kerr MR & MRS Alexander (Margaret C Wilson) | ☎ (215) 242-8323
Sa.Ph.Rc.Y.'67 . . . . | 505 W Chestnut Hill
MISS Cecily W . . . . | Av, Philadelphia,
MISS Susannah W . . . . | PA *19118*
Kerr MR & MRS Andrew P (Marjorie A McVicar) | ☎ (503) 223-2448
OreSt'69.PortSt'82.Dth'66.Willa'69 . . . . | 2831 SW Labbe Av,
MISS Allison S . . . . | Portland, OR *97221*
MR Robert M . . . . |
Kerr MRS Constance B (Constance J Barkan) Cal'68
☎ (415) 349-9621 . . 5 Creekridge Court, San Mateo, CA *94402*
Kerr REV DR & MRS Donald C (Nora M Lloyd) P'37.Tor'42
☎ (941) 371-2750 . . 5220 Manz Place, Sarasota, FL *34232*
Kerr MR & MRS E Coe 3d (Anne K Edmonson) Pr.Lic.Bost'73
☎ (516) 922-1610 . . "Waterlot" Roger Canoe Hollow Rd, Mill Neck, NY *11765*
Kerr MISS Elizabeth
☎ (904) 285-8214 . . 1000 Vicar's Landing Way, Box G209, Ponte Vedra Beach, FL *32082*
Kerr MR & MRS John D (Marion Conboy) Y'37
☎ (406) 586-5023 . . 658 Coulee Dv, Bozeman, MT *59715*
Kerr MR John Hoare—Y'55 . . . . | of "Derrydown"
MR Ian A N MacD—StA.Snc.Cw.Nu'85.Nu'86. | RD 1, Newport, RI
Cl'89—at 173 Av A, New York, NY *10009* . . . | *02840*
MR Colin A MacK VanK—RISD'89—at | 1111—30 St NW,
94 St Marks Place, New York, NY *10009* . . . . . | Washington, DC
MR Alan A MacM-G—Snc.Cw.Mass'91—at | *20007*
405 W 48 St, Apt 2R, New York, NY *10036* . . . |
Kerr MISS Marion F . . see P Lewis
Kerr MRS Wendell (Soule—Barbara Wendell) Cs.
☎ (212) 348-2186 . . 127 E 92 St, New York, NY *10128-1603*
Kersey MR & MRS James W JR (Miriam W Wadick) Va'79.Va'77
☎ (310) 274-6539 . . 416 N Oakhurst Dv, Beverly Hills, CA *90210*
Kershaw MR & MRS Warren E (Ida Marshall) Colg'47
☎ (914) 226-5011 . . "Windswept" Box 253, Clinton Corners, NY *12514*
Kestler MRS Manuel S (Kneedler—Pauline Perry)
☎ (510) 947-5558 . . 1580 Geary Rd, Apt 148, Walnut Creek, CA *94596*
Ketcham MRS Gordon (Marion L Bischoff)
☎ (619) 435-4096 . . 612 Glorietta Blvd, Coronado, CA *92118*
Ketcham MRS Howard (Gardner—Elisabeth C Tappen) Dar.
☎ (561) 659-5552 . . 3800 Washington Rd, West Palm Beach, FL *33405*
Ketcham MR & MRS James B (Ira C Davisson) | ☎ (516) 239-6740
Ey.Y'45 . . . . | 298 Ocean Av,
MISS Laurie C—Hartw'75—at 210 E 36 St, | Lawrence, NY
New York, NY *10016* . . . . | *11559*
Ketcham MR & MRS William T JR—Rc.B.Plg.Chr.Cw.Snc.Coa.Y.'41.Y'48
☎ (212) 421-6971 . . 411 E 53 St, New York, NY *10022*
Ketchum MR & MRS Perry D (Helen W Metz) V'75.Cl'81.Cl'66.Minn'76
☎ (612) 479-6580 . . 6760 Fogelman Rd, Independence, MN *55359-9790*

Ketner MR & MRS D Scott (Elizabeth Brown) | ☎ (212) 369-1873
V'72.Ln.Fic.Cly.Y'69.Pa'73 . . . . | 1120 Fifth Av,
MISS Barbara L—at Stanford | New York, NY
MR D Scott JR—at Princeton . . . . | *10128*
JUNIORS MISS Elizabeth P—at Groton . . . . |
Kew MISS Christina E . . see MISS L B Watson
Key MR & MRS Albert L (Julia I Bowdoin) Rc.Pr.Cly.H'50
☎ (516) 676-9027 . . 67 Dogwood Lane, Locust Valley, NY *11560*
Key MR & MRS Albert L JR (Monica A Ray) Sth'84.Csh.LakeF'80
☎ (212) 426-5134 . . 8 E 96 St, Apt 8A, New York, NY *10128*
Key MRS C S King (Coralie S King) NTexSt'83
☎ (817) 737-3342 . . 4433 Fletcher St, Ft Worth, TX *76107*
Key MRS Frank L (Ann V Jones)
☎ (314) PA5-7201 . . 6367 Ellenwood Av, St Louis, MO *63105*
Key MISS Julia Bowdoin (Albert L JR) . . . . Born at New York, NY Dec 5'94
Key MR Timothy S—Rm'79
☎ (516) 626-3196 . . 68 Wheatley Rd, Brookville, NY *11545*
Keyes MRS Alexander L (Josephine T Adrian) Yn.
☎ (201) 425-3806 . . RD 1, Box 124, Bailey's Mill Rd, Basking Ridge, NJ *07920*
Keyes MR Austin D . . see P H Briger
Keyes MR & MRS Charles Griffith (E Kenan Jones) RMWmn'68.Rhodes'66
☎ (501) 664-1814 . . 2904 N Pierce St, Little Rock, AR *72207*
Keyes MR Eben Wight 2d—Plg.Myf.Ne.Snc.Cw.H.'55.Cl'57
☎ (212) 369-5717 . . 16 E 96 St, New York, NY *10128*
Keyes MR & MRS Fenton (Elizabeth D Dix) V'36.Y'37
☎ (215) 968-7893 . . Pennswood Village E102, Newtown, PA *18940*
Keyes MR & MRS George T (Lucy B Stone) H'35
☎ (508) 433-5711 . . 55 River Rd, Box 589, Pepperell, MA *01463*
Keyes MRS Henry M (Stires—Jane S Nelson) . . . . . | ☎ (207) 586-5711
MR Henry W—at 507 Main St, Apt B66, | Juniper Hill,
Worcester, MA *01608* . . . . | RR 1, Box 606,
 | Alna, ME *04535*
Keyes MR & MRS Jonathan M (Judith S Button) Un.Chi.H'57
☎ (508) 369-3485 . . 91 Liberty St, Concord, MA *01742*
Keys MR A de Forest—Pn.P'40 | ☎ (011-44-1380)
MR David de F—Bost'93—at ☎ (213) 954-1343 | 828-518
1226 S Highland Av, Los Angeles, CA *90019* . . | Cleeve Lodge,
 | SEEND, Wiltshire
 | SN12 6PG, England
Keys MR & MRS William A 3d (Natalie Jaeger) | ☎ (914) 337-7834
Ny.Myf. . . . . | 57 Summit Av,
MR Tyler W . . . . | Bronxville, NY
 | *10708*
Keyser MR & MRS Campbell Dirck (Weedon—Collamore—Joan M Kirkland) P'49.Va'95 . . of
☎ (804) 823-1208 . . 2645 White Hall Rd, Crozet, VA *22932*
☎ (941) 493-6362 . . 729 N Manasota Key Rd, Englewood, FL *34223*
Keyser MRS W Fenwick (Barbara Longcope) BMr'38.Gv.Csn.
☎ (410) 833-3100 . . "Jones Contrivance" Box 33, Reisterstown, MD *21136*
Keyser MR W McHenry . . see W Adamson JR
Khan MR & MRS Mohamad W (Frost—Rosemary Layne) Cal'69.Cal'76.Cal'57.Cal'58
☎ (330) 668-2767 . . 225 Lake Point Dv, Bath, OH *44333*

Khatami MR & MRS S Abulqasim (Marie Hoguet) Rdc'46.Mds.Teh'45 . . . . ☎ (212) 759-7308 200 E 66 St, New York, NY 10021
   MR James L—at 2771 Bryant St, San Francisco, CA 94110 . . . .

Kiaer MRS Herman S (Fearing—Stubbs—Vera W Howell) D.C.Chi. . . . . ☎ (617) 326-0268 590 Gay St, Westwood, MA 02090
   MR Travers Fearing . . . .

Kidd MR Barron du P (Barron U) . . . . Married at Italy, TX
   Taylor MISS Tammy Lee (Terry) . . . . Apr 27'96

Kidd MR & MRS Barron U (Jane deD du Pont) V'61.Fic.Tex'58 . . . . of ☎ (214)528-8506 4315 Glenwood Av, Dallas, TX 75205
   MISS Ellet deL—MtVern'94 . . . . ☎ (214) 483-6903 Five Points Farm, RFD 2, Italy, TX 76651

Kidde MR Robert L G
   ☎ (213) 661-4347 . . 1942½ N Kenmore Av, Los Angeles, CA 90027-1812

Kidder MRS Catherine E (Catherine E Taylor) Syr'73
   ☎ (212) 535-4106 . . 240 E 76 St, New York, NY 10021

Kidder MR Christopher H—W&M'87
   ☎ (011-44-171) 924-7008 . . 1 Battersea Bridge Rd, London SW11 3BZ, England

Kidder MR & MRS Howard C (Bettibelle Heslop) Cr'53.Y'49 . . . . ☎ (703) 536-6715 3941 N Glebe Rd, Arlington, VA 22207
   MISS Elizabeth K—Br'90 . . . .
   MR James T—Va'93 . . . .

Kidder MRS Jerome H T (Frances L Turnbull) Cda.
   ☎ (410) 435-0595 . . Cross Keys, 34 Olmsted Green Court, Baltimore, MD 21210

Kidder MR Timothy J
   Sandy Hill Rd, Oyster Bay, NY 11771

Kiefer DR & MRS William F JR (Clément-Bayard—Melinda M Moon) Paris'76.Pn.P'67.Ill'75 . . . . . ☎ (314) 434-6673 "Yellowood" 1047 Tidewater Place, Town & Country, MO 63017-5933
   JUNIORS MR William F 3d . . . .
      MISS Allegra Clément-Bayard—Ken'95 . . . . .
      MISS Aurelie Clément-Bayard—at U of Paris Sorbonne

Kieffer MR A Christopher . . see MRS B Duval

Kieffer MISS Jenifer W—JMad'88.AGSIM'92 . . see MRS B Duval

Kieffer MISS Phebe W—MmtVa'91.CentFla'95 . . see MRS B Duval

Kiendl MR & MRS Philip R (Audrey G Ochs) Cw.Cly.Y'49
   ☎ (802) 496-4040 . . Box 125, RR 1, German Flats, Waitsfield, VT 05673

Kiendl MR & MRS Theodore JR (PRCSS Elizabeth A Poniatowska) Cw.Rv.Y'43.H'49 . . of
   ☎ (011-33-1) 42-65-89-31 . . 22 rue de la Boëtie, 75008 Paris, France
   ☎ (011-33-93) 77-37-03 . . 79 Chemin des Ribes, 06650 Le Rouret, France

Kientz MR & MRS William A 3d (Janis R Dorris) Ark'74.Ark'72.Ark'74 . . . . ☎ (601) 366-5656 151 Glen Way, Jackson, MS 39216
   MISS Julia V

Kiernan MR & MRS Gregory F (Vera E Habich) Aht'79.H'82
   ☎ (914) 241-2159 . . 300 Millwood Rd, Chappaqua, NY 10514

Kiernan MR & MRS John S (Lisa Edmondson) Ws'77.Cl'81.Cl'83.H'76.H'80
   ☎ (914) 738-2328 . . 17 Black St, Pelham Manor, NY 10803

Kiernan MISS M Carroll—Geo'79.Y'85 . . see R F Callahan

Kiernan DR Michael J—Wms'81.Cl'85 . . see R F Callahan

Kiernan MR & MRS Peter de L 3d (R Eaddy W Hayes) Duke'76.Tul'80.Wms'75.Va'79
   ☎ (914) 967-3697 . . "The Ledges" 16 Justin Rd, Harrison, NY 10528

Kiernan MR & MRS Stephen P G (Amy L Wright) Mid'86.Mid'82.JHop'83
   ☎ (802) 425-4409 . . RR 1, Box 1138, Charlotte, VT 05445

Kiersted MR & MRS Christopher W (Parthenia Ross) Bost'76.Eyc.JHop'71
   ☎ (508) 627-9060 . . Box 1537, 60 North St, Edgartown, MA 02539

Kiesel MR & MRS Michael T (Precourt—Helen B Wallace) Briar'67.Chr.Bm.Cly.Myf.Ncd.P.'69.Pa'72.Nu'79
   ☎ (212) 988-3162 . . 211 E 70 St, New York, NY 10021-5218

Kieser MR & MRS John F (Valerie J Tognazzini) Mls'59
   ☎ (510) 531-4836 . . 3437 Crane Way, Oakland, CA 94602

Kiesewetter MISS Patricia J—Ty'73
   ☎ (970) 845-5075 . . Box 1996, Vail, CO 81658

Kiesewetter MR & MRS William B JR (Murphy—Barton—E Jayne Howard) Ky'65.NCar'68.Fcg.Pg.Rr.Y'69.Duq'76
   ☎ (561) 791-0273 . . Meadow Brook C104, 13254 Polo Club Rd, West Palm Beach, FL 33414

Kilborne MR & MRS George B (Mahoney—Jean W W Bronson) V'52.BtP.Evg.Ri.Myf.Y'52
   ☎ (561) 655-9045 . . 4 Major Alley, 417 Peruvian, PO Box 2717, Palm Beach, FL 33480

Kilborne MISS Sarah S (George B) . . . . Married at Deerfield, MA
   de Bienville MR Michael LeM (Peter) . . . . Aug 28'95

Kilborne MRS William S (Egbert—Virginia G Wylie) V'34.Nu'41
   ☎ (609) 448-0944 . . Meadow Lakes 49-04, Hightstown, NJ 08520

Kilborne MR & MRS William S JR (Irene C McDonald) Nw'56.Nw'60.Y'58.Nu'64 . . . . ☎ (817) 926-0388 2200 Huntington Lane, Ft Worth, TX 76110
   MR William S 3d—Nw'84—at 1811 Hurley Av, Ft Worth, TX 76110 . . . .

Kilbourn MRS Samuel V D (Louise H Tucker)
   ☎ (203) 655-2163 . . 7 Prospect Av, Darien, CT 06820

Kilbourne MRS Susan L (Susan B Lowe) . . . . ☎ (416) 486-0103 9 Doncliffe Dr, Toronto, Ontario M4N 2E5, Canada
   MISS Laura I—at ☎ (416) 922-6841 44½ Birch Av, Toronto, Ontario M4V 1C8, Canada . . . .

Kilbourne MR & MRS Thomas L (Carolyn S Douglas) Bishops'86
   ☎ (416) 222-6080 . . 28 Beechwood Av, Toronto, Ontario M2L 1J1, Canada

Kilbourne MR & MRS William T 3d (Lynn Wolverton) Y'84.H'91
   ☎ (415) 621-0275 . . 1338 Masonic Av, San Francisco, CA 94117

Kilburn MR & MRS H Thomas JR (Peck—Potter—Victoria D Tyner) Ln.P'53.Cl'59 . . of
   ☎ (212) 758-1196 . . 139 E 63 St, New York, NY 10021
   ☎ (203) 869-1845 . . 48 Walsh Lane, Greenwich, CT 06830

Kilduff MRS Delanie (Delanie Madison) . . . . Died at San Francisco, CA Oct 24'95

Kilduff MR & MRS William Dobson (Petersen—Catherine Randel) Bhm.Pcu.Sfg.P'41 . . of
   ☎ (415) 771-7314 . . 2250 Hyde St, San Francisco, CA 94109
   ☎ (808) 822-1172 . . "Lae Nani" 410 Papaloa Rd, Kapaa, Kauai, HI 96746

Kiley MRS Eugene J (H Jessie Hadley) Wa.Dar . . .of
☎ (847) CE4-4569 . . 130 E Foster Place, Lake Forest, IL *60045*
☎ (305) 367-2090 . . Ocean Reef Club, 86, Snapper Lane, Key Largo, FL *33037*

Kilgore MISS Constance P—Col'73.Nu'86 . . of
☎ (212) 925-3596 . . 130 Mulberry St, New York, NY *10013*
☎ (860) 599-0906 . . 14 Pinewoods Rd, North Stonington, CT *06359*

Kilgore MRS Emilie S (Gilbreath—Emilie de Mun Smith) Sth'57 . . . .   ☎ (713) 522-8529
MR Alexander G—at 98 Summit St, Brooklyn,   3239 Avalon Place,
NY *11231* . . . .   Houston, TX *77019*

Kilgore MR & MRS John E JR (Rassman—Annie J de Montel)
RMWmn'42.Unn.Aht'41.H'44
☎ (207) 667-3351 . . "Birchwood" Box 127, Surry, ME *04684*

Kille MR & MRS John E (Joanna P White) Denis'85.Miami'85
☎ (410) 757-8118 . . 1319 Farley Court S, Arnold, MD *21012*

Killea MR & MRS John W (Suzanne M Willoughby)
P'83.Stan'91.CalTech'80.Pa'84
☎ (415) 343-9010 . . 1601 Willow Av, Burlingame, CA *94010*

Killeen MR & MRS Henry W 3d (Allithea E Lango)
Wheat'70.Syr'80.H'68.Bost'75
☎ (716) 655-9982 . . "Kilhaven Farm" 502 Jewett-Holmwood Rd, East Aurora, NY *14052*

Killefer MR Tom . . . . Died at
Portola Valley, CA Jun 16'96

Killefer MRS Tom (Carolyn Clothier) Ri.Ln.Sl.Hn.
☎ (415) 948-5827 . . 708 Los Trancos Rd, Portola Valley, CA *94028*

Killhour MR & MRS Gilson E (Caroline M McGlynn) Pa'79
☎ (207) 985-9800 . . 22 Blueberry Pines Dv, Kennebunk, ME *04043*

Killhour MR & MRS William G (Josephine Q Greenwood) Myf.Ncd.Pa'47
☎ (803) 681-4207 . . "The Wells" 4 Brams Point Rd, Hilton Head Island, SC *29926*

Killiam MR Paul—Hn.H'37 . . . .   ☎ (203) 966-2479
MR Timothy S—at Kerkstraat 211, 1017 GJ   115 Bayberry Rd,
Amsterdam, The Netherlands . . . .   New Canaan, CT
MR Theodore R—at ☎ (203) 458-3922   *06840*
185 Dennison Dv, Guilford, CT *06437* . . . .

Killian MRS (DR) Marianne L (Marianne Legato)   ☎ (212) 838-7629
Man'vl'56.Nu'62.Bcs.Cs. . . . .   200 E 66 St,
MISS Christiana I—Bnd'90.H.'92.Cantab'94 . . . .   New York, NY
MR Justin P *10021*

Killion MRS Marion P (Marion M Payne) IaSt'62 . .   ☎ (602) 706-5772
MISS Karen L . . . .   16217 S 34 Way,
MISS (DR) Susan L—ArizSt'89.Ariz'93 . . . .   Phoenix, AZ *85044*

Kilmer MR & MRS Joyce P (M Catesby Halsey)
Bcs.Cly.Fla'80.Fla'82.Fla'84 . . of
☎ (212) RE4-0995 . . 315 E 70 St, Apt 3E, New York, NY *10021*
☎ (516) 283-0088 . . "The Banks" 64 S Magee St, Southampton, NY *11968*

Kilmer MRS Norman Joyce (Margaret E S Prentice) FlaAtl'83
☎ (561) 640-1055 . . "The Carriage House-Spunk Cottage" 601 S Cleary Rd, West Palm Beach, FL *33413*

Kilpatrick MR & MRS Charles O (Margie A Partin) Austin'46.A.Austin'42
☎ (210) 226-1130 . . 262 Losoya St, Apt 300, San Antonio, TX *78205*

Kilpatrick MR & MRS Ringland F JR (Nesbitt—Alicia N Shea) Rm.Y'38
☎ (561) 746-2043 . . 810 Saturn St, Apt 16, Jupiter, FL *33477*

Kilroy MR & MRS Edward A JR (Angela McCrory) Kt.Un.It.Y'49 ⚓
☎ (216) 932-5547 . . 2701 Chesterton Rd, Cleveland, OH *44122*

Kilroy MR Gregory T—Y'82
14909 Clifton Blvd, Apt 1, Lakewood, OH *44107*

Kilroy MR & MRS William S (Jeanie Spiegelhauer)   of ☎ (713)850-8850
Y'49 . . . .   3696 Willowick Rd,
MR William S JR—at 5110 San Felipe St,   Houston, TX *77019*
Apt 171W, Houston, TX *77056* . . . .   Kilroy Ranch,
6107 H'way 60 S,
Wallis, TX *77485*

Kimball MR & MRS Arthur L (Davenport—Effie L Brewer) UWash'59
☎ (907) 789-9438 . . PO Box 210147, Auke Bay, AK *99821*

Kimball MISS Catherine A (Scar—Catherine A Kimball) AmU'69
☎ (212) 988-7138 . . 401 E 74 St, New York, NY *10021*

Kimball MRS Cynthia F (Merriam—Cynthia F   7 Thoreau Rd,
Kimball) . . . .   Lexington, MA
MISS Priscilla A F Merriam *02173*
JUNIORS MR Scott R K Merriam . . . .

Kimball MR & MRS Daniel M (Lydia C Fitler)
Mid'84.H.'92.Nf.Me.Conn'63 . . of
☎ (207) 276-3700 . . PO Box 514, Northeast Harbor, ME *04662*
☎ (617) 354-6768 . . 6 Poplar Rd, Cambridge, MA *02138*

Kimball MRS Frederick M (Rachel R Coolidge) Stan'34.Un.
☎ (617) 862-6424 . . Brookhaven E316, 1010 Waltham St, Lexington, MA *02173*

Kimball MR & MRS Geoffrey D (Romia Bull) BMr'57.Y.'55.Cl'61
☎ (212) 688-2889 . . 420 E 55 St, New York, NY *10022*

Kimball MR & MRS John K (Margaret A McWilliams) H'85.Ill'68
Heald St, Pepperell, MA *01463*

Kimball MISS Katharine W . . see MRS (DR) M A White

Kimball MRS Mary Eliza (Stanley—Mary Eliza   of ☎ (860)928-7689
Kimball) Sth'73.GeoW'76 . . . .   "Jericho"
JUNIORS MR Arthur E Kimball-Stanley—at Taft   Seth Kimball Rd,
Pomfret Center, CT
06259
☎ (212) 688-4516
303 Rivercross,
531 Main St,
New York, NY
10044

Kimball MR & MRS Nicholas H (Lynn C Cuthbert) Colg'79.Ec.H'79
☎ (508) 526-4118 . . "Seawold" 450 Summer St, Manchester, MA *01944*

Kimball MR Richard A—C.Y'22
☎ (914) 234-3944 . . Pleasant St, Bedford, NY *10506*

Kimball MR & MRS Richard A JR (Hopeton D   ☎ (914) 677-9366
Kneeland) BMr'54.Un.C.Cly.Y'52 . . . .   RR 1, Box 123,
MISS Sylvia K—Y'91 . . . .   Fraleigh Hill Rd,
MR Samuel W—Y'84 . . . .   Millbrook, NY
12545

Kimball MR & MRS W Geoffrey (Joan Alice Wood)   ☎ (315) 853-6846
Sth'53.Y'52 . . . .   23 Fountain St,
MISS Nina J—Y'80—at ☎ (508) 371-1708   Clinton, NY *13323*
14 Union St, Concord, MA *01742* . . . .
MR Andrew W—Box 146, Williamstown, VT
05679 . . . .

Kimball-Stanley JUNIORS MR Arthur E . . see MRS M E Kimball

Kimber MR & MRS W Lawrence (Caroline Letchworth) Hav'37 . . of
☎ (716) 652-2233 . . 106 Elmwood Av, East Aurora, NY *14052*
☎ (315) 364-5545 . . ''Meadow Cottage'' W Lake Rd, Box 179, Auburn, NY *13021*

Kimberly MR & MRS John R (Barbara L Christy) Wells'68.Y'64.Cr'70
MISS Laura L—at Yale
JUNIORS MR John F
☎ (215) 242-6461
9225 Germantown Av, Philadelphia, PA *19118*

Kimberly MR Oliver A 3d . . see MRS B Gray 3d

Kimbro MRS Robert Willis (Smith—Marion A Yturria) Smu'49.A.
☎ (210) 828-8678 . . 122 Chester St, Apt 1, San Antonio, TX *78209*

Kimmick MR & MRS Adam O (Katharine L Schwab) Ty'85.Nu'89.Pr.Ty'86
☎ (516) 922-6552 . . 20 Northern Blvd, Oyster Bay, NY *11771*

Kincaid MR Brian McK—H'67.Stan'75
PO Box 12721, Berkeley, CA *94701*

Kincaid MRS Margaret Gray (Margaret Anne Gray) Stan'70.Stan'73
MISS Eleanor Zoe—H'96
JUNIORS MR Christopher McK
☎ (510) 525-7801
1438 Grant St, Berkeley, CA *94703*

Kindred MRS Joan H (F Joan Hover) Cly.Cs.
MISS Drewry A—at ☎ (212) 988-1869
300 E 71 St, Apt 8S, New York, NY *10021*
☎ (212) 986-1815
330 E 38 St, New York, NY *10016*

Kindred MR John J III—Snc.Coa.W&L'52.Va'55
☎ (212) 679-3181 . . 121 Madison Av, New York, NY *10016*

Kineon MR & MRS James C (Forsyth Watson) Unn.Yn.Y'44
MISS Forsyth P—Colby'89
☎ (203) 869-8030
26 Meadow Lane, Greenwich, CT *06831*

Kineon MR James C JR (James C) . . . . Married at Otis, MA
Perry MISS Ashley B (Ralph H 3d) . . . . Aug 24'96

Kineon MR & MRS James C JR (Ashley B Perry) Skd'89.Un.Gettys'87
☎ (212) 861-7859 . . 1365 York Av, Apt 18M, New York, NY *10021*

Kinerk MR & MRS Burton J (Nancy L Burton) Ariz'62.Ariz'57.Ariz'62
☎ (520) 326-8382 . . 2103 E Hampton St, Tucson, AZ *85719*

Kinerk MR Kevin B (Burton J) . . . . Married at Portland, OR
Lewin MISS Jennifer (Kenneth) . . . . Apr 29'95

Kinet MRS Henry R L (Virginia S Unsell) V'42
☎ (860) 536-0493 . . 147 Pequot Av, Mystic, CT *06355*

King MRS Alfred F JR (Gorman—Frances P Barton) MdInst'44.L.Elk.Md.Snc . . .of
☎ (561) 546-4101 . . PO Box 2026, Hobe Sound, FL *33475*
☎ (410) 321-4841 . . 17 Seminary Dv, Lutherville, MD *21093*

King MR Alfred F 3d—L.Col'64
21 Bayberry Rd, Westport, CT *06880*

King MISS Alice Gore—BMr'37.Lm.
☎ (203) 248-1593 . . 200 Leeder Hill Dv, Apt 641, Hamden, CT *06517*

King MISS Anna Talcott (MRS Catharine H) . . . . Born at Fletcher, NC Dec 20'95

King MR & MRS Bayard LeR (Joyce E Mallinger) Minn'51.Snc.Cc.H'44
☎ (505) 828-1774 . . 9731 Village Green NE, Albuquerque, NM *87111*

King DR & MRS (DR) Caleb K (Louise B Rambo) NCar'88.H'93.NCar'82.H'93
☎ (617) 566-6286 . . 131 Freeman St, Apt 3A, Brookline, MA *02146*

King MISS Carole A—Aub'76.WKy'82
☎ (334) 265-7144 . . 18 S Capitol P'kway, Montgomery, AL *36107*

King MRS Catharine H (Laffoon—Catharine L Hollerith) Pitzer'76. . . . .
JUNIORS MISS Catharine A Laffoon . . . .
JUNIORS MR Nathan P Laffoon JR . . . .
☎ (704) 859-7016
214 Hogback Mountain Rd, PO Box 484, Tryon, NC *28782*

King MR & MRS Charles H JR (Karla L Besozzi) Y'57 . . . .
MR Locke H . . . .
☎ (203) 762-0884
20 Cannon Rd, Wilton, CT *06897*

King MR & MRS Charles H 3d (Elizabeth R Buck) Va'81.Y'81
☎ (203) 698-0119 . . 7 Hearthstone Dv, Riverside, CT *06878*

King MR & MRS Clarence H JR (Toni Richards) Y'52 ⚓
☎ (941) 964-1419 . . Box 340, 1624 Gaspar Dv S, Boca Grande, FL *33921*

King MR & MRS Clarence H 3d (Mary S Hoagland) Bow'80.H'78
☎ (617) 295-2051 . . 35 Beverly Rd, Wellesley, MA *02181*

King MR Daniel J—Rc.Me. . . . .
LT D J Winsor—USA.—at Frankfurt, Germany .
☎ (610) 525-0716
''Pied à Terre'' 1050 Sentry Lane, Gladwyne, PA *19035*

King MRS David R (Mary S Griffith) . . . .
MISS Elizabeth P—Leh'79—at ☎ (214) 922-7032
2427 Allen St, Dallas, TX *75204* . . . .
MISS Melissa M—Cl'91 . . . .
MR Nicholas R—Leh'82.Cl'89—at
☎ (212) 534-3149 . . 17 E 97 St, New York, NY *10029*
☎ (908) 232-2398
139 Wells St, Westfield, NJ *07090*

King MR & MRS Edmund T 2d (Diane Raoul-Duval) Bhm.Bur.Pcu.Stan'58
☎ (415) 579-1787 . . 670 Woodstock St, Hillsborough, CA *94010*

King MR & MRS Frank-Paul A (Eugenia Hudson) SanDiego'87.MontSt'85.Duke'91
☎ (214) 559-4865 . . 4605 Arcady Av, Dallas, TX *75209*

King MR & MRS Frederick J JR (Rosemarie H Daly) Geo'66.Tul'70
☎ (504) 895-0425 . . 1021 Fourth St, New Orleans, LA *70130*

King MRS Garfield (Mary M Rice)
☎ (808) 878-6685 . . Box 186, Kula, Maui, HI *96790*

King MR & MRS George G (Sarah S King) Bost'79.Rc.Cc.Cda.MdArt'77
27 E 95 St, Apt 3E, New York, NY *10128*

King MRS Gilbert W (Abigail Adams)
☎ (310) 476-3681 . . 700 Halliday Av, Los Angeles, CA *90049*

King MR & MRS H Barnard 3d (Margaret A Landes) Denis'67.Denis'65 . . . .
MISS Caroline H—OWes'90—at
☎ (415) 775-1671 . . 1265 Bay St, San Francisco, CA *94123* . . . .
MR Tyler L . . . .
MR S Jamison—Denis'93—at ☎ (773) 248-2642
2110 N Sheffield Av, Apt 2, Chicago, IL *60614*
☎ (847) 559-1725
1501 Walters Av, Northbrook, IL *60062*

King MR & MRS Henry L (Sokolov—Margaret Gram) H'64.Nu'76.Un.Ri.Fic.Fiy.Lic.C.Cs.Cl'48.Y'51
☎ (212) 734-1993 . . 115 E 67 St, New York, NY *10021*

King MR James D JR
☎ (410) 662-8290 . . 4300 N Charles St, Apt 4C, Baltimore, MD *21210*

King DR & MRS (DR) James Jung-Kan (Cash—Martha S Nolte) Ws'73.Pa'77.Csp.W.Wis'70.Wis'71.Cwr'77
☎ (415) 386-1266 . . ''Thalatta'' 641—48 Av, San Francisco, CA *94121*

King MRS James M JR (Helen L Prichard) Bgt. . . . . | ☎ (914) 276-2305
MISS H Justine—at ☎ (914) 279-8164 | 355E Heritage Hills,
7 Carmel Av, Brewster, NY 10509 . . . . | Somers, NY 10589
MR Timothy W—at ☎ (401) 846-8519
2 Admiralty Dv, Apt 8, Middletown, RI 02842 .

King MR & MRS John Andrews JR (Rheault—M Cristina Carega) H'40 . . of
☎ (202) 462-2566 . . 2230 California St NW, Apt 5AE, Washington,
DC 20008
☎ (601) 283-1164 . . "Tolten" Rte 1, Stewart, MS 39767

King MRS John Lord (F Theodora Shaw)
☎ (415) 435-4866 . . 7 Windward Rd, Belvedere, CA 94920

King MR & MRS John S (Payne—Carolyn Nason) Sth'60.Chi.H.'51
☎ (617) 923-9630 . . 131 Coolidge Av, Apt 728, Watertown, MA 02172

King REV & MRS Jonathan LeR (Jacqueline P | ☎ (201) 444-6105
Esmerian) BMr'51.Mo.Plg.StJ.H'51 . . . . | 340 Godwin Av,
MR Edward LeR—BostColl'86 . . . . | Ridgewood, NJ
MR Frederic R—H'88—at ☎ (201) 652-7267 | 07450-3619
341 E Ridgewood Av, Ridgewood, NJ 07450 . .

King MISS Katharine H
☎ (215) 836-7173 . . 519 Filbert Rd, Oreland, PA 19075

King MRS Kerryn (Maytag—Shirley N Latham) Witw'48.Ny.Ri . . .of
☎ (212) 688-4777 . . 17 E 63 St, New York, NY 10021
☎ (407) 740-7767 . . 907 Old England Av, Winter Park, FL 32789

King MR & MRS Kimball (Harriet R Lowry) V'53.Myf.JHop'56
☎ (919) 942-4224 . . 610 North St, Chapel Hill, NC 27514

King MISS Kristina van B—Mar'vil'76 | ☎ (719) 372-0101
MISS (DR) Victoria van B—Stan'75.Mo'79 . . . . . | 1210 Apple Lane,
| Penrose, CO 81240

King MRS Le Roy (Woodbury—Pamela Sutherland) Cly.
☎ (011-44-1721) 721443 . . 59 High St, Peebles EH45 8AN, Scotland

King MR & MRS Ludlow (Elizabeth E Stovall) Cvc.Mt.Sl.USA'30
☎ (202) 541-0376 . . 6200 Oregon Av NW, Apt 376, Washington,
DC 20015

King MR Ludlow 3d—Mt.Cvc.Md'69.GeoW'72 . . . | ☎ (301) 229-7673
MR Seann P . . . . | 6410 Wishbone
| Terr, Cabin John,
| MD 20818

King MR & MRS MacLellan E JR (Elizabeth C | ☎ (702) 882-8800
Hellyer) USN'59.Ch'72 . . . . | 5575 Franktown Rd,
MISS Stephanie L . . . . | Carson City, NV
MR Blair M . . . . | 89704

King MRS Margo Miller (Margo L Miller) | ☎ (301) 983-8835
NotreDMd'65.Md'69.Sl . . . . | 8900 Potomac
JUNIORS MR Ludlow 4th . . . . | Station Lane,
| Potomac, MD 20854

King MRS Mary S (A Mary Sturges) Fic.Cly . . . . . . | ☎ (212) 744-5032
MISS Eleanor S . . . . | 175 E 79 St,
MR Andrew L . . . . | New York, NY
MISS Alexa S Bator—Stan'94—at Yale Law . | 10021
MR Timothy C Bator—at Kenyon . . . .

King MR & MRS Matthew A (Llew Ann Murray) WakeF'83.WakeF'82
☎ (615) 665-0518 . . 802 Lynwood Blvd, Nashville, TN 37205

King MR & MRS Matthew H (Elizabeth B L'Hommedieu)
Mid'89.Wes'81.Cl'91
☎ (415) 751-2805 . . 150 Palm Av, Apt 4, San Francisco, CA 94118

King MR Michael B—Dth'57.Bost'85 . . . . | of ☎ (508)975-5476
MR Stephen W—at U of Mass Amherst . . . . . . | Brooks School,
| 1160 Great Pond
| Rd, North Andover,
| MA 01845
| ☎ (603) 563-8066
| "Stonefields"
| PO Box 374,
| Dublin, NH 03444

King MRS Moya B (Moya B Shields)
☎ (202) 338-5159 . . 2500 Q St NW, Washington, DC 20007

King MRS Nicholas Le R (King—Canfield—Joan H | ☎ (212) 988-4058
Auerbach) BMr'51.Cda. | 39 E 79 St,
MR Bayard Le R 2d—at ☎ (212) 427-6967 | New York, NY
17 E 97 St, Apt 2A, New York, NY 10029 . . . . | 10021

King MR & MRS Paul K (Edith H G Joy) Ne'70 . . . . | of ☎ (508)475-7596
MISS Melissa van B—at St Lawrence U . . . . | "Twin Ridge"
MISS Sarah H J—at Dickinson . . . . | 1 Burton Farm Dv,
| Andover, MA 01810
| ☎ (207) 596-7349
| Rockport, ME 04856

King MR & MRS Richard H (Reta P Schoonmaker)
Wh'lck'60.H'55 ⚓ . . of
☎ (860) 633-8255 . . 75 Willow Green Lane, Glastonbury, CT 06033
☎ (508) 548-3635 . . "Sea Barker" 11 Snug Harbor Lane,
West Falmouth, MA 02574

King MR & MRS Robert M (Laura T Bethea) | ☎ (203) 762-9926
Cly.P'57.CTech'58.H'65 . . . . | 9 English Dv,
MISS Caroline P—at DePaul . . . . | Wilton, CT 06897
MR Donald M—at ☎ (203) 838-5708
208 Flax Hill Rd, Apt 9, Norwalk, CT 06854 . .

King MR & MRS Rufus Middleton (Anne K | ☎ (334) 264-5588
Danziger) Y'50.Ala'56 . . . . | 2468 Wildwood Dv,
MISS Anne M . . . . | Montgomery, AL
MR William R . . . . | 36111

King MR & MRS Samuel G (Jean L Macleod) Cw.Hb.H'49
☎ (401) 635-8767 . . "Windsong" 55 Quicksand Pond Rd,
Little Compton, RI 02837

King MR & MRS Samuel G JR—U'74
☎ (617) 326-8723 . . 5 Mt Hope Place, Dedham, MA 02026

King MR & MRS Scottow A (Rosso—Camille Cooley) Cal'72.Y'79
☎ (310) 471-8077 . . 11360 Waterford St, Los Angeles, CA 90049

King MR & MRS Timothy P (Diana B Niles) Hob'77.Pa'69 . . of
☎ (212) 517-3547 . . 157 E 75 St, New York, NY 10021
☎ (518) 398-6614 . . PO Box 498, Pine Plains, NY 12567

King Virginia F (Kimball) . . . . Married at Chapel Hill, NC
Nicholson DR Nigel J (Anthony) . . . . Jun 22'96

King MR & MRS W Griffin JR (Mary C Floyd) | ☎ (305) 367-2892
Uncl.Kt.Cwr'48 ⚓ . . . . | 19 Bay Ridge Rd,
MR William B B—at ☎ (703) 379-4835 | Key Largo, FL
5040—7 Rd S, Apt 302, Arlington, VA 22204 . . | 33037

King MRS Willard van B (Holmes—King—D'Wolf—Frances H Lewis) Cy.
☎ (314) 721-3700 . . 709 S Skinker Blvd, Apt 302, St Louis, MO 63105

King MR & MRS William A (Barbara S Beard) Nw'52.Ny.Wes'50 ⚓
☎ (203) 637-3164 . . 8 Indian Point Lane, Riverside, CT 06878

King MR & MRS William C (Anne D Van Slyck) StLaw'56
☎ (617) 354-7066 . . 14 Old Dee Rd, Cambridge, MA 02138

Kingery DR & MRS Frederick A J (Anne W Maloon) Y'48
☎ (503) 635-2755 . . 11641 SW Military Rd, Portland, OR *97219*

Kingman MR & MRS Abner (Diana E Davis)
Cl'64.Me.McG'51.Mich'62 . . . .
MISS Alexandra—Vt'93 . . . .
MR Abner JR—ColC'92 . . . .
☎ (610) 296-7913
2253 Buttonwood
Rd, Berwyn, PA
19312

Kingsbury MRS Frederick H JR (O'Donnell—Eleanor Bried)
MaryMt'30.Cly.Dh . . .of
☎ (212) 861-2635 . . 655 Park Av, New York, NY *10021*
☎ (941) 676-6435 . . PO Box 832, Mountain Lake, Wales,
FL *33859-0832*

Kingsbury MR H Neal—Geo'91 . . see F M Pope

Kingsbury MRS Henry A (Elizabeth F Hobart)
☎ (813) 584-6502 . . 101 Sarasota Rd, Belleair, Clearwater, FL *34616*

Kingsbury MR Howard T (Ellen M Wales) Ncd.
☎ (508) 287-0931 . . 301 Newbury Court, Concord, MA *01742*

Kingsbury MISS Macy T . . see F M Pope

Kingsbury-Smith MR & MRS Joseph (Eileen O'Neil) B.Mt.Km.Lond'29
☎ (540) 882-3327 . . Bantry Hill, PO Box 96, Waterford, VA *20197*

Kingsland MRS Elizabeth C (Finlay—Elizabeth E
Corbin) Srb. . . . .
MR Nicholas C—K.Ox'78.Geo'81—at
☎ (202) 338-6061 . . 2501 Q St NW,
Washington, DC *20007* . . . .
of ☎ (212)722-0762
57 E 92 St,
New York, NY
10128
☎ (516) 267-6551
18 Sandpiper Lane,
Amagansett, NY
11930

Kingsland MR & MRS James A (Auchincloss—Eve Grantham)
Rdc'44.K.C.Y'48
☎ (212) 777-2313 . . 5 Gramercy Park W, New York, NY *10003*

Kingsland MRS Mary E (Fairclough—Mary E Kingsland) Blackstone'48
☎ (561) 626-6226 . . 7 Oyster Bay, North Palm Beach, FL *33408*

Kingsley MRS John McC (Elizabeth H Curry) V'31.Ne.
☎ (203) 869-2007 . . "Hickory Hill" 599 Round Hill Rd, Greenwich,
CT *06831*

Kingsley MR & MRS John McC JR (Ines
Hinckeldeyn) MtH'61.Mds.Y'53.H'55 . . . .
MISS Kate A—at 2856 S Buchanan St, Arlington,
VA *22206* . . . .
☎ (203) 661-4437
16 Will Merry Lane,
Greenwich, CT
06831

Kingsley MR John McC 3d—CarnM'91
☎ (310) 543-1508 . . 508 Av F, Redondo Beach, CA *90277*

Kingsley MR & MRS Leonard E (Hunter—Sylvia C Morton)
Bhm.Bur.Sfg.Tcy.StJ.Hn.Ham'51.H'55
☎ (415) 567-6909 . . 2310 Broadway St, San Francisco, CA *94115*

Kingsley MR & MRS Robert L (Sarah F Du Bois) F&M'79
☎ (301) 897-5388 . . 5431 Lincoln St, Bethesda, MD *20817*

Kingston MRS C John (Kingston—Toms—Emily R Fuller)
Tufts'66.Myf.Dc.
☎ (212) 726-0048 . . 305 E 24 St, Apt 17F, New York, NY *10010*

Kingston MR Samuel S R—Plg.Cw.CtCol'94
☎ (212) 816-1616 . . 28 E 18 St, New York, NY *10003*

Kinkade MRS Charles E (Doucette—Patricia G
King) Cyb.Ec. . . . .
MISS Sheila A . . . .
MISS Susan M . . . .
MISS Nancy A . . . .
MISS Patricia H (Boymer—Patricia H Kinkade) .
MR Donald F Doucette JR . . . .
☎ (207) 985-7928
16 Grove St,
Kennebunk, ME
04043

Kinnaird MRS Eleanor F (Eleanor Foster)
☎ (813) 360-7436 . . 3520 E Maritana Dv, St Petersburg Beach,
FL *33706*

Kinne MR & MRS Wisner P (Barbara Bremer) . . . . . .
MR Cornelius . . . .
☎ (607) 869-2864
"Woodland Farm"
6858 Kinne Rd,
Ovid, NY *14521*

Kinney MR & MRS Douglas M (Smyth—Elizabeth
Hummel) On.Cho.H'52 . . . .
MISS Martha S . . . .
MISS Hilary S . . . .
MISS Elizabeth E Smyth . . . .
MR John E Smyth . . . .
of ☎ (561)624-6362
Seminole Landing,
12476 Ridge Rd,
North Palm Beach,
FL *33408*
☎ (847) 234-0832
920 E Deerpath Rd,
Lake Forest, IL
60045

Kinney MR & MRS Douglas M JR (Kimberly R Booth) Pom'81.On.Clare'79
☎ (847) 234-6414 . . 57 Franklin Place, Lake Forest, IL *60045*

Kinney MRS Francis S (Mary D Fowler) Csh.Pr.Cly.
☎ (516) 671-9362 . . 7 Rabbit Run, Matinecock Farms, Glen Cove,
NY *11542*

Kinney MR & MRS Gilbert H (Ann B Rasmussen)
V'53.Unn.Cvc.Mt.Nf.Sl.Y'53 . . . .
MISS Eleanor H—Y'90—at ☎ (401) 423-3333
90 Cedar Hill Dv, Jamestown, RI *02835* . . . . . .
of ☎ (202)965-5176
1231—31 St NW,
Washington, DC
20007
☎ (207) 244-5186
"TOP"
Pretty Marsh,
Mt Desert, ME
04660

Kinney MR & MRS Jeremy F (McNulty—Holly
Arnold) Rc.Ng.Ny.Y'68.H'73 . . . .
MR Oren T McNulty—at U of Colo . . . .
of ☎ (303)757-4516
2420 S Clayton St,
Denver, CO *80210*
☎ (212) 580-2203
33 W 70 St,
New York, NY
10023

Kinnicutt MRS G Hermann (Solmsen—Irène Jena) .
MR Michael T—H'72 . . . .
☎ (212) BU8-9696
169 E 69 St,
New York, NY
10021

Kinnicutt MRS Roger JR (Janet Heywood)
☎ (508) 842-0630 . . Southgate, 30 Julio Dv, Shrewsbury, MA *01545*

Kinsella MR & MRS Eugene Benoist (Lindsey—Ethel
P du Pont) BtP.Cda. . . . .
MISS Marina H Lindsey—ColC'91 . . . .
☎ (561) 659-2436
243 Seaspray Av,
Palm Beach, FL
33480

Kinsella MR & MRS Stephen R JR (Angela A
Wittenberg) Wash'58 . . . .
JUNIORS MR Stephen P . . . .
☎ (314) 962-3709
3 Danfield Rd,
St Louis, MO *63124*

Kinsella MR & MRS William A 3d (Eleanor L
Watson) Van'79.Va'81.D.Ncd.Conn'72 . . . .
MR William S—at Hamilton . . . .
JUNIORS MR Christopher B—at Yale . . . . | ☎ (508) 785-0207
14 Juniper Lane,
Dover, MA *02030*

Kinslow MRS Pamela M S (Pamela M Scott) Cal'76
☎ (011-44-1488) 648683 . . Jasmine Cottage, East Garston,
nr Hungerford, Berkshire RG17 7EX, England

Kinsolving MRS Arthur L (Mary K Blagden) Fic.StJ.
☎ (410) 377-0559 . . 17 Parliament Court, Baltimore, MD *21212*

Kinsolving MR & MRS Augustus B (Monique O H
Bérard) Paris'68.Cl'73.Ny.Y'61.Ox'63 ⚓ . . .
JUNIORS MISS Isabelle . . . .
JUNIORS MR Arthur B . . . . | ☎ (212) 794-2489
150 E 73 St, Apt
6D, New York, NY
10021

Kinsolving MR Herbert Leigh—Y'28.H'34
☎ (410) 224-2867 . . 5105 River Crescent Dv, Annapolis,
MD *21401-7273*

Kinsolving MR & MRS Lucien L (Mary Cole) Lm.H'45.Va'50
☎ (203) 458-6067 . . 929 Nut Plains Rd, Guilford, CT *06437*

Kip MRS R Delafield (Marquand—Robbins—Smith—Ayer—
Rita Delafield Kip) SL'75.Nyc.
☎ (508) 228-2562 . . 7 Mamack Lane, Nantucket, MA *02554*

Kipp MR & MRS Donald B (Jessup—Kellogg—
Wilhelmina van Neyenhoff) Ny.Nf. . . . .
MR Henry S Jessup—Br'74.Cl'79—at
☎ (212) 580-8059 . . 17 W 71 St, Apt 4B,
New York, NY *10023* . . . . | of ☎ (203)869-4466
PO Box 373,
Cos Cob, CT *06807*
☎ (561) 659-5259
2600 N Flagler Dv,
West Palm Beach,
FL *33407*

Kipp MR & MRS John P (Jean W Smith) Hl.P'31
☎ (561) 286-6854 . . 1429 SW Shoreline Dv, Palm City, FL *34990*

Kipp MR & MRS John P JR (Hewitt—Phyllis P
Myers) P'66 . . . .
MISS Jessica S . . . .
JUNIORS MISS Brooks S . . . .
JUNIORS MISS Kate H . . . .
JUNIORS MISS Anna G Hewitt . . . .
JUNIORS MISS Carolina A Hewitt . . . . | ☎ (207) 781-5458
17 Falmouth Rd,
Falmouth, ME
04105

Kipp MR & MRS Wilson (Jean M Creely) . . . .
MISS Donna L—Swb'78.Pitt'81—at
☎ (412) 741-3425 . . 93 Merriman Rd,
Sewickley Heights, PA *15143* . . . . | 875 Golf View Rd,
Moorestown, NJ
08057

Kippax MR & MRS John E (Helen F Frech) Ws'76.Rol'74
☎ (914) 834-8193 . . 18 Mayhew Av, Larchmont, NY *10538*

Kippax MR & MRS Lynn (Margaret L Good)
Penn'44.Penn'43 . . . .
MR Lynn JR—Box 57, Kennebunkport, ME *04046*
MR Jeffrey M—at 962 N 2 St, Philadelphia, PA
19123 . . . . | ☎ (610) 543-4356
915 Westdale Av,
Swarthmore, PA
19081

Kirby MR & MRS James Lewis JR (Ann S Kirby)
K.StJ.Ofp.Myf.Cw.Rv.Wt.P'46. . . . .
MISS Annette S—at 3224 Avenham Av, Roanoke,
VA *24014*. . . . .
MR Roger H W—at 4112 Hanover Av, Richmond,
VA *23221*. . . . . | ☎ (757) 866-8904
Claremont Manor,
Mansion Rd,
Claremont, VA
23899

Kirby MR & MRS James W (Rex—Cynthia Robinson)
☎ (401) 846-1154 . . ''Saltwood'' 15 Sachuest Dv, Middletown,
RI *02842*

Kirk MR & MRS Alan G 2d (P Joan Carr)
Cal'52.Cvc.Mt.P'50.Pa'56 . . . .
MISS Alison G. . . . .
MR Augustus G. . . . . | ☎ (703) 356-2762
827 Turkey Run Rd,
McLean, VA *22101*

Kirk MR & MRS Carey H (M Elizabeth B Gordon)
Van'71.Van'72.P'64.Va'67.Van'72
☎ (319) 266-2239 . . 1720 Cottage Lane, Cedar Falls, IA *50613*

Kirk MR Charles Avery—Ind'83.Ind'90
☎ (317) 253-4136 . . 5326 Central Av, Indianapolis, IN *46220*

Kirk MR & MRS Clarence L JR (Mary E Jones) Ncd.Ariz'39
☎ (317) 251-9880 . . 8442 Shoreway Dv, Indianapolis, IN *46240*

Kirk MRS Donald G (Maureen V Shanley) Ty'58.Mds.Cly . . .of
☎ (212) 988-4929 . . 131 E 69 St, New York, NY *10021*
☎ (516) 324-4075 . . Further Lane, East Hampton, NY *11937*

Kirk MR Eleanor H (Eleanor L Huser) V'49
☎ (914) 961-7411 . . 67 Rockledge Rd, Bronxville, NY *10708*

Kirk CAPT G G Ely—USN. . . . . Died at
Arlington, VA May 22'96

Kirk MRS G G Ely (Jean F von Schrader)
☎ (703) 536-9536 . . 4616 N 38 St, Arlington, VA *22207*

Kirk MRS Grayson L (Marion Sands) . . . . Died at
Washington Court House, OH May 17'96

Kirk MR Grayson L—C.Plg.StJ.Miami'24
☎ (914) 793-0808 . . 28 Sunnybrook Rd, Bronxville, NY *10708*

Kirk MR L Harvey . . of
☎ (516) 537-2868 . . PO Box 2184, Southampton, NY *11969*
''The Run'' 7 Guyers Rd, Water Mill, NY *11976*

Kirk MR Robert L JR
☎ (212) 752-0373 . . 58 W 58 St, New York, NY *10019*

Kirk MR & MRS Roger (Madeleine E Yaw) Mls'52.Mt.Cvc.P'52
☎ (202) 625-1096 . . 3230 Woodley Rd NW, Washington,
DC *20008-3334*

Kirkbride MR Chalmer G—An.Mich'30 . . . .
MR Chalmer G JR . . . . | ☎ (202) 686-1278
4000 Massachusetts
Av NW,
Washington, DC
20016

Kirkbride MRS Malcolm C (Sheridan—Adelaide D Soles)
☎ (415) 851-7414 . . 1550 Portola Rd, Woodside, CA *94062-1227*

Kirkbride MR & MRS Nicholas L S (Leggatt—
Margaret E Sherston-Baker) Plg.Y'59 . . . .
MISS Adele T—at ☎ (011-44-171) 738-7745
44 Regen Rd, London W1 9PN, England . . . . . .
MR Nicholas S—at ☎ (212) 627-5894
10 Morton St, Apt 10, New York, NY *10014* . . . | ☎ (561) 833-2535
1801 S Flagler Dv,
West Palm Beach,
FL *33401*

Kirkham MR & MRS Francis R (Ellis Musser)
Bhm.Sfg.Pcu.Tcy.GeoW'31 . . of
☎ (415) 931-7033 . . 3245 Pacific Av, San Francisco, CA *94118*
☎ (707) 944-2505 . . ''Little Farm'' 1591 Oakville Grade Rd, Oakville,
CA *94562*

Kirkham MR & MRS James F (Katherine D Dibblee)
Sth'58.Pcu.Y'54.Cal'57 . . . .
MR James D . . . . | ☎ (415) 922-4969
2239 Green St,
San Francisco, CA
94123

Kirkham MRS Kate B (Kate H Bicknell) . . . . | 7325 Stump Hollow
MISS Samantha—at 2 Crecienta Dv, Sausalito, CA | Lane, Chagrin Falls,
94965 . . . . | OH *44022*
MR W Gates—at Sinkola Plantation, Thomasville,
GA *31792*. . . . .

Kirkland MRS Alma de B W (Alma de B Walsh) | ☎ (212) 966-5772
Dar. . . . . | Box 2110, Times
MISS Bonnie J de B . . . . | Square Station,
| New York, NY
| *10036*

Kirkland MR Benjamin B—Hn.H'39 . . . . | ☎ (908) 996-2845
MISS Caroline M . . . . | PO Box A,
| Frenchtown, NJ
| *08825*

Kirkland MR & MRS Bruce A (Pollock—Cynthia | ☎ (303) 674-4079
Berkley) McG'55 . . . . | 33118 Alta Vista
MISS Tricia F . . . . | Dv, Evergreen, CO
| *80439*

Kirkland MR Charles McM—Hp.H'34
☎ (201) 567-9759 . . 119 Lydecker St, Englewood, NJ *07631*

Kirkland MR & MRS David S (Lila Wilmerding) | ☎ (561) 833-0280
Rcn.Pr.Ln.Mb.StLaw'62 . . . . | 235 Wells Rd,
MISS Amanda R . . . . | Palm Beach, FL
| *33480*

Kirkland MR & MRS F Russell JR (Cheri L Laughner) Nw'79.Me.StLaw'77
☎ (919) 471-3547 . . ''Fabula Farm'' 9402 Hampton Rd, Rougemont,
NC *27572*

Kirkland LT COL & MRS Faris Russell (Emelyn S Ewer)
USA.BMr'55.BMr'73.Me.Ph.Rv.Fw.P'53.Pa'70.Pa'82
☎ (610) 525-9909 . . 121 Kennedy Lane, Bryn Mawr, PA *19010*

Kirkland MISS Lila Webb—Vt'84
☎ (703) 516-2182 . . 1200 N Veitch St, Apt 335, Arlington, VA *22201*

Kirkland MRS Nancy B (Nancy C Bromley) | ☎ (410) 321-1137
JHop'80 . . . . | 310 Alabama Rd,
MISS Emilie S . . . . | Towson, MD *21204*

Kirkland DR & MRS Theo N 3d (Haltermann—Susan | ☎ (619) 454-5022
K Lesser) Pa'72.Ala'76 . . . . | 7704 Ludington
JUNIORS MISS Perry R . . . . | Place, La Jolla, CA
| *92037*

Kirkpatrick MR & MRS Alexander L (Elizabeth C | ☎ (303) 744-2513
Tieken) P'66. . . . . | 2141 E Alameda St,
MR Taylor C . . . . | Denver, CO *80209*
MR David F . . . .

Kirkpatrick MRS Crawford N JR (Elizabeth R Gross) BMr'42
☎ (410) 823-4535 . . 309 Greenwood Rd, Baltimore, MD *21204*

Kirkpatrick MR & MRS Hugh R JR (Frances Grauer) P'59
☎ (201) 425-1310 . . Grandview Farm, PO Box 335, New Vernon,
NJ *07976*

Kirkpatrick MR & MRS Miles W (Anna P Skerrett) P'40
☎ (610) 688-3144 . . 624 Knox Rd, Strafford, PA *19087-2016*

Kirkpatrick MR & MRS Thomas W (Anne G More)
☎ (803) 363-5802 . . 10 Acorn Lane, Hilton Head Island, SC *29928*

Kirkwood MR & MRS John H (Amanda C Hayne) Tcy.Stan'72
☎ (415) 346-7482 . . 2636 Union St, San Francisco, CA *94123*

Kise MR & MRS James Nelson (Sarah L O Smith) | ☎ (215) VI8-0008
Sth'64.Ch'68.LuthSem'92.Ph.Fi.Pc.Pe.Cs.Pa'59. | ''Lane's End''
Pa'62.Pa'63 . . . . | 3031 School House
MISS L L Susanna . . . . | Lane, Philadelphia,
MR C Curtis—Curry'87—at 2132 Penmar Av, | PA *19144*
Apt 6, Venice, CA *90291* . . . .
JUNIORS MR A L Triplett . . . .

Kissel MR & MRS Frank A (Sylvia B Talmage) | ☎ (908) 439-3076
Eh.Rol'73 . . . . | PO Box 841,
JUNIORS MISS Abbey T—at Brooks . . . . | Far Hills, NJ *07931*
JUNIORS MR Frank A JR—at Brooks. . . . .

Kissel MR & MRS Lester (Alice F MacRae)
Bnd'33.Un.C.Plg.StJ.Wis'25.H'31
☎ (212) 722-6495 . . 1170 Fifth Av, New York, NY *10029-6527*

Kissel MR & MRS Michael Case (Elena M Thornton) Br'81.Rc.Nrr.Srb.
☎ (212) 288-7999 . . 106 E 85 St, Apt 3S, New York, NY *10028-0982*

Kissel MRS Peter F F (Phyllis Ashburn) . . . . Died at
Peapack, NJ Apr 26'96

Kissel MR & MRS Peter F F JR (Katharine D Moyer) . | ☎ (904) 285-7132
MISS Frances D . . . . | 117 Teal Pointe
JUNIORS MR Peter F F 3d . . . . | Lane, Ponte Vedra
| Beach, FL *32082*

Kissel MR W Thorn JR—Rcn.Gv.Md.Cc.H'44
☎ (410) 363-1565 . . 223 Valley Rd, Owings Mills, MD *21117*

Kissinger DR & MRS Henry A (Nancy Maginnes)
MtH'55.Bhm.C.Mt.Ri.Cly.H'50.H'54
350 Park Av, New York, NY *10022*—(Henry A Kissinger)

Kissinger MASTER Samuel Fulton (g—Henry A Kissinger) . . . . . . Born at
Los Angeles, CA Jun 28'94

Kissinger MISS Sophia Frances (g—Henry A Kissinger) . . . . Born at
Los Angeles, CA Apr 30'96

Kistler MRS John S (Anita N Harding) Pa'43
☎ (610) 696-8020 . . 1421 Ship Rd, West Chester, PA *19380*

Kistner MR & MRS Stephen B (Olivia L Haydock) Skd'76.D.H.'74
☎ (508) 785-2055 . . 33 Haven St, Dover, MA *02030*

Kitchel MR & MRS Denison (Naomi M Douglas) Cly.Y'30.H'33
☎ (602) 585-1635 . . ''Casa Mirador'' 9735 E Vereda Solana, Scottsdale,
AZ *85255*

Kittell DR & MRS John C (Melinda Marvin) | ☎ (518) 677-3589
Myf.Cr'73 . . . . | Box 220B, Center
MISS Heather . . . . | Cambridge Rd,
MISS Shayna . . . . | Valley Falls, NY
| *12185*

Kittredge MR & MRS Charles J (Ogden—Clucas— | ☎ (413) 243-0176
Celia C de Gersdorff) Lx.Cy.Chi.Y'43 . . . . | ''Merrybrook''
MISS Catherine de G Clucas . . . . | Main Rd,
| Tyringham, MA
| *01264*

Kittredge MR & MRS Harvey Gaylord JR (Elizabeth J | ☎ (803) 524-1578
Houston) Bnd'47 . . . . | 28 Lucy Creek Dv,
MISS Clare B—Sth'71—at ☎ (603) 433-3939 | Beaufort, SC *29902*
27 Franklin St, Portsmouth, NH *03801* . . . .
MISS Sophie B—at ☎ (201) 798-8921
205 Clinton St, Hoboken, NJ *07030* . . . .

Klapp MR Edward M K JR—Me.Ste.Rv.Cspa.Ll.
☎ (954) 467-1200 . . 801 NE 19 Terr, Ft Lauderdale, FL *33304-3033*

Klapp MR Joseph W—Me.Rv.Ll. 🐚
☎ (610) 649-6116 . . 450 Old Lancaster Rd, Apt 8, Haverford, PA *19041*

Klapp MRS Nina S (Nina C Scheidt) Me. . . . . | ☎ (610) 687-6771
MISS Christina S—at 445 Old Lancaster Rd, | 9 Gwen Lane,
Haverford, PA *19041* . . . . | Devon, PA *19333*

Klapp MRS Wilbur P (Higgins—Elizabeth H Orr) . . . . Died in
Pennsylvania Apr 14'96

Klapp MR Wilbur P 2d—Me.Rv.Ll . . see MRS C H Heed

Klaus MR Charles—Kt.Cr'56.Cr'61
''The Gatehouse'' 9195 Baldwin Rd, Kirtland Hills, OH *44060*

Klaus MRS Gwendolen W (Gwendolen C Wendell) | ☎ (610) 279-0910
V'74.Ncd. . . . . | 1130 Dairy Lane,
JUNIORS MR John L . . . . | Blue Bell, PA *19422*

Klaussmann MISS Elizabeth M . . see J H Grummon

Klaussmann MR Eric K—Bost'94 . . see J H Grummon

Kleberg MR & MRS Richard M 3d (Olive A | ☎ (210) 822-2348
Musgrave) A.Dar.Ty'65 . . . . | PO Box 17777,
MISS Christina L . . . . | San Antonio, TX
MR Richard M 4th . . . . | *78217*

Klebnikov MASTER Alexander (Paul) . . . . Born Feb 5'95

Klebnikov MR & MRS George (Sarah D Coffin) | of ☎ (212)289-1537
Y.'73.Cl'75.Au.Cl'60 . . . . | 12 E 97 St, PH-D,
MISS Anne—at 64 E 86 St, New York, NY *10028* | New York, NY
MR Peter—at 64 E 86 St, New York, NY *10028* | *10029*
| ☎ (518) 239-4814
| Oak Hill, NY *12460*

Klebnikov MASTER Gregory (Paul) . . . . Born May 14'96

Klebnikov MR & MRS Michael (Alexandra Ourusoff)
☎ (212) 427-4086 . . 1326 Madison Av, New York, NY *10128*

Klebnikov MR & MRS Paul (Helen Train)
130 W 79 St, New York, NY *10024*

Klein MR & MRS Donald R (Karen B Loucks)
☎ (212) 772-1718 . . 501 E 87 St, Apt 18D, New York, NY *10128*

Klein MR & MRS G Robert (Mary E Fisher) OWes'31.Un.It.Mit'32 . . of
☎ (216) 464-1336 . . 23699 Shaker Blvd, Shaker Heights, OH *44122*
☎ (561) 588-6764 . . 3300 S Ocean Blvd, Palm Beach, FL *33480*

Klein MR & MRS Gilbert W (Marybelle P Ziesing) Me.Ac.Hav'50
☎ (610) LA5-3696 . . 1432 Orchard Way, Rosemont, PA *19010*

Klein MISS Joan Mathilde . . . . | ☎ (718) 229-1132
MR Louis F JR . . . . | 38-30 Douglaston
| P'kway, Douglaston,
| NY *11363*

Klein MR Thomas H—Me.NEng'85
☎ (610) 525-7636 . . ''The Caboose'' 1432 Orchard Way, Rosemont, PA *19010*

Kleiner MISS Margaret E S (Cederberg—Margaret E S Kleiner) Ga'90
☎ (513) 561-8702 . . 8820 Old Indian Hill Rd, Cincinnati, OH *45243*

Kleiner MR & MRS Scott A (Heather Lee Smith) | ☎ (706) 769-0525
Sth'61.Lynch'69.Wms'60.Ch'61.Ch'68 . . . . | 1061 Greystone
MISS Catherine B—Ws'88.Duke'89—at | Lane W,
Sandia Park, NM *87047* . . . . | Watkinsville, GA
| *30677*

Kleinhans MR & MRS Lewis C 3d (Lucie L Guernsey)
Wheat'77.Eyc.P.'53 . . of
☎ (212) 876-9123 . . 1755 York Av, Apt 5D, New York, NY *10128*
☎ (860) 567-3498 . . PO Box 419, Litchfield, CT *06759*

Kleinsorge MRS William P (Evelyn McKisick) | ☎ (916) 927-7081
Tcy.Dar.Cp. . . . . | 849 Commons Dv,
MR Edward R . . . . | Sacramento, CA
MR Alanson H—Ore'73 . . . . | *95825*

Kleinsorge MR & MRS William Peter (Kathryn D | ☎ (770) 971-2599
Vincent) Cp.Nev'64 . . . . | 2809 Meadow Dv,
MISS Elizabeth L . . . . | East Cobb, GA
| *30062*

Klenk MRS Eugene L (Anne C Stribling) | ☎ (303) 333-3114
Rdc'57.Sim'67.Ncd. . . . . | 325 Eudora St,
MISS Rebecca M—ColC'85.UWash'90—at | Denver, CO *80220*
U of Wash'n . . . . |
MISS Melissa S—DU'91 . . . . |
MR Christian W . . . . |

Klick MRS Walter H (Edith L Clark)
618 Nantucket Dv, Chula Vista, CA *92011*

Klimley MR & MRS Brooks J (Laura S Eimicke) Bnd'80.Cl'81.Cl'79.Ox'81
☎ (212) 486-4652 . . 444 E 57 St, New York, NY *10022*

Kline MR & MRS C Tomlinson 3d (Catherine Hanlon | ☎ (610) 687-6878
W Zaro) Me.Rv.DU'75 . . . . | 990 Brower Rd,
JUNIORS MISS Laura L . . . . | Radnor, PA *19087*
JUNIORS MR C Tomlinson 4th . . . . |

Kline MR Charles T JR—Me.Rv.Pa'43
1400 Waverly Rd, Andrews 215, Gladwyne, PA *19035*

Klinefelter MR & MRS Harry F (Moss—Amy B Carr) | ☎ (410) 323-4430
Elk.Mv. . . . . | 108 Castlewood Rd,
MR Harry F 3d—at ☎ (817) 926-6403 | Baltimore, MD
3721 Bellaire Dv S, Ft Worth, TX *76109* . . . . . | *21210*
MISS Anne M Moss—at ☎ (513) 221-0698 |
2709 Euclid Av, Cincinnati, OH *45219* . . . . . |

Klinefelter MR & MRS Stanard T (Sarah Cross) | ☎ (410) 823-0989
Elk.Md.Mv.Pa'69.Md'72.Geo'75 . . . . | 530 Greenwood Rd,
MR Christopher T—at Loyola . . . . | Baltimore, MD
JUNIORS MISS Amanda M. . . . . | *21204*

Kling MR Daniel W—Un.W&L'59
☎ (216) 321-8567 . . 2736 Claythorne Rd, Shaker Heights, OH *44122*

Kling MRS John A 2d (Lois Paxton) Rol'51.Cwr'53 | ☎ (703) 836-3196
MISS Elizabeth B—W&M'86.Bost'90—at | 433 Monticello
☎ (703) 998-0830 . . 3763 Keller Av, Alexandria, | Blvd, Alexandria,
VA *22302* . . . . | VA *22305*

Klingenstein MR Christopher . . see P B Holmes

Klipstein MR & MRS Kenneth H II (Pierrepont—Priscilla E Haack)
Shcc.Cly.Rut'88
PO Box 490, Oldwick, NJ *08858*

Kloman MR & MRS Christopher R (Pamela W | ☎ (703) 356-9142
Brown) GeoW'69 . . . . | 1403 Kurtz Rd,
MISS Sibyl W—P'94—at Boston, MA . . . . | McLean, VA *22101*
MR Christopher A T—at U of Va . . . . |
JUNIORS MR Peter J—at Potomac Sch . . . . |

Kloman MRS E Felix (Olivia R Pragoff) Louis'27.Sl.Cda.
☎ (703) 578-1000 . . Goodwin House E, 4800 Fillmore Av, Alexandria, VA *22311*

Kloman MR & MRS Erasmus H (Roosevelt—Suzanne Perrin)
Cos.P'43.H'47.Pa'62
☎ (202) 244-6142 . . 3065 University Terr NW, Washington, DC *20016*

Kloman MR & MRS H Felix 2d (Ann B Stern) Pn.P'55 ⚓ . . . . ☎ (860) 434-5356 61 Ely's Ferry Rd, Lyme, CT *06371*
MISS Sarah P—at ☎ (718) 856-1895 369 Parkside, Brooklyn, NY *11226* . . . .
MR Edward F—Ty'81—at ☎ (508) 463-6904 14 Buck St, Newburyport, MA *01950* . . . .

Klose MRS Willard (Virginia Taylor) . . . . ☎ (914) 758-3131 Echo Valley Farm, PO Box 292, Red Hook, NY *12571*
MISS Deborah . . . .
MISS Victoria—Mich'71—at 7 E 14 St, New York, NY *10003* . . . .

Klose MR & MRS Woody N (Elizabeth Smithers) Cr'60.Albany'71. . . . . ☎ (914) 758-6161 ''Carriage House'' Echo Valley Farm, RD 3, Box 188, Red Hook, NY *12571*
MISS Elizabeth . . . .
MR Woody N JR—StLaw'91 . . . .

Klots MRS Trafford P (Isabel S Hulings) Gv.
☎ (410) 685-6918 . . 1101 St Paul St, Baltimore, MD *21202*

Klotz MRS Annie K V (Annie K Vauclain) Me.Ncd. ☎ (610) 525-7646 138 Montrose Av, Apt 6, Rosemont, PA *19010*
MISS Ann V—Y'82.Ncd.—at ☎ (212) 794-0126 80 East End Av, Apt 4F, New York, NY *10028*.

Klotz MR George Meredith
☎ (904) 775-6264 . . 120 Southlake Dv, Apt 319C, Orange City, FL *32763*

Klotz MR John R—Me.Sa.Pa'45 . . of
☎ (610) 527-7766 . . D1 Mayflower Square, 922 W Montgomery Av, Bryn Mawr, PA *19010*
☎ (954) 749-9434 . . 7720 NW 50 St, Bldg 14, 208, Lauderhill, FL *33351*

Klotz MISS Leslie R . . see MRS C E Hallenborg

Knable MR & MRS John P 2d (M Cynthia Boyle) Lv.Y'50.CTech'59 . . . . ☎ (301) 299-7593 9117 Cherbourg Dv, Potomac, MD *20854*
MISS Eliza M . . . .
MR John P 3d . . . .
MR Geoffrey L . . . .

Knapp MRS Alexander Payson (May G Nelson) . . . . Died at New Orleans, LA Jly 17'96

Knapp MR & MRS Audenried W (Agatha M Krantz) Wash'58.Creigh'70
☎ (815) 469-1280 . . 10592 Brookridge Dv, Frankfort, IL *60423*

Knapp MR Audenried W JR—Loy'83
406 Wilcox St, Joliet, IL *60435*

Knapp MR & MRS Brian P (Cleaver L White) Red'90.Red'87
401 Succabone Rd, Mt Kisco, NY *10549*

Knapp MR C Evan . . see W M Boulos

Knapp MR & MRS George F (Mary Ann Hofheins) MoSt'53.Hob'51 . . . . of ☎ (301)694-3337 1301 N Market St, Frederick, MD *21701* ''Shaki Shanti'' Cranberry Lake, NY *12927*
MISS Katharine K . . . .
MR Robert H . . . .
MR George F JR . . . .
MR Geoffrey L . . . .

Knapp MRS George O 2d (Martha Gratwick) Sth'37 ☎ (203) 655-0700 250 Mansfield Av, Darien, CT *06820*
MISS Susan D . . . .

Knapp MR & MRS Harry K (Hinds—Marie L E Weidemann) NCar'55.Ty'50 . . . . ☎ (860) 535-3255 18 Tipping Rock Rd, Stonington, CT *06378*
MISS Alexandra K—Ken'90 . . . .

Knapp MISS Laura I (Whitman E) . . . . Married at Cohasset, MA Davidson MR Simon M (Peter) . . . . Jun 29'96

Knapp MR & MRS Lawrence W 3d (Genoveva de Carvalho Dias) Srr.Rr.Ariz'62
☎ (011-55-16) 851-1211 . . ''Fazenda Cruzeiro'' Caixa Postal 56, Morro Agudo, SP 14640-000, Brazil

Knapp MR & MRS Robert H (Faith Thoron) Cs.Chi.H.'36
☎ (315) 655-9552 . . ''Old Trees'' Box 433, Rippleton Rd, Cazenovia, NY *13035*

Knapp MRS Theodosia B (McLanahan—Watkins— Barnes—Theodosia B Knapp) . . . . ☎ (860) 535-4060 22 Elm St, Stonington, CT *06378*
MISS Amanda K Barnes . . . .
MR Duer McLanahan 3d . . . .

Knapp MR & MRS Whitman (Ann M Fallert) C.Cs.Y'31.H'34 . . . . ☎ (212) 226-4703 134 Greene St, New York, NY *10012*
MISS Marion E—at ☎ (715) 834-0687 611 Second Av, Eau Claire, WI *54703* . . . .
MR Gregory W—at ☎ (216) 231-8772 11477 Mayfield Rd, Cleveland, OH *44160* . . . . .

Knapp MR & MRS Whitman E (Ruth W Chute) Cy.Yn.Y'62 . . . . ☎ (617) 735-9221 120 Codman Rd, Brookline, MA *02146*
MR Whitman G S—Mid'89.Va'93—at
☎ (212) 986-2298 . . 245 E 40 St, New York, NY *10016* . . . .
MR Richard C—at Harvard . . . .

Knapp MR & MRS William B (La Bar—Judith L Mundy) Rr.Pars'67 . . . . ☎ (412) 238-3234 ''Deer Hill'' 229 Old Forbes Rd, Ligonier, PA *15658*
MISS Evelyn W . . . .
MR William B JR—at Pittsburgh, PA . . . .
MR James W La Bar—at San Diego, CA . . . .
MR Adam G La Bar—at Pittsburgh, PA . . . .

Knauft MRS Robert W (Mary E De Bus) Cin'31
☎ (513) 271-3740 . . 3939 Erie Av, Apt T6, Cincinnati, OH *45208*

Knauss MISS Katherine E
3601—39 St NW, Washington, DC *20016*

Knauth MR John A—Mich'61 . . . . ☎ (203) 852-1690 10 E Beach Dv, Rowayton, CT *06853*
MISS Jennifer E—EverSt'82 . . . .
MISS Alison F—BMr'82 . . . .
MISS Marianna M—Stph'85 . . . .

Kneass MRS Dudley (Louise Dudley Hines)
☎ (610) 644-0646 . . 411 Conestoga Rd, Apt 33, Devon, PA *19333*

Kneass MRS George B (Clement—Anita K Wood) . ☎ (610) 688-1037 429 Timber Lane, Devon, PA *19333*
MISS Susan B—at 3 Tammy Hill Rd, Wallingford, CT *06492* . . . .
MR De Witt C—at 512 Post Oak Rd, Annapolis, MD *21401* . . . .
MR Strickland L . . . .

Knechtle MR & MRS Emilio B (Ann Johnston) . . . . . ☎ (203) 966-9707 639 Smith Ridge Rd, New Canaan, CT *06840*
MISS Heidi P—Wheat'82 . . . .
MISS Grace A . . . .
MR John C—Wheat'81.Emory'86 . . . .
MR David M—Wheat'87 . . . .

Kneedler DR W Harding—P'22.Pa'26
The Pines, Apt 142, Davidson, NC *28036*
Kneeland MISS Deborah Van D—Sth'55
☎ (914) 265-4186 . . ''Deep Hollow'' Rte 301, Cold Spring, NY *10516*
Kneen MR & MRS Alfred T JR (Kay—Sally Parker Mohn) Skd'76.Dar.Cl'64
☎ (203) 966-6565 . . 281 Old Stamford Rd, New Canaan, CT *06840*
Kneen MR & MRS Thomas Beaudry (Sturges—   of ☎ (914)679-6963
Elizabeth W Betz) Pa'31 . . . .   ''Avanti''
MISS Judith F—BMr'58.Rdc'60—at   Box 136A,
10008 Stedwick Rd, Gaithersburg, MD *20879* . .   Byrd Cliffe,
   Woodstock, NY
   12498
   ☎ (508) 775-9097
   PO Box 225,
   West Hyannisport,
   MA *02672*
Knehr MR Charles A . . . . Died Apr 26'96
Knerly MR & MRS Stephen J JR (CTSS Catherine A H C A de Bravura)
☎ (216) 285-0979 . . 10390 Mitchells Mill Rd, Chardon, OH *44024*
Knewstub MR John C . . . . 934 County Line
MR Edwin O . . . . Rd, Bryn Mawr, PA
   19010
Kniest MR & MRS Bernard J (Joan C Vogler)   ☎ (314) 432-5614
Wash'57.Wash'81.Dar.StL'50   12040 Conway Rd,
MISS Joan M—StL'89 . . . . St Louis, MO *63131*
MISS Holly J—at N'east Mo . . . .
MR William L—Mo'94 . . . .
Kniffin MRS Edgar A (Jean Nolan)
☎ (516) JU4-7337 . . 176K Horse Race Lane, St James, NY *11780*
Kniffin MR & MRS Edgar A JR (Anne M Peper)   ☎ (203) 966-0730
Ws'58.Mid'54.Y'61 . . . . 129 Gerdes Rd,
MISS Catherine A—OWes'91—at   New Canaan, CT
☎ (203) 977-7742 . . 103 Holcomb Av, Stamford,   *06840*
CT *06906* . . . .
MR Edgar A 3d . . . .
Kniffin MRS Leonard D (Louise W Rogers) Ncd.
☎ (860) 232-4790 . . 331 N Steele Rd, West Hartford, CT *06117*
Kniffin MR & MRS Robert S (Leta W Pyne) Ny.Pa'67 ⚓
☎ (617) 729-7447 . . 94 Church St, Winchester, MA *01890*
Knight MR & MRS C Foster (Kathryn J Scott)   ☎ (617) 721-2118
Cal'66.GeoW'80.Y'62.Cal'68 . . . . 16 Hillside Av,
MISS Jessica P . . . . Winchester, MA
JUNIORS MISS Alexa S *01890*
Knight MR & MRS Charles C (Mary L Franz)   ☎ (610) MI9-4131
Rose'63.Me.Ala'65 . . . . 536 Montgomery
MISS Lisa M—Colg'91—at ☎ (212) 924-7968   Av, Haverford, PA
7 Jane St, Apt 3F, New York, NY *10014* *19041*
MR Charles C 3d—Penn'95—at
☎ (603) 523-7136 . . RD 2, Box 276, Rte 118,
Rumney, NH *03266* . . . .
Knight MRS Charles Carroll (Ruth W Greene) . . . . Died Jun 13'96
Knight MR & MRS Charles F (Joanne Parrish) Cy.Cho.Ln.Lc.Cr'58
☎ (314) 991-0802 . . 24 Foreway Dv, St Louis, MO *63124*
Knight MR & MRS G Morgan D (Mary J Wright) Penn'60
☎ (207) 829-6986 . . 8 Hillcrest Dv, Cumberland Center, ME *04021*

Knight MR & MRS George C (Meghan M Walsh)
Mid'90.Man'vl'95.Pn.P'89.Y'95
☎ (203) 562-4952 . . 26 Academy St, New Haven, CT *06511*
Knight MASTER George Craig JR (George C) . . . . Born at
New Haven, CT Apr 17'96
Knight MR & MRS George W (Adelaide C Hardenbergh) Cly.Paris'30.H'33
☎ (212) BU8-7830 . . 120 E 81 St, Apt 14F, New York, NY *10028*
Knight JUNIORS MR Hunter H . . see T A McGraw JR
Knight MR & MRS James A (Cynthia F Olney)
Bost'82.GoldG'87.Msq.Yn.Bost'75.Dth'84
☎ (847) 735-1156 . . ''Coach House'' 606 Tiverton Rd, Lake Forest,
IL *60045*
Knight MR & MRS James E (Alison W Rogers) StLaw'91
☎ (212) 966-2500 . . 115 E 90 St, Apt 5E, New York, NY *10128*
Knight MASTER James Edward JR (James E) . . . . Born at
Greenwich, CT Jly 28'95
Knight MRS Jesse JR (Kathryn C Whittemore) Sim'37
☎ (812) 333-0649 . . 2455 Tamarack Trail, Apt 011, Bloomington,
IN *47408-1294*
Knight MR & MRS Lawrence A (Linda J Augustine)
☎ (610) 668-1581 . . 144 Rockland Av, Belmont Hills, PA *19004*
Knight MR Mark W—Me.Cc.Vt'81
☎ (610) 964-9559 . . ''The Alcove'' 117 Glynn Lane, St Davids,
PA *19087*
Knight MRS Peyton H (Claudine M Tillier)   ☎ (212) 861-4336
Bnd'50.Un.Cly.Y. . . . . 325 E 79 St,
MISS Cornelia C—Man'vl'93.Cly. . . . . New York, NY
   10021
Knight MR & MRS Richard N JR (Ann H Philbrick) V'45.Rc.Gm.Fst.Cr'41
☎ (610) 649-2641 . . 1010 Merion Square Rd, Gladwyne, PA *19035*
Knight MR & MRS Ridgway B (Dupont—Christine Saint-Léger)
HESl'52.B.Mt.Sar.Paris'29.H'31
☎ (011-33-1) 45-48-09-18 . . 32 rue de Varenne, 75007 Paris, France
Knight MR & MRS Robert C (Sara A Marshall) . . . . | ☎ (860) 523-8410
MISS Sara E—Cr'91 . . . . | 18 High Farms Rd,
MISS Kathryn A—NH'92 . . . . | West Hartford, CT
   | *06107*
Knight MR & MRS Robert H (Gibson—Rosemary Costikyan)
Lx.Ln.Ri.Ct.L.Mt.Plg.Cs.Y'40.Va'47 . . of
☎ (212) 838-0961 . . 570 Park Av, New York, NY *10021*
☎ (203) 869-8997 . . ''The Knoll'' 12 Knollwood Dv, Greenwich,
CT *06830*
Knight MR & MRS Robert P (Andrea Saladine) Cyc.Ih.Y'48
851 Bryant St, Winnetka, IL *60093*
Knight MRS Roma W (Roma L Wickwire)
☎ (610) 964-8905 . . 117 Glynn Lane, St Davids, PA *19087*
Knight MR & MRS Thomas S JR (Kathleen C Craig) | ☎ (203) 661-2511
BMr'52.Unn.Chr.Plg.Pn.P'52 . . . . | 340 North St,
MR Thomas S 3d—CtCol'88 . . . . | Greenwich, CT
MR Peter A—Ty'93 . . . . | *06830*
Knight MR & MRS Townsend J (Margaret Elise Heck) Snc.Cs.H.'49.Cl'52
☎ (212) 876-5318 . . 1158 Fifth Av, New York, NY *10029*
Knipe MR & MRS Peter R (Nancy L Rodgers) Y'60 . | ☎ (609) 466-0630
MR Peter G—U'96 . . . . | 156 Spring Hill Rd,
MR Daniel R . . . . | Skillman, NJ *08558*

Knipe MR & MRS T Wetherill (Gilchrist—Wainwright—Mary G Harris)
Un.Mds.Gr.Plg.Fw.Myf.Cw.Cly.P'43
☎ (212) RE7-2281 . . 530 E 72 St, New York, NY *10021*

Kniskern MR & MRS Philip N (Anne S Cooper) Pa'57.Ncd.Swth'49.Dth'51
☎ (954) 943-5049 . . 2961 NE 27 Av, Lighthouse Point, FL *33064*

Kniskern MR Thomas R (Philip N) . . . . . Married at Lighthouse Point, FL
Christenson MISS Julie A . . . . Mch 12'94

Knode MR & MRS Ralph H (Judith M O'Neill)
☎ (307) 674-8933 . . 11 Pintail Rd, Sheridan, WY *82801*

Knoll MR David H
☎ (513) 321-3585 . . 3650 Shaw Av, Cincinnati, OH *45208*

Knollenberg MR & MRS Peter S (Pieternel Stoop)
Sim'85.BtP.S.Sar.Hb.Nu'73.H'88
☎ (918) 481-1155 . . 6117 E 82 Place S, Tulsa, OK *74137*

Knoop MR & MRS Frederick G (Grace E Gilmore) | ☎ (415) 324-2455
Bur.Pcu.Cal'51 . . . . | 127 Isabella Av,
MISS Katherine D . . . . | Atherton, CA *94027*
MR Robert G . . . . |

Knoop MR Frederick W—SCal'78
☎ (415) 364-9224 . . 920 Pleasant Hill Rd, Redwood City, CA *94061*

Knop MR Peter J—Mt.Ct.Ty'62.Va'66 . . . . . . | of ☎ (703)525-4499
MISS Alexandra B—at "The Cottage" | 1200 N Nash St,
26314 Ticonderoga Rd, Chantilly, VA *20152* . . . | Apt 529, Arlington,
MR Peter R Q—at 26314 Ticonderoga Rd, | VA *22209*
Chantilly, VA *20152* . . . . | ☎ (703) 754-4484
JUNIORS MR William J W . . . . | Ticonderoga Farm,
| 26175 Ticonderoga
| Rd, Chantilly, VA
| *20152*

Knopf MR & MRS Alfred JR (Alice M Laine) C.U'42
☎ (203) 227-9365 . . Bayberry Ridge, Westport, CT *06880*

Knott MRS Carolan (Carolan Poett) . . . . | ☎ (208) 726-4243
MISS Carolan . . . . | Box 832,
| Ketchum, ID *83340*

Knott MR David H—Rcn.Mid'60
☎ (208) 726-3093 . . Box 1242, Sun Valley, ID *83353*

Knott MR & MRS Francis X (Johnson—Susan W | ☎ (410) 526-0756
Miller) Cy.Md.Mv. | "Hazard"
MISS Aimee E . . . . | 2300 Geist Rd,
MR Francis X . . . . | Glyndon, MD *21071*
MISS Jesse K Johnson . . . . |
JUNIORS MR Marshall B Johnson . . . . |

Knott MRS James (Whitney—Adelaide Weld) Pr.
☎ (516) 676-8660 . . 18 Matinecock Farms Rd, Glen Cove, NY *11542*

Knott MRS James (Susan F Gordon)
☎ (717) 529-2920 . . 63 Maple Shade Rd, Christiana, PA *17509*

Knowles DR & MRS David S (Marion P Hewson) Ithaca'82.Cr'82.Mit'91
☎ (619) 792-5192 . . 12535 Montellano Terr, San Diego, CA *92130*

Knowles MR Francis E . . see MRS G A Sawyer

Knowles MR & MRS Gorham B (Hickingbotham—Diana Dollar)
Bur.Cal'40.H'42 . . of
☎ (415) 751-1811 . . 3725 Washington St, San Francisco, CA *94118*
☎ (408) 624-5569 . . Pebble Beach, CA *93953*

Knowles MRS James H (Reed—Elizabeth McCullough) Pg.Rr . . .of
☎ (520) 684-5484 . . Rancho de los Caballeros, 1551 S Vulture Mine Rd,
Wickenburg, AZ *85390*
☎ (412) 238-6261 . . "Three Chimneys" RR 2, Box 343, Ligonier,
PA *15658*

Knowles MR & MRS James H JR (Sherin Hetherington)
Fcg.Pg.Rr.Y'62.H'64 . . of
☎ (412) 681-2444 . . 206 Schenley Rd, Pittsburgh, PA *15217*
☎ (412) 238-6400 . . "Dragonswood" Box 36, Ligonier, PA *15658*

Knowles MR & MRS Robert W (Barbara M | ☎ (803) 649-2626
Rutherfurd) . . . . | 504 Berrie Rd,
MISS Alice R . . . . | Aiken, SC *29801*

Knowles MISS Sarah M
☎ (617) 235-8708 . . 72 Standish Rd, Wellesley Hills, MA *02181*

Knowlton MRS Eben (Helen M Foote) Ncd . . .of
☎ (561) 746-5519 . . Jupiter Inlet Apt I106, 755 Saturn St, Jupiter,
FL *33477*
☎ (860) 824-7321 . . "The Chimneys" 71 Belden St, Falls Village,
CT *06031*

Knowlton MR & MRS Frank W (Hélène Sigourney) | ☎ (941) 966-1887
Myf.Ht.Hb.H'35 . . . . | 1615 Bayhouse
MISS Lindsay—at Concord Green 7, | Court, Apt BA113,
1024 Main St, Concord, MA *01742* . . . . | Sarasota, FL *34231*

Knowlton GEN & MRS William A (Marjorie A | ☎ (703) 841-0140
Downey) An.Cw.Myf.Rv.USA'43.Cl'57 . . . . . . | 4520—4 Rd N,
MR Davis D—FlaSt'74—at US Embassy, | Arlington, VA
Bangkok, APO AP, *96546* . . . . | *22203-2342*

Knox MR & MRS Andrew S (Claire N White) . . . . . . | ☎ (803) 650-5764
MR Gary S . . . . | 203 Misty Pine Dv,
| Myrtle Beach, SC
| *29575*

Knox MRS Arthur JR (Hubby—Margaret N Fisher) Cly.Myf.Ncd.
☎ (860) 767-7026 . . 125 Essex Meadows, Essex, CT *06426*

Knox MISS Cynthia B—SL'83 . . see MRS J G Harcum

Knox MRS D Thoma (Kaiser—Diana Thoma) Flor'53
☎ (410) 268-3614 . . 71 Bay Dv, Annapolis, MD *21403*

Knox DR & MRS J H Mason 3d (Frances Apthrop Vaughan)
Mv.Ncd.Y'34.JHop'38
☎ (410) 823-3089 . . 1407 W Joppa Rd, PO Box 23, Riderwood,
MD *21139*

Knox MR N Rulison JR—H'43
☎ (410) 923-2323 . . 402 Tulip Trail, Crownsville, MD *21032*

Knox MR & MRS Northrup R (Lucetta G Crisp) Rc.St.Ts.B.G.Cly.Y'50
☎ (716) 652-3366 . . 437 Buffalo Rd, East Aurora, NY *14052*

Knox MR & MRS Northrup R JR (Victoria A Beers) Stet'83.D.Aht'76.Y'84
☎ (617) 329-2953 . . 32 Farm Lane, Westwood, MA *02090-1108*

Knox MASTER Northrup Rand 3d (Northrup R JR) . . . . Born at
Boston, MA Nov 28'94

Knox MR & MRS Peter G (Lilla T Davison) H'48
☎ (610) 820-5883 . . 2634 Washington St, Allentown, PA *18104*

Knox MRS Richard G (Edwards—M Stevenson Murdoch)
Temp'41.Cvc.StA.
☎ (404) 266-1439 . . 3060 N Pharr Court NW, Atlanta, GA *30305*

Knox MR Seymour H 3d . . . . Died at
East Aurora, NY May 22'96

Knox MRS Seymour H 3d (Jean Read) Cy.Ts.St.B.G.Cly.Ncd.Myf.
☎ (716) 652-1999 . . 437 Buffalo Rd, East Aurora, NY *14052*

Knox MR & MRS Seymour H 4th (Constance M Jewell)
StJFisher'85.Cy.St.LakeF'78
☎ (716) 873-1006 . . 250 Middlesex Rd, Buffalo, NY *14216-3118*
Knox MR & MRS William A Read (Nancy M | ☎ (410) 771-4742
Griswold) JHop'79.Md.Gv.Cly.Mv.Y'78 . . . . . . | 3613 Hess Rd,
JUNIORS MISS Arabella R . . . . | Monkton, MD
JUNIORS MISS Avery H . . . . | *21111*
Knox-Johnston MR & MRS John A (Lovell—Beatrice Sweney-Borden)
Geo'79 . . of
☎ (508) 228-5090 . . "Corner House" 49 Center St, Box 1828,
Nantucket, MA *02554*
☎ (011-44-171) 589-8784 . . 3A Egerton Gardens, London SW3 2BS,
England
☎ (805) 969-6331 . . 1338 E Valley Rd, Montecito, CA *93108*
Knoy MRS Maurice G (Hurley—Gwendolyn L Juergens) Rcch.Cas.Cnt.
☎ (317) 463-9435 . . 2741 N Salisbury St, Apt 2415, West Lafayette,
IN *47906*
Knutsen MRS Otto F JR (Betty Nichols) Cv.
☎ (216) 423-3163 . . Cedar Rd, Hunting Valley, Gates Mills, OH *44040*
Kobelt MR & MRS Peter R (Laura A Munson) Denis'88.Myf.Suff'89
☎ (406) 862-7912 . . 113 Park Knoll Lane, Whitefish, MT *59937*
Koberg MR & MRS Heino C F (Charlotte W Baker) | ☎ (610) 525-4373
OsnU'63 . . . . | 217 Landover Rd,
MR Heino F—at Pottsville, PA *17901* . . . . | Bryn Mawr, PA
MR David S—at Blue Bell, PA *19422* . . . . | *19010*
MR Franz P—at San Diego, CA . . . . |
Kobusch MR Nicholas Cabell—Cysl.Lc.TCU'87
see Dilatory Domiciles
Kobusch MRS Richard B (Clarkson—Margaret M Wightman) Cy.Lc.
☎ (314) 994-0140 . . 215 S Warson Rd, St Louis, MO *63124*
Kobusch MR Richard B JR
☎ (314) 994-0140 . . 215 S Warson Rd, St Louis, MO *63124*
Koch MR David H (late Fred C) . . . . Married at Southampton, NY
Flesher MISS Julia M (Fredric C) . . . . May 25'96
Koch MR Frederick R—C.Mto.Gr.H.'55.Y'61 . . of
☎ (212) 838-0800 . . 825 Fifth Av, New York, NY *10021*
"Elm Court" Polk St, Butler, PA *16001*
Koch MR & MRS Robert S (Kimberly A Eversole) ColC'86
☎ (773) 348-1312 . . 711 W Gordon Terr, Apt 821, Chicago, IL *60613*
Kock MR & MRS E James JR (Mary R Foster) Tul'49
☎ (504) 899-4862 . . 1530 State St, New Orleans, LA *70118*
Koehler MR & MRS Carl A (Barbara French) Y'51 . . . | ☎ (203) 869-1387
MISS Jennifer W—Vt'87—at 1407 Francisco St, | 8 Hobart Dv,
San Francisco, CA *94123* . . . . | Greenwich, CT
                                                        | *06831*
Koehler MISS Ellen F . . . . | 15 Grosset Rd,
MR H William D . . . . | Riverside, CT *06878*
Koehler MR & MRS Henry W (Mason—Audrey T Carey)
B.C.So.Bcs.Srr.Y'50 . . of
☎ (516) 283-3179 . . 80 N Main St, Southampton, NY *11968*
☎ (212) 744-2672 . . 218 E 70 St, New York, NY *10021*
Koëhn MR & MRS André O (Potter—Brenda A Timpson) Cly.Gen'33
☎ (212) 752-6917 . . 200 E 66 St, New York, NY *10021*
Koekkoek MR & MRS Byron J (Martha D Park) Ol'49.Vien'53
☎ (716) 839-3240 . . 32 Bernhardt Dv, Apt 10, Amherst, NY *14226*
Koekkoek MR & MRS Peter Mannes (Martha P Soper) Vt'81.Hob'79
☎ (508) 443-6282 . . 141 Morse Rd, Sudbury, MA *01776-1714*

Koenig MR R Julian—Csh.LakeF'73.H'75 . . . . | ☎ (516) 624-9153
JUNIORS MISS Elizabeth P . . . . | 115 Cove Neck Rd,
                                                        | Oyster Bay, NY
                                                        | *11771-1822*
Koenig MRS Robert P (Angela R Pow) Ox'41.Cly.
☎ (516) 624-9376 . . "Fair Winds" 115 Cove Neck Rd, Oyster Bay,
NY *11771*
Kohle MR Christopher F . . see La Besse CTE de
Kohle MISS Patricia J . . see La Besse CTE de
Kokesh MR & MRS Michael O (Sandra J Stockton)
SantaC'76.SantaC'78.Sfy.Col'74.Hast'79
☎ (415) 661-2233 . . 20 San Pablo Av, San Francisco, CA *94127*
Kolachov MRS Sergei P (Sophie L Walcott) . . . . | ☎ (610) 975-9189
MR Nicholas P—LakeF'89 . . . . | 301 Drummers
MR Paul W—StLaw'91 . . . . | Lane, Wayne, PA
                                                        | *19087*
Kole MR & MRS Michael U (Kelly A Murray) Rich'90.ECar'90
☎ (804) 360-7929 . . 5936 Park Forest Lane, Glen Allen, VA *23060*
Kole MISS Riley Hope (Michael U) . . . . Born at
Richmond, VA Jly 12'96
Kolowitz MISS Emma H . . see W P C Hudson
Koob MR & MRS Daniel J (Elizabeth B Walton)
V'68.Cal'79.H.NotreD'67.Clare'69
☎ (212) 874-7345 . . 125 Riverside Dv, New York, NY *10024*
Koons MRS Benjamin H B JR (Violette R Mann) . . . | 133 Lee Circle,
MR Charles B—Temp'76 . . . . | Bryn Mawr, PA
MR Garner M . . . . | *19010*
Koons MR Tilghman B—P.'49.Paris'52 . . of
☎ (212) 989-2027 . . 462 W 23 St, New York, NY *10011*
☎ (516) 324-2358 . . 40 Egypt Close, East Hampton, NY *11937*
Koontz MR & MRS James W 2d (Florence D Harris)
Rol'65.Md.Rv.Cw.Wt.Dar.Va'52.W&M'79
☎ (561) 844-5456 . . 232 La Puerta Way, Palm Beach, FL *33480*
Kopp MR & MRS Bradford B (Jean S Rath)
CtCol'74.Ford'80.Msq.Cly.Ncd.Ht.Myf.H'73.H'77 . . of
☎ (401) 272-7592 . . 43 Congdon St, Providence, RI *02906*
☎ (401) 596-5625 . . 10 Sunset Av, Watch Hill, RI *02891*
Koppelman MRS John Van C (Nannie P Mitchell) Gi.
☎ (410) 377-8765 . . 6006 Hunt Ridge Rd, Baltimore, MD *21210*
Koppelman MRS Walter JR (Barbara R M Tschudi) | ☎ (410) 435-0703
Mv. . . . . | 100C Cross Keys
MR Jay Van C—Frost'82 . . . . | Rd, Baltimore, MD
MR Baker R—Guil'90 . . . . | *21210*
Koppelman MR & MRS Walter 3d (Deborah J Steinmetz) Md'89
☎ (410) 239-7387 . . Windswept Farm, 18515 Gunpowder Rd,
Hampstead, MD *21074*
Kopper MRS John M (Lula H Bowen) . . . . Died at
Baltimore, MD Feb 27'96
Kopper MR John M—Cw.JHop'33
☎ (410) 235-0267 . . 512 Woodlawn Rd, Baltimore, MD *21210*
Kopper MRS Juliette Starr (Bidlack—Juliette Starr Kopper)
Ober'52.AmU'78
☎ (301) 972-7425 . . PO Box 217, 22331 Mt Ephraim Rd, Dickerson,
MD *20842*
Kopper MISS Lula B—Ws'71
☎ (617) 646-1918 . . 153 Waverly St, Arlington, MA *02174*

Kopper MR & MRS Philip D (Hallett—Mary S Carll) AmU'77.Y'59
☎ (301) 652-2383 . . 4610 DeRussey P'kway, Chevy Chase, MD *20815*

Korff BRNSS Serge A (Mittendorf—Brett—Marcella C Heron) BMr'42.Cly.
☎ (212) 535-4508 . . 333 E 68 St, New York, NY *10021*

Korosi MR & MRS Dana A (Johnston—Barbara C Caldwell)
Cwr'76.Cwr'86.Bost'71
☎ (216) 247-0882 . . 35945 Jackson Rd, Moreland Hills, OH *44022*

Korrick MR & MRS Edgar L (Helen L Weins) Wis'48.Stan'48
☎ (602) 941-6743 . . 2225 E Marshall Av, Phoenix, AZ *85016*

Korth MR & MRS Fred (Williams—Charlotte Brooks)
An.A.Tex'32.GeoW'35.GeoW'60 . . of
☎ (202) 223-3630 . . 4200 Massachusetts Av NW, Apt 101, Washington,
DC *20016-4744*
☎ (915) 584-7060 . . 6041 Torrey Pines Dv, El Paso, TX *79912*

Korybut-Daszkiewicz MR Alexis . . see R D O'Connor

Korybut-Daszkiewicz MR Michael . . see R D O'Connor

Kosmak MISS Katharine L—V'29
☎ (609) 426-6119 . . Meadow Lakes 18-06, Hightstown, NJ *08520*

Kostmayer MISS Ashley A . . see MISS S de L Whitlock

Kostmayer JUNIORS MISS Mary . . see MISS S de L Whitlock

Kostmayer MISS Virginia K . . see MISS S de L Whitlock

Kountze MRS Thorne (Pierce—Leslie Thorne) . . . . . | ☎ (207) 372-8039
MR Hallett P . . . . | Walston Rd,
| HCR 35, Box 289A,
| St George, ME
| *04857*

Kouwenhoven MR & MRS William G (Alexandra | of ☎ (410)323-4418
Stein) Gi.Ny.Rv.Snc.Mv.Dc.JHop'44.H'51 . . . . | 17 Midvale Rd,
MR William B—Gi.JHop'85.JHop'86 . . . . | Baltimore, MD
| *21210*
| ☎ (410) 360-1612
| Skywater Rd,
| Gibson Island, MD
| *21056*

Kovas MR & MRS Ronald A (Patricia L Bond) | 269 Oak Grove Av,
Nw'65.Stan'64.Nw'66 . . . . | Atherton, CA *94027*
MISS Allyson E . . . . |
JUNIORS MR Peter B . . . . |
JUNIORS MR Charles A . . . . |
JUNIORS MR Joseph S . . . . |

Koven MR & MRS Theodore Gustav (Stephanie | ☎ (908) 832-2562
Van Rensselaer) . . . . | 6 Saw Mill Rd,
MISS Stephanie H—GeoW'89—at | Mountainville,
☎ (212) 572-2889 . . 73 W 11 St, Apt 3S, | Lebanon, NJ *08833*
New York, NY *10011*
MR Theodore G 2d—Stv'87—at
☎ (610) 749-0686 . . 130 Spruce St, PO Box 543,
Riegelsville, PA *18077* . . . .

Kozumbo DR & MRS Walter J (Jamie Miller) P'67.Purd'72.JHop'83
☎ (410) 323-2139 . . 7 W Melrose Av, Baltimore, MD *21210*

Krafft MR & MRS Frederic B (Sesaly Gould) Mit'49. | ☎ (410) 758-1627
MISS Susan—at ☎ (804) 979-2462 | 300 Oak Farm Lane,
27 University Circle, Apt 2, Charlottesville, VA | Centreville, MD
22903 . . . . | *21617*

Kraft MR & MRS F Gordon (Suzanne B Henry) | of ☎ (412)784-0807
Fcg.Pg.Va'64 . . . . | 807 Delafield Rd,
MISS Kendall B—Va'85.Fcg.Pg.—at | Pittsburgh, PA
☎ (412) 363-8881 . . 6810 Juniata Place, | *15215*
Pittsburgh, PA *15208* . . . . | ☎ (561) 266-3700
MISS A Barclay—Va'89—at ☎ (202) 686-9534 | 10 Little Club Rd,
3970 Langley Court NW, Apt B614, Washington, | Gulf Stream, FL
DC *20016* . . . . | *33483*

Kraft MRS John F JR (Mary S Gordon) Pg.Fcg.
☎ (941) 262-6422 . . 102 Moorings Park Dv, Apt 204, Naples, FL *34105*

Kraft MR & MRS John F 3d (Mary J West) Fcg.Rr.Ty'62 . . of
☎ (412) 521-2951 . . 5433 Kipling Rd, Pittsburgh, PA *15217*
☎ (508) 627-5841 . . ''Mattakesett'' Edgartown, MA *02539*

Kraft MR John F 4th—Fcg.Br'91
☎ (415) 968-6786 . . 1200 Dale Av, Apt 32, Mountain View, CA *94040*

Kraft MR Peter A—Fcg.Yn.W&M'92.Va'93
☎ (609) 448-7335 . . The Peddie School, PO Box A, S Main St,
Hightstown, NJ *08520*

Kraft MR & MRS William B 3d (Mentzer—Cathy A Crowl) Me.
☎ (610) 296-9819 . . 750 Old Lancaster Rd, Apt A510, Berwyn,
PA *19312-1339*

Kraftson MR & MRS Donald W (Ann H Madara) W&M'89.Me.Rc.W&M'89
☎ (610) 664-7967 . . PO Box 413, 1319 Hagy's Ford Rd, Penn Valley,
PA *19072-0413*

Kraftson MR & MRS Raymond H (Marguerite O | ☎ (610) 525-6257
Knewstub) VillaN'87.Ph.Me.Ac.Pa'62.W&M'67 | 501 Candace Lane,
MISS Marguerite O . . . . | Villanova, PA *19085*
JUNIORS MISS Audrey E . . . . |
JUNIORS MISS Michele S . . . . |

Krag MR & MRS W Brace JR (Kristen B Peterson) Denis'89.Ac.Denis'88
☎ (203) 255-9782 . . 365 Old Mill Rd, Fairfield, CT *06430*

Kramer MR & MRS Henry T (Janet P Bunyan) CtCol'41.Y'40
☎ (908) 526-5531 . . 51 Village Way, Somerville, NJ *08876*

Kramer DR & MRS John F JR (Beverly J Granger) Br'61.Wis'73
☎ (610) 827-7402 . . Upland Farm, PO Box 529, Chester Springs,
PA *19425-0529*

Kramer JUNIORS MISS Katherine A . . see A L Cushman

Kramer MR Le Roy JR—Cho.Cw.Cc.
☎ (616) 347-7200 . . 184 Beach Rd, Harbor Springs, MI *49740*

Kranz MR & MRS Thomas F (Travis D Barton) | ☎ (310) 471-6151
Cal'72.Bhm.K.Mt.Mto.Stan'60 . . . . | 245 Strada Corta
JUNIORS MR Alexander B . . . . | Rd, Los Angeles,
JUNIORS MR Francis E . . . . | CA *90077*

Kratovil MRS Elizabeth S (Elizabeth J Stetson) | ☎ (609) 451-5453
Cly.Ncd. . . . . | PO Box 211,
MR Emil A 3d . . . . | Bridgeton, NJ *08302*
MR deWolf H . . . . |

Kratovil MR Emil A JR—Unn.San.Eyc.Wms'62
☎ (203) 532-1171 . . 206 W Lyon Farm Dv, Greenwich, CT *06831-4353*

Kratovil MR & MRS Stephen C (Barbara Werner) | ☎ (212) 628-5618
Rc.Eyc.Ny.Cly.Pa'69 ⚓ . . . . | 167 E 82 St,
JUNIORS MR S Carr JR . . . . | New York, NY
JUNIORS MR Werner DeW . . . . | *10028*

Krech MRS Minette G (Minette D Grand)
☎ (203) 972-7431 . . 130 South Av, New Canaan, CT *06840*

Krech DR & MRS Shepard (Nora Potter) Y'41.Cl'44
☎ (410) 822-0128 . . "Whitehouse Farm" PO Box 779, Easton, MD 21601
Krech MR & MRS Shepard III (Sheila ffolliott) V'67.Pa'79.Y'67.Ox'69.H'74 . . . .
MISS Teal C . . . .

of ☎ (401)351-4559 84 Keene St, Providence, RI 02906
☎ (202) 234-5818 2311 Connecticut Av NW, Washington, DC 20008

Kreger MR & MRS Charles S (Lynch—Whitaker—Mary B Brown) Why.Cw.Ncd.Cda.Hn.H'46 . . .
MISS Mary B Lynch—at U of Alaska . . . . . .
MISS Elizabeth W Lynch—Cly.—at Sharon, CT 06069 . . . .

of ☎ (561)588-6430 7601 Pine Tree Lane, West Palm Beach, FL 33406
☎ (401) 348-0035 "Caboose II" 4 Camelback Way, Watch Hill, RI 02891

Kreimer MISS Mary S—Sth'48.Tufts'49 . . . .
MRS Barbara K Stuart (Christenson—Barbara S Kreimer) Cin'45 . . . .

☎ (202) 244-0108 4443 Ellicott St NW, Washington, DC 20016-4070

Kreimer MRS Ralph C (Jill C Martyn) . . . .
MISS Kathryn S . . . .

☎ (561) 746-7577 19538 Trails End Terr, Jupiter, FL 33458

Kreizel JUNIORS MR Justin A . . see G G Herrick
Krementz MR & MRS Richard (Margaret S Guckes) Y'49
☎ (201) 539-4037 . . Red Gate Rd, Morristown, NJ 07960
Kremer MRS J Lee (Joan F Lee) Me.
☎ (610) 527-8886 . . 1100 Beech Rd, Rosemont, PA 19010
Kremer MR & MRS John 4th (Erika Holly Lederman) Mid'86.Cl'91.Mid'86.JHop'91
see Dilatory Domiciles
Kress MRS Rush H (Canning—Virginia H Watkins) Cly.
☎ (212) 288-7200 . . 1020 Fifth Av, New York, NY 10028
Kribben MR Delafield . . see MRS W M Dixon
Kridel MRS James A (Margaret M Mayne) . . . .
MR Geoffrey M—at ☎ (404) 364-9036 519 Old Ivy Rd NE, Atlanta, GA 30342 . . . .

☎ (305) 666-2270 66 N Prospect Dv, Coral Gables, FL 33133

Krimendahl MISS (DR) Elizabeth K (Wolf—Elizabeth K Krimendahl) Duke'82.Nu'92.Mds . . .of
☎ (212) 689-0405 . . 220 Madison Av, New York, NY 10016
☎ (516) 324-4552 . . PO Box 218, 40 West End Rd, East Hampton, NY 11937

Krimendahl MR H Frederick 2d—Ri.Ln.Dyc.Mds. OState'50.H'52 . . . .
MISS Nancy C—Duke'83—at ☎ (213) 656-9729 2148 Stanley Hills Dv, Los Angeles, CA 90046 .

of ☎ (212)288-2607 834 Fifth Av, New York, NY 10021
☎ (516)324-4552 PO Box 218, 40 West End Rd, East Hampton, NY 11937

Krisel MR & MRS William E (Donna S Zilkha) P'76.Hn.H'76
☎ (011-33-1) 46-37-56-27 . . 57 blvd du Commandant Charcot, 92200 Neuilly, France
Kriz MR Christopher J—Myf.Rich'91 . . . .
MR Andrew S—Rich'93 . . . .

☎ (212) 288-0137 425 E 76 St, Apt 11A, New York, NY 10021

Kroeger MISS Alexa G—Ws'74.Cly.Ncd.
☎ (212) 570-1956 . . 201 E 66 St, New York, NY 10021
Kroeger MR & MRS Arthur F (Hammond—Alexa C Daley) Ncd.Br'33.H'36 . . of
☎ (561) 231-9426 . . 891 Rainbow Lane, John's Island Club, Vero Beach, FL 32963
☎ (704) 963-6732 . . Hound Ears Club, Shulls Mill Rd, Blowing Rock, NC 28605
Kroeger MR & MRS Harold A JR (Carole D Ferris) P'62.H'64 . . . .
MR Hal R—at Princeton . . . .
JUNIORS MR George F—at U of Ore . . . .

☎ (314) 991-1967 "The Woodlands" 9625 Ladue Rd, St Louis, MO 63124

Krogstad MRS Henry Pichon (Buffum—Sarah S Landers) Pa'51.Pe.Sdg.Ll.Cspa.Cw.Dll. . . . .
MR Garry B—Ll.Rv.Pa'83 . . . .
☎ (609) 869-4598 . . 256A Chrystal Lake Av, Haddonfield, NJ 08033 . . . .
MR Edwin C Buffum—at ☎ (602) 470-1220 5638 S 41 Way, Phoenix, AZ 85040 . . . .

☎ (215) 643-0991 1021 Stevens Dv, Ft Washington, PA 19034

Krogstad MR & MRS Robert B 2d (Diane M Kemler) Ll.Rv.Dll.Temp'88
☎ (610) 432-9035 . . 4312 Clear Way, Allentown, PA 18103
Krone MRS Robert C (Mary L Ewing) Bv.
230 S Brentwood Blvd, Apt 8A, St Louis, MO 63105
Kroon MR & MRS Johannes A (Erica B Hopkins) Delft'83.Delft'86
☎ (011-31-45) 423762 . . Vrusschemigerweg 157, 6417 PK Heerlen, The Netherlands
Kroos MR & MRS Arthur G JR (Fuller—Barbara Brooks) Lawr'38
☎ (414) 351-0330 . . 1765 W Bradley Rd, Milwaukee, WI 53217
Krout MR & MRS John E (Heppe—H Anne Merriman) Gchr'53.Me.Sar.Ac.Ncd.P'41.H'44 . .
MR Robert E—Ithaca'78.Cl'83—at 84 Dug Rd, New Paltz, NY 12561 . . . .

of ☎ (610)525-9613 1214 Weybridge Lane, Radnor, PA 19087
☎ (242) 366-0153 "Sand Lily" Hope Town, Abaco, Bahamas

Krueger MR & MRS John W (Sarah G Hudson) Vt'76.SUNY'78.Ty'90.Cly.Ncd.Bost'72.Vt'75. SUNY'81 . . . .
JUNIORS MISS Sarah G . . . .
JUNIORS MR Christopher C—at Deerfield . . . .

☎ (802) 658-6526 203 Meadowood Dv, South Burlington, VT 05403

Kruesi DR & MRS Oscar R (Elizabeth N Potter) U'47
☎ (908) 766-0321 . . 69 Old Army Rd, Bernardsville, NJ *07924*

Kruger MRS Erich (Charlotte Gunn)
☎ (707) 539-3619 . . 428 Oak Brook Lane, Santa Rosa, CA *95409*

Krulak LT GEN & MRS Victor H (Amy Chandler) | *see*
USMC.Bhm.USN'34 . . . . | *Dilatory Domiciles*
CDR REV Victor H JR—USN'59. . . . . |

Krulak REV & MRS William M (Mae M Spence) | The Rectory,
Gchr'63.GMason'75.Y'92.USN'62.Roch'72.Y'91 | 403 Water Lane,
MR William H JR—Dth'89—at | Tappahannock, VA
4303 Plaza Gate Lane, Apt 201, Jacksonville, FL | *22560-0336*
32207 . . . . |

Krumbhaar MR Peter D—Pc.Sa.Pa'49.VillaN'69
☎ (610) 828-7966 . . 515 Plymouth Rd, Apt E6, Plymouth Meeting,
PA *19462*

Krummel MRS Ann H (Ann B Hiemenz) . . . . | ☎ (303) 986-9953
MISS Julia A—at 1510 Jenifer St, Madison, WI | 2174 S Field Way,
53703 . . . . | Lakewood, CO
MR Charles J—at 16343 E Rice Place, Aurora, | *80227*
CO *80015* . . . . |

Krummel MR William J JR
☎ (303) 986-4938 . . 8557 W Hampden Av, Apt 4-108, Lakewood,
CO *80227-4795*

Kubal MR & MRS Lawrence A (Patricia C Tobin)
Stan'77.Bur.Duke'74.Stan'82
☎ (415) 327-2000 . . 97 Elena Av, Atherton, CA *94027*

Kuczynski MISS Alexandra L—Bnd'90
☎ (212) 684-4592 . . 235 E 22 St, Apt 7N, New York, NY *10010*

Kuczynski MR Pedro P de G—Pg.Rcn.Pn.Ox'59. | ☎ (305) 285-7995
P'61 . . . . | 3 Grove Isle Dv,
MR John-Michael—at U of Cal Los Angeles . . . | Apt 301, Miami, FL
 | *33133*

Kuehn MR Alfred L—Cy.Nyc.Bost'62
☎ (617) 630-9039 . . 17 Hemlock Rd, Newton, MA *02174*

Kuehn MR & MRS George W (Katherine Rust) Un.Cy.Cho.Chi.Hn.H'32
☎ (617) 329-4852 . . 10 Longwood Dv, Apt 146, Westwood, MA *02090*

Kuehn MRS Martha (Martha A Ronan) Ty'69.Cy. . . | ☎ (617) 235-1346
JUNIORS MISS Winifred O . . . . | 403 Grove St,
 | Needham, MA
 | *02192*

Kuensell MR & MRS Scott L (Elizabeth C Gowen)
Wash'82.Me.Fst.Ac.Pn.P'76
☎ (610) 649-4451 . . 120 Orchard Lane, Haverford, PA *19041*

Kuhl MR & MRS Nevin E (Elizabeth DeLong)
V'47.Cvc.Mt.Ken'46 . . of
☎ (202) 462-4462 . . 2029 Connecticut Av NW, Washington, DC *20008*
☎ (410) 745-9775 . . Thornton Rd, Royal Oak, MD *21662*

Kuhn MR & MRS Dixon S (Cecilia Browne) Cr'70
☎ (415) 331-7160 . . 1135 Meadowsweet Dv, Corte Madera, CA *94925*

Kuhn MR Jay C—Y'57
3450 Pierce St, San Francisco, CA *94123*

Kuhn MR & MRS John L (Anita C Jones) | ☎ (860) 824-7363
Ncd.Stan'35 . . . . | Sugar Hill Rd,
MISS Jacqueline H—Cl'84 . . . . | Falls Village, CT
 | *06031*

Kuhn MRS Lyman (Edith F Lyman)
☎ (415) 851-7227 . . 455 Old La Honda Rd, Woodside, CA *94062*

Kuhn MISS Marian—Ty'77
☎ (202) 667-0168 . . 1916—17 St NW, Apt 406, Washington, DC *20009*

Kuhn MR & MRS R Parker JR (Farr—Anne Witherspoon) Cr'43
☎ (914) 277-8412 . . 515D Heritage Hills, Somers, NY *10589*

Kuhn MRS Spencer F (Ada M Dixon)
☎ (513) 321-9206 . . 1213 Hidden Wood Place, Cincinnati, OH *45208*

Kuhns MR Benjamin F JR—Mor.Rol'35
☎ (513) 435-0175 . . 5311 Himes Lane, Dayton, OH *45429*

Kuhns MISS Jennifer D . . see W H Corson 2d

Kuhns MR & MRS Matthew W (Margaret C Crimmins) Cal'82.SCal'87
☎ (213) 939-5076 . . 1315 S Tremaine Av, Los Angeles, CA *90019*

Kuhns MISS Pamela G . . see W H Corson 2d

Kulikowski MRS Edward (F Lorillard Ronalds) . . . . | ☎ (813) 896-4455
MISS M Josephine L . . . . | MLS Towers Apt
 | 709, 540 Second Av
 | S, St Petersburg, FL
 | *33701*

Kulikowski MR & MRS Léon T (Pollack—Frances Eberlin)
Rc.Sc.Yn.Y'42 . . of
☎ (619) 454-6722 . . 7270 Carrizo Dv, La Jolla, CA *92037*
☎ (312) 337-3359 . . 175 E Delaware Place, Apt 5917, Chicago,
IL *60611*

Kundtz MR & MRS John M (Susan L Manning) Denis'83.Kt.Denis'82
☎ (216) 247-7149 . . 148 High St, Chagrin Falls, OH *44022*

Kunhardt MRS Edith W (Edith L Woodruff) . . . . . . | ☎ (212) 472-0104
MR Timothy W—at ☎ (212) 385-1366 | 500 E 85 St,
324 Pearl St, New York, NY *10038* . . . . | New York, NY
 | *10028*

Kuper MRS Charles A (Kathleen Jersig) A.
☎ (210) 824-8475 . . 122 Chester St, Apt 6, San Antonio, TX *78209*

Kuper MR Charles A JR
☎ (210) 822-8602 . . 6606 N New Braunfels Av, San Antonio,
TX *78209*

Kuper MR & MRS George Henry (Danielle E Pienaar)
Pqt.Ny.Ll.JHop'63.Lond'64.H'70 ⚓
☎ (313) 663-0086 . . 431 Highland Rd, Ann Arbor, MI *48104*

Kurtz MR & MRS Charles H (Jeannette A Pollard) Vt'76.DU'73
☎ (303) 761-5809 . . 31 Sunset Dv, Englewood, CO *80110*

Kurtz MR Henry K 3d . . . . | ☎ (215) CH7-5627
MISS Elizabeth A—at ☎ (215) 233-3176 | 214 E Willow Grove
923 Pleasant Av, Wyndmoor, PA *19038* . . . . . . | Av, Philadelphia,
 | PA *19118*

Kurtz MR & MRS Paul B 3d (Katherine B Neilson)
RMWmn'76.Ncd.W&L'75
☎ (314) 727-6377 . . 6178 Kingsbury Av, St Louis, MO *63112*

Kurtz MR Robert Fulton—Nf.H'44
☎ (207) 276-4073 . . Box 127, Northeast Harbor, ME *04662*

Kusack JUNIORS MR Alastair G . . see MISS A Truitt

Kusack JUNIORS MR Samuel D . . see MISS A Truitt

Kuser MR & MRS John E (Eleanor C Will) P'46 . . . . | ☎ (609) 924-0380
MISS Caryl H—at 55 Palmer Square, Princeton, | 175 Lambert Dv,
NJ *08540* . . . . | Princeton, NJ *08540*
MISS Eleanor C—at ☎ (213) 228-1988 |
Box 86572, Los Angeles, CA *90086-0572* . . . . |

Kuser MISS Suzanne D—Cvc.Sl.
☎ (202) FE8-1849 . . 2225—46 St NW, Washington, DC *20007*

Kuser MRS Walter G (Teresa de Quesada) . . . .
MR W Timothy—Leh'64 . . . . | ☎ (609) 298-0050
"Fernbrook"
Georgetown Rd,
Rte 545,
PO Box 648,
Bordentown, NJ
08505

Kusserow MR & MRS Paul B (Serena Reed) Wes'83.Cly.Wes'85.Ox'88
☎ (203) 869-2121 . . 591 Riversville Rd, Greenwich, CT *06831*

Kust MRS Leonard E (Henrietta B Logan) . . . . | ☎ (212) 876-9108
NCar'41.Chr.Cs.Dar.Ncd . . . . | 1115 Fifth Av,
MISS Andrea L—Skd'76.Ncd.Dar.—at | New York, NY
☎ (212) 988-8966 . . 435 E 79 St, New York, NY | *10128*
10021 . . . . |

Kyle DR & MRS G Clayton (Barbara J McDowell) Pc.Sg.Ac.P'45.Pa'47
☎ (215) CH7-1614 . . 8009 Navajo St, Philadelphia, PA *19118*
Kyle MR Robert J JR—Dth'89 . . see J R Sherwood 3d

Kysely MR & MRS Arvy F (Elizabeth G Coxe) Col'63.NCol'75
☎ (719) 576-1082 . . 3011 E Springlake Circle, Colorado Springs,
CO *80906*

Kyser MR & MRS Emery K (Judith C Clark) | of ☎ (334)263-2686
Aub'64.Dar.Aub'61 . . . . | 2224 Fernway Dv,
MISS Kristin C . . . . | Montgomery, AL
MR E Kyle JR—at 3035 Thirteenth Av S, | *36111*
Birmingham, AL *35205* . . . . | ☎ (334) 584-7140
JUNIORS MISS Caroline C . . . . | Salem Plantation,
| Rte 3, Troy, AL
| *36081*

Kyte MRS Lawrence H (Mary E Williams) Man'vl'28.Qc.Cw.
☎ (513) 231-7511 . . 7803 Ayers Rd, Cincinnati, OH *45255-4610*
Kyte MR & MRS Lawrence H JR (Marjorie A Meyer) | ☎ (513) 561-5180
Qc.NotreD'60.Va'63 . . . . | 5805 Mohican Lane,
MISS Megan E . . . . | Cincinnati, OH
MR Ryan L—at 535 Tusculum Av, Cincinnati, | *45243*
OH *45226* . . . . |

L

La Bar MR Adam G . . see W B Knapp
La Bar MR James W . . see W B Knapp
LaBarre MR & MRS Dennis W (Camille H Dickinson)
Nw'65.Kt.Rr.Eyc.Cv.Nw'65.Va'68
☎ (212) 744-3953 . . 188 E 70 St, New York, NY *10021-5168*
La Besse CTE & CTSSE de (Kohle—Jane B | of ☎ (011-33)
Boardman) Mls'54 . . . . | 45-91-10-34
MISS Patricia J Kohle . . . . | 34 Rond Point du
MR Christopher F Kohle . . . . | Bois, Cidex 663,
| 16730 Linars par
| Fleac, France
| ☎ (510) 947-1264
| 870 Terra California
| Dv, Apt 5,
| Walnut Creek, CA
| *94595*

La Bonte MR & MRS Walter O JR (Rosanna E Agnew) Mid'80.Mid'81
☎ (508) 257-4572 . . "Canine Mutiny" 32 Morey Lane, Box 701,
Siasconset, MA *02564*
Labouisse MRS Henry R (Eve D Curie) Ri.Mt.Cs.Sl . . .of
☎ (212) 751-4156 . . 1 Sutton Place S, New York, NY *10022*
☎ (516) 537-7719 . . Beach Lane, Box 616, Wainscott, NY *11975*
Labouisse MR & MRS John P (Westfeldt—Hayne—Katherine A Phillips)
Ncmb'42.Tul'30 . . of
☎ (504) 835-7988 . . 12 Pelham Dv, Metairie, LA *70005*
☎ (601) 795-2223 . . Straw Hill Farm, 2352 Ford's Creek Rd,
Poplarville, MS *39470*
Labouisse MR & MRS John Peter 3d (Meredith T | ☎ (504) 897-1605
Janvier) GaTech'64 . . . . | 1203 Marengo St,
JUNIORS MISS Mary-Frances J . . . . | New Orleans, LA
JUNIORS MR Charles J . . . . | *70115*

La Branche MISS Elizabeth—SL'40
☎ (202) 337-5535 . . 3335 Dent Place NW, Washington, DC *20007*
Labrot MR & MRS Andrew G (Marguerite E | of ☎ (912)233-5481
Wilford) Ithaca'71.Srr.Ayc.Y'53 . . . . | 23 W Charlton St,
JUNIORS MISS Sarah H . . . . | Savannah, GA
JUNIORS MR William H . . . . | *31401*
| ☎ (803) 757-2618
| 844 May River Rd,
| Bluffton, SC *29910*

Labrot MRS Elizabeth B (Elizabeth J Buell) CtCol'55
☎ (303) 839-1156 . . 614 Emerson St, Denver, CO *80218*
LaCasse MR & MRS William O (Lucy O Lee) Bow'80.Bow'78
☎ (207) 883-3637 . . 67 Burnham Rd, Scarborough, ME *04074*
La Cava MR & MRS Gregory (Andrea C B B | ☎ (508) 428-4498
Humphreys) Bow'50 . . . . | PO Box 1850,
MISS Victoria H . . . . | Cotuit, MA *02635*
MR Gregory R . . . . |

Lacey MR Brent P . . see M A Gordon
Lacey DR & MRS Stephen H (Kathleen O'N Henney) | ☎ (216) 321-2287
Ws'64.May.Y'64 . . . . | 2277 Chatfield Dv,
MISS Margaret C—at 154 W 70 St, Apt 3A, | Cleveland Heights,
New York, NY *10023* . . . . | OH *44106-3655*
MISS Elizabeth H . . . . |

Lackey MRS Howard J JR (Girvin—Meyer—Alexandra Field) Bur.
☎ (415) 851-0889 . . 515 Manzanita Way, Woodside, CA *94062*
Ladd MR & MRS Carleton R (Adelaide L Lutz) | ☎ (508) 785-1480
Cal'64.D.Cda.Pars'65 . . . . | 48 Miller Hill Rd,
MISS Alexandra C—at Little Compton, RI *02837* | Dover, MA *02030*
Ladd MR & MRS Charles Haven (Phyllis A Howe) D.H.'39
☎ (617) 329-8086 . . 10 Longwood Dv, Apt 538, Westwood, MA *02090*
Ladd MR William—Hb.H'34 . . . . | ☎ (603) 239-4468
MR William E 2d . . . . | "Spring Hill Farm"
| 421 Manning Hill,
| Winchester, NH
| *03470*

La Farge DR & MRS C Grant (Heartt—Patricia Arscott)
Rdc'53.Tvb.Hn.H'51
☎ (505) 983-5104 . . PO Box 4760, Santa Fe, NM *87502-4760*

La Farge MRS Edward H (Anne S Woolsey) V'32 .
MISS Elizabeth—at 219 E Broad St, Quakertown,
PA *18951* . . . .
☎ (860) 421-3624
''Woodcock''
214 Green Hill Rd,
Killingworth, CT
06419

La Farge MR & MRS Edward T (E F Maida Williams)
GeoW'73.GeoW'78.Ny.DU'72.GeoW'78
☎ (202) 328-1830 . . 2916—29 St NW, Washington, DC *20008*

La Farge MRS Henry A (M Lathrop Allen)
Man'vl'41
MISS Beatrice—Man'vl'70.Frankf'84.
Frankf'90—at Frankfurt, Germany . . . .
☎ (203) 966-9758
''Rocky Run''
721 N Wilton Rd,
New Canaan, CT
06840

La Farge MR John Pendaries—Bost'74
☎ (505) 983-8377 . . 647 Old Santa Fe Trail, Santa Fe, NM *87501*

La Farge MISS Louisa R H (late William E R) . . . . Married at
Saunderstown, RI
Rosston MR Steven J (John W) . . . . Jun 29'96

Lafferty MR & MRS F Wayne JR (Hilary C Eddy)
Duke'87.Cc.Duke'82.Duke'86
☎ (203) 268-7864 . . 62 Wells Rd, Monroe, CT *06468*

Laffey MRS E Heard (Elizabeth S Heard) PineM'78
☎ (908) 439-3930 . . Box 474, Oldwick, NJ *08858*

Laffey MRS Edwin W (Shirley Ann Collette) Shcc. .
MR Edwin W JR . . . .
of ☎ (908)234-0377
PO Box 185,
Far Hills, NJ *07931*
☎ (242) 333-2205
''Briland House''
Harbour Island,
Bahamas

Laffon MRS Penrose S (Penrose Stovell) . . . .
MISS Alexandra P—Geo'90 . . . .
☎ (011-44-171)
589-3260
21 Onslow Gardens,
London SW7 3AL,
England

Laffoon JUNIORS MISS Catharine A . . see MRS C H King
Laffoon JUNIORS MR Nathan P JR . . see MRS C H King
Laffoon MR & MRS Polk (Stanley—Susan Morris
Steman) Y'42 . . . .
MR Ethan T Stanley—Nw'93—at
☎ (606) 572-0963 . . 100 Gettysburg Square
Rd, Ft Thomas, KY *41075* . . . .
☎ (513) 871-5566
18 Weebetook Lane,
Cincinnati, OH
45208

Laflin MRS Lloyd Alan (Brady—Patricia A Sweeney)
Wis'49.Wis'51.On.Cho.
☎ (360) 834-9373 . . 3624 NW MacIntosh Rd, PO Box 1035, Camas,
WA *98607*

Laflin MRS Louis E 3d (Carolyn Robbins)
☎ (602) 952-1667 . . 4450 E Camelback Rd, Villa 8, Phoenix, AZ *85018*

La Forte MR & MRS William N (Susan S Rupp)
Wells'70.Colg'70.Syr'74 . . . .
MISS Jennifer L . . . .
☎ (716) 586-5473
23 Country Club Dv
N, Rochester, NY
14618 . . MR absent

Lagercrantz MR Eric G—Stock'30
☎ (914) 352-1957 . . 241 Hungry Hollow Rd, Apt 2, Chestnut Ridge,
NY *10977*

La Haye Jousselin MR & MRS Edmond de (Anne G
Manice) . . . .
MISS Alix de . . . .
MISS Amélie de . . . .
JUNIORS MR George de . . . .
of ☎ (011-33-1)
47-20-98-46
17 rue de l'Amiral
d'Estaing, 75116
Paris, France
☎ (011-33)
32-35-87-01
Château de St Aubin
d'Ecrosville,
27110 St Aubin
d'Ecrosville, France
France

Lahourcade MR & MRS J Lance (Gretchen
Perryman) Tex'75.A.Ty'75. . . . .
MISS Ashley LaR . . . .
JUNIORS MISS Erin L . . . .
☎ (210) 824-3097
123 Rockhill Dv,
San Antonio, TX
78209

Laidlaw MRS David K (Ruth Welch) StA.
☎ (914) 234-7228 . . 350 Cantitoe St, Bedford Hills, NY *10507*

Laidlaw MR & MRS Douglas B (Louise Storck)
USMMA'70 . . . .
MISS Jennifer S . . . .
MR Douglas A . . . .
☎ (908) 753-1541
94 Meadowbrook
Rd, North Plainfield,
NJ *07062*

Laidlaw MR & MRS Robert S (Amy E Connard)
MtH'61.Y.'58. . . . .
MISS Amy H—Cal'92 . . . .
MISS Heather S . . . .
MISS Robin W . . . .
MR David K—Reed'89.Rut'94 . . . .
☎ (914) 764-4786
14 Doe View Lane,
Pound Ridge, NY
10576

Laidlaw MR William C . . see W S Emmet

Laidler DR & MRS Keith J (Mary C Auchincloss)
Ox'38.P'40. . . . .
MR James R—at 15 Birch Av, Ottawa, Ontario,
Canada . . . .
☎ (613) 749-3316
734 Eastbourne Av,
Ottawa, Ontario
K1K 0H7, Canada

Laimbeer MR & MRS Richard B (Mary A Kotecki)
Cata'67. . . . .
MR Jonathan W . . . .
JUNIORS MISS Kate A . . . .
☎ (810) 932-3362
30465 Rushmore
Circle, Franklin, MI
48025

Laing MR & MRS C Christopher (Diana Whitehill) Sm.H'53.H'54
☎ (011-44-1353) 661091 . . 4 Barton Square, Ely, Cambridgeshire
CB7 4DF, England

Laird MR & MRS Edwin C 3d (Edith McK Rockefeller) Bost'66
☎ (206) 522-2883 . . 5646 NE Keswick Dv, Seattle, WA *98105*

Laird MR & MRS Walter J JR (Antonia V Bissell) Wil.Cw.Ncd.P'48.Mit'50
☎ (610) 388-6341 . . ''Treetops'' 1202 Stockford Rd, Chadds Ford,
PA *19317*

Laird MR & MRS Walter J 3d (Gail S Dixon) Vt'81.Bgt.Wil.Vt'81
☎ (914) 666-5085 . . 45 Hillside Av, Mt Kisco, NY *10549*

Lake MISS Amanda R—Ham'91.StJ'95 . . see B B Woodger

Lake MISS D Elise—MidTennSt'87
☎ (334) 832-9878 . . 710 Cloverdale Rd, Apt C, Montgomery, AL *36106*

Lake MRS Henri Z (Baker—Audrey Jaeckel) So.Cly.
☎ (516) 283-2271 . . 107 Wickapogue Rd, PO Box 5010, Southampton,
NY *11969-0726*

Lake MRS J Douglas (Elizabeth N Talbott) Dar. . . . .
MR Anthony C T . . . .
JUNIORS MR James D T—at Tallulah Falls Sch . .
☎ (404) 231-2055
2800 Atwood Rd
NE, Atlanta, GA
30305

Lake MR & MRS Rutherford C JR (Mary A Mead) ☎ (757) 930-2925
ChrNew'77.Va'50.Va'57 . . . . 1 Fishers Landing,
MR Rutherford C 3d—ChrNew'83—at Newport News, VA
291 E Queens Dv, Williamsburg, VA *23185* . . . *23606*
CAPT Stephen M—USA.E&H'82—at
1200 St Andrews Rd, Apt 610, Columbia, SC
29210 . . . .
Lake MR Whitney B . . see B B Woodger
Lakeman MR & MRS David J (Susanne E Collier)
W'mont'80.Birm'ham'86.Lond'76
2546 E Lynwood St, Simi Valley, CA *93065*
Lakin MR & MRS Charles B (Mary Wight) H'30
☎ (803) 689-2070 . . 77 Bird Song Way, Apt 111, Hilton Head Island,
SC *29926*
Lakusta MR Alexis M
☎ (415) 851-5814 . . 633 Old La Honda Rd, Woodside, CA *94062*
Lakusta MR Boris H JR
☎ (707) 965-3022 . . Meadowcreek Farm, Box 44, Pope Valley,
CA *94567*
Lalire MR & MRS Rex P (Greta S Nettleton) Duke'79.Tex'86.Pratt'76 . . of
☎ (914) 359-0513 . . Heyhoe Woods Rd, Box 75, Palisades, NY *10964*
☎ (914) 856-7702 . . Hartwood Club, Box 210, RD 1, Forestburgh,
NY *12777*
Lally MRS John (Franca M Pironti) Cs.
☎ (212) 628-8690 . . 132 E 65 St, New York, NY *10021*
Lalor MR & MRS R Peter (Deborah B Miller)
V'73.Va'81.Ny.Duke'71.Duke'73.Va'82 . . of
☎ (757) 787-2991 . . 33457 Bradford's Neck Rd, Quinby, VA *23423*
☎ (910) 295-6893 . . ''Little Cabin'' Azalea Rd, Pinehurst, NC *28374*
La Marche MASTER Matthew Proctor (Stephen W) . . . . Born at
Melrose, MA Nov 9'93
La Marche MISS Renée Fortiere (Stephen W) . . . . Born at
Melrose, MA Nov 13'95
La Marche MR & MRS Stephen W (Amy L Walther) CtCol'86
☎ (617) 334-5022 . . 9 Charing Cross, Lynnfield, MA *01940*
Lamb MR & MRS Charles Anthony (Beverly J Barrie)
Cal'49.Rv.Cw.Yn.Y'45w
☎ (203) 655-2896 . . 8 Woods End Rd, Darien, CT *06820*
Lamb MR & MRS David R (Daria K Pace) Ch'86.Ck.Pars'79.Pa'84
☎ (516) 922-6478 . . PO Box 391, 52 Frost Mill Rd, Mill Neck,
NY *11765-0391*
Lamb MRS F Madeline H (F Madeline Hartsell) ☎ (610) 647-5530
Duke'62.VillaN'78 . . . . 333 Paoli Woods,
MISS Amanda H—Duke'88—*see* Paoli, PA *19301*
Dilatory Domiciles
MR Joshua H—at 1111 Crab Orchard Dv, Apt 1B,
Raleigh, NC *27606* . . . .
Lamb MR & MRS Faron C (Lucy A Muckerman) Rich'88
☎ (703) 317-1817 . . 3707 Fort Hill Dv, Alexandria, VA *22310*
Lamb MR & MRS Gordon E (Anita B Dryselius) ☎ (516) 692-9596
NewSchSR'84.P'52 . . . . 175 Turkey Lane,
MISS Faith B—Mid'88 at ☎ (303) 447-0974 Cold Spring Harbor,
401 Alpine Av, Boulder, CO *80304* . . . . NY *11724*
MR Bradford S—Leh'82—at ☎ (011-852)
812-0906 . . Hong Kong Parkview, Tower 14,
Apt 0877, 88 Tai Tam Resevoir Rd, Hong Kong

Lamb MR & MRS James R (Brigid Shanley) ☎ (201) 543-6221
BostColl'69.S'Hall'76.Shcc.Eh.Mds.Pa'64. RD 2, Pleasant
Mich'67 . . . . Valley Rd,
JUNIORS MISS Abigail . . . . Mendham, NJ *07945*
JUNIORS MR Sean T . . . .
JUNIORS MR Seamus S . . . .
Lamb MR & MRS Kip K (Isabel H Morian) Lamar'82.Cda.Bay'80
☎ (409) 892-6356 . . 635 Belvedere Dv, Beaumont, TX *77706*
Lamb MR & MRS Lawton S (H Heathcote McIlvaine) ☎ (914) 232-3941
Bgt.Nyc.Cly.P'55 . . . . 63 Katonah's Wood
MR Dana L—Mid'88 . . . . Rd, Katonah, NY
10536
Lamb MASTER Nicholas Morian (Kip K) . . . . Born at
Beaumont, TX Nov 21'95
Lamb MASTER William Miner (David R) . . . . Born Jly 13'95
Lambart MR Eric C—Cl'29
☎ (904) 384-3738 . . 5075 Charlemagne Rd, Jacksonville, FL *32210*
Lambart MR & MRS Harry S (Alison H Williams) Leh'69
☎ (970) 879-2838 . . PO Box 773960, Steamboat Springs, CO *80477*
Lambert MRS Adrian (Mary Alice Bacon)
☎ (212) 744-6992 . . 150 E 77 St, New York, NY *10021*
Lambert MR & MRS Adrian JR (Sandia E Dain) . . of
☎ (617) 329-4497 . . 751 East St, Dedham, MA *02026*
☎ (860) 739-0753 . . 20 Great Wight Way, Old Black Point, Niantic,
CT *06357*
Lambert MR Arthur G . . . . Died Jun 6'91
Lambert MRS Arthur G (Mary L Sipple) Cvc.Mt. . . 5215 Cedar Lane,
MR Arthur G JR—at 33 W 9 St, New York, NY Bethesda, MD
10011 . . . . *20814*
Lambert MRS Barron P (Ingram—Mary F Rudigier) Rose'38.Mv.Elk.
830 W 40 St, Apt 815, Baltimore, MD *21211*
Lambert DR & MRS Brent W (Katharine P Merrill) ☎ (617) 749-0657
Sth'62.Cy.H'61 . . . . 17 Martin's Cove
MISS Rebecca—H'92 . . . . Rd, Hingham, MA
MR Luke—H'90 . . . . *02043*
Lambert MR & MRS J Laird (M Susan Mahoney) Fontb'77.Wash'73
☎ (815) 633-3231 . . 2505 Bradley Rd, Rockford, IL *61107*
Lambert MR John T (Marjorie N Richmond) . . . . . ☎ (860) 739-8941
MISS Frances N . . . . 208 Old Black Point
MR John T JR . . . . Rd, Niantic, CT
06357
Lambert MR & MRS Paul C (Mary Lee) ☎ (212) 369-1279
Bnd'57.Un.Stc.Rm.Ri.Y'50.H'53 . . . . 1088 Park Av,
MR John C—at ☎ (212) 533-7297 . . 324 E 19 St, New York, NY
Apt 52, New York, NY *10003* *10128*
Lambert MR & MRS Samuel W III (Louisa B ☎ (609) 896-0029
Garnsey) Col'61.Y'60.H'63 . . . . 1 Carter Rd,
MISS Sarah H—at ☎ (415) 381-4940 Princeton, NJ *08540*
148 California Av, Mill Valley, CA *94941* . . . . .
Lambert MRS Scott (Cleo Clawson) Sfg.Fr . . .of
☎ (415) 771-5011 . . 1400 Geary Blvd, Apt 4F, San Francisco,
CA *94109*
☎ (707) 226-1186 . . 140 Bonnie Brook Dv, Napa, CA *94558*
Lambert MR & MRS Scott C JR (Laura A Martin)
L&C'78.GoldG'82.Stan'63.Cal'67.Cal'70
☎ (415) 921-0555 . . 2578 Pine St, San Francisco, CA *94115*

Lamberton MR & MRS Benjamin Paulding 3d (Mary P Riches) AmU'66.U'62.Va'65 . . . . ☎ (202) 362-3997 | 4418 Lowell St NW, Washington, DC 20016
MISS Eleanor M B . . . .
JUNIORS MR Derek H R . . . .

Lamberton MRS Harry C (Anne H Michie)
☎ (804) 984-4961 . . Martha Jefferson House, 1600 Gordon Av, Charlottesville, VA 22903

Lamberton MR & MRS Harry C JR (Margaret M Schaefer) Ct . . .of
☎ (202) 483-6161 . . 2230 Massachusetts Av NW, Washington, DC 20008
☎ (717) 794-2493 . . ''Margaret's Place'' Charmian Lane, Blue Ridge Summit, PA 17214

Lamberton MR & MRS Harry C 3d (A Meredith Davis) Mich'90.NH'90
☎ (404) 888-9564 . . 890 Virginia Circle NE, Atlanta, GA 30306

Lamberton MASTER Harry Clabaugh 4th (Harry C 3d) . . . . Born at Atlanta, GA Feb 13'96

Lamberton MR & MRS Ian K (M Lewis Barroll) Ncd.Stan'38.H'40 . . . . ☎ (910) 762-0244 | 2516 Canterbury Rd, Wilmington, NC 28403
MR Rolland H—at ☎ (703) 532-0693 4601 N 41 St, Arlington, VA 22207 . . . .

Lamberton MR & MRS Richard D (Barbara J Douglas) Cal'54.Aht'53.Stan'58
☎ (503) 636-5137 . . 16625 Pacific H'way, Lake Oswego, OR 97034

Lamblé MR & MRS William E (Richards—Florence Garth) Md.Cy.Elk.Gv.Mv.JHop'39
☎ (410) 377-2828 . . 15 Devon Hill Rd, Baltimore, MD 21210

Lambros MRS C Ryan (Cynthia F Ryan) . . . . 17 E 89 St, New York, NY 10128
MISS Olivia W . . . .
MR John F . . . .

Lamdin MRS C Ridgely (Elizabeth S Moore) An.Ncd. . . . . 385 Buckskin Way, Monument, CO 80132
MISS Patricia M—Ncd. . . . .

Lame MR & MRS Anthony C (Judith A Taulane) Sth'68.Me.Wes'67.Cl'68 . . . . ☎ (610) 896-6037 | 420 Wister Rd, Wynnewood, PA 19096
MISS Elizabeth P . . . .
MISS Eleanor T . . . .
JUNIORS MISS Jennifer C . . . .

Lame DR Edwin L—Me.Mit'26.Pa'33
☎ (610) 645-8697 . . Waverly Heights Villa 48, 1400 Waverly Rd, Gladwyne, PA 19035

Lammers MRS Suzanne K (E Suzanne Kaiser) Buck'55.Me.Rd. . . . . ☎ (610) 525-3538 | ''Moro Manor'' 1618 Hepburn Dv, Villanova, PA 19085
MISS Suzanne K—Temp'81.Nw'92.Me.—at 214 Park Av, Apt 3L, Hoboken, NJ 07030 . . . . .
MISS Alexandra V—Franklin'88.Mich'90.Rd.Me.

Lammert MR & MRS Martin 5th (Karen A Snodgrass) Ark'77.Cy.CtCol'77
☎ (314) 997-4276 . . 209 Graybridge Rd, St Louis, MO 63124

Lammert MR & MRS Warren B JR (Susan Robinson) Y'56.H'60
☎ (314) 961-8768 . . 8 Overbrook Dv, St Louis, MO 63124

Lammot MISS Elizabeth B
Clara Burke Home, 251 Stenton Av, Plymouth Meeting, PA 19462

Lamont MRS Austin (Lieber—Roll—A Bodine Moon) Csp.
☎ (207) 781-2491 . . 64 Foreside Common, Falmouth, ME 04105

Lamont MR Donald B—Rcn.Sfg.Ln.Pcu.Ri.Yn. Y'42.H'47 . . . . ☎ (561) 546-4445 | 145 S Beach Rd, Hobe Sound, FL 33455
MISS Pamela J—at Los Angeles, CA . . . .
MISS Susan R—at Wilton, CT . . . .

Lamont MR & MRS Edward M (Camille H Buzby) H'48
☎ (516) 692-8736 . . PO Box 1234, Moores Hill Rd, Syosset, NY 11791

Lamont MR & MRS Lansing (Ada Jung) Nw'53.C.Cly.H.'52.Cl'58
☎ (212) 249-6266 . . 133 E 80 St, New York, NY 10021

Lamont MR & MRS Nicholas S (Gillespie—Jean G Gear) Mid'66.Hn.H'60.P'66 . . . . ☎ (203) 865-8505 | 145 Cliff St, New Haven, CT 06511
MR Ian A—HWSth'90—at 962 Lexington Av, New York, NY 10021 . . . .
MR Colin P
MR David H Gillespie—at Hobart-Wm Smith
MR Timothy A Gillespie—at Middlesex . . . .

L'Amoreaux MRS Paul C (Katharine B Littlefield) . . . . Died at Winnetka, IL Mch 26'96

L'Amoreaux MR Paul C—Wab'37
☎ (847) 446-2024 . . 603 Elm St, Winnetka, IL 60093-2620

LaMothe MR & MRS John D JR (Cynthia K Lewis) Sth'62.W.Ty'60.Cl'63 . . . . ☎ (508) 369-9676 | 51 Autumn Lane, Lincoln, MA 01773
MISS K Barrett—Ty'91 . . . .
MR John D 3d—Cl'89—at 5057 Broadway, Apt 43, New York, NY 10034 . . . .

LaMothe MISS Kimerer L . . see G K Gee

La Motte MR & MRS Ferdinand 3d (June Mitchell) DelB.
☎ (561) 276-1504 . . St Andrews Club 407, 4475 N Ocean Blvd, Delray Beach, FL 33483

La Motte MR Ferdinand 4th—Me.Cry.P'58
☎ (610) 695-0871 . . PO Box 101, Wayne, PA 19087

La Motte MR & MRS Louis H 3d (Anne E Shryock)
☎ (803) 681-5502 . . 14 Millwright Dv, Hilton Head Island, SC 29926-1234

La Motte MR & MRS Nicholas H (Susan P Wright) Skd'68.Ste.Cry.Rc.Me.Gm.Ac.Pa'68 . . . . ☎ (610) 896-6638 | ''Camaraderie'' 401 Mulberry Lane, Haverford, PA 19041
MISS Whitney F—Ty'95—at ☎ (212) 861-2843 200 E 72 St, Apt 18G, New York, NY 10021 . .
JUNIORS MR Gardner H—Princeton . . . .

La Motte MR & MRS W Mitchell (Anne E Ewing) Cry.Cho.Ih.P'61 . . . . ☎ (847) 446-5615 | 109 Old Green Bay Rd, Winnetka, IL 60093
MISS Anne H . . . .
MISS Nicole . . . .

Lamour MR Marcel F—R.Pa'65 . . . . ☎ (610) 687-5126 | 660 Shoemaker Lane, Gulph Mills, PA 19406
MR Theodore A . . . .
MR Joshua M . . . .

L'Amoureaux MR Paul C JR
☎ (203) 245-7782 . . 875 Boston Post Rd, PO Box 301, Madison, CT 06443

Lampen LT CDR (RET) & MRS Ambrose M D (Elizabeth Grubb) RN.Tcy.Ncd. . . . . ☎ (415) 346-4673 | 2930 Jackson St, San Francisco, CA 94115-1007
MR Michael D—at 36 Union St, San Francisco, CA 94133 . . . .

Lampen MR Stephen H (Ambrose M D) . . . Married at San Francisco, CA Belleci MISS Debra . . . . Nov 18'95

Lamport MRS Richard M (Soper—Marjorie J Swenson)
☎ (805) 484-0303 . . 30106 Village 30, Camarillo, CA 93012

Lampshire MR & MRS Nicholas P (d'Aquin—Pauline B Williams) Tulsa'79.Br'71
☎ (803) 432-0021 . . 202 Greene St, Camden, SC 29020

Lampson MRS Edward T (Mary C Wright)
☎ (202) 338-6645 . . 1527—30 St NW, Washington, DC *20007*
Lampton MRS Nancy (Cox—Ray—Nancy Lampton) Ws'64
☎ (502) 228-3665 . . Tirbracken Farm, 3915 Tirbracken Lane, Goshen, KY *40026*
Lamy MR & MRS James Pierre (Eileen C O'Sullivan) Mit'33
☎ (816) 826-2161 . . Rte 4, Sedalia, MO *65301*
Lamy MISS Julia M (Anstey—Julia M Lamy)
Newt'59.Cy. . . . . | ☎ (314) 993-1930
MR Christopher L Anstey. . . . . | 1 Wickersham Lane, St Louis, MO *63124*
Lancaster MR David P—Van'82
☎ (415) 435-1542 . . 24 San Rafael Av, Belvedere Tiburon, CA *94920*
Lancaster MR & MRS Henry Carrington JR (Martha G Roe)
MdArt'85.JHop'48
☎ (410) 323-5222 . . 1113 Bellemore Rd, Baltimore, MD *21210*
Lancaster MISS M Alden—Duke'77.GeoW'79
☎ (301) 270-2222 . . 6708 Poplar Av, Takoma Park, MD *20912*
Lancaster MR & MRS W Lloyd JR (Stewart—Roxie C Grace)
Birm'ham'53.Jones'74.Aub'51 . . of
☎ (334) 265-7446 . . 2052 Myrtlewood Dv, Montgomery, AL *36111*
☎ (205) 825-4463 . . ''The North Forty'' Riverboat Rd, Lake Martin, Dadeville, AL *36853*
Land MR & MRS Thomas W (S Randolph Burnam) Pitzer'72.Cda.NCar'70
☎ (615) 373-5487 . . 6038 Sherwood Court, Nashville, TN *37215*
Land MR & MRS William G (McAvoy—Frances B Chisolm)
BMr'29.Csn.Hb.H'28
☎ (202) 333-5511 . . 4418 Greenwich P'kway NW, Washington, DC *20007*
Landen MR & MRS Gerald C (Elizabeth Stevens) . . . | ☎ (307) 322-3196
MISS Jennifer S—ColSt'95 . . . . | 349 W Fairview Rd,
MR G Calvin JR . . . . | Wheatland, WY *82201*
Lander MR & MRS Richard E (Patricia B Riter) Tufts'48
☎ (610) 687-2649 . . 6 Forest Rd, Wayne, PA *19087*
Lander DR & MRS William W (Nancy G Bomberger) Me.Cs.Ursin'46.Pa'49
☎ (610) 525-1046 . . 201 Broughton Lane, Villanova, PA *19085*
Landguth MISS Ashley Page (gg—MRS James A Wise) . . . . Born at Knoxville, TN Jan 3'96
Landis MRS Philip F (Barbara S Olney) Ncd.
☎ (415) 221-3848 . . 3855 Washington St, San Francisco, CA *94118*
Landon MR & MRS Russell W (Jennifer Mann) FIT'80.Yn.Y'79.Cl'85
☎ (617) 659-1868 . . 793 Main St, Norwell, MA *02061*
Landon MRS Stephen L JR (Frances V Sweat) . . . . Died Aug 30'96
Landon MR Stephen L JR—Y'45w . . . . | ☎ (860) 868-7655
MR Stephen Scudder . . . . | 156 Calhoun St,
MR Matthew Jay . . . . | Washington Depot, CT *06794*
Landreth MRS Betty W (Stevens—Landreth—
O'Neill—Betty A Wright) . . . . | ☎ (212) 355-7004
MISS Ann W—at ☎ (847) 475-9966 | 325 E 57 St,
820 Grey Av, Evanston, IL *60202* . . . . . . | New York, NY *10022*
MISS Nancy W—Box 586463, Oceanside, CA *92058-6463* . . . . |
Landreth MR Charles B—Pc.Rv.Lea'70 . . . . | ☎ (215) 592-8398
MISS Kirsten E H—at Mt Holyoke . . . . | 731 Spruce St,
JUNIORS MR Charles A B—at Trinity . . . . | Philadelphia, PA *19106*

Landreth MR Charles H—Pc.Cw.Rv.
☎ (215) 248-1883 . . 8833 Stenton Av, Philadelphia, PA *19118*
Landreth MR & MRS Chase W (Laurie G Greaves)
Skd'69.Pr.Va'70.Ch'72 . . of
☎ (212) 737-3657 . . 174 E 74 St, New York, NY *10021*
☎ (516) 671-9349 . . 20 Shelter Lane, PO Box 426, Locust Valley, NY *11560*
Landreth MR David C—Cl'95 . . see S G White
Landreth MRS Diana C (Childs—Altschul—Diana C Landreth)
SL'68.Cr'79.Cs.
☎ (212) 875-8686 . . 610 West End Av, New York, NY *10024*
Landreth MR Edward S—Rv.Cspa.Cw.W.Pa'33
☎ (212) 535-0162 . . 544 E 86 St, New York, NY *10028*
Landreth MR & MRS Edward S JR (Dorrie P | ☎ (213) 934-6620
Kavanagh) NewSchSR'66.H'64 . . . . | 1211 S Genesee Av,
MISS Audrey P—at Columbia . . . . | Los Angeles, CA
MR Jonathan S—Cal'92—at ☎ (212) 645-3178 | *90019*
137A Christopher St, New York, NY *10014* . . . |
Landreth MR John Colt—Rc.Sr.Bost'73
☎ (312) 642-2051 . . 1448 N Lake Shore Dv, Chicago, IL *60610*
Landreth MR & MRS John T (Webbe—Katherine H Maher) Cho.On.
☎ (619) 728-2479 . . 3944 La Canada Rd, Fallbrook, CA *92028*
Landreth MR & MRS John T JR (Jeanne L Martineau) DU'83.Pac'83
☎ (847) 441-0690 . . 2299 Drury Lane, Northfield, IL *60093*
Landreth MRS Rodney N 2d (Marie Steketee) Cvc. . | ☎ (860) 767-8363
MR Oliver L—Nu'77.Pa'82—at via Belmeloro 11, | 85 River Rd,
40126 Bologna, Italy . . . . | Essex, CT *06426*
Landreth MISS Sarah P . . see S G White
Landstreet MR & MRS Beverly W IV (Julia N Fry)
SL'81.Van'92.Msq.NCar'80
☎ (615) 297-9628 . . 4318 Sunnybrook Dv, Nashville, TN *37205*
Lane MR Charles A
☎ (314) 361-0004 . . 4540 Laclede Av, St Louis, MO *63108*
Lane MR & MRS Charles E JR (Ethel M Vincent) | ☎ (212) 838-0536
Un.Chr.Cw.P.'30 . . . . | 200 E 66 St, Apt
MRS Ann L Breit (Ann B Lane) | D1601, New York,
B'gton'64.Ncd.Ne. | NY *10021-6728*
Lane MR Christopher T—Rcn.Ny.Dth'62.H'65
☎ (415) 441-8043 . . 1067 Broadway St, San Francisco, CA *94133*
Lane DR & MRS Daniel K (Janet G Knight) Hlns'56.Cy.P'55
☎ (314) 994-7903 . . 18 S McKnight Rd, St Louis, MO *63124*
Lane MRS Edward D (Downe—Wisner—Elaine Bellins)
☎ (305) 864-5334 . . 9821 E Bay Harbor Dv, Bay Harbor Island, FL *33154*
Lane MR & MRS Garrison Fairfield (Marcia Huhn) | of ☎ (203)661-6026
Ny.Chr.Plg.Coa.Cc.Cw.Ne.Ofp.Fw.Rv.Sar.Wt. | ''Lafayette Cottage''
Vca.Myf.P'57.Cl'60 . . . . | Bush Av,
MISS Marcia Fairfield—at ☎ (516) 283-6222 | Greenwich, CT
PO Box 958, Southampton, NY *11969* . . . . | *06830*
MISS K Madeleine Huhn—Me'95 . . . . | ☎ (941) 966-5411
MR Garrison Sewall—at ☎ (203) 625-9384 | 2821 Casey Key,
249 Milbank Av, Greenwich, CT *06830* . . . . . . | Nokomis, FL *34275*
Lane MR George Bliss JR
☎ (617) 277-5225 . . 258 Harvard St, Apt 303, Brookline, MA *02146-2904*

Lane MR Glenn—Okla'41
☎ (503) 299-4514 . . 2545 SW Terwilliger Blvd, Apt 514, Portland, OR 97201

Lane MR & MRS Hugh C JR (Croft Whitener) NCar'78.Pa'70
☎ (803) 577-4440 . . 30 Church St, Charleston, SC 29401

Lane MR & MRS John A S (Melita B Renfert) V'41
☎ (414) 352-6925 . . 7740 N Rivers Edge Dv, Milwaukee, WI 53209

Lane MR & MRS John K (Sandra A Beech)   ☎ (847) 256-2975
Ih.Br'62.Mich'65 . . . .   157 Kenilworth Av,
MR James R—Ih.Colg'91.Nw'96—at   Kenilworth, IL
333 E Ontario St, Apt 1708B, Chicago, IL 60611   60043
MR Brandon B—Lynch'93—at
600 W Washington Av, Apt 3B, Lake Bluff, IL
60044 . . . .

Lane MR & MRS K J Winton (Tyrwhitt—Delia G Scott)
☎ (011-44-171) 584-8018 . . 125 Cranmer Court, Whitehead's Grove, London SW3 3HE, England

Lane MRS Peggy O (Peggy A Offutt) Pn. . . . .   ☎ (941) 263-5872
MISS Heather W—Dth'91.Va'96—at New York,   4796 Crayton Court,
NY . . . .   Naples, FL
MR Christopher—Ham'93—at 119 W 71 St,   34102-3012
New York, NY 10023 . . . .

Lane REV DR & MRS Warren W (Virginia Penney)
SL'48.St.G.Ch'46.DU'49.EpiscTheo'52.P'69 . . of
☎ (716) 885-4254 . . 194 Windsor Av, Buffalo, NY 14209
☎ (905) 468-3475 . . "Far End" 369 Niagara Blvd, Niagara-on-the-Lake, Ontario L0S 1J0, Canada

Lane MRS Wendy C H (Curll—Surtees—Wendy C   of ☎ (212)751-2586
Henry) LakeF'69   575 Park Av,
MISS Campbell N—at 1060 Paseo Del Mar,   New York, NY
San Pedro, CA 90731   10021
MISS Heather H—P'87 . . . .   ☎ (203) 431-6617
     "Serendipity"
     452 Silver Spring
     Rd, Ridgefield, CT
     06877

Lane MR & MRS William H (Elizabeth L Nesbitt) Cl'31
☎ (941) 263-8802 . . 114 Moorings Park Dv, Apt A504, Naples, FL 34105

Lane MR William N 3d—On.P'65 ⛵

☎ (847) 234-0470 . . 349 N King Muir Rd, Lake Forest, IL 60045

Laney MR & MRS James C R (Curtis—Margaret A Johnson)
Swb'62.W&M'67
☎ (423) 821-1405 . . 319 Park Rd, Lookout Mountain, TN 37350

Laney MR & MRS Lynn M JR (Jean C Kennedy) Stph'51.Ariz'57
☎ (602) 840-2874 . . 4031 E San Miguel Av, Phoenix, AZ 85018

Lang MR & MRS Cecil Y (Violette N Guérin-Lésé) InstCath'48.Duke'41
☎ (804) 293-4673 . . University Village 1507, 2401 Old Ivy Rd, Charlottesville, VA 22903-4860

Lang MR & MRS François-Michel (Elizabeth D Hunter) RMWmn'79.P'81
☎ (301) 652-1172 . . 7202 Denton Rd, Bethesda, MD 20814

Lang MR & MRS Gordon JR (Clara B Van Derzee)   ☎ (312) 337-0544
Cho.On.Rc.Wa.Cnt.Y'54.Ariz'58.H'60 . . . .   1520 N Astor St,
MISS Elizabeth K—at N'western . . . .   Chicago, IL
MISS Harriet B—at Brooks   60610-1610
MR Gordon III—at Emory . . . .

Lang MR Victor J JR—Ph.Tex'60
see Dilatory Domiciles

Langan MR & MRS John J (Caroline W Savage)   ☎ (508) 369-6512
Wheat'57.Mid'61.MassArt'52.Tufts'58 . . . .   260 Oak Hill Circle,
MISS Catherine A—Hartw'88 . . . .   Concord, MA 01742

Langan MR & MRS Michael W (Candace B Register) Ny.Webb'77
☎ (203) 454-1519 . . 5 Pilgrim Lane, Weston, CT 06883

Langdon MR Campbell B—H'83.H'89
☎ (212) 315-1684 . . 124 W 60 St, Apt 33B, New York, NY 10023

Langdon MRS George D (Anne C Zell) Ncd.
☎ (860) 435-0386 . . Salisbury, CT 06068

Langdon MR & MRS George D JR (Domandi—Agnes Körner)
V'59.Nu'66.C.H'54.Y'61
124 W 60 St, Apt 17H, New York, NY 10023

Langdon MRS Hepburn (Tracy—Culbertson—Cora M Hepburn) Dar.
11141 W Arizona Av, Apt D102, Youngtown, AZ 85363

Lange MISS Ann—Cda . . .see W B Hopkins

Lange MR & MRS Kenneth R (Biddle—Geraghty—Elizabeth R Clay)
MooreArt'66.Penn'58
☎ (203) 322-3805 . . 1887 Newfield Av, Stamford, CT 06903

Lange MR & MRS Richard A (Catherine H Meyer)
Pa'70.MichSt'74.A.Cda.Pa'68.MichSt'75
7 Elmcourt St, San Antonio, TX 78209

Langenberg MR & MRS John F (Alice T Chaplin) Cl'33
☎ (314) 994-1730 . . 8701 Delmar Blvd, Apt 3A, St Louis, MO 63124

Langenberg MRS Margaret M (Quinn—Margaret M Langenberg)
☎ (212) 674-3772 . . 60 Gramercy Park, New York, NY 10010

Langenberg MR & MRS Oliver M (Evans—Polk—Mary E Booth)
Cy.Rc.P'35
☎ (314) 863-3072 . . 6419 Ellenwood Av, St Louis, MO 63105

Langenberg MR & MRS Roy T (Patricia I Cole) Wash'62.K.Br'60
☎ (603) 772-9093 . . 140 High St, Exeter, NH 03833

Langhorne MR & MRS W Keene (Skillern—Jane T Cobb) Va'41
☎ (415) 854-5938 . . 127 Ash Lane, Portola Valley, CA 94028

Langley MR & MRS Ralph G (Doris J Kellam) Tex'37
☎ (210) 492-9600 . . 3527 Hunter Circle, San Antonio, TX 78230

Langmann DR & MRS Robert D (Toulmin—   ☎ (860) 677-1001
Saraellen Merritt) BMr'55.Au.Ncd.H'50.Cl'55 . .   23 Vine Hill Rd,
MR Henry C Toulmin—Vt'88—at   Farmington, CT
☎ (617) 661-7207 . . 52 Kelly Rd, Apt 1,   06032
Cambridge, MA 02139 . . . .

Langworthy MR & MRS David C (Norma J Shea) Me . . .of
☎ (212) 260-4180 . . 18 W 11 St, New York, NY 10011
☎ (802) 297-9756 . . Fairway Meadow 12, Stratton Mountain, VT 05155

Lanier MR & MRS Addison 2d (M Elizabeth Kilcullen)
Sth'73.Cl'77.Rcn.B.Qc.Wms'76.H'80
☎ (513) 321-6570 . . 4 Elmhurst Place, Cincinnati, OH 45208

Lanier MR & MRS Henry D (Catherine H Bragg)   ☎ (212) 431-6071
Sth'74.Y'78.H'65.Y'78 . . . .   335 Greenwich St,
JUNIORS MISS Lauren B . . . .   New York, NY
     10013

Lanier MISS Katherine C
see Dilatory Domiciles

Lanier MRS Kimberly H (Kimberly H Putnam) Au. . ☎ (802) 878-1185
JUNIORS MISS Courtney H . . . . 8 Spruce Lane,
Essex Junction, VT
05452-4387

Lanius MR P Baxter 3d—Rc.Ub.Y.Dth'72
30 E 95 St, Apt 7A, New York, NY *10128*

Lankenau MISS Catherine A—P'89
☎ (212) 787-7102 . . 225 Central Park W, Apt 1616, New York,
NY *10024*

Lankenau MR & MRS John C (Alison D Lanckton) ☎ (212) 799-0074
CUNY'64.Cs.Cr'52 . . . . 20 W 86 St,
MISS Christine R—at U of Colo Boulder . . . . . . New York, NY
10024

Lannamann MRS Margaret P (Margaret A Payne) ☎ (203) 637-1078
Sth'69. . . . . 16 Druid Lane,
MR Thomas C—P'96 . . . . Riverside, CT *06878*
JUNIORS MR Edward P—at Vanderbilt . . . .
JUNIORS MR John S . . . .

Lannamann MR Richard S—Ln.Yn.Y'69.H'73
☎ (203) 637-9337 . . 21 Willowmere Circle, Riverside, CT *06878*

Lanni MRS Allison D (Allison B Day) Duke'85
☎ (610) 526-9955 . . 900 Montgomery Av, Apt 602, Bryn Mawr,
PA *19010*

Lansbury MR & MRS Edgar G (Rose A Kean) ☎ (212) 874-7536
V'53.Cos.C.Cly. . . . . 211 Central Park W,
MISS Katharine Rose . . . . New York, NY
MR Brian McI—at ☎ (212) 662-1123 *10024*
127 W 96 St, New York, NY *10025* . . . .

Lansbury MR & MRS George W (Emily A Bickford) Skd'87.Skd'85
☎ (212) 362-5669 . . 151 W 85 St, New York, NY *10024*

Lansbury MR & MRS James E (Susan A Snorf) SCal'78
☎ (310) 459-8900 . . 16388 Shadow Mountain Dv, Pacific Palisades,
CA *90272*

Lansdowne MRS F Mackinnon (Mary A Grigsby) SanJ'75.Dar.Cda . . .of
☎ (408) 626-4824 . . 8545 Carmel Valley Rd, Carmel, CA *93923*
☎ (408) 659-2344 . . 6 La Rancheria, Carmel Valley, CA *93924*

Lansing MR & MRS Gerrit L (M Suydam ☎ (203) 869-7300
Rosengarten) Rcn.Mds.Nf.Snc.Hl.Nu'66 ⛵ . . 30 Husted Lane,
MR Gerrit L JR—Duke'95—at ☎ (212) 426-1584 Greenwich, CT
40 E 88 St, New York, NY *10128* *06830*

Lansing MR & MRS John T (Mary S Harrison) ☎ (612) 653-8562
NTex'87.Pa'69 . . . . 20 Doral Rd,
MR Charles B 4th . . . . Dellwood, MN
MR John T JR *55110*

Lapey DR & MRS Allen (Wallis—Janet E Dundee) ☎ (617) 696-8288
Rdc'59.Wms'61 . . . . 59 Randolph Av,
MISS Sarah E—Wms'93—at Harvard Med . . . . . Milton, MA *02186*

Lapey MR & MRS John D (Jennifer L Monachino)
Sth'91.StJ'96.Wms'90.Ne'91
☎ (718) 575-3750 . . 1 Station Square, Apt 202, Forest Hills Gardens,
NY *11375*

Lapey MRS Paul W (Elisabeth W Allen) St.
☎ (561) 220-3293 . . 5333 SE Miles Grant Rd, Apt I204, Stuart,
FL *34997*

Lapham MR & MRS Anthony A (Burks Y Bingham) ☎ (202) 387-7120
Rdc'60.Cly.Y'58.Geo'61 . . . . 2919 Woodland Dv
MR Nicholas P NW, Washington,
MR David A . . . . DC *20008*

Lapham MISS Ellen V B (Ludwick—Ellen V ☎ (415) 917-8017
Brown) Syr'66.Stan'77 . . . . ''The Denizens''
MR Dennis K Ludwick—Cal'93 . . . . 4017 Page Mill Rd,
Los Altos Hills, CA
94022

Lapham MRS Lewis A (Jane A Foster) Ln.Cly.
☎ (203) 869-5522 . . ''Windover'' 170 John St, Greenwich, CT *06831*

Lapham MR & MRS Lewis H 2d (Joan B Reeves) ☎ (212) 439-1998
Y'56. . . . . 19 E 72 St,
MISS Elizabeth D D. . . . . New York, NY
MR Lewis A P. *10021*
JUNIORS MR Winston P . . . .

Lapham MR & MRS Roger D (de Clara—Phyllis Kyrides)
Pcu.Bur.B.Ri.H'40 . . of
☎ (408) 624-5154 . . Porque Lane, Box 721, Pebble Beach, CA *93953*
☎ (310) 278-1789 . . 8822 Dorrington Av, Los Angeles, CA *90069*

Lapin MR & MRS David A (Phyllis Teti) ClareMcK'74.Cl'75
☎ (310) 859-9373 . . 1080 Woodland Dv, Beverly Hills, CA *90210*

Lapin MISS Elizabeth J—SL'77
☎ (212) 489-1790 . . 235 W 56 St, Apt 42K, New York, NY *10019*

Laplante MR & MRS Paul A (Elizabeth A Wiley) 274 White Oak
Rens'54 . . . . Ridge Rd,
MR Andrew P—Miami'87 . . . . Short Hills, NJ
MR David A—Van'90. *07078*
MR John P—Buck'92 . . . .
MR Christopher S—Van'96. . . . .

Laporte MR & MRS William F (Ruth W Hillard) Ri.Cly.Ncd.P'36.H'38 . . of
☎ (212) 593-1919 . . 435 E 52 St, New York, NY *10022*
☎ (717) 595-2298 . . ''The Spruces'' Buck Hill Falls, PA *18323*

Laporte MR & MRS William F 3d (Virginia D Schrum)
Wes'82.WakeF'79.Babcock'83
2200 Sherwood Av, Charlotte, NC *28207-2122*

Lapsley MR & MRS John W (Hope Whitney) ☎ (516) 922-3699
LIU'65.Ng.Pr.Ln.H'57 . . . . Mill River Rd,
MR Howard. . . . . Oyster Bay, NY
11771

Lardi MISS Lisa C—AmU'88
☎ (305) 538-6004 . . 800 West Av, PH-15, Miami Beach, FL *33139*

Lardi MR & MRS (DR) Paul F (Elizabeth Coryllos) of ☎ (516)671-6815
Bnd'49.Cr'53.Ford'53.NYLaw'57 . . . . 8 Jaegger Dv,
MR Gordon C . . . . Glen Head, NY
11545
☎ (518) 672-7368
Mountain Brook
Farm, 106 Clum Rd,
Hillsdale, NY *12529*

Large MISS Barsha P—Eck'93 . . see MRS B B Lloyd
Large MR & MRS Henry W (Emily N Ingersoll) Sg.Rb.Ac.P'28
☎ (215) 646-0255 . . 4 Spring House Lane, Blue Bell, PA *19422*

Large MR & MRS James M JR (Blossom—Carole A Elkins) Pr.Cry.P'54 . . . . | ☎ (516) 671-1626
MR James M 3d . . . . | 14 Underhill Rd,
MR Richard C . . . . | Locust Valley, NY
  MISS Virginia Blossom. . . . . | 11560
  MR Jonathan Blossom . . . . |

Large MISS Nina L . . see MRS B B Lloyd

Large MRS W Mifflin (Wade—Ann Gray Dolan) Gm.
  ☎ (610) 933-8510 . . Larchwood Farm, RD 2, Phoenixville, PA 19460

Larkin DR & MRS Charles L JR (Anne R Meigs) V'44.Y'44.Cl'47
  ☎ (203) 758-9183 . . PO Box 326, Wooster Rd, Middlebury, CT 06762

Larkin MRS Edith G (Edith P Garver) Pl.Cs . . .of
  ☎ (212) 980-2032 . . 125 E 63 St, New York, NY 10021
  ☎ (516) 325-0379 . . Rogers Lane, Remsenburg, NY 11960

Larkin MR & MRS Frank Y (Smith—June Noble) Ln.Mds.C.Plg.Cly.Sl.Ncd.P'37 . . of
  ☎ (203) 869-6716 . . 600 Lake Av, Greenwich, CT 06830
  ☎ (212) 249-8131 . . 115 E 67 St, New York, NY 10021

Larkin MR & MRS Fred C (Lucetta D Makepeace) Neb'57.Neb'56.DU'60 . . . . | ☎ (303) 794-4923
MISS Molly D—at 77 Bleecker St, Apt 830, | 1 Cove Lane,
New York, NY 10012 . . . . | Bow Mar, CO
 | 80123

Larkin MR & MRS H Robert (Evelyn Coltharp) MissStW'43.Wash'49
  ☎ (805) 969-3344 . . 8 Seaview Dv, Montecito, CA 93108

Larkin MRS Jeannette M (Jeannette Marsh) . . . . | ☎ (716) 652-0530
MISS Mary—at 3260 Seneca St, Apt 12, | 2800 Bowen Rd,
West Seneca, NY 14224 . . . . | Box 176, Elma, NY
 | 14059

Larkin MRS Marian R (Prince—Marian R Larkin) Wheat'69.Btn.Cy.
  ☎ (617) 965-4345 . . 729 Dedham St, Newton, MA 02159

Larkin MISS Paige M (Fred C) . . . . Married at Denver, CO
Zangrillo MR Robert L (Robert P) . . . . Jun 24'95

Larkin MR & MRS Richard W (Morgan—Mary B Fiedler) H'53
  ☎ (847) 446-3624 . . 461 Maple St, Winnetka, IL 60093

Larkin MISS Sarah (Fred C) . . . . Married at Denver, CO
Lundy MR Sean H (Jack) . . . . Aug 14'93

Larkin MRS Sarah M (Harvey—Sarah M Larkin) Ty'82
  ☎ (860) 535-3395 . . 17 Wamphassuc Point Rd, Stonington, CT 06378-2815

Larkin MR Thomas B JR—Cvc.Va'40
  ☎ (714) 675-5152 . . 1573 E Ocean Blvd, Balboa, CA 92661

Larm MR & MRS Richard P (Jona C Vieta) Wheat'68.H'67.H'70
  ☎ (212) 794-1499 . . 301 E 66 St, New York, NY 10021

Larned MR & MRS Michael C (Beatrice M Litchfield) Rv.Ll.Myf.Wt.Pace'70 . . . . | ☎ (203) 322-0294
MISS Marguerita S—MtH'96. . . . . | ''June House''
MISS Emily K—at Wesleyan . . . . | 178 Farms Rd,
 | Stamford, CT 06903

La Roche MRS Chester J (Rasmussen—Warren— Clark—Ritchey C Farrell) Evg.BtP.Cly. . . . . . . | ☎ (561) 655-9333
MISS Leslie Warren . . . . | 529 S Flagler Dv,
 | Apt 25E,
 | West Palm Beach,
 | FL 33401

La Rochefoucauld CTE Patrice de & CTSSE de (Stephanie W Parrish) NH'75.Me'86.Paris'74.Wid'80 . . of
  ☎ (011-33-1) 46-03-73-24 . . 58 rue de Silly, 92100 Boulogne, France
  ☎ (011-33) 54-98-01-04 . . ''Château de Douy'' 41320 Chatres-sur-Cher, France

Larocque MRS Joseph (Callaway—Edna Strangfeld)
  ☎ (609) 448-4100 . . Meadow Lakes 43-07, Hightstown, NJ 08520

Larrabee MR & MRS Stephen F (Marka H Truesdale) | of ☎ (860)928-0217
Wh'lck'66.Conn'85.Dar.H'61.H'63.Bab'79 . . . . | 7 Bradley Rd,
MISS Elizabeth M . . . . | Pomfret Center, CT
MR Jonathan F . . . . | 06259
 | ☎ (207) 985-8090
 | 21 Rosewood Circle,
 | Kennebunk, ME
 | 04043

Larsen MR & MRS Carter L (Caroline Martin) | of ☎ (415)346-8500
Pcu.Rv.Fr.Hn.Buck'40.H'47. . . . . | 3621 Washington St,
MR M Scott. . . . . | San Francisco, CA
MR Carter L JR . . . . | 94118
MR Brett F M . . . . | ☎ (707) 433-1273
 | Larsen Vineyards,
 | 4420 W Sausal
 | Lane, Healdsburg,
 | CA 95448

Larsen MRS H Irgens (Patricia C Pike)
  ☎ (617) 661-8873 . . 8 Hubbard Park Rd, Cambridge, MA 02138

Larsen REV & MRS Lawrence B JR (Marion D | ☎ (914) 763-8981
Hines) Hlns'65.Ty'58.Gen'lTheo'61.Tenn'89 . . | ''The Meadows''
MISS Hannah H—at Savannah Art & Design . . . . | 17 Briar Court,
MISS Sarah A . . . . | Cross River, NY
MR Lawrence B 3d—Buck'93 . . . . | 10518

Larsen MR & MRS Robert R (Vaast—Constance L Cheney) Pqt.Ny.Nyc.Cly.H'54 . . of
  ☎ (203) 259-2212 . . 504 Sasco Hill Rd, Fairfield, CT 06430
  ☎ (561) 234-9965 . . 131 Silver Moss Dv, Vero Beach, FL 32963

Larson MRS Carl B (Houston—M Bayard Thompson)
  ☎ (619) 437-1516 . . 1720 Avenida del Mundo, Apt 1206, Coronado, CA 92118

Larson MR & MRS Daniel L JR (Graziano—Laura T | ☎ (617) 720-1164
Hobson) Ariz'77.Va'91.Ln.Sm.Cly.H'70.H'75 . . | 92 Mt Vernon St,
JUNIORS MISS Jessica D Graziano . . . . | Boston, MA 02108

Larson MR & MRS Daniel M (Catherine L McNeal) Hlns'74.GeoW'73
  ☎ (703) 360-1384 . . 1601 Cool Spring Dv, Alexandria, VA 22308

Larson MRS E Carruthers (Rebhun—Minor—Elizabeth P Carruthers) . . of
  ☎ (954) 765-1251 . . 1801 SE 21 Av, Ft Lauderdale, FL 33316
  ☎ (616) 526-5938 . . Box 800, Cottage 41, Harbor Point, MI 49740

Larson MR & MRS James W (Blunt—Susan H | ☎ (512) 345-7525
Bunting) Valp'66.MichSt'68 . . . . | 4104 River Place
MR Christopher C Blunt—at | Blvd, Austin, TX
  ☎ (805) 646-3297 . . 10239 Ojai-Santa Paula | 78730
  Rd, Ojai, CA 93023 . . . . |
  MR Alexander R Blunt—at U of Tex . . . . |

Larson MRS Susan Foley (Susan M Foley) | ☎ (508) 369-7705
Wheat'70 . . . . | 63 Monument St,
MISS Alexandra C—at Trinity . . . . | Concord, MA 01742
MISS Charlotte W—at Wesleyan . . . . |
JUNIORS MISS Anna F—at Phillips Andover . . . . . |

Larson MRS Wadsworth (Hughes—Nancy E | ☎ (212) 876-0911
Wadsworth) Cly. | 215 E 68 St,
MISS Eleanor B . . . . | New York, NY
 | 10021-5718

Larson MR & MRS Wilfred J (Joan J Tilford) Bf.Pa'51 . . of
☎ (716) 881-2708 . . 88 Oakland Place, Buffalo, NY *14222*
☎ (941) 649-7255 . . 2321 Gulf Shore Blvd N, Apt 708, Naples,
FL *34102*

Larzelere MR & MRS William E JR (Kathleen F Chace) Ariz'75.U'71
☎ (914) 234-6798 . . "Twin Oaks" 120 Fox Lane, Bedford Corners,
NY *10549*

Lasell MR & MRS Chester H (Hite—Elizabeth E Grant) Csn.Wms'30
☎ (203) 869-4777 . . 19 Doverton Dv, Greenwich, CT *06831*

Laserson MR & MRS Stephen A (Frances M Griffith) | of ☎ (212)289-7676
Swb'70.Un.Cly.Hob'66 . . . . | 1130 Park Av,
JUNIORS MISS Tenley L . . . . | New York, NY
JUNIORS MISS Galen G . . . . | *10128*
| ☎ (516) 653-9555
| "Tuckaway"
| Ocean Av, Quogue,
| NY *11959*

Lashley MR & MRS William A (Chadwick—Elinor A | ☎ (757) 220-3133
Huston) HampSydney'40.Va'42 . . . . | 8 Whittaker's Mill
MR William A JR—at 36 W 22 St, New York, NY | Rd, Williamsburg,
10011 . . . . | VA *23185*
MR Claiborne—USN.—at Rte 5, Box 123, |
Hedgesville, WV *25427* . . . . |
MR Barham—VPI'78—at 574 Honey Pot Rd, |
Candor, NY *13743* . . . . |
   MISS Elizabeth A Chadwick . . . . |

Laskow MR & MRS Mark J (Lisa H Childs) Pa'71.Rr.Pg.Fcg.Pa'71.Pitt'74
☎ (412) 421-3638 . . 6693 Kinsman Rd, Pittsburgh, PA *15217*

Lasry MR & MRS David P (Evelyn M Day) Ty'85.Cal'82.Y'.'85
☎ (212) 988-2699 . . 245 E 72 St, New York, NY *10021*

Lassen MR Christian K II—Myf.
PO Box 1603, New York, NY *10021*

Lassen MR & MRS John Kai (Flanagan—Marion duP McConnell)
Wh'lck'70.Wil.Cw.Myf.Yn.Y'64.Pa'67
☎ (302) 652-7222 . . "Crooked Billet" PO Box 3712,
3510 Kennett Pike, Wilmington, DE *19807*

Lastavica MR & MRS (DR) John (Sears—Catherine Coolidge)
Rdc'53.JHop'58.Chi.Sm.H.Catol'56.Y'58
☎ (508) 526-1641 . . PO Box 1443, 9 Coolidge Point,
Manchester-By-The-Sea, MA *01944-0853*

Latham MRS Robert E (M Ella Jesse) Ncd.
☎ (703) 538-4636 . . 3601 N Glebe Rd, Arlington, VA *22207*

Lathrop MR & MRS Philippe G W (M Michele MacDonald) Leh'79.Leh'77
☎ (205) 967-1779 . . 4224 Caldwell Mill Rd, Birmingham, AL *35243*

Lathrop MR & MRS Walter W JR (Anne Alexander) | of ☎ (419)893-7650
Mich'64.Cr'56 . . . . | "Grassy Creek"
MISS Susan C—at London, England . . . . | 9684 Carnoustie Rd,
MR John E—at 180 Beacon St, Apt 8A, Boston, | Perrysburg, OH
MA *02116* . . . . | *43551*
MR George W—at 8609 Ponte Vedra, Holland, | ☎ (941) 964-1260
OH *43528* . . . . | "Osprey Nest"
| Boca Grande Club,
| PO Box 476,
| Boca Grande, FL
| *33921*

Latimer MR & MRS William H (Kelly—Natalie A Mercer) Fcg.H'43
1000 Lowry St, Apt 5C, Delray Beach, FL *33483*

Latini MR & MRS Francesco B (Viléne—Merryl P | ☎ (707) 935-9795
Lackey) Stock'65.Mit'54 . . . . | 1651 Point Dv,
MISS Gabriella M . . . . | Sonoma, CA *95476*
MR Alessandro W . . . . |

Latos MR & MRS Eric B (Susan P Rath)
K.Sg.Cly.Ncd.Myf.Ht.MichSt'69 . . of
☎ (212) 996-7671 . . 1158 Fifth Av, New York, NY *10029*
☎ (860) 567-8100 . . PO Box 520, Litchfield, CT *06759*

Latta MRS Cuthbert H (Deborah Bradley)
Cathedral Village G319, 600 E Cathedral Rd, Philadelphia, PA *19128*

Lattimer DR & MRS John K (Jamie E Hill) | ☎ (201) 567-0055
Ofp.Rv.Sar.Fw.Snc.Cw.Wt.Cl'35.Cl'38.Cl'43 . . | 56 Beech Rd,
MISS B Evan—at 4203 Holly St, Kansas City, MO | Englewood, NJ
64111 . . . . | *07631*
DR D Gary—Rv.Snc.Cl'75.Cl'78.Cl'79.Cl'84—at |
Honolulu, HI . . . . |

Lattu RR ADM (RET) & MRS Onnie P (Arlene M Ringer) USN.Myf.Cal'30
☎ (202) WO6-4891 . . 3600 Ordway St NW, Washington,
DC *20016-3176*

Lau DR & MRS Frederick T 2d (Patricia G Cochran) | ☎ (602) 948-6154
Ariz'66 . . . . | 8201 N Charles Dv,
MISS Amy M . . . . | Paradise Valley, AZ
MISS Megan A . . . . | *85253*
MISS Kathryn E . . . . |
MR Matthew C . . . . |

Laub MR David C—Cy.Bf.Br'60.Buf'65
☎ (716) 877-0479 . . 81 Middlesex Rd, Buffalo, NY *14216*

Laub MRS George C (Phipps—Buchanan—Brewster—
Josephine E Greer) Sg.
☎ (610) 645-8951 . . 1400 Waverly Rd, Apt A120, Gladwyne, PA *19035*

Lauck MR & MRS Gerold McK JR (Renehan—Marian L McLeod) Rv.Y'38
☎ (941) 263-2565 . . 1900 Gulf Shore Blvd N, Apt 605, Naples,
FL *34102*

Lauck MRS Peter (Annette Campbell) V'40
☎ (609) 924-3298 . . 882 Lawrenceville Rd, Princeton, NJ *08540*

Lauder MRS George (Bedford—DuPuy—Jessie Cook) Ihy.BtP.Evg.
☎ (561) 655-7996 . . 137 Australian Av, Palm Beach, FL *33480-4434*

Lauer MRS Harry I (Ketcham—Ruth Van Sciver) Pc.Ncd.
☎ (215) 283-7273 . . 808 Foulkeways, Sumneytown Pike, Gwynedd,
PA *19436*

Laughlin MR & MRS Alexander M (Judith Walker)
Rc.Mds.Rr.Mto.Cly.Sl.Y'49
☎ (212) 861-9330 . . 3 E 77 St, Apt 14A, New York, NY *10021*

Laughlin MR & MRS Alexander M JR (Veronica P Whitlock)
Duke'83.NYSID'89.Cly.
☎ (203) 637-8898 . . 64 Stirrup Lane, Riverside, CT *06878*

Laughlin MR Alexander M JR—B.Rr.Mds.GeoW'77
☎ (203) 637-3046 . . 276 Palmer Hill Rd, Riverside, CT *06878*

Laughlin MR & MRS Leighton H (Carin E Moore) P'49
☎ (609) 921-9544 . . 142 Winant Rd, Princeton, NJ *08540*

Laumont MR & MRS Philippe E (Anne C Adams) Cal'67.Au.Louvain'65
☎ (212) 222-9357 . . 945 West End Av, New York, NY *10025*

Laurendeau MASTER James Thomas JR (gg—MRS Ward S Curtiss) . . . Born
at Boston, MA Feb 8'96

Lauricella MR & MRS Francis E JR (Mary B Pickering)
H'75.H'76.H'88.H'76.Stan'79.Y'83
☎ (415) 921-3157 . . 2360 Vallejo St, San Francisco, CA *94123*

LaValle MR Irving H—Ty'60.H'63.H'66
☎ (504) 899-8110 . . 726 Foucher St, New Orleans, LA *70115*
LaValley MR & MRS Frederick J M (Christine Dengler)
Pa'67.Ph.Ac.Dar.Stan'69.Pa'72
☎ (215) 627-1563 . . 315 S 12 St, Philadelphia, PA *19107*
Laverack MR & MRS William (Persis E Gleason) V'49.H'40
☎ (207) 879-1077 . . 45 Eastern Promenade, Apt 9D, Portland,
ME *04101*

Laveran-Stiebar DR & MRS Rudolf F (Deirdre B	☎ (610) 525-1683
Harder) Gm.Me.Vien'51	235 Pennswood Rd,
MISS Maria C—at 3611 University Dv, Durham,	Bryn Mawr, PA
NC *27707*	*19010*
MR Peter A	

Laveran-Stiebar DR & MRS Rudolf L (Harriet J Peabody) Ky'90.Gm.Vt'87
☎ (717) 854-0725 . . 917 McKenzie St, York, PA *17403*

Lavin CDR & MRS Charles V (Barbara J Hofheins)	☎ (757) 255-2211
Cr'55.J'ville'67.Rich'89.Myf.Dar.USN'52.	1850 Cherry Grove
GeoW'69	Rd N, Suffolk, VA
MR Robert C—Va'88.Ch'95	*23432*

Lavin MASTER Henry William (Michael D) . . . . Born at
Stamford, CT Dec 7'94
Lavin MR & MRS Michael D (Nancy A McKernan)
Ty'83.Ny.GeoW'80.GeoW'83
☎ (203) 333-7727 . . "Suncourt" 274 Balmforth St, Bridgeport,
CT *06605*
Lavin MR Peter C—ODom'92
☎ (860) 767-1174 . . 97 Book Hill Rd, Essex, CT *06426*

Lavine MR & MRS Henry W (White—Martha P	☎ (202) 333-7765
Cathcart) Sth'70.UWash'77.Mt.Pa'57.Pa'61	3224 Cleveland Av
MISS Lindsay A	NW, Washington,
	DC *20008*

Lavino MRS E George (Virginia Vail) CtCol'33.Cs.
☎ (610) 584-3915 . . 73 Spruce Run, Lansdale, PA *19446*

Law MR & MRS Hugh R (Katherine B Gatch)	☎ (314) 863-2159
LSU'72.Nd.H'69	6208 Pershing Av,
JUNIORS MISS Sarah P G	St Louis, MO *63130*

Law MRS Wilbur S (Anne M Gerrish) MtH'41
☎ (303) 681-2663 . . 7035 Perry Park Blvd, Larkspur, CO *80118*
Lawlor MISS Andrea Michelle (g—David C Streett 2d) . . . Born Jan 7'93
Lawrence MR & MRS A Brewster JR (Lathrop—Nancy L Lambie) Lm.
☎ (516) 584-7545 . . PO Box 205, St James, NY *11780-0205*

Lawrence MR & MRS A Brewster 3d (Jennifer	☎ (713) 578-1106
Townsend Bielaski) MtH'72.Lm.Dar.TCU'72.	20402 Kelliwood
Nw'75	Lakes Court, Katy,
MISS Fairlie Townsend—at Knox	TX *77450*
JUNIORS MISS Allison Paige	

Lawrence MR Alexander K—Pc.Colg'35
☎ (610) 584-3874 . . Meadowood at Worcester, 22 Hickory Heights,
Lansdale, PA *19446*
Lawrence MISS Alida S
460 Cold Springs Av, West Springfield, MA *01089*

Lawrence MR Arthur Burtis—U'38	☎ (703) 777-8132
MR Reed K—VPI'82	Burnwood Farm,
	Rte 2, Box 120,
	Leesburg, VA *20175*

Lawrence MISS Barbara K (Train—Barbara K Lawrence)
B'gton'65.Nu'69 . . of
☎ (617) 247-9474 . . 34 Upton St, Boston, MA *02118*
☎ (207) 276-5108 . . PO Box 168, Northeast Harbor, ME *04662*

Lawrence MR & MRS David B (Hannele Robinson)	of ☎ (212)517-5183
Sth'50.Y.'51	800 Park Av,
MR George F 2d—Bard'85—at 111—76 St,	New York, NY
Forest Hills, NY *11370*	*10021*
MR David B JR—Ham'85—at 22F Citibank	☎ (516) 288-1735
Tower, 3 Garden Rd, Central Hong Kong	"Ambunti"
	8 Delafield St, Box
	1368, Westhampton
	Beach, NY *11978*

Lawrence MR & MRS David T (Susan L Hadden)	of Regent Court
Wh'lck'69.Pr.K.Cly.H'67	16B, 4 Sankuaiban
MISS Katharine P—at Colby	Yonganli,
MR John H—at Trinity	Jianguomenwai,
JUNIORS MISS Sarah T—at Groton	Dajie, Beijing
	100022, China
	☎ (516) 364-2995
	"Orchard House"
	202 Brookville Rd,
	Glen Head, NY
	11545

Lawrence MR E Alexander—Lm.Tufts'81.Cl'83
☎ (212) 595-1082 . . 140 Riverside Dv, Apt 17C, New York, NY *10024*

Lawrence MR & MRS J Townsend (Janet B Walling)	☎ (203) 762-7288
Y'44	269 Nod Hill Rd,
MR J Townsend JR—Emer'72—at	Wilton, CT *06897*
☎ (510) 254-8248 . . 45 Oak Dv, Orinda, CA	
94563	

Lawrence MRS James (Hallowell—Frances L Weeks) Cy.Tv.Ub.Chi.Ncd.
535A Gay St, Westwood, MA *02090*

Lawrence DR & MRS James 3d (Jane S Burgin)	☎ (410) 337-8017
Rdc'62.Cy.Mv.H'58	6137 Barroll Rd,
MR Langdon S—Y'89	Baltimore, MD
MR James 4th—H'93	*21209*

Lawrence MRS James F (Barbara R Childs) Yh.Cly.Cda.
☎ (860) 542-5495 . . "South Pole Farm" 57 Windrow Rd, Norfolk,
CT *06058*
Lawrence MR & MRS James R (Jill A Owesny) BMr'76.Mid'77
☎ (914) 241-1353 . . 12 Overlook Dv, Bedford Corners, NY *10549*
Lawrence MR & MRS John E (Barnes—Janet White) Sbc.Sm.Tv.My.H'31
☎ (508) 468-1750 . . Winthrop St, South Hamilton, MA *01982*
Lawrence MR & MRS John T JR (Anne T Ingalls) Y'50
☎ (513) 831-6300 . . 8100 Buckingham Rd, Cincinnati, OH *45243*

Lawrence MR & MRS John W (Reba R Carruthers)	☎ (214) 521-4202
AmU'74	4527 Arcady Av,
JUNIORS MISS Elizabeth R	Dallas, TX *75205*

Lawrence MR & MRS L Peter (Susan C Upton)	☎ (203) 655-7981
Bost'73.Cl'79.Hn.Ty'71.H'76	110 Five Mile River
JUNIORS MR John U	Rd, Darien, CT
	06820

Lawrence MR Lewis R M—Y.'53
☎ (212) 288-7829 . . 240 E 76 St, Apt 12K, New York, NY *10021*

Lawrence MR & MRS Peter G (Sandra Bartolini)
Me'71.Ne'72.Sm.Laf'67.RISD'74
☎ (617) 277-5676 . . 19 Colchester St, Brookline, MA *02146*

Lawrence MR & MRS Philip S (Jill A Peklo) Duke'86.Cl'87
☎ (914) 666-5193 . . 60 Darlington Rd, Mt Kisco, NY *10549*

Lawrence MR & MRS Richard H (C Starr Oliver) BMr'53.Y'50
☎ (914) 666-8640 . . 60 Darlington Rd, Mt Kisco, NY *10549*

Lawrence MR & MRS Richard S (Marjorie A Brown)
Ithaca'78.Geo'83.Pc.Pa'76.DU'87
☎ (610) 279-7578 . . 1610 Jennifer Lane, Blue Bell, PA *19422*

Lawrence MR Richard W JR—Au.P.'31.Cl'34
☎ (518) 873-6532 . . PO Box 427, Elizabethtown, NY *12932*

Lawrence MR & MRS Robert A (Patricia Perrin) D.Sm.Tv.Y'47
7 Jackson Pond Rd, Dedham, MA *02026*

Lawrence MRS Robert C JR (Genevieve R Kellogg) Rm.
☎ (908) 291-3619 . . 7 Black Point Horseshoe, Rumson, NJ *07760-1928*

Lawrence MR & MRS Robert C 3d (Mary R Stout) | ☎ (908) 747-0071
V'63.Rm.Stc.Ri.Plg.StJ.Cr'60.Nu'63.Nu'66 . . . . | 7 Black Point
MISS Kendra S—Y'90—at ☎ (216) 371-2484 | Horseshoe, Rumson,
2611 Shaker Rd, Cleveland Heights, OH *44118* . | NJ *07760-1928*

Lawrence MR Robert C 4th—Rc.Stc.Y'89
☎ (212) 807-9639 . . 615½ Hudson St, Apt 9, New York, NY *10014*

Lawrence MR & MRS Robert L (Joan E Hilseberg) Seton'65
☎ (910) 256-0230 . . 1221 Arboretum Dv, Wilmington, NC *28405*

Lawrence MRS Sidney S JR (Polly Ghirardelli) Cal'43
550 S Carlin Springs Rd, Arlington, VA *22204*

Lawrence MR Sidney S 3d—Ct.Cp.Cal'72.Cal'80
☎ (202) 342-6353 . . 1240—29 St NW, Washington, DC *20007*

Lawrence MR & MRS Solon L N (Matlack—Elizabeth Buchanan) Colg'44
☎ (603) 927-4540 . . RR 1, Box 137, Sutton, NH *03221*

Lawrence MRS Stuart N (Emerson—Christine L Allen)
☎ (954) 942-2994 . . 260 SE 3 St, Pompano Beach, FL *33060*

Lawrence MRS Suzanne (Suzanne Were) NotreD'80 | ☎ (410) 329-3050
MISS Denise G . . . . | 812 Walters Lane,
MR Mark T . . . . | Glencoe, MD *21152*

Lawrence MRS Suzanne S (Suzanne Spear) Bgt. . . . | ☎ (914) 234-6763
MR Christopher C—Wms'93 . . . . | PO Box 651,
JUNIORS MR Arthur W—at Colo Coll . . . . | Bedford, NY *10506*

Lawrence MRS Virginia M (Virginia M Maloney) | ☎ (617) 720-1984
Ws'64.Br'94.Cy. | 77 Pinckney St,
MISS Eloise P—Stan'95—at ☎ (508) 465-1763 | Boston, MA
Governor Dummer Academy, 1 Elm St, Byfield, | *02114-4303*
MA *01922* . . . . |
MR Abbott W—H'93—☎ (617) 720-1978 . . . . . |

Lawrence MR W Jeffrey—Lm.JHop'77.JHop'78.Cl'81
☎ (011-44-171) 823-4877 . . 46 Chester Row, London SW1W 8JP, England

Lawrence MR & MRS Wayne B (Elizabeth B Smith)
Sbc.Eh.Shcc.My.Hob'77
☎ (508) 468-6686 . . 144 Larch Row, Wenham, MA *01984*

Lawrence MR William—Cc.H'37.Y'40 . . . . | ☎ (508) 548-2265
MR William 3d—at ☎ (412) 922-3951 | 197 Nobska Point
120 Oakville Dv, Apt 1A, Pittsburgh, PA *15220* | Rd, Box 11,
| Woods Hole, MA
| *02543*

Lawrence MR & MRS William Goadby (Nathalie Brown)
☎ (207) 882-7300 . . "Creekside" RR 1, Box 2920, Edgecomb, ME *04556*

Lawrence MRS William Van D (Jones—Downer—Jean Hibbard) V'44
☎ (603) 868-7071 . . 27 Bucks Hill Rd, Durham, NH *03824*

Laws MISS Elizabeth
☎ (215) PE5-7776 . . 1907 Spruce St, Philadelphia, PA *19103*

Lawson MRS Carol S (Carol H Skinner) Ncd. . . . . . | ☎ (804) 983-3021
MISS Susanna V R . . . . | West Farm,
| Rte 1, Box 184,
| Dillwyn, VA *23936*

Lawson MR & MRS Frank B (Margaret K Farnsworth) H'36
☎ (617) 934-2138 . . Box 96, 34 Sunset Rd, Duxbury, MA *02331*

Lawson MR & MRS Joel S JR (Libbey—Ann Koover)
Occ'52.Cos.Ncd.Wms'45.Ill'49.Ill'53 . . of
☎ (808) 921-9924 . . 3089 La Pietra Circle, Honolulu, HI *96815*
☎ (301) 652-2840 . . 5301 Westbard Circle, 118, Bethesda, MD *20816*

Lawson MR & MRS Richard L (Carolyn P Thomas) OState'68.H'71 . . of
☎ (704) 553-8603 . . 3500 Kylemore Court, Charlotte, NC *28210*
☎ (704) 664-4327 . . "El Nido" 120 Newark Lane, Mooresville, NC *28115*

Lawson MR & MRS Robert F A (Andria F Rowley) Cy.H'52.H'56
☎ (617) 277-6060 . . 37 Cedar Rd, Chestnut Hill, MA *02167*

Lawson MR & MRS Thomas S JR (Sarah H Clayton) | ☎ (334) 264-9682
Ala'59.Ala'57.Ala'63 . . . . | 1262 Glen Grattan,
MISS Rose G . . . . | Montgomery, AL
MISS Gladys R . . . . | *36111*
MR Thomas S 3d . . . . |

Lawson MR & MRS W David IV (Constance T Carter)
Nw'79.Cvc.Rr.W&L'75
☎ (212) 426-1346 . . 1150 Fifth Av, New York, NY *10128*

Lawson-Johnston MR & MRS Peter O (Dorothy S Hammond)
Err.Ri.C.Md.Gv.Va'51
☎ (609) 921-6250 . . 215 Carter Rd, Princeton, NJ *08540*

Lawton MRS Edward P (Elizabeth Rounds) . . . . | ☎ (941) 278-0842
MISS Daphne E . . . . | 36 Barkley Place,
| Apt 145, Ft Myers,
| FL *33907*

Lawton MR & MRS Frank B (Madonna Marty) | ☎ (314) 993-8388
DePaul'76 . . . . | 8200 Gannon Av,
JUNIORS MISS Ellen B . . . . | University City, MO
| *63132*

Lawton MR Robert E . . see MISS C F Whitney

Lawton JUNIORS MISS Whitney A . . see MISS C F Whitney

Lawton MR William J JR
☎ (314) 692-0024 . . 1 Jaccard Lane, Frontenac, MO *63131*

Lay MR & MRS David (Mary L Pollard) H'53 . . . . . . | ☎ (703) 435-1271
MISS Martha P—Ty'87 . . . . | Box 711,
| Kilmarnock, VA
| *22482*

Lay MR Mark P—Ct.Va'83
☎ (703) 356-5857 . . 6601 Georgetown Pike, McLean, VA *22101*

Layng MR & MRS John G (Amanda La M Barney) | ☎ (203) 966-2587
PineM'74.Laf'75 . . . . | 150 Rosebrook Rd,
JUNIORS MISS Katherine S . . . . | New Canaan, CT
JUNIORS MR Andrew G . . . . | *06840*

Layton MRS Buxton Lawn JR (Ruth D Ellis) GaTech'37.Cda.
☎ (504) 897-0582 . . 6112 Hurst St, New Orleans, LA *70118*
Layton MR & MRS Buxton Lawn 3d (Carolyn Wente)
4800 Arroyo Rd, Livermore, CA *94550*
Lea MRS A Stevens (Avice M Stevens) Swth'50.Ncd.
☎ (203) 661-9834 . . 1 Putnam Hill, Apt 3G, Greenwich, CT *06830*
Lea MR Churchill P—Y'32
☎ (513) 321-0648 . . 7 Rennel Dv, Cincinnati, OH *45226*
Lea MR Edward E—Y'26
☎ (513) 321-1148 . . 3350 Shaw Av, Apt 255, Cincinnati, OH *45208*
Lea MRS Francis C JR (Carolyn M Coady)
☎ (610) 993-9275 . . 1023 Derwydd Lane, Berwyn, PA *19312*
Lea MISS Jane J . . see B L O'Neill
Lea MR & MRS Robert C JR (Nancy H Kellogg) V'39.Ph.Rcp.Ac.H'37.Pa'40
☎ (410) 822-0021 . . ''Langshaws'' 12814 Ocean Gateway, Queen Anne, MD *21657-3022*
Lea MR & MRS Robert C 3d (Boright—Thérèse L de Nagy)
JohnSt'74.H'64.H'74.H'83
☎ (410) 822-8060 . . ''Langshaws'' 12812 Ocean Gateway, Queen Anne, MD *21657*
Leach MISS Ambler P—UMiami'94 . . see J E Colen JR

Leach MR & MRS Edwin F II (Deborah N Woodward) Wheat'72.Dth'69.	☎ (508) 222-1277 ''Long Haul'' 80 Ridgewood Rd, Attleboro, MA *02703*
MISS Haverhill A	
MR Jedediah W	

Leach MISS Jennifer M—Ty'92 . . see J E Colen JR

Leach MR & MRS Paul C (Dorsey—Bates—Sheila W Jackson) V'64.Pcu.Dth'67.Stan'71	of ☎ (415)563-2460 2935 Pacific Av, San Francisco, CA *94115*
MISS Barclay P Bates	☎ (707) 938-5860 ''Pool House'' 1221 Sobre Vista Dv, Sonoma, CA *95476*

Leach MR Percival H E
☎ (201) 347-2032 . . Waterloo Village, Stanhope, NJ *07874*

Leach MR & MRS Peter T (Lee H Davidson) Me.Wis'67	☎ (610) 649-0453 274 Hathaway Lane, Wynnewood, PA *19096*
JUNIORS MR Alexander D—at Colby	
JUNIORS MR Christopher T—at Holderness	

Leach MR & MRS Peter T (Patricia S Smythe) MaryB'83.RochTech'82
☎ (717) 267-4980 . . 501 Walnut St, Denver, PA *17517*

Leach MR & MRS Richard M (Wheelock—Cornelia S McElroy) D.Ny.Ty'55	☎ (603) 763-9191 Maple Lane, Box 1888, New London, NH *03257*
MISS Virginia P	
MR Nathaniel B—at U of NH	

Leach MRS Richard P (Katherine Thatcher) . . of
☎ (518) 584-9294 . . ''River Run Farm'' 149 Fitch Rd, Saratoga Springs, NY *12866*
☎ (212) 755-0940 . . 10 Mitchell Place, New York, NY *10017*
Leach MRS Virginia F (Virginia C Ferguson)
☎ (617) 383-1362 . . 50 Red Gate Lane, Cohasset, MA *02025*

Leachman MR & MRS William H 3d (Kelsey K Drowne)
MtVern'85.Unn.Cvc.W&L'83
1312—35 St NW, Washington, DC *20007*

Leahy MR & MRS Robert B (Marie Louise Slidell) Mt.Cvc.P'59	☎ (301) 656-0781 6921 Woodside Place, Chevy Chase, MD *20815*
MR William H 2d	
MR Christopher B	

Leake MISS Joan A
☎ (212) 769-3547 . . 150 W 79 St, New York, NY *10024*
Leake MR & MRS John B (Jane Whitridge)
Ph.Rb.Gm.Srb.Yh.Ac.Y'34.Ford'38
☎ (610) 525-1782 . . 1113 Brynlawn Rd, Villanova, PA *19085*

Leale MR & MRS Douglas M (Harvie-Watt—Olivia M Smith) V'66.Cal'57 ⚓	of ☎ (206)524-0471 5427 NE Penrith Rd, Seattle, WA *98105*
MISS Jennifer Harvie-Watt—Pitzer'91	☎ (360) 376-5291 Linden Tree Farm, PO Box 98, Olga, WA *98279*

Leaman MR & MRS Benjamin F (Richmond—Blake—Monique A Pflieger)
M.Cry.Rr.Pkg.Penn'44
☎ (610) 827-9256 . . Stone Hedges Farm, PO Box 228, Birchrunville, PA *19421*
Lear MR John B JR
☎ (215) 247-2248 . . 201 W Evergreen Av, Apt 414, Philadelphia, PA *19118*

Leary MR & MRS Brian F (M Thana Caldwell) P'73.UMiami'78	☎ (954) 566-5643 2870 NE 28 St, Ft Lauderdale, FL *33306*
JUNIORS MR Thomas F	

Leary MRS H Fairfax (Sarah L O'Neill) Cts.Ac.Me.W.Myf.Ncd.
☎ (610) 525-8096 . . 1404 Mt Pleasant Rd, Villanova, PA *19085*
Leary MR & MRS H Michael B (Catherine L Collins) Rol'76.Me.
☎ (610) 525-2876 . . 1 Fawn Lane, Haverford, PA *19041*
Leas MISS Ann P . . see A L Wermuth
Leas MISS Samantha B . . see MRS L S Shaw
Leas MRS Thompson (Stephens—Mary Grace Black) Ncd.
☎ (603) 643-1578 . . 131 Brook Hollow, Hanover, NH *03755*
Leavens MRS William B (Gibson—Margaret P Reynolds) Ws'31.Dar.
☎ (201) 736-0030 . . Llewellyn Park, West Orange, NJ *07052*
Leavenworth MR & MRS Coman (Ellen Kupfer)
Myf.Cw.Snc.Ht.Rv.Y.'43.Cl'48
☎ (516) 537-3072 . . ''ElCo'' Box 24, Wainscott, NY *11975*

Leavitt MR & MRS Gregory A (Lydia Thompson) CtCol'72.DU'70	☎ (610) 358-4378 ''Malster's House'' 476 Valley Brook Rd, Wawa, PA *19063*
MISS Camille—at Pa Acad of Fine Arts	
JUNIORS MR Benjamin P	

Leavitt MR & MRS W Bradbury (Galvin—Anne Lochridge) Sth'65.NH'63
☎ (541) 485-7362 . . 1609 Washington St, Eugene, OR *97401*
Le Baron DR & MRS Charles Wade (Tessa H Merritt)
Col'74.Myf.Hn.P'66.H'80.H'84
☎ (770) 270-1417 . . 2297 LaVista Woods Dv, Tucker, GA *30084*
Leber MR & MRS Edward C JR (Jean A Eugene) Gettys'69.Colg'68
☎ (704) 846-1407 . . 6101 Providence Country Club Dv, Charlotte, NC *28277*

Le Blanc MRS Bertrand (Noël Kennerly)
☎ (415) 346-5734 . . 3140 Pacific Av, San Francisco, CA *94115-1016*
LeBlanc MR & MRS Stewart A JR (Jeanne T Alvarez) Ala'45.At.Ala'43
☎ (334) 433-7703 . . 304 S Georgia Av, Mobile, AL *36604*
Le Blond MR Richard Emmett . . . . Died at
Cincinnati, OH Dec 14'95
Le Bourgeois MRS John D (C Muriel Chisholm)
☎ (718) 478-5989 . . 139-66—135 Av, Flushing, NY *11354*
LeBourgeois MR & MRS Louis P 3d (Mary W Selman) FIT'90.Tul'91
6124 Annunciation St, New Orleans, LA *70118*
LeBourgeois MISS Mary Wilder Claiborne (Louis P 3d) . . . Born Jly 19'96
Le Boutillier MR & MRS Benjamin H (Elizabeth Ann Newbold) Rv.
☎ (610) 644-0551 . . 2287 S Valley Rd, Berwyn, PA *19312*
Le Boutillier MR C Pierre R . . . . | ☎ (610) MU8-8815
MISS Jeanine E—Shippens'94 . . . . | 407 Conestoga Rd,
MISS Ondraya M—at U of Del . . . . | Wayne, PA
| *19087-4811*
Le Boutillier MR Charles P
5 Mary Bell Rd, Audubon, PA *19407*
Le Boutillier MR & MRS John (Susanna Shore) H'86.H'86
☎ (212) 289-2147 . . 1170 Fifth Av, Apt 1C, New York, NY *10029*
Le Boutillier MRS Philip JR (Felia Ford)
☎ (419) 666-9606 . . 29819 E River Rd, Perrysburg, OH *43551*
LeBoutillier MRS Thomas (Secor—Pamela Tower)
☎ (516) 626-0831 . . PO Box 230, Old Westbury, NY *11568*
Lebow MR & MRS Jeffrey A (Laurel M Lavin) Emory'77.Mich'80.Mich'81
☎ (770) 333-0214 . . 3110 Brandy Station NW, Atlanta,
GA *30339-4406*
LeBrecht MRS Brown (Maxwell—Sheila T Brown) Mds.
☎ (212) BU8-6605 . . 66 E 79 St, New York, NY *10021*
Jan 15 . . ☎ (941) 262-1580 . . 4001 Gulf Shore Blvd N, Naples,
FL *34103*
LeBrecht MRS Robert (Carol C Straton)
☎ (914) 986-4414 . . ''Meadowlark'' 263 Bellvale Lakes Rd, Warwick,
NY *10990*
LeBreton MR & MRS David H (Moore—Ann C | ☎ (617) 326-1859
Boothby) Bost'73.D.Cvc.Eyc.Nu'75 . . . . | 38 Wampatuck Rd,
JUNIORS MISS Hadley H Moore . . . . | Dedham, MA *02026*
JUNIORS MISS Colby D Moore . . . . |
Le Breton MRS Edward Francis JR (Gladys L Gay)
☎ (504) 525-2651 . . 1441 Jackson Av, New Orleans, LA *70130*
Leckie MR & MRS Frederick A (A Elizabeth | ☎ (805) 563-9189
Wheelwright) Stan'56.StAndr'49.Stan'58 . . . . . . | 1177 N Ontare Rd,
MR Gregor W—at ☎ (847) 948-0957 | Santa Barbara, CA
945 Hemlock Av, Deerfield, IL *60015* . . . . | *93105*
MR Sean C . . . . |
Leckie MR & MRS Gavin F (Elizabeth A O'Donnell) Ox'84.Camb'81.Ill'88
☎ (914) 738-0414 . . 226 Highbrook Av, Pelham, NY *10803*
Leclerc MR & MRS Ivor (Thayer—Joan Pirie) | Cranmer Court,
H'75.Chi.Hb.Lond'49 . . . . | Apt 36, Whitehead's
MISS Margaret P Thayer . . . . | Grove, London
| SW3 3HG, England
LeComte MR & MRS Jonathan B (Denise E Alexandre) Swb'76
☎ (203) 531-4365 . . 1375 King St, Greenwich, CT *06831*

Leddy MR & MRS Thomas F (Studebaker—Newell— | of ☎ (212)288-7126
Tamara L B Newell) UMiami'72.Me.Nf.Rd. | 1000 Park Av,
Ford'68.Pa'70 . . . . | New York, NY
JUNIORS MISS Alexandra Newell . . . . | *10028*
| ☎ (561) 881-9208
| ''Il Tocai''
| 1291 N Ocean Way,
| Palm Beach, FL
| *33480*
Lederer MRS A McGrath (Anne D McGrath) | of ☎ (804)973-1171
Geo'57.Cda. . . . . | 2250 Earlysville Rd,
MISS Sloane W—Va'87 . . . . | Earlysville, VA
MR Andrew W—Wis'96 . . . . | *22936-9667*
| ☎ (540) 347-9233
| PO Box 1063,
| Warrenton, VA
| *20188*
Lederer MRS Henry A 3d (Maria S Gamble) Cybl. . | ☎ (954) 462-6332
MISS Maria G—at 19029 Brick Store Rd, | 1956 S Ocean Lane,
Hampstead, MD *21074* . . . . | Ft Lauderdale, FL
| *33316*
Lederer MR & MRS Steven E (Wiles—M Alden Murray)
MtVern'86.Tufts'83.Tufts'85
☎ (707) 252-1912 . . 3062 Soda Canyon Rd, Napa, CA *94558*
Ledes MR & MRS George M (Allison M Eckardt) V'75.Bgt.Cly.GeoW'80
☎ (212) 734-6304 . . 315 E 80 St, New York, NY *10021*
Ledes MR & MRS John G (Sara M Chapman) | ☎ (914) 232-5716
Bgt.Mv.Cda.Y.'45 | ''Twin Oaks''
MISS L Bayly—at ☎ (011-33-1) 45-49-35-38 | RD 1, Katonah, NY
3 rue du Sabot, 75006 Paris, France . . . . | *10536*
Ledes MR Richard C (John G) . . . . Married at New York, NY
Jaharis MISS Kathryn M (Michael JR) . . . . Sep 8'96
Ledes MR & MRS Richard C (Kathryn M Jaharis) Nw'83.Aht'79
☎ (212) 799-7506 . . 110 Riverside Dv, PH-A, New York, NY *10024*
Ledoux MISS Jeanne-Nicole (Chase—Jeanne-Nicole Ledoux) . . of
☎ (914) 245-6938 . . 2977 Meadowcrest Court, Yorktown Heights,
NY *10598*
☎ (914) 534-3487 . . Deer Hill Rd, PO Box 397, Cornwall-on-Hudson,
NY *12520*
Ledoux MR & MRS L Pierre (Joan Fernegg) C.H.'35 . . of
☎ (802) 362-1833 . . Dorset Hill Rd, RD 1, Box 690, East Dorset,
VT *05253*
☎ (212) 751-3077 . . 200 E 66 St, Apt D1605, New York, NY *10021*
☎ (914) 534-3487 . . Deer Hill Rd, PO Box 397, Cornwall-on-Hudson,
NY *12520*
Ledyard MR Jason—B'gton'91 . . see MISS L V Mattlage
Ledyard MRS Lewis Cass (Pell—Eve Mortimer) Srr.
☎ (610) 869-9422 . . 372 Lamborntown Rd, West Grove, PA *19390*
Ledyard MR & MRS Michael M (Offut—Catherine S | ☎ (610) 869-8466
Davis) Del'79.Wil.Hawaii'70 . . . . | 500 Wilson Rd,
JUNIORS MISS Eve . . . . | West Grove, PA
| *19390*
Lee MASTER Andrew Hebberd (Bruce H R H) . . . . Born Nov 6'95
Lee MRS Augustus W (E Brooke Conley) Mv.Cda.
☎ (561) 276-2162 . . 4227 N County Rd, Gulf Stream, FL *33483*

Lee MR & MRS B Herbert (Margery B Peterson)
BMr'51.Me.Ac.Cs.Va'48 .. of
☎ (610) 525-1029 .. 305 Gatcombe Lane, Bryn Mawr, PA *19010*
☎ (561) 265-4838 .. 790 Andrews Av, Apt H301, Delray Beach,
FL *33483*

Lee MRS Bain S (M Bain Severn) . . . . | ☎ (215) 233-2772
MR Clifford A—Rich'85 . . . . | 127 Erdenheim Rd,
Erdenheim, PA
19038-7807

Lee MRS Blair 3d (Mathilde Boal) BMr'42 . . . . | ☎ (301) 622-0876
MR Christopher G—at Boal Mansion, Box 116, | 400 Warrenton Dv,
Boalsburg, PA *16827* . . . . | Silver Spring, MD
20904-2851

Lee MR & MRS Bruce (Janetta Macpherson) QnsLond'62.S.Ny.Rol'54
☎ (212) 861-2984 .. 115 E 67 St, New York, NY *10021*

Lee MR & MRS Bruce H R H (Sarah D Forbush) Wh'lck'86
☎ (301) 949-7978 .. 4105 Franklin St, Kensington, MD *20892*

Lee DR & MRS Burton J 3d (Jennings—Mary Ann Kelly) Rcn.Y'52.Cl'56
☎ (508) 627-3371 .. "Leeway" PO Box 2477, 20 Shurtleff Way,
Edgartown, MA *02539*

Lee MR & MRS Charles C (Sally S White) Chr.Shcc.Eh.Ln.Y'50
☎ (908) 234-1104 .. PO Box 577, Far Hills, NJ *07931*

Lee MR Charles O'D 3d—Cal'45 . . . . | ☎ (805) 969-8334
MISS Jenifer—at ☎ (714) 854-7314 | Casa Dorinda,
19461 Sierra Porta Rd, Irvine, CA *92715* . . . . . . | 300 Hot Springs Rd,
Santa Barbara, CA
93108

Lee MR & MRS Charles P (Camilla Wall) Ny.Pa'66 .. | ☎ (212) 439-9359
MR Christopher . . . . | 215 E 79 St,
MR John . . . . | New York, NY
10021

Lee DR & MRS Charles T JR (Caroline T Lawson) Au.Rb.Sg.Ac.Pa'47
☎ (215) 247-8189 .. 8882 Norwood Av, Philadelphia, PA *19118*

Lee MR & MRS Charles T 3d (Elizabeth P Hyland) Au.Pc.Buck'78
☎ (215) 247-7009 .. 8412 Navajo St, Philadelphia, PA *19118*

Lee MR & MRS Chong S (Jacqueline Vaughan) | ☎ (512) 345-2896
Seoul'64 . . . . | 7205 Running Rope
MISS Jennifer—at Bowdoin . . . . | Circle, Austin, TX
MR Christopher J—Bow'95—at Stanford . . . . . . | *78731*

Lee MR & MRS D Day (Nancy A Mills) Sth'49.Au.H'45.Pa'56
☎ (505) 299-6292 .. 10821 Central Park Dv NE, Albuquerque,
NM *87123*

Lee MR & MRS David S (M Lucinda Hopkins) | ☎ (617) 731-4430
Sm.Cy.H.'56 | 27 Laurel Rd,
MISS Madeline J . . . . | Chestnut Hill, MA
MISS Alice I . . . . | *02167*
MR Alexander P . . . . |

Lee MISS Denise M S—Cda . . .of
☎ (561) 655-1618 .. 400 S Ocean Blvd, Palm Beach, FL *33480*
☎ (908) 234-9378 .. Poverty Pocket Farm, PO Box 5, Bedminster,
NJ *07921*

Lee MR & MRS Edward F (Tracie Anne Morrissey) Ken'83.Fst.Gm.Ken'83
☎ (610) 687-8419 .. 54 Deepdale Rd, Strafford, PA *19087-2608*

Lee MRS Frederick B (Jane Pillow Rightor) Sth'30.Mt.Cvc.C.Csn.Hn.
☎ (703) 356-7549 .. 1327 Potomac School Rd, McLean, VA *22101*

Lee MR & MRS George Terry JR (Natalie B | of ☎ (214)363-4067
Henderson) Stan'59.Smu'82.Y'57.Stan'60 . . . . . | 3101 Greenbrier Dv,
MISS Blythe . . . . | Dallas, TX *75225*
MISS M Rebecca . . . . | ☎ (903) 338-2356
MR Hamilton S . . . . | "Koon Kreek"
Rte 1, Athens, TX
75751

Lee MR & MRS Gerald J (Heather A Scarlett) VillaN'73
☎ (610) 793-3633 .. 1167 Arrowhead Dv, West Chester, PA *19382*

Lee DR & MRS Harry G (Sarah F Hadden) | ☎ (904) 389-4049
Wms'62.Cr'66 | 4132 Ortega Forest
MISS Sarah C . . . . | Dv, Jacksonville, FL
MR Harry G JR . . . . | *32210*
MR Robert H . . . . |

Lee MR & MRS Henry (Joan C Metcalf) Sm.Tv.Mt.H'48
☎ (617) 227-7227 .. 90 Mt Vernon St, Boston, MA *02108*

Lee MR & MRS Henry C (Phyllis A Miller) Cr'56.Cda.
☎ (802) 362-4522 .. PO Box 1033, Manchester, VT *05254*

Lee MR & MRS J Philip (Amy W Roberts) Pa'66 . . . . | ☎ (508) 636-5262
JUNIORS MISS Frances P . . . . | Sweetwater Farm,
587 River Rd,
Westport, MA
02790

Lee MR & MRS J Wayne (Anne W Dulany) Pc.Pa'56 | ☎ (215) CH7-8293
MISS Anne W—Laf'82 . . . . | 320 W Mermaid
MR J Wayne JR . . . . | Lane, Philadelphia,
MR Henry R . . . . | PA *19118*

Lee MRS Jacqueline (Hanley—Allen—Jacqueline | ☎ (540) 347-0607
Lee) Ncd.Dar. | 216 Fairfield Dv,
MR Michael W Hanratty . . . . | Warrenton, VA
MR John L Allen . . . . | *20186*

Lee MR James H—Unn.Chr.Plg.Cc.Cw.Myf.NCar'41.Va'49
☎ (704) 274-1280 .. 27 White Oak Rd, Asheville, NC *28803-2922*

Lee MR & MRS James W 2d (Foote—Holmes—
May Katharine Strangfeld) P'28
☎ (802) 867-5344 .. RR 1, Box 30, Dorset, VT *05251*

Lee MR & MRS John N (Mary H Subers) Pa'52
☎ (610) 434-4993 .. 745 N 30 St, Allentown, PA *18104*

Lee MRS John P (Nancy G Peabody) Cy.Ncd.
☎ (617) 329-9067 .. 10 Longwood Dv, Apt 312, Westwood, MA *02090*

Lee MR & MRS John R (Lucy W Abendroth) | ☎ (205) 880-6032
ClevSt'71.Pa'72 . . . . | 1427 Chandler Rd,
MISS Bryneth W . . . . | Huntsville, AL
MR Todd G . . . . | *35801*
MR Dylan H . . . . |

Lee MISS Julia R
see Dilatory Domiciles

Lee MR & MRS Knute D (Nancy Wellington) Ny. . . . | of ☎ (212)673-2006
MR Robin A . . . . | 2 Fifth Av,
New York, NY
10011
☎ (516) 286-2292
"Leeward"
Baycrest Av,
Bellport, NY *11713*

Lee MISS Latané Lisle (Martini—Latané Lisle Lee) OState'72
☎ (707) 762-7177 .. 120 Eastside Circle, Petaluma, CA *94954*

Lee MR & MRS Lewis H JR (Jean E Andrews) W&M'43
4039 Evergreen Rd, Allentown, PA *18104*
Lee MR & MRS M L Dawson (Letitia S Roberts) Md.Cvc.Va'44
☎ (410) 730-8955 . . Mountjoy Farm, 499 Columbia Pike,
Ellicott City, MD *21043*

Lee MR & MRS P O'Donnell (Jean R Gibb)   ☎ (410) 228-3892
Elk.Pr.Mv. . . . . 5301 Cassons Neck
MISS Virginia D . . . . Rd, Cambridge, MA
MR O'Donnell *21613*

Lee MR & MRS R Bland 5th (Marsh—White—M Ann Carter)
Cvc.Sl.Ncd.Va'55 . . of
☎ (804) 435-3636 . . "Cedar Point" PO Box 288, White Stone,
VA *22578*
☎ (804) 435-0984 . . "Cobbs Hall" Rte 1, Box 1777, Kilmarnock,
VA *22482*
Lee MRS Rensselaer W (Stella W Garrett) . . . . Died at
Princeton, NJ Jly 12'96
Lee MR & MRS Robert E IV (Rice—Jane C Cotton)
Cvc.Elk.Ct.Mt.Sl.W&L'49
☎ (301) 229-3355 . . 4418 Chalfont Place, Bethesda, MD *20816*
Lee DR & MRS Robert Earl (Viek—Elaine K D Chapleau)
Rdc'47.StJ.Ac.Colg'48.Cr'52
☎ (215) 862-3106 . . 9 Old Windy Bush Rd, New Hope, PA *18938*

Lee MR & MRS Robert H (Sandra Cummings) Nu'62 | ☎ (941) 394-4424
MR James H—Buck'90 . . . . 524 Yellowbird St,
MR Jeffrey B—Buck'91.AGSIM'94 . . . . Marco Island, FL
  33937

Lee MR & MRS Robert H JR (Holt—Mary Clay Platt) | ☎ (610) 649-6032
V'53.Gm.Me.Pn.P'56 . . . . 9 Llanalew Rd,
MR John W P Holt—Bow'79.Y'88 . . . . Haverford, PA
MR Henry M R Holt—Col'84 . . . . *19041*

Lee MISS Sara M . . of
☎ (212) 924-8795 . . 53 W 21 St, New York, NY *10010*
☎ (207) 526-4277 . . Swan's Island, Atlantic, ME *04608*
Lee MR Stephen S—Pc.Leh'90
☎ (215) 732-0051 . . 226 W Rittenhouse Square, Apt 2312, Philadelphia,
PA *19103*
Lee MRS Thomas D (Susan D Randall) Pn.
☎ (304) 636-0318 . . PO Box 508, Elkins, WV *26241*
Lee MR & MRS Thomas G (Anna T Petite) Ty'83
☎ (914) 961-8936 . . 41 Sturgis Rd, Bronxville, NY *10708*
Lee MR Thomas S—H'59
☎ (212) LE5-0370 . . 176 E 77 St, New York, NY *10021*
Lee MR & MRS W Ashton (Barbara E Whiting) Dy.Cnt.P'39.H'41 ⚓ . . of
☎ (303) 322-3207 . . 1111 Race St, Apt 14A, Denver, CO *80206*
☎ (970) 468-2762 . . The Moorings, Apt B, PO Box 1513,
316 E LaBonte St, Dillon, CO *80435*
Lee MR & MRS W Brewster 3d (Victoria West) NH'81.Ub.Tr.Y'79.Cr'84
☎ (508) 921-2166 . . Bulrush Farm, 343 Dodge St, Beverly, MA *01915*
Lee MRS William Colin (Helen E Hebard) Bgt.
5700 Williamsburg Landing Dv, Apt 119, Williamsburg, VA *23185*
Lee MR William Justice—R.Me.Fw.
☎ (610) 359-1035 . . 3500 West Chester Pike, Apt E205,
Newtown Square, PA *19073*
Leech MR Spencer J
☎ (516) 221-3384 . . 294 Twin Lane S, Wantagh, NY *11793-1949*

Leeds MR & MRS Roland O (Mary D L Boersma) | ☎ (313) 971-3708
Mich'66.Mich'69.Dar.Mich'66.Mich'73 . . . . . . 1140 Chestnut Rd,
JUNIORS MR Anthony R L . . . . Ann Arbor, MI
  48104

Leeds MR & MRS Ronald P E (Damgard—Darcy A | of ☎ (212)472-8777
Mead) Bcs.Pa'62 . . . . 1035 Fifth Av,
MISS Natalie . . . . New York, NY
MISS Julie M Damgard—Y'93 . . . . *10028*
  ☎ (011-41-82)
  33284
  "Villa Eichberg"
  21 via Johannes
  Badrutt, 7500
  St Moritz,
  Switzerland

Leedy MRS Larry L (Harriett E Veale) | ☎ (216) 423-1059
Cent'y'62.Cv.Un. . . . . Epping Rd, Box
MR Christian V . . . . 263, Gates Mills,
  OH *44040*

Leefeldt MR & MRS Robert C (Mary-tom Henshaw)
Stan'50.Bhm.Pcu.Fr.Stan'49
☎ (415) 460-9788 . . 1 Morrison Rd, Ross, CA *94957-1590*
Leeper MR & MRS Harry G JR (Rossana M Sollitto) Denis'79.Unn.A.
☎ (210) 735-1528 . . 250 Laurel Heights Place, San Antonio, TX *78212*
Lees MISS Aubrey (Polk—Aubrey Lees) Nu'73
☎ (212) 645-5184 . . 80 Perry St, Apt 3E, New York, NY *10014*
Lees MRS Charles A (Achelis—Mary C Harlow)
☎ (212) LE5-2345 . . 145 E 74 St, New York, NY *10021*
Lees MR & MRS Robert W (Wood—Elizabeth S Cooper)
V'44.Rcp.Ph.P'41.Pa'49
☎ (609) 235-4208 . . 131 Chestnut St, Moorestown, NJ *08057*

Leeson MR & MRS A Dix (Nancy A Browne) | of ☎ (617)329-9659
D.Ac.H'43 . . . . 10 Longwood Dv,
MISS Melinda K—Lawr'76.Brand'78—at Apt 169, Westwood,
899 Brentwood Dv, Venice, FL *34292* . . . . MA *02090*
  ☎ (508) 994-4304
  16 Broadway,
  Cuttyhunk, MA
  02713

Leeson MR Richmond T—H'59.Va'64 . . . . | ☎ (508) 994-1933
MR Richmond T JR—Col'86.Cal'90 . . . . PO Box 6,
MR William A—Mid'86 . . . . Dartmouth, MA
MR Thomas E—Mass'90 . . . . *02714*
JUNIORS MISS Gwendolyn G—at St Mark's . . . . .

Leeson MRS Robert (Evelyn O Talbot) . . of
☎ (401) 521-5677 . . 355 Blackstone Blvd, Apt 435, Providence,
RI *02906*
☎ (401) 783-4279 . . Hazard Av, Narragansett, RI *02882*
Leeson MR & MRS Robert JR (Margaret H Goddard) | ☎ (401) 783-3881
Pemb'61.H'55 ⚓ . . . . "Indian Rock"
MISS Margaret H—Br'85—at Boston, MA . . . . 4 Hazard Av,
MR Benjamin D—at Taos Ski Valley, NM *87525* Narragansett, RI
  02882

Leeson MR & MRS Robert 3d (Laura H Dennison) LakeF'84.LakeF'83
☎ (617) 631-6280 . . 78 Beacon St, Marblehead, MA *01945*
Leet MRS John D (Irene J Haines) Ncd.Dar.
☎ (316) 321-9570 . . 330 W Central Av, El Dorado, KS *67042*

LeFeaver MR & MRS James H JR (Olivia B Swaim) Sth'45.Cvc.Cal'39
☎ (415) 492-2660 . . Villa Marin 266, 100 Thorndale Dv, San Rafael, CA *94903*

LeFevre MR & MRS A Scott (Susan H Toland) Cal'83.Bhm.Pcu.Cp.Cal'82
☎ (415) 386-0570 . . 3751 Clay St, San Francisco, CA *94118*

Leff MRS William C (Caroline A Platt) BMr'27.Tv.Ncd.
☎ (773) 561-1383 . . 909 W Foster Av, Apt 902, Chicago, IL *60640*

Lefferts MR & MRS Gillet (Lucia B Hollerith) CtCol'47.C.Wms'47.P'50
☎ (203) 655-2327 . . 177 Leroy Av, Darien, CT *06820*

Lefferts MISS Kate C—BMr'33.Cly.Cs.
☎ (610) 645-8688 . . Waverly Heights Villa 39, 1400 Waverly Rd, Gladwyne, PA *19035*

Lefferts MR & MRS Leffert (Hubbard—Judith A Baldwin) Mich'63.Rcn.L.San.Sar.Hl.Ht.Cl'62 . . | ☎ (540) 592-3839 1272 Dunvegan Dv, Upperville, VA *20185*
  MISS Alexandra B—at Boston U . . . . |
  MR Leffert JR—Pa'92—at ☎ (617) 247-6386 403 Marlborough St, Apt 10, Boston, MA *02115* |

Lefkowitz MR & MRS Alan L (Potter—Elizabeth Franzen) Rdc'63.H'66.Cy.H.'53.H'58 . . . . | of ☎ (617)547-8528 975 Memorial Dv, Cambridge, MA *02138*
  MISS Hope E Potter—at ☎ (617) 492-7672 10 Agassiz St, Cambridge, MA *02140* . . . . . . |
  | ☎ (508) 636-8712 1133 Horseneck Rd, Westport, MA *02790*

Leftwich MISS M Edith
☎ (914) 337-9351 . . 900 Palmer Rd, Bronxville, NY *10708*

Legaré MR & MRS T Allen JR (Virginia I Green) SCar'39.Winth'39
☎ (803) 723-1692 . . 142 Tradd St, Charleston, SC *29401*

Legendre MISS Bokara H (Patterson—Bokara H Legendre) . . of
361 E Strawberry Dv, Mill Valley, CA *94941*
"Tashmarkhan" 55425 H'way 1, Big Sur, CA *93920*

Legendre MRS Sidney J (Weeks—Gertrude Sanford) Fic.Yh.Cly.
☎ (803) 553-1121 . . Medway Plantation, 300 Medway Rd, Goose Creek, SC *29445*

Legg MR Eugene Monroe—Cvc.Wes'70.H'81
☎ (703) 759-3690 . . 9018 Old Dominion Dv, McLean, VA *22102*

Leggett MR & MRS Anthony L (Claire E Cosner) Hampshire'79.H.'76 ⚓
☎ (914) 833-5007 . . 19 Forest Park Av, Larchmont, NY *10538*

Leggett MRS John D JR (O'Connell—Catharine M Bracher) Swb'43.Yh.Ncd.
☎ (860) 767-8952 . . 257 Essex Meadows, Essex, CT *06426*

Leggett MRS Mary Lee (Mary Lee Fahnestock) Ia'73.Ia'76.Cs.
☎ (212) 879-9263 . . 520 E 89 St, Apt 1, New York, NY *10128*

Legier MR & MRS David A JR (Jane Cunningham) StMDom'74.SoLa'68
☎ (504) 897-2682 . . 1401 Exposition Blvd, New Orleans, LA *70118-6037*

Legvold MR Paul A—Ln.Mto.Chr.StJ.SCal'72
☎ (805) 969-3108 . . 1525 Bolero Dv, Santa Barbara, CA *93108*

Lehmann MR Frederick W 4th . . of
☎ (512) 480-9499 . . 1800 Lavaca St, Apt 311, Austin, TX *78701*
"Love's Cabin" Current River, Rte 5, Salem, MO *65560*

Lehmann MR & MRS George P (Margaret D Johnson) Mo'36.Cspa.Rv.Cw.Ofp.Fw.Dc.Ncd.IaState'34 ·
☎ (610) 642-0680 . . 432 W Montgomery Av, Apt 401, Haverford, PA *19041*

Lehmann MR & MRS Kennett L (Dixie Tenny) UWash'85.Wash'85
☎ (206) 821-0760 . . 13304—69 Av NE, Kirkland, WA *98034*

Lehmann MRS Mary L (Mary P Love) V'46.Cda. . . | ☎ (314) 621-1432 1845 S 10 St, St Louis, MO *63104*
  MISS Phoebe S Love—at ☎ (314) 361-5949 4552 McPherson Av, St Louis, MO *63108* . . . |

Lehrman MR & MRS Lewis E (Louise L Stillman) Rc.Au.Ri.Cly.Y'60.H'63 . . . . | of ☎ (212)717-4218 620 Park Av, New York, NY *10021*
  MISS Eliza D . . . . |
  MR Leland . . . . |
  MR John S . . . . | ☎ (203) 629-7994 77 Cherry Valley Rd, Greenwich, CT *06831*
  MR Thomas D . . . . |
  JUNIORS MR Peter R . . . . |

Leib MR Franklin A—Stan'66.Cl'71 ⚓
☎ (203) 259-1899 . . 251 Greens Farms Rd, Greens Farms, CT *06436*

Leib MR G Bruce—Un.So.Nrr.Pl.Va'53 . . . . | ☎ (212) 861-4607 239 E 79 St, New York, NY *10021*
  MISS Cara I—at ☎ (212) 980-9536 359 E 62 St, New York, NY *10021* . . . . |
  MR G B Eric—at ☎ (212) 249-7421 434 E 84 St, New York, NY *10028* . . . . |

Leib MR & MRS John H (Danforth—Du Bois—Mary I Bryan) Rcn.Pr.Nu'50
☎ (561) 231-6750 . . 901 Bay Rd, Apt 103, Vero Beach, FL *32963*

Leibert MR McGurrin Seton . . see MRS A McGurrin

Leibert MISS Meighan . . see MRS A McGurrin

Leidy MR & MRS Carter R JR (Hamilton—Antonia Wallace) Sth'62.Va'68.Mich'71.Ph.Rd.Ste.Rv.Ll.Pa'61
☎ (610) 430-3843 . . 358 N Church St, West Chester, PA *19380*

Leidy MRS Frances A Hufty (Frances A Hufty) V'65.Rc.Ph.Rd.BtP.Ste.Cvc. . . . . | ☎ (610) 692-8735 Springhouse Farm, 1145 W Strasburg Rd, West Chester, PA *19380*
  MISS Frances A . . . . |
  MR Carter R 3d . . . . |
  MR Page R . . . . |

Leidy MR & MRS Robert P P (Terry—Liza D Pulitzer) UMiami'58.B.Evg.BtP.Ll.Rv. . . . . | ☎ (561) 832-0123 PO Box 589, Palm Beach, FL *33480*
  MR Robert P P JR . . . . |
  MR Christopher P . . . . |

Leigh MR & MRS Anthony M (Eleanore T Speer) Gi.Va'55
☎ (941) 262-4144 . . 640 Ketch Dv, Naples, FL *34103*

Leigh MRS Egbert G (Lucinda L Kinsolving) . . . . . | ☎ (202) 333-3369 3023 P St NW, Washington, DC *20007*
  MR Catesby M—Pn.P'79 . . . . |

Leighton MR & MRS Charles M (Vaughan—Sanderson—Roxanna B McCormick) Mid'67.Ny.Hn.Bow'57.H.'60.Bow'89 ⚓
☎ (508) 779-5390 . . 51 Vaughn Hill Rd, PO Box 247, Bolton, MA *01740-0247*

Leighton MASTER David Stewart (g—MRS Willem F van Vliet) . . . . Born at Minneapolis, MN Jly 26'95

Leinberger MR & MRS Christopher B (Madeleine Le M McDougal) Swth'72.SCal'74.Swth'72.H'76
☎ (505) 983-9475 . . "Las Milpas" Box 489, Tesuque, NM *87574*

Leininger MISS Linda L—Hlns'82.Nw'95.Bm.Pc.
☎ (212) 717-0604 . . 422 E 72 St, Apt 21B, New York, NY *10021*

Leininger MR Robert D—Rcp.Pc.Sar.Aht'87.Pa'93
☎ (203) 531-5658 . . 328 Pemberwick Rd, Apt 1, Greenwich, CT *06831*

Leininger MRS Robert L (Augusta Y Ulmer) Pc.Ac.
☎ (215) 242-4714 . . 206 Whitemarsh Av, Philadelphia, PA *19118*

Leiper MR & MRS Edwards F 3d (Betsy J English) Pn.P'49
  ☎ (603) 284-7785 . . ''Strathaven'' North Sandwich, NH *03259*
Leiper MR & MRS John A JR (Susan J Scott) Pa'54
  ☎ (215) 887-6229 . . 612 Willow Grove Av, Custis Woods, Glenside,
  PA *19038*
Leisenring MR & MRS Edward B (Julia du P Bissell) Pa'70.Ph.Cs.Y'49
  ☎ (610) 644-0715 . . Leopard Rd, Berwyn, PA *19312*

Leisenring MR & MRS Edward W (Maider—Lindsay	☎ (610) 408-9009
N Scott) Vt'84.Gm.Ph.U'76.Pa'88	2575 White Horse
MISS Aida F—at Brown	Rd, Berwyn, PA *19312*

Leisure MR & MRS George S JR (Joan Casey)
  CarnM'49.Ri.Chr.C.Rr.Mb.Y'48.H'51
  ☎ (912) 638-0102 . . PO Box 30221, Sea Island, GA *31561*

Leisure MR & MRS Peter K (Kathleen Blair)	☎ (212) 791-0927
Sth'54.Chr.Plg.Y'52.Va'58	608 US Courthouse,
MISS M Blair—Col'85.Y'90	40 Centre St,
MISS Kathleen K—Sth'92	New York, NY *10007*

Leitch MR & MRS Dynes L (Mochwart—Mary Jane Offutt)
  Cvc.Sl.Pn.Cent'50 . . of
  ☎ (561) 746-4473 . . 17137 Waterbend Dv, Villa 203, Jupiter, FL *33477*
  ☎ (301) 229-3813 . . 4411 Chalfont Place, Bethesda, MD *20816-1812*
Leith MR & MRS Alexander K (Eileen Bellardini) SUNY'80.D.CtCol'77
  ☎ (617) 326-3533 . . 136 Village Av, Dedham, MA *02026*
Leith MISS Anne G—Mls'83.Pa'89.Me.
  ☎ (011-33-1) 42-36-31-75 . . 2 rue Tiquetonne, 75002 Paris, France
Leith MRS Donald E (Krause—Delphis B King) Cly.Mds . . of
  ☎ (212) TE2-8421 . . 563 Park Av, New York, NY *10021*
  ☎ (516) 324-0289 . . 29 Dunemere Lane, East Hampton, NY *11937*
Leith MR & MRS R Willis (Barbara A Bell) D.Sm.Chi.Bow'50 . . of
  ☎ (617) 326-7533 . . 115 Common St, Dedham, MA *02026*
  ☎ (802) 763-7113 . . ''Mountain Meadow'' Pomfret, VT *05067*
Leith MRS Virginia B (Virginia G Bullitt) Me.
  ☎ (610) 527-6507 . . 2060 Matsons Circle, Villanova, PA *19085-1814*
Lejeune MRS Patrick A (Mary C Carleton) Scripps'49.Vh.
  ☎ (818) 799-3563 . . 1920 Edgewood Dv, South Pasadena, CA *91030*
Leland MRS Caroline C (Caroline C Cadwalader)
  see MRS H Cadwalader
Leland MR & MRS S Tudor (Phyllis Forbes) My.Myc.
  ☎ (508) 922-0176 . . 783 Hale St, Beverly Farms, MA *01915*
Leland MR & MRS Timothy (Hatfield—Julie A Stockwell)
  Mich'62.H.'60.Cl'61
  ☎ (617) 437-0748 . . 617 Tremont St, Boston, MA *02118*
Lemaitre MRS Victor A (Jean R Spencer)
  ☎ (212) TR6-4374 . . 15 E 91 St, New York, NY *10128*
Lemann MR & MRS Nicholas (Dominique Browning)
  22 Nyac Av, Pelham, NY *10803*
Lemann MR & MRS Thomas B (Barbara London) Ws'48.Hn.H'49
  ☎ (504) 891-2430 . . 6020 Garfield St, New Orleans, LA *70118*

Lembo MR & MRS Gregory L (Carole R Neri)	☎ (561) 655-1356
Man'vl'57.Evg.Geo'57	100 Royal Palm
MISS Joanne G—at 5 Quad Way, Durham, NH	Way, Palm Beach,
03824	FL *33480*
MISS Eleanor R—at Georgetown	

le Menestrel MR Charles . . see MRS H D Paxson
le Menestrel MISS Geneviève . . see MRS H D Paxson

le Menestrel MISS Marie-Adèle . . see MRS H D Paxson
Lemmon MR & MRS George B JR (Elise K Harrison)
  H'83.M.Me.Gm.Rc.H'83
  ☎ (610) 525-6218 . . 2000 Montgomery Av, Villanova, PA *19085*
Lemmon DR & MRS Mark L (Thomas—Barbara Bogy) Tex'46
  ☎ (214) 351-3177 . . 4618 Watauga Rd, Dallas, TX *75209*
Lemmon MRS Nancy O (Nancy Overton)
  4251 Westway Av, Dallas, TX *75205-3725*
Lemon MR & MRS George F JR (Zouck—Mary R B Groff) Hawaii'35
  ☎ (410) 823-7672 . . 1207 Boyce Av, Baltimore, MD *21204*
Lemon MR & MRS L Gene (Catherine D Lanier)
  Salem'63.ArizSt'95.Ill'62.Ill'64
  ☎ (602) 997-0568 . . 1136 W Butler Dv, Phoenix, AZ *85021-4428*
Leness MISS Amanda V—HRdc'89.Cl'93
  PO Box 339, Quogue, NY *11959*
Leness MR Anthony H—Ham'94 . . see D W Peck JR

Leness MR & MRS Anthony V (Beuerlein—Maureen	of ☎ (212)752-5054
F Geraty) Un.Lic.Ng.B.Csh.H.'61	30 Sutton Place,
MISS Pamela Beuerlein—Les'90	Apt 3A, New York,
MISS Sandra Beuerlein—MtVern'91	NY *10022*
MR Robert Beuerlein—BostColl'92	☎ (516) 653-4031
	23 Penniman Point
	Rd, PO Box 669,
	Quogue, NY *11959*

Leness MRS George J (Christine C Gibbs) Cly.	☎ (212) 737-1304
MR George C—D.H'58.Cl'61—at	31 E 79 St,
☎ (212) 794-9521 . . 220 E 72 St, New York,	New York, NY
NY *10021*	*10021*

Leness MR & MRS John G (Jean R Southworth)	of ☎ (212)722-8958
V'57.Ng.Lic.Cly.Cs.H.'56	1192 Park Av,
MR Thomas G—at Mich State	New York, NY
	10128
	☎ (516) 653-4661
	Penniman Point Rd,
	PO Box 192,
	Quogue, NY *11959*

Leness MISS Susan B—Mid'91 . . see D W Peck JR
Lengfeld MR Lewis F—Stan'41
  ☎ (415) 344-3191 . . 250 Woodridge Rd, Hillsborough, CA *94010*
Lennig MR Charles K JR—Sg.Cc.
  ☎ (215) 283-7368 . . 1316 Foulkeways, Sumneytown Pike, Gwynedd,
  PA *19436-1032*
Lennig MR Frederick—P'32
  ☎ (215) 639-0460 . . ''Roseneath'' Box 148, Andalusia, PA *19020*

Lennig MR & MRS Frederick III (Carol A Shertz)	☎ (610) 399-1545
Me.Cc.	PO Box 147,
MISS Anne M—☎ (610) 399-1528	Westtown, PA
MISS Leslie F—☎ (610) 399-1528	*19395*

Lennon MR & MRS Kenneth N (Catharine R Pilling) Pc.Pa'42
  ☎ (215) 233-3195 . . 8014 Flourtown Av, Wyndmoor, PA *19038*
Lennon MASTER Riggs McConnell (g—Samuel Eells JR) . . . . Born
  May 26'94

Lenos MRS Anna E (Anna E Gould) . . see A P Gould
Lenos MR Daniel E . . see A P Gould
Lenos MISS Heidi . . see A P Gould
Lenssen MRS I Mann (Isabel Mann)
  ☎ (805) 541-4221 . . PO Box 14925, San Luis Obispo, CA *93406*

Lenssen MRS Nicholas F (Edith L Barratt)
☎ (904) 439-2711 . . 2801 John Anderson H'way, Flagler Beach, FL *32136*

Lenssen MRS Nicholas F JR (Madlene C E von Glasow) . . . .
☎ (242) 322-1024
''Landfall''
Box N1709,
Nassau, Bahamas
MISS Charlotte N—Rol'87—at ☎ (561) 832-2282
322 Cranes Nest Way, West Palm Beach, FL *33401* . . . .
MR Mathias B—Clark'88—at ☎ (203) 655-0762
PO Box 26, Darien, CT *06820* . . . .

Lenssen MR & MRS Nicholas F 3d (Joan M Golaszewski)
Bryant'83.Bryant'90.Bryant'82.Bryant'86
4 Greenview Court, Johnston, RI *02919*

Lenssen MISS Sandra T—Cal'85.Rcp.
see Dilatory Domiciles

Lenssen MR & MRS William (Mary Patalak) Bow'61
☎ (904) 439-2711
2801 John Anderson
H'way, Flagler
Beach, FL *32136*
MISS Ann—ColC'92
MISS Sarah A—at Northern Ariz U . . . .
MR William A—Bow'91 . . . .

Lentz MRS Horace D (Eleanor P Murphy) . . . .
☎ (941) 649-6953
4255 Gulf Shore
Blvd N, Apt 105,
Naples, FL *34103*
MISS Barbara L (Akins—Barbara L Lentz) . . . . .

Lentz MRS Joseph S (Carry—M Trigg Waller)
☎ (602) 451-2270 . . 12000 N 90 St, Apt 1073, Scottsdale, AZ *85260*

Lentz MR Martin M—ArizSt'64
☎ (602) 943-8826 . . 10 E Butler Dv, Phoenix, AZ *85020*

Leo VERY REV & MRS James R (Patricia Y Elliman)
Sth'61.Un.Qc.StJ.Myf.Ht.Ncd.Buck'56.Gen'lTheo'62
☎ (513) 369-0944 . . 550 E 4 St, Cincinnati, OH *45202*

Leo REV & MRS Jason E (Jeanne E Folts) Buck'88
☎ (614) 885-1544 . . 695 Hartford St, Worthington, OH *43085*

Leo MR & MRS Jonathan T (Susan J Lundeen) Macalester'85.Macalester'86
see Dilatory Domiciles

Leonard MR & MRS Anthony C JR (Helen C Brumback) Van'90
☎ (407) 644-9431 . . 531 Brechin Dv, Winter Park, FL *32792*

Leonard MR Anthony N
1106—2 St, Encinitas, CA *92024*

Leonard MR & MRS Buchanan R (Joyce G Wynkoop) Wes'71
☎ (401) 295-5378 . . 24 Johnson Av, North Kingstown, RI *02852*

Leonard MR Charles R JR—Rc.Pr.H'42
☎ (516) 674-2040 . . 26 W 4 St, Locust Valley, NY *11560*

Leonard MR & MRS Craigh (Evelyn du P Irving)
Rc.Bcs.Y'65.Cl'68.Nu'78 . . . .
of ☎ (212)249-4157
955 Lexington Av,
New York, NY
10021
☎ (516) 283-8237
PO Box 39,
107 Breese Lane,
Southampton, NY
11969
MR Nicholas M . . . .
JUNIORS MISS Alix I . . . .

Leonard MISS Cynthia Elyse—PineM'74.Bvl . . .of
691 S York St, Denver, CO *80209*
☎ (508) 748-1960 . . 185 Converse Rd, Marion, MA *02738*

Leonard MR & MRS Daniel (S May Morey) Dth'24
☎ (847) 492-2928 . . 1 Calvin Circle, Apt A412, Evanston, IL *60201-1928*

Leonard MR & MRS Daniel JR (Elizabeth D Chamberlain) Myf.Ofp.Ht.Dar.Aht'57.Ch'61 . . .
☎ (603) 673-5055
21 Cricket Hill Dv,
Amherst, NH *03031*
MISS Ashley F—Wheat'87—at ☎ (630) 665-7639
11 Kensington Circle, Wheaton, IL *60187* . . . . .
MISS Elizabeth C—Bow'84.Mit'85.Sim'90—at
☎ (617) 332-7969 . . 43 Philbrick Rd,
Newton Center, MA *02159* . . . .
MR Danford C—NH'87—at ☎ (401) 782-1363
64 Beach Plum Rd, Harbour Island, Narragansett,
RI *02882* . . . .

Leonard MR & MRS Edward M (Victoria A Fay)
Cal'71.B.Bur.Sfg.Y'63.Stan'71 . . . .
☎ (415) 759-8149
87 Farnsworth Lane,
San Francisco, CA
94117
MISS Cynthia H—Ty'95 . . . .
MR Andrew W—Stan'93 . . . .

Leonard MR & MRS James G (Henning—Cavanagh —Anne Butler) Y'39
MISS Kimberly V Henning—Box 22125,
Santa Fe, NM *87502* . . . .
MR Geoffrey B Henning—at
☎ (206) 527-5369 . . 10224 Fischer Place NE,
Seattle, WA *98125* . . . .
of ☎ (212)752-4568
201 E 62 St,
New York, NY
10021
☎ (203) 245-4020
20 Kingsbridge
Way, Madison, CT
06443

Leonard MRS James H (Margot R Donald) Rcch. . .
MR John H . . . .
☎ (713) 965-0176
PO Box 56182,
Houston, TX *77256*

Leonard MRS James R (Elizabeth de Rham) . . of
☎ (860) 767-7068 . . 202 Essex Meadows, Essex, CT *06426*
☎ (508) 548-0463 . . Chappaquoit Island, West Falmouth, MA *02574*

Leonard MRS Jeanne P (Jeanne G Poett)
☎ (415) 464-0311 . . 456 Old Quarry Rd N, Larkspur, CA *94939*

Leonard MR & MRS John D (Dorothy M Hummel)
CtCol'66.Adelphi'77.Pn.P'67.H'69
☎ (011-44-171) 266-4529 . . 23 Vale Court, 28 Maida Vale, London W9 1RT, England

Leonard MISS Lindsay M
☎ (415) 927-4227 . . 36 Parkview Circle, Corte Madera, CA *94925*

Leonard MISS Margot D
☎ (503) 245-4571 . . 5003 SW Taylors Ferry Rd, Portland, OR *97219*

Leonard MR & MRS Nelson J (Phelps—Margaret Taylor) SL'48.Vh.
☎ (818) 449-1669 . . 389 California Terr, Pasadena, CA *91105*

Leonard MR Nicholas A—Rv.EmbRid'69 🏇
☎ (210) 535-4823 . . Rte 1, Box 1173, Pipe Creek, TX *78063*

Leonard MR & MRS Richard G (Patricia Dermody) Pe.Fw.Ac.Pa'34
☎ (215) 546-1766 . . 1917 Spruce St, Philadelphia, PA *19103*

Leonard MR & MRS Richard H (Lily Richardson)
Bow'78.Unn.Ub.Cyb.Colg'52.Geo'55.Cl'58
☎ (011-852-2) 524-7692 . . Hillview Apt 304, 23 MacDonnell Rd, Hong Kong

Leonard MR & MRS Richard R (Gayle K Turk) H'94.Rc.H'94
☎ (212) 427-9625 . . 111 E 88 St, New York, NY *10128*

Leonard MR & MRS Robert M (Mary M Dalzell)
Pitt'50 . . . .
MISS Nancy A . . . .
MR Gerard . . . .
☎ (201) 779-0394
44 Brantwood Place,
Clifton, NJ *07013*

Leonard MR Spencer H . . see G W Smith

Leonard MISS Stephanie—Wells'69.Nu'73
☎ (415) 331-8020 . . 24A Cazneau Av, Box 2613, Sausalito, CA *94966*

Leonards MR & MRS Thomas C JR (Barbara Baketel) ☎ (610) 644-1336
Me.Pa'48 . . . . 1308 Berwyn-Paoli
MISS Sherry K—at ☎ (610) 942-0255 Rd, Berwyn, PA
35 Ramblewood Dv, Glenmoore, PA *19343* *19312*
MR James B . . . .

Le Pelletier MR & MRS Franck (Monica Behn) . . MR absent
see W C Behn

Lerch MR & MRS Dana Thompson (Gretchen A of ☎ (610)642-6473
Young) Me.Ac.H.Cr'59 . . . . "Whispering
MR Richard Jones T—Me.Ty'94—at Winds" 526 N Rose
☎ (212) 488-8117 . . 375 South End Av, Lane, Haverford, PA
Apt 25S, New York, NY *10280* *19041*
☎ (518) 674-3217
"Lerches Birches"
Bowman Lake,
Taborton Rd,
Sand Lake, NY
12153

Lerch MR Robert Bond (Dana Thompson) . . . . Married at Wellesley, MA
Laucks MISS Elizabeth J . . . . Sep 7'96

Lerner MISS Adeline Page (Jay B) . . . . Born at
Houston, TX Feb 28'96

Lerner MR & MRS Jay B (Daphne P Seaman) Br'92.Br'90.Tex'92
☎ (713) 663-6632 . . 2712 Fenwood Rd, Houston, TX *77005*

LeRoux MR & MRS Jacques J (E Shelley Earhart) of ☎ (610)642-1592
Me.Sfh.Fw.Va'46 . . . . "Dove Lake
MR James J 3d—Me.Fw.VillaN'85.VillaN'89 . . . House" Dove Lake
Rd, Gladwyne, PA
19035
☎ (207) 633-3710
"Bay Ledge"
Boothbay Harbor,
ME *04538*

Le Roy MR & MRS G Palmer (Kyra Hawkins) ☎ (914) 234-9339
K.Bgt.Nyc.Plg.H'51 . . . . 444 Cantitoe Rd,
MISS Pamela . . . . Bedford, NY *10506*

Le Roy MRS J Livingston (Kathryn F Shepherd)
☎ (561) 737-2286 . . 2100 SW Lake Circle Dv, Boynton Beach,
FL *33426*

Le Roy MISS Kyra
☎ (617) 262-7273 . . 135 Marlborough St, Boston, MA *02116*

LeRoy MR & MRS Michael D (Kathleen A Wright) ☎ (818) 793-0206
SCal'72.Vh.SCal'70 . . . . 1260 Wentworth Av,
MISS Kathleen V . . . . Pasadena, CA *91106*
MISS Kelley M . . . .
JUNIORS MISS Lisa E . . . .
JUNIORS MISS Amanda E . . . .

Le Roy MRS Newbold (Dorothy M Woods)
☎ (860) 953-2285 . . 67 Avery Heights, Hartford, CT *06106*

Le Roy MR & MRS Newbold 3d (Nancy G Mangan) ☎ (603) 524-6554
Y'62.Y'63 . . . . 1388 Old N Main
MISS Elizabeth Everts—at U of NH . . . . St, Laconia, NH
MR Robert Otis—at 54 Brooks St, Medford, MA *03246*
02155 . . . .

Le Sauvage MR & MRS George R JR (Faith R Davies) Chr.Pa'39.Ch'47
☎ (516) PO7-1698 . . 1 Willow Dv, Port Washington, NY *11050*

Leschen MR & MRS Harry J 3d (Anne H Goddard) . . of ☎ (314)993-0227
MR H John 4th . . . . 12 Dromara Rd,
MR Elliott F—Van'94—at ☎ (615) 292-8795 St Louis, MO *63124*
2903 Belmont Blvd, Nashville, TN *37212* . . . . . ☎ (561) 234-1138
1616 S Ocean Dv,
Vero Beach, FL
32963

Lesemann MISS Elise C—Ga'90 . . see MRS E D Porcher
Lesemann MR & MRS Ellis R—SCar'94 . . see MRS E D Porcher
Lesesne MR & MRS Eugene F (Anne B Johnson) Char'ton'78.Cw.Cit'59
☎ (803) 881-3061 . . 216 Williams St Ext, Mt Pleasant, SC *29464*
Lesesne MRS Thomas P 3d (Doris A Clary) ☎ (803) 884-7076
SCar'54.Ht.Cw. . . . . 310 Bennett St,
MISS Caroline C—Char'ton'87.Ht.Ncd . . . . Mt Pleasant, SC
MR Thomas P 4th—Cw. *29464-5302*
Lesher MR Stephen H—Vt'75.Ariz'78
☎ (520) 795-4800 . . 5667 N Via Salerosa, Tucson, AZ *85715*
Leslie MRS Clarissa C (Clarissa Cady) Pr. . . . . ☎ (561) 881-0182
MISS Charlotte B—at ☎ (516) 367-7754 2516 Timber Run N,
40 Goosehill Rd, Cold Spring Harbor, NY *11724* West Palm Beach,
FL *33407*
Leslie MR & MRS George R (Smith—Catherine M McIntire)
Fic.Fiy.Cly.Dar.Ht.Ncd.
10 Longwood Dv, Apt 309, Westwood, MA *02090*
Leslie MRS James JR (Hackett—Lela L Ottley) V'57.Pr. . .of
☎ (516) 671-6698 . . 17 Matinecock Lane, Locust Valley, NY *11560*
☎ (561) 234-5684 . . 70 Paget Court, Vero Beach, FL *32963*
Leslie MR James JR—Pr.Y.'51.Y'55
☎ (516) 674-5132 . . PO Box 365, Mill Neck, NY *11765*
Leslie MR John E (Emmet—Ryan—Miriam U Paul) Sth'38.Cly.Ncd.
☎ (301) 216-5669 . . 438 Russell Av, Gaithersburg, MD *20877*
Leslie MR & MRS Seaver W (Anne C Rogers) P'78.RISD'69.RISD'71
☎ (207) 882-5037 . . Old Stone Farm, Wiscasset, ME *04578*
Lester MR & MRS Anthony M (Katrina W Williams) ☎ (203) 245-2134
MR Timothy W . . . . 55 Wyndy Brook
MR Geoffrey W . . . . Lane, Madison, CT
06443
Lester MR & MRS Robin D (Helen S Doughty) of ☎ (773)404-5956
Pep'61.Ch'66.Ch'74 . . . . 2230 N Lincoln Park
MR Robin D . . . . W, Chicago, IL
MR James R *60614*
"Trespassers W"
Old Rte 55, Pawling,
NY *12564*
Letchworth MRS Edward H JR (Jane J Jehle) G.
☎ (716) 884-6415 . . 176 Chapin P'kway, Buffalo, NY *14209*
Letchworth MR Geoffrey J JR . . . . Died at
Stuart, FL Jun 18'96
Letchworth MRS Geoffrey J JR (Margaret S Fry) . . . 1848 SE Coronado
MR Thomas F . . . . Lane, Stuart, FL
34996
Letchworth MR George C—Wms'32.H'35
☎ (704) 885-2625 . . 1 College Walk, Brevard, NC *28712*
Letson MR Walter Neil—Ox'53.Geo'57
PO Box 2026, Palm Beach, FL *33480*
Letsou MR & MRS Peter V (Felicity Harper) HRdc'85.H'83.Ch'86
☎ (703) 536-8309 . . 2125 N Huntington St, Arlington, VA *22205*

Letteron MR Edward H—Unn.Myf.Cw.Rv.Roch'55
☎ (860) 364-0757 . . PO Box 72, Cornwall Bridge, CT *06754*
Levering MRS C Rowland (Cornelia Rowland) Gv.Mv.
☎ (410) 363-0761 . . 117 Garrison Forest Rd, Owings Mills, MD *21117*

Levering MR & MRS C Tilghman (Rebecca H
Cromwell) Cw.W&M'50 . . . . | of ☎ (410)377-8461
MR C Tilghman JR—Duke'76 . . . . | 7347 Brightside Rd,
Baltimore, MD
21212
☎ (410) 822-4965
''Little Gross
Coate'' 11249 Gross
Coate Rd, Easton,
MD *21601*

Levering MR & MRS Edwin W 4th (Mary W
Hauprich) JHop'73.Gv.F&M'73 . . . . | ☎ (410) 363-7541
JUNIORS MISS Courtney W . . . . | 115 Garrison Forest
JUNIORS MR Christopher R . . . . | Rd, Owings Mills,
JUNIORS MR Whitaker K . . . . | MD *21117*

Levering MR & MRS Frederick A 3d (Brown—
Frances M Gullion) Elk.Swth'38 . . . . | ☎ (410) 825-6313
MISS Martha S—at 815 Orangedale Av, | 1713 Circle Rd,
Charlottesville, VA *22903* . . . . | Baltimore, MD
MR Frederick A 4th—at 2010 Indian Head Rd, | *21204*
Baltimore, MD *21204* . . . . |

Levering MR & MRS J P Wade (Hundley—Davis—L Louise La Montagne)
Elk.Cry.Cda.
☎ (941) 964-2585 . . PO Box 1403, Boca Grande, FL *33921*
Levick MR & MRS Dudley A JR (Lucy D Dunham) Mit'38
☎ (606) 781-5127 . . 63 W Kimberly Dv, Ft Thomas, KY *41075-1258*
Levick MISS Stephanie S—Drew'80
☎ (908) 234-0623 . . Dunwalke Farm, 1215-2 Larger Cross Rd N,
Far Hills, NJ *07931*

Levin MRS Mercedes (Mercedes B Bograd) . . . . | ☎ (212) 737-9478
MISS Rachel S . . . . | 1000 Park Av,
JUNIORS MR Peter B . . . . | New York, NY
10028-0934

Levin MR & MRS Michael B (Sally M Chapin)
H'64.Rut'67 . . . . | ☎ (860) 673-6382
MISS Emily C . . . . | 118 Fox Den Rd,
Avon, CT *06001*

Levine MR & MRS Andrew S (Julia H Mills) AmU'87.AmU'86
☎ (410) 363-3336 . . 3681 Ashley Way, Owings Mills, MD *21117*
Le Vine MR & MRS D Christopher (M Victoria McNeil) MtH'79.Rc.Pa'79
☎ (610) 527-7539 . . 506 Old Gulph Rd, Bryn Mawr, PA *19010-3642*
Levine MISS Jessica Rachel (Andrew S) . . . . Born at
Baltimore, MD Jun 5'95
Levine MISS Samantha Brooke (Andrew S) . . . . Born at
Baltimore, MD Jun 5'95
Le Viness MRS G Denmead (Hamilton—Barbara A Tulloch)
Rdc'54.Md.Dar.Hb . . .of
☎ (410) 323-8594 . . 5510 Lombardy Place, Baltimore, MD *21210*
''Beach House'' 22 Henlopen Av, Rehoboth Beach, DE *19971*

Levis MR & MRS Frederick H JR (Mercedes W
Zoller) Me.Cw.Rv.Y'50 . . . . | ☎ (610) 469-0426
MISS Lisa B—at Dallas, TX . . . . | Flowing Springs Rd,
MR Frederick Z . . . . | Birchrunville, PA
MR Christian W . . . . | *19421*

Levit MISS Alison J—Wis'90
☎ (415) 931-9472 . . 3535 Fillmore St, Apt 102, San Francisco,
CA *94123*

Levit MR & MRS William H JR (Mary E Webster) | ☎ (414) 351-6699
Gchr'66.Ncd.Y'60.H'67 . . . . | 1061 E Thorne
MISS Alexandra Bradley—at U of Wisc Madison | Lane, Fox Point, WI
MISS Laura E F—at Lake Forest Coll . . . . | *53217*
MISS Amalia E W—at U of Mich Ann Arbor . . . |
JUNIORS MR William H 3d—at St George's . . . . . |

Levy MR & MRS Eugene P (Gertrude W Cromwell) Hlns'59.Va'59
☎ (501) 663-8668 . . 5415 Sherwood Rd, Little Rock, AR *72207-5333*
Levy MR Irvin L (late Milton P) . . . . Married at Houston, TX
Schnitzer MRS Joan W (Joan Weingarten) . . . . Jun 1'96
Levy MR & MRS Irvin L (Schnitzer—Joan Weingarten) Smu'50
☎ (214) 599-9885 . . 2801 Turtle Creek Blvd, Apt 11, Dallas, TX *75219*
Lewallen DR & MRS John D (Deborah Smith)
ECar'73.NCar'82.Duke'77.WVa'84.WVa'89
☎ (919) 682-6617 . . 908 Urban Av, Durham, NC *27701*

Lewin MR & MRS John H JR (Jean T T Brown) | of ☎ (410)435-0123
Gchr'70.Elk.Mv.P'61.Md'63 . . . . | 1020 St Georges Rd,
MISS Janet T—at ☎ (415) 681-6221 | Baltimore, MD
358 Frederick St, Apt 5, San Francisco, CA | *21210*
94117 . . . . | ☎ (302) 539-1408
MR John H 3d—at ☎ (410) 563-9262 | ''Somersault''
713 S Bond St, Apt 1R, Baltimore, MD *21231* . | 36 Cove Way,
Cotton Patch Hills,
Bethany Beach, DE
19930

Lewis MR & MRS A Churchill (Marjorie A Gavin) | ☎ (617) 566-1847
Bost'74.Cvc.Mv.Stan'73 . . . . | 348 Walnut St,
JUNIORS MISS Anna . . . . | Brookline, MA
02146

Lewis MR Adam
☎ (212) 987-1161 . . 115 E 90 St, Apt 5C, New York, NY *10128*
Lewis MR & MRS Andrew A (Virginia K Boone) Swth'86.Me.Dar.Swth'85
☎ (610) 543-0836 . . 503 Walnut Lane, Swarthmore, PA *19081*
Lewis MR Andrew C . . see MISS C L Smythe
Lewis MR & MRS Andrew L 4th (Joanna P McNeil)
P.'81.Me.M.Sg.Laf'79.Pa'83
☎ (610) 658-0878 . . 214 Glenn Rd, Ardmore, PA *19003*
Lewis MR & MRS Arthur L 2d (Ellen B Gibbs) Rich'80.D.Nh.Vt'75
☎ (508) 359-8825 . . 329 North St, Medfield, MA *02052*
Lewis MR & MRS Burton O JR (Dorothy L Crane) Ws'50.USA'45
☎ (202) 362-0787 . . 3714 Corey Place NW, Washington, DC *20016*
Lewis MRS Carolyn C (Carolyn I Coble) . . . . | ☎ (212) 753-7093
JUNIORS MR Warner M—at Trinity . . . . | 200 E 66 St,
JUNIORS MR John F—at Choate Rosemary . . . . . . | New York, NY
10021

Lewis MISS Catherine T . . see MRS E Auchincloss
Lewis MRS Charles W (I Maria Bonzi) Cly.Cda.
☎ (203) 259-5031 . . 1081 Redding Rd, Fairfield, CT *06430*
Lewis MR Charles W JR—Hn.
1081 Redding Rd, Fairfield, CT *06430*
Lewis MR Christopher F . . see MRS P J Wheaton
Lewis MRS Clarence J JR (Georgiana C Wetherill) Me.Ac.Sdg.Sl.Ncd.
☎ (610) 642-2957 . . 526 New Gulph Rd, Haverford, PA *19041*

Lewis MR & MRS Clifford 3d (Pitz—Mary W Wood)
PhilaArt'35.Ph.Fi.R.Cspa.Rv.Cw.Cc.Wt.Pa'28
☎ (215) 836-2595 . . 2008 Hilltop Rd, Flourtown, PA *19031*
Lewis MR & MRS Craig (Katherine Hunner) Elk.Md.P'52
☎ (410) 828-1637 . . 1000 Rolandvue Rd, Baltimore, MD *21204*
Lewis MR & MRS David P (Leslie A Flail) Duke'94.Dth'90.Duke'94
see Dilatory Domiciles
Lewis MRS David W (Rebecca Perry) D.Hn. . . . . . . | ☎ (508) 785-0217
   MISS Joan P . . . . | 1 Pegan Lane,
    | Dover, MA *02030*
Lewis MR David W JR—Nh.Sm.H'65.Geo'68
☎ (508) 785-1346 . . 28 Farm St, Dover, MA *02030*
Lewis MRS Davies (Maryon L Davies) Bur.
☎ (415) 567-5776 . . 2900 Broadway St, San Francisco, CA *94115*
Lewis MR & MRS Davis L (L Eugenie Harshbarger)
Swth'33.Cw.Cspa.W.Swth'32
☎ (302) 239-6553 . . Cokesbury Village 710, 726 Loveville Rd,
Hockessin, DE *19707*
Lewis MISS Diana J . . see MRS P J Wheaton
Lewis MRS E Mower 3d (Mary E Pilling) . . . . | ☎ (215) 242-2846
   MR Ross . . . . | 23 Station Lane,
    | Philadelphia, PA
    | *19118*
Lewis MR & MRS Edward D (Elvira Bonaccorsi | ☎ (610) 649-0122
di Patti) Pa'51 . . . . | 942 Youngsford Rd,
   MISS Domenica L . . . . | Gladwyne, PA
    | *19035*
Lewis MISS Emily A . . see MRS E Auchincloss
Lewis MRS Francis A (Willcox—Joyce L Cochrane) | ☎ (610) NI4-0380
Gm.Ac.Ncd.W.Lm. . . . . | "Nannau"
   MISS Louisa L Willcox—at ☎ (406) 222-1485 | 744 Providence Rd,
   Rte 38, Box 2013, Livingston, MT *59047* . . . | RD 2, Malvern, PA
    | *19355*
Lewis MR Frederick W 3d—NCar'86
☎ (910) 799-2640 . . 2032 Albert Circle, Wilmington, NC *28403*
Lewis MRS Geoffrey W (Elizabeth M Locke) Sth'34.Chi . . . of
☎ (207) 354-6670 . . Rte 68, Box 104, Cushing, ME *04563*
☎ (617) 275-9811 . . 56 Dartmouth Court, Bedford, MA *01730*
Lewis MR George P . . see MRS E Auchincloss
Lewis MR & MRS George R (Carolyn Cantwell) | ☎ (214) 526-6551
Tex'60.Cvc.P'59.H'61 . . . . | 3604 Princeton St,
   MISS Dorothy . . . . | Dallas, TX *75205*
   MR James . . . . |
Lewis MR & MRS Griffith E (Anne M Kiernan) CtCol'85.Bab'85
☎ (518) 436-5960 . . 19 Wildwood Dv, Loudonville, NY *12211*
Lewis MR & MRS H H Walker (Eleanor R Nelson) V'36.P'25.H'28
☎ (410) 243-7371 . . 822 W 40 St, Baltimore, MD *21211*
Lewis MR & MRS H Hunter (Elizabeth Sidamon-Eristoff)
Y'83.Mt.K.Ub.H'69
☎ (804) 973-9003 . . Trearne Farm, 6747 Blackwells Hollow Rd, Crozet,
VA *22932*
Lewis MRS Henry 3d (Meyer—Georgie Williams) Msq.Pr.Mb.Cly.
☎ (516) 674-3538 . . 3 Cherrywood Rd, Locust Valley, NY *11560*

Lewis MR & MRS Howard H (Maxine M | ☎ (610) 687-0850
de Schauensee) BMr'58.Srr.Ph.Ac.H'56. | 120 S Devon Av,
JHop'58.H'62 . . . . | Devon, PA *19333*
   MR J Rodolphe M de S—Cr'88 . . . . |
   MR Howard H JR—Syr'91 |
Lewis MR & MRS J Curtis JR (Nancy Nelson) Ga'48
☎ (912) 598-0271 . . 502 McWhorter Dv, Savannah, GA *31411*
Lewis MR & MRS J Curtis 3d (Carol S Smith) Emory'79.Ga'74.Ga'75.Ga'78
see Dilatory Domiciles
Lewis DR & MRS J Eugene (Elizabeth B McKee)
V'47.H'51.Rv.Dar.Ncd.Mo'38.H'42 . . of
☎ (314) 726-0658 . . 625 S Skinker Blvd, St Louis, MO *63105*
☎ (203) 272-5741 . . "Brooks Homestead" 532 S Brooksvale Rd,
Cheshire, CT *06410*
Lewis MR & MRS J Sheldon (Mary A Hildebrand) Elmira'45.NCar'45
☎ (203) 966-1527 . . 36 Sunrise Av, New Canaan, CT *06840*
Lewis MR & MRS James E 3d (Kenna M Bratcher) WmJewel'79.Lawr'73
☎ (816) 941-3811 . . 11600 Pennsylvania Av, Kansas City, MO *64114*
Lewis MISS Jennifer T . . see MISS C L Smythe
Lewis MISS Joan K
☎ (703) 533-0255 . . 5901 N 10 Rd, Arlington, VA *22205*
Lewis MRS John B (Cuyler—Margery P Merrill) . . of
☎ (609) 924-3075 . . 13 Edgehill St, Princeton, NJ *08540*
☎ (609) 426-6127 . . Meadow Lakes 17-11L, Hightstown, NJ *08520*
Lewis MR & MRS John B JR (Kirsten N Hansen) | ☎ (011-44-171)
Rcn.P'57 . . . . | 352-0236
   MR David L—Ham'91—at 1377 Lexington Av, | 57 Glebe Place,
   Apt 2B, New York, NY *10128* . . . . | London SW3 5JB,
    | England
Lewis MR John G JR—Br'64 . . . . | ☎ (802) 234-6600
   MR Barrett H . . . . | North Rd
    | Schoolhouse,
    | PO Box 235,
    | Barnard, VT *05031*
Lewis MR & MRS John H (Harding—Joan Harding) D.Nh.H.'40
10 Longwood Dv, Apt 222, Westwood, MA *02090*
Lewis MR & MRS John Van D (Faith Greenfield) | of ☎ (011-33)
BMr'70.CathU'83.Cvc.Sl.Cl'69.Y'79 . . . . | 96-92-92-16
   MISS Mathilde G . . . . | Manoir de Pors Ker
   MISS Eleanore F . . . . | Derrien, sur les
   JUNIORS MR Samuel Van D . . . . | quais, Place General
    | De Gaulle, Tréguier,
    | 22220 Côtes
    | d'Armor, France
    | ☎ (202) 829-0503
    | 4511—17 St NW,
    | Washington, DC
    | *20011*
Lewis MR & MRS Joseph W (Anne C Beech) Stan'41.Vh.CalTech'41 . . of
☎ (909) 624-5965 . . 941 W Bonita Av, Claremont, CA *91711-4193*
☎ (619) 756-1828 . . 7021 Las Colinas Rd, Rancho Santa Fe, CA *92067*
Lewis MR Julius—Rc.Cas.Yn.Ch'50
☎ (312) 337-1747 . . 1524 N Dearborn P'kway, Chicago, IL *60610*

Lewis MRS Mary Hope (Ford—Mary Hope Lewis)
Ws'50.Au.Cly.Cda. . . . . | ☎ (203) 869-4588
   MISS Mariah Hope Ford—Champ'88 . . . . | "Meadowbrook"
   MR F Richards Ford 4th—Ithaca'79—at | 72 Doubling Rd,
   428 N Orange Grove Av, Los Angeles, | Greenwich, CT
   CA 90036 . . . . | 06830

Lewis MISS Mary Key—Ncd.
   ☎ (804) 262-2877 . . 1711 Bellevue Av, Apt D1018, Richmond,
VA 23227

Lewis MR Millard JR
   ☎ (214) 526-6551 . . 3604 Princeton St, Dallas, TX 75205

Lewis MR & MRS Ogden Northrop (Adams—Susan S | of ☎ (212)794-2306
   High) NCar'65.Rc.Plg.Cly.H'65.Ox'67.H'73 . . . | 955 Lexington Av,
   JUNIORS MR Ogden N JR . . . . | New York, NY
    | 10021
    | ☎ (516) 653-4665
    | PO Box 798,
    | 21 Ocean Av,
    | Quogue, NY 11959

Lewis MR & MRS Orme JR (Elizabeth Bruening) V'63.Geo'74.Mt.Ariz'58
   ☎ (602) 840-6497 . . 4325 E Palo Verde Dv, Phoenix, AZ 85018-1127

Lewis MR & MRS Perry (Kerr—Elizabeth Wright) | ☎ (508) 842-8112
   Il.Pa'65 . . . . | 7 Eastwood Rd,
   MISS Elizabeth Story—at ☎ (401) 272-2914 | Shrewsbury, MA
   56 Ivy St, Providence, RI 02906 . . . . | 01545
      MISS Marion F Kerr—at Wrightsville Beach,
   NC 28480 . . . .

Lewis MR & MRS R Brian (Sarah M Wood) Rdc'73.SimonF'70
   ☎ (604) 731-0782 . . 2724 W Fourteenth Av, Vancouver, BC V6K 2X2,
Canada

Lewis MRS R Warner (Rosalind B Warner) | ☎ (207) 244-0005
   Ncd.Myf. . . . . | Oak Hill Rd,
   MISS Molly MacK—at New York, NY . . . . | Somesville, ME
    | 04660

Lewis MR & MRS Ralph D (Virginia O Gates) Skd'80 . . of
   ☎ (415) 566-9282 . . 88 Ashbury Terr, San Francisco, CA 94117
   ☎ (212) 736-6972 . . 335 W 38 St, New York, NY 10018

Lewis MR Raymond P
   see Dilatory Domiciles

Lewis MR & MRS Robert D 2d (Mathews—Maryan O | ☎ (561) 220-1733
   Adams) . . . . Rcsl. | 5411 SW Turtle
   MISS Patricia A Mathews—at | Shell Way,
   ☎ (510) 881-4776 . . 5299 Proctor Rd, | Palm City, FL
   Castro Valley, CA 94546 . . . . | 34990
      MR Thomas A Mathews—at
   ☎ (210) 690-1418 . . 11707 Vance Jackson Rd,
   Apt 509, San Antonio, TX 78230 . . . .

Lewis MR & MRS Ronald B (Anne McCutcheon) | ☎ (202) 333-4388
   Rdc'65.H'62 . . . . | 3400 Reservoir Rd
   MR Matthew Van D—at Harvard . . . . | NW, Washington,
   JUNIORS MR Oliver McC—at Harvard . . . . | DC 20007

Lewis MISS S Tyler—RI'89
   ☎ (401) 274-8412 . . 21 Russo St, Apt 2R, Providence, RI 02504

Lewis MR & MRS Stanley P (Julia N Beals) | ☎ (203) 259-0730
   V'52.Ihy.Cly.Myf.Br'47 . . . . | 1252 Pequot Av,
   MISS Julia P—Ham'77—at ☎ (212) 289-5810 | Southport, CT 06490
   51 E 90 St, New York, NY 10128 . . . .
   MR Douglas B—StLaw'86 . . . .

Lewis MRS Stuart A (Elizabeth R Fankhauser) | ☎ (202) 363-9225
   Cal'43.Cvc. . . . . | 5035 Lowell St NW,
   MISS Mary Margaret—at 2984 Clay St, | Washington, DC
   San Francisco, CA 94115 . . . . | 20016

Lewis MRS William (Victoria Potter)
   Kimball Farms 118, 235 Walker St, Lenox, MA 01240

Lewis MR William Draper—Ne.P'26
   ☎ (215) 699-0396 . . Normandy Farms Estates, Apt D208, Box 1108,
Blue Bell, PA 19422

Lewis MR & MRS Winslow JR (Thompson—Lucina H | ☎ (609) 924-2309
   Johnson) Rcp.Ph.Pn.P'59 . . . . | 641 Princeton-
   JUNIORS MR Winslow 3d—at Hun . . . . | Lawrenceville Rd,
    | Princeton, NJ 08540

Lewisohn MISS (DR) Marjorie G—Mich'40.JHop'44.Cs.
   ☎ (212) 427-8340 . . 15 E 91 St, New York, NY 10128-0648

Lex MR & MRS John B (Sherri A Broderick) Me.Ds.Lm.Rv.
   ☎ (610) 524-5363 . . 263 Monmouth Terr, West Chester, PA 19380

Lex MR & MRS William B JR (Mary Lee Hillhouse)
   Me.R.Rv.Sdg.Ds.Cc.Ncd.Lm.Y . . .of
   ☎ (610) 527-0134 . . 840 Montgomery Av, Apt 805, Bryn Mawr,
   PA 19010
   ☎ (561) 272-0934 . . 122 Andrews Av, Delray Beach, FL 33483

Leydon MRS E Yerger (Elizabeth D Yerger) Me.Ac.
   ☎ (610) 642-4903 . . 137 Rose Lane, Haverford, PA 19041

Leys MR & MRS Dirck F (Osborn—Mary E Wilson) | ☎ (518) 734-3414
   Cl'49 . . . . | Back-A-Bit Farm,
   MISS Lida E O . . . . | PO Box 952,
    | Windham, NY
    | 12496

Libby MRS Scott L JR (Eleanor I Waddell)
   ☎ (602) 991-5127 . . 110 Mountain Shadows W, 5525 E Lincoln Dv,
Paradise Valley, AZ 85253

Lichty MR & MRS Roger H (Priscilla B Ripley) | ☎ (303) 394-4685
   DU'72.Myf.Dar.P'67.Col'70 . . . . | 15 Elm St, Denver,
   JUNIORS MISS Elizabeth R—Myf . . . . | CO 80220

LickDyke MR & MRS Jay C (Nagle—Priscilla Cunningham)
   Sth'58.Ec.Cs.StBona'58 . .of
   ☎ (212) 535-0838 . . 200 E 72 St, Apt 34K, New York, NY 10021
   ☎ (516) 283-5009 . . "Beekhaven" 40 Oakhurst Rd, Hampton Bays,
   NY 11946

Lickle MR Garrison duP—Rr.BtP.Rol'76.Rich'80
   ☎ (561) 833-7111 . . 400 S Ocean Blvd, Apt 209E, Palm Beach,
FL 33480

Lickle MR & MRS William C (Renee C Kitchell)
   Srr.Wil.Evg.BtP.Sar.Cw.Va'51.Va'53 . . of
   ☎ (561) 655-0919 . . 568 Island Dv, Palm Beach, FL 33480
   ☎ (302) 652-5457 . . 300 Rockland Rd, Montchanin, DE 19710
   ☎ (212) 879-3900 . . 1 E 66 St, Apt 10A, New York, NY 10021

Liddell MR & MRS D Roger B (Florence J Wofford) | ☎ (212) 988-0220
   Un.Bm.Snc.Ll.Lm.Cw.P'67 . . . . | 520 E 86 St,
   MISS Alice E E—at Bowdoin . . . . | New York, NY
   JUNIORS MR Torrey B W—at Hotchkiss . . . . | 10028-7534

Liddell MR & MRS Donald M JR (Jane Hawley Hawkes)
Sth'31.Un.Chr.Plg.Coa.Ll.Cw.Fw.Rv.
Lm.StJ.Ht.Bm.Cly.Ncd.Cda.Dc.Dh.P'28
☎ (212) BU8-9608 . . 930 Park Av, New York, NY *10028*

Lidgerwood MR & MRS William van V (King—Harriet L Barney) Hn.H'39
☎ (860) 677-1429 . . 25 Mountain Spring Rd, Farmington, CT *06032*

Liebau MR F Jack JR—Vh.Stan'85 . . of
☎ (818) 821-9859 . . 1014 Fairview Av, Apt 5, Arcadia, CA *91007*
☎ (619) 755-5067 . . 2929 Camino Del Mar, Apt 20, Del Mar, CA *92014*

Lieber MRS Francis (Hagar—Elizabeth A Greer) . . of
Bentley Village, 426 Bentley Dv, Naples, FL *34110*
☎ (215) 646-2083 . . Whitpain Farm, 12 Hounds Run Lane, Blue Bell, PA *19422*

Liebolt MR & MRS Frederick Lee JR (Suzanne L Lloyd)
Un.Plg.B.Snc.Cly.Pa'63.NCar'66
☎ (212) 369-8067 . . 115 E 90 St, New York, NY *10128*

Ligamari MR & MRS Anthony B (Robinette—Juana M Schurman)
Hampshire'77
☎ (415) 921-0657 . . 1717 Green St, San Francisco, CA *94123*

Ligget MISS Frances C—VPI'76 . . see MRS R D Torrey

Ligget MR & MRS Robert C (Joy T Morris) | ☎ (801) 968-8620
Utah'81.Rv.GeoW'75 . . . . | 4293 Tidwell St,
JUNIORS MISS Amy J . . . . | Salt Lake City, UT
| *84118*

Liggett MRS Alexander C (Priscilla W Watson) Cvc.Sl.Ncd.
☎ (202) 332-9517 . . 2339 Massachusetts Av NW, Washington, DC *20008*

Liggett MR & MRS Alexander P (Kimberly L Knapp) Fla'87.Clem'87
see Dilatory Domiciles

Liggett MRS Alexander W (Jane P Bowers) | ☎ (813) 251-4443
Cly.Myf.Ht.Ncd . . . . | 2419 Bayshore Blvd,
MR Ambler W—at ☎ (305) 861-5859 | Tampa, FL *33629*
233 Sunny Isles Blvd, North Miami Beach, FL
33160 . . . . |

Liggett MR & MRS David K (M Ellen Harris) WCar'88.NCar'88
☎ (919) 782-3412 . . 2504 Beechridge Rd, Raleigh, NC *27608*

Liggett MR & MRS Frank R 3d (Mildred L Le Blond)
Cm.NCar'61.NCar'63.NCar'66
☎ (919) 782-0094 . . 1917 Lewis Circle, Raleigh, NC *27608*

Liggett MR & MRS Frank R 4th (Kimberly A Maultsby) NCar'86
☎ (401) 351-8046 . . 259 Williams St, Providence, RI *02906*

Liggett MASTER Frank Rahm 5th (Frank R 4th) . . . . Born at
Providence, RI Apr 25'96

Liggett MR & MRS Hiram S JR (Margaret M | ☎ (314) 532-1404
McGinness) Mar'vil'61.Wash'72.Wash'77.Str. | 64 Chesterfield
ColC'53 . . . . | Lakes Rd,
MISS Lucille G—at 832 Queen Anne Place, | Chesterfield, MO
St Louis, MO *63122* . . . . | *63005*
MISS Frances S . . . . |

Liggett MRS Keith S (Shirley I Phillips) Bvr'83
☎ (215) 542-2328 . . 552 Grouse Court, Blue Bell, PA *19422*

Liggett MR Keith S—Penn'77.Bvr'83 . . . . | ☎ (215) 279-1826
JUNIORS MISS Jaclyn M . . . . | 1147 McKelvey
JUNIORS MR Glendon S . . . . | Lane, Blue Bell, PA
| *19422*

Liggett MR & MRS Kevin L (Rodica I Mihalea) Bucha'73.Mich'72.Temp'77
321 Ashbourne Rd, Elkins Park, PA *19117*

Liggett MISS Louise H—NCarSt'92
☎ (919) 834-7371 . . 1611 Sutton Rd, Raleigh, NC *27605*

Liggett MISS Ruth Le Blond (David K) . . . . Born at
Raleigh, NC Mch 15'96

Liggett MR & MRS Thomas 3d (Eleanor B Dustin) Leh'34
☎ (215) 886-2321 . . Rydal Park 302, The Fairway, Rydal, PA *19046*

Light MR & MRS J Thomas (Irene du Pont) Y'63
☎ (860) 435-2752 . . 94 White Hollow Rd, Lakeville, CT *06039*

Light MR & MRS Richard B JR (Deborah S Franklin) | ☎ (610) 687-2619
StAndr'68.Me.Fst.Nf.Ds.Ac.StAndr'68 . . . . | 173 Ladderback
MISS Ashley W F . . . . | Lane, Devon, PA
| *19333*

Lightfoot MRS Richard W 3d (Carolyn I Gleaves) | ☎ (334) 262-7008
Aub'54.Dar . . . . | 3362 Walton Dv,
MISS Martha A—at 1217 Druid Oaks Dv NE, | Montgomery, AL
Atlanta, GA *30329* . . . . | *36111*

Lihme MR Edward H—Va'34
☎ (561) 283-3351 . . 2045 SE St Lucie Blvd, Stuart, FL *34996*

Lihme MISS Heidi L—LIU'37
☎ (516) 686-2216 . . PO Box 95, East Norwich, NY *11732*

Likins MR & MRS Robert C (Hayne—Anna Walcott)
Tcy.Ncd.SanDiegoSt'56
☎ (541) 857-6683 . . 1323 Peartree Lane, Medford, OR *97504*

Lilien MR & MRS Robert D (Georgiana W Lewis) Un.Chr.Cs.Ncd.P'48
☎ (212) 876-0733 . . 70 E 96 St, Apt 3B, New York, NY *10128-0745*

Lilienthal MR & MRS John G (June Roberts) | of ☎ (415)221-7322
Bhm.Pcu.Cp.Stan'50 . . . . | 3903 Washington St,
MISS Brett A—SCal'88 . . . . | San Francisco, CA
MR Christopher R—SCal'89 . . . . | *94118*
| ☎ (415) 868-2404
| 197 Seadrift Rd,
| Stinson Beach, CA
| *94970*

Lillard MR & MRS John S (Paula L Polk) | ☎ (847) 295-2098
Sth'53.Xav'70.On.Cm.Tvcl.Va'52.Xav'64 . . . . . | 1300 N Waukegan
MISS Pamela P—at Los Angeles, CA . . . . | Rd, Lake Forest, IL
MISS Angeline S—at San Francisco, CA . . . . . . | *60045*
MISS Paula P . . . . |

Lillard MRS Margarita F (Margarita Fuller) Mass'47
☎ (513) 831-4425 . . 714 Yale Av, Terrace Park, OH *45174*

Lilley MRS Genevieve G (Abberley—Genevieve G Caldecutt)
1000 Vicar's Landing Way, Ponte Vedra Beach, FL *32082*

Lilley MISS Madeline—Colg'89 . . see A E Newbold 4th

Lilley MISS Sarah W—Cal'88 . . see A E Newbold 4th

Lilley MR & MRS William 3d (Eve La G | ☎ (202) 966-5371
Auchincloss) Me.Cvc.Cos.Mt.Ri.Cly.Pa'59.Y'61. | 4941 Glenbrook Rd
Y'65 . . . . | NW, Washington,
MR Buchanan M—Leh'82—at Dartmouth . . . . . | DC *20016*
MR Justin W—Ty'86—at London Sch of Econ . . |

Lilly DR & MRS Douglas R (Ann W Rubicam) Cy.P'52
☎ (314) 997-7437 . . 9540 Clayton Rd, St Louis, MO *63124*

Limberg MR & MRS Charles F (Suzanne Shapleigh) Cy.P'39
☎ (314) 721-1708 . . 200 S Brentwood Blvd, Apt 17D, Clayton, MO *63105*

Limberg MR & MRS Edward A (Sarah B Perry) Rcsl.P'37
☎ (941) 465-3666 . . 140 Eventide Av, Lake Placid, FL *33852*

Limbocker MR & MRS Derek L (Nicole du Pont) ☎ (212) 794-2525
B.Srb.BtP.Ny.Ncd.Y'62 . . . . 925 Park Av,
MISS N Ridgely . . . . New York, NY
10028

Limbocker MR & MRS John JR (Ritter—Wilson—Rosen—
Cynthia N M Blyth) Cv.It.Tv.Y'55
☎ (216) 721-4188 . . 12407 Fairhill Rd, Cleveland, OH *44120*

Limpert MRS John H JR (Michelle Van der Leur) . . ☎ (718) 601-7589
MISS Alexandra Michelle—at ☎ (718) 387-9126 2475 Palisade Av,
63 S 3 St, Brooklyn, NY *11211* . . . . Apt 5D, Bronx, NY
MR John H 3d—Cl'91—at ☎ (212) 539-1472 *10463*
315 E 12 St, New York, NY *10003* . . . .

Limpert MR John H JR—H'55
☎ (908) 753-7289 . . 1111 Park Av, Plainfield, NJ *07060*

Lincoln MR Alexander JR—H'32
☎ (603) 528-4064 . . 4 Ledgecroft Place, Laconia, NH *03246*

Lincoln MR & MRS Alexander 3d (Isabel F Ross)
DU'69.Myf.Ofp.Ncd.DU'67
☎ (303) 399-3238 . . 121 S Dexter St, Denver, CO *80222*

Lincoln MRS B Larsen (Barbara B Larsen) Skd'57
☎ (617) 277-8099 . . 132 Middlesex Rd, Chestnut Hill, MA *02167*

Lincoln MRS B Tyler (Bell—B Tyler Lincoln) ☎ (610) 376-1220
NCar'69.VillaN'88.Ncd. . . . . 1315 Parkside Dv N,
MISS Mary-Knight T Bell—at U of Fla . . . . . Wyomissing, PA
JUNIORS MISS Barbara L Bell *19610*
JUNIORS MR C Branson Bell 3d . . . .

Lincoln MRS Carolyn R (Carolyn T Ream) . . of
☎ (203) 869-5733 . . 351 Round Hill Rd, Greenwich, CT *06831*
☎ (212) 838-0800 . . 825 Fifth Av, New York, NY *10021*

Lincoln MR & MRS Daniel W (Katherine K Kruesi) Sth'78.Ty'76.Pa'79
☎ (908) 204-0088 . . 150 Seney Dv, Bernardsville, NJ *07924*

Lincoln MR & MRS Edmond L (Pamela Wick) ☎ (212) 472-2665
Gr.Wil.H'71.H'74 . . . . 161 E 79 St,
JUNIORS MISS Lucy A . . . . New York, NY
JUNIORS MISS Emily L *10021*

Lincoln MR & MRS George J 3d (Nelly J Keffer)
BMr'48.Me.M.Pe.Sa.Ll.Rv.Cspa.Cw.Y'48
☎ (610) LA5-3655 . . 1428 Old Gulph Rd, Villanova, PA *19085*

Lincoln MR & MRS Gilbert (Le Boutillier—Polly Kinnear) . . of
☎ (860) 232-8522 . . 30 Braintree Dv, West Hartford, CT *06117*
☎ (860) 739-6315 . . Old Black Point, Niantic, CT *06357*

Lincoln MR & MRS J Alden (Elaine E Fairman) ☎ (508) 887-2214
Y'58.Pa'63 . . . . Sprucewood Circle,
MISS Lista A . . . . Boxford, MA *01921*
MR Stephen E . . . .
MR Benjamin B . . . .

Lincoln MR John J JR . . . . Died Apr 8'96

Lincoln MRS John J JR (Jean G Wise) Sth'25
☎ (803) 686-4960 . . 300 Woodhaven Dv, Apt 3402,
Hilton Head Island, SC *29928*

Lincoln MRS L W Thompson (Strickland—Barbara B Tyler) M.Ac.Ncd.
☎ (610) 645-8993 . . 1400 Waverly Rd, Andrews 317, Gladwyne,
PA *19035*

Lincoln MR & MRS L W Thompson JR (Bonnie J ☎ (508) 385-6133
Beggs) Roch'72.M.Me.Rv.Roch'72 . . . . 273 Cranview Rd,
JUNIORS MISS Jean T . . . . Brewster, MA *02631*
JUNIORS MR L W Thompson 3d . . . .

Lincoln MR & MRS Richard K (Roberts—Margaret ☎ (617) 547-8035
M Simonds) Wheat'64.Ub.Cw.Ncd.H'53 . . . . . 59 Fresh Pond Lane,
MISS Caroline G P Roberts—Br'94.Ncd.— Cambridge, MA
at ☎ (212) 780-9208 . . 213 E 15 St, Apt 5, *02138-4644*
New York, NY *10003* . . . .
MR Nathaniel P Roberts—Cal'94 . . . .

Lincoln DR & MRS Thomas L (Catherine ☎ (310) 828-2174
de La Prée) Cos.Y'51.Y'60 . . . . 802 Franklin St,
MISS Elizabeth C . . . . Santa Monica, CA
MISS Iris S—CalSt'89 . . . . *90403*
MR John L—Cal'91 . . . .

Lind MR & MRS Albert W (Sterling—Mueller—Virginia Lee Roberts Boyce)
So.BtP.Ncd.H'29.H'31
☎ (561) 655-1573 . . 231 Chilean Av, Palm Beach, FL *33480*

Lind MR & MRS Gerard G (Carolyn C Rittenour) ☎ (561) 655-4004
Unn.Evg.Mds.BtP.Cly.Cda.Bab'62 . . . . 149 Via Palma,
MISS Elizabeth L—B'gton'91 . . . . Palm Beach, FL
MISS Alexandra G—MtVern'92 . . . . *33480*

Lind MR & MRS H Robert (Lorna T Jaques) ☎ (561) 229-2131
Cal'67.Pa'68 . . . . 9550 S Ocean Dv,
MISS Cameron M—at 11 Thomas Park, Apt 6, Apt 905,
Boston, MA *02127* . . . . Jensen Beach, FL
MR Jamieson C *34957*
MR Adam T . . . .

Lind MR & MRS Jon R (Jane P Langfitt) ☎ (847) 446-3105
Wells'57.Ih.H'57.H'60 . . . . 644 Walden Rd,
MISS Susan P . . . . Winnetka, IL *60093*

Lindblad MRS Elizabeth T (Abbott—Elizabeth L ☎ (212) 722-2559
Tysen) Cl'84 . . . . 27 E 95 St,
JUNIORS MR Justin T—at St George's . . . . New York, NY
10128

Lindburg MR & MRS A Clinton (Carol T Hughes)
☎ (314) 994-7575 . . 75 Randelay Dv, St Louis, MO *63124*

Linden MRS Carvel C (Jones—Oakes—Knight— ☎ (305) 866-2476
Mary Sue McCulloch) Dar.Ht. . . . . 17 Indian Creek
MISS Daphne V N Oakes—at Island, Surfside, FL
161 Camden Dv, Bal Harbour, FL *33154* *33154*

Linder MR Brian W . . see D J Masoner

Linder MR Charles K . . see D J Masoner

Linder MRS Fay M—Tufts'49.Penn'56
☎ (909) 626-1986 . . 619 Alden Rd, Claremont, CA *91711*

Linderman MR & MRS Robert P 3d (Greeff—Arrel of ☎ (617)267-4569
Parson) Cy.Sm.P'52 . . . . 301 Berkeley St,
MISS Nicole F S . . . . Boston, MA *02116*
☎ (508) 283-8632
''Head of the Cove''
4 Lane Rd,
Annisquam, MA
01930

Lindgren MR & MRS Robert K (Victoria T Cleveland) Ty'89.Cvc.Cly.Ty'88
☎ (212) 861-0529 . . 150 E 73 St, New York, NY *10021*

Lindh MR & MRS David E P (Lynda Yost) ☎ (817) 665-5030
Unn.Nrr.Srb.BtP.Snc.Cw.Ht.Ne.Cly.Cda.Y'54 . . Sycamore Creek
MR Kenneth M P—Ht.Smu'93 . . . . Ranch, Box 678,
Gainesville, TX
76241

Lindh MR & MRS Henry C B (Kathleen Davis)
Stan'54.Unn.Snc.Cw.Ne.Ht.Y'52.Cl'54 . . . .
MISS Jennifer D—at 3490 Scott St, Apt 306,
San Francisco, CA *94123* . . . .
MR Andrew S P—Hart'93—at ☎ (860) 231-7703
32 Lorraine St, Hartford, CT *06105* . . . . |
☎ (203) 869-8669
North Rock Ridge,
Greenwich, CT
06831

Lindley MRS Daniel A (Marion Miller)
☎ (860) 739-5277 . . 235 Old Black Point Rd, Niantic, CT *06357*

Lindley MR & MRS Daniel A JR (Lucia W Woods)
Swb'59.C.Y'55.H'59.FlaSt'70 . . of
☎ (847) 864-9283 . . 1217 Ridge Av, Evanston, IL *60202*
☎ (212) 477-1822 . . 45 Gramercy Park N, New York, NY *10010*

Lindley MR & MRS Daniel F (Sydney C Lickle)
Wil.Cw.Cda.Wms'72.Va'75 . . . .
MR Peyton F—at U of Va . . . .
JUNIORS MISS Blair C . . . .
JUNIORS MR Hunter duP—at U of Del . . . . |
☎ (302) 656-1463
10 Pheasants Ridge,
Centerville, DE
19807

Lindon MR & MRS Christopher A (Diana B Gaston) Wheat'83.Prov'81
☎ (203) 255-1684 . . 69 Parkway, Fairfield, CT *06430*

Lindsay MR & MRS Alvin F (Jameson—Webster—Helen V Kiendl)
Srr.Cly.Dc.Ncd.Mo'43
☎ (305) 864-5903 . . 6645 Pinetree Lane, Miami Beach, FL *33141*

Lindsay MR & MRS Alvin F III (Mayra Peña)
Aht'87.UMiami'92.SCal'83.UMiami'91
☎ (305) 361-8669 . . 177 Ocean Lane Dv, Apt 202, Key Biscayne,
FL *33149*

Lindsay MRS George N (Mary S Dickey) . . of
☎ (212) 593-0634 . . 16 Sutton Place, New York, NY *10022*
☎ (516) 692-7388 . . PO Box 1462, Laurel Hollow, Syosset, NY *11791*

Lindsay MR & MRS John V (Mary A Harrison)
V'47.C.StA.StJ.Y'44.Y'48 . . . .
MISS Anne R—at 33-2 Joshua Lane, Lyme, CT
06371 . . . . |
of 215 E 68 St,
New York, NY
10021
"Highlands" Box
233, Joshuatown Rd,
Lyme, CT *06371*

Lindsay MR & MRS Robert D (Teresa T Elms)
Stan'78.Pr.Wk.Ln.Mb.Cly.H.'78
☎ (516) 671-9795 . . 322 Duck Pond Rd, Locust Valley, NY *11560*

Lindsay MR & MRS Robert V (Nancy A Dalley) Ln.Wk.L.Plg.Cs.Y'48
☎ (914) 677-3111 . . Highlands Farm, Altamont Rd, RR 3, Box 219,
Millbrook, NY *12545*

Lindsey MISS Anne Y—Exet'76
☎ (416) 489-0251 . . 38 Hillholm Rd, Toronto, Ontario M5P 1M3,
Canada

Lindsey MRS Chisholm (Jean G Chisholm) Sth'48
☎ (212) 879-5558 . . 136 E 79 St, New York, NY *10021*

Lindsey MRS (DR) Ethel du P (Denton—Ethel du P Lindsey)
TexA&M'88.Fla'92
☎ (561) 659-2436 . . 243 Seaspray Av, Palm Beach, FL *33480*

Lindsey MR & MRS James H (Charlotte Roesler) Cly.Pn.P'55
☎ (805) 688-3532 . . 2875 Ridge Rd, Santa Ynez, CA *93460*

Lindsey MISS Marina H—ColC'91 . . see E B Kinsella

Lindsley MRS Dorothy S (Way—Dorothy G Sills)
☎ (212) 289-3033 . . 12 E 88 St, New York, NY *10128*

Lindsley MRS Hope C (Hope C Lewis) . . . .
MR Coleman . . . . |
416E S Hutchinson
St, Philadelphia, PA
19147

Lindsley MR Robert C—LakeF'66
☎ (610) 687-3665 . . 222 W Lancaster Av, PO Box 205, Devon,
PA *19333*

Lindsley MR Winston J
☎ (703) 273-8131 . . 4913 Tydfil Court, Fairfax, VA *22030*

Lineaweaver MR F Ridgway . . . . Died in Sep 1995

Lineaweaver MR & MRS Timothy H (Teresa Adelaide Morgan)
CtCol'81.Mass'90
☎ (508) 548-7482 . . 410 Woods Hole Rd, Woods Hole, MA *02543*

Lineberger MRS Walter F JR (Coakley—Patricia Hunkin) Cv.It.Un.Kt.
☎ (216) 423-0515 . . PO Box 333, Gates Mills, OH *44040*

Lineberry MR & MRS William D (Sally M Dommerich) Van'89.Van'89
☎ (205) 879-6317 . . 9 Gaywood Circle, Birmingham, AL *35213*

Lingelbach MR & MRS David C (Jeannette A Wentz) Hav'85.Mit'84
☎ (215) 247-2113 . . 18 E Abington Av, Philadelphia, PA *19118*

Lingelbach MR & MRS William E (Litchfield—Alice W Sailer)
Sth'25.Rc.Sg.Cw.Pa'25.Ox'29
☎ (215) 233-3394 . . 503 Auburn Av, Glenside, PA *19038*

Link MRS Edwin Cary (Franchelle H Watson)
☎ (713) 622-5802 . . 5602 Wickersham St, Houston, TX *77056*

Link MR & MRS George H (Betsy Leland)
Pac'61.Cal'89.Bhm.Cal'61.H'64 . . . .
MR Thomas H . . . .
MR Christopher L . . . . |
☎ (310) 476-7730
315 N Carmelina
Av, Los Angeles,
CA *90049*

Link MR & MRS Roger W (Pamela B Purdon) WestMich'68
☎ (410) 867-3007 . . Foxdown Farm, 429 Harwood Rd, Harwood,
MD *20776*

Link MR & MRS Theodore C (Vlk—Catherine V
Goode) Houst'66 . . . .
MISS Stephanie L—at U of Tex Pan America . . . |
2100 Pecos,
Mission, TX *78572*

Linke MR & MRS Gordon F (Jocelyn B Allan) Cvc.Mt.Bow'50
☎ (301) 229-5765 . . 5115 Cammack Dv, Bethesda, MD *20816*

Lins MR & MRS John P (Marion K Stewart) Plg.Cly.Dc.Ncd.Wms'37
☎ (212) 288-8086 . . 1040 Fifth Av, New York, NY *10028*

Linsley MISS Julia W—CtCol'50.Cly. . . . .
MISS Julia R—Br'85 . . . .
MR Graham S—USN.—at North Island,
San Diego, CA *92135* . . . . |
☎ (203) 259-5620
425 Pequot Av,
Southport, CT *06490*

Linthicum MR & MRS Edward B (Murchison—C Virginia Long)
☎ (214) 357-3275 . . 9785 Audubon Place, Dallas, TX *75220*
Feb 1 . . La Quinta Gina, 9 Almendros, Las Brisas, Acapulco,
GRO, Mexico

Linzee MR & MRS Thomas E JR (Roeann P Wilkins) Rol'76
☎ (617) 489-4052 . . 39 Chester Rd, Belmont, MA *02178*

Lionberger MR & MRS John S JR (Erle T Lund) V'55.Cy.Ncd.P'50
☎ (314) 863-4077 . . 21 Dartford Av, St Louis, MO *63105*

Lipman MR & MRS Lawrence M (Alexandra J Viehmann)
Smu'73.Tul'74.MempSt'70
☎ (615) 665-0358 . . 5906 Hillsboro Rd, Nashville, TN *37215*

Lippincott MR & MRS Barton H (Earle—Carol H Helms) Pc.Ph.Y'46
☎ (215) 247-1817 . . 727 Glengary Rd, Philadelphia, PA *19118*

Lippincott MR & MRS Bertram JR (Margaret Bruun)
Gm.Cw.Myf.Dar.Dc.Cda.P.'45 . . of
☎ (212) 254-6481 . . 431 E 20 St, New York, NY *10010-7502*
☎ (401) 423-1013 . . 272 Highland Dv, PO Box 404, Jamestown,
RI *02835*

Lippincott MR & MRS Bertram 3d (Jane R Coxe)
RI'81.Nrr.Tr.Myf.Cw.Ncd.Pn.RI'80
☎ (401) 423-0305 . . 10 Walcott Av, PO Box 194, Jamestown, RI *02835*
Lippincott MRS C Seebohm (Smith—Caroline Seebohm) Ox'61.C.
☎ (609) 737-7648 . . 19 River Dv, Titusville, NJ *08560*
Lippincott MRS Christopher B—V'88
230 Garden St, Hoboken, NJ *07030-3706*
Lippincott MRS David McC (Joan S Bentley) Sth'54.Cs.Ncd.
☎ (212) RE4-9271 . . 53 E 66 St, New York, NY *10021*
Lippincott MRS Eleanor H (Lapsley—Boucher—Eleanor H Hallowell)
☎ (609) 924-3570 . . 68 Westerly Rd, Princeton, NJ *08540*
Lippincott MR John L—Tul'76
☎ (203) 532-1723 . . 7 Moshier St, Greenwich, CT *06831*
Lippincott MRS Joseph W (Mathieson—Virginia Jones)
☎ (941) 966-2797 . . 2405 Casey Key Rd, Nokomis, FL *34275*
Lippincott MR & MRS Joseph W JR (Thomas—Marie L Beck)
Me.Fi.Rv.Ac.Pn.P'37
☎ (561) 234-8717 . . 970 Sandfly Lane, Vero Beach, FL *32963*
Lippincott MRS R Schuyler (Jones—Elizabeth W Hanger)
Swb'42.Pc.Sg.Ac.Ncd.
☎ (215) 233-3792 . . 560 E Evergreen Av, Wyndmoor, PA *19038*
Lippincott MR & MRS Richard (Niessen—Angela Heckscher) Rc.Swth'28
☎ (610) 645-8650 . . 1400 Waverly Rd, Villa 1, Gladwyne,
PA *19035-1254*

Lippincott MR Walter H JR—C.K.P'60 . . . . | ☎ (609) 737-3762
MISS Sophie E . . . . | 1 River Knoll Dv,
JUNIORS MR Hugh . . . . | Titusville, NJ *08560*

Lippincott MR William D'O 2d—Buck'91 . . . . | of ☎ (212)337-0803
MR Alexander H—Denis'92 . . . . | 4 E 12 St,
New York, NY
10003
"Palimpsest"
Rte 209,
Stone Ridge, NY
12484

Lippman MR & MRS L Max JR (Fordyce—Zoé Desloge) Mls'46.Web'68
☎ (314) 837-3225 . . "Beau Eaux" 2705 Shackelford Rd, Florissant,
MO *63031*
Lipscomb DR & MRS A Brant JR (Susan M Dunkel) Van'80.Van'75
☎ (713) 364-0542 . . 58 Acorn Cluster Court, The Woodlands,
TX *77381-4840*

Lipson MRS Howard S (Katharine S Cammann) . . . | ☎ (603) 823-5251
Ncd. . . . . | Maplehurst Farm,
MR Peter S—Sap.NCar'68—at Raleigh, NC . . . . | Sugar Hill, NH
03585

Lirakis MR & MRS W Stephen (Bernadette Sabatier) | ☎ (401) 846-5364
Srb.Ny.Cw. . . . . | "Elm Lodge"
MISS Isabelle C M . . . . | Newport, RI *02840*
JUNIORS MR W Stefan
JUNIORS MR Pierre B . . . . |

Lischer MRS Carl E (Noel—Christine C Jones) Cy.
☎ (314) 725-1065 . . 1 McKnight Place, St Louis, MO *63124*
Lisle MRS Clifton (Anna H Hayward) Sfh.
☎ (610) 827-7516 . . "Melbrook" 1120 Lower Pine Creek Rd,
Chester Springs, PA *19425*
Lisle REV & MRS John (Quick—Hettie J Paull) Ph.Leh'35
☎ (941) 349-4137 . . 759 Norsota Way, Sarasota, FL *34242*

Lisle MR & MRS John JR (Elaine K Moynihan) Pa'76.Ph.Me.Rc.Pa'68
☎ (610) 525-0798 . . 626 Winsford Rd, Bryn Mawr, PA *19010*
Lissner MISS Elaine A . . see A E Siegman
Litchfield MRS Edward S (Jacobi—Marjorie de Greeff) Bgt.
☎ (914) 232-3366 . . "Talisman Hill" 168 Mt Holly Rd, Katonah,
NY *10536*
Litchfield MRS Isabel C (H Isabel Crouse) . . . . | ☎ (203) 531-5086
MR Christopher S—at ☎ (203) 622-6060 | 513 W Lyon Farm
52 Lafayette Place, Apt 4B, Greenwich, CT | Dv, Greenwich, CT
06830 . . . . | *06831*
Litchfield MR & MRS Philip A (Hamill—Sarah A Richardson) Bgt.
☎ (914) 764-8433 . . 29 Bender Way, Pound Ridge, NY *10576*
Litchfield MR William G—P'46
☎ (518) 434-8916 . . 40 Willett St, Albany, NY *12210*
Litsas MRS Ann P (Ann E Poor) Skd'68.Nu'83
☎ (212) 737-1541 . . 315 E 72 St, New York, NY *10021*
Littell MR Andrew—Cl'92.EcolePoly'93
☎ (617) 497-3970 . . 1137 Massachusetts Av, Cambridge, MA *02138*
Littell MR Hardin H 2d . . . . Died at
Tucson, AZ Jun 14'96
Littell MISS Lisa
☎ (520) 298-0945 . . 2025 Camino De La Cienega, Tucson, AZ *85715*
Littell MRS Saxe (Mary Van R Saxe) Ncd.
☎ (561) 655-1138 . . 400 N Flagler Dv, Apt 801, West Palm Beach,
FL *33401*
Littell MR Walter D—C.H'55
☎ (617) 628-4517 . . 87 Clarendon Av, Somerville, MA *02144*
Little MRS David B (Goldsborough—Marjorie | ☎ (508) 369-3427
English) . . . . | 100 Newbury Court,
MR Peter B—at Salem, MA *01970* . . . . | Concord, MA *01742*
MR Benjamin—Tufts'70—at Nashua, NH *03061* |
Little MR & MRS David J (Beverly Y Lindh) Y.'88.Srb.Cly.Ht.Cl'87
☎ (212) 288-5406 . . 55 E 72 St, Apt 12N, New York, NY *10021-4149*
Little MRS Donald C (Jane L Milliken) . . . . Died at
Glen Cove, NY Aug 10'96
Little MR Donald C—Ny.Pr.S.Va'41
☎ (516) 626-0591 . . 56 Wolver Hollow Rd, Glen Head, NY *11545*
Little MR & MRS Gary R (Leslie F Moffat) Swth'83.Pa'91.Cal'81.H'86
619 Cotton Av, Menlo Park, CA *94025*
Little MR & MRS George F 2d (Claudia A Randel) | of ☎ (212)988-6094
Skd'74.Bgt.Cw.Ham'71 . . . . | 1 Gracie Square,
JUNIORS MR Bradford C . . . . | New York, NY
10028
☎ (203) 655-9889
57 Contentment
Island Dv, Darien,
CT *06820*
Little MR & MRS Henry A 3d (Sarah E Hicks) Rk. . . | ☎ (804) 276-9462
MISS Elizabeth A—W&M'95 . . . . | 7616 Millcreek Dv,
MR James H—VaCmth'93 . . . . | Richmond, VA
23235
Little DR & MRS John B (Françoise Cottereau) | ☎ (617) 232-2022
Paris'56.H'51 . . . . | 307 Warren St,
MR Frédéric—at ☎ (415) 661-4331 | Brookline, MA
200 Carl St, Apt 104, San Francisco, CA *94117* | *02146*

Little MRS Juliana P (Juliana P von Kienbusch) BMr'47.Ncd.
☎ (207) 244-7930 . . ''The Homestead'' Oak Hill Rd, PO Box 396, Somesville, ME *04660*
Little MR Lawrence S
☎ (860) 521-6481 . . 38 N Main St, West Hartford, CT *06107*
Little MISS Melinda L—Wes'75.Nw'78
☎ (518) 891-0197 . . 18 Shepard Av, Saranac Lake, NY *12983*
Little DR & MRS Robert A (Gammill—Phyllis A Starnes)
Ark'70.Miss'51.Tul'60
☎ (601) 896-1620 . . 6 Mockingbird Lane, Gulfport, MS *39501*
Little MR & MRS Robert A 2d (Catherine A Derdeyn)
Va'86.Tul'91.Miss'85.Tul'90
1910 Claremont St NW, Atlanta, GA *30318*
Little MR Robert Forsyth (Riegel—Susan Richards) Pr.P'39.Cl'42
☎ (516) 367-9778 . . 1294 Ridge Rd, Laurel Hollow, Syosset, NY *11791*
Little MR & MRS Warren M (Jean E Hardy) Rdc'55.Cc.Myf.H'55
☎ (617) 491-3937 . . 35 Brewster St, Cambridge, MA *02138-2203*
Littlefield MR & MRS Arthur S JR (Schoenbrod—Blossom—Mary L Harden)
Purd'63.Ch'65.Nw'41
☎ (847) 251-1797 . . 1046 Seneca Rd, Wilmette, IL *60091*
Littlefield MR & MRS Arthur S 3d (Cecelia M Blaine) Det'84.DeP'73.Ind'75
213 W 9 St, Hinsdale, IL *60521*
Littlefield MR & MRS Durwood E (Elizabeth P Hyde) | ☎ (609) 921-3454
Wab'69.JHop'77 . . . . | 40 Battle Rd,
JUNIORS MISS Catherine H . . . . | Princeton, NJ *08540*
Littlefield MR & MRS Edmund W (Jeannik M C Méquet)
Wells'41.Mls'42.Bhm.Bur.Pcu.StJ.Ln.Sfg.Stan'36
☎ (619) 568-3666 . . 74-185 Quail Lakes Dv, Indian Wells, CA *92210*
Littlefield MRS Jameson (Margaret D Jameson)
☎ (201) 652-3038 . . 39 Bradford St, Glen Rock, NJ *07452*
Littlefield MR John S—Bab'86 . . see D M Payne
Littlehales MRS G Reber (Dorothy Bell Warren) Sl.Mt.Cvc.
☎ (603) 643-1491 . . 80 Lyme Rd, Apt 268, Hanover, NH *03755*
Littlejohn MRS Angus C (Riggs—Mercedes Daly)
☎ (516) 676-8304 . . 44 Overlook Rd, Locust Valley, NY *11560*
Littlejohn MR & MRS Angus C JR (Leslie W Butcher) Conn'75.Pa'73
☎ (203) 966-0625 . . 648 Smith Ridge Rd, New Canaan, CT *06840*
Littlejohn MRS Jacqueline S (Jacqueline A Smith) RISD'76
☎ (212) 744-4360 . . 245 E 72 St, New York, NY *10021*
Littlejohn MR & MRS R Duncan (Sonia A Feijóo) Strasbourg'77.Pa'76
☎ (011-55-11) 523-3084 . . Rua Cassiano Ricardo, Apt 38, Jardim Cordeiro, 04640 São Paulo, Brazil
Littlejohn MR Robert M—Cw.Y'50
☎ (413) 637-1630 . . 37 Morgan Manor, Lenox, MA *01240*
Littleton MR & MRS Peter D (Andrea N Garwood) | ☎ (603) 643-2353
Pc.Myf.Elm'74.Pa'78 . . . . | 16 Haskins Rd,
JUNIORS MR Peter D JR—at St George's . . . . | Hanover, NH *03755*
Littleton MR & MRS William G 2d (Maud Hardwick) | ☎ (215) 247-1223
Pc.Sg.Myf.Ac.Pa'48 . . . . | 700 Glengary Rd,
MR Richard S—Pc.Myf.Ithaca'77—at | Chestnut Hill, PA
☎ (011-44-171) 376-4236 . . 8 Elm Park | *19118*
Mansions, Park Walk, London SW10 0AN,
England . . . .

Livens MR John H—Sm.Cy.Btn.Hn.H'55.H'60 . . . . | of ☎ (617)720-4590
MISS Elizabeth Ann—Colby'90 . . . . | 27 Beaver Place,
MR John H JR—Bates'93 . . . . | Boston, MA
| *02108-3303*
| ☎ (561) 833-6456
| Trump Plaza 20G,
| 525 S Flagler Dr,
| West Palm Beach,
| FL *33401*
| ☎ (603) 236-4477
| Village Condos
| O-91, Waterville
| Valley, NH *03223*
Livens MRS M A Harris (Mary Ann Harris) Au.Chi.Ncd . . .of
☎ (508) 287-0232 . . 168 Sunset Rd, Carlisle, MA *01741*
☎ (603) 968-7140 . . ''Willoughby Point'' Box 573, Holderness, NH *03245*
Livermore MR & MRS David P (Rebecca L Oliver) Cal'80.RISD'83.Wms'77
1960 Hubbard Av, Salt Lake City, UT *84108*
Livermore MISS Francesca G
☎ (415) 388-9529 . . 447 Molino Av, Mill Valley, CA *94941*
Livermore MR George S—Bhm.Pcu.Stan'36.Y'40
☎ (415) 421-7705 . . 414 Mason St, San Francisco, CA *94102*
Livermore MR & MRS Norman B (Virginia M | of ☎ (415)453-9229
Pennoyer) Pcu.Stan'33 . . . . | 141 Mountain View
MISS Edith P—at 1735 Chicago Av, Apt 903, | Av, San Rafael, CA
Evanston, IL *60201* . . . . | *94901*
| ☎ (707) 942-4069
| ''Montesol''
| 5500 Lake County
| H'way, Calistoga,
| CA *94515*
Livermore DR & MRS Norman B 3d (Sproul—Marion N Orrick)
Cal'73.Dth'70.Cal'74
☎ (510) 376-1254 . . 1070 Bollinger Canyon Rd, Moraga, CA *94556*
Livermore MR & MRS Richard C (Patricia A Mulford)
Cal'71.GeoW'78.Stan'69.SantaC'73.SanJ'75
☎ (415) 321-4018 . . 1010 Almanor Av, Menlo Park, CA *94025-2302*
Livermore MRS Robert (Farley—Isabel Kernan) . . . | ☎ (617) 259-8045
MR David B—at ☎ (541) 386-3327 | 19 Baker Farm,
601—13 St, Hood River, OR *97031* . . . . | Lincoln, MA *01773*
Livermore MR & MRS Samuel M (Cynthia R Saranec)
CtCol'73.SFrSt'81.Dth'73.Lond'74.Stan'78
☎ (415) 457-9019 . . PO Box 973, 2 Ames Av, Ross, CA *94957*
Liversidge MR & MRS Thomas K (Mary C Parsons) | of 4 Crescent Surf,
Me.Colg'41 . . . . | Kennebunk, ME
MISS Laurie E—at 100036 Hellingley Place, | *04043*
Gaithersburg, MD *20879* . . . . | ☎ (610) 827-9206
| ''Rabbit Run''
| Chester Springs, PA
| *19425*

Livingood MR Charles A—Stan'59
1221 Darien Club Dv, Darien, IL *60561*
Livingood DR & MRS (DR) John M (Amy S | ☎ (301) 229-4130
Bookman) SUNY'71.H'62 . . . . | 5940 Searle Terr,
JUNIORS MR Jason J . . . . | Bethesda, MD
| *20816*

Livingston MR & MRS Clayton C (Susanna Soutter) RSage'55.Rens'52
☎ (914) 279-9448 . . ''Otter Hill'' Putnam Lake Rd, Brewster, NY *10509*

Livingston MR & MRS Deryck Van V (Serena T Ritter) Gordon'83.Iona'92 ⚓
☎ (860) 355-5404 . . 191 Carmen Hill Rd, Apt 2, New Milford, CT *06776*

Livingston MISS Eleanor M—V'41.Wyo'69.Lm.
☎ (303) 499-8234 . . 2625 Table Mesa Court, Boulder, CO *80303*

Livingston MR & MRS Henry H (Maria M Burroughs) Swb'40.Plg.Snc.StA.Rv.Hl.Myf.Lm.Ncd.Y'40.Y'41 . . of
☎ (212) 348-2926 . . 115 E 90 St, New York, NY *10128-1509*
☎ (518) 828-6183 . . 184 Oak Hill Rd, Hudson, NY *12534*

Livingston MR & MRS James A JR (Margaret M Gresham) V'45.Ala'46.Mich'40.Mich'41
☎ (205) 879-3061 . . 12 Country Club Rd, Birmingham, AL *35213*

Livingston MR & MRS James A 3d (Susan B Bevill) Ithaca'72.Cy.Ala'74
☎ (205) 969-1542 . . 3423 E Briarcliff Rd, Birmingham, AL *35223*

Livingston MRS John H (Elisabeth S Pratt) Ck.Pr.
☎ (516) 922-0409 . . PO Box 78, 380 Berry Hill Rd, Syosset, NY *11791*

Livingston MR & MRS Kipp B (Susan E Rexford) Mich'81.Ub.Ey.Col'76
☎ (508) 371-2116 . . 39 Wilson Rd, Concord, MA *01742*

Livingston MISS Lorna M—Lm.
☎ (212) RH4-1322 . . 531 E 72 St, New York, NY *10021*

Livingston MRS Madeleine B (Madeleine B Bullock) . . . .
MR Harry J JR—at Haddonfield, NJ *08033* . . . . .
MR Steven M—at ☎ (407) 868-2435
211 Chandler Dv, Apt 313, Cape Canaveral, FL *32920* . . . .
| ☎ (908) 349-3313
| 14 Maple St,
| Toms River, NJ
| *08753*

Livingston MR & MRS Ralph E (Lucia B Buchanan) Hlns'43.H'39 . . of
☎ (561) 272-0727 . . 123C Venetian Dv, Delray Beach, FL *33483*
☎ (508) 369-3948 . . 106 Milldam Square, 100 Keyes Rd, Concord, MA *01742*

Livingston MR & MRS Richard H B (Elizabeth Dubben) V'69.Y'69 . . . .
MISS Elizabeth T . . . .
JUNIORS MISS Catharine C . . . .
| ☎ (203) 966-9831
| 17 Hampton Lane,
| New Canaan, CT
| *06840*

Livingston MRS Susan W (Susan J Weidenkopf) OState'85
☎ (216) 228-2704 . . 17202 Hilliard Rd, Lakewood, OH *44107*

Livingston DR & MRS William H 3d (Julie C Hall) Myf.Penn'70.PennOpt'78
☎ (617) 639-0090 . . 18 Cypress St, Marblehead, MA *01945*

Livingstone MR & MRS Seabourn S (Mettler—Salant—Kay Will) Y'45w
☎ (561) 546-5280 . . PO Box 816, Hobe Sound, FL *33475*

Lizars MR & MRS Rawson G JR (E Rosemary Camp) Hlns'57.Va'55 . . . .
MISS H Mabry—Rol'88 . . . .
MR Rawson G 3d—WashColl'91 . . . .
| ☎ (561) 283-0951
| 4 Island Rd,
| Sewalls Point,
| Stuart, FL *34996*

Llewellyn MR & MRS David S (Barbara L Mayo) Mass'73.Coe'68 . . . .
JUNIORS MR Mark S . . . .
| ☎ (510) 254-7383
| 100 Overhill Rd,
| Orinda, CA *94563*

Llewellyn MR Parker B—Rcn.Hn.Stan'66.H.'68
☎ (617) 523-3931 . . 68 Beacon St, Boston, MA *02108*

Llewellyn MR & MRS Timothy D (Elizabeth Hammond) Rdc'68.Camb'69
☎ (011-44-171) 373-2333 . . 160 Gloucester Rd, London SW7 4QF, England

Llopis MR & MRS Jose Maria (Garrigues—Frances G Aldrich) Cly.Jesuit'54
☎ (011-34-1) 561-98-91 . . Francisco Asis Mendez, Casariego 4, 28002 Madrid, Spain

Lloyd MRS Barsha B (Large—Barsha Baugh) . . . . .
MISS Barsha P Large—Eck'93—in Florida . .
MISS Nina L Large . . . .
| ☎ (215) 836-1394
| 1727 E Willow
| Grove Av,
| Laverock, PA *19038*

Lloyd MR & MRS Bruce M (Elinor S Jackson) Mt.Br'69.Pa'77 . . . .
MISS Sandra S . . . .
| ☎ (818) 799-7159
| 1054 S Arroyo Blvd,
| Pasadena, CA *91105*

Lloyd MR & MRS Charles E G JR (Sally B Hill) Unn.DU'71 . . . .
MISS Jennifer H—at Georgetown . . . .
JUNIORS MR Ewing McA—at Lawrenceville . . . .
| ☎ (201) 379-6143
| 39 Knollwood Rd,
| Short Hills, NJ
| *07078*

Lloyd MR & MRS Charles F JR (Nancy E Landon) Fcg.Va'42 . . of
☎ (412) 963-8743 . . 604 Squaw Run Rd, Pittsburgh, PA *15238*
☎ (561) 278-8743 . . 3860 Bermuda Lane, Gulf Stream, FL *33483*

Lloyd MR & MRS David (Hollenbeck—Susan B Lattner) Msq.Why.Ty'66 . . . .
MR Jordan S—at 246 Tulip Tree Rd, Blue Bell, PA *19422* . . . .
| of ☎ (215)836-0458
| 6009 Cricket Rd,
| Flourtown, PA
| *19031*
| ☎ (401) 348-8989
| ''Bluffit''
| 8 Bluff Av,
| Watch Hill, RI
| *02891*

Lloyd MRS Francis V JR (Elisabeth Boardman)
☎ (508) 398-3823 . . 222 Pleasant St, Box 38, South Yarmouth, MA *02664*

Lloyd MR & MRS Francis V 3d (Lida L Thompson) Sth'65.Cy.H.Y'59.Wash'64 . . . .
MISS Lida L—Sth'89 . . . .
MR Stratton C—at Yale . . . .
| ☎ (617) 734-9562
| 59 Hilltop Rd,
| Chestnut Hill, MA
| *02167*

Lloyd MR H Gates—P'50.Cl'52
☎ (610) 642-0103 . . 3300 Darby Rd, Apt 2202, Haverford, PA *19041-1068*

Lloyd MR H Gates 4th—Ken'81
☎ (970) 468-0212 . . PO Box 2366, Dillon, CO *80435*

Lloyd MR J Palmer JR—CalSt'60
☎ (805) 684-8801 . . 3375 Foothill Rd, Apt 111, Carpinteria, CA *93013*

Lloyd MR & MRS John S (Florence A Hubbard) V'59.Rc.Cc.Wes'59 . . . .
MISS Maria B—Br'88—at ☎ (203) 772-1402
83 Cottage St, New Haven, CT *06511* . . . .
MISS Rebecca C—at U of Cal Berkeley . . . .
DR John H—Aht'86.Cwr'91—at
☎ (617) 864-3538 . . 22 Bigelow St, Cambridge, MA *02139* . . . .
MR Thomas P—at Columbia . . . .
| ☎ (215) 925-2250
| 321 Spruce St,
| Philadelphia, PA
| *19106*

Lloyd MR John Strawbridge—Ph.Msq.Pn.P'73
☎ (215) VE6-5776 . . 1777 E Willow Grove Av, Laverock, PA *19038*

Lloyd MRS L Herman (Beatson—Linda Herman) . . .
JUNIORS MR Oliver M—at Salisbury . . . .
| ☎ (212) 249-2340
| 69 E 82 St,
| New York, NY
| *10028*

Lloyd MRS Morris (Hope Starr) Sg.
☎ (215) 836-4648 . . 1777 E Willow Grove Av, Laverock, PA *19038*

Lloyd MR & MRS Morris JR (Eleanor R Price) | ☎ (215) CH7-6745
Sg.Ph.Ty'60 . . . . | 8300 Navajo St,
MR Anthony M—Wit'91 . . . . | Philadelphia, PA
MR Edward B—Ty'94 . . . . | *19118*
Lloyd MR & MRS R McAllister 3d (Margaret A | ☎ (617) 329-6026
Ewing) Br'75.WIT'75 . . . . | 505 Washington St,
JUNIORS MR Robert McA 4th . . . . | Dedham, MA *02026*
Lloyd MR & MRS Reese B (Kathleen Antoine)
☎ (215) TU7-2672 . . Rydal Park, Woodside Apt 477, Rydal, PA *19046*
Lloyd MRS Richard W (Margaret C P Hebard) | of 911 Kirkwood
Nu'79 . . . . | Circle, Camden, SC
MR O H Perry—EverSt'84 . . . . | *29020*
| ☎ (212) 734-0304
| 524 E 72 St,
| New York, NY
| *10021*
Lloyd MR & MRS Robert McA JR (Barbara Burroughes) Y'48
☎ (603) 323-8696 . . "Timberlea II" Chocorua, NH *03817*
Lloyd MR & MRS Robin M (Georges—Tamara L | ☎ (301) 656-7469
Hall) Cal'68.Nu'76.P'73.Cl'76 . . . . | 6215 Kennedy Dv,
JUNIORS MISS Marisa E D . . . . | Chevy Chase, MD
| *20815*
Lloyd MRS Stacy B (Virginia Boy Ed) Mt.Ri.Gi.Sl.
☎ (540) 955-3226 . . PO Box 267, Berryville, VA *22611*
Lloyd MR Stacy B 3d—Cvc.Mt.Mid'60 . . . . | of ☎ (202)232-1836
MR Thomas L—at St Mark's . . . . | 1836—24 St NW,
JUNIORS MR Stacy B 4th—at Kents Hill Sch . . . . | Washington, DC
| *20008*
| ☎ (540) 592-3214
| "Oak Spring"
| Upperville, VA
| *20185*
Lloyd MRS Tangley C (Quinn—DeLaney—Tangley | of ☎ (203)629-3435
C Lloyd) . . . . | 150 Stanwich Rd,
MISS Demarest L Quinn—at Geo Wash'n . . . | Greenwich, CT
MR James P Quinn—at Rollins . . . . | *06830*
| ☎ (561) 225-3542
| "Kokomo Palms"
| Sailfish Point, 6740
| SE South Marina
| Way, Stuart, FL
| *34996*
Lloyd MR & MRS Thomas (Susan M Campbell) | ☎ (215) CH2-2931
Pc.Ty'62.Pa'67.Rut'79 . . . . | 9417 Meadowbrook
MISS Ellen C . . . . | Lane, Philadelphia,
MR Thomas B . . . . | PA *19118*
Lloyd MR & MRS Whitney (Georgia G Llop) | ☎ (216) 321-8202
SUNY'67.H'65 . . . . | 2647 Berkshire Rd,
MISS Marion W . . . . | Cleveland Heights,
MR Robert H—H'92 . . . . | OH *44106*
Lloyd MR & MRS William W (Margaret A Coyne) Spgfd'82.Colby'84
☎ (716) 226-3010 . . Haverford Farm, 4285 S Avon Rd, Avon,
NY *14414*
Lloyd MR & MRS Wingate (Janet West)
GeoW'55.GeoW'77.CathU'81.P'53.JHop'55
☎ (202) 244-6924 . . 4500 Cathedral Av NW, Washington, DC *20016*

Lloyd-Butler MR & MRS Thomas O (Diane L Butler) Cal'82
☎ (415) 776-8285 . . 3209 Jackson St, San Francisco, CA *94118*
Lobaugh MR & MRS Garry M (Diane H Beales) | 529 E Snow Rd,
Cent'y'68.Rcch.IaState'67 . . . . | Baroda, MI *49101*
MISS Molly B . . . .
MR Christopher M . . . .
JUNIORS MISS Caroline E . . . .
JUNIORS MR Timothy J . . . .
Lobel MR & MRS Elliot D (Lenore R F Zug) Ws'70.Tufts'70.Nu'73.Suff'81
☎ (617) 893-3155 . . 31 Love Lane, Weston, MA *02193*
Lober MR William D—Gettys'71.Rut'75
☎ (610) 688-1758 . . "Windy Hill" King of Prussia Rd, PO Box 8102,
Radnor, PA *19087-8102*
Loberg MISS Ingrid A—Ore'82 . . see L M Weld JR
Loberg MISS Karen Q—ArtCtr'83 . . see L M Weld JR
Lobkowicz PRCSS Anita O (Cossé Brissac—PRCSS Anita O Lobkowicz)
☎ (011-33) 37-26-78-69 . . 2 rue de la Croix Blanche, 28190
St Luperce, France
Lobkowicz PRC Edouard A de & PRCSS de (PRCSS | ☎ (011-33-1)
Françoise de Bourbon de Parme) B.Paris'49. | 47-23-99-47
H'51 . . . . | 30 av de New York,
PRCSS Marie-Gabrielle de . . . . | 75116 Paris, France
PRC Charles-Henri de . . . .
Lobkowicz MR & MRS Martin G (M Brooks Juett) | ☎ (508) 785-0864
Ws'52.D.H'51 . . . . | 280 Dedham St,
MISS Margaret S . . . . | Dover, MA *02030*
Locher MR & MRS Paul R (Wick—Anne C Farrelly)
Rose'49.NotreD'38.H'41.Paris'49
☎ (202) 363-5201 . . 4833 Rodman St NW, Washington, DC *20016*
Lochridge MISS Georgia P—Sth'67
☎ (312) 787-9126 . . 222 E Pearson St, Apt 1404, Chicago, IL *60611*
Lochridge MR & MRS Lloyd P (Frances Potter) P'38
☎ (512) 452-1221 . . 3400 Hillview Rd, Austin, TX *78703*
Locke REV Bradford B—Va'49.VaTheo'52 . . . . . . | ☎ (203) 453-2479
MISS Suzanne G—at ☎ (203) 453-1376 | 75 Stepstone Hill
23 Davis Dv, Guilford, CT *06437* . . . . | Rd, Guilford, CT
MISS Nancy A—at ☎ (203) 838-0384 | *06437-2021*
11 Winthrop Av, Norwalk, CT *06851* . . . .
Locke MR & MRS Curtis H (Penelope I Wheeler) St.G.Penn'35
☎ (716) 884-8108 . . 664 Lafayette Av, Buffalo, NY *14222*
Locke MRS F Howell (Frances Howell)
see Dilatory Domiciles
Locke MRS Henry W (Margaret M R Howell) Ncd. . | ☎ (617) 471-6543
MR Charles H—at Syracuse, NY . . . . | 540 Hancock St,
| Apt 314, Quincy,
| MA *02170*
Locke MR & MRS John R (Grace Walker) A.Va'15
☎ (210) 822-1424 . . 700 E Hildebrand Av, San Antonio, TX *78212*
Locke MR & MRS John S (Constance M Beardsell) | ☎ (703) 356-8066
GeoW'69.BFklin'69.AmU'77 . . . . | 8180 Greensboro
MISS Constance M . . . . | Dv, McLean, VA
| *22102*
Locke MISS Katharine B—Hampshire'83
☎ (802) 223-9834 . . PO Box 1519, Montpelier, VT *05601*
Locke MISS Margaret Chase—Earl'47.Sth'49.Spgfd'59
☎ (607) 734-7653 . . 337 Glen Av, Elmira, NY *14905-1227*

Locke DR & MRS Mark D (Sarah F Bovaird) DeP'87.Cwr'91
2139 N Bissell St, Chicago, IL *60614*
Locke MRS T Ferguson (Millar—Mary B Lex) Sth'40
☎ (617) 444-5970 . . North Hill K205, 865 Central Av, Needham,
MA *02192*
Locke MR & MRS T Ferguson JR (Patricia B
Rasinski) Nw'71. . . . .
MISS Anna B . . . .
JUNIORS MISS Elizabeth F . . . .
☎ (414) 961-7195
1908 E Cumberland
Blvd, Whitefish Bay,
WI *53211*
Lockee CAPT & MRS Garette E (Sears—Sarah D Storm)
USN.Pa'62.SCar'43.GeoW'66
☎ (901) 878-1168 . . PO Box 664, La Grange, TN *38046*
Lockhart MISS A Whitney . . see F L Patterson 3d
Lockhart MISS Emily R . . see A A Yort JR
Lockwood MR & MRS Charles H (Jeannine M Nowack)
Wash'83.Cr'88.Naz'86.Syr'96
☎ (716) 654-5633 . . 210 Salisbury St, Rochester, NY *14609*
Lockwood MR & MRS George S JR (Lee Wilson) Ws'37.Un.Cv.Y'33
☎ (216) 561-6586 . . 13415 Shaker Blvd, Cleveland, OH *44120*
Lockwood MRS H Winthrop (Lucille Schlesinger) Cvc.
☎ (561) 778-1330 . . Royal Palm Center, Rm 32, 2180 Tenth Av,
Vero Beach, FL *32960*
Lockwood MR Hamilton de F JR—H'25
☎ (617) 266-4135 . . 180 Beacon St, Boston, MA *02116*
Lockwood MRS John Edwards (Henrietta E Sedgwick) C.Plg.Cs.Cly . . .of
☎ (212) 737-3080 . . 215 E 72 St, New York, NY *10021*
☎ (914) 234-7173 . . 32 St Mary's Church Rd, RD 2, Box 192, Bedford,
NY *10506*
Lockwood MR John M 2d—Vt'86
☎ (310) 581-1000 . . 20 Beverly Park Terr, Beverly Hills, CA *90210*
Lockwood MRS Lois K (Lois L Kinnicutt) V'55
☎ (505) 466-1953 . . HC 75, Box 306, Lamy, NM *87540*
Lockwood MR & MRS Myron E (Marion L McGlinn)
WakeF'66. . . . .
MR Frank McG . . . .
MR Robert C . . . .
☎ (912) 477-4356
580 Commanche
Place, Macon, GA
31210
Lockwood MR & MRS Roy H (Nina S Hunsicker)
Dick'61.Dick'59.AmU'64 . . . .
MISS Christina C—Dick'94—at
☎ (716) 256-1921 . . 2141 East Av, Rochester,
NY *14610*. . . . .
☎ (716) 385-1232
48 Astor Dv,
Rochester, NY
14610
Lockwood MR Thomas W—⚓
☎ (561) 778-4656 . . 7275—45 St, Vero Beach, FL *32967*
Lodge MR & MRS John A (Katherine F J Sherman) H.'50
☎ (508) 228-2560 . . 94 Main St, Nantucket, MA *02554*
Loeb MR John L JR—Plg.Sar.Rv.Snc.Fw.H.'52 . . . .
MR Nicholas M . . . .
☎ (914) 328-0078
''Ridgeleigh''
194 Anderson Hill
Rd, Purchase, NY
10577
Loebs MRS Edith S S (Edith Shaw Safe) Sl.Srb.Il.
☎ (401) 847-2026 . . 267 Indian Av, Middletown, RI *02842*
Loebs MR Peter S S—Srb.CtCol'82 . . of
☎ (540) 456-6988 . . ''Sundance'' Rte 1, Box 346, Afton, VA *22920*
☎ (540) 456-6989 . . ''Point de Vue'' Rte 1, Box 347, Afton, VA *22920*
Loebs MR Richard C JR—Srb.Nrr.Il.Wes'80
☎ (401) 849-7667 . . 207 Third Beach Rd, Middletown, RI *02842*

Loening MR & MRS George S (Louise L Eastman) Sth'88.Lm.Cl'89
☎ (212) 677-7975 . . 28 E 4 St, New York, NY *10003*
Loening MR & MRS J Michael (Edith S Twiss)
Wms'53.H'56. . . . .
MR M Brooke—Cw.Lm.CtCol'86—
☎ (212) 517-5725 . . 164 E 72 St, New York, NY
10021. . . . .
☎ (212) 988-0076
215 E 72 St,
New York, NY
10021
Loewenstein MRS Pamela (Pamela B Amberg)
Ober'58.Nw'91 . . . .
MR David M—at 306 W 12 St, Lawrence, KS
66044. . . . .
☎ (847) 328-5287
1311 Maple Av,
Apt 3W, Evanston,
IL *60201*
Löfberg MR & MRS Per G H (Margaret P McDowell)
Rc.Cy.Sm.Stock'71.CarnM'73 . . . .
JUNIORS MR John P . . . .
of ☎ (212)410-4725
63 E 92 St,
New York, NY
10128
☎ (508) 992-5501
''Ricketson's Point''
110 Elm St,
South Dartmouth,
MA *02748*
Loftheim MISS Inger M (Jon W) . . . . Married at Winter Park, FL
Rood MR Douglas M . . . . Feb 17'96
Lofting MR & MRS Colin M (Ida M E Kerr)
☎ (610) 869-9837 . . 341 Lamborndown Rd, West Grove, PA *19390*
Lofting MRS Wendy W (Wendy R Winslow). . . . . .
JUNIORS MISS Elliott R . . . .
JUNIORS MR Hugh . . . .
☎ (610) 444-4794
113 Meadow View
Lane, Kennett
Square, PA *19348*
Lofton MISS Melissa . . see W A Burkett
Logan MISS Alice L—NCar'43
☎ (919) 918-3472 . . 750 Weaver Dairy Rd, Apt 2106, Chapel Hill,
NC *27514*
Logan MRS Constance E (Constance T Etz) Swb'90
☎ (912) 355-0510 . . 2411 Easy St, Savannah, GA *31406*
Logan MR & MRS Francis D (Claude Rivière
de Colommès) Vh.Ch'50.Ox'54.H'55 . . . . . .
MR Francis D JR—Dth'86 . . . .
☎ (818) 796-8020
1726 Linda Vista
Av, Pasadena, CA
91103
Logan MR & MRS Frank G 2d (Sally J Stephens)
Cr'55.Rv.Dar.Cr'54.Cr'55 . . . .
MR Thomas D—Cr'82.Cr'84—at
☎ (510) 838-0799 . . 78 Larkstone Court,
Danville, CA *94526* . . . .
☎ (508) 875-1490
18 Travis Dv,
Framingham, MA
01701
Logan MRS George T (Frances G Stewart) Cs.
☎ (215) MA7-0761 . . 210 Locust St, Philadelphia, PA *19106-3926*
Logan MR & MRS John A JR (de Forest—Ann D Orr) C.Ncd.Yn.Y'45
☎ (203) 481-7990 . . Evergreen Woods 353, 88 Notch Hill Rd,
North Branford, CT *06471*
Logan MRS John G JR (Anne H Clarke) SL'46. . . . .
MISS Edith S (McLean—Edith S Logan)—at
5 Birch Brook Rd, Bronxville, NY *10708* . . . . .
☎ (607) 547-2476
PO Box 147,
Cooperstown, NY
13326
Logan MR & MRS Kevin M (Saxenmeyer—Nathalie F Compton) Ty'57
☎ (203) 245-3411 . . 26 Fairfield Rd, Madison, CT *06443*

Logan MR & MRS Wade Hampton JR (Virginia Watson)
AScott'38.Ncd.Cit'35
☎ (803) 722-8529 . . 1873 Camp Rd, Apt 67, Charleston, SC *29412-3567*

Logan MR Walton M—Cal'59
14 Beach Rd, Apt G, Belvedere Tiburon, CA *94920*

Logothetis MR & MRS Anestis L (Constance R Booth) MaryW'61.Del'67.Grin'55.Mit'58 . . . . . | ☎ (302) 478-4425 "Talleybrook"
MR Michael L—Laf'94—at U of Tex Austin . . . | 2816 Kennedy Rd, Wilmington, DE *19810*

Logothetis MISS Elaine A (Anestis L) . . . . . Married at Gibson Island, MD
Jack MR Matthew F (Richard M) . . . . May 4'96

Lohmann MISS Catherine N . . . . Married at Lewiston, ME
Ripley MR Steven . . . . Sep 7'96

Lohmann MR & MRS Charles P 3d (Jennifer W Smith) Mil'vl'84.Juniata'78
☎ (610) 431-3190 . . "Breeze Hill" 208 Laydon Lane, West Chester, PA *19380*

Lohmann MRS Powell (Elizabeth P Powell) Eastern'86.Ncd.
☎ (610) 687-2828 . . 304 N Valley Forge Rd, Devon, PA *19333*

Lohmann MR & MRS Richard P (Susan S Hastings)
Gettys'81.WChesU'83.Mariet'81
☎ (609) 758-1683 . . 226 Schoolhouse Rd, Wrightstown, NJ *08562*

Loizeaux MISS Christine
☎ (805) 683-1315 . . 1459A Tunnel Rd, Santa Barbara, CA *93105*

Loizeaux MISS Sonia—Tufts'72
☎ (617) 523-4585 . . 112 Pinckney St, Boston, MA *02114*

Loizeaux DR & MRS Theodore (Cecily W Flanagan) Rut'41
☎ (908) 756-5091 . . 1689 Woodland Av, Edison, NJ *08820*

Lolli-Ghetti MRS Dwight (Cassandra Dwight) Cly. . | ☎ (212) 348-0323
MISS Mara . . . . | 8 E 96 St,
JUNIORS MISS Beatrice . . . . | New York, NY
JUNIORS MR Glauco . . . . | *10128*

Lombard MRS Barbara C (Twaddell—Barbara C Hooton)
☎ (407) 255-3333 . . 380 Bay Point Dv, Melbourne, FL *32935*

Lombard MRS Eleanor G (Eleanor G Little) . . Married at Washington, DC
Roberts MR Thomas M (late James T) . . . . Jun 27'96

Lombard MR James M—B.Mt.Sm.H'61 . . . . | ☎ (941) 955-6161
MISS Hillary S—at Kenyon . . . . | 888 Blvd of the
MR Laurence M 2d—H'95—at ☎ (212) 752-5166 | Arts, Sarasota, FL
401 E 63 St, Apt 6, New York, NY *10021* . . . . . | *34236*

Lombard MR & MRS Langdon F (Nancy W Regan) | ☎ (617) 489-4555
Mass'64 . . . . | 134 Mill St,
MISS Catharine E . . . . | Belmont, MA *02178*
MR Langdon F JR . . . . |

Lombard MR Laurence C
☎ (704) 743-9009 . . PO Box 1713, Cashiers, NC *28717*

Lombard MRS Susan Sweet (Susan Sweet)
☎ (941) 966-6161 . . 140 Sugarmill Dv, Osprey, FL *34229*

Lombardi MR & MRS David E JR (Susan C | ☎ (415) 386-0133
Woodbury) Pcu.Cal'62.Y'66 . . . . | 1650 Lake St,
MISS Sara Ennis . . . . | San Francisco, CA
JUNIORS MR Eric D . . . . | *94121*

Lombardo MR & MRS Fabio (Catharine B McGuire) WashColl'89
☎ (011-39-41) 526-5046 . . via Lorenzo Marcello 12, 30126 Lido, Venezia, Italy

Londen MR & MRS Jack W (Dodie M Isaacson)
☎ (602) 956-7971 . . 33 Biltmore Estates, Phoenix, AZ *85016*

Lonergan MR & MRS Pierce J (Berdan—Joan C | 5971 Kugler Mill
Frail) P'53 . . . . | Rd, Cincinnati, OH
MISS Amy—Nw'85.Tul'90 . . . . | *45236*

Loney MR & MRS Frederick R (Nancy H Shevers) Msq.Cly.Wms'51
☎ (212) 831-3271 . . 70 E 96 St, Apt 12A, New York, NY *10128*

Long MR & MRS Bruce C (Deborah L Daniel) Cin'72.Cin'71
☎ (513) 831-8726 . . 810 Lexington Av, Terrace Park, OH *45174*

Long MRS Claxton A (O'Connell—Judith G | of ☎ (415)922-2311
Shepard) Pcu.Bur. . . . . | 2218 California St,
JUNIORS MISS Lydia S . . . . | San Francisco, CA
MR Courtney O'Connell . . . . | *94115*
MR Robin S O'Connell . . . . | ☎ (707) 252-1501
| "Rancho Valdera"
| 1300 Wooden
| Valley Rd, Napa,
| CA *94558*

Long MR & MRS David A (Alice P St Claire)
V'71.TrentSt'78.Pn.Wes'71.Cal'75.P'83 . . of
☎ (609) 921-1533 . . 241 Snowden Lane, Princeton, NJ *08540*
☎ (215) 545-4846 . . 1420 Locust St, Apt 31J, Philadelphia, PA *19102*

Long MRS Donna M (Woods—Donna M Wilson) | *see*
Peab'yCons'69.CalSt'71 . . . . | *Dilatory Domiciles*
MISS Diantha L Woods . . . . |
MR Douglas R Woods . . . . |

Long MRS John C (Mary C Parsons)
☎ (617) 275-8132 . . 16 Bedford Court, Bedford, MA *01730*

Long MR & MRS John G (Fitler—M Elizabeth E Parker)
Me.Ncd.Dar.Dc.Ht.W.Colg'33
☎ (610) 642-9070 . . 3300 Darby Rd, C101, Haverford, PA *19041*

Long MISS Karen (Dwight—Karen Long) NCar'67 . | ☎ (201) 292-5244
MISS Anne V Dwight . . . . | "Stonewood"
JUNIORS MR John K Dwight JR . . . . | PO Box 48,
| Long Hill Rd,
| New Vernon, NJ
| *07976*

Long MR & MRS Phillip C (M Whitney Rowe) | ☎ (513) 561-4795
Qc.Tul'65 . . . . | 4795 Burley Hills
MISS Charlotte C . . . . | Dv, Cincinnati, OH
MR Elisha W . . . . | *45243*
JUNIORS MR Elliot S . . . . |

Long MR & MRS Robert E (Price—Patricia H Bane) Mt.Ind'53.GeoW'59
☎ (703) 765-8525 . . 7608 Southdown Rd, Alexandria, VA *22308*

Long MRS Syida H (Syida G Haas) . . . . | ☎ (415) 931-2277
MISS Syida C . . . . | 2727 Filbert St,
MR Claxton A JR—☎ (415) 553-2534 . . . . | San Francisco, CA
| *94123*

Long MR & MRS Thad G (Carolyn F Wilson) | ☎ (205) 870-0171
Hlns'63.Ala'65.Cy.Rv.Dar.Cl'60.Va'63 . . . . | 2880 Balmoral Rd,
MISS Louisa F—Va'95 . . . . | Birmingham, AL
MR Wilson A . . . . | *35223*

Long MR & MRS Thomas F JR (Deborah M Dey) | ☎ (303) 449-1393
DU'72.DU'71 . . . . | "North House"
MISS Adrienne H . . . . | 4935 Lee Hill Dv,
| Boulder, CO *80302*

Long MR & MRS Walter T (Patricia M Weizer) Gm. . | ☎ (610) 527-3193
  MISS Katharine J—at Wm & Mary . . . . | 35 Aldwyn Lane,
  MR W Thayer JR—at Davidson . . . . | Villanova, PA *19085*
Longaker MISS Bettina . . see MRS A B de Szinay
Longcope MR & MRS Thomas M 3d (Elizabeth Lefferts) Pn.P'41
  ☎ (203) 767-2404 . . Essex Meadows, Bokum Rd, Essex, CT *06426*
Longmaid MRS David D (McKelvie—Dale N | ☎ (610) 793-1208
  Ellsworth) . . . . | Longmeadow Farm,
  MISS Karen E . . . . | 520 Broad Run Rd,
  MR David N . . . . | RD 4, Marshallton,
  MR Christopher N . . . . | PA *19382*
Longmaid MR & MRS John H—Nf.PugetS'72
  ☎ (616) 938-7924 . . 3238 Holiday View Dv, Traverse City, MI *49686*
Longmaid MRS Penelope (Penelope J Shumaker) | ☎ (207) 244-5772
  Kent'68.RI'71.Nf.Dar. . . . . | ''Invermeade''
  JUNIORS MR Ashley J S—at Roger Williams . . . . | 56 Fernald Point Rd,
  | PO Box 765,
  | Southwest Harbor,
  | ME *04679-0765*
Longman MR & MRS Tremper 3d (Alice L Scheetz) | ☎ (215) 233-3352
  OWes'74.Pc.Rv.W.OWes'74.W'minsterTheo'77. | 7803 Froebel Rd,
  Y'83 . . . . | Laverock, PA *19038*
  JUNIORS MR Tremper 4th—at Clemson . . . .
  JUNIORS MR Timothy S . . . . |
Longmire MR & MRS C Henry (Mary V W Osgood)
  Franklin'72.NMex'71.AGSIM'79
  ☎ (508) 468-4919 . . 317 Highland St, South Hamilton, MA *01982*
Longmire MR & MRS David R (Carolyn G Love) | ☎ (303) 795-6054
  Mit'47.Mich'50.Wis'58 . . . . | 4696 W Lake Circle,
  MISS Ellen K—P'82.Stan'85.Stan'90—at | Littleton, CO *80123*
  ☎ (612) 823-8901 . . 3121 S Emerson Av,
  Minneapolis, MN *55408* . . . . |
  MR John R—Bow'87 . . . . |
Longmire MISS Helen M
  ☎ (314) 692-1182 . . 2 McKnight Place, Apt 315, St Louis,
  MO *63124-1900*
Longmire MR Richard E M—Y'50.SCal'64
  ☎ (310) 822-4483 . . 4121 Via Marina, Marina Del Rey, CA *90292*
Longnecker MRS H Reed (MacDonnell—Sarah J Wagner) Skd'65.Me.
  ☎ (508) 468-3403 . . 874 Bay Rd, Box 464, Hamilton, MA *01936*
Longnecker MR Henry C—Hav'38
  ☎ (603) 383-4360 . . Box 506, Thorn Hill Rd, Jackson, NH *03846*
Longshaw MR & MRS Nigel P (M Lucille Koch) Tufts'77.Aston'76
  ☎ (609) 683-5716 . . 107 Laurel Rd, Princeton, NJ *08540-2709*
Longstreth MR & MRS Peter S (Elizabeth E Steel) | ☎ (215) CH8-2547
  BMr'83.Rc.Pc.P'66 . . . . | 301 W Gravers
  MISS Hadley H . . . . | Lane, Philadelphia,
  MISS Amanda C . . . . | PA *19118*
  JUNIORS MR John S . . . . |
Longstreth MR & MRS Richard W (Lucinda E Train) Au.Pa'68
  ☎ (202) 328-3965 . . 1803 Irving St NW, Washington, DC *20010*
Longstreth MR & MRS W Thacher (Anne S Claghorn) P'41
  ☎ (215) 247-5747 . . 530 Telner St, Philadelphia, PA *19118*
Lonsdale MRS John W (Elsie J Peterson) Bgt.Chr.
  ☎ (203) 531-1335 . . 1165 King St, Greenwich, CT *06831*

Lonsdorf DR & MRS Richard G (Alice W Belew) Tex'44.Me.Scran'43.Pa'46
  ☎ (610) 664-9797 . . 415 Old Gulph Rd, Penn Valley, Narberth,
  PA *19072*
Look MRS Allen M (Maria S Auchincloss)
  ☎ (508) 693-2558 . . PO Box 43, West Tisbury, MA *02575*
Look MR & MRS David T (Charlotte G Cleveland) | ☎ (207) 729-3614
  Pn.P'51 . . . . | Box 3054,
  MISS Ellen D—Ty'81—at ☎ (207) 775-0205 | Mere Point Rd,
  88 Edgeworth Av, Portland, ME *04103* . . . . . . | Brunswick, ME
  | *04011*
Loomis MR & MRS A Worthington (Louise H Earle) | ☎ (860) 233-8966
  BMr'50.Hart'78.Mass'94.C.Tvcl.Cc.Y'45.Nu'55 | 70 Terry Rd,
  MISS Charlotte E—V'87—at ☎ (203) 458-3811 | Hartford, CT *06105*
  1641 Durham Rd, Guilford, CT *06437* . . . . . . |
Loomis MR & MRS Alfred F 2d (Stephanie A Neuhaus)
  Cin'88.Cc.Roch'80.Nu'94
  ☎ (212) 734-9791 . . 420 E 79 St, Apt 15B, New York, NY *10021*
Loomis MRS Alfred L JR (Hosmer—Virginia N | of ☎ (516)922-6851
  Davis) Ri.Ny.S.Mt.Cly.Ncd.Cc. . . . . | Cove Neck Rd,
  MISS V Sabra—H'60—at ☎ (212) 645-5131 | Oyster Bay, NY
  136 Waverly Place, New York, NY *10014* . . . . . | *11771*
  | ☎ (803) 757-2202
  | Bull Island
  | Plantation, Bluffton,
  | SC *29910*
Loomis MRS Ann M (Ann Menge) | ☎ (504) 893-2007
  Monticello'66.Mds. . . . . | 508 E Tenth Av,
  JUNIORS MR A Landon . . . . | Covington, LA
  JUNIORS MR I Dodd . . . . | *70433*
Loomis MR Harvey B—Y'53
  ☎ (212) 737-0730 . . 315 E 77 St, New York, NY *10021*
Loomis MR & MRS Henry (Williams—Jacqueline A | ☎ (904) 384-8620
  Chalmers) Mt.H'41 . . . . | ''Tarn Haven''
  MR Robert W Williams—Va'81 . . . . | 4661 Ortega Island
  | Dv, Jacksonville, FL
  | *32210*
Loomis MRS Macleod (Mary P Macleod) My.
  ☎ (508) 526-9652 . . 37 Forster Rd, Manchester, MA *01944*
Loomis MR & MRS N Barton (Stone—Virginia MacIntyre) Mds.Pa'68
  ☎ (504) 733-4871 . . 5825 Plauche St, New Orleans, LA *70123*
Loomis MR & MRS Robert L—Y'50 . . . . | ☎ (860) 738-2721
  MISS Julia W—V'83—at ☎ (773) 274-7882 | PO Box 210,
  6307 N Lakewood Av, Chicago, IL *60660* . . . . . | Colebrook, CT
  MR Timothy L . . . . | *06021*
Loomis MR & MRS Thomas H (Lorenz—Alice W | of ☎ (508)526-4840
  Ingraham) Chi.DavEl'64 . . . . | 11 Smith's Point Rd,
  MISS Jennifer M—at Columbia, MO . . . . | Manchester, MA
  MISS Elizabeth A—at Seattle, WA . . . . | *01944*
  MR Christopher P Lorenz—at Boston, MA . . | ☎ (605) 685-6900
  | Star Rte 2, Box 5A,
  | Martin, SD *57551*
  | ☎ (941) 472-6170
  | 11530 Chapin Lane,
  | Captiva Island, FL
  | *33924*
Looram MR & MRS Matthew J (Bettina de Rothschild) Mt.H'43
  ☎ (011-43-7480) 259 . . 3294 Langau bei Gaming, NÖ, Austria

Loose MRS Clyde E (Margaret Jenkins) Ncd.
☎ (410) 435-2626 . . 6307 Blackburn Court, Baltimore, MD *21212*

Lopez JUNIORS MISS Laura V . . see R W Hill JR

Lorber JUNIORS MISS Augusta H B . . see MISS J de M Foster

Lorber MR D Martin H B—K.Rc.NCar'65
☎ (212) 260-3809 . . 304 E 20 St, New York, NY *10003*

Lorber JUNIORS MR Giraud van N F . . see MISS J de M Foster

Lord MISS Ann O—Bvr'72.NCar'74
☎ (617) 277-4545 . . 46 Carlton St, Apt 4, Brookline, MA *02146*

Lord MRS Charles E (Margaret A Plunkett) V'51.Ny.Cvc.Myf.Yn.
☎ (561) 546-7848 . . 114 N Beach Rd, Hobe Sound, FL *33455*

Lord MRS Clarence A (Celestine Bonner) LakeF'43
☎ (847) 446-0643 . . 235 Riverside Dv, Northfield, IL *60093*

Lord MR & MRS Edward C (Elena M Echarte) Nu'71.Ri.Ng.BtP.Pa'71.Cl'78
☎ (212) 876-3704 . . 1070 Park Av, New York, NY *10128*

Lord MRS Edwin C E (Mary P Draper) Cly.Ncd.
☎ (302) 652-7229 . . 813 Greenwood Rd, Wilmington, DE *19807*

Lord DR & MRS George de F JR (Sharon M Allen) GaSt'86.Emory'90.Wash'76.LCC'80 . . . . | ☎ (706) 678-1863 116 S Elijah Clark Dv, Washington, GA *30673*
JUNIORS MISSES Amelia T & Juliette K—at
☎ (860) 691-0538 . . 11 S Ridge Rd, Niantic, CT *06357* . . . .
JUNIORS MR Miguel W—at ☎ (860) 691-0538
11 S Ridge Rd, Niantic, CT *06357* . . . .

Lord MR & MRS Hambleton D (Michelle M Grigas) BostColl'84.Br'83
☎ (617) 237-0633 . . 21 Rockridge Rd, Wellesley, MA *02181*

Lord MR Henry—Mass'86 . . see J G Holmes

Lord MR & MRS Henry Robbins (Sarah Fenno Williams) AmU'69.Ant'75.Elk.Md.Mv.Pn.P'60.Va'63
☎ (410) 828-4355 . . "Revelry" 6134 Barroll Rd, Baltimore, MD *21209*

Lord MRS Herbert G (Norton—Anne D Bingham) V'23
North Hill D307, 865 Central Av, Needham, MA *02192*

Lord MR & MRS J Couper (Barbara S Hartley) St.So.H'41.Duke'48 . . . . | ☎ (516) 283-1882 PO Box 1446, S Hill St, Southampton, NY *11969*
MR J Couper JR—Rol'72 . . . .

Lord DR & MRS Jere W JR (Margaret H Graham) Bgt.P'33.JHop'37
☎ (914) 234-7253 . . 179 Greenwich Rd, Bedford, NY *10506*

Lord MRS Paul E (Mabel A Strong) MtH'18.Sim'20 | of ☎ (212)289-4156 60 E 96 St, New York, NY *10128* ☎ (207) 622-2653 Webber Pond Rd, RFD 1, Box 786, Augusta, ME *04330*
MISS Barbara Gile . . . .

Lord MISS Sarah (late Charles E) . . . . Married at Wakefield, RI
Field MR R Gregory (R Henry) . . . . Jun 22'96

Lord MRS Stackpole (Susan M Stackpole)
☎ (803) 797-6161 . . 9163 Spring Branch Court, North Charleston, SC *29418-9130*

Loree MR & MRS Leonor F 3d (Pamela Van D Bucher) Hood'65.Va'65.Va'70 . . . . | ☎ (804) 285-1256 26 E Glenbrooke Circle, Richmond, VA *23229*
MISS Gretchen Van D—Mid'91—at Atlanta, GA
MR Leonor F 4th—at U of Va . . . .
JUNIORS MR Austin C . . . .

Lorentzen MRS Hans L (Morris—Gerd K Wiese) Me.Ac.
☎ (610) 642-5206 . . 506 Hillbrook Rd, Bryn Mawr, PA *19010*

Lorentzen MRS Herbert T (Ferrell—Lydia H Goodwyn) Snc.Myf.Ds.
☎ (804) 358-1037 . . 211 Locke Lane, Richmond, VA *23226*

Lorenz MRS Barbara S (Barbara P Strong) . . . . | 130 E 94 St, New York, NY *10128*
MISS Anne E . . . .

Lorenz MR Christopher P . . see T H Loomis

Lorenz MR Keith JR—Hn.H'58 . . of
☎ (808) 732-6627 . . Box 61081, Manoa Valley, Honolulu, HI *96822*
☎ (207) 342-5156 . . "Gudanya House" Box 123, Morrill, ME *04952*

Lorenze DR & MRS Edward J 3d (Margit Hintz) Chr.StJ.StA.Cl'44.Nu'46 . . of
☎ (212) 980-9382 . . 200 E 66 St, New York, NY *10021*
☎ (561) 747-2015 . . 300 Ocean Trail Way, Jupiter, FL *33477*

Lorenzen MR & MRS Phillip H JR (Elizabeth P S Hunter) Cal'65.Col'69.DU'62.DU'70 ⚓ . . . . . | ☎ (206) 232-7444 7827 SE 73 Place, Mercer Island, WA *98040*
MISS Hayley P . . . .
MISS Susannah B . . . .
MISS Kathryn H . . . .

Lorillard MRS Alice C (Augustus—Alice Cavedon) Srb.Dar . . .of
☎ (561) 588-2707 . . "Chateau Cheverny" Ibis Isle Rd, Palm Beach, FL *33480*
☎ (401) 847-3767 . . "Belair" 50 Old Beach Rd, Newport, RI *02840*

Lorillard MRS Screven (Alice Whitney) . . of
☎ (908) 234-0951 . . Bindon Farm, PO Box 219, Larger Cross Rd, Far Hills, NJ *07931*
☎ (212) 935-6322 . . 30 E 62 St, New York, NY *10021*
☎ (970) 728-5289 . . 150 Elk Way, Raspberry Patch, Telluride, CO *81435*

Lorillard MR Screven Peter (late Screven) . . . Married at Front Royal, VA
Hall MISS Victoria A . . . . Apr 27'96

Loring MR & MRS Augustus P (Elisabeth J Blake) My.Chi.Ncd.
☎ (508) 927-0088 . . PO Box 220, 502 Hale St, Prides Crossing, MA *01965*

Loring MISS Elizabeth Atherton (Ian K) . . . . Born at Boston, MA Jly 31'94

Loring MR & MRS Ian K (Isabelle C Parsons) Ty'89.Ty'88
☎ (617) 326-5864 . . 15 Glenridge Rd, Dedham, MA *02026*

Loring MR Jonathan B—Sm.Myc.CtCol'75
☎ (508) 921-0088 . . PO Box 182, 502 Hale St, Prides Crossing, MA *01965*

Loring MR & MRS Peter B (Elizabeth E Shennan) Bost'69.Tufts'71.My.Myc.Un.Bost'67.Va'76
☎ (508) 927-4450 . . "Burnside" Box 218, 573 Hale St, Prides Crossing, MA *01965*

Loring MR & MRS Robert W (Elizabeth Madeira) Mid'76.Ub.Nf.Hob'73 . . . . | ☎ (617) 934-5143 61 Cedar St, Box 123, Snug Harbor, Duxbury, MA *02331*
JUNIORS MISS E Amory . . . .

Loring MRS Thacher (Helene P Abell) BMr'50.Ncd.
☎ (520) 721-7119 . . 2739 N Camino Valle Verde, Tucson, AZ *85715*

Loring MR & MRS Thomas B (Parnum—Patricia Hibben) H'52 . . . . ☎ (617) 770-9759
MR Edward B—at ☎ (508) 228-0636 . . 3 Mill St, Nantucket, MA *02554* . . . . | 5 Brigantine Lane, Quincy, MA *02171*
MR Christopher B—LakeF'81—at ☎ (617) 742-0791 . . 97 W Cedar St, Boston, MA *02114* . . . .

Loring MR & MRS William C (Agnes Waller) Myc.Cc.Chi.Ncd.H'50 ⚓ . . . . ☎ (508) 927-0184
MR Timothy G—Utah'84 . . . . | 140 Hart St, PO Box 23, Prides Crossing, MA *01965*

Loring MR & MRS William C JR (Mary Copley Felton) My.Chi.Cc.Bow'73
☎ (508) 927-0265 . . Preston Place, Beverly Farms, MA *01915*

Lortz MR Edward K—Cr'66
☎ (415) 695-0369 . . 1242—19 St, San Francisco, CA *94107*

Lortz MRS Russell E (Feuerbacher—Virginia Weidemueller)
☎ (314) 725-0603 . . 816 S Hanley Rd, St Louis, MO *63105*

Lortz MR & MRS William C (Helene N Stehlin) Wh'lck'60.Van'60 . . . . | 2 Oakleigh Lane, St Louis, MO *63124*
MISS Jennifer C . . . .
MR Michael E—at 522 Briar Hill Lane NE, Atlanta, GA *30324* . . . .

Losee MR & MRS David B (Joan N Marshall) Ws'76.Wes'68
25 Linnard Rd, West Hartford, CT *06107*

Losee MR & MRS Thomas P JR (Muriel F Hahn) Csh.Ck.Duke'63 . . of
☎ (516) 367-3885 . . 20 Saw Mill Rd, Box 471, Cold Spring Harbor, NY *11724*
2613 N Ocean Blvd, Gulf Stream, FL *33483*

Lothrop MR & MRS Francis B JR (Kristin L Curtis) B'gton'51.Sm.H'50
☎ (508) 526-7100 . . 71 Bridge St, Manchester, MA *01944*

Lotsch MISS Pamela King . . of
400 E 59 St, New York, NY *10022*
Carysbrook Plantation, RR 1, Box 57D, Fork Union, VA *23055*

Lott MRS Edward M JR (Sigrid K Freudenberg) Col'56.R.
☎ (510) 935-2031 . . 775 Palmer Rd, Walnut Creek, CA *94596*

Lott MR & MRS Edward M 3d (Tamara J Neufeld) Biola'84.Biola'86
☎ (510) 661-9391 . . 2222 Valorie St, Fremont, CA *94539*

Lott MR & MRS John Benjamin (Monica L Sims) Htdon'90.Htdon'89
☎ (334) 244-9340 . . 1812 Llanfair Rd, Montgomery, AL *36106*

Lott MRS Sinclair R (F Jeanice Uhrich)
☎ (213) 681-8552 . . 111 S Orange Grove Blvd, Pasadena, CA *91105*

Loucks MR & MRS Thomas A (Dominique M S Chesneau) SteCroix'73.Dth'71
☎ (303) 781-2918 . . 5270 S Logan Dv, Littleton, CO *80121*

Loucks MRS William D JR (Carolyn Bade)
☎ (914) 337-6375 . . 32 Sturgis Rd, Bronxville, NY *10708*

Loud MR & MRS Douglass N (Smith—Erin H Farrell) Ck.Y'64.Cal'67 . . . . | 23 Abbott Lane, Wilton, CT *06897*
MR Douglass N JR . . . .
MR Thurston H Smith 3d—at Lynchburg Coll
MR Townsend U Smith—at Trinity . . . .

Loud MR Nelson M—Pr.Rby.Y.'35
340 E 57 St, Apt 9C, New York, NY *10022*

Loud MR & MRS Theodore E (Deering—Eager— R Keith Kerr) Ne.Cly.Yn.Y'57.Pa'60 . . . . ☎ (804) 295-4242
MISS Amanda K . . . . | 1253 Maple View Dv, Willow Lake, Charlottesville, VA *22902*

Lough DR & MRS Lawrence R (Amanda W Whitaker) SCar'85.MedSCar'80
☎ (803) 699-3292 . . 112 Duck Pond Rd, Columbia, SC *29223*

Loughborough REV Robert H R—Y'49
☎ (717) 275-4938 . . 8 Tower View Circle, Danville, PA *17821*

Loughlin MISS Anna M . . see J T Witherspoon

Loughlin MISS Clare M . . see J T Witherspoon

Loughlin MR John J JR . . see J T Witherspoon

Lounsbery MRS DeWitt (Carol Batchelder) Dar.
☎ (512) 343-7817 . . 3517 N Hills Dv, C204, Austin, TX *78731-3120*

Lounsbery MRS Phillips (Barbara Butler) Bgt.
☎ (914) 234-9371 . . Guard Hill Rd, Bedford, NY *10506*

Lourié MISS Elizabeth S . . see MRS G J Johnson 2d

Louthan MRS Sterling C (Allyson B Crawford) . . . . | ☎ (513) 439-4772
MISS Amy T . . . . | 7675 Duffield Circle, Centerville, OH *45459*

Louthan MR & MRS Thomas C (Paige R Gillette) Nu'81.Bcs.Clark'70.Wid'75
☎ (703) 790-5911 . . ''Toyland'' 1431 Layman St, McLean, VA *22101*

Love MR Brett J . . see F M Graff JR

Love MR Charles A
☎ (609) 884-8326 . . 1509 New Jersey Av, Cape May, NJ *08204*

Love MRS Eleanor J (Ammermann—Eleanor J Love) Cl'68
Karl-Theodor-Strasse 2, 82343 Pöking, Possenhofen, Germany

Love MR & MRS George H (Lindenmeyr—McClintic—Lorraine McArthur)
☎ (561) 278-0776 . . 3524 Oleander Way, Delray Beach, FL *33483*

Love MR & MRS Howard McC (Jane Vaughn) Fcg.Rr.Ln.Pg.Cly.Colg'52.H'56
☎ (412) 621-4881 . . 1440 Bennington Av, Pittsburgh, PA *15217*

Love MR & MRS Howard McC JR (Harriet P Van Ingen)
☎ (415) 347-7850 . . 2889 Adeline Dv, Burlingame, CA *94010*

Love MR & MRS J Kenneth (E Faye Blankenship) Aub'66
☎ (334) 272-4754 . . 1359 Pine Ridge Rd, Montgomery, AL *36109*

Love MISS Kathryn S . . see H G Berg JR

Love MR Kennett F P—Ny.C.P.Cl'48
☎ (516) 725-7856 . . 127 Bay St, PO Box 2663, Sag Harbor, NY *11963*

Love MISS Mary K (Moskey—Mary K Love) Pr. . . . | ☎ (970) 926-0026
MISS Marina L Moskey—Bow'95 . . . . | The Ranch at
JUNIORS MR Matthew L Moskey—at Trinity . . | Cordillera, Box 1479, 151 Red Draw, Edwards, CO *81632*

Love MISS Nathalie C P . . . . | ☎ (505) 982-4113
MISS Lily P . . . . | 304 E Berger St, Santa Fe, NM *87501*

Love MR & MRS Norris (Marcena P Waterman) Rr.Cho.P'58.Stan'60 . . . . | ☎ (847) 446-6903
MISS Sara N—at ☎ (773) 871-3537 | 1175 Pelham Rd, Winnetka, IL *60093*
609 W Stratford Place, Apt 7C, Chicago, IL *60657* . . . .

Love MISS Phoebe S . . see MRS M L Lehmann

Love MRS Robert M (MacLaren—Knowles—Elizabeth Morgan Firth) Ncd...of
☎ (941) 966-9249 . . Bayhouse 150, 1520 Pelican Point Dv, Pelican Cove, Sarasota, FL *34231*
☎ (860) 928-3647 . . "Tyrone Farm" 89 Tyrone Rd, Pomfret, CT *06258*
Love MR Steven S . . see F M Graff JR
Love MISS Suzanna P (Lommel—Suzanna P Love) V'73 . . of
☎ (207) 734-8891 . . "The Jap House" HCR 60, Box 62, Dark Harbor, ME *04848*
☎ (207) 734-2244 . . "Tiffany Cottage" HCR 60, Box 82, Dark Harbor, ME *04848*

Love MR W Kimbrough—Va'71 . . . . | ☎ (307) 674-7878
MR Edwin A . . . . | 336 W Alger,
JUNIORS MISS Elizabeth A . . . . | Sheridan, WY *82801*

Lovejoy MR & MRS George M JR (Ellen W Childs) Sm.Chi.Ncd.H'51
☎ (617) 742-4973 . . 81 Beacon St, Boston, MA *02108*

Lovejoy MISS Janet P (Taylor—Janet P Lovejoy) . . | ☎ (508) 369-9133
MISS Caryl P Taylor—at 47 Walcott Valley | 621 West St,
Rd, Hopkinton, MA *01748* . . . . | Carlisle, MA *01741*
MISS Hilary Taylor . . . . |

Lovejoy MR Philip W—Ty'83
☎ (617) 425-0034 . . 160 Beacon St, Apt 1, Boston, MA *02116*

Lovejoy MRS Sherrylyn P (Sherrylyn Patecell) . . . . | *see*
MISS Kindra H . . . . | *Dilatory Domiciles*

Lovejoy MR & MRS Thomas B (Patricia A M | ☎ (203) 661-6765
O'Connell) BMr'70.Geo'74.H'80.Ct.Hn.Mit'59. | 48 Burying Hill Rd,
H'61 . . . . | Greenwich, CT
MR T Curvin—at Lake Forest Coll . . . . | *06831*

Lovelace MR & MRS Richard S (Whitney—Caroline | ☎ (860) 767-2534
S Oveson) Pn.P'40.Mit'42 . . . . | Foot of Main,
MISS Caroline S—Bost'70.Bost'73—at | 48 Main St, Essex,
172 E 90 St, Apt 3E, New York, NY *10128* . . . . | CT *06426*
MR Richard S JR—RISD'75.RISD'77 . . . . |

Loveland MR & MRS William A (Katharine A von Hafften) Stan'71.Rut'77.Ncd.Stan'71.Rut'75.Rut'79
☎ (510) 210-1345 . . 3280 Diablo Shadow Dv, Walnut Creek, CA *94598*

Lovell MR & MRS A Buffum (Amanda L Norris) | ☎ (914) 764-0141
Br'60.K.Br'59.Cl'62 . . . . | 91 Pound Ridge Rd,
MR Jonathan R . . . . | Pound Ridge, NY
| *10576*

Lovell MR & MRS John E (Margaret Essock) | ☎ (203) 661-6163
Myf.Rv.Cw.Ne.Cl'52.Cl'59 . . . . | 29 Carlton St,
MISS Susan M E—at Manhattanville Grad . . . . . | Greenwich, CT
MISS Allison A S—Cl'82 . . . . | *06830*

Lovell MR & MRS Jonathan H (Margaretta J Markle) | ☎ (510) 524-1261
Sth'66.Del'75.Y'80.Wms'67.Ox'69.Y'80 . . . . . . | 1160 Amador Av,
MISS Stephanie J . . . . | Berkeley, CA *94707*
MISS Helen W . . . . |

Lovell MISS Katherine G . . see MRS W R Huntington
Lovell MR & MRS Lane (Patricia White) Eyc.P'31
☎ (508) 627-4447 . . PO Box 414, 123 N Water St, Edgartown, MA *02539*
Lovell MR William B N (A Buffum) . . . . Married at Bedford, NY
Cutler MISS Cheryl (Thomas) . . . . May 27'95
Lovering MRS Charles T 2d (A Margaret Murray) Dc.
☎ (516) 374-3023 . . 120 Ocean Av, Woodmere, NY *11598*

Lovering MR & MRS Joseph S (Eleanor T Dunning) Rc.Ac.
551 E Evergreen Av, Wyndmoor, PA *19038*
Lovering MR & MRS Richard S (Errol Cropper) An.H'37
☎ (803) 795-3854 . . 45 Wappoo Creek Place, Charleston, SC *29412-2121*
Lovering MR & MRS Richard S 3d (Arleen R Burke) JMad'79.Ty'76.Va'80
☎ (614) 855-1989 . . 7754 Arboretum Court, New Albany, OH *43054*

Lovett MR & MRS H Malcolm JR (Mary N Jeffers) | ☎ (713) 963-0022
Tex'67.Nyc.Rice'67.H'69 . . . . | 105 Broad Oaks
MISS Kate M . . . . | Trail, Houston, TX
| *77056*

Lovett MR Laurence Dow—B.K.H'51.H'54 . . of
☎ (011-39-41) 523-7942 . . "Palazzo Sernagiotto" Canareggio 5723, 30131 Venice, Italy
☎ (011-44-171) 584-4008 . . 30 Cadogan Square, London SW1X 0JH, England

Lovett MRS Robert S 2d (Dorothy deHaven) | ☎ (302) 656-6713
Ws'57.Cly. . . . . | PO Box 3657,
MISS Virginia Q—NYTech'89—at | Greenville, DE
☎ (617) 734-0606 . . 255 St Paul St, Brookline, | *19807*
MA *02146* . . . . |
MR Robert A 2d—at Trinity . . . . |

Lovett MR & MRS W Radford 2d (Lisa S Borie) MtH'83.Hn.H'82
☎ (904) 285-4039 . . 4039 Duval Dv, Jacksonville Beach, FL *32250*

Low MR & MRS Anthony (Pauline I Mills) H'57 . . . . | ☎ (203) 438-4672
MISS Elizabeth . . . . | 7 Christopher Rd,
MISS Catherine . . . . | Ridgefield, CT
MISS Alexandra . . . . | *06877*
JUNIORS MISS Nicholas . . . . |

Low MR & MRS Christian C (O'Brien—Julie F Chu) Hawaii'81.H'82
26 Ewen-Alison Rd, Devonport, Auckland, New Zealand

Low MR & MRS E Holland (Marilyn C Crane) | ☎ (413) 567-6125
Nyc.Un.Va'53 . . . . | 91 Colony Rd,
MISS Elizabeth Holland . . . . | Longmeadow, MA
MISS Loretta Ann—at Lake Forest Coll . . . . | *01106*
MR Charles Crane . . . . |

Low MR Francis H . . . . Died Jun 27'96
Low MRS Francis H (Susanne W Murray) Cly.Ncd...of
☎ (410) 822-3666 . . 27029 Miles River Rd, Easton, MD *21601*
☎ (941) 964-2500 . . "Bayou" Box 1401, Boca Grande, FL *33921*
Low MR & MRS Frank H (Clara B Everett) Mit'46.H.'47.H'49
☎ (914) 666-3247 . . 33 Joan Dv, Chappaqua, NY *10514*
Low MR & MRS John M (Julie S Henderson) Me.StLaw'82
☎ (203) 259-4220 . . 110 Figlar Av, Fairfield, CT *06430*

Low MR & MRS K Prescott (Susan Tucker Boaz) | of ☎ (561)832-0794
Cyb.Evg.BtP.Cc.Myf.Mid'63 . . . . | "Lowkey"
MISS Lisa Tucker—Br'92—at Block Island, RI | 577 S County Rd,
02807 . . . . | Palm Beach, FL
MR Seth Prescott—at Tufts . . . . | *33480*
| ☎ (242) 332-2538
| Windermere Island,
| Eleuthera, Bahamas

Low MR & MRS Malcolm S (Pecci-Blunt—Joan R | ☎ (207) 363-1786
Russell) Sm.Y'51.Cl'54 . . . . | "The Cottage"
MR Abbot A—at ☎ (714) 842-8529 | 4 Scotland Bridge
7701 Warner Av, Apt Q240, Huntington Beach, | Rd, York, ME
CA 92647 . . . . | *03909-5208*

Low MRS S Hastie (Logan—Sara C Hastie)
☎ (803) 577-9535 . . 45 E Battery, Charleston, SC *29401*

Low MR Seth JR
☎ (516) 364-3898 . . 66 Calvin Av, Syosset, NY *11791*

Low MRS W Gilman JR (Frances J Larrabee) Sth'50 | ☎ (401) 831-2174
MR David B—Duke'77—at 6127 N Fairhill St, | 60 Stimson Av,
Philadelphia, PA *19120* . . . . | Providence, RI
MR J Gilman—Vt'77—at 7551—33 Av NE, | *02906*
Seattle, WA *98115* . . . . |
MR Abbot F—PortArt'89—1550 Thompson Av, |
Santa Cruz, CA *95062* . . . . |

Lowder MR & MRS James K (Margaret Berry) | ☎ (334) 834-6609
Aub'72 . . . . | 3332 Stratford Lane,
MISS Anna C . . . . | Montgomery, AL
JUNIORS MISS Emily E . . . . | *36111*

Lowdon MISS Catherine Bowman (Todd H) . . . . Born at
San Francisco, CA May 4'95

Lowdon MR & MRS Todd H (C Victoria Bowman)
Cal'83.Stan'91.Duke'85.Stan'90
☎ (415) 343-0434 . . 1440 Carlos Av, Burlingame, CA *94010*

Lowdon MASTER Todd Hunter JR (Todd H) . . . . Born at
San Francisco, CA May 4'95

Lowe MISS Avery Higbie (David M) . . . . Born Oct 17'95

Lowe MISS Barbara . . see MRS P S Foster JR

Lowe MR & MRS David M (Katrina K Higbie) AmU'83.Law'81
☎ (617) 639-0317 . . 132 Front St, Marblehead, MA *01945*

Lowe MR & MRS George H III (Katherine Newbold) Y'38
☎ (617) 585-5566 . . 290 Kings Town Way, Apt 267, Duxbury,
MA *02332*

Lowe MR & MRS James J (Tatiana Litchfield) | ☎ (914) 234-7130
Bgt.Cyb. . . . . | 100 Clinton Rd,
MISS Penelope S—at ☎ (802) 748-1975 . . RR 1, | Bedford Hills, NY
Box 109D, Danville, VT *05828* . . . . | *10507*

Lowe MR & MRS James R 3d (Streed—Jerilyn K Miller) Mt.LakeF'87
☎ (612) 822-6589 . . 303 W Elmwood Place, Minneapolis, MN *55419*

Lowe MR & MRS James Rowland (Elizabeth A | ☎ (202) 363-9443
Murphy) Bhm.Cvc.Mt.StJ.Y'59.Y'64 . . . . . | 4615 Cathedral Av
MISS Elizabeth McIntyre—Scripps'92 . . . . | NW, Washington,
MISS Amanda B—at U of Maine . . . . | DC *20016*
MR E Garrett—Pa'88—at ☎ (202) 337-2372 |
4812 Hutchins Place NW, Washington, DC *20007* |

Lowe MRS Jean H (Jean S Holmes) Cal'62 . . . . | ☎ (703) 754-2669
MISS Carol B . . . . | "CALEDAN"
MR Edward D . . . . | 3704 Sanders Lane,
| Catharpin, VA
| *20143-1023*

Lowe MR Stephen . . . . | ☎ (510) 835-8424
MR Stephen G . . . . | 424—2 St, Oakland,
MR Oliver W . . . . | CA *94607*

Lowe MR & MRS W Courtney (Daphne B Norfleet)
Rol'88.Man'vl'92.OWes'86
☎ (802) 867-0438 . . 1298 Danby Mountain Rd, Dorset, VT *05251*

Lowe MR & MRS William L (Margaret Sloss) Fmy.Pcu.Stan'36.Stan'39 . . of
☎ (415) 363-0676 . . 14 Alverno Court, Redwood City, CA *94061*
☎ (702) 749-5384 . . 2045 Pray Meadow Rd, Glenbrook, NV *89413*

Lowell MR & MRS Frederick K (Lisa K Freeman) Stan'78.Pcu.Sfy.Cl'71
☎ (415) 435-4647 . . 201 Golden Gate Av, Belvedere Tiburon,
CA *94920*

Lowell MR & MRS John (Eleanor Trumbull) | ☎ (617) 581-0232
Un.Cc.H.'42 . . . . | 10 Vernon St,
MISS Mary W—at ☎ (215) 345-5082 | Nahant, MA *01908*
6-5 Aspen Way, Doylestown, PA *18901* . . . . . . |
MISS Eleanor—at ☎ (508) 832-3355 |
3 Tuck Farm Rd, Apt 5, Auburn, MA *01501* . . . |

Lowell MR & MRS Ralph JR (Joan MacDuffie) H.'45 . . of
☎ (508) 627-9653 . . 45 Mill St, Edgartown, MA *02539*
☎ (617) 581-0126 . . 11 Swallow Cave Rd, Nahant, MA *01908*

Lowery MRS James L (Mary Rhodes)
☎ (303) 752-1225 . . Treemont Apt 350, 10200 E Harvard Av, Denver,
CO *80231*

Lowndes MR & MRS Tasker G (Roberts—Sprague—Sydney M Huey)
Rcn.Evg.BtP.Yn . . .of
☎ (561) 832-5797 . . 232 Coral Lane, Palm Beach, FL *33480*
☎ (610) 896-6572 . . 155 Booth Lane, Haverford, PA *19041*

Lowndes MRS W Bladen (Hepburn—Eleanor W Macgill) Gi.Ncd.
☎ (410) 243-6616 . . Roland Park Place, Apt 257, 830 W 40 St,
Baltimore, MD *21211*

Lowney MR & MRS John P JR (Dakin—Kay F | ☎ (415) 927-1066
Sutton) Cal'56 | 5 Madrono St,
MISS Alicia Dakin . . . . | Corte Madera, CA
MISS Karla Dakin . . . . | *94925*
MISS Cary Dakin . . . . |

Lowrance MR & MRS Hughes W (Sara St J Selman)
☎ (706) 548-4093 . . 280 Southview Dv, Athens, GA *30605*

Lowrey MR & MRS Charles F (Mary C Rentschler)
V'51.Bhm.Sfy.Pcu.StJ.Fr.Cly.Y'50 ⚓
☎ (415) 346-7634 . . 2609 Scott St, San Francisco, CA *94123-4634*

Lowrey MR & MRS Charles F JR (Susan T Rodriguez)
Cr'81.Cl'85.P'79.Y'82.H'88
☎ (212) 496-8226 . . 136 W 75 St, New York, NY *10023-1923*

Lowry MR & MRS Arthur S (Julie A Smith)
Ty'84.H'88.Hav'81.Roch'82.Va'85
☎ (703) 525-5107 . . 4268 N 25 St, Arlington, VA *22207*

Lowry MRS (DR) Barbara S (Barbara H Sawyer) | ☎ (717) 646-2807
BMr'46.Temp'54.Jef'77.JHop'90 . . . . | "The Hermit"
MR John B 3d—Penn'92.Drex'94—at | Pocono Lake
36 Sequoia Court, Marlton, NJ *08053* . . . . | Preserve, PA *18348*
MR Peter A |
MR Charles W—Penn'93 |

Lowry MRS David A (Finch—Barbara B Black)
☎ (860) 354-8136 . . "Naromiyock" 39 Rte 39 N, Sherman, CT *06784*

Lowry MR & MRS Edward G (Ruth Driver)
V'26.Cly.Chi.Ncd.H'25.Ox'28.Cl'29
☎ (941) 365-0124 . . 700 John Ringling Blvd, Apt 2114, Sarasota,
FL *34236*

Lowry MR Philip H—P'39 . . . . | ☎ (703) 893-8812
MISS Marion H—at 120 S Granville Av, Apt 22, | "Difficult"
Los Angeles, CA *90049* . . . . | 8701 Georgetown
| Pike, McLean, VA
| *22102*

Lowry MR & MRS Ritchie P (Betty Trishman) Cal'48.Cal'52 . . . . ☎ (508) 358-4098
MISS Robin E—Box 15, RD 1, Fitzwilliam, NH *03447* . . . . 79 Moore Rd, Wayland, MA *01778*

Lowry MR & MRS William C 3d (Affel—Kristin J Freeman) Sg.Wis'68
☎ (215) 233-2351 . . 21 Franklin Av, Flourtown, PA *19031*

Lowry MR & MRS William C 4th (Aurelia M Whitney) MooreArt'74.Sg.Syr'73 . . . . ☎ (215) 242-0166
JUNIORS MR W Tyler . . . . 25 W Sunset Av, Philadelphia, PA *19118*

Lowsley-Williams MR & MRS Paul J (Elizabeth C Allyn) Va'86.Va'86
☎ (415) 749-1141 . . 1872 Bush St, San Francisco, CA *94109*

Lowther MR & MRS George 4th (Kathleen F Burns) OWes'87.Skd'80
☎ (203) 637-9128 . . Lowther Point, 34 Indian Point Lane, Riverside, CT *06878*

Loyd MR & MRS Mark R (Narmont—Frances Dail Mudd) MmtLoy'66.Str.Ncd.Ga'58 . . . . ☎ (314) 878-4808
MISS Elizabeth R—at Washington U . . . . 311 Ladue Oaks Dv, St Louis, MO *63141*
JUNIORS MISS Catherine D . . . .

Lubowski MISS Alicia E . . see MRS M Bograd

Lubowski MR Rubén N . . see MRS M Bograd

Lubrano MR & MRS Steven D (Allegra G Biggs) Hampshire'85.Hampshire'91.StLaw'81.Dth'87
☎ (603) 643-1213 . . 30 Goodfellow Hill Rd, Hanover, NH *03755*

Lucas MISS Diana D
☎ (609) 924-5595 . . 261 Moore St, Princeton, NJ *08540*

Lucas MRS James D (Joan Bissell) Rice'48.Cda. . . . ☎ (803) 722-8976
MISS Elizabeth F—at 1 Rutledge Blvd, Charleston, SC *29401* . . . . 27½ Wentworth St, Charleston, SC *29401*

Lucas MRS M Clare (Sawyer—Marcia H Clare) DU'71.Nf.Csn.Ncd.Ne.Myf. . . . . ☎ (803) 722-1474
JUNIORS MISS Christina C . . . . 24 Limehouse St, Charleston, SC *29401*
JUNIORS MR Ryan C . . . .

Lucas MRS M Virginia (M Virginia Whetstone)
☎ (610) 565-1453 . . 801 Manchester Av, Media, PA *19063*

Lucas MR & MRS Morton J 3d (Ann T Key)
☎ (314) 863-4131 . . 7534 Teasdale Av, St Louis, MO *63130*

Luce MRS Ann R (Baird—Campbell—Ann Raymond) V'46.Col'75
☎ (303) 642-7252 . . PO Box 1882, Boulder, CO *80306*

Luce MRS Elisabeth R (Hagenbuch—Elisabeth R Luce) Briar'77
☎ (415) 922-1737 . . 3476 Jackson St, San Francisco, CA *94118*

Luce MR & MRS Henry 3d (Hadley—Smitter—Musham—Leila Eliott Burton) Fic.Plg.Y'45 . . of
☎ (212) 759-8640 . . 4 Sutton Place, New York, NY *10022*
☎ (516) 922-0356 . . "Wychwood" Mill Hill Rd, Mill Neck, NY *11765*

Lucey MR & MRS Denis (Carla H McKay) Cork'75
☎ (203) 961-8424 . . 22 Radio Place, Apt 5, Stamford, CT *06906*

Luckie MR & MRS Robert E 3d (Jill Harris) Ala'71.Ala'91.Cy.Ala'69
☎ (205) 970-2226 . . 137 Queensberry Crescent, Birmingham, AL *35223*

Ludgate-Fraser MRS Verity M (Holmstrom—Meacham—Verity M Ludgate) P'cpia'59 . . . . . . ☎ (818) 445-4463
MR Geith St John Fraser—at Pasadena Comm Coll . . . . 819 Fairview Av, Apt 6, Arcadia, CA *91007*

Ludington MISS Anne C—Ken'82
☎ (314) 991-0745 . . 7 Anfred Walk, St Louis, MO *63132*

Ludington MR Hoyt W—Wms'88.Duke'92
☎ (617) 367-3566 . . 1 Devonshire Place, Apt 3303, Boston, MA *02109*

Ludington MR & MRS Martin L (Baum—Betty L Carico) Rcsl.Br'56 . . . . ☎ (809) 778-7386
MR David B—at 632 W Deming Place, Chicago, IL *60614* . . . . "Sandpiper II" Cotton Valley 5075, Christiansted, St Croix, VI *00820*

Ludington MR Nicholas L—B.Chr.Plg.Cw.Rv.Br'55 of ☎ (212)877-7239
MR Leland H—StAndr'90.Nu'94 . . . . 365 West End Av, New York, NY *10024*
☎ (516) 583-8218 75 Ridge Rd, Point O'Woods, NY *11706*

Ludington MR & MRS Nicholas S (Cassandra K Van Alen) Rc.Cts.H'56
☎ (914) 398-2621 . . 36 Lawrence Lane, PO Box 63, Palisades, NY *10964*

Ludington MR & MRS William F (van Otterloo—Betty A Erickson) Wh'lck'60.Wes'58 . . of
☎ (561) 231-9653 . . "Windsong" 301 Sable Oak Dv, Vero Beach, FL *32963*
☎ (508) 696-8719 . . "East View" RFD 475D, Edgartown, MA *02539*

Ludlow MR Alden R JR—Y'34
☎ (516) 239-0364 . . 100 Ocean Av, Lawrence, NY *11559*

Ludlow MISS Amy C—Hart'82
☎ (212) 579-5226 . . 308 W 91 St, Apt 4, New York, NY *10024*

Ludlow MR & MRS George C (Louise H McGuinness) Ty'51
☎ (518) 873-6899 . . "Friendship Hill" Box 847, Lincoln Pond Rd, Elizabethtown, NY *12932*

Ludlow MR & MRS George C JR (Amy A Veit) Col'87.NCar'86.Pace'90
☎ (214) 789-1520 . . 5707 Williamstown Rd, Dallas, TX *75230*

Ludlow MISS (DR) Jeanne C—Pa'88
☎ (215) 361-0340 . . 712 Walnut St, Apt 3, Lansdale, PA *19446*

Ludlum MRS Samuel A (Shippee—Anne B Miles)
☎ (908) 747-9487 . . 132 South St, Red Bank, NJ *07701*

Ludwick MR Dennis K—Cal'93 . . see MISS E V B Lapham

Luebbermann MR & MRS Henri A JR (Susan L Emley) Cl'69.Ariz'74 . . of
☎ (520) 299-4953 . . 6154 N Zorrela Segundo, Tucson, AZ *85718*
☎ (520) 357-6196 . . Watermelon Farm, Box 4310, Aravaipa Canyon, Dudleyville, AZ *85292*

Luebke MISS Marie K . . see G Schwab 5th

Luers MR & MRS William H (Turnbull—Wendy W Woods) Stan'61.Ham'51.Cl'58 . . . . of ☎ (212)288-0034
MISS Ramsay F Turnbull—Geo'92—at 695 Noe St, Apt 2A, San Francisco, CA *94114* 993 Fifth Av, New York, NY *10028*
MISS Connor E Turnbull—Br'94 . . . . ☎ (860) 868-1285 44 Upper Church Hill Rd, Washington Depot, CT *06794*

Luetkemeyer MR & MRS John A JR (Suzanne Frey) Elk.Md.Cy.Wms'63 . . . . ☎ (410) 377-4077
MISS Mary A . . . . 910 Applewood Lane, Baltimore, MD *21212*
MISS Julia B . . . .
MISS Anne F . . . .

Lufkin MRS Blakeslee Cook (F Blakeslee Cook) ☎ (615) 292-3860
SL'56.Nyc. . . . . 2140 Golf Club
MR H Christopher—at ☎ (410) 742-8451 Lane, Nashville, TN
1514G Sharen Dv, Salisbury, MD 21801 . . . . . . | 37215
Lufkin MR Dan W—Y'53
see Dilatory Domiciles
Lufkin MR Peter W SR—Nyc.Yn.Y'49
☎ (615) 356-0372 . . 2303 Hillmeade Dv, Nashville, TN 37221
Lugar MR & MRS Norman O JR (Mary E ☎ (313) 632-5322
Mollenhauer) Wayne'63 . . . . 1252 Long Lake
MISS Kristin S . . . . Court, Brighton, MI
48116
Lukacs MR & MRS John A (Segal—Stephanie C Harvey) Camb'39.Buda'46
☎ (610) 933-7495 . . "Pickering Close" Valley Park Rd, Phoenixville,
PA 19460
Lukacs MR & MRS Paul B (M Karen Johnson) Ken'79.Ken'78
☎ (410) 323-8155 . . 5102 Norwood Rd, Baltimore, MD 21212
Luke MR & MRS David L 3d (Sweetser—Fanny R Curtis)
Rdc'51.Pr.Ln.Ri.Cly.Y'45
☎ (212) 249-7039 . . 775 Park Av, New York, NY 10021
Luke MR & MRS Douglas S (Sarah C Mullen) of ☎ (305)669-3249
V'79.Au.B.Sa.Va'64.Va'66 . . . . "French Cottage"
MISS Lindsay H—at 2905 E Lester St, Tucson, 1004 Cotorro Av,
AZ 85716 . . . . Coral Gables, FL
MR D Russell 33146
☎ (518) 576-4411
"The Lean-To"
Ausable Club,
St Huberts, NY
12943
Luke MR & MRS John A (Joy Carter) Y'86.Y'48 . . of
☎ (203) 972-3524 . . 377 Oenoke Ridge, New Canaan, CT 06840
☎ (561) 231-6117 . . 660 Indian Harbor Rd, John's Island, Vero Beach,
FL 32963
Lukens MR & MRS Alan W (Susan Atkinson) ☎ (301) 652-7538
Cvc.Pn.P'46 . . . . 18 Grafton St,
MR Timothy E—Colg'91 . . . . Chevy Chase, MD
20815
Lukens REV Alexander M—Y'26
Park Manor Apt 601, 1801 E Nineteenth Av, Denver, CO 80218
Lukens MR E Benjamin C—P'56 . . . . ☎ (207) 846-5740
MR Peter G . . . . 14 Summer St,
Yarmouth, ME
04096
Lukens MISS Elizabeth B . . see C A Day
Lukens MRS John Brockie (Amy Austin) Sth'39.Ste.Cda.
☎ (610) 828-3139 . . 3012 Park Av, Lafayette Hill, PA 19444-1710
Lukens MISS Margaret A (Harrington—Margaret A Lukens) Rdc'77
17 Pierce St, Orono, ME 04473
Lukens MR & MRS Robert A (Elizabeth S Taylor) ☎ (215) 836-7328
CtCol'66.Pc.Ph.Rb.P'62.H'65 . . . . 8221 Ardmore Av,
MISS Alice L—P'95 . . . . Wyndmoor, PA
MR David C—V'92 19038-8401
MR J Nicholas—at Yale . . . .
Lum MR & MRS Jack Brady (Jill W Morehouse) Va'89.Va'89.H'93
☎ (404) 237-8862 . . 2870 Elliott Circle NE, Atlanta, GA 30305

Lum MR & MRS William Douglas JR (Deborah E Dulaney)
SoMiss'82.MissCol'76.MissState'91
☎ (601) 437-4798 . . Van Dorn House, 103 Van Dorn Dv, Port Gibson,
MS 39150
Lumbard MR Dirk—CentWashSt'74
☎ (212) 757-1366 . . 320 W 56 St, Apt 2D, New York, NY 10019
Lumbard MR & MRS J Edward (Polly Poindexter) Sth'27.C.Rv.Hn.H'22
☎ (203) 259-0054 . . "Barley Hill" 490 Hillside Rd, Fairfield, CT 06430
Lummis MR Dayton M JR—Me.Myf.Rv.Y'59 . . of
☎ (505) 820-1711 . . 318 W Houghton St, Santa Fe, NM 87501
☎ (610) 688-1681 . . 129 Aberdeen Terr, St Davids, PA 19087
Lumpkin MR & MRS Richard A (G Gail Gawthrop) ☎ (217) 234-4422
V'59.Cho.Y'57.H'63 . . . . 5 Lafayette Av,
MISS Elizabeth A—DeP'92 . . . . Mattoon, IL 61938
MR Benjamin—Yale . . . .
Lundgren MR & MRS Richard J (Nancy W Truslow) ☎ (508) 785-1533
Sm.Cy.Rens'64.H.'90 . . . . 48 Center St, Dover,
JUNIORS MISS Elizabeth W . . . . MA 02030
JUNIORS MR Andrew A . . . .
Lundy MASTER Fred Mason (g—Fred C Larkin) . . . . Born at
Denver, CO May 16'95
Lunny MRS Robert M (BRNSS Liane von Wallenberg) Gr.
☎ (908) 439-2121 . . "Fieldcote" Far Hills, NJ 07931
Lunt MRS Dudley C (Margaret F Duane) Ncd.Ds. . . ☎ (302) 239-5120
MISS Anne D—at ☎ (603) 878-3443 . . East Rd, Cokesbury Village
RFD 1, Wilton, NH 03086 . . . . 408, 726 Loveville
Rd, Hockessin, DE
19707
Lupfer MISS Caroline H (Edgar B) . . . . Married
Kurtz MR Willis O'C . . . . Jun 1'96
Lupfer MR & MRS Edgar B (Sarah S Henry) ☎ (513) 399-6276
V'45.Csn.P'42 . . . . 2851 Burrwood Rd,
MR Jonathan B—P'85—at 836 Centre St, Springfield, OH
Jamaica Plain, MA 02130 45503
Luppen MR & MRS Luppe Ridgway (Paula Busch) ☎ (213) 581-8121
Stan'66.Stan'65 . . . . 10309 Seabury
MISS Karye C . . . . Lane, Los Angeles,
MISS Cynthia A . . . . CA 90077
JUNIORS MR Luppe B . . . .
Lupton MR & MRS John Thomas 2d (Alice M Probasco) Ln.NCar'50 . . of
☎ (423) 821-6561 . . "Stonedge Point" Lookout Mountain, TN 37350
☎ (561) 546-8528 . . 157 S Beach Rd, Hobe Sound, FL 33455
Luquer MRS Evelyn P (Frances M N Jones) V'26.Ncd.Dc.
Kendal at Hanover 351, 80 Lyme Rd, Hanover, NH 03755
Luquer MR & MRS Peter Van C (Deborah B ☎ (802) 436-3340
Morgan) Ty'56.Pa'64 . . . . PO Box 72,
MISS Heidi P—Vt'85.AGSIM'91—Box 1770, Hartland Four
Manomet, MA 02345 . . . . Corners, VT 05049
MR Peter S—at 849 Beacon St, Apt 10, Boston,
MA 02215 . . . .
Lurie MR & MRS David V (Sally W Johnson) Skd'78
☎ (617) 773-9487 . . Marina Bay, 16 Schooner Lane, North Quincy,
MA 02171
Lurie MISS Katherine C—Bost'91 . . see M M Backerman
Lurie MISS Renée C—StL'89 . . see M M Backerman

Lusk MR & MRS Charles T (Anne C Durgee) O'70.Vt'74 . . . . ☎ (802) 253-7758 RD 2, Box 3780, Stowe, VT *05672*
MISS Katharine A . . . .
MR Nathaniel C . . . .

Lusk MR & MRS James H (Janet L Armstrong) Y'60. of ☎ (847)251-5823
MISS Wendy P—Dick'94 . . . . 2025 Chestnut Av,
MR Andrew P—Buck'95 . . . . Wilmette, IL *60091*
☎ (815) 777-1609 17 North Ridge, Galena, IL *61036*

Luther MR Crocker—Hn.H'62 . . . . ☎ (203) 655-3134
MISS Sandra B—Conn'83—at ☎ (202) 547-0996 1 Nolen Lane,
112—4 St SE, Apt 1, Washington, DC *20003* . . Darien, CT *06820*

Luther MISS Elizabeth A . . see H N Slater

Luther MISS Frances R—Ncd.
☎ (513) 321-6352 . . 3580 Shaw Av, Apt 427, Cincinnati, OH *45208*

Luther MR & MRS Michael (Imogene R Pratt) Wms'51 . . . . ☎ (203) 387-4972 "Anchorground"
MISS Sarah P—OWes'87.Nu'96—at 128 Northrup Rd,
☎ (212) 586-5778 . . 330 W 45 St, New York, Woodbridge, CT
NY *10036* . . *06525*

Luther MRS Schulze (Elizabeth R Schulze) LIU'63.Nu'76.Dc.
☎ (212) 879-9359 . . 311 E 71 St, New York, NY *10021*

Lutken MR & MRS Donald C JR (Nell I Breed) *see*
SoMiss'75 . . . . *Dilatory Domiciles*
MR Donald C 3d . . . .
MR John B . . . .
JUNIORS MR Christian R . . . .

Lutton MRS Robert (Newson—Grace W Schroeder) Cda.
☎ (610) 688-0224 . . 500 E Lancaster Av, Apt 130A, St Davids, PA *19087*

Lutz MRS Kenneth C (Orr—Marjorie Brunhoff)
☎ (518) 854-3287 . . Toddhunter Farm, PO Box 14, Shushan, NY *12873*

Lybrand MRS John E (M Terry Da Costa) . . . . ☎ (610) SU9-6180
MR Walter J Da C . . . . 805 Terwood Rd,
MR Stephen E . . . . Drexel Hill, PA *19026*

Lyden DR & MRS John P (Engelhardt—Carol S Murphy) Geo'77.Un.Cly.H.'61
☎ (212) 879-7812 . . 148 E 65 St, New York, NY *10021*

Lydon MRS Alicia K (Wasson—Alicia L Kircher) Btc.
☎ (847) 295-5802 . . 1350 N Western Av, Apt 208, Lake Forest, IL *60045*

Lydon MR Douglas K—Wash'77
☎ (312) 943-1133 . . 301 W Superior St, Chicago, IL *60610*

Lyle MR & MRS James Arthur (Martha L Gale) ☎ (915) 533-1754
Tex'74.Rv.Dar.Cda.GaTech'68 . . . . 626 Blacker Av,
MR Cory J G . . . . El Paso, TX *79902*

Lyman MRS Arthur T (Joan M Lincoln)
☎ (803) 648-8658 . . 1290 Richardson Lake Rd, Aiken, SC *29803*

Lyman MR Arthur T 3d—Ny.Cl'68.H'71
☎ (617) 523-3321 . . 85 E India Row, Boston, MA *02110*

Lyman MR & MRS Cabot (Heidi Hoffman) Vt'67 . . . ☎ (207) 354-6865
MR Zachary C . . . . 11 Knox St,
JUNIORS MR Alex C . . . . Thomaston, ME
JUNIORS MR Drew H *04861*

Lyman MR & MRS Charles P (Jane H Cheever) Tv.D.H.'36
☎ (617) 828-1202 . . 105 Elm St, Canton, MA *02021*

Lyman MISS Charlotte P—Y'82 . . see P Van Slyck

Lyman MR & MRS Frederick W (Mary S Freeman) Ty'77.Cw.Myf.Bow'70.H'74
☎ (617) 729-7623 . . 21 Washington St, Winchester, MA *01890*

Lyman MR & MRS Huntington (Lineaweaver—Chastain— Anne A Tilghman) BMr'53.Cc.Y'45 . . of
☎ (860) 739-5282 . . 267 Old Black Point Rd, Niantic, CT *06357*
☎ (508) 457-1871 . . 5 Old Homestead Rd, Falmouth, MA *02540*

Lyman MRS John L (Cynthia Forbes) Chi.Ncd.
☎ (617) 235-0351 . . "Descrie" 636 Charles River St, Needham, MA *02192*

Lyman MRS Laura R (Venetti—Laura Robbins) . . . ☎ (813) 596-9393
MR Joseph JR . . . . 14449 Oakglen Dv N, Largo, FL *33774-5029*

Lyman MR & MRS Lincoln P (Barbara L Putnam) of ☎ (212)369-0075
Rdc'76.Bgt.Nf.Cly.H.'74.H'82 . . . . 1067 Fifth Av,
JUNIORS MISS Daphne W . . . . New York, NY *10128*
☎ (914) 234-9414 "Green Acres" 56 Indian Hill Rd, Bedford, NY *10506*

Lyman MISS Lorraine
☎ (617) 864-7255 . . 10 Soden St, Apt 42, Cambridge, MA *02139*

Lyman MISS Lydia W
☎ (207) 276-3296 . . Joy Rd, Northeast Harbor, ME *04662-0875*

Lyman MR Ronald T—K.Sm.Ub.Cc.H'76
☎ (202) 362-5425 . . 4740 Connecticut Av NW, Apt 409, Washington, DC *20008*

Lyman MRS Ronald T JR (Shaw—Susan J Storey) Rdc'49.Sm.Yh.
☎ (803) 747-7882 . . Yeamans Hall Club, PO Box 9455, Charleston, SC *29410*

Lymburn MASTER Spencer Clarkson (g—Arthur L Kelly) . . . . Born Mch 20'94

Lynch MR & MRS Alexander P (Sally K Woolworth) Fic.Pa'74
☎ (203) 869-9859 . . 5 Woodside Rd, Greenwich, CT *06830*

Lynch MISS Alexandra D . . see J P Bradley

Lynch MR C Bruton (R Vincent) . . . . Married at Dallas, TX
Foster MRS Shannon (Shannon R Savage) . . . . Jun 22'96

Lynch JUNIORS MR Charles H . . see J P Bradley

Lynch MR & MRS Christopher C (Laura B Vastine) Ken'85.Me.Bates'84
☎ (203) 972-8732 . . 545 Smith Ridge Rd, New Canaan, CT *06840*

Lynch MR & MRS David B (Bretherton—Josephine A ☎ (610) 658-0218
Dexter) Y'50 . . . . 828 Black Rock Rd,
MISS Linda—at San Francisco, CA . . . . Gladwyne, PA
MR David B JR—at Buckfield, ME *04220* *19035*

Lynch MRS Edmund A (Florence D Sullivan)
☎ (516) CE9-3447 . . "Holly House" 206 Sage Av, Lawrence, NY *11559*

Lynch MR & MRS Edmund C JR (Braff—Teller—Alice Treibick) Ny.B.Pr.Srb.Plg.Y'48
☎ (561) 546-7005 . . 406 S Beach Rd, Hobe Sound, FL *33455*

Lynch MR & MRS Edmund C 3d (Deborah A Brown) Pr.
☎ (516) 759-2911 . . 12 Matinecock Farms Rd, Glen Cove, NY *11542*

Lynch MISS Elizabeth T . . see J P Bradley
Lynch MISS Elizabeth W—Cly . . .see C S Kreger
Lynch MRS Frank C (Emily H Todd)
 ☎ (860) 535-1195 . . 188 Water St, PO Box 449, Stonington, CT *06378*
Lynch MR & MRS G Philip (Horner—Sylvia W Maitland) Rc.
 ☎ (516) 569-4849 . . 175 Briarwood Crossing, Lawrence, NY *11559*
Lynch MR Hampton S—Y'48.Nu'57
 ☎ (011-33-1) 47-04-59-72 . . 8 Villa Spontini, 75116 Paris, France
Lynch MRS Hilary G (Marian P Tenaglia) Pg.Rr. . . . | ☎ (412) 683-3266
 MR Kevin McK. . . . . | Royal York Apt
 MISS Michelle G (Asselineau—Michelle G Lynch) | 816, 3955 Bigelow
 | Blvd, Pittsburgh, PA
 | *15213*
Lynch CDR & MRS Hubbard (Diana W Webster) | ☎ (619) 789-0288
 USNR.Sth'59.Y'55.Cl'63 . . . . | 15926 Arena Dv,
 MR Kevin H . . . . | Ramona, CA *92065*
Lynch MR & MRS John D (Emily S Montgomery) | ☎ (307) 739-0540
 Hn.H'52.Nu'58. . . . . | PO Box 7615,
 MR John M—Col'91 . . . . | Jackson, WY *83002*
 MR Michael D—CtCol'93 . . . . |
Lynch MISS Lindsay R . . see J P Bradley
Lynch MISS Mary B . . see C S Kreger
Lynch MR & MRS Michael P (Catherine R Parker)
 Buck'77.VillaN'83.Temp'78.Pa'81
 ☎ (610) 431-3204 . . 1226 Upton Circle, West Chester, PA *19380*
Lynch MRS Nell Orand (F Nell Orand) . . . . Married at Dallas, TX
 Beck MR Henry C JR (late Henry C) . . . . Apr 27'96
Lynch MR Peter C (R Vincent) . . . . Married at Dallas, TX
 Nady MISS Elizabeth A (Gary) . . . . Feb 24'96
Lynch MISS Phoebe R . . see O P Burden
Lynch MRS R Parsons (Rose P Parsons)
 ☎ (203) 966-7990 . . 23 Hathaway Common, New Canaan, CT *06840*
Lynch MR R Vincent—Fic.Cvc.Y'45 . . . . | *see*
 MR Joseph B—Miss'88 . . . . | *Dilatory Domiciles*
Lynch MR & MRS R Vincent JR (Rebecca P | ☎ (011-44-171)
 Hathaway) DU'73.Fic.P'72 . . . . | 581-2823
 JUNIORS MISS Rebecca P . . . . | 27 Pelham Crescent,
 JUNIORS MR Redington B . . . . | London SW7,
 | England
Lynch MR & MRS Robert F 3d (Robin M Keefe) Tul'78.Cda.Colg'73
 ☎ (718) 543-6362 . . 4663 Palisades Av, Bronx, NY *10471*
Lynch MRS Sylvia Leland (Hilmer—Sylvia Leland Lynch) RISD'72
 ☎ (860) 535-1195 . . 188 Water St, PO Box 449, Stonington, CT *06378*
Lynch MR & MRS William R (Mary P Grant) | ☎ (203) 661-0047
 Sth'57.Y'51.Cl'58 . . . . | 100 Bedford Rd,
 MISS Elizabeth B—Mid'84—at Emory Law . . . . | Greenwich, CT
 MISS Cynthia P—at San Francisco, CA. . . . . . . | *06831*
 MISS Kimberly T—at 825 West End Av, |
 New York, NY *10025* . . . . |
 MISS Sarah P—at Conn Coll . . . . |
Lynd MR & MRS Richard B (Susan C Thompson) Ncd.H.'57 . . of
 ☎ (718) JA2-3820 . . 200 Hicks St, Brooklyn, NY *11201*
 ☎ (518) 286-2833 . . "Windward" Box 358, Rensselaer, NY *12144*
Lynn MR B Stanley—Stan'38
 ☎ (408) 722-7714 . . Pajaro Dunes H11, 2661 Beach Rd, Watsonville, CA *95076*

Lynn MR Henry S JR—K.Cy.Cc.Rv.Cw.Wt.StJ.Pn.P'66.H'71
 ☎ (205) 871-3440 . . "Hickory Hill" 2878 Shook Hill Rd, Birmingham, AL *35223*
Lynn MR Jeffrey R—LIU'71
 ☎ (516) 283-2104 . . . "Wyndecote Cottage" 45 Gin Lane, PO Box 5072, Southampton, NY *11969*
Lynn MISS Letitia C . . see D R Valiunas
Lynn MR & MRS Seth McC JR (Hélène Martin) | ☎ (914) 234-9700
 Briar'72.Cl'80.Bgt.Y'71.Pa'75 . . . . | 87 Clinton Rd,
 JUNIORS MISS Ashley R . . . . | Bedford Hills, NY
 JUNIORS MR Seth McC 3d . . . . | *10507*
Lyon MRS Alice E (Auchincloss—Thompson—Alice E Lyon)
 ☎ (516) 725-5269 . . 28 Palmer Terr, Sag Harbor, NY *11963*
Lyon BRIG GEN (RET) & MRS Archibald W (Abbott—Frances E Dowdle)
 USA'32.CTech'35
 ☎ (703) 799-9674 . . 9110 Belvoir Woods P'kway, Apt J414, Ft Belvoir, VA *22060*
Lyon MRS Cecil T F B (Elizabeth S Grew) B.Mt.Hn.
 ☎ (603) 525-3375 . . "On the Rocks" 301 Kings H'way, Hancock, NH *03449-5110*
Lyon MR & MRS Richard A M (A Remsen Franklin) | ☎ (617) 333-0709
 MdArt'73.Cy.Bost'73 . . . . | 1084 Brush Hill Rd,
 JUNIORS MISS Addison F . . . . | Milton, MA *02186*
Lyon MR & MRS Robert B (Jo Ann Vestal)
 ☎ (540) 338-7776 . . Rte 2, Box 578, Purcellville, VA *20132*
Lyon MR & MRS Robert B JR—Ayc.Cw.SCar'70
 ☎ (410) 263-8404 . . 9 Steele Av, Annapolis, MD *21401-2840*
Lyon MR & MRS William W (Nina LeR Miller) DelB.Ht.Ncd.H'55
 ☎ (561) 278-7950 . . 2150 S Ocean Blvd, Delray Beach, FL *33483*
Lyon MR & MRS William W 3d (Kathleen M Mitchel) OWes'67
 ☎ (707) 584-3083 . . 6460 Meadow Pines Dv, Rohnert Park, CA *94928*
Lyons MR & MRS Donald J (Melinda A Bradford) | ☎ (503) 636-7350
 MichSt'63.Myf.Nw'67 . . . . | 17769 Overlook
 MISS Anne E . . . . | Circle,
 | Lake Oswego, OR
 | *97034*
Lyons MR & MRS Dudley E (Volina F Valentine) | ☎ (212) 222-4401
 Sth'63.Aht'62.H'65 . . . . | 390 Riverside Dv,
 MISS Victoria R—Denis'90.Bridgept'95—at | New York, NY
 11631 Charter Oak Court, Reston, VA *20190* . . | *10025*
 MR Gregory N—Aht'94 . . . . |
Lyons MR & MRS George R (Anne Starr) | of ☎ (215)836-5164
 Cent'y'58.Ncd.Pa'67 . . . . | 545 Spring Lane,
 MR George A 2d—NCar'87—at | Wyndmoor, PA
 ☎ (617) 969-0764 . . 36 Central Av, Newtonville, | *19038*
 MA *02160* . . . . | ☎ (941) 964-0553
 | PO Box 864,
 | Boca Grande, FL
 | *33921*
Lyons DR & MRS George V (Maureen Foster) McG'47.StJ.Siena'50.Cl'53
 ☎ (802) 773-4162 . . "Robinwood" HCR 34-14, Killington, VT *05751*
Lyons MR & MRS Henry W (Winifred Runton) | ☎ (508) 256-2430
 BMr'50.Ll.H'45 . . . . | 48 Grandview Rd,
 MR David A—Ne'76 . . . . | Chelmsford, MA
 MR Robert W—Ll.H'79 . . . . | *01824*

Lyons MR Matthew B (Donald J) . . . . Married at Portland, OR
    Lundin MISS Kristi A (Robert) . . . . Jun 8'96
Lytle MR & MRS John H (Kindred—Jean Heath) | of ☎ (513)293-7732
    Hob'33 . . . . | 1212 Lytle Lane,
    MR John H 3d . . . . | Dayton, OH 45409
    | ☎ (602) 977-6883
    | 10663 W Tropicana
    | Circle, Sun City, AZ
    | *85351*

M

McAdoo MRS Annie T (Annie C Taussig) . . see MRS J T Taussig
McAdoo MR & MRS Davis F (Patricia B Durbin) . . . . | ☎ (301) 530-1655
    MISS Heather D . . . . | 10416 Farnham Dv,
    MR Scott D—Ogle'75 . . . . | Bethesda, MD
    | *20814-2220*
McAdoo MR & MRS Francis H JR (Cynthia S Heffron) Rcn.Md.P'38
    ☎ (908) 439-2651 . . 58 Fox Hill Rd, Califon, NJ *07830*
McAdoo MR & MRS Henry M JR (Marion Markell) V'41.Ph.Rb.
    ☎ (215) MI6-0514 . . "Patteran" 1300 Gypsy Hill Rd, Penllyn,
    PA *19422*
McAdoo MR & MRS Malcolm R JR (Yvonne | ☎ (301) 229-5278
    Christlieb) Cal'49 . . . . | 7201 Crail Dv,
    MRS Jean McA Miler (Jean M McAdoo) | Bethesda, MD
    SCar'79—☎ (301) 320-2945 . . . . | *20817*
McAdoo MISS Marguerite de H—Cly.
    ☎ (212) 355-3595 . . 480 Park Av, New York, NY *10022-1613*
McAdoo MR & MRS McKinley Campbell (Elsie Heard)
    Chath'74.Me.Rr.Gm.P'71.Temp'75
    ☎ (610) 525-8187 . . 237 Ladbroke Rd, Bryn Mawr, PA *19010*
McAdoo MR & MRS Richard B (Mary Wigglesworth) Tv.Hn.H'42
    ☎ (617) 868-2628 . . 7 Lincoln Lane, Cambridge, MA *02138*
McAdoo MR & MRS Robert C (Hancock—Mary L Cheston)
    Rc.Me.Gm.Ac.Aht'43.Pa'48
    ☎ (610) 649-0119 . . 1421 Waverly Rd, Gladwyne, PA *19035*
McAfee MRS Horace J (Wright—Christine Parker) Plg.Chr.StJ.Ncd.Dar.
    ☎ (914) 591-7204 . . "Stoneleigh" Matthiessen Park,
    Irvington-on-Hudson, NY *10533*
McAfee MISS Mary Ann (Baxter—Mary Ann | ☎ (212) 580-9564
    McAfee) SL'64 . . . . | 171 W 71 St, Apt
    MR James A Baxter . . . . | 3E, New York, NY
    | *10023-3837*
McAfee MR & MRS W Gage (Linda Ho) | ☎ (011-852)
    McG'71.Cl'73.H'65.Cl'68 . . . . | 2849-6014
    JUNIORS MISS Dallas—at Phillips Andover . . . . . | 3 Severn Rd,
    JUNIORS MR Zachary R G—at Phillips Andover . | The Peak,
    JUNIORS MR Horace M . . . . | Hong Kong

McAleenan MRS Clifford C (Stewart—Sheronas— | ☎ (207) 594-0660
    Marian Farrel) Ncd. ⚓ | "Bear House"
    MISS Marian Stewart—at 3850 Delaware Lane, | 38 Wellington Dv,
    Las Vegas, NV *89109* . . . . | Rockport, ME
    | *04856-4022*
    | Jan 1 . .
    | ☎ (970) 925-6441
    | PO Box 9939,
    | 0137 Northway Dv,
    | Aspen, CO
    | *81612-7306*

McAllister MR & MRS Alexander B (Owen—Elizabeth M Ustvedt)
    Cal'54.Bur.Bhm.Sfg.Cp.
    ☎ (619) 341-6242 . . 46-795 E El Dorado Dv, Indian Wells, CA *92210*
McAllister MR & MRS Bruce R (Maxwell—Claire E Ruple) Nw'70.H'58
    ☎ (303) 444-5052 . . 2330 Linden Av, Boulder, CO *80304*
McAllister MRS Helen Borie (Helen S Borie) Sg.
    ☎ (610) 645-8836 . . 1400 Waverly Rd, Blair 126, Gladwyne, PA *19035*
McAllister MRS Walter W JR (Edith L Scott) Tex'38.A.
    ☎ (210) 826-1005 . . 203 Terrell Rd, San Antonio, TX *78209*
McAllister MRS William B (Nancy B Barth)
    ☎ (203) 777-8547 . . 34 Deepwood Dv, Hamden, CT *06517*
McAlpin MR & MRS Benjamin B 3d (Jeanie P Gerst)
    Man'vl'60.K.Coa.Snc.StA.Vca.Fw.Myf.Cw.Cc.StJ.Rv. Wt.P'51.Nu'80
    ☎ (203) 661-0914 . . 24 N Porchuck Rd, Greenwich, CT *06831*
McAlpin MR & MRS Charles N (Anne M Stupp) | ☎ (314) 993-1884
    Swb'68.Cy.Rc.Nd.P'69 . . . . | 2 Upper Ladue Rd,
    JUNIORS MR Charles N JR . . . . | St Louis, MO *63124*
McAlpin MR & MRS David Hunter (Stewart—Sarah Sage) G.B.Cly.Myf.
    ☎ (609) 924-1019 . . PO Box 670, Princeton, NJ *08542-0670*
McAlpin MISS Dorothy P
    ☎ (914) 963-8608 . . 117 DeHaven Dv, Apt 247, Yonkers,
    NY *10703-1313*
McAlpin MR & MRS Malcolm M (Judith A | ☎ (908) 766-6774
    Rohrbacher) Duke'69.Shcc.Duke'67 . . . . | 20 Post Kennel Rd,
    MISS Joann C—at ☎ (201) 426-0189 | Far Hills, NJ *07931*
    55 S Village Green, Budd Lake, NJ *07828* . . . . . |
    MISS Marian M . . . . |
    MR Andrew M—at ☎ (412) 441-9462 |
    370 S Negley Av, Apt 7, Pittsburgh, PA *15232* . |
McAlpin MRS William R (Williams—Lawrence—
    Kathleen E Middleton) Yh.
    ☎ (410) 778-1866 . . Land's End Farm, 23629 Land's End Rd,
    Chestertown, MD *21620*
McAnerney MISS Lisa T . . see MRS H C Slack
McAnerney MR Robert M—Snc.Wms'45.Va'53 . . of
    ☎ (203) 838-8530 . . 2 Pin Oak Lane, West Norwalk, CT *06850*
    ☎ (941) 649-0442 . . La Maison Club, 3450 Gulf Shore Blvd N, Naples,
    FL *34103*
McAniff MR & MRS John Edward (Carey Theresa Lewis)
    SCal'81.Vh.HolyC'83
    ☎ (818) 796-4818 . . 1406 Wellington Av, Pasadena, CA *91103*
McAshan MRS Samuel A (Phelps—Marie C Lee)
    see Dilatory Domiciles

McAtee MRS Swoyer (Susan E Swoyer). . . . . | ☎ (215) 836-0533
MR Nathan Stuart—LaS'94. . . . . | 8101 Eastern Av,
| Wyndmoor, PA
| *19038*

McAuliffe MRS Dorothy Buck (Dorothy Weekes | ☎ (212) 744-4396
Buck). . . . . | 170 E 78 St,
MISS Thirza D. . . . . | New York, NY
MISS Dorothy L. | *10021*
MR George B 3d—Cl'89. . . . . |
McAuliffe MR E Timothy JR—Cr'95 . . see L S Jackson
McAvoy MR & MRS Norman M (Helen C Arndt) | ☎ (610) 527-4892
Wheat'56.Ncd.Swth'54.H'57 . . . . | 601 Winsford Rd,
MR Norman M JR—Rich'82—at | Bryn Mawr, PA
☎ (610) 688-6364 . . 490 General Washington | *19010*
Rd, Wayne, PA *19087* . . . . |
MR William M—Ty'83—at ☎ (617) 367-6225
2 Hawthorne Place, Apt 8E, Boston, MA *02114*
MR Henry C—Del'88 . . . . |
McBain MR & MRS Angus W (Bell—Lucy A Q | ☎ (213) 938-0186
Toberman) Cal'61.Stan'64.Stan'76. . . . . | 227 Muirfield Rd,
MISS Barbara E . . . . | Los Angeles, CA
    MR Jeffrey M Bell . . . . | *90004*
    MR Charles Derek Bell. . . . . |
    MR Christopher A Bell. . . . . |
McBaine MR & MRS J Patterson (Susan Swinerton) | ☎ (415) 387-1883
Wheat'68.Bur.H'65 . . . . | 20 Presidio Terr,
MISS Amanda—V'95 . . . . | San Francisco, CA
JUNIORS MR Justin T . . . . | *94118*
McBean MR & MRS Peter (Helmer—Nancy N Hoguet)
Srr.Srb.Fic.K.Pcu.Bur.Sfg.StJ.
☎ (415) 344-3629 . . 25 Downey Way, Hillsborough, CA *94010*
McBee MRS Keith W (Lucy H Banks) . . . . | ☎ (410) 823-3403
MR Keith W JR . . . . | 1207 Berwick Rd,
MR Andrew A D—Nu'77 . . . . | Baltimore, MD
MR Edward V—MdArt'83 . . . . | *21204*
McBride MR Andrew Gore—SFrArt'92
see Dilatory Domiciles
McBride MRS Davis (Isabelle S Davis)
☎ (914) 679-8496 . . 6 Cedar Way, Woodstock, NY *12498*
McBride MR Harman W . . . . Died at
Mayfield Heights, OH Apr 11'96
McBride MR James Bradley—TexA&M'82
☎ (713) 888-0659 . . 5001 Woodway Dv, Apt 1404, Houston, TX *77056*
McBride MR John G JR—Bhm.Cal'81
☎ (510) 841-2945 . . 55 Alvarado Rd, Berkeley, CA *94705*
McBride MR & MRS Jonathan E (Emilie E Dean) | ☎ (301) 656-1359
Mt.Cvc.Yn.Y'64. . . . . | 3704 Blackthorn
MISS Morley E . . . . | Court, Chevy Chase,
JUNIORS MR Webster D—at Yale. . . . . | MD *20815*
McBride MISS Lucia—Cwr'36.Plg.Cda.Dar.Myf.
☎ (212) 876-4045 . . 201 E 87 St, New York, NY *10128*
McBride DR Raymond A . . . . Died May 13'96
McBryde MR & MRS J Bolton (Landreth—Tinney—Ethel M Wilson)
☎ (803) 521-9034 . . 821 Ribault Rd, Beaufort, SC *29902*

McBurney MRS Andrew M (Lidie L Sloan) SL'36.Cly.Ncd.Y . . .of
☎ (212) 737-0147 . . 190 E 72 St, New York, NY *10021*
☎ (518) 523-3245 . . "River Ranch" Adirondack Loj Rd, Box 1271,
Lake Placid, NY *12946*
McCabe MRS Annette P (Annette J Prophet) | ☎ (617) 237-9851
Km.Dar. . . . . | 137 Hampshire Rd,
MR Edward J 3d . . . . | Wellesley Hills, MA
| *02181*
McCabe MR & MRS Calvert C JR (Grace F Koppelman) Cy.Gi.JHop'35
☎ (410) 321-5454 . . Blakehurst 5, 1055 W Joppa Rd, Towson,
MD *21204*
McCabe MR & MRS Fred A (Ramsay—Elizabeth J Wiel) Stan'34.Pitt'32
☎ (307) 733-2203 . . Circle EW Ranch, Box 648, Jackson, WY *83001*
McCabe MR & MRS James L (Louise Beachboard) | ☎ (610) 526-0639
Sth'63.Y'66.H.'78.Me.Ph.Ac.Ncd.Colby'65.Pa'70 | 701 Williamson Rd,
MISS Sarah B . . . . | Bryn Mawr, PA
JUNIORS MR William L . . . . | *19010*
McCabe MRS N Vastine (Nelle A Vastine) Pa'49.Me.M.Ncd.
☎ (610) MI2-4076 . . 244 Hathaway Lane, Wynnewood, PA *19096-1903*
McCabe MR & MRS Thomas B 3d (Anne M | ☎ (610) 642-5228
Edwards) Rose'77.M.Me.Ph.Mds.Stan'75.Pa'78. | 613 College Av,
MISS Katherine E . . . . | Haverford, PA
MISS Christina M . . . . | *19041*
JUNIORS MR Thomas B 4th . . . . |
McCabe MR & MRS Walter C (Norment—Nancy A | ☎ (301) 229-7436
Richards) Cvc. | 5500 Albemarle St,
    MISS Elizabeth L Norment—at 565 E Howard | Bethesda, MD
    St, Pasadena, CA *91104* . . . . | *20816*
    MISS Katherine B Norment—at 35 Bedford St,
    New York, NY *10014* . . . . |
McCaffree MRS Burnham C (Averill—Margaret StJ Sidway)
3620 Buckwood Court, Annandale, VA *22003-1951*
McCain MR Charles S 3d . . see MRS C D Heddens
McCain MISS Claudia V . . see MRS C D Heddens
McCain MR & MRS David W (Eleanor M O'Brien) Hlns'57.W&L'55.H'60
☎ (706) 268-3424 . . 184 Big Canoe, Big Canoe, GA *30143*
McCain MRS Samuel A (Jane Murtagh)
☎ (910) 962-0244 . . Penick Home, Box 2004, Southern Pines,
NC *28388-2004*
McCall MISS Alison G (Cushman—Alison G | ☎ (212) 410-6097
McCall) MtH'76.Pr. . . . . | 70 E 96 St, Apt 8D,
JUNIORS MR Blinn L Cushman . . . . | New York, NY
| *10128*
McCall MR & MRS David B JR (Abigail F Stackpole) Bnd'84.Rc.Conn'81
☎ (212) 289-3971 . . 139 E 94 St, New York, NY *10128*
McCall MRS Doy Leale JR (Margaret T Kohn) | of ☎ (334)872-6161
Hln'60.Ncd. | 11 Pine Acres,
MISS Margaret T . . . . | Selma, AL *36701*
MR Doy L 3d . . . . | ☎ (334) 962-7184
MR John P. . . . . | "Tear Down
| House" 30650
| Magnolia St,
| Perdido Beach, AL
| *36530*
McCall MR Edgar S (Robert H) . . . . Married at S'Agaro, Spain
Comas MISS Rosa M (Francesc) . . . . Jly 8'95
McCall MISS Frances F . . see J N Dill JR

McCall MR & MRS Harry JR (Evelyn B Peck) P'36.Tul'39
☎ (504) 891-2212 . . 1427 Fourth St, New Orleans, LA *70130*

McCall MR & MRS J Bartow (Leilani J Fairman) | ☎ (215) CH2-1736
Pc.Pa'52 . . . . | 9502 Wheel Pump
MISS Florence E . . . . | Lane, Philadelphia,
| PA *19118*

McCall MR John P—B'gton'79 . . see C P Cox 2d

McCall MR & MRS Jonathan C (Jane A Walker) | ☎ (504) 891-3990
P'72.Tul'77 . . . . | 1420 Harmony St,
MISS Alston W—at Georgetown . . . . | New Orleans, LA
MR Jonathan C JR—at Middlebury . . . . | *70115-3407*

McCall MISS Monica Comas (g—Robert H McCall) . . . . Born at
Guadalajara, Mexico Jun 5'96

McCall MR & MRS Peter C (de St Phalle—Susan K Collingwood)
Fic.Rc.Sa.Cl'81 . . of
☎ (212) 988-1519 . . 165 E 72 St, Apt 20G, New York, NY *10021*
☎ (860) 434-0016 . . ''Maison Skootee'' 25 Johnny Cake Hill Rd,
Old Lyme, CT *06371*

McCall DR & MRS Richard E (Ingrid Marical) P'65.Tul'69
Rte 2, Box 80, Elm Grove, LA *71051*

McCall MR Robert D—L&C'84
☎ (206) 860-2139 . . 1111 E John St, Seattle, WA *98102*

McCall MR & MRS Robert H (Carol A Sawyer) | ☎ (503) 228-5600
Col'62.Col'62 . . . . | 1808 SW Laurel St,
MR Robert C . . . . | Portland, OR *97201*

McCall MR & MRS S Carter JR (Thornton—Sandra H Rex) Pa'56
1714 Newbridge Court, Reston, VA *20191-3500*

McCall MR Thomas C—Ore'91 . . see C P Cox 2d

McCallum MR & MRS David K (Katherine E | ☎ (212) 371-5134
Carpenter) Cly. . . . . | 40 E 62 St,
MISS Sophie R—at U of Vt . . . . | New York, NY
MR Peter W—Van'93 . . . . | *10021*

McCammon MR & MRS Joseph K 4th (Katherin G | ☎ (610) 932-4300
Armstrong) Mt. . . . . | ''Etcetera Farm''
MISS Abbie B . . . . | 101 Newark Rd,
MR Joseph K 5th. . . . . | Lincoln University,
MR David G . . . . | PA *19352*

McCance MISS Catherine Emma Burlingame (William H) . . . . . . Born at
Winchester, MA May 14'96

McCance MR & MRS Thomas JR (Francine Jaques) Lx.Yn.Y'55.Cl'58
☎ (413) 637-0143 . . 16 Cliffwood St, Lenox, MA *01240*

McCance MR & MRS William H (Suzanne M Biette) NH'86
☎ (617) 241-5872 . . 65 Pearl St, Charlestown, MA *02129*

McCandless MR & MRS Hugh D (Dorothy C Andrew)
☎ (203) 281-7200 . . 200 Leeder Hill Dv, Apt 434, Hamden, CT *06517*

McCandless MRS Rosemary Van L (Ross—Fri—Rosemary Van L
McCandless) ColC'71.Tex'88.Dar.W.
☎ (216) 449-9483 . . PO Box 192, Chagrin Falls, OH *44022*

McCann MR & MRS Donald Fraser (Fairchild—Joy E Vietor)
☎ (602) 991-4168 . . 7759 Bowie Rd, Scottsdale, AZ *85258*

McCann MISS Helen M . . . . | ☎ (011-41-21)
MISS Frances. . . . . | 728-44-93
| ''Beau-Rêve''
| 27 Ch de
| Chamblandes, Pully,
| CH 1009 Vaud,
| Switzerland

McCargo MR & MRS Grant (McLean—Chew—Audrey S Holding)
Eyc.Rr.Edg.BtP.Err.Evg.Br'52 ⚓
☎ (412) 741-8832 . . Audubon Rd, Sewickley, PA *15143*

McCargo MR Thomas W—Eyc.
☎ (412) 749-0565 . . Little Sewickley Creek Rd, Sewickley, PA *15143*

McCarley MR & MRS Thomas P (Hedges—Diana B | ☎ (617) 698-5235
Roberts) Drake'71.Ga'67 . . . . | 332 Blue Hills
MISS Page R . . . . | P'kway, Milton, MA
JUNIORS MISS Diana P . . . . | *02186*

McCarrens MRS Arthur D (Constance Alexander)
☎ (561) 278-2171 . . 821 Seasage Dv, Delray Beach, FL *33483*

McCarrens MISS Constance (Schwerin—Constance McCarrens) Man'vl'71
☎ (617) 742-1416 . . 66 Chestnut St, Boston, MA *02108*

McCarter MR Thomas N 3d—Bcs.Ri.B.Ln.Rc.So.Plg.Ll.Snc.P'52
☎ (212) 319-8331 . . 188 E 64 St, New York, NY *10021*

McCarthy MR & MRS David G (Helen W Jordan) Vt'85.Cal'85
☎ (201) 267-7444 . . 48 Kitchell Rd, Morristown, NJ *07960*

McCarthy MR & MRS John G (Fleming—Lily Lambert)
Rcn.B.Err.Eyc.Evg.BtP.Plg.StJ.Cly.Dar.Cda. Wms'30.H'32
☎ (561) 659-4379 . . 1801 S Flagler Dv, Apt 1602, West Palm Beach,
FL *33401*

McCarthy MR & MRS Louis B JR (Judith M Warner)
Gchr'46.Cy.Gi.Rv.Mv.Myf.Ncd.P'47.NH'54
☎ (410) 235-7127 . . 615 W University P'kway, Baltimore, MD *21210*

McCarthy MR & MRS Michael J (Charlotte B Miller)
Ty'79.Rcn.Au.Elk.Md.Dth'79.Cl'82
☎ (410) 771-0710 . . Crooked Fence Farm, 2200 Geist Rd, Glyndon,
MD *21071*

McCauley MRS Clayton C (Heinz—Joan Diehl) Sfy.
☎ (415) 931-7757 . . 2750 Vallejo St, San Francisco, CA *94123*

McCauley MR & MRS Hugh J (Katharine G Vaux) McG'67.Pa'72 . . of
☎ (610) LA5-4517 . . 320 Caversham Rd, Bryn Mawr, PA *19010*
☎ (609) 884-1911 . . 809 Sewell Av, Cape May, NJ *08204*

McCawley DR & MRS (DR) Christopher L (Susan E Gehman)
Penn'79.Pa'83.Penn'79.Del'81.Pa'85
☎ (860) 434-8150 . . 57 Bill Hill Rd, Lyme, CT *06371*

McCawley MR & MRS Edmund S JR (McMullen—Janet F Cruikshank)
CtCol'46.Pa'43
☎ (508) 693-1851 . . 250 Franklin St, Box 1661, Vineyard Haven,
MA *02568*

McCawley MR & MRS William M (Sarah A Fisher) Ds.Pa'41
☎ (610) 431-0136 . . 1203 Princeton Lane, West Chester,
PA *19380-5741*

McCay MR Andrew T . . see W G von Weise JR

McChord MR & MRS John S (Barbara L Simmelink) | ☎ (216) 291-0941
MISS Janet L . . . . | 3550 Woodridge Rd,
MISS Susan Sawyer—Gchr'92—at | Cleveland Heights,
☎ (410) 821-6687 . . 904 Dulaney Valley Court, | OH *44121*
Apt 904, Towson, MD *21204*. . . . . |

McClain MR & MRS Allan (Charlotte R Williams) | ☎ (540) 632-8720
Hlns'65.P'63 . . . . | 1715 Meadowview
MR James 2d. . . . . | Lane, Martinsville,
| VA *24112*

McClain MR & MRS Carson (Nancy Lewis) V'47.Me.Mich'47
☎ (610) 525-0299 . . Andover House B307, 975 Mill Rd, Bryn Mawr,
PA *19010*

McClean MR J Devereux E—P'74
☎ (617) 734-9364 . . 1443 Beacon St, Brookline, MA *02146*
McCleary MR Benjamin P—F&M'94 . . see R E Watson
McCleary MR & MRS Benjamin W (Jean L Muchmore) DU'72.P.'66 . . of
☎ (212) 831-5461 . . 114 E 90 St, New York, NY *10128*
☎ (401) 783-6223 . . PO Box 5236, Wakefield, RI *02880*
McCleary MISS Katherine C—Br'95 . . see R E Watson
McClellan MISS Alice B . . see R G Powers
McClellan MRS Constance S B (Constance R Seely Brown)
☎ (860) 434-1900 . . 2-1 Lee St, Old Lyme, CT *06371*
McClellan MRS Emilie S (Wood—Emilie R Stevenson)
☎ (804) 973-1161 . . Four Seasons, 64 Woodlake Dv, Charlottesville,
VA *22901*
McClellan MR Gerald C
☎ (212) 752-2786 . . 125 E 63 St, New York, NY *10021*
McClellan MR Gordon S . . see R G Powers
McClellan MR James B . . see R G Powers
McClellan JUNIORS MISS Lucy S . . see R G Powers
McClellan MR Maxwell C . . see R G Powers
McClellan MRS Otey (Frances P Traylor) . . . . Died at
New York, NY Jun 30'96
McClellan MRS Robert (A Jeanette Banta) . . . . Died at
Geneseo, NY Jun 21'96
McClellan MR Robert—Srr.Y.'38 . . . . | of ☎ (716)243-1361
MR Robert 3d—Box 638, Potsdam, NY *13676* . . | "Meikleknox"
MR Gordon B . . . . | 5230 Reservoir Rd,
| PO Box 218,
| Geneseo, NY *14454*
| ☎ (518) 677-3158
| "Northwood"
| 41 N Union St,
| Cambridge, NY
| *12816*
McClellan MR Stephen A JR—Br'54 . . . . | of ☎ (757)481-6112
MR Stephen J . . . . | 2005 Compass
| Circle, Virginia
| Beach, VA *23451*
| ☎ (207) 282-2791
| "The Shack"
| 96 Mile Stretch Rd,
| Biddeford Pool, ME
| *04006*
McClellan MR William Traylor . . see R G Powers
McClelland MR & MRS Donald R (Janet N | of ☎ (202)338-2286
Legendre) Mich'54 . . . . | 2903 N St NW,
MISS Sylvia Marina . . . . | Washington, DC
MISS Janet Newbold . . . . | *20007*
| ☎ (410) 651-0426
| "School Ridge
| Farm" Box 137,
| Upper Fairmount,
| MD *21867*
McClenahan MISS Ann B (Le Breton—Ann B McClenahan)
☎ (202) 244-4773 . . 6240 Utah Av NW, Washington, DC *20015*
McClenahan DR & MRS John L (Cheek—Mary Tyler Freeman)
V'37.Pc.StJ.Cs.Cda.Y'37.Pa'41
☎ (804) 359-4376 . . 4703 Pocahontas Av, Richmond, VA *23226*

McClenahan MR John M . . . . Died at
Bryn Mawr, PA Nov 26'95
McClenahan MRS John M (Barbara Brown) Me.Ncd.
☎ (610) 649-1220 . . 449 Montgomery Av, Apt 112, Haverford,
PA *19041*
McClenahan MR & MRS Robert W JR (Ann Rebecca | ☎ (203) 782-0459
Freeman) NCar'69.Ty'58.NCar'74 . . . . | 72 Cottage St,
MISS Amanda W—at ☎ (212) 370-1078 | New Haven, CT
300 E 46 St, Apt 4J, New York, NY *10017* . . . . | *06511*
JUNIORS MR Edward P—at Ohio Wesleyan . . . . . |
McClendon MR & MRS Burwell B JR (Grace J Gillespie) Miss'52.Miss'52
☎ (601) 366-3791 . . 4163 Dogwood Dv, Jackson, MS *39211*
McClintic MASTER Alasdair William Stanley (Richard D) . . . . . . Born at
London, England May 15'95
McClintic MR & MRS David W (Denise L Arcand)
Tufts'80.Suff'83.Bost'86.Rr.Pg.Ne'84.NH'92
☎ (603) 523-7876 . . RR 2, PO Box 56A, Canaan, NH *03741*
McClintic MR & MRS Richard D (Katherine A A Murphy)
Pom'77.AmUParis'82
☎ (011-44-171) 224-3130 . . 66 Harley House, Marylebone Rd,
London NW1 5HR, England
McClintock MR & MRS Edward A 3d (Iris Fitzhugh | ☎ (520) 297-5055
Gordon) Ariz'72.Purd'68 . . . . | 11680 N Dragoon
JUNIORS MISS Lauren A . . . . | Springs Dv, Tucson,
JUNIORS MR Reade A . . . . | AZ *85737*
McClintock MR & MRS John T (Mary B Mitchell) | ☎ (212) 860-3471
Plg.Cly.Cs.Ncd.Y'31.H'33 . . . . | 1220 Park Av,
MISS Elizabeth S (Istel—Elizabeth S McClintock) | New York, NY
—at ☎ (212) 431-5244 . . 53 Crosby St, | *10128*
New York, NY *10012* . . . . |
McCloskey MR & MRS M Wayne JR (Frances C | ☎ (860) 242-5635
Sherman) Hood'69.Chi.NMex'72 . . . . | 246 Duncaster Rd,
MISS Lee A—at Ohio U . . . . | Bloomfield, CT
MR Mark B—at Ariz State . . . . | *06002*
McCloskey MR & MRS Paul N JR (Helen V Hooper) Ant'75.Stan'51.Stan'53
☎ (415) 851-0218 . . 580 Mt Home Rd, Woodside, CA *94062*
McCloskey MR Paul W—Pa'48
☎ (301) 652-8033 . . 3405 Cummings Lane, Chevy Chase, MD *20815*
McCloud MR & MRS Kimball P (Claire Swain | ☎ (909) 392-9504
Huntington) Stan'73.Bur.Stan'73 . . . . | 25553 Brassie Lane,
MISS Casey H . . . . | La Verne, CA *91750*
MISS Ashley H . . . . |
McCloud MRS Kimberly S (Kimberly A Sherman) | ☎ (415) 434-3419
CalInst'82 . . . . | 22 Vandewater St,
MR Cory S—Reed'92—at Paris, France . . . . | Apt 108,
| San Francisco, CA
| *94133*
McCloy MR & MRS John J II (Laura H McGehee) | ☎ (203) 629-2324
V'63.Ln.P'59 . . . . | "Hunter's Rest"
MR John J III—Van'94—at ☎ (011-49-89) | 313 Stanwich Rd,
986289 . . Fr Herschelstrasse 5, Munich, Germany | Greenwich, CT
MR Rush M—at U of Va . . . . | *06830*
McClughan DR & MRS Joseph F (Annette M Stahl) | 28 Highland
Sth'35.Colg'31.Cl'35 . . . . | Mountain Rd,
MISS Joanne F . . . . | Northfield, NH
| *03276*

McCluney MR & MRS Henry N (Carolyn Lansing) Sth'40.Cysl.Aht'39
☎ (561) 231-2712 . . 271 Indian Harbor Rd, John's Island, Vero Beach, FL *32963*

McClung MR & MRS S Alfred 3d (Adelaide B Smith) V'41.Pg.Cda.Pitt'53
☎ (412) 826-5722 . . Longwood at Oakmont CH22, 500 Rte 909, Verona, PA *15147*

McClure MR & MRS Archibald (Downey—Anna G Cunningham) Sth'44.Cho.Ih.Bur.Tcy.Y'44
1 Arbor Lane, Apt 405, Evanston, IL *60201*

McClure MRS William H (Sarah S Gibbs) Me.
☎ (610) LA5-6981 . . 1430 County Line Rd, Rosemont, PA *19010*

McColley MR Sutherland—Plg.Coa.Snc.Cw.Cspa.
W'minster'60.W'minster'62 . . of
☎ (516) 324-3373 . . PO Box 155, Wainscott, NY *11975-0155*
☎ (212) 861-8420 . . 420 E 80 St, New York, NY *10021*

McCollum MR Gordon
☎ (212) 260-1846 . . 203 Prince St, New York, NY *10012*

McCollum MRS Leonard F (Whitney—Eleanor Searle) Ln.
☎ (713) 622-2755 . . 3435 Westheimer Rd, Houston, TX *77027*

McCollum MR Otis R—Cvc.NCar'52
☎ (301) 654-6847 . . 5500 Friendship Blvd, Apt 2110N, Chevy Chase, MD *20815*

McCollum MR & MRS T Bonner (Edwene Stevens) Ark'60.Ark'55
☎ (501) 633-3622 . . 2 Ridgewood Lane, Forrest City, AR *72335*

McComas MR & MRS Louis G JR (Patricia E Garmer) NotreDMd'54.Loy'54 . . . .
MR Mark E—at 10 Killadoon Court, Timonium, MD *21093* . . . .
MR John H—at 6408 Eastern P'kway, Baltimore, MD *21214*
☎ (410) 321-8232 915 Breezewick Circle, Towson, MD *21286-3302*

McComas MR & MRS Oliver P JR (Chamberlain—Goodnow—Peggy B Caldwell) P'52
☎ (415) 328-4872 . . 380 Santa Margarita Av, Menlo Park, CA *94025*

McComas MR Richard C . . . . Died at New Brunswick, NJ Jly 23'95

McComb MR & MRS David F (Frances B Wharton Elek) H'89.VillaN'92.Ac.Van'78.Pitt'81
☎ (215) 732-2241 . . 1837 Lombard St, Philadelphia, PA *19146*

McCombs MRS Robert P (Dorothy E Reist) . . . .
MISS Patricia A . . . .
☎ (803) 681-2198 150 S Port Royal Dv, Hilton Head Island, SC *29928*

McComic MR & MRS R Barry (Judith J Joseph) Sdy.U'61.Tul'64.Freib'65 ⛵
☎ (619) 459-7799 . . 2032 Via Casa Alta, La Jolla, CA *92037*

McConihe MRS F Moran (Marguerite C Hagner) Mt.Cvc.Sl.
☎ (301) 299-4132 . . 11501 Piney Meeting House Rd, Potomac, MD *20854*

McConnaughey MR & MRS David T (Linda A Munn) Br'74.Bcs.Cly.Br'74
☎ (212) 689-5030 . . 137 E 38 St, Apt 10E, New York, NY *10016*

McConnel MR & MRS W Bruce 3d (Margaret P Sutton) M.Ph.Rr.P'65 . . . .
MISS Mary Blair—Cr'96 . . . .
MR W Bruce 4th . . . .
MR Ian Roberts—at Middlebury . . . .
☎ (610) 527-4097 604 Pembroke Rd, Bryn Mawr, PA *19010*

McConnell MISS (DR) Carol J . . . . Married at Long Beach, CA
Benoit MR James P . . . . Jan 26'96

McConnell MRS E Riggs (McCook—Cornelia B Sloane) V'42
525 Latona Av, Ewing, NJ *08618*

McConnell MRS Frederick S (Ann S Hitchcock) Sth'48.Un.Cv.Kt.
☎ (216) 255-8993 . . 8724 King Memorial Rd, Mentor, OH *44060*

McConnell MRS Julia C (Waterbury—Julia L Chieppo) Ford'77
☎ (561) 832-4240 . . 128 Seabreeze Av, Palm Beach, FL *33480*

McConnell MR & MRS Scott K (Ulrike H Lwowski) APac'89.APac'90.HMudd'88
☎ (219) 875-3101 . . 22371 W Briarhill Dv, Goshen, IN *46526-8410*

McConney MR & MRS Gerald E (Polly P Fagen) P'45
☎ (310) 476-2162 . . 470 Robinwood Dv, Los Angeles, CA *90049*

McConoughey MISS Caitlin H—Hlns'91 . . see M B Weir

McCord MR A Jamison . . see P S Rawlings

McCord MR & MRS Paul C JR (Sarah G Freeman)
3344 Bell St, New Orleans, LA *70119*

McCormack MR & MRS Brian P (Barbara D Juergens) Prov'65 . . . .
MR M Scott—H'90 . . . .
MR Brian P JR—H'92 . . . .
☎ (512) 392-5568 2912 Maravillas Loop, Austin, TX *78735*

McCormick MR Brooks—Cas.Cho.Rc.Y'40
☎ (312) 944-4242 . . 1530 N State P'kway, Chicago, IL *60610*

McCormick MR Brooks JR
"Troubled Waters" PO Box 1801, Barrington, IL *60011*

McCormick MR & MRS Christopher L (Tanya Irving) LakeF'82.LakeF'81.Nw'91
☎ (847) 295-2430 . . 29 Oak Terr, Lake Bluff, IL *60044*

McCormick MRS Clement T (Cordova—Hannah L Jisa) . . . .
MISS Catherine E—at 3313 Virgo St, Sacramento, CA *95827* . . . .
MISS Jennifer B—Stan'94 . . . .
MR Michael T . . . .
MR Robert A Cordova JR—at U of Cal Berkeley . . . .
of ☎ (415)665-0158 1520 Monterey Blvd, San Francisco, CA *94127-2019* "Surfside" 21 Calle Del Embarcadero, Stinson Beach, CA *94970*

McCormick MRS Cross (I Balene Cross) Mds.
☎ (505) 984-8479 . . 209 Tano Rd, Santa Fe, NM *87501*

McCormick MR David W
☎ (201) 445-1081 . . 143 Union St, Ridgewood, NJ *07450*

McCormick MR & MRS Ernest O 3d (Cynthia Romaneck) Bur.Pcu.Cp.SantaC'54 . . . .
JUNIORS MR Christopher R . . . .
of ☎ (415)347-9050 85 Falkirk Lane, Hillsborough, CA *94010*
☎ (408) 688-5526 767 Las Olas Dv, Sea Cliff Beach, Aptos, CA *95003*

McCormick MISS Frances
☎ (415) 931-8571 . . 2500 Pacific Av, San Francisco, CA *94115-1126*

McCormick MR & MRS John S (Bertha B Brooks) P'35
☎ (802) 362-1578 . . "Hillborn Farm" RR 2, Box 3120, Manchester Center, VT *05255-9604*

McCormick MISS Laura L—Cal'91 . . see F H Grau

McCormick MR & MRS Levering (Brown—Judith L Talcott) Denis'71.DU'74.Vt'69 . . . . | ☎ (802) 362-3201 PO Box 116, West Rd, Manchester, VT 05254
MISS Wynne K—Vt'94—at 327 NE 57 St, Seattle, WA 98105 . . . .
MR John W—at Ohio Wesleyan . . . .

McCormick MISS Mary K
☎ (415) 931-0122 . . 2944 Pierce St, San Francisco, CA 94123

McCormick MR Matthew B—Tul'83
☎ (202) 265-5100 . . 2430 Wyoming Av NW, Washington, DC 20008

McCormick MR Michael H—H'50
Elmwood Park, IL 60635

McCormick MR & MRS Peter H (Fair Alice S Bullock) BMr'59.Chi.H'59 ⚓ . . . . | ☎ (508) 748-2055 13 Cove St, Marion, MA 02738
MR Alexander H—in Slovakia . . . .
MR Benjamin G . . . .

McCormick MASTER Peter Leander (Christopher L) . . . . . Born Sep 19'94

McCormick MR & MRS Thierry L (Mari Bahe) SL'49.Fy.Ch'43
☎ (910) 295-5515 . . "Tremont" 15 Maple Rd, Box 1761, Pinehurst, NC 28374

McCoun MR Bruce T . . . . Died at Quogue, NY Jly 23'96

McCoun MR Peter T
☎ (516) 653-4714 . . 9 Deer Path, Quogue, NY 11959

McCown MR John A . . see MRS P T Stowe

McCown MISS Susan G
736 Stoke Rd, Villanova, PA 19085

McCoy MR & MRS Charles W (Peschel—Gloria J Shepherd) NCar'67.Purd'60 . . . . | ☎ (619) 454-9434 1441 Inspiration Dv, La Jolla, CA 92037
MISS Lisa R . . . .
MR Jeffrey W . . . .
MISS Shana C Peschel . . . .
MISS Neile E Peschel . . . .

McCoy MR Peter A—Bhm.Paris'70.Cal'71.Cal'76
☎ (707) 942-0515 . . "Clos des Pierres" 17050 H'way 128, Calistoga, CA 94515

McCoy MR & MRS Timothy J (Linda B Lewis) Sth'77.Mar'vil'84.Wash'95
☎ (314) 298-7832 . . 12121 Jeannette Mary, Maryland Heights, MO 63043

McCracken MR David Jackson Beekman—Ht.Drew'73
☎ (814) 459-5303 . . 1324 S Shore Dv, Erie, PA 16505

McCracken MRS Jackson (Clara S Jackson) Cly.Cda.Ht.Dh.
☎ (212) PL3-6519 . . 36 Sutton Place S, New York, NY 10022

McCracken MR & MRS John E (Jeanne M Smith) Un.Plg.Coa.Snc.StA.Cw.Rv.Cs.P'36.Y'39
☎ (212) 876-5166 . . 1199 Park Av, New York, NY 10128-1711

McCracken MRS Stewart (Joan A Fernley) Pa'47.Pc.Ac.Ncd. . . . . | ☎ (610) 828-2504 "Meadow Run" 2300 Hickory Rd, Plymouth Meeting, PA 19462
MR James C—Sar. . . . .

McCready MR & MRS Joseph M 3d (Sheryl A Fisher) Hood'63.Pa'63 . . . . | ☎ (610) 527-3951 1013 Longview Rd, Gulph Mills, PA 19406
MR Joseph M 4th . . . .
MR H Robert . . . .

McCready MR & MRS Richard F JR (Jane C Houston) Bost'69.K.Cly.P'63.Va'66.Lond'67 . . | ☎ (606) 299-6584 3150 Cleveland Rd, Lexington, KY 40516
MISS Sarah H—at Bowdoin. . . . .

McCreary MR & MRS Pierce N (Elizabeth M Smith) Ny.Y'49.Va'52 ⚓
☎ (914) 834-2942 . . 90 Valley Rd, Larchmont, NY 10538

McCreary MR & MRS Pierce N JR (Holly L Bartlett) RSage'77.Ny.CtCol'76
☎ (914) 762-2535 . . 1305 Eagle Bay Dv, Ossining, NY 10562

McCreery MR & MRS Lawrence K (Lorraine Sampson)
☎ (561) 588-9061 . . 1980 S Ocean Blvd, Manalapan, FL 33462

McCrindle MR Joseph F R—Rc.Gr.C.H'44.Y'48
☎ (212) 362-4052 . . 91 Central Park W, Apt 14A, New York, NY 10023

McCrum DR & MRS Edward A (Hope Griswold) Sth'52.Dth'45 . . . . | ☎ (415) 332-1021 830 Spring St, Sausalito, CA 94965
MISS Elizabeth C—at 28 Lovejoy Way, Novato, CA 94949 . . . .
MR Edward G . . . .

McCuaig MR & MRS Victor C JR (Robb—Fell—Cordelia D Reid) Lic.Ck.Hl.StA.P'51.Cl'58
☎ (516) 676-9339 . . 24 Matinecock Farms Rd, Glen Cove, NY 11542

McCue MRS Allen L (Gertrude L Peabody) Ncd.
☎ (207) 846-5387 . . 35 Applegate Lane, Falmouth, ME 04105

McCullagh MR & MRS Grant G (Suzanne D Folds) Sth'73.H'74.H'81.Cho.Ih.Cas.Cnt.Cda.Ill'73.Pa'75. Ch'79
☎ (847) 446-0499 . . 43 Locust Rd, Winnetka, IL 60093

McCulloch MR & MRS Andrew C (Joan G Houston) Bnd'50.Dth'47.Cl'56
☎ (203) 661-5354 . . 4 Augustus Lane, Greenwich, CT 06830

McCulloch MISS Jeanne R (Taylor—Jeanne R McCulloch)
see A W Wadsworth

McCulloch MRS John I B (Van Devere—Patricia Robineau) Ri.Mds.Dyc.Cly.Cs.StJ. . . . . | ☎ (212) 737-3171 151 E 79 St, New York, NY 10021
MISS P Darcy—at ☎ (212) 473-7409
24 Gramercy Park, New York, NY 10003 . . . . .

McCulloch MR & MRS Owen (Julia M Lyons) OreSt'89.Myf.OreSt'89
☎ (503) 228-0849 . . 1020 NW Front Av, Apt N10, Portland, OR 97209

McCulloch MR & MRS Paul L (Helen E Widmaier) Cho . . .of
☎ (561) 735-3277 . . 3574 Royal Tern Circle, Boynton Beach, FL 33436
☎ (847) 724-2189 . . "Carriage Hill on the West Fork" 1500 Palmgren Dv, Glenview, IL 60025

McCulloh MRS Davidson (Elizabeth H Davidson) . . | ☎ (203) 359-3304 1900 Summer St, Apt 21, Stamford, CT 06905
MISS Amy G—at ☎ (914) 921-6838
184 Purchase St, Apt 13, Rye, NY 10580 . . . . . .
MR James S 2d—at ☎ (914) 699-1088
111 N Third Av, Apt 1M, Mt Vernon, NY 10550
MR Davidson—SUNY'96 . . . .

McCulloh MR & MRS Hamilton (Maureen A Twomey) StA.
☎ (206) 938-1982 . . 1729—41 Av SW, Seattle, WA 98116

McCullough MR Andrew D JR—Smu'92 . . see R N Murray

McCullough MR & MRS C Hax JR (Jean G Humason) V'51.Pg.Y'46 . . . . | ☎ (412) 963-9414 240 W Chapel Ridge Rd, Pittsburgh, PA 15238
MR Malcolm M—Y'79—at ☎ (508) 456-9828
PO Box 233, 6 Littleton Rd, Harvard, MA 01451
MR Alexander R—Y'85—at ☎ (718) 369-1918
94 Prospect Park SW, Brooklyn, NY 11218 . . . .

McCullough DR & MRS Charles T JR (Shirley A Freeman) Van'62.Ky'57 . . . . ☎ (704) 253-1178 57 Woodland Rd, Asheville, NC 28804
   MISS Leslie C—NCar'86—at ☎ (423) 673-3755 1611 Laurel Av, Apt 1212, Knoxville, TN 37916

McCullough MR George F—Rr.Rol'82 . . see G McK Blair

McCullough MR & MRS George R (Henshaw— Elisabeth G Briant) Ws'58.Rr.Pg.Y'51 . . . . of ☎ (412)683-9440 305 Schenley Rd, Pittsburgh, PA 15217
   MR John H Henshaw 3d—Mass'83.Tufts'85— at 1718 P St NW, Washington, DC 20005 . . . ☎ (412) 238-7733 ''Deer Springs'' Box 7, Rector, PA 15677

McCune MR & MRS John R 5th (Nancy J Raymond) . ☎ (405) 751-1137 3301 Quail Creek Rd, Oklahoma City, OK 73120
   MISS Molly C—at 1211 Belford Av, Oklahoma City, OK 73120 . . . .
   MISS Carrie N

McCune MR John R 6th
   ☎ (405) 842-2892 . . 7208 Waverly Av, Oklahoma City, OK 73120

McCurdy DR & MRS Alexander 3d (Tyson—Stroud—Patricia J Peterson) Sth'55.Cts.Nf.Ac.Wes'60.EpiscDiv'64 ⚓
   ☎ (610) 687-4827 . . ''Box Hill'' 613 Maplewood Rd, Wayne, PA 19087

McCurdy MR & MRS Ian A (Jane Byrd Sargeant) S.Ny.Rens'73.Mich'75 . . . . ☎ (516) 922-1861 5 Seawanhaka Place, Oyster Bay, NY 11771
   MR Peter J—at Georgetown . . . .
   JUNIORS MR J Morgan—at Kildonan . . . .

McCurdy MRS James A (Faith T Higgins) V'45.Pr.S.Cs. ⚓
   ☎ (516) 692-7344 . . PO Box 206, Cold Spring Harbor, NY 11724

McCurdy MR & MRS John G (Johnson—Marion L Schaefer) Pc.Y'49
   ☎ (215) 233-2765 . . 8811 Montgomery Av, Wyndmoor, PA 19038-8309

McCutcheon MR & MRS Benjamin K (Sarah S Defty) V'84.Cl'85
   ☎ (217) 947-2769 . . RR 1, Box 56, Elkhart, IL 62634

McCutcheon MISS Corwen . . see D Cavalla

McCutcheon MR & MRS George Barr 2d (Paula E Wilms) Rc.Fy.H'48 . . . . of ☎ (773)327-6464 2400 N Lakeview Av, Apt 1903, Chicago, IL 60614
   MR Ian—Ch'85.IIT'91 . . . . ☎ (803) 524-5242 601 Prince St, Beaufort, SC 29902

McCutcheon MR & MRS John T JR (Susan M Dart) Conn'42.On.Fy.H'39 . . of
   ☎ (704) 894-2707 . . 99 Holbert Cove Rd, Saluda, NC 28773-9502
   ☎ (847) 234-0898 . . PO Box 689, Lake Forest, IL 60045-0689

McCutcheon MISS Mary—Rice'69.Ariz'81
   ☎ (703) 243-3643 . . 2115 N Rolfe St, Arlington, VA 22209

McDaniel MRS David Jamison (Martha K Eyre) Tcy.
   ☎ (415) PR6-1451 . . 1250 Jones St, San Francisco, CA 94109

McDaniel MRS John S JR (Pulling—Emily K Platt) Ws'43.Sim'51.Cda. ☎ (410) 889-5723 105 Millbrook Rd, Baltimore, MD 21218-1018
   MR John S 3d—Cr'82.Balt'89 . . . .

McDaniel MRS Nancy M (Nancy L Moss) Swb'65 . ☎ (203) 438-4571 189 Barry Av, Ridgefield, CT 06877
   MISS Catherine B . . . .
   MISS Sarah V . . . .
   JUNIORS MR William B . . . .

McDaniel MR & MRS R Chase 2d (Barbara Santora) Me.Myf.Ac.Pa'54 . . . . ☎ (610) MI2-7013 337 Laurel Lane, Haverford, PA 19041
   MISS Sarah D—at London Sch of Business . . . . .
   MR R Chase 4th . . . .

McDermott MRS Clare Peterkin (Clare Peterkin) . . . ☎ (904) 285-3062 505 Rutile Dv, Ponte Vedra Beach, FL 32082
   MISS Stephanie A—at U of Fla . . . .

McDermott MRS Edward H (Ingersoll—Kelly—Mildred B Wetten) Cas.Wa.Ct.Myf.Ncd.
   ☎ (312) 787-2881 . . 237 E Delaware Place, Chicago, IL 60611-1713

McDermott MRS Eugene (Margaret Milam)
   ☎ (214) 521-1498 . . 4701 Drexel Dv, Dallas, TX 75205

McDermott MISS Jennifer J . . . . Married at Darien, CT Clarke MR Scott R (Robert) . . . . May 11'96

McDermott MR & MRS John H (Ann E Pickard) Cho.Cm.Ih.Wa.Wms'53 . . . . ☎ (847) 446-2022 330 Willow Rd, Winnetka, IL 60093
   MISS Elizabeth A . . . .
   MISS Mary L . . . .
   MR Edward H . . . .

McDermott BRIG GEN (RET) Robert F—A.USA'43
   ☎ (210) 828-6493 . . PO Box 33366, San Antonio, TX 78265

McDermott DR William V JR—Cy.Rv.H'38 . . . . . . ☎ (617) 326-5798 570 Bridge St, Dedham, MA 02026
   MISS Blanche A—☎ (617) 326-2498 . . . .

McDevitt MRS Gwynne C G (Rhodes—Severance—Gwynne C Garbisch) Rd . . .of
   ☎ (610) 356-2184 . . Covered Bridge Farmhouse, 4111 Goshen Rd, Newtown Square, PA 19073
   ☎ (302) 227-4926 . . 46 Pine Reach Rd, Henlopen Acres, DE 19971

McDevitt MR & MRS John J 3d (Elkins—Elizabeth Downes) Ac.
   ☎ (215) 886-5328 . . 1515 The Fairway, Apt 476, Rydal, PA 19046

McDevitt MR & MRS Joseph T (Suzanne B Jackson) Skd'76.Me.StJos'74
   ☎ (610) 649-8889 . . 414 Berkley Rd, Haverford, PA 19041

McDill MRS Laura (Gratwick—Laura McDill) Rdc'64 . . . . of ☎ (207)781-7117 7 Studley St, Falmouth, ME 04105-1612
   MISS Laura B Gratwick—Wes'95 . . . .
   MISS Katharine Gratwick—at Columbia . . . . . ☎ (802) 457-1725 ''Line Farm'' Woodstock, VT 05091

McDonald MISS Alexandra T . . see R H Norweb 3d

McDonald MR & MRS Donald (Jean Pettis) Ws'47.Me.Ncd.H'39 . . . . ☎ (610) LA5-2692 916 Oak Ridge Rd, Rosemont, PA 19010
   MISS Diane—at 510 Forest Glen St, Ames, IA 50014 . . . .

McDonald MR & MRS Ellice JR (Hayward—Rosa P Laird) Au.Cry.Ac.Swth'38
   ☎ (302) 652-4745 . . ''Invergarry'' Box 92, Montchanin, DE 19710

McDonald MISS Frances B—Col'84.StLaw'87
   ☎ (303) 623-3737 . . 1551 Larimer St, Apt 3103, Denver, CO 80202

McDonald MISS Hadley P . . see R H Norweb 3d

McDonald MR J Fairley JR—H'49
   ☎ (334) 264-6522 . . 2963 Old Farm Rd, Montgomery, AL 36111

McDonald MRS Mary M (Mary B Mix) Nw'46.Cas.
   ☎ (847) OR4-1742 . . 6739 Longmeadow Av, Lincolnwood, IL 60646

McDonald MR & MRS Matthew D (Eugenie L Mackey)
Duke'83.Duke'85.NCar'89
☎ (219) 432-9056 . . 6227 Tolbert Court, Ft Wayne, IN *46804*

McDonald MRS Nancy M (Raphael—Nancy M McDonald) Cly.
☎ (904) 285-2863 . . 34 Tifton Way S, Ponte Vedra Beach, FL *32082*

McDonald MR & MRS Samuel J (Alice M Soule)
Br'38 . . . . | ☎ (617) 894-2230
MISS Jeanne W—at ☎ (610) 458-8768 | 15 Pinecroft Rd,
Turning Point Farm, 390 Milford Rd, | Weston, MA *02193*
Downingtown, PA *19335* . . . .
MISS Nancy S—at ☎ (508) 872-8947
15 Weld St, Framingham, MA *01701* . . . .

McDonnell MISS Elaine B
☎ (201) 316-5009 . . 182 River Dv, Lake Hiawatha, NJ *07034*

McDonnell MR & MRS Hubert (Aline M M Elwes) . .
MISS Aline A L . . . . | ☎ (203) 869-1408
MISS Rosamond B J . . . . | 43 Buckfield Lane,
| Greenwich, CT
| *06831-2656*

McDonnell MR & MRS James S 3d (Elizabeth M | 40 Glen Eagles Dv,
Hall) Hlns'62.Bgy.Rr.Cy.P'58 . . . . | St Louis, MO *63124*
MISS Katherine H . . . . |

McDonnell MRS Kenneth (May Sandoz) . . . . . . Married at Greenwich, CT
Brittain MR Alfred 3d . . . . Jly 20'96

McDonnell MR Lawrence B
☎ (703) 533-8428 . . 2212 Boxwood Dv, Falls Church, VA *22043*

McDonnell MRS Lawrence E (Coralie B Barry) . . . . Died at
Hightstown, NJ May 6'96

McDonough MRS J Martin (L Norton Carroll) . . . . . | ☎ (410) 771-4579
MR Henry C—P'70.Va'78 . . . . | ''Duddington''
| 14936 Carroll Rd,
| Sparks, MD *21152*

McDonough MR John R
☎ (216) 521-5994 . . 17225 Clifton Blvd, Lakewood, OH *44107*

McDonough MR & MRS Michael P (Florence T | of ☎ (212)249-3232
Strawbridge) Srb.Rens'60 . . . . | 130 E 67 St,
MR Michael L—Denis'92 . . . . | New York, NY
MR David Lucas—ColC'95 . . . . | *10021*
| ☎ (802) 824-3742
| Hell's Peak Rd,
| Weston, VT *05161*

McDonough MR & MRS Paul H (Lynne Madden)
Geo'87.Geo'90.Geo'86.Ch'91
☎ (312) 573-1858 . . 1366 N Dearborn St, Apt 5A, Chicago, IL *60610*

McDougal MR & MRS Brent P (Jennifer E Lee) Emory'93.Emory'92
☎ (205) 870-2185 . . Samford University, Box 2309, Birmingham,
AL *35229*

McDougal DR & MRS David B JR (Dryden—Barbara | ☎ (314) 742-2862
S Price) P'45.Ch'47 . . . . | ''Ivyneck''
MISS Sarah H . . . . | 1033 Fiddle Creek
| Rd, Labadie, MO
| *63055-1801*

McDowell MR & MRS Putnam B (Lee—Lee—Rosamond Brooks)
BMr'46.Pg.Cy.Yh.Hn.H.'46
☎ (617) 326-3775 . . 21 Old Farm Rd, Dedham, MA *02026*

McDowell MR & MRS William W JR (Anne B | ☎ (203) 661-9167
Perkins) Rcn.P'58 . . . . | 754 Lake Av,
MISS Stewart L . . . . | Greenwich, CT
MISS Susan H . . . . | *06830*
MISS Abigail A . . . . |

McDuffie MR & MRS Charles H (E Ann | ☎ (914) BE4-3124
Van Norden) Y'50 . . . . | 74 David's Hill Rd,
MISS Carrington H—at ☎ (206) 284-0736 | Bedford Hills, NY
3213 W Wheeler St, Apt 304, Seattle, WA *98199* | *10507*
MISS Katharine W B—at 170 Irvington Av,
Apt 201, South Orange, NJ *07079* . . . . |
MISS Margaret Van N . . . . |

McDuffie MR & MRS Malcolm (MacLeod—Mary S leBrun de Surville)
Stan'40
☎ (818) 795-0348 . . 2060 Lombardy Rd, San Marino, CA *91108*

McElhiney MR & MRS Richard L (Lucie Lee Kinsolving)
Br'75.Nu'88.Y'75.Y'79
☎ (212) 316-3203 . . 7 W 96 St, New York, NY *10025*

McElroy MISS Ansley Fry (Malcolm N) . . . . Born at
Cincinnati, OH Feb 4'96

McElroy MR & MRS David B (Iglehart—Marjorie Le Boutillier) Mb.P'30
☎ (561) 546-4040 . . 210 S Beach Rd, Hobe Sound, FL *33455*

McElroy MISS Lauren Gooding (Malcolm N) . . . . Born at
Cincinnati, OH Feb 4'96

McElroy MR & MRS Malcolm N (Lori J Wigor)
Rol'78.Qc.Hn.H'70.Nw'72 . . of
☎ (513) 321-5611 . . 3575 Bayard Dv, Cincinnati, OH *45208*
☎ (513) 722-1406 . . ''Long Branch Farm'' 6883 Gaynor Rd, Goshen,
OH *45122*

McElroy MR W Finley . . . . Died at
Clayton, MO Jan 25'96

McEvoy MRS Nan Tucker (Phyllis A Tucker) Bur.Ri.
☎ (415) 398-5162 . . 611 Washington St, San Francisco, CA *94111*

McEvoy MR & MRS Thomas M 3d (Constance Tirrell)
Wms'76.Wms'76.Emory'76
☎ (011-44-1932) 222339 . . 28 Broadlands Av, Shepperton,
Middlesex TW17 9DQ, England

McEwan MRS Allerton J A (Ruth J Bell) V'34
☎ (805) 969-8397 . . 300 Hot Springs Rd, Apt 108, Montecito,
CA *93108-2038*

McEwen MR & MRS Lawrence C JR (Luntz—Joan K Hall) Fr.Mit'40
☎ (707) 963-1024 . . 1290 Sylvaner Av, St Helena, CA *94574*

McFadden MR & MRS Ashton S dos S (Camilla Corballis) Rol'88.Rc.Cr'88
☎ (212) 280-0208 . . 3 E 71 St, Apt 5E, New York, NY *10021*

McFadden MISS Elizabeth C—Br'93 . . see MRS L E Taylor

McFadden MR & MRS George (Moreton—Carol Owsley)
Tex'79.Ng.Mb.Van'63.Cl'66
☎ (212) 831-7878 . . 54 E 92 St, New York, NY *10128*

McFadden MR & MRS John H (Deirdre M | ☎ (011-44-171)
Whiteside) Bnd'74.Cl'75.Pr.Ph.H'70.Cl'73. | 935-1798
Ford'78 . . . . | 2 Chester Terr,
JUNIORS MR William V W . . . . | London NW1 4NL,
| England

McFadden MR John J W F—Fi.Ll.
269 S 21 St, Philadelphia, PA *19103*

McFarlan MRS Ronald L (Ethel W White) Ws'31.Ncd.
☎ (617) 721-2048 . . 299 Cambridge St, Apt 245, Winchester, MA *01890-2390*

McFarland MRS Alan R (Elizabeth M Mathieu) Sg.Fw.Ncd.
☎ (610) 645-8946 . . 1400 Waverly Rd, Andrews 112, Gladwyne, PA *19035*

McFarland MR & MRS Alan R JR (Kathleen M Troia) GeoW'73.Ox'78.Un.Rc.Mt.So.B.Ln.Ng. Cly.Y.'64.Y'67 . . . . | of ☎ (212)628-7540 770 Park Av, New York, NY *10021*
MR Andrew R—Cl'91 . . . . | ☎ (516) 283-9660 "The Pump House" Ram Island, PO Box 825, Southampton, NY *11969*
MR Gavin R—Va'94 . . . . | ☎ (202) 483-1725 2122 California St NW, Washington, DC *20008*

McFarland MR & MRS Duncan M (Ellen R Bromley) Pc.Cy.Y'65
☎ (617) 329-3361 . . 299 Clapboardtree St, Westwood, MA *02090*

McFarland MR & MRS George C JR (Elizabeth L Kennedy) NH'81.Me.Rc.P.'81.Duke'84
☎ (610) 689-8848 . . 215 Cheswold Lane, Haverford, PA *19041*

McFarland MRS H Barclay JR (Eleanor S Wood) . . | ☎ (215) 542-7090 111 Orchard Court, Blue Bell, PA *19422*
MISS Eleanor W—at ☎ (206) 329-9633 863 E Gwinn Place, Seattle, WA *98102* . . . . |

McFarland MRS Malcolm T (Marjorie T Hays) Cent'y'64.ClevSt'85.ClevSt'91 | ☎ (216) 247-6983 160 Glenn Rd, Moreland Hills, OH *44022*
MR Malcolm 3d—ColSt'90—Box 21, Kelly, WY *83011* . . . . |
MR Gregory H—at W Va Wesleyan . . . . |
JUNIORS MR Braddock A . . . . |

McFerran MR & MRS Alexander Y (Frederica P French) Cy.Chi.P'64.Wes'69 . . . . | ☎ (617) 326-8117 423 Sandy Valley Rd, Westwood, MA *02090*
MISS Brooke A—at Groton . . . . |
MR Alexander Y JR—at Colgate . . . . |
MR Christopher D—at Cornell . . . . |
JUNIORS MR Frederick P—at St George's . . . . . . |

McGarr MR & MRS Cappy R (Jane E Strauss) Tex'75.Tex'73
☎ (214) 352-3966 . . 5338 Wenonah Dv, Dallas, TX *75209*

McGaughy MR & MRS T Elkin (Barbara Crossette) Tex'50
☎ (210) 826-7865 . . 307 Encino Av, San Antonio, TX *78209*

McGee MISS Dorothy H—Pr.Cly.Sl.Cda.
☎ (516) 676-2332 . . Piping Rock Club, 150 Piping Rock Rd, Locust Valley, NY *11560*

McGee MR & MRS Joseph H (Evelyn B Moore) Conv'57.Ne.W&L'50.W&L'52 . . . . | ☎ (803) 722-3049 72 Anson St, Charleston, SC *29401*
MISS Madeleine S . . . . |

McGehee MRS C Coleman (Caroline Y Casey) Swb'49.Ncd. . . . . | of ☎ (804)282-3910 6128 St Andrew's Lane, Richmond, VA *23226*
MISS Margaret F V—at ☎ (804) 750-9937 8951 Bellefonte Rd, Richmond, VA *23229* . . . . | ☎ (804) 529-6642 "Faunroy" Bon Harbors, Lottsburg, VA *22511*

McGehee MR & MRS Carden C JR (Kristine E Miller) Hlns'78.Dar.Skd'76.Va'80
☎ (301) 320-2858 . . 4907 Rockmere Court, Bethesda, MD *20816*

McGehee DR & MRS Edward H (Carolyn Dunn) Pc.Ph.Cs.Pa'42.Jef'45 . . . . | ☎ (215) 233-0232 527 E Gravers Lane, Wyndmoor, PA *19038*
MISS Virginia McD—at ☎ (802) 655-5764 500A Dalton Dv, Colchester, VT *05446* . . . . . . |
MR Edward McD—Ty'84—at ☎ (860) 659-3537 . . 554 Hopewell Rd, South Glastonbury, CT *06073* . . . . |

McGehee MR & MRS Michael H (Ann Bacot C Igoe) Mid'84.Va'65
☎ (803) 723-0529 . . 21 Legare St, Charleston, SC *29401*

McGehee MR & MRS Stephen Y (Ruth Antell) CtCol'74.W&L'79
☎ (404) 233-4021 . . 924 Buckingham Circle NW, Atlanta, GA *30327*

McGehee MR & MRS Thomas C (Stallworth—Lucile R Smith) At.Sar.Ga'81
☎ (334) 478-8271 . . 6 Elizabeth Place, Mobile, AL *36606*

McGennis MR & MRS William J (Winifred J Wetherald)
☎ (941) 261-7243 . . 2777 Gulf Shore Blvd N, Apt N1, Naples, FL *34103*

McGeorge MR & MRS Arthur JR (Patricia L Fenn) Sth'50.Wil.Ncd.Pa'42 . . . . | ☎ (302) 652-7921 900 Barley Dv, Wilmington, DE *19807-2532*
MISS Judith F—Pa'77—at RFD 5, Box 264, Ellsworth, ME *04605* . . . . |

McGeorge MRS Edward B JR (Oberweiser—Ambler— Dorothy L Newsome) Mds.Cly.Cda.
☎ (212) PL3-0470 . . 200 E 66 St, New York, NY *10021*

McGettigan MR & MRS Charles C JR (Meriwether L Stovall) Rcn.Sfg.Bhm.Pcu.Bur.B.Pr.Cp.Geo'66. Pa'69 . . . . | of ☎ (415)921-6890 3375 Clay St, San Francisco, CA *94118*
JUNIORS MISS Meriweather L F . . . . | ☎ (707) 253-2662 McGettigan Ranch, 4740 Monticello Rd, Napa, CA *94558*

McGhee MR & MRS George C (Cecilia J DeGolyer) Bhm.Mt.B.Cos.Sl.Okla'32.Ox'36
☎ (540) 687-3451 . . "Farmer's Delight" 36276 Mountville Rd, Middleburg, VA *20117*

McGinn MR Michael E—Bost'84
☎ (415) 931-9817 . . 2139½ Pierce St, San Francisco, CA *94115*

McGinty MR & MRS (DR) John E (Sarah E Myers) Bates'67.Nw'71.Nu'84.Nw'68.Ch'70 . . . . | ☎ (617) 262-0056 322 Marlborough St, Boston, MA *02116*
JUNIORS MISS Sarah . . . . |
JUNIORS MR John W . . . . |

McGleughlin MISS Julie P—Hampshire'82 . . see C L Austin JR

McGleughlin MR & MRS Peter T (Sally E L Theakstone) Br'82
☎ (011-44-171) 486-6409 . . 11 Marylebone Mews, London W1, England

McGleughlin MR & MRS William R 3d (Gzchwind—Aleksandra Badanjak) Wes'82
☎ (011-41-1) 493-3095 . . Hirzelstrasse 4, 8004 Zürich, Switzerland

McGlinn MR & MRS Francis C P (Louise C Lea) | ☎ (610) MI2-2876
Me.W.NCar'37.Pa'40 . . . . | 729 Millbrook Lane,
MISS Ann C (Barnes—Ann C McGlinn) Me.—at | Haverford, PA
☎ (404) 355-0994 . . 1902 Defoors Landing NW, | *19041-1210*
Atlanta, GA *30318* . . . . |

McGoodwin MR & MRS Robert R 3d (Jacqueline L | ☎ (617) 934-6475
Franks) Rv.Cw.Suff'68 . . . . | 140 Onion Hill Rd,
MR Robert R 4th—at U of RI . . . . | Duxbury, MA *02332*

McGoodwin MISS Whitney L (Robert R 3d) . . . . Married at Chatham, MA
Fulmer MR Stephen T (David H) . . . . Aug 31'96

McGovern MR & MRS David T (Owen—Margery | ☎ (011-33-1)
White) Ws'51.Cl'54.Ln.Y'49.Cl'55 . . . . | 45-00-20-98
MISS M Alexandra—Y'83 . . . . | 22 Villa Said,
| 75116 Paris, France

McGovern MR & MRS James W (Deborah Berns)
☎ (212) 996-4752 . . 65 E 96 St, New York, NY *10128*

McGovern MR & MRS John E JR (Karen A Osborne) | ☎ (847) 234-0131
Cho.Rc.On.P'53.H'59 . . . . | 79 N Mayflower Rd,
MISS Courtney O—at Colgate . . . . | Lake Forest, IL
MR John E 3d—P'91 . . . . | *60045*

McGovern MRS Meston (Susan Meston)
☎ (540) 635-3063 . . PO Box 576, Front Royal, VA *22630*

McGowan MR & MRS Gerard F (Claire M Miller) | of ☎ (716)875-3232
Man'vl'58.St.G.Cl'54 . . . . | 761 W Ferry St,
MISS Claire K—Cr'85—at New York, NY . . . . . | Buffalo, NY *14222*
MR Gerard A—Ham'87—at Brooklyn, NY . . . . . | ☎ (905) 894-1984
MR Edwin M—Bow'88—at Ft Montgomery, NY | Grey Grove Farm,
| Erie Rd, Bay Beach,
| Ridgeway, Ontario
| L0S 1B0, Canada

McGowan MR John F JR—Va'30
☎ (912) 921-8078 . . 78 Pine Knoll Court, Savannah, GA *31406*

McGowin MRS Julian F (Betty D Rossell) MaryB'38.B.
☎ (334) 376-9783 . . ''Rossellini'' PO Box 86, H'way 31, Chapman, AL *36015*

McGowin MRS Nicholas S (Elizabeth B Smith) Lime'43.At.
☎ (334) 342-8557 . . 3604 Springhill Av, Mobile, AL *36608*

McGowin MR & MRS Norman F JR (Rosa J Tucker) Y'53
☎ (334) 376-2625 . . PO Box 35, Chapman, AL *36015*

McGrady MR & MRS Arthur L (Louise B Gilliam) Swb'87.Rm'87
☎ (703) 729-1224 . . 43572 Blacksmith Square, Ashburn, VA *20147*

McGrail MISS Anne L . . see MRS G Gwathmey JR

McGrail MR Thomas H . . see MRS G Gwathmey JR

McGrail MR & MRS William P 3d (Martine V Victor) B'gton'83.Pr.Bost'76
☎ (802) 362-4968 . . ''Equinox-on-the-Battenkill'' Manchester, VT *05254*

McGrath MRS Gordon R (Grace M Cutting) Pr.Mb. | ☎ (516) 626-1096
MR Gordon R JR—☎ (516) 626-3596 . . . . | 154 Wheatley Rd,
| Glen Head, NY
| *11545*

McGraw MR & MRS David D (Elizabeth L Frank) Duke'88.Ford'82
☎ (415) 441-9147 . . 3080 Jackson St, Apt 6, San Francisco, CA *94115*

McGraw MRS Diana Dent (Diana G Dent) Ky'77.Ri.L.
☎ (212) 535-5526 . . 177 E 75 St, New York, NY *10021*

McGraw MISS Elizabeth Scheerer (James H 4th) . . . . Born at
New York, NY Jan 11'96

McGraw MR & MRS James H 4th (Jane V Love)
LakeF'86.Rcn.Rr.Cly.DU'77.Ford'91
☎ (201) 376-3989 . . 70 Stewart Rd, Short Hills, NJ *07078*

McGraw MR & MRS Theodore A (Helen R Stoepel) Sth'44.L.Ri.Cly.Y'39
☎ (313) 882-3942 . . 83 Vendome Rd, Grosse Pointe Farms, MI *48236*

McGraw MR & MRS Theodore A JR (Knight— | ☎ (212) 570-0204
Christy Hamilton) DU'75.Fic.Ri.L.Cly.Y.'77. | 130 E 75 St, Apt
Nu'84 ⛵ . . . . | 11D, New York, NY
JUNIORS MR Hunter H Knight . . . . | *10021*

McGreevy MR & MRS Michael Neil (Michael E | 736 Tarento Dv,
Taylor) SantaC'71.Sdy.SantaC'71 . . . . | San Diego, CA
MISS Taylor M . . . . | *92106*

McGregor MRS C Dangerfield (Carol Dangerfield) Cvc.
☎ (203) 255-1530 . . PO Box 552, Southport, CT *06490-0552*

McGuckin MISS Alice C
☎ (415) 852-1270 . . 3117 Middlefield Rd, Palo Alto, CA *94306*

McGugan MR & MRS Vincent J (Joyce H Wyman)
Ws'72.Bost'78.H'72.H'76
☎ (617) 731-0607 . . 36 Arlington Rd, Chestnut Hill, MA *02167*

McGuigan MR & MRS E Gayle (Alice Montant) Cly.H'35
☎ (212) 288-1889 . . 333 E 68 St, New York, NY *10021-5693*

McGuigan MR E Gayle JR—Unn.Pa'66.Pa'70
see Dilatory Domiciles

McGuigan MR & MRS Philip Palmer—Unn.Br'66.Minn'69
☎ (312) 573-1134 . . 1310 N Ritchie Court, Chicago, IL *60610*

McGuinness MR & MRS Aims C JR (Susan Norton) | ☎ (303) 798-0392
Pa'65.Au.Pa'65.GeoW'70.Syr'79 . . . . | 4988 W Fair Av,
MR Alexander W—StOlaf'92 . . . . | Littleton, CO *80123*

McGuire MISS Amanda K . . see W R Reagan

McGuire MR & MRS Edward L (Deborah M O'Connell) Va'89
☎ (508) 443-1326 . . 32 Pennymeadow Rd, Sudbury, MA *01776*

McGuire DR & MRS Hunter H JR (Alice B Reed) Fic.Va'51.VaMed'55
☎ (804) 355-0422 . . 1218 Rothesay Circle, Richmond, VA *23221-3809*

McGuire MRS Lockhart B (Anne T Kane)
☎ (804) 296-2539 . . 1801 Westview Rd, Charlottesville, VA *22903*

McGuirk MR & MRS Hugh D (Flick—Amy H Ziesing) Md.Va'82.H'91
☎ (410) 472-1299 . . 1120 Western Run Rd, Butler, MD *21023*

McGuirk MR & MRS William E (Mary T Paige) | ☎ (410) 838-4828
Md.USN'39 . . . . | ''Marylea Farm''
MR Ian . . . . | 2211 Pennington Rd,
| Bel Air, MD *21015*

McGurk MR & MRS John J 3d (Deidre A Cheney) | ☎ (561) 586-6331
Cw.Ht. . . . . | 227 Elwa Place,
JUNIORS MR John J 4th . . . . | West Palm Beach,
JUNIORS MR A Whitney . . . . | FL *33405*

McGurrin MRS Alexa (Leibert—Alexa M P | *see*
McGurrin) . . . . | *Dilatory Domiciles*
MISS Meighan Leibert . . . . |
MR McGurrin Seton Leibert . . . . |

McGusty MR & MRS James Constable (Hudson—Phyllis Forster)
Pa'49.Pc.Chr.Plg.Rv.Va'42
☎ (215) 836-9439 . . 7801 Ardmore Av, Wyndmoor, PA *19038*

McHugh MRS Burton P (June W Fiske) Dar. . . . . . . | ☎ (717) 595-2843
MISS Gail F—P'85—at ☎ (215) 732-4412 | "Hobby House"
1530 Locust St, Apt 5G, Philadelphia, PA *19102* | Box 216, Skytop,
MR John W F—Cw.—at 200 E 75 St, Apt 5A, | PA *18357*
New York, NY *10021* . . . . |

McHugh MR & MRS Burton P JR (Jennifer James)
Ty'88.Pc.Rc.Sg.Cw.Ac.Pa'85
☎ (215) 732-7708 . . 2044 Bainbridge St, Philadelphia, PA *19146*

McHugh MRS Ernestine L (Suwal—Poole—Ernestine L McHugh)
Cal'76.Cal'85
☎ (716) 473-4928 . . 120 Hampshire Dv, Rochester, NY *14618*

McIlhenny MR & MRS Alan (Gwinn—Kennedy—Vittoria Vitelli)
Cry.Nf.P'42.Pa'49
☎ (207) 276-3040 . . Asticou Way, Northeast Harbor, ME *04662-0848*

McIlvain MR & MRS Alan (Elizabeth L Claghorn) Rr.Rv.Ac.Ncd.
☎ (803) 846-0521 . . Bray's Island Plantation, Box 30, Sheldon,
SC *29941*

McIlvain MR & MRS Alan JR (Ann Havens) | ☎ (610) 527-2692
Me.Rv.OWes'71. . . . . | 314 Airdale Rd,
MISS E Coryell . . . . | Rosemont, PA
JUNIORS MR Alan 3d . . . . | *19010*
JUNIORS MR J Wick . . . . |

McIlvain MRS J Gibson JR (Anne E Stone) . . . . Died at
Honey Brook, PA Apr 4'96

McIlvain MR J Gibson JR . . . . Died at
Honey Brook, PA Feb 6'95

McIlvain MR & MRS J Gibson 3d (Marian Ashton) | ☎ (610) 869-4936
Dick'73.Me.Ac.NEng'71 . . . . | "Thomaston"
JUNIORS MISS Caroline A . . . . | Box 1005,
| 1966 Newark Rd,
| New London, PA
| *19360*

McIlvain MR Joshua M . . see D S Traxel

McIlvain MR Samuel S . . see D S Traxel

McIlvain MR & MRS T Baird (Mary L Boles) Me.M.Ac . . .of
☎ (912) 638-3172 . . Cottage 172, Box 31172, Sea Island, GA *31561*
☎ (610) 645-8696 . . 1400 Waverly Rd, Villa 47, Gladwyne, PA *19035*

McIlvaine MISS Allan—Ncd.
☎ (802) 863-5797 . . RD 2, 315 Dorset Heights, South Burlington,
VT *05403*

McIlvaine MR & MRS Charles L 3d (Susan Merritt) | ☎ (215) 233-3168
Pc. | 1414 Firethorne
MR C Lee 4th—at Lehigh . . . . | Lane, Wyndmoor,
MR Edward M—at New England Coll . . . . | PA *19038*

McIlvaine MISS Diana
☎ (212) UN1-6268 . . 157 E 72 St, New York, NY *10021*

McIlvaine MR & MRS Leighton H JR (Probst—Karin | ☎ (203) 629-4460
M Rose) StMarys'75.Ty'59.Nu'67 . . . . | 1 Ridgeview Av,
MR L Reed—L&C'94—at ☎ (503) 452-7426 | Greenwich, CT
7604 SW Capital Hill Rd, Portland, OR *97219* . | *06830*

McIlvaine MR & MRS William B (Whitebrook—Ross—
Nancy M Newman) On.Rc.Sc.P'49.H'51
☎ (312) 266-9869 . . 55 W Goethe St, TH-1248, Chicago,
IL *60610-2233*

McIlwain MR & MRS John K (Wende L Sheffield) | ☎ (301) 951-4454
S.P'65 . . . . | 3605 Underwood St,
MR Knox L . . . . | Chevy Chase, MD
| *20815*

McInerney MRS Mallan (Mary Stuart Mallan) | ☎ (904) 241-7196
Stph'53.Miami'62 . . . . | 2707 Colonies Dv,
MR Sean M—Frost'85—at Palm Beach, FL *33480* | Jacksonville Beach,
| FL *32250*

McInerney MR & MRS Mark J (Hilary K Colgate) Mid'88.Bgt.Mid'85
☎ (914) 232-8273 . . 33 Lyon Ridge Rd, Katonah, NY *10536*

McInnes MR & MRS William W (Betsy Vinson) | ☎ (615) 352-1638
Hn.Van'70.H'77 . . . . | 604 Westover Dv,
JUNIORS MR William V . . . . | Nashville, TN *37205*

McInnis MR & MRS John W (Hannah D Proctor) Cyc.Dar.Pa'54
☎ (847) 251-7836 . . 144 Tudor Place, Kenilworth, IL *60043*

McIntire MR & MRS Henry Dickson (Taylor— | ☎ (203) 966-7583
Jocelyn D Keith) Franklin'71.H'80 . . . . | 105 Thayer Pond
MISS Ashley C Taylor . . . . | Rd, New Canaan,
JUNIORS MR Ashton K Taylor . . . . | CT *06840*

McIntire MR & MRS William Tredick 3d (Elisabeth R Witte)
Sim'79.H'77.Cl'81
☎ (203) 972-6909 . . 29 Church St, New Canaan, CT *06840*

McIntosh MR Andrew D JR—Y'31
☎ (860) 567-8888 . . 234 Looking Glass Hill Rd, Bantam,
CT *06750-1044*

McIntosh MR & MRS Angus (Williamson—Karina Side) Ox'34.H'37
☎ (011-44-131) 667-5791 . . 32 Blacket Place, Edinburgh EH9 1RL,
Scotland

McIntosh MISS Ann L . . see MRS E N Hower

McIntosh MR Christian C . . see W N Bucklin 3d

McIntosh MR & MRS De Courcy E (Susan R Bell) | ☎ (412) 781-4468
Ws'65.StThos'81.C.Pg.H'65 . . . . | 4 St James Place,
MISS Madeline E—H'91—at New York, NY . . . | Pittsburgh, PA
MR David G—H'94—at Cambridge, MA . . . . . | *15215*

McIntosh MR & MRS Henry P 4th (Susan D Riggs) BtP.Evg.Tul'60 . . of
☎ (561) 659-2995 . . 124 Via Bethesda, Palm Beach, FL *33480*
☎ (970) 925-1788 . . Aspen Alps Club, Aspen, CO *81611*

McIntosh MRS Rustin (M Millicent Carey) BMr'20
☎ (413) 243-0459 . . "Mountain Brook Farm" Tyringham, MA *01264*

McIntosh MRS Susan Upham (Susan M Upham) | ☎ (617) 277-9530
Wells'68.Cy. | 17 Devon Rd,
JUNIORS MR Forgan C . . . . | Chestnut Hill, MA
| *02167*

McIntyre MR & MRS Angus P (Barbara R Eckhardt) | of ☎ (516)667-4437
Cly.Y.'49 . . . . | 640 Half Hollow
MISS Rebecca P—H'80.BostColl'85—at | Rd, Dix Hills, NY
Cambridge, MA . . . . | *11746*
MISS Anne P—Y'83.Ox'85—at Los Angeles, CA | ☎ (802) 253-7602
| Cottage Club Rd,
| Stowe, VT *05672*

McIntyre DR & MRS Angus P JR (Carol Littlefield) | ☎ (508) 468-2018
Stan'77.My.Myc.H.'74.Stan'79 . . . . | 3 Patton Dv,
JUNIORS MR A Duncan . . . . | South Hamilton, MA
| *01982*

McIntyre MR & MRS Frederic S (Anne Huber) ☎ (617) 237-9760
Ht.Cda.Dar.Bost'60 . . . . 81 Royalston Rd,
MISS Deborah C—at Dallas, TX . . . . Wellesley Hills,
MISS Dianne U . . . . MA *02181*
MISS Donna F—at Geneva, Switzerland . . . . . .
MISS Stephanie A . . . .
MR Frederic S 3d—at Geneva, Switzerland. . . . .

McIntyre MR & MRS Henry L (Winifred Wheeler) Stan'56.Bur.P'33.Nw'36
☎ (415) 323-1031 . . 55 Serrano Dv, Atherton, CA *94027*

McIntyre MR & MRS James Bigelow (Juliana S of ☎ (609)924-5931
Cuyler) Ws'57.H'63.Plg.Rv.Ht.Ofp.Sar.Cw.Myf. 34 Edgehill St,
Hp.Hn.Nw'50.H'53 . . . . Princeton, NJ *08540*
MR James B—ColC'93 . . . . ☎ (802) 533-2247
"Weathervane"
Main St,
Greensboro, VT
05841

McIntyre MISS Juliana S C (James Bigelow) . . . . Married at
Greensboro, VT
Sowles DR Nicholas P (James H) . . . . Jly 6'96

McIver MRS Katherine W (Katherine K Wood) . . . . ☎ (713) 464-0300
MISS Kelly H . . . . 9940 Memorial Dv,
JUNIORS MR Douglas W . . . . Apt 15, Houston,
TX *77024-3400*

McIver MRS Renwick S (Conklin—Marcella S ☎ (561) 231-1167
Babbitt) M.Me. . . . . 550 Riomar Dv,
MR Renwick S JR—Me.Ty'65 . . . . Apt 21, Vero Beach,
FL *32963*

McKay MRS George F (Marybeth O'Reilly) Geo'40 ☎ (314) 367-4903
MR George F JR—at 4475 W Pine Blvd, 4525 Lindell Blvd,
St Louis, MO *63108* . . . . Apt 303, St Louis,
MO *63108*

McKay MISS Isabel D (Robert) . . . . Married at Newburgh, ME
Thompson MR Richard C (Richard) . . . . Oct 8'95

McKay MRS James C (Thompson—E Jane Reeves) ☎ (412) 238-9369
Pg.Fcg.Rr. . . . . "Smallwonder"
MR Arthur R Thompson—Rr.—at Rector, PA *15677*
☎ (303) 449-4442 . . Poorman's Rd, Feb 1 . .
Sunshine Canyon, Boulder, CO *80302* . . . . . . ☎ (941) 472-4469
"La Casita de
Bahia" Box 486,
16131 San Cap Rd,
Captiva, FL *33924*

McKay MR & MRS Lawrence (Elizabeth A Slocum) Rr.Bab'37
☎ (412) 238-9306 . . RD 2, Box 354, Ligonier, PA *15658*

McKay MR & MRS Robert (Emily A Baldwin) ☎ (203) 966-4049
Wis'55.P'50 . . . . 46 Benedict Hill Rd,
MR Robert B—Wis'94 . . . . New Canaan, CT
06840

McKay MR & MRS Thomas A (Elizabeth R Remington)
V'73.T.Rcn.P'69.H'74
☎ (201) 447-5784 . . 147 Hamilton Rd, Ridgewood, NJ *07450*

McKay MRS William C (Gail H Wright) Cly . . .of
☎ (561) 835-0106 . . 2600 N Flagler Dv, West Palm Beach, FL *33407*
193 Stuyvesant Av, Rye, NY *10580*

McKean MR Henry P 2d—B.Rcn.My.Ec.H'50.Stan'52
☎ (561) 231-3250 . . 300 Harbour Dv, Apt 201A, Vero Beach, FL *32963*

McKean MR John W—My.H'71
☎ (910) 295-6743 . . Sandy Woods Farm, PO Box 309, Pinehurst,
NC *28374*

McKean MRS M Fisher (Margaret A Fisher) ☎ (410) 363-0720
Gchr'66 . . . . "Walnutwood"
MR Benjamin F . . . . 2919 Caves Rd,
Owings Mills, MD
21117

McKean MR Paul F—Gv.Md.Rr.Tex'58
☎ (717) 993-3979 . . RR 1, Box 1490, Stewartstown, PA *17363*

McKean MR & MRS Paul F JR (Ann E Ziegler) Ariz'86.Rr.Md.Ariz'86
☎ (941) 649-0405 . . 451 Rudder Rd, Naples, FL *34102*

McKean MRS Q A Shaw (Katharine Winthrop) ☎ (910) 295-6743
Unn.My. . . . . Sandy Woods Farm,
MR Robert W—at 299 Bronwood Av, PO Box 309,
Los Angeles, CA *90049* . . . . Pinehurst, NC *28374*

McKean MR & MRS Q A Shaw JR (Linda H Borden)
Unn.Rm.Stc.H'48.Cl'51
☎ (908) 842-2074 . . 70 W River Rd, Rumson, NJ *07760*

McKechnie MR D Eric—Rd.Nyc.
☎ (508) 228-9163 . . 76 N Liberty St, Nantucket, MA *02554*

McKechnie MRS Deborah S (Deborah N Smith) ☎ (610) 647-4284
Rd.Nyc. . . . . 707 Hillview Rd,
MR Christopher W—at ☎ (415) 921-8363 Malvern, PA *19355*
1801 Beach St, San Francisco, CA *94123* . . . . .
MR Gregory E . . . .
MR Andrew N . . . .

McKee MR & MRS A Kingston (Veva M Eilers) SCal'56.Vh.Stan'54
☎ (818) 792-8052 . . 1240 Patton Way, San Marino, CA *91108*

McKee MRS E Bates (Rowell—Tanja Ramm) Ayc.Mv.Yn.
☎ (410) 224-4631 . . 6305 River Crescent Dv, Annapolis, MD *21401*

McKee MR & MRS Julien D (Goodyear—Mary Van R Robins) H'41
☎ (603) 563-8534 . . PO Box 247, Dublin, NH *03444-0247*

McKee MISS M Jean—V'51.Ncd . . .of
☎ (202) 363-2602 . . 3001 Veazey Terr NW, Apt 1225, Washington,
DC *20008-5407*
☎ (203) 272-5741 . . "Brooks Homestead" 532 S Brooksvale Rd,
Cheshire, CT *06410*

McKee MR Paul W—Mich'58
☎ (202) 333-1108 . . 2502 I St NW, Washington, DC *20037-2210*

McKee MR & MRS Richard G (Gärd E Ölund) Mit'54 ☎ (706) 453-4818
MISS Hope E—at ☎ (503) 288-7808 1200 Oconee Way,
4551 NE 32 Av, Portland, OR *97211* . . . . Greensboro, GA
30642

McKee MISS Susan E
☎ (215) 732-7393 . . 2028 Delancey St, Philadelphia, PA *19103*

McKeever MRS Chauncey (Lasker—Doris Lachman) . . . . Married at
San Francisco, CA
Keenan MR Henry C . . . . Jun 4'96

McKeever MRS John B (Iorio—Adèle M A Harvey) ☎ (508) 228-3781
Ncd.Dar. . . . . 47 Centre St,
MR Christopher W—Rv.Ken'72—at Nantucket, MA
☎ (617) 899-1854 . . 79 Hall St, Waltham, MA *02554*
02154 . . . .
MR Mark W—Rv.LakeF'79—at
☎ (617) 891-3010 . . 19 Chestnut St, Waltham,
MA *02154* . . . .

McKeever MISS M Barbara—VillaN'76
☎ (609) 397-0059 . . 28 Seabrook Rd, Stockton, NJ *08559*
McKeever MR & MRS William W (G Virginia Schley) M.Me.Cr'39
☎ (610) 527-3468 . . 721 Harriton Rd, Bryn Mawr, PA *19010*
McKellar MR & MRS Donald McC (Dorothy W Pierce) Sr.Cho.H'38
☎ (602) 997-2000 . . 1301 E Gardenia Dv, Phoenix, AZ *85020-5114*
McKellar MR & MRS Winston P (Victoria Valdes) Sr.LakeF'73
☎ (602) 266-3114 . . 311 E Rose Lane, Phoenix, AZ *85012*
McKelvey MR & MRS Thomas H JR (Amy C Scruggs)
☎ (615) 352-3108 . . 5128 Boxcroft Place, Nashville, TN *37205*

McKelvy MRS F Shepard (Francine J Shepard) V'52 | ☎ (303) 753-0969
MISS Karen S—at ☎ (303) 722-5501 | 2005 S Monroe St,
1294 S Josephine St, Denver, CO *80210* . . . . . . | Denver, CO *80210*
MR Douglas S JR—at ☎ (617) 259-9466
9 Bedford Lane, Lincoln, MA *01773* . . . . |

McKelvy MR & MRS John E JR (Nancy G Woodrow) | ☎ (617) 329-4435
Chi.Ty'60.Pa'63 . . . . | 848 High St,
MISS Laura G . . . . | Dedham, MA *02026*

McKelvy MR & MRS William G (Nancy C Henry)
☎ (561) 546-4908 . . 324 S Beach Rd, Hobe Sound, FL *33455*
McKenna MR Andrew S . . see J H Fridy
McKenna MISS Constance—Bnd'37
☎ (520) 684-3134 . . Flicker Lane, Box 2749, Wickenburg, AZ *85358*
McKenna MR & MRS David M (Elizabeth C Whipple) Vt'80.LakeF'80
☎ (203) 966-2555 . . Deer Park Rd, New Canaan, CT *06840*
McKenna MR Douglas H—Del'52
Rte 100 & Lakewood Dv, Killington, VT *05751*
McKenna MR John J III—Col'90 . . see J T Carpenter
McKenna MR Todd A—WVa'93 . . see J T Carpenter
McKenna MR Trevor C—WVa'93 . . see J T Carpenter
McKenna MR William R . . see J H Fridy
McKenrick MR S Eyre JR—Cw.Cl'75 ⛵
☎ (410) 263-6256 . . PO Box 344, Annapolis, MD *21404*
McKenrick MRS Stratford Eyre (Keith McC Price) Md.Cw.Myf.Cda . . .of
☎ (954) 491-6457 . . 5820 NE 22 Way, Ft Lauderdale, FL *33308*
☎ (410) 224-5668 . . 930 Astern Way, Apt 407, Annapolis, MD *21401*
McKenzie MR Garfield A—Y'31
☎ (717) 278-3101 . . 1 Cherry St, Montrose, PA *18801-1104*

McKenzie MR & MRS Thomas L (Mary L Scott) . . . . | of ☎ (904)893-7388
MR Edson S . . . . | 3010 Trestwick
Way, Tallahassee,
FL *32312*
☎ (904) 267-1318
''Altus Donus''
27 Gulf Dunes Lane,
Santa Rosa Beach,
FL *32459*

McKeon MR Daniel M—Km.Y'28 . . . . | ☎ (203) 438-2304
MR Daniel M JR . . . . | 11 Old Stage Coach
MR Denis C . . . . | Rd, Ridgefield, CT
06877

McKeon MR & MRS Robert M (Véronique Meyer) | ☎ (011-33-1)
Rv.Pn.P'56.CalTech'57.Paris'60 . . . . | 46-34-18-91
MISS Anne S . . . . | 17 rue St Louis en
MISS Caline . . . . | l'Ile, 75004 Paris,
MR Robert A . . . . | France
MR Thomas D . . . . |

McKim MISS Charlotte W . . see G R Furse
McKinley MRS (REV) Ellen B (Ellen A Bacon) | ☎ (609) 497-2329
BMr'51.Y'76.UTheo'88.Sl. . . . . | 59 Dorann Av,
MR David T—Br'81—at Stamford, CT . . . . | Princeton, NJ *08540*
McKinley MISS Ellen G (Wynkoop—Ellen G McKinley)
Y'76.W'minster'83
☎ (609) 683-4060 . . 391 Franklin Av, Princeton, NJ *08540*
McKinley MR & MRS John K (Helen G Heare) Tex'45.Ln.B.Ny.Cly.Ala'40
☎ (203) 655-3729 . . 5 Searles Rd, Darien, CT *06820*

McKinley MRS Silas Bent (Nancy M Wallace) . . . . | ☎ (314) 993-1146
MISS Nancy M—V'60.T.Bm.—at | 18 Pine Valley Rd,
☎ (914) 351-2653 . . 58 Club House Rd, | St Louis, MO *63124*
Tuxedo Park, NY *10987* . . . . |
MR Silas B—Cy.Str.Cw.Wash'61 |

McKinney MR Christopher R—Laf'80.Bost'86
☎ (414) 731-4403 . . 1725 S Outagamie St, Appleton, WI *54914-4407*

McKinney MR & MRS James E (Ann M Marrow) | of ☎ (212)427-2279
Cs.Y.'55.Va'62 . . . . | 125 E 87 St,
JUNIORS MR Robin L . . . . | New York, NY
10128
☎ (860) 567-5648
''Kilbourn Farm''
37 Saw Mill Rd,
Litchfield, CT *06759*

McKinney MR Reynold M—Bost'70 . . . . | ☎ (310) 540-1152
JUNIORS MR Reynold L . . . . | 306 Vista Del Mar,
JUNIORS MR Travis R . . . . | Redondo Beach, CA
90277-5845

McKinney MR & MRS Richardson (Elizabeth F | ☎ (513) 871-2533
McLane) CtCol'52.H'49.SanM'50 . . . . | 3251 Hardisty Av,
MR Jonathan—Y'84—at ☎ (406) 582-0315 | Cincinnati, OH
420 W Koch, Bozeman, MT *59715-4545* . . . . . . | *45208-3006*

McKinney MR & MRS Robert M (de Montmollin—Marie Louise
Ehrmann-Egry) B.K.Ln.Ri.C.Cvc.Mt.StJ.Okla'32 . . of
☎ (212) 535-9510 . . 720 Park Av, Apt 17B, New York, NY *10021*
☎ (540) 687-5207 . . Wind Fields Farm, 39850 Snickersville Tpke,
Middleburg, VA *20117-9411*
McKinney MR & MRS W Richardson (Jie Cao)
Sichuan'84.Guam'90.Pa'79.Cal'81.ColSt'92
☎ (414) 830-2226 . . 1321 Montclaire Court, Appleton, WI *54915*
McKinnie MRS Ralph E (Everett—Gwendolen Shethar)
☎ (619) 756-3450 . . PO Box 2493, Rancho Santa Fe, CA *92067*

McKinnon MR & MRS Ian Neil (Rebecca Webster) | ☎ (416) 481-4103
Ws'68.Pn.P'67.Cl'69 . . . . | 32 Ridge Dv,
MISS Michelle—at U of W Ontario . . . . | Toronto, Ontario
MISS Laura—at Princeton . . . . | M4T 1B7, Canada

McKinnon MR & MRS James M (Marthe W Tribble)
Ac.Cw.Cda.Ncd.Ht.Yn.P'61
☎ (609) 921-3732 . . ''Woodslea House'' 91 Edgerstoune Rd, Princeton,
NJ *08540*

McKittrick MRS John (Grace Fagerstrom) . . . . | ☎ (201) 664-3957
MISS Judith—at ☎ (516) 671-7592 | 23 Holiday Court,
12A Maple St, Glenwood Landing, NY *11547* . . | River Vale, NJ
07675

McKleroy MR & MRS Bruce G (Mary Jo Gi_v_iné) Man'vl'71.Stan'70 . . . . ☎ (415) 567-4823 244 Laurel St, San Francisco, CA *94118*
JUNIORS MR B Gardiner JR . . . .

McKnight MRS Agnes H (Agnes Hanes) 3 Coniston Dv, West Chester, PA *19382*

McKnight MRS Diana A (Diana G Appleton) Bost'67 . . . . ☎ (303) 447-2398 1550 Hawthorne Av, Boulder, CO *80304*
MR Ian R—at ☎ (617) 282-6004 797 Columbia Rd, Apt 1, Dorchester, MA *02125*
MR Christopher I . . . .

McKnight MR & MRS Frank G (Sara Stevens) Hlns'46.Ncd.Tex'42 ☎ (915) 581-5101 . . 612 Satellite Dv, El Paso, TX *79912*

McKnight MR & MRS H Turney JR (Elizabeth Pearce) Md.Cr'65.Mich'69 . . . . ☎ (410) 557-9273 2520 Lemon Rd, White Hall, MD *21161*
JUNIORS MR E Phillip . . . .

McKnight MISS Leila L ☎ (202) 337-2405 . . 3900 Cathedral Av NW, Washington, DC *20016*

McKnight MR & MRS Philip R (Kathleen E Lord) V'66.Rcn.Wms'65.Ch'68 . . . . ☎ (860) 435-2068 59 Old CNE Rd, Lakeville, CT *06039*
MISS Sarah L—Wms'93.Man'vl'95 . . . .

McKnight MRS Roy H JR (Beatrice C Bartlett) Fcg.Tc. ☎ (412) 441-1885 . . 114 Woodland Rd, Pittsburgh, PA *15232*

McKnight MR & MRS Stephen H (Peggy L Thomas) Rr.Fcg.Pa'74.Pitt'75 ☎ (412) 963-1723 . . 203 Fairview Rd, Pittsburgh, PA *15238*

McKnight MRS William G JR (Le Brun C Rhinelander) Bcs. ☎ (561) 833-3815 . . PO Box PH-4B, 400 N Flagler Dv, West Palm Beach, FL *33401*

McKnight MR & MRS William G 3d (Katherine W Ewart) Rc.Bcs.Cly.Ty'62 . . . . ☎ (212) 628-9373 200 E 71 St, New York, NY *10021*
MR William R . . . .

McKone MR & MRS Michael E R (Elvira D Pope) Bgt.Lond'32 ☎ (914) 276-2831 . . 60A Heritage Hills, Somers, NY *10589*

McKown MR & MRS Alexander P (Pamela H Brigg) Pa'65.Fic.Pa'65 ☎ (914) 238-6225 . . 35 Florence Dv, Chappaqua, NY *10514*

McKown MR & MRS David R (Ann F Gasque) Bgt.Bost'65 . . . . ☎ (713) 558-6947 12729 Hollandale Dv, Houston, TX *77082*
MISS Hilary B—at Georgetown . . . .
MR Matthew W—at St George's . . . .

McKown MRS Frank B (Helen M Pendleton) Bgt. ☎ (914) 276-2248 . . Heritage Hills, 361A West Hill Dv, Somers, NY *10589*

McKown MR & MRS Frank B JR (Nancy C Bird) B.Bgt.StA.Snc.Y'54 . . . . ☎ (914) BE4-7735 462 Succabone Rd, RD 2, Mt Kisco, NY *10549-9802*
MISS Alice B—Mid'95 . . . .

McKown MRS Gilbert C (Biggers—Hamilton—Suzanne W White) V'36.Cly.Sl. ☎ (540) 955-1789 . . Norwood Farm, Berryville, VA *22611*

McKoy MR Thomas H 4th . . . . Married at San Francisco, CA White MISS Ellen . . . . Jan 2'96

McLallen MR Scott W—Ill'90 ☎ (212) 410-4938 . . 201 E 86 St, Apt 7A, New York, NY *10028*

McLallen CAPT (RET) & MRS Walter F (Kathleen M Klewitz) USN.Nw'55 ☎ (847) 367-6665 . . 77 Oak Lane, Lake Forest, IL *60045*

McLanahan MR Alexander G—P'76.Stan'81 ☎ (405) 752-4610 . . 12831 N Stratford Dv, Apt 217, Oklahoma City, OK *73120*

McLanahan MR & MRS Alexander K (Mary A Caldwell) Tex'51.K.Y'49 ☎ (713) 523-2323 . . 1507 Kirby Dv, Houston, TX *77019*

McLanahan MR & MRS Bruce (Ellen J Mahoney) Y'57.H'60 . . . . ☎ (203) 966-4895 81 Woodway Ridge Lane, New Canaan, CT *06840*
MISS Elizabeth S—Dth'93—at Duke . . . .
MR John H B—at ☎ (617) 437-1322 458 Beacon St, Apt 4, Boston, MA *02115* . . . . .
MR Jeremiah B—Y'91—at Pembroke Coll England . . . .

McLanahan MRS Duer (Martha M Bloch) Bcs. ☎ (212) 535-5291 . . 215 E 72 St, New York, NY *10021*

McLanahan MR Duer 3d . . see MRS T B Knapp

McLanahan MR & MRS Morgan C (Elizabeth A Markham) Ken'85.Rc.Ng.Bcs.Vt'86 38 E 85 St, New York, NY *10028*

McLanahan MR & MRS W Alexander (Barbara E Eddy) Rc.Rv.StA.Y.'52 ☎ (212) 988-8871 . . 200 E 74 St, New York, NY *10021*

McLanahan MR & MRS William Dyer (Lara Brook Schefler) Bost'90.Rc.Ng.Bcs.Geo'87.Cl'94 ☎ (212) 427-3885 . . 49 E 96 St, New York, NY *10128*

McLane MRS Allan (Jean Marianne Spottiswoode) Srb . . .of ☎ (011-33-1) 48-08-78-53 . . 20 rue des Coutures St Gervais, 75003 Paris, France
☎ (401) 849-6887 . . ''The Glen House'' Glen Farm Rd, Portsmouth, RI *02871*

McLane MRS Elizabeth (Jennison—Elizabeth Heed) Bnd'52.Cl'74.Csn. ☎ (011-33-1) 45-27-35-92 . . 75 rue de l'Assomption, 75016 Paris, France

McLane MR John H—Carl'93 ☎ (212) 737-2843 . . 415 E 82 St, Apt 4C, New York, NY *10028*

McLane MR & MRS Robert M (Camilla Merritt) Pr.Ln.Y'52 ☎ (516) 671-3466 . . 4 Cherrywood Rd, Locust Valley, NY *11560*

McLane MR & MRS Robert M JR (Gratia L Robertson) MtH'83.Pr.Tr.My.StLaw'81 ☎ (508) 468-2161 . . 33 Elm St, South Hamilton, MA *01982*

McLane MRS Shirley J (Pfeifer—Shirley J McLane) . . . . Married at Chevy Chase, MD
Putnam MR David E (Charles S) . . . . Jun 15'96

McLane MISS Sophia F—Occ'94 . . see MRS P Forbes

McLane MR & MRS Thomas L (Judith H Anthony) Ny.Yn.Y'54 ⚓ ☎ (203) 966-9901 . . ''Sprucewood'' 37 Dunning Rd, New Canaan, CT *06840*

McLarty MR & MRS Thomas F 3d (Donna Cochran) Ark'68.Ark'68 . . of ☎ (202) 462-7218 . . 2323 Wyoming Av NW, Washington, DC *20008* 3 Greenbrier Rd, Little Rock, AR *72202*

McLaughlin MR Daniel J—Tufts'74 . . see MRS K R Ellicott

McLaughlin MR & MRS Edward H 3d (Denise J Barrena) Stan'69 . . . . ☎ (818) 441-4903 2150 Ashbourne Dv, San Marino, CA *91108*
MISS Meegan B . . . .
JUNIORS MR Edward H 4th . . . .

McLaughlin MRS Frederic T (Kettering—Jane Woodhouse) B'gton'36.Col'48 ☎ (303) 733-9573 . . 100 Park Av, Apt 2007, Denver, CO *80205-3245*

McLaughlin MR & MRS George H 2d (Charlotte Heyl) ColbyS'60.P'58.H'63 . . . . MR George H 3d—Bost'87—at Quito, Ecuador . MR J Wolcott—at Pepperdine U . . . . ☎ (609) 924-4190 263 Mercer Rd, Princeton, NJ 08540

McLaughlin MR & MRS Ian M W (Mary G Makrianes) Rcn.Eh.Shcc.H'68 . . . . JUNIORS MR Gavin M K . . . . JUNIORS MR Callum M W . . . . JUNIORS MR Ian A Van D . . . . ☎ (908) 234-1829 Windfall Farm, PO Box 407, Peapack, NJ 07977

McLaughlin MR & MRS Marcellus H JR (Sandra L Houck) Wt.Rv.Cr'42.Dick'50 . . . . MR Marcellus H 3d—Wt.Rv.East'76.VillaN'78. VillaN'84 . . . . ☎ (610) MI9-6864 232 Winsor Place, Haverford, PA 19041

McLaughlin MR Robert T—Denis'77 . . see MRS K R Ellicott

McLaughlin MR & MRS Timothy R (Linda B Holmes) Briar'70.Wash'75.Rcsl.Ck.Hn.Geo'69. H'71 . . . . MISS Blair C . . . . MISS Brooke T . . . . ☎ (603) 837-9215 Mountain View Rd, Whitefield, NH 03598

McLaury MR & MRS William Walker (Catherine McDermott) Ch'38 ☎ (847) 256-4558 . . 152 Robsart Place, Kenilworth, IL 60043

McLean DR & MRS Donald A JR (Susan C Gould) Hob'70.NH'74.ColSt'83.Bost'94 ☎ (210) 981-4581 . . Stirrup Cup Farm, 10056 Dos Cerros Loop, Boerne, TX 78006-5125

McLean MR & MRS Donald G (Kennedy—Mona Townsend) Nf.Sg.P'51 ☎ (215) 646-0879 . . 274 Woodcock Lane, Ambler, PA 19002

McLean MR & MRS Edward B 4th (Carolyn N Hager) Mo'90 32 Glen Eagles Dv, Rear, St Louis, MO 63124

McLean DR & MRS Ephraim R 3d (Jane J Ruckert) Cr'58.Mit'67.Mit'70 . . . . MISS Janet . . . . MISS Susan . . . . 2257 Old Brooke Point, Dunwoody, GA 30338

McLean MRS Gale (Mary P Gibson) Cvc.Ct.Mt.Cly.Sl . . .of ☎ (202) 332-7830 . . 1806 Kalorama Square NW, Washington, DC 20008 ☎ (941) 964-2662 . . PO Box 484, Boca Grande, FL 33921

McLean MRS Hirons (Cornelia P Hirons) Dc.Myf. ☎ (860) 399-7881 . . PO Box 340, Westbrook, CT 06498

McLean MR & MRS J Kenneth JR (Barbara A Atkins) Hlns'74.StAndr'65 . . . . MR James K III . . . . ☎ (334) 928-8997 PO Box 769, Point Clear, AL 36564

McLean MRS James (Imbrie—Violet B Grubb) . . . . MR & MRS James (Mary T Horky)— ☎ (410) 836-3544 . . . . JUNIORS MISS Rebecca S . . . . JUNIORS MR Alexander C . . . . ☎ (410) 836-3554 "Fairland" 3160 Deths Ford Rd, Darlington, MD 21034

McLean MR James H 3d—Ny.Chap'70⚓ PO Box 244, Mantoloking, NJ 08738

McLean MR James M 3d ☎ (908) 899-3142 . . 1517 Ocean Av, Mantoloking, NJ 08738

McLean MR & MRS Locke (Sara P Ridgway) V'71.Ln.Fic.Plg.Myf.Cly.P'59 . . . . JUNIORS MISS Emily R—at Downe House . . . . . . JUNIORS MR George R—at Radley Coll . . . . ☎ (011-44-171) 937-3005 25 Argyll Rd, London W8 7DA, England

McLean CDR (RET) & MRS Michael A (Faith Ford) USN.Bates'68.An.Ty'67.SCal'74 . . . . MR Michael A JR—Bates'94 . . . . MR Scott F—WestMd'95 . . . . 113 High St, Somersworth, NH 03878

McLean MR & MRS Robert 2d (Susan D Johnson) Sg.Rc.Pc.Br'76 . . . . JUNIORS MISS Clare S . . . . ☎ (215) 643-7765 100 Spruce Rd, Ambler, PA 19002

McLean MR & MRS Robert 3d (Elizabeth M Lewis) Rcp.Rr.Gi.Mt.Cly.Cda.Y'50 . . . . MISS Mary S—ColC'88 . . . . MR John S P—at Georgetown . . . . of ☎ (703)893-5599 867 Canal Dv, McLean, VA 22102 ☎ (410) 360-6995 Gibson Island, MD 21056

McLean COL (RET) & MRS Robert L (Linda K Durfee) USA.DU'67.Rc.An.L.Lic.Bcs.StA.Vca. P'52 . . . . MISS Elissa S—Vt'95 . . . . MISS Margaret T—at Wesleyan . . . . of ☎ (212)755-7318 870 United Nations Plaza, Apt 16D, New York, NY 10017 ☎ (516) 283-8698 18 Ochre Lane, Southampton, NY 11968

McLean MISS Sarah H—V'30 ☎ (860) 868-2193 . . 145 Kinney Hill Rd, New Preston, CT 06777

McLean MRS Stafford (Manice—Josephine Coster) T.Cly. Jan 1 . . ☎ (912) 638-0722 . . Box 30395, Sea Island, GA 31561 May 1 . . ☎ (914) 351-2270 . . Tuxedo Club, PO Box 602, W Lake Rd, Tuxedo Park, NY 10987

McLean MR & MRS Stafford 3d (Elizabeth H Archer) Bost'76.Wh'lck'81.CathU'86.Bost'74.P'82 ☎ (860) 572-8295 . . 368 Mistuxet Av, Stonington, CT 06378

McLean MR & MRS Stephen T (Caroline G Wilson) Va'76.Va'79.P'72 ☎ (804) 295-9033 . . 401 Bloomfield Rd, Charlottesville, VA 22903

McLean MR Stuart L—Rcn.Fic.Ham'91 ☎ (212) 517-9672 . . 321 E 79 St, New York, NY 10021

McLean MR & MRS William H (Vesta B Tittmann) Unn.Bg.Cysl.Plg.Hn.Stv'31.H'33 ☎ (201) 379-2017 . . 50 Birch Lane, Short Hills, NJ 07078

McLean MR & MRS William L 3d (Elizabeth D Peterson) Pa'51.Pa'53.Me.Rc.W.Ncd.P'49 . . . . . MISS Elizabeth R—Pa'78—at ☎ (610) 668-9374 216 Hampden Av, Narberth, PA 19072 . . . . MISS Sandra L—Guil'84—at ☎ (610) 668-0865 438 Old Forge Crossing, 1027 Valley Forge Rd, Devon, PA 19333 . . . . ☎ (610) MI2-4196 139 Cherry Lane, Wynnewood, PA 19096

McLellan MR & MRS Douglas Buckingham (Callie B Tilden) Cal'53.Bhm.Pcu.Sfg.Fr.Stan'51.Cal'54 ☎ (415) 752-6711 . . 67 Jordan Av, San Francisco, CA 94118

McLemore MR & MRS Bryan Simmons (Margaret Pope) SoMiss'34.Dar.MissState'33 ☎ (601) 894-2608 . . 23099 Dentville Rd, Hazlehurst, MS 39083

McLenegan MRS Alan G (Janet Scott) ☎ (415) 461-0122 . . 501 Via Casitas, Apt 610, Greenbrae, CA 94904

McLennan MRS Juliette C (Juliette N Clagett) Cvc.Ny.Mt. . . . .
MISS Stephanie W—at 1080 Wisconsin Av NW, Apt 2005, Washington, DC *20007* . . . .
JUNIORS MR Christopher T . . . . | of ☎ (202)234-3090 1809 Kalorama Square NW, Washington, DC *20008*
☎ (410) 820-9595 ''Innisfree'' 27833 Waverly Rd, Easton, MD *21601*

McLennan MR & MRS William L (Alice P Warner) Rr.Cho.Fy.Cnt.Y'45
☎ (704) 859-5688 . . 32 Hunting Country Trails, Tryon, NC *28782*

McLeod DR & MRS Alexander C (Dorothy Woods) Swb'58.Gr.Pn.P'56
☎ (615) 383-1276 . . ''Tayburn'' 203 Evelyn Av, Nashville, TN *37205-0451*

McLeod MRS Norman C JR (Joan D Whitehouse) Gchr'51 . . . .
MISS Jean H—NAriz'84—at 4910 Aztec Court NE, Albuquerque, NM *87111* . . . .
MISS Margaret W—NAriz'85—at 1119 E Wahalla Lane, Phoenix, AZ *85024* . . . . . | ☎ (520) 445-6343 323 Forest Hills Circle, Prescott, AZ *86303*

McLucas MR & MRS Don H (Cudahy—Annie M Henry) Sr.On.Nw'32
☎ (847) 234-0540 . . 390 N Green Bay Rd, Lake Forest, IL *60045*

McLucas MR & MRS Don H JR (Pepper—Lloyd—Anne Emmet) Rcn.Mt.S.Cvc.Cly.Sl.P'62.Ox'64
⚓ . . . .
MISS Edith M Pepper . . . . | ☎ (202) 686-5454 4426 Cathedral Av NW, Washington, DC *20016*

McMahan MR & MRS James Albert (Jacqueline Logan-Jones)
☎ (310) 472-5911 . . 2 Oakmont Dv, Los Angeles, CA *90049*

McMahon MR & MRS Bernard J JR (Frances A Kelly) Cysl.Wash'57
☎ (970) 453-1949 . . PO Box 7897, Breckenridge, CO *80424*

McMahon MR & MRS Bernard J 3d (Laura L McManus) Cysl.NCol'85
☎ (970) 668-1378 . . 32 Hawn Dv, PO Box 1892, Frisco, CO *80443*

McMahon MR & MRS Frederic G (Elizabeth A Pflug) Skd'58.Rv.Cw.Snc.Dh.Ncd.Bow'50.Pa'57 . . . . .
MR Frederic C—at Princeton . . . . | ☎ (516) 365-7823 11 North Dv, Plandome, NY *11030*

McMahon MR & MRS Michael W (Sarah M Disston) Skd'84.Duke'79
☎ (214) 239-5331 . . PO Box 670588, Dallas, TX *75367-0588*

McMakin MR & MRS Leigh A (Kemble—P Mimi Maddock) Briar'69.BtP.Rich'64 . . . .
MISS Cecilia L Kemble . . . .
JUNIORS MISS Phoebe P Kemble . . . . | ☎ (561) 842-7079 549 N Lake Trail, Palm Beach, FL *33480*

McManigal MR Roderick A—Bhm.Sfy.Cl'48.Sorb'54.Ox'56
☎ (415) 392-8848 . . 840 Powell St, San Francisco, CA *94108*

McManus MR & MRS Charles J JR (Press—Esther T Azran) Nw'72.Ph.R.Rc.Pc.Fi.Pe.Pa'49 . . . .
MR Barton C—Penn'83 . . . . | ☎ (215) 732-9050 2102 Spruce St, Philadelphia, PA *19103*

McManus MISS Clare E D . . see T E Miller
McManus JUNIORS MR Henry J . . see T E Miller

McMath MR John N JR—L.Myf.Wms'52 . . . .
MISS Sandra B . . . .
MISS Lesley . . . .
MR Andrew . . . . | *see Dilatory Domiciles*

McMeel DR & MRS J Wallace (Elizabeth C Wetherill) Cy.Sm.Btn.Cvc.GeoW'50 . . . .
MR W Cortright—at Columbia Grad . . . . | ☎ (617) 227-4480 22 W Cedar St, Boston, MA *02108*

McMeen MR & MRS Albert R JR (Wilson—Janet Haines) Myf.Laf'39 . . of
☎ (610) 430-0828 . . 536 Franklin Way, Hershey's Mill, West Chester, PA *19380*
☎ (941) 625-1658 . . 21300 Brinson Av, Apt 107, Port Charlotte, FL *33952*

McMenamin MRS Edward B (Joan B Stitt) Cs . . .of
☎ (516) 537-0768 . . Box 768, 172 Church Lane, Bridgehampton, NY *11932*
☎ (561) 746-3072 . . 350 Beach Rd, Tequesta, FL *33469*

McMillan MRS H George JR (Jean E Croker) Swb'54 . . . .
MISS Deborah J . . . . | ☎ (802) 297-2927 PO Box 686, Manchester Center, VT *05255*

McMillan MR & MRS Harold D JR (Judith G Place) Geo'83.CUNY'84
☎ (203) 384-0447 . . 290 Lake Av, Black Rock, CT *06605*

McMillan MR & MRS S Sterling (Elizabeth H Mather) Kt.Un.Ncd.P'29.H'32.Ind'48
☎ (216) 942-6484 . . Mountain Glen Farm, RD 1, Mentor, OH *44060*

McMillan MR & MRS S Sterling 3d (Judith E Knight) Un.Tv.P'60.H'63
MISS Victoria M—at ☎ (206) 643-0722 16061 E 16 St, Bellvue, WA *98008* . . .
MR S Sterling 4th—at ☎ (773) 327-0504 434 W Roscoe St, Apt 5A, Chicago, IL *60657* . . | ☎ (216) 256-8224 9044 Metcalf Rd, Waite Hill, OH *44094*

McMillan MR & MRS William JR (M Elizabeth Myer) BMr'61.Elk.Lm.Mv.Cda.P'57 . . . .
MISS Martha G . . . .
MISS Virginia H . . . .
MISS Eleanor W . . . . | ☎ (410) 429-2991 PO Box 3603, Glyndon, MD *21071*

McMillen MR James JR—Va'53 . . . .
MISS Shelley—Les'91—at ☎ (617) 783-1243 56 Brighton Av, Apt 48, Allston, MA *02134* . . .
MR Bryan—Ariz'90—at ☎ (213) 851-2650 1605 W Martel Av, Apt 18, Los Angeles, CA *90046* . . | ☎ (516) 749-0255 29 Nostrand P'kway, PO Box 545, Shelter Island Heights, NY *11965-0545*

McMillen MRS Julie C (Julie A Cadoret) . . of
☎ (617) 497-6292 . . 6 Dunstable Rd, Cambridge, MA *02138*
☎ (305) 743-7193 . . 269 Morton St, Marathon, FL *33050*

McMillen MR Louis A—Sm.Y'40.H'47
☎ (508) 768-6138 . . ''Rudder Grange'' 80R Eastern Av, PO Box 490, Essex, MA *01929*

McMorris MR & MRS Howard 2d (Clare B Tweedy) Mid'67.Rc.Me.Ri.Cs.P'66
☎ (212) 534-1120 . . 1120 Park Av, New York, NY *10128*

McMorris MISS Mary A
☎ (609) 924-3920 . . Heathcote Farm, 14 Spruce Lane, Princeton, NJ *08540*

McMullen MRS George R (Jane T Garesché) . . . . . .
MR George R JR . . . . | ☎ (313) 885-8055 16832 St Paul Av, Grosse Pointe, MI *48230-1526*

McMullen MR & MRS Greerson G (Ann E Cogswell) Clem'80.SCar'83.Geo'83.Va'88
7565 Seth Raynor Av, Sarasota, FL *34240*

McMullin MR & MRS David B (Sandra F Keefe)
Pa'62.Me.P.'59.Va'64 . . . .
  MISS Anita L—Pa'85.Me.—at ☎ (410) 997-7464
1034 Hickory Ridge Rd, Apt 337, Columbia, MD
21044 . . . .
  MISS (DR) Dana F—W&M'87.Penn'96—at
☎ (717) 531-8852 . . Hershey Medical Center,
38 University Manor E, Hershey, PA 17033 . . .
  MR David B JR—Me.Denis'92—at
☎ (610) 526-2868 . . 1429 County Line Rd,
Rosemont, PA 19010 . . . .
  ☎ (610) 356-5633
  813 Malin Rd,
  Newtown Square,
  PA 19073-3515

McMullin MR & MRS Hunter B (Pamela E Powell)
Fst.Me.Ll.Denis'62 . . . .
  MR H Brooke JR—Pa'86—at ☎ (610) 642-6683
208 Linwood Av, Ardmore, PA 19003 . . . .
  MR Scott P—at ☎ (610) 520-9968
322 Avon Rd, Haverford, PA 19041 . . . .
  ☎ (610) 525-1808
  661 Mill Rd,
  Villanova, PA 19085

McMullin MR & MRS Kimball R (Laura E M
Mullins) Briar'68.Cy.Aht'67.Me'74 . . . .
  MISS Katherine G . . . .
  JUNIORS MISS Anne McA F . . . .
  JUNIORS MR Birch O M . . . .
  JUNIORS MR Christopher K . . . .
  ☎ (314) 994-0059
  7 Fordyce Lane,
  St Louis, MO 63124

McMunn MRS William M (Helen K Hoeveler) Pitt'35.Dar.
☎ (904) 673-2658 . . 596 N Nova Rd, Apt 311, Ormond Beach,
FL 32174

McMurtry MRS John G (Virginia B Symes)
Ncd.Myf. . . . .
  MISS Katharine S . . . .
  MR John G 3d—at Park City, UT 84060 . . . .
  MR Michael G . . . .
  ☎ (303) 781-5859
  2890 S Clarkson St,
  Englewood, CO
  80110

McNabb MR & MRS Mark Hopkins (Hotle—Phoebe
D Hickingbotham) Bhm. . . . .
  JUNIORS MISS Chelsea C H . . . .
    MISS Mercedes E J Hotle . . . .
  ☎ (213) 933-5008
  5008 W 2 St,
  Los Angeles, CA
  90004

McNally MR Andrew 3d—Cho.Rc.Cas.Sc.Yn.Y'31
☎ (773) 477-9330 . . 2430 N Lakeview Av, Chicago, IL 60614-2720

McNally MR & MRS Brian J (Margaret T Corbin) Bost'80.Eh.Srb.Bost'80
☎ (908) 234-9434 . . Box 611, Holland Rd, Far Hills, NJ 07931

McNally MR & MRS Edward C (Margaret McGann)
Barat'65.Rc.Sc.R'velt'66.Ch'78 . . . .
  MISS Heather C . . . .
  JUNIORS MR E Gray . . . .
  ☎ (773) 472-5551
  2920 N
  Commonwealth Av,
  Chicago, IL 60657

McNally MRS Frederick G (Berkey—Martha R
Fleming) Sr. . . . .
  MR Charles P Berkey—at ☎ (303) 355-9157
450 N Josephine St, Apt A, Denver, CO 80206
  ☎ (011-52-73)
  12-79-66
  Cuahtemotzin 403,
  Cuernavaca, Mexico

McNamara MR & MRS J Daniel (Kim York)
Cent'y'66.Curry'71 . . . .
  JUNIORS MISS Ashley Y . . . .
  ☎ (703) 759-6889
  503 Arnon Lake Dv,
  Great Falls, VA
  22066

McNamara MRS John J (Hazel Dionne)
☎ (508) 369-2563 . . 257 Lowell Rd, Carlisle, MA 01741

McNamara MR & MRS John J JR (Ryan—Ann
Johnson) Rcn.Wk.Eh.Nrr. . . . .
  MISS Caroline O Ryan . . . .
  MISS Jean Ryan—at Belmont Abbey Coll . . .
  MR Clendenin J Ryan—at Boston Coll . . . . .
  MR Thomas F Ryan . . . .
  MR Nathaniel J Ryan—at Rensselaer . . . . .
  ☎ (908) 234-1131
  PO Box 809,
  Liberty Corner Rd,
  Far Hills, NJ 07931

McNamara MR William W . . see MRS M Meehan

McNaughton MR & MRS Donald B (M Alison Pyne)
P'82.Dth'90.Pr.Dth'81.Dth'89
☎ (607) 732-4733 . . Strathmont Park, Elmira, NY 14905

McNeal MISS Darby E . . see F R Thompson

McNeal MRS Thomas F (Grace H Smith) Mv . . . of
☎ (410) 235-9020 . . 4219 Wickford Rd, Baltimore, MD 21210
☎ (207) 359-8377 . . ''Kill Kare Kamp'' Rte 15-175, Box 281,
Sargentville, ME 04673

McNealy MR & MRS Dean B (Jones—Ann B Wheeler)
Stan'30.Sfy.Tcy.Ncd.Stan'28 . . of
☎ (415) 492-2427 . . Villa Marin Apt 270, 100 Thorndale Dv,
San Rafael, CA 94903
☎ (619) 767-5449 . . Box 480, Borrego Springs, CA 92004

McNear MR & MRS Donald C (Nancy A Johnston)
Fmy.Cal'52 . . . .
  MR Andrew E . . . .
  MR Frederick W 3d . . . .
  ☎ (415) 386-4443
  11 Seventeenth Av,
  San Francisco, CA
  94121

McNee MRS James (French—Carson—Joan F Remick)
☎ (704) 859-5567 . . 118 Country Club Heights, Tryon, NC 28782

McNeely MR & MRS George H 3d (Wister—Alta D Eisenhauer)
Ph.Gm.Ny.Srb.Me.JHop'53.Pa'56
☎ (610) MI2-9322 . . 635 Dodds Lane, Gladwyne, PA 19035

McNeely MISS Melissa F (Prentice J 3d) . . . . . Married at Greenwood, VA
Kattmann MR Mark H (Ted) . . . . May 25'96

McNeely MRS Prentice J (Powell—Rosalean
Rothermel) Me. . . . .
  MISS Margot McCoy Powell . . . .
  MISS Laura Johnson Powell . . . .
  MR Sheppard T Powell 2d . . . .
  ☎ (610) 525-7131
  77 Middle Rd,
  Apt 260,
  Bryn Mawr, PA
  19010

McNeely MR & MRS Prentice J 3d (Susan H Finney)
Va'69 . . . .
  MR Prentice J 4th—at Harrisonburg, VA 22801 .
  MR Grayson C . . . .
  JUNIORS MR John W . . . .
  ☎ (804) 823-2325
  March Mountain
  Farm, Rte 1,
  Box 547, Crozet,
  VA 22932

McNeil MR & MRS Collin F (Virginia W Judson)
Denis'85.Srr.Ph.Rv.Sdg.Ac.Laf'73
☎ (610) 527-7858 . . 400 Fisher's Rd, Bryn Mawr, PA 19010

McNeil MRS Henry S (Lois A Fernley) Ac.Ncd. ⚓ . . of
☎ (610) 828-1706 . . Hickory Farm, 2300 Hickory Rd, PO Box 211,
Plymouth Meeting, PA 19462
☎ (242) 334-6221 . . ''Claneil'' Cotton Bay Club, Rock Sound,
Eleuthera, Bahamas

McNeil MR Henry S JR—Sg.W&L'68
☎ (215) 790-2486 . . 2104 Delancey Place, Philadelphia, PA 19103

McNeil MR & MRS Robert D (Jennifer P Cox)
Vt'81.NewHaven'84.Sg.Pc.So'73
☎ (610) 857-5097 . . Springbank Farm, RD 3, Coatesville, PA 19320

McNeil MR & MRS Robert L JR (Jones—Nancy M McKinney)
Pc.Ph.Rv.Sar.Ac.Ncd.Y'36 . . of
☎ (215) 836-1044 . . 601 E Evergreen Av, Wyndmoor, PA *19038*
☎ (561) 546-1555 . . 110 Gomez Rd, Hobe Sound, FL *33455*
McNeill MISS Leslie C . . see W P Stedman
McNeill MRS Russell B (Rebecca E Duncan) Cy.G.
☎ (716) 626-4201 . . 61 Briar Row, Williamsville, NY *14221*
McNicol MR & MRS Paul M (Christena C Luce) Elmira'78.Pr.H.'79.Ford'82
☎ (516) 922-3148 . . ''The Pumpkin Patch'' 305 Oakley Court,
Mill Neck, NY *11765*
McNulty MR Oren T . . see J F Kinney
McNulty MR & MRS T Stanley JR (Jean G Hartsell) Cl'59.Ark'57
☎ (501) 535-8025 . . 605 W 34 Av, Pine Bluff, AR *71603*
McPherson MR & MRS Aaron F (Amy B Lankenau) Ws'93.Mit'89.Mit'95
☎ (617) 787-1726 . . 16 Ransom Rd, Apt 14, Brighton, MA *02135-4914*
McPherson MR & MRS J Bruce (Susan H Shea)
MmtVa'81.Ny.Va'63
JUNIORS MISS Ellen B
☎ (609) 896-0190
51 Willow Rd,
Lawrenceville, NJ
08648
McPherson MRS John B (Barbara Chadwick) Sth'35.Exy.
☎ (860) 434-2428 . . 40 Smith's Neck Rd, Old Lyme, CT *06371*
McPherson MR & MRS John W (Rupp—Jane M Dubbs)
V'36.Me.Rc.Gm.Cw.Rv.Cc.Ac.H.'29
☎ (610) 527-1818 . . 79 Pasture Lane, Bryn Mawr, PA *19010*
McPhillips MR & MRS Julian L JR (J Leslie Burton)
LErie'71.P'68.Cl'71
MISS Rachel S
JUNIORS MISS Grace B
☎ (334) 263-4916
831 Felder Av,
Montgomery, AL
36106
McQuade MR & MRS Lawrence C (Margaret Osmer)
Cr'60.C.Mt.Ri.Plg.Cs.Y'50.Ox'52.H.'54
MR Andrew P
☎ (212) 570-0009
125 E 72 St,
New York, NY
10021
McQuiddy MR & MRS Arthur R (Aleen F Hinkle)
Gchr'48.Ncd.Mo'47
MISS Marian E—Purd'74.Ncd.Dar.—at
Alamogordo, NM *88310*
☎ (505) 623-6350
''Hacienda de la
Vista'' 5061 Bright
Sky Rd, Roswell,
NM *88201*
McQuilkin MR G J Geoffrey—H'91
☎ (619) 647-6393 . . 57—4 St, Lee Vining, CA *93541*
McQuilkin MISS Hilary B . . see MRS S A Barngrove
McShane MR & MRS Creighton (Louise L Parry)
Ck.Cl'53.
MISS Suzanne P.
MISS Margot L
MISS Nina C
of ☎ (516)676-2820
224 Lattingtown Rd,
Locust Valley, NY
11560
☎ (561) 231-1382
8735 Lakeside Blvd,
Vero Beach, FL
32963
McShane MR & MRS John L (Suzanne B Deeds) Md.Gv.P'52
13731 Falls Rd, Cockeysville, MD *21030*
McSweeney MISS A Thayer . . see W J Strawbridge JR
McSweeney JUNIORS MISS Catherine B D . . see W J Strawbridge JR
McSweeney MISS Christine S . . see W J Strawbridge JR

McSweeney MRS Edward F (Ramsay—Newman—
Eleanor Walton Newman) Va'71.Cly.Ncd.
MISS Eleanor H Williamson
DR Brandt H Williamson—Mid'88.Va'92—at
Portsmouth, VA *23702*
of ☎ (561)835-4283
300 S Ocean Blvd,
Palm Beach, FL
33480
☎ (757) 484-7151
3101 Riveredge Dv,
Portsmouth, VA
23702
McVeigh MR Charles S—B.H'38.Va'41
MISS Evelyn B—at ☎ (212) 929-4783
99 Bank St, New York, NY *10014*
☎ (516) 922-1948
367 Split Rock Rd,
Syosset, NY *11791*
McVickar MRS Grenville K (Slater—Nancy Wiggin) ColbyS'47.Myf.
☎ (617) 585-9581 . . 7E Treetop Lane, Kingston, MA *02364*
McVickar MR & MRS Malcolm (Bullard—Marion E
Kelly) Sfy.Cl'38
MR Morgan
MR Brian B Bullard
☎ (707) 967-9009
2636 Colombard
Court, St Helena,
CA *94574*
McVickar MRS Ronald (Mary G Filley)
☎ (619) 741-2646 . . PO Box 460775, Escondido, CA *92046*
McVitty MRS Reginald L M (Honoria A Livingston)
☎ (941) 955-9139 . . 700 John Ringling Blvd, Sarasota, FL *34236*
McVoy MRS Eugene J (Constance L Florian) Ch'44.On.Cnt.Fy.
☎ (847) 234-2916 . . 620 Washington Rd, Lake Forest, IL *60045*
McWhinney MR William F . . see MRS J B L Orme
McWilliams MRS Hugh L JR (Margaret McP Adreon)
☎ (508) 433-0614 . . 21 Heald St, Pepperell, MA *01463*
McWilliams MR & MRS James K (Anne M Giannini)
Stan'53.Sfg.Pcu.Fr.Stan'52
MR Kevin S
☎ (415) 931-7162
1940 Vallejo St,
San Francisco, CA
94115
McWilliams MRS John P (Priscilla G Morse)
☎ (505) 989-8185 . . 640 Alta Vista St, Apt 109, Santa Fe, NM *87505*
McWilliams MR John P JR—P'67
☎ (415) 775-5330 . . 1945 Jefferson St, Apt 303, San Francisco,
CA *94123*
McWilliams MISS Marcia Reed
☎ (603) 964-5534 . . PO Box 476, Rye Beach, NH *03871-0476*
McWilliams MISS Saba—SL'59
☎ (719) 539-7486 . . 949 F St, Salida CO *81201-2501*
Maas MRS Walter M JR (Cecelia B Moore)
☎ (608) 233-2387 . . 4029 Council Crest, Madison, WI *53711*
Mabon MR & MRS Charles K (Fredericka A
Galuppo) Cad'61.Ford'68.Cs.Va'64
MISS Francesca H—at Barnard
MR Charles D—at NYU
☎ (212) 472-2835
325 E 72 St,
New York, NY
10021
Mabrey MR & MRS Roy E JR (Edith P MacAusland)
Mid'76.Cy.NCar'75.Kent'79
☎ (617) 455-8023 . . 46 Pheasant Landing Rd, Needham, MA *02192*
MacArthur MR & MRS Bowman McC (Perrin—DiFiore—
Kathleen M Gray) Cvc.Cc.H'30
☎ (561) 439-0918 . . 437 Davis Rd, Palm Springs, FL *33461*
MacArthur MRS Cynthia W (Preble—Hutchison—Cynthia W Wirtz)
☎ (561) 744-8510 . . 104 Waters Edge Dv, Jupiter, FL *33477*
MacArthur MRS Douglas (Jean Faircloth)
☎ (212) 355-3100 . . Waldorf Towers, 301 Park Av, New York,
NY *10022*

MacArthur MR Douglas 2d—Cvc.Mt.Y'32
 ☎ (202) 387-5662 . . 2101 Connecticut Av NW, Washington, DC *20008*
MacArthur MR & MRS Edward S (Wright—Billie S Rowley) On.Cyc. ⚓
 ☎ (847) 234-2792 . . 245 E Vine Av, Lake Forest, IL *60045*
Macarthur-Stanham MR & MRS R Quentin (Barnard—Schumacher—
 Diana Kissel) BtP.Evg.Cly.Cda . . .of
 ☎ (401) 847-3320 . . ''Cannon Hill'' 469 Bellevue Av, Newport,
 RI *02840*
 ☎ (011-61-46) 556425 . . ''Camden Park'' Menangle, NSW 2568,
 Australia

Macauley MRS Edward 3d (Dorothy S Mahana) . . .	☎ (202) 338-6336
MISS Cathleen	3314 O St NW,
MR Edward 4th	Washington, DC
	20007

Macauley MR & MRS John C W (Margaret A Long) NCar'76.NCar'74
 ☎ (203) 834-2592 . . 54 Canterbury Lane, Wilton, CT *06897*
Macauley MR & MRS Michael (Barbara J Cart) B'gton'49.Cal'44
 ☎ (919) 967-3998 . . 318 McCauley St, Apt 4, Chapel Hill, NC *27516*
MacAusland MISS Robin—SacredH'94
 ☎ (203) 656-0429 . . 11 Cliff Av, Darien, CT *06820*
MacAusland MR W Russell 3d—StA.H'70.Stan'73
 ☎ (212) 254-6315 . . 446 E 20 St, Apt 6G, New York, NY *10009*
Macbeth MR Pierre de StJ—SantaC'51
 800 Powell St, San Francisco, CA *94108*
MacBride MISS Abigail A
 ☎ (305) 538-7339 . . 1835 W 27 St, Miami Beach, FL *33140*
MacBride MR & MRS Thomas J JR (Derith R Wallace) Bhm.Cal'71.Cal'73
 ☎ (510) 547-1330 . . 1 Crocker Av, Piedmont, CA *94611*
MacCain MR & MRS James P 2d (Mygatt—Mary Ann Barrett)
 Pc.Pe.Cspa.Sdg.Aht'38
 ☎ (610) 940-9834 . . ''Rebel Hill'' 94 Lemonton Way, Radnor,
 PA *19087-4664*

MacCallum MR & MRS David H (N Lee Neill)	of ☎ (212)737-3324
DU'72.Rc.Mds.Dyc.Br'59.Nu'63	151 E 79 St,
JUNIORS MISS Alexandra Y	New York, NY
JUNIORS MR Neill McL	*10021*
	☎ (516) 324-5549
	19 Amy's Lane,
	East Hampton, NY
	11937

MacColl MR & MRS E Kimbark (Leeanne Gwynne) P'47
 ☎ (503) 223-7664 . . 2620 SW Georgian Place, Portland, OR *97201*

MacColl MR & MRS Eugene K JR (Melinda Bishop)	☎ (503) 227-3058
Ariz'72.P'72	2823 NW
MISS Gretchen B	Cumberland Rd,
MR Eugene K 3d	Portland, OR *97210*
MacColl MR J Roberton 4th—Susq'69.Pa'72	3 Highland Court,
MISS Heather D—at U of NCar Chapel Hill	Needham, MA
JUNIORS MR Douglas R—at 3107 Old Towne	*02192*
Lane, Chattanooga, TN *37415*	

MacColl REV DR & MRS James R 3d (Cynthia Doyle) Rb.Ph.Gm.P.'41
 ☎ (610) 527-7322 . . 74 Pasture Lane, Apt 114, Bryn Mawr,
 PA *19010-1934*
MacColl MR & MRS Malcolm (Dorothy B McAdoo)
 Ty'74.Cy.Me.Gm.Sap.Ty'73
 ☎ (617) 455-0760 . . 54 Pheasant Landing Rd, Needham, MA *02192*

MacColl MR & MRS N Alexander JR (Nancy F Herron) Chi.Ncd.Bab'56
 ☎ (860) 521-0601 . . 37 Sunset Farm Rd, West Hartford, CT *06107*
MacColl MR & MRS Norman A 3d (Mary L Mamulski) StLaw'86.Ty'86
 ☎ (215) 884-1361 . . 1256 Red Rambler Rd, Rydal, PA *19046*

MacCracken MRS Constable (Van Deren—Harriet	☎ (203) 966-2002
B Lyons) Myf.Hn.	630 Oenoke Ridge,
MISS Nancy Van Deren—at ☎ (212) 229-1218	New Canaan, CT
123 Bank St, New York, NY *10014*	*06840*

MacCracken MRS Eleanor D (Eleanor G Dickson) V'40.Dyc.Cs.
 ☎ (212) 249-2591 . . 115 E 67 St, New York, NY *10021*
MacCracken MISS Nell E
 ☎ (919) 398-4222 . . 420 Lakeview Dv, Murfreesboro, NC *27855*

MacDermid MR & MRS Lindsay (Jean K Wilkinson)	☎ (415) 386-1593
Cl'62.Stv'60	335 Maple St,
MISS Jessica G—Cal'89—at ☎ (011-852)	San Francisco, CA
2803-0567 . . 6F Park Height, Apt A, 12A Park	*94118*
Rd, Mid Levels, Hong Kong	
MR L Wallace—Cal'91—*see Dilatory Domiciles*	

MacDonald MISS Catherine . . see MRS S A Trundle JR

MacDonald MR & MRS Christopher W (Nicole M	☎ (415) 851-4612
de Sugny) Bhm.Bur.Pcu.Tufts'66.Pa'68	40 Hayfields Rd,
MR Christopher G	Portola Valley, CA
	94028

MacDonald MISS Cybille A . . see C W Bardin
MacDonald DR & MRS Douglas G (Diane Driscoll) Wh'lck'72.Pa'69.Vt'81
 ☎ (603) 529-1980 . . Poor Farm Rd, Weare, NH *03281*
MacDonald MR & MRS Edmund B (Virginia T Vandever)
 Bhm.Pcu.Sfg.Fr.Stan'36
 ☎ (415) 221-3332 . . 3730 Washington St, San Francisco, CA *94118*
MacDonald MR & MRS Edmund B JR (Vivien A Hickman) Sfg.
 ☎ (415) 386-5151 . . 263—28 Av, San Francisco, CA *94121*
MacDonald MR & MRS Graeme K (Phyllis Welch) Bhm.Pcu.Bur.Stan'33
 ☎ (415) 348-3363 . . 1 Fern Court, Hillsborough, CA *94010*
Macdonald REV CANON & MRS John A (Gail T Hastings)
 MtH'78.Les'79.Dick'79.TyEpisc'86
 ☎ (011-504) 32-4473 . . Apdo 4008, Tegucigalpa, Honduras
MacDonald MRS John E (Margaret Clark) Skd'51.Cda.Dar.Ncd.Ofp.
 333 NE 92 St, Miami, FL *33138*
MacDonald MR Joseph . . see MRS S A Trundle JR

MacDonald MR & MRS Kirkpatrick (Jory—Lee A	of ☎ (212)580-7990
Fahey) ArtInst'73.Bhm.K.Y.'62.Ox'64.Gen'67 .	114 W 78 St,
MR Bryce E A—Geo'92	New York, NY
JUNIORS MISS Alexis A—at Thacher Sch	*10024*
	☎ (914) 534-9690
	''Deerhill Point''
	Cornwall-on-
	Hudson, NY *12520*

| **Macdonald** MRS Neil M (Eleanora von Meister) Eh. | *see* |
| JUNIORS MISS Susannah C . . . . | *Dilatory Domiciles* |

Macdonald MR & MRS Palmer C (Ireland—Martha D Robbins) Fr.Cal'43
 ☎ (415) 325-5433 . . 50 Barry Lane, Atherton, CA *94027*
MacDonald MISS Patricia A—Cly.Ncd.
 ☎ (212) 988-4862 . . 26 E 84 St, New York, NY *10028*
MacDonald MR & MRS Reid V (Ann B Reppert)
 Wh'lck'78.Stan'70.Minn'76
 ☎ (612) 374-5455 . . 1620 Mt Curve Av, Minneapolis, MN *55403*

Macdonald MR & MRS Robert S JR (Leola Armour) | ☎ (212) 369-1341
Sth'60.Rc.Mds.H'58 . . . . | 157 E 94 St,
MR Ian R . . . . | New York, NY
JUNIORS MR Colin S . . . . | *10128*

Macdonald MRS Sheilah E (Gunnin—Sheilah E Kernan) . . . .
name changed to Kernan

Macdonald MR & MRS William M (Kennedy—Hickenlooper—
Anne D Morris) V'42.Sfh.H'48
☎ (610) MU8-5008 . . 104 Devonwood Lane, Devon, PA *19333*

MacDonnell MR & MRS Robert A (Adams—Susan E | ☎ (610) 399-6875
Johnson) SCal'73.Br'65.Pa'67.Pa'72 . . . . | 200 W Street Rd,
MISS Caroline C Adams . . . . | West Chester, PA
MR Brinton H Adams. . . . . | *19382*

MacDougall MRS Allan (Rella M Gammon) Lind'26.Cly.
☎ (212) 758-0089 . . 480 Park Av, New York, NY *10022*

MacDuffie MR John 2d . . . . Died at
Westwood, MA Jan 25'96

Mace DR & MRS Myles L JR (Susan B Andrews) | ☎ (508) 785-0760
Bost'64.D.Chi.Myf.H'62 . . . . | 124 Farm St, Dover,
MISS Alexandra R—at ☎ (212) 366-4340 | MA *02030*
55 W 14 St, Apt 7E, New York, NY *10011* . . . .
MISS Alison A—at ☎ (415) 346-7870
2056 Vallejo St, Apt 4, San Francisco, CA *94123*

MacElree MISS Ellen W
☎ (212) 288-2262 . . 415 E 80 St, New York, NY *10021*

MacElree MR & MRS Lawrence E (Hill—Jane Cox) | of ☎ (610)353-7787
Laf'43.Pa'49 . . . . | Fairy Hill Farm,
MISS Charlotte Hill—at ☎ (415) 824-2083 | 7080 Goshen Rd,
3380A 22 St, San Francisco, CA *94110* . . . . . | Newtown Square,
MISS Ann Hill—at ☎ (410) 658-9159 | PA *19073*
1089 Nesbitt Rd, Colora, MD *21917* . . . . | ☎ (207) 374-5465
| Chase House,
| Box 792, Union St,
| Blue Hill, ME
| *04614*

MacEslin MR & MRS Donald R JR (Nancy Lee Dismukes) Temp'54
☎ (717) 428-1059 . . "Tree House" RD 1, Seven Valleys, PA *17360*

MacEwan MRS A Jones (Alison M Jones) . . . . . . name changed to Jones

MacEwan MISS Elizabeth P . . see MRS A M Jones

MacEwan MR & MRS Nigel S (Elliman—Beavers—Judith G Sperry)
Ln.Ny.Yn.Y'55.H'59 ⚓
☎ (203) 972-9253 . . 153 Oenoke Lane, New Canaan, CT *06840*

MacEwan MR Nigel S JR—GeoW'89
☎ (703) 739-7781 . . 212 N Fairfax St, Alexandria, VA *22314*

MacEwan MISS Pamela T . . see MRS A M Jones

MacEwen MR & MRS Peter W (Elizabeth T Rhinelander) McG'85.McG'85
☎ (508) 927-6415 . . 17 High St, Beverly Farms, MA *01915*

MacEwen MASTER William Templeton (Peter W) . . . . Born Apr 20'94

MacFadyen MR & MRS John A JR (de Mailly—Babcock—
Diane L Beersman) Wms'45.Cl'62
☎ (860) 535-0539 . . 98 Water St, Stonington, CT *06378*

Macfarlane MISS Jean P . . see MRS H Brown

MacFarlane MR & MRS S Neil (Anne C Bigelow)
Dth'78.Camb'80.Dth'76.Ox'82
4 Winchester Rd, Oxford, England

MacGaffin MR & MRS Norman J (Jane Thayer) Rol'36.Rol'37
☎ (904) 247-6837 . . 4110 Fleet Landing Blvd, Atlantic Beach,
FL *32233*

Macgill MRS James (Jackson—Elizabeth Rawson) Mv.
☎ (410) 321-0675 . . Blakehurst 518, 1055 W Joppa Rd, Towson,
MD *21204*

Macgregor MRS James Verry (Gregg—Virginia Wyckoff) Csn.Ncd.
☎ (203) 655-0860 . . 2 Queen's Lane, Darien, CT *06820*

MacGuigan MRS V Duncan (Virginia C Duncan) Cda.Dar.
☎ (212) RE4-3781 . . 136 E 76 St, New York, NY *10021*

MacGuire MR & MRS John T (Betty L Moor) Tex'48.Sdy.Tex'43
☎ (915) 584-7111 . . 1209 Thunderbird Dv, El Paso, TX *79912*

MacGuire MISS Mary J—Man'vl'87 . . . . | see F R Reinecke
MR Sean M . . . . |

Machold MR & MRS Roland M (Pamela W Pulleyn) | ☎ (609) 921-2627
Au.Wt.Y'57.H'63 . . . . | 1091 Princeton-
MISS Alyssa M—Ch'94. . . . . | Kingston Rd,
MR Roland P . . . . | Princeton, NJ
MR Robert P—Y'91—at MIT . . . . | *08540-4129*

Machold MR William D—Miami'69.Wash'76
☎ (212) 741-2286 . . 458 W 22 St, New York, NY *10011*

Machold MR William F . . . . Died at
Newtown Square, PA Feb 28'96

Mack MRS Charles J (Alice C Brown) . . . . | ☎ (518) 584-5268
MISS Honour D . . . . | 165 Union Av,
MR George M—at Hamilton . . . . | Saratoga Springs,
| NY *12866*

Mack MR & MRS Harold L JR (Maria C Moore)
☎ (415) 573-0433 . . 155 Flying Mist St, Foster City, CA *94404*

Mack MR & MRS John D (Etter—Lorna U Carey) Rdc'52.StJ'48.H'50
☎ (609) 466-1256 . . 339 Rileyville Rd, Ringoes, NJ *08551*

Mack MISS Linda C (FitzSimmons—Linda C Mack) Ariz'72.Nw'77.Cas.
☎ (312) 951-8365 . . 1100 N Lake Shore Dv, Chicago, IL *60611*

Mack MR & MRS M Wakefield (Sandra A | ☎ (503) 223-1201
MacGregor) Col'71.NotreD'63. . . . . | 1201 SW Highland
MISS Elizabeth W . . . . | Rd, Portland, OR
JUNIORS MISS Annie M . . . . | *97221*

Mack MR Norman E 2d—St.P'50
☎ (803) 723-0045 . . 16 Atlantic St, Charleston, SC *29401*
Dec 15 . . ☎ (561) 655-0976 . . 6 Via Vizcaya, Palm Beach, FL *33480*

Mack MRS Ralph B (Katharine E Roberts) Ncd.
31004 Aliso Circle, South Laguna, CA *92677*

Mack MISS Suzanne (Beck—Suzanne Mack)
☎ (714) 249-8269 . . 23667 Brockton Court, Laguna Niguel, CA *92677*

Mack MR & MRS Walter M (Suzanne Charbonneau) Sr.Cas.Cnt.Ch'48 . . of
☎ (847) 446-4231 . . 334 Woodley Rd, Winnetka, IL *60093*
☎ (561) 234-4605 . . John's Island Club, 450 Beach Rd, Vero Beach,
FL *32963*

Mack MR & MRS William L (Jennifer L McLean)
☎ (716) 377-3975 . . 44 Halburt Av, Fairport, NY *14450*

Mackall MISS Lucy H—Ncd.
☎ (202) 965-5140 . . 1413—30 St NW, Washington, DC *20007*

Mackall MRS William W (Mary E Hoxton) Sl . . .of
☎ (804) 288-2492 . . 28 Chatham Square, 6161 River Rd, Richmond,
VA *23226*
☎ (540) 554-8545 . . Bruce Farm, Bluemont, VA *20135*

MacKay MRS Edward H (Whitman—Cynthia Vansittart) StJ. . . . .
☎ (415) 346-5625
2655 Clay St, San Francisco, CA 94115
MR Edward H 3d—at ☎ (510) 256-6347
275 Stevenson, Pleasant Hill, CA 94523 . . . . . .
MR Robert V—at ☎ (707) 776-2701
1609 Andover Way, Petaluma, CA 94954 . . . . .

Mackay MR & MRS Ian D (Susan Marckwald) StA.Hlns'62.Rut'72 . . . .
☎ (908) 234-9169
137 Mosle Rd, Far Hills, NJ 07931
MISS Heather N—at 6503 N Military Trail, Boca Raton, FL 33496 . . . .
MISS Holly P—at 5701-310 Chapman Mill Dv, Rockville, MD 20852 . . . .
MR Ian A B—Menlo'95 . . . .

Mackay MRS Jacqueline deF (Jacqueline deF Meyler)
☎ (212) 535-4826 . . 120 East End Av, Apt 11A, New York, NY 10028-7552

MacKay MRS John F (Helen Pflug) Pr.
☎ (516) 674-3863 . . Box 618, Buckram Rd, Locust Valley, NY 11560

MacKay MR & MRS John F JR (Lisa Robins) P'57 . .
☎ (516) AR1-4945
Lloyd Lane, Huntington, NY 11743
MR Hugh G . . . .

MacKay MR & MRS John F 3d (Kelly A Brazill)
☎ (516) 692-9680 . . 11 Spring St, Cold Spring Harbor, NY 11724

Mackay MRS John W (Gwendolyn Rose) Pr.Cly.
☎ (516) 671-0664 . . 31 Factory Pond Rd, Locust Valley, NY 11560

MacKay MR & MRS (DR) Malcolm (Cynthia N Johnson) Rdc'64.SUNY'77.Pr.C.Cs.P'63.H'66 .
☎ (718) 625-4021
2 Montague Terr, Brooklyn, NY 11201
MISS Hope L . . . .
MR Robert L . . . .

Mackay MRS Malcolm S (V Gray von Grebenstein)
☎ (612) 473-8302 . . PO Box 667, Long Lake, MN 55356

Mackay MISS Melinda L
☎ (516) 922-5771 . . 10 Shutter Lane, Oyster Bay, NY 11771

Mackay MR & MRS (DR) Michael W (Meggan C Quigley) StLaw'79.NYMed'91.Y'79
☎ (914) 738-2414 . . 214 Fifth Av, Pelham, NY 10803

Mackay MR & MRS Patrick H (Duryea—Elise B Bradley) CtCol'68.Pr.Srr.
☎ (516) 676-2230 . . PO Box 383, Locust Valley, NY 11560

MacKay MR & MRS Robert B (Anna A von Raits) LakeF'74.S.Csh.Ny.Cw.Snc.StA.Bost'68.H'72.Bost'80
☎ (516) 271-1905 . . 18 Pennington Dv, Huntington, NY 11743

Mackay MR & MRS Rupert (Hillary D Bidwell) Y'88.Lond'92.Yn . . .of
☎ (011-44-171) 793-8180 . . 5 Albert Square, London SW8 1BU, England
☎ (011-44-1983) 761-428 . . The Wight House, High St, Yarmouth, Isle of Wight, England

MacKay MISS Victoria Anne (Rupert) . . . . Born at London, England Mch 2'96

Mackay-Smith DR & MRS Matthew P (Wingate Eddy) H'53.Ga'58.Pa'63
☎ (540) 837-1787 . . "Greenwood" Rte 1, Box 31, White Post, VA 22663

Mackel MR & MRS James P JR (Judith A Coleman) Vh.SCal'56.SCal'60
☎ (541) 420-0110 . . PO Box 1573, Bend, OR 97709-1573

MacKenzie MR & MRS David O (Deborah W Williams) On.Sr.Cas.Ncd.Ty'54 . . . .
☎ (847) 234-9249
1180 N Elm Tree Rd, Lake Forest, IL 60045
MR Douglas S—at Chicago, IL . . . .
MR David W—Col'92. . . . .

MacKenzie MR & MRS Donald D (Suzanne P Grant) Ken'88.Wa.Mid'85
☎ (303) 782-0614 . . 3850 S Albion St, Cherry Hills Village, CO 80110

Mackenzie MR & MRS Duncan H (Clemson—Anne H Stick) Gchr'50.Lm.Mv.Cda.Dc.Br'49.Md'52 .
☎ (410) 734-4536
"Kintail Glebe" 3019 Goat Hill Rd, Bel Air, MD 21015-6619
MISS Suzanne S (Stearns—Suzanne S Mackenzie) MaryW'78 . . . .
MR G Scott Clemson—H'77 . . . .

Mackenzie MRS G Norbury 4th (Dorothy Yorke Beaman)
☎ (610) 525-5859 . . 156 Pennsylvania Av, Bryn Mawr, PA 19010

Mackenzie MR & MRS Guy David (Blynn—Nancy A McAvity) Yn.Y'58
☎ (203) 255-3348
505 Merwins Lane, Fairfield, CT 06430
MISS Frances A Blynn—at ☎ (415) 563-1638
325 Walnut St, San Francisco, CA 94118 . . . .
MISS Alexandra P Blynn—at 66 Simpson Av, Apt 1, Somerville, MA 02144 . . . .

MacKenzie MR & MRS Jared D (Margaret Faesy) SL'87
☎ (508) 693-6787 . . "Peace Gate" off State Rd, Tisbury, MA 02568

MacKenzie MRS Phoebe C (Phoebe Ann Connor) V'56
☎ (203) 655-7201
21 Canoe Trail, Darien, CT 06820
MR W Gair JR—at 75 Monmouth St, Brookline, MA 02146 . . . .
MR Scott Anderson—at ☎ (618) 374-4789 Principia College, Elsah, IL 62028 . . . .

Mackenzie MR & MRS William G (Weaver—Shirley E Fetterolf) Sg.
☎ (408) 624-6016 . . 3331 Ondulado Rd, Pebble Beach, CA 93953

Mackey MR B Franklin JR—Nw'57.Ark'73
900 N Lake Shore Dv, Apt 1802, Chicago, IL 60611

Mackey DR & MRS Barton L (Eugenie H Lewis) Wil.W.Cw.Cda.F&M'59.Pa'69 . . . .
☎ (302) 652-8015
2205 Kentmere P'kway, Wilmington, DE 19806
MR Dwight D—at Eatons Ranch, Wolf, WY 82807 . . . .
MR Scott L—at Berklee Col of Music . . . .

Mackey MR & MRS Barton L JR (Jennifer L Manthorpe) MaryB'82
☎ (302) 656-3935 . . PO Box 381, Montchanin, DE 19710

Mackey MRS Diane (Diane G Stoakes) Nw'58.Ark'78
☎ (501) 664-3020 . . 3404 Cedar Hill Rd, Apt 3, Little Rock, AR 72202

Mackey MR & MRS Michael V (Wendy E Dorsaneo) WChesU'85
☎ (610) 449-4637 . . 127 Strathmore Rd, Havertown, PA 19083

Mackey MISS Taylor Marie (Michael V) . . . . Born at Bryn Mawr, PA Jun 8'95

Mackie MR & MRS Charles L (Rosanne McCaffrey) Tul'73.Tul'73.Tul'76
11124 Marden Lane, Austin, TX 78739

Mackie MRS Donald (Valdes—M Fleury Velie) . . . .
☎ (609) 924-5383
566 Princeton-Kingston Rd, Princeton, NJ 08540
MISS F Kelly Valdes—at ☎ (610) 353-2303
1615 E Strasburg Rd, West Chester, PA 19380

Mackie DR & MRS Julius A JR (O'Malley—Joan T M Wheeler) Me.Rc.Ac.NCar'47.Pa'50
☎ (610) 687-3303 . . 800 Godfrey Rd, Villanova, PA 19085

Mackintosh MR & MRS Ian (Victoria Cobb) Camb'61 . . . . ☎ (011-44-1962) 734182
MISS Alexandra . . . . 9 Grange Rd,
MISS Juliet . . . . Alresford,
JUNIORS MISS Evelyn . . . . Hampshire SO24 9HB, England

Mackroth MRS John R (Alice G McKnight) Sth'38.Ncd. . . . . ☎ (904) 384-3610 2970 St Johns Av, Apt 12C,
MISS Garland—at ☎ (312) 943-7977 260 E Chestnut St, Chicago, IL *60611* . . . . Jacksonville, FL *32205*

MacLaren CAPT (RET) & MRS William F (Martha A Wilson) USN.Ws'67.H'67 . . . . ☎ (860) 963-0077 PO Box 272,
MISS Catharine P—Va'91 . . . . Pomfret, CT *06258-0272*
MR W Morgan—at 1107 Locust Grove Lane, Charlottesville, VA *22901* . . . .
MR Ian L—at 1107 Locust Grove Lane, Charlottesville, VA *22901* . . . .

MacLaren MRS Wistar H (Louisa B Phillips) Me.Gm.Cs.Ac.Cda.
☎ (610) 527-9147 . . 76 Middle Rd, Bryn Mawr, PA *19010*

Maclaurin MR Peter J—Lawr'67
☎ (617) 423-5930 . . 9 Melrose St, Apt 3, Boston, MA *02116*

MacLaury MR Ian G . . see MRS E A Riley

Maclay MRS Archibald (Truslow—Jennifer A Bearcroft)
☎ (561) 833-2616 . . 240A Worth Av, Palm Beach, FL *33480*

Maclay MR & MRS John B JR (Joyce Moore) Gchr'66.JHop'66 . . . . ☎ (410) 235-7985 4504 Roland Av, Baltimore, MD *21210*
MR David M—Cr'95 . . . .

Maclay MR John B 3d—Hav'90.H'94
☎ (212) 496-0584 . . 101 W 81 St, Apt 317, New York, NY *10024*

MacLean MR & MRS Angus Lloyd JR (Virginia Willingham Arnold) Bhm.Bur.Pcu.Sfg.Fr.Ncd. Br'53 . . . . ☎ (415) 342-8257 510 N San Raymundo Rd, Hillsborough, CA *94010*
MISS Lowrie H . . . .
MISS Virginia C . . . .
MR Angus L 3d . . . .

MacLean MR & MRS Babcock (M Cynthia Gannon) Daemen'73.Cwr'74.S.Sa.Y.'67.Cl'70.Cwr'75.Nu'87 ⚓ . . of
☎ (212) 956-4090 . . 27 W 55 St, New York, NY *10019*
☎ (516) 424-5675 . . 44 Knollwood Av, Huntington, NY *11743*

Maclean MISS Barbara J
☎ (212) 751-8609 . . 200 E 66 St, Apt D901, New York, NY *10021*

MacLean MRS Charles C (Lee S Howe) Ws'31.Cly . . .of
☎ (212) 838-1647 . . 200 E 66 St, New York, NY *10021*
☎ (516) 423-3258 . . 40 Lloyd Lane, Lloyd Neck, Huntington, NY *11743*

MacLean MR & MRS Charles C 3d (Salsbery—Barbara A Weathers) Y'60.Y'63
☎ (602) 956-6222 . . 2102 E Marshall Av, Phoenix, AZ *85016*

Maclean REV CANON & MRS Dougald L (Mary W Patterson) Adelphi'67.SUNY'71.Un.Chr.Plg.StA.StJ.Cly.Ne.Dar. B'klyn'35.PhilaDiv'42 . . of
☎ (718) 359-4641 . . 32-30—160 St, Flushing, NY *11358-1345*
☎ (860) 536-3028 . . "Waukeya" 24 Whitehall Landing, Mystic, CT *06355*

MacLean MISS Heather L (Charles C 3d) . . . . Married at Huntington, NY
Blok MR Christiaan J (Hendrik C) . . . . May 18'96

MacLean MR Ian W—StLaw'87.Nu'92
☎ (212) 535-4478 . . 517 E 87 St, Apt 4E, New York, NY *10128*

MacLean MR & MRS Malcolm O (Honor L Banks) Lic.Cw.P'50 ⚓ . . . . ☎ (516) 239-3085 240 Causeway Rd, Lawrence, NY *11559*
MR Malcolm O JR—WashColl'77—at 1835 Ocala Rd, Juno, FL *33408* . . . .

MacLean MISS Nancy L
☎ (415) 923-1643 . . 2999 California St, Apt 45, San Francisco, CA *94115*

MacLean DR William A H—Y'61.Cl'65 . . . . 2305 English Village Lane, Birmingham, AL *35223-1732*
MISS Kathryn E—Wms'93.Cl'94—at 1401 St Andrew St, Apt 109, New Orleans, LA *70130* . . . .
MISS Stephanie H—Ty'96—at 401 Holland Av, San Antonio, TX *78212* . . . .

MacLear MR & MRS Frank R (Suzanne G Gardner) Ny.R.Mich'43 . . . . ☎ (212) 988-2940 117 E 72 St, New York, NY *10021*
MISS Lydia A—at 165 E 60 St, New York, NY *10022* . . . .
MR Malcolm G—at 301 W Eugenie St, Chicago, IL *60614* . . . .
MR Bruce A . . . .

MacLeish MRS Lenore Guest (Platt—Lenore Guest MacLeish) ChHill'81
☎ (215) 753-1004 . . 732 Wolcott Dv, Apt A1, Philadelphia, PA *19118*

Maclennan MR & MRS Robert A R (Noyes—Helen Cutter) Rdc'57.Ox'59.Ox'58.Camb'60 . . . . of ☎ (011-44-171) 937-5960 74 Abingdon Villas, London W8 6XB, England
MISS Ruth B I—Camb'91 . . . .
MR Adam L R—at Edinburgh U . . . .
MR Nicholas H Noyes—Cl'84—at
☎ (212) 865-4889 . . 315 Riverside Dv, Apt 19B, New York, NY *10025* . . . . ☎ (603) 466-3857 "Little House" Durand Rd, Randolph, NH *03570*

MacLennan DR & MRS W Donald (Mildred M Godwin) Edin'44
☎ (011-44-1620) 843314 . . "Aros House" Templar Place, Gullane, East Lothian EH31 2AH, Scotland

Macleod MR & MRS Cameron (Beatrice Endicott) . . . ☎ (207) 864-5134 "Skye Fields" Box 686, Rangeley, ME *04970*
MISS Beatrice M . . . .

MacLeod MR Hugh D T . . see MISS V L Pierpont

MacLeod MR & MRS Ian D (Brooke M Steinmetz) Wit'87.Wit'88
☎ (206) 822-3258 . . 523 Fifteenth Av, Kirkland, WA *98033-5608*

MacLeod MRS Lynette A (Lynette J Abbott) Ws'70.Pr.
☎ (516) 674-5155 . . 6 Poppy Lane, Glen Cove, NY *11542*

Macleod MR & MRS Robert W (Barbara B Wilmerding) Cy.Ny.Fic.Nh.Ty'62 . . . . ☎ (508) 359-8353 "Shepherds Plains" 331 North St, Medfield, MA *02052*
MISS Avery W . . . .
MR Ian R . . . .
MR Morris W . . . .

MacLeod MRS Rosemary H (Ingram—E Rosemary Hood)
☎ (202) 244-4861 . . 4000 Massachusetts Av NW, Apt 924, Washington, DC *20016*

MacLeod MISS Sarah T . . see MISS V L Pierpont

MacLeod MR Sayre 3d—Pr.Syr'66
☎ (516) 676-9503 . . PO Box 342, Mill Neck, NY *11765*
MacLeod MR William—Aberdeen'61
3418 Wickersham Lane, Houston, TX *77027-4134*
MacMahon MISS Alexandra Heurich (g—MRS Benjamin C Evans JR) . . . . .
Born at Washington, DC May 10'96
MacMahon MR & MRS Edward G (Noelle L Greabell) StLaw'88.StLaw'88
☎ (508) 897-0990 . . 19 Demars St, Maynard, MA *01754*
MacMaster MR & MRS Donald F (Frances W Carey)
AmU'82.Temp'85.Bridgept'89
☎ (201) 593-8247 . . 10 Hunter Dv, Madison, NJ *07940*
MacMillan MR & MRS A Bryan (Brauer—Hunter—Jane Franklin)
Bv.Wash'43 . . of
Hunter Farms, 13501 Ladue Rd, St Louis, MO *63141*
825 Fifth Av, New York, NY *10021*
MacMillan MR & MRS Richard J (Josephine B | 29 Webster St,
Worcester) . . . . | Hudson, NH *03051*
MISS Josephine B—NH'90 . . . . |
MR Donald S—at Babson . . . . |
MacMorris MR & MRS John W 3d (Abramson—Elizabeth S Nicholson)
Pa'71.OklaSt'69.Minn'75
☎ (415) 323-0591 . . 205 Colorado Av, Palo Alto, CA *94301*
MacMullan JUNIORS MR Chace T . . see E D Pearre
MacMullan MR Russell J SR—Me.Pa'34
☎ (610) 325-9686 . . Dunwoody Village C216, 3500 West Chester Pike,
Newtown Square, PA *19073*
MacMullan JUNIORS MR Russell J 3d . . see E D Pearre
MacNair MR Andrew P—Pn.P'69.Cl'73
☎ (212) 334-2132 . . 426 W Broadway, New York, NY *10012-3775*
MacNair MISS Caroline P (Tauranac—Caroline P MacNair) BMr'65
☎ (212) 388-7188 . . 141 E 88 St, Apt 2C, New York, NY *10128*
MacNair MRS Cynthia P (Cynthia H Parrott)
☎ (212) 674-3704 . . 23 E 10 St, New York, NY *10003*
MacNair MR Pierce (Margaret H Prichitt)
☎ (601) 467-3792 . . 117 DeMontluzin Av, Apt 50, Bay St Louis,
MS *39520*
Macneil MRS James D (Warner—R Lee Drummond) | ☎ (818) 441-9050
Vh. . . . . | 1230 Hillside Rd,
MISS Nina E Warner—at ☎ (310) 453-2822 | Pasadena, CA *91105*
1217—25 St, Santa Monica, CA *90404* . . . . . |
MacNeish MR & MRS William Jack JR (Marion S | ☎ (610) 525-6054
Madara) Grin'67.Ihy.Cry.Me.Br'68 . . . . | "Larkhall"
MISS Marion Madara . . . . | 427 Garden Lane,
MISS Anna Jack . . . . | Bryn Mawr, PA
| *19010*
Macomb MRS Alexander (Lake—Edna Wilson)
☎ (757) 428-0928 . . 4800 Atlantic Av, Virginia Beach, VA *23451*
Macomb MR & MRS J de Navarre JR (Marjorie R Street)
Ih.Cw.Ds.Ll.Lm.Snc.StA.Cnt.Ncd.P'35
☎ (847) 446-1037 . . 588 Arbor Vitae Rd, Winnetka, IL *60093-2302*
Macomber MR & MRS John De W (Caroline | ☎ (202) 338-3677
Morgan) BMr'54.Unn.Ri.Ln.Mt.StJ.Sl.Csn. | 2806 N St NW,
Y'50.H'52 . . . . | Washington, DC
MISS Elizabeth C—Wes'88—at | *20007*
☎ (206) 784-1224 . . 4502 Second Av NW, |
Seattle, WA *98107* . . . . |
MR William B 2d . . . . |

Macomber MR & MRS William B (Phyllis D Bernau)
Sim'45.C.Csn.Sl.Y'44.H'47.H'49.Ch'51
☎ (508) 228-0594 . . "Blowing Clear" 27 Monomoy Rd, Nantucket,
MA *02554*
Macon DR & MRS William L 4th (Mary L Schilling) | ☎ (410) 323-9454
Cy.P'59.H'63.Syr'64 . . . . | 805 St Georges Rd,
MR William H—Ty'93 . . . . | Baltimore, MD
MR Christopher B—at Johns Hopkins . . . . | *21210*
JUNIORS MR Stewart M—at Johns Hopkins . . . . . |
Macpherson MISS Marian . . see P L Payson
MacPherson MR & MRS Robert W B (Joan B Wallace) H.'46
130 Mt Auburn St, Cambridge, MA *02138*
MacRae MR Cameron F—Bcs.Plg.Myf.StA.StJ.NCar'27 . . of
☎ (561) 546-3355 . . PO Box 1905, Hobe Sound, FL *33475*
☎ (516) 283-6707 . . PO Box 1267, Southampton, NY *11969*
MacRae MR & MRS Cameron F 3d (Ann W Bedell) | of ☎ (212)734-2109
Rc.Ln.Cly.P'63.Y'66 . . . . | 125 E 72 St,
MISS Catherine F . . . . | New York, NY
JUNIORS MISS Ann C . . . . | *10021*
| ☎ (516) 283-5792
| Meadow Lane,
| Southampton, NY
| *11968*
Macrae MRS John (Solley—Niedringhaus—Jane Switzler)
Nyc.Chi.Cysl.Ncd . . . of
☎ (561) 278-4679 . . 1111 N Ocean Blvd, Delray Beach, FL *33483-7229*
☎ (508) 228-1760 . . 45 Cliff Rd, Nantucket, MA *02554*
Macsherry MRS Bernard S (Barbara D Wise) An . . . | ☎ (301) 299-6465
MISS Helen D—Wells'78 . . . . | 10316 Crown Point
MR Bernard S JR—Geo'75 . . . . | Court, Potomac, MD
MR Richard M—Wms'75 . . . . | *20854*
MacVeagh MR & MRS Charles P 3d (Patricia K | ☎ (703) 759-3109
Williams) Cr'51.An.Nd.H'53.Ox'55 . . . . | 9418 Brian Jac
MR Charles P 4th—at First Dollar Farm, | Lane, Great Falls,
PO Box 420, Washington, VA *22747* . . . . | VA *22066*
MacVeagh MR & MRS Charlton (Diana S Greeff) Hn.H'57
☎ (603) 876-3330 . . "Cloudlands" Marlborough, NH *03455*
MacVeagh MR Colin L—H'70.Cl'78
☎ (212) 734-4883 . . 444 E 75 St, New York, NY *10021*
MacVeagh MRS Francis W (Ellen W Thoron)
☎ (707) 963-4209 . . La Herradura Ranch, 970 Conn Valley Rd,
St Helena, CA *94574*
MacVeagh MRS Lincoln (Coats—Virginia Ferrante di Ruffano)
☎ (315) 655-9560 . . 9 Sullivan St, Apt 8, Cazenovia, NY *13035*
MacVeagh MISS Martha W—Cr'84
☎ (314) 962-5734 . . 119 E Frisco Av, Webster Groves, MO *63119*
MacWilliams MR & MRS John J (M Lee Elliott) | ☎ (408) 625-4003
Cly.Hob'51 . . . . | PO Box 43,
MISS Cameron L—Col'87—at ☎ (415) 928-6870 | Pebble Beach, CA
2101 Beach St, San Francisco, CA *94123* . . . . . | *93953*
MR W Brewster—Cr'82—at ☎ (310) 454-2215 |
17250 Sunset Blvd, Pacific Palisades, CA *90272* |
MR P Huntington—Menlo'84—at |
1305 Chelsea Way, Redwood City, CA *94061* . . |

Macy MR & MRS A Martin (Hutchinson—Bona Comel di Socebran) Sl.Cr'51.. of
☎ (713) 961-7780.. 19 E Briar Hollow Lane, Houston, TX *77027*
Mill Reef Club, Antigua

Macy MRS Gay Fessenden (Gay Mesta Fessenden)
see Dilatory Domiciles

Macy MRS Henry R (Katharine L Hartman) . . . . | ☎ (516) 692-7034
MISS Victoria R—at 32 Pearson Rd, Apt 1, | 240 Jennings Rd,
Somerville, MA *02144* . . . . | Cold Spring Harbor,
MISS Mary—at 125 Washington Place, | NY *11724*
New York, NY *10011* . . . . |

Macy MRS J H Dick (Elizabeth B Bacon) Rc.
☎ (309) 836-3226.. "South Farm" Macomb, IL *61455*

Macy MRS J Noel (Kohler—Elena de R Aldcroftt) Csn.
☎ (202) 337-3339.. 3339 N St NW, Washington, DC *20007*

Macy MR & MRS John H D JR (Janice A Kettley) Cyb.
☎ (602) 391-9833.. 9209 N 117 Way, Scottsdale, AZ *85259*

Macy MRS Josiah JR (Mary C Emerson) Au. . . . . . . | of ☎ (201)538-8492
MR Josiah 3d—at Vail, CO *81658* . . . . | Jockey Hollow Rd,
MR Michael E F—Box 1043, Juneau, AK *99802* | Morristown, NJ
| *07960*
| ☎ (518) 576-9742
| "Running Fox"
| Keene Valley, NY
| *12943*

Macy MR & MRS Thomas G (Natalie Morgan) | ☎ (215) 836-1108
ChHill'84.Pc.LakeF'73 . . . . | 4115 Fields Dv,
JUNIORS MISS Louisa M . . . . | Lafayette Hill, PA
JUNIORS MR Alexander G . . . . | *19444*

Madara MRS Edward S (Ann W Hessenbruch) Me.Ac.
☎ (610) 645-8917.. Waverly Heights 329B, 1400 Waverly Rd,
Gladwyne, PA *19035*

Madara MR & MRS Edward S JR (Rosalinda B | ☎ (610) 664-2738
Roberts) MaryB'63.Me.Ncd.Pa'63 . . . . | "Rabbit Run"
MR Edward S III—Emory'86.W&L'89—at | PO Box 413,
☎ (212) 431-8907.. 145 Spring St, New York, | Narberth, PA *19072*
NY *10012* . . . . |

Madden MRS James E (Betty Mae Hamilton) Ncd. . | ☎ (860) 435-0007
MISS Anne Marie—V'78—at 779 Fourteenth Av, | "Bobolink Hill"
San Francisco, CA *94118* . . . . | Lakeville, CT *06039*
MR Peter C—Marl'88.NH'92—Box 892, Calais, |
ME *04619* . . . . |

Madden MISS Paula M—Ncmb'75.Reed'95
☎ (503) 777-2779.. "Far Outlook" 10862 SE Idleman Rd, Portland,
OR *97266*

Madden MR & MRS Robert L (Frazer—Butler—Diana Dunning)
Dll.Ncd.Myf.Pitt'37
☎ (561) 286-2711.. 1600 SE St Lucie Blvd, Apt 115, Stuart, FL *34996*

Maddock MR & MRS Paul L JR (Dewing—Read— | of ☎ (561)844-9231
Cythlen Cunningham) Evg.BtP.Br'72 . . . . | 1160 N Ocean Blvd,
MISS Cythlen A Dewing . . . . | Palm Beach, *33480*
JUNIORS MR Zachary B Read . . . . | ☎ (970) 728-6145
| "Polecat Palace"
| 150 Polecat Lane,
| Telluride, CO *81435*

Maddock MRS Victoria N (Victoria K Neumann) . . | ☎ (561) 833-6629
MR Paul L 3d . . . . | 227 Australian Av,
JUNIORS MR Charles N . . . . | Apt 2A,
| Palm Beach, FL
| *33480*

Maddux MR Fielding L—Geo'73
☎ (561) 832-4934.. 2800 N Flagler Dv, West Palm Beach, FL *33407*

Maddux MR & MRS H Cabell JR (Yolanda M Alfaro) Cvc.Sl.Va'39
☎ (703) 356-6260.. 1140 Chain Bridge Rd, McLean, VA *22101*

Maddux MR H Cabell 3d—Cvc.Va'73 . . . . | ☎ (540) 349-4653
JUNIORS MR H Cabell 4th . . . . | Rte 1, Box 55H,
JUNIORS MR Victor H . . . . | Broad Run, VA
| *20137*

Madeira MRS C Bradley (Constance Bradley) Nf.
☎ (207) 276-5815.. "Madhouse" Northeast Harbor, ME *04662*

Madeira MR & MRS Crawford C JR (Homan—Hélène de Baubigny)
Stan'52.Me.Gm.Cts.Rb.Nf.Cly.Ac.P.'40
☎ (610) 649-5221.. 414 Old Lancaster Rd, Haverford, PA *19041*

Madeira MRS Dashiell L (Elizabeth Ambrose) V'21.Cda.Ncd.
☎ (757) 428-8083.. 3810 Atlantic Av, Apt 903, Virginia Beach,
VA *23451*

Madeira MR & MRS Edward W JR (Grace T Luquer) | ☎ (610) MU8-3490
Ph.Rc.Sa.Nf.Cry.Pa'49 ⚓ | 227 Atlee Rd,
MISS Martha L—at ☎ (610) 649-8742 | Wayne, PA
113 Walnut Av, Ardmore, PA *19003* . . . . | *19087-3835*
MISS Amanda T—Box 305, Manchester, MA |
01944 . . . . |

Madeira MISS Elizabeth—Ac.Cs.
☎ (610) 525-2661.. "Tuckaway" 337 Avon Rd, Bryn Mawr,
PA *19010-3655*

Madeira MR & MRS George W P (Mary H Rivinus) Temp'76
☎ (215) 233-0927.. 602 Wyndmoor Av, Wyndmoor, PA *19038*

Madeira MR Harry R—Me.Nf. ⚓
☎ (207) 276-3788.. "Mainstream" Box 506, Rock End Rd,
Northeast Harbor, ME *04662*

Madeira MR & MRS Harry R JR (Harriet W Goss)
WmSth'77.Ph.Me.Cts.Gm.Nf.Hob'76
☎ (610) 648-0989.. 1143 Edgewood Av, Berwyn, PA *19312*

Madeira MR & MRS Lewis N (Hay—Joan Dillon) Pr.Chr.Cly.Pa'43 .. of
☎ (561) 546-2575.. 18 Riverview Rd, Hobe Sound, FL *33455*
on board Tern II" Jupiter Island, Hobe Sound, FL *33455*

Madeira MRS Louis C (Helen Tyson) Ac.Cs.
☎ (610) 642-2678.. 1600 Monk Rd, Gladwyne, PA *19035-1318*

Madeira MISS Margaret C—Br'67
☎ (610) 296-7316.. 226 Joseph's Way, 1 Park Place, Frazer, PA *19355*

Madeira MRS Mary V (Mullet—Mary V Madeira) Pac'76
☎ (408) 626-6585.. 25500 Shafter Way, Carmel, CA *93923*

Madeira MRS Nathalie W (Nathalie P Wagnon) Hampshire'84
☎ (404) 685-9601.. 745 Argonne Av NE, Atlanta, GA *30308*

Madeira MR & MRS Percy C (Stevenson—Ann M Ellicott)
BMr'42.P'36.Penn'39
☎ (301) 320-4155.. 6620 River Rd, Bethesda, MD *20817*

Madeira MR & MRS Peter M (Carol J Cox) . . . . | ☎ (215) 248-3025
MR William P—Pa'67 . . . . | 8011B Germantown
MR David—Col'79.Col'81 . . . . | Av, Philadelphia,
| PA *19118*

Madill MISS Delphine A
☎ (314) 965-0258 . . 10342 Manchester Rd, St Louis, MO *63122*

Madsen MISS Christie M
☎ (916) 725-8088 . . 6418 Denton Way, Citrus Heights, CA *95610*

Madsen MR & MRS Stephen S (Rebecca W Howard)
P.'78.Camb'82.Va'83.Un.Myf.Rv.Cw.Ac.Dll.Cda. H'73.Cl'80
☎ (212) 348-8525 . . 1185 Park Av, New York, NY *10128*

Maebius MR & MRS Jed B JR (Nancy B Kingsland) | ☎ (210) 822-3651
Mich'63.Tex'90.Mich'63.GeoW'66.Tex'67 . . . . | 200 Belvidere Dv,
MISS Elizabeth F—at 1527—1 St, Coronado, CA | San Antonio, TX
92118 . . . . | *78212*
MR Stephen B—at 1114—21 St S, Arlington, VA |
22202 . . . . |
MR Brian G—at 1756 E 4620 S, Salt Lake City, |
UT *84117* . . . . |
MR Andrew K—at 200 McCauley St, Chapel Hill, |
NC *27516* . . . . |

Maechling MR & MRS Charles JR (Janet G Leighton)
SL'44.Ct.Cos.Y'41.Va'49
☎ (202) 244-8923 . . 3403 Lowell St NW, Washington, DC *20016*

Maffitt MRS Edward P (Mann—Nancy S Beale) Mt.Cvc.Sl.
☎ (202) 332-1239 . . 2700 Calvert St NW, Apt 711, Washington, DC *20008*

Magee MRS Harry H (Ruth O Julian) . . . . | ☎ (702) 463-5341
MISS Julie . . . . | "Edgewood"
| 19 Maple Dv,
| Yerington, NV
| *89447*

Magee MR Jerome . . . . Died at
Oakland, CA Dec 28'95

Magee MRS Jerome (Barbara J Hansen)
☎ (510) 547-4337 . . 8 Requa Place, Piedmont, CA *94611*

Magee MR & MRS John A 4th (Barbara Montross) | ☎ (410) 467-2572
Md.Cy.Cw.Y'52.Md'55 . . . . | 504 Overhill Rd,
MR James M . . . . | Baltimore, MD
| *21210*

Magee MRS John B M (Elizabeth C Bradshaw) | ☎ (408) 624-1435
Stan'29 . . . . | PO Box 1501,
MISS Sally M . . . . | Carmel, CA *93921*

Magee MRS Rice (Helen J Rice) . . . . | ☎ (310) 477-6747
MISS Martha R—SCal'77—at ☎ (310) 399-7488 | 1370 Kelton Av,
202 Third Av, Venice, CA *90291* . . . . | Apt 204,
MISS Daisy M—L&C'84—at ☎ (801) 359-8331 | Los Angeles, CA
366 N Center St, Apt 1, Salt Lake City, UT | *90024*
84103 . . . . |
MR David B JR—Y'79—at ☎ (213) 658-5996 |
238 Tower Dv, Apt 103, Beverly Hills, CA |
90211 . . . . |
MR John G 3d—SCal'79—at ☎ (213) 655-5031 |
6532½ Olympic Blvd, Los Angeles, CA *90048* . |

Magendantz DR & MRS Henry G (Ann S Rotch) | ☎ (401) 724-0179
BMr'59.H'58 . . . . | 1896 Old
MISS Elisa M—at U of Pa . . . . | Louisquisset Pike,
MR Eric A—Tampa'90—at ☎ (352) 860-0060 | Lincoln, RI *02865*
9295 E Moccasin Slough Rd, Inverness, FL |
34450 . . . . |
MR Christopher L—Bates'91—at |
☎ (617) 391-0899 . . 50 Water St, Apt 18, |
Medford, MA *02155* . . . . |
MR Nicholas A—Wheat'96 . . . . |

Magie MRS William A (Margaret J MacGregor) | ☎ (847) 492-7748
Rdc'28 . . . . | Westminster Place,
MR John Q 2d—H'61 . . . . | 603 Trinity Court,
| Evanston, IL *60201*

Maginnis MR Duncan . . of
☎ (860) 354-0124 . . "Tamlaght" PO Box 96, Sherman, CT *06784*
49 W 88 St, Apt 4, New York, NY *10024*

Maginnis MR Gordon Hobson
☎ (504) 522-0831 . . 831 Dauphine St, New Orleans, LA *70116-3018*

Maginnis MR & MRS Malcolm G (H Octavia Wilson)
☎ (504) 892-2211 . . 19296 Mulberry Grove, Covington, LA *70435*

Magnuson MR & MRS Mark G JR (Elise C Gray) . . . | ☎ (561) 231-4605
MR & MRS Charles L Siemon (Laura S | 2636 Ocean Dv,
Magnuson) . . . . | Apt 303,
| Vero Beach, FL
| *32963*

Magnussen MISS Carey L . . see J S Pfeiffer
Magnussen MISS Kendall L . . see J S Pfeiffer

Magoun MR & MRS William C B (Patricia C | ☎ (602) 443-9097
Lavezzorio) On.Fy.H'50 . . . . | Desert Highlands
MISS Margaret B—*see Dilatory Domiciles* . . . . | 2021, 10040 E
MISS Mary N . . . . | Happy Valley Rd,
| Scottsdale, AZ
| *85255*

Magowan MISS Estelle S—Cly.Bcs . . .of
☎ (212) 897-3900 . . 1 E 66 St, New York, NY *10021*
☎ (516) 283-1341 . . "Caerleon" 659 Hill St, Southampton, NY *11968*

Magowan MR & MRS Merrill L (Cynthia C Hooton) | of ☎ (415)347-1831
Cal'78.Sfg.Bur.Pcu.StJ.Y'60 . . . . | 735 Bromfield Rd,
MR Charles M—Y'85—at ☎ (415) 346-2648 | Hillsborough, CA
1200 Francisco St, San Francisco, CA *94123* . . . | *94010*
| ☎ (408) 626-8161
| "Gabion"
| 1572 Riata Rd,
| Pebble Beach, CA
| *93953*

Magowan MRS Robert A (Doris Merrill) Ri.Cly.BtP.Ng.Evg.So.StJ. . . . . | of ☎ (415)563-5581 2100 Washington St, San Francisco, CA *94109*
MR Stephen C—Y'68—at ☎ (212) 787-7921 1 W 72 St, New York, NY *10023* . . . . | ☎ (212) 737-2113 46 E 69 St, New York, NY *10021* Jan 15 . .
☎ (561) 844-5183 589 N County Rd, Palm Beach, FL *33480*

Magowan MR & MRS Thomas C (Rúna L Engel) Hawaii'85.Sfg.Bur.Ty'86
☎ (415) 347-1809 . . 774 Edgewood Rd, San Mateo, CA *94402*

Magro MR & MRS John L (Nancy L Post) Sb.Hn.H'32 . . . . | ''Belore'' 27 Sea St, Camden, ME *04843-1732*
MISS Nancy L . . . . |

Magruder MRS Joseph Hull (Marjorie E Saunders) Myf.Pn.
☎ (401) 849-3045 . . ''Benjamin Howland House'' 6 Bridge St, Newport, RI *02840*

Magruder MR Roy M—Tex'87 . . see MRS T Barrett JR

Maguire MRS Edward (Mary L Todd) Cly. . . . . . . | ☎ (516) 324-0007 87A Buell Lane, East Hampton, NY *11937*
MR Edward JR—Mds.H'54—at
☎ (212) BU8-9185 . . 139 E 66 St, New York, NY *10021* . . . . |

Maguire MRS Elizabeth J (McClure—Elizabeth J Maguire) Sl.
☎ (202) 333-8849 . . 1655—32 St NW, Washington, DC *20007*

Maguire MRS Henry C (Marjorie G Mitchell) . . . . . | ☎ (860) 421-4132 154 River Rd, Killingworth, CT *06419*
MISS Jean H—at Santa Fe, NM *87504*
MR Joseph G—at 713 E Cottonwood, Bozeman, MT *59715* . . . . |

Maguire MR & MRS J Robert (Pauline Thayer) Ln.Cly.Ncd.P'46.Y'53
☎ (802) 897-7221 . . Hands Cove, Shoreham, VT *05770*

Maguire MR & MRS John P (Mary-Emily Jones) Sth'42.Cy.Pr.P'41.Y'43 . . . . | ☎ (314) 997-6804 8 Chatfield Place Rd, St Louis, MO *63141*
MISS Joan G—P'81—at 425 Larkhill Court, St Louis, MO *63119* . . . . |

Maguire MISS Pauline T—P'78.Cl'95.Ac.Cly.
☎ (202) 686-7254 . . 3000 Tilden St NW, Apt 403I, Washington, DC *20008*

Maguire MR & MRS Walter L JR (Martha S Phipps) HRdc'82.Hn.H'75
☎ (203) 453-6335 . . 160 Uncas Point Rd, Guilford, CT *06437*

Magyar, Mark J & Parker, Elizabeth K—Ken'75.TEdison'84
☎ (908) 647-6784 . . 16 Overlook Rd, Millington, NJ *07946*

Mahaffey MR & MRS Daniel M (Barbara B Kamm) Stan'73
☎ (714) 536-2965 . . 1015 Park St, Huntington Beach, CA *92648*

Maher MR & MRS John Francis (Helen Lee Stillman) Bhm.Ln.Menlo'65.Pa'67 . . . . | of ☎ (818)775-3494 11456 Bellagio Rd, Los Angeles, CA *90049*
JUNIORS MISS Helen C . . . . |
JUNIORS MR Michael S . . . . | ☎ (970) 845-7007 Strawberry Park 604, PO Box 724, Avon, CO *81620*

Maher MRS Richard J (Avery Poor) BMr'86.H'89 . . | ☎ (617) 235-3133 45 Seaward Rd, Wellesley Hills, MA *02181*
MISS Kathleen E—at U of Cal Los Angeles . . . .
MR Richard J—Laf'96 . . . . |
MR J Sheppard—at U of Va . . . . |

Mahon MISS Marinna (Fairbank—Marinna Mahon) Rose'63 . . . . | ☎ (216) 420-7086 12493 Cedar Rd, Apt 16, Cleveland Heights, OH *44106*
MISS Elsa Fairbank . . . . |
MISS Wendy Fairbank (Hatch—Wendy Fairbank) . . . . |

Mahoney MISS Barbara A—Skd'84.SL'88
☎ (516) 726-4608 . . PO Box 1197, 89 Little Noyack Path, Water Mill, NY *11976*

Mahoney MR & MRS David J (Merrill—Hildegarde M W Ercklentz) Rc.Evg.Ng.Cly.Pa'45 . . of
☎ (212) 223-4567 . . 800 Fifth Av, New York, NY *10021*
☎ (561) 832-6485 . . ''Hilago'' 1296 S Ocean Blvd, Palm Beach, FL *33480*

Mahoney MR & MRS Jerome J (Rebecca P Gay) Smu'77.Colg'74 . . . . | ☎ (215) 297-0432 5968 Sheffield Dv, Doylestown, PA *18901*
JUNIORS MISS Margaret P . . . . |

Mahoney MR William J 3d—So'65
☎ (334) 272-3000 . . 4317 Remington Court, Montgomery, AL *36116*

Mahony MRS Cummings (Philomena B Cummings)
☎ (410) LA3-2708 . . 1333 Bolton St, Baltimore, MD *21217*

Maier MR James S—Me.Hav'29
☎ (610) 642-1252 . . 3300 Darby Rd, Elm 3103, Haverford, PA *19041*

Maier MR Robert C (Ward R) . . . . Married at Villanova, PA
Casey MISS Jennifer L (Joseph C) . . . . Aug 10'96

Maier DR & MRS Ward R (Christine Walker) Pa'64.Ste.Pa'64.Va'69 . . . . | ☎ (617) 484-6058 346 Marsh St, Belmont, MA *02178*
MISS Sarah E—SCal'93—at Columbia Phys & Surg . . . . |

Mail MRS G Allen (Beal—Constance La M Davison) Sth'30 . . . . | ☎ (360) 438-5306 Panorama City, 3994 Holladay Park Lane, Lacey, WA *98503*
MISS Patricia D—Y'67—at ☎ (301) 340-1416 142 Monroe St, Rockville, MD *20850* . . . . |

Mailliard MR & MRS Howard (Tonya C Wildman) . . | ☎ (415) 457-0334 135 Van Winkle Dv, San Anselmo, CA *94960*
MISS Jean H . . . . |

Maisey MISS Hilary L . . see MRS C Hooper

Maitland MR & MRS Peter J (Nancy W Strange) Camb'56. . . . . | ☎ (011-44-171) 937-6948 50 Stanford Rd, London W8 5PZ, England
MISS Melissa S . . . . |
MISS Alison C . . . . |
MISS Annabel R . . . . |

Major MR & MRS Howard B JR (Eleanor Gontier) Unn.BtP.Wms'48.H'50 . . . . | of ☎ (561)659-6938 455 Australian Av, Palm Beach, FL *33480*
REV Howard B 3d—StOlaf'72.UnTheo'75—at 97 Huguenot St, New Paltz, NY *12561* . . . . . . | ☎ (216) 247-4553 15005 County Line Rd, Chagrin Falls, OH *44022*

Makepeace MRS Lloyd B (Jean Thompson) . . . . | ☎ (203) 869-5089
MISS Marilyn A—at 955 Garcia Rd, | 32 Grahampton
Santa Barbara, CA *93103* . . . . | Lane, Greenwich,
                   | CT *06830*

Makiver MR & MRS John S P JR (Yancey—Linda Hale) Pa'52
  ☎ (207) 967-3299 . . 14 Governors Way, Kennebunk Beach, ME *04043*

Makrianes MR & MRS James K (Judith A Erdmann) Rc.Mds.Ln.Aht'49
  ☎ (212) 371-4042 . . 415 E 52 St, New York, NY *10022*

Malabre MR & MRS Alfred L JR (Mary P | ☎ (516) 653-4431
Wardropper) Durham'53.Ng.Un.Plg.Cs.Y'52 . . . | PO Box 208,
MISS E Ann—Ty'85.Sim'90—at | Quogue, NY *11959*
  ☎ (207) 824-3050 . . PO Box 1097, Bethel, ME |
04217 . . . . |
MR John A—at ☎ (212) 772-2328 |
1587 Second Av, New York, NY *10028* . . . . . . |

Malabre MR Richard C—Unn.Ty'82.Mit'91
  see Dilatory Domiciles

Malarkey MRS Thomas B JR (Catharine B Hord) | ☎ (415) 386-1363
V'57.Fr.Sfg. . . . . | 84 Commonwealth
MISS C Tucker—Geo'85—at New York, NY . . . | Av, San Francisco,
MISS Sarah E—Cl'90—at New York, NY . . . . . | CA *94118*
MR Thomas W—Wms'84—at ☎ (415) 441-5652 |
1661 Grove St, San Francisco, CA *94117* . . . . . |

Malcom MR & MRS John W (Judith C Walsh) | ☎ (212) 724-2827
Sth'55.Rc.Plg.Cc.Wms'52 . . . . | 255 W 88 St,
MISS Lily C W—Tul'92—at ☎ (212) 229-2294 | New York, NY
208 W 23 St, New York, NY *10011* . . . . | *10024*
MR Benjamin W—at ☎ (212) 769-4066 |
41 W 86 St, New York, NY *10024* . . . . |

Malcom MR & MRS William S (Elinor Bliss) Ncd.H'45
  ☎ (508) 369-3683 . . 395 School St, Carlisle, MA *01741*

Mali MR & MRS Frederick J (Lucretia Simmons) Un.Y'53 . . of
  ☎ (212) 861-2659 . . 39 E 79 St, New York, NY *10021*
  ☎ (860) 379-8927 . . ''Wendigo'' Grantville Rd, Winchester, CT *06098*

Mali MR & MRS Pierre (Millicent W Satterlee) Bnd'53.Cl'66.Y'50.Mid'65
  ☎ (401) 884-6461 . . 210 Spring St, Box 377, East Greenwich, RI *02818*

Mallace MR & MRS Alexander D (Simon— | ☎ (818) 440-1429
Maria-Luz Miro) StMarys'84.Vh.Roch'52 . . . . . | 1485 Lomita Dv,
MISS Mercedes A Simon—at Vanderbilt . . . . | Pasadena, CA *91106*
MR Gregory S Simon—Cal'96 . . . . |

Mallery MR & MRS Bayard M (Virginia | ☎ (215) 242-8827
Reichenbach) Ac.Csn.Y'42.Pa'48 . . . . | 8702 Seminole Av,
MR John C . . . . | Philadelphia, PA
                  | *19118-3708*

Mallery MISS (DR) Berrell E—YeshivaU'80 . . see P B Street

Mallery MR & MRS David (Judith Chappell) | ☎ (215) CH7-3113
Temp'56.Pc.Hav'45.Mid'52 . . . . | 9006 Crefeld St,
MR Roger—Eck'81 . . . . | Philadelphia, PA
                  | *19118*

Mallinckrodt MRS Charles O (Martha L Graves)
  ☎ (714) 581-3633 . . 3193A Via Buena Vista, Laguna Hills, CA *92653*

Mallinckrodt MISS Jane A—Bnd'83.S.
  900 Third Av, New York, NY *10022*

Mallinckrodt MISS Rosalie R . . see E V Dickson

Mallon MRS Henry Neil (Thayer—Anne Wrightson)
  ☎ (214) 521-6660 . . 3800 Turtle Creek Blvd, Dallas, TX *75219*

Mallory MR Blaine W—Dth'38 . . . . | ☎ (508) 693-2198
MISS Sarah B—at ☎ (213) 655-1834 | PO Box 1644,
647 N La Jolla Av, Los Angeles, CA *90048* . . . | Oak Bluffs, MA
                  | *02557*

Mallory MR & MRS C King 3d (Smith—Florence B | of ☎ (301)654-7902
Marshall) Stan'63.Mt.Cvc.Y'58 . . . . | 17 Magnolia
MR C King 4th—at ☎ (011-44-171) 730-8124 | P'kway,
26 Lower Sloan St, Apt D, London SW1 W8BJ, | Chevy Chase, MD
England . . . . | *20815*
JUNIORS MR Richard C M—at St Mark's . . . . . . | ☎ (717) 794-5301
                  | Monterey Circle,
                  | Blue Ridge Summit,
                  | PA *17214*

Mallory MR Charles—Ihy.Ny.Unn.Clare'73 ⚓
  ☎ (203) 532-1107 . . 137 Weaver St, Greenwich, CT *06830*

Mallory MR & MRS Clifford D (Pauline Cropper) Unn.Ny.StJ.Cly.
  ☎ (860) 535-2258 . . 76 Water St, Stonington, CT *06378*

Mallory MRS Diane Driggs (Adair—Diane M Driggs) Va'75
  ☎ (203) 629-5282 . . 999 Lake Av, Greenwich, CT *06831*

Mallory MRS Margaret P (Leary—Margaret W Pierson)
  1602 Wethersfield Rd, Austin, TX *78703*

Mallory MISS Margaret P
  ☎ (805) 969-1195 . . 305 Ortega Ridge Rd, Santa Barbara, CA *93108*

Mallory MR Raburn M (C King 3d) . . . . Married at New Orleans, LA
  Dunbar MISS Lisa A (Franklin H) . . . . Apr 13'96

Mallory MR & MRS Raburn M (Lisa A Dunbar)
  32 Cook Rd, Prospect, CT *06712*

Mallory MR & MRS Robert 4th (Deanne D Harts) | ☎ (201) 444-3282
Bow'63 . . . . | 828 Bernard Place,
MISS Robin L—Pep'92—at ☎ (310) 471-2742 | Ho Ho Kus, NJ
11611 Chenault St, Apt 313, Brentwood, CA | *07423*
90049 . . . . |

Mallory MR & MRS Thomas D JR (Eleanor Berry Bingham)
Tufts'82.StLaw'82
  ☎ (404) 816-8824 . . 2940 Mabry Rd NE, Atlanta, GA *30319*

Malloy DR & MRS Bernard M (Davidge—Patricia Appel)
AmU'73.CathU'76.Mt.Cvc.Lambuth'50.Van'54
  ☎ (202) 363-3991 . . 3716—49 St NW, Washington, DC *20016*

Malloy MISS Elizabeth G—H'89.Cvc.
  ☎ (415) 986-4252 . . 490 Lombard St, Apt 5, San Francisco, CA *94133*

Malone MRS Frances M (Frances L Martin) | 1820 N Scott St,
NCar'63.Gv. . . . . | Wilmington, DE
MISS Alexandra M—Tul'95 . . . . | *19806*

Malone MRS Frederick R (Jean Hamilton) Me . . .of
Fieldway Lane, Prouts Neck, ME *04074*
  ☎ (610) 645-8912 . . 1400 Waverly Rd, Blair 319, Gladwyne, PA *19035*

Malone MR & MRS (DR) Frederick R 3d (Biddle—Carol M Collins)
Pa'75.H'mannMed'87.Ste.Cry.Rcp.Pa'65
  ☎ (011-44-171) 581-2114 . . 26 Thurloe Square, London SW7 2SD,
England

Malone DR Laurence A—Cc.JCar'35.Geo'44.
Ch'67.ColSt'72
MR Michael H L—Ursul'94 . . . .
| of ☎ (216)247-3670
''Rosehenge''
332 Hamlet Hills
Dv, Chagrin Falls,
OH *44022*
☎ (301) 387-6571
''Meadowood''
Deep Creek Lake,
Swanton, MD *21561*

Malone MR & MRS Stuart H (Mary A Dorrance)
Ariz'72.Me.Roan'68 . . . .
JUNIORS MISS Mary A D . . . .
| ☎ (610) 383-4717
''Iron Spring Farm''
RD 3, Stottsville Rd,
Coatesville, PA
19320

Maloney MR & MRS Paul (Virginia Wells) R.Sg.Me.Pe.Ph.Ac.P'30.Pa'33
☎ (610) 525-0783 . . 720 Morris Av, Bryn Mawr, PA *19010-2925*

Maloumian MR & MRS Royden M (Carey M Thomas) LaS'65.Temp'71
☎ (215) 247-9618 . . ''Mill Pond'' 15 W Bells Mill Rd, Philadelphia,
PA *19118*

Maloy MR Laurence . . . .
MR Andrew B—USMC. . . . .
| ☎ (212) 832-3919
337 E 50 St,
New York, NY
10022

Man MRS Christine (M Christine White) Mid'50 . . .
MISS Stephanie C—at ☎ (716) 289-4669
40 E Main St, Shortsville, NY *14548* . . . .
MR William P—at ☎ (203) 882-8043
23 Melba St, Milford, CT *06460* . . . .
| ☎ (904) 471-8402
509 F St,
St Augustine, FL
32084

Manace DR & MRS E David (Kathryn A Cole)
Tor'66.Tor'64 . . . .
MISS Leslie C . . . .
| of ☎ (415)386-2559
3957 Sacramento St,
San Francisco, CA
94118
☎ (707) 963-7229
Forest Hill
Vineyard, PO Box
96, St Helena, CA
94574

Manchester DOWAGER DUCHESS OF (Coleman—Crocker—
Elizabeth Fullerton) Cly . . .of
☎ (408) 624-4025 . . PO Box 303, Pebble Beach, CA *93953*
☎ (011-39-41) 5207-746 . . ''Ca Vendramin'' 13 Giudecca,
30123 Venice, Italy

Manchester MRS M Whitham (Margaret H R Whitham) Sth'47.Emory'77
☎ (404) 351-4337 . . 2570 Ridgewood Terr NW, Atlanta, GA *30318*

Mander MISS Melanie R (Sevastopoulo—Melanie R Mander) . . of
☎ (212) 534-7272 . . 120 E 86 St, Apt 3C, New York, NY *10028*
☎ (213) 852-0774 . . 620 N Sweetzer Av, Apt 8, Los Angeles, CA *90048*

Manée MR Monte Stewart—Sa.Rv.Cl'55 . . . .
MISS Amanda B—CtCol'94 . . . .
| ☎ (914) SC3-2661
6 Fenimore Rd,
Scarsdale, NY
10583

Mangan MRS Thomas J (Elsie E Haas) Me.Ri.Km.
☎ (904) 261-6024 . . 3301 Fairway Oaks, Amelia Island, FL *32034*

Manganaro MRS E Morris (Ellen N W Morris) Ac.Ds.W.
☎ (610) 399-0131 . . ''Wexford'' PO Box 55, Westtown, PA *19395*

Manganaro MR Nicholas W—Rcp.Ds.W.Reed'79.Mit'84
☎ (212) 346-9546 . . 105 Duane St, Apt 46G, New York, NY *10007*

Manger DR & MRS William M (Lynn S Sheppard)
Bcs.Ne.Rv.Cw.Ds.Lm.Myf.Cly.Ncd.Dh.Dc.
Y'44.Cl'46.Minn'58 . . . .
MR William M JR . . . .
MR S Sheppard . . . .
MR Charles S . . . .
| of 8 E 81 St,
New York, NY
10028
☎ (516) 283-3365
''Top O'Dunes''
Fairlea Rd,
Southampton, NY
11968

Manheim JUNIORS MR Francis B C M . . see MISS A P Reath
Manheim MR Grant C—Pa'67 . . of
☎ (011-44-171) 280-5000 . . New Court, St Swithin's Lane,
London EC4P 4D4, England
☎ (212) 744-1600 . . 35 E 76 St, New York, NY *10021*
Manheim MR Joseph P R . . see MISS A P Reath
Manice MR Alexis C—Ph.Rc.
☎ (610) 525-2386 . . 315 Gatcombe Lane, Bryn Mawr, PA *19010*

Manice MRS Hayward F (Beatrice Goelet) . . . .
MISS Pamela . . . .
| ☎ (212) 737-2569
4 E 72 St,
New York, NY
10021-4144

Manice MR & MRS John H (Anne P de La
Rochefoucauld) Rc.K. . . . .
MR Peter . . . .
JUNIORS MR Christopher . . . .
JUNIORS MR Charles . . . .
| ☎ (212) 753-3463
201 E 62 St,
New York, NY
10021

Manice MR & MRS Oliver A (Mathilde A Zara) DU'74
☎ (802) 672-5215 . . PO Box 27, Bridgewater, VT *05043*

Manice MR & MRS Robert G (Heidi G Knollenberg)
RISD'80.Bost'76 . . . .
JUNIORS MISS Emily P . . . .
| ☎ (508) 785-8068
229 Dedham St,
Dover, MA *02030*

Manice MRS William DeF (Olivia Ames)
Srb.Cy.Chi.Ncd. . . . .
MR William DeF 3d . . . .
| ☎ (617) 893-3047
92 Orchard Av,
Weston, MA *02193*

Manierre MRS Alfred Lee (Cornelia C Colt) Cda.
☎ (315) 655-3150 . . 61 Lincklaen St, Cazenovia, NY *13035*
Manierre MR George A (late Francis E) . . . . Married at Ocala, FL
Puckett MRS Elizabeth E (Dangerfield—Elizabeth E Keithline) . . . .
Apr 6'96
Manierre MR & MRS George A (Dangerfield—Puckett—
Elizabeth E Keithline)
☎ (352) 236-4171 . . 920 NE Fiftieth Av, Ocala, FL *34470*
Manierre MRS Nancy R (Manierre—McVitty—Nancy E Redmond)
☎ (540) 687-5420 . . ''Waycroft'' 3655 Landmark Rd, The Plains,
VA *20198*
Manigault MRS Landine (Wood—Landine S Legendre)
☎ (860) 535-3511 . . PO Box 57, Stonington, CT *06378*
Manigault MR & MRS Pierre (Elizabeth L Van Alen) Bnd'92
☎ (803) 722-8787 . . 33 King St, Charleston, SC *29401-2734*

Maniha MR & MRS John K (Barbara Brinser)
Tul'62.Mich'70 . . . .
MR John C—Rad'91.GeoM'94 . . . .
MR Gregory B—at Berklee Coll of Music . . . . .
| ☎ (703) 860-9693
11459 Purple Beech
Dv, Reston, VA
20191

Manley MISS Alexandra C . . see J J G Cameron
Manley MISS Jennifer A . . see J J G Cameron

Manlove DR & MRS Francis R (Kluber—Margaret Perkins) BMr'42.Dick'34.Temp'38 . . . . ☎ (610) 525-0790
MR Charles F—Col'85—at 2827—10 St, Boulder, CO *80304* . . . . 77 Middle Rd, Apt 363, Bryn Mawr, PA *19010*

Manly-Power MR & MRS John K (Kelly A Sinon) Pc.
☎ (610) 828-1922 . . 3182 Mayflower Rd, Plymouth Meeting, PA *19462*

Mann MR Benjamin H R—Bf.OState'80
☎ (216) 473-3348 . . 5723 York Dv, Lyndhurst, OH *44124*

Mann MR & MRS Donald S (Cornelia E Wight) Sth'52.Aht'52
see Dilatory Domiciles

Mann MR & MRS Donegan (Jenkins—Frances M Mann) Cvc.GeoW'47.GeoW'50
☎ (301) 424-6466 . . 9312 Overlea Dv, Rockville, MD *20850-3733*

Mann MISS Frances R—Pc.
Roland Park Place, 830 W 40 St, Baltimore, MD *21211-2115*

Mann MR & MRS Henry B (Nancy L Mersfelder) Skd'67.Conn'70.Yn. . . . . ☎ (203) 245-7627
MR David W . . . . PO Box 940,
JUNIORS MR Michael L . . . . Madison, CT *06443*

Mann DR Henry B—Yn.Tufts'60.Y'66
☎ (860) 873-3510 . . "The Old Bank House" 90 Main St, PO Box 482, East Haddam, CT *06423-0482*

Mann MRS J Herbert (de Mello—Joyce Herbert) Cl'81.BtP.Cly.Cda.StJ. . . . . ☎ (212) 838-2948
MISS Joanne—Bnd'90—☎ (212) 888-6617 . . . . 31 E 63 St, New York, NY *10021*

Mann MRS James E (Nancy A Riddle) Bf.
☎ (512) 454-3397 . . 29 Woodstone Square, Austin, TX *78703-1159*

Mann MR & MRS Thomas D JR (Susan T Porter) Qns'69.Ober'69.Pa'71.Suff'81 . . . . ☎ (617) 698-7757
MISS Lauren P—at U of Pa . . . . 28 Dudley Lane,
JUNIORS MISS Leslie C—at Milton . . . . Milton, MA *02186-3505*

Mann MR Walter—BtP.K.Y'43.H'48
☎ (561) 655-3234 . . 525 S Flagler Dv, West Palm Beach, FL *33401*

Mann MRS William F (Dora S Foss) D. . . . . ☎ (617) 326-0347
MR William T—P'63—at 754 N George Mason Dv, Arlington, VA *22203* . . . . 10 Longwood Dv, Apt 556, Westwood, MA *02090*

Mann MR & MRS William H (Wilkins—Sewall—Patricia Leighton) Ncd.Ch'40 . . of
☎ (603) 563-8371 . . "Spur House II" PO Box 273, Dublin, NH *03444*
☎ (561) 744-7351 . . 353 US H'way 1, Jupiter, FL *33477*

Mannal MRS Janice H (Peake—Janice H Mannal)
☎ (215) 233-4299 . . 7809 Pine Rd, Wyndmoor, PA *19038*

Manning MRS Alice V—Ws'69
☎ (212) 472-0492 . . 305 E 72 St, New York, NY *10021*

Manning MRS Florence T H (Carroll—Mundhenk—Florence T H Manning) . . . . ☎ (415) 854-4225
MR James R T H Carroll—Denis'84.SFr'95 . 1240 Sharon Park Dv, Box 7585, Menlo Park, CA *94025*

Manning MISS Julia W—Duke'78.Nw'82
☎ (215) 546-5912 . . 2112 Pine St, Philadelphia, PA *19103*

Manning MR & MRS William D JR (Carol R Gillis) Kt.Cv.Tv.FlaSt'56
☎ (216) 423-0861 . . 650 Racebrook Rd, Gates Mills, OH *44040*

Manning MR & MRS William P JR (Peachey W Lillard) Me.Wms'48.Y'51 . . of
☎ (610) 526-2688 . . 1102 St Andrews Rd, Bryn Mawr, PA *19010*
☎ (941) 261-5180 . . 3450 Gulf Shore Blvd N, Apt 201, Naples, FL *34103*

Mannion MRS Hartley S (E Hartley Shedd)
☎ (203) 255-2165 . . 360 Veres St, Fairfield, CT *06430*

Mannion MRS William F (H Langdon Manley) Ty'59
☎ (561) 234-1515 . . 761 Manatee Cove, Vero Beach, FL *32963*

Mannion MR William F JR—Gm.Me.Mid'83
☎ (610) 688-7262 . . 724 Newtown Rd, Villanova, PA *19085*

Manny MR & MRS James C (Abigail Adams) Rdc'58.Ny.Ht.Y'54.H'58 . . . . ☎ (207) 725-9062
MISS Abigail L—at Harvard . . . . 2161 Pinkham Point
MISS Ailsa B—at Trinity . . . . Rd, Brunswick, ME
MR Timothy S—H'93 . . . . *04011*

Manoogian MR & MRS Richard A (Jane A Cameron) Y'59 . . of
☎ (313) 886-1500 . . 204 Provencal Rd, Grosse Pointe Farms, MI *48236*
☎ (561) 234-5005 . . 602 Ocean Rd, John's Island, Vero Beach, FL *32963*

Manou MRS Dorothy R B (Manou—Glebe—Dorothy R Brinley) . . . . ☎ (215) 247-1850
MISS Alexandra W F—at Solebury . . . . 212 W Highland Av, Philadelphia, PA *19118*

Manou MR Laurence
☎ (215) 684-2999 . . 2008 Fairmount Av, Philadelphia, PA *19130*

Mansbridge MR & MRS F Ronald (van Duyn—Janet Dunning) V'32.C.Camb'28 . . of
☎ (011-44-1580) 753281 . . "Gun Green Farm" Hawkhurst, Kent TN18 5DE, England
☎ (203) 227-2324 . . "Corner House" 306 Lyons Plain Rd, Weston, CT *06883*

Mansell MR & MRS Frank L (Miller—Edmona Lyman) Ln.Mds.Bur.Srr.
☎ (561) 546-1458 . . 161 Gomez Rd, Hobe Sound, FL *33455*

Mansfield MR John H—Hn.H'52
☎ (617) 491-8182 . . 225 Walden St, Cambridge, MA *02140*

Manss MRS Robert W (Welch—Kruse—Barbara Kruttschnitt)
☎ (513) 321-2555 . . 2444 Madison Rd, Apt 810, Cincinnati, OH *45208*

Mansson MISS Wendy W . . see MRS C L Myrin

Manternach MISS Josie C (Gemmill—Josie C Manternach) . . . . ☎ (603) 226-3432
MISS Helen J Gemmill . . . . 9 Auburn St, Concord, NH *03301*

Mantius MR & MRS Ernest R (Helen E Menzel) Cly.
☎ (212) 288-2467 . . 122 E 76 St, New York, NY *10021*

Mantz MRS Nancy B (Nancy A Bodman) Syr'72 . . . *see*
MISS Jessica A . . . . *Dilatory Domiciles*
MR John R . . . .

Manuel MRS David B (Anne C Meyer) Kt.Un.Cv.
☎ (216) 423-3579 . . 1760 County Line Rd, Box 38, Gates Mills, OH *44040*

Manuel MR & MRS John S (Eileen Eyre) Cv. . . . . ☎ (216) 423-3265
MISS Susan E—Cal'72.Cal'78 . . . . 1970 Woodstock Rd, Gates Mills, OH *44040*

Manuel MR & MRS Richard A (Constance Curtiss) Sim'40.Cwr'45.Kt.Cv.Tv.Y'38
☎ (216) 442-0360 . . 34750 Cedar Rd, Gates Mills, OH *44040*

Manuel MR & MRS William S 3d (J Christian Inkley) ☎ (713) 681-0462
V'67.Y'64.RI'70 . . . . | 9321 Oakford Court,
MR William S 4th . . . . | Houston, TX *77024*
Manzanares MR & MRS Daniel (Emily T Nomer) V'76.Lond'78
☎ (212) 995-9167 . . 200 E 16 St, Apt 10D, New York, NY *10003*
Mapes MR & MRS H Jeffrey (Margaret E Sloan) ☎ (714) 858-5797
Cal'42.Aht'39 . . . . | 60 Via Andorra,
MR Jeffrey S—Stan'75—at ☎ (415) 364-3906 | Coto de Caza, CA
555 Sequoia Av, Redwood City, CA *94062* . . . . | *92679*
Mapes MR & MRS Pierson G (Patricia A Carlson) Mich'64.Norw'59 . . of
☎ (914) 753-5405 . . Cranberry Lake, Pierson Lakes, Sterlington,
NY *10974*
☎ (809) 523-3189 . . Costa Verde 1, Casa de Campo,
Dominican Republic
Marani MR & MRS Paul P (Carole du P Wickes) F&M'87.Ford'85
☎ (615) 377-6248 . . 9008 Demery Court, Brentwood, TN *37027*
Marano MR & MRS Peter D (Elena Bowes) Cal'84.Rcn.Cal'81
☎ (011-44-171) 235-1508 . . 1 Belgrave Place, London SW1, England
Marble MR & MRS William Baird 3d (Moffett—Hillary Hilken)
Cal'80.Vh.Fr.Menlo'82
☎ (818) 799-4585 . . 1790 Ramiro Rd, San Marino, CA *91108*
Marburg MRS Charles L (Morgan—Nancy Iselin) . . ☎ (410) 377-3363
MISS Barbara I . . . . | 101 Charlesbrooke
| Rd, Baltimore, MD
| *21212*
Marburg MR & MRS Charles L (Louise D White) . . of
☎ (212) 431-3007 . . 548 Broadway, Apt 4D, New York, NY *10012*
☎ (860) 526-4524 . . PO Box 151, Hadlyme, CT *06439*
Marburg MRS F Grainger (Mary R Hocking) Mv.Ncd.
☎ (410) 823-7227 . . 7 Sunset Knoll Court, PO Box 310, Riderwood,
MD *21139*
March MRS Albert P (Margaret Ash) Pc.Dar . . . . . . ☎ (802) 457-2764
MR & MRS Robert M (Patricia Derr) | 15 Rose Hill,
BMr'54.Hav'54.H'56 . . . . | Woodstock, VT
MR A Paul—Cr'83 . . . . | *05091*
Marckwald MR & MRS A Hunt (Catherine Palumbo) ☎ (516) 653-4795
SHall'74.Rol'74 . . . . | 11 Club Lane,
MISS Morgan N . . . . | PO Box 879,
JUNIORS MR A Hunt JR . . . . | Quogue, NY *11959*
JUNIORS MR Nicholas K . . . . |
Marckwald MRS Andrew K (Clarissa T Price) Shcc.
☎ (908) 234-2684 . . "Cloud Croft" Mosle Rd, PO Box 838, Far Hills,
NJ *07931*
Marcus MR & MRS Richard C (Heather Johnson) ☎ (214) 528-1555
Kas'61.H'60 . . . . | 16A Turtle Creek
MR Charles A . . . . | Bend, Dallas, TX
| *75204*
Marcy MRS George H (Elizabeth A Comins) ☎ (716) 884-3114
Buf.St.G. . . . . | 45 Lexington Av,
MR Barton C—at 91 W Roma Dv, Tucson, AZ | Buffalo, NY *14222*
85737-7920 . . . . |
Marcy MRS William L JR (Katharine T Richard) ☎ (716) 876-1131
Skd'62.G.St. . . . . | 90 Dana Rd,
MISS Carrie E . . . . | Buffalo, NY *14216*
MR William L 4th—at 51-636 Kam H'way,
Kaawa, Honolulu, HI *96730* . . . . |

Marden MRS William G (Buchet—Nina S Taylor) ☎ (516) 265-1105
Lm. . . . . | "Meadowlands"
MR Robert F Buchet—Lm.Snc.—at | RFD 2,
☎ (212) 864-3583 . . 216 W 100 St, Apt 609, | 192 River Rd,
New York, NY *10025* . . . . | St James, NY *11780*
Mare MR & MRS Charles A (Carryl B Brewster)
☎ (201) 569-5244 . . 55 Elm St, Tenafly, NJ *07670*
Maresi MR & MRS Henry J (Priscilla H Mapes) ⚓ . ☎ (561) 231-2410
MISS Belinda H—Lynch'91—at 103 Turtle Creek | 185 Springline Dv,
Rd, Apt 2, Charlottesville, VA *22901* . . . . | Vero Beach, FL
| *32963*
Maricle MR & MRS Earle F (Weld—Carolyn L Niedringhaus) Rc.Cy.Nyc.
☎ (314) 993-2202 . . 20 Conway Lane, St Louis, MO *63124*
Maricle MR John F—CalTech'77
☎ (314) 991-1797 . . 24 Burroughs Lane, St Louis, MO *63124*
Marié MR Camille S—JHop'43 ☎ (410) 486-6049
MISS Olivia D | 3121 Old Court Rd,
MR Richard M . . . . | Pikesville, MD
| *21208*
Marin JUNIORS MISS Carmen R . . see J D Saunders
Marine MR & MRS Jeffrey A (Lee C Gowen)
Va'86.Cal'90.Mds.Va'86.Pa'90
☎ (212) 427-5772 . . 145 E 92 St, Apt 4D, New York, NY *10128*
Mariner MR & MRS Michael H (Marion H Mauran) | of ☎ (401)751-5435
Colby'77.Aga.Ncd.Y'68 . . . . | 87 Williams St,
JUNIORS MISS Madeleine A . . . . | Providence, RI
JUNIORS MR Edward H . . . . | *02906*
| ☎ (207) 363-1317
| 6 Lilac Lane,
| York Harbor, ME
| *03911*
Marion MR & MRS John L (Meeker—Phillips—Sowell—
Anne B Windfohr) Ford'56
☎ (817) 332-6666 . . 1400 Shady Oaks Lane, Ft Worth, TX *76107*
Mark MR Christopher W—RogerW'88
☎ (508) 252-6425 . . 41 French St, Rehoboth, MA *02769*
Mark MR Gordon Griffith—Nyc.StOlaf'83.Duke'85
☎ (312) 787-1701 . . 1360 N Lake Shore Dv, Apt 1612, Chicago,
IL *60610*
Mark MR & MRS Gordon St G (Barbara L Wedelstaedt) Nyc.Cho.Ih.H'52
☎ (847) 446-6262 . . 661 Blackthorn Rd, Winnetka, IL *60093*
Mark MR Michael C—Ken'87.DePaul'89
☎ (312) 944-6369 . . 1360 N Lake Shore Dv, Apt 1511, Chicago,
IL *60610*
Mark MR Peter C—Woos'90
☎ (312) 944-4422 . . 1120 N Lake Shore Dv, Apt 9A, Chicago, IL *60611*
Mark DR & MRS W Steven (Charlotte L Wolf) | ☎ (610) 296-2506
Bvr'65.Wcc.Rv.Dar.Colg'65.H'mannMed'69 . . . | 26 Salem Way,
MR W Steven JR—Rv.Hob'94 | RD 5, Malvern, PA
MR James D—Rv.—at U of Richmond . . . . | *19355*
Markham MRS John Jay (Alice R Utley) | ☎ (847) 251-3243
Nw'47.Wa.Cda.Ncd. . . . . | 1435 Sheridan Rd,
MISS Caroline B—TCU'79 . . . . | Wilmette, IL *60091*
Markle MR & MRS Alvan 3d (Frances M Johnston)
Me.R.Fw.Cw.Ht.Rv.Ac.Ncd.Dar.Y'41
☎ (610) 642-8195 . . "Hollybrook" 305 Mill Creek Rd, Ardmore,
PA *19003-1507*

Markle MR & MRS Alvan 4th (Anne D Wadsworth)
Bost'70.CalArts'77.R.Me.Fw.Cw.Laf'65.Geo'68.
Temp'80. . . . . ☎ (610) 964-1910
MR Andrew B—Susq'91 . . . . 110 Sugartown Rd,
Devon, PA
19333-1610

Markle MR & MRS John JR (Kathryn E Wheeler) M.Y.'53.H'58
☎ (610) 363-2342 . . 205 Cambridge Chase, Exton, PA *19341*

Markle MR & MRS Mary McL (Mary B McLean) Wcc.
☎ (610) 430-7630 . . 970 Kennett Way, West Chester, PA *19380*

Marks MR & MRS C Caldwell (Jeanne A Vigeant) Benn'40.So'42 . . of
☎ (205) 871-3913 . . 2828 Cherokee Rd, Birmingham, AL *35223*
☎ (561) 231-3674 . . 450 Beach Rd, John's Island, Vero Beach,
FL *32963*

Marks MR & MRS Charles P (Tanya Sanderson) JackSt'80.Tul'75
☎ (205) 870-5541 . . 3140 Pine Ridge Rd, Birmingham, AL *35213*

Marks MISS Heather Ann (Randolph A) . . . . Married
Palmer MR Marc . . . . Oct 23'94

Marks MR & MRS John P JR (Joan F Horrell) . . . . . . 5526 Castle Way,
MISS Natalie R . . . . San Antonio, TX
MISS Emily K *78218*
MR John P 3d . . . .

Marks MRS Laurence M (de Bosdari—Martin—Herzer—
Marjorie Greenan) Pr.Chr.Cly.
☎ (516) 922-6269 . . 12 Frost Mill Rd, Mill Neck, NY *11765*

Marks MR & MRS Randolph A (Abell—Sally
McConnell) Evg.Bf.St.Cy.Leh'57 . . . . of ☎ (716)652-8240
MR Joshua R . . . . "Welcome"
  MISS Alice O'M Abell—at 176 Ludlow St, Porterville Rd,
  New York, NY *10002* . . . . East Aurora, NY
  MR Charles L Abell 3d—at 6682 W Gulick *14052*
  Rd, Naples, NY *14512* . . . . ☎ (561) 655-4808
  MR Edward S G Abell—at 20 Clinton St, 221 El Bravo Way,
  New York, NY *10002* . . . . Palm Beach, FL
  33480

Marlette MRS John E (Rosemary H Smith) Juilliard'47.G.St.Ts.
☎ (716) 832-5563 . . 150 Brantwood Rd, Buffalo, NY *14226-4370*

Marlette MR John E—Dth'84
☎ (415) 669-1101 . . PO Box 804, Inverness, CA *94937*

Marlette MISS Mary C (late John E) . . . . Married at Buffalo, NY
Smith MR Sidney V JR (Sidney V) . . . . Jun 29'96

Marlow MR & MRS Michael J (Jean E Clark) Pitt'50. | ☎ (301) 299-4625
MISS Jean A—at ☎ (606) 276-1272 10407 Riverwood
2504 Larkin Rd, Apt 66, Lexington, KY *40503* . Dv, Potomac, MD
20854

Marlowe MRS Walter G (Patrick—L Clare Foster)
☎ (202) 462-2330 . . 3133 Connecticut Av NW, Washington, DC *20008*

Maroney MR & MRS Samuel P JR (Reisky de Dubnic—Ehrenpreis—
Mary Louise Kemp) BMr'57.Wes'50.Duke'57
☎ (804) 977-3054 . . 2108 Morris Rd, Charlottesville, VA *22903*

Marovic MR & MRS Joseph J (Arinno—Susan L Hartig) ArizSt'78.ArizSt'72
☎ (602) 820-6188 . . 721 E Citation Lane, Tempe, AZ *85284-1409*

Marr MR & MRS John Stewart (Andrea R Gilman) Vt'77.Cc.P'67.Pa'70
☎ (540) 364-2339 . . "Soldier's Rest" Orlean, VA *20128*

Marr MRS William G (Mary W Speer) Md.Gv.Elk.Mv.Cda . . .of
☎ (410) 363-0088 . . 231 Green Spring Valley Rd, Stevenson, MD *21153*
☎ (941) 261-4517 . . 2011 Gulf Shore Blvd N, Apt 42, Naples, FL *34102*

Marrack MRS Richard M (A Verlinda Glidden)
☎ (770) 667-6353 . . 3820 Stepney Way, Cumming, GA *30131*

Marran MR & MRS Jack F (Theodora W Morris)
Ken'84.Nu'87.YeshivaU'91
☎ (516) 472-2680 . . 175 S Snedecor Av, Bayport, NY *11705-2132*

Marrin DR & MRS (DR) Charles A S (Marian A | ☎ (802) 436-2060
Bruen) Cl'73.Plg.Ht.Lond'71 . . . . "Juniper Hill"
JUNIORS MISS Minet A B . . . . RFD 1, Hartland,
VT *05048*

Marrin MR & MRS James M (Hamilton—Phebe E
Thorne) Cl'64.Pace'82.Au.Cly.Ford'65.Ford'69 . of ☎ (518)576-4306
MR John P T—Colg'92 . . . . "The Uplands"
JUNIORS MISS Helena Thorne—at St George's . . . Keene Valley, NY
  MR Lewis Thorne Hamilton—at Marymount . *12943*
☎ (212) 265-5575
75 West End Av,
Apt P19E,
New York, NY
10023

Marriner MR & MRS Kenneth W JR (Judith Cabot) | ☎ (508) 369-6621
Rdc'60.Ty'53 . . . . 350 Lowell Rd,
MISS Miriam—Ham'92—at San Francisco, CA . Concord, MA *01742*
MR Nathaniel K—Earl'89—at 297 Mt Auburn St,
Watertown, MA *02172* . . . .

Marriner MR William C—L&C'86
see Dilatory Domiciles

Marron MR & MRS Donald B (Catherine D Calligar) | of ☎ (212)988-6262
Ws'77.Ri.Mds.B.Ng. 720 Park Av,
MR Donald B JR—H'87 . . . . New York, NY
10021
☎ (516) 283-7744
PO Box 2573,
174 Coopers Neck
Lane, Southampton,
NY *11969*

Marron MRS Gloria S (Gloria A Swope) Ws'52
☎ (212) 288-5423 . . 180 E 79 St, New York, NY *10021*

Marrow MRS Macklin (Knapp—Julie Orthwein)
☎ (212) 722-4116 . . 1192 Park Av, New York, NY *10128*

Marsh MISS A Carter—Cvc . . .of
☎ (804) 282-4296 . . 8260 W Greystone Circle, Richmond, VA *23229*
☎ (804) 435-3838 . . "Cedar Point" PO Box 288, White Stone,
VA *22578*

Marsh MISS Adrienne A (Maloney—Bentien—Adrienne A Marsh)
☎ (011-33-93) 20-33-39 . . 2 Allée du Puy, 06270 Villeneuve-Loubet,
France

Marsh MR & MRS Alan R JR (Mary M Farnsworth) ColC'82.H'86.P'82.H'86
☎ (914) 793-8289 . . 2 Studio Lane, Bronxville, NY *10708*

Marsh MR Clifford B JR—Ts.Cy.Wms'27
28 Lancaster Av, Buffalo, NY *14222-1402*

Marsh MR & MRS H Newman JR (Marion Carhart) Bow'45
☎ (413) 354-9697 . . Misty Mountain Farm, 70 Ingell Rd, Chester,
MA *01011*

Marsh MR & MRS Harry A JR (Susan C Kendall) Ncd.Cent'51
☎ (610) 649-4935 . . 23 Railroad Av, Haverford, PA *19041*

Marsh MRS Helen H (Helen C Hewitt) Sth'52.Cl'73
☎ (203) 661-7730 . . 3 Cat Rock Rd, Cos Cob, CT *06807*

Marsh MR & MRS Howard D (Helen Joy Jones) Y'73
15 Orchard Hill Lane, Greenwich, CT *06831*

Marsh MR Michael—K.Rc.Ph.Cl'93 . . . . | ☎ (212) 799-9786
MISS Sarah K . . . . | 101 Central Park W,
JUNIORS MR William A . . . . | New York, NY
10023

Marsh MR Peter D
☎ (617) 242-1631 . . 40 Shipway Place, Charlestown, MA *02129*

Marsh MR & MRS Richard S T (Joan S Ferguson) Cvc.Sl.Y'43
☎ (301) OL6-5135 . . 101 E Kirke St, Chevy Chase, MD *20815*

Marsh MR & MRS Theron L (Willetts—Vogel—Mary L Wiener)
Shcc.Pn.P'33
☎ (201) 543-4334 . . 44 Hampshire Dv, Mendham, NJ *07945*

Marsh MR & MRS Tom Fariss (Charlene Cline) | ☎ (214) 352-1173
Nu'76.P'63 . . . . | 5007 Seneca Dv,
JUNIORS MISS Charlene C. . . . . | Dallas, TX *75209*
JUNIORS MR Charles . . . . |

Marsh DR & MRS (DR) William McN (Stefanie C Cann)
Bow'79.Dth'86.Dth'79.Dth'82
☎ (603) 569-6382 . . ''The Old Cotton Tavern'' 412 Cotton Valley Rd,
Wolfeboro, NH *03894*

Marsh MR & MRS William T (Mary L McNaugher) | ☎ (412) 963-9016
Fcg.Tc.Y'53.Pa'59 . . . . | 801 Fairview Rd,
MR Robert McN—at Bucknell . . . . | Pittsburgh, PA
15238

Marshall MR Alexander R—Vt'76
☎ (914) 762-1970 . . 61 Prospect Av, Ossining, NY *10562*

Marshall MR & MRS Allerton D (Pollard—Mary Markley)
Nw'58.Cl'65.P'53 ⚓
☎ (803) 689-6263 . . 33 Old Fort Dv, Hilton Head Island, SC *29926*

Marshall MR Andrew . . . . Died at
San Antonio, TX Mch 17'96

Marshall MRS Andrew (Sayre—Margaret F | ☎ (719) 634-6025
Lincoln) . . . . | 2370 Wood Av,
MR Andrew 3d—Marl'62—at ☎ (415) 621-5739 | Colorado Springs,
187A Corbett St, San Francisco, CA *94114* . . . . | CO *80907*

Marshall MRS Barbara M (Barbara Morss) Chi.Cy.
☎ (617) 734-4375 . . 172 Chestnut Hill Rd, Chestnut Hill, MA *02167*

Marshall MRS Benjamin H JR (Evelyn Chapuis)
☎ (847) 446-2224 . . 1044 Cherry St, Winnetka, IL *60093*

Marshall MISS Blair C . . see MRS B Green

Marshall MR & MRS Charles N (Ann S Donovan) | ☎ (610) 527-4416
Me.Ac.P'63.Mich'67 . . . . | 633 Winsford Rd,
MISS Elizabeth B . . . . | Bryn Mawr, PA
MISS Caroline B . . . . | *19010*
MISS Cornelia L . . . . |

Marshall MRS Charles R (Duke—Dolores Carrillo de Albornoz) Cly.
☎ (914) 677-9086 . . Millbrook Meadows 102, 560 Flint Rd, Millbrook,
NY *12545*

Marshall MR & MRS Claiborne T (Pamela J Duca)
Skd'86.Sar.Snc.Dc.Skd'86
☎ (210) 824-2324 . . 321 Rosemary Av, San Antonio, TX *78209*

Marshall MR Donald W
☎ (610) 584-3664 . . Meadowood at Worcester, 130 Laurel House,
Lansdale, PA *19446-5878*

Marshall MRS Duncan L (Mary S Osborn)
☎ (860) 567-4924 . . Box 1143, Woodruff St, Litchfield, CT *06759*

Marshall MRS Dwight (Gertrude A Nolan)
☎ (203) 322-0127 . . 46 Brookdale Rd, Stamford, CT *06903*

Marshall MRS Edward Le B (Jean Zimmermann) . . | ☎ (508) 775-5348
MR John C . . . . | ''Edge Hill House''
97 Edge Hill Rd,
Hyannis Port, MA
02647

Marshall DR & MRS (DR) Edward W 3d (Joanna M Bassert)
MtH'81.Pa'89.Temp'73.Pa'88
☎ (215) 242-4829 . . 8101 Winston Rd, Philadelphia, PA *19118*

Marshall MRS Fenton (Elinor S Fenton) Sim'57.Md. | ☎ (410) 728-7147
MR Edward T F . . . . | 1419 Park Av,
MR Ragan S . . . . | Baltimore, MD
21217

Marshall MR & MRS Frederick W JR (Pauline S Foraker) Gm.Rb.H.
☎ (610) 525-3373 . . 1395 Montgomery Av, Rosemont, PA *19010*

Marshall MR & MRS George K JR (Dorothy T Hirst) | ☎ (610) 688-6243
Me.Pa'60 . . . . | 140 S Devon Av,
MISS Priscilla M—at Yale . . . . | Devon, PA *19333*
MR George C—at Union Coll . . . . |

Marshall MR & MRS Harry R JR (Claire S Whitman) | ☎ (301) 652-1735
Briar'71.Cvc.Nyc.Va'61.Pa'65.Camb'67 . . . . . . | 7307 Maple Av,
MISS Katharine S—at U of Va . . . . | Chevy Chase, MD
MR Harrison R—at Wash'n U . . . . | *20815*

Marshall MR & MRS J Paull (Jane S Dwire) Cvc.Aht'34.Y'37
☎ (301) 571-0880 . . 9707 Old Georgetown Rd, Apt 2502, Bethesda,
MD *20814*

Marshall MR & MRS James R L (Helfinstine—Jan E Bragg)
Ariz'50.ArizSt'76.Ariz'51
☎ (602) 995-4967.7212 N Fifteenth Av, Phoenix, AZ *85021*

Marshall DR & MRS James S (Elizabeth Rockwell)
Sth'49.Cv.Tv.It.Rr.Pn.P'46.Cl'48 . . of
☎ (216) 423-3162 . . Epping Rd, Gates Mills, OH *44040*
☎ (207) 236-2066 . . ''Owl House'' PO Box 912, Beaucaire Rd,
Camden, ME *04843*

Marshall MR & MRS Jeffrey E (Jane Dumaresq Whitney)
Chi.W&M'64.H'66
☎ (617) 536-3123 . . 192 Commonwealth Av, Boston, MA *02116*

Marshall MR & MRS John (Cynthia G Churchman) . . | ☎ (610) 688-6873
MR William B—Ken'81 . . . . | 48 Hunters Lane,
Devon, PA *19333*

Marshall MR John A JR—Stan'57
☎ (212) 758-7546 . . 400 E 57 St, New York, NY *10022*

Marshall MR John H (Eickhoff—Constance E Leighton)
☎ (410) 363-7581 . . 2707 Greenspring Valley Rd, Owings Mills,
MD *21117*

Marshall MR John Hunt—Ny.H'29 ⚓
☎ (941) 964-2221 . . PO Box 1106, Boca Grande, FL *33921*

Marshall MR & MRS John R (Virginia N Corbett) | of ☎ (703)821-2249
RMWmn'64.Cc.Ncd.P'60.Va'65.Geo'95 . . . . . . | ''Crow's Nest''
MISS Peyton M—Reed'96—at ☎ (503) 239-5707 | 7508 Royal Oak Dv,
21 SE 18 St, Portland, OR *97214* . . . . | McLean, VA *22102*
MR Fielding C—Va'93—at ☎ (703) 521-0187 | ☎ (804) 529-5435
519 S Courthouse Rd, Arlington, VA *22204* . . . | Bright Meadow
Farm, Lodge Creek,
PO Box 80,
Lottsburg, VA
22511

Marshall MR John R (Julian McI) . . . . Married at Watertown, CT
Bullock MRS Deborah R (Deborah L Reilly) . . . . Jly 12'96
Marshall MR & MRS Joseph R (Jane D Wylie) DU'53.Y'50
☎ (203) 458-1065 . . 265 Dromara Rd, Guilford, CT *06437*
Marshall MR & MRS Julian McI (Henrietta A Harrison) Ac.Ncd.
☎ (610) 642-5357 . . 3300 Darby Rd, Apt 7217, Haverford,
PA *19041-1075*
Marshall MISS Katherine Payson—Pars'78.Cly.
☎ (212) 737-5090 . . 47 E 64 St, New York, NY *10021*
Marshall MRS Lawrence C (Sylvia Hitch)
☎ (803) 689-6916 . . The Cypress, 7 Birdsong Way, Hilton Head Island,
SC *29926*
Marshall MR & MRS Leonard L JR (Elizabeth F Phillips)
LIU'70.Adelphi'72.Ck.Snc.StJ.Y.'46
☎ (516) 922-1177 . . "Woodsong" 358 Ridge Lane, Mill Neck,
NY *11765*
Marshall MR & MRS Linton S JR (Morse—Cummins—Browning—
Diane D Morrell) P'49.Geo'52 . . of
☎ (410) 213-1295 . . 12616 Rumgate Rd, Ocean City, MD *21842*
☎ (410) 758-2157 . . 251 Bulle Rock Rd, Centreville, MD *21617*
Marshall MISS Mary W—Sth'78.Cr'84
☎ (508) 791-2399 . . 46 Flagg St, Worcester, MA *01602*
Marshall MISS Melissa R—Sth'72.H'75.Rr.
☎ (412) 362-9306 . . 428 Denniston Av, Pittsburgh, PA *15206*
Marshall MR & MRS Norman S (Marilyn Matter)
Occ'57.CalSt'55.SCal'62.SCal'80
☎ (818) 282-0290 . . 1735 Chelsea Rd, San Marino, CA *91108*
Marshall MRS Patricia T (Patricia A Taussig) CtCol'53.Cs.
☎ (212) 988-0513 . . 120 E 81 St, New York, NY *10028*
Marshall MRS Pendleton (MacDonald—Frances Townsend) V'30 . . of
☎ (941) 262-4413 . . 122 Moorings Park Dv, Naples, FL *34105*
☎ (802) 824-6309 . . Riverside Farm, Boynton Rd, RR 1, Box 97B,
Londonderry, VT *05148*

Marshall MR & MRS Peter E (Wood—Laurette B Milask) Pa'76.Ck.Y'74 . . . . JUNIORS MR Jonathan P	of ☎ (516)676-2745 "The Barn" 10 Frost Pond Rd, Locust Valley, NY *11560* ☎ (561) 833-7097 1515 S Flagler Dv, West Palm Beach, FL *33401*

Marshall MISS Rebecca S—BMr'21.Ncd.
☎ (410) 366-7798 . . 3900 N Charles St, Apt 1114, Baltimore,
MD *21218*

Marshall MR & MRS Robert B (Walthraut G Moecke) Mercy'81.LIU'85.Dth'40 . . . . MR Hauke H	☎ (914) 962-9888 "Forestfarm" 1710 Baptist Church Rd, Yorktown Heights, NY *10598*
Marshall MRS Ruth S (Ruth R Sizer) . . . . MR Ryland S	☎ (313) 994-3179 2364 Leslie Circle, Ann Arbor, MI *48105*

Marshall MR & MRS Samuel R (Laura K Buck) Vt'78.M.Me.Rc.Hav'77
☎ (610) 527-9552 . . 122 Kennedy Lane, Bryn Mawr, PA *19010*

Marshall MR & MRS Samuel S 3d (Laura G Chandler) Y'45 . . . . MISS Marguerite R—at 16 W 16 St, Apt 12H-S, New York, NY *10011* . . . . MR André C—at 165 E 90 St, Apt 5B, New York, NY *10128*	"Lemon Tree" Box 147, Harbour Island, Bahamas
Marshall MR & MRS Thomas C (Barbara F Wilson) Ws'57.Cyc.Fy.Carl'52.Wis'65 MR Thomas C JR—at 15 Kidder St, Somerville, MA *02144* . . . . MR David W—at 334 W Menominee St, Apt B2, Chicago, IL *60614* . . . . MR Stephen T—at 1600 N Hinman Av, Apt 1M, Evanston, IL *60201*	☎ (847) 234-9563 1345 W Deerpath, Lake Forest, IL *60045*

Marshall MR & MRS Thomas H (Eleanora O'D Lee) Cc.Rv.JHop'35
see Dilatory Domiciles

Marshall MR & MRS Thornton W (Farrell—Carolann Frost) Snc.Cw.Ds.Y'57. MISS Courtney D'E—at St Paul's . . . . MISS Kristin A Farrell—V'91	☎ (516) 271-6708 37 Briarfield Lane, Huntington, NY *11743*

Marshall MRS Thurgood (Cecilia A Suyat)
6233 Lakeview Dv, Falls Church, VA *22046*

Marshall MR & MRS William P (Susan L Nelson) Wh'lck'61.Bab'63.Seton'67 . . . . MISS Jill L—PineM'89 . . . . MR James P—RI'93	☎ (203) 655-8623 358 Hollow Tree Ridge Rd, Darien, CT *06820*

Marso MR & MRS Robert D JR (Anne T Love) Bab'86.Bates'75
☎ (517) 278-4797 . . 56 N Circle Dv, Coldwater, MI *49036*
Marsteller MR & MRS Robert W (Maralyn A Elmore) Van'84.Va'81
☎ (202) 966-7139 . . 4230 Fordham Rd NW, Washington, DC *20016*

Marsters MRS Katherine S (Katherine C Stillman) . . MISS Amy V—Ham'81—at ☎ (303) 692-8325 2446 S Monroe St, Denver, CO *80210*	☎ (617) 577-8782 4 Canal Park, Cambridge, MA *02141*

Marston MR & MRS Anthony Heselton (Brown—Peabody—
Marilynn Morse) Evg.BtP.
☎ (561) 655-2332 . . 140 Brazilian Av, Palm Beach, FL *33480*
Marston MR & MRS Hunter S 3d (Helen D Williams)
Cy.Msq.Okla'76.Okla'78 . . of
☎ (617) 566-4855 . . "Sunset Hill" 271 Goddard Av, Brookline,
MA *02146*
☎ (401) 348-8904 . . "Aloha Cottage" Aloha Rd, Watch Hill, RI *02891*
Marston MR John B—CentCtSt'79
see Dilatory Domiciles
Marston MRS Lauren O (Lauren Albee Oakford)
☎ (919) 380-1207 . . 107 Picker Lane, Cary, NC *27511*
Marston MRS M Marshall (Patricia I Power) Dar.Ncd.
☎ (561) 286-2477 . . 624 St Lucie Crescent, Stuart, FL *34994*
Marston MR & MRS Thomas Atherton (Josephine Heron Jellett)
☎ (954) 772-1532 . . 3050 NE 47 Court, Apt 607, Ft Lauderdale,
FL *33308*
Martenstein MR & MRS Thomas B (Carolyn K Turner) At.Vmi'54
☎ (334) 342-5024 . . 4761 Bexley Lane, Mobile, AL *36608*
Martin MR Alastair B—Rc.Bgt.P'38
☎ (914) 232-3052 . . PO Box 642, Katonah, NY *10536*

Martin MR Benjamin—Ph.Pkg.Sa.Ty'53.Pa'61 .... | ☎ (610) 933-8015
MISS Anne T . . . . | ''Glenbryte''
MISS Roberta E . . . . | Box 130,
MR Briton . . . . | Chester Springs, PA
| *19425*

Martin MR & MRS Brandon C (Alice T Squires) | ☎ (804) 861-8621
StAndr'71.W&L'69.W&L'72 . . . . | 1546 Berkeley Av,
JUNIORS MR John C . . . . | Petersburg, VA
| *23805*

Martin MISS Candyce—Stan'63
☎ (202) 337-6219 . . 3334 Reservoir Rd NW, Washington, DC *20007*

Martin MRS Carroll (Marilee de B Chadeayne) | ☎ (314) 962-8210
StL'50 . . . . | 1421 Peacock Lane,
MR Henry C . . . . | St Louis, MO *63144*

Martin MRS Charles C (Barbara Brunker) Myf.
☎ (504) 524-8432 . . 1009 Burgundy St, New Orleans, LA *70116-2403*

Martin MR & MRS Christopher H (Chloé A Drake) Y'90.Y'90
☎ (203) 776-7278 . . 24 Bishop St, New Haven, CT *06511*

Martin MR Crozer W . . see H B W Hoffman

Martin MR & MRS David B H JR (Martha Bacon) | ☎ (703) 836-4915
Mt.Y'69 . . . . | 318 Mansion Dv,
MISS Charlotte . . . . | Alexandria, VA
MISS Jessica . . . . | *22302*

Martin MRS David C (Helen L Wright) Cs.
☎ (610) 642-2832 . . 12 Booth Lane, Haverford, PA *19041*

Martin MISS Duart M . . see MRS E M Pollock

Martin MR & MRS Edward J (Schwefel—Chambers—Grace L Beer)
Mto.Nu'34
☎ (561) 655-6722 . . 389 S Lake Dv, Palm Beach, FL *33480*

Martin MRS Francis A JR (Consuelo Tobin) Bur.
☎ (415) 343-3591 . . 851 Sharon Av, Hillsborough, CA *94010*

Martin MR Franklin N—Cal'77.Cal'81.Cal'84
☎ (352) 377-0983 . . 4415 NW 70 Terr, Gainesville, FL *32606*

Martin MR George W—C.Hn.H'48.Va'53 . . of
☎ (610) 388-0529 . . 21 Ingleton Circle, Kennett Square, PA *19348*
☎ (941) 676-3540 . . 1616 S Highland Park Dv, Lake Wales,
FL *33853-7465*

Martin MR & MRS Guy (Edith K Gould) | ☎ (202) 338-3890
Mt.Ct.B.K.Sl.Yn.Ox'34.Y'37.Ox'44 . . . . | 3300 O St NW,
MISS Theodosia Burr . . . . | Washington, DC
| *20007*

Martin MR & MRS Guy 3d (Ellen B Fishwick) | ☎ (202) 745-7474
Ws'70.Cvc.Mt.Sl.Ncd.P'70 . . . . | 3117 Woodley Rd
JUNIORS MR Isaiah G 4th . . . . | NW, Washington,
JUNIORS MR John B F . . . . | DC *20008*

Martin MR & MRS H Curtiss (Virginia W Drewry)
Wms'75.Va'82.Tufts'75.Va'81
☎ (703) 548-2810 . . 118 Prince St, Alexandria, VA *22314*

Martin DR Harris W—Cw.Ll.Ant'79.Del'83.Fla'90. | ☎ (302) 427-8444
JUNIORS MISS Rachel E . . . . | 229A Presidential
| Dv, Greenville, DE
| *19807-3351*

Martin MRS Hollinshead T (Abbott—Elinor R Hay)
☎ (941) 485-2977 . . 50 Inlets Blvd, Nokomis, FL *34275-9704*

Martin MISS Holly H—Bost'80
☎ (617) 277-4383 . . 27 Englewood Av, Apt 27-6, Brookline, MA *02146*

Martin MR & MRS J Stanwood (Mary E Newkirk)
Fw.Cc.Rv.Ll.Cw.Cspa.Y'38
☎ (610) 431-1435 . . 308 Devon Lane, West Chester, PA *19380-6823*

Martin MR & MRS James F (Hope H McCulloch) | ☎ (847) 998-4549
Syr'67.MichSt'68 . . . . | 1115 Normandy
MISS Faith Hamilton . . . . | Lane, Glenview, IL
JUNIORS MISS Aimee Leavenworth . . . . | *60025*

Martin MR & MRS James S (Forsyth—Tilton—Grace D Wilson)
☎ (541) 772-0079 . . 228 Black Oak Dv, Medford, OR *97504*

Martin MRS John M (Helen Barker)
☎ (860) 726-2193 . . Duncaster, Talcott 414, 20 Loeffler Rd, Bloomfield,
CT *06002-2262*

Martin MRS John R (Charlotte A Nourse) Stan'50 . . | ☎ (408) 484-9364
MISS Priscilla S . . . . | 45 Paseo Hermoso
MR John R JR . . . . | St, Salinas, CA
| *93908*

Martin MR John T . . see G F Ford

Martín MR & MRS José (Lou Ella Oakes)
☎ (561) 684-4894 . . PO Box 16515, West Palm Beach, FL *33416*

Martin MR Joseph JR—Pcu.Bur.Y'36.Y'39
☎ (415) 434-4000 . . 2879 Woodside Rd, Woodside, CA *94062*

Martin MISS Josephine C . . of
☎ (703) 812-8055 . . Cardinal House C510, 3000 Spout Run P'kway,
Arlington, VA *22201*
☎ (540) 687-4147 . . ''Sweet Grass'' Rte 1, Box 165, Middleburg,
VA *20117*

Martin MISS Katharine W . . see G F Ford

Martin MR Lee Gwynne—Ll . . . . | ☎ (212) RE7-0133
MISS Martha K—Wash'79—at ☎ (718) 788-1949 | 7 Gracie Square,
221A 22 St, Brooklyn, NY *11232* . . . . | New York, NY
MISS Mary A—Sth'81—at ☎ (212) 787-0507 | *10028*
2211 Broadway, New York, NY *10024* . . . . . . |

Martin MISS Leslie—MtH'58
18 Bissell Lane, Norwalk, CT *06850*

Martin MR & MRS Malcolm Van D (Moffit—Nancy B Webb)
Evg.Y'41 . . of
☎ (561) 798-6433 . . 12373 Quercus Lane, Wellington, FL *33414*
☎ (441) 293-2479 . . ''Calico House'' 7 Glebe Hill, Tucker's Town
HS 02, Bermuda

Martin MISS Margaret Brodie (Paul E) . . . . Born at
San Francisco, CA Mch 15'96

Martin MRS Mary Vincent (Hanke—Mary Vincent | *see*
Martin) Y'61.AmU'71.Ri.Cda.Myf.Ht.Yn. . . . . | *Dilatory Domiciles*
MISS Christine Flagler Hanke . . . . |
MR G F Robert Hanke JR . . . . |
MR John Vincent Hanke . . . . |

Martin MR & MRS Middleton Ansley (Anne K | ☎ (703) 356-5577
Newhard) Cvc.Mt.P'66 . . . . | 1030 Pine Hill Rd,
MISS Anne W—Va'94 . . . . | McLean, VA *22101*
MISS Virginia U—Ham'95 . . . . |
MISS Margot H . . . . |
MR Middleton A JR—F&M'91 . . . . |

Martin MRS Milward W (Fletcher—Mary L Thurman) BMr'19.Pr.
☎ (516) 676-1481 . . 15 Shelter Lane, Locust Valley, NY *11560*

Martin MRS Nancy R (Nancy E Reakirt) Stph'48
☎ (704) 859-5850 . . 22 Mimosa Rd, PO Box 598, Tryon, NC *28782*

Martin MR & MRS Oliver (Ellen Allen) Me.Gm.Pa'41.. of
☎ (610) 642-0320.. 3300 Darby Rd, Beech 2221, Haverford, PA *19041-1068*
☎ (508) 428-6138.. "Bayberry" 1267 Main St, Cotuit, MA *02635*

Martin MR & MRS Paul E (Georgia W Remington) StLaw'80.P'80.Ch'84
☎ (415) 731-9829.. 201 Magellan Av, San Francisco, CA *94116*

Martin MR & MRS Peter B (Victoria H Viot) Y'61.Cl'65 | ☎ (561) 483-5160
MISS Elise C—Colg'93—at ☎ (617) 720-4903 | 3080 Canterbury Dv,
50 Pinckney St, Boston, MA *02114* .... | Boca Raton, FL *33434*

Martin MR & MRS Peter R (Isabella M Edwards) Rdc'64.H'64 .... | ☎ (802) 899-3166
MISS Isabella W .... | Field's Lane, Box 235, Jericho,
MR Andrew W—at American Embassy, Harare, Zimbabwe, Dept of State, Washington, DC *20010* | VT *05465*
MR Pieter L—Macalester'90

Martin MR & MRS Peter S (Deirdre W Scudder) Ty'84.Ty'78
☎ (617) 444-1720.. 204 Fair Oaks Park, Needham, MA *02192*

Martin MR & MRS Pierre E (Gertrude L Whitall) Ant'77.Paris'39
☎ (603) 673-3042.. "Farmlands" 5 Fellows Farm Rd, Amherst, NH *03031-1502*

Martin MRS Prudence S W (Prudence S White) V'44 .... | ☎ (215) 843-5266
MISS Laurie S—☎ (215) 844-7008 .... | 6300 Greene St, Philadelphia, PA *19144*

Martin MR & MRS R David (Bonnie J Allen) MichSt'68 .... | ☎ (602) 945-2100
MISS Leslie C .... | 6020 E Calle Del Media, Scottsdale,
MR Robert D 3d .... | AZ *85251*

Martin MR & MRS Richard S (Cynthia Blodgett) Sth'49.Ty'48
☎ (908) 273-0839.. 135 Hobart Av, Summit, NJ *07901*

Martin MR & MRS Robert I M (Caroline W M Wauchope) P'77.Va'79 ...... | ☎ (212) 349-5453
JUNIORS MISS Margaret M—at Brearley...... | 366 Broadway, Apt 8D, New York, NY
JUNIORS MISS Harriet W—at Grace Church Sch . | *10013*

Martin MRS Robert W (Black—Virginia Uihlein) Cly...of
☎ (406) 586-5278.. 2212 Spring Creek Dv, Bozeman, MT *59715*
☎ (406) 995-4908.. Trapper's Cabin Ranch, PO Box 267, Gallatin Gateway, MT *59730*

Martin MR & MRS Theodore R P (Frances C Thomas) Cy.Lc. .... | ☎ (314) 993-1128
MR Thomas R .... | 782 Kent Rd, St Louis, MO *63124*
MR Theodore R ....

Martin MR & MRS Thomas W (Lynn A Specker) ColbyS'76.NH'76
☎ (508) 264-0179.. 57 Washington Dv, Acton, MA *01720*

Martin MRS W Swift (Marguerite G Prewer) Sl.
☎ (202) 333-0876.. 2915 Q St NW, Washington, DC *20007*

Martin LT COL & MRS W Swift (Ellen M Wills) Van'58.An.Cc.Ncd.USA'60.Bost'77.Bost'80
☎ (202) 362-3148.. 4955 Glenbrook Rd NW, Washington, DC *20016-3222*

Martin MR William R
☎ (941) 964-2528.. Waterways, Box 854, Boca Grande, FL *33921*

Martin MR William W .... Married at Wayne, PA
Bates MISS Laura L .... Jun 1'96

Martindell MRS Anne C (Scott—Anne B Clark) Au.
☎ (609) 924-1260.. 40 Constitution Hill W, Princeton, NJ *08540*

Martineau MRS Glenn B (Louisa B Gibson) Pa'56.Cl'58.Vh.
☎ (818) 793-6280.. 3535 E California Blvd, Pasadena, CA *91107*

Martinelli MR Peter J—Cal'86.. see MRS L B Jenkins

Martinet MR & MRS Robert Thomas (Elizabeth A Brown) Sdy.
☎ (619) 272-0656.. 1069 E Briarfield Dv, San Diego, CA *92109*

Martinez MISS Gabriela M .. see E E Hastings

Martinez MR & MRS James M JR (Kathleen M Gurren) VaCmth'83.W&L'74.Va'77
☎ (804) 359-2735.. 1504 Palmyra Av, Richmond, VA *23227*

Martinez MR & MRS John M 2d (Teleha—Judith Brubaker) Va'70.Va'72.Syr'75 .... | ☎ (214) 351-2391
MISS Sloan .... | 10015 Dale Crest, Dallas, TX *75229*
MR Michael L ....

Martinez MR & MRS Oscar R (Margaret Tyson) Pa'67.Sg.Pa'66 .... | ☎ (215) 646-7830
MISS Sarah T—at Yale .... | 265 Mathers Rd, Ambler, PA *19002*
JUNIORS MR Brook T ....

Martinez MISS Patricia (Baker—Patricia Martinez) Alf'73 .... | ☎ (805) 834-4118
MISS Carmen M Baker .... | 5807 Stacey St, Bakersfield, CA
MISS Casey E Baker .... | *93313*

Martinez MR Peter M—CtCol'78
☎ (617) 326-7852.. "Lowder Brook Hollow" 82 Highland St, Dedham, MA *02026*

Martinez MR & MRS Roman 4th (Helena E Hackley) Bnd'76.Rc.Ln.Ri.Pr.Bost'69.Pa'71 | of ☎ (212)750-7567
JUNIOR MISS Helena C—at Groton . | 555 Park Av, New York, NY *10021*
JUNIOR MR Roman 5th—at Groton .... | ☎ (516) 922-2149 Planting Fields Rd, Upper Brookville, NY *11771*

Marting MRS Walter A (Margaret Brown) Ky'34.Kt.
☎ (216) 831-2009.. 3911-3 Lander Rd, Chagrin Falls, OH *44022-1328*

Marty MRS Kenneth B (Westerlind—Huppman—Beatrice H Hooker) .... | ☎ (410) 821-9580
MISS Elizabeth R H Huppman .... | 7525 Bellona Av, Ruxton, MD *21204*
MR George H Huppman ....

Marty MR & MRS Kenneth M (Susanne C Grasty) Va'62 .... | 1809 Indian Head Rd, Baltimore, MD
MR John G .... | *21204*

Maruca MR & MRS Samuel M (Linda C McKoy) Y'77.Y'77
☎ (202) 966-4221.. 3432—34 St NW, Washington, DC *20008*

Marvel MR & MRS Hunter M (Camilla S McKisson) StLaw'67.Msq.Ty'63.Cl'66 .... | ☎ (203) 637-3646
MISS Genevieve M—at Greenwich Acad ...... | 197 Riverside Av, Riverside, CT *06878*
MR Hunter M JR—at Hamilton Coll ....

Marvel MR James M D .. see W B Denham JR

Marvel MISS Jennifer V—Denis'90.Msq.Why.
☎ (617) 536-6116.. 182 Beacon St, Apt 2, Boston, MA *02116*

Marvel MR & MRS Robert (Mary J Stiles) CtCol'61.Why.Msq.Cl'66 .... | ☎ (401) 596-5990
MR H Jackson—at Bates .... | "Robin's Nest" 1 Turtleback Rd, Watch Hill, RI *02891*

Marvel MRS William (Boggs—Laura L Blair) Wil.
☎ (302) 654-5516.. PO Box 3683, Greenville, DE *19807*

Marvin MRS A Bryan (Alexa L Evans) Myf.Cw.Cda.
☎ (941) 349-4008 . . 5377 Shadow Lawn Dv, Sarasota, FL *34242*
Marvin MRS Beverley H (Anness—Beverley J Hooker) Ws'46 . . . . | *see Dilatory Domiciles*
   MR Peyton R Anness 3d . . . .
   MR Frederick H Anness . . . .
Marvin MRS Camilla (Behn—Weinmann—Camilla Marvin)
☎ (202) 333-5741 . . 3014 P St NW, Washington, DC *20007*
Marvin MR & MRS Timothy S (Jones—D Faye Mann) Myf.Emory'79
☎ (205) 978-9360 . . 2638 Greenmont Dv, Birmingham, AL *35226*
Marwedel MISS Elsie C—Cal'52
☎ (415) 776-2313 . . 1270 Lombard St, San Francisco, CA *94109*
Marx MR Alexander R (Graham A) . . . . Married at Winnetka, IL
  von Oppen MISS Stephanie C (Dieter) . . . . Sep 16'95
Marx MR & MRS Graham A (Louise McVickar) | ☎ (610) 642-5300
Eyc.M.Me.Err.O'67 . . . . | 521 N Rose Lane,
  MISS Elizabeth McK—Y'94 . . . . | Haverford, PA
| *19041*
Marx MR Graham E—Cm.Cr'38
☎ (513) 321-7484 . . 2472 S Rookwood Court, Cincinnati, OH *45208*
Marx MR & MRS Louis JR (Helen Zanetti) Sth'60.Ri.K.Ln.Cly.P'53
☎ (212) 427-1025 . . 1115 Fifth Av, New York, NY *10128*
Marzin MRS Jean E (Anne A Doub) Sth'57 . . . . . . | ☎ (011-33)
  MISS Sophie—at 8 rue Ferdinand Fabre, 75015 | 78-35-23-30
Paris, France . . . . | 88 Chemin de la
  MISS Catherine . . . . | Torchetière,
  MISS Josephine . . . . | 69760 Limonest,
  MR Paul—at 10 rue Miollis, 75015 Paris, France | France
Maschal MR & MRS John R (Maribell R Whetstone) | ☎ (305) 745-2871
Denis'58 ⚓ . . . . | PO Box 294,
  MR John Bell . . . . | Sugarloaf Shores,
  MR Peter Roberts . . . . | FL *33044*
Mascheroni MR & MRS Mark (Eleanor F Earle) Br'77.Dc.CarnM'77.Y'81
☎ (212) 371-5335 . . 435 E 57 St, New York, NY *10022*
Mashek MR & MRS Chandler C (Montgomery—A | of ☎ (561)659-4999
Chandler Cox) Smu'72.BtP.Evg.Srb.Cly. . . . . . . | 1290 S Ocean Blvd,
  JUNIORS MR Grant E . . . . | Palm Beach, FL
| *33480*
| ☎ (212) 223-2044
| 40 E 61 St, Apt
| 19B, New York, NY
| *10022*
Mashek MR John D JR—BtP.Evg.NTexSt'65 . . . . . . | ☎ (561) 833-7247
  MISS Lauren L . . . . | 82 Middle Rd,
| Palm Beach, FL
| *33480*
Masland MRS James G (Godsman—Emma Gillinder) Il.
☎ (401) 847-5478 . . 129 Spring St, Newport, RI *02840*
Masland MR Michael S—Pc.H'95
☎ (617) 527-3083 . . 11 Lombard St, Newton, MA *02158*
Mason MR & MRS Austin B (Connie M Bell) Cy.Chi.H'44
☎ (508) 433-6382 . . "Chick-a-Tee Farm" 63 Prescott St, Pepperell, MA *01463*
Mason MR & MRS Charles E (Geraldine Ridgway) Rad'62.Sewanee'61
☎ (301) 248-3806 . . 7518 Glade Dv, Ft Washington, MD *20744*

Mason MR & MRS Charles E JR (Ada B Trafford) | ☎ (617) 320-0529
Cy.Tv.H'30 . . . . | 10 Longwood Dv,
  MR Charles E 3d—Y'60—at 16 Joy St, Boston, | Westwood, MA
MA *02114* . . . . | *02090*
Mason MRS Charles J (Palmer—Katharine H Post) Cly.Cda.Dc.
☎ (860) 535-1779 . . "The Wing" 4 Temple St, Stonington, CT *06378*
Mason MRS Dandridge K (Elizabeth MacKie) | ☎ (214) 361-9229
Cda.Ncd. . . . . | 10566 High Hollows
  MISS Mary S . . . . | Dv, Apt 155, Dallas,
| TX *75230-4707*
Mason MR & MRS Dwight N (Sue E Wheeler) | 7307 Broxburn
Ws'62.Cos.Br'61.Cal'62.P'72 . . . . | Court, Bethesda,
  MR Nathaniel D—at U of Redlands . . . . | MD *20817*
Mason MR & MRS Eugene W JR (Mary Young) | ☎ (908) 234-1190
Sm.Cly.Ncd.P'42 . . . . | Box 275,
  MR Eugene W 4th—at ☎ (914) 626-7763 | Willow Av,
PO Box 326, Kerhonkson, NY *12446* . . . . | Peapack, NJ *07977*
Mason MRS Francis de L (Bull—Margaret Parker) Dar.
☎ (516) PI6-1055 . . 67 Hilton Av, Apt A4, Garden City, NY *11530*
Mason MRS Grey (Anne Miller)
☎ (516) 676-1286 . . Pound Hollow Rd, Glen Head, NY *11545*
Mason MRS Harold F (Cary P Gravatt) Cda. . . . . . . | ☎ (813) 251-5138
  MISS Junia S . . . . | 717 S Orleans Av,
| Apt 5, Tampa, FL
| *33606*
Mason MR & MRS Henry L 3d (Elaine J Bobrowicz) H'63.H'67
☎ (312) 664-2892 . . 1555 N Astor St, Chicago, IL *60610*
Mason MRS John A (Phyllis M Little) . . . . | ☎ (508) 945-0949
  MR John A JR—at Wyoming Seminary College, | 33 Marcus Lane,
201 N Sprague Av, Kingston, PA *18704-3593* . . | West Chatham, MA
| *02669-0237*
Mason MR & MRS John H (Smith—Barbara B | ☎ (617) 969-6251
Boeger) V'68.BostColl'72.H'67.Pa'73 . . . . | 47 Hancock Av,
  JUNIORS MISS Abigail van S Smith . . . . | Newton Center, MA
| *02159*
Mason MRS M Ashley (McMakin—Martha E | ☎ (410) 263-1258
Ashley) . . . . | 2125 Beach Village
  MR George G 3d . . . . | Court, Apt T2,
| Chesapeake Harbor,
| Annapolis, MD
| *21403*
Mason MRS Mary T (Mary E Terry) . . . . | ☎ (202) 537-8066
  MISS Alexandra T . . . . | 6015 Broad Branch
  MISS Peyton R . . . . | Rd NW,
| Washington, DC
| *20015*
Mason MR Newell O—Br'27.H'30
☎ (609) 443-5962 . . Meadow Lakes 15-03L, Hightstown, NJ *08520*
Mason MR & MRS Randolph D (Hyder—Patty K Lowdon)
Tex'69.Cvc.Srb.Cc.Va'64.Va'67
☎ (817) 732-5757 . . 505 Alta Dv, Ft Worth, TX *76107*
Mason MR & MRS Robert C (Martha A Goodyear)
☎ (603) 525-3507 . . Main & School Sts, Box 310, Hancock, NH *03449*
Mason MR & MRS Scott C (Carolyn Amos) Va'56
☎ (508) 994-3217 . . 194 Rockland St, South Dartmouth, MA *02748*

Mason MRS Thomas F (Reed—Patricia Goodall)
☎ (215) 627-2076 . . 604 S Washington Square, Apt 717, Philadelphia, PA *19106*

Mason MR W Beverley JR . . . . Died at Leesburg, VA Jly 29'96

Mason MRS W Beverley JR (Camp—McCanless—Helen A Prather) Smu'52.Cvc.
☎ (540) 592-3812 . . "Locke Farm" PO Box 183, Upperville, VA *20185*

Masoner DR & MRS David J (Linder—Barbara A Smith) Pitt'59.Pitt'70 . . . . | *see*
MISS Nancy Lash . . . . | *Dilatory Domiciles*
MR Brian W Linder . . . . |
MR Charles K Linder . . . . |

Massey MR & MRS Calvin R (Martha C Miller) Nu'67.Whit'69
☎ (415) 928-5985 . . 2539 Vallejo St, San Francisco, CA *94123-4640*

Massey MRS Jack C (Armistead—Alyne Queener) Bcs.BtP.Evg.Cly.Dar.Ncd . . .of
☎ (615) 269-0917 . . "Brook House" 4431 Tyne Blvd, Nashville, TN *37215*
☎ (561) 832-7000 . . "The Beachouse" 1125 S Ocean Blvd, Palm Beach, FL *33480*

Massey MR Jay Richardson JR—Ph.Wt.HolyC'60.BMr'62.Lond'94 . . of
☎ (215) 732-6565 . . 2017 Waverly St, Philadelphia, PA *19146*
☎ (011-44-171) 835-1234 . . 17F Nevern Square, London SW5 9PD, England

Massey MR & MRS (DR) Jon G (McCarthy—Hildreth J Bigham) BemidjiSt'74.Dc.Tul'71
☎ (504) 891-4589 . . 4920 Coliseum St, New Orleans, LA *70115*

Massey MRS Linton R (Mary Ord Preston) Ncd.
☎ (804) 296-6201 . . 2401 Old Ivy Rd, Apt 1303, Charlottesville, VA *22903*

Massey MRS Paul H (Dorothy T Doubleday) Csn. . . | ☎ (505) 982-6170
MISS Mary Elizabeth—Pom'91 . . . . | 939 Acequia Madre
MR Paul D—at 744 Spruce, Boulder, CO *80302* . | St, Santa Fe, NM *87501*

Massey MR & MRS Richard W JR (M Ann Hinkle) | ☎ (205) 969-2161
Aub'53.Cy.Rv.Va'39.Van'60 . . . . | 1304 Kingsway
MISS Dale E—at Jackson, MS . . . . | Lane, Birmingham, AL *35243*

Massey MR Robert Valentine JR—M.Y.'28
☎ (610) 642-2292 . . 221 Cheswold Lane, Haverford, PA *19041*

Mast MR & MRS Robert D JR (Katharine DeW Cheek) CtCol'90.Rv.Penn'88
☎ (617) 723-7933 . . 152 Mt Vernon St, Apt 2, Boston, MA *02108*

Masten MR John E—Dth'33.Y.'36
☎ (914) 967-1086 . . 81 Oakland Beach Av, Rye, NY *10580*

Master DR & MRS John Reis (Janet A Crawford) | ☎ (215) 794-2086
Hough'64.P.Hough'67.DallasTheo'69. | 2481 Furlong Rd,
DallasTheo'73 . . . . | Doylestown, PA *18901*
MR Daniel M . . . . |
JUNIORS MR Jonathan L . . . . |

Master MR & MRS Lawrence L (Nancy A Sweet) | ☎ (617) 647-9311
Mich'75.StLaw'68.Mich'72.Mich'77 . . . . | 1 Lantern Lane,
MISS Kathryn I—at Stanford . . . . | Weston, MA *02193*
MR Peter O—at Skidmore . . . . |

Master MR & MRS William O JR (Judith J | ☎ (206) 232-6730
Leutzinger) Col'60 . . . . | 7800 SE 70 St,
MR John L . . . . | Mercer Island, WA *98040*

Masters MR & MRS Francis R JR (Patricia J Klumpp) Wcc.Me.Y.'51
☎ (610) NI4-8513 . . 15 Andrews Rd, Malvern, PA *19355*

Masters DR & MRS William H (Becker—Oliver—Geraldine H Baker) G.Ham'38.Roch'43 . . of
☎ (520) 299-9381 . . 4970 E Oakmont Dv, Tucson, AZ *85718-1707*
☎ (518) 891-0988 . . "Serenescene" Gabriels Rd, Box 10, Onchiota, NY *12989*

Masters MR & MRS William H 3d (Victoria M Baker) Ham'74.Mich'75
225 W 80 St, Apt 6C, New York, NY *10024*

Masterson MR & MRS Carlos B (Josephine Y Smith)
☎ (011-52-415) 2-02-01 . . Sollano 44, San Miguel de Allende, GTO 37700, Mexico

Masterson MR & MRS Harris 3d (Winston—Cowan—Isla C Sterling) Rice'55
☎ (713) 523-0524 . . 1406 Kirby Dv, Houston, TX *77019*

Masterson DR & MRS Thomas J (Adelaide A Drew) | ☎ (860) 887-5310
Dar.RI'42.Tufts'45 . . . . | 31 Tanglewood Dv,
MISS Anne L—Conn'86.FP'90 . . . . | Norwich, CT *06360*

Mastin MRS Carroll S (Laura Baumgarten) Sth'39.Cy.
☎ (314) 367-9808 . . 25 Westmoreland Place, St Louis, MO *63108*

Mastin REV & MRS Charles O'F (Georgann Logsdon) Ill'46.Sar.Ncd.Del'59.VaTheo'61
3925 Muhlenberg Court, Burlington, NC *27215*

Mateer MR & MRS G Diehl JR (Hentz—Eldredge—Ann N Lohmann) Cda . . .of
☎ (941) 378-2251 . . 3321 Highlands Bridge Rd, Sarasota, FL *34235*
☎ (540) 364-3101 . . Tirvelda Farms, PO Box 111, Middleburg, VA *20118*

Mather MRS Charles E 2d (Miller—Catherine M Haas) Rd.Me.
☎ (610) 642-6209 . . "Hillside" 425 Mulberry Lane, Haverford, PA *19041*

Mather MR & MRS Charles E 3d (Mary A MacGregor) Rdc'55.Srr.Fi.Ph.R.B.Pe.K.Mt.Rby.Plg.Cw.Myf.Rv.W. Ac.Cs.H'56.Pa'59
☎ (215) VI8-9842 . . 3819 The Oak Rd, Philadelphia, PA *19129*

Mather MR & MRS Charles E 4th (Elizabeth M Sigler) B.Srr.Pe.Ph.Pc.R.Pr.Br'82.Penn'86
30 Lincoln Plaza, Apt 4J, New York, NY *10023*

Mather MR & MRS Thomas W (Gatch—Brodhead— Elizabeth A Lamy) Wis'43
☎ (941) 953-3449 . . 3953 Red Rock Way, Sarasota, FL *34231*

Mathers MR & MRS William H (Myra T Martin) Pr.Ny.Csh.Sm.Csn.Dth'35.Y'38
☎ (802) 467-3414 . . "Gordon Farm" RR 1, Box 83, Sutton, VT *05867-9721*

Matheson MR & MRS Charles T (Bonnie R | ☎ (540) 253-5249
Buchanan) Mt.Cvc.Nrr.Sl.Va'64 . . . . | "Heathfield"
MR Robert R—at George Mason U . . . . | PO Box 1,
MR Murdoch B—Denis'96 . . . . | The Plains, VA *20198*

Matheson MR & MRS Finlay L (Lucretia G Brooks) V'41.Geo'40
☎ (305) 661-6859 . . 4940 Sunset Dv, Miami, FL *33143*

Matheson MR & MRS William L (Bard—Marjorie Anderson)
Pr.Mb.Ln.Emory'47.Va'50
☎ (561) 546-8430 . . 430 S Beach Rd, Jupiter Island, Hobe Sound, FL *33455*

Mathews MR & MRS Adam A (Cheryl A Beach) Vt'80
☎ (954) 389-9369 . . 555 Cambridge Dv, Ft Lauderdale, FL *33326*

Mathews MR Alexander S—K.Dth'76.Miami'79
☎ (202) 332-6509 . . 1749 Q St NW, Washington, DC *20009*

Mathews MISS Barbara R . . see D R Arthur

Mathews MR & MRS Charles P (Wendy E Graham)
Denis'83.Mid'85.Dar.CtCol'80.Nu'91
☎ (201) 701-9424 . . 74 Fairmount Av, Chatham, NJ *07928*

Mathews MISS Charlotte Bakkeby (Charles P) . . . . Born at Morristown, NJ Mch 8'96

Mathews MRS Dorothea S (Dorothea S Smith) Cda.
☎ (203) 323-2947 . . 77—3 St, Stamford, CT *06905*

Mathews MR Harry B 3d—Rc.
☎ (314) 994-1604 . . 45 Overhills Dv, St Louis, MO *63124*

Mathews MR & MRS Hayden (Ross—Elizabeth S Baker) Cly.Ncd.Rut'53
☎ (203) 359-4112 . . 585 Westover Rd, Stamford, CT *06902*

Mathews MRS Henderson (Holder—Marion W Speakman)
☎ (561) 832-2538 . . 315 Cocoanut Row, Palm Beach, FL *33480*

Mathews MISS Patricia A . . see R D Lewis 2d

Mathews MR & MRS Richard A (Anne P Powell) Sth'54.Cr'55
☎ (908) 775-6422 . . 709B Ocean Av, Avon-By-The-Sea, NJ *07717*

Mathews MRS Rita W (Thompson—Rita M White) Cl'67.CUNY'73.Csn.
☎ (413) 229-7738 . . ''Stoneridge'' E Hill Rd, PO Box 237, Southfield, MA *01259-0237*

Mathews MRS Robert F (Allen—Ruth Deibel)
☎ (602) 948-5975 . . 5525 E Lincoln Dv, Paradise Valley, AZ *85253*

Mathews MR & MRS Robert W (Margaret B Prindle) Sth'57.Bow'56
☎ (207) 729-9117 . . 63 Federal St, Brunswick, ME *04011*

Mathews MR & MRS Sidney (Harrison—Allen—Phyllis Dickinson) BtP.P'33
☎ (561) 844-1132 . . 1141 N Lake Way, Palm Beach, FL *33480-3248*

Mathews MR Thomas A . . see R D Lewis 2d

Mathews MRS Walter M (Anna E Klecka)
☎ (847) 438-3358 . . 21511 Pine Lake Court, Kildeer, IL *60047*

Mathewson MR & MRS William G JR (Sally A Olhausen) Y'61.H'65 . . . .
JUNIORS MISS Christina B . . . .
☎ (908) 766-7124
40 Sunnybrook Rd,
Basking Ridge, NJ *07920*

Mathey MR & MRS Timothy W (Diana O Batchelder)
see Dilatory Domiciles

Mathias MR & MRS Charles McC JR (Ann Hickling Bradford) V'51.Cc.Mv.Hav'44.Md'48 . . . .
MR Charles B—H'81.Va'85—at
☎ (202) 338-6881 . . 2803 Dumbarton St NW, Washington, DC *20007* . . . .
☎ (301) 986-1620
3808 Leland St,
Chevy Chase, MD *20815*

Mathias MR & MRS Richard L (Bennett—Lynn Hellyer) Nat'lCollEd'80.Ih.Denis'61.Mich'64 . .
MISS Emily R . . . .
MR David H—at 2443 N Burling St, Chicago, IL *60614* . . . .
☎ (847) 256-0393
422 Cumnor Rd,
Kenilworth, IL *60043*

Mathieu MRS Charles L JR (Barbara Bedford)
☎ (516) 283-1835 . . 21 Huntting St, Southampton, NY *11968*

Mathieu MR Charles L JR
☎ (561) 659-7596 . . PO Box 2511, Palm Beach, FL *33480*

Matisse MRS S Barrett (Sarah S Barrett) . . . .
MR George P B . . . .
MR Michael A C . . . .
MR Robert A P . . . .
☎ (617) 547-8104
21 Avon St,
Cambridge, MA *02138*

Matsch MR Tilman H—Cl'50
☎ (516) 287-1441 . . S Main St, Southampton, NY *11968*

Mattei MRS Albert C (Ferne Orchard) Tcy.Bur.
☎ (510) 838-5830 . . 151 Sonora Av, Danville, CA *94526*

Mattei MR & MRS Peter O (Shewell—Carmelita Romano) Pcu.Stan'45.Cal'49 . . . .
MISS M Ayn—at ☎ (773) 286-0322
5340 W Belle Plaine Av, Chicago, IL *60641* . . .
MISS Lyn O—at ☎ (916) 583-4157 . . Box 2647, Olympic Valley, CA *95730* . . . .
of ☎ (510)837-4061
24 Mott Dv, Alamo,
CA *94507*
☎ (011-52-322)
25282
''Casa Fontana Sur''
259 Matamoros,
Puerto Vallarta,
Jalisco, Mexico

Mattes MRS Edward C (Minnie W Fite) T.Cly.Dar.
☎ (914) 351-4442 . . PO Box 794, Ridge Rd, Tuxedo Park, NY *10987*

Mattes MR Edward C JR—Pa'79
☎ (212) 995-9498 . . 76 Irving Place, Apt 4C, New York, NY *10003*

Mattes MR & MRS John B (Sarah E Lindsley) MtH'85.Unn.T.Geo'84
☎ (617) 934-3209 . . 15 Old Mill Lane, Duxbury, MA *02332*

Mattes MISS Laura L—Sth'82.Cly.Dar.
☎ (914) 835-4681 . . 40 Bradford St, Harrison, NY *10528*

Matteson MISS Claire C . . see MISS K G Pollock

Matteson JUNIORS MR Oren P . . see MISS K G Pollock

Matteson JUNIORS MR Robert K . . see MISS K G Pollock

Matthai MR & MRS George M (M Keene Barroll)
Hlns'83.Elk.Ny.Ncd.Rm'71
11129 Falls Rd, Lutherville, MD *21093*

Matthews MRS A Bruce (Dalley—Dale Porter Pfohl)
☎ (416) 929-4418 . . 70 Rosehill Av, Apt 506, Toronto, Ontario M4T 2W7, Canada

Matthews MR & MRS A Pierce JR (Ann-Patton Biddle) Cin'46
☎ (513) 831-5188 . . 132 Windingbrook Lane, Terrace Park, OH *45174*

Matthews MR & MRS Charles L 3d (Barbara S Standish) . .
MISS Mary B . . . .
MR Charles L—NH'89 . . . .
☎ (313) 884-0745
313 Mt Vernon St,
Grosse Pointe, MI *48236*

Matthews MR & MRS Fontaine M (Knight—Mary L Scudder)
Wash'76.Cy.Nd.Pa'70.Pa'74
12 Upper Ladue Rd, St Louis, MO *63124-1630*

Matthews MR & MRS L Churchill JR (Martha Culver) Cy.Wash'61 . . . .
MISS Martha E . . . .
☎ (314) 991-5727
9440 Old
Bonhomme Rd,
St Louis, MO *63132-3407*

Matthews MISS Mary-Morse
☎ (513) 831-4809 . . 601 Myrtle Av, Terrace Park, OH *45174*

Matthews MR & MRS Wilbur L (Prichard—Davis—Helen Pruit)
LMorris'30.A.Tex'26
☎ (210) 822-5638 . . 200 Patterson Av, Apt 806, San Antonio, TX *78209*

Matthews MRS William Dunham (Sherman—Mary L Doherty)
☎ (619) 435-8765 . . 135 E Av, Coronado, CA *92118*

Matthias MR Daniel R (William W) . . . . Married at Phoenix, AZ
  Smith MISS Kristina M (William) . . . . Jun 29'96
Matthias MR & MRS William W (Angela A Ely) Y'61.Nw'69
  ☎ (303) 795-7708 . . 13 Dutch Creek Rd, Littleton, CO 80123
Matthiessen MR Erard A—Y'24
  ☎ (941) 472-1049 . . 4619 Rue Bayou, Sanibel, FL 33957
Mattis MISS Nancy R—Ne'96
  ☎ (617) 738-1415 . . 669 Washington St, Apt 3, Brookline, MA 02146
Mattis MR Richard B—Drake'69 . . . . | ☎ (314) 863-5705
  JUNIORS MR R Brent JR . . . . | 940 Audubon Dv,
    | Clayton, MO 63105
Mattis MR & MRS Stephen van S (Mary Christy | ☎ (314) 991-3172
  Bohn) Mar'vil'71.Rc. . . . . | 9219 Ladue Rd,
  JUNIORS MISS Virginia B . . . . | St Louis, MO 63124
  JUNIORS MISS Hilary H . . . . |
Mattison MR & MRS Joseph JR (Elizabeth Moir) V'41.Cy.Chi.H.'39
  ☎ (617) 232-2297 . . 339 Hammond St, Chestnut Hill, MA 02167
Mattison MR & MRS Joseph 3d (Alice C Donahue)
  Briar'72.Eyc.Ny.P'68.Va'77 ⚓
  ☎ (508) 428-6767 . . 501 Eel River Rd, Osterville, MA 02655
Mattison MR & MRS Mark H (Karel D Oliver) | ☎ (203) 966-3730
  V'63.Rcn.Unn.Err.Eyc.Ny.Ford'64 . . . . | 40 River Wind Rd,
  MISS Delphine—at 18 Follen St, Boston, MA | New Canaan, CT
  02116 . . . . | 06840
  MISS Alissa—at Boston U . . . . |
  MR Graham—in Hong Kong . . . . |
Mattison MR & MRS Peter D (Rebecca G Wells) Bates'72.H'68
  ☎ (508) 369-8150 . . 631 Strawberry Hill Rd, Concord, MA 01742
Mattlage MISS L Valerie (Ledyard—L Valerie | ☎ (203) 259-7397
  Mattlage) . . . . | PO Box 286,
  MR Jason Ledyard—B'gton'91—at Ben'gton | Southport, CT 06490
  Grad . . . . |
Mattmiller MR & MRS Arthur W 3d (Ramsden— | ☎ (415) 461-2101
  Bayles—Suzanne C Bowman) DU'65.CalSt'72. | 398 N Almenar Dv,
  Cal'73 . . . . | Greenbrae, CA
  MR Arthur W 4th . . . . | 94904
  MR Charles D Bayles . . . . |
Mattson MR & MRS (DR) John E (Louisa B Hasen) Mich'71.Bost'76
  523 Autumn Lane, Carlisle, MA 01741
Mattsson MR & MRS N Christer (Lynch—Deborah W Lippincott) Pa'76
  ☎ (011-44-171) 730-3729 . . 67 Eaton Terr, London SW1, England
Maull MRS Baldwin (Flora Davis) | ☎ (609) 426-6085
  V'25.Plg.Cly.Ncd.Dc.Cw.Ht.Pn. . . . . | Meadow Lakes
  MISS Diana—at ☎ (212) 877-8919 | 17-09U, Etra St,
  142 West End Av, New York, NY 10023 . . . . . | Hightstown, NJ
    | 08520
Maulsby MR Allen F—Chr.Plg.StJ.Ne.Wms'44.Va'46 . . of
  ☎ (203) 629-4624 . . 392 North St, Greenwich, CT 06830
  ☎ (603) 532-4595 . . ''Twin Meadows'' Dublin Rd, Jaffrey Center,
  NH 03454
Maulsby MR Allen F JR
  ☎ (508) 745-9482 . . 17 Heritage Dv, Apt 26, Salem, MA 01970
Maulsby MR & MRS David L JR (Sara A Hadeler) | ☎ (410) 523-2737
  Md.Y'65.Cr'68 . . . . | 1424 Park Av,
  MISS Lucy M—at Clare Coll, England . . . . | Baltimore, MD
  MISS Catherine H—at Colgate . . . . | 21217

Mauran MR & MRS Duncan H (Louise K S Safe) Cc.Chi.H'50
  ☎ (401) 751-8819 . . 35 Charlesfield St, Providence, RI 02906
Mauran MR & MRS Frank (Esther E Metcalf) SL'53.Cc.Csn.Y'49
  ☎ (401) 861-0612 . . 109 Benefit St, Providence, RI 02903
Maurer MR & MRS Donald E (Clark—Ann L | ☎ (410) 381-7432
  Outhwaite) Briar'68.Col'64.CalTech'68 . . . . . . | 7160 Lasting Light
  MISS Stephanie L—at Moore Coll of Art . . . . . | Way, Columbia, MD
  JUNIORS MISS Laura A . . . . | 21045
Maurer DR & MRS Richard K (Alexandra W Strawbridge)
  L&C'88.OreCol'74.Nat'lC'94
  ☎ (207) 721-0750 . . 97 Pennellville Rd, Brunswick, ME 04011
Maurice MISS Kiffin
  ☎ (803) 649-4136 . . 620 Barnwell Av NW, Aiken, SC 29801
Maurice MISS Michelle
  ☎ (404) 875-0171 . . 200 Montgomery Ferry Dv NE, Apt 21, Atlanta,
  GA 30309
Maury MR & MRS John M (Rosalie L Brown) Ny. . . | ☎ (203) 838-0218
  MR Richard L—San.NCar'68—at | 24 Indian Spring Rd,
  ☎ (307) 687-7750 . . 813 Wagon Trail, Gillette, | Rowayton, CT
  WY 82716 . . . . | 06853
Maus MR & MRS William D JR (Kneeland—June McIntosh) Bhm.Va'45
  ☎ (707) 963-7559 . . PO Box 1029, St Helena, CA 94574-0529
Mause MR & MRS Philip J (Cheryl C Wyman) AmU'71.Gi.Geo'65.H'68
  ☎ (202) 966-6508 . . 5108 Palisade Lane NW, Washington, DC 20016
Maushardt MR & MRS Peter W (Lucinda Kent) Ore'81.Ncd.Cal'76
  ☎ (707) 996-5215 . . 121 Madrid Way, Sonoma, CA 95476
Mautz MISS Elizabeth A . . see MRS S B Johnson
Mautz MISS Jennifer N . . see MRS S B Johnson
Mauzé MR & MRS James F (Sondra B Seeger)
  WmWds'62.Cy.Nd.W'minster'61
  ☎ (314) 997-7779 . . 91 Pointer Lane, St Louis, MO 63124
Mawicke MISS Adele R . . see S E Brinckerhoff
Mawicke MR Andrew D—Mich'89 . . see S E Brinckerhoff
Mawicke MR Frederick H . . see S E Brinckerhoff
Maxfield MR C James 3d . . of
  ☎ (212) 242-1917 . . 201 W 16 St, New York, NY 10011
  ☎ (610) 644-9094 . . ''Littlebrook'' 416 Littlebrook Rd, Devon,
  PA 19333
Maxson MRS William B (Audrey Arnold) . . . . | ☎ (717) 394-4323
  MR William B 3d—at Ruidoso, NM 88345 . . . . . | 314 Cornell Av,
  MR Michael—Mil'vl'81—at ☎ (703) 791-4884 | Lancaster, PA 17603
  8471 Jacqueline Av, Manassas, VA 20112 . . . . . |
Maxwell MR & MRS David B (Kathryn A Winkhaus) | ☎ (703) 821-0855
  Pr.Hof'72.Cl'81 . . . . | 901 Walker Rd,
  MR David B JR | Great Falls, VA
  JUNIORS MISS Marcia W . . . . | 22066
  JUNIORS MR James C . . . . |
  JUNIORS MR Ian W . . . . |
Maxwell MR & MRS Dennis G 3d (Robin C Tucker) | ☎ (203) 259-9544
  Myf.Yn.Y'50 . . . . | 66 High Point Rd,
  MR D Gray 4th—Stan'82—at ☎ (202) 966-0503 | Westport, CT 06880
  3887 Rodman St NW, Apt E71, Washington, DC |
  20016-2837 . . . . |
Maxwell MISS Elizabeth C—Pars'77.Myf.
  ☎ (212) 532-3203 . . 41 Park Av, Apt 14C, New York, NY 10016
Maxwell MR F Rollins 3d—H'62
  ☎ (212) 628-8265 . . 860 Fifth Av, New York, NY 10021

Maxwell DR & MRS G Patrick (Caldwell—Katherine C Follin)
Van'76.Van'68
☎ (615) 292-8662 . . 4416 Gerald Place, Nashville, TN *37205*

Maxwell MR George L—Co.Un.Ny.Plg.An.Vca.StA.Fw.Pa'63 ⚓
☎ (212) 988-1057 . . 53 E 66 St, New York, NY *10021*

Maxwell MR & MRS Irving McC (Mary M McKee)
☎ (513) 271-1036 . . 3817 Indianview Av, Cincinnati, OH *45227*

Maxwell MR & MRS John C JR (Adrienne d'A Leichtle)
V'61.Cw.Cly.Pn.P'50 . . of
☎ (804) 359-4608 . . 4703 Rolfe Rd, Richmond, VA *23226*
☎ (207) 244-9073 . . ''Linn Mor'' Mt Desert, ME *04660*

Maxwell MR & MRS John C 3d (Carol M Barrett) FairD'88
☎ (713) 362-9924 . . 78 Red Sable Dv, The Woodlands, TX *77380*

Maxwell MISS Linda S
177 E 75 St, New York, NY *10021*

Maxwell MISS Margaux Monroe (John C 3d) . . . . Born at
Greenwich, CT Nov 22'94

Maxwell MISS Mary Brooke—Skd'66
☎ (508) 448-2205 . . 3 Highland Rd, Groton, MA *01450*

Maxwell MR R Bruce—Wms'58
☎ (202) 338-9275 . . 1613—35 St NW, Washington, DC *20007*

Maxwell MRS Walburga W (Walburga Walsh)
☎ (215) CH8-2047 . . 8800 Germantown Av, Philadelphia, PA *19118*

May MR Albert C—CarnM'21
☎ (216) 226-8477 . . 1341 Marlowe Av, Apt 610, Lakewood, OH *44107*

May MR Andrew—Ken'81 . . see MRS L Hawkins

May MR Brian—SimR'83 . . see MRS L Hawkins

May MR & MRS Edward L (Mary F Waterfall)
Sth'52.Mich'55.Dth'54.Mich'57
☎ (313) 769-5485 . . 3005 Geddes Av, Ann Arbor, MI *48104*

May MR & MRS Edward L JR (Genet T Case) Ober'85.Dth'82
☎ (216) 331-8943 . . 19851 Saranac, Fairview Park, OH *44126*

May DR & MRS George A JR (Beth H Butler)
Cy.Y'58.H'62 . . . . | ☎ (617) 332-4637
MISS Sarah K . . . . | 80 Berkeley St,
MR Peter F . . . . | West Newton, MA
| *02165*

May MRS Henry 3d (Eleanor L Goldsborough)
☎ (716) 883-7280 . . 141 Highland Av, Buffalo, NY *14222*

May MR & MRS Herbert A 3d (Julia W Barnes) HWSth'86.Va'87
☎ (410) 581-0914 . . 301 Golf Course Rd, Owings Mills, MD *21117*

May MR & MRS Irénée du P (Reese—Katherine L Evans)
Stan'52.Wil.Ac.Wms'50 . . of
☎ (610) 388-7141 . . 4 Frog Pond Rd, Chadds Ford, PA *19317*
☎ (803) 723-7928 . . 8 St Michaels Alley, Charleston, SC *29401*

May MR & MRS J Denny (Meriam—Kathryn Arns) Kt.It.Chi.W&J'28
☎ (561) 276-8980 . . Harbour's Edge 617, 401 E Linton Blvd,
Delray Beach, FL *33483*

May MR & MRS James G G (Michele M Georger)
St.Colg'66 ⚓ . . . . | ☎ (716) 833-5818
MISS Michele G—at Middlebury . . . . | 191 Woodbridge Av,
MR James G G JR . . . . | Buffalo, NY *14214*

May MR & MRS James Q JR (Eleanor G Locke) Gv.Md.JHop'79
☎ (410) 653-0048 . . 1535 Hillside Rd, Box 115, Stevenson, MD *21153*

May MR Laurence . . see MRS L Hawkins

May MR Oliver—Ny.Y'30
☎ (860) 388-9024 . . Watrous Point, Box 413, Essex, CT *06426*

May DR & MRS (DR) Stuart T 3d (Cain—Amy R Renfro)
Htdon'74.Aub'78.Htdon'68.Tul'72
☎ (334) 272-2689 . . 3132 Fieldcrest Dv, Montgomery, AL *36106*

May MR & MRS William B JR (Wiles—Jeanne C | ☎ (410) 778-4273
Atkinson) K.Fic.Fiy.Dar.Ncd.U'43 . . . . | 25830 Collins Av,
MR William T . . . . | Chestertown, MD
| *21620*

May MR & MRS William F (Kathleen H Thompson)
Wis'47.Roch'37.H'49 ⚓ . . of
☎ (203) 661-2551 . . 35 Lauder Lane, Greenwich, CT *06831*
☎ (207) 236-8157 . . ''Liberty Cottage'' 90 Beauchamp Point Rd,
PO Box 62, Rockport, ME *04856*

Maybank MR Francis P—H'55 . . . . | ☎ (864) 876-3176
MISS Alexis M—at Harvard . . . . | 455 Cheek Rd,
MISS Helena E R—at Charleston . . . . | Gray Court, SC
| *29645*

Maybank MR & MRS John P F (Marina Rancic) SUNY'83.SUNY'83
☎ (213) 935-0359 . . 814 S Sierra Bonita, Los Angeles, CA *90036*

Maycock MR & MRS Joseph F JR (Margaret L Shaw) | ☎ (313) 884-6239
Mich'63.Oakland'88.Ham'52.Mich'55 . . . . | 301 Touraine Rd,
MISS Suzannah S—Ham'91—at | Grosse Pointe, MI
111 Winthrop Rd, Brookline, MA *02146* . . . . . . | *48236*
MISS Mary C—Duke'93—at 407 Wilkes St,
Alexandria, VA *22314* . . . .
MR John F—at Middlebury . . . .

Mayer MR Charles A—Purd'71.Temp'78
☎ (610) 642-4132 . . 602 Love's Lane, Wynnewood, PA *19096*

Mayer MISS Elizabeth L—Rdc'58
☎ (011-33-66) 85-44-19 . . Château de Malerargues, 30140 Thoiras,
Anduze, Gard, France

Mayer MR & MRS Frederick R (Jan MacC Perry)
Ariz'55.Ny.Cho.Yn.Y'50 ⚓
☎ (303) 781-3727 . . 37 Sunset Dv, Englewood, CO *80110*

Mayer DR & MRS George L (Ruth P Page) | ☎ (904) 388-7949
NCar'68.Ark'72 . . . . | 4539 Bass Place S,
MR Stewart R . . . . | Jacksonville, FL
JUNIORS MR Russell P . . . . | *32210*

Mayer MRS John (Helen E Shumway)
☎ (203) 869-4204 . . 264 Taconic Rd, Greenwich, CT *06831*

Mayer MRS John A (Effie F Disston) Rr.
☎ (561) 276-0906 . . 4475 N Ocean Blvd, Apt 7C, Delray Beach,
FL *33483*

Mayer MRS Mary Elizabeth (Mary Elizabeth | ☎ (410) 377-6138
Baetjer) Mid'76.Mid'82.Gv . . . . | 209 Gaywood Rd,
JUNIORS MISS Josephine E . . . . | Baltimore, MD
| *21212*

Mayfield MR & MRS E Scott (Margaret Redfield) Wms'81.Wms'81.Pa'87
☎ (508) 785-2370 . . 166 Pine St, Dover, MA *02030*

Mayfield MR & MRS Glover B (Soule—Gale Smith)
Swth'45.Rol'51.Tufts'52.Ec.H.'50
☎ (617) 259-8927 . . ''Winter Island'' 15 Winter St, Lincoln, MA *01773*

Mayhew MRS Clarence W W (Joan Rapp) Stan'36.Sfy.Tcy.
☎ (415) 492-2518 . . 100 Thorndale Dv, Apt 424, San Rafael, CA *94903*

Mayhew MR & MRS Timothy P JR (Elizabeth J Schecter) Geo'90.Br'90
☎ (212) 873-4296 . . 23 W 68 St, Apt 4, New York, NY *10023*

Maynard DR & MRS Edwin P (Elizabeth S Simonds)
Sth'51.Cy.Chi.Ncd.Wms'49.Cl'53
☎ (617) 277-1676 . . 47 Lawrence Rd, Chestnut Hill, MA *02167*

Maynard MR & MRS John (Penelope Kirton)   ☎ (914) 234-7572
Rc.Fiy.H'62.H'65 . . . .   210 Hook Rd,
MR Geoffrey . . . .   Bedford, NY *10506*
MR Nicholas . . . .

Maynard MRS Walter (Agnew—Billings—Augusta M Poe)
☎ (516) 283-7483 . . PO Box 1502, Southampton, NY *11969*

Maynard MR & MRS Walter JR (Swords—Jane F   ☎ (212) BU5-5766
Henderson) Rc.Mds.Ri.Cly.Cs.H'54.H'58 ⚓ .   19 E 72 St,
MR W Alexander—CtCol'80—at   New York, NY
☎ (516) 324-6570 . . 65 Toylsome Lane,   *10021*
East Hampton, NY *11937* . . . .
     MISS Deirdre H Swords—HRdc'86.HRdc'95—
     at ☎ (718) 388-9536 . . 432 Driggs Av,
     Brooklyn, NY *11211* . . . .

Maynard MISS Wendy G
☎ (617) 242-1205 . . 9A Monument Square, Charlestown, MA *02129*

Mayne MR Leslie S—Camb'24
☎ (415) 492-2526 . . 100 Thorndale Dv, Apt 418, San Rafael, CA *94903*

Mayne MR & MRS Stephen A (Linda Furst)   ☎ (415) 931-0900
Cal'75.Bhm.Br'63.Geo'66 . . . .   2240 Jackson St,
MR Michael . . . .   San Francisco, CA
                                       94118

Mayor MR & MRS André G (Sally K Reichner) . . . .   ☎ (011-41-27)
MISS Patricia A   483-50-00
MISS Adrienne S . . . .   Beau Soleil Est 6-7,
                                       3962 Crans-
                                       Montana, Valais,
                                       Switzerland

Mayosmith MR & MRS Worthington C (Margaret S Collette)
Sth'49.Bgt.Aht'49.H'51
☎ (914) 666-3578 . . 406 Croton Lake Rd, Mt Kisco, NY *10549*

Mead MR & MRS Donald E (Hopkins—Cynthia   ☎ (201) 825-8670
Redmond) Cr'42 . . . .   49 Hillcrest Dv,
     MISS S Antoinette Hopkins—at   Upper Saddle River,
     1249 Beacon St, Waban, MA *02168* . . . .   NJ *07458*
     MISS Jennifer Hopkins—Box 623, Newport,
     VT *05855* . . . .

Mead MR & MRS Frederick G (Helen E Hale) Skd'79
☎ (603) 876-4644 . . "Frost Hill" PO Box 312, Marlborough,
NH *03455*

Mead MR & MRS James G (Maria Martinez) Ub.H.'59
180 Beacon St, Boston, MA *02116*

Mead DR & MRS Lawrence M 3d (Robin E Brady)
V'78.Nu'83.Co.Aht'66.H'72
☎ (212) 475-1070 . . 4 Washington Square Village, Apt 9P, New York,
NY *10012-1906*

Mead MR & MRS Nelson S (Ruth D Cummings) V'51.Mvh.Mor.
☎ (561) 546-2128 . . 216 S Beach Rd, Hobe Sound, FL *33455*

Mead MR & MRS Robert H (Henrietta W Mills) V'76.Yn.Y'54
☎ (860) 824-5002 . . Yale Farm, Norfolk, CT *06058*

Mead MR Whittaker W—Ant'78
5702 Elbon Rd, Waynesville, OH *45068*

Mead MR & MRS William G (Mary-Chilton   of ☎ (718)625-2762
Winslow) Aht'54.Va'60 . . . .   22 Willow St,
MR Malcolm G—Roch'92 . . . .   Brooklyn, NY *11201*
                                       PO Box 176,
                                       Middleville, NJ
                                       07855

Meade MR Everard Kidder JR—BtP.C.An.StJ.Cw.Sar.USA'43
☎ (212) TE8-3632 . . 45 E 62 St, New York, NY *10021*

Meade MRS John P (Nancy M Underhill)   ☎ (914) 666-5405
SL'46.Ayc.Co.P. . . . .   "Ballymartle"
MISS Elizabeth E—SL'83.Ill'86—at Berkeley, CA   703 Croton Lake
MR John P JR—P'74—at Santa Fe, NM . . . . . .   Rd, RFD 4,
MR Andrew M—EmpSt'83—at Brooktondale, NY   Mt Kisco, NY
14817 . . . .   *10549-9693*

Meaders MR & MRS Paul Le Sourd (Jane Dickely)   ☎ (914) 793-6150
Chr.Plg.Vca.Va'52.Tex'57.Nu'61 . . . .   Southgate 6C,
MR Paul Le S 3d—Va'83 . . . .   Bronxville, NY
                                       10708

Meador MR & MRS Daniel J JR (Mary L Bowen) Va'86.Va'87.Va'92
☎ (804) 977-6448 . . "Lilac Cottage" 2227 Owensville Rd,
Charlottesville, VA *22901*

Meadows MR & MRS Bryan G (Donna J Schmidt)
LakeF'65.Barat'84.R'velt'87.LakeF'66
☎ (847) 945-1761 . . 1246 Gordon Terr, Deerfield, IL *60015*

Meadows MR & MRS Curtis W JR (Patricia A Blachly) Tex'60.Tex'62
☎ (214) 871-8984 . . 2707 State St, Dallas, TX *75204*

Meagher MRS Judith H (Judith J Humphreys)   ☎ (214) 349-1419
Ash'70 . . . .   10248 Vistadale Dv,
MR John P 3d . . . .   Dallas, TX *75238*
JUNIORS MR Joseph P . . . .

Means MRS Blanchard W (Louise C Rich) Myf. . . .   ☎ (508) 867-3844
MISS Louise B . . . .   Elm Hill Farm,
                                       24 E Main St,
                                       Brookfield, MA
                                       01506

Means MRS James Howard (Butler—Carol V Lord) Sth'26
☎ (617) 523-3436 . . 60 Mt Vernon St, Boston, MA *02108*

Means MRS Marian D (Marian Donald) . . . .   ☎ (401) 751-2391
MR Graeme D—at Aspen, CO . . . .   Laurelmead 116,
                                       355 Blackstone
                                       Blvd, Providence, RI
                                       02906

Means MR & MRS Robert L (Joan I Braddon) Hn.H'46
☎ (508) 352-6420 . . 410 Andover St, Georgetown, MA *01833*

Means MR & MRS William M 2d (Melinda D Johnson)
Ty'83.Drex'87.Me.Cwr'84.Temp'87
☎ (610) 941-5482 . . 14 Forsythia Court, Lafayette Hill, PA *19444*

Mecaskey MR & MRS Jeffrey W (Marie A Center) H'88.Hampshire'80.H'90
860 Tenth Av, Apt 5R, New York, NY *10019-2920*

Mecaskey MR & MRS Richard G (Cathryn A Wendler) It.Myf.Dar.Ty'51
☎ (216) 795-0082 . . 11428 Cedar Glen P'kway, Apt C1, Cleveland,
OH *44106*

Mecray MR Christopher H . . see E L Ruegg

Mecray MISS Ellen L . . see E L Ruegg

Medearis DR & MRS Donald N JR (Mary Ellen Marble) V'55.Bost'81.Kas'49.H'53 . . . . 3 Seal Harbor Rd, Apt 536, Winthrop, MA *02152-1060*
MISS Jennifer M—H'94—at New York, NY . . . .
MR Donald H—Ch'81.Bost'84—at Los Angeles, CA . . . .

Medearis MR & MRS Roger N (Sterling—Elizabeth L Burrall) Occ'51.Vh.KCAI'41
☎ (818) 281-5834 . . 2270 Melville Dv, San Marino, CA *91108*

Medina MR & MRS Harold R 3d (Pamela C Huck) P.'60. . . . . | ☎ (610) 565-0502 / 12 Hilltop Rd, Wallingford, PA *19086*
MR Scott A—at Boulder, CO . . . . |

Medina MR Standish Forde—P'37.Cl'40 ⚓ . . of
☎ (201) 377-2446 . . 23 Loantaka Lane S, Morristown, NJ *07960*
☎ (516) 288-1655 . . 1 Apaucuck Point Lane, Westhampton, NY *11977*

Medina MR & MRS Standish Forde JR (Kathryn L Bach) Sth'65.Nu'92.C.Cs.P'62.Cl'65.Cl'66 . . of
☎ (212) 831-0897 . . 1105 Park Av, Apt 9A, New York, NY *10128-1236*
☎ (516) 288-3873 . . ''Still To Windward'' Box 210, 5 Apaucuck Point Lane, Westhampton, NY *11977*

Medlin MR & MRS John G JR (Pauline W Sims) NCar'57.Ncd.NCar'56
☎ (910) 724-5023 . . 1056 Kenleigh Circle, Winston-Salem, NC *27106*

Mee MR & MRS John Hubert JR (Sally Cheek) Mls'42.Cal'39 . . . . | ☎ (916) 456-9870 / 1217—46 St, Sacramento, CA *95819*
MISS Catherine—Cal'77—at ☎ (406) 683-6803 PO Box 1396, Dillon, MT *59725* . . . . |
MR John H 3d—at ☎ (916) 455-5778 460 Lovella Way, Sacramento, CA *95819* . . . . . |

Meech MISS Louise B—MooreArt'74
☎ (215) 988-1221 . . The Touraine, PH-03, 1520 Spruce St, Philadelphia, PA *19102*

Meehan MR Alexander D . . see MRS A T Fessenden

Meehan MRS Mary (McNamara—Barbusse—Mary E McClain). . . . . | ☎ (212) 772-6644 / 215 E 72 St, New York, NY *10021*
MR William W McNamara. . . . . |

Meehan MRS Mary Ellen (Driver—Solley—Ely—Sterba—Mary Ellen Meehan) Man'vl'58
☎ (212) 734-5683 . . 980 Fifth Av, New York, NY *10021*

Meehan MR & MRS Michael J 2d (Jenkins—Carr—Sandra Gotham) Stan'70.Stan'71.Rc.B.Ln.Ng.So.Pa'63 . . of
☎ (212) 734-1249 . . 220 E 73 St, Apt 5H, New York, NY *10021*
☎ (516) 283-7585 . . ''Mungo Hall'' 451 Hill St, Southampton, NY *11968*

Meehan MR Michael J 3d . . see MRS A T Fessenden

Meek MR & MRS George H (Cynthia A Martin) Cal'67.Pac'65 . . . . | ☎ (209) 827-4125 / 1621 S 6 St, Los Banos, CA *93635*
MISS Lissa H—at ☎ (702) 869-4599 9105 W Desert Inn Rd, Apt B205, Las Vegas, NV *89114*. . . . . |
MISS Tally A—at ☎ (916) 546-7103 5060 Nevada St, PO Box 704, Carnelian Bay, CA *96140* . . . . |
JUNIORS MR John M—at U of Cal San Diego . . . |

Meek MRS Samuel W (Priscilla Mitchel)
☎ (203) 869-2020 . . 88 Doubling Rd, Greenwich, CT *06830*

Meek MR & MRS Samuel W JR (Dunn—Appleby—Marjorie Meacham) Rcn.Evg.BtP.K.Plg.Sar.StJ.Y'46
☎ (561) 655-0759 . . 11 Via Vizcaya, Palm Beach, FL *33480*

Meek MR & MRS Samuel W 3d (Marguerite A Holgate) Rcn.B.BtP.Rol'77
☎ (208) 622-7930 . . 258 Elkhorn Rd, Sun Valley, ID *83353*

Meeker JUNIORS MISS Alena M . . see MRS M L Fairbanks

Meeker MR & MRS James B (Cynthia B McKay) DU'74.Denis'73
☎ (203) 531-1329 . . 530 W Lyon Farm Dv, Greenwich, CT *06831*

Meeker JUNIORS MISS Jessica C . . see MRS M L Fairbanks

Meeker MR William V—Vh.NotreD'64
☎ (805) 969-0254 . . 368 Lambert Rd, Carpinteria, CA *93013*

Meeks MR Benjamin W JR—JHop'31
☎ (410) 243-5353 . . 830 W 40 St, Apt 660, Baltimore, MD *21211-2126*

Meeks MISS Natalie B (Bryant—Natalie B Meeks) Gchr'63
☎ (703) 979-8564 . . 817 S Monroe St, Arlington, VA *22204*

Meem MR & MRS Gilbert S JR (Knight Patterson) Rol'78.Un.Ct.Sar.Cly.W&L'72. . . . . | of ☎ (212)410-7685 / 170 E 87 St, New York, NY *10128* / ☎ (516) 283-0503 ''Four Walls'' 30 Wall St, Southampton, NY *11968*
JUNIORS MR Gilbert S 3d . . . . |

Meenan MRS Marion M (Marion D Morey) Br'64.Bab'83 . . . . | ☎ (617) 259-0874 / 34 Windingwood Lane, Lincoln, MA *01773*
MISS Loraine L . . . . |

Meers MR & MRS Henry W (Evelyn Huckins) Ln.Cho.On.Sr.Fy.Cda.Ill'30 . . of
☎ (847) 234-5011 . . 550 N Green Bay Rd, Lake Forest, IL *60045*
☎ (561) 546-4474 . . Beach Rd, Box 907, Hobe Sound, FL *33475*

Meers MR & MRS Henry W JR (M Cecilia Barnett) Miami'73.LakeF'73 . . . . | ☎ (815) 469-5741 / 20500 S 84 Av, Frankfort, IL *60423*
JUNIORS MR Henry W 3d . . . . |

Megear MRS Bayard H (Winifred M Wadbrook) Pr.Cly.
☎ (516) 626-0453 . . 29 Meadowood Lane, Glen Head, NY *11545*

Megear MR & MRS Thomas J (Sally A Hill) NH'74.Rcn.Pr.San.Pa'72
see Dilatory Domiciles

Megowen MR & MRS William J (Alicia Barbour) NH'78.Mich'80.Mich'84.Myf.Ripon'78
☎ (508) 369-2795 . . 244 Independence Rd, Concord, MA *01742*

Mehegan MR Eben J—Ham'92
☎ (203) 221-0843 . . 1 Weathervane Hill, Westport, CT *06880*

Mehegan MRS Gay (Gay Griscom) . . . . Died Dec 19'95

Mehlman DR & MRS Robert D (Mary A Caner) Rdc'53.Cy.Ec.Btn.H.'52
☎ (617) 566-8185 . . 20 Netherlands Rd, Brookline, MA *02146*

Mehran MR Alexander R—Bur.Pcu.Sfg.H'72 . . of
☎ (415) 386-0600 . . 3680 Jackson St, San Francisco, CA *94118*
☎ (707) 944-9000 . . ''Nonesuch Place'' 1380 Walnut Dv, Oakville, CA *94562*

Mehran JUNIORS MR Alexander R JR . . see MISS L B Watson

Mehran MISS Annabel M . . see MISS L B Watson

Mehrtens LT COL (RET) & MRS Donald J (Vroom—Joan Dunstan) Dar.USA'43.Cr'48
☎ (915) 562-6225 . . 2435 McKinley Av, Apt 63, El Paso, TX *79930*

Mehta MR & MRS Ved P (Linn F C Cary)
Y.'77.Ox'79.C.Cly.Pom'56.Ox'59.H'61 ⚓
☎ (212) 737-7487 . . 139 E 79 St, New York, NY *10021*

Mehurin MRS Chester Arthur (Evelyn M Grace)
☎ (504) 899-4168 . . 1524 Third St, New Orleans, LA *70130*

Meier MRS Duncan I JR (Marie P Ball)
☎ (314) 256-7788 . . 1131 Jo Carr Dv, Town & Country,
MO *63017-8401*

Meier CAPT & MRS Louis L (DONNA Eleanora
Tomacelli-Filomarino) Mt.Cvc.Ny.USN'42.
Geo'51 . . . . | of ☎ (301)495-4851
MISS Catherine F—at 349 E 49 St, New York, | 5132 Baltan Rd,
NY *10017*. . . . . | Bethesda, MD
MISS Marina P—☎ (301) 229-2367 . . . . | *20816*
| ☎ (212) 486-6765
| 10 Mitchell Place,
| New York, NY
| *10017*

Meier MR & MRS Roger S (Laura Schwartz) Hlns'49.Y'50
☎ (503) 222-5329 . . 2011 SW Carter Lane, Portland, OR *97201*

Meigs CAPT & MRS Charles H (Keel—Irwin—Frances K Bradford)
Fw.USN'37.Mit'43
☎ (617) 271-0820 . . 79 Essex Court, Bedford, MA *01730-1270*

Meigs MR & MRS Henry (Sara L Willis) | ☎ (502) 895-2930
SL'44.Sl.Ky'49 . . . . | 2811 Rainbow Dv,
MR John B Averell. | Louisville, KY
| *40206*

Meigs MRS Hildreth (Elizabeth Cuendet) Cyb.Ncd. . | ☎ (603) 431-6973
MISS Martha—at ☎ (603) 431-3959 | 245 Washington Rd,
12 Stonecroft, Lang Rd, Portsmouth, NH *03801* | Rye, NH *03870*

Meigs DR & MRS J Wister (Camilla K Riggs) P'36.H'40
☎ (203) 488-8000 . . Brewster 272, 88 Notch Hill Rd, North Branford,
CT *06471*

Meigs DR & MRS James B (Julia M Talcott) Wms'80.Wms'81.H'89
☎ (617) 630-0377 . . 74 Elmhurst Rd, Newton, MA *02158*

Meigs MR & MRS John Forsyth 2d (Walsh—Faith C | ☎ (215) 247-3837
Watson) Pa'87.Pc.Ph.Y'64 . . . . | 6 Norman Lane,
MISS Oona H Walsh. . . . . | Philadelphia, PA
| *19118*

Meigs MR John V
☎ (508) 468-5236 . . 304 Old Country Rd, Wenham, MA *01984*

Meigs MR & MRS S Willis (Deborah R Wyatt) | ☎ (804) 740-0393
VaCmth'76.Trans'73.W&M'76 . . . . | 405 Wishart Court,
JUNIORS MISS Lauren W—at Richmond Collegiate | Richmond, VA
| *23229*

Meigs MISS Wendy L—Bradford'75
☎ (508) 740-1096 . . 21 Wisteria St, Salem, MA *01970*

Meihuizen MR Nicolaas J van
☎ (212) MU9-8139 . . 30 Waterside Plaza, New York, NY *10010*

Mein MR Robert Nickel . . . . Died at
Woodside, CA Jan 17'96

Mein MR William W—Pcu.Bur.Ri.H'32
☎ (415) 851-1834 . . 1308 Canada Rd, Woodside, CA *94062*

Meinfelder MR & MRS Edmond L 2d (Anderson— | of ☎ (610)933-3597
Edith S Blake) Eyc.Rd.Madrid'63 . . . . | "Gunncroft"
MISS Elizabeth S Anderson—Ty'95.Eyc.—at | PO Box 61,
☎ (617) 367-1286 . . 2 Brimmer St, Apt B, | Kimberton, PA
Boston, MA *02108* . . . . | *19442*
| "The Crow's Nest"
| Barrio Florida,
| PO Box 1521,
| Vieques,
| Puerto Rico *00765*

Meinfelder MR Edmond L 3d . . see MRS B L Wheat

Meinfelder MR Jason J . . see MRS B L Wheat

Mejia MR Arthur—Pcu.Bhm.Stan'56
☎ (415) WA2-0727 . . 2105 Bush St, San Francisco, CA *94115-3103*

Mejia MRS Edwin J (Elise Harbaugh) Sfg.
☎ (415) 771-0648 . . 1042 Chestnut St, San Francisco, CA *94109*

Mejia-Hernandez MR & MRS Alberto (Taliaferro— | of ☎ (212)751-0233
Margaret C Hooker) Ri.B.Pr.Myf.P.'69.Pa'72 . . | 435 E 52 St,
JUNIORS MR Alexander H . . . . | New York, NY
| *10022*
| ☎ (516) 626-0678
| Friendly Rd,
| Upper Brookville,
| NY *11771*

Melano MRS Mario (Maria d'Antona) Bnd'33.Cs. . . | ☎ (212) 722-6628
MR Fabrizio—Cl'58—at 159 W 74 St, | 1175 Park Av,
New York, NY *10023* . . . . | New York, NY
| *10128*

Melby MR & MRS Charles B (Meta C Dunning) Ncd.Wis'42.H'48 . . of
☎ (630) 323-5075 . . 152 Easton Place, Burr Ridge, IL *60521-6480*
☎ (602) 488-1300 . . "The Boulders at Carefree" PO Box 2782,
Carefree, AZ *85377-2782*

Melby MR M Schuyler
☎ (602) 990-7044 . . 4032 N Parkway Av, Scottsdale, AZ *85251*

Melby MR & MRS Scott E (Louise A Root)
Pa'77.Pa'78.Rcp.Pc.Hob'77.Cr'81
☎ (301) 770-2372 . . 6106 Tilden Lane, North Bethesda, MD *20852*

Melcher MISS Pamela
☎ (207) 276-3340 . . "The Yellow House" Rockend Rd,
Northeast Harbor, ME *04662*

Melcher MRS Ursula W (de Fontaines de Logères—Ursula W Melcher)
☎ (011-33) 31-92-69-41 . . Ferme de La Chauleuse, Le Jardin du
Pressoir, 14400 Subles, France

Melcher MRS William Cramp (Clarissa Smythe)
☎ (215) 482-7625 . . Cathedral Village H402, 600 E Cathedral Rd,
Philadelphia, PA *19128*

Meldrum MR & MRS Donald N (E Florianne Greer) Wcc.Hav'47
☎ (610) NI4-9210 . . 6 Shepherd Rd, Malvern, PA *19355*

Mele MR & MRS Joseph F (Butler—M Victoria | ☎ (301) 656-2323
Leiter) Cvc.Srb.Dyc.Wag'71 . . . . | 40 Grafton St,
JUNIORS MR Nicholas L . . . . | Chevy Chase, MD
MR Desmond O Butler. . . . . | *20815*
MR Tyssen W Butler . . . .

Melen DR & MRS Roger D (Williams—Arlene H Camm) Stan'73.Stan'74.Stan'78.Stan'71 . . . . . . | ☎ (415) 941-5546 12992 Vista Del Valle Court, Los Altos Hills, CA 94022
    JUNIORS MISS Michelle A. . . . .
      JUNIORS MR Samuel A F Williams—Box 4051, Stanford, CA 94305
      JUNIORS MR Nicholas C Williams . . . .

Melhado MR & MRS Frederick A (Tydings—White—Virginia Campbell) Rc.K.Ng.Elk.Y'51.Cl'53
    ☎ (212) 288-8758 . . 720 Park Av, New York, NY 10021

Melhado MR & MRS William A (Trask—Barbara J Burch) Mid'59.Y'51
    ☎ (802) 867-5370 . . Box 507, Cheney Rd, Dorset, VT 05251

Mellen MISS Abigail (Rothschild—Abigail Mellen)
    ☎ (212) 982-5289 . . 44 Gramercy Park, New York, NY 10010

Mellen MR de Forest
    ☎ (415) 467-8689 . . 1485 Bayshore Blvd, San Francisco, CA 94124-3002

Mellen MR & MRS Henry L 3d (Mary C Phelps) Aub'69.Aub'71 . . . . | ☎ (205) 871-2261 24 Country Club Rd, Birmingham, AL 35213
    MISS Katherine S . . . .
    JUNIORS MISS Mary R . . . .

Mellen MR & MRS Henry W (Bell—Harriette B Allen) Cc.
    ☎ (860) 927-3164 . . 52 Treasure Hill Rd, South Kent, CT 06785

Mellen MRS Loudon (Constance Loudon) Csn.
    ☎ (202) 338-8916 . . 2911 O St NW, Washington, DC 20007

Mellgard MR & MRS David M (Georgiana J Slade) Duke'82.H'85.Ri.Mds.Cly.Colg'81.Duke'84
    ☎ (212) 755-1663 . . 417 Park Av, New York, NY 10022

Mellick MR R Drew JR . . . . | ☎ (908) 534-5076 36 Hunter's Glen, Box 106, Oldwick, NJ 08858
    MISS Helen H—Box 9121, Aspen, CO 81611 . . .

Mellon MR & MRS Armour N (Sophie C Annibali) StL'87.Rr.Pg.LakeF'88
    ☎ (412) 682-5707 . . 201 Gladstone Rd, Pittsburgh, PA 15217

Mellon MRS Charles H 3d (Katherine P Hopkins) . . | ☎ (908) 234-1850 340 Larger Cross Rd, Box 487, Far Hills, NJ 07931
    MR Charles H JR . . . .

Mellon MRS Gertrud A (Gertrud M F Altegoer)
    ☎ (212) 734-0578 . . 1035 Fifth Av, New York, NY 10028

Mellon MR Henry C S—DelB.HWSth'90 ⚓
    ☎ (561) 265-3749 . . 4 Driftwood Landing, Gulf Stream, FL 33483

Mellon MRS Marian Carroll (Derrickson—M Carroll Mellon) . . . . | ☎ (941) 774-6919 186 Harrison Rd, Naples, FL 34112
    MR Edward M Derrickson—Ithaca'80—at
    ☎ (305) 530-3780 . . 100 Sun Rise Dv, Key Biscayne, FL 33149 . . . .

Mellon MR Matthew T . . see J R Bright

Mellon MR & MRS Paul (Lloyd—Rachel Lambert) Rcn.Ln.Ri.Gr.K.Mt.Cly.Y'29.Camb'31
    "Oak Spring" 8554 Oak Spring Rd, Upperville, VA 20185

Mellon MR & MRS Seward P (Stout—Sandra J Springer) Rr.Susq'65 . . . . | Huntland Downs, Box K, Ligonier, PA 15658
    MISS Catharine L—at 59 W 70 St, New York, NY 10023 . . . .
    MISS Constance E—at 1120D John St, Charlottesville, VA 22903 . . . .

Mellor MR Douglas W—Roan'69
    ☎ (610) 527-9040 . . 1020 Mt Pleasant Rd, Bryn Mawr, PA 19010

Mellor MRS Mary-Audrey W (Mary-Audrey Weicker) Adelphi'74.Cly. . . . . | ☎ (602) 423-0810 6711 E Camelback Rd, Scottsdale, AZ 85251
    MISS Jennifer S—at 11670 Sunset Blvd, Apt 208, Los Angeles, CA 90049 . . . .
    MR Andrew W—at U of Ariz . . . .

Melly MR & MRS L Thomas (Alice G Pack) V'56.Hob'52 . . . . | ☎ (203) 869-2023 25 Meadowcroft Lane, Greenwich, CT 06830
    MISS Laura A—at 320 Spencer, Devon, PA 19333
    MR David R—at 1021 Broadway, 225, San Pablo, CA 94804 . . . .

Melone MR & MRS Drury (Mary F Temple) Cal'30
    ☎ (808) 621-6777 . . 103 Nakeke Place, Wahiawa, HI 96786

Melone MR & MRS Jonathan (Margaret D Salm) Cal'70.SCal'76
    ☎ (209) 957-5329 . . 2162 Piccardo Circle, Stockton, CA 95207

Melone MR & MRS Robert Woodward (Uta M E Burstenbinder) WWilhelms'91.SanJ'76
    ☎ (415) 892-2762 . . 100 Deer Trail, Novato, CA 94947

Melone MR & MRS Woodward (Joy Peskay) Stan'33
    ☎ (415) 892-2762 . . 100 Deer Trail, Novato, CA 94947

Melville MRS Charlotte L (Charlotte S Landreth) . . . | ☎ (215) 788-8008 6308 Radcliffe St, Bristol, PA 19007
    MISS Ann S—at Jakarta, Selatan 12160, Indonesia
    MISS Linda L—at ☎ (412) 421-4964 344 Connor St, Pittsburgh, PA 15207 . . . .

Melville MR & MRS John A (Lee A Deters) NKy'83.Duke'69.Xav'78
    ☎ (606) 341-1426 . . 232 Edgewood Rd, Ft Mitchell, KY 41011

Melville MR & MRS John W (Jane Akin) Cin'32.Cin'35
    ☎ (513) 821-3070 . . 3113 Evergreen Ridge Dv, Cincinnati, OH 45215

Melvin MRS Mary M (Mary A Morrow) . . . . | ☎ (410) 268-1811 989 Melvin Rd, Annapolis, MD 21403
    MISS Elizabeth P—at ☎ (410) 974-8223 1001 Melvin Rd, Annapolis, MD 21403 . . . .
    MR John B JR—at 4941 September St, San Diego, CA 92110 . . . .

Melvin MR & MRS Norman C (Virginia B Lester) JHop'53.Sar.Cw.Dar.JHop'39.H'42
    ☎ (410) 467-2108 . . 4202 Wickford Rd, Baltimore, MD 21210

Mendle MRS Milton C (Roberta W Pierce) Dar.
    ☎ (314) 872-7962 . . 1 McKnight Place, Apt 120, St Louis, MO 63124

Meneely MRS George R (Van der Leur—M Leslie Stewart) Cos. . . . . | ☎ (816) 322-2420 1500 W Foxwood Dv, 117B, Raymore, MO 64083
    MISS Suzanne Van der Leur—at
    ☎ (816) 966-0978 . . PO Box 9609, Kansas City, MO 64134-0609 . . . .

Menefee MR & MRS John C (Jane K Torney) UWash'84.UWash'82 2187 SW Kings Court, Portland, OR 97205-1119

Meneghin MR & MRS Brian C (Julia I Mathews) DeP'83.SUNY'85
    ☎ (303) 393-6048 . . 1640 Dahlia St, Denver, CO 80220

Menendez MRS Lydia S (Lydia L Saltus) Sth'62 . . . | ☎ (561) 625-1406 2368 Flamingo Rd, Palm Beach Gardens, FL 33410
    JUNIORS MISS Lydia L
    JUNIORS MISS Melanie . . . .

Menges MR & MRS Carl B (Cordelia Sykes) V'60.Un.Mds.Ng.Cly.Ham'51.H'53 . . . . | ☎ (212) 472-2299 215 E 72 St, New York, NY 10021
    MR Benjamin W . . . .
    MR Samuel G . . . .

Menges MR & MRS James C (Devon M Smith) Mds.NEng'93
325 E 72 St, New York, NY *10021*

Menken MR & MRS Kenneth A (Joan H Buck)
An.Un.Mds.Rv.Ne.Cly.Ncd.Duke'52.Pa'56
☎ (212) 288-8063 . . 111 E 80 St, New York, NY *10021*

Menocal MR & MRS Alberto V (Joan E Hallanger) | ☎ (215) 242-2133
Luther'68.PaArt'51 . . . . | 7147 Ardleigh St,
MISS Carmen E—Bnd'96 . . . . | Philadelphia, PA
MR Alexis C—at Wash'n U . . . . | *19119-1211*

Menocal MR & MRS Enrique V (Rosa E Delmás) Havana'50
☎ (610) 688-2934 . . 23 Fariston Rd, Wayne, PA *19087-3414*

Mentz MR George F M JR—Va'55
☎ (757) 481-6542 . . 2105 Cricket Court, Virginia Beach,
VA *23454-2805*

Menzies MR John T 3d (John T JR) . . . . Married at Owings, MD
Ware MISS Penelope (Peter) . . . . Sep 23'95

Menzies MRS Julia B (Julia M Baker) Tufts'69.Md. | 926 Fell St,
MISS Mary C . . . . | Baltimore, MD
MR John B . . . . | *21231*

Mercer MR & MRS Douglas (Pauline L Tobey) V'42.Cy.H'40
☎ (617) 893-6902 . . 115 Chestnut St, Weston, MA *02193-1504*

Mercer MISS Kathryn B—Briar'70.MFArts'73
☎ (561) 231-3821 . . 1100 Beach Rd, Apt 3K, John's Island,
Vero Beach, FL *32963*

Mercer MR & MRS Richard D (Nancy C Brown) | ☎ (561) 231-7803
Rr.P'49 . . . . | 1100 Beach Rd, Apt
MISS Laura S—at ☎ (714) 494-9630 | 3K, John's Island,
1285A Roosevelt Lane, Laguna Beach, CA *92651* | Vero Beach, FL
| *32963*

Mercer MR Richard D JR—Pitt'81
☎ (412) 682-0399 . . 5532 Claybourne St, Pittsburgh, PA *15232*

Mercer MR & MRS Richard J (O'Connor—Harriet A Jopson)
Roan'64.ODom'72.W&M'75.Bost'77.Bost'86
☎ (508) 785-1831 . . 2 Oak Circle, Dover, MA *02030*

Merck MR & MRS Albert W (Katharine M Evarts) Mo.Eh.Shcc.Csn.Hn.H'43
☎ (201) 543-4694 . . "Turtle Hill" 26 Corey Lane, Mendham, NJ *07945*

Merck MR & MRS Albert W JR (Margaret E Warnecke) Stan'75.Cl'89
☎ (212) 393-9773 . . 57 Warren St, New York, NY *10007*

Merck MR & MRS Antony M (Julia P Hazzard) | of ☎ (803)577-7440
K.Va'66 . . . . | 16 Legare St,
JUNIORS MISS Elizabeth M . . . . | Charleston, SC
| *29401*
| ☎ (803) 844-2753
| Paul & Dalton
| Plantation,
| Green Pond, SC
| *29446*

Merck MR & MRS George F (Adele W Shook)
☎ (561) 848-2123 . . 244 Palmo Way, Palm Beach, FL *33480*

Merck MRS George Wall (Elizabeth A Mead)
☎ (908) 234-1167 . . "The Fields" Box 35, Bedminster, NJ *07921*

Meredith MR William Morris—C.P'40
see Dilatory Domiciles

Merkley MAJ & MRS Bart N (Patricia T Vincent) | ☎ (703) 335-9528
USA.BrigY'75.BrigY'91.BrigY'76.Utah'86 . . . . | 9638 Shannon Lane,
JUNIORS MISS Andrea J . . . . | Manassas, VA
JUNIORS MISS Deamond L . . . . | *20112*

Merle MRS Leo V (Tuttle—Clotilde A Fargo)
☎ (415) 567-1181 . . 2275 Broadway, Apt 104, San Francisco, CA *94115*

Merle MR Michael V—SFrColl'68
☎ (707) 935-9095 . . 18700 Melvin Av, Sonoma, CA *95476*

Merle MR Thomas O V—Geo'65.Ch'74
☎ (415) 392-5656 . . 30 Miller Place, San Francisco, CA *94108*

Merle-Smith REV & MRS Van Santvoord JR (Combs—Katherine P N Smith)
MdArt'42.Au.P'40.Cl'50.UnTheo'64
☎ (610) 691-1202 . . 51 Wall St, Bethlehem, PA *18018*

Merna MR Thomas F JR—Mass'77.Tufts'79
☎ (617) 934-2275 . . 569 Washington St, Box 265 SHS, Duxbury,
MA *02331*

Merow MR & MRS John E (Mary Alyce Smith)
Sth'54.Un.Ln.Pr.Mto.Chr.Plg.StJ.Cly.Cs.Mich'52. H'58 . . of
☎ (212) RE7-8197 . . 350 E 69 St, New York, NY *10021*
☎ (516) 626-0357 . . 51 Fruitledge Rd, Brookville, NY *11545*

Merrell MR & MRS Cyrus W JR (Clark—Ewald—Katharina deF Möller)
Paris'59.Va'51
☎ (406) 642-3073 . . Duck Creek Ranch, PO Box 818, Victor,
MT *59875*

Merrell MR & MRS Stanley W 2d (L Lynn Stuart) P.'51.H'57
☎ (716) 385-4462 . . 3437 Elmwood Av, Rochester, NY *14610*

Merrell MR & MRS Stanley W 3d (Lynne S Stamp) Ken'80
☎ (716) 482-5409 . . 524 Humboldt St, Rochester, NY *14610*

Merriam MISS Priscilla A F . . see MRS C F Kimball

Merriam JUNIORS MR Scott R K . . see MRS C F Kimball

Merriam MR William R—Cvc.Mt.Leh'34
☎ (202) 338-7756 . . 2512 Q St NW, Washington, DC *20007*

Merrick MRS Edward S (Beatrice E Bolton) Cwr'32.May.
☎ (216) 321-0896 . . 2514 Wellington Rd, Cleveland, OH *44118*

Merrick MRS John (Friend—Kenworthey—Jessica W Holton)
☎ (561) 272-9036 . . 401 E Linton Blvd, Apt 524, Delray Beach,
FL *33483*

Merrifield MR & MRS D Bruce (Paula D Sorensen)
Cos.Chr.G.P'42.Ch'48.Ch'50
☎ (202) 223-6518 . . 1316 New Hampshire Av NW, Apt 701,
Washington, DC *20036*

Merrill MISS Anne Stewart (George V) . . . . Born at
New York, NY Jun 5'96

Merrill MR Arthur C—Rc.Pr.H'45
☎ (516) 676-9166 . . 11 Valley Rd, Locust Valley, NY *11560*

Merrill MR & MRS Arthur C JR (Monique J Vos)
Mich'82.Rc.Bcs.B.So.Ng.Pr.Ford'77 . . of
☎ (516) 626-1725 . . 1892 Muttontown Rd, Muttontown, NY *11791*
☎ (516) 283-0805 . . 2 Whitefields, 155 Hill St, Southampton,
NY *11968*

Merrill MR & MRS Barrant V (Martha E Page) | of ☎ (561)276-5954
Unn.Why.Msq.Yh.Cr'53 . . . . | 3525 Polo Dv,
MISS Elizabeth M—at ☎ (212) 772-8737 | Gulf Stream, FL
156 E 79 St, New York, NY *10021* . . . . | *33483*
MR William D—at ☎ (212) 772-8737 | ☎ (401) 348-3036
156 E 79 St, New York, NY *10021* . . . . | "Crows Nest"
| 11 Nepun Rd,
| Watch Hill, RI
| *02891*

Merrill MRS C McCormick (Christina D McCormick)
☎ (415) 563-2724 . . 2724 Lyon St, San Francisco, CA *94123*

Merrill MR & MRS George V (Janice A Humes)
MtH'77.Mid'78.Rcn.Unn.Sm.B.Fw.Plg.Cly.H'68.H'72. Cl'74
☎ (305) 740-9076 . . 4011 Granada Blvd, Coral Gables, FL *33146*

Merrill MRS J Barba (Joan S Barba) Wheat'75 . . . . | 120 Old Short Hills
JUNIORS MR Andrew V—at Hotchkiss . . . . | Rd, Short Hills, NJ
JUNIORS MR Scott J—at Westminster . . . . | *07078*

Merrill MISS Jane M—Tcy.
☎ (011-44-171) 589-3652 . . 7 Onslow Gardens, London SW7 3LY,
England

Merrill MRS Janet S (Janet B Sawyer) . . . . | 34 Londonderry Rd,
JUNIORS MISS Dorothy I . . . . | Grafton, MA *01519*
JUNIORS MR John L 4th . . . . |

Merrill MR & MRS John L JR (Helen B R Swan) D.Chi.Ncd.H'50 . . of
☎ (617) 329-3369 . . 151A Grove St, Westwood, MA *02090*
Seabrook Island, SC *29455*

Merrill MRS John Lenord (Josephine S Logan)
☎ (207) 967-4724 . . ''High Seas'' Sea Rd, Kennebunk Beach,
ME *04043*

Merrill MR & MRS John O (Elizabeth A Martin) | ☎ (415) 435-3658
Sfy.Fmy.Mit'49 . . . . | 2514 Mar East St,
JUNIORS MISS Ross E M . . . . | Tiburon, CA *94920*

Merrill MR & MRS Joseph A JR (Ann S Gregory) | ☎ (847) 362-4261
BMr'47.Nw'51.Myf.Ht.Ofp.Rv.Sar.Cw.Dar.Ncd. | 1409 Victory Dv,
MR Joseph A 3d . . . . | Box 186,
MISS Janet G (Staszak—Janet G Merrill) . . . . . . | Libertyville, IL
 | *60048*

Merrill MISS Mary D—Man'vl'48.Pa'51.Ncd.
☎ (207) 284-7938 . . River Bend Farm, 184 Simpson Rd, Saco,
ME *04072*

Merrill MR & MRS Nathaniel S (Sally A MacIntyre) | of ☎ (617)326-9024
Ober'54.Hav'55 . . . . | 23 Willow St,
MR Stuart M . . . . | Westwood, MA
MR Douglas S . . . . | *02090*
 | ☎ (207) 236-8840
 | Rockbrook Dv,
 | Camden, ME *04843*

Merrill MR & MRS Peter K (Harriette A Mauran) Mid'83.Ey.Ncd.Mid'83
☎ (617) 631-2661 . . 16 Washington Square, Marblehead, MA *01945*

Merrill MR Randolph S JR . . . . Died at
Boca Raton, FL Apr 5'96

Merrill MRS Randolph S JR (Anne A Barnett) Ncd. . | ☎ (561) 392-2360
MR R Searing 3d—at ☎ (813) 831-5136 | 1717 Sabal Palm
4002 Barcelona St, Tampa, FL *33629* . . . . | Dv, Boca Raton, FL
MR William R B . . . . | *33432*

Merrill MR & MRS Robert A (Christina O Bushkin) Drew'88.Pr.H'81
☎ (212) 593-4281 . . 435 E 52 St, New York, NY *10022*

Merrill MR & MRS Robert G (Vernon Lynch) Pr.Cly.H'47
☎ (516) 671-2811 . . 17 Cherrywood Rd, Locust Valley, NY *11560*

Merrill MR & MRS Steven L (Judy P Stewart) | ☎ (415) 666-3762
L&C'73.Bhm.Bur.B.Pcu.Stan'64 . . . . | 13 Presidio Terr,
JUNIORS MR John S . . . . | San Francisco, CA
 | *94118*

Merrill DR Thomas S—Col'58.Hawaii'78.Tex'81 . . | ☎ (808) 949-3300
MISS Kirsten E . . . . | 1441 Kapiolani
MISS Kimberly A . . . . | Blvd, Apt 909,
 | Honolulu, HI *96814*

Merrill MR & MRS William B 2d (Cynthia W | of ☎ (847)735-8252
Buescher) DU'70 . . . . | ''The Club House''
JUNIORS MISS Jessie M . . . . | 1036 Estate Lane,
 | Lake Forest, IL
 | *60045*
 | ☎ (603) 447-8457
 | Merrill Farm,
 | Mill St,
 | Center Conway, NH
 | *03813*

Merrill DR & MRS William Dickey (Martin—Evelyn G Selfridge)
V'26.Cal'30.H'32.Hawaii'57.Edin'74
☎ (408) 624-1281 . . 8545 Carmel Valley Rd, Carmel, CA *93923*

Merrill MR & MRS Charles H JR (Alice Searcy) RMWmn'26
☎ (804) 295-9568 . . 6 Ivy Lane, Farmington, Charlottesville, VA *22901*

Merrill MR Charles H 3d—Rcn.Va'56
☎ (804) 285-3729 . . 5507 Cary Street Rd, Richmond, VA *23226*

Merriman MR & MRS David W (Virginia Anderson) | of ☎ (011-44-171)
Finch'71.Rcn.Ri.Pa'63.Pa'66 . . . . | 373-6424
MISS Serena A . . . . | 3 Tregunter Rd,
JUNIORS MR Charles A . . . . | London SW10 9LS,
 | England
 | ☎ (401) 635-8579
 | ''Sealands''
 | 82 Warren's Point
 | Rd, Little Compton,
 | RI *02837*

Merriman MR & MRS John C (Laura L Balboni) StMarys'78.Ariz'78
86 Beach St, Bloomfield, NJ *07003*

Merriman MRS M Heminway (Natalie-Smith Rowbottom) . . . . Died at
Waterbury, CT May 1'96

Merriman MR & MRS M Heminway 2d (Linda J | ☎ (860) 274-5228
Lane) NewHaven'72 . . . . | 57 Academy Hill,
MISS Hillary C . . . . | Watertown, CT
MR M Heminway 3d . . . . | *06795*

Merriman MISS Natalie-Smith—Cda.
☎ (860) 274-1807 . . ''Overlea'' 212 Woodruff Av, Watertown,
CT *06795*

Merriman MR & MRS Richardson T (Pamela | ☎ (610) 688-3460
Beardsley) U'75.Me.Ac.Ncd.Rol'71.Nu'75 . . . . | 288 Upper Gulph
JUNIORS MR Edward W . . . . | Rd, Radnor, PA
JUNIORS MR Peter H . . . . | *19087*

Merritt MR & MRS Christopher J (Katherine L Meyer) CtCol'87.SUNY'86
☎ (516) 364-2404 . . 36 Crestwood St, Syosset, NY *11791*

Merritt MR & MRS Henry F (Hamilton—Jane La Rowe) Ny.Pn.P'48
''Garuda'' RD 1, West Redding, CT *06896*

Merritt CAPT (RET) Robert G—An.Rv.Ny.USN'39
☎ (301) 530-6267 . . 10101 Grosvenor Place, Apt 1216, Rockville,
MD *20852*

Merryman MR & MRS Adrian H (Moylan—Joan M Corrigan)
☎ (410) VA3-8998 . . ''Briar Patch'' Box 26, Falls Rd, Brooklandville,
MD *21022*

Merryman LT COL & MRS L James (Andrea F Tallmadge)
USA.Rol'81.JHop'89.Ark'73.SCal'79.Col'81
☎ (703) 548-5269 . . 304 Kentucky Av, Alexandria, VA *22305*

Merryman MR & MRS Nicholas B (of J) (Nell A Williams) Mv.Md'35 . . of
☎ (410) 343-0085 . . Clover Hill Farm, 19635 Eagle Mill Rd, Parkton, MD *21120*
Mariner Village, Tarpon Springs, FL *33589*

Merryman MR & MRS Nicholas B 3d (Virginia E M Thompson) Ncd.
☎ (410) 885-5260 . . Herring Creek Farm, 2 Shady Dv, Chesapeake City, MD *21915*

Merryman LT COL & MRS Pitt McL (Elizabeth K Keating) Bost'80.USAF'78
☎ (505) 437-8830 . . 2316 Cherry Hills Dv, Alamogordo, NM *88310*

Merwin MR Davis U—H'50 . . . . | ☎ (520) 455-5692
MISS Laura H—at ☎ (309) 829-2871 | PO Box 546,
PO Box 8, Bloomington, IL *61702* . . . . | Sonoita, AZ *85637*

Merwin MISS Delight—NewHaven'73.Fairf'85.Ht.
☎ (203) 255-0126 . . 439 Beach Rd, Fairfield, CT *06430*

Merwin MR & MRS John D (Spaulding—Marjorie A Davis) Cos.Yn.Y'43.GeoW'48
☎ (603) 823-7171 . . "Foxwood" Ridge Rd, PO Box 778, Franconia, NH *03580*

Merwin MRS S Newbury (Sylvia Newbury) Sth'49.Ncd.
☎ (203) 869-0544 . . 1 Putnam Hill, Greenwich, CT *06830*

Meserve MRS F Leighton (Kathleen Kelloggo) Csn.Cda.Myf.
☎ (561) 231-9194 . . 300 Harbour Dv, Apt 102B, Vero Beach, FL *32963*

Meserve MR & MRS Frederick L JR (Patricia A | ☎ (610) 869-4194
Boyce) Wil.Unn.P'60.Cl'62 . . . . | 551 West Street Rd,
JUNIORS MR Andrew E | Kennett Square, PA *19348*

Mesker MR & MRS David W (Susan C Priest) | ☎ (314) 991-0195
V'58.Cy.Rc.Aht'53 . . . . | 5 Fair Oaks,
MISS Elizabeth A—Wheat'83—at | St Louis, MO *63124*
☎ (212) 861-4454 . . 220 E 73 St, New York, NY *10021* . . . .
MR David W JR . . . .

Mesnard DR & MRS (DR) William J (Ann W Lucas) Reed'70.Pa'75.Au.Cly.Ncd.Va'77.Va'82
☎ (908) 439-2824 . . 13 Dinnerpot Rd, Califon, NJ *07830*

Messenger MRS Robert W (Jones—Josephine C Cochrane) Vil Vue 31, Box 767, Park St Ext, Moravia, NY *13118*

Messimer MRS W Gilbert (Juliet W Harrison) Cal'35 . . of
☎ (914) 677-5218 . . Millbrook Meadows 211, 560 Flint Rd, Millbrook, NY *12545-6413*
☎ (802) 375-9716 . . "Tory Lane" PO Box 556, Arlington, VT *05250*

Messiqua MRS Gail P (McKinney—N Gail Price) | ☎ (011-33-1)
SL'61 . . . . | 45-27-12-70
MISS Alice L—Ty'94—at U of Perugia Italy . . . | 100 av Paul
MISS Diane N—at Brown . . . . | Doumer,
| 75116 Paris, France

Mestres MR & MRS Anthony G (Sarah B Ingersoll) Dick'92.Dick'92
☎ (206) 324-6918 . . 2428 E Calhoun St, Seattle, WA *98112*

Mestres MR & MRS Ricardo A JR (Ann Farnsworth) Ln.Cs.P'55.H'61
☎ (212) 628-2721 . . 133 E 80 St, New York, NY *10021*

Met DR & MRS Philippe C F (Katherine D Robbins) Dom'82.Paris'86.Cal'94
☎ (610) 524-8166 . . 440 S Saddlebrook Circle, Chester Springs, PA *19425*

Metcalf MISS Amelia Marie (Stephen C) . . . . Born at Boston, MA Aug 23'95

Metcalf MISS Barbara E (Heydt—Barbara E | ☎ (419) 882-0978
Metcalf) Tol'82.Mich'83 . . . . | 6031 Barkwood
JUNIORS MR Charles E Heydt . . . . | Lane, Sylvania, OH *43560*

Metcalf MR & MRS John Brockway (Elizabeth C Scott) Wes'80.Cal'82.Cal'81.SFrSt'84
14005 SW Tooze Rd, Sherwood, OR *97140*

Metcalf MR & MRS John R (Catherine J Rolph) Pcu.Sfg.Bur.Stan'37
☎ (415) FI6-8337 . . 2864 Broadway St, San Francisco, CA *94115*

Metcalf MR & MRS Jonathan M (Jane A Brassard) Cal'72.Cr'80.V'78.Nu'87
32 Garrison St, Boston, MA *02116*

Metcalf MRS Lawrence V (Susan Stimmel) Cal'47.Bur.Sfg.Tcy.StJ.
☎ (415) WE1-7839 . . 2990 Vallejo St, San Francisco, CA *94123*

Metcalf MR & MRS Manton B 3d (Teresa D | ☎ (212) 288-0445
Peabody) Un.Rm.Stc.Myf.Cly.H'45 . . . . . | 21 E 79 St,
MR John P—at ☎ (970) 626-5399 . . PO Box 517, | New York, NY
Ridgway, CO *81432* . . . . | *10021*

Metcalf MRS Michael P (Charlotte L Saville) | ☎ (508) 636-8156
V'62.B. . . . . | 813 River Rd,
MISS Hannah S . . . . | Westport, MA
MISS Lucy D . . . . | *02790*
MR Jesse P . . . . |

Metcalf MISS Pauline C—SI'60.Cs . . .of
☎ (212) 831-2486 . . 19 E 88 St, New York, NY *10128*
☎ (401) 295-8442 . . 375 Mail Rd, Exeter, RI *02822*

Metcalf MR & MRS Philip A (Diana H Allen) | ☎ (610) 642-9955
Tor'70.Pa'71.M.Me.Ripon'67.NCar'69 . . . . . . | 243 Cheswold Lane,
MISS Julia A—at Syracuse U . . . . | Haverford, PA
MR James L A . . . . | *19041*
JUNIORS MR Christopher A . . . . |

Metcalf MRS Richard G (Dorothy R Anson) Rm.
☎ (410) 226-5425 . . "Attica" 4270 Windrush Rd, Oxford, MD *21654*

Metcalf MR Robert A
☎ (407) 330-8075 . . PO Box 1627, Sanford, FL *32772-1627*

Metcalf MR & MRS Robert Treat Paine (Barbara P Smith) Sth'53.Sbc.Ec.Chi.H'51
☎ (508) 927-0148 . . "West Beach Hill" 894 Hale St, Beverly Farms, MA *01915*

Metcalf MR & MRS S Warren (Joan Pressprich) Sth'52.Cs.P'46 . . of
☎ (212) 289-4884 . . 1185 Park Av, New York, NY *10128*
☎ (203) 259-1399 . . 92 Center St, Southport, CT *06490*

Metcalf MR & MRS Stephen C (Virginia M Cassella) Tufts'82
☎ (617) 964-6334 . . 16 Adella Av, West Newton, MA *02165*

Metcalf MR & MRS Thomas N JR (Patricia A Thompson) Gen'47.Cyb.Ct.H'44
☎ (803) 838-7418 . . 205 Odingsell Court, Dataw Island, SC *29920*

Metcalf MR & MRS William 3d (Edith A Binney) | ☎ (412) 741-4298
Edg.Rr.P'46 . . . . | RD 1, Blackburn
MISS Christine F—at Middlebury, VT *05753* . . . | Rd, Sewickley, PA
MISS Brooks H—at Fraser, CO *80442* . . . . . . | *15143*

Metcalfe MR & MRS David D (Orthwein—Ann P | ☎ (314) 994-0149
Thornley) Cy.P'44 . . . . | 13 Black Creek
MR David T Orthwein—Cy.Cr'81—at | Lane, St Louis, MO
☎ (314) 862-7341 . . 7536 Forsyth Blvd, | *63124*
St Louis, MO *63105* . . . . |

Metcalfe MR & MRS James W (Elizabeth C Brokaw) | ☎ (314) 962-8481
Wash'62.Ncd.Wash'57.StL'67 . . . . | 65 Berry Road Park,
MISS Elizabeth C—at Colby . . . . | St Louis, MO *63122*
MR James K B—K'zoo'95—at ☎ (011-42-47)
526-3287 . . Pension Spolchemie 26, Klisská 53,
400 01 Ústí nad Labem, Czech Republic . . . . . .

Methmann MISS Cheyanne Skye (gg—MRS Hugo H Methmann) . . . Born at
Los Angeles, CA Feb 4'96

Methmann MRS Hugo H (Wehr—Alicia M Compton)
Cal'21.Cp.Wt.Dar.Ncd.Lm.Dcw.
☎ (510) 653-6781 . . Piedmont Gardens Apt 1015, 110—41 St, Oakland,
CA *94611-5250*

Mettler MISS Ellen
51 Seacape Dv, Muir Beach, Sausalito, CA *94965*

Mettler MR & MRS John W III (Goodrich—Cornelia | ☎ (212) 734-3529
Daley) Rc.Fic.Cly.Stan'63 . . . . | 215 E 72 St,
MISS Melinda W—at Deerfield . . . . | New York, NY
MISS Catherine D Goodrich—Duke'96 . . . . . | *10021*

Mettler MRS Nancy K (Nancy K King) Fic.Cly.
☎ (203) 661-4226 . . 190 Clapboard Ridge Rd, Greenwich, CT *06831*

Metz MR & MRS Richard E (Muriel Gurdon Howells) K.Rc.Cly.H'35
☎ (212) TE8-1954 . . 580 Park Av, New York, NY *10021*

Metz REV & MRS Ronald I (Helen Chapin) | ☎ (202) 244-2923
V'49.Beirut'54.Cal'44.Beirut'54.Y'69 . . . . | 3001 Veazey Terr
MISS Grace C—at ☎ (202) 332-4207 | NW, Apt 334,
2070 Belmont Rd NW, Washington, DC *20009* . | Washington, DC
| *20008-5455*

Metzger MR & MRS J William JR (Perry—Anne D | ☎ (561) 842-0224
Grant) Pa'71.BtP.P'71 . . . . | 277 Esplanade Way,
MR Nathaniel D Perry . . . . | Palm Beach, FL
JUNIORS MR David H Perry . . . . | *33480*

Metzger MR & MRS Kurt P (Wendy J Pollard) Br'81.Br'81 ⚓
☎ (011-65) 469-0181 . . 33 Chee Hoon Av, Singapore 299758

Meyer MISS Beverly V (Malham—Beverly V Meyer) Duke'73.A.Ncd.
☎ (210) 805-0318 . . 208 Primera Dv, San Antonio, TX *78212*

Meyer MR Charles A . . . . Died at
Lake Forest, IL Aug 12'96

Meyer MRS Charles A (Suzanne Seyburn) On.Sr.Rc.B.
☎ (847) 234-5185 . . 1320 N Sheridan Rd, Lake Forest, IL *60045*

Meyer MR & MRS Charles G JR (Katherine Baehr) | ☎ (516) 922-5623
V'59.Pr.B.Myf.Y'60.Y'65 . . . . | 518 Centre Island
MR Robert P . . . . | Rd, Centre Island,
| Oyster Bay, NY
| *11771*

Meyer MR & MRS Charles G 3d (Susan B Campbell)
Va'88.Va'92.Yn.Y'88.Camb'89.Va'92
☎ (804) 288-6230 . . 5408 Cary Street Rd, Richmond, VA *23226*

Meyer MR Christopher H . . see MRS R Ducas

Meyer MR & MRS Douglas C (Mary L Froehlich) Ck.Hof'76
☎ (516) 676-4480 . . 100 Midway Av, Locust Valley, NY *11560*

Meyer MR Edward B 3d—Pr.Rc.S.LakeF'82
☎ (516) 676-9564 . . 71 Midway Av, Locust Valley, NY *11560*

Meyer MISS Eliza F . see W G von Weise JR

Meyer MISS Elizabeth Alker—Cly.Csh.
☎ (212) 288-3962 . . 157 E 72 St, New York, NY *10021*

Meyer MR Ernest W . . . . Died at
San Francisco, CA Apr 19'96

Meyer MR & MRS G Christian 3d (Bailey Logan) | ☎ (415) 579-6522
Cal'61.Pcu.Bur.Sfg.Y'62 . . . . | 2855 Ralston Av,
MR Christian L . . . . | Hillsborough, CA
MR Nicholas B . . . . | *94010*

Meyer MRS George C JR (Esther P Blodgett) Sth'37.Ck.
135 Beach Bluff Av, Swampscott, MA *01907*

Meyer MR & MRS George F (Helen J Whitaker) | ☎ (314) 991-0431
Bv.Wash'51 . . . . | 43 Pointer Lane,
MISS Elizabeth P . . . . | St Louis, MO *63124*

Meyer MR & MRS George F JR (Suzanne L Hater) | ☎ (314) 432-0309
Mar'vil'71.Bv.Wash'69.Wash'72 . . . . | 2 Ellsworth Lane,
MISS Heather H . . . . | St Louis, MO *63124*
MR George F 3d . . . . |

Meyer MR & MRS George S (Sarah F Glenn) | ☎ (516) 624-6020
V'63.S. ⚓ | 84 Cove Neck Rd,
MISS Edith L—Leh'91 . . . . | Oyster Bay, NY
MR Willets Symington—CtCol'88.Tul'93 . . . . . | *11771*
MR David S—Hof'96 . . . . |

Meyer MRS Henry L 2d (Anne G Taylor) Kt.
☎ (216) 321-0205 . . 2318 Delamere Dv, Cleveland, OH *44106*

Meyer MR & MRS Henry von L JR (Babinski—Barbara E Osborn) . . of
☎ (914) 357-0295 . . 56 Viola Rd, Suffern, NY *10901*
☎ (516) 537-0972 . . 20 Beach Lane, Box 660, Wainscott, NY *11975*

Meyer MR & MRS Herbert R (Frances H Lengfeld) | ☎ (702) 826-8386
Cl'36.Stan'42 . . . . | 4480 Plumas St,
MISS Christina R—at 1160 Ash Lane, | Reno, NV *89509*
Erwin Lake, CA *92314* . . . . |

Meyer MR & MRS J Edward JR (Carolyn Starring) Myf.
☎ (803) 939-0212 . . ''Still Hopes'' 100—7 St Ext, Box 186,
West Columbia, SC *29169*

Meyer MRS John M JR (Windisch—Helen Baker) . . . . Died at
Greenwich, CT Mch 28'96

Meyer MR John M JR . . . . Died at
Greenwich, CT Jly 4'96

Meyer MR & MRS John M 3d (Rodd—Elizabeth H | ☎ (617) 329-0312
Channing) Ty'62 . . . . | 162 Highland St,
MISS Katherine D—at Hobart-Wm Smith . . . . . | Dedham, MA *02026*
MR F Morgan Rodd JR—Wes'86.Pa'94—at |
☎ (415) 567-0178 . . 1725 Lyon St, |
San Francisco, CA *94115* . . . . |

Meyer MISS Margaret Fleet (Charles G 3d) . . . . Born Mch 30'96

Meyer MRS Mary Ann (Mary Ann Sawyer) Cwr'56. | ☎ (315) 446-4538
MR William B—Wms'83 . . . . | 7 Bradford St,
| Syracuse, NY *13224*

Meyer MR Richard W—Ck.Y'42
☎ (516) 676-4404 . . 7 Peacock Pond Rd, Matinecock Farms,
Glen Cove, NY *11542*

Meyer MR & MRS Richard W JR (Carol A | ☎ (516) 671-1852
Brittingham) Ck.Buck'70 . . . . | 650 Chicken Valley
MISS Tara B—Lynch'91—at ☎ (212) 580-4931 | Rd, Matinecock, NY
107 W 86 St, Apt 7D, New York, NY *10024* . . . | *11560*
MISS Michelle A—at Gettysburg Coll . . . . |
JUNIORS MR Richard W 3d . . . . |

Meyer MRS Robert B JR (Maria T de Zaldo) V'49.S. | ☎ (301) 299-8236
MISS Katharine M—BMr'76 . . . . | 9800 Sotweed Dv,
MR Carlos R B—Y'82—at ☎ (703) 777-4365 | Potomac, MD *20854*
PO Box 189F, Leesburg, VA *20178* . . . . |

Meyer LT COL (RET) Robert J—USA. . . . . Died at
Chesterfield, MO Feb 13'96
Meyer MRS Robert J (M Joan Fischer) Bv.
☎ (314) 434-5229 . . 18 Brook Mill Lane, Chesterfield, MO *63017*

Meyer MR & MRS Thomas H (H Elizabeth Catron) | ☎ (914) 234-7826
Denis'63. . . . . | 333 Bedford Center
MR Thomas H JR—Ham'89 . . . . | Rd, Bedford Hills,
MR William A—CtCol'91—at | NY *10507*
☎ (212) 717-4140 . . 212 E 83 St, Apt 1D, |
New York, NY *10028* . . . . |

Meyer MR & MRS Ulrich D (Marion C Schoellkopf) | of ☎ (011-41-1)
ParisCons'57 . . . . | 781-38-33
MISS Ulrike A—at Princeton . . . . | Halbinsel Au,
| CH 8804 Au,
| Zürich, Switzerland
| ☎ (011-41-81)
| 34-12-94
| ''Cresta Stguoira''
| CH 7078
| Lenzerheide,
| Switzerland

Meyer MR & MRS Vaughan B (Reynolds—Alice G K | ☎ (210) 820-0552
Kleberg) Tex'49.A.Rv.Ll.Cw.Ncd.Myf.Rice'41 . | 200 Patterson Av,
MISS Katherine B Reynolds . . . . | Apt 906,
MISS Alice K Reynolds (Tatum—Alice K | San Antonio, TX
Reynolds) Cr'80 . . . . | *78209*

Meyers MR & MRS Peter (Kathleen Ogden) | On the Green,
Ty'61.ColSt'59. . . . . | Redding, CT *06875*
MR William O. . . . . |
MR John P. |

Meyers MR & MRS Philip G (Constance M Grant) Nw'48
☎ (715) 887-4142 . . 1650 Spring Hill Lane, Port Edwards, WI *54469*

Meynell MR & MRS David B (Margaret A Shotton) | ☎ (416) 922-4897
Tor'55.Acadia'53.Dalh'56 . . . . | 42 Scholfield Av,
MISS Andrea M . . . . | Toronto, Ontario
MISS Christina M . . . . | M4W 2Y3, Canada
MR Robert A S . . . . |

Meynell MRS Gerard Balfour (Aulsbrook—Dorothy | ☎ (573) 325-8253
J Bowell) Pn. . . . . | New Liberty Horse
MR Richard Balfour—at 3511 Floral Dv, | Farm, HCR 89,
Santa Cruz, CA *95062* . . . . | Box 385, Winona,
| MO *65588*

Michael MR & MRS Charles A SR (Carole W Neff) . . | of ☎ (717)626-8816
MR Todd W—at 2013 Harbour Gates Dv, | 209 Oxford Dv,
Apt 163, Annapolis, MD *21401* . . . . | Lititz, PA *17543*
| ☎ (410) 723-9042
| Bay Watch 2,
| 11618 Seaward Rd,
| Ocean City, MD
| *21842*

Michael MR Charles A JR (Charles A SR) . . . . . . Married at Lancaster, PA
Hilton MISS Nicole (Rodney) . . . . Aug 20'94
Michael MRS Dorothea F (Smith—Slayton—Dorothea F Michael)
☎ (802) 229-4576 . . RR 1, Box 33G, Worcester, VT *05682*

Michael MR & MRS Leslie W (Alison A Carnahan) | ☎ (847) 295-3078
Mls'65.Y'60.H'66 . . . . | 544 Ravine Av,
MISS Susannah T—at Ithaca Coll . . . . | Lake Bluff, IL
MR Henry B—Y'93—at Duke Law . . . . | *60044*
JUNIORS MISS Lucy A . . . . |

Michael MR Peter Cannon—Cal'94 . . see MISS B V Bowles
Michael MR Timothy B (Charles A SR) . . . . Married at Lancaster, PA
Sides MISS Tori (Terry) . . . . Nov 25'95
Michaels MR Wilkinson S . . see N M Montgomery
Michaelsen MRS Alwin C (Rita E S Patzner)
☎ (212) AT9-6451 . . 103 E 86 St, New York, NY *10028*

Michahelles MRS Caroline Burton E (Caroline B | of ☎ (011-39-55)
Ewing) Pa'51.FIT'53.Ac. . . . . | 225-478
MR Alexis . . . . | via Bellosguardo 20,
MR Alexander . . . . | 50124 Florence,
| Italy
| ☎ (212) 581-0252
| 17 W 54 St,
| New York, NY
| *10019*

Michalis MR & MRS Clarence F (Cora D Bush) Ln.Un.Pr.S.Ny.Cly.H'44
☎ (516) 676-7777 . . 273 Bayville Rd, Locust Valley, NY *11560*
Michel MR Clifford F—Y'90
☎ (212) 226-6138 . . 17 White St, Apt 5A, New York, NY *10013*

Michel MR & MRS Clifford L (Betsy Shirley) | of ☎ (908)234-0343
Sth'63.P'61 . . . . | St Bernard's Rd,
MISS Katherine B . . . . | Gladstone, NJ *07934*
MR Jason L—at 3032 Q St NW, Washington, DC | ☎ (508) 257-4128
20007 . . . . | PO Box 231,
| Siasconset, MA
| *02564*

Michel MISS Julienne M
☎ (202) 986-2996 . . Kalorama Square 1808, 1824 Phelps Place NW,
Washington, DC *20008*
Michell MR & MRS Henry F 3d (Wheeler—Elizabeth Van B Baxter)
Gm.Me.Pa'50
☎ (610) 688-1232 . . 100 Quail Lane, Radnor, PA *19087*
Michell MRS Robert W (Evangeline C Greeff)
☎ (203) 227-6323 . . 57 Compo Beach Rd, Westport, CT *06880*
Michelsen MRS Katherine K (Katherine Ann Killgallon) Bel'67
☎ (203) 255-8736 . . 3113 Bronson Rd, Fairfield, CT *06430*
Michie MRS Alethea N (Alethea N Riggs) BMr'50
☎ (914) 868-7606 . . Bulls Head Rd, Stanfordville, NY *12581*
Michotte MR & MRS Eloy U P G (Letitia L M Erler)
Ty'77.JHop'83.Me.Louvain'71.Ch'72
☎ (011-44-171) 584-3598 . . 18 South Terr, London SW7, England
Mickel MR & MRS Paul J (Thayer C Tolles) Wms'87.Del'90.Ham'87 . . of
☎ (908) 508-9426 . . 17 Division Av, Summit, NJ *07901*
☎ (603) 284-7028 . . Coolidge Farm Rd, Center Sandwich, NH *03227*
Mickle MISS Anne R—CtCol'89.Col'90
☎ (413) 253-1467 . . 35 Salem Place, Amherst, MA *01002*
Mickle MR & MRS John C (Jocelyn A Haven) CtCol'53
☎ (212) 722-1365 . . 145 E 92 St, New York, NY *10128*
Middendorf MR Henry S—Un.Plg.Rv.Cw.H.'45
☎ (212) 575-0350 . . 175 W 12 St, New York, NY *10011*
Middendorf MRS W Kennedy B (Mary G Reynolds) Plg.Rc.Hn.
☎ (314) 991-0038 . . 56 Clermont Lane, St Louis, MO *63124*

Middlebrook MRS George (Alice E Caruthers)
☎ (310) 277-7089 . . 341 Peck Dv, Beverly Hills, CA *90212*

Middlebrook MRS Robert W (Georgianna S Leslie) Mich'45.K.Pn.
☎ (860) 868-7075 . . Sprain Brook Farm, 204 Nettleton Hollow Rd, Washington Depot, CT *06793*

Middleton DR & MRS Blackford (Ursula G King)
Roch'84.Col'79.Yn.Y'81.SUNY'85.Stan'91
see Dilatory Domiciles

Middleton MR & MRS Charles B (Barbara F Reichner) . . . .
MR Charles B JR . . . .
☎ (301) 942-1576
10220 Carroll Place, Kensington, MD *20895*

Middleton MR & MRS Charles F (Elizabeth C Tillman) Cw.Cc.Ht.SCar'64 . . . .
MISS Elizabeth K
MISS Felicia McR . . . .
☎ (803) 577-4849
14 Logan St, Charleston, SC *29401*

Middleton MR Daniel T—Stan'87 . . see J W Aldrich

Middleton MR & MRS David (Reed—Joan Bartlett) Cos.Sar.Cs.H.'42 . . . .
MISS Susan T—Mass'84—at ☎ (413) 628-4039 PO Box 26A, Norton Hill Rd, Ashfield, MA *01330* . . .
MISS Leslie B—RI'82—at ☎ (804) 823-6913 General Delivery, White Hall, VA *22987* . . . . .
  MR Christopher H Reed—H'70—at
☎ (212) 427-5410 . . 213 E 89 St, New York, NY *10128* . . . .
  MR Henry H Reed—Ithaca'76.Ithaca'79—at
13 rue André Antoine, 75018 Paris, France . .
  MR Andrew B Reed—StJColl'74—
☎ (212) 663-3437 . . . .
☎ (212) 410-9298
127 E 91 St, New York, NY *10128*

Middleton MISS Ellen Alice (Thieringer—Ellen Alice Middleton)
Bow'74.Cardozo'81
☎ (914) 868-7889 . . RR 1, Box 429B, Amenia, NY *12501*

Middleton DR & MRS (REV) Elliott JR (Elizabeth Blackford)
Cl'48.Col'68.G.P'47.Cl'50
☎ (207) 846-6411 . . RR 1, Box 596, Chebeague Island, ME *04017*

Middleton MR & MRS Elliott 3d (Valerie J Gramberg) Y'73
☎ (612) 435-8088 . . 231 S Oak Shore Dv, Burnsville, MN *55337*

Middleton MR & MRS Henry B (Condon—Payne W Payson) B.Ny.Cs.
MISS Alison H—at ☎ (011-39-55) 854-7970 ''Le Caselle'' 50022 Greve in Chianti, Italy . . . .
of ☎ (212)486-0684
1 Sutton Place S, New York, NY *10022*
☎ (803) 387-5422
Venture Plantation, PO Box 96, Lane, SC *29564*

Middleton MR James J—Roch'83
☎ (303) 778-6149 . . 1630 S Ogden St, Denver, CO *80260*

Middleton MISS Laura D R—Sth'86.Wash'87.AmU'94 . . see J W Aldrich

Middleton MR & MRS Philip A (Judith Hanckel) SCar'69.Cw.Char'ton'66 . . . .
MISS Martha I . . . .
MR Philip A JR . . . .
☎ (803) 722-7546
86 Church St, Charleston, SC *29401*

Middleton MR & MRS William (Frances G Hanahan)
☎ (803) 722-3416 . . 83 Tradd St, Charleston, SC *29401*

Mifflin MR John Wright—Chr.
☎ (513) 984-9400 . . 7100 Dearwater Dv, Cincinnati, OH *45236*

Mikell MRS Thomas P (Alma H Karr) Pc.
☎ (215) 653-0116 . . 31 Cavendish Dv, Ambler, PA *19002*

Mikell MR & MRS Thomas P JR (Ellen Glendinning) Pc.So'76
83 Fourth Av, Broomall, PA *19008*

Milbank MR & MRS David L (Sally L Thomas) Pa'58.P'51.JHop'67
MISS Michelle R—Box 404, Dayton, VA *22821* .
MR Thomas L—at Bryn Mawr . . . .
☎ (801) 942-9525
9712 Quail Ridge Rd, Sandy, UT *84092*

Milbank MR & MRS Jeremiah (Sheppard—Rose D Jackson)
B.Ri.Ds.Cda.Y'42
☎ (203) 869-3744 . . ''Longleat'' 535 Lake Av, Greenwich, CT *06830*

Milbank MR & MRS Jeremiah 3d (Caroline K Rennolds)
B'gton'77.Ln.K.Bhm.Cly.Cda.Ty'70.Stan'73.Va'80
☎ (212) 570-6807 . . 53 E 66 St, New York, NY *10021*

Milbank MR & MRS Joseph H (M Sabina Martin) Sth'84.Va'85
☎ (804) 971-3066 . . ''Braeside'' 960 Old Ballard Rd, Charlottesville, VA *22901*

Milbank MRS Robbins (Helen P Kirkpatrick) Sth'31
☎ (757) 229-6467 . . 3022 Willow Spring Court, Williamsburg, VA *23185*

Milbank MR & MRS Samuel L (Dominique Detay) Un.Myf.Lm.Cl'64.Dth'67 . . . .
MISS Nathalie . . . .
JUNIORS MR Thomas . . . .
of ☎ (212)348-5201
19 E 88 St, New York, NY *10128*
☎ (518) 589-6272
Onteora Park, Tannersville, NY *12485*

Milbank MRS Wetmore (Marian L Wetmore) Cly.Lm.
☎ (212) 744-6492 . . 1 East End Av, New York, NY *10021*

Milburn MR & MRS Devereux (Elizabeth C Hinckley) Mb.Ln.Rc.Ox'38 . . . .
MISS Nancy G—at New York, NY . . . .
MR Devereux 3d—H'63—at Los Angeles, CA . .
☎ (516) 334-3733
Box 144, 69 Hitchcock Lane, Old Westbury, NY *11568*

Milburn MR & MRS Frank H (Hirsch—R Maria Vicien)
☎ (212) 249-5007 . . 501 E 87 St, New York, NY *10128*

Milbury MR & MRS Edwin Van R (Henderson—Cassandra K Mellon)
Evg.BtP.Rr.Rd.Pg.Ny . . .of
☎ (412) 238-5653 . . ''Stirling Hall'' Ligonier, PA *15658*
☎ (561) 832-3186 . . 356 Worth Av, Palm Beach, FL *33480*
☎ (268) 460-4142 . . ''Weatherside'' Mill Reef, Antigua

Milbury MR & MRS K David (Edith E Nelson) Bhy.BostColl'59 . . of
☎ (617) 566-2299 . . 12 Kilsyth Terr, Brookline, MA *02146*
☎ (207) 288-9544 . . ''Villa Mary'' 77 Eden St, Bar Harbor, ME *04609*

Miler MRS Jean McA (Jean M McAdoo) SCar'79 . . see M R McAdoo JR

Miles MR & MRS Charles R (Jean Carpenter) H'39
☎ (207) 878-3433 . . 2 Poplar Ridge, Falmouth, ME *04105*

Miles MRS Clarence W (Lanahan—Eleanor Addison Williams) Mv.Cda.
☎ (410) 827-8000 . . ''White Banks'' PO Box 21, Queenstown, MD *21658-0021*

Miles MRS James A (Mary F Graham) BMr'44 . . . .
MISS Elizabeth E—Cal'77 . . . .
MR James A JR—Bow'75 . . . .
☎ (209) 227-2847
PO Box 5182, Fresno, CA *93755-5182*

Miles MR & MRS Paul W (Mary D Clarke) Hlns'59.Emory'57
☎ (334) 263-7610 . . 744 Cloverdale Rd, Montgomery, AL *36106*

Miles MRS Serena W (O'Shaughnessy—Serena W | ☎ (302) 226-0245
Miles) Gchr'89 . . . . | 70 Park Av,
 MR Robert M O'Shaughnessy—at Boston U . | Rehoboth Beach, DE
 JUNIORS MR William A O'Shaughnessy . . . . . | *19971*

Milford MR & MRS James L (Charlotte M Kunz) Rv.
☎ (215) 672-5315 . . 1026 Davis Grove Rd, Ambler, PA *19002-1106*

Milholland MR & MRS James JR (Pamela M Burden)
SL'50.Cv.Penn'47.JHop'51
☎ (814) 237-0976 . . 423 W Park Av, State College, PA *16803*

Milinowski MR & MRS Arthur S JR (Alice E Wade) | ☎ (905) 871-3472
H'32 . . . . | 19 High St,
 MR Curtis C—at 13 Patch St, Danbury, CT *06810* | Apt A101, Ft Erie,
  | Ontario L2A 5W7,
  | Canada

Millar MR & MRS Dodd R (Rose A Di Luzio) | ☎ (708) 771-3736
Grin'60 . . . . | 1027 N Keystone
 MR Eric T—StOlaf'89 . . . . | Av, River Forest, IL
 MR Anthony R . . . . | *60305*

Millar MR Goodwin W
☎ (617) 232-9079 . . 61 Hedge Rd, Brookline, MA *02146*

Millar MR James
☎ (508) 398-3980 . . 19 Fairway Rd, South Yarmouth, MA *02664-2304*

Millar MR & MRS Robert G (Anna C Benedict) Chi.Mit'40
☎ (617) 934-2113 . . Box 234, 315 King Caesar Rd, Duxbury,
MA *02331*

Millar MR & MRS (DR) Robert G 3d (Mary Ann Lucyk)
Ws'81.ECar'88.Pa'87
☎ (508) 475-1150 . . 64 Central St, Andover, MA *01810*

Millard MISS Elizabeth B
57 Charles St, New York, NY *10014*

Millard MRS Everett Lee JR (Mary P Hyde) R'velt'74
019 Picket Pin Lane, Snowmass, CO *81654-9221*

Millard MR Everett Lee JR—H'31 . . . . | ☎ (847) 432-2769
 MISS (DR) Mary C—Ch'81.Ill'87 . . . . | "Log House"
  | 1623 Sylvester
  | Place,
  | Highland Park, IL
  | *60035*

Millard MR J Alden JR (John A) . . . . Married at St Louis, MO
Sommer MISS Jane B (Charles S) . . . . May 11'96

Millard MR & MRS J Alden JR (Jane B Sommer) Dick'92.Nu'95.H'91.Cl'96
☎ (212) 426-8757 . . 130 E 94 St, New York, NY *10128*

Millard MR & MRS John A (Carey B French) | of ☎ (212)288-1875
Sth'65.Un.Cs.H'63 . . . . | 755 Park Av,
 MR James G—at ☎ (213) 939-1862 | New York, NY
430 S Cloverdale Av, Apt 26, Los Angeles, CA | *10021*
90036 . . . . | ☎ (516) 537-0337
 MR Alexander F—at U of Pa . . . . | Matthews Lane,
  | Bridgehampton, NY
  | *11932*

Millard MISS Olivia P—Col'81.Cr'84
☎ (914) 669-8517 . . "Moss Hollow" Titicus Rd, North Salem,
NY *10560*

Millard MR & MRS Peter de F (Dudensing—Anne | ☎ (212) 879-0908
Lalor) Un.Cly.Y'54.H'58 . . . . | 150 E 73 St,
 MISS Anne . . . . | New York, NY
 MR Hugh . . . . | *10021*
 MR Peter de F JR . . . . |

Millard MR & MRS Richard D (Kathleen S Traynor) P'83.Un.Cly.Geo'83
☎ (212) 517-8914 . . 222 E 71 St, New York, NY *10021*

Millard MR & MRS Richard T (Amory A Hubbard) AmU'78
☎ (212) 308-3717 . . 435 E 57 St, Apt 4C, New York, NY *10022*

Millard MR Richard T—Br'74.Pa'78 . . of
☎ (212) 794-1260 . . 3 E 85 St, Apt 5A, New York, NY *10028*
☎ (413) 528-9692 . . Rowe Rd, North Egremont, MA *01252*

Millard MR & MRS Stephens F (Hale—Knight—Linda L S Dyer)
Mls'65.Fmy.Pa'55.Nw'63
☎ (415) 851-3747 . . 5 Fremontia St, Portola Valley, CA *94028-8032*

Millard MRS Suzanne T (H Suzanne Taylor) Col'56 | ☎ (513) 438-1017
 MR William C—PugetS'90 . . . . | 970 Deer Run Rd,
  | Centerville, OH
  | *45459*

Millen MR Frederic—Pa'67 . . see P A Drury 3d

Millen MR R Woodward—Pr.Va'64
☎ (803) 648-1219 . . 1014 Holly Lane, Aiken, SC *29801*

Miller MISS (DR) Amanda B—Minn'87
☎ (408) 257-7247 . . 104 Golden Gate Circle, Napa, CA *94558*

Miller MR & MRS Andrew J (Charlotte P Taylor) Swb'55.Cda.Hn.H'54
☎ (540) 554-8281 . . Foxhall Farm, PO Box 412, Round Hill,
VA *20142*

Miller MRS Andrew Otterson JR (Jeanne L White) Un.Pr.BtP.Evg.Cw . . .of
☎ (561) 833-7322 . . Rapallo North Apt 1602, 1701 S Flagler Dv,
West Palm Beach, FL *33401*
☎ (516) 692-2893 . . "Ducks Landing" 1452 Ridge Rd, Laurel Hollow,
Syosset, NY *11791*

Miller MRS Barbara Duff (Barbara D Duff) . . . . | 224 Dolphin Cove
 MR Prescott C—at U of SCar . . . . | Quay, Stamford, CT
 JUNIORS MR Barclay St J . . . . | *06902*

Miller MR & MRS Barton H (Marion J Becker) CtCol'58.Lx.Rr.Y'58 . . of
☎ (617) 267-2522 . . 40 Commonwealth Av, Apt H, Boston, MA *02116*
☎ (413) 243-0112 . . "Red House" Spring St, Lee, MA *01238*

Miller MR & MRS Bradford P (Pamela M McCain) BtP.Rc.
☎ (314) 991-4001 . . 11 Fordyce Lane, St Louis, MO *63124*

Miller MR Caleb N (Philippus JR) . . . . Married at Bolinas, CA
Hershman MISS Terri L (Nelson) . . . . Sep 7'96

Miller MR & MRS Cameron A (Mary H Ames) IllSN'87.Aquinas'83
☎ (616) 245-8485 . . 1333 Philadelphia Av SE, Grand Rapids,
MI *49506*

Miller MISS Caroline Ann (Charles J JR) . . . . Born at
Hartford, CT Oct 2'95

Miller MRS Carroll JR (Nancy L Milligan)
☎ (412) 781-1035 . . 110 West Dv, Pittsburgh, PA *15215*

Miller MR & MRS Carroll T (Inganni—Sachs—Carroll R | ☎ (617) 423-2088
Townsend) Ub. . . . . | 50 Fayette St,
 MISS Sarah T . . . . | Boston, MA *02116*
 JUNIORS MR Andrew D . . . . |
 JUNIORS MR Jared W . . . . |

Miller MRS Charles Duncan (Jeanine de Croze S Matthews) Cs.StA.Snc.Y.
☎ (516) 862-9322 . . "Harbor View" Box 100D, Long Beach Rd,
St James, NY *11780*

Miller MR Charles Duncan 3d—Snc.Y'74
☎ (516) 584-7965 . . 455 N Country Rd, St James, NY *11780-1704*
Miller MR & MRS Charles J JR (Abigail B Chase) MassArt'92
☎ (860) 657-9280 . . 19 Cutter Lane, Glastonbury, CT *06033*
Miller MR & MRS Clay Lowell (Ellen E Green) Stan'73.Cp.Stan'69
☎ (707) 433-5467 . . 532 College St, Healdsburg, CA *95448*
Miller MR & MRS Cleaveland D (Margot W Tabb) | ☎ (410) 323-1254
Md.Mv.JHop'60.H'63 . . . . | 811 W Lake Av,
MISS Margot T—at Corvallis, OR . . . . | Baltimore, MD
MISS Elizabeth L—at San José, Costa Rica . . . . . | *21210*
Miller MR & MRS Corbin R (Kathryn A Anderson)
V'72.Rc.K.B.Mto.StJ.Cly.P'71
☎ (212) 534-8326 . . 1165 Fifth Av, New York, NY *10029*
Miller MR & MRS Courtlandt G (Gina M Salvatore)
Geo'79.Loy'81.Rcn.Ri.Evg.BtP.Pr.Snc.Cly.Ford'76. Tul'80
☎ (561) 833-4446 . . 177 Clarke Av, Palm Beach, FL *33480*
Miller MR & MRS D Livingston JR (Patricia O'Donohue) Rcn.Snc.Y'68
☎ (203) 629-2531 . . 281 Stanwich Rd, Greenwich, CT *06830*
Miller MRS Danforth JR (Bisset—Helen Fuller) Ny.Why.Fic.San.
☎ (561) 231-4513 . . 875 Bowline Dv, Vero Beach, FL *32963*
Miller MR David C
see Dilatory Domiciles
Miller MR & MRS David F (Margaret H Porter) | 208 S Hanson St,
OState'72.GeoW'77.Del'96.Ncd.Va'67 . . . . | Easton, MD *21601*
JUNIORS MISS Cynthia G . . . . |
JUNIORS MR Neil P . . . . |
Miller DR & MRS David H (Patricia C Hancock)
Hlns'79.Ny.H'72.Va'76 . . of
☎ (212) 472-0343 . . 435 E 70 St, Apt 31D, New York, NY *10021*
☎ (802) 824-4330 . . PO Box 143, Peru, VT *05152*
Miller MR & MRS Decatur H (Sally B Smith) | ☎ (410) 366-3394
Elk.Mv.Y'54.H'59 . . . . | 26 Whitfield Rd,
MISS Clémence M K . . . . | Baltimore, MD
| *21210*
Miller DR & MRS Don Robert (Cynthia J Thomas) | ☎ (805) 541-3217
OState'69.OState'65.OState'69.OState'73 . . . . . | 2340 Sunset Dv,
MISS Tara E . . . . | San Luis Obispo,
JUNIORS MISS Ramey K . . . . | CA *93401*
Miller MR & MRS Donald F (Pamela S Jayne) | ☎ (203) 869-0764
Unn.Unb.Ne.Minn'50 . . . . | 543 North St,
MR Malcolm E—Ty'90.NCar'95 . . . . | Greenwich, CT
| *06830*
Miller MR & MRS Donald K (Priscilla C Barker) Rc.Myf.Cr'54.H.'59 . . of
☎ (203) 622-0544 . . ''Jamais Fini'' 588 Round Hill Rd, Greenwich,
CT *06831*
☎ (212) 722-6932 . . 40 E 94 St, New York, NY *10128*
Miller DR & MRS Donald McE (Evelyn R Swett) H'88.P'86.Dth'91
☎ (502) 339-6366 . . 3071 Running Deer Circle, Louisville, KY *40241*
Miller MR & MRS Dwight A (Ewell—Keithley Rose) | ☎ (314) 991-5001
Swb'69.Rc.Ny.Y'67.Va'73 . . . . | 67 Briarcliff,
JUNIORS MISS Victoria S . . . . | St Louis, MO *63124*
JUNIORS MR Christopher G . . . . |
Miller MR & MRS Edward B (Phillips—Anne H Chase)
☎ (847) 729-2857 . . 632 Chatham Rd, Glenview, IL *60025*
Miller MR & MRS Edward M (Barbara Brady) Pr.Y.
☎ (516) 626-1076 . . 1254 Cedar Swamp Rd, Old Brookville, NY *11545*

Miller MR & MRS Edward M (Janet R Henning) | ☎ (804) 977-5761
Pr.TexA&M'68.H'72 . . . . | Rosemont Farm,
JUNIORS MISS Kristen S . . . . | RR 10, Box 272,
| Charlottesville, VA
| *22903*
Miller REV & MRS Edward O (Ann H Lackman) C.Csn.H'37
☎ (207) 326-8594 . . Perkins St, Box 197, Castine, ME *04421*
Miller MR & MRS Edward Terhune (Noël C Clark) | ☎ (202) 338-3954
BMr'62.Au.Mt.Cvc.P'58.Y'63 . . . . | 3109 N St NW,
MISS Virginia C—Tul'89—*see Dilatory Domiciles* | Washington, DC
MR Edward G S—Reed'92—at ☎ (360) 676-2510 | *20007*
1000B Jersey St, Bellingham, WA *98225* . . . . . |
Miller MR & MRS Eric T (Spencer—Susan Williams) | ☎ (415) 397-0936
Unn.Dth'50 . . . . | 155 Jackson St,
MISS Holly Spencer—at 406 S Sherman St, | Apt 1307,
Denver, CO *80209* . . . . | San Francisco, CA
| *94111*
Miller MR & MRS F Keene (Luanne Fields) Montevallo'85.Emory'83
☎ (404) 352-9157 . . 2373 Alton Rd NW, Atlanta, GA *30305-4001*
Miller MRS Francesca M (Francesca Moulton)
☎ (415) 364-5161 . . 2409 Hampton Av, Redwood City, CA *94062*
Miller MR & MRS Frederick R (Nancy McDaniel) Rv.Y'52
☎ (520) 398-9215 . . PO Box 1503, Tubac, AZ *85646*
Miller MR G Russell—P'67
Cedar Pond Dv, Warwick, RI *02886*
Miller MRS Garfield L (Johanne Cunningham) Cy.G. | ☎ (716) 836-7925
MR Stephen L—Mid'73—at ☎ (212) 349-1553 | 47 Four Seasons W,
70 Fulton St, New York, NY *10038* . . . . | Eggertsville, NY
| *14226*
Miller MR Gavin—H'50 . . . . | ☎ (818) 577-7478
MISS Emily S . . . . | 371 W Bellevue Dv,
MISS Louise H . . . . | Pasadena, CA *91105*
MISS Catherine S . . . . |
Miller MR & MRS George B B (Dale M Price) | ☎ (412) 363-8413
Rol'72.Rr.Rol'66.AmU'70 . . . . | 1171 Murray Hill
JUNIORS MR Corbin P—at Woodberry Forest . . . . | Av, Pittsburgh, PA
JUNIORS MR Edward McC—at Taft . . . . | *15217*
Miller MR & MRS George G (Mary Richardson | ☎ (305) 860-9111
Buck) Me.Ste.Pa'59.Pa'68 . . . . | Brickell Bay Club,
MISS Cassandra C . . . . | Apt 1506,
MR Alexander C—Col'93 . . . . | 2333 Brickell Av,
| Miami, FL *33129*
Miller MRS George J (Mary M Donald) Dar.
☎ (904) 477-0729 . . 8876 Burning Tree Rd, Pensacola, FL *32514*
Miller MR & MRS George J (Louise P Wilde) | ☎ (610) 642-4237
Bvr'64.VillaN'83.Gm.Me.P'53.Pa'56 . . . . | 209 Booth Lane,
MR Paul V II—Col'85—at ☎ (415) 637-1030 | Haverford, PA
6 Calypso Lane, San Carlos, CA *94070* . . . . . | *19041*
MR Jonathan S—Bard'92—☎ (610) 642-7465 . . |
Miller MR George S—H'51
☎ (718) 857-0828 . . 409 Bergen St, Brooklyn, NY *11217*
Miller MR & MRS Gerald A (Gail C Benedict) | ☎ (847) 234-1041
On.Rc.Sc.Cas.Wa.Miami'69 . . . . | ''Blyth Field''
JUNIORS MISS Brooke B—at St George's . . . . . . | 1701 Kennedy Rd,
JUNIORS MISS Christina P—at St George's . . . . . | Box 936,
JUNIORS MR Stuart H—at Vanderbilt . . . . | Lake Forest, IL
| *60045*

Miller MR Gordon E—Mds.
☎ (505) 757-2361 . . River House, Los Trigos Ranch, Rowe, NM *87562*
Miller MRS Guenn S (Dixon—Guenn S Miller) . . . . | ☎ (516) 862-8168
   MISS Lisette B Miller-Dixon . . . . | 69 Moriches Rd,
   JUNIORS MR Sorrel S Miller-Dixon . . . . | St James, NY *11780*
Miller MRS H Wisner JR (Riley—Palmer—Barbara Clapp) Sth'46
☎ (561) 283-8870 . . 4245 Centerboard Lane, Stuart, FL *34997-6165*
Miller MR Harold C—Mo'37 . . . . | 364 Antlers Dv,
   MISS Elizabeth F . . . . | Rochester, NY
   | *14618-2102*

Miller MR Harry E 3d—Y'62.H'65
☎ (415) 931-1841 . . 2375 Broadway St, San Francisco, CA *94115*
Miller MISS Helen Candler—Occ'70.Cal'86.Vh.
see Dilatory Domiciles
Miller MISS Helen H— Hlns'77.Cs.
☎ (212) 879-7568 . . 340 E 74 St, New York, NY *10021*
Miller MR & MRS Henry S (Martha O Stengel) | ☎ (215) 646-2353
   Pc.Fw.Ll.Rv.Ac.H.'35.H'38 . . . . | 6317 Joshua Rd,
   MR Henry S JR—H'73—at 46 Greenville St, | Ft Washington, PA
   Somerville, MA *02143* . . . . | *19034*
Miller MR & MRS Henry S JR (Juanita Lewis) Okla'33.A.Smu'34
100 Highland Park Village, Apt 370, Dallas, TX *75205*
Miller MRS Hugh K (Bubendey—Sarah Barrows) . . of
☎ (860) 767-3424 . . 155 Essex Meadows, Essex, CT *06426*
☎ (619) 328-5335 . . 40-140 Via Buena Vista, Rancho Mirage,
CA *92270*
Miller MR & MRS J Norris (Suzanne Sturgis)
☎ (603) 643-6364 . . Quail Dv, Etna, NH *03750*
Miller MR & MRS Jeffrey C (Susanne Jackson) | ☎ (203) 866-4596
   Y'65.Cr'68 . . . . | 1 Valley Rd,
   MISS Katherine . . . . | Norwalk, CT *06854*
   MR Gordon Q . . . . |
   MR Andrew D . . . . |
   JUNIORS MR Eric M . . . . |
Miller MR & MRS Jeffrey K (Mary Armour Reid) Br'83.Br'83
☎ (203) 972-6144 . . 92 Woodland Rd, New Canaan, CT *06840*
Miller MR & MRS Jo Zach 4th (Bonnyman—Mercer—Virginia Hunter)
S.Ny.Pr.Y'40 ⚓
☎ (941) 366-7203 . . 434 Meadow Lark Dv, Sarasota, FL *34236*
Miller MR & MRS John A (Hoëfle—M Elizabeth Latimer)
Wheat'59.Wcc.Colg'45
☎ (610) 296-2435 . . 1770 Horseshoe Trail, Box 424, Paoli, PA *19301*
Miller MR & MRS John A 3d (Schoettle—Gainor B Ingersoll)
Ws'51.Swth'52
☎ (215) 844-1147 . . 720 Westview St, Philadelphia, PA *19119-3532*
Miller MR & MRS John D (Barbara C Leovy) Cw.Tul'28
☎ (504) 525-2974 . . 1441 Jackson Av, Apt 3C, New Orleans, LA *70130*
Miller MR & MRS John F (Jo Anne Edwards) Stan'47.Fr.Stan'46.H'49
☎ (415) 368-8838 . . 71 Ralston Rd, Atherton, CA *94027*
Miller MR & MRS John G (Elizabeth G Snyder) Pa'38.Sdg.Dar.
☎ (215) 248-2244 . . 21 Waterman Av, Philadelphia, PA *19118*
Miller MR & MRS Jonathan R (M Rawlings Lamberton) U'92.Bost'93
Redondo Towers 8G, 425 W Paseo Redondo, Tucson, AZ *85701*
Miller MRS Joseph A (Charlotte F Lee) . . . . | ☎ (410) 889-1717
   MR Joseph O'D—at ☎ (410) 768-4785 | 123 Hawthorne Rd,
   6453 Heritage Hill Dv, Glen Burnie, MD *21061* | Baltimore, MD
   | *21210*

Miller MR & MRS Joseph S (Odessa R Schipfer) Y'36
☎ (505) 522-3095 . . 3045 Buena Vista Circle, Apt 209E, Las Cruces,
NM *88011*
Miller DR & MRS Jule P JR (Desmond—Anne B | ☎ (314) 993-8843
   Hoge) Wash'49 . . . . | 476 N Warson Rd,
   MISS Leslie F Desmond . . . . | St Louis, MO *63124*
   MR Christopher T Desmond . . . . |
Miller DR & MRS (DR) Jule P 3d (Sharon T LaRose)
Mo'81.StL'86.Mo'81.StL'85
☎ (601) 436-9359 . . 1293 Kensington Dv, Biloxi, MS *39530-1623*
Miller MR & MRS K Dexter JR (Barbara F Beranger) V'42.P'43.P'48
☎ (713) 781-5225 . . 338 Tynebridge Lane, Houston, TX *77024*
Miller MRS K Gill (Kathleen L Gill) Sth'66 . . . . . . | ☎ (914) 472-2305
   JUNIORS MISS Emelie B . . . . | 48 Church Lane,
   | Scarsdale, NY
   | *10583*
Miller DR Kennon S—Wms'82.Dth'87
☎ (716) 854-6302 . . 11 Marina Park S, Buffalo, NY *14202*
Miller MR L Don
☎ (602) 947-6441 . . 4821 N 70 St, Scottsdale, AZ *85251*
Miller MR L Garrison JR (Lindley G) . . . . Married at Old Greenwich, CT
Barr MISS Carrie S (Donald J) . . . . Jun 22'96
Miller MR & MRS L Garrison JR (Carrie S Barr) Denis'81.Rcn.BostColl'85
☎ (203) 637-1140 . . 64 S Park Av, Old Greenwich, CT *06870*
Miller MRS L Vernon (Katherine L Baum) Mv . . . . . | ☎ (410) 527-1133
   MR James H—at 1221 Patapsco St, Baltimore, | 13801 York Rd,
   MD *21230* . . . . | Apt T371,
   | Cockeysville, MD
   | *21030*
Miller MR & MRS Leigh M (Lynden R Breed) | of ☎ (212)722-5497
   Sth'60.Mt.Cs.Y'48.Y'52 . . . . | 1170 Fifth Av,
   MR Ethan D—Hob'83.Nw'89—at | New York, NY
   ☎ (312) 988-9625 . . 2002 N Howe St, Apt 2N, | *10029*
   Chicago, IL *60614* . . . . | ☎ (860) 364-0244
   MR A Gifford—P'92—at ☎ (212) 348-9849 | Calkinstown Rd,
   200 E 90 St, New York, NY *10128* . . . . | Sharon, CT *06069*
   MR Marshall L—Y'93—at Yale Law . . . . |
Miller MR & MRS Leverett S (Linda P Bartlett) | ☎ (352) 591-1673
   BtP.Srr.Y'53.Cl'57 . . . . | ''T-Square Stud''
   MISS Whitney M—at Vanderbilt . . . . | Box 900, Fairfield,
   JUNIORS MISS Penelope P—at Deerfield . . . . | FL *32634*
Miller MR & MRS Lindley G (Patricia M Cromwell) | ☎ (516) MA6-1082
   Pr.P'43.Va'49 . . . . | 1203 Pine Valley
   MISS Patricia R—at ☎ (212) 355-3530 | Rd, Oyster Bay, NY
   141 E 55 St, New York, NY *10022* . . . . | *11771*
Miller MRS Louisa H (Louisa M Howland) | ☎ (330) 759-2636
   Bnd'70.Lm. . . . . | 4073 Sampson Rd,
   JUNIORS MISS Katherine H . . . . | Youngstown, OH
   | *44505*
Miller MR & MRS Ludlow (Barbara S Baldwin) | ☎ (215) 247-0908
   MtH'61.Pc.Au.Br'58 | 215 W Gravers
   MISS Elizabeth S—Ham'90—at | Lane, Philadelphia,
   ☎ (415) 775-5866 . . 2351 Washington St, | PA *19118*
   Apt 104, San Francisco, CA *94115* . . . . |
   MR L Clarke—Br'95—at ☎ (415) 759-6643 |
   106 Ortega St, San Francisco, CA *94122* . . . . . . |

Miller MRS M Benson (Marion F Benson) Pa'64 . . . ☎ (860) 599-1514
MISS Julia I—at U of Pa . . . . 449 Pendleton Hill
MR Peter B—Nw'90 . . . . Rd, North Stonington, CT 06359

Miller MRS M Hummel (Margaret E Hummel) ☎ (011-44-1203)
Sth'63.Y'64 677320
MISS Jennifer D . . . . 7 Spencer Av,
MISS Sonia H . . . . Coventry, Warwickshire CV5 6NQ, England

Miller MR & MRS Malcolm F (Elizabeth M Craig) ☎ (504) 275-7904
P'58 . . . . 14642 Stoneberg
MR Donald C—USMC . . . . Av, Baton Rouge,
MR Ian A . . . . LA 70816

Miller MISS Margery K (Van Buskirk—Margery K Miller) Sth'68.Pa'72
☎ (215) 854-6939 . . 2020 Walnut St, Apt 27H, Philadelphia, PA 19103

Miller MR & MRS Marshall B JR (Claudia P Huntington) Stan'74.A.W&L'71
☎ (210) 490-7975 . . 319 Limestone Creek, San Antonio, TX 78232

Miller MR & MRS Matthew R (Kathleen A Dodds) Vt'75.Vt'76
☎ (503) 242-1305 . . 2141 SW Hillcrest Place, Portland, OR 97201

Miller MRS Merle M (Mather—D Buvel Folwell) Pc.
☎ (215) CH7-7665 . . 16 Waterman Av, Philadelphia, PA 19118

Miller MR & MRS Michael (Edith duP Riegel) ☎ (301) 229-6257
Fic.Sl.Cc.Cw.Ds.Ncd.Y'54 . . . . 4402 Boxwood Rd,
MISS Edith H—at 31 Beechcroft St, Brighton, MA Bethesda, MD 20816
02135 . . . .

Miller MR & MRS Michael JR (Elsie White) Bow'83.Fic.Fiy.Y'79.H'83
☎ (714) 640-4077 . . 1644 Marguerite Av, Corona Del Mar, CA 92625

Miller MASTER Michael 3d (Michael JR) . . . . Born at Boston, MA Sep 17'95

Miller MRS Mitchell H (Helen T Knox) V'37
☎ (410) 243-4583 . . 830 W 40 St, Apt 415, Baltimore, MD 21211

Miller MR & MRS Norman H (Haight—Nellie I ☎ (215) 248-5836
Fitzgerald) Pc.Myf.Ncd.Pn.Pa'39 . . . . 720 Wolcott Dv,
MR David C Haight . . . . Chestnut Hill, PA 19118

Miller MR & MRS Norman W (Chapin—Bette Frampton) Tcy.Stan'33
☎ (408) 659-2762 . . Upper Circle Dv, Carmel Valley, CA 93924

Miller MR & MRS Otto N (Merrill—Natalie O'Maley) Bur.Pcu.StJ.
☎ (415) 397-5896 . . 1000 Mason St, San Francisco, CA 94108

Miller MR & MRS Patrick D (Cynthia M Coates) ☎ (501) 664-9220
Ark'72.Ark'70 . . . . 2512 N Taylor St,
JUNIORS MISS Marian M . . . . Little Rock, AR
JUNIORS MR Mathews M 72207

Miller MR & MRS Paul L (Adèle Olyphant) ☎ (201) 539-2575
Ln.Ri.Shcc.Nf.P'41 ⚓ . . . . ''Still Pond''
MISS Hilary—at ☎ (212) 249-0542 . . 19 E 73 St, Young's Rd,
New York, NY 10021 . . . . New Vernon, NJ 07976

Miller MRS Paul L JR (M Kathryn Callaghan) 541 Exmoor Rd,
Man'vl'74 . . . . Kenilworth, IL
JUNIORS MISS Kathryn A 60043

Miller MR & MRS Peter F (Ridgely—Julie D S ☎ (203) 838-0733
Ripley) Duke'75.F&M'73 . . . . PO Box 233,
JUNIORS MISS Mary McN . . . . Norwalk, CT
JUNIORS MR Peter D 06853-0233
JUNIORS MISS Laura L Ridgely . . . .

Miller MR & MRS Philippus JR (Sally Wistar Winsor) ☎ (610) 527-9669
Ph.Me.Cc.TyDub'52 . . . . ''Unter Den Linden''
MR Philippus 3d—Cr'83—at ☎ (607) 256-5455 126 N Roberts Rd,
1126 E Shore Dv, Ithaca, NY 14850 . . . . Bryn Mawr, PA 19010

Miller MRS R Bleecker JR (Marie C Dyckman) Cly.
☎ (212) 570-1007 . . 200 E 74 St, New York, NY 10021

Miller MR & MRS Randolph L (Janet K Warner) of ☎ (503)222-2224
KasSt'70.Bost'69 . . . . 4100 SW Arthur
MISS Kelsey A . . . . Way, Portland, OR
MISS Haley E 97221
☎ (503) 738-9330
101—5 St, Gearhart, OR 97138

Miller MR Richard C—Ithaca'67
☎ (617) 749-8154 . . 15 Hemlock Rd, Hingham, MA 02043

Miller MR & MRS Richard F (Suzanne S Sumner) ☎ (818) 449-9002
Utah'65.Vh.Stan'59.Stan'63 . . . . 705 Chaucer Rd,
MR Sumner C . . . . San Marino, CA 91108

Miller MRS Robert (Victoria E Pearson) Rdc'56 . . . ☎ (212) 769-2317
MR Robert P—P'87—at ☎ (212) 987-1937 277 West End Av,
201 E 87 St, New York, NY 10128 . . . . New York, NY 10023
MR Christopher Y—Geo'93—at
☎ (202) 543-9492 . . 714 A St NE, Washington, DC 20002 . . . .

Miller JUNIORS MR Robert B . . see W P Jones

Miller MR Robert F—Bur.Pcu.SFr'55
☎ (415) 579-7091 . . 101 Robin Rd, Hillsborough, CA 94010

Miller MR & MRS Robert H (Quarton—Cynthia E PO Box 4124,
Swanson) Cal'68.Wms'70.Stan'74 . . . . McLean, VA 22103
MISS Carolyn D . . . .
JUNIORS MR Robert H JR . . . .
MISS Anne K Quarton . . . .
JUNIORS MR Bradley R Quarton . . . .

Miller MR & MRS Robert J (Adrienne Agardy) MtH'70.Unn.Aht'67
☎ (203) 226-1608 . . 10 Bluewater Hill S, Westport, CT 06880

Miller MR Robert J 3d . . see D G Anderson

Miller MR & MRS Robert John (Deborah G Ratliff) ☎ (513) 683-6514
Miami'67.Cr'67 . . . . 808 Woodlands
MISS Emily G . . . . Lane, Loveland, OH
JUNIORS MR Robert H 45140

Miller MRS Robert L (Marsh—Hull—Nancy Demarest) Gi.
☎ (410) 437-2678 . . Box 31, Oxbury Rd, Gibson Island, MD 21056

Miller MRS Robert N 3d (Elizabeth T Broome) ☎ (805) 969-9398
An.Ny. . . . . 944 Hot Springs Rd,
MR & MRS James J Chrismen (Leslie S Miller) Santa Barbara, CA 93108

Miller MR Robert N 4th—Sfy.Ny.
☎ (805) 969-5803 . . 489 Scenic Dv, Santa Barbara, CA 93108

Miller MR & MRS Samuel C (Eliza S Myers) Aht'41 . | ☎ (610) MU8-1720
MR Mark S . . . . | 427 Midland Av,
| Wayne, PA *19087*

Miller MR & MRS Stanley R JR (Stillman—Frances M Mason)
T.Chr.Cly.Hn.H'36
☎ (860) 767-0096 . . Riversedge, Box 772, Essex, CT *06426*

Miller MR & MRS Thomas B (Ethel B Guthrie) Baylor'38.Tcy.
☎ (011-52-73) 12-72-32 . . "Casa Mia" Matamoros 106,
Cuernavaca 62440, Morelos, Mexico

Miller MR & MRS Thomas E (McManus—Emery M | ☎ (216) 423-0713
Norweb) GeoW'71.It. . . . . | 2020 Berkshire Rd,
JUNIORS MISS Eleanora J . . . . | Gates Mills, OH
JUNIORS MR Thomas E JR . . . . | *44040*
MISS Clare E D McManus
JUNIORS MR Henry J McManus . . . . |

Miller MR & MRS Thomas W C (Miller—Loraine | ☎ (212) 289-1376
Laughlin MacDougall) Pa'65.Un.Rr.Chr.Msq. | 161 E 90 St,
Why.Plg.Ll.Cly.P.Hav'60.Cl'64 . . . . | New York, NY
MISS Katherine A—SCal'90.Rr.—at | *10128*
☎ (310) 450-8544 . . 2010—3 St, Apt 106,
Santa Monica, CA *90405*
MR T Wilson C—Unn.Why.Plg.J&W'89—at
☎ (704) 362-3745 . . 196 Providence Square Dv,
Charlotte, NC *28270* . . . .
MR Jason E B—Rr.Un.Plg.HWSth'92—at
☎ (212) 477-9303 . . 220 Park Av S, Apt 9D,
New York, NY *10003*

Miller MR & MRS Victor B (Elizabeth C Thurston) | ☎ (203) 878-0921
Y'62 . . . . | 144 W River St,
MR Joshua G—at ☎ (510) 841-2404 | Milford, CT *06460*
1937 Dwight Way, Apt 27, Berkeley, CA *94704*

Miller MRS W Howard (Ringe—Bertolet—Clementine B C Brick) Ncd.
☎ (610) 645-9270 . . The Quadrangle 6102, 3300 Darby Rd, Haverford,
PA *19041*

Miller MRS W Tyler (Elizabeth Mann) Kt.
☎ (216) 921-6862 . . 13615 Shaker Blvd, Apt 3B, Shaker Heights,
OH *44122*

Miller MRS Walter P JR (Anne P Prichard) Pc.
☎ (215) 984-8928 . . Cathedral Village G417, 600 E Cathedral Rd,
Philadelphia, PA *19128*

Miller MR & MRS Walter P 3d (Nuissl—Binney B | ☎ (201) 515-4457
Bromley) Ws'66.Me.Wes'59 . . . . | 610 S Beverwyck
MR Rudolph F H Nuissl JR—Colby'89 . . . . . . | Rd, Parsippany, NJ
| *07054*

Miller MR & MRS Walter R JR (Joan M Groark) | ☎ (203) 773-0168
Pg.Rr.Yn.Dth'55.Cl'57.Nu'65 . . . . | 2 Marshall Rd,
MISS Kathryn A . . . . | Hamden, CT *06517*
MISS Meghan E . . . . |
MISS Jennifer M . . . . |
JUNIORS MR Walter R 3d . . . . |

Miller MR & MRS William C (Susan B Daoust) Cal'48
☎ (510) 935-0187 . . 3361 Reliez Highland Rd, Lafayette, CA *94549*

Miller MR & MRS William G (Florence M Hornsby) Sar.Stv'27
☎ (617) 275-1228 . . 32 Concord Court, Bedford, MA *01730*

Miller MR & MRS William H (Martha O Clarke) V'32.Gm.P'31
☎ (610) 645-8800 . . 1400 Waverly Rd, Blair 033, Gladwyne, PA *19035*

Miller MR & MRS William H JR (Jean McK Piersol) | ☎ (203) 866-2347
Cl'66.Ny.P'61.Syr'66 . . . . | 4 Valley Rd,
MR William H 3d—StLaw'92 . . . . | Wilson Point,
MR Thomas P—Mont'95 . . . . | South Norwalk, CT
| *06854*

Miller MRS William J (Muriel McKaig) Msq.Pg.Myf.
☎ (401) 596-7204 . . "Prospect" 35 Pasadena Av, Watch Hill, RI *02891*

Miller MRS William R (Rosa D C Williams) Gchr'34.Mv.Ncd.
☎ (410) 243-4861 . . 830 W 40 St, Apt 515, Baltimore, MD *21211*

Miller MR & MRS William R (Fowler—Black—Emma Gillespie)
Un.Plg.Coa.Myf.Snc.Cw.Cs . . .of
☎ (212) 751-7381 . . 139 E 63 St, New York, NY *10021*
☎ (516) 239-5823 . . 121 Berkshire Place, Lawrence, NY *11559*

Miller MR & MRS William R JR (Barbara J Bott) | ☎ (513) 294-1871
Penn'67.P'61.Cl'62.Cl'65 . . . . | 249 Chatham Dv,
MISS Laura B . . . . | Kettering, OH *45429*
JUNIORS MR William R 3d . . . . |

Miller MR & MRS William S (Anne D Hopkins) Rc.Coa.Fw.Ll.Snc.Cw.Y.'41
☎ (914) 234-3956 . . "The Pond House" 657 Harris Rd, Box 133,
Bedford Hills, NY *10507*

Miller MRS Willis McCook (Margaret B Berger) Pg.Fcg.Rr.Ncd.
☎ (412) 681-5954 . . 631 Pitcairn Place, Pittsburgh, PA *15232*

Miller MR Willis McCook JR—Pg.Fcg.Rr.Ln.Y'63.Cl'70
☎ (412) 355-0838 . . 1171 Murray Hill Av, Pittsburgh, PA *15217*

Miller-Dixon MISS Lisette B . . see MRS G S Miller

Miller-Dixon JUNIORS MR Sorrel S . . see MRS G S Miller

Millet MR & MRS David F (Christina W Moore) | ☎ (617) 449-6997
Pa'72.Cy.Cry.H.'66 ⚓ . . . . | 623 Chestnut St,
MR Alexander C . . . . | Needham, MA
JUNIORS MISS Katharine W . . . . | *02192*

Millet MR Francis D—Hn.H.'40
☎ (617) 696-3370 . . 170 Centre St, Milton, MA *02186*

Millet DR & MRS J Bradford (Kurtz—Constance H Dallas) H'38
☎ (315) 392-4780 . . "Hemlock Hill" 3 Newell Rd, Forestport,
NY *13338*

Millett MR & MRS Daniel C (Mary Allison) Y'41
☎ (203) 264-4941 . . 124 Pomperaug Woods, Southbury, CT *06488*

Milliken MR & MRS Christopher C (Nancy Ryerson) | ☎ (847) 615-9496
Rc.Cyb.On.Fic. . . . . | 105 E Laurel Av,
MISS Kate R—at ☎ (212) 245-0901 | Lake Forest, IL
62 W 62 St, Apt 4B, New York, NY *10023* . . . . | *60045*
MR Christopher C JR—at ☎ (970) 479-1942
PO Box 5438, Vail, CO *81658* . . . .

Milliken MR & MRS Gerrish H (Winslow—Phoebe T Goodhue) Ll.Csn.
☎ (203) TO9-7969 . . 39 Pierson Dv, Greenwich, CT *06831*

Milliken MR & MRS Henry O JR (Sheila E S Inglis) | ☎ (617) 934-2994
Bnd'49.Bard'51 . . . . | 125 Abrams Hill,
MISS Susan I—at ☎ (617) 639-4314 | Duxbury, MA *02332*
10 Village St, Marblehead, MA *01945* . . . .
MR Henry O 3d—at ☎ (401) 782-6257
804 Point Judith Rd, Narragansett, RI *02882* . . .

Milliken MR & MRS John F (Elizabeth P Willcox) Y'42
☎ (919) 545-0133 . . 687 Fearrington Post, Fearrington Village,
Pittsboro, NC *27312*

Milliken MR & MRS Minot K (Hovey—Clark—Norris—Armene Lamson)
Ln.P'37
☎ (212) 249-8370 . . 19 E 72 St, New York, NY *10021*

Milliken MRS Peter H 2d (Susan P Johnstone) Dh.Cda.
☎ (212) 749-7949 . . 423 W 120 St, New York, NY *10027*

Milliken MR & MRS Roger (Justine V R Hooper) | ☎ (864) 585-5251
Ln.Yh.Y'37 . . . . | 627 Otis Blvd,
MISS (DR) Nancy—Duke'81 . . . . | Box 3167,
MR Weston F . . . . | Spartanburg, SC
| *29304*

Milliken MRS Seth M (Knapp—Gloria Walker) Ny . . .of
☎ (212) 751-8147 . . 30 Sutton Place, New York, NY *10022*
☎ (207) 633-4747 . . ''Two Deck Wonder'' West Southport, ME *04576*

Millington MR & MRS George P JR (Patricia Cooney)
StCath'44.Sg.Ht.Rv.Cc . . .of
☎ (561) 234-4729 . . 2060 Las Ramblas, Vero Beach, FL *32963-3097*
☎ (610) 645-8678 . . Waverly Heights Villa 29, 1400 Waverly Rd,
Gladwyne, PA *19035*

Millonzi MRS Robert I (Eleanor V Verduin) Cy.St.G.
☎ (716) 873-0076 . . 75 Meadow Rd, Buffalo, NY *14216*

Mills MR & MRS Bradford Alan (Carol McIntyre) Rut'82.Stan'77.Stan'79
☎ (510) 284-5259 . . 3692 Happy Valley Rd, Lafayette, CA *94549*

Mills MRS Elizabeth L (Elizabeth D Leisk) Sth'46.Cvc.Cly.
☎ (609) 924-3318 . . ''Brook House'' 840 Pretty Brook Rd, RD 2,
Princeton, NJ *08540*

Mills MR & MRS Gordon Lawrence (Read—Signa J Lynch)
B'gton'79.Ln.Snc.P'54.H'58
☎ (802) 824-6847 . . Three Meadows Farm, Box 8, Peru, VT *05152*

Mills MRS James Paul (Alice F du Pont) Ri.Srr.
☎ (561) 546-5617 . . 190 Gomez Rd, Hobe Sound, FL *33455*

Mills MR & MRS John T (Priscilla W Liggett) | of ☎ (704)328-3409
Mt.Sl.Myf.Ncd.W&L'63 . . . . | 960 Eighteenth Av
MISS Priscilla—at U of NCar Chapel Hill . . . . . | Circle NW, Hickory,
JUNIORS MR John W . . . . | NC *28601*
| ☎ (704) 898-6439
| Raven Ridge 38,
| Elk River Club,
| Banner Elk, NC
| *28604*

Mills MRS Marcey D (Marcey C Davis) . . . . | ☎ (520) 455-5724
MISS Kimberly C . . . . | PO Box 95, Sonoita,
MR David D—at 4431 N Summer Place, Tucson, | AZ *85637*
AZ *85749* . . . . |

Mills MRS Margaret A (Margaret D Aydelotte) V'55.Csn.
☎ (203) 869-8358 . . 18 Maher Av, Greenwich, CT *06830*

Mills MR & MRS Ralph J JR (Helen D Harvey) | ☎ (312) 943-5940
ArtInst'78.Cas.Fy.LakeF'54.Nw'56 . . . . | 1451 N Astor St,
MISS Brett H . . . . | Chicago, IL *60610*
MR Julian H . . . . |

Mills MR & MRS Ross D (Avril H Cox) . . of
☎ (908) 788-5495 . . Mile Away Farm, 143 Copper Hill Rd, Ringoes,
NJ *08551*
☎ (011-353-78) 33047 . . ''Lettren'' Elphin Rd, Strokestown,
Co Roscommon, Ireland

Mills MR & MRS Samuel W JR (Elizabeth Y A Ferguson)
Cal'74.Stan'77.Pr.Drex'65
1958 Vallejo St, San Francisco, CA *94123*

Mills MR & MRS William N (Barbara Toms) . . . . | ☎ (415) 931-5891
MR Robert M . . . . | 3471 Washington St,
| San Francisco, CA
| *94118*

Millspaugh MR & MRS Gordon A JR (Joan F | 40 Overleigh Rd,
Wakefield) Sth'56.Mo.P'56 . . . . | Bernardsville, NJ
MISS Julia W . . . . | *07924*

Millspaugh MR & MRS Robert P (Mary F Bishop) Dll.Y'52
☎ (561) 234-1015 . . 8846 Lakeside Circle, Vero Beach, FL *32963*

Millspaugh MR & MRS S Kirk (Eleanor M P Smith)
Elk.Gi.Gv.Md.JHop'55 ⚓ . . of
☎ (410) 366-4789 . . 3908 N Charles St, Apt 403, Baltimore, MD *21218*
☎ (212) 832-7662 . . 480 Park Av, New York, NY *10022*

Milne MR MRS David 4th—R.Ste.Rv.Pa'58 . . . . | ☎ (215) 922-3311
MR Caleb . . . . | 118 Church St,
| Philadelphia, PA
| *19106*

Milne MRS Walgren (Karen Walgren) Ac. . . . . | ☎ (610) 527-2331
MR David 5th—at Miller Rd, Chester Springs, PA | 332 Greenbank Rd,
19425 . . . . | Rosemont, PA
| *19010*

Milner COL (RET) & MRS James W (Margaret B Wiebusch) USA'40.Mich'54
☎ (703) 536-6891 . . 3830 N Woodrow St, Arlington, VA *22207*

Milroy LT GEN (RET) & MRS William A (Ann de K Tilton) CA.
☎ (613) 736-0614 . . 138 Chambord Court, Ottawa, Ontario K1V 0L4,
Canada

Milstead MR & MRS William C (Jacqueline Wheeler) Tex'55.A.Rice'43
☎ (512) 477-4784 . . 2516 Tanglewood Trail, Austin, TX *78703*

Miltenberger MR & MRS Eugene F JR (Barbara J Holbrook)
☎ (908) 291-2200 . . 60 Pine Cove Rd, Fair Haven, NJ *07704*

Miltenberger MR & MRS Henry J JR (Cheryl A Graddy)
☎ (504) 892-5145 . . 105 Blackburn Place, Covington, LA *70433*

Milton MR & MRS A Fenner (Stanton—Ina M | ☎ (202) 686-5376
Orwicz) Ct.Cos.Wms'62 . . . . | 5200 Reno Rd NW,
MISS Elizabeth H—at Columbia . . . . | Washington, DC
| *20015*

Miner MR & MRS Charles JR (Mae D Hoffman) Mds.P'43 . . of
☎ (561) 231-9276 . . 1150 Beach Rd, Apt 3M, Vero Beach, FL *32963*
☎ (203) 655-4145 . . 40 Horseshoe Rd, Darien, CT *06820*

Miner MR & MRS Granville T M (Mary Elizabeth Shoemaker) Dth'44 . . of
☎ (941) 349-5121 . . 104 Whispering Sands Dv, Sarasota, FL *34242*
☎ (802) 425-4489 . . RR 2, Box 2104, Charlotte, VT *05445*

Minett MR & MRS Irving Jerome (Dorothy E Scott) K.Purd'34
☎ (810) 646-0649 . . 535 N Williamsbury Rd, Bloomfield Hills,
MI *48301*

Minevitz MR & MRS Bruce H (Katherine R Cunningham)
BostColl'78.D.Tr.Bvl.Chi.H.'75
☎ (617) 749-8181 . . 754 Main St, Hingham, MA *02043*

Mingoli MR & MRS Andrea (Anne B McAdoo) Skd'72
☎ (011-39-6) 30889750 . . ''Villa Rotta'' Largo Olgiata 15, isola 70-G-2,
00123 Rome, Italy

Minich CANON & MRS Henry N F (Helen de Russy Morris) Va'53.VaTheo'58.So'68.UMiami'76 . . .
  MISS Catherine E—Nu'81—at ☎ (804) 353-9603
  509 N Meadow St, Apt 201, Richmond, VA 23220 . . . .
  MR Stephen B—OState'79—at
  ☎ (207) 799-4876 . . 34 Deake St, South Portland, ME 04106 . . . .
  | ☎ (804) 975-0569
  "Falconest"
  3115 Dundee Rd, Earlysville, VA 22936

Minnis MRS Samuel C (Mary M Campbell) . . . . . .
  MISS Evelyn C . . . .
  MR Samuel C JR . . . .
  MR Stephen Y . . . .
  | ☎ (314) 361-3015
  5123 Westminster Place, St Louis, MO 63108

Minor MR Edward T—Y'53 . . . .
  MISS Susan D . . . .
  MISS Ann N . . . .
  | 115—5 St NE, Washington, DC 20002

Minor MR & MRS R Lance (Mary H Gregg) Ithaca'87.Cr'94
  ☎ (212) 650-0583 . . 414 E 84 St, New York, NY 10028

Minot MR & MRS David T W (Maynard—Marjorie A Cromer) Mid'74
  ☎ (802) 899-4903 . . Box 1044, Bolger Hill Rd, Jericho Center, VT 05465

Minot DR & MRS Henry D JR (Jacobson—Joan E Lochner) H'40
  ☎ (203) 438-8020 . . 6 W Mountain Rd, Ridgefield, CT 06877

Minot MR & MRS Henry W JR (Elizabeth M Cabot) Nh.H'46 . . . .
  MR Henry W 3d—at 4555 RR 1, Dresden, ME 04342 . . . .
  MR James J 2d—at 41 Park St, Medfield, MA 02052 . . . .
  | ☎ (508) 785-0577
  19 Wilsondale St, Dover, MA 02030

Minot MASTER Joshua Robert (David T W) . . . . Born at Burlington, VT May 15'94

Minot MRS Otis N (E Louise Gross) Sth'42
  ☎ (207) 729-0606 . . 1082 Merepoint Rd, Brunswick, ME 04011

Minot MRS William (Hill—Virginia K Harrington) .
  MR David H Hill . . . .
  MR Andrew B Hill . . . .
  | ☎ (508) 295-1445
  Bourne Point, Wareham, MA 02571

Minot MRS Winthrop G (Gale O Winslow) Wheat'75.Cy.Chi. . . . .
  JUNIORS MISS Hilary R . . . .
  | ☎ (617) 566-6267
  43 Valley Rd, Chestnut Hill, MA 02167

Minot MR Winthrop G—Sm.Cy.Eyc.H.'73.Ox'75.H'79
  ☎ (617) 242-7399 . . Flagship Wharf 603, 197—8 St, Charlestown, MA 02129

Minott MR Geoffrey D—Rc.Pa'75.Cal'82
  ☎ (215) 569-0589 . . 2201 Pennsylvania Av, Apt 707, Philadelphia, PA 19130

Minott MR & MRS Joseph A JR (Lorraine D Lukens) BMr'46.H'45 . . . .
  MISS Elizabeth—HRdc'82—at Harvard . . . . . .
  MR John H C—Stan'74 . . . .
  | ☎ (215) 248-1644
  8028 Roanoke Court, Philadelphia, PA 19118

Minott MR & MRS Joseph O (Wells—Louise Pangborn) Pa'77.Pa'78.VillaN'82 . . . .
  JUNIORS MR James P Wells . . . .
  | ☎ (215) 836-4379
  810 Abington Av, Philadelphia, PA 19118

Minott MR & MRS Owen W (Mary S Vermilye) P'81.Ec.H'80
  ☎ (617) 444-3430 . . 1196 Central Av, Needham, MA 02192

Minton MASTER Alexander Field (MISS Susan) . . . . Born Jun 27'96

Minton MR & MRS Dwight C (Marian H Haines) Rcn.Myf.S.Y'59
  ☎ (609) 683-0116 . . 130 Hodge Rd, Princeton, NJ 08540

Minton MR & MRS G V Morton (Lloyd McKee) TCU'60.Tex'54.Tex'57 . of
  ☎ (817) 737-8938 . . 1407 Hillcrest Rd, Ft Worth, TX 76107
  ☎ (970) 641-1032 . . 12855 Taylor River Rd, H'way 742, Almont, CO 81210

Minton MRS Henry M (Helen D Church) Pr.Cly.Myf.
  ☎ (516) 671-3646 . . 28 Edwards Lane, Glen Cove, NY 11542

Minton MISS Susan—TCU'85.TexA&M'86
  ☎ (817) 737-8655 . . 5724 Birchman Av, Ft Worth, TX 76107

Minton MASTER Timothy Edward (MISS Susan) . . . . Born Jun 27'96

Minturn MR & MRS Richard S (Suzanne T Freeman) H'71
  JUNIORS MISS Mary W . . . .
  | ☎ (508) 526-1398
  22 Brook St, Manchester, MA 01944

Minturn MR Robert B JR—Sm.My.Ln.Hn.H.'61
  ☎ (617) 423-6760 . . 53 Clarendon St, Boston, MA 02116

Miranda MRS Arlinda W (Arlinda F Willkie) SL'68
  MISS Julia T . . . .
  | ☎ (203) 966-6512
  106 Mariomi Rd, New Canaan, CT 06840

Miranda MR César
  ☎ (212) 534-8544 . . 9 E 96 St, New York, NY 10128

Miree DR & MRS Aubrey S 3d (Mary A Oliver) Ala'59.OState'64.David'52
  ☎ (205) 967-1870 . . 4228 Caldwell Mill Rd, Birmingham, AL 35243

Mirick MRS Henry D (Marion Winsor) . . . . Died at Bryn Mawr, PA Mch 20'96

Mirick MR Henry D—Me.Ph.P.'27.Pa'31
  ☎ (610) MI2-7948 . . 101 Cherry Lane, Box 671, Ardmore, PA 19003

Mirkil MR John M—Rc.Me.Gm.Sa.Cspa.Fw.Rv.Cw.Ll.Pa'50
  2 Hopeton Lane, Villanova, PA 19085

Mirkil MR William I JR—BtP.Me.Rr.Sa.Ll.Cw.Rv.Fw.Pa'50
  ☎ (610) EL6-3094 . . "Woodsedge" 628 Andover Rd, Newtown Square, PA 19073

Missett MR & MRS Joseph V 3d (Topping—Nancy Lu Davenport) Va'65.Mb.Cly.Geo'57.Geo'61 . .
  MR Joseph V 4th—Emory'87—at
  ☎ (212) 988-5314 . . 23 E 74 St, Apt 8E, New York, NY 10021 . . . .
  MR Stephen T
    MISS Samantha S Topping—at
    ☎ (212) 472-8631 . . 203 E 72 St, Apt 3H, New York, NY 10021 . . . .
    MR Henry J Topping 4th—Smu'91—at
    ☎ (804) 979-9318 . . 134 Ivy Dv, Apt 3, Charlottesville, VA 22903 . . . .
  | of ☎ (212)744-5319
  115 E 67 St, New York, NY 10021
  ☎ (011-33-1)
  47-20-12-73
  28 av Montaigne, 75008 Paris, France

Mitch DR & MRS William E JR (F Alexandra Fisher) Ws'65.Mid'84.Cda.H'63.H'67
  MISS Eleanor B—Pa'90.Paris'96.Dar.—at
  23 rue Rosenwald, 75015 Paris, France . . . .
  MR William Armistead—H'93—at 1240—7 St, Apt 12, San Francisco, CA 94122 . . . .
  | ☎ (404) 239-9064
  3330 W Andrews Dv NW, Atlanta, GA 30305

Mitchell MRS Albert H (Grace T Davis)
  ☎ (513) 321-3143 . . 2444 Madison Rd, Apt 1103, Cincinnati, OH 45208

Mitchell MISS Anne F
☎ (215) 545-8207 . . 301 S 19 St, Apt 8B, Philadelphia, PA *19103*
Mitchell MISS Anne G—Cin'78 . . of
☎ (513) 871-1451 . . 3416 Custer St, Cincinnati, OH *45208*
☎ (803) 649-2639 . . 426 Orangeburg St, Aiken, SC *29801*
Mitchell MR & MRS Charles D (Mary C Carrick) Y'34
☎ (606) 266-6402 . . 250 Holiday Rd, Lexington, KY *40502*
Mitchell MR Charles W 3d—Cybl.Gi.Ds.
☎ (011-44-1494) 488-318 . . Stonygreen Hall, Prestwood,
Buckinghamshire HP16 0PQ, England
Mitchell DR & MRS Daniel R (Cynthia C Thornton) Van'84.Van'82.Van'86
☎ (406) 652-5533 . . 1145 Bluegrass Dv W, Billings, MT *59106*
Mitchell MR & MRS David H (Michaelyn A Bush) Cr'73.Cr'75
☎ (212) 874-3594 . . 107 W 86 St, New York, NY *10024*

Mitchell MR & MRS David L (Frances S Binger)	☎ (212) 348-4769
BMr'48.Ln.C.Cs.Y'44	174 E 93 St,
MISS Janet E—Reed'83.CathU'92—at	New York, NY
☎ (202) 462-6220 . . 1321 Corcoran St NW,	*10128-3711*
Washington, DC 20009	
MISS Anne B—at ☎ (201) 795-1142	
815 Willow Av, Hoboken, NJ *07030*	

Mitchell MR & MRS David R (Kathleen M Coleman) Sth'79.Ga'79
☎ (773) 528-1377 . . 560 W Roscoe St, Apt 2W, Chicago, IL *60657*
Mitchell MR & MRS Davis van B (Marguerite Marvin-Smith)
Snc.Bridgept'52
☎ (203) 869-1684 . . "Little Cliff" Cliffdale Rd, Greenwich, CT *06831*
Mitchell MR Edward B . . see MRS W M Austin
Mitchell MRS Francesca . . see MRS W M Austin

Mitchell MRS Frank P (Stanley—Louise A	☎ (202) 541-0332
Tittmann) An.Cvc.Cc.Cw.Wt.Ncd.Dar.Dc	6200 Oregon Av
MISS Elizabeth A Stanley	NW, Apt 332,
	Washington, DC
	20015

Mitchell MR & MRS Franklin O (Katharine Howard)	☎ (215) 947-6269
GaTech'46	840 Fettersmill Rd,
MISS Mary N—at Washington, DC	Huntingdon Valley,
	PA *19006*

Mitchell MR & MRS George B (Lynne Nesbitt)	☎ (301) 656-1937
Cvc.Cc.Ds.Va'59.Pa'64.GeoW'76	4109 W Leland St,
MISS Suzanne R	Chevy Chase, MD
MR Douglas B—Br'94	*20815*
MR Carter W—at Brown	

Mitchell DR & MRS George W JR (Mary E McKay)	☎ (210) 496-1989
Ws'49.JHop'38.JHop'42	105 Village Circle,
MISS Katharyne W—P'83	San Antonio, TX
MR George W 3d—at 17 Wallingford Rd,	*78232*
Brighton, MA *02135*	

Mitchell MR & MRS Henry B (Diana C H	☎ (713) 528-5817
Learmont) Pn.P'37.H'40	3606 Lake St,
MR James L—Tex'88	Houston, TX *77098*

Mitchell MR Henry B 3d . . see MRS W M Austin
Mitchell MR & MRS James F 3d (Judith A McNeely)
Rc.Me.Cry.Sa.Fw.Pa'60
☎ (610) LA5-8890 . . 726 Waverly Rd, Bryn Mawr, PA *19010*
Mitchell MR John J 4th—Me.Fcg.Rv.H'50 . . of
☎ (412) 683-3245 . . 4716 Ellsworth Av, Pittsburgh, PA *15213*
☎ (910) 295-4226 . . PO Box 3587, Pinehurst, NC *28374*

Mitchell MR & MRS John Wright (Carol A Clifford)	☎ (608) 274-2580
Stan'57.Stan'56	6114 Piping Rock
MISS Sarah L	Rd, Madison, WI
	53711

Mitchell MR & MRS MacNeil (Katherine McGowin)
Mds.Dyc.Chr.Ne.P.Y'26.Cal'29
☎ (212) 288-2121 . . 755 Park Av, New York, NY *10021*
Mitchell MRS Michael C (H Hope Dechert)
☎ (941) 383-6380 . . 350 Gulf of Mexico Dv, Apt 219A, Longboat Key,
FL *34228*
Mitchell MR & MRS Paul R (Davidson—Susan V Stanger)
Ws'64.Ny. ⚓ . . of
☎ (401) 423-2069 . . PO Box 408, Jamestown, RI *02835*
on board Elenoa'' Sydney, Australia
Mitchell MRS Rand (Mitchell—Murphy—Jeanette H Rand) . . . . . . Died at
St Louis, MO Jun 15'96

Mitchell MR & MRS Richard B (Deborah M Boas)	☎ (203) 762-3730
Nu'69	43 Collinswood Rd,
MISS Rebecca B—Van'96	Wilton, CT *06897*
MISS Jessica B	

Mitchell MR & MRS Robert P (Tucker C Leslie) Pr.S.OWes'74
☎ (516) 922-3373 . . 42 Tooker Av, Oyster Bay, NY *11771*

Mitchell MR & MRS Roland G (Virginia S Watkins)	☎ (540) 837-1118
Sl	"Saratoga"
MISS Virginia P—at 2748 S Langley Court,	Box 155, Boyce, VA
Denver, CO *80210*	*22620*

Mitchell MR & MRS S Alexander (Sally J Howells) BMr'51.S.Y'50
☎ (803) 838-3742 . . "Palmetto Point" 200 Millstone Dv, Frogmore,
SC *29920*
Mitchell MRS Samuel S JR (Martha Worrall) Sth'45.St.G.
☎ (716) 873-1891 . . 125 New Amsterdam Av, Buffalo, NY *14216*
Mitchell MR & MRS Timothy L P (Mary K Mower) Br'77.Pa'71.Nu'82
☎ (914) 337-3032 . . Westbourne, Alger Court, Bronxville, NY *10708*

Mitchell MR & MRS W Garry (Valerie Nield)	☎ (508) 362-9794
Alta'62.Nu'88	450 Main St,
MISS Heather McC—at Cornell	Yarmouth Port, MA
	02675

Mitchell MR & MRS Walter B (Nancy A Denebeim)
Cal'77.GoldG'88.Gi.USMMA'79
☎ (242) 327-6368 . . PO Box CB13445, Nassau, Bahamas
Mitten MR & MRS Roger C (Barbara Hobart) Br'54.Br'55.Nw'61
☎ (602) 840-5765 . . 6204 Hogahn Circle, Paradise Valley, AZ *85253*
Mittendorf MRS W Frederick (Canham—Eleanor R Shaw) BMr'38.Yn . . .of
☎ (908) 766-1390 . . 131 Mt Harmony Rd, Bernardsville, NJ *07924*
☎ (242) 327-7261 . . Islands Club, W Bay St, Box N424, Nassau,
Bahamas

Mittendorf MR & MRS William F (Joan Cahill)	☎ (415) 921-0696
Stan'69.Pcu.Cal'71	75 Raycliff Terr,
JUNIORS MR Constantine R	San Francisco, CA
	94115

Mittnacht MRS Lisa A (Elizabeth A Asche) Bost'75
☎ (904) 268-8230 . . 5312 Morgan Horse Dv N, Jacksonville, FL *32257*
Mittnacht MR Stewart JR—P'74.Duke'83
☎ (610) 527-6614 . . 200 David Dv, Apt A1, Bryn Mawr, PA *19010*

Mitton MR & MRS Michael A (Marilyn K Bowen) Ore'67.Wyo'70 . . of
☎ (503) 295-1184 . . 5826 SW River Point Lane, Portland, OR *97201*
☎ (541) 994-9539 . . ''Casa Pacifica'' PO Box 982, Lincoln City, OR *97367*

Mitton MRS Ralph W (Stone—Ann-Louise von Pilarz) Cly.An. . . . . | ☎ (212) 861-7768
MR Jeffrey C . . . . | 8 E 83 St, New York, NY *10028-0418*

Mix MR & MRS B John JR (Nancy M Stevens) Nw'53 . . . . | ☎ (773) 286-4622
MISS Katherine S—Nw'78—at 2526 N Princeton Av, Evanston, IL *60201* . . . . | 6070 N Forest Glen Av, Chicago, IL *60646*
MR B John 3d—L&C'81—at 1555 N Vail Av, Arlington Heights, IL *60004* . . . . |
MR William S—Quinn'84 . . . . |
MISS Katharine F Stevens . . . . |

Mixson MR & MRS James Franklin JR (Rhonda A Hoggett) Miss'74.Dar.Va'73 . . . . | ☎ (601) 981-3221
JUNIORS MR Laurence D . . . . | 2317 E Northside Dv, Jackson, MS *39211*

Mixter MR & MRS David M (Ives—Stephanie Leonard) Y'45
☎ (203) 655-1673 . . 20 Greenleaf Av, Darien, CT *06820*

Mixter LT CDR (RET) Henry F JR—USN.Bost'68
10 Shamrock Dv, Mary Esther, FL *32569*

Mixter MRS Nancy W (Nancy Van H Wagner) . . . . | ☎ (904) 651-8652
MISS Paige R . . . . | 28 Poplar Av, Shalimar, FL *32579*
MISS Heather E . . . . |

Mixter MR & MRS Peter J (Nancy G Schaefer) Occ'75.Ri.Vt'74
☎ (212) 570-0237 . . 171 E 73 St, New York, NY *10021*

Mocek MR & MRS Gregory G (Avery S Miller) P'90.SwLa'85.Tul'91.Bost'92
☎ (504) 387-3072 . . 634 Louisiana Av, Baton Rouge, LA *70802*

Model MISS Faith . . see J E Nielson

Model MR Robert—B.Elon'64
☎ (307) 587-8106 . . Mooncrest Ranch, PO Box 158, Cody, WY *82414*

Model MR Robert JR . . see J E Nielson

Moe MASTER Jack Elliot (John C JR) . . . . Born at Berkeley, CA Aug 21'95

Moe MR & MRS John C JR (Beatrice C Thys) Col'83.Cal'72
☎ (510) 547-2135 . . 5863 Chabot Court, Oakland, CA *94618*

Moeller DR & MRS Mark B (Phoebe Sands Montgomery) Dth'75.Dth'77 . . . . | ☎ (919) 633-4482
JUNIORS MR Peter S . . . . | 303 Wexford Place, New Bern, NC *28562*

Moffat MR Abbot Low . . . . Died at Hightstown, NJ Apr 17'96

Moffat MISS Jane-Kerin—Ox'52
☎ (203) 629-1248 . . 98 Valley Rd, Apt 12, Cos Cob, CT *06807*

Moffat MR & MRS Jay P (Pamela M Dawson) Mt.H'53
☎ (202) 363-2192 . . 4341 Forest Lane NW, Washington, DC *20007*

Moffat MR & MRS Keith M (M Frances Seidel) Un.Pr.Chr.Cly.Ncd.Y'44 . . of
☎ (212) 289-3894 . . 1088 Park Av, New York, NY *10128*
☎ (516) 692-5061 . . Box 96, 471 Woodbury Rd, Cold Spring Harbor, NY *11724*
☎ (941) 472-0998 . . 4206 Old Banyan Way, Sanibel, FL *33957*

Moffat MR & MRS Nathaniel C (Abby A Spencer) Mt.Ty'91
☎ (301) 718-2806 . . 4805 Dover Court, Bethesda, MD *20816*

Moffett MR & MRS George H JR (Sabine R Bethge) StA.StOlaf'68.ANewton'74 . . . . | ☎ (860) 572-7145
JUNIORS MISS Jessica R . . . . | 11 Linden Lane, Ledyard, CT *06339*

Moffett MR & MRS George M 2d (Kilborne—Lucie W Peck) TCob'59.BtP.Cry.Pa'62 . . . . | ☎ (561) 845-5259
MR J Andrew—at Palm Beach Gardens, FL . . . . | 245 List Rd, Palm Beach, FL *33480*

Moffett MRS James A (Retallack—Williams—Elizabeth F M L Bayley)
☎ (011-44-171) 352-5496 . . 26B Elm Park Rd, London SW3 6AX, England

Moffett MRS Karen K (Karen W Kipp) Hof'63
☎ (561) 743-7695 . . 300 Moccasin Trail W, Jupiter, FL *33458*

Moffett MISS Margaret Elizabeth . . see MRS T Whipple

Moffett MR & MRS Warren C (Anne V Dort) Sm.Ncd. . . . | ☎ (617) 367-1671
MISS Sarah de R—at ☎ (508) 429-6998 | 101 Chestnut St, Boston, MA *02108*
9 Franklin St, Holliston, MA *01742* . . . . |
MR Jonathan C—at ☎ (510) 522-1914 |
2019 Clinton Av, Apt C, Alameda, CA *94501* . . |
MR Samuel C—at ☎ (617) 275-2459 |
26 South Rd, Bedford, MA *01730* . . . . |

Moffitt MRS Anne P (Wickersham—Lawton—Anne P Moffitt) Wheat'64.Cly . . .of
☎ (941) 346-8200 . . 333 Island Circle, Sarasota, FL *34242*
☎ (516) 624-2224 . . ''Orchard II'' 101 Blair Rd, Oyster Bay, NY *11771*

Moffitt MR & MRS George W JR (Ann W Jones) Pa'48.Pa'51 . . . . | ☎ (610) 525-4985
MISS Nancy A R—BMr'75 . . . . | 262 S Roberts Rd, Bryn Mawr, PA *19010*

Moffitt DR & MRS Herbert C (Gwynne Reed) Pcu.Tcy.Cal'38.H'40
☎ (415) 771-7339 . . 1170 Sacramento St, San Francisco, CA *94108*

Moffly MR & MRS John W 4th (Donna J Clegg) Ws'57.Ny.P'49
☎ (203) 637-0691 . . 100 Meadow Rd, Riverside, CT *06878*

Mogan MR & MRS Richard F 3d (Gross—Keon—Sally Tuttle)
160 S Rockingham Av, Los Angeles, CA *90049*

Mohl MR & MRS Anthony S (Alix de Nicolay) CtCol'81.Nu'86.Rc.Wes'84.Cl'87
☎ (212) 794-6378 . . 27 E 65 St, Apt 12E, New York, NY *10021*

Mohl MISS Catherine M—V'81 . . see MRS A R de Laire

Mohlman MR & MRS Theodore A JR (Roberta L Lundgren) Nw'64.Chap'83 . . . . | ☎ (707) 864-0252
MISS Amy E . . . . | ''Possum Hill West'' 1490 Rockville Rd, Suisun City, CA *94585*
MISS Stephanie L . . . . |
JUNIORS MISS Marcia M . . . . |

Mohn MISS Anne Mercier M (Bradley—Anne Mercier M Mohn) Bnd'71.Ne'82
☎ (617) 876-4415 . . 10 Channing St, Cambridge, MA *02138*

Mohn MISS Susan W . . see W M Brazer

Mohr MISS Ann—Ind'79
☎ (610) 779-2975 . . 617 Orchard View Lane, Reading, PA *19606*

Mohr MR & MRS George F (Sarah P Jamison) Sar. . . | ☎ (610) 688-3886
MISS Barbara J—Gettys'82—at | 217 Gulf Creek Rd, Radnor, PA *19087-3886*
☎ (610) 688-3826 . . 500 E Lancaster Av, St Davids, PA *19087* . . . . |

Mohun MR Charles A
☎ (011-61-75) 304-990 . . Mt Nimmel Rd, Lot 2, Neranwood, Queensland 4213, Australia

Mohun MR & MRS Charles Leon (Ann C Harris) | of ☎ (011-61-75)
StM'58 . . . . | 304-990
MISS Dorothy B—at 117B Planet St, Carlisle, WA | 2 Mt Nimmel Rd,
6101, Australia . . . . | Mudgeeraba,
MR Edwin H—at 158 Johnson St, Southport, | Queensland 4213,
Queensland 4215, Australia . . . . | Australia
| ☎ (011-61-66)
| 857-513
| ''The Hawk''
| Pandanus Place,
| Wategos Beach,
| Byron Bay, NSW,
| Australia

Moir MISS Heather Coolidge . . see MISS S H Perkins
Moir MISS L Skye . . see MISS S H Perkins
Mollaioli MISS Diana Le G . . see MRS E Le G Hellyer
Mollaioli MRS E Hellyer (Eloise Le G Hellyer) . . . . name changed to Hellyer
Mollaioli MISS Lucia C . . see MRS E Le G Hellyer
Mollenberg MR & MRS Henry Van (Trudy S Adam) | ☎ (716) 836-2718
Skd'69.Bf.Ts.Alf'68 . . . . | 130 Morris Av,
MISS Wende A . . . . | Buffalo, NY *14214*
JUNIORS MR Richard A . . . . |
Moller MR & MRS Kenneth JR (Marion Collin) H.'45
☎ (610) 525-1135 . . 129 Upper Gulph Rd, Radnor, PA *19087*
Möller MR & MRS Mikael C L (Alicia Rand) LakeF'81.Pr.Cly.
☎ (212) 410-6571 . . 1150 Fifth Av, New York, NY *10128*
Moloney MR & MRS Philip J (Bidwell—Gimbel— | of ☎ (203)869-4024
Gail G Sheppard) V'60.Cly.Pa'51 . . . . | 19 Stanwich Rd,
MISS Kimberley W Bidwell— Les'90 . . . . . . | Greenwich, CT
MISS Courtney E Bidwell— Br'92.Br'93 . . . . | *06830*
| ☎ (561) 234-1552
| 331 Shores Dv,
| Vero Beach, FL
| *32963*
Molthan MISS (DR) Marian E—Cl'52 . . see MRS M Wurts
Moltke MISS Victoria A
☎ (011-353-1) 284-1150 . . 30 Temple Park Av, Blackrock, Co Dublin, Ireland
Molyneux MR & MRS Edward F (Pamela Brewer) Y'54
☎ (914) 876-4821 . . Mountain View Rd, RD 2, Box 306, Rhinebeck, NY *12572*
Monck MRS Harvey R (Madge S Day)
☎ (941) 485-0309 . . 873 Whitecap Circle, Venice, FL *34285-1137*
Moncrief MR & MRS Richard W (G Marsland Buck) | ☎ (817) 731-4119
Tex'70.K.Tex'65 . . . . | 1900 Spanish Trail,
MISS Georgina M . . . . | Ft Worth, TX *76107*
MR R Wesley . . . . |
Moncrief MR & MRS William Alvin JR (Johnson—Deborah Beggs) . . of
☎ (817) 732-1451 . . 4920 Crestline Rd, Ft Worth, TX *76107*
☎ (619) 346-0608 . . 46-980 Agate Court, Indian Wells, CA *92260*
Moncrieff MR & MRS Ernest V JR (Audrey M Cox)
StLaw'53.Ny.Nrr.Cw.StA.StLaw'54.Nu'64 ⚓
☎ (401) 295-8990 . . 11 Fountain St, Wickford, RI *02852*

Mondale MR & MRS Walter F (Joan Adams) Minn'50.Macalester'52
☎ (011-81-3) 3224-5560 . . US Embassy, Tokyo, Japan, Unit 45004, Box 200, APO AP, *96337-5004*
Monell MR & MRS Ambrose K (Lili Crichton) Rcn.B.Bcs.BtP.Va'76
☎ (561) 882-9947 . . 635 Crest Rd, Palm Beach, FL *33480*
Monell MRS R Harron (Renée J Harron) . . . . | ☎ (212) 832-1328
JUNIORS MISS Nina V . . . . | 415 E 54 St,
| New York, NY
| *10022*
Moneta MR & MRS John A (Leslie A Schwarz) | ☎ (610) 525-5912
Ht.VillaN'67.Pa'74 . . . . | 718 Old Lancaster
JUNIORS MR Jonathan W—at St Andrew's . . . . . . | Rd, Bryn Mawr, PA
JUNIORS MR Christopher W—at St Andrew's . . . | *19010*
Moneta MISS Judith A (Dillon—Judith A Moneta) Dick'63.Me.Ht.
☎ (610) 525-6233 . . 1617 Montgomery Av, Villanova, PA *19085*
Monge MRS Julia Burdick (Julia T Burdick) . . . . . . | ☎ (212) 737-1439
MR Justin P—H'92 . . . . | 200 E 72 St,
MR Lindsay N—Cr'95 . . . . | New York, NY
| *10021*
Mongendre MR & MRS Gérard (Sandra P Smith) | of ☎ (011-33-1)
Cly.FacdeDroit'62 . . . . | 45-04-61-39
JUNIORS MISS Nina . . . . | 2 rue Paul Saunière,
| 75116 Paris, France
| ☎ (011-33)
| 30-55-94-34
| 4 rue Maurice
| Barrés, La Boissière,
| 78370 Plaisir,
| France
Monjauze MRS Susan S (Susan H Sterling) Stan'63 . | ☎ (415) 854-5237
MISS Valerie—Paris'91—in Hong Kong . . . . . . | 1151 Orange Av,
MR Thierry C . . . . | Menlo Park, CA
| *94025*
Monmonier MR Raymond F
☎ (305) 448-2156 . . 1805 Ferdinand St, Coral Gables, FL *33134*
Monroe MR & MRS Alexander G (Mary S Gillespie) | ☎ (804) 358-8300
Swb'67.W&M'70.Va'64.W&M'69 . . . . | 1826 Grove Av,
MISS Alison G—at Wm & Mary . . . . | Richmond, VA
JUNIORS MISS Anne K . . . . | *23220*
Monroe MR & MRS Andrew P (Mary E McCoun) P'45
☎ (941) 383-4336 . . 3130 Bayou Sound, Longboat Key, FL *34228*
Monroe MR Daniel G
☎ (305) 294-1602 . . 1221 Olivia St, Key West, FL *33040*
Monroe THE REVS John W 3d & Elizabeth W (Elizabeth W Johnson)
VillaN'75.UnTheo'85.David'79.P'84
☎ (602) 992-8720 . . 2845 E Calavar Rd, Phoenix, AZ *85032*
Monroe MR William F—Cw.Pa'48
☎ (513) 221-8680 . . 2200 Victory P'kway, Cincinnati, OH *45206*
Montague DR & MRS Albert C W (Serena B Briscoe)
V'58.Elk.Md.Mv.Ncd.JHop'53.JHop'58
☎ (410) 377-5150 . . 6006 Charlesmeade Rd, Baltimore, MD *21212*
Montague MR & MRS Alexander B (Caroline F Armstrong)
Pa'84.Md.Cc.Rich'83
421 Garrison Forest Rd, Owings Mills, MD *21117*
Montague MR & MRS Andrew A (Walton—Dorothy Frey) Bur.Friedrichs'32
☎ (415) 343-2437 . . 1 Baldwin Av, Apt 709, San Mateo, CA *94401*

Montague MR & MRS Edward (Dianne C Tankoos)
☎ (212) RE4-8023 . . 12 E 86 St, New York, NY *10028*

Montague MRS F Breckinridge (BRNSS Anna M D van Lynden)
24 Arnold St, Providence, RI *02906*

Montague MR F Breckinridge—HampSydney'70.
GeoW'75.RI'76 . . . .
MISS Ada C G . . . .
MR Robert B . . . .
of ☎ (804)693-3042 Toddsbury, PO Box 695, Gloucester, VA *23061-0695*
☎ (508) 693-2717 "The Nest" RFD 413, Lambert's Cove Rd, Vineyard Haven, MA *02568*

Montague MRS H Williams (Helen B Williams) Sth'81.H'87
☎ (802) 765-4811 . . Justin Smith Morrill H'way, Strafford, VT *05072-4811*

Montague MR Richard A JR—Cl'65
☎ (802) 765-4546 . . 1 Main St, Strafford, VT *05072*

Montague MR Robert L 3d—An.Cc.Va'56 . . . .
MISS Anne S M . . . .
MR Robert L 4th . . . .
of ☎ (703)836-0670 207 Prince St, Alexandria, VA *22314*
☎ (804) 758-2663 "Sandwich" PO Box 327, Urbanna, VA *23175*

Montant MRS A Philippe (Laura H Brown) . . . .
MR P Townsend—at ☎ (561) 288-2665 120 Lonita St, Stuart, FL *34994* . . . .
MR Tilden H—at ☎ (302) 537-0641 Box 1136, Ocean City, MD *21842* . . . .
☎ (561) 286-1127 1600 SE St Lucie Blvd, Apt 302, Stuart, FL *34996*

Montant MRS J Smallwood (Jane Smallwood)
☎ (212) 249-3847 . . 500 E 77 St, New York, NY *10021*

Monteagle MRS Paige (Whittell—Louise Kaye) . . . . Died at San Francisco, CA May 4'96

Montgelas MRS Rudolph (Rafferty—Barbara J Trowbridge) Yn.
☎ (203) 655-0691 . . 75 Hanson Rd, Darien, CT *06820*

Montgomerie MRS Patricia C (Patricia Corey) Pr.
☎ (212) 722-2508 . . 55 E 86 St, New York, NY *10028*

Montgomerie MR Robert S—K.Nrr . . .see MRS O H Hammond

Montgomery MR & MRS Archibald R 3d (Anita C Packard) V'52.Rb.Sa.Me.Cc.Pa'49 . . . .
MISS Anita P—at ☎ (206) 324-6910 1608 E Republican St, Seattle, WA *98112* . . . . .
MISS Carolyn C . . . .
☎ (610) 933-7283 328 Campwood Rd, Phoenixville, PA *19460*

Montgomery MR & MRS Archibald R 4th (Phyllis C Sponberg)
OklaSt'74.Pa'75.Tex'82
☎ (410) 323-3800 . . 5407A Roland Av, Baltimore, MD *21210*

Montgomery MRS Austin P JR (Eleanor Whitney) Sth'54 . . . .
MISS Susan K—Wms'76.Cs.—at ☎ (212) 831-7970 . . 1435 Lexington Av, New York, NY *10128* . . . .
MR Austin P 3d—H'80.Cal'85.Roch'89—at ☎ (301) 990-1020 . . 16810 Chestnut St, Gaithersburg, MD *20877* . . . .
☎ (518) 658-2267 PO Box 256, Berlin, NY *12022*

Montgomery DR & MRS Charles H (Mary L Pratt) MtH'60.Y'56.Cwr'61 . . . .
MR David P—Y'89—at Georgetown . . . .
☎ (508) 548-2939 19 Gunning Point Rd, Falmouth, MA *02540*

Montgomery MR & MRS Daniel Binney (Maria L Tamborrel) Mex'49.Ofp.Sar.Mex'49 . . . .
MRS Louise M Snyder (M Louise Montgomery) . . . .
☎ (210) 896-6475 701 Oakland Hills Lane, Kerrville, TX *78028*

Montgomery MR Donnell Harry—Vh.SCal'53
☎ (818) 795-8093 . . 2040 E Walnut St, Pasadena, CA *91107*

Montgomery MR & MRS Edward A JR (Susan H Oliver) Buf'60.Cs.Ty'56 . . . .
MISS Margaret E—Ty'91—at ☎ (860) 408-1376 Westminster School, 995 Hopmeadow St, Simsbury, CT *06070* . . . .
☎ (215) 639-3155 "Wharf Cottage" 536 Wharf Rd, Andalusia, PA *19020*

Montgomery MR George G JR—C.Unn.Ln.Pcu. Y'55.H'59
MR Jonathan W—at 1 Christopher St, New York, NY *10014* . . . .
☎ (414) 441-7927 1170 Sacramento St, San Francisco, CA *94108*

Montgomery MRS Haddon B (Farrell—Montgomery—McAdam—Haddon F Bowen) . . . . Married at Santa Barbara, CA Dillon MR Herbert L JR (late Herbert L) . . . . May 27'96

Montgomery MR & MRS Hugh (Esther Howland) V'26.Y'32
☎ (610) 645-8869 . . Waverly Heights 220B, 1400 Waverly Rd, Gladwyne, PA *19035*

Montgomery MR & MRS Hugh (Patricia A Martin) Ithaca'80.W&L'80
☎ (203) 259-5242 . . 269 Parkwood Rd, Fairfield, CT *06430*

Montgomery MR & MRS J Anthony (Virginia E Haynes) Rc.Un.Plg . . .of
☎ (212) 832-8699 . . 420 E 55 St, New York, NY *10022-5139*
☎ (914) 666-5611 . . "Crows Nest" Crow Hill Rd, Mt Kisco, NY *10549*

Montgomery MR & MRS J Anthony JR (Christina M Swanson) Colg'85.Rc.Ne.Skd'85
☎ (914) 967-1681 . . 22 Lakeside Dv, Rye, NY *10580*

Montgomery MRS J Pauley (Julia Sanford Pauley)
☎ (214) 350-2007 . . 4138 Woodcreek Dv, Dallas, TX *75220*

Montgomery MR & MRS John L 2d (Natalie M Moore) Wheat'48.Cc.H'51
☎ (610) 688-7932 . . 445 Robinwood Rd, Strafford, PA *19087-5428*

Montgomery MRS John R (Helen E Fyke) Ih.
☎ (847) 256-0119 . . 1500 Sheridan Rd, Wilmette, IL *60091*

Montgomery MR John R 3d—Ih.Wms'52.Ch'59
☎ (847) 446-6321 . . 315 Birch St, Winnetka, IL *60093*

Montgomery MISS Martha O (Edward A JR) . . Married at Philadelphia, PA Napolitana MR Duane J (Patrick J) . . . . Aug 26'95

Montgomery MR & MRS Neil M (Michaels—Anne W Satterthwaite) . . . .
MR Wilkinson S Michaels—at ☎ (716) 884-5273 . . 144 Chapin P'kway, Buffalo, NY *14209* . . . .
☎ (802) 348-7938 Timson Hill Rd, Williamsville, VT *05362*

Montgomery MR & MRS Parker G (Yorke—Lane Harvey) NCar'56.Pcu.Bgt.Ri.H.'49.H'53
☎ (212) 288-2307 . . 812 Park Av, New York, NY *10021*

Montgomery MRS Philip S (Kelly—Elizabeth L Jones)
☎ (716) 634-8391 . . 267 MacArthur Dv, Williamsville, NY *14221*

Montgomery MR Robert Alexander—Ph.Myf.Fw.Rv.Cw.H'33
☎ (610) 688-0570 . . "Murray House" 801 Newtown Rd, Villanova, PA *19085*

Montgomery MR Rodman B JR—Bgt.
☎ (212) 535-4534 . . 333 E 66 St, New York, NY *10021*

Montoro MQS (DR) & MQSE Rafael de (Elrick—Ploch—Marianne Crocker)
Fic.Ri.Havana'46
610 Valencia Av, Apt 501, Coral Gables, FL *33134*

Montross MR & MRS Franklin 3d (Helen L Mohr)
Miami'69.Bgt.Nyc.Duke'50
☎ (508) 945-4145 . . PO Box 215, North Chatham, MA *02650-0215*

Montross MR & MRS Franklin 4th (Laura Lee Eifert)
FP'79.Bgt.Nyc.Lm.Ncd.H.'78
☎ (914) 234-9343 . . 60 Davids Hill Rd, Bedford Hills, NY *10507*

Montross MRS J Oliver (Joan H Oliver) Duke'52
☎ (914) 234-7023 . . 525 Bedford Center Rd, Box 136, Bedford Hills, NY *10507*

Moody MR & MRS Dempsey W (Meri Wood)
2312 Woodley Rd, Montgomery, AL *36111*

Moody MR & MRS Douglas MacM (Jordan—Emily H Alsop) My.Yn.
☎ (508) 922-4763 . . "Rochamar" 12 Curtis Point, Beverly, MA *01915*

Moody MR & MRS Kenneth M (Moody—Ruth E McAnulty) FlaSt'36.IIT'32
☎ (941) 676-1829 . . 1103 Sunset Dv, Lake Wales, FL *33853*

Moon MR Frederick F 3d—Aht'64.H'66 . . . . | ☎ (415) 776-8582
MISS Julia D . . . . | 2727 Pacific Av, San Francisco, CA *94115*

Mooney MRS Alan P (Jean McK Connelly) Cly.
☎ (707) 433-1711 . . 14645 Grove St, Healdsburg, CA *95448*

Mooney MR Christopher B—Pars'83
☎ (503) 233-5805 . . 8332 SE Sixteenth Av, Portland, OR *97202*

Mooney MR & MRS James D JR (Van Bomel—Gloria R Shoninger)
Ny.S.Pr.USN'44.P'47
☎ (516) 922-5758 . . "Hillfield" 527 Centre Island Rd, Oyster Bay, NY *11771*

Mooney MR Michael M JR . . . . Died at
St Petersburg, FL May 31'96

Moore MR & MRS A Preston (Nathalie C Hague) Myf.Sar.Dth'43.H'49 . . of
☎ (212) 737-9696 . . 20 E 74 St, New York, NY *10021*
☎ (508) 349-2783 . . 975 Chequesset Neck Rd, Wellfleet, MA *02667*

Moore MRS André Brown (Calvert—Mary E Rodenhauser) Van'34
☎ (615) 352-4495 . . 4487 Post Place, Apt 121, Nashville, TN *37205*

Moore MR & MRS Arthur B (Rita Vegter) Ind'66 . . . | ☎ (011-31-70)
MISS Caroline M . . . . | 3932252
JUNIORS MR Kevin A . . . . | Bous de Jongpark l6, 2283 TH Rijswijk, ZH, The Netherlands

Moore MR & MRS Arthur Cotton (Patricia K Stefan) Mt.Cvc.P'58
☎ (202) 337-9081 . . 3633 M St NW, Apt 5, Washington, DC *20007*

Moore MASTER Baker Chase (Charles P) . . . . Born at
Concord, MA Feb 22'96

Moore MRS Beatriz B (Beatriz B Bermejillo) Cly.
☎ (011-52-5) 45-56-17 . . 47 Calle de Comte, Colonia Anzures, Mexico, DF 11599, Mexico

Moore MR & MRS Beverly C (Irene W Mitchell) NCar'31.Y'34
☎ (910) 274-6519 . . 906 Country Club Dv, Greensboro, NC *27408-5602*

Moore MR & MRS C Atwell JR (Erica E Bauer) | ☎ (941) 486-0225
Penn'65 . . . . | 712 Valencia Rd, Venice, FL *34285*
MISS Erica F—at ☎ (941) 488-2032
608 Armada Rd S, Venice, FL *34285* . . . .
MR C Atwell 3d—at U of Va Law . . . . |

Moore MR & MRS C Bradley (Penelope W Percival) | ☎ (510) 524-1714
H'60.Cal'62 . . . . | 936 Oxford St, Berkeley, CA *94707*
MISS Megan Bradley . . . . |
MR Scott W . . . . |

Moore MR C Wickham—H'30 . . of
☎ (561) 655-6228 . . 1801 S Flagler Dv, West Palm Beach, FL *33401*
☎ (212) 838-0800 . . 825 Fifth Av, New York, NY *10021*

Moore MISS Caroline D
☎ (212) 472-0453 . . 165 E 72 St, New York, NY *10021*

Moore MRS Charles A 3d (HON Sheila Digby) . . of
☎ (404) 256-9222 . . 5310 Chemin De Vie NE, Atlanta, GA *30342*
☎ (011-353-22) 21568 . . Bearforest House, Mallow, Co Cork, Ireland

Moore MR & MRS Charles P (Alison R Chase) Tufts'86.U'84
☎ (508) 358-9507 . . 17 Draper Rd, Wayland, MA *01778*

Moore JUNIORS MISS Colby D . . see D H LeBreton

Moore MR & MRS David A C (Christiane H Citron) Y'71.StJ'67
☎ (303) 777-2242 . . 373 Marion St, Denver, CO *80218*

Moore MR & MRS David D (Kirsten C McL Severson) Ariz'92.Ariz'92
☎ (310) 306-1931 . . 2201 Ocean Av, Apt 9, Venice, CA *90291-4685*

Moore MR & MRS Douglas G (Margaret G Gibbs) | ☎ (415) 921-5570
Pcu.Bhm.Cal'59.H'65 . . . . | 15 Walnut St, San Francisco, CA *94118*
MR Mark A . . . . |

Moore MRS E Townsend (Elizabeth C Cuddy) NCar'40.Rd.
☎ (610) GL9-3162 . . 434 Darlington Rd, Media, PA *19063*

Moore MRS Edward P (Barbara Bingham) An.Cvc.Sl.Ncd.Dar.
☎ (202) 338-1464 . . 2500 Virginia Av NW, Washington, DC *20037*

Moore MRS Edward Parsons (Martha Richardson) Ws'29.Yn.
☎ (203) 977-7094 . . Water Ridge 506, 26 Mill River St, Stamford, CT *06902*

Moore MISS Elise H (G Dwight) . . . . Married at Newton, MA
Kelley MR Brian J (Francis) . . . . Jun 1'96

Moore MR & MRS Eugene M (Edith B Dent) Rcn.Yn.Y'40
☎ (203) 259-4502 . . 1050 Old Academy Rd, Fairfield, CT *06430*

Moore MRS Francis G (Hewlett—Elizabeth Lorraine Werlein)
☎ (601) 255-1438 . . "Holly Forest" 22180 Moore Rd, Picayune, MS *39466*

Moore MR Franklin H—Ty'68 . . . . | of ☎ (617)236-6407
MISS Margaret O—at ☎ (212) 529-9621 | 188 W Canton St, Boston, MA *02116*
134 E 17 St, New York, NY *10003* . . . .
MISS Natalie H—at ☎ (508) 248-9783 | ☎ (508) 255-7914
65 Worcester Rd, Charlton, MA *01507* . . . . | 310 Windjammer Lane, Eastham, MA *02642*

Moore MRS G Dwight (Roberts—Josephine C Brodhead)
Pa'71.Pitt'96.Rr.Pg.Ac.
☎ (412) 687-8216 . . 515 Amberson Av, Pittsburgh, PA *15232*

Moore MR G Dwight—Rr.Hiram'64 . . . . | ☎ (412) 441-3870
JUNIORS MR G Dwight JR—at 422 Woodland Rd, | 100 Denniston Av, Sewickley, PA *15143* . . . . | Apt 220, Pittsburgh, PA *15206*

Moore MR & MRS George B (Katharine F Lipson) ☎ (203) 966-5363
Bhm.Ln.Ncd.Y'61.Stan'64 . . . . 579 Frogtown Rd,
MISS Tanya F—WashColl'93 . . . . New Canaan, CT
MR George B JR—Colby'91 . . . . *06840*

Moore MR & MRS George C (Audrey Connell)
Man'vl'55.NYSID'62.Evg.Msq.BtP.Why.Cly.Y.Bow'53 . . of
☎ (212) 988-5129 . . 875 Park Av, New York, NY *10021*
☎ (401) 348-8258 . . ''Cove Cottage'' 7 Pawcatuck Av, Watch Hill,
RI *02891*
☎ (561) 659-6951 . . 1515 S Flagler Dv, West Palm Beach, FL *33401*

Moore JUNIORS MISS Hadley H . . see D H LeBreton

Moore MRS Henrietta Ayres (Hendrickson— ☎ (773) 784-6852
Henrietta Ayres Moore) CtCol'63.Ch'66.DeP'76 1616 W
MISS Katherine Ayres Hendrickson—at Summerdale Av,
Ben'gton . . . . Chicago, IL
MISS Rebecca Clark Hendrickson—at *60640-2027*
Wesleyan . . . .

Moore MR & MRS J Bart (Lynn A McGovern) Cal'75.Bhm.Myf.Cal'67
☎ (707) 255-0639 . . ''The Compound'' 45 Burning Tree Court, Napa,
CA *94558*

Moore MR & MRS J Hunter (Elizabeth C Creel) Skd'79.JHop'87.Sap.Pa'83
☎ (202) 546-5669 . . 737—10 St SE, Washington, DC *20003*

Moore MRS J Max (Mary E Cowles) Stan'41.Tcy.Sfg.Ncd.Myf.
☎ (415) 921-1283 . . 2200 Sacramento St, Apt 1701, San Francisco,
CA *94115*

Moore MR & MRS J Thomas (Maribeth R Hamilton) Penn'79.Sdg.Ac.Pa'75
☎ (304) 343-1223 . . 1223 Bougemont Rd, Charleston, WV *25314*

Moore DR James A—Dav'30.H'34 . . . . ☎ (212) RE4-5694
MR J Douglas MacL—Dav'66.Aub'68 . . . . 504 E 87 St,
New York, NY
10128

Moore MR James R—Bhm.Pcu.Cal'33 . . . . ☎ (510) 283-2788
MR Ronald S . . . . 3802 Happy Valley
Rd, Lafayette, CA
94549

Moore MR & MRS James R (Christine Watters) Stan'87.Cal'87
☎ (916) 729-4775 . . 8172 Talbot Way, Citrus Heights, CA *95610*

Moore MR & MRS James W (Elizabeth Hunter) ☎ (617) 899-0086
CtCol'49.Dth'50.Pa'56 . . . . 116 Meadowbrook
MISS Sandra K—Van'87—at ☎ (415) 221-3856 Rd, Weston, MA
188 Arguello Blvd, San Francisco, CA *94118* . . *02193*

Moore MISS Jayne Thaler
24801 Santa Fe St, Carmel, CA *93923*

Moore MR & MRS Jerome T JR (Bonnie A Beall) ☎ (334) 264-9408
BowlG'62.Ala'60 . . . . 3033 Boxwood Dv,
MR Jerome T III . . . . Montgomery, AL
36111

Moore MR John C 3d—B.Md.Elk.Ham'60.Va'63
☎ (212) 541-6388 . . 100 Central Park S, New York, NY *10019*

Moore MR & MRS John Clark JR (Helen N Brandt) Dth'43
☎ (704) 743-3601 . . PO Box 586, 210 Preston Rd, Cashiers,
NC *28717*

Moore MR & MRS John L JR (Hope Trumbull) H'51
☎ (561) 234-3806 . . 1955 Mooringline Dv, Vero Beach, FL *32963*

Moore MR & MRS John W (Isabel T Disbrow) Cy.P'48
☎ (314) 994-3156 . . 10426 White Bridge Lane, St Louis, MO *63141*

Moore MR John W JR—Cysl.CtCol'76.H'80
☎ (508) 693-3885 . . PO Box 840, West Tisbury, MA *02575*

Moore MR & MRS Joseph Alexander (Gladys Gillig)
Stan'31.Bhm.Pcu.Sfg.Fr.Cal'29.Stan'31
☎ (415) 776-6226 . . 2000 Washington St, Apt 5, San Francisco,
CA *94109*

Moore MR & MRS Joseph G (Barbara Bliss)
☎ (415) 344-8888 . . 2145 Geri Lane, Hillsborough, CA *94010*

Moore MRS Marian S (Geary—Ford—Marian B Smithers) Cly.
☎ (212) 737-5565 . . 165 E 72 St, New York, NY *10021*

Moore MR & MRS Martin L JR (Graves—Mary O ☎ (412) 741-5292
Sutton) Y'33 . . . . Davis Lane,
MISS Margaret C . . . . Sewickley, PA
15143

Moore MR & MRS Matteo P (Judy A Toussel) AppSt'77.NMex'77
☎ (770) 551-0824 . . 8305 Ison Rd, Atlanta, GA *30350*

Moore DR & MRS Matthew R (Alison C Chapman)
Ws'82.H'89.Ncd.H'81.Y'86 ⚓
☎ (561) 392-7435 . . 1793 Sabal Palm Dv, Boca Raton, FL *33432*

Moore MR & MRS Maurice T (Elisabeth M Luce) Cs.StJ. . ☎ (212) 288-3384
MR M Thompson JR—at Provincetown, MA 1000 Park Av,
02657 New York, NY
MR Michael *10028*

Moore MISS Melissa (Robert J) . . . . Born at
Evanston, IL Jly 16'96

Moore MR Michael B
☎ (011-44-181) 870-2597 . . 298 Trinity Rd, London SW18 3RG,
England

Moore MISS Nancy C—Wash'68
☎ (212) 348-2449 . . 7 E 93 St, Apt 1B, New York, NY *10128*

Moore DR & MRS Nicholas K (Eleanor H Vermillion) Hlns'60.SCar'59
☎ (803) 254-1896 . . 1330 Adger Rd, Columbia, SC *29205*

Moore MR Peter V—JHop'73
☎ (603) 526-4373 . . ''The Moorings'' Little Sunapee Rd, New London,
NH *03257*

Moore DR & MRS Peter Van C (Pamela P Harris)
V'46.Unn.Cos.Cly.Cl'53.Va'57
☎ (202) 966-4613 . . 4901 Hillbrook Lane NW, Washington, DC *20016*

Moore MRS Pohl (Rust—Jane Pohl) . . see MRS H H Pohl

Moore MRS R McCreery (Renée McCreery) Bur. . . . ☎ (415) 851-0101
MISS Sheila—at ☎ (415) 345-9254 255 Mountain Wood
408 W 25 Av, San Mateo, CA *94403* . . . . Lane, Woodside, CA
MR Thomas G—at ☎ (415) 598-9933 *94062*
339 Chesham, San Carlos, CA *94070* . . . .

Moore MR & MRS Robert J (Annabel Cochran) MtH'82.Tex'83
☎ (847) 501-3847 . . 385 Provident Av, Winnetka, IL *60093*

Moore MR Robert McA—Pcu.Stan'39
☎ (415) 921-1593 . . 2453 Filbert St, San Francisco, CA *94123*

Moore MR S Harbaugh 3d—NCar'66.Nat'l'83 . . . . . ☎ (703) 440-5923
MISS Elizabeth H—at Hollins . . . . 8008 Ferncliff
MISS Amanda S—at Hollins . . . . Court, Springfield,
VA *22153*

Moore MRS Sandra Sizer (Moore—Sandra Sizer)
☎ (941) 729-0141 . . 4322—15 Way W, Palmetto, FL *34221*

Moore MRS Springer H (Elizabeth B Scott) Sth'35
☎ (561) 567-2175 . . 2695 Tropical Av, Vero Beach, FL *32960*

Moore MR & MRS Sumner Kittelle JR (Ann Hollister Hamilton) Va'74
☎ (804) 358-5813 . . 4311 N Ashlawn Dv, Richmond, VA *23221*

Moore MR & MRS Thomas A (Avril M Barton) P'73.Dar.P'73 . . . .
JUNIORS MR Thomas B . . . .
☎ (513) 281-1188
750 Old Ludlow Av, Cincinnati, OH *45220*

Moore MR Thomas E 3d—Rc.Mto.Stan'81 . . of
☎ (516) 537-5301 . . 61 Summerfield Lane, PO Box 1271, Bridgehampton, NY *11932*
☎ (212) 686-6167 . . 45 E 25 St, Apt 29A, New York, NY *10010*

Moore MR & MRS Thomas G (Cassandra Chrones) Rdc'56.Cvc.GeoW'57 . . . .
MISS Antonia L—at 192A Duncan St, San Francisco, CA *94110* . . . .
☎ (415) 493-7358
3766 La Donna Av, Palo Alto, CA *94306*

Moore MR & MRS Thomas M (Dorothy Alexander) LSU'65.Smu'68.Tex'62 . . . .
MISS Margaret L . . . .
☎ (214) 369-5946
4730 Irvin Simmons Dv, Dallas, TX *75229*

Moore MR & MRS Thomas O JR (Gray—Katherine T Condon) NCar'61.Cda.NCar'56.Va'60 . . . . .
MR Bowman Gray 4th—at ☎ (612) 377-9915 2823 Wayzata Blvd, Minneapolis, MN *55405*
of PO Box 1547, Kernersville, NC *27285-1547*
"Bearlocks" 2028 Coquina Trail, Bald Head Island, NC *28461*

Moore MR & MRS Thomas R (Margaret C King) CtCol'54.Plg.Chr.Myf.StJ.Y'54.H'57 . . . .
MISS E M Clarissa—Y'82.Dth'88—at
☎ (203) 847-1616 . . 66 Hills Lane, Westport, CT *06880* . . . .
MR Charles R H—Tul'85—at ☎ (970) 728-9717 PO Box 847, Telluride, CO *81435* . . . .
☎ (212) 427-8675
1170 Fifth Av, New York, NY *10029*

Moore MRS W Bedford 3d (Jane T Smith) RMWmn'39.Cc.Ncd.
☎ (804) 973-6113 . . "Shack Mountain" 1790 Lambs Rd, Charlottesville, VA *22901*

Moore MR W Bion—Mit'28.Y'32
☎ (915) 544-0175 . . 801 Turney Dv, El Paso, TX *79902*

Moore DR & MRS Walter L (Carpenter—Dorothy J Mahaffey) Str.Cw.StL'35
☎ (314) 441-3409 . . Three Creek Farm, 71 Wolfram Rd, St Charles, MO *63304*

Moore MR & MRS Wesley D (Kathleen M McMahon) SantaC'80.Br'79
☎ (415) 921-5565 . . 200 Laurel St, San Francisco, CA *94118*

Moore MR & MRS Willard S (Margaret E Nelson) Bost'75.Bost'83.Y'81.Cal'84
☎ (212) 787-2065 . . 230 W 79 St, New York, NY *10024*

Moore MR & MRS William C (Helga Davis) Berlin'58.Duke'61 . . . .
MISS Andrea E . . . .
MISS Sabrina G . . . .
MR Charles W . . . .
☎ (770) 993-3448
9725 Nesbit Ferry Rd, Alpharetta, GA *30201*

Moore MRS William E JR (Margaret J Shanks) V'50.Cly.
☎ (212) 879-3900 . . 1 E 66 St, New York, NY *10021*

Moore MR & MRS William H (Edith McKnight) Ln.Ny.Cly.Y'37
☎ (561) 546-5122 . . 426 S Beach Rd, Hobe Sound, FL *33455*

Moore MRS William H 3d (Mabelle Symington) Md.Cw.
☎ (561) 278-2905 . . 2727 N Ocean Blvd, Gulf Stream, FL *33483*

Moore MR & MRS William H 3d (Dorothy B Martin) Y'62
☎ (203) 661-8258 . . Fort Hill Lane, Greenwich, CT *06831*

Moorhead MISS Allison F—SCal'93 . . see MISS C E Wood

Moorhead MR Dudley T 3d . . see MISS C E Wood

Moorhead MRS Fahnestock (Clare H Fahnestock) BMr'49.Sl . . .of
☎ (802) 297-1816 . . "Shilly Chalet" 38 W Hill Rd, Box 376, Stratton Mountain, VT *05155*
☎ (617) 547-0495 . . 336 Harvard St, Apt 1B, Cambridge, MA *02139-2002*

Moorhead MRS Horace R (Scott—Morris—Virginia L Brock)
☎ (610) 527-6953 . . 74 Pasture Lane, Apt 325, Bryn Mawr, PA *19010*

Moorhead MRS J Upshur (Regan—Virginia Paschall) Pa'45.Stc. . . . .
MISS Linda J Regan—Br'78—at
☎ (802) 254-8477 . . 5 School St, Apt 4, Brattleboro, VT *05301* . . . .
☎ (561) 747-0544
186 Turtle Creek Dv, PO Box 3637, Tequesta, FL *33469*

Moorhead MR & MRS J Upshur 2d (Mari A Kilroy) Hlns'76.Va'82.Rc.Ri.Cvc.Pr.Cly.Vt'75
☎ (212) 996-3035 . . 70 E 96 St, New York, NY *10128*

Moorhead MR & MRS Rodman W 3d (Alice B Kerr) V'65.Cl'74.Rc.H'66.H'68 . . . .
JUNIORS MR Rodman W 4th. . . . .
JUNIORS MR Clay W . . . .
of ☎ (212)861-1567
53 E 66 St, New York, NY *10021*
☎ (610) 869-5869 Buttonwood Farm, 361 Lamborntown Rd, West Grove, PA *19390*

Moorhead MR Thomas B—Yn.Y'56.Pa'59.Nu'64 . .
MISS Hannah C—OWes'93—at 215 W 10 St, Apt 2E, New York, NY *10014* . . . .
MISS Rachel McG—at Kenyon . . . .
☎ (203) 966-0627
148 Ramhorne Rd, New Canaan, CT *06840*

Moorhead MR & MRS Thomas C JR (Elizabeth S Hundt) Vt'83.Pa'70
☎ (412) 741-7397 . . Farmhill Rd, Sewickley, PA *15143*

Moorhead MRS William S (Lucy K E Galpin) V'46.Sl.Cvc . . .of
☎ (202) 338-7078 . . 1312—31 St NW, Washington, DC *20007*
PO Box 1508, Middleburg, VA *20118*

Moorhouse MR & MRS Leslie C (Woodward—Wendy A Attee) Pkg. ⛵
☎ (610) 935-1589 . . "Creekview" Box 106, Kimberton, PA *19442*

Moorhouse MISS Meghan Marie (Leslie C) . . . . Born at Phoenixville, PA Mch 10'96

Moorhouse MR Richard T . . see B Barstow JR

Moorhouse MR & MRS William H JR (Margaret C Pew) M.Sfy.Fmy.Me.Fr.Va'70 . . . .
MISS Nina E—at 2080 Filbert St, Apt 3, San Francisco, CA *94123* . . . .
of ☎ (610)649-6066
719 Black Rock Rd, Gladwyne, PA *19035*
☎ (415) 435-3042 85 Mt Tiburon Rd, Tiburon, CA *94920*

Moot MR & MRS John R (Ellen Guild) Rdc'52.Y'55.H.'43.H'48 . . . .
MISS Amey D—H'84—at 76 W Cedar St, Boston, MA *02114* . . . .
☎ (617) 491-8120
44 Coolidge Hill Rd, Cambridge, MA *02138*

Moot MR & MRS Richmond D (Hazel R Matzinger) Wis'43.H'44 . . . . ☎ (802) 485-6800
"Moot Point"
RD 1, Box 350, Northfield, VT 05663
MISS Candace—at 48 E State St, Montpelier, VT 05602 . . . .
MISS Heidi—at 121 Chebacco Rd, Hamilton, MA 01982 . . . .

Moppert MR & MRS Philip E (Gay E Young) Ind'76.Tulsa'74 . . . . ☎ (314) 961-2761
144 S Rock Hill Rd, St Louis, MO 63119
MISS Kristin E . . . .
JUNIORS MISS Elizabeth D . . . .

Moran MR Alfred Jay JR—Rcn.B.NCar'67.H'69
☎ (310) 271-1678 . . 8811 Burton Way, Los Angeles, CA 90048

Moran MRS Bernard A (Helen Gary) Cly.Cda.
☎ (212) RH4-0216 . . 834 Fifth Av, New York, NY 10021

Moran MR & MRS E Leonard JR (Dolores A Matushak) Wis'49
☎ (602) 866-7755 . . 514 W Wakonda Lane, Phoenix, AZ 85023

Moran MR J Douglas JR . . see C McG Hepburn

Moran MR James B—Pa'87 . . see C McG Hepburn

Moran MR & MRS John P (Margaretta B Knorr) Wms'64 . . . . ☎ (307) 632-0316
3571 Hynds Blvd, Cheyenne, WY 82001
MR John P JR—at ☎ (970) 482-6293
2606 Wyandotte Dv, Ft Collins, CO 80526 . . . .

Moran MR Joseph H 2d—Pr.BtP.Bcs.Wms'33.H'36 . . of
☎ (561) 655-5600 . . 160 Royal Palm Way, Palm Beach, FL 33480
☎ (516) 671-8257 . . 24 Prospect Av, Sea Cliff, NY 11579-1004
☎ (970) 923-2420 . . Stonebridge Inn, PO Box 5008, 300 Carriage Way, Snowmass Village, CO 81615

Moran REV (MRS) Lansing S (Lansing Simonds)
☎ (561) 655-5472 . . 230 S County Rd, Palm Beach, FL 33480

Moran MISS Margaretta G—Geo'88
☎ (212) 874-1625 . . 2109 Broadway, Apt 892, New York, NY 10023

Moran MISS Thirza T—Denis'91
☎ (773) 665-2631 . . 519 W Deming Place, Apt 2S, Chicago, IL 60614

Moran DR & MRS Thomas J (Phillips—Katharine B Fetterman) Pitt'36 . . . . ☎ (804) 793-0669
2 Creekside Dv, Danville, VA 24541
MR Thomas J JR—at ☎ (415) 826-2983
1213 Sanchez St, San Francisco, CA 94114 . . . .

Morang MRS Diane D (Diane G Damon) . . . . ☎ (914) 357-0488
10 Sussex Court, Suffern, NY 10901
MISS Laura L—at M W Farms, Star Rte 2, Box 299, Twentynine Palms, CA 92277 . . . .
MR Kevin D—at M W Farms, Star Rte 2, Box 299, Twentynine Palms, CA 92277 . . . .

Moravec MR & MRS F Joseph (Augusta C Off) LakeF'72.Mt.Rr.Cvc.H'73 . . . . ☎ (301) 469-0248
9224 Vendome Dv, Bethesda, MD 20817
JUNIORS MISS Alexandra C . . . .

More MR & MRS Douglas McL (Bucknall—Pamela B Marr) H'47.Cl'50
☎ (203) 869-0663 . . 27 Skylark Rd, Greenwich, CT 06830-4624

More MR & MRS Timothy T (Rebecca W Sherrill) Va'70.Br'86.Chi.Y'67.Va'70 . . . . ☎ (401) 751-4641
135 Benefit St, Providence, RI 02903
MISS Eleanor S—at Brown
MR Henry Brooks—Vt'95—at Siena, Italy . . . . .

Morehouse MR & MRS Alexander G (Elizabeth W Rasch) Emory'63 . . . .
Burge Plantation, 200 Morehouse Rd, Mansfield, GA 30255
MISS Nancy A . . . .
MISS Eve G . . . .

Morehouse MR & MRS M Dutton JR (Young—Joyce L Clasen) Cal'56.Cw.Y'59 . . . . ☎ (810) 645-0963
520 Lone Pine Rd, Box 801, Bloomfield Hills, MI 48303-0801
MISS Alison L Young . . . .

Morehouse MR & MRS W Bradley (Blow—Marian A Bradley) Bnd'58.Dth'45.Y'51
☎ (203) 255-1140 . . 345 Mill Hill Rd, Southport, CT 06490

Moreland MISS Elaine S
☎ (212) 255-8374 . . 95 Horatio St, New York, NY 10014

Moreland MR & MRS W Ford 2d (Ellen M Zook) Pg.Y'58 . . . . ☎ (412) 621-5676
917 St James St, Pittsburgh, PA 15232
MR Raymond F 2d—at ☎ (412) 431-1875
2027 Carey Way, Pittsburgh, PA 15203 . . . .

Moreland MR W Theodore
☎ (212) 987-1381 . . 319 E 92 St, Apt 3W, New York, NY 10128

Morello MR Stephen J—Ne.Fw.Pace'55
☎ (212) 751-0364 . . 300 E 51 St, New York, NY 10022-7806

Morey MR Joseph H JR—St.Ts.Y'34
☎ (716) 882-2062 . . 20 Clarendon Place, Buffalo, NY 14209

Morgan MISS Alexandra W . . see MRS D S Helie

Morgan MR & MRS Alfred Y 3d (Virginia E Toomey) Man'vl'62.Mds.Ri.BtP.Cly.HolyC'60 .
of ☎ (212)744-5840
850 Park Av, New York, NY 10021
MISS Muriel C . . . .
MISS Charlotte M . . . .
☎ (516) 324-6730
"The Tyler House"
217 Main St, East Hampton, NY 11937

Morgan MR Cecil—Cc.LSU'19
☎ (504) 522-5758 . . 1435 Jackson Av, New Orleans, LA 70130

Morgan MRS Charles Baird (Isobel D Lincoln)
☎ (610) 647-2943 . . 296 Bair Rd, Berwyn, PA 19312-1406

Morgan MR Charles E
☎ (602) 948-2023 . . 6702 E Shea Blvd, Scottsdale, AZ 85254

Morgan MR & MRS Charles F (Sarah B Lambert) Ny.S.G.Cly.Cda.H'50 . . of
☎ (212) 879-0773 . . 520 E 86 St, New York, NY 10028
☎ (516) 922-6911 . . 154 Cove Rd, Oyster Bay, NY 11771

Morgan MR Chauncey G—Dth'86.Nu'91
☎ (203) 852-1829 . . 14 Juniper Rd, Rowayton, CT 06853

Morgan MR Edwin Ernest (Freer—Jane B Walker) Vh.
☎ (818) 792-7884 . . 842 E Villa St, Apt 323, Pasadena, CA 91101

Morgan MISS Eugenia B—Elk.Ncd.
☎ (410) 377-6953 . . 223 Overbrook Rd, Baltimore, MD 21212

Morgan MR F Corlies 2d—H'83
☎ (703) 521-1242 . . 1164 S Thomas St, Apt 21, Arlington, VA 22204

Morgan MR & MRS G Frederick (Paula Deitz) Sth'59.K.Sm.Rv.Fw.Cw.Cs.P.'43
☎ (212) 831-7019 . . 1220 Park Av, New York, NY 10128

Morgan MRS G Walker (Dorothy S Wegg) Cnt.
☎ (518) 465-3337 . . 145 Broadway, Apt 1A, Menands, NY 12204

Morgan MR & MRS George O (Maria Madarkova) Pn.P'38
☎ (011-34-6) 687-5241 . . "Chalet Morgan" La Sierra 21, Carretera de Monte Casino, 03530 La Nucia, Alicante, Spain

Morgan MR & MRS George O JR (Marianela
Martinez de Eguiluz) Laf'72.Iese'74 . . . . | ☎ (305) 663-5607
MR George O 5th . . . . | 11345 SW 62 Av,
JUNIORS MISS Marianela . . . . | Miami, FL
33156-4943

Morgan MRS George W (M Carolyn Nichols)
☎ (216) 247-8386 . . 20 Mill Creek Lane, Chagrin Falls, OH *44022*

Morgan MR H Vaughan JR (Susan E Manimon)
☎ (904) 439-7945 . . 900 Ocean Marina Dv, Flagler Beach, FL *32136*

Morgan MRS Hallowell V (Sellers—Helen S Chance) Ph.Me.Ac.Cc.
☎ (610) 692-1773 . . 283 Devon Way, Hershey's Mill, West Chester,
PA *19380*

Morgan MR & MRS Henry (Susan L De Laney)
Skd'73.Wes'78.Ny.S.Csh.Roch'72
☎ (516) 759-5791 . . 11 Cherrywood Lane, Lattingtown, NY *11560*

Morgan RR ADM (RET) & MRS Henry S (Flather—J | ☎ (410) 360-3432
Alexandra McCain) USN.Br'56.GeoW'78.Gi. | 641 Stillwater Rd,
Ny.Mt.H'44.GeoW'78 . . . . | PO Box 173,
MISS Katherine McC—MaryB'89—at | Gibson Island, MD
☎ (703) 691-4052 . . 9509 Barcellona Court, | *21056*
Fairfax, VA *22031* . . . . |
MISS (DR) Alexandra W Flather-Morgan— |
P'85.Y'89—at ☎ (617) 876-6782 |
38 Dana St, Cambridge, MA *02138* . . . . |

Morgan MR & MRS Hewitt JR (J Rose Converse) | ☎ (508) 356-3824
Sth'58.Ec.H'52 . . . . | 7 Waldingfield Rd,
MISS Laura K . . . . | Ipswich, MA
01938-2732

Morgan MISS Holly Anna (Seth A) . . . . Born at
Washington, DC Mch 20'96

Morgan MR & MRS Howard R (Elizabeth B Trudeau) | ☎ (610) 254-9686
Pe.M.Sdg.Ncd.Wes'61.Pa'63 . . . . | 234 Pembroke Av,
MISS Anna E—at Roanoke Coll . . . . | Wayne, PA *19087*
MR H Randall JR—*see Dilatory Domiciles* . . . . . |
MR Carl G—Rich'90—at 2514 Page Terr, |
Alexandria, VA *22302* . . . . |

Morgan MR & MRS Ivan J (Keith R Deering) Pom'81.Clare'85.Pom'84
☎ (310) 434-8322 . . 1030 Loma Av, Apt 103, Long Beach, CA *90804*

Morgan MR & MRS Jeffery B (Virginia R Turnure) Vt'85.ColSt'83
☎ (802) 644-2412 . . Smugglers Notch Inn, Church St, Jeffersonville,
VT *05464*

Morgan MR & MRS John A (Coldren—Loise | of ☎ (310)275-0200
Abrahamson) Rcch. . . . . | 702 N Foothill Rd,
MISS Lindsay Coldren—at 206 Sierra View | Beverly Hills, CA
Rd, Pasadena, CA *91105* . . . . | *90210*
☎ (619) 324-1946
''Los Conejos''
70465 Sunny Lane,
Rancho Mirage, CA
92270

Morgan MR & MRS John M (Andrew—Elizabeth M McPherson)
Strat'64.Gi.Elk.Mv.Rv.Cw.Ncd.JHop'51 . . of
☎ (410) 532-6771 . . 115 Cross Keys Rd, Baltimore, MD *21210*
☎ (561) 231-7022 . . 203 N Carmel Court, Vero Beach, FL *32963*

Morgan MR John M JR . . see A A Duer

Morgan MR & MRS John P 2d (Claire B Ober) Ny.Pr.S.Cly.Cda.H'40
☎ (516) 922-7456 . . 247 Cleft Rd, Mill Neck, NY *11765*

Morgan MR John S—H'39
☎ (212) GR3-4055 . . 40 E 10 St, New York, NY *10003*

Morgan MR John S C—H'60
☎ (617) 332-3253 . . 29 Morseland Av, Newton Center,
MA *02159-1151*

Morgan MR & MRS Jonathan C (Carol S Frigo) Ill'84.JHop'96.Ill'83
☎ (410) 435-8223 . . 5006 Broadmoor Rd, Baltimore, MD *21212*

Morgan MISS Josephine M—Hlns'64
☎ (011-30-1) 751-4403 . . Damareos 102-104, Pangrati, 11633 Athens,
Greece

Morgan MR & MRS Junius S 2d (Patricia A Milton) LakeF'69
☎ (703) 356-7195 . . 7600 Timberly Court, McLean, VA *22102*

Morgan MISS Laila Maria (g—Charles F Morgan) . . . . . Born May 12'96

Morgan MRS Laurence W (Ann Clarke). On. . . . . . | ☎ (847) 234-1104
MR William O . . . . | 930 S Green Bay
Rd, Lake Forest, IL
60045

Morgan MRS LeRoy Tuttle (Carolyn Diana Mary | ☎ (301) 972-1612
Makins) GeoW'75.Cvc. . . . . | 25214 Peach Tree
MISS Cecilia Hay—AmU'87 . . . . | Rd, Clarksburg, MD
MISS Maria Abell—Mass'89—at NYU . . . . | *20871-9101*
MISS Olivia Dudley—Wes'94 . . . . |

Morgan MRS Margaret C (Frothingham—Fisher—Margaret C Morgan)
☎ (609) 924-8844 . . 105 Audubon Lane, Princeton, NJ *08540*

Morgan MISS Margaret Eiluned—Sth'72.Ford'86.Cly.Cs.
☎ (212) 753-8744 . . 245 E 63 St, New York, NY *10021*

Morgan MR & MRS Matthew (Rosalinda A Rosales) | ☎ (516) 922-6399
H'50.Nu'65 . . . . | 51 Tooker Av,
MR Matthew R . . . . | Oyster Bay, NY
MR Alexander R . . . . | *11771*
MRS Marianna C (Lansbury—Marianna C |
Morgan) Skd'85 . . . . |

Morgan MR Miles—Ny.H'50
☎ (011-33) 93-32-77-36 . . 616 chemin des Allègres,
06480 La Colle-sur-Loup, France

Morgan MRS Randal (Mary E Roberts) Ac.
☎ (610) 645-8689 . . 1400 Waverly Rd, Villa 40, Gladwyne, PA *19035*

Morgan MRS Reed A JR (Lucille E Smith) Pc.
☎ (404) 255-6846 . . 4620 W Wieuca Rd NE, Apt 60, Atlanta,
GA *30342*

Morgan MR & MRS Reginald H T 3d (Sara E Brown) CtCol'81
☎ (919) 967-8700 . . 160 Kingston Dv, Chapel Hill, NC *27514*

Morgan MR & MRS Robert F (Mary E Howard) P'52 | ☎ (514) 737-4869
MR Robert F JR—McG'80 . . . . | 219 Chester Av,
MR Jonathan E H . . . . | Mt Royal, Quebec
H3R 1W4, Canada

Morgan MISS Rose B (Hewitt JR) . . . . Married at Ipswich, MA
Daignault MR David A . . . . Apr 20'96

Morgan DR & MRS (DR) Seth A (Heloise E De Rosis) CtCol'74.CtCol'76
5417 Center St, Chevy Chase, MD *20815*

Morgan MRS Stewart McK (Kennedy—Geraldine G Dryer)
☎ (561) 231-2324 . . 5601 N A1A, Apt 106S, Vero Beach, FL *32963*

Morgan MR Thomas M—Ariz'53 . . . . | 1315 E Mabel St,
MISS Amy K . . . . | Tucson, AZ *85719*
MR McKee E . . . . |

Morgan MR & MRS Walter L (Helen Dugan) Rc.Me.M.Ph.Gm.Ac.Pn.P.'20
☎ (610) LA5-3368 . . 440 Garden Lane, Bryn Mawr, PA *19010*

Morgan DR & MRS Walter McN 3d (Anne McK Zimmerman)
P'78.Van'81.Elk.P'78.Van'82
☎ (615) 383-0438 . . ''Greenspring'' 200 Evelyn Av, Nashville,
TN *37205*

Morgan MR & MRS William B 2d (Burnham—Helen Foster)
Gm.Fst.Sg.Yh.Ac.Pa'32
1400 Waverly Rd, Blair 131, Gladwyne, PA *19035*

Morgan MR & MRS William J (Melissa C Jackson) Pa'74.Ford'81.Csh.H.'68
☎ (516) 692-5923 . . 7 Kennedy Lane, Cold Spring Harbor, NY *11724*

Moriarty MRS George M (Elizabeth B Moore) . . . . | of ☎ (617)441-3813
MISS Caroline W . . . . | 75 Richdale Av, 17,
MISS Sarah C . . . . | Cambridge, MA
MR Bradley M—Geo'91 . . . . | *02140*
| ☎ (207) 882-4010
| McCarty Cove Rd,
| Westport Island, ME
| *04578*

Moriarty MR George M—Sm.Tv.Mt.H.'64
☎ (508) 927-7302 . . ''Old Fort Barn'' Paine Av, Prides Crossing,
MA *01965*

Morison MRS Elting E (Tilghman—Elizabeth D Forbes) Chi.
☎ (603) 924-3218 . . 343 Old Sharon Rd, Peterborough, NH *03458*

Morley MR & MRS Christopher J (Melissa K Slingluff)
Denis'85.Bgt.Stc.Ken'83
☎ (914) 234-0822 . . 479 Cantitoe St, Bedford, NY *10506*

Morley MR & MRS Daniel F (Evans—Ruth F Oliver) | ☎ (617) 354-7804
Sm.Chi.Yn.Dth'67.Lond'69 . . . . | 148 Brattle St,
JUNIORS MISS Amanda W—at St Paul's . . . . . . | Cambridge, MA
MR Jeremy A M Evans—StAndr'93 . . . . | *02138*

Mormoris MR & MRS Stephen C (Jean A Sampson) Tufts'79.Nu'82.S.P.'79
☎ (516) 922-6652 . . 73 Cove Rd, Oyster Bay, NY *11771*

Moroney MR & MRS William M (Rosemary Newman) An.Minn'32.Minn'34
☎ (202) 966-5323 . . 2913 University Terr NW, Washington, DC *20016*

Moroney MR & MRS William R (Tracy Mullin) Cc.Bost'67
☎ (301) 229-7107 . . 6505 River Rd, Bethesda, MD *20817*

Morosani MR & MRS John W (Joan C Devine) SL'75.Rc.Mid'74.Dth'76
☎ (212) 410-1755 . . 1619 Third Av, New York, NY *10128*

Morosani MISS Katherine C—Rol'91 . . of
☎ (212) 645-7735 . . 210 W 10 St, Apt 3C, New York, NY *10014*
☎ (860) 567-8122 . . ''Laurel Ridge'' 164 Wigwam Rd, PO Box 1235,
Litchfield, CT *06759*

Morosani MRS Rémy E (Mackoy—Virginia Warrington)
☎ (860) 567-8122 . . ''Laurel Ridge'' 164 Wigwam Rd, Litchfield,
CT *06759*

Morosani MR & MRS Reto W (Marana L Brooks) | ☎ (860) 567-4292
Nu'73.Nu'74.Dar.Mid'67 . . . . | 88 Wigwam Rd,
JUNIORS MR Reto N . . . . | PO Box 1045,
| Litchfield, CT *06759*

Morosi MR & MRS Donald J (Dominga E Vance) | ☎ (415) 883-0168
SFr'63 . . . . | 35 Corte Alta,
MISS Elena D . . . . | Ignacio, CA *94949*
MR Vance J—at 413 E Van Ness Place,
Salt Lake City, UT *84111* . . . . |

Morosi MR & MRS Justin I (Marji O Gilles) CalPoly'95
☎ (317) 259-0546 . . 7469 Somerset Bay, Indianapolis, IN *46240*

Morphy MR & MRS James C (Priscilla W Plimpton) Ws'80.T.H.'76.H'79
☎ (203) 637-2511 . . 191 Riverside Av, Riverside, CT *06878*

Morrel MR & MRS W Griffin JR (Sandra V Coats) | ☎ (410) 323-2529
RMWmn'57.Md.Elk.Mv.Yn.Y'55 . . . . | 6 Beechdale Rd,
MISS Elisabeth W—at 4407 Clydesdale Rd, | Baltimore, MD
Baltimore, MD *21211* . . . . | *21210*
MR Jere C—at Lafayette . . . . |

Morrill MR Amos—Y'48 | ☎ (268) 461-2100
MR Amos JR | ''Turtle Gate''
| PO Box 171,
| Antigua

Morrill MR & MRS Benjamin B (Morgan—Elizabeth | ☎ (508) 927-1359
R Choate) L.My.Myc.Myf.Bost'54 . . . . | 68 West St,
MISS Amelia C . . . . | Beverly Farms, MA
MR Benjamin B 2d . . . . | *01915*

Morrill MR & MRS C Ford (Conway—Constance | ☎ (314) 966-6379
Bradshaw) Stph'55.Wash'58.Nd.Cy.H'34 . . . . . | 7 Deacon Dv,
MISS Constance F . . . . | St Louis, MO *63131*
MR Frederick W B . . . . |

Morrill MR & MRS F Gordon (Elizabeth Hunter) H'32 . . of
☎ (011-39-55) 2480711 . . 73 Costa San Giorgio, 50125 Florence, Italy
Dorchester Apt 5S, 200 N Ocean Blvd, Delray Beach, FL *33483*

Morrill MR & MRS Henry Leighton (Irene N Randolph) Cy.H'32
☎ (314) 993-3445 . . 917 S Warson Rd, St Louis, MO *63124*

Morrin MR & MRS Gerard F (Lisa Lowell Hay) CtCol'79
☎ (310) 459-0544 . . 911 Fiske St, Pacific Palisades, CA *90272*

Morrin MRS Kevin C (Helen L Clanton) . . . . | ☎ (314) 367-0291
MR Kevin C JR—Wash'61—at | 1 McKnight Rd,
Columbus Academy, 4300 Cherry Bottom Rd, | Apt 131, St Louis,
PO Box 30745, Gahanna, OH *43230* . . . . | MO *63124*

Morrin DR & MRS Peter A F (Mariella C Coe) | ☎ (613) 546-2880
Wells'58.Dub'55 ⚓ . . . . | 209 Fairway Hill
MR Hugh F—at Port Washington, NY *11050* . . . | Crescent, Kingston,
MR Robin D . . . . | Ontario K7M 2B5,
| Canada

Morrin MR & MRS Peter P (Carolyn J S Brooks) | ☎ (502) 456-2397
MtH'67.H'68.P'73 . . . . | 1288 Bassett Av,
JUNIORS MR Matthew B—at Harvard . . . . | Louisville, KY
| *40204*

Morris MISS Adrienne C—Geo'84.Cda.
☎ (212) 974-0650 . . 405 W 57 St, Apt 6B, New York, NY *10019*

Morris MRS Albert L (Craig Dorchester) G.
☎ (716) 875-4650 . . 23 Dana Rd, Buffalo, NY *14216*

Morris MR & MRS Anthony (A Elizabeth S Wingerd) Denis'72.Dick'71
☎ (610) 692-7363 . . 700 N Walnut St, West Chester, PA *19380*

Morris MR Bingham W . . . . Died at
Southampton, NY May 28'96

Morris MR & MRS Charles W JR (Pamela H Sattley) | ☎ (313) 886-9553
Mich'56.Va'50 . . . . | 181 Earl Court,
MISS Lindsay M—at ☎ (516) 329-3652 | Grosse Pointe
37 Harbor View Lane, East Hampton, NY *11937* | Farms, MI *48236*
MISS Carrington C—at ☎ (212) 982-3585 |
2 Bleecker St, New York, NY *10012* . . . . . . |
MR Charles W 3d . . . . |
MR Stuart H . . . . |

Morris MRS Daniel I (Sarah L Lorimer) Cs....... | ☎ (610) 649-0418
MISS Faith M—at ☎ (610) 873-0386 | 934 Remington Rd,
500 Campbell Circle, Apt H15, Downingtown, | Wynnewood, PA
PA *19335* .... | *19096*
MR Francis G—Temp'81 ....
MR Nicholas H—at ☎ (617) 426-6962
62 Boylston St, Apt 115, Boston, MA *02116* . . .

Morris MISS Deirdre L E—Vt'83
☎ (802) 459-6389 . . 15 Pine St, Proctor, VT *05765*

Morris MRS Edward W (Ruth Gibson) V'30.Cc.
☎ (803) 689-3558 . . 22 Meadowlark Lane, Hilton Head Island,
SC *29926*

Morris MR & MRS Frederic H (Elizabeth A Bisso) | ☎ (508) 526-4490
GeoW'71.My.Myc.Sm.Y'68.H'74 ⚓ ...... | 18 Boardman Av,
JUNIORS MISS Elizabeth D .... | Manchester, MA
JUNIORS MR Frederic H JR—at St Paul's ...... | *01944*

Morris MRS Frederick W 3d (Mildred D Dickinson) Sg.
☎ (561) 835-3529 . . 400 N Flagler Dv, Apt 1205, West Palm Beach,
FL *33401*

Morris MR & MRS Galloway C 3d (Elizabeth L Boyd) Rv.Ht.Ncd.Cr'21
☎ (610) 584-3811 . . Meadowood at Worcester, 135 Laurel House,
Lansdale, PA *19446*

Morris MR & MRS Galloway C 4th (Sandra Bromley) | ☎ (610) 933-6580
Rv. .... | 55 Buckwalter Rd,
MISS Rebecca M—MtH'88.Cda. .... | Phoenixville, PA
MR G Cheston 5th....................... | *19460*

Morris MRS Gelston B JR (Weir—Helen D Harmonson) .... Died at
Pittsburgh, PA Feb 24'96

Morris MR & MRS George C (Mary L Cook) Mich'63.Ts.Bf.P'61
☎ (716) 655-2932 . . 1600 N Davis Rd, East Aurora, NY *14052*

Morris MR & MRS George F (Gaston—Diane A Day) | ☎ (203) 869-1650
MR G Renick .... | 544 Round Hill Rd,
MISS G Kemper Gaston .... | Greenwich, CT
MR Talbot F Gaston.................... | *06831*

Morris MR George H
☎ (908) 782-0044 . . "Hunterdon" 680 Sidney Rd, Pittstown, NJ *08867*

Morris MR & MRS Grinnell (Cornelia R Kellogg) BMr'39.Plg.Ncd.Yn.Y'32
☎ (941) 643-1406 . . 108 Moorings Park Dv, Apt B301, Naples,
FL *34105*

Morris MISS Helen S—Cl'76.Lond'78
☎ (212) 288-7836 . . 925 Park Av, New York, NY *10028*

Morris MR & MRS I Wistar JR (Foust—Gerda Haller) Ph.Me.Cts.P.'36
☎ (610) MU8-0289 . . 500 Conestoga Rd, Villanova, PA *19085*

Morris MR & MRS I Wistar 3d (Martha F Hamilton) | ☎ (610) LA5-6659
Me.Ac.Cr'64.H'70 .... | 234 Broughton
MISS Melissa H—Duke'95 .... | Lane, Villanova, PA
MISS Lydia P—at Harvard .... | *19085*
JUNIORS MISS Eleanor W

Morris MR & MRS J L Malcolm (Meriwether W Hudson) Duke'85.Pc.Pa'85
☎ (410) 363-1292 . . 405 Garrison Forest Rd, Owings Mills, MD *21117*

Morris MR & MRS James S (Eleanor K Smith) | of ☎ (215)248-4553
Rdc'56.Pa'59.Pc.Cs.Ac.Edin'55.Pa'57 .... | "Sugar Loaf
MR S Houston—H'89—at 30 Brechin Place, | Orchard"
London SW7, England .... | 31 W Bells Mill Rd,
Philadelphia, PA
19118
☎ (011-44-1875)
833-789
"Woodcote Park"
Fala & Soutra,
Midlothian EH37
57G, Scotland

Morris MR & MRS Jeffrey J (Sharon P Hadley) Stan'67
☎ (415) 929-9580 . . 1463 Jefferson St, San Francisco, CA *94123*

Morris MRS John A (Edna Brokaw) Srr.Cly.Ht.Cda.
☎ (212) BU8-2196 . . 4 E 72 St, New York, NY *10021*

Morris DR & MRS John A JR (Julia W Caldwell) | ☎ (615) 292-0483
Ky'72.Ky'82.Unn.Cly.Ty'69.Ky'77 .... | 870 Tyne Blvd,
JUNIORS MISS Jessie C .... | Nashville, TN *37220*

Morris MR & MRS John D 2d (Susan Brooks) | ☎ (207) 832-7607
Rdc'65.Pa'67 .... | Storer Mountain
MR Joshua B—at Colby .... | Farm, 222 Storer
MR Samuel W—at Berklee Coll of Music...... | Mountain Rd,
North Waldoboro,
ME *04572*

Morris MRS John McL (Marjorie S Austin) Cda.
☎ (203) 562-5070 . . 4 Edgehill Rd, New Haven, CT *06511*

Morris MR & MRS John W (Catherine B Urban) | ☎ (202) 966-8596
Newt'64.Cvc.P'61 .... | 5155 Macomb St
MISS Caroline S—at Colby .... | NW, Washington,
JUNIORS MR Giles R .... | DC *20016*

Morris MRS Joseph J (Elizabeth M Buckley) ...... | ☎ (415) 325-1116
MISS Nancy M—at 21 Willow Rd, Menlo Park, | 92 Flood Circle,
CA *94025* .... | Atherton, CA *94027*

Morris MR & MRS Joseph Paul JR (Rebecca P | ☎ (610) TA8-8268
Darnall) Rv.Wt.Fw.W.Cspa.Ncd. .... | 1551 Butler Pike,
MISS Sarah P W—W.Ncd. .... | Blue Bell,
PO Box 218,
Ambler, PA *19002*

Morris MR & MRS Lewis (Patricia B Carr) Pqt.H'47
☎ (203) 259-5144 . . Box 386, 1074 Sturges H'way, Southport,
CT *06490*

Morris MR & MRS Martin Van B (Sara E Layman) | of ☎ (305)245-4488
Br'61 .... | 25300 SW 187 Av,
MISS Heather de R .... | Homestead, FL
MR Martin Van B 3d................... | *33031*
JUNIORS MR Courtney de R .... | ☎ (516) 288-8676
47 Beach Rd,
Westhampton
Beach, NY *11978*

Morris MRS Nicholas W (Margaret Pancoast)
☎ (610) 429-4961 . . 760 Inverness Dv, West Chester, PA *19380*

Morris MR & MRS Peter V C (Carlotta M Noël) Cly.H'53
☎ (212) 289-2590 . . 1170 Fifth Av, New York, NY *10029*

Morris MRS Priscilla P (Priscilla P Perry) Rdc'63.H.
MISS Sarah P—H'91—at ☎ (617) 497-1240
177 Hancock St, Cambridge, MA *02139* . . . . . .
MR Edward H—Wes'94 . . . . | of ☎ (617)326-9815
10 Campus Dv,
Dedham, MA *02026*
☎ (508) 255-3017
55 Deborah Doane
Way, PO Box 501,
Eastham, MA *02642*

Morris MR & MRS Robert F JR (Margaret J
Fenimore) Pe.Rv.Cspa.Dar.P'62 . . . .
MR Robert F—Pa'94—at Vanderbilt Law . . . . . . | 5 Broadacres Court,
Moorestown, NJ
08057

Morris MR & MRS Robert M (Nellie Terzian)
Bnd'76.VillaN'80.Rc.Sa.Bost'77.VillaN'86 . . of
☎ (610) NI4-4004 . . 201 Three Rivers, Berwyn, PA *19312*
☎ (610) 399-1521 . . ''The Bungalo'' 1275 Westtown-Thornton Rd,
Westtown, PA *19395*

Morris MR & MRS Roland (Sally J Fageol)
Au.Ph.Gm.Me.P'55.Pa'60 . . . .
MISS Heather H—Tufts'85—at
☎ (617) 267-3633 . . 118 Newbury St, Boston,
MA *02116* . . . . | of ☎ (610)525-2893
301 N Ithan Av,
Rosemont, PA
19010
☎ (518) 962-4975
''Meadow Springs''
Rte 1, Box 1140A,
Westport, NY *12993*

Morris MR & MRS Roland JR (Karen L Kummerer)
Barat'79.Ch'83.Gm.Me.Vt'80
☎ (914) 793-8161 . . 56 Dellwood Rd, Bronxville, NY *10708*

Morris MR & MRS Samuel W (Eleanor M Jones) H'40.Pa'49
☎ (610) 469-6268 . . Lundale Farm, RD 7, Box 360, Pottstown,
PA *19464*

Morris MR & MRS Samuel W JR (Hatcher—Carolyn V N Foster)
Ga'72.Rc.Me.H.'66.GeoW'69
☎ (610) 525-5240 . . 1451 County Line Rd, Rosemont, PA *19010*

Morris MR & MRS Seymour JR (Gabriela Dordai)
Romania'69.B.Hn.H'68.H'72
☎ (011-40-1) 323-2731 . . 133-135 Calea Victoriei, Etaj 6, Apt 3,
401 Bucharest, Romania

Morris MRS Stephen V C (Persis W Mason) Mt.
☎ (703) 538-2546 . . 6133 Brook Dv, Falls Church, VA *22044*

Morris MR Theodore H 3d . . . . Died at
Bryn Mawr, PA May 8'96

Morris MRS Theodore H 3d (Nancy L Crockett)
Bates'36.Me.Gm.Ac.Fw.W.Myf.
☎ (610) LA5-1425 . . 1425 Morris Av, Villanova, PA *19085*

Morris MR Thomas—Bost'47 . . . .
MR Bradford T . . . . | ☎ (860) 669-7300
24 Commerce St,
Clinton, CT *06413*

Morris MR & MRS Thomas B JR (Ann Peirce)
Pc.Sg.Ph.Rc.P.'58.H'62
MISS Lauren A—at ☎ (215) 893-1258
1500 Locust St, Apt 2812, Philadelphia, PA
19102 . . . .
MR Thomas B 3d—at ☎ (617) 625-0913
12 Lovell St, Somerville, MA *02144* . . . .
MR Richard T—Hob'92—at ☎ (617) 666-3781
29 Pearson Rd, Apt 2, Somerville, MA *02144* . . | ☎ (215) CH7-2449
8320 Seminole Av,
Philadelphia, PA
19118

Morris MR & MRS Warren L 2d (Elizabeth H Swift)
Macalester'81.Kt.Macalester'80
☎ (216) 423-0903 . . 901 Chagrin River Rd, Gates Mills, OH *44040*

Morris MR William B—Rc.Me.H'65 . . of
☎ (212) 988-8204 . . 315 E 70 St, New York, NY *10021*
☎ (860) 535-1107 . . 8 Broad St, Stonington, CT *06378*

Morris MR & MRS William H (Arvia B Crosby)
Ws'50.Cs.Cda.Y'52
MISS Arvia E—Nw'79—at 283 Bleecker St,
New York, NY *10014* . . . . | of ☎ (212)861-9203
137 E 66 St,
New York, NY
10021
☎ (914) 876-3231
''Cedar Heights
Orchards'' Crosby
Lane, Rhinebeck,
NY *12572*

Morrisey MISS Florence Earle—Grenoble'76.CUNY'77
☎ (516) 283-0120 . . 135 Corrigan St, Southampton, NY *11968*

Morrisey MRS John L (Piers—Frances E Gensler) . . of
☎ (516) 283-0866 . . PO Box 1209, Southampton, NY *11969*
162 E Inlet Dv, Palm Beach, FL *33480*

Morrish MR David H (late Frederick D) . . . . . Married at Palm Beach, FL
Walthew MRS K Conway (Bier—Karen M Conway) . . . . Jun 22'96

Morrish MR & MRS David H (Bier—Walthew—Karen M Conway)
Cw.Myf.Ne.Fla'55.Cl'59
☎ (561) 655-5322 . . 1 Royal Palm Way, Palm Beach, FL *33480*

Morrison MISS Barbara—Woos'77.Cl'79.UWash'86
☎ (217) 422-0595 . . 854 W William St, Decatur, IL *62522*

Morrison MR & MRS Bart W (Marguerite E Howard)
JHop'78.Md'81.Lm.Dar.Ncd.Dc.Tex'74.Pa'76 . . of
☎ (212) 769-2847 . . 20 W 86 St, Apt 6A, New York, NY *10024*
☎ (203) 746-0374 . . 20 Woods Rd, Candlewood Knolls, New Fairfield,
CT *06812*

Morrison MR D Craig JR—So'65 . . . .
MISS Heather E . . . .
MR Donald C 3d . . . . | ☎ (404) 876-5520
1437 Wessyngton
Rd NE, Atlanta, GA
30306

Morrison MR David J—Rv.Leh'73 . . of
☎ (717) 234-5757 . . 936 N 2 St, Harrisburg, PA *17102*
☎ (717) 646-0818 . . Biddle-Morrison Camp, Pocono Lake Preserve,
PA *18348*

Morrison MRS Donald C (Natalie P Gates) Ncd.
☎ (513) 321-4663 . . 2444 Madison Rd, Apt 504, Cincinnati, OH *45208*

Morrison MR & MRS Edward A (Rodker—Barbara
MacKenzie-Smith) Ox'29 . . . .
MR Thomas A . . . . | ☎ (011-44)
Dolgellau 422611
Maes-y-Bryner,
Dolgellau,
Gwynedd,
North Wales
LL40 2NF, UK

Morrison MRS Eric H (Christine S Duncan) Me.
☎ (610) 359-1203 . . Dunwoody Village, 3500 West Chester Pike,
Newtown Square, PA *19073-4168*

Morrison MR & MRS George H (Marie A Tramelli) .
MR William K 2d . . . . | ☎ (314) 361-7052
5026 Westminster
Place, St Louis, MO
63108

Morrison MRS George Le R (Martha B Gross) BMr'47
☎ (717) 599-5077 . . 430 Fishing Creek Valley Rd, Harrisburg, PA *17112*

Morrison MR & MRS Gordon M (Barbara J Lee) Wheat'54.H.'52
☎ (508) 655-6391 . . 32 Old Orchard Rd, Sherborn, MA *01770*

Morrison MR & MRS James A (Anne N Wilbur) Geo'87.Cal'82.Dth'87
☎ (415) 459-1747 . . 501 Oak Av, San Anselmo, CA *94960*

Morrison MR & MRS James R (Anne Sloan) V'55.Bow'47
☎ (719) 471-3046 . . 1514 Mesa Av, Colorado Springs, CO *80906*

Morrison MISS Joan Van D—NH'76 . . see C M Biddle 3d

Morrison MRS John McF (Eleanor B Morris) V'38
☎ (011-44-131) 447-6373 . . The Elms 23, 148 Whitehouse Loan, Edinburgh EX9 2EZ, Scotland

Morrison MR & MRS Langdon G (Ellen D Ferrari) Elmira'73.So'67
68 York River Rd, Williamsburg, VA *23188-4012* . . MRS absent

Morrison MR & MRS Mills Lane (Lucille P Orr)	☎ (912) 233-5842
Swb'67.Ncd.NCar'67	Lebanon Plantation,
MISS Augusta O	5745 Ogeechee Rd,
MR Mills L JR	Savannah, GA
JUNIORS MR Hugh C	*31405*
Morrison MR & MRS Peter (Susanne E King)	☎ (415) 507-9246
Tcy.Pcu.Y'50	200 Deer Valley Rd,
MR Stephen B	Apt 3L, San Rafael,
	CA *94903*

Morrison MR Reid B—Nrr.Cw.H.'54
☎ (617) 247-0154 . . 180 Beacon St, Boston, MA *02116-1455*

Morrison MR & MRS Roger A (Beatrice A Reed) Br'83.Cly.Dth'83
☎ (213) 931-6408 . . 236 S Irving Blvd, Los Angeles, CA *90004*

Morrison MR & MRS Thompson (Louise Douglas) Van'38.Cwr'72
☎ (615) 269-6548 . . Royal Oaks Apt 168, 4505 Harding Rd, Nashville, TN *37205*

Morrissett DR Leslie E—Chr.An.Rv.Va'30
☎ (804) 232-0109 . . 310 W 31 St, Richmond, VA *23225*

Morrissey MR Robert N
☎ (314) 781-8508 . . 7452 Wise Av, St Louis, MO *63117*

Morrow MR & MRS A J Donelson (Sears—Suzanne	☎ (505) 466-0126
Roy) P'60	1 Lime Kiln Rd,
MR Andrew J—P'90	General Delivery,
MR Nathaniel R Sears—Y'90—at	Lamy, NM *87540*
☎ (415) 703-0360 . . 120 Pierce St,	
San Francisco, CA *94117*	
MR Sebastian C Sears—Cl'93—at	
☎ (208) 726-2038 . . PO Box 4384, Ketchum,	
ID *83340*	

Morrow MRS Anne P (Vorndran—Perkins—Anne Powers)
☎ (561) 743-2219 . . Jupiter O & R Club, B2 Apt 112, 1605 US H'way 1 S, Jupiter, FL *33477*

Morrow MR & MRS J Peter (Brewer—Melanie A	☎ (602) 997-0222
Atkinson) NMex'84.Hb.H'69	7145 N 11 Place,
MISS Amelia	Phoenix, AZ *85020*
JUNIORS MISS Kimberly	
JUNIORS MR Charles	

Morse MISS Alice H—MtH'70
☎ (610) 827-7308 . . 1201 Conestoga Rd, Chester Springs, PA *19425*

Morse MR & MRS Breton B (Thomas—Doré M Martin) GeoW'53.RISD'53
☎ (407) 628-2480 . . 1049 Aragon Av, Winter Park, FL *32789*

Morse MR & MRS David H (McNeely—Susan P McWhinney)
Sth'55.Au.Ub.Sm.H'56.Cl'59 . . of
☎ (617) 227-1570 . . 13 Temple St, Boston, MA *02114*
☎ (617) 698-6870 . . 397 Hillside St, Milton, MA *02186*

Morse MRS David Hunnewell (Nancy M Balis)
☎ (617) 876-4595 . . 17 Buckingham St, Cambridge, MA *02138*

Morse MR & MRS Edmond H (Barbara R White) Conn'72.Br'71
☎ (610) 293-9018 . . 507 Askin Rd, St Davids, PA *19087*

Morse MR & MRS Edmond N (Sidney H Phillips)	of ☎ (203)655-9190
Hn.Br'43.H'47	Ridge Acres,
MR David F—Br'74.Pa'81—at	Darien, CT *06820*
☎ (215) 627-0732 . . 726 Fitzwater St,	☎ (802) 824-6622
Philadelphia, PA *19147*	Windy Hill Farm,
	Peru, VT *05152*

Morse MRS Edward Clarke (Nealley—Eleanor L	*see*
Scott) Ober'27	*Dilatory Domiciles*
MR Alexander B	

Morse MRS Gardner S (Eleanor Rice) Lx.Chi.
☎ (413) 637-4213 . . Kimball Farms 103, 235 Walker St, Lenox, MA *01240*

Morse MR Henry P (Louise R Davis)
☎ (915) 598-5744 . . 8905 El Dorado Dv, El Paso, TX *79925*

Morse MR John B—Cr'87
☎ (607) 273-8455 . . 309 N Aurora St, Ithaca, NY *14850*

Morse MISS Judith B—Beloit'76
☎ (207) 829-4252 . . 33 Winterberry Court, Cumberland, ME *04021*

Morse MRS Judith S (Judith R Sterling) Vh.	369 California Terr,
MR James W	Pasadena, CA *91105*
JUNIORS MR Frank P	

Morse MR & MRS Murray H JR (Eleanor L Peters)	☎ (203) 255-4903
Ty'60	324 Mine Hill Rd,
MR Murray H 3d	Fairfield, CT *06430*
MR Stephen L—at U of Bridgeport	
MR Christopher P—at Skidmore	

Morse MR & MRS Richard C (Theodora H P Cronin)
☎ (212) 228-2552 . . 9 Stuyvesant Oval, New York, NY *10009* . . MR absent

Morse MRS Robert Hosmer (Helen S Beck) Evg.BtP.Cda.
☎ (561) 655-2388 . . 140 Brazilian Av, Palm Beach, FL *33480*

Morse MR & MRS Robert P (Sarah M Cumings)	☎ (516) 922-2114
Bost'74.Un.Ln.S.Csh.Ny.Vca.Myf.Snc.Pa'67 . . .	96 Cove Rd,
JUNIORS MISS Sarah S	Oyster Bay, NY
JUNIORS MR Robert B StC	*11771*
JUNIORS MR Parker M	

Morse DR Stephen S—Wis'77
☎ (212) 724-7543 . . 275 Central Park W, Apt 11F, New York, NY *10024*

Morse MRS Thomas R JR (Suzanne Rice)	☎ (508) 263-7230
RISD'50.Tufts'73	61 Meetinghouse
MR Thomas R 3d—at ☎ (617) 639-2639	Lane, Boxborough,
11 Beacon St, Marblehead, MA *01945*	MA *01719-1129*

Morsell MRS John B (Amelia B Thomas) Dar.Ncd.
☎ (410) 535-0351 . . Rte 1, Box 124G, Prince Frederick, MD *20678*

Morshead MRS Brandon (Elaine Brandon) Stan'51.Stan'78
☎ (415) 854-3739 . . 2161 Sterling Av, Menlo Park, CA *94025*

Morshead MR & MRS Jeffory S (Henderson—
Catherine von Warton) Bhm.B.Sc.Stan'52.
Stan'61 . . . .
    MR Mark W Henderson—at 55 Norfolk St,
Apt 302, San Francisco, CA *94124* . . . .
   ☎ (415) 461-5480
   635 Goodhill Rd,
   Kentfield, CA *94904*

Morsman MR & MRS Joseph J 3d (Laura C
DeYoung) Err.Y'59 . . . .
MISS Laura W . . . .
MISS Virginia H . . . .
MR Joseph J 4th . . . .
   ☎ (413) 665-0504
   Box 81, Deerfield,
   MA *01342*

Morsman MR & MRS Kimball H (Ingrid A
Thompson) Fst.M.Me.Y'69.H'74 . . . .
MISS Kristin K . . . .
MISS Whitney H . . . .
   ☎ (610) 527-1444
   820 Potts Lane,
   Bryn Mawr, PA
   19010

Morss MR & MRS Anthony W (Carolyn Charles) H'53
   ☎ (212) 595-1165 . . 473 West End Av, New York, NY *10024*

Morss MR Christopher—H'62
   ☎ (508) 655-4144 . . 11 Peckham Hill Rd, Sherborn, MA *01770*

Morss MRS Everett (Anne Wentworth) Ncd.
   ☎ (508) 526-4653 . . ''Oakwood'' 601 Summer St, Manchester,
MA *01944*

Mortensen MR & MRS Dan S (Motch—Warner—Dorothy C Stearns)
Tvcl.Purd'39 ⛵
   ☎ (561) 231-4583 . . Riomar, 914 Lady Bug Lane, Vero Beach,
FL *32963-2105*

Mortimer MR & MRS Averell H (Jean H Newhard) Rc.Col'80
   ☎ (212) 772-7590 . . 117 E 72 St, New York, NY *10021*

Mortimer MR E Nicholas . . see S G Chapin

Mortimer MR & MRS E Paul (Lee—Nancy F Hatch)
Unn.Ng.Csn.Witw'54.Ox'59.H'61
   ☎ (203) 531-0615 . . 610 W Lyon Farm Dv, Greenwich, CT *06831*

Mortimer MRS Henry T (Linda M Metcalfe) . . . . . .
MR John M . . . .
MR Alexander D . . . .
   ☎ (561) 844-0944
   ''Keewaydin''
   239 Tangier Av,
   Palm Beach, FL
   33480

Mortimer MR & MRS Henry T JR (Bierbaum—Susan
E Lewis) CedarC'76.Rc.Bcs.B.So.H'64 . . . .
MISS Caroline E . . . .
MR Henry T 3d . . . .
   JUNIORS MISS S Caroline Bierbaum . . . .
   JUNIORS MR Richard L Bierbaum . . . .
   102 Boulder Trail,
   Bronxville, NY
   10708

Mortimer MR & MRS J Thomas (Sarah V G
Watterson) ColbyS'61.TexTech'64.Cit'65.Cwr'68
MISS Elizabeth Van G—Buck'92 . . . .
MISS Katherine S—Cr'94 . . . .
JUNIORS MISS Anne W . . . .
   ☎ (216) 423-0836
   13753 County Line
   Rd, Chagrin Falls,
   OH *44022*

Mortimer MISS Liza . . see S G Chapin

Mortimer MR & MRS Richard (Coulter—Madeline H Brown)
Rc.Bcs.B.So.H'54 . . of
   ☎ (212) 988-7311 . . 130 E 75 St, New York, NY *10021*
   ☎ (516) 283-3778 . . Breese Lane, PO Box 1089, Southampton,
NY *11969*

Mortimer MR & MRS Richard I (Cynthia T E Henderson)
   ☎ (516) 676-0563 . . PO Box 193, Duck Pond Rd, Locust Valley,
NY *11560*

Mortimer MR & MRS Stanley G (Kathleen L Harriman) Rc.T.Srr.So.Cs.H'36
   ☎ (212) TR9-1779 . . 149 E 73 St, New York, NY *10021*

Mortlock MR & MRS David H JR (Elizabeth C Early)
Wells'69.Y'94.Cr'69.Va'75 . . . .
MR David H 3d . . . .
JUNIORS MISS Christine . . . .
   of ☎ (203)966-2522
   34 Whiffletree Lane,
   New Canaan, CT
   06840
   ☎ (207) 236-2841
   85 Bayview St,
   Camden, ME *04847*

Morton MRS Charles I (Winslow—Morton—Sabin—
Elizabeth L Nickerson)
   ☎ (860) 535-1153 . . 23 Water St, Stonington, CT *06378*

Morton MR & MRS Edward C (Snell—Florence D Smith)
Cy.Elk.Rv.Mv.P'37
   ☎ (410) 323-3050 . . 200 Cross Keys Rd, Apt 68, Baltimore, MD *21210*

Morton LT CDR (RET) & MRS John Lindman (Arlis B Cowan)
USN.Cal'35.Vh.
   ☎ (818) 799-1011 . . 788 S Grand Av, Pasadena, CA *91105*

Morton MR & MRS Robert S (Elizabeth V Evans) V'45.Fic.Vh.StJ.Y'44
   ☎ (818) 793-2459 . . 1280 Shenandoah Rd, San Marino, CA *91108*

Morton MR & MRS Thomas M (Carver—Elizabeth A
Coffell) . . . .
JUNIORS MR Robert L 4th . . . .
   ☎ (713) 499-4106
   2911 Del Monte
   Court, Missouri
   City, TX *77459*

Morton MR & MRS W Hugh M (Diana H Manton)
Sth'60.Un.Wms'59 . . . .
MISS Sandra T—Dth'90—at ☎ (212) 765-2129
235 W 56 St, Apt 41B, New York, NY *10019* . .
   ☎ (508) 358-4928
   74 Glezen Lane,
   Wayland, MA *01778*

Morton MR & MRS W Merriman (Kandel—Dorothy J Drummer)
Sth'70.A.Sw'63
   ☎ (512) 452-4425 . . 3604 Mt Bonnell Rd, Austin, TX *78731*

Morton-Smith MR James M—Unn.Rcn.Pr.SDak'34
   ☎ (805) 565-1358 . . 970 Brooktree Rd, Santa Barbara, CA *93108*

Morton-Smith DR & MRS William S (Rhodabel S Fletcher)
NCar'71.SCal'78
   ☎ (805) 969-4334 . . 797 Park Lane W, Santa Barbara, CA *93108*

Mosbrook MR & MRS Robert C (Jean J Nugent)
ClarkTech'61 . . . .
MISS Mary W—at ☎ (602) 941-5644
2636 N Fiesta Dv, Scottsdale, AZ *85257* . . . . . .
MR Robert W . . . .
   ☎ (910) 295-9149
   ''Five Points''
   PO Box 70,
   225 Magnolia Rd,
   Pinehurst, NC
   28374-0070

Mosden MR & MRS F William (Eleanor L Graupner) Cal'40.Tcy.Glasg'38
   ☎ (415) 461-2306 . . 501 Via Casitas, Greenbrae, CA *94904*

Moseley MRS David Bogue (Fernow—M Carolyn
Roberg) . . . .
   MISS Carola B Fernow—Ga'87—at
   Boston, MA . . . .
   MR Steven D Fernow—Y'74—at
   ☎ (860) 673-7197 . . Avon Old Farms School,
   500 Old Farms Rd, Avon, CT *06001* . . . .
   ☎ (602) 423-1959
   ''Finisterre''
   6258 E Avalon Dv,
   Scottsdale, AZ
   85251-7006

Moseley MR & MRS Frederick S 3d (Elizabeth H Perkins) My.Sm.Ln.H'51
   ☎ (508) 468-2516 . . 38 Gardner St, Hamilton, MA *01936*

Moseley MR & MRS George T 3d (Robb—Francisco—Elizabeth R Keating)
Cw.G.H'41.Buf'48
   ☎ (716) 886-0865 . . 17 Cleveland Av, Buffalo, NY *14222*

Moseley MISS Georgia B—Boca'78
☎ (716) 689-4868 . . 1205 Youngs Rd, Williamsville, NY *14221*
Moseley MR & MRS James B (J Patricia Little) Rcn.Srr.Ny.My.Myc.B.H'55
☎ (508) 468-1014 . . ''Ardboe'' Hamilton, MA *01936*
Moseley MRS Marcia L (Marcia E Lovegrove). . . . . | ☎ (203) 259-0138
MR William R 3d . . . . | 184 Figlar Av,
| Fairfield, CT *06430*
Moses DR & MRS Hamilton 3d (Alexandra McC Gibson)
Gchr'72.Sap.Md.Gv.Ac.Ncd.Pa'72.Rush'75
☎ (804) 984-2010 . . ''Oakmont'' Rte 1, Box 549, North Garden,
VA *22959*
Moses MR & MRS Philip C (Christina W Clothier) Del'82.Me.Tufts'82
☎ (508) 653-8060 . . 2 Apple Ridge Dv, South Natick, MA *01760*
Moskey MISS Marina L—Bow'95 . . see MISS M K Love
Moskey JUNIORS MR Matthew L . . see MRS M K Love
Moskey MR Stamatis—Pr.Cin'61.Cwr'64 . . of
☎ (011-44-1962) 779-424 . . Avington Park House, Avington,
Hampshire SO21 1DD, England
☎ (011-44-171) 351-5608 . . 10 Rossetti Gardens Mansions, Flood St,
London SW3, England
Mosle MR A Henry—Y'60.H'66 . . . . | ☎ (609) 396-7811
MISS Cassandra L—Occ'91—at 137 Spruce St, | 132 Mercer St,
Princeton, NJ *08542* . . . . | Trenton, NJ
| *08611-1724*
Mosle MISS Anne B (late William B JR) . . . . | Married at Pecos, NM
Whitney MR James (William) . . . . | May 26'96
Mosle MISS Cornelia B—Cda. . . . . | 37 Thibault P'kway,
MR Daniel B . . . . | Burlington, VT
| *05401*
Mosle MR Douglas C—Drew'93 . . see MRS L O'Shaughnessy
Mosle MR & MRS John L JR (Paula Meredith) Rice'52.Y'51
☎ (214) 526-4818 . . 6125 Westwick Rd, Dallas, TX *75205*
Mosle MR & MRS William B JR (Frances A O'Neill) | ☎ (412) 471-0473
V'61.Fcg.Rr. . . . . | 1100 Liberty Av,
LT Edward B—USN.Y'87—at ☎ (847) 266-0543 | Apt 805, Pittsburgh,
610 Sheridan Rd, Apt 3D, Highwood, IL *60040*. | PA *15222*
Moss MR & MRS Ambler H JR (Serena Welles) | 5711 San Vicente
An.Y'60.GeoW'70 . . . . | St, Coral Gables,
MISS Serena M . . . . | FL *33146*
MR Ambler H 3d—Cal'88—at 167 S Arden Blvd, |
Los Angeles, CA *90004* . . . . |
JUNIORS MR Benjamin S . . . . |
Moss MISS Anne M . . see MRS H F Klinefelter
Moss MR & MRS Arthur H (Gaston—E Leslie Fritz) | ☎ (610) 688-0983
M.Wms'52.Pa'55 . . . . | 200 Walnut Av,
MR Robert F Gaston—at ☎ (718) 834-9045 | Wayne, PA *19087*
104 Butler St, Brooklyn, NY *11231* . . . . |
Moss MRS Cyndi L (Robert E) . . . . | Married at Abilene, TX
Rusnack MR Gary . . . . | Jly 29'95
Moss REV & MRS Frank H 3d (Elizabeth W | ☎ (219) 436-5649
McDaniel) Bost'68.Ant'76.P'67.EpiscDiv'70 . . . | 3525 Willowdale
MISS Elizabeth W—at Wittenberg. . . . . | Rd, Ft Wayne, IN
MR F Hazlett 4th—at Hobart-Wm Smith . . . . . . | *46802*
Moss MR & MRS George K (Joyce K Leonard) | ☎ (212) 737-0862
Pa'65.Pr.B.Ny.Cly.Va'55 . . . . | 10 Gracie Square,
MR Richard B . . . . | New York, NY
| *10028*

Moss MR & MRS Hunter (Peake—Helen G Clegg) P'35
☎ (610) 645-8887 . . 1400 Waverly Rd, Blair 245, Gladwyne, PA *19035*
Moss MR Hunter V—Presby'71
☎ (202) 232-8405 . . 1628D Beekman Place NW, Washington,
DC *20009*
Moss MR & MRS John H (Margaret Stewart) Sth'42. . . . . . | ☎ (717) 394-4735
MISS Barbara H—at ☎ (212) 867-4241 | 23 Conestoga
2 Tudor City Place, New York, NY *10017*. . . . . | Woods Rd,
MISS Jane S—at ☎ (212) 865-4074 | Lancaster, PA *17602*
417 Riverside Dv, New York, NY *10025* . . . . . . |
Moss MISS Margaret P—Sth'66
☎ (610) 692-3885 . . 34 Ashton Way, West Chester, PA *19380*
Moss MR & MRS Michael P (Jill L Chasens) NTexSt'83.OWes'77
6001 Timber Creek Lane, Dallas, TX *75248*
Moss MRS Patricia C (Sargent—Shober—Patricia Conrad)
☎ (716) 243-3363 . . 3986 Avon Rd, Geneseo, NY *14454*
Moss MR & MRS Peter B (Sherrer—Anne Bordley) V'59.Pr.Pn.P'54
☎ (410) 778-0275 . . Rock Point Farm, 23665 Lovely Lane, Chestertown,
MD *21620*
Moss MR Peyton H—C.Br'36.H'40 . . . . | ☎ (212) 289-2248
MR Peyton H JR—H'78—☎ (212) 860-0882 . . . | 1150 Fifth Av,
MR John W—H'81—at ☎ (212) 753-3243 | New York, NY
354 E 51 St, New York, NY *10022* . . . . | *10128*
Moss MR & MRS Philip A (Penelope A Scott) SCal'87.Bg.
☎ (212) 758-3498 . . FDR Station, PO Box 7053, New York,
NY *10150-1908*
Moss MR & MRS Robert A JR (Laurie McL Watson) | of ☎ (508)475-9191
Ty'67.Ty'82 . . . . | 38 Phillips St,
MISS Laurie McL—at U of Mass Amherst . . . . . | Andover, MA *01810*
MISS Sarah B—at Union Coll . . . . | ☎ (508) 945-2806
| 204 Countryside Dv,
| Chatham, MA *02633*
Moss MR & MRS Robert E (Ross—Kathleen Browne) | ☎ (202) 337-5283
V'66.Cal'66 . . . . | 1626 Foxhall Rd
MISS Paige M . . . . | NW, Washington,
MISS Elizabeth F Ross . . . . | DC *20007*
MR Matthew K Ross . . . . |
Moszka MR & MRS Stanley J (Peters—Marriott L | ☎ (508) 888-8216
Welch) Bost'54 . . . . | ''Cuil-Lodair''
MISS Whitney L Peters—Bost'80—at | 34 Marshview
65 Langdon St, Cambridge, MA *02138* . . . . . . | Circle,
MR Robert E Peters JR—Bost'83—at | East Sandwich, MA
☎ (213) 933-1372 . . 324 Curson St, | *02537*
Los Angeles, CA *90036* . . . . |
Motch MR & MRS Elton F JR (Patricia A Pecor) | ☎ (802) 425-2423
Duke'65.Tvcl.Duke'65 . . . . | ''Wings Point''
MISS Lauren S—Sth'87—at ☎ (617) 241-8852 | RR 2, Box 2442,
33 Mystic St, Apt 3, Charlestown, MA *02129* . . | Charlotte, VT *05445*
MR E Franklin 3d—StLaw'91—at |
☎ (802) 865-0153 . . 350 Maple St, Apt E, |
Burlington, VT *05401* . . . . |
Motherwell MRS Robert (Renate Ponsold) Munich'59
909 North St, Greenwich, CT *06830*
Motley MRS Catherine H (Catherine R Hamlen)
☎ (508) ST5-0494 . . Haven St, Dover, MA *02030*
Motley MR & MRS Frank R (Johnson—Renate I Mayer) Ulm'61.San.Va'50
☎ (423) 288-8115 . . 121 Columbine Rd, Kingsport, TN *37660*

Motley MR & MRS George B (Priscilla H Olive) Ty'75.H'74.H'78
☎ (508) 653-9139 . . 28 Nason Hill Rd, Sherborn, MA *01770*

Motley MRS Herbert J (Catharine A Little)
☎ (941) 263-7760 . . 225 Fifth Av S, Apt 201, Naples, FL *34102*

Motley MR & MRS Herbert J JR (Pamela M | ☎ (617) 581-0109
Kinnicutt) Ws'66.H.'65.Mich'72 . . . . | ''Dashing Rock''
MISS Kendra J—at Conn Coll . . . . | Nahant, MA *01908*

Motley MR & MRS John L (Strickler—Maureen M Erwin)
MaryW'66.Syr'71.H'46
☎ (508) 540-3318 . . 24 Gilbert Lane, PO Box 353, West Falmouth, MA *02574*

Motley MR & MRS John L 3d (Deborah E Benton) VillaN'81.Dar.Vt'73
☎ (703) 734-8588 . . 7703 Carlton Place, McLean, VA *22102-2150*

Motley MR Thomas—H.'63.Cl'66 . . . . | ☎ (508) 263-4054
MISS Sarah P—NH'93 . . . . | 115 School St,
MISS Elisabeth C—at Columbia . . . . | Acton, MA
MR Thomas 3d—McG'91 . . . . | *01720-4415*

Motley MR William C—Sm.Denis'84
☎ (617) 241-0241 . . 12 Washington St, Apt 4, Charlestown, MA *02129*

Motlow MR & MRS (DR) John G (Elena A Gates) Y'75.Cal'81.Pcu.Cal'69
☎ (415) 752-6934 . . 52 W Clay St, San Francisco, CA *94121*

Mott MR & MRS Colter W (Steffanie R Griffis) Va'77 . . of
☎ (206) 285-0569 . . 2724 W Blaine St, Seattle, WA *98199*
☎ (206) 884-9862 . . ''Tu Tucy'' 5012 Mahncke Rd KPS, Longbranch, WA *98349*

Mott MR & MRS Garret JR (Cornelia Hadsell) CtCol'37.P'32
☎ (802) 985-5494 . . 3118 Wake Robin Dv, Shelburne, VT *05482-7572*

Mott MR Garret 3d
☎ (802) 453-3232 . . Box 1812, McCollough Tpke, Buels Gore, VT *05487*

Mott MR & MRS John G (Leslie Alt) | ☎ (202) 244-5299
Ws'58.Mt.P'51.H'57 . . . . | 3406 Lowell St NW,
MISS Julie G—P'85—at ☎ (408) 457-1018 | Washington, DC
118 Sacramento Av, Santa Cruz, CA *95060* . . . . | *20016*
MR John W—Y'82.Y'89—at ☎ (718) 267-2847 |
32-63—43 St, Astoria, NY *11103* . . . . |

Mott MR Lawrence H—Vt'85 ⚜ . . of
☎ (802) 985-3122 . . Shelburne Farms, Shelburne, VT *05482*
''Antler Lodge'' Old County Rd, Buels Gore, VT *05487*

Motter MRS William C (Ellen M Gorham)
☎ (612) 227-3905 . . 756 Fairmount Av, St Paul, MN *55105*

Moulding MRS Arthur T (Mary C Baker) Ih.Wa.Ncd.
☎ (847) 446-1818 . . 82 Woodley Rd, Winnetka, IL *60093*

Moulton MR & MRS Anthony K (Arden Green) DU'66.Au.Ri.DU'70
☎ (203) 966-9141 . . 86 Gerrish Lane, New Canaan, CT *06840*

Moulton MR & MRS Henry H (Elizabeth W Day) Rdc'46.Sm.Csn.H'46
☎ (617) 864-2437 . . 989 Memorial Dv, Apt 491, Cambridge, MA *02138*

Mount MR & MRS Edson H (Anne G Taylor) Sth'62 . . . | ☎ (203) 281-3272
MISS Katherine A—Syr'92—at Los Angeles, CA | 220 Blue Trail,
MR Howard C—OWes'93—at Wayne, PA *19087* | Mt Carmel, CT
| *06518-1615*

Mountain MR & MRS Robert P JR (Marjorie C Pile) | ☎ (203) 661-1776
Pars'67.H'83 . . . . | Khakum Wood,
MISS Leila C—at Westminster . . . . | Greenwich, CT
JUNIORS MR Robert P 3d—at Westminster . . . . . | *06831*
JUNIORS MR T Chadbourne . . . . |

Mountain MRS Worrall F (Oram—Grace H Dewes) BMr'32
☎ (609) 426-6152 . . Meadow Lakes 45-07, Hightstown, NJ *08520-3350*

Movius MRS Hallam L (Nancy Champion de Crespigny)
☎ (617) 876-1022 . . 17 Larchwood Dv, Cambridge, MA *02138-4617*

Movius MRS K Kirkham (Katherine Kirkham) | 3245 Pacific Av,
Rdc'62 . . . . | San Francisco, CA
MISS Katherine de C—Cl'89 . . . . | *94118-2026*
MR Hallam L 2d—H'87 . . . . |
JUNIORS MR John K . . . . |

Movius MR & MRS Lee W (Gwynne Lewis) | ☎ (704) 366-9409
Cr'69.H'69 . . . . | 4801 Howland Lane,
JUNIORS MISS Diana R . . . . | Charlotte, NC *28226*

Mower MR & MRS Grove N (Brooke Hummer) Wes'85.Br'80
☎ (773) 871-4419 . . 829 W George St, Chicago, IL *60657*

Moyer MR & MRS F Stanton (Ann P Stovell) Sa.Rc.Me.Gm.Pa'51
☎ (610) 527-5010 . . 445 Caversham Rd, Bryn Mawr, PA *19010*

Moyer MR & MRS Timothy B (Wilhelmina R Bolling) B.Eh.Stan'73.H'77
☎ (908) 439-2823 . . PO Box 165, Oldwick, NJ *08858*

Muckerman MR & MRS Edward C (Toni Marie Andrews) Md'82
☎ (703) 799-7864 . . 1008 DeWolfe Dv, Alexandria, VA *22308*

Muckerman MR & MRS John C (Mildred C | ☎ (314) 822-1040
Bakewell) . . . . | 453 Cloister Walk,
MR Stephen A—Mo'85 . . . . | St Louis, MO *63122*

Muckerman COL (RET) & MRS Joseph E 2d (Anne J Butler) USA'49
☎ (703) 329-1075 . . 2103 Woodmont Rd, Alexandria, VA *22307*

Muckerman MR & MRS Peter M (Stephanie R Dimond)
VPI'82.VPI'91.MtStMary'83
☎ (703) 836-2376 . . 6 W Maple St, Alexandria, VA *22301*

Muckerman DR & MRS Richard I C (Barbara L Hagnauer)
Geo'43.StL'45 . . of
☎ (314) 863-3425 . . 816 S Hanley Rd, 7A, St Louis, MO *63105-2678*
☎ (970) 949-3290 . . 918 Deer Blvd, Eagle Vail, CO *81657*

Mucklé MRS C Kendrick (Christine M Kendrick) Me.
☎ (610) 645-8976 . . Waverly Heights A224, 1400 Waverly Rd, Gladwyne, PA *19035*

Mucklé MRS Craig W (Scheetz—Katherine E Jones) Me.Ac.W.Ncd.
☎ (610) LA5-3562 . . 1221 Mt Pleasant Rd, Villanova, PA *19085*

Mucklé MR & MRS Craig W JR (Amanda E Barnes) Me.Vca.Rv.Ll.Ht.Dll.
☎ (610) MO4-7902 . . 424 S Woodbine Av, Penn Valley, Narberth, PA *19072-1540*

Mudd MR & MRS Dayton H (Dorothy R Morse) | ☎ (314) 569-2710
Ncd.SpgH'35.Bab'36 . . . . | 3 Chatfield Place,
MR Dayton H JR—at ☎ (314) 821-4338 | St Louis, MO *63141*
1451 Topping Rd, St Louis, MO *63141* . . . . . . |

Mudge MR & MRS Edmund T 4th (Joan K Weidlein) | of ☎ (410)337-9414
Gchr'69.Gv.Md.Rr.Rm'68 . . . . | PO Box 477,
MISS Margaret C . . . . | Riderwood, MD
JUNIORS MR Edmund T 5th . . . . | *21139*
| ☎ (412) 238-2202
| ''Rumbling Bridge''
| Rector, PA *15677*

Mudge MR & MRS L Taylor (Dale Sperry) | of ☎ (207)236-3873
Me'93.Rr.Sm.Pg.Chi.Bost'70 . . . . | 101 Chestnut St,
MR Webster T—Geo'93 . . . . | Camden, ME *04843*
MR Matthew S—at U of Vt . . . . | ☎ (617) 723-8342
JUNIORS MISS Sarah A—at Middlesex . . . . | 92 Beacon St,
JUNIORS MR Samuel A—at Brooks . . . . | Boston, MA *02108*

Mueller MR Bret A . . see E T H Talmage 3d
Mueller MR & MRS Donald V (Elizabeth U Whiteman)
GreenMt'75.Laf'77.Y'80
☎ (908) 665-9496 . . ''Tall Oaks'' 11 Kendrick Rd, Summit, NJ *07901*
Mueller MR J Adrian . . see E T H Talmage 3d
Mueller MR & MRS John M (Emily Hartwell) Tv.Un.
☎ (216) 752-9459 . . 19513 Shaker Blvd, Shaker Heights, OH *44122*
Mueller MISS Lydia W—Mid'80
☎ (505) 820-7813 . . PO Box 9433, Santa Fe, NM *87504*
Mueller MR & MRS Michael H H (Elizabeth H Jones)
Conn'77.SConn'82.Ncd.Wis'76
☎ (203) 544-9509 . . 144 Florida Rd, Ridgefield, CT *06877*
Mueller MR & MRS Paul R (Margaretta P Blair) NotreD'55
☎ (415) 941-4334 . . 630 Kingswood Way, Los Altos, CA *94022*
Mueller MR & MRS Robert S JR (Alice Truesdale) Pn.P'38
☎ (603) 569-6088 . . 2 Mountain West Dv, Apt 21, Wolfeboro,
NH *03894*
Mueller MR & MRS Werner D (Margaret C Reid) Sth'51.Kt.Dar.H'49.H'54
☎ (216) 338-3857 . . 8848 Music St, Russell, Novelty, OH *44072*
Muench MRS Alfred G (Freeman—Sarah Ellmaker McIlvaine) Ncd.Dc.
☎ (717) 569-9616 . . 2305 Fruitville Pike, Lancaster, PA *17601*

Muenter MRS Knud B (Eirin T Münter) Medaille'75.SUNY'80 . . . . MISS S Merete—SUNY'86—at ☎ (212) 315-2045 . . 415 W 47 St, Apt 5E, New York, NY *10036* . . . . MR Knud B JR—SUNY'86.LawrTech'92—at ☎ (412) 276-8777 . . 607 Bank St, Upper Carnegie, PA *15106*	of ☎ (716)839-3738 225 Roycroft Blvd, Snyder, NY *14226* ☎ (716) 941-5909 ''Knudahei'' 8009 Lower E Hill Rd, Colden, NY *14033*
Mugnaini MR & MRS Renzo (Marie L Musto) . . . . . . MR Enrico	☎ (011-39-55) 232-0913 via B Umiliana 83, 50124 Florence, Italy

Muhlenberg MR & MRS Kobi (Mary E Kearns) Wid'81.Wid'87.Ac.
☎ (610) 544-7056 . . 315 Cornell Av, Swarthmore, PA *19081*

Muhlhofer MR & MRS F William JR (Clarinda Schmidlapp) Cin'58.Cda.Cin'55 . . . . MR F William 3d—at 2259 Spinningwheel Lane, Cincinnati, OH *45244*	☎ (513) 871-2196 1265 Hayward Av, Cincinnati, OH *45208*

Muir MR Charles G
☎ (610) 584-8472 . . 1901 Whitehall Rd, RD 3, Norristown, PA *19403*

Muir MRS D Delafield (Newbold—Diana F Delafield) . . . . MR T A Scott Newbold—Vt'93—at US Peace Corps, PO Box 93, Gaborone, Botswana	☎ (215) 643-5530 211 Madison Av, Ft Washington, PA *19034*
Muir MR & MRS J Dapray (Louise R Pierrepont) Col'65.Cvc.Mt.Cda.Wms'58.Va'64 MISS Sophie S—Wms'91—at 310 E 55 St, New York, NY *10022* . . . . MR Christopher B—at U of Vt	☎ (202) 337-0289 3104 Q St NW, Washington, DC *20007*
Muir MR & MRS James JR (Marjorie Flynt) . . . . MISS Helen G . . . . MR Henry F . . . . MR Frederick G	☎ (203) 869-5431 504 North St, Greenwich, CT *06830*

Muir MRS Malcolm JR (Nancy H Jones)
☎ (212) 877-5980 . . 1 W 67 St, New York, NY *10023*

Mulcahy MR & MRS Charles W JR (Mary F O'Day) My.H'43 . . . . MR Charles W 3d	☎ (508) 468-3808 49 Myles River Rd, Hamilton, MA *01936*
Mulder MR & MRS Gary C (Eleanor G Elliot) Vt'60.BowlG'70 . . . . JUNIORS MR Theodore H	☎ (614) 764-3806 4802 Inisheer Court, Dublin, OH *43017*

Mulford MR & MRS William (Wells—Mary J Williams) Pa'40.Me.H.'28
983 Railroad Av, Bryn Mawr, PA *19010*
Mullally MR Kevin M
33 Schooner Court, Richmond, CA *94804*
Mullally MRS Mandeville (Mellen—Putnam—Mary T Pratt)
☎ (516) 239-5175 . . 5 Stable Lane, Lawrence, NY *11559*
Mullan DR & MRS Hugh (Mariquita P MacManus) Cos.Sl.USN'34.Cr'39
☎ (202) 667-1077 . . 2126 Connecticut Av NW, Washington, DC *20008*

Mullan MRS Nancy D (Nancy De V Field) Cly . . . . . MR Peter D—P'91—at ☎ (203) 865-2335 8 Edgewood Av, New Haven, CT *06511*	of ☎ (212)628-4629 333 E 68 St, Apt 6F, New York, NY *10021* ☎ (516) 653-4315 49 Quaquanantuck Lane, Box 47, Quogue, NY *11959*

Mullen MR & MRS Robert W (Lucy M Reiss) Ne.SetonH'55.NYLaw'59
☎ (212) 535-6602 . . 36 E 72 St, New York, NY *10021*
Mullen MR & MRS Robert W JR (Kathleen E Slusser)
Stan'77.Ford'81.Pa'77.Ford'80
21 Sturgis Rd, Bronxville, NY *10708*

Mullen MR & MRS T David (Joan K Berg) Ng.Cly.P.Roch'50.Cr'54 . . . . MISS Joan H	☎ (516) 653-5552 7 Club Lane, Box 928, Quogue, NY *11959-0928*
Muller MR & MRS E Nicholas (Mary F Clay) Y'37 . . MR Richard C	☎ (520) 760-1066 9225 E Tanque Verde Rd, Apt 13104, Tucson, AZ *85749-8715*

Muller MRS Frederick B (Stevenson—Jeanette Steele)
☎ (619) 340-4477 . . 46-200B Cottage Lane, Palm Desert, CA *92260*
Muller MR & MRS L Philip (Elizabeth Wallace) Wms'42
☎ (610) 376-4470 . . 1423 Parkside Dv N, Wyomissing, PA *19610*

Muller MR & MRS Scott W (Caroline S Adams) GeoW'71.Mt.Nyc.Ny.Cvc.P'71 ⚓ . . . . JUNIORS MISS Robin McP . . . . JUNIORS MR Christopher A	☎ (301) 657-4363 20 Magnolia P'kway, Chevy Chase, MD *20815*

Mullet MR & MRS Daniel (Olive Gale Moore)
Col'65.Wis'73.Cwr'64.Purd'67
☎ (616) 796-3211 . . ''Tanglebank II'' 9402 Nine Mile Rd, Big Rapids,
MI *49307-9103*

Mulligan MR & MRS Charles A (Susan W Abendroth) Kent'65 MISS Melinda E—at Bowdoin . . . . MR William C—CtCol'94—at ☎ (203) 481-6833 20 Second Av, Branford, CT *06405*	☎ (216) 321-1347 2596 Ashton Rd, Cleveland, OH *44118*

Mulligan ENS & MRS Nikolai F (Tracey D Righter) CtCol'91.USN'92
☎ (011-81-468) 211-911-4435 . . PSL 473, Box 2025,
FPO AP, *96349-5555*

Mulliken MR & MRS Alfred D (Margaret Kelly)
☎ (561) 229-8986 . . 8880 S Ocean Dv, Apt 201, Jensen Beach,
FL *34957*

Mullin MR & MRS Francis J R JR (Chapman— | ☎ (207) 592-7962
Margaret Jane Loblein) NH'58 . . . . | PO Box 54,
  MR Scott W Chapman . . . . | Owls Head, ME
  MR Robert W Chapman . . . . | *04854*

Mullins MR & MRS Fristoe (Elizabeth C Mahaffey)
Rcn.Bv.Nd.Rr.Rc.Cw.Rv.Mo'36 . . of
☎ (314) 725-1300 . . 200 S Brentwood Blvd, Apt 4E, St Louis,
MO *63105*
☎ (441) 238-2140 . . Burnt House, Box 534, Warwick WK BX, Bermuda

Mullins MR & MRS Thomas D 2d (Corinne A McLaughlin) Rr.Pa'58 ⚓
☎ (617) 576-4740 . . 23 Berkeley St, Cambridge, MA *02138*

Mullins MR William E G—Edin'91
☎ (617) 547-7638 . . 77 Hancock St, Apt 5, Cambridge, MA *02139*

Mulvany MISS Dana—Wms'80
☎ (408) 379-6065 . . 350 Budd Av, Apt A1, Campbell, CA *95008*

Muma MRS John R (Edith Smith Noyes) B'gton'36.Cs . . .of
☎ (212) 628-2144 . . 1 E 66 St, New York, NY *10021*
☎ (516) 727-0145 . . "Chain Hill" 41½ Sound Av, PO Box 1048,
Riverhead, NY *11901*

Mumford MR & MRS (DR) George S III (Elizabeth Levenson)
ColSt'91.ColSt'91
☎ (970) 484-8479 . . 3621 W Bingham Hill Rd, Ft Collins, CO *80524*

Mumford MR & MRS Manly W (Louise T Horne) | ☎ (773) 525-7791
Cr'59.H'46.Nw'50 . . . . | 399 W Fullerton
  MISS Shaw . . . . | P'kway, Chicago, IL
  MR M Dodge . . . . | *60614*

Mumma MR & MRS Kenneth B (Moira H Forbes) Aberdeen'77.F&M'80
☎ (610) 827-9232 . . Box 254, Merlin Rd, Chester Springs, PA *19425*

Munch MR & MRS Ernest R (Anne C Rossbach) | ☎ (503) 224-8210
SL'72.Ore'70.Cl'71 . . . . | "Bailiwick"
  MISS Lucia E M . . . . | 1515 SW Myrtle St,
   | Portland, OR *97201*

Mundy MR & MRS Edward S (Sarah E Hooper) | ☎ (914) 234-6587
Y'67.Cl'72 . . . . | 4 Loop Rd, Bedford,
  JUNIORS MR William H . . . . | NY *10506*
  JUNIORS MR Nathaniel E . . . . |

Mundy MR & MRS Gardner M (Diana Vietor) | ☎ (516) 671-2057
Cl'62.Un.Y.'63.H'66 . . . . | 140 Linden Farms
  MISS Catherine E—at Denison . . . . | Rd, Locust Valley,
  MR Philip G—Y'95—at ☎ (011-61-2) 361-5679 | NY *11560*
5 Stanley St, Darlinghurst 2010, Sydney, NSW,
Australia . . . . |

Mundy MRS William G (Riley—Isabel S Marsh) V'42.Pr.
☎ (802) 824-6630 . . PO Box 201, Weston, VT *05161*

Mungall MR & MRS Daniel JR (Edith D Smith) | ☎ (610) 688-0491
Sg.Me.Y'37.H'40 . . . . | 11 Meadowcrest Rd,
  MISS Joanne D . . . . | Radnor, PA *19087*

Mungall MR & MRS Stephen B (Linda E Burton)
Roan'85.Me.Roan'84.Emory'88
see Dilatory Domiciles

Munger MR & MRS Harold N JR (Vietor—Dorothy K Burghard)
Cy.P'41 . . of
☎ (508) 428-9094 . . 173 Starboard Lane, Osterville, MA *02655*
☎ (802) 867-2210 . . PO Box 681, Dorset, VT *05251*

Munn MRS Charles A (Dupuy—McCarthy—Dorothy C Spreckels) . . of
☎ (561) 844-6766 . . "Amado" 455 N County Rd, Box 269,
Palm Beach, FL *33480*
22 rue Barbet de Joux, 75007 Paris, France

Munn MRS Ector O (Abbott—Virginia C Robinson) B.
☎ (561) 655-6526 . . 311 Cocoanut Row, Palm Beach, FL *33480*

Munn MRS Mark S (McKelvy—Patricia M Pyke) | ☎ (561) 546-4877
Ri.L. . . . . | 324 S Beach Rd,
  MISS Mary L . . . . | Hobe Sound, FL
   | *33455*

Munn MR & MRS Orson D (Patricia A Geoghegan) Cly.P'47 . . of
☎ (212) 348-4836 . . 25 E 86 St, New York, NY *10028*
☎ (516) 283-2501 . . "Dividend" Gin Lane, Southampton, NY *11968*

Munn MR & MRS Orson D 3d (Christine Jue) Bnd'79.Cl'81.Bcs.Rv.Col'76
☎ (212) 570-6378 . . 225 E 70 St, Apt 10C, New York, NY *10021*

Muñoz MRS W P Custis (Gillet—A Elizabeth | ☎ (410) 889-2545
Bowland) Sth'39.Cy.Dar. . . . . | Winthrop House,
  MR Nairn' Bowland Gillet—at | 4100 N Charles St,
☎ (941) 359-3696 . . 5046 Barrington Circle, | Baltimore, MD
Sarasota, FL *34234* . . . . | *21218*

Munroe MRS Andrew T H (Susan H Spalding) . . . . | ☎ (202) 638-1971
  MISS Nicoletta L—at ☎ (213) 413-7025 | 1026—16 St NW,
748 Parkman Av, Apt 4, Los Angeles, CA *90026* | Apt 202,
  MR Antonio W—at ☎ (202) 986-2062 | Washington, DC
1910—16 St NW, Washington, DC *20009* . . . . . | *20036*

Munroe COL Charles L—USAF.CTech'28
☎ (210) 675-2323 . . 4917 Ravenswood Dv, Apt 1786, San Antonio,
TX *78227*

Munroe MISS Dorothy F (Houglan—Dorothy F | ☎ (330) 928-8849
Munroe) . . . . | 873 Gaylord Grove
  MR Timothy E Houglan 2d . . . . | Rd, Cuyahoga Falls,
   | OH *44221*

Munroe MRS Henry (Hughes—Juliet Garrett) BMr'29
☎ (415) 348-3930 . . 850 N El Camino Real, San Mateo, CA *94401*

Munroe MR & MRS Henry W (Enid C Hughes) | ☎ (203) 255-0528
Pqt.Csn.H'43.Cl'47 . . . . | 131 Fleming Lane,
  MISS Alexandra K—Sophia'81.Nu'93—at | PO Box 784,
☎ (212) 757-6080 . . 146 W 57 St, Apt 55C, | Southport,
New York, NY *10019* . . . . | CT *06490-0784*

Munroe MR John—H'46
☎ (914) 677-8197 . . PO Box 137, Tyrell Rd, Millbrook, NY *12545*
Dec 15 . . ☎ (809) 956-5588 . . "Flint River House" Sandy Bay,
Hanover, Jamaica

Munroe MRS Paul (Edith L Breslow)
☎ (401) 847-2563 . . PO Box 339, Newport, RI *02840-0339*

Munroe MR & MRS Walter L (Alma F Evans) Penn'30
☎ (330) 923-3592 . . 540 E Portage Trail, Apt 609, Cuyahoga Falls,
OH *44221*

Munson MR & MRS Charles S JR (Harts—Celia B Deming)
Ln.Rcn.Unn.Cc.Y'37.Camb'38
☎ (561) 546-4571 . . 101 South Trail, Hobe Sound, FL *33455-2314*

Munson MR & MRS George R (Victoria T Kilbourn) RISD'63.Hart'65 . . . . ☎ (860) 658-1626 | 35 Woodside Circle,
MISS Mimi L—at Columbia . . . . | Simsbury, CT *06070*

Munson MR & MRS John C (Virginia D Aldrich) On.Cw.Cnt.Ncd.Myf.Ill'40 . . . . ☎ (847) 234-2672 | 140 E Ridge Lane,
MR John C JR . . . . | Lake Forest, IL
60045

Munson MRS John H G (Ruth F Blake) . . . . ☎ (617) 461-5786 | 30 Court St,
MISS Marianna C A. | Dedham, MA *02026*

Munson MISS Marjorie S (de Milhau—Marjorie S Munson)
☎ (415) 346-2332 . . 1063 Lombard St, San Francisco, CA *94109*

Murchison MISS Anne A . . see MRS W J Watson

Murchison MR & MRS Burk C (Christine E Keeney) | 5400 Montrose Dv,
Tex'75.Wes'71 . . . . | Dallas, TX
JUNIORS MR Burk C JR. . . . . | *75209-5618*
JUNIORS MR David L . . . . |

Murdoch MRS Allison H (Allison L Hammond)
☎ (215) 643-2520 . . 309 Elliger Av, Ft Washington, PA *19034*

Murdoch MR & MRS Britton (Harrison—Joan S | ☎ (610) 525-5678
Humpton) Me.M.Pa'53 . . . . | 101 Sproul Rd,
MISS Holly N Harrison—Denis'93—*see* | Villanova, PA *19085*
Dilatory Domiciles . . . . |

Murdoch MRS Lawrence C (Barbara M Boyd) . . . . Died at
Ambler, PA Jun 17'96

Murdoch MR & MRS Lawrence C JR (O'Neill—Eleanor M Egan) Cc.Pa'48
☎ (215) CH7-5814 . . 115 Hilltop Rd, Philadelphia, PA *19118*

Murdoch-Muirhead MR & MRS Thomas (Baugh—Murr S Sinclair) BA.Rby.
☎ (706) 746-2546 . . 27 Big Bear Trail, 176 Sky Valley, Dillard,
GA *30537*

Murdock MISS Catherine C . . of
☎ (202) 244-9364 . . 3267D Sutton Place NW, Washington, DC *20016*
☎ (540) 687-3604 . . PO Box 943, Middleburg, VA *20118*

Murdock MISS Frances N
☎ (212) 496-5129 . . 145 W 71 St, Apt 3A, New York, NY *10023*

Murdock MRS James G (Marie L de Chadenédes)
☎ (301) 229-1534 . . 4948 Sentinel Dv, Apt 306, Bethesda, MD *20816*

Murdock MR & MRS Lewis C (Madeleine D Huntington) Eh.B.
☎ (908) 234-0117 . . ''Hopeland'' Holland Rd, Peapack, NJ *07977-9999*

Murdock MISS Pamela H
see Dilatory Domiciles

Murfey MR & MRS Latham W 3d (Marion E Thompson)
BethanyWVa'72.Kt.Rr.Tv.Col'76
☎ (216) 352-5324 . . 7184 Pinehill Rd, Concord, OH *44077*

Murkland MRS John C (T Jane Magee) . . . . | of ☎ (203)661-9247
MISS Elizabeth G—Wheat'81—at | 53 Round Hill Rd,
☎ (617) 269-9234 . . 135 Marlborough St, | Greenwich, CT
Boston, MA *02116* . . . . | *06831*
☎ (508) 228-1361
Gull Island,
Nantucket, MA
02554

Murley MR & MRS Robert S (Mary B Pivirotto)
P'76.Cl'81.Sr.Rc.On.Cho.P'72.Cal'74.LondEc'75
☎ (847) 234-0994 . . 994 Meadow Lane, Lake Forest, IL *60045*

Murphy JUNIORS MR E Evan C . . see G A Johnson

Murphy MR & MRS E Hanlon (Joan Daly) Cy.Md'51 | ☎ (410) 235-2489
MISS Joan D—Md'84 . . . . | 3521 Newland Rd,
MR Timothy C—Md'83 . . . . | Baltimore, MD
21218

Murphy MRS Edward D (Harrell—Mary E Beedy)
☎ (703) 860-0738 . . 2231 Colts Neck Rd, Apt 801, Reston, VA *20191*

Murphy MR Emmett R—Ny.P'45
2 Sutton Place S, New York, NY *10022*

Murphy MISS Esmé C—H'81 . . see E E Vose

Murphy MR & MRS George A (Ruth B Milliken)
Unn.Chr.Plg.Csn.Hn.Ogle'27.H'31.Nu'42
☎ (860) 868-7795 . . East St, PO Box 1281, Washington, CT *06793*

Murphy MRS Grayson M P (Mary E Warren) Cly.Cs.
☎ (212) 838-8096 . . 1 E 66 St, New York, NY *10021*

Murphy MR Howland D—Fic.K.Rc.Pr.Ln.H'75
☎ (212) 517-3331 . . 175 E 79 St, New York, NY *10021*

Murphy MR & MRS James R (Margaret S Garrison) Pac'93.Ariz'87
☎ (602) 614-5957 . . 9225 N 119 Way, Scottsdale, AZ *85259*

Murphy MR & MRS Jonathan J (Jane T Luke) Briar'76.StLaw'73.Pace'79
☎ (203) 259-6390 . . 88 Hillside Rd, Fairfield, CT *06430*

Murphy, Joseph F 3d & Ward, Hilary H—Geo'90.H'85.Pa'90
☎ (914) 921-2782 . . 289 Milton Rd, Rye, NY *10580*

Murphy MR & MRS Joseph G (Grace H Trammell) Stph'48.Van'50.Van'47
☎ (615) 665-1781 . . 4400 Tyne Blvd, Nashville, TN *37215-4538*

Murphy MR & MRS Lewis C (Carol J Carney) Ariz'56.Ariz'55.Ariz'61
☎ (520) 327-0553 . . 3134 Via Palos Verdes, Tucson, AZ *85716*

Murphy MISS Margaret J—Ia'84 . . . . | ☎ (773) 404-1622
MR George J 3d . . . . | 2658J N Southport
Av, Chicago, IL
60614

Murphy MR & MRS Mark (Potter—Suzanne Simonin) ⚓
☎ (814) 455-5229 . . 322 Crescent Dv, Erie, PA *16505*

Murphy MR Martin N . . see MRS V J Stevenson

Murphy MRS R Montgomery (Ruth C Montgomery) | ☎ (914) 241-2319
Bgt. . . . . | 77 Buxton Rd,
MR Justin G—Col'92 . . . . | Bedford Hills, NY
10507

Murphy MRS Richard C (Nelson—Elizabeth C McCune) StA . . .of
☎ (203) 869-3725 . . 90 Oneida Dv, Indian Harbor, Greenwich,
CT *06830*
☎ (603) 756-4345 . . PO Box 432, Wentworth Rd, Walpole,
NH *03608-0432*

Murphy MR & MRS Richard W (Anne H Cook) | ☎ (212) 319-6541
Rdc'53.Cs.H'51 . . . . | 16 Sutton Place, Apt
MR Richard M . . . . | 9A, New York, NY
10022-3057

Murphy MR & MRS Robert E (Elizabeth M Shedd) | ☎ (847) 446-5017
Wa.Cnt.Ncd.UMiami'55 . . . . | 1501 Tower Rd,
MISS Margaret E . . . . | Winnetka, IL *60093*
MISS Suzanne E . . . . |

Murphy MR & MRS Robert E (A Kinzie Selfridge) Cal'64
809 Cobble Cove Lane, Sacramento, CA *95831*

Murphy MR & MRS Russell W JR (Patricia B | ☎ (314) 432-4692
Farrelly) SFr'75.Wash'62 . . . . | 21 Georgian Acres,
MISS Elizabeth F . . . . | St Louis, MO *63131*
MR Christopher M. . . . . |
JUNIORS MISS Adrian L . . . . |

Murphy MISS Sarah P C—Smu'95 . . see MRS K H Straus
Murphy MISS Stephanie Chouteau—StL'68.Dar. . . . . ☎ (954) 943-6880
  MRS Edwynne P (Jeanne C Chouteau) Dar. . . . . 133 N Pompano Beach Blvd, Apt 709, Pompano Beach, FL *33062*
Murphy MR Stephen C . . see G A Johnson
Murphy MISS Virginia M . . see MRS V J Stevenson
Murray MR & MRS A Brean (Sands—Bettina B Patterson) Cl'70.Cl'83.T.Cly.P.VillaN'61 . . . . . . of ☎ (212)288-2388 925 Park Av, New York, NY *10028*
  MR Stephen F . . . . ☎ (914) 534-7154 "Sengen" Deer Hill Rd, Box 234, Cornwall-on-Hudson, NY *12520*
  MR Christopher B—Mont'94—at U of Mich . . . ☎ (208) 622-4506 PO Box 2594, Sun Valley, ID *83353*
Murray MR & MRS Albert F 3d (Shelly E M Portner) Cvc.Rm'68 . . . . ☎ (301) 469-9091 8814 Bellwood Rd, Bethesda, MD *20817*
  MISS Valaer E . . . .
  MR Alexander F . . . .
  MR Andrew P . . . .
Murray MR & MRS Archibald (Anna C Mattison) V'33 ☎ (508) 428-2328 . . 1331 Main St, Cotuit, MA *02635-3538*
Murray MRS Arthur M JR (MacLeod—Rayma L Whittemore) ColbyS'52 . . . . ☎ (203) 967-3015 94 Liberty St, Apt 11, Stamford, CT *06902*
  MISS Penelope B . . . .
Murray MISS Daphne C . . see A Gawthrop JR
Murray MR & MRS David S (Margaret L Kennedy) V'41.SCar'42 ☎ (703) 780-2091 . . 1905 Hackamore Lane, Alexandria, VA *22308*
Murray MR & MRS Edwards B (McKinney—Pyles—Nancy Mann) Dth'47 ☎ (212) 327-2304 . . 196 E 75 St, Apt 18B, New York, NY *10021*
Murray MR & MRS Emmet Van A (Jeanne A Beatty) Cly . . .of ☎ (212) 472-0300 . . 524 E 72 St, New York, NY *10021* ☎ (516) 288-1171 . . Quiogue, NY *11978*
Murray MR & MRS F Wisner 4th (Betts Howes) Br'77.Ny.CtCol'79 ☎ (617) 383-9444 . . 8 Westgate Lane, Cohasset, MA *02025*
Murray MISS Felicia C—Franklin'74 ☎ (212) 674-0148 . . 131 E 19 St, New York, NY *10003*
Murray MRS Ford (Hutton—Weed—Noyes—Jill B Ford) PO Box 10099, Toledo, OH *43699*
Murray MR & MRS Francis Key (Marvel—Clara A Showell) JHop'50.Md'57 ☎ (610) 388-1124 . . PO Box 217, Mendenhall, PA *19357*
Murray MR & MRS Francis W 3d (Ames—Higginson—Shirley A Foerderer) Adelphi'81.Csh.Mt.Ac.Cly.Y'50 . . of ☎ (941) 472-3950 . . 993 Fish Crow Rd, Sanibel, FL *33957* ☎ (516) 692-4824 . . 86 White Hill Rd, Cold Spring Harbor, NY *11724*
Murray MR & MRS G Donald 3d (Edna Harrison) V'51.Rcn.Bhm.Fr.P'54 . . . . ☎ (707) 226-5614 Wild Horse Valley Ranch, PO Box 126, Napa, CA *94559*
  MISS Alexandra W—MtVern'89 . . . .
  MR J Angus—SonSt'88 . . . .

Murray MRS Henry Alexander (Davis—Fish—Caroline Chandler) Sth'42.Nyc. ☎ (508) 228-1119 . . "Fayaway" 11 Lincoln Av, Nantucket, MA *02554-3412*
Murray MR & MRS James B (Jean M Brundred) San.Km.Ncd.Geo'41.Y'43 . . . . ☎ (804) 973-5268 Panorama Farms, 333 Panorama Rd, Earlysville, VA *22936*
  MR Timothy B—Wms'84—at ☎ (510) 644-1548 1624 Tyler St, Berkeley, CA *94703* . . . .
Murray MR & MRS James B JR (Bruce D Randolph) Va'68.W&M'74 . . . . ☎ (804) 293-7653 "Greenmont" Keene, VA *22946*
  MISS Meghan R—at U of Va . . . .
  JUNIORS MR James B 3d—at Williams . . . .
Murray MR & MRS James G JR (Mary S Hinkle) Pa'77.Plg.Cw.Ne.Snc.StA.Pa'77 . . . . ☎ (011-44-181) 940-2403 Stokes House, Ham St, Richmond, Surrey TW10 7HR, England
  JUNIORS MISS Sarah P . . . .
Murray MR James Gordon—Rc.Plg.Chr.Snc.Cw.Ne.StA . . .of ☎ (941) 964-0720 . . 4 Park Place Colony, PO Box 716, Boca Grande, FL *33921* ☎ (212) 535-1787 . . 201 E 66 St, New York, NY *10021*
Murray MRS Jayne B (Jayne A Blodgett) Dar. . . . . . ☎ (914) 252-7220 Commodore Murray House, 58—5 St, Narrowsburg, NY *12764*
  MISS Jayne B . . . .
Murray MR & MRS John V A (Francesca P Hersloff) Ng.Nrr.Cda.Myf.Br'74.Conn'77 ☎ (203) 655-6797 . . 14 Dorchester Rd, Darien, CT *06820*
Murray MR & MRS Karl S (Mary Brooke Norris) Hav'86.VillaN'85.Drex'87 ☎ (215) 887-4019 . . 1068 Beverly Rd, Rydal, PA *19046*
Murray MISS M Piper (G Donald 3d) . . . . Married at Napa, CA
  Quinones MR Paul (Francisco) . . . . May 4'96
Murray MR & MRS M Timothy (Eugenia B Jessup) NEng'85.NEng'83 ☎ (561) 220-2927 . . 4230 SE Kubin Av, Stuart, FL *34997*
Murray MRS Mary S (Cuddihy—Mary R Smiley) ☎ (423) 577-4520 . . 2523 Fox Chase Hill, Knoxville, TN *37920*
Murray REV & MRS Michael H (Eliane Cadilhac) H'48.JHop'50.EpiscTheo'64 ☎ (410) 226-5311 . . 209 Tred Avon Av, PO Box 517, Oxford, MD *21654*
Murray MISS Olivia A—Stan'74.Stan'78 ☎ (212) 288-5567 . . 220 E 67 St, Apt 12E, New York, NY *10021*
Murray MR & MRS Palmer N (Stephanie A Booth) SCal'90.Tex'87 1221 Stone Canyon Dv, Los Angeles, CA *90077*
Murray MR R Nelson JR—Va'86 . . see A Gawthrop JR
Murray MR & MRS Robert A (Meredith H Medina) V'65.Y'62 . . . . ☎ (609) 466-8610 117 Rolling Hill Rd, Skillman, NJ *08558*
  MISS Amanda M—Cr'91—at ☎ (212) 254-0353 99 MacDougal St, Apt 5, New York, NY *10012*
  MISS Kimberly T—Cal'93 . . . .
Murray MR & MRS Robert N (McCullough—Bettyann Asche) Col'61.Rcn.Rr.P'60 . . . . ☎ (713) 622-0505 10 S Briar Hollow, Apt 8, Houston, TX *77027*
  MR Andrew D McCullough JR—Smu'92 . . . .

Murray MR & MRS Russell 2d (Sally T Gardiner) Mit'49
☎ (703) 683-4018 . . 210 Wilkes St, Alexandria, VA *22314*

Murray MISS Sally T (William T 3d) . . . . Married at Easley, SC
Bradberry MR Jesse . . . . May 26'95

Murray MISS Suzanne S (Vanaria—Suzanne S Murray) WmSth'76
☎ (860) 651-5885 . . 26 Elaine Dv, Simsbury, CT *06070*

Murray MR & MRS Thomas A (Lauren R Ingersoll) Wms'80.Wms'79
☎ (703) 734-4925 . . 6316 Hunting Ridge Lane, McLean, VA *22101*

Murray MR & MRS Thomson C (Roberta E Purvis) | ☎ (516) 922-4408
V'56.Pr.StA.P'56 . . . . | 220 Cleft Rd,
MR Thomson C JR . . . . | Mill Neck, NY
| *11765*

Murray MR & MRS W Stephen (Amory—Muffie W S Bancroft)
L.Pqt.Rr.Cly . . .of
☎ (203) 259-2334 . . "Bearlea" 86 Beachside Av, Greens Farms,
CT *06436*
☎ (212) 744-3087 . . 163 E 81 St, New York, NY *10028*

Murray MR William E—SCar'45.H'49 ⚓ . . of
☎ (212) 879-9582 . . 200 E 61 St, Apt 4G, New York, NY *10021*
☎ (803) 722-0400 . . 156 Tradd St, Charleston, SC *29401*

Murray MR & MRS William T JR (Jane M A | ☎ (212) 722-5577
Sheridan) GaTech'67 . . . . | 17 E 96 St,
MR William T 3d—at Babson . . . . | New York, NY
| *10128-0783*

Murray MR & MRS William T 3d (Clagett—Virginia | ☎ (410) 867-1550
L Parker) Sth'65.Elk.Ncd.Ty'54 . . . . | "Ivy Neck" Box 1,
MISS Linda H . . . . | West River, MD
| *20778*

Murrie MR & MRS Richard W (Finley—Rita R Toohey)
Cw.Rv.StA.P'39.Y'42
☎ (212) 888-7521 . . 200 E 66 St, New York, NY *10021*

Muse MR & MRS Albert C (Nancy B Trainer) Rr.Fcg.Pg.P'58 . . of
☎ (412) 621-7384 . . 5208 Pembroke Place, Pittsburgh,
PA *15232-1429*
☎ (412) 238-2454 . . "Laurel Glen" Rte 381, Rector, PA *15677*

Muse MISS Alexandra V—Geo'89.Rr.Pg.Fcg.
☎ (212) 875-0463 . . 322 W 87 St, Apt 1, New York, NY *10024*

Muse MISS Martha T—Bnd'48.Cl'55.Cly.Chr.Ht.Ncd.StJ . . .of
☎ (561) 287-6014 . . 3664 SE Fairway E, Stuart, FL *34997*
312 Harvest Commons, Westport, CT *06880*

Muse MISS Nancy C—SCal'92.Rr.Pg.Fcg.
☎ (213) 933-8705 . . 630 S Masselin Av, Apt 403, Los Angeles,
CA *90036*

Musgrave MAJ GEN & MRS Thomas C JR (Josephine Bennett)
Cvc.A.Mt.Sl.Ncd.USA'35
☎ (202) 537-1378 . . 4640 Garfield St NW, Washington, DC *20007*

Musgrave MR & MRS William G (Elizabeth R | ☎ (617) 698-6625
Sweetland) H'42 . . . . | 222 Highland St,
MISS Jane G R . . . . | Milton, MA *02186*

Muspratt MRS Sara McGuire (Sara J McGuire) | ☎ (617) 327-2401
Rdc'61.Camb'63 . . . . | 10 Linnet St,
MR Matthew . . . . | West Roxbury, MA
JUNIORS MR James A . . . . | *02132*

Musser MISS Lisa D . . see R B Ewart

Mustin MISS Josephine E—Me.Dar.
☎ (610) 359-0186 . . Dunwoody Village CH29, 3500 West Chester Pike,
Newtown Square, PA *19073*

Musto MRS Clarence E (Louise Van Fleet) Bur. . . . . | Stratford Apt 205,
MR Clarence E 3d . . . . | 601 Laurel Av,
| San Mateo, CA
| *94401*

Musto MISS Marguerite L
☎ (415) 368-2701 . . 535 Sunset Way, Redwood City, CA *94062*

Musto MR Peter Johnson—Bhm.Bur.Nrr.Pcu.Cp.StJ.Stan'63
☎ (415) 885-1640 . . 2644 Larkin St, San Francisco, CA *94109-1513*

Mutart MR & MRS Steven Lewis (Hundley—Lynne | of ☎ (610)793-4648
M Stockton) Wilkes'63.Penn'62.VillaN'65 . . . . | 803 Paine Dv,
MR Lee S—at U of Richmond . . . . | West Chester,
MISS Laura L Hundley—at Jacksonville, FL . | PA *19382*
MR J Douglas Hundley 2d—at Atlanta, GA . . | ☎ (609) 884-3245
| 1145 Maryland Av,
| Cape May, NJ
| *08204*

Muzzy MR & MRS Gray H (Phoebe LeM Welsh) Van'78.Y'76
☎ (713) 621-1249 . . 3679 Inwood Dv, Houston, TX *77019*

Myer MISS Georgia M—B'gton'75
☎ (802) 425-4169 . . 137 Popple Dungeen Rd, Charlotte, VT *05445*

Myer MR & MRS Lynford R (Marion S Stallard) VillaN'48
☎ (610) 828-8376 . . 3008 Joshua Rd, Lafayette Hill, PA *19444*

Myer MR & MRS Samuel C (M Josefa C Whitman) Lm.P'43
☎ (805) 647-9891 . . Nutwood Farm, 12168 Darling Rd, Ventura,
CA *93004*

Myer MR & MRS Theodore H (Mary E Hartmann) | ☎ (202) 333-1198
Rdc'60.H'77.S.Snc.Hl.Lm.Csn.H.'59.Mit'63 ⚓ | 2721 N St NW,
MR John W . . . . | Washington, DC
MR Frederick H . . . . | *20007*
MR Arthur R . . . . |

Myer MR & MRS Thomas J (Mary Anne A McNelis) | ☎ (215) CH8-1079
Pa'49.R.Pc.Rc.Rv.Cspa.VillaN'49 . . . . | 109 W Mermaid
MISS A Anastasia—Wils'84 . . . . | Lane, Chestnut Hill,
| PA *19118*

Myers MISS Barbara Q . . see MRS T A Ball

Myers MR C Twiggs—P'52
Berkshire School Rd, Sheffield, MA *01257*

Myers COL (RET) & MRS Eugene E (Ritchie—Florence M Hutchinson)
USAF.An.Ct.Evg. Ht.Ncd.Dar.Hn.NDak'36.NDak'38.Nw'40.Cl'47 . . of
☎ (202) FE7-1715 . . 3320 Volta Place NW, Washington, DC *20007*
☎ (561) 655-3334 . . 1 Royal Palm Way, Palm Beach, FL *33480-4249*

Myers MR John Woods (Elinor Eberhard)
☎ (508) 462-6055 . . 217 High Rd, Newbury, MA *01951*

Myers MR Paul D—Msq.NMo'42.H'47
☎ (513) 751-7446 . . 2121 Alpine Place, Apt 1503, Cincinnati,
OH *45206*

Myers MR R Graham—Hn.H'66 . . of
☎ (307) 778-7117 . . 515 E Pershing Blvd, Box 152, Cheyenne,
WY *82001*
☎ (860) 927-4534 . . 251 Kent Rd, Kent, CT *06757*

Myers MR & MRS Rem Van A (Marion Parker) Csh.Pn.P'37
☎ (203) 264-5039 . . 541A Heritage Village, Southbury, CT *06488*

Myers MR & MRS Rem Van A JR (Susan M Oelerich) Col'83.Ey.Denis'81
☎ (617) 595-1162 . . 84 Ocean Av, Swampscott, MA *01907*

Myers MR & MRS Robert A (Barbara W Stilson) V'59.Ri.T.Cly.Ncd.H.'58
☎ (212) 861-2374 . . 60 East End Av, Apt 9A, New York, NY *10028*

Myers DR & MRS W P Laird (Katharine Van Vechten) C.Ofp.Yn.Y'43.Cl'45
☎ (802) 295-9664 . . Four Winds Farm, Norwich, VT *05055*

Myers MRS Walter K (E Carol Grosvenor) Cvc.Ncd.
☎ (202) 363-4747 . . 3900 Cathedral Av NW, Washington, DC *20016*
Jan 1 . . ☎ (305) 444-2608 . . 3975 Douglas Rd, Coconut Grove,
FL *33133*

Myers MR & MRS William A (Harriet L Robey) | ☎ (203) 421-4404
SL'54.USA'52 . . . . | 131 Summer Hill
MR William T—at ☎ (617) 424-0027 | Rd, Madison, CT
406 Marlborough St, Apt 5, Boston, MA *02115* . | *06443*

Mygatt MR & MRS Donald L (Mary O Winslow) P'39
☎ (206) 747-1828 . . 472 W Lake Sammamish Rd N, Bellevue,
WA *98008*

Myles MR & MRS Robert C (Francine P Berth) | ☎ (212) 799-7181
Ws'57.Myf. . . . . | 325 W 86 St,
MISS Robin P—at Boston Coll . . . . | New York, NY
| *10024-3114*

Myles MISS Sarah Lindsay (Jaeger—Sarah Lindsay Myles)
SCar'92.Cit'95.Myf.
☎ (803) 768-2207 . . Heron Point, Seabrook Island, SC *29455*

Myles MR & MRS Thomas F (Star Paris) H'37.H'41 . | ☎ (508) 358-2513
MISS Barbara R—Br'80.Sim'84 . . . . | 110 Glezen Lane,
MISS Loring—Mass'82 . . . . | Wayland, MA *01778*

Myrin MRS Cuthbert L (Mansson—Louisa T | ☎ (307) 733-5998
Stephenson) Me.Fic. . . . . | PO Box 75, Wilson,
MISS Wendy W Mansson . . . . | WY *83014*

Myrin MR Cuthbert L JR—Me.DWeb'90
☎ (970) 925-2691 . . 300 Puppy Smith St, Apt 205, Aspen, CO *81611*

Myrin MR & MRS F A Wilhelm 2d (Janet Van A | ☎ (401) 635-2786
Olsen) StLaw'64 . . . . | 40 Grange Av,
MISS Arden V A—at ☎ (212) 501-9783 | Little Compton, RI
70 W 83 St, Apt DA, New York, NY *10024* . . . | *02837*
MR F Alarik W 3d—at ☎ (718) 260-9248
177 Columbia Heights, Apt 21, Brooklyn, NY
11201 . . . .

Myrin MRS Leslie du P (Leslie D du Pont) Me. . . . . | ☎ (610) 642-2804
MISS Mimi du P . . . . | 101 Cheswold Lane,
| Apt 4C, Haverford,
| PA *19041*

N

Nachman MR & MRS M Roland JR (Sadler—Martha Street)
Cal'57.H'43.H'48
☎ (334) 263-0197 . . 3261 Thomas Av, Montgomery, AL *36106*

Nadai MR & MRS Christopher M (Deirdre E Pennoyer) ColC'77
68 Grove St, Essex, MA *01929*

Nadai MRS Judith B (Judith D Beal) V'45.Tcy.Ncd. | ☎ (415) 931-1608
MISS Cynthia M—Cal'77.Ne'85—at Sydney, | 2619 Divisadero St,
Australia. . . . . | San Francisco, CA
| *94123*

Nadal MRS Carlos (Green—Lansing—Joan C Brander) . . Died Aug 27'96

Nadal MR Carlos—Cl'32
☎ (516) 283-0151 . . "La Casa" PO Box 796, 315 Narrow Lane,
Southampton, NY *11969*

Nadal MR David W—BaldW'69
☎ (516) 283-3031 . . 11 Little Neck Rd, PO Box 796, Southampton,
NY *11969*

Nadherny MR & MRS Ferdinand (Elinor N Case)
SL'50.Ih.Cho.Cnt.Yn.Y'50.H'52 . . of
☎ (847) 251-2470 . . 1630 Sheridan Rd, Apt 4A, Wilmette, IL *60091*
72 Country Rd S, Village of Golf, FL *33436-5603*

Nadler MR & MRS Charles F JR (Louise K Mauran) Bost'79.Ncd.Dth'78
☎ (508) 748-2885 . . 237 Converse Rd, Marion, MA *02738*

Nagel MRS Charles (Lucie L Oliver)
☎ (508) 748-0831 . . 18 Sippican Lane, Marion, MA *02738*

Nagel MRS Frederick W (Lisa Gratwick) BMr'37.G.
☎ (716) 243-2748 . . 3500 Main St, Piffard, NY *14533*

Nager DR & MRS George T (Mathilde Hofstetter) | ☎ (410) 366-6778
Elk.Zur'39 . . . . | 4403 Bedford Place,
MR Thomas R—Rich'78 . . . . | Baltimore, MD
| *21218*

Nagle MR Peter D
PO Box 221, Cable, WI *54821*

Nagy MR & MRS Gabriel F (Jones—Bell—Wendy S | ☎ (215) 247-4059
Lutkins) Macq'73.UNEng'75.AusNat'79.Pc.Rc. | 3 Druim Moir Court,
P.'63.H'66 . . . . | Philadelphia, PA
MISS Frances P—at Princeton . . . . | *19118*
MR J Estep—Y'92 . . . . |
JUNIORS MR Alexander K—at Choate Rosemary . |

Nagy MR & MRS Gregory B (Olga M Davidson) | ☎ (617) 523-5664
Bost'75.P'83.Tv.Chi.Ind'62.H'66 . . . . | 84 Revere St,
JUNIORS MISS Antonia . . . . | Boston, MA *02114*
JUNIORS MR Laszlo |

Nahigian MR & MRS James M (Alice A Evans) Pac'77.Pac'77
☎ (310) 395-7190 . . 513 Euclid St, Santa Monica, CA *90402*

Naimi DR & MRS Shapur (Amy C Simonds) | of ☎ (617)731-0439
Cy.BirmEng'53 . . . . | 265 Woodland Rd,
MISS Susan L—Dth'87 . . . . | Chestnut Hill, MA
DR Timothy S—H'86.Mass'91 . . . . | *02167*
MR Cameron L—H'91 . . . . | ☎ (617) 383-1466
| 55 Lothrop Lane,
| Cohasset, MA *02025*

Nalle MR & MRS Alexander B (Alison B Tracy) Vt'85.P'83
☎ (215) 248-1420 . . 7920 Crefeld St, Philadelphia, PA *19118*

Nalle MISS Ann B
4204 Maple Terr, Chevy Chase, MD *20815*

Nalle MR & MRS David (Dickey—Margaret B | ☎ (202) 466-8410
Shumaker) Sth'47.Cvc.Cos.P'46 . . . . | 1402—21 St NW,
MISS Susan T—at 206—10 St, Hoboken, NJ | Washington, DC
07030 . . . . | *20036*

Nalle MR & MRS Edwin N B (Karen Dotrice) P'76.Pa'78
☎ (310) 451-0007 . . 12751 Evanston St, Los Angeles, CA *90049*

Nalle MASTER Griffin Benson Dotrice (Edwin N B) . . . . Born at
Los Angeles, CA May 2'96

Nalle MR & MRS Horace D (Ethel Benson) Sg.Ph.P'44
☎ (215) 248-1417 . . 218 Lynnebrook Lane, Philadelphia, PA *19118*

Nalle MR & MRS Horace D JR (Patricia S Marlette) NH'82.Pc.Sg.H'78.Pa'83
☎ (201) 984-2656 . . 44 Springbrook Rd, Morristown, NJ *07960*

Nalle MR & MRS Jesse (Alice H Scott)
Ph.Ny.Pqt.San.NCar'43.Pa'59 ⛵
☎ (203) 259-6938 . . 494 Harbor Rd, Southport, CT *06490*

Nalle MISS Nina Louisa (Alexander B) . . . . Born at
Philadelphia, PA Dec 4'95
Nalle MR & MRS Richard T JR (Joan Thayer) Gm.Me.Rb.P'42.H'55
☎ (610) 525-4589 . . 915 Mt Pleasant Rd, Bryn Mawr, PA *19010*
Nammack MR & MRS Thomas W (Alexandra F Noble)
P'81.Pa'93.Br'80.Pa'93
☎ (610) 565-3096 . . 611 W Rosetree Rd, Media, PA *19063*
Nancarrow MR John William—HWSth'85 . . see G R Baer JR
Nancarrow MISS Melissa A—PineM'91 . . see G R Baer JR
Napier LT COL (RET) & MRS John H 3d (Cameron M Freeman)
USAF.Ala'55.StA.Cw.Fw.Ofp.Rv.Sar.Vca.Wt.StJ.Dar.
Ncd.Dcw.Miss'49.Aub'67
☎ (334) 281-0505 . . ''Kilmahew'' Rte 2, Box 614, Ramer,
AL *36069-9245*
Naquin MR & MRS David W D (Carola L Higby) NCar'71.NCar'70.NCar'84
☎ (505) 271-8751 . . 2926 La Palomita St NE, Albuquerque, NM *87111*
Naquin MR Stuart G A—Elk.Br'72 . . see R W Sharp
Narten MISS Martha C
☎ (617) 383-6201 . . 20 Church St, Cohasset, MA *02025*
Narten MR & MRS Peter B (Doris Ann Wright)
☎ (216) 338-5776 . . 213 Manor Brook, Chagrin Falls, OH *44022*
Narten MR Thomas W
☎ (617) 383-6201 . . 20 Church St, Cohasset, MA *02025*
Nash DR & MRS (DR) A E Keir (Marguerite
Bou-Raad) NCar'62.H'58 ⚓ . . . .
MR William E . . . .
☎ (805) 687-9315
1033 N Ontare Rd,
Santa Barbara, CA
93105
Nash MR Bradley De L—Cvc.Mt.Hn.H'23
☎ (304) 535-6876 . . High Acres Farm, Box 122, Rte 3, Harpers Ferry,
WV *25425*
Nash MR & MRS Edmund W (Ruth P Coffin) Bhm.Pcu.Sfg.Y'39
☎ (415) 435-9783 . . 16 Crest Rd, Belvedere, CA *94920*
Nash MISS Elizabeth Le Noir (g—Paul Le N Nash) . . . . Born at
Cincinnati, OH Jan 18'96
Nash MR & MRS F Philip JR (Lilia R Gherardi) Nyc.Ty'51
☎ (401) 751-2085 . . 41 Everett Av, Providence, RI *02906*
Nash MR & MRS John 2d (Hellyer—Joan G Le Grand) Bel'72.Cr'44
☎ (704) 859-9653 . . PO Box 1480, Tryon, NC *28782*
Nash MR & MRS Paul Le N (Nancy A Thouron)
V'56.Drew'96.Y'53.H'58 . . . .
MISS Laurie Le N—Y'88.Nw'96 . . . .
MISS Daphne T—GeoW'92 . . . .
☎ (201) 538-0524
4 Westminster Place,
Morristown, NJ
07902
Nash MR & MRS Peter W II (Sandra B Nichols) LakeF'84.Nyc.Ken'83
☎ (508) 266-0013 . . 216 School St, Acton, MA *01720-4468*
Nash MR & MRS Philip V (Renate E E Ambrosius)
Plg.P'46 . . . .
MR Philip M—at ☎ (617) 969-3277
19 Circuit Av, Newton, MA *02161* . . . .
☎ (212) 662-9403
360 Central Park W,
New York, NY
10025
Nash MR Stephen E—Y'42
☎ (412) 741-7614 . . Backbone Rd, Sewickley, PA *15143*
Nason MR & MRS John W (Knapp—Elizabeth Mercer)
Bnd'37.C.Cos.Csn.Carl'26.H'28.Ox'31
☎ (610) 388-1392 . . Crosslands 12, Kennett Square, PA *19348*
Nassau MR & MRS Henry N (Catharine A Mather)
Dick'77.Ph.Sa.Pa'76.Dick'79
☎ (610) 648-0494 . . Wilson Farm, 113A Swedesford Rd, Malvern,
PA *19355*

Nassau MR & MRS William L 3d (Caroline C
Rodenbaugh) Pa'49.Pa'48 . . . .
MISS Sarah C . . . .
☎ (610) 296-2531
1625 Le Boutillier
Rd, RD 3, Malvern,
PA *19355*
Naudé MR & MRS Klaus (Virginia B Norton)
BMr'60.Ph. . . . .
MISS Alice H—Y'87 . . . .
MR Philip W—SL'90 . . . .
☎ (215) 836-1170
752 Germantown
Pike, Lafayette Hill,
PA *19444*
Naughton MR & MRS A Stephen JR (Cynthia L Cannon) Aub'88
☎ (334) 826-0875 . . 303 E Samford Av, Auburn, AL *36830*
Naughton MR & MRS Albert S (Dorothy J Preuit) Aub'55.Cy.Aub'55
☎ (205) 967-4153 . . 2613 Caldwell Mill Lane, Birmingham, AL *35243*
Nauman MR & MRS Spencer G JR (Helen G Trimble)
V'55.Rc.Pn.P.'55.Pa'61 . . . .
MISS Helen G—HWSth'89—at 639 Lyndon St,
Monterey, CA *93940* . . . .
MR Spencer G 3d—Shippens'91—at
4117 S 570 E, Salt Lake City, UT *84107* . . . . . .
MR John T—at ''Spring House'' Box 83,
Bowmansdale, PA *17008* . . . .
☎ (717) 766-0936
Creek Farm,
Bowmansdale, PA
17008
Navarro MR Carlos F . . see J C Keene
Navarro MISS Gabriela (Rául A) . . . . Born Jan 29'94
Navarro MR & MRS Mario E (Wendy Chamberlain) Ky'79
Ulysses 79, Lomas de Axomitla, Mexico DF 02820, Mexico
Navarro MR & MRS Rául A (Marta Cabané) Me.Ky'81
☎ (305) 442-8351 . . 900 Cotorro St, Coral Gables, FL *33146*
Navarro MR René R—Ky'78 . . see J C Keene
Naylon MRS Henry M 3d (Patricia A Hopkins) Bf. .
MR Peter C—Cy.SFla'79—at
☎ (716) 837-7260 . . 211 Brantwood Rd, Snyder,
NY *14226* . . . .
☎ (941) 964-2502
150 Gilchrist Av,
PO Box 3,
Boca Grande, FL
33921
Neagle MRS Francis E JR (Julia M Snow) Mds . . .of
☎ (212) 861-6657 . . 103 E 75 St, New York, NY *10021*
☎ (516) 324-1717 . . 72 James Lane, East Hampton, NY *11937*
Neagle MRS John A (Mann—Cabot—Natalie Harris)
☎ (617) 862-7640 . . 265 Lowell St, Lexington, MA *02173*
Neal MR & MRS Bernard N JR (Elizabeth D Kennard)
BMr'49.Ncd.Emory'50 . . . .
MISS Elizabeth F . . . .
☎ (706) 291-7181
301 E Fourth Av,
Rome, GA *30161*
Neale MR & MRS Sterling L (Barber—H Virginia Fairbanks) Cycl.Cwr'34
☎ (561) 286-5932 . . 5625 SE Miles Grant Rd, Stuart, FL *34997*
Neblett MRS Cary H (Mary H G West) Hlns'66 . . . .
MISS Berkeley H . . . .
MISS Dabney C H . . . .
MR Brandon H . . . .
☎ (410) 235-6062
Roland Park,
7 Elmhurst Rd,
Baltimore, MD
21210
Needham MR Howard F
☎ (415) 389-9821 . . 137 Seminary Dv, Mill Valley, CA *94941*
Neel MISS Cynthia P—Ursinus'67.VillaN'74.VillaN'86
☎ (610) 644-3967 . . PO Box 42, Malvern, PA *19355*
Neel MR & MRS Richard (Constance M Hoguet)
Sth'65.Ri.Cs.Cl'61.Cl'64 . . . .
MISS Olivia D . . . .
MISS Antonia H . . . .
MISS Alexandra H . . . .
JUNIORS MISS Victoria A . . . .
☎ (212) 472-0337
333 E 68 St,
New York, NY
10021

Neel MR & MRS Samuel E (Mary Wilson) Mt.Ny.Sl.Ncd.Yn.Y'38
☎ (703) 356-3866 . . 1157 Chain Bridge Rd, McLean, VA 22101

Neely MRS Homer E (Marjorie McKie) Sth'35
☎ (513) 232-0222 . . 6153 Wasigo Dv, Cincinnati, OH 45230

Neff MR Christopher W (James L) . . . . Married at Summit, NJ
Takizawa MISS Shino . . . . Apr 6'96

Neff MR & MRS Edward B (A Virginia Beidler) May.It.Dth'30.Cwr'32
☎ (216) 991-5488 . . 3240 Green Rd, Beachwood, OH 44122

Neff MISS Hilary H—GeoW'93
☎ (212) 288-8946 . . 203 E 74 St, New York, NY 10021

Neff MR & MRS James L (Barney—Frederica S Auerbach)
V'49.Cs.Cda.P.'53 . . of
☎ (212) 288-5672 . . 150 E 73 St, New York, NY 10028
☎ (518) 589-5761 . . "Skyhigh" Onteora Park, Tannersville,
NY 12485

Neff MR & MRS Morton Gibbons JR (Florence M Chance) Cry.
☎ (410) 778-0775 . . Clovelly Farm, 401 Clovelly Lane, Chestertown,
MD 21620

Neff MR & MRS Richard B (Mary Alice Jester) Ga'34.Chr.H.Ga'35
☎ (212) RH4-0011 . . 114 E 84 St, New York, NY 10028

Neff MR & MRS Richard B JR (Joan E Russell) Nu'66.Evg.Pa'65.Cl'67
☎ (561) 842-8051 . . 250 Palmo Way, Palm Beach, FL 33480

Neff DR & MRS Richard S (Margot Ardlie) H'33
☎ (209) 435-7191 . . 5312 N Colonial Av, 102, Fresno, CA 93704

Neff MASTER Spencer Leene (g—W Perry Neff) . . . . Born at
Salem, MA Oct 27'95

Neff MR & MRS W Perry (Michele D Dubois) | of ☎ (802)824-6485
SL'62.S.Wms'50.Wis'54 . . . . | Little Holden Farm,
DR Taylor E—Cl'88—at ☎ (612) 822-5001 | 96 Holden Hill Rd,
3132 Freemont Av S, Minneapolis, MN 55408 . | Weston, VT 05161
MR Michael W P—Mid'87—at ☎ (212) 265-4552 | ☎ (516) 671-7490
235 W 48 St, New York, NY 10036 . . . . | Dogwood Lane,
| PO Box 364,
| Mill Neck, NY
| 11765

Neidecker MR & MRS Peter C (Dora D Shaw)
Sth'51.DU'70.Pn.Br'45.P'47 . . of
☎ (303) 744-1100 . . 820 S Garfield St, Denver, CO 80209
☎ (719) 395-6960 . . Box 32011, H'way 24, Buena Vista, CO 81211

Neiger MR Henry M
☎ (212) 865-4717 . . 285 Riverside Dv, New York, NY 10025

Neiley MR & MRS Richard B JR (Patricia L McClenahan) P'48
☎ (215) 348-3498 . . 606 Hampton Court, Doylestown, PA 18901

Neill MR & MRS J Kerby (Julia D Stewart) | 3767 Winchester Rd,
MissStw'34.StL'40.Geo'28.JHop'35 . . . . | Lexington, KY
MR Paul W . . . . | 40509-7510

Neill MR Michael S de L—Snc.Lm.Rv.Ht.Cw.
☎ (212) 689-8139 . . 30 Waterside Plaza, Apt 7J, New York, NY 10010

Neill MRS Robert (Nancy Mitchell) Bgy.
Evergreen Woods, 88 Notch Hill Rd, North Branford, CT 06471

Neill MR & MRS William 3d (Henrietta S Hopper)
Wheat'49.Md.Rv.JHop'50.Pa'52
☎ (410) 823-4827 . . 1809 Circle Rd, Ruxton, MD 21204

Neilson REV & MRS Albert P (Julie Hopkins) | ☎ (610) 942-2585
Bost'50.Yn.Y'52.Gen'lTheo'57 . . . . | RD 1, Box 622,
MISS Katharine B F . . . . | Honey Brook, PA
| 19344

Neilson MR & MRS Benjamin R (Grace—Meta B | ☎ (610) 527-0497
Lewis) Rc.Ph.Hn.H'60.H'63 . . . . | 917 Sorrel Lane,
MR Eugene Grace . . . . | Bryn Mawr, PA
| 19010

Neilson MR & MRS Carl L (Anne S Nimick) Ty'78.Me.Ac.Ncd.Bates'79
☎ (610) 971-9588 . . 257 Chester Rd, Devon, PA 19333

Neilson MR Harry R JR (Haack—Janneke Seton) Me.Nf.Cts.Gm.Ac.
☎ (610) 644-9618 . . Spring Meadow Farm, RD 2, Malvern, PA 19355

Neilson MRS James C (Marguerite H Coe) Dc.Ncd. . | ☎ (314) 725-5226
MISS Margaret J (Podhorn—Margaret J Neilson) | 6249 Pershing Av,
Gchr'67.Ncd. . . . . | St Louis, MO 63130

Neilson MRS Judith R (Judith Rawle) Rdc'60 . . . . . | ☎ (610) 688-2939
MISS Theodora C . . . . | 112 Steeplechase
MISS Alberta R—at 1408 California St, | Rd, Devon, PA
San Francisco, CA 94109 . . . . | 19333
MR Marshall R . . . . |

Neilson MRS Lewis L (Barbara S Leech) Au.Sa.Sfh.Me.Sdg . . . of
☎ (610) 827-7367 . . Chantilly Farm, Horseshoe Trail, Chester Springs,
PA 19425
☎ (518) 576-9846 . . "Windy Brow" Ausable Club, St Huberts,
NY 12943

Neilson MR & MRS Lewis L JR (Carol H Newhall)
Wms'84.Drex'94.Au.Me.Ph.Coa.Cc.Cspa.Cw.
Ll.Rv. Sar.Fw.W.Dar.Bab'71.Del'78.Temp'81
☎ (215) 836-7959 . . 8004 Gladstone Rd, Wyndmoor, PA 19038

Neilson MR & MRS Louis (Stanton—Rosamond G Wilfley) Ws'42.H'39
☎ (802) 325-3066 . . Dorset, VT 05251

Neilson MISS Ruth W—Ken'79 . . see M A M Wall

Neilson MR Silas W M—Br'91.Cal'95 . . see M A M Wall

Neilson MISS Susanna M (late Harry R JR) . . . . . Married at Malvern, PA
Du Bois MR Richard S . . . . Jun 29'96

Neilson MRS Thomas R JR (Florence A Schenck) | ☎ (610) 644-0616
VillaN'85.Rd.Nyc. . . . . | 2 Porteous Rd,
MISS Susan (Madigan—Tutolo—Susan Neilson) | Berwyn, PA 19312
Rd.—at ☎ (610) 296-3675 . . 330 Spring House |
Lane, West Chester, PA 19380 . . . . |

Neilson MR & MRS William L (Pia Bundgaard) Y'77
☎ (914) 833-3706 . . 6 Rockhill Terr, Larchmont, NY 10538

Neilson MRS Winthrop C (Frances Fullerton Jones)
☎ (717) 273-5320 . . Cornwall Manor, Mansion Annex B7, Cornwall,
PA 17016-0125

Nelidow MISS Irina—BMr'50
☎ (314) 725-1445 . . 701 S Skinker Blvd, St Louis, MO 63105-3226

Nelms MR & MRS Frank C (Suzanne Rodgers)
☎ (713) 621-4274 . . 4515 Banning Dv, Houston, TX 77027

Nelsen MR & MRS Peter R (Charlotte R Hundley) CtCol'75.GeoW'69
☎ (703) 385-8124 . . 3167 Lindenwood Lane, Fairfax, VA 22031

Nelson MR Albert L 3d—Wash'60.Wash'62.GeoW'64
☎ (520) 577-3116 . . 5352 Via Entrada, Tucson, AZ 85718

Nelson MRS Anne R (Anne W Rankin) . . . . | ☎ (941) 378-3171
MR Barclay D—at ☎ (314) 773-9022 | 3382 E Chelmsford
2108 Allen Av, St Louis, MO 63104 . . . . | Court, Sarasota, FL
| 34235

Nelson MR & MRS Arthur H (Eleanor Thomas) V'53.H'54.Kas'43.H.'49
☎ (617) 894-6583 . . 75 Robin Rd, Weston, MA 02193

Nelson MR & MRS B Gordon 3d (A Kennedy Beckwith) Vt'77.Rr.Fcg.Skd'74.Pitt'79
☎ (412) 441-9257 . . Hood Farm, PO Box 188, Stahlstown, PA *15687*

Nelson MR & MRS Charles 3d (Mary M Bass) Nw'80.Van'86.NCar'72
☎ (615) 665-1950 . . 2704 Tyne Blvd, Nashville, TN *37215*

Nelson MR & MRS Douglas A (Mary E Johnson) Swb'64.Va'61.Va'64 . . . .
MR Douglas A JR . . . .
JUNIORS MISS Cynthia M . . . .
of ☎ (423)821-1368 | 719 E Brow Rd, | Lookout Mountain, | TN *37350* | Cottage 332, | Sea Island, GA | *31561*

Nelson MISS E Pegge—PugetS'80.Pitt'96.Me . . .see S B Dunn JR

Nelson MR & MRS Edward G (Carole O F Minton) Van'60.Ri.So'52 . . . .
MISS Carole G—at 4505 Harding Rd, Apt 155, Nashville, TN *37205* . . . .
MISS Ellen P—at 327 Villages at Vanderbilt, Nashville, TN *37212* . . . .
☎ (615) 383-7822 | 1305 Chickering Rd, | Nashville, TN *37215*

Nelson MRS Edward H (Martha E Leavitt) Myf.Ncd. 1833 Clifton Rd NE, Apt 301, Atlanta, GA *30329*

Nelson MR & MRS George A 3d (Elizabeth A Pyles) Chr.Cl'69 . . . .
JUNIORS MR Alexander P—at St Andrew's Scotland . . . .
☎ (212) 628-0823 | 12 E 86 St, | New York, NY | *10028*

Nelson DR & MRS James A (Katherine R Metcalf) Stan'62.H'61 . . . .
MISS Julie H . . . .
MR John M . . . .
☎ (206) 523-4546 | 5655 NE | Windemere Rd, | Seattle, WA *98105*

Nelson MR & MRS Lathrop B JR (Hillman—Lorna A Dea) Me.Pa'63
☎ (610) 527-4938 . . 13 Courtney Circle, Bryn Mawr, PA *19010*

Nelson MRS Lewis C (Dorothy M Dean) Mo'30
☎ (314) 863-7390 . . 7525 Wellington Way, St Louis, MO *63105*

Nelson MISS Lori A—Miami'90
6251 Southwood Av, Apt 25, St Louis, MO *63105*

Nelson MISS (REV) Nancy F—Ant'79.SFrTheo'84
☎ (508) 228-2864 . . 10 Lincoln Av, Nantucket, MA *02554*

Nelson MR & MRS Norman F 2d (Sally L Hutt) Syr'58.Snc.Syr'57 ⚓
☎ (201) 934-1238 . . 145 Old Woods Court, Mahwah, NJ *07430*

Nelson MRS Pamela E (Pamela R Eakins) Hlns'63 . .
MISS Holly R—Ty'96 . . . .
JUNIORS MISS Amy B—at Choate Rosemary . . . .
☎ (330) 867-8474 | 154 Durward Rd, | Akron, OH *44313*

Nelson MR & MRS Paul A (Margaret Piper)
☎ (413) 268-7533 . . 60 Old Goshen Rd, Williamsburg, MA *01096*

Nelson MR Robert M—Ore'75 ⚓
☎ (508) 655-4820 . . Nelson Farm, Christmas Tree Lane, South Natick, MA *01760*

Nelson MR & MRS Thomas E JR (Carol Corley) Tex'58.A.Tex'57
☎ (512) 472-6157 . . 2422 Wooldridge Dv, Austin, TX *78703*

Nelson MR & MRS Thomas F (Barbara McDowell) Cal'58.SFr'57 . . . .
MISS Karen F . . . .
MR Gregory A . . . .
☎ (415) 941-5377 | 11550 Old Ranch | Rd, Los Altos, CA | *94024*

Nelson MR Trevor C (John H) . . . . Married at Friday Harbor, MA
Davis MISS Margaret W (Robert G) . . . . Aug 24'96

Nelson MR & MRS Valle R (Pamela M Bosten) Ec.Myc.Bab'73 . . . .
MISS Sarah R—at Rollins . . . .
JUNIORS MISS Vanessa R . . . .
of ☎ (508)526-7529 | 23 Ocean St, | Manchester, MA | *01944* | ☎ (603) 236-9940 | 8 Tyler Springs, | Waterville Valley, | NH *03215*

Nelson MRS Warren G (Dorothy Q Beckwith) . . . . .
MISS Abigail T . . . .
☎ (617) 899-4462 | 9 Montvale Rd, | Weston, MA *02193*

Nelson MRS Wenley D (Wickwire—Roma L Austin)
☎ (610) 645-8718 . . Waverly Heights, 1400 Waverly Rd, Gladwyne, PA *19035*

Nemazee MR & MRS Hassan (Sheila Kashanchi) SCal'72.Rc.Bgt.H.'72 . . . .
MISS Yasmine F . . . .
JUNIORS MR Kamyar M . . . .
of ☎ (212)744-3061 | 770 Park Av, Apt | 14A, New York, NY | *10021* | ☎ (914) 232-4243 | Old Apple Farm, | Box 136, | Mt Holly Rd, | Katonah, NY *10536*

Nesbit MRS Thorpe (Jarrett—Elizabeth N Bland) Mv.
☎ (410) 827-7215 . . "Walsey Farm" 222 Bunny Rabbit Lane, Queenstown, MD *21658*

Nesbit MR Thorpe JR—H.'49
☎ (610) 642-3259 . . 170 Lakeside Rd, Apt A11, Ardmore, PA *19003*

Nesbitt MRS M Huppman (Bealmear—Moore—Mary L Huppman)
☎ (410) 433-5296 . . 4909 Falls Rd, Baltimore, MD *21210*

Ness MR & MRS Peter S (Williams—Christine Vanderwarker) Csn.Y'60.Cl'63 . . . .
MISS Ashley Williams . . . .
MR Alexander H Williams 4th . . . .
MR James D Williams-Ness . . . .
☎ (203) 622-6569 | 51 North St, | Greenwich, CT | *06830*

Ness MR & MRS Philip W (Anne T F Semple) JHop'29 . . of
☎ (941) 922-5442 . . 7979 S Tamiami Trail, Sarasota, FL *34231*
☎ (508) 428-6779 . . 449 Eel River Rd, Osterville, MA *02655*

Ness MR & MRS Philip W JR (Jessop—Susan E Kinnear) NB'68.Bgt.Y'58 . . . .
MISS Alexandra S—Nw'92—at 340 E 90 St, New York, NY *10128* . . . .
MISS Stephanie E G Jessop . . . .
MISS Heidi S R Jessop . . . .
☎ (203) 869-6640 | 9 Mead Point Dv, | Greenwich, CT | *06830*

Nettl MR & MRS Stephen A (Pratt—Noël S Butcher) Dick'75.Rc.Me.LondEc'75 . . . .
JUNIORS MISS Christine S Pratt . . . .
☎ (610) 525-7625 | "Little Garden | House" 318 | Thornbrook Av, | Rosemont, PA | *19010*

Neubauer DR & MRS Darwin W (Virginia C Withington) Wash'35.Wash'35.Wash'39
☎ (520) 885-5948 . . 7218 E Camino Valle Verde, Tucson, AZ *85715*

Neuhaus MR & MRS James Harrison (Kathryn H Gaffney) Yn.Y'50 . . . .
MISS Mary H—at ☎ (404) 237-7116 2298 Briarwood Hills Dv NE, Atlanta, GA *30319*
☎ (713) 622-4947 | 10 S Briar Hollow | Lane, 48, Houston, | TX *77027-2809*

Neuhaus MR & MRS Joseph R (Margaret L Elder) Y'40 . . . . MR Charles E—Rr.Y'83 . . . . ☎ (713) 522-2220 2125 Pine Valley Dv, Houston, TX 77019

Neuhaus MR & MRS Joseph R JR (Lisa E Keeper) Va'70 ☎ (713) 665-1669 . . 2804 University Blvd, Houston, TX 77005

Neuhaus MR & MRS William O 3d (E Kay Ficklen) GaBap'64.GaTech'67 . . . . MISS Kimberly Sautelle—Cl'79.Pa'92—at ☎ (212) 477-5810 . . 111 Fourth Av, Apt 11H, New York, NY 10003 . . . . of ☎ (713)524-2402 3266 Locke Lane, Houston, TX 77019 461 Acequia Madre St, 2, Santa Fe, NM 87501

Neuhauser MR & MRS Charles W (Liane Lunny) Md.Coa.Cw. ☎ (410) 472-4839 . . 14836 Carroll Rd, Phoenix, MD 21131

Neuhoff MISS Christie B—StL'88 ☎ (314) 962-8861 . . 2521 Bremerton Av, St Louis, MO 63144

Neuhoff MISS Donna . . see J S Josey

Neuhoff MISS Emily P . . see J S Josey

Neuhoff MR Joe O 3d . . see J S Josey

Neuhoff MISS Virginia F . . see J S Josey

Neumann MRS Anne Rittershofer (Anne F Rittershofer) Sth'58 . . . . MISS Helen K—Cal'84—at ☎ (415) 494-1433 360 Shasta Dv, Palo Alto, CA 94306-4541 . . . . of ☎ (513)321-4415 Madison House Apt 203, 2324 Madison Rd, Cincinnati, OH 45208-2638 ☎ (508) 645-9934 ''Studio House'' Middle Rd, PO Box 148, Chilmark, MA 02535-0148

Neumann MRS Charles P (Saranne King) ☎ (520) 886-2253 . . 7269 E Camino Vecino, Tucson, AZ 85715

Neumann DR Peter G—H'54 . . of ☎ (415) 494-1433 . . 360 Shasta Dv, Palo Alto, CA 94306-4541 PO Box 148, Chilmark, MA 02535-0148 Madison House Apt 203, 2324 Madison Rd, Cincinnati, OH 45208-2638

Neumann MRS Theodore W (Hanson—Grace T Middleton) ☎ (914) NE6-8240 . . 425 Wilmot Rd, New Rochelle, NY 10804

Neumeyer MRS William E (Carpenter—Julia B Snowden) Swb'52 ☎ (703) 356-3232 . . 1033 Savile Lane, McLean, VA 22101

Nevill MR & MRS Hugh T A (Patricia M Harris) Brdgwtr'68.Va'64 . . . . MR Hugh E C—Va'91 . . . . MR Lowell S W—Va'94 . . . . ☎ (540) 364-1440 ''Carswell'' 6422 Swains Rd, Marshall, VA 20115

Neville MISS Betsey B (Bright—Betsey B Neville) Nu'72.Ant'85 ☎ (603) 464-3474 . . RFD 1, Box 176, Hillsborough, NH 03244

Neville MR & MRS Francis W (Sally A Nenner) V'50.Cy.Cwr'48 ☎ (216) 292-6728 . . 3741-3 Lander Rd, Chagrin Falls, OH 44022

Neville MR & MRS James D (Anne McM Biggar) Sth'77.Cy.Tv.Dth'72 ☎ (216) 765-0922 . . 2762 Inverness Rd, Shaker Heights, OH 44122

Neville MR & MRS Robert J (Ruby Brown) MtH'46.Cy.Case'38 ☎ (216) 321-4922 . . 2766 Belvoir Blvd, Shaker Heights, OH 44122

Neville MR & MRS Warwick F (Walley—Pamela R Rowe) BtP.Cc.Cw.P'52.Pa'55 . . . . MISS Hope V . . . . MR George R—at 227 Australian Av, Palm Beach, FL 33480 . . . . MR Noah J Walley—Ox'84.Stan'90 . . . . MR Matthew B Walley—Ox'87 . . . . of ☎ (561)659-4310 153 Australian Av, Palm Beach, FL 33480 ☎ (910) 295-1357 ''Holly House'' PO Box 1827, Pinehurst, NC 28374 ☎ (011-44-171) 235-4917 55 Eaton Square, London SW1, England

Nevius MR & MRS Garrett W (Antich—Mary E Peltz) V'48.Ty'91.P'36.Cl'39 . . . . MISS Mary E—Tufts'85 . . . . ☎ (860) 674-9794 The Barn, 45 Mountain Rd, Farmington, CT 06032

Nevius MR & MRS John G (Alison A Hess) Sth'82.Ariz'85.Conn'83.Pa'87.Pace'96 ☎ (718) 638-5253 . . 235 Lincoln Place, Apt 2H, Brooklyn, NY 11217-3734

Newbegin MRS Robert (Katharine Slade) ☎ (202) 337-6091 . . 3900 Cathedral Av NW, Apt 503A, Washington, DC 20016

Newberry MR Alexander S ☎ (941) 349-2289 . . 5750 Midnight Pass Rd, Siesta Key, FL 34242

Newberry MR Gardner C—Bates'96 . . see R Gignoux

Newberry JUNIORS MR James W . . see R Gignoux

Newberry MR & MRS John S IV (MacGuigan—Edith McBean) Wheat'73.My.Nrr.Ri.Srb.Pa'72 . . of ☎ (508) 927-0264 . . ''Lee's Crossing'' 175 West St, PO Box 5620, Beverly Farms, MA 01915 ☎ (212) 744-4395 . . 155 E 72 St, New York, NY 10021

Newbold MR Arthur E 3d . . . . Died at West Chester, PA Feb 23'96

Newbold MRS Arthur E 3d (Swartley—Emily Trefz) Eastman'65.Temp'69.Combs'87.Nf.Ph.Rb. ⚓ MR J Christopher Swartley—at U of Rochester ☎ (610) 935-7887 ''Fair Kleyona'' 605 Cherry Lane, Phoenixville, PA 19460

Newbold MR & MRS Arthur E 4th (Lilley—Douglass A Wallace) Ph.Rd.H.'64.Pa'67 . . . . MISS Gerda P—Nw'86—at ☎ (310) 450-9980 2821—3 St, Santa Monica, CA 90405 . . . . MISS Eliza B—Col'93—at 3600—20 St, Apt 404, San Francisco, CA 94110 . . . . MISS Sarah W Lilley—Cal'88—at 236 Lafayette St, Apt 5, New York, NY 10012 MISS Madeline Lilley—Colg'89—at 823 Ashbury St, Apt 1, San Francisco, CA 94117 . . . . ☎ (610) 296-0463 ''Frog Hollow'' 764 Hillview Rd, RD 2, Malvern, PA 19355

Newbold MR Christopher H—Pa'70 ☎ (213) 483-6764 . . 1616 Angelus Av, Los Angeles, CA 90026

Newbold MR & MRS Clement B JR (Virginia A Dunkerton) Penn'61.Temp'81.Penn'61 . . . . | of ☎ (941)676-1939 Mountain Lake, PO Box 832, Lake Wales, FL 33859-0832
MISS Pamela deWindt—Box 464275, Lawrenceville, GA 30246 . . . .
MR Clement B 3d . . . . | ☎ (704) 295-4441 ''Eastern View'' Box 1910, 1125 Old John's River Rd, Blowing Rock, NC 28605

Newbold MISS Daisy D . . see H C Bishop

Newbold MRS FitzEugene D JR (Sarah F Vaughan)
☎ (757) 220-1409 . . 225A Woodmere Dv, Williamsburg, VA 23185

Newbold MR & MRS J Cheston M (Ann E Brown) | ☎ (603) 675-2394 Dingleton Hill Farm, RR 3, Box 24, Cornish, NH 03745
JHop'62 . . . .
MISS Elise M . . . .
JUNIORS MISS Amanda G . . . .

Newbold MR J Cheston M JR (J Cheston M) . . . . Married at Cornish, NH
Schriver Kristine (Edward J) . . . . Aug 26'95

Newbold MR James F . . see W B Garrison JR

Newbold MISS Jennifer H—Vt'82
☎ (301) 585-6022 . . 10017 Pratt Place, Silver Spring, MD 20910

Newbold MR & MRS John L (Judith A Bourne) | ☎ (908) 277-4293 47 Hillcrest Av, Summit, NJ 07901
V'59.Mt.Yn.Y'57.Nu'63 . . . .
MR Timothy B—Duke'85.Ch'91—at
333 E Ontario St, Apt 1305B, Chicago, IL 60611

Newbold MRS John S (Mary Ernestine Dexter) | ☎ (610) 525-6503 34 Wistar Rd, Villanova, PA 19085
Ac.Gm. . . . .
MR Clinton C . . . .

Newbold MR & MRS Michael JR (Marion E Rothbart) Wid'87.Penn'87
☎ (302) 234-2353 . . 815 Benge Rd, Hockessin, DE 19707

Newbold MISS Noel T . . see H C Bishop

Newbold MR Richard C (Margery E Lawler)
☎ (610) 692-3889 . . 449 Eaton Way, West Chester, PA 19380

Newbold MR T A Scott—Vt'93 . . see MRS D D Muir

Newbold MR & MRS Thomas (M Noreen Maxwell) | ☎ (617) 259-8584 58 Todd Pond Rd, Lincoln, MA 01773
Sm.H'38 . . . .
MR Robert H . . . .

Newbold MR Thomas D . . see W B Garrison JR

Newbold MR William D
see Dilatory Domiciles

Newbold MR & MRS William F (Wolf—Elinor Kemper)
Bost'38.Cts.Csp.P'46
☎ (941) 383-0882 . . 3630 Gulf of Mexico Dv, Apt 201B, Sarasota, FL 34228

Newbold MRS William T 2d (Mary K Simmons) Ala'80.Temp'94
☎ (205) 547-8858 . . 280 Alpine View, Gadsden, AL 35901

Newbold MR William T 2d—Ala'79.Drex'86.Drex'92
☎ (215) 233-9072 . . 401 Hillcrest Av, Wyndmoor, PA 19038

Newcomb MRS J Stephen (Louisa B Martinelli) Cal'91
☎ (415) 868-9811 . . Paradise Valley Ranch, PO Box 347, Bolinas, CA 94924

Newcomb MR J Stephen—Cal'72
☎ (011-55-11) 240-6604 . . Avenida Jurucê 873, 04080 São Paulo, Brazil

Newcomer MR & MRS Francis R (Andrea A Martinovic) Vt'78.Char'ton'75
☎ (212) 627-9069 . . 29 King St, New York, NY 10014

Newcomer MR & MRS Waldo (Linda L Moon) | 31 Grey Wing Pointe, Naples, FL 34113-8404
UMiami'59.Ec.Mit'52 . . . .
MR John W—at ☎ (508) 281-2611
29 Rockholm Rd, Annisquam, MA 01930 . . . . .

Newell JUNIORS MISS Alexandra . . see T F Leddy

Newell MR & MRS Clifford A JR (Jane H Badger) | ☎ (617) 762-3601 522 Pond St, Westwood, MA 02090
Myf. . . . .
MR Walter C—at ☎ (617) 628-7521
255 Medford St, Apt 46, Somerville, MA 02143

Newell MISS Frances T . . see R S Perkins

Newell MR George P—Stan'47

Newell MRS George T (Jelke—Teal—Elizabeth M Clarke) Cly.
☎ (203) 743-0516 . . ''Windsong'' Saw Mill Rd, Danbury, CT 06810

Newell MR & MRS John O 3d (Barbara Hoblitzelle) Bnd'60.Cl'58
☎ (860) 236-3425 . . 144 Pioneer Dv, West Hartford, CT 06117

Newell MR & MRS John O 4th (Cornelia S Worsley)
HRdc'79.Cl'83.Myf.Mid'80.Nu'84
9 Bradyll Rd, Weston, MA 02193

Newell MR & MRS Robert M JR (Judith Ann Reynolds) Stan'66.Vh.Stan'66 . . . . | 1645 Euclid Av, San Marino, CA 91108
MISS Angela G—Stan'95 . . . .
MR Robert M 3d—Cal'94—at
3533 Keystone Av, Apt 2, Los Angeles, CA 90034 . . . .

Newell MR & MRS Charles Mercer (Brock—Priscilla Jenks) Pa'31
☎ (610) 356-8246 . . Dunwoody Village, 3500 West Chester Pike, Newtown Square, PA 19073

Newhall MR & MRS Charles W 3d (Amy L Liebno) | ☎ (410) 363-1552 2803 Caves Rd, Owings Mills, MD 21117
Sm.Rr.Gv.Cc.Mv.Pa'67.H'71 . . . .
MR Charles A . . . .
JUNIORS MR Adair B . . . .

Newhall MR & MRS Daniel T (Tracey E Baldwin) PCTS'81.Myf.Wilm'78
☎ (215) 646-6321 . . 310 Walker Rd, Ambler, PA 19002

Newhall MR George A III—Sfy.Cp.SFr'67 ⚓
☎ (415) 332-2666 . . 69 Prospect Av, Sausalito, CA 94965

Newhall MISS Jane
☎ (415) 346-4744 . . 2950 Pacific Av, San Francisco, CA 94115

Newhall MISS Jane
☎ (203) 869-0805 . . 41 Fairfield Rd, Greenwich, CT 06830

Newhall MRS John A (Dorothy M Todd) V'46.Pc.
☎ (215) 247-2143 . . 8701 Shawnee St, Philadelphia, PA 19118

Newhall MR & MRS John H (Jane C Ward) | ☎ (610) 664-6566 414 Righters Mill Rd, Penn Valley, PA 19072
BMr'62.BMr'84.BMr'87.Me.Gm.Wms'55.H'60 . . .
MR Daniel W—Wms'91—at U of Va . . . .

Newhall MR Paul K (late William Price) . . . . Married at Naples, FL
Plumb MRS Andrew (Betty L Ball) . . . . Jun 22'96

Newhall MR & MRS Paul K (Plumb—Betty L Ball)
☎ (941) 597-4251 . . 2615 Magnolia Park Lane, Apt W202, Naples, FL 34109

Newhall MRS Scott (Ruth Waldo) Cal'31.Pcu.
☎ (805) 521-1441 . . 829 Park St, PO Box 409, Piru, CA 93040

Newhall MR & MRS Thomas B (Sarah S Shelburne)
HWSth'90.Me.Wms'88 ⚓
☎ (617) 383-2934 . . 155 Sohier St, Cohasset, MA *02025*

Newhall MRS William P (Ann M Clifford)   2454—39 St NW,
SConnSt'70.Y'75 . . . .   Washington, DC
    MISS Katharine C *20007-1703*
    MR William P JR

Newington MRS John C (Barbara Steinschneider) . .   Field Point Circle,
    MISS Barbara B . . . .   Box 1098,
                                                       Greenwich, CT
                                                       06836

Newkirk MISS Martha B
    ☎ (610) LA5-1499 . . 223 Curwen Rd, Rosemont, PA *19010*

Newland MRS Nanette (Duerr—Plamondon—   ☎ (619) 673-9566
Van Antwerpen—Nanette Newland) . . . .   15635 Caldas de
    MR Dana M Duerr . . . .   Reyes, San Diego,
                                                       CA *92128*

Newlin MR & MRS John E JR (Barbara C Newhall)   ☎ (610) 375-8778
Rc. . . . .   1511 Meadowlark
    MISS E Noël—at ☎ (206) 789-6328   Rd, Wyomissing,
7045 Eleventh Av NW, Seattle, WA *98117* . . . .   PA *19610*

Newlin MR & MRS John E 3d (Johnson—Dorothy K   ☎ (302) 655-2339
Kimmel) Ariz'66.Spgfd'68.Pa'70 . . . .   1611 Tower Rd,
    MR Nicholas A . . . .   Wilmington, DE
    JUNIORS MR Christopher R *19806*
    JUNIORS MR Andrew deR . . . .
        JUNIORS MR Christopher E Johnson . . . .
        JUNIORS MR E Reed Johnson . . . .

Newlin MRS Virginia S (Kline—Virginia N Strong)   ☎ (610) 692-9106
StJColl'74.Ant'79 . . . .   299 Devon Lane,
    MR Alfred S—StJColl'81.Pa'84—at 201 W 77 St,   West Chester, PA
    Apt 15G, New York, NY *10024* *19380*

Newlin MR & MRS William V P (Louisa Lawrence   ☎ (202) 362-1038
Foulke) Rdc'60.Nf.Mt.Cc.H'55 . . . .   3026 Newark St
    MR Nicholas—H'82—at ☎ (301) 888-1281   NW, Washington,
14411 Baden-Westwood Rd, Brandywine,   DC *20008*
MD *20613* . . . .

Newman REV & MRS Andrew H (Carmichael—Mary M Allen) P'47
    ☎ (513) 653-7279 . . 724 S Main St, Urbana, OH *43078*

Newman MR & MRS Charles H JR—T.Y.'60
    ☎ (212) 262-3687 . . 161 W 61 St, Apt 35E, New York, NY *10023*

Newman MR & MRS Charles I (Anglesea A Parkhurst)
Montclair'86.Rut'92.Geo'50
    ☎ (201) 228-0633 . . 12 Inwood Rd, Essex Fells, NJ *07021*

Newman DR & MRS Clyde F JR (Sheila V   ☎ (610) MU8-6929
Dougherty) W.Ac.Pa'43.Pa'76 . . . .   601 Maplewood Rd,
    MR Peter V . . . .   Wayne, PA *19087*

Newman MR & MRS George W 3d (Mary E Kyte)   ☎ (513) 561-8118
Man'vl'63.Xav'65.Cal'72.My.Ec.Qc.Geo'61.   9825 Cunningham
Cin'64 . . . .   Rd, Cincinnati, OH
    MR George W 4th *45243*
    JUNIORS MISS Mary E K . . . .
    JUNIORS MR Charles L . . . .

Newman MR & MRS John Winslow (Anne Lansdale Sasscer)
Va'81.LakeF'73
    ☎ (610) 293-4929 . . 27 Paper Mill Rd, Newtown Square, PA *19073*

Newman MRS Leslie H (Walker—Leslie M Hailand)   ☎ (847) 295-5161
Nu'72.On. . . . .   260 E Onwentsia
    MISS Whitney H Walker—Duke'95 . . . .   Rd, Lake Forest, IL
                                                       60045

Newsom MR & MRS Noble (Boldemann—Marjorie S   ☎ (619) 759-0717
Behneman) Stan'44.Cal'38 . . . .   4023 Avenida Brisa,
    MR Roger Van S—at ☎ (954) 963-3460   Rancho Santa Fe,
3331 Farragut St, Apt 8D, Hollywood, FL *33021*   CA *92091-4297*

Newsom MR & MRS Samuel B (C Damon Herkness) Colg'81
    ☎ (540) 389-4441 . . 6625 Hidden Woods Court, Roanoke, VA *24018*

Newton MISS Barbara L (White—Barbara L Newton) Cal'84
    ☎ (714) 650-3065 . . 543 Aliso Av, Newport Beach, CA *92663*

Newton MR & MRS Charles I (Sarah L Hodges) Br'89
    ☎ (310) 822-5357 . . 2326 Clement Av, Venice, CA *90291*

Newton MR & MRS Edwin Anthony T (Meredith D Morris) Evg.Sg.BtP.H'58
    ☎ (561) 848-2697 . . 217 Debra Lane, Palm Beach, FL *33480*

Newton MR & MRS Harold R (Margaret A Turner)   of ☎ (818)792-4514
Vh. . . . .   377 W Bellevue Dv,
    MISS Priscilla A—at 305 San Vicente Blvd,   Pasadena, CA *91105*
    Apt 202, Santa Monica, CA *90402* . . . .   ☎ (714) 494-1303
                                                       "El Parador"
                                                       156 Emerald Bay,
                                                       Laguna Beach, CA
                                                       92651

Newton MRS Howard M (Hallock—Juliet Townshend) Ncd.
    621 Maple Av, Wilmette, IL *60091*

Newton MR & MRS Howard Pardue (Mary E Miller)   ☎ (210) 736-9130
Tex'74.A.H'67.Bost'73 . . . .   138 E Gramercy
    JUNIORS MISS Roxana D . . . .   Place, San Antonio,
                                                       TX *78212*

Newton MR & MRS Matthew K (Victoria L Carver) So'76
    RR 4, Box 212, Salem Rd, Pound Ridge, NY *10576*

Newton MISS Meredith M—Pa'85.Geo'89
    ☎ (213) 851-6684 . . 1633 N Gardner St, Hollywood, CA *90049*

Nice MISS Sidney P . . see R L Cover

Nicholas MR Frederick S—Rd.H'33 . . of
    ☎ (610) 696-1969 . . 496 Eaton Way, West Chester, PA *19380*
    ☎ (207) 374-2230 . . "1798" East Blue Hill, ME *04629*

Nicholas MR & MRS Frederick S JR (Jacomina M de Ru) H'57.H'58
    ☎ (860) 535-4567 . . 9 Church St, Stonington, CT *06378*

Nicholas MR Harry I (Betner—Josephine L Auchincloss) Gm.
    ☎ (610) 687-3627 . . 861 Lesley Rd, Villanova, PA *19085-1117*

Nicholas MISS Nancy . . . . Died at
                                                       Gladwyne, PA Jly 16'95

Nicholas MRS Peter H (Mattison—Gretchen Ridder) Cly.Cs . . .of
    ☎ (212) RE7-6938 . . 131 E 69 St, New York, NY *10021-5158*
    ☎ (860) 739-8457 . . "White Shutters" 5 Francis Lane, Old Black Point,
    Niantic, CT *06357*

Nicholl MRS Helen Dale (Helen D Kulik) Bvr'67 . . .   of ☎ (212)745-4282
    MISS Ashley A—at St Mark's . . . .   435 E 79 St,
    JUNIORS MR Maynard C 3d—☎ (212) 517-4017 .   New York, NY
                                                       10021
                                                       ☎ (516) 287-5281
                                                       "Sparrow's Nest"
                                                       399 Canoe Place Rd,
                                                       Southampton, NY
                                                       11968

Nicholl MRS Maynard C (White—Ann W Turner) An.Sl.Ncd.
☎ (410) 268-0724 . . ''Heron Watch'' 842 Bywater Rd, Annapolis, MD *21401*
Nicholl MR Maynard C JR—Va'53.Balt'60
☎ (301) 972-6661 . . 12409 Deoudes Rd, Boyds, MD *20841-9022*
Nicholls MISS Jamie C—Aht'88.H'92 . . see MRS J C Cormier
Nicholls MR Samuel S 3d—Yn.Ham'89
☎ (203) 624-1368 . . 255 Whitney Av, Apt 20, New Haven, CT *06511*
Nichols MR & MRS Alan H JR (Jennifer W Ehrhard) Colg'82.Stan'81
☎ (415) 381-5913 . . 128 Locust Av, Mill Valley, CA *94941*
Nichols MR & MRS Brett E (D Reed Wessells) Ken'88.RochTech'86
☎ (908) 719-7738 . . 39 Cedar Ridge Rd, Bedminster, NJ *07921*
Nichols MR & MRS C Walter 3d (Anne S Sharp) | ☎ (914) 232-4421
Bgt.Plg.Cly.Cda.Va'59 . . . . | 69 Maple Av,
MR C Walter 4th—Br'89 . . . . | Katonah, NY *10536*
Nichols MRS (DR) Charles W (Chrysler—Marguerite P Sykes)
Nu'48.Nu'63.Ri.Cly.StJ.
☎ (212) PL5-4583 . . 45 Sutton Place S, New York, NY *10022*
Nichols MR & MRS Clifford JR (Edson—Mary M Butler) Pitt'54.Edg.Hob'40
☎ (412) 741-5824 . . 505 Grove St, Sewickley, PA *15143*
Nichols MRS Elizabeth M (O'Keefe—Elizabeth M | ☎ (617) 237-0724
Nichols) Wh'lck'70.Mds.Dyc. . . . . | 33 Valley Rd,
MISS Shannon E O'Keefe—Woos'91 . . . . | Wellesley Hills, MA
MR Michael T O'Keefe 2d—at Colgate . . . . . | *02181*
MR Berkeley H O'Keefe—at Union Coll . . . . |
Nichols MR Floyd G . . . . Died at
Denver, CO May 11'96
Nichols MR Frank B . . . . Died Apr 23'96
Nichols MR & MRS George Q (Audrey F Coleman) | ☎ (215) AD3-1877
Rb.Tvb.Sg.Hn.H'52 . . . . | 730 Andorra Rd,
MR Jonathan T—Wes'88 . . . . | Lafayette Hill, PA
MR Benjamin T—Br'93 . . . . | *19444*
Nichols MR & MRS George Q JR (Audrey L Smith) LakeF'85.Ub.StLaw'86
☎ (615) 386-7333 . . 211 Craighead Av, Nashville, TN *37205*
Nichols MASTER George Quincy 3d (George Q JR) . . . . Born at
Berkeley, CA May 31'94
Nichols MR & MRS Gouverneur M (Cates—Marjorie S Handy)
Co.Ny.Lm.Cly.Dc.
☎ (203) 966-2245 . . 634 Carter St, New Canaan, CT *06840*
Nichols MASTER Grantland Taggart (George Q JR) . . . . Born at
Nashville, TN Jun 7'96
Nichols MR & MRS Grosvenor G (Sarah A Willets) Stan'77
3611 Arden Creek Rd, Sacramento, CA *95825*
Nichols MR & MRS H Gilman (Swigert—Ellen Ford)
Rdc'48.Sm.Cc.H'52 🚣
☎ (508) 768-6987 . . 90 Apple St, Essex, MA *01929*
Nichols MR & MRS H Gilman 3d (Polly C Bakewell)
Me'82.Franklin'76.Ore'79
☎ (207) 688-4931 . . 1026 Hodsdon Rd, Pownal, ME *04069*
Nichols MR & MRS J Donald (Hackett—Elizabeth G Litterer)
Tenn'75.WakeF'65 . . of
☎ (615) 298-3610 . . 416 Jackson Blvd, Nashville, TN *37205*
☎ (404) 231-0599 . . 3131 Slaton Dv NW, Apt 32, Atlanta, GA *30305*
Nichols MR & MRS J Jay (Roberta R Vilas) Cnt.Ncd.Myf.Cr'45.H'49
☎ (847) 446-3946 . . 150 Dickens Rd, Northfield, IL *60093*
Nichols COL (RET) & MRS John D (Kathleen Gayer) USAF.Bow'39
☎ (703) 356-8609 . . 6027 Orris St, McLean, VA *22101*

Nichols MRS John S (Jarvis Gilbert) Cly.Dc.
☎ (516) 692-6018 . . 572 Cold Spring Rd, Syosset, NY *11791*
Nichols MR & MRS John S JR (Alice A Marshall) | ☎ (401) 331-4084
H'69.H'74 . . . . | 94 Congdon St,
MR James T . . . . | Providence, RI
MR Christopher G . . . . | *02906*
Nichols MRS John T G (Mary Alice Thomas)
64 Matthew Dv, Brunswick, ME *04011*
Nichols MRS Katharine M (Katharine F Merriman) | ☎ (203) 263-2711
West'66 . . . . | 212 Main St N,
MISS Ashley M—at Syracuse U . . . . | Woodbury, CT
JUNIORS MR C Houk—at Forman. . . . . | *06798*
Nichols MR Michael W—BtP.Hills'94.JCar'95
☎ (561) 361-1458 . . 5645 Pacific Blvd, Apt 2803, Boca Raton, FL *33433*
Nichols MR & MRS Milton G (Margaret J Adams) | ☎ (612) 452-6990
Macalester'56.ColC'56 . . . . | 1794 Summit Lane,
MR M Griggs JR . . . . | Mendota Heights,
MR Peter A . . . . | MN *55118*
Nichols MRS (DR) N Taylor (Nancy Taylor Pinks) V'42.Cl'45
☎ (410) 435-4991 . . 17 Cross Keys Rd, Baltimore, MD *21210*
Nichols MR & MRS Osgood M (Roberts—Eleanor L Patterson)
C.Lm.Hn.H'32
☎ (203) 762-2461 . . 16 Belden Hill Lane, Wilton, CT *06897*
Nichols MR Robert John—Conn'66.Conn'69
59 Valley View Dv, Meriden, CT *06540*
Nichols MR William Ichabod—C.H'26.Ox'27
☎ (011-33-1) 42-61-14-92 . . 21 rue de Verneuil, 75007 Paris, France
Nicholsen MR Hamilton R . . see R Kelham
Nicholsen MR Ronald C . . see R Kelham
Nicholson MR & MRS Frederic A (Betty A Easton) | ☎ (602) 951-3360
Me.Ac.Pn.P'52.Pa'72 . . . . | 8216 N 54 St,
MISS Ann E—at Mt Vernon Coll . . . . | Paradise Valley, AZ
MR Edward A—at Claremont Grad . . . . | *85253*
Nicholson MRS G J Guthrie JR (Baumgartner—Klara Weibel)
☎ (307) 864-5312 . . PO Box 828, Thermopolis, WY *82443*
Nicholson MRS Jesse T (Edith Rose) | ☎ (610) MI2-3595
BMr'37.Me.Cs. . . . . | 516 Oakley Rd,
MISS Virginia—Col'74—at 67 Walker St, | Haverford, PA
Cambridge, MA *02138* . . . . | *19041*
Nicholson MR & MRS John B (Marnie A Miller) | ☎ (202) 338-7434
Ct.P'59 . . . . | 1429—44 St NW,
MISS Wendy A . . . . | Washington, DC
MR Peter B . . . . | *20007*
Nicholson DR & MRS John W (Elizabeth S Nash)
V'40.Csp.Dc.P'37.Pa'41.Minn'51
☎ (609) 953-2712 . . Medford Leas, 643 Rushmore, Medford, NJ *08055*
Nicholson BRIG GEN (RET) & MRS John W (Brawner | 608 Pollard Park,
—Sophie S Marshall) Cvc.Sl.USA'56 . . . . | Williamsburg, VA
MISS Mary L . . . . | *23185*
Nicholson DR & MRS Nigel J (Virginia F King) Y'86.Ox'90.Pa'94
☎ (503) 775-8744 . . 3703 SE Woodstock Blvd, Portland, OR *97202*
Nicholson MR & MRS Oliver P (Caroline A Smitter)
Wash'81.GeoW'84.BMr'85.Ox'72.Ox'76.Ox'82
☎ (612) 922-7849 . . 5312 York Av S, Minneapolis, MN *55410*

Nickel MR & MRS George W JR (Selfridge—Adele D Rock)
Cal'40.Pcu.Tcy.Cal'38
☎ (805) 872-5225 . . PO Box 60679, Bakersfield, CA *93386-0679*

Nickel MR & MRS James L (Kathleen M McGrath) | ☎ (805) 872-5050
O'68.Ariz'66 . . . . | PO Box 60679,
MISS Erin D . . . . | Bakersfield, CA
MISS Heidi K . . . . | *93386-0679*
MR James C . . . . |

Nickerson MR & MRS Adams H (Bateson—Virginia | of ☎ (212)288-5943
Moffat) V'47.Rc.Un.Pr.Cs.Cly.Ncd.H.'46 . . . . . | 136 E 79 St,
MR William M Bateson—W&M'87—at | New York, NY
☎ (212) 348-6369 . . 360 E 88 St, New York, | *10021*
NY *10128* . . . . | ☎ (516) 692-7652
| 10 Dock Hollow Rd,
| Cold Spring Harbor,
| NY *11724*

Nickerson MRS Albert L (Elizabeth Perkins) Cy.Hn. | ☎ (617) 259-9664
MR Albert W—at 115 Mt Auburn St, Cambridge, | 3 Lexington Rd,
MA *02138* . . . . | Box 346,
| Lincoln Center, MA
| *01773*

Nickerson MR E Carleton—Myf.H'32.H'34
☎ (508) 428-8328 . . 21A Village Square N, 39 Tower Hill Rd,
PO Box 717, Osterville, MA *02655*

Nickerson MR & MRS Eugene H (Marie-Louise Steiner) Pr.H'41.Cl'43
☎ (516) MA1-8098 . . 495 Bryant Av, Roslyn Harbor, NY *11576*

Nickerson MR Joshua B—Geo'92 . . see W M Riegel

Nickerson MR & MRS Martinus H (Sheila Bunker) | ☎ (907) 586-6553
BMr'64.U'85.Rv.Ofp.Ty'64.Col'66 . . . . | 540 W 10 St,
MR Thomas M . . . . | Juneau, AK *99801*
JUNIORS MR Samuel B—at Reed . . . . |

Nickerson MRS Pauline M (Dearborn—Pauline H Moore)
☎ (508) 468-1420 . . Dearborn Farm, 91 Cedar St, Wenham, MA *01984*

Nickerson MR & MRS William H (Jane M | ☎ (203) 661-0597
McPherson) H'61.Cl'64 . . . . | 35 Quail Rd,
MISS Sarah S—H'90—at New Orleans, LA . . . . | Greenwich, CT
MR W Storm—H'88—at ☎ (212) 876-5622 | *06831*
120 E 89 St, Apt 2A, New York, NY *10128* . . . |

Nicodemus DR & MRS Christopher F (Elizabeth Pingchang Chow)
Ws'79.H'79.SUNY'84
☎ (603) 823-5342 . . 13 Sunset Lane, PO Box 429, Franconia,
NH *03580*

Nicodemus MR & MRS Richard T (Elisabeth Marchet) Camb'48
☎ (516) 265-1070 . . ''Ships' Hole'' PO Box 428, Smithtown,
NY *11787*

Nicol MR & MRS Arthur C A (Margaret R Finch)
Rc.Eyc.Bab'71.Suff'74 . . of
☎ (212) 744-8260 . . 133 E 80 St, New York, NY *10021*
☎ (508) 627-8313 . . ''Katama'' Edgartown, MA *02539*

Nicolaus MR Edward A . . . . Died at
Greenbrae, CA Jan 21'96

Nicolaus MRS Edward A (Dorothea Holden)
☎ (415) 461-5519 . . 501 Via Casitas, Greenbrae, CA *94904*

Nicolaus MR Edward A 3d—Pac'62.Mich'69
☎ (415) 922-5115 . . 2557 Filbert St, San Francisco, CA *94123*

Nicolaus-Zacher MRS Nancy (Zacher—Nancy H | ☎ (510) 547-5384
Nicolaus) Cal'63 . . . . | 104 Requa Rd,
MISS Katherine A Zacher—Geo'91.Cal'96—at | Piedmont, CA *94611*
2557 Filbert St, San Francisco, CA *94123* . . . |
MR Peter A Zacher—Col'90—at |
2567 Filbert St, San Francisco, CA *94123* . . . |
JUNIORS MR Edward G Zacher . . . . |

Nicoll MR & MRS De Lancey 3d (A Virginia Vose) | ☎ (603) 279-4300
Adelphi'70.Pn.P'47 . . . . | RFD 2, Box 16,
MISS Jessica F—Sth'83.Del'85—at | Terrace Av,
☎ (413) 585-0213 . . 163 Prospect St, | Meredith, NH *03253*
Northampton, MA *01060* . . . . |

Nicoll MRS E D Vere (Molly McIntosh)
☎ (804) 293-3534 . . 3150 Ridge Rd, Charlottesville, VA *22901*

Nicoll MISS Eileen—Pitzer'83
☎ (202) 546-1423 . . 313 C St SE, Washington, DC *20003*

Nicoll MISS Margaret—Nu'83
☎ (310) 394-8212 . . 858—14 St, Apt 5, Santa Monica, CA *90403*

Nicoud MISS Barbara McN . . see MRS R E Reynolds
Nicoud MR George B . . see MRS R E Reynolds
Nicoud MR Louis JR . . see MRS R E Reynolds
Nicoud MISS Sarah L . . see MRS R E Reynolds

Niedermayer MR & MRS Theodore E (Virginie T Soubiran)
Paris'83.Pa'86.Y.HWSth'84.Dth'88
☎ (212) 831-1581 . . 139 E 94 St, New York, NY *10128*

Niedringhaus MR & MRS George W 3d (Cynthia L | ☎ (314) 966-8979
Wichite) Wash'62 . . . . | 32 Deacon Dv,
MR John H . . . . | Huntleigh, MO
| *63131*

Niedringhaus MR George W 4th—Van'86
☎ (212) 717-5363 . . 555 E 78 St, Apt 8E, New York, NY *10021*

Niedringhaus MRS W Delafield (Effie V Zeibig) . . . | ☎ (314) 569-2466
MISS Adaline H—at ☎ (314) 991-0768 | 10379 Tuxford Dv,
979 Rue De La Banque, Apt 1, St Louis, MO | Apt 2, St Louis, MO
63141 . . . . | *63146*

Niedringhaus MR & MRS W Delafield JR (Linda | ☎ (314) 997-6751
Van Eck) BostColl'72.BostColl'73.Cy.W&L'66 | 4 Wyndtop Lane,
MISS Alicia A . . . . | St Louis, MO *63141*
MR Charles H—W&L'90—at 8121 Whitburn Dv, |
St Louis, MO *63105* . . . . |

Niedringhaus MR & MRS William F (Helen P Cizek)
☎ (206) LA2-0327 . . 6007 NE Windermere Rd, Seattle, WA *98105*

Niehoff MR K Richard B JR . . see MRS L S Walker
Niehoff MISS Kelly B . . see MRS L S Walker

Nield MRS Walter K (Williams—Lord—Helen | ☎ (203) 245-1911
Curran) . . . . | Box 1026,
MR Ogden—at 205 E 77 St, New York, NY | 153 Five Field Rd,
10021 . . . . | Madison, CT *06443*

Nields MRS Benjamin 3d (Brown—Sheila A Moore)
☎ (914) 967-2684 . . Highland Ridge Lane, Rye, NY *10580*

Nields MR Benjamin 4th—Y'76
☎ (202) 337-2135 . . 2922 N St NW, Washington, DC *20007*

Nields MR & MRS Henry C (S Olivia Marshall) Y'45 | 1184 Monument St,
MISS Nancy C . . . . | Concord, MA *01742*
MR Henry M . . . . |

Nielsen MR & MRS Arthur C JR (Patricia McKnew)
BMr'43.Ih.Rc.Cho.Cas.Fy.Wis'41
☎ (847) 446-4636 . . 1122 Pelham Rd, Winnetka, IL *60093*
Nielsen MR & MRS J Christopher (Laurie G Cherbonnier) Camb'75.H'71
☎ (504) 891-1879 . . 2901 Chestnut St, New Orleans, LA *70115*
Nielsen MR & MRS Robert J JR (Michelle I Olds)
☎ (510) 828-3642 . . 6407 Tassajara Rd, Pleasanton, CA *94566*

Nielson, James E & Young, Anne N (Model—Anne | ☎ (307) 587-5821
N Young) Pa'63.Cly.Wyo'54 . . . . | Sage Creek Ranch,
  MISS Faith Model—at Cornell . . . . | PO Box 1507, Cody,
  MR Robert Model JR—at U of Wyo . . . . | WY *82414*

Nigh MR William H 3d
2151 Angel Camp Court, Cool, CA *95614*

Nigra DR & MRS Thomas P (Jane H Brawley) | of ☎ (410)822-8885
Sth'67.Cl'69.Au.Cvc.Mt.Cly.Pa'67 . . . . | 27151 Bailey's Neck
  MISS Jane H—at Rhodes Coll . . . . | Rd, Easton, MD
  MR Peter T—Ty'95 . . . . | *21601*
  | ☎ (202) 965-5656
  | 1515—31 St NW,
  | Washington, DC
  | *20007*

Nigro MR & MRS Robert A (Nancy P Rath) | ☎ (203) 622-0434
Myf.Ht.Cly.Ncd.Va'71 . . . . | 15 Midwood Rd,
  JUNIORS MISS Lillian P . . . . | Deer Park,
  JUNIORS MR John W . . . . | Greenwich, CT
  | *06830*

Niles MR Andrew E (late John D) . . . . Married at Worcester, MA
  Tsandikos MISS Stephanie (Solon) . . . . Apr 27'96
Niles MRS Barbara E (Barbara H Elliott) Cs . . .of
☎ (212) 628-4563 . . 170 E 79 St, New York, NY *10021*
☎ (860) 435-9994 . . ''Sow's Ear'' Selleck Hill Rd, Salisbury, CT *06068*
Niles MISS Catherine E—Ws'85
see Dilatory Domiciles
Niles MR & MRS John A (Carolyn M Wende) Y'58
☎ (603) 643-5139 . . PO Box 235, Three Mile Rd, Etna, NH *03750*
Niles MR & MRS John Cutler (Cara M Bertrand) StLaw'87.Ey.StLaw'85
☎ (617) 639-0561 . . 19 Waldron Court, Marblehead, MA *01945*
Niles MR Jonathan B—Nu'79
☎ (617) 566-7634 . . 669 Washington St, Apt 2, Brookline, MA *02146*
Niles MRS Nicholas (Marian L Freeman)
☎ (908) 604-9280 . . 4115 Fellowship Rd, Basking Ridge, NJ *07920*
Niles MR & MRS Nicholas (Varick Katzenbach)
Sth'61.Nrr.Cw.Cc.Myf.P'56
☎ (203) 259-2396 . . 533 Merwin's Lane, Fairfield, CT *06430*
Niles MR & MRS Nicholas 3d (Lois C Duke) Sim'90.Colby'87
☎ (203) 256-9178 . . 533 Merwin's Lane, Fairfield, CT *06430*
Niles MR & MRS Robert L (Virginia A Moore) Cy.Ub.Cw.
☎ (617) 259-8384 . . 23 Blueberry Lane, Box 6153, Lincoln Center,
MA *01773-6153*
Niles MR Samuel V—Cw.Ham'88
☎ (617) 969-4826 . . 174 Cabot St, Newton, MA *02158*
Niles MISS Wende L—NCar'92
☎ (617) 566-0949 . . 457 Washington St, Apt 3, Brookline, MA *02146*

Niles MR & MRS William F (Ann Boughton Thorne) | ☎ (212) 876-8868
Ws'66.Cly.Ty'63 . . . . | 49 E 96 St,
  MR David T—Wes'94 . . . . | New York, NY
  JUNIORS MR Peter C—at Groton . . . . | *10128-0782*

Nimick MRS A Corkran (Anne S Corkran) BMr'50.Me.Ac.Ncd.
☎ (610) 527-2048 . . 542 Maison Place, Bryn Mawr, PA *19010*
Nimick MR & MRS C Lockhart Howe (Lisa A J De Cardona)
StJos'86.Rr.Pn.P'83.Wash'89
☎ (703) 533-2921 . . 2101 Reynolds St, Falls Church, VA *22043*
Nimick MISS Eleanor Howe—Sth'42
115 Beacon Hill Dv, Coraopolis, PA *15108*
Nimick MR & MRS Francis B JR (Leighton—Katharine C Knight)
Ncd.P'39.H'41
☎ (412) 741-5584 . . Darlington Lane, Sewickley, PA *15143*
Nimick MR & MRS Reade B JR (Laura L Weisbrodt)
☎ (716) 624-3245 . . 85 W Main St, Honeoye Falls, NY *14472*

Nimick MR & MRS Thomas M H JR (Whiteside— | of ☎ (412)238-4240
Hunt—Theresa M Listowska) Cl'62.Pg.Rr.P'45. | Forbesway,
H'50 . . . . | PO Box 377,
  MR George A Whiteside 3d—H'87—at | Ligonier, PA
  ☎ (617) 625-7053 . . PO Box 1653, | *15658-0377*
  Cambridge, MA *02238* . . . . | ☎ (412) 621-9861
  | 1424 Bennington
  | Av, Pittsburgh, PA
  | *15217-1139*

Nimick MASTER Thomas Marshall Howe 3d (C Lockhart Howe) . . . . . Born
at Falls Church, VA Apr 5'95
Nitze MISS Heidi—Ws'56.Cs.H.
☎ (212) 787-3901 . . 1 W 72 St, New York, NY *10023*
Nitze MR & MRS Paul H (Porter—Elisabeth Scott) Mt.B.C.H'28
☎ (202) 588-0800 . . 2416 Tracy Place NW, Washington, DC *20008*

Nitze MR & MRS William A (Ann K Richards) | of ☎ (202)337-4263
Ln.Mt.Cvc.H'64.H'69 . . . . | 1336—30 St NW,
  JUNIORS MR Paul K . . . . | Washington, DC
  | *20007*
  | ☎ (970) 920-1179
  | 420 W North St,
  | Aspen, CO *81611*
  | ☎ (212) 717-5260
  | 157 E 74 St,
  | New York, NY
  | *10021*

Niven MRS James G (Fernanda Wanamaker | ☎ (212) 744-5339
Wetherill) BtP. . . . . | 160 E 72 St,
  MISS Fernanda W . . . . | New York, NY
  MISS Eugenie R . . . . | *10021*

Niven MR James G—K.Ng.Sg.BtP.Plg.StJ.H'67
4 E 66 St, New York, NY *10021*

Niven MRS William S D (Jeanne L C Skinner) | ☎ (516) 922-4168
Pr.Cly. . . . . | 8 Sagamore Hill Rd,
  MISS Susan McK—at 301 E 75 St, New York, | Cove Neck,
  NY *10021* . . . . | Oyster Bay, NY
  MR William S D JR—at Rte 3, Box 315, Orange, | *11771*
  VA *22960* . . . . |
  MR John B—at 169 E 78 St, New York, NY |
  10021 . . . . |

Nixon MISS Allison Elizabeth (Jeffrey S) . . . . Born Nov 24'95
Nixon MISS Amy Catherine (Jeffrey S) . . . . Born May 31'94
Nixon MISS Diane A—Sth'57.Cly.
☎ (212) 289-2063 . . 21 E 87 St, New York, NY *10128*

Nixon MRS E Ward (Emily A Ward) Ill'57.Sc.
☎ (618) 242-1784 . . 1816 Richview Rd, Mt Vernon, IL *62864*
Nixon MR & MRS F Ward (Sarah L Sedgwick) OWes'87.Tul'82.Ch'88
☎ (847) 570-0553 . . 2408 Ridgeway St, Evanston, IL *60201*
Nixon MR & MRS G Stuart (Clara F Taft) . . . . | ☎ (415) 344-1830
  MISS Florence T—at ☎ (415) 594-9552 | 925 Culebra Rd,
  600 Park Av, San Carlos, CA *94070* . . . . | Hillsborough, CA
  MISS Clarissa H—at ☎ (415) 347-4147 | *94010*
  1120 El Camino Real, Burlingame, CA *94010* . . |
  MR John S . . . . |
Nixon MR & MRS Jeffrey S (Holly B Walker) Les'89.NewHaven'89
☎ (908) 219-6646 . . 4 Forrest Av, Rumson, NJ *07760*
Nixon MR & MRS Justin W (Anne Fletcher) | ☎ (203) 637-9105
  Rdc'47.Sim'50.Wyo'55.McG'59 . . . . | 6 North St,
  MR Robert E—H'line'82.Tufts'88 . . . . | Old Greenwich, CT
  | *06870*
Nixon MR & MRS Robert G (Toni A Alexander) | ☎ (847) 441-5497
  Ariz'69 . . . . | 480 Provident,
  MISS Sarah E . . . . | Winnetka, IL *60093*
  MR Geoffrey A . . . . |
Nobel MR & MRS Robert D (Cowen—Cecilia Van Strum)
  Cal'60.Cry.Pa'62 ⚓
☎ (410) 822-5598 . . ''Greybarn'' 7718 Bloomfield Rd, Easton,
MD *21601*
Noble MRS Carol Tyler (Carol E Tyler) | ☎ (508) 526-7962
  Bradford'63.Sim'88.Ec.Btn. . . . . | 5 University Lane,
  MISS Lisa L . . . . | Manchester, MA
  MR George W JR—at Rollins . . . . | *01944*
  JUNIORS MR Alexander T—at Berkshire . . . . . . |
Noble MR & MRS Cary L (Mary E Haile)
☎ (601) 445-4114 . . 412 S Commerce St, Natchez, MS *39120*
Noble MR & MRS Charles H JR (Sara McNeel) | ☎ (210) 822-0432
  A.Rice'51 . . . . | 401 Wildwood Dv
  MISS Laura L—Swb'82 . . . . | E, San Antonio, TX
  MR Samuel M—at Wash'n & Lee . . . . | *78212*
Noble MRS Charles L J (Susan Means) . . . . | ☎ (603) 585-6687
  MISS Susan Weare—at 25 Elizabeth Rd, Sandown, | Box 371, W Lake
  NH *03873* . . . . | Rd, Fitzwilliam, NH
  | *03447*
Noble MR Christopher—Ec.Pars'64
  abroad
Noble MR & MRS Christopher V (Merrill E Williams) LakeF'78.LakeF'77
☎ (508) 264-4945 . . 1147 Liberty Square Rd, Boxboro, MA *01719*
Noble DR Cyrus B (John) . . . . Married at New York, NY
  Biggs MISS (DR) Robin B (Jeremy H) . . . . Apr 27'96
Noble DR & MRS (DR) Cyrus B (Robin B Biggs) Y'91.Cl'95.H'90.Cl'95
☎ (203) 629-7008 . . ''The Cottage'' 390 Riversville Rd, Greenwich,
CT *06831*
Noble MR & MRS Daniel S (Elizabeth A Ream) LakeF'90.LakeF'89
☎ (847) 251-4352 . . 2334 Greenwood Av, Wilmette, IL *60091*
Noble MR Duncan . . . . Died at
  Sugar Land, TX Dec 11'95
Noble MRS Duncan (Anne M Griswold)
☎ (713) 242-4447 . . 16 Charleston St N, Sugar Land, TX *77478*
Noble MR George W—Ec.Bost'64
☎ (508) 526-7040 . . 21 Pine St, Apt 3, Manchester, MA *01944*

Noble MISS Helen Rike (Daniel S) . . . . Born at
  Wilmette, IL Jan 3'96
Noble MR & MRS Henry S (Elizabeth L Brewer) Ny.Y'38
☎ (203) 966-1425 . . 190 Huckleberry Hill Rd, New Canaan, CT *06840*
Noble MRS John Van Arsdale (McKee—Suzanne Eddy) Ec.
☎ (508) 526-7394 . . 59 Forest St, Manchester, MA *01944*
Noble MR & MRS John W JR (Pembroke T France) Elk.Yh.P'51 . . of
☎ (410) 822-2025 . . 6184 Shipyard Lane, Easton, MD *21601*
☎ (803) 744-7118 . . Yeamans Hall Club, PO Box 9455, Charleston,
SC *29410*
Noble MRS Joyce G (Wickware—Joyce E Gafke) | ☎ (212) AT9-5019
  MISS Margaret H—Sth'81 . . . . | 1240 Park Av,
  | New York, NY
  | *10128*
Noble MRS Lawrence M (Louise S McLanahan)
☎ (860) 535-1781 . . 21 Main St, Stonington, CT *06378*
Noble MR Lawrence M JR—Yn.Y'53.H'64
☎ (203) 248-2971 . . 35 Fennbrook Dv, Hamden, CT *06517-1607*
Noble MR Lawrence R—Denis'84
  6334 Broad St, Bethesda, MD *20816*
Noble MR & MRS Marshall H (Hollingsworth—Harris—Carolie F Woods)
  Scripps'47.Cvc.Ri.Pn.P'44
☎ (860) 599-3828 . . 219 Osbrook Point, Pawcatuck, CT *06379*
Noble MR & MRS Richard E (Clayton—Janice A | ☎ (508) 485-8910
  Pryor) San.Ty'80.Ty'82 . . . . | Fay School,
  MISS Martha A Clayton—at Boston, MA . . . . | Box 9106,
  | 48 Main St,
  | Southborough, MA
  | *01772-9106*
Noble MR Robert W . . see MRS A Hutchinson
Noble MR Timothy E—Wes'62
☎ (212) 249-7095 . . 354 E 66 St, New York, NY *10021*
Noble DR & MRS W Morris H (Winifred Brady) | of ☎ (415)922-3630
  Pcu.Tcy.Cp.H'54 . . . . | 3095 Pacific Av,
  MR Morris H . . . . | San Francisco, CA
  MR William L . . . . | *94115*
  | ☎ (707) 935-3616
  | Sonoma, CA *95476*
Noël MRS Auguste L (Theodora M Winslow)
☎ (212) 535-5281 . . 142 E 71 St, New York, NY *10021*
Noel MR & MRS Edwin L (Nancy C Simpson) | ☎ (314) 991-4471
  Cy.Nd.Br'68.StL'74 . . . . | 301 S McKnight Rd,
  MISS Caroline C . . . . | St Louis, MO *63124*
  JUNIORS MR Edwin C . . . . |
Noel MR & MRS Lee F (Lois E Jordan) | ☎ (615) 383-0878
  Van'70.Van'69 . . . . | 305 Lynwood Blvd,
  MISS Andrea C . . . . | Nashville, TN *37205*
  JUNIORS MR Lois E . . . . |
Noell MR & MRS Charles P JR (Virginia J Evans) Mar'vil'53.Dar.Ncd.StL'52
☎ (314) 725-6997 . . 7701 Shirley Dv, St Louis, MO *63105*
Noell MR Charles Preston 3d
☎ (703) 892-1810 . . 4107 N 27 Rd, Arlington, VA *22207*
Nolan MR & MRS Gaillard R (Meryl E Richardson) MaryB'60.Cvc.Mit'58
☎ (305) 235-4448 . . 8200 SW 115 St, Miami, FL *33156*
Nolan MR Merlyn R (Gaillard R) . . . . Married at Denver, CO
  Falk MISS Heather J (Donald P) . . . . Jly 20'96

Nolen MR & MRS Christian (Anson E Wright) H'81.H'84.Y'82.Cl'89
☎ (617) 864-8640 . . 19 Bellevue Av, Cambridge, MA *02140*
Nolen MR & MRS Malcolm Chace (Mary Ellen Donovan) Dth'76.Y'83.Cl'90
☎ (212) 645-3073 . . 327 W 19 St, New York, NY *10011*
Nolen MR & MRS Wilson (Eliot Chace) Sth'54.Ln.Ri.C.Cly.Y'48.H'51
☎ (212) 831-4330 . . 1120 Fifth Av, New York, NY *10128*
Nolte MRS Ann L (Ann Lipscomb) Pr.Cly.
☎ (516) 671-1943 . . 23 Matinecock Farms Rd, Glen Cove,
NY *11542-3343*
Nolting MRS Frederick E JR (Olivia Lindsay Crumpler)
231 Wellington Dv, Charlottesville, VA *22903*
Nomer MRS Howell F (Genevieve L Trevor) | ☎ (210) 895-2765
Bnd'48.GlasSt'74 . . . . | 424 East Lane,
MR Lawrence H—P'78—at ☎ (919) 554-4256 | Kerrville, TX *78028*
62 Brick St, Wake Forest, NC *27587* . . . .
MR Timothy P—at ☎ (818) 403-1876
406 Monterey, Apt N, South Pasadena, CA *91030*
Noojin MR & MRS Ray O JR (Janice D Skinner) | ☎ (205) 879-8079
Ala'66.Cy.Ala'67.Ala'70 . . . . | 38 Stonehurst Green,
MISS Catherine E—at 2517 Mountain Brook | Birmingham, AL
Circle, Birmingham, AL *35223* . . . . | *35213*
MISS Allison D—at 2564 Beverly Dv,
Birmingham, AL *35223* . . . .
MR Ray O 3d . . . .
Noonan MR Stephen M—Rv.Sar.StL'85.CUNY'94
☎ (212) 496-0159 . . 666 West End Av, New York, NY *10025*
Noonan CAPT Timothy R—USMC.USN'88
☎ (215) 236-9834 . . 2122 Mt Vernon St, Philadelphia, PA *19130*
Noone MR & MRS Robert J (Vehlow—Harriet V Hillyer) Cal'63.Cal'47
☎ (904) 247-8853 . . 118 Fleet Landing Blvd, Atlantic Beach, FL *32233*
Noone MRS Robert Scott (Johnson—Hallock—Ruth H Gordon) Myf.Ncd.
☎ (513) 771-7595 . . 890 Forest Av, Glendale, OH *45246*
Norberg MR Charles R—Mt.Rcp.Hn.Cr'34.Pa'37.H'39
☎ (202) 333-4324 . . 3104 N St NW, Washington, DC *20007-3413*
Nord MR & MRS Philip M (Elizabeth A Strawbridge) Me.Ncd.OreSt'71
☎ (610) 525-4230 . . 267 S Roberts Rd, Bryn Mawr, PA *19010*
Nordeman MR & MRS Jacques C (Anne W Stillman) | ☎ (212) 289-5587
Un.Ng.So.Cly.Dc.Myf.Ncd.Colg'58.H'64 . . . . . . | 21 E 87 St,
MR Landon S—at U of Va . . . . | New York, NY
MR John H—at Wesleyan . . . . | *10128*
JUNIORS MISS Eliza P—at Kent Sch . . . .
Norden MR & MRS Carl F (Archer—Vivian Nichol) | ☎ (202) 966-1714
Cvc.Cos.Sl.Dth'29 . . . . | 2724 Chain Bridge
MISS Susan W—at 2940 Eagle Way, Boulder, CO | Rd NW,
80302 . . . . | Washington, DC
MISS Bettina—at 91565 Donna Rd, Springfield, | *20016-3404*
OR *97478* . . . .
MISS Elaina—at 2219 California St NW, Apt 22,
Washington, DC *20008* . . . .
MISS Caroline—at ☎ (207) 846-1580
27 Cumberland St, Yarmouth, ME *04096* . . . . . .
Nordmann MR & MRS Gary A (Brune—Caroline S | ☎ (516) 673-4787
Crary) Mich'63.Cl'65.Purd'64.H'70 . . . . | 15 Lloyd Harbor Rd,
MISS Constance T Brune . . . . | Huntington, NY
MR William H N Brune 2d—StLaw'91—at | *11743*
765 Ottawa St, Harbor Springs, MI *49740* . . .
MR Timothy H C Brune . . . .

Nordstrom MR & MRS John N (Sally E Boid) UWash'60.UWash'58
☎ (206) 454-6118 . . 4227 Hunts Point Rd, Bellevue, WA *98004*
Nordt MR & MRS Paul W 3d (Sydney P Henshaw) | ☎ (540) 387-0629
Cal'64.Leh'63 . . . . | 1569 Dunrovin
MISS Alison A . . . . | Lane, Salem, VA
MISS Elizabeth MacG . . . . | *24153*
Norfleet MR & MRS Charles C (Elizabeth H Stachnik) Pars'81
☎ (203) 629-3819 . . 6 Glen Rd, Greenwich, CT *06830*
Norfleet MR & MRS Christopher McC (Joan A Nelson) UMiami'82
☎ (203) 762-8276 . . 29 Dorado Court, Wilton, CT *06897*
Norfleet MR & MRS John Van R SR (Sarah F Edwards)
Wheat'83.Sar.Cw.Rv.Myf . . . .
☎ (617) 585-9062 . . ''Evergreen'' 14 Summer St, Kingston, MA *02364*
☎ (508) 487-2253 . . Cottage at Captain Lysander Inn, 96 Commercial
St, Provincetown, MA *02657*
Norfleet MR Philip S—Myf.Sar.Colby'70
☎ (619) 793-5401 . . 12960-132 Carmel Creek Rd, San Diego, CA *92130*
Norfleet MISS Valerie W (late Norwood) . . . . . . Married at Greenwich, CT
McMorrow MR Patrick J (Edward J) . . . . Jun 22'96
Norling MR & MRS Barry Allen (Abigail B Chandler) | ☎ (207) 474-2738
Bost'67.Bost'67 . . . . | RFD 1, Box 5190,
MISS Alesia Fay—RISD'94—at | Beech Hill Rd,
☎ (401) 351-4895 . . 27 Sycamore St, | Norridgewock, ME
Providence, RI *02909* . . . . | *04957*
JUNIORS MISS Rebecca M . . . .
Norling MR & MRS John C (Katherine C Barr) Ne'95
☎ (617) 738-3341 . . 2 Washburn Place, Brookline, MA *02146*
Norman MR Frederick C—Ihy.Ny.Yn.Y'32
☎ (954) 782-8219 . . 2800 NE 30 Av, Apt 12D, Lighthouse Point,
FL *33064-8251*
Norman MR & MRS James T (Bierman—Caroline T Hooff) Sl.David'63
☎ (703) 683-2355 . . 104 Cameron Mews, Alexandria, VA *22314*
Norman MISS Jessye
PO Box S, Crugers, NY *10521*
Norman DR & MRS Ruskin C (Karen A Roitsch) Tex'85.A.Nw'45.TexL'63
☎ (210) 492-1295 . . 11331 Whisper Falls, San Antonio, TX *78230*
Norment MISS Elizabeth L . . see W C McCabe
Norment MISS Katherine B . . see W C McCabe
Norris MR A Mercer Biddle—
☎ (610) 687-5746 . . 680 Glenmary Rd, Radnor, PA *19087*
Norris MRS Albert F (Eleanor A Miller) V'34.Myf.
☎ (617) 659-7771 . . 53 River St, Box 128, Norwell, MA *02061*
Norris MR & MRS Alfred D JR (Marguerite A | ☎ (610) 647-1941
Scadding) NatCollEd'59.WChesU'79 . . . . | 6 Reynard Rd,
MISS Karen L—at 1138 Old Forge Rd, | Malvern, PA *19355*
New Castle, DE *19720* . . . .
Norris MR Charles C 2d (late John) . . . . Married at Andalusia, PA
Dougherty MISS Mary C . . . . Jun 16'96
Norris MR Charles H—Ph.Pkg.Evg.Rr.K.Cy.Pa'63 . . of
☎ (617) 236-7606 . . 214 Commonwealth Av, Boston, MA *02116*
☎ (970) 476-2801 . . Forest Rd, Vail, CO *81657*
Norris DR Frank—Stan'32 . . . . | 758 Bounty Dv, Apt
MR Charles G 2d—at ☎ (415) 355-1238 | 5808, Foster City,
415 Inverness St, Pacifica, CA *94044* . . . . | CA *94404*
Norris MISS Katharine H—LakeF'74
☎ (215) 732-5123 . . 1420 Locust St, Apt 27M&O, Philadelphia,
PA *19102*

Norris MR & MRS Kingsley C 2d (Katherine A Lobdell) Skd'71.Aht'70 . . . . | St Mark's School, 25 Marlborough Rd,
MISS Carolyn L—at Dickinson . . . . | Southborough, MA
MR Kingsley F—at Hobart | 01772

Norris MISS Margaret D . . see W R Wister JR

Norris MR & MRS Paul S (June E Taylor) Pa'59.Rut'55
☎ (215) TU4-1670 . . 1853 Harte Rd, Jenkintown, PA 19046

Norris MRS Robert F (Mary M Scattergood) CtCol'29.Me.
☎ (610) 356-9295 . . Dunwoody Village CH109, 3500 West Chester Pike, Newtown Square, PA 19073

Norris MRS Sandra L (Mullaney—Sandra L Norris) Cly.
☎ (610) 254-9377 . . 435 Beaumont Rd, Devon, PA 19333

Norris MR & MRS William K (Patricia S Gates) BtP.Y'52.Pa'54
☎ (561) 655-0688 . . 220 Jungle Rd, Palm Beach, FL 33480

Norris MR William Pepper JR . . . . Died Feb 10'96

North MR & MRS Peter W (Dorothy K West) Bvr'73.Ub.Nrr.Cc.Cw.Myf.Conn'66.Bost'78
☎ (203) 266-0550 . . 148 Tuttle Rd, Woodbury, CT 06798

North MRS William S (Donald—Margaret B Reid) Cas.On.Ncd.
☎ (847) 234-1451 . . 485 N Oakwood, Lake Forest, IL 60045

Northrop MISS Abby W—Cl'75
☎ (202) 363-3879 . . 3707 Woodley Rd NW, Washington, DC 20016

Northrop MR Edward H . . . . Died Jly 16'96

Northrop MRS Edward H (Christine E B Mueller) . | PO Box 808,
MISS Marjorie C . . . . | Fraser, CO 80442
MR Wilhelm E |

Northrop MR & MRS Johnston F (Gray—Lucile R Ralston) Ihy.Nyc.Chr.Ne.Cly.Yn.Y'43
☎ (203) 869-9243 . . 665 Steamboat Rd, Greenwich, CT 06830

Northrop MR & MRS Johnston W (Jill L Weissinger) SCal'80.Yn.Y'76.Cl'83
☎ (203) 329-8461 . . "Sagamore Hill" 1839 Newfield Av, North Stamford, CT 06903

Norton MRS Garrison (Emily E McMullan) C.Csn.Sl.Hn.
☎ (202) 667-2101 . . 2101 Connecticut Av NW, Washington, DC 20008

Norton CAPT & MRS Gerald S (Mary K Hewitt) CtCol'44.GeoW'69.GeoM'74.USN'39.GeoW'60
☎ (410) 268-2322 . . 398 Ridgely Av, Annapolis, MD 21401

Norton DR & MRS Lawrence A (Mary C Hammond) Ws'54.D.Cda.Y'52.NYMed'56
☎ (617) 326-7385 . . 942 High St, Dedham, MA 02026

Norton MR & MRS Lawrence A JR (Melissa S Warner) Conn'76.Dth'80
☎ (203) 254-8118 . . 24 Lee Dv, Fairfield, CT 06430

Norton MR & MRS Marshall L (Alison G Byers) Pr.LakeF'70 . . . . | ☎ (804) 784-5523 "Kinloch"
MR Marshall L JR . . . . | 282 Vinita Rd,
JUNIORS MR Adam B . . . . | Richmond, VA 23233

Norton MRS Nathaniel R (Trina C Marshall) Cly.
☎ (804) 288-6242 . . 300 Ridge Rd, Apt 66, Richmond, VA 23229

Norvell MISS Emme O—Belm'84
☎ (615) 665-0298 . . 2804 Tyne Blvd, Nashville, TN 37215

Norvell MISS Margaret P (Ward—Margaret P Norvell) Ala'66.Cda.
☎ (615) 297-8855 . . 25 Washington Park, Nashville, TN 37205

Norweb MRS R Henry JR (Elizabeth Gardner) Kt.Un.It.Cly.
☎ (216) 951-8044 . . 9595 Kirtland-Chardon Rd, Kirtland, OH 44094-9515

Norweb MR & MRS R Henry 3d (McDonald—Pamela W Taylor) Bvl.Uncl.Bel'70 ⚓ . . . . | ☎ (508) 748-0512 339 Point Rd,
JUNIORS MISS Elizabeth H . . . . | Marion, MA 02738
MISS Alexandra T McDonald—at 3210 Wisconsin Av NW, Washington, DC 20016 . . . .
MISS Hadley P McDonald—Box 8, Narragansett, RI 02882 . . . .

Notebaert MRS Charles C (Marie Cannon)
☎ (613) 241-2449 . . 40 Boteler St, Apt 903, Ottawa, Ontario K1N 9C8, Canada

Notides MR & MRS Russell J (Ellanor T Roberts) Bur.Bgt.Nf.LakeF'73 . . . . | ☎ (011-852) 2868-4410
JUNIORS MISS Elizabeth C . . . . | Tavistock 602,
JUNIORS MR Alexander B . . . . | 10 Tregunter Path, Hong Kong

Notman MASTER Alexander Goodrich (Donald D JR) . . . . Born at Baltimore, MD Nov 11'95

Notman MR & MRS Donald D (Gertrude L M Raynor-Smith) Mt.Cvc.Sl.Ncd.Y'49
☎ (207) 967-5129 . . PO Box 527, 15 Summit Av, Kennebunkport, ME 04046

Notman MR & MRS Donald D JR (Pamela G Bowers) Bates'84.Md.Mv.Mid'82.Dth'88
☎ (410) 825-1401 Curving Lane, Ruxton, MD 21204

Nott MR & MRS Thomas E 4th (Anne C Phillips) Sg.Clem'50.Pa'57
☎ (305) 445-7326 . . 4010 El Prado Blvd, Coconut Grove, Miami, FL 33133

Nott MISS Victoria—V'60
☎ (212) 254-6039 . . 118 Waverly Place, New York, NY 10011

Nottebohm MR & MRS Johann D (Mary H Burchenal) Rdc'62.Mv.Cly.Ncd.H'61 . . . . | ☎ (011-502-2) 69-10-14
MISS Barbara H—H'89—at ☎ (212) 410-3073 1021 Park Av, New York, NY 10028 . . . . | 21 Avenida 3-84, Zona 15,
MISS Margaret F—at ☎ (212) 410-3073 1021 Park Av, New York, NY 10028 . . . . | Guatemala City, Guatemala

Nottebohm MR & MRS Johann D JR (Sheila A Tellier) StLaw'92.Mid'89
☎ (011-502-2) 37-36-53 . . Jardin de Oakland 15A, 17 Calle 16-89, Zona 10, Guatemala City, Guatemala

Nottingham MR & MRS Charles Denmead (E Catherine Casey) RMWmn'89.Tul'94.Wes'88.GeoM'94
☎ (540) 371-3279 . . 300 Princess Anne St, Fredericksburg, VA 22401

Nottingham MR & MRS R Kendall (Elizabeth H Le Viness) Bg.Ste.Cvc.Mv.Cly.Ncd.Pn.JHop'59 ⚓
☎ (201) 763-8531 . . 393 Charlton Av, South Orange, NJ 07079

Nottingham MR Robinson K JR—Ct.Wes'83.Va'86
☎ (202) 337-7257 . . 2813 Bellevue Terr NW, Washington, DC 20007

Notz MR & MRS Edward U (Sandra Keep) Rc.On.Y'57.Nw'60 . . . . | of ☎ (847)295-2226 580 S Rockefeller
MISS Isabel Stephanie—Nw'93—at Chicago, IL . | Rd, Lake Forest, IL 60045
☎ (520) 762-5345 Andrada Ranch, 17000 S Old Sonoita H'way, Vail, AZ 85641

Notz MR Edward U JR (Edward U) . . . . Married at Lake Forest, IL
  Edwards MISS Tiffany S . . . . Jun 29'96
Notz MR & MRS John K JR (Janis L Wellin) | ☎ (773) 348-5196
  Rc.Wa.Wms'53.Nw'56. . . . . | 399 W Fullerton
  MISS Jane Elinor—Pa'90. . . . . | P'kway, Chicago, IL
  MR John Wellin—Dth'93 . . . . | *60614*
Nouri MR & MRS Edmond J (Redington—Diana H | ☎ (212) 838-7689
  Crocker) Rdc'48.Un.K.Ri.B.Pr.Plg.Bur.Geo'41 . | 435 E 52 St,
  MISS Ruth M Redington. . . . . | New York, NY
   | *10022*

Nourie MR Bruce L—Bry'64.Bost'72
  ☎ (203) 498-9849 . . 26 Gail Dv, New Haven, CT *06473*
Nowland MR & MRS David T (Cathleen B Cotter) W&M'89
  ☎ (212) 832-0998 . . 349 E 49 St, Apt 6K, New York, NY *10017*
Nowland MRS Philip J (Sandra A Robertson) Wil. . . | ☎ (302) 654-7556
  MISS Elizabeth B—Del'88—at ☎ (302) 427-0454 | 2311 Ridgeway Rd,
  817 Bayard Av, Wilmington, DE *19805*. . . . . . | Wilmington, DE
  MR Philip C . . . . | *19805-2628*
Nowotny MR & MRS Walter W JR (Mary C | ☎ (314) 863-3445
  Roudebush) Wells'68.Mo'58 . . . . | 27 Dartford Av,
  MISS Molly J. . . . . | St Louis, MO *63105*
  MISS Anna L. . . . . |
Noyes MRS Blancke (Margaret T Talbott)
  ☎ (203) 655-9138 . . 373 Brookside Rd, Darien, CT *06820*
Noyes MR & MRS David C JR (Elizabeth Bull) | ☎ (516) 692-6311
  V'44.Ny.Csh.H.'43. | 243 Jennings Rd,
  MR Robert M—Y'76—at ☎ (208) 726-8557 | Cold Spring Harbor,
  PO Box 76, Ketchum, ID *83340*. . . . . | NY *11724*
Noyes MR & MRS Jansen JR (M Dorothy O'Day) Ln.Fic.Fiy.Cr'39 ⚓
  ☎ (203) 655-1338 . . 299 Hollow Tree Ridge Rd, Darien, CT *06820*
Noyes MR & MRS José W (Grace E Gammino) | ☎ (212) 355-5495
  Rc.Un.L.Plg.Sa.Vca.Cly.Cl'61 . . . . | 116 E 63 St,
  MR José W JR . . . . | New York, NY
  JUNIORS MR Prentiss G . . . . | *10021-7343*
Noyes MR & MRS Joseph C 4th (Laura A Talbot) Bost'92
  ☎ (617) 527-2678 . . 96 East Side P'kway, Newton, MA *02158*
Noyes MRS Julius W (McCallum—Rosita de Texada) Cly.Dll.
  ☎ (212) 753-5417 . . 1 Sutton Place S, New York, NY *10022*
Noyes MR Nicholas H—Cl'84 . . see R A R Maclennan
Noyes MR William M—Unn.RogerW'86 ⚓ . . of
  ☎ (305) 361-2303 . . 151 Crandon Blvd, Key Biscayne, FL *33149*
  "Quinta Encantada" Val de Gosh, Armansil, Portugal
Nuckols MR & MRS Samuel C 3d (Ella S Jackson) | PO Box 218,
  Dth'61.Pa'66 . . . . | Merry Point, VA
  MISS Margaret Z—at 730 Bedford Rd, Concord, | *22513*
  MA *01742* . . . . |
  MISS Paige S—at Hollins . . . . |
Nugent MRS William B (Jean J W Darrow)
  ☎ (910) 295-6256 . . "Essex Cottage" PO Box 448, Pinehurst,
  NC *28374*
Nuissl MISS Binney H . . . . Married at Bryn Mawr, PA
  Huffman MR Jeffrey J (Jay E) . . . . May 18'96
Nuissl MR Rudolph F H JR—Colby'89 . . see W P Miller 3d

Nunan MR & MRS Alfred B (Beverly E McLaughlin) | of ☎ (908)892-8628
  Upsala'60 . . . . | 720 East Av,
  MISS Elizabeth D . . . . | Box 15,
  MR Alfred B JR . . . . | Bay Head, NJ *08742*
   | ☎ (717) 289-4561
   | "Meadowbound"
   | PO Box 37,
   | Hop Bottom, PA
   | *18824*
Nunan MRS Maurice G (Virginia Bedell)
  ☎ (908) 892-0316 . . 700 East Av, Bay Head, NJ *08742*
Nunan MR & MRS Neil M (Louisa W Lipp) . . . . | ☎ (207) 499-7939
  MISS Marilla P—at ☎ (207) 947-5308 | "Beechbrook"
  532D Hammond St, Bangor, ME *04401* . . . . . . | 8 Hill Rd, Lyman,
   | ME *04005*
Nunan MRS Steinman (Caroline M H Steinman) Sl. . | ☎ (717) 394-9944
  MISS Louise T—Box 292, Norwich, VT *05055* . . | 2171 New Holland
   | Pike, Lancaster, PA
   | *17601*
Nusrala MR & MRS Edward J (Mimika L Garesché) | 2101 S Warson Rd,
  Mar'vil'62.HolyC'61 . . . . | St Louis, MO *63124*
  MISS Amelia L . . . . |
Nuti-de Biasi MR & MRS Pierluigi (Merlin Elliot) | ☎ (561) 791-8448
  AccNaw'53.BelleArti'55 . . . . | 15129 Sunnyland
  MISS Charis . . . . | Lane, Palm Beach
  MR Alexis . . . . | Point, West Palm
   | Beach, FL *33414*
Nutt MR & MRS William J (Deborah D Stout) | ☎ (617) 631-8038
  Roan'73.Me.Ey.My.Grove'67.Pa'71. . . . . | 20 Foster St,
  MISS Caroline D—at Colby . . . . | Marblehead, MA
  JUNIORS MR Alexander J—at St George's . . . . . . | *01945*
  JUNIORS MR William M—at Deerfield . . . . |
Nutting MR & MRS Raymond J (Katherine McC | ☎ (510) 654-2639
  Marwedel) Cal'49.Cal'47. . . . . | 122 Dracena Av,
  MISS Nancy K . . . . | Piedmont, CA *94611*
  MR Raymond J 3d . . . . |
Nutting MR & MRS William C (Pauline H Bray) Sl.Wms'59.H'63
  ☎ (561) 546-7929 . . 3 Isle Ridge W, Hobe Sound, FL *33455*
Nuttle MR & MRS John C (Colegate N Woodward) | ☎ (410) 825-6567
  Mv.Gv.JHop'42 . . . . | 1021 Wagner Rd,
  MISS Elizabeth C—at 10104 Falls Rd, Box 586, | Ruxton, MD *21204*
  Brooklandville, MD *21022* . . . . |
Nyce MR & MRS Fletcher E (Katharine B Thomas) Cm.Qc.Y'30
  ☎ (513) 791-1521 . . 8800 Blome Rd, Cincinnati, OH *45243*
Nycum MR & MRS R Scott JR (Joan L Burchenal) | ☎ (203) 655-6209
  V'72.Ox'73.Wms'71.Ox'73 . . . . | 5 Lantern Lane,
  JUNIORS MISS Rebecca H . . . . | Darien, CT *06820*
Nye MR & MRS Richard B (Milbank—Amory— | of ☎ (212)996-7777
  Elizabeth H Griffis) V'71.Rc.Ri.B.H'61.H'64 . . | 1120 Fifth Av,
  MISS Amy J—at 235 E 73 St, New York, | New York, NY
  NY *10021* . . . . | *10128*
  MR Timothy U—at 476 Broadway, New York, | ☎ (516) 537-5164
  NY *10013*. . . . . | Beach Lane,
   | Wainscott, NY
   | *11975*

Nyland MRS Katherine S (Katherine S McLenegan). ☎ (415) 441-7408
  MISS Leslie S . . . . 2325 Northpoint St,
  MR Matthew W—Cal'95. . . . . San Francisco, CA
                                                                                    | 94123

Nype MR & MRS Russell H (Mander—Diantha Lawrence) LakeF'43
  ☎ (212) BU8-6808 . . 151 E 83 St, Apt 4D, New York, NY 10028

Nype MR & MRS Russell L (Martha E Foley) Wheat'79.Br'77 . . of
  ☎ (212) 988-3363 . . 829 Park Av, New York, NY 10021
  ☎ (207) 967-3531 . . Pear Tree Farm, Kennebunkport, ME 04046

O

Oakes MISS Daphne V N . . see MRS C C Linden

Oakes COL & MRS John Hawley (Carol V Dunn) | 505 North St,
  Cvc.USA'56. . . . . | Chapel Hill, NC
  MISS Sue McKinley—NCar'83—at | 27514
  ☎ (404) 248-0484 . . 524 Clairmont Circle,
  Apt 8, Decatur, GA 30033 . . . .

Oakes MISS Sarah L
  59 W 12 St, New York, NY 10011

Oakes MRS Thomas F (Elinor Righter)
  ☎ (860) 767-1045 . . 353 Essex Meadows, Essex, CT 06426-1526

Oates MASTER Gage Garat (g—MRS George Temple Bowdoin) . . . Born at
                                                          St Petersburg, FL Mch 2'96

Oates MR & MRS William A JR (Elizabeth D Macy) | ☎ (617) 326-9359
  DeP'64.Cy.Sm.Chi.Colby'65.H'72 . . . . | 201 Village Av,
  MISS Elizabeth N—Vt'93—at San Francisco, CA | Dedham, MA 02026
  MISS Katherine M—at Middlebury . . . .
  JUNIORS MISS Emily E A—at Groton . . . .

Ober MR & MRS David G (Polly F Norris) LakeF'76.B.BtP.Cly.
  ☎ (561) 844-0174 . . 248 West Indies Dv, Palm Beach, FL 33480

Ober MR & MRS Frank B JR (Alice J Parker) Mv.
  ☎ (410) 557-7141 . . ''Bryarly'' 3818 Beatty Rd, Monkton, MD 21111

Ober MR Gustavus—P'40
  ☎ (212) 535-4060 . . 500 E 77 St, Apt 2425, New York, NY 10021

Oberdorf MR & MRS John G (Elizabeth van B Joy) | ☎ (610) 347-0370
  AmU'68.Gi.Stan'65.Md'80 . . . . | 724 Northbrook Rd,
  JUNIORS MISS Laura McC . . . . | Kennett Square, PA
                                                     | 19348

Oberholtzer MR & MRS Wendell W (Wentz—Deborah Bradley)
  Pa'51.Hav'52
  ☎ (215) 247-2113 . . 18 E Abington Av, Philadelphia, PA 19118

Obermeyer MRS Louise T (Louise L Towles) . . . . . | ☎ (314) 991-0304
  MISS Lindsay B—at 2035 W Shakespeare Av, | 11 Black Creek
  Chicago, IL 60647 . . . . | Lane, St Louis, MO
  MR Charles M JR . . . . | 63124

Obolensky PRC & PRCSS Alexis N (Selene R Smith) | ☎ (202) 244-4728
  Bnd'50.Siena'53.Flor'45.Flor'47.Rome'49 . . . . . | 4501 Connecticut
  PRC Dimitri S—Cal'91—at U of Moscow . . . . . | Av NW, Apt 523,
                                                     | Washington, DC
                                                     | 20008-3725

Obolensky MRS Serge (Breer—Marilyn F Wall) So . . .of
  ☎ (212) PL5-5000 . . 465 Park Av, New York, NY 10022
  ☎ (313) 886-5848 . . ''Rose Hill House'' 45 Preston Place,
  Grosse Pointe Farms, MI 48236

O'Boyle MRS Edwards C (Katharine B Thurber) Bgt.
  ☎ (914) 277-8783 . . 367E Heritage Hills, Somers, NY 10589

Obregón-Peña MR & MRS Eduardo (Micaela Prescott) Techol'84.Techol'85
  ☎ (011-52-415) 22541 . . Chiquitos 1, CP 3700 San Miguel de Allende,
  GTO, Mexico

Obregón-Peña MASTER Eduardo Franco (Eduardo) . . . . . Born Nov 25'95

O'Brien MR Andrew J 3d . . see C H Cox

O'Brien MRS Averyl C (Averyl Vaux Craven) Rd. . | ☎ (610) 793-3031
  MISS Emily S—at 1735 Dogwood Dv, Alexandria, | 1058 General
  VA 22302. . . . . | Sullivan Dv,
  MISS Elizabeth C—at Wake Forest U . . . . | West Chester, PA
                                                     | 19382

O'Brien MRS Catherine L (James—Noel—Catherine L O'Brien)
  Dyc.Syc.Mds.Chr.Fw.Ne.Cda.Dar.Dc.Myf. ⚓ . . of
  ☎ (212) 535-4967 . . 605 Park Av, New York, NY 10021
  ☎ (516) 324-1045 . . ''Sea Cote'' Lily Pond Lane, Box 1488,
  East Hampton, NY 11937

O'Brien MR & MRS Clarence J 2d (Butt—Agnes M Pancoast) Ram'76
  ☎ (610) 869-3305 . . 241 Upland Rd, West Grove, PA 19390

O'Brien MR & MRS Daniel B (Wendy Wilson) | ☎ (914) 373-8506
  Rd.Geo'68 . . . . | Trout Walk Farm,
  MISS Timoney M—at Colo Coll . . . . | 133A Amenia Union
  MISS Caroleana M—at Bost Coll . . . . | Rd, South Amenia,
  MR D Bryce—Vt'94—at 1705 First Av, Apt 5RN, | NY 12592
  New York, NY 10128 . . . .
  JUNIORS MR Christopher G . . . .

O'Brien MRS Francis T (Stone—Frances Dunn McKee) Cda.
  ☎ (410) 266-0509 . . Scotch Broom Point, 1829 Cove Point Rd,
  Annapolis, MD 21401

O'Brien MR & MRS Frank JR (Marianna H Mead) Err.Ey.Cy.Chi.H.Yn.Y'44
  ☎ (617) 266-3217 . . 90 Commonwealth Av, Boston, MA 02116

O'Brien MRS Hugh E (Nancy M Drinkwater) . . . . . | ☎ (610) MU8-3496
  MISS Rachel S—Dick'73.Drex'74—at | 102 Old Lancaster
  ☎ (803) 686-2698 . . PO Box 2001, | Rd, Devon, PA
  Hilton Head Island, SC 29925 . . . . | 19333
  MR Ward J—Dick'76—at ☎ (610) 495-6733
  RD 4, Grubb Rd, Pottstown, PA 19464 . . . .

O'Brien MR & MRS Jonathan B (Joan Dominick) | St Andrew's School,
  Wms'60.Cl'63 . . . . | Noxontown Rd,
  MISS Jennifer C—Wms'83—at ☎ (617) 367-1910 | Middletown, DE
  73 Charles St, Boston, MA 02114 . . . . | 19709

O'Brien MR & MRS Lawrence F 3d (Helen M | ☎ (703) 536-1607
  Powell) Ri.H'67.Cl'72 . . . . | 4701 N 34 St,
  MR Luke . . . . | Arlington, VA
  JUNIORS MR Peter . . . . | 22207

O'Brien MR & MRS Michael S (van Gerbig—Lois A | of ☎ (516)922-6896
  Hochschwender) Pr.Mb.B.Y'63 . . . . | Shutter Lane,
  MISS Hilary H . . . . | Oyster Bay, NY
  MR Michael S JR . . . . | 11771
    MISS Dorothy F van Gerbig . . . . | ☎ (212) 517-8211
                                                     | 222 E 71 St,
                                                     | New York, NY
                                                     | 10021

O'Brien MR & MRS Patrick C JR (Elizabeth C
Farrelly) Kt.Tv.Rr.Geo'58 . . . .
☎ (216) 951-9412 "Merrifields" Hobart Rd, Waite Hill, OH 44094
    MISS S Carbery—JCar'90.Rr.—at 1051 Second
Av, Apt 3, New York, NY 10022 . . . .
    MISS Josephine G—StLaw'94.Rr. . . . .
    MISS Margaret R—Rr. . . . .
    MR Patrick C 3d—Kt.Rr.HWSth'91 . . . .

O'Brien MR & MRS Robert E (Smith—Marian S Achilles)
Sth'56.An.StL.'46.StL'47
☎ (508) 945-0612 . . "The Baxter House" 117 Old Wharf Rd, Chatham,
MA 02650

O'Brien MR & MRS Thomas C JR (Webster—Doris E Reimers)
Buf.G.BryStratton'36
☎ (716) 839-1229 . . 52 Greenbrier Rd, Snyder, NY 14226

O'Brien MR & MRS W Gardnar (Kathryn C McHugh) Stph'74.Mo'74
☎ (714) 738-5519 . . 1100 W Las Palmas Dv, Fullerton, CA 92635

Ocampo MR & MRS Juan M (Anne K O'Neil)
Duke'80.Rc.Mds.Cs.Mit'76.H.'79 . . of
☎ (212) 879-0891 . . 445 E 80 St, New York, NY 10021
☎ (516) 537-0776 . . Wainscott Stone Rd, Wainscott, NY 11975

Ochsner DR & MRS John L (Mary Lou Hannon) Tul'52
☎ (504) 866-9922 . . 84 Audubon Blvd, New Orleans, LA 70118

O'Connell MR Courtney . . see MRS C A Long

O'Connell MR & MRS J Ryan (Janet B Keyes)
MtH'74.Nu'82.Mds.H.'73.Pa'77
☎ (914) 833-3568 . . 13 Bayard St, Larchmont, NY 10538

O'Connell DR & MRS James R (Elizabeth C
Robinson) Me.StJos'61 . . . .
☎ (610) 353-5551 3319 Saw Mill Rd, Newtown Square, PA 19073
    MISS Elise S . . . .

O'Connell MR & MRS Matthew McG (Elizabeth S Haight)
Tufts'76.Va'87.Csh.Ty'74.Va'79
☎ (516) 549-8551 . . 228 Southdown Rd, Lloyd Harbor, NY 11743-1719

O'Connell MR Robin S . . see MRS C A Long

O'Connell MRS Walter Francis (Morrison—Fraser—
Pauline P Forney) Ln.Cly.Dar.
☎ (803) 681-5059 . . "Casa Llennoco" Cypress Bay Club,
9 Hadley Lane, Hilton Head Island, SC 29926

O'Connor MR & MRS Anthony M (Suzanne De G
Perry) V'57.Eyc.Cs.P'50 . . . .
☎ (212) 289-0620 1158 Fifth Av, New York, NY 10029
    MR Edward R—at ☎ (802) 496-5260
PO Box 1246, Waitsfield, VT 05673 . . . .

O'Connor MR & MRS Anthony M JR (M Susan Kearing)
StLaw'89.Cl'94.Eyc.P'81.Nu'86
☎ (817) 329-0690 . . 1907 Hartford Rd, Grapevine, TX 76051-7137

O'Connor MISS Elisabeth H—Bnd'47.Cly.Ds . . of
☎ (212) 737-2687 . . 163 E 81 St, New York, NY 10021
☎ (413) 229-8836 . . PO Box 55, Ashley Falls, MA 01222

O'Connor MR & MRS Francis F JR (Cynthia L Ruff) Okla'81.Va'82
☎ (212) 534-6431 . . 61 E 86 St, Apt 64, New York, NY 10028

O'Connor MRS Joan D (Joan P Dunbar) . . . .
2531 Tupelo Dv, Augusta, GA 30909
    MISS Sallie H D—RMWmn'87—at
☎ (804) 346-4437 . . 4701G Four Seasons Terr,
Glen Allen, VA 23060 . . . .
    MR Gregory C . . . .

O'Connor MR & MRS Michael J (Serena Van R Koven) Eh.
☎ (908) 439-3116 . . 7 Church St, PO Box 513, Oldwick, NJ 08858

O'Connor MRS Molly M (Molly Meyer) BMr'37
☎ (206) 329-0770 . . 1630—43 Av E, Apt 906, Seattle, WA 98112

O'Connor MR & MRS Richard D (Korybut—
Unger—Katherine C Maffitt) V'55.Ln.Cly.Dar.
Mich'54 . . . .
of ☎ (212)535-3423 320 E 72 St, New York, NY 10021
    MR Timothy J . . . .
    MR John P. . . . .
        MR Michael Korybut-Daszkiewicz—at
☎ (810) 642-6292 235 Barden Rd, Bloomfield Hills, MI 48304
        ☎ (415) 968-5452 . . 1921 California St,
Mountain View, CA 94040 . . . .
        MR Alexis Korybut-Daszkiewicz—
☎ (212) 794-0114 . . . .

O'Connor MRS Robert Barnard (Mary Wistar Morris)
☎ (914) 666-5067 . . RD 2, Box 153, Baldwin Rd, Mt Kisco, NY 10549

O'Connor MR & MRS Robert J (Noëlle W King)
Cal'74.Cl'85.Cs.Ford'82.Cl'84.PolyNY'89
☎ (516) 922-2597 . . 158 Ivy St, Oyster Bay, NY 11771

O'Connor MR & MRS William F (Callans—Mary Jane Merle) Rc.Ill'51
☎ (312) 337-2499 . . 1500 N Lake Shore Dv, Chicago, IL 60610

O'Day MR & MRS John C (Coyne—Sheila G Doyle)
DomSR'48.USMMA'43
☎ (415) 563-2341 . . 2662 Union St, San Francisco, CA 94123

Odell MISS Alison W . . see J A Evans

Odell MRS David Dallas (Watson—Roberta M Martin)
CtCol'45.Rd.Rc.Fcg.Pg.Rr.
☎ (610) 793-1119 . . "Skirmish Hill" 1050 Meeting House Rd,
West Chester, PA 19382

Odell MR & MRS Henry R (Branigan—Evelyn B Christiansen) H'46
☎ (804) 296-8046 . . 2200 Croydon Rd, West Leigh, Charlottesville,
VA 22901

Odell MR & MRS I Gordon (Jane A Schaff) Vh.P'44 . .
☎ (818) 799-8046 655 S Orange Grove Blvd, Pasadena, CA 91105
    MR Gordon T . . . .

Odell MISS Suzanne W . . see J A Evans

O'Dell MR & MRS W H Sterg (Perot—Frances L Heublein)
V'35.Rc.Me.Cs.Ac.Ncd.Hn.Ia'40.H.'48
☎ (610) MU8-9310 . . "Hilltop House" Waterloo Rd, Devon, PA 19333

Odén MISS Lisbeth N (DeLorme—Lisbeth N Odén) ColMtn'93
☎ (970) 925-3548 . . PO Box 660, Aspen, CO 81612

Odén DR & MRS Robert R (Edwards—Nancy N
Clow) Ill'43.Nw'46
of ☎ (970)925-3548 PO Box 660, Aspen, CO 81612
    MR M Beach C Edwards—at
☎ (970) 382-0500 . . 230 Blue Sky Dv,
Durango, CO 81301 . . . .
☎ (941) 472-2964 "Sanderling" Box 172, Captiva Island, FL 33924

Odgers MR & MRS John B (Pamela B Prout)
Cw.Rv.Cp.Myf.Ll.Pa'60.Cl'62 . .
☎ (614) 457-3350 4401 Sussex Dv, Columbus, OH 43220
    MISS Eloise W—Miami'90—at
☎ (513) 553-3145 . . 441 Missouri Av, Apt 6,
Cincinnati, OH 45226 . . . .

Odom MR & MRS John G (E Lee Scott)
Va'76.An.Cw.Ncd.Y'73.Ox'75.Va'78.Ox'81 . . of
☎ (504) 837-8883 . . 105 Northline St, Metairie, LA 70005
☎ (912) 794-3420 . . "Old Home Place" 5502 Hall Rd, Hahira,
GA 31632

O'Donnell MISS Nancy S—Srb . . .of
☎ (415) 474-7539 . . 3196 Pacific Av, San Francisco, CA *94115*
☎ (561) 655-5947 . . 325 S Lake Dv, Palm Beach, FL *33480*
O'Donnell MR & MRS Robert J (Sue L Dodson) BtP.Me.Srb.Can'52 . . of
☎ (561) 655-5947 . . 325 S Lake Dv, Palm Beach, FL *33480*
☎ (401) 846-0075 . . "Crossways" 83 Ocean Av, Newport, RI *02840*
O'Donnell MR Robert J JR (Carol Befanis)
Skd'78.Cardozo'81.Unn.Srb.RISD'79
☎ (203) 254-7755 . . 540 Joan Dv, Fairfield, CT *06430*
O'Donnell MR & MRS William T 3d (Kemble C Lickle)
Colby'79.H'84.Ub.Rr.Vt'83 . . of
☎ (203) 655-7550 . . 37 Knollwood Lane, Darien, CT *06820*
☎ (802) 297-3002 . . Fairway Meadows 3, Stratton Mountain, Stratton,
VT *05155*
O'Donoghue MR & MRS Sidney L (Csango—Ilona Kacser) H'44
☎ (904) 261-8319 . . 3429 Fiddler's Bend, Amelia Island,
FL *32034-5059*

O'Donovan DR & MRS Charles 3d (H Gail Brewington) Gchr'61.Md.Cw.Y'58.JHop'63. Van'65 . . . . | ☎ (410) 296-5177 "Garryowen" 600 Greenwood Rd,
MR E Patrick H—Cw . . . . | Baltimore, MD *21204*

O'Donovan MR & MRS Charles 5th (Mary M Whitaker) Md.Rich'84
504 Highland Av, Baltimore, MD *21204*

O'Donovan MR & MRS Hugh J (Achsah C Stettinius) Gv.Md.Va'40 . . . . | ☎ (410) 833-0271 Grasslands Farm,
MISS Achsah S—Temp'74.Gchr'79.Gv. . . . . | 4243 Mt Zion Rd, Upperco, MD *21155*

O'Dowd MRS John B (Ellen Marie H Sande)
☎ (520) 298-1035 . . 311 N Elena Maria St, Tucson, AZ *85715*
O'Dunne MRS Eugene (Elsie W Ekengren) Cvc.Sl.
☎ (202) 333-2486 . . 3900 Cathedral Av NW, Washington, DC *20016*
Oehmig MR & MRS Daniel West (Matilda L Thomas) V'48.Va'48
☎ (423) 821-1835 . . 503 Pine Av, Lookout Mountain, TN *37350*
Oehmig MR & MRS Von Daniel (Margaret I Chenoweth) Dth'36.Va'40
☎ (706) 820-0268 . . 1230 Scenic H'way, Box 144, Lookout Mountain,
GA *30750*

Oelsner MR & MRS W James (Carol Perkins) Ri.BtP.S.Evg.Ck.Pa'51 . . . . | of ☎ (561)659-1620
MISS Christine E—Rol'89 . . . . | 110 Clarke Av, Palm Beach, FL
MR Robert C—at ☎ (504) 649-5169 | *33480*
6 Mills Lane, Slidell, LA *70460* . . . . | ☎ (516) 922-7417 "Seacroft" Centre Island, Oyster Bay, NY *11771*

Oesch MR Peter I . . see MRS W N Frank JR
Oesch MISS Stephanie E . . see MRS W N Frank JR
Oestreich MR & MRS George H 3d (Susan A Loney) Wheat'77.Msq.Syr'76
☎ (513) 321-9088 . . 3581 Raymar Blvd, Cincinnati, OH *45208*
Oestreich MR William A—StL'76
☎ (561) 686-9549 . . 6204 Glenmoor Dv, West Palm Beach, FL *33409*
O'Farrell MR & MRS William J (E M Noreen Drexel)
Br'83.Srb.Cly.Br'84.H'88
☎ (401) 272-6228 . . 76 Taber Av, Providence, RI *02906*

Off MR & MRS Clifford JR (Fromm—Mary G Fields) P'41 . . . . | PO Box 575, Library, PA *15129*
MISS Linda H—Box 8339, Pittsburgh, PA *15218*
Off MR & MRS Robert B (Marjorie W Warner) Hlns'70.Rr.Susq'70 . . . . | ☎ (513) 561-4884 4645 Burley Hills
JUNIORS MISS Eleanor B | Dv, Cincinnati, OH *45243*
Off MR Robert W—Pg.Rr.Va'42
☎ (412) 687-7779 . . 5023 Frew St, Pittsburgh, PA *15213*
Off MR & MRS Samuel W (Mary D Hays) Rr.Wms'38
☎ (412) 593-2911 . . "Cherry Hill" 141 Jefferson School Rd, Ligonier,
PA *15658-2035*
Off MR & MRS Samuel W JR (Barbara B Childs) ColSt'79.Rr.Curry'70
☎ (412) 593-7478 . . Topsfield Farm, 159 Caven Rd, Ligonier, PA *15658*
Offenhiser MR Andrew B—Sar.Myf.Colby'49.Stan'55
☎ (815) 232-8721 . . 614 Woodbridge Lane, Apt 4, Freeport,
IL *61032-4459*
Offenhiser MISS Nancy L—Purd'87
☎ (503) 246-3104 . . 7833 SW 34 Av, Portland, OR *97219*
Offield MRS Wrigley (Edna J Headley) Cnt.
☎ (619) 767-4063 . . PO Box 2155, Borrego Springs, CA *92004*
Offutt MR & MRS Robert L Bentley (Ann Harrison) Bost'63.Gv.Md.Mv.Leh'60.GeoW'68 . . . . | ☎ (410) 429-4499 "Locust Hill"
MISS Emily J W—Duke'90 . . . . | 3515 Butler Rd, Glyndon, MD *21071*
Offutt MR & MRS Thomas W (Josephine Bentley) Gv.Mv.Cda.
☎ (410) 494-0772 . . 604 Brightwood Club Dv, Lutherville, MD *21093*
Offutt MR & MRS Thomas W 3d (Madeleine McMillan) Ws'62.Kt.JHop'55 . . . . | ☎ (216) 255-5143 "Little Glen"
MISS Katherine B—JHop'88—at | 9071 King Memorial
226 W Rittenhouse Square, Apt 803, | Rd, RR 1, Mentor,
Philadelphia, PA *19103* . . . . | OH *44060*
MR Thomas W 4th—Colby'89—at
101 W 69 St, Apt 2D, New York, NY *10024* . . .
Ogan MR & MRS M Sean (Nina K Merrill)
☎ (303) 320-5979 . . 560 Circle Dv, Denver, CO *80206*
Ogan MASTER Taylor Lynch (M Sean) . . . . Born at Denver, CO Nov 24'95
O'Gara MR & MRS Gordon C (Kribs—Elizabeth Schardt) P'42
☎ (305) 666-3831 . . 6220 Leonardo St, Coral Gables, FL *33146*
Ogburn MR & MRS Hugh B (Petersen—Nancy Wrenn) Ws'48.Me.Pcu.Pn.P'44 ⚓
☎ (808) 732-6503 . . 4340 Pahoa Av, Apt 16A, Honolulu, HI *96816*
Ogden MR Alfred—C.Cos.Plg.StJ.Cw.Y.'32.H'35
☎ (212) RE7-7138 . . 150 E 73 St, New York, NY *10021*
Ogden MR & MRS Alfred T 2d (Tyler—Susan R Clark) Pa'66.Ri.Y.'62.Cr'65 ⚓ . . . . | ☎ (212) 722-9093 200 E 90 St,
MISS Alix R—Ty'90—at ☎ (206) 523-7150 | New York, NY
743 N 86 St, Seattle, WA *98103* . . . . | *10128*
MISS Mary Fell P—at Yale
MR Alfred T 3d—Y'93—at 520 E 86 St,
New York, NY *10028* . . . .
MISS Mary T Tyler—Ty'94
MISS Cecily W Tyler—at Sarah Lawrence . . .
JUNIORS MR Wat H Tyler—at Trinity . . . .

Ogden MR & MRS Dayton (Elizabeth C Pinneo)
Sth'40.Wms'36 . . . . ☎ (203) 966-2050
MISS Katharine P—Y'72—at 2741 Regent St, | 83 Orchard Dv,
Berkeley, CA *94705* | New Canaan, CT
| *06840*
Ogden MR & MRS Dayton JR (Margaret P Reid)
Bost'68.Rcn.Y'67 . . . . ☎ (203) 966-7598
MISS Margaret P—at Boston U . . . . | 17 Toquam Rd,
MR Dayton R—at Wittenberg . . . . | New Canaan, CT
| *06840*
Ogden MR & MRS Elliott M JR (Mary Stuart) Rc.P'44 | ☎ (516) 537-0922
MR Gordon S—at ☎ (212) 249-8742 | PO Box 137,
12 E 86 St, New York, NY *10028* | Wainscott, NY
MR Henry M—at 2347 Arlington Ridge Rd, | *11975*
Arlington, VA *22202* |
MR Jacob B—at Goucher . . . . |
Ogden MR & MRS Elliott M 3d (Santhea Manos) Bklyn'80.Rc.StLaw'72
☎ (914) 273-2153 . . 7 Willow Pond Lane, Armonk, NY *10504*
Ogden MR & MRS Henry M (Mary G Wells) CedarC'81.OWes'82
☎ (908) 277-1137 . . 83 Maple St, Summit, NJ *07901*
Ogden MR & MRS Jeffrey E (Morse—Doris E Haug) Vt'78.Vt'93.Hob'72
☎ (802) 658-2836 . . 37 Simms St, Burlington, VT *05401*
Ogden MR & MRS John (Elizabeth Harnischfeger) Cr'39
☎ (414) 352-8998 . . 1300 E Fox Lane, Milwaukee, WI *53217-2850*
Ogden MISS Margaret—Sth'28.Cs.
☎ (212) 744-4870 . . 226 E 70 St, Apt 2C, New York, NY *10021-5429*
Ogden MR & MRS Robert M 3d (Maureen M Black)
Bg.Yh.Plg.Coa.Cw.W.Myf.Rv.Csn.DU'48
☎ (201) DR6-7118 . . 59 Lakeview Av, Short Hills, NJ *07078*
Ogden MR & MRS Thomas P (Cynthia McL Porter)
P'80.Rc.Bgt.P.'78.Ch'82 . . of
☎ (212) 289-1157 . . 1165 Fifth Av, New York, NY *10029*
☎ (914) 234-9593 . . 760 Old Post Rd, Bedford, NY *10506*
Ogelsby MR & MRS Charles Warwick JR (Carol R | ☎ (610) 525-5387
Long) Me.Gm.Temp'69.Temp'73 . . . . | 933 Old Gulph Rd,
MISS Alison D . . . . | Bryn Mawr, PA
MR Matthew W . . . . | *19010*
Ogilby MR & MRS Henry McF (Anne C Phillips)
H'80.Va'84.Cyb.Unb.Ht.Myf.Chi.Dc.Cda.
☎ (207) 439-0161 . . "Goose Crossing" 70 River Rd, Eliot, ME *03903*
Ogilvy MR & MRS L Phippen (Lydia R Phippen) | ☎ (603) 466-2008
CtCol'42.Bost'67.Ncd.Myf. . . . . | Randolph, NH
DR J David—H'74.Bost'79 . . . . | *03570*
Ogilvie MR & MRS Andrew J (Ann F Godfrey) | ☎ (415) 752-1610
Bur.H'70 . . . . | 215 Cherry St,
MISS Sarah H . . . . | San Francisco, CA
MR Charles P . . . . | *94118*
Ogilvie MR & MRS John G (Silvia E Tortorelli) Un.Y'64.H'66 . . of
☎ (212) 996-9787 . . 1075 Park Av, New York, NY *10028*
☎ (413) 528-3046 . . Jug End Rd, Box 193, South Egremont, MA *01258*
Ogilvie-Laing MR & MRS Gerald (Meyer—Adaline H Frelinghuysen)
Ri.Cly.StMartin'65 . . of
☎ (212) 772-6268 . . 901 Lexington Av, New York, NY *10021*
☎ (011-44-1349) 861485 . . Kinkell Castle, Conon Bridge,
Ross & Cromarty IV7 8AT, Scotland
Ogilvy MRS Anne (Cabot—Anne R Flint) Rdc'51.Hn.H.
☎ (215) 247-7057 . . 12 W Willow Grove Av, Philadelphia,
PA *19118-3952*

Ogilvy MR & MRS David F (Hanson—Jeannette | ☎ (203) 869-0040
Model) Cly.Va'64 . . . . | 34 Field Point
MR J Stillman Hanson—WakeF'94 . . . . | Circle, Greenwich,
| CT *06830*
O'Grady MR & MRS Bradford S (Alexandra H Wolffe) LakeF'85
☎ (609) 921-8496 . . 95 Crestview Dv, Princeton, NJ *08540*
O'Hara MRS Charles E (Brewster—Theodora L Oakes)
☎ (401) 635-4765 . . "Londonderry" 560 W Main Rd, Box 571,
Little Compton, RI *02837-0571*
O'Hara MR & MRS David O (Janet L McIlvain) | PO Box 107,
Bost'76.My.Ac.Br'73.Bab'82 ⚓ . . . . | Farrington Lane,
JUNIORS MISS Elizabeth L . . . . | Hamilton, MA
JUNIORS MISS Caroline B . . . . | *01936*
O'Hara MISS Isabelle F—CtCol'94 . . see F B Seggerman
O'Hara MR & MRS Peter J (Edna H Taylor) SFr'64 . | ☎ (415) 931-0812
MISS Lindsay E . . . . | 2651 Green St,
| San Francisco, CA
| *94123*
O'Hara MR & MRS Robert S JR (McSweeney— | ☎ (212) 734-2530
Bonnie Ann Durkin) Ri.Cly.P'60.Pa'63 ⚓ . . . | 850 Park Av,
MISS Alison—at ☎ (907) 235-7571 | New York, NY
PO Box 2319, Homer, AK *99603* . . . . | *10021*
MISS Jennifer L—at ☎ (203) 865-9247 |
627 Whitney Av, Apt 7, New Haven, CT *06511* |
MISS Katherine D—at ☎ (212) 807-9829 |
404 W 22 St, New York, NY *10011* . . . . |
MISS A Brett—at ☎ (415) 641-0876 |
99 Jersey St, Apt 12, San Francisco, CA *94114* . |
O'Hara MISS Whitney H (Peter J) . . . . Married at St Helena, CA
O'Keefe MR Peter G (Philip J) . . . . Jun 29'96
Ohl MR & MRS Charles B (Shirley T Cugeber) Unb.Col'59
☎ (603) 383-4003 . . Box 1207, Victoria Ledge Rd, Glen, NH *03838*
Ohl MRS Edwin N (Harriet H Boyden) D. | ☎ (617) 326-1298
MR Edwin—Un.H'67.H'75—☎ (617) 320-9277 | 181 Highland St,
| Dedham, MA *02026*
Ohler MRS David (Caroline W Hardenbergh) . . . . . . | ☎ (914) 764-8430
MR Philip E—HWSth'82—at ☎ (213) 653-0692 | 20 Tatomuck Rd,
740 N Kings' Rd, Apt 218, Los Angeles, CA | Pound Ridge, NY
90069-5472 . . . . | *10576*
Ohmer MR & MRS Frederic L (Martha J Kemper) Day'50 . . of
☎ (513) 434-1454 . . 489 Jenny Lane, Dayton, OH *45459*
☎ (813) 867-8916 . . 4961—59 Av S, Bayway Isles, St Petersburg,
FL *33715*
Ohmer MR & MRS Frederic L 3d (Cheryl L Huber) | ☎ (513) 299-3219
FlaSo'76.Day'74 . . . . | 1300 Raleigh Rd,
JUNIORS MISS Jennifer H . . . . | Dayton, OH *45419*
Ohrstrom MR & MRS Christopher F (Lilla Y Matheson)
☎ (607) 293-7945 . . RR 1, Box 93B2, Hartwick, NY *13348*
Ohrstrom MR George L—Rcn.P'50
Whitewood Farm, The Plains, VA *20198*
Ohrstrom MASTER Gustav Oskar (Mark J) . . . . Born at
Stockholm, Sweden Sep 25'95
Ohrstrom MR Kenneth M
☎ (561) 655-6507 . . 150 Chilean Av, Palm Beach, FL *33480*
Ohrstrom MR & MRS Mark J (Karin S J Broomé) Shen'92.Shen'92
☎ (540) 837-1466 . . Rte 1, Box 163MM, Boyce, VA *22620*

Ohrstrom MRS Ricard R (Rosse—Allen G Dunnington)
Bnd'50.Cvc.Cly.Ncd . . .of
☎ (540) 253-5056 . . ''Hill House'' PO Box 446, 4008 Milestone Rd,
The Plains, VA 20198
3237B Sutton Place NW, Washington, DC 20016

Ohrstrom MR & MRS Ricard R JR (Rochelle Steiner) | ☎ (212) 717-6099
Cin'72.Pa'72 . . . . | 1025 Fifth Av,
JUNIORS MISS Lysandra A—at Chapin . . . . | New York, NY
| 10028

Ohrstrom MISS Winifred E A . . MRS S S Wright

Ohrstrom MR Wright R S—Ken'93 . . see MRS S S Wright

O'Keefe MR Berkeley H . . see MRS E M Nichols

O'Keefe MR John E—Y'60 . . see J W Walker

O'Keefe MR Michael T 2d . . see MRS E M Nichols

O'Keefe MISS Shannon E—Woos'91 . . see MRS E M Nichols

Okie MR Charles T—Pa'38
☎ (610) 644-5679 . . Hillside Farm, 1070 Darby-Paoli Rd, Box 103,
Devon, PA 19333-0103

Olcott MRS A Van Santvoord JR (Diana M Morgan) | ☎ (802) 362-1570
Snc. . . . . | ''Glebelands''
MISS Leslie H—at ☎ (802) 375-9734 | Rte 7A, Box 476,
Box 171, Old Mill Rd, East Arlington, VT 05252 | Manchester, VT
| 05254

Old MRS William Hayes (Louisa P Clark) V'31
☎ (410) 795-4186 . . 7200 Third Av, C061, Sykesville, MD 21784

Oldberg MRS Eric (Mary E Swissler) V'36.On.Cas.
☎ (847) 234-4242 . . 901 Hawthorne Place, Lake Forest, IL 60045

Oldenburg MR & MRS Richard E (H Lisa Turnure) H'54
☎ (212) 753-8674 . . 447 E 57 St, New York, NY 10022

Oldham MRS Diana T (Diana Thompson)
☎ (011-44-1453) 860-605 . . 21 Green Close, Uley, Dursley,
Gloucestershire GL11 5TH, England

Olds MR & MRS John T (Candace Rose) Bgt.Pa'65 . . | ☎ (914) 234-6484
MISS Samantha . . . . | 7 Plateau Lane,
| Bedford, NY 10506

Olds MR William L JR—SFr'70
☎ (415) 567-7077 . . 3569 Washington St, San Francisco,
CA 94118-1848

Olds MR William L 3d—L&C'81
☎ (415) 921-0848 . . 1355 Francisco St, San Francisco, CA 94123

O'Leary MR & MRS Robert S (Eleanor M Ruggles) V'38.H.'40
☎ (617) 868-7535 . . 985 Memorial Dv, Apt 203, Cambridge, MA 02138

Oler REV & MRS Clarke K (Wendy Salmond) C.Y'49
☎ (818) 796-6567 . . 407 W Walnut St, Orange Grove Village, Pasadena,
CA 91103

Oler DR & MRS (DR) Wesley M 3d (Virginia C Craemer)
Pa'45.Pa'49.Cvc.Mt.Sar.Cos.Y'40.Cl'43
☎ (301) 913-9261 . . 8101 Connecticut Av, Apt N612, Chevy Chase,
MD 20815-2805

Olhausen MRS Joseph H (Neall—Marie L Adams) Dar.
☎ (908) 234-0631 . . PO Box 456, Far Hills, NJ 07931

Olinger MR & MRS Chauncey G JR (Carla R Dragan)
Rut'75.C.Chr.Plg.Coa.Cw.StJ.StA.Va'55.Cl'71
☎ (718) 549-5518 . . 4455 Douglas Av, Bronx, NY 10471

Oliphant MR & MRS Andrew E (Lara M Hall) NCar'87
☎ (704) 849-7949 . . 4514 Candalon Way, Matthews, NC 28105

Oliphant MR & MRS Bryan M (Katherine H Maguire) Man'vl'70.NCar'70
☎ (914) 234-9322 . . 752 Old Post Rd, Bedford, NY 10506

Oliphant MR John L—Cvc.Mt.Stv'45 . . . . | ☎ (202) 338-3616
MR Cortright Wetherill . . . . | 4816 W St NW,
MR Christopher H—at Wesleyan . . . . | Washington, DC
| 20007

Oliphant MR & MRS Robert T (Diana A Marston) | ☎ (520) 282-9071
Pa'57 . . . . | 254 Lynx Dv,
MR Alexander M—NAriz'86—at | Sedona, AZ 86336
☎ (602) 955-5696 . . 3547 E Monterosa St,
Phoenix, AZ 85018 . . . .

Oliphant MR & MRS S Parker (Martha Carmichael) | ☎ (202) 244-7749
Ws'57.Cvc.Mt.Sl.P'49 . . . . | 4977 Glenbrook Rd
MR Samuel D . . . . | NW, Washington,
| DC 20016

Oliva MR George JR—Cv.Pn.P'43
☎ (912) 377-4677 . . Beverly Plantation, Rte 3, Thomasville, GA 31792

Oliva MR & MRS Mark (Victoria McKittrick) CtCol'81.CtCol'82
☎ (617) 864-1876 . . 40 Blakeslee St, Cambridge, MA 02138

Olive MR & MRS John C (Patricia L Paul) | ☎ (212) 369-0665
Sth'73.Cly.H'71 . . . . | 49 E 96 St,
JUNIORS MISS Elizabeth L . . . . | New York, NY
| 10128

Oliver MRS A Douglas (Elizabeth G Lea) Ncd.
☎ (410) 889-6281 . . 3801 Canterbury Rd, Baltimore, MD 21218

Oliver MR Andrew (Ruth Blake) Chi.Ncd . . .of
☎ (617) 536-5094 . . 274 Beacon St, Boston, MA 02116
☎ (508) 758-6469 . . ''The Parsonage'' 36 Water St, Mattapoisett,
MA 02739

Oliver MRS Charlotte O'N (Van Akin—Charlotte D | of ☎ (203)329-7440
O'Neil) Bgt.Pg. . . . . | 789 Riverbank Rd,
MR Stoddard M—Curry'88—at | Stamford, CT 06903
☎ (401) 621-9734 . . 333 Morris Av, Providence, | ☎ (307) 733-6632
RI 02906 . . . . | PO Box 1125,
| Wilson, WY 83014

Oliver MR & MRS Daniel (A Louise Vietor) | ☎ (202) 328-2304
Sth'66.Tvb.Mt.C.Cvc.Myf.Cda.H'61.Ford'67 . . . | 3105 Woodley Rd
MISS A Louise—H'90 . . . . | NW, Washington,
MISS Susan F—at Bowdoin . . . . | DC 20008
MR Andrew II—H'92 . . . .
MR Daniel JR—at Vanderbilt . . . .
JUNIORS MR Peter A—at Groton . . . .

Oliver MR & MRS David B 2d (Laura S Liggett) Rr.Y'38
6845 N Ocean Blvd, Mews 2, Ocean Ridge, FL 33435

Oliver MR & MRS Edward O'N (Catherine Doykos) OWes'84
14 Fairfield Rd, Greenwich, CT 06830

Oliver MR George P—Pg.Stet'92
☎ (412) 688-9275 . . 3955 Bigelow Blvd, Pittsburgh, PA 15213

Oliver MRS Henry JR (Emily B Frew) Pg.Rr.
☎ (412) 741-6362 . . Blackburn Rd, Sewickley, PA 15143

Oliver MR & MRS J Harvey JR (Pohl—Anne B McMorrow)
☎ (910) 485-5579 . . 401 Mirror Lake Place, Fayetteville, NC 28303

Oliver CDR James H—USN . . .see G P O'Neil

Oliver MISS Joan Duncan
☎ (212) 794-0337 . . 315 E 68 St, New York, NY 10021

Oliver MR & MRS Joseph W (C Edwina Pickrell) Fcg.Y'30
100 Glenview Place, Naples, FL 34108

Oliver MR & MRS Paul W (Dern—Caroline E Wickett) Ih.Cnt.
☎ (561) 231-4926 . . 917 Lady Bug Lane, Vero Beach, FL *32963*
Oliver MR & MRS Persifor S (Eleanor McC Maxwell) Rr.H'38
☎ (412) 238-2380 . . Box 111, Ligonier, PA *15658*
Oliver MR & MRS Samuel W JR (Anne Marshall) Ala'61.Cy.Ala'59.Ala'62
2913 Overton Rd, Birmingham, AL *35223*
Ollivier MR & MRS Jacques M (Shirley D Carse)
Mon'69.Cl'79.Brest'78 . . of
☎ (011-33) 33-53-62-52 . . Domaine de Beaurepaire, 50690 Martinvast,
France
☎ (011-33) 98-26-21-72 . . Kerlouantec, 29160 Crozon, France

Olmi MR Eugene J JR—⚓ . . . . MISS Natalie S—at 4101 Dunwoody Club Dv, Dunwoody, GA *30338*	☎ (703) 329-1085 2100 Windsor Rd, Alexandria, VA *22307*

Olmstead MR & MRS William W (Higgins—Marillyn M Maxted)
CtCol'40.M.Rcp.Dth'38 . . of
☎ (410) 778-5184 . . 438 Heron Point, Chestertown, MD *21620*
☎ (410) 275-1246 . . ''Mt Harmon'' Earleville, MD *21919*
Olmstead DR Charles M—Ark'69
Rte 1, Box 186A, Tazewell, VA *24651*
Olmsted MRS Conway H (Mary E Johnston) On.Cas.Fy.
☎ (847) 234-2246 . . 1086 Valley Rd, Lake Forest, IL *60045-2968*

Olmsted MR & MRS Garrett S (Hope T McCurdy) Rdc'68.H'68.H'76 . . . . MR John B 3d—H'94—at 1400 Narrow Lane, Johnson City, TN *37604* . . . . JUNIORS MR Charles M—at Phillips Exeter . . . . . JUNIORS MR James B	☎ (540) 988-6948 Crabtree Farm, Rte 1, Box 605, Tazewell, VA *24651*

Olmsted MR Jeffrey S—Y'76
15 W 64 St, New York, NY *10023*
Olmsted MISS Mary M
☎ (703) 527-1616 . . 2136 N Military Rd, Arlington, VA *22207*

Olmsted MR & MRS Robert G (Louise MacCracken) V'32.Cly.Y'31.H'33 . . . . MISS (DR) Nancy—V'60.Y'69—at 6004 Vista de la Mesa, La Jolla, CA *92037*	☎ (561) 220-0637 1469 SW Shoreline Dv, Palm City, FL *34990*
Olmsted MR Robert MacC—Au.Pr.Ri.P'63.Cl'65 . . MISS Alexandra MacC—P'94—at 166 Máy Dèn, Chuong Duong, Hanoi, Vietnam	☎ (212) TR6-8668 1100 Park Av, New York, NY *10128*

Olney MR John C—H'51.Cal'94
☎ (310) 392-6650 . . 2512 Beverly Av, Santa Monica, CA *90405*
Olney MISS Katrina—ColbyS'84
☎ (914) 241-6337 . . PO Box 713, Bedford Hills, NY *10507*

Olney MR & MRS Richard 3d (Linda Paul) Ey.Sm.Ny.Chi. . . . . MISS Robin P . . . . MR Alexander D . . . . MRS Richard JR (Isabel F Potter) Ncd.	☎ (617) 631-8884 13 Goldthwait Rd, Marblehead, MA *01945*

Olney MR Richard D (Richard 3d) . . . . Married at Concord, MA
Nichols MISS Katherine W (Samuel Q) . . . . Jun 29'96

Olney MR & MRS William S (Rogers—Diana S Forbes) Cy.Cw.Rv.Hn.H.'46 . . . . MISS Diana S—H'79	☎ (617) 329-5747 10 Longwood Dv, Apt 215, Westwood, MA *02090*

Olsen MR & MRS Burton A JR (Hughes—Mary P Ziel) Cal'57.Cp.Ncd.Cal'52
☎ (916) 682-6188 . . 10808 Chambeau Way, Elk Grove, CA *95624*
Olson MR & MRS Douglas L (Mary K Womrath) Cr'75.Wis'76
☎ (203) 966-7712 . . 229 W Hills Rd, New Canaan, CT *06840*

Olson MR & MRS John F (Elizabeth H Callard) MtH'61.Mt.Bhm.Cal'61.H'64 . . . . MISS Emily M . . . . MR Timothy C . . . . MR Peter J . . . . MR Matthew E . . . . JUNIORS MR Nicholas P	☎ (301) 654-1209 3719 Bradley Lane, Chevy Chase, MD *20815*
Olson DR & MRS Robert M (Megan E Thomas) Dth'79.Pa'89.Yn.Dth'71.Pa'74 . . . . JUNIORS MR Robert H	of ☎ (609)281-7243 181 Canal Rd, RD 1, Princeton, NJ *08540* ☎ (908) 281-7249 ''Stepping Stones'' RD 1, Griggstown, NJ *08540*

Olson MISS Sonjia Martin Goodwin (Robert M) . . . . Born Dec 13'95
Olyphant MRS David (Tatyana Doughty) BMr'70.Rut'73 . . of
☎ (212) 570-9885 . . 210 E 73 St, New York, NY *10021*
☎ (201) 377-3391 . . New Vernon, NJ *07976*

Olyphant MR David—Plg.StA.H.'58 MISS Elgin—at U of Colo Boulder . . . . MISS Flora—at ☎ (406) 285-3296 1200 Buffalo Jump Rd, Three Forks, MT *59752*	☎ (212) 255-4211 145 W 13 St, New York, NY *10011*

O'Malley MISS Alixine F . . see MRS F D Burden

O'Malley MR C Hooker—H'59.Cl'63 . . . . MR Niall H . . . . MR Oisin L . . . . JUNIORS MR M Douglas	☎ (203) 655-8408 25 Rockwell Lane, Darien, CT *06820*
O'Malley MR & MRS Cormac K H (Moira Kennedy) H.'65.Cl'70 . . . . MISS Bergin . . . . JUNIORS MR Conor H—at Pomfret	156 E 79 St, New York, NY *10021*
O'Malley MRS E Campion (Louise R Twining) Pa'93 . . . . MISS Aideen M T	☎ (610) 688-3676 407 St Davids Rd, St Davids, PA *19087*

O'Malley MR Hilaire
☎ (212) 348-0652 . . 401 E 88 St, New York, NY *10128*

O'Malley MR & MRS James JR (Marcella Butler) Cly.P.'32.H'35 . . . . MISS Anne B—Pa'77—at 141 E 89 St, New York, NY *10128* . . . . MR Malcolm B—Ham'66.Syr'72—at ☎ (315) 331-9301 . . 112 Grant St, Newark, NY *14513*	☎ (212) BU8-2060 131 E 69 St, New York, NY *10021*

O'Malley MR & MRS John P (Hutchinson—Margaret L Parlin)
BMr'61.VillaN'89.VillaN'50.CathU'69
☎ (610) 688-5589 . . 64 Crestline Rd, Strafford, PA *19087*
O'Malley MISS Justine B . . see MRS F D Burden

O'Malley MR & MRS Michael A H (Elisabeth W
Peters) Cal'61.CalTech'59.Mich'64 . . . .
  MISS Sara S—Bnd'85 . . . .
  MISS Rachel E—Swth'86 . . . .
  MISS Elizabeth H—Ober'92 . . . .
| 2910 Ashby Av,
Berkeley, CA *94705*

O'Malley MR & MRS Shaun F (S Julia Bernard)
BMr'65.B.Ri.Pc.Pa'59 . . . .
  MISS Sibyl H—at 74 Fayette St, Cambridge, MA
02139 . . . .
  MISS Aine B—at NYU . . . .
| ☎ (215) 247-7785
725 Glengary Rd,
Philadelphia, PA
19118

O'Malley MR W Gresham 3d—Ph.Rc.Cts.Me.K.
Pe.Pa'61 . . . .
  MISS Inez B M—BostColl'91—at
  ☎ (307) 672-3198 . . 318 W Burkitt St, Sheridan,
WY *82801* . . . .
  MR W Gresham 4th—M'vian'93 . . . .
  MR Andrew W . . . .
| ☎ (610) MU8-4248
''Hickory Hall''
Ithan, PA *19085*

O'Mara MR & MRS John M (Margot Murray)
Man'vl'58.B.P'49 . . . .
  MISS Deirdre M . . . .
| ☎ (203) 661-4193
623 Lake Av,
Greenwich, CT
06830

O'Neil MR & MRS George P (Oliver—Constance C
Hillman) Rr.Edg.Ac.Y'36 . . . .
  CDR James H Oliver—USN. . . . .
| ☎ (412) 741-4771
Spanish Tract,
Sewickley, PA
15143

O'Neil MR & MRS J Pierce (Ashley M Lickle)
Va'82.Bost'84.Bgt.BostColl'80
  ☎ (203) 966-6025 . . 370 Wahackme Rd, New Canaan, CT *06840*

O'Neil MR & MRS James M (Anne Kennedy) Man'vl'51.Cs.H.'50
  ☎ (212) 289-4827 . . 60 E 96 St, New York, NY *10128*

O'Neil MR John H—StBrieuc'51 . . . .
  MISS Sandra P . . . .
  MR John 3d . . . .
  MR Gordon P . . . .
| ☎ (561) 395-3223
2408 E Maya Palm
Dv, Boca Raton, FL
33432

O'Neill MR & MRS Bertram L (Lea—E Jane Jordan)
Rc.Ph.Sg.Myf.W.Cs.Ac.P'42 . . . .
  MISS Jane J Lea—at ☎ (508) 487-0234
  Box 744, Sylvan Lane, Truro, MA *02666* . . . .
| of ☎ (215)242-3800
8703 Seminole Av,
Philadelphia, PA
19118-3707
☎ (207) 796-2908
Munson Island,
Grand Lake Stream,
ME *04637*

O'Neill MR & MRS Bertram L JR (Thrall—Debra A Drashpil)
Ga'73.Ga'76.Rc.Rr.Myf.Rol'72
  ☎ (610) 793-3256 . . ''Brandybend'' 1573 Camp Linden Rd,
West Chester, PA *19382*

O'Neill MR & MRS George D (Abby R Milton) Ck.Pr.Km.Ncd.H.'50
  ☎ (516) 922-6144 . . 200 Sunset Rd, Oyster Bay, NY *11771*

O'Neill MR & MRS George D JR (Amy E Whittlesey) Bhm.Ny.
  ☎ (941) 676-2992 . . Mountain Lake, Lake Wales, FL *33859*

O'Neill MR & MRS Grover JR (Mackay—Elizabeth H MacLean)
Pr.Cly.H'44 . . of
  ☎ (212) 308-0625 . . 200 E 66 St, New York, NY *10021*
  ☎ (516) 922-5771 . . 10 Shutter Lane, Oyster Bay, NY *11771*

O'Neill DR Hugh—Me.Cts.P'45.Pa'54 . . . .
  MISS Maria L . . . .
| ☎ (215) 928-9168
226 Pine St,
Philadelphia, PA
19106-4314

O'Neill MRS Kathryn D (Kathryn Dunscombe) Cly.
  ☎ (212) 421-0220 . . 200 E 66 St, New York, NY *10021*

O'Neill MR & MRS W Paul JR (Caroline K Slutter)
V'42.P'38 . . . .
  MISS Phebe W . . . .
| ☎ (202) 244-9377
2940 Chain Bridge
Rd NW,
Washington, DC
20016

Oppedahl MR & MRS John F (Gillian Coyro) Wayne'78.Cal'67.Cl'68
  ☎ (602) 952-8546 . . 4565 E Lafayette Blvd, Phoenix, AZ *85018*

Oppenheimer MR & MRS Jesse H (Susan Rosenthal)
Ws'45.A.Ariz'39.H'42 . . of
  ☎ (210) 826-5809 . . 312 E Hermosa Dv, San Antonio, TX *78212*
  ☎ (210) 224-2855 . . ''Halycion Place'' Pearsall, TX *78206*

Oppersdorff MR & MRS Anthony T (Goodale—
Whitney C Wing) SL'61.Cl'65.Cl'71 . . . .
  JUNIORS MR M Wing Goodale—at Colo Coll .
| ☎ (207) 763-3664
Box 606, RR 2,
Lincolnville, ME
04849

Oppersdorff MR Mathias
  ☎ (401) 783-5389 . . ''Hawk Hill'' PO Box 590, Wakefield,
RI *02880-0590*

Oppmann MR & MRS Harvey G (Patricia H Coakley)
Briar'72.Cv.Rr.Un.O'69 . . . .
  MR Justin C—at Georgetown . . . .
  JUNIORS MISS Alexandra F . . . .
  JUNIORS MR Patrick P—at West'n Reserve Acad .
| of ☎ (216)423-3500
Sunshine Farm,
Foxboro Rd,
Gates Mills, OH
44040
☎ (242) 333-2075
''Blue Ruin''
Harbour Island,
Bahamas

Oram MRS James W (Kathryn L Murphy) Me.M.Cnt.Ac.
  ☎ (610) 525-6605 . . 74 Pasture Lane, Apt 229, Bryn Mawr, PA *19010*

Oram MRS Joan S (Joan B Shippee)
  ☎ (410) 745-9415 . . 708 East Side Dv, St Michaels, MD *21663*

Oram MR Peter D—H.'60.H'63
  ☎ (212) 873-4304 . . 185 West End Av, Apt 1B, New York, NY *10023*

Orbegoso MR & MRS Alfonso G (Margaretta M
Keyes) Sth'62.Lima'62.Cl'68 . . . .
  MR Ricardo G—Carl'93—at 5669 Camden Place,
Goleta, CA *93117* . . . .
  MR Alfonso K G—at U of Iowa . . . .
  MR Geoffrey G—at U of NH . . . .
| ☎ (617) 444-8126
39 Barbara Rd,
Needham, MA
02192

Orcutt MRS Robert S (Elizabeth M Lummis) . . . . . .
  MISS Anne M—at 122 Palapu St, Kailua, HI
96734 . . . .
  MR William P—at 624A Kalolina St, Kailua, HI
96734 . . . .
| ☎ (203) 453-3389
457 Podunk Rd,
Guilford, CT *06437*

Ordway MRS Samuel H (Anna Wheatland) Cs.Ncd.
  MISS Ellen—at ☎ (612) 589-1648 . . 915 W 4 St,
Morris, MN *56267* . . . .
| ☎ (212) 288-2336
155 E 72 St,
New York, NY
10021

O'Rear MRS William G (Jane Johnson) Aub'58
  ☎ (334) 271-1904 . . 2123 Vaughn Lane, Montgomery, AL *36106*

O'Rear MR & MRS William G JR (Rebecca B Marley)
1479 Watson Av, Montgomery, AL *36106*
O'Reilly MR & MRS Brian J JR (Rebecca T Ecton) Van'91.Van'91
☎ (504) 891-2045 . . 1226 Napoleon Av, New Orleans, LA *70115*
O'Reilly MISS Catherine W . . . . | ☎ (314) 361-4985
MISS Jane . . . . | 5272 Westminster
Place, St Louis, MO
63108
O'Reilly MR & MRS Gerald A (Mary Seton Lindsay) | ☎ (860) 567-3243
Sth'58.NotreD'47 . . . . | 199 Meadow St,
MISS Patricia E—Dick'81 . . . . | Box 1156,
MISS Priscilla L—Geo'82 . . . . | Litchfield, CT *06759*
MR Gerald A JR—Y'83 . . . . |
MR William F B . . . . |
MR Peter L—at Notre Dame . . . . |
O'Reilly MR J Archer—Cc.Hn.H'29
☎ (314) 997-2875 . . 9 Ladue Hills, St Louis, MO *63132*
O'Reilly MRS Mary E (Sowinski—Mary E O'Reilly) Nu'91
☎ (203) 849-9747 . . 91 Fawn Ridge Lane, Norwalk, CT *06851-1138*
O'Reilly MR & MRS Maurice F (Harper—Dorothy A | ☎ (540) 672-2676
Riley) V'45 . . . . | 13097 Hackberry
MR Duncan T Harper—Box 5042, | Rd, Orange, VA
Santa Barbara, CA *93150* . . . . | *22960*
O'Reilly MRS Nicholas S (Sutton—Trudy Hawkins) | ☎ (214) 824-3032
JUNIORS MISS Megan C . . . . | 4826 Swiss Av,
MR Cameron Sutton . . . . | Dallas, TX *75204*
O'Reilly MR Noël S—Cc.Myf.Cw.H'31.H'33
☎ (214) 827-0002 . . 4826 Swiss Av, Dallas, TX *75204*
O'Reilly MR & MRS Terence J (Katharine van D | of ☎ (415)364-2224
Wallace) Bhm.Bur.Tcy.Cal'69 . . . . | 119 Selby Lane,
MR Tobin C | Atherton, CA *94027*
JUNIORS MR Matthew W . . . . | ☎ (702) 749-5435
"The Rock Pile"
PO Box 503,
Glenbrook, NV
89413
Oriel MRS S Parsons (Sarah L Parsons) DelB.Cly.Ht.Lm.Cda.
☎ (212) 759-8060 . . 10 Mitchell Place, New York, NY *10017*
Jan 1 . . ☎ (561) 278-0705 . . 86 MacFarlane Dv, Delray Beach,
FL *33483*
O'Riley MR & MRS J Michael (Lynn McB Beach) | ☎ (714) 645-0859
JCar'57 . . . . | 1221 W Coast
MSRS Michael McB & Nicholas G R—at | H'way, Apt 420,
3024 N Evergreen St, Phoenix, AZ *85014* . . . . . | Newport Beach, CA
92663-5001
Orlandini MRS Edward (Elizabeth P Mason) Hn.
☎ (202) 965-3256 . . 1659—34 St NW, Washington, DC *20007*
Orlowski MR & MRS David W (Hannah L Wise) Aub'89.WakeF'87.Ga'91
☎ (912) 436-1116 . . 119 Lavender Lane, Leesburg, GA *31763*
Orme MR & MRS Edgar J JR (Nancy L Luttrell) V'39.Cvc.Mt.Sl . . .of
☎ (703) 777-2143 . . "Greenfield Farm" 41284 Hogeland Mill Rd,
Leesburg, VA *20175*
☎ (268) 460-4168 . . "Palo Santo" Mill Reef Club, St Johns, Antigua

Orme MRS James B Lockwood (Gentry—Orme— | ☎ (561) 833-4383
De Veau—Violet D Young) So.Evg.Myf.Ncd. | 315 S Lake Dv,
Dar. . . . . | Palm Beach, FL
MR William F McWhinney—at 938—5 St, | *33480*
Apt 6, Santa Monica, CA *90403* . . . . |
Orme MR & MRS Nathaniel L (Mildred A Reynolds) Cvc.SCar'69
☎ (301) 469-5490 . . 7622 Royal Dominion Dv, Bethesda, MD *20817*
O'Rourk DR & MRS Thomas R (Maria N Digges) | ☎ (410) 433-9060
Cy.Ncd.Md'56.Md'62 . . . . | 5605 St Albans
MISS Maria Digges—Md'91—*see* | Way, Baltimore,
Dilatory Domiciles . . . . | MD *21212*
Orr MR & MRS Charles P (Paula G Welles) V'48.Pg.Rr.Y'49
☎ (412) 682-6105 . . 5452 Aylesboro Av, Pittsburgh, PA *15217*
Orr MR & MRS Henry S 2d (Nannette B Foss) | ☎ (914) 232-3334
Sa.Pa'62 . . . . | Holly Hill Lane,
MR John C—at 307 Fountain St, New Haven, CT | Katonah, NY *10536*
06515 . . . . |
Orr MRS Isaac C (Mary C Sloan) Sth'25
☎ (314) 567-7958 . . Gatesworth, 1 McKnight Place, St Louis,
MO *63124*
Orr MISS Jean A—Bnd'79 . . of
☎ (203) 531-6179 . . 18 Connecticut Av, Greenwich, CT *06830*
☎ (518) 854-3287 . . "Todd Hunter Farm" Robinson Rd, Shushan,
NY *12873*
Orr MR John C 3d—Br'56.Clark'66
☎ (914) 276-2211 . . 24C Heritage Hills, Somers, NY *10589*
Orr MR & MRS P Welles (Ann S Young) Y'80.Pg.Rr.Denis'82
☎ (202) 342-7130 . . 4823 Reservoir Rd NW, Washington, DC *20007*
Orr MR & MRS Robert A (Marjorie L Bolton) Fw.Ac.Ncd.Cal'42.H'47
☎ (215) 242-2711 . . 600 St Andrews Rd, Philadelphia, PA *19118*
Orr MR & MRS William Pratt (Sullivan—Pauline Gerli) Bcs.Cs.Okla'40 . . of
☎ (212) 759-6358 . . 200 E 66 St, Apt B804, New York, NY *10021*
☎ (407) 876-0037 . . 6029 Lexington Park, Orlando, FL *32819*
Orrick MR & MRS A Downey (Marjorie H Soule) | ☎ (415) 391-3033
Pcu.Sfg.Tcy.Y'40 . . . . | 850 Powell St,
MR Andrew D JR . . . . | Apt 803,
MR Winsor S . . . . | San Francisco, CA
MR Murray S . . . . | *94108*
MR Samuel W—DU'82 . . . . |
Orrick MR DeCourcy W 3d—Va'73
☎ (404) 816-9179 . . 1180 Kendrick Rd NE, Apt A, Atlanta, GA *30319*
Orrick MR & MRS Peter M (Cynthia S Cotton) Vt'77.Syr'71
☎ (203) 834-2429 . . 100 Indian Hill Rd, Wilton, CT *06897*
Orrick MR & MRS Stuart S (Kathleen W Young) Gi.
☎ (804) 980-9350 . . 250 Pantops Mountain Rd, Charlottesville,
VA *22901*
Orrick MR & MRS William H JR (Rogers—Suzanne | ☎ (415) 567-8324
V Bensinger) BMr'45.Bhm.Pcu.Sfy.Bur.Tcy. | 250 Locust St,
Y'37.Cal'41 . . . . | San Francisco, CA
MISS Diana V Rogers—at ☎ (510) 548-8433 | *94118*
20 Stonewall Rd, Berkeley, CA *94705* . . . . . . |
Orth MR John C—CalW'72
☎ (602) 998-5504 . . 4839 E Horseshoe Rd, Paradise Valley, AZ *85253*
Orth MR & MRS Philip W (Mariette R Clark) Aht'40.H'42
☎ (414) 764-5500 . . 2623 N Terrace Av, Milwaukee, WI *53211*

Orthwein MR & MRS Adolphus B JR (Judith A Baring-Gould) Y'65 .... ☎ (404) 355-1451
MR Adolphus B 3d—Cr'91 .... 4647 Polo Lane
NW, Atlanta, GA
30339

Orthwein MR David T—Cysl.Cr'81 .. see D D Metcalfe

Orthwein MR & MRS James B JR (Jane R Ross) Wash'76.Rcsl.
☎ (561) 243-0567 .. 3500 Polo Dv, Gulf Stream, FL *33483*

Orthwein MR & MRS Peter B (Beverly Miller) ☎ (203) 629-9540
Pratt'77.Cr'68 .... Conyers Farm,
JUNIORS MISS Jennifer .... 154 Guards Rd,
Greenwich, CT
06831

Osborn MR & MRS Charles S (Lynn Rajacich)
P'79.H'84.Ub.P'77.Pa'86.H'92
66 Watson Rd, Belmont, MA *02178*

Osborn MR F Henry 4th (Frederick H 3d) ..... Married at Garrison, NY
Nelson MISS Krista L (Thomas) .... Jun 22'96

Osborn MR & MRS F Henry 4th (Krista L Nelson) Rut'95
Tabor Academy, Front St, Marion, MA *02738*

Osborn MRS Frederick H JR (Anne DeW Pell) Dc.P.
☎ (914) 424-3710 .. Snake Hill Rd, RR 1, Box 492, Garrison,
NY *10524*

Osborn MR & MRS Frederick H 3d (Anne H de P ☎ (914) 424-3683
Todd) C.Ny.P.Colby'71 ⚓ "Cat Rock"
MISS Alice-Elisabeth Van C—at Wellesley ..... PO Box 347,
JUNIORS MR Graham L—at Tabor Acad........ Garrison, NY
10524-0347

Osborn MR & MRS Henry C 3d (Mary W ☎ (610) 458-5912
Stephenson) Cry.Rc.Pa'66.Pa'68 .... 124 Nantmeal Rd,
MISS Mary W—P'cpia'93 .... Glenmoore, PA
MR David S *19343*

Osborn MRS James E 2d (Taggart—Dorothy J Harris) Ws'49.Csn.
☎ (203) 869-1909 .. 15 Pinecroft Rd, Greenwich, CT *06830*

Osborn MRS James W (Catherine A Bill) BMr'35
☎ (860) 435-0197 .. Noble Horizons, Salisbury, CT *06068*

Osborn MR John B—Dth'88
☎ (212) 866-8363 .. 316 W 98 St, Apt 5, New York, NY *10025*

Osborn MR & MRS (DR) John J JR (Emilie H Sisson) Rdc'69.H'67
☎ (415) 282-1629 .. 14 Fair Oaks St, San Francisco, CA *94110*

Osborn MRS Katherine Page (Case—Edwards— ☎ (617) 523-5095
Katherine P Osborn) Chi.Ncd. .... 10 Emerson Place,
MISS Dana H—Conn'90—at ☎ (617) 367-1180 Boston, MA *02114*
9 Hawthorne Place, Apt 11K, Boston, MA *02114*

Osborn MR & MRS O'Neill (Michelle Pynchon) Sth'48.Cal'41
☎ (610) 642-1535 .. 751 Millbrook Lane, Haverford, PA *19041*

Osborn CAPT & MRS Philip R (Caryl M Elliott) Sar.USN'29
☎ (410) 224-0720 .. 8206 River Crescent Dv, Annapolis, MD *21401*

Osborn MR & MRS Steele Bartley (Gogolak— ☎ (612) 475-0304
Harriet G Van Kennen) D.Sm.Ncd.Dth'61 ..... 360 Orono Orchard
JUNIORS MR Bowen B .... Rd, Wayzata, MN
55391

Osborn MRS Weld (Ada R Weld)
☎ (203) 966-8416 .. 6 Fieldcrest Rd, New Canaan, CT *06840*

Osborn MASTER William de Peyster (g—MRS L Todd Ambler)...... Born
Dec 11'95

Osborn MRS William H JR (Ryus—Stewart—Barry Martin) Pr.Cly.
☎ (516) 676-0564 .. "Billy Goat Hill" Chicken Valley Rd, Box 545,
Locust Valley, NY *11560*

Osborne MISS Elizabeth
☎ (617) 497-5135 .. 9 Chauncy St, Apt 52, Cambridge, MA *02138*

Osborne MR & MRS Frederik R-L (May Minturn ☎ (315) 252-6533
Sedgwick) Tufts'49.Rc.C.H'50.Syr'60 .... 32 Owasco St,
MISS Elizabeth E—H'80.Cl'88—at Auburn, NY *13021*
☎ (212) 866-5378 .. 246 W 106 St, Apt 4W,
New York, NY *10025* ....

Osborne MRS H Thomas (Alice Manegold) Cly.
☎ (011-44-171) 351-3160 .. 46B Redcliffe Gardens,
London SW10 9HB, England

Osborne MRS Lithgow (Sara T Tenney)
☎ (413) 458-3836 .. 10 Porter St, Williamstown, MA *01267*

Osborne MR Lithgow 2d—SL'84
☎ (212) 353-1664 .. 168 Av B, New York, NY *10009*

Osborne DR & MRS (DR) Maurice M JR (Marion T Shikamura)
Stan'51.Stan'56.Tvb.H'45.Cl'47
☎ (415) 948-9103 .. 26050 Torello Lane, Los Altos Hills, CA *94022*

Osborne MR & MRS Minturn S (R Starr Collins) Y.'85.Ncd.Ken'84.Syr'89
☎ (315) 252-4121 .. 111 South St, Auburn, NY *13021*

Osborne MR & MRS Raymond B (McReynolds—Dorothy C Fox)
Me.M.Gi.Nott'44
☎ (610) MI2-0113 .. 141 Rose Lane, Box 116, Haverford,
PA *19041-1724*

Osborne MRS Richard (Ames—Olga de Bottari)
☎ (408) 624-4160 .. PO Box 1652, Pebble Beach, CA *93953*

Osborne MR Stanley de J—Ri.B.H'26 .. of
☎ (212) 288-3404 .. 1 East End Av, New York, NY *10021*
☎ (802) 533-2364 .. E Craftsbury Rd, Greensboro, VT *05841*

Osborne MR W Irving JR—On.Cho.Y'26
☎ (847) 234-1404 .. 347 Bluffs Edge Dv, Lake Forest, IL *60045*

Osgood MRS Alice C K (Keeble—Alice O Collins) ☎ (410) 226-5255
GeoW'72 .... 4340 Bachelors
MR G Hudson—at U of Pa .... Point, Oxford, MD
21654

Osgood MR & MRS Edward H (Peters—Virginia W Cook)
Sbc.Un.Sm.My.Chi.Cda.H'38
☎ (508) 468-2488 .. 675 Bay Rd, Hamilton, PO Box 2118,
South Hamilton, MA *01982-0118*

Osgood MR & MRS Edward H JR (Bunker—Antonia T O'Riley) Exy. ⚓
☎ (860) 767-2260 .. PO Box 281, Essex, CT *06426*

Osgood MR Hamilton—Cy.Ox'28
☎ (617) 566-0266 .. 12 Kingsbury Rd, Chestnut Hill, MA *02167*

Osgood MR & MRS Thomas H (Dorothy B Hull) Geo'86.Ty'76
106 Sheridan Av, Takoma Park, MD *20912*

Osgood MR & MRS William B (Nancy R Patton) ☎ (802) 649-3416
Sb.Sm.Cyb.Chi.H'49 .... PO Box 331,
MR David S .... Norwich, VT *05055*
MR Christopher P ....

O'Shaughnessy MISS Elise M—H.'80
☎ (212) 932-1301 .. 610 W 110 St, New York, NY *10025*

O'Shaughnessy MR & MRS James P (Melissa L Walker)
StThos'82.Sm.Minn'83
☎ (203) 661-2547 .. 4 Jennifer Lane, Cos Cob, CT *06807*

O'Shaughnessy MRS Lynn (Mosle—C Lynn O'Shaughnessy) . . . .
  MR Douglas C Mosle—Drew'93—at
  ☎ (802) 244-5627 . . 170 S Main St,
  Waterbury, VT 05676 . . . .
| ☎ (609) 924-5972 269 Snowden Lane, Princeton, NJ 08540

O'Shaughnessy MR Phillips P—Md.H'69
1102 Terrace Glen, Baltimore, MD 21210-1200

O'Shaughnessy MR Robert M . . see MRS S W Miles

O'Shaughnessy JUNIORS MR William A . . see MRS S W Miles

O'Shea MR Sean T—Rcp.Pc.F&M'70 . . of
  ☎ (303) 604-6235 . . PO Box 20430, Boulder, CO 80308-3430
  ☎ (970) 544-0806 . . 160 Pitkin Mesa Dv, Aspen, CO 81611

Oshei MRS Mary B (Dillaway—Mary E Bayliss) . . .
  MISS Mary E B—OWes'78 . . . .
  MR William B—Buf.
  MISS Kimberly H—StLaw'95—at
  ☎ (716) 885-8089 . . 201 Cleveland Av, Buffalo, NY 14222
| of ☎ (716)834-0360 360 Depew Av, Buffalo, NY 14214
☎ (941) 472-3915 Middle Gulf Dv, Sanibel Island, FL 33957

Oshei MR & MRS Robert C JR (Mary M Magee)
  Barat'71.St.Hob'69 . . . .
  MISS Mary E P . . . .
  MISS Claire M F . . . .
  JUNIORS MISS M Elizabeth B . . . .
  JUNIORS MR Robert C 3d . . . .
| ☎ (716) 833-6549 82 Morris Av, Buffalo, NY 14214

Osler MISS Lois B—BMr'79.Va'84
3925 Huntington St NW, Washington, DC 20015

Osmond MR & MRS Arthur S (Dorothy E Wilson) Cin'41
  ☎ (513) 871-4449 . . 14 Far Hills Dv, Cincinnati, OH 45208

Ostergard MR & MRS Derek E (Lillian H Hoffman)
GeoW'73.B.Cly.AmU'74
  ☎ (212) 750-9837 . . 405 E 56 St, New York, NY 10022

Osterhus MRS Robert J (M Meredith Moffitt)
  Wheat'61.Csh. . . . .
  MISS Elizabeth T—Ty'89—at ☎ (847) 492-9814
  634 Sherman Av, Apt 1S, Evanston, IL 60202 . .
  MR Edward M E—Ck.Denis'86—at
  ☎ (212) 570-6846 . . 12 E 86 St, New York, NY 10028 . . . .
| ☎ (516) 427-2947 18 Garden Court, Huntington, NY 11743

Osterhus MR Robert J—Csh.Y.'61.Mit'63
  ☎ (516) 624-8926 . . 62 Private Rd, Mill Neck, NY 11765

Ostermann MISS Katharine H—Sl.
  ☎ (703) 356-3906 . . 1052 Waverly Way, McLean, VA 22101

Ostheimer MR & MRS Anthony McI (Mary B Parke)
  H'57 . . . .
  MISS Caroline P—at 84-770 Upena, Waianae, HI 96792 . . . .
  MR Richard K—at 420 E Broadway, Missoula, MT 59807 . . . .
  MR William B—at 246 Ridgeway, Lolo, MT 59847 . . . .
| ☎ (406) 745-4125 Moss Ranch, Rte 1, Box 145, St Ignatius, MT 59865

Ostheimer MR & MRS J Gibson (Debra M McCormick) Ariz'91
  ☎ (715) 268-4114 . . 1326—140 Av, Balsam Lake, WI 54810

Ostheimer MR & MRS John M (Nancy J Cushing)
Man'vl'60.Myf.Dar.Y'60.Y'67 . . . .
  MR William A . . . .
| 3615 Canada Goose Crossing, Racine, WI 53403

Ostrom MRS Vincent F (Davol—Roesler—Dorothy Miller)
  ☎ (203) 869-3109 . . 51 Mooreland Rd, Greenwich, CT 06831

Oswald MRS Clinton (Pile—Audrey G Clinton)
  Srb.Cly. . . . .
  MISS Diana S T—at ☎ (212) 724-5533
  321 W 90 St, Apt 5B, New York, NY 10024 . . .
| of ☎ (401)849-7246 ''Treehaven'' Ledge Rd, Newport, RI 02840
☎ (212) 439-9769 163 E 81 St, New York, NY 10028

Oswald MR & MRS David D C (Abigail F Rowe)
  ☎ (203) 329-9559 . . 674 Den Rd, Stamford, CT 06903

Oswald MR & MRS Frank G 3d (Laurinda P Middleton) Nrr.RISD'79 . . of
  ☎ (212) 967-4400 . . 448 W 37 St, Apt 11B, New York, NY 10018
  ☎ (520) 398-2883 . . Reventone Ranch, Box 504, Amado, AZ 85645

Otis MR & MRS Elliott N (Jane Dielhenn)
  ColbyS'63.P'57 . . . .
  MISS Wendy M—at 6 W 90 St, New York, NY 10024 . . . .
  MISS Marcia L . . . .
| ☎ (847) 272-5122 1216 Western Av, Northbrook, IL 60062

Otis MRS J Sanford (Spencer—Violetta L Berry) On.Ncd . . . of
  ☎ (207) 772-6211 . . 45 Eastern Promenade, Apt 5E, Portland, ME 04101
  ☎ (207) 781-5574 . . ''Fairways'' 17 Foreside Rd, Falmouth Foreside, ME 04105-1925

O'Toole MR & MRS John J 3d (Suzanne Black) Geo'77.GeoW'77.CathU'80
  ☎ (630) 920-8046 . . 424 N Garfield Av, Hinsdale, IL 60521

Ott MR & MRS James Forgan (Edna Cassinerio)
  Cas.Br'58.Nw'61 . . . .
  MISS Emily F—at Chicago, IL . . . .
  MR Michael F—at Evanston, IL . . . .
| ☎ (847) 234-3872 25 Warrington Dv, Lake Bluff, IL 60044-1322

Ott MR & MRS John Nash 3d (Brenda A Lees) . . . . .
  MISS Letitia G . . . .
  MR Anthony E . . . .
| ☎ (201) 376-6558 35 Barnsdale Rd, Short Hills, NJ 07078

Ott MRS John R (Louise Parsons) Gm.
  ☎ (610) 525-2565 . . 74 Pasture Lane, Apt 121, Bryn Mawr, PA 19010

Ott MR & MRS Lambert B (Suzanne Austin) Me.P'44.P'49
  ☎ (610) MI2-6024 . . 135 Cheswold Lane, Haverford, PA 19041

Ott MR & MRS Robert B (Mary P Kelley) Ty'48.Qc.Cm.
  ☎ (513) 871-1802 . . 2943 Alpine Terr, Cincinnati, OH 45208

Ott MR Wendel Fentress—Rcch.
  ☎ (619) 233-0235 . . Box 124799, San Diego, CA 92112-4799

Otter MR & MRS Richard C (Sibyl A Wiper)
  Stan'57.Bhm.Fr.Cal'56 . . . .
  MISS Sibyl A—at 117 Mallorca Av, San Francisco, CA 94123 . . . .
| ☎ (415) 435-0563 69 Beach Rd, Belvedere, CA 94920

Ottley MR & MRS E Granger (Smith—Judith Morton)
  Wms'51 . . . .
  MR Garrett M Smith—at ☎ (212) 535-0933
  510 E 85 St, New York, NY 10028 . . . .
| ☎ (207) 655-2947 132 Mountain Rd, PO Box 783, Raymond, ME 04071

Ottley MISS Heidi H—Vt'90
  ☎ (208) 726-9447 . . PO Box 1444, Sun Valley, ID 83353

Ottley MR Henry G—Hartw'79
170 W 81 St, Apt 7B, New York, NY 10024

Ottley MR & MRS Philip G (Glenna R Holleran) CtCol'59 ⚓
☎ (561) 546-5465 . . on board Noble Falcon'' PO Box 8530,
Hobe Sound, FL *33475*

Ottley MR Philip G JR—Vt'93
☎ (208) 726-9447 . . PO Box 1444, Sun Valley, ID *83353*

Ottman MR & MRS John B (Joan S Kennedy) | ☎ (203) 869-6176
Sth'51.Cly.Y'44.H'47 . . . . | 10 North St,
MISS Josephine K—Mid'77—at | Greenwich, CT
☎ (609) 924-8864 . . 154 Prospect Av, Princeton, | *06830*
NJ *08540* . . . . |

Otto MRS George J (Marie Kendrick) Cal'28.Pcu.Sfg.Fr.
☎ (415) FI6-2116 . . 2701 Pierce St, San Francisco, CA *94123*

Otto MR & MRS John 3d (Deans—Sallie G Kenefick)
☎ (716) 885-5054 . . 778 W Ferry St, Apt 1, Buffalo, NY *14222-1678*

Otto Marie Luise—Cal'59.Dom'81.Fr.
☎ (415) 346-1206 . . 1070 Green St, Apt 602, San Francisco, CA *94133*

Otto MR & MRS Robert E JR (Mary T Jones) Swb'82.Nd.Va'85
☎ (314) 721-7087 . . 3 Harcourt Dv, St Louis, MO *63105-3034*

Ottum MR Philip K—Ore'73 . . . . | ☎ (503) 226-0433
JUNIORS MISS Katherine McI . . . . | 2377 NW Overton
| St, Portland, OR
| *97210*

Oudin MR C Folger JR—Wms'51.H'59
☎ (561) 288-3873 . . Mariner Sands, 5270 SE Burning Tree Circle,
Stuart, FL *34997*

Oughton MR James H JR . . . . Died at
Kankakee, IL Jun 11'96

Ours JUNIORS MR Adam S . . see M Everett JR

Ours MISS Alice C . . see M Everett JR

Ours MR John W JR . . see M Everett JR

Ourusoff MRS Leonide (Katherine Carlisle)
☎ (603) 526-6332 . . Burpee Hill Rd, New London, NH *03257*

Outerbridge MR & MRS David E (Lilias L Hollins) | ☎ (207) 338-2530
Nu'57.H'55 . . . . | Snow Valley Farm,
MR Benoni L—at ☎ (212) 662-9722 | RD 1, Box 673,
510 W 110 St, New York, NY *10025* . . . . | Belfast, ME *04915*
MR Oliver W—at ☎ (207) 734-6543 |
PO Box 201, Islesboro, ME *04848* . . . . |
MR Thomas B—at ☎ (212) 982-5974 |
430 E 9 St, New York, NY *10009* . . . . |
MR Joshua E . . . . |

Outerbridge MISS Elizabeth W (McMenamin—Elizabeth W Outerbridge)
NYSID'82.Ac.
☎ (215) 242-6560 . . 109 W Willow Grove Av, Chestnut Hill, PA *19118*

Outerbridge MR & MRS Yeaton D (Betsey Coste) | of ☎ (441)293-0822
Rby. . . . . | ''Mermaid Cottage''
MISS Louisa Y—Tufts'89 . . . . | 46 N Shore Rd,
| Hamilton Parish
| FL 04, Bermuda
| ☎ (401) 423-1710
| ''Clove Hitch''
| 28 Hawthorne Rd,
| Jamestown, RI
| *02835*

Outhwaite MRS Leonard (Lucille Conrad) Srb.Unn.
☎ (401) 847-5656 . . ''Beachmound'' Bellevue Av, Newport, RI *02840*

Outten MISS Amanda B (Ewald—Amanda B Outten) SFr'83
☎ (415) 459-3579 . . 333 C St, San Rafael, CA *94901*

Outwater MR & MRS John O (Alice H Davidson)
V'51.Vt'74.UnInst'90.Snc.Hl.Chi.Camb'43.Mit'50. Camb'76 . . of
☎ (802) 862-2089 . . 62 Overlake Park, Burlington, VT *05401-4012*
☎ (802) 425-2012 . . ''Pebble Beach'' Thompson's Point, Charlotte,
VT *05445*

Outwater MR Thomas D—Wheat'93
☎ (860) 379-9566 . . ''The Pond House'' 376 Platt Hill Rd, Winchester,
CT *06098*

Ouwerkerk MR & MRS Pieter C (Edith R McLaughlin) Hlns'77
☎ (610) 363-2326 . . 603 French Creek Lane, Chester Springs, PA *19425*

Overaker DR Lewis J—Unb.Cw.Myf.MacMurray'64.Ind'66.OState'71
☎ (603) 536-3916 . . Holderness School, Rte 175, RFD 3, Plymouth,
NH *03264*

Overall MISS (REV) Martha R—Rdc'69.Nu'76.UnTheo'91.H.
☎ (212) 996-5244 . . 345 E 86 St, New York, NY *10028*

Overall MRS Mary Jane O'R (Mary Jane O'Reilly) | ☎ (301) 656-0944
Cvc. . . . . | 119 E Melrose
MR Curtis F B—at U of Ariz . . . . | Court,
| Chevy Chase, MD
| *20815*

Overall CAPT & MRS Sidney R (Hill—Dean Hanly)
USN.Rut'48.Cvc.Cysl.Y'45
☎ (912) 638-4301 . . 134 Alder Circle, St Simons Island, GA *31522*

Overdurff MISS Megan . . see MRS W Cates

Overholser MR & MRS Adrian L (Elizabeth P Ballantine)
Bnd'82.Cl'86.Myf.Ncd.Cda.
☎ (718) 402-1015 . . 828 Gerard Av, Bronx, NY *10451*

Overland MR & MRS Mark Eric (Barbara L Cosgriff) | ☎ (310) 459-4289
Cal'66.Loy'62 . . . . | 515 Chapala Dv,
MISS Christina J . . . . | Pacific Palisades,
MISS Candace M . . . . | CA *90272*
MISS Courtney A . . . . |

Overton MRS J Woodhull (Havemeyer—Joan Blair) T.
☎ (914) 561-6369 . . 78 Balmville Rd, Newburgh, NY *12550*

Overton MR John B (late J Woodhull) . . . . . . Married at San Rafael, CA
Tower MISS Ruth E (late James A) . . . . Aug 10'95

Overton MISS Natalie Elizabeth (g—MRS J Woodhull Overton) . . Born at
Mill Valley, CA May 18'96

Owen MISS Caroline Bright (John E) . . . . Born at
Greenwich, CT Dec 17'95

Owen MR & MRS David J SR (Jean F Malcomson) | ☎ (407) 644-2175
Ncd.Dc.Nw'45 . . . . | 860 Park Av N,
MISS Ruth McK . . . . | Winter Park, FL
MR David J . . . . | *32789*

Owen MR & MRS David R (Adams—Eleanor S Abell)
MdArt'65.MdArt'67.Elk.Mv.Cda.Ncd.Va'37
☎ (410) 825-0259 . . 8028 Thornton Rd, Towson, MD *21204*

Owen MRS Dudley (Lillian M Dudley) Sth'31.Sl.
☎ (202) 338-5837 . . 3015 P St NW, Washington, DC *20007*

Owen BRIG GEN (RET) & MRS Edgar R (Jeffords—H Sidney Dixon)
USAF.Rc.Pkg.Fw.
☎ (717) 278-9240 . . Lake Shore Dv, PO Box 531, Montrose,
PA *18801*

Owen MISS Frances T
☎ (407) 841-7935 . . 514 W Harvard St, Orlando, FL *32804*

Owen MRS Frederick H JR (Dayton—Jeanne P Comey) Sth'47.Dyc.
☎ (561) 978-0911 . . 2727 Tenth Av, Vero Beach, FL *32960*

Owen MRS George H (Sofia I Antuña) . . . . | ☎ (202) 337-1518
MISS Isabella M—StJ'78 . . . . | 3018 P St NW,
| Washington, DC
| *20007*

Owen MISS Helen H
☎ (202) 530-0538 . . 725—24 St NW, Washington, DC *20037*

Owen MR & MRS Hugo A (Sally Waterman) Sth'76.GeoW'76
☎ (508) 462-6766 . . 60 High Rd, Newbury, MA *01951*

Owen MR & MRS John E (Margaret K Harding) Mid'85.Mid'85
☎ (203) 316-8141 . . 2 Briar Brae Rd, Darien, CT *06820-3001*

Owen MR & MRS John G (Hope Henshaw) P'40
☎ (602) 274-1151 . . 2901 E Manor Dv, Phoenix, AZ *85014*

Owen MR & MRS Mitchell (Alma F Chapin) St.
☎ (716) 537-9179 . . 9764 Savage Rd, Holland, NY *14080*

Owen MR Stephen B—Rc.Duke'85
☎ (212) 879-4399 . . 860 Fifth Av, New York, NY *10021*

Owen MR & MRS Stephen C JR (Evelyn D Bates) Rc.Cly.NCar'56
☎ (212) 879-6768 . . 19 E 72 St, New York, NY *10021*

Owen MR & MRS Thomas G (Helena Hitchcock)
☎ (203) 373-6504 . . 3030 Park Av, Apt 6E12, Bridgeport, CT *06604*

Owen MR & MRS William H (Denise Colonna d'Istria)
EcoleNS'78.Unn.StJColl'77 . . of
US Consulate Gen'l, Milan, Italy, Box M, PSC 59, APO AE, *09624*
☎ (011-33-86) 41-13-02 . . "Eyguilles" Commune de Beauvoir, Egleny,
France

Owens MRS Courtenay W (Kulikowski—Courtenay Weems Owens) Cda.
Apartado Postal 1311, Cuernavaca, Morelos 62000, Mexico

Owens MRS Seymour D (Patricia S Donavin)
☎ (704) 859-5130 . . Hillside Farm, 719 Newmarket Rd, Tryon,
NC *28782*

Owens MR & MRS Seymour K (Carol A Falise) OState'65.Jaccard'58
☎ (704) 859-9202 . . "Many Levels" Box 1151, Tryon, NC *28782*

Owings MR George C
☎ (410) 823-5330 . . PO Box 185, Riderwood, MD *21139*

Owings MRS Nathaniel A (Millard—Margaret Wentworth) Mls'34
☎ (408) 667-2254 . . "Wild Bird" Grimes Point, Big Sur, CA *93920*

Owings MRS Robert E (Gwendolyn E Moore)
☎ (410) 889-2412 . . Keswick, 700 W 40 St, Baltimore, MD *21211*

Owsley MR David T—K.H'51.Nu'64
☎ (212) 288-1845 . . 116 E 68 St, New York, NY *10021-5956*

Owsley REV & MRS Randolph Gibson JR (Barbara A | 122 Carlyle Dv,
Jones) SFla'51 | Palm Harbor, FL
MISS Laura A . . . . | *34683*
MISS Barbara A . . . . |
MR R Gibson 3d . . . . |

Owsley MR Richard P (Clark—Alexander—Anne Paul)
☎ (561) 278-0967 . . 790 Andrews Av, Apt G201, Delray Beach,
FL *33483*

Oyler MR & MRS Thomas T (Thayer—Barbara Thornton) Mich'37.Cin'39
☎ (619) 673-1691 . . 18755 W Bernardo Dv, Apt 1049, San Diego,
CA *92127-3011*

P

Pace MR Eric D—C.Y'57.JHop'59
☎ (212) 662-0334 . . 697 West End Av, New York, NY *10025*

Pack MR & MRS Lewis Gerald (Elizabeth B Morgan)
☎ (704) 894-8127 . . Stoney Knoll Farm, Fox Mountain Rd,
PO Box 575, Columbus, NC *28722*

Packard DR & MRS A Gibson JR (Vernon—Mary F | ☎ (410) 822-4737
Reeves) Cy.JHop'50.Md'54.Cl'59 . . . . | 7302 Waverly Island
MISS M Tracy . . . . | Rd, Easton, MD
| *21601*

Packard MISS Elise B . . see B D Jones

Packard MR & MRS George W W (Louise C Burnham) Y'83.Mid'88.Y'87
2920 Jackson St, San Francisco, CA *94115*

Packard MR Kent
☎ (610) 933-4114 . . "Fox Glen" RR 5, Box 297, Malvern,
PA *19355-9651*

Packard MR & MRS Parker W (Smith—Jane F | ☎ (610) 649-3364
deLedesma) Stan'62 . . . . | 17 Llanfair Rd,
MISS Elizabeth W—at Antioch . . . . | Apt 302, Ardmore,
MISS Hillary W Smith—Nu'94 . . . . | PA *19003*

Packard MRS Peter F (Jarmila de Daubek) K.
☎ (212) TR9-7965 . . 162 E 80 St, New York, NY *10021*

Packard MRS Thomas W (Sandra B Grove) . . . . | ☎ (212) 722-1821
MISS Amanda B . . . . | 108 E 86 St,
MR Timothy W . . . . | New York, NY
| *10028*

Packard MR Thomas W—Sa.
☎ (212) 772-0512 . . 315 E 65 St, New York, NY *10021*

Packer MRS Charles Wallace (Virginia C | ☎ (847) 446-5876
Whittemore) Ws'43 . . . . | 425 Linden St,
MISS Mary Bliss—at ☎ (312) 642-2711 | Winnetka, IL *60093*
1830A N Dayton St, Chicago, IL *60614* . . . . . . |
MR Charles W JR—Cal'81—at ☎ (847) 869-5641 |
1728 Seward St, Evanston, IL *60202* . . . . |

Packer MRS John B (Eunice R Rodman) Pa'67.Pa'79
☎ (610) 525-6344 . . 404 Cheswick Place, Apt 406, Rosemont,
PA *19010*

Paddock MR & MRS Anthony C (Wendy E Brewer)
Un.H.'57.H'60.Cl'61 ⚓
☎ (914) 834-0935 . . 14 N Chatsworth Av, Larchmont, NY *10538*

Paddock MRS Franklin K (Frances P Clucas) Lx. . . | ☎ (413) 637-0181
MR Lowell C—Y'82 . . . . | 680 East St, Lenox,
| MA *01240*

Page MR & MRS Allison F (Margaret B Lucas) H'45.Va'51
☎ (303) 791-1918 . . 8850 S Blue Mountain Place, Highlands Ranch,
CO *80126*

Page MRS Anderson (Burwell—Katharine G | ☎ (908) 781-5851
Despard) . . . . | 4128 Fellowship Rd,
MISS Lesslie B Burwell—at ☎ (206) 729-0829 | Basking Ridge, NJ
326 NE 54 St, Seattle, WA *98105* . . . . | *07920*
MR John T Burwell 3d—H'72—at |
☎ (508) 460-0040 . . St Mark's School, |
25 Marlborough Rd, Southborough, MA *01772* |

Page MR Arthur W . . . . Died May 24'96

Page MRS Arthur W (Anita P Hadden) Cly.H.
　☎ (516) 385-8743 . . 406 W Neck Rd, Huntington, NY *11743*
Page MR & MRS Benjamin G JR (Elizabeth W Robinson) Tul'76.Ga'74
　☎ (615) 385-9539 . . 3801 Richland Av, Nashville, TN *37205*
Page MR Blakely C—Smu'96 . . see C T Cudlip
Page MR C Donald—C.Hn.BlackMt'41.H'48
　☎ (508) 645-3361 . . PO Box 365, Chilmark, MA *02535*
Page MRS Charles (M Catherine Hall) . . . . Died at
　Kentfield, CA Jun 16'96
Page MR Charles—Pcu.Yn.Y'26
　☎ (415) 461-6326 . . 501 Via Casitas, Kentfield, CA *94904*
Page MR & MRS Charles H (Mayer—Garril C Goss)　of ☎ (415)456-3933
　Pcu.Mt.Cp.Y'60.Pa'69 . . . . PO Box 182, Ross,
　MISS Atlantic F—CtCol'93—at　CA *94957*
　☎ (202) 966-3889 . . 3401—38 St NW,　☎ (702) 749-5443
　Washington, DC *20016* . . . . "Fafolly"
　MR Charles 3d—at Bates　PO Box 173,
　Glenbrook, NV
　89413
Page MR & MRS David Arthur (Anne P Blaxter) Rr.Pg.Rens'56.H'65
　☎ (412) 621-8760 . . 3955 Bigelow Blvd, Pittsburgh, PA *15213*
Page MR & MRS David N (Lee Porter)　of ☎ (603)883-1314
　Bost'79.Ds.Br'59.Y'63 . . . . 78 Concord St,
　MR David A—Wit'91 . . . . Nashua, NH *03060*
　MR Andrew D—Woos'92 . . . . ☎ (603) 763-2577
　Woodland Rd,
　Sunapee, NH *03782*
Page MRS Edward C (Elizabeth W Griffith) . . . . Died at
　Newtown Square, PA Apr 16'94
Page MRS Elsie H (Elsie M Hellyer) Ncd.
　☎ (401) 331-2134 . . 259 Benefit St, Providence, RI *02903*
Page MR F Le Moyne—T . . . see MRS D F Darlington
Page MR Harry D—Stan'62.H'65
　16 Yellow Ferry Harbor, Sausalito, CA *94965*
Page MRS Harve H (Margaret H Morsman)
　☎ (847) 492-4889 . . 1 Calvin Circle, Apt B211, Evanston, IL *60201*
Page MRS Hollace T (Hollace E Triller) Syr'69
　☎ (914) GR1-0241 . . 139 Academy St, Poughkeepsie, NY *12601*
Page MR Holt W JR . . of
　☎ (713) 529-9969 . . 1601 S Shepherd St, Apt 111-112, Houston,
　TX *77019*
　☎ (305) 294-1253 . . 324 Elizabeth St, Key West, FL *33040*
Page MRS Hope Austen (Hope Austen) V'63 . . . . . . | ☎ (415) 221-8473
　MR Thomas S . . . . | 21 Sixth Av,
　MR Michael E . . . . | San Francisco, CA
　94118
Page DR & MRS James A (Richards—Edith B Whetstone) Gm.Lond'51
　☎ (941) 434-7912 . . 103 Clubhouse Lane, Apt 182, Naples, FL *34105*
Page MRS James K (Perkins—Kathleen E Maynard)
　☎ (802) 867-5316 . . 12 Meadow Lane, Box 213, Dorset, VT *05251*
Page MR Jay J—Un.Srb.SlII'65 . . of
　☎ (212) 737-4217 . . 155 E 73 St, New York, NY *10021*
　☎ (401) 847-8142 . . 34 Golden Hill St, Newport, RI *02840*
Page MRS John H (Susan C Simonds) Pr.Csh. . . . . . | ☎ (516) AR1-3194
　MISS Julia L—at ☎ (406) 848-7571　| 395 W Neck Rd,
　PO Box 608, Gardiner, MT *59030* . . . . | Huntington, NY
　| *11743*

Page MRS John R (Galloway—Mary Menzies)
　☎ (408) 626-4827 . . 8545 Carmel Valley Rd, Carmel, CA *93923*
Page MR Kimball M—Nw'51
　☎ (919) 542-1139 . . 641 Fearrington Village, Pittsboro, NC *27312*
Page MR & MRS L Rodman (Atterbury—Mary Stafford) P'41
　☎ (610) 525-2958 . . 37 Pond Lane, Bryn Mawr, PA *19010*
Page MR & MRS L Rodman 3d (Smith—Diane　| ☎ (610) 688-1792
　Davies) Ithaca'66.Me.Cr'73 . . . . | 318 Midland Av,
　MISS Katherine P Smith . . . . | Wayne, PA *19087*
　MISS Elizabeth D Smith . . . . |
Page MRS Marguerita S (Lewis—Marguerita S Hunter) Temp'70.Rut'72
　☎ (707) 746-7758 . . 1750 Stuart Court, Benicia, CA *94510*
Page MISS Olivia M . . see C T Cudlip
Page MR Peter F . . see MRS D F Darlington
Page MR & MRS Richard K (Martha Rivinus) Cry.Me.Ph.Gm.
　☎ (610) 527-9511 . . 46 Rosemont Av, Rosemont, PA *19010*
Page MR & MRS Richard K JR (Priscilla W　| ☎ (610) 527-2466
　Bradshaw) Me.P'65.H'67 . . . . | 721 Waverly Rd,
　MISS Wendy B . . . . | Bryn Mawr, PA
　MR Richard K 3d . . . . | *19010*
Page MRS Robert Holmes (Mary N Lea)
　235 Lancaster Av, Devon, PA *19333*
Page MR & MRS Shelby H (Roberta G Raworth) Hn.H'43
　☎ (803) 681-6474 . . 15 Outerbridge Circle, Hilton Head Island,
　SC *29926*
Page MISS Susan M . . see MRS D F Darlington
Page MRS Sylvia M (Sylvia W Morss)
　☎ (413) 443-1345 . . 177 Dawes Av, Pittsfield, MA *01201*
Page MR & MRS Thomas S (Mattern—A Jean　| ☎ (202) 363-3219
　Jepson) Sth'46.An.Yn.Y'38.H'42 . . . . | 3219 Chesapeake St
　MISS Margot E—at 409 Columbia Rd,　| NW, Washington,
　Santa Cruz, CA *95060* . . . . | DC *20008*
　MISS Victoria A . . . . |
Page MR & MRS Walter H (Jane N Nichols) BMr'40.Ny.Cs.H'37
　☎ (516) 692-6937 . . 255 Lawrence Hill Rd, PO Box 278,
　Cold Spring Harbor, NY *11724-0278*
Page MRS Wheeler H (Dolan—Edith Hutchinson) Ncd.
　☎ (610) MU8-0755 . . 221 Chester Rd, Devon, PA *19333*
Page MRS William H JR (Frances W Bicknell)
　☎ (303) 794-6484 . . Hallmark, 3701 W Radcliff Av, Denver, CO *80236*
Page MR & MRS William H 2d—Wis'53.Loy'62　| ☎ (847) 446-1458
　MISS Jennifer W—at 4232 Latona Av NE, Seattle, | 786 Foxdale Av,
　WA *98105* . . . . | Winnetka, IL *60093*
　MISS Mary A—at 1 E Scott St, Apt 1001,　|
　Chicago, IL *60610* . . . . |
　MR Christopher K—at 616 Michigan Av,　|
　Evanston, IL *60202* . . . . |
Pagel MR & MRS Alex B (Luisa M LaViola)　| ☎ (212) PL8-3533
　V'64.Cl'70.Un.Rc.Mto.Mds.Cly.Y.'59.Va'62 . . . | 555 Park Av,
　JUNIORS MISS Allegra LaV . . . . | New York, NY
　| *10021*
Pagel MRS Alex J (Elinor R Bronaugh) Mds.Cda.Dar.
　☎ (212) 988-9310 . . 29 E 64 St, New York, NY *10021*
Pagenstecher MR Bernard—Y'29
　5711 Timber Lake Dv, Sarasota, FL *34243*
Pagenstecher MR & MRS John A (Alexandra E Syms) Mid'52 ⚓
　☎ (301) 299-9321 . . 9726 The Corral Dv, Potomac, MD *20854*

Paige MR & MRS Donald G (Louisa D Keller) Lawr'78.Cy.H'68.Va'71
☎ (617) 367-3360 . . 8 Walnut St, Boston, MA *02108*
Paige MR & MRS Francis U (Judy E Andresen) Cy.Ey . . .of
☎ (617) 631-3670 . . 4 Sargent Rd, Marblehead Neck, MA *01945*
☎ (305) 367-4233 . . 50 Clubhouse Rd, Key Largo, FL *33037*
Paige MR & MRS Francis U JR (Linda A Ball) FlaAtl'94
☎ (954) 764-5681 . . 1114 SE 7 St, Ft Lauderdale, FL *33301*
Paige MR & MRS Peter (Natalie F Lambing) Chath'41
☎ (516) 286-0284 . . ''Meadowedge'' 2 Gerard St, Bellport, NY *11713*
Paige MRS Richard S (Margery E Gibby) Cyb.
☎ (561) 276-0697 . . 401 E Linton Blvd, Apt 201, Delray Beach,
FL *33483*
Paige MISS Taylor Lowa (Francis U JR) . . . . Born at
Ft Lauderdale, FL Mch 24'96

Paine MRS Alix E (Seymore—O'Shea—Alix E | of ☎ (212)988-6671
Paine) SL'69.ChHill'91 . . . . | 157 E 72 St,
  MISS Chloë B Seymore—RISD'96 . . . . | New York, NY
  | *10021*
  | ☎ (518) 398-5601
  | ''Old Orchard''
  | PO Box 162,
  | Pine Plains, NY
  | *12567*
Paine MR Andrew S—Un.Ty'84
☎ (718) 520-2958 . . 72-81—113 St, Forest Hills, NY *11375*
Paine MR David L—Hn.H'88 . . of
☎ (011-852) 2987-0881 . . Greenmont 20F, Discovery Bay,
Lantau Island, Hong Kong
☎ (207) 371-2229 . . ''Timberlea'' MacMahan Island, ME *04548*
Paine MR Hugh E JR—Un.Plg.StA.StJ.Y'52 . . . . . . | ☎ (718) 268-0975
  MR William D—Un.Ty'81—at | 150 Burns St,
  ☎ (718) 476-3773 . . 86-30—55 Av, Elmhurst, | Forest Hills, NY
  NY *11373* . . . . | *11375*
Paine MRS J Haskell (Julia K Haskell) Bnd'56
☎ (212) 369-4006 . . 345 E 86 St, New York, NY *10028*
Paine MISS Louise M (Sheerin—Baldwin—Louise | ☎ (808) 373-3991
M Paine) . . . . | 1035 Kaimoku
  MR Cedric B Baldwin 3d . . . . | Place, Honolulu, HI
  | *96821*
Paine DR & MRS Michael P W H (Cornelia T Clark) Sth'61.Lond'61
☎ (011-44-1329) 662124 . . 6 Hill Head Rd, Hill Head, Fareham,
Hampshire PO14 3JH, England
Paine MR & MRS Peter S (Ellen C Lea) B.Pc.Ac.Cly.P'32 . . of
☎ (561) 546-3638 . . 240 S Beach Rd, Hobe Sound, FL *33455*
☎ (215) 248-3117 . . 404 W Springfield Av, Philadelphia, PA *19118*
Paine MR & MRS Peter S JR (Constance M Murphy) | of ☎ (212)249-0166
Rdc'59.C.Cly.P'57.Ox'59.H'61 . . . . | 16 Henderson Place,
  MR Alexander G—at U of Vt . . . . | New York, NY
  | *10028*
  | ☎ (518) 963-4081
  | Red Farm,
  | 30 River Rd,
  | Willsboro, NY
  | *12996*

Paine MR & MRS Peter S 3d (Els M Neukermans)
P'86.Pa'92.Pc.P'85.Ox'87.Van'90
☎ (215) 248-4652 . . 116 W Springfield Av, Philadelphia, PA *19118*
Paine MR & MRS Richard P (Dickison—Dragonas— | ☎ (603) 888-6945
Martha L Parsons) Cw.Hb.H'54 . . . . | 45 Green Heron
  MISS Sara E Dickison—at 25 Fayette St, | Lane, Nashua, NH
  Apt 1, Boston, MA *02116* . . . . | *03062*
  MR Matthew P Dickison—at |
  ☎ (703) 313-0352 . . 7471 Towchester Court, |
  Alexandria, VA *22315* . . . . |
Paine MR & MRS Richard P JR (Cathleen F Ross) Vt'85.Vt'84
☎ (617) 863-1521 . . 20 Avon St, Lexington, MA *02173*
Paine MR & MRS Thomas M (Lynda S Sharp) | ☎ (617) 431-9759
Sth'71.Ox'74.H'79.H'70.H'74.Va'85 . . . . | 2 Cushing St,
  JUNIORS MR Sumner B . . . . | Wellesley Hills, MA
  JUNIORS MR Mallory . . . . | *02181*
Painter MR & MRS Charles A 3d (Potter—Barbara N | ☎ (714) 494-3209
Baker) . . . . | 1665 Viking Rd,
  MR William H—Va'72—at ☎ (702) 873-8291 | Laguna Beach, CA
  3778 Prosperity Lane, Las Vegas, NV *89117* . . . | *92651-3246*
Painter MRS Clarke (Adèle L Gilbert) Bnd'28 . . . | ☎ (310) 476-4550
  MISS Tamera A—P'72.Pn.—at ☎ (713) 358-4728 | 427 N Bundy Dv,
  1600 Walnut Lane, Kingwood, TX *77339* . . . . . | Los Angeles, CA
  | *90049*
Painter MISS Cornelia B
4125 N Tripp Av, Chicago, IL *60607*
Painter MR & MRS David L (Harriet E Roberts) | ☎ (610) LA5-0886
Drex'45.Me.Rv.Dar.Y'43 . . . . | 201 Morlyn Av,
  MISS Sally H | Bryn Mawr, PA
  MISS Suzanne R . . . . | *19010*
Painter MRS Edward H (Katherine E Saltus) NH'86
18 Kilmer Rd, Short Hills, NJ *07078*
Painter MR Edward H—IllWes'83.Ill'85
30 E 81 St, Apt 10D, New York, NY *10028*
Painter MRS J L Dawson (Eleanor C Hall)
☎ (508) 362-3064 . . 2204 Heatherwood, Yarmouth Port, MA *02675*
Painter MR John L (David L) . . . . Married at West Chester, PA
Giordano MRS Gale A (Gale A Spina) . . . . Jly 11'96
Painter MRS Nancy J (Nancy J Bowser) Susq'77
16 Regents Court, Kennett Square, PA *19348*
Painter MR & MRS Richard W (Karen J Lindsley)
Y'87.Cl'90.Myf.Yn.Hb.H'84.Y'87
☎ (603) 643-5849 . . 34 MacDonald Dv, Hanover, NH *03755*
Painter MR & MRS William H (Marion S Homer) Sth'50.Cos.P'49.H'54
☎ (202) 966-3458 . . 6652—32 St NW, Washington, DC *20015*

Pakenham HON & MRS Michael Aidan (Lavine— of ☎ (011-33-1)
Meta L Doak) Ty'64.Tex'65 42-66-91-42
JUNIORS MISS Alexandra Clio I B . . . . British Embassy,
35 rue du Faubourg
St Honoré, 75383
Paris Cedex 08,
France
☎ (011-44-1580)
860-494
Bernhurst,
Hurst Green,
East Sussex
TN19 7QN, England
☎ (011-44-171)
727-8956
34 Aldridge Rd
Villas, London
W11 1BW, England

Pakradooni MR & MRS Dikran S (Ann L Jacobs)
Me.Ac.Hav'38 . . . . ☎ (610) 525-1339
MISS A Virginia A—at ☎ (617) 964-8618 ''The Greenhouse''
115 Commonwealth Av, Chestnut Hill, 808 Castlefinn Lane,
MA 02167 . . . . Bryn Mawr, PA
MR D Loyd—Va'69—at ☎ (610) 993-9789 19010
1000 Conestoga Rd, Berwyn, PA 19312 . . . . . .

Palache MR & MRS John G JR (Sally Biscoe) Nyc.Cly.Yn.Y'52.H'57
☎ (203) 661-7454 . . 35 Ridgeview Av, Greenwich, CT 06830

Palache MISS Lucy B—Rdc'49.Cl'70
☎ (212) 663-1478 . . 380 Riverside Dv, New York, NY 10025

Palen MR & MRS Frederick P (Harriette H Adams) Bnd'39.Hl.Y'36
☎ (610) 584-7579 . . Meadowood at Worcester, 503 Center Bridge,
Lansdale, PA 19446-5886

Palfrey MR & MRS George G (Martha A Macdonald) ☎ (617) 934-5147
BMr'47.H.'51 . . . . 101 St George St,
MISS Ellen D—Ne'82—at ☎ (617) 268-1348 Duxbury, MA 02332
59 Gates St, South Boston, MA 02127 . . . .

Palfrey MR & MRS John C (Debra L Wonkka) ☎ (617) 934-2443
AldB'79.AldB'79 . . . . 101 St George St,
JUNIORS MISS Emily S . . . . Duxbury, MA 02332
JUNIORS MR Christopher W . . . .

Palmer MR & MRS A Wright P (Anna Maria ☎ (212) 752-6477
Caracciolo di Brienza) Un.Cly.Y'57 . . . . 136 E 64 St, PH-B,
MISS Katharine P—Y'92 . . . . New York, NY
MISS Elizabeth C—Y'92 10021

Palmer MR & MRS Alexander S (Margaret Allen) ☎ (615) 383-0186
MaryB'68.Van'68 . . . . 1009 Belle Meade
MISS Elizabeth B . . . . Blvd, Nashville, TN
MR Alexander S JR 37205

Palmer MR & MRS Anthony G W (A Barbara Jürgensen)
MtH'81.Bow'81.Pa'90 . . of
☎ (011-49-89) 724-1489 . . Schoettlstrasse 3, 81369 Munich, Germany
☎ (413) 243-1558 . . Hickory Farm, Tyringham, MA 01264

Palmer MRS Arthur E (Julia C Reed) . . of
☎ (212) 744-7202 . . 157 E 81 St, New York, NY 10028
☎ (207) 244-3915 . . HCR 62, Box 76, Pretty Marsh Pond, Mt Desert,
ME 04660

Palmer MISS Blair W—HWSth'95 . . see H L Bogert 3d

Palmer MR & MRS C Harvey JR (Elizabeth H Machen) MtH'47.Cda.H'41
☎ (410) 549-6731 . . Fairhaven C102, 7200 Third Av, Sykesville,
MD 21784

Palmer MR & MRS C Scott (Susan Tobian)
10553 Pagewood Dv, Dallas, TX 75230

Palmer GEN & MRS Charles D (Murray—Eugenia Kingman)
An.Cvc.USA'24
☎ (703) 578-7479 . . 3440 S Jefferson St, Falls Church, VA 22041

Palmer MR Christopher D—Colg'86.Nu'88 . . see P M Hammett

Palmer MR & MRS Edward L (Margaret Preston)
Rc.B.Pr.Ck.Ri.Plg.Pcu.Ng.Ln.Lic.Cly.Br'38 . . of
☎ (516) 922-5135 . . 108 Horseshoe Rd, Mill Neck, NY 11765
☎ (212) 838-3840 . . 200 E 66 St, New York, NY 10021

Palmer MRS Elisabeth G (CTSS Elisabeth Gatterburg) Cs.
☎ (212) 753-0534 . . 405 E 51 St, New York, NY 10022

Palmer MRS Elliott P (Elizabeth L Heizer)
☎ (513) 321-6373 . . 3939 Erie Av, Cincinnati, OH 45208-1954

Palmer MR & MRS Everett A JR (Margaret A Niedringhaus)
CarnM'36.Vh.Cr'37.H'39 . . of
☎ (818) 792-6481 . . 1350 Linda Ridge Rd, Pasadena, CA 91103
☎ (316) 843-2551 . . Palmer Ranch, Beaumont, KS 67012
700 W Bay Av, Balboa, CA 92661

Palmer MR & MRS F Morgan (Susan P Battelle) Rc.P'29
☎ (212) TR9-4109 . . 139 E 79 St, New York, NY 10021

Palmer MR & MRS F Morgan JR (Helen C Potts) ☎ (212) FI8-4026
Sth'62.Ty'60 . . . . 315 E 88 St,
MISS Susan B—Rm'95—at Dallas, TX . . . . New York, NY
10128

Palmer MR F Timothy—S.Occ'66 . . . . ☎ (970) 468-5049
MR Brett T—David'94 . . . . PO Box 9000,
MR Todd C . . . . Silverthorne, CO
80498

Palmer MR H Meredith—CarnM'58
☎ (412) 439-1005 . . PO Box 952, Uniontown, PA 15401

Palmer MRS Henry (Mary C King)
☎ (610) 558-1499 . . White Horse Village 206A, 535 Gradyville Rd,
Newtown Square, PA 19073-2815

Palmer MISS Isabelle D
☎ (914) 986-4433 . . ''1810 House'' 80 Main St, Warwick, NY 10990

Palmer MRS James K (Mickelson—E Joan Ramsay) of ☎ (415)851-0288
MISS Elizabeth W—at Hollins . . . . 150 Fox Hollow Rd,
JUNIORS MR James R . . . . Woodside, CA
94062
☎ (707) 433-3790
Palmer Ridge
Ranch,
3369 West Rd,
Healdsburg, CA
95488

Palmer MRS Jane S (Jane A Strauss) Sth'69.Stan'74
☎ (206) 325-7990 . . 624—37 Av, Seattle, WA 98122

Palmer MRS Lansing R (Voehl—Patricia A Saville) ☎ (212) 744-7111
RISD'62.Csh.Nrr. . . . . 205 E 83 St,
MISS Allison H Voehl—Duke'91 . . . . New York, NY
10028

Palmer MR Lansing R—Un.Ri.Pr.Plg.Snc.Coa.Cw.Myf.Y'66.Bost'71
☎ (212) 794-3131 . . 210 E 73 St, New York, NY 10021

Palmer MR Lansing R JR—HWSth'90 . . see H L Bogert 3d

Palmer MR & MRS Lucius N (Muriel A Castadot) Ty'85.Ty'87
☎ (212) 360-5199 . . 425 E 86 St, Apt 9D, New York, NY 10028

Palmer MR Morgan—H'55
☎ (508) 650-3586 . . PO Box 133, Natick, MA 01760

Palmer MR Morton M—My.Sm.
☎ (508) 468-2204 . . PO Box 346, Hamilton, MA 01936

Palmer MISS Natalie Beekman (Lucius N) . . . . Born Jun 15'95

Palmer MISS Pamela G—SL'79
☎ (617) 749-9890 . . 402 Main St, Hingham, MA 02043

Palmer MR & MRS Philip (Louisa W Jones) | ☎ (212) 369-1938
Rdc'58.H.'57.H'62 . . . . | 1160 Park Av,
MR Jedediah—at ☎ (718) 596-8529 | New York, NY
5 Montague Terr, Brooklyn, NY 11231 . . . . | 10128

Palmer MR & MRS Potter (Diane R Parker) | ☎ (847) 234-0029
LakeF'87.Cas.On.Cho.Rc.B.H'56 . . . . | 45 S Sheridan Rd,
MR Potter JR—SCal'85 . . . . | Lake Forest, IL
| 60045

Palmer MRS R Dean (Leslie K Powell) . . . . . . Married at Mill Creek, WA
Siggs MR Roland W (Arthur) . . . . May 18'96

Palmer MRS R Movius (Renshaw—Rose S Movius) Cas.
☎ (305) 666-1303 . . 5840 SW 117 St, Miami, FL 33156

Palmer MR & MRS Raymond N (Joan M Starkey)
Ty'75.H'84.P'68.H'78.Bost'85
☎ (512) 263-1879 . . 10012 Circleview Dv, Austin, TX 78733

Palmer MRS Richard M (Amanda V Street)
☎ (718) UL5-9099 . . 41 Sidney Place, Brooklyn, NY 11201

Palmer REV Richard R—Cw.DU'53.Nash'59
☎ (303) 377-8629 . . PO Box 18949, Denver, CO 80218

Palmer MR & MRS Stewart L (Camilla T Knapp)
☎ (914) 764-9404 . . 82 Hack Green Rd, Pound Ridge, NY 10576

Palmer MRS Vincent (Lucie C Mackay)
☎ (314) 367-8080 . . 5399 Lindell Blvd, St Louis, MO 63112

Palmer MR & MRS William F (Christine B Childs) | ☎ (415) 388-0478
DU'70.SFrSt'76.Cal'70 . . . . | 339 Melrose Av,
JUNIORS MISS Emily G . . . . | Mill Valley, CA
JUNIORS MISS Claire C . . . . | 94941

Palsgrove MR & MRS James L 3d (Phyllis R Leidy) | ☎ (212) 831-5005
SCal'56.Cda.Wes'48.Y.'54 . . . . | 21 E 90 St,
MR J Lincoln 4th—at NYU . . . . | New York, NY
| 10128

Paluck MISS Elizabeth A . . see J C Bright

Paluck JUNIORS MR Ronald T . . see J C Bright

Palumbo MR & MRS Jonathan B (Leslie K Hunt) Bost'88.Cas.NCar'87
☎ (773) 278-3183 . . 2228 W Charleston St, Chicago, IL 60647

Panarese MR & MRS Mark J (Alexandra T Dodge) Wheat'81.Cy.H.'78
☎ (617) 333-6996 . . 75 Milton St, Milton, MA 02186

Pancoast MR & MRS Charles E III (Mary V Riter) Hav'45
☎ (610) 948-4098 . . 111 Alackness Rd, Spring City, PA 19475

Pancoast MRS Howell W (Katherine J Class)
☎ (502) 895-3201 . . 247 Stonehenge Dv, Louisville, KY 40207

Pancoast MR & MRS Richard M (Agnes M Horan)
☎ (610) 933-7484 . . Chester Springs Rd, PO Box 353, Kimberton,
PA 19442

Pancoast MR & MRS Ross (Margaret J Bailey) Reed'41.Cwr'43.JHop'32
☎ (301) 942-7338 . . 2902 Sheraton St, Silver Spring, MD 20906

Panetta MR & MRS Vincent J JR (Eunice C Johnson)
H'90.H'72.Sth'84.H'88.H'91
☎ (617) 235-3289 . . 84 Standish Rd, Wellesley Hills, MA 02181

Pannell MRS Leigh M (Leigh E K Morfit)
☎ (916) 692-0412 . . PO Box 35, Oregon House, CA 95962

Panon Desbassayns de Richemont JUNIORS MISS Amélie
see C F Smithers JR

Panon Desbassayns de Richemont JUNIORS MR Philippe
see C F Smithers JR

Pantaleoni MR & MRS Anthony (Emily A Patterson) | ☎ (212) 535-7836
Rc.H'61 . . . . | 850 Park Av,
MR Michael T . . . . | New York, NY
| 10021

Pantaleoni MR & MRS Jonathan R (S Jane Worley) WmW'ds'78.H'68
128 N Bemiston Av, St Louis, MO 63105

Pantaleoni MRS Nancy N (Nancy E Nutter) . . . . | see
MR Matthew . . . . | Dilatory Domiciles
MR Tad . . . . |

Paolella MR & MRS John S (Elliot Davis)
P.'84.Nu'85.Cl'92.Cly.P.'84.Y'86.H.'90
☎ (212) 249-8687 . . 170 E 77 St, Apt 3G, New York, NY 10021

Paolozzi CTSS Lorenzo (Alice Spaulding) Cly.Cda.
870 United Nations Plaza, Apt 18F, New York, NY 10017

Papamarkou MR Alexander P—Syr'50.P'52.LondEc'61
☎ (212) 755-9177 . . 800 Fifth Av, New York, NY 10021

Papanicolaou MR & MRS Nicholas F (Alexandra | ☎ (203) 869-3317
Gardner) Ri.Hn.H'70 . . . . | 19 Brookridge Dv,
MISS Tatiana G—at Harvard . . . . | Greenwich, CT
JUNIORS MISS Alexandra E . . . . | 06830
JUNIORS MR S Nicholas . . . . |

Pape JUNIORS MISS Katrina V . . see MISS M T Vitagliano

Papin MR Allen A
9350 Sunshine Av, Flagstaff, AZ 86004

Papin MR & MRS Gerard A (Suzanne Mann) | 249 Middleton Rd,
Wms'56 . . . . | Boxford, MA 01921
MISS E Kellogg . . . . |
MISS Megan L . . . . |
MR Nicholas . . . . |

Papin MRS Pierre L (Lilly Allen)
☎ (603) 778-2611 . . Langdon Place of Exeter, 17 Hampton Rd, Exeter,
NH 03833

Pappas MR & MRS Paul T (Esther D Marshall) BowlG'73.Del'75
☎ (207) 846-0714 . . 16 South St, Yarmouth, ME 04096

Papps MR John . . see C S Cheston JR

Papy MR & MRS Hugh R (Jeanne H Dixon) . . . . | ☎ (912) 355-9820
MR Richard W . . . . | 5714 Sweetbriar
| Circle, Savannah,
| GA 31406

Papy MR & MRS Hugh R JR (Ghia Mahany) Rm'78
☎ (912) 355-5470 . . 26 Island Dv, Savannah, GA 31406

Paquet MR & MRS Raymond M (Jane S Braff) Conn'80.Conn'79.Hart'89
☎ (860) 675-6670 . . 8 Dunne Wood Court, Farmington, CT 06085

Pardee MR & MRS S Trevor (Erdice Rockhill) | ☎ (401) 846-1934
V'49.S.P'43 ⛵ . . . . | ''Boone House''
MISS Margaret T—at ☎ (610) 630-1403 | 422 Thames St,
710 Willowbrook Dv, Norristown, PA 19403 . . . | Newport, RI 02840

Pardee MR S Trevor JR—S.P.'81.H'86 ⚓
☎ (212) 535-8956 . . 36 E 69 St, Apt 5B, New York, NY *10021*

Parham MR & MRS Duncan de P (Harriet M Davis) Ncmb'60.Tul'60
☎ (504) 895-5313 . . 3435 Camp St, New Orleans, LA *70115*

Paris MR & MRS Francklyn Wynne (Grace L Gale)
Rv.Cc.Cspa.Cw.Myf.Ofp.Wt.
☎ (407) 242-8278 . . 1914 Ford Circle N, Melbourne, FL *32935*

Paris COL & MRS William F 2d (Rosmarie G Fischer) USA.An.Cc.Ofp.Rv.Cw.Wt.Myf.W. Roan'58 . . . . | ☎ (703) 250-5370
MR F Wynne 2d . . . . | 10831 Burr Oak
MR William F 3d—Gettys'90 . . . . | Way, Burke, VA *22015*

Parish MISS A Meredith (Franck—A Meredith Parish) Skd'67
☎ (904) 654-1759 . . 734 Legion Dv, Apt 24, Destin, FL *32541*

Parish MRS Ann Dickinson (Ann M Dickinson) BtP. | ☎ (864) 457-4980
MISS Linda D . . . . | Fox Run Farm, PO Box 38, Campobello, SC *29322*

Parish MR & MRS Edward C JR (Joan de F Brush) H'36
☎ (603) 924-7539 . . 13 Windy Row, Peterborough, NH *03458*

Parish MISS Jessica . . see J Bechtle

Parish MR & MRS Richard Laurence JR (Lowther—Joan H Reijmers) Bg.Evg.Rcn . . .of
☎ (561) 622-1008 . . 100 Lake Shore Dv, L7, North Palm Beach, FL *33408*
☎ (203) 637-0226 . . Lowther Point, Indian Point Lane, Riverside, CT *06878*

Parisot MRS Ellen Lewis (Ellen J Lewis)
☎ (203) 762-3737 . . 56 Hillbrook Rd, Wilton, CT *06897*

Parisot MR & MRS Ricardo (Katherine Throckmorton)
☎ (203) 834-9679 . . 274 Nod Hill Rd, Wilton, CT *06897*

Park MASTER Alexander Hay (Philip J) . . . . Born at Annapolis, MD Apr 25'96

Park MR David D . . see R F Batchelder

Park MR & MRS David M (Torrey—Edith C Davis) P'50.MichSt'51
☎ (803) 884-9611 . . 1141K Shadow Lake Circle, Mt Pleasant, SC *29464*

Park MR & MRS H Halsted JR (Virginia G Semlow) Bgt.Ny.Plg.Rv.
☎ (941) 261-4845 . . 1010 Oriole Circle, Naples, FL *34105-7425*

Park MR & MRS Howard C (Newcombe—Anne S Appleton) OState'29
☎ (614) 252-8935 . . 407 Northview Dv, Columbus, OH *43209*

Park MR & MRS John N (Trimble—Carol A Kirkman) Wheat'54.Aht'53
☎ (610) 644-4490 . . 46 Manchester Court, Berwyn, PA *19312*

Park MR John N JR—Pc.Rc.Rv.Hav'79
☎ (215) 247-7875 . . 8015 Navajo St, Philadelphia, PA *19118*

Park MR & MRS Joseph F JR (Susan C Pund) Ub.Cy.Bab'64
☎ (617) 536-5557 . . 166 W Canton St, Boston, MA *02118*

Park MR & MRS Peter G (Mary G Pearson) Mit'40
☎ (011-61-6) 295-2709 . . 21 Scarborough St, Red Hill, Canberra 2603, Australia

Park MR & MRS Peter G JR (McPherson—Joy J Medley) NEng'74.CathU'75.Wis'67.GeoW'74
1909 Earldale Court, Alexandria, VA *22306-2715*

Park MR & MRS Philip J (Elizabeth L Thomson) Leh'84.JHop'95.OState'81
☎ (410) 626-0157 . . 1263 Crummell Av, Annapolis, MD *21403*

Park MR & MRS Richard G 3d (Charlotte E Pearson) Ds.P'37
☎ (941) 485-1425 . . 204 Louella Lane, Nokomis, FL *34275*

Parke MRS Thomas (Caroline L Hoopes) Ac.
P Patch Farm, PO Box 476, Downingtown, PA *19335*

Parker MRS Allan D (Elizabeth Chick) Cyb.Chi.Ncd.
☎ (912) 638-5064 . . PO Box 30233, Sea Island, GA *31561*

Parker MR & MRS Allan D 3d (Margery D Cahoon) Ws'80.Cy.Chi.Bab'73.Bab'74 . . . . | ☎ (617) 834-6873
MR Allan D 4th . . . . | PO Box 1369, 295 S River St, Marshfield, MA *02050-1369*

Parker MR & MRS Anthony W (Margaret C Alexander) NCar'80.Cvc.Mt.Ny.H'68 . . . . | ☎ (202) 333-6543
JUNIORS MR Preston W . . . . | 4881 Potomac Av NW, Washington, DC *20007*

Parker MR Arthur M JR—Me.Nat'l'38
☎ (803) 722-8439 . . 135 S Battery St, Charleston, SC *29401*

Parker MRS Augustin H (Reynolds—Judith McKean) Sth'47 ⚓ | of ☎ (617)723-6095
MISS Pamela D—Colby'88—at | 40 Joy St, Apt 8, Boston, MA *02114*
☎ (207) 582-8209 . . RR 2, Box 663, Augusta, ME *04330* . . . . | ☎ (207) 326-4677 Box 11, Rte 1,
MR Jonathan McK Reynolds—H'77.Stan'89— | Brooksville, ME *04617*
at ☎ (313) 996-0829 . . 1604 Westminster Place, Ann Arbor, MI *48104* . . . . |

Parker MR & MRS Brainard W 2d (Susan H Oliver) Ayc.Cvc.Ncd. | ☎ (410) 268-6096
MISS Blair O . . . . | 900 Arbutus Rd,
JUNIORS MISS Lida T . . . . | Annapolis, MD *21403*

Parker MISS Caroline D (Allan D 3d) . . . . Married at Boston, MA
Alexandre MR J Henry 5th (late J Henry 4th) . . . . Oct 7'95

Parker MR & MRS Christopher W (Merry J Brashares) Sth'59.Y'54 . . . . | ☎ (215) 248-0955
MISS Pamela . . . . | 420 W Allens Lane,
MR Christopher W JR . . . . | Philadelphia, PA *19119*

Parker MRS Comfort T (O'Connor—Lord—Stuart—Comfort T Parker) Cly.
☎ (561) 655-6323 . . The Australian, 429 Australian Av, Palm Beach, FL *33480*

Parker MR & MRS Cortlandt (Nancy Knowles) Srb.Hn.H'43 . . of
☎ (908) 776-1391 . . PO Box 962, Far Hills, NJ *07931*
☎ (401) 847-3268 . . Greenvale Farm, 582 Wapping Rd, Portsmouth, RI *02871*

Parker MR Douglas S—P'46 . . . . | ☎ (941) 676-0400
MISS C Cary—at Spring City, PA *19475* . . . . . . | 555 Clubhouse Dv, Lake Wales, FL *33853*

Parker DR Edward F—Duke'33
☎ (803) 723-1931 . . 128 Tradd St, Charleston, SC *29401*

Parker MRS Edward P (Natalie Stevens) Chi.My.Ncd.
☎ (508) 927-0197 . . 45B West St, Beverly Farms, MA *01915*

Parker MISS Elizabeth Day (Harry S 3d) . . . . Married at Fishers Island, NY
Waters MR Thomas J (James D) . . . . Aug 10'96

Parker MISS Elizabeth K . . see M J Magyar

Parker MR & MRS Ellis J 3d (Haase—Nancy E Bealer) MaryW'59.Cvc.Mt.Md.USA'57.Ala'60 . MR Ellis S—at U of Ala . . . . MISS Debra L Haase—at 6 Sprinklewood Court, Potomac, MD *20854* . . . . | of ☎ (301)881-9398 11133 Stephalee Lane, Rockville, MD *20852* ☎ (205) 349-4824 Third St 229, Northport, AL *35476*

Parker MRS Esther G (Esther Grew)
☎ (508) 653-6323 . . 177 Lake St, Sherborn, MA *01770*

Parker MRS Fitzgerald (Terry—Madeline Blackman) Ncd.
☎ (615) 292-3395 . . 504 Elmington Av, Apt 404, Nashville, TN *37205*

Parker MR & MRS Foxhall A (Helen P Walker) Bgt.Cly.Dth'48 . . . . MISS Mary M . . . . | ☎ (914) 763-3856 "Spring House" 205 Honey Hollow Rd, Pound Ridge, NY *10576-1109*

Parker MR Francis Hill—Md.Cc.Ky'92
☎ (606) 527-3524 . . 7547 Athens-Boonesboro Rd, Lexington, KY *40509*

Parker MR & MRS Francis LeJau II (Briggs—Elizabeth W Middleton) Char'ton'78.Ht.Ncd.Char'ton'35
☎ (803) 571-5923 . . 844 Sheldon Rd, Charleston, SC *29407*

Parker MR & MRS Frederick A JR (Susan N Embree) Un.Bm.Plg.Rv.Coa.Fw.Snc.Cw.Ne.Ac.H'51 . . of
☎ (212) BU8-9592 . . 219 E 69 St, New York, NY *10021*
☎ (203) CI5-4333 . . 91 Middle Beach Rd, Madison, CT *06443*

Parker MR & MRS Garth R (Rosalie C Seely-Brown) Hav'55.Cr'57
☎ (305) 661-2344 . . 1520 Av Lugo, Coral Gables, FL *33156*

Parker MR & MRS Garth R JR (Karen J Fenic) BMr'84.Hav'81.CalTech'88
☎ (215) 361-1512 . . 107 Twinings Rd, Lansdale, PA *19446*

Parker MR George JR—A.K.B.P'43.Mich'49 . . of
☎ (214) 692-6360 . . 10340 Strait Lane, Dallas, TX *75229*
☎ (210) 822-5697 . . 779 Terrell Rd, San Antonio, TX *78209*

Parker MR & MRS George F (Virginia Millspaugh) BaldW'76.Cy.Myf.Cw.Ken'75.Dth'81
☎ (617) 326-0326 . . 47 Bemis Rd, Dedham, MA *02026*

Parker MR & MRS George M (Susan P Bissell) Rby.Plg.Y'58.H'62 . . . . MISS Julia Du P—Bnd'92—at ☎ (212) 873-1618 251 W 81 St, New York, NY *10024* . . . . MR Angus M—Pa'90—at ☎ (215) 731-0384 252 S 23 St, Apt 1R, Philadelphia, PA *19103* . . | ☎ (441) 236-9466 Skye Point, McGalls Bay Rd, Smiths Parish, Bermuda

Parker MR & MRS Harry S 3d (Ellen M McCance) V'58.C.H'61 . . . . MISS Catherine A . . . . MR Thomas B—Ken'89—at ☎ (212) 387-7853 21 E 10 St, New York, NY *10003* . . . . MR Samuel F—at ☎ (415) 474-3216 2576 Washington St, San Francisco, CA *94115* . | ☎ (415) 681-5577 171 San Marcos Av, San Francisco, CA *94116*

Parker MRS Henry S JR (Ruth Weyburn)
☎ (207) 596-0866 . . 11 Jameson Point Rd, Rockland, ME *04841*

Parker MR & MRS Henry S 3d (M Susan Barrow) H'66
☎ (410) 626-7560 . . 12 Brice Rd, Annapolis, MD *21401*

Parker MR & MRS J Hutchison (Rebecca J Pollack) Cal'86.P'86
☎ (310) 451-5225 . . 517 Lincoln Blvd, Santa Monica, CA *90402*

Parker MR James—Un.Nrr.H'46
☎ (212) 427-5746 . . 17 E 89 St, New York, NY *10128*

Parker MR James M JR—R.H'60.BMr'70
☎ (302) 656-0110 . . Centreville, 5718 Kennett Pike, Wilmington, DE *19807*

Parker MR & MRS James W C (Katherine H Glass) Cy.Ne'71 . . . . MR James W C JR . . . . JUNIORS MR Charles D . . . . | 44 Court St, Dedham, MA *02026*

Parker CAPT (RET) & MRS Jefferson D (Louisa B Barbour) USN'35
☎ (703) 356-4382 . . 6209 Loch Raven Dv, McLean, VA *22101*

Parker MR John MacRea JR—Cc.Y'45
☎ (215) 297-5872 . . "Laurelton" PO Box 93, Solebury, PA *18963*

Parker MR & MRS John O (Olivia C Hood) Ws'63.Un.Ec.Chi.Dth'58 . . . . MISS Helen E—at 2828 N Pine Grove Av, Apt 312, Chicago, IL *60657* . . . . MR John O JR—at 131A Commonwealth Av, Boston, MA *02116* . . . . | ☎ (508) 526-7344 "Hemlock Hill" 229 Summer St, Manchester, MA *01944*

Parker MR & MRS Jonathan W (Heidi J Smith) Tex'81.Nu'84.Ct.Gi.Cc.Wes'66.Cl'70
☎ (301) 913-9210 . . 14 Farmington Court, Chevy Chase, MD *20815*

Parker MR & MRS Joseph S W (Joan Falvey) Ey.Myf. . . . . MISS Elizabeth W—Ty'80 . . . . | ☎ (617) 631-5466 Nashua Av, Marblehead, MA *01945*

Parker MRS Judith A (Westin—Judith A Parker) Rdc'66 . . . . MISS Anne M . . . . JUNIORS MR William S . . . . | ☎ (215) 545-6828 2317 Naudain St, Philadelphia, PA *19146*

Parker MR & MRS Michael R (Virginia W Reynolds) Duke'80.Rcn.Ng.Cly.Mid'79
☎ (203) 622-8694 . . 1110 Lake Av, Greenwich, CT *06831*

Parker MRS Mills (Dorothy Telfair Mills) Ncd.
☎ (202) 966-7695 . . 3040 Idaho Av NW, Apt 313, Washington, DC *20016*

Parker MRS Patricia Gross (Dempsey—Patricia L Gross) . . . . MISS Victoria D . . . . MISS Elizabeth S . . . . MR John E JR . . . . | ☎ (314) 361-0959 4944 Lindell Blvd, St Louis, MO *63108*

Parker MRS Paul E JR (Kathleen C Oliver) B'gton'47.Cs.
☎ (212) 348-3167 . . 1170 Fifth Av, New York, NY *10029*

Parker MR Peyton Bradford—PaArt'82 . . see H M Denault

Parker JUNIORS MR R Jeffrey (James W C) . . . . Died at Southborough, MA May 4'96

Parker MR & MRS Richard Lee (Eveline Dunham) Cr'84
☎ (415) 731-7572 . . 1581 Masonic Av, San Francisco, CA *94117*

Parker MR & MRS Richard S JR (Kirstie L Alley) KasSt'74.P'76 ⚓
4875 Louise Av, Encino, CA *91316*

Parker MR & MRS Robert B (Lorenzen—Brenda Sweet)
☎ (603) 547-2749 . . Juniper Hill Farm, Francestown, NH *03043*

Parker COL (RET) & MRS Robert M (Lilly Pang) USA.Unn.Mt.Cw.H'37 . . . . MISS Elizabeth van C—Va'91.AmU'95 . . . . MR John MacD—P'89 . . . . | ☎ (703) 356-2792 7309 Dulany Dv, McLean, VA *22101*

Parker MISS Sarah Grace (J Hutchison) . . . . Born Mch 15'94

Parker MRS Sherman C (Horne—Kathleen Sheldon) Pg.Chi.Cc.
☎ (202) 625-2920 . . 2512 Q St NW, Apt 316, Washington, DC *20007*

Parker MR & MRS (DR) Stephen W (Elizabeth V Hillyer)
Y'78.Tufts'83.Rcn.Nrr.H'78.Cl'83
  ☎ (908) 439-3383 . . Church St, PO Box 617, Oldwick, NJ *08858*

Parker MR & MRS Thomas J (Hilary B Higgins) Wms'75.Bost'80
  ☎ (540) 672-5259 . . Woodberry Forest School, Box 22,
Woodberry Forest, VA *22989*

Parker MRS Thornton J JR (Margaret H Kerr) Ncd. . | ☎ (301) 652-6848
MR John W—Cc.Y'60.Pa'63 . . . . | 3502 Hamlet Place,
                                 | Chevy Chase, MD
                                 | *20815*

Parker MR & MRS Todd K (Sandra L Douglas)
  ☎ (703) 536-4514 . . 6230—19 St N, Arlington, VA *22205*

Parker MR & MRS William E (Rowland—Ruth Bentley)
  ☎ (416) 481-2453 . . 350 Lonsdale Rd, Apt 210, Toronto,
Ontario M5P 1R6, Canada

Parker MRS William Henry (Anne Wetherill) Ac.Ncd.
  ☎ (215) 283-7307 . . 1016 Foulkeways, Sumneytown Pike, Gwynedd,
PA *19436*

Parker MR & MRS William Merrick (Mackall—Virginia Lawrence)
Mt.Cvc.Cc.Ncd.GeoW'24
  ☎ (301) 654-7879 . . 108 E Melrose St, Chevy Chase, MD *20815*

Parker MRS William Montrose (Geraldine Page) . . . | ☎ (813) 799-0126
MISS Melanie S—at ☎ (209) 527-4545 | 2331 Finlandia
717 Wright St, Modesto, CA *95354* . . . . | Lane, Apt 21,
MR Douglas P—at 4200 Bay St, Apt 279, | Clearwater, FL
Fremont, CA *94538* . . . . | *34623*

Parkerson MR & MRS Godfrey R (Joan B Schwing)
  ☎ (504) 835-1644 . . 307 Rue St Ann, Metairie, LA *70005*

Parkin MR & MRS R Rex JR (Eliza McCawley) | ☎ (216) 247-4767
Kt.Rc.DU'70.DU'73.Mich'83 . . . . | 10 Old SOM Lane,
JUNIORS MISS Phebe E . . . . | Moreland Hills, OH
JUNIORS MR Henry McC . . . . | *44022*

Parkinson JUNIORS MR A Troup . . see MRS J H Briggs

Parkinson MISS Dana R . . see MRS J H Briggs

Parkinson MR & MRS James T 3d (Molly O Owens)
Swb'61.Cs.Va'62.Pa'64 . . of
  ☎ (212) 427-4112 . . 1170 Fifth Av, New York, NY *10029*
  ☎ (717) 646-3271 . . Pocono Lake Preserve, PA *18348*

Parkinson MR James T 4th (James T 3d) . . . . Married at
                                          Paradise Valley, AZ
  Monahan MISS Susan L (late Thomas R) . . . . Apr 13'96

Parkinson MR & MRS James T 4th (Susan L Monahan)
Ariz'91.Pa'95.Rc.Gettys'90.Pa'94
  ☎ (215) 569-2250 . . 2112 Chancellor St, Philadelphia, PA *19103*

Parkinson MR & MRS Robert (Porter—Francesca Nagle) WIT'35
  ☎ (508) 563-5787 . . 106 Bay Rd, Box 366, North Falmouth, MA *02556*

Parkman MR & MRS Samuel (Mary K Simonds) Sth'55.Ncd.H'54
  ☎ (212) 369-3183 . . 22 E 89 St, New York, NY *10128*

Parkman MR & MRS Theodore B (Winslow—G Floyd-Jones Harrison)
Bard'49.H'49
  ☎ (603) 778-0102 . . 7 River Woods Dv, Apt F112, Exeter,
NH *03833-4376*

Parks MISS Frances S
  ☎ (508) 428-0353 . . 1441 Old Post Rd, Marstons Mills, MA *02648*

Parks MR & MRS Nicholas R (Carole S Leonard) | ☎ (516) 367-3642
Ws'67.Pr.Ny.Csh.P.Mich'66 . . . . | 1560 Laurel Hollow
MISS Whitney S—at Middlebury . . . . | Rd, Syosset, NY
MR Gregory G—at Pepperdine U . . . . | *11791*
JUNIORS MR Nicholas R JR—at Boston U . . . . . . |

Parks MRS Thomas J (Blanton Sanders) S.Plg.
  ☎ (516) 922-4441 . . "Captured Brook" 157 Cove Rd, Oyster Bay,
NY *11771*

Parks MR & MRS William O 3d (Gael A Neugebauer) ArizSt'69.Ariz'66
  ☎ (602) 861-1850 . . 1130 E Palmaire Av, Phoenix, AZ *85020*

Parlange MR & MRS Walter C JR (Lucy M Brandon) | ☎ (504) 638-8410
Rv.Cw.Wt.Ncd.LSU'43 . . . . | Parlange Plantation,
MISS Angèle M—at ☎ (504) 895-2383 | New Roads, LA
5114 Pitt St, New Orleans, LA *70115* . . . . | *70760*

Parlee MISS Elizabeth J—V'63 . . see J A Bauer JR

Parmele MR & MRS Charles Roome 3d (Jacquelyn V | ☎ (609) 466-0526
White) Mds.Snc.Pn.P'49 . . . . | "Dog Woods"
MR Charles R 4th—Snc.Louis'79—at | 131 Rolling Hill Rd,
  ☎ (609) 466-1975 . . 148 N Greenwood Av, | Skillman, NJ *08558*
Hopewell, NJ *08525* . . . . |

Parmele MR James W—Snc.Ken'83
  ☎ (609) 466-1874 . . 11 S Lanning Av, Hopewell, NJ *08525*

Parmenter MRS Marian N (Wintersteen—Marian N Horwitz)
  ☎ (415) 388-4201 . . 21 Tamalpais Av, Mill Valley, CA *94941*

Parmley MR & MRS John R (Shyamala Murugesan)
  ☎ (808) 247-6094 . . 45-082 Wiape Place, Kaneohe, HI *96744*

Parmley MRS M Gilsey (Mary H Gilsey)
  ☎ (207) 563-5872 . . 70A River Rd, Newcastle, ME *04553*

Parnell MR & MRS C Nichols 3d (Sandra L Finch) | ☎ (334) 272-1470
Ala'73.Ala'70.Ala'73 . . . . | 2153 Vaughn Lane,
JUNIORS MR Justin M . . . . | Montgomery, AL
                                   | *36106*

Parr MR & MRS Edward John JR (Adair D Freeman)
Duke'88.Geo'93.Nu'86.Geo'93
  ☎ (540) 592-3690 . . 22378 Trappe Rd, PO Box 438, Upperville,
VA *20185*

Parr MR & MRS Thomas D R (Jenepher L Burton) | ☎ (410) 429-8947
Gv.Md.Elk.Mv.P'55 . . . . | 13800 Longnecker
MISS Amanda . . . . | Rd, Glyndon, MD
MR Crawford B . . . . | *21071*

Parrack MR & MRS Edward T (Elizabeth R Felix) Rr.Pg.Fcg.Cly.Pitt'36
  ☎ (412) 621-5744 . . Park Mansions, 5023 Frew St, Pittsburgh,
PA *15213*

Parriott MR Foster B 2d—SCal'82
  ☎ (314) 645-2980 . . 6625 Clayton Av, Apt 215, St Louis, MO *63139*

Parriott MR & MRS Jackson C (Sally C Lambert) Sth'56.Cy.Mo'54 . . of
  ☎ (314) 997-1197 . . 500 S Price Rd, St Louis, MO *63124*
  ☎ (561) 735-9155 . . 6880 N Ocean Blvd, Ocean Ridge, FL *33435*

Parriott MR & MRS Jackson C JR (Ashley A Roodhouse)
Van'87.Cysl.Van'87
  ☎ (410) 823-6358 . . 1404 Ruxton Rd, Baltimore, MD *21204*

Parris MRS S Nye (Sally B Nye) Nw'68 . . . . | ☎ (203) 698-3003
MISS Samantha R . . . . | 51 Stirrup Lane,
                                   | Riverside, CT *06878*

Parrish MRS Anthony R (Anne M Riegel)
  ☎ (904) 241-9019 . . 5306 Fleet Landing Blvd, Atlantic Beach, FL *32233*

Parrish MR & MRS Brainerd S (Kathleen F Moore) Tex'64.Tex'67 . . . . | of ☎ (915)533-4347
MISS Christine H—Tex'92.Tex'95—at | 516 Blacker Av,
☎ (713) 783-9495 . . 6444 Ella Lee Lane, | El Paso, TX 79902
Houston, TX 77057 . . . . | ☎ (505) 682-2164
MR David B—Tex'95—at U of Houston Law . . | ''Los Tres
    | Hermanos''
    | Cloudcroft, NM
    | 88317

Parrish MR & MRS Hugh M (Therese P Sellers) NH'67.Ph.An.Cry.Aga.Cw.Cc.Fw.Ac.Ncd. . . . . . | ☎ (207) 846-9675
MR Hugh R 3d—Cc. . . . . | ''Cousins Island''
    | RR 1, Box 323C,
    | Sea Meadows Lane,
    | Yarmouth, ME
    | 04096

Parrish MR & MRS John C (Parrott—Susan N Jones) B'gton'70.Pa'68.Pa'72 | ☎ (415) 922-4747
JUNIORS MR John R—at Tabor Acad . . . . | 2275 Broadway,
  MISS Amy L Parrott—at 216 Miller Av, Apt 4, | Apt 415,
Mill Valley, CA 94941 . . . . | San Francisco, CA
    | 94115

Parrish MRS Linda R (Linda K Riley) . . . . | ☎ (212) 876-9353
JUNIORS MR T Kirkpatrick 4th . . . . | 9 E 97 St, Apt 1C,
    | New York, NY
    | 10029

Parrish MR T Kirkpatrick—P'52
☎ (212) 879-0986 . . 215 E 73 St, New York, NY 10021

Parrish MR & MRS Thomas McC (Elizabeth D Wilson) Swb'87.HampSydney'87
☎ (804) 282-4123 . . 811 Horsepen Rd, Richmond, VA 23229

Parrott MISS Amy L . . see J C Parrish

Parrott MR & MRS Thomas A (Barbara Brown) Mt.Cvc.Fic.Cly.Sl.P'36
☎ (202) 337-3512 . . 3312 R St NW, Washington, DC 20007

Parrott MR & MRS William G JR (Hazard—Mary F Pitney) Bur.Pcu.Y'40 . . . . | ☎ (408) 646-0661
MR Gregory H . . . . | 200 Glenwood
    | Circle, Apt F6,
    | Monterey, CA
    | 93940

Parry MISS Allison J (Edward Owen JR) . . . Married at Charlottesville, VA
Hall MR Joseph M (James) . . . . Dec 2'95

Parry MR & MRS David A (A Beverley B Wilson) SL'68.Emer'73.Mit'79 . . . . | ☎ (802) 649-5151
MISS Blair A . . . . | Dutton Hill Rd,
JUNIORS MR Wilson S—at Hotchkiss . . . . | Norwich, VT 05055

Parry MR & MRS David L (Reeser—Susan Baumbach) LErie'61.Sar. . . . . | ☎ (814) 838-7740
  MR J Weston Reeser—at 513 S Walnut St, | 339 Shorehaven Dv,
West Chester, PA 19380 . . . . | Erie, PA 16505

Parry MR & MRS Edward O (Virginia Lloyd) Rv.Myf.Hav'36
☎ (412) 963-7580 . . 894 Locust Lane, Pittsburgh, PA 15238

Parry MR & MRS Edward Owen JR (Haycock—Susan J Fedor) Va'65 . of
☎ (212) 545-9051 . . 139 E 33 St, Apt 2-O, New York, NY 10016
☎ (201) 729-3536 . . ''Windfall'' 14 Island Trail, Sparta, NJ 07871

Parry COL (RET) & MRS Francis Fox (Thomas—Alice G Wurst) USMC.Pc.USN'41.GeoW'65
☎ (215) 233-5675 . . 6009 W Valley Green Rd, Flourtown, PA 19031

Parry DR & MRS H Frazer (Shaffer—Kathleen L Anderson) Pa'40.Pc.Ac.Hav'36.Pa'40
☎ (215) 646-8184 . . Whitpain Farm, 2 Bridge Lane, Blue Bell, PA 19422

Parry MR & MRS John C (Madeleine M Tiers) Ste.Ll.Pa'41
☎ (803) 881-0550 . . 1039 Loyalist Lane, Mt Pleasant, SC 29464

Parry MR & MRS John C JR (Vicki M Keller) SUNY'79.Man'vl'81.SCar'66.Pace'80 . . . . | of ☎ (914)628-7820
MISS Liana L—Tufts'91.Pace'93— | 11 Muscoot N,
☎ (914) 628-6114 . . . . | Mahopac, NY 10541
MISS Alicia T—at Dickinson . . . . | ☎ (441) 292-5445
    | ''Anne''
    | 22 Cavendish Rd,
    | Hamilton HM 12,
    | Bermuda

Parry MRS Richard (Buchan—Nesta I Crozier) Ac.
☎ (215) 247-3925 . . 8862 Towanda St, Philadelphia, PA 19118-3628

Parry MR William L—Duke'72 . . . . | ☎ (919) 876-8081
MISS Emily E—at Duke . . . . | 4553 Hargrove Rd,
    | Raleigh, NC 27604

Parshall MISS Barbara B (late H Baldwin) . . . . . . Married at Jericho, VT
Koier MR John C . . . . Aug 10'96

Parshall MR C Ward—Pg.Cl'63.Va'65.Y'74
☎ (011-44-1865) 512743 . . 2A Park Town, Oxford OX2 6SN, England

Parshall MISS Pamela W
☎ (802) 899-2994 . . Rte 1, Box 680, Range Rd, Underhill, VT 05489

Parson MRS Frederick P (Fardy—Helen Wolcott)
☎ (207) 374-8867 . . PO Box 31, Blue Hill, ME 04614

Parson MR & MRS Joseph (McWilliams—Penelope P Griswold) ColbyS'68.Grenoble'69.Dean'68
☎ (207) 767-5220 . . 9 Avon Rd, Cape Elizabeth, ME 04107

Parson MR & MRS Timothy P (Elizabeth B Toulmin) H'82.H'79
☎ (508) 369-0782 . . 190 Lowell St, Carlisle, MA 01741

Parsons MR & MRS Charles W (Margaret J Hill) Bgt.Snc.Hob'60 . . . . | ☎ (914) 234-3142
MR Justin J . . . . | Rte 2, Box 62,
    | Pound Ridge, NY
    | 10576

Parsons MR David McI—H'71.Stan'79
☎ (914) 777-2617 . . ''Lounsberry'' 240 Boston Post Rd, Rye, NY 10580-1126

Parsons MR & MRS Eugene M (Lucy McKinney) Htdon'58.Aub'56
☎ (334) 262-3127 . . 1672 Gilmer Av, Montgomery, AL 36104

Parsons MR & MRS Harris M (Elsie M White) Fic.
☎ (401) 245-8039 . . 63 Chapin Rd, Barrington, RI 02806

Parsons MR & MRS I Manning 3d (Fehsenfeld—Cynthia Riley) Sth'56.JHop'63.Nyc.Gv.Mv. Ty'52.Md'79 . . . . | ☎ (410) 329-3747
MISS Caroline Harvey E—at ☎ (508) 257-6785 | 1701 Western Run
PO Box 471, Siasconset, MA 02564 . . . . | Rd, Cockeysville,
MR Ira Manning IV—at Columbia Phys & Surg . | MD 21030

Parsons MR & MRS J Lester 3d (Estella P Day) Fic.Fiy.Shcc.Pn.P'61.H'65.Nu'69.FairD'86 . . . | ☎ (908) 766-5845
MR James S . . . . | 52 Chapin Rd,
MR Charles S . . . . | Bernardsville, NJ
    | 07924

Parsons MRS John J (Olive Whitman) Dc.Dar.Ncd.
☎ (410) 266-7127 . . ''Ginger Cove'' 1306 River Crescent Dv, Annapolis, MD 21401

Parsons DR & MRS John M (Dorothy A Vietor)
Laf'60
MR Timothy V—Laf'91 . . . .
☎ (413) 586-3982
324 Audubon Rd,
Leeds, MA *01053*

Parsons MR Marselis C—Plg.Pn.P'28
☎ (603) 795-2570 . . River Bend Farm, 498 River Rd, Lyme,
NH *03768*

Parsons MR & MRS Marselis C 3d (Julie E McVeigh)
Vt'69.Plg.Laf'66 . . . .
MISS Susan W . . . .
''Clearwater''
8 Pinehurst Dv,
Shelburne, VT
05482

Parsons MISS Michele—Sth'85 . . see B H Grove JR

Parsons MR & MRS Robert White (Suzanne de C
Warner) Fic. . . . .
JUNIORS MISS Rebecca H . . . .
JUNIORS MISS Emily W . . . .
☎ (401) 421-8882
90 Congdon St,
Providence, RI
02906

Parsons MR Stephen C—P'72
☎ (847) 295-9065 . . 177A Washington Circle, Lake Forest, IL *60045*

Parsons MRS Thomas III (Boice—Sheila Crimmins) C.
☎ (203) 655-4637 . . 171 Pear Tree Point Rd, Darien, CT *06820*

Parsons MR & MRS Todd M (Kasi McGhee)
3145 Partridge Rd, Montgomery, AL *36111*

Parsons MR & MRS William (Louise Bigelow) Cly.Ncd.Yn.Y'31.Y'34
☎ (207) 985-3918 . . ''Crescent Surf'' PO Box 97, Kennebunk,
ME *04043*

Parsons MR & MRS William JR (Marie Thérèse
Foley) Newt'73.Mb.Pr.Cly.Y.'65.Cl'68 . . . .
MISS Louise W . . . .
MR William C . . . .
MR Charles B . . . .
of ☎ (516)676-0032
16 Cherrywood Rd,
Locust Valley, NY
11560
☎ (212) 628-9660
985 Fifth Av,
New York, NY
10021

Parvis MR & MRS Peter P (Mary L Pendleton) Md'67.Md'77
☎ (410) 377-2390 . . 7011 Copeleigh Rd, Baltimore, MD *21212*

Paschal MR & MRS Guy (Helen M Weld) Snc.H'55 .
MISS Elizabeth W—at ☎ (914) 381-0196
412 Munro Av, Apt 1E, Mamaroneck, NY *10543*
JUNIORS MISS Emilie B
☎ (803) 886-3294
411 Pelican Flight
Dv, Dewees Island,
SC *29451*

Pascoe MR & MRS Llewellyn P (Mary V Gibb) Cvc.Cl'61
☎ (202) 686-3155 . . 4515 Cathedral Av NW, Washington, DC *20016*

Passano MR & MRS Edward M JR (Helen C
Marikle) NotreDMd'69.JHop'78.StA.Ds.Rv.Cw.
JHop'67.JHop'69 . . . .
MISS Catherine M . . . .
MISS Tamara A . . . .
JUNIORS MISS Sarah R . . . .
☎ (410) 889-1853
3925 Linkwood Rd,
Baltimore, MD
21210

Passano MR & MRS L Baldwin (Julia E Evans) Sg.Fst.Cw.JHop'32
☎ (410) 632-2449 . . ''Cherrystone'' 208 W Federal St, Snow Hill,
MD *21863*

Passano MR & MRS William M JR (Helen V Addington)
Gi.Md.Cw.Rv.Mv.HampSydney'52 ⚓ . . of
☎ (410) 523-2764 . . 251 W Lanvale St, Baltimore, MD *21217*
☎ (410) 255-6776 . . Cooley's Pond Rd, Box 40, Gibson Island,
MD *21056*

Passano MR & MRS William M 3d (Terry E Dennis)
Hlns'80.Gi.Cy.Cw.Roan'78 ⚓
☎ (410) 433-2729 . . 5502 Lombardy Place, Baltimore, MD *21210*

Paston-Bedingfeld MR & MRS Henry E (Mary K
Ambrose) StGeoSwitz'65 . . . .
MISS Katherine M . . . .
MISS Charlotte A . . . .
MR Richard E A . . . .
JUNIORS MR Thomas H . . . .
☎ (011-44-1366)
328269
Oxburgh Hall,
King's Lynn,
Norfolk PE33 9PS,
England

Patcévitch MRS Iva S V (Tullis—Hall—Amory—
Chesbrough Lewis) Bcs.So.BtP.Evg . . .of
☎ (561) 659-0148 . . 141 Brazilian Av, Palm Beach, FL *33480*
☎ (516) 283-1709 . . 31 Foster Crossing, PO Box 5077, Southampton,
NY *11969*

Patch MR & MRS Benjamin T (Ellen J Coniglio) SUNY'88.Mid'89
☎ (011-44-181) 788-1534 . . Elmley Cottage, 81 Wimbledon Parkside,
London SW19 5LP, England

Patch MASTER Benjamin Woodward (Benjamin T) . . . . Born at
New York, NY Jly 5'95

Patch MRS Howard R JR (Kathryn V Woodward)
Ws'46.Co.Hn. . . . .
MR David S R—Cr'88—at ☎ (419) 472-3878
2034 Berdan Av, Toledo, OH *43613* . . . .
☎ (860) 434-2450
25 McCurdy Rd,
Old Lyme, CT
06371

Patch MR Peter B—H'71
22 Brush Hill Rd, Newton, MA *02161*

Pate MR & MRS Carlton O JR (Ida Louise Tobey) . . . .
MR William T—Rv. . . . .
☎ (203) 481-7280
88 Notch Hill Rd,
Apt 153,
North Branford, CT
06471

Pate MR & MRS Carlton O 3d (Anne C Nelson)
Mon'72.Mon'69 . . . .
MISS Lesley A . . . .
JUNIORS MR Carlton O 4th . . . .
☎ (860) 633-2052
285 Forest Lane,
Glastonbury, CT
06033

Patel MR & MRS Sanjay H (Leslie S Dickey) Ws'83.Cs.H.'83.Stan'87
☎ (212) 288-6599 . . 125 E 72 St, Apt 10D, New York, NY *10021*

Paternotte MR & MRS William L (Nancy D
Brewster) Md'84.Au.Md.Mv.Gv.P'67.Pa'69 . . .
MISS Nancy M . . . .
MR William B . . . .
MR Christopher B . . . .
of ☎ (410)581-2686
2 Chetwick Court,
Owings Mills, MD
21117
☎ (518) 576-9734
''Bear-in-Mind''
Rte 73, Box 567,
Keene Valley, NY
12943

Paterson MRS Thomas H (Alexander—Barney—Virginia E Ely) May.
☎ (216) 382-3818 . . 1659 Sheridan Rd, Cleveland, OH *44121*

Paterson MR Thomas H JR—Hampshire'78
☎ (401) 624-4217 . . 191 Hilton St, Tiverton, RI *02878*

Paton DR & MRS David (Beardmore—Brokaw—Diane D Johnston)
Mds.C.Cly.P'52.JHop'56
☎ (516) 324-3979 . . 24 Cove Hollow Farm Rd, PO Box 5015,
East Hampton, NY *11937*

Paton MR Kenneth H
☎ (803) 671-4454 . . 31 Twin Pines Rd, Hilton Head Island, SC *29928*

Patricola MR & MRS Steven L (Lucy B Baker)
Pa'79.Conn'84.Pe.Cly.Pa'79.Pa'87
☎ (914) 698-0317 . . 491 S Barry Av, Mamaroneck, NY *10543*

Pattee MR & MRS Gordon B (Dailey Jones)
B.Un.K.Pr.Ri.Ng.Cly.Stan'70.H'75 . . . . ☎ (212) RE4-0360
JUNIORS MISS Mary D . . . . 812 Park Av,
JUNIORS MISS Ashleigh L . . . . New York, NY
10021

Pattee MRS W Burleigh (Dorothy E Evans) Bur.Tcy.
☎ (423) 821-7506 . . 224 W Brow Oval, Lookout Mountain, TN *37350*

Patterson MR & MRS A Willing (Leila Delano) Gm.Me.H'32
☎ (610) 645-8812 . . 1400 Waverly Rd, Blair O32, Gladwyne,
PA *19035*

Patterson MISS Abby Ann (Swenson—Cammann—
Abby Ann N Patterson) KHam'tn'72
☎ (617) 965-9461 . . 15 Francis St, Newton Center, MA *02159*

Patterson MRS Alexander E (Eleanor Morgan) V'18
☎ (914) 967-4100 . . Osborn Home, 501 Theo Fremd Av, Rye,
NY *10580*

Patterson MR & MRS Alexander E JR (Mary R
McPherson) V'54.Rv.Cw.Ncd.P'45 . . . . ☎ (203) 869-1394
MISS Joan M—Cal'81 . . . . 291 Stanwich Rd,
MISS Wynne McP—RISD'83.Y'88 . . . . Greenwich, CT
MISS Jill R—V'87.Y'90 *06830*

Patterson MR & MRS Alexander E 3d (Carol Ann Johnson)
☎ (515) 472-8690 . . 1203 S Main St, Fairfield, IA *52556*

Patterson MR & MRS Arthur C (Louise Muhlfeld)
3135 Pacific St, San Francisco, CA *94115*

Patterson MRS C Campbell (Margaret S Bent) Cy.Cda.
☎ (617) 461-8575 . . 10 Longwood Dv, Apt 276, Westwood, MA *02090*

Patterson MR & MRS David C (Considine—Maria C
Wall) Rdc'70.K.Fic.H'70 . . . . ☎ (212) 439-9103
MISS Eloise C . . . . 162 E 66 St,
JUNIORS MR David G . . . . New York, NY
10021

Patterson MR & MRS David S (Emelyn L Whiton)
Rdc'62.H.'57.Cl'61 . . . . ☎ (212) 472-0448
MR David S JR . . . . 165 E 65 St,
MR James W . . . . New York, NY
MR Philip C *10021*

Patterson MR Edward—Pr.Y'43
☎ (212) 586-6474 . . 24 W 55 St, New York, NY *10019*

Patterson MR & MRS Edward M (Beverly A Smith)
Ala'70.Ala'71.Dar.Ala'70.Ala'73 . . . . ☎ (334) 265-9772
MISS Kathryn E . . . . 3103 Boxwood Dv,
MISS Erin E . . . . Montgomery, AL
36111

Patterson MR & MRS Ellmore C (Anne H Choate) Ln.Fic.Fiy.Cly.Ch'35
☎ (561) 546-7025 . . 17 S Beach Rd, Box 775, Hobe Sound, FL *33475*

Patterson MR & MRS F Lytton 3d (Betty L Leggett) ☎ (302) 328-7469
MR Francis L 4th—Cw.—at ☎ (302) 984-1684 28 E 3 St,
1907 Van Buren St, Wilmington, DE *19802* . . . New Castle, DE
MISS A Whitney Lockhart *19720*

Patterson MR & MRS George W 3d (Harding— ☎ (508) 475-6564
Frances D Walker) V'49.USN'50.Mit'56 . . . . . . 75 Cheever Circle,
MISS Frances F—Ws'85.Spgfd'89—at Andover, MA *01810*
Scripps College, 1030 Columbia Av, Claremont,
CA *91711* . . . .
MISS Brenda B Harding—at Winnemucca, NV
89445 . . . .

Patterson MR & MRS Henry D 2d (Ann McCartin) Ncd.
☎ (619) 281-8338 . . 941 G Av, Coronado, CA *92118*

Patterson MR Henry Stuart 2d—Csn.P'44 . . . . ☎ (609) 924-4342
MR Henry S 3d—F&M'75—at ☎ (908) 354-4393 46 Westcott Rd,
1 Elizabethtown Plaza, Elizabeth, NJ *07202* . . . . Princeton, NJ *08540*

Patterson MISS (DR) J Ritchie (Russel H JR) . . . . . . Married at Alpine, NY
Gibbons DR Lawrence K (Earl D) Aug 17'96

Patterson MR & MRS James B (Audrey R Hagen) ☎ (860) 355-1078
Ne.Tulsa'60 . . . . PO Box 2548,
MISS Dorothy H—at Syracuse U . . . . New Preston, CT
06777

Patterson MR James G
778 N Pleasant St, Amherst, MA *01002*

Patterson MRS Jefferson (M Marvin Breckinridge) Cly.Csn.Sl.
☎ (202) 333-5251 . . 3108 Woodland Dv NW, Washington, DC *20008*

Patterson MR & MRS Jere W (Healey—Betty of ☎ (212)PL1-2888
Muggleton) Un.Plg.So.Bcs.Cs.P.'38.Ox'39 . . . . 480 Park Av,
MR Jere W JR—P'74 . . . . New York, NY
10022
☎ (516) 283-7050
30 Wall St,
Southampton, NY
11968

Patterson MRS John McC (Hope C Wood) Csn.
☎ (202) 338-1258 . . 4832 Hutchins Place NW, Washington, DC *20007*

Patterson MR & MRS Lloyd A (Judith I Carroll)
Sth'74.Nu'82.Tex'70.Tex'74
☎ (512) 263-5878 . . 702 Commons Ford Rd, Austin, TX *78733*

Patterson MRS Marion D JR (Tamia J Biddle)
☎ (814) 696-4050 . . 5 Blairmont Terr, Hollidaysburg, PA *16648*

Patterson MR & MRS Michael E (Elena A Carrillo) of ☎ (212)628-9549
Wheat'64.Ri.H'64.Cl'67 . . . . 530 E 86 St,
MISS Anne—at Westbrook, CT *06498* . . . . New York, NY
MR Michael E JR—Wes'95 . . . . *10028*
☎ (860) 434-0650
''La Folie''
Lord Hill Lane,
Box 4009,
Old Lyme, CT
06371

Patterson MR & MRS Oliver M (Donnelley—Cynthia K Coffey)
Cas.Cnt.Wis'50
☎ (520) 577-0667 . . 7348 E Calle Alba Serena, Tucson, AZ *85750*

Patterson MRS Patricia M (Barlerin—Lebermann— ☎ (214) 521-9940
Patricia M Patterson) Sth'60.Cl'70.Ri. . . . . 3831 Turtle Creek
MISS Caroline P Barlerin—V'95—at Blvd, Apt 23C,
329—25 Av, Apt 2, San Francisco, CA *94121* Dallas, TX *75219*

Patterson MRS Patricia S (Norris—Patricia Shephard) Bcs.Ri.Cly.
☎ (212) 744-5690 . . 1 E 66 St, New York, NY *10021*

Patterson MR & MRS Remington P (E Duane Lloyd) Bnd'55.Y'50.Y'57
☎ (212) 662-3233 . . 280 Riverside Dv, New York, NY *10025*

Patterson MR & MRS Robert E (Christina F Balboni) ☎ (415) 326-1016
CtCol'69.Bhm.Fr.Ncd.Cal'64.Stan'72 . . . . 176 Tuscaloosa Av,
JUNIORS MR Victor E . . . . Atherton, CA *94027*

Patterson MR & MRS Robert E (Jane E Manopoli)
Rdc'70.Cal'73.Cy.Fic.Ln.Sm.H'67.H'71
☎ (617) 262-3789 . . 370 Beacon St, Boston, MA *02116*

Patterson MRS Robert E (Whitall—Pamela B Payne) . . . . ☎ (860) 572-9932 Bishops Cove,
MISS Pamela B . . . . 5 Canberra Court, Mystic, CT *06355*

Patterson DR & MRS Robert J (Patricia A Moore) Ws'47.Buf.G.SUNY'50
☎ (716) 839-2744 . . 10 Rankin Rd, Amherst, NY *14226*

Patterson MRS Robert Lee JR (Margaret D Sloane)
☎ (914) 666-4258 . . PO Box 59, Mt Kisco, NY *10549*

Patterson MR & MRS Robert P JR (Bevin Daly) of ☎ (212)826-9268
C.Chr.Cs.H'45.Cl'50 . . . . 200 E 66 St,
MISS Katherine E A . . . . New York, NY
MR Paul—GeoW'86 . . . . *10021*
☎ (914) 265-3008 Fair Oaks Farm, Cold Spring, NY *10516*

Patterson MR & MRS Robert R (Edith B Sheerin) Va'78.Vmi'71.Gen'84
☎ (703) 548-7617 . . 2933 Eddington Terr, Alexandria, VA *22302-3503*

Patterson MRS Rushmore (Peyton S Kirk) P.Pr.Cly . . .of
☎ (212) RE7-7452 . . 142 E 71 St, New York, NY *10021*
☎ (516) WA2-0539 . . "Little House" East Norwich, NY *11732*

Patterson DR & MRS Russel H JR (Juliet R Boyd) of 146 W 57 St,
K.Stan'48.Cr'52 . . . . New York, NY
MR Alexander C *10019*
☎ (802) 482-2234 Rte 116, Hinesburg, VT *05461*

Patterson MISS Shirley C
☎ (202) 537-0861 . . 4200 Cathedral Av NW, Apt 917, Washington, DC *20016*

Patterson MRS Susan H (Petschek—Churchill—Susan H Patterson) Cly.H.
☎ (212) 838-4927 . . 455 E 57 St, New York, NY *10022*

Patterson MR Thomas—Wms'50
☎ (212) 289-8757 . . 120 E 90 St, New York, NY *10128-1549*

Patterson MR & MRS Thomas G (Nancy T Pollock) Coe'76.Sc.Mich'60
☎ (773) 348-5919 . . 2128 N Fremont St, Chicago, IL *60614*

Patterson MRS V A Bookhart (Virginia A Bookhart) Mlsp'60.Ncd.
☎ (601) 982-3939 . . 4546 Kings H'way, Jackson, MS *39206*

Patterson MR & MRS William C (Carolyn S Leigh) Bgt.NCar'63.Cl'68
☎ (212) 831-0272 . . 1050 Park Av, New York, NY *10028-1031*

Patteson MR Charles J—Ht.Cw.WKy'64
☎ (212) 744-2914 . . 823 Madison Av, New York, NY *10021*

Pattishall MR & MRS Beverly W (Mashek—Dorothy M Daniels)
Wa.Nw'38.Va'41 . . of
☎ (773) 883-1377 . . 2244 N Lincoln Park W, Chicago, IL *60614*
☎ (616) 469-0448 . . "Swift Cottage" 14156 Swift Lane, Lakeside, MI *49116*
☎ (970) 728-4297 . . 285 Beaver Pond Lane, Telluride, CO *81435*

Pattison MR Frederick Woodworth—Gr.Chr.Sar.Rv.Ofp.
Coa.Cw.Ne.Ll.Snc.Ty'53.Cwr'54
☎ (212) CH3-5656 . . 10 W 16 St, New York, NY *10011*

Patton MR & MRS J Stiles (Joan S Gilmore) ☎ (215) 643-2417
Bvr'65.Temp'70 . . . . 342 Mattison Av,
MISS Anna S—at Munich, Germany . . . . Ambler, PA
MISS Katherine L—at Drexel *19002-4656*
MR R Price—at Raleigh, NC . . . .

Patton MR & MRS James R JR (Mary M Maughan)
B.Mt.Sl.NCar'48.H'51 . . of
☎ (970) 923-4028 . . 58 Fox Lane, PO Box 6627, Snowmass Village, CO *81615*
☎ (703) 759-2970 . . 456 River Bend Rd, Great Falls, VA *22066*

Patton MR & MRS Paul L (Kimble—Judith A ☎ (415) 459-1277
Thomas) Cal'69.Cal'70 . . . . 20 Hill Dv,
MISS Jennifer L . . . . Kentfield, CA *94904*
JUNIORS MR Nicholas B . . . .

Patton MR & MRS Richard C (Robin B Ingram) DU'88
1600 Chickering Rd, Nashville, TN *37215*

Patton MR & MRS Stuart T (Susan B Richardson) ☎ (334) 279-0987
Aub'78.Aub'78 . . . . 3856 Colline Dv,
JUNIORS MR S Timothy . . . . Montgomery, AL *36106*

Pattou MR & MRS A Brace (Grant—Suzanne Pirie) Ch'45
☎ (312) 337-7961 . . 1448 N Lake Shore Dv, Chicago, IL *60610*

Patty MISS Eleanor J—Rol'86
305 S Valley Forge Rd, Devon, PA *19333*

Patty MR William A 4th . . see MRS K E Jackson

Paul MR & MRS A J Drexel JR (Margaret Delano)
Gm.Ph.Ssk.H'37.Va'41 . . of
☎ (610) 688-2874 . . 1275 Upper Gulph Rd, Radnor, PA *19087*
☎ (561) 336-0798 . . 12458 Harbour Ridge Blvd, Palm City, FL *34990*

Paul MRS A Johnson (Virginia Ann Johnson) Ac.
☎ (317) 781-8552 . . 5808 Quail Chase Dv, Indianapolis, IN *46237*

Paul MR & MRS Anthony M (Anne W Carse) Ws'62. ☎ (011-66-2)
MR A Brodie—Macalester'89 439-5322
MR Bruce B—NCar'89 . . . . Tridhos City Marina 148, 1867 Charoen Nakorn Rd, Klongsarm, Bangkok 10600, Thailand

Paul MR & MRS Douglas L (McMullen—Elizabeth A of ☎ (212)832-1790
Curtis-Setchell) Rc.Pr.B.Chr.StJ.Ri.F&M'65. 570 Park Av,
Cl'70 . . . . New York, NY
JUNIORS MR Nicholas L *10021*
☎ (516) 671-9284 Meadow Farm, Sheep Lane, Lattingtown, NY *11560*

Paul MRS Frances E (Frances E Clark) Cly.
☎ (610) 353-2714 . . Featherfield Farm, 15 Marlborough Rd, Newtown Square, PA *19073*

Paul MRS J H Haywood-Reuben (J Hope Haywood-Reuben) Wa.Sc.Cas.
13045 Biggin Church Rd, Jacksonville, FL *32216*

Paul MRS Lawrence O (Louise L Carr)
☎ (703) 578-7633 . . 3440 S Jefferson St, Apt 1110, Falls Church, VA *22041*

Paul MRS Margaret S (Margaret L Smith) ☎ (215) 646-0495
PCTS'77.Neumann'89 . . . . 905 Valley Rd,
MISS Letitia L—KutzU'89 . . . . Blue Bell, PA *19422*
MISS Marianne H . . . .

Paul DR & MRS Oglesby (Hatch—Paul—Jean D Lithgow) Sb.Sm.Cw.StJ.Csn.H'38.H'42 . . . . . . | 10 Longwood Dv, Apt 322, Westwood, MA *02090*
  MISS Marguerite—at ☎ (404) 377-4871 269 Mt Vernon Dv, Decatur, GA *30030*. . . . . .

Paul MR & MRS Robert H 3d (Pamela D Yardley) Yn.Y'57
  ☎ (904) 285-5653 . . PO Box 1188, Ponte Vedra Beach, FL *32082*

Paul MISS Ruth U—Sth'38.Cvc.Ct.Ncd.
  ☎ (202) 966-3920 . . 4301 Massachusetts Av NW, Washington, DC *20016*

Paul MRS Wendy D (Vincent—Wendy D Paul) Gm. | ☎ (610) 688-0918
  MISS Margaret D . . . . | ''Mouse Acre'' 1259 Upper Gulph Rd, Radnor, PA *19087*

Pauley MR & MRS J Renard (Frances Carton) StL'59 | 1442 Christmas Creek Rd, Chesterfield, MO *63005*
  MISS Elizabeth C . . . .
  MISS Julia B . . . .
  MR Christopher R—at 112 Lewis Place, St Louis, MO *63135* . . . .
  MR Daniel J . . . .

Paull MR & MRS Robert C (Heather B Fick) Cal'87.Cal'86
  ☎ (408) 335-2875 . . 498 Fall Creek Dv, Felton, CA *95018*

Paulson MR John F . . see E G Cumming

Pauly MRS Elizabeth L (Elizabeth L von Weise)
  ☎ (513) 561-7100 . . 4610 Burley Hills Dv, Cincinnati, OH *45243*

Paumgarten MR & MRS Nicholas B (Carol Marshall) Pa'68.Rc.Ri.Ln.Pa'67.Cl'71 . . . . | of ☎ (516)624-8141 411 Centre Island Rd, Oyster Bay, NY *11771*
  MR Nicholas B JR—P'91 . . . .
  MR Alexander M—Pa'94 . . . . | ☎ (212) 628-0526 130 East End Av, New York, NY *10028*

Paumgarten-Hohenschwangau-Erbach MR & MRS Harald (Barbara Rowinska) War'60.Ste.B.Cc. Pa'60.Cal'64 . . . . | of ☎ (718)834-9569 298 Hicks St, Brooklyn, NY *11201*
  MISS Christina—at U of Pa . . . . | ''The Farm'' Saranac, NY *12981*

Pawlick MR & MRS Albert (Douglass—Tyler—Marian Phelps) V'47.Cho.On.Sr.Cas.StJ.Wms'45
  ☎ (847) 234-4951 . . Box 522, 100 Crabtree Lane, Lake Bluff, IL *60044*

Paxton MR & MRS Henry Douglas (Adèle Warden) Ac.Ncd. | ☎ (215) 794-8144 ''Elm Grove'' Holicong, PA *18928-0125*
  MISS Marie-Adèle le Menestrel—at ☎ (540) 822-4176 . . Rte 3, Box 68, Lovettsville, VA *20180* . . . .
  MISS Geneviève le Menestrel . . . .
  MR Charles le Menestrel—at Paris, France . .

Paxton MR & MRS Frank Roberts (Stein—Prowell—Leonora H Parsons) Sth'36.Cly.
  ☎ (860) 526-9089 . . ''Merecote'' 150 Ferry Rd, Hadlyme, CT *06439*

Paxton MISS Isabel Larkin (John C) . . . . Born at San Francisco, CA Mch 19'96

Paxton MR & MRS John C (Elizabeth L O'Brien) Br'77.Cal'71
  ☎ (415) 563-0886 . . 330 Presidio Av, San Francisco, CA *94115*

Payne MR & MRS David M (Littlefield—Sally Shore) Sth'53.Csn.Yn.Y'41.Cl'48 . . . . | of ☎ (860)434-1679 53-2 Brockway Ferry Rd, Lyme, CT *06371*
  MR John S Littlefield—Bab'86 . . . . | ☎ (207) 372-6615 CR 35, Box 765, Glenmere Rd, Tenants Harbor, ME *04860*

Payne MRS Harold (Norris—Abeles—Catherine Fuller)
  ☎ (941) 966-2019 . . 222 N Casey Key, Osprey, FL *33559*

Payne MR & MRS Jackson Middleton (N Suzanne Trimm) Aub'67 . . . . | ☎ (205) 969-0013 3428 Brookwood Rd, Birmingham, AL *35223*
  MISS Jennifer M . . . .
  JUNIORS MISS Sarah S . . . .
  JUNIORS MR Jesse J . . . .

Payne DR & MRS John W (Jane Champe) Sth'64.Md.JHop'57.JHop'61 . . . . | ☎ (410) 889-8644 4311 Underwood Rd, Baltimore, MD *21218*
  MR David F C . . . .
  JUNIORS MR J Kimball C . . . .

Payne LT COL (RET) & MRS Thomas C (Ellison—Ruth A Sharrett) BA.Sth'37.Tufts'71.Lond'32 . . | ☎ (617) 262-2744 81 Marlborough St, Boston, MA *02116*
  MR Brooks E—McG'68.Bost'73—at 185 W Canton St, Boston, MA *02116* . . . .

Payne MISS Victoria M (Vizcaino—Victoria M Payne) Rich'83.VPI'86
  ☎ (910) 922-6050 . . 2813 Bethabara Park Blvd, Winston-Salem, NC *27106*

Paynter MR & MRS Grenville H (Tehan—Sally Gooch) Sth'55.Cs.P.'53 . . . . | ☎ (212) 371-7341 333 E 57 St, New York, NY *10022*
  MR Bradford G—at ☎ (203) 324-9326 34B Dora St, Stamford, CT *06902* . . . .
  MR Nathaniel C . . . .

Paynter MR & MRS Raymond A JR (Elizabeth Storer) Bow'46.Y'48 . . . . | ☎ (617) 899-3533 74 Sunset Rd, Weston, MA *02193*
  MISS Dorothy S—Mid'87—at ☎ (212) 570-2395 418 E 83 St, Apt 5D, New York, NY *10028* . . .
  MR Raymond A 3d—H'89 . . . .

Payson, Parker L & Macpherson, Marian—So'88.Tul'91.GeoW'96. So'87.Ch'93
  ☎ (703) 768-3676 . . 2403 Daphne Lane, Alexandria, VA *22306*

Payson MR & MRS Phillips H (Kilburn—Sarah H Taylor) Pn.P'53 . . . . | ☎ (860) 868-2285 PO Box 1234, Washington, CT *06793*
  MISS Elizabeth W—Vt'92—at ☎ (805) 772-9798 PO Box 373, Morro Bay, CA *93443* . . . .

Payson MRS Rosalind S (Becker—Rosalind B Spong) SCar'47.Cly.Cda. . . . . | ☎ (203) 259-7517 227 Main St, PO Box 943, Southport, CT *06490*
  MR Laurence G 2d—Ty'78 . . . .
  MR Blakeney D—NewSchSR'80 . . . .
  MR Eliot K . . . .

Payson MR & MRS Samuel R (Laura Richardson) Wh'lck'51.H'57.Un.Cw.Ncd.H.'38
  ☎ (617) 899-1802 . . PO Box 318, Weston, MA *02193*

Payson MISS Sandra (Meyer—Weidenfeld—Sandra H Payson) Sl.Cly . . .of
  ☎ (202) 667-7892 . . 2210 Kalorama Rd NW, Washington, DC *20008*
  ☎ (540) 364-3132 . . ''Ashley'' PO Box 55, Delaplane, VA *20144*

Peabody MR Alexander B (John D JR) . . . . Married at Santa Barbara, CA Hanssen MISS Jennifer B . . . . Oct 2'93

Peabody MR & MRS Alexander B (Jennifer B Hanssen)
BostColl'88.KeeSt'86
☎ (714) 854-2013 . . 6 Baycrest Court, Newport Beach, CA *92660*
Peabody MR & MRS Endicott (Barbara W Gibbons) H'42 ⚓ . . of
☎ (603) 465-7771 . . Box 1078, 33 Main St, Hollis, NH *03049*
☎ (441) 293-0215 . . "Tigh-Na-Creige" 15 Tucker's Town Rd,
Tucker's Town HS 02, Bermuda

Peabody MR & MRS Endicott JR (Andrea L Lamp) | ☎ (617) 738-7236
Ws'74.Cy.H'71 . . . . | 2 Perrin Rd,
MR Endicott 4th—at U of Vt . . . . | Brookline, MA
| *02146*

Peabody MR & MRS Francis W (Ward—Swetzoff—Sara T Weeks)
Cy.Hn.H'46
☎ (617) 277-8656 . . 99 Clyde St, Chestnut Hill, MA *02167*

Peabody MR Henry L—Ec. . . . . | ☎ (508) 768-7941
JUNIORS MR Henry L JR . . . . | 136 Eastern Av,
JUNIORS MR John G . . . . | Essex, MA *01929*

Peabody MR & MRS Howard B JR (Margaret G Pipes) V'48.Cly.USMMA'44
☎ (504) 840-9935 . . 309 Rue St Ann, Metairie, LA *70005*
Peabody MRS James B (Ann C Reinicke) Cly.Cda.Km.
☎ (212) 755-8757 . . 250 E 65 St, New York, NY *10021*

Peabody MR & MRS John D JR (Wall—Elizabeth | ☎ (603) 525-3564
Frazier) PhilaArt'50.Ty'47 . . . . | 111 Middle Rd,
MR James B—NH'89—at 223 N Guadalupe St, | Hancock, NH *03449*
Box 247, Santa Fe, NM *87501* . . . . |
MR Michael A P Wall—Col'90—at |
112 Myrtle St, Boston, MA *02114* . . . . |

Peabody MR & MRS John D 3d (John D 3d) . . . . Married at Peterborough, NH
Green MISS Kathryn L (Michael) . . . . May 30'96
Peabody MR & MRS John D 3d (Kathryn L Green) UWash'87.Ty'83.NH'89
☎ (703) 979-3346 . . 1125—20 St S, Arlington, VA *22202*
Peabody MR & MRS Julian L (Bowles—Hart—Constance E Crowley)
SL'37.C.Gr.Bur.Fr.P'37.Cl'42 . . of
☎ (415) 346-3324 . . 3410 Jackson St, San Francisco, CA *94118*
☎ (209) 826-3175 . . "Water Tower" 11609 S Hereford Rd, Los Banos,
CA *93635*

Peabody MR & MRS Malcolm E (Pamela O Rowe) | ☎ (202) 333-5715
V'57.H'50 . . . . | 2811 Dumbarton St
MR Carter E—at ☎ (213) 655-2361 | NW, Washington,
7940 Blackburn Av, Los Angeles, CA *90048* . . . | DC *20007*

Peabody MISS Mina B . . see M Cox 3d
Peabody MRS Pamela T (Lee—Pamela T Dix) | ☎ (508) 526-1191
Bnd'48.Cl'62.Ec.Myc. . . . . | 22 Friend St,
MISS Virginia S—Ken'79—at ☎ (508) 468-1127 | Manchester, MA
324 Forest St, South Hamilton, MA *01982* . . . . . | *01944*

Peabody MR & MRS Samuel P (Judith A | ☎ (212) 861-0056
Dunnington) Rc.Cly.H'50 . . . . | 990 Fifth Av,
MISS Elizabeth T—at 450 E 52 St, New York, NY | New York, NY
10022 . . . . | *10021-0141*

Peace MRS E Coleman (Large—Lee R Edwards) Me.Ncd.
☎ (610) 933-1965 . . "Stoney Hollow" Box 283, RD 5, Malvern,
PA *19355*

Peace MR & MRS William H 3d (Tufari—Anna E M | ☎ (011-44-1494)
Venturi) IstArte'70.Y'60 . . . . | 712213
JUNIORS MISS Letizia Tufari . . . . | "Orchard Cottage"
JUNIORS MISS Ilaria Tufari . . . . | Cockpit Rd,
| Great Kingshill,
| Buckinghamshire
| HP15 6ER, England

Peake MR & MRS David V (Cameron A McAdoo) | ☎ (215) 836-2745
OWes'77.Sa.Gm.Fst.Rv.Ty'66.Pa'74 . . . . | 1003 Quill Lane,
JUNIORS MR David V JR . . . . | Oreland, PA *19075*
JUNIORS MR R Liggett M . . . . |

Peake MR & MRS David W (Ann D Journeay) Sth'47.StA.Yn.Y'50
☎ (713) 622-8529 . . 5304 Shady River Rd, Houston, TX *77056*
Peake MR & MRS David W JR (Katherine B Fordyce)
NMex'75.DU'80.DU'76
☎ (210) 644-2767 . . Luckenbach Rte, Box 1A, Fredericksburg,
TX *78624*

Peake MR & MRS Frederick R (Preston—Gertrude E Bradford)
Cw.Yn.Y'35.Y'38
☎ (561) 746-1348 . . 219 Golf Club Circle, Tequesta, FL *33469*
Peake MR & MRS J H Cameron (Brunschwig—Doris Cordts)
IllColl'56.Ey.Yn.
☎ (860) 767-1140 . . 146 Saybrook Rd, Essex, CT *06426*
Peake MISS Susan S—Hlns'83
☎ (713) 529-8455 . . 2417 San Felipe St, Houston, TX *77019*

Peale MR & MRS James (Jean J Darling) | ☎ (914) 337-4637
Rdc'59.H'55 . . . . | 12 Lee Place,
MISS Frances A—H'88—at 4801 Connecticut Av | Bronxville, NY
NW, Washington, DC *20008* . . . . | *10708*
MISS Christie E—H'93 . . . . |
MR James G D—V'91 . . . . |

Peale MRS Patricia (Keesee—Valando—Patricia Peale)
68 Birch Lane, Greenwich, CT *06830*
Peale MR & MRS William Allen 3d (Hill—Evelyn D Miller)
SoMiss'63.LSU'70
☎ (601) 446-7134 . . 406 S Rankin St, Natchez, MS *39120*

Pearce MRS Arthur W (Marion Gengler) . . . . | ☎ (203) 259-5864
MISS Marion—at 40 W 75 St, New York, NY | 2870 Burr St,
10023 . . . . | Fairfield, CT *06430*

Pearce MR & MRS John I JR (Jane S Ely) Y'61 . . . . . | of ☎ (919)929-8666
JUNIORS MISS Sarah E . . . . | 632 Brookview Dv,
JUNIORS MR James I. . . . . | Chapel Hill, NC
| *27514*
| ☎ (516) 267-3651
| "Hedge-Gate"
| Further Lane,
| Amagansett, NY
| *11930*

Pearce MR Richard I—Yn.Y'38
☎ (860) 434-9037 . . Box 426, Sill Lane, Old Lyme, CT *06371*
Pearce MR & MRS Samuel D (Stephanie D Shepherd) TexWmnU'89.TCU'86
☎ (970) 259-5208 . . 111 Pine Ridge Loop, Durango, CO *81301-7506*
Pearce MR & MRS William H (Elizabeth Ward) Cy.Bf.St.Rut'43.H.'46
☎ (716) 688-7507 . . 101 Farmington Rd, Williamsville, NY *14221*

Pearman LADY (Trott—Antoinette Aiguier) Cs.Rby.Cda . . .of
☎ (212) 753-3282 . . 575 Park Av, New York, NY *10021*
☎ (441) 292-1125 . . "Palmetto Cove" 15 Lone Palm Dv,
Pembroke HM 05, Bermuda

Pearman MR & MRS Richard S L (Newhard—Jean   of ☎ (212)879-3900
McW Hamilton) Ox'56 . . . . 1 E 66 St,
MR R Scott—at Merton Coll Oxford . . . . New York, NY
10021
☎ (441) 236-5122
"Callithea"
9 Bellevue Dv,
Paget PG 06,
Bermuda
☎ (011-44-171)
589-6035
9 Ennismore
Gardens, London
SW7 1NL, England

Pearre MR & MRS Aubrey (Dorothy C Jenkins) Mv.Cda.P'40
☎ (410) 584-8383 . . 2040 Geist Rd, Glyndon, MD *21071*

Pearre MR Aubrey 4th—Conn'78
☎ (410) 342-1251 . . 1634 Shakespeare St, Apt 5-6, Baltimore,
MD *21231*

Pearre MR & MRS Edward D (MacMullan—Wendy J | ☎ (617) 332-9071
Thorsen) Denis'81 . . . . | 250 Waltham St,
JUNIORS MR Russell J MacMullan 3d . . . . | West Newton, MA
JUNIORS MR Chace T MacMullan . . . . | *02165*

Pearson MR & MRS Alexander C (Kristin A Lindgren) Dth'81.H'82
☎ (610) 668-0933 . . 156 Idris Rd, Merion, PA *19066*

Pearson MR & MRS Arthur N (Barbara Harris) Dth'78.H'91
52 Lewis Rd, Belmont, MA *02178*

Pearson MRS Brooke (Elizabeth L Morrill)
16500 Victoria Crossing Dv, Wildwood, MO *63040*

Pearson MR Brooke—P'68.Geo'75 . . . . | ☎ (802) 229-9888
MISS Elizabeth M—at Deerfield . . . . | 30 Murray Hill Dv,
MR Peter G—at Vanderbilt . . . . | Montpelier, VT
| *05602*

Pearson MISS Caroline C . . see MRS W B Smith 2d

Pearson MR Charles 3d . . . . | ☎ (716) 839-3691
MISS Charlotte T . . . . | 49 Harwood Dv,
MR Charles W . . . . | Snyder, NY *14226*

Pearson MRS Corning (Marian L Davis) Pc.
☎ (215) 643-2379 . . 1 Farrier Lane, Blue Bell, PA *19422*

Pearson MR & MRS Eric Garfield (Virginia B Riddle) | ☎ (215) 247-1287
Ws'68.Pc.Ac.P'66.Pa'76 . . . . | 701 W Gravers
MR Forrest Marshall . . . . | Lane, Philadelphia,
MR Duncan Riddle . . . . | PA *19118*
JUNIORS MISS Alexandra V C . . . . |
JUNIORS MR Eric Garfield JR . . . . |

Pearson MR & MRS F Gardiner (Charlotte E H | ☎ (610) 964-9536
Pennypacker) Sth'38.Ste.Rv.Cw.Hav'36.Pa'42 . . | 92 Hillside Rd,
MR David R . . . . | Strafford, PA *19087*

Pearson MR & MRS G Burton JR (Riegel—Edith | ☎ (302) 652-7641
du Pont) Wil.Fic.Cw.Cc.Ncd.P'27.Pa'31 . . . . . | PO Box 68,
MISS Margaret C—Del'73.Ncd. . . . . | Montchanin, DE
| *19710*

Pearson MR & MRS Gardiner P (Laura B Watts) | US Embassy, Paris,
Cw.P'67.P'73 . . . . | France, APO AE,
JUNIORS MISS Eleanor B . . . . | *09777*
JUNIORS MR Nicholas G . . . . |

Pearson MR James A JR . . . . Died at
Phoenix, AZ Aug 27'95

Pearson MRS James A JR (Buchanan—Myra Ann Graf) Ws'40
☎ (602) 948-0923 . . 5030 Desert Jewel Dv, Paradise Valley, AZ *85253*

Pearson MR & MRS Joshua L (Tracy M Brown) RISD'86.RISD'88
☎ (401) 273-8228 . . 96 Larch St, Apt 2ND, Providence, RI *02906-2602*

Pearson MR & MRS Lawrence D (Meyer—Linda Lowry) Rcn.Cr'58.Y'61
☎ (203) 254-0879 . . 19 Old Redding Rd, Easton, CT *06612-1514*

Pearson MR & MRS Nathan W (Kathleen P McMurtry)
Stan'38.Rr.Edg.Dth'32.H'34
☎ (412) 741-6282 . . 10 Woodland Rd, Sewickley, PA *15143*

Pearson MR & MRS Philip Y (Stephanie E LoRusso) P'90.P'91
"Corgimara Cottage" Rte 5, Box 272, Charlottesville, VA *22901*

Pearson MR Richard E—Cspa.Cw.Rv.Pa'50.Tufts'54
☎ (202) 363-1968 . . 2844 Wisconsin Av NW, Washington, DC *20007*

Pearson MISS Sarah B . . see MRS W B Smith 2d

Pearson MR Stanley W JR—Rc.Pc.Ssk.P'41
☎ (215) 836-9268 . . 551 E Evergreen Av, Apt C318, Wyndmoor,
PA *19038*

Pearson MR & MRS Stanley W 3d (Lynne M | ☎ (908) 322-7063
Shropshire) Dick'70 . . . . | 180 N Martine Av,
JUNIORS MISS Courtney L . . . . | Fanwood, NJ *07023*

Pearson MR & MRS Stephen (Margaret Y Newbold) Sg.Ph.P'43
☎ (215) 233-4259 . . 502 Cresheim Valley Rd, Wyndmoor, PA *19038*

Pearson MR & MRS Stephen JR (Irwin—Elizabeth N Dunning)
Penn'73.Rc.Pc.Dll.P'73
☎ (215) 233-5723 . . 108 Haws Lane, Flourtown, PA *19031*

Pearson MRS Stillman (Pearson—Riggio—Nancy B Stillman)
☎ (307) 672-2516 . . 2516 Coffeen Av, Sheridan, WY *82801*

Pearson MR Theodore JR—Fiy.H'61
☎ (619) 574-1055 . . 1043 University Av, 141, San Diego, CA *92103*

Pease MR Matthew P—Laf'73
☎ (212) 472-0567 . . 421 E 84 St, New York, NY *10028*

Pease MISS Pauline T—Ac.
☎ (610) 356-3766 . . Dunwoody Village CH2, 3500 West Chester Pike,
Newtown Square, PA *19073*

Pease MR Roland F—Un.Chr.Mto.Plg.Myf.Vca. | 45 E 72 St,
Rv.Cw.Ne.StJ.Cl'48 . . . . | New York, NY
MISS Deborah S . . . . | *10021*

Peaslee MRS Amos J JR (Barbara A Shedden) . . . . . | ☎ (609) 423-5756
MISS Sharon D—at ☎ (310) 399-6289 | "Windswept"
425 Marine St, 6, Santa Monica, CA *90405* . . . . | 344 Kings H'way,
| Clarksboro, NJ
| *08020*

Peaslee MISS Charlotte H—Dc.Ds.
☎ (212) 861-2619 . . 165 E 72 St, New York, NY *10021*

Peaslee MR & MRS Edmund W JR (Sally S Dunn) | ☎ (212) 861-7482
Lynch'52.Y'48 . . . . | 168 E 74 St,
MISS Elizabeth K—at ☎ (516) 668-4292 | New York, NY
PO Box 1133, Montauk, NY *11954* . . . . | *10021-3561*
MR Edmund W 3d—Box 832392, Richardson, TX |
75083-2392 . . . . |

Peck MRS Arthur K (Coleman—Jane Cochran) Cly . . .of
☎ (713) 627-0678 . . 3711 San Felipe, PH-D, Houston, TX *77027*
☎ (516) 569-4151 . . ''Eastview'' 221 Polo Lane, Lawrence, NY *11559*

Peck MR & MRS David Bell 3d (Fay C Gunderson)
UMiami'53.On.Rc.Ty'43 . . . .
MISS Adair F—at 1935 W Wellington Av, Chicago, IL *60657* . . . .
MR Neil W—at 59 Clinton St, Newport, RI *02840* . . . .
| ☎ (847) 234-4368
| 334 Circle Lane,
| Lake Forest, IL
| *60045*

Peck MR & MRS David Bell 4th (Lauren Hermann) Ill'84.On.NEng'79
☎ (847) 295-6838 . . 231 Washington Circle, Lake Forest, IL *60045*

Peck MR & MRS David W JR (Leness—Susan B Harfield) Uncl.Lic.Cly.P'54.H.'59 . . . .
MISS Susan B Leness—Mid'91—at 111 E 80 St, Apt 9A, New York, NY *10021* .
MR Anthony H Leness—Ham'94—at 110 W 96 St, Apt 3A, New York, NY *10024* .
| ☎ (516) 653-9641
| ''Brigadune''
| PO Box 349,
| Quogue, NY *11959*

Peck MRS F Taylor (Monica B Gaillard) Sth'49.Sl.Myf.Ht.Ncd. . . . .
MISS Catherine D—at Santa Fe, NM . . . .
MISS Sarah G—at Gaithersburg, MD . . . .
| ☎ (410) 224-8187
| 970 Shadewater
| Way, Heritage
| Harbour, Annapolis,
| MD *21401-6848*

Peck MR Frederick W G—Sg.Pa'33
☎ (215) 247-2262 . . 8420 St Martin's Lane, Philadelphia, PA *19118-3724*

Peck MR & MRS Girvan (Schurz—Nancy L Mailliard) Cal'57.Tcy. . . . .
MR Alexander M—Laf'91 . . . .
| ☎ (415) 921-7807
| 2741 Union St,
| San Francisco, CA
| *94123*

Peck MRS H Rollinson JR (Consuelo M Lembcke) Cw.
☎ (561) 231-6447 . . 1402 Club Dv, Vero Beach, FL *32963*

Peck MRS Hubert R (Barbara F Smith) Me.
☎ (610) 525-3031 . . 1250 Denbigh Lane, Radnor, PA *19087-4645*

Peck MR & MRS Jeffrey E (Abigale H McKean) Mich'85.Fic.Tr.Ken'77
☎ (504) 899-4496 . . 2222 Jefferson Av, New Orleans, LA *70115*

Peck MRS John Wheeler (Jean McNeil) . . . . Died at Palm Beach, FL Nov 24'95

Peck MRS Lee Wallace (Kristey A Gunnell) DU'68.Cly. . . . .
JUNIORS MISS Alix Knowlton—at Groton . . . . . .
| ☎ (212) 772-3767
| 30 E 72 St,
| New York, NY
| *10021*

Peck MRS Pamela R (Pamela A Read) Rdc'56
☎ (540) 554-8554 . . PO Box 1024, Middleburg, VA *20118*

Peck MISS Pamela S—Col'72.Fic.Ncd.
☎ (860) 651-0028 . . 110 Library Lane, Simsbury, CT *06070*

Peck MR Philip F W—Y'41
☎ (860) 232-5256 . . 9 Timberwood Rd, West Hartford, CT *06117*

Peck MR & MRS Philip F W 3d (Sandra G Hawkey) Pa'70
☎ (508) 369-6074 . . 190 Elsinore St, Concord, MA *01742*

Peck DR & MRS Robert G (Cleaves—Leila C Patterson) SanDiegoSt'60.Me.Y.'56.H.'71 . . . . .
MR Richard F—Roch'81.BostColl'93—at
☎ (410) 357-0016 . . 114 Stablers Church Rd, Parkton, MD *21120* . . . .
| ☎ (610) 687-4795
| 104A Lantoga Rd,
| Apt 6, Wayne, PA
| *19087*

Peck MR Robert McC—Ph.Ssk.P'74
☎ (215) 242-2071 . . 55 W Springfield Av, Philadelphia, PA *19118*

Peck MRS Thomas H (Jean T Nalle) Pa'75.Me.Rc.
☎ (610) 688-7109 . . 240 Church Rd, Devon, PA *19333*

Peck MR & MRS William F (Anne S Neill) Denis'78.Pa'79.Md.Cda.Denis'79
☎ (410) 252-0075 . . Deep Run Farm, 12207 Boxer Hill Rd, Cockeysville, MD *21030*

Peck MR & MRS William H (Mary Q Weeks) Y'36.H'39 . . . .
MR William H 3d—Y'68 . . . .
| ☎ (203) 264-1861
| 632B Heritage
| Village, Southbury,
| CT *06488*

Peckham MISS Mary S
☎ (704) 252-7992 . . 31 Blackwood Rd, Asheville, NC *28804*

Peckham MR Rufus W JR—Mt.K.Sar.Ofp.Myf.AmU'53.Wash'57
☎ (202) 965-1466 . . 2501 Q St NW, Washington, DC *20007-4303*

Peddle MRS James B (Day—Mary Alice Clark)
☎ (314) 997-3226 . . 1 Watch Hill Rd, Ladue, MO *63124*

Pedersen MISS Amy R—Me'93
☎ (603) 891-1355 . . 41 Royal Crest Dv, Apt 1, Nashua, NH *03060*

Pedersen MR & MRS (DR) Eric W (Bettina C McAdoo) P'71.Stan'78.Cal'72.Stan'75
☎ (415) 851-0734 . . 3366 Tripp Rd, Woodside, CA *94062*

Pedersen MR & MRS (DR) Matthew H (Theresa T Kudlak) Bnd'71.Cl'72.ClP&S'79.MeMarit'84 ⚓
☎ (207) 781-2707 . . 20 Longmeadow Rd, Cumberland Foreside, ME *04110*

Pedersen MR & MRS Oskar H (T M Redette Cornell) Temp'51
☎ (207) 326-8708 . . Main St, PO Box 312, Castine, ME *04421*

Pedley MR & MRS Eric A (Jane Leland) Bhm.Fr. . . . .
MISS Alison . . . .
MR Dean A . . . .
| ☎ (415) 387-1354
| 3961 Washington St,
| San Francisco, CA
| *94118*

Peebles MR & MRS Emory B 3d (Celeste H Hodges) Qns'66.At.Van'65
☎ (334) 473-4733 . . 2465 Venetia Rd, Mobile, AL *36605*

Peebles MR & MRS Emory Bush JR (Butler—Ford—Barbara W Cowan) Ala'45.Dar.Cit'39
☎ (334) 476-0546 . . 110 Canongate, 2404 Springhill Av, Mobile, AL *36607*

Peeples MR Joseph C . . see G B Pickett JR

Peeples MISS Melanie S—Ala'90 . . see G B Pickett JR

Peet MR & MRS E Chester JR (Mary G Prime) Hlns'63.Myf.Geo'52 ⚓ . . . .
MR E Chester 3d . . . .
| ☎ (516) 749-4056
| ''Burro Hall''
| PO Box 2002,
| 31 N Menantic Rd,
| Shelter Island, NY
| *11964*

Peet MRS Robert M (Mleczko—Florence Farley) Wis'40.Hn.
☎ (603) 643-3124 . . 80 Lyme Rd, Apt 337, Hanover, NH *03755*

Peet MRS W Creighton (Austen—Helen T Hope) . . .
MR William Creighton 3d . . . .
MR David Austen . . . .
| ☎ (415) 567-7575
| 2635 Green St,
| San Francisco, CA
| *94123*

Peipers MR David H—K.Shcc.Ln.H'78.H'81
☎ (212) 397-4088 . . 146 W 57 St, Apt 72E, New York, NY *10019*

Peirce MR John W—Sb.H'33
☎ (508) 887-2022 . . 9 Garden St, Topsfield, MA *01983*

Peirce MR & MRS W Grant 3d (Vanessa J Lawton) Sg.Pc. ... ☎ (215) VE6-5285
109 E Mill Rd,
Flourtown, PA
19031
MR Brian G—F&M'80 ....
MR Dana L ....
MR Robin J ....
MR W Grant 4th ....

Peirce MR & MRS William H (Jamesina Bathgate)
Mit'46.Wis'51.Wis'56 .... of ☎ (561)499-7806
2168 SW 36 Terr,
Delray Beach, FL
33445
MISS Margaret H ....
MISS Kittson B ....
☎ (207) 864-3726
Loon Camp,
PO Box 1008,
Rangeley, ME
04970

Pelaez MR & MRS Jorge L (Carmen E Navarro) StJos'84.Me.NH'83
☎ (610) 293-9106 . . 676 Glenmary Rd, St Davids, PA *19087*

Pell MISS Allison M . . see E N Cutler 3d

Pell MR & MRS Anthony D (Katharine Ludington Murphey)
BMr'63.H'76.Mt.Au.Cy.Chi.Cda.P'60.GeoW'66
☎ (617) 899-7327 . . 2 Willow Rd, Weston, MA *02193*

Pell MR & MRS Christopher T H (Janet Alexander)
RI'96.Nrr.Srb.K.Il.Lm.Cly.Dc.Br'70.RI'80 . . . . . ☎ (401) 847-1162
"Telegraph Hill"
129 Brenton Rd,
Newport, RI *02840*
MISS Tripler—H'96—at Oxford ....
JUNIORS MR Nicholas L—at Duke ....

Pell MR & MRS Claiborne (Nuala O'Donnell)
Rcn.Mt.K.Nrr.Srb.B.Plg.Lm.Cw.Cc.StJ.P'40.Cl'46
☎ (202) 333-3425 . . 3425 Prospect St NW, Washington, DC *20007*

Pell MR & MRS Clarence C (King—Francesca L Hinckley) Rcn.Nrr.Lm.H'33
☎ (401) 783-2434 . . 72 Cormorant Rd, Narragansett, RI *02882-3154*

Pell MRS Francis L JR (Clarissa Wardwell) Sg.Csn.
☎ (215) 233-0736 . . 551 E Evergreen Av, Apt C304, Wyndmoor,
PA *19038*

Pell MRS H Williamson (McGurrin—Elizabeth A Ulman) Ri.Sfg.Shcc.
☎ (908) 766-2123 . . Claremont Rd, PO Box 772, Bernardsville,
NJ *07924*

Pell MR & MRS Haven N B (Mina M Stockman)
Pa'71.B.Mt.Rcn.Cvc.H'68 .... ☎ (202) 298-7355
3900 Fulton St NW,
Washington, DC
20007-1374
MR Haven N B II ....
JUNIORS MISS Mina M ....
JUNIORS MR E William J ....

Pell MR & MRS Herbert C 3d (Eugenia S Diehl)
Nrr.Srb.Il.Cc.Lm.RISD'69 .... ☎ (520) 615-9405
2820 E Cerrado Los
Palitos, Tucson, AZ
85718-4220
MISS Christina O'D ....
JUNIORS MR Herbert C 4th ....

Pell MR John Bigelow—Hn.SUNY'91 . . of
☎ (520) 284-2904 . . 5 Soldier Basin Dv, Sedona, AZ *86351*
☎ (401) 847-2462 . . "Pelican Place" 579 Bellevue Av, Newport,
RI *02840*

Pell MISS Julia L W—RI'81.Srb.Lm.
☎ (401) 683-4561 . . 82 Glen Rd, Portsmouth, RI *02871*

Pell MRS L Jeffcott (Lucy B Jeffcott)
☎ (011-39-564) 83-52-32 . . Piazza Galliano 19, 58018 Porto Ercole,
Grosseto, Italy

Pell MR & MRS Peter J (Corey—Christine Benson)
Post'84.Rc.Pr.Post'67 .... ☎ (516) 671-1971
6 Libby Dv,
Glen Cove, NY
11542
MISS Christine M Corey—at
☎ (360) 943-4010 . . 1262 NE Glass St,
Olympia, WA *98506*
MISS Cynthia E Corey—at 6 Windsor Dv,
Old Westbury, NY *11568*
MR Alan L Corey 4th ....
MR R William Corey ....

Pell JUNIORS MR Peter J JR . . see E N Cutler 3d

Pell MR & MRS Stuyvesant B (Patricia C Doom)
V'56.Pn.P'53 .... ☎ (609) 924-7336
697 Rosedale Rd,
Princeton, NJ *08540*
MISS Sarah B—at 906 Eagles Chase Dv,
Lawrenceville, NJ *08648* ....

Pell MRS W H Dannat (Elisabeth P Haldane) Cda.
☎ (914) 265-2403 . . 61 Chestnut St, Cold Spring, NY *10516*

Pell-Dechame MR Robert R—Fi.Cw.Lm.Ford'80
☎ (518) 585-2556 . . Fort Rd, PO Box 7, Ticonderoga, NY *12883*

Pellegrini MRS George (Sheila Cudahy)
Bnd'43.Cl'94.P. .... ☎ (505) 988-9760
333 Calle Loma
Norte, Santa Fe,
NM *87501*
MR Edward C—Ri. ....

Pellenc BRNSS (Frances M Kier)
☎ (011-33-1) 43-59-93-14 . . 38 av Gabriel, 75008 Paris, France

Pellet MR & MRS Benoit J F X (Anita B Strawbridge) DU'90.EcolePSI'84
☎ (011-33-1) 47-71-33-12 . . 6 rue du Commandant de Larienty,
92210 St Cloud, France

Pellet MISS Florence Strawbridge (Benoit J F X) .... Born at
Paris, France Aug 29'96

Pelliconi MR & MRS Richard R (Ingraham—Page T Phelps)
Dar.CathU'74.CathU'76
☎ (703) 548-6006 . . 110 W Myrtle St, Alexandria, VA *22301-2425*

Peltier MR & MRS Alec M (Catherine A Morgan)
GeoM'84.GeoM'96.Occ'67 .... ☎ (703) 734-1286
1320 Alps Dv,
McLean, VA
22102-1502
MISS Patricia G ....
MISS Amy A ....

Peltz MR & MRS George M Dallas (Fassnacht—M Dorothy Vermeer)
Rcn.Pa'68
☎ (201) 784-3272 . . 206 County Rd, Demarest, NJ *07627*

Peltz MR & MRS Henry S (Katharine B Sallé) H'49 . . ☎ (802) 362-4156
PO Box 717,
Manchester, VT
05254
MR Henry B ....
MR John S ....

Peltz DR & MRS William L (Margaret R Adams) Chi.Y'31.H'36
☎ (508) 693-7488 . . RFD Box 407, Lamberts Cove Rd,
Vineyard Haven, MA *02568*

Pelzer MRS Cornelia H (Cornelia E Hines) Cw.Ncd.
MR Francis J 5th—Dth'93—at ☎ (404) 252-5144
2060 Chastain Park Court NW, Atlanta, GA
30342 .... ☎ (803) 853-8224
70½ Tradd St,
Charleston, SC
29401

Pelzer MR & MRS Felix C (Carol N Cole)
Swb'65.Yh.So'64 .... ☎ (803) 722-1313
11 Legare St,
Charleston, SC
29401
MR Felix C JR—Van'94 ....
MR Arthur C ....

Pemberton MISS Catherine W—LakeF'83
☎ (610) 688-1661 . . 1027 Valley Forge Rd, Devon, PA *19333*

Pemberton DR & MRS Clifford H (Ellen P Bailey) | ☎ (610) 526-9297
Me.H'74.Jef'78 . . . . | 502 Lynmere Rd,
JUNIORS MISS Caroline K . . . . | Bryn Mawr, PA
| *19010*

Pemberton MRS John C (Catherine Watjen) Cly.Cs.
    ☎ (212) BU8-3841 . . 116 E 66 St, New York, NY *10021*

Pemberton MR & MRS John C JR (Mary W Belcher) Sa.Me.Pa'51
    ☎ (610) LA5-2591 . . 1448 County Line Rd, Rosemont, PA *19010*

Pemberton MISS Julia (Louis W) . . . . Married at West Tisbury, MA
    Hellums MR Jay D (J David) . . . . Sep 23'95

Pemberton MRS LeRoy (Ruth B Longnecker) H.
    ☎ (610) 645-8831 . . Waverly Heights B138, 1400 Waverly Rd,
    Gladwyne, PA *19035*

Pemberton MR & MRS Louis W (Suzanne Grace) Un.Plg.Cly.P'51
    ☎ (212) 348-8468 . . 170 E 87 St, Apt W18A, New York, NY *10128*

Pemberton MRS Robert (Carroll R Young)
    ☎ (215) 247-3360 . . 7654 St Martin's Lane, Philadelphia,
    PA *19118-4210*

Peña MRS Katherine D (Katherine M Donohoe) Cp.
    ☎ (510) 830-4797 . . 1368 Silverwood Court, Danville, CA *94526*

Penati MR Giannotto . . see C F Adams

Pendar MR Oliver A—Cc.H'27
    ☎ (516) 537-0942 . . 200 Church Lane, PO Box 863, Bridgehampton,
    NY *11932-0863*

Pendergast MRS Edward S H JR (Madeleine Herrmann)
    ☎ (330) 493-3913 . . 5020 Violet Knoll NE, Canton, OH *44705*

Pendergast MR & MRS George H JR (Ellen McK Draper) Ore'78.Ham'73
    59 Wellesley St, Weston, MA *02193*

Pendergast MR Jeffrey R
    ☎ (610) 525-0768 . . 17 Hawthorne Lane, Rosemont, PA *19010*

Pendergast MR & MRS Stephen H (Rosalind M | ☎ (610) 896-8445
Torrillo) VillaN'68 . . . . | 142 Cricket Av,
MISS Mary H—BostColl'89—at | TH-7, Ardmore, PA
    ☎ (203) 226-4284 . . 128 Bayberry Lane, | *19003*
Westport, CT *06880* . . . . |

Pendergast MR & MRS Stephen W (Britt F Woolhiser) AmU'84
    ☎ (203) 227-1801 . . 7 Hidden Hill Rd, Weston, CT *06883-2808*

Pendergrass DR & MRS Henry P (Roberts—Carol Y Minster)
    M.Me.Ac.P'48.Pa'52.H'69
    ☎ (610) 527-3002 . . 512 Fishers Rd, Bryn Mawr, PA *19010*

Pendl MR & MRS Ulrich G (Mary Van R Cruger) T.Cly . . .of
    ☎ (212) UN1-9367 . . 167 E 82 St, New York, NY *10028*
    ☎ (914) 351-4470 . . Ridge Rd, Tuxedo Park, NY *10987*

Pendleton MR & MRS Brian G (Bigby—Susan Wichman)
    Sonoma'72.ColC'78
    ☎ (206) 833-6513 . . 37407—188 Av SE, Auburn, WA *98002-8902*

Pendleton REV Dudley D—CarnM'35
    ☎ (609) 234-1336 . . 4 E Azalea Lane, Mt Laurel, NJ *08054*

Pendleton MR & MRS Edmund E (Kyoko Makino)
    Cvc.Pa'42.Geo'48.GeoW'50
    ☎ (703) 848-0717 . . 6915 Lemon Rd, McLean, VA *22101*

Pendleton MR Edmund S JR—WakeF'84
    5 Ashfield Lane, Blythewood, SC *29016*

Pendleton MR & MRS Miles S JR (Elisabeth A | ☎ (202) 363-2601
Morgan) Sth'62.H'67.Csn.Y'61.H'67 . . . . | 3410 Lowell St NW,
MISS Constance M—at U of Va Law . . . . | Washington, DC
MR Nathaniel P . . . . | *20016*

Pendleton MRS Nancy S (Nancy T L Scott) | of ☎ (410)732-5903
Towson'71.Loy'73 . . . . | 10 N Wolfe St,
MR T Scott . . . . | Baltimore, MD
| *21231*
| ☎ (302) 645-7599
| ''Trespassers W''
| Plantations Resort
| 6A, Lewes, DE
| *19958*

Pendleton MR & MRS Nathan S 3d (Pamela T | ☎ (561) 234-8285
Taylor) Mon'72.Cw.Md'63 . . . . | 1775 Sand Dollar
MR Nathan S 4th—Fla'93 . . . . | Way, Vero Beach,
JUNIORS MR Matthew S . . . . | FL *32963*

Pendleton MR & MRS Philip R (Dean J Loose) Ncd. . | ☎ (410) 435-2626
MR Philip R JR . . . . | 6307 Blackburn
| Court, Baltimore,
| MD *21212*

Penfield MRS Elizabeth F (Elizabeth V Few) Swb'60.Duke'62.Cly . . .of
    ☎ (504) 566-7457 . . 1009 St Ann St, New Orleans, LA *70116*
    ☎ (970) 963-3206 . . 1204 County Rd 170, Carbondale, CO *81623*

Penhallow MR & MRS David P (Patricia A Mallan) . . | ☎ (804) 282-8824
MISS Anna K . . . . | 2018 Milbank Rd,
| Richmond, VA
| *23229*

Penhallow MISS Sarah M (David P) . . . . Married at Richmond, VA
    Vostal MR Kenneth N (Robert T) . . . . Oct 28'95

Peniston MR & MRS E Winchester (S Lyerly Spöngberg)
    see E de Cordova JR

Peniston MR & MRS Eric W JR (Deborah P Haslam) | of ☎ (212)722-0733
Swb'66.Rc.Ri.Y.Cr'60 . . . . | 1185 Park Av,
MR Nathaniel F—at U of Miami . . . . | New York, NY
| *10128*
| ☎ (860) 364-1212
| ''Penbrook Hill''
| PO Box 1404,
| Sharon, CT *06069*
| ☎ (561) 231-6693
| 505 River Dv,
| Vero Beach, FL
| *32963*

Penn MR John Rogers
    ☎ (818) 761-4043 . . 5144 Cahuenga Dv, North Hollywood, CA *91601*

Penna MR & MRS Antonio (Maria Antonietta Poggi-Cavalletti)
    Ht.Dh.Bologna'80
    ☎ (011-39-51) 304608 . . via Tambroni 9, 40137 Bologna, Italy

Pennebaker MR & MRS Charles D JR (Quay—Katharine Brooks)
    Geo'30.H'33
    ☎ (610) 388-7805 . . 37 Kendal at Longwood, Kennett Square,
    PA *19348*

Pennell MR & MRS Henry B 3d (Marion H Lowry) Wms'43.Va'67
    ☎ (860) 868-7654 . . ''Four Winds'' 33 Fenn Hill Rd,
    Washington Depot, CT *06794*

Penney MR & MRS John S JR (Celeste O'D Smith) Cysl.Bg.Y'41
    ☎ (508) 636-6041 . . PO Box 411, Adamsville, RI *02801*

Penniman MR & MRS Caleb J (Anne Winchester) | ☎ (860) 767-1184
Fy.Va'49 . . . . | 85 River Rd, Essex,
MR Caleb J JR . . . . | CT *06426*

Penniman MR & MRS George W (Anne K Lacouture) Y'80.Va'81.Va'86
☎ (860) 767-7439 . . 16 Curiosity Lane, Essex, CT *06426*

Penniman MR & MRS H Dawson (Eleanor L Thompson)
Ph.Cw.Ofp.Ac.Cda.Dc.JHop'51.Md'57
☎ (215) 646-7084 . . 149 Splitrail Lane, Blue Bell, PA *19422*

Penniman MRS Nicholas G 3d (Foster—Pattie Symington) Elk.Yh . . .of
☎ (410) 356-6323 . . "Welshes Cradle" 12427 Park Heights Av,
Owings Mills, MD *21117*
☎ (207) 276-5050 . . "The Havoc" Northeast Harbor, ME *04662*

Pennington MR & MRS James S JR (Eleanor Wetten)
Ws'35.Ih.Myf.Wa.Cda.Ncd.Aht'30.Ch'32
☎ (561) 231-1232 . . 180 Oleander Way, Vero Beach, FL *32963*

Pennington MR & MRS James Sutton 3d (Jennie R Collis) Stan'65.Stan'64
☎ (518) 372-7503 . . 2276 Sweetbriar Rd, Niskayuna, NY *12309*

Pennington MRS Richard H (Genevieve P Hart) V'42.Cin'50
☎ (513) 321-0824 . . 2918 Observatory Av, Cincinnati, OH *45208*

Pennington MR & MRS Stuart W (Mary Melonakis) | ☎ (206) 885-1054
DU'70.DU'69 . . . . | 14502 NE 61 St,
MR Mark . . . . | Redmond, WA
JUNIORS MISS Christine . . . . | *98052-4680*
JUNIORS MR Daniel . . . . |

Pennink MR & MRS Karel B (Elizabeth M Barclay) | of ☎ (561)229-9657
V'47.Csn. | Atlantis 412B,
MISS Carol B—at ☎ (011-31-10) 422-7591 | 10152 S Ocean Dv,
Willem v Hillegaersbergstraat 106B, 3051 RP | Jensen Beach, FL
Rotterdam, The Netherlands . . . . | *34957*
                                                     | ☎ (203) 264-4053
                                                     | 708A Heritage
                                                     | Village, Southbury,
                                                     | CT *06488*

Pennisi MR & MRS Mario C (Alexandra C Whitcraft) Col'71
☎ (516) 367-9401 . . 27 Titus Lane, Cold Spring Harbor, NY *11724*

Pennock MRS Caspar W A (Gabriella P Davis)
☎ (215) 860-3589 . . Pennswood Village H112, Newtown, PA *18940*

Pennock MR & MRS J Liddon JR (Alice Herkness)
Ph.Cry.Cspa.Sg.Ac.Cs.Ncd.
☎ (215) 884-4440 . . Meadowbrook Farm, PO Box 3007, Meadowbrook,
PA *19046*

Pennoyer MR & MRS Paul G JR (Cecily Henderson) | ☎ (516) 676-8349
B'gton'49.Ny.C.H.'42.H'48 ⚓ . . . . | "The Stables"
MR William M—Me'86 . . . . | PO Box 315,
                                                   | Locust Valley, NY
                                                   | *11560*

Pennoyer MR & MRS Peter M (Katherine L Ridder) SCal'84.K.Cl'80
☎ (914) 337-3022 . . 38 Dellwood Rd, Bronxville, NY *10708*

Pennoyer MR & MRS Robert M (Victoria L Parsons) H'44.Cl'50 . . of
☎ (212) 988-8098 . . 33 E 70 St, New York, NY *10021*
☎ (914) 232-8267 . . PO Box 299, Cross River, NY *10518*

Pennoyer MR & MRS Russell P (Helen E Bearn) | ☎ (212) 360-7544
Sth'76.K.Msq.Cly.H'73.Cl'82 . . . . | 17 E 97 St,
JUNIORS MR Gordon S . . . . | New York, NY
                                                 | *10029*

Pennoyer MR & MRS Sheldon K (Penelope G Beal)
Wms'85.RISD'84.RISD'85
☎ (508) 768-7439 . . 68 Grove St, Essex, MA *01929*

Pennypacker MISS Joanna—BMr'52
☎ (212) 650-0407 . . 301 E 64 St, New York, NY *10021*
Mch 1 . . ☎ (610) 647-6854 . . 220 W First Av, Malvern, PA *19355*

Pennypacker MR N Ramsay—R.Cc.Rv.Pa'43 . . . . . | ☎ (610) LA5-6511
MISS Cary B—Drex'84.Ac . . . . | 915 Sorrel Lane,
MR D Ramsay—Pa'81 . . . . | Bryn Mawr, PA
                                                    | *19010*

Penovich MR & MRS Joseph (Eleanor T Redwood)
StMarys'43.Ncd.Dc.Belgrade'41
☎ (410) 268-8730 . . 920 Melvin Rd, Annapolis, MD *21403-1316*

Penovich MISS Katherine Redwood (Joseph) . . Married at Washington, DC
Clark DR Jonathan C D (Ronald J) . . . . Apr 27'96

Penrose MRS A Melvin (Anna M Melvin) Rdc'49 . . | ☎ (610) 527-0395
MR Boies 3d—Rol'74 . . . . | 737 S Roberts Rd,
                                                    | Bryn Mawr, PA
                                                    | *19010*

Penrose MR & MRS Charles JR (Ann L Cantwell) Plg.StJ.
☎ (203) 655-9674 . . 81 Mansfield Av, Darien, CT *06820*

Penrose MR & MRS James C (Mary Buff Hunter) Cr'76.Un.Plg.Pa'72
☎ (212) 427-2750 . . 22 E 88 St, New York, NY *10128*

Penrose MR & MRS Julian d'E (Elvia Martin) Ac . . . . | ☎ (215) 568-6029
MISS Christine—at ☎ (215) 790-9914 | 2031 Locust St,
301 S Chadwick St, Philadelphia, PA *19103* . . . | Apt 903,
MR Timothy . . . . | Philadelphia, PA
MR Julian d'Este JR—Pitzer'83—at | *19103*
☎ (206) 632-9488 . . 3843 Fremont Av N, |
Apt 201, Seattle, WA *98103* . . . . |

Penrose MR Thomas—SUNY'80 . . of
☎ (203) 866-9381 . . 166 Rowayton Av, Rowayton, CT *06853*
Briar Farm, North Sandwich, NH *03259*

Penson MR & MRS John Gordon (Nancy E Penn) Ws'45.H'42.H'47
☎ (214) 528-1322 . . 3756 Armstrong P'kway, Dallas, TX *75205*

Penton MR & MRS Hugh V (Janis Robertson) P'cpia'49.Vh.Cal'46
☎ (619) 433-5270 . . 45 St Malo Beach, Oceanside, CA *92054*

Penton MR & MRS Hugh V JR (Mary A Blount) CalPoly'81.Vh.CalPoly'79
☎ (619) 436-4670 . . 1740 Hygeia Av, Leucadia, CA *92024*

Penton MRS J Randolph JR (Jean A Evans)
☎ (334) 271-6355 . . 3123 Gatsby Lane, Montgomery, AL *36106*

Pepper MR & MRS B Franklin (Helen S Warner) P'51
☎ (703) 960-9239 . . 5959 Wilton Rd, Alexandria, VA *22310*

Pepper MR & MRS Charles W (McLean—Anne H Crockett)
☎ (561) 832-4863 . . 333 Seaspray Av, Palm Beach, FL *33480*

Pepper MRS D Sergeant (Hester Laning) Me.Ac.Ncd.
☎ (610) 645-8947 . . Waverly Heights 112A, 1400 Waverly Rd,
Gladwyne, PA *19035*

Pepper MISS Edith M . . see D H McLucas JR

Pepper MR & MRS G Willing (Elizabeth J G Guest) Ph.Rb.
☎ (610) 566-2747 . . 128 Springton Lake Rd, Media, PA *19063*

Pepper MRS George W 3d (Whitman—Meyer—Margaret E Morgan) . . of
☎ (803) 869-2844 . . Botany Bay Plantation, Box 6, Edisto Island,
SC *29438*
☎ (207) 244-7226 . . "Causeway House" Causeway Lane N, Box 1253,
Southwest Harbor, ME *04679*

Pepper MR & MRS H L Perry (E March Wier) | ☎ (610) MI9-5997
Ph.Me.Myf.Wt.Pa'67.Pa'73 . . . . | 901 Black Rock Rd,
MISS Meredith F . . . . | Gladwyne, PA
MISS Page C . . . . | *19035*

Pepper MR & MRS T Sergeant (Marion Schultze-Rhonhof) BMr'85.Ph.Pe.Ssk.Myf.Cw. Pa'66.VillaN'70 . . . . | of ☎ (610)642-6548 1412 Stony Circle, Gladwyne, PA *19035*
MISS Anita S-R—Cr'95—at NYU . . . .
MISS Marion L—Wms'96 . . . . | Peppercorn Farm, Still Pond, MD *21667*
MR J Sergeant—Me.Gchr'93 . . . .

Pepper MRS William (Margaret Royer)
☎ (215) 283-7085 . . GH8 Foulkeways, Sumneytown Pike, Gwynedd, PA *19436*

Pepper MRS Wright (Anna H Wright) V'47 . . . . | ☎ (610) 828-9880 2309 S Gilinger Rd, Lafayette Hill, PA *19444*
MR William S JR . . . .

Percival MR & MRS J Nicholas (Camden G White) Cyb.H'64 . . . . | ☎ (203) 438-9307 193 Peaceable St, Ridgefield, CT *06877*
MISS Arlen R—Bates'94—at Boston U Law . . . .
MR Eric S—at Conn Coll . . . .

Percy MR & MRS Charles H (Loraine Guyer) Ct.Ch'41
☎ (202) 337-1691 . . 1691—34 St NW, Washington, DC *20007*

Percy MR & MRS Roger D (Penelope Chambers) Stan'70.Wash'73.Stan'70.Wash'72
☎ (206) 622-3244 . . 4727 NE 36 St, Seattle, WA *98105*

Pereira MR & MRS Gaston E (Claire S Benacerraf) Nu'70 . . . . | ☎ (011-56-2) 243-4004 Pedro Lira Urquieta 11568, La Dehesa, Santiago, Chile
JUNIORS MR Alejandro E . . . .

Pereira MR & MRS William C (H Caroline Farrell) Cal'89.Cal'88
☎ (208) 853-6603 . . 4770 Riverine Place, Boise, ID *83703*

Perera MR Guido R—Tv.Cy.Sm.Mt.B.H'24
☎ (617) 523-4185 . . 12 W Cedar St, Boston, MA *02108*

Perera MR & MRS Guido R JR (Joan W Hulme) Stan'62.H'53 . . . . | ☎ (617) 259-8944 Old Concord Rd, Lincoln, MA *01773*
MISS Jessica H—Mid'88 . . . .
MISS Helen T—Mid'92 . . . .
MISS Margaret S—at Millbrook . . . .

Perera MR & MRS Lawrence T (Elizabeth A Wentworth) Sm.Tv.Ub.Cy.H'57 . . . . | ☎ (617) 262-4176 18 Marlborough St, Boston, MA *02116*
JUNIORS MR Lawrence T JR—at U of Vt . . . .

Perera MISS Lucy E (Lawrence T) . . . . Married at Yarmouth, MA
Adams MR Matthew J (James T 2d) . . . . Jun 8'96

Perera DR & MRS Richard D (Evelyn F Lewis) Rdc'61.P'54 . . . . | ☎ (413) 448-8066 219 S Mountain Rd, Pittsfield, MA *01201-8153*
MISS Rosemary L—Br'85—at ☎ (206) 868-2571 22112 NE 9 Place, Redmond, WA *98053* . . . . .
MISS Jane F—Ober'92—at 72 Seaman Av, Apt 4H, New York, NY *10034* . . . .
MR Richard D JR—Br'87—at 207 Lansdowne Av, Decatur, GA *30030* . . . .

Perera MR & MRS Ronald C (Judith A Weed) Bost'65.Tv.H'63 . . . . | ☎ (413) 586-2970 30 Lyman Rd, Northampton, MA *01060*
MISS Lisa D—at 85 Carl St, Apt 8, San Francisco, CA *94117* . . . .
MISS Katherine T . . . .
MISS Rosalind P . . . .

Pergande MR & MRS John F (F Frasher Hudson) Hlns'85.Smu'94.Y'85.Nw'91
☎ (214) 363-2163 . . 6754 Prestonshire Lane, Dallas, TX *75225*

Perin MRS Lawrence (Smith—Margaret G Vogel) Md.Elk.Cvc.Cw.
☎ (410) PL2-4851 . . 1031 N Calvert St, Baltimore, MD *21202*

Perkin MRS Marianne (Marianne H K de Lidertejed) Ri . . . . | *see Dilatory Domiciles*
MR Nicholas R . . . .

Perkin MR & MRS Richard T (Leslie M Bergesch) Un.Snc.Plg.Cly.H'54 . . . . | ☎ (212) 744-0345 36 E 72 St, New York, NY *10021*
JUNIORS MISS Caroline S . . . .

Perkins MISS Anne R—B'gton'78 . . see MRS E P W Edmunds

Perkins MRS Charles B (Hodgson—Adeline Hazard)
☎ (401) 783-7604 . . Wilderness Farm, PO Box 29, 839A Ministerial Rd, Wakefield, RI *02880*

Perkins MR & MRS Charles M JR (Gwendolen N Everett) Dick'63 . . . . | ☎ (508) 887-8847 10 Lawrence Rd, Boxford, MA *01921*
MISS Heather S—ColbyS'84—at 9C Kent St, Newburyport, MA *01950* . . . .
MR Matthew E—Bab'91—at 201 E 86 St, Apt 12E, New York, NY *10028* . . . .

Perkins MR & MRS Chiswell D L (Mary T Bryan) Sth'58.Gm.Me.Va'49
325 Charmian Rd, Richmond, VA *23226*

Perkins MISS Courtney Leeanne (Jason F) . . . . Born at Austin, TX Mch 10'95

Perkins MR & MRS Edward C (Louise D DuBois) Bnd'46.C.Hn.H'42.Cl'48 . . of . .
☎ (610) 868-3061 . . 449 High St, Bethlehem, PA *18018*
☎ (413) 243-0681 . . "Glencote" Box 365, Tyringham, MA *01264*

Perkins MR & MRS Eric B (A Joyce Cottrell) Syr'70.BtP.Ck.Ny.Eyc.Syr'71 . . . . | ☎ (561) 625-8933 39 Balfour Rd W, Palm Beach Gardens, FL *33418*
MISS Carolyne B . . . .
JUNIORS MISS Alison J . . . .
JUNIORS MR Eric H T . . . .

Perkins MRS Evelyn M (Harley—Evelyn M Perkins) Pars'64
☎ (617) 354-6455 . . 328 Prospect St, Cambridge, MA *02139*

Perkins MR & MRS Francis E JR (Edith M Bradley) H'64.Va'67 . . . . | ☎ (508) 485-0006 65 Sears Rd, Southborough, MA *01772*
MR William S—H'93 . . . .

Perkins MR Frederic B . . . . | ☎ (409) 836-0998 Rte 1, Box 298, Brenham, TX *77833*
MISS Jennifer L—at U of Tex Austin . . . .
MR Joshua B—at 3700 Balfour Place, Carrollton, TX *75007* . . . .

Perkins MR G Holmes—Pc.H'26
☎ (215) 247-2424 . . 82 Bethlehem Pike, Philadelphia, PA *19118*

Perkins MR & MRS George W JR (Nancy Foster) Me'49
☎ (914) 677-3947 . . Walbridge Farm, Rte 1, Box 30, Millbrook, NY *12545*

Perkins MR & MRS Gilman (Rebecca D Mastin)
☎ (716) 264-9985 . . 14 Tobey Court, Pittsford, NY *14534*

Perkins MR & MRS Gilman C (Deborah S Hower) Van'84.StLaw'77 . . of
☎ (203) 222-0663 . . 375 Sasco Hill Rd, Fairfield, CT *06430*
☎ (207) 967-0027 . . RR 2, Box 985, Kennebunkport, ME *04046*

Perkins MRS Gladys Lovering (Gladys Lovering Swasey) . . . . | ☎ (508) 369-8824 Middlesex School, 1400 Lowell Rd, Concord, MA *01742*
MISS Sarah N—at ☎ (617) 522-4434 20 Newton St, Brookline, MA *02146* . . . .
Perkins MRS Grete L (Adair—Grete L Perkins)
☎ (907) 733-2354 . . PO Box 243, Talkeetna, AK *99676*
Perkins MISS Isabel C (Roberts—Isabel C Perkins) Mid'68
☎ (508) 526-1483 . . 11 Highland Av, Manchester, MA *01944*
Perkins MR James G B 3d—Tex'70.Temp'73
7925 Ridge Av, Apt 36, Philadelphia, PA *19128*
Perkins MR & MRS James H JR (Judith O'Connell) D.Chi.H'58.Va'69 . . . . | ☎ (617) 329-1622 510 Clapboardtree St, Westwood, MA *02090*
MISS Edith G—Ant'94 . . . .
MR Elliott K—ColC'93 . . . .
MR Alexander H—at U of Mont . . . .
Perkins MR & MRS Jason F (Toni Jo Siegel)
☎ (512) 206-0350 . . 3302 Oakmont Blvd, Austin, TX *78703*
Perkins MR & MRS John A (Lydia B Cobb) Tv.D.H'40
☎ (617) 326-0631 . . 203 Highland St, Dedham, MA *02026*
Perkins MR & MRS John M C (Eleanor G James) Au.Pr.USN'48
☎ (516) 692-7151 . . 1424 Ridge Av, Laurel Hollow, NY *11791*
Perkins MR & MRS L Parker 3d (Sarah S Hollister) Rice'96.JMad'89
☎ (804) 799-1646 . . 130 Sutherlin Av, Danville, VA *24541*
Perkins MISS Marguerite C (Sorum—Marguerite C Perkins) Wash'77
☎ (202) 966-4284 . . 4341 Verplanck Place NW, Washington, DC *20016*
Perkins MRS Palfrey (Linda Wellington) Sm.
☎ (617) 227-8355 . . 68 Beacon St, Apt 3, Boston, MA *02108*
Perkins MR & MRS Paul F JR (Mary W McCagg) My.Tv.Ncd.H'45
☎ (508) 468-1916 . . PO Box 87, Hamilton, MA *01936*
Perkins MR & MRS R Forbes (Florence B Cushing) V'42.My.Chi.H'40
☎ (508) 526-1492 . . "Owl's Nest" Box 398, Manchester, MA *01944*
Perkins MRS R Marlin (Cotsworth—Carol M Morse) Minn'37
52 Aberdeen Place, St Louis, MO *63105*
Perkins MRS Ralph JR (Nancy B Fenton)
☎ (603) 563-8553 . . Box 258, Upper Jaffrey Rd, Dublin, NH *03444*
Perkins MR & MRS Richard S (Newell—Audrey T Walker) Rc.Ri.Ln.Rm.Stc.Plg.Cs. . . . . | ☎ (561) 546-3887 30 Riverview Rd, Hobe Sound, FL *33455*
MISS Frances T Newell . . . .
Perkins MR & MRS Richard S JR (Mildred D Baxter) Ub.Tv.Y'58
☎ (508) 887-8891 . . 82 River Rd, Topsfield, MA *01983*
Perkins MR Robert F JR—H'74
☎ (617) 868-2751 . . 18 Hawthorne St, Cambridge, MA *02138*
Perkins MRS Robert W (Margaret H Edwards) Ws'46. . . . . | ☎ (203) 288-2911 202 Centerbrook Rd, Hamden, CT *06518*
MR Charles B 2d—at ☎ (202) 332-2816 1855 Calvert St NW, Apt 402, Washington, DC *20009* . . . .
MR Morgan B—at Hangzhou, China . . . .
Perkins MR Robert W—H'43
☎ (410) 820-7325 . . 640 Goldsborough St, Easton, MD *21601*
Perkins MR & MRS Roswell B (Joan Titcomb) Rc.K.C.Mt.Plg.Myf.Cs.H.'47 . . of
☎ (212) SA2-3673 . . 1120 Fifth Av, New York, NY *10128*
☎ (401) 635-4444 . . 125 Sakonnet Point Rd, Little Compton, RI *02837*

Perkins MR Rufus M—H'62.Cal'65
☎ (617) 864-7012 . . 415 Broadway, Cambridge, MA *02138*
Perkins MISS Sarah H (Moir—Sarah H Perkins) Les'80.Cda. . . . . | ☎ (508) 369-6161 292 Musketaquid Rd, Concord, MA *01742*
MISS Heather Coolidge Moir . . . .
MISS L Skye Moir . . . .
Perkins MR & MRS Stephen L (Vause—Paula J Wiltshire) Va'74.Me.Cry.Ac.Pa'89. . . . . | ☎ (610) 293-1001 609 S Valley Forge Rd, Wayne, PA *19087*
MR Ryan W . . . .
Perkins MR Thomas H—Ham'60
☎ (805) 688-8659 . . 2575 Latigo Dv, Solvang, CA *93463*
Perkins MR & MRS Thomas H (Lydia L Smith) Bost'76.Myc.Ne'87
☎ (508) 356-7726 . . 6 East St, Ipswich, MA *01938*
Perkins MR Thomas J—Ln.Ny.Pcu.Sfy.Mit'53.H'57 . . of
☎ (415) 435-9551 . . 345 Golden Gate Av, Belvedere, CA *94920* Plumpton Place, East Sussex BN7 3AF, England
Perkins MR & MRS Walter B (Caroline S Darlington) H'41 . . . . | ☎ (310) 476-6048 1428 Tigertail Rd, Los Angeles, CA *90049*
MR W Bryn—at Carleton . . . .
JUNIORS MR Paul D—at Beloit . . . .
Perkins MR & MRS William S (Anne Volger Darst) SWMoSt'82.StP'81
☎ (314) 963-9102 . . 8657 Rosalie Av, Brentwood, MO *63144*
Perkins MR William S . . see MRS E P W Edmunds
Perkins MR & MRS William Whittington (Betty A Malvaney) LSU'49
☎ (601) 833-1748 . . 1595 Smith Lake Rd NE, Brookhaven, MS *39601*
Perlberg MR Edward B—Ng.Br'60 . . of
☎ (212) 744-6839 . . 180 E 79 St, New York, NY *10021*
☎ (516) 537-0614 . . Sagaponack, NY *11962*
Perlberg MRS Hope Brown (Acquavella—Hope Brown) . . . . | ☎ (212) 289-6668 1021 Park Av, New York, NY *10028*
JUNIORS MR Frederick A B . . . .
MISS Eleanor H Acquavella . . . .
Perlitz MR & MRS William C (Gloria A Lobraico) Nat'lCollEd'71.Geo'71.Nw'72 . . . . | ☎ (847) 446-8962 380 Linden St, Winnetka, IL *60093*
MISS Anne Marie . . . .
MR William C JR . . . .
Pernoud DR & MRS Michael J (Christine Costello) StL'71.Mo'75.Wash'81.Str.StL'71.Mo'75. Wash'79 . . . . | ☎ (314) 537-0435 43 Chesterfield Lake Rd, Chesterfield, MO *63005*
MISS Cathleen . . . .
MISS Elizabeth . . . .
JUNIORS MR Michael J . . . .
JUNIORS MR Matthew J . . . .
Pero MRS Roderick E (Marie T Werlemann)
☎ (206) 881-9520 . . 3037—122 Place NE, Bellevue, WA *98005*
Perot MR A Morris JR—StLaw'90 . . see MRS W J Dixon 3d
Perot MRS Henry F (Helene W King) R.
☎ (610) LA5-7727 . . 917 Field Lane, Villanova, PA *19085*
Perot MISS Jocelyn M—Buck'94 . . see MRS W J Dixon 3d
Perot MRS S Baird (Suzanne W Baird) V'65.Pa'80.Ac.Me.
☎ (215) 641-9499 . . 807 Spring Av, Ft Washington, PA *19034*
Perot MRS T Morris 3d (Merritt—Mary F Lennig) Sg.
☎ (215) 283-7186 . . B13 Foulkeways, Sumneytown Pike, Gwynedd, PA *19436*

Perrin MR & MRS Anthony L (Beecher—Marie L Barney) Dick'70.Nyc.On.Ds.Y'45w . . . .
    MISS Olivia S Beecher
    MR Henry G Beecher—Ds. . . . .
    JUNIORS MISS Lucile G Beecher . . . .
    JUNIORS MISS Katherine P Beecher . . . .
☎ (847) 295-1655 995 Maplewood Rd, Lake Forest, IL 60045-2469

Perrin MISS Gail—Ws'60
    ☎ (617) 891-0013 . . 27 Rolling Lane, Weston, MA 02193-2438

Perrin MRS John (Gardner—Esther Coffin)
    ☎ (305) 443-9757 . . 4000 Ventura Av, Coconut Grove, FL 33133

Perrin DR & MRS Mark (Ursula M Gutmann) Sth'56.P'56 . . . .
    MR Thomas M—J&W'88—at 1011 Massachusetts Av, Arlington, MA 02174 .
    MR Christopher . . . .
☎ (908) 362-9125 Brick Kiln Farm, 26 E Crisman Rd, Blairstown, NJ 07825

Perrott MISS Isabel Antonio (g—MRS William L Hires) . . . . Born at Sacramento, CA Oct 9'95

Perrott MR & MRS Robert S JR (Elizabeth G Hagar) D.Wms'55 . . . .
    MR Jeffrey H—Wms'88—at Yale Sch of Art . . .
    MR Andrew S—Wms'90. . . . .
☎ (508) 785-2421 4 Hunt Dv, Dover, MA 02030

Perry MRS A Dean (Helen W Greene) Kt.Tv.Cv.Un.It.
    ☎ (216) 932-7131 . . 14607 Shaker Blvd, Cleveland, OH 44120

Perry MR Alexander T—Emory'92
    ☎ (215) 567-2388 . . 2214 St James St, Apt 3, Philadelphia, PA 19103

Perry MR & MRS Allen Wade (Black—Judith Sinclair) Bost'68.Cv.H.'62.Cl'65.Y'72 . . . .
    MISS Heather S Black—at ☎ (212) 535-1469 1360 York Av, Apt 3D, New York, NY 10021
    MR Andrew A Black—at Colby . . . .
☎ (617) 259-0336 97 Lincoln Rd, Lincoln, MA 01773

Perry MRS Barbara M (Barbara F Moon) FlaAtl'76
    ☎ (954) 785-2257 . . 771 SE Seventh Av, Pompano Beach, FL 33060

Perry MRS Bertha S (Bertha D Scott) Ncd.Dar.
    ☎ (601) 798-0071 . . 604 Hide-a-Way Lane, Carriere, MS 39426

Perry MR & MRS Chad A (Julie B Lerner) SFrSt'89.Atlantic'93.PortSt'96
    ☎ (617) 934-2411 . . "Perrydise" 66 Elder Brewster Rd, Duxbury, MA 02332-5129

Perry MR & MRS Charles S (Julie R Boothe) Swb'58.GeoW'60
    ☎ (207) 633-5177 . . "Longview" PO Box 0176, Boothbay Harbor, ME 04538

Perry MR Christopher D—Wes'90
    70 Strathmore Rd, Apt 11B, Brighton, MA 02135

Perry MR & MRS David G (Julia T Bohlen) P'86.Colby'80
    ☎ (301) 320-6838 . . 4517 Wetherill Rd, Bethesda, MD 20816

Perry JUNIORS MR David H . . see J W Metzger JR

Perry MR & MRS E Lee (Slocumb D Hollis) SL'71.Kt.Cy.Chi.Ncd.Dc.Roch'69.Bost'71
    ☎ (617) 739-1298 . . 112 Dudley St, Brookline, MA 02146

Perry MR & MRS Finley H (Sylvia Stokes) V'44.H.'39.H'42
    ☎ (508) 785-0063 . . 40 Pleasant St, Dover, MA 02030

Perry MR & MRS H Bradlee (Virginia Reimers) H'50
    ☎ (508) 529-9910 . . 5 Bradish Farm Rd, Upton, MA 01568

Perry MRS Hart (Beatrice Gaidzik) Ri.Cs.
    ☎ (518) 537-6431 . . "Southwood" 726 Woods Rd, Germantown, NY 12526

Perry MR Henry E—Y'43.Nw'52 . . . .
    MR Henry E 3d—at 223 Yesler Way, Seattle, WA 98104 . . . .
    MR George F—NH'80—at 2447—61 St NW, Seattle, WA 98107 . . . .
of ☎ (206)324-3825 3215 E Morley Way, Seattle, WA 98112 "Winter Sun" Winthrop, WA 98862

Perry DR J Mitchell—Fy.Pac'80 . . . .
    JUNIORS MISS Marlowe H . . . .
☎ (209) 477-9494 3379 Fairway Dv, Stockton, CA 95204-1107

Perry MISS Julia W . . see T M Claflin 2d

Perry MR & MRS Lee R (Barbara A Mitchell) Ariz'55
    ☎ (602) 996-1292 . . 10838 N 38 Place, Phoenix, AZ 85028-3416

Perry MR & MRS Lewis JR (Russell—Mary L Peltz) H'36.Ox'38
    ☎ (719) 633-7927 . . 107 W Cheyenne Rd, Colorado Springs, CO 80906

Perry MRS Lewis F (Alice de V Ware) Cy.Ncd.Myf.
    MISS Alice de V—at ☎ (203) 397-1908 14 Burton St, New Haven, CT 06515 . . . .
☎ (617) 444-5154 North Hill G402, 865 Central Av, Needham, MA 02192

Perry MR & MRS Lyman S A (Kate T Driggs) Sth'60.Me.USN'60.Pa'68
    ☎ (610) 353-1122 . . 311 N Newtown Street Rd, Newtown Square, PA 19073

Perry MR Matthew McC
    ☎ (805) 962-6553 . . PO Box 954, Santa Barbara, CA 93102

Perry MR Nathaniel D . . see J W Metzger JR

Perry MRS Oliver H (Woods—Louise H Colie) Sth'41.Mv . . .of
    ☎ (410) 494-0214 . . Blakehurst 209, 1055 W Joppa Rd, Towson, MD 21204
    ☎ (954) 943-9851 . . 1600 N Ocean Blvd, Apt 706, Pompano Beach, FL 33062

Perry MRS Parker D (Elizabeth McCord)
    see Dilatory Domiciles

Perry MR Parker D JR
    ☎ (520) 327-8140 . . 3933 E Hampton Place, Tucson, AZ 85712

Perry MR & MRS Richard G (Lawrence—Allene P Ferguson)
    ☎ (914) 763-3836 . . Schoolhouse Rd, Waccabuc, NY 10597

Perry MRS Roger A (Elizabeth Bradlee) V'23.Cy.
    ☎ (617) 444-4518 . . North Hill B503, 865 Central Av, Needham, MA 02192

Perry MR & MRS Samuel D (Lanigan—Elizabeth A Shaw) Ub.Cy.H'65 . . . .
    MISS Elizabeth L . . . .
☎ (617) 566-3454 26 Old Orchard Rd, Chestnut Hill, MA 02167

Perry MR & MRS Walter E 3d (Mary E G Kennard) Man'vl'71.K.San.Ncd.Cl'74.TyDub'78 . . . .
    MISS Diana B . . . .
    JUNIORS MR Sam H P . . . .
    JUNIORS MR Benjamin R H . . . .
of ☎ (201)761-0580 32 Maple Terr, Millburn, NJ 07041 Box 25, Esmont, VA 22937

Perry MR & MRS Warren W (Gregory—Joan McGeoch) BMr'52.Cal'51 . . . .
    MISS Ann C Gregory—at ☎ (415) 921-7587 2028 Beach St, San Francisco, CA 94123 . . .
    MR Robert W Gregory—at ☎ (916) 345-6734 9492 Perkins Rd, Dayton, CA 95928 . . . .
☎ (415) 921-8941 2500 Green St, San Francisco, CA 94123

Perry MR William Haggin JR—Coa.Cw.Snc.Juilliard'59 . . of
☎ (212) TE1-1489 . . 1111 Park Av, New York, NY *10128*
☎ (860) MO3-3262 . . "Maple Hill" 67 Roast Meat Hill Rd,
Killingworth, CT *06419*
☎ (561) MA7-5739 . . "Gator Hollow" 1104 Mahogany Place,
PGA National, Palm Beach Gardens, FL *33418*

Perry MR & MRS Winston C (Zahnzinger—Andrea J Hiller) Ty'58
☎ (617) 934-2411 . . "Perrydise" 66 Elder Brewster Rd, Duxbury,
MA *02332-5129*

Pershing COL & MRS John W (Lloyd—Bergen—Sandra Sinclair)
USA.An.B.Un.L.Wk.Why.So.Pr.Ll.Rv.Vca.Ck.Bost'64 . . of
☎ (516) 671-8240 . . 9 Ludlam Lane, Locust Valley, NY *11560-1724*
☎ (212) 734-1133 . . 3 E 77 St, New York, NY *10021*

Person MR & MRS Solon A 3d (Dyane R Nelson) W&L'57
☎ (412) 963-8894 . . 130 Field Club Rd, Pittsburgh, PA *15238*

Person MR & MRS Solon A 4th (Josita L de G Károlyi) LakeF'81.Leh'81
34 Windsor Rd, Pittsburgh, PA *15215-1813*

Persons MR & MRS Alan R (Rosa C Miller) | ☎ (716) 223-1335
Ncd.Ham'53.Cr'56 . . . . | 58 Nettlecreek Rd,
MISS Elizabeth A—at N'western . . . . | Fairport, NY *14450*
MR Robert D—Buck'84—at 185 Pine St,
Apt 516, Manchester, CT *06040* . . . .
MR William S—Rich'89—at 6807 Bonnie Ridge
Dv, Baltimore, MD *21209* . . . .

Persse MRS John W JR (Mary Louise Flockhart) Pn. | of ☎ (203)281-7658
MR John W 3d—Cw.Syr'80 ⚓—at | Whitney Center 537,
☎ (203) 562-5680 . . 115 Deepwood Dv, | 200 Leeder Hill Dv,
Hamden, CT *06517* . . . . | Hamden, CT *06517*
| ☎ (802) 446-2523
| Roxborough,
| Persse Park,
| Butterworth Rd,
| Wallingford, VT
| *05773*

Pervere MR Peter F—Stan'70
☎ (408) 688-5385 . . 753 Oakhill Rd, Aptos, CA *95003*

Peschel MISS Neile E . . see C W McCoy

Peschel MISS Shana C . . see C W McCoy

Peter MR Jeffrey C—Sdy.SCal'89
☎ (619) 226-7557 . . 3851 Bernice Dv, San Diego, CA *92107*

Peter MR & MRS Oliver Bernard (Cameron E Brown) SCal'60.Sdy.Pom'52
☎ (619) 225-1715 . . 976 Scott St, San Diego, CA *92106*

Peter MR & MRS Phillips S (Jania J Hutchins) | of ☎ (301)299-2006
SFr'61.Cvc.Va'54.Va'59 . . . . | 10805 Tara Rd,
MR Phillips S JR . . . . | Potomac, MD *20854*
| ☎ (561) 231-6999
| 1000 Beach Rd, Apt
| 198, John's Island,
| Vero Beach, FL
| *32963*
| 690 Ocean Rd,
| John's Island,
| Vero Beach, FL
| *32963*

Peter MRS Walter G JR (Evelyn Booth) Ct.Cvc. . . . . | ☎ (202) 333-4288
MISS Martha Custis—Ncd. . . . . | 3024 Dumbarton Av
| NW, Washington,
| DC *20007*

Peterkin MR & MRS (DR) Christopher M (Joanna M Janoska)
Ty'80.LIU'81.NewCMed'86.Ken'80.Durham'85
☎ (619) 689-1342 . . "Le Petit Belsay" 9948 Cummins Place,
San Diego, CA *92131*

Peterkin MR & MRS DeWitt JR (Katharine Urban) | ☎ (203) 655-9887
Sth'41.StA.Yn.Y'37 . . . . | 224 Long Neck
MISS Kate—Sth'76.Yn.—at ☎ (970) 204-0321 | Point Rd, Noroton,
730 Sandpiper Point, Ft Collins, CO *80525* . . . . | CT *06820*
MR DeWitt 3d . . . . |
MR George U |

Peterkin MR & MRS George A JR (Watson—Nancy J Girling) Tex'48
☎ (713) 785-5545 . . 5787 Indian Circle, Houston, TX *77057*

Peterkin MR & MRS Patrick O'B (Jennifer M Wieland)
CarnM'86.Nu'95.Yn.W&L'85
☎ (203) 655-0359 . . 33 Brookside Rd, Darien, CT *06820*

Peterkin MASTER William Patrick O'Brien (Patrick O'B) . . . . Born
Mch 17'96

Peters MR Alexander C 2d—Bost'82
34 Marshview Circle, East Sandwich, MA *02537*

Peters MR & MRS Alton E (Fisher—Elizabeth I | of ☎ (212)873-8657
Berlin) V'58.K.Gr.Chr.C.Plg.StJ.H.'55 . . . . | 211 Central Park W,
MISS Rachel C—at ☎ (212) 535-6430 | New York, NY
50 E 72 St, New York, NY *10021* . . . . | *10024*
| ☎ (860) 824-5206
| Falls Village, CT
| *06031*

Peters MRS Franklin Woodson (Christopher—Marian A Peters) An.
☎ (804) 296-2509 . . "Liberty Hall" Rte 5, Box 341, Charlottesville,
VA *22901*

Peters MR & MRS Frederick W (Mary I Gores) | ☎ (202) 363-3049
Ws'70.Mit'76.H'68.Lond'73.H'76 . . . . | 3250 Highland Place
MISS Mary I | NW, Washington,
MISS Elizabeth H . . . . | DC *20008*
JUNIORS MISS Margaret E . . . . |

Peters MR & MRS Frederick W (Alexandra T Lally) | of ☎ (212)362-4610
Cl'75.Y'74 . . . . | 262 Central Park W,
MISS Clelia W . . . . | New York, NY
JUNIORS MR John F . . . . | *10024*
| ☎ (914) 763-8685
| 137 Boway Rd,
| South Salem, NY
| *10590*

Peters MRS George B (Marion C McClelland) | ☎ (610) MO4-7856
Sth'42 . . . . | 47 Penarth Rd,
MR George McC—at 20 Brookline Blvd, | Bala-Cynwyd, PA
Havertown, PA *19083* . . . . | *19004*
DR James C—Pa'77.Pa'83 . . . . |

Peters MRS Horace W (Edith C Colt) Sth'29.Sl.Myf.
☎ (202) 483-6149 . . 2335 Ashmead Place NW, Washington, DC *20009*

Peters MR James G
☎ (520) 648-8314 . . 501 La Posada Circle, Apt 190, Green Valley,
AZ *85614*

Peters MRS Jane H (Jane S Hallenborg)
☎ (707) 967-0644 . . 1095 Crinella Dv, St Helena, CA *94574*
Peters MRS John L D (Eleanor T Carpenter)
☎ (941) 349-4288 . . 4822 Ocean Blvd, Sarasota, FL *34242*
Peters MISS Marjorie S—Bab'89
☎ (703) 836-2178 . . 801 N Pitt St, Alexandria, VA *22314*
Peters MR & MRS Merz K (Nancy Champe) | ☎ (212) 535-3303
Sth'61.Cs.Y'55.H.'57 . . . . | 520 E 86 St,
MISS Julie E—H'91 . . . . | New York, NY
MISS Cynthia C . . . . | *10028*
MR Craig T—H'93 . . . . |
Peters MR Preston H—Cl'64
☎ (860) 824-5088 . . 2 Puddlers Lane, Falls Village, CT *06031*
Peters MR & MRS Ralph F (Threatt—Diana J | ☎ (609) 397-5968
Clayton) Ln.L.P'51 . . . . | Laogaland Farm,
MR Richard C . . . . | 55 Strimples Mill
Rd, Stockton, NJ
08559-1703
Peters MR & MRS Richard (Gribbel—Elizabeth T | ☎ (804) 296-3907
Fehr) San.Sap.Cw.Pa'47 . . . . | 4 Sunset Circle,
MISS Julie—at ☎ (970) 925-2994 . . PO Box | Farmington,
1643, Aspen, CO *81612* . . . . | Charlottesville, VA
22901-1920
Peters MR Robert E JR—Bost'83 . . see S J Moszka
Peters MR Robeson—H'42
☎ (617) 661-3895 . . 18A Forest St, Cambridge, MA *02140*
Peters MR & MRS Warren A (V Elizabeth Stith) P'34
☎ (510) 428-2786 . . 150 Brookside Dv, Berkeley, CA *94705*
Peters MISS Whitney L—Bost'80 . . see S J Moszka
Petersen MR & MRS Erroll M (Romaine—Elisabeth S Howe)
Sth'59.ArizSt'61
☎ (520) 684-3362 . . PO Box 21221, Wickenburg, AZ *85358*
Petersen MRS Howard C (Elizabeth A Watts) DeP'32.Mt.C.Plg.Ac . . .of
☎ (610) MU8-2737 . . PO Box 8253, Radnor, PA *19087-8253*
☎ (202) 342-1739 . . 3900 Watson Place NW, Apt A2C, Washington,
DC *20016*
Petersen MR & MRS James L (M Merryfield | ☎ (610) 388-2353
Laimbeer) Temp'61 . . . . | "Wood's Edge"
MISS Pamela W—Nev'92 . . . . | 26 Sapling Dv,
MISS Elizabeth M . . . . | Kennett Square, PA
MR David L . . . . | *19348*
Petersens MR & MRS Carl F af (Alice A Hooper) Lund'42
☎ (011-44-171) 235-7301 . . 110 Eaton Square, London SW1W 9AA,
England
Peterson MR & MRS Charles M JR (Patricia F | ☎ (215) 836-4208
Lennig) Pe.Pc.Sa.Rv.Ty'55 . . . . | 8307 Stenton Av,
MR Charles M 3d—at Roanoke Coll . . . . | Wyndmoor, PA
MR Frederick L—at Wash'n Coll . . . . | *19038*
JUNIORS MR Nicholas H . . . . |
Peterson MISS Charlotte R—Denis'90.Ac.Cda.
☎ (610) 296-5997 . . 802 Weatherstone Dv, Paoli, PA *19301*
Peterson MR & MRS David S (Cynthia L Cruice)
ColC'81.DU'85.Neb'83.DU'85
☎ (303) 797-2935 . . 5171 S Juniper St, Littleton, CO *80123-1533*
Peterson MRS Eleanor R (Eleanor F W Reeve) Me.Rd.Ac.Cda.
☎ (610) 975-9981 . . 220 Hedgemere Dv, Devon, PA *19333*

Peterson MR & MRS Frederick A (Elisabeth McC | of ☎ (617)367-9068
Thomas) Rdc'60.Ub.Y'38 . . . . | 19 Temple St,
MISS Nancy Lee—at 53-1 Summer St, Gloucester, | Boston, MA *02114*
MA *01930* . . . . | ☎ (207) 627-4335
MR Robert B—at 112 Varnum St, Arlington, MA | Box 5035, RFD 1,
02174 . . . . | Oxford, ME *04270*
MR John T . . . . |
Peterson MRS G Baltzer (Terbell—Cowles—Louise Boone) Bur.
☎ (805) 969-8236 . . Casa Dorinda B45, 300 Hot Springs Rd,
Santa Barbara, CA *93108*
Peterson MR & MRS George 3d (Anne C Gamble) | ☎ (908) 766-6223
Sap.Ac.Pa'58 . . . . | 301 Claremont Rd,
MR Clark G . . . . | Bernardsville, NJ
MR George V . . . . | *07924*
Peterson MR John H—Pc.Rv.Sar.
☎ (941) 263-3449 . . 501 Forest Lake Blvd, Naples, FL *34105-5560*
Peterson MR & MRS Robert L (Evelyn C Fry) | ☎ (203) 661-7315
V'41.BtP.Evg.Cly.Myf.Dar.GeoW'45 . . . . | 644 Lake Av,
MR William P . . . . | Greenwich, CT
06830
Peterson MR Robert N—Minn'42
☎ (302) 426-8297 . . "The Country House" 4830 Kennett Pike,
Wilmington, DE *19807*
Petó MR Alexander T . . see S M Summers
Petrasch MR & MRS John G (Olivia H Rutter) | of ☎ (508)785-2504
Nyc.Rv.Y'61 . . . . | 3 Claybrook Rd,
JUNIORS MISS Anne S . . . . | Dover, MA *02030*
JUNIORS MR John G JR . . . . | ☎ (508) 228-2585
"Shawkemo"
10 Berkeley Av,
Monomoy,
Nantucket, MA
02554
Petri MR Camillo F—Ham'39
☎ (207) 326-8677 . . Perkins St, PO Box 244, Castine, ME *04421*
Petri MR & MRS Hector D (Deborah S Shepard) | ☎ (508) 877-0882
Hob'49 . . . . | 384 Edmands Rd,
MR Ogden W . . . . | Framingham Center,
MA *01701*
Petri MR & MRS Pitt JR (Anne J Weedon) SUNY'80.Ham'61
☎ (716) 627-3464 . . S 5555 Truscott Terr, Lake View, NY *14085*
Petrie MR John E . . . . Died at
Solebury, PA May 9'96
Petrie MRS John E (Gribbel—Katherine E Wiedersheim) Ac.
☎ (215) 297-8155 . . "Crossroads" PO Box 119, Solebury, PA *18963*
Petsas MR & MRS William D (Kathryn Pappas) Ariz'85.Valp'80.Ind'86
☎ (602) 955-2897 . . 4131 E Patricia Jane Dv, Phoenix, AZ *85018*
Pettengill MR & MRS Charles A (Lisa K Raushenbush) Miami'89.Colg'89
☎ (513) 321-4772 . . 1000 Crest Circle, Cincinnati, OH *45208*
Pettengill MR & MRS Daniel A (Clarinda B Huntington) Sth'53.Wms'48
☎ (941) 591-1965 . . 804 Rue de Ville, Naples, FL *34108*
Pettengill MR & MRS Kroger (Kathryn W Mitchell) Cm.Qc.P'44 . . of
☎ (513) 561-6732 . . 4750 Willow Hills Lane, Cincinnati, OH *45243*
☎ (941) 261-7926 . . 1785 Gulf Shore Blvd N, Naples, FL *34102*

Petter MR Stanley DuB JR—Srr.Wk.Va'56 . . . . . . | ☎ (606) 255-8707
MISS Anna Webb . . . . | ''Hurricane Hall''
PO Box 11220,
Lexington, KY
40574

Pettibone MR & MRS Peter J (Jean Kellogg) | of ☎ (212)289-0045
Ws'64.Au.Cc.Cly.P'61.H'64 . . . . | 1158 Fifth Av,
MISS Victoria K—at Stanford . . . . | New York, NY
MR Stephen P—Mid'94 . . . . | *10029*
☎ (516) 749-0957
''Woodbine''
Shelter Island
Heights, NY *11965*

Petticrew MR & MRS William K JR (E Andreé Abell) Ncd.USN'46
☎ (512) 261-4366 . . ''The Crews' Croft'' 114 Barbie Court, Austin,
TX *78734-4559*

Pettit MR & MRS Jeffrey (Brigitte E Pasewark) | ☎ (212) 534-0444
Rc.Un.Stc.Y'50 . . . . | 1088 Park Av,
MISS Priscilla M . . . . | New York, NY
MISS Jennifer E . . . . | *10128*

Pettit MISS (DR) Mary De W . . . . Died May 5'96
Pettit MR & MRS William D (Stetson—Elizabeth J McChristie)
V'41.Err.Eyc.Cly.P'41 . . of
☎ (609) 921-9148 . . 68 Drake's Corner Rd, Princeton, NJ *08540*
☎ (508) 627-5869 . . 4 Armstrong Lane, PO Box 5037, Edgartown,
MA *02539*

Pettus MRS Charles P (Stella R Cartwright) Cy. . . . | of ☎ (314)997-4220
MISS Georgia—at ☎ (314) 647-6649 | 8 Treebrook Lane,
7018 Forsythe Blvd, St Louis, MO *63105* . . . . . | St Louis, MO *63124*
MR Charles P JR—at 626 S Hanley Rd, St Louis, | ☎ (505) 988-5898
MO *63105* . . . . | 151 Gonzales Rd,
Santa Fe, NM *87501*

Pettus MR & MRS Robert C (Sharon A Wright) | of ☎ (314)968-8631
Wash'63 . . . . | 6 Daniel Rd,
MISS Airlia W—at 9515 Park Lane, St Louis, MO | St Louis, MO *63124*
63124 . . . . | ☎ (520) 624-5330
''La Casa del
Escorpión'' PO Box
85293, Tucson, AZ
85754-5293

Pettus MRS Thruston (F Virginia Cave) Cysl.
☎ (904) 285-6349 . . PO Box 358, Ponte Vedra Beach, FL *32082*
Pettus MR & MRS Thruston W (Susan F Fouke) | ☎ (201) 538-4667
Mt.Mg.Cysl.P'63 . . . . | Glen Alpin Rd,
MISS Katherine K . . . . | New Vernon, NJ
JUNIORS MR Thruston W JR . . . . | *07976*

Petty MRS Elizabeth B (Elizabeth M Bucknall) Pitzer'76.Les'82
☎ (508) 465-7429 . . 57 Purchase St, Newburyport, MA *01950*
Petty MRS James M (Tschudy—Mary L Hunt)
☎ (410) 268-1382 . . 113 Wardour Dv, Annapolis, MD *21401*
Petty MR & MRS James Marshall 3d (Allen—Linda S Perry) MdArt'78
☎ (410) 263-5792 . . 1970 Fairfax Rd, Annapolis, MD *21401*
Petty MR & MRS L Talmage (Elizabeth D Sands) Wes'82.Tr.Nu'82
☎ (301) 320-9492 . . 5004 Rodman Rd, Bethesda, MD *20816*

Petty MRS Lee M (H Lee Mills) V'52.Cvc.T. . . . . . | ☎ (301) 654-1813
MISS Victoria L—at ☎ (503) 635-4378 | 37 W Lenox St,
1 Jefferson P'kway, Apt 105, Lake Oswego, OR | Chevy Chase, MD
97035 . . . . | *20815*

Petty MR & MRS Robert de S (Sydney S Johnson) WashColl'76.Md'75
☎ (410) 266-7854 . . 134 Summer Village Dv, Annapolis, MD *21401*
Petty MR & MRS Scott JR (Egan—Weed—Eleanor T Oliver)
Ty'66.A.Tex'60.Tex'61
☎ (210) 826-2795 . . 202 La Jara Blvd, San Antonio, TX *78209-4444*

Pew MR & MRS G Thompson JR (Sandra L Kennedy) | ☎ (610) 527-7407
Ph.Me.Rc.Cts.R.Ste.Gi.Cry.Rd.Pa'71 ⚓ . . . . . | ''La Cachette''
MR G Thompson 3d . . . . | 310 Caversham Rd,
Bryn Mawr, PA
19010

Pew MR & MRS George L (Sally D Chinn) Cts.Yn.Y.'58.Drex'68 . . of
☎ (610) 687-1764 . . ''Wayside'' 569 Conestoga Rd, Ithan, PA *19085*
☎ (207) 633-4942 . . Mouse Island, PO Box 475, Boothbay Harbor,
ME *04538*

Pew MR James S—Me.Stan'84.Camb'87.Pa'89
311 N Edgewood St, Arlington, VA *22201*

Pew MR & MRS Joseph N 3d (Doris E Myers) | ☎ (610) 642-3080
Me.M.Rc.Gm.Ac.Stan'45 . . . . | 701 Merion Square
MISS (DR) M Catharine—Y'75.Pa'83—at | Rd, Gladwyne, PA
☎ (206) 328-4490 . . 102 Maiden Lane E, Seattle, | *19035*
WA *98112* . . . . |
MR Thomas A—at ☎ (610) 254-9330 |
164 Pugh Rd, Strafford, PA *19087* . . . . |

Pew MISS Katherine N (Thomas W JR) . . . . | Married at Tucson, AZ
Hollar MR Troy E (Earl E 3d) | . . . . Jun 1'96

Pew MRS Margaret W (Sunderland—Delano—Margaret Wiberg) Ac.
☎ (410) 778-7559 . . ''Fowl Play'' 7886 Airy Hill Rd, Chestertown,
MD *21620*

Pew MR & MRS Richard Ford (Scott—Jepson—M | ☎ (406) 388-2450
Thérèse Rakestraw) Bvl.Ny.ArizSt'66 ⚓ . . . . | North Ridge Ranch,
JUNIORS MR Weston C . . . . | 28500 Rocky
MR Edward B Jepson—at ☎ (406) 586-1220 | Mountain Rd,
111C Gallatin Dv, Bozeman, MT *59715* . . . . | Belgrade, MT *59714*

Pew MR & MRS Thomas W JR (Laura Neuhaus) . . . . . | 5445 N Camino
MR Thomas W . . . . | Escuela, Tucson, AZ
MR David R . . . . | *85718*

Peyton MR & MRS Bernard 3d (Susanne G Tilney) Ty'75.H'72
☎ (510) 549-9661 . . 2841 Forest Av, Berkeley, CA *94705*
Peyton MR & MRS F Bradley 3d (Sargent—Gertrude B Breckinridge)
Ky'43.Sl.Cda.Va'38
☎ (540) 456-6151 . . ''Seven Oaks'' PO Box 305, Greenwood,
VA *22943*

Peyton REV & MRS F Bradley 4th (Joan A D'Adamo) | ☎ (301) 609-8596
Md'81.Md'89.Cc.Va'72.Va'75.VaTheo'84 . . . . . | 1020 Wiltshire Dv,
MISS K Ashby . . . . | La Plata, MD
JUNIORS MR F Bradley 5th . . . . | *20646-3510*

Peyton MR & MRS Scott B (M Page Edwards) Cc.VPI'76
☎ (540) 456-6418 . . ''The Hilltop'' PO Box 5, Greenwood, VA *22943*
Peyton MR & MRS Theodore S (Elizabeth A Lord) | ☎ (609) 921-2666
P'60 . . . . | 73 Drakes Corner
MISS Elizabeth A—at 405 W 23 St, Apt 6A, | Rd, Princeton, NJ
New York, NY *10011* . . . . | *08540*

Pfaelzer MR Arthur Goodhue—Sm.D.Cy.H'59 .... | of ☎ (617)738-7983
MISS Christine E . . . . | 33 Chestnut Hill Rd,
MISS Diane E . . . . | Chestnut Hill, MA
02167
☎ (802) 867-5746
"Castile"
Lower Hollow Rd,
Dorset, VT *05251*

Pfaelzer MR Carter P—Cy.H.'55.Mit'82 ⚓
☎ (617) 899-0429 . . 20 Rolling Lane, Weston, MA *02193*

Pfau MRS E Spencer (Elizabeth L Spencer) | ☎ (415) 567-3214
Sth'49.Tcy. . . . . | 250 Laurel St,
MISS Elizabeth Churchill . . . . | Apt 202,
San Francisco, CA
94118

Pfau MR & MRS George H JR (Anne E Mayhew) Cal'62.Bhm.Y'48
☎ (415) 931-1067 . . 2298 Vallejo St, San Francisco, CA *94123*

Pfeffer MR Charles A 3d—San.Cl'65.Pa'67 . . . . | ☎ (207) 781-5382
MISS Amy-Louise A—at 428 Thoreau Dv, | 15 Coveside Rd,
Branford, CT *06405* . . . . | Cumberland, ME
MISS Elizabeth A—at ☎ (207) 799-2418 | *04110*
51 Willow St, South Portland, ME *04106* . . . . .
MR Richard A—at ☎ (207) 871-7173
88 Park St, Portland, ME *04101* . . . .

Pfeffer MR & MRS James L (Jane E Macy) | ☎ (860) 767-0263
Conn'73.AmInt'l'74.Ny.Ne.JHop'73.Bost'75 ⚓ | "Eight Bells"
JUNIORS MISS Abigail S . . . . | 10 Meigs Lane,
JUNIORS MISS Eliza M . . . . | Essex, CT *06426*
Pfeifer MISS Emma Beatty (g—Herbert W Hansen) . . . . . . Born Jly 25'95
Pfeiffer MR & MRS John S (Magnussen—Pfeiffer— | ☎ (303) 660-1612
Susan C Browne) Cda.Ncd.ColC'51.DU'54 . . . . | 2515 Tournament
MR Edward C . . . . | Dv, Castle Pines
MISS Carey L Magnussen . . . . | Village,
MISS Kendall L Magnussen . . . . | Castle Rock, CO
80104-9095

Pfeiffer MR & MRS Timothy A (Sophia D Wells) V'39.P'37 . . of
☎ (207) 729-7502 . . 15 Franklin St, Brunswick, ME *04011*
"Saltim Shingle" Ripley Neck, Harrington, ME *04643*

Pfeil MR & MRS Roy S (Jamali—Juliana Post) | ☎ (203) 656-0897
Wis'73.Cl'80.Dth'55.H'59 . . . . | 436 Brookside Rd,
JUNIORS MISS Samar Jamali . . . . | Norwalk, CT *06850*

Pfeil MRS (REV) Susan M (Susan Magro) Y'94.Yn. . . | ☎ (203) 966-7271
MISS Anneliese—Dth'92—at 284 Mott St, | 275A Park St,
Apt 9P, New York, NY *10012* . . . . | New Canaan, CT
06840

Pfingst MR & MRS Osborne JR (Eleanor F Cannon) Pc.
☎ (215) 643-7388 . . 9 High Gate Lane, Blue Bell, PA *19422*

Pfingst MR & MRS William C (Barbara J Jack) Temp'78.Pc.
☎ (215) 646-6160 . . 1351 W Butler Pike, Blue Bell, PA *19422*

Pfisterer MR & MRS Scott McKenna (Elizabeth S Gay) Smu'82.Miami'83
☎ (630) 325-2041 . . 119 N Grant St, Hinsdale, IL *60521*

Pflager MR & MRS Godfrey H (Susan C Denious) | ☎ (212) 362-7853
Wash'63.Bost'66 . . . . | 257 Central Park W,
MISS Dorothy H . . . . | New York, NY
10024

Pflieger MR & MRS John E (Donna R Carlson) Rcn.Cvc.Rr.Ri.Lic.Y'53 . . of
☎ (202) 244-5424 . . 4204—48 Place NW, Washington, DC *20016*
☎ (410) 745-5316 . . "Westlea" PO Box 335, Royal Oak,
MD *21662-0335*

Pflueger MR & MRS Edward M (Neighbour—Kathleen I Powers)
Rc.K.Mto.Lm.Ht.Cs.Cly.Dh.Cda.Dc . . .of
☎ (212) BU8-8385 . . 760 Park Av, New York, NY *10021*
☎ (914) 221-2692 . . Kiyiwana Farm, 440 Hosner Mountain Rd,
Stormville, NY *12582-5326*

Phelan MR & MRS Arthur J JR (Kathleen A Butler) | ☎ (301) 656-9315
Cvc.Mt.Yn.Y'56.Y'57 . . . . | 6300 Brookville Rd,
MISS Margaret A—at Wellesley . . . . | Chevy Chase, MD
MR Arthur J 3d—at U of Mich . . . . | *20815*

Phelps MISS Ann Naile—Ac.Pc.Dll.Myf.Cda.W.
☎ (215) VI4-4148 . . 4000 Gypsy Lane, Apt 506, Philadelphia,
PA *19144*

Phelps MR & MRS Ashton JR (Mary E Sanders) | ☎ (504) 895-3443
LSU'75.Y'67.Tul'70 . . . . | 1457 State St,
MISS Cary C . . . . | New Orleans, LA
MISS Mary L . . . . | *70118*

Phelps MR Gouverneur M—Rcn.H'31
☎ (413) 268-9472 . . 7 Nash Hill Place, Apt 202, Williamsburg,
MA *01096*

Phelps MRS Irene S (Irene D Siragusa) Tul'75
☎ (310) 453-4363 . . 1435—26 St, Apt 10, Santa Monica, CA *90404*

Phelps MR & MRS Irving P (Patricia Burke) My.L.B. | of ☎ (508)927-1773
MR John J . . . . | 176 Hale St,
Beverly, MA
01915-3846
☎ (803) 642-1967
460 Sumter St SE,
Aiken, SC *29801*

Phelps MR Mason JR—On.Srb . . .of
☎ (561) 790-4695 . . 13368 Polo Rd W, Apt 203C, West Palm Beach,
FL *33414*
☎ (970) 925-4589 . . 401 North St, Aspen, CO *81612*

Phelps MR Reginald H—H'30 . . . . | ☎ (617) 864-2847
MR Henry C . . . . | 107 Irving St,
Cambridge, MA
02138

Phelps MR & MRS Stowe C (Charlton Y Jacobs) C.Gm.Fic.Fiy.Cs.Y.'39
☎ (212) 570-9113 . . 149 E 73 St, New York, NY *10021*

Phifer MR & MRS Thomas M 3d (Murphy—Jean C Parker)
Y'74.Cl'77.C.Gi.Clem'75.Clem'77 . . of
☎ (212) 496-0590 . . 565 West End Av, Apt 14A, New York, NY *10024*
447 Craryville Rd, Hillsdale, NY *12529*

Philbin MRS Brisbane (Kelley—Elinor Brisbane) B'gton'46.Dyc.Cly.
☎ (212) 831-5305 . . 1150 Fifth Av, New York, NY *10128-0724*

Philbin MR & MRS Ewing R JR (Andrew—Seelye—Susan C Ott) Y'47
☎ (707) 525-0551 . . 4650 Montecito Av, Santa Rosa, CA *95404*

Philbin MISS Florence S
☎ (860) 693-2581 . . PO Box 99, Canton, CT *06019*

Philbrick MISS Ann M—NCar'78
☎ (202) 686-4532 . . 4601 Connecticut Av NW, Apt 620, Washington,
DC *20008*

Philbrick MR & MRS John A 3d (Marion F Broadbent)
Mich'52.Me.Ph.Ssk.Cs.Y'49
☎ (610) 527-2074 . . 201 Ladbroke Rd, Bryn Mawr, PA *19010*
Philbrick MR & MRS Richard B (Ruth A Rowe) Wa.Cnt.Sl.Ch'43
☎ (301) 309-0196 . . 118 Monroe St, Apt 307, Rockville, MD *20850*
Philip MR John Van Ness 3d—P'76
☎ (212) 873-4069 . . 260 W 91 St, New York, NY *10024*
Philip MR & MRS Peter S (Victoria S Rockefeller) Mid'85.Cly.Yn.Y'85 . . of
☎ (860) 435-0549 . . The Hotchkiss School, PO Box 800, Lakeville,
CT *06039*
☎ (207) 885-0224 . . ''Greywalls'' 494 Black Point Rd, PO Box 3055,
Prouts Neck, ME *04074*
Philip MR & MRS Peter V N (Sabina FitzGibbon)
Bnd'48.Rc.Ln.Bgt.Plg.Sa.Rv.Cly.Y.'45w
☎ (914) 234-7229 . . ''Fairways'' Box 395, Bedford, NY *10506*
Philip MR & MRS Thomas W (Lela R Schaus) Denis'83.Rc.Bgt.Y.Buck'84
☎ (914) 234-6634 . . 748 Guard Hill Rd, Bedford, NY *10506*
Philip MR & MRS William V N (Jennifer C Brainard) Y'83.Yn.Y'83 . . of
☎ (860) 658-6754 . . Westminster School, 995 Hopmeadow St,
Simsbury, CT *06070*
☎ (802) 867-5365 . . West Rd, Dorset, VT *05251*
Phillips MR & MRS Arthur H (Elizabeth E Sass) H'42 . . of
☎ (803) 723-7333 . . 86 King St, Charleston, SC *29401*
☎ (508) 356-4870 . . 174 Argilla Rd, Ipswich, MA *01938*
Phillips MRS (DR) Asa E JR (Anne Wight) BMr'39.Pa'43.Cy.Chi.Myf.Ncd.H.
☎ (617) 232-8836 . . 80 Sargent Rd, Brookline, MA *02146-7571*
Phillips MISS Caroline A (Adams—Caroline A | ☎ (203) 782-1743
Phillips) Sth'80 . . . . | 377 St Ronan St,
MR Alexander D Adams . . . . | New Haven, CT
| *06511*
Phillips MR Christopher H—Mt.H'43
☎ (202) 333-4996 . . 2801 New Mexico Av NW, Apt 924, Washington,
DC *20007*
Phillips MR Christopher L—Tex'91
☎ (212) 481-3461 . . 401 E 34 St, Apt N21E, New York, NY *10016*
Phillips MR D Colin—Van'90
☎ (212) 627-0806 . . 232 W 16 St, Apt 1FR, New York, NY *10011*
Phillips MR & MRS (REV) Daniel A (Diana Walcott) | ☎ (617) 491-2435
Ws'78.H'82.H'60 . . . . | 975 Memorial Dv,
MR Bradford L—Va'89 . . . . | Apt 903, Cambridge,
MISS Lisa W (Meyer—Lisa W Phillips) Ty'86 . . | MA *02138*
Phillips MISS Deborah C . . see MRS P K Bell
Phillips MR Derek A—Cal'89.Pac'93 . . see G R Henry JR
Phillips MRS Donald B (Mary N R Gunnell)
☎ (540) 463-1957 . . Rte 2, Box 114B, Lexington, VA *24450*
Phillips MRS Drayton (Pier—Reinette Plimpton) Chi.
☎ (508) 468-1053 . . 14 Dodges Row, Wenham, MA *01984*
Phillips MR & MRS Duncan B (Katherine McKinney) | ☎ (910) 686-9448
Sth'52 . . . . | 271 Beach Rd N,
MR Duncan McK—at 304—36 St, | Figure Eight Island,
Newport Beach, CA *92663* . . . . | Wilmington, NC
MR Peter R—at 3320A Steppes Court, | *28405*
Falls Church, VA *22041* . . . . |
Phillips MRS Elizabeth B (Elizabeth S Brown) Man'vl'65.Houst'77
☎ (713) 522-7667 . . 9 Waverly Court, Houston, TX *77005*
Phillips MISS Elizabeth Piper (g—Broaddus Johnson) . . . Born May 30'95

Phillips MR & MRS Ellis L JR (Marion E Grumman) | ☎ (561) 234-5164
Adelphi'81.Ck.C.Pn.P'42 . . . . | 1855 Bay Rd, Apt
MR Ellis L 3d—at 233 Commonwealth Av, | 302D, Vero Beach,
Boston, MA *02116* . . . . | FL *32963*
Phillips MRS Frances H L (Frances H Locke) | ☎ (011-502-2)
Wheat'64 . . . . | 336582
MISS Leila G—at Georgetown . . . . | 20 Calle 22-18,
| Zona 10, Guatemala
| City, Guatemala
Phillips MR & MRS Francis F (Chara D Church)
☎ (908) 363-8858 . . Harrogate B2200, 400 Locust St, Lakewood,
NJ *08701*
Phillips MR Frederick F—Rc.LakeF'69.Pa'73
☎ (312) 922-0092 . . 53 W Jackson Blvd, 1752, Chicago, IL *60604*
Phillips MR & MRS George F JR (Kohlmeyer—Carin Wyckoff) St.
☎ (716) 884-5442 . . 80 Chapin P'kway, Buffalo, NY *14209*
Phillips MR & MRS Gerald B (Maria B Lewis) | ☎ (212) 535-1922
P'46.H'48 . . . . | 196 E 75 St,
MISS Abigail S—Y'93 . . . . | New York, NY
MISS Elizabeth B—P'95 . . . . | *10021*
Phillips MISS Harriet M—Me.
74 Pasture Lane, Apt 321, Bryn Mawr, PA *19010*
Phillips MR & MRS Harry H S (Munson—Marr—Martha J Potter) Bgt.
☎ (561) 278-3860 . . 1002 Vista Del Mar, Delray Beach, FL *33483*
Phillips MR & MRS J Ormsby (Harriet S Pullen) | ☎ (412) 782-1341
Swb'43.Ncd.Leh'42 . . . . | 105 Fahnestock Rd,
MISS M Virginia . . . . | Pittsburgh, PA
MR Charles P . . . . | *15215*
Phillips MRS Jeffrey B (Susan L Morgan) Hood'71 . | ☎ (954) 564-6599
MISS Christie . . . . | 1524 NE Eighteenth
MR Jeffrey B JR . . . . | Av, Ft Lauderdale,
| FL *33304*
Phillips MR Jeffrey B—Ty'70
173 Union St, South Weymouth, MA *02190*
Phillips MRS John Goldsmith (Giovanna M Sodi) C.
☎ (561) 655-2760 . . Portofino South Apt 205, 3800 Washington Rd,
West Palm Beach, FL *33405*
Phillips MRS Laughlin (Cafritz—Jennifer Stats) Rr.Mt.Cos.Ch'49
☎ (202) 333-1337 . . 3044 O St NW, Washington, DC *20007*
Phillips MRS Lewis G (Butler—Jessie V Ewing) Dyc.Cly.Cda.
☎ (516) 922-0002 . . 40 Cove Woods Rd, Oyster Bay, NY *11771*
Phillips MRS M Jackson (Mary B Jackson) Ht.
☎ (303) 973-1195 . . 11500 Park Range Rd, Littleton, CO *80127*
Phillips MR & MRS Peter L (H Leigh Keyser) | ☎ (802) 425-3259
Pa'72.VillaN'76.Hawth'69 . . . . | RD 2, Box 2368,
MISS Helen H . . . . | Charlotte, VT *05445*
JUNIORS MR Brent C . . . . |
Phillips MR & MRS Peter M (Mary A Coulson) H'54 | ☎ (415) 435-0135
MISS Deborah . . . . | 98 Main St, Tiburon,
| CA *94920*
Phillips DR Philip—Wms'22
☎ (508) 779-2289 . . 43 Old Sugar Rd, Bolton, MA *01740*
Phillips MR & MRS R Wendell JR (Elizabeth D Moss) | ☎ (603) 526-8054
Sb.Myf.Cw.Ncd.Br'50.Mit'52.Ill'53 . . . . | 173 County Rd,
MR R Wendell 3d—Bost'79—at Bethlehem, NH | New London, NH
03574 . . . . | *03257*

Phillips MRS Ralph E JR (Caroline A Luce) Cal'50.Vh.
☎ (818) 441-3383 . . 307 Arlington Dv, Pasadena, CA *91105*

Phillips MRS Sandra L H (Eddy—Sandra L H | ☎ (303) 972-2398
Phillips) BMr'66 | 7599 Storm
   MISS Nathalie K Eddy—at U of Colo Boulder | Mountain, Littleton,
   MR Philip S Eddy—at U of Colo Boulder . . . | CO *80127*

Phillips MR & MRS Silas B JR (Frances M Rau) H'37 . . of
☎ (915) 698-1574 . . 5 Trafalgar Square, Abilene, TX *79605*
☎ (011-52-415) 2-24-30 . . Revueltas 19, San Miguel de Allende,
GTO, Mexico

Phillips MRS Stephen (Bessie G Wright) | ☎ (508) 744-2028
Chi.Ey.Un.Ncd. | 30 Chestnut St,
   MISS Jane A | Salem, MA *01970*

Phillips MR & MRS Stephen (Barbara Piattelli) Rc.B.BtP.So.Bcs.
☎ (212) LE5-6886 . . 900 Fifth Av, New York, NY *10021*

Phillips, Steven P & Siegman, Jessica L—Cal'80.SanJ'88
☎ (916) 971-0878 . . 4220 Boone Lane, Sacramento, CA *95821*

Phillips MISS Susan C . . see MRS P K Bell

Phillips MR & MRS W Robert (Alexandra Kelham) | ☎ (707) 944-2868
Pcu.Stan'47 | Vine Hill Ranch,
   MR Robert B | PO Box 2066,
 | Yountville, CA
 | *94599*

Phillips MR & MRS Walter J (Harrison—Nancy N Ashbridge)
☎ (215) 242-6077 . . 8420 Ardleigh St, Philadelphia, PA *19118*

Phillips MRS William (Barbara I Holbrook) Sth'41
☎ (207) 563-8866 . . Glidden St, Newcastle, ME *04553*

Phillips MR William A—Br'50.Conn'54
☎ (203) 629-1755 . . 40 Bruce Park Dv, Greenwich, CT *06830*

Phillips MRS William M (Elizabeth P Colahan)
☎ (215) 984-8355 . . Cathedral Village I505, 600 E Cathedral Rd,
Philadelphia, PA *19128-1933*

Phillips MR William Wightman
☎ (301) 320-2682 . . 5820 Durbin Rd, Bethesda, MD *20817*

Philp MR & MRS Sanborn F (Christine Trump) | 85 Crofut St,
MtH'64.Sar.Mit'50 | Pittsfield, MA *01201*
   MR John N S |

Philson DR & MRS Arthur De L (Pogue—Gourd—Nancy W Hadra)
Unn.Snc.Rv.Ht.Cly.Cda.
200 Greytwig Rd, Vero Beach, FL *32963*

Phinizy MR & MRS James G (Elin C Myrin) Wk.Cal'71
☎ (603) 835-6074 . . ''Blethering Heights'' Acworth, NH *03601*

Phipps MR & MRS Frank H 3d (Averyl B McComb) Sg.Sa.Fw.Ac.
☎ (610) 645-8803 . . Waverly Heights, Blair 039, 1400 Waverly Rd,
Gladwyne, PA *19035*

Phipps MR Frank H 4th
☎ (904) 362-3015 . . 11193—198 Terr, O'Brien, FL *32071*

Phipps MR & MRS Howard JR (Mary N Stone) | ☎ (516) 333-0051
Pr.Lic.Ln.Mb.Sm.Plg.Yh.Cly.H'55 | ''Erchless''
   MR George D—Rc.H.'86—at ☎ (212) 674-4416 | PO Box 531,
143 Av B, Apt 4B, New York, NY *10009* | Westbury, NY
 | *11590-0531*

Phipps MR & MRS Howard 3d (Terry R A Beesley)
Australia'81.Pr.Unn.Denis'80
☎ (604) 228-0474 . . 4770 W Second Av, Vancouver, BC V6T 1B9,
Canada

Phipps MRS John H H (Elinor Klapp)
☎ (904) 562-2068 . . PO Box 3048, Tallahassee, FL *32315*

Phipps MR Ogden—Srr.Rcn.Pr.Yh.Mto.H'31 . . . . . . | of 1286 N Lake
   MISS Cynthia—Srr. . . . . | Way, Palm Beach,
 | FL *33480*
 | 208 Sumpter St,
 | Summerville, SC
 | *29483*

Phleger MRS Atherton M (Klein—Jean Cameron) | ☎ (415) 931-0614
Bur.Pcu. . . . . | 2728 Green St,
   MISS Mary K . . . . | San Francisco, CA
 | *94123*

Phyfe MR & MRS Churchill B (Bloom—Jean Corris) | ☎ (941) 263-3124
Co.Ny.Snc.Y'38 . . . . | 550 Harbor Dv,
   MR Duncan A . . . . | Naples, FL *34103*

Phyfe DR & MRS Henry Pinkney (J Ellis Taussig) Cc.H.'33.Cl'41
☎ (212) 348-1405 . . 118 E 91 St, New York, NY *10128-1672*

Phyfe MR Henry Pinkney JR—Van'91 . . see D Roberts

Phyfe MR & MRS James D (Herrick—Winifred | ☎ (212) 987-9180
Swoyer) Ln.Co.Ny.Chr.Plg.Snc.Cs.H.'64 ⚓ . . | 1075 Park Av,
   MISS Gaelen B—at Harvard . . . . | New York, NY
   MR James D 3d—at US Merchant Marine Acad . | *10128*
     MISS Robin F Herrick—at Hobart-Wm Smith |
   MR Trevor S Herrick—Occ'93—at |
319 Sixth Av, New York, NY *10012* . . . . |

Piasecki MR & MRS Frank N (Vivian O | ☎ (610) 642-6164
Weyerhaeuser) Rc.M.Me.Cry.Ac.Pa'41 . . . . . . | Tunbridge Rd,
   MISS Lynn W—at ☎ (212) 737-8604 | Haverford, PA
175 W 93 St, New York, NY *10025* . . . . | *19041*
   MISS Nicole W—at ☎ (206) 324-8102 |
1422—37 Av, Apt 6, Seattle, WA *98122* . . . . . |
   MR Frank W—at ☎ (212) 249-7977 |
155 E 77 St, Apt 1D, New York, NY *10021* . . . |
   MR John W . . . . |
   MR Michael W . . . . |
   MR Gregory W . . . . |

Piasecki MR Frederick W (Frank N) . . . . . . Married at Wynnewood, PA
Wolferth MISS Catherine F (Charles C JR) . . . . Jun 24'95

Piasecki MR & MRS Frederick W (Catherine F Wolferth)
Va'84.H'mannMed'88
☎ (610) 658-2431 . . 1 Buck Lane, Haverford, PA *19041*

Picard MR & MRS Geoffrey W (Lynne Peterson) | of ☎ (916)581-1726
T.H'66 | ''Runnemor''
   MISS Alexandra H—H'94—at ☎ (212) 877-2555 | 2020 W Lake Blvd,
50 Central Park W, New York, NY *10023* . . . . | Tahoe City, CA
   MISS Caroline J—at Santa Catalina Sch . . . . . . | *96145*
   MR Peter W L—H'96 . . . . | ☎ (415) 789-5151
 | 12 Leeward Rd,
 | Belvedere, CA
 | *94920*

Piccoli MR & MRS Joseph G 3d (Breitenbach—Mary L McGraw)
RSage'58.HRdc'83.NCol'78
☎ (307) 733-2100 . . ''Cottonwood House'' Star Rte, Wilson, WY *83014*

Pickands MR Henry S JR—Leh'62
☎ (941) 455-6465 . . ''Bassethaven'' 2850—4 St NE, Naples, FL *34120*

Pickard MR & MRS Frank A (Carrie N Augustine) Myf.Ncd.H'29.H'31
☎ (804) 282-6652 . . 501 Henri Rd, Richmond, VA *23226*

Pickard MR & MRS Frank A JR (Anne McI Gilman)
Sth'79.Cc.Rv.Cw.H'75.Va'77
☎ (303) 721-7133 . . 4991 S El Camino Dv, Englewood, CO *80111*

Pickering MR & MRS Kendall A (Catherine C Wiles) V'75.Cp.Cal'66
☎ (415) 389-8836 . . 12 Eucalyptus Knoll, Mill Valley, CA *94941*

Pickering MR Kirk R—Var'85
☎ (615) 662-5577 . . 4502 Scenic View Dv, Pegram, TN *37143*

Pickering MR R Alexander—Cp.P'40 . . . . | ☎ (415) 921-7087
MR John A—P'79 . . . . | 2360 Vallejo St,
San Francisco, CA
94123

Pickering REV & MRS William (Lee A Bunnell) | ☎ (412) 854-0834
O'69.Rm'68.Gen'lTheo'71 . . . . | 126 Boxfield Rd,
MISS Amy M . . . . | Pittsburgh, PA
MR Matthew T . . . . | *15241*
JUNIORS MR David M . . . . |

Pickett MR Barrett N—Pr.Rc.Ty'90.Ford'94
☎ (212) 861-8381 . . 325 E 72 St, Apt 15A, New York, NY *10021*

Pickett MAJ GEN (RET) & MRS George B JR (Peeples— | ☎ (334) 277-1497
Rachel L Copeland) USA'41 . . . . | 3525 Flowers Dv,
MISS Melanie S Peeples—Ala'90 . . . . | Montgomery, AL
MR Joseph C Peeples—at ☎ (334) 269-6054 | *36109*
526 Federal Dv, Montgomery, AL *36107* . . . . |

Pickett MISS Jocelyn M—Ty'93 . . see W I Hollingsworth 3d

Pickett MR & MRS John O 3d (Alexandra H Hamm)
Geo'88.Rc.Pr.Cly.Fr.H'88 . . of
☎ (212) 628-8285 . . 178 E 80 St, Apt 22C, New York, NY *10021*
☎ (415) 922-3281 . . 3281 Jackson St, San Francisco, CA *94118*

Pickhardt MRS Thomas K (Alice Frazer)
☎ (803) 881-6605 . . 1050 Hunter's Trace, Mt Pleasant, SC *29464*

Pickhardt MR William P—Y'45
☎ (302) 764-5723 . . 1005 River Rd, Wilmington, DE *19809-2430*

Pickman MR & MRS Anthony P (Alice P Loring) | ☎ (617) 259-9033
H'39 . . . . | 213 Concord Rd,
MR Allan L—Nu'71—at ☎ (603) 878-3332 | Lincoln, MA *01773*
PO Box 90, Temple, NH *03084* . . . . |

Pickman MR & MRS David (Elizabeth Van Ausdel) | ☎ (617) 275-7199
Tv.Sm.H'42 . . . . | 240 Dudley Rd,
MISS Stephanie . . . . | Bedford, MA *01730*
MISS Elizabeth . . . . |
MR Edward M . . . . |

Pickrell MRS Claude D (Marie D Pittman) . . . . | ☎ (314) 725-9813
MISS Marie F . . . . | 329 N Central Av,
Clayton, MO *63105*

Pidot MR & MRS Whitney D (F Jeanne Stoddard) | of ☎ (516)759-9389
StJos'71.Pr.Ln.Un.Cly.H'66.Cl'70 . . . . | Piping Rock Rd,
MR Whitney D JR—at Harvard . . . . | Locust Valley, NY
MR Philip M—at Notre Dame . . . . | *11560*
JUNIORS MR Seth T—at Georgetown . . . . | ☎ (561) 546-7375
25 Gomez Rd,
Hobe Sound, FL
33455

Pier DR & MRS Arthur S (Anna J Blake) Tv.H.'35 . . | ☎ (617) 566-1942
MR Richard B—at ☎ (630) 355-2499 | 21 Hawthorn Rd,
1053 Ogden Av, Apt 349, Naperville, IL *60540* . | Brookline, MA
02146

Pierce MRS Allen B (Helen Lee Lawrence) . . . . | ☎ (617) 864-8491
MR W Shelby—Hart'88 . . . . | 229 Huron Av,
MR Allen L—Drew'90 . . . . | Cambridge, MA
02138

Pierce MASTER Andrew Corvus (Roger) . . . . Born Aug 6'95

Pierce MISS Anne—Bost'67.NH'79
☎ (603) 424-4720 . . 30 Turkey Hill Rd, Merrimack, NH *03054*

Pierce MR & MRS Benjamin R (Cynthia A Woodcock) Wells'74.Me.H'74
☎ (610) 964-1527 . . 56 Steeplechase Rd, Devon, PA *19333*

Pierce MR & MRS Benjamin T (Josephine Wells Browning)
Sl.Y'39.Cl'41 . . of
☎ (202) 232-8378 . . 2540 Massachusetts Av NW, Washington,
DC *20008*
☎ (011-33) 59-26-13-72 . . ''Menda Belateia'' Vieille rte de St Pée,
64500 St Jean-de-Luz, France

Pierce MR & MRS C Eliot (Dora M Redway) H'36
☎ (207) 276-3218 . . PO Box 665, Northeast Harbor, ME *04662*

Pierce MR & MRS Charles E JR (Barbara G Hanson) | of ☎ (212)996-1828
Rdc'68.Cl'82.C.K.Gr.H'64.H'70 . . . . | 14 E 90 St,
MISS Sheila H—Ken'94—at ☎ (212) 645-2399 | New York, NY
45 W 11 St, Apt 1D, New York, NY *10011* . . . . | *10128*
MR C Eliot 3d—at Brown . . . . | (914) 266-3505
RD 1, Box 189,
Clinton Corners Rd,
Salt Point, NY
12578

Pierce MISS Cynthia W . . see MRS P G Boorman

Pierce MR & MRS Daniel (May P Harding) Cy.Sm.H.'56
☎ (617) 329-1390 . . 354 Westfield St, Dedham, MA *02026*

Pierce MRS Frederick S (Phyllis E Wendt) SL'47.Cy.St.Bf.G.Ln.
☎ (716) 885-8294 . . 36 Tudor Place, Buffalo, NY *14222*

Pierce MR & MRS Guy C 3d (Elaine F Fowler) Rc.Sg.Cda.Penn'61
☎ (215) 542-8998 . . 6 Hunter's Run, Spring House, PA *19477*

Pierce MR Henry H—Pl.Camb'31
☎ (203) 624-0693 . . 200 Leeder Hill Dv, Apt 130, Hamden,
CT *06517-2725*

Pierce MR John B JR—Sm.H'45
☎ (617) 523-3320 . . 65 E India Row, Boston, MA *02110*

Pierce MR Julius E—Cysl.Geo'25 . . . . | ☎ (305) 666-0016
MR Jay P Havre . . . . | 6040 Moss Ranch
Rd, Miami, FL
33156

Pierce MR & MRS Leo W JR (Eve S Bullitt) NH'76.Me.LaS'67
☎ (610) 688-9104 . . 122 E Beechtree Lane, Wayne, PA *19087*

Pierce REV & MRS Nathaniel W (Buchanan—Audrey Byam)
Cr'66.CDSP'72.GTheo'72 ⚓
☎ (410) 228-3210 . . 107 High St, Cambridge, MD *21613*

Pierce MRS Norman (Adèle C Eells) Ncd.
☎ (802) 388-6773 . . 33½ Weybridge St, Middlebury, VT *05753*

Pierce MRS Robert B (Ewers—Constance A Jamison)
Nu'69.Wt.Dar.NotreDSI'48
☎ (914) 949-7593 . . 111 E Hartsdale Av, Hartsdale, NY *10530-3201*

Pierce MR & MRS Roger (Felicia P Havre)
☎ (207) 244-5624 . . PO Box 897, Southwest Harbor, ME *04679*

Pierce MR & MRS Stephen B (Catherine Calvé) | of ☎ (011-33-1)
Paris'71.Unn.Cl'68 . . . . | 42-94-29-80
MISS Pauline C . . . . | 3 rue de
JUNIORS MISS Susan P . . . . | Copenhague,
JUNIORS MR Philip C . . . . | 75008 Paris, France
☎ (011-33-3)
44-07-68-77
60 rue Nicolas
Fortin, 60250
Mouchy-la-Ville,
France

Pierce MR & MRS William Curtis (Elizabeth N Gay)
Bnd'29.Chr.Cw.Ne.Cc.Myf.Cly.Ncd.Bow'28.H'31 . . of
☎ (207) 625-3942 . . ''The Pierce Place'' Rte 1, Box 5140,
West Baldwin, ME 04091
☎ (212) 534-8676 . . 1088 Park Av, New York, NY 10128-1172

Pierce MRS William G (Bunting—Susan H Sayen)
☎ (610) 644-4126 . . ''Woodsedge'' 444 Waynesbrooke Rd, Berwyn,
PA 19312

Pierotti MISS Emma Frances (g—William N Ashbey) . . . . Born at
Berkeley, CA May 30'96

Pierpoint MR & MRS Powell (Margaret S Sagar) C.Chr.Plg.Cly.Y'44
☎ (212) RH4-1910 . . 155 E 72 St, New York, NY 10021

Pierpont MRS Donald W (Anne J Tyler) W&M'39
☎ (914) 946-4639 . . 9 Windward Av, White Plains, NY 10605

Pierpont MR & MRS Douglas C (Elizabeth G Miller) CtCol'86.Rr.Conn'85
☎ (303) 794-9171 . . 933 W Longview Av, Littleton, CO 80120

Pierpont MR & MRS Harlan T JR (Georgia W Simmons) Chi.H'35 . . of
☎ (561) 231-9417 . . 4049 Ocean Dv, Apt 301, Vero Beach, FL 32963
☎ (617) 934-6786 . . 70 Peterson Rd, Duxbury, MA 02332

Pierpont MR & MRS Richard H (Stebbins—Leslie W | ☎ (203) 966-4736
Hughes) ColC'71.Ec.Cda.Dar.Aht'67.Emory'72. | 84 Stonehenge Dv,
JUNIORS MISS Laurel H—at Middlesex . . . . | New Canaan, CT
JUNIORS MR Hunter S—at Groton . . . . | 06840

Pierpont MR & MRS Thomas H—Tr.Emory'83
☎ (617) 266-9635 . . 334 Beacon St, Apt 1, Boston, MA 02116

Pierpont MISS Virginia L (MacLeod—Virginia L | ☎ (011-44-171)
Pierpont) Bost'71 . . . . | 371-6627
MISS Sarah T MacLeod . . . . | 10 Royal Crescent,
MR Hugh D T MacLeod—at | London W11 4SL,
344 W Chestnut St, Chicago, IL 60610 . . . . . | England

Pierrepont MR & MRS John (Dewey—Nancy Weller) K.Eh.C.Cly.Y'39
☎ (212) 755-8939 . . 201 E 62 St, New York, NY 10021

Pierrepont MISS Margaret
☎ (212) 645-3239 . . 376 Bleecker St, New York, NY 10014

Pierrepont MRS R Stuyvesant JR (Mary O Shriver) Pr.Cly . . .of
☎ (561) 546-5232 . . 106 Black Bear Trail, Jupiter Island, Hobe Sound,
FL 33455
☎ (516) 671-4291 . . 336 Duck Pond Rd, Locust Valley, NY 11560

Pierrepont MR & MRS R Stuyvesant 3d (Davol—Virginia L Crawford)
RISD'81.Rc.Pr.UMiami'78
23 Davis St, Locust Valley, NY 11560

Pierrepont MR & MRS Seth Low (Consuelo D Wilson)
Skd'75.On.Rc.Cly.Pa'74.Cl'79
1280 N Sheridan Rd, Lake Forest, IL 60045

Piersol MR George Morris JR—Co.Cry.Y'38 ⚓
☎ (516) 749-0419 . . 51 Peconic Av, PO Box 3021,
Shelter Island Heights, NY 11965-3021

Piersol MRS J Marshall (Wolf—Elysbeth A Neill) Sfy.
☎ (415) 751-2265 . . 140 El Camino Del Mar, San Francisco, CA 94121

Pierson MR Daniel B 5th—Me.Rc.Dth'58.Temp'61 . | 1810 Rittenhouse
MISS Jane W . . . . | Square, Apt 1501,
MR Daniel B . . . . | Philadelphia, PA
19103

Pierson MR & MRS Daniel H (Wendy M Watts) | ☎ (508) 546-3078
SFrSt'69.Hav'61 . . . . | PO Box 2358,
MISS Nina L—at Portland, OR 97202 . . . . | 3 Curtis St,
Pigeon Cove,
Rockport, MA
01966

Pierson MR & MRS Henry L (Johnson—Cecile E Ryden)
Aug'ana'37.P'30.Cl'33 . . of
☎ (914) 753-2715 . . ''Cranberry Weir'' PO Box 5, Sloatsburg,
NY 10974
☎ (212) 496-7374 . . 1 W 67 St, New York, NY 10023

Pierson MR & MRS Mitchell JR (Louisa W Hunsicker)
SUNY'70.Roch'73.Roch'89.Pa'58
☎ (716) 924-2514 . . 1661 Murray Rd, Victor, NY 14564

Pierson MR & MRS R Hunter (Catherine H Deming) | of ☎ (504)866-5465
Tul'73.LSU'73 . . . . | 456 Audubon St,
JUNIORS MR R Hunter 3d . . . . | New Orleans, LA
70118
☎ (601) 452-3477
102 W 1 St,
Pass Christian, MS
39571

Pierson DR & MRS Richard N JR (Dunn—Alice W Roberts)
Ws'51.Bost'56.C.P'51.Cl'55 ⚓
☎ (201) 569-3562 . . 60 Lincoln St, Englewood, NJ 07631

Pierson DR & MRS Richard N 3d (Allene G Russell) P'81.P'78.Cl'83
☎ (615) 385-4665 . . 3419 Hampton Av, Nashville, TN 37215

Pietsch REV DR & MRS (REV DR) William V (Weld— | ☎ (203) 438-9310
Louise Parsons) Cl'63.UnTheo'82.Drew'88. | 16 Craigmoor Rd N,
Nw'45.P'52.ANewton'81 . . . . | Ridgefield, CT
MISS Ashley N Weld . . . . | 06877

Pigford MRS Robert T (Lavinia S Harris) Cda.
☎ (910) 762-5020 . . 301 Colonial Dv, Wilmington, NC 28403

Pignatelli di Montecalvo PRCSS (Barbara Eastman)
☎ (212) 988-3578 . . 165 E 72 St, New York, NY 10021

Pigott MR & MRS Charles F JR (Janet F Jarrett) Cho.Marq'51.IIT'53.H'58
☎ (847) 509-8123 . . 2535 Stonebridge Lane, Northbrook, IL 60062

Pigott MR & MRS James S G (Wyckoff—Oscarsson | ☎ (203) 629-6287
—Constance A H Robinsson) Unn.Plg. | Bellehaven,
Reading'28 . . . . | 40 Mayo Av,
MR Richard I—Cw.Snc.Pace'76—at | Greenwich, CT
4 Country Club Dv, Apt C, Coram, NY 11727 . . | 06830

Pike MR & MRS F Norris (Nancy S Devine) Bnd'80.WIT'75
☎ (401) 466-2284 . . PO Box 306, Southwest Point, Block Island,
RI 02807

Pike REV & MRS Thomas F (Lys McLaughlin) ☎ (212) 260-2442
Nu'67.C.Plg.Coa.Snc.Sar.SUNY'60.Y'63 . . . . . 61 Gramercy Park,
MISS Jean L—Y'86 . . . . New York, NY
CAPT Thomas F JR—USA.Eyc.An.Vca.GeoW'89 *10010*
—at Defense Intelligence Coll . . . .

Pilcher MR & MRS William F (Mary Elizabeth Killiam)
Unn.Coa.Cw.Rv.Cly.Cda.Dar.
☎ (203) 262-6244 . . 708B Heritage Village, Southbury, CT *06488*

Pile MR & MRS Edward B (Jacqueline S Johnson) GeoW'78
☎ (703) 481-3067 . . 1536 Malvern Hill Place, Herndon, VA *20170*

Pile MR Roger S JR . . see MRS G F B Johnson JR

Pile MR & MRS Sterling JR (Leila Chadbourne) Pr.
☎ (516) 626-0635 . . 74 Wheatley Rd, Brookville, Glen Head,
NY *11545*

Pile MR Sterling 3d—Bost'74
☎ (310) 575-4401 . . 2122 Kelton Av, Los Angeles, CA *90025*

Pile MR & MRS Wilson H JR (M Susan Williams) . . . ☎ (617) 383-6088
JUNIORS MR W Hunt W . . . . 65 Elm St, Cohasset,
MA *02025*

Pilgrim MR & MRS James F (Katharine B Baetjer)
Rdc'67.Nu'70.Elk.Wms'63.Nu'67
☎ (410) 889-5632 . . 501 Overhill Rd, Baltimore, MD *21210*

Pilkington MR & MRS Charles F (Katherine B Scott)
StLaw'92.Rcn.Mb.WashColl'91
☎ (610) 975-0705 . . 20 Aldwyn Lane, Villanova, PA *19085*

Pilkington MR & MRS Robert (Helen S Cutting) of ☎ (516)626-0209
Rc.B.Mb.Pr.Ox'66 152 Wheatley Rd,
MISS Justine . . . . Glen Head, NY
JUNIORS MISS Lisa *11545*
☎ (212) 861-2913
222 E 71 St,
New York, NY
10021

Pilling MRS Frank B (Frances C Lee) Sa.Pc.Ac.Sdg.Cda.Ds.
☎ (215) 247-1994 . . 7835 Winston Rd, Chestnut Hill, PA *19118*

Pilling MRS George Platt 4th (Barbara Bosworth) Sth'44.Ac . . .of
☎ (215) 283-7301 . . 1010 Foulkeways, Sumneytown Pike, Gwynedd,
PA *19436*
☎ (717) 646-2722 . . "Lake's End" Pocono Lake Preserve, PA *18348*

Pilling CAPT (RET) J Ross—USN.H'47
☎ (610) 645-8975 . . 1400 Waverly Rd, Apt A223, Gladwyne, PA *19035*

Pilling MRS Janet K (Janet L Kavanaugh) OWes'73.Mo'76.VillaN'86.Me.
☎ (216) 234-9570 . . 454 Woodridge Circle, Berea, OH *44017*

Pilling MR & MRS John F (Constance Earle)
☎ (908) 892-3693 . . 1 Arnold St, Mantoloking, NJ *08738*

Pilling MR & MRS Robert B (Elizabeth J Ludzinski) W&L'74.Tenn'82
☎ (904) 269-2776 . . 3427 Inlet Lane, Orange Park, FL *32073*

Pilling MR & MRS William S 2d (Helen d'A Holt) H'45
☎ (406) 777-5994 . . "Meadows" 763 S Sunset Bench Rd, Stevensville,
MT *59870*

Pillsbury MRS Charles S B . . see J B Britton

Pillsbury MRS Donald M (Moore—Cooper—Susan V Peebles) Dar.Ncd.
☎ (610) 525-2144 . . 77 Middle Rd, Apt 155, Bryn Mawr, PA *19010*

Pillsbury MRS Evans S 2d (Gardner—Catherine A Wheeler)
☎ (805) 969-2423 . . 2141 Ten Acre Rd, Santa Barbara, CA *93108*

Pillsbury MR & MRS John S JR (Katharine H Clark) Y'35
☎ (612) 473-8223 . . "Bayhurst" 1280 Bracketts Point Rd, Wayzata,
MN *55391*

Pillsbury MRS Louise Rollins (Sterling—Louise PO Box 631,
Rollins) Ots'64.Vh.Cda. . . . . La Jolla, CA
MR Graham Lee Sterling 4th *92038-0631*

Pillsbury MR & MRS Philip W JR (Caroline E ☎ (202) 363-6108
Hannaford) Ct.Cvc.Cc.Y'57 . . . . 5036 Sedgwick St
MISS Caroline H—Br'93—at ☎ (212) 779-0774 NW, Washington,
16 Park Av, Apt 9D, New York, NY *10016* . . . . DC *20016*
MR Philip W 3d—Col'95—at ☎ (612) 824-6032
4203 Pillsbury Av, Minneapolis, MN *55409* . . .

Pinckney MR & MRS Alfred G (Julianna French) ☎ (803) 723-9708
Cc.Cw.Ht.Dar.Dc. . . . . 26 New St,
MISS Anne F—at 2141 Selwyn Av, Apt 206, Charleston, SC
Charlotte, NC *28207* *29401*
MISS Caroline G

Pinckney MISS Elizabeth R—Char'ton'45.NCar'49.Ncd.
☎ (803) 723-5749 . . 11 Meeting St, Charleston, SC *29401*

Pinckney MISS Julia D (Alfred G) . . . . Married at Charleston, SC
Frenzel MR Michael A (Robert P) . . . . Apr 28'95

Pindar MR & MRS Duncan M (Therese B Forrester)
488 Beaulieu Av, Rte 3, Box 488, Savannah, GA *31406*

Pindar MISS Mary S
162 Lehigh Av, Savannah, GA *31406*

Pingeon MR & MRS Hendon C (Kate C Mali) Ken'84.Roan'84
☎ (617) 259-8849 . . 9 Baker Bridge Rd, Lincoln, MA *01773*

Pingeon DR & MRS René A (Frances D Parsons) ☎ (201) 543-4494
Mo.Csn.Gen'45.Cl'50. . . . . Kennaday Rd,
MR James R—at ☎ (617) 259-8681 Mendham, NJ *07945*
Lincoln Rd, Lincoln, MA *01773* . . . .

Pingeon MR & MRS Robert R (Emily S Lodge) Geo'75.Bost'73
☎ (011-33-1) 43-06-10-27 . . 21 rue Monsieur, 75007 Paris, France

Pingree MR & MRS Sumner JR (Brush—Virginia L of ☎ (803)524-8063
Caswell) . . . . 53 Stuart Towne Dv,
MR Richard C . . . . Beaufort, SC *29902*
☎ (803) 846-3100
Brays Island
Plantation, Sheldon,
SC *29941*

Pingree MR & MRS Sumner 3d (Sally Engelhard) Ore'75 . . of
☎ (202) 686-3877 . . 4636 Garfield St NW, Washington, DC *20007*
☎ (410) 745-5802 . . Deep Neck Farm, Deep Neck Rd, Royal Oak,
MD *21662*

Pinkard MRS Walter D (Anne M Merrick) Gchr'46.Elk.Md.Mv.
☎ (410) 823-2809 . . 613 Brightwood Club Dv, Lutherville, MD *21093*

Pinkerton MR & MRS Charles JR (Lucy M Blatchford) Rv.Wms'45
☎ (203) 847-2565 . . 6 Crocus Lane, Norwalk, CT *06851*

Pinkerton MR & MRS Peyton R H (Slaughter— ☎ (914) 769-4261
Roxana E Baker) Winth'52.SL'92.Sa.Rv.Cl'55 . 54 Sunnyside Av,
MR Peyton R H JR—Hampshire'94—at Pleasantville, NY
☎ (413) 582-0686 . . 12 Linden St, Northampton, *10570*
MA *01060* . . . .

Pinkham MR & MRS Arthur D JR (Margaret H Merker)
Rcn.Cly.Chi.Ncd . . .of
☎ (617) 266-8885 . . 160 Commonwealth Av, Boston, MA *02116*
Pumpkin Hill Farm, 106 Colts Pond Rd, Ashford, CT *06278*

Pinkham MR & MRS David J (Virginia G Erickson) Pcu.Ncd.Stan'41 . . . . ☎ (415) SK1-8954
MR David E—*abroad* . . . . 550 El Camino del Mar, San Francisco, CA *94121*

Pinkham MR & MRS Richard A R (Mary G Struthers) Y'36
☎ (561) 546-6907 . . 182 S Beach Rd, Hobe Sound, FL *33455*

Pinnell MR & MRS Raymond A JR (Mary R Waller) StJ.Tex'51
☎ (210) 494-5446 . . 118 Rio Bravo, San Antonio, TX *78232*

Piñon MR & MRS Horacio J (Maria V Sanchez-Elia) Nu'77
☎ (011-54-1) 42-1933 . . Avenida Alvear 1654, Buenos Aires 1014, Argentina

Pinson MR & MRS Pablo C (Winifred Wisner) Dar.Mex'59 . . . . of ☎ (713)629-7733 3435 Westheimer Rd, Apt 1707, Houston, TX *77027*
MISS Cecilia—Rice'87.Pars'91—at 217 E 86 St, Apt 4A, New York, NY *10028* . . . .
MR Pablo—Nw'88.Tex'91 . . . . ☎ (011-52-5) 282-5542 Alencastre 99, 202, Lomas Virreyes, Mexico DF 11000, Mexico
MR George—LaS'93 . . . .

Pinto MR & MRS Maurice E (Elizabeth A Cooley) Sth'58.Y'55 . . . . of 55 S Edwardes Square, London W8 6HP, England Hascombe Court, West Godalming, Surrey, England
MISS Lisa—at 1065 Park Av, New York, NY *10128* . . . .

Pirie MRS Gordon L (Nancy B Palmer) Ih.Wa.Cas.
see Dilatory Domiciles

Piro DR & MRS Philip A JR (Marion W Jones) Hlns'75.Bcs.So.Unn.Syc.Myf.Cda.Y'74
☎ (203) 661-0802 . . Conyers Farm Dv, Greenwich, CT *06831*

Pirrung MR & MRS C Mark (Mary D Gargaro) Rcsl.Va'73.Wash'78 . . of
☎ (404) 264-9411 . . "Whitehall" 3425 Tuxedo Rd NW, Atlanta, GA *30305*
☎ (912) 246-3158 . . Aragon Farms, Bainbridge, GA *31717*

Pischel MRS Janet K (Janet Kirk)
☎ (415) 454-1793 . . PO Box 856, Ross, CA *94957*

Pistell MR & MRS Christopher A (Louise H Wharton) P'78.Cda.P'78
☎ (410) 653-9379 . . St Timothy's School, Stevenson, MD *21153*

Pitarys MR & MRS Peter S (Nancy H Leggett) Sth'65.Sim'70.Aht'59.Pa'61 . . . . ☎ (617) 899-6641 21 Autumn Rd, Weston, MA *02193*
MISS Katherine—at Oberlin . . . .
MISS Laura—at Colby . . . .

Pitcairn MRS James F (Hicks—Ellen I Cook) Fcg.Pg.
☎ (412) 622-9174 . . Canterbury Place 318, 310 Fisk St, Pittsburgh, PA *15201*

Pitcher MRS William H (Virginia G Stein) Ncd.Dc. . ☎ (407) 677-9983 1620 Mayflower Court, B401, Winter Park, FL *32792-2570*
MR William T B . . . .

Pitocchelli MRS Francis J (Barbara A Mangan) Me. . ☎ (610) 525-5558 1016 Great Springs Rd, Rosemont, PA *19010*
MISS Johanna—Ty'82.Me.—at
☎ (415) 928-6884 . . 2010 Chestnut St, Apt 308, San Francisco, CA *94123* . . . .
MISS Elsie A—DU'86.Me.—at ☎ (717) 397-9529 917 Columbia Av, Apt 124, Lancaster, PA *17603*
MR Francis J—Me.Hob'79.Mem'l'81.CUNY'88

Pitou MR David W—Wag'56 . . . . ☎ (718) 984-0900 20 Edgewood Rd, Staten Island, NY *10308*
MR Jeremy D . . . .

Pitt MR & MRS Stephen McC (Sarah S K Johnson) MaryB'82.A.TexTech'72
see Dilatory Domiciles

Pitt MR William H—B.Rcn.Evg.BtP.Ng.So.
☎ (561) 842-1536 . . 320 Tangier Av, Palm Beach, FL *33480*

Pittman MRS A Smith (Thompson—Adele C Smith)
☎ (561) 231-3358 . . "Off Course" 281 Sabal Palm Lane, Vero Beach, FL *32963*

Pitts MR & MRS Clinton P (M Claire Conley) Elk.Cw.Cda.
☎ (410) 557-7883 . . 2830 Pocock Rd, Monkton, MD *21111*

Pitts JUNIORS MISS Frances E (Henry C) . . . . Died at Lexington, KY Aug 6'95

Pitts MR & MRS Henry C (Jennifer J Haig) Cw. ⚓ ☎ (410) 472-4578 15757 Irish Av, Monkton, MD *21111*
MISS Susanna C . . . .

Pitts MR & MRS Paris T (Lynn E Ferrarini) Whit'91.Van'88
☎ (206) 957-0428 . . 16949 NE 19 Place, Bellevue, WA *98008*

Pitts MR Tilghman G (Fitje L Pitts) Sth'39.Mv.
☎ (410) 377-4564 . . 2 Knoll Ridge Court, Baltimore, MD *21210*

Pivirotto MR & MRS Richard R (Mary P Burchfield) Fcg.Rr.Pn.P'52.H'54 . . . . ☎ (203) 661-4048 111 Clapboard Ridge Rd, Greenwich, CT *06830*
MISS Jennifer P . . . .

Pizzicaria MRS Jean H (Jean E Hope) . . . . of ☎ (011-39-6) 321-8952 via Monti Parioli 53, 00197 Rome, Italy ☎ (860) 675-7107 12 Mystic Court, Avon, CT *06001*
MISS Sabrina . . . .
MR Marco . . . .

Pizzinat MR & MRS Arthur Franklin (Julia Wingfield) Stan'62.Vh.Stan'56
☎ (805) 969-3868 . . 1419 Sea Meadow Place, Montecito, CA *93108*

Place MR & MRS David E (Susanna M Badgley) P'75.Y'79.Sm.H.'43.H'48 ⚓
☎ (617) 696-0643 . . 224 Adams St, Milton, MA *02186*

Place MR George T—Syr'78
☎ (914) 677-3811 . . N Tower Hill Rd, Millbrook, NY *12545*

Place MR & MRS H Calvin (Nancy L Hacker) Bentley'81.Sim'91.Cy.Dar.H'57.H'61
☎ (617) 235-7697 . . 51 Curve St, Wellesley, MA *02181*

Place MR & MRS H Curtis (Patricia M Miller) Ncd.Cr'49
☎ (914) 677-3811 . . N Tower Hill Rd, PO Box 737, Millbrook, NY *12545*

Place MR & MRS John B M (Katharine Smart) Pcu.Unn.Bur.Fr. . . . . ☎ (415) 771-8166 1100 Union St, San Francisco, CA 94109
MISS Marian R—at 215 San Andres Av NW, Albuquerque, NM 87107 . . . .
MR J Bassett M JR—at 40 Laurel Place, Bridgeport, CT 06604 . . . .

Place MRS Julie L (Julie C Lewis) Wheat'59.Nh.Cy. ☎ (617) 237-5289 108 Clarke Rd, Needham, MA 02192
MR H Calvin JR . . . .
MR Jonathan C . . . .

Place MR & MRS Richard M (Maireda S Seaman) Bnd'82.Cl'91
☎ (212) 663-2337 . . 711 Amsterdam Av, Apt 15D, New York, NY 10025
Place MISS Sabrina C—Skd'89 . . see MRS C S-H Bowers
Placenti MR & MRS Frank M (Barbara A McNemar) OState'76.OState'75
☎ (602) 265-3570 . . 6040 N 5 Place, Phoenix, AZ 85012
Plant MR John—Gm.Ox'37
☎ (610) 525-8693 . . Benson House Apt 303, Montgomery Av, Bryn Mawr, PA 19010
Plate MRS H Robinson (Huard—Mildred D Mersich)
☎ (415) 321-5529 . . 332 Austin Av, Atherton, CA 94027
Plate MR James M—Pac'83
☎ (415) 363-1022 . . 244 Selby Lane, Atherton, CA 94027
Plater MR & MRS David D (Sheela G Burke) of ☎ (504)446-8908 425 Easy St, Thibodaux, LA 70301 "Ballingrobe" Covington, LA 70433
Tul'60.Wms'58.Tul'61 . . . .
MISS Juliana H . . . .
MR Bryan B . . . .
MR Christopher S . . . .

Plater MR & MRS Richard C JR (Pamela Q Robinson) Ncmb'35.Wms'31
☎ (504) 447-3427 . . Acadia Plantation, PO Box 110, Thibodaux, LA 70302

Platt MR & MRS Charles A (Joan Mathieson) Rdc'58.C.H'54 . . . . ☎ (212) TR6-9228 1261 Madison Av, New York, NY 10128
MISS Sylvia—H'84—Box 1643, Port Townsend, WA 98368 . . . .
MISS Virginia L—Y'88 . . . .

Platt MR & MRS David N (Marguerite L E Beer) Un.Ri.Plg.Cw.Cly.Y'51.H'53 . . . . of ☎ (212)517-3381 340 E 72 St, New York, NY 10021 ☎ (516) 653-6630 25 Quaquanantuck Lane, Quogue, NY 11959
MISS Marguerite F—at Georgetown . . . .
MR David S—Denis'96 . . . .

Platt MRS Diana D (Rappel—Diana Drum) . . . . ☎ (415) 347-6787 1821 Ralston Av, Burlingame, CA 94010
MISS Laura H Rappel . . . .
MR Richard W Rappel JR . . . .

Platt MRS Frank H (Audrey Achelis)
☎ (203) 869-4690 . . 31 Evergreen Rd, Greenwich, CT 06830
Platt MRS Geoffrey (Holbrook—Alice Doubleday) . . . . Died at Bedford Hills, NY May 29'96

Platt MR & MRS Geoffrey JR (Hope G Forsyth) V'66.C.Mt.H'63.H'73 . . . . ☎ (804) 740-5043 100 Williamson Court, Richmond, VA 23229
MISS Lucy F . . . .
JUNIORS MR Rufus C . . . .

Platt MR & MRS Graham L (Ann Lethbridge) Va'52
☎ (516) MY2-7682 . . 40 Walnut Tree Lane, Cold Spring Harbor, NY 11724-1202
Platt MR H Lee
☎ (809) 773-2568 . . Estate Pearl, Box 242, Christiansted, St Croix, VI 00821
Platt MR Henry—Y.'45w
☎ (212) 838-0800 . . 825 Fifth Av, New York, NY 10021
Platt MR Hermann K—Hav'58.Rut'63
☎ (201) 434-8884 . . 2672 Kennedy Blvd, Apt 302, Jersey City, NJ 07306
Platt MR John W S
☎ (503) 292-8982 . . 4550 SW Humphrey Blvd, Portland, OR 97221
Platt MR & MRS Lucian B (Kathrin Straumann) Cos.Me.Y'53 . . . . ☎ (610) 525-0807 306 N Ithan Av, Rosemont, PA 19010
MR David W . . . .
MR Martin B—Br'83 . . . .

Platt MR & MRS Nicholas (Sheila Maynard) Ty'70.CathU'73.H'57.JHop'59 . . . . of ☎ (212)717-4951 131 E 69 St, New York, NY 10021 ☎ (202) 333-4337 1313—28 St NW, Washington, DC 20007
MR Adam—at 225 Central Park W, New York, NY 10024 . . . .

Platt MR & MRS Oliver (M Camilla B Campbell) Bost'85
29 E 9 St, New York, NY 10003
Platt MRS Richard (Mary S Gordon) Ncd.
☎ (912) 233-4874 . . 417 E 44 St, Savannah, GA 31405
Platt MR Richard B—Cc.Yn.Y'69 . . . . of ☎ (313)886-3014 381 Country Club Lane, Grosse Pointe Farms, MI 48236-2904 ☎ (809) 773-9353 16 N Grapetree, St Croix, VI 00820
JUNIORS MISS Anne D—at Phillips Andover . . . .
JUNIORS MR R Booth JR—at Proctor Acad . . . . . .

Platt MR & MRS Roger (Christie Mercer) Pitzer'73.CalPsych'92.H'81
☎ (202) 363-8533 . . 6653 Barnaby St NW, Washington, DC 20015
Platt MR & MRS S Phelps (Smithers—Margaret McClure) Cda.Yn.Y'40
38 Aylesbury Circle, Madison, CT 06443
Platt MR & MRS Thomas C (A Byrd Symington) Csh.Y.'45w ⚓ . . . . ☎ (516) 427-0944 "Low Bridge" 448 W Neck Rd, Lloyd Harbor, Huntington, NY 11743
MISS Heather—at 8 Irvine Rd, Old Greenwich, CT 06870 . . . .

Platt MR William—Cc.Fw. of ☎ (610) 525-8824 245 Broughton Lane, Villanova, PA 19085
MR Benjamin C . . . .

Platt MR & MRS William R (Heather T Strawbridge)
Ursinus'89.Co.Ursinus'91
☎ (215) 248-5158 . . 800 Longfield Rd, Erdenheim, PA *19038*

Plauché MR & MRS Walter F (Joy Clay) Ncmb'43.Tul'48
☎ (504) 488-6927 . . 5929 General Diaz St, New Orleans, LA *70124*

Player MISS Elizabeth C—Ty'93 . . see J L Adams

Player MR Samuel L—Wes'91 . . see J L Adams

Pleasants MR & MRS W Shepard JR (Fleming—Mary Marguerite Bouden)
Ncmb'53.Tul'51
1837 State St, New Orleans, LA *70118-6219*

Pless MR & MRS John A (Helena P Hallock)
Enschede'52 . . . . | ☎ (802) 867-0314
MISS Katriena M . . . . | West Rd,
MR Anthony J 3d—at Middlebury . . . . | PO Box 512,
Dorset, VT *05251*

Plimpton DR & MRS Calvin H (Ruth Talbot)
C.Tvb.Plg.Myf.Cs.Chi.Aht'39.H'43
☎ (718) KI3-3242 . . 4600 Palisade Av, Bronx, NY *10471-3508*

Plimpton MR & MRS Francis T P JR (Susan Wadsworth) Aht'50
☎ (904) 672-8711 . . "The Whim" 186 S Beach St, Ormond Beach, FL *32174-6437*

Plimpton MR & MRS George A (Sarah W Dudley)
Cl'81.Rc.B.C.Ri.Dyc.Cs.H'50.Camb'52 . . . . | ☎ (212) 861-0016
MISS Medora A—Hampshire'93 . . . . | 541 E 72 St,
MR Taylor A—at Reed . . . . | New York, NY
10021

Plimpton REV DR & MRS Hollis W JR (Peggy Lucas)
Duke'54.Sm.BtP.Cy.Chi.Myf.Ncd.Duke'52.Ore'58. EpiscDiv'88
☎ (617) 232-2021 . . 39 Clyde St, Chestnut Hill, MA *02167*

Plimpton MR & MRS Hollis W 3d (Constance G Smith)
Rich'82.Cy.W&L'82.Bost'83
☎ (617) 237-0481 . . 91 Mayo Rd, Wellesley, MA *02181*

Plimpton MRS Jane Z (Jane Zimmerman) Chi.
☎ (609) 924-7335 . . 31 Richard Court, Princeton, NJ *08540*

Plimpton MR & MRS John (Katharine Sawtell) Bow'43
☎ (508) 653-5335 . . 115 N Main St, Box 489, Sherborn, MA *01770*

Plimpton MRS Leslie E K (Leslie E Kloville) Wash'66.BostColl'82.Btn.
☎ (617) 227-4899 . . 83 Mt Vernon St, Boston, MA *02108*

Plimpton MR & MRS Samuel (Isabel M Shattuck)
NECons'75.Bost'80.Btn.Cy.Stan'71.H'78.H'80
☎ (617) 364-9946 . . 1383 Brush Hill Rd, Milton, MA *02186*

Plimpton MR Stephen W—Cw.Myf.
☎ (617) 423-9666 . . 10 Temple Place, Apt 510, Boston, MA *02111-1333*

Plowden-Wardlaw MR & MRS James C (Weldon—
Angela M H Hill) SL'66.Rc.Va'58.Cl'64 . . . . . . | ☎ (212) 753-8858
JUNIORS MR Henry L Weldon 3d—at Salisbury | 116 E 63 St,
New York, NY
10021

Plowden-Wardlaw MR & MRS Thomas C (Mason—Stanton—
Mary D Francis) Chi.Cda.Ncd.Ox'30.Cl'34 . . of
☎ (508) 992-0862 . . "Boxwood House" Box 164P, South Dartmouth, MA *02748*
☎ (561) 234-4724 . . 300 Harbour Dv, Apt 302B, Vero Beach, FL *32963*

Plum MR & MRS John E (Mimi Kim)
Sth'74.Hn.Mit'74 . . . . | Homat Sharon, Apt
JUNIORS MISS Sabrina M . . . . | 501, 4-9-3 Minami
JUNIORS MISS Tamina M . . . . | Azabu, Minato-ku,
Tokyo 106, Japan

Plum MR & MRS Matthias JR (Morris—Margaret E R
White) Syr'56.Ny.Sm.Cy.Chi.Ncd.P'56.H.'64 . . | of ☎ (617)266-6077
MISS Arabella G . . . . | 172 Beacon St,
MR Matthias M . . . . | Boston, MA *02116*
☎ (508) 945-0286
"Appleway"
114 Cedar St,
Chatham, MA *02633*

Plum MISS Nancy T—AmU'75.TrentSt'89
☎ (215) 321-0647 . . 1111 Yardley Commons, Yardley, PA *19067*

Plum MR Robert R—M'vian'75
☎ (201) 538-8122 . . PO Box 213, Convent Station, NJ *07961*

Plum MR & MRS Roy R (Horn—Katherine F Foshay)
Ng.Cly.Y'60 . . . . | ☎ (561) 546-7646
MR Richard R—at ☎ (212) 879-6146 | 6 Isle Ridge W,
340 E 72 St, New York, NY *10021* . . . . | Hobe Sound, FL
MR Fraser M Horn—at ☎ (970) 827-9353 | *33455*
PO Box 75, Minturn, CO *81645* . . . .

Plumb MR & MRS Fayette R 2d (Patricia H Walker) Rv.Myf.Va'44
☎ (215) 646-3166 . . "Troll House" 910 Valley Rd, Blue Bell, PA *19422*

Plumb MRS Marilyn McC (Marilyn E McClure)
Bgt. . . . . | ☎ (914) 234-1266
MISS E Wendell—Ham'93—at ☎ (212) 879-5424 | 39 Stonehill Rd,
176 E 81 St, Apt 3B, New York, NY *10028* . . | Bedford, NY *10506*
MR Peter C JR—Vt'88—at ☎ (802) 655-6325
155 Weaver St, Winooski, VT *05404* . . . .
MR William K—Bgt.Ham'89—at
☎ (212) 362-4302 . . 48 W 68 St, Apt 2A,
New York, NY *10023* . . . .

Plumb MR Peter C—Bgt.
☎ (802) 297-9366 . . PO Box 333, Bondville, VT *05340*

Plumb MR & MRS Robert J 3d (Laura H Fergusson) Ty'80.Au.Ty'80
☎ (617) 235-8740 . . 55 Wingate Rd, Wellesley, MA *02181*

Plumer MR & MRS Davenport (Susan B Heist) Ll.P'28
☎ (215) 646-2483 . . 2 Spring House Lane, Blue Bell, PA *19422*

Plumer MR & MRS William R (Audrey Capen) H'57 . | of ☎ (617)235-1739
MISS Pamela—at Riviera Beach, FL *33404* . . . . | 20 Alden Rd,
MISS Julie . . . . | Wellesley Hills, MA *02181*
☎ (508) 945-9460
252 Stage Harbor
Rd, Chatham, MA *02663*

Plummer MRS H Pierson (Atherton—Roberta Stevenson) Cal'42.Fr.A.
☎ (210) 824-7234 . . 119 Paddington Way, San Antonio, TX *78209*

Plummer MR & MRS Morgan H JR (Jean MacHale) Chi . . .of
☎ (617) 326-2838 . . 583 Gay St, Westwood, MA *02090-1731*
☎ (508) 758-2833 . . "Tupelo House" 13 Shipyard Lane, Mattapoisett, MA *02739*

Plummer MR Robert S . . see MRS J H Allen

Plummer MRS William L (Merrill—Hellen Ingram) Evg.Ncd . . .of
☎ (404) 233-8680 . . 3131 Slaton Dv NW, 28, Atlanta, GA *30305*
☎ (561) 655-5268 . . 340 S Ocean Blvd, Palm Beach, FL *33480*

Plunkett MRS William C (Eleanore A Kennedy) Sth'27.Myf.
☎ (561) 546-7848 . . 114 N Beach Rd, Hobe Sound, FL *33455*

Poccianti CT Guido & CTSS (Allegra Corsini di Laiatico) Sth'85
☎ (011-39-55) 250015 . . via Poccianti, 1 Scandicci, 50018 Firenze, Italy

Pochna MRS Priscilla T (Priscilla P Tilt) Fic.
☎ (212) 262-7055 . . 15 W 53 St, New York, NY *10019*

Pocock MR & MRS Richard H (Kathryn M Tanner)
BMr'47.Me. . . . . | ☎ (610) LA5-3663
MR David MacH—Va'79—at Rutherfordton, NC | 1147 Brynllawn Rd,
28139 . . . . | Villanova, PA *19085*

Podles MR & MRS Leon J (Mary E A Smith) | ☎ (410) 435-8140
Ws'72.Cl'75.Cl'78.Prov'68.Va'71.Va'75 . . . . . . | 104 Longwood Rd,
JUNIORS MISS Mary E A . . . . | Baltimore, MD
JUNIORS MR James R . . . . | *21210*

Poe MR E Allan 4th . . see MRS W H Brett

Poe MR & MRS Edgar A 3d (Rojahn—Christina F Zuray)
Towson'72.JHop'75.Gv.Me.Cc.Va'47 . . of
☎ (410) 363-1259 . . ''Oakland'' Garrison Forest Rd, Box 3, Garrison,
MD *21055*
''Ravens Cliff'' Tesuque, NM *87574*

Poe MR L Harvey JR—B.Mt.Cc.Va'41.Ox'57 . . of
☎ (410) 263-6245 . . 139 Market St, Annapolis, MD *21401*
☎ (202) 338-7849 . . Watergate East, 2500 Virginia Av NW,
Washington, DC *20037*

Poggi-Cavalletti MR & MRS Antonio (Moycah A B Korée) Dh.Cda.Dar.Ht.
☎ (011-39-51) 333225 . . via Castiglione 81, 40124 Bologna, Italy

Poggio DR Gian F—Genoa'51
☎ (410) 377-0502 . . 10 Over Ridge Court, Baltimore, MD *21210*

Pogue MR & MRS Shelton L (Brooks—Marion Phillips) Dth'46
☎ (919) 636-2153 . . 504 Fairway Dv, New Bern, NC *28560*

Pohl MRS Herman H (Jane C Andrews) . . . . | ☎ (703) 777-1575
MRS Pohl Moore (Rust—Jane Pohl) . . . . | Rte 2, Box 165,
| Leesburg, VA *20175*

Pohlers MRS Mary Judith B (Mary Judith Butler)
☎ (314) 361-2960 . . 4642 Pershing Place, St Louis, MO *63108-1908*

Pohlers MRS Paige Catharine (Marsh—Paige Catharine Pohlers) MaryB'87
☎ (703) 836-5058 . . 1118 Powhatan St, Alexandria, VA *22314-1304*

Poillon MAJ GEN (RET) & MRS Arthur J (Garrett—Virginia R Mouchett)
USMC.An.Hl.Ht.Cw.P'47
☎ (207) 236-2695 . . PO Box 638, Rockport, ME *04856*

Poinier MRS John (Lawrence—Lois P Wodell) Shcc.Msq.
☎ (908) 781-6522 . . ''Vixen's Lair'' PO Box 192, Gladstone,
NJ *07934*

Poitevent MR & MRS Eads 3d (Deborah Roulhac) | of ☎ (504)897-0437
NOlns'63.Tul'94.Nd.Tul'68 . . . . | 1432 Pleasant St,
MISS Evelyn S . . . . | New Orleans, LA
MR Eads 4th . . . . | *70115*
| ☎ (615) 924-2488
| ''Wayside Cottage''
| Monteagle
| Assembly,
| Monteagle, TN
| *37356*

Poitevent MR & MRS Edward B 2d (Julia D Baños)
StMarDom'72.Tul'71.Tul'74
☎ (504) 897-2463 . . 2006 Jefferson Av, New Orleans, LA *70115*

Poland MR William B JR—Cvc.Leh'48
☎ (202) FE3-4378 . . 1701 Hoban Rd NW, Washington, DC *20007*

Polese MR & MRS James K (Adeline L Bradlee) | ☎ (508) 927-1709
Wh'lck'56.Ec.H'57 . . . . | 809 Hale St,
MR William Trippe—Pitzer'89—at | Beverly Farms, MA
☎ (214) 321-6164 . . 7000 Wildgrove Av, Dallas, | *01915*
TX *75214* . . . . |

Polhemus MR & MRS Henry Martin JR (Curtis—Brown—
Cynthia J Bassett) CtCol'53.Aht'49
☎ (516) 537-1611 . . PO Box 356, 468 Sagg Main St, Sagaponack,
NY *11962*

Politzer REV & MRS Jerome F (Beverly J Reeves) Stan'48
☎ (408) 624-9721 . . 3770 Whitman Circle, Carmel, CA 93923

Politzer MR & MRS Jerome F JR (Rosemarie Indjayan) Cal'77.Cal'78
☎ (408) 484-9008 . . 34 Paseo Hermoso, Salinas, CA *93908*

Polk MR & MRS David C S (Amy Brown) | ☎ (215) 248-0340
B'gton'60.Gc.Dth'53.Pa'56 . . . . | 91 E Bells Mill Rd,
MISS Julia M P—Bnd'89—at ☎ (215) 546-8230 | Philadelphia, PA
1911 Pemberton St, Philadelphia, PA *19146* . . . | *19118*

Polk MISS Davin Mary Butler (F Lyon 3d) . . . . Born at
New York, NY Jly 1'96

Polk MR & MRS F Lyon 3d (Hilary B Edson) Tufts'84.Hartw'84
50 E 89 St, Apt 28F, New York, NY *10128*

Polk MR & MRS Frank L JR (Nancy H Wear) | ☎ (516) MA6-1882
Pr.Y.'58 . . . . | 31 Old Wheatley
MISS Pamela . . . . | Rd, Glen Head, NY
MR Potter . . . . | *11545*
MR J Bucky . . . . |

Polk MISS Grace Connors (g—David C S Polk) . . . . Born at
Salem, MA Aug 28'95

Polk MR & MRS Samuel S (Anne Page Homer) | of ☎ (914)234-3261
Fic.Fiy.Ri.Bgt.Ty'59.Va'62 . . . . | 634 Guard Hill Rd,
MR Thomas S—DU'94 . . . . | Bedford, NY *10506*
MR Samuel H—at St Lawrence U . . . . | ☎ (212) 308-2283
| 200 E 66 St,
| New York, NY
| *10021*

Polk MR William Julius JR—Rc.Cy.K.Cc.Y'33
☎ (314) FO1-6982 . . 4969 Pershing Place, St Louis, MO *63108*

Polk MR & MRS William M (Lu Ann Smith) | ☎ (508) 448-6391
Ty'62.UnTheo'66 . . . . | Groton School,
MISS M Malinda . . . . | Box 991, Groton,
MISS E Gillian . . . . | MA *01450*

Pollak MR & MRS Julian A JR (Elisabeth H Hicks) Swb'45.Mid'49
☎ (703) 538-2637 . . 1129 N Ivanhoe St, Arlington, VA *22205*

Pollard MR & MRS Charles F JR (Mary E Fritze)
Geo'89.Cl'94.Mid'88.Van'93
☎ (212) 874-8825 . . 107 W 86 St, Apt 3C, New York, NY *10024*

Pollard MR & MRS John D JR (M Hope Smith) | ☎ (410) 433-2276
Syr'64.Loy'75 . . . . | 6015 Bellona Av,
MR John D 3d . . . . | Baltimore, MD
JUNIORS MR Timothy A V . . . . | *21212*

Pollard MR Mark R—Emory'87.Ga'91
☎ (404) 607-9510 . . 980 Lanier Blvd NE, Atlanta, GA *30306*

Pollard MR & MRS Robert A (Nancy E Marshall) | ☎ (518) 758-2123
Suff'60 . . . . | Box 462,
MISS Linda M—at ☎ (617) 242-3539 | 33 Hudson St,
34 Mead St, Apt 2, Charlestown, MA *02129* . . . | Kinderhook, NY
| *12106*

Pollard MR & MRS William A (Jeannette Jones)
Br'48.Cry.Csp.Dar.Br'50 . . of
  ☎ (860) 767-1839 . . 26 Main St, Essex, CT *06426*
  ☎ (970) 476-5560 . . ''Far East Shelter'' G2 All Seasons Club,
434 Gore Creek Dv, Vail, CO *81657*

Pollard MR & MRS William R (Jennifer B Hildebran) L&C'85.L&C'85
  ☎ (206) 454-6301 . . 4425—94 Av NE, Bellevue, WA *98004*

Pollock MRS Elizabeth Maclean (Martin—Elizabeth | ☎ (212) 832-6773
O Maclean) Cly.Ncd. . . . . | 45 E 62 St,
  MISS Duart M Martin . . . . | New York, NY
     | *10021*

Pollock MR & MRS Eugene P (Mary C Weedon) Skd'60
  ☎ (804) 293-7755 . . 417 Ednam Dv, Charlottesville, VA *22903*

Pollock MRS James 3d (Neel—Bessie E Norris)
  ☎ (610) 688-8268 . . 501 Chandler Lane, Villanova, PA *19085*

Pollock MRS James H (Susan S Van Winkle) | ☎ (860) 567-5000
CtCol'68. . . . . | ''Lane's End''
  MR Christopher H—at Georgetown. . . . . | 271 N Lake St,
     | Litchfield, CT *06759*

Pollock MISS Katherine G (Matteson—Katherine G | ☎ (773) 248-7524
Pollock) Occ'74.Sc. . . . . | 743 W Bittersweet
  MISS Claire C Matteson . . . . | Place, Chicago, IL
  JUNIORS MR Oren P Matteson . . . . | *60613*
  JUNIORS MR Robert K Matteson . . . . |

Pollock MR & MRS Thomas Hood (Donna Hart) | ☎ (803) 669-6961
Pa'46.Leh'74.Pc.P'43 . . . . | 455 Harborough
  MISS Patricia T . . . . | Court, Florence, SC
     | *29501*

Pomeroy MR & MRS Burdette (Julia M Richmond) | ☎ (914) 961-5551
V'45w.Plg.P. . . . . | 87 Tanglewylde Av,
  MR James B—Plg.Ty'81 . . . . | Bronxville, NY
     | *10708*

Pomeroy MRS Lawrence A (Lucia Chamberlain) It.
  ☎ (216) 283-6259 . . 13710 Shaker Blvd, Apt 1004, Cleveland,
OH *44120*

Pomeroy MR & MRS Robert W 3d (Giblin—Jane G | ☎ (207) 637-2873
A Ramsay) McG'52.Stan'58 . . . . | RR 1, Box 679,
  MR Seth B—at ☎ (773) 880-2053 | Cornish, ME *04020*
2300 N Lincoln Park W, Chicago, IL *60614* . . . |

Pomeroy MR William A C
  ☎ (704) 863-4247 . . Winterbrook Farm, Rte 2, Box 1461, Columbus,
NC *28722*

Ponce MR & MRS Joseph L (M Anne Gates)
  ☎ (505) 984-9903 . . 150 Estrada Maya, Santa Fe, NM *87501*

Ponce MR & MRS Michael C (Jennifer C Teodecki) Rc.Bost'79
  ☎ (215) 836-4365 . . ''Le Matarie'' 510 Spring Lane, Wyndmoor,
PA *19038*

Pond MR Thomas T—H'51 . . . . | PO Box 61,
  MR Francis T . . . . | Hancock, NH *03449*

Pons MR & MRS John P (Yvonne G Archer) Ac.Cda. | of ☎ (410)877-7769
  MISS Deborah P A—Schil'74.Cda.—at | Country Life Farm,
238 Grove St, Auburndale, MA *02166* . . . . | Box 107,
  MISS Louise B—Cda.—at Mt Vernon Coll . . . . . | Bel Air, MD *21014*
  MR John P JR—at ☎ (401) 397-7189 | ☎ (609) 368-5529
17 Club House Rd, West Greenwich, RI *02186* . | 184—70 St, Avalon,
     | NJ *08202*

Ponti MR & MRS Andrea (Hilary L L Graham) Colg'85.B.NCar'85
  ☎ (011-44-171) 602-8312 . . 34 Royal Crescent, London W11 4SN,
England

Ponti MRS Ettore (Anne K Riggins) NCar'58
  ☎ (011-39-6) 536781 . . via Vitellia 89, 00152 Rome, Italy

Ponvert MRS Nancy B (Wilkinson—Nancy Borger) | ☎ (617) 227-3219
Buck'62 . . . . | 131 Charles St,
  MR Kent K Wilkinson JR—Tufts'89—at | Boston, MA *02114*
Boston U . . . . |

Ponvert MR Warren N—Unn.
  ☎ (561) 659-7053 . . 310 Australian Av, Palm Beach, FL *33480*

Pool MR & MRS Beekman H (Elizabeth Shallcross) | ☎ (603) 563-8428
C.Hn.H'32.Cl'35 | Snow Hill, Dublin,
  MISS Felicity M—V'71.Cr'74—at | NH *03444*
  ☎ (413) 498-5081 . . Northfield-Mt Hermon |
School, Northfield, MA *01360-1046* . . . . |

Pool MR Charles Chauncey—Y'35
Caller 9000, Water Mill, NY *11976*

Pool MR & MRS Eugene H (L Parrish Dobson) | ☎ (617) 489-2829
Y'71.Brand'80.H.'64 | 263 Payson Rd,
  MR Nathan B—at San Ramon, CA *94583* . . . . | Belmont, MA *02178*

Pool MRS G Hansen (Gillette K Hansen) . . . . . . | ☎ (303) 333-2220
  MR Fred W 3d . . . . | 401 Gilpin St,
  MR Henry B . . . . | Denver, CO *80218*
  JUNIORS MR Wyllys L . . . . |

Pool DR J Lawrence—C.H'28.Cl'32
  ☎ (860) 672-6910 . . 41 Cherry Hill Rd, West Cornwall, CT *06796*

Pool MR & MRS James L S (Kathryn L Sass) | ☎ (508) 655-0102
DU'74.Mds.DU'76.Bab'86 | 130 Maple St,
  JUNIORS MISS Kathryn M . . . . | Sherborn, MA
     | *01770*

Pool DR & MRS John L (Quigley—Amy W Wing) Sth'48.P'30.ClP&S'34
  ☎ (203) 762-3537 . . 37 Cannon Rd, Wilton, CT *06897*

Pool MRS Philip B (Dick—Virginia M French) Srb.Cly.Lm.Ht.Ncd.Dc.
  ☎ (242) 32-77205 . . ''Casa Rosa'' PO Box N3912, Nassau, Bahamas

Pool MR & MRS Philip B JR (Joan H Barnes)
NCar'75.Rc.Mb.Pr.Lm.Ht.Va'76.Cl'80
  ☎ (516) 676-6006 . . 8 Eyre Lane, Locust Valley, NY *11560-2202*

Pool MR & MRS W Henry 2d (Mary P Heller) Unn.DU'74.Nu'80
  ☎ (203) 629-8250 . . 587 North St, Greenwich, CT *06830*

Poole MR & MRS Alan C (Anne S Norris) Pn.P'37
  ☎ (609) 924-0694 . . 75 Alexander St, Princeton, NJ *08540*

Poole MR & MRS Allan K JR (Alice C Ehrenclou) | ☎ (203) 799-2151
V'53.Cl'54.P'49.H'54 . . . . | PO Box 1219,
  MR William A. . . . . | Orange, CT *06477*

Poole MR & MRS David W (Diane T Miller) Ore'83.Fr.Stan'79.Stan'80
  ☎ (415) 327-5417 . . 427 Alma St, Palo Alto, CA *94301*

Poole MR & MRS Edward G (Lynn A Anderson)
Stan'82.Cal'87.Tcy.Bow'82.Pac'85
  ☎ (415) 775-3926 . . 2737 Vallejo St, San Francisco, CA *94123*

Poole MISS Elisabeth C—Colby'90.Tcy.
  ☎ (212) 639-1792 . . 240 E 76 St, Apt 2A, New York, NY *10021*

Poole MR Fitz John P—Nu'68.Cr'70.Cr'76
  ☎ (619) 944-9668 . . 2366 Cambridge Av, Cardiff-By-The-Sea,
CA *92007*

Poole MRS George A (Ellen Stuart) Cho.Rc.On.Sr.Cas.Myf.Ncd.
  ☎ (847) 234-0761 . . 66 N Mayflower Rd, Lake Forest, IL *60045*

Poole MR & MRS Gordon L (Lois C Teasdale) Stan'49.Bhm.H'49.H'52
☎ (415) 366-9624 . . 2280 Stockbridge Av, Woodside, CA *94062*

Poole MR & MRS Lenwood H (Nancy S Ginn) Md'64 | ☎ (770) 992-6679
MISS Dana G . . . . | 295 Seventeenth
MR Craig D . . . . | Fairway, Roswell,
| GA *30076*

Poole DR & MRS Mark K (Sara A Day) JHop'35.StJ.Tex'29.JHop'34
☎ (409) 245-4000 . . 2420 Av K, Bay City, TX *77414*

Poole MRS Nicholas V (Peggy Porter) . . . . | ☎ (914) 723-2110
MR David D P . . . . | 49 Barry Rd,
| Scarsdale, NY
| *10583*

Poole MR & MRS Parker JR (Victoria Simes) CtCol'49
☎ (207) 799-2062 . . 442 Old Ocean House Rd, Cape Elizabeth,
ME *04107*

Poole MR & MRS Peter A (Rosemary F Sullivan) Cl'56.Y'57.AmU'68
☎ (703) 281-0530 . . 10526 Marbury Rd, Oakton, VA *22124*

Poole MR & MRS Peter R (Sebelle H von Hafften) Stan'77.Laf'68
☎ (203) 637-3645 . . 168 Riverside Av, Riverside, CT *06878*

Pooley MR & MRS John A (Mary L Gardner) D.
☎ (704) 884-5645 . . 17 Tsisdu Court, Connestee Falls, Brevard,
NC *28712*

Poor MR & MRS Charles L (Greene—Edith F Cowles)
Cvc.K.Ct.Ayc.Sl.H'41 ⚓ . . of
☎ (202) 333-7530 . . 1615—35 St NW, Washington, DC *20007*
☎ (508) 992-4696 . . Box P290, Nonquitt, South Dartmouth, MA *02748*

Poor MR & MRS Frederic H JR (Elizabeth L Hart) Hn.H'34.H'37
☎ (303) 798-7047 . . 71 Fairway Lane, Columbine Valley, CO *80123*

Poor MR & MRS J Sheppard (Jordan L Avery) | ☎ (908) 291-4748
Ny.Plg.H'47 . . . . | "Leeward"
MISS Deborah (Bernard—Karlsson—Deborah | 828 Navesink River
Poor)—at ☎ (401) 272-2568 . . 143 Cypress St, | Rd, Locust, NJ
Providence, RI *02906* . . . . | *07760*

Poor MISS Penelope (Bickley—Penelope Poor)
☎ (908) 872-7432 . . PO Box 17, Rumson, NJ *07760*

Poor MRS Richard W (Anne H Benson) Sth'38
☎ (201) 445-4534 . . 242 Fairmount Rd, Ridgewood, NJ *07450*

Pope MISS Adrianna M—SCal'83.Bur.
☎ (415) 861-2666 . . 117 Frederick St, San Francisco, CA *94117*

Pope MR & MRS Albert A (Renata M S Borsetti) Milan'80.H'67
☎ (914) 868-1233 . . Stone Oaks Farm, PO Box 557, Bangall, NY *12506*

Pope MR & MRS Christopher M (Sarah H Hand) Cy.Chi.Pa'75
☎ (617) 329-5789 . . 220 Stoney Lea Rd, Dedham, MA *02026*

Pope MRS Edward J (Horkan—McConnell—Evelyn H Maddox)
Sl.Ncd . . of
☎ (202) 966-4883 . . 3245B Sutton Place NW, Washington, DC *20016*
☎ (540) 687-5884 . . "Rockmere" PO Box 915, Middleburg, VA *20118*

Pope MR & MRS Frank M (Kingsbury—Sylvia M | ☎ (617) 731-8805
Thorndike) Chi.H'69 . . . . | 4 Monmouth St,
MISS Rosamond T . . . . | Brookline, MA
JUNIORS MR Albert A—at St Paul's . . . . | *02146*
MISS Macy T Kingsbury—at 65 E India Row,
Boston, MA *02110* . . . .
MR H Neal Kingsbury—Geo'91—at
541—16 St, Miami, FL *33139* . . . .

Pope MR Frederick C B . . see E Hoffman

Pope MRS George A (Coleman—Pope—Andrews— | ☎ (209) 674-8506
Patricia Moffat) Tcy. . . . . | El Peco Ranch,
MISS Patricia M . . . . | 10462 Road 21,
| Madera, CA *93637*

Pope MISS Geraldine (Warren—Geraldine Pope)
☎ (360) 834-2220 . . 4230 NW McIntosh Rd, Camas, WA *98607*

Pope MR Guy B—Pcu.P'58
☎ (360) 834-2000 . . 20109 SE 40 St, Camas, WA *98607*

Pope MR Guy W . . see E Hoffman

Pope MR & MRS John A (Nancy Mabrey) Briar'72.Cy.Ec.Bost'69
☎ (617) 227-5006 . . 10 Lime St, Boston, MA *02108-1103*

Pope MRS Ralph L JR (Thelma E Morales) Emman'42
☎ (617) 333-0469 . . 1421 Brush Hill Rd, Milton, MA *02186*

Pope MISS Sarah A . . see J R Cook JR

Pope MR Thomas M
4000 Via Marisol, Apt 101, Los Angeles, CA *90042-5151*

Pope MR & MRS Wilmot T (Margery P Montgomery) | ☎ (617) 566-6493
Sbc.Cy.Ec.My.Chi.Y'41.H'48 . . . . | 80 Heath St,
MR Geoffrey J—Cy.My.Y'82— | Brookline, MA
☎ (617) 566-1039 . . . . | *02146-5926*

Porcher MRS Elise Dillman (Lesemann—Elise C | *see*
Dillman) SCar'64.SCar'85.Ncd. . . . . | *Dilatory Domiciles*
MISS Elise C Lesemann—Ga'90 . . . .
MR Ellis R Lesemann—SCar'94—at
U of SCar Grad . . . .

Porteous MISS Alexandra K . . see W J Thomas JR

Porteous MRS Jane D (Vale—Jane B Drexel) BtP . . . | of ☎ (561)832-4299
MR Louis D . . . . | 3800 Washington
| Rd, PH-7,
| West Palm Beach,
| FL *33405*
| ☎ (207) 288-2348
| Acadian Farm,
| 1 Youngs Mountain
| Rd, Bar Harbor, ME
| *04609*

Porteous MRS Robert E (Ellen P Stephenson)
☎ (412) 621-6397 . . 238 Gladstone Rd, Pittsburgh, PA *15217-1112*

Porteous MR William D . . see W J Thomas JR

Porter MR & MRS A Hobart (Pamela J DeGraff)
Ws'82.Me.Gm.Sl.Ty'76.Pa'82
☎ (610) 527-6933 . . 318 N Ithan Av, Rosemont, PA *19010*

Porter MR & MRS Andrew W JR (Heath B McCawley)
Me.Gm.Rb.Cc.P.Pa'51
☎ (610) MU8-3530 . . 743 Parkes Run Lane, Villanova, PA *19085*

Porter MISS Barbara Hamilton
☎ (401) 423-0756 . . 70 Whittier Rd, Box 322, Jamestown, RI *02835*

Porter MR & MRS Barkley N (Lisa D Davis) Ariz'81.MmtPV'79
☎ (310) 433-1771 . . 150 Glendora Av, Belmont Shore, CA *90803*

Porter MR & MRS Clark Willard (Kathryn Anne Thrall) Cal'84.Cal'85
☎ (310) 454-6448 . . 1412 Via Anita, Pacific Palisades, CA *90272*

Porter MR & MRS Frank B JR (Bisbee—Ann M | ☎ (617) 492-3605
Giese) Rdc'62.Sim'75.Sm.Ds.Y'59.H'65 . . . . . . | 6 Mercer Circle,
MISS Dorothy W Bisbee—Br'86.Va'94 . . . . . | Cambridge, MA
MR John B Bisbee—Alf'90 . . . . | *02138*
MR Samuel M Bisbee—Cl'90 . . . .

Porter MRS Gail (Torres—Gail Porter)
☎ (203) 966-9828 . . 345 Main St, New Canaan, CT *06840*
Porter DR & MRS George H 3d (Virginia Pillow)
Duke'54.Duke'58.C.Mto.Sar.Duke'54.Duke'58
☎ (504) 842-3232 . . 1330 Eleonore St, New Orleans, LA *70115-4316*
Porter MR & MRS Grant A (Christina C French) Bost'73.Pr.Mb.Br'73
☎ (516) 676-6730 . . 141 Skunks Misery Rd, Locust Valley, NY *11560*
Porter MRS Henry H (Mary L Kinney) Cvc.Sl.Mt.Cos.
☎ (202) FE3-3107 . . 3107 Woodland Dv NW, Washington, DC *20008*

Porter MR & MRS Henry H JR (Louisa C Perkins) B'gton'57.Mt.Yn.Y'56.H'62 . . . . | ☎ (502) 426-6181 5806 River Knolls
MISS Catherine—at 2020 Floral Dv, Boulder, CO *80304* . . . . | Dv, Louisville, KY *40222*

Porter MR & MRS Joseph H 3d (Beth W Hall) FlaSt'74.ArizSt'67 . . . . . . | ☎ (602) 949-5840 6039 E Calle Del
MISS Elizabeth B . . . . | Paisano, Scottsdale,
JUNIORS MISS Lindsey C . . . . | AZ *85251*

Porter MRS Lewis Morgan (Alberta E M Gillespie)
☎ (860) 643-5640 . . 70 Westminster Rd, Manchester, CT *06040*
Porter MISS Linda M
☎ (847) 441-6547 . . 840 Tower Rd, Winnetka, IL *60093*
Porter MISS Mary K
☎ (305) 296-0970 . . 1616 Atlantic Blvd, Key West, FL *33040*
Porter MRS Richard L (Joan M Klots) Csn.
☎ (941) 488-8768 . . 250 Santa Maria St, Apt 121C, Venice, FL *34285*
Porter MRS Richard P (Barbara H Spangler)
☎ (212) 988-0285 . . 535 E 87 St, New York, NY *10128*
Porter MR & MRS Robert H (Atwater—Joan Hamill) Sfg.SCal'47
☎ (619) 454-1879 . . 2521 Via Viesta, La Jolla, CA *92037*
Porter MR & MRS S Prentice (Burrage—Hope Wallach) Y'31
☎ (540) 347-0720 . . ''Willow Spring'' PO Box 1126, Warrenton, VA *20188*

Portner MRS John A D (Erveane D Massey) Cvc. . . | of ☎ (202)966-6304 2917 Glover Dv
MR John A D JR . . . . | NW, Washington, DC *20016*
| ☎ (919) 441-2565 ''Marslanding'' Kill Devil Hills, NC *27948*

Poschl MR & MRS Nicholas F (Judith A Knight) Ty'60 . . . . | ☎ (201) 539-3664 16 Herms Place,
MR Christopher W . . . . | Convent Station, NJ
JUNIORS MR Mark A . . . . | *07961*
Posselius MR Edward J JR . . . . | ☎ (313) TU4-3663 160 Lewiston Rd,
MISS M Christy . . . . | Grosse Pointe, MI
MISS Patricia E . . . . | *48236*

Post MISS Barbara St C . . see C W Chatfield
Post MISS Caroline C . . see C W Chatfield
Post MR & MRS Christopher C (Jennifer Fortenbaugh) Hlns'76.Wash'77
☎ (518) 851-5950 . . PO Box 521, Claverack, NY *12513*
Post MISS Diana—Pa'71.Pa'81
☎ (215) 222-2682 . . 1008 S 46 St, Philadelphia, PA *19143*

Post MR & MRS Edward Everett (Smith—Harriet C Bottomley) V'40.C.Csn.Hn.H'33.Nu'41 . . . . . . | ☎ (802) 985-9242 610 Wake Robin
MISS Dorothy S—at ☎ (617) 527-1862 24 Brookdale Rd, Newtonville, MA *02160* . . . . | Dv, Shelburne, VT *05482*

Post MR & MRS George B (Linda Moore) Man'vl'81.C.Dc.H'45
☎ (203) 866-5810 . . ''Poppasquash'' 18 Stephen Mather Rd, Norwalk, CT *06850*
Post MR & MRS George B JR (Sarah H Skeele) MtH'83.H'73
☎ (803) 524-7717 . . ''The Little Taj'' 401 King St, Beaufort, SC *29902*
Post MASTER James Richardson (George B JR) . . . . Born at Beaufort, SC Dec 8'95
Post MR Joel S (George B) . . . . Married at Saratoga, CA Christopher MISS Lori A (Frank A) . . . . Aug 31'96
Post MR & MRS Joel S (Lori A Christopher) Cal'90.Pa'95.H'89.Pa'95
☎ (011-44-171) 221-0010 . . 218 Westbourne Grove, London W11 2RH, England

Post MRS Sarah W (Sarah M Wood) . . . . | ☎ (203) 762-0112 58 Horseshoe Rd,
JUNIORS MR Alexander O . . . . | Wilton, CT *06897*
JUNIORS MR R Tucker . . . . |
Post MR & MRS Waldron K 2d (Sheila M Margey) SUNY'63.SUNY'64 . . . . | ☎ (914) OR9-6403 PO Box 1187,
MISS Kirsten A—Box 715, Normal, IL *61761* . . . | Woodstock, NY *12498*

Post MR & MRS William S (Pamela Peyton) Cly.Roan'74
☎ (203) 966-2507 . . 97 Overlook Dv, New Canaan, CT *06840*
Postley MRS Clarence S (Kebaili—Marilynn L Dinneen) Cly.Pr.S . . .of
☎ (516) OR6-1546 . . ''Ranley House'' Piping Rock Rd, Locust Valley, NY *11560*
☎ (415) 771-4286 . . 1980 Jackson St, San Francisco, CA *94109*

Potter MISS Barbara F—ColC'71.Sc.
☎ (312) 787-5460 . . 1440 N State P'kway, Apt 16A, Chicago, IL *60610*

Potter MR & MRS C Nicholas (Clare E Prentice) Ln.Pr.Mb.Y'61 . . . . | ☎ (516) 922-7957 Horseshoe Rd,
MR Christopher K . . . . | Mill Neck, NY
JUNIORS MISS Jennifer—at St Mark's . . . . | *11765*

Potter MR & MRS Cary (Harding—Harrison—Mary L Rice) V'44.Rcn.Cy.Y'37
☎ (617) 326-1923 . . 10 Longwood Dv, Apt 122, Westwood, MA *02090*
Potter MR & MRS Charles S (Barbara O McClurg) Sth'46.Rc.Cho.Cas.On.Cnt.Fy.Ncd . . .of
☎ (312) 944-1911 . . 1500 N Lake Shore Dv, Apt 18C, Chicago, IL *60610-1624*
☎ (561) 546-1739 . . 476 S Beach Rd, Hobe Sound, FL *33455*
Potter MR & MRS Charles S JR (Julia B Peabody) DU'83.On.Rcch.Nw'82
☎ (406) 655-9155 . . ''The Rims'' 4626 Arapaho Lookout, Billings, MT *59106*
Potter MR & MRS Clarkson N (Helga Maass) Cl'65.Nrr.C.U'50
☎ (401) 423-1720 . . 5 Westwood Rd, Jamestown, RI *02835*
Potter MR & MRS David (Elizabeth A Lyman) Pcu.Tcy.Ncd.Cal'36
1400 Geary Blvd, Apt 2010, San Francisco, CA *94109*
Potter DR & MRS (DR) David S (Ellen A Bauerle) Ober'80.Mich'84.Mich'90.H'79.Ox'84
☎ (313) 747-6337 . . 1331 White St, Ann Arbor, MI *48104*
Potter MR & MRS E Clifford (Towne—Matthews—Jacklyn O Meek) Rcn.Ariz'50 . . of
☎ (207) 594-7502 . . PO Box 316, Spruce Head, ME *04859*
''Mussel Cove'' Rte 73, South Thomaston, ME *04858*

Potter MR & MRS Edward E (Penelope Stoddart) Y'81
☎ (810) 932-3116 . . 5197 Wing Lake Rd, Bloomfield Hills, MI *48302*

Potter MR & MRS Eugene W JR (M Melinda Rice) | ☎ (914) 961-3865
Cc.Y.'50. . . . . | 43 Elm Lane,
MISS Peyson W—Ty'85—at ☎ (508) 228-0534 | Bronxville, NY
PO Box 15, Nantucket, MA *02554* . . . . | *10708*
MR Winslow W . . . . |

Potter MR & MRS Gordon (Riker—Nancy Quirk) | ☎ (908) 842-1656
Rm.Ty'43 . . . . | 10 Broadmoor Dv,
MISS Louise—at ☎ (508) 456-3476 | Rumson, NJ *07760*
267 Littleton Rd, Harvard, MA *01451* . . . . |
MR Henry C . . . . |
MISS Elizabeth Q Riker—at ☎ (202) 966-0414
4601 Connecticut Av NW, Apt 619,
Washington, DC *20008* . . . . |

Potter MR & MRS Gregory C (Isota T Epes) | ☎ (609) 589-8026
Cda.Pa'64.VillaN'68.Rut'81 . . . . | 70 Pitman Av,
MISS Melissa H—at Rutgers . . . . | Pitman, NJ *08071*
MR Gregory C JR . . . . |

Potter MR & MRS H David (Elizabeth F Stone) | of ☎ (212)831-5234
Ws'53.Rc.K.H.'53.H'58 . . . . | 1160 Fifth Av,
MR Nicholas F—Rc.H'85.H'88—at | New York, NY
☎ (212) 924-6941 . . 43 Fifth Av, Apt 1A, | *10029-6936*
New York, NY *10003* . . . . | ☎ (860) 542-5448
| 220 Mountain Rd,
| Norfolk, CT *06058*

Potter MRS H Spencer (Margaret Allen) Fw.Dar. . . . | ☎ (941) 778-1738
MR Charles A 3d . . . . | 521—75 St,
| Holmes Beach, FL
| *34217*

Potter MR & MRS Hamilton F JR (Maureen E Cotter) Cs.H'50 . . of
☎ (212) 737-4225 . . 325 E 65 St, New York, NY *10021*
☎ (516) 584-7589 . . 99 Long Beach Rd, RFD 1, Box 99, St James,
NY *11780*

Potter MR Hamilton F III (Hamilton F JR) . . . . Married at New York, NY
Turner MISS Jennifer . . . . Mch 29'96

Potter MRS Hitt (Romaine—Diana Hitt) SL'55.Lx.
☎ (413) 243-4354 . . ''Dragonfly Hill'' PO Box 238, South Lee,
MA *01260*

Potter MISS Hope E . . see A L Lefkowitz

Potter MR & MRS Horatio R (Elizabeth G O'Connell) Cl'91.Rcn.V'87
☎ (406) 686-4406 . . Clementine Ranch, 55 Briggs Lane, Wilsall,
MT *59086*

Potter MR Jack R H . . see MRS N W Gumprecht

Potter MR James M—Ham'92 . . see A J Casner JR

Potter MR Jeffrey D—Ham'89 . . see A J Casner JR

Potter MASTER Jeffrey Gunn Bigelow (Horatio R) . . . . Born at
Livingston, MT Apr 4'96

Potter MRS John C (Mary P Davis)
☎ (508) 362-6493 . . Tonela Rd, Cummaquid, MA *02637*

Potter MR & MRS John H N 2d (Kimberly D McKinley)
Ga'83.Y'85.Nw'95 . . of
☎ (216) 752-5779 . . 3330 Glencairn Rd, Shaker Heights, OH *44122*
☎ (401) 423-1369 . . 191 Narragansett Av, Jamestown, RI *02835*

Potter MR & MRS John S JR (Joan C Wall) Eyc.H'46 | ☎ (011-852)
MR John S 3d . . . . | 872-6558
MR William N H . . . . | F at J4,
MR Robert L C . . . . | 20 Scenic Villa Dv,
| Victoria Rd,
| Hong Kong

Potter MISS Molly M (g—Andrew J Casner JR) . . . . Born Jun 8'96

Potter MR & MRS Nicholas B (Jane Stevenson) | ☎ (630) 325-2894
Cly.H'54 . . . . | 721 Cleveland Rd,
MISS Laura A . . . . | Hinsdale, IL *60521*

Potter MR & MRS Nicholas S (Susan P Kuniholm) Cr'88.H'86
2324 Bellfield Rd, Cleveland Heights, OH *44106*

Potter MR & MRS Philip C JR (Letitia D McClure) | ☎ (203) 869-6069
V'59.H'48.H'52 . . . . | 44 Rockwood Lane,
MISS Clarissa H—Vt'89 . . . . | Greenwich, CT
MR Alexander G—Vt'88 . . . . | *06830*
MR James P T—Vt'95 . . . . |

Potter MRS Richard M B (Maxwell—Sylvia A Lathrop)
☎ (508) 675-4864 . . 500 Wilbur Av, Somerset, MA *02725*

Potter MR Robert B—K.H'81
☎ (212) 753-2653 . . 141 E 56 St, New York, NY *10022-2713*

Potter MR & MRS Robert G JR (Edith Welch) H'50
☎ (508) 627-4667 . . Star Rte 149, Edgartown, MA *02539*

Potter MRS Robert S (Isabel D Russell) C.
☎ (212) 734-8991 . . 116 E 66 St, New York, NY *10021*

Potter DR & MRS Robert T (Helena A Wolfe) Sth'52.H'46.H'52
☎ (941) 475-6385 . . 8270 Manasota Key Rd, Englewood, FL *34223*

Potter MRS Ruth (Waters—Ruth Saxer)
☎ (415) 922-0346 . . 2446 Washington St, San Francisco, CA *94115*

Potter MRS Sheldon III (Eleanor P Wood)
☎ (561) 498-1143 . . 711 Av Chaumont, Delray Beach, FL *33445*

Potter MRS Sheldon F (Hillyer—Marie S Ritter)
☎ (302) 645-9125 . . Mill Pond Acres, 4 Sherbrooke Rd, Lewes,
DE *19958*

Potter MR & MRS Spencer W (Cornelia V H Ferber) | of ☎ (617)742-7979
V'67.GeoW'71.Bost'85.U'58 . . . . | 67 Revere St,
JUNIORS MISS Diana L . . . . | Boston, MA *02114*
JUNIORS MISS Lydia L . . . . | ☎ (401) 423-1369
| 191 Narragansett
| Av, Jamestown, RI
| *02835*

Potter MR & MRS Stephen W (A Lynn Peloubet)
Wh'lck'77.Eyc.Mass'79.H'89
596 Locust St, Winnetka, IL *60093-2174*

Potter MR Trevor A McC—Mt.H'78.Va'82
☎ (540) 364-3681 . . ''Poke House'' Whiting Rd, Marshall, VA *20115*

Potter MRS Virginia P (Virginia F Patterson) | ☎ (212) 289-0731
Sth'52.Ncd. . . . . | 125 E 87 St,
MISS Elizabeth S—H.'90 . . . . | New York, NY
| *10128*

Potter MISS (DR) Virginia P—Mit'77.Mit'78.Chti'90.Chti'95.Ncd.
☎ (011-39-85) 380176 . . via del Circuito 111, 65124 Pescara, Italy

Potter DR & MRS William H (Lighthill—Agnes E Hawkins)
Sth'54.Hb.Y'37.H'41 . . of
☎ (203) 637-1091 . . "Primrose Cottage" 49 Edgewater Dv,
Old Greenwich, CT *06870*
☎ (941) 434-0531 . . "Chaconne Rue" 338 Fourth Av N, Naples,
FL *34102-8424*

Pottharst MR Russell C
☎ (504) 861-8273 . . 6319 S Prieur St, New Orleans, LA *70118*

Pottle MR & MRS Willard M JR (Donna Atwill) | ☎ (716) 836-0035
St.G.Ham'61 . . . . | 186 Woodbridge Av,
MISS Deirdre A . . . . | Buffalo, NY *14214*
MR Willard M 3d . . . . |
JUNIORS MISS Louise A . . . . |

Potts DR & MRS Daniel T (H Hildreth Burnett) H'77.H'75.H'80
☎ (011-62-2) 369-1617 . . 29 Henry St, Queens Park, Sydney,
NSW 2024, Australia

Potts MRS Elisabeth B (Gannon—Elisabeth B Potts) Siena'80.SUNY'85
44 Westchester Dv, Clifton Park, NY *12065*

Potts MRS Frederic A JR (Karen A Braley) V'66 . . . | ☎ (818) 796-7922
MISS Jennifer B . . . . | 1130 S Oakland Av,
JUNIORS MR Frederic A 3d . . . . | Pasadena, CA *91106*

Potts MR & MRS Herbert J (Minnis—Mary E Ervin) P'32
☎ (334) 928-5583 . . 455 S Mobile St, Fairhope, AL *36532*

Potts MR & MRS Robert H (E Halsey Ligget) | of ☎ (941)263-2496
Me.Gm.Yp.Y'45w . . . . | 336 Bowline Bend,
MR David L . . . . | Naples, FL *34102*
 | ☎ (603) 253-4537
 | RR 1, Box 185,
 | Center Harbor, NH
 | *03226*

Pough MR & MRS Edward W (Marguerite A Teyssandier) Tark'64.Ga'70
☎ (206) 282-0932 . . 2550 Westmont Way W, Seattle, WA *98199-3720*

Pough MR Harold B—Me.
☎ (610) MI2-1295 . . 329 Cherry Lane, Wynnewood, PA *19096*

Pough MR Richard H—C.Mit'26.Hav'70
☎ (914) 738-0198 . . 33 Highbrook Av, Pelham, NY *10803*

Poulden MR Richard O'D—Ox'73
☎ (011-44-1452) 813220 . . "Tibbiwell House" Painswick,
Gloucestershire GL6 XX, England

Poutiatine MR & MRS Michael (Marcia Meserve) | ☎ (561) 231-5830
Srr.Y'57 ⛵ . . . . | 2095 Mooring Line
MISS Allison M . . . . | Dv, Vero Beach, FL
MISS Jennifer M . . . . | *32963*

Powel MR & MRS John H (Ann C Ellis) H'42 . . . . . . | ☎ (206) 842-4140
MR Michael W H—at 1210 Sawdust Hill Rd, | 15254 Broom St
Poulsbo, WA *98370* . . . . | NE, Bainbridge
 | Island, WA *98110*

Powell MASTER Arthur Gray 4th (g—George M Wood JR) . . . . Born
Dec 16'94

Powell MRS Charles S (Marguerite B Shannon) RSage'27.Y'28 . . of
☎ (201) 644-2455 . . 7 Humphrey Rd, Morristown, NJ *07960*
☎ (809) 773-2660 . . "Little Whim" Estate Boetzberg, Christiansted,
St Croix, VI *00820*

Powell GEN (RET) & MRS Colin L (Alma V Johnson) | ☎ (703) 847-0455
USA.Fisk'57.CUNY'58.GeoW'71 . . . . | 1317 Ballantrae
MISS Linda . . . . | Farm Dv, McLean,
MISS Annemarie . . . . | VA *22101*
MR Michael . . . . |

Powell MISS Frances E . . . . Married at Atlanta, GA
Clark MR W Wayne (Charles M) . . . . Oct 24'94

Powell MR & MRS Humbert B 3d (Shala Afshar) | ☎ (201) 912-9634
Salem'66 . . . . | 33 Brooklawn Dv,
MISS Elizabeth Price—at 8650 Southwestern | Short Hills, NJ
Blvd, Dallas, TX *75206* . . . . | *07078*
MISS Victoria Remington . . . . |
MISS Catherian R . . . . |

Powell MR & MRS Irwin A (Myles—Edith B Harlan) Pr.Cs . . .of
☎ (212) 734-3919 . . 955 Lexington Av, PH-A, New York,
NY *10021-5107*
☎ (516) OR6-8306 . . "Woods Harbor" 40 Frost Creek Dv, Lattingtown,
Locust Valley, NY *11560*

Powell MISS Jane L
☎ (410) 885-5033 . . 71 Port Herman Rd, Chesapeake City, MD *21915*

Powell MR & MRS John (Margaret L Proper) Mid'56.Colg'52.Cl'58
☎ (602) 991-0212 . . 5347 E Royal Palm Rd, Paradise Valley, AZ *85253*

Powell MR & MRS John B JR (Susan V Baker) | ☎ (410) 323-1744
Ws'63.Elk.P'59 . . . . | 5508 Normandy
MISS Julia C—Dth'89 . . . . | Place, Baltimore,
MR Brentnall M—Wms'91 . . . . | MD *21210*
MR David B—at Bowdoin . . . . |

Powell MRS John G (Alcorn—Sara A Deacon) Me.M . . .of
☎ (610) MI9-7456 . . 101 Cheswold Lane, Haverford, PA *19041*
☎ (561) 655-6087 . . 300 S Ocean Blvd, Palm Beach, FL *33480*

Powell MRS John W G (Janet G Travell)
☎ (202) 363-9090 . . 4525 Cathedral Av NW, Washington,
DC *20016-3564*

Powell MISS Laura Johnson . . see MRS P J McNeely

Powell MRS Lewis F JR (Josephine P Rucker) . . . . Died at
Richmond, VA Jly 24'96

Powell MISS Margot McCoy . . see MRS P J McNeely

Powell MISS Marguerite McD . . see G M Wood JR

Powell MR Peter Irwin A . . . . | ☎ (212) 832-8427
MR R Augustus—at Oberlin . . . . | 331 E 58 St,
 | New York, NY
 | *10022*

Powell MR & MRS Philip N (Margaret G Morris)
Swb'54.Ncd.Va'52.JHop'60
☎ (410) 828-9511 . . 7523 L'Hirondelle Club Rd, Ruxton, MD *21204*

Powell MR & MRS Robert E (Janet B Strahorn)
Wils'57.Gchr'58.JHop'57.Md'60
☎ (410) 337-0703 . . 518 Charles Street Av, Towson, MD *21204*

Powell MR Robert F JR . . . . Died at
New York, NY May 5'96

Powell MR Sheppard T 2d . . see MRS P J McNeely

Powell DR & MRS William E 3d (Elizabeth O'N | ☎ (334) 271-3485
Crawford) Aub'67.Aub'68.Aub'66.Aub'70 . . . . | 3549 Melton Rd,
MR William E 4th . . . . | Montgomery, AL
MR Gregory S . . . . | *36106*
JUNIORS MR Matthew C . . . . |

Powelson MR & MRS Douglas V N (Carolyn H
Hughes) SoSem'65.Va'68 . . . . ☎ (864) 573-7123
  MR Randall V N—Va'90—at ☎ (773) 275-5191 | 357 Twin Oaks Dv,
4731 N Kenmore Av, Chicago, IL 60640 . . . . . . | Spartanburg, SC
| 29306
Powers MR F Thomas 3d
Skunk's Misery Rd, Locust Valley, NY 11560
Powers MR Francis F S—B.Pr.Gm.Me.Pa'75
  ☎ (610) 642-6014 . . 101 Mill Creek Rd, Ardmore, PA 19003
Powers MR & MRS H Burton (Anne Lyman)
V'45-4.Sbc.Cw.H'33 . . . . ☎ (617) 235-0476
  MISS Katherine B—at ☎ (212) 734-9877 | 57 Benvenue St,
218 E 82 St, New York, NY 10028 . . . . | Wellesley, MA
  MISS Eleanor H—at ☎ (212) 675-6950 | 02181
15 W 11 St, New York, NY 10011 . . . . |
Powers MRS John M (Marie J Drew) V'40.Un.Cly.Dc.Ncd.Cda.Dar.
  ☎ (212) 861-4579 . . 190 E 72 St, New York, NY 10021
Powers MRS John M JR (Marian B Stevens) Cent'y'50.Me.M.Pn.
  ☎ (610) 688-6415 . . 20 Ridgewood Rd, Radnor, PA 19087
Powers MR John Michael JR—Un.Pl.Ste.Cw.Cc.Ne.Rv.Pa'73
  ☎ (212) 308-0262 . . 333 E 56 St, New York, NY 10022
Powers MR & MRS Joshua B JR (Cynthia F Titus) Me'58.LondEc'60
  ☎ (802) 763-8087 . . 97 Broad Brook Rd, South Royalton, VT 05068
Powers MR & MRS Ronald G (McClellan—Elizabeth
C Braislin) Pa'56 . . . . ☎ (802) 824-4557
  MISS Alice B McClellan . . . . | 137 Piper Hill Rd,
  MR William Traylor McClellan . . . . | Weston, VT 05161
  MR James B McClellan . . . . |
  MR Maxwell C McClellan . . . . |
  MR Gordon S McClellan . . . . |
  JUNIORS MISS Lucy S McClellan—at Hotchkiss |
Powning MRS Kimball C (Carolyn Walker) Chi.Ncd.
Carlton-Willard Village, Llewsac Lodge 109, Bedford, MA 01730
Poynter MR & MRS William F (McFarland—
Helengrace Sawyer) Stan'32 . . . . ☎ (707) 546-9647
  MR James T—at ☎ (415) 665-0700 | 283 Oak Tree Dv,
3045—23 St, San Francisco, CA 94110 . . . . . . | Santa Rosa, CA
| 95401
Pracht MR & MRS Frederick R JR (Hope Mason)
Mls'59.Cal'55 . . . . ☎ (717) 697-8417
  MR Nicholas A—Ga'87 . . . . | 315 E Main St,
| Mechanicsburg, PA
| 17055
Pradier MR & MRS Laurent S (Mary C Politzer)
Cal'85.Nw'88.EcoleCen'84.Cal'89
  ☎ (011-33-1) 45-88-41-23 . . 5 bis rue d'Alesia, 75014 Paris, France
Prado MRS Christine T (Christine S Tiffany) . . . . . . ☎ (207) 734-6867
  MISS Maria C—at 1337 California St, | Mill Creek Rd,
San Francisco, CA 94109 . . . . | Islesboro, ME 04848
  MR Manuel D . . . . |
Pratt MR & MRS Albert (Morgan—Fanny Gray Little)
Ny.Chi.Ncd.H'33 . . of
  ☎ (305) 367-2382 . . Anglers Club 40, 50 Clubhouse Rd,
North Key Largo, FL 33037
  ☎ (508) 428-8218 . . ''Dam Pond House'' Box 508, Osterville,
MA 02655
Pratt MR & MRS Alexander (Barbara Sexton) Sth'56.Pa'57
  ☎ (207) 883-6274 . . 24 Piper Rd, Scarborough, ME 04074
Pratt MISS Anne Biddle (Jackson—Cress—Anne Biddle Pratt)
  ☎ (609) 884-5453 . . PO Box 2422, Cape May, NJ 08204

Pratt MR & MRS Carl E (M Julie Hogan)
Cin'70.Xav'77.Cc.Xav'67.Xav'75.Cin'77.Xav'86 | ☎ (513) 231-6332
  JUNIORS MR Carl E JR . . . . | 1159 Sutton Rd,
  MRS Everard D JR (Susan C Slough)— | Cincinnati, OH
  ☎ (513) 231-7930 . . . . | 45230
Pratt MR & MRS Charles McC (Helen H Forson)
Hlns'63.H'61 . . . . | ☎ (212) 289-2569
  MR Eliot F—H'94—at ☎ (212) 737-2896 | 1165 Fifth Av,
221 E 83 St, New York, NY 10028 . . . . | New York, NY
  JUNIORS MR Charles E—at Geo Wash'n . . . . . . | 10029
Pratt JUNIORS MISS Christine S . . see S A Nettl
Pratt MR Edward L—Yn.Y'46 . . . . | ☎ (203) 227-9312
  MISS Wendy F—at 6210½ S San Vicente Blvd, | 171 Newtown Tpke,
Los Angeles, CA 90048 . . . . | Westport, CT 06880
Pratt MRS H Irving (Ellen R Hallowell) Cs.Ny.
  ☎ (212) 751-2503 . . 200 E 66 St, New York, NY 10021
Pratt MR & MRS Harold I (Frances H Gillmore)
CtCol'60.Cy.Un.H.'59.H'63 . . . . | ☎ (617) 491-0132
  MISS Frances H—Duke'86—at | 157 Coolidge Hill,
  ☎ (703) 683-1965 . . 610 N West St, Alexandria, | Cambridge, MA
VA 22314 . . . . | 02138-5508
  MR Charles Q A—Duke'89—at |
  ☎ (401) 831-8538 . . 26 S Angel St, Providence, |
RI 02906 . . . . |
Pratt MR Harold I JR (Harold I) . . . . Married at Little Compton, RI
Emery MISS Marjorie T (Hiram W) . . . . Jun 15'96
Pratt REV & MRS James L (Nancy L May) . | ☎ (860) 536-7129
Ws'60.H'55.Y'58.Y'60 . . . . | 26 Cathedral
  MR Clark M 3d—H'87 . . . . | Heights, Noank,
| CT 06340
Pratt MR & MRS John T (Jane S Stone)
BMr'51.Rcn.Ny.Ncd.H'55 . . . . | ☎ (561) 546-9072
  MISS Jane S—at ☎ (212) 226-1692 | 7817 SE Loblolly
55 Prince St, New York, NY 10012 . . . . | Bay Dv,
| Hobe Sound, FL
| 33455
Pratt MRS M Melville (Mary M Melville) Cin'66 . . | ☎ (513) 761-5058
  MR Lanier W 3d . . . . | 531 Laramie Trail,
  JUNIORS MR Jonathan M . . . . | Wyoming, OH
  JUNIORS MR Charles A . . . . | 45215
Pratt MRS Maud W (Maud T Walker) . . . . | ☎ (610) 688-9349
  MISS Abby T—at Tufts . . . . | 2 Fairview Dv,
  MR Elisha W—Hartw'96 . . . . | St Davids, PA
| 19087
Pratt MR & MRS Richardson (Mary E Offutt) C.Pr.Cly.Wms'45.H'48
  ☎ (516) 692-8308 . . 30 Dock Hollow Rd, Cold Spring Harbor,
NY 11724
Pratt MRS Sally D (Sally L Davis) . . . . | ☎ (941) 261-5085
  MISS Pamela D . . . . | 4005 Rum Row,
| Naples, FL 34102
Pratt MRS Sherman (Manville—Ethel B Schniewind) Pr.Ht.
  ☎ (516) 676-0357 . . ''Still Pond'' Horse Hollow Rd, PO Box 421,
Locust Valley, NY 11560
Pratt MR & MRS Stanley E (Maryanne Thomas) | ☎ (617) 235-6715
Br'55.Br'53 . . . . | 51 Abbott Rd,
  MISS Johanna L . . . . | Wellesley Hills, MA
| 02181

Pratt DR T Dennie—H'34.Y'37
☎ (207) 244-7090 . . Stafford-Pratt Farm, Box 250, Bass Harbor, ME *04653*

Pratt MR & MRS Vaughan W (Caroline W Malone) Strat'71.Me.Rcp.Dick'64 ⚓ . . . . | ☎ (207) 871-0066
48 Neal St,
MISS Katherine B—at ☎ (617) 566-4990 | Western Promenade,
19 Mt Hood Rd, Brighton, MA *02135* . . . . | Portland, ME *04102*
MR Jon V M—at ☎ (410) 576-0411
7A W Lee St, Baltimore, MD *21201* . . . .
JUNIORS MISS Chauncey H—at Waynflete . . . . . .

Pratt MISS Virginia L—NH'81
6 Larkspur Way, Apt 5, Natick, MA *01760*

Pratt MR William C JR (Patricia C Morey)
☎ (413) 567-5179 . . 293 Merriweather Dv, Longmeadow, MA *01106*

Pray MISS Melanie B . . see F R Ford 3d

Pray MR Samuel Wendell—Plg.Y'41
☎ (011-44-171) 584-5620 . . 5 Egerton Place, London SW3, England

Preble MR & MRS Wallace L (Elizabeth L Ward) | ☎ (503) 645-1520
SL'65.Wms'61 ⚓ . . . . | 13805 NW
MR Thomas Ward—Linf'90—at 200 Greenridge | Thompson Rd,
Dv, Lake Oswego, OR *97035* . . . . | Portland, OR *97229*
MR Mark E—Cal'91—at 2249 Fulton St,
San Francisco, CA *97117* . . . .

Prentice MRS Bryant H JR (Jeanne Crowley)
☎ (805) 969-4860 . . 468 Crocker Sperry Dv, Santa Barbara, CA *93108*

Prentice MISS Colette—Franklin'89.MmtVa'93
☎ (202) 625-2223 . . 1539 Foxhall Rd NW, Washington, DC *20007*

Prentice MR & MRS Colgate S (Pamela Davis)
BMr'50.Wes'78.Swth'49.P'51
☎ (508) 636-3879 . . 185 Howland Rd, Westport, MA *02790*

Prentice MR & MRS Ezra P (Anderson—Sarah M Benjamin) P'39 . . of
☎ (704) 669-2099 . . 43 Wagon Trail Rd, Black Mountain, NC *28711*
☎ (941) 472-5624 . . 4221 Old Banyan Way, Sanibel, FL *33957*

Prentice MR Robert D (McMillen—Virginia Donald) Plg.Dar.
☎ (407) 783-9702 . . 235 Jamaica Dv, Cocoa Beach, FL *32931*

Prentice MR & MRS Sheldon E (Nancy M Reilly) | ☎ (011-44-171)
Bcs.B.Ln.Ng.Cc.Y'63 . . . . | 589-9142
MISS Alison P—at 215 E 73 St, New York, NY | 8 Ennismore St,
10021 . . . . | London SW7 1JE,
JUNIORS MISS Katherine S . . . . | England
JUNIORS MISS James E . . . . |

Prentice DR & MRS Theodore C (Mary-Kent Jewett)
SL'45.Cy.Ts.G.Colg'43.Buf'45
☎ (716) 882-7405 . . 18 Lincoln Woods Lane, Buffalo, NY *14222*

Prentice MR & MRS William C H (Elsie B Doty) Swth'37.H'42
300 Harbour Dv, Apt 100A, Vero Beach, FL *32963*

Prentice MR William C H JR—Macalester'68
☎ (508) 487-2173 . . 54 Commercial St, Provincetown, MA *02657*

Prentis MR & MRS Peter D (Lorraine Johnson)
25 Cross Lane, Cos Cob, CT *06807*

Prescott MISS Charleen B
see Dilatory Domiciles

Prescott MASTER Ivan William (g—MRS James McC Truitt) . . . . Born
Nov 1'94

Prescott DR & MRS Richmond (Dwight—Pamela Sedgwick)
H'49.H'52.Cl'59
☎ (415) 931-9204 . . 2633 Green St, San Francisco, CA *94123*

Pressley MR & MRS James F (Marion Dondero) Cp.
☎ (415) 461-3109 . . 755 S Eliseo Dv, Apt 6, Greenbrae, CA *94904*

Pressly MR & MRS James G (Anna Finn) Ers'29.Cl'31
☎ (561) 626-0256 . . 181 Green Point Circle, Palm Beach Gardens, FL *33418*

Prestegord MR & MRS Adam (Karen W Van Gulick)
Del'86.Dll.Dar.Penn'87
19 Cricket Dv, Holland, PA *18966*

Preston MRS Charles D (Sylvia Peter) On.Cnt.
☎ (847) 234-0580 . . 501 Oakwood Av, Lake Forest, IL *60045*

Preston MISS Frances L—Gchr'69
☎ (609) 466-3287 . . 17 Dunwald Lane, Hopewell, NJ *08525*

Preston MR John D—Rc.H'44.Cl'49
☎ (212) 628-4462 . . 125 E 72 St, New York, NY *10021*

Preston MRS John McA (Alsup—Caroline D Jackson) Bur.
☎ (415) 343-2059 . . 80 DeSabla Rd, Hillsborough, CA *94010*

Preston MR Kendall JR—Cyb.H'49
☎ (520) 795-3160 . . 3180 Hill Farm Dv, Tucson, AZ *85712*

Preston MRS Lewis T (Bartlett—Gladys M Pulitzer) K.BtP.
☎ (202) 483-3280 . . 3025 Whitehaven St NW, Washington, DC *20008*

Preston MR & MRS Ord (Marjorie H Ellis) Cvc.Va'39
☎ (619) 454-4019 . . 1963 Paseo Dorado, La Jolla, CA *92037-3332*

Preston MR Percy JR—Nf.Chr.K.Md'69
☎ (212) 595-8979 . . 311 W 91 St, New York, NY *10024*

Preston MRS Richard (Brown—Carolyn Crandall) | ☎ (508) 468-2712
My.Chi.Hn. . . . . | 454 Bay Rd,
MR Robert G . . . . | Box 427, Hamilton,
| MA *01936*

Preston MRS Seymour (Thorne—Barbara A Grassi) Bgt.
☎ (914) 234-7935 . . 34 Middle Patent Rd, Armonk, NY *10504*

Preston MR & MRS Seymour JR (Suzanne Gregory) | ☎ (914) 234-7824
Au.P'66.Nu'69 . . . . | 339 Cantitoe Rd,
JUNIORS MISS Eliot . . . . | Bedford Hills, NY
| *10507*

Preston MRS Seymour S JR (Mary A Harper)
☎ (610) 361-2022 . . White Horse Village, Apt A113, 535 Gradyville Rd, Newtown Square, PA *19073*

Preston MR & MRS Seymour S 3d (Jean E Holman) | ☎ (610) NI4-5317
Denis'55.Rd.Wms'56.H'58 . . . . | ''Mill Race''
MISS Katherine E—at ☎ (212) 628-4798 | 330 Dutton Mill Rd,
35 E 85 St, Apt 2AN, New York, NY *10028* . . . | West Chester, PA
MISS Alicia D—Denis'84—at ☎ (610) 647-0329 | *19380*
808 S Warren Av, Malvern, PA *19355* . . . . |
MISS Shelley S—at ☎ (718) 965-4330 |
424—4 St, Brooklyn, NY *11215* . . . . |

Preston MR & MRS Thomas P (Helen C Davis) | ☎ (302) 888-2018
Sth'68.Ac.Y'68.Va'75 . . . . | 805 Berkeley Rd,
MISS Barbara P . . . . | Wilmington, DE
| *19807*

Prettyman MISS Eleanor B—Ncd.Dar.
☎ (215) 242-0142 . . 201 W Evergreen Av, Apt 1104, Philadelphia, PA *19118*

Prettyman MRS James M H (Barbara Rolfe) . . . . . . of ☎ (410)523-1414
  MISS A Yardley—NEng'79 . . . . 1414 Bolton St,
Baltimore, MD
21217
☎ (302) 227-7692
1 Pennsylvania Av,
Rehoboth Beach, DE
19971

Preucel MRS Robert W (Ruth B Garrett) Swb'49.Ph.
  ☎ (610) 525-2028 . . 1147 Norsam Rd, Gladwyne, PA *19035*

Preucel MISS Ruth B G—Pa'82
  ☎ (415) 292-5964 . . 2411 Webster St, Apt 7, San Francisco, CA *94115*

Prewitt MRS Russe (Prewitt—Eaton—Ann H Russe)
  ☎ (905) 468-0724 . . ''Walnut Tree Cottage'' 22 Johnson St,
PO Box 251, Niagara-on-the-Lake, Ontario L0S 1J0, Canada

Preyer MR & MRS Britt Armfield (Alice C Dockery) ☎ (910) 275-6442
  Salem'77.Cda.David'75 . . . . 1508 Kirkpatrick
  JUNIORS MR Britt A JR . . . . Place, Greensboro,
NC *27408*

Prezioso MR & MRS Giovanni P (Elizabeth H Mathews)
Duke'83.Ncd.H'79.H'82
  ☎ (301) 229-1447 . . 5116 Cammack Dv, Bethesda, MD *20816*

Prezioso MR & MRS Michael S (Miranda Griscom Smith)
CtCol'85.CtCol'84.CtCol'86
  ☎ (518) 899-7252 . . 65 Pepperbush Place, Ballston Spa, NY *12020*

Pribble MR & MRS Robert (McIntyre—Emily T Gilbert) Cly.Nu'72
152 Old Black Point Rd, Niantic, CT *06357*

Price MR & MRS Boyce P (Elizabeth B Williams) Dth'36
  ☎ (603) 643-5803 . . Kendal at Hanover 216, 80 Lyme Rd, Hanover,
NH *03755*

Price MR & MRS C Michael (Hope van B Wood) ☎ (301) 229-3167
  Mt.Cvc.GeoW'65 . . . . 5402 Spangler Av,
  MISS Natasha de N—*see Dilatory Domiciles*. . . . Bethesda, MD
  MISS Alonsa B—at James Madison U *20816*

Price MRS Constance M (Constance Mather)
  ☎ (216) 451-7754 . . 19 Oakshore Green, Bratenahl, OH *44108*

Price MR & MRS Dwight L (Susan D W Stith) StL'87.Y'80
  ☎ (904) 448-2070 . . 3022 Bridlewood Lane, Jacksonville, FL *32257*

Price MISS Elizabeth W . . see C C Whitaker III

Price MRS Gregory F (Helen Piersol)
Mediplex, 162 S Britain Rd, Southbury, CT *06488*

Price MRS Hickman JR (Meacham—Eyre—Dorothy Hurt) BtP.
  ☎ (561) 655-5983 . . 10 Via Vizcaya, Palm Beach, FL *33480*

Price MR & MRS John S (Martha E Stokes) BMr'47.Rc.Me.Cw.Ac.Csn.P'44
  ☎ (610) 525-2096 . . Landover & Coopertown Rds, PO Box 187,
Bryn Mawr, PA *19010-0187*

Price MR & MRS John S (Sarah M Smith) Aub'56
  ☎ (334) 272-8076 . . 1820 Croom Dv, Montgomery, AL *36106*

Price MR & MRS Joseph A (Weeks—Barbara A Benedict)
NewSchSR'72.SUNY'74 . . of
  ☎ (212) 772-8942 . . 168 E 74 St, New York, NY *10021*
  ☎ (802) 824-3916 . . 111 Landgrove Rd, Weston, VT *05161*

Price MISS Margaret B—Aht'91.Mich'96
  ☎ (313) 665-6253 . . 1790 Country Club Rd, Ann Arbor, MI *48104*

Price MRS Martha A (Cost—Laidlaw—Foote— ☎ (860) 434-9359
  Martha A Price) Conn'84 . . . . 86 Bill Hill Rd,
  MISS Catherine A Cost—at U of Colo . . . . . . PO Box 718,
Old Lyme, CT
06371

Price MRS Philip (Sarah M Harrison) Ac.Cda.
  ☎ (215) 233-0833 . . 551 E Evergreen Av, Wyndmoor, PA *19038*

Price MR & MRS Philip JR (Sarah B Dolan) ☎ (215) 247-5681
  Sth'60.BMr'87.Ph.Pc.Ac.H'56.Pa'61 . . . . 8003 Navajo St,
  MISS Alexandra G—Pa'87 . . . . Philadelphia, PA
  MISS Emilie A—Cr'89 . . . . *19118*
  MR Philip 3d—Br'95 . . . .

Price MR & MRS Richard H SR (Mary K Beecher) ☎ (313) 665-6287
  Lawr'62.Lawr'62.Ill'66 . . . . 1790 Country Club
  MR M Daniel . . . . Rd, Ann Arbor, MI
48105

Price MR Richard H JR—Carl'90
  ☎ (708) 445-8956 . . 1151B S Oak Park Av, Oak Park, IL *60304*

Price MRS Robert M (O'Hara—Mary C Arkell) . . . . Died Aug 14'96

Price MR Robert M—Sg.Pc.Cry.DelB.Sap.Cc.Pp.P'37.Pa'39 ⚓ . . of
  ☎ (908) 899-1567 . . 84 Bay Point Harbour, Point Pleasant, NJ *08742*
  ☎ (561) 272-2855 . . 1117 Island Dv, Delray Beach, FL *33483*

Price MR Robert R JR (late Robert R) . . . . . . Married at Centreville, MD
  Hammond MRS Nancy R (Nancy T Robinson) . . . . Oct 22'95

Price MR & MRS Robert R 3d (Judith Marie Warfield)
WestMd'76.Md'79.Md.Gi.Ste.Pa'76.Md'79 ⚓
  ☎ (410) 827-6286 . . 325 Sayers Forest Dv, Queenstown, MD *21658*

Price MRS Sidney L (Morrow—Macfarland—Ailene E Wharton) Dar.
  ☎ (561) 655-5799 . . 311 Cocoanut Row, Apt 101, Palm Beach,
FL *33480*

Price MRS Theodore H JR (Price—Ewoldt—Nancy A Heckscher)
105 N Will Scarlett Lane, Queen's Lake, Williamsburg, VA *23185*

Price MR & MRS Theodore W (Carol L Bayne) ☎ (804) 288-5651
  Hlns'66.Rich'93.B.Cc.Va'64.Va'68 . . . . 6709 River Rd,
  MISS Sibyl W—Ty'92—at 1924 Waverly St, Richmond, VA
  Philadelphia, PA *19146* *23229*
  MISS Nancy D—at Denison . . . .
  MR Theodore C—P'90—at 180 E Walnut St,
  Apt 305, Pasadena, CA *91103* . . . .
  JUNIORS MR Thomas W—at Denison . . . .

Price DR & MRS Thomas Ransone (Nancy W ☎ (410) 337-0177
  Franklin) RMWmn'58.Sar.Mv.Dar.Va'56.Va'60 ''Hilcote''
  MR F Ransone—Va'86—at 5712 Garrow Point 7841 Ellenham Rd,
  Court, Richmond, VA *23228* . . . . Ruxton, MD *21204*

Price MR & MRS Willard L (Marsha E Crew)
Ash'65.IndSt'72.Ash'64.IndSt'72
  ☎ (812) 726-4627 . . RR 3, Box 70A, Vincennes, IN *47591*

Price MR & MRS William A (Rosalie Pettus)
B'hamS'35.Cy.Sar.Wt.Cw.Ala'31
  ☎ (205) 326-1041 . . 2831 Highland Av S, Apt 616, Birmingham,
AL *35205*

Price MR & MRS William R (Christine C Goodman) Rol'82.Geo'74 . . of
  ☎ (201) 612-0887 . . 57 N Hillside Place, Ridgewood, NJ *07450*
  ☎ (516) 288-6387 . . 52 Griffing Av, Westhampton Beach, NY *11978*

Prichett MR & MRS Wilson JR (Harriet F Vaughan) ☎ (215) 283-7381
Sg.Rv.Fw.P'43 . . . . Foulkeways, 5,
   MISS Frances F—at ☎ (619) 283-0368 Rowntree, 1120
5235—35 St, San Diego, CA 92116 . . . . Meetinghouse Rd,
   MISS Vaughan de B—at ☎ (215) 646-5908 Gwynedd, PA 19436
413 Marie Rd, Ambler, PA 19002 . . . .

Prichett MR & MRS William (du Pont—Caroline ☎ (410) 755-6880
MacL Johnstone) P'47.H'51 . . . . Great House Farm,
   MISS Allaire du Pont . . . . PO Box 403,
Chesapeake City,
MD 21915

Priddy MR & MRS Richard V (Finn—Cameron V Noble)
StLaw'76.JHop'80.Mv.Ncd.Clem'70.Ia'79
   ☎ (410) 828-6201 . . 6507 Darnall Rd, Ruxton, MD 21204

Prideaux-Brune MR & MRS Rowland D C of ☎ (415)474-5426
(Genevieve P McLaren) Pcu.Bur.Camb'50 . . . . . 1100 Union St,
   MISS Diana E . . . . San Francisco, CA
94109
☎ (408) 625-9756
PO Box 1761,
Pebble Beach, CA
93953

Priebe MR & MRS Frank A JR (Juliet L Kuehnle) On.Cnt.Nw'54
   ☎ (847) CE4-3217 . . 710 N Mayflower Rd, Lake Forest, IL 60045

Prien MR & MRS Henry I (Elizabeth A Peterson) Sfy.Cp.Cal'40 ⚓ . . of
   ☎ (415) 346-0725 . . 2275 Broadway St, San Francisco, CA 94115
''Casa Alvarado'' Punta Pescadero, Baja California Sur, Mexico

Priest MR H Samuel (Margaret B McDonald) SL'46.Ncd.
   ☎ (314) 361-1526 . . 5122 Westminster Place, St Louis, MO 63108

Priester DR & MRS William D (Cortesi—Smith— ☎ (212) 799-1923
Leslie Armstrong) Br'62.Cl'66.Un.Cly.Stan'70. 333 W 70 St,
Ia'77 . . . . New York, NY
     MISS Vanessa L Cortesi 10023
     MR S Scott Smith . . . .

Priestley MR & MRS William T 3d (Gina B Arsena)
Cwr'65.Kent'67.Cwr'65.Mich'69
   ☎ (847) 397-1984 . . 1 Pepperell on Asbury, Rolling Meadows, IL 60008

Prime MRS J Kerr (Jane L Kerr) . . . . ☎ (914) 764-0420
   MISS Eve D—Nu'89 . . . . 249 Stone Hill Rd,
   MISS Alexandra K—ColC'93 . . . . Pound Ridge, NY
   MR William Corry—at Ft Lewis Coll 10576

Prime MRS Johnston (Elizabeth B Johnston)
   ☎ (212) 861-1704 . . 136 E 76 St, New York, NY 10021

Primm MRS A Timon 3d (Nancy Russell) Cy . . . . . ☎ (314) 993-3541
   MISS Susan R—at Watertown, MA 02272 . . . . . 750 S Hanley Rd,
   MR Alexander T 4th—at ☎ (573) 341-2464 Apt 44, St Louis,
Rte 4, Box 23, Rolla, MO 65401 . . . . MO 63105

Prince MR & MRS Donough (Jeanne Lawson) V'39.Coa.H'31
   ☎ (904) 285-2696 . . 1000 Vicar's Landing Way, Apt B108,
Ponte Vedra Beach, FL 32082

Prince MR & MRS Frederick H (Diana A Cochrane) ☎ (202) 342-2026
Rcn.Rcch.Mt.Cas.B.Srb.Nrr.Sl.Cl'69 . . . . 2812 N St NW,
   MISS Daisy . . . . Washington, DC
   JUNIORS MR Octavius 20007

Prince MRS Frederick H 3d (J Fay de Danek d'Esse)
   ☎ (011-41-21) 107-10-06 . . ''Le Manoir'' 7 Abbesses, 1026 Echandens,
Vaud, Switzerland

Prince CAPT & MRS Howard R (Mary B Mackall) An.Ncd.USN'32
7105 River Crescent Dv, Annapolis, MD 21401

Prince MRS James (Monique James) . . . . 2101 Coldwater
   MISS Pamela . . . . Canyon,
Beverly Hills, CA
90210

Prince MR Patrick B Wood . . see E T Chewning JR

Prince MRS Peirce (Helen E A Peirce) BMr'42.Srb.Cs.
   ☎ (212) TE8-1307 . . 116 E 63 St, New York, NY 10021

Prince MR Scott C Wood . . see E T Chewning JR

Prince MR William N W—Rcn.Rc.Cho.Srb.Sr.Van'64
   ☎ (312) 787-2832 . . 303 W Wisconsin St, Chicago, IL 60614

Prince MR & MRS William Wood (de Ricou— ☎ (773) 348-2430
Eleanor Edwards) Rcn.Rc.Sr.Cas.Cho.On.Ln.K. 2430 N Lakeview
Ri.P'36 . . . . Av, Chicago, IL
   MR Edward A W—Rc.—at ☎ (312) 787-3200 60614
1425 N Dearborn St, Chicago, IL 60610 . . . . . .

Prindle MR Kirk M—Cal'84.Pac'88
2050 Keller Springs Rd, Apt 1516, Carrollton, TX 75006

Prindle MR & MRS Walter K (Noreen E Doyle) ☎ (214) 380-2903
Dth'57 . . . . 5610 Bent Trail,
   MISS Susan D . . . . Dallas, TX 75248

Pringle MR & MRS Ashmead F JR (Helen M Johansen)
SCar'74.Char'ton'27.H'29
   ☎ (803) 722-1984 . . 109 E Bay St, Charleston, SC 29401

Pringle MRS E Covington JR (Janet Walter)
   ☎ (916) 662-7700 . . 908 W Cross St, Woodland, CA 95695

Pringle MR & MRS Robert C (Margaret R Ely) ☎ (415) 323-6601
Ore'75.Stan'77.Myf.Stan'72.Nw'80 . . . . 4 Hesketh Dv,
   JUNIORS MISS Abigail E . . . . Menlo Park, CA
94025

Prioleau MR & MRS Charles H (Miriam W Payne)
Tex'82.Ht.W&L'82.Tex'87
   ☎ (713) 666-5762 . . 3514 Albans Blvd, Houston, TX 77005

Prioleau MR & MRS H Frost (Diane H Thys) ☎ (510) 547-5041
Ws'55.Ht.P'50.H'52 ⚓ . . . . 111 Woodland Way,
   MISS Michelle H—P'83—at ☎ (415) 771-3876 Piedmont, CA 94611
990 Bay St, Apt 604, San Francisco, CA 94109 .

Prioleau MASTER Lucas Daniel (Marc T R) . . . . Born at
Palo Alto, CA Jly 27'94

Prioleau MASTER Mack Frost (g—H Frost Prioleau) . . . . Born at
Oakland, CA Aug 12'94

Prioleau MR & MRS Marc T R (Sally J Sweetman)
Cal'80.TCU'89.Cal'81.H'86
   ☎ (415) 494-7577 . . 140 Iris Way, Palo Alto, CA 94303

Prioleau MR & MRS Robert M (Patricia C Green) ☎ (713) 975-7449
Sth'55.Ht.P'55.H'57 . . . . 6011 Deerwood Rd,
   MISS Caroline E—David'93 . . . . Houston, TX 77057

Prioleau MR & MRS Robert P (A Rachel Matthews)
Van'89.GaTech'93.Ht.Van'87.Tex'92
   ☎ (404) 815-0886 . . 760 Penn Av NE, Atlanta, GA 30308

Prioleau MR & MRS William F JR (Paul—Roberta M Maybank)
Rdc'46.Cit'46.SCar'49
   ☎ (803) 787-4556 . . 4210 Woodleigh Rd, Columbia, SC 29206

Prior MR & MRS Cornelius B JR (Sandra E Pierson)
Ws'62.Cl'77.HolyC'56.H'62 . . . . | ☎ (718) 768-0548
547—3 St,
MISS Sarah M . . . . | Brooklyn, NY
11215 . . MR absent

Priory MR & MRS Joseph D (Sheila A McNeil) | *see*
MmtMhn'69.Rcp.Geo'66.VillaN'69 . . . . | *Dilatory Domiciles*
MISS Jennifer K . . . . |
MISS Colleen B . . . . |
MISS Sheila D . . . . |

Pritchard MRS Anne L S (M Anne L Snyder) Cda.
☎ (610) 687-2112 . . St Davids Park 124A, 500 E Lancaster Av,
St Davids, PA 19087

Pritchard MR & MRS Donald B JR (Mary B Long)
Duke'71.Pa'76.Pa'73.Dick'76
204 Barrie Rd, Narberth, PA 19072

Pritchard MR & MRS William S JR (Ann B Adams)
Ala'49.Cy.Ala'47.Ala'50
☎ (205) 967-3588 . . 303 Easton Circle, Lockerbie, Birmingham,
AL 35223

Prochnow MR & MRS Herbert V JR (Lucia Boyden)
BMr'56.Cho.On.Hn.H'53 . . . . | ☎ (847) 234-8785
949 Woodbine
MISS Laura S—Duke'93 . . . . | Place, Lake Forest,
MR Thomas H—H'89—at ☎ (212) 675-9453 | IL 60045
22 W 15 St, Apt 12D, New York, NY
10011-6845 . . . .

Prockop MR & MRS David J (Hope S Nichols) H'90.Wms'87.Tufts'93 . . of
☎ (860) 651-4336 . . Westminster School, 995 Hopmeadow St,
Simsbury, CT 06070
☎ (802) 365-9105 . . River Rd, Box 448, Newfane, VT 05345

Proctor MR & MRS Kenneth C (Baker—Margaret Leonard)
Swb'42.Mv.JHop'28.Md'32
☎ (410) 323-8081 . . 101 Cross Keys Rd, Apt B, Baltimore, MD 21210

Proctor MISS Mattina R—Chi.
☎ (207) 763-3683 . . "Stone Point" PO Box 339, Camden,
ME 04843-0339

Proctor MR & MRS Robert A 3d (Cynthia M Collin) B.Rr.Bgt.Louis'68
☎ (914) 234-3710 . . "Oak Hill" 701 S Bedford Rd, Bedford Corners,
NY 10549

Proctor MR & MRS Robert W (Monica U Sobek) Fur'82.Ty'81
☎ (860) 651-9738 . . 1 Cricket Lane, Simsbury, CT 06070

Proctor MR & MRS Schuyler J (Lorinda B Martel)
Conn'85.Mariet'79.SConn'83
☎ (203) 966-7302 . . 8 Nubel Lane, New Canaan, CT 06840

Proctor MR & MRS Waldron W (Helen J Kobbé) | ☎ (203) 966-0213
Y'44.Va'51 . . . . | 140 Carter St,
MISS Patricia W—Pace'92 . . . . | New Canaan, CT
06840-5007

Proctor MR & MRS William Ross JR (Mary Jane Keck)
Man'vl'61.Ford'69.Wk.
☎ (941) 472-8202 . . 820 Sand Dollar Dv, Sanibel Island, FL 33957

Proffitt MRS Claire B M (Claire J B Miller) Sth'63 . | ☎ (301) 299-3748
MR William B M—StLaw'92 . . . . | 12400 Piney Glen
Lane, Potomac, MD
20854

Proffitt MISS Ruth S—V'51.Cly.
☎ (212) 722-5377 . . 1021 Park Av, New York, NY 10028

Prosser MRS Camilla S (Camilla H Spalding) . . . . . | ☎ (303) 368-8808
MISS Marian H—at ☎ (970) 925-3375 | 1590 S Syracuse St,
PO Box 10513, Aspen, CO 81612 . . . . | Denver, CO 80231
MR John A 3d—at ☎ (505) 438-0063 . . Rte 10,
Box 88A, Santa Fe, NM 87501 . . . . |
MR Andrew B—NCol'83.Drake'86—at
☎ (319) 752-3201 . . 9303 Gaslight Dv,
Burlington, IA 52601 . . . . |

Prosser MR & MRS Robert L (Stanley—Judith L
McKinlay) Wheat'62.Ny.Why.Cl'53 . . . . | ☎ (561) 234-4869
MISS Lindsay B Stanley . . . . | 205 Sago Palm Rd,
MR Edwin J C Stanley . . . . | John's Island,
Vero Beach, FL
32963

Prout DR Curtis—Tv.H'37.H'41
☎ (508) 526-1271 . . 115 School St, Manchester, MA 01944

Prout MRS Francis J (Rackus—Tomiyo Tomita) . . . | ☎ (212) 289-0391
MISS Catharine B—AmU'92 . . . . | 17 E 96 St,
REV Thomas S—Ham'80—at ☎ (212) 288-6200 | New York, NY
53 E 83 St, New York, NY 10028 . . . . | 10128

Prout MR & MRS John R (Weldon—Judith de Barany)
Ws'77.H'80.Cly.H'75 . . of
☎ (011-33-1) 47-42-22-69 . . 52 rue du Faubourg St Honore,
75008 Paris, France
☎ (011-33) 37-47-20-99 . . 2 rue des Ormes, Vilsix, 28800
Pré-St-Evroult, France

Prout MR & MRS William W (Betts—Evelyn Ohman) Sth'41.H'36
☎ (561) 546-5064 . . 34 N Beach Rd, Hobe Sound, FL 33455

Prouty MR & MRS Charles N 3d (Wright—Thorne—Helen P Ellis) Au.H'31
☎ (203) 488-3025 . . 88 Notch Hill Rd, Apt 123, North Branford,
CT 06471

Prouty MISS Honor H—Pitzer'93
☎ (310) 278-2324 . . 445 N Doheny Rd, Apt B, Beverly Hills,
CA 90210-2642

Prouty MR Nicholas A—B.Pitzer'92
☎ (212) 987-9829 . . 55 E 93 St, Apt 2E, New York, NY 10128

Prouty MR & MRS Norman R JR (Chapin—Allison L | of 5 Mountain Wood
Simmons) B'gton'68.Rcn.B.Fic.Cly.Y'61 . . . . . . | Dv, Greenwich, CT
MR Brooks S—Snc.—at Columbia . . . . | 06830
☎ (212) 861-3270
120 E 80 St,
New York, NY
10021

Prouty MR & MRS Richard (Ann Jenkins) Cy.H.'35
☎ (508) 799-0798 . . 770 Salisbury St, TH-202, Worcester,
MA 01609

Prouvost MR & MRS Amédée S (Clare H Cushman)
Mid'84.Paris'94.Paris'82.Pa'90 . . of
☎ (301) 654-4611 . . 3615 Spring St, Chevy Chase, MD 20815
☎ (508) 790-7863 . . "Halftide Rock" 875 Great Island Rd,
West Yarmouth, MA 02673

Prowell MRS Leonora P (Meusnier—Leonora P Prowell) Cly.
☎ (860) 434-9512 . . "Cove House" 33 Joshuatown Rd, Lyme,
CT 06371

Pruden MR & MRS Terry A (Nancy Paris) | 2402 Reba Dv,
Ga'68.TCU'67.Nw'70 . . . . | Houston, TX 77019
MISS Tully K—at Dartmouth . . . . |
JUNIORS MR Benjamin P . . . . |

Prugh MR & MRS Clayton A (Eleanor M H Hately)
Pitzer'78.Rc.K.Mto.Cly.H.'76.Va'81
☎ (516) 922-2849 . . 367 Split Rock Rd, Syosset, NY *11791*

Pruyn MRS John A (Hellyer—La Verne Louer) Chr.Mto.Cs.Wa.Ncd.
☎ (212) 755-9029 . . 200 E 66 St, New York, NY *10021*

Pryal MR & MRS Mark A (Andrea H Price) Char'ton'93.Ct.Bay'89
☎ (301) 657-2781 . . 5301 Westbard Circle, Apt 223, Bethesda, MD *20816*

Pryce-Jones MR Alan—C.Srb.K.Nrr.Ox'27
46 John St, Newport, RI *02840*

Pryor MR & MRS Edward R (Beverly B Jones) Va'56
☎ (860) 536-9746 . . 6 Hickory Ledge, Mason's Island, Mystic, CT *06355*

Pryor MRS Luanne W (Van Norden—Luanne R Williamson)
CalSt'71.H'84.Cly.H.
☎ (617) 247-2366 . . 181 Marlborough St, Boston, MA *02116*

Pryor MR & MRS William B (Beverly J Holland) Coa.Cw.Snc.Ht.Wt.
☎ (201) 228-2154 . . 30 Francis Place, Caldwell, NJ *07006*

Pryor MR William Y—Cw.Snc.StA.Rv.Wt.Sar.Ne.
Coa.Ht.Cspa.Pn.Cl'31.Nu'34 . . . . | ☎ (201) 226-2254
MISS Ann L—Ht.Dar.—at ☎ (201) 697-0408 | 64 Fellswood Dv,
73 Sugar Maple Rd, Newfoundland, NJ *07435* . | Essex Fells, NJ *07021*

Psoroyannis MISS Ioanna R . . see MRS P A Taylor

Puckett MR & MRS Thomas D (Mary A Johndroe) | ☎ (713) 952-2883
TCU'69.TCU'69.GeoW'72.Paris'74 . . . . | 9539 Highmeadow
MISS Eve E . . . . | Dv, Houston, TX *77063*
JUNIORS MR James C |

Pugh MRS Charlotte R (Charlotte C Reed) . . . . | ☎ (513) 321-1296
MR R Reed—at ☎ (617) 431-9593 | 3428 Traskwood
6 Summit Rd, Wellesley, MA *02181* . . . . | Lane, Cincinnati, OH *45208*

Pugh MR & MRS Douglas B (Margaret E Kaufman) OreSt'72.OreSt'79
4005 Tempest Dv, Lake Oswego, OR *97035-1930*

Pugh MISS (DR) Elizabeth W (Schwarckoff—Elizabeth W Pugh)
Rens'80.Tul'89.Tul'93
☎ (410) 666-5276 . . 10702 Cardington Way, Apt 202, Cockeysville, MD *21030*

Pugh MR & MRS William W (Elizabeth J Ritter) Sth'41.Mit'44
☎ (513) 533-4476 . . 3509 Forestoak Court, Cincinnati, OH *45208*

Pujol MR & MRS Raoul H (Evgenia Gagarin) Ri.VillaN'58.Cl'69 . . of
☎ (212) 688-5766 . . 2 Sutton Place S, New York, NY *10022*
☎ (011-33-1) 40-50-37-88 . . 7 rue le Tasse, 75116 Paris, France
Lugar do Monte Tapado, Balazar, 4490 Póvoa de Varzim, Portugal

Pulitzer MR & MRS Frederick D (Adele G Millar) HolyC'74.NH'77
☎ (603) 659-8183 . . 5 Toon Lane, Lee, NH *03824*

Pulitzer MRS Joseph JR (Emily S Rauh) Nd.Cy.Rc.
☎ (314) 361-3212 . . 4903 Pershing Place, St Louis, MO *63108*

Pulitzer MR & MRS Joseph 4th (Delano—Flynn— | ☎ (314) 533-8363
Jennifer A Williams) Wash'73.Rc.Nd.H'72 . . . . | 4456 Maryland Av,
MISS Elkhanah—at Berkeley, CA . . . . | St Louis, MO *63108*
MISS Bianca—at Santa Cruz, CA . . . . |
  MISS Abigail W Flynn . . . . |

Pulitzer MR & MRS Michael E (Eisenbeis—J Cecille | ☎ (314) 863-5774
Stell) Cy.H'51 . . . . | 625 S Skinker Blvd,
MR M Culver Eisenbeis . . . . | St Louis, MO *63105*
MR William H S Eisenbeis . . . . |
MISS Christina H Eisenbeis (Zane—Christina H Eisenbeis) . . |

Pulleyn MRS Robert F (Peggy Wattles)
☎ (908) 439-2114 . . PO Box 87, Oldwick, NJ *08858*

Pulling MR Edward L—P'89
☎ (011-852) 2849-7451 . . 3-5 Plunketts Rd, Modreenagh Apt 3A, The Peak, Hong Kong

Pulling MRS S Sonne (Sheila B A Sonne) | of ☎ (212)348-9110
V'87.Chr.Cly.Ncd. | 8 E 96 St, PH,
MISS Diana D—CtCol'95 . . . . | New York, NY *10128-0706*
JUNIORS MR Christopher C—at Phillips Andover . | ☎ (516) 537-5890
 | ''Higgledy''
 | Box 456,
 | Bridgehampton, NY *11932*

Pulling MR & MRS Thomas L (Odelfelt—Youngman | of ☎ (516)922-6267
—Eileen Kingsbury-Smith) Pr.Mto.C.Plg.StJ. | ''Woodhouse''
P'61 . . . . | 34 Yellowcote Rd,
  MISS Helen I Youngman—P'93—at | Oyster Bay, NY *11771*
  2378 Vallejo St, San Francisco, CA *94123* . . . | ☎ (305) 891-9570
 | 11111 Biscayne
 | Blvd, Miami, FL *33161*

Pulling MISS Victoria S (Thomas L) . . . . Married at
Cold Spring Harbor, NY
Allen MR Christopher J L (Jon S L) . . . . Jun 22'96

Pulling MISS Wendy—P'85.Stan'90 . . see R B Semple JR

Pullman MR & MRS Frederick Childs (Alice E Brown) Cho.Wms'50
☎ (401) 635-2209 . . 31 Patten Dv, Little Compton, RI *02837*

Pulsifer MR & MRS Nathaniel (F Holliday Miller) | ☎ (508) 356-3655
BMr'59.Unn.My.Cc.U'59 . . . . | 11 Waldingfield Rd,
MISS Alicia H—ColC'93—at 143 Spurwink Rd, | Ipswich, MA *01938*
Scarborough, ME *04074* . . . . |
MR Nathaniel M—ColC'96 . . . . |

Pulsifer MR & MRS Richard S (Lynn C Outhwaite) | ☎ (207) 725-5457
Unn.Bow'62 . . . . | ''Woodmere''
MISS Katherine O—at U of NMex | 3045 Mere Point Rd,
MR Leonard Hale—at Brown | Brunswick, ME *04011*
JUNIORS MR Richard T S—at
North Yarmouth Acad . . . . |

Pulsifer MR & MRS Stephen Mackintosh (Mary C | ☎ (914) 232-8830
Hanna) Ariz'68.Un.S.Cly.Bow'68.Nu'79 . . . . . . | Upper Hook Rd,
MISS Mary C R—at Kent . . . . | Katonah, NY *10536*
MR William H—at U of Vt . . . . |

Pulver MR & MRS George M (Penelope A Spencer) StAndr'63.Cathdel'Ouest'65.Cvc.GeoW'50. H'52 ⚓ . . . . MISS Caroline—at Leicester U . . . . of ☎ (011-44-1398) 361-476 Huntsham House, Huntsham, nr Tiverton, Devon EX16 7NA, England ☎ (011-44-171) 828-6587 68 Marsham Court, Marsham St, London SW1, England

Pumphrey MR & MRS Edward A 3d (Elisabeth A A Ehrhorn) Cda.Ithaca'76 537 Aberdeen Rd, Frankfort, IL *60423*

Punnett MISS Sarah S ☎ (508) 228-7833 . . 5 Equator Dv, Nantucket, MA *02554*

Punnett MRS William M (Alexandra S Loder) ☎ (508) 228-2425 . . ''Enterprise'' 11 Old North Wharf, Nantucket, MA *02554*

Purdon MR & MRS Eric StC (Godfrey—Cheryl A Tillotson) WashColl'66 . . . . JUNIORS MR Edward S . . . . JUNIORS MISS Kristin D Godfrey . . . . JUNIORS MISS Cori T Godfrey . . . . JUNIORS MR Mark A Godfrey . . . . ☎ (410) 867-4822 ''Beechwood'' 459 Harwood Rd, Harwood, MD *20776*

Purdon MR & MRS Henry P (Kathleen Shine) SanDiegoSt'77.Sdy.Aub'67 ⚓ ☎ (619) 222-0330 . . 1025 Albion St, San Diego, CA *92106*

Purdy MR Christopher H—Carl'88.Cr'92 ☎ (212) 662-0976 . . 285 Riverside Dv, Apt 2A, New York, NY *10025*

Purdy MR & MRS Peter J (Susan S Fisher) Cal'59.Cl'78.Cl'84.Minn'58.Cal'65.Mich'73 . . . MISS Mary S—Ober'92—at ☎ (212) 662-2737 310 Riverside Dv, New York, NY *10025* . . . . . . ☎ (212) 662-0976 285 Riverside Dv, New York, NY *10025*

Purdy MR & MRS Richard W (Nancy W Stevens) CtCol'57.Cy.Ty'57 ☎ (508) 999-3051 . . 14 Chestnut St, South Dartmouth, MA *02748*

Purinton MR & MRS Harold G (Karr—Jane M C Iglehart) Cda. . . . . MISS Mary I . . . . ☎ (410) 823-5916 1501 W Joppa Rd, Towson, MD *21204*

Purnell MRS Bundy Marshall (Julia Bundy Marshall) ☎ (212) 861-3840 . . 308 E 79 St, New York, NY *10021*

Purnell MR & MRS John Hurst JR (Gummey—Yerkes—Eleanor Clark) Md.Gv.Ncd.P'41 ☎ (410) 778-0313 . . ''Buttonwood'' 25860 John Hanson Rd, Chestertown, MD *21620-9715*

Purnell MR & MRS John Hurst 3d (M Claire McDonnell) Swb'81.Md.Gv.Rens'80 ☎ (410) 267-9433 . . 4 Thompson St, Annapolis, MD *21401*

Purnell MISS Marguerite W—P'82.Cly.Fic. ☎ (860) 868-6624 . . 5 Old Litchfield Rd, Washington, CT *06793*

Purnell MR & MRS Richard I (Marguerite W Hillman) B.Ri.Pr.Fic.Mb.Rr.Cly.P'40 . . of ☎ (516) 671-7128 . . Piping Rock Rd, Locust Valley, NY *11560* ☎ (212) TR9-3900 . . 1 E 66 St, New York, NY *10021*

Purser MR & MRS Carr R JR (Susan W Hunter) Pa'66 . . . . MR Carr R 3d . . . . ☎ (941) 379-6496 4511 Windsor Park, Sarasota, FL *34235*

Purtell MR & MRS Edward A JR (Harriet R McMahon) Wis'84.Wis'55 . . . . MISS Ellen C . . . . MR Edward A 3d . . . . ☎ (414) 352-4148 7775 N River Rd, Milwaukee, WI *53217*

Purves MR & MRS Alexander (Drika N Agnew) Y'58 ☎ (203) 777-3427 . . 18 Lincoln St, New Haven, CT *06511-6212*

Purves MRS Dale (Louise E Allen) ☎ (610) 896-9346 . . The Quadrangle, Elm 3309, 3300 Darby Rd, Haverford, PA *19041*

Purves MRS John C (Mary Temple Bradley) . . . . Died at Lexington, MA Jly 18'96

Purviance MRS Akeroyd (Edith Akeroyd) Sg. ☎ (610) 645-8842 . . 1400 Waverly Rd, Apt 116, Gladwyne, PA *19035*

Purviance MR & MRS James A (Virginia Pepper) P'52 ☎ (401) 847-7586 . . 47 Kane Av, Middletown, RI *02842*

Purvis MR & MRS J Oliver JR (Clover Du Val) StJ'34 ☎ (410) 832-1736 . . Pickensville Apt 1422, 615 Chestnut Av, Towson, MD *21204*

Purvis MR & MRS Terry L (Elizabeth L Webster) Roan'69 . . . . JUNIORS MISS Katharine C . . . . JUNIORS MISS Elizabeth D . . . . ☎ (410) 583-8232 7319 Yorktowne Dv, Baltimore, MD *21204*

Putnam MRS Alfred W (Anne Beale) Au.Ssk.Rc.Ph.Rb.Sg.Pe.Sa.Ac.Cc.Cw.H. MISS Anne L—Pa'71—at ☎ (215) 836-7133 717 Wyndmoor Av, Wyndmoor, PA *19038* . . . . ☎ (215) CH7-6166 8500 Seminole Av, Philadelphia, PA *19118*

Putnam MR & MRS Alfred W JR (Kathleen A Gordon) Rdc'73.Pa'76.Au.Ph.Me.Ac.H'73. Ox'75.Pa'78 . . . . JUNIORS MISS Clare T . . . . ☎ (610) MI9-7166 124 Bleddyn Rd, Ardmore, PA *19003*

Putnam MR & MRS Augustus L (Schmitz—Barbara Blake) Wash'60.Y'61.H'49.Tufts'55 ☎ (212) 289-2406 . . 1261 Madison Av, New York, NY *10128*

Putnam MR & MRS Bruce M (Titus—Elizabeth S Cushman) V'55.Cda.Stan'52.Stan'61.H'61 . . of ☎ (802) 442-4004 . . Manatuck Farm, RR 1, Box 354, Shaftsbury, VT *05262* ☎ (603) 763-2775 . . PO Box 628, New London, NH *03257*

Putnam MR & MRS Carleton (Auchincloss—Esther McK Willcox) Cvc.Cos.Cly.P'24.Cl'32 ☎ (804) 295-0885 . . 4 Brook Hill, Farmington, Charlottesville, VA *22901*

Putnam MISS Carley P . . see MRS J M P Wilson

Putnam MR & MRS Charles S (Nancy P King) H'43 ☎ (912) 598-8480 . . 14 Marsh Tower Lane, Savannah, GA *31411*

Putnam MR & MRS David E (Charles S) . . . . Married at Chevy Chase, MD McLane MRS Shirley J (Pfeifer—Shirley J McLane) . . . . Jun 15'96

Putnam MR & MRS David E (Pfeifer—Shirley J McLane) Sth'78.Wes'66.Bost'69 ☎ (301) 656-2127 . . 7209 Pomander Lane, Chevy Chase, MD *20815*

Putnam MR & MRS Frederic P (Penny C Johnson) H'69.Cl'72 ☎ (203) 869-5125 . . 477 Field Point Rd, Greenwich, CT *06830*

Putnam MR & MRS George (Boardman—Nancy Burrows) Lasell'52.Myc.Nf.Ec.Sm.H'49 . . . . . . MISS Susan W—HRdc'79.H'92 . . . . ☎ (508) 526-1891 ''Ausolus'' 36 Proctor St, Manchester, MA *01944*

Putnam MR George 3d—Ec.Myc.Nf.Rcp.Sm.H'73
☎ (508) 526-4404 . . 52 Proctor St, Manchester, MA *01944*

Putnam MR & MRS George E (Elizabeth St Goar) My.Cw.Plg.H'43
☎ (508) 468-2336 . . 78 Gardner St, PO Box 89, Hamilton, MA *01936*

Putnam MRS Gerald R (Nancy A Darsie) Au. . . . . . | of ☎ (603)526-4700
MR Gerald R JR—Box 1382, New London, NH | 88 Knights Hill Rd,
03257 . . . . | PO Box 1088,
MR John D—at Eldora Star Rte, Nederland, CO | New London, NH
80466 . . . . | *03257*
 | ☎ (518) 576-4445
 | "Hielan Home"
 | Ausable Club,
 | St Huberts, NY
 | *12943*

Putnam MRS Harrington (Violeta Maldonado)
☎ (914) 266-3014 . . "Woodsedge" Meadowbrook Lane, RR 1,
Box 171B, Staatsburg, NY *12580*

Putnam MRS Harrington (Wilkins—Gail M Brinn)
M'dith'61.NYSID'79.Pars'80 . . of
☎ (704) 376-1177 . . 717 Queens Rd, Charlotte, NC *28207*
30 Beach Rd S, Figure 8 Island, Wilmington, NC *28405*

Putnam MR & MRS Haven (Holmes—Marguerite | ☎ (423) 639-3487
Ballantine) Ncd.Dar. . . . . | "Villa Turicum"
MR David B—at ☎ (770) 435-8129 | E Allen's Bridge
2127A Lake Park Dv, Smyrna, GA *30080* . . . . . | Rd, PO Box 968,
 | Greeneville, TN
 | *37744*

Putnam MR & MRS Hugh T (Anne R Gallagher) V'39.H'38
☎ (802) 457-2765 . . PO Box 175, South Woodstock, VT *05071*

Putnam MR & MRS Hugh T JR (Heather A | ☎ (617) 696-2885
McCusker) Hlns'65.H'63.Syr'65 . . . . | 242 Highland St,
MISS Robin A—at U of Ariz . . . . | Milton, MA *02186*
MR Hugh T 3d—at Geo Mason U . . . . |

Putnam MR James E . . see MRS J M P Wilson

Putnam MR James W W—RochTech'89
☎ (703) 830-6832 . . 14410 Newton Patent Court, Apt 3F, Centreville,
VA *20120*

Putnam MR & MRS John G JR (Thekla W Polley)
Wh'lck'53.St.Ts.Buf.Myf.Duke'51.Buf'57
☎ (716) 874-5485 . . 332 Middlesex Rd, Buffalo, NY *14216-3139*

Putnam MR & MRS John K (Lynch—Noble—Mary L Wasem) H'50
☎ (602) 922-7748 . . 7345 E Solano Dv, Scottsdale, AZ *85250*

Putnam MRS Lyonel H (Julia T Doolittle) Ncd.
☎ (860) 521-8389 . . 1044 Farmington Av, West Hartford, CT *06107*

Putnam DR Michael C J—H'54
Brown University, Providence, RI *02912*

Putnam MISS Rebecca D—PineM'77.Ncd.
☎ (508) 744-6343 . . 27 Broad St, Salem, MA *01970*

Putnam DR & MRS Richard C (Tase—Jean E | ☎ (610) 687-1489
Sheperd) Sth'45.Gm.Ph.Me.Ac.H.'47.Temp'51 . | 787 Valley Forge
MISS Eliza R—Ant'79—at Stockholm, Sweden . | Rd, Devon, PA
MISS Nancy W—at Tallahassee, FL . . . . | *19333*
MISS Meredith H—OWes'85—at Medfield, MA |
02052 . . . . |

Putnam DR Robert M—Myf.Cw.Y'30.H.'33.McG'44
North Hill I307, 865 Central Av, Needham, MA *02192-1342*

Putnam MR & MRS Sumner C (Jane H Bishop) | ☎ (908) 719-2757
Eyc.Eh.H'71.Cl'73 . . . . | PO Box 105,
MR Sumner C JR . . . . | 1741 Lamington Rd,
JUNIORS MISS Katherine P . . . . | Bedminster, NJ
JUNIORS MR Nicholas B . . . . | *07921*

Putnam MR & MRS Timothy (Nancy C Lionberger) Bvl.H'36
☎ (508) 748-0445 . . 562 Point Rd, Marion, MA *02738*

Putnam MR William L—Eyc.H'45
1400 W Mars Hill Rd, Flagstaff, AZ *86001*

Putnam-Farr MISS Eleanor L . . see T G Delaney

Putney MR & MRS Lacey E JR (Laura M Mason) Hlns'81.Rich'78
☎ (757) 496-9328 . . 1729 Cooper Rd, Virginia Beach, VA *23454*

Pyle MRS Charles McA JR (Margot H Copeland) | ☎ (617) 326-1291
Sth'56.Sbc.Cy.My. . . . . | 53 Stoney Lea Rd,
MR Stuart H . . . . | Dedham, MA *02026*
MR Russell T—P'91—at ☎ (617) 859-0952 |
76 Commonwealth Av, Apt 6, Boston, MA *02116* |

Pyle MR & MRS Charles McA 3d (Sarah Ford Hibbard)
Skd'77.Cyb.Myf.LakeF'74.Bentley'88
☎ (603) 547-3934 . . New Boston Rd, Francestown, NH *03043*

Pyle MR & MRS James Tolman (Ann Finlay) P.'35 . . of
☎ (516) 922-5321 . . "Carriage House" 52 Sandy Hill Rd, Oyster Bay,
NY *11771*
☎ (207) 276-3794 . . "Over Sea" Seal Harbor, ME *04675*

Pyle MRS John H (Fairman—Smith—J Carolyn Ely) On.Vh.
☎ (619) 756-2903 . . PO Box 673, 6748 Las Colinas, Rancho Santa Fe,
CA *92067*

Pyle MR & MRS Mark C (Melanie J McCall) Pc.Dick'76
8708 Winthrop Dv, Alexandria, VA *22308*

Pyle MR & MRS Robert M JR (C Page Neville) | ☎ (201) 376-5632
Sth'61.Rcn.Plg.Wms'60.Va'63 . . . . | 16 Delwick Lane,
MISS Cynthia N—Wms'93 . . . . | Short Hills, NJ
☎ (212) 463-0053 . . 120 W 23 St, Apt 2A, | *07078*
New York, NY *10011* . . . . |
MISS Laura C—Wes'95 . . . . |

Pyle MR & MRS Robert N (Crosier—Claire Thoron) | ☎ (202) 338-9039
B'gton'65.Ct.Dick'48 . . . . | 2613 Dumbarton St
MR Louis M Crosier—Dth'87 . . . . | NW, Washington,
 | DC *20007*

Pynchon MISS Patricia—Cs.
☎ (212) 737-0209 . . 737 Park Av, New York, NY *10021*

Pyne MR & MRS Benjamin N (Janet E Auchincloss) Geo'82.P'81
☎ (212) 595-8333 . . 321 W 78 St, New York, NY *10024*

Pyne MR & MRS Eben W (Beebe—Gray—Nancy Maguire)
Rc.Pr.Ln.Ri.Ng.Mb.Plg.Lm.Cly.P'39 . . of
☎ (516) 333-2084 . . PO Box 195, 134 Willets Rd, Old Westbury,
NY *11568*
☎ (212) 688-1978 . . 200 E 66 St, New York, NY *10021*
☎ (561) 546-2891 . . 231 S Beach St, Hobe Sound, FL *33455*

Pyne MRS Grafton H JR (Mary W Van Pelt) Cly.
☎ (212) 288-3162 . . 220 E 67 St, New York, NY *10021*

Pyne MRS H Rivington JR (Lydia M Fulweiler) . . of
☎ (242) 333-2158 . . "Dugdale" Harbour Island, Bahamas
☎ (207) 529-5564 . . "Pine Island" Box 200, Medomak, ME *04551*

Pyne MR & MRS John S (Ann Wilkinson Sherrill) | of ☎ (212)751-9650
SL'73.Rc.Ln.Ng.Bcs.StA.Cly.NCar'69 . . . . | 580 Park Av,
JUNIORS MISS Elizabeth S . . . . | New York, NY
JUNIORS MR John S JR . . . . | *10021*
    | ☎ (516) 283-8971
    | 449 Hill St,
    | Southampton, NY
    | *11968*

Pyne MR & MRS M Taylor (Shyamoli Sen-Gupta) Br'70.Rc.DU'73
☎ (212) 996-4005 . . 1150 Park Av, New York, NY *10128*

Pyne MR & MRS Percy R 3d (Evelyn Sloane) Bnd'47.Ri.StA.Cda.P'37
☎ (908) 234-0275 . . Vanishing Brook Farm, PO Box 55, Far Hills,
NJ *07931-0055*

Pyne MR & MRS Percy R 4th (Alison H Warner) | of ☎ (203)966-2280
Ln.StA.DU'70.Cl'73 . . . . | 96 Lambert Rd,
MISS Amalia S—at Vanderbilt . . . . | New Canaan, CT
JUNIORS MR Rawleigh W . . . . | *06840*
    | ☎ (212) 223-2929
    | 424 E 52 St,
    | New York, NY
    | *10022*

Pyne MR & MRS Robert W (Lisa A Emmons) Va'75.Ln.Pn.P'75.Cl'80
☎ (203) 869-9110 . . 77 Park Av, Greenwich, CT *06830*

Pyne MR & MRS Russell B (Helen D Cooke) Mid'78.Ln.P'77.Stan'81
☎ (415) 326-4913 . . 69 Stern Lane, Atherton, CA *94027*

Pyne MR Schuyler N (Jane L Martin) Ny.Cc.Ds.Ht.Ncd.
☎ (313) 741-1322 . . 1200 Earhart Rd, Ann Arbor, MI *48105*

Pyott MR & MRS Albert E (Elizabeth S Thorne) | ☎ (847) 446-2052
Mund'88.Ih.Fy.Cr'53 . . . . | 666 Spruce St,
MISS Sheila S—Sth'85—at ☎ (617) 864-6959 | Winnetka, IL *60093*
19 Lancaster St, Cambridge, MA *02140* . . . . |
MISS Marianne S—Presc'92 . . . . |

Pyott MR Albert R (Albert E) . . . . Married at Agadir, Morocco
Mouali MISS Khadija (Ahmed) . . . . May 20'95

Q

Quarré MRS Harriet M (Harriet W Meyer) Fr.
☎ (415) 929-9007 . . 2307 Scott St, San Francisco, CA *94115*

Quarton MISS Anne K . . see R H Miller

Quarton JUNIORS MR Robert H JR . . see R H Miller

Quasha MR & MRS Alan G (Diana V Ronan) Rc.Un.Ck.Cly.H'72.H'76
☎ (212) 517-6597 . . 720 Park Av, New York, NY *10021*

Quasha MISS Jennifer C . . see J R French

Quayle MR & MRS J Danforth (Marilyn Tucker) | 11711 N
DeP'69.Ind'74 . . . . | Pennsylvania St,
MISS Mary Corinne . . . . | Carmel, IN
MR Tucker D . . . . | *46032-4559*
MR Benjamin E . . . . |

Queen MR & MRS John R (Patricia F Earl) | ☎ (415) 851-7985
Col'62.StMarys'61 . . . . | 810 Los Trancos Rd,
MR John R 3d—Purd'89 . . . . | Portola Valley, CA
MR Christopher P—SanDiegoSt'92 . . . . | *94028*

Quick MR William Jay
☎ (941) 924-2906 . . 3837 Torrey Pines Blvd, Sarasota, FL *34238*

Quillen MR & MRS Cecil D 3d (Mary S Humes) H'85.B.Plg.H.'85.Va'88
☎ (212) 987-1364 . . 9 E 96 St, Apt 5A, New York, NY *10128*

Quillen MRS Jacqueline L (Elizabeth Jacqueline | ☎ (202) 333-2383
Loomis) Rdc'64.Sl.Cly.Mds. . . . . | 3507 R St NW,
MR Whitney S—Mds.—at 1080 Madison Av, | Washington, DC
New York, NY *10028* . . . . | *20007*
MR Barton H . . . . |

Quillen MR & MRS Parker L (Bronwyn T Maloney) V'86.Un.Mds.Nu'87
☎ (212) 650-9833 . . .200 E 74 St, New York, NY *10021*

Quillman MRS D Scott (Diane Scott Darby) Ac.Ncd.Myf.
☎ (610) 827-7657 . . ''Deerbrook'' Birchrunville, PA *19421*

Quillman MR & MRS R Scott (Meredith J Borst)
Swb'78.Myf.Rv.Dar.Merc'76
☎ (610) 374-9014 . . 1400 Dauphin Av, Wyomissing, PA *19610*

Quillman MR Richard E—Pkg.Rv.Leh'52
☎ (610) 466-7453 . . 210 Buck Run Rd, East Fallowfield, PA *19320*

Quinby MR & MRS Jonathan S (Maria K Norrman) Uppsala'86.P'77.Cal'82
☎ (415) 851-1100 . . 308 Glenwood Av, Woodside, CA *94062*

Quinby DR & MRS William C (Susan Whiteley) H'36
☎ (617) 333-0328 . . 45 Brush Hill Lane, Milton, MA *02186-1303*

Quinlan MISS Kimberley L . . see P A Bakker

Quinley MR E Wayne—Sar . . .see MRS H L Smith JR

Quinn MRS Arthur H JR (Constance C Jones) BMr'27
☎ (610) 353-3973 . . Dunwoody Village E210, 3500 West Chester Pike,
Newtown Square, PA *19073*

Quinn MR & MRS Bruce M (Carolyn G Lewis)
Pa'79.Pa'85.Bgt.Ncd.Myf.Geo'76.Pa'81
☎ (914) 234-3230 . . Pea Pond Rd, Bedford, NY *10506*

Quinn MISS Demarest L . . see MRS T C Lloyd

Quinn MR & MRS E Frederick (Charlotte A Smith) | 5702 Kirkside Dv,
BMr'56.Cal'64.Cal'67.Cos.Alleg'57.Cal'66. | Chevy Chase, MD
Cal'67.Cal'70 . . . . | *20815*
MISS Alison M—Sth'93—at 114 W 16 St, |
New York, NY *10011* |
MR Christopher E V—at 9042 N Swan Circle, |
Brentwood, MO *63144* . . . . |

Quinn MR & MRS J Eugene (Trevor—I Marguerite | ☎ (202) 337-8196
Slocum) Srb.Cly.Sl.Cda.Prov'61 . . . . | 3664 Winfield Lane
MISS Evelyn J B Trevor—at Harvard Grad . . | NW, Washington,
MISS Sophia A B Trevor—at New York, NY . | DC *20007*
MISS Irene S Trevor—at Brown . . . . |

Quinn MR James P . . see MRS T C Lloyd

Quinn MR & MRS John J (Joan Agajanian) SCal'58.SCal'54 . . of
☎ (310) 274-4938 . . 621 N Alta Dv, Beverly Hills, CA *90210*
☎ (212) 744-7538 . . 311 E 71 St, Apt 5C, New York, NY *10021*

Quinn MISS Tara E—Col'95
☎ (212) 410-1406 . . 120 E 88 St, Apt 1R, New York, NY *10128*

Quintal MR & MRS Richard M (Catherine B Wriston) | ☎ (203) 655-1512
Finch'69.Eyc.Y'67.Va'70 . . . . | 3 Roland Dv,
JUNIORS MR Christopher W . . . . | Darien, CT *06820*

Quintal MRS Theodore G (Muriel F Smith) Dar.
☎ (914) 921-9001 . . The Osborn, 101 Theall Rd, Rye, NY *10580-1406*

Quintana MR & MRS Nicolas I (Diane N Norfleet) Wash'77.Wash'76
☎ (011-65) 462-0778 . . 27 Sian Tuan Av, Singapore 588301

Quist MR & MRS Gunnar H (Keen—Jeanne L Schloesser) . . . . ☎ (610) MI9-7649
20 Coopertown Rd,
   MISS Kristen W Keen . . . . Haverford, PA
19041

Quist MR & MRS Robert L (Leslie P Madeira) ☎ (415) 851-7572
Cal'75.Bhm.Pcu.Cal'75 . . . . 219 Albion Av,
JUNIORS MISS Lauren S . . . . Woodside, CA
JUNIORS MR William G *94062*

R

Raab MR & MRS Henry R (Deborah Wylie Gibson)
Nu'73.Ac.Cly.Ncd.Muhl'68
  ☎ (610) 439-0977 . . 42 N West St, Allentown, PA *18102*
Rabbe MR & MRS George W (Theodora V Aspegren) Wheat'74.Cly.SCar'71
  ☎ (914) 232-0510 . . 65 Todd Rd, Katonah, NY *10536*
Rabenberg MR & MRS Steven N (Anne Marie Auffenberg)
StMarys'88.Ty'86.Web'91
  ☎ (314) 966-3555 . . 831 Garland Place, St Louis, MO *63122*
Rabenberg MASTER Timothy Conrad (Steven N) . . . . Born at
St Louis, MO Mch 12'96
Rabenberg MRS William V (Ruth L North) Bv.Dar.
  ☎ (314) 991-1300 . . 1 Woodbridge Manor Rd, St Louis,
MO *63141-8237*
Raby MR & MRS Victor (Carmen Valenzuela) ☎ (516) 676-5415
Ln.Pr.Cly. . . . . Piping Rock Rd,
MISS Alexandra . . . . Locust Valley, NY
MR George V *11560*
Rackemann MISS Dorothy . . . . Died at
Westwood, MA Aug 17'96
Rackemann MR Ford S—Tufts'81
PO Box 116, Concord, MA *01742*
Radcliffe MR & MRS Charles E C (Sarah D F Jeffords)
GeoW'76.BostColl'74
  ☎ (212) 206-1244 . . 140 Fifth Av, New York, NY *10011*
Radcliffe MR & MRS George M (Augusta H Boggs) Md.P'43.Md'48
  ☎ (410) 228-5471 . . ''Spocott'' 1625 Hudson Rd, Cambridge,
MD *21613*
Radloff MR & MRS Robert A (Ann M Beha) Ws'72.Mit'75.Sm.Cly.Bost'69
  ☎ (617) 227-6999 . . 75 Revere St, Boston, MA *02114*
Radsch MR & MRS Richard T (Lottie Lee Haines) ☎ (908) 522-9157
Y'62 . . . . ''Westwinds''
MISS Amanda W—at Randolph-Macon . . . . 19 Rotary Lane,
MR Christopher B . . . . Summit, NJ *07901*
JUNIORS MISS Gwendolyn M . . . .
Radsch MR & MRS Robert W (Mary Louise G Stalter)
AmU'67.Pr.Un.Bm.Ne.Cw.StA.Cly.Ncd.Y.'65.Cl'67
  ☎ (212) 348-5405 . . 1435 Lexington Av, New York, NY *10128*
Radziwill MR & MRS John S (Marchessini—Eugenie ☎ (212) 628-6446
M Carras) Rc.K.Dyc.Ox'68 . . . . 834 Fifth Av,
JUNIORS MR John M S . . . . New York, NY
JUNIORS MR Philip C W *10021*

Rae MR & MRS James M (Bradbury—Ann S Rippin) ☎ (203) 966-0811
Brad'63.Yn.Y'56.H'59 . . . . 122 Rosebrook Rd,
MR Matthew A—at Curry . . . . New Canaan, CT
06840
Rae MR Thomas N—Y'52
  ☎ (212) 249-1943 . . 163 E 81 St, New York, NY *10028*
Rafferty MR & MRS Bernard (Natalie C Rice) Rcn.B.Fic.Yn.Y'43
  ☎ (860) 677-9547 . . 37 Mountain Spring Rd, Farmington, CT *06032*
Rafferty MRS Brendan G (Cullen—Betty S Clark) ☎ (203) 869-9493
Fic. . . . . 2 Birch Lane,
MISS Betty S Cullen . . . . Greenwich, CT
06830
Rafferty MR & MRS John P (Emily H Kernan) Bost'71.P.'70
  ☎ (212) 877-9430 . . 20 W 77 St, Apt 13A, New York, NY *10024*
Raffetto REV & MRS Edward C JR (Elizabeth D ☎ (410) 778-6694
Purnell) Gv.Geo'64 . . . . 301 Main St,
JUNIORS MR Charles P . . . . Church Hill, MD
21623-1278
Ragan MR & MRS Dennis O (Hess—Stephanie Berrien) Hlns'57.Iowa'67
  ☎ (540) 896-9020 . . 293 N Main St, Timberville, VA *22853*
Ragland MRS Tom R JR (de Sibour—Valerie S Prochnik)
  ☎ (410) 745-2502 . . ''Onion Hill'' 24743 Ray's Point Rd, St Michaels,
MD *21663*
Raibourn MRS Gerald R (Diana Drexel) . . . . ☎ (011-33-1)
MISS Lelia—at ☎ (212) 627-7238 40-67-70-96
201 W 16 St, Apt 16A, New York, NY *10011* . . 15 rue de Presbourg,
MISS Claire—L&C'93—at ☎ (212) 387-8908 75116 Paris, France
31 E 12 St, New York, NY *10003* . . . .
MR Jay—P'88—at ☎ (212) 627-7238
201 W 16 St, Apt 16A, New York, NY *10011* . .
Raiguel MRS Walter M (Margaret E Schuder) Ht.
  ☎ (410) 398-6750 . . 4873 Telegraph Rd, Elkton, MD *21921*
Rainer MR & MRS James W 3d (Mary A Gates) of ☎ (205)933-6217
Aub'65.Aub'65 . . . . 2828 Berwick Rd,
MISS Mary G . . . . Birmingham, AL
MR James W 4th *35213*
☎ (801) 649-1123
2675 Telemark Dv,
Park City, UT *84060*
Raines MR & MRS Victor K (Lily L C Bedford) Tul'80.USMMA'80.Van'86
  ☎ (410) 337-8436 . . 8143 Clyde Bank Rd, Baltimore, MD *21234-5105*
Rainey MR John Crews—Ht.Tex'57.Mit'58
  ☎ (212) PL8-7913 . . 310 E 55 St, New York, NY *10022*
Raley MR & MRS Robert L (Mary C Fenn)
Nyc.Wil.Lm.Cw.Csn.Ncd.Pa'51 . . of
  ☎ (302) 654-2781 . . 800 Center Mill Rd, Greenville, DE *19807*
  ☎ (603) 827-3028 . . ''Hayward House'' Harrisville, NH *03450*
Rambo MR & MRS Joseph S (Pamp—Maree L Frisby) Rc.Pc.Fst.Sg.
  ☎ (215) 248-9555 . . 9507 Wheel Pump Lane, Philadelphia, PA *19118*
Ramer MRS Rex J (Locke—Dorothy Clark)
  ☎ (703) 578-7547 . . 3440 S Jefferson St, Apt 833, Falls Church,
VA *22041*
Ramsay MISS Ann M—Occ'65
  ☎ (415) 366-1355 . . 290 Polhemus Av, Atherton, CA *94027*
Ramsay MR Gustavus R—C.P'58
  ☎ (212) 362-8681 . . 115 Central Park W, New York, NY *10023*

Ramseur MR & MRS Thomas M (Suzanne H Tompkins) P'45.Cl'50
☎ (203) 966-3633 . . 584 West Rd, New Canaan, CT 06840

Ramsey MR & MRS John F (Virginia P Farr) | ☎ (713) 520-7980
Bnd'75.Cal'71 . . . . | 4447 Mt Vernon St,
JUNIORS MISS Elsie O . . . . | Houston, TX 77006
JUNIORS MISS Mary R . . . . |

Ramsey MRS Norman C (Rosalie A Christie) Rm.
☎ (908) 842-1200 . . 45 Ridge Rd, Rumson, NJ 07760

Ramsing MR & MRS Byron L (Annette H Reynolds) K.Ln.BtP.Evg.Cly.Y'41
☎ (561) 655-4577 . . 232 Emerald Lane, Palm Beach, FL 33480

Ramstad MR & MRS Dean D (Marion McKinney) V'45.Minn'44
☎ (805) 964-3207 . . 4452 Via Esperanza, Santa Barbara, CA 93110-2342

Ranck MR & MRS J Hutchison (Annabelle L B | ☎ (011-61-2)
Walker) Pa'71 . . . . | 960-1884
JUNIORS MISS Josephine S . . . . | 19 The Grove,
JUNIORS MISS Rosemary B . . . . | Mosman, NSW
| 2088, Australia

Ranck MRS J Richard (Anne M Scott) Me.
☎ (610) MI2-6328 . . 363 Youngsford Place, Gladwyne, PA 19035

Rand MRS Adaline H (Perkins—Adaline Havemeyer) Cly.Chi.Cda . . .of
☎ (617) 444-1222 . . 865 Central Av, Apt O-405, Needham, MA 02192-1345
☎ (508) 997-4421 . . ''Whale House'' 112 Mishaum Point Rd, South Dartmouth, MA 02748-1294

Rand MR & MRS Frank C 3d (Elizabeth B Hobson)
☎ (805) 969-4713 . . 1647 Posilipo Lane, Apt F, Montecito, CA 93108

Rand MR & MRS Frank C 4th (Lois A Sullivan) Pom'82.Clare'82
☎ (201) 783-7480 . . 247 Midland Av, Montclair, NJ 07042-3022

Rand MRS George F 3d (Carroll—JoAnn P Hayden) WOnt'49.Cy.Bf.G.
☎ (716) 882-9375 . . 94 Lexington Av, Buffalo, NY 14222

Rand MR & MRS John F (Clement—H Penn Gardner)
Pa'71.Pratt'79.Unn.Rcn.Pr.Fic.NCar'69.H'77
☎ (303) 781-6660 . . 10 Meadow Lane, Englewood, CO 80110

Rand MR Laurance B—Y'31
☎ (617) 449-2044 . . 865 Central Av, Apt M202, Needham, MA 02192

Rand MRS Mary F (Wohltman—Troy—Mary F Rand)
☎ (212) 744-4972 . . 42 E 73 St, New York, NY 10021

Rand MRS Renée de R A (Nourse—Renée de R | ☎ (704) 297-3700
Allen) Dar.Myf. . . . . | ''Serendipity Acres''
MISS Christina C—Greens'96 . . . . | 8018 Rominger Rd,
MISS Courtney C—Van'96 . . . . | Sugar Grove, NC
MR Richard N 3d—Cr'89—at Philadelphia, PA . | 28679

Rand MR & MRS Richard A (Elizabeth L Hartmann) | ☎ (205) 759-4693
Sth'63.Hn.H'62 . . . . | 1612 Dearing Place,
MISS Ilona T . . . . | Tuscaloosa, AL
MR Sebastian G—Wes'95 . . . . | 35401
JUNIORS MR Paul H—at Groton . . . . |

Rand MISS Whitney S (Richard N JR) . . . . Married at Linville, NC
Franz MR Jason G (Manfred R) . . . . Aug 18'96

Rand MR & MRS William (Paula M Coudert) | ☎ (212) 369-8841
BMr'57.Rc.Pr.S.Cly.H'48.Cl'51 . . . . | 1150 Fifth Av,
MISS Paula B—H'93—☎ (212) 427-6614 . . . . . | New York, NY
MR William C—H'87—☎ (212) 996-6453 . . . . . | 10128

Randall DR & MRS Peter (Rose G Johnson) BMr'47.Pc.Ac.P'44.JHop'46
☎ (215) 247-1797 . . 20 Laughlin Lane, Philadelphia, PA 19118

Randall MR & MRS Peter G (Louisa G Borie) Roan'82.Pc.P'73.P'74
☎ (215) 247-0397 . . 718 St Andrews Rd, Philadelphia, PA 19118

Randall MASTER Quinn Coerper (Ross G 2d) . . . . Born Apr 19'96

Randall MR & MRS Ross G 2d (Lois P Coerper) Denis'83.An.CentWash'84
☎ (703) 339-6195 . . ''Gunston Hall'' Mason Neck, VA 22079

Randell MR Thomas W . . see H Cutting

Rando MR John S JR—Rby.Sfy.Ey.Un.Bost'86 ⛵
☎ (508) 281-0300 . . 34 Eastern Point Blvd, Gloucester, MA 01930

Randol MISS Eliza P . . see MRS J P Gordan

Randol MISS Lucinda L . . see MRS J P Gordan

Randol MR & MRS Mark A (Sandra L Fuller) | ☎ (216) 932-9093
Ty'66.Cv.StMarys'57 . . . . | 2742 Belvoir Blvd,
MISS Elizabeth F . . . . | Shaker Heights, OH
MISS Adrienne La B . . . . | 44122

Randolph MRS Archibald Cary (Winthrop—Theodora Ayer) . . . . . Died at
Upperville, VA Jun 11'96

Randolph MRS Archibald Cary JR (Markette—Betty J Cook)
☎ (540) 364-1617 . . PO Box 57, Marshall, VA 20115

Randolph MRS David S (Hannah W Sullivan) Ac.Cda.
☎ (610) MU8-0752 . . 235 Chamonix Rd, St Davids, PA 19087

Randolph MR & MRS David S JR (Mayer—Joyce M | ☎ (215) 476-7780
Mayeda) Tor'65.Tor'67.Tor'71.Cl'73 . . . . | 411 S 46 St,
JUNIORS MISS Elizabeth M . . . . | Philadelphia, PA
| 19143

Randolph MR & MRS Evan (Frances L Beale) Ph.W.Ac.H'31
☎ (215) WA3-3180 . . 318 St James Place, Philadelphia, PA 19106

Randolph MR & MRS Evan 4th (Penelope H Dixon) | ☎ (508) 526-7060
Sth'63.H.'57 . . . . | Spy Rock Hill,
MISS Camilla C—SCal'89 . . . . | Manchester, MA
MISS Lisa L—MontSt'94 . . . . | 01944

Randolph MR & MRS Francis F JR (Dickey—Catherine A Meyers)
Ws'58.Un.Cs.Y'50.Cl'53 . . of
☎ (212) 628-8063 . . 770 Park Av, Apt 18D, New York, NY 10021
☎ (203) 438-8995 . . Rippowam Farm, 177 Rippowam Rd, PO Box 538, Ridgefield, CT 06877

Randolph MR & MRS John (Alice D Moffat) | ☎ (215) 732-2012
PhilaArt'70.Gc.Pa'69.P'71 . . . . | 253 S 25 St,
MISS Rachel—at NYU . . . . | Philadelphia, PA
JUNIORS MISS Kathrine—at Germantown Friends | 19103

Randolph MRS Larned D (Angulo—Carolyn L Bonin)
☎ (804) 293-2823 . . 1618 Kenwood Lane, Charlottesville, VA 22901

Randolph MRS M Elliott (A Pickett Davis) Elk.Mv.
☎ (410) 243-4241 . . 830 W 40 St, Apt 354, Baltimore, MD 21211

Randolph MR & MRS Malcolm M (Olivia L Gilliam) | ☎ (804) 288-3163
StMarys'65.Va'64 . . . . | 6508 Three Chopt
MISS Olivia L . . . . | Rd, Richmond, VA
MISS Margaret M . . . . | 23226
MISS Beverly V . . . . |
JUNIORS MR Malcolm M JR . . . . |

Randolph DR & MRS Peter B F (Helen Garside)
Sth'56.Tv.Chi.Dc.Y'56.H'61 . . . .
MISS Helen Tod—Juilliard'88—at 366 W 11 St,
New York, NY *10014* . . . .
MISS Sarah French Robinson—Rice'86—at
57 Charter St, Boston, MA *02113* . . . .
MISS Eliza C F—Ham'95—at 1647 Lincoln St,
Berkeley, CA *94703* . . . .
MR Christopher B F—Bost'82.Cal'85—at
3110 Highland St, Santa Monica, CA *90405* . . .
MR Nicholas D F—at 5412 Lawton Av, Oakland,
CA *94618* . . . .
☎ (617) 497-4537
22 Craigie St,
Cambridge, MA
02138

Randolph MR & MRS Philip S P 3d (Ulrica D Hubbard) Ph.Rb.Ssk.Ac.
☎ (610) LA5-0533 . . 7 Cushman Rd, Rosemont, PA *19010*

Randolph MRS Pickett D (Hulley—Pickett D Randolph) Wheat'60
☎ (202) 966-9346 . . 3130—38 St NW, Washington, DC *20016*

Randolph MR & MRS Richard R III (Natasha M Blinov)
Lynch'61.Ala'61 . . of
☎ (205) 871-6541 . . 4149 Winston Way, Birmingham, AL *35213*
☎ (704) 526-5135 . . "Homewoods" Highlands, NC *28741*

Randolph MR & MRS Richard R IV (Patricia A Farmer) Ala'87.Aub'89
☎ (205) 822-1983 . . 2115 Shades Av, Vestavia, AL *35216*

Randolph MR & MRS Robert L (Welling—Mary Lou
Hollaman) SL'51.Elk.Y'50 . . . .
MISS Lucy McH . . . .
☎ (410) 435-6850
5711 Stony Run Dv,
Baltimore, MD
21210

Randolph MR Ryland M—Montevallo'92
☎ (205) 699-5827 . . 108 Tramway Court, Leeds, AL *35094*

Randt MRS Ann E (Ann C English) . . . .
JUNIORS MISS Christie Ann . . . .
☎ (602) 585-0131
10464 E
Candlewood Dv,
Scottsdale, AZ
85255

Randt MR Thomas A—OState'66.Pa'68 . . of
☎ (619) 456-6678 . . 1363 Caminito Diadema, La Jolla, CA *92037*
253 Bonair St, La Jolla, CA *92037*

Raney MISS Jordan Reese (Kristopher M) . . . . Born at
Santa Monica, CA Jun 2'96

Raney MR & MRS Kristopher M (Kristina L Kluth)
Cal'87.Cal'89.Cal'90 . . of
410—21 St, Manhattan Beach, CA *90266*
Raney Ranch, Springville, CA *93265*

Rankin MR & MRS Alfred M JR (Victoire C Griffin)
Man'vl'64.Kt.Mt.Cv.Tv.Un.Rr.Sl.Y'63 . . . .
MISS Clara T—at 2600 N Southport Av, Chicago,
IL *60614* . . . .
☎ (216) 269-8222
7421 Markell Rd,
Waite Hill, OH
44094

Rankin MR & MRS Douglas W (Mary L B Backus)
Ws'56.H'66.Cos.Colg'53.H'61 . . . .
MISS Katharine N . . . .
MISS Andrea L . . . .
☎ (202) 337-8659
1614—44 St NW,
Washington, DC
20007

Rankin MRS Harley L (Anna-Binney Hancock) . . . . Died at
Bryn Mawr, PA Nov 30'95

Rankin MR & MRS Harley L JR (Lucy H Wallace)
Sth'63.H'67.Quinn'93.Me.P'61.H'67
66 Stanton Rd, Darien, CT *06820*

Rankin MR & MRS Henry P JR (Clark—Hook—Louise C Morgan)
Pk.Cv.Cly.Y'33 . . of
☎ (216) 423-4556 . . Rake Mill Farm, 7545 Old Mill Rd, Box 336,
Gates Mills, OH *44040*
☎ (941) 262-1385 . . 55 Gulf Shore Blvd N, Naples, FL *34102*

Ranlet MR & MRS Robert (Suzanne Hanckel) Va'27 . . of
☎ (941) 261-2597 . . "The Billows" 2601 Gulf Shore Blvd N, Naples,
FL *34102*
☎ (804) 286-2369 . . "The Rectory" Keene, VA *22946*

Ranney MR F Garner—H'42
☎ (410) 837-3382 . . 807 Cathedral St, Baltimore, MD *21201*

Ransom MISS Ashley B—Mid'88 . . see V H Brown JR

Ransom MISS Louise
☎ (212) 879-9809 . . 245 E 72 St, New York, NY *10021*

Rantoul MISS Harriet I
☎ (508) 758-4624 . . 15 Shady Oak Dv, Mattapoisett, MA *02739*

Rantoul MRS Robert (Norma F Shortt)
☎ (519) 824-0106 . . 147 Norfolk St, Guelph, Ontario N1H 4J7, Canada

Raoul MR & MRS Gaston C 3d (Ellen M Exum)
1427 Appallo Rd, Lookout Mountain, GA *30750*

Rapalyea MRS Angela J (Clark—Angela M Jaekle) Myf.
☎ (215) 233-0825 . . "Roaring Corners" 501 E Gravers Lane,
Wyndmoor, PA *19038*

Rapalyea MR Richard G—Col'70 . . . .
MISS Sarah G . . . .
MISS Lydia B . . . .
402 Arthur's
Roundtable,
Wynnewood, PA
19096

Raphael MR & MRS Kenneth G (Helen H Osterhaus)
HolyN'66.StM'65.StM'78 . . . .
MISS Patricia W—Chap'93 . . . .
MR Andrew D . . . .
☎ (510) 547-1788
6055 Wood Dv,
Oakland, CA *94611*

Rappel MISS Laura H . . see MRS D D Platt

Rappel MR Richard W JR . . see MRS D D Platt

Rappleye MR & MRS Willard C JR (Doherty—Tankoos—Marita Crofton)
Pr.C.Y'45
☎ (516) 671-4685 . . 84 Bayville Rd, Locust Valley, NY *11560*

Rasin MR & MRS Rudolph S (Joy Peterkin)
Cho.Wa.Rut'53 . . . .
MR James Stenning—at 20 E 13 St, New York,
NY *10003* . . . .
of ☎ (630)323-8250
328 E 8 St,
Hinsdale, IL *60521*
☎ (414) 248-8011
"Flowerside Inn"
N2261 Mallory
Lane, Lake Geneva,
WI *53147*

Rasmussen MR & MRS David J (Helen L Bird) Ga'73.Cl'78.Nu'71.Cl'74
☎ (914) 939-8541 . . 11 Central Av, Port Chester, NY *10573*

Rasmussen MR & MRS Garret G (Banus—Jean R
Middendorf) Sim'72.Cvc.Sl.Mt.Dth'71.H'74 . . .
JUNIORS MISS Lisa G . . . .
JUNIORS MR William M . . . .
☎ (202) 337-3396
3321 Q St NW,
Washington, DC
20007

Rasmussen MR & MRS Harold F (Sara W Jackson) V'39.Ht.Dth'38
☎ (203) 698-2282 . . 8 Shore Rd, Old Greenwich, CT *06870*

Rast MR & MRS Holt (Wilson—Elizabeth Wilkinson)
Htdon'47.Cy.Ala'42 . . of
☎ (205) 967-3397 . . 2908 Overton Rd, Birmingham, AL *35223*
☎ (205) 329-0605 . . "Lake House" Pike Creed Rd, Lake Martin,
Alexander City, AL *35010*

Rastetter DR & MRS William H (Lucy S Dillon) Sim'76.Mit'71.H'75
Puerta Del Sol, PO Box 2804, Rancho Santa Fe, CA *92067*

Ratchuk MR & MRS Gregory R (Carol Whiting) WmW'ds'78.SanDiegoSt'78
4060 Tynebourne Circle, San Diego, CA *92130*

Ratcliff MR & MRS John P (Katherine A Joy) . . . . . .

MISS Nancy J—at 44 Central St, West Boylston,
MA *01583* . . . . | of ☎ (510)254-5959
7 El Sueno,
Orinda, CA *94563*
☎ (707) 884-3433
Slick Rock Creek
Ranch, 31101 S
Coast H'way 1,
Gualala, CA *95445*

Ratcliffe MRS Myron F (Margaret E Archibald) Cho.Ih.Cas.Cnt . . .of
☎ (847) 251-7126 . . 82 Indian Hill Rd, Winnetka, IL *60093*
''La Casa Pequeña'' 1008 Fairway Rd, Montecito, CA *93108*

Rath MR John S—Cw.Rv.Stan'39
☎ (860) 567-8222 . . 15 Sarcka Lane, Box 455, Litchfield,
CT *06759-0455*

Rath MR & MRS M Peter (S Hilary Straat) Ind'84.Syr'77
☎ (702) 829-1937 . . 3604 Grand Teton Court, Reno, NV *89509*

Rath MRS Patricia R (Graffin—Patricia Ruhl) ClevInst'50
☎ (212) 744-8527 . . 165 E 72 St, New York, NY *10021*

Rathbone MR & MRS Perry T (Euretta de Cosson) Tv.Sm.C.H.'33
☎ (617) 864-1542 . . 130 Mt Auburn St, Cambridge, MA *02138*

Rathbone MR & MRS Peter B (Teissier—G Alanna
Chesebro) Nu'75.Bost'71 . . . .

JUNIORS MISS Sarah T . . . . | ☎ (203) 972-2860
24 Llewellyn Dv,
New Canaan, CT
06840

Rathborne MRS Carol S (Carol Simmons) Man'vl'69.Mds . . .of
☎ (212) 223-0022 . . 485 Park Av, New York, NY *10022*
☎ (516) 329-1212 . . ''Thither 'n Yon'' 54 Hither Lane, East Hampton,
NY *11937*

Rathborne MR J Cornelius—Ng.Y'58 . . . .

MISS Diana W—at ☎ (612) 377-4786
1722 Fremont Av S, Minneapolis, MN *55403* . . | ☎ (504) 368-6355
PO Box 157,
Harvey, LA *70059*

Rathborne MR & MRS J Cornelius JR (Elizabeth E Rogers)
Denis'90.StThom'88
☎ (773) 549-2453 . . 717 W Roscoe St, Apt 1, Chicago, IL *60657*

Rathborne MISS Nancy Winship (Schniewind—
Roberts—Nancy W Rathborne) . . . .

MR Henry E Schniewind 3d—at
☎ (011-33) 79-06-16-58 . . 36 Residence Les
Andes, 73150 Val d'Isère, France . . . .

MR Nelson R Schniewind—at
☎ (401) 823-0243 . . 20 Quaker Dv, Apt 18,
West Warwick, RI *02893* . . . .

MR Edward P Roberts 3d—at N'western . . . . | ☎ (970) 920-6908
PO Box 4933,
Aspen, CO *81612*

Rathbun MR & MRS Dean A (Helen O Hance)
Dth'48 . . . .

MISS Anne P . . . . | 25 Rhetts Bluff Rd,
Kiawah, SC *29455*

Rather MRS Margaret B (Margaret J Bakewell)
☎ (713) NA2-5808 . . 3853 Del Monte St, Houston, TX *77019*

Ratliff MR & MRS Thomas A JR (Lucy L Graydon) Cin'40
☎ (513) 771-6197 . . 755 Greenville Av, Cincinnati, OH *45246*

Rauch MR & MRS Alfred JR (Mary Belle Scott)
Swb'62.M.Me.Ph.Ac.Cr'61.Pa'64 . . . .

MISS M Brearley—Nw'94 . . . .

MR J Scott—Duke'92 . . . . | ☎ (610) MI9-1990
308 Brentford Rd,
Haverford, PA
19041

Rauch MR & MRS Alfred 3d (Elaine T Petrossian)
Va'91.Va'94.Mg.Me.Va'89.VillaN'92
338 Fitzwater St, Philadelphia, PA *19147*

Rauch MR Benjamin B—Ri.P'78
☎ (212) 702-0821 . . 309 E 49 St, New York, NY *10017*

Rauch MR & MRS R Stewart (Frances S Brewster)
Ph.Gm.Me.Fic.Rb.Ri.Pn.P.'36
☎ (610) 527-3321 . . 13 Pond Lane, Bryn Mawr, PA *19010*

Rauch MISS Susan P . . of
☎ (307) 733-0549 . . PO Box 960, Wilson, WY *83014-0960*
☎ (011-33-1) 43-26-96-64 . . 5 rue Bréa, 75006 Paris, France

Rauch MR & MRS Thomas M (Jean Ballinger) Ph.Dar.P'44
☎ (410) 822-3477 . . ''Land's End'' 27461 Travelers Rest Court, Easton,
MD *21601*

Rauh MR & MRS Stephen S (Louise R Dix) Ty'95.Ty'68.Dth'72
☎ (802) 223-6727 . . RD 1, Box 122H, Murray Rd, East Montpelier,
VT *05651*

Raurell-Soto MR A Miguel . . see R L Forbes

Rauscher MR & MRS John Howard JR (Vaughn—Mary J McCorkle)
Smu'51.Tex'50
☎ (214) 368-4741 . . 10573 Inwood Rd, Dallas, TX *75229*

Rava MR & MRS John A (Susan D'A Roudebush)
Nd.H'58.JHop'60.H'63 . . . .

MISS Carol E—H'92 . . . .

MR William C—H'91 . . . . | ☎ (314) 863-1927
7129 Washington
Av, St Louis, MO
63130

Raven MR & MRS Peter H (Tamra Engelhorn)
SanDiegoSt'66.Stan'72.Cy.Cos.Cal'57.Cal'60
☎ (314) 726-2344 . . 7632 Westmoreland Av, St Louis, MO *63105*

Ravenel MR & MRS Charles du F (Williamson—
Susan G Woodward) SCar'64.Unn.Yh.H'61.
H'64 . . . .

MISS Susan G Williamson . . . .

MR Thomas B Williamson JR . . . . | ☎ (803) 577-7518
9 Legare St,
Charleston, SC
29401

Ravenel MR Curtis deSt Julien . . see J H Fair JR

Ravenel MR & MRS Daniel (Linda Compton)
Fur'71.Cit'75.Cw.Ht.Char'ton'72 ⚓ . . . .

JUNIORS MISS Elizabeth H . . . . | of ☎ (803)577-4453
68 Broad St,
Charleston, SC
29401
☎ (704) 692-7087
''Piedmont''
Middleton Rd,
Box 147,
Flat Rock, NC
28731

Ravenel MR & MRS Lee B (Anne A Dickson)
Wheat'66.Gchr'67.Cvc.Aht'59 . . . .

MISS Renee St Julien—at Catawba Coll . . . . . . | ☎ (202) 333-0052
3528 Fulton St NW,
Washington, DC
20007

Ravenel MISS Margaret Benoist (Lee B) . . . . . Married at Washington, DC
Elliott MR David R JR (David R) . . . . Apr 20'96

Ravenel MR Ramsay M . . see J H Fair JR

Ravenel DR & MRS René (L Marion Rivers) Conv'65.Ht.Char'ton'65
☎ (803) 722-1856 . . 11 Gibbes St, Charleston, SC *29401*

Ravenel MISS Tiphaine T . . see J H Fair JR
Ravenscroft MR & MRS Jackson P (C Day Ely) | ☎ (520) 299-9484
Ws'51.Strayer'39 . . . . | 5240 Camino
MISS Virginia C—H'92 . . . . | Apolena, Tucson,
| AZ *85718*
Ravenscroft MR & MRS Richard S (Susan H | ☎ (610) LA5-9762
Davidson) Rdc'60.Pa'67.Ph.Y'59 . . . . | 622 Carisbrooke Rd,
MISS Allison M . . . . | Bryn Mawr, PA
MISS Catherine H . . . . | *19010*
MR Philip M . . . . |
Rawle MR & MRS David (Cynthia S Woodward) Ac.H'33
☎ (610) 644-5050 . . 515 Newtown Rd, Berwyn, PA *19312*
Rawlings MR & MRS Peter Sayres (McCord—Sarah | ☎ (610) 520-4474
M Parker) Gm.Ac.Va'64 . . . . | 1610 Old Gulph Rd,
JUNIORS MR Peter Sayres JR . . . . | Villanova, PA *19085*
MR A Jamison McCord |
Rawlings MR & MRS Phillip O (Gloria A Derrick) | ☎ (334) 265-5352
Aub'70.Aub'70 . . . . | 2610 Fernway Dv,
JUNIORS MR Phillip O 2d . . . . | Montgomery, AL
| *36111*
Rawls MR Henry P—Pc.LaS'73
☎ (215) 247-7401 . . 234 W Willow Grove Av, Philadelphia, PA *19118*
Rawls MR & MRS William H (Mary M Holmes) H'57 | Beaver Pond,
MR Timothy F—at ☎ (206) 782-3998 | Beverly, MA *01915*
2641 NW 57 St, Seattle, WA *98107* . . . . |
Rawls MR & MRS William S (Hope Knowles) Pc.P'37.H'40
☎ (215) 247-7401 . . 234 W Willow Grove Av, Philadelphia, PA *19118*
Rawson MR & MRS David W (Therese G Casadesus) | ☎ (610) 647-3548
Paris'63.P'63.Pa'66 . . . . | "Crum Creek
MR Carter C . . . . | House"
MR Ramsay C . . . . | Berwyn, PA *19312*
Rawson MRS Kennett L (MacMannis—Eleanor Stierhem) C.Cs.Y. ⚓
☎ (212) 535-0547 . . 150 E 69 St, New York, NY *10021*
Rawson MISS Rebecca H—BMr'69.Ch'72
☎ (212) 769-2667 . . 100 W 89 St, New York, NY *10024-1932*
Ray MR E Tinsley JR—LakeF'67.Pa'79
☎ (203) 655-2098 . . 43 Blueberry Lane, Darien, CT *06820*
Ray MRS George L (McCollum—Stelling—Elizabeth H Fisher) Cly.Cda.
☎ (212) 688-7942 . . 200 E 66 St, Apt 706, New York, NY *10021*
Ray MR & MRS William F (Helen A Payne) | of ☎ (617)461-2560
Ws'37.Unn.Fic.Fiy.Plg.Cy.Sm.Rv.Km.Ncd. | 10 Longwood Dv,
Cin'35.H'37 . . . . | Apt 468, Westwood,
MISS Susan E—at ☎ (617) 293-5461 | MA *02090-1146*
664 School St, Pembroke, MA *02359* . . . . | ☎ (941) 676-7297
| "Trimanor"
| Mountain Lake,
| Lake Wales, FL
| *33859*
Ray MR & MRS Wilson K JR (Virginia H Stafford) Rcp.P'50
☎ (207) 967-4227 . . 15 Port Arundel, PO Box 1205, Kennebunkport,
ME *04046*
Rayfield MISS Sophie Alexander (g—Louis I Kane) . . . . Born at
Lebanon, NH Nov 18'95
Raymer MR & MRS John H JR (Nancy T Barry)
StJos'86.VillaN'90.WChesU'87
☎ (610) 896-8314 . . 213 Harrogate Rd, Wynnewood, PA *19096*

Raymer MR & MRS John Hutcheson (Mary L | ☎ (610) 688-6547
Snodgrass) Sar.Dar.Wes'60 . . . . | 466 Upper Gulph
MR Andrew B—Bost'89 . . . . | Rd, Radnor, PA
| *19087*
Raymond MRS Charles H (Elena R Salvatore) . . . . . | ☎ (718) 852-6756
MISS Louise R . . . . | 148 Clinton St,
MR Richard V . . . . | Brooklyn, NY *11201*
Raymond MR & MRS David A (Dorothy C Dillon) Ty'73.Mt.P'69 . . of
☎ (301) 299-6039 . . 9026 Bronson Dv, Potomac, MD *20854*
☎ (508) 257-6517 . . "Rugosa Cottage" Baxter Rd, Siasconset,
MA *02554*
Raymond MR & MRS Edward H (Katherine B Channing) Col'58.H'58
☎ (617) 329-9095 . . 986 High St, Dedham, MA *02026*
Raymond MRS Fairfield E (Fanny Bemis Chandler) Chi.Ncd.
☎ (603) 924-6938 . . "Fair Fields" 81 Crosby Rd, Peterborough,
NH *03458*
Raymond MRS Irving W (Henrietta D Skinner) . . . . | ☎ (212) 628-9264
MISS Henrietta D—at ☎ (904) 253-2439 | 238 E 84 St,
935 N Halifax Dv, Apt 409, Daytona Beach, FL | New York, NY
32018 . . . . | *10028*
Raymond MR M Whitridge (Virginia H Parsons)
☎ (203) 637-3053 . . 81 Silo Circle, Silo Hill, Riverside, CT *06878*
Raymond MR & MRS Peter D (Blossom—Christina | ☎ (914) 337-8144
A Morris) Sth'75.V'76 . . . . | 52 Summit Av,
JUNIORS MISS Anne R Blossom . . . . | Bronxville, NY
| *10708*
Rayner MR & MRS William P (Kornbluth—Katharine A Johnson)
SL'68.Bcs.K.Ri.Ng.Cly.Va'52
☎ (212) 794-2046 . . 11½ E 76 St, New York, NY *10021*
Raynolds MR & MRS David R (Mary Alice Kean) Sth'49.Lm.Cly.Cda.Dth'49
☎ (307) 332-9067 . . Table Mtn Ranch, 30 Field Station Rd, Lander,
WY *82520*
Raynor MASTER Alexander Louis (Andrew B) . . . . Born at
New York, NY Dec 11'95
Raynor MR & MRS (REV) Andrew B (Andrea L Ruehrwein)
Denis'83.H'86.Denis'83.Cl'90
96 Douglas Place, Mt Vernon, NY *10552*
Raynor MISS Sarah M—Boca'87 . . see M S Gibbons
Raynor-Smith MR & MRS Murray (Virginia | ☎ (215) 233-1842
Robbins) Temp'91.Y.'48 . . . . | 408 Penn Oak Rd,
MISS Kimberly . . . . | Flourtown, PA
MISS Alison . . . . | *19031*
Rea MISS Alison B—Pa'74.Nu'82
☎ (212) 787-9153 . . 110 Riverside Dv, New York, NY *10024*
Rea MR & MRS C Cary (Nancy B Robbins) | ☎ (410) 263-4849
Wheat'69.Bow'67 ⚓ . . . . | 413 Schley Rd,
MR Charles C—at Wheaton . . . . | Annapolis, MD
| *21401*
Rea MRS Elizabeth Beach (Sterling—Elizabeth B K Beach) Sl.Cda.
☎ (202) 362-2205 . . 4255 Fordham Rd NW, Washington, DC *20016*
Rea MRS James C JR (Mary C Cary) Sth'39.Ncd.
☎ (207) 846-4478 . . 59 Blueberry Cove, Yarmouth, ME *04096*
Rea MRS John M (E Ellida Davison) BMr'32
☎ (516) 741-0934 . . 14 Damson St, Garden City, NY *11530-6208*
Rea MR Malcolm D—Stan'70
☎ (303) 722-4421 . . 145 S Clarkson St, Denver, CO *80209*
Read MISS Carolyn A—Colby'94 . . see G N Valentine

Read MRS Charles A (Green—Katherine H Ayers)
see Dilatory Domiciles
Read MR David W—H'44
229 Willardshire Rd, East Aurora, NY *14052*
Read MR Duncan H—Mt.Hn.H'19
☎ (540) 687-6762 . . "Dundrillin" PO Box 185, Middleburg,
VA *20118*
Read MR & MRS Edward Sears JR (Norma A | 103 Indian Hill,
Webster) Ws'91.H'49. . . . . | Carlisle, MA *01741*
MR Edward Sears 3d . . . . |
Read DR & MRS J Harleston 6th (Karin P Bartsch) | ☎ (609) 358-2791
Cc.P'67.Jef'71 . . . . | "Belle-Rivè North"
MR J Harleston 7th . . . . | 62 Remsterville Rd,
JUNIORS MISS Ashley B . . . . | Elmer, NJ *08318*
JUNIORS MR Robert G . . . . |
Read MISS Priscilla A (Crane—Priscilla A Read) . . . . Married at
Barnstable, MA
Romeiser DR David E (William) . . . . Sep 29'93
Read MR & MRS Robert O JR (Alden H Calmer) | ☎ (412) 683-0620
Bnd'52.Pg.P'50 . . . . | 614 Pitcairn Place,
MR Jonathan B . . . . | Pittsburgh, PA
| *15232*
Read MISS Sandra L (Foley—Sandra L Read) Wms'73.Cl'80
☎ (970) 349-1551 . . PO Box 1305, 506 Butte Av, Crested Butte,
CO *81224*
Read MR & MRS William A JR (Collier—Isabel | ☎ (561) 655-4242
Uppercu) Evg.BtP.B.Rr. . . . . | 850 S County Rd,
MR Inglis U Collier . . . . | Palm Beach, FL
| *33480*
Read MR & MRS William B 3d (Susan W Hayne) | ☎ (610) 525-7704
VillaN'86.Me.Cry.Cc.DU'70 . . . . | 1140 Ginkgo Lane,
MISS Kim A . . . . | Gladwyne, PA
MISS Lori M . . . . | *19035*
Read JUNIORS MR Zachary B . . see P L Maddock JR
Reagan MR & MRS Brian P (Abigail E Crocker) Br'82.PugetS'82
☎ (415) 333-6105 . . 735 Urbano Dv, San Francisco, CA *94127*
Reagan MR & MRS Bruce V 3d (Allison T Scudder) | ☎ (206) 363-9331
Seattle'73 . . . . | 17360 Beach Dv
MISS Christina A—at Geo Fox Coll . . . . | NE, Seattle, WA
JUNIORS MISS Laurel B . . . . | *98155*
Reagan MR & MRS Ronald W (Nancy Davis) Eureka'32
668 St Cloud Rd, Los Angeles, CA *90077*
Reagan, William R & McGuire, Amanda K—Ken'88.Va'92.VaCmth'93
☎ (540) 925-2426 . . Rte 1, Box 131, Millboro, VA *24460*
Reakirt MRS Charles Coleman (Mary E Colby)
"Laurel Hills" PO Box 1311, Tryon, NC *28782*
Reals DR & MRS William J (Norma R Monahan)
StMarys'42.An.Cos.StJ.Cw.Dar.Creigh'45 . . of
☎ (316) 681-3692 . . 706 Stratford Rd, Wichita, KS *67206-1455*
Cherokee Farm, PO Box 8, Scammon, KS *66773*
Ream MRS John W (Barbara Borden)
☎ (508) 775-3058 . . 85 Ocean Av, Hyannis Port, MA *02647*
Feb 1 . . 264 Dunbar Rd, Palm Beach, FL *33480*
Ream MR & MRS Miller JR (Chonita M Bovet) | ☎ (415) 343-5806
Bur.Sfg.P'57. | 25 New Place Rd,
MISS Suzanne B . . . . | Hillsborough, CA
MR Miller 3d. | *94010*

Reaper MR & MRS J Anthony (Laura D Neff) Rby.Ny.
☎ (516) 922-8063 . . 110A Horseshoe Rd, Mill Neck, NY *11765*
Reardon DR & MRS James J JR (Miller—Robin A | of ☎ (212)722-2152
Arbon) S.Ck.Mto.Cly.StJ'61.SUNY'65 . . . . . . | 128 E 95 St,
JUNIORS MISS J Alexes—at Marymount Sch . . . . | New York, NY
JUNIORS MR J Ashe—at Browning . . . . | *10128*
| ☎ (516) 676-0380
| "Cymbidium"
| Box 188,
| Locust Valley, NY
| *11560*
Reardon MR & MRS Mark C (Elizabeth K Rich) Pac'89.Pac'87.Cal'93
☎ (847) 735-1321 . . 775 E Illinois Rd, Lake Forest, IL *60045*
Reath MISS Alberta P (Manheim—Alberta P Reath) | ☎ (609) 737-8632
MR Joseph P R Manheim—at St John's Coll . | 614 Scotch Rd,
JUNIORS MR Francis B C M Manheim . . . . . . | Pennington, NJ
| *08534*
Reath MRS George (Isabel D West) Ac.
☎ (215) CH2-8446 . . 8000 Seminole Av, Philadelphia, PA *19118*
Reath MRS J Pancoast (Sarah A Mitchell)
☎ (610) 325-9387 . . Dunwoody Village CH120,
3500 West Chester Pike, Newtown Square, PA *19073*
Reath MR & MRS Thomas JR (E Joyce Borie) Pa'39
☎ (603) 722-0300 . . PO Box 203, Stratham, NH *03885*
Reath MRS Timothy (Dinah H Guernsey) Bgt.
3811 Canterbury Rd, Apt 404, Baltimore, MD *21218-2317*
Reback MR & MRS Forbes R (Charlotte D Buttrick)
Swb'76.Hlns'79.Rv.Cda.Cr'58.Va'64
☎ (804) 823-2540 . . "Dogpatch" PO Box 20, Charlottesville, VA *22902*
Reber MRS Miles (Hawfield—Julia Stott) An.
☎ (413) 243-1822 . . "Little House" Main Rd, Tyringham, MA *01264*
Rebmann MRS Paul C (F Irene Jackson) Me.Sdg.
☎ (610) MI2-4125 . . 130 St George's Rd, Ardmore, PA *19003*
Reboul MR & MRS Edward L (Laura K Heath) | ☎ (617) 729-4841
Bnd'61.H.'62 . . . . | 32 Myrtle Terr,
MISS Kathryn A—WNe'88 . . . . | Winchester, MA
| *01890*
Reboul MR & MRS John W (Josée Vrignon) | ☎ (212) 289-3654
Paris'70.Nu'76.Rc.Un.H'59.H'63.Paris'64 . . . . . | 1165 Fifth Av,
JUNIORS MISS Alexandra . . . . | New York, NY
JUNIORS MR John M. . . . . | *10029*
Record DR & MRS Eugene E (Emily C Davis) Cy.H.'32
☎ (617) 631-4303 . . Crowninshield Rd, Peaches Point, Marblehead,
MA *01945*
Redding MR & MRS George H JR (Buck—Margaret | ☎ (847) 446-1198
Le M Whiting) Rdc'55.Ncd.W&J'43.Nw'48 . . . | 365 Chestnut St,
MR Graham W . . . . | Winnetka, IL *60093*
Redfield MR & MRS Christopher McK (Carol A Holmes)
Duke'83.Mit'87.P'85.Mit'87
☎ (415) 917-8754 . . 1101 Los Altos Av, Los Altos, CA *94022*
Redfield MISS Elizabeth C (Cowles—Elizabeth C Redfield)
see W W Atterbury 3d
Redfield MR & MRS LeGrand S (Susan T White) | ☎ (773) 975-0525
Cw.Ll.Aht'49 . . . . | 519 W Dickens Av,
MR Prescott L . . . . | Chicago, IL
JUNIORS MR Whitney T . . . . | *60614-4520*

Redfield MRS R Bruce (Anne J Elavsky)
135 E Varnum, Munising, MI *49862*
Redfield MR & MRS Robert Latimer 3d (K Renate Beckmann) Bnd'55.Wms'52 .... | PO Box 18895, Fountain Hills, AZ *85269-8895*
   MISS (DR) Christina—Ws'79.H'80.H'84—at
   ☎ (011-44-1865) 52704 . . 1 Park Close, Oxford OX2 8NP, England. . . . .
   MISS Isobel—Wy'83.Wh'lck'89—at
   ☎ (617) 575-1640 . . 18 Bailey Court, Canton, MA *02021* . . . .
Redhead MRS Duncan N (Charlotte E Marlinière) LSU'33.Dar.
   ☎ (601) 442-2725 . . 6 Spanish Court, Natchez, MS *39120*
Redington MRS Ruth M . . see E J Nouri
Redmond MR Bruns D'Aunoy—Rv.Loy'41
   ☎ (504) 866-1134 . . 10 Trianon Plaza, New Orleans, LA *70125*
Redmond MR & MRS J Woodward (Elizabeth B Aldrich) Ri.Mt.Cvc . . .of
   ☎ (202) 966-2498 . . 2960 Chain Bridge Rd NW, Washington, DC *20016*
   ☎ (207) 734-6479 . . "One Way" Dark Harbor, ME *04848*
Redmond MRS Roland L (Macy—di San Faustino—Lydia P Bodrero) . . of
   ☎ (914) 757-2521 . . PO Box 100, Tivoli, NY *12583*
   ☎ (805) 969-2130 . . 825 Rockbridge Rd, Santa Barbara, CA *93108*
Redmond MRS Thomas J L (Mary R Millard) Bur. . | ☎ (505) 983-2918 1045½ Camino San Acacio, Santa Fe, NM *87501*
   MISS Maria L—at Santa Cruz, CA . . . .
   MR Johnston L—at 306 E 15 St, New York, NY *10003* . . . .
   MR Hugh M . . . .
Redpath MR Frederick L . . . . Died May 22'96
Redpath MRS Frederick L (Long—Deborah B Law) Pn. . . . . | ☎ (610) 645-8652 1400 Waverly Rd, Villa 3, Gladwyne, PA *19035*
   MR Bruce L . . . .
Redpath MRS Robert U JR (Nancy S Miller) Sth'29
123 Lincoln Rd, Lincoln, MA *01773*
Feb 1 . . 3502 Estero Blvd, Ft Myers Beach, FL *33931*
Redway MR & MRS David D (Bennetts—Anita M Barbey) Stan'71.Tex'78.Tex'81.Ncd.Bost'72. JHop'74 . . . . | *see Dilatory Domiciles*
   MISS Irene G . . . .
   JUNIORS MISS Charlotte S . . . .
Redway MR & MRS Laurance M (Annabelle Loud) Syr'64.Mt.Pa'62 . . . . | ☎ (202) 362-9715 5035 Macomb St NW, Washington, DC *20016*
   MISS Merrell . . . .
   MISS Annabelle . . . .
Reece MR & MRS Christopher S (Elizabeth L Riemer) Ty'78.Cy.San.Cw.Chi.Pa'72 . . of
   ☎ (617) 320-8577 . . 1061 High St, Dedham, MA *02026*
   ☎ (207) 276-5376 . . "Stone's Throw" Northeast Harbor, ME *04662*
Reece MR & MRS Franklin A 3d (Joyce Reath) Wheat'64.H'76.Cy.H'68 . . . . | ☎ (617) 354-5206 45 Garden St, Cambridge, MA *02138*
   JUNIORS MR Franklin T . . . .
Reece MR & MRS J Brooks JR (Judith D Strohmeier) Skd'70.Cy.Nf.San.Cw.Pa'69 . . . . | ☎ (617) 277-1176 218 Middlesex Rd, Chestnut Hill, MA *02167*
   JUNIORS MR J Brooks 3d . . . .

Reece MRS John B (Helm—Peabody—Barbara Ginn) BtP.Bvl.Cy.Chi . . .of
   ☎ (561) 659-0421 . . 353 Seaspray Av, Palm Beach, FL *33480*
   ☎ (508) 748-0783 . . 114 Point Rd, Marion, MA *02738*
Reed MR & MRS A Lachlan (Martha W Sweatt) Ers'41.B.BtP.Evg.Yn.Y'39
   ☎ (561) 844-7690 . . 1545 N Ocean Way, Palm Beach, FL *33840*
Reed MR & MRS Adrian P (Nancy J Austin) Unn.Cly.USA'53 . . . . | ☎ (410) 758-0800 Lands End Farm, 1464 Lands End Rd, Centreville, MD *21617*
   MISS Margery P . . . .
   MR Austin. . . . .
Reed MR & MRS Alan L (C Louise Herron) Me.Gm.Eyc.Err.Cts.Wms'55.H'61 . . . . | ☎ (610) 525-2890 1106 Spring Mill Rd, Villanova, PA *19085*
   MR Edward L—at 520 High St, Apt 10A, Medford, MA *02156* . . . .
Reed MR Andrew B—StJColl'74 . . see D Middleton
Reed MRS C Lawson (Dorothy Whittaker) Qc.Cm.Yn.
   ☎ (513) 321-6833 . . 419 Torrence Court, Cincinnati, OH *45202*
Reed MR & MRS Charles C (Lorna Young) SCal'58.Vh.Stan'55.Stan'60
   ☎ (818) 795-6965 . . 1250 Oxford Rd, San Marino, CA *91108*
Reed MR Charles V . . see O de la Renta
Reed MR Christopher H—H'70 . . see D Middleton
Reed MR & MRS David John JR (Barry—Brenda K Rockwell) SCal'57 . . of
   ☎ (310) 476-8828 . . 11559 Bellagio Rd, Los Angeles, CA *90049*
   ☎ (619) 340-2956 . . 75-605 Painted Desert Rd, Indian Wells, CA *92210*
Reed MISS Diana L—BMr'78
   ☎ (412) 222-2141 . . 140 LeMoyne Av, Washington, PA *15301*
Reed MRS Edward A (Savera—Pfann—Polak— Annelies B M Tischer) Gm.
   ☎ (610) 649-4880 . . 102A Montgomery Av, Ardmore, PA *19003*
Reed MR & MRS Frank Fremont 2d (Matthiessen— Cox—Jaquelin Silverthorne) Rcch.Wa.Mich'52 . | ☎ (805) 969-4409 1944 E Valley Rd, Santa Barbara, CA *93108*
   MISS Nancy de F—Cal'87. . . . .
   MISS Sarah C . . . .
Reed MR & MRS G Peter Q (Mary E Gamwell) Bgt.H'48 . . . . | ☎ (914) 232-5421 3 Mt Holly Rd E, Katonah, NY *10536*
   MR Benjamin . . . .
Reed MR & MRS H Mason JR (Marguerite Mann) Rr.P'54
   ☎ (203) 966-5494 . . 141 Hemlock Hill Rd, New Canaan, CT *06840*
Reed MR Henry H—Ithaca'76.Ithaca'79 . . see D Middleton
Reed MR James—Stan'32 . . . . | ☎ (707) 538-1045 301 White Oak Dv, Apt 318, Santa Rosa, CA *95409*
   MR James 3d . . . .
   MISS Laura L (Drown—Laura L G Reed) . . . . . .
Reed MR James H IV—MempArt'72
   ☎ (615) 665-0912 . . 2026 Priest Rd, Nashville, TN *37215*
Reed MR & MRS John (Helen E Anderton) Bnd'50.Ct.H'45
   ☎ (301) 654-1162 . . 35 W Irving St, Chevy Chase, MD *20815*
Reed MR & MRS John S (Marjorie Lindsay) Cho.On.Sr.Y'39 . . . . | ☎ (847) 234-4086 301 W Laurel Av, PO Box 112, Lake Forest, IL *60045*
   MISS Helen S—at 109 av de la République, 94300 Vincennes, Frances . . . .
   DR Peter S—Pa'89—at ☎ (212) 744-7963 180 E 79 St, Apt 6G, New York, NY *10021* . . .

Reed MR & MRS Joseph Verner JR (Marie M Byers) Ri.Ln.Gr.Mt.Plg.Myf.Cw.Sar.Cly.Y'61 . . . . ☎ (203) 869-2121 Denbigh Farm, 73 Sterling Rd, Greenwich, CT 06831
MISS Electra—Cly.—at 3101 Clay St, San Francisco, CA 94115 . . . .

Reed MR & MRS Nathaniel (G Dabney Freeman) Bcs.Ec.Y'55.Y'64 ☎ (508) 526-1648 9 Harold St, Manchester-By-The-Sea, MA 01944-1258
MISS Wrenn D—at ☎ (617) 232-4807 100 Naples Rd, Brookline, MA 02146 . . . .
MR Timothy N—at ☎ (617) 425-8642 150 Huntington Av, NL8, Boston, MA 02115 . .

Reed MR & MRS Nathaniel P (Alita D Weaver) Ln.Ty'55 . . . . ☎ (561) 546-5323 6 River View Rd, Hobe Sound, FL 33455
MISS Alita D—Ty'89 . . . .

Reed MR & MRS Nathaniel P JR (Emily K Thomas) Va'88.StM'93.Va'96 ☎ (804) 293-9830 . . 1629 Inglewood Dv, Charlottesville, VA 22901

Reed MISS P J Eliza—Br'92 . . see O de la Renta

Reed MR & MRS P Loring JR (Truesdale—Ann M Soule) Cy.D.Hn.H'40 ☎ (508) 785-0449 . . 6 Strawberry Hill St, Dover, MA 02030

Reed MR & MRS Pendennis W JR (Smith—Barbara W Cutchins) Sth'52.Ncd.Mid'56 ☎ (802) 867-4038 . . Kirby Hollow Rd, Dorset, VT 05251

Reed MISS Phyllis A—Evg.BtP.Mds. ☎ (561) 832-6978 . . 369 S Lake Dv, Apt E1, Palm Beach, FL 33480

Reed MR Samuel P—K.Ri.Ty'58 ☎ (212) 744-5963 . . 953 Fifth Av, New York, NY 10021

Reed MR & MRS Stanley F (Harriet T Dyer) Srb.BtP.Evg.Cc.Cly.Cda.Y'35.H'38 . . of ☎ (561) 659-6950 . . 389 S Lake Dv, Palm Beach, FL 33480 ☎ (401) 847-0402 . . Bonnie Crest Apt B8, 111 Harrison Av, Newport, RI 02840

Reed MISS Susan K—V'78 ☎ (718) 965-9129 . . 459—12 St, Brooklyn, NY 11215

Reed MR & MRS William G JR (Victoria S Nicol) Stan'63.Pcu.Duke'61 PO Box 31, Medina, WA 98039

Reed MR William M—H'46 ☎ (214) 526-1933 . . 2601 Hudnall St, Apt 122, Dallas, TX 75235

Reed MR William S—Stan'67 . . . . ☎ (415) 851-0369 328 Highland Terr, Woodside, CA 94062
JUNIORS MISS Alexandra J . . . .

Reeder MR & MRS Henry S (Susan B Carnes) Skd'63.Cy.Chi.P'61.Mit'63.H'64 . . . . ☎ (617) 899-0274 16 Saddle Hill Rd, Weston, MA 02193
MISS Liza C—ColC'93 . . . .
MR Nathaniel S—Mont'88 . . . .

Reeder MR & MRS Oliver H (Nancy H Fisher) Md.Elk.Ny.Gi.Wt.Cw.Mv.Dh.Cc.Cda.Pn.P'39 ⚜ ☎ (410) VA3-5544 . . 1300 Dulaney Valley Rd, Towson, MD 21286

Rees MR & MRS Homer McK (L Coverly Roche) Cly.Cda.Yn.Y'52.H'61 . . . . ☎ (203) 869-6661 Hilltop Farm, 816 North St, Greenwich, CT 06831
MISS Sarah C—at 254 W 10 St, New York, NY 10014 . . . .
MISS Nancy McK—at 15 Colborne Rd, Brighton, MA 02135 . . . .

Rees MR & MRS Malcolm C JR (Gail K Swanson) P'55 . . . . ☎ (508) 475-2878 5 Bridle Path Rd, Andover, MA 01810
MR Malcolm C 3d . . . .
MR Stuart M—Cal'92—at Harvard Law . . . .

Rees MR & MRS Morgan Van A (Joanna J Wallis) McG'58 ☎ (512) 261-4036 9 Swiftwater Trail, Austin, TX 78738
MR J Eliot . . . .

Rees MRS Richard Lee SR (Jane Davis) . . . . of ☎ (415)775-7055 1333 Jones St, Apt 403, San Francisco, CA 94109
MR Richard L JR . . . . ☎ (011-81-3) 265-1111 New Otani Hotel, 4 Kioi-cho, Tokyo, Japan

Rees MR & MRS William M (Marianna Adair) Bhm.Ln.Cly.Y'37 ☎ (203) 531-7652 . . 623 W Lyon Farm Dv, Greenwich, CT 06831

Rees MR & MRS William M JR (Nancy C Donohue) Geo'77.Yh.Y.'76 ☎ (914) 967-9275 . . 164 Grandview Av, Rye, NY 10580

Reese MRS Addison H (Gertrude R Craig) ☎ (410) 243-5506 . . 830 W 40 St, Apt 715, Baltimore, MD 21211

Reese MR & MRS Alexander S (Marina E Killery) Unn.Y'75.Cl'79 ☎ (011-44-171) 792-2332 . . 16 Denbigh Rd, Nottinghill Gate, London W11 2SN, England

Reese MR & MRS Algernon B 3d (Lyman—Catherine S Mallinckrodt) Wash'87.Y'88.Y.'66.Cr'69 . . of ☎ (914) 373-9165 . . 144 Amenia Union Rd, Amenia, NY 12501 ☎ (212) 260-6598 . . 71 Washington Place, Apt 2A, New York, NY 10011

Reese MISS Anne H . . see C E Anagnostopoulos

Reese DR & MRS Charles L 4th (Sara C Holliday) TJef'76.Wil.P'73.Jef'78 PO Box 469, Unionville, PA 19375

Reese MRS Charles Lee (Bush—Annette E Mason) . . . . Died at Hockessin, DE May 21'95

Reese MR & MRS Charles W JR (Olsen—Jill Fritschi) Mls'66.Pcu.Tcy.W&L'66.Cal'69 . . . . ☎ (510) 547-4745 89 LaSalle Av, Piedmont, CA 94611
MISS Clarissa J . . . .
JUNIORS MISS Alexandra R—☎ (510) 547-0613 .

Reese MR & MRS George B (Elizabeth A Stolba) V'72.Un.Y.'70.Cl'73 ☎ (212) 737-1057 . . 830 Park Av, New York, NY 10021

Reese MR & MRS George Marlow JR (Ann B Covey) Aub'62 . . . . ☎ (334) 834-7116 2619 Wildwood Dv, Montgomery, AL 36111
MISS Margaret A . . . .
MISS Letitia A . . . .
MR Pickett R . . . .
JUNIORS MISS Carol M . . . .

Reese MR & MRS John R (L Hope Wells) Rc.Pr.Ng.Csh.Pa'65.Pa'67 . . . . of ☎ (212)517-2491 30 E 76 St, New York, NY 10021
MISS Augusta B . . . . ☎ (516) 367-3985 86 Shore Rd, Cold Spring Harbor, NY 11724

Reese MR & MRS John S 4th (Mary A Ranken) Cw.Ncd.P'27.JHop'31
☎ (302) 652-5455 . . The Devon Apt 1114, 2401 Pennsylvania Av, Wilmington, DE *19806-1418*
Reese MR Morgan C—Cc.Rv.
☎ (212) 529-8204 . . 738 Broadway, New York, NY *10003*
Reese MR Peter P . . see C E Anagnostopoulos
Reese MR & MRS Rigdon L (Hanson—Candace Cain) | of ☎ (401)846-5901
Nf.Ny.Pa'67.Cr'70 . . . . | 590 Bellevue Av,
MISS Remington C—at Dean Coll . . . . | Newport, RI *02840*
MISS Dillon B—at Dean Coll . . . . | ☎ (207) 244-5394
  MISS Ashley C Hanson—at Wheaton . . . . . . | Kings Lane, Manset,
  MR Brewster B Hanson 3d—at Wheaton . . . . | ME *04656*
Reese MR & MRS William Willis (Sonia L van Voorhees)
Rc.Un.K.Plg.Bcs.Chr.Bm.Pl.Mto.Cw.Fw.Ne.Lm.Vca.
Coa.Snc.StA.Rv.Ht.Sar.Myf.StJ.Wt.Ty'63.Cl'70 . . of
☎ (212) 737-2223 . . 910 Park Av, New York, NY *10021*
☎ (561) 659-3232 . . 1515 S Flagler Dv, West Palm Beach, FL *33401*
Reese MRS Willis L M (Frances G Stevens) C.Cly.Dc.
☎ (914) 297-2213 . . ''Obercreek'' PO Box 220, Hughsonville, NY *12537*
Reeser MR J Weston . . see D L Parry
Reeve MR & MRS Alfred Roosevelt (Elizabeth B Kent) H'86
☎ (508) 526-8750 . . 5 Washington St, Manchester, MA *01944*
Reeve MRS Brooke JR (Virginia D Williams)
☎ (912) 354-7277 . . Sylvan Island, Savannah, GA *31404*
Reeve MISS Cintra Lowell (Rossi—Cintra L Reeve) Briar'68
☎ (508) 927-3994 . . ''Rockmarge'' Prides Crossing, MA *01965*
Reeve MR & MRS Lawrence Lowell (Eleanor Swift)
Nf.Sm.Chi.H'35.Mit'41 ⚓ . . of
☎ (508) 526-1105 . . ''Wyck'' Smith's Point, PO Box 311, Manchester, MA *01944*
☎ (207) 288-3037 . . ''Deep Cove'' Mt Desert, ME *04660*
Reeve MRS Richard H (Jacob—Josephine F R Thomas) Sdy.Ncd.
☎ (520) 398-2081 . . San Cayetano Farm, PO Box 37, Tumacacori, AZ *85640*
Reeve MRS Rowland S (Mary G Pancoast) M.Ncd.Dar.
☎ (610) 642-6620 . . 449 Montgomery Av, Apt 412, Haverford, PA *19041*
Reeve MR & MRS Stuart A (Mary Elizabeth B Mitchell)
Beloit'74.SUNY'78.Ill'85.SUNY'71.SUNY'76.SUNY'86
☎ (203) 938-0456 . . 124 Gallows Hill Rd, West Redding, CT *06896*
Reeves MR & MRS C E Graham (Joan U Mallory) Ws'43.Csn.Ncd.Pn.P'34
☎ (803) 546-5970 . . Annandale Plantation, Rte 2, Box 188, Georgetown, SC *29440*
Reeves MR Charles B JR—Gv.Elk.Md.P'45
☎ (410) 235-3937 . . 4406 Greenway, Baltimore, MD *21218*
Reeves MRS Elizabeth L (Elizabeth L Gould) . . . . . . | see A P Gould
MISS Elizabeth L . . . . |
Reeves MISS Elizabeth S
☎ (212) 734-4385 . . 1 Gracie Terr, New York, NY *10028*
Reeves MR & MRS H Van Kirk (Ann Murchison) | ☎ (011-33-1)
B.Snc.H'61.H'64 . . . . | 43-21-37-37
MISS Daisy F—at 7 Wyatt St, Somerville, MA | 240 blvd Raspail,
02143 . . . . | 75014 Paris, France
MR Evander J—at Leicester U . . . . |

Reeves MR Laurence E 3d—Syr'72 . . . . | ☎ (802) 785-4985
JUNIORS MISS Caitlin De G . . . . | PO Box 201,
   | Thetford Center, VT
   | *05075*
Reeves MISS Lydia L—Penn'87
☎ (302) 456-0630 . . 373 W Chestnut Hill Rd, Newark, DE *19713*
Reeves MRS Morris (Lydia L Morris)
☎ (610) MU8-1324 . . 252-2D Iven Av, St Davids, PA *19087*
Reeves MR & MRS William H 4th (Suzanne Evans) | of ☎ (401)621-8848
Swb'68.NCar'66.Pa'71 . . . . | 175 Upton Av,
MISS Elizabeth S—at ☎ (415) 673-7427 | Providence, RI
1550 Bay St, Apt 258, San Francisco, CA *94123* | *02906*
MR William Evans—at ☎ (415) 292-7369 | ☎ (415) 775-8848
1312 Fulton St, San Francisco, CA *94117* . . . . . | 1895 Jackson St,
   | Apt 506,
   | San Francisco, CA
   | *94109*
Reeves MR William P—Pc.Penn'59
☎ (860) 824-0112 . . ''Wenlock Edge'' 285 Norfolk Rd, East Canaan, CT *06024-0666*
Regalbuto MR & MRS Jason R (Wilder O Bishop) PineM'91.BtP.
☎ (561) 655-1886 . . 160 Seabreeze Av, Palm Beach, FL *33480*
Regan MR & MRS Donald T (Ann G Buchanan) Mt.An.Ncd.H'40 . . of
136 John Wickham, Williamsburg, VA *23185*
7864 Chick Evans Place, Sarasota, FL *34240*
Regan MR Glen B . . . . | ☎ (415) 851-3000
JUNIORS MISS Elyse E . . . . | 305 Lindenbrook
   | Court, Woodside,
   | CA *94062-2445*
Regan MRS Gordon S (Baltazar—Elba V Campos) . | ☎ (540) 832-3343
MR Gordon B—Rol'65 . . . . | ''Inverness''
  MR J Rafael Baltazar-Campos . . . . | 10226 Inverness Dv,
   | Gordonsville, VA
   | *22942-8355*
Regan MISS Linda J—Br'78 . . see MRS J U Moorhead
Regan MR & MRS Robert J (Susan T Matthews) CalSt'93.SonSt'92
☎ (805) 685-9758 . . 7632 Hollister Av, Apt 248, Santa Barbara, CA *93117*
Regan MR & MRS T Winston (Courtney K Armour) | ☎ (803) 853-5111
B.Mds.Ri.Ty'72.Ty'73 . . . . | 55 E Bay St,
JUNIORS MISS Chauncey B . . . . | Charleston, SC
   | *29401*
Regan MR & MRS William J JR (Barbara Leahy) St.Cy.G.Wms'55
☎ (716) 885-0234 . . 46 Penhurst Park, Buffalo, NY *14222*
Reger MR Robert J JR—Ford'70.Va'73
☎ (212) 744-7824 . . 163 E 81 St, Apt 5D, New York, NY *10028*
Register MR & MRS Albert L 3d (Costikyan—Hope | ☎ (508) 627-7948
M Kingsbury) V'57.Eyc.Err.USN'50 . . . . | ''Telescope Hill''
  MR Warren K Costikyan—at | 15 Atwood Circle,
44 Kirkham Place, Apt 3, Stamford, CT *06890* | PO Box 1247,
  MR Timothy W Costikyan—at | Edgartown, MA
178 Rowayton Woods Dv, South Norwalk, CT | *02539-1247*
06854 . . . . |
  MR Kent R Costikyan 3d—at |
178 Rowayton Woods Dv, South Norwalk, CT |
06854 . . . . |

Register MISS Alison S
☎ (609) 758-7007 . . 23 Hutchinson Rd, Allentown, NJ *08501*
Register MR & MRS Frederick L (Constance E Jordan) Md'89
☎ (804) 273-9017 . . 3924 Freeport Place, Apt 11, Richmond, VA *23233*
Register MR & MRS John M (Joanna G Logan) H'51
☎ (919) 946-1330 . . 111 River View Dv, Washington, NC *27889*
Register MR & MRS John S (Catherine Richards)
Cal'61 . . . . | ☎ (310) 457-7367
MISS Kathryn S . . . . | 7031 Fernhill Dv,
MR David C . . . . | Malibu, CA *90265*
Register MR & MRS Peter E (Karen L Shumaker) Ken'88.Ken'88
☎ (310) 391-4341 . . 4318 Moore St, Los Angeles, CA *90066*
Reich MR & MRS Christopher V (Eleanor M Paschal) Nu'91.Dth'80
☎ (914) 253-8336 . . 70 Westerleigh Rd, Purchase, NY *10577*
Reich MR & MRS David R (Elisabeth L Gant) Ala'82.SpgH'83
☎ (205) 933-2843 . . 2616 Lanark Rd, Birmingham, AL *35223*
Reich MASTER George Scoville (Christopher V) . . . . Born at
New York, NY Feb 5'94
Reich MR & MRS Ronald E (Camille A Timberlake)
CalSt'66 . . . . | ☎ (415) 563-6464
MR Christopher Guittard . . . . | 46 Presidio Av,
MR Alexander Sommer . . . . | San Francisco, CA
MR Marc La Fore | *94115*
Reichel MR & MRS Frank H JR (Beatrice A Hinson) Me.Ln.Y'48
☎ (970) 728-4761 . . 207 N Oak St, PO Box 1526, Telluride, CO *81435*
Reichel MR & MRS Frank H 3d (Suzanne L Schott)
Dth'85.Me.Cry.Dth'86.Pa'93
☎ (610) 525-2268 . . 601 Harriton Rd, Bryn Mawr, PA *19010*
Reichner MRS Aiken (Erika Bogner)
☎ (011-41-22) 735-28-30 . . 1 Chemin de le Planta, 1223 Cologny, Geneva, Switzerland
Reichner MR Aiken—Cw.Sar.Cc.P'47 . . . . | ☎ (561) 659-7479
MISS Cristina—P'95—at Georgetown Med . . . . . | LaFontana Apt 105,
| 2800 N Flagler Dv,
| West Palm Beach,
| FL *33407*
Reichner MRS C Fraser (Mary C Watters)
☎ (609) 859-3315 . . 31 Pulham Lane, Southampton, NJ *08088-1017*
Reichner COL & MRS Henry H JR (Julia A Spencer) USMC.Pc.Wt.Rv.Pa'40
☎ (215) 247-1566 . . 8005 Crefeld St, Philadelphia, PA *19118*
Reid MR Alexander B
☎ (415) 665-4682 . . 1460 Eighteenth Av, San Francisco, CA *94122*
Reid MR & MRS Andrew C (Jessie H Leonard) Pr.Hob'81
☎ (508) 356-9819 . . 3 S Village Green, Ipswich, MA *01938*
Reid MR Andrew V—CalArts'87
☎ (503) 238-5761 . . 3333 SE 39 Av, Apt 26, Portland, OR *97202-1760*
Reid MRS B Trowbridge (Sheriff—White—Barbara W Trowbridge) . . . . . .
Married at Stonington, CT
Barnes MR Chaplin Bradford (late Irston R) . . . . Apr 13'96
Reid MR Bagley—Fic.Va'59 . . of
☎ (212) 371-0821 . . 400 E 57 St, New York, NY *10022*
☎ (516) 788-7882 . . PO Box 475, Fishers Island, NY *06390*
Reid MR & MRS Bruce S (Emilie C Hobbs)
NCar'75.Cy.Ala'76 . . . . | ☎ (334) 281-7654
JUNIORS MR Bruce S JR . . . . | 3541 Thomas Av,
| Montgomery, AL
| *36111*

Reid MR & MRS C Nash (Perrault—Elizabeth T Willis) Dar. ⚓ . . of
☎ (561) 276-0904 . . 400 Seasage Dv, Apt 904, Delray Beach, FL *33483*
☎ (914) 273-3123 . . "Dier Hill" 31 N Greenwich Rd, Armonk, NY *10504*
Reid LT & MRS Daniel F M (Andrea R McEuen)
USN.SwTex'86.CalSt'89.Leh'85
3323 Hickory Falls Dv, Kingwood, TX *77345*
Reid MR David W—ColC'89
☎ (212) 246-6649 . . 427 W 51 St, Apt 5H, New York, NY *10019*
Reid MR Dorian F—Aht'38
☎ (415) 368-6902 . . 47 Shearer Dv, Atherton, CA *94027*
Reid MRS Fergus JR (Etheldreda W Seabury) Cly.Cda.Ncd.
☎ (207) 363-8281 . . PO Box 76, Stage Neck Rd, York Harbor, ME *03911-0076*
Reid MRS Horace W (Augusta McC Forker) . . . . Died at
Cincinnati, OH Feb 10'96
Reid MR & MRS Horace W JR (Ann G Becker) Sth'52.Wms'50
☎ (513) 561-6554 . . 8780 Old Indian Hill Rd, Cincinnati, OH *45243*
Reid MR & MRS James G (Elizabeth D Key) Rol'90.Fic.Rol'90
☎ (804) 358-9415 . . 341 Lexington Rd, Richmond, VA *23226*
Reid MRS John (Denyse E Van Hove) Mds.
☎ (609) 924-5755 . . 26 Westcott Rd, Princeton, NJ *08540*
Reid MR & MRS John M (Louise P Ott) Rcn.Ny.Wms'49 . . of
☎ (203) 966-4425 . . 28 Buttery Rd, New Canaan, CT *06840*
☎ (717) 775-7371 . . "Cousin's Cove" Blooming Grove Hunt & Fish Club, Hawley, PA *18428*
Reid MRS Marian V (Marian M Vilas) Cnt.Wa.
☎ (630) 377-0234 . . 26 Lakewood Circle, St Charles, IL *60174*
Reid MR & MRS Ogden R (Mary L Stewart) Bnd'46.Cl'48.Ny.Cly.Y'50
☎ (914) 763-5337 . . Mead St, Waccabuc, NY *10597*
Reid MR & MRS Samuel S (Juliet C Weber) Br'92.Ty'85 . . of
☎ (401) 886-4448 . . 1 Cedar Rock Meadows, East Greenwich, RI *02818*
☎ (207) 439-0118 . . "Heron Hill" PO Box 161, Kittery Point, ME *03905*
Reid MR & MRS William S (Ala M O'N Hencken) Rdc'60.Y'56
☎ (207) 363-4824 . . "Birch Hill" Box 738, 496 York St, York Harbor, ME *03911*
Reidy MR James T . . see W A Jaicks JR
Reidy MR John S—Cyb.Sm.H.'61
☎ (212) 249-4764 . . 151 E 79 St, New York, NY *10021-0421*
Reigart MRS John M (Dorothy Chandler)
☎ (803) 768-0088 . . 2745 Seabrook Island Rd, Johns Island, SC *29455*
Reigate LADY (Emily Cross) Csn.
☎ (011-44-171) 235-6506 . . 36 Eaton Square, London SW1W 9DH, England
Reigeluth MR & MRS Robert S (Mary C Applegate) Yn.Y'39
☎ (203) 776-4666 . . 123 Ogden St, New Haven, CT *06511*
Reilley MRS Ewing W (Soffer—Clawson—Elizabeth M Kals) S.Gr.Cs.
☎ (516) WA2-0225 . . "Little Orchard" PO Box 175, East Norwich, NY *11732*
Reilly MR Christopher C
☎ (703) 820-6711 . . 3464 Martha Custis Dv, Alexandria, VA *22302*
Reilly MISS Elena C—Stan'93 . . see J R Shoch 3d
Reilly MR George D—AmU'86
☎ (212) 249-0973 . . 424 E 77 St, Apt 2C, New York, NY *10021*

Reilly MR John H JR—Ihy.Ny.S.USMMA'48.
StJ'52 ⚓ . . . .
  MISS Margaret M—at Fordham . . . .
  JUNIORS MISS Elizabeth A—at Deerfield . . . .
  JUNIORS MR John H 3d—at Fordham . . . .
☎ (914) 855-9010
331 Quaker Hill Rd,
Pawling, NY *12564*

Reilly MR Matthew T . . see J R Shoch 3d
Reilly MR & MRS Robert D (Martha B Baldwin) Nw'46.Nw'47
  ☎ (847) 446-5860 . . 985 Pine Tree Lane, Winnetka, IL *60093*
Reilly DR & MRS Robert J (Diane T Tiffany) Cl'62.Cl'57
  ☎ (520) 299-1193 . . 4477 E Saranac Dv, Tucson, AZ *85718*
Reily MR & MRS Stephen R (Emily S Bingham) H'87
  see Dilatory Domiciles
Reily MR & MRS W Boatner III (Edwinna Griswold)
Ncmb'58.Err.Ny.Eyc.Tul'50 ⚓
  ☎ (504) 523-1031 . . 2221 Prytania St, New Orleans, LA *70130*
Reimer MR & MRS J Squier (Donna V Webster) Bgt.P'54
  ☎ (914) 234-3328 . . 46 Hook Rd, Bedford, NY *10506*
Reimers DR & MRS Carl D 3d (Pamela G Polcini)
Syr'83.Macalester'84.NJMed'88
  ☎ (212) 879-9346 . . 500 E 77 St, Apt 1531, New York, NY *10162-0005*
Reimers MRS Warren D (Lorna M Anderson) Nw'35
  ☎ (601) 352-8793 . . 1020 Carlisle St, Jackson, MS *39202*
Reinecke MR Robert M . . see MRS R J Bates
Reineman MR & MRS Joseph V JR (Sarah B Polese) LakeF'84.Ty'82
  ☎ (508) 927-2206 . . 788 Hale St, Beverly Farms, MA *01915*
Reiner MR & MRS John P (Mary E Wells) Mid'53.
Nu'55.Cl'60.T.Km.Cly.Dar.Ford'54.Cl'55.Cl'60
  MISS Mary E A—Bnd'84.Ford'88.Nu'92.Cly.
Mto.Dar.
  MR Clark B—Mid'86 . . . .
of ☎ (212)628-2341
340 E 72 St,
New York, NY
10021
☎ (914) 351-2673
Tuxedo Club,
W Lake Rd,
Tuxedo Park, NY
10987

Reinhardt MRS G Frederick (Lillian L Tootle)
  ☎ (212) 988-9699 . . 29 E 64 St, Apt 11C, New York, NY *10021-7043*
Reinicke MR & MRS F Rogers (Dalais—Judith A
MacGuire) Woos'49.Cl'51 . . . .
  MISS Mary J MacGuire—Man'vl'87 . . . .
  MR Sean M MacGuire . . . .
☎ (212) 427-3681
1100 Park Av,
New York, NY
10128

Reiniger MASTER Alexander Graham (Harlan deC) . . . . Born at
Winchester, MA Mch 16'95
Reiniger MR & MRS Harlan deC (Jane D Maurer) AMag'78.Bost'80.Emer'87
  ☎ (617) 631-3180 . . 4 Linden St, Marblehead, MA *01945*
Reiniger MR & MRS Scott H (Grace deCernea) Nyc.
  ☎ (914) 234-7188 . . "The Cottage" 326 Cantitoe Rd, Bedford Hills,
NY *10507*
Reisinger MR & MRS Ronald B (Carolyn J Gall)
MtH'82.Cysl.FairD'67 . . . .
  MISS Hope B . . . .
  MR Christopher B . . . .
of ☎ (813)541-4244
9441 Beachberry
Place, Pinellas Park,
FL *34782*
☎ (616) 846-1738
PO Box 612,
25 Stickney Ridge
Rd, Grand Haven,
MI *49417*

Reisky de Dubnic MR & MRS John S P (Karen A Thorsey)
Va'85.Va'85.Va'91
  ☎ (617) 431-8658 . . 37 Park Av, Wellesley Hills, MA *02181*
Reitter MR & MRS Frank R (Gail G Linzee)
Tenn'92.NotreD'59 . . . .
  MISS Stefani A—BostColl'94 . . . .
  MISS Kirsten M—Tenn'96 . . . .
of ☎ (508)650-0974
1 Phillips Pond,
South Natick, MA
01760
☎ (802) 422-8067
''Villa Reitter''
Weathervane Rd,
Killington, VT
05751

Reksten MRS Astrid J (Hoyer-Ellefsen—Astrid J Reksten) V'55
  ☎ (954) 752-9518 . . 6450 NW 80 Dv, Parkland, FL *33067-2485*
Remer MR & MRS John H (Ketcham—Frances C Edmunds) Wil.Y'48
PO Box 3720, Wilmington, DE *19807*
Remer MRS John H JR (Mary F Scott) Bost'73
  ☎ (610) 688-0516 . . ''Ardrossan'' 811 Newtown Rd, Villanova,
PA *19085*
Remer MR John H JR—Col'73 . . of
  ☎ (302) 995-1559 . . PO Box 3720, Wilmington, DE *19807*
  ☎ (212) 355-1214 . . 340 E 52 St, New York, NY *10022*
Remick MR Fenton M—Y'56 . . . .
  MISS Elisabeth L . . . .
  MISS Charlotte B . . . .
  MR Fenton M 2d . . . .
  MR Jerome H 4th . . . .
☎ (313) TU2-0043
457 Lexington Rd,
Grosse Pointe
Farms, MI *48236*

Remington MR & MRS David F (Chelsey A Carrier)
Br'61.H'64 . . . .
  MISS Chelsey A—Br'89.Pa'95—at
1840 Jefferson St, Apt 201, San Francisco, CA
94123 . . . .
☎ (508) 456-8889
3 Depot Rd,
General Delivery,
Still River, MA
01467

Remington MRS George C T (Nemota—Kamila M Formanek) Me.Rcp.
  ☎ (561) 655-4689 . . 520 Island Dv, Palm Beach, FL *33480*
Remington MRS James F—Br'92
  ☎ (415) 274-5425 . . 770 California St, Apt 106, San Francisco,
CA *94108*
Remington MR & MRS Thomas R (Frances Whitehead)
Cysl.Nd.P'51.H'56 . . of
9 Cedar Crest, St Louis, MO *63132-4205*
  ☎ (941) 697-5985 . . ''Tween Waters Cottage'' Palm Island,
7092 Placida Rd, Cape Haze, FL *33946*
Remmel MR & MRS H Lawrence (Helen L Victor)
SL'81.Ln.Pr.Cly.P'75.W&L'78
  ☎ (212) 288-3754 . . 106 E 85 St, New York, NY *10028*
Renault MR & MRS Robert (Tallmadge Starr) Sth'65.Msq.AmInt'l'68
  ☎ (860) 434-0168 . . Sandpiper Point Rd, Old Lyme, CT *06371*
Renchard MR & MRS William S (Alice M Fleming) Ck.Cly.P.
  ☎ (516) 674-3877 . . 7 Matinecock Farms Rd, Glen Cove, NY *11542*
Rende MR & MRS Giandomenico (Kathleen
Mailliard) Stph'61.Juilliard'62.Fmy.Fr.Rome'59
  MISS Giuliana—Cal'91—at Vail, CO . . . .
  DR Robert—Stan'85.Tul'89—at
US Army Hospital, Heidelburg, Germany . . . . .
  MR John Ward—Sfg.Clare'89.Cal'96 . . . .
☎ (415) 461-1865
45 Via Barranca,
Greenbrae, CA
94904

Renehan MR & MRS Peter L (Diana R MacLear) Skd'86
  ☎ (212) 734-2506 . . 10 East End Av, Apt 3H, New York, NY *10021*

Rennie MRS William R (Jean Tower) V'35.BtP.Evg.Cly.Ncd . . .of
☎ (561) 655-4693 . . 136 Kings Rd, Palm Beach, FL *33480*
☎ (414) 271-8554 . . 2105 E Lafayette Place, Milwaukee, WI *53202*
Reno DR & MRS Stephen J (Catherine R Motley)
Elmira'74.StJColl'65.Cal'66
☎ (541) 482-3044 . . 610 Elkander St, Ashland, OR *97520*
Renshaw MR Frederick W—Rc.
☎ (312) 944-4489 . . 222 E Pearson St, Chicago, IL *60611*

Renshaw MISS Jeanette W . . . . MR Bache McE—Ny.Y'48—at Rice Blvd, New Bedford, MA *02745*	☎ (508) 369-7877 Garfield Rd, Concord, MA *01742*
Renshaw MRS John P (Nichols—Lolita Berns) Stan'52.Bur.Fr. . . . . MISS Corinne McC—at 123 W 900 St, Apt 4, Logan, UT *84321*	☎ (415) 342-3161 1808 Floribunda Av, Hillsborough, CA *94010*

MISS Allison H—at ☎ (415) 578-9853
8209 Admiralty Lane, Foster City, CA *94404* . .
Renshaw MR & MRS Robert H 3d (Mildred A Hoke) WestMd'43.Sar.StJ'38
☎ (941) 455-4549 . . 2269—50 Terr SW, Naples, FL *34116-6917*

Rentschler MR & MRS Charles E M (Suzanne S Snowden) Ln.Fic.P'61.H'64 . . . . MISS Marie K—at St Lawrence U . . . . MR Adam S—Nw'96 . . . . MR Charles F—at Tulane	☎ (812) 546-5975 2375 North 1050 East, Hartsville, IN *47244*

Rentschler MRS Frances B (Krumbhaar—Frances D Banes)
☎ (610) 644-4276 . . 16 Leopard Rd, Paoli, PA *19301*
Rentschler MRS Frederica S (Frederica P Schlaff) Mds.Cly.
☎ (212) 249-1761 . . 108 E 66 St, Apt 2A, New York, NY *10021*

Rentschler MR George Adam—Rc.P'59 . . . . MISS Farley M—at Purnell . . . . JUNIORS MISS Mary M	☎ (212) 980-1928 136 E 64 St, Apt 2D, New York, NY *10021-7360*

Rentschler MR Henry A—Wcc.P.'50
☎ (610) 644-5343 . . 1880 Fox Hill Lane, PO Box 962, Paoli, PA *19301-0962*
Renwick MR & MRS Edward Shield (Gloria A Rainey)
Cal'59.SCal'88.Vh.Stan'56.Stan'58
☎ (818) 796-6820 . . 1500 Normandy Dv, Pasadena, CA *91103*

Renwick MRS Frank W (Ethel P Hulbert) . . . . MISS Margaret M . . . . MR George W . . . . MR Robert H	☎ (602) 488-2884 PO Box 5007, Carefree, AZ *85377*
Renwick MRS John P—Bgt. MR David R—at ☎ (508) 252-9838 232 New St, Rehoboth, MA *02769*	☎ (914) 234-7125 "Dower House" PO Box 42, Bedford, NY *10506*
Renwick MR & MRS John P 3d (Meryl C Smith) Bgt.Pa'69 . . . . MISS Whitney V—Vt'93—at ☎ (212) 879-5424 176 E 81 St, New York, NY *10028* . . . . MR Nicholas C—at Wash'n & Lee	☎ (914) 232-5549 357 Mt Holly Rd, Katonah, NY *10536*
Renzy MR & MRS Bernard T III (Sandra J Welborn) Mt.Sl.Ncd.Dar.Cit'59.SCar'63 . . . . MISS Ann K—CtCol'94	1327 Carper's Farm Way, Vienna, VA *22182*

Repp MRS Herbert N (Rike—Catharine B Conklin) Mor.Mvh.DelB.
1475 Ridgegate Rd, Apt G, Dayton, OH *45429*

Repplier MISS (DR) Ann D—Buck'72.Temp'76.Temp'86
☎ (215) 843-5761 . . Manor 407A, 5500 Wissahickon Av, Philadelphia, PA *19144*

Repplier MRS Sidney N (Eleanor T Dill) . . . . MISS Constance N—at New York, NY	☎ (908) 341-2569 317 Huntington Av, Pine Beach, NJ *08741*
ReQua MR & MRS Michael C (Patricia Corscaden) FlaTech'73 . . . . JUNIORS MR Haven C	of ☎ (207)563-5649 RR 2, Box 60, River Rd, Newcastle, ME *04553* ☎ (207) 864-5421 130 Rock Pond Rd, Sandy River Plantation, Rangeley, ME *04970*

ReQua MRS Patrick A (Joan Smith) Carl'44 . . of
☎ (207) 633-2397 . . Dover Rd, RR 1, Box 354, Boothbay, ME *04537* Squirrel Island, ME *04570*

Reque DR & MRS Paul G (Barbara T Britton) Duke'33 . . . . MR Peter A—at 1073 Bush St, San Francisco, CA *94109* . . . . MISS Susan B (Aldridge—Susan B Reque)—at 312 E Glenwood Dv, Birmingham, AL *35209* . .	3850 Galleria Woods Dv, Apt 215, Birmingham, AL *35244*

Resnik MR & MRS David B (Susan M Preston) NCar'87.David'85.NCar'90
☎ (307) 742-8585 . . 1326 Thomes St, Laramie, WY *82070*

Resnik MR & MRS Michael D (Janet M Depping) V'60.Y'60 . . . . MISS Sarah L—NCar'92 . . . . MR Dimitri—NCar'88	☎ (919) 929-3324 Pegasus Farm, 132 Collins Mountain Rd, Chapel Hill, NC *27516*

Resor MRS Clifford (Hanson—Mabel F James)
☎ (520) 297-4280 . . 7317 N Yucca Via, Tucson, AZ *85704-6226*
Resor MR Stanley R—C.Yn.Y'39
☎ (203) 966-9889 . . 809 Weed St, New Canaan, CT *06840*
Resor MR & MRS Thomas S (Tamsen T Cudahy) Tufts'81.D.Wms'82
☎ (617) 329-9307 . . 18 Guild Rd, Dedham, MA *02026*
Ressler MR & MRS Harold Kirkby (Gabriella Plimpton)
Hlns'76.Y.'66.H'69 . . of
☎ (011-41-22) 750-0712 . . 47 Chemin des Princes, 1253 Vandoeuvres, Geneva, Switzerland
☎ (516) 749-3095 . . Shore Rd, PO Box 293, Dering Harbor, Shelter Island Heights, NY *11965*

Reuben MR & MRS Don H (Haywood—Jeannette Hurley) Nw'51 . . . . MR Howard E—at San Diego State U	☎ (619) 324-0619 20 Jill Terr, Rancho Mirage, CA *92270*

Reuben MR & MRS Jeffrey L (Kelley J FitzGerald) OreSt'87.Wes'82.Ch'85
☎ (818) 386-1232 . . 16379 Mandalay Dv, Encino, CA *91436*
Reuben MR & MRS Michael B (Susan B Miller)
Ford'76.H'79.H'73.Stan'77.Stan'80.H'82
☎ (212) 570-9486 . . 70 E 77 St, Apt 7A, New York, NY *10021*

Reuben MR & MRS Timothy D (Katherine M Semones) Cal'87.H'77.H'80
☎ (818) 343-3442 . . 4745 Yarmouth Av, Encino, CA *91316*

Reusch MR & MRS Dennis S (Timpson—Margret R Smith)
SanDiego'82.CPI'72
☎ (619) 942-6412 . . 2112 Bulrush Lane, Cardiff-By-The-Sea, CA *92007*

Reuter MRS Walter H JR (Roberta T Speller)
☎ (704) 625-4274 . . Rte 1, Box 529A, Lake Lure, NC *28746*

Revell MR & MRS Alexander H 3d (Priscilla Morrill) Me.Ac.Nw'48.Mid'55
☎ (610) 323-8599 . . 201 Moyer Rd, Box 316, Pottstown, PA *19464*

Reventlow CTSS Court Haugwitz (Van Laer—Davis—Brent—
Margaret A Drayton) Cly . . .of
☎ (212) 355-4738 . . 570 Park Av, New York, NY *10021*
☎ (860) 567-9000 . . ''Pineholm Farm'' Duck Pond Rd, PO Box 1046,
Litchfield, CT *06759*

Rex MR & MRS A Perry (Adèle Augustine Perry)
Col'66.Bab'78 . . . . ☎ (617) 527-9261
MR Daniel F 2d . . . . 24 George St,
  Newton, MA *02158*

Rex MISS Rebecca—Col'89
☎ (401) 846-1154 . . ''Saltwood'' Sachuest Dv, Middletown, RI *02842*

Rex MRS Robert McC (Struthers—Lilly S Ferrell) Ncd . . .of
☎ (561) 272-1456 . . 200 Little Club Rd, Apt 9, Delray Beach,
FL *33483-7556*
5 Sessions Dv, Columbus, OH *43209*

Rexford MR & MRS Stephen C JR (Elizabeth M Corbin)
GeoW'91.Skd'87.Fairf'90.Mid'95
☎ (203) 371-6242 . . 220 Old Black Rock Tpke, Fairfield, CT *06430*

Reynal MR Anthony—Un.H'62
☎ (212) 289-3245 . . 245 E 87 St, New York, NY *10128*

Reynal MR & MRS Eric Y (Carmen Quintana) H'58 . ☎ (011-44-1451)
MISS Carmen L 821947
MR Michael L . . . . Keyneton Hayes,
  Upper Slaughter,
  Gloucestershire
  GL54 2JG, England

Reynders MR & MRS Charlton JR (Knowlton Ames) ☎ (914) 234-7337
Bgt.Plg.Cly.P.'59 . . . . 326 Cantitoe Rd,
MISS Alys Ames—Ham'89.Cly.—at Bedford Hills, NY
☎ (617) 437-0520 . . 6 Marlborough St, Boston, *10507*
MA *02116* . . . .

Reynders MR & MRS (DR) Charlton 3d (Claudia R Showalter)
P'88.Y'92.Bgt.P'88.P'92
☎ (617) 262-7240 . . 39 Marlborough St, Apt 4, Boston, MA *02116*

Reynders MR & MRS John V W 3d (Mary F Neven)
Morehd'83.Tex'85.Rens'86.P'92
2928 Calle De Ovejas, Santa Fe, NM *87505*

Reynolds MR & MRS A William (Joanne McCormick)
Kt.Un.Pk.H'55.Stan'57 . . of
☎ (216) 423-3433 . . Old Mill Rd, Gates Mills, OH *44040*
950 Beach Rd, Apt 391, Vero Beach, FL *32963*

Reynolds MISS Alice K (Tatum—Alice K Reynolds) Cr'80
see V B Meyer

Reynolds MRS Bartow (Prudence M Bartow) ⚓ . . ☎ (201) 376-1034
MR Philip B . . . . 123 River Edge Dv,
  Chatham, NJ *07928*

Reynolds MR & MRS Christopher H (H Bredt Handy) Ober'80.Dth'82
☎ (508) 358-7757 . . 6 Holiday Rd, Wayland, MA *01778*

Reynolds MR & MRS George I (Love—Royds— of ☎ (561)659-2939
Nancy R Sullivan) GeoW'50.NECons'52. 400 N Flagler Dv,
Man'vl'77.Evg.BtP.Ncd.Wes'38.H.'47 . . . . Apt 2001,
MISS Janet—at ☎ (202) 534-6876 West Palm Beach,
3110 Quebec Place NW, Washington, DC *20008* FL *33401*
  ☎ (203) 661-7249
  Khakum Wood,
  Greenwich, CT
  06831
  ☎ (607) 547-5208
  96 Lake St,
  PO Box 128,
  Cooperstown, NY
  13326

Reynolds MR & MRS Hal W (Elizabeth I McLean) Ithaca'84.Va'80
☎ (213) 661-2100 . . 5000 Ambrose Av, Los Angeles, CA *90027*

Reynolds MR & MRS J Donald (Alice D Derrick) RMWmn'57.Wash'59
☎ (334) 269-2764 . . 2030 S Hull St, Montgomery, AL *36104*

Reynolds MRS J W Stoddard (Guanda M Carter) Cal'51
☎ (818) 709-2808 . . 8801 Eton Av, Apt 17, Canoga Park, CA *91304*

Reynolds MR & MRS James A (Joan K Jefferson) Col'52.Sdy.
☎ (619) 223-7313 . . 2833 Talbot St, San Diego, CA *92106*

Reynolds MR James R—Tv.My.Hn.H.'23
☎ (508) 468-1580 . . 38 Larch Row, Wenham, MA *01984*

Reynolds MR & MRS Jeffrey T (Joanne M Gaderick)
OWes'82.Wh'lck'87.Denis'82.H'87
☎ (203) 421-5096 . . 443 Bartlett Dv, Madison, CT *06443*

Reynolds MR & MRS John D JR (Alexandra R Boardman)
☎ (212) 535-9551 . . 200 E 72 St, Apt 35H, New York, NY *10021*

Reynolds MR Jonathan McK—H'77.Stan'89 . . see A H Parker

Reynolds MISS Katherine B . . see V B Meyer

Reynolds MR & MRS Michael M (Deborah K White) Tex'76
☎ (512) 477-4252 . . 2305 Bonita St, Austin, TX *78703*

Reynolds MRS Nourse (Martha E Nourse)
☎ (352) 873-3393 . . 353 NW 125 Av, Ocala, FL *32675*

Reynolds MR & MRS Oliver C (Mildred Ellis) Rdc'21 . . of
☎ (203) 374-5611 . . 3030 Park Av, Health Center 208, Bridgeport,
CT *06604*
☎ (860) 868-7585 . . Old Litchfield Rd, Washington, CT *06793*

Reynolds MR R Roland—P'93 . . see MRS M Ballentine

Reynolds MRS Ralph E (Nicoud—A Jane ☎ (415) 435-9423
Hendrickson) . . . . 18 Paseo Mirasol,
MISS Barbara McN Nicoud . . . . Tiburon, CA *94920*
MISS Sarah L Nicoud . . . .
MSRS Louis JR & George B Nicoud . . . .

Reynolds MRS Richard S (Virginia Sargeant)
☎ (804) 288-4072 . . 5621 Cary Street Rd, Richmond, VA *23226*

Reynolds MR & MRS Russell S JR (Deborah A Toll)
Cal'55.Ihy.Ri.Ln.Ny.Y'54 ⚓
☎ (203) 869-8823 . . 39 Clapboard Ridge Rd, Greenwich, CT *06830*

Reynolds MR & MRS Russell S III (Lynda C Low)
Me'83.Unn.GeoW'82.Poly'96
☎ (203) 625-0219 . . 4 Ridge Rd, Greenwich, CT *06807*

Reynolds MISS (DR) Susan F (Frost—Root—Susan F Reynolds)
V'70.Cal'74.Cal'76
☎ (310) 454-4933 . . 652 Jacon Way, Pacific Palisades, CA *90272*

Rezny MRS Catherine M (Read—Catherine Minnick) Pa'41 . . . . | 2120 Sonoma Av, Apt 19, Santa Rosa, CA *95405*
MISS Karen K—at ☎ (512) 472-3329
2500 Nueces St, Austin, TX *78705* . . . . |

Rezny MISS Catherine M
☎ (916) 451-0405 . . 55 Aiken Way, Sacramento, CA *95819*

Rhame DR & MRS Harold E JR (Joan Williams)
Sth'49.Ht.Ny.Pqt.Sar.Cw.P'47 ⚓
☎ (203) 259-2220 . . 501 Mine Hill Rd, Fairfield, CT *06430*

Rhame MRS Lucy S (Pyle—Lucy S Rhame) Bost'78.GeoW'80
☎ (703) 836-3532 . . 508 S Fairfax St, Alexandria, VA *22314*

Rhea MR & MRS Alexander D 3d (Suzanne Menocal) | of ☎ (212)838-2494
K.Sar.Cly.P'41 . . . . | 580 Park Av,
MR Mark A—at 1217 Roaring Springs Rd, | New York, NY
Ft Worth, TX *76114* . . . . | *10021*
| ☎ (817) 731-3214
| 949 Roaring Springs
| Rd, Ft Worth, TX
| *76114*

Rhea MR & MRS Edward J (Signe L Girgus) | ☎ (703) 979-4824
VaCmth'72.Dar.Pn.P'61.Paris'64 . . . . | 1425 S Eads St, Apt
MR Alexander J—CathU'91—at Hautes Etudes | 1603, Arlington, VA
Commerciales Paris . . . . | *22202*

Rhea MR Kenneth A—Rol'94
301 W 53 St, Apt 25C, New York, NY *10019-5766*

Rhein MRS Francis B (Jane A Foster) . . . . | ☎ (540) 667-2023
MISS Jane F—Bow'78—at ☎ (401) 294-2724 | 2717 Blue Ridge
PO Box 403, Saunderstown, RI *02874* . . . . | Terr, Winchester,
| VA *22601*

Rhein MRS Jean-Pierre F (Wills—BRNSS Ludmilla M Forani)
Brussels'59.Duke'66.Rut'72 . . of
☎ (011-33-1) 42-23-51-91 . . 102 Chemin du Puy du Roy,
13090 Aix-en-Provence, France
☎ (011-33-16) 92-18-95-91 . . ''Les Terrasses du Soleil''
40 rte des Bréguières, 06110 Le Cannet, France

Rhein MR & MRS John H W 3d (Phyllis J Betz) | ☎ (516) 248-6642
Hob'53 . . . . | 127 Cherry Valley
MISS Deborah B—at 20 Union Place, Northport, | Av, Garden City,
NY *11768* . . . . | NY *11530*

Rhein MR John H W 4th (John H W 3d) . . . . | Married at
Cold Spring Harbor, NY
Kettler MISS Petra (Hans) . . . . | Oct 20'95

Rhein MR Peter Van R—Va'74 . . of
☎ (617) 367-0030 . . 6 Whittier Place, Apt 2K, Boston, MA *02114*
☎ (401) 294-6816 . . ''Bayberry Cottage'' 195 Waterway, Saunderstown,
RI *02874*

Rhett MR & MRS H Moore 3d (Lynne Smith) Van'79.Van'77
☎ (615) 385-3345 . . 1223 Nichol Lane, Nashville, TN *37205*

Rhett MR Harry M . . . . Died at
Huntsville, AL Feb 3'96

Rhett MR & MRS W Warren B (Ellen MacElvain)
Van'78.Ala'81.W&L'83 . . of
☎ (205) 871-9777 . . 2517 Canterbury Rd, Birmingham, AL *35223*
☎ (904) 747-0590 . . 324 E Beach Dv, Apt 100, Panama City, FL *32401*

Rhett REV DR & MRS William P JR (Dorothy I Carson)
Cc.Cw.Char'ton'53.VaTheo'59.Temp'68.Aub'73
☎ (803) 723-6359 . . 2 St Michaels Alley, Charleston, SC *29401*

Rhinelander MISS Clare H (Kenney—Clare H Rhinelander) Cal'84.Cal'86
☎ (415) 441-4244 . . 1265 Washington St, Apt 3, San Francisco,
CA *94108*

Rhinelander MRS Frederic W (Julie C Hale)
Shorecliffs, 341 Avenida Vaquero, San Clemente, CA *92672*

Rhinelander MR & MRS John B (Jeanne E Cattell) | of ☎ (703)356-0825
Y'55.Va'61 . . . . | 6115 Ramshorn
MISS Margaret T—at 724 S St Asaph St, | Place, McLean, VA
Apt B203, Alexandria, VA *22314* . . . . | *22101*
MISS Katherine P . . . . | ☎ (508) 283-1478
| 10 Cove Way,
| Rust Island,
| Gloucester, MA
| *01930*

Rhinelander MR & MRS John R (Amy M Dixon) Sth'92.Aht'85.Nw'91
☎ (201) 635-8228 . . 1 Williams Rd, Chatham, NJ *07928*

Rhinelander MRS Laurens H (Louise M Reed) Wells'31.Sl.Ncd.
☎ (804) 293-3124 . . 1819 Edgewood Lane, Charlottesville, VA *22903*

Rhinelander MR & MRS Nicholas T (Emily D Hewitt) Wes'87.H'88
see Dilatory Domiciles

Rhinelander MASTER Peter William (John R) . . . . Born at
Summit, NJ Mch 17'96

Rhinelander MR & MRS Philip M (Sonzski—Sears— | ☎ (207) 846-4970
Susannah White) Sth'62.H'65 | RR 3, Box 403D,
MISS Katharine C Sears—at Stanford . . . . | Browns Point Rd,
MR Edmund H Sears JR . . . . | Yarmouth, ME
| *04096*

Rhinelander MISS Phyllis M—Dc.Cda.Dar.
157 E 72 St, New York, NY *10021*

Rhoades MR & MRS James C (Mary B Rogers) Skd'85.Skd'84
☎ (214) 361-1159 . . 3921 Greenbrier Av, Dallas, TX *75225-5405*

Rhoades MRS John H (Bird—Alice M Heye)
3925 Greenbrier Dv, Dallas, TX *75225*

Rhoades MISS Patricia Gridley—Camb'71.Bard'75
☎ (508) 429-5327 . . 102 Church St, Apt 5, Holliston, MA *01746*

Rhoades MR Stephen P N
☎ (561) 689-8772 . . PO Box 545, Palm Beach, FL *33480*

Rhoads MRS C Brewster (Priscilla C Stevens) Ac.
☎ (215) WI7-0347 . . 2400 Washington Lane, Huntingdon Valley,
PA *19006*

Rhoads MRS Owen B (Brooks—Emily C Scott) Rc.Rd.Ph.Ac.Cspa.
☎ (610) 644-2077 . . ''Hollystone'' 333 S Valley Rd, Paoli, PA *19301*
Jan 1 . . ☎ (910) 692-8168 . . ''Moccasin Crossing'' PO Box 426,
Southern Pines, NC *28387*

Rhodes MRS Augustine J (McKinney—Augustine W Janeway) Pa'51
520 Fearrington Post, Pittsboro, NC *27312*

Rhodes DR & MRS C Harker 3d (Anne W Symington)
H'72.Geo'75.Hb.H'75.Cr'82.Rock'82
☎ (603) 643-5209 . . ''Tirtiganga'' 5 Curtiss Rd, Hanover, NH *03755*

Rhodes MR & MRS Clarence J (Hellmuth—Dorothy A Marshall)
Skd'49.Kt.GaTech'39
☎ (216) 932-7565 . . 2360 Delamere Dv, Cleveland Heights, OH *44106*

Rhodes MRS Robert E (Wheaton—Jaquith Jackson) Vh.
☎ (818) 799-6820 . . 691 S Orange Grove St, Pasadena, CA *91105*

Rial MRS William S JR (Sally L Wentling) S'Hill'35.Fcg.
☎ (412) 776-8414 . . Sherwood Oaks 403, 100 Norman Dv,
Cranberry Township, PA *16066-4238*

Rianhard MISS Elizabeth B (Lockwood) . . . . . Married at Morristown, NJ
  McCartney MR Kenneth E (Kenneth H) . . . . May 11'96
Rianhard MR & MRS Lockwood (Mary E Wurst) | ☎ (201) 895-2189
  Mo.Y'53.Mit'54.H'58 | 103 Shady Lane,
  MR Edward N—at 46 Davenport Place, | Randolph, NJ *07869*
  Morristown, NJ *07960* . . . . |
Rianhard MR & MRS Perry D (Susan M Colloty) | 37 Dogwood Lane,
  Ty'63 . . . . | Trumbull, CT *06611*
  MR Jonathan McK—LakeF'88—at |
  ☎ (773) 327-5247 . . 2040 N Clifton St, Chicago, |
  IL *60614* |
Rianhard MR & MRS Thomas McM JR (Chapman—Phyllis Leavenworth)
  ☎ (203) 263-3443 . . 6 Old Flanders Rd, Woodbury, CT *06798*
Ribbel MR & MRS Frank E (Merrilee J Steege) | ☎ (415) 457-9948
  SIll'71.Menlo'65 | 28 Mountain View
  MISS Emily C . . . . | Av, San Rafael, CA
   | *94901*
Ribeiro MR Elpidio W . . . . Died at
   | Boston, MA Apr 12'95
Ribeiro MRS Elpidio W (Linda Sturgis) Bost'68.Nh. | ☎ (508) 785-1739
  MISS Jenny L . . . . | 9 Wildwood Rd,
  MR Mark S . . . . | Dover, MA *02030*
  MR Eric P . . . . |
Riblet MISS Abigail H (Roy J 3d) . . . . Married at Seattle, WA
  Hartman MR Alan E . . . . Oct 7'95
Riblet MR Andrew W (Roy J 3d) . . . . . . Married at Santa Cruz, CA
  Martinez MISS Cynthia L . . . . Sep 16'95
Riblet MR & MRS Roy J 3d (Edwina E Peters) | ☎ (619) 755-2854
  Stan'65.CalTech'64.Stan'71 . . . . | 13746 Mira
  MR Christian M—at 651 NW 84 St, Seattle, WA | Montana Dv,
  98103 . . . . | Del Mar, CA *92014*
Rice MISS Alice H—Cl'90
  ☎ (212) 831-5698 . . 12 E 97 St, Apt 7C, New York, NY *10029*
Rice MR & MRS Donald S (M Edgenie Higgins) | ☎ (212) 427-0021
  Bost'65.Ri.Ny.C.Cs.H.'61 ⚓ | 1120 Fifth Av,
  MISS Edgenie R—at ☎ (212) 427-0018 | New York, NY
  12 E 97 St, Apt 9C, New York, NY *10029* . . . . | *10128*
Rice MR & MRS Francis B (Lynn W Wanamaker) | ☎ (516) 271-8685
  Bcs. | 147 Huntington Bay
  MISS Amy L—PineM'92 . . . . | Rd, Huntington, NY
  MR Francis R—O'92 . . . . | *11743*
Rice MR & MRS L Rushton (Martha B Chambers) Miss'86.Ala'84
  ☎ (334) 834-5333 . . 3343 Allendale Place, Montgomery, AL *36111*
Rice MR & MRS Richard C (Mary A Brooke) | ☎ (301) 953-7262
  Cc.Sl.Ncd.JHop'54.Md'60 . . . . | 409 Prince George
  MR Kennedy C—StMarys'95 . . . . | St, Laurel, MD
   | *20707*
Rich MRS B McNabb (McAllister—Betty McNabb) LakeF'49
  ☎ (847) 615-0151 . . 30 E Deerpath Rd, Lake Forest, IL *60045*
Rich MRS Edward L JR (Alexandra Russell) Gi.Cda.
  ☎ (410) 323-4027 . . 5105 Roland Av, Baltimore, MD *21210*
Rich MRS G Barrett 3d (Ruth I Jenkins) GeoKy'21.Yn.
  ☎ (203) 373-6210 . . 3030 Park Av, Bridgeport, CT *06604*
Rich MR & MRS George S (Isabel C Barrett) | ☎ (410) 653-9080
  Md.Gi.Cw.Hob'70.Pa'74 . . . . | 2016 Wiltonwood
  MISS Alexandra B . . . . | Rd, Stevenson, MD
  JUNIORS MR David B . . . . | *21153*

Rich MR & MRS Robert S (Myra Lakoff) | of ☎ (303)321-4965
  H'61.Y'65.Yn.Cr'59.Y'63 . . . . | 458 Grape St,
  MISS Rebecca A . . . . | Denver, CO
  MR David M—Box 884, Telluride, CO *81435* . . | *80220-5232*
  JUNIORS MISS Sarah C . . . . | ☎ (970) 968-2882
   | ''Copper Valley''
   | PO Box 3440,
   | Copper Mountain,
   | CO *80443*
Rich MR & MRS Russell P (Stephanie B Lassotovitch)
  Va'75.Gi.Md.Hob'68.JHop'83
  ☎ (410) 323-4574 . . 902 W Northern P'kway, Baltimore, MD *21210*
Richard MRS Auguste (Clark—Rita M Conway) Cly.
  ☎ (212) 421-8827 . . 480 Park Av, New York, NY *10022*
Richard MR & MRS Harold Van B (Jane Schmeltzer) Pr.Cly.P'36
  ☎ (561) 231-3471 . . 181 Oleander Way, Vero Beach, FL *32963*
Richard MR & MRS Peter L (Virginia A Rynne) | ☎ (914) 753-5568
  T.Cly.DU'69.DU'74 . . . . | Box 168,
  MR W Zachary—at San Fran Art Inst . . . . | 6 Sterlington Rd,
  JUNIORS MISS Cecily J C—at Groton . . . . | Sloatsburg, NY
  JUNIORS MR Travis Van B—at Kimball-Union . . | *10974*
Richards MRS Alexander (Elizabeth F Alexander) BMr'41
  ☎ (212) 662-7669 . . 905 West End Av, Apt 142, New York, NY *10025*
Richards MR & MRS Alfred N 3d (Karen R Knipp) | ☎ (610) 647-8733
  ColC'73 . . . . | 10 Pine Rd,
  MISS Katherine O . . . . | Malvern, PA *19355*
  JUNIORS MR Andrew W . . . . |
Richards MR & MRS Barry G (Katherine A Casey) . . | ☎ (864) 654-2721
  MR Kevin F . . . . | 323 Lancelot Dv,
   | Clemson, SC *29631*
Richards MISS Christine Louise
  see Dilatory Domiciles
Richards MRS Cordelia C (Cordelia G Creamer) | of ☎ (212)534-8467
  Sth'52.Cs.Ncd.Myf.Dc. . . . . | 70 E 96 St,
  MISS Cordelia Loomis—Br'83.Myf.Ncd.— | New York, NY
  ☎ (212) 876-1251 . . . . | *10128*
   | ☎ (860) 677-1803
   | 100 Main St,
   | Farmington, CT
   | *06032*
Richards MRS David E (Nancy B Lane)
  ☎ (801) 467-9905 . . 1151 E Brickyard Rd, Salt Lake City, UT *84106*
Richards MR Eben—H'52
  ☎ (703) 883-9639 . . 934 Mackall Av, McLean, VA *22101*
Richards MR & MRS Eric P (Cheryle L Kitchen) | ☎ (203) 966-7605
  Cl'67.Cl'69.Plg.Ny.Cly.Ncd.Dar.Cl'67 . . . . . . | 23 Pond View Lane,
  MISS Caroline E—Denis'96 . . . . | New Canaan, CT
  MISS Cynthia L—at Bucknell . . . . | *06840*
Richards MR & MRS Francis M JR (M Gaynor Wynne)
  MtH'45.Me.W.Dar.Ncd.Aht'45.Pa'49
  ☎ (610) LA5-7438 . . 359 Thornbrook Av, Rosemont, PA *19010*
Richards MR & MRS Frederick 3d (Suzanne E Thompson)
  Ws'84.Van'86.Wash'92
  ☎ (202) 537-7143 . . 4417—48 St NW, Washington, DC *20016*
Richards MR & MRS George J (Patricia Farrelly) Va'50
  ☎ (908) 234-0617 . . Fowler Rd, PO Box 401, Far Hills, NJ *07931*

Richards MR & MRS John H JR (Mary E Melville)
Me.Rd.Pkg.Sar.Ac.Ncd.Dar.Buck'33
☎ (610) 429-9986 . . 254 Chatham Way, West Chester, PA *19380-6816*
Richards MR & MRS John H 3d (Susan J | ☎ (610) 687-8332
MacCallum) MooreArt'66.VaTheo'94.Me. | 280 Pugh Rd,
Buck'64 . . . . | Wayne, PA *19087*
MR John H 4th—at ☎ (518) 587-1356
7 White Farms Rd, Saratoga Springs, NY *12866*
MR Bradley N—at ☎ (215) 829-4364
1110 Lombard St, Apt 16, Philadelphia, PA
19147 . . . .
Richards MRS John L (Sanford—Elizabeth W | of ☎ (561)626-9293
Prosser) BankSt'43 . . . . | 500 Ocean Dv,
MISS Holly L—Wes'80.Cl'83.SUNY'89—at | Apt W2D,
76 Jackson St, Apt 3, Hoboken, NJ *07030* . . . . . | Juno Beach, FL
| *33408-1919*
| ☎ (203) 869-8730
| 98 Valley Rd,
| Apt 8, Cos Cob, CT
| *06807-2224*
Richards MR & MRS John T L (Nancy J Gascoigne) Va'50 . . of
☎ (703) 683-7498 . . 210 N Royal St, Alexandria, VA *22314*
☎ (207) 563-5195 . . High St, Newcastle, ME *04553*
Richards MR & MRS Lee S 3d (Bonnie S Lyons) | ☎ (718) 624-5842
Va'81.Ncd.Aht'72.Cl'75 . . . . | 226 Warren St,
JUNIORS MR Matthew C . . . . | Brooklyn, NY *11201*
Richards MRS LeRoy JR (Jeannetta M Burpee) Me.Ncd.
☎ (610) 642-7212 . . 221 Kent Rd, Ardmore, PA *19003*
Richards MRS MacMullan (Eleanor P MacMullan)
☎ (215) 568-1474 . . 1901 Walnut St, Apt 300, Philadelphia,
PA *19103*
Richards MRS Murray (Harriet Welling) V'38.An.Fy.Ncd.
☎ (415) 453-3993 . . PO Box 1039, Ross, CA *94957*
Richards MRS R Draper (Ayer—Betty Jenney) Mds.
☎ (516) 324-5610 . . ''Little too Close'' 81 Ocean Av, PO Box 684,
East Hampton, NY *11937*
Richards MRS Ralph S JR (McConnell—Shelagh B Bertschmann)
☎ (412) 741-4471 . . 520 Osborne Lane, Sewickley, PA *15143*
Richards MR & MRS Reuben F (Elizabeth H Brady) Rcn.Ln.Eh.H'52
☎ (908) 439-2527 . . Black River Rd, Far Hills, NJ *07931*
Richards MR & MRS Rowland JR (Martha L Marcy) | ☎ (716) 884-3115
Vt'62.G.P'57 . . . . | 45 Lexington Av,
MISS Christine K—at Cornell . . . . | Buffalo, NY *14222*
MISS Jean L—at U of Vt . . . . |
MR Rowland 3d—at U of Vt Law . . . . |
LT George M—USA. |
Richards MR Thomas R—Cl'60 . . . . | ☎ (212) 472-0259
MISS Diana M—at Vassar . . . . | 160 E 84 St,
LT Anthony R—USN.—at ☎ (619) 435-1211 | New York, NY
562 I Av, Coronado, CA *92118* . . . . | *10028*
Richards MR & MRS Warren (Constance H Babcock) | ☎ (410) 235-9865
Elk.H'36. . . . . | 4316 Roland Av,
MISS Constance H—at ☎ (207) 733-2401 | Baltimore, MD
RR 1, Box 248A, Pembroke, ME *04666* . . . . . . | *21210*

Richards MR William B—Me.Denis'67 . . . . | ☎ (212) 684-7595
MR William B JR—at ☎ (916) 925-5003 | 38 E 37 St, PH,
1100 Howe Av, Apt 426, Sacramento, CA *95825* | New York, NY
MR Robert A—at U of Cal Santa Barbara . . . . . . | *10016*
Richards MR & MRS William P JR (Deborah L | ☎ (818) 792-9510
Daves) Col'62.Hn.Stan'58.H'62 . . . . | 1024 Armada Dv,
MISS Dana A . . . . | Pasadena, CA *91103*
Richards MR & MRS Artemas P 2d (Frederica | ☎ (603) 679-8177
McAfee) SCal'40.FramSt'67.Wms'40.IaState'47 | 106 North Rd,
MR David R . . . . | Fremont, NH *03044*
Richardson MRS Blanchard (Ann E Blanchard) Ncd.
☎ (510) 839-9851 . . 1555 Lakeside Dv, Apt M1, Oakland, CA *94612*
Richardson MR C Tiffany—H'39
☎ (516) 671-0512 . . 16 Highland Mews, Glen Cove, NY *11542*
Richardson MRS Charles S JR (Janet Bane) | ☎ (617) 241-7279
LakeF'67 . . . . | 20 Concord St,
MR Samuel S . . . . | Charlestown, MA
JUNIORS MISS Hannah B . . . . | *02129*
Richardson MR Charles S JR—Bost'67
☎ (617) 241-0244 . . 9 Monument Av, Charlestown, MA *02129*
Richardson MR David—Hn.H'40
☎ (202) 338-3523 . . 3338 Dent Place NW, Washington, DC *20007*
Richardson MR & MRS Derek (Barbara Proctor) Camb'38
☎ (203) 255-3740 . . 41 Sasco Creek Rd, Westport, CT *06880*
Richardson MR & MRS Donald H (Plumley—Charlotte A Brown)
B.Cvc.Mt.Mds.Rr.Sl . . .of
☎ (561) 546-2002 . . 275 S Beach Rd, Hobe Sound, FL *33455*
☎ (202) 337-1001 . . 2700 Virginia Av NW, Apt 1001, Washington,
DC *20037*
Richardson MRS Edmund E JR (Elinor Bright)
2100 St Charles Av, New Orleans, LA *70140*
Richardson DR & MRS Edward P JR (Margaret S Eustis) Cy.Chi.H'39
☎ (617) 277-7569 . . 617 Boylston St, Brookline, MA *02146*
Richardson MR & MRS Edward W (York—Margaret W Clinton)
R.Cw.Rv.Ac.Ncd.Myf.GaTech'46
☎ (610) 687-0155 . . 460 Highview Dv, Radnor, PA *19087*
Richardson MRS Eugene S JR (Southwell—Priscilla | ☎ (610) 388-8421
L Cox) Fy.W.Cda. | 112 Kendal at
MISS Priscilla L Southwell (Spettel—Priscilla | Longwood,
L Southwell) Col'74.Col'77.NCar'82—at | Kennett Square, PA
☎ (541) 344-8962 . . 2740 Fairmount Blvd, | *19348*
Eugene, OR *97403* . . . . |
MR Benjamin Sharvy—Reed'90—at
☎ (541) 687-0822 . . 2447 Kincaid St, Eugene,
OR *97405* . . . .
JUNIORS MISS Sara E Spettel—at
☎ (541) 344-8962 . . 2740 Fairmount Blvd,
Eugene, OR *97403* . . . .
Richardson MR Frank E JR . . . . Died Apr 22'96
Richardson MRS Frank E JR (Rosamound T Fitch) Rr.Edg.Cly.Ncd.
☎ (412) 741-4081 . . ''Edgewise'' Chestnut Rd, Sewickley, PA *15143*
Richardson MRS Frederick L W (Hughes—Ross—Rebecca G Brock)
☎ (804) 296-4794 . . 2401 Old Ivy Rd, Apt 2105, Charlottesville,
VA *22903*

Richardson DR & MRS George S (Rebekah Ketchum) Tv.H'43 . . . . 58 Winter St, Nahant, MA *01908*
MR Jonathan M . . . .
MR Frederick S . . . .

Richardson MR Harris S JR
☎ (617) 729-1606 . . 11 Ledgewood Rd, Winchester, MA *01890*

Richardson MR & MRS Henry H (Hildegard Berg) Cy.H'30
☎ (617) 566-0605 . . 25 Cottage St, Brookline, MA *02146*

Richardson MR & MRS Henry H JR (Mariana C Weaks) Van'74.Cyb.Ncd.Wms'71
☎ (615) 385-9878 . . 313 Sutherland Av, Nashville, TN *37205*

Richardson MR & MRS John D (Nina M Leake) Sl.H'64
☎ (202) 965-1398 . . 1516—34 St NW, Washington, DC *20007*

Richardson MR & MRS John L (M Margaret Milner) V'65.GeoW'68.Mt.Ct.Mich'62.Va'67 . . . . ☎ (202) 244-0516 5121 Tilden St NW, Washington, DC *20016*
MISS Margaret L—at U of Va . . . .

Richardson MRS Julian H (Winsor—Diana Beebe) Ec . . .of
☎ (508) 927-1305 . . PO Box 123, 13 Thissell St, Prides Crossing, MA *01965*
☎ (802) 457-3701 . . 12 River St, Woodstock, VT *05091*

Richardson MR & MRS Maurice H 3d (June P Childs) Wheat'50.Cy.H.'51 . . . . ☎ (617) 232-9641 82 High St, Brookline, MA *02146*
DR Maurice H 4th—H'76.Va'80—at Jupiter, FL

Richardson MRS Melody Sawyer (Kidd—Chabris— Sturcke—R Melody Sawyer Richardson) Cin'65.OState'67.Rut'81.Qc. . . . . ☎ (513) 321-1444 "River High" 16 Elmhurst Place, Cincinnati, OH *45208*
MR Peter D Chabris JR—Geo'96 . . . .

Richardson REV & MRS Peter T (Billings—Eleanor Motley) Brand'70.Tufts'62.StLaw'65.Brdgwtr'76 . . . ☎ (508) 470-1006 199 Chestnut St, Andover, MA *01810*
MISS Elise J Billings—at U of Mass Med . . .

Richardson MR & MRS Peter W (Wendy C Morgan)
☎ (508) 468-6254 . . 81 Berry Circle, South Hamilton, MA *01982*

Richardson BRIG GEN (RET) & MRS Robert C 3d (Anne W Taylor) USAF.V'45-4.An.Ac.W.Ncd.USA'39
☎ (703) 836-0541 . . 212 S St Asaph St, Alexandria, VA *22314*

Richardson MRS Roberts (Elizabeth J Roberts)
☎ (508) 468-1277 . . 887 Bay Rd, PO Box 458, Hamilton, MA *01936*

Richardson MR & MRS Thomas F (Joyce L Sentman) Wells'66.P'64. . . . . ☎ (212) 876-0341 1112 Park Av, New York, NY *10128*
JUNIORS MR Thomas M . . . .

Richardson MR & MRS Tolbert N 3d (Nancy C Bojarski) Rut'69. . . . . ☎ (860) 928-4676 Pomfret School, Rte 44, Pomfret, CT *06258*
MISS Katherine P . . . .
JUNIORS MISS Genevieve S . . . .

Richardson DR & MRS William C (Nancy Freeland) Sth'62.Cos.Ty'62.Ch'67.Ch'71
☎ (616) 671-5175 . . 4392 E Gull Lake Dv, Hickory Corners, MI *49060*

Richardson MR & MRS William S (Rosamond Simes) CtCol'46.Mit'44
☎ (207) 799-0911 . . "House of the Eagle" 440 Old Ocean House Rd, Cape Elizabeth, ME *04107*

Richardsson MR Peter K . . see H E Alleman JR

Richardsson MR Richard K . . see H E Alleman JR

Richardsson MR Richmond H . . see H E Alleman JR

Richey MR & MRS John M (Barbara Bray) Gchr'56.Rcn.Mds.Ty'43
2810 Cardinal Dv, Vero Beach, FL *32963*

Richey MR & MRS Sheffield C JR (Jeannetta Murray Richards) Denis'73.Ncd.Yn.Y'72.Emory'75. Geo'79.Geo'85. . . . . ☎ (703) 836-6827 3203 Alabama Av, Alexandria, VA *22305*
JUNIORS MISS Heather D . . . .

Richey MR & MRS Thomas W JR (Janet D Neuberg) Y'54 . . . . ☎ (713) 467-4590 115 Willowend Dv, Houston, TX *77024*
MISS Rue Doyé—V'93 . . . .

Richey MR & MRS Walter N (Alice Plunkett Mitchell)
☎ (803) 671-3684 . . 391 Briarwood Villa, 15 Calibogue Cay Rd, Hilton Head Island, SC *29928*

Richmond MRS Beirne W (Rose—M Beirne Waters) LIU'79.Ncd.
☎ (520) 284-2063 . . 875 Verde Valley School Rd, Sedona, AZ *86351*

Richmond MISS Janet V V M (Braekman—Janet V V M Richmond) NCar'70.Cal'80 . . . . ☎ (818) 905-1964 13207 Weddington St, Sherman Oaks, CA *91401*
JUNIORS MISS Heather M . . . .

Richmond DR & MRS Stewart S (Carolyn B Lewis) MtH'62.NotreD'78.W.Aht'62.Cr'66. . . . . ☎ (603) 472-3293 13 Buttonwood Rd, Bedford, NH *03102*
MISS Cynthia E—Aht'93 . . . .
MR Davis L—NH'91

Richmond MR & MRS Stewart S JR (Tanya S Goff) Colby'89.FP'93.Colby'88.BostColl'96
91 Fordway Extension, Derry, NH *03038*

Richmond MR & MRS Thomas T (Eleanor Angle) Sth'38.Y'35.Y'38
☎ (941) 676-2033 . . "Sunninghill" PO Box 832, Mountain Lake, Lake Wales, FL *33859-0832*

Richter MR & MRS Dudley C (Peggy W Steine) Ncmb'71.Tul'71 . . . . ☎ (615) 356-1186 200 Brookhollow Rd, Nashville, TN *37205*
MISS Ashley B . . . .
MISS Jennifer E . . . .
JUNIORS MISS Samantha D . . . .

Richter MR & MRS Stephen T (Pennell—Marjorie Holmes) Br'43
☎ (941) 465-3079 . . 662 Enos Av NW, Lake Placid, FL *33852*

Rick MRS Alan J (Nancy B Moss) WKy'50.NotreD'55.WinSt'66.ClPac'85 . . . . ☎ (702) 747-8473 PO Box 13117, Reno, NV *89507*
MISS Margaret M—Weber'88—at 1380 Carlin St, Reno, NV *89503* . . . .

Ricketson MRS Frances D (Frances E Dechert) D.
☎ (508) 984-5323 . . PO Box P125, South Dartmouth, MA *02748*

Ricketson MR & MRS Scott (Balding—Elizabeth T Whitman) Cy.D.Sm.Hn.H'53
☎ (617) 329-7572 . . "HonahLee Pond" 585 Gay St, Westwood, MA *02090*

Ridder MR & MRS Bernard H JR (Jane W Delano) P'38 . . . . of ☎ (561)732-8902 6861 N Ocean Blvd, Apt 103, Ocean Ridge, FL *33435*
MISS Jill Delano—at ☎ (707) 433-0213 2490 Mill Creek Rd, Box 1429, Healdsburg, CA *95448* . . . . ☎ (612) 452-3992 1775 Lexington Av S, Apt 9, St Paul, MN *55118*

Ridder MRS Bernard J (Georgia G Buck) Cly.
☎ (818) 441-2181 . . 612 S San Rafael Av, Pasadena, CA *91105*

Ridder MR & MRS Daniel H (Ackerman—Frani Cooper)
Sim'54.Bhm.P'43 . . of
☎ (310) 597-4461 . . 5531 Bryant Dv, Long Beach, CA *90815*
☎ (408) 624-8150 . . 3251 Alvarado Lane, Pebble Beach, CA *93953*
Ridder MR Eric . . . . Died at
Locust Valley, NY Jly 23'96
Ridder MR L Michael—P'62 . . of
☎ (212) 722-7493 . . 40 E 88 St, New York, NY *10128*
☎ (011-33-93) 01-05-06 . . ''Le Bristol'' 4 rue Lt Colonelli,
06310 Beaulieu-sur-Mer, France
Ridder MISS Susan L . . see R A Roosevelt
Ridder MRS Tucker (Ethelette Tucker) Cly.Ne.
☎ (212) PL5-8884 . . 350 E 57 St, New York, NY *10022*
Ridder MRS Virginia (Virginia Dunne) Cly.
☎ (805) 969-1158 . . 2120 Forge Rd, Santa Barbara, CA *93108*
Riddle VERY REV DR & MRS Sturgis L (Elisabeth P Sloan)
Srb.Un.Plg.Cly.Stan'31
☎ (212) 794-2270 . . 870 Fifth Av, New York, NY *10021*
Ridenhower MISS Elizabeth Miller—Bay'51.Cl'58
☎ (210) 735-2802 . . PO Drawer 12139, San Antonio, TX *78212*
Ridge DR Bradley Bateman—Coa.Snc.Cw.Fw.
Ht.Sar.Tex'48.Stan'55.Temp'64
☎ (415) 673-2655 . . 1062 Sutter St, Apt 10, San Francisco,
CA *94109-5827*
Ridgely JUNIORS MISS Laura L . . see P F Miller
Ridgway MRS William C JR (Emily F Parsons) Bg.Fic.Pn.
☎ (201) 379-3377 . . 250 Hartshorn Dv, Short Hills, NJ *07078*
Ridley MR & MRS Frank M (Walker—Wallace— | ☎ (941) 262-4855
Camilla M Gimbernat) GaTech'34 ⛵ . . . . | 696 Spyglass Lane,
  MISS Michelle McC Walker—at | Naples, FL *34102*
☎ (941) 261-3934 . . 750 Mooringline Dv,
Naples, FL *34105* . . . .
  MR James G Walker—at ☎ (404) 350-0045
2509 Warren Rd NW, Atlanta, GA *30318* . . . .
  MR Jonathan S Walker—at ☎ (301) 907-8596
7500 Woodmont Av, Apt S1011, Bethesda,
MD *20814* . . . .
  MR Robert L Walker—at ☎ (904) 656-5946
267 Whetherbine Way, Tallahassee, FL *32301*
  MR Raymond R Walker—at
☎ (713) 580-7404 . . 2431 FM 1960 Rd W,
Apt 1616, Houston, TX *77068* . . . .
Ridruejo MR & MRS Epifanio (Monique B Timbal) | ☎ (011-34-1)
V'58.Madrid'55.H'58 . . . . | 563-6556
MISS Susana . . . . | Hermanos Pinzon 4,
MR Ignacio . . . . | 28036 Madrid, Spain
Rieck MR John E
☎ (212) 879-0134 . . 176 E 71 St, New York, NY *10021*
Riefler MR & MRS Donald B (Patricia A Hawley) | ☎ (561) 234-4251
Cin'49.Ck.Aht'49 . . . . | 512 Bay Dv,
MISS Barbara A—Wms'83—at 125 Beacon St, | Vero Beach, FL
Apt 3R, Boston, MA *02116* . . . . | *32963*
Riefler MR & MRS Duncan W (Wendy T Wheatley)
Hlns'84.Ck.Mds.Denis'81
☎ (516) 676-4655 . . 59 Simonson Rd, Old Brookville, NY *11545*
Riegel MISS Anne Alexandrine de M—CarnM'95.Fic.
☎ (202) 884-0070 . . 2138 California St NW, Washington, DC *20008*

Riegel MR & MRS Guy R (Harriet M Smith) BostColl'80.Ken'80
☎ (203) 656-3630 . . 2 Woods End Rd, Darien, CT *06820*
Riegel MR & MRS John E (A Deborah du Pont) | ☎ (302) 656-3282
Fic.Wil.Del'68.Del'71 . . . . | PO Box 1,
MISS Deborah du P—at Rollins . . . . | Montchanin,
MR John E JR—Ken'94—at Westminster School, | DE *19710*
995 Hopmeadow St, Simsbury, CT *06070* . . . . |
Riegel MISS Laura Cushing (Richard E JR) . . . . Married at Greenville, DE
Curry MR Patrick D (late Daniel J) . . . . Apr 27'96
Riegel MR & MRS Lawrence M (Jeanne A Ballentine) | ☎ (212) BU8-7338
Ri.P'55 . . . . | 129 E 69 St,
MISS Cynthia B—Swb'89 . . . . | New York, NY
    | *10021*
Riegel MR & MRS Richard E JR (Law—Barbara C Ives)
Wil.Fic.Fiy.Cry.Cc.Cly.
☎ (302) 655-0083 . . PO Box 250, 5 Guyencourt Rd, Montchanin,
DE *19710*
Riegel MR & MRS Richard E III (Amanda J Thompson)
Bnd'92.Un.Fic.Fiy.Mid'88
☎ (212) 570-9620 . . 179 E 79 St, New York, NY *10021*
Riegel MR & MRS William M (Nickerson—Nancy C | of ☎ (617)934-5161
Bailey) V'57.H.'61.Chi.Wms'50 . . . . | 14 Surplus St,
MR Joshua B Nickerson—Geo'92—at | Duxbury, MA *02332*
U of Va Law . . . . | ☎ (602) 481-6024
  | 5101 N Casa Blanca
  | Rd, Scottsdale, AZ
  | *85253*
  | ☎ (901) 761-4328
  | 5400 Park Av,
  | Apt 217, Memphis,
  | TN *38119*
Riegel MR & MRS William M JR (Elizabeth A Lyman) . . of
☎ (212) 794-8509 . . 108 E 81 St, Apt 5B, New York, NY *10028*
☎ (860) 868-9381 . . ''Achness'' 29 Mallory Brook Rd, Washington,
CT *06794*
Rieger MR & MRS Brian L (Sharon L Zick) | ☎ (847) 291-9632
Simp'73.Ill'72.DePaul'75 . . . . | 2429 Partridge Lane,
JUNIORS MISS Megan B . . . . | Northbrook, IL
JUNIORS MISS Rebecca A . . . . | *60062*
Riemer MRS Karl (Louise Crowninshield) Cy.Chi.
☎ (617) 731-8555 . . 17 Fairgreen Place, Chestnut Hill, MA *02167*
Rienhoff MRS Coke (Kathryn L Coke) | ☎ (410) 323-7595
Smu'49.Mv.Elk. | 8 Palmer Green
MISS Alexandra C—Roan'81—at | Court, Baltimore,
☎ (704) 386-8953 . . 518 N Pine St, Charlotte, | MD *21210*
NC *28202* . . . . |
DR Hugh Y JR—Wms'75.JHop'82—at |
☎ (410) 472-2397 . . 15016 Priceville Rd, Sparks, |
MD *21152* . . . . |
Rienhoff MRS MacCallum (Oldberg—Joanne Winkenwerder)
Rdc'60.JHop'63.Mv.
☎ (970) 887-2861 . . Ouray Ranch, 13 County Rd 6203, Granby,
CO *80446*
Riepe REV Charles K—Elk.Md.Innsbruck'60
☎ (410) 877-8118 . . Hollingsworth Farm, 1401 Hollingsworth Rd,
Joppa, MD *21085*

Riepe MR & MRS James S (Gail N Petty)
Pa'68.Gv.Md.Mv.Pa'65.Pa'67 . . . . | ☎ (410) 329-3925
MISS Christina N . . . . | 14921 Tanyard Rd,
MR James S JR . . . . | Sparks, MD *21152*

Rigby MR & MRS Henry S (MacMullan—Marjorie S Holt)
☎ (610) LO6-1344 . . 635 Bobbin Mill Rd, Media, PA *19063*

Rigg MRS Horace A JR (Ruth B Lyman)
☎ (207) 236-4846 . . 19 Rockbrook Dv, Camden, ME *04843-1616*

Riggs MRS Benjamin C (Bergesen—Elizabeth C Dekle)
Fla'51.Fla'53.Fla'55
☎ (803) 884-9895 . . Thickett Apt P6, 1900 H'way 17 N Bypass,
Mt Pleasant, SC *29464*

Riggs MR & MRS Francis Graham (Mary F
Henderson) Gv.Md.Mv.NCar'60 . . . . | ☎ (410) 363-0912
MISS Charlotte S—at Skidmore . . . . | 405 Chattolannee
MR Dudley G—at Coll of Charleston . . . . | Hill, Owings Mills,
JUNIORS MISS Melissa H H—at Calvert . . . . | MD *21117*

Riggs MRS Lawrason JR (Jeanne H West)
Mv.Nyc.Ncd. . . . . | ☎ (508) 228-0874
MR John W—Char'ton'93—*see* | 18 Meadowview Dv,
Dilatory Domiciles . . . . | Nantucket, MA
| *02554*

Riggs MRS Richard C (Eleanor A Reifsnider) Ncd.
☎ (410) 821-0745 . . 507 Brightwood Club Dv, Lutherville, MD *21093*

Riggs MR & MRS Richard C JR (Sheila B Kayser)
Bost'65.Md.Elk.Mv.P'61.H'65 ⚓ . . of
☎ (410) 433-3943 . . 907 Poplar Hill Rd, Baltimore, MD *21210*
☎ (970) 845-8455 . . Beaver Creek, CO *81620*

Righi DR & MRS David F (Elysabeth M Borie) Tufts'81.Nyc.Tufts'79.H'84
☎ (602) 264-4538 . . 5620 N 4 St, Phoenix, AZ *85012*

Righter MR & MRS Brewster A McN (Soutter—Julie
Hattersley) V'57.H'57 . . . . | ☎ (516) 676-1305
MISS Lucy Soutter—H'90 . . . . | 760 Chicken Valley
| Rd, Locust Valley,
| NY *11560*

Righter MRS Elizabeth (Elizabeth H Carleton)
Rdc'59.Rdc'61.Rd. . . . . | ☎ (809) 776-5287
MISS Amy L—at U of Cal Berkeley . . . . | 5-1 Estate
MISS Daphne—Vt'86—at Breckenridge, CO | Lerkenlund,
80424 . . . . | Box 304629,
| St Thomas, VI
| *00803*

Righter MR & MRS James V (Alice A Robinson) H'58.Y'70
☎ (617) 720-0606 . . 72 Pinckney St, Boston, MA *02114*

Righter MR & MRS Volney F (Sarah E Williams) Bgt.Fic.H.'26 . . of
☎ (914) BE4-3540 . . 125 Davids Hill Rd, Bedford Hills, NY *10507*
☎ (212) BU8-9537 . . 1 E 66 St, New York, NY *10021*

Riginos MR & MRS Vasilis E (Alice Swift)
Ch'63.Stv'65 . . . . | ☎ (202) 342-1069
MISS Cynthia—at U of Ariz . . . . | 2400—44 St NW,
MISS Corinna . . . . | Washington, DC
| *20007*

Rihm MR & MRS Roger S (Christina R Sprague) Geo'75.Rut'79
☎ (202) 244-0704 . . 5511—30 St NW, Washington, DC *20015*

Riker MISS Audrey—Cly.Stc.Rm.
☎ (410) 329-6305 . . ''Patchwork II'' 2952 Bradenbaugh Rd, Whitehall,
MD *21161*

Riker MISS Elizabeth Q . . see G Potter

Riker MRS Grace F (Grace H Fischbeck)
ColbyS'62.Dar.Myf. . . . . | ☎ (941) 924-8908
JUNIORS MISS Ann F . . . . | 4050 Via Mirada,
JUNIORS MISS Sara T . . . . | Sarasota, FL *34238*

Riker MR John L—An.Un.Rm.Stc.Ny.Hl.Plg.Snc.Myf.H.'61.H'66 . . of
☎ (212) 879-1556 . . 47 E 64 St, New York, NY *10021-7044*
☎ (908) 291-4194 . . 440 Locust Point Rd, PO Box 236, Rumson,
NJ *07760-0236*

Riker MR Richard J—Stc.H'54.Cl'60 . . . . | ☎ (908) 291-3877
MR William J . . . . | 6 Third Av,
| Atlantic Highlands,
| NJ *07716*

Riker CDR & MRS Robert T (Burt—Lucretia H Hill)
USN.Ken'61 ⚓ . . . . | ☎ (941) 346-1714
MR Christopher K Burt . . . . | 767 Tropical Circle,
MR Russell B Burt . . . . | Sarasota, FL *34242*

Riker MRS Samuel (Anne T Cox)
☎ (941) 349-5618 . . 1208 South View Dv, Sarasota, FL *34242*

Riker MR & MRS Samuel 3d (Sarah J Pilcher)
Cc.SFrSt'65 . . . . | ☎ (441) 293-0848
MR Anthony T—Bost'82—at ☎ (441) 293-2721 | Fairland,
''Aloha'' 10 Skyline Rd, Smith's Parish FL 08, | 14 Glebe Hill,
Bermuda . . . . | Tucker's Town
MR Andrew E—at Dartmouth . . . . | HS 02, Bermuda

Riley MR & MRS C Madison JR (Marie Louise Vanneman) Me.P.'43
☎ (610) EL6-7394 . . 633 Andover Rd, Newtown Square, PA *19073*

Riley MR & MRS C Madison 3d (Laura Alden Hewitt)
Ty'82.Sap.Ty'81.Va'85
☎ (617) 235-6524 . . 61 Livingston Rd, Wellesley, MA *02181*

Riley MRS Cathleen D (Proctor—Cathleen P Dugan) Sth'44.Cl'45
☎ (203) 245-0045 . . 47 Wilshire Rd, Madison, CT *06443*

Riley MRS Edgar A (Johnson—MacLaury—Daphne
R Nowell) Csn.Yn. | ☎ (505) 438-3048
MR Ian G MacLaury—at ☎ (860) 536-2394 | PO Box 22753,
PO Box 296, Noank, CT *06340* . . . . | Santa Fe, NM *87502*

Riley MISS Elizabeth M—Nu'28.Cl'30.Cs.Gr.Chr.
☎ (212) 534-4401 . . 1140 Fifth Av, New York, NY *10128*

Riley MR & MRS J Barton (Martha Gretchen Pfaff)
Pa'70.Me.M.Rc.Pa'70 . . . . | ☎ (610) 896-7718
JUNIORS MISS M Quincy—at Phillips Exeter . . . . | 526 Avonwood Rd,
JUNIORS MISS H Barton—at U of Pa . . . . | Haverford, PA
| *19041*

Riley MR & MRS J Gregory (Carol P Spier)
Csh.Myf.Y.'55 . . . . | ☎ (516) 427-7666
MISS Elizabeth T . . . . | Lloyd Lane,
JUNIORS MISS Caitlin P—at Phillips Exeter . . . . . | Lloyd Neck, RD 3,
| Huntington, NY
| *11743*

Riley BRIG GEN (RET) & MRS James L (Coad—Ethel
Worthington) USAF.Cvc.Sl.Ncd.Emory'32.H'35 | ☎ (904) 273-9152
MR W James Coad 3d—at Chicago, IL . . . . . | 1000 Vicar's
| Landing Way,
| Apt I-109, Ponte
| Vedra Beach, FL
| *32082*

Riley MRS James W (Ethridge—Carragan—Ann E McIntyre) . . . . . Died at
Ft Myers, FL Feb 20'96

Riley MR James W—Myf.Y'44
☎ (207) 363-3701 . . ''Seaward'' 22 Aldis Lane, PO Box 51,
York Harbor, ME *03911*

Riley MR & MRS James W 3d (Campagna—Holly A Harcourt) Myf.Pa'67 . . . . ☎ (212) 987-4470
MISS Elizabeth H . . . . 146 E 89 St,
New York, NY
10128

Riley MISS Mary L—Cal'74.H'76.Cl'87.Csn . . .of
☎ (011-852) 987-9379 . . 13E Verdant Court, Peninsula Village, Discovery Bay, Lantau, Hong Kong
☎ (508) 724-6654 . . ''Blueberry Park'' 32 Sunset Lane, Petersham, MA *01366-0066*

Riley MR & MRS Phelps T (Mary L Pacent)
Man'vl'67.Me.Y'68.Temp'74.Temp'81 . . . . ☎ (610) 373-7840
MISS Eleanor W . . . . 1220 Parkside Dv S,
MR Phelps T JR—at Yale . . . . Reading, PA *19611*

Riley MR Richard B
59 rue Chardin Lagache, 75016 Paris, France

Riley DR & MRS Richard L (Mary V Catesby Jones)
B'gton'39.H'33 . . . . ☎ (508) 724-6654
MISS Susan H . . . . 32 Sunset Lane,
Petersham, MA
01366-0066

Riley MR & MRS Thomas A 3d (Barbara W Johnson)
Sth'88.Gm.Geo'87.VillaN'90.Geo'93
☎ (301) 657-2682 . . 4609 Merivale Rd, Chevy Chase, MD *20815*

Riley MR & MRS W Phelps (Emilie K Townsend) Me.Gm.Y'37
☎ (610) MI2-4769 . . 938 Black Rock Rd, Gladwyne, PA *19035*

Rimmer MR & MRS Charles P JR (Clare H Curtis) Ec.Ncd.H'50
☎ (508) 526-7090 . . 39 Forster Rd, Manchester, MA *01944*

Rinaker MRS Alice Bentley (Alice Wrenn Bentley)
☎ (909) 925-8202 . . 2200 W Acacia Av, Apt E121, Hemet, CA *92545*

Rinaldini MR & MRS Luis E (Talbert—Julie S Short)
Pars'72.Rc.Pr.Mb.Cly.P'74.H'80 . . of
☎ (212) 355-5506 . . 124 E 64 St, New York, NY *10021*
☎ (516) 759-2784 . . ''Two Sheds'' West Island, Glen Cove, NY *11542*

Rinehart MR & MRS Edmon L (Barbara Y Lutz) Pn.P'42
☎ (334) 272-8745 . . 1725 Croom Dv, Montgomery, AL *36106*

Rinehart MR & MRS Robert B (Fairlie G Haynes) StMarys'74.Aub'78.So'75
☎ (334) 264-2480 . . 1580 Gilmer Av, Montgomery, AL *36104*

Ring DR & MRS Edward M (Wilson—Claudine M Vincent) Geo'52.StL'56
☎ (207) 777-6262 . . 216 Nottingham Rd, Auburn, ME *04210*

Ring MR & MRS Thornton D (Pierce—Moody—Elizabeth M Barker) Myf.Ncd.Norw'68 . . . . ☎ (207) 865-3177
JUNIORS MISS Caroline E . . . . Smelt Brook Farm,
JUNIORS MR Thornton D JR . . . . PO Box 54,
South Freeport,
ME *04078-0054*

Ringe MR & MRS Henry Ralph 2d (Sarah T Funk)
RI'71.Sap.F&M'62 . . . . ☎ (609) 596-0599
MISS Jennifer T—Mid'88 . . . . 605 Westerly Dv,
MISS V Alexandra—Wes'92—at 272 Sixth Av, Marlton, NJ *08053*
Apt 2L, Brooklyn, NY *11215*
MR Benjamin Rhoads—Del'93—at 1026 Pine St,
Apt 3, Philadelphia, PA *19107* . . . .

Ringe MR & MRS Thomas B K (Cynthia K Steward)
Rv.Ac.Ncd.Dth'50.Pa'57
☎ (610) 687-2557 . . 2 Highfield Lane, Wayne, PA *19087*

Ringe MR & MRS Thomas B K 3d (Patricia M McGuinn)
Penn'84.VillaN'88.Gm.Rv.Duke'79.UMiami'82
☎ (610) 341-9370 . . 303 Dundee Place, Devon, PA *19333*

Ripley MRS Bradford (Priscilla W Bradford)
Cly.Ht.Myf.Dar.Cda.Dc.Dh.Dll.
☎ (203) 966-3764 . . 62 Heritage Hill Rd, New Canaan, CT *06840*

Ripley MR & MRS Edward F (Elizabeth R Tucker)
Ws'52.Cw.Fw.Myf.Cda.Laf'50.Cl'53 . . . . ☎ (215) 248-5246
MISS Elizabeth S—Ty'90.Pc. . . . . 300 W Gravers
☎ (212) 439-9481 . . 219 E 77 St, Apt 5C, Lane, Philadelphia,
New York, NY *10021* . . . . PA *19118*

Ripley MR & MRS Henry B H 3d (Dianne M Dean) Ill'76.DU'75.DU'78
☎ (303) 756-2446 . . 3200 E Flora Place, Denver, CO *80210*

Ripley MR & MRS John C (Nancy H Gould) Ncd.Y'42.Mit'47
☎ (410) 822-2430 . . 210 S Harrison St, Easton, MD *21601-2910*

Ripley MR & MRS Malcolm P (Fenwick—Bettie J Boatman)
Unn.Rcn.Cw . . .of
☎ (619) 564-5413 . . 78-023 Lago Dv, PO Box 1745, La Quinta, CA *92253*
☎ (619) 673-4318 . . 12347 Fairway Pointe Row, San Diego, CA *92128*

Ripley MR Peter H (Edward F) . . . . Married at Chestnut Hill, PA
Smith MISS Hillary E (Eric N) . . . . Jun 1'96

Ripley MISS Rosemary L (Lanius—Rosemary L Ripley)
Y.'76.Y'80.Cly . . .of
☎ (212) 860-9051 . . 55 E 86 St, New York, NY *10028*
☎ (860) 567-4375 . . 32 Duck Pond Rd, Litchfield, CT *06759*

Ripley MRS S Dillon 2d (Eddy—Mary M Livingston) . . . . Died at
Litchfield, CT Apr 15'96

Ripley MR S Dillon 2d—K.Cos.Mt.C.Plg.Cc.Lm.Y'36.H'43 . . of
☎ (202) 232-3131 . . 2324 Massachusetts Av NW, Washington, DC *20008*
☎ (212) 935-7289 . . 125 E 63 St, New York, NY *10021*
☎ (860) 567-8208 . . ''Paddling Ponds'' PO Box 210, 63 Duck Pond Rd, Litchfield, CT *06759*

Rippel MRS G Crivelli (Colapinto—Gioconda M C Crivelli) . . of
☎ (212) 988-8872 . . 117 E 71 St, Apt 5C, New York, NY *10021*
☎ (011-39-55) 47-42-17 . . ''I Colombi'' Vicolo San Marco Vecchio 34, La Pietra, 50139 Firenze, Italy

Rippel MR & MRS Mark L (Mary L Hancock)
MtH'77.Pa'79.Pa'77.VillaN'87
☎ (610) 688-9323 . . 340 Oak Terr, St Davids, PA *19087*

Rippin MR Charles—An.P'61.Va'68 . . . . ☎ (609) 497-9245
MISS Allyn S—at Vassar . . . . College Rd W,
Apt 65H, Princeton,
NJ *08540*

Rise MR & MRS P Carter (Louise S Lionberger) Va'82.Va'82
☎ (212) 769-4880 . . 235 W 76 St, Apt 11C, New York, NY *10023*

Risk MRS Sharon Clay (Louise G Brown) BMr'46.Pn.
☎ (301) 320-0197 . . 6604 Tulip Hill Terr, Bethesda, MD *20816*

Risom MR & MRS C Nicholas (Martha Bush-Brown)
Ty'86.Ck.S.LakeF'85.Cl'95
☎ (516) 676-0336 . . 57 High St, Locust Valley, NY *11560*

Ritchie MR & MRS Charles L (Mary A Starr) Y'45
☎ (518) 891-4288 . . HC 1, Box 38A, Saranac Lake, NY *12983*

Ritchie MRS Ethel Y (Ethel R Young) SL'46
☎ (908) 766-1378 . . 34 Lindabury Av, Bernardsville, NJ *07924*

Ritchie MR & MRS Haiden (Zanze—Jane F Olds)
Fr.Dth'44.Y'48 . . . . ☎ (415) 563-3132
MR William I Zanze . . . . 2700 Pacific Av,
San Francisco, CA
94115

Ritchie MR & MRS John B (Suzanne Raisin) B.Fr.Y'46.Cal'49 . . . .
MR Randolph B . . . .
MR Mark H—at ☎ (415) 771-9474 1055 California St, San Francisco, CA *94104* . .
MISS Charlotte S (Hogan—Charlotte S Ritchie) —at 21 Marinero Circle, Apt 203, Tiburon, CA *94920* . . . .
of ☎ (415)921-2250 1201 Greenwich St, Apt 400, San Francisco, CA *94109*
☎ (808) 926-5515 Niihau PH, 247 Beach Walk, Waikiki, Honolulu, HI *96815*

Ritchie MR & MRS Thomas M JR (Jean W Baldwin) Bg.P'54 . . . .
MISS Katherine W—StLaw'92 . . . .
MR Robert B—Vt'89 . . . .
☎ (908) 273-6163 28 Cedric Rd, Summit, NJ *07901*

Ritchie MRS William L (Eleanor C Preston) Sl. . . . .
MR William L JR . . . .
of ☎ (202)332-3626 34 Kalorama Circle NW, Washington, DC *20008*
☎ (508) 257-6720 Baxter Rd, Siasconset, MA *02654*

Rittenhouse MR Peter D—Del'72 . . of
☎ (610) 388-6424 . . 3 Cardinal Lane, Chadds Ford, PA *19317*
☎ (302) 645-5343 . . "Sand Castles" 114 E 4 St, Lewes, DE *19958*

Rittenour MR & MRS Charles A (Calder—Maralyn Christie-Miller) Dyc.BtP.L.Cw.W'burn'60
☎ (212) 289-1293 . . 1700 York Av, New York, NY *10128*

Ritter MISS Deborah C—Sdg.Ncd.Myf.Dc.
☎ (215) 885-5940 . . 1007 Edann Rd, Oreland, PA *19075*

Ritter MR & MRS Edmund U (Priscilla Rich) BMr'44.Cy.Cw.Myf.Phi.Ncd.Mit'47
☎ (617) 566-7648 . . 413 Hammond St, Chestnut Hill, MA *02167*

Ritter MR & MRS John D (Ellen R Neiley) Ken'81.Ken'80.Cwr'85
☎ (216) 653-8542 . . 2801 Hudson Aurora Rd, Hudson, OH *44236*

Ritter MR & MRS Philip O (Barbara G Ringe) Gchr'58.Myf.Rv.Cw.W.Ty'56 . . . .
MR John S—Pa'85.Pa'93 . . . .
☎ (610) 647-0235 421 Daventry Rd, Berwyn, PA *19312*

Ritter MR & MRS William B (Barbara T Barclay) Myf.Pa'57
☎ (561) 288-0687 . . 5751 Winged Foot Dv, Stuart, FL *34997*

Rittershofer MRS Clare R (Mary C Swing)
☎ (513) 321-4415 . . Madison House Apt 203, 2324 Madison Rd, Cincinnati, OH *45208-2638*

Rittershofer MRS John S (Gloria Virtucio)
☎ (914) 423-3889 . . 117 De Haven Dv, Yonkers, NY *10703*

Rivers MR & MRS John M JR (Elebash—M Kathleen Hudson) Yh.NCar'67 . . . .
MISS Alice Palmer Elebash—at San Francisco, CA . . . .
☎ (803) 577-2509 20 Church St, Charleston, SC *29401*

Rives MRS George L (E Jane Eyre) . . . .
MR Christopher L—Y'80.Pace'87—at
☎ (718) 658-7664 . . 143-25—84 Dv, Briarwood, NY *11435*. . . . .
☎ (912) 638-7474 403 Couper Av, St Simons Island, GA *31522*

Rives MR Lloyd M—Rcn.Srb.Sm.P'44
☎ (617) 536-8970 . . 2 Commonwealth Av, 10B, Boston, MA *02116*

Riviere MRS Himes (Marilynn Himes) Sl . . .of
☎ (803) 649-0358 . . PO Box 1319, Aiken, SC *29802*
☎ (803) 648-7373 . . "Hidden Stables" 534 Marion St, Aiken, SC *29801*

Riviere MR Scott D . . of
PO Box 593, Miami, FL *33170*
☎ (305) 258-5858 . . "Gator Pear Grove" 22400 Naranja Rd, Redland, FL *33170*

Rivinus MR & MRS F Markoe (Anne L Hutchins) Ph.H'38
☎ (215) 242-1181 . . 201 W Evergreen Av, Apt 604, Philadelphia, PA *19118*

Rivinus MR & MRS J Willis M (Anne M Gaither) P'50 . . . .
MISS Elizabeth M . . . .
MR Jonathan W M JR . . . .
☎ (215) 297-5559 "Lindencroft" 6832 Paxson Rd, New Hope, PA *18938*

Rizk MR Khalil R—K.Cr'78
☎ (212) 772-9510 . . 106 E 71 St, New York, NY *10021*

Rizzo MRS Joan N (Joan Nichols) . . . .
MISS Marguerite D—Geo'88—at
☎ (415) 661-0344 . . 822 Clayton St, Apt 3, San Francisco, CA *94117* . . . .
of ☎ (212)628-8982 520 E 86 St, New York, NY *10028*
☎ (914) 763-9384 1 Hunt Farm, Waccabuc, NY *10597*

Rizzo MR Peter Cyrus 4th—Skd'86
☎ (847) 295-6222 . . 369 Lincoln Av, Lake Bluff, IL *60044*

Roach MRS Caryl L M (Caryl L Miller) Wheat'65 . .
MISS Janis E . . . .
☎ (916) 583-1320 PO Box 2450, Olympic Valley, CA *96146*

Roach MR Isaac—Bvl.
☎ (561) 231-2717 . . 800 Date Palm Rd, Vero Beach, FL *32963*

Roach CAPT & MRS J Ashley (Pamela S Patterson) USN.GeoW'83.An.Cda.Pa'60.Pa'63.GeoW'71 . .
MISS Christina K—at U of Tex Austin . . . .
MR Ashley P—at U of Pa . . . .
☎ (703) 521-8849 820 S Quincy St, Arlington, VA *22204-1562*

Roach MR & MRS Lloyd B (Jacqueline Laplace) Barat'67.Me.Emer'70 . . . .
MISS Geneviève—HRdc'94 . . . .
☎ (610) 793-2552 1025 Meeting House Rd, West Chester, PA *19382*

Roach MR Pemberton H (Lloyd B) . . . . Married at Wantagh, NY Campfield MISS Marybeth . . . . Apr 27'96

Roark MRS M Worman (Mignon D Worman) . . name changed to Worman

Robb MR & MRS Charles S (Lynda B Johnson) . . . . .
MISS Lucinda D . . . .
MISS Catherine L . . . .
JUNIORS MISS Jennifer W . . . .
☎ (202) 224-4024 154 Russell Senate Office Bldg, Washington, DC *20510*

Robb MR & MRS David B (Sarah W Carson) R.Pe.Cw.Ncd.
☎ (610) 645-8957 . . 1400 Waverly Rd, Andrews 123, Gladwyne, PA *19035*

Robb MISS Eugenia Van D—Gv.Sl.Lm.Ncd.Cda.
☎ (202) 332-6327 . . 2935 Cathedral Av NW, Washington, DC *20008*

Robb MR & MRS G B Garrett (Kathleen Tetreault) Mis'dia'71.Denis'76
☎ (717) 646-8955 . . 37 Crocketts Crescent, Timber Trails, Pocono Pines, PA *18350*

Robb MRS J Hampden JR (Audrey C Wagstaff) Cly. ☎ (212) 879-7119
  MISS Christy C . . . . 163 E 81 St,
                                                New York, NY
                                                10028

Robb MR & MRS Russell (Davis—Leslee W Hables). ☎ (508) 369-4174
  MR C Ian . . . . Pippin Tree Farm,
                                                635 Monument St,
                                                Concord, MA *01742*

Robbins MRS Chandler 2d (Sarah Fraser) BMr'34.Csn.Chi.
  ☎ (508) 283-1044 . . 5 Aileen Terr, Eastern Point, Gloucester,
  MA *01930*

Robbins MR & MRS Donald M (Allison Privett) ☎ (714) 673-5378
  Cal'70.Cal'72.Vh.Cal'69.Hast'73 . . . . 828 Via Lido Soud,
  MISS Lindsay M . . . . Newport Beach, CA
  JUNIORS MR Hunter S *92663*

Robbins MRS Edward C (Hatfield—Mary Stewart Hodge)
  ☎ (610) 353-5656 . . Dunwoody Village G311, 3500 West Chester Pike,
  Newtown Square, PA *19073*

Robbins COL (RET) & MRS Edwinston L ☎ (610) LA5-1421
  (Loughborough—Loughborough—Biddle— 1207 Club House
  Margaret S B Atkinson) USAF.An.Rr.Gm.Ac. . . Rd, Gladwyne, PA
  MISS Margaret G A Biddle *19035*

Robbins MISS Frances K (Hanson C) . . . . Married at Seattle, WA
  Bauer DR Faron J . . . . Aug 20'94

Robbins MRS George A (Eleanor Hart) . . . . ☎ (215) 283-7152
  MISS Eleanor A—at ☎ (011-44-171) 727-7412 79 Foulkeways,
  47 Northumberland Place, London W2 5AS, Sumneytown Pike,
  England . . . . Gwynedd, PA *19436*

Robbins MR & MRS Hanson C (Chase—Linda H ☎ (617) 266-1321
  Morrison) MaryW'63.H'59.Cl'64 . . . . 207 Commonwealth
  MISS Christine D Chase—at New York, NY . Av, Apt 9, Boston,
  MR Eric H Chase—at Bethlehem, NH *03574* . MA *02116*

Robbins MISS Helen A R—Pom'85 . . see R C Wheeler

Robbins MR & MRS James M (Schwartzburg—Mary ☎ (914) BE4-3567
  Brooks) Srr.Bgt.Myf.Cly.Dar.P'26 . . . . Bayberry Lane,
  MR John A Schwartzburg—Myf.Lawr'64. . Box 389, Bedford,
  Mid'66.Mid'72—Box 6225, Lawrenceville, NY *10506*
  NJ *08648* . . . .

Robbins MR & MRS James O (Deborah H Clark) ☎ (404) 355-3551
  Denis'70.Pa'65.H'70 . . . . 3185 Nancy Creek
  MISS Jane B . . . . Rd NW, Atlanta,
  MISS Payson C . . . . GA *30327*
  MISS Hilary C . . . .

Robbins MR & MRS Joseph F (Coolidge—Jayne C Edington) My.H'36
  ☎ (508) 468-2744 . . 217 Larch Row, Wenham, MA *01984*

Robbins MISS Katherine F (Hanson C) . . . . . . Married at Gloucester, MA
  Garbus MR Peter A . . . . Aug 7'94

Robbins MR & MRS Kip M (Glenaan M Elliott)
  NEng'74.Nyc.Miami'77 . . of
  ☎ (561) 848-3053 . . 1440 N Ocean Way, Palm Beach, FL *33480*
  ☎ (508) 228-5802 . . "Mandalay" 13 Goldfinch Dv, Nantucket,
  MA *02554*

Robbins MISS Letitia M—OWes'83 . . see R C Wheeler

Robbins MRS Louise N (Louise S Nash) Wells'49.Cv.
  ☎ (520) 577-7444 . . 6907 E Nuthatch Trail, Tucson, AZ *85715*

Robbins MRS Noel (Hope B Saunders) San.Yn.
  ☎ (201) 635-8931 . . 6 Edgehill Av, Chatham, NJ *07928*

Robbins MRS Rowland Ames (Margaret C Paterson) . . . . . . Died Jly 5'96

Robbins MRS Sabin (Harriet T Galt)
  ☎ (561) 278-3665 . . 401 E Linton Blvd, Apt 400, Delray Beach,
  FL *33483*

Robbins MRS Thomas H (Barbara Little)
  ☎ (860) 535-1277 . . 2 Cannon Square, Stonington, CT *06378*

Robbins MR & MRS Thomas N (Elizabeth W Custis) Cw.Bost'71
  ☎ (415) 772-8716 . . 92 Palm Av, San Francisco, CA *94118*

Robbins MRS Whitney K (M Whitney Kemble) ☎ (505) 466-6225
  Wheat'60 . . . . 204 Apache Trail,
  MISS Whitney C—at 20 Montfern Av, Brighton, Santa Fe, NM *87505*
  MA *02135* . . . .

Robbins MRS William Bradford (Giles—Belle O'D Wildrick) Cly.Ncd.Myf.
  ☎ (803) 785-6243 . . 300 Wood Haven Dv, Apt 3306,
  Hilton Head Island, SC *29928*

Robbins MR & MRS William C 3d (Scott—Jane F ☎ (510) 540-8365
  Gillespie) Stan'76.Y'63 . . . . 260 Panoramic Way,
  MISS Schuyler B . . . . Berkeley, CA *94704*
  MISS Courtney Q . . . .
  MR W Christopher—at 303 Green St, Apt 303,
  San Francisco, CA *94133* . . . .
  MISS Alexandra C Scott . . . .

Robbins MR & MRS William LeB (Elizabeth H Ward)
  H.'90.B.Ncd.H.'90.H'95
  ☎ (212) 496-7243 . . 20 W 72 St, Apt 206, New York, NY *10023*

Robbins MRS William Moore (Dodge—Lyda F Plunkett)
  Cly.Myf.Ncd . . .of
  ☎ (203) 869-0649 . . 218 Old Mill Rd, Greenwich, CT *06830*
  ☎ (242) 362-4088 . . Box N7776, Lyford Cay, Nassau, Bahamas

Robbins REV DR William Randolph—Unn.Rby. ☎ (203) 248-4651
  Plg.Coa.Snc.Cw.Cc.Fw.Ll.Ofp.Ht.Myf.StJ.Pn. 24 Battis Rd,
  P'34.Y'41 . . . . Hamden, CT
  MR Henry C—Cc.Fw. *06514-2908*

Robe MRS Robert S JR (Lucy B Barry) . . . . Died at
  Ft Lauderdale, FL May 13'96

Robe MR Robert S JR—S.StA.Va'56.NYTech'76. ☎ (561) 627-6815
  LIU'86 . . . . 509 Sea Oats Dv,
  MISS Parrish C—Rol'95 . . . . Apt D1,
                                                Juno Beach, FL
                                                33408-1433

Roberson MR & MRS Robert S (Barbara C Drane) ☎ (757) 595-6600
  RMWmn'67.Unn.Plg.Fic.Ny.Fiy.Chr.Snc.Cw. "Kipsberry"
  StJ.Cda.Dar.Nu'64.W&M'73 ⚓ 58 James Landing
  MISS Merritt Brooke—RMWmn'92.Van'94 . . . . Rd, Newport News,
  MISS Barbara D—Va'94.Cl'95 . . . . VA *23606*

Roberts MRS A Addison (Doris L Lawrence) Rc.Pe.Me.Gm.Ph.Ac.
  ☎ (610) 527-1421 . . 1140 Grandview Terr, Radnor, PA *19087*

Roberts MR & MRS A Sydney (Andrews—Baird—Mary S Dempwolf)
  Evg.BtP.Cda.Y'36
  ☎ (561) 659-2841 . . 684 Pelican Lane, Palm Beach, FL *33480*

Roberts MR & MRS A Sydney JR (Christine E Gibbons)
  Wheat'82.Srb.BtP.Evg.Chi.Cda.Marl'86 ⚓
  ☎ (561) 835-0444 . . PO Box 2953, Palm Beach, FL *33480*

Roberts MR & MRS Alan Y (Sally W Gordon) Gchr'64.Va'64 . . of
  ☎ (914) 763-8372 . . Box 69, 41 Chapel Rd, Waccabuc, NY *10597*
  ☎ (561) 588-4629 . . 1255 Lands End Rd, Point Manalapan, FL *33462*

Roberts MRS Albert S (Marie L Slocum) Rr.
☎ (412) 238-9296 . . ''Penllyn'' Star Rte, Rector, PA *15677*

Roberts MRS Algernon (Elizabeth Kurtz) Sth'39 . . . | ☎ (610) 525-3352
MISS Letitia—Sth'64—at ☎ (212) 249-4094 | 7 Pond Lane,
200 E 72 St, New York, NY *10021* . . . . | Bryn Mawr, PA
| *19010*

Roberts DR & MRS Andrew B (Susan Bradford) Bost'78.P'70.Minn'75
149 W Meade St, Philadelphia, PA *19118*

Roberts MISS Anne C—Pitzer'73.Nw'78
☎ (773) 477-9819 . . 3031 N Clifton Av, Chicago, IL *60657*

Roberts MR & MRS Bayard H (M Louise McIlhenny)
Ph.Gm.Rb.Ac.P.'34.Pa'37 . . of
☎ (610) 527-6517 . . 53 Pasture Lane, Bryn Mawr, PA *19010*
☎ (207) 276-5427 . . ''Grasslands'' PO Box 523, Northeast Harbor,
ME *04662*

Roberts DR & MRS Brooke (Anna W Ingersoll) V'43. Rb.Ph.Ac.P'39.Pa'43
☎ (610) 520-1670 . . 20 Pond Lane, Bryn Mawr, PA *19010*

Roberts MR & MRS Bruce L (Sulger—Marie R | of PO Box 2270,
Connors) Yn.Y'47 . . . . | New London, NH
MISS Sarah P Sulger—at ☎ (773) 404-2987 | *03257*
3229 N Wilton Av, Chicago, IL *60657* . . . . . . | ☎ (561) 234-3550
| 936 Seagrape Lane,
| Vero Beach, FL
| *32963*

Roberts MR & MRS Cameron B (Eve L Ross)
BostColl'79.Cy.Sm.Cw.H'75.Ore'77.H'82
☎ (508) 921-6467 . . Paine Av, Box 146, Prides Crossing, MA *01965*

Roberts MISS Caroline G P—Br'94.Ncd . . .see R K Lincoln

Roberts MR Clarence L . . . . Died at
Bryn Mawr, PA Dec 24'95

Roberts MR & MRS Clarence L JR (Frances H Gibby) Hlns'65.Y'56.AmU'62
☎ (860) 364-0285 . . 5 Sharon Mountain Rd, Box 601, Sharon,
CT *06069*

Roberts MRS Cornelia C (Cornelia Van R Clark) | ☎ (508) 653-0257
Wheat'65.Nh.Sm. | 202 Lake St,
MISS Isabel P—Ch'91—at 647 President St, | Sherborn, MA
Apt 4A, Brooklyn, NY *11215* . . . . | *01770*
MR Nathaniel T—Pa'88—at 810 Flamingo Dv, |
West Palm Beach, FL *33401* . . . . |

Roberts DR & MRS Dale M (Patricia E Santa Maria) | ☎ (502) 897-1275
Pa'68.Louis'86.Ore'63.Pa'67.Albany'72 . . . . . . | 3 Indian Hills Trail,
MR John A—Mich'90.Ia'93—at 405 N Wabash | Louisville, KY
Av, Apt 4902, Chicago, IL *60611* . . . . | *40207*
JUNIORS MR Jeffrey S—at Princeton . . . . |

Roberts DR & MRS David 4th (Beebe Eileen | ☎ (205) 979-2429
Bromeyer) Rol'66.Rol'65 . . . . | 2217 Vestavia Dv,
MISS Kathryn J . . . . | Birmingham, AL
MR David 5th . . . . | *35216*

Roberts MR & MRS Donald M (Mary A Gordon) Sth'60.Ln.Fic.Y'57 . . of
☎ (212) 288-1086 . . 10 Gracie Square, New York, NY *10028*
☎ (413) 528-1984 . . Tullar Farm, Sheffield Rd, South Egremont,
MA *01258*

Roberts MR & MRS Dudley (Fitch—Phyfe—Laura | of ☎ (516)324-0330
Serra-Garibaldi) Mds.Dyc. ⚓ . . . . | PO Box 1077,
MR Henry Pinkney Phyfe JR—Van'91 . . . . . . | Further Lane,
| East Hampton, NY
| *11937*
| ☎ (242) 334-6188
| Sanderling,
| Cotton Bay Club,
| Rock Sound,
| Eleuthera, Bahamas
| ☎ (212) 832-7424
| 10 Mitchell Place,
| New York, NY
| *10017*

Roberts MR & MRS Edward P (Alice Jaques) My.H'39
☎ (508) 468-3351 . . 201 Main St, Wenham, MA *01984*

Roberts MR Edward P 3d . . see MISS N W Rathborne

Roberts MR & MRS Edward W (Keeler—Squibb—M | ☎ (401) 423-0001
Thayer Eliason) Ac.Ncd. . . . . | 196 Highland Dv,
MR Marston W Keeler JR . . . . | PO Box 596,
| Jamestown, RI
| *02835*

Roberts MR & MRS Elzey M (Rachel L Anderson) | ☎ (314) PA5-6789
Wash'45.Nd.P'42 . . . . | 22 Wydown Terr,
MISS Lila L . . . . | St Louis, MO *63105*

Roberts MRS Eugene B (Marie-Bonne de Viel-Castel) Ct.K.Sl.
☎ (301) 390-6288 . . ''Fairwood'' 12215 Annapolis Rd, Glenn Dale,
MD *20769*

Roberts MR & MRS Eugene B JR (Lynn E Springer)
Wash'65.Nrr.Mt.Srb.Csn.Y'64.Ch'75
☎ (301) 627-8622 . . Patuxent Farm, 4700 Old Crain H'way,
Upper Marlboro, MD *20772*

Roberts MISS Frances Carolina (g—Robert Earl Kelso) . . . . Born at
San Antonio, TX Jan 31'95

Roberts MR Frederick E—Hn.Dth'62.H'72
☎ (713) 965-9588 . . 2500 McCue Rd, Houston, TX *77057-0036*

Roberts MISS Gainor
☎ (610) 525-6885 . . 635 Old Gulph Rd, Bryn Mawr, PA *19010-1805*

Roberts MRS George (Kramer—Esther S Schoellkopf)
☎ (203) 869-3436 . . 253 Round Hill Rd, Greenwich, CT *06831*

Roberts MR & MRS George B JR (Zara Bentley) Y'52
☎ (215) 242-8738 . . 429 W Allens Lane, Philadelphia, PA *19119-2805*

Roberts MRS George Brooke (Mary H Howland) Cda.
☎ (215) 242-8738 . . 429 W Allens Lane, Philadelphia, PA *19119-2805*

Roberts MR & MRS George R (Leanne Bovet) | of ☎ (415)326-8708
Bhm.Clare'66.Hast'69 . . . . | 260 Atherton Av,
MISS Courtney A . . . . | Atherton, CA *94027*
MR Eric B . . . . | Stone Canyon
MR Mark B . . . . | Ranch, 20328
| Airline H'way,
| Paicines, CA *95043*

Roberts MRS H Radclyffe (E Hazel Warden)
☎ (610) 645-8653 . . Waverly Heights, Villa 4, 1400 Waverly Rd,
Gladwyne, PA *19035*

Roberts MR & MRS Harold M (Jill L Curry) Y'49 . . .
MISS Stephanie E B—at Nightingale-Bamford . .
☎ (212) PL5-7096
325 E 57 St,
New York, NY
10022

Roberts MR & MRS Henry B (Paton Rauch) D.Sm.Chi.Ncd.P'36
☎ (508) 653-7532 . . 202 Farm Rd, Sherborn, MA *01770*

Roberts MR & MRS Henry P (Catherine E Savage)
Keuka'72.Bvl.Hob'73 . . . .
MISS Sarah W . . . .
☎ (508) 763-5260
"Shadow Farm"
171 Mendell Rd,
Rochester, MA
02770

Roberts MR & MRS Howard H (Joan L Church)
Rose'87.Rb.P'50 . . . .
MISS Elisabeth P—Mariet'74.JHop'85 . . . .
MR Owen B—Dick'88 . . . .
☎ (610) LA5-4731
1319 Wendover Rd,
Rosemont, PA
19010

Roberts MR & MRS Isaac W 2d (Debra A Disch) Wis'72.Sg.Pa'69
☎ (215) 233-5278 . . 501 Auburn Av, Wyndmoor, PA *19038*

Roberts MR & MRS Jared I (Katherine M Sherwood) Cal'76.P'68.Va'74
☎ (703) 538-4343 . . 3607 N Glebe Rd, Arlington, VA *22207*

Roberts MRS John A (Patricia Hennecart) Cs.Cw.
☎ (212) 288-8312 . . 75 East End Av, New York, NY *10028-7974*

Roberts MR & MRS John L M (Irène E Crofut)
Br'65.Br'66 . . . .
JUNIORS MISS Serena van S . . . .
JUNIORS MR Nicholas de C . . . .
☎ (610) 294-8054
2—2 St, Erwinna,
PA *18920*

Roberts DR John M—Pc.Y'49.Y'52
☎ (215) CH8-4788 . . 234 W Allens Lane, Philadelphia, PA *19119*

Roberts MR & MRS John R (Barbara Wilbanks)
Ala'67.Cysl.Bgy.Nd.Ala'63 . . . .
MISS Allison W—Duke'92—at ☎ (703) 841-9221
4650 N Washington Blvd, Apt 516, Arlington,
VA *22201* . . . .
MISS Sarah E—Aub'94—at ☎ (901) 324-3320
3685 Johnwood Dv, Memphis, TN *38122* . . . . .
☎ (901) 323-6888
65 W Chickasaw
P'kway, Memphis,
TN *38111*

Roberts MR & MRS John S JR (Helen I Martindale)
Cr'66.Y.'60.Pa'68 . . . .
MR Christopher V—Y'92 . . . .
MR Alexander I—Leh'94 . . . .
250 Bell Rd,
Wynnewood, PA
19096

Roberts MR & MRS Laurance P (Isabel M Spaulding)
V'33.C.K.Csp.Ac.Mv.P'29
☎ (410) 383-2294 . . 1310 Bolton St, Baltimore, MD *21217*

Roberts MISS Lily Elizabeth Shao (MISS Anne C) . . . . Born in
Hunan Province, China May 16'95

Roberts MISS Lucy C . . see W Byrd

Roberts LT COL (RET) & MRS Malcolm JR (M Nancy Tattersall) USA.
☎ (757) 564-0675 . . 3800 Treyburn Dv, 4506, Williamsburg,
VA *23185-2875*

Roberts CHAPLAIN (COL) & MRS Malcolm 3d (Mary L
Simpson) USA.NCar'69.W'ham'66.
VaTheo'75 ⚓ . . . .
JUNIORS MISS Mary L . . . .
JUNIORS MR Jonathan E . . . .
☎ (757) 868-0072
10 Saunders Dv,
Poquoson, VA
23662

Roberts MR Nathaniel P—Cal'94 . . see R K Lincoln

Roberts MISS Noma Ann (Bohlen—Noma Ann Roberts) Me.
☎ (610) 525-8733 . . 1216 Spring Mill Rd, Villanova, PA *19085*

Roberts MR & MRS Philip R (Lorraine H Lipscomb)
Pqt.Rr.H'64 . . . .
MISS Margaret C—at 3931 Cabinet Way,
Pittsburgh, PA *15201* . . . .
MR Frederick W 2d—at 5 Grandview Rd,
Pittsburgh, PA *15237* . . . .
MR Charles L . . . .
☎ (412) 967-0732
750 Fairview Rd,
Pittsburgh, PA
15238

Roberts MR & MRS Ralston P (Virginia McKee)
Ariz'65.Bur.Stan'65 . . . .
MISS Hilary E—Ariz'92—at ☎ (415) 441-7607
2828 Greenwich St, Apt 5, San Francisco, CA
94123 . . . .
MR Ralston P JR . . . .
JUNIORS MR John L . . . .
☎ (415) 375-1920
595 Hayne Rd,
Hillsborough, CA
94010

Roberts MR & MRS Stephen F (Elizabeth D Lewis)
Del'78 . . . .
JUNIORS MR Eli L . . . .
☎ (802) 623-6461
"Mountain View"
Miller Hill, Sudbury,
VT *05733*

Roberts MR & MRS T Williams JR (Clement—Jane B Savage)
Rb.Ncd.P'50.Penn'82
☎ (610) 525-8791 . . 669 Conestoga Rd, Villanova, PA *19085*

Roberts MR & MRS T Williams 3d (Emma H Rymer) Denis'88.Ub.Denis'87
☎ (617) 424-9939 . . 121 Marlborough St, Boston, MA *02116*

Roberts MR & MRS Thomas C W (Sally C Rutherfurd) Sth'50.Csn.Ch'50
☎ (609) 921-6114 . . 16 Stony Brook Lane, Princeton, NJ *08540*

Roberts MR & MRS William C (Lisa M Potter) . . . .
MISS George-Anne—at ☎ (516) 324-3916
130 Gerard Dv, East Hampton, NY *11937* . . . . .
☎ (212) 737-2245
308 E 79 St,
New York, NY
10021

Roberts MR & MRS William D (Caroline P Moody) Swb'53.Edg.Va'55
☎ (412) 741-6558 . . 531 Boundary St, Sewickley, PA *15143*

Roberts MR & MRS William J O (Ann E Vail) Sth'50.On.Br'42
☎ (847) 234-1884 . . 280 Bluffs Edge, Lake Forest, IL *60045*

Robertson MR Charles S JR—Mit'55 ⚓ . . . .
MR Charles S 3d—Y'83—at 983-1 Belmont Terr,
Sunnyvale, CA *94086* . . . .
☎ (513) 831-4251
505 Marietta Av,
Terrace Park, OH
45174

Robertson MRS Charles Stuart (Elizabeth Swing) Cy.Ny.
☎ (508) 822-0547 . . 48 Church Green, Taunton, MA *02780*

Robertson DR Charles W—Cy.Syr'36
☎ (617) 696-0326 . . 43 Randolph Av, Milton, MA *02187*

Robertson MR & MRS David A JR (Fisher—Frothingham—
Harriet W Cooper) BrM'53.C.Au.P'36.P'40
☎ (609) 924-5252 . . 75 Arreton Rd, Princeton, NJ *08540*

Robertson MRS Edward L JR (Pearsall—Jean Taussig)
☎ (561) 278-6469 . . Harbour's Edge 461, 401 E Linton Blvd,
Delray Beach, FL *33483*

Robertson MR & MRS George W JR (Elizabeth F
Lindsley) Rc.Rd.Wyo'61 . . . .
MISS Alexandra H—StAndr'96 . . . .
MR George W 3d—Rut'94 . . . .
☎ (610) NI4-0679
22 Laurel Circle,
Malvern, PA *19355*

Robertson MR & MRS Harrison M JR (Burnham—Barbara N Bumgarner) Md'52.Md.Elk.Cy.Cw. Cda.Va'42 . . . . of ☎ (561)842-4756 134 Seagate Rd, Palm Beach, FL 33480
MR Harrison M 3d . . . .
MISS Kim N Burnham—Gchr'80 . . . . ☎ (410) 435-8903 124C E Melrose Av, Baltimore, MD 21212

Robertson MISS Isabel A—Ober'89 . . see N Abeel

Robertson MRS James L 3d (Sanford—Genevieve B Sullivan) Cly.
☎ (561) 276-9716 . . 4475 N Ocean Blvd, Delray Beach, FL 33483

Robertson MRS James Y (Sara R Stewart) CtCol'61.AmU'69.Wa . . .of
☎ (561) 832-4081 . . 122 Peruvian Av, PH, Palm Beach, FL 33480-4477
☎ (773) 248-7628 . . 1243 W Barry Av, Chicago, IL 60657

Robertson MR & MRS Jaquelin T (Marianna Neese) K.Mds.Y'55.Ox'57.Y'61 . . of
☎ (516) 323-1906 . . 11 Dunemere Lane, East Hampton, NY 11937-2705
☎ (212) 744-6465 . . 211 E 70 St, New York, NY 10021

Robertson MR & MRS John O (Sonia A Bill) V'65.Br'63 ⚓ . . . . ☎ (207) 774-1288 "The Vespiary" 336 Danforth St, Portland, ME 04102
JUNIORS MISS Caroline I B . . . .

Robertson MR & MRS John T 3d (Nancy V Plummer) WChesSt'64.Balt'63 ⚓
☎ (410) 221-0381 . . 6208 Castle Haven Rd, Cambridge, MD 21613

Robertson MRS Kenneth D (Howard—Natalie B Merrill) . . . . Died at Stockbridge, MA Jun 5'96

Robertson MR & MRS Noel D (Laura L P Fahy) Ws'62.Tor'58.Cr'64 . . . . of ☎ (905)685-7943 3 Towering Heights Blvd, Apt 1107, St Catherines, Ontario L2T 4A4, Canada
MISS Eva L—at 102 E 7 St, New York, NY 10009 . . . .
MISS Emily A—at 503 S Texas St, Silver City, NM 88061 . . . .
MISS Laura I—at McGill . . . . ☎ (603) 539-2271 "Indian Point" Connor Pond, Center Ossipee, NH 03814
MR Samuel A—at 102 E 7 St, New York, NY 10009 . . . . ☎ (905) 627-8244 82 Victoria St, Dundas, Ontario L9H 2C2, Canada

Robertson MRS Norman F (Mary K McCoy) Mt.Eyc.Cly.Ncd.Dh.
☎ (201) 731-3885 . . Llewellyn Park, West Orange, NJ 07052

Robertson MR & MRS Philip McR (Hanna—Mary Lawrence) Bhm.Pcu.Bur.
☎ (360) 468-3381 . . "Whale Point" PO Box 830, Shaw Island, WA 98286

Robertson MR & MRS R Bruce (Sarah O Wells) Bnd'68.Nu'78.Ri.P'65.H.'69
☎ (212) 877-2394 . . 210 W 90 St, New York, NY 10024

Robertson MR R Emmett 3d—Gi.Ct.Md.Hn.Hb.H'64
☎ (804) 784-2668 . . Commonwealth House, PO Box 27281, Richmond, VA 23261

Robertson MR Samuel D—Bard'92 . . see N Abeel

Robertson MISS Susan . . see H A Wise JR

Robertson MR W James—StMarys'39 3400 Wagner Heights Rd, Apt 104, Stockton, CA 95209

Robertson MR & MRS William D (D Scarlett Leas) Rdc'74.Rc.So.B.Paris'72 . . . . ☎ (212) 980-3183 415 E 52 St, New York, NY 10022
MISS Scarlett Leas . . . .
JUNIORS MISS Alexis Virginia . . . .

Robertson MR & MRS William R (Anne Tuck) Sth'36.Cw.Cr'34
☎ (603) 924-8654 . . 55 Colonial Square, Peterborough, NH 03458

Robeson-Miller MR Stephen A—San.Myf.Rv.Ty'78
☎ (508) 877-5941 . . PO Box 183, Brookline, MA 02146

Robinette MR & MRS G Todd (Sally J Ames) SanJ'78.Hampshire'77
☎ (415) 348-5202 . . 415 Concord Way, Burlingame, CA 94010

Robinette MRS George Earle (Jane U Butler) Me.M.
☎ (610) 527-5316 . . 735 Harriton Rd, Bryn Mawr, PA 19010-2907

Robinette MRS J Todd (Joan Todd) Ac.Me.
☎ (610) LA5-5919 . . 1114 Wyndon Av, Bryn Mawr, PA 19010

Robins MR & MRS Alfred LeC (Barbara A Randle) OklaSt'62.Okla'63 ⚓ . . . . ☎ (713) 496-7513 14818 Broadgreen Dv, Houston, TX 77079
MISS Elizabeth H—at 5211 Beaverbrook Dv, Houston, TX 77084 . . . .

Robins MISS Josephine K—Br'92
☎ (212) 229-9871 . . 104-106 Bedford St, Apt 2D, New York, NY 10014

Robins MR & MRS Seth S (Sarah J Scrymser) Sth'77.CUNY'77
☎ (212) 932-0150 . . 245 W 107 St, Apt 8E, New York, NY 10025

Robins MR & MRS Thomas 3d (Jean E Bergland) P'58.H'66 . . . . ☎ (206) LA3-7410 4114—37 Av NE, Seattle, WA 98105
MISS Martha J—SantaC'94 . . . .

Robins MRS William R JR (Lucille M LeCocq)
☎ (713) 932-8574 . . Memorial City Terrace Apt 7127, 11900 Barryknoll Lane, Houston, TX 77024

Robins MR & MRS William R 3d (Nancy L Hood) Okla'61.Cc.Hn.Okla'60.Pa'62.H'63 . . . . ☎ (609) 924-9105 696 Princeton-Kingston Rd, Princeton, NJ 08540
MISS Mary H H—at 1226 Seventeenth Av E, Seattle, WA 98112 . . . .

Robinson MR & MRS A Pitts 2d (Carla G Digges) Ncd.JHop'61
☎ (410) 825-7518 . . 7810 Chelsea St, Ruxton, MD 21204

Robinson MR A Pitts 3d—Loy'87.GeoW'93
☎ (212) 721-0708 . . 50 W 77 St, Apt 6G, New York, NY 10024

Robinson MRS Agnes C (Wales—Agnes C Adams) Bnd'41
☎ (415) 321-3162 . . 1765 Fulton St, Palo Alto, CA 94303

Robinson MRS Alexander C 4th (Patricia R Davin) Swb'49
☎ (810) 644-4230 . . 3949 Oakhills Dv, Bloomfield Hills, MI 48301

Robinson MR & MRS Alexander L JR (Ann Lenher) Myf.Ncd.Y'52 . . . . ☎ (804) 985-4350 "Still Pond" Rte 1, Box 147, Stanardsville, VA 22973
MR Alexander L 3d—Lynch'88—at
☎ (203) 259-8907 . . 848 Surrey Lane, Fairfield, CT 06430 . . . .

Robinson MR & MRS Barclay JR (Katharine H McCagg) Sth'56.Conn'83.Y'56.Y'63
☎ (860) 535-4433 . . 229 Wamphassuc Point Rd, Stonington, CT 06378

Robinson MR & MRS Beverley (Hattler—Roselène Briceño) DU'81.Cc.Cl'57.JHop'61.Mid'67 . . . . of ☎ (303)773-0451 6180 E Briarwood Circle, Englewood, CO 80112
MR John B . . . . ☎ (303) 440-7361 2137—4 St, Boulder, CO 80302

Robinson MR & MRS Blake W (Marjorie F Merritt) H'70 5 Meadow Rd, Darien, CT 06820

Robinson MR & MRS C David (Mary P Leonard) ☎ (415) 332-1470
Bur.P'57.Pa'65 . . . . 54 Spencer Av,
MISS Anne H—P'88.H'92—at 223 N Guadalupe Sausalito, CA *94965*
St, Santa Fe, NM *87501* . . . .
MR Edward B . . . .
MR Steven L—Colg'95—at 30 W 63 St,
New York, NY *10023* . . . .

Robinson MR & MRS Caldwell C (Greiner—Dick— ☎ (561) 833-5450
Jane B Cunningham) Cc. . . . . 2600 N Flagler Dv,
MISS Nicole de G—at ☎ (212) 628-9321 West Palm Beach,
303 E 83 St, New York, NY *10028* . . . . FL *33407*
JUNIORS MR C Colt JR—at 215 El Bravo Way,
Palm Beach, FL *33480* . . . .

Robinson MISS Carol
☎ (860) 364-5700 . . 20 Amenia Union Rd, Sharon, CT *06069-0126*

Robinson MR & MRS Christopher J (Barbara Gisel) *see*
Wheat'72.Me.Gm.M.DU'73 . . . . *Dilatory Domiciles*
JUNIORS MISS Katherine G . . . .

Robinson MR & MRS D Patrick M (Elisabeth T Howell) Hav'47
☎ (610) 866-1375 . . 333 Pine Top Trail, Bethlehem, PA *18017*

Robinson MR & MRS David G (M Susan de Gruchy) ☎ (561) 234-8449
Av'tt'67.Cw.Chi.Dar.P'67.H'72 . . . . 545 Coconut Palm
MISS Anne Fisher . . . . Rd, Vero Beach, FL
MR D Graham JR *32963*

Robinson MR & MRS Davis R (Suzanne Walker) ☎ (202) 362-0556
Mt.Cvc.Myf.Y'61.H'67 . . . . 3729 Fordham Rd
MISS Gracyn W . . . . NW, Washington,
DC *20016*

Robinson MRS Dorothy F (Dorothy Fay) Ri. . . . . . . ☎ (212) 289-0437
MISS Victoria A—B'gton'93—at 1155 Park Av,
☎ (212) 529-2825 . . 50 E 3 St, New York, NY New York, NY
10003 . . . . *10128*

Robinson MR & MRS Dwight C (Anne S Grosvenor) V'40.UWash'71.Cly.Ncd.
☎ (206) 324-3340 . . 4245 E Lee St, Seattle, WA *98112*

Robinson MRS Dwight P JR (Mary H Gass) Cy.Chi.Ncd.
☎ (617) 320-9584 . . Fox Hill Village 508, 10 Longwood Dv, Westwood,
MA *02090*

Robinson MR & MRS Edward T (Mary E Lipscomb) ☎ (617) 332-1712
Roch'62.Roch'69.Myf.Ncd.H'65 . . . . 11 Leighton Rd,
MISS Elizabeth B—at Smith . . . . Auburndale, MA
JUNIORS MR Lloyd S—at Middlebury *02166*

Robinson MRS Eileen G (Cumming—Eileen Garrity)
☎ (561) 547-5327 . . PO Box 2814, Palm Beach, FL *33480*

Robinson MISS Elizabeth C—Col'90
☎ (212) 628-9321 . . 303 E 83 St, Apt 105, New York, NY *10028*

Robinson MISS Elizabeth D—RISD'88.Dar.
☎ (415) 389-9830 . . 321 Corte Madera Av, Mill Valley, CA *94941*

Robinson MISS Evelyn Brown (J Howland) . . . . Born at
New York, NY Aug 18'95

Robinson MR & MRS Francis W (H Shirley Coffey) Me.Fw.Nich'38
☎ (610) MU8-0319 . . 272 Abraham's Lane, Villanova, PA *19085-1129*

Robinson MR & MRS Frank Brooks (Jean C Ackerman)
Fic.Pg.Rr.Y'54.CarnM'60
☎ (412) 683-6590 . . 1414 Bennington Av, Pittsburgh, PA *15217-1139*

Robinson MR Gardner J H—Denis'88
☎ (212) 650-0541 . . 425 E 85 St, Apt 4B, New York, NY *10028*

Robinson MRS George D F JR (Margaret W Wood) Elk.
☎ (410) 243-5322 . . Roland Park Place, Apt 305, 830 W 40 St,
Baltimore, MD *21211*

Robinson MR George H—Bab'86
8 Park Plaza, Apt 269, Boston, MA *02116*

Robinson MR & MRS H Ivens (Dodge Hobson) Ncmb'74.H'73
☎ (504) 895-7555 . . 6028 Pitt St, New Orleans, LA *70118*

Robinson MRS Hamilton (Nancy M Brereton) Cvc.Mt.Sl.Ncd.
☎ (202) 265-4332 . . 84 Kalorama Circle NW, Washington, DC *20008*

Robinson MR & MRS Hamilton JR (Alger—Roxana of ☎ (212)421-8598
Barry) Ri.Bgt.C.P'55.H'60 ⚓ . . . . 400 E 52 St,
MISS Roxana S Alger—at ☎ (718) 768-8581 New York, NY
425—14 St, Brooklyn, NY *11215* *10022*
☎ (914) 232-9061
Willow Green Farm,
159 N Salem Rd,
Katonah, NY *10536*

Robinson MISS Helen Harper (Marc C) . . . . Born at
New York, NY Apr 27'96

Robinson MR & MRS Horace B B (Henrietta Truesdell)
Sth'38.Un.Plg.Coa.Myf.Ne.Cw.StJ.Cs.Ncd.H'34
☎ (212) 722-5022 . . 1170 Fifth Av, New York, NY *10029*

Robinson MR & MRS J Howland (Janet E Sproul)
Colg'77.Cw.Myf.Ncd.Dar.Hampshire'73.Geo'77
☎ (914) 234-6763 . . 519 Bedford Center Rd, Bedford Hills, NY *10507*

Robinson MR & MRS Kevin T C (Ann H Swift) ☎ (603) 253-8363
D&E'71.Bab'72.Ws'73 . . . . PO Box 493,
MISS Jennifer L . . . . 5 Reedy Rd,
MR Kevin T C 2d . . . . Moultonborough,
JUNIORS MR Geoffrey S . . . . NH *03254*

Robinson MRS Lauretta D (Plentl—Lauretta D Robinson) Cr'34.Cr'44
Harbour's Edge 328, 401 E Linton Blvd, Delray Beach, FL *33483*

Robinson MR & MRS Marc C (Helen Van V Corroon) CtCol'80.Smu'73
☎ (212) 249-4805 . . 229 E 79 St, Apt 10F, New York, NY *10021*

Robinson DR & MRS Marc L (April A Bernard) H'78.Ham'84.Y'90.Y'92
☎ (212) 645-1228 . . 18 Grove St, Apt 2, New York, NY *10014*

Robinson MRS Mary L K (Mary L Kendall) Tul'50.Cly.
☎ (504) 899-0990 . . 1439—7 St, New Orleans, LA *70115*

Robinson MR Michael W—Myf.Syr'85
☎ (202) 686-0451 . . 4849 Connecticut Av NW, Washington, DC *20008*

Robinson MR & MRS Patrick M (Jennifer G Slingluff)
Hlns'84.Rcn.Stc.W&L'81
☎ (203) 656-3549 . . 25 Andrews Dv, Darien, CT *06820*

Robinson MR & MRS Patrick W (Ann D Fletcher) Cly.Camb'49 . . of
☎ (011-44-171) 352-9089 . . 127 Swan Court, Flood St,
London SW3 5RY, England
☎ (011-44-196) 324-0243 . . Lovington Mill, nr Castle Cary,
Somerset BA7 7PS, England

Robinson MR & MRS Paul J (Woodruff—Marie S ☎ (508) 420-1300
Crompton) . . . . 157 Saddler Lane,
JUNIORS MR William D . . . . PO Box 279,
West Barnstable,
MA *02668-0279*

Robinson MR & MRS Peter C (Hardie—Howard— Sarah L Lingham) Aub'91.Geo'61.Bab'63.H'86 | ☎ (334) 263-2601
MISS Andrea S—McG'90.McG'92 . . . . | 1822 Galena Av,
DR Edward T L Hardie—Y'85.Stan'89. | Montgomery, AL
Stan'92 . . . . | *36106*

Robinson MR & MRS Randall S (Charlotte U Hitchcock) Mit'55
☎ (410) 472-4633 . . 12 Sparks Station Rd, Sparks, MD *21152*

Robinson MR & MRS Robert W A (D Ann Harding)
Chr.Plg.Un.Mt.Yh.StJ.Km.StA.Cs.Br'50.Br'52.
Ill'54.EpiscTheo'71.So'72 . . of
☎ (203) 966-3426 . . 2 Hathaway Common, New Canaan,
CT *06840-5737*
☎ (518) 758-1861 . . "Kinder Kane" 1374 Old Post Rd, Valatie,
NY *12184*

Robinson MISS Rosemary T
☎ (216) 354-4701 . . 301 High St, Fairport Harbor, OH *44077*

Robinson MRS Samuel S (Carolyn L Fotterall)
☎ (908) 439-2623 . . Homestead Rd, Pottersville, NJ *07979*

Robinson MR & MRS Samuel S JR (Hess—Kristin A Meade)
☎ (908) 234-1206 . . PO Box 1011, Bedminster, NJ *07979*

Robinson MR & MRS Sanger P (Baur—Martha Fishback) Cas.Sc.Eyc.
1430 N Lake Shore Dv, Chicago, IL *60610*

Robinson MR Sanger P II . . see H G Cummings

Robinson MR Terence P—Pace'84.Man'vl'86
100 Diplomat Dv, Apt 7A, Mt Kisco, NY *10549*

Robinson DR & MRS Thomas D (Anne S Jeffers) V'76.P'68
☎ (212) 427-4052 . . 21 E 90 St, Apt 7A, New York, NY *10128*

Robinson MR & MRS Thomas R (Laura C Clements) P'84.H'89.P'84
☎ (617) 749-1206 . . 297 Main St, Hingham, MA *02043*

Robinson MR & MRS Timothy T (Marianna Merritt Ashmead)
LakeF'86.Ny.Srb.Hob'87
☎ (401) 848-2644 . . 56 Farewell St, Newport, RI *02840*

Robinson MRS W Champlin (Olivia E Frick) Mv.Cda.
☎ (410) 823-6989 . . 514 Brightwood Club Dv, Lutherville, MD *21093*

Robinson MR Winthrop A—Dth'84
☎ (203) 622-4074 . . 18 Putnam Park, Greenwich, CT *06830*

Robinson MR & MRS Wolcott de W (Pew—Marjorie Mason)
☎ (610) 527-6365 . . 1004 Broadmoor Rd, Bryn Mawr, PA *19010*

Robinson MR Wolcott de W JR—Sap.Rv.Pa'63
☎ (212) 725-0952 . . 40 Park Av, New York, NY *10016*

Robson MASTER Frederick William Lawrence (Rupert W) . . . . . . Born at
London, England Jly 14'95

Robson MR & MRS Robert K (Bartlett—Anne M Kemp) Wes'42
☎ (410) 226-5155 . . Holly Harbor Rd, Box 67, Oxford, MD *21654*

Robson MR & MRS Rupert W (E K Alexandra G Morris)
Camb'91.Stan'93.Camb'89.Stan'94
☎ (011-44-171) 603-1084 . . 15 Hofland Rd, London W14, England

Roby MRS Cynthia H (Cynthia H Higgins) Bost'68 . | ☎ (415) 332-6556
MR Joseph 4th . . . . | 40 Cable Roadway,
JUNIORS MR Nicholas C . . . . | Sausalito, CA *94965*

Roche MR & MRS Robert P (Priscilla C Longstreth) Me.Hav'46.Pa'48
☎ (610) 642-9242 . . 305 Wister Rd, Wynnewood, PA *19096*

Roche MR & MRS Thomas K (Knapp—Beverly Brady) S.P'39.Y'41 ⚓ . . . . | ☎ (516) WA1-7543
MISS Barbara M . . . . | "Poverty Pocket"
| RD Box 1782,
| 1782 Oyster Bay
| Rd, Syosset, NY
| *11791*

Rochester MR Andrew D—Ne'78
"Morrill School House" HC 64, Box 720, Black Mountain Rd,
West Sumner, ME *04292*

Rochfort COL & MRS Robert E (Elizabeth B Larkin) An.USA'45
☎ (210) 826-1396 . . 447 Burr Rd, San Antonio, TX *78209*

Rockafellow MR & MRS Daniel B (Virginia A Logan)
Laf'81.VillaN'84.Laf'81
☎ (610) 525-1971 . . 121 Browning Lane, Rosemont, PA *19010*

Rockefeller MRS David (Margaret McGrath) . . . . Died at
New York, NY Mch 26'96

Rockefeller MRS Deborah (Deborah C Sage) Ox'69 | ☎ (805) 379-2587
MISS Andrea D—at 2401 Lakeview Dv, Apt O-2, | 1014-14 Westlake
North Little Rock, AR *72116* . . . . | Blvd, Apt 177,
MISS Katherine C . . . . | West Lake Village,
JUNIORS MR Winthrop P JR . . . . | CA *91361*

Rockefeller MR & MRS Godfrey A (Margaret N Kuhn)
NCar'50.Gi.Md.Mt.Sl.Yn.Y'45 ⚓ . . of
☎ (410) 255-5022 . . PO Box 204, Gibson Island, MD *21056*
☎ (561) 272-7704 . . 1127 Vista Del Mar, Delray Beach, FL *33483*

Rockefeller MRS J Sterling (Paula Watjen) Yh.Cly.
☎ (203) 869-0156 . . 375 E Middle Patent Rd, Greenwich, CT *06831*

Rockefeller MR J Stillman—Mt.Y'24
☎ (203) 869-4330 . . "Rockfields" 1 Indian Spring Rd, Greenwich,
CT *06831-4430*

Rockefeller MR & MRS Laurance S (Mary French) B.K.Mt.Cos.Cs.Cly.P'32
834 Fifth Av, New York, NY *10021*

Rockefeller MRS Mary Clark (Mary T Clark) Cs.
810 Fifth Av, New York, NY *10021*

Rockefeller MRS Nelson A (Murphy—Margaretta L | Pocantico Hills,
Fitler) . . . . | Tarrytown, NY
MR Nelson A JR . . . . | *10591*
MR Mark F . . . . |

Rockefeller MR O Stillman—AmU'82
560 W 43 St, Apt 27J, New York, NY *10036*

Rockefeller MR & MRS Rodman C (Sascha von Metzler) Ri.Dth'54 . . of
☎ (212) 421-6778 . . 435 E 52 St, New York, NY *10022*
☎ (914) 631-0910 . . "Winterburn" 48 Raafenberg Rd, Pocantico Hills,
Tarrytown, NY *10591*

Rockefeller MRS William (Mary D Gillett) Ri.Ny.Mto.Cly.Plg.Ncd.
☎ (914) 967-3967 . . 84 Grandview Av, Rye, NY *10580*

Rockwell MR Alan W—Gm.Hn.H'40
☎ (415) 435-1296 . . 76 Red Hill Circle, Tiburon, CA *94920-1773*

Rockwell MR & MRS Charles E JR (Madeline B | ☎ (802) 325-3534
Neilson) Mid'71.Mid'71 . . . . | Sykes Hollow Rd,
JUNIORS MISS Katherine L . . . . | Pawlet, VT *05761*

Rockwell MR Charles Embree
☎ (516) 584-5324 . . "Woodcrest" 43R Moriches Rd, St James,
NY *11780-9709*

Rockwell MR & MRS Dean M 3d (Murray—Suzanne Spaulding)
Cy.St.G.Mich'43
☎ (716) 992-9376 . . 9716 Knoll Rd, Eden, NY *14057*

Rockwell MRS Matthew L (Mary Hill) V'42 . . of
☎ (847) 446-4487 . . 393 Fairview Av, Winnetka, IL *60093*
6700 Gulf of Mexico Dv, 108, Longboat Key, FL *34228*

Rockwell MR & MRS Robin Markle (Barbara J Russell) . . . . | ☎ (561) 833-7777
MISS Stephanie O—at Boston U . . . . | 3140 Washington Rd, West Palm Beach, FL *33405-1645*

Rockwell MR & MRS Steven A (Helen M Suarez)
NotreDMd'78.Gv.Md.Pa'77
☎ (410) 363-0404 . . 240 Hopkins Lane, Owings Mills, MD *21117*

Rockwell MR & MRS Stuart W (Rosalind H Morgan) Ws'47.Cvc.Mt.H'39 . . . . | ☎ (202) 363-0545
MISS Susan C—H'84 . . . . | 5001 Sedgwick St NW, Washington, DC *20016*
MR Stephen W—ColC'84 . . . . |
MR Geoffrey M—Mass'85 . . . . |

Rockwell MR Thomas E—Hob'54.DU'58
PO Box 371, Franktown, CO *80016*

Rockwell MR & MRS Thorson (Melinda de W Highley)
F'klinSwitz'82.Nyc.Srb.
☎ (212) 288-8167 . . 28 E 73 St, New York, NY *10021*

Rockwood MISS Allison C . . see MRS R Crimmins

Rockwood JUNIORS MR John A . . see MRS R Crimmins

Rockwood MAJ & MRS Robert K (Margaret E Dolan)
Geo'89.Ill'91.USA'82.Ill'91
☎ (913) 784-3787 . . 435 Carpenter Av, Apt A, Ft Riley, KS *66442*

Rockwood MR & MRS William R (Elizabeth B Kirkland)
Ncd.Cda.TexA&M'40
☎ (210) 824-6124 . . 127 Haverhill Way, San Antonio, TX *78209*

Rodd MR F Morgan JR—Wes'86.Pa'94 . . see J M Meyer 3d

Rodd MR Thomas—Y'35
☎ (603) 938-2777 . . PO Box 522, Marshall Hill Rd, Bradford, NH *03221*

Roddy MR & MRS Gilbert M JR (Susan B Guild)
Wheat'78.Ub.Bow'78.Dth'83
☎ (508) 369-5004 . . 101 Barnes Hill Rd, Concord, MA *01742*

Rode MR & MRS Stephen W (Sletvold—Patricia L Bryant)
Pa'73.Temp'75.Vien'78.Penn'79.Pa'88
☎ (610) 649-5858 . . 1136 Waverly Rd, Gladwyne, PA *19035*

Rodemyer MISS Jeannette C—Myf.Ncd.Ofp.
☎ (314) 993-0302 . . 8 Sunnymeade Lane, St Louis, MO *63124*

Roden MR & MRS Lincoln 3d (Geralyn Winner) Y'52 . . . . | ☎ (215) 659-4856
MISS Valerie-Clark (Abraham—Valerie-Clark Roden) Hlns'85.Ncd. . . . . | 2535 Edgehill Rd, Huntingdon Valley, PA *19006*

Rodgers MR & MRS Christopher R P (Parson—Katharine S Bolton)
Au.Chi.Ncd.P'42
☎ (561) 265-0668 . . 555 Palm Way, Gulf Stream, FL *33483*

Rodgers MR H S Taylor—Nd.Cy.Y'45 . . . . | ☎ (314) 991-1051
MR H S Taylor JR . . . . | 16 Narragansett Dv, St Louis, MO *63124*

Rodgers MRS J Walter (Spencer—Joan Maloney)
☎ (910) 998-6672 . . 2327 Bermuda Village, Advance, NC *27006*

Rodgers MR & MRS James J (Hill—Eleanor C Musser) Fcg.Rr.Tc.
☎ (412) 826-5991 . . Longwood at Oakmont CH41, 500 Rte 909, Verona, PA *15147*

Rodgers MRS John B (Ruth Easton) Sth'31.Bur.Tcy.Cly.Ncd.Myf.
☎ (415) 851-7634 . . 501 Portola Rd, Box 8030, Portola Valley, CA *94028*

Rodgers MR & MRS John C (Barbara A Johnston) ColbyS'53
☎ (603) 863-2781 . . PO Box 583, Grantham, NH *03753*

Rodgers MR & MRS John L 3d (Charlotte T Landreth) . . . . | ☎ (215) 836-5313
MISS Margaret T—W&M'93 . . . . | 96 S College Av, Flourtown, PA *19031*
MR John L 4th—Cr'90 . . . . |

Rodgers MRS Julia O'Connor (Julia T O'Connor) Bnd'59
☎ (212) 628-9627 . . 446 E 86 St, Apt 10G, New York, NY *10028*

Rodiger MR & MRS Albert A (Jennifer H Watts) Sim'88.Bost'87.Bost'90
☎ (617) 749-4510 . . 3 Eastgate Lane, Hingham, MA *02043*

Rodiger MASTER Charles Gregory (W Gregory 3d) . . . . Born at Norwalk, CT Jly 25'96

Rodiger MASTER Jonathan Amory (William K) . . . . Born at Newton, MA Jan 11'95

Rodiger MR & MRS W Gregory 3d (Beverly J Bodnar)
MtH'83.Conn'87.StLaw'82
☎ (203) 834-2735 . . 8 Spicewood Lane, Wilton, CT *06897*

Rodiger MR & MRS Walter G JR (Elizabeth D King) SL'88.Yn.Y'43
☎ (203) 966-3671 . . 585 Silvermine Rd, New Canaan, CT *06840-4322*

Rodiger MR & MRS William K (Heather L McKinney)
Roch'86.SUNY'88.Dick'84.Syr'86
☎ (508) 443-9435 . . 193 Morse Rd, Sudbury, MA *01776*

Rodner MR & MRS Henry F JR (Alejandra Aquirre-Aquiso)
Mt.USN'43 ⚓
☎ (011-58-2) 752-93-84 . . Quinta Los Rodner, Av Chula Vista, Bello Monte, Caracas, Venezuela

Rodner MR & MRS James O (Felicity A Maxwell-Bresler) Ox'68.H'76.Cal'67.H'72 . . . . | ☎ (011-58-2) 751-51-70
MISS Maria R . . . . | Res Valser,
MISS Victoria L . . . . | Calle Suapure, Col B Mono, Caracas 1010A, Venezuela

Rodocanachi MR Paul S
☎ (212) 787-7055 . . 150 Central Park S, Apt 1506, New York, NY *10019-1566*

Rodocanachi MR Stephen J (Paul S) . . . . Married at New York, NY
DeVito MISS Antoinette V (late Rocco) . . . . Jun 29'96

Rodzianko MR & MRS Paul (Putnam—Chauncie McKeever)
SL'74.T.Ne.P'67
☎ (914) 351-2458 . . E Lake Rd, PO Box 757, Tuxedo Park, NY *10987*

Roe MISS Hilda L
☎ (415) 749-0285 . . 1221 Greenwich St, Apt 6, San Francisco, CA *94109*

Roe MR & MRS Ralph C (Stacy N Wardrop) Briar'73.DU'68.Cl'78
☎ (203) 869-8209 . . Cherry Valley Rd, Greenwich, CT *06831*

Roebling MR & MRS Wainwright R (Eudora N J DeRenne)
MtH'50.Ncd.Ga'53
☎ (941) 383-2341 . . 501 Hornblower Lane, PO Box 8834, Longboat Key, FL *34228*

Roehrs MRS Walter E JR (Brent Wolcott) Ncd.
☎ (610) 687-2352 . . 111 Steeplechase Rd, Devon, PA *19333*

Roell REV Rudolph—D.P.'33 . . of
☎ (561) 231-5268 . . 600 Riomar Dv, Apt 5, Vero Beach, *32963*
☎ (617) 326-2342 . . 52 Village Av, Box 223, Dedham, MA *02026*

Roenisch MR & MRS Clinton A (Cynthia D Carter)
Mid'87.Ch'90.Ih.Ken'83.Ch'88
16 Hillside Dv, Kentfield, CA *94904*

Roesler MRS Anne M (Slocum—Anne M Roesler)
210 Delespine Dv, De Bary, FL *32713*

Roesler MRS Edward JR (Marshall—Frances E Kerr)
☎ (415) 851-1930 . . 501 Portola Rd, Box 8007, Portola Valley,
CA *94028-7601*

Roessler MR & MRS Carl C (Mary F Rousseau)
Rcn.Bab'65.StL'71 . . . . ☎ (203) 762-0799
MISS Rebecca C . . . . 34 Ryder's Lane,
Wilton, CT *06897*

Rogers MR Andrew Y—Unn.Yn.Y'33
☎ (207) 883-2325 . . Winslow Homer Rd, Prouts Neck, Scarborough,
ME *04074*

Rogers DR & MRS Arthur M (Marguerite W MacCoy) Y'33
☎ (941) 676-4034 . . PO Box 832, Mountain Lake, Lake Wales,
FL *33859*

Rogers MR & MRS Arthur M JR (Barbara Whitney)
Ln.Mb.Csh.Y'63 ⚓ . . . . ☎ (516) 922-0366
MISS Whitney M—P'94 . . . . Sagamore Hill Rd,
MR Arthur M 3d—Ham'89 . . . . Oyster Bay, NY
11771

Rogers MR Bernard F 3d—Rcch.Cho.Y'53
see Dilatory Domiciles

Rogers MR Berry B
1008 Poplar Hill Rd, Baltimore, MD *21210*

Rogers MRS C Boyd (Ruth Donnell)
☎ (314) 962-0298 . . 420 Yorkshire Place, St Louis, MO *63119*

Rogers DR & MRS (DR) David Price (Helen E
Johnson) NCar'73.NCar'80.Duke'62.Duke'70 . . ☎ (919) 942-8064
MISS Cinnamon . . . . 3222 Tipi Lane,
MISS Ariel . . . . Durham, NC *27705*

Rogers MISS Diana V . . see W H Orrick JR

Rogers MR & MRS Edmund H JR (Joyce H Hendren)
San.Rr.Rv.Ll.Fw.Cw.Pa'44
☎ (805) 969-2093 . . 529 Las Fuentes Dv, Santa Barbara, CA *93108*

Rogers MR Edward S 2d—Va'54
☎ (719) 527-1724 . . 440D Autumn Ridge Circle, Colorado Springs,
CO *80906*

Rogers MR & MRS Frank H (Alice W Myers) Vt'80.Tow'79
☎ (610) 388-0430 . . 124 W Thomas Court, Kennett Square, PA *19348*

Rogers MR Frank L . . of
☎ (609) 662-8022 . . "Penn Oak" PO Box 771, Moorestown,
NJ *08057*
☎ (540) 837-1828 . . "Norwood Cottage" PO Box 70, Boyce,
VA *22620*

Rogers MR & MRS Glenn R (Jennifer O Johnston)
NMex'68.Clare'65.Stan'67 . . . . ☎ (510) 531-0287
MISS Catherine L . . . . 72 Inverleith Terr,
JUNIORS MR Christopher G . . . . Piedmont, CA *94611*

Rogers MR & MRS H Elliott JR (Gail M Underwood)
Pa'73.Pa'75.Rc.Pa'72.Pa'75
☎ (212) 734-6817 . . 325 E 72 St, New York, NY *10021*

Rogers MASTER Henry Weldon (M Weldon 4th) . . . . Born at
St Louis, MO Jly 20'95

Rogers MR & MRS Howland P (Chace—Zosia Znamiecka)
V'44.Rcn.T.Cly.H'44
☎ (561) 546-6257 . . 89 S Beach Rd, Hobe Sound, FL *33455*

Rogers MRS Hugh F (Arline B Dickson) . . . . ☎ (818) 753-4915
MISS Marilyn C . . . . 10805 Camarillo St,
North Hollywood,
CA *91602*

Rogers MR & MRS James G (Barbara M Baird)
Hood'75.Me.Ac.W&L'73.AmU'75 . . . . ☎ (610) 687-5152
JUNIORS MR Andrew B . . . . 308 Chamounix Rd,
JUNIORS MR Benjamin B . . . . St Davids, PA
19087

Rogers MR & MRS James H (Henrietta L Owens) CtCol'28.Yn.Y'31
☎ (203) 966-2433 . . 48 Rosebrook Rd, New Canaan, CT *06840*

Rogers MRS James Gamble 2d (Evelyn C Smith)
☎ (407) 645-2662 . . 1011 Temple Grove, Winter Park, FL *32789*

Rogers MR & MRS James H 3d (Margaret Frost)
Col'59.Br'56.H'65 . . . . ☎ (207) 326-8020
MISS Jessica H—Br'93—at 247 W 87 St,   "Dotten House"
Apt 10J, New York, NY *10024* . . . .   Perkins St,
PO Box 281,
Castine, ME *04421*

Rogers MRS James Webb (Anna P Clarke) Dar.Myf. ☎ (301) 773-6937
MR Joseph Shepperd . . . . "Beall's Pleasure"
PO Box 1268,
Landover, MD
20785

Rogers MR John A—Wms'51.Ox'53
☎ (505) 983-8000 . . "Mireposo" 211 Camino Del Norte, Santa Fe,
NM *87501-0789*

Rogers MR & MRS John C (Anne C Read)
Gchr'47.P'40 . . . . ☎ (413) 567-7233
MISS Amy R—P'76—Box 1200, Wiscasset, ME   788 Longmeadow
04578 . . . . St, Longmeadow,
MA *01106*

Rogers MR John G 3d (M Katherine Comegys)
☎ (410) 465-1522 . . 8700 Ridge Rd, Ellicott City, MD *21043-4104*

Rogers MR & MRS Lawrence H 2d (Suzanne H Long)
CtCol'46.B.Ny.Rr.Cly.P'43
☎ (513) 561-4212 . . 4600 Drake Rd, Cincinnati, OH *45243*

Rogers MRS Leslie Woods (Woods—Leslie J Pasch) LakeF'69 . . of
☎ (212) 860-9114 . . 1060 Park Av, New York, NY *10128*
☎ (970) 923-5124 . . "River Run" 118 Woods Rd, Box 176,
Woody Creek, CO *81656*

Rogers MR & MRS M Weldon 3d (Billman—
Penelope A Short) Mo'66.Cy.Str.Yn.Y'63 . . . . . ☎ (314) 997-0805
MISS Caroline B . . . . 13 Clermont Lane,
JUNIORS MISS Sarah L . . . . St Louis, MO *63124*

Rogers MR & MRS M Weldon 4th (Kathleen A Vild)
Duke'83.H'90.B.Rc.Bur.Cy.Duke'84.H'89
☎ (314) 993-6865 . . 5 McKnight Lane, St Louis, MO *63124*

Rogers DR & MRS Malcolm P (Susan E Atkins)   of ☎ (617)661-2095
Skd'66.H'88.Y'65.H'69 . . . . 7 Concord Av,
MISS Lauren A . . . . Cambridge, MA
MR Stuart A *02138*
☎ (603) 764-5246
"Studio Barn"
Warren, NH *03279*

Rogers MR & MRS N Pendleton (Laurie C Jarrett)
So'85.Duke'90.Fb.So'72.StJ'77.Nu'79
☎ (804) 285-8989 . . 7721 Hollins Rd, Richmond, VA *23229*

Rogers MRS Paul D (Frances L Clarkson) . . . . . . Married at St Louis, MO
Breckner MR Kenneth D . . . . Mch 23'96

Rogers MR & MRS Paul H (Frances McL Emmons) OWes'81.Conn'80
☎ (610) 688-1668 . . 1180 Radnor Hill Rd, Wayne, PA *19087*

Rogers MR Peter M—H'76
☎ (860) 379-3932 . . 153 Chapel Rd, Winchester Center, CT *06094*

Rogers MR & MRS Richard M (Joan R Gerdau) | ☎ (203) 426-0216
Sth'59.Hob'63 | ''Jubilee''
MR Gregory T—at Camphill Soltane, Nantmeal | 44 Taunton Lake
Rd, Box 300, Glenmoore, PA *19343* . . . . | Dv, Newtown, CT
MR Alec N M—at 3945 SE Cora St, Portland, OR | *06470*
97202 . . . . |

Rogers MR & MRS Robert G JR (Dora S Lewis) | ☎ (610) 525-7250
Pa'71.Ncd.SCal'67.Pa'69 . . . . | 221 N Ithan Av,
MISS Dorothy B . . . . | Rosemont, PA
JUNIORS MR Robert G 3d . . . . | *19010*

Rogers LT COL (RET) & MRS Robert V (Harle—Leslie A Stuart) USAF.
☎ (510) 945-7588 . . 16 Swan Court, Walnut Creek, CA *94596*

Rogers MISS Susan F
☎ (203) 324-0890 . . 410 West Av, Apt 107, Darien, CT *06820-3938*

Rogers MRS Suzanne W (Suzanne Wilson) . . . . | ☎ (954) 772-2405
MISS Stephanie L—Va'89—*see* | 5231 NE 33 Av,
Dilatory Domiciles . . . . | Ft Lauderdale, FL
MR Christopher C—Va'92—at | *33308*
☎ (804) 971-5530 . . 910A Cottage Lane, |
Charlottesville, VA *22903* . . . . |

Rogers MR & MRS Sydney H (Harriet L Gould) Ny.Ncd.Y'43
☎ (860) 536-6199 . . 30 Cove Rd, Stonington, CT *06378*

Rogers MR & MRS Theodore B 3d (Mary E Denney) Bvr'31
4 Carolina Meadows 106, Apple Tree Lane, Chapel Hill, NC *27514-8524*

Rogers MR & MRS Theodore O (Susan P Windle) Ws'60.Pa'63.Pa'37.Pa'40
☎ (610) 692-6048 . . ''Amarna'' 351 Sunset Hollow Rd, West Chester,
PA *19380-3841*

Rogers MR & MRS Theodore O JR (Hope T Scott) HRdc'76.K.Rv.H'76.H'79
☎ (212) 628-1977 . . 535 E 86 St, New York, NY *10028*

Rogers CAPT (RET) & MRS Thomas W (Kristina | ☎ (703) 448-7633
Cunningham) USN.Pa'69.Pa'68 . . . . | 1636 Wrightson Dv,
MISS Frances E . . . . | McLean, VA *22101*
MR Thomas A . . . . |

Rogers MISS Whitney H—Br'88
☎ (401) 846-3255 . . 45 Tilden Av, Newport, RI *02840*

Rogers MRS William F 3d (Angela S Dunham) Ncd.
☎ (203) 264-2918 . . 1025B Heritage Village, Box 412, Southbury,
CT *06488*

Rogerson MRS John E (Jean R Porter)
☎ (617) 698-6522 . . 114 Canton Av, Milton, MA *02186*

Rogerson MR & MRS Thomas C (Catherine M Munson)
OWes'79.Cy.Ub.Myf.Ncd.Ithaca'79 ⚓
☎ (617) 934-2029 . . PO Box 2201, Duxbury, MA *02332*

Rogerson MR William G—H.'66.Pa'69 ⚓
☎ (617) 227-9722 . . 103 Pinckney St, Boston, MA *02114*

Rohlfs MRS Otto D JR (Madeline Denison Jenkins) Gi.Myf.Ncd.Dar.
☎ (410) 366-8941 . . 3601 Greenway, Apt 606, Baltimore,
MD *21218-2439*

Rohner MR & MRS Henry John 3d (Lucy A Polese)
LakeF'86.Me.Ec.LakeF'86
☎ (508) 927-8032 . . 26 High St, Beverly Farms, MA *01915*

Rohrbach MISS (DR) Augusta (Johnson—Augusta Rohrbach)
NewSchSR'83.Cl'86
☎ (216) 774-7036 . . 20 N Pleasant, Oberlin, OH *44074*

Rohrbach MR Brison C—Mt.Ariz'86 . . see J G Grayson

Rohrbach MR & MRS Gammon E (Mary E Carmichael) V'81
☎ (540) 255-9460 . . 9927 Steeple Run Court, Vienna, VA *22181-3157*

Rohrer MR & MRS John B (Marilynne M Morshead) Ore'86
☎ (408) 253-5298 . . 11732 Trinity Springs Court, Cupertino, CA *95014*

Rolfe MISS Barbara H—Stan'48
☎ (415) 397-8456 . . 550 Battery St, Apt 610, San Francisco,
CA *94111-2320*

Rolfe MISS Leslie Welch (Robert O) . . . . Born Mch 23'95

Rolfe MR & MRS Robert O (Kathy G Welch) Ala'82.Ala'82.Van'88
☎ (615) 385-4346 . . 505 Park Center Dv, Nashville, TN *37205-3429*

Rolin MR & MRS Harry M (Churchman—Chapman—Agnes E Kendig)
Sa.Fw.Pa'29
☎ (610) 584-3871 . . Meadowood at Worcester, 15 Dogwood Knolls,
Lansdale, PA *19446*

Roll MR & MRS Walter G (Jane H Choremi) Wheat'79.StLaw'81
☎ (516) 922-7654 . . 350 Centre Island Rd, Oyster Bay, NY *11771*

Rollhaus MISS Natalie—Bow'90.Mid'91.Myf.
☎ (714) 376-2008 . . 557 Lombardy Lane, Laguna Beach, CA *92651*

Rollhaus MR & MRS Philip E JR (Childs—Barbara L Walker)
WestMich'71.Bhm.Rc.Cho.BtP.Myf.Wes'56 ⚓ . . of
☎ (312) 787-2875 . . 1500 N Lake Shore Dv, Apt 11A, Chicago,
IL *60610*
☎ (219) 787-8942 . . ''Dune Acres'' Chesterton, IN *46304*

Rollhaus MR Philip E 3d—Ty'92
☎ (617) 491-7599 . . 22 Prince St, Cambridge, MA *02139*

Rollins MRS Deborah F (Sanderson—Deborah J | ☎ (610) 688-1351
Fowler) . . . . | 431 Newtown Rd,
JUNIORS MISS Alexandra F . . . . | Berwyn, PA *19312*
JUNIORS MISS Emily R . . . . |

Rollins MR Joseph R III—Penn'69
☎ (610) 647-6979 . . 502 Weatherstone Dv, Paoli, PA *19312*

Rollins MR & MRS Richard 2d (M Shannon Oster) Rich'77.Me.
☎ (610) 688-1168 . . 204 Devon Blvd, Devon, PA *19333*

Rollins MRS Sherwood JR (Anne Alger)
☎ (603) 868-5444 . . Stone House Farm, 315 Durham Point Rd, Durham,
NH *03824*

Rollinson MR & MRS Simeon H 3d (Julia B | ☎ (201) 425-0821
Hefferan) Eh.Shcc.P'61 . . . . | Bailey's Mill Rd,
MR Christopher H . . . . | PO Box 371,
MR Augustin W . . . . | New Vernon, NJ
MR James H . . . . | *07976*
MR William H . . . . |

Rollman MRS Frances M (Frances N Merryman) Edg.
☎ (412) 741-7203 . . ''The Gatehouse'' Blackburn Rd, Sewickley,
PA *15143*

Rollow MR & MRS J Douglas JR (Miesse—Loblein—Bergen—
Marie D Lawrence) Eh.Hl.
☎ (561) 738-9594 . . 5900 Old Ocean Blvd, Apt 6B, Ocean Ridge,
FL *33435*

Roloson MRS Sarah F (Sarah H Freeman) On. . . . . . of ☎ (847)234-5558
MISS Helen T . . . . 280 Overlook Dv,
MISS Wendy C . . . . Lake Forest, IL
MISS Natalie R *60045*
MISS Cary B . . . . ''The Lake House''
MR Robert M 4th . . . . Leland, MI *49654*
MR Edward W . . . .

Rolph CAPT & MRS H Renton JR (Mary M MacRae) ☎ (415) 435-1695
USNR.Stan'70.Cal'76 . . . . 95 Reed Ranch Rd,
JUNIORS MR James R—at Marin Cath Prep . . . . . Tiburon, CA *94920*
JUNIORS MR John MacR—at Redwood Sch . . . . .
JUNIORS MR Ronald S—at St Ignatius . . . .

Rolph JUDGE & MRS Henry R (Barbara D Sherwood) ☎ (415) 921-2626
Stan'41.Bhm.Sfg.Stan'36.Stan'40. . . . . 2626 Lyon St,
MISS Barbara J—Stan'72—at ☎ (415) 381-0647 San Francisco, CA
256 Sycamore Av, Mill Valley, CA *94941* *94123*

Rom MR & MRS Paul R (Helen Gray) Nw'71 . . . . . . ☎ (630) 858-9503
JUNIORS MISS Holly G . . . . 957 Highland Av,
Glen Ellyn, IL
60137

Romaine MR & MRS Arthur C (Deborah Vaughan) Barat'73.H'59 . . of
☎ (212) 996-1751 . . 139 E 94 St, New York, NY *10128*
☎ (516) 537-1626 . . Bridgehampton, NY *11932*

Romaine MR David F—BaldW'68.Nw'70
☎ (804) 649-2216 . . 104 W Franklin St, Apt 405, Richmond, VA *23220*

Romaine MR & MRS Henry S (Susan Donaldson) Conn'72.Ln.Hn.H'54
☎ (803) 883-9472 . . 7 Conquest Av, Sullivans Island, SC *29482*

Romaine MR & MRS Theodore C JR (Elaine Scherer) ☎ (212) 860-0652
Cly.Va'54. . . . . 1230 Park Av,
MISS Pamela T—Va'88 . . . . New York, NY
MISS Ashley C—Br'91 . . . . *10128*

Roman MR Mafeo—StM'50 . . . . of ☎ (415)342-3672
MISS Marisa de S . . . . 416 Roehampton
MR Marco de S . . . . Rd, Hillsborough,
CA *94010*
☎ (415) 343-1782
PO Box 117217,
Burlingame, CA
94011

Roman MR & MRS Stephen H (Isabelle T Morris) Ariz'79.Ariz'82.Ky'75
☎ (602) 264-1609 . . 3022 N Manor Dv E, Phoenix, AZ *85014*

Romano MR & MRS Mark S (C Leigh Upson) StLaw'83.Va'82.Cwr'90
☎ (412) 221-2760 . . 1798 Tyris Dv, Upper St Clair, PA *15241*

Romanoff MRS S Cook (Stephena V Cook) Sth'60.On.
☎ (847) 295-3353 . . 207 E North Av, Lake Bluff, IL *60044*

Romeiser MASTER Kohl William (g—Edward Sears Read JR) . . . . Born at
Boston, MA May 2'95

Romeiser MASTER Trevor Read (g—Edward Sears Read JR) . . . . . Born at
Boston, MA May 2'95

Romine MR & MRS David E (Kathryn A Kopple)
B'gton'84.Nu'94.Hn.Cl'86.H'93
☎ (610) 617-7980 . . 300 N Essex Av, Apt 210B, Narberth, PA *19072*

Romine MR & MRS John R JR (Laura Estabrook) BMr'39.WVa'44
☎ (610) 688-5419 . . 990 Ivycroft Rd, Wayne, PA *19087-2014*

Romine MR John R 3d (John R JR) . . . . Died at
Los Angeles, CA Feb 28'96

Romley MR Frederick J JR—H'57.Y'64.Y'65 . . of
☎ (504) 586-1011 . . 502B St Peter St, New Orleans, LA *70116*
☎ (508) 394-8894 . . 100 Centre St, RR 1, South Dennis, MA *02660*

Ronaldson MR Walker Y JR—W&L'63.Tul'65.Tul'68
☎ (504) 891-8211 . . 1119 Delachaise St, New Orleans, LA *70115*

Ronan MR & MRS William J (Elena V de Poblet y ☎ (561) 833-5396
Vinadé) K.Ck.Evg.Csn.Syr'34.H'35.Nu'40 . . . . 525 S Flagler Dv,
MRS Monica V (Montoya—Nourie—Monica V TH-2F,
Ronan) MaryMt'85.Nu'87 . . . . West Palm Beach,
FL *33401*

Rood MRS Armistead B (Margaret Suter) B'gton'36.Hb.Hn.
☎ (202) EM3-7275 . . 3520—35 St NW, Washington, DC *20016*

Rooke MR & MRS Christopher D (Cynthia M Azoy)
PO Box 39, Village Rd, New Vernon, NJ *07976*

Roome MISS Barbara S (González—Barbara S Roome) Tul'82
PO Box 4882, Greenwich, CT *06830*

Roome MR & MRS Howard Le C (Ann S Fox) . . of
☎ (847) 272-3338 . . 9 Court of Hidden Bay, Northbrook, IL *60062*
☎ (813) 461-0376 . . 6 Belleview Blvd, Belleair, FL *34616-1965*

Roome REV & MRS Howard R (Lisa J Ratko) Nw'80.Ken'75.VaTheo'82
☎ (847) 253-2511 . . 205 N Wille St, Mt Prospect, IL *60056*

Roome MR & MRS Peter W (Hartranft—Stitzer—Phyllis D Jones)
Sm.Yn.Y'49
63 N Beach Rd, Hobe Sound, FL *33455*

Roome DR & MRS Peter W JR (Serrell—Marie M Mulhall)
ColbyS'73.Conn'75.Smu'79.SwTex'85
☎ (609) 924-7725 . . 50 Scott Lane, Princeton, NJ *08540*

Roome MR & MRS Reginald JR (Healey—Joan Edmondson)
Man'vl'54.FairF'88.Yn.Y'43
☎ (941) 923-7728 . . 1707 Starling Dv, Sarasota, FL *34231*

Roop MR Guy Russell . . . . Died at
Santa Barbara, CA in Jly 1995

Roosevelt MISS (DR) Anna C—Stan'68.Cl'77
☎ (847) 869-0422 . . 1028 Judson Av, Evanston, IL *60202*

Roosevelt MR & MRS Christopher du P (Rosalind ☎ (914) 234-3729
Havemeyer) Bgt.Fic.Fiy.Cly.Va'64.Geo'68 . . . . 14 Middle Patent
MISS Kate—at 1011—32 Av E, Seattle, WA Rd, Armonk, NY
98112 . . . . *10504*
MISS Emily—at 34 Fessenden St, Portland, ME
04103 . . . .
MR Christopher H . . . .

Roosevelt MISS Elizabeth E—DU'62.S.Cly.
☎ (516) WA2-6243 . . ''The Bilge'' Cove Neck Rd, Oyster Bay,
NY *11771*

Roosevelt MRS Franklin D JR (Weicker—Linda McK Stevenson) Cly.
☎ (212) 759-2827 . . 200 E 66 St, New York, NY *10021*

Roosevelt MRS H Latrobe (Vera F Story)
☎ (610) 793-1131 . . Round Hill Farm, Pocopson, PA *19366*

Roosevelt MR & MRS Henry L (Janice E Clark) Minn'74.Pitt'68
☎ (610) 793-2770 . . 2585 Brinton's Bridge Rd, Pocopson, PA *19366*

Roosevelt MR & MRS James A 2d (Mary S Duvall) Col'81.Col'81
☎ (303) 442-0421 . . 730 Pine St, Boulder, CO *80302*

Roosevelt MRS John E (Helen C Sparrow) S.Cly....
MISS Cordelia—Hn.—at ☎ (213) 969-9778
1301 N Spaulding Av, Los Angeles, CA *90046* .
MR Robert E—at ☎ (212) 861-8159
160 E 85 St, New York, NY *10028* ....
MR Andrew E—Cl'88—☎ (212) 752-9782 ....
| ☎ (212) PL2-6613
235 E 61 St,
New York, NY
10021

Roosevelt MRS Julian K (Scholle—Margaret F Schantz) S.Ny.Rby.Cda.
☎ (516) 674-4565 . . "Bonnie Brae" 38 Horse Hollow Court,
Locust Valley, NY *11560*

Roosevelt MISS (REV CANON) Nancy A (Taylor—
Cecil—Nancy A Roosevelt) Hlns'69.
Gen'lTheo'85 . . . .
  MISS Jennifer H Taylor . . . .
  MISS Constance M Taylor . . . .
| ☎ (716) 377-7701
11 Cambridge Court,
Fairport, NY *14450*

Roosevelt MR & MRS Nicholas S (Winsor—Karin E Perman). Me.
☎ (717) 529-2596 . . Tweed Run Farm, 3802 Bethel Rd, Oxford,
PA *19363*

Roosevelt MR & MRS P James (Philippa D Buss)
S.Ny.Hl.H'50 . . . .
  MISS P Jean . . . .
  MR Michael J . . . .
| ☎ (516) 922-6499
1 Cove Neck Rd,
Oyster Bay, NY
11771

Roosevelt MR & MRS Peter K (Marjorie Snyder)
Col'56.Nyc.S.Hl.Col'56 . . . .
  MISS Christine—Box 632, Old Lyme, CT *06371*
  MISS Margaret—at U of Colo . . . .
| ☎ (303) 789-3900
39 Sunset Dv,
Englewood, CO
80110

Roosevelt MR Robin A . . . .
  MISS Susan L Ridder . . . .
| ☎ (212) 867-2446
25 E 40 St, Apt 32F,
New York, NY
10016

Roosevelt MR & MRS Theodore 3d (Anne M Babcock) Ph.Hp.H'36
☎ (207) 244-5222 . . "Whalesback" PO Box 265, Mt Desert, ME *04660*

Roosevelt MR & MRS Theodore 4th (Constance L
Rogers) V'66.Ln.Hl.Hl.'65 . . . .
  MR Theodore 5th—at Princeton . . . .
| ☎ (718) 237-9172
1 Pierrepont St,
Brooklyn, NY *11201*

Roosevelt MR & MRS Thomas D (Frances G Humphreys)
Va'77.Y'81.Ncd.Conn'78.Penn'82
☎ (610) 869-2537 . . 1115 N Chatham Rd, Coatesville, PA *19320*

Roosevelt MR & MRS Tweed (Candace C MacGuigan)
Bnd'70.Cr'74.Nu'79.Cl'82.K.Sm.Cy.Snc.Hl.Cda.H.'64. Cl'77
☎ (617) 367-0161 . . 1 Acorn St, Boston, MA *02108*

Roosevelt MR W Emlen—S.Chr.Unn.Bg.Hl.Pn.
☎ (908) 435-6972 . . 68 Broad St, Elizabeth, NJ *07207*

Root MR & MRS Anthony (Pamela J Peglau) BMr'76.Nu'80.Hav'75.Nu'82
☎ (011-852) 2849-8233 . . Mt Austin Estates H-D, 5 Mt Austin Rd,
The Peak, Hong Kong

Root MR & MRS Henry W (Marilyn B Seabury) Scripps'76.Pc.DU'75.DU'82
☎ (310) 454-0416 . . 16970 Avenida de Santa Ynez, Pacific Palisades,
CA *90272*

Root MRS Oren (Daphne D Skouras) Man'vl'44.Bgt.Cs.
☎ (914) 234-7081 . . PO Box 565, Bedford, NY *10506*

Root MR & MRS Oren JR (Barbara A Schruth)
Man'vl'69.Cl'69 . . . .
  MISS Micaela K . . . .
| ☎ (212) 662-0415
43 W 93 St,
New York, NY
10025

Root MR & MRS Stanley W JR (Joan L Schimpf)
Skd'47.Sg.Pc.Fw.Ll.Ac.Sdg.P.'47.Pa'50 . . of
☎ (215) 646-3676 . . 16 Hounds Run Lane, Blue Bell, PA *19422*
☎ (941) 262-8932 . . Admiralty Point II, Apt 103,
2400 Gulf Shore Blvd N, Naples, FL *34102*

Rooth MR & MRS Robert S (Ann C Rogers) P'71 . . .
JUNIORS MISS Carroll L . . . .
| of ☎ (504)899-6936
1221 Soniat St,
New Orleans, LA
70115
☎ (809) 458-3277
"Longpoint"
Moonhole, Bequia,
St Vincent &
Grenadines

Roper MRS William Winston JR (S Katharine Blue) Pp.
see Dilatory Domiciles

Rorbach MRS E Monteath (Elizabeth Monteath
Hubbell) Ariz'79 . . . .
JUNIORS MISS Erin G . . . .
| ☎ (602) 951-8554
9000 N 60 St,
Paradise Valley, AZ
85253

Rorem DR & MRS David A (Sarah G Burkham) Wash'70.Ant'63
☎ (210) 490-5814 . . 211 Bluff Hollow, San Antonio, TX *78216*

Rorer MR & MRS Edward C (Sarah H Bradbury)
Wheat'68.Err.Eyc.Pc.Me.Sg.Rc.Ty'65.Pa'70 . . .
  MISS Amélie Marshall . . . .
| ☎ (610) 520-1215
1109 Brynllawn Rd,
Villanova, PA *19085*

Rorer MR & MRS Gerald B (Elizabeth A Keator)
Me.Cry.M.Rv.Cspa.W.P.'64.H'66 ⚓ . . . .
  MISS Carrie A . . . .
  MR Jonathan B . . . .
  JUNIORS MISS Elizabeth C . . . .
  JUNIORS MR Christopher K . . . .
| ☎ (610) 688-4626
761 Newtown Rd,
Villanova, PA
19085-1027

Rorer MRS Gerald F (M Amélie Runk) V'32.M.Me.Cts.Ac.Ncd.
Beaumont, Bryn Mawr, PA *19010*

Rorer MR & MRS Herbert T (Linda M Hibbins)
M.Me.Ac.Nath'lH'70 . . . .
  MISS Heather A—at Yale . . . .
  JUNIORS MR Edward T . . . .
| ☎ (610) 642-9971
655 Dodds Lane,
Gladwyne, PA
19035

Rorer MISS Sarah Brooke (Edward C) . . . . . . Married at Edgartown, MA
Brown MR Eric C (Christopher C) . . . . Jun 22'96

Rorick MR & MRS Richard P (Herrlinger—Marcia
Van E Pearsall) Mvh.BtP.Mich'50 . . . .
  MISS Gretchen A—at ☎ (212) 769-1482
100 W 92 St, New York, NY *10025* . . . .
| ☎ (561) 655-1741
218 Seaspray Av,
Palm Beach, FL
33480

Rorimer MRS James J (Katherine N Serrell) Ws'29.Cs.Ncd . . .of
☎ (216) 543-4419 . . "Bigsbluff" 18173 Geauga Lake Rd, Chagrin Falls,
OH *44023*
☎ (212) 288-7873 . . 1000 Park Av, New York, NY *10028*

Rorimer MR & MRS Louis (Helen Savery Fitz-Gerald)
Stph'65.CleveArt'70.Cwr'75.H'69.Cwr'75
☎ (216) 295-1105 . . 17900 S Park Blvd, Shaker Heights,
OH *44120-1717*

Rork MR & MRS Allen Wright (Marilyn Greene) Sth'67.Nu'71.Ford'95.Wms'66.H'68 . . . . | of ☎ (203)259-5322 410 Galloping Hill Rd, Fairfield, CT *06430*
MISS Jennifer—Wms'95—at 181 North St, Williamstown, MA *01267* . . . .
MISS Tamara—at Lafayette . . . . | ☎ (802) 464-8910 "Greenspring" Rte 100, West Dover, VT *05356*

Rosborough MR Robert S—Y'82.Stan'85
☎ (415) 673-5081 . . 44 Macondray Lane, Apt 4W, San Francisco, CA *94133-2602*

Rose MR & MRS Andrew B (Sarah E Walsh) Wheat'85.Nu'91.Fic.Fiy.Ny.Colg'86
☎ (212) 628-9318 . . 1 Gracie Terr, New York, NY *10028*

Rose MR & MRS Andrew C (Ann S Copeland) Pa'90.B.Srr.Gr.Mds.Cly.Pn.P'82
☎ (302) 421-5719 . . PO Box 4357, Greenville, DE *19807*

Rose MR & MRS Benjamin H 3d (Roberta A Simkins) Juniata'60 . . . . | ☎ (415) 387-9785 2515—15 St, San Francisco, CA *94114*
MR Benjamin H 4th—at U of San Fran . . . .

Rose MR & MRS Bernd P (Ann C Heumann) P'46
☎ (970) 245-9018 . . 479 Tiara Vista Dv, Grand Junction, CO *81503*

Rose MRS C Bowie (Kathryn M Wells) Md'37.MdArt'66.Md'70.Ayc.
☎ (410) 641-3135 . . Gull Creek Estates, 12 Meadow St, Berlin, MD *21811*

Rose MR & MRS C Bowie (Mary J Scally) Ayc.Sar.Rv. ⚓ . . . . | ☎ (410) 974-4182 "Whitehall Manor" 600 Canal Lane, Annapolis, MD *21401*
MISS Margaret C—Del'95 . . . .
MISS Elizabeth A . . . .

Rose MR & MRS George H (Wregg—Daphne Persse-Sealy) Pr.Cly.H'54
☎ (516) 676-0825 . . 111 Walnut Rd, Glen Cove, NY *11542* . . MR absent

Rose MR & MRS J Harden (Georgia S Rockefeller) V'55.Mds.Cly.Dar.P.'51.Cl'56
☎ (212) RH4-5940 . . 155 E 70 St, New York, NY *10021-5109*

Rose MR & MRS James McK JR (Anne L Bourne) Sth'57.Cvc.Bm.Coa.Cw.Snc.Pn.P'51.H'54 . . . . . | ☎ (202) 362-1324 4913 Rodman St NW, Washington, DC *20016*
MISS Anne C—Bow'86—at ☎ (207) 729-6219 5 High St, Brunswick, ME *04011* . . . .
MISS Louise B—Mid'89 . . . .

Rose MR & MRS Jonathan Chapman (Susan Porter) Earl'63.Mt.Cvc.Uncl.Tvcl.Y'63.H'67 . . . . | ☎ (703) 683-2931 501 Slaters Lane, 1001, Alexandria, VA *22314*
JUNIORS MR Benjamin C . . . .

Rose MR Middleton JR—Cw.Y'51
☎ (802) 672-5537 . . PO Box 119, Bridgewater Corners, VT *05035*

Rose MR & MRS Milton C (Emily W Mason) Lx.C.G.Csn.Wms'27.H'30
☎ (413) 528-1096 . . PO Box 427, Great Barrington, MA *01230*

Rose MR & MRS Peter B (Jocelyn C White) Algon'80
☎ (203) 938-2538 . . 15 Indian Hill Rd, West Redding, CT *06896*

Rose MR & MRS Peter H (Alexandra Pietrasanta) Ty'58.Ham'57.Pa'58 . . . . | ☎ (212) 759-8173 200 E 58 St, Apt 20C, New York, NY *10022*
MISS Catherine B . . . .
MISS Mary H . . . .

Rose MR & MRS R Peter (Duval—Jeanne H Chick) Elms'64.Pr.H'51 . . . . | ☎ (520) 749-8773 13540 E Camino La Cebadilla, Tucson, AZ *85749*
MR Bradford B Duval—L&C'95—at ☎ (619) 459-1013 . . 7341 Eads Av, La Jolla, CA *92037* . . . .

Rose MASTER Robert Carter (Andrew B) . . . . Born at New York, NY Mch 21'96

Rose MR & MRS Walter B (Kate R Luppen) Cal'66.Y'71
☎ (818) 441-6796 . . 1877 McFarlane St, San Marino, CA *91108*

Rose MR & MRS William Duncan (Juliette C Loizeaux) Syr'76.StA.Ind'75
☎ (908) 439-3594 . . 61 Saw Mill Rd, Lebanon, NJ *08833*

Rose MR & MRS William I JR (Alexandrine G Rust) Sth'66.Dth'66 . . . . | ☎ (906) 482-6613 6 Woodland Rd, Houghton, MI *49931*
MR Christopher McK . . . .
MR Jason G . . . .

Rosebrook MRS John B (Stevenson—Partridge—Virginia J Doering) Sl.
☎ (804) 295-0206 . . 29 Ednam Village, Charlottesville, VA *22903*

Rosekrans MISS Cordelia . . see F G Chambers

Rosekrans MR & MRS John N JR (Topham—Georgette Naify) Bur.Stan'50
☎ (415) 921-6115 . . 2840 Broadway St, San Francisco, CA *94115*

Rosen MRS M Patiño Treat (Treat—Marita C Patiño) Pa'61.VillaN'79
☎ (215) 473-1124 . . 5937 Overbrook Av, Philadelphia, PA *19131*

Rosenberg MISS Amelia Reeves (Martin E) . . . . Born at San Francisco, CA Jun 28'96

Rosenberg MR & MRS Martin E (Ann E Politzer) Cal'77.Cal'76
☎ (415) 775-4127 . . 3825 Scott St, Apt 202, San Francisco, CA *94123*

Rosenberry MRS Samuel L (Cicely L Kershaw) Sth'30.Cs.
☎ (212) 879-2289 . . 116 E 66 St, New York, NY *10021*

Rosenblad MISS A Mikaela—Rad'90.RingArt'93
☎ (404) 266-9051 . . 114 Peachtree Hills Circle NE, Atlanta, GA *30305*

Rosenblad MR & MRS Eberhard M (Sandra J Sayen) UAmericas'67
☎ (941) 349-4179 . . 5207 Cape Leyte Dv, Sarasota, FL *34242*

Rosenblad MISS Nicole L—RingArt'92
☎ (404) 266-9051 . . 114 Peachtree Hills Circle NE, Atlanta, GA *30305*

Rosenblum MR & MRS John W (Carolyn E Jones) Br'65.Br'65
Eaglehurst Farm, Rte 3, Box 530, Crozet, VA *22932*

Rosenfeld MR & MRS Michael A (Bettina I Wulfing) Wash'83.Wes'83
☎ (213) 467-2372 . . 920 N Wilcox Av, Los Angeles, CA *90038*

Rosengarten MRS Adolph G JR (Denison—Virginia F Smith) Gm.Me.
☎ (610) 688-0191 . . "Minder House" PO Box 347, Wayne, PA *19087*

Rosengarten MR & MRS Frederic JR (Miriam B Osterhout) Ph.BtP.P'38 . . of
☎ (561) 655-8090 . . 247 Jungle Rd, Palm Beach, FL *33480*
88 Battle Rd, Princeton, NJ *08540*

Rosengarten MR & MRS Peter K (Christine M Muckle) Me.P'58.Pa'70 . . . . | ☎ (802) 824-8190 Mountain Pond Farm, Box 37, 74 Obed Moore Rd, Weston, VT *05161*
MR Mitchell J . . . .

Rosengarten MRS T Jeffries (Chalker—Carolyn English) Gm.Me.
☎ (610) 525-8154 . . 1245 Lafayette Rd, Gladwyne, PA *19035*

Ross MRS Abby D (Abby A L Doolittle) Rr.
☎ (412) 238-2937 . . Box 53, Star Rte E, Ligonier, PA *15658*

Ross MRS Andrea C (Andrea G Courchene)
Shcc.Eyc.Mo.Eh. . . . . | ☎ (201) 543-2551
MISS Allyson H . . . . | 14 Corey Lane,
JUNIORS MISS Dana T . . . . | Mendham, NJ *07945*

Ross MRS Anthony O (Rosalie K Sullivan) MtH'65 . | ☎ (202) 965-7437
MISS Christina D . . . . | 730—24 St NW,
MISS Vanessa M . . . . | Washington, DC
| *20037*

Ross MRS B Lloyd (B Lloyd Boland)
☎ (301) 854-6984 . . 2700 Duvall Rd, Daisy, MD *21797*

Ross MR Dennis B—Snc. . . . . | ☎ (203) 966-8252
MR Dennis B JR—at 123D Heritage Hill Rd, | 75 Thayer Dv,
New Canaan, CT *06840* . . . . | New Canaan, CT
| *06840*

Ross MR & MRS Donald F (Elizabeth H Boardman)
Stan'42.Bhm.Fr.Cal'41.Stan'47 . . of
☎ (415) 854-4031 . . 125 Alta Vista Dv, Atherton, CA *94027*
☎ (916) 583-4705 . . 2065 Big John Rd, Bear Creek, Alpine Meadows,
Tahoe City, CA *96145*

Ross DR & MRS Donald F JR (Jeanne F Martin) | ☎ (617) 244-3592
Woos'69.Wms'65.Tufts'66.Tufts'67.Tufts'74 . . | 211 Winslow Rd,
JUNIORS MISS Elizabeth S . . . . | Waban, MA *02168*
JUNIORS MISS Anne N . . . . |

Ross MR & MRS Donald O (Susan S West) | of 530
Rcn.B.Srb.Nrr.NCar'70.Pa'72 . . . . | Clapboardtree St,
JUNIORS MISS Fraser S—at St George's . . . . | Westwood, MA
JUNIORS MR James W O—at Hamilton . . . . | *02090*
| ☎ (401) 847-4671
| Gravel Court,
| Clay St, Newport,
| RI *02840*

Ross MR Donald P JR—Y'54 . . . . | ☎ (610) 268-3469
MISS Susanna L Dent . . . . | PO Box 155,
| Chatham, PA *19318*

Ross MR E Burke JR—Rcn.Shcc.Eyc.Mo.Eh.Pn.P'73.Ch'82
☎ (908) 766-0083 . . 85 Crest Dv, Bernardsville, NJ *07924*

Ross MR & MRS Edmund B (Margaret R Haskell) | ☎ (908) 766-0588
Rcn.Err.Eyc.Shcc.Eh.Mo.Cda.Pn.P'41 . . . . | 135 N Maple Av,
MR Benson T—Eh.Shcc.Eyc.Bost'84—at | Basking Ridge, NJ
☎ (201) 538-9550 . . PO Box 581, Featherbed | *07920*
Lane, New Vernon, NJ *07976* . . . . |

Ross MR Edward Humes—U'60
☎ (802) 244-6148 . . PO Box 114, Waterbury Center, VT *05677*

Ross MISS Elizabeth—Nw'69.Ncd.
☎ (805) 684-7975 . . 4800 Sawyer Av, Carpinteria, CA *93013*

Ross MISS Elizabeth F . . see R E Moss

Ross MR & MRS George S (M Anne Bryant) Sth'55.Bg.Hn.H'56
☎ (908) 273-0490 . . 69 Hobart Av, Summit, NJ *07901*

Ross MR & MRS George S 3d (Cinthia C Deatly) StLaw'84.Bg.StLaw'81
☎ (201) 701-0109 . . 108 Fairmount Av, Chatham, NJ *07928*

Ross MR H Lawrence 3d (Henry L JR) . . . . Married at Fishers Island, NY
Albrittain MRS James S (Andrea C Robinson) . . . . Jly 27'96

Ross MR & MRS H Lawrence 3d (Albrittain—Andrea C Robinson)
Pa'79.Pa'81.Rcn.Fic.Y'79
☎ (203) 259-4509 . . 405 Sasco Hill Rd, Fairfield, CT *06430*

Ross MRS Henry A (Alice T FitzPatrick) . . . . Died Oct 15'95

Ross MR & MRS John G (Patricia A Edgar) P'58
☎ (908) 766-0593 . . 66 Childsworth Av, Bernardsville, NJ *07924*
Jan 1 . . ☎ (305) 367-2281 . . Ocean Reef Club, 39 Moorings, A,
Key Largo, FL *33037*

Ross MR Laurence Seton—Y.Cl'71 . . of
☎ (212) 688-3982 . . 400 E 57 St, Apt 12G, New York, NY *10022-3020*
☎ (203) 329-1919 . . ''Chez Reynard'' 690 Riverbank Rd, Stamford,
CT *06903*

Ross MRS Leroy W (Anne Eisenmayer)
☎ (305) 661-9764 . . 1150 Madruga Av, Coral Gables, FL *33146*

Ross MR & MRS Lewis C (Cecilia S Lanahan) Syr'77.H'74
☎ (610) 268-3423 . . RR 2, Box 322A, Indian Run Rd, Avondale,
PA *19311*

Ross MR & MRS Llewellyn G (Katharine C Leyman) | ☎ (609) 924-6577
Col'70.P'58 | 167 Edgerstoune Rd,
MISS Jennifer B—at 7 E 86 St, New York, NY | Princeton, NJ *08540*
10028 . . . . |

Ross MRS Mary Anna (Mary Anna Wiley) Ursinus'43
☎ (215) 242-6576 . . Hill Tower Apt 18C, 7600 Stenton Av,
Philadelphia, PA *19118*

Ross MR Matthew K . . see R E Moss

Ross MR & MRS Paul C (Kathryn H Karol) Ober'53
☎ (212) 427-4567 . . 1160 Park Av, New York, NY *10128*

Ross MR & MRS Paul H (Patricia S Allen)
Wheat'67.Cl'68.Cs.Ne.Pa'68.Nw'69
☎ (212) 427-9595 . . 1125 Park Av, Apt 11C, New York, NY *10128*

Ross MRS Robert S (Janet Burk) . . of
☎ (215) 546-0214 . . 1830 Rittenhouse Square, Philadelphia, PA *19103*
☎ (508) 994-0641 . . ''The Farm House'' Nonquitt, South Dartmouth,
MA *02748*

Ross MR & MRS Robert S JR (Louise R Potter) | ☎ (202) 362-2306
Bnd'77.Mt.Rcp.P'66 . . . . | 4434 Westover
MISS Jennifer P—at ☎ (203) 483-5141 | Place NW,
275 Northford Rd, Branford, CT *06405* . . . . | Washington, DC
MR Robert S 3d—at NYU . . . . | *20016*

Ross MRS Robyn (Beauchamp—Robyn Place | ☎ (215) 233-9190
Kenney) PAFA'69.Pc. | 7921 Eastern Av,
MISS Waverley C B—Drex'94—at Madras, India | Wyndmoor, PA
MR Blaik P—at U of Pa . . . . | *19038*

Ross MR & MRS Samuel S (Ann F Nelligan) Bost'84.P'84
☎ (301) 230-2241 . . 5605 Dowgate Court, Apt T3, Rockville,
MD *20851*

Ross MR & MRS Stuart C (Wendy W Flickinger) Bab'77.Bgt.Srb.Y.'74.Y'77
☎ (914) 232-7450 . . Katonah's Wood Rd, Katonah, NY *10536*

Ross MR & MRS Thomas E (Suzanne F Hancock) | ☎ (610) 647-8354
Gm.Ph.P'70.VillaN'74 . . . . | 551 Conestoga Rd,
MISS Nina W . . . . | Berwyn, PA *19312*
JUNIORS MR T Eliot JR . . . . |

Ross MR & MRS Thomas H (Susan Read Wickham)
Dick'77.Sa.Ds.Pa'75.Pa'79
☎ (610) 695-9927 . . 153 Woodgate Lane, Paoli, PA *19301-1447*

Ross MR & MRS W Ogden (Ogburn—Anne P Wotherspoon)
V'44.Nrr.Srb.Cw.Ncd.Y'43
☎ (401) 846-5706 . . ''Beechbound'' Brenton Cove, Newport, RI *02840*

Ross MR Walter L—Y'45
PO Box 454, Laughlintown, PA *15655*

Ross MRS Walter L 2d (Sarane B Hickox) Pr.StJ.
☎ (516) 626-1854 . . 81 Linden Lane, Glen Head, NY *11545*
Ross MR & MRS Walter L 3d (Pamela J Cooper) DU'80
☎ (561) 588-6161 . . 6 Indigo Terr, Lake Worth, FL *33460*
Ross MR & MRS Wilson Sharpless (Catharine E Shober) Y'50
☎ (412) 741-9122 . . 114 Centennial Av, Sewickley, PA *15143*
Rossbach MRS Richard M (Susan M Goodman) V'41.Cly.
☎ (212) RE4-4677 . . 830 Park Av, New York, NY *10021*
Rossi DR & MRS Joseph G (Cornelia L Cogswell)
Skd'54.Nf.Csn.Yn.Ty'43.Geo'50
☎ (203) 787-2796 . . 594 Prospect St, Apt B1, New Haven, CT *06511*
Rossiter MR & MRS (DR) A Wickes (Leila M Schueler) GaMed'86.Cl'70
☎ (617) 237-6406 . . 17 Cypress Rd, Wellesley, MA *02181*
Rossiter MR Arthur W (M Frances Allen)
☎ (617) 329-9670 . . Fox Hill Village 165, 10 Longwood Dv, Westwood, MA *02090*

Rossmassler MR & MRS Peter R (Frances B Scott) Ncd.Pn.P'54 . . . . | ☎ (609) 466-3211 Windy Top Farm, 149 Mountain View Rd, Princeton, NJ *08540*
MR William R III—Vt'87 . . . .
MR Thomas B S—Wis'95 . . . .
MR Richard R—HWSth'95 . . . .

Rotch MR & MRS A Lawrence (Emily B Roe) Rdc'64.H'61 ⚓
☎ (207) 845-2250 . . RFD 1, Box 2275, Liberty, ME *04949*
Rotch MR Edward C—Bost'67
☎ (207) 845-2536 . . PO Box 255, Washington, ME *04574*
Rotch MR & MRS William (Jane C Whitehill) Rdc'53.Sm.Hn.H'51 ⚓
☎ (804) 293-7034 . . 808 Fendall Terr, Charlottesville, VA *22903*

Roth MR & MRS William V JR (Jane K Richards) Sth'56.H'65.Wil.Ore'45.H'49 . . . . | ☎ (302) 658-7654 2206 Old Kennett Rd, Wilmington, DE *19807*
MISS Katharine K—at Harvard . . . .
MR William V 3d—at U of Mont Law . . . .

Rothe MR & MRS Ernst (Nancy Louise Eberhart) Bm.Srb.Cly.Cw.Rv.Sar.StA.Ofp.Myf.Ne.Br'63 . | of ☎ (212)348-1557 1158 Fifth Av, New York, NY *10029*
MR Ernst JR—Tufts'93—at ☎ (011-45) 3315-5933 . . Fredericiagade 50, 3TH, 1310 Copenhagen, Denmark . . . .
JUNIORS MR Alden Augustus—at Hotchkiss . . . . | ☎ (401) 849-6281 "Posapaug" 80 John St, Newport, RI *02840*

Rother MR & MRS W Klaus H (Christine Yandell) NYSID'72.Nu'67 . . . . | ☎ (215) 925-8449 715 Bradford Alley, Philadelphia, PA *19147-1326*
JUNIORS MR Sloan C Y . . . .

Rothermel MR & MRS Peter F (Beatrice D Alexander) Ncd.P'42
☎ (803) 838-2155 . . 127 Otter Lane, Fripp Island, SC *29920*
Rothstein MRS Harriet (Harriet Elsom) . . see MRS K A Elsom
Rothwell MRS William H 2d (Kelley—Mann—Nancy Porter) Ncd.Dar.Dcw.H.
☎ (617) 631-1515 . . "Oceanspray" Ft Glover, 77 Bubier Rd, Marblehead, MA *01945-3630*

Roudebush MR & MRS George M 3d (Nancy A Ball) Cwr'54.Denis'49.Cr'51 . . . . | ☎ (216) 286-4121 11706 Sycamore Rd, PO Box 777, Chardon, OH *44024-0777*
MISS Kristin F—at Chardon Rd, PO Box 140, Chardon, OH *44024* . . . .

Roudebush MR & MRS George Shotwell (Dorothy J Coleman) Nd.P'31.H'34 . . . . | ☎ (314) 432-5269 2127 N Ballas Rd, St Louis, MO *63131*
MR George S JR—*abroad* . . . .

Roulette REV & MRS Philip Burwell (Clover D Purvis) Md.Gv.Ds.Cw.W&L'64.VaTheo'67 . . . . | ☎ (410) 833-3284 St John's Rectory, 3738 Butler Rd, Glyndon, MD *21071*
MR Carter B—Gv.Ds. . . . .
MR Randolph B D—Gv.Ds. . . . .

Roulston MR & MRS Thomas H (Lois E Mueller) Sth'54.Unn.Pk.Cy.It.Dth'55 . . of
☎ (216) 932-5427 . . 2627 Fairmount Blvd, Cleveland, OH *44106*
☎ (970) 926-3233 . . "Arrowhead at Vail" 97 Hillside Court, Edwards, CO *81632*
Rounds MR Stowell . . . . Died at Ukiah, CA Jun 12'96
Rounds MRS Stowell (Caroline C Curtis) Cl'29.Cc.
☎ (707) 463-2939 . . 1380 Sanford Ranch Rd, Ukiah, CA *95482*
Rouner DR & MRS Leroy S (Rita Rainsford) Sth'48.Hb.H'53
☎ (603) 284-6635 . . High Meadow Farm, Center Sandwich, NH *03227*
Rouse DR & MRS Ernest T (Eleanor Scott) Aub'39.Cy.Aub'39.Wash'43 . . of
☎ (561) 231-5003 . . 2636 Ocean Dv, Apt 201, Vero Beach, FL *32963*
☎ (314) 725-5978 . . 710 S Hanley Rd, Apt 5C, St Louis, MO *63105*

Rousmaniere MR & MRS James A (Jessie B Pierce) Hn.H'40 . . . . | ☎ (203) 262-6345 624C Heritage Village, Southbury, CT *06488*
MISS Kate B—at ☎ (513) 523-5101 107 Ardmore, Oxford, OH *45056* . . . .

Rousseau MRS Henry H (Mary Bullard) Cly.
☎ (203) 259-1492 . . "The Cottage" 449 Mill Plain Rd, Fairfield, CT *06430*
Rouvina MISS Julia E—Mich'83 . . see C R Harvey
Rowan MASTER Avery Scott (John F JR) . . . . Born at New Orleans, LA Jan 22'96
Rowan MISS Dorothy G—Br'82
☎ (212) 627-8578 . . 99 Bank St, Apt 4L, New York, NY *10014-2125*
Rowan MR & MRS John F JR (Virginia Scott Freeman)
☎ (504) 899-6656 . . 3803 Camp St, New Orleans, LA *70115*

Rowan DR & MRS Joseph E (Diana M Pyle) Un.Ncd.StMichaels'61.Geo'65.Nu'68 . . . . | of ☎ (212)722-7677 1140 Fifth Av, New York, NY *10128*
MISS Victoria C—at ☎ (212) 570-1997 57 E 78 St, New York, NY *10021* . . . .
MR Ian McA—Ken'95 . . . . | ☎ (860) 868-0282 "Knoll" 7 North Shore Rd, New Preston, CT *06777*
MR Edward Van S—at Colby . . . .

Rowan MR Paul . . of
☎ (410) 819-8193 . . 27337 Rest Circle, Easton, MD *21601*
☎ (561) 231-0944 . . 550 Beach Rd, John's Island, Vero Beach, FL *32963*
Rowe MR & MRS A Loring (Barbara A Bastien) Err.Rc.Eyc.Cas.Cnt.Chi.P'34 . . of
☎ (312) 944-0140 . . 1365 N Dearborn St, Chicago, IL *60610*
☎ (508) 627-5003 . . 82 N Water St, Box 595, Edgartown, MA *02539*
Rowe MR & MRS George W (Kate R Munson) V'64.Ln.Bur.Pcu.Cly.H'62
☎ (415) 775-6166 . . 2785 Vallejo St, San Francisco, CA *94123*
Rowe MR & MRS James L (Pauline P Stone) Purd'40.P'39.Ch'47.Ind'68
☎ (317) 251-0077 . . 7775 Spring Mill Rd, Indianapolis, IN *46260*

Rowe MR & MRS John J (Diana V Cutler) Mds.Dyc.Cs.H'40
☎ (516) 267-2300 . . PO Box 7112, Amagansett, NY *11930*
Rowe MRS Marian Sanzone (Marian A Sanzone) | ☎ (513) 561-4987
Sth'51 . . . . | 5320 Miami Rd,
MR Basil H . . . . | Cincinnati, OH
MR Charles W . . . . | *45243*
Rowe MR Peter J—Ga'70 . . of
☎ (803) RA2-2254 . . ''Carriage House'' 46 Society St, Charleston,
SC *29401*
☎ (941) 748-3193 . . 1610—30 St W, Bradenton, FL *34205*
Rowe MRS William S (Martha P Whitney) Qc.
☎ (513) 561-7822 . . 4765 Burley Hills Dv, Cincinnati, OH *45243*
Rowe MR & MRS William S 2d (Eliza H Sprague) OWes'92
☎ (617) 536-8796 . . 136 Beacon St, Apt 8, Boston, MA *02116*
Rowe MRS William Wallace (Elizabeth F Woodin) Ncd . . .of
955 Riomar Dv, Vero Beach, FL *32963*
☎ (513) 561-7388 . . 8605 Camargo Club Dv, Cincinnati, OH *45243*
Rowland MISS Anne—Ac.
☎ (757) 220-1206 . . 5701 Williamsburg Landing Dv, Apt 2,
Williamsburg, VA *23185*
Rowland MR & MRS Benjamin A JR (M Wendy Gartner) Sth'58.Ey.Y'57
☎ (617) 631-5414 . . 27 Waldron St, Marblehead, MA *01945*
Rowland MR & MRS George R (Carolyn C Crossett)
B'gton'37.Cy.Chi.Ncd.Y'33 . . of
☎ (617) 266-1855 . . 2 Commonwealth Av, Apt 12F, Boston, MA *02116*
☎ (508) 428-6348 . . ''Innisfree'' PO Box 246, Fox Island Rd, Osterville,
MA *02655*
Rowland MR & MRS James H JR (Henderlite—Olga | ☎ (410) 472-4490
de Sparré) Hlns'52.Y'49 . . . . | 15424 Duncan Hill
MR Robert L Henderlite—Penn'87—at | Rd, PO Box 613,
5011C Cherry Crest Lane, Charlotte, NC *28217* | Sparks, MD *21152*
Rowland MRS Paul C (Clement—Mary E Deacon)
☎ (609) 298-5992 . . 4 Fireside Circle, Columbus, NJ *08022*
Rowlands MR & MRS Eliot W (Marguerite T Di Gangi)
GeoW'72.Cp.Bard'71.Rut'83
☎ (913) 722-5944 . . 5307 Falmouth Rd, Shawnee Mission, KS *66205*
Rowlands MISS Penelope I—Bard'73.Stan'85 . . see P D White
Rowley MR & MRS Charles F (Van Leer—Christiane Timbal) On.Sr.H'43
☎ (910) 295-2275 . . Twin Meadow Farm, PO Box 2138, Pinehurst,
NC *28374*
Rowley MR & MRS E Davis JR (Maria Cristina Pope) Cy.
☎ (617) 469-0443 . . 42 Ogden Rd, Chestnut Hill, MA *02167-3732*
Rowley MR & MRS Edward D (Lusk—Adelaide E Storer) Cy.Chi.Ncd.H'40
☎ (617) 566-5830 . . 117 Woodland Rd, Chestnut Hill, MA *02167*
Rowley MR & MRS Eric B (Marcia E Neal) Kas'75.On.DU'76
☎ (847) 234-5935 . . 382 Basswood, Lake Forest, IL *60045*
Rowley MR & MRS Henry N JR (Francine Roselli) | of ☎ (212)861-4835
Cly.Y.'52 . . . . | 155 E 72 St,
MISS Maria F—Nu'92—at Bank Street Grad . . . | New York, NY
MISS Alexandra—Ken'94 . . . . | *10021*
| ☎ (619) 771-0111
| ''Casa Serena''
| 52-135 Eisenhower
| Dv, La Quinta, CA
| *92253*
Rowley MR John C—Y.'85.Pa'89
☎ (212) 737-4858 . . 36 E 69 St, Apt 5A, New York, NY *10021*

Rowley MR & MRS Peter W (Terez De Tuboly) | ☎ (212) 734-8784
Plg.Un.K.Cly.Cl'73 . . . . | 815 Park Av,
JUNIORS MISS Caroline . . . . | New York, NY
| *10021*
Rowse MISS Flavia . . see G L Smith
Roxby MAJ GEN (RET) & MRS William C JR (Corinne | ☎ (215) 836-0121
T Romig) USAF.MtH'57.R.Pc.Rv.Wt.P. | ''Chantilly''
Leh'53.Cl'59 | 701 Hunt Lane,
MISS Elisabeth C—P.'89.Pp.—at | Flourtown, PA
☎ (212) 243-3501 . . 9 E 13 St, Apt 2J, | *19031-1001*
New York, NY *10003* . . . . |
MISS Susanna T—Roan'92.Pc.P.—at |
☎ (215) 283-3258 . . 200 Tupelo Grove, Ambler, |
PA *19002* . . . . |
Royall MRS William L 3d (Smith—Kates—Ane Louise Waterhouse) Pa'53
☎ (954) 566-6692 . . 1706 NE 19 St, Ft Lauderdale, FL *33305-3233*
Royce MISS Amanda B . . see T F Bundy JR
Royce MR & MRS Charles M (Karen P Free)
Cal'73.Un.K.Why.L.Msq.Cs.Br'61.Cl'63 . . of
☎ (203) 869-3603 . . 67 Harbor Dv, Greenwich, CT *06830*
☎ (518) 589-5246 . . ''Witchwood'' Onteora Club, Tannersville,
NY *12485*
Royce MR Charles M JR . . see T F Bundy JR
Royce MRS Frank A (Margaret Newlin) . . . . Died at
Needham, MA Jan 2'96
Royce MISS Jennifer H . . see T F Bundy JR
Royce MR & MRS Robert C (Willoughby K Ellis) | ☎ (516) 968-8635
LIU'83.Chr.Br'61.Br'64.Dick'67 . . . . | 74 Garner Lane,
MR Charles J—Bost'92—at ☎ (561) 395-1984 | Bay Shore, NY
575604 Arbor Club Way, B3, Boca Raton, FL | *11706*
33433 . . . . |
Royce MR & MRS Stephen W 2d (Brigitte Bernhardt) Cal'77 🏛
☎ (011-33-92) 98-69-30 . . Villa Les Cerisiers, 41 rue du Pont, St Victor,
06400 Cannes, France
Royer MR & MRS David L (Elizabeth L Crane)
☎ (410) 523-3545 . . 235 W Lanvale St, Baltimore, MD *21217*
Royer MRS Elizabeth D (Royer—Diffenderffer— | ☎ (610) 642-4466
Elizabeth J Dripps) Me.Cda . . . . | 510 N Rose Lane,
MISS Isabel R . . . . | Haverford, PA
| *19041*
Royer MR Theodore W—Me . . .see MRS E W Van Pelt
Royster MRS Hubert A JR (Elizabeth Rutan)
☎ (207) 374-2779 . . Parker Point Rd, PO Box 322, Blue Hill,
ME *04614*
Royster DR & MRS Thomas S JR (Caroline M Henry) | of ☎ (561)231-9761
Ng.Ri.Plg.Csn.NCar'40.Pa'43 . . . . | 231 Indian Harbor
MR John S—at ☎ (910) 256-0800 | Rd, John's Island,
7221 Gray Gables Lane, Wilmington, NC *28403* | Vero Beach, FL
| *32963*
| ☎ (919) 438-3321
| ''La Grange''
| PO Box 166,
| Henderson, NC
| *27536*
Rubin MR & MRS Howard (Mary J Henry) Occ'73.H.'82.Laf'77.H.'82 . . of
☎ (212) 734-8171 . . 120 East End Av, New York, NY *10028*
☎ (516) 537-2435 . . 120 Bay Lane, Mecox Bay, Water Mill, NY *11976*

Rubin MR & MRS Vaughn P (Sara E Sterling) Ws'49.Kt.Cv.Cr'46
☎ (216) 991-5154 . . 19500 S Woodland Rd, Shaker Heights, OH *44122*

Rublee MR & MRS George 2d (Gallagher—Gilbert— | of ☎ (202)298-9120
Ellen M MacVeagh) Mt.Cvc.Ct.Sl.H'48.H'53 . . | 3042 N St NW,
MR Francis H Gilbert . . . . | Washington, DC
| *20007*
| ☎ (603) 675-2778
| "The Crossways"
| HCR 75, Box 6,
| Platt Rd, Cornish,
| NH *03745*

Rudd MR & MRS Eldon (Ann Merritt) ArizSt'47.Ariz'49
☎ (602) 945-3066 . . PO Box 873, Scottsdale, AZ *85252*

Rudkin MRS Dorothy S (Dorothy S Smith) Ri.BtP.Pqt.Dc.Ncd.
☎ (561) 964-8284 . . Florida Gardens, Box 6885, Lake Worth, FL *33461*

Rudman MR & MRS Stephen M (Alexandra W de Erney)
☎ (561) 392-6299 . . 1230 Spanish River Rd, Boca Raton, FL *33432*

Rue MR & MRS Francis J JR (Rosina E Bateson) Nu'50.Csh.Rv.Ncd.P'43
☎ (941) 472-2816 . . 957 Cabbage Palm Court, Sanibel, FL *33957*

Rue MR Howard S JR—Me.Wt. . . . . | ☎ (610) 520-9992
MR James M—Bethany'79 . . . . | 74 Pasture Lane,
| Apt 134,
| Bryn Mawr, PA
| *19010*

Ruebensaal MRS Clayton F (M Virginia Latrobe)
☎ (203) 259-6164 . . 3 Rustic Lane, Greens Farms, CT *06436*

Ruebhausen MR Oscar M—Ri.C.Dth'34.Y'37
☎ (212) 688-3134 . . 450 E 52 St, New York, NY *10022*

Rueckert DR & MRS Frederic (Joan Dodge) Ham'45.Cl'47
☎ (603) 643-4106 . . 18 Berrill Farm Lane, Hanover, NH *03755*

Ruegg MR & MRS Edward L (Mecray—Priscilla E | of ☎ (602)488-5004
Jackson) Ncd.Hb.Aht'55.H'56 . . . . | The Boulders,
MISS Laura W—at New York, NY . . . . | 77 Desert Bloom
MISS Ellen L Mecray . . . . | Circle, Scottsdale,
MR Christopher H Mecray—at Baltimore, MD | AZ *85262*
| ☎ (207) 867-4472
| "The Red House"
| North Haven, ME
| *04853*

Ruehlmann MR & MRS Eugene P (Virginia Juergens)
Cin'46.Cin'48.Cm.Qc.Cin'48.H'50
☎ (513) 451-4939 . . 1150 Gleneagles Court, Cincinnati, OH *45233-4865*

Rueter MISS Katherine B
☎ (508) 283-3048 . . 7 Taylor St, Gloucester, MA *01930-2921*

Rueter MISS Margaret B—Aht'78
☎ (617) 661-3897 . . 3 Sumner Rd, Cambridge, MA *02138*

Rueter MR Matthew C—Mass'76.Ch'81.Geo'88
☎ (201) 963-5855 . . 932 Willow Av, Hoboken, NJ *07030*

Rueter MR & MRS William G JR (Sarah L Edwards) | ☎ (617) 242-4041
H'47.Mich'50 . . . . | 27 Mt Vernon St,
MR John L—H.'83.Bost'89—at | Charlestown, MA
☎ (617) 643-3350 . . 315 Ridge St, Arlington, | *02129-3410*
MA *02174* . . . . |

Ruffin MR & MRS Sidney M (Harriet Martin) | ☎ (412) 781-0146
Fcg.Va'39. . . . . | 107 Westchester Dv,
MISS Caryanne R . . . . | Pittsburgh, PA
MR Nicholas C . . . . | *15215*

Ruffing MISS Anne S—Brdgwtr'91 . . see J F St Georges

Ruffing MR James McI—CarnM'89 . . see J F St Georges

Ruffing MR John J JR—WChesSt'57
☎ (610) 370-1057 . . Crestwood Cliffs, B4 Alpine Court, Reading, PA *19606-3010*

Rugg MRS J Samuel (Sara S Lewis) Bnd'49
☎ (805) 969-0830 . . 1510 Monte Vista Rd, Santa Barbara, CA *93108*

Rugg MR & MRS Peter (Meredith C Phelps) | of ☎ (214)369-4464
SL'70.Fic.Ny.Cs.Cl'69 . . . . | 4 Glenheather Court,
MISS C Caroline . . . . | Dallas, TX *75225*
MR Charlton A—Br'95 . . . . | ☎ (212) 734-3495
| 176 E 71 St,
| Apt 18B,
| New York, NY
| *10021*

Ruggieri MRS Tenney (Hearst—Patricia L Tenney) . | ☎ (516) 726-4734
MISSES Christina P & Kate T—at | "Wood's Hole"
☎ (212) 517-5980 . . 501 E 87 St, New York, NY | 506 Edge of Woods
10128 . . . . | Rd, PO Box 616,
| Water Mill, NY
| *11976-0616*

Rulon-Miller MR Berkeley T—Elk.U'74.Va'78 ⛵
☎ (610) 975-0238 . . 500 E Lancaster Av, Apt 116D, St Davids, PA *19087*

Rulon-Miller MR & MRS Christopher (Laura L Edwards) Cal'83.Un.P'78
☎ (914) 793-2046 . . 120 Park Av, Bronxville, NY *10708*

Rulon-Miller MR & MRS Patrick (Davis—Judith S | ☎ (609) 921-1076
Rollinson) Yn.Y'63 . . . . | PO Box 431,
MISS Sarah—Colg'94 . . . . | 13 Academy St,
MR Ian Davis—at Breckenridge, CO *80424* . . | Kingston, NJ *08528*

Rulon-Miller MRS Richmond (Frances E McCarthy)
☎ (410) 243-5319 . . Roland Park Place, Apt 652, 830 W 40 St, Baltimore, MD *21211*

Rulon-Miller MR & MRS Samuel F (Patricia Lippincott) Rb.P'47
☎ (610) MI9-0679 . . 1 Craig Lane, Haverford, PA *19041*

Rulon-Miller MR & MRS Samuel F JR (Cornelia M McEneaney)
BostColl'82.Ripon'74
☎ (508) 475-1727 . . 69 Park St, Andover, MA *01810*

Rulon-Miller MISS Virginia—Pa'70
☎ (415) 381-3045 . . 383 Molino Av, Mill Valley, CA *94941*

Rulon-Miller MR & MRS William L (A Catherine Seely) Hood'73.Ph.P'70
☎ (610) 525-3169 . . 330 Highland Lane, Bryn Mawr, PA *19010*

Rumbough MR & MRS Douglas M (Laura J ten Broeke)
Mid'82.Au.Rv.Denis'79
☎ (203) 853-0696 . . 110 Highland Av, Rowayton, CT *06853*

Rumbough MR & MRS J Wright JR (Melissa Moffett) Au.B.Pr.Plg.Rv.Y.'52
☎ (516) 671-2726 . . 271 Piping Rock Rd, Glen Head, NY *11545*

Rumbough MR & MRS J Wright 3d (Jennifer S McCartney)
LakeF'75.My.Au.Rv.LakeF'76
☎ (508) 922-1318 . . 103 Hart St, Beverly Farms, MA *01915*

Rumbough MRS Margaretha W (Srybnik—Margaretha Wagstrom) BtP.
☎ (561) 844-3568 . . 318 Caribbean Rd, Palm Beach, FL *33480*

Rumbough MR & MRS Stanley M JR (Janson—Janne Herlow)
Copen'64.Rc.BtP.Mds.Ng.Evg.Y'42 . . of
☎ (561) 659-2230 . . 655 Island Dv, Palm Beach, FL *33480*
☎ (516) 324-0563 . . PO Box 1053, 22 Terbell Lane, East Hampton, NY *11937*

Rumery MR & MRS John R (Hall—Nancy Kluge) B'gton'46.Va'40
☎ (910) 295-6376 . . PO Box 1584, Linden Rd, Pinehurst, NC *28374*

Rumford MR & MRS Lewis 2d (M Rose Clymer) | ☎ (410) 527-1362
Elk.Mv.Ncd.P'26 . . . . | 13801 York Rd,
MISS Beatrix T—at Tayloe House, | Apt K16,
207 E Nicholson St, Williamsburg, VA *23185* . . | Cockeysville, MD
| *21030*

Rumsey MRS Daniel L (Luella M Nitterauer) BufSt'29.G.St.
☎ (716) 884-6447 . . 50 Windsor Av, Buffalo, NY *14209*

Rumsey MRS Lee M (Grange—Catharine B Clothier) Gm.
☎ (610) 353-7709 . . Dunwoody Village CH17, 3500 West Chester Pike,
Newtown Square, PA *19073*

Rumsey MR & MRS R Douglas (Elizabeth F Smith) | 148 Summer St,
Ts.G.H'41 . . . . | Buffalo, NY *14222*
MR Theodore B—at 26 Linnaean St, Cambridge, |
MA *02138* . . . . |
MR Nicholas P . . . . |

Rumsey MR & MRS Roger C (Barbara Johnson) . . . . | ☎ (818) 794-9078
MR Roger C JR . . . . | 2545 Boulder Rd,
| Altadena, CA *91001*

Rumsey MISS Tessa A S—SL'92 . . see P M Jeanrenaud

Rundlett MASTER Crawford Billington (Raymond C 2d) . . . . Born at
Williamsburg, VA Sep 24'94

Rundlett MRS Donald H (Mary Jane Keller) Skd'57 | ☎ (561) 694-6750
MISS Elizabeth H—at ☎ (212) 982-9512 | 11666 Lost Tree
7 Lexington Av, Apt 7C, New York, NY *10010* | Way, North Palm
| Beach, FL *33408*

Rundlett MR Donald H JR—SL'91
☎ (503) 221-6239 . . 2014 NW Glison St, Apt 404, Portland, OR *97209*

Rundlett MR & MRS Raymond C 2d (Leslie H May)
SUNY'84.Ng.Denis'85.W&M'95
☎ (804) 230-5750 . . 5204 Devonshire Rd, Richmond, VA *23225*

Rundlöf MRS Margaret M (Margaret S Mueller) . . . | ☎ (203) 270-0530
MISS Dana C . . . . | 9 Antler Pine Rd,
MR Christer S . . . . | Sandy Hook, CT
JUNIORS MISS Katrine P . . . . | *06482*
JUNIORS MR John W . . . . |

Runnells MR & MRS Clive (Firestone—Garwood— | ☎ (713) 622-1469
Nancy J Morgan) A.B.Cly.Y'48 . . . . | 3649 Chevy Chase
MR Thomas Pierce—at ☎ (512) 322-0933 | Dv, Houston, TX
1400 Scenic Dv, Apt 2, Austin, TX *76703* . . . . . | *77019*
MR David M Firestone . . . . |
MR John M Garwood—at 5225 Agnes Av, |
Apt 206, North Hollywood, CA *91607* . . . . . |

Runnells MR & MRS John S 2d (Louise O Gale) | of ☎ (847)234-3636
Sth'50.Cho.On.Fy.Y'50 . . . . | 89 Warrington Dv,
MISS Gale P—Wa.—at ☎ (312) 944-0792 | Lake Bluff, IL
1730 N Clark St, Chicago, IL *60614* . . . . | *60044*
MR John S 3d—at Rte 1, Box 32, Bay City, TX | ☎ (561) 546-2176
77404 . . . . | 57 S Beach Rd,
| Hobe Sound, FL
| *33455*

Runnette MR & MRS Robert G (Margaret W Sloan) | ☎ (412) 963-9422
Rr.Fcg.Buck'60 . . . . | 114 Hillcrest Rd,
MISS Martha S—F&M'91 . . . . | Pittsburgh, PA
MR A Creighton 2d—NEng'94 . . . . | *15238*

Runyeon DR & MRS William K (Jane W Williams) | ☎ (610) 375-1219
P'46.Pa'48 . . . . | 8 Hummingbird Rd,
MISS Jane W—Ind'77.Cin'81 . . . . | Wyomissing, PA
| *19610*

Runyon MRS C Randolph 3d (Anne C Van Alstyne) Dar.
☎ (908) 295-4849 . . 977 Barnegat Lane, Mantoloking, NJ *08738*

Runyon MR & MRS Charles 3d (Mary Robbins) Sth'34.Hn.H'36.Y'39
☎ (919) 928-5811 . . PO Box 85, Ocracoke, NC *27960*

Rupp MRS Albert G (Rupp—Lowell—Baxter— | ☎ (561) 844-2944
Cynthia C Foy) Pr.BtP. . . . . | 275 Tradewind Dv,
MR Byron C—at ☎ (602) 949-2639 | Palm Beach, FL
Pavo Real 28, 6711 E Camelback Rd, Scottsdale, | *33480*
AZ *85021* . . . . |

Rupp MR & MRS Christopher Foy (Carolyn G Logan) Duke'81.Nu'85
☎ (212) 831-6960 . . 1133 Park Av, New York, NY *10128*

Rupp MR & MRS Richard W (Frances O'Neil) | ☎ (716) 876-2129
Cy.St.G.Colg'41 . . . . | 21 New Amsterdam
MR William R . . . . | Av, Buffalo, NY
| *14216*

Rusch MRS Henry A (Frances M Williams) Dar.H. . | ☎ (212) BU8-2927
MISS (DR) Valerie W—V'71.Cl'75—at | 129 E 69 St,
☎ (212) 744-9609 . . 203 E 72 St, Apt 22B, | New York, NY
New York, NY *10021* . . . . | *10021-5041*

Rush MISS Deborah N
☎ (610) 459-5923 . . 18 Webb Rd, Chadds Ford, PA *19317*

Rush MRS Kenneth (Jane G Smith)
☎ (561) 276-5939 . . Dorchester Apt 8N, 200 N Ocean Blvd,
Delray Beach, FL *33483*

Rush MRS Lockwood (Hendrick—Jacklyn B Ewing) P'55 . . of
☎ (202) 333-1446 . . 2920 N St NW, Washington, DC *20007*
☎ (610) 347-0437 . . ''Mostly Cottage'' PO Box 535, Unionville,
PA *19375*

Rush MR & MRS R Stockton (Said—Jane W Simpkins) Ln.Bhm.Cc.P'53
☎ (415) 771-1084 . . 790 Bay St, San Francisco, CA *94109*

Rush MR & MRS R Stockton 3d (Wendy H Weil) P'84.P'84
☎ (206) 392-7371 . . 12031 Issaquah-Hobart Rd, Issaquah, WA *98027*

Rush MRS Richard (Mary S Conover) . . . . | ☎ (860) 354-6143
MISS Susan B . . . . | 245 Second Hill Rd,
| New Milford, CT
| *06776*

Rusmisel JUNIORS MISS Margo A . . see MISS B Donaldson

Russe MR Roger D—Cc.Hn.H'75.Tul'78
☎ (703) 352-5860 . . 4011 Locust St, Fairfax, VA *22030*

Russell MR & MRS A David (Lois A Robinson)
Ws'47.Snc.Rv.Cw.Y'45w.Y'51
☎ (203) 938-9305 . . 9 Little River Lane, Redding, CT *06896*

Russell MR & MRS A Douglas JR (Marie-Caroline M | ☎ (301) 299-5920
Masson) Paris'70.P'55.Pa'60 . . . . | 9709 Sotweed Dv,
MISS Eugenie Isabelle C . . . . | Potomac, MD *20854*
MR Alexis A Douglas |
JUNIORS MR Adrien Philippe M M . . . . |
JUNIORS MR Pierre-Alexandre O . . . . |

Russell DR & MRS A Preston (Nancy M Gibson) | ☎ (912) 352-2718
Van'63.Cw.Tul'62 . . . . | 4617 Lansdowne
MISS Lindsay B . . . . | Place, Savannah,
MR Alexander P JR . . . . | GA *31405*

Russell MRS Angelica L (Macdonald—Russell—Clagett—
Angelica Lloyd) Sl. ♨
☎ (508) 636-4582 . . Barney's Joy Farm, 14 Barney's Joy Rd,
South Dartmouth, MA *02748*

Russell MR & MRS Angus M (Elisabeth A
Waterworth) Sth'59.Me.Csp.Ncd.Dth'52.Pa'55 .
MR Alexander M—VillaN'91—at
☎ (406) 586-8154 . . 5610 Violet, Bozeman, MT
59715 . . . .
MR John D—Vt'94—at ☎ (802) 863-5184
30½ Dans Court, Burlington, VT *05401* . . . .
| ☎ (802) 649-5430
| 11 Cossingham Rd,
| Norwich, VT *05055*

Russell MRS Caroline G (R Caroline Gardiner) Me.
☎ (610) 526-1797 . . 74 Pasture Lane, Apt 127, Bryn Mawr, PA *19010*

Russell MR & MRS Charles T JR (Catharine Olney) H'30
☎ (508) 945-1324 . . PO Box 433, Chatham, MA *02633*

Russell MR Charles T 3d—Pa'63
☎ (617) 326-4245 . . 30 Court St, Dedham, MA *02026*

Russell MASTER Corlis Ashbey (Rudolph A) . . . . Born at
Walnut Creek, CA Jly 8'96

Russell MRS D Fenton (Diane Sawyer Fenton)
☎ (212) TR6-6344 . . 1150 Park Av, New York, NY *10128*

Russell MISS Diana—BMr'65.S.Ny . . .see MRS A Farwell

Russell MR & MRS Edward JR (Louise Carpenter)
Rcn.B.So.StJ.Cly. . . . .
MISS Lesley C—at 671 Prospect St, New Haven,
CT *06511* . . . .
| ☎ (803) 722-8040
| 5 Legare St,
| Charleston, SC
| *29401*

Russell MR & MRS Edward T JR (M Charlotte
Emery) Denis'59.Mass'61 . . . .
MISS Aldis—at Oberlin . . . .
MISS Bradley . . . .
| ☎ (617) 646-7464
| 6 Chapman St,
| Arlington, MA
| *02174*

Russell MR & MRS Edwin F (Van Pelt—Cynthia Cary) B.Pr.Mb.Ng.Srb.P'37
☎ (516) 759-2109 . . PO Box 526, 5 Overlook Rd, Locust Valley,
NY *11560*

Russell MR & MRS Francis P (Ellen E Fabe) V'83.H'89
☎ (513) 321-2200 . . 3240 Hardisty Av, Cincinnati, OH *45208*

Russell MRS George S (Allan—Baldwin—Margaret S Aspinwall) Tcy.
☎ (415) 851-1420 . . 3900 Sandhill Rd, Woodside, CA *94062*

Russell MR & MRS Grant E JR (Stella N Slater) Wash'38
☎ (408) 735-8838 . . 1033 Havre Court, Sunnyvale, CA *94087*

Russell MR & MRS Harold S (Margo Stratford)
Rcp.Pc.Fy.Y'57.Ch'62.Ch'64 . . . .
MR Nathan W—Knox'85—at ☎ (773) 883-1743
2253 W Addison St, Chicago, IL *60618* . . . .
MR Peter L—at RI Sch of Design . . . .
| ☎ (202) 338-1538
| 1532—31 St NW,
| Washington, DC
| *20007*

Russell MR & MRS Hollis F (Griffin—Alice B Forster)
Sth'82.Rcn.BtP.Cw.P'75.Cr'78
☎ (561) 848-5501 . . 224 Colonial Lane, Palm Beach, FL *33480*

Russell MR & MRS James B (Joan Anderson)
"Strawberry Fields" 34 Bourne Lane, PO Box 2082, Ogunquit,
ME *03907*

Russell MR & MRS James S (Léonore Upham) Cal'39.P'34 . . of
☎ (415) 453-7921 . . PO Box 287, Ross, CA *94957*
☎ (415) 669-1073 . . Inverness, CA *94937*

Russell MR & MRS John B JR (Cynthia Lee)
Rcn.Rm.Y'45 . . . .
MISS Jenny de W—at ☎ (617) 825-6469
26 Harley St, Dorchester, MA *02122* . . . .
| ☎ (919) 932-5853
| 334 Carolina
| Meadows, Villa,
| Chapel Hill, NC
| *27514-7520*

Russell MRS John C (Lewine Hoefer) Ch'28.Ac.
☎ (610) NI4-1181 . . "76 Farm" 2495 White Horse Rd, Box 155,
Devon, PA *19333*

Russell MRS John E JR (Brumfield—Sara E S Weymouth) Ncd.
☎ (410) 457-5162 . . "Owl Hill" Trappe Church Rd, Darlington,
MD *21034*

Russell MR John Mosby—CathU'50.GeoW'71
☎ (301) 229-8893 . . 5029 Allan Rd, Bethesda, MD *20816*

Russell MRS Mary E—MoVal'70
☎ (415) 771-5787 . . 1580 Filbert St, Apt 15, San Francisco, CA *94123*

Russell MR & MRS Munro C (Bayne Peyton)
Strat'69.MaryB'92.Lynch'69 . . . .
MISS Genevieve B—at U of Vt . . . .
MR M Cannon JR—at New River Coll . . . .
| ☎ (804) 973-4947
| "Rivercroft"
| PO Box 5581,
| Charlottesville, VA
| *22905*

Russell MRS Nancy Clark (Nancy R Clark) . . . .
MR E Cheston—Box 271, Almont, CO *81210* . .
MR Marshall H—at 123 Price St, West Chester,
PA *19382* . . . .
| ☎ (610) 436-4489
| 440 N High St,
| West Chester, PA
| *19380*

Russell MR & MRS Norman F S (Vivianne L
Hooppaw) GeoW'45.Cw.Pn.P'43 . . . .
MISS Anne G—P'79.Dth'91—at ☎ (011-60-3)
456-0522 . . Kuala Lumpur Intern'l School, Jalan
Kolam Air, 68000 Ampong, Selangor Darul
Ehsan, Malaysia . . . .
| ☎ (908) 782-5196
| Applestone Farm,
| 78 Rocktown Rd,
| Ringoes, NJ
| *08551-1211*

Russell MR & MRS Paris Scott (Turnbull—Dalton—Berckemeyer—
Elizabeth D Manning) Ncd.
☎ (941) 966-4495 . . 500 Webb's Cove, Osprey, FL *34229*

Russell MRS Renouf (Lily Warren) Sm . . .of
☎ (803) 649-3316 . . 220 Walker Av SE, Aiken, SC *29801*
☎ (603) 532-7023 . . "Wesselhoeft Farm" 4 Gilson Rd, Jaffrey,
NH *03452*

Russell MR & MRS Rudolph A (Katharine Van D Ashbey)
L&C'85.Mls'90 . . of
☎ (916) 842-4033 . . 3300 Delphic Rd, Montague, CA *96064*
☎ (510) 595-1761 . . 3432 Magnolia St, Oakland, CA *94607*

Russell MR Stuart A (Cody—Blyth—Jane Steinwedell)
see Dilatory Domiciles

Russell MR & MRS Theodore A (Sidney B
MacDonald) Cal'66.Cal'69 . . . .
JUNIORS MISS Virginia V . . . .
| ☎ (415) 752-0356
| 133 Thirtieth Av,
| San Francisco, CA
| *94121*

Russell MR & MRS Thomas W JR (Mary Ferguson)
Fic.Fiy.Csn.Yn.Y'39 . . . .
MISS Jennifer—at ☎ (212) 535-3375
176 E 77 St, New York, NY *10021* . . . .
MR Thomas W 3d . . . .
| ☎ (860) 767-2850
| Heritage Cove J4,
| 85 River Rd, Essex,
| CT *06426*

Russell MR William Francis . . . . Died at
New York, NY Apr 9'96

Russell MRS William Francis (Miller—Hatch—Mary W Vander Poel) Chr.Pr.Cly.StJ.
☎ (516) 922-0842 . . 411 Mill River Rd, PO Box 330, Oyster Bay, NY *11771-0330*

Russell REV & MRS William Hamilton (Elizabeth B Truslow) Cl'64.StA.Va'51.Merc'81 . . . . | ☎ (516) 475-4376
MR James T . . . . | 31 Rider Av, Patchogue, NY *11772*

Russo MRS Jeremy W (Jeremy Warburg) V'57 . . . . | ☎ (773) 288-3349
MISS Condée N . . . . | 5421 S Cornell Av, Apt 16, Chicago, IL
MR Alexander W W . . . . | *60615*

Rust MR David E—K.H'51 . . . . | of ☎ (202)333-1383
MISS Marina M—Duke'87 . . . . | 2812 P St NW, Washington, DC *20007*
☎ (305) 294-9833 306 Elizabeth St, Key West, FL *33040*

Rust MR & MRS Edgar C 3d (Loraine L Morey) Rdc'62.Cal'71.Wms'61.Mit'63.Cal'75 . . . . | ☎ (510) 652-0551
MISS Marion L—H'85—at 709 Roble Av, Apt 2, | 67 Parkside Dv, Berkeley, CA *94705*
Menlo Park, CA *94025* . . . . |

Rust MR Edgar F (Langbourne W) . . . . Married at Seattle, WA
Franzen MISS Ruth A (James) . . . . Aug 31'96

Rust MR George W JR . . . . | ☎ (415) 924-8712
MISS Jennifer A—at ☎ (516) 224-1216 | 22 Skylark Dv,
262 Rockaway St, Islip Terrace, NY *11752* . . . . | Apt 323, Larkspur, CA *94939*

Rust MR & MRS John M (Margaret A Bryant) Pg.Ck.Leh'72 . . of
☎ (516) 427-5541 . . 19 Carnegie Av, Cold Spring Harbor, NY *11724*
☎ (207) AT4-5131 . . Box 101, Granite Point, Fortunes Rocks, Biddeford, ME *04005*

Rust MR & MRS Langbourne W (Frances P O'Connell) Man'vl'66.Man'vl'70.Cl'84.H.'65.Cl'66.Cl'71
☎ (914) 769-8866 . . 96 Round Hill Dv, Briarcliff Manor, NY *10510*

Rust MR & MRS S Murray JR (Hill—Elinor Q Cowdrey) Pg.Leh'34
☎ (941) 262-1376 . . 138 Ninth Av S, Naples, FL *34102*

Rust MISS Susanne L—Bnd'94
☎ (608) 259-9066 . . 301 Norris Court, Apt 8, Madison, WI *53703*

Rust MR & MRS William A (Alexandrine McKennan) H'29
☎ (719) 475-1146 . . 2120 Hercules Dv, Colorado Springs, CO *80906-1136*

Rutan MR & MRS Frank E 3d (Crandall—Beverly A | ☎ (610) MU8-1429
Tuthill) Me.Fst.Why.Va'52 . . . . | 270 Chamounix Rd, St Davids, PA
MISS Eleanor H (Schilling—Eleanor H Rutan)—at | *19087*
430 Brookhurst Av, Narberth, PA *19072* . . . . . . |

Rutan MR Nicholas W
☎ (401) 348-8279 . . 7 Yosemite Valley Rd, Watch Hill, RI *02891*

Rutgers MR & MRS Anthony L (Diane G Lipshultz) | ☎ (970) 925-8229
Cal'75.Cal'75 . . . . | 512 Spruce St,
JUNIORS MR Anthony L JR . . . . | Aspen, CO *81611*

Rutgers MR & MRS Nicholas G JR (Nancy E Hall) Rcn.Rut'50
☎ (303) 753-0311 . . 5400 Nassau Circle E, Cherry Hills Village, CO *80110-5134*

Ruth MRS Sarah S (Madsen—Sarah P Stewart)
☎ (216) 338-1891 . . 14030 Caves Rd, Novelty, OH *44072*

Ruth MR & MRS Thomas N (M Virginia Pioda) | ☎ (408) 624-7618
Hav'52.Cal'55 . . . . | 25851 Tierra Grande
MR Michael De C—Box 31, Lincoln, VA *22078* | Dv, Carmel, CA
MR Jonathan P . . . . | *93923*

Rutherford DR & MRS Charles L JR (Harriet Kelly) | ☎ (334) 344-2330
At.Cda.David'59.Ala'63 . . . . | 204 Oakland Av,
MISS Nell S . . . . | Mobile, AL *36608*

Rutherford MR & MRS Edwin K (Nona H Conger) | ☎ (910) 692-4856
Myf.Sar.Ds.StA.Ncd.Dth'48.Mich'49.Del'57 . . . | 101 Cliff Court,
MISS (REV) Ellen C—Duke'77.Ch'79. | Southern Pines, NC
Gen'lTheo'89—at ☎ (517) 872-5624 | *28387*
6432—7 St, Cass City, MI *48726* . . . . |
MR Bruce K—Wms'84.Tufts'88 . . . . |

Rutherford MR & MRS James D (Hirtz—Nancy J Coleman) Hlns'60.Kas'61
☎ (713) 461-4374 . . 1124 Green Valley Dv, Houston, TX *77055*

Rutherfurd MR & MRS Alan L (Susan E McMurtrie) SCar'79
1530 Canal Dv, Columbia, SC *29210*

Rutherfurd MR & MRS Duncan (Sheeley—Diane Mace)
☎ (803) 649-7498 . . 190 Dogwood Rd, Aiken, SC *29801*

Rutherfurd MR & MRS Edward C (Oakes—Patricia A O'Shields) Evg.BtP.Cw.Lm.Snc.
☎ (561) 842-8540 . . 257 Tradewind Dv, Palm Beach, FL *33480*

Rutherfurd MR & MRS Guy G (Georgette Whelan) Rc.Fic.Yh.Cly.P'38
☎ (212) 369-9130 . . 40 E 88 St, New York, NY *10128*

Rutherfurd MR & MRS Guy G JR (CTSS Marie T | ☎ (212) 570-0108
Seilern-Aspang) Rc.Ln.P'62.H'68 . . . . | 156 E 79 St,
MISS Elizabeth F . . . . | New York, NY
MR Guy Christopher . . . . | *10021*

Rutherfurd MR Hugo—P'34
☎ (561) 546-4171 . . 106 South Trail, Hobe Sound, FL *33455-2313*

Rutherfurd MR & MRS Hugo JR (Merike Aro) | 8 Cottonwood Lane,
SCar'67 . . . . | Greenwood Village,
JUNIORS MISS Lisa . . . . | CO *80121-1410*

Rutherfurd MR & MRS James P (M Tracy Pearce) StLaw'79.Rc.Fic.Cly.P'78.Va'81
☎ (914) 793-9185 . . 26 Courseview Rd, Bronxville, NY *10708*

Rutherfurd MR & MRS Jay (Brown—Sarbacher—Blakemore—Griffis— Elizabeth S Kampmann) Evg.BtP.So.
☎ (561) 833-8341 . . 485 S County Rd, Palm Beach, FL *33480*

Rutherfurd MR Jay 2d
☎ (301) 330-5784 . . 444 N Frederick Av, Apt 203, Gaithersburg, MD *20877*

Rutherfurd MR & MRS John JR (Caroline L Gordon) Ws'79.Cy.Au.Cly.P'62.H'66 . . of
☎ (617) 566-7833 . . 248 Dudley St, Brookline, MA *02146*
☎ (518) 576-9816 . . ''Hill Station'' St Huberts, NY *12943*

Rutherfurd MR & MRS John M L 2d (Jennifer M Ryan) Sth'88.Cw.Snc.Stet'87
257 Tradewind Dv, Palm Beach, FL *33480*

Rutherfurd MISS Leslie H (Winthrop JR) . . . . . Married at New York, NY
Coleman MR Kevin C (Robert J) . . . . Jun 8'96

Rutherfurd MR Morton A—Nf.Ny. . . . . | ☎ (203) 389-4878
MR Oliver M—at U of Vt . . . . | 3 Westward Rd,
JUNIORS MISS Victoria M—at Indian Mtn Sch . . . | Woodbridge, CT
JUNIORS MR Nicholas M—at Bowdoin . . . . | *06525*

Rutherfurd MRS Winthrop (Alice Polk) Fic.Cly . . .of
☎ (212) 369-4422 . . 1088 Park Av, New York, NY *10128*
☎ (516) 788-7640 . . Fishers Island, NY *06390*

Rutherfurd MR & MRS Winthrop JR (Mary S Kernan) Rc.Fic.Cly.P'64.Va'67 . . . . | ☎ (212) 348-6051 1115 Fifth Av, New York, NY *10128*
MISS Elizabeth P—P'93 . . . .
MISS Emily K—at U of So Cal . . . .

Ruthrauff MRS F Bourne (Nancy Ewing) Rm.
☎ (609) 426-6209 . . Meadow Lakes 21-04, Hightstown, NJ *08520*

Ruthrauff MR & MRS Wilbur Bourne (Lynn N Williams) Pa'67.Drex'76.Sa.Pa'64.Pa'67
☎ (215) 247-4890 . . 6 Caryl Lane, Philadelphia, PA *19118*

Rutland MR & MRS Gregory W (Susan H Thomson) Ncmb'85.SoMiss'79 . . of
☎ (601) 896-4131 . . 9170 Ridge Rd, Gulfport, MS *39503*
☎ (904) 837-7601 . . Shoreline Towers W, 970 Gulf Shore Dv, Destin, FL *32541*

Rutland MR & MRS James W JR (Lucile F Herbert) Dar.Aub'41
☎ (334) 263-3555 . . Rte 2, Box 332, Old Selma Rd, Montgomery, AL *36108*

Rutledge MISS Diana—Vt'85.Temp'95
☎ (215) 732-5031 . . 1926 Pine St, Apt 2, Philadelphia, PA *19103*

Rutter MR & MRS David M (Kristie M Mapes) Me'78
☎ (847) 382-7410 . . 248 Beverly Rd, Barrington, IL *60010-3406*

Rutter MR J Wood 2d—Unn.Pn.W&L'65.NCar'67
☎ (860) 435-5704 . . Salisbury School, Salisbury, CT *06068*

Rutter MR & MRS John A (Ann K Scharman)
☎ (910) 924-1852 . . 3865 Lakeview Dv, Pfafftown, NC *27040*

Rutter MR & MRS John A JR (Williams—Suzin V Hay) Stph'70.Tv.Ken'66 . . . . | ☎ (216) 831-3122 3740 Greenwood Dv, Pepper Pike, OH *44124*
MISS Cynthia P—at 3445 Superior Park Dv, Apt 12, Cleveland Heights, OH *44118* . . . .
MISS Catherine Grier—at 18 Isabella St, Apt 2, Boston, MA *02116* . . . .

Rutter MR & MRS N Edward C (Penelope S Ball) Mo. . . . . | ☎ (201) 543-2212 44 Essex Dv, Mendham, NJ *07945*
MR N Edward C 3d—at ☎ (415) 586-1357 215 Hearst Av, San Francisco, CA *94131* . . . . .

Ruxton MISS Mary L—V'47
☎ (614) 876-8852 . . 3301 Kilwinning Place, Columbus, OH *43221*

Ruzicka MR & MRS Jeffrey F (Pamela Barnard) Rcch.Msq.Plg.Wa.Colg'64 . . . . | ☎ (011-44-171) 351-5404 12 Mallord St, London SW3 6DU, England
MISS Alexa—SL'92 . . . .
MISS Christina . . . .

Ryan MRS A Park (Trefts—Anne T Park) . . . . | ☎ (510) 254-5592 40 Las Palomas St, Orinda, CA *94563*
MR Sean C . . . .
MR Park E Trefts—at U of Cal San Diego . . .

Ryan MR Allan A 3d—Ln.Y'54 . . . . | ☎ (212) SA2-6431 17 E 89 St, New York, NY *10128*
MISS Melissa R F . . . .

Ryan MR & MRS Allan A IV (Maria C Fanjul) UMiami'84.BtP.Evg.HWSth'82
☎ (561) 845-0927 . . 230 Miraflores Dv, Palm Beach, FL *33480*

Ryan MR C Gregg—Rcn.StLaw'83
☎ (540) 253-7402 . . 7234 Fleming Farm Rd, The Plains, VA *20198*

Ryan MISS Caroline O . . see J J McNamara JR

Ryan MRS Charlotte B (Charlotte Boettger) Me.
☎ (610) 645-8685 . . 1400 Waverly Rd, Villa 36, Gladwyne, PA *19035*

Ryan, Christopher & Baddour, Cynthia A—V'77.Mass'79
28 Myrick Lane, Harvard, MA *01451*

Ryan MR & MRS Christopher W (Lloyd—Moira O'C Graham) . . . . | ☎ (011-353-667) 5293 Derrynane Cross, Caherdaniel, Co Kerry, Ireland
MISS Cynthia F—at U of Paris Sorbonne Rm.
JUNIORS MISS Jessica F—at St Columbas . . . .

Ryan MR Clendenin J . . see J J McNamara JR

Ryan MISS Elizabeth . . . . | 3814 W Roscoe St, Apt 1, Chicago, IL *60618*
MISS Carolyn . . . .
MISS Nancy . . . .
MR Michael B . . . .

Ryan MR & MRS James J (Patricia A Connolly) Vh.Nw'46.Cal'49.Va'51 . . of
☎ (818) 792-6417 . . 770 S Oak Knoll Av, Pasadena, CA *91106*
☎ (619) 437-4996 . . 1108 F Av, Coronado, CA *92118*

Ryan MRS James U C (Hope P McLoughlin) . . . . . . | ☎ (718) 601-0205 3640 Johnson Av, Apt 4D, Bronx, NY *10463*
MR Joseph Croston . . . .
MR John T . . . .

Ryan MISS Jean . . see J J McNamara JR

Ryan MR John B
☎ (415) 661-2533 . . 1233 Willard St, San Francisco, CA *94117*

Ryan MRS John T JR (M Irene O'Brien) Fcg.Rr.Pg.
☎ (412) 521-3210 . . 20 W Woodland Rd, Pittsburgh, PA *15232*

Ryan MISS Lucinda F (late Clendenin J) . . . . Married at Oxford, MD
Stewart MR William L (late H Dorn JR) . . . . Apr 20'96

Ryan MRS McA Donald (Madeleine C Hemingway)
☎ (011-44-171) 245-9003 . . 93 Eaton Place, London SW1X 8L, England

Ryan MR & MRS Michael (Debora D Gilbert) Ws'73.Cl'75.H.'72 . . of
☎ (212) 995-5945 . . 28 E 10 St, New York, NY *10003*
☎ (518) 851-9140 . . 41 van Hoesen Rd, Craryville, NY *12521*

Ryan MISS Muriel L—MaryMt'26
☎ (305) 573-2341 . . 3301 NE Fifth Av, Miami, FL *33137*

Ryan MR Nathaniel J . . see J J McNamara JR

Ryan MISS Saville (late Theodore S) . . . . Married at Aspen, CO
Marsh MR Charles S (late Charles) . . . . May 4'96

Ryan MISS Sharon
☎ (919) 286-7890 . . 2303 Pershing St, Durham, NC *27705*

Ryan MR & MRS Stephen D 3d (Evelyne R Handy) Bost'77.Bgt.Aht'73.Ox'75.Bost'78 . . . . | ☎ (914) 764-4785 48 Horseshoe Hill Rd, Pound Ridge, NY *10576-1609*
JUNIORS MISS Amanda M B . . . .

Ryan MR Thomas F . . see J J McNamara JR

Ryan MR & MRS W Hurley (Speakman—Isabella T Pearson) Mds.Rcp.Wil.Ncd. . . . . | of ☎ (302)658-3930 1025 Kent Rd, Wilmington, DE *19807*
MISS Isabella P Speakman . . . .
☎ (516) 324-1430 1 Amy's Court, PO Box 2539, East Hampton, NY *11937*

S

Ryan MR W Hurley JR—Geo'86
☎ (912) 232-8850 . . 233 Abercorn St, Savannah, GA *31401*

Ryan MR & MRS William F JR (Elise E H Jeffress) P'76.Ncd.Dc.Pn.P'76
☎ (410) 323-2004 . . 5423 Purlington Way, Baltimore, MD *21212*

Ryan MRS William H (Jane Kales) Lx.K. . . . . | ☎ (413) 298-3466
MISS Nina F—Pa'80—at 42 Barrow St, | ''Old Place''
New York, NY *10014* . . . . | Stockbridge, MA
MISS Laura B—at 52 Chestnut St, Boston, MA | *01262*
02108 . . . . |

Ryburn MR & MRS Samuel M (M Beverly Huse) Sth'43.D.Chi.Sl.Vien'38
☎ (508) 785-0575 . . 33 Wilsondale St, Dover, MA *02030*

Ryder MR & MRS Geoffrey Strawbridge (Gina M Laakman) Ind'81.Roan'81
☎ (704) 362-0004 . . 535 Medearis Dv, Charlotte, NC *28211*

Ryder MR & MRS Harry V JR (Phyllis L Jones) Cy.Rv.Fw.Cp.Myf.Pa'50
☎ (508) 432-3750 . . 53 Chase St, PO Box 564, West Harwich,
MA *02671*

Ryerson MR & MRS Joseph T 3d (Barbara I Hyde) Cy.DU'70.Suff'74
☎ (617) 232-0617 . . 27 Conant Rd, Chestnut Hill, MA *02167*

Ryerson MRS M Ducey (Maria B Ducey) Cy. . . . . . | ☎ (617) 734-0660
MISS Maria D—at ☎ (617) 327-5854 | 347 Woodland Rd,
44 Hackensack Rd, Chestnut Hill, MA *02167* . . | Chestnut Hill, MA
 | *02167*

Ryerson MRS Margaret H (Margaret Hutchins) Sr.On.Cas.
☎ (847) 234-0973 . . 49 S Negaunee Lane, Lake Forest, IL *60045*

Ryland MR & MRS G Neal (Marjorie K Gerry) | ☎ (508) 927-9066
Sbc.My.H'63.Nu'67 . . . . | Beaver Pond Rd,
MISS Alexandra . . . . | Beverly Farms, MA
MR Nelson . . . . | *01915*
JUNIORS MISS Averell T—at St Paul's . . . . |
JUNIORS MISS Elizabeth G . . . . |

Ryland MRS Judith D (Judith Y Dubben) CtCol'67
☎ (619) 459-9438 . . 409 Dunemere Av, La Jolla, CA *92037*

Ryland MR W Bradford 2d—Cw.Cc.Br'62
☎ (619) 360-9139 . . ''Castello Rylando'' 77120 Delgado Dv,
Indian Wells, CA *92210*

Ryland MR & MRS William H (George Ann H Doty) StLaw'58.Mt.Cvc.Y'57
☎ (301) 654-7306 . . 3511 Hamlet Place, Chevy Chase, MD *20815*

Ryle MRS Robert W (Anne L Thouron) Ncd.
☎ (520) 886-7846 . . 6560 E Paseo Dorado, Tucson, AZ *85715-4717*

Rynning MR & MRS Eivind P (Baker—Virginia L | ☎ (215) 242-8286
Busser) SL'57.SUNY'70.Nor'66.GaTech'68. | 7827 Winston Rd,
Rens'71 ⚓ . . . . | Philadelphia, PA
MR Ralph E—Bow'94 . . . . | *19118*
JUNIORS MR Lars E . . . . |

Ryon MR & MRS Mortimer (Cornell—E Sandra Lipson) Laf'51.Cr'57
☎ (215) 297-0459 . . Centre Hill Farm, PO Box 378, Solebury,
PA *18963*

Ryus MR & MRS David D 3d (Martin—Mary Louise Ward)
Sbc.Ln.My.Tv.Stan'39
☎ (508) 468-1749 . . Wheeler Farm, 466 Bridge St, South Hamilton,
MA *01982*

Sabater MR Eldredge F—Syr'56
☎ (954) 781-7126 . . 361 SE Nineteenth Av, Apt 12, Pompano Beach,
FL *33060-7658*

Sabet JUNIORS MR Amman H . . see MRS S H Cole

Sabin MR & MRS Robert C (Helen B Zimmermann) Bow'77.Y'71.B'gton'74
☎ (914) 232-7955 . . 37 Woodfield Rd, Katonah, NY *10536*

Sabo MR & MRS John P (Margaret F Clattenburg) | 6038 Cannon Hill
Cwr'67.Cl'68.Pc.Rv.Cda.Cwr'69.Drex'74 . . . . . | Rd, Ft Washington,
MISS Jennifer E—at Gettysburg Coll. . . . . | PA *19034-1802*
JUNIORS MR J Erik—at Syracuse U . . . . |

Sachs MR Stephen F—O'68 . . . . | ☎ (202) 362-3117
MISS Natasha . . . . | 4536 Macomb St
MR Shamus F—at Wash'n U . . . . | NW, Washington,
 | DC *20016*

Sachs MR & MRS William R JR (Elizabeth Le D Kidd) Tex'91.Tex'84
☎ (214) 361-2183 . . 6607 Norway Rd, Dallas, TX *75230*

Sack MR & MRS A Albert (Maguire—Susan S | ☎ (441) 293-2202
Van Wyck) Unn.L.Cda.Dar. . . . . | ''Cedarhurst''
MISS Carter Van W—at ☎ (617) 776-8332 | Bailey's Bay,
16 Josephine Av, Somerville, MA *02144* . . . . . | Bermuda
MR A Albert VI—at Roanoke Coll . . . . |

Sackett MR & MRS L Hugh (Davis—Eleanor Stuart | ☎ (508) 448-5205
Childs) BMr'59.Ht.Lm.Ncd.Dh.Ox'53 . . . . | Groton School,
MISS Ruth Gardner Davis—at 309 E 9 St, | PO Box 991,
New York, NY *10003* . . . . | Groton, MA *01450*
MR Rodman Townsend Davis JR—at |
219 W 16 St, New York, NY *10011* . . . . |

Sackett MRS Nelson B (Elizabeth Noble Gray) | ☎ (212) 288-0434
Myf.Ncd. . . . . | 860 Park Av,
MR Nelson B JR . . . . | New York, NY
MR George O 2d . . . . | *10021*
MR Paul R G . . . . |

Sadler MRS Julius T JR (Jacquelin D Jones) . . . . Died at
Gracefield, Quebec, Canada Jun 4'96

Sadler MR Julius T JR—Va'45 . . . . | ☎ (860) 567-8804
MISS S Garrett . . . . | ''Carolina House''
MR Julius T 3d . . . . | PO Box 55,
 | Litchfield, CT *06759*

Sadron MRS Alexandra (Alexandra Sellar) . . . . | ☎ (970) 925-5107
MR Nicholas . . . . | PO Box 7814,
 | Aspen, CO *81612*

Sadtler MRS G Lewis (Alice L Rogers)
☎ (404) 256-3345 . . Mt Vernon Towers A909, 300 Johnson Ferry Rd
NE, Sandy Springs, GA *30328*

Sadtler MR & MRS Philip (Traude Hagel) Leh'34
☎ (215) 849-8499 . . 3555 W School House Lane, Philadelphia,
PA *19144*

Sadtler MR & MRS Philip B (Julia E Gallup) Pa'67 . . | ☎ (610) 687-3790
MISS Sarah E G—at ☎ (617) 964-7504 | 631 Newtown Rd,
457 Washington St, Apt 3, Newton, MA *02158* . | Berwyn, PA *19312*
MISS Catherine B—at Hamilton . . . . |

Sadtler MR & MRS Samuel B (Laura J Cline)
NCar'69.Sth'77.Cry.Leh'60 ⚓
☎ (215) 923-3714 . . 340 S 4 St, Philadelphia, PA *19106*

Sadtler MR & MRS Stephen C (Jean A Johnson) Roan'63 . . . . | of ☎ (215)557-0092 1924 Brandywine St, Philadelphia, PA *19130*
MR Stephen C JR—ODom'84.Alaska'93 . . . .
MR Thomas MacL—VaCmth'91 . . . .
MR Benjamin B—at Va Com'wth U . . . . | ☎ (757) 787-7320 ''Folly Creek'' PO Box 614, Accomac, VA *23301*

Sadtler MR & MRS Thomas M (Jane E Wells) Pa'74.Bost'83.Tufts'73.H'81
☎ (508) 369-7929 . . 51 Chestnut St, Concord, MA *01742*

Saer DR & MRS J Kenneth (Audrey P Emling) Ncmb'52.Tul'51.Tul'54.Mich'60
☎ (504) 866-5666 . . 582 Audubon St, New Orleans, LA *70118*

Safe MR & MRS Kenneth S JR (Elizabeth Kelley) Sm.Cy.Cw.Cc.Chi.H'51
☎ (617) 934-5034 . . 207 King Caesar Rd, Duxbury, MA *02332*

Saffelle MR & MRS Robert N (Constance P M Hall) Bab'78.NCar'80
☎ (804) 355-8929 . . 202 Gun Club Rd, Richmond, VA *23221*

Safford MR & MRS Thomas H (Leila D Cleaves) Colg'85.Me.Hartw'85
2392 Pineview Dv, Malvern, PA *19355-2310*

Safrin MRS Louise P (Louise G Peck)
☎ (215) 984-8992 . . Cathedral Village I-304, 600 E Cathedral Rd, Philadelphia, PA *19128*

Safrin MR & MRS Robert W (Darlington—Silvana R A Lubini) BtP.Evg.Cly.Pa'48
☎ (561) 655-4422 . . 2 Four Arts Plaza, Palm Beach, FL *33480-4102*

Sage DR & MRS Louis E (Honor M Fox) Cry.Vt'63.Leh'72 . . . . | ☎ (207) 633-5793 PO Box 537, Boothbay, ME *04537-0537*
MISS Kristin B . . . .
MR Brian D . . . .
MR Jonathan W . . . .

Sage MR & MRS Nathaniel McL JR (Dorothy A Blair) Pemb'51.San.Mit'41
☎ (401) 789-6307 . . PO Box 3726, 957 Saugatucket Rd, Peace Dale, RI *02883*

Sagendorph MR Frank E 3d—M.P.'31.Pa'36
☎ (610) 642-6336 . . 225 Elbow Lane, Haverford, PA *19041*

Sailer MR & MRS Christopher A (C Christina Berg) Louis'91.Pa'73 . . . . | ☎ (502) 896-4774 315 Jarvis Lane, Louisville, KY *40207*
MR Christopher A JR—at Brown . . . .
JUNIORS MR Samuel C—at Middlesex . . . .

Sailer MISS Jacqueline—Sth'85.StJ'90
see Dilatory Domiciles

Sailer MR & MRS John JR (Pamela W Steffens) Wil.Pa'65 . . . . | ☎ (302) 654-1213 2502 Willard St, Wilmington, DE *19806*
JUNIORS MR John 3d . . . .

Sailer MR Joseph—Del'91
☎ (302) 324-1508 . . 509 Cherry St, New Castle, DE *19720*

Saint MR & MRS Kelsey Y (Elizabeth C Marsh) Y'35
☎ (301) 925-7326 . . Collington 3111, 10450 Lottsford Rd, Mitchellville, MD *20721*

Saint-Amand DR & MRS Nathan E (Cynthia W Chisholm) Sth'59.Rc.B.Ri.Bgt.Fic.Fiy.Cly. Duke'59.Duke'63 . . . . | of ☎ (212)722-7522 2 E 88 St, New York, NY *10128*
MISS Elizabeth . . . .
MR Alexander . . . . | ☎ (914) 666-2518 Guard Hill Farm, Bedford Hills, NY *10507*

St Claire REV & MRS E Kyle JR (Teresa A M Whidden) Pe.Myf.Hav'68.EpiscDiv'71.Y'74 . . . | 1650 Franklynn Dv, Furlong, PA *18925*
MISS Ann W . . . .
MR Elbert K 3d . . . . |

St Claire REV & MRS Elbert K (Schmidt—Jean Maxwell) Syr'50.Me.P'41.EpiscDiv'43 . . . . | ☎ (610) 658-0220 The Quadrangle H101, 3300 Darby Rd, Haverford, PA *19041*
MISS Helène M Schmidt—Fla'86—at
☎ (610) 688-5683 . . 796 Godfrey Rd, Haverford, PA *19041* . . . . |

St Georges MR & MRS Joseph F (Ruffing—Patricia McIlvain) Duke'62.Yn.Y'48 . . . . | ☎ (610) 458-1945 164 Finney Rd, Glenmoore, PA *19343*
MISS Anne S Ruffing—Brdgwtr'91—at
☎ (540) 828-4641 . . 112 Old River Rd, Bridgewater, VA *22812* . . . .
MR James McI Ruffing—CarnM'89—at
☎ (215) 321-1823 . . 7505 Spruce Mill Dv, Yardley, PA *19067* . . . . |

St Goar DR & MRS Walter T (Anne F Godley) Cy.Sb.Chi.Cal'44.Roch'49 . . . . | ☎ (617) 232-5775 21 Sargent Crossway, Brookline, MA *02146*
MISS Elizabeth—at 2232 La Mesa Court, Davis, CA *95616* . . . . |

St John MR & MRS Fordyce B JR (Lisa S Polhemus) P'45
☎ (203) 966-5440 . . 62 Norholt Dv, New Canaan, CT *06840*

St John MR & MRS Warren Jackson (Irma Claire Frech) Brenau'65.GaTech'59 ⚓ . . . . | ☎ (205) 967-5556 3833 Williamsburg Circle, Birmingham, AL *35243*
MISS Mary C . . . .
MISS Susanna H . . . .
MR Warren J JR . . . . |

Salant MRS Robert S (Marilyn Moffat) Pr.
☎ (516) 671-1002 . . Ludlam Lane, Locust Valley, NY *11560*

Salas MRS Caroline W (Caroline W Trevor) Ws'78.Mb.Pr.Cly.Dc.Ht. . . . . | ☎ (516) 922-0620 367 Split Rock Rd, Syosset, NY *11791-1508*
JUNIORS MISS Caroline T . . . . |

Salas MR Peter E—Mb.H'78
☎ (516) 466-3059 . . 8 W Mill Dv, Great Neck, NY *11021*

Salem MR & MRS David A (Eleanor B Shannon) Dth'79.H'84.Hn.Mid'78.H'83
☎ (603) 643-2004 . . 6 Rope Ferry Rd, Hanover, NH *03755*

Salembier MRS Harold P (Townsend—Anita van L Higgins) Pr.Mds.Cly . . .of
☎ (516) 759-1734 . . 2 Wood Lane, Locust Valley, NY *11560-1629*
☎ (212) 988-8036 . . 116 E 66 St, New York, NY *10021*

Saliba MR & MRS Robert G (Jenifer Newhall) Pa'66.Nu'69.Wes'62.Cr'65 . . . . | ☎ (201) 895-4823 1 Andrews Rd, Randolph, NJ *07869*
MISS Lynne N—CtCol'94 . . . .
JUNIORS MR George N . . . . |

Salisbury MR D Austin JR—Dyc.Nu'84 . . of
  ☎ (212) 777-2121 . . 20 E 9 St, New York, NY *10003*
  ☎ (516) 324-5731 . . 105 Main St, East Hampton, NY *11937*

Salisbury MR & MRS John F (Nancy W Furlong)   of ☎ (203)322-3330
  Stan'55.VillaN'52.Pa'58 . . . .   "Springbank"
  MISS Adrienne H—Duke'87—at   484 Old Long Ridge
  ☎ (212) 663-0284 . . 155 W 95 St, Apt 2,   Rd, North Stamford,
  New York, NY *10025* . . . .   CT *06903*
  MISS Philippa R . . . .   ☎ (208) 622-3330
  MISS Anne W—Tufts'87.Pa'91—at   617-20 Wildflower,
  ☎ (212) 663-0284 . . 155 W 95 St, Apt 2,   Sun Valley, ID
  New York, NY *10025* *83353*
  MISS Eugenia F—Bost'88—at ☎ (212) 663-0284
  155 W 95 St, Apt 2, New York, NY *10025* . . . .

Salisbury MRS Lorraine L (Burke—Salisbury—Colvin—
  Lorraine Littlefield)
  ☎ (561) 655-0704 . . 1001 S Flagler Dv, Apt 201, West Palm Beach,
  FL *33401*

Salisbury MRS Robert E (Kirkland—Nancy L Hoadley) B.
  ☎ (561) 231-7940 . . 191 Silver Moss Dv, John's Island, Vero Beach,
  FL *32963-3317*

Sallee MISS Caroline S—Col'91
  40 E 94 St, New York, NY *10128*

Sallee MRS George J (Suzanne D Rumbough)
  ☎ (561) 582-7468 . . Newport Place 404, 4735 NW 7 Court, Lantana,
  FL *33462*

Sallee MR & MRS John C (Esther S Lee) Rcn.Va'67 . | ☎ (011-63-2)
  MR Bradford C   818-2397
  JUNIORS MISS Samantha L . . . .   1155 Tamarind Rd,
  JUNIORS MR George L . . . .   Dasmarinas Village,
                                             Makati, Metro
                                             Manila, Philippines

Salm MR H Alexander—Un.T.Dth'41
  ☎ (914) 351-2417 . . 25 Tower Hill Loop, Tuxedo Park, NY *10987*

Salmons MR & MRS Richard W JR (Angela H Dillard)
  StMarys'82.Cw.W&L'81
  ☎ (803) 556-8337 . . 18 Logan St, Charleston, SC *29401*

Salsbery MR Eric B (Otto H) . . . . Married at Grindstone Island, NY
  Anderson MISS Julie A (Terry N) . . . . Jly 6'96

Salsbury MR & MRS Richard L (Miller—Veronica M Hughes) Fcg.P'42
  ☎ (412) 963-0871 . . 1120 Fox Chapel Rd, Pittsburgh, PA *15238*

Salsbury MR & MRS William B (Hepburn—Barbara Cooper) Fcg.
  ☎ (941) 366-6033 . . 1762 Bay St, Sarasota, FL *34236*

Salter MRS Margaret S (Margaret C Stage)   ☎ (706) 324-0249
  Ws'62.Cr'64 . . . .   2902 Madden Dv,
  MR James G—P'86.Stan'87—at Carrer Cardedeo   Columbus, GA
  24, 08023 Barcelona, Spain *31906*
  MR Michael E—Stan'90.GaSt'96—at
  2392 Melinda Dv NE, Atlanta, GA *30345* . . . . .
  MR Benjamin T—Ga'91—at 2392 Melinda Dv
  NE, Atlanta, GA *30345* . . . .

Saltonstall MR David P (Endicott P JR) . . . . . Married at Palm Springs, CA
  Brumley MISS Eva . . . . May 21'94

Saltonstall MR & MRS Endicott P JR (Cabot—Susan   231 Chestnut Hill
  M Brock) Bost'74.Ne'66 . . . .   Rd, Chestnut Hill,
  MSRS Charles D, John N & Peter E—at   MA *02167*
  ☎ (602) 438-2592 . . 4424 E Baseline Rd,
  Apt 1181, Phoenix, AZ *85440* . . . .
  JUNIORS MR Matthew P Cabot . . . .
  JUNIORS MR Christopher C Cabot . . . .

Saltonstall MR & MRS John L 2d (Maria L Schubert) Rose'82.Mass'83
  ☎ (908) 604-9768 . . 148 E Spring Brook Dv, Gillette, NJ *07933*

Saltonstall MR & MRS Robert (Hannah G Ayer) H.'33
  Carleton-Willard Village, Essex 77, 100 Old Billerica Rd, Bedford,
  MA *01730*

Saltonstall MR & MRS William L (Jane Chandler) V'51.H'49
  ☎ (508) 526-7111 . . 388 Summer St, Manchester, MA *01944*

Saltsman MR & MRS James A (E Brooks Johnstone) Cvc.Sl.W&L'39
  ☎ (301) 654-3481 . . 8101 Connecticut Av, Apt N307, Chevy Chase,
  MD *20815*

Saltus MR Ralph W H
  ☎ (415) 726-1392 . . PO Box 2140, El Granada, CA *94018*

Saltus MISS Sarah
  ☎ (203) 869-2859 . . 43 Maple Av, Greenwich, CT *06830*

Saltus MR & MRS Seymour S (Sarah A McDougall)   ☎ (908) 879-6281
  Cc.Yn.Y'63 . . . .   89 Pleasant Hill Rd,
  MR Edward A—Rens'94—at ☎ (201) 216-0464   Chester, NJ *07930*
  108—14 St, Apt 1RW, Hoboken, NJ *07030* . . . .

Saltzman MRS Charles E (Sierstorpff—Waycott—McCormick—
  Clotilde Knapp) Cly.Un.
  ☎ (212) PL9-5655 . . 30 E 62 St, New York, NY *10021*

Salyard MISS (DR) Lann B—Mit'78.Pa'83
  ☎ (610) 645-0767 . . Hunter House 405, 449 W Montgomery Av,
  Haverford, PA *19041*

Salyard MR & MRS Robert R (Ann B Barriger) Ws'52.Me.Nw'47.H'51
  ☎ (610) 642-4020 . . 530 Mulberry Lane, Haverford, PA *19041*

Saman MR & MRS Alain-Constantin (Anita E Alig)
  Pa'75.Rc.K.Cly.Pa'66 . . of
  ☎ (212) 860-5655 . . 115 E 87 St, Apt 7D, New York, NY *10128*
  ☎ (860) 542-5112 . . "Torrington House" 127 Old Goshen Rd, Norfolk,
  CT *06058*

Sammis MR & MRS Jesse F 3d (Jean McA Tilt)   of ☎ (203)661-5143
  Rcn.StL'60 . . . .   432 Round Hill Rd,
  MISS Suzanne Tilt—Vt'91 . . . .   Greenwich, CT
  MR Jesse F 4th *06831*
                                             ☎ (802) 728-9122
                                             "Stoneleigh"
                                             Green Mountain
                                             Stock Farm,
                                             Randolph, VT *05060*

Sample MR & MRS Charles W (Jana Bowerman)   ☎ (847) 835-4062
  Gchr'59.Md'69.JHop'58.Ch'59 . . . .   706 Country Lane,
  MISS Jana B—at Wellesley Hills, MA . . . .   Glencoe, IL *60022*
  MR Charles F—at Boston, MA . . . .

Sample MR & MRS Joseph S (Willing—Miriam Tyler) Stph'40.Y'45 . . of
  ☎ (406) 252-8662 . . 606 Highland Park Dv, Billings, MT *59102-1909*
  ☎ (941) 263-2911 . . "Pirates Landing" 940 Admiralty Parade E,
  Naples, FL *34102*

Sampson MRS Susan J (Borneman—Susan J Sampson) Cin'69.Qc.
  ☎ (606) 581-2419 . . 312 Garrard St, Covington, KY *41011*

Samuel MR & MRS Aderton P (Elizabeth A Mullen) StL'59 . . . . | ☎ (910) 686-0376 2 Surf Court, Figure Eight Island, Wilmington, NC 28405
MR Christopher R . . . .

Samuel MRS Edward (Hutchinson—Anne Hurd) Me. . . . . | ☎ (610) 527-4449 1062 Lancaster Av, Apt 722, Rosemont, PA 19010-1552
MR Mahlon Hutchinson 3d—Me. . . . .

Samuel MRS James R (Louise G Primm)
☎ (314) 862-1305 . . 8109 Stratford Dv, St Louis, MO 63105
Samuel MR & MRS James R JR (M Jane C Murphy) Mar'vil'73.StL'68 . . . . | ☎ (314) 993-4145 2800 Stonington Place, St Louis, MO 63131
JUNIORS MISS Clara P . . . .
JUNIORS MISS Catherine L . . . .
Sanchez-Elia MR Diego
432—15 St, Santa Monica, CA 90402-2232
Sanden MR & MRS Robert V (White—Diana St John Rose) WmJewel'51 . . . . | of ☎ (847)234-6641 685 Burton Dv, Lake Forest, IL 60045
MISS Elizabeth A St J . . . . | 2526 Muir Circle, West Palm Beach, FL 33414

Sander MRS Cintra Carter (Huber—Cintra H Carter) PhilaArt'51
☎ (904) 285-7950 . . 24618 Deer Trace Dv, Ponte Vedra Beach, FL 32082-2112
Sanders MR Algernon W R . . see H T Snowdon JR
Sanders MR & MRS Cameron H JR (M Elizabeth Tucker) V'57.Mt.Ncd.Ken'55 . . . . | ☎ (202) 362-9476 3117—35 St NW, Washington, DC 20016
MISS Marcia B—Br'89—at U of Pa . . . .
MR Cameron H 3d—Y'88 . . . .
MR Nicholas T—Br'93 . . . .
Sanders MISS Catherine Legaré (David L) . . . . Born at Mobile, AL Jan 5'96
Sanders MR & MRS David I (Hatfield—H Celeste Pogue) Eyc.Miami'53 ⚓ . . . . | ☎ (513) 561-7475 6405 Given Rd, Cincinnati, OH 45243
MISS Susan E . . . .
MR David I JR . . . .
Sanders MR & MRS David L (Elizabeth P Stevens) Char'ton'85.At.SoAla'79.SoAla'82
☎ (334) 433-5097 . . 202 George St, Mobile, AL 36604
Sanders MR & MRS David R (Laurie T Shields) Ty'90.Ty'91.Ty'90.Ty'95
☎ (210) 828-5285 . . 217 Alta Av, San Antonio, TX 78209
Sanders JUNIORS MR Henry C C B . . see H T Snowdon JR
Sanders MISS Joan Gillespie (William B 3d) . . . . Born May 4'94
Sanders MISS Marietta P C . . see H T Snowdon JR
Sanders MRS Terence R B (Deborah Donoghue)
☎ (011-44-171) 589-4756 . . 124 Cranmer Court, Whiteheads Grove, London SW3 3HE, England
Sanders MR & MRS Theodore R (Elizabeth D Parker) G.Buf'50
☎ (716) 886-7653 . . 50 Cleveland Av, Buffalo, NY 14222
Sanders MR & MRS William B 3d (Julia H Gillespie) Denis'86.Cvc.So'86
☎ (301) 949-5350 . . 3901 Saul Rd, Kensington, MD 20895
Sanders MASTER William Barlow 4th (William B 3d) . . . Born May 10'96

Sanderson MISS Alexandra E—Cr'86
☎ (607) 266-0133 . . 4 The Strand, Ithaca, NY 14850
Sanderson MR & MRS James A (Mary G Esty) Dth'55 . . . . | of ☎ (607)257-6234 3 Lisa Lane, Ithaca, NY 14850
MR Nicholas B—at ☎ (508) 741-8943 2 Cheval Av, Salem, MA 01970 . . . . | ☎ (941) 964-2828 PO Box 83, 251 Park Av, Boca Grande, FL 33921
Sanderson MRS Lloyd B (Ardelle V Kloss)
☎ (518) 523-3073 . . 9 Marcy Rd, Lake Placid, NY 12948
Sandman MR & MRS J Bertheau (Becky S Baldra) Cal'70.Cp.Cal'70 . . . . | ☎ (209) 727-5738 Box 371, Lockeford, CA 95237
MISS Anna K . . . .
MISS Molly S . . . .
MISS Nellie M . . . .
MR Mark C . . . .
Sandreuter MR Gregg E—Ham'84.H'88 . . see C R Smith
Sandreuter MISS Heidi—Wms'92 . . see C R Smith
Sandreuter MR Jeffrey R—LakeF'88 . . see C R Smith
Sands MR A Jay C—Me.Pa'48
☎ (610) 525-7359 . . 359 Wyldhaven Rd, Rosemont, PA 19010
Sands MR & MRS Benjamin F (Dana E Allen) Y'83.Nu'90.Geo'74
☎ (914) 631-3530 . . 131 Neperan Rd, Tarrytown, NY 10591
Sands MISS Elizabeth—Swth'75
☎ (410) 964-6408 . . 5191 Columbia Rd, Columbia, MD 21044
Sands MR & MRS Geoffrey K (Elena Kugler) Aht'87.Y'91.Sa.Y.'84.Y'92
☎ (212) 977-9754 . . 45 W 60 St, Apt 8H, New York, NY 10023
Sands MR & MRS James (MacCoy—Adèle G Griffin) V'41.VillaN'70.Ph.R.Sa.Fw.Mt.Ncd.Bow'35
☎ (610) 459-3270 . . "Sunnyside" 1452 W Baltimore Pike, Wawa, PA 19063
Sands MR & MRS James JR (Barbara L Beckley) Pa'78.Wid'74
☎ (610) 642-1805 . . 441 Berkley Rd, Haverford, PA 19041
Sands MR John K—Pr.NCar'48
☎ (212) 744-0271 . . 300 E 75 St, Apt 15K, New York, NY 10021
Sands MR & MRS John O (Geales Gavin) LSU'75.Ty'71.Del'73.GeoW'80
☎ (757) 220-1448 . . 159 Dennis Dv, Williamsburg, VA 23185
Sands MRS Joseph E 3d (C Melissa Marsh)
☎ (717) 322-2751 . . "Bald Eagle's Nest" 1145 Four Mile Dv, Williamsport, PA 17701
Sands MISS Lily Ashenden (Benjamin F) . . . . Born at New York, NY Jun 10'96
Sands MRS Patricia P (Patricia Pulling) V'53
☎ (516) 922-0872 . . 33 Yellowcote Rd, Oyster Bay, NY 11771
Sands MRS Robert J (Otis—Doris B Livingston) . . . | ☎ (610) MI2-5309 1123 Maplecrest Circle, Gladwyne, PA 19035
MR Robert J JR—Gettys'77.VillaN'79—at ☎ (514) 499-1480 . . 3 Ontario Place, Montreal, Quebec H3G 1E9, Canada . . . .
MRS Blair L (Browne—Blair L Sands) . . . .
Sands MR & MRS S Stevens JR (Rosa H L Beckwith) NCar'65.Md.Gv.Mv.Ncd.JHop'69 . . . . | ☎ (410) 833-7035 "Sheldrake House" Mantua Mill Rd, Glyndon, MD 21071
MR S Stevens 3d—Rol'92 . . . .
MR W Page—at Rollins . . . .

Sands MR & MRS William D (Henny E van Beek) | 314 Ardmore Court,
UAmericas'70.NatL'92.Tulsa'79 . . . . | Vernon Hills, IL
MISS Jean P. . . . . | *60061*
MR William D JR . . . . |
MR R Blake . . . . |

Sanford MISS Camilla R—Occ'78
☎ (415) 921-7900 . . PO Box 274, Ross, CA *94957-0274*
Sanford MR & MRS Lawrence H (Mary Patience Rood) Ariz'50.Cr'55
☎ (513) 931-2295 . . 9852 Lorelei Dv, Cincinnati, OH *45231-2608*
Sanford MR & MRS Terry (Margaret R Knight)
NCar'41.Cos.NCar'39.NCar'46
☎ (919) 489-0700 . . 2500 Auburn St, Durham, NC *27706*

Sanger MR & MRS Christopher D (Jane F Biggs) Bates'83
☎ (302) 892-9664 . . 503 Wooddale Rd, Wilmington, DE *19807-2445*
Sanger MRS Richard H (Marion Child) Cvc.Sl.
☎ (301) 229-7137 . . 4425 Boxwood Rd, Bethesda, MD *20816-1817*
Sanger MR Richard H JR—Ty'67.Va'73 . . . . | ☎ (409) 762-7802
MR Patrick M . . . . | 2908 Av O,
| Galveston, TX
| *77550*
Sanger MR & MRS Richard H 3d (Anne T Rockage) PtPark'90
☎ (804) 360-7463 . . 2801 Ashley Glen Dv, Richmond, VA *23233*
Sanger MR & MRS Wilson (Adèle R Wilson)
☎ (508) 785-0047 . . 46 Farm St, Dover, MA *02030*
San Román MR & MRS José L (Pauline F Marshall) | Calle Adelfas 53,
Madrid'56 . . . . | Monteprincipe,
MISS Lola . . . . | Boadilla del Monte,
MR José F . . . . | 28668 Madrid, Spain
MR David . . . . |
MR Jacabo . . . . |
Sant MR & MRS John T (Almira S Baldwin) StL'82.Cy.Nd.P'54.H'57
☎ (314) 994-0340 . . 9 Ridgewood Rd, St Louis, MO *63124*
Santa Maria MR & MRS Ernesto D (Josephine A | ☎ (215) CH7-5716
Swope) . . . . | 180 E Willow Grove
MR Stephen M . . . . | Av, Philadelphia,
| PA *19118*
Santry MR & MRS Peter T (Marilyn J Willoughby) P'85.Ny.Unn.Wms'81
☎ (704) 365-9357 . . 4213 Dumbarton Place, Charlotte, NC *28211*
Santy MR & MRS Albert C JR (Stefani Glasgow) Duke'71.Duke'71
☎ (301) 490-0453 . . 9703 Polished Stone, Columbia, MD *21046*
Santy MR & MRS Ross C (Lucia L Elmore) | ☎ (207) 439-4649
P'60.H'63 . . . . | 42 Goodwin Rd,
MISS Leigh—at U of Cal Santa Cruz . . . . | Kittery Point, ME
| *03904*
Sarabia MRS McVoy (Fellowes—Conger—Jean D McVoy) LakeF'64
☎ (303) 777-9655 . . 480 S Marion P'kway, Apt 1904A, Denver,
CO *80209*
Sargeant MR & MRS Ben J (Katherine E Moon) Wash'53.Ncd.Va'52
☎ (804) 295-3528 . . 2691 Free Union Rd, Charlottesville, VA *22901*
Sargent MR & MRS Christopher S (Anne MacGaffin) | ☎ (301) 986-0773
Cvc.Mt.Sl.Wms'62 . . . . | 11 W Melrose St,
JUNIORS MISS Thayer A . . . . | Chevy Chase, MD
JUNIORS MR Christopher S 3d . . . . | *20815*
Sargent MR E Rotan . . . . Died at
Haverford, PA Jan 28'96
Sargent MRS Edward C (Nancy B Lawrence) Cv.
513 Fearrington Post, Pittsboro, NC *27312*

Sargent MRS F Porter (Jane K Culver) V'45-4 . . . . . | ☎ (617) 232-5645
MISS Cornelia E—Sth'92 . . . . | 26 Weybridge Rd,
MISS Hannah C H—at Springfield, MA . . . . | Brookline, MA
MISS Roslyn . . . . | *02146*
Sargent MR & MRS Fitzwilliam (Mercedes Muguiro) | of ☎ (011-34-1)
Sbc.H'38.Va'41 . . . . | 247-2885
MR Antonio M . . . . | Cruzada 4, 28013
| Madrid, Spain
| ☎ (508) 526-4438
| 202 Beach St,
| Manchester, MA
| *01944*
Sargent MR & MRS Francis W (Jessie Fay) Tv.Mit'39
64 Farm St, Dover, MA *02030*
Sargent MRS George Lee (Hester Lloyd Jones) Cy.Sm.
☎ (617) 723-7233 . . 300 Commercial St, Boston, MA *02109*
Sargent MR & MRS Hugh A A (Wetherill—Cheryl | ☎ (215) 542-8985
Repp) Sg.Ph.H'56.Camb'57.Pa'60 . . . . | 812 Brushtown Rd,
MISS Ashley F Wetherill—at Beaver Coll . . . | Lower Gwynedd,
JUNIORS MISS Leason R Wetherill—at | PA *19002*
Germantown Acad . . . . |
Sargent MR & MRS Ignatius (Frances W Moffat) | ☎ (202) 667-7931
Rcn.Mt.Cvc.Sl. . . . . | 2344 California St
MISS Sarah M—at Heinestrasse 14-11, | NW, Washington,
1020 Vienna, Austria . . . . | DC *20008*
Sargent MR & MRS James C (Rebecca P Jackson) | ☎ (212) YU8-8248
Chr.Lm.Cs.Va'38.Va'40 . . . . | 310 E 84 St,
MISS Sarah B—Ws'79—at ☎ (804) 971-3575 | New York, NY
521½ N 1 St, Charlottesville, VA *22902* . . . . . | *10028*
Sargent MR & MRS James C JR (Elizabeth McM Godley) Y'71.Va'74
☎ (610) 347-0239 . . PO Box 610, Unionville, PA *19375*
Sargent MISS Jessie (Flynn—Gorman—Jessie | ☎ (401) 841-5667
Sargent) Bost'72 . . . . | 330 Indian Av,
MISS Kristen S Gorman . . . . | Middletown, RI
| *02842*
Sargent MRS John A (Shirley B Owen)
☎ (203) 661-7838 . . 2 Rockwood Lane Spur, Greenwich, CT *06830*
Sargent MR & MRS John T (Kelly—Elizabeth Nichols) Mich'62.C.K . . .of
☎ (516) 726-4554 . . Crescent Av, PO Box 32, Water Mill, NY *11976*
☎ (212) 486-1531 . . 5 Beekman Place, New York, NY *10022*
Sargent MRS Ruth S (Ruth V Sargent)
☎ (610) LA5-4692 . . 108 Charles Dv, Apt D1, Bryn Mawr, PA *19010*
Sargent MR & MRS Thomas A (Allison D Ijams) Al.Fic.Conn'82
☎ (617) 235-5302 . . The Waterway, Wellesley Farms, MA *02181*
Sarkowsky MR & MRS Herman (Faye V Mondschein) UWash'49
☎ (206) 328-6022 . . 917 Harvard Av E, Seattle, WA *98102*
Sarpy MISS Courtney A—Man'vl'61
☎ (504) 861-3519 . . 455 Walnut St, New Orleans, LA *70118*
Sarran MRS Wallace E SR (M Estelle Rapp)
☎ (513) 539-7070 . . 114 Northwestern Av, Monroe, OH *45050-1131*
Sarran MR & MRS William R (Janet S Walker) | 808 Poplar Av,
Miami'77.Miami'76 . . . . | Terrace Park, OH
JUNIORS MISS Lisa M . . . . | *45174*
JUNIORS MISS Jennifer A . . . . |

Sasso MRS Leonard P (Anna W Bockius) Gv.Pkg. . . ☎ (610) 983-9089
MISS Josephine A—Srb.Rd.—at Anderson Place
☎ (212) 348-8668 . . 205 E 95 St, Apt 10D, Farm, Valley Park
New York, NY *10128* . . . . Rd, Phoenixville,
MR Michael W—Rd.—at ☎ (011-39-6) 687-5669 PA *19460*
Piazza Rondanini 52, 00186 Rome, Italy . . . . . .
MR Anthony B—at ☎ (516) 267-6108
Box 1893, 67 Cross H'way, Amagansett, NY
11930 . . . .
MR Paul N—at ☎ (520) 751-9428
6830 E 3 St, Tucson, AZ *85710* . . . .
MR Alfred B—at ☎ (302) 892-2951
927 Centre Rd, Wilmington, DE *19807* . . . .

Satterthwaite MISS Ann—Rdc'53.Y'60
☎ (202) 342-0203 . . 1615—34 St NW, Washington, DC *20007*

Satterthwaite MR & MRS Franklin B JR (Goodwin—Martha L Werenfels)
Cr'84.P'65.Y'68.Y'75
☎ (401) 461-9806 . . 81 Strathmore Rd, Cranston, RI *02905*

Satterthwaite MR & MRS Franklin Bache (Emily Vaux Cresson)
Plg.Snc.Lm.Ht.Rv.Cw.Ds.Cly.Ncd.Cda.Dh.P'38.Nu'49 . . of
☎ (212) 935-0828 . . 439 E 51 St, New York, NY *10022-6473*
☎ (819) 842-2620 . . "Willow Wood Cottage" North Hatley,
Quebec J0B 2C0, Canada
☎ (803) 671-6821 . . Sea Pines Plantation, Lighthouse Villa 8,
Hilton Head Island, SC *29928*

Satterthwaite COL (RET) George 2d—USA.Pa'57. ☎ (301) 292-2312
JHop'65 . . . . 513 Holly Rd,
MR Livingston L—Cr'82.Stan'88 . . . . Ft Washington, MD
20744

Satterthwaite MR & MRS Henry B (Jonson—Anne of ☎ (203)854-5229
W Stambaugh) Cl'62.Yn.Y'64 . . . . 109 Maywood Rd,
MR James D—Colg'90 West Norwalk, CT
MISS Dana A Jonson—Fairf'95 . . . . *06850*
MR Randolph S Jonson—HWSth'94 . . . . . . ☎ (011-353-65)
74351
"Luogh South"
Coast Rd, Doolin,
Co Clare, Ireland

Satterthwaite MR & MRS James B (Natica Bates) Rdc'51.Chi.Y'37.Camb'39
☎ (207) 865-3856 . . "Tidebrook" 38 Bartol Island Rd, Freeport,
ME *04032*

Satterthwaite MR Sheafe—Va'62
☎ (802) 823-7290 . . North Pownal, VT, PO Box 596, Williamstown,
MA *01267*

Satterthwaite MRS T Wilkinson (Anne T Stewart) Cly.
☎ (802) 254-5684 . . RR 2, Box 1008, East-West Rd, Putney, VT *05346*

Saul MR & MRS B Francis 2d (Elizabeth Patricia of ☎ (301)652-2633
English) Mt.Cvc.B.Sl.VillaN'54.Va'57 ⚓ . . . . 1 Quincy St,
MISS Elizabeth W—at 3194 Alika Av, Honolulu, Chevy Chase, MD
HI *96817* *20815*
MISS Patricia E . . . . ☎ (410) 639-2587
"Bungay Hill"
Chestertown, MD
21620

Saulnier MRS Woodcock (Frances E Woodcock) Temp'64.Me.
☎ (610) 296-8898 . . 423 Waynesbrooke Rd, Berwyn, PA *19312*

Saunders MRS Arnold C 3d (Furrer—Patricia ☎ (216) 541-4123
Crofts) . . . . One Bratenahl Place,
MR Arnold C 4th . . . . Bratenahl, OH
MR John L *44108*

Saunders MR Benjamin H—Dth'92.Wyo'95
☎ (307) 742-0186 . . 471 N 9 St, Apt 1, Laramie, WY *82070*

Saunders MR & MRS Donald H (Eleanor F Hall) of ☎ (202)363-0076
GeoW'29.Il.Ht.Dcw.Cda.Dar. . . . . 4922 Quebec St
MISS Patricia G—Il. ⚓—at ☎ (202) 244-0194 NW, Washington,
4616 Sedgwick St NW, Washington, DC *20016*. DC *20016*
☎ (401) 847-4683
42 Elm St,
Newport, RI *02840*

Saunders MR & MRS E Randolph (Amy E Gaffney) Rol'93
☎ (508) 257-6154 . . PO Box 466, Siasconset, MA *02564*

Saunders MISS Elenore Holden (E Randolph) . . . . Born at
Hyannis, MA Jan 19'96

Saunders MRS Harriet M (Harriet A Martin) . . . . . . ☎ (516) 759-3301
MISS Sydney F—at ☎ (617) 227-5381 PO Box 120,
63 W Cedar St, Boston, MA *02114* . . . . Locust Valley, NY
11560

Saunders MR & MRS Jesse D (Marin—Rikki D "The Hollow"
Morley) Cts.Roan'70 . . . . 227 Jackson Rd,
JUNIORS MISS Carmen R Marin . . . . Cochranville, PA
19330

Saunders MR & MRS Morton T (Deirdre L Dixon) Me.Gi.Cry.Wms'57
☎ (610) MI2-7535 . . 112 Old Gulph Rd, Gladwyne, PA *19035-1615*

Saunders MISS Paige W—see R E Stetson JR

Saunders MR & MRS Preston H (Rebecca J Bulkley)
Ws'61.D.Sm.Dth'52.H'55
☎ (617) 326-5148 . . 480 Summer St, Westwood, MA *02090*

Saunders MISS Sally Love (Craigie—Sally L Saunders) GeoWms'65
☎ (415) 673-7213 . . 2030 Vallejo St, Apt 501, San Francisco,
CA *94123-4854*

Saunders MR & MRS Stuart M (Anne B Lukens) ☎ (401) 783-0939
V'46 . . . . 2464 Commodore
MISS Anne M—at 3509 Dixon Cove Dv, Perry H'way,
Ft Collins, CO *80526* . . . . Wakefield, RI *02879*
MR Douglas S—at 2 Church St, Warren, RI
02885 . . . .

Saunders MR & MRS Stuart T JR (Susanna K Terrell) ☎ (610) 642-0888
CtCol'67.BMr'74.Ph.Me.Ln.NCar'64.Va'67 . . . 411 N Rose Lane,
MR Stuart T III—at Brown Haverford, PA
JUNIORS MR Charles T—at Trinity *19041*

Saunders MR & MRS Thomas A III (M Jordan of ☎ (516)671-4143
Horner) VaCmth'64.Ln.Pr.Ri.Cly.Vmi'58.Va'67 180 Piping Rock Rd,
MR Thomas A IV—Cc.—at ☎ (212) 734-2752 Locust Valley, NY
176 E 77 St, New York, NY *10021* *11560*
☎ (212) 288-1236
130 E 75 St,
New York, NY
10021

Saunders MR & MRS Thomas R (Margaret E Jennings) Pa'50.Me.Swth'49 . . . .
MISS Katharine G—CtCol'88—at 2010 Hamilton St, Abington, PA *19001* . . . .
MR James J—Me.CtCol'91—at 506 Maplewood Av, Wayne, PA *19087* . . . .
MR Samuel V L
☎ (610) MU8-2868
15 Fairview Dv, St Davids, PA *19087*

Saunders MR & MRS W Grier (Vanaman—Patricia A Chamberlin) GwynM'53.Me.Sdg.Rich'59 . . . . .
MISS Patricia A Vanaman . . . .
☎ (610) 942-2242
Glengelly Farm, RD 1, Honey Brook, PA *19344*

Saunderson MR & MRS Alexander (Mdivani—Louise A Van Alen) Rcn.Cly.Camb'38
☎ (805) 969-2646 . . Birnam Wood Golf Club, 1984 Inverness Lane, Santa Barbara, CA *93108*

Saurel MRS Paul (Louise R Hoguet) . . . .
MISS Christine . . . .
☎ (212) 744-1429
152 E 81 St, New York, NY *10028*

Saurel MR & MRS Paul L (Leonora de Sola) SL'68.K.Cly.P'64.Cl'68 . . . .
MISS Leonora—at French Am Int'l Sch . . . .
JUNIORS MISS Gabriela L—at Calvin Geneva . . . .
☎ (011-41-22) 736-1890
6 Rte du Guignard, 1223 Cologny, Geneva, Switzerland

Sause MR & MRS John W JR (Julia B Browne) Gi.Elk.Mv.Cda.Wms'55.Va'58 . . . .
MR R Barkley—Gi. . . . .
☎ (410) 758-1775
202 S Liberty St, PO Box 70, Centreville, MD *21617-0070*

Sauvayre MR & MRS Pascal E (Sarah C Chubb) H.'82.Ford'81
☎ (212) 874-2652 . . 2166 Broadway, Apt 20A, New York, NY *10024*

Savage MR & MRS Arthur V (Harriet B Hawes) Sth'57.C.P.'48.H'52 . . of
☎ (914) 738-1832 . . 221 Corona Av, Pelham, NY *10803-2305*
☎ (518) 576-2223 . . "All Seasons" St Huberts, NY *12943*

Savage MRS Betsy P (Betsy B Pitman)
☎ (603) 497-3918 . . 24 Portage Rd, RD 3, Goffstown, NH *03045*

Savage MR Charles C—P'64.Nu'77
☎ (212) 989-4401 . . 127 W 26 St, 1201, New York, NY *10001-6808*

Savage MRS Elizabeth O (Elizabeth M Oberschall) Geo'66.Fst.Gm. . . . .
MR Joseph F 4th—Ty'93 . . . .
MR Edmund T—Vt'95 . . . .
☎ (610) 995-2655
308 Conestoga Rd, Wayne, PA *19087*

Savage MR & MRS Ernest C JR (Sarah F Trowbridge) P'46.H'52
☎ (610) 388-6834 . . 18 McCarthy Rd, Chadds Ford, PA *19317*

Savage MR Frederick Van C—Myf.
☎ (603) 647-5948 . . 117 Avon St, Manchester, NH *03102*

Savage MRS Henry L (Mary Radclyffe Furness) Ac.
☎ (609) 924-1444 . . 210 Prospect Av, Princeton, NJ *08540*

Savage MISS Margaret L—Laf'79.Ga'82.Au.
☎ (508) 359-5042 . . 55 West St, Apt 3, Medfield, MA *02052*

Savage MR & MRS Michael D (Remp—Ann S Tweedy) Ws'69.Ri.Cs.Y'68.Geo'73
☎ (212) 223-3274 . . 400 E 52 St, Apt 15F, New York, NY *10022*

Savage MR & MRS Stephen M (Lois S Palestine) V'68.Pa'68 . . . .
MISS Meredith A . . . .
JUNIORS MR Samuel H . . . .
☎ (602) 266-6945
3002 E Manor Dv, Phoenix, AZ *85014*

Savage MR & MRS Thomas L (Patricia A Burke) Leh'84.Ty'82.Pa'88
☎ (609) 234-4726 . . 428 Paul Dv, Moorestown, NJ *08057*

Savage MR William Halsted—Un.StA.Plg.Snc. Lm.Myf.Ne.H'41
MR William H JR—Myf.—at ☎ (505) 877-8396 1856 Patton Rd SW, Albuquerque, NM *87105* . .
of ☎ (212)734-1813
333 E 68 St, New York, NY *10021*
☎ (518) 251-3816
North Woods Club, PO Box 905, Minerva, NY *12851*

Savard MR & MRS Edward L (Molly C Houston) Tufts'69.H'81.Cly.Hb.Bates'68.H'76 . . . .
JUNIORS MR Nicholas H—at Salisbury . . . .
JUNIORS MR Turner H—at St Mark's . . . .
☎ (860) 343-0625
76 Ryefield Rd, Middletown, CT *06457*

Saveri MR & MRS Guido (Catherine A Yoell) Mls'52.Bhm.Fr.SFr'47 . . . .
MISS Francesca—Cal'79 . . . .
MISS Andrea—H'84 . . . .
MR Richard A—Tex'90 . . . .
☎ (415) 563-5819
2662 Vallejo St, San Francisco, CA *94123*

Saverin MR & MRS Kenneth A (Laura M Childs) Y'76.Stan'81.Rr.Clare'76.Ford'79
☎ (203) 972-2123 . . 24 Oenoke Ridge Rd, New Canaan, CT *06840*

Saviano MRS Diana M (Diana Morris) Wheat'70.Tcy.Dar. . . . .
MR Mark J . . . .
JUNIORS MR John A . . . .
☎ (415) 668-4746
190—25 Av, San Francisco, CA *94121*

Savory MR & MRS Wallace E (Charlotte Macy) Pa'68.Curry'87.Br'64 . . . .
MISS Caroline—at Colby . . . .
MR Richard—Dick'96 . . . .
☎ (617) 784-8323
295 Mountain St, Sharon, MA *02067*

Sawers MRS William B (Amy B Hayward) Gchr'31.Ncd.
☎ (410) 377-7572 . . 830 W 40 St, Baltimore, MD *21211*

Sawin MISS Janet L—Carl'84.Tufts'93
☎ (603) 253-7780 . . "Tree Tops" Box 174, RR 1, Center Harbor, NH *03226*

Sawtelle MR Chester M—Ey.U'32
☎ (617) 631-2641 . . 1 Ft Sewall Terr, Marblehead, MA *01945*

Sawyer MR & MRS Baldwin (Dorothy A Straker) AmCM'47.JCar'82.Cv.Y'44.CTech'51 . . . .
MISS D Carol—at 3491 Edison Rd, Cleveland Heights, OH *44121* . . . .
MR Charles B 2d—at 143 Freeman St, Apt 1, Brookline, MA *02146* . . . .
☎ (216) 423-3849
"The Spruces" 1659 Berkshire Rd, Gates Mills, OH *44040*

Sawyer MISS Eloise McLaran—Dar.
☎ (314) 533-8568 . . 4440 Lindell Blvd, Apt 202, St Louis, MO *63108*

Sawyer MRS Geoffrey A (Knowles—Elizabeth C Pennock) Cy.
MR Francis E Knowles . . . .
☎ (617) 894-3101
37 Webster Rd, Weston, MA *02193*

Sawyer MR & MRS Henry W 3d (Grace P Scull) Pa'40 . . . .
MISS Rebecca—at San Francisco, CA . . . .
☎ (215) VI8-4660
3033 School House Lane, Philadelphia, PA *19144*

Sawyer MR & MRS Henry W 4th (Leila V Bickford)
☎ (215) 849-7359 . . 5444 Morris St, Philadelphia, PA *19144*
Sawyer MR & MRS Jonathan S (Elizabeth A Hennessy) Wms'87.Y'78
☎ (215) 438-1495 . . 5436 Morris St, Philadelphia, PA *19144*
Sawyer MR R Curtis JR—StAndr'76.Adelphi'85
☎ (516) 671-7850 . . Portledge School, 355 Duck Pond Rd,
Locust Valley, NY *11560*
Sawyer MRS Richard C (Sylvia Ward)
☎ (410) 778-4629 . . 221 Birch Run Rd, Chestertown, MD *21620*

Sawyer MR & MRS S Prentiss (Mary S Roach)   ☎ (847) 491-1764
Y'56.Pa'63.OState'68 . . . .   2915 Grant St,
MISS Mary Tamzin—Sth'94 . . . .   Evanston, IL *60201*

Sawyer MISS Sally B
☎ (212) 787-2960 . . 20 W 77 St, New York, NY *10024-5127*
Sawyer MR William B H (Fannette B Horner) V'40.Ts.Cy.Nyc.St.G . . .of
☎ (716) 883-2138 . . 27 Oakland Place, Buffalo, NY *14222*
☎ (508) 228-1954 . . 37 Hulbert Av, Nantucket, MA *02554*
Saxton MRS A Clifford (Catherine A Weber)
☎ (314) 725-0160 . . 816 S Hanley Rd, Apt 2B, St Louis, MO *63105*

Saxton MR & MRS A Clifford JR (Gail Suzedell)   ☎ (314) 821-7917
Ws'69.Wes'68 . . . .   12363 Federal Dv,
MISS Laura V . . . .   Des Peres, MO
                                             63131

Sayad MRS Homer E (Elizabeth F E Gentry)   ☎ (314) 367-4030
Wash'55.Nw'58.Rc.Bv.Dar. . . . .   41 Westmoreland
MISS Helene E T . . . .   Place, St Louis, MO
MR E W Gentry *63108*

Sayen DR & MRS John J (Anne E Read)   ☎ (610) 642-3680
Cspa.Rv.P'35.Pa'39 . . . .   506 Montgomery
MR John J JR—Rv.Cit'70.SCar'80—at   Av, Haverford, PA
☎ (703) 640-0304 . . 504 Broadway St, Apt 4,   *19041*
Quantico, VA *22134* . . . .

Sayler MR & MRS Bentley S (Elizabeth M Jubitz) Y'91.Y'89.Y'91
4308 Second Av NE, Seattle, WA *98105*

Sayler MR & MRS John M (Elizabeth K Miller)   of ☎ (912)233-7797
Swb'55.An.Cw.Ncd.USA'49 . . . .   4 Sandy Point Rd,
MISS Elizabeth K—Ncd.—at ☎ (202) 333-1897   Savannah, GA
4649 Q St NW, Washington, DC *20007* *31404*
                                             ☎ (941) 964-2131
                                             Boca Grande Club,
                                             GM 102,
                                             PO Box 1086,
                                             Boca Grande, FL
                                             33921

Sayler MR & MRS John M JR (Linda K Mottice) Aub'85.Cc.Cw.Ga'85
☎ (205) 918-0049 . . 2535 Aberdeen Rd, Birmingham, AL *35223*
Saylor MR & MRS Harold D 2d (Genevieve M Gutt)
M'wd'76.Au.Rv.Wt.Ll.Cw.Cspa.Dar.Dll.Mariet'80
☎ (610) 948-3222 . . Saylor Farm, 191 W Linfield-Trappe Rd, Limerick,
PA *19468*
Saylor MR & MRS Harry T (Dorothy M Johnson)
☎ (610) 353-7080 . . Dunwoody Village E209, 3500 West Chester Pike,
Newtown Square, PA *19073*

Saylor MR & MRS J Michael (M Jeanette Bullman)   ☎ (610) 527-4289
M. . . . .   315 Thornbrook Av,
JUNIORS MISS Megan M . . . .   Rosemont, PA
JUNIORS MR Todd J *19010*

Saylor MR & MRS Peter M (Caroline W Metcalf)   ☎ (215) 233-4232
Pa'63 . . . .   "Iverton"
MISS Elizabeth B . . . .   500 E Evergreen
MR Thomas S . . . .   Av, Wyndmoor, PA
                                             19038

Sayre DR & MRS Richard W (Elene R Owen)   ☎ (510) 284-2235
H'57.Cwr'65 . . . .   3500 Springhill Rd,
MISS Robin W—at Sweet Briar . . . .   Lafayette, CA *94549*
MR Owen T—at Alfred U . . . .

Sayre MR & MRS Robert W (Lucy B McCoy) Wells'39.Rc.Cs.P'37
3300 Darby Rd, Apt C902, Haverford, PA *19041*
Scaife MR Curtis S—Rr.Ariz'56
☎ (520) 299-2793 . . 4530 N Hacienda Del Sol, Tucson, AZ *85718*
Scaife MR David N—Rr.Pitt'89
☎ (412) 621-5033 . . 1444 Inverness St, Pittsburgh, PA *15217-1158*

Scaife MRS Frances G (Frances L Gilmore) V'56.Rr.   of ☎ (412)681-4097
MISS Jennie K . . . .   5023 Frew Av,
                                             Pittsburgh, PA
                                             15213
                                             ☎ (212) 472-1904
                                             2 E 67 St,
                                             New York, NY
                                             10021

Scaife MR & MRS Richard Mellon (Battle—Margaret   of ☎ (412)687-4333
Ritchie Rhea) Qns'69.Pg.Rr.Pitt'57 . . . .   613 Pitcairn Place,
MR T Westray Battle . . . .   Pittsburgh, PA
                                             15232
                                             ☎ (408) 625-0124
                                             "Wit's End"
                                             3392 Seventeen
                                             Mile Dv, PO Box
                                             1153, Pebble Beach,
                                             CA *93953-1153*

Scannell MR Christopher G—Geo'91.CathU'92
☎ (703) 960-7954 . . 5990 Richmond H'way, Apt 1109, Alexandria,
VA *22303*

Scannell MR & MRS David G (Susan M Lloyd)   of ☎ (203)966-7957
Mls'68.Ant'74.Bridgept'87.Geo'61.Cl'64 . . . . . .   110 Turtleback Rd
MISS Anik E . . . .   S, New Canaan, CT
MISS Kirsten M *06840*
                                             ☎ (508) 420-0247
                                             101 Vineyard Rd,
                                             Cotuit, MA *02635*

Scarbrough MRS Roberta Raworth (Roberta G   ☎ (601) 445-8228
Raworth) MissCol'90 . . . .   500 Orleans St,
JUNIORS MISS Ella G . . . .   Natchez, MS *39120*

Scarff DR & MRS Timothy B (Lindley L Hunter) Pitt'74.Pg.P'61.Va'65
☎ (770) 461-5376 . . 1055 Wedgewood Dv, Fayetteville, GA *30214*
Scarlett MR Cedric C F—RNC'40
☎ (610) 687-0624 . . 221 S Wayne Av, Wayne, PA *19087*
Scarlett MISS L Landon—Pa'64.Cl'67.Pa'84
☎ (615) 377-3999 . . 1133 Holly Tree Farms Rd, Brentwood, TN *37027*

Scarlett MR & MRS Lindley C (Christine P   ☎ (201) 267-9822
Kenworthy) Cent'y'69.Ty'66 . . . .   Tempe Hollow
MISS Whitney B—at Trinity . . . .   Farm, Tempe Wick
MR Beecher C—at Denison . . . .   Rd, Morristown, NJ
                                             07960

Scarlett MR & MRS William J 4th (Alexandra Story) MaryW'89
31 Eastman Farm Rd, Burlington, VT *05401*

Scattergood MR & MRS J Henry (M Augusta Russel) | ☎ (201) 635-7370
NCar'67.NCar'67 . . . . | 53 Lincoln Av,
MISS Caroline I—Tul'89—at 1219 Peniston St, | Chatham, NJ *07928*
New Orleans, LA *70115* . . . . |
MISS Katharine C . . . . |

Schabacker MR C Edgar JR
☎ (207) 967-3910 . . 27 Fairfield Dv, PO Box F, Kennebunkport,
ME *04046-1695*

Schabacker MRS C Hendy (Carole StC Hendy) . . . . | ''Sunnybank''
MISS Sarah P . . . . | 26 Christchurch Hill,
MISS Anne C . . . . | London NW3,
                                                          | England

Schabacker MR & MRS Christopher E 3d (Carol A | ☎ (914) 533-6216
Eichenholtz) Hob'65 . . . . | Wakeman Farm,
MISS Emily W . . . . | Rte 4, Box 73,
MR Christopher E 4th . . . . | South Salem, NY
JUNIORS MR John K . . . . | *10590*

Schabacker MR & MRS Peter H (Norris—Jennifer A Cowan)
Bard'65.H'68.H'72
☎ (011-44-1959) 522344 . . ''Water House'' Shoreham, Sevenoaks,
Kent TN14 7SE, England

Schade MR & MRS Wilbert C JR (Florence M Allen) . | ☎ (317) 288-8118
MR Bradford D—at ☎ (616) 582-2634 | 4501 N Wheeling
02190 Pleasant Valley Rd, Boyne City, MI *49712* | Av, Apt 2-314,
                                                 | Muncie, IN *47304*

Schaefer MR & MRS Charles H (Cornelia C Guerrini) | ☎ (215) WI7-1677
Ac.Ncd.P'52.Mit'53 . . . . | 1405 Grasshopper
MR George H—Cr'87—at ☎ (215) 957-9517 | Rd, Huntingdon
89 Ash Stoker Lane, Horsham, PA *19044* . . . . . | Valley, PA *19006*

Schaefer MR & MRS Frederic M (Imelda Avila)
Toledo'69.Cyb.Ny.Pitt'42 ⚓
☎ (207) 781-4093 . . 103 Foreside Rd, Cumberland Foreside, ME *04110*

Schaefer MRS Henry R (Betty Wilcox)
☎ (905) 871-6410 . . 373 Garrison Rd, Ft Erie, Ontario L2A 1N1,
Canada

Schaefer MRS Henry W (Nancy V Crecca) . . . . | ☎ (301) 986-8793
MISS Judith K—SantaC'89—at ☎ (970) 453-5448 | 3722 Manor Rd, Apt
PO Box 3882, Breckenridge, CO *80424* . . . . . . | 3, Chevy Chase, MD
MISS Susan A—Tufts'91 . . . . | *20815*
MR Henry C—Pratt'93 . . . . |

Schaefer MR & MRS Herman A (Montaldo—Marie-France Fosset)
Paris'63.Rcn.Mb.Pa'43.P'48
☎ (305) 661-2342 . . 4117 Santa Maria St, Coral Gables, FL *33416*

Schaefer DR & MRS (DR) John P (Helen M Schwarz)
Mich'55.Ill'57.Ill'78.Gr.C.PolyNY'55.Ill'58
7401 E Kenyon Dv, Tucson, AZ *85710*

Schaefer MR Paul S—Duke'83
☎ (410) 825-7503 . . 445 Range Rd, Baltimore, MD *21204*

Schaeffer MRS Marcia M (Marcia A Meehan) Cly. . | ☎ (212) 688-2441
MISS Georgina B—at Boston U . . . . | 485 Park Av,
                                                     | New York, NY
                                                     | *10022*

Schafer MISS Elizabeth King—Hlns'86.GeoW'93.Rr.
☎ (202) 686-3678 . . 3130 Wisconsin Av NW, Apt 801, Washington,
DC *20016*

Schafer MR & MRS Gilbert P (Frances King) Kt.Un.Tv.It.Mich'20
☎ (216) 974-8030 . . 9777 Little Mountain Rd, Mentor, OH *44060*

Schafer MR & MRS John H (Edith T Nalle) | ☎ (202) 337-4856
Mt.Cvc.Wms'48.Va'54 . . . . | 1530—30 St NW,
MISS Alison T . . . . | Washington, DC
MISS Nancy C—at Austin, TX . . . . | *20007*
MR John R—at New Orleans, LA . . . . |

Schafer MISS Margaret MacG—Colby'88.Rr.
☎ (212) 535-6885 . . 311 E 75 St, Apt 3E, New York, NY *10021*

Schafer MRS Robert (Ann Shelly) Me . . . . | 425 Glyn Wynne
MR Robert S—H'76—Box 164, Granite Springs, | Rd, Haverford, PA
NY *10527* . . . . | *19041*
MISS Elizabeth A (Vale—Elizabeth A Schafer) . . |

Schafer MR & MRS Robert K (Dorothy E Whittemore) Kt.Rr.
☎ (216) 255-3113 . . 8501 King Memorial H'way, Mentor, OH *44060*

Schaff MR & MRS David S 3d (Sarah I Hosack) Ofp.P'47
☎ (412) 741-4754 . . 605 Maple Lane, Sewickley, PA *15143*

Schaff MR & MRS John H (Mary Elder) Mont'81.DU'80
☎ (616) 956-0912 . . 1344 Winterwood Dv NE, Grand Rapids,
MI *49546*

Schaff MRS Norman JR (Florence Bigelow) Cly.
☎ (203) 255-2528 . . 152 Regents Park, Westport, CT *06880*

Schaff MR & MRS Philip H JR (Mary G Johnson) | ☎ (847) 446-6086
Ih.Cho.Ncd.P'42 . . . . | 6 Indian Hill Rd,
MISS Nancy B . . . . | Winnetka, IL *60093*
MISS Susan H . . . . |
MR Philip D . . . . |
MR S Johnson . . . . |

Schaff MR Walter JR—P'44 . . . . | ☎ (330) 746-2316
MISS Anne H—at ☎ (207) 773-6357 | 2326 Selma Av,
713 Washington Av, Portland, ME *04103* . . . . . | Youngstown, OH
                                                    | *44504*

Schaffer MR & MRS Jeffrey P (Tara A Verkuil) SCal'85.Pa'95
☎ (714) 760-3174 . . 320 Hazel Dv, Corona Del Mar, CA *92625*

Schager MR Franz—Pr.Grenoble'28.DipAcadWien'30.WienLaw'37
☎ (516) 676-3380 . . 21 Wood Lane, PO Box 485, Locust Valley,
NY *11560-0485*

Schaller MR William A . . see S G Simmons

Schaperkotter MR & MRS John D (Cary R White)
StLaw'77.Cy.Nd.Nyc.Ncd.Mo'74.Va'77
☎ (314) 993-3943 . . 12 Brazilian Court, St Louis, MO *63124*

Scharffenberger MR & MRS George T (Marion A Nelson) B.Cl'40 . . of
☎ (310) 377-5964 . . 4 Appaloosa Lane, Rolling Hills, CA *90274*
☎ (212) 996-4429 . . 40 E 94 St, New York, NY *10128*

Scharlotte MR Robert B—ClevSt'42
☎ (216) 656-2150 . . 2199 Fairway Blvd, Hudson, OH *44236*

Scharnberg MR & MRS James Fagan (Patricia L | ☎ (610) 827-1037
Colladay) Fi.Sfh.Sa.Rv.Cw.Y'59 . . . . | 73 Bodine Rd,
MR Eric C . . . . | Malvern, PA *19355*
MR Alexander M—Hob'95 . . . . |

Schatz MR & MRS David R (Elizabeth H North) | ☎ (941) 355-0329
CtCol'66.P'66.H'69.Mich'82 . . . . | 5071 Bay Shore Rd,
MISS Elizabeth H . . . . | Sarasota, FL *34234*

Schatz MISS Sarah N (David R) . . . . Married at New York, NY
Deschenes MR Stephen L (Donald) . . . . Mch 9'96

Schaub MR James Carter—R.Pe.Rcp.Fw.Vca. Laf'59.Pa'61 . . . . — PO Box 2300, Delray Beach, FL *33447-2300*
MR Joseph L—at 401 Hilltop Rd, Strasburg, PA *17579-9771* . . . .

Schauffler MR Frederick A—Vca.Wt.SUNY'82 . . — ☎ (212) 410-1806 66 E 93 St, Apt 2R, New York, NY *10128*
MISS Nancy A—Ober'81—at ☎ (212) 876-1791 66 E 93 St, Apt 5R, New York, NY *10128* . . . .

Schaupp DR & MRS Willis C (Pinger—Joan H Whitney) Bhm.Fr.H'50 . . of
☎ (415) 346-7890 . . 2000 Baker St, San Francisco, CA *94115*
☎ (415) 868-1657 . . PO Box 641, Stinson Beach, CA *94970*

Schechter DR & MRS Stephen L (Head—Kendra D Blodgett) Rdc'65.Mich'81.Ncd.Mich'65.Geo'69 — ☎ (301) 984-8960 6 Hitching Post Court, Rockville, MD *20852*
MISS Rebecca B . . . .
JUNIORS MISS Elizabeth B . . . .

Scheerer MR Thomas I—Mds.CooperU'85 . . of
☎ (803) 723-0210 . . 60 Anson St, Charleston, SC *29401*
☎ (516) 324-0586 . . PO Box 1248, West End Rd, East Hampton, NY *11937*

Scheerer MR & MRS William 2d (Idoline W Crabbe) Cl'81.Un.Mds.Cly.P'45 . . of
☎ (212) 987-2338 . . 49 E 86 St, New York, NY *10028*
☎ (516) 324-0586 . . PO Box 1248, West End Rd, East Hampton, NY *11937*

Scheetz MR & MRS Edwin F JR (Theresa Larson) Ws'56.Ln.Fcg.Rr.Pg.Leh'54 . . . . — ☎ (412) 782-3143 300 Hampton Rd, Pittsburgh, PA *15215*
MISS Nancy B—Chath'84.Rr.Fcg.—at
☎ (334) 272-4017 . . 5756B Arbor Station Rd, Montgomery, AL *36117* . . . .
MISS Elizabeth H . . . .
MR Peter L—Rr.Fcg.Colby'83—at
☎ (714) 251-9235 . . 134 Murica Aisle, Irvine, CA *92714* . . . .
MR Edwin F 3d . . . .

Scheetz MRS Edwin Freed (Eleanor Baton) Ws'27.Fcg.Rr.Pg.Tc.Ndc. Longwood at Oakmont A327, 500 Rte 909, Verona, PA *15147*

Scheetz MR & MRS J Paul (Alice C Rust) Sth'31.Pg.Rr.Tc.Ncd.Mo'29 . . of
☎ (412) 682-1783 . . 5023 Frew Av, Pittsburgh, PA *15213*
☎ (703) 777-1139 . . "Murray Hill" PO Box 289, Leesburg, VA *20178*

Scheetz MR William Cramp JR . . . . Died at West Chester, PA May 13'96

Scheetz MRS William Cramp JR (Snyder—Stouffer—Mary A Biddle) Me.Pe.Ac.Sdg.Ncd.
☎ (610) 359-1314 . . 3500 West Chester Pike, CH124, Newtown Square, PA *19073-4168*

Schefer MR Anton E B—Va'67
☎ (703) 532-4167 . . "Woodland House" 610 Fulton Av, Falls Church, VA *22046*

Scheie MR Eric Glendon—Cal'78.SFr'82 . . see P T Tryon

Scheie MISS Nancy Ware . . see P T Tryon

Schell REV & MRS Donald J (Ellen S Phelps) Y'76.StJ'68 . . . . — ☎ (415) 647-8149 877 Rhode Island St, San Francisco, CA *94107*
MISS Patience A . . . .
MISS Maria R . . . .
JUNIORS MR Peter StG . . . .

Schellenbach MR & MRS Peter W (Dorothy S Platt) Sth'62.Nw'64.Miami'67 . . . . — ☎ (847) 835-0634 634 Drexel Av, Glencoe, IL *60022*
MR Peter W JR . . . .
MR John S—Miami'96 . . . .
MR David P . . . .
JUNIORS MR Michael E . . . .

Schellenberg MR & MRS Robert P (Masterson—Hunter—Ann G Fisher) Mis'dia'92.Wilkes'96.Sg.Me.Ac.W&L'42
☎ (717) 472-3091 . . "Grouse Cottage" PO Box 218, Bear Creek, PA *18602*

Schenck MRS J Cornell (Doris C Dibble) Sth'33.Cl'37.C.
☎ (203) 264-9503 . . East Hill Woods, 107 Dogwood, Southbury, CT *06488*

Schenck MR & MRS John C JR (Hollis A McCollum) Hl.Y.'65 . . . . — ☎ (212) 876-2204 49 E 96 St, New York, NY *10128*
MISS Elizabeth G—V'88—at ☎ (718) 643-2082 412 Clinton St, Brooklyn, NY *11231* . . . .
MR Charles E—Skd'92—at ☎ (212) 832-2047 420 E 64 St, New York, NY *10021* . . . .
MR Edward L—at Antioch . . . .

Schenck MR William C—Bow'89
☎ (718) 802-1757 . . 241 President St, Brooklyn, NY *11231*

Schenkel MR & MRS John L H (Suzanne Chance) Tufts'62.Gi.W&L'59
☎ (410) 974-6857 . . 1052 Carriage Hill P'kway, Annapolis, MD *21401*

Schenkel MR & MRS John L H (Joan H McIlvaine) Dick'88.Gi.Dick'87
☎ (410) 433-1808 . . 6006 Pinehurst Rd, Baltimore, MD *21212*

Schepens DR & MRS Charles L (Marie G vander Eecken) Sm.H.Ghent'35
☎ (617) 227-5867 . . 68 Beacon St, Boston, MA *02108*

Schepens MR & MRS Luc J (Hester Garfield) Sm.Ub.H.'62 . . . . — ☎ (508) 485-4849 9 Parkerville Rd, Southborough, MA *01772*
MR Augustin P—at Brown . . . .
MR Charles A—at U of Cal Berkeley . . . .
JUNIORS MISS Alexandra—at St Paul's . . . .
JUNIORS MR Marc N—at St Paul's . . . .

Scherbatow PRC Alexis & PRCSS (E Kathleen C McLoughlin) Brus'34
☎ (212) 876-8497 . . 345 E 86 St, Apt 11G, New York, NY *10028*

Scherbatow PRCSS Kyril (Hamlin—Palmer—Lucile Forman) Cly. . . . . — ☎ (212) 759-7538 570 Park Av, New York, NY *10021*
MISS Lucile Hamlin—SL'62—at
☎ (914) 693-7467 . . 81 S Lawn Dv, Dobbs Ferry, NY *10522* . . . .

Scherer MRS Albert G (Clara Legg) Cly.Ncd.Dar.
☎ (212) 534-3723 . . 1192 Park Av, New York, NY *10128*

Schermerhorn MR James—Stan'54 . . . . — ☎ (415) 924-4791 317 Oakdale Av, Corte Madera, CA *94925*
MR James 4th . . . .

Schermerhorn MR & MRS John E (Farwell—Barbara Knowlson) Syr'51 — ☎ (803) 837-6610 21 Wax Myrtle Lane, Hilton Head Island, SC *29926*
MISS Anne E—StThos'92 . . . .

Scherrer MR & MRS Frederick W (M Kim Kahle) Nd.Wes'61.Wash'64 . . . . — ☎ (314) 993-8062 903 S Warson Rd, St Louis, MO *63124*
JUNIORS MISS Stacy B . . . .
JUNIORS MISS Nicole A . . . .

Schieffelin MR G Richard—Pn.Hob'53 . . of
☎ (813) 832-4219 . . 2905 Euclid Av, Tampa, FL *33629*
☎ (406) 245-2770 . . "Stage Halt" 3014 Joan Lane, Billings, MT *59102*
Schieffelin MRS John Jay (Lois L Smith)
☎ (212) 744-0652 . . 209 E 66 St, New York, NY *10021*
Schieffelin MR & MRS John S (Linda L Wall)
Wheat'70.Ny.LIU'73.Cl'79 . . . . | ☎ (401) 423-0133
MR Cooper L—at Wesleyan . . . . | 4 Ranger Court,
JUNIORS MISS Julia S . . . . | Jamestown, RI
JUNIORS MR Peter L—at Kimball Union . . . . | *02835*
JUNIORS MR Nicholas W—at Middlesex . . . .
Schieffelin DR & MRS John W (Marion C Lohman)
Hn.H'54.Cl'59 . . . . | ☎ (510) 283-3943
MR John S—at Corps de la Paix, BP 43, Domoni, | 691 Old Jonas Hill
Anjouan, Comoros . . . . | Rd, Lafayette, CA
| *94549*
Schieffelin MISS Julia C—Rdc'65.Cl'68.Cs . . .of
☎ (212) 734-8540 . . 222 E 71 St, New York, NY *10021*
☎ (860) 672-0113 . . PO Box 152, Cornwall Bridge, CT *06754*
Schieffelin MISS Mary S—Nu'44
☎ (860) 672-6046 . . Popple Swamp Rd, Cornwall Bridge,
CT *06754-0035*
Schieffelin MR & MRS Timothy P (McParland—Susan E Utley)
NH'81.Rcn.Plg.Dar.Myf.W&J'77
☎ (203) 861-4130 . . "The Ledges" 42 Bruce Park Dv, Greenwich,
CT *06830*
Schieffelin MRS William Jay (Annette Markoe) Cly.
☎ (212) 289-4541 . . 1220 Park Av, New York, NY *10128*
Schieffelin MRS William Jay III (Joy W Proctor) Ny.Plg.Ht.
☎ (914) 666-5548 . . Darlington Rd, RD 2, Mt Kisco, NY *10549*
Schiff MR & MRS David T (Martha E Lawler) | of ☎ (212)535-1575
Ri.B.C.Plg.Y.'58 . . . . | 770 Park Av,
MISS Ashley R—Y'96—at ☎ (212) 988-0392 | New York, NY
214 E 74 St, New York, NY *10021* . . . . | *10021*
DR Andrew N—Rc.Ri.Y.Br'87.Cr'90—at | ☎ (970) 925-1340
☎ (212) 396-1881 . . 860 Fifth Av, New York, | "Serendipity"
NY *10021*. . . . . | 214 Lake Av,
MR David B—Lic.Y.Ty'91—at | Aspen, CO *81611*
☎ (212) 249-2784 . . 230 E 73 St, New York, NY
10021 . . . .
Schiff MRS John M (Fell—Josephine L Laimbeer) Pr.Ck.Mb . . .of
☎ (212) 355-2125 . . 475 Park Av, New York, NY *10022*
☎ (516) 759-9522 . . 135 Piping Rock Rd, Locust Valley, NY *11560*
Schiff MR & MRS Peter G (Elizabeth B Peters) | ☎ (516) 922-1542
LakeF'75.Mb.Rc.Pr.Srr.LakeF'74.Ch'76 . . . . . . | "FoxRidge"
JUNIORS MR Edward T . . . . | 70 Sandy Hill Rd,
JUNIORS MR James G . . . . | Oyster Bay, NY
| *11771*
Schiffeler DR & MRS John Wm (Katherine Y Chang)
Cc.Myf.Cal'66.Cal'67.Hawaii'69.Ind'74.Cal'79 . . of
☎ (415) 221-0511 . . 511 El Camino Del Mar, San Francisco,
CA *94121-1041*
☎ (011-86-21) 5854-6712 . . Jianping-21st Century High School,
275 Gu Shan Rd, Pudong, Shanghai 200135, China
Schiffer MR & MRS Herbert F (Margaret Berwind) Ac.Ncd.
☎ (610) 696-4504 . . 1469 Morstein Rd, West Chester, PA *19380*

Schiffer MR & MRS Peter B (Nancy J Nutt) | ☎ (610) 593-7070
Wells'69.GeoW'71.Rv.Cspa.W.Godd'71 . . . . . . | 77 Lower Valley
MR Herbert N . . . . | Rd, Atglen, PA
JUNIORS MR Peter N . . . . | *19310*
Schiffner MR & MRS Charles R (Burchett—Carney— | ☎ (602) 952-1375
Adrienne A McAndrews) | 5202 E Osborn Rd,
MISS Anita G . . . . | Phoenix, AZ *85018*
MISS Arianne S . . . .
Schildhauer MRS C Henry JR (Helen L Hurlock) | 411 E Lake Av,
Gv. . . . . | Baltimore, MD
MR C Henry 3d . . . . | *21212*
Schildhauer MRS Clarence H (Carmita Kennedy) Gv.
☎ (919) 331-2116 . . 600 W Main St, Elizabeth City, NC *27909*
Schilling MR Robert E
☎ (415) 854-1976 . . 1969 Palo Alto Way, Menlo Park, CA *94025*
Schipper MRS A Evarts (Alice C Evarts) . . . . name changed to Evarts
Schirmer MR & MRS Rudolph E (M Raffaela Mormino
di San Vincenzio Ferreri) Rome'59.K.Mto.
☎ (212) 355-4690 . . 555 Park Av, Apt 3W, New York, NY *10021*
Schlaff MR Richard J—An.MichSt'59
☎ (517) 856-3750 . . 9635 Crescent Beach Rd, PO Box 494, Caseville,
MI *48725*
Schlafly MR & MRS Daniel L (Adelaide Mahaffey)
StL'56.Cy.Nd.Km.Geo'33
☎ (314) 361-1543 . . 26 Westmoreland Place, St Louis, MO *63108*
Schlafly MISS Eleanor L
☎ (314) 993-1249 . . 5 Edgewood Rd, St Louis, MO *63124*
Schlafly MR & MRS Robert F (Maie B Kimball) | ☎ (314) 994-7062
Mar'vil'85.Cy.StL'36.H'39 . . . . | 9265 Clayton Rd,
MR Robert A—at 911 St Rita Av, St Louis, MO | St Louis, MO *63124*
63105 . . . .
Schlafly MR & MRS Thomas F (Ulrike G Kärst)
Cologne'77.Rc.Nd.Cy.Geo'70.Geo'77
☎ (314) 361-0361 . . 8 Portland Place, St Louis, MO *63108*
Schleussner MRS Robert C JR (Grehan—Elisabeth G | of ☎ (410)377-8338
Stevens) Ws'51.Cl'56.Gi. ⚬ . . . . | 6604 Walnutwood
MISS Laura S—Br'93 . . . . | Circle, Baltimore,
| MD *21212*
| ☎ (315) 859-0980
| "Bardscroft"
| 15 Marvin St,
| Clinton, NY *13323*

Schley MRS Diana R (Clucas—Diana A Reeder)
☎ (011-39-6) 807-0115 . . via Castellini 13, 00197 Rome, Italy
Schley MRS Gertrude—Cly.
☎ (860) 364-5214 . . 3 West Woods Rd, Sharon, CT *06069*
Schley MR John P—Eh.Y'61
☎ (908) 534-6351 . . PO Box 181, Whitehouse, NJ *08888*
Schley MR & MRS Kenneth B JR (McKinley—Yvonne Queripel) P'41
☎ (908) 234-0053 . . 260 Holland Rd, Far Hills, NJ *07931*
Schley MRS Reeve JR (Elizabeth D Boies) Sth'30.Ln.Eh.Yn.
☎ (908) 439-2234 . . PO Box 165, Whitehouse, NJ *08888*
Schley MR & MRS Reeve 3d (Georgia R Terry) | ☎ (908) 534-2473
Skd'67.Y'59 . . . . | PO Box 254,
MISS Marie B—Vt'94 . . . . | Whitehouse, NJ
JUNIORS MR Reeve T—at Hamilton . . . . | *08888*

Schley DR & MRS Richard L JR (Marjorie D Christian) P'38
☎ (912) 232-7490 . . 238 E Oglethorpe Av, Savannah, GA *31401*
Schley DR & MRS W Shain (Stephanie A Titus) | ☎ (212) 628-7987
Cly.Emory'62 . . . . | 320 E 72 St,
MISS Alexandra . . . . | Apt 3C,
MR William S JR . . . . | New York, NY
JUNIORS MISS Caroline . . . . | *10021-4769*
JUNIORS MR James T . . . . |
Schloss MR & MRS B Stephen (Jean A Tomasco) Pa'76.Pa'76.Ala'78
☎ (334) 281-8354 . . 3572 Thomas Av, Montgomery, AL *36111*
Schloss MR S Adam—Va'86.Van'88
☎ (334) 265-3029 . . 1460 Woodley Rd, Montgomery, AL *36106*
Schloss MR & MRS Samuel L (Burke H Klein) GaTech'47.Cl'48 . . of
☎ (334) 262-4674 . . 3305 Boxwood Dv, Montgomery, AL *36111*
☎ (904) 231-4990 . . Grayton Beach, FL *32459*
Schlossberg MR & MRS Edwin A (Caroline B Kennedy) Cl'88
see Dilatory Domiciles
Schlumberger MR & MRS Pierre Marcel (Mary L McCary)
Houst'78.A.Yn.Y'63.Smu'66
☎ (210) 629-8003 . . 350 Lakeview Blvd, New Braunfels, TX *78130*
Schmader MR & MRS J Peter (Rachel L Ijams) WmSth'81.VillaN'73
☎ (410) 727-5935 . . 38 E Montgomery St, Baltimore,
MD *21230* . . MRS absent
Schmeisser MR William C JR—Elk.Cvc.Y'38.H'41 . | ☎ (301) 299-6751
MISS C Avery . . . . | 11606 River Rd,
MR Christopher W . . . . | Potomac, MD *20854*
Schmid MR & MRS Johannes A (Failey—Elisabeth A Boyd) Ariz'60
☎ (011-852) 2987-7758 . . 9D Haven Court, Discovery Bay,
Lantau Island, Hong Kong
Schmid MR & MRS Leo B (Ann R Morrill) Lind'77.Cy.Van'76
☎ (314) 993-1713 . . 20 Clermont Lane, St Louis, MO *63124*
Schmidlapp MR & MRS Allan (Jane Jenkins) LIU'70 | ☎ (516) 922-1663
JUNIORS MR Allan C—at Lawrenceville . . . . | Cove Neck Rd,
| Oyster Bay, NY
| *11771*
Schmidlapp DR & MRS Carl J 2d (Barbara McKissock) Pr.L.S.P'35.Cr'40
☎ (516) 922-4808 . . 538 Centre Island Rd, Oyster Bay, NY *11771*
Schmidlapp MRS W Horace (McClintock—Olson—Patricia Kennedy)
Evg.BtP.
☎ (561) 655-1592 . . 695 S County Rd, Palm Beach, FL *33480*
Schmidt MR & MRS Adolph W (Helen S Mellon)
SL'36.Pg.Rr.Ln.Mt.P'26.H'29
☎ (412) 593-2621 . . RD 4, Ligonier, PA *15658*
Schmidt MR & MRS Eric C (Valerie F Thirkell) | ☎ (916) 525-6920
SCal'65.Rcn.SCal'66 . . . . | "Snowflake"
MISS Angela M—Pac'94—at ☎ (415) 343-1198 | PO Box 191,
834 Acacia Dv, Burlingame, CA *94010* . . . . . . | Homewood, CA
MR Alexis C—StMarys'93—at ☎ (415) 343-1198 | *96141*
834 Acacia Dv, Burlingame, CA *94010* . . . . . . |
Schmidt MISS Helène M—Fla'86 . . see E K St Claire
Schmidt MRS J Armstrong (Joan P Armstrong) | ☎ (617) 277-2428
Knox'54.Myf. . . . . | 57 Laurel Rd,
MR Robert E JR—Occ'79 . . . . | Chestnut Hill, MA
MR Andrew H—Syr'85.CalInst'88 . . . . | *02167*
Schmidt MR & MRS Jeffrey D (Elizabeth A Barnett) Ac.Ncd.Tul'80.Tul'82
☎ (203) 862-9409 . . 15 Carriage Rd, Cos Cob, CT *06807*

Schmidt MISS Joeanne Foskett—Wa.BtP.
☎ (773) 477-8787 . . 3270 N Lake Shore Dv, Chicago, IL *60657*
Schmidt MR & MRS Louis H 3d (Katharine B Pool) | ☎ (203) 259-0145
ArizSt'73.Pqt.ArizSt'74 . . . . | 1506 Burr St,
JUNIORS MISS Mary B—at Greens Farms . . . . . . | Fairfield, CT *06430*
Schmidt MASTER Samuel Aaron (g—Elbert K St Claire) . . . . Born
Feb 27'95
Schmidt MR & MRS Thomas M (Susan E Scott) | ☎ (412) 441-7409
Chath'81.Pitt'88.Pg.Rr.P'62.H'65 . . . . | 1060 Highmont Rd,
MISS Elizabeth W—BMr'87—at | Pittsburgh, PA
☎ (215) 724-7845 . . 4817 Trinity Place, | *15232*
Philadelphia, PA *19143* . . . . |
MISS Helen M—SL'89—at ☎ (802) 348-7130 |
Box 73, South Newfane, VT *05351* . . . . |
MISS Josie H—Bnd'92—at ☎ (718) 398-7964 |
234 Fifth Av, Apt 2, Brooklyn, NY *11215* . . . . . |
Schmitt MR & MRS Michael A 3d (Joan P Eldredge) | ☎ (802) 586-9619
BMr'59.Unn.P'58.Nu'64 . . . . | Craftsbury Common,
MISS Elizabeth T—at 5923 E 136 St, Grandview, | VT *05827*
MO *64030* . . . . |
Schmitt MR Roger M L—An.Bm.My.Sa.Plg.Lm. | of "Woodbine
Myf.Ds.Snc.Cw.Ofp.Vca.Rv.Hl.Fw.Ne.Ll.Cp. | House" PO Box
Coa.Sar.Ht.W.Cspa.Cc.Wt. . . . . | 231, Mill Neck, NY
MR John F 2d—Mt.Lm.Myf.Sar.Cc.Ds. . . . . | *11765*
MR James E—Rd.Cw.Myf.Lm.Cc.Ds.Rv.Ofp. . . | "Greensliegh Park"
| Abingdon-Winsley
| Way, Whitchurch,
| nr Banbury,
| Oxfordshire,
| England
Schmitz MR & MRS Richard D (Ellen T Goodwin) | ☎ (212) 580-0663
Sth'70.Cl'65 . . . . | 59 W 71 St,
MISS Catherine . . . . | New York, NY
MR Jeffrey D . . . . | *10023*
Schmitz MR & MRS Walter D (Marie Lenfest) Swth'52.Cl'59.Nd.Bv.Swth'52
☎ (314) 721-8296 . . 6 Crestwood Dv, St Louis, MO *63105*
Schmokel MISS Clarissa S—Vt'90
☎ (802) 253-6814 . . PO Box 1501, Stowe, VT *05672*
Schneeberger MR & MRS John A (Heather I Dickey) NotreD'72.Mo'75
☎ (212) 534-0564 . . 425 E 86 St, New York, NY *10028*
Schneider MR & MRS (DR) Barton T (M Elizabeth Uhrig)
Purd'81.Ind'85.Ty'74.Ch'82
☎ (703) 519-7983 . . 4100 Orleans Place, Alexandria, VA *22304*
Schneider MRS Edward J (Yvonne M Sbarboro) Sfg.Fr.
☎ (415) 776-7345 . . 1400 Geary Blvd, Apt 5J, San Francisco, CA *94109*
Schneider MR & MRS Edward J 3d (Fidela N | ☎ (415) 326-0642
Zanetta) Stan'68.Pcu.Bur.Stan'67.Cl'69 . . . . . . | 92 Atherton Av,
MISS Elena A—at Harvard . . . . | Atherton, CA *94027*
MR Edward J 4th—at Princeton . . . . |
Schneider DR & MRS George T (Ann Le Jeune) Tul'41.Tul'44
☎ (504) 866-4444 . . 218 Audubon Blvd, New Orleans, LA *70118*
Schneider MISS Laura T—BMr'63.Mich'66.Cvc.
☎ (202) 333-3184 . . 4000 Cathedral Av NW, Apt 231B, Washington,
DC *20016*
Schneider MRS Mark Lockyer (Irien Knapp) Un.
☎ (212) 986-7262 . . 111 E 39 St, New York, NY *10016*

Schneider MR & MRS Richard G (Margaret P Fritz) Me.M.Y.'52.Pa'57
☎ (610) 649-3087 . . 918 Merion Square Rd, Gladwyne, PA *19035*

Schneider MR & MRS Thomas J (Cynthia Perrin)
H'75.H'84.H'73.Ox'77.H'80
☎ (301) 570-4782 . . 17201 Norwood Rd, Sandy Spring, MD *20860*

Schneider MR & MRS Thomas P (Lee Ann McNabb) Geo'81
☎ (203) 761-0736 . . 50 Sturges Ridge Rd, Wilton, CT *06894*

Schneithorst MR & MRS James E (Caro N Smith)
Bv.Cr'64 . . . . | ☎ (314) 821-3288
MR Christopher C—at 800 Victoria Av, St Louis, | 5 Squires Lane,
MO *63122* . . . . | Huntleigh Village,
| MO *63131*

Schneithorst MR James E JR—Bv.Smu'91
435 Quan Av, Kirkwood, MO *63122*

Schniewind MRS Henry E (Helen Ball) Pr.
☎ (617) 862-6464 . . Brookhaven D435, 1010 Waltham St, Lexington,
MA *02173*

Schniewind MR Henry E 3d . . see MISS N W Rathborne

Schniewind MRS Julia W (Julia R Wight) Bost'81 . | ☎ (617) 723-5854
MISS Helena L—Cal'94 . . . . | 76 Chestnut St,
| Boston, MA *02108*

Schniewind MR Nelson R . . see MISS N W Rathborne

Schock MR & MRS William C (Dian C Chandler) Cy.Rc.Ncd.P'47.Va'51
☎ (314) WO2-6813 . . 9559 Litzsinger Rd, St Louis, MO *63124*

Schoder MR & MRS Andrew O (Ann M Freeman) Y'79.Yn.Dth'79.Pa'83
☎ (203) 966-0645 . . 10 Dew Lane, New Canaan, CT *06840*

Schoeffer MR & MRS Peter A V (Jeannine B | ☎ (413) 528-5596
Rhinelander) Lx.Br'70 . . . . | ''Coppertops''
JUNIORS MR Frederic B R . . . . | West Rd, Alford,
JUNIORS MR Peter A S . . . . | MA *01266*

Schoelkopf MR & MRS Thomas R (Parker—Patricia F Masters)
StLaw'78.AmInt'l'84.WWash'82
☎ (901) 758-0045 . . 3069 Mon Cheri Lane, Memphis, TN *38119*

Schoeller MR & MRS K Christian (C Brewer Mullins)
LakeF'88.Pg.Rr.Cc.LakeF'89
☎ (412) 682-6180 . . 586 Moorhead Place, Pittsburgh, PA *15232*

Schoellerman MR & MRS Jack L (Katharine Tucker) | ☎ (714) 640-8790
Scripps'68.Clare'73.Clare'68.SanDiego'71 ⚓ . | 2845 Cassia St,
MR John M—H'96 . . . . | Newport Beach, CA
JUNIORS MISS Anne T . . . . | *92660*

Schoellkopf MRS J Frederick 4th (Patricia C Calkins) SL'34.St.G.Ncd.
☎ (716) 627-3558 . . 6252S Old Lake Shore Rd, Lake View, NY *14085*

Schoellkopf MR Walter H 3d
☎ (970) 927-4203 . . PO Box 188, Snowmass, CO *81654*

Schoen DR & MRS (DR) Robert T (Cynthia B French) Ws'72.Y'80.H'72.Cl'76
☎ (203) 254-1280 . . 115 Main St, Box 73, Southport, CT *06490*

Schoenfeld MR & MRS Benjamin F (Susan H McWilliams) North'60
Short Creek Ranch, PO Box 181, 1240 CR 45, Coaldale, CO *81222*

Schoenly MR & MRS Newton C JR (Barbara S Hammond)
Mid'75.H'82.Cda.Ncd.Hn.
☎ (860) 435-4810 . . ''Mountain Meadows'' 46 Logan Rd, Salisbury,
CT *06068*

Schoettle MR Douglas Abbott—Mich'78.Mich'81
☎ (212) 932-0535 . . 243 Riverside Dv, Apt 1005, New York, NY *10025*

Schoettle MR Ferdinand P—Ayc.P'55.H'60.H'78. | ☎ (410) 263-1804
H'83 . . . . | ''Shearwater''
MR Michael K . . . . | 15B3 Spa Creek
MR Derek C . . . . | Landing, PO Box
| 4935, Annapolis,
| MD *21403-6935*

Schoettle MRS Karl R (Margaret L Diss) Me.Gm.Yh.Ac.
☎ (610) 527-3349 . . 49 Pasture Lane, Bryn Mawr, PA *19010*

Schoettle MR & MRS Karl R JR (Katherine Illoway) | ☎ (617) 326-2878
Me.Rd.Ac. ⚓ . . . . | 8 School Master
JUNIORS MISS Sarah E . . . . | Lane, Dedham, MA
| *02026*

Schoettle MRS Marc Clarkson (Carole J Springer) Cs.Ac.Sdg.
☎ (215) CH7-2920 . . 8610 Millman Place, Philadelphia, PA *19118*

Schoettle MR & MRS Michael B (Marcia Dornin) | of ☎ (310)541-6374
Dick'59.Me.Y'58.H'63 . . . . | 24 Eastfield Dv,
MR Timothy W—at U of Mich Ann Arbor . . . . . | Rolling Hills, CA
MR William D—at 200 E 66 St, New York, NY | *90274*
10021 . . . . | ☎ (207) 359-2368
| ''The Belfry''
| Harding's Lane,
| Sargentville, ME
| *04673*

Schoettle MR & MRS Philip A (Merritt—Adele Biddle) Pc.Myf . . .of
☎ (215) CH7-4831 . . 7830 Winston Rd, Philadelphia, PA *19118*
☎ (908) TW9-0257 . . 510 East Av, Bay Head, NJ *08742*

Schoettle MR & MRS Robert C (Julia A Kavanagh) Va'81.Va'80.Stan'86
☎ (415) 948-5068 . . 876 Carmel Av, Los Altos, CA *94022*

Schoettle MRS Robert M (Elisabeth D Abbott)
☎ (757) 787-2651 . . 23255 Court House Av, Accomac, VA *23301*

Schoettle MR William Clarkson
☎ (757) 253-1262 . . 5700 Williamsburg Landing Dv, Apt 200,
Williamsburg, VA *23185*

Schoettler MR & MRS James R (Douglass—Ann A Odell) Purd'46.Lawr'51
☎ (603) 964-7788 . . 9 Bradley Lane, North Hampton, NH *03862*

Schofield MR R Hayden JR—Cr'84
☎ (212) 535-8638 . . 230 E 73 St, Apt 8E, New York, NY *10021*

Schofield MR & MRS Robert H (Barbara F Porter) | ☎ (561) 832-3219
V'56.Evg.Csn.Ncd.P'55.Mit'59 . . . . | 369 S Lake Dv,
MR Porter H—FP'87—at Beaver Creek, CO . . . . | Palm Beach, FL
| *33480*

Schofield MRS Sarah C (Sarah Ann Caner) BMr'50 . | ☎ (215) 247-5712
MISS Sarah A—at U of Chicago . . . . | 34 W Southampton
MISS Mary A . . . . | Av, Philadelphia,
MR J Dobson 4th—at ☎ (219) 464-8552 | PA *19118*
210 Logan St, Apt 2, Valparaiso, IN *46383* . . . . |

Schofield MISS Sarah H (Robert H) . . . . Married at Little Compton, RI
Herzog MISS Frank W (Werner) . . . . Aug 24'96

Scholle MR & MRS Oliver C (Diana deB Parsons) | ☎ (415) 347-8790
Bur.Cc.H'49 . . . . | 535 Laurent St,
MR Palmer H—at 21 Kinross Rd, Apt 1R, | Hillsborough, CA
Brighton, MA *02135* . . . . | *94010*

Scholle MR & MRS Oliver C JR (Elizabeth R Haffenreffer)
Dth'82.Pa'87.Bgt.Fiy.Hn.H'76
see Dilatory Domiciles

Schoonmaker MR James M 2d—Pg.Ny.Rby.
☎ (305) 667-6626 . . 4055 Douglas Rd, Miami, FL *33133*

Schorr MR & MRS Paul C 4th (Mary Burwell Espy)
Van'92.Cly.Geo'89.H.'93
☎ (212) 752-3952 . . 424 E 52 St, Apt 4F, New York, NY *10022*

Schottland JUNIORS MR David N . . see C A Ernst 3d

Schottland MR Fletcher B . . see C A Ernst 3d

Schottland JUNIORS MR Joshua S . . see C A Ernst 3d

Schottland JUNIORS MISS Katherine M . . see C A Ernst 3d

Schotz MR & MRS Jon P (Patricia F Wheeler) Y'77.Y'77
☎ (310) 458-9402 . . 148 Georgina Av, Santa Monica, CA *90402*

Schoyer MR & MRS Edward H (Elizabeth B Foster) Pg.H'39
☎ (412) 421-1488 . . 5524 Dunmoyle St, Pittsburgh, PA *15217*

Schoyer MR Timothy R
☎ (512) 992-0268 . . 4645 Ocean Dv, Apt 1B, Corpus Christi, TX *78412*

Schoyer MR & MRS Wayne A (Florence L Sloan) Stph'53.San.Ty'54
☎ (207) 282-2379 . . "Willowlawn" PO Box 163, Biddeford Pool, ME *04006*

Schrade MR & MRS Randolph R A (Vera Holschneider) Y'83
☎ (212) 472-4521 . . 121 E 77 St, Apt 2W, New York, NY *10021*

Schrade MR & MRS Robert W (Rolande M Young) Dar.Man'48 . . . . | of ☎ (212)288-4261
MISS Rhonda-Lee . . . . | 30 East End Av,
MISS Rolisa M . . . . | New York, NY
MISS Rorianne C—Juilliard'85—at | *10028*
☎ (212) 472-0396 . . 80 East End Av, New York, | ☎ (413) 238-5854
NY *10028* . . . . | Sevenars,
| Ireland St S,
| Worthington, MA
| *01098*

Schrauff MR & MRS Hamilton P (Carol J Wesley) | ☎ (214) 661-9739
P'57.Cl'59 . . . . | 6849 Midcrest Dv,
MISS Catherine L . . . . | Dallas, TX *75240*
MR William P . . . . |
MR Christopher W . . . . |

Schreiber MRS Bennett (Schreiber—Rock—Madeleine E Bennett)
☎ (203) 264-2627 . . 111 Pomperaug Woods, Southbury, CT *06488*

Schrier DR & MRS Michael D (Lorna J Vermeer) Hope'63.Hope'65
☎ (334) 269-5193 . . 3215 Brentwood Dv, Montgomery, AL *36111*

Schroeder MR & MRS A Reed (Ann H Williams) Ty'45
☎ (412) 741-7594 . . Persimmon Rd, Sewickley Heights, Sewickley, PA *15143*

Schroeder MRS Carol T (Carol Thayer)
Willow Valley Lakes Manor, Willow Street, PA *17584-9491*

Schroeder MR & MRS Frederic S (Sandra L | ☎ (610) 459-5096
Cadwalader) Sth'69.Temp'74.PennM'69 . . . . . . | "Aberfeldy"
MR Frederic S JR—StMarys'93—at | 200 Wawa Rd,
1000 Valley Dv, Alexandria, VA *22307* . . . . . . | Wawa, PA *19063*
MR N Thayer . . . . |

Schroeder MRS Gilliat G (Margaret Wood) Ac.
☎ (610) 459-2051 . . "White Oak" 186 Wawa Rd, Wawa, PA *19063*

Schroeder MR & MRS J Howison (Elisabeth G Millspaugh)
WmSth'78.Cl'85.Hob'78.Pa'83
☎ (207) 846-9388 . . 80 Pleasant St, Yarmouth, ME *04096*

Schroeder MRS Neil R (Margaret S Comey)
☎ (216) 791-8539 . . 1801 Chestnut Hills Dv, Apt 116, Cleveland Heights, OH *44106*

Schroeder MR Seaton 4th—Pa'64
417 Sheffield Dv, Wallingford, PA *19086*

Schroeder MRS William F (Jane B Smyth) Col'45
☎ (503) 537-9391 . . PO Box 58, Newberg, OR *97132*

Schubert MISS Lisa A (Thomas—Lisa A Schubert) Swb'76
☎ (212) 595-4630 . . 17 W 67 St, Apt 9D, New York, NY *10023*

Schuette MRS William (Emily G Parker) . . . . Died Aug 21'96

Schultz MR & MRS Jackson Le R (Fitzpatrick—Lachman—Rhoda Welch) Bur.Pcu.
☎ (415) 342-2816 . . 1780 Manor Dv, Hillsborough, CA *94010*

Schultz MR & MRS John F (Patricia A Kelsey) | ☎ (804) 673-1005
Tufts'64.Cl'66.NCar'65.UnTheo'70.Cl'74 . . . . . | 606 Horsepen Rd,
MISS Frances E—at U of Va . . . . | Richmond, VA
MISS Joanna K . . . . | *23229*
MR Christopher B—Va'96 . . . . |

Schulze MR & MRS Richard G—SCal'64.SCal'65
☎ (203) 625-0122 . . 28 Dublin Hill Rd, Greenwich, CT *06830*

Schulze MR & MRS Robert C (Barbara M Buckley) Cal'36
☎ (916) 678-5561 . . PO Box 580, Dixon, CA *95620*

Schumacher MR & MRS Dick L (Henrietta G Boyce) OState'36
☎ (210) 598-5487 . . 107 Silver Spur, PO Box 8168, Horseshoe Bay, TX *78654-9203*

Schumacher MR & MRS H Richard (Ware—Katherine E Yager) Nu'86.Bm.Un.Chr.Plg. | ☎ (212) 289-3056
Y'51.H'58 . . . . | 47 E 88 St,
MR Richard S—at 33 Le Thanh Tong, Hanoi, | New York, NY
Vietnam . . . . | *10128*
MR Garry K—at 402 W California, Urbana, IL |
61801 . . . . |

Schurman MRS Jacob G 3d (Juanita Hill) Bur.Fr. . . | ☎ (415) 776-1914
MR Jacob G 4th—at 16180 Greenwood Lane, | 1750 Taylor St,
Monte Sereno, CA *95030* . . . . | San Francisco, CA
| *94133*

Schurz MR Franklin D JR—Hb.H'52.H'56
225 W Colfax Av, South Bend, IN *46626*

Schurz MR & MRS James M (Julie L Ruskin) Cal'83.Stan'84
☎ (415) 388-8432 . . 25 Coronet Av, Mill Valley, CA *94941*

Schuster MR & MRS Charles B (Felicia R S Taylor)
☎ (212) 517-0085 . . 3 E 71 St, New York, NY *10021*

Schuster MRS Charles J (Amanda A Cecil) Pr.
☎ (516) 676-1748 . . 78 Weir Lane, Box 75, Locust Valley, NY *11560*

Schutt MR & MRS C Porter (Layton—Greta B Brown)
Wil.Cry.Ny.Ac.Cly.Ncd.Va'35
☎ (302) 658-4421 . . PO Box 3694, 302 Hillside Rd, Greenville, DE *19807*

Schutt MR & MRS Charles P JR (Katharine R Draper) | ☎ (610) 388-6943
Pa'66.Cry.Wil.Nf.Cw.Ac.Ncd.Del'64 ⚓ . . . . . | 419 Burnt Mill Rd,
MISS Katharine D—at Harvard . . . . | Chadds Ford, PA
MR Jacob F—Col'94 . . . . | *19317*
MR C Porter 3d—Va'92—in Hong Kong |

Schuyler MR & MRS David B (Lynn E McCormac) NIll'85.NIll'85
☎ (847) 726-1106 . . 6 Summit Terr, Lake Zurich, IL *60047*

Schuyler MR Peter G . . . . | ☎ (505) 258-5683
MR Peter G JR—Ill'83—at 3040 E Shea Blvd, | 203 Heath Dv,
Apt 2037, Phoenix, AZ *85028* . . . . | Ruidoso, NM *88345*

Schuyler MR & MRS William M (Katherine K Groman)
Ch'31.Hl.Cnt.Dth'31.Ch'39
☎ (312) 573-1456 . . 680 N Lake Shore Dv, Apt 518, Chicago, IL *60611-4414*

Schwab MRS D Johnson (Deborah R Johnson)
☎ (203) 855-8078 . . PO Box 462, New Canaan, CT *06840*
Schwab MR & MRS George B (Katherine E Whelahan)
StMarys'84.Va'87.Un.Pr.Cly.Y'83.Va'86
☎ (718) 788-9570 . . 494—13 St, Brooklyn, NY *11215*

Schwab MR & MRS Gustav 5th (Luebke—Mary E	of ☎ (904)285-7309
Klein) Col'60.Y'36	The Carlyle 407,
MISS Marie K Luebke—at 108 E 38 St,	600 Ponte Vedra
Apt 200, New York, NY *10016*	Blvd, Ponte Vedra
	Beach, FL *32082*
	☎ (860) 535-4568
	21 Quanaduck Cove
	Rd, Stonington, CT
	06378

Schwab MR & MRS Hermann C (C Meteer Shanks)
V'52.Lic.Pr.StJ.Cly.Y'41 . . of
☎ (516) 922-0362 . . 34 Northern Blvd, Oyster Bay Cove, Oyster Bay,
NY *11771*
☎ (212) 879-3900 . . 1 E 66 St, New York, NY *10021*
Schwab MR & MRS John C—Me.Vt'86
☎ (610) 664-6684 . . 114 Rockland Av, Merion, PA *19066*
Schwab MR & MRS Matthew R (Kathleen M Feeley) Sth'89.Sth'90.Aht'88
☎ (313) 475-4341 . . 345 Elm St, Chelsea, MI *48118*
Schwab MR & MRS Nelson JR (Kelly—Sylvia C Lambert) Qc.Cm.Y'40.H'43
☎ (513) 321-4114 . . 2470 W Rookwood Court, Cincinnati, OH *45208*
Schwab MR & MRS Stuart T (Vicki A McClendon) Tex'83.Duke'81.Tex'86
☎ (210) 828-0135 . . 112 Sheraton Dv, San Antonio, TX *78209*
Schwab MR & MRS Winthrop D de V (Patricia B Thurston)
Ws'43.Me.Ac.Ncd.Y'40.H'42
☎ (610) 649-9516 . . 367 Aubrey Rd, Wynnewood, PA *19096-1812*
Schwabacher MRS Albert E JR (Philbin—Cynthia C Soles)
☎ (415) 851-0181 . . PO Box 620067, 250 Whiskey Hill Rd, Woodside,
CA *94062*
Schwaner JUNIORS MR Mark A . . see MISS R E Boykin
Schwartz MR & MRS Alexander C JR (Perry—Glorvina H Rodewald)
Wk.T.K.BtP.Cl'56
☎ (561) 848-6238 . . 995 Adam Rd, Palm Beach, FL *33480*

Schwartz MR & MRS Arthur W (Virginia A	☎ (413) 298-5225
Haggerty) CtCol'65.Lx.P'63	PO Box 418,
MISS Julia C—LakeF'92	Main St,
MR Arthur W JR—at San Francisco, CA	Stockbridge, MA
	01262

Schwartz MR & MRS Edwin J (Elisa K Escamilla)	of ☎ (415)929-7119
SL'60.Bhm.Rut'55	3325 Jackson St,
MISS Victoria B—SFrSt'88—at	San Francisco, CA
☎ (415) 550-8844 . . 510B Hill St,	*94118*
San Francisco, CA *94114*	☎ (415) 669-7566
	200 Via De La
	Vista, Inverness, CA
	94937

Schwartz MR & MRS James P (Mary L Moseley) Pc.	☎ (215) 836-5584
MR Marshall L—Elmira'93	512 E Gravers Lane,
	Wyndmoor, PA
	19038

Schwartz MRS P Kay (Nancy H Putnam) Dar.
☎ (215) 563-1800 . . Logan Square E, Apt 2103, 2 Franklin Town Blvd,
Philadelphia, PA *19103*
Schwartz MR Peter A—Pn.P'36
☎ (803) 559-2251 . . 2151 River Rd, Johns Island, SC *29455*
Schwartz MRS Philip W (Seabury—Bright—Mary L Peck) . . of
☎ (941) 964-0283 . . 1030—10 St, PO Box 713, Boca Grande, FL *33921*
☎ (860) 434-3200 . . "Eight Mile River House" 20 Old Hamburg Rd,
Lyme, CT *06371*
Schwartz MRS Walter M JR (Backus—Rosina D Malpass) Pc.Sg.Ac.
☎ (215) 248-0961 . . 7516 McCallum St, Philadelphia, PA *19118*
Schwartzburg MR John A—Myf.Lawr'64.Mid'66.Mid'72
see J M Robbins
Schwarz MRS Andrew A (K Searcy Carr)
☎ (212) 961-1013 . . 265 Riverside Dv, Apt 11F, New York,
NY *10025*
Schwarz MR Andrew A
☎ (212) 663-8479 . . 501 Cathedral P'kway, Apt 6G, New York,
NY *10025*

Schwarz DR & MRS Fred R (Carol Larner)	☎ (803) 736-0804
Laf'62.NJMed'70	2114 Bermuda Hills
MISS Lesley A—SCar'94	Rd, Columbia, SC
MR Jeffrey R—SCar'92.Fla'96	*29223*
MR Jason B—at U of Fla	
JUNIORS MISS Allyson L M	

Schwarz MR & MRS Horace W (Ann Haydock) Me.Ht.P'43
PO Box 467, Wynnewood, PA *19096*
Schwefel MR Charles A—Tufts'77
120 Wildflower Lane, Fairfield, CT *06430*
Schweppe MR & MRS Charles H (Chapman—Susan L Macke) Ia'67.Bel'71
☎ (303) 530-7221 . . 4790 Old Post Court, Boulder, CO *80301*
Schweppe MR & MRS David P (Valerie Graham) AugCol'75.Bost'74
☎ (970) 925-1808 . . 0750 Meadowood Dv, Aspen, CO *81611*
Schweppe MR & MRS John S (Lydia H Elliott) Ih.Cho.Cnt.H'39.Nw'43
☎ (847) 446-7727 . . 30 Indian Hill Rd, Winnetka, IL *60093*
Schwerin MISS Christina P—Vt'90 . . see MRS P P Brown
Schwering MR & MRS Harley E (Gamble—Rispah A Dowse)
Carroll'50.Bv.DelB.StL'57.Wash'60 . . of
33 Upper Ladue Rd, St Louis, MO *63124*
☎ (561) 276-6516 . . 2613 N Ocean Blvd, Gulf Stream, FL *33483*

Sclufer MR & MRS Nicholas G (Anne H Sprague) . . .	☎ (610) 649-3980
MISS Karen A	725 Dodds Lane,
	Gladwyne, PA
	19035

Scoll MRS David E (M Patricia Mason) . . . . Died at
New York, NY in Nov 1993

Scott MRS A Thornton (Catherine Little) BMr'35 . .	☎ (606) 266-8362
DR Robert A T—H'60	1386 Lakewood Dv,
	Lexington, KY
	40502

Scott MR Alexander L (Alfred L) . . . . Married at Palm Beach, FL
Ballentine MISS Mary W (James M JR) . . . . May 18'96
Scott MISS Alexandra C . . see W C Robbins 3d

Scott MR & MRS Alfred L (Jacks—Elizabeth Bond Hunter) V'62.Ch'65.UnTheo'89.CUNY'92.Ri.Un. Myf.Cs.Cly.Ncd.Dc.U'53.Nu'56 . . . . | of ☎ (212)534-5148 1160 Park Av, New York, NY *10128*
   MISS Elizabeth B Jacks—Duke'91.Nw'96 . . . | ☎ (518) 851-6220 "The Hill" 65 Bells Pond Rd, Box 92, Hudson, NY *12534*
   MR Robert LeRoy Jacks JR—Duke'94.Stan'95 —at ☎ (910) 251-7711 . . 201½ S Front St, Wilmington, NC *28401* . . . .

Scott MRS Amélie (Amélie Sigourney) Ncd. . . . . . . | ☎ (860) 232-4162 275 Steele Rd, Apt B115, West Hartford, CT *06117*
   MISS Nancy C—at 711 Farmington Av, West Hartford, CT *06119* . . . .

Scott MR Andrew F . . see M M Jeanes

Scott MR Ashton T JR—Me.Laf'57
   ☎ (610) 687-4389 . . 817 Weadley Rd, Radnor, PA *19087*

Scott MR & MRS Bobby Clay (Pauline Tarver) Carey'62.Dar.Carey'63
   ☎ (601) 442-3315 . . 11 Thorn Rd, Natchez, MS *39120*

Scott MR & MRS C Howell (Lalitte Carusi) Mds.Y'59 | ☎ (516) 329-5489 15 Windmill Lane, East Hampton, NY *11937*
   MISS Cecil C—Stan'84 . . . .

Scott MR & MRS Daniel W 2d (Beard—Alice K Hollister) Ky'37
   ☎ (606) 299-1646 . . 2470 Russell Cave Rd, Rte 3, Lexington, KY *40511-9509*

Scott MR & MRS Daniel W 3d—Rcch.Trans'64 | 417 Torrence Court, Cincinnati, OH *45202*
   MISS Stephanie I . . . .
   MR Daniel W 4th . . . .

Scott MRS Davenport (Sally C Staley)
   ☎ (407) 896-4449 . . 2550 Lake Shore Dv, Orlando, FL *32803*

Scott MRS David J (Blanid M Ennis) Wt.Cw.Cc. . . . | ☎ (215) 862-3495 249 Windy Bush Rd, New Hope, PA *18938*
   MISS Bridgett L—at 40-50 E 10 St, New York, NY *10003* . . . .
   MR Peter M—Geo'82—at ☎ (212) 242-4156 119 Bank St, New York, NY *10014* . . . .

Scott MR & MRS David R (Ruth E Wardle) Rdc'61.Y'63.Me.H'60.H'65 . . . . | ☎ (609) 683-1733 255 Russell Rd, Princeton, NJ *08540*
   MISS Cintra W—H'93—at ☎ (212) 929-9095 395 West St, New York, NY *10014* . . . .
   MR D Rodman—at U of Vt . . . .

Scott MRS Delia J (Delia Jaramillo) . . . . | ☎ (610) LO6-7047 34 E 2 St, Media, PA *19063*
   MISS Edith M R . . . .

Scott MISS Diana M—LakeF'78.Nyc.
   ☎ (508) 228-2651 . . 4 Capaum Rd, Nantucket, MA *02554*

Scott MRS Donald JR (Margaret J Dilworth) . . . . Died at Harvard, MA Jun 18'96

Scott MR Donald JR—H.'30 . . . . | ☎ (508) 456-6845 165 Littleton County Rd, Harvard, MA *01451*
   MR Jonathan M . . . .

Scott MR & MRS Donald A (Jeanne M Cooper) Rut'50.P'51.H'56
   ☎ (215) 247-7793 . . 714 W Mt Airy Av, Philadelphia, PA *19119*

Scott MR & MRS Donald B JR (Patience F Stevenson) Gi.Pr.Cly.
   58 Peacock Lane, Locust Valley, NY *11560-1019*

Scott MR & MRS Edgar JR (Lindsay C Febiger) Srr.Ph.H'49
   ☎ (610) 347-2235 . . PO Box 431, Unionville, PA *19375*

Scott MR & MRS Edgar 3d (Lindsay Scott) Ph.Rcp.Wil.Pa'77
   ☎ (302) 654-8404 . . 107 Twaddell Mill Rd, Wilmington, DE *19807*

Scott MR & MRS Eugene L (Mary van L Eastman) OWes'81.Rc.Ri.Y'60.Va'65
   ☎ (212) 752-8450 . . 439 E 51 St, New York, NY *10022*

Scott MR & MRS G Gordon (Elinor Hult) Syr'72
   PO Box 281, Girdwood, AK *99587*

Scott MR & MRS George C (Mary J Chadbourne) Rm.Stc.
   ☎ (908) 291-0621 . . 904 Navesink River Rd, Locust, NJ *07760*

Scott MR & MRS George C JR (Boyle—Helen R Shepard) BMr'38.Ub.Ey.Chi.Ncd.H'34 ⚓ . . . | ☎ (508) 356-2272 "Warners" PO Box 466, 35 Mill Rd, Ipswich, MA *01938*
   MISS Mary A—at 7845 Lampley Rd, Primm Springs, TN *38476* . . . .

Scott MR & MRS Hardie (Jackson—Scott—Almira G Rockefeller) Rc.M.Rd.Ac.Cly.Y'30
   ☎ (610) EL6-0400 . . Kirkwood Farm, PO Box 325, 6101 Goshen Rd, Edgemont, PA *19028*

Scott MR & MRS Harlan (Skelly—Ann S Layton) Y'39
   ☎ (302) 658-9517 . . 1105 Nottingham Rd, Wilmington, DE *19805*

Scott MR & MRS Harold W JR (Dorothy C Cumming) Rm. . . . . | ☎ (908) 747-2693 14 Alden Terr, Little Silver, NJ *07739*
   MISS Laura C . . . .
   MR Harold W 3d . . . .

Scott MR & MRS Henry C JR (Elizabeth M Pendergrass) Y'51 | ☎ (203) 775-2535 Barkwood Falls, 17 Signal Hill Rd, Brookfield, CT *06804-1318*
   MISS Diane M—DU'79—at ☎ (415) 389-6352 8 Robertson Terr, Mill Valley, CA *94941* . . . . .
   MISS Elizabeth B—at ☎ (406) 586-2904 8363 Forswall Rd, Belgrade, MT *59714* . . . . . .
   MISS Melinda M—Conn'90 . . . .
   MISS Penelope C—Y'95 . . . .

Scott MRS Henry P 3d (Elizabeth T Shepherd) Wil . . .of
   ☎ (304) 876-3440 . . 204 W New St, PO Box 2054, Shepherdstown, WV *25443*
   ☎ (302) 654-1082 . . Rockford Tower Apt J14, 7 Rockford Rd, Wilmington, DE *19806*

Scott MR & MRS Hugh 3d (Ann R Cady) Drake'71.Mo'72.Cy.Lc.Cc.Y'71 . . . . | ☎ (314) 991-1443 565 Barnes Rd, St Louis, MO *63124*
   MISS Sara C—at Yale . . . .
   MR Hugh 4th—at Boston U . . . .

Scott MR & MRS Hugh Lenox 2d (Mary Celeste McAshan) Rice'41.Rice'34
   401 Emerson St, Houston, TX *77006-4506*

Scott MR & MRS Hugh N (Alexandra Korff) BMr'60.Cvc.Au.Mt.P'50 . . . . | ☎ (202) 965-1064 1318—30 St NW, Washington, DC *20007*
   MISS Eliza R—Br'91—at 106 E 30 St, New York, NY *10016* . . . .
   MISS Laura H—at Princeton . . . .

Scott MR & MRS James H JR (Shelah K Kane) Bnd'56.Va'75.Cc.Ncd.Va'51.Cl'58 . . . . | ☎ (804) 293-7939 1863 Winston Rd, Charlottesville, VA *22903*
   MR Keith K . . . .

Scott MR James H 3d—Unn.Va'82.Va'91
   ☎ (804) 295-4135 . . 2850 Locust Hill Dv, Charlottesville, VA *22901*

Scott MR & MRS James W McA (Ellen M Bates)
Ty'80.StL'89.Cy.Mo'84.Cl'88
☎ (314) 727-0667 . . 109 Aberdeen Place, St Louis, MO *63105*
Scott MR Jeffrey F—Cr'91 . . see MRS A Z Gammon
Scott MR & MRS John H (Avern—Jean McDougall) | ☎ (412) 361-2556
Pg.P'45.Cr'51 . . . . | 1275 Beechwood
MR Hugh McD—Nyc.Ken'80 . . . . | Blvd, Pittsburgh, PA
| *15206*
Scott MR & MRS John J (Evelyn Attwood) Sth'41.Ncd.Dth'28.Bklyn'33 . . of
☎ (203) 869-5518 . . 8 Beechcroft Rd, Greenwich, CT *06830*
☎ (941) 964-2049 . . 140 Gilchrist Rd, Boca Grande, FL *33921*
Scott MR & MRS John T (Haas—Elizabeth M Knight) H'50
☎ (610) 933-4423 . . Pickering Rd, RD 2, Phoenixville, PA *19460*
Scott MR & MRS John T JR (Karen W Fraley)
☎ (610) 469-9258 . . Box 142, Hilltop Rd, Birchrunville, PA *19421*
Scott MR & MRS Joseph A 3d (Elizabeth K Atkinson) | ☎ (610) 827-7588
Colby'57.Pa'54 . . . . | Bodine Rd, RD 1,
MISS Elizabeth B—LorHgts'82—at | Malvern, PA *19355*
2710 Folsom St, Philadelphia, PA *19130* . . . . . . |
Scott MR Joseph A 4th—Rc.W&L'80 . . of
2316 Manning St, Philadelphia, PA *19103*
☎ (212) 447-6509 . . 7 E 35 St, Apt 1B, New York, NY *10016*
Scott MISS Katherine B (Boyd—Katherine Scott Busselle) MtH'95
☎ (508) 540-4822 . . Box 27, 24 Bowline Rd, West Falmouth,
MA *02574*
Scott MR & MRS Laurence S (Parker—F Jane Wykle) Stph'48.Hof'51
237 Springs Av, Gettysburg, PA *17325*
Scott MR M Simon . . see M M Jeanes
Scott MRS Margaret (Wickes—Margaret F Jones) | ☎ (610) 527-3733
Me. . . . . | 138 Montrose Av,
MR Christopher P Wickes—Me.—at | 34, Rosemont, PA
☎ (610) 892-0308 . . 225 W Jefferson St, | *19010*
Apt 1A, Media, PA *19063* . . . . |
Scott MR Norman—Pcu.Mt.Bur.USN'43
2164 Hyde St, San Francisco, CA *94109*
Scott MRS Patricia K (Patricia Kennedy) Tcy. . . . . . | ☎ (415) 921-8984
MR Norman 3d—at 63390 Overtree Rd, Bend, OR | 23 Presidio Av,
97701 . . . . | San Francisco, CA
| *94115*
Scott MR & MRS Philip W (Amy H Saulnier) Tul'86.Me.Hob'83
☎ (610) 993-9237 . . 1549 Sugartown Rd, Paoli, PA *19301*
Scott MR & MRS R Stewart (Bowman—Sheila | ☎ (561) 276-6614
Williams) Fcg.StA. . . . . | 2910 Gulfstream Rd,
MR Timothy W Bowman . . . . | Gulf Stream, FL
MR J Hunt Bowman 3d—Nath'lH'75 . . . . | *33483*
MR Bradford L Bowman . . . . |
MISS Tracey Bowman (Geczik—Tracey |
Bowman) Edin'79—at |
973 W Dobyns Lane, Tucson, AZ *85704* . . . . |
Scott MR Ralph M S—Rv.
☎ (609) 829-8900 . . 139 E Warren St, Edgewater Park, NJ *08010*
Scott MR Robert L—Sm.Btn.Hn.H'31 . . of
600 Charles River St, Needham, MA *02192*
☎ (617) 235-6455 . . ''Barnstable'' PO Box 812026, Wellesley,
MA *02181*

Scott MRS Robert Montgomery (H Gay Elliot) Rdc'51.Ac.
☎ (610) 688-7010 . . ''Hopelands'' 705 Church Rd, Wayne, PA *19087*
Scott MR Robert Montgomery—Nyc.Ph.K.Myf.H'51.Pa'54 . . of
☎ (610) 688-2401 . . ''Ardrossan'' 807 Newtown Rd, Villanova,
PA *19085*
☎ (215) 985-4102 . . 1701 Locust St, Apt 812, Philadelphia, PA *19103*
Scott MR & MRS S Buford (Susan E Bailey) Va'55
☎ (804) 320-7664 . . 7612 Hill Dv, Richmond, VA *23225*
Scott MRS S Lytton (Underhill—Dorothy Sullivan) Ri.Cly.
☎ (212) 355-1815 . . 435 E 52 St, New York, NY *10022*
Scott MASTER Samuel Lytton (Eugene L) . . . . Born at
New York, NY Jun 1'96
Scott MR & MRS Sean D (Lindsay S Cullen) Col'91.Me.Col'91
255 Price Av, Berwyn, PA *19312*
Scott MISS Sheila N—Bnd'73
☎ (212) 228-2573 . . 50 E 10 St, Apt 2A, New York, NY *10003*
Scott MR & MRS Sidney JR (Evelyn T Price) Wil.Yn.Y'45
☎ (302) 656-2695 . . PO Box 3755, Greenville, DE *19807*
Scott MR & MRS Sidney 3d (Elaine R Steinacker) Ant'73.Pa'79.Pa'75.Del'84
33 Deer Path, Kennett Square, PA *19348*
Scott MR & MRS Stephen H (Charlotte L | ☎ (602) 955-4704
Vandeweghe) Ariz'69.Clare'66 . . . . | 3631 E Pasadena
MISS Haley A . . . . | Av, Phoenix, AZ
JUNIORS MISS Mary F . . . . | *85018*
Scott MR & MRS Stephen H JR (Marcia L Harris) Fla'92.Fla'91
☎ (404) 355-7332 . . 732 Channing Dv NW, Atlanta, GA *30318*
Scott MR Stuart—Rc.Bgt.H.'33
☎ (914) 232-8160 . . 60 Girdle Ridge Dv, Box 420, Katonah, NY *10536*
Scott MRS W Frazier (Marion E Carmichael)
see Dilatory Domiciles
Scott MR & MRS Warren T (Ellen V Kittredge) Pa'78.Pa'76
☎ (610) 645-5473 . . 128 St Georges Rd, Ardmore, PA *19003*
Scott MISS Wendy V . . see M M Jeanes
Scotten MRS Robert McG (Crain—Ann Boyd) Cly.
☎ (609) 443-7597 . . Meadow Lakes 40-06, Hightstown, NJ *08520*
Scott-Paine MRS Elizabeth B (Elizabeth A Baker) . . | ☎ (805) 565-5920
MR Mark H—☎ (805) 566-9984 . . . . | 900 Hot Springs Rd,
| Montecito, CA
| *93108*

Scovil MR & MRS Alexander C (Katharine P Oliva) | ☎ (216) 423-0317
Conn'78.Tv.Cv.Pk.Y'76 . . . . | PO Box 279,
JUNIORS MISS Katharine H . . . . | 1139 W Hill Dv,
JUNIORS MISS Diana K . . . . | Gates Mills, OH
| *44040*
Scovil MRS Janet MacL (Janet MacL Fates) Y'73 . . | ☎ (919) 774-6237
MISS Amanda J . . . . | 1712 Lord Ashley
JUNIORS MR R Malcolm . . . . | Dv, Sanford, NC
JUNIORS MR Matthew H . . . . | *27330*
Scovil MRS Richard Malcolm (Jeffrey—Florence H Crocker) . . . . . Died at
Columbus, OH Apr 4'95
Scovil MR & MRS Samuel K (Barbara C Baker) Sth'45.Kt.Tv.Un.Cv.Pk.Y'45
☎ (216) 423-3322 . . 1809 Berkshire Rd, Gates Mills, OH *44040*
Scovil MR & MRS Samuel K 3d (Katherine R Sullivan) Skd'82.Rr.Y'73
☎ (414) 242-3620 . . 5309 W River Trail, Mequon, WI *53092*

Scribner MRS Charles JR (Joan Sunderland)   ☎ (212) 744-3942
Shcc.Cly. . . . .   211 E 70 St,
   MR Blair S—at ☎ (212) 794-1515   New York, NY
   215 E 68 St, New York, NY *10021* *10021*
   MR John—at ☎ (212) 777-0185 . . 105 E 16 St,
   New York, NY *10003* . . . .

Scribner MR & MRS Charles 3d (Ritchie H Markoe) Nu'75.Pr.Rc.Cly.P'73
   ☎ (212) 744-3462 . . 655 Park Av, New York, NY *10021*

Scribner MRS David (Grant—Marjorie Perez)
   ☎ (212) GR5-6687 . . 230 E 15 St, New York, NY *10003*

Scribner MR & MRS David H (Kathleen M Wisdom)
   Fox Den Farm, RR 1, Box 348, Myers Rd, Shaftsbury, VT *05262*

Scripps MR & MRS Barry H (Gail L DeVane) SanDiegoSt'78.Sar.Ariz'69
   1318 Caminito Laura, Olivenhain, CA *92024*

Scripps MR & MRS Edward W (McDonnell—Betty J Knight)
   BtP.Sfy.Evg.Cly.Cda.Dar.Pom'29
   ☎ (561) 844-8962 . . ''Karnak'' 947 N Ocean Blvd, Palm Beach,
   FL *33480*

Scudder MR & MRS Barrett (Hyde—Aljean Thomas) H'27
   ☎ (941) 964-0242 . . PO Box 38, Boca Grande, FL *33921*

Scudder MR & MRS David W (Marie Louise Sibley) Rdc'59.Un.Chi.H'57
   ☎ (508) 356-3236 . . 248 Argilla Rd, Ipswich, MA *01938*

Scudder MR & MRS Edward W JR (Perrin—Louise B Fry) SCar'41.Rm.P'35
   ☎ (561) 272-3209 . . 1171 N Ocean Blvd, Gulf Stream, FL *33483*

Scudder MR & MRS Edward W 3d (Lucretia A McDougal) Fla'74.P'71
   ☎ (609) 737-9030 . . 12 Benjamin Trail, Pennington, NJ *08534*

Scudder MR & MRS George W (Holly L Winant)   ☎ (610) MU8-3548
PaMil'66 . . . .   17 Forest Rd,
   MISS Jennifer L—Bates'88 . . . .   Wayne, PA *19087*

Scudder MRS Mason (Celia Vandermark) Chi.Cysl.Ncd.
   ☎ (941) 262-7490 . . 2215 Southwinds Dv, Naples, FL *34102-7657*

Scudder MR Rogers V—H'34
   ☎ (508) 448-6736 . . Groton School, Box 991, Groton, MA *01450*

Scudder MISS Saidie E—V'29
   ☎ (516) 922-4332 . . ''Deep Woods'' Cleft Rd, Mill Neck, NY *11765*

Scull MISS Anna C—Br'63
   ☎ (617) 661-9029 . . 240 Brattle St, Apt 42, Cambridge, MA *02138*

Scull MRS David (Patricia Grant)
   ☎ (207) 276-3921 . . Northeast Harbor, ME *04662*

Scull MRS Edward B (Anna C Keen) Atown'96
   ☎ (610) 282-1409 . . 5185 W State St, Coopersburg, PA *18036*

Scull MR & MRS John L JR (Elizabeth H Stulb) Ncd.Dar.Pa'48
   ☎ (803) 797-8507 . . The Elms, 9102 Lafayette Court,
   North Charleston, SC *29406-9131*

Scull MR Theodore C—Me.Gm.
   ☎ (610) 645-8659 . . 1400 Waverly Rd, Villa 10, Gladwyne, PA *19035*

Scull MR & MRS Theodore W (Preston—Suellyn M Barton)
   Qnslnd'66.Ty'63.Lond'67.BankSt'76
   ☎ (212) 535-6860 . . 325 E 72 St, New York, NY *10021*

Sculley MR & MRS Arthur B (Jill Jensen)   ☎ (201) 263-0447
Ln.Rby.Pa'67 . . . .   289 Morris Av,
   MR Arthur B JR . . . .   Mountain Lakes, NJ
     07046

Sculley MR & MRS David W (Kahrl—Paula Cook)   of ☎ (412)741-5396
Sth'66.H'68 . . . .   Blackburn Rd,
   MR David W 2d . . . .   Sewickley, PA
     15143-8386
     ☎ (516) 584-5315
     ''Gamewood''
     Harbor Rd,
     St James, NY *11780*

Sculley MR & MRS John S 3d (Hersh—Carol L Adams)
   End'64.Bur.Ln.Br'61.Pa'63
   ☎ (212) 755-9624 . . 580 Park Av, New York, NY *10021*

Scullin MR & MRS Albert J (Sherrill H Warner) Bab'63
   ☎ (617) 729-2952 . . 31 Canal St, Winchester, MA *01890*

Scullin MISS Barbara B—Ty'87 . . see M P Erdman

Scullin MR & MRS John R (McAdams—Janice J Micka) Ub.H'60
   70 Miller Rd, Newton Center, MA *02159*

Scullin MISS Josephine S
   ☎ (505) 982-9955 . . 523 E Alameda St, Santa Fe, NM *87501*

Scully MR & MRS Arthur M (Eleanor A Foster)   ☎ (412) 521-3270
Pg.Rr.Pitt'50. . . . .   5558 Aylesboro Av,
   MR Arthur M 3d . . . .   Pittsburgh, PA
   MR Timothy I *15217*

Scully MR & MRS David B (Erika Christensen) HWSth'91.B.Shcc.Rcn.Ty'83
   ☎ (011-44-171) 721-3574 . . 20 Campden St, London W8 7EP, England

Scully MISS Elizabeth A
   ☎ (212) 475-7176 . . 330 E 19 St, Apt 5D, New York, NY *10003*

Scully MR & MRS Henry C (Louise W O'Brien)
   ''Glenross House'' 9 Crada Glen, Paget PG 03, Bermuda

Scully MR & MRS John A (Josephine W Pepper)   ☎ (908) 766-2506
B.Eh.Shcc.Yn.Y'53 . . . .   110 Post Kunhart
   MR Benjamin P . . . .   Rd, PO Box 371,
     Bernardsville, NJ
     07924-0371

Scully MR & MRS John A JR (Samantha G Chapin) Mid'88.Tul'87.Brand'90
   ☎ (718) 852-5097 . . 150 Montague St, Apt 5, Brooklyn, NY *11201*

Scully MR & MRS Kevin M (Hope G Henchey)
   Conn'88.Pratt'95.SCar'82.CUNY'95
   ☎ (914) 285-9597 . . 37 Lynton Place, White Plains, NY *10606*

Scully MR & MRS Leonard Tyson (Jean T Jackson)
   K.Chr.Plg.Fw.StJ.Cl'32.Nu'39
   ☎ (212) AL5-8399 . . 45 Fifth Av, New York, NY *10003*

Scully MR & MRS Thomas A (Ann E Hoffmann)
   WmSth'80.Fcg.Va'79.CathU'86
   ☎ (703) 683-3429 . . 2915 King St, Alexandria, VA *22302*

Seabright MR & MRS Thomas W (Ann T Smith)   ☎ (216) 257-5198
Ws'78.JCar'88.Cin'72.Ill'74.JCar'88 . . . .   9498 Headlands Rd,
   JUNIORS MISS Elizabeth J . . . .   Mentor, OH *44060*
   JUNIORS MISS Clare H . . . .
   JUNIORS MISS Anne T . . . .

Seabrook MR & MRS de Lacy H (Joan S Schullinger)   ☎ (201) 376-8542
Y'45w . . . .   304 Forest Dv S,
   MR Randall de L—Denis'86—at   Short Hills, NJ
   ☎ (508) 463-9229 . . 6 Hallisey Dv,   *07078*
   Newburyport, MA *01950* . . . .

Seal MRS Henry Kendall (Margaret I Kester) . . . . Died at
   Newtown Square, PA May 16'96

Seale MR & MRS William (Lucinda L Smith) of ☎ (703)549-4086
Salem'63.Cos.Sar.Sl.Dar.Ncd.Sw'61.Duke'65 . . 805 Prince St,
MR William 3d . . . . Alexandria, VA
MR John Henry B *22314*
☎ (409) 384-5269
"Ant Hill" Rte 2,
Box 507, Jasper, TX
75951

Seaman MRS Dixon (Madeleine C Dixon) Mds.Cly.Dyc . . .of
☎ (212) 988-0032 . . 315 E 72 St, Apt 19L, New York, NY *10021*
☎ (516) 324-4723 . . Town House East, 18 Cross H'way, East Hampton,
NY *11937*

Seaman MR & MRS Douglas (Eleanor H Remick) of ☎ (414)351-0524
Cc.Cly.Cda.Yn.Y'43 . . . . 800 W Bradley Rd,
MISS Eleanor H—Ken'89.Cly.Cda.—at Milwaukee, WI
201 E 86 St, New York, NY *10028* *53217*
MISS Sarah M—Geo'95—at 3777 Peachtree Rd ☎ (561) 546-6201
NE, Atlanta, GA *30319* . . . . 164 Gomez Rd,
MR Douglas JR—Rc.On.Bost'91—at Hobe Sound, FL
1448 N Lake Shore Dv, Chicago, IL *60610* *33455*

Seaman MR & MRS Irving JR (June Carry) ☎ (847) 234-1457
Cho.On.Sr.Rc.Y'45 . . . . 946 N Elm Tree Rd,
MISS Anne D. . . . . Lake Forest, IL
60045

Seaman MR & MRS Peter S (Margaret W Swift) Tufts'75.Rcch.H'74
☎ (805) 684-9566 . . 805 Sand Point Rd, Carpinteria, CA *93013*

Seamans DR & MRS Robert C JR (Eugenia A Merrill)
Myc.Ec.Cvc.Chi.Mt.H.'40.Mit'42.Mit'50 ⚓
☎ (508) 927-0212 . . "Sea Meadow" 675 Hale St, Beverly Farms,
MA *01915*

Seamans MR & MRS Robert C 3d (Stella M ☎ (508) 922-1392
Renchard) Swb'67.Myc.Ey.Cl'72 . . . . 840 Hale St,
MISS Rebecca M . . . . Beverly Farms, MA
MR Robert C 4th. *01915*
JUNIORS MISS Eve R . . . .
JUNIORS MR Adam B . . . .

Searle MISS Marion S (Chandler—Marion S Searle)
see D C Bermingham

Searle MR & MRS Robert S (Davie—Urling S Iselin) Nu'76
☎ (203) 869-4805 . . 66 Old Church Rd, Greenwich, CT *06830*

Searle MR & MRS William L (Sally D Burnett) Sr.Cho.On.Cas.Mich'50
☎ (847) 234-3971 . . 171 W Laurel Av, Lake Forest, IL *60045*

Sears MRS Alexandra W (Alexandra P Whelen) ☎ (011-51-14)
So.Cly. 477085
MISS Alexandra B—AmU'94—at Vasco Nuñez de
☎ (202) 342-5479 . . 3850 Tunlaw Rd NW, Balboa 586,
Apt 815, Washington, DC *20007* . . . . Lima 18, Peru
MR Russell A 3d—Tul'82—at ☎ (202) 362-1577
3287D Sutton Place NW, Washington, DC *20016*
MR Richard W—Bradford'86—at
☎ (803) 785-4355 . . 94 Forest Cove,
Hilton Head Island, SC *29928* . . . .

Sears MISS Alice G
☎ (202) 362-1577 . . 3287D Sutton Place NW, Washington, DC *20016*

Sears MR & MRS Daniel H (Robin deP Dodge) V'86.Sbc.Tr.Bost'91
☎ (508) 468-0077 . . 6 Cedar St, Wenham, MA *01984*

Sears MR Edmund H JR . . see P M Rhinelander

Sears MR Edmund H 3d—H'59
☎ (508) 358-2172 . . 187 Pelham Island Rd, Wayland, MA *01778*

Sears MR & MRS Francis P (Barbara Iselin) Sbc.My.Sm.
☎ (508) 468-3339 . . 25 Gardner St, PO Box 579, Hamilton, MA *01936*

Sears MR Frederick F JR—Bost'90
☎ (617) 639-8530 . . 66 Front St, Marblehead, MA *01945*

Sears MR Frederick R
☎ (011-51-14) 679605 . . Las Magnolias 160, Barranco, Lima, Peru

Sears MR & MRS Herbert T (Ann Goodyear Mason) ☎ (603) 772-4497
TyU'69.Bost'69.Wash'73 . . . . 33 Pine St, Exeter,
MISS Hannah T . . . . NH *03833*
JUNIORS MISS Emily G. . . . .
JUNIORS MR H Mason . . . .

Sears MR John W—Sm.Tr.Cy.Sb.H'52.Ox'55.H'57
☎ (617) 227-6664 . . 7 Acorn St, Boston, MA *02108*

Sears MISS Katharine C . . see P M Rhinelander

Sears MISS Marguerite Dodge (Daniel H) . . . . Born at
Boston, MA Mch 25'96

Sears MR Nathaniel R—Y'90 . . see A J D Morrow

Sears MR & MRS R Buford (Suzanne M Marlette) NCar'77.Buf.NCar'77
☎ (716) 837-3806 . . 240 Middlesex Rd, Buffalo, NY *14216*

Sears MR Richard—Sm.H'38 . . . . ☎ (011-33-1)
MISS Stephanie 47-23-49-11
2 rue Gaston de St
Paul, 75016 Paris,
France

Sears MR Richard D 3d—Cyb.H'50 . . . . ☎ (803) 649-6378
MISS Page E Kelleher. . . . . "Rosewall"
607 Colleton Av SE,
Aiken, SC *29801*

Sears MR & MRS Richard M (Theresa Grace) Ford'80.Pr.Vt'76
☎ (516) 627-4086 . . 7 Plandome Dv, Plandome, NY *11030*

Sears MR & MRS Robert M (Erica B Leisenring)
Pa'74.Ant'77.Nf.ColC'68.Bost'71
☎ (314) 361-1478 . . 5095 Westminster Place, St Louis, MO *63108*

Sears MRS Sally (Wechsler—Sally S Thayer)
☎ (212) 924-1387 . . 387½ Bleecker St, New York, NY *10014-2452*

Sears MISS Sarah Eleanor (g—Garette E Lockee) . . . . Born Nov 27'95

Sears MR Sebastian C—Cl'93 . . see A J D Morrow

Sears MR Stephen T—Rc.W&L'88.Duke'94
☎ (212) 737-8244 . . 315 E 65 St, New York, NY *10021*

Sears MASTER Timothy Duncan (g—Garette E Lockee) . . . . Born
Mch 12'94

Seat MRS Ward F (Cornelia Garrott) Miss'25
☎ (334) 626-8663 . . Westminster Village 263, 500 Spanish Fort Blvd,
Spanish Fort, AL *36527*

Seaton MRS Henry D (Newbold—Jo Walker)
☎ (941) 676-4747 . . PO Box 832, Mountain Lake, Lake Wales,
FL *33859-0832*

Seaton MR & MRS Hugh Van (Lucille C Pendleton) ☎ (904) 262-2314
Conn'74.Nu'84.Mo'65.StL'69 . . . . 11287 Scott Mill
MISS Dana A—at Syracuse U . . . . Rd, Jacksonville, FL
MR Hugh G—at Tainan, Taiwan *32223*

Seavey MR & MRS William A (Mary van Beuren) Rdc'56.Pcu.Tcy.P'52.H'55
☎ (510) 547-4656 . . 303 Pacific Av, Piedmont, CA *94611*

Seawell BRIG GEN (RET) & MRS William T (Judith T Alexander)
Ws'40.Cly.Ncd.USA'41.H'49
☎ (501) 536-4819 . . 21 Westridge Dv, Pine Bluff, AR 71603

Sebring MR & MRS Orvel (Margaret Dulles) Ph.Ac.P.'26.H'33
☎ (610) 353-2635 . . Dunwoody Village CH111,
3500 West Chester Pike, Newtown Square, PA 19073

Secor MR & MRS James Jay 3d (Christine L | ☎ (540) 433-5078
Robinson) VaWes'73.VaWes'73.JMad'95 . . . . . | 218 Franklin St,
MISS Virginia M—at Kenyon . . . . | Harrisonburg, VA
JUNIORS MISS Caroline R—at St George's . . . . . | 22801
JUNIORS MR Jay K M—at Phillips Exeter . . . . . . |

Secor MR & MRS W Fielding (Sheila M Coy) | ☎ (203) 263-4710
SL'68.Ny.Y'64 . . . . | 167 Sycamore Av,
MISS Sarah E . . . . | Woodbury, CT
JUNIORS MR Casey McA . . . . | 06798 . . MR absent

Seddon MRS James A (Joan Krieger) . . . . | ☎ (314) 991-1006
MR Scott . . . . | 410 S McKnight Rd,
MR Douglas . . . . | St Louis, MO 63124

Seden MR & MRS Theodore R (Susan E Stampley) | ☎ (714) 723-5766
Vh.SanDiegoSt'67 . . . . | 111 Via San Remo,
MISS Tiffany L—Cal'91.Cal'94—at | Newport Beach, CA
1011—4 St, Apt 101, Santa Monica, CA 90403 . | 92663
MISS Alyson M—Cal'93 . . . . |

Sedgwick REV Harold Bend—Sb.Ds.Cw.Ofp.H.'30.EpiscTheo'35 . . of
☎ (617) 863-0840 . . Brookhaven F24, 1010 Waltham St, Lexington,
MA 02173
☎ (617) 423-4948 . . 151 Tremont St, Boston, MA 02111

Sedgwick MR & MRS Henry D (Auchincloss—Robin | of ☎ (212)427-9380
Dike) Wheat'65.Hb.H'51.MgmtInst'53 . . . . | 163 E 94 St,
MR Robert B . . . . | New York, NY
MR Nicholas J . . . . | 10128
MISS Hilary M Auchincloss . . . . | ☎ (860) 434-2114
MR Conrad McI Auchincloss . . . . | 23 Ferry Rd,
| Old Lyme, CT
| 06371

Sedgwick MR & MRS Jonathan de F (Anne M Kirst) | ☎ (208) 664-2378
H'62.Cal'67.NAriz'73 . . . . | 3961 Nicklaus Dv,
MR Shane de F . . . . | Coeur D'Alene, ID
JUNIORS MISS Hana-Lee . . . . | 83814

Sedgwick MRS William P 3d (Margaret Allen) | ☎ (212) SP7-4007
V'53.Mds.Dyc.P. . . . . | 11 Gramercy Park,
MR Mitchell W—at Fletcher . . . . | New York, NY
| 10003-1753

Sednaoui MR & MRS M Kent (Jennifer S Wettlaufer)
LakeF'83.Fic.Bgt.LakeF'81
☎ (914) 234-0250 . . 28 Middle Patent Rd, Bedford, NY 10506

See MR & MRS Alva B JR (Nancy Gay) Ncmb'67.Ncd.Ty'55
598 Chestnut Oak Court NW, Atlanta, GA 30327

See MR & MRS Alva B 3d (Alison B Davis) Tul'83
☎ (504) 899-9041 . . 6030 Camp St, New Orleans, LA 70118

See MISS E Bailey—MassArt'94
☎ (508) 921-1233 . . 26 High St, 2, Beverly Farms, MA 01915

See MR Richard E—Ty'82
☎ (212) 860-6674 . . 121 E 90 St, New York, NY 10128

Seed MRS Barbara B (Barbara A Buchanan) Nat'l'59.StJ.
☎ (561) 640-0693 . . 945 Bear Island Circle, West Palm Beach,
FL 33409

Seed DR & MRS William T (Smith—E Dorsey Ivey) | of ☎ (914)234-9757
Duke'60.Cl'75.Bgt.Wms'54.Cr'62 . . . . | ''Pondside''
MISS Betsy Smith—Van'88 . . . . | 349 Harris Rd,
MR Nelson C Smith—Tul'89 . . . . | Bedford Hills, NY
| 10507
| ☎ (212) 570-6563
| 985 Fifth Av, Apt
| 2A, New York, NY
| 10021

Seegers MR F Scott—Fr'69
☎ (540) 788-4452 . . Walnut Hill Farm, 10593 Shenandoah Path, Catlett,
VA 20119

Seeley MRS de Benneville K (Lydia M Clothier)
☎ (610) 353-7252 . . Dunwoody Village CH126,
3500 West Chester Pike, Newtown Square, PA 19073

Seeley MR de Benneville K JR—Mid'52 . . . . | ☎ (801) 278-9755
MISS Ellen F . . . . | 3872 Parkview
JUNIORS MR Morris C . . . . | Circle,
| Salt Lake City,
| UT 84124

Seeley MR & MRS Franklin M (Suzanne E Fotterall) | ☎ (610) 642-3109
Skd'73.Me.Fst.Ofp.Temp'50 . . . . | PO Box 190,
MISS Olivia F—at Randolph-Macon . . . . | Gladwyne, PA
MISS Cordelia M—at Dickinson . . . . | 19035

Seeley MR & MRS James H (Elizabeth La M Tilton) Dar.Dc.Kas'30
☎ (503) 588-2306 . . 294 Hrubetz Rd SE, Salem, OR 97302-4985

Seeley MR & MRS James H JR (Deborah A Johnson) | ☎ (503) 635-6823
OreSt'76.OreSt'76 . . . . | 555 Atwater Rd,
JUNIORS MR Peter T . . . . | Lake Oswego, OR
| 97034

Seeley MR & MRS Leonard P (Karin M Smith) Cv. . . | ☎ (205) 828-3389
MISS Margaret J . . . . | 102 Leesburg St,
MR R Scott . . . . | Meridianville, AL
| 35759

Seeley MR Nathaniel Keim—Myf.Mid'90
☎ (802) 247-4422 . . 18 Pearl St, Brandon, VT 05733

Seely-Brown MRS Horace JR (Rosalie H Slack) Cly.Ncd.
☎ (561) 272-4936 . . Harbour's Edge 257, 401 E Linton Blvd,
Delray Beach, FL 33483

Seely-Brown MR & MRS Horace 3d (Hood Yeilding) | ☎ (847) 948-0971
FlaSt'67.SCal'63 . . . . | 2950 Cherokee
MISS Melissa H—BowlG'94 . . . . | Lane, Riverwoods,
MR Horace 4th—at Miami U . . . . | IL 60015
JUNIORS MISS Emily Coe . . . . |

Seelye MRS Mary S (Mary S Sickels) SL'50
☎ (215) 646-4947 . . 5 Mullen Rd, Ambler, PA 19002

Segerstrom MRS Yvonne de C (Yvonne de C Perry) | ☎ (310) 557-0673
Fr. . . . . | 2222 Av of the
MR Toren H . . . . | Stars, Apt 2001E,
MR Anton D . . . . | Los Angeles, CA
| 90067

Seggerman MR & MRS Frederick Bonsal (O'Hara— | ☎ (860) 345-3441
Isabelle F Douglas) Pr.P'43 . . . . | Bonsal Douglas
MISS Isabelle F O'Hara—CtCol'94—at | House, Walkley Hill
7709 Random Run Lane, Apt 203, | Rd, Haddam, CT
Falls Church, VA 22042 . . . . | 06438

Seggerman MR & MRS Frederick E (Ingeborg E Blaurock) T. . . . . ☎ (011-49-6172) 33674 Weidebornweg 24, 61348 Bad Homburg, Germany
MISS Natalia C A . . . .
MISS Maja T . . . .
MR Alexander F E . . . .
Seggerman MR & MRS Harry G A (Anne P Crellin) P'49 . . . . ☎ (203) 255-4459 "Deer Meadow" 5060 Congress St, Fairfield, CT 06430
MISS Patricia S . . . .
MISS Marianne G C. . . . .
MR John E G . . . .
Seggerman MR Kenneth M—P'47.Cl'51 . . . . ☎ (212) TR9-4439 520 E 86 St, New York, NY 10028
MISS Sarah A—at 1112 Melvina Hill Rd, Boulder, CO 80302. . . . .
MISS Victoria M—Box 973, Santa Cruz, CA 95061 . . . .
Seggerman MRS Rosemary L (Rosemary McV Lawrence) ☎ (805) 969-4555 . . PO Box 5887, Santa Barbara, CA 93150
Seherr-Thoss MRS C Hutton (Consuelo V Hutton) . . . . . name changed to Hutton
Seherr-Thoss MR Henry W . . . . Married at Alford, MA
Hanlon MISS Elizabeth A . . . . Jun 15'96
Seherr-Thoss MR & MRS Henry W (Elizabeth A Hanlon) Pratt'85.Rc.Bgt.Syr'59 . . of
☎ (914) 764-6464 . . 15 Honey Hollow Rd, Pound Ridge, NY 10576
☎ (413) 232-4323 . . "Blueberry Hill" W Alford Rd, West Stockbridge, MA 01266
Seibert MR & MRS Edward P (Winifred Rouillion) Au.Ty'61.Stan'63 . . . . ☎ (914) 763-5967 Redcoat Lane, Waccabuc, NY 10597
MISS Katharine P—StLaw'88.Bost'92—at ☎ (617) 367-4829 . . 44 Joy St, Boston, MA 02114. . . . .
MISS Elizabeth S—at Trinity . . . .
MR Timothy R—Ty'90—at ☎ (617) 742-7026 68 N Margin St, Boston, MA 02133. . . . .
MR William D—StLaw'92
Seibert MRS Elvin (BRNSS Christina Beck-Friis) . . . . ☎ (914) 677-3649 Front St, Apt 24, PO Box 626, Millbrook, NY 12545
MISS Angela M—☎ (914) 868-7001 . . . .
Seidler MR & MRS Francis F (Hately—Patricia C Martin) Pcu.Sfg.Innsbruck'35 . . . . of ☎ (415)567-5948 1333 Jones St, San Francisco, CA 94109
MISS Jennifer W Hately . . . .
☎ (707) 257-3866 170 Westgate Dv, Napa, CA 94558
Seidlitz MR & MRS Charles N 3d (Woodle—Anne T Spence) Ct.Rcch.Sc.Cvc.Stan'68.Nw'72
☎ (202) 966-9664 . . 5014 Lowell St NW, Washington, DC 20016
Seidner MR Irving Morton
☎ (303) 722-9882 . . 420 S Marion P'kway, Apt 203, Denver, CO 80209
Seipp MR & MRS Edwin A (P Anne Wieboldt) Bur.Pcu.Tcy.On.Pn.P'40
☎ (415) 323-3197 . . 49 Tuscaloosa Av, Atherton, CA 94027-4014
Seitz MR Daniel Ward—Rm.Snc.StJ.H'53
☎ (908) 291-0661 . . "Portland Place" 220 Hartshorne Rd, Locust, NJ 07760

Sekera MR Jeffrey O—Tufts'92 . . see E H Bennett 3d
Sekera MISS Katherine H—Loy'94 . . see E H Bennett 3d
Selby MR Frederick P—Ri.Pa'59
☎ (212) 988-9539 . . 36 E 72 St, New York, NY 10021
Selby MR John H—P'41
☎ (415) 776-9121 . . 1170 Sacramento St, San Francisco, CA 94108
Selby MRS Linn Howard (Linn Howard) Ri. . . . . of ☎ (212)996-3128 1060 Fifth Av, New York, NY 10128
MISS Andrea H—Pars'87—at ☎ (212) 675-6239 225 W 12 St, Apt 4B, New York, NY 10011 . . .
MISS Stephanie M—Wes'89—Box 271, Bethlehem, CT 06751. . . . .
☎ (307) 587-3917 Hawkeye Ranch, 4148 S Fork Rd, Cody, WY 82414
Selby MR & MRS Norman C (Melissa G Vail) Y'74.Nu'80.Rc.Bgt.Y'74.H'78 . . of
☎ (212) 877-5756 . . 262 Central Park W, New York, NY 10024
☎ (914) 666-7435 . . 205 Wood Rd, Mt Kisco, NY 10549
Selden MR & MRS George D (Patricia M FitzPatrick) Cc.Cw.Y'48
☎ (860) 536-0563 . . 14 Brandon Lane, Mystic, CT 06355
Selden MR & MRS George L (Ann L Arnold) Cly.Ncd.H.'49.H'52
☎ (212) 744-5997 . . 164 E 72 St, New York, NY 10021
Seldon MRS M Robert (Mervyn W Adams) Cl'64.CalSt'95
☎ (818) 919-1297 . . 909 S Fircroft St, West Covina, CA 91791
Selfe MR & MRS Edward M (Simon—Jane C Bowron) Va'50 . . of
☎ (205) 933-0427 . . Arlington Crest 84, 2600 Arlington Av S, Birmingham, AL 35205
☎ (970) 925-7281 . . 700 Ute Av, Aspen, CO 81611
Selfridge MISS Cynthia B
☎ (415) 461-7256 . . 18 Laderman Lane, Greenbrae, CA 94904
Seligman MR & MRS Joseph L JR (Peggy Van Horne) Mls'43.Mit'34.Y'38 . . . . ☎ (415) 868-1421 127 Seadrift Rd, PO Box 565, Stinson Beach, CA 94970
MR Edward S—Y'69—at ☎ (202) 265-5154 1838 Ingleside Terr NW, Washington, DC 20010
Seligman MR & MRS Thomas K (Rita Barela) NMex'69.Stan'65 . . . . ☎ (415) 552-8846 34 Woodland Av, San Francisco, CA 94117
MR Christopher A . . . .
JUNIORS MR Timothy A . . . .
Selke MR Edward D—Mass'84
☎ (404) 377-1919 . . 1653A McLendon Av NE, Atlanta, GA 30307
Selke MR & MRS Whitney F (Christian P Laidlaw) Vt'85.Wes'78
☎ (413) 698-2212 . . 317 Cone Hill Rd, Richmond, MA 01254
Selke MR & MRS William A (Martha W Floyd) Lx.Mit'43.Y'49
☎ (413) 298-4975 . . "Meetinghouse" Box 506, Stockbridge, MA 01262-0506
Selke MR William A JR—Hampshire'77
☎ (206) 882-1199 . . 56 Swan Lake, 6421—139 Place NE, Redmond, WA 98052
Selkirk MR & MRS Bruce B JR (Lauren N Goessling) Rc.Geo'67
☎ (314) 997-1524 . . 34 Upper Ladue Rd, St Louis, MO 63124
Sellar MRS Rita Dolan (Rita Dolan) Srb.Il. . . . . ☎ (401) 847-5362 "Seaweed" 740 Bellevue Av, Newport, RI 02840
MR Owen N . . . .

Selleck DR & MRS Nathaniel (Ross—Emily C Lanier)
Cl'69.Au.Conn'51.SUNY'55
☎ (203) 938-3633 . . 285 Poverty Hollow Rd, Redding, CT *06896*

Sellers MR & MRS Coleman VI (Louisa W Wright)
Ty'85.Me.Pe.Rv.Cc.Ac.Ithaca'85
☎ (302) 655-1976 . . 710 Coverdale Rd, Wawaset Park, Wilmington, DE *19805*

Sellers MR & MRS Emory R JR (MinnieBelle Fry) H'60.GeoW'65.GeoW'67
☎ (407) 645-0563 . . 325 Park North Court, Winter Park, FL *32789*

Sellers MRS Eva G (Eva A Geiger) . . . . | ☎ (610) 948-4659
MISS Elizabeth A . . . . | 570 King Rd,
Royersford, PA
19468

Sellers MR & MRS Frank R S (Julia D Wood) Me.Rv.USN'42
☎ (610) 640-0827 . . 422 Waynesbrooke Rd, Berwyn, PA *19312*

Sellers MR & MRS Frank R S JR (Coonley—Suzanne | ☎ (610) 525-6097
DuBarry) Briar'67.Ithaca'79 . . . . | 132 Browning Lane,
MISS Deborah B Coonley—at Lafayette . . . . . | Rosemont, PA
MR Howard Coonley 3d—at Davidson . . . . . . | *19010*

Sellers MR & MRS John F (Grace E Pifer) . . . . | 4385 Kenson Dv,
MISS Mary E . . . . | Allison Park, PA
MISS Jacqueline F . . . . | *15101*

Sellers MR Nicholas—An.Ph.Cc.Rv.Pa'53.Pa'60.Pa'74
☎ (610) 964-1754 . . "Longstone" PO Box 8141, Radnor, PA *19087-8141*

Sellers MRS William (Hall—Gadd—Annah Colket McKaig)
Rd.Me.Ac.W.Ncd.
☎ (610) 687-8612 . . "The Fox Box" 560 Red Fox Lane, Strafford, PA *19087*

Sellers MR & MRS William B (Lucille L Grant) Ala'88.Hills'85
☎ (334) 284-6784 . . 3405 Thomas Av, Montgomery, AL *36111*

Sellers MR & MRS William W (Nancy W Fields)
Pa'49.Me.Sa.Fw.Cc.Rv.Ac.Pa'43
☎ (610) MU8-2981 . . 701 Eagle Rd, Wayne, PA *19087-3409*

Sellman MR & MRS Charles R (Patricia M M Barroll) Va'86.Pom'87
☎ (212) 875-1614 . . 114 W 70 St, New York, NY *10023*

Selman MR & MRS James L 2d (Wilder | ☎ (504) 895-7549
Breckenridge) Ncmb'59.Tul'93.Tul'57.Tul'59 . . | 1910 Jefferson Av,
MR J Larkin 3d—NOlns'83—at New York, NY . | New Orleans, LA
70115

Selman MR & MRS John B (Susan L Lightsinger) Ala'84.Ala'85.Ala'86
☎ (409) 860-5243 . . 7880 Blue Bonnet Lane, Beaumont, TX *77725*

Selnick MR & MRS R Bruce (Sarah H Warrington) Lawr'83.Geo'82
☎ (513) 561-2425 . . 5820 Miami Rd, Cincinnati, OH *45243*

Seltman MR & MRS Arthur J (Nathalie F Runyon) | ☎ (703) 521-7909
Camb'40 . . . . | 619 S 23 St,
MISS I Frances—at ☎ (703) 276-9574 | Arlington, VA
1710 N Glebe Rd, Arlington, VA *22207* . . . . . . | *22202*

Seltzer DR & MRS Jonathan H (Elizabeth D Nickerson)
Geo'84.Tufts'88.Hav'80.Mich'82.Pa'88
216 Pine St, Philadelphia, PA *19106*

Semans DR & MRS James H (Trent—Mary D Biddle) | ☎ (919) 489-5194
Ri.Cos.Md.P'32.JHop'36 . . . . | 1415 Bivins St,
MR James D B T . . . . | Durham, NC *27707*

Semans MR & MRS Truman T (Nellie M Merrick) | ☎ (410) 823-1935
Md.Gv.B.Cly.P'48 . . . . | PO Box 827,
MR Truman T JR . . . . | Brooklandville, MD
MR William M . . . . | *21022-0827*

Semerjian MR George G—Hof'54 . . of
☎ (516) 283-0264 . . "Brigadune" Gin Lane, PO Box 112, Southampton, NY *11969*
35 E 76 St, New York, NY *10021*

Semple MRS Harton S (Phyllis A Keister)
☎ (412) 741-7013 . . 519 East Dv, Sewickley, PA *15143*

Semple MISS Heather H (Reynolds—Heather H Semple) MtVern'82
☎ (412) 741-2630 . . Quaker Hollow, Sewickley, PA *15143*

Semple MR & MRS Nathaniel M (Patricia Maguire) | of ☎ (202)342-9649
Md'70.Mt.Gi.Cl'68. | 3604 Davis St NW,
JUNIORS MR Nathaniel M JR—at Landon . . . . . . | Washington, DC
20007
☎ (540) 364-2305
Pohick Farm,
Delaplane, VA
20144

Semple MRS Robert B (Fowler—Holly R Reid) Rdc'48
☎ (804) 984-3641 . . 2205 Whippoorwill Rd, Charlottesville, VA *22901*

Semple MR & MRS Robert B JR (Pulling—Elizabeth | ☎ (212) 734-1972
F Canby) Sth'61.Nu'68.C.Cly.Ncd.Y.'59.Cal'61 | 135 E 74 St,
MISS Wendy Pulling—P'85.Stan'90 . . . . | New York, NY
10021

Sendax MRS Deborah de L (Webster—Deborah | ☎ (212) 570-6296
de Land Cobb) . . . . | 244 E 77 St,
JUNIORS MISS Jennifer R . . . . | New York, NY
10021

Sengelmann MR Erich P—Col'87.LondEc'88
☎ (415) 441-6041 . . 2363 Greenwich St, San Francisco, CA *94123*

Sengelmann MR Peter S . . see R K Simmons

Sengelmann MISS (DR) Roberta D—Mid'88
☎ (713) 664-2378 . . 7500 Kirby Dv, Apt 1331, Houston, TX *77030*

Senior MR & MRS Enrique F (Robin S Gimbel) ⚓ | of ☎ (516)367-8239
EsmodGL'75.LIU'90.B.Pr.Y'64.Y'67.H'69 | "Pheasant's Rest"
JUNIORS MISS Tailer F . . . . | 1290 Ridge Rd,
JUNIORS MISS Heather S . . . . | Laurel Hollow, NY
JUNIORS MISS Fern D . . . . | *11791*
☎ (804) 979-4356
Forest Hill
Plantation,
Box 20A, Rte 9,
Charlottesville, VA
22901

Senior MR & MRS Richard J L (Diana T Morgan) | ☎ (312) 337-3420
SL'62.Y'64.ArtInst'92.Rc.Cho.Cas.Wa.Ox'62. | 1420 N Lake Shore
Y'64 | Dv, Chicago, IL
MISS Alicia M—Y'93—at 2256 N Orchard St, | *60610*
Apt 1D, Chicago, IL *60614* . . . . |
MISS Amanda T—at Museum of Fine Arts Sch. . |
MR Alden L—Ken'92.DePaul'94—at
☎ (312) 951-1979 . . 1350 N Lake Shore Dv,
Apt 1118S, Chicago, IL *60610* . . . . |

Senseman DR & MRS David M (Kathleen McClune) Norw'79.P'76
☎ (210) 545-1823 . . 703 Slate Rock St, San Antonio, TX *78232*

Sensenbrenner MR & MRS F James JR (Cheryl L Warren) Lawr'72.Stan'65.Wis'68 . . . .
JUNIORS MR F James 3d . . . .
☎ (703) 751-1508 609 Ft Williams P'kway, Alexandria, VA 22304

Serfaty MR & MRS Simon H (Daly—Gail H Fitzgerald) JHop'67 . . . .
JUNIORS MR Alexis L . . . .
of ☎ (202)234-9022 2009 Kalorama Rd NW, Washington, DC 20009
☎ (757) 622-2903 ''The Pier'' 40 Rader St, Norfolk, VA 23517

Servick MRS K Hannah (Katharine M Hannah) . . . .
MR Edward Ross 2d—Pg.Rr.Denis'91—at
☎ (216) 421-9377 . . 2119 Lenox Rd, Apt 9, Cleveland Heights, OH 44106 . . . .
MR Douglas Todd . . . .
☎ (404) 233-5139 280 Rumson Rd NE, Atlanta, GA 30305

Sesnon MRS Jacqueline K (Jacqueline Keesling) . . .
MR Jackson K—Pcu.Stan'63 . . . .
☎ (310) 271-1787 707 N Maple Dv, Beverly Hills, CA 90210

Sessions MRS Robert E (Janice C de la Croix) Ala'32.Dar.Ncd.
☎ (610) 649-4284 . . Wynnewood Park Apt 28C, Wynnewood, PA 19096

Sessions MR & MRS Robert E JR (Sarah A Taunton) .
MISS Gemma L—at Bedford Coll . . . .
JUNIORS MISS Miranda J—at More House Sch . . .
☎ (011-44-171) 834-4180 33 Eccleston Square, London SW1, England

Sethness MRS Charles H JR (Mary G Buckley) Sc.Wa.Cas.
☎ (312) 787-9199 . . 1500 N Lake Shore Dv, Chicago, IL 60610

Sethness MRS Mary F (Mary Fahrner) . . . .
MR C Brian . . . .
☎ (847) 866-9144 525 Grove St, Apt 2B, Evanston, IL 60201

Seus MR & MRS Thomas E (Sheila M G Warnock) Y.'70.VillaN'76
☎ (215) 884-0208 . . 1100 Country Club Dv, Oreland, PA 19075

Sevcenko MRS Nancy P (Nancy Patterson) Sth'60.Cl'73 . . . .
MISS Elisabeth A—at 359—11 St, Brooklyn, NY 11215 . . . .
☎ (617) 492-0643 6 Follen St, Cambridge, MA 02138

Severson MR & MRS Edward E (Jacqueline C L McLean) Ariz'64 . . . .
MISS Kimberly L McL . . . .
MR Edward J McL . . . .
MR Courtney A McL . . . .
☎ (520) 744-2328 8820 N Scenic Dv, Tucson, AZ 85743

Sévigny MR & MRS J P Albert (Laurel L Delamater) McG'79.Concordia'74 . . . .
JUNIORS MISS Catherine M . . . .
☎ (514) 488-9437 2060 Grand Blvd, Montreal, Quebec H4B 2W8, Canada

Sévigny COL HON & MRS Pierre (Corinne A R Kernan) CA.Laval'37 . . . .
MR Robert K . . . .
☎ (514) 847-5260 3495 rue de la Montagne, Apt 909, Montreal, Quebec H3G 2A5, Canada

Sewall MRS George T (Mary H Bossidy) Lx.
☎ (212) LE4-4624 . . 1212 Fifth Av, New York, NY 10029

Sewall MR Harold Marsh—Dyc.Myf.Bow'51
☎ (207) 729-7495 . . 11 Appletree Dv, Brunswick, ME 04011

Sewall MRS L Roosevelt (Lucy M Roosevelt) Wheat'64
☎ (617) 731-1891 . . 19 Thatcher St, Brookline, MA 02146

Sewall MISS Margaret H R (Tingey H) . . . . . . Married at Middletown, CT
Boogaard MR Thomas C (late Tom) . . . . May 18'96

Sewall MRS Nancy Anne (Nancy A McClellan) Westbrook'59
☎ (704) 859-5247 . . ''The Green House'' Fox Trot Lane, Tryon, NC 28782

Sewall MR Tingey H—Ub.Bow'62
☎ (617) 383-6086 . . 11 Spindrift Lane, Cohasset, MA 02025

Seward MR Dwight T—Cy.Nd.Br'58
☎ (314) 721-3055 . . 710 S Hanley Rd, Apt 11C, St Louis, MO 63105-2654

Sexson MR & MRS Timothy J (Elizabeth Wilmer) Ariz'62.Ariz'63 . . of
☎ (602) 277-7872 . . 310 E Keim Dv, Phoenix, AZ 85012
☎ (520) 367-1731 . . 3244 Bullfrog Loop, Pinetop, AZ 85935

Sexton MRS Eric H L (Beryl M D Partridge)
☎ (207) 236-2118 . . ''Berwick Hill'' Rockport, ME 04856

Sexton MRS Mason Speed (Twachtman—May Mason Speed) ConsAm'28.Cda.Ht.
☎ (804) 971-1955 . . 1420 Grove Rd, Charlottesville, VA 22901

Sexton MR & MRS Peter R L (Esther E Page) R.Pa'65
☎ (207) 763-3348 . . HC 62, Box 124, Hope, ME 04847

Sexton MR Richard H L—Plg.H'32
☎ (207) 596-6269 . . Elm St, South Thomaston, ME 04858

Seybolt MR Calvert H—Cyb.Sm.Cc.Mid'80.Geo'88
☎ (757) 665-7959 . . ''Cedar Grove'' PO Box 297, Mappsville, VA 23407

Seybolt MISS Edwina P (Granelli—Edwina P Seybolt) MassArt'75 . . . .
JUNIORS MISS Alexis Granelli . . . .
☎ (902) 479-3648 230 Spinnaker Dv, Halifax, Nova Scotia B3N 3C6, Canada

Seybolt MR & MRS G Crossan JR (Margaret McC Meyer) Vt'80.Rc.B.Plg.Mid'77
☎ (212) 861-8279 . . 520 E 86 St, New York, NY 10028

Seybolt MRS George C (Hortense E Kelley) NCar'42.Cy.Sm.Chi.Ncd. . . . .
MRS Reva B (McNally—Reva B Seybolt) Mid'72.H'75—at ☎ (860) 928-0754 . . Box 29, Woodstock, CT 06281 . . . .
☎ (617) 326-3359 699 High St, Dedham, MA 02026

Seydel MISS Florence Vasser (gg—MRS Sumner S Sollitt) . . . . Born at Atlanta, GA Apr 10'95

Seymore MISS Chloë B—RISD'96 . . see MRS A E Paine

Seymour MR & MRS Allyn JR (Karen A Mayfield) Mid'80.Ec.V'75.Hart'77
☎ (860) 233-4363 . . 42 Westwood Rd, West Hartford, CT 06117

Seymour MRS Caroline C (Harloff—Caroline W Cole) BtP.Cda.Dc.Myf. . . . .
MISS Melanie R—OWes'88.Cda.—at
☎ (203) 222-8218 . . 32 Harbor Rd, Westport, CT 06880 . . . .
☎ (561) 659-5904 1701 S Flagler Dv, West Palm Beach, FL 33401

Seymour MR & MRS Charles W JR (Edith D Hardin) Bur.Nw'51
☎ (415) 343-1302 . . 25 Buckthorn Way, Hillsborough, CA 94010

Seymour MR & MRS Christopher H (Barbara Quinn) Man'vl'76.Ford'79.P'76
☎ (914) 834-5961 . . 104 Beach Av, Larchmont, NY 10538

Seymour MR & MRS David L (Sylvia E Middleton)
V'58.Me.Sfh.Pa'58 . . . . | ☎ (814) 362-2815
MR Andrew L—Curry'89—at ☎ (610) 296-7729 | 59 Stone Av,
1201 Sugartown Rd, Malvern, PA *19355* . . . . . . | Bradford, PA *16701*

Seymour MISS Holly M (David L) . . . . Married at Bryn Mawr, PA
Yerkes MR John R (John B JR) . . . . Jun 1'96

Seymour MR Peter A (late James A) . . . . . . Married at Brussels, Belgium
Vaisière MISS Anne . . . . May 4'96

Seymour MR Richard S
☎ (216) 423-4549 . . Box 115, Old Mill Rd, Gates Mills, OH *44040*

Seymour DR & MRS Robert J (Ann H Ribbel) Pcu.Tcy.Ncd.Stan'55
☎ (415) 693-9651 . . 840 Powell St, Apt 501, San Francisco, CA *94108*

Seymour MR & MRS Thaddeus (Polly Gnagy) C.Cal'50.NCar'55
☎ (407) 644-1180 . . 1350 College Point, Winter Park, FL *32789*

Seymour MR & MRS Whitney N JR (Catryna)
Ten Eyck) C.StJ.Cs.P'45.Y'50 . . . . | ☎ (212) CH3-4273
MISS Tryntje . . . . | 290 W 4 St,
MISS Gabriel . . . . | New York, NY
                                                            | *10014*

Seymour MR William B (Florence Scafe)
☎ (216) 247-5862 . . 618 Bell St, Chagrin Falls, OH *44022*

Shackelford MR & MRS Virginius R JR (Carroll Kem)
V'40.Va'64.Sl.Va'36.Va'38
☎ (540) 672-2256 . . ''Brampton'' PO Box 871, Orange, VA *22960*

Shackelford MR & MRS Virginius R 3d (Jane L Schwarzschild) Sth'71.P'68
☎ (540) 672-5211 . . PO Box 871, Orange, VA *22960*

Shackford MRS Waylett (Anna P Waylett)
☎ (617) 235-6933 . . 12 Fells Rd, Wellesley, MA *02181*

Shackleton MRS William H (Elsa A Milota)
☎ (212) 861-3657 . . 301 E 66 St, New York, NY *10021*

Shadd MR & MRS Robert W (Stewart—Catherine C Hill)
Mich'47.Mich'50 . . of
☎ (401) 245-6762 . . 25 Knapton St, PO Box 390, Barrington, RI *02806*
☎ (603) 539-2632 . . Freedom Point Rd, Box 483, Freedom, NH *03836*

Shafer MR & MRS Donald L Peter 3d (Catherine L Hatfield)
WashColl'88.WashColl'86
☎ (410) 296-1833 . . 241 Ridge Av, Towson, MD *21286*

Shafer MAJ G Carlton 3d—USMC. (George C JR) . . . . Married at
                                                            Bryn Mawr, PA
MacBean MISS Janet E (David) . . . . Dec 30'94

Shafer MAJ & MRS G Carlton 3d (Janet E MacBean)
USMC.SimonF'94.Me.Woos'79.TroySt'93
☎ (604) 439-0490 . . 6055 Nelson Av, 208, Burnaby, BC V5H 4L4,
Canada

Shafer MRS Gail P (Gail C Patterson) Ws'52 ⚓
☎ (941) 966-5636 . . PO Box 1274, Osprey, FL *34229-1274*

Shafer MR & MRS George C JR (Louise S Hoopes) | ☎ (610) 353-0844
Me.Cspa.W.P'51.Cl'52 . . . . | 860 Briarwood Rd,
MISS Elizabeth T . . . . | Newtown Square,
                                                            | PA *19073*

Shafer MASTER George Chapman (G Carlton 3d) . . . . Born at
                                                            Richmond, BC, Canada Sep 13'95

Shafer MR & MRS J Bradley (Cynthia A Cozad)
Hlns'81.Sc.Wa.Ill'73.Ill'75.Ch'79
☎ (847) 441-4076 . . 365 Shadowood Lane, Northfield, IL *60093*

Shafer MR & MRS Robert L (Ellen A Schlafly) | ☎ (914) 967-9454
Man'vl'62.Plg.Km.Cly.StJ'54.Geo'61 . . . . | 96 Evergreen Av,
MISS Adelaide . . . . | Rye, NY
MISS Katherine . . . . | *10580-2005*
JUNIORS MR Daniel . . . . |

Shaffer MR & MRS William B JR (Law—Mary F | ☎ (513) 321-3055
Morrison) Sth'53.Y'50.H'55 . . . . | 5 E Rookwood Dv,
MISS Dorothy P—Y'87 . . . . | Cincinnati, OH
MR W Bakewell 3d—Ripon'82—at Tucson, AZ. | *45208*
MR Robert M M—Y'90 . . . . |

Shahzada MR & MRS Sohail (Rebecca Jensen) IFAC'76.Syr'76
☎ (904) 221-7006 . . 2002 St Martins Dv W, Jacksonville, FL *32246*

Shanahan MR & MRS James D (Harriett B Hare) | ☎ (334) 288-2963
Ala'66.Dar.Ala'58 . . . . | 2606 Knollwood Dv,
MISS Virginia B—Ala'90 . . . . | Montgomery, AL
                                                            | *36116*

Shand MRS James JR (Corina C Guild) Nyc.
☎ (717) 397-7996 . . 206 N President Av, Apt C4, Lancaster, PA *17603*

Shand MR James JR—Cyb.P'74
☎ (717) 390-0830 . . 240 E Marion St, Lancaster, PA *17602*

Shands MRS Courtney (Elizabeth W Jones) Swb'28.Ncd . . .of
☎ (314) 966-3710 . . 507 N Taylor Av, Kirkwood, MO *63122*
''Hilltop'' PO Box 527, Warrenton, MO *63383*

Shands MR & MRS Courtney JR (Nancy B Lewis)
Br'65.Sim'68.Rc.Nd.Wash'51.H'54 . . of
☎ (314) 822-7952 . . 507 N Taylor Av, Kirkwood, MO *63122*
''Hilltop'' PO Box 527, Warrenton, MO *63383*

Shands MR & MRS E F Berkley (Pamela M Leahy) Wash'83.Pitzer'80
☎ (314) 965-0416 . . 603 Meadowridge Lane, Kirkwood,
MO *63122-3021*

Shank MR & MRS Howard C (Pattou—Hollis L McLaughlin)
Sth'49.On.Fy.LakeF'42
☎ (847) 234-1660 . . 777 Washington Rd, Lake Forest, IL *60045*
Nov 1 . . ☎ (619) 345-2173 . . 38071 Tandika Trail, Palm Desert,
CA *92211-7038*

Shanley MR Brendan—Ithaca'71
☎ (941) 642-0624 . . 620 Rockport Court, Box 1939, Marco Island,
FL *33969-1939*

Shanley MR & MRS Kevin (Eleanor S Canham) | ☎ (908) 234-9048
Bhm.Ng.Cly.Pa'64 . . . . | 4 Jackson Av,
MISS Alison P . . . . | PO Box 201,
MISS Katy S . . . . | Gladstone, NJ *07934*
MISS Julie S . . . . |
MISS Elizabeth S . . . . |

Shanley MR Seton—L.Lx.Mds.Dyc.Pa'62
☎ (516) 324-6686 . . ''The Old Post Office'' 54 Buells Lane,
East Hampton, NY *11937-3212*

Shanner MR & MRS Robert W (Caughlan—Elizabeth | ☎ (717) 846-7219
F Page) Briar'70.SFrSt'75.Stan'76 . . . . | 987 Brockie Lane,
JUNIORS MISS Jessica P . . . . | York, PA *17403*

Shannon MR James J JR—Rv.Cw.Wt.Cumberland'55 . . of
☎ (606) 623-6036 . . 224 W Main St, Richmond, KY *40475*
☎ (954) 772-0893 . . 5230 NE 28 Av, Ft Lauderdale, FL *33308*

Shannon MRS James R (Katharine W Street)
☎ (303) 733-9600 . . 111 Emerson St, Apt 1743, Denver, CO *80218*

Shantz MRS Lois W (Lois W Beebe)
☎ (516) 921-8667 . . 378 Woodbury Rd, Woodbury, NY *11797*

Shapley MR & MRS Scott D (Laura C Hoover)
☎ (011-7-95) 255-9720 . . 2 Pushechnaya St, Moscow 103012, Russia

Sharkey MR & MRS Thomas R 6th (Kehe— | ☎ (415)854-4031
Anderson—Fleddermann—Katherine C Ross) | 125 Alta Vista Dv,
CalArts'69.CalArts'71 . . . . | Atherton, CA *94027*
MR Erin . . . . |
JUNIORS MR Eaman . . . . |
JUNIORS MR T Ryan 7th. . . . . |
  MR Bodhi M Anderson—USN.—at |
US Naval Hospital Corps, Great Lakes, IL |
60088 . . . . |

Sharon MISS Barclay N—Hlns'94.Cvc.
☎ (704) 372-4064 . . 1500-2 Euclid Av, Charlotte, NC *28302*

Sharon MRS Corsini (Ruth A Corsini)
☎ (301) 656-5248 . . 8101 Connecticut Av, Apt N206, Chevy Chase, MD *20815*

Sharon MRS John H (Frances W Virgin) | ☎ (202) 364-4937
SL'62.Cvc.Mt.Sl. . . . . | 4500 Klingle St
MR Edward W—at American U . . . . | NW, Washington, DC *20016*

Sharp MR Frederick D 3d—Cc.Bard'40
☎ (207) 846-4663 . . 3 Fairwind Lane, Yarmouth, ME *04096*

Sharp MR & MRS George B (Lucy B Hufstader)
Rol'63.Y'95.K.Plg.Y'63.Cl'69
☎ (914) 232-4550 . . 76 Girdle Ridge Rd, Katonah, NY *10536*

Sharp MRS George C (Ruth Baldwin) Bgt.Cly.K.Cda.StJ . . .of
☎ (914) 232-3566 . . "Cantitoe Corners" Box L, Katonah, NY *10536*
☎ (212) TE8-0800 . . 825 Fifth Av, New York, NY *10021*

Sharp MRS H Parker (Emma E Ochiltree) Pg.Lv.Tc.
☎ (412) 682-6363 . . Park Mansions Apt 3A, 5023 Frew Av, Pittsburgh, PA *15213*

Sharp MRS James L JR (Elena de Martini) Cal'29.Wa . . .of
☎ (510) 254-3563 . . 325 Village View Court, Orinda, CA *94563*
☎ (916) 743-6495 . . Honcut Ranch, 1933 Ramirez Rd, Marysville, CA *95901*

Sharp MR & MRS M Rust (Nancy C Day) | ☎ (610) 527-1811
Me.M.Rc.Sa.Ph.Ncd.NCar'62.Temp'68 . . . . | 41 Wistar Rd,
MISS Emily De F . . . . | Villanova, PA *19085-1512*

Sharp MR & MRS Robert W (Naquin—Mary G | of ☎ (410)435-5971
Miller) Swb'40.Sim'42.Gi.Elk.Md.Mv. | 2 Gittings Av,
Miami'39.OState'40 ⚓ . . . . | Baltimore, MD
MR Stuart G A Naquin—Elk.Br'72 . . . . | *21212*
 | ☎ (410) 255-1881
 | Gibson Island, MD *21056*

Sharp MRS Walter B (Huldah W Cheek) BMr'38
☎ (615) 373-8126 . . 666 Beech Creek Rd, Brentwood, TN *37027*

Sharpe MR & MRS William P (Soule—Emily F Moser)
Il.Co.Wms'52.Dth'54.Bost'61
☎ (401) 846-5523 . . 93 Annandale Rd, Newport, RI *02840*

Sharples MR & MRS Hendrik J W (Karen D Hawkins)
Ore'83.OreSt'85.Reed'77
3226 NE Glisan St, Portland, OR *97232*

Sharples MR & MRS Philip Price (Morse—Shelton—Jane C Loew)
Cvc.Cry.Rv.H'42
☎ (520) 398-2274 . . PO Box 1600, Tubac, AZ *85646*

Sharples MR & MRS Russell P (Pamela S Danielson)
W'minsterC'83.W'minsterC'91.Me.Colg'82.Va'86
☎ (609) 443-0975 . . 3 Sheffield Rd, East Windsor, NJ *08520*

Sharples MR & MRS Thomas D (Renate H A Backhausen)
SFr'75.SFr'77 . . of
☎ (415) 324-4848 . . 128 Heather Dv, Atherton, CA *94027*
☎ (541) 998-6090 . . 91448 Steinmetz Rd, Junction City, OR *97448-9540*

Sharretts MRS Amos B (Louise H Hoy)
☎ (516) 367-3732 . . 18 Dock Hollow Rd, Box 458, Cold Spring Harbor, NY *11724*

Sharretts MR & MRS Amos B JR (Jeanne M McMillan) Vt'80.CasSt'79
☎ (201) 644-0674 . . 76 Washington Av, Morristown, NJ *07960*

Sharvy MR Benjamin—Reed'90 . . see MRS E S Richardson JR

Shattuck MR & MRS George H JR (Isabel D Closson) Sm.Ri.Cly.
☎ (212) 753-1274 . . 350 E 57 St, New York, NY *10022*

Shattuck MR & MRS George H 3d (Janet L Patenaude) Wells'83.Cr'83
see Dilatory Domiciles

Shattuck MR H Francis JR—Yn.Y'42.H'48
242 E 68 St, New York, NY *10021*

Shattuck MRS Jennifer B (Jennifer W Budge) | ☎ (415) 342-6711
Wms'75.Nu'78.Bur.Gv.Mv. . . . . | 671 Brewer Dv,
JUNIORS MISS Kathleen E . . . . | Hillsborough, CA
JUNIORS MR Mayo A 4th . . . . | *94010*

Shattuck MR & MRS Peter H (Elizabeth J Horr) Cal'59.Y'56.Cal'60 . . of
☎ (916) 482-6503 . . 4627 Ashton Dv, Sacramento, CA *95864*
☎ (707) 964-9548 . . "Ojala" Mendocino, CA *95460*

Shaw MR & MRS Alan W 3d (Ingree A Griffin) | ☎ (615) 353-7900
LSU'66.SwLa'66 . . . . | 3802 Hillmeade
MR Alan W 4th . . . . | Court, Nashville, TN *37221*

Shaw MR & MRS Alexander A 2d (Sally N Ryan) Ty'80.Un.DU'75
☎ (212) 772-9036 . . 151 E 83 St, Apt 3H, New York, NY *10028*

Shaw MISS Amidie E—Austin'95
☎ (214) 521-8871 . . 3911 Holland Av, Apt 105, Dallas, TX *75219*

Shaw MISS (DR) Deborah S (Passarella—Hickox— | ☎ (303) 322-2828
Tankoos—Deborah S Shaw) Ga'75.Ga'79 . . . . . | 450 Clermont St,
JUNIORS MR James A B Hickox . . . . | Denver, CO *80220*

Shaw MISS Elizabeth R—Pa'92 . . see MRS E G S Wills

Shaw MISS Emily T . . . . | ☎ (603) 352-2912
CDR Herbert B 3d—USN.NH'65 . . . . | RR 3, Box 400,
MISS Tommi deV . . . . | 712 Court St, Keene,
MISS M Elizabeth . . . . | NH *03431*

Shaw MR & MRS Francis G (Ruth B Wellington) | ☎ (617) 566-4683
Rdc'33.Cy.Sb.Cc.Cw.Chi.Ncd.H'31 . . . . | 272 Woodland Rd,
MR Robert G—H.'61 . . . . | Chestnut Hill, MA *02167*

Shaw MR & MRS George T (Anna B Draper) | ☎ (508) 526-1057
Cl'66.Ty'62.H.'65 . . . . | 9 Spy Rock Hill Rd,
MISS Rebecca B—Colby'94—at 500½ E 84 St, | Manchester, MA
Apt 4A, New York, NY *10028* . . . . | *01944*

Shaw MR & MRS Harry L (Jocelyn Thomas) | ☎ (203) 259-1847
V'53.David'26.SCar'27 . . . . | 476 Old Mill Rd,
MR T Gray—Clark'80—at 1135 Addison St, | Fairfield, CT *06430*
Berkeley, CA *94702* . . . . |

Shaw MRS Henry D (Janet L Kittredge) Albion'42
☎ (714) 675-1127 . . 208 Via Lido Nord, Newport Beach, CA *92663*

Shaw MRS Howard S (Cooke—Joan Sullivan)
☎ (508) 748-0380 . . 61 Lewis St, PO Box 652, Marion, MA *02738*

Shaw MRS James C (Perkins—Elizabeth H Riley)
☎ (603) 835-6052 . . Scrimshaw Farm, Pleasant St, Box 57, Alstead,
NH *03602*

Shaw MR Jerome T 2d—Col'88
☎ (206) 325-5863 . . 1401 E Harrison St, Apt 104, Seattle,
WA *98112-5189*

Shaw MR John I JR—Pr.Y'57
☎ (212) 288-7637 . . 1009 Park Av, New York, NY *10028*

Shaw MR & MRS John K 3d (Fredericka A Savage) | ☎ (410) 833-2888
Gv.Md. . . . . | 3737 Butler Rd,
  MISS Elizabeth W . . . . | Glyndon, MD *21071*
  MR John K 4th |

Shaw MR & MRS L Edward JR (Irene M Ryan) | of ☎ (914)698-9528
Mds.Ng.Geo'66.Y'69 . . . . | 9 Carriage House
  MISS Hope E . . . . | Lane, Mamaroneck,
  MISS Hillary A . . . . | NY *10543*
  MISS Julia J . . . . | ☎ (516) 329-2331
  MR Christopher B . . . . | PO Box 416,
  JUNIORS MR Rory E . . . . | Middle Lane,
 | East Hampton, NY
 | *11937*

Shaw MRS Leverett S (Leas—Johanna C Snyder) | ☎ (561) 659-7065
Evg.BtP. . . . . | 220 Brazilian Av,
  MISS Samantha B Leas . . . . | Palm Beach, FL
 | *33480*

Shaw MISS Louise C (Herbert B 3d) . . . . Married at Sacramento, CA
  Wieser MR Karl W . . . . Jun 30'96

Shaw MRS Mary H (Mary L Hackett) D. . . . . | ☎ (617) 326-4772
  MISS Louisa H—at 1628 Sul Ross St, Houston, | 216 Village Av,
TX *77006* . . . . | Dedham, MA *02026*
  MR Howard S—Box 269, Lubec, ME *04652* . . . |

Shaw MR & MRS Norman F JR (Virginia C Spencer) Ariz'72.Ariz'74
☎ (520) 722-5167 . . 7910 E Garland Rd, Tucson, AZ *85715*

Shaw MR Patrick—Rc.H'55 . . . . | ☎ (312) 664-8090
  MR Alfred M—at Ariz State . . . . | 860 N Lake Shore
 | Dv, Apt 13K,
 | Chicago, IL *60611*

Shaw MRS Phyllis E (Nash—Shepard—Phyllis E | ☎ (508) 945-1581
Shaw) Cly. | ''Delphinus''
  MR James MacM Shepard . . . . | 36 Harding Lane,
 | Chatham, MA *02633*

Shaw MRS Quincy A (Marjory B Cheney) Cy.
☎ (617) 566-6898 . . 96 Sears Rd, Brookline, MA *02146*

Shaw MR & MRS Robert G (Cass L Ruxton) | of ☎ (914)351-2210
Un.T.Lm.Myf.Cly.Dc.Cda.Dh.Ty'51 . . . . | ''Highland''
  MISS (REV) Cass L—Sth'77.PTheo'80 . . . . . . | PO Box 106,
 | Tuxedo Park, NY
 | *10987-0106*
 | ☎ (212) 751-1912
 | 200 E 66 St,
 | New York, NY
 | *10021*

Shaw MR & MRS Robert H JR (Elizabeth Kirksey) | ☎ (205) 349-5293
MissStW'75.Ala'78.USN'61.Duke'76.Ala'84 . . | 12 Ridgeland,
  MR Robert H 3d—at U of Ala . . . . | Tuscaloosa, AL
  JUNIORS MR William W—at U of Ala . . . . | *35406*
  JUNIORS MR George L—at U of Ala . . . . |

Shaw MR & MRS Robert J (Davis—Patricia N French) Cr'40
☎ (941) 676-1784 . . Mountain Lake, Lake Wales, FL *33853*

Shaw MR & MRS S Parkman JR (Lisa A Geissenhainer) NH'80.Sm.H'66
☎ (617) 731-5261 . . 89 Carlton St, Brookline, MA *02146*

Shaw MR Timothy T (George T) . . . . Married at Akron, OH
  Rensel MISS Elizabeth A (John D) . . . . Aug 10'96

Shaw MR & MRS William D JR (C Tobey Gilmore) | ☎ (203) 629-6022
Swb'72.Gv.Cal'70 . . . . | 194 Otter Rock Dv,
  JUNIORS MR Carroll G . . . . | Greenwich, CT
  JUNIORS MISS Katherine B . . . . | *06830*

Shaw MR & MRS William V (Osborne—Mary Morse) Stan'42.Cal'43
☎ (408) 624-1336 . . PO Box 1614, Pebble Beach, CA *93953*

Shaw MRS Wyman B (Rosamond L Grenfell) McG'39
Dunwoody Village CH10, 3500 West Chester Pike, Newtown Square,
PA *19073*

Shaw MR & MRS Z George (Bingham—Mary Ann Pearce) Dar.
☎ (601) 453-5734 . . 406 Crockett Av, Greenwood, MS *38930*

Shea MR & MRS Daniel J (P Stephanie Stokes) Geo'81.Clark'81
☎ (504) 488-0327 . . 115 Maryland Dv, New Orleans, LA *70124*

Shea MR & MRS Peter L (Nancy W Sage) | of ☎ (212)876-3555
Cl'64.Lic.Ln.Pr.Cly.P.'55.Stan'59 . . . . | 1220 Park Av, Apt
  JUNIORS MR James DeW . . . . | 13A, New York, NY
 | *10128*
 | ☎ (516) 676-8863
 | PO Box 384,
 | Locust Valley, NY
 | *11560*

Shea MRS Stephanie W (Stephanie Wilds) Cly . . .of
☎ (011-55-11) 247-2937 . . Rua Cassiano Riccardo 83, São Paulo
04640-020 SP, Brazil
☎ (212) 249-8383 . . 20 E 68 St, Apt 10G, New York, NY *10021*

Sheaffer MRS Charles M (Fisher—Dorothy M Rumpf) Me.
☎ (610) 525-2261 . . 74 Pasture Lane, Apt 217B, Bryn Mawr, PA *19010*

Sheaffer MR Theodore C—Rc.Gm.Ph.Y'25
☎ (610) NI4-2342 . . Gaylea Farm, 7126 Goshen Rd,
Newtown Square, PA *19073*

Shearer MR & MRS Hartley P (Linda Balding) SL'68.Nu'68
☎ (413) 458-4082 . . 202 Pine Cobble Rd, Williamstown, MA *01267*

Shearer MISS Joy B—Fla'75
610 Toxaway Dv, West Palm Beach, FL *33413*

Sheble MR & MRS John W (Barbara Lovett) Pc.P'51
☎ (215) 233-3621 . . 829 Andorra Rd, Lafayette Hill, PA *19444*

Shedd MR & MRS Carl B Ely (Barton—Isabel | Farm Rd,
McIlvain) Sth'66.Y'54 . . . . | PO Box 840,
  MISS Elisabeth H Ely . . . . | Sherborn, MA
 | *01770*

Shedd MISS Eliza C—Col'87
see Dilatory Domiciles

Shedd MRS Patricia T (Patricia J Truxell) Alleg'52 . | ☎ (561) 234-0484
  MISS Patricia A—at ☎ (203) 359-2981 | 2131 Via Fuentes,
  50 Aquila Rd, Stamford, CT *06902* . . . . | Vero Beach, FL
 | *32963*

Sheehan MR & MRS David N (Elizabeth E Meuller) Ty'84.Pg.Ken'85
☎ (212) 727-7947 . . 56 Seventh Av, Apt 17F, New York, NY *10011*

Sheehan MR Mark A—Pg.Rc.Va'84.Pitt'89
☎ (215) 545-2268 . . Academy House 28P, 1420 Locust St, Philadelphia, PA *19102-4217*

Sheehan MR & MRS Robert W (Pauline O Vietor) Un.Err.Eyc.Cly.Cda.Ncd.Y.'67.Nu'74 . . . . | ☎ (212) 289-0939
MR William B—at Columbia Law . . . . | 1220 Park Av,
MR Thomas V—at Yale . . . . | New York, NY
JUNIORS MR Arthur W—at St Paul's . . . . | *10128*

Sheehan MR & MRS Thomas E (Mary F Anderson) Pg.VillaN'54
☎ (412) 242-7881 . . 499 Locust St, Pittsburgh, PA *15218*

Sheerin MR Charles M—Va'84
☎ (202) 537-3165 . . 3283C Sutton Place NW, Washington, DC *20016*

Sheerin REV & MRS Charles W JR (Edith P Barton) Ws'52.Va'50.VaTheo'55
☎ (518) 438-7676 . . 57 Lenox Av, Albany, NY *12203*

Sheerin MR & MRS J Laurence (Halff—Betty L | ☎ (210) 829-7501
Burton) Tex'57.Srb.Evg. . . . . | 555 Ivy Lane,
MISS Andrea Kate . . . . | San Antonio, TX
MR J Laurence JR . . . . | *78209*

Sheets MRS M Brennig (Margaret M Brennig)
''Brenlair'' 1333 Rutledge Lane, Lebanon, TN *37087*

Sheffield MRS Anne (Anwyl—Anne Sheffield) V'51 | ☎ (212) 319-4232
  MISS Pandora H C Anwyl—at | 136 E 64 St,
  ☎ (305) 867-0429 . . 710—86 St, | New York, NY
  Miami Beach, FL *33141* . . . . | *10021*

Sheffield MR & MRS David P (di Rende—Carole A Bray) PhilaArt'74.Temp'85.Pc.Ac.Temp'80.Temp'96
☎ (215) 233-4286 . . 8116 Flourtown Av, Wyndmoor, PA *19038*

Sheffield MR & MRS Edwin S (Dorothy G Yerger) | ☎ (215) 247-9165
Pc.Ph.Sg.Pe.Srb.Ac.Wms'44 . . . . | 510 E Evergreen
MR Edwin S JR—at ☎ (212) 644-3894 | Av, Wyndmoor, PA
400 E 59 St, New York, NY *10022* . . . . | *19038*

Sheffield MRS Frederick (Carolyn C Blair) Cs.
☎ (212) 737-3312 . . 215 E 72 St, New York, NY *10021*

Sheffield MRS Sandra S (Sandra W Shelvey) Sth'61.On.
☎ (847) 234-3718 . . 385 E Westminster Av, Lake Forest, IL *60045*

Sheffield MR & MRS Thomas C JR (Austin—Pamela S Starry) SFr'79.SFr'81.On.Rc.Wa.H'58.H'60
☎ (312) 787-1121 . . 1500 N Lake Shore Dv, Chicago, IL *60610*

Shehan MR John T—Cy.Loy'55 . . . . | 505 Epsom Rd,
MISS Margaret H . . . . | Apt 2A, Towson,
  | MD *21286*

Shelby MR & MRS Thomas W (Gail P Gebhart) | ☎ (520) 886-2806
SDakSt'66.SDak'68 . . . . | 4000 N Ridgecrest
MR Steven G . . . . | Dv, Tucson, AZ
JUNIORS MISS Suzanne G . . . . | *85715-2464*

Sheldon MRS Frank R (Foster—Marjorie Capen) Cy.
☎ (314) 726-2238 . . 825 S Hanley Rd, St Louis, MO *63105*

Sheldon MR & MRS George W 3d (Elizabeth W Bowen) MtVern'83.Va'78.AmU'82
☎ (202) 362-4373 . . 5212 MacArthur Blvd NW, Washington, DC *20016*

Shellenberger MISS Elisabeth—Pc.Ncd.
☎ (215) 438-4775 . . 107 School House Lane, Philadelphia, PA *19144-3348*

Shellenberger MR & MRS James A (Ann W Howard) Pa'37
☎ (203) 869-1757 . . ''Shellwood'' 650 Lake Av, Greenwich, CT *06830*

Shellenberger MR Thomas D—Del'82.WNe'85
☎ (302) 571-0392 . . 1809 Washington St, Wilmington, DE *19802*

Shellenberger MR William C—Nasson'82
☎ (207) 646-5084 . . PO Box 1362, Wells, ME *04090*

Shellenberger DR & MRS William D (Barbara A | ☎ (302) 656-0459
Chantler) Wms'46.Temp'51 . . . . | 4101 Kennett Pike,
MISS Susan A—MaryB'84 . . . . | Wilmington, DE
  | *19807*

Shelly MR & MRS James N JR (Julia E Jorgensen) CUNY'70.Penn'74
☎ (941) 594-7242 . . 7045 Barrington Circle, Naples, FL *34108*

Shelmerdine MRS William (Juliet B Upson) . . . . . . | 115 Coolidge Hill,
MISS Susan C—Sth'76—at 2500 Shady Lawn Dv, | Cambridge, MA
Greensboro, NC *27408* . . . . | *02138*

Shelnutt MRS Budd (Martha L Budd)
☎ (302) 654-9882 . . Devon Apt 711, 2401 Pennsylvania Av, Wilmington, DE *19806*

Shelton MISS Frances E—Cda.Dar.Dcw.Ht.
☎ (212) 799-1856 . . 155 W 68 St, New York, NY *10023*

Shelton MRS Richard D (Catherine P McKay) Cy.
☎ (314) 991-2441 . . Gatesworth, 1 McKnight Place, St Louis, MO *63124*

Shelton MRS Robert R (Fronie Kempe) Stph'65.A. . | ☎ (210) 896-8282
MISS Sarita M . . . . | PO Box 1834,
MISS Katherine R—at Ft Worth, TX . . . . | Kerrville, TX *78029*
MISS Susan A . . . . |
MISS S Saphronia . . . . |
MR Robert R JR—at College Station, TX . . . . . . |

Shennan MR & MRS James G JR (Janna L Osmond) | ☎ (415) 854-6494
Cal'64.Fr.P'63.Stan'65 . . . . | 75 Kilroy Way,
MISS Elizabeth R . . . . | Atherton, CA *94027*
JUNIORS MR William G . . . . |

Shepard MRS Addison (Margaret L Addison) | ☎ (202) 965-9514
MaryB'71 . . . . | 3612 S St NW,
JUNIORS MISS Margaret D . . . . | Washington, DC
JUNIORS MR David A . . . . | *20007*

Shepard DR & MRS Edward M (Avery—Flanigan—E Joan Pulling) V'52.Pr.Cly.Wms'36.Cr'40
☎ (802) 457-1770 . . RR 2, Box 487, Church Hill, Woodstock, VT *05091*

Shepard MR Francis B—K.Eh.Plg.Cw.Mid'63 . . . . . | ☎ (908) 766-3644
MR Robert C—at U of NCar Chapel Hill . . . . . . | Box 641,
JUNIORS MR Clark D—at Hotchkiss . . . . | Bernardsville, NJ
  | *07924*

Shepard MRS I Minot (Frances E Burge) Sth'39 . . . | ☎ (617) 237-9225
MR Irving M 3d—H'72—at ☎ (617) 731-9169 | 150 Adams House,
60 Longwood Av, Apt 308, Brookline, MA | 65 Grove St,
02146 . . . . | Wellesley, MA
  | *02181*

Shepard MR James MacM . . see MRS P E Shaw

Shepard MISS Josephine R—GeoW'65
☎ (301) 365-3106 . . 8044 Cindy Lane, Bethesda, MD *20817*

Shepard MISS Mary H—GeoW'63
☎ (301) 365-4855 . . 7901 Carteret Rd, Bethesda, MD *20817-1919*

Shepard MRS Merrill (Voight—Brenda Forbes) Cs.
☎ (212) 644-8215 . . 430 E 57 St, New York, NY *10022*

Shepard MR & MRS William B JR (Marguerite P AuWerter) CtCol'68.Conn'93.Wes'68.Cl'73 . . . ☎ (203) 655-9199 9 Beach Dv, Darien, CT *06820-5609*
   MISS Susan E . . . .
   MR William B 3d—Tufts'96 . . . .
   MR Jay A—at Boston U . . . .

Shephard MISS Geraldine L—Ri.Bcs . . .of
   ☎ (212) 861-9656 . . 137 E 66 St, New York, NY *10021*
   ☎ (516) 283-5722 . . "Tucked Away" PO Box 1024, Southampton, NY *11969*

Shepherd MR & MRS Everett JR (Catherine Jones) MaryW'52.SEBible'80.Mtvlo'86.Vmi'50
   ☎ (205) 969-1022 . . 3312 E Briarcliff Rd, Birmingham, AL *35223*

Shepley MRS Ethan A H JR (Meyer—Margaret Bragdon) Nd.Cy.
   ☎ (314) 862-3260 . . 329 N Bemiston Av, St Louis, MO *63105*

Sheppard MR & MRS Carl F JR (Carroll A Hogan) Pa'69.Ox'71.Cspa.W.Ac.Pa'68.Pa'71 ⚓
   ☎ (215) CH7-9610 . . "Hollies" 8039 Seminole Av, Philadelphia, PA *19118*

Sheppard MR & MRS Edgar M JR (Mary A Smythe)
   ☎ (215) 233-5012 . . 601 E Moreland Av, Wyndmoor, PA *19038*

Sheppard MRS Penelope L (Penelope A Lofting) . . . ☎ (302) 426-1616 1501 Hancock St, Wilmington, DE *19806*
   MISS Diana R . . . .
   MR Daniel E—at 103 W Street Rd, Kennett Square, PA *19348* . . . .

Sheppard MR & MRS W Stevens (Bloom—Patricia Gillis) CalSt'72.Ny.Pqt.Va'53 ⚓ . . . ☎ (203) 255-1660 PO Box 543, Southport, CT *06490*
   MR Gregory Bloom—Cr'92 . . . .
   MR J Derek Bloom—Cr'94—at MIT . . . .

Sheppard MRS Walter Lee JR (Kendall—Boudinot A Oberge) . . . . Died at Havertown, PA Feb 20'96

Sheppard MR Walter Lee JR—W.Fw.Myf.Cr'32. Pa'33 . . . . ☎ (610) HI9-2167 923 Old Manoa Rd, Havertown, PA *19083*
   MR Charles H Kendall JR—Gc.W.Rv.Stan'63

Sheppard MR & MRS Winston C (Olive C Pearson) Pc.
   ☎ (215) 248-2622 . . 413 W Mermaid Lane, Philadelphia, PA *19118*

Sheridan MR & MRS John Edward (Herbert—Mary A Hemry) Pqt.Hn.Dth'56.H'62 ⚓
   ☎ (203) 454-3890 . . 421 Sasco Hill Rd, Fairfield, CT *06430*

Sheriff MISS Nathalie H . . see C B Barnes

Sherk DR & MRS Henry H (Lea Carson) Bnd'65.P'52.Jef'56 . . . . ☎ (215) WA3-3020 624 Spruce St, Philadelphia, PA *19106*
   MISS Mary H—Ken'90—*see Dilatory Domiciles*
   MISS Julia S—Nw'95—at ☎ (773) 348-7720 1253 W Newport Av, Chicago, IL *60657* . . . . . .

Sherk MISS Katherine L (Henry H) . . . . Married at Philadelphia, PA
   Simons MR Victor W (Victor) . . . . Jun 8'96

Sherley MR Thomas H—GeoW'43
   ☎ (301) 656-7925 . . 8014 Custer Rd, Bethesda, MD *20814*

Sherlock MISS Valerie J—Wis'67
   ☎ (713) 965-0828 . . 5050 Ambassador Way, Apt 101, Houston, TX *77056*

Sherman MRS Dallas B (Glass—Beatrice Schaenen) Nu'32.Nu'67 . . . . ☎ (619) 454-5545 Seville Apt 10D, 1001 Genter St, La Jolla, CA *92032* Apr 15 . .
   MISS Cordelia C—V'71—at 111 Elm St, Somerville, MA *02144* . . . .
   MR Laurence d'A M Glass—P'58.P'59—at 704 Cathedral St, Baltimore, MD *21201* . . . . . ☎ (516) 283-4263 64 Down East Lane, Southampton, NY *11968*

Sherman MR Edward D—Sbc.Ec.Al.
   ☎ (617) 566-4346 . . 25 Essex Rd, Chestnut Hill, MA *02167*

Sherman MR & MRS Eric (Eugenia B Dillard) Y'68 . ☎ (213) 466-4348 2427 Park Oak Dv, Los Angeles, CA *90068*
   JUNIORS MR L Cosimo . . . .
   JUNIORS MR Daniel T . . . .

Sherman MRS George C JR (Natalie Hyde) Cly. . . . ☎ (212) 288-6415 117 E 72 St, New York, NY *10021* Nov 15 . .
   MR Michael G C—at Berkeley, CA . . . . ☎ (561) 276-9832 "Bahia" 3818 Bermuda Lane, Gulf Stream, FL *33483*

Sherman MR & MRS Michael (Agnes D Bull) Bnd'54.P'45 . . . . ☎ (609) 921-1193 55 Battle Rd, Princeton, NJ *08540*
   MISS Caroline W—Bow'83—at 2400 E Valley St, Seattle, WA *98112* . . . .

Sherman MR Michael T—H.'72
   ☎ (617) 876-7726 . . 46 Shepard St, Apt 31, Cambridge, MA *02138*

Sherman MR & MRS Roger F (Judith A Young) Nat'lCollEd'63.MichSt'60 . . . . ☎ (810) 626-2048 1631 Apple Lane, Bloomfield Hills, MI *48302*
   MISS Ingrid A—WestMich'93 . . . .

Sherman MR Roger F JR—MichSt'88
   ☎ (510) 235-6922 . . 30144 Lakemont Dv, San Ramon, CA *94583*

Sherman MISS Wendy
   ☎ (212) 876-6654 . . 1435 Lexington Av, New York, NY *10128*

Sherman MRS William B (Catherine B McKecknie) Cl'68.Nyc.
   3300 Darby Rd, Apt 2213, Haverford, PA *19041*

Sherman MR Wilson R . . see R R Hanna

Sherrer MR & MRS Roland C JR (Moss—Thelma T Cremer) S.Fic.Fiy. . . . . of ☎ (516)922-4369 Cove Neck Rd, Oyster Bay, NY *11771*
   MR Charles D—Fic.Rc.Ne'91 . . . . ☎ (516) 788-7637 "White Wings" Fishers Island, NY *06390*

Sherrerd MR & MRS John J F (Kathleen Compton) Sth'54.Me.M.Ac.Pn.P.'52.Pa'56
   ☎ (610) LA5-8942 . . 833 Muirfield Rd, Bryn Mawr, PA *19010*

Sherrill MR & MRS Charles H (Christine Hayward) L. . . . . ☎ (508) 927-3700 858 Hale St, Beverly Farms, MA *01915*
   MR Christopher G . . . .

Sherrill MR & MRS H Sinclair (Alexandra V Cooper)
PineM'92.Myc.Rby.Hn.H.'80.PugetS'85
☎ (508) 921-0941 . . PO Box 5494, Beverly Farms, MA *01915*
Sherrill MR & MRS H Virgil (Betty L Stevens) Rc.Bcs.B.Ng.Cly.Y'42
☎ (212) 753-3604 . . 1 Sutton Place S, New York, NY *10022*
Sherrill REV & MRS Henry W (Martha S Weeks) Cin'69.Chi.Yn.Y'45
☎ (520) 529-0513 . . 5434 N Via Papavero, Tucson, AZ *85750*
Sherrill MISS Jane W . . see MRS W D English
Sherrill MR & MRS M David (Mary Alice Hoyt)
FIT'85.Un.Cw.Ht.Snc.Myf.Rv.Sar.Cal'83
☎ (212) 787-2605 . . 255 W 88 St, New York, NY *10024*
Sherrill MISS Mary Sayre (M David) . . . . Born at
New York, NY Sep 14'94
Sherrill MISS Sarah B . . see MRS W D English
Sherrill MR & MRS Stephen C (Katherine S Duncan)
H'79.Rc.B.Ng.Bcs.Cly.Y'75.Cl'78
☎ (212) 737-0375 . . 765 Park Av, New York, NY *10021*

Shertenlieb MR & MRS William B (Elizabeth T B
Allen) Skd'64.U'64 . . . . | ☎ (410) 228-6778
MISS Elizabeth T B . . . . | "Brelsmir Haven"
MR William B JR . . . . | 6212 Castle Haven
   Rd, Cambridge, MD *21613*

Sherwin MR & MRS John JR (Clara C De Mallie) | ☎ (216) 951-6775
LErie'62.Kt.Un.Tv.It.JCar'68 . . . . | "Windrush"
MISS Heather—at 7071 Waite Hill Rd, | 9400 Smith Rd,
Willoughby, OH *44094* . . . . | Waite Hill, OH
MISS Laura—at 2773 Hampshire Rd, Apt 5, | *44094*
Cleveland Heights, OH *44106* . . . . |
MR Tyler . . . . |

Sherwin MR Peter M—Bgt.Bab'47.Bab'51 . . . . . . | ☎ (540) 456-8857
MISS Carolyn C—at ☎ (914) 666-0743 | "Rockfish Orchard"
208 Harris Rd, Bedford Hills, NY *10507* . . . . . . | Rte 2, Box 586,
   Afton, VA *22920*

Sherwin MR Peter M JR
☎ (408) 625-9652 . . PO Box 381, Carmel, CA *93921*
Sherwin MRS Robert P (Thayer—Katherine V Barr)
☎ (610) 525-5891 . . 312 Thornbrook Rd, Rosemont, PA *19010*
Sherwood MRS Arthur M (Marjorie F Catron) BMr'42
☎ (609) 921-0361 . . 53 Castle Howard Court, Princeton, NJ *08540*

Sherwood MR & MRS John R 3d (Kyle—Elisabeth L | ☎ (410) 269-1907
Dobbin) BMr'61.Ayc.Gi.Mv.Dth'58.NCar'64 . . | 51 Southgate Av,
MISS Anne D—P'92 . . . . | Annapolis, MD
  MR Robert J Kyle JR—Dth'89 . . . . | *21401*

Sherwood MRS Thorne (Nancy D Chapman)
☎ (860) 567-8075 . . 291 W Morris Rd, Morris, CT *06763*
Shettle MISS Ann B . . see MISS H R Tyson
Shettle MR Arthur F 2d . . see MISS H R Tyson
Shettle MR & MRS William M 2d (Renée M Wellford)
Del'72.Rcp.Me.Gm.Fst.Sap.NCar'62
☎ (410) 957-1549 . . 808 Beverly Lane, Pocomoke City, MD *21851*
Shields MR & MRS Charles W (Catherine C Kernott) Pep'85.Pep'86
☎ (805) 969-4417 . . 558 San Ysidro Rd, Montecito, CA *93108*
Shields MR & MRS D Leet (Betty G Young) Edg.Leh'39
☎ (412) 741-9420 . . 436 Beaver Rd, Edgeworth, Sewickley, PA *15143*

Shields MR & MRS David V (Margaret Barney) | ☎ (212) 249-0739
Rc.Msq.Why.Pa'61 ⚓ . . . . | 131 E 69 St,
MISS Elizabeth L . . . . | New York, NY
MR D Larus . . . . | *10021*

Shields MR & MRS Day R (M Elaine Hamrick) Y'69 . . of
☎ (203) 762-9849 . . 155 Hulda Hill Rd, Wilton, CT *06897-1814*
☎ (242) 332-6003 . . "Sundowner" Windermere Island, Eleuthera,
Bahamas
Shields MRS Edward M (Hathaway—Marjorie C Huston)
222 Lansdowne Av, Wayne, PA *19087*

Shields MR & MRS Francis A (Auchincloss—Diana B | ☎ (561) 655-8969
Lippert) Pr.BtP.Pa'63 . . . . | 149 Clarke Av,
MISS Marina T—Geo'93—at 210 E 68 St, | Palm Beach, FL
New York, NY *10021* . . . . | *33480*
MISS Cristiana T . . . . |
JUNIORS MISS Olympia T . . . . |

Shields DR & MRS Joseph Dunbar JR (Kendall—Goodrich—
Mary L Netterville) So.Cly.Dar.Tul'33
☎ (601) 445-5674 . . "Montaigne" PO Box 886, 200 Liberty Rd,
Natchez, MS *39121*
Shields MR & MRS Joseph V JR (Maury deG Flowers)
Rc.Pr.Ln.Cly.Geo'61 . . of
☎ (212) 421-2727 . . 715 Park Av, New York, NY *10021*
☎ (516) 626-1232 . . 152 Wheatley Rd, Brookville, NY *11545*
Shields MISS Katharine . . see MRS R G Blaine

Shields MR & MRS Leighton (Gail P Sisson) | ☎ (617) 749-6930
Bates'64.Br'65.Bates'48.H'50 . . . . | 54 Old County Rd,
MISS Hilary W . . . . | Hingham, MA
   02043

Shields MR & MRS Thomas J (Janet S Lawrence) | ☎ (415) 853-1593
Lyc'64 . . . . | 510 Washington Av,
MISS Jennifer A . . . . | Palo Alto, CA
   94301

Shields MISS Victoria G . . . . | ☎ (510) 485-1518
MR James K—in Thailand . . . . | 785 Rose Av,
  Pleasanton, CA
   94566

Shields MR & MRS W Dickinson (Schmeltzer—Betty M Wike) Edg.Leh'40
☎ (941) 921-7681 . . 4476 Deer Trail Blvd, Sarasota, FL *34238*
Shields MR William X . . see MRS R G Blaine
Shiland MR & MRS Scott DeF (Heather G Matheson)
Au.B.My.Srb.BostColl'79
☎ (508) 468-4147 . . "Rabbit Ridge" 33 Essex St, South Hamilton,
MA *01982*
Shiland MR & MRS William McA JR (Patricia J Netter)
Cr'83.Un.Pr.Reed'78.Cr'83
☎ (212) 288-2295 . . 129 E 69 St, New York, NY *10021*
Shinkle MRS Andrew J (Schneidenbach—Suzanne Sinclair)
☎ (314) 965-0457 . . 749 W Jewel St, St Louis, MO *63122*
Shinkle MR & MRS Jackson J (Judith B Cutler) Cy.Va'35
☎ (314) 991-2294 . . 29 Oakleigh Lane, St Louis, MO *63124*
Shinn VICE ADM & MRS Allen M (Sevilla H Shuey)
Err.Cos.Ny.Eyc.Myf.Ncd.USN'32.Cal'36 . . of
☎ (415) 492-2633 . . Villa Marin, Apt 330, 100 Thorndale Dv,
San Rafael, CA *94903*
☎ (508) 627-8693 . . 46 Cooke St, Box 9, Edgartown, MA *02539*

Shinn MR & MRS George Latimer (Clara L Sampson) | of ☎ (201)267-5558
Ln.Ri.C.Mg.StA.Aht'45 .... | 55 Pippins Way,
MISS Deborah S—at 100 W 80 St, Apt 10F, | Morristown, NJ
New York, NY 10024 .... | 07960-7011
MISS Amy L—at 40 Atlantic Dv, Scarborough, | ☎ (802) 362-2090
ME 04074 .... | "High Meadows"
| Manchester Center,
| VT 05255

Shinn MR & MRS Jonathan H (Yates—Isabel B | ☎ (415) 435-4268
Lenssen) UWash'83.Sfy.Cal'67 ⚓ .... | 65 Beach Rd,
MR Alexander L .... | Belvedere, CA
JUNIORS MR Jonathan M .... | 94920

Shipley MR & MRS Paul E (Burkhart—Caroline M | ☎ (610) 388-0929
Cheston) BMr'53.BMr'86.Pc.W.Hav'51.Pa'56.. | PO Box 4295,
MISS Catherine M C Burkhart—at | Wilmington, DE
☎ (703) 931-4857 .. 4323—32 Rd S, | 19807-0295
Arlington, VA 22206 .... |
MISS Clarissa A Burkhart .... |

Shipley MR & MRS Samuel R 3d (Hannah Hope | ☎ (610) 687-3324
Randolph) V'68.Ph.Me.Nyc.W.Ac.Temp'63 ... | "Oakland"
MISS Julia R—Les'96 .... | 250 Woodland Rd,
MR Upton S .... | PO Box 419,
| Strafford, PA 19087

Shippen MRS Edward (Natalie Brooks Sears)
☎ (203) 637-1164 .. 5 Terrace Av, Riverside, CT 06878

Shiras MR & MRS Winfield 3d (Sherrill L Joyce)
Chath'55.Ih.Cr'48.H'50 .. of
☎ (847) 446-0057 .. 42 Indian Hill Rd, Winnetka, IL 60093
☎ (619) 340-0443 .. Ironwood Country Club, 48-978 Foxtail Lane,
Palm Desert, CA 92677

Shiverick MR & MRS Asa JR (Patricia Coombe) Kt.Un.Cv.Cly.
☎ (216) 247-6218 .. 2710 Chagrin River Rd, Chagrin Falls, OH 44022

Shiverick MR & MRS David G (Sandra A Bergsten)
Mich'85.Cl'90.Cv.T.Alleg'75
☎ (216) 991-1034 .. 3038 Woodbury Rd, Shaker Heights, OH 44120

Shiverick MR Nathan C—Sm.H'52
☎ (617) 864-0056 .. 215 Brattle St, Cambridge, MA 02138

Shiverick MR & MRS Paul C (Margaret R Brown)
WmSh'76.H'84.Ln.Y.Nw'75.Dth'83
☎ (914) 961-9265 .. 11 Argyle Place, Bronxville, NY 10708

Shiverick MR & MRS Reginald C (C Lynn Creviston)
Br'80.Cl'84.Un.Cyb.Buck'78.Dth'87
☎ (716) 248-2782 .. 1250 Clover St, Rochester, NY 14610

Shober MR Edward W 3d .. see C de Rham

Shober MISS Jorie Butler
☎ (512) 328-8131 .. 815 The High Rd, Austin, TX 78746

Shober MRS Nancy C (Nancy D Campbell) Rdc'56
☎ (201) 635-6322 .. 20 Pine St, Chatham, NJ 07928

Shober MRS Pemberton H (Georgiana F Harris)
301 Stenton Av, Plymouth Meeting, PA 19462

Shober MR & MRS Pemberton H JR (M Elizabeth | ☎ (773) 235-5205
Doretti) Loy'63.Nw'83.Mit'56.FairD'75 ...... | 2632 N Sawyer Av,
MISS Elizabeth C—Bost'84—at | Chicago, IL 60647
☎ (714) 588-6230 .. 243 Cinnamon Teal, |
Aliso Viejo, CA 92656 .... |
MR Samuel L—Emory'87—at ☎ (404) 373-4586 |
597 Seminole Av NE, Atlanta, GA 30307 ..... |
JUNIORS MISS Evelyn D .... |
JUNIORS MR Nathaniel W .... |

Shober MR & MRS Wharton (Diffenderffer—Sandra Metcalf) B.Srb.P'50
☎ (011-44-1666) 822-518 .. Hankerton Field Farm, Crudwell Rd,
Malmesbury, Wiltshire SN16 9RY, England

Shoch MR & MRS James R III (Reilly—Elena Miller) | ☎ (818) 799-4232
Stan'63.Me.Tcy.Va'63 .... | 335 Wigmore Dv,
MISS Alexandra—Va'93—at 418 W Shore Dv, | Pasadena, CA 91105
Madison, WI 53715 .... |
MISS Gillian—at U of Va .... |
MISS Elena C Reilly—Stan'93—at |
☎ (415) 775-9477 .. 1150 Union St, |
San Francisco, CA 94108 .... |
MR Matthew T Reilly—at U of Cal Berkeley . |

Shoemaker MISS Alexis Ann (Peter R) .... Born at
Portland, OR Sep 7'95

Shoemaker DR & MRS B Dawson (Cheryl H Linn) | ☎ (609) 845-1712
Yn.Y'54 .... | 1064 Ollerton Rd,
MISS Elizabeth J—at U of Vt .... | Woodbury, NJ
| 08096

Shoemaker MR & MRS Peter R (Leslie A McCall) L&C'93.PortSt'93
☎ (503) 297-1281 .. 4170 SW Parkview Av, Portland, OR 97225

Shoemaker MR & MRS William Reed (Sarah C Lange)
Dick'79.CUNY'84.Cda.Buck'79.Camb'91
"Coxefield" Willisbrook Farm, 266 Boot Rd, Malvern, PA 19355

Sholes MRS Justin Grant JR (Summerlin—Damaris | ☎ (805) 969-3445
Veitch) .... | 13 Seaview Dv,
MISS Piper E Summerlin—at | Santa Barbara, CA
☎ (805) 682-8337 .. 2616 Orella St, | 93108
Santa Barbara, CA 93105 .... |
MR Laird B Summerlin—at 322 College St, |
Amherst, MA 01002 .... |

Sholes MISS Natalie
3880 San Rafael Av, Los Angeles, CA 90065

Shonnard MRS Elizabeth F (E Elizabeth Fox)
94 Ebury St, London SW1, England

Shoop MRS Hugh K (Jean H Hall) .... | ☎ (716) 592-4633
MISS Sandra J .... | 30 East Av,
MR Hugh K JR—Cal'85—at ☎ (707) 939-0569 | Springville, NY
1071 W Watmaugh Rd, Sonoma, CA 95476 ... | 14141

Shore MISS Barbara G (Goff—Barbara G Shore) RingArt'77
☎ (561) 498-3472 .. 3742 Arelia Dv N, Delray Beach, FL 33445

Shore MR F Croft JR—W&J'75
☎ (513) 241-7138 .. 231 W 4 St, Apt 501A, Cincinnati, OH 45202

Shore MR & MRS Frank C (Ruth P Gibson) Va'50
☎ (941) 639-6078 .. 526 Via Cintia, Punta Gorda, FL 33950

Shore MR Howard Everett 4th—Reed'72.CalPsych'92
☎ (503) 650-7075 .. PO Box 29091, Portland, OR 97210

Shores MR & MRS Terrell D (Sylva Swenson) . . . . . . ☎ (415) 322-7815
 MISS Susan E . . . . 853 Forest Av,
  Palo Alto, CA
  94301-2105
Short MISS Caroline T (R Carter N) . . . . . Married at Charlottesville, VA
 Beisswanger MR William J (William C) . . . . Jun 15'96
Short MRS J Simonds (Hurd—Janet Simonds)
 ☎ (941) 262-3424 . . Pier 8, Apt 3A, 780 Thirteenth Av S, Naples,
 FL *34102*
Short MR & MRS Jeffrey R JR (Barbara Allen) Ih.Hn.H'36
 ☎ (847) 446-2264 . . 630 Pine Lane, Winnetka, IL *60093*
Short MR & MRS R Carter N (Ann C Kelley) ☎ (201) 825-1733
 Va'68.Snc.Va'67 . . . . 123 Park Av,
 MISS Ann C—at ☎ (415) 922-9868 Allendale, NJ *07401*
 1767 Union St, Apt 303, San Francisco, CA
 94123 . . . .
Short MR & MRS Winthrop A JR (Andrea E ☎ (757) 460-3922
 McClintock) Penn'69.P'68.BostColl'80 . . . . 4205 White Acres
 MISS Leslie M . . . . Court,
 JUNIORS MISS Amanda L . . . . Virginia Beach,
  VA *23455*
Shotzberger MR & MRS Samuel T (Elisabeth B Delano)
 Berry'81.Del'80.Pa'88
 ☎ (610) 268-8499 . . Landhope Farm, 640 Newark Rd, Kennett Square,
 PA *19348*
Shoumatoff DR Nicholas—Mit'39
 ☎ (914) 234-7165 . . Old Post Rd, Bedford, NY *10506*
Shrady MR & MRS Alexander J S (Suzanne M ☎ (203) 567-5896
 Gaspar) NRoch'75.Ford'72 . . . . "Windridge"
 JUNIORS MISS Annamaria L . . . . 298 Kenyon Rd,
  Bethlehem, CT
  06751
Shrady MRS Frederick C (Maria ☎ (203) 268-5027
 Likar-Waltersdorff) Cly. . . . . "Easterfields"
 MISS Marina . . . . 190 Maple Rd,
  Easton, CT *06612*
Shrady MR Henry M 3d—C.Pl.S.Snc.SFrArt'65. ☎ (212) 254-5606
 Cl'67 . . . . 72 E 1 St,
 MISS Francesca L—NMex'94—at New York, NY
 ☎ (505) 873-8162 . . 1801½ Neat Lane, *10003*
 Albuquerque, NM *87105* . . . .
Shrady MR Lewis B—Rens'59
 ☎ (914) 591-8007 . . Harriman Rd, Irvington, NY *10533*
Shrady MRS Nicholas C F (Ghislaine Anne de Rochefort) Geo'80
 ☎ (011-34-3) 204-52-86 . . Paseo Bonanova 109, C-4-1,
 08017 Barcelona, Spain
Shrady MR Nicholas C F—Geo'81
 ☎ (011-34-1) 469-5330 . . Calle Gumersindo Azcárate 23,
 28026 Madrid, Spain
Shrady MR Theodore G N—StL'61
 6 Canal Park, Apt 210, Cambridge, MA *02141*
Shreve MR & MRS Levin Gale (Barbara Harris) Elk.Md.Mt.Cw.Cc.JHop'32
 ☎ (410) 296-4653 . . 205 Brightwood Club Dv, Lutherville,
 MD *21093-3640*
Shreve MR & MRS Richard S (Watson—Eloise J Honnet)
 ☎ (508) 428-6473 . . 39 Tower Hill Rd, 21B, Osterville, MA *02655*

Shriver MR & MRS Beverley Randolph JR (Abigail Alden Smith)
 Sth'53.Fcg.Ty'53
 ☎ (540) 839-2083 . . "Wilcuma" PO Box 845, Hot Springs,
 VA *24445*
Shriver MRS George M JR (Virginia S Warren) Sth'28
 ☎ (410) 795-8432 . . 7200 Third Av, Apt 212A, Sykesville, MD *21784*
Shriver MR H Patrick
 ☎ (011-44-1303) 259084 . . 4 Coolinge Rd, Folkestone,
 Kent CT20 1EW, England
Shriver MR & MRS Robert Sargent JR (Eunice M Kennedy)
 Cvc.Rcch.Yn.Y'38
 9109 Harrington Dv, Potomac, MD *20854*
Shriver MR & MRS Timothy P (Linda Potter)
 ☎ (203) 787-9273 . . 54 Cleveland Rd, New Haven, CT *06515*
Shriver MR & MRS Van Lear P 3d (M Patricia ☎ (520) 445-3682
 Roberts) . . . . 1891 Holly Dv,
 MISS Deborah A . . . . Prescott, AZ *86301*
 MR William M . . . .
Shrock MRS John F (Matthews—Phyllis E Peter) Cnt.
 ☎ (847) 234-5067 . . 1290 N Western Av, Apt 111, Lake Forest,
 IL *60045*
Shrock MR Peter J—Wes'87
 ☎ (773) 338-0331 . . 7010 N Ashland Av, Apt 305, Chicago, IL *60626*
Shuey MR & MRS Hayden (Mary E Hiller) Cp.Ncd.Cal'38
 ☎ (415) 461-2520 . . 4 Rock Rd, Kentfield, CA *94904*
Shufeldt MISS Alexina
 ☎ (914) 265-1023 . . "The Toll House" 328 Main St, Nelsonville,
 NY *10516*
Shuford MISS Anna Louise (Robert A) . . . . Born at
  Atlanta, GA Feb 21'96
Shuford MR & MRS Robert A (Margret S Tingue) Van'85.Ga'85
 ☎ (404) 351-1594 . . 710 Longwood Dv NW, Atlanta, GA *30305*
Shuford MR & MRS Sydney H (Sheila C Smith) ☎ (201) 927-5591
 NCar'58 . . . . 12 Sorman Terr,
 MR Andrew P—Nu'92 . . . . Randolph, NJ
  07869-3433
Shuman MR & MRS Stanley S (Gould—Sydney M ☎ (212) 644-1320
 Roberts) Ri.Hb.H.'56.H'59.H'61 . . . . 25 Sutton Place,
 MR David L—Wms'93—at ☎ (212) 879-9612 New York, NY
 17 E 73 St, New York, NY *10021* *10022*
 MR Michael A—Cl'96 . . . .
  MR Gordon R Gould—Pitzer'93—at
  ☎ (212) 647-1153 . . 463 W 21 St, New York,
  NY *10011* . . . .
   MR Howard B Gould—at ☎ (212) 288-1467
   17 E 73 St, New York, NY *10021* . . . .
Shuman MR & MRS Stephen E (Anne H Sweeney) Ds.
 ☎ (410) 377-8822 . . 4 Over Ridge Court, Apt 3812, Baltimore,
 MD *21210*
Shumate DR C Albert—Km.Sar.Cp.SFr'27.Creigh'31.SFr'76
 ☎ (415) 921-0232 . . 1901 Scott St, San Francisco, CA *94115-2613*
Shumate MR John T M—Rv.Ty'69.CarnM'73
 ☎ (703) 241-1217 . . 1821 N Tuckahoe St, Arlington, VA *22205*
Shumlin MR & MRS Jeffrey P (Evelyn deH Lovett) Wes'88.Wes'82
 ☎ (802) 387-2706 . . RD 3, Putney, VT *05346*
Shurcliff MR & MRS William A (Joan Hopkinson) H'30
 ☎ (617) 876-0764 . . 19 Appleton St, Cambridge, MA *02138*

Shurtleff MR & MRS John L (Victoria E Hurd)
V'47.Cl'54.San.Mo.Hn.H'46.Cl'48 . . . . | ☎ (201) 543-4605
MR Matthew M—at New York, NY . . . . | Green Bank Farm,
| 25 Cold Hill Rd,
| Morristown, NJ
| *07960*

Shute MRS Benjamin R (Katherine Van Varick) Sth'33.Csn.
☎ (203) 938-2932 . . 9 Turney Rd, Box 43, Redding Ridge, CT *06876*

Shute MR & MRS Benjamin R JR (Janet M MacDonell) Pemb'66.Cs.H.'59
☎ (212) 628-2769 . . 150 E 73 St, New York, NY *10021*

Shutt MR & MRS George Austin (Nancy W Perkins) Tex'55.Ln.Yn.Y'54
☎ (214) 363-1123 . . 5310 Park Lane, Dallas, TX *75220*

Shy MR & MRS DeWitt M (Sarah B Johnson)
Finch'67. . . . . | ☎ (901) 324-8334
MISS S Genevieve . . . . | 76 Lombardy Rd,
MR D F Sellers | Memphis, TN *38111*

Sias MRS Roane T (Charlotte M Sherman) . . . . Died at
San Anselmo, CA Mch 20'96

Sias MR Roane T—Wash'48
☎ (415) 453-6589 . . 160 Sturdivant Av, San Anselmo, CA *94960*

Sibley MAJ GEN (RET) & MRS Alden K (Drake—V Elvira Trowbridge)
BMr'34.An.Plg.Sar.Cs.USA'33.Ox'36
☎ (212) 737-3946 . . 969 Park Av, New York, NY *10028*

Sibley MR & MRS Horace H (Beverly Bryan)
Van'61.Ga'63 . . . . | ☎ (404) 261-7178
MISS Beverly Clare . . . . | 3056 E Pine Valley
MISS Barbara E . . . . | Rd NW, Atlanta,
MR J Holden . . . . | GA *30305*

Sibley MRS John Adams (Barbara S Thayer)
☎ (404) 233-5122 . . 165 W Wesley Rd NW, Atlanta, GA *30305*

Sibley MR & MRS John B (Heiserman—Shirley D
Cook) Pa'45 . . . . | ☎ (610) 353-2523
MISS Mariah W—OWes'87—at | 627 Glendale Rd,
☎ (610) 356-9322 . . 618 Andover Rd, | Newtown Square,
Newtown Square, PA *19073*. . . . . | PA *19073*
| MISS Blake Chandler . . . . |
| MR Robert B Heiserman 3d—at |
| ☎ (212) 749-0382 . . 878 West End Av, |
| Apt 2D, New York, NY *10025* . . . . |

Sibley MR & MRS Stephen T (Lisa A Czarick)
Lind'80.Van'70.Tenn'82 ⚓
☎ (423) 894-9327 . . 1109 N Concord Rd, Chattanooga, TN *37421*

Sibley MR & MRS Thomas (Jean C Eagleson)
Fla'67.H'62 . . . . | ☎ (941) 688-9802
MISS Erin W—at New York, NY . . . . | 1400 Grasslands
MR Thomas S—at Chicago, IL . . . . | Blvd, Lakeland, FL
| *33803*

Sidamon-Eristoff MR Andrew (Constantine) . . . Married at New York, NY
Baxter MISS Catherine E (C Cash) . . . . Mch 30'96

Sidamon-Eristoff MR & MRS Andrew (Catherine E Baxter) P'85.Geo'89
☎ (212) 935-1361 . . 480 Park Av, Apt 16J, New York, NY *10022*

Sidamon-Eristoff MR & MRS Constantine (Anne Phipps)
BMr'54.Rc.C.K.Cly.Cs.Ncd.P'52.Cl'57
☎ (212) 988-2261 . . 120 East End Av, New York, NY *10028*

Sidamon-Eristoff MR & MRS Simon (Nancy B Zabel) P'81.P'80
☎ (202) 338-5973 . . 4420 Dexter St NW, Washington, DC *20007*

Sides MR & MRS Frederick H (Louise B Whitehouse) K.Bgt.
☎ (914) 234-3726 . . Baldwin Rd, Mt Kisco, NY *10549*

Sidley MR & MRS William F (Cornelia L Krause)
Y'47. . . . . | 5700 E First Av,
MR Peter F . . . . | Denver, CO
| *80220-5812*

Siebens MRS Allen C (Margaret M Dunn) B'gton'45
☎ (609) 924-2766 . . 4 Hunter Rd, Princeton, NJ *08540*

Siebens MR & MRS Geoffrey A (Cyrice L Griffith) SCal'88.Va'78.Cl'81
☎ (213) 462-1154 . . 6433 Deep Dell Place, Los Angeles, CA *90068*

Siedlarz MRS Joseph B JR (Nancy D England) | ☎ (610) LA5-8687
Drex'51.Me.Pe.Ac.W.Ncd.Dar.Dll. . . . . | 26 Meadows Lane,
MISS Abigail H—Me.W.Dar.Ncd. . . . . | Haverford, PA
| *19041-1128*

Siedlarz MR & MRS Joseph B 3d (Eugenia M C Warnock)
Pa'95.Me.Pe.Sfh.Ll.Rv.W.Cw.Cspa.Drex'91.Del'94
☎ (610) 688-2752 . . 20 Matlack Lane, Villanova, PA *19085*

Siedler DR & MRS H Duane (Nancy C Miller) | ☎ (415) 388-4464
Wash'54.P'51 . . . . | 501 Tamalpais Av,
MISS Bridget A . . . . | Mill Valley, CA
MISS Hillary M—at 147 rue d'Aboukir, | *94941*
75002 Paris, France . . . . |
MR Lucian D—at ☎ (415) 564-9915 |
228 Hugo St, San Francisco, CA *94122* . . . . . . |

Siegel JUNIORS MR Henry W 4th . . see S E Slagsvol

Sieglaff MR & MRS Peter M JR (Victoria L Sanderson) Cr'94.Denis'91
☎ (941) 964-2365 . . 260 Palm Av, PO Box 1771, Boca Grande,
FL *33921*

Siegman MR & MRS Anthony E (Carney—Lissner— | of ☎ (415)326-6669
Virginia W Howard) Stan'65.Cp.H'52.Cal'54. | 550 Junipero Serra
Stan'57 . . . . | Blvd, Stanford, CA
MISS Elaine A Lissner . . . . | *94305*
| ☎ (916) 546-3239
| Cedar Summit,
| PO Box 1516,
| Carnelian Bay, CA
| *96140*

Siegman MISS Jessica L . . see S P Phillips

Siemon MR & MRS Charles L (Laura S Magnuson) . . see M G Magnuson JR

Siems MISS Shelby D—Mid'84
☎ (206) 528-4746 . . 8060 Ridge Dv NE, Seattle, WA *98115*

Sierck MR & MRS Alexander W (Susan S Arthur) | ☎ (202) 333-7224
CtCol'63.Unn.Mt.Cvc.Va'62.Va'65 . . . . | 3216 Cathedral Av
MISS Sarah S—at U of Va . . . . | NW, Washington,
| DC *20008*

Sierck MISS Carsten W (Atterbury—Carsten W Sierck) Cl'88.Va'92
☎ (202) 237-8254 . . 5177 Fulton St NW, Washington, DC *20016*

Sigety MR & MRS Cornelius E (Virginia White)
H'86.Unn.Cly.Hn.Roch'80.H'85 ⚓
7145 Old Easton Rd, PO Box 369, Pipersville, PA *18947*

Sigety MR & MRS Robert G (Elizabeth P Donnem)
Y.'86.Ch'89.Duke'80.H.'90 . of
☎ (215) 766-2300 . . 3820 Secondwoods Rd, PO Box 1090, Doylestown,
PA *18901*
☎ (212) 517-6208 . . 333 E 80 St, Apt 6F, New York, NY *10021*

Sigler MR Frederick G 4th . . see E G Thomas

Sigler MISS Gretchen C . . see E G Thomas

Siglow MR Jesse W JR—KeeSt'92 . . see D N Adams JR

Siglow MR Zachary H . . see D N Adams JR

Silbersack MR & MRS John W (Elionora van T Wilking) Duke'80.Br'77
☎ (516) 883-8456 . . 5 Harbor Rd, Sands Point, NY *11050*
Silbert THE REVS John C R & Marion N (Marion G Nimick)
NH'76.PTheo'82.Gordon'78.PTheo'82
☎ (412) 327-5826 . . 4016 Remaley Rd, Murrysville, PA *15668*
Sill MRS James Mather (Grieves—Posey—Frances R Kefauver) Elk.
615 Chestnut Av, Towson, MD *21204*
Sill MR & MRS Louis F (Joan B Boucher) Ck.USA'63.Nu'74
☎ (203) 622-6542 . . 11 Grant Av, Old Greenwich, CT *06870*
Sillcocks MR H Jackson—Yn.Y'28.H'31
☎ (508) 945-6045 . . Chatham House 10, 33 Cross St, Chatham,
MA *02633*
Sills MR Charles F—Mt.Ne.P'65.Tufts'67
see Dilatory Domiciles

Silva-Sadder MR & MRS Adolfo (Anita G Messimer) | ☎ (914) 265-9422
Cl'69 . . . . | Lake Valhalla,
MR Andre R . . . . | Valley View Dv,
                                      | Cold Spring, NY
                                       | *10516*

Silva-Sadder MR Alexander G
☎ (305) 445-0263 . . 2772 SW Thirtieth Av, Miami, FL *33133*
Silver MR Duncan M—FairD'82 ⚓
☎ (716) 626-9085 . . 12 Spindrift Dv, Apt 3, Williamsville, NY *14221*

Silver DR & MRS Stuart R (Patricia Dunn) | ☎ (941) 953-4402
B'gton'48.Cl'77.Dth'48.Cr'52 . . . . | 480 Meadow Lark
MISS Alexander B—at U of Edinburgh Scotland . | Dv, Sarasota, FL
                                       | *34236*

Silverthorne MRS John H (Mary L Rose) ⚓
☎ (214) 361-9595 . . 10640 Lennox Lane, Dallas, TX *75229*
Simenstad MRS Susan O (Susan A Oyster) Stph'65
☎ (415) 454-9553 . . 366 Forbes Av, San Rafael, CA *94901*

Simmons MR & MRS Cheston (Bakewell—Emily A | ☎ (610) 933-8576
Ames) Pa'70.Y'51 . . . . | "Pickering House"
MISS Jenifer J Bakewell—at 76 Strawberry | RD 2, Phoenixville,
Lane, Yarmouth Port, MA *02675* . . . . | PA *19460*

Simmons MR & MRS Grant G JR (Darlington—F Elizabeth Richardson)
Au.B.Mto.Plg.Myf.Y'42
☎ (803) 671-3296 . . 35 Baynard Park Rd, Villa 410,
Hilton Head Island, SC *29928*

Simmons MRS Harry C B (Mary O Blair) Pg.Rr. . . . | ☎ (412) 361-2851
MISS Lisabeth B—Wheat'81.Emory'86 . . . . | 109 Conover Rd,
MISS Nancy L—CathU'92 . . . . | Pittsburgh, PA
MR John T B—Norw'88 . . . . | *15208*
MR Harry C—at Duquesne . . . . |

Simmons DR & MRS Heber S JR (Jean E Frazer) MempSt'57.Tenn'57
☎ (601) 982-4313 . . 646 Seneca Av, Jackson, MS *39216*
Simmons MRS James L (Annison—Urbahn—Allyn D Smith)
Cly.Myf.Ht . . .of
45-215 Camino Dorado, Indian Wells, CA *92210*
☎ (508) 428-5706 . . 10 Crossway, Osterville, MA *02655*
Simmons MR & MRS John Farr (Caroline H Thompson) BMr'31
☎ (202) 965-5470 . . 1508 Dumbarton Rock Court NW, Washington,
DC *20007*

Simmons MRS Rebecca K (Sengelmann—Rebecca S | ☎ (805) 542-9226
Kendall) . . . . | PO Box 1183,
MR Peter S Sengelmann—☎ (805) 773-2390 | San Luis Obispo,
                                       | CA *93406*

Simmons MR & MRS Richard De L (Mary De W Bleecker)
Cl'60.Adelphi'78.Cvc.Mt.H'55.Cl'58 . . of
☎ (540) 987-9205 . . "Poortown Hill" PO Box 242, Sperryville,
VA *22740*
☎ (703) 548-5585 . . 715½ S Lee St, Alexandria, VA *22314-4331*
Simmons MRS Richard W (Goodwin—Charlotte B Head) Cho.On.Sr.
☎ (847) 234-0038 . . 105 E Laurel Av, Lake Forest, IL *60045*

Simmons MR & MRS Sanford G (Schaller—Marie J | of ☎ (203)869-5469
Harms) Msq.Dar.Y'45w . . . . | "Rabbit Hill"
MR William A Schaller—at U of RI . . . . | 70 Porchuck Rd,
                                       | Greenwich, CT
                                       | *06831*
                                       | ☎ (912) 355-9761
                                       | "Vernon View"
                                       | Rte 3, Box 290,
                                       | Center Dv,
                                       | Savannah, GA
                                       | *31406*

Simmons MR & MRS William E 3d (Bolles—Eliza A Atkinson)
SoMiss'69.Cda.Dar.Mlsps'78
☎ (601) 736-1763 . . 1 Hugh White Place, Columbia, MS *39429*
Simon MR Gregory S—Cal'96 . . see A D Mallace
Simon MR James E—Bow'92.Cl'93
☎ (312) 280-0863 . . 1300 N Astor St, Apt 8D, Chicago, IL *60610*
Simon MISS Mercedes A . . see A D Mallace

Simon MR & MRS Robert S (Margaret D Turnbull) | ☎ (415) 986-3642
SL'68.Tcy.Cl'64 . . . . | 45—21 Av,
JUNIORS MISS Abigail T . . . . | San Francisco, CA
                                       | *94121*

Simonds MR & MRS Albert R (Frances M Lamar) W&M'35.NCar'34 . . of
☎ (803) 723-3556 . . 18 Lamboll St, Charleston, SC *29401*
☎ (803) 844-2562 . . White House Plantation, Green Pond, SC *29446*

Simonds MR & MRS Albert Rhett JR (Struse—Marie | ☎ (703) 683-6778
C Baker) Pa'68.Md'73.NCar'65.Pa'68 . . . . | 624 S Lee St,
MISS Caroline L—at U of Pa . . . . | Alexandria, VA
JUNIORS MISS Frances R—at Holton-Arms . . . . . | *22314*

Simonds MRS Cassandra G (Cassandra Goss) | ☎ (207) 729-5027
CtCol'58.Cly.Ncd. . . . . | 29 Birch Meadow
MR Reade H—at ☎ (301) 593-9358 | Rd, Brunswick, ME
720 University Blvd W, Silver Spring, MD *20901* | *04011*

Simonds MR Charles S—Y'56.H'64 . . . . | ☎ (203) 222-3847
MISS Melissa G—Y'83—at Tabor Academy, | 34 Edgewater
Front St, Marion, MA *02738* . . . . | Hillside, Westport,
MR C Sprague JR—Conn'86 . . . . | CT *06880*

Simonds MRS Gifford K JR (Lyons—Ingalls— | ☎ (617) 631-0414
Virginia Wells) Ey.Cda.Dar. . . . . | "The Mooring"
MR John J Ingalls—at 12 Kesswick St, Boston, | 27 Ballast Lane,
MA *02215* . . . . | Marblehead, MA
                                       | *01945*

Simonds MRS John H (Patricia T Spencer) Chi.
☎ (603) 924-3969 . . 129 Riverhead, Peterborough, NH *03458*
Simonds MR & MRS John L (Mary F Trafton)
MtH'40.Cw.Chi.Cda.Ncd.Y'40.H'43
☎ (617) 489-4710 . . 20 Tyler Rd, Belmont, MA *02178*

Simonds MR & MRS Jonathan O (Marcia T
Rowbotham) NECons'52.H'52 . . . .
MISS Jane B—Cr'82.Wis'92—at
☎ (301) 891-2441 . . 121 Sherman Av,
Takoma Park, MD *20912* . . . .
MISS Rebecca Lawrence—HWSth'83—at
☎ (617) 354-7521 . . 45 Langdon St, Cambridge,
MA *02138* . . . .
| ☎ (508) 540-0516
| 8 Benefit St,
| East Falmouth, MA
| *02536*

Simonds MR & MRS Peter K (Elizabeth S Colt)
2406 N Catalina St, Los Angeles, CA *90027*

Simonds MR & MRS Robert L (Ann S Bainbridge)
Colby'68.LakeF'70.WorPoly'70 . . . .
JUNIORS MISS Caroline F . . . .
JUNIORS MISS Rebecca T . . . .
JUNIORS MR Alden B . . . .
| ☎ (617) 489-3708
| 63 Rutledge Rd,
| Belmont, MA
| *02178-2631*

Simonds MR & MRS Robinson (Leonard—Jane C Mellon) Me.Y'30
☎ (610) 645-8843 . . 1400 Waverly Rd, Apt B114, Gladwyne, PA *19035*

Simonin MR & MRS L Taylor (Tina M Mucci) StLaw'78.StLaw'78 . . of
☎ (860) 364-1608 . . PO Box 42, 120 Calkinstown Rd, Sharon,
CT *06069*
☎ (212) 206-9402 . . 275 Greenwich St, New York, NY *10007*

Simonin MRS Robert W (Virginia A Taylor) Dar.
☎ (215) 233-4181 . . 8520 Ardmore Av, Wyndmoor, PA *19038*

Simons MR & MRS Albert JR (Caroline P Mitchell) Cc.Cw.Pn.P'40.Y'47
☎ (803) 723-3350 . . 1 King St, Apt 207, Charleston, SC *29401-2719*

Simons MR & MRS Albert 3d (Theodora B Wilbur)
K.Va'72.Va'76 . . . .
MR Albert 4th . . . .
| of ☎ (212)628-7426
| 830 Park Av,
| New York, NY
| *10021*
| ☎ (518) 828-3416
| PO Box 134,
| Livingston, NY
| *12541*
| ☎ (803) 853-8951
| 8 S Battery St,
| Charleston, SC
| *29401*

Simons MR & MRS Cotesworth P (Elizabeth A Salmon) Hlns'80.W&L'79
☎ (803) 883-3166 . . 1763 Atlantic Av, Sullivans Island, SC *29482*

Simons MR D Brenton—Ht.Myf.Rv.Sar.Wt.Cc.Bost'88.Bost'94
142 Chandler St, Boston, MA *02116-6061*

Simons MR & MRS Julian M (Davis—Deborah K
Martin) . . . .
JUNIORS MR Robert K Davis 3d . . . .
| ☎ (803) 883-3745
| 1754 I'On Av,
| Sullivans Island, SC
| *29482*

Simons MR & MRS Langdon S JR (Anne W McBride) Occ'49.Hn.H'45
☎ (206) 621-1981 . . 98 Union St, Apt 1000, Seattle, WA *98101*

Simons MR & MRS S Stoney (Virginia L Cooke) Ph.Sg.Rb.Cc.P'42
☎ (215) 233-3946 . . 540 E Evergreen Av, Wyndmoor, PA *19038*

Simons MR & MRS William L JR (Susan Willingham)
Ws'.64.GaTech'57 . . . .
MISS Susan W . . . .
MISS Adele C . . . .
MISS Dorothy A . . . .
| 227 Deer Park Dv,
| Nashville, TN *37205*

Simpkins DR & MRS (DR) C Alexander (Annellen
Minkin) USInt'l'83.USInt'l'83 . . . .
MISS Alura L—at Cal Polytech . . . .
JUNIORS MR Charles A JR—at Bishop's Sch . . . .
| ☎ (619) 488-0907
| 727 Salem Court,
| San Diego, CA
| *92109*

Simpkins MRS Nathaniel S 3d (Carmen E F Zitelmann) . . of
☎ (561) 388-5972 . . 9422 US 1, Apt 302, Sebastian, FL *32958-6398*
☎ (207) 236-2579 . . "Wishbone Point" RR 1, Box 4250, Beaucaire Rd,
Camden, ME *04843*

Simpkins MRS Willard S (de Watteville-Berckheim—
Jacqueline P de Neuflize) Cly.Chi.
☎ (508) 362-3824 . . "Onion Acre" PO Box 302, Barnstable, MA *02630*

Simpson MR & MRS Andrew W 3d (Bowman—Ann M Nathan)
Cal'35.Fmy.Stan'35
☎ (408) 625-2416 . . 2416 Bayview, Carmel, CA *93923*

Simpson MR & MRS C Morgan (Linda McD Tourison) Gm.Ph.Smu'73
☎ (610) 889-3887 . . 1 Martin's Lane, Berwyn, PA *19312*

Simpson MRS Charles J (Ann I Townsend)
☎ (301) 365-2918 . . 7535 Spring Lake Dv, Bethesda, MD *20817*

Simpson MR & MRS Charles J JR (Pamela A Raymont)
Bost'75.Geo'83.Gi.Tufts'74.Geo'79
☎ (301) 654-5853 . . 125 Grafton St, Chevy Chase, MD *20815*

Simpson MR David E—Rc.Sa.Rcch.Wms'50
☎ (516) 653-4221 . . 4 Jessup Lane, Quogue, NY *11959*

Simpson MR Davis JR . . see F L Barton

Simpson COL (RET) & MRS Frank H 2d (Shirley
Hollingsworth) USMC.Dth'41 . . . .
MR Aaron H—NH'86—at U of Vt Law . . . .
| ☎ (603) 763-5121
| "Balla Macree"
| 270 Stagecoach Rd,
| Sunapee, NH *03782*

Simpson MR G Northrup JR—Aht'51.Ch'52
☎ (773) 493-7723 . . 5500 S Shore Dv, Apt 607, Chicago, IL *60637*

Simpson MR George W . . see F L Barton

Simpson MR & MRS Harry E (Elizabeth C Hettler)
Wa. . . . .
MISS Erminnie H . . . .
MISS Kathryn H . . . .
| ☎ (847) 446-5634
| 1355 Hackberry
| Lane, Winnetka, IL
| *60093*

Simpson MRS Howard K (Susan H Kephart) . . . . . .
MR Christopher K—WmSth'80 . . . .
| ☎ (610) 649-9541
| 616 Argyle Rd,
| Wynnewood, PA
| *19096*

Simpson MR James A—Gm.Bab'87
☎ (610) 975-0577 . . 132 Plant Av, Wayne, PA *19087*

Simpson JUNIORS MISS Melanie S . . see MRS M Trevor

Simpson MR & MRS Michael (Barbara A Bodtke)
Rc.Sr.On.Mich'65 . . . .
MISS Elizabeth McL—at Purdue . . . .
| ☎ (847) 234-6895
| 765 W Westleigh
| Rd, Lake Forest, IL
| *60045*

Simpson MR & MRS Michael H (Marion H Brown)
Br'83.Dth'89.Denis'75.Dth'81.Ant'84
☎ (603) 863-6006 . . HCR 63, Box 74, Grantham, NH *03753*

Simpson MRS Sandra S (Sandra Stingily) Swb'57
3796 Glencoe Dv, Birmingham, AL *35213*

Simpson MR & MRS William (Curtis—Barbara H Gatins)
Rc.Pr.Ln.Ri.Cly.H'34
☎ (516) 674-3855 . . 14 Cherrywood Rd, Locust Valley, NY *11560*

Simpson MR & MRS William 4th (Charlene Amidon) Tex'43.Gm.Rc . . .of
☎ (610) 296-4004 . . 38 Manchester Court, Berwyn, PA *19312*
☎ (602) 471-7536 . . 18810 Chinle Dv, Rio Verde, AZ *85263*

Simpson MR William K—Ub.Bgt.Mto.Ri.Un.C.Rv.Y'47.Y'48.Y'54
☎ (914) 232-4221 . . Katonah's Wood Rd, Katonah, NY *10536*
Simpson MR William S—Pars'67.AIFT'68.AGSIM'75
☎ (610) 993-2181 . . 38 Manchester Court, Berwyn, PA *19312*
Simpson DR & MRS Zachary A (Dorothy C Weeder) V'47.Duke'46.Duke'48
☎ (904) 267-3346 . . 1143 Troon Dv, Sandestin, FL *32541*
Sims MRS John C (Lucile Caldwell) Pa'43.Pa'45
☎ (603) 643-3576 . . Kendal at Hanover 203, 80 Lyme Rd, Hanover, NH *03755*
Sims MR Joseph P JR—Ph.Fst.Cc.Cw.Pa'40
☎ (215) 561-0756 . . 2031 Locust St, Apt 1405, Philadelphia, PA *19103*
Sims MRS Richard B (Antoinette M Grau) . . . . | ☎ (415) 931-7442
MISS Diana M—at ☎ (509) 779-4756 | 1400 Geary Blvd,
Box 46, Malo, WA *99150* | San Francisco, CA
MR Richard K—at ☎ (515) 469-5020 | *94109*
1000 N 4 St, Apt 331, Fairfield, IA *52557* . . . . .
MR Donald W—at ☎ (707) 275-0238
PO Box 211, 1703 Hunter Point Rd, Upper Lake, CA *95485* . . . .
Sims MR & MRS Sanders S (Jaeckel—Jenifer G Coward) Ph.
☎ (518) 854-7248 . . ''Flax Mill House'' RD 1, Scotch Hill Rd, Cambridge, NY *12816*
Sims MR William S . . . . Died at Shelburne, VT Jly 9'96
Simson MRS Prudence G (Prudence A Goodman) Roch'75.Nu'84.Cly.
☎ (919) 419-0353 . . 106 Timber Ridge Dv, Durham, NC *27713*
Sincerbeaux MRS Richard M (Katherine A Connell) | ☎ (212) 860-2973
Ws'66.Cly. . . . . | 1088 Park Av,
MISS Caroline C—at Princeton . . . . | New York, NY | *10128*
Sincerbeaux MR Richard M—Ck.P'64 . . . . | ☎ (212) 734-4053
MR Richard M JR—Vt'90 . . . . | 520 E 76 St, Apt | 6B, New York, NY | *10021*
Sinclair MR & MRS David W (Lilliana Ćuković) Sarajevo'79.Nu'79
☎ (212) 534-0598 . . 201 E 87 St, Apt 15K, New York, NY *10128*
Sinclair MR & MRS James P (Margaret K Nieland) | ☎ (212) 534-0611
Cald'62.Rc.T.Mto.Eyc.Plg.P'59.Va'65 . . . . | 4 E 95 St,
MR James W 2d—at ☎ (203) 254-1396 | New York, NY
1727 Fairfield Beach Rd, Westport, CT *06430* . . | *10128*
MR Ian R L—at ☎ (415) 921-6929
2930 Webster St, San Francisco, CA *94123* . . . .
JUNIORS MR Duncan McA S—at St Paul's . . . . . .
Sinclair MRS Winkler (Gretchen A Winkler)
☎ (802) 457-1249 . . 17 High St, Apt 1, Woodstock, VT *05091*
Singer MR & MRS F R Forbes (Anne M | ☎ (011-44-171)
de Lapeyrouse) Rcn.K.B.Pa'69. . . . . | 235-3151
JUNIORS MR Mortimer M . . . . | 36 Chapel St,
JUNIORS MR Oliver G L . . . . | London | SW1X 7DD, | England
Singer MR & MRS G Harton 3d (Susan P Lyon) | ☎ (412) 741-7224
Rr.Y'47 . . . . | Spanish Tract,
MISS Anna P—at 328 W 96 St, Apt 3C, | Sewickley, PA
New York, NY *10025* . . . . | *15143*
MR William H—Box 325, Gorham, ME *04038* . .

Singer MR & MRS James W 3d (Mary S Swarts) | ☎ (202) 363-6785
V'63.H'57.Va'60 . . . . | 2920—44 Place
MISS Lindsay K . . . . | NW, Washington,
MISS Lauren F . . . . | DC *20016*
MISS Mary B . . . .
Singer MRS Sandra Clothier (Sandra L Clothier) | ☎ (610) 688-7848
Pa'63 . . . . | Regency Apt 314,
MR Nathanael L—at 654 Rosemont Av, La Jolla, | 313 Creek Dv,
CA *92037* . . . . | Radnor, PA *19087*
Singer MR & MRS Thomas E (Ellen Colt) | ☎ (617) 566-6831
Ec.Chi.Hn.GeoW'50.H.'52 . . . . | 30 Heath St,
MISS M Forbes—at 131 Freeman St, Brookline, | Brookline, MA
MA *02146* . . . . | *02146*
MISS Dominique R—at 579 Broadway,
New York, NY *10012* . . . .
MR Henry A—at 11 Colville Mews, London
W11 2DA, England . . . .
Singleton MR Edwin T . . . . | ☎ (802) 824-8137
MISS Deirdra B—Mid'89 . . . . | 3 Evergreen Lane,
MR Edwin J 2d—at Sheridan, MI *48884* . . . . . . | Londonderry, VT | *05148*
Singmaster MR & MRS Lawrence G (Barbara L | ☎ (617) 237-5960
Barnes) Ub.Cy.P'64.Pa'69.Bost'78 . . . . | 19 Indian Springs
MISS Dara W—L&C'92 . . . . | Way, Wellesley
JUNIORS MISS Carlen H—at Tabor Acad . . . . | Hills, MA *02181*
JUNIORS MR Ross B . . . .
Sinkinson MR & MRS Mark C (Anne H Warden) | ☎ (508) 475-9143
WashColl'72.RI'76. . . . . | 187 Chestnut St,
JUNIORS MISS Elizabeth S . . . . | Andover, MA *01810*
Sinkler MR & MRS David D (Rebecca W Pepper) Pa'75.Rb.Ph.Ac.P'56 . . of
☎ (215) 735-3542 . . 2128 Pine St, Philadelphia, PA *19103*
☎ (603) 284-6366 . . 14 Bickford Crossroad, Center Sandwich, NH *03227*
Sinkler MR G Dana JR . . see J P Kassebaum
Sinkler MR & MRS George Dana (Pritchard—Sallie S McPherson)
Char'ton'83.Yh.Va'57
☎ (803) 722-4668 . . 39 Church St, Charleston, SC *29401*
Sinkler MR Huger 2d . . see J P Kassebaum
Sinkler MR & MRS J Marshall (Charlotte I Fuller)
☎ (415) 457-4530 . . 96 Laurel Av, Fairfax, CA *94930*
Sinkler MR & MRS Richard K (Nancy McL Steel) . . . | ☎ (401) 364-9777
MISS Nancy McL—Box 554, Trinidad, CA *95570* | PO Box 246,
MR R Knowles JR . . . . | Shannock, RI *02875*
Sinkler REV DR & MRS Wharton 3d (Bass— | ☎ (612) 476-2267
Margherita G Harris) Cal'61.Cal'67.H'60. | PO Box 67,
CDSP'65.Cwr'72 . . . . | Crystal Bay, MN
JUNIORS MISS Ianna Marie H . . . . | *55323*
Sinnott MRS John JR (Marjorie V White) Rm.
☎ (908) 842-1293 . . 7 Rutgers Dv, Fair Haven, NJ *07704-3142*
Sinnott MR & MRS Robert V (Rosa Lee Kendall) Bost'76.Cda.Va'71.H'76
☎ (310) 394-8038 . . 214—22 St, Santa Monica, CA *90402*

Sinton MRS Stanley H JR (Gantner—Florence W Erskine) Rdc'39 . . . . of ☎ (415)673-0159 1170 Sacramento St, San Francisco, CA *94108*
    MR Stephen E Gantner—at 1855 Vernon St NW, Washington, DC *20009* . . . .
    MR Anthony F Gantner—at 235 Chestnut St, San Francisco, CA *94133* . . . . ☎ (707) 963-7330 3600 Spring Mountain Rd, St Helena, CA *94574*

Sinwell MR Andrew E—Elk.P'87 . . see R L De Groff JR

Sinwell MR & MRS John W (Hart—Suzanne Gerard) Me.W&L'57.Va'60 . . . . ☎ (610) 525-8935 1110 Ivymont Rd, Rosemont, PA *19010*
    MR Christopher P Hart—Ty'93 . . . .

Sinwell MISS Marion B (John W) . . . . Married at Baltimore, MD
    Smith MR Charles E W (C Edgar JR) . . . . Jun 8'96

Sioussat MR & MRS Pierce S (Abigail H Ross) Hlns'81.NECons'80
    ☎ (212) 987-8406 . . 114 E 90 St, Apt 9A, New York, NY *10128*

Sipe MR & MRS Richard G (Deborah L MacArthur) Briar'68.VillaN'68 . . . . ☎ (847) 234-7992 441 E Westminster Rd, Lake Forest, IL *60045*
    MR Christopher S . . . .

Siphron MR & MRS Joseph R (Mary John Wilson) Sth'57.Un.Cly.Y.'55
    ☎ (212) 628-8491 . . 50 E 72 St, New York, NY *10021*

Sise MRS Charles Carpenter (Anna Belle Sewell) Sg.
    ☎ (215) CH7-2565 . . 135 W Willow Grove Av, Chestnut Hill, PA *19118*

Sise MR & MRS Daniel H (Cornelia D Ford) Cly.Ncd.Col'52
    ☎ (203) 281-6694 . . 25 High Meadow Rd, Hamden, CT *06517*

Sise MR & MRS John Sewell (Peyton W Bird) Sg.Pa'66. . . . . ☎ (212) 831-6261 520 E 90 St, New York, NY *10128*
    JUNIORS MR Christopher J—at Kent. . . . .

Sisson DR & MRS Warden B (Georgia L Kendall) Rdc'61.Pom'59 . . . . ☎ (209) 439-5410 1339 W San Madele Av, Fresno, CA *93711*
    MISSES Anne L & Mary B—at 31-25—33 St, Apt 2D, Astoria, NY *11106* . . . .
    MR Franklin K—at 7522 Campbell Rd, Apt 113-161, Dallas, TX *25248* . . . .

Sivy MRS John (Louise S Gwinn) Chath'52.Myf.Cda. . . . . ☎ (410) 757-2935 807 Holly Dv, Rte 10, Amberley, Annapolis, MD *21401*
    MR Michael B—at 391 Volley Court, Arnold, MD *21012* . . . .

Sizemore MR & MRS James M JR (Smith—Brenda K Champlin) Aub'71.Aub'75.Aub'88.Sam'63. Va'66.Ala'78 . . . . ☎ (334) 277-5341 3123 Fieldcrest Dv, Montgomery, AL *36106-3334*
    MISS Charlotte C Smith . . . .
    JUNIORS MR John A Smith 5th . . . .

Sizemore MISS Rebecca L (James M JR) . . . . . Married at Tuscaloosa, AL
    Henderson MR William B JR (William B) . . . . Aug 26'95

Sizer MISS Wendy R (Hayden—Wendy R Sizer) Madrid'67
    ☎ (540) 891-8908 . . 10006 Sand Wedge Court, Fredericksburg, VA *22408*

Skallerup MRS Walter T JR (Hull—Margaret S Perkins) Sth'52.Mt.Ct. . . . . ☎ (703) 528-1470 1155 Crest Lane, McLean, VA *22101*
    MR Edward L Hull . . . .

Skeele MR & MRS James B (Constance E C Moss) Fic.
    ☎ (508) 541-1422 . . 76 Cleveland St, Norfolk, MA *02056*

Skelly MRS Ann T (Townsend—Ann L Skelly) NCar'65
    4 Hunt Rd, Peterborough, NH *03458*

Skelly MR & MRS T McFarland (Patricia F Peterson) Cda.Wil.NCar'67 . . . . ☎ (561) 655-3450 223 Seminole Av, Palm Beach, FL *33480*
    MR Christopher L—Ty'93—at New York Med Coll . . . .
    JUNIORS MISS Marriner L N . . . .

Skewes-Cox MR & MRS Martin V (Elizabeth A Dunne) MtH'48.Cal'48
    ☎ (707) 935-0425 . . "Escalera" 1229 Sobre Vista Dv, Sonoma, CA *95476-3233*

Skidmore MR & MRS Louis H JR (Margaret B Cooke) Chath'60.StLaw'58.Y'63 . . . . ☎ (713) 464-7134 302 Litchfield Lane, Houston, TX *77024*
    MISS Elizabeth P—at 72 Adamson St, Allston, MA *02134* . . . .
    MISS Heather C . . . .
    MR Christopher A—at 1917½ Banks St, Houston, TX *77098* . . . .

Skiff MRS A Harrington (Ann P Harrington) . . . . Died at Chevy Chase, MD Nov 23'95

Skillern MRS Ross P (Lia A Martucci)
    ☎ (610) 272-8582 . . "Holly Hill" PO Box 659, Plymouth Meeting, PA *19462*

Skillin JUNIORS MISS Adele E . . see MISS M T Vitagliano

Skinner MRS Claiborne A (Meeker—E Olivia Little)
    ☎ (505) 989-9617 . . 984 Acequia Madre St, Santa Fe, NM *87501*

Skinner MRS Donald M (Eleanor Stineman)
    ☎ (214) 526-8021 . . 6033 Hillcrest Av, Dallas, TX *75205*

Skinner MR & MRS E Lemoine 3d (Kathleen A Malley) Cal'84.Cal'85.P'66.Hast'72.Nu'83
    ☎ (415) 566-1365 . . 1334 Eighth Av, San Francisco, CA *94122*

Skinner MR & MRS James F 3d (Sharon L Davin) Stan'56.Stan'56
    ☎ (805) 528-4121 . . 1566—9 St, Los Osos, CA *93402*

Skinner MR & MRS Jeffrey A (Katherine S Cookson) Cal'68.Tcy.Cal'64.Hast'68 . . . . ☎ (415) 457-3716 5 Walters Rd, Box 1342, Ross, CA *94957*
    MISS Courtney C . . . .
    MR Samuel D . . . .

Skinner MRS Roberts K (Elizabeth Steele)
    ☎ (904) 255-7080 . . 721 S Beach St, Apt A203, Daytona Beach, FL *32114*

Skowronek MR & MRS Lawrence J JR (Cynthia W Cass) Wms'92.Wms'92
    1700 Russell St, Nashville, TN *37206*

Skvarch MR & MRS Jeffrey P (Cynthia A Bradford) Stph'86
    ☎ (616) 335-3364 . . 4766 Wildwood Rd, Holland, MI *49423*

Slack MRS Henry Campbell (McAnerney—Mona H Tjäder) Ncd.Pn. . . . . of ☎ (203)655-1062 Tokeneke Trail, Darien, CT *06820*
    MISS Lisa T McAnerney . . . . ☎ (561) 278-8891 1700 S Ocean Blvd, Delray Beach, FL *33483*

Slack MR & MRS W Cameron (Riedel—Erika O Muehlen) Elk.Gi.P'50. . . . . ☎ (410) 255-5747 627 Ayrlie Water Rd, Box 41, Gibson Island, MD *21056*
    MR Randall D—*abroad* . . . .

Slade MRS A Patterson (Alice R Patterson) Cly.
☎ (212) 935-1768 . . 200 E 66 St, New York, NY *10021*

Slade MR Brayton H—Y'30.H'32
☎ (203) 483-1685 . . Evergreen Woods 362, 88 Notch Hill Rd, North Branford, CT *06471*

Slade MRS Howard (Cecily S Work) Csn.
☎ (860) 767-0578 . . Hanna Lane, Essex, CT *06426*

Slade MR & MRS Jarvis J JR (Carmen B Torruella) H.'87.H'91.Ri.Mds.Stan'85
☎ (212) 874-8871 . . 205 West End Av, Apt 16L, New York, NY *10023*

Slagsvol MR & MRS Steven E (Siegel—Mae A Cavanagh) Syr'80 . . . . | ☎ (914) 635-8283 PO Box 736, Traver Rd, Pleasant Valley, NY *12569*
    MR Henry W Siegel 4th—at SUNY New Paltz |

Slater MR & MRS Alexander B (Murray—Steinmann —Dionne K Ryan) L.Pr.Lic.Va'55 . . . . | ☎ (516) 676-0274 "Holly House" Duck Pond Rd, PO Box 491, Locust Valley, NY *11560*
    MR Alexander B JR . . . . |

Slater MR & MRS Clifford E JR (Nelson—Anne D Sallee) Ht.Br'57
☎ (310) 459-4162 . . 1312 Marinette Rd, Pacific Palisades, CA *90272*

Slater MR & MRS H Nelson (Brenda Luther) Cly.Mit'50 . . . . | ☎ (860) 435-0024 45 Slater Rd, Taconic, CT *06079*
    MISS Elizabeth A Luther . . . . |

Slater MR John G T JR—Ham'83.Cl'92 . . see J A Day

Slater MR & MRS Samuel (Eleanor H Forbes) Md'83.K.Pa'72
☎ (610) 383-4155 . . Box 309, RD 3, Gum Tree Rd, Coatesville, PA *19320*

Slattery MRS E Hodges (Elizabeth W Hodges) . . name changed to Hodges

Slattery MRS Price W (M Elizabeth M Rawle) Ncd. | ☎ (610) 525-1881 831 Castlefinn Lane, Bryn Mawr, PA *19010*
    MISS Rebecca W—HWSth'84 . . . . |
    MR James R . . . . |

Slaughter MRS Charles (Leary—Eugenia Peabody)
☎ (203) 762-7578 . . 430 Nod Hill Rd, Wilton, CT *06897*

Slaughter MR & MRS D French 3d (Marcie L Mott) MtVern'80.Va'77.Va'80 . . . . | ☎ (804) 979-0331 "Holly Hollow" 2330 Owensville Rd, Charlottesville, VA *22901*
    JUNIORS MISS Caroline M . . . . |
    JUNIORS MISS Karin E . . . . |

Slaughter MR & MRS Frank G JR (Taylor S Barnett) Pitt'73.H'61.Duke'66
☎ (412) 963-8137 . . 608 Dorseyville Rd, Pittsburgh, PA *15238*

Slaughter MR & MRS William M (Diana B Rediker) Swb'66.H'61.Va'66 . . . . | ☎ (205) 871-9011 2942 Cherokee Rd, Birmingham, AL *35223*
    MR B Hanson—Va'94—at 215 E 95 St, New York, NY *10128* . . . . |
    MR William C—H'95—at U of Ala |

Slaughter MR William V—Cw.Rv.Cc.P'36.LaS'50 900 W Franklin St, Richmond, VA *23220*

Slaymaker MR & MRS R Barrie (Sandra H McIlvain) Sfh.P'51 Box 505, Clothier Spring Rd, RD 5, Malvern, PA *19355*

Slaymaker MR & MRS R Barrie JR (Elizabeth A Prothero) CarnM'90 1648 Jancey St, Pittsburgh, PA *15206*

Slaymaker MR Samuel Cochran 3d (late Samuel R 2d) . . . . . Married at Lancaster, PA
Lyon MISS Laura A (Thomas) . . . . May 27'95

Slaymaker MR & MRS Samuel Cochran 3d (Laura A Lyon) Del'89.Dick'92.Cw.Cc.Wt.Rv.Ty'86.Dick'89
☎ (717) 442-4026 . . "White Chimneys" 5117 Lincoln H'way, Gap, PA *17527*

Slaymaker MRS Samuel R 2d (Sarah E Hazzard) Ncd.
☎ (717) 390-0710 . . 124 Deer Ford Dv, Lancaster, PA *17601*

Slaymaker MASTER Samuel Redsecker 3d (Samuel Cochran 3d) . . . . . Born at Lancaster, PA Jun 6'96

Slaymaker DR & MRS William W (Diana J Washburn) Ws'83.Va'82.Pa'87
☎ (610) 407-9070 . . 8078 Goshen Rd, Malvern, PA *19355-3332*

Slidell MRS John R (Hallie M Brooke) Cvc.Ncd.
☎ (202) WO6-7361 . . 3542 Porter St NW, Washington, DC *20016*

Slingluff MR & MRS Charles H JR (Gail K Grant) Evg.Rm.Ny.Stc.Cly.Yh.Va'51 . . . . | of ☎ (908)842-2815 20 Av of Two Rivers S, Rumson, NJ *07760* ☎ (561) 833-3424 350 S Ocean Blvd, Palm Beach, FL *33480*
    MR Charles H 3d . . . . |

Slingluff MR & MRS J Kernan (Gertrude S G Sessions) Elk.Ham'31
☎ (410) 467-4540 . . 411 Woodlawn Rd, Baltimore, MD *21210*

Slingluff MR & MRS John K JR (Paula M Peruzzi) MtStAg'66.JHop'66 . . . . | ☎ (410) 366-6741 104 W Oakdale Rd, Baltimore, MD *21210*
    MISS Jennifer D—Va'92 . . . . |
    MISS Laura K—Woos'95 . . . . |
    MISS Rebecca K—at U of Md . . . . |
    MISS Kathleen K—at U of Del . . . . |

Slingluff MRS Patricia K (Patricia D'A de Koranyi) Il. ⚓ . . . . | ☎ (212) 289-5106 125 E 87 St, New York, NY *10128*
    MR David D JR—RI'82 ⚓ —at ☎ (619) 273-5809 . . 4073 Kendall St, Pacific Beach, San Diego, CA *92109* . . . . |
    MR Peter de K—StLaw'82—at ☎ (617) 787-5613 . . 2 Appian Way, Allston, MA *02134* . . . . |

Slingluff MRS T Rowland (Gibson—Pamela Lloyd) Nf.Mv. ⚓ . . of 616 Brightwood Club Dv, Lutherville, MD *21093*
☎ (207) 244-5801 . . "Rock Point" PO Box 124, Mt Desert, ME *04660*

Sloan MISS Amanda W (Gurney P JR) . . . . . Married at Lumberville, PA
Richter MR Thomas L (late LeRoy H) . . . . Sep 9'95

Sloan MRS Benson B (Virginia F Stephens)
☎ (615) 292-5355 . . Richland Place Apt 420, 500 Elmington Av, Nashville, TN *37205*

Sloan MR & MRS David R (Amy E North) Conn'85.Juniata'84
☎ (914) 677-6750 . . "Pheasantcrest" RR 2, Box 124, South Rd, Millbrook, NY *12545*

Sloan MISS Edith J—Rdc'50.Nu'57.Bm.Dh.Ht.Ncd.
☎ (914) 677-6191 . . Millbrook Meadows 419, 560 Flint Rd, Millbrook, NY *12545-6419*

Sloan MR & MRS Edward W JR (Josephine Rudolph) Sth'27.Un.Pk.Cv.Cwr'29
☎ (216) 247-7343 . . 344 Hamlet Hills Dv, Chagrin Falls, OH *44022*

Sloan MISS Emily Cecilia (g—Robert N Sloan) . . . . Born at Stamford, CT Jly 9'96

Sloan MRS Eugene W (Grace E Switzer)
☎ (573) 546-2784 . . 412A Cayce St, Farmington, MO *63640*

Sloan MR & MRS Gurney P JR (Faith Rorer)
Sg.Rc.Ste.Ll.Rv.Ncd.Leh'53.Pa'66
☎ (215) 297-5679 . . ''Deer Walk'' Lumberville, PA *18933*

Sloan MISS Holly M—LakeF'93 . . see T L Elsberry

Sloan MR & MRS James R (Mimmu M A Hartiala) | ☎ (508) 456-8295
Lx.Y'59.H'61 . . . . | 16 Fairbank St,
MISS Eva-Jo E . . . . | PO Box 124,
MR Martti R T . . . . | Harvard, MA *01451*
MR Peter-Pike J . . . . |
JUNIORS MISS Anna-Laura A . . . . |
JUNIORS MR Richard A . . . . |

Sloan MRS John E (Margaret Howe) Cly.
☎ (615) 373-5209 . . Box 2027, Maple Grove, 9116 Concord St, Brentwood, TN *37027*

Sloan MRS John E JR (Delphine M Oman) | ☎ (615) 794-7346
Ws'63.Mt. . . . . | Cloverdale Farm,
MISS Catherine J B—at Middlebury . . . . | PO Box 466,
MR John Elliott 3d—Van'90—at | Franklin, TN *37065*
101 Deerfield Lane, Franklin, TN *37069* . . . . . . |
MR John Oman—Mid'94 . . . . |

Sloan MR & MRS Julian R (Cecile C Kelly) Br'51 . . . | ☎ (508) 945-3639
MISS H Edesse—Conn'80—at ☎ (203) 454-1915 | ''Wicked Hill Barn''
12 Wild Rose Rd, Westport, CT *06880* . . . . | 106 Highland Av,
MISS Margot S—at ☎ (508) 240-0595 . . RR 2, | Box 453, Chatham,
Herringbrook Rd, Eastham, MA *02640* . . . . | MA *02633*
MR Julian R 3d—WNEng'82—at |
☎ (513) 923-1612 . . 3473 Oakmeadow Lane, |
Apt 2, Cincinnati, OH *45239* . . . . |

Sloan MRS (REV) M Treadway (Margaret M Treadway)
V'40.Br'66.CDSP'82.Cda . . .of
☎ (520) 325-5376 . . ''A Place Apart'' 5233 E Woodspring Dv, Tucson, AZ *85712*
☎ (520) 720-4218 . . ''Spirit Journey'' 56 Sabin St, St David, AZ *85630*

Sloan MISS Margaret S—LakeF'91 . . see T L Elsberry

Sloan MISS Marion B—Syr'79
☎ (212) 243-2192 . . 10 W 15 St, Apt 819, New York, NY *10011*

Sloan MR Peter G JR—Bryant'73
☎ (615) 371-9085 . . 522 Belair Way, Nashville, TN *37215*

Sloan MR & MRS Peter Gordon (Helen Underhill Wick)
6035 Hillsboro Rd, Nashville, TN *37215-5003*

Sloan MR & MRS Robert N (Caroline L Talmage) | ☎ (803) 524-6215
Hof'62 . . . . | ''The Rookery''
MR Prentice E—SCar'90—at ☎ (704) 376-1681 | 2 Rush St,
2512 Kenmor Av, Charlotte, NC *28204* . . . . | Cat Island, Beaufort,
MR Lockwood T—Wheat'92—at | SC *29902*
☎ (212) 348-9169 . . 304 E 90 St, Apt 1D, |
New York, NY *10128* . . . . |

Sloan MR & MRS Samuel (Titus—Marion D Baker) Rm.Snc . . .of
☎ (561) 746-1714 . . 162 Beacon Lane, Jupiter, FL *33469*
☎ (908) 741-3434 . . 65A Cheshire Square, Little Silver, NJ *07739*

Sloan MRS William Lytle 2d (Virginia B Lyne) Ncd. | ☎ (561) 278-1108
MISS Barbara McC—at 308 E 79 St, New York, | 3860 Bermuda Lane,
NY *10021* . . . . | Apt 2,
MISS Laura G—at ☎ (212) 879-6349 | Gulf Stream, FL
200 E 69 St, Apt 5D, New York, NY *10021* . . . | *33483*

Sloane MR & MRS James R W (Stowe—Elizabeth B Davidson)
Wheat'74.Y'77.Wms'76.Y'84
135 Bainbridge Rd, West Hartford, CT *06119*

Sloane MRS James Ross (Hammond—Helen C Stuart) Sth'45.Csn.Lx.
☎ (413) 443-4625 . . 311 Washington Mountain Rd, Becket, MA *01223*

Sloane MRS John Edison (Jule M Day)
215 Crosslands Dv, Kennett Square, PA *19348-2021*

Sloat MR & MRS Jonathan W (DeGraff—Jane E Roberts) Mt.Cvc.Sl.Y'50
☎ (202) 362-3746 . . 3006—45 St NW, Washington, DC *20016*

Slocum MR Brooks K
☎ (516) 676-2681 . . 125 Duck Pond Rd, Glen Cove, NY *11542*

Slocum MR John J 3d . . see N L D Firth

Slocum MR & MRS John Jermain (Eileen S S Gillespie)
Unn.Cos.Nrr.C.K.Mt.Sm.Plg.Srb.Cc.Cly.G.Sl.Cda.H'36
☎ (401) 847-3276 . . 459 Bellevue Av, Newport, RI *02840*

Slocum MR & MRS John Jermain JR (Diana H Roberts)
Unn.Nrr.Sm.Srb.H'64.H'69
☎ (401) 849-7660 . . 431 Bellevue Av, Newport, RI *02840*

Slocum MISS M Olivia J . . see N L D Firth

Slocum MISS Marie-Louise C . . see N L D Firth

Slocum MISS Suzanne
☎ (516) 759-9196 . . PO Box 234, Mill Neck, NY *11765*

Sloneker MR & MRS John Goodman (Mary W Sauer) Qc.Msq.Evg.Y'44
☎ (513) 561-0049 . . 8400 Camargo Club Dv, Cincinnati, OH *45243*

Slowinski MRS Walter A (Annette C Roberts)
GeoW'51.Mt.Cos.Ncd.Dc . . .of
☎ (301) 320-6110 . . 4405 Tournay Rd, Bethesda, MD *20816*
☎ (301) 259-2392 . . ''Yatten'' Mt Victoria, MD *20661*

Sluder DR & MRS (DR) Greenfield (Patricia M O'Connor)
Bost'76.Cal'82.Sim'89.Mid'68.Pa'76
☎ (508) 443-6615 . . 161 Plympton Rd, Sudbury, MA *01776*

Sluder MRS John C (Elizabeth C Bradley) Rdc'44.Cly.
☎ (914) 273-3127 . . 9 Half Mile Rd, Armonk, NY *10504*

Slusser MR & MRS Willis S (Macey—Marion Bridgman)
BMr'36.Bhm.Pcu.Cal'38.Cal'41
200 Deer Valley Rd, Apt 1D, San Rafael, CA *94903*

Small MR Clifford T . . . . Died at Hayward, CA Aug 4'96

Small MRS Clifford T (Humphreys—Susan J Wright) CalSt'90.Dar.
☎ (510) 581-2412 . . 21187 Locust St, Hayward, CA *94541-1525*

Smallhouse MR & MRS David C (Sarah M Brown)
UWash'82.Ariz'88.Cal'79.Ariz'82
☎ (520) 290-1231 . . PO Box 31597, Tucson, AZ *85751-1597*

Smart MR Allen R 2d—P'56.H'61
☎ (312) 944-3310 . . 1732 N North Park Av, Chicago, IL *60614*

Smart MR & MRS Jackson W JR (Suzanne Tobey) | ☎ (847) 446-0227
Cho.Ih.Cnt.Mich'52.H'54 . . . . | 1090 Westmoor Rd,
MR Jackson W 3d—at ☎ (312) 751-8962 | Winnetka, IL *60093*
1313 N Ritchie Court, Chicago, IL *60610* . . . . . |

Smart MR & MRS S Bruce JR (Edith M Merrill) Ln.H'45.Mit'47
☎ (540) 554-8302 . . Trappe Hill Farm, 20561 Trappe Rd, Upperville, VA *20185*

Smartt MR & MRS James M (Fleitas—Priscilla C McIlvaine) M.Me.Fst.Cry.Ac.Ncd.Stet'67 . . . . . ☎ (610) 525-7633 1114 Beech Rd, Rosemont, PA
MR James M JR . . . .
MR W Polk *19010*
MISS Garrett H Fleitas . . . .
MR Albury N Fleitas JR . . . .

Smela MR & MRS Stephen J (Cordelia S C Pierson) P'86.Minn'93.P'87
☎ (612) 379-8196 . . 621—5 St SE, Minneapolis, MN *55414*

Smethurst MRS Lucy C (Lucy C Cabot) Wheat'56
☎ (404) 843-1395 . . 1144 Evergreen Dv NE, Atlanta, GA *30319*

Smid MR & MRS Derek J (Rebecca L Dudley)
GaSt'91.GaTech'91.GaTech'93
3577 Bishop Dv, Tucker, GA *30084*

Smidt MRS Thomas R (Davis—Camilla R Cole) Bgt.
☎ (914) 273-3635 . . Chestnut Ridge Rd, Mt Kisco, NY *10549*

Smith MR & MRS A Ledyard JR (Jacqueline Walker) H'55 . . . . ☎ (508) 779-2715 197 Century Mill Rd, Bolton, MA *01740-0800*
MISS Margaret F—at ☎ (508) 779-2715 PO Box 391, Hudson, MA *01749* . . . .
MISS Josette W—at ☎ (508) 779-2934 PO Box 800, Bolton, MA *01740-0800* . . . .
MR Robert E 2d—at ☎ (406) 585-0654 PO Box 6731, Bozeman, MT *59771* . . . .

Smith MR & MRS A Warren JR (Bloss—Gretchen A Leeds) Ts.St. . . . . ☎ (716) 883-4395 269 Highland Av, Buffalo, NY *14222*
MISS Jennifer L—Norw'79—at
☎ (203) 531-0149 . . 40 Glenville St, Greenwich, CT *06831* . . . .
MISS Caroline A Bloss—Ithaca'75—at
☎ (702) 828-7532 . . 4500 Mira Loma Dv, Apt 354, Reno, NV *89502* . . . .

Smith JUNIORS MISS Abigail van S . . see J H Mason

Smith MR & MRS Alaister G (Valentine—Consuelo Ashe) Tcy.Cp.H'47
PO Box 2088, Mill Valley, CA *94942*

Smith DR & MRS Alexander B (Emily B Griffin) StJ'40.Cl'43 ⚓ . . . . of ☎ (305)367-3393 Ocean Reef Club A, 67 Anchor Dv, Key Largo, FL *33037*
MISS Kathryn R—at ☎ (910) 871-2966 PO Box 274A, Sandy Ridge, NC *27046* . . . .
MR Kirkland B . . . . ☎ (914) 723-1533 26 Walworth Av, Scarsdale, NY *10583-1434*

Smith MR & MRS Alexander J (Alice L Grau) Stan'74.Un.Pr.Snc.Br'66 . . . . ☎ (516) 626-1922 58 Wheatley Rd, Brookville, NY *11545*
JUNIORS MISS Katherine M—at Phillips Andover .
JUNIORS MR Cameron A—at Brown . . . .

Smith MISS Alexandra D . . see F L Bissinger JR

Smith MR & MRS Anderson P (Susan J Costa)
Pac'80.TexA&M'82.TexA&M'80.TexA&M'82
☎ (713) 980-6602 . . 4526 Ranger Run, Sugar Land, TX *77479*

Smith MR Andrew L . . see A P Huntington

Smith MISS Ann A . . see MRS G A Cluett JR

Smith MR Antony C—H'56
☎ (561) 694-2940 . . 100 Lakeshore Dv, North Palm Beach, FL *33408*

Smith MISS Bailey H . . see F P Day JR

Smith MR & MRS Baldwin JR (Suzanne E Young) Pr.Mb.Ln.H'65 . . . . ☎ (516) 676-8621 High Farms Rd, Glen Head, NY *11545*
MR Baldwin 3d—StLaw'92 . . . .
MR Jonathan B . . . .

Smith DR & MRS Barry H (Carley Eldredge) Un.Cly.Cda.H.'65.Mit'68.Cr'72 ⚓ . . . . of ☎ (212)289-6609 1192 Park Av, Apt 10B, New York, NY *10128-1314*
MR Christopher R—H'95 . . . .
JUNIORS MISS Sara R . . . . ☎ (207) 883-2018 79 Sandpiper Cove, Scarborough, ME *04074*

Smith MR & MRS Bayard W (Susanna A McClary) . . ☎ (802) 674-6537 Gilnocky Farm, Horseback Ridge, Box 762, Windsor, VT *05089*
MR Nathaniel A—at ☎ (970) 870-9278 PO Box 774151, Steamboat Springs, CO *80477* .

Smith MR & MRS Bernard E JR (Bellamy—Jean S Ford)
BMr'48.Bhm.Yh.Cly.USN'47 . . of
☎ (803) 554-4584 . . 900 Yeamans Hall Rd, Hanahan, SC *29410*
☎ (212) 752-4017 . . 200 E 66 St, Apt D2103, New York, NY *10021*

Smith MISS Betsy—Van'88 . . see W T Seed

Smith MR & MRS Blair W (C Stirling Cassidy)
NCar'82.Lm.Cly.Dc.Ncd.Dh.GeoW'80.Cl'85 ⚓
☎ (212) 427-9225 . . 17 E 89 St, Apt 6D, New York, NY *10128*

Smith MR & MRS Bradford D (B Billings Day) Rol'86.Rcn.Cl'84
☎ (912) 897-9183 . . 277 Turners Rock Rd, Savannah, GA *31410*

Smith COL & MRS Bradish Johnson II (Ruth Alexander)
An.Rv.Sar.Cw.Cda.Dar.USA'41.GeoW'66
☎ (703) 960-4385 . . 2059 Huntington Av, Apt 115, Alexandria, VA *22303*

Smith MR Bradley W—Nu'62 . . of
☎ (207) 781-2736 . . 6 Coveside, Cumberland Foreside, ME *04110*
☎ (207) 925-6253 . . "Pinecrest" Severance Lodge Club, Center Lovell, ME *04016*

Smith MR & MRS Brice R JR (Medart—Jane W Currie)
Ariz'53.Lc.Bv.Mo'50.Mit'52
☎ (314) 991-1149 . . 15 Fielding Rd, St Louis, MO *63124*

Smith MR Burchell P . . see F L Bissinger JR

Smith MR & MRS C Carter JR (Elizabeth Covington) V'59.C.Csn.So'51
☎ (860) 364-0503 . . Box 125, 20 W Woods Rd, Apt 1, Sharon, CT *06069*

Smith MR & MRS C Edgar JR (Dorothy L Williams) Md.Elk.P'37
☎ (410) 377-8107 . . 6 Brooke Court, Baltimore, MD *21212*

Smith MR C H Sabin—H'57
☎ (805) 687-5687 . . 1816 De La Vina St, Apt 1, Santa Barbara, CA *93101*

Smith MR & MRS Cabanné C (Carole Jacobson)
Pa'66.Drex'79 . . . . of ☎ (610)896-0506 47 Tunbridge Rd, Haverford, PA *19041*
MISS Betty K—Pa'93—at ☎ (212) 501-8302 420 West End Av, Apt 8B, New York, NY *10024*
MR Joshua C—Pa'90.Wash'92—at
☎ (214) 443-0845 . . 4147 Druid Lane, Apt 2, Dallas, TX *75205* . . . . ☎ (561) 833-3876 1801 S Flagler Dv, West Palm Beach, FL *33401*

Smith MRS Carleton Sprague (Elisabeth C Sperry) C.Plg.Csn.G.Hn.
☎ (860) 868-0395 . . Waldingfield Farm, Washington, CT *06793*

Smith MR & MRS Cary C (Virginia V Knowles) Syr'77
☎ (860) 677-4571 . . 426 Main St, Farmington, CT *06032*

Smith MRS Catherine Z (Catherine B Zick) Smu'75
☎ (703) 528-2667 . . 1506 N 22 St, Arlington, VA *22209*

Smith MR & MRS Chadbourne B (Vivian A Anderson) Cr'47.W&L'47
☎ (512) 267-2067 . . Point Venture, 220 Lakefront Dv, Leander, TX *78645*

Smith MR Charles E W (C Edgar JR) . . . . Married at Baltimore, MD
Sinwell MISS Marion B (John W) . . . . Jun 8'96

Smith MR & MRS Charles E W (Marion B Sinwell) Buck'85.Md.Mv.
☎ (410) 377-4483 . . 124 Hopkins Rd, Baltimore, MD *21212*

Smith MISS Charlotte C . . see J M Sizemore JR

Smith MISS Christina L—SCal'91
☎ (310) 827-4765 . . 13603 Marina Pointe Dv, Apt A621, Marina Del Rey, CA *90292-5589*

Smith MR & MRS Clayton G (Nathalie Letchworth)
☎ (716) 633-6110 . . 47 Arlington Rd, Williamsville, NY *14221*

Smith MRS Clifford G 2d (Kathryn A Fail) . . . . | ☎ (602) 277-9452
MISS Lindsay K . . . . | 147 W Rose Lane,
JUNIORS MISS Hayley A . . . . | Phoenix, AZ *85013*

Smith MR Clifford G 2d—LSU'74
11070 N 24 Av, Phoenix, AZ *85029*

Smith MR & MRS Colin L M (Diana M Dennison) | ☎ (617) 259-9759
V'68.Lond'57.H'59 . . . . | Library Lane,
MISS F Isabel—at Havard . . . . | PO Box 6294,
MR Adrian C M—at Middlebury . . . . | Lincoln Center, MA *01773*

Smith MR & MRS Courtney C JR (Margaret P | 238 Monroe St,
Remington) H.'64.Ox'66.Pa'69 . . . . | Philadelphia, PA
MISS Margaret Dabney—Ken'91 . . . . | *19147*
MISS Elizabeth C—Hav'94 . . . . |
MISS Emily R—Swth'94 . . . . |
JUNIORS MR Courtney C 3d—at Friends Select . . |

Smith MR & MRS Crosby Rogers (Sandreuter— | ☎ (203) 966-9428
Sandra Rhines) Wms'57 . . . . | 69 Sherwood Lane,
MISS Cynthia R—Mid'88 . . . . | New Canaan, CT
MISS Shelby T—CtCol'90 . . . . | *06840*
MISS Lindsay A—Mid'92 . . . . |
  MISS Heidi Sandreuter—Wms'92 . . . . |
  MR Gregg E Sandreuter—Ham'84.H'88 . . . . |
  MR Jeffrey R Sandreuter—LakeF'88 . . . . |

Smith MRS Crosby Tuttle (Vernon M R Siems) Cda. | ☎ (203) 966-9381
MR Christopher V—Mid'65—at | 20 Hathaway
☎ (212) 861-2569 . . 1317 First Av, New York, | Common,
NY *10021* . . . . | New Canaan, CT
MR Geoffrey R—Mid'74—at ☎ (802) 453-4663 | *06840*
Mt Pleasant Farm, Box 2660, RD 1, Bristol, VT |
05443 . . . . |

Smith MR & MRS David A (Camilla R Lloyd) | ☎ (610) 838-0471
Norw'39 . . . . | 1822 Friedensville
MISS Lucinda R—Sth'79—at ☎ (970) 667-8545 | Rd, Bethlehem, PA
1118 E 7 St, Loveland, CO *80537* . . . . | *18015*

Smith MR & MRS David L (Leslie A Gerardo)
Va'84.AmU'87.Dick'82.Bost'87
☎ (703) 671-6852 . . 4618A S 36 St, Arlington, VA *22206*

Smith MR & MRS David Milne (Bielaski—Audrey Fairlie MacAllister)
☎ (713) 395-0002 . . 1122 Wellshire Dv, Katy, TX *77494*

Smith MR & MRS David N (Heckler—Young—Ruth M Bauman)
Syr'47.Nu'62
☎ (011-44-142) 475-1497 . . Capricorn Kennels, Chowns Hill, St Helens, Hastings, East Sussex TN35 4PA, England

Smith MR David O
300 Gray Av, Webster Groves, MO *63119*

Smith MR David O JR . . see A P Huntington

Smith MR & MRS David S (Mary M Kaercher) LErie'50
☎ (216) 991-7295 . . 3265 Dorchester Rd, Shaker Heights, OH *44120*

Smith MR & MRS David S J (Mary I Claytor) | ☎ (610) 687-2437
Me.Rb.Ste.Cts.Pa'63 . . . . | 501 Montgomery
MISS Eliza W—Vt'90 . . . . | Lane, Radnor, PA
MR D Brinton—Vt'88—at 4710 Aurora Av N, | *19087*
Apt 102, Seattle, WA *98103* . . . . |
MR Norris M—NH'93—at 9556 Sandpoint Way |
NE, Apt 7, Seattle, WA *98115* . . . . |

Smith MR & MRS David Shiverick (Mary H Edson)
B.Mt.Cvc.Plg.BtP.Evg.Cc.Myf.Cly.Dth'39.Cl'42
☎ (561) 655-0010 . . 525 S Flagler Dv, Apt 20C, West Palm Beach, FL *33401*

Smith REV & MRS Du Bois T (Frances W Noble) | ☎ (516) 537-0753
Cr'67 . . . . | PO Box 673,
MISS Dorothy M . . . . | Bridgehampton, NY *11932*

Smith MR & MRS Dudley Renwick (Juliana Buros) | ☎ (603) 863-8856
Dth'60 . . . . | 60 Fairway Dv,
MR Bradley R—StLaw'89—at ☎ (315) 426-0273 | PO Box 1335,
100 Victoria Place, Syracuse, NY *13210* . . . . . | Grantham, NH
MR Gregory D—BostColl'93—at | *03753-1335*
☎ (617) 796-8948 . . 379 Linwood Av, Newton, |
MA *02160* . . . . |

Smith MR & MRS E Newbold (Margaret L du Pont)
Gm.Cry.Wil.Ny.Sa.Cw.Ac.USN'48.Pa'56
☎ (610) 688-7664 . . 871 Lesley Rd, Villanova, PA *19085*

Smith MR & MRS Edmund D 3d (Renee W Minnick)
☎ (212) 421-3406 . . 201 E 62 St, New York, NY *10021*

Smith MRS Edmund P 2d (Carolyn A Ross)
1700 Embassy Dv, Apt 103, West Palm Beach, FL *33401*

Smith MR Edmund P 2d—Y'57 . . . . | 206 E Mason St,
MISS Suzanne B . . . . | Bozeman, MT
MR David H . . . . | *59715*
MR Daniel S . . . . |

Smith MR Edward Byron—Cas.Cm.Cho.Sr.Rc.On.Ri.Myf.Y'32 . . of
☎ (847) CE4-0435 . . 1133 Lake Rd, Lake Forest, IL *60045*
☎ (561) 546-7654 . . ''Fantaisie'' PO Box 125, Hobe Sound, FL *33475*

Smith MR & MRS Edward Byron JR (Maureen F | ☎ (847) 234-7997
Dwyer) Newt'66.Cho.On.Rc.K.Cas.Fy.Y'66. | 90 Ahwahnee Rd,
Cl'69.Cl'70.Nu'74 . . . . | Lake Forest, IL
MR Edward Byron 3d—at Harvard . . . . | *60045*
JUNIORS MR Peter Byron—at Yale . . . . |

Smith MISS Elinor L—Ariz'79.Cit'94
☎ (803) 762-3791 . . 2069 Medway Rd, Charleston, SC *29412*

Smith MISS Elizabeth Curtiss—Ty'80.Me.
☎ (703) 836-1923 . . 505 Duke St, Alexandria, VA *22314*

Smith MISS Elizabeth D . . see L R Page 3d

Smith MRS Elodie H (Ballantine—Elodie B Huntley)
 ☎ (561) 231-1134 . . 1515 Orchid Dv, Vero Beach, FL *32963*

Smith MR & MRS Emery P (A Claire Pike) GeoW'50 | ☎ (301) 229-1861
 MISS C Alexandra—*see Dilatory Domiciles* . . . . | 5522 Parkston Rd, Bethesda, MD *20816-3326*

Smith MR & MRS Emmet Carter (Martine F Cappuyns) Rcsl.Cysl.Mo'70.Mo'71
 ☎ (011-44-171) 602-5922 . . 84 Addison Rd, London W14 8ED, England

Smith MR & MRS Endicott (Steele—Jeanne E Fellows) Cy.Un.Chi.Dth'39
 ☎ (617) 566-5467 . . 29 Fairgreen Place, Chestnut Hill, MA *02167*

Smith MR Eugene C—Ky'57
 ☎ (502) 897-1110 . . 130 N Peterson Av, Louisville, KY *40206*

Smith MRS Everett Ware (Ruth H Tyler) Sth'36.Uncl.Cv.Cyb.
 ☎ (561) 231-6593 . . 1875 Bay Rd, Apt 215, Vero Beach, FL *32963*

Smith MRS F Grosvenor (Hodges—Hester S Codman)
 121 Lincoln Court, Nashville, TN *37205*

Smith MR Forrester C—My.Lm.Hb.Ty'53 . . . . | ☎ (207) 372-8888
 MR Forrester C JR—EmbRid'84—at | ''The Bickmore''
 ☎ (508) 921-4846 . . 200 Hart St, Beverly Farms, | Hart's Neck,
 MA *01915* . . . . | Box 568, Tenants Harbor, ME *04860*

Smith MISS Frances R—Ty'79
 ☎ (410) 771-4219 . . 1018 Belfast Rd, Sparks, MD *21152*

Smith MR & MRS Frank C JR (Sadler—Katherine B Fay) Ny.CalTech'44
 ☎ (713) 780-2514 . . 3330 Bering Dv, Houston, TX *77057*

Smith MR Frederick M R—Ri.Ln.Fic.Y.'63
 ☎ (212) 879-1213 . . 784 Park Av, New York, NY *10021*

Smith MR & MRS G E Kidder (Dorothea F Wilder) BMr'37.C.Ds.Cs.Cda.P'35.P'38 . . of
 ☎ (212) 535-0904 . . 163 E 81 St, New York, NY *10028*
 ☎ (607) 547-9298 . . ''The Manor House'' Springfield Center, NY *13468*

Smith MR G Stevenson—Me.Gm.Y'40 . . . . | ☎ (610) 688-4784
 MISS Catherine—at 1350A Filbert St, | 1 Sugar Knoll Dv,
 San Francisco, CA *94109* . . . . | Devon, PA *19333*
 MR G Stevenson JR . . . . |

Smith MR & MRS Gardiner F (Durstine—Claudia A | ☎ (615) 684-4964
 H Street) Cr'58 . . . . | Eastfield Farm,
 MISS Narcissa A B—Ober'89.Cal'91—at | 200 Huffman Lane,
 ☎ (703) 317-0084 . . 5843 Monticello Rd, | Shelbyville, TN
 Alexandria, VA *22303* . . . . | *37160*

Smith MR Garrett M . . see E G Ottley

Smith MR & MRS Geoffrey W (Leonard—Nancy W | ☎ (617) 523-3258
 Spencer) CtCol'63.Bost'66.Al.Cy.Cr'67.Bost'72 | 29 W Cedar St,
 MR Spencer H Leonard . . . . | Boston, MA *02108*

Smith MR & MRS George D (Carolyn S E Koenig) | ☎ (314) 961-5538
 Mo'58 . . . . | 13 Litzsinger Lane,
 MISS Cynthia E . . . . | St Louis, MO *63124*
 MR Charles F . . . . |
 MR Nicholas E . . . . |

Smith MRS George G (Elizabeth G Galloway) Roch'37.Cy.
 ☎ (716) 662-3772 . . ''Pinehome'' 7220 E Quaker Rd, Orchard Park, NY *14127*

Smith MR & MRS George Putnam (Llewellyn S | ☎ (508) 526-1935
 Parsons) Sth'60.Sbc.Y'58.H'67 . . . . | ''Masconomo
 MISS Abigail A—Bow'91—at Harvard Divinity . | House''
 MR G Putnam JR—Bow'94 . . . . | 8 Masconomo St, Manchester, MA *01944*

Smith MRS George T (Sarah H Liggett)
 ☎ (919) 787-1924 . . 525 Marlowe Rd, Raleigh, NC *27609*

Smith MR & MRS George T JR (Margaret E Holdford) M'dith'82.NCar'82
 ☎ (919) 787-0744 . . 2316 Gaddy Dv, Raleigh, NC *27609*

Smith MR George V 3d—Gm.Me.Msq.Fst.Why.
 ☎ (561) 278-1090 . . 3023 Polo Dv, Gulf Stream, FL *33483*

Smith MR & MRS George W H JR (Susan L Plummer) Cc.
 ☎ (508) 758-2427 . . 4 Ned's Point Rd, Mattapoisett, MA *02739*

Smith MR & MRS Gerald K (Jane E Venard) KasSt'61.KasSt'57.Nu'61
 ☎ (602) 265-4384 . . 3203 N Manor Dv W, Phoenix, AZ *85014*

Smith MR & MRS Gerard L (Carr—Rowse—Isabel | ☎ (212) 861-4826
 de Rancougne) Rc.Bcs.B.Ng.Y'68.H'74 . . . . . . | 150 E 73 St,
 MISS Hadley L—at Yale . . . . | New York, NY
  MISS Flavia Rowse—at U of East Anglia | *10021*
 England . . . . |
  MR Michael Carr—Brist'87 . . . . |

Smith MR & MRS Gerard W (Patricia B Mohun) . . . . | ☎ (860) 672-0330
 MISS Catherine C . . . . | 235 College St,
 MISS Sarah M C . . . . | Litchfield, CT *06759*
 MR Gerard S 2d—at 349 Park Av, Torrington, CT |
 06790 . . . . |
 MR Christopher G . . . . |

Smith MR & MRS Gordon (Bent—Harding—Charlotte Boyer) Sth'39.Ne'75.Un.Cy.Nyc.Chi.Ncd.
 ☎ (617) 735-9245 . . 15 Fairgreen Place, Chestnut Hill, MA *02167*

Smith MR & MRS Gordon H (Eunice Hale) Cho.On.Cas.Fy.P'36.Y'39
 ☎ (847) 234-5381 . . 1302 N Green Bay Rd, Lake Forest, IL *60045*

Smith MR & MRS Gregory Little 2d (Frazer—Clara H Little) Ncd.Ala'38
 ☎ (334) 342-4382 . . 1 Hillwood Rd, Mobile, AL *36608*

Smith MR & MRS H Brooks (Meredyth M Hull) Aht'79.Pr.Ne.Va'76
 ☎ (516) 671-2043 . . 42 Ryefield Rd, Locust Valley, NY *11560*

Smith MR & MRS H Cortelyou (Barbara J DeLaney) DU'75.Stc.DU'73
 ☎ (908) 946-2431 . . 5 Old Mill Rd, Holmdel, NJ *07733*

Smith MR & MRS H Morgan (Katharine V Darmanin) | ☎ (610) 964-9446
 OWes'82.Me.Cry.M.Rv.Me'66 ⚓ . . . . | ''Skytop''
 MISS Julia T—at Lynchburg Coll . . . . | 409 Upper Gulph
 MR H Morgan JR—at Penn State . . . . | Rd, Radnor, PA *19087*

Smith MRS H Webster (Coffin—Sallie O Gorman) Mv.Cda.
 ☎ (207) 372-8843 . . ''Hart House'' PO Box 555, Tenants Harbor, ME *04860*
 Jan 1 . . ☎ (410) 323-5726 . . Cross Keys, 36 Olmsted Green, Baltimore, MD *21210*

Smith MR & MRS Harold P (Mary P Frederick) Pc.H'56
 ☎ (215) 643-7277 . . 308 Bangor Lane, Gwynedd Hunt, Lower Gwynedd, PA *19002*

Smith DR Harton S—Reed'75
 ☎ (617) 964-4769 . . 24 Aspen Av, Newton, MA *02166*

Smith MR & MRS Henry B duP (June Marshall) F&M'86.Me.Rc.Gm.Cw.F&M'84
 350 Millbank Rd, Bryn Mawr, PA *19010*

Smith MR & MRS Henry H JR (Julia J Hildt) Me.Dth'36
☎ (610) 688-5676 . . 94 Hunters Lane, Devon, PA *19333*

Smith MR & MRS Henry J (Judith Adams) Cly.P'45.H'50 . . of
☎ (207) 867-4408 . . Box 805, RR 1, North Haven, ME *04853*
☎ (011-33-1) 45-03-27-79 . . 24 rue Desbordes-Valmore, 75116 Paris, France

Smith MR & MRS Henry O 3d (Pamela Shields)
Y.'68 . . . . | ☎ (914) 967-6286
MISS Loren F . . . . | 75 Glendale Rd,
MR Nicholas F . . . . | Rye, NY *10580*
JUNIORS MR H Oliver 4th . . . . |

Smith MRS Herbert L JR (Hill—Quinley—Phillis— | ☎ (813) 584-3357
Maggiore—Nancy V Wurts) Ac.Cda.Dar. . . . . . | 612 Pineland Av,
MR E Wayne Quinley—Sar. . . . . | Belleair, FL *34616*

Smith MR & MRS Herbert L 3d (Virginia W Mackoy)
B'gton'54.Sa.Pr.L.Cly.Wms'53
☎ (516) 922-4165 . . 116 Horseshoe Rd, Mill Neck, NY *11765*

Smith MR & MRS Herbert L 4th (Marianna McD Murnane)
Wheat'85.Pr.Cly.Wms'82
☎ (516) 759-2731 . . 444 Oyster Bay Rd, Locust Valley, NY *11560*

Smith MISS Hillary W—Nu'94 . . see P W Packard

Smith MR & MRS Howard W JR (Marion H Norris) Cvc.Rv.Sl.Dar.Nat'l'38
☎ (703) 548-0151 . . 200 S Fairfax St, Alexandria, VA *22314*

Smith MR & MRS Howard W 3d (E Page Lane) NCar'83.Cvc.Mt.W&L'80
☎ (202) 362-3531 . . 2915—44 St NW, Washington, DC *20016*

Smith MR & MRS Hugh M (Chata Robinson) | ☎ (410) 822-6970
Franklin'74.Mt.Ac.AmU'77 . . . . | 27525 Westpoint
JUNIORS MISS Courtland C—at Country Sch . . . . | Rd, Easton, MD
| *21601*

Smith MRS Hugh R H (Marianne M Moses) Sl.
☎ (301) 654-6426 . . 6803 Meadow Lane, Chevy Chase, MD *20815*

Smith DR & MRS Hugo Dunlap (Helen L Lewis) Y'45.H'47
☎ (215) 836-7992 . . 526 E Evergreen Av, Wyndmoor, PA *19038*

Smith MRS Irving T (Florence W Bolton) Evg.BtP.Cly.
☎ (561) 655-2021 . . 1 Royal Palm Way, Palm Beach, FL *33480*

Smith MRS J Marshall (Linell C Nash) Mv.Cda.
☎ (410) 771-4219 . . 1018 Belfast Rd, Sparks, MD *21152*

Smith MR J Quincy—Y'93 . . see G T Vincent

Smith MR & MRS J Somers (Lichte—Evelyn R Poole) Hawaii'67.Pa'46
☎ (207) 372-8503 . . HCR 35, Box 286A, Watts Cove, St George, ME *04857*

Smith MR & MRS James Dale (Patricia S Stone) SAla'80.At.SAla'80
☎ (334) 478-1412 . . 2308 Ashland Place Av, Mobile, AL *36607*

Smith MR & MRS James G 3d (Cynthia Denham) Va'87.Del'82
☎ (302) 652-6442 . . 103 Dickinson Lane, Wilmington, DE *19807*

Smith MRS James P (Smith—Sally Shonk) StA.
☎ (904) 285-3217 . . 22 Maria Place, Ponte Vedra Beach, FL *32082-2314*

Smith MR & MRS James P JR (Catherine T Wilson) | ☎ (904) 285-6677
Sth'66.Pn.P'65.Stan'70 . . . . | 552 Ponte Vedra
MISS Catherine H . . . . | Blvd, Ponte Vedra
MR James P 3d . . . . | Beach, FL *32082*

Smith MR & MRS James R (Miranda P M McClintic) | of ☎ (212)996-3292
SL'69.Rr.Van'63 . . . . | 1060 Fifth Av,
JUNIORS MISS Logan McC—at Brearley . . . . | New York, NY
| *10128-0104*
| ☎ (518) 392-6309
| ''Willow Rise''
| General Delivery,
| Ghent, NY *12075*

Smith DR & MRS James W JR (Nancy G Keck) | ☎ (203) 869-8204
Ncd.Cwr'48.Cl'52 . . . . | 100 Meadow Wood
MR Peter F—Ty'86.Pa'92 . . . . | Dv, Greenwich, CT
| *06830*

Smith JUNIORS MR John A 5th . . see J M Sizemore JR

Smith MR & MRS John C 3d (Randall Tindle) Dth'63 | ☎ (610) 687-0496
MISS Rebecca K . . . . | 309 Warner Rd,
MR Christopher S . . . . | Wayne, PA *19087*

Smith MR & MRS John Cram (Dianne P Shiland)
Rc.Ln.Pr.Ng.Lm.BostColl'77
☎ (516) 626-2613 . . Cedar Ridge Rd, Upper Brookville, Oyster Bay, NY *11771*

Smith REV & MRS John Cutrer (Mary A Gregg) | ☎ (212) YU8-0884
V'56.Rc.Cly.Ncd.Va'48 . . . . | 45 E 85 St,
MISS Alexandra G . . . . | New York, NY
MR John Clark . . . . | *10028*

Smith MR John H 3d—Cw.Mo'91 . . see W W Spivy

Smith MR & MRS Jonathan T (Larkin—Moira K Holden) Cal'79.Wms'66
☎ (415) 461-2293 . . 65 Redwood Dv, Kentfield, CA *94904-2528*

Smith MRS June D (June E Dickinson) Kent'56
☎ (216) 761-5955 . . 30 Oakshore Green, Bratenahl, OH *44108*

Smith MR K Hart—Bhm.Cp.Cal'40 ⚓
☎ (415) 392-2913 . . 850 Powell St, Apt 902, San Francisco, CA *94108*

Smith DR & MRS (REV) Kaighn (Ann G Robb)
Pa'50.LuthTheo'90.H.'90.Pa'54
☎ (610) 525-2231 . . 816 Castlefinn Lane, Bryn Mawr, PA *19010*

Smith MR & MRS Kaighn JR (Audrey Maynard) Cal'79.Cal'79
☎ (207) 871-1407 . . 86 Pitt St, Portland, ME *04103*

Smith MR & MRS Karl B (Ross—Diana Lanier)
Bnd'45.Srb.Cw.Cda.P'39 . . of
☎ (401) 423-0671 . . 47 Longfellow Rd, Jamestown, RI *02835*
☎ (941) 395-1271 . . 4248 Old Banyan Way, Sanibel, FL *33957*

Smith MR & MRS Katherine K (Dean—Van Duzer—Katherine B Kling)
☎ (717) 566-8483 . . 599 Cook Court, Hummelstown, PA *17036*

Smith MISS Katherine P . . see L R Page 3d

Smith MISS Kathleen—Cl'32
☎ (908) 273-8027 . . 35 Druid Hill Rd, Summit, NJ *07901*

Smith MR Kennedy . . . . Died at
Sherwood, MD Jan 3'96

Smith MRS Kennedy (Mary E Rutter) Pg.Tc. . . . . . . | ☎ (412) 361-8008
MR Kennedy JR—Cr'69 . . . . | 5834 Walnut St,
DR Frederick F A—H'71.Geo'74—at | Pittsburgh, PA
☎ (773) 283-5800 . . 5800 N Keating Av, | *15232*
Chicago, IL *60646* . . . . |
MR Mark T V O—H'75.Stan'78—at |
☎ (412) 683-8448 . . 5090 Warwick Terr, |
Pittsburgh, PA *15213* . . . . |

Smith MR & MRS Langhorne B (Valerie G Lamb) Sth'58.Ph.Gm.Rd.T.Y.'58 . . . . | ☎ (610) 353-4345 7036 Goshen Rd, Newtown Square, PA *19073*
   MISS Averil S—at 2209 Walnut St, Philadelphia, PA *19103* . . . . |
   MR Philip R—at 316 Hamilton St, Evanston, IL *60201* . . . . |

Smith MR & MRS Lathrop W JR (Garland Wingfield Cook) Livingston'63 . . . . | of ☎ (205)967-6841 4060 Old Leeds Rd, Birmingham, AL *35213* "Sterrett-McWilliams House" Camden, AL *36726*
   MR Lathrop W 3d . . . . |
   JUNIORS MISS Lindsay S . . . . |

Smith MR & MRS Lawrence D JR (Nancy C Fitzgerald)
   ☎ (602) 488-2317 . . PO Box 2012, Carefree, AZ *85377*

Smith MRS Linda Ball (Linda M Ball) Me.
   ☎ (610) 964-0168 . . 219 Poplar Av, Wayne, PA *19087*

Smith MRS Linda P (Linda A C Pancoast)
   ☎ (502) 895-3201 . . 247 Stonehenge Dv, Louisville, KY *40207*

Smith MR Lloyd H—B.Ri.Rcn.Ng.Evg.Y'29
   ☎ (561) 833-7939 . . 101 El Vedado Way, Palm Beach, FL *33480*

Smith MR & MRS Logan M (Margaret L Yocum) Ithaca'76.Cspa.Cw.F&M'73.VillaN'85
   ☎ (215) 643-3614 . . 1066 Hemlock Dv, Blue Bell, PA *19422*

Smith MRS Lois Shethar (Lois Shethar)
   ☎ (520) 299-3212 . . 6250 Cerrada Moreno, Tucson, AZ *85718*

Smith MRS Louise H (Louise A Hagemann) Scripps'66 . . . . | ☎ (615) 353-0683 123 Westover Dv, Nashville, TN *37205*
   MISS Louise A . . . . |
   MR Shepley P . . . . |
   JUNIORS MISS Susannah S . . . . |

Smith MRS Marcel A (Emilie Béra) . . . . | ☎ (860) 567-9162 45 Fern Rd, PO Box 1029, Litchfield, CT *06759*
   MR Leonard Bacon—Dick'82.ColM'86—at
   ☎ (860) 651-7880 . . 5 Oak Glen Court, Simsbury, CT *06070* |

Smith MR & MRS Marcus W (Strawbridge—Alexandra White) Pr.Dth'56 . . . . | of ☎ (516)676-3088 16 Valley Rd, Locust Valley, NY *11560*
   MR Robert E Strawbridge 4th . . . . |
| ☎ (207) 883-2751 25 Massacre Lane, Prouts Neck, ME *04074*
| ☎ (561) 274-8963 725 Palm Trail, Delray Beach, FL *33483*

Smith MRS Margaret Henry (Cunningham—Margaret R Henry) Cly.Ht.Lm. . . . . | ☎ (207) 781-3648 19 Stornoway Rd, Cumberland Foreside, ME *04110*
   JUNIORS MR Bradley W JR . . . . |
   JUNIORS MR Malcolm P . . . . |

Smith MISS Margaret Le B 230 E 15 St, New York, NY *10003*

Smith MRS Mary Coxe Miller (Humphreys—Bruce—Mary Coxe Miller) Chr.Cly.Cda.Dh.
   ☎ (212) 308-1293 . . 200 E 66 St, New York, NY *10021*

Smith MRS McCain (Helen N Crean) Cda.
   ☎ (202) 232-2876 . . 2126 Connecticut Av NW, Washington, DC *20008*

Smith MR & MRS McKelden 3d (Diana K Donnelley) Van'80.Ri.Wms'74
   ☎ (203) 972-0570 . . 226 Lambert Rd, New Canaan, CT *06840*

Smith MR & MRS Michael S (Anne M Murray) Ty'81.Eh.Sm.Ty'81
   ☎ (908) 234-2502 . . PO Box 56, Far Hills, NJ *07931*

Smith MRS Montgomery M (Anne Fairchild P Bowler) Cly.Cda.Dc.Ht.Dar.
   ☎ (212) SA2-8266 . . 49 E 86 St, New York, NY *10028*

Smith MRS Morgan K (Beatrice Stewart) Au.Chi.
   ☎ (508) 369-3719 . . 100 Newbury Court, Apt 113, Concord, MA *01742*

Smith MISS Nancy de W . . see MRS F L Wehr

Smith MRS Nancy M (Nancy Morgan) . . . . | ☎ (303) 333-8371 18 Polo Field Lane, Denver, CO *80209*
   MISS Sandra—at 3059—103 Rd, Carbondale, CO *81623* . . . . |
   MISS Dinah—at 1720 Chapala St, Santa Barbara, CA *93101* . . . . |

Smith MISS Natalie B (Hines—Natalie B Smith) . . see A W Coolidge

Smith MR Nelson C—Tul'89 . . see W T Seed

Smith MR Nicholas O—HWSth'95 . . see G T Vincent

Smith MR & MRS Olcott D (Swett—Catharine Carton) Csn.Ncd.Y'29.H'32
   ☎ (860) 677-1495 . . 67 Mountain Spring Rd, Farmington, CT *06032*

Smith MR & MRS Page W (Teagle—Boggs—Jane Will) Evg.BtP.Cal'35 . . of
   ☎ (561) 655-5945 . . 350 Island Rd, Palm Beach, FL *33480*
   ☎ (410) 822-2390 . . Crowe Point Farm, PO Box 1192, Easton, MD *21601*

Smith MR Perry E H—Coa.Snc.Cw.Ht.Rv.Ne.P'57.H'58 . . of
   ☎ (011-91-22) 220-262 . . Cricket Club of India, Box 11059, Bombay 400-020, India
   ☎ (011-44-171) 581-2781 . . 27 Queen's Gate Gardens, London SW7 5RP, England

Smith MR Peter de W . . see MRS F L Wehr

Smith MR & MRS Peter L (Marie L Shrady) Mds.Ri.Cly.Hob'64.Syr'67 . . . . | of ☎ (212)879-3636 640 Park Av, New York, NY *10021*
   MISS Maria Alexandra . . . . |
   JUNIORS MISS Maria Elizabeth . . . . |
| ☎ (516) 537-3560 "Hearthstone" PO Box 81, Sagg Main St, Sagaponack, NY *11962*

Smith MR & MRS Philip C F (Stevenson—G G Meredith Smith) Hlns'61.Ac.Lm.Ncd.H'61
   ☎ (207) 443-6070 . . 985 High St, Bath, ME *04530-2216*

Smith MR & MRS Philip MacAulay (Keenan—Mariana Casserly) Pcu.Sfg.Stan'62
   ☎ (415) 332-2141 . . 98 San Carlos Av, Sausalito, CA *94965*

Smith MR Philip Meade (A Brita I Svensson)
   ☎ (410) 348-5478 . . "White Lodge" PO Box 107, Still Pond, MD *21667*

Smith MR & MRS Philip W JR (Sheila M Scott) Eh.H'52
   ☎ (908) 234-0789 . . Box 176, 2000 Larger Cross Rd, Far Hills, NJ *07931*

Smith MR & MRS Philip W III (Hillary C Bailey)
   ☎ (908) 439-3050 . . Long Lane, PO Box 944, Far Hills, NJ *07931*

Smith MR & MRS Philo (Ann D Valkenburgh) Yn.Y'48.Nu'55
   ☎ (203) 869-9586 . . 113 Patterson Av, Greenwich, CT *06830*

Smith MR & MRS Prentice K (Patricia Ford) Rcn.Cly.P'42 . . of
☎ (508) 627-5965 . . Pierce Lane, Edgartown, MA *02539*
☎ (242) 333-2185 . . PO Box 75, Harbour Island, Bahamas

Smith MR & MRS Prentice K JR (Sheilah L Thorn) Nw'73.DU'73
abroad

Smith MR Presley A L (Howard W JR) . . . . . . Married at Broad Run, VA
Sebree MISS Laura L (Frank) . . . . Mch 30'96

Smith MR & MRS R Andrew (Karen A Grace) Mo'83
☎ (314) 567-5127 . . 1299 McKnight Rd, St Louis, MO *63117*

Smith MR & MRS R Gordon (Bockmann—Catherine | ☎ (804) 288-2658
C Baird) Va'60.H'64 . . . . | 5 Spicer Rd,
  MISS Jill O Bockmann—Bow'89—at | Richmond, VA
  ☎ (203) 699-1213 . . 1308 S Meridan Rd, | *23226*
  Cheshire, CT *06410* . . . . |
  MR Nathaniel V Bockmann—at |
  ☎ (503) 235-7361 . . 3022 SE Main St, |
  Portland, OR *97217* . . . . |

Smith MR & MRS R Leigh JR (Miraed M Peake) BMr'49.W&L'49
☎ (212) 861-2121 . . 225 E 66 St, New York, NY *10021*

Smith MRS R Witham (Anne Thomson)
☎ (513) 321-5370 . . 2482 W Rookwood Court, Cincinnati, OH *45208*

Smith MR Ralph O . . see MRS G A Cluett JR

Smith MRS Ralston F (Billie E Feddery) Cwr'45
☎ (216) 561-0652 . . 20800 Almar Dv, Shaker Heights, OH *44122*

Smith MRS Rayburn Clark (Janet L Bullitt)
Crosslands 102, Kennett Square, PA *19348*

Smith MR & MRS Richard A (Catherine C | ☎ (011-82-2)
Munnell) Ws'64.Cvc.Sl.Ty'65 . . . . | 397-4114
MR Carter McC . . . . | American Embassy,
 | Seoul, Korea, Unit
 | 15550, APO AP,
 | *96205-0001*

Smith MR & MRS Richard Austin (Kathleen Knox) Pg.An.Sar.Cly.Pn.
☎ (860) 536-8182 . . Cove Nook Farm, PO Box 9191, 243 Brook St,
Noank, CT *06340*

Smith MR Richard B—Pn.P'34
☎ (908) 842-1447 . . 11 Linden Lane, Rumson, NJ *07760*

Smith MR & MRS Richard C (Elisabeth L Patterson)
☎ (412) 266-5557 . . ''Scariff'' PO Box 51, Sewickley, PA *15143*

Smith MR & MRS Richard F JR (Anna G Cooke) Wells'86.Pc.StJos'82
☎ (215) 844-8127 . . 3239 W Queen Lane, Philadelphia, PA *19129*

Smith MR Richard J 2d—Tul'83
☎ (203) 259-4122 . . 139 Main St, Southport, CT *06490*

Smith MR Richard L—Pc.Stan'52.Stan'56 . . . . | ☎ (215) 248-1555
MISS B Blossum . . . . | 566 St Andrews Rd,
MR Miles V—Van'87.AGSIM'92—at San José, | Philadelphia, PA
Costa Rica . . . . | *19118*
MR R Tyson—Cal'96 . . . . |

Smith MR & MRS Robert A K (Mary F Carter) Cy.
☎ (314) 725-5949 . . 625 S Skinker Blvd, Apt 603, St Louis, MO *63105*

Smith MR & MRS Robert A K JR (Katharine D | ☎ (810) 540-7490
Southworth) V'64.Rcsl.Cysl.P'62.H'70 . . . . | 651 Bennington Dv,
MISS Katie S—at Dartmouth . . . . | Bloomfield Hills, MI
MR R Angus K 3d—Dth'90 . . . . | *48304*

Smith MR & MRS Robert B (Nancy L Morrill) Cy.Nd.Pn.
☎ (314) 993-2410 . . 3 Glenview Rd, St Louis, MO *63124-1307*

Smith MRS Robert S (Blossom—Gertrude H Scribner) . . . . Died at
Vero Beach, FL Oct 3'95

Smith MR & MRS Rodney W (Phyllis G Fiske) Adelphi'49.Cly.Cl'49 ⚓
☎ (941) 474-2045 . . 7770 Manasota Key Rd, Englewood, FL *34223*

Smith MR & MRS Roger D (Kathleen W Tener) | of ☎ (212)787-2188
V'65.H'68.Cw.Y. | 54 Riverside Dv,
MISS Jocelyn T—at U of Mich Ann Arbor . . . . . | New York, NY
ENS Silas W—USN.Y'94—at Johns Hopkins Med | *10024*
JUNIORS MR Luke E T—at Denison . . . . | ☎ (914) 255-7435
 | LeFevre Bontecou
 | Farm,
 | 454 Rte 32 N,
 | New Paltz, NY
 | *12561*

Smith MRS Ruth U (Ruth R Urban) V'71 . . . . | ☎ (540) 882-3627
JUNIORS MISS Anna D—at Lawrenceville . . . . . . | ''Magnolia House''
 | PO Box 53,
 | Waterford, VA
 | *20197*

Smith MR S Scott . . see W D Priester

Smith MR & MRS S Yeardley (Doris L Buker) Md.Gi.JHop'29
☎ (410) 437-0991 . . Gibson Island, MD *21056*

Smith MISS Sallie Dorsey—Ws'76.Mv.Cda. ⚓
☎ (212) 777-1179 . . 245 E 19 St, Apt 3D, New York, NY *10003*

Smith MRS Sarah D (Sarah D Schumacher) Ncd.
☎ (212) 249-2458 . . 510 E 84 St, Apt 5A, New York, NY *10028*

Smith MRS Sarah Hoffman (Sarah Harvey Hoffman) | ☎ (212) 734-7224
Fic.Cly.Ncd. | 215 E 72 St,
MISS Margaret L . . . . | New York, NY
MR Frederick M R JR . . . . | *10021*
JUNIORS MR Charles L . . . . |

Smith MR & MRS Scott C (Martha E Reilly) Col'72.Y'73
☎ (954) 522-2270 . . 2533 Aqua Vista Blvd, Ft Lauderdale, FL *33301*

Smith MR & MRS Scott F (Nancy A Brown)
Denis'80.Pa'85.H.'76.Tex'80 . . of
☎ (212) 362-0332 . . 600 West End Av, Apt 3B, New York, NY *10024*
☎ (203) 245-3675 . . 32 Neptune Av, Madison, CT *06443*

Smith MR Sebastian M von B—Edin'90
☎ (011-7-95) 243-3923 . . Agence France-Presse, 13 place de la Bourse,
BP20, 75061 Paris, France

Smith MR & MRS Sherman H (McGehee—Elizabeth L Weldon)
MtVern'81.Ncd.
☎ (334) 928-8501 . . ''Point of View'' 19493 Scenic H'way 98,
PO Box 231, Point Clear, AL *36564*

Smith MRS Sidney S (Louise F Clark) Cda.Ht . . . . . . | ☎ (203) 966-4918
MR Sidney S 3d—at ☎ (413) 774-1681 | 127 Middle Ridge
PO Box 231, Deerfield, MA *01342* . . . . | Rd, New Canaan,
MR Douglas V C—Ty'96 . . . . | CT *06840*

Smith MR Sidney V JR (Sidney V) . . . . Married at Buffalo, NY
Marlette MISS Mary C (late John E) . . . . Jun 29'96

Smith MR & MRS Sidney V JR (Mary C Marlette)
Dth'87.SUNY'90.Rc.M.Pa'78
☎ (610) 664-0356 . . 24 Narbrook Park, Narberth, PA *19072*

Smith DR & MRS (DR) Stanley L (Susan Cabot Goodale)
Denis'80.Cl'82.GaMed'86.Emory'82.GaMed'86
☎ (612) 222-7230 . . 808 Goodrich Av, St Paul, MN *55105*

Smith MRS Starbuck JR (Mary C McLain)
☎ (513) 561-8804 . . Deupree House E, Apt 402, 3939 Erie Av, Cincinnati, OH *45208*

Smith MR & MRS Stephen A (Phoebe E MacKenzie)
P'cpia'79.NYSID'82.Kas'79
☎ (314) 727-8204 . . 8044 Crescent Dv, Clayton, MO *63105*

Smith MR & MRS Stephen B (Mary C Sehnert)
Cas.Cho.Cw.Cnt. . . . . | ☎ (847) 381-1338
  MISS Mary C H—LakeF'89—at | PO Box 52,
  2650 N Lakeview Av, Chicago, IL *60614* . . . . . | Barrington, IL
  MISS Gillian B H—Lynch'92 . . . . | *60011*

Smith MR & MRS Stephen H (Ann B Holmes) L&C'75.Cal'74
☎ (503) 651-2520 . . 8462 S Heinz Rd, Canby, OR *97013*

Smith MR & MRS Stephen J (Catharine McK Gould)
Man'vl'72.Bgt.Stc.StLaw'68 . . . . | ☎ (914) 234-3533
  MR Stephen J JR—at Humboldt State . . . . | 589 Guard Hill Rd,
  JUNIORS MISS Eliza McK . . . . | Bedford, NY *10506*
  JUNIORS MR Elliott M—at San Fran State . . . . . . |

Smith MR & MRS Stockton N (Sallie B Spence) Van'77.Me.Wil.Cw.Va'77
☎ (804) 977-7575 . . Rte 5, Box 427B, Charlottesville, VA *22901*

Smith MRS Suzette de M (Faux—Bensinger—Suzette de M Smith)
Ri.Cly.Myf.Cda.
☎ (212) 348-8246 . . 1115 Fifth Av, New York, NY *10128*

Smith MR & MRS T Gunter (Bradley Goodyear)
SpgHill'63.At.GaTech'59 . . . . | of ☎ (334)343-1999
  MISS Jeanette G . . . . | 603 Fairfax Rd W,
  MISS Susanne R . . . . | Mobile, AL *36608*
  | ☎ (607) 547-9375
  | "Cary Mede"
  | PO Box 188,
  | Springfield Center,
  | NY *13468*

Smith MRS Taylor R (Jean N Dunn) Bnd'48 . . . . . . | 1815 Brookwood
  MISS Robin S . . . . | Dv, Akron, OH
  MISS Sarah L . . . . | *44313*
  MISS Margaret D . . . . |
  MR Taylor M . . . . |

Smith MR & MRS Templeton (Nellie M Fergus)
MtH'41.Pitt'43.Dar.H'40.H'43.H'47
☎ (412) 341-9993 . . 776 Valleyview Rd, Pittsburgh, PA *15243*

Smith MR & MRS Templeton JR (Lea E Anderson)
WVa'76.WVa'79.W&L'74.Pitt'77
☎ (412) 561-6515 . . 829 White Oak Circle, Pittsburgh, PA *15228*

Smith MRS Thomas W M (Jane S McDill) Mt. . . . . | ☎ (202) 333-4426
  MISS Ann L M—Hav'87 . . . . | 4426 Hadfield Lane
  | NW, Washington,
  | DC *20007*

Smith MRS Thurston H (Ruth E Mooney) My.
☎ (561) 274-2266 . . 1111 George Bush Blvd, Apt K, Delray Beach, FL *33483*

Smith MR Thurston H 3d . . see D N Loud

Smith MISS Tiffany Louise—SCal'88
☎ (603) 646-7379 . . Dartmouth College, 419 Byrne Hall, Hanover, NH *03755-9100*

Smith MR & MRS Timothy D (Marie N Holmes)
BMr'54.Msq.Y'51 . . . . | ☎ (202) 537-1517
  MISS Patience B . . . . | 4342 Reno Rd NW,
  MR Jabish G . . . . | Washington, DC
  | *20008-4235*

Smith MR & MRS Timothy H (Fredrica B Stoddard)
Wheat'58.Ln.Yn.Wms'58 . . . . | ☎ (203) 259-5340
  MISS Sibley L . . . . | 65 Verna Field Rd,
  MR Richard J 2d—Tul'83 . . . . | Fairfield, CT *06430*
  MR Timothy W . . . . |

Smith MR Townsend U . . see D N Loud

Smith DR & MRS Trent W (Eileen Ebert) CapU'36.OState'33.OState'37
☎ (614) 464-1110 . . 155 W Main St, Columbus, OH *43215*

Smith MR & MRS W N Harrell 4th (Mary Oakes
Skinner) Sth'63.Mit'77.Cvc.Mt.Sl.Wms'60. | of ☎ (202)338-2630
Ox'62.H'65 . . . . | 2630 Foxhall Rd
  MISS Caroline Doswell—at 1611 Anacapa St, | NW, Washington,
  Apt 6, Santa Barbara, CA *93101* . . . . | DC *20007*
  MR W N Harrell 5th . . . . | ☎ (540) 775-7373
  | "Nanzatico" Rte
  | 698, King George,
  | VA *22485*

Smith MR & MRS W S Burges (Cynthia G Pillsbury)
Stan'83.Cp.Cc.Myf.P'84
☎ (707) 963-8436 . . 1761 Stockton St, St Helena, CA *94574*

Smith MR & MRS W Scott JR (Kathleen E Stull) M.Syr'50
☎ (610) 356-0797 . . PO Box 310, Newtown Square, PA *19073-0310*

Smith MR & MRS W Watt (M Jacqueline Vance)
PUCRio'68.S.Snc.Br'60 . . . . | ☎ (516) 692-6139
  MISS Adriana W . . . . | 23 Glen Way,
  MISS Carolina W . . . . | Cold Spring Harbor,
  | NY *11724*

Smith MRS Wallace H (Mary A Kelsey) Cy. . . . . . . | ☎ (314) 991-1286
  MR Jay Herndon—Bard'51.Y'58—at London, | 51 Pointer Lane,
  England . . . . | St Louis, MO *63124*

Smith MRS Walter Burges 2d (Pearson—Nancy
Clark) OWes'62.Cal'65.Mt.Nrr.Cc.Snc.Dh. . . . . | ☎ (301) 986-8659
  JUNIORS MISS Lydia W S . . . . | 7007 Connecticut
  MISS Sarah B Pearson . . . . | Av, Chevy Chase,
  MISS Caroline C Pearson . . . . | MD *20815*

Smith MR & MRS Warren L JR (Linda B McHale)
Newt'69.Drex'71.Va'61 . . . . | ☎ (610) 649-6049
  JUNIORS MR Reid T . . . . | 459 Montgomery
  | Av, Haverford, PA
  | *19041-1712*

Smith MRS Warren Lister (Marcia E Wilson) M.Ac.
☎ (610) 527-4192 . . 601 Montgomery Av, Bryn Mawr, PA *19010*

Smith MR & MRS Warren W (Ruth S Lee)
V'47-8.Y'44 . . . . | ☎ (011-58-2)
  MISS Roxa L—Bow'84 . . . . | 261-38-54
  MISS Kora M—SCal'87 . . . . | Apartado 14230,
  MISS Ruth S—at Evergreen Coll . . . . | Caracas 1011A,
  | Venezuela

Smith MISS Wendell C . . see MRS F L Wehr

Smith MR William B . . see C E Baum

Smith MR William G S—U'71 ⛵
☎ (203) 438-3408 . . 17 Keeler Close, Ridgefield, CT *06877*

Smith MR & MRS William Marion (Carolyn J Vance)
MissWmn'60.Van'65.Miss'55 . . . . | ☎ (601) 445-5955
  MR William M JR . . . . | Glen Mary
  | Plantation,
  | 270 Foster Mound
  | Rd, Natchez, MS
  | *39120*

Smith MR & MRS William P R (Reese—Mitchell—Cherie J Sharp)
Ariz'66.Ty'50
☎ (520) 577-3567 . . 4490 N Via De La Granja, Tucson, AZ *85718*

Smith MRS William W (Elizabeth C Watt) Dar.Cda.
☎ (516) 676-3887 . . 157 Factory Pond Rd, Mill Neck, NY *11765*

Smith MR & MRS William Wharton (Claire W Shoemaker) Hav'34
''Juneberry'' 40 Pennsylvania Av, Jamestown, RI *02835*

Smith MRS William Whitney (Morris—Joyce C Plumb) Me.Myf.Ncd.
☎ (610) 896-1613 . . 100 Grays Lane, Apt 102, Haverford, PA *19041*

Smith MRS Wilson L (Barbara A Koehrman)
Toledo'76.Cw.Cspa.Denis'76.Van'80
☎ (610) 648-0824 . . 109½ S Valley Rd, Paoli, PA *19301-1425*

Smith MR Winthrop
☎ (212) 228-7638 . . 261 W 22 St, Apt 4, New York, NY *10011*

Smith MR & MRS Winthrop D (Claire V A de Tarr)
Mid'74.Mid'80.Mid'75.Mit'81 . . of
☎ (603) 436-5516 . . 485 FW Hartford Dv, Portsmouth, NH *03801-5890*
☎ (603) 278-5516 . . 100 Mt Washington Place, Bretton Woods, NH *03595*

Smith MRS Winthrop H (Linke—McVay—Boslo—Vivian G Brown) Cly.
☎ (561) 276-3459 . . Harbour's Edge 556, 401 E Linton Blvd, Delray Beach, FL *33483*

Smith MR & MRS Winthrop H JR (Margaret D Smith) Wheat'73.Ln.Aht'71.Pa'74 . . . . | of 3 MacPherson
  MISS Heather C . . . . | Dv, Greenwich, CT *06830*
  MISS Christina B . . . . | ☎ (860) 567-8703
  JUNIORS MR Winthrop H 3d . . . . | Winvian Farm,
  JUNIORS MR Cameron W . . . . | Alain White Rd, Morris, CT *06763*

Smith MR & MRS Winthrop S (Susan L Clay) MidTenn'91
☎ (615) 684-7326 . . 300 Lee Lane, Shelbyville, TN *37160-2535*

Smith MRS Zimri Luce (Elizabeth S Hornung) . . . . | ☎ (518) 587-9499
  Ws'60.SUNY'79 . . . . | 3 Collins Terr,
  MR Robert T—Col'87 . . . . | Saratoga Springs, NY *12866*

Smith MR Zimri Luce JR—Br'92
☎ (212) 580-5198 . . 102 W 79 St, Apt 4A, New York, NY *10024*

Smithers MR & MRS Austin L (Bartram—Anstiss H McCormick-Goodhart) Err.
☎ (603) 795-4845 . . PO Box 246, 19 Cutting Hill Lane, Lyme, NH *03768*

Smithers MRS C Francis (Eleanor V Thibaut) . . . . . | ☎ (540) 839-5853
  MISS M Vey—Pa'72—at ☎ (011-502-9) 320-280 | Rte 2, Box 593,
  6A Calle Oriente 12, Antigua Guatemala, | Hot Springs, VA
  Guatemala . . . . | *24445*

Smithers MR & MRS Charles F JR (Panon | ☎ (212) 753-0785
  Desbassayns de Richemont—Anne M Hart | 570 Park Av,
  Green) Un.Chr.Ny.Plg.Hob'52 . . . . | New York, NY
    JUNIORS MISS Amélie Panon Desbassayns | *10021*
    de Richemont—at Wycombe Abbey England .
    JUNIORS MR Philippe Panon Desbassayns
    de Richemont—at Winchester Coll England . .

Smithers MR & MRS Charles F 3d (Elizabeth H Adam)
WmSth'81.WmSth'78
☎ (203) 661-3117 . . 14A Mead Av, Cos Cob, CT *06807*

Smithers MR & MRS Francis C (Virginia L Pearson) Ck.
☎ (561) 231-3260 . . 121 Stingaree Point, Vero Beach, FL *32963*

Smithers MR & MRS P Christopher (Jane H Eversman)
☎ (303) 733-2656 . . 540 S Franklin St, Denver, CO *80209*

Smithers SIR Peter & LADY (Lane—Dojean Sayman) | of ☎ (011-41-91)
  Evg.BtP.Ox'34 . . . . | 69-19-73
  MISS Sarah Otway—at ☎ (941) 488-4206 | 6921 Vico Morcote,
  1031 Albee Farm Rd, Venice, FL *34292* . . . . . . | Switzerland
  MISS Amelia F Otway—Lond'78 . . . . | Everglades Club, 356 Worth Av, Palm Beach, FL *33480*

Smithers MRS Ruth H (Ruth A Hall) | of ☎ (203)966-2986
  TexWmn'49.Man'vl'77 . . . . | 25 Kimberly Place,
  MISS Claire H . . . . | New Canaan, CT *06840*
  | ☎ (212) 532-1763
  | 10 Park Av, New York, NY *10016*

Smith-Petersen MRS Pettengill (Mary E Pettengill)
☎ (941) 591-3005 . . 6621 Trident Way, Naples, FL *34108*

Smithwick MRS A Patrick (Suzanne de S Whitman) | ☎ (410) 771-4723
  Gv. . . . . | 15385 Manor Rd,
  MISS Sallie B—at 36 Vermont St, | Monkton, MD
  Saratoga Springs, NY *12866* . . . . | *21111*

Smithwick MR & MRS A Patrick JR (Ansley Dickinson) Hlns'75.JHop'73
☎ (410) 472-4282 . . ''The Pond House'' Sparks Glencoe, MD *21152*

Smithwick MR Reginald H—Cy.Ey.Br'53 . . of
☎ (561) 746-2187 . . 151 Beacon Lane, Jupiter, FL *33469-3504*
☎ (617) 631-0555 . . ''Boat House'' Foster St, Marblehead Neck, MA *01945*

Smoot MR & MRS William S (Katharine Smull) Pr.Cs.H'36
☎ (516) 692-7413 . . 1270 Ridge Rd, Syosset, NY *11791*

Smylie MR & MRS Charles A (Green—Marguerette S Sheridan) Pa'50.USN'42
☎ (941) 964-0266 . . 4020—40 St, PO Box 1238, Boca Grande, FL *33921*

Smyth MR & MRS Constantine J 3d (Waitt—Anne W Pilson) GeoW'55
105 Pebble Cove, 3833 Banana River Blvd, Cocoa Beach, FL *32931*

Smyth MR & MRS D Grahame (Leu—Louisa Zimmerman) Pg.Snc.Ds.Ac.Ncd.Hn.H'45
☎ (412) 683-4127 . . 5023 Frew St, Pittsburgh, PA *15213-3829*

Smyth MISS Elizabeth E . . see D M Kinney

Smyth MRS Gordon S (G Louise Davenport) . . . . Died at Gwynedd, PA Feb 14'95

Smyth MR John E . . see D M Kinney

Smyth MR & MRS William R JR (Eleanor N | ☎ (305) 666-1341
  Churchman) USMMA'54.Geo'57 . . . . | 9385 Gallardo St,
  MISS Eleanor N . . . . | Coral Gables, FL
  MISS Ellen L . . . . | *33156*
  MR William R 3d . . . . |
  MR Daniel A—at 104 Racquet Rd, Jamestown, RI *02835* . . . . |
  MR David R . . . . |

Smythe MISS Cameron Sinclair (Christopher W) . . . . Born Mch 2'96

Smythe MISS Christine L (Lewis—Christine L | ☎ (703) 522-9142
  Smythe) Wells'67.Bost'75.Myf. . . . . | 2607 Arlington
  MISS Jennifer T Lewis . . . . | Blvd, Apt 102,
  MR Andrew C Lewis . . . . | Arlington, VA *22201*

Smythe MR & MRS Christopher W (Bryn M Johnston) ECar'83.OWes'82
☎ (610) 789-3308 . . 33 Sycamore Rd, Havertown, PA *19083*

Smythe MR & MRS J L Nevill (Ann V Stout) Wms'49
3 Huntingwood Retreat, Savannah, GA *31411*

Smythe MR & MRS J L Nevill 3d (Karen A Strain) V'82.Va'87.Wms'81
☎ (514) 939-3817 . . 8 Ch DeCasson, Westmount, Quebec H3Y 2H1, Canada

Smythe LT CDR & MRS T H Butler 2d (Maria L Farris) USN.Ithaca'77 ⛴
☎ (619) 575-8544 . . 826 Orange Av, Box 147, Coronado, CA *92118*

Snead MR Phillip H—W&M'55
☎ (860) 525-2227 . . 525 Crown St, B9 Apt 193, Meriden, CT *06450*

Snead MR Phillip H 3d . . of
☎ (212) 794-7260 . . 187 E 80 St, New York, NY *10021-0447*
☎ (508) 228-6827 . . "All Myne" 36 Monomoy Rd, Nantucket, MA *02554-2312*

Snedeker MR & MRS Robert D (Frances H Muth)	☎ (914) 834-3081
Duke'64.P.'64.H'66	20 Linden Av,
MISS Kate G—at Princeton	Larchmont, NY *10538*

Snedeker MR & MRS Sedgwick (McGrath—Elizabeth G Naudin) Evg.Pr.Hl.Cly.P.'33.Cl'36 . . of
☎ (561) 655-3051 . . 369 S Lake Dv, Palm Beach, FL *33480*
☎ (516) 367-9172 . . 568 Cold Spring Rd, Laurel Hollow, Syosset, NY *11791*

Snider MR & MRS Ronald A (Virginia C Smith) Emory'71.At.Ala'70
☎ (334) 433-9455 . . 407 Church St, Mobile, AL *36601*

Snodgrass MR & MRS Francis R (Anne L Darneille)	of ☎ (202)337-8914
V'69.Cvc.Mt.P'61.H'64	2804—34 St NW,
JUNIORS MISS Virginia W	Washington, DC *20008*
JUNIORS MISS Anne W	☎ (207) 647-2072
JUNIORS MR Francis D	"Nawandyn" Rte 3, Box 1075, Bridgton, ME *04009*

Snodgrass MR & MRS John D'Arcy (Toner—Ellen L Carlson) Ck.NH'78
☎ (516) 944-6403 . . 16 Leeds Dv, Port Washington, NY *11050*

Snodgrass MRS Russell L (Helen Walker) Cvc.Ncd.
☎ (410) HO7-9213 . . 3909 Cloverhill Rd, Baltimore, MD *21218*

Snow MR & MRS Crocker (Smith—Little—Janice Vaughan) Sbc.My.H'26
☎ (508) 356-2277 . . 126 Topsfield Rd, Ipswich, MA *01938-1665*

Snow MRS E Douglas (Gucker—Ellen H Douglas) BMr'30.Cda.
☎ (617) 326-6776 . . 195 Mt Vernon St, Dedham, MA *02026*

Snow MRS Elliot (Mary E Merrill)	☎ (603) 563-8718
MR Nathaniel M—Bow'95	PO Box 27, 9 Boulder Dv, Dublin, NH *03444*

Snow MR & MRS J Roberts (Jennifer J Jameson) Woos'89.Bost'92.Myf.Dar.Mid'89
☎ (508) 476-3369 . . 182 Perry St, Douglas, MA *01516*

Snow MRS Robert B (Mary Welman)
☎ (573) 651-8326 . . 3120 Independence St, Apt 326, Cape Girardeau, MO *63703*

Snowden MRS George G 3d (Ann W Hoare)	☎ (401) 348-8203
MISS Annabel H—Wheat'93	4 Ocean View H'way, Watch Hill, RI *02891*
MISS Susannah H—Wheat'95	
MISS Melissa S—at Wheaton	
MISS Charlotte L—at Wheaton	

Snowden MRS James M (Marie S Kiely) Fic.Cly.
☎ (212) 832-8982 . . 1 Sutton Place S, New York, NY *10022*

Snowden MR & MRS James M JR (Katherine B G	☎ (314) 997-3310
Orthwein) Msq.Rc.Ln.Cy.Why.Pa'65	12 Fordyce Lane,
MISS Katherine K—at Wash'n U	St Louis, MO *63124*
MISS Suzanne O'F—at Vanderbilt	

Snowden MISS Joan P
☎ (215) 551-8054 . . 244 Queen St, Philadelphia, PA *19147*

Snowden MISS Mary Anna
☎ (215) 247-0207 . . 7708 McCallum St, Philadelphia, PA *19118-4308*

Snowden MR Richard Wood—Rc.Fi.Ph.Ken'79 . . of
☎ (215) 639-2164 . . "Andalusia" Andalusia, PA *19020*
☎ (215) 248-1395 . . "Hollowood" 8847 Norwood Av, Chestnut Hill, PA *19118*

Snowden MRS Henry Taft (Nancy C Buckingham) Mt.Cvc.Ncd.
☎ (202) 337-6316 . . 4000 Cathedral Av NW, Apt 852B, Washington, DC *20016*

Snowdon MR & MRS Henry Taft JR (Sanders—	☎ (202) 829-4780
Philippa C J Hohler) NCar'69.GeoW'73	1606 Varnum St NW, Washington, DC *20011*
MISS Marietta P C Sanders—at ☎ (011-44-171) 352-1690 . . 79 Ifield Rd, London SW10 9AU, England	
MR Algernon W R Sanders—at ☎ (011-852) 855-8741 . . 1 Victoria Rd, Hong Kong	
JUNIORS MR Henry C C B Sanders	

Snyder DR & MRS Howard McC 3d (Mary C	☎ (610) 649-9634
Woodville) Ws'67.Pa'83.Ub.Me.Cyb.P'65.H'69	330 Laurel Lane, Haverford, PA *19041*
MISS Emily C	
JUNIORS MR Laurence C	

Snyder MR & MRS J Brandon (Jean R Stiles) Pitt'75 .	☎ (412) 741-9350
MISS Heather L	PO Box 85, Blackburn Rd, Sewickley, PA *15143*
MISS Margaret B	
JUNIORS MR J Brandon JR	

Snyder MRS John A (Huntington—Mary B Kniffin) Ln.Cly.
133 E 64 St, New York, NY *10021*

Snyder MRS John Avery (Dietzen—Elizabeth R	☎ (610) 645-6324
Marshall) Van'77.Ncd.	626 Railroad Av, Haverford, PA *19041-1222*
JUNIORS MISS Cassin A	
JUNIORS MISS Alexandra McI	

Snyder MR John Avery—Rv.Wt.Ty'69
☎ (610) 293-0720 . . 452 Inveraray Rd, Villanova, PA *19085-1138*

Snyder MR & MRS John H (Anna S Carter) Bost'57.Y'54
☎ (540) 672-1530 . . 12574 Chicken Mountain Rd, Orange, VA *22960*

Snyder MRS Louise M (M Louise Montgomery) . . see D B Montgomery

Snyder MR & MRS Martin Avery (Ann P Cauffman)	☎ (610) MU8-4825
OWes'76.Sa.Me.Ph.Rv.Wt.Ac.Mit'64.Nu'66 . . .	"Camp Woods" 745 Newtown Rd, Villanova, PA *19085*
MISS Rebecca S—F&M'92	
MR Martin C—at Cornell	

Snyder MR Martin P—Ph.Wt.Rv.Cw.W.Hav'35.Pa'38
☎ (610) 645-8977 . . 1400 Waverly Rd, Andrews 225, Gladwyne, PA *19035*

Snyder MR & MRS Paul H H (Margaret G Whiteman) Swth'40.Swth'41
☎ (202) 298-7013 . . 3900B Watson Place NW, Apt 5C, Washington, DC *20016*

Snyder MRS Philip M (Eleanor H Mullally) . . . . ☎ (516) 239-4934
  MR Philip M JR—P'72 . . . . 238 Causeway,
  Lawrence, NY *11559*

Snyder MR & MRS Robert M (Barbara A E Carson) ☎ (914) 557-8160
  SanDiegoSt'78.NCar'73 . . . . 171 County Rd 21,
  JUNIORS MISS Elizabeth . . . . Barryville, NY *12719*

Snyder MR & MRS Roy H JR (Millicent J Lennig) Me.Myf.Ac.Cda.P.'30
  ☎ (610) 642-4254 . . 405 Penn Rd, Wynnewood, PA *19096-1305*

Snyder MR & MRS William P 3d (Jean E Rose) Rr.Ny . . .of
  ☎ (412) 741-4351 . . PO Box 85, Blackburn Rd, Sewickley,
  PA *15143*
  ☎ (561) 276-5869 . . 601 S Ocean Blvd, Delray Beach, FL *33483*

Sobel MRS William S (Joubert—Clement— ☎ (203) 227-8801
  Wilhelmina H Young) . . . . 1 Charcoal Hill Rd,
  MISS Louise Y Clement . . . . Westport, CT *06880*

Sodi MR & MRS Marco (M Ariane Noel) Geo'88.Cr'80
  ☎ (212) 486-8233 . . 320 E 57 St, Apt 10C, New York, NY *10022*

Sodi MR Mario (Sodi—Damon—Diana D ☎ (561) 546-9100
  Hutchinson) . . . . 9438 SE Mast Terr,
  MISS Daniela . . . . Hobe Sound, FL
  MR Alessandro *33455*
  MR Michele—at ☎ (914) 365-4890
  265 River Rd, Grandview-on-Hudson, NY *10960*

Soffel MISS Christie A—EMich'77
  4607 Kenmore Dv NW, Washington, DC *20007*

Sohier MR W Davies 3d—Rcb.Sm.H'77.Macalester'79
  American Embassy, Manila, Philippines, APO AP, *96440*

Sohier MRS William D JR (Gladys E Arias) Sbc.BtP.Evg . . .of
  ☎ (561) 833-2596 . . 240 Clarke Av, Palm Beach, FL *33480*
  ☎ (508) 526-1944 . . 43 Proctor St, PO Box 1542, Manchester,
  MA *01944*

Sokoloff MRS Boris T (Bijur—Lee—Alice St J Hunt)
  ☎ (914) 277-4340 . . 63A Heritage Hills, Somers, NY *10589*

Sokoloff MRS Kiril (Catherine H Miller) Bgt.Ri.
  Cider Mill Farm, Bouton Rd, South Salem, NY *10590*

Sokoloff MR Kiril—Rcn.Bgt.Ri.Geo'69 . . . . ☎ (208) 726-4334
  JUNIORS MISS Emily D—at Kent Sch . . . . 109 Boulder View
  JUNIORS MR Kiri St J . . . . Lane, PO Box 6191,
  Ketchum, ID *83340*

Solacoff DR & MRS (DR) David K (Margaret L du Pont)
  Wms'89.JHop'94.OState'88.JHop'93
  ☎ (410) 583-1878 . . 1921 Old Court Rd, Baltimore, MD *21204*

Soleri MR Paolo—TorinoPolytec'46
  ☎ (602) 948-6145 . . 6433 E Doubletree Ranch Rd, Paradise Valley,
  AZ *85253*

Sollers MR Joseph S JR (C Carter Middleton) Gi.
  ☎ (410) 252-5306 . . 11425 Greenspring Av, Lutherville, MD *21093*

Solley MRS Nancy F (Eastburn—Nancy D Farr)
  ☎ (860) 868-7452 . . "Holliecroft Farm" Washington, CT *06793*

Solley MR & MRS Nicholas N (Keogh—Wierdsma— ☎ (860) 868-0092
  Pamela D Clark) IaWes'72 . . . . Apple Lane Farm,
  MISS Emily F Wierdsma . . . . 17 Judea Cemetery
  MR George P Keogh—at Columbia Med . . . . Rd, Washington, CT
  MR Clark R Wierdsma *06793*

Sollitt MRS Sumner S (Nye—Bettye Herb)
  ☎ (312) 642-3637 . . 1350 N Astor St, Chicago, IL *60610*

Solomon MRS Emmett G (Tognazzini—Page P Pressley) Bur.StJ.Tcy.
  ☎ (415) 343-0636 . . 20 Bayberry Place, Hillsborough, CA *94010*

Somers MR & MRS George W JR (Judith F Hansen) Cp.
  ☎ (707) 433-0253 . . 15909 Norton Rd, Healdsburg, CA *95448*

Somers MRS George Willard (Katherine R Stent) Bur.
  ☎ (415) 548-1885 . . 601 Laurel Av, San Mateo, CA *94401*

Somers MASTER George Willard 3d (John W) . . . . Born at
  Woodland, CA Mch 22'96

Somers MR John W (George W JR) . . . . Married at Monterey, CA
  Horan MISS Laura J (Laurence) . . . . Aug 6'94

Somers MR & MRS John W (Laura J Horan) Pac'89.Cal'90
  ☎ (707) 433-1626 . . 237 Grant Av, Healdsburg, CA *95448*

Sommaripa MRS Ann K (Ann C Kuhn) Pa'86
  ☎ (215) 247-8622 . . 8117 Shawnee St, Philadelphia, PA *19118*

Sommaripa MR & MRS George (Eva A Coifman) of ☎ (617)661-3800
  Ws'63.H'51.Cl'60 . . . . 17 Bishop Allen Dv,
  MR Leo M—at Corps de la Paix, BP 1282, Cambridge, MA
  Cidex 01, Abijan 06, Côte d'Ivoire *02139*
  JUNIORS MR Nicholas C R—at ☎ (508) 636-5869
  Northfield-Mt Hermon . . . . "Eva's Garden"
  105 Jordan Rd,
  South Dartmouth,
  MA *02748*

Sommer MR & MRS Charles S (Jane M Hamill) of ☎ (314)991-5527
  Swb'65.EdenTheo'92.Cy.Nd.Aht'65.Va'67 . . . . 11 Upper Ladue Rd,
  MR Graydon H—at Washington U . . . . St Louis, MO *63124*
  ☎ (809) 496-0244
  "Aslantic House"
  Little Bay,
  Long Look, Tortola,
  BVI

Sommer MISS Jane B (Charles S) . . . . Married at St Louis, MO
  Millard MR J Alden JR (John A) . . . . May 11'96

Sommerfield MRS Mark J (Carvette—Katharine K ☎ (908) 449-2256
  Gold) UMiami'69.Ac.Chr.Sdg.Dll.Dar.Ht.Ne. . . 501 Jersey Av,
  MISS Megan A . . . . Spring Lake, NJ
  JUNIORS MISS Laura B *07762*

Sommerfield MR Mark J—Pe.Pars'69
  ☎ (704) 556-7141 . . 6332-3C Cameron Forest Lane, Charlotte,
  NC *28210*

Sones DR & MRS James Q 2d (Donna L Kennedy) ☎ (601) 355-1234
  Miss'67.Miss'68 . . . . 4029 Northeast Dv,
  MR James Q 3d . . . . Jackson, MS
  MR Frederick K *39211-6331*
  JUNIORS MISS Megan L . . . .

Soniat MR & MRS Robert U (Ann H Hobson) ☎ (504) 897-0140
  Nu'75.Va'61.Tul'64.GeoW'66 . . . . 1011 Jefferson Av,
  MR Robert S . . . . New Orleans, LA
  MR Ashton H *70115*

Sonne MR & MRS Christian R (Sara E Barnes) Sth'62.T.K.Y.'57 . . . . ☎ (914) 351-5635
  "Sunny Rock"
  MISS Edith C—at Yale . . . . PO Box 777,
  MR Peter C—at 215 E 95 St, New York, NY Tuxedo Park, NY
  10128 . . . . *10987*
  MR Matthew M—at 2801 N Glade St NW,
  Washington, DC *20016* . . . .
  MR Nicholas B

Sonntag MR Joseph K—Mich'39.H'48
  5858 Midnight Pass Rd, Siesta Key, Sarasota, FL *34242*

Soper MR & MRS Brian McK (Vaughan—F Jane Todd) Camb'46 . . of
  ☎ (410) 822-1052 . . PO Box 1494, Easton, MD *21601*
  ☎ (011-44-1983) 293947 . . "The Gables" Egypt Hill, Cowes,
  Isle of Wight PO31 8BP, England

Soper MR & MRS John W (Parsons—Martha K Davis) Y'45.Mit'56
  ☎ (860) 388-4764 . . 48 Cromwell Place, Old Saybrook, CT *06475*

Soroko MR & MRS John J (Cameron C Adams)
  OWes'81.Pc.Rc.Ac.Hav'73.Nu'77
  ☎ (215) 247-6399 . . 8730 Germantown Av, Philadelphia, PA *19118*

Sortwell MR & MRS Daniel R JR (Nancy H Bascom) of ☎ (508)653-1268
  Chi.H'39 . . . . 113 S Main St,
  MISS (DR) Cynthia G—Bost'75.Wash'79—at Sherborn, MA
  31 Cliff Rd, South Portland, ME *04106* *01770*
  ☎ (207) 882-7393
  Willow Lane Farm,
  Wiscasset, ME
  04578

Sortwell MR Daniel R 3d—Rut'73
  Division del Norte 215, Casa 17, Col Lomas de Memetla,
  05330 Mexico, DF, Mexico

Sorum MR Peter H—Ct.MichSt'68
  ☎ (202) 296-7891 . . 2601 Woodley Place NW, Apt 1113, Washington,
  DC *20008*

Souder MISS Margaret L—Ncd.
  ☎ (610) 527-9427 . . 1062 Lancaster Av, Apt 407, Rosemont, PA *19010*

Soule MR & MRS Augustus W (Mary W Rogers) Ws'43.Cw.Myf.H.'40
  ☎ (617) 326-5196 . . 15 Common St, Dedham, MA *02026*

Soule MR Christopher W—Cl'60
  ☎ (212) 247-6087 . . 345 W 58 St, Apt 11C, New York, NY *10019*

Soule MR & MRS Edgar W (Elizabeth C Wheeler) Cr'85.HWSth'84
  27 Ivy Rd, Wellesley, MA *02181*

Soule MR & MRS Horace H (Sarah H Foster) Chi.Cy. . . . . ☎ (617) 329-6568
  MR Horace H JR—at 2425 University Heights, 151B Grove St,
  Boulder, CO *80302* . . . . Westwood, MA
  02090-1027

Soule MISS Martha R—Bost'76
  ☎ (617) 431-1429 . . 3 Upson Rd, Wellesley, MA *02181*

Soule MR & MRS Richard H (Cooper—Virginia L ☎ (603) 526-6769
  Anthony) Mid'49.H'50.H'52 . . . . 2 Homan Lane,
  MR Alan A Cooper—McG'84 . . . . New London, NH
  MR Douglas C Cooper *03257*

Soule MR & MRS Richard H JR (Kimberly Anne Beede)
  Wes'83.H'94.Hb.Br'82
  ☎ (011-65) 777-2805 . . 8 Rochester Park, Singapore 139219

Soule MASTER Samuel Ellington (Richard H JR) . . . . Born at
  Singapore May 16'96

Soule MR Timothy W (Richard H) . . . . . Married at Pacific Palisades, CA
  Hayden MISS Samantha (Glenn) . . . . May 4'96

Soutendijk MR & MRS Dirk R (Mary M Tremaine) Chath'77.Y'60 . . of
  ☎ (201) 334-9237 . . 52 Briarcliff Rd, Mountain Lakes, NJ *07046*
  ☎ (212) 722-0726 . . 1755 York Av, New York, NY *10128*
  ☎ (705) 732-0000 . . Humphrey Township, Little Lake Joseph, Muskoka,
  Ontario P0B 1G0, Canada

Southam MR & MRS Gordon L (Browne—Young—Mary W Patterson)
  ☎ (813) 785-3621 . . 245 Cypress Lane, East Lake Woodlands, Oldsmar,
  FL *34677*

Southwell MISS Priscilla L (Spettel—Priscilla L Southwell)
  Col'74.Col'77.NCar'82 . . see MRS E S Richardson JR

Southwell MRS Hamilton (Katharine R Jones) ☎ (212) 744-2214
  Gr.C.Cs. . . . . 200 E 66 St,
  MR Thomas S—Y'63 . . . . New York, NY
  10021

Southworth MR & MRS Hamilton JR (Eleanor W Ewart)
  Sth'59.Cs.Y'56.Mit'57.Cl'64.Nu'75 . . of
  ☎ (212) 369-6579 . . 1133 Park Av, New York, NY *10128*
  ☎ (516) 653-4369 . . PO Box 277, Quogue, NY *11959*

Soutter DR & MRS Lamar (Mary C Bigelow) Sm.Chi.Hn.H'31
  ☎ (508) 369-1345 . . 100 Newbury Court, Apt 314, Concord,
  MA *01742-4156*

Soutter MISS Lucy—H'90 . . see B A McN Righter

Sowanick MR & MRS Thomas J (Stone—Christine Wainwright)
  Ty'79.Pa'84.AmU'76
  ☎ (212) 517-8825 . . 870 Fifth Av, New York, NY *10021*

Sowles DR & MRS Nicholas P (Juliana S C McIntyre)
  Wheat'91.Ub.Ken'88.Tufts'95
  ☎ (617) 983-2982 . . 44½ Burroughs St, Jamaica Plain, MA *02130*

Spaeth MR & MRS Christopher P (Julie L Bartelme) ColSt'94.Pc.ColSt'95
  ☎ (215) 848-9396 . . 2822 Midvale Av, Apt A, Philadelphia, PA *19129*

Spaeth MR & MRS Karl H (Ann D Wieland) ☎ (610) 828-2357
  Ph.Pc.Fw.Hav'51.H.'58 . . . . 2129 Harts Lane,
  CAPT Karl H JR—USMCR.StLaw'88 . . . . Miquon,
  MR Edmund A—StLaw'90 . . . . Conshohocken, PA
  19428

Spaeth MR & MRS Otto L JR (Ann C Barringer) P'55.H'63
  ☎ (914) 967-7670 . . N Kirby Lane, Rye, NY *10580*

Spahr MR Boyd Lee—Rc.R.Ph.Dick'32.Pa'35
  ☎ (215) MI6-3009 . . "Rogues Roost" 1009 Walton Rd, Blue Bell,
  PA *19422*

Spahr MR & MRS Boyd Lee 3d (Sandra L Welsch) Dick'63
  ☎ (215) TU4-4699 . . 601 Oreland Mill Rd, Oreland, PA *19075*

Spahr MR & MRS C Stewart W (Sidney F Bohlen) ☎ (610) 353-3539
  Beloit'69.Dick'69 . . . . 3523 Caley Rd,
  MISS Catherine E . . . . Newtown Square,
  JUNIORS MR Murray H 2d . . . . PA *19073*

Spahr MR & MRS Robert N (Julia W Darling) ☎ (610) 644-6422
  Me.Ty'60 . . . . 136 Grubb Rd,
  MISS Stephanie N . . . . Malvern, PA *19355*
  MISS Nöel W . . . .

Spalding MR Alfred B JR—Sar.Ds.Stan'36.Cal'39
  ☎ (415) 453-0658 . . PO Box 2, Ross, CA *94957*

Spalding MRS Charles F (Janet F Haskell)   ☎ (914) 424-3030
CUNY'65.Marist'76 . . . . | PO Box 139,
MISS Bethany P—Wms'89.H'93—Box 84619, | Garrison, NY *10524*
Fairbanks, AK *99708* . . . . |
MR Mark F—Ken'91.FlaIT'94 . . . . |

Spalding MR Hobart A (late Philip L) . . . . Married at Washington, DC
Long MISS Constance M (Raymond F) . . . . Dec 16'95

Spalding MR & MRS Hobart A (Constance M Long) Ws'46.Mt.H'34
☎ (202) 362-2846 . . 3726 Connecticut Av NW, Apt 420, Washington,
DC *20008-4547*

Spalding MRS Jean S (Jean U Scharin)
☎ (804) 973-8939 . . 48 Lake Forest Dv, Charlottesville, VA *22901*

Spangler MRS James L—Pa'42
☎ (520) 326-9618 . . 151 N Camino Del Norte, Tucson, AZ *85716*

Spangler MR & MRS John L JR (Elsie M Lindeman)
Temp'45.Fw.Hp.Ty'41.H'42
☎ (609) 829-5067 . . 212 Maureen Dv, Cinnaminson, NJ *08077*

Sparkman MISS Elliott W (Thorne JR) . . . . . . Married at Bryn Mawr, PA
Walker MR S Sloan 3d (late Samuel S JR) . . . . Apr 27'96

Sparkman DR & MRS Thorne JR (Marban E   ☎ (610) 688-4535
McGraw) Sth'62.H'61.Temp'65 . . . . | 351 Church Rd,
MR J Alexander—Pa'92 . . . . | Devon, PA *19333*

Sparkman MR & MRS Thorne 3d (Lane H Talbot) P'89.H'89
☎ (510) 848-7261 . . 2912 Claremont Av, Apt 32, Berkeley, CA *94705*

Spaulding MISS Esther W—G.
☎ (212) 369-0246 . . 17 E 89 St, New York, NY *10128*

Spaulding MR & MRS Frederick A (Karen L Lee)   ☎ (716) 992-9776
SL'74.St.ArtInst'73 . . . . | 9195 Sandrock Rd,
MISS Alexandra P . . . . | Eden, NY *14057*
JUNIORS MISS Eliza R . . . . |

Spaulding MRS Josiah A (Helen H Bowdoin) Sbc.Sm.My.Chi.
☎ (508) 526-1747 . . 19 Smith's Point Rd, Manchester, MA *01944*

Spaulding MR & MRS Josiah A JR (Victoria R Reeve) | ☎ (508) 468-4200
My.Bow'74 . . . . | 860 Bay Rd, Box
JUNIORS MR Josiah A 3d . . . . | 210, Hamilton, MA
                                        | *01936*

Speakes MR & MRS Charles Cooke (Vera J Jacobs)
LSU'45.Ncd.Dar.GaTech'43
☎ (601) 742-3313 . . Waveland Plantation, Benoit, MS *38725*

Speakman MISS Isabella P . . see W H Ryan

Spears MR & MRS Daniel B (Margaret E Williams) Bow'81.Gv.Bow'81
☎ (410) 584-2904 . . Old Orchard Farm, 14640 Falls Rd, Cockeysville,
MD *21030*

Speck MR Robert H JR—Myf.Rv.Cr'58
☎ (215) 925-1375 . . 423 S 3 St, Philadelphia, PA *19147*

Speed MRS James R (Peard—Nancy L Wheeler) Sth'26.Mv.
☎ (410) 243-4750 . . Roland Park Place, Apt 854, 830 W 40 St,
Baltimore, MD *21211*

Speer MRS Louise P (Louise P Leetch)
558 Twelfth Av S, Naples, FL *34102*

Speers REV & MRS T Guthrie JR (Susan Savage)
BMr'51.C.Csn.P'50.UnTheo'53
☎ (603) 284-7770 . . 36 Taylor Rd, Center Sandwich, NH *03227-3129*

Speers REV & MRS Thomas G 3d (Elizabeth M Cromwell)
Mid'86.CtCol'80.Y'87
☎ (410) 448-3173 . . 5116 Wetheredsville Rd, Baltimore, MD *21207*

Speers MR & MRS William S (Donna E Kinney)
Mid'83.Mid'87.Pp.P'79.Mid'84
☎ (302) 378-4205 . . 350 Noxontown Rd, Middletown, DE *19709*

Speese MR & MRS John JR (Margaret C Clark) Pa'48
☎ (912) 635-3049 . . 17 Glynn Av, Jekyll Island, GA *31527*
Apr 15 . . ☎ (706) 896-4371 . . 7066 Speese Dv, Hiawasse, GA *30546*

Speidel MR & MRS Russell F 2d (Sophie C Carpenter) Va'85.Va'89.Va'82
☎ (804) 295-4214 . . 1636 Meadowbrook Heights Rd, Charlottesville,
VA *22901*

Speight MR & MRS Randolph L (June P Danglade) | of ☎ (212)628-1771
Md'48.Rc.Rby.NCar'41 . . . . | 740 Park Av,
MISS June Jacqueline D . . . . | New York, NY
MR Randolph L 2d . . . . | *10021*
MR Craig M P . . . . | ☎ (441) 293-8088
                                    | "Camalot"
                                    | 39 Knapton Estates
                                    | Rd, Smiths Parish
                                    | HS 01, Bermuda

Speir MRS (DR) Betty Ruth (Smith—Betty Ruth Speir) Ala'61.AlaMed'63
☎ (334) 990-9161 . . 21 Magnolia Trace, PO Box 109, Point Clear,
AL *36564*

Speir MRS Lydia P (Elissabide—Lydia M Pratt) | ☎ (212) 288-8771
V'52.Cs.Bm. . . . . | 333 E 68 St,
MR R Wade JR—Wes'87 . . . . | New York, NY
                                    | *10021*

Speller MR & MRS John L (Lydia M Agnew)
BMr'75.Ox'80.Bristol'75.Ox'77
4716 Clifton Av, St Louis, MO *63109*

Spellman MR & MRS James Whitney (Anne W Nairn) CalW'68
☎ (602) 241-9423 . . 333 W Berridge Lane, Phoenix, AZ *85013*

Spence MR & MRS Donald P (Mary N Cross) | ☎ (609) 921-1483
BMr'47.H'47.Cl'55 . . . . | 9 Haslet Av,
MISS Katherine B . . . . | Princeton, NJ *08540*

Spence MRS F Amberg (Frances A Amberg) | ☎ (312) 664-9520
Sth'44.Cas.Cnt. . . . . | 179 E Lake Shore
MR William T JR . . . . | Dv, Chicago, IL
                                    | *60611*

Spencer MR Carlton W—Un.Al.Bost'27
☎ (617) 244-9662 . . 121 Valentine St, West Newton, MA *02165*

Spencer MRS Charles H JR (Beatrice H Marsh)
Sherwood Oaks 271, 100 Norman Dv, Cranberry Township, PA *16066*

Spencer MR & MRS Clayton B (Susan J Fischer) Nu'62.Y'60.Ty'72
☎ (860) 567-8221 . . 219 Chestnut Hill Rd, Litchfield, CT *06759*

Spencer MR & MRS Duncan C (Megan D Rosenfeld) Ant'69.Fb.Y'62 ⚓
☎ (202) 544-4185 . . 643 E Capitol St SE, Washington, DC *20003*

Spencer MR & MRS F Gilman (Isabel C Brannon) | ☎ (212) 629-6120
BMr'62 . . . . | 11 W 30 St,
MISS Amy A—at 3726 School Lane, Drexel Hill, | Apt 12F, New York,
PA *19026* . . . . | NY *10001*
MISS Isabel C . . . . |

Spencer MR & MRS George C (Molly Palmer) Ore'63.Ore'63.Ore'66
☎ (503) 292-2988 . . 4232 SW Greenhills Way, Portland, OR *97221*

Spencer MR & MRS H Allen (Suzanne C Moorhead) SL'62.Syr'93.Cda.Wms'61.Roch'76 . . . . ☎ (716) 442-6161 125 Old Mill Rd, Rochester, NY *14618*
DR Upshur M—Bates'87.Geo'96—at ☎ (617) 899-6163 . . 5709 Stearns Hill Rd, Waltham, MA *02154* . . . .
MR G Parke—Wms'89—at ☎ (212) 727-1266 117 Christopher St, Apt 18, New York, NY *10014* . . . .

Spencer MR & MRS Harold R (Martha J Hamm) . . . . ☎ (540) 347-0225 PO Box 12, Warrenton, VA *20188*
MISS Sarah C—at 108 Graymont Rd, Richmond, VA *23229*. . . . .
MR Hawes C—at 108 Graymont Rd, Richmond, VA *23229*. . . . .

Spencer MR & MRS Henry B 2d (Phillips—Helen M Walker) K.Mt.Cvc.H'62 ☎ (203) 662-0869 . . ''The Greenhouse'' Great Island, Darien, CT *06820*

Spencer MISS Holly . . see E T Miller

Spencer MRS Horatio N JR (Harriet V Edwards) Rcsl. ☎ (561) 231-4319 . . 526 Riomar Dv, Vero Beach, FL *32963*

Spencer DR Jamieson—P'66.Sussex'67.Wash'72 . . . ☎ (314) 961-4122 1725 Redbird Cove, St Louis, MO *63144*
MISS Kate W . . . .
MR Jamieson JR . . . .

Spencer MR & MRS John (Cushing—Natalie L Fell) Bhm.Ri.Mds.P'53 . . . . ☎ (802) 388-2946 PO Box 727, Painter Rd, Middlebury, VT *05753*
MISS Natalie C . . . .

Spencer MR & MRS John M (Diana C Davis) Wheat'60.Ht.Myf.Cl'58 . . . . ☎ (617) 237-3459 19 Ridge Hill Farm Rd, Wellesley, MA *02181*
MISS Kimberly F . . . .

Spencer MRS K Lambart (Karen H Lambart) ColC'66.PugetS'81 ☎ (719) 635-0519 . . 1513 Cheyenne Blvd, Colorado Springs, CO *80906*

Spencer MISS Katherine King (Scott R) . . . . Born at Bernardsville, NJ May 18'95

Spencer MR & MRS Robert A (Anne B Robertson) Ws'66.Ty'64.UnTheo'67.Wash'84 . . . . ☎ (011-41-22) 755-6313 2 chemin Mégard, CH 1290 Versoix, Geneva, Switzerland
MISS Amanda M . . . .
MR Nathaniel R . . . .

Spencer MR & MRS Samuel (Byrne—June Beakes) Mt.Cvc.Cc.Sl.H'32 ☎ (301) 657-8204 . . 5904 Cedar P'kway, Chevy Chase, MD *20815*

Spencer MR Samuel 3d—ColC'92 ☎ (415) 292-6185 . . 2001 Pierce St, Apt 56, San Francisco, CA *94115*

Spencer MR & MRS Scott R (Elizabeth K Ballantine) Gettys'87.Smu'85 ☎ (908) 953-0324 . . 9 Bodnar St, Bernardsville, NJ *07924*

Spencer MISS Shayla (Provost—Shayla Spencer Fine) ☎ (808) 261-1164 . . ''Lanikite'' 1226 Mokulua Dv, Kailua, HI *96734*

Spencer MR & MRS Stephen W (Marjorie L Potts) Un.Srb.Cly.H'47 . . . . ☎ (212) 744-5194 103 E 75 St, New York, NY *10021-2848*
MR Stephen L—Nrr.V'83—at ☎ (212) 688-5706 200 E 66 St, New York, NY *10021* . . . .

Spencer MR William H F—Nrr.Srb.Y'51.Bridgept'63 ☎ (401) 849-7382 . . 1 Janet Terr, Newport, RI *02840*

Sperling MRS Peter R (Lewis—Edwina W Van Winkle) . . . . ☎ (914) 666-9391 PO Box 432, Bedford, NY *10506*
MISS Ridley W . . . .

Sperling MR & MRS Peter R—Rc.Ub.Bgt.H'53.Y'56 ☎ (914) 234-3498 . . 11 Homestead Lane, Bedford, NY *10506*

Sperry MR & MRS G Brooks (Murphy—Margaret E McMahon) SFr'84.Sfy.CalSt'73 ☎ (518) 449-4757 . . 21 Newell Court, Menands, NY *12204*

Sperry MR & MRS Paul S (Beatrice H Mitchell) Y.'78.Cl'80.Sa.Cs.Ty'80.Cl'82 ☎ (212) 427-2022 . . 167 E 94 St, New York, NY *10128*

Sperry MR & MRS Richard S (Nancy E Collins) Bow'76.My.H.Y'68 ☎ (610) 642-7951 . . 14 S Buck Lane, Haverford, PA *19041*

Spettel JUNIORS MISS Sara E . . see MRS E S Richardson JR

Spicer MR & MRS John S (Rebecca S Hanna) Ncd.Dar. . . . . ☎ (301) 845-4719 Johnny-Reb Farm, 10302 Coppermine Rd, Woodsboro, MD *21798*
MR John S JR—at U of Md . . . .

Spiel MR & MRS Robert E JR (Gail R Brown) Occ'75.Ch'77.On.Y'65.Nw'68 ☎ (847) 234-0381 . . 270 E Westleigh Rd, Lake Forest, IL *60045*

Spiess MR & MRS Dominik F (Anne H Wagnière) Laus'86.Laus'85 ☎ (011-41-21) 807-42-81 . . En Chaperon, CH 1164 Buchillon, Switzerland

Spiller MR & MRS Raymond M (La Salvia—Miriam M Britton) PhilaArt'52 ☎ (215) 849-2888 . . ''Belvedere'' 1025 Westview St, Philadelphia, PA *19119*

Spiller MRS Robert E (Wright—Anna H Moss) Fi. ☎ (215) 483-5903 . . Cathedral Village BWL 102, 600 E Cathedral Rd, Philadelphia, PA *19128*

Spilman MRS Edward D (Altizer—Ida R Bumstead) An.Cly.Myf. ☎ (561) 272-9891 . . 2727 N Ocean Blvd, Gulf Stream, FL *33483*

Spink MRS Charles C (Edith S Jenkin) Wash'45.Wash'46.Cy. ☎ (314) 997-0405 . . 9 Log Cabin Dv, St Louis, MO *63124*

Spiro MR & MRS Herbert J (Adler—Marion Ballin) Hn.H'49.H'50.H'53 ☎ (512) 472-5304 . . Towers of Town Lake 4B3, 40 IH35 North, Austin, TX *78701*

Spivy MR & MRS William W (Smith—Ann A Clarke) Nd.Cy.Dc.Wash'49. . . . . ☎ (314) 993-0969 8507 Gannon Av, St Louis, MO *63132*
MR John H Smith 3d—Cw.Mo'91 . . . .

Spoehel MISS Elizabeth Schuyler (Ronald R) . . . . Born at Melbourne, FL Apr 19'96

Spoehel MR & MRS Ronald R (Percy—Deborah E Bell) Van'80.Sam'85.Mt.Ac.Cly.Pa'79.Pa'80 ☎ (407) 777-3122 . . 826 Loggerhead Island Dv, Satellite Beach, FL *32937*

Spofford MR & MRS C Nicholas (Martha F McKown) Bgt.Fic.Y.'56 ☎ (914) 234-7924 . . 472 Bedford Center Rd, Bedford, NY *10506*

Spofford MRS Charles M (Luddy—Sydney R Brewster) CUNY'35.Plg.Myf. ☎ (810) 364-8566 . . 1954 Michigan Av, Marysville, MI *48040*

Spofford MR & MRS Charles McK (Sherin W Knowles) Fic.Vt'88 ☎ (617) 924-7792 . . 9 Gay Rd, Watertown, MA *02172*

Spofford MISS Jennifer B—Vt'92 ☎ (617) 354-4285 . . 24 Chauncy St, Apt 15, Cambridge, MA *02138*

Spofford MR & MRS John L (A Virginia Smythe) OWes'78.Me.Gm.OWes'78 ☎ (610) 254-9288 . . 435 St Davids Av, St Davids, PA *19087*

Spofford MR & MRS John S W (Mélie B Truesdale) | ☎ (914) 234-3477
Ln.Bgt.Fic.Plg.Y.'64.Stan'66 . . . . | 167 Hook Rd,
MISS Daphne B—Br'93 . . . . | Bedford, NY 10506
MR Jeremy S W—at Lynn U . . . . |

Spofford MRS Margaret W (Margaret M Walker) V'26.Fic.Cs.
☎ (212) AT9-7482 . . 1088 Park Av, New York, NY 10128-1132
Spradley MR & MRS James W JR (Frances S Berry) Tenn'79.Van'78
☎ (615) 269-5372 . . 3725 Richland Av, Nashville, TN 37205
Spradling LT & MRS Brock A (Hannah A T Lee) Md'93.USN'93
☎ (360) 598-6995 . . 6004 Gudgeon Av, Apt A, Silverdale, WA 98315
Spragins DR & MRS Melchijah (Betsey Rochester) | 13801 York Rd,
Sth'44.Cw.Mv.JHop'39 . . . . | Cockeysville, MD
MR James S B—Wms'77—at 7 Nightingale | 21030
Court, Lutherville, MD 21093 . . . . |
MR William S—StLaw'80—at 5360 Highline |
Place, Denver, CO 80222 . . . . |

Sprague MR & MRS Carl J (Rockwell—Susan LeR Merrill)
B'gton'64.Mass'86.Lx.
☎ (413) 298-4723 . . 11 Yale Hill, Stockbridge, MA 01262
Sprague MR & MRS Charles G JR
☎ (603) 447-5717 . . Odell Falls Dv, Center Conway, NH 03813
Sprague MR & MRS Charles W (Kearney—Mary P Hamilton)
MaryB'73.Va'74.Rcn.Yn.Y'71.Nu'75
☎ (414) 365-1686 . . 8180 N Green Bay Rd, River Hills, Milwaukee,
WI 53217
Sprague MR & MRS George R (R Lee Thorndike) | ☎ (617) 742-8989
Sm.Chi.H'60.Bost'64 . . . . | 89 Mt Vernon St,
MISS Lucy R—Tul'88—at ☎ (773) 883-0713 | Boston, MA 02108
3170 N Sheridan Rd, Apt 429, Chicago, IL 60657 |
MISS Cynthia N—MtH'94—at 8695 NW 6 Lane, |
Apt 201, Miami, FL 33126 . . . . |
MR Alexander T—Pitzer'91—at |
☎ (617) 965-1515 . . 27 Herrick Rd, |
Newton Center, MA 02159 . . . . |

Sprague MR & MRS Howard B JR (Margaret C | ☎ (508) 927-0315
Ricketson) Cw.H'46 . . . . | 675 Hale St,
MISS Sallie G—Mid'73.Mass'78.Mass'81—at | PO Box 144,
2095 N Shore Rd, Bellingham, WA 98226 . . . . . | Prides Crossing, MA
| 01965-0144
| Feb 15 . .
| ☎ (912) 269-3605
| Cumberland Island,
| PO Box 900,
| Fernandina Beach,
| FL 32035-0900

Sprague MR & MRS J Christopher (Margot A Lyman)
Wheat'78.Mit'85.Bab'78.Mit'89
189 Mystic Valley P'kway, Winchester, MA 01890
Sprague MRS J Hume (Clifford—Jeanette T Hume) Chi.
52 Falmouth Rd, Apt 223, Falmouth, ME 04105
Sprague MR & MRS John A (Dorothy S Whitmarsh)
Br'78.Nu'80.Ln.Ri.Bg.Cly.H.'74.Stan'80 . . of
☎ (212) 288-7080 . . 770 Park Av, New York, NY 10021
☎ (518) 398-5343 . . Conklin Hill Rd, Stanfordville, NY 12581
Sprague MR & MRS John L (Mary Jane Whitney)
Sth'53.Myf.Pn.P'52.Stan'59
☎ (413) 458-4698 . . 175 Bee Hill Rd, Williamstown, MA 01267-2703

Sprague MR & MRS John S (Marianne Litkei) Ts.Buf.G.P.'46
☎ (716) 876-0172 . . 31 Edge Park, Buffalo, NY 14216
Sprague MR & MRS Jonathan D (Mary B Willis) Ga'77.Ga'77
14 Tidewater Way, Savannah, GA 31411-2110
Sprague MR Juan H
☎ (011-45-33) 15-90-97 . . Larsbiornsstraede 15, 1454 Copenhagen,
Denmark
Sprague MRS Julie H (Minot—Talmage—Julie H Sprague)
☎ (561) 833-4944 . . 354 Chilean Av, Apt 2A, Palm Beach, FL 33480
Sprague MRS Penelope A (Penelope Andrews) . . see MRS W E Andrews
Sprague MR & MRS Phineas (Mary L Thomas) BMr'50.Chi.Bow'50
☎ (207) 799-5999 . . Spurwink Farm, 500 Fowler Rd, Cape Elizabeth,
ME 04107-2515
Sprague MRS Robert C JR (Geraldine H Lapham) | ☎ (413) 458-5091
TCU'58.Myf. . . . . | ''Grayling''
MR Michael M . . . . | PO Box 7,
MR Steven W . . . . | Williamstown, MA
| 01267

Sprague MR & MRS Wallace A (Mary L Dull)
Ober'38.Cl'39.Mt.Bg.Plg.Hn.Ober'38.H'39
☎ (201) 379-4869 . . 33 Birch Lane, Short Hills, NJ 07078-3247
Sprague MR & MRS William W 3d (Taryn E Winner) Col'79
15 Bransby Dv, Savannah, GA 31406
Sprague-Smith . . see Smith
Sprayregen MR & MRS Peter H (Lucy P Eshleman) | ☎ (617) 259-0690
Ub.Pa'68 . . . . | Baker Farm,
JUNIORS MR Peter R . . . . | Box 14,
JUNIORS MR Benjamin F . . . . | Lincoln Center, MA
| 01773

Sprecher MR Alexander—Vt'94 . . see MISS N Brown
Sprecher MISS Alexandra—LakeF'91 . . see MISS N Brown
Sprecher DR Armant Grant 3d—Br'89.TJef'94 . . see MISS N Brown
Sprengnether MR Ronald J—StL'67.Mo'84 . . see MRS V B Harris
Spring MR & MRS Herbert A (Katherine H Baker)
Sth'43.Kt.Un.Cho.Pk.It.Wms'43
☎ (216) 991-6286 . . 19300 S Park Blvd, Shaker Heights, OH 44122
Spring MR & MRS Robert E (Cornelia A Beshar)
Sth'78.Cl'85.Kt.Ln.Pr.Wms'74.Duke'77
☎ (212) 734-5929 . . 332 E 74 St, New York, NY 10021
Spring MR & MRS William C (Barbara R Lovejoy) Rol'76.DU'73.Bab'76
☎ (508) 369-6208 . . 1195 Lowell Rd, Concord, MA 01742
Spring MR William P—Kt.Wms'83
☎ (212) 517-6519 . . 404 E 66 St, Apt 8L, New York, NY 10021
Springer MR & MRS Alfred 3d (Pogue—Jean M Mohrman)
☎ (513) 321-7670 . . 3439 Berry Av, Cincinnati, OH 45208
Springs MISS Clare H—Mls'65.Cal'72
☎ (415) 982-1400 . . 1960 Broadway St, San Francisco, CA 94109
Springs MISS E Bleecker—Skd'70.Wes'75.Pa'86
☎ (801) 645-9117 . . PO Box 681814, Park City, UT 84068
Springs MR & MRS Orlando W (Mary Lee Woolsey)
Emory'75.Gv.Md.Hl.Sar.Mv.P'67
☎ (410) 296-2824 . . 1915 Ruxton Rd, Ruxton, MD 21204
Springs MRS Richard A (Kate M Rubin) Pn.
☎ (410) 745-9622 . . Holland Point Farm, 24082 Deep Neck Rd,
PO Box 308, Royal Oak, MD 21662

Springstead MR & MRS Wallace Couts (Cynthia M Howes)
SCal'74.Sdy.SCal'73
☎ (619) 459-3116 . . 6111 Beaumont Av, La Jolla, CA *92037*
Sproul MASTER Charles Farnsworth (George F) . . . . Born at
Princeton, NJ Apr 25'95
Sproul MR & MRS George F (Margaret F Paige) LakeF'86.Ithaca'86
☎ (609) 466-8468 . . 211 Pennington Rocky Hill Rd, Pennington,
NJ *08534*
Spruance MR & MRS W Halsey JR (Samantha McLean)
Ham'87.Fic.Wil.Del'86
☎ (202) 338-4762 . . 1657—31 St NW, Washington, DC *20007*
Spruance MASTER William Halsey 3d (W Halsey JR) . . . . Born Sep 20'95
Spurdle MR & MRS John William JR (Cynthia W Stauffer)
K.Fic.Ln.Stc.Rm.Plg.Wes'59.H'61
☎ (212) 289-4439 . . 1150 Fifth Av, New York, NY *10128*
Spurgeon MR & MRS Edward V R (Patricia T Flynn) | ☎ (203) 655-4794
Dth'53 . . . . | 35 Raiders Lane,
MR Edward V R JR—at ☎ (310) 278-6416 | Darien, CT *06820*
140 S Canon Dv, Apt 206, Beverly Hills, CA
90212 . . . . |
Spurgeon MISS Elizabeth D (Heinrici—Elizabeth D Spurgeon) Hlns'77
☎ (541) 687-0301 . . 2784 Central Blvd, Eugene, OR *97403*
Spurzem MR & MRS Karl R (Louisiana S Foster) Cal'82.Cal'81
☎ (415) 924-6131 . . 73 Lakeside Dv, Corte Madera, CA *94925*
Squibb MR & MRS George R (C Fay Irving) CtCol'37.Mich'33 . . of
☎ (810) 646-5385 . . 3568 Bloomfield Club Dv, Bloomfield Hills,
MI *48301*
☎ (941) 263-4911 . . 110 Wilderness Dv, Apt 129, Naples, FL *34105*
Squiers MR & MRS James D (Virginia M Barrie) Sar.Ncd.Ken'50
☎ (941) 355-0020 . . 4749 Oak Run Dv, Sarasota, FL *34243*
Srodes MRS W Glenn (Jean Henninger) Ws'29.Tc.
Canterbury Place 509, 310 Fisk St, Pittsburgh, PA *15201-1708*
Stabler MR & MRS C Norman 3d (Elizabeth S Finnie) Stan'81.Stan'82
☎ (011-44-1444) 482-420 . . ''West View House'' West View, Lindfield,
West Sussex RH16 2LL, England
Stackelberg MRS Constantine (Gardiner—Garnett Butler)
☎ (202) 667-6520 . . 1673 Columbia Rd NW, Apt 709, Washington,
DC *20009*
Stackpole MR & MRS William (Gregg—Willa Mackey) C.H'49.Cl'52
☎ (609) 896-4985 . . 2705 Main St, Lawrenceville, NJ *08648*
Stackpole MR William JR
☎ (212) 348-2897 . . 1065 Park Av, New York, NY *10128*
Stadler MR & MRS George B (Julia A Carell) Hlns'81.W&L'81.Van'91
☎ (615) 385-0771 . . 1235 Nichol Lane, Nashville, TN *37205*
Staempfli MR & MRS George W (Barbara Dierich) | ☎ (212) 744-6696
Erl'35 . . . . | 40 E 78 St,
MR G Gamble . . . . | New York, NY
| *10021*
Stafford MR & MRS Mark MacLeod (Holly F Cooke) Eliz'tn'82.PacLuth'82
☎ (610) 650-0878 . . 23 Firethorn Dv, Collegeville, PA *19426*
Stafford MRS Robert (Brookfield—Sidney F Bacon)
☎ (516) 286-4028 . . 2793 Montauk H'way, Brookhaven, NY *11719*
Stafford MR & MRS Robert T (Helen Kelley) Mid'35.Bost'38 ⚓
☎ (802) 773-1620 . . RD 1, Box 3954, Rutland, VT *05701*

Stafford DR & MRS Sam 3d (Ann M Webb) | ☎ (803) 884-6759
Char'ton'70.Ncd.Char'ton'68.SCar'71 . . . . | 301 Pitt St,
MISS Adele P . . . . | Mt Pleasant, SC
MISS Ann L . . . . | *29464*
Stagg MR & MRS Eduardo J (Daugherty—Barbara V Roome)
☎ (203) 966-9895 . . 76 Heritage Hill Rd, New Canaan, CT *06840*
Stagg MISS Hilary A—Hlns'85
☎ (508) 257-6943 . . PO Box 867, Siasconset, MA *02564*
Stahl MR & MRS William C (Lurline H Nisbet) | 801 Adrian Dv,
Myf.Pa'42 . . . . | Virginia Beach, VA
MISS Jennifer L . . . . | *23452*
Stahl MR & MRS William W JR (Nancy Ireland) | of ☎ (914)677-8006
Hlns'77.Rc.B.Cly.Ty'74 . . . . | ''Rose Cottage''
JUNIORS MISS Jacqueline McN . . . . | PO Box 1031,
| Millbrook, NY
| *12545*
| ☎ (212) 628-1804
| 170 E 78 St,
| New York, NY
| *10021*
Stahlgren MRS LeRoy H (Wray—Anita D Elliott) . . . . Died Nov 1'95
Stahlgren DR LeRoy H—Gm.Pa'48
☎ (303) 777-3302 . . 377 Race Court, Denver, CO *80206*
Stahr MR & MRS Elvis J JR (Dorothy H Berkfield) | ☎ (203) 869-8166
Plg.An.Sar.Ky'36.Ox'39 . . . . | 16 Martin Dale N,
MR Bradford L . . . . | Greenwich, CT
| *06830-4719*
Staley MR & MRS David R (Brynne A Montgomery) Cal'80.Cal'83
☎ (510) 834-5934 . . 4107 Lake Shore Av, Oakland, CA *94610*
Stallings MR & MRS John H (Jeanne S Reynolds) Pa'37
☎ (215) CH2-0176 . . 7660 St Martin's Lane, Philadelphia, PA *19118*
Stallwort MR & MRS F Dennis JR (Dianne Owens) . . of
☎ (334) 564-2114 . . PO Box 38, Beatrice, AL *36425*
☎ (334) 928-3838 . . 7 Molokai Lane, Fairhope, AL *36532*
Stallworth MR Nicholas Jack—At.LSU'42
☎ (334) 432-1878 . . 1604 Springhill Av, Mobile, AL *36604*
Stalter MRS David E (Mary L H Graves) . . . . Died Apr 16'96
Stalter MR David E—Rv.Cr'35 . . . . | ☎ (206) 322-0963
MR David E 4th—Rv. . . . . | 1235—39 Av E,
| Seattle, WA *98112*
Stamell MR & MRS Neal A (L Trimble Hoblitzelle) Tufts'80.Tufts'81
☎ (847) 475-5544 . . 1422 Elmwood Av, Evanston, IL *60201-4308*
Stamm MRS John D (Sara B Babbitt) Cly.Ncd.Myf . . .of
☎ (212) 794-2780 . . 875 Park Av, New York, NY *10021*
☎ (516) 537-5124 . . 1 Montauk H'way, PO Box 1113, Bridgehampton,
NY *11932*
Stamp LADY (Frances D Bosworth) . . . . | ☎ (011-44-171)
HON J Richard—at ☎ (011-44-171) 435-6207 | 435-1625
11 Lymington Rd, Apt B, London NW6 1HX, | 12 Crediton Hill,
England . . . . | London NW6 1HP,
| England
Standish MRS Pery R C (Wallace—Joan H Lloyd) Cly.
☎ (011-44-171) 720-3175 . . 14 Albert Bridge Rd, Apt B,
London SW11 4PY, England
Standley MR & MRS Burgess P (Caroline J Dabney)
V'52.Chi.Ncd.Dth'49.H'80
☎ (508) 359-8800 . . 75 Elm St, Medfield, MA *02052*

Staneluis MR & MRS James M (Kim Ely Peck) ☎ (419) 893-8432
Bost'69.Bost'71.Day'63.Cwr'66. . . . . 611 W Harrison St,
MR Christian N . . . . Maumee, OH *43537*

Stanger MRS John H (Georgena Wetherill) ☎ (401) 423-2069
Me.Ac.Ncd. . . . . PO Box 408,
MISS Jean H (Metcalfe—Jean H Stanger) . . . . . . Jamestown, RI *02835*

Staniford MR & MRS Foye F JR (Williams—Ellen W ☎ (212) RE4-0634
Breed) Srr.Va'53 . . . . 901 Lexington Av,
MR William M—USMC. . . . . at New York, NY
MISS Louise B Williams—at *10021*
752 West End Av, New York, NY *10025*. . . .

Staniford MR & MRS Foye McK (Melissa T Collier) Woos'91.Woos'91
☎ (817) 763-8855 . . 3812 Potomac Av, Ft Worth, TX *76107*

Staniford MRS Robert H JR (Eleanor C Wilson) ☎ (516) 759-9609
Ri.Pr.Lic. . . . . Peacock Point,
MISS Winifred C . . . . PO Box 584,
MR Daniel A . . . . Locust Valley, NY *11560*

Staniland MR William G 3d—ErieTech'64
☎ (716) 839-2732 . . 115 Parkwood Dv, Snyder, NY *14226*

Stanley MR & MRS Edward L (Mary E Gaylord) Sg.Ph.Wms'37
☎ (215) 984-8374 . . Cathedral Village K001, 600 E Cathedral Rd,
Philadelphia, PA *19128*

Stanley MR Edwin J C . . see R L Prosser

Stanley MISS Elizabeth A . . see MRS F P Mitchell

Stanley MISS (DR) Elizabeth K—Aht'82.Pa'93
☎ (508) 476-2724 . . 803 NW Main St, Douglas, MA *01516*

Stanley MISS (DR) Emily H—Y'84.ArizSt'93
☎ (405) 372-5743 . . 2108 N Husband St, Stillwater, OK *74075*

Stanley MR Ethan T—Nw'93 . . see P Laffoon

Stanley MR & MRS Frank L (Elizabeth C Kingsley) Y'53.H'58
☎ (860) 693-2074 . . 150 Barbourtown Rd, Collinsville, CT *06022*

Stanley MR & MRS Harlan F (Margaret K Carton) ☎ (847) 501-4323
Tufts'74.Ill'80.Ih.Fy.Wes'71.Ch'74 . . . . 156 Chestnut St,
JUNIORS MISS Melinda C . . . . Winnetka, IL *60093*
JUNIORS MR Bradford C—at Deerfield . . . .

Stanley MR & MRS John B (Patricia A Houdry) ☎ (610) 687-5346
Ithaca'73.Me.Penn'73. . . . . 677 Knox Rd,
MISS Nina P . . . . Strafford, PA *19087*
MR Spencer J—at U of Richmond . . . .

Stanley MR & MRS Jonathan L (Deborah L Meagher) Ty'79.Ty'79.Cl'84
323 Pinebrook Rd, Bedford, NY *10506*

Stanley MR Joseph W—Cvc.Mt.An.Rv.Ll.Cw.H'35 . ☎ (202) 333-3636
MISS Florence C—Dll. . . . . 4600 Reservoir Rd
NW, Washington,
DC *20007-1917*

Stanley MRS Julian Carr (Margaret M Schniewind) Pr.
88 Notch Hill Rd, Apt 262, North Branford, CT *06471-1846*

Stanley MR & MRS Justin A (Helen L Fletcher) Wells'34.Cho.Ih.Dth'33
☎ (847) 251-6297 . . 1630 Sheridan Rd, Apt 5A, Wilmette, IL *60091*

Stanley MISS Lindsay B . . see R L Prosser

Stanley MR & MRS Peter G (Susan P Hine) ☎ (215) 247-9727
Rc.Sg.Dick'66 . . . . 610 W Gatehouse
MISS Susannah P . . . . Lane, Philadelphia,
MISS Elizabeth G . . . . PA *19118*

Stanley MISS Torrey M—Sth'81.A.
☎ (210) 826-7749 . . 900 Burr Rd, San Antonio, TX *78209*

Stanton MRS Dixon La F (H Barbara Hadley) V'57.Cl'64.Cly.Un.
☎ (212) 288-6004 . . 133 E 64 St, New York, NY *10021*

Stanton MR & MRS Gordon R (Catherine Duer Brown)
Colby'86.Cly.Y'82.Nu'92
☎ (212) 249-6160 . . 230 E 73 St, New York, NY *10021*

Stanton MR & MRS Henry B (Mitchell—Elizabeth Monroe) Sb.H'44
☎ (508) 356-1939 . . 7 Ipswich Woods Dv, Ipswich, MA *01938*

Stanton MRS L Lee (Helen P La Fétra) Cly.
☎ (212) 988-0679 . . 129 E 69 St, New York, NY *10021*

Stanton MR & MRS L Lee 3d (Elizabeth R Rose) ☎ (206) 725-4272
Skd'75.Cl'78.Y'74.Cl'78 2659 Cascadia Av S,
JUNIORS MISS Penelope R . . . . Seattle, WA *98144*

Stanton MR & MRS Louis L JR (Brattnäs—Berit E ☎ (212) BU8-7046
Rask) Plg.Cc.Lic.Y'50.Va'55 . . . . 116 E 68 St,
MR Fredrik S . . . . New York, NY *10021*

Stanton MR & MRS Myron E (Ann C Dawson) ☎ (941) 992-0579
Ill'56.Ch'61 . . . . 27125 Kindlewood
MISS Sarah A . . . . Lane,
MISS Margaret A . . . . Bonita Springs, FL
MR John R *33923*

Stanton MR & MRS Peter W (Judith A Crawford) ☎ (617) 891-7465
Cal'60.Stan'62.H'60.Stan'62 . . . . 17 Fields Pond Rd,
MISS Cornelia C . . . . Weston, MA *02193*
MR Peter W JR . . . .

Stanton MRS Phoebe R (Phoebe Rentschler) V'50.Cly.
☎ (212) 876-1751 . . 1021 Park Av, New York, NY *10028*

Stanton DR & MRS Vincent P JR (Genevieve C Fisher)
Pa'77.Ox'79.Mit'77.Pa'81
☎ (617) 489-6459 . . 32 Royal Rd, Belmont, MA *02178*

Stanwood MR & MRS Charles F (Buell—Eleanor Little) Bow'32.Ox'34
☎ (603) 224-6905 . . 149 East Side Dv, Box 262, Apt 27E, Concord,
NH *03301*

Staples MRS Charles R (Farnell—Margaret R Carpenter)
☎ (716) 882-4649 . . 1088 Delaware Av, Buffalo, NY *14209*

Starbuck MR & MRS John W (Margaret Easton) Yn.Y'39
☎ (203) 655-9211 . . 7 Parson's Walk, Darien, CT *06820*

Stark MR & MRS Charles B JR (Frances W Ames) ☎ (415) 387-8216
Fr.Rut'59.Stan'65 . . . . 52 Jordan Av,
MISS Marianna A—Cal'93 . . . . San Francisco, CA
MISS Frances W—at U of So Cal *94118*

Stark MR Frederic W 2d . . . . Died Oct 17'94

Stark MR & MRS J Edward JR (Agnes A Gordon) ☎ (901) 458-2354
Va'51.CTech'62 . . . . 3598 Cowden Av,
MR Gordon Metcalf—Col'91 . . . . Memphis, TN *38111*

Stark MR & MRS Louis B (Edith A Monks) Col'30 . . ☎ (516) 749-0504
MR Louis J . . . . 20 Clinton Av,
MR Charles H . . . . Shelter Island
Heights, NY *11965*

Stark MRS Nora R (Nora Robinson)
☎ (520) 795-7570 . . 3892 N Paseo de Las Canchas, Tucson, AZ *85716*

Starkey MISS Alison B (George W B) . . . . Married at Norfolk, CT
Morosovsky MR Matthew A (late Bohdan) . . . . Jun 29'96

Starkey MR & MRS Charles P (Sandra S Gordon) Myf.Cw.Cl'72.Cal'75
☎ (503) 224-9871 . . 3841 SW Mt Adams Dv, Portland, OR *97201*

Starkey MR & MRS Craig Alvah (Dorothy L Alderson)
Scripps'57.Sdy.CalW'59.AGSIM'60.USInt'l'71
☎ (619) 756-2692 . . PO Box 1122, Rancho Santa Fe, CA *92067*
Starkey MRS Earle J (Ambler—Eleanor Nash) V'29.Cs.Myf.Cda . . .of
☎ (561) 276-0586 . . Harbour's Edge 654, 401 E Linton Blvd,
Delray Beach, FL *33483*
☎ (212) 289-3626 . . 1075 Park Av, New York, NY *10128*
Starkey DR & MRS George W B (Lois Van A MacMurray)
BMr'46.Tv.Cy.Ty'39.H.'43
☎ (617) 277-3760 . . 87 Fairmount St, Brookline, MA *02146*
Starr MISS Charlotte C . . . . Died Mch 28'96
Starr MR Donald Carter (Polly R Thayer) Chi.Csn . . .
☎ (617) 266-1591 . . 198 Beacon St, Boston, MA *02116*
☎ (617) 749-1684 . . 140 Turkey Hill Lane, Hingham, MA *02043*
Starr MR & MRS Edward 3d (Antoinette Nolan)
Err.Eyc.Gm.Cts.Me.Cw.Y'45
☎ (610) 525-1063 . . 300 Landover Rd, Bryn Mawr, PA *19010*
Starr MRS George R 3d (H Paige Milliken) . . . . Married at Duxbury, MA
Vinal MR Arthur H JR (late Arthur H) . . . . Jly 12'96
Starr MRS H Danforth (L Kathryn Siedenburg) Cly.
☎ (203) 869-1867 . . 14 Ft Hills Lane, Greenwich, CT *06831*

Starr MR & MRS Harold P (Emily W Churchman) Rdc'59.Y'54.H'61	☎ (215) AD3-4224 8411 Stenton Av, Philadelphia, PA *19150-3433*
MR Isaac B	
Starr MR & MRS I Tatnall 2d (Mary M Detweiler) Van'62.Ph.Ac.Y'61.Pa'67	☎ (215) 836-7268 877 Andorra Rd, Lafayette Hill, PA *19444*
MISS Emily L—Skd'90	
MISS Elise L—Skd'93	
MR William F—at 34232 Colorado Lake Dv, Corvallis, OR *97333*	

Starr MR & MRS Louis (Abbey T Kissel) Unn.Cly.
☎ (908) 234-0035 . . 830 Holland Rd, Far Hills, NJ *07931*
Starr MRS Martha H (Lee—Martha T Houghton) V'50
☎ (202) 966-4340 . . 3500 Newark St NW, Washington, DC *20016-3168*
Starr MR & MRS Michael M (Clarice M C Rote)
☎ (268) 462-4457 . . PO Box 45, St John's, Antigua
Starr MRS Nathan C (Nina Howell) Bnd'26
☎ (212) 879-8756 . . 333 E 68 St, New York, NY *10021*
Starr MR & MRS Ogden P (Patricia Morrill)
☎ (268) 460-4165 . . Mill Reef Club, Antigua
Starr MR Ogden P JR—Pratt'78
☎ (860) 350-6443 . . PO Box 55, Sherman, CT *06784*
Starr MR & MRS Ralph T (Borie—Joan Gilbert) Sg.Y'50
☎ (215) 247-2298 . . 18 Waterman Av, Philadelphia, PA *19118*
Starr MRS Theodore D (Mackey—Gloria Willard Drew)
☎ (561) 832-4996 . . Villa del Lago 3B, 1617 N Flagler Dv,
West Palm Beach, FL *33407*
Starring MR & MRS Mason B 3d (Nancy B Donaldson) . . of
☎ (603) 431-2327 . . Tidewatch 9, 579 Sagamore Av, Portsmouth,
NH *03801-5567*
☎ (268) 460-4127 . . ''On the Rocks'' Mill Reef Club, Antigua
Stason MR E Blythe JR—An.Mich'46.Mich'47.Mich'56.H'57
☎ (815) 758-8902 . . 6190 W Twombley Rd, De Kalb, IL *60115*
Statter MR & MRS Humphrey (Lowell—Julia E Brokaw)
Un.Plg.Ht.Cly.Cda.H'29
☎ (212) 838-2414 . . 521 Park Av, New York, NY *10021*

Staub MR & MRS E Norman (Mary Ann Dilley) Ws'37.Cho.Ih.P'37.H'39
☎ (847) 835-3809 . . 135 Sheridan Rd, Winnetka, IL *60093*
Staub MR & MRS John H 2d (Faith Hussey) Geo'51
☎ (860) 567-5250 . . ''Et Cetera'' PO Box 655, Wolcott St, Litchfield,
CT *06759*
Staub MR John H 3d—Cw.Va'74 . . of
☎ (212) 644-3510 . . 721 Fifth Av, Apt 46H, New York, NY *10022*
☎ (215) 598-7072 . . ''Boxwood'' 62 Thompson Mill Rd, Wrightstown,
PA *18940*

Stauffer MR & MRS Charles R JR (Susan A Dripps) Rc.Pc.Sg.Ac.W&J'67	☎ (215) 247-6035 100 W Mermaid Lane, Philadelphia, PA *19118*
MR C Winthrop—Pc.Rut'89	
Stauffer MR & MRS James W (Sherryn E Kenworthy) Bentley'74	☎ (804) 285-4360 6612 Westham Station Rd, Richmond, VA *23229*
MR Andrew L	
JUNIORS MISS Shapley S—at St Catherine's	

Stauffer MR & MRS John C (Cynthia J Learn) Leh'87.P'84
☎ (914) 834-9462 . . 8 Summit Av, Larchmont, NY *10538*

Stauffer MR & MRS John E (Valerie V Brown) Ws'56.K.Pn.P'54	of ☎ (203)869-7451 6 Pecksland Rd, Greenwich, CT *06831*
MR Peter E—at Duke	☎ (802) 297-1971 Middle Ridge Rd, Stratton Mountain, VT *05155*

Stauffer MRS John H (von Reischach—Eunice Bennett)
Ws'28.Ox'30.Cly.Dar.Ncd.Cda.
☎ (212) 737-4909 . . 190 E 72 St, Apt 19A, New York, NY *10021-4370*
Stautberg MR & MRS Aubrey Theodore JR (Susan Berwind Schiffer)
Wheat'67.GeoW'69.Un.Nrr.Srb.Ct.Cly.StJ.Ncd.Tex'68. Tex'72
☎ (212) 996-4449 . . 17 E 89 St, New York, NY *10128*

Stayman DR Joseph W JR—Pa'38.Jef'42 . . . . MISS M Wendy—Box 33, Haydenville, MA *01039*	☎ (864) 457-4635 322 Hearthstone Ridge, Landrum, SC *29356*

Steadman MR & MRS Charles W (Artini—Consuelo Matthews)
Rcn.Uncl.Evg.Hn.Neb'35.H'38 . . of
☎ (561) 833-2487 . . 425 Worth Av, Apt 3E, Palm Beach, FL *33480*
☎ (202) 333-1770 . . 700 New Hampshire Av NW, Apt 1202,
Washington, DC *20037*
Stearns MR & MRS David G (Carol M Dwyer) Wheat'62.Cl'56
☎ (860) 355-9028 . . 135 Davenport Rd, Washington, CT *06793*
Stearns MR & MRS James B (Hester Hewlett)
☎ (561) 276-4645 . . 1101 Vista Del Mar, Delray Beach, FL *33483*

Stearns MR & MRS James P JR (Margaret Byard) Sth'57.Csn.H'54.Mich'59	☎ (860) 927-1320 PO Box 2006, Kent, CT *06757*
MISS Katherine D—Ty'91	
Stearns MR & MRS John P (Winifred C Anthony) Mid'49.Dth'49.H'52	☎ (603) 643-8242 5 Dorrance Place, Hanover, NH *03755*
MR Malcolm K—Bab'81—at 4057 Sussex Av, Lake Worth, FL *33461*	
MR J Anthony—Dth'86—at 3821 Everett Av, Oakland, CA *94602*	

Stearns MR & MRS Peter C (Cordelia P Dunlaevy) Pr.Ri.Chr.Ncd.Ne.Y'56 . . . . of ☎ (307)733-8090
MR John C—Va'85 . . . . 3465 Arrowleaf Lane, E4, Jackson, WY *83001*
☎ (212) 249-3959
785 Park Av, New York, NY *10021*

Stearns MRS Russell B (Ryan—Andrée Beauchamp) Cy.Sm.D.Chi.
50 Haven St, Dedham, MA *02026*

Steavenson MR & MRS David H M J (Foshay—Wendell E Miller) B. . . . . ☎ (011-44-181) 960-9172
MISS M Wendell E—Camb'92—at 23 Bassett Rd, London W10 6LA, England
☎ (212) 614-0666 . . 245 E 10 St, New York, NY *10009* . . . .
MR D H Michael McL—at ☎ (212) 614-0666 245 E 10 St, New York, NY *10009* . . . .
MR Alexander M H . . . .

Stebbins MRS Frederick C (Wainwright—Helen Rae) Swb'37.Dar.
☎ (412) 741-3859 . . 610 Poia Place, Sewickley, PA *15143-1047*

Stebbins MRS H Lyman (Madeleine Froelicher)
☎ (914) 235-8962 . . 40 Oxford Rd, New Rochelle, NY *10804*

Stebbins MR & MRS James F (Cynthia R Rossbach) B.Srr.Rby.Au.Pr.L.Vca.Wk.Lic.Rv.Ll.Cly.Ty'54
☎ (516) 921-5028 . . White Oak Farm, Box 1792, Rte 106, Muttontown, NY *11791*

Stebbins MRS James H (Williams—Loudon—Beatrice C Cobb) StJ.
☎ (904) 477-1206 . . 7461 Baywood Lane, Pensacola, FL *32504-6700*

Stebbins MR & MRS John B (Lisa Carney) Sc.LakeF'67 . . . . ☎ (312) 751-1844
JUNIORS MISS Meredith P . . . . 1855 N Howe St, Chicago, IL *60614*

Stebbins MR & MRS Morgan (Alison Morgan Henning) Sth'66.Nu'72 . . . . ☎ (401) 273-1563
MR Rowland—Ty'95 . . . . 109A Benefit St, Providence, RI
JUNIORS MR Cameron D *02903*

Stebbins MR Richard R—AmU'84
☎ (703) 892-9026 . . 1200 S Courthouse Rd, Arlington, VA *22204*

Stebbins MRS Rowland (Josephine F Small) Cly.Un.
☎ (212) 737-5965 . . 955 Lexington Av, New York, NY *10021*

Stebbins MR & MRS Rowland 3d (Dick—Carla M Cole) K.Plg.Y'59.H'62
☎ (607) 936-8952 . . 1 North Rd, Corning, NY *14830*

Stedman MR & MRS Derek C (Stahlgren—Amory H Zantzinger) Br'55.Cl'67
☎ (617) 659-0545 . . "Heartstone" 253 River St, Norwell, MA *02061*

Stedman MR & MRS Theodore W (McDonell—Patricia Hallowell) Fic.Fiy.Cly.H'33
☎ (860) 677-9083 . . 30 Mountain Rd, Farmington, CT *06032*

Stedman MR & MRS William Preston (McNeill—K Leslie Clark) Pac'75.TexC'44.Roch'53 . . . . ☎ (310) 694-5022
MISS Leslie C McNeill . . . . 731 Avocado Crest Rd, La Habra Heights, CA *90631*

Steeble MISS L Maris—Ncd.
☎ (415) 961-5209 . . 2280 Latham St, Apt 14, Mountain View, CA *94040*

Steeger MRS Henry 4th (Betsey S Brown) Ws'57.Cl'58 . . . . ☎ (212) 427-5507
MISS Marie S . . . . 1623 Third Av, New York, NY *10128*

Steel MR Alfred . . . . Died at Philadelphia, PA Feb 28'96

Steel MRS Alfred (Nancy McL Boyd) Sg.Pc.Ac.Ncd.
☎ (215) 283-7168 . . 113 Foulkeways, Sumneytown Pike, Gwynedd, PA *19436-1018*

Steel MR & MRS Alfred JR (Hannah D Butler) Ty'64 . ☎ (860) 521-3557
MISS Loretta D—Bow'95 . . . . 147 Stoner Dv,
MISS Amy H—at Bowdoin . . . . West Hartford, CT *06107*

Steel MR & MRS Francis P (Sinkler—Nina Knowles) R.Pc.Ph.Cry.Il.Nrr.Cw.Ac.Cda.Y'33 . . of
☎ (215) 247-0105 . . 201 W Evergreen Av, Apt 710, Philadelphia, PA *19118*
☎ (401) 253-8490 . . "Lee Shore" 24 Monkey Wrench Lane, PO Box 108, Bristol, RI *02809*

Steel MR & MRS Francis P JR (Elizabeth W Flint) Del'82.Pc.Cry.Y'81
☎ (215) 247-5564 . . 8005 Navajo St, Philadelphia, PA *19118*

Steele MR & MRS Crittenden P (Ridder—Mary L Hoyt) Wash'37
☎ (206) 453-1237 . . 101—101 Av SE, Apt 104B, Bellevue, WA *98004*

Steele DR & MRS David V Q (R Lorraine Harrison) Y'47 . . . . of ☎ (814)834-6440
MR David V Q JR—in St Thomas, VI . . . . 638 Sherry Rd, St Marys, PA *15857*
MR William S 3d . . . . ☎ (412) 593-7803
MR Charles W . . . . Pike Run Country Club, Jones Mills, PA *15646*

Steele MR & MRS Edward C (Joan Markey) Man'vl'49.B.Ng.So.Evg.Cly.Geo'47 . . . . ☎ (561) 546-2200
MR Edward L—at Phoenix, AZ . . . . 196 Gomez Rd, Hobe Sound, FL *33455*

Steele MR & MRS John F JR (Jeanine E Mullen) MtStJ'79.Rol'75.Xav'84
☎ (513) 321-9846 . . 3522 Principio Av, Cincinnati, OH *45208*

Steele MR & MRS Kilman (Carol L Knowles) Ec. . . . ☎ (508) 526-1339
MR Lockhart—Br'96 . . . . 22 Sea St,
JUNIORS MR George F—at U of Colo Boulder . . . Manchester, MA *01944*

Steele MR & MRS Rodney R (Minter—Frances M Blair) Htdon'62.Dar.
☎ (334) 265-0367 . . 1227 Magnolia Curve, Montgomery, AL *36106*

Steele MR & MRS Roger D (Linda M Lucas) Swb'75.Va'74
☎ (703) 922-3733 . . 1740 Roanoke Rd, Daleville, VA *24083*

Steele MR & MRS William Alexander (Saundra J Rucker) NCar'71 . . . . ☎ (615) 370-9006
JUNIORS MISS Britt G . . . . "Owl's Hill" 565 Beech Creek Rd, Brentwood, TN *37027*

Steen MR & MRS John T JR (Ida L Clement) TyU'74.A.P'71 . . . . ☎ (210) 824-7999
JUNIORS MISS Ida L—at St Mary's Hall . . . . 207 Ridgemont Av,
JUNIORS MR John T 3d—at Deerfield . . . . San Antonio, TX *78209-5431*

Steeper MRS Richard B (Poth—Wayne Hansell) JHop'73
☎ (410) 825-2427 . . 7 Ruxview Court, Apt 201, Baltimore, MD *21204*

Steere MR & MRS Bruce M (Harper—Anne MacC S Bullivant) Smu'78.Smu'85.BtP.Evg.Ny.Chi.Y'42.H'43
☎ (561) 842-2512 . . "Tahiti" 1177 N Lake Way, Palm Beach, FL *33480*

Steere MR & MRS David T (Ewing—Margaret de V Lawson) Ncd.Wms'40 . . . . | ☎ (610) MO4-6779
MR Andrew de V . . . . | 310 Berkeley Rd, Merion, PA *19066*

Steers MR & MRS Charles R C JR (Margaret L Hamilton) Ncd.
☎ (914) 967-1078 . . 12 Boxwood Lane, Rye, NY *10580*

Steers MR & MRS Charles R C 3d (Shawn Holmes) Rol'84.VillaN'73
☎ (914) 967-5204 . . 55 Glendale Av, Rye, NY *10580*

Steers MR & MRS Henry 2d (Martha A Whitney) . . . | ☎ (912) 598-0671
MR Henry 3d . . . . | 36 Wiley Bottom Rd, Skidway Island, Savannah, GA *31411*

Steers MR & MRS J Rich JR (Patricia K McGrath) Y'87.Cly.P'48
☎ (212) 794-1421 . . 117 E 72 St, New York, NY *10021*

Steers MR & MRS John C (Claudia A Peaquin) McG'53.Ford'49
☎ (203) 531-9330 . . 200 Byram Shore Rd, Greenwich, CT *06830*

Steers MRS Judith (Judith Harvey) Pr.
☎ (516) 626-1038 . . 70 Wheatley Rd, Brookville, NY *11545*

Steers MR & MRS William M (Diana S Walker) Ithaca'79.Man'vl'79 . . . . | ☎ (914) 967-6631
JUNIORS MISS Caroline G . . . . | 14 Boxwood Lane, Rye, NY *10580*

Steever MR Edgar Z 4th—Y'36 . . . . | ☎ (610) 687-3376
MR Theodore B—Cr'66 . . . . | 317 Dorset Rd, Devon, PA *19333*

Steever MR N Beaumont—Syr'70
☎ (401) 466-8843 . . ''Cielo'' 781 Lakeside Dv, Box 1281, Block Island, RI *02807*

Steever DR Sanford B—Cr'74.Ch'79.Ch'83
☎ (203) 966-9149 . . ''Boomerang'' 724 Old Stamford Rd, New Canaan, CT *06840*

Stefani MR & MRS Jeffrey J (Emily E Todd) Stph'79.Cda.Purd'79
☎ (513) 624-7449 . . 5926 Lengwood Dv, Cincinnati, OH *45244*

Steffan MR & MRS Andrew P (Patricia V Andrews) Sth'60.Un.Mds.P'59.H'61 . . . . | ☎ (212) 249-7530
MR Alexander P—F&M'93 . . . . | 215 E 72 St, New York, NY *10021*

Steffens MR George V—Il.
5440 Magnolia Grove, Memphis, TN *38119*

Steffens MR & MRS George V 3d (Virginia G Golden) . . . . | ☎ (901) 761-1819
JUNIORS MR George V 4th . . . . | 418 Avon Woods Cove, Memphis, TN
JUNIORS MR Andrew G . . . . | *38117*

Stege MR & MRS John B (Lelia S Taylor) Pa'70.IllWes'70
☎ (970) 925-2761 . . 830 Cemetery Lane, Aspen, CO *81611*

Stehli MISS Emma Huntington (g—Peter H Stehli) . . . . . . | Born Feb 1'96

Stehli MR & MRS Peter H (Manly—Annabel W Stearns) V'61.Y'55 . . . . | ☎ (203) 227-5468
MR Mark W—at U of Vt . . . . | 7 Northgate, Westport, CT *06880*
JUNIORS MISS Sarah S—at St Paul's

Stehlin MRS Morton (Jones—Elizabeth G Morton) Ncd.
☎ (404) 261-7125 . . 2820 Peachtree Rd NW, Apt 1313, Atlanta, GA *30305*

Steiger MR & MRS Frederick M (Martha S Watkins) Wash'79 . . . . | ☎ (618) 288-5360
JUNIORS MR Alexander M . . . . | 100 Lakewood Dv, Glen Carbon, IL *62034*

Steigerwalt MRS John L (Hancock—Suzanne W Fuguet) Me.Ac.Ncd.
☎ (610) 525-8055 . . 64 Middle Rd, Bryn Mawr, PA *19010*

Stein MR & MRS Charles F 3d (Ilse Ann Farinholt) Md'60.SCal'67.Cy.Gi.Cw.Cc.Sar.Wt.Rv.Mv. P'55.Va'60 ⚓ . . . . | ☎ (410) 437-8610
MISS Laura H—Van'92.Gi.Cc. . . . . | ''Bay Meadows'' PO Box 206, Gibson Island, MD
MR Charles F 4th—Gi.Cc.Dick'94 . . . . | *21056*

Stein MR & MRS Julian S JR (Schwab—Emory B Phillips) H'41 . . . . | ☎ (410) 775-2587
MISS Sarah E . . . . | 205 Hoff Rd, Union Bridge, MD *21791*

Steinbreder MRS Harry J (Cynthia A Means) . . . . | ☎ (203) 259-5057
MISS Gillett—at ☎ (415) 563-5299 | 931 Mine Hill Rd, Fairfield, CT *06430*
2025 Broderick St, Apt 1, San Francisco, CA *94115* . . . .
MISS Sarah C—at ☎ (415) 474-8134
1830 Beach St, San Francisco, CA *94123* . . . . .

Steinert MR Robert S—Dth'49 . . . . | ☎ (310) 498-3000
MISS Lucy P C—Cal'85 . . . . | 5250 Los Flores St, Long Beach, CA
MISS Cornelia A—at ☎ (508) 768-6110 | *90815*
9 Harlow St, Essex, MA *01929* . . . .

Steinmetz MRS Judith C (Judith J Chapman) Hlns'63.Fmy. . . . . | PO Box 2301, Mill Valley, CA
MISS Melinda—at ☎ (202) 224-3121 | *94942*
308—2 St SE, Apt 3, Washington, DC *20003* . .

Steinmetz MRS & MRS Robert C (Louise W Yeomans) Cr'59 . . . . | Mermaid Beach Club 218,
MR Douglas C . . . . | PO Box WK250, Warwick WK BX, Bermuda

Steinmetz MR William Q—Hn.Cr'53.H'67 . . . . . . | ☎ (415) 383-7167
MR Robert . . . . | 610 Wanda Lane, Mill Valley, CA
MR James . . . . | *94941*
JUNIORS MISS Liana . . . .

Steinway MR & MRS Frederick (Mary K Castle) Rdc'46.Csn.Cl'42.H'47 . . . . | ☎ (413) 549-5438
MR Frederick E—Nu'74 . . . . | 197 Amity St, Amherst, MA
MR Robert C—at 170 Juniper Heights Av, | *01002-2202*
Golden, CO *80403* . . . .

Stemberg MR & MRS Thomas G (Hamilton—Zarins —Dola S Davis) V'74.Pa'H.'71.H'73 . . . . . . | ☎ (617) 227-5293
JUNIORS MR Rylan Hamilton . . . . | 5 Louisburg Square, Boston, MA *02108*

Stemmler MRS Sandra H (Sandra Humphreys) . . . . | ☎ (314) 993-6559
MR George L 3d—at 7719 Lile Av, St Louis, MO | 9715 Conway Rd, St Louis, MO *63124*
63117 . . . .
JUNIORS MR Michael P . . . .

Stenbeck MR & MRS Jan H (Scott—Merrill MacLeod) Pr.Ri.Upsala'66.H'70 . . . . | ☎ (516) 671-8910
MISS Cristina M . . . . | Mayville Farm, 867 Cedar Swamp Rd, Old Brookville, NY
JUNIORS MISS Sophie M—at St Andrew's . . . . . | *11545*
JUNIORS MR Hugo E—at Episcopal . . . .

Stengel MR & MRS Geoffrey (M Louise Roberts) Me.Gm.Cts.P'37.Pa'40
☎ (610) 645-8741 . . 1400 Waverly Rd, Villa 2, Gladwyne, PA *19035*

Stengel MR & MRS Geoffrey JR (Alice L Taylor) Pa'66.Me.Gm.P'65 . . . . | 460 Glyn Wynne Rd, Haverford, PA
MISS Whitney R—Va'93 . . . . | *19041-1748*
MR Geoffrey 3d—P'90 . . . .

Stenson MRS Julia Butler (Julia M Butler). . of
☎ (216) 591-9343 . . 3791-3 Lander Rd, Orange Village, OH *44022*
☎ (540) 839-5010 . . Deepwood Lane, North Ridge, Hot Springs,
VA *24445*
Stent MRS Ferdinand R (Nancy S Couch)
☎ (415) 921-7543 . . 1860 Jackson St, San Francisco, CA *94109*
Stent MR & MRS Ferdinand T (Margaret R De Bord) Bur.Y'61.H'68 . . of
☎ (770) 491-1297 . . 1846 Chartwell Trace, Stone Mountain, GA *30087*
8200 Royal St E, Park City, UT *84060*
Stent MR James P—Cal'68
☎ (011-66-2) 679-4837 . . 7 Soi Prapinij, Thungmahamck, Yannawa,
Bangkok, Thailand
Stephaich MRS Louise H (Louise E Hitchcock)
Cly.BtP. . . . . of ☎ (561)655-7768
MISS Pauline M. . . . . 265 Emerald Lane,
MR Paul M—Rc. . . . . Palm Beach, FL
33480
☎ (212) 734-9510
117 E 72 St,
New York, NY
10021
Stephaich MR & MRS (DR) Peter H (Rachel M Daher) Nu'85.Mid'78.Nu'89
☎ (212) 734-9510 . . 117 E 72 St, Apt 14, New York, NY *10021*
Stephanoff MR & MRS Alexander N (Emilie P Forte)
Wheat'80.Me.Sfh.Ste.Ncd.Pa'74
☎ (610) 527-3987 . . 830 Montgomery Av, Apt 314, Bryn Mawr,
PA *19010*
Stephanoff MRS Nicholas N (Patricia Duncan) Nyc.Sfh.Ncd.
☎ (610) 649-0790 . . 6 Coopertown Rd, Haverford, PA *19041-1013*
Stephens MR & MRS Bradley H (Ann K Schmidlapp) Dar.Cin'60
☎ (804) 438-5350 . . "Treetops" King Carter Dv, Irvington,
VA *22480*
Stephens MRS Charles H (Janet T Urian)
Man'vl'49.Cy. . . . . ☎ (314) 993-5754
MISS Mary M . . . . 1 Westridge Court,
MR Charles H 4th—at 822 N McKnight Rd, St Louis, MO *63124*
St Louis, MO *63132* . . . .
Stephens MR Clay G 4th—Hartw'83
☎ (518) 962-4869 . . PO Box 205, Westport, NY *12993*
Stephens MR & MRS Craig A (Sara K Callander)
Stan'74.Bhm.Sfg.SCal'70 . . . . ☎ (415) 751-2199
JUNIORS MR John T . . . . 16 Seventeenth Av,
JUNIORS MR Clark A . . . . San Francisco, CA
94121
Stephens MR & MRS F Scott (Woodruff—Joanna D
Beal) Bab'70 . . . . ☎ (617) 598-1630
MISS Darrow A . . . . 25 Lincoln Circle,
MISS Joanna B . . . . Swampscott, MA
MR Clayton L *01907*
Stephens MR & MRS James Thomas (Julia F
McDonald) Y'61.H'64 . . . . ☎ (205) 322-5279
MISS Trent McD . . . . 3710 Redmont Rd,
MISS Alys F . . . . Birmingham, AL
MR Bryson D D *35213*
MR Bart W R . . . .
Stephens MR John K—Wright'89 . . see MRS H S Widmer
Stephens MR & MRS John Krey (Dorothy Manewal) Mar'vil'45.Evg.
☎ (314) 993-2500 . . 25 Trent Dv, St Louis, MO *63124*
Stephens MISS Laura L . . see D M Haffner

Stephens MRS Simone S (Simone M Smith) . . . . . . ☎ (518) 962-8220
MISS Alexandra H . . . . "Viewpoint"
Westport, NY *12993*
Stephenson MR & MRS Charles G (Tracy E Innes)
Cal'60.Cal'63.Cal'57.Stan'63 . . . . ☎ (415) 387-4734
MISS Kate T—at 86 Parker Av, Apt 301, 240—32 Av,
San Francisco, CA *94118* . . . . San Francisco, CA
MR Anthony I—at 1549 Vallejo St, *94121*
San Francisco, CA *94109* . . . .
Stephenson MR & MRS David C (Julia M
Weatherman) Cvc.Cc.Sl.P'47.NCar'62 . . . . ☎ (202) 338-7472
MISS Julia W . . . . 3410 Q St NW,
MISS Evelyn C . . . . Washington, DC
20007
Stephenson MR & MRS Garrick C (Obolensky—
Claire McGinnis) Rc.B.Evg.Pr.BtP.Ng.So.Y'48 . of ☎ (212)734-7701
MISS Claire E—at Deauville, France . . . . 1 E 66 St,
MISS Christina C—at Paris, France . . . . New York, NY
10021
☎ (561) 659-6926
133 Gulfstream Rd,
Palm Beach, FL
33480
Stephenson MR & MRS J Clayton (Sarah H Taylor)
Ln.Rr.Cly.Sl.Y'54 . . . . ☎ (203) 622-1387
MR Robert W—at U of Colo Boulder . . . . 19 Meadow Lane,
Greenwich, CT
06831
Stephenson MRS John G 3d (Elizabeth Cashman) Ws'31
2861 Calle Trafalgar, Green Valley, AZ *85614*
Stephenson MISS L Parker—Tufts'90.Y.
☎ (212) 496-8038 . . 263 West End Av, Apt 9C, New York, NY *10023*
Stephenson MR & MRS Lowry C (Nancy I S Downs) Rc.Sa.Pa'40
☎ (610) LA5-7690 . . "Glenvale" 711 County Line Rd, Box 356,
Villanova, PA *19085*
Stephenson MRS Robert C (Joan Wilson)
Gm.Fic.Fiy. . . . . ☎ (610) 566-0257
MR William H . . . . 111 Mansion Dv,
Media, PA *19063*
Stephenson MR & MRS Robert L (Madeline Lewis)
CarnM'36.P'35 . . . . ☎ (412) 421-6620
MR Robert L JR—Duq'87 . . . . 1309 Shady Av,
Pittsburgh, PA
15217-1339
Sterling MRS Deborah P (Deborah Platt) Cly.Eyc. . . ☎ (203) 622-9077
MR Robert Livingston—GeoW'90.Pa'95 . . . . 16 Pheasant Lane,
MR Cameron P—at Kenyon . . . . Greenwich, CT
06830
Sterling MR Graham Lee 4th . . see MRS L R Pillsbury
Sterling MR Ian W—Va'87
PO Box 69, 53501 Lappeenranta, Finland
Sterling MR & MRS Keir B (Anne C Diller)
V'60.Cw.Cl'61.Cl'73 . . . . ☎ (804) 285-8354
MSRS Duncan D & Warner S—at 9604—48 Av, 7104 Wheeler Rd,
College Park, MD *20740* . . . . Richmond, VA
MR Theodore C—at U of Cal Berkeley *23229*
Sterling MR & MRS Robert Lee JR (Milner—Joyce Lanier)
Ga'53.BtP.Eyc.Plg.Srb.Evg.StA.Cc.Snc.Ne.Br'56. Cl'62 . . of
☎ (212) 288-1379 . . 907 Fifth Av, Apt 5C, New York, NY *10021*
☎ (561) 655-5981 . . 200 Regent Park, Palm Beach, FL *33480*
"Wakefield" 2724 Peachtree Rd NE, Atlanta, GA *30305*

Sterling MRS Spalding (Jean M Spalding) . . . . | ☎ (561) 686-9129
MISS Ann M . . . . | 1700 Embassy Dv,
MR Robert D . . . . | Apt 105,
                                       | West Palm Beach,
                                       | FL *33401*

Sterling MR & MRS T K Nelson (Linthicum—Anna Garey Bready)
Ayc.Ht.Cw.Rv.Sar.Wt.Dar.Md'30
☎ (407) 779-1285 . . 520 Palm Springs Blvd, Apt 410,
Indian Harbor Beach, FL *32937-2657*

Sterling MR & MRS William Lee (Renée L Sands)
Dick'92.Cl'94.Pn.StLaw'92 . . of
☎ (212) 717-1528 . . 168 E 74 St, Apt 1B, New York, NY *10021*
☎ (914) 534-7154 . . "Sengen" PO Box 234, Cornwall-on-Hudson,
NY *12520*

Stern DR W Eugene—Cal'41.Cal'43
☎ (310) 393-6976 . . 435 Georgina Av, Santa Monica, CA *90402*

Stern MR & MRS Walter E 3d (Mary E Mannion)
WmSth'79.Ne'81.BostColl'84.Cal'78.BostColl'82
☎ (505) 898-9155 . . 925 Guadalupe Court NW, Albuquerque,
NM *87114*

Sterne MR & MRS Richard J (Nicholas—Eleanor M Moore)
Ws'72.Rc.Ri.Pr.Cly.H.'68.Stan'70 . . of
☎ (212) 861-7155 . . 117 E 72 St, New York, NY *10021-4249*
☎ (914) 234-0176 . . "Thistle Hill" 89 Hook Rd, Bedford, NY *10506*

Sterrett MR & MRS Frank G (Patricia H Griffin) | ☎ (301) 229-8244
Cvc.Geo'37 . . . . | 5008 Keokuk St,
MISS Judith C—at ☎ (803) 884-0407 | Bethesda, MD
1523 Barquentine Dv, Pirate's Cove, | *20816*
Mt Pleasant, SC *29464* . . . . |

Sterrett MR & MRS Malcolm M B (Joan P | ☎ (301) 229-0676
De Chant) Cvc.Mt.P'64.Van'67 . . . . | 4516 Wetherill Rd,
MISS Anne B . . . . | Bethesda, MD
                                       | *20816*

Sterrett JUDGE & MRS Samuel B (Jeane McBride) | of ☎ (301)656-4630
Sth'47.Mt.Cvc.Ln.Chr.Aht'47.Va'50 . . . . | 133 Hesketh St,
MISS Robin D—StLaw'84.GeoW'90 . . . . | Chevy Chase, MD
MR Samuel B JR—Aht'82.Va'87—at | *20815*
711 Oronoco St, Apt 4, Alexandria, VA *22314* . | ☎ (518) 523-3863
MR Douglas McB . . . . | 1 Chipmunk Place,
                                       | Lake Placid, NY
                                       | *12946*

Sterrett MR & MRS William D JR (Kolek—Annette Tregler)
Cc.Sar.GeoW'32.Nat'l'38 . . of
1150 Eighth Av SW, Apt 2504, Largo, FL *33770-3142*
☎ (813) 796-9492 . . 2294 Belgian Lane, B67-34, Clearwater,
FL *34623-2549*

Stetson MR & MRS Basil W JR (Alice B Griswold) Cda.Ht.Myf.DU'76
☎ (206) 232-8488 . . 4841 W Mercer Way, Mercer Island, WA *98040*

Stetson MRS Brewster (Nancy K Andrews) . . of
☎ (561) 220-0598 . . 1605 SW Egret Way, Palm City, FL *34990*
☎ (617) 934-6535 . . PO Box 1086, Duxbury, MA *02332*

Stetson MR & MRS Charles P (Barbara Brown) | ☎ (203) 259-1013
Ny.Y'42 . . . . | 160 Morehouse
MISS Barbara B—at ☎ (212) 486-0846 | Lane, Southport, CT
401 E 50 St, New York, NY *10022* . . . . | *06490*

Stetson MR & MRS Charles P JR (Emilie Codoner) | ☎ (212) 688-8236
Un.Ln.Ny.Pcu.Cly.Y.'67 . . . . | 115 E 62 St,
MISS Amanda de S . . . . | New York, NY
JUNIORS MISS Brooke E . . . . | *10021*

Stetson MR & MRS E William 3d (Heyl—Jane W | of ☎ (802)649-3738
Watson) Hn.H'82 . . . . | 139 Elm St,
JUNIORS MISS Nancy H Heyl . . . . | Norwich, VT *05055*
                                       | ☎ (802) 457-3724
                                       | "Guest House"
                                       | Gully Rd,
                                       | Woodstock, VT
                                       | *05091*

Stetson MR Eugene W JR . . . . Died at
                                     Hobe Sound, FL May 1'96

Stetson MRS Eugene W JR (Nicoll—Walbridge—Kathryna H Ray)
☎ (561) 546-4949 . . PO Box 1190, Hobe Sound, FL *33475*

Stetson MRS G Richardson (Lambert—Grace S | ☎ (203) 259-1302
Richardson) . . . . | 109 Field Point Dv,
MISS Nancy P—at ☎ (203) 227-3430 | Fairfield, CT *06430*
Weathervane Hall, Westport, CT *06880* . . . . |

Stetson MISS Iola L—Col'82.Eyc.
☎ (206) 392-9710 . . 1420 NW Gilman Blvd, Apt 2287, Issaquah,
WA *98027*

Stetson MR & MRS Rufus E JR (Saunders—Janette W | ☎ (207) 563-8374
Cole) Unb.Myf.Dc.Ncd.Bow'47.GeoW'49 . . . . . | Bristol Rd,
   MISS Paige W Saunders—at ☎ (207) 563-7891 | Damariscotta, ME
Church St, Damariscotta, ME *04543* . . . . | *04543*

Stettinius MR Edward R—Va'84 . . see MRS M Ballentine
Stettinius MR Joseph JR . . see MRS M Ballentine
Stettinius MISS Mary Stuart—Va'89 . . see MRS M Ballentine

Stetzer MR & MRS John J 3d (Mary Anne M | ☎ (610) LA5-5299
Maguire) Ri.Mds.M.Ac.Cda. . . . . | 767 Mt Pleasant Rd,
MISS Alexandra P—Hlns'94.Cda. . . . . | Bryn Mawr, PA
MISS Susanne W—Cda.—at Trinity . . . . | *19010*

Stevens MR & MRS Barrett W (Mary Louise Herrick) Gen'lTheo'82.H'29
☎ (207) 967-3867 . . 16 Larboard Lane, Kennebunk, ME *04043*

Stevens MR & MRS Bayard M (Mary L Whitney) Cw.P'39.Nu'54
☎ (561) 231-2475 . . 1485 Treasure Cove Lane, Vero Beach, FL *32963*

Stevens MR & MRS Benjamin McC 3d (Susan H Crawford)
MontSt'86.MontSt'84
☎ (601) 584-8507 . . 509 Court St, Hattiesburg, MS *39401*

Stevens MRS Borden B (M Borden Burck) . . . . | see MRS B D Dixon
MISS Joelle B |
MR Scott B—Ia'90 . . . . |

Stevens MRS Brooks JR (McMillan—Harris—Caroline Cutter)
☎ (508) 371-0868 . . "Belknap House" 207 Main St, Concord,
MA *01742*

Stevens MR & MRS Byam K JR (Priscilla G Lucas) LIU'96.Pr.Cc.Y'52
☎ (516) 921-1976 . . Kirby Hill, Jericho, NY *11753*

Stevens MR & MRS Charles J (Tobey—Mary H Reisinger)
☎ (954) 524-7151 . . 2406 Laguna Dv, Ft Lauderdale, FL *33316*

Stevens MR & MRS Charles J (Diana L Byrd) | ☎ (602) 991-1095
Ariz'76.Ariz'76 . . . . | 12593 N 72 Place,
JUNIORS MISS Courtney J . . . . | Scottsdale, AZ
                                       | *85260*

Stevens MISS Courtney Jean (g—Byam K Stevens JR) . . . . Born at
                                     Fairfield, CT May 3'95

Stevens MR & MRS Edward M (Susan P Collins) ☎ (610) 688-3493
Denis'66.Pa'69 . . . . 724 Clovelly Lane,
MISS Heather C . . . . Devon, PA *19333*
MISS Lindsey N . . . .

Stevens MRS Edwin A 4th (M Susanne Leake)
☎ (310) 393-8930 . . 12919 Montana Av, Apt 103, Los Angeles,
CA *90049*

Stevens MR Edwin A 5th
☎ (310) 829-4917 . . 2439 Chelsea Place, Apt 3, Santa Monica,
CA *90403*

Stevens MISS Hannah Hurd (Benjamin McC 3d) . . . . Born at
Hattiesburg, MS Oct 27'94

Stevens MRS Henry W (Margaret J Holden)
☎ (941) 261-6104 . . 114 Moorings Park Dv, Apt 211A, Naples,
FL *34105*

Stevens MR & MRS J Earle (Mary Rose Hamilton Jackson)
Plg.H'29.Camb'37
☎ (914) 351-2497 . . Tower Hill Rd, Tuxedo Park, NY *10987*

Stevens MR & MRS James H (Joan H Coulborn) ☎ (610) 667-3467
Pa'64.BMr'73.P.'61.Pa'64 . . . . 302 Berkeley Rd,
MR J Alexander—Cr'94—at 2710 Windwood Dv, Merion Station, PA
Apt 127, Ann Arbor, MI *48105* *19066*
MR Russell McI . . . .
JUNIORS MR Geoffrey F . . . .

Stevens MISS Katharine F . . see B J Mix JR

Stevens MISS Larkin E—Pa'74.Nu'80
☎ (212) 721-9150 . . 109 W 89 St, Apt 3A, New York, NY *10024*

Stevens MR & MRS Lawrence L JR (Howard—Gertrude R Tiers)
Pe.Coa.Cw.Rv.Ll.Cspa.Ofp.Lm.Wt.Ht.Snc.Sdg.Ac.Dll. Ncd.Pa'38
☎ (609) 387-0396 . . ''Riverbank'' Edgewater Park, NJ *08010*

Stevens MR & MRS Lemuel B JR (Caroline A Boyd) Van'54.H'56
☎ (615) 665-2811 . . 4422 Warner Place, Nashville, TN *37205*

Stevens MR & MRS Norton (Wright—Margaret McC Love)
V'53.Ri.Ln.Cs.Y.'52.H'58
☎ (212) 628-3323 . . 770 Park Av, New York, NY *10021*

Stevens MR & MRS Raymond D JR (V Aline Larkin) of ☎ (716)876-3363
SUNY'81.St.G.Pa'51 . . . . 81 Hallam Rd,
MR Hunter H—at ☎ (941) 434-0275 Buffalo, NY *14216*
545 First Av N, Naples, FL *34102* . . . . ☎ (941) 434-0212
185 Third Av N,
Naples, FL *34102*

Stevens MR & MRS Robert G (Carol K Flagg) Col'58
☎ (208) 726-8839 . . PO Box 308, Sun Valley, Ketchum, ID *83340*

Stevens MR & MRS Robert L (Sydney A Davis) ☎ (610) 296-5539
Ph.Me.Cry.Myf.Nw'59 . . . . 403 Waynesbrooke
MISS Dina B . . . . Rd, Berwyn, PA
19312

Stevens MRS Stevan I (Edith Sidway) Sth'34.Nu'38.Ht.
Pennswood Village C203, Newtown, PA *18940*

Stevens MR & MRS William H JR (Alyce McC Stone) ☎ (212) 737-8571
Y.'41 . . . . 925 Park Av,
MR William H 3d—at ☎ (212) 737-9725 New York, NY
1590 Second Av, New York, NY *10028* *10028*

Stevens MRS William J JR (Kathleen A T Harris)
☎ (610) 942-2818 . . ''Bally Cloon'' 221 Highspire Rd, Glenmoore,
PA *19343-1711*

Stevens MR & MRS William J 3d (Nancy L Braden)
☎ (610) 942-2892 . . PO Box 258, Lyndell, PA *19354*

Stevenson MRS Anne H (Anne M Hollister)
☎ (212) 838-0544 . . 200 E 66 St, New York, NY *10021*

Stevenson MISS Annette P—PineM'84.Leh'92
☎ (011-33-1) 44-05-13-92 . . 19 rue Greuze, 75116 Paris, France

Stevenson MR Borden W—H'55 . . of
☎ (212) 737-3626 . . 44 E 67 St, New York, NY *10021*
☎ (208) 726-9591 . . 108 Walnut St, Ketchum, ID *83340*

Stevenson MR & MRS Charles P (Rogers—Barbara J Franklin)
Bcs.So.Ng.St.Sar.Y'41
☎ (561) 546-8765 . . ''Winterlude'' 104 Bassett Creek Trail,
Hobe Sound, FL *33455*

Stevenson MISS Elizabeth Holly—Hlns'90
☎ (212) 838-6112 . . 200 E 66 St, Apt A404, New York,
NY *10021-6728*

Stevenson MRS Elizabeth T (Elizabeth M Tarasi) Pitt'82.Duq'91
☎ (412) 741-8909 . . 620 Sewickley Heights Dv, Sewickley, PA *15143*

Stevenson MR & MRS Eric Van C (Judith A K Herrick) Rdc'54.Y'47.Y'50
☎ (202) 363-8534 . . 3502—36 St NW, Washington, DC *20016*

Stevenson MR & MRS Frederick J JR (Sally B Wheat) ☎ (412) 741-8543
Chath'81.Pitt'92.Edg.P'55.H'61 ⚓ 607 East Dv,
MISS Elizabeth B—Col'95—at ☎ (970) 728-1881 Sewickley, PA
PO Box 3278, Telluride, CO *81435* *15143*
MR William E—Ober'85.Cl'89—at
☎ (212) 627-8707 . . 134 W 15 St, New York,
NY *10011* . . . .

Stevenson MR Frederick J 3d
312 Breading Av, Ben Avon, Pittsburgh, PA *15202*

Stevenson MR & MRS G Barnes (Brown—Josephine E Reilly)
☎ (908) 892-6705 . . 547 W Lake Av, Bay Head, NJ *08742*

Stevenson MR & MRS G Barnes 3d (Diane Kapsimalis)
Ill'78.Cr'80.Conn'85.StLaw'78.Cr'80
☎ (203) 762-5605 . . 276 Newtown Tpke, Wilton, CT *06897*

Stevenson MISS Gertrude Gouverneur (Pickering—
Gertrude Gouverneur Stevenson) Van'85.Ac.
☎ (615) 791-0175 . . 3264 Southall Rd, Franklin, TN *37064-9259*

Stevenson MR James H 3d—Cspa.Cw.Rv.Pa'60
☎ (561) 835-8044 . . 1200 S Flagler Dv, Apt 605, West Palm Beach,
FL *33401*

Stevenson MRS Joan C (Joan H Clement) On.
☎ (847) 234-1361 . . 1500 N Sheridan Rd, Lake Forest, IL *60045*

Stevenson MR & MRS John R (Johnson—Ruth Carter)
SL'45.Ln.Mt.Cvc.Cly.Sl.P'42
☎ (817) 737-9582 . . 1200 Broad Av, Ft Worth, TX *76107*

Stevenson MR Kennedy—K.P.'47
☎ (212) 753-7714 . . 30 E 62 St, New York, NY *10021*

Stevenson MR & MRS Richard D (Joanne H Harrison)
☎ (941) 966-8218 . . Bay Village Apt 510, 8400 Vamo Rd, Sarasota,
FL *34231-7899*

Stevenson MRS Robert 3d (Dorothy Duval) Sc. . . . . . ☎ (773) 929-2645
MISS Ann E—at ☎ (773) 883-1337 2437 N Southport
3440 N Lake Shore Dv, Chicago, IL *60657* . . . . Av, Chicago, IL
60614

Stevenson MRS Robert L (Fronk—Katherine Wallace) Hills'70 . . . . ☎ (716) 875-3154 40 Dana Rd, Buffalo, NY *14216*
   JUNIORS MISS Margaret L . . . .
   JUNIORS MISS Emily E . . . .
   MISS Katherine C Fronk . . . .

Stevenson MR Robert L—Cy.Bf.Ts.St.Y'73 . . . . . . ☎ (716) 877-2235 87 Nottingham Terr, Buffalo, NY *14216*
   MISS Alexa S . . . .
   MR R Trevor . . . .

Stevenson MR Robert M McC JR—Eyc.Ty'57 . . . . . ☎ (617) 863-6157 3 Lois Lane, Lexington, MA *02173*
   MISS Anna Louise G . . . .
   MISS Mamie McC . . . .

Stevenson MR & MRS Roy (Polly Shepard) H'78.Emory'92
   ☎ (770) 813-9718 . . 1812 Ballybunion Dv, Duluth, GA *30136*

Stevenson MRS Stuart D (Margaret D Roberts) Ws'48.Me.Ncd. . . . . ☎ (610) 896-9732 The Quadrangle C903, 3300 Darby Rd, Haverford, PA *19041-1065*
   MISS Irene D—P'83 . . . .

Stevenson MRS Thomas S (Harriet I Butler) CarnM'37
   ☎ (941) 474-9056 . . 2985 N Beach Rd, Apt BV3, Englewood, FL *34223*

Stevenson MRS Virginia J (Murphy—Virginia J Stevenson) . . . . ☎ (804) 979-3709 500 McIntire Rd, Apt 2, Charlottesville, VA *22901*
   MISS Virginia M Murphy—at
   ☎ (610) 983-3607 . . PO Box 524, Kimberton, PA *19442* . . . .
   MR Martin N Murphy—at 411 King St, Beaufort, SC *29902* . . . .

Stevenson MR Wade 2d
   132 Cleveland Av, Buffalo, NY *14222*

Stevenson MR & MRS William H 3d (Davis—Evelyn V Cheek) NCar'46 . . . . ☎ (410) 745-3481 "Deep Enuff" 25969 Goose Neck Rd, Royal Oak, MD *21662*
   MR William H 4th—at ☎ (410) 745-3311 The Old Mill, St Michaels, MD *21663* . . . .

Stevenson MR & MRS William W (Carol R Wheeler) MaryB'62.P'50.Va'59
   ☎ (804) 293-6731 . . 406 Wellington Dv, Ednam Forest, Charlottesville, VA *22903*

Stevenson MR William Wheeler—Denis'92
   ☎ (804) 285-1961 . . 605 Silver Spring Dv, Richmond, VA *23229*

Steves MR & MRS Albert 4th (Martha E Monier) Smu'60.W&L'58
   ☎ (210) 826-8062 . . 7919 Kings Reach, San Antonio, TX *78209*

Steves MISS Gale C (Stocker—Gale C Steves) Cr'64.Nu'66
   ☎ (212) 799-8942 . . 185 West End Av, New York, NY *10023*

Steward MR & MRS Campbell (Fairfield—Grace H Vanner) CtCol'63.Sbc.Cvc.Ny.My.Sm.BtP. Cda.Myf.H'56 . . . . of ☎ (508)887-3901 "Grasslands" 65 Asbury St, Topsfield, MA *01983* ☎ (561) 655-4960 "Birdsnest" 441 Australian Av, Palm Beach, FL *33480*
   MISS Eleanor C . . . .
   MISS Diana A . . . .

Steward MRS Gilbert L (Coolidge—Victoria S Tytus) My.
   ☎ (508) 741-5700 . . Grosvenor Park, 7 Loring Hills Av, Salem, MA *01970-4267*

Steward MR & MRS Gilbert L JR (Sally Jay) My.
   ☎ (508) 468-4688 . . 116 Grapevine Rd, Wenham, MA *01984*

Steward MR Nicholas—My.CtCol'90
   ☎ (508) 927-6982 . . 45 Folly Pond Rd, Apt 32, Beverly, MA *01915*

Steward MR Scott C—Sb.Hn.H'86
   ☎ (617) 868-6834 . . 1556 Cambridge St, Cambridge, MA *02139*

Stewardson MISS Caroline C—Bost'87 . . see J Ford 3d

Stewardson MR & MRS Dana H (Alice E Moyer) OWes'84.Gm.Me.OWes'84
   ☎ (610) 527-9030 . . 626 Morris Av, Bryn Mawr, PA *19010*

Stewart MISS A Leigh—OWes'75
   ☎ (202) 362-9014 . . 3101 New Mexico Av NW, Apt 233, Washington, DC *20016*

Stewart MR Andrew M—Colg'90
   ☎ (212) 496-7837 . . 18 W 83 St, Apt B, New York, NY *10024*

Stewart MRS Anne Lee (Anne Lee Rose) Temp'44 . ☎ (314) 458-2411 1333 Pond Rd, Glencoe, MO *63038*
   MISS Amy H—Dth'85—at U of Iowa Grad . . . .

Stewart MISS Caroline Grace (g—W Lloyd Lancaster JR) . . . . Born at Montgomery, AL Dec 30'95

Stewart MRS Charles L (Sharon P Campbell) Cly.Ne.Y. . . . . ☎ (212) 744-1621 80 East End Av, New York, NY *10028*
   MISS Marjorie L . . . .
   MR Charles L 3d—at Denison . . . .
   JUNIORS MR Campbell L—at Hotchkiss . . . .

Stewart MR & MRS Charles P 3d (Frances H Todd) Wms'79.Fcg.Pg.Rr.Ty'76
   ☎ (412) 238-6694 . . RD 2, Barron Rd, Ligonier, PA *15658*

Stewart MR & MRS Charles Wesley 2d (Margaret H Lewis) Tul'75 . . . . ☎ (504) 899-1703 5934 Chestnut St, New Orleans, LA *70115*
   MISS Jean M . . . .
   JUNIORS MISS Margaret McK . . . .

Stewart MR David E—Il.Ny.Ne'72 ⚓
   ☎ (401) 624-9168 . . "Cedar Brook Ledge" Box 79, Highland Rd, Tiverton, RI *02878*

Stewart MISS Elizabeth B (Brown—Elizabeth B Stewart) Canis'87.SUNY'91 . . . . 99 St James Place, Buffalo, NY *14222*
   JUNIORS MR Clinton S Brown—at Georgetown
   JUNIORS MR Peter H Brown . . . .

Stewart MR & MRS Floyd M (Carol A Pfeifer)
   ☎ (216) 562-8579 . . 445 Pioneer Trail, Aurora, OH *44202*

Stewart MRS James (Dwight—Martha E Terry) BtP.Evg.So.Sl. . . . . ☎ (212) 753-3500 42 W 58 St, New York, NY *10019*
   MR James E T Dwight . . . .

Stewart MR & MRS James M (Hunter—Joly Walton) Nyc.Sg.Ac.Ty'50 . . . . ☎ (215) 646-2698 Forge Farm, 701 W Butler Pike, Ambler, PA *19002*
   MISS Lea A—at ☎ (603) 968-3526 . . RFD 2, Box 279D, Plymouth, NH *03264* . . . .
   MR James M JR—at ☎ (215) 641-1442 10 Morris Av, Ambler, PA *19002* . . . .
   MR Mahlon K—Ty'91—at ☎ (212) 780-9144 40-50 E 10 St, Apt 2E, New York, NY *10003* . .
   MISS Elizabeth S Hunter—at
   ☎ (970) 221-2979 . . 208 N Roosevelt Av, Ft Collins, CO *80521* . . . .

Stewart MR James P . . . . Died at Hightstown, NJ Dec 22'95

Stewart MRS James P (Hackl—Faith D Severance) Dyc.
☎ (609) 426-6274 . . Meadow Lakes 17-10U, Hightstown, NJ *08520-3315*

Stewart MR John A (Catherine C Hill) . . . . . Married at Barrington, RI Shadd MR Robert W (late Harold C) . . . . Jun 29'96

Stewart MR & MRS John A JR (Carol A Geiger) MmtVa'73.Co.Ayc.RI'69 ⚓
☎ (410) 268-5403 . . 2705 Willow Hill Rd, Annapolis, MD *21403*

Stewart MR & MRS John E (Bishop—Barbara B Adams) Mich'64.BtP.Evg.Rcch.Sar.Rv.Tc.
☎ (561) 835-1679 . . 315 S Lake Dv, Palm Beach, FL *33480*

Stewart MR & MRS John E (Bonnie M Phillips) Evg.Fla'70
☎ (910) 725-9293 . . 2545 Wakewood Hill, Winston-Salem, NC *27106*

Stewart MR & MRS John G (Gould—Linda C McKoy) Stc.Hn.H'40
☎ (908) 741-1391 . . 18 Osprey Lane, Rumson, NJ *07760*

Stewart MR & MRS John G (Sarah A F Canby) NCar'65.BritCl'69 . . . . | ☎ (604) 531-3742
MISS Maggie | 2818 Gordon Av,
MISS Katherine C | Crescent Beach, Surrey, BC, Canada

Stewart DR & MRS John M 3d (Melissa McL Ricci) Ck.Y'70.Va'74 . . . . | ☎ (516) 922-9083
JUNIORS MR John M 4th . . . . | W Shore Rd, Oyster Bay, NY *11771*

Stewart MISS Marian . . see MRS C C McAleenan

Stewart MRS Michael M (Anne L Fritts) Cl'62.Chr. | ☎ (212) 987-7393
MISS Mary C | 1235 Park Av, Apt
MR Christopher J B | 16A, New York, NY
MR Michael C | *10128*

Stewart MRS Potter (Mary A Bertles) Cvc.Sl.
☎ (202) 362-0211 . . 5136 Palisade Lane NW, Washington, DC *20016*

Stewart MR & MRS R Bruce (Margaret T Morgan) Stan'60.Cal'59
☎ (818) 449-6148 . . 250 La Mirada Rd, Pasadena, CA *91105*

Stewart MR Robert W
☎ (508) 540-1600 . . 339 Gifford St, Falmouth, MA *02540*

Stewart MR & MRS Thomas A (Amanda H B Vaill) Rdc'70.C.H'70 . . . . | ☎ (212) 427-8204
JUNIORS MISS Pamela A V . . . . | 60 E 96 St, New York, NY *10128*

Stewart MRS Thomas C (McIlvaine—Katherine E Mein) Ac.Me.Ncd.
☎ (610) 642-5521 . . Thacher Court 10, 251 Montgomery Av, Haverford, PA *19041*

Stewart MR Timothy F—ColSt'68
☎ (303) 443-0328 . . 525 Hawthorn Av, Boulder, CO *80302*

Stewart MR & MRS W Parker (Eileen Eshleman) . . see C L Eshleman JR

Stewart MR & MRS William A W 3d (Cutter— | ☎ (212) 734-7487
Elizabeth H Whittemore) Rc.Cl'61 . . . . | 901 Lexington Av,
MR Christian A S | New York, NY
MISS Kimberly E Cutter . . . . | *10021*
MISS Amanda H Cutter . . . . |

Stewart MRS William H (Watson—Mary S Hayes)
☎ (617) 899-3401 . . 8 Partridge Hill Rd, Weston, MA *02193*

Stewart MR & MRS William H (M Amy Geer) Miss'77.Miss'78.NCar'74.Cl'86
☎ (202) 966-9301 . . 2825 Rittenhouse St NW, Washington, DC *20015*

Stewart MRS William Steele (Bunts—Mary W Corbin) May. Hamlet Manor, 150 Cleveland St, Chagrin Falls, OH *44022*

Stewart MRS William T JR (Bertish—Cecile B | ☎ (908) 534-6918
Bridgett) Eh.Shcc. . . . . | "Hedgerow"
MISS Suzanne C Bertish . . . . | PO Box 116,
MISS Jane M Bertish | Far Hills, NJ *07931*

Stewart MR & MRS Zeph (Diana Childers) | ☎ (617) 926-2515
Cos.C.Y'43 . . . . | 85 Garfield St,
MISS (DR) Sarah B—HRdc'83.MassPsych'91—at | Watertown, MA
☎ (617) 876-6735 . . 263 Concord Av, | *02172*
Cambridge, MA *02138* . . . . |
DR Christopher C—Y'85.H'96 . . . . |

Stewart-Clark MRS Alan (Stevenson—Shaw—Jane Morris)
☎ (011-44-1340) 810-202 . . "Carron House" Carron, Aberlour, Banffshire AB38 7RE, Scotland

Stick MR Gordon M F JR—Rv.Cc.Wt.Cw.Lm.Ht. | ☎ (410) 243-5555
JHop'57.Nw'70 . . . . | A308 Evans Chapel
MISS Anne H F . . . . | Rd, Baltimore, MD
MISS Sarah W . . . . | *21211-1616*
JUNIORS MISS Fair E B . . . . |
JUNIORS MISS Margaret G W . . . . |

Stick MRS Joyce Y (Carr—Joyce Yeargin) Va'57 . . | ☎ (610) 649-7081
MR Richard F Carr JR—Md'82 . . . . | 1534 Monticello Dv,
MR John N Carr—WakeF'88.SantaC'92 . . . . | Gladwyne, PA *19035*

Stick MR & MRS T Howard F (Easter—Alyce C | of ☎ (610)642-1946
Cushing) ColbyS'64.Bost'66.Me.Rv.Cc.Cw.Wt. | "Sticky Wicket"
Lm.Ll.Y.'60.Pa'65 . . . . | 1501 Monticello Dv,
MR Edward M—Ty'84 . . . . | Gladwyne, PA
MR Alexander W—W&L'83.Miami'87 . . . . . . | *19035*
MR David F—VillaN'94 . . . . | ☎ (603) 823-8841
 | "Butternut"
 | Blake Rd,
 | Sugar Hill, NH
 | *03585*

Stickle MRS David Van R (Helen C Wellman) Cwr'39
☎ (410) 584-1230 . . 13801 York Rd, Apt F5, Cockeysville, MD *21030*

Stickney MR & MRS Albert III (Susan K King) | ☎ (914) 764-5193
Bgt.L.Fic.Fiy.H.'67 . . . . | 70 West Lane,
MISS Katharine K—at F'klin & Marshall . . . . . | Pound Ridge, NY
JUNIORS MISS Anna N . . . . | *10576*

Stickney MR & MRS Charles E JR (Anita S Cooper) V'47.Myf.Cda.Me'44
☎ (207) 846-5765 . . "Cutter House" Gilman Rd, RR 3, Box 16, Yarmouth, ME *04096*

Stiff MR & MRS S Bertram 3d (Margaret D Wood) | ☎ (610) 688-4913
Me.Gm.Roan'68 . . . . | 629 S Valley Forge
MISS Elisabeth L . . . . | Rd, Wayne, PA
JUNIORS MISS Alexander W . . . . | *19087*

Stiger MR & MRS William M (Hughes—Virginia Quinn) S.Ny.Pr.Y'36
☎ (516) 922-7588 . . 320 Yacht Club Rd, Centre Island, Oyster Bay, NY *11771*

Stiles MRS Bradford W (Mary I S Brown) Cda.Dc.
☎ (512) 263-2331 . . 1101 Crystal Creek Dv, Austin, TX *78746*

Stiles MR & MRS Ned B (Deborah Fiedler)
Rdc'69.H'74.Ri.Miami'53.Cin'58 . . . . | of ☎ (203)622-1664
MR Andrew J . . . . | 12 Creamer Hill Rd,
MR Peter S . . . . | Greenwich, CT
JUNIORS MISS Jessica B . . . . | 06831
 | ☎ (516) 653-4120
 | 58 Quaquanantuck
 | Lane, Quogue, NY
 | 11959
 | ☎ (561) 795-4428
 | 12582 Mallet Circle,
 | West Palm Beach,
 | FL 33414

Stillman MR Alfred 3d—Y.'80.H'91
 ☎ (212) 645-0198 . . 46 Downing St, New York, NY 10014
Stillman MRS Charles L (Peters—Marjorie Hodgsdon) Cly.
 ☎ (203) 259-0121 . . PO Box 633, Southport, CT 06490-0633
Stillman MR & MRS J Whitney (Irene Pérez-Porro) Barc'76.H.'73
 ☎ (212) 274-1016 . . 81 Greene St, New York, NY 10012
Stillman MR & MRS John S (Jackson—Amelia di C | of ☎ (914)534-4365
Pasquini) C.Nf.H.'40.Cl'47 . . . . | 72 Maple Rd,
MR John J . . . . | Cornwall-on-
 | Hudson, NY
 | 12520-1801
 | ☎ (242) 333-2017
 | ''Tabebuia Terrace''
 | PO Box EL27092,
 | Harbour Island,
 | Bahamas
Stillman MRS Margaret R (Margaret D Riley) Cs.
 ☎ (212) 831-4625 . . 145 E 92 St, Apt 6D, New York, NY 10128
Stillman MR Mark C—H'76.Cl'87
 ☎ (914) 534-3439 . . 9 Stillwood Rd, Cornwall-on-Hudson, NY 12520
Stillman MR & MRS Peter G (Adelaide H Villmoare)
Sth'67.Nu'70.Nu'77.Y'66.Y'73
 ☎ (914) 473-0186 . . 106 Academy St, Poughkeepsie, NY 12601
Stillman MRS Peter Gordon B (Eugenia Watters) Chr.Un.Cly.Dc.Ncd.
 ☎ (212) 517-8968 . . 201 E 66 St, New York, NY 10021-6453
Stillman MR & MRS Waddell W (Kristina E Weisenstein)
Y.'83.P'85.Chr.StJ.Myf.Y.'83.H.'88
 ☎ (212) 787-0187 . . 2166 Broadway, Apt 5B, New York,
NY 10024-6670
Stillman MR William R—Rv.
 ☎ (941) 349-6258 . . 1215 S Portofino Dv, Apt 104, Sarasota, FL 34242
Stilson MR & MRS Colby (Georgia B Fauls) | ☎ (516) 543-5643
StLaw'63 . . . . | 6 Iroquois Lane,
MISS Hilary P W . . . . | Commack, NY
MR Colby 3d . . . . | 11725-4209
Stimpson MR & MRS Alexander F (Danah C Frederick) On.Cw.Vt'85.Nw'88
 ☎ (847) 234-4964 . . 301 E Rose Terr, Lake Forest, IL 60045
Stimpson MR & MRS John W (Patricia R Sudler)
Sth'57.Cyb.Fy.Ncd.Hn.H'58
 ☎ (860) 435-2370 . . ''Greybarn'' 23 Valley Rd, Lakeville, CT 06039
Stimpson MR & MRS Phillip E (Brita E Schlosser) Rc.Y.Vt'81 . . of
 ☎ (212) 996-7271 . . 115 E 87 St, Apt 30A, New York, NY 10128
 ☎ (516) 287-0564 . . 201 Towd Point Rd, Southampton, NY 11968
Stimpson MASTER William Emory (Alexander F) . . . . Born Apr 11'96
Stimson MR David G . . see R G Barnes

Stimson MISS Faith A . . see R G Barnes
Stimson MR & MRS Frederick B 3d (Amanda S Fowler)
StJColl'71.Cr'74.San.NCar'71
 ☎ (415) 864-4729 . . 3628—16 St, San Francisco, CA 94114
Stimson MR William A—Pcu.Snc.Sar.Cw. . . . . | ☎ (415) 346-2927
MISS Alexandra L . . . . | 3256 Washington St,
MISS Charlotte P . . . . | San Francisco, CA
 | 94115
Stinchcomb MR Carl J—K.F&M'60 . . of
 ☎ (561) 744-9276 . . 400 Beach Rd, Apt 201, Tequesta, FL 33469
 ☎ (212) 838-4910 . . 14 Sutton Place S, New York, NY 10022
Stinchcomb MRS Elizabeth H (Elizabeth P Haneman)
 ☎ (212) 877-5373 . . 101 W 81 St, New York, NY 10024
Stinchcomb MR Lawrence S—Buck'62 . . . . | 2171 N Pierce St,
MR Joshua S—Mid'95 . . . . | Arlington, VA
JUNIORS MR Matthew S—at Oberlin | 22209
Stine MR & MRS Jonathan E (M Susan Bee) | ☎ (610) 688-9245
OWes'63.Sfh.Leh'63 . . . . | 1 Weirwood Rd,
MISS Cynthia B—at Wesleyan . . . . | Radnor, PA 19087
MR Daniel E—Mit'94.Mit'95—at
1346 Pacific Beach Dv, San Diego, CA 92109 . .
Stine MRS M Peters (Schaldach—Marion A Peters) | ☎ (908) 766-0026
Shcc. . . . . | 380 Claremont Rd,
MR Thomas H . . . . | Bernardsville, NJ
 | 07924
Stineman MRS J Wilbur (Margaret G Morris) . . . . . | ☎ (610) LA5-5298
MISS (DR) Margaret G—Temp'74.Drex'81. | 16 Wistar Rd,
H'mannMed'83—at ☎ (215) 473-0401 | Villanova, PA 19085
2647 Lenape Rd, Philadelphia, PA 19131 . . . . .
Stinson MISS (DR) Nell L—Cal'74.Guad'80
 ☎ (415) 344-7539 . . 1508 Arc Way, Burlingame, CA 94010
Stires MRS Ernest Van R (Guntharp—Nell Kilgore). | ☎ (912) 638-4628
MR Alfred E Guntharp JR . . . . | 28 E DeSoto,
 | PO Box 30006,
 | Sea Island, GA
 | 31561-0006
Stirling MR & MRS E Tillman (Genevieve Ruffner)
Mt.Cvc.Cc.GeoW'51.GeoW'53
 ☎ (301) 656-3519 . . 7012 Beechwood Dv, Chevy Chase, MD 20815
Stirling MRS Elizabeth Cole (Cole—Elizabeth L Stirling)
 ☎ (505) 989-8664 . . 3101 Old Pecos Trail, 426, Santa Fe, NM 87505
Stirling MR & MRS James P (Ellen A Foster) | ☎ (847) 234-1970
Rc.Cho.On.Cas.P'63.Stan'65 . . . . | 165 N Green Bay
MISS E Ginevra—at Kenyon . . . . | Rd, Lake Forest, IL
MISS D Leslie—at Princeton . . . . | 60045
JUNIORS MISS Alexandra C—at Lake Forest Sch .
Stith LT COL (RET) & MRS J Denvir (Susan Wilkinson) USMC.StL'42
 ☎ (803) 736-2093 . . 122 Beaver Dam Rd, Columbia, SC 29223
Stith MR & MRS Richard T JR (Ann C See) Nd.StL'40
 ☎ (314) 725-4379 . . 37 Aberdeen Place, St Louis, MO 63105
Stobaugh MR & MRS Clay E (Mary B Gallatin) Pa'80.Un.Pr.Tul'80.H'84
210 E 68 St, New York, NY 10021
Stobs MRS Constance W (Constance Wick) . . . . . . | ☎ (602) 996-9024
MISS Wendy W . . . . | 4225 E North Lane,
MISS Natalie . . . . | Phoenix, AZ 85028
Stock DR & MRS Richard J (Eleanor M Schwarz) C.Cs.Y'45.Cl'47
 ☎ (212) TR9-9485 . . 155 E 72 St, New York, NY 10021

Stockbridge MR & MRS John J (Wardman—Anita S de Bragança) Mls'69.Bgt.P'65.Cl'67 . . . . | ☎ (914) 241-0407
191 Sarles St,
MISS Jennifer K—Stan'93—at 345 E 81 St, | Mt Kisco, NY
New York, NY *10028* . . . . | *10549*
MISS Katherine W—StLaw'96 . . . .
  MISS Tiffany A Wardman—Cal'95—at
  308—1 St, Crested Butte, CO *81224* . . . .
  MR George S Wardman—Me'92—at
  308—1 St, Crested Butte, CO *81224* . . . .

Stocker MRS David B (Wendy Townsend) Pa'74
  ☎ (508) 369-0317 . . 702 Lowell Rd, Concord, MA *01742-5510*

Stocker MR David B—H'57.H'59
  ☎ (206) 453-9959 . . 10022 Meydenbauer Way SE, Apt 217, Bellevue, WA *98004*

Stockly MR & MRS A Holmes (Doris du P Silliman) | ☎ (207) 781-4254
Br'47.Cr'54 . . . . | 186 Falmouth Rd,
MISS Elise—at Portland, ME . . . . | Falmouth, ME
  | *04105*

Stockly MR & MRS John G (Elizabeth I Boethelt) Rdc'49.Cw.
  ☎ (201) 635-1898 . . 270 Washington Av, Chatham, NJ *07928*

Stockman MR & MRS Henry C (Jeanne E Monroe) Pr.Snc.Pa'39
  ☎ (516) 676-2142 . . Piping Rock Rd, Locust Valley, NY *11560-0107*

Stockman MR Henry C 3d—Stan'75.Pa'78
  ☎ (415) 776-7867 . . 3171 Sacramento St, San Francisco, CA *94123*

Stockman MR & MRS Robert B (Lisa A Russell) | ☎ (609) 924-3005
Ws'74.H'76.Dth'80.Srb.Cly.H'76.Dth'81 . . . . . . | Green Valley Farm,
JUNIORS MISS Lily R . . . . | 286 Carter Rd,
  | Princeton, NJ *08540*

Stockmar MR J Brian—Pn.P'72.DU'76 . . of
  ☎ (303) 778-8593 . . 400 Lafayette St, Denver, CO *80218*
  ☎ (970) 476-4833 . . "Stream Side" 4096 Columbine Lane, Vail, CO *81657*

Stockmar MR & MRS Ted P JR (Suzanne Harl) Col'45.ColM'43.DU'48 . . of
  ☎ (303) 744-6555 . . 2552 E Alameda Av, Apt 8, Denver, CO *80290*
  ☎ (970) 476-5103 . . "Vail Retreat" 4192 Columbine Way, Vail, CO *81657*

Stockton MR & MRS Cleveland J JR (Jeanne H | 6812 Corte De Oro,
Herrmann) Nw'41.H'48 . . . . | Modesto, CA *95356*
MISS Nadine Y—at ☎ (415) 776-5057
2140 Hyde St, San Francisco, CA *94109-1704* . .

Stockton MR & MRS H Haines (Merkel—Janet McLaughlin) San.Snc.Ds.Cw.NCar'40 . . of
  ☎ (908) 974-1940 . . 33 Walnut Dv, Spring Lake Heights, NJ *07762*
  ☎ (941) 475-3037 . . 1531 Placida Rd, Apt 1-101, Englewood, FL *34223*

Stockwell MR & MRS D Hunt JR (Margaret S Good) Cw.Cr'62.Pa'64
  ☎ (609) 683-5670 . . 48 Glen Dv, Princeton, NJ *08540*

Stockwell MR David H—Wil.Pe.Ll.Cspa.Cw.Rv.Wt.Pa'30.H'31
  ☎ (302) 658-5685 . . 1001 Barley Dv, PO Box 3711, Greenville, DE *19807*

Stockwell MR & MRS David H 3d (Catherine C Morgan) Duke'89.Va'92.Duke'89
  ☎ (212) 472-4228 . . 420 E 70 St, Apt 15L, New York, NY *10021*

Stockwell MR & MRS John F (Dorothea C Baker) | ☎ (508) 887-6397
Ec.Y'57 . . . . | 22 Herrick Rd,
MISS Stephanie R . . . . | Boxford, MA *01921*
MR John F JR—at 23 Nineteenth Av, Apt 5,
Venice, CA *90291* . . . .
MR William A—at ☎ (508) 922-8284
45 West St, Beverly Farms, MA *01915* . . . .

Stockwell MISS Katharine W—H'92
  ☎ (617) 666-1172 . . 26 Campbell Park, Somerville, MA *02144*

Stoddard MISS Alexandra B . . see P M Brown

Stoddard MISS Brooke G . . see P M Brown

Stoddard MR & MRS Ezekiel G (Mary Alice Waller) Mt.Cvc.Y'31
  ☎ (202) 338-2601 . . 2108—48 St NW, Washington, DC *20007*

Stoddard MISS Margery P—Myf.Dc.Dh.Ncd.Dll. | ☎ (212) 861-1244
Ne.Ht. . . . . | 340 E 72 St,
MR Dudley W—Snc.Cc.Ht.Myf.Cw.Ll.Rv.— | New York, NY
☎ (212) 249-6790 . . . . | *10021*

Stoddard MR & MRS Whitney S (Russell—Jensvold—Elizabeth Fish) Wms'35.H'41
  ☎ (413) 458-4077 . . 43D Gale Rd, Williamstown, MA *01267*

Stoddart MR & MRS Alexander N (Emilie M Cole) My.
  ☎ (912) 232-0386 . . 413 E Jones St, Savannah, GA *31401-4707*

Stoddart MISS Jane W (John T JR) . . . . | Married at Denver, CO
Wilcox MR Ronald L (Floyd K) . . . . | Jun 1'96

Stoddart MRS John O (Mary E Gruber) Swb'37.Sg.Ncd.
  ☎ (215) 233-5633 . . "Dogwoods" 3028A Church Rd, Lafayette Hill, PA *19444*

Stoddart MR & MRS John T JR (Lenore M Thomas) | ☎ (303) 698-1474
Y'43 . . . . | 27 Polo Field Lane,
MISS Anne E . . . . | Denver, CO *80209*

Stoddart MR & MRS John T 3d (Laura M Gardner)
  ☎ (303) 388-7927 . . 1340 Poplar St, Denver, CO *80220*

Stokes MR & MRS Alexander C (Tiernan—Lynda Scheerer) Rd.Rc.Gm.Me.Mds . . of
  ☎ (561) 276-7336 . . 3550 Polo Dv, Gulf Stream, FL *33483*
  ☎ (610) LA5-1913 . . 418 Colebrook Lane, Bryn Mawr, PA *19010-2904*

Stokes MRS Anson Phelps JR (Hope Procter) Lx.Cy.Chi.Ncd.
  ☎ (617) 232-1474 . . 99 Codman Rd, Brookline, MA *02146*

Stokes MR & MRS Edward B (Catherine Merritt) Me.Pa'44
  ☎ (610) 687-2041 . . 820 Lawrence Lane, Newtown Square, PA *19073*

Stokes MR Edward B JR—Ste. . . . . | ☎ (610) 689-4083
MISS Elizabeth A . . . . | Loder Rd,
JUNIORS MR John L B . . . . | Birdsboro, PA
  | *19508*

Stokes MR & MRS Isaac Newton Phelps (Huntington—Katrina T Roelker) C.Y'29
80 Lyme Rd, Apt 106, Hanover, NH *03755*

Stokes MRS J Tyson (L Gurney Fuguet)
  ☎ (610) 356-6864 . . Dunwoody Village CH122,
3500 West Chester Pike, Newtown Square, PA *19073*

Stokes MR John S 3d—Lind'73
  ☎ (619) 298-2438 . . 3645 Seventh Av, San Diego, CA *92103*

Stokes MR & MRS John W 2d (Alice H Enos) | ☎ (203) 259-2750
Me.Nrr.Hn.H'54.H'58 . . . . | 221 Willow St,
MISS Ellery T—Vt'89.JHop'95 . . . . | Southport, CT *06490*
MISS Anne Kemble—Wash'95 . . . .

Stokes MRS Patricia S (Patricia Schriever) . . . . | ☎ (215) 836-1283
MISS M Elizabeth—at 3594 Indian Queen Lane, | 703 E Willow Grove
Philadelphia, PA *19129* . . . . | Av, Wyndmoor, PA
MR Thomas E—at 416 E Mt Airy Av, | *19038*
Philadelphia, PA *19119* . . . . |

Stokes MR & MRS Richard W (Betty-Anne Levis) Cy.H'50
☎ (617) 326-0106 . . 75 Thatcher St, Westwood, MA *02090*

Stokes MRS Sarah Lee (Stokes—Sarah Lee Stokes)
see Dilatory Domiciles

Stokes MR & MRS Turner van C (Kinehan—La Verne M Utterback)
☎ (703) 777-4611 . . 13674 Hidden Hollow Lane, Leesburg,
VA *20176-6108*

Stokes MR Walter H—Bost'89
☎ (305) 531-7959 . . 20 Island Av, Apt 1406, Miami Beach, FL *33139*

Stokes MRS Walter Watson (Hannah Lee Sherman) Cly.Cda.
☎ (607) 547-9266 . . Lee's Hill Farm, PO Box 26, Oriole Rd,
Cooperstown, NY *13326*

Stokes MR & MRS William S 3d (Mary F Merchant) . | ☎ (540) 592-3533
MISS Susan B—at ☎ (212) 633-8389 | ''Ayrshire''
149 W 10 St, Apt 5, New York, NY *10014* . . . . | Upperville, VA
MR William S 4th—at ☎ (703) 522-5246 | *20185*
601 N Lincoln St, Arlington, VA *22201-2308* . . |
MR Claiborne M—at U of Ala Tuscaloosa . . . . . |

Stokes MR & MRS William Standley (Sarah Lee Biddle) Ssk.Gm.Me.Cyc.Fw.
☎ (610) 356-0430 . . 800 Grubbs Mill Rd, Berwyn, PA *19312*

Stone MRS Alexander Graham (Hagan—Dolly O'Neile Corbin)
Evg.Cvc.Sl . . .of
☎ (561) 655-1340 . . ''Dolly's Folly'' 50 Middle Rd, Palm Beach,
FL *33480*
☎ (202) 338-3856 . . Colonnade Apt 1422, 2801 New Mexico Av NW,
Washington, DC *20007*

Stone MR & MRS Charles Lanier (Jacqueline B Hekma) Y'52 ⚓ . . of
☎ (203) 661-7120 . . 870 North St, Greenwich, CT *06831*
☎ (508) 993-8284 . . Nonquitt, South Dartmouth, MA *02748*

Stone MRS David L (Patricia A Dugall) Sth'65 . . . . | ☎ (540) 547-9881
MR Paul D—Skd'91—at ☎ (201) 366-4320 | Listening Heart
44 Center Grove Rd, Apt P30, Randolph, NJ | Farm at Rose Hill,
07869-4421 . . . . | Rte 1, Box 235,
| Reva, VA *22735*

Stone MR Edward C—M.Me.Dick'82
☎ (610) 525-4765 . . 924 Deer Rd, Bryn Mawr, PA *19010*

Stone MR & MRS Edward L (Cassandra S Reeve)
Rdc'63.Sm.Srb.Nrr.Chi.Y'58
☎ (401) 847-8883 . . ''The Poplars'' 12 Leroy Av, Newport, RI *02840*

Stone MR & MRS Franz T (Katherine D Jones)
Bf.Cybf.St.Ts.Mt.G.Ncd.H'29
☎ (561) 278-9914 . . El Cortijo, Apt 4CS, 1171 N Ocean Blvd,
Gulf Stream, FL *33483*

Stone MR & MRS Galen L (Anne Brewer) Mt.B.Chi.H'43 . . of
☎ (617) 326-3140 . . 214 Lowder St, Dedham, MA *02026*
☎ (508) 748-0293 . . ''Great Hill'' Marion, MA *02738*

Stone MR & MRS George E (Charlotte C Harper) | ☎ (864) 585-4769
Ln.Sm.Hn.H'56 . . . . | 17 Springdale Lane,
MISS Ruth G—at 123 Queen St, Charleston, SC | Spartanburg, SC
29401 . . . . | *29302*
MR Eliot—at 103 Brixton Court, Spartanburg, SC |
29301 . . . . |

Stone MRS Henry A JR (Elizabeth R Kindleberger) | ☎ (910) 251-9465
BMr'33 . . . . | E14 Oleander Court
MR Nicholas B—at 7631 Beck Rd, Belleville, MI | Apts, Wilmington,
48111 . . . . | NC *28403*
MR Crosby—at 1295 Buck St, Eugene, OR *97402* |

Stone MR & MRS James C (Dorothy A Brett) Cin'40.Cin'40.Stan'49
☎ (510) 837-5159 . . PO Box 374, Diablo, CA *94528*

Stone DR & MRS Lawrence A (Marnette Butler) Van'54.Van'54
☎ (210) 824-5402 . . 2638 Brookhurst Dv, San Antonio, TX *78209*

Stone MRS Melville E (Naomi C Burton)
188 Jones Av, Apt 109, Portsmouth, NH *03801-5516*

Stone MR & MRS Richard B (Marlene L Singer) | ☎ (011-45)
Van'57.Mt.H'49.Cl'54 . . . . | 31-42-31-44
MISS Amy—at 1315½ N Curson Av, | American Embassy,
Los Angeles, CA *90046* . . . . | Copenhagen,
MR Elliot—at 161 Shore Dv S, Miami, FL *33133* | Denmark, APO AE,
| *09716*

Stone MR & MRS Richard H (Blackiston—Wilson— | ☎ (860) 824-5980
Isabel C Livingston) Bradford'77.Rens'65 . . . . . | PO Box 234,
MR Alexander H Blackiston—at Ohio State . . | Falls Village, CT
MR H Schuyler Blackiston—at | *06031*
Johnson & Wales . . . . |
JUNIORS MR Nathaniel L Wilson—at |
Woodberry Forest . . . . |

Stone MRS Robert G (Bertha Lea Barnes)
North Hill E210, 865 Central Av, Needham, MA *02192*

Stone MR & MRS Roger D (Florence O Smith) | ☎ (202) 337-6286
V'60.C.Y'55 . . . . | 3403 O St NW,
MISS Leslie B . . . . | Washington, DC
| *20007*

Stone MR & MRS Timothy J (Cleveland—Nancy S Morehead)
Wheat'62.Y'48
☎ (212) 988-4208 . . 301 E 69 St, New York, NY *10021*

Stone MR & MRS Warren T (Sally M Warden) M.Me.Sa.Pa'54 . . of
☎ (610) 525-1344 . . 1234 Ridgewood Rd, Bryn Mawr, PA *19010*
☎ (941) 378-1517 . . 7612 Donald Ross Rd W, Sarasota, FL *34240*

Stoner MR & MRS Frank R 3d (Sarah H Sutherland) P'50
☎ (410) 819-6939 . . 6065 Hedges Lane, Easton, MD *21601*

Stoner MR & MRS John N (E Louise C Putnam) Va'80.Va'79
☎ (804) 296-7501 . . 230 Chestnut Oak Lane, Charlottesville, VA *22901*

Stonesifer DR & MRS Geary L JR (Ann Carter Kennedy)
Gchr'59.Elk.Gv.Mv.Pn.P'54
☎ (410) 363-8400 . . 3107 Golf Course Rd W, Owings Mills, MD *21117*

Stonesifer MR & MRS Geary L 3d (Shelley A Bowen)
Duke'88.O'91.Gv.Duke'86.Tul'92
☎ (410) 429-4341 . . 2750 Butler Rd, Glyndon, MD *21071*

Stonor HON Julia M C M (Saunders—HON Julia M C M Stonor)
☎ (011-44-171) 385-8528 . . ''Stonor Lodge'' 90 Burnthwaite Rd,
Fulham, London SW6 5BG, England

Stookey MR & MRS John Hoyt (Katherine E Emory) | of ☎ (212)769-4658
Un.Lx.C.Cw.Cc.Cly.Ncd.Aht'52 . . . . | 80 Central Park W,
MR Hunt E—at ☎ (203) 656-0360 | New York, NY
164 Old Kings H'way S, Darien, CT *06820* . . . . | *10023*
MR Anson G P—at ☎ (415) 771-7630 | ☎ (203) 259-5857
1 Charlton Court, Apt 304, San Francisco, CA | 1155 Sasco Hill Rd,
94123 . . . . | Southport, CT
| *06490-0434*

Storer MISS Ethel T
☎ (413) 229-8168 . . 2105 S Under Mountain Rd, Sheffield, MA *01257*

Storer MR & MRS Francis E (Dinet—Bankier—Nancy Bruce Fulton)
Rdc'47.Rv.Csn.Cl'58
☎ (941) 434-7242 . . "The Billows" 2601 Gulf Shore Blvd N, Naples, FL *34102*

Storer MR & MRS Robert T P JR (Margaret Amory) Ec.H.'45
MISS Susan P—Mid'75.Dth'80—at
☎ (513) 321-8953 . . 3068 Portsmouth Av, Cincinnati, OH *45208* . . . .
MISS Margaret A—at ☎ (617) 266-4429
128 Marlborough St, Boston, MA *02116* . . . . . .
| ☎ (508) 927-0058 PO Box 5263, Beverly Farms, MA *01915*

Storer MR & MRS Robert T P 3d (Donna J Bussema) ArizSt'78.Cy.H.'79
☎ (508) 655-7636 . . 10 Ward Lane, Sherborn, MA *01770*

Storey MR & MRS Anderson (Joan A Butkowsky) Gen'68.Cc.Nasson'67
☎ (508) 768-6826 . . Giddings Farm, 143 John Wise Av, Essex, MA *01929*

Storey MR & MRS Bayard T (Frances M Elliot) Rdc'56.Ph.Ac.H'53
☎ (215) 557-8183 . . 1919 Brandywine St, Philadelphia, PA *19130*

Storey MR & MRS Charles Mills (Marie-Armide L Ellis)
Br'81.Va'87.H'82.H'89
☎ (508) 768-6300 . . Giddings Farm, 143 John Wise Av, Essex, MA *01929*

Storey MR & MRS Charles P (Helen H Stephens) Tex'48
☎ (214) 522-2292 . . 4400 Rheims Place, Dallas, TX *75205*

Storey MRS Forbes-Johnson (Polly Forbes-Johnson)
☎ (207) 244-7791 . . "Farm House" Cranberry Isles, ME *04625*

Storey MR & MRS James M (von Steiger—Evans—Isabelle H Boeschenstein)
Nf.Sm.Tv.C.Chi.Hn.H'53 ⚓ . . of
☎ (617) 720-0603 . . 89A Mt Vernon St, Boston, MA *02108*
☎ (207) 244-4108 . . Cranberry Isles, ME *04625*

Storey MR John C—Cy.H'35
☎ (617) 333-0440 . . 175 Milton St, Apt 12, Milton, MA *02186-2344*

Storey MRS Patricia P (Patricia V S Pruyn) . . . .
MR Peter Van S . . . .
MR John H . . . .
MR Philip B . . . .
| ☎ (617) 320-9436 45 Old Farm Rd, Dedham, MA *02026*

Stork MR Francis Wharton—Pc.Hav'34.Temp'40.Temp'47
☎ (215) 233-2516 . . 6195 W Mill Rd, Flourtown, PA *19031*

Storm DR & MRS George (Jane R Shoemaker)
Yh.Y'55.Cl'59 . . . .
MR Anthony R—at 42—8 St, Apt 5405, Charlestown, MA *02129-4228* . . . .
| ☎ (603) 772-4812 110 Pickpocket Rd, Brentwood, NH *03833*

Storment MR & MRS F Page (Marie C Zuloaga)
Sth'54.Pr.Ck.Cly.Y.Cal'48.H'50 . . . .
MISS Claire H—at ☎ (617) 783-2153
16 Ransom Rd, Boston, MA *02135* . . . .
| ☎ (516) OR1-7252 Feeks Lane, Mill Neck, NY *11765*

Storment MR Peter M—H.'85
☎ (212) 355-0923 . . 412 E 55 St, Apt 6A, New York, NY *10022*

Storrow MRS James J (Stephenson—Brooke—Edythe M Geissinger)
CtCol'43.Ey.Rby.Hb.
☎ (941) 263-7346 . . Horizon House 602, 3951 Gulf Shore Blvd N, Naples, FL *34103*

Storrs MR & MRS David K (Young—Landon R Thorn) Ny.Pqt.Yn.Y'67.H'71 . . . .
MR David K JR—at 330 W 72 St, New York, NY *10023* . . . .
| ☎ (203) 255-4969 65 Southgate Lane, Southport, CT *06490*

Storrs MRS Gervas McE (Helen B Hawkins) Cda.
☎ (410) 669-5893 . . 208 Bolton Place, Baltimore, MD *21217*

Storrs MR Richard S (Frances Rousmaniere) Pr.
☎ (516) 922-4391 . . 6 Cove Neck Rd, Oyster Bay, NY *11771*

Story MR & MRS Howard C JR (Eaton—Barstow—Fritzi T Glauser)
NotreD'57.Unn.Evg.Pa'42
☎ (561) 848-4597 . . 620 N Lake Way, Palm Beach, FL *33480*

Story MR & MRS Julian R (Patricia M Adams)
Cc.Ox'59 . . . .
MISS Jane P—at ☎ (011-44-171) 352-2398
48A Redcliffe Gardens, London SW10, England
MISS Sarah A F . . . .
| ☎ (011-44-1306) 882075 Old Bury Hill House, Westcott, Dorking, Surrey RH4 3JU, England

Story CAPT & MRS William F (Martha van Beuren)
Ws'62.An.Ny.USN'62 ⚓
☎ (804) 725-9134 . . "Holly Cove" Cricket Hill Rd, PO Box 117, Hudgins, VA *23076*

Stott MRS Alan E (Norman—Scott—Harriman—Marion Morrow) Cal'40
☎ (011-44-1491) 575732 . . 8 Rupert Close, Henley-on-Thames, Oxfordshire RG9 2JD, England

Stott MR Donald B—B.P.'60
☎ (212) 879-1533 . . 700 Park Av, New York, NY *10021*

Stott MR & MRS Gordon D (H Elizabeth Hubbard) V'41.Cl'59.Nu'89.Csn.
☎ (860) 677-4678 . . 20 Devonwood Dv, Apt 267E, Farmington, CT *06032-1471*

Stott MR & MRS James L JR (E Nivin Snyder)
W&L'63 . . . .
MISS Anne N—at Barnard . . . .
MR James G—at Colgate . . . .
| ☎ (612) 473-6888 1850 Fox Ridge Rd, Long Lake, MN *55356*

Stott MRS Joan Johnson (Quinn—Joan W Johnson) Evg.BtP.
☎ (717) 226-3346 . . "Rockwood Acres" Daniels Rd, PO Box 8, Lakeville, PA *18438*
Dec 1 . . ☎ (561) 691-3919 . . 11301 Turtle Beach Rd, North Palm Beach, FL *33408*

Stott MR & MRS Robert L JR (Fell—Heidi M Bingham) B.Pr.Ng.Cly.P'52 . . . .
MR David W W—Nu'91—at ☎ (212) 598-1014
172 E 4 St, Apt 10C, New York, NY *10009* . . .
MR Lawrence L B—F&M'90—at
☎ (212) 982-0714 . . 316 E 11 St, Apt 3C, New York, NY *10003* . . . .
| of ☎ (212)288-6278 3 E 77 St, Apt 9A, New York, NY *10021*
☎ (561) 234-5897 129 Island Creek Dv, John's Island, Vero Beach, FL *32963*

Stouch MR & MRS Bruce C (Patricia A Heppe 2d) Ty'82.Me.Laf'81
☎ (610) 356-8658 . . 3211 Saw Mill Rd, Newtown Square, PA *19073*

Stout MRS A Varick (Simonds—Elizabeth S Sprague)
☎ (802) 985-8600 . . 52 Harbour Rd, Shelburne, VT *05482*

Stout MR & MRS Bayard D (Parker—M Ruth Maney) Rm.Stc.Rv.
☎ (908) 747-1081 . . 3 Orchard Lane, Rumson, NJ *07760*

Stout MR & MRS Charles L (Gatchell—Margaret B Parsons) Sth'57.Elk.Md.P'53 . . . .
MISS Margaret P Gatchell . . . .
| ☎ (410) 825-7346 8 Malvern Court, Baltimore, MD *21204*

Stout MR Frank D—Cho.Bhm.Cr'44
☎ (707) 963-4515 . . 800 Greenfield Rd, St Helena, CA *94574*
Stout MRS J Jeppson (Julie Jeppson) Sl. . . . . | ☎ (202) 965-1225
MISS Antonia A—at ☎ (212) 505-0048 | 3016 O St NW,
131-133 Thompson St, Apt A1, New York, NY | Washington, DC
10012 . . . . | *20007*
MISS Julie S—at St Paul's . . . . |
MR Carder J—at ☎ (212) 929-0709 |
81 Bedford St, Apt 5C, New York, NY *10014* . . |
Stout MR Joseph C 3d . . see D C Fuchs
Stout MRS Joseph Suydam (Barbara H Donaldson)
354 W Neck Rd, Lloyd Harbor, Huntington, NY *11743*
Stout MR Mark W H—Rr.CarnM'82
☎ (206) 836-2503 . . 18666 Redmond Way, Apt D1027, Redmond,
WA *98053*
Stout MR & MRS Merrell L JR (Madge B Lohmeyer) | ☎ (706) 738-7207
Elk.Md.Mv.Duke'58 . . . . | 3403 Walton Way,
MISS Anne L . . . . | Augusta, GA *30909*
MISS Barry L . . . . |
Stout MR & MRS Morris A 3d (Deborah D Melcher) Pc.Br'46
☎ (215) CH7-6316 . . 112 W Springfield Av, Philadelphia, PA *19118*
Stout MR & MRS Morris A 4th (Anne C Woodruff) Van'79.Pc.AmU'75
☎ (215) 886-0291 . . 540 Custis Rd, Glenside, PA *19038*
Stout MR & MRS Prentice K (Margaret A Rice) Denis'56
☎ (401) 783-0838 . . 15 Dockray Rd, Wakefield, RI *02879*
Stout MISS Susan A—V'72.NCar'80
☎ (202) 745-5803 . . 1210 Euclid St NW, Washington, DC *20009*
Stout MR William C . . see D C Fuchs
Stovell MR & MRS James B (Snyder—Thompson—Katharine G Randolph)
Rcn.Ny.
☎ (941) 676-5465 . . Mountain Lake, Lake Wales, FL *33853*
Stovell DR & MRS Peter B (Helen P Stockman) | ☎ (203) 255-4696
Ny.Pqt.Rby.Yn.H'64.Cl'68 ⚓ . . . . | 164 Greenfield Hill
MISS Helen P—H'95—at Columbia Phys & Surg | Rd, Fairfield, CT
MR James B 2d—H'91—at San Francisco, CA . . | *06430*
MR Peter M—H'93—at New York, NY . . . . |
JUNIORS MISS Mary C . . . . |
Stovell MR & MRS Thomas P (Alice B Wilson) Me.
☎ (610) MI2-3592 . . 230 Booth Lane, Haverford, PA *19041*
Stowe MR & MRS Charles R B (Laura L Everett)
DBU'76.Van'71.Dallas'76.Houst'82
☎ (409) 295-0010 . . 564 Akridge Dv, Huntsville, TX *77340*
Stowe MR David B—Ny.H'39 . . . . | PO Box 2144,
MR Richard A M—at Santa Barbara, CA . . . . . . | Huntsville, TX
MR Henry B—at Pensacola, FL . . . . | *77341-2144*
Stowe MRS Putnam T (McCown—Juliana Wright) | ☎ (610) LA5-1171
Sth'49.Me.Gm.Ac.Myf.Ncd. . . . . | 736 Stoke Rd,
MR John A McCown—at Salt Lake City, UT | Villanova, PA *19085*
Stowell MRS Edward Esty (Helen D'Olier) Ncd.Hn.
☎ (201) 425-3866 . . RD 1, Baileys Mill Rd, Basking Ridge, NJ *07920*
Straat MR & MRS Kent L (Donna Miller) | ☎ (203) 324-5121
Snc.Rv.Hl.Leh'58 . . . . | 14 Cresthill Place,
MR Theodore K . . . . | Stamford, CT *06902*

Strachan MR & MRS F Duncan M 3d (Camille Jones) | ☎ (504) 523-2697
Rol'64.Tul'67.Fic.Cw.Ht. . . . . | 1717 Coliseum
MISS Felicity S F . . . . | Place, New Orleans,
MR Frank G 2d . . . . | LA *70130*
JUNIORS MR Minor S P . . . . |
JUNIORS MR F D Macperson 4th . . . . |
JUNIORS MR Eric C P . . . . |
Stradella MRS Charles G (Marilyn Carter) Ln.
☎ (954) 941-1948 . . 945 Hillsboro Mile, Pompano Beach, FL *33062*
Strader MR & MRS John J 4th (Joan E Ganne)
3650 Clifton Av, Cincinnati, OH *45220-1704*
Straehley MRS Erwin M (Margaret V Cureton)
☎ (513) 271-5310 . . 7010 Rowan Hill Dv, Apt 441, Cincinnati,
OH *45227*
Strain MRS Martha B (Martha B Bitner) | ☎ (516) 889-6015
SL'67.Adelphi'68.Nyc. . . . . | 76 Dalton St,
MISS Amanda B . . . . | Long Beach, NY
MR Robert M 3d . . . . | *11561*
Strain MR Robert M JR—Ny.Cin'64.Cin'65
☎ (516) 371-6731 . . 1635 Ocean Blvd, PO Box 476, Atlantic Beach,
NY *11509*
Stralem MR Pierre—Pn.P'32
651 Bering Dv, Apt 1202, Houston, TX *77057*
Strand MR & MRS John G (Amanda S Bidlack) Nu'88.Mass'80
☎ (301) 607-4127 . . 3812 Pippins Place, Point Of Rocks, MD *21777*
Strandberg MR A David 3d—Duke'84.Mich'88 . . see J R Wierdsma
Strandberg MR & MRS Robert S (Robin L Fancher) RMWmn'87.Pr.Ham'86
☎ (404) 222-9500 . . 828 Ralph McGill Blvd NE, 300 & 302, Atlanta,
GA *30306*
Strang MR & MRS Michael L (Kathleen Sherry) | of ☎ (970)963-2319
V'56.Pn.P'51.P'56 . . . . | Mill Iron Lazy M
MISS Laura—Vt'86 . . . . | Ranch, 0393 County
MISS Bridget S—Del'90 . . . . | Rd 102, Carbondale,
MR Michael L JR—Col'86 . . . . | CO *81623*
| ☎ (202) 544-0470
| 218—2 St SE,
| Washington, DC
| *20003*
Strange MRS A Bruton (Burns—Dugdale—Jane Kennedy) Yn.
☎ (561) 659-7494 . . 1801 S Flagler Dv, 903, West Palm Beach,
FL *33401-7346*
Strange MR & MRS Andrew H (Mary G Lawrence) Roan'82.U'82
515 Church Rd, Eagleville, PA *19403*
Strange MR Robert H—Sm.Nrr.Stan'36.Ox'38
☎ (619) 756-8160 . . PO Box 2021, Rancho Santa Fe, CA *92067*
Stransky MR & MRS Thomas M (Hillary Olyphant) Hartw'84.GeoW'85
☎ (908) 439-3431 . . 14 New Bromley Rd, Whitehouse Station,
NJ *08889*
Strasenburgh MR & MRS J Griffin (Suzanne C | ☎ (603) 643-1529
Thompson) Eh.Cda.Mid'70 . . . . | PO Box 5156,
MR John G JR—at Ridley . . . . | Hanover, NH *03755*
JUNIORS MISS Allison W . . . . |
JUNIORS MR Blair B—at Avon Old Farms . . . . . . |

Strate MR & MRS Norman F JR (Ann M Latimer) | ☎ (203) 227-6757
Susq'64.Leh'62.Pa'65 . . . . | 11 Glenwood Rd,
MISS Margaret A . . . . | Weston, CT *06883*
MISS Mary E—at St Andrew's . . . . |
MISS Amanda I—at Museum of Fine Arts Sch . . |

Strater MR & MRS Edward P (Blanche Frenning) | ☎ (860) 742-5800
Rdc'51.Cw.H'50 . . . . | 248 Goose Lane,
MR William E 2d—at ☎ (860) 632-0603 | Coventry, CT *06238*
18 Trolley Crossing Lane, Middletown, CT *06457* |

Stratford MRS Herbert R (Margo J Wyeth) Cho.Cas.Fy.
☎ (307) 587-3903 . . Lazy Bar F Ranch, 576 Hunter Creek Rd, Cody,
WY *82414*

Straton MR & MRS John C JR (Marion S Holder) | of ☎ (914)351-4424
T.Fw.Plg.Va'54 . . . . | Ledge Rd,
MISS Sara S—at 237 Tappan Rd, Norwood, NJ | Tuxedo Park, NY
07698 . . . . | *10987*
MISS Ashley H . . . . | ☎ (212) PL8-9687
MR John C 3d—at 237 Tappan Rd, Norwood, NJ | 155 E 47 St,
07698 . . . . | New York, NY
| *10017*

Stratton MISS Lucinda—Tufts'89.Cl'92 . . see W E Boom

Stratton MR Walter L—Ihy.Yn.Y'48.H'51 . . | ☎ (203) 869-8294
MR John E—at 15 Westview Lane, Riverside, CT | 434 Round Hill Rd,
06878 . . . . | Greenwich, CT
| *06831*

Straub MR & MRS W Watson (Cheryl L Sterner) FlaSo'88.M.Me.FlaSo'91
☎ (610) 527-3339 . . 103B Summit Dv, Bryn Mawr, PA *19010*

Straub MRS William C (Piel—Crouse—Mary K Loomis)
☎ (860) 364-0147 . . ''Okeden'' Sharon, CT *06069*

Straube DR & MRS William L (Paula F P Henry)
Reed'77.Md'85.Knox'77.Md'89
☎ (301) 474-1874 . . 47F Ridge Rd, Greenbelt, MD *20770*

Straus MR Edward K . . . . Died at
New York, NY Aug 21'96

Straus DR & MRS Francis H 2d (Helen L | ☎ (773) DO3-7145
Puttkammer) Rdc'55.Ch'62.H'53.Ch'57. . . . . . | 5642 S Kimbark Av,
MISS (DR) Helen E—Ch'84.Ch'90 . . . . | Chicago, IL *60637*
MR Francis H 3d—H'81 . . . . |
DR Christopher M—Ch'88.Ch'92 . . . . |
MR Michael W—MichSt'92 . . . . |

Straus MR Kenneth H . . . . Died at
New York, NY Jly 24'96

Straus MRS Kenneth H (Murphy—Brenda V | of ☎ (212)288-5278
Neubauer) Br'61.Nu'86.Un.Pr.StJ.Myf.H. . . . . . | 60 East End Av, Apt
MISS Sarah P C Murphy—Smu'95 . . . . | 40C, New York, NY
| *10028*
| ☎ (561) 844-7886
| 745 N Lake Way,
| Palm Beach, FL
| *33480*

Straus MR & MRS Michael S (Philippa McC Bainbridge)
3004 Brookwood Rd, Birmingham, AL *35223*

Straus MRS Ralph I (Maffitt—Katherine Mulvane) Mt.Cs . . .of
☎ (212) 935-6197 . . 14 Sutton Place S, Apt 13F, New York, NY *10022*
☎ (602) 488-1651 . . 36402 N Derringer Rd, Box 922, Carefree,
AZ *85377*

Straus MR & MRS Thomas P (Carol A Herschel) | ☎ (914) 835-0355
Wil'58.Myf.Y'58.H'64 . . . . | 66 Barlow Lane,
MR Stephen D—Colg'87—at Cambridge, MA . . | Rye, NY *10580*
MR Douglas B—at Austin, TX . . . . |

Straus MR Timothy von F—Ub.Nrr.Ste.JHop'76
☎ (617) 859-9984 . . 224 Marlborough St, Boston, MA *02116*

Strauss RR ADM & MRS Elliott B (Beatrice S Phillips)
Mt.An.Cvc.Ny.Sl.USN'23
☎ (202) 332-5042 . . 2945 Garfield Terr NW, Washington, DC *20008*

Strauss MR & MRS Elliott MacGregor (Tower— | of ☎ (212)861-3521
Luise E von Mayrhauser) Un.Mt.Nrr.Srb.H'50 . . | 201 E 79 St,
MISS Caroline H Tower—CtCol'95—at | New York, NY
H1058 Budapest, Belgrad rakpart 27 I-3A, | *10021*
Hungary . . . . | ☎ (401) 847-1786
MISS Lydia M Tower—at Conn Coll . . . . | ''Bridge House''
| 485 Paradise Av,
| Middletown, RI
| *02842*

Strauss MR & MRS Theodore H (Annette L Greenfield) Tex'44.Cl'45.Tex'46
☎ (214) 368-6821 . . 3510 Turtle Creek Blvd, Apt 4A, Dallas, TX *75219*

Strawbridge MR & MRS David W (Mary E Burke) | ☎ (610) 397-1976
Me.Ty'62 . . . . | 298 Militia Dv,
MR Christopher W—Wms'90 . . . . | Radnor, PA *19087*
MR Geoffrey D—Ty'93 . . . . | . . MRS absent

Strawbridge MR & MRS Francis R 3d (Mary Jo | ☎ (610) 664-5096
Beatty) Gm.Me.W.Ac.P.'59 . . . . | 25 Merion Station,
MISS Elisabeth D . . . . | Merion, PA *19066*
MISS Margaret B . . . . |

Strawbridge MRS Frederic H JR (Emily E Clothier)
☎ (610) 642-1165 . . ''Ballytore'' Wynnewood, PA *19096*

Strawbridge MR & MRS G Stockton (Mary T Lowry) Ph.Gm.Me.Rd.Ncd.
☎ (610) NI4-2236 . . Cross Brook Farm, 928 Garrett Mill Rd,
Newtown Square, PA *19073*

Strawbridge MR & MRS George JR (Neilson—Nina G Stewart)
Srr.Ph.Rcp.Ty'60
☎ (302) 571-8340 . . 3801 Kennett Pike, B100, Greenville, DE *19807*

Strawbridge MR & MRS John 3d (Suzanne K Foley) | ☎ (860) 263-2373
Me.Cry.Yn.Y'65 . . . . | PO Box 1058,
MISS Samantha Jones—at ☎ (307) 733-2435 | Washington, CT
PO Box 917, Wilson, WY *83014* . . . . | *06793*
MR Welsh Oak |

Strawbridge MR & MRS John N (Catharine D Stryker) Rcp.Dh.
☎ (203) 855-8030 . . 61 Lockwood Lane, Norwalk, CT *06851*

Strawbridge MR & MRS Peter S (Elizabeth H Blagden) Rd.Ham'60
☎ (610) 647-7343 . . 8002 Goshen Rd, Newtown Square, PA *19073*

Strawbridge MR Richard V—Pa'67 . . . . | ☎ (610) 363-5622
MR Andrew V—at ☎ (312) 397-0224 | PO Box 563,
1924 N Burling St, Chicago, IL *60614* . . . . | Chester Springs, PA
| *19425*

Strawbridge MR Robert E III—B.Rc.Ln.H'62 . . of
☎ (307) 733-8810 . . PO Box 25002, Jackson, WY *83001*
☎ (610) 869-2101 . . Chatham Farm, PO Box 156, Chatham, PA *19318*

Strawbridge MR Robert E 4th . . see M W Smith

Strawbridge MRS Welsh (Margaret E Marshall) Ac.Ncd.
☎ (215) DI3-6577 . . ''Graeme Park'' Horsham, PA *19044*

Strawbridge MRS William J (Finch—Powers—Marjorie S Flagg) Pr.Cly.
☎ (516) 674-0789 . . 10 Quail Ridge Rd, Glen Cove, NY *11542*

Strawbridge MR & MRS William J JR (McSweeney—
Christine S Penniman) Nf.Chr.Cly.Br'60 . . . . .
☎ (410) 822-8228
"Hippo"
6860 Travelers Rest
Circle, Easton, MD
21601-7668
MISS Sabrina V—at 90 Victoria St, Windsor, CT
06095 . . . .
MR Geoffrey T . . . .
MR Michael R—at 812 Gerald St, Missoula, MT
59801 . . . .
MISS A Thayer McSweeney—at 206 E 81 St,
New York, NY 10028 . . . .
MISS Christine S McSweeney—at
Roanoke Coll . . . .
JUNIORS MISS Catherine B D McSweeney . . . .

Strebeigh MISS Katherine Waring
☎ (818) 505-1835 . . 10153½ Riverside Dv, Apt 212, Toluca Lake,
CA 91602

Strebeigh MR Robert M—P'45 . . . .
☎ (813) 398-1129
PO Box 718,
Bay Pines, FL
33744-0718
MSRS T Lee & Thomas T—at ☎ (415) 898-2466
851 Hayden Av, Novato, CA 94928 . . . .

Strebeigh MRS Waring C (Nancy G Marshall)
Sth'41 . . . .
☎ (508) 994-9332
29 Fremont St,
South Dartmouth,
MA 02748
MR Waring M—Y'74—at ☎ (203) 495-8749
53 Edgehill Rd, New Haven, CT 06511 . . . .

Strebeigh MR Woodruff F
☎ (813) 398-1129 . . PO Box 718, Bay Pines, FL 33504-0718

Street MR & MRS David P (Gretchen Behre)
☎ (404) 875-0973 . . 1083 High Point Dv NE, Atlanta, GA 30306

Street MR & MRS Jeffrey R (Maryann T Mercer) LakeF'80.St.LakeF'80
☎ (508) 369-2764 . . 69 Lexington Rd, Concord, MA 01742

Street MR & MRS Phillips B (Mallery—Berrell
Evans) Rc.Me.Wt.Cr'35 . . . .
☎ (610) 647-8324
1102 Signal Hill
Lane, Berwyn, PA
19312
MISS Anne P—at Denver, CO . . . .
MISS (DR) Berrell E Mallery—YeshivaU'80—at
89 Bleecker St, New York, NY 10012 . . . . . .

Street MR & MRS Thomas A (Sylvia Bassett) St.
☎ (404) 355-8548 . . 915 Hawick Dv NW, Atlanta, GA 30327

Street MASTER Thomas Mercer (Jeffrey R) . . . . Born at
Concord, MA Mch 23'95

Streeter MR & MRS Frank S (Nancy E Angell) Ws'50.Un.Gr.C.Cs.H.'40
☎ (212) LE5-0525 . . 141 E 72 St, New York, NY 10021

Streeter MR & MRS Henry S (Mary Ann Dexter)
Sm.My.Chi.Ncd.H'42 . . . .
☎ (508) 468-2262
"Old Farm"
Maple St, Wenham,
MA 01984
MISS Natalie T—HWSth'88—Box 4377,
Park City, UT 84060 . . . .

Streett REV & MRS David C 2d (Dunlap—
Betty Lou Evans) Aug'67.Tenn'96.Cw.JHop'42.
StJ'50.NashSm'52.So'53.VaTheo'54 . . . .
☎ (601) 627-4496
"The Duck Walk"
1923 Woodlawn
Circle, Clarksdale,
MS 38614-2617
JUNIORS MISS Corbin R G . . . .

Streett MRS J Clark (Frances B Harris)
3604 Dryden Rd, Ft Worth, TX 76109

Streibert MR & MRS Marshall G (Elizabeth A Tweedy)
Carl'61.Minn'65.Y'62 . . of
☎ (212) 289-1623 . . 155 E 93 St, New York, NY 10128
☎ (516) 726-7509 . . 336 Head of Pond Rd, Water Mill, NY 11976

Strekalovsky MR & MRS Vcevold O (M Jane Cram)
Mid'61.Mid'60.Pa'63 . . . .
of ☎ (617)749-0127
47 Fearing Rd,
Hingham, MA
02043
☎ (802) 545-2241
"Gooseneck Bend"
Box 172, RD 1,
Middlebury, VT
05753
MISS Anna B . . . .

Strelinger MRS Gilbert P (Elizabeth Wright)
☎ (314) 863-1663 . . 709 S Skinker Blvd, St Louis, MO 63105

Strelinger MR & MRS Richard W (Margaret P Belt)
Dar.Mo'71 . . . .
☎ (314) 725-5080
6366 Alamo Av,
St Louis, MO 63105
MISS Elizabeth P . . . .
JUNIORS MISS Margaret S . . . .
JUNIORS MR Richard W JR . . . .

Strickland MR & MRS Seth DeV (Katherine J
Fulenwider) Dth'60.Dth'61 . . . .
☎ (203) 869-4813
14 Stanwich Lane,
Greenwich, CT
06830
MISS Cynthia S . . . .
MISS Elizabeth J . . . .

Strickler MR & MRS Richard S JR (Diana B Hole)
Wms'73.Cl'79.H'70.Pa'76.Pa'76 . . . .
of ☎ (804)979-9493
"Woodbine"
6 Sunset Circle,
Charlottesville, VA
22901
☎ (203) 245-7093
20 Grove Av,
Madison, CT 06443
JUNIORS MISS Margaret E H . . . .

Stride MR & MRS William F A (Caroline B McGlennon)
Sth'54.Ec.Chi.USN'53
☎ (508) 283-3255 . . "Indian Spring" Elm Av, Eastern Point,
Gloucester, MA 01930

Stringham MR Elliott L—Un.Chr.Coa.Snc.Cw.Rv.Gettys'68.LIU'74 . . of
☎ (212) 861-1682 . . 124 E 71 St, New York, NY 10021
☎ (516) 627-2163 . . 62 Valley Rd, Plandome, NY 11030

Stringham MR & MRS John K (Alice F Petersen)
Wash'56.Cr'59 . . . .
☎ (573) 766-5647
HC 65, Box 32,
Belgrade, MO 63622
MR John Fell . . . .
MR George E . . . .

Stroh MISS Elizabeth Rutledge Weyerhaeuser Day (John William III) . . . . .
Born Apr 25'96

Stroh MR & MRS John William III (Vivian Weyerhaeuser Day)
Rich'85.OWes'82
☎ (313) 881-5416 . . 516 Shelden Rd, Grosse Pointe Shores, MI 48236

Stroh MR & MRS Peter W (Nicole E
Fauquet-Lemaitre) Nyc.P'51 . . . .
☎ (313) 886-9099
26 Waverly Lane,
Grosse Pointe
Farms, MI 48236
MR Pierre A—at 201 E 69 St, Apt 3G, New York,
NY 10021 . . . .
MR Frederic C—at 1416—30 St NW,
Washington, DC 20007 . . . .

Stroh MR & MRS Samuel E (Emmie K King) Conv'82
☎ (334) 277-7033 . . 4512 W Lisa Court, Montgomery, AL 36106-3522

Strong MR & MRS Benjamin W (Christina M Woodward)
Skd'85.Rut'88.Lm.Ds.Thiel'80
☎ (609) 497-9310 . . 46A Haverhill Court, Princeton, NJ 08540

Strong MRS Bonsall (Katharine B Bonsall) Swb'39.Lm.Cda.Dh.
☎ (860) 536-2427 . . 54 Morgan Point, Noank, CT 06340

Strong MR & MRS Frederick S 3d (White—Leary—Elizabeth N Shontz) Ws'41.Pr.Cw.P'35.H'37 . . of
☎ (561) 231-5491 . . 300 Harbour Dv, Apt 103A, Vero Beach, FL *32963*
☎ (810) 646-9164 . . 56 Vaughn Ridge, Bloomfield Hills, MI *48304*

Strong MR & MRS George V 3d (Ann P Hiestand)
Pa'83.Pa'88.Me.Duke'78.Nw'81
☎ (610) 527-2979 . . 5 Haymarket Lane, Bryn Mawr, PA *19010*

Strong MR & MRS Harry B (Connie R Brunner) NMont'84.Ds.Rut'78
☎ (406) 273-2306 . . 308 Tyler Way, Lolo, MT *59847*

Strong MISS Juliana M—OWes'87.Pc.
☎ (610) 660-8060 . . 219 Grayling Av, Apt 5, Narberth, PA *19072*

Strong MISS Lucy L
☎ (773) 244-2376 . . 652 W Waveland Av, Chicago, IL *60613*

Strong MRS Nancy J (de Rohan—Nancy S Jones)
☎ (908) 234-2077 . . PO Box 986, Far Hills, NJ *07931*

Strong MR & MRS Newbold (Anne S Ashton) Pc.Sg.M.P'51
☎ (215) 242-0778 . . 105 W Mermaid Lane, Philadelphia, PA *19118*

Strong MISS Nina Altair Livingston (Benjamin W) . . . . Born at Lawrenceville, NJ Apr 4'96

Strong MR & MRS Peter B (Lindsey M Callen) Mid'83.OWes'85
☎ (617) 266-5272 . . 25 Marlborough St, Boston, MA *02116*

Strong MRS Phebe (Phebe Drayton) Pc.
☎ (215) 836-9217 . . 8125 Eastern Av, Wyndmoor, PA *19038*

Strong MR & MRS Philip L (Sally A Borthwick) | ☎ (609) 395-0820
Lm.Snc.Ds.Hn.H'40.Cl'47 . . . . | 93 N Main St,
MR Thomas L—Lm.Ds. | Cranbury, NJ *08512*

Strong MRS Raymond B JR (Ann Schroedel) | ☎ (516) 751-9485
Sth'61.Plg.Lm. . . . . | 34 Brewster Lane E,
MR Raymond B 3d—Mid'91 . . . . | Setauket, NY *11733*
MR Benjamin B—Colby'94 |

Strong MR & MRS Robert L (Mary J Sutherland)
Gchr'46.Bg.Lm.Ds.Snc.Cly.Sl.H'36.Cl'39
☎ (617) 320-0602 . . 10 Longwood Dv, Apt 447, Westwood, MA *02090-1145*

Strong MISS Sally H—Laf'82
☎ (610) 525-3878 . . 1557 County Line Rd, Rosemont, PA *19010*

Strong MR Stephen W—Ne.Cal'63 ⛵ . . . . | ☎ (203) 661-5011
MISS Katerina M . . . . | 1117 E Putnam Av,
MR Stewart W—at U of Conn . . . . | Riverside, CT *06878*

Strong MR & MRS Trowbridge (Alice T Wadsworth) | of ☎ (610)664-8792
Me.Rd.Bow'50 . . . . | 401 S Woodbine
MISS Alice T—UArts'89.Me.—at | Av, Narberth, PA
Rosemont, PA *19010* . . . . | *19072*
| ☎ (716) 243-4191
| "Hartford House"
| Box 236, Geneseo,
| NY *14454*

Strong MR & MRS William L 3d (Beverly C Brand) Rm.Stc.Yn.Y'55
☎ (908) 842-8856 . . 137 Ridge Rd, Rumson, NJ *07760*

Strong MR & MRS William S (Hendel—Ann E Reinke)
Wis'65.K.Sm.H'73.H'77
☎ (617) 491-4905 . . 31 Gray St, Cambridge, MA *02138*

Strong MR & MRS Woodbridge (Joumine de Viry) | ☎ (413) 637-0703
Lx.Lm.Ds.H'32 . . . . | 97 Cliffwood St, PO
MR Alan H—Lm. | Box 491, Lenox,
MR Timothy de V—Lm. . . . . | MA *01240*

Strother MRS Corneille O (Suzanne Moot)
☎ (914) 693-5773 . . 57 Bellewood Av, Dobbs Ferry, NY *10522*

Stroud MR & MRS Samuel S (Judith M Chamberlin) Rb.Ph.Ncd.Pa'50
☎ (215) 233-1007 . . 8500 Ardmore Av, Wyndmoor, PA *19038*

Stroud MRS William D (Agnes H Shober) Ncd.
Dunwoody Village F203, 3500 West Chester Pike, Newtown Square, PA *19073*

Stroud MR & MRS William D 2d (Nancy S Webb)
Va'79.PhilaArt'81.PAFA'81
☎ (610) 687-4263 . . 761 Valley Forge Rd, Wayne, PA *19087*

Strough MRS Ivan C (Anson—Pool—Elizabeth Rogers) Cda.
☎ (609) 426-6684 . . Meadow Lakes, Health Center 10C, Hightstown, NJ *08520*

Strubing MRS Philip H (Elizabeth L Hanes)
☎ (901) 327-4407 . . Trezevant Manor, 177 N Highland St, Memphis, TN *38111-4735*

Struse MR & MRS C Richard (Frederica G K | ☎ (410) 268-5560
Richards) Bost'77.Sl.Pa'67 . . . . | 120 Duke of
JUNIORS MISS Elizabeth L K . . . . | Gloucester St,
| Annapolis, MD
| *21401*

Stryker MR & MRS A Bartlett JR (Catharine F Duane) P'53
☎ (302) 984-1444 . . 3911 Ardleigh Dv, Greenville, DE *19807*

Stuart MR & MRS Alexander D (Nostrand—Ann R Peake) DU'73.P'72.H'75
☎ (847) 615-8208 . . 366 Scott St, Lake Forest, IL *60045*

Stuart MRS Barbara K (Christenson—Barbara S Kreimer) Cin'45
see MISS M S Kreimer

Stuart MRS Edward T JR (Mildred P Sinkler) | of ☎ (610)688-4250
Cw.Fw. . . . . | 19 Sugar Knoll Dv,
MR Edward T 3d. | Devon, PA *19333*
| ☎ (410) 778-4056
| Patience Reward
| Farm, Quaker Neck
| Landing Rd,
| Chestertown, MD
| *21620*

Stuart MRS Errett F (Berry P Meyer)
☎ (619) 749-1594 . . 18218 Paradise Mountain Rd, Apt 107, Valley Center, CA *92082*

Stuart MR & MRS John D (Mildred H Dent) Va'72
☎ (606) 885-5525 . . Cavalier Farm, 6289 Harrodsburg Rd, Nicholasville, KY *40356*

Stuart MR & MRS Mose W 3d (Eva M Stuckey) | of ☎ (334)272-8537
Ala'56.Aub'52 . . . . | 1708 Croom Dv,
MR William B . . . . | Montgomery, AL
| *36106*
| ☎ (334) 857-3450
| Nero's Point,
| Elmore, AL *36025*

Stuart MR & MRS Robert D JR (Lovenskiold—Ingegjerd Andvord)
Bhm.Mt.Cho.On.Sr.Cas.Ri.Myf.P'37.Y'46 . . of
☎ (847) 234-3894 . . Topsfield Farm, 1601 Conway Rd, Lake Forest, IL *60045*
"Vaekero" Drammensveien 250, 0277 Oslo, Norway

Stuart MR Robert W W—Unn.Evg . . .of
☎ (561) 334-6268 . . 1424 SE Macarthur Blvd, Stuart, FL *34996*
☎ (011-34-52) 448-206 . . ''Villa Monterrey'' Benalmadena,
Malaga, Spain

Stubbins MR Hugh A JR—C.Hb.GaTech'33.H'35
☎ (561) 737-3626 . . 6110 N Ocean Blvd, Ocean Ridge, FL *33435*

Stubbins MRS Sam G (Billie J Malm) Rc. . . . . | ☎ (216) 321-4280
MISS MacKenzie—B'gton'84 . . . . | 13606 Ardoon Av,
Cleveland, OH
44120

Stubblefield DR & MRS Earl T (Ann C Williamson) | of ☎ (601)982-1434
Mlsps'66.Miss'70 . . . . | 2025 Heritage Hill
MISS Ann E . . . . | Dv, Jackson, MS
MISS Holly L . . . . | *39211*
JUNIORS MR Earl T JR . . . . | ☎ (601) 856-5377
''Lake Cavalier
Retreat''
550 Lake Cavalier
Rd, Madison, MS
39110

Stubbs MR & MRS Donald F (Gretel M Bailey) | ☎ (908) 277-3064
Mich'60.Mich'52 . . . . | 68 Woodland Av,
MISS Emily A—Swth'92—at U of Cal Berkeley | Summit, NJ *07901*
Law . . . . |
MISS Christina S—Ober'95 . . . . |

Stubbs MRS John D (Margaret McD Winsor) . . . . . . | ☎ (617) 894-4315
MISS Anne D . . . . | 12 Meadowbrook
Rd, Weston, MA
02193

Stubbs MR & MRS Michael B (Veronica S Mallory) | ☎ (212) 769-2828
Briar'70.Un.K.Ny.Cly.Pa'70 ⚓ . . . . | 88 Central Park W,
MISS A Merrill—at Brown . . . . | New York, NY
MISS Abigail M—at Groton . . . . | *10023*

Stubenbord DR & MRS William T (Jane C | ☎ (212) 879-5327
MacDougall) Cr'62.Ny.Y'58.Cr'62 . . . . | 179 E 70 St,
MISS Elizabeth J—Emory'86.Cda. . . . . | New York, NY
MISS Pamela T—Bost'88.GeoW'91—at | *10021*
860—24 Av, San Francisco, CA *94121* . . . . . . |

Stuckey MR & MRS Jay C JR (Mary S Samples) TexTech'68.Ariz'64
☎ (602) 991-0428 . . 5301 E Desert Vista Rd, Paradise Valley,
AZ *85253*

Studwell MR & MRS James R (Virginia M Healy) Skd'84.Wes'83
☎ (415) 781-7990 . . 665 Greenwich St, San Francisco, CA *94133*

Studwell MISS Susanna Healy (James R) . . . . Born at
San Francisco, CA Jun 30'95

Study MR & MRS Lomax (Phyllis Taft) Wash'49 . . . . | ☎ (310) 472-8361
MISS Simone A—☎ (310) 440-0329 . . . . | 440 Denslow Av,
Los Angeles, CA
90049

Stuebe MR & MRS William H (Isabel M Combs) | ☎ (212) LE5-4218
Duke'64.Nu'78.Leh'63 . . . . | 164 E 72 St,
MISS Alison M—Duke'95 . . . . | New York, NY
JUNIORS MR David A—at Fieldston . . . . | *10021*

Stuhl MR & MRS Harold M JR (Conchita G Werner) Cy.Wes'83.Ch'86
☎ (314) 991-3651 . . 3 Loren Woods, St Louis, MO *63124*

Stulb MR & MRS Edwin H 3d (E Elaine Garrabrant) V'45-4.Pc.Rv.Sdg.
☎ (215) 654-1750 . . 143 Culpepper Dv, Penllyn, PA *19422*

Stulb MR & MRS Edwin H 4th (Laura W Krecker) Swb'74.Pc.Rv.Rm'74
☎ (215) 641-9427 . . 1048 Gypsy Hill Rd, PO Box 93, Penllyn,
PA *19422*

Stulb MR & MRS Joseph 5th (Mary A Pfingst) | ☎ (215) 646-2229
Pc.W&J'49 . . . . | 501 N Bethlehem
MR David O . . . . | Pike, Apt 5D,
Ambler, PA *19002*

Stull MR & MRS Lee T (Elizabeth D Brooks) P'48
☎ (610) 647-4681 . . ''The School House'' S Valley & Whitehorse Rds,
Paoli, PA *19301*

Sturgeon MR Alonzo Holmes 3d—Miss'88
☎ (601) 888-6152 . . PO Box 1175, Woodville, MS *39669*

Sturges MRS Charles P (Lucy Key Miller) . . . . Died at
Palm Beach, FL Apr 8'96

Sturges MR George David—Cal'63 . . of
☎ (818) 799-3555 . . 1155 Hermosa Rd, Pasadena, CA *91105*
☎ (805) 684-3663 . . 4587 Sandyland Rd, Sandyland Cove, Carpinteria,
CA *93013*

Sturges MR Hollister 3d—Cr'62.Cal'65
☎ (203) 869-4012 . . 40 Field Point Park, Greenwich, CT *06830*

Sturges MR John M (Alice Schumacher) So.Cly.Bcs.
☎ (212) 744-8132 . . 215 E 68 St, Apt 19B, New York, NY *10021-5727*

Sturges MR & MRS John P (Davis—Alice C Ellsworth) Y'36
☎ (401) 521-2067 . . 51 Manning St, Providence, RI *02906*

Sturges MR W Delafield
☎ (818) SY9-2105 . . 730 La Loma Rd, Pasadena, CA *91105*

Sturgis MR & MRS John C (Loretta M Howard)
☎ (941) 262-3102 . . 595—3 St N, Naples, FL *34102*

Sturgis MISS Josephine G
☎ (617) 648-8109 . . 35 Wellington St, Arlington, MA *02174*

Sturgis MR & MRS Nathaniel R (Ecaterini Satolias) | 53 Greer St,
Bost'60.Myf.Ne. . . . . | Waltham, MA
MISS Christine—at 837—3 St, Apt 208, | *02154*
Santa Monica, CA *90403* . . . . |

Sturgis MR & MRS Norman R (Linda Terry) Csn.
☎ (941) 466-4240 . . 14830 David Dv, Ft Myers, FL *33908*

Sturgis MR & MRS Robert M (Katharine A Ray) D.Fic.
☎ (508) 653-8416 . . 38 Hunting Lane, Sherborn, MA *01770*

Sturtevant MR & MRS Albert D (Emily D Byron) | ☎ (202) 966-8176
V'63.Mt.Cvc.Y'63.Y'67 . . . . | 3408 Lowell St NW,
MR Albert D 3d . . . . | Washington, DC
MR David B . . . . | *20016*
JUNIORS MR Charles C . . . . |

Sturtevant MISS Brereton—Ws'42.Temp'49
☎ (703) 765-8598 . . 1227 Morningside Lane, Alexandria,
VA *22308-1042*

Sturtevant MR & MRS Charles L (Frances Carter) Cvc.Ct.
☎ (202) 337-5723 . . 3231 Reservoir Rd NW, Washington, DC *20007*

Sturtevant MR & MRS Peter A (Marriott—Linda L Webber)
MtH'60.Cvc.Rol'53.GeoW'62.Vt'67 ⚓
☎ (410) 778-6746 . . ''River House'' 107 N Water St, Chestertown,
MD *21620*

Sturtevant MRS Theodore C (Dane—Barbara H | ☎ (401) 847-0074
Welch) . . . . | ''Swallows Cave''
MISS Eleanor H Dane—at ''San Marco'' | 101 Indian Av,
Center Harbor, NH *03226* . . . . | Middletown, RI
02842

Stuurman MRS John H G 3d (Margaret M Carnese) ☎ (516) 921-2805
Ht. . . . . 35 White Oak Tree
MISS Linda A—V'77.Cl'79. . . . . Rd, Syosset, NY
11791

Succop MR & MRS John C (Susan M Laird) ☎ (214) 680-8027
Pitt'74.Pitt'75.W&J'69 . . . . 2425 Canyon Creek
JUNIORS MR John S . . . . Dv, Richardson, TX
JUNIORS MR Benjamin T *75080*

Sudderth MR & MRS Joe R (Mary A Poole) ☎ (817) 776-1610
Austin'59.JHop'62.Austin'63.FlaSt'66 . . . . 7301 Brentwood
MISS Sara C . . . . Circle, Waco, TX
76712

Sudler MR Carroll H 4th . . see J G Henry
Sudler MISS Elizabeth E . . see J G Henry
Sudler MR Louis C (Virginia F Brown) Ch'33.Ch'34.Sc.Cho.Cas.Cw.
☎ (312) 944-0359 . . 229 E Lake Shore Dv, Chicago, IL *60611-1307*
Sudler MR & MRS Louis C JR (Ames—Laura of ☎ (773)880-5614
Fairbank) Ih.Cw.Fy.Y'53 . . . . 2355 N
MR John W E—at ☎ (802) 563-6016 . . RFD 1, Commonwealth Av,
Box 259A, Cabot, VT *05647* . . . . Chicago, IL *60614*
MR S Zachariah . . . . ☎ (219) 232-4044
MISS Nathalie E Ames—Vt'89 . . . . 62322 Oak Rd,
South Bend, IN
46614

Sulger MISS Sarah P . . see B L Roberts
Sullivan MR & MRS A Gary (Carley A Miller) BostColl'79
☎ (203) 348-7649 . . 39 Intervale Rd, Darien, CT *06820*
Sullivan MR & MRS A Michael JR (Beverly S Bissell) Srb.Ct.Sl . . .of
☎ (202) 965-5697 . . 2817 N St NW, Washington, DC *20007*
☎ (540) 364-1110 . . Guin Mill Farm, PO Box 71, Middleburg,
VA *20118*
☎ (561) 659-0099 . . 124 Australian Av, Palm Beach, FL *33480*
Sullivan MR Arthur Thomas . . . . Died at
Chevy Chase, MD Feb 28'94
Sullivan MR & MRS Barry R (Fagan—Ann S Ebbert) Pitt'62.Pg.Rr.Y'59 . . of
☎ (412) 683-7830 . . 102 Schenley Rd, Pittsburgh, PA *15217*
☎ (412) 238-6083 . . Foxglove Farm, Laughlintown, PA *15655*
Sullivan MR & MRS Benjamin J JR (Charlotte V Mullen)
Sth'76.Cly.NCar'75.Va'82
☎ (914) 967-6438 . . 267 Locust Av, Rye, NY *10580*
Sullivan MRS E Murray (Sarah O M Whitall) Gi.Ncd.
☎ (410) 323-0031 . . Cross Keys, 11B Hamill Rd, Baltimore, MD *21210*
Sullivan MISS Eugenia C—Ac.
☎ (215) 542-9122 . . 239 Tulip Tree Court, Blue Bell, PA *19422*
Sullivan MR Geoffrey P
☎ (301) 654-5372 . . 8904 Kensington P'kway, North Chevy Chase,
MD *20815*
Sullivan MR & MRS Henry P (Joan G Blair) ☎ (412) 741-5357
Ac.Pa'48 . . . . 640 Canterbury
MR Jeremiah J 4th—Hav'78 . . . . Lane, Sewickley, PA
MR H Paul JR—Pitt'84 . . . . *15143*
Sullivan MR J Langdon . . . . Died at
Newport, RI Dec 17'95
Sullivan MRS J Langdon (Griswold—Denny Prager) Plg.Hb.H . . .of
☎ (212) 879-7090 . . 127 E 80 St, New York, NY *10021*
☎ (203) 227-3082 . . "Kettle Creek Farm" 127 Kettle Creek Rd,
Weston, CT *06883*

Sullivan DR & MRS James R (Mary F Ferguson) V'42.Cybf.G.Dth'40.Buf'44
2150 S Ocean Blvd, Apt 7C, Delray Beach, FL *33483*
Sullivan MR & MRS Jeremiah J 3d (Jane Mather)
☎ (610) 793-1157 . . "Cockaigne" 1046 Birmingham Rd,
West Chester, PA *19382*
Sullivan MR & MRS John C (Molly S Mugler)
Pa'73.Bost'80.Tufts'72.Bost'76
☎ (508) 470-0793 . . 6 Osgood St, Andover, MA *01810*
Sullivan MR & MRS John F (Lilley—M Beverly Knight)
GeoW'82.Yn.Y'66.Cl'68 . . of
☎ (202) 338-6986 . . 1412—28 St NW, Washington, DC *20007*
☎ (540) 364-2814 . . Poe's Run Farm, PO Box 202, Flint Hill,
VA *22627*
Sullivan MR & MRS John McN JR (Susan L Pelland) ☎ (516) 624-7641
LIU'86.Rc.Pr.Ng.StJos'69 . . . . 50 Moores Hill Rd,
MISS Jessica G—at Wheaton . . . . Oyster Bay, NY
MISS Samantha L—at Lake Forest Coll *11771*
Sullivan MRS John S (Jane Doering) Sdy.
☎ (619) 435-8463 . . 1051 Adella Av, Coronado, CA *92118-2907*
Sullivan MR & MRS Joseph V (Elizabeth T Coats) Cal'62
☎ (818) 368-3278 . . 10807 Blucher Av, Granada Hills, CA *91344*
Sullivan MR & MRS Leonard (Margo M Blackley) ☎ (301) 320-7548
Cvc.San.Sl.Mit'49 . . . . 4401 Boxwood Rd,
MISS M Dianne—Pa'83.Va'87—at Bethesda, MD
☎ (703) 370-4090 . . 1214 Quaker Hill Dv, *20816-1817*
Alexandria, VA *22314* . . . .
Sullivan MR Mark C—LakeF'82
☎ (410) 783-4599 . . 401 Warren Av, Baltimore, MD *21230*
Sullivan MR & MRS Mortimer A JR (Maryanne Calella) St.Buf'54
☎ (716) 662-3270 . . 19 Knob Hill Rd, Orchard Park, NY *14127*
Sullivan MR & MRS Richard P JR (Karen C Gustafson)
☎ (540) 955-4244 . . "Riverview" Rte 606, Box 555, Bluemont,
VA *20135*
Sullivan MRS S Perkins (Sallie Perkins) CtCol'59
Borderline Plantation, Rte 4, Box 283, Thomasville, GA *31792*
Sullivan MR & MRS Walter H (Dagmar dePins) Pcu.Bur.Stan'39
☎ (415) 929-1221 . . 1170 Sacramento St, San Francisco, CA *94108*
Sullivan MRS Ward (Adele K Baehr) Rd.Dar. . . . . . ☎ (610) NI4-2137
MISS Natalie . . . . "Court-Yard"
MR Robert . . . . 647 S Warren Av,
MR William W . . . . Malvern, PA *19355*
JUNIORS MR Mark W . . . .
Sullivan MR & MRS William H L (Thomas—Sallie C Blake)
Sg.LaS'41.Pa'46
☎ (215) 643-3541 . . 126 Splitrail Lane, Blue Bell, PA *19422*
Sultan MR & MRS Arthur P (Evelyn G Miller) ☎ (203) 966-5829
Pars'63.Ne.Sar.Rv.Snc.Wt.Dar.Bridgept'63. 788 South Av,
Hof'66 . . . . New Canaan, CT
MISS Katharine G—at Skidmore *06840*
MR Graham P—at U of Mich Ann Arbor . . . . . .
Sulzer MRS John R (Wehrli—Mary Knowlton) Pr.Cs.
☎ (516) 676-3395 . . 8 Overlook Rd, Matinecock Farms, Glen Cove,
NY *11542*
Summerlin MR Laird B . . see MRS J G Sholes JR
Summerlin MISS Piper E . . see MRS J G Sholes JR

Summers MRS M Elizabeth M (M Elizabeth Moore) | ☎ (561) 659-7464
BtP.Evg. . . . . | 334 Barton Av,
MISS Bliss E—JHop'95—at ☎ (212) 674-5549 | Palm Beach, FL
89 Bleecker St, New York, NY *10012* . . . . | *33480*
MR G Ellis JR . . . . |
Summers MR & MRS Paul D JR (Jill Faulkner) USA'51
☎ (804) 823-2255 . . Knole Farm, RFD 2, Charlottesville, VA *22901*
Summers DR & MRS Roland S (Sylvia S Newton) | ☎ (912) 354-6240
Wes'64.Nw'66.JHop'61.Nw'66 . . . . | 104 Johnston St,
MISS Sidney N—at 2793 Atwood Rd NE, Atlanta, | Savannah, GA
GA *30305* . . . . | *31405*
MISS Lane N—at Vanderbilt . . . . |
MR Roland S JR—at 85 Sheen Rd, London, |
England . . . . |
JUNIORS MISS Sarah A P . . . . |
JUNIORS MR Phillip T—at Salisbury . . . . |
Summers MR & MRS S Martin (Petó—Anne C | ☎ (011-44-171)
Tysen) . . . . | 352-8535
JUNIORS MISS Tara S . . . . | 55 Glebe Place,
MR Alexander T Petó . . . . | Chelsea, London
| SW3 5JB, England
Sumner MR Jason—Mds.Colg'40 ⚓ |
☎ (203) 886-4883 . . PO Box 841, Norwich, CT *06360-0841*
Sumner MR & MRS Lawrence C (Marilyn C Roth) | ☎ (314) 994-0658
Man'vl'62.StL'54 . . . . | 42 York Dv,
MR Lawrence C JR . . . . | St Louis, MO *63144*
MR Paul E . . . . |
Sumner MR & MRS William O (Nancy Dry) | ☎ (602) 488-5767
Sth'57.Bur.H'54 . . . . | Sincuidados 27,
MISS Allison F . . . . | 30600 N Pima Rd,
MR Robert M . . . . | Scottsdale, AZ
MR Stephen S . . . . | *85262-1856*
Sunderland MRS Cynthia H (Cynthia Heath) Rdc'55 | ☎ (617) 661-3277
MISS Susannah—Skd'87 . . . . | 35 Bowdoin St,
| Cambridge, MA
| *02138*
Sunderland REV & MRS Edwin S S (Choumenkovitch—Phyllis Gardner)
Sm.H'49
☎ (804) 977-5989 . . 1611 Grove Rd, Charlottesville, VA *22901*
Sunderland MR & MRS Thomas E (Mary L Allyn) . . . . . . | ☎ (602) 948-7745
MISS Anne R—at 515 W Briar Place, Apt 402, | 5840 E Starlight
Chicago, IL *60657* . . . . | Way, Paradise
| Valley, AZ *85253*
Sundlun MRS Joyanne T (Carter—Joyanne B | ☎ (202) 332-1221
Thomas) Cl'48 . . . . | 2700 Calvert St
MISS Cintra E Carter . . . . | NW, Washington,
MR Michael R E Carter . . . . | DC *20008*
Sundt MR & MRS H Wilson (Dorothy L Van Gilder) Ariz'54.Ariz'54
☎ (520) 298-2797 . . 6002 E San Leandro, Tucson, AZ *85715*
Sundt MR & MRS Robert S (Frances E Schmidt) Ariz'50
☎ (520) 299-0459 . . 7181 E Grey Fox Lane, Tucson, AZ *85715*
Supper MRS Frederick M (Green—Chace—Patricia McKeon) Cho.Ihy.
☎ (561) 659-6046 . . "Villa Maggiore" 260 Via Bellaria, Palm Beach,
FL *33480*
Supplee MR & MRS Cochran B (Angela T Place)
C.Snc.Lm.Cly.Cda.P'46.Nu'52
☎ (805) 969-8072 . . 300 Hot Springs Rd, Santa Barbara, CA *93108*

Supplee MR & MRS Edward A (Mary C Wilson) Cy.Cw.Ncd.P'43.Md'49
☎ (410) 467-5971 . . 3 Hillside Rd, Baltimore, MD *21210*
Supplee MR & MRS Edward A JR (Sarah E Sawhill) | ☎ (415) 327-3284
Fla'71.Stan'77.W&L'67.Emory'72 . . . . | 1901 Birch St,
MR Edward A 3d—Cal'87.Stan'95 . . . . | Palo Alto, CA
| *94306*
Supplee MRS Henderson JR (Mary O Baker) Gm.
☎ (610) 353-3773 . . Dunwoody Village CH113,
3500 West Chester Pike, Newtown Square, PA *19073*
Supplee DR & MRS (DR) W Scott (Gail P Cunningham)
Md'82.Geo'83.Geo'87.Cy.Wms'76.Md'86
"High Meadows" 13020 Gent Rd, Reisterstown, MD *21136*
Surer MISS Josephine Mary Anne (Thibault M) . . . . Born at
Paris, France Jly 25'96
Surer MR & MRS Thibault M (M Cassandra Myer) SL'87.Pc.HEC'85
☎ (011-33-1) 45-67-43-68 . . 27 rue Rousselet, 75007 Paris, France
Sutherland MRS Beverley W (Sutherland—Swerz— | ☎ (203) 762-8022
Beverley M Waud) . . . . | 15 Nod Hill Rd,
MISS Claire P—StLaw'85 . . . . | Wilton, CT *06897*
MISS Beverley M—at 501 Cathedral P'kway, |
New York, NY *10025* . . . . |
MR Robert B JR—LakeF'88—at |
☎ (603) 431-5318 . . 67 S South St, Portsmouth, |
NH *03801* . . . . |
Sutherland MR & MRS Donald J (Denise S Jackson) | ☎ (516) OR1-1973
Ck.Ln.P'53.H'58 . . . . | High Farms Rd,
MISS Paige C—at ☎ (212) 877-9117 | Glen Head, NY
1 Nevada Plaza, New York, NY *10023* . . . . | *11545*
MISS Shelley W—at ☎ (606) 266-9448 |
204 Woodspoint Rd, Lexington, KY *40502* . . . . |
Sutherland MR & MRS Malcolm J JR (Elizabeth C McDaniel)
VillaN'83.Me.Ken'81.Wayne'84
☎ (610) 527-1427 . . 505 Old Gulph Rd, Bryn Mawr, PA *19010*
Sutherland REV & MRS Malcolm R JR (Mary Anne | of ☎ (508)456-3900
Beaumont) Wells'36.ClevInst'37.Miami'38. | 21 Woodside Rd,
Cwr'41.Ch'45 . . . . | Harvard, MA
MISS Maryanne B—at Fox Glen Farms, | *01451-1616*
12495 Germany Rd, Fenton, MI *48430* . . . . | ☎ (207) 326-4743
MR Malcolm R 3d—at 6043 W Crain, | "Dunrobin"
Morton Grove, IL *60053* . . . . | Timothys Lane,
| South Brooksville,
| ME *04617*
Sutor MR & MRS James F (Helme—Flora Van Sciver) Pc.Sg.Fw.Ac.Hav'46
☎ (215) 233-3377 . . "Glenwood" 740 W Thomas Rd, Philadelphia,
PA *19118-4601*
Sutphin MR & MRS Stuart B JR (Jean C Webber) Err . . .of
☎ (513) 561-3377 . . 4685 Burley Hills Dv, Cincinnati, OH *45243*
☎ (941) 427-4913 . . 4979 Joewood Dv, Sanibel, FL *33957*
Sutro MRS John A (Elizabeth L Hiss) Tcy.Fmy.StJ.
☎ (415) 563-3433 . . 3598 Jackson St, San Francisco, CA *94118*
Sutro MR & MRS John A JR (Loulie G Hyde) | ☎ (415) 453-5878
Conn'57.Tcy.Ncd.Stan'57.H'60 . . . . | 35 Toussin Av,
MISS Loulie E—Nw'95 . . . . | Kentfield, CA *94904*
MISS Sarah H—CtCol'94 . . . . |

Sutro MRS Katharine B (Katharine S Barbour) Mds. | ☎ (561) 231-8436
MR Andrew H—Skd'93—at ☎ (617) 288-6323 | 600 Indian Harbor
56 Granite Av, Dorchester, MA 02124 . . . . | Rd, Vero Beach, FL
| 32963

Sutro MR & MRS Nicholas S (Suzanne Nolan)
☎ (914) 472-8679 . . 26 East P'kway, Scarsdale, NY 10583

Sutro MR & MRS Ogden W (Nettleton—G Susanna | ☎ (203) 453-8636
Small) Tex'44.Y'46.Cl'81.Snc.Myf.Yn.Y'36 . . . | 53 Long Hill Farm,
MR Curtis de W—Van'80—at ☎ (203) 966-9769 | Guilford, CT 06437
76 Oak St, New Canaan, CT 06840 . . . .

Sutro MR & MRS Paul N (Mary Long) | 814 Sabot Hill Rd,
Van'56.Wes'52 . . . . | Manakin-Sabot, VA
MISS Martha L—Wes'87 . . . . | 23103-3008
MR Paul N JR—Wes'85 . . . . |
MR Thomas W—Denis'89 . . . . |
MR John A S—at U of Colo Boulder . . . . |

Sutro MR & MRS Peter C (Marina C Johnson) | ☎ (508) 228-2190
Cly.Y'52 . . . . | 12 Milk St,
MISS Sabrina D—at ☎ (508) 228-6091 | Nantucket, MA
PO Box 2030, Nantucket, MA 02584 . . . . . . | 02554

Sutro MR & MRS Porter H (Myra Solby) Y'61 . . . . . | ☎ (914) 723-0690
MR David D . . . . | 9 High Point Terr,
| Scarsdale, NY
| 10583

Sutro MR & MRS Stephen H (Ann W Busse) Ty'92.Ty'91.SantaC'94
☎ (415) 563-6631 . . 2765 Gough St, Apt 8, San Francisco, CA 94123

Sutro MRS Victor H (Julia L Delafield) Nu'47.Dh.Ds.
☎ (516) 288-2131 . . "Gleneen" PO Box 125, Westhampton Beach, NY 11978

Sutter MR & MRS William P (Helen Y Stebbins)
Duke'51.Ih.Ncd.Y'45.Mich'50 . . of
☎ (847) 446-6637 . . 96 Woodley Rd, Winnetka, IL 60093
☎ (561) 734-1169 . . Pelican Cove Apt 36, 6110 N Ocean Blvd, Ocean Ridge, FL 33435

Sutterley MR & MRS Edmund L JR (Reed—Ruth Mary Williams) Elmira'42
☎ (520) 326-2896 . . 417 Stratford Dv, Tucson, AZ 85716-5616

Sutterley MR Roger E
☎ (602) 581-8541 . . 3737 W Morrow Dv, Glendale, AZ 85308

Suttle MRS Harold L (Virginia Liggett) Snc.
☎ (212) 838-3452 . . 125 E 63 St, New York, NY 10021

Sutton MR Cameron . . see MRS N S O'Reilly

Sutton MR & MRS David A (Whitney C Smith) Va'86.Va'85.GeoW'94
☎ (404) 842-9472 . . 3352 Kilby Place NW, Atlanta, GA 30327

Sutton MR & MRS David Charles (Elizabeth H Scull) | ☎ (864) 297-9836
Dar.Tenn'62 . . . . | 201 Pruitt Dv,
MISS Elizabeth H—Winth'91.Dar.—at | Greenville, SC
921 N Nevada Av, Apt 1, Colorado Springs, | 29607
CO 80903 . . . . |
MISS Whitney W—Belm'96.Dar.—at |
☎ (615) 292-1813 . . 1626 Sixteenth Av S, |
Apt A4, Nashville, TN 37212 . . . . |
MR David L—at ☎ (864) 370-0924 |
260 Pelham Rd, Apt F12, Greenville, SC |
29615-2508 . . . . |

Sutton MASTER David Wheeler (David A) . . . . Born at Atlanta, GA May 10'96

Sutton MR & MRS Edmund H (Grace B Stevens) | ☎ (212) 348-3063
BMr'61.Ri.H.'60 . . . . | 1185 Park Av,
MR Robert H—H'93 . . . . | New York, NY
MR Charles S . . . . | 10128

Sutton MRS F Michael (Elizabeth A Holt) ⚓ . . . . | ☎ (408) 646-1315
MR M Joseph—at ☎ (408) 462-3705 | Dartington Ridge,
1141 El Dorado Av, Santa Cruz, CA 95062 . . . . | Big Sur, CA 93920

Sutton MRS Gardner (Cowden—Elizabeth Southworth)
☎ (617) 523-0840 . . 42 Mt Vernon St, Boston, MA 02108

Sutton MR & MRS Howard D (D Selden Womrath) Va'53.Cl'58 . . of
☎ (212) 410-1382 . . 4 E 88 St, New York, NY 10128
☎ (860) 535-9221 . . 13 School St, Stonington, CT 06378

Sutton MRS James A (Eloise Chadwick Collins) BMr'39
☎ (610) 525-1138 . . 322 Caversham Rd, Bryn Mawr, PA 19010

Sutton MR & MRS James P (Laurie Grimm) | ☎ (203) 264-7052
Emory'39 . . . . | 57 Curt Smith Rd,
MR John C . . . . | Southbury, CT
| 06488

Sutton MR & MRS John B JR (Knipe—Salvesen—Ann D Gross)
Fcg.Pg.Rr.Pratt'39
☎ (561) 278-2530 . . 4475 N Ocean Blvd, Apt 105, Delray Beach, FL 33483

Sutton MR & MRS Roger B (Caroline H Craig) . . . . . | ☎ (412) 441-6246
MISS Judith C—at 325 E 80 St, New York, NY | 5829 Elwood St,
10021 . . . . | Pittsburgh, PA
| 15232-2509

Suydam MRS Henry W JR (Wheeler—Jane G Eustis) Sl.Cda.
☎ (202) 332-1234 . . 2917 Garfield St NW, Washington, DC 20008

Suydam MR Joseph W—Rens'38
☎ (410) 778-1715 . . 7138 Pomona Rd, Chestertown, MD 21620

Suydam MR & MRS Lispenard (Margaret B Card) | ☎ (207) 644-8286
Snc.Cw.Hl.Dar.Colg'42 . . . . | "Fox Den Hill"
MR W Lispenard 3d—LakeF'66—at | South Bristol, ME
59 Harbor Av, Marblehead, MA 01945 . . . . . . | 04568
MR Bryce C—Colg'69.Bost'73—at |
2 Driftwood Lane, Marblehead, MA 01945 . . . . |

Swaim MRS Stanley W (Bancroft—Jean Tuckerman) D.
☎ (508) 359-6281 . . 66 Foundry St, Medfield, MA 02052

Swain MR & MRS Anthony (Susan E Rudd) Y'68.Pa'71
☎ (617) 723-4317 . . 1A Acorn St, Boston, MA 02108

Swain MR & MRS Clifford H (Rebecca M | ☎ (215) CH2-6898
Conderman) Rc.Pc.Y'63.Pa'68 . . . . | 710 W Allen's Lane,
MISS Rebecca M . . . . | Philadelphia, PA
MR Clifford H JR . . . . | 19119
JUNIORS MR Theodore H |

Swain MR & MRS David S (Christina Wood)
☎ (860) 658-1347 . . 5 Madison Lane, West Simsbury, CT 06092

Swain MR & MRS Edward (Anne Benedict) Swb'39.Pa'34
☎ (610) 645-8945 . . 1400 Waverly Rd, Andrews 111, Gladwyne, PA 19035

Swain MR & MRS Edward 3d (Ruth W Freeman)
☎ (610) 688-4844 . . PO Box 7420, St Davids, PA 19087

Swain MRS Francis R D (Sarah M LeFevre)
☎ (352) 377-5642 . . 1730 NW 11 Rd, Gainesville, FL 32605

Swain MR & MRS Joseph W JR (Mary V Brownback)
Ph.Me.Nyc.Sa.Fw.Pa'39.Pa'42
☎ (610) MI2-6479 . . 261 Laurel Lane, Haverford, PA 19041

Swain MISS Sally W—Me.
☎(610) 525-5278 . . 16 Barley Cone Lane, Rosemont, PA *19010*
Swain JUNIORS MISS Sarah E . . see A K Wheelock JR
Swain MR & MRS Thomas S (Anne Mehan)
Penn'70.Lond'78.R.Del'71.Pa'74
☎(718) 624-3853 . . 295 Henry St, Brooklyn, NY *11201*
Swain MR & MRS William M (Lawton—Shaw—Saylor—
Audrey P S Hutchinson) Pc.Ac.Pa'35
☎(610) 527-3940 . . Beaumont 213, 74 Pasture Lane, Bryn Mawr,
PA *19010-1766*
Swan MISS Catharine R—Hartw'82 . . see W D Hart JR
Swan MRS Channing S (Elise Rutledge) Ncd.
☎(617) 863-9497 . . Brookhaven, Exeter 221, 1010 Waltham St,
Lexington, MA *02173*
Swan MR Elliot G—P'78.Ch'84
☎(202) 686-6785 . . 2501 Porter St NW, Apt 118, Washington,
DC *20008-1249*
Swan MR & MRS Henry (Freda Theopold) Stph'55.Bost'57.Me'57.H'63
☎(603) 353-9834 . . Butternut Farm, 133 Breck Hill Rd, Lyme,
NH *03768*
Swank MR & MRS Mark F (Cynthia G Whitman) Vt'84.Bgt.Vt'82
☎(914) 232-8677 . . "Gardener's Cottage" 65 Girdle Ridge Dv,
Katonah, NY *10536*

Swann MR John B—H'28	☎(413) 298-3535
MISS Clover	"Cherry Hill"
MR Robert H	Stockbridge, MA
MR Nicholas	*01262*
Swanson MRS Elizabeth F (Elizabeth Farwell)	☎(203) 966-3697
MR Matthew B	125 Fox Run Rd,
	New Canaan, CT
	06840

Swartley MR J Christopher . . see MRS A E Newbold 3d
Swarts MRS Frederick B (Elizabeth von P Keeler) Cy.
☎(314) 993-0654 . . 2 Buckhammon Place, St Louis, MO *63124*
Swartwood MR Alexander B—Denis'89
☎(617) 247-0029 . . 354 Commonwealth Av, Boston, MA *02115*

Swartwood MR & MRS Charles B 3d (Judith K	☎(617) 491-6792
Farrington) Hl.Br'61.Bost'64	19 Centre St, 1,
MR Thayer F—Hl.—at Vanderbilt	Cambridge, MA
	02139

Swartwood MISS Heather W (Slater W)	Married at Cotuit, MA
Dazet MR Michael E (Ralph A)	Jun 22'96

Swartwood MR & MRS Slater W (Kathryn H Pécot)	☎(404) 255-2980
Tr.SELa'67	13 Ridgemere Trace
MR Slater W JR—at U of Ala	NE, Atlanta, GA
JUNIORS MISS Effie B	*30328*

Swartz MR & MRS A Wakelee JR (Deborah Disston) Gm.Cda.Wms'36
☎(610) 645-8874 . . Waverly Heights 230, 1400 Waverly Rd,
Gladwyne, PA *19035*

Swartz MR & MRS Thomas B (Ann Wright)	☎(510) 547-8666
Bhm.Tcy.Y'54	17 Sierra Av,
MR Anthony C	Piedmont, CA *94611*

Swartz MRS W Hamilton (Margaret Mac I Farmer) . . . . Died at
New York, NY May 21'96

Swayze MR & MRS Douglas A 2d (Van Hecke—Marie E Holman)
NCar'47.Miss'42 . . of
☎(601) 366-3114 . . 149 Woodland Circle, Jackson, MS *39216*
☎(601) 388-1231 . . 134 Barq Av, Biloxi, MS *39531*
16281 Perdido Key Dv, 1102W Eden, Pensacola, FL *32507*
Swayze MRS John L (Phyllis Smith) Csn.
☎(609) 426-6714 . . Meadow Lakes 48-08L, Hightstown, NJ *08520*
Swayzee MR & MRS Cleon O 2d (Ulstrup—Mary E King) Bnd'51.Wash'56
☎(314) 994-7068 . . 11 Pebble Creek Rd, St Louis, MO *63124*
Swearingen MR & MRS Patrick H JR (de Marigny—Gail T Hall)
Swb'52.A.P'46
☎(210) 822-1695 . . 262 Geneseo Rd, San Antonio, TX *78209*
Sweeney MRS F Graves (Frances C Graves) . . . . Died
Sweeney MR John A H—Y'52.Del'54
☎(302) 762-1307 . . 207 Hoiland Dv, Wilmington, DE *19803*

Sweeney MR & MRS John F JR (Rhetta A Boyd)	☎(508) 468-1536
My.Bow'62	"Rock Maple"
MISS Alicia B	24 Meyer Lane,
MISS Faith A	Hamilton, MA
	01982

Sweeny MR & MRS Bradley P (Cynthia M	☎(914) 967-7389
Davenport) Un.Ln.Cly.U'62	20 Griswold Rd,
MISS Heather G—Denis'86.Cly.—at	Rye, NY *10580*
☎(212) 628-6711 . . 120 E 79 St, New York, NY	
10021 . .	
MISS Hilary B—Roan'93—at ☎(212) 369-3689	
201 E 87 St, Apt 5C, New York, NY *10128* . . .	

Sweet MR & MRS Philip W K JR (Nancy Frederick)	☎(847) 234-4582
On.Sr.Cho.Cas.Cw.Myf.H'50	990 Ringwood Rd,
MR David A F—at ☎(310) 372-8899	Lake Forest, IL
90 N Morningside Way, Manhattan Beach, CA	*60045*
90266 . .	
MISS Sandra H (Gedge—Sandra H Sweet)—at	
☎(847) 724-4799 . . 1960 Spruce Av, Glenview,	
IL *60025*	

Sweet MR & MRS Philip W K 3d (Carol Monek)	☎(713) 461-3269
Loy'76.Nw'78	6146 Bordley Dv,
JUNIORS MISS Stephanie F	Houston, TX *77057*
JUNIORS MISS Stacy B	

Sweet MRS Stanley A (Barbara W McGraw) Cly.
☎(518) 523-3712 . . Mirror Lake Dv, PO Box 310, Lake Placid,
NY *12946*
Sweetser MR & MRS John A 3d (Druanne Blackmore) Ty'42
☎(612) 377-2761 . . 1501 Mt Curve Av, Minneapolis, MN *55403*
Sweney MR John E—Br'79 . . see R Borden
Swenson MRS Roderic B (Macdonald—Hope Hollister) Myf.
☎(203) 438-4981 . . 371 Wilton Rd W, Ridgefield, CT *06877*
Swensson MR & MRS Earl S (Suzanne Dickenson)
FlaSo'53.VPI'52.VPI'53.Ill'55
☎(615) 373-9780 . . 1122 Harpeth Ridge Dv, Franklin, TN *37064*

Swetland MR & MRS Eli B (Michelle Garnette)	☎(011-571)
Miami'71.NMex'70	341-9059
MR Eli B JR—at Tex Christian U	Carrera 13,
JUNIORS MR Luke V—at Mercersburg	27-98 Torre B,
	Apt 1701, Bogotá,
	Colombia

Swetland MR & MRS Frederick L JR (Anita M Fellner) V'40.Wms'35 . . of
☎ (513) 767-2541 . . Hawk Hill Farm, 170 E Hyde Rd, Yellow Springs,
OH *45387*
☎ (508) 228-1327 . . 16 N Liberty St, Nantucket, MA *02554*

Swett MR & MRS Bradford N (Holly B McAllister) H.'57
☎ (212) 534-0647 . . 49 E 96 St, New York, NY *10128*

Swett MR & MRS Nicholas (Alice H Harvey) Wyo'65 | ☎ (307) 745-7158
MISS Alice E—at Trinity . . . . | 318 S 15 St,
MR Shane H . . . . | Laramie, WY *82070*
JUNIORS MR William N—at St John's Acad . . . . . |

Swett MR & MRS Steven C (Shiela L Chanler) Rdc'57.C.Hn.H'56
☎ (802) 649-2121 . . 1062 Bragg Hill Rd, Norwich, VT *05055*

Swett MR & MRS Thomas C (Baker—Carolyn Gordy) | ☎ (610) 347-2425
Del'58.Ph.Pa'64 . . . . | PO Box 838,
MR David A Baker . . . . | Unionville, PA
| *19375*

Swift MASTER Alexander Harvey (Donald S) . . . . Born Sep 5'94

Swift MISS Alison C—NCar'81.Sim'90
☎ (408) 293-2380 . . 216 Milbrae Lane, Los Gatos, CA *95030*

Swift MASTER Benton Gillespie (Thomas B) . . . . Born May 10'96

Swift MISS Byrd G
☎ (617) 262-3406 . . 68 Commonwealth Av, Boston, MA *02116*

Swift MR & MRS Carleton B JR (Seebach—Schwartz—Patricia C Waring)
Mt.H'41 . . of
☎ (202) 363-4624 . . 2738 Chain Bridge Rd NW, Washington, DC *20016*
☎ (410) 778-2241 . . 114 Ryan Court, Chestertown, MD *21620*

Swift MRS Catherine Van S (Montgomery—Catherine Van S Swift) Bost'77
☎ (207) 773-0330 . . 71 Carleton St, Portland, ME *04102*

Swift MR & MRS Donald S (Marjorie M Harvey) NEng'83.Mg.Eh.Denis'79
☎ (908) 781-2465 . . PO Box 205, Old Farm Rd, Bedminster, NJ *07921*

Swift MR & MRS E Kent JR (Arlette B Steel) | ☎ (508) 548-0451
Sim'75.Bost'86.Cy.Cw.Chi.H.'46 . . . . | 98 Gansett Rd,
MISS Jeannine S—Chi.—at ☎ (703) 739-9778 | PO Box 27,
655 S Colombus St, Alexandria, VA *22314* . . . . | Woods Hole, MA
MR E Kent 3d—Cw.—at ☎ (617) 225-2027 | *02543*
10 Rogers St, Apt 907, Cambridge, MA *02142* . |

Swift MR & MRS Edward F 3d (Whipple—Carol M Coffey)
Cho.On.Rc.Cnt.Y'45
☎ (847) 234-9444 . . 531 N Mayflower Rd, Lake Forest, IL *60045*

Swift MR & MRS George H 3d (Gayle A Humberstone) Bost'71.Bridgept'85
see Dilatory Domiciles

Swift MRS Gustavus F (Eleanor B Ransom) Rdc'39
☎ (773) 753-4647 . . 5550 S Shore Dv, Apt 1013, Chicago, IL *60637*

Swift MRS H M Steel (Catherine Van S Dugan)
☎ (617) 698-4528 . . 31 Canton Av, Milton, MA *02186*

Swift MR & MRS Hampden M (Margaret | ☎ (847) 234-5239
Muckerman) Cho.Rc.On.Y'36 . . . . | 770 N Washington
MISS Laura C . . . . | Rd, Lake Forest, IL
MISS Maria M—at 2050 N Racine Av, Chicago, | *60045*
IL *60614* . . . . |
MISS Constance J . . . . |
MR Stephen M—at 605 W Madison St, Chicago, |
IL *60605* . . . . |
MR Stewart G—LakeF'89 . . . . |

Swift MR & MRS Humphrey H (Pamela A Whitney) | ☎ (617) 749-2336
V'44.Co.San.Chi.Ncd.NCar'39 ⚓ . . . . | 38 Cottage St,
MISS Edith S—at ☎ (011-61-4) 267-1300 | Hingham, MA
9 Corbett Av, Thirroul, NSW 2515, Australia . . | *02043*

Swift MISS Lindsay C . . see G R Wright

Swift MISS Madeleine B . . see MRS J D Kelsey

Swift MR Matthew S—Mit'91.Hlns'92.Bost'95
☎ (617) 739-6157 . . 59 Brainerd Rd, Apt 202, Allston, MA *02134*

Swift MR & MRS Nathan B (Stitgen—Melinda A Sherman)
Col'68.Nw'73.Wa.LakeF'68 ⚓
☎ (312) 266-2848 . . 1560 N Sandburg Terr, Apt 4012, Chicago,
IL *60610*

Swift MR & MRS Peter W (Austin—Sandra Schmidlapp)
☎ (919) 942-6039 . . 604 Cedar Run Lane, Chapel Hill, NC *27514*

Swift MR & MRS Phelps H (Bartholomay—Sara H Taylor) Cho.Sr.Y'50
☎ (307) 537-5491 . . Circle 9 Ranch, PO Box 38, Pinedale,
WY *82941*

Swift MR & MRS Shepard C (Patricia H McHugh) DePaul'94.Rc . . .of
6556 Diamond Lake Rd, Long Grove, IL *60047*
1540 W Wrightwood Av, Chicago, IL *60614*

Swift MR & MRS Stephen Hathaway (Gallaudet—Sally B Smith)
Ws'41.Vmi'41
☎ (508) 994-3653 . . 32 Mishaum Point, South Dartmouth, MA *02748*

Swift MR & MRS Thomas B (Joan O'N Gillespie)
Va'82.Stan'86.Cvc.Pcu.Pa'64 . . of
☎ (415) 460-0240 . . 32 Shady Lane, PO Box 21, Ross, CA *94957*
☎ (707) 942-9526 . . High Ridge Ranch, 10500 Franz Valley Rd,
Calistoga, CA *94515*
☎ (208) 788-9400 . . Greenhorn Ranch, 151 Greenhorn Rd,
PO Box 3610, Ketchum, ID *83340*

Swift MR William F—ColC'85
☎ (310) 395-7864 . . 1527—9 St, Apt 202, Santa Monica, CA *90401*

Swiggart MRS C Rudisill (Carolyn C Rudisill)
Ws'80.Conn'83.Cly.Dc.Ncd.Dh.
☎ (203) 655-4840 . . PO Box 941, Darien, CT *06820*

Swindell MR Douglas C (Robert H JR) . . . . Married at Baltimore, MD
Schmidt MISS L Tracy (Theodore) . . . . Oct 1'94

Swindell MR & MRS Robert H JR (Nancy D Cotton) Elk.Md.Mv.Va'55
☎ (410) 377-8684 . . 109 Charlesbrooke Rd, Baltimore, MD *21212*

Swindell MR & MRS Robert H 3d (Elizabeth C O'Herron)
☎ (203) 698-2745 . . 10 Club Rd, Riverside, CT *06878*

Swindells MR & MRS Theodore H (Phyllis S Evans) Col'81
☎ (415) 750-0177 . . 139—24 Av, San Francisco, CA *94121*

Swinerton MR & MRS William A (Mary N Clark) Rdc'39.Pcu.Bur.Y'39
☎ (415) 851-7743 . . 279 Albion Av, PO Box 620265, Woodside,
CA *94062*

Swing MRS Leonard (Goes—I Jane Leonard) | ☎ (561) 832-6575
BtP.Myf.Cda.Dar. . . . . | 168 Kings Rd,
MISS Susan J . . . . | Palm Beach, FL
MR Edward A . . . . | *33480*

Swint MR & MRS Samuel H JR (Ann H Brede) | ☎ (516) 283-9171
Bcs.So.Cly. . . . . | ''Eastlake''
MISS Amy H . . . . | 137 S Main St,
| PO Box 5073,
| Southampton, NY
| *11969-5073*

Switz DR & MRS Donald MacL (Elise Hurd) . . . . | of ☎ (804)358-7676
Sth'64.VaCmth'79.Hn.Carl'58.Ch'62 . . . . | 19 Maxwell Rd,
MISS Katherine L—at Dartmouth . . . . | Richmond, VA
MR Neil A—at Stanford . . . . | 23226
MR Geoffrey MacL—at Hampden-Sydney . . . . . | ☎ (804) 325-9078
| "Windfall"
| Wintergreen, VA
| 22938

Switz MISS Susan K . . see MRS M S Hepburn
Swope MR & MRS Gerard L (Mary G Carlton) . . . . | of ☎ (202)363-1394
Rdc'59.H'66.Un.Csn.Bab'61.H'70 . . . . | 3927 Idaho Av NW,
MR Timothy W C . . . . | Washington, DC
MR Ian G—at ☎ (215) 925-8562 | 20008
329 S 12 St, Philadelphia, PA 19107 . . . . | ☎ (508) 548-0625
| 90 Church St,
| Woods Hole, MA
| 02543

Swords MISS Deirdre H—HRdc'86.HRdc'95 . . see W Maynard JR
Swords MRS Gerard S (Cherry Shaw) Csn.Ncd.
☎ (203) 865-6292 . . 17 Briar Lane, New Haven, CT 06511
Swoyer MR & MRS George R (Thompson—E Patricia | ☎ (609) 884-2371
Hale) F&M'44.Pa'51 . . . . | 1044 Idaho Av,
MR Allan H—LaS'84 . . . . | Cape May, NJ
| 08204

Sykes MISS Barbara M'Cready
☎ (508) 432-1798 . . "Esmond Cottage" Harwich Port, MA 02646
Sykes MR & MRS Richard M (Greenleaf—Jane E | ☎ (516) 922-7565
Stebbins) Au.Ny.S.Pr.Cly.Wms'61.Cl'63 . . . . . . | 37 Frost Mill Rd,
MR Colin M . . . . | Mill Neck, NY
| 11765

Sylvester MRS John (Mandell—Geraldine Clark) Cvc.Chi.Sl.
☎ (202) 244-8381 . . 4708 Yuma St NW, Washington, DC 20016
Sylvester MR & MRS Michael S (Allatt—Louise Macy)
Kt.Rr.Tv.Colby'64.H'70
5109 Hamilton Av, Cleveland, OH 44114
Symington MR & MRS Charles H JR (Bailey Walker) | ☎ (212) 308-5957
Rc.Pr.Ln.Cly.Wms'53.H'56 . . . . | 570 Park Av,
MR Randolph W—at 21 W 10 St, New York, NY | New York, NY
10011 . . . . | 10021

Symington MR J Fife—Elk.Gv.B.Md.P'33
☎ (410) 833-3632 . . 3717 Butler Rd, Glyndon, MD 21071
Symington GOV & MRS J Fife III (Ann O Pritzlaff) | 4450 E Camelback
Md.Gv.B.H'68 . . . . | Rd, 9, Phoenix, AZ
MISS Whitney O . . . . | 85018
MR Scott H . . . . |
JUNIORS MR Richard E . . . . |

Symington MR J Fife IV (J Fife III) . . . . Married at San Antonio, TX
Billups MISS Marcella (James S JR) . . . . Mch 16'96
Symington MR & MRS J Fife IV (Marcella Billups) Smu'91.AGSIM'95.H'92
4614 N 40 St, Phoenix, AZ 85018
Symington MRS James H (Valeria M Harris)
☎ (703) 777-2532 . . "Birdsey Hall" 301 North St NE, Leesburg,
VA 20176-2313
Symington MRS James McKim (Mary T Norris) Cvc.Cw.Ll.Ncd.Yn.
☎ (202) 667-5783 . . 2937 Garfield Terr NW, Washington, DC 20008

Symington MR & MRS James McKim JR (Susan M Ratcliff)
NwColl'76.AmU'78.Y'74.Geo'82
☎ (703) 356-2340 . . 1712 Birch Rd, McLean, VA 22101-4729
Symington MR & MRS James W (Sylvia C Schlapp)
SL'53.Wash'58.Bhm.Mt.Cos.Sl.Y'50.Cl'54
☎ (202) 338-4304 . . 3900 Watson Place NW, Washington, DC 20016
Symington DR & MRS (DR) John S (Margaret J McFarland)
Y'82.P'84.P'87.Y'82.StL'86
4674 Garfield St NW, Washington, DC 20007
Symington MRS Lloyd (Nancy E Glover)
☎ (301) 320-2842 . . 4400 Tournay Rd, Bethesda, MD 20816
Symington MRS M Frick (Martha H Frick) Mv . . . of
☎ (602) 948-2516 . . 14 Colonia Miramonte, Paradise Valley, AZ 85253
☎ (410) 583-8005 . . 2 Old Boxwood Lane, Lutherville, MD 21093
Symington MRS Maud L (Van Alen—Ives—Gray—Crosby—
Maud L Symington)
☎ (602) 314-0714 . . PO Box 12414, Scottsdale, AZ 85267-2414
Symington MR & MRS Sidney S (Nancy J Rothman)
Y'78.Nu'84.C.Yn.Y'78.Nu'84
☎ (203) 259-7377 . . 42 Ludlowe Rd, Fairfield, CT 06430
Symington MR & MRS Stuart (Watson—Ann C Hemingway) Cly.Cvc.Mt.
☎ (203) 966-3515 . . PO Box 1087, New Canaan, CT 06840
Symington MR & MRS Stuart (Jane Studt) V'50.H'59.Cy.Y'50.H'53
☎ (314) 994-3233 . . 745 Cella Rd, St Louis, MO 63124
Symington MR & MRS W Stuart 4th (Susan Ide) Bnd'74.Br'74 . . of
☎ (314) 994-3233 . . 745 Cella Rd, St Louis, MO 63124
☎ (703) 256-7913 . . 6423 Lakeview Dv, Falls Church, VA 22041
Symmers MR Benjamin K JR—Va'84.H'93
☎ (757) 626-1001 . . 300 Yarmouth St, Apt 320, Norfolk, VA 23510
Symmers MR William Garth—Ny.Ihy.StA.Va'33. | ☎ (212) 758-3916
Va'35 . . . . | 444 E 52 St,
MISS Deborah K—at ☎ (203) 661-4813 | New York, NY
34 Alexander St, Greenwich, CT 06830 . . . . | 10022

Symmes MR & MRS Laurence M (Beryl J Boyce) | ☎ (415) 388-2294
Tcy.Dth'38.H'39 . . . . | 309 Tamalpais Av,
MISS Marilyn F—at 1199 Park Av, Apt 7G, | Mill Valley, CA
New York, NY 10128 . . . . | 94941
MR Anthony G—at 1850 June Way, Paradise, CA |
95969 . . . . |
MR William C—at 1817 California St, Apt 305, |
San Francisco, CA 94109 . . . . |
MR Jonathan H . . . . |

Symon MR & MRS Robert O (Moulder—Anne B Cope) Tcy.Camb'28
☎ (415) 492-2590 . . 100 Thorndale Dv, Apt 259, San Rafael, CA 94903
Symonds MR & MRS David P (Anne Worthington) | Vineyard Rd,
RISD'67.Mid'68 . . . . | Saunderstown, RI
MISS Adrienne Worthington—HWSth'96 . . . . . . | 02874
MISS Margaret Preston |

Symonds MR & MRS George W D (Margaret Preston) Y'34
☎ (203) 762-3569 . . 114 Vista Rd, Wilton, CT 06897
Symonds MR & MRS Jonathan T (Anne Allen) | ☎ (713) 520-0770
Swb'62.Ln.Pcu.Stan'61.H'65 . . . . | 2509 Westgate St,
MR Allen G . . . . | Houston, TX
MR Jonathan T 2d . . . . | 77019
MR David B—at Tex Christian U . . . . |

Symonds MRS Samuel M (Anderson—Deborah S Lee) Tex'71 . . . . ☎ (713) 627-0107
JUNIORS MISS Courtenay B . . . . 3729 Wickersham
JUNIORS MISS Samantha L . . . . Lane, Houston, TX 77027
Symons MISS Natalie C (Thomas W) . . . . Married at Derby, NY
Bjornholm MR Shayn . . . . Aug 3'96
Sypher MRS Eleanor K (Eleanor C Kramer) Ncd.Dc. | ☎ (212) 410-3536
MISS Eleanor H . . . . 515 E 89 St, Apt 2F,
New York, NY 10128

Sypher MR Francis J—Cos.Snc.Rv.Cw.Cl'63.Cl'64.Cl'68
☎ (212) 568-6740 . . 730 Ft Washington Av, New York, NY 10040
Szabo-Imrey MISS Celia C A (George Z) . . Married at West Tisbury, MA
Culbert MR Timothy G (William E) . . . . Jun 24'95
Szabo-Imrey MRS Diane L (Diane B D Leroy) | ☎ (617) 497-9390
Bnd'59.H'63.Ey. . . . . 9 Channing St,
MR G Christopher . . . . Cambridge, MA
MR Thomas R—Ne'93.Wh'lck'95 . . . . | 02138

Szabo-Imrey MR George Z—H.Hn.Mit'56
122 Bowdoin St, Boston, MA 02108

T

Taber MR & MRS George H (Janet Beebe) | ☎ (412) 683-4082
Rcn.Pg.Rr.Cly.H'50 5315
MR Stephen H—at 1326 Madison Av, Apt 63A, | Northumberland St,
New York, NY 10028 . . . . Pittsburgh, PA
MR John . . . . | 15217

Tabler MR & MRS William B (Phyllis M Baker) Ws'36.Pr.Myf.Ncd.H.'36
☎ (516) 626-1199 . . 44 Wolver Hollow Rd, Glen Head, NY 11545
Tabler MR & MRS William B JR (Carol A Forman) | ☎ (516) 676-2275
Ws'65.Pr.H'65 . . . . PO Box 358,
MR William B 3d—at Vanderbilt . . . . Town Cocks Lane,
Locust Valley, NY 11560

Taft MR & MRS Arthur T (Venning—Linda C H Frech) Wheat'75.Ht.Cr'75
☎ (908) 874-7190 . . 11 Bridgewood Court, Belle Mead, NJ 08502
Taft MR & MRS David D (Sara Leonard) | ☎ (415) 854-6288
MichSt'62.Ken'60.MichSt'63 . . . . 45 Melanie Lane,
MISS Amy R—Sth'86—at 1708 Sanborn Av, | Atherton, CA 94027
Los Angeles, CA 90027 . . . .
MISS Elisabeth K—Buck'91—at
1250 Sherman Av, Menlo Park, CA 94025 . . . .

Taft MR Kingsley A (Louise Dakin) Sth'27.Un.
☎ (614) 486-1905 . . 1840C Riverside Dv, Columbus, OH 43212
Taft MRS Robert JR (Swift—Warner—Joan McKelvy)
SL'46.Cm.Sr.Cvc.Fy.Sl . . .of
☎ (513) 561-8977 . . 4300 Drake Rd, Cincinnati, OH 45243
☎ (202) 265-2541 . . 2541 Waterside Dv NW, Washington, DC 20008
Taft MR Robert W—Aht'59.Y.'62 . . of
☎ (212) 988-9711 . . 53 E 66 St, New York, NY 10021-6112
☎ (305) 296-5867 . . 418 William St, Key West, FL 33040
Taft MR & MRS Sheldon A (Rebecca S Rinehart) OState'57.Aht'59.H'62
☎ (614) 253-1412 . . 317 Stanbery Av, Columbus, OH 43209-1468

Taft MR & MRS William H JR (Leanne Hansen) | ☎ (201) 425-1425
Cl'61.Rut'52 . . . . Young's Rd,
MR William P . . . . Box 122B,
MR Timothy E—Hartw'94 . . . . Basking Ridge, NJ 07920

Taft MR & MRS William H 4th (Malone—Julia A | ☎ (202)338-2754
Vadala) Col'64.Col'67.Cos.Y'66.H'69 . . . . 3245 Cleveland Av
MISS Maria C . . . . NW, Washington,
JUNIORS MISS Julia H . . . . DC 20008
JUNIORS MR William H 5th . . . . | ☎ (703) 550-0618
Indian Springs Farm,
PO Box 227, Lorton,
VA 22199

Taft MRS William Howard 3d (Barbara H Bradfield)
Mich'38.BMr'42.Mt.Cos.
☎ (202) 363-4685 . . 3101—35 St NW, Washington, DC 20016
Taft MR & MRS William W (Edith Gress) | ☎ (216) 751-9438
Kt.Aht'54.H'59 . . . . 2932 Courtland
MISS Linda R—Pitzer'89 . . . . Blvd, Cleveland, OH 44122

Taft MR & MRS William W JR (Lisa A Fuller) Emory'85
218 Flora Av NE, Atlanta, GA 30307-2716
Tagatac MR & MRS Christopher J (Ashley H Jones)
Geo'86.Rc.Bcs.Cly.Col'86
☎ (212) 475-0428 . . 34 Gramercy Park E, New York, NY 10003
Taggart MRS John V 3d (Theodora J Lannon) C.Bgt.Cs.
☎ (914) 234-3793 . . 371 Greenwich Rd, Bedford, NY 10506-1738
Taggart MR & MRS Rush 3d (Dorothy L Bedford)
P'78.H'82.Ny.Ihy.Pn.Ant'75.H'86
☎ (609) 683-0981 . . 492 Prospect Av, Princeton, NJ 08540
Tailer MRS T Suffern (Thompson—Clark—Jean Sinclair)
Cly.So.Evg.Ng.Dar . . .of
☎ (212) 832-1797 . . 475 Park Av, New York, NY 10022
☎ (561) 832-1511 . . 1 N Breakers Row, Palm Beach, FL 33480
Tait MR & MRS Thomas (Patricia E Ritter) ArizSt'64
☎ (602) 944-6667 . . 511 W Northview Av, Phoenix, AZ 85021
Tait MR & MRS William E (Jill S Maurer) NAriz'91.NAriz'89
☎ (602) 861-2979 . . 65 W State Av, Phoenix, AZ 85021
Tait MASTER William Matthew (William E) . . . . Born Mch 14'95
Talamo MRS L Rutherfurd (Carter—Leith W W | ☎ (212) 535-8293
Rutherfurd) . . . . 210 E 73 St, Apt
MR Gerard . . . . 4B, New York, NY
JUNIORS MR Lupo R . . . . | 10021

Talbot MR & MRS Bradford C (Mary H Clark) DU'77.F&M'72
☎ (303) 789-9488 . . 1875 Cherryville Rd, Littleton, CO 80121
Talbot DR & MRS C Conover (Sylvia V Martin) P'34.Nw'38
☎ (312) 787-4411 . . 441 E Erie St, Apt 4904, Chicago, IL 60611
Talbot MRS C Meredith (Carlotta Haines) Stan'41 . . | ☎ (508) 922-0016
MISS Carlotta F . . . . 84 West St,
MISS Cynthia D . . . . Beverly Farms, MA 01915

Talbot MR & MRS Fraser H (Virginia S Thomas) Rice'92
☎ (713) 974-5966 . . 2301 Hayes Rd, Apt 7220, Houston, TX 77077
Talbot DR & MRS (DR) George H (Sheryl Flaschen)
GeoW'75.Nu'79.Wes'70.Y'75
☎ (610) 964-0946 . . PO Box 7440, St Davids, PA 19087-7440

Talbot MR & MRS Harold R (M Louise Lane) CtCol'60.Bgt.K.P'58.Va'65 . . . . | ☎ (914) 232-5149
MR James S—at Boston Coll Law . . . . | 67 Mt Holly Rd, Katonah, NY *10536*

Talbot MR & MRS James M II (Nina Sinkler) Pc.Sg.Cda.NCar'65.Pa'85 . . . . | ☎ (610) 275-7222
MR John D II—P'94 . . . . | 1906 Johnson Rd, Norristown, PA *19401*

Talbot MR & MRS Lee M (Martha W Hayne) Cos.Cal'52 . . . . | ☎ (703) 734-8576
MR Lawrence H—Cal'93 . . . . | 6656 Chilton Court, McLean, VA *22101*
JUNIORS MR Russell M—at Dartmouth . . . . |

Talbot MISS Lorna (Atkins—Lorna Talbot) Fr . . .of
☎ (540) 592-9545 . . Ross Farm, 20821 Trappe Rd, Upperville, VA *20185*
☎ (415) 775-7223 . . 30 Pleasant St, San Francisco, CA *94108*

Talbot MRS Nathan B (Anne Perry) Cy.Chi.Sb.
☎ (617) 566-3288 . . 176 Warren St, Brookline, MA *02146*

Talbot MR & MRS Richmond deP JR (Alice L Spruance) Swb'66.Fiy.Va'66 . . . . | ☎ (203) 762-0851
MISS Margaret H—at Davidson . . . . | 901 Ridgefield Rd, Wilton, CT *06897*
MR Richmond deP 3d . . . . |

Talbot MR & MRS Robert B (Caroline Allen) Fiy.Y'39
☎ (860) 233-6115 . . 23 Plymouth Rd, West Hartford, CT *06119*

Talbot MRS Susan S (Driscoll—Susan R Smith) Pa'69 . . . . | ☎ (508) 768-7160
JUNIORS MISS Samantha L . . . . | 78 Western Av, Essex, MA *01929*

Talbot MR & MRS Timothy R 3d (N Allison Davies) Wells'67.Ty'67 . . . . | ☎ (908) 879-8596
MISS Nancy L—at Drew . . . . | 17 Warren Cutting, Chester, NJ *07930*
JUNIORS MR Timothy D . . . . |

Talbot MR & MRS William R (Elizabeth F Hall) Cc.Ty'63 . . . . | ☎ (513) 530-9434
MR William R 3d—Bab'89 . . . . | 11050 Sycamore Grove Lane, Cincinnati, OH *45241*
MR Charles MacD—at U of Cincinnati . . . . |

Talcott MR & MRS Hooker JR (Jane C McCurrach) Sim'79.Eyc.Ub.Cy.P'54
☎ (617) 734-6279 . . 420 Warren St, Brookline, MA *02146*

Taliaferro MR & MRS C Champe (Polk—Margaret S Salvage) Pr . . .of
☎ (561) 546-5529 . . 478 S Beach Rd, Hobe Sound, FL *33455*
☎ (516) 759-3887 . . 20 Highland Mews, Glen Cove, NY *11542*

Taliaferro MR & MRS George W JR (Elizabeth L Wilson) Sth'78.Cly.Hn.P'64
☎ (513) 561-1193 . . 5600 Pamlico Lane, Cincinnati, OH *45243*

Taliaferro MR & MRS John C III (Audrey F Wilson) Elk.H'39
☎ (410) 366-5036 . . 4300 N Charles St, Apt E3, Baltimore, MD *21218*

Taliaferro MR & MRS Scott L (Patty B Nixon) Sth'50.Y'44
☎ (915) 692-7878 . . 1414 Tanglewood Rd, Abilene, TX *79605*

Talley DR & MRS (DR) David K (Karin A Johnson) B'hamS'85.Ala'90.NCar'84.Ala'88
☎ (918) 456-6265 . . Rte 4, Box 473, Tahlequah, OK *74464*

Talley MR & MRS Truman M (Madelon DeVoe) B.Mds.P'47 . . . . | ☎ (212) 988-3127
MISS Marina . . . . | 876 Park Av, New York, NY *10021*
MR Macdonald—at 192 Sloat Av, Pacific Grove, CA *93950* . . . . |

Tallmadge MRS Edward S (Marie I Amberg) Man'vl'54
☎ (414) 367-2940 . . Pine Lake, PO Box 303, Hartland, WI *53029*

Tallman MRS D Rex (Brownlee—Frances V Waggaman) An.Sl.Ncd.
☎ (619) 435-8311 . . 1155 Star Park W, Apt 3A, Coronado, CA *92118*

Talmage MR & MRS E T Hunt 3d (Mueller—Kathrin L Johnson) Mt.Rv.Col'68.Geo'71 . . . . | of ☎ (011-66-2) 266-6485
MR E Taylor H . . . . | 20 N Sathorn Rd, Bangkok 10500, Thailand
MR J Adrian Mueller . . . . | ☎ (916) 546-7305
MR Bret A Mueller . . . . | 5845 Sudan Rd, PO Box 241, Carnelian Bay, CA *96140*
☎ (011-33-1) 42-67-34-82
11 Cité de Pusy, 75017 Paris, France

Talmage MR Edward T H JR
☎ (303) 733-8733 . . 90 Corona St, Apt 1105, Denver, CO *80218*

Talmage MR John F—Lic.Hof'61 . . . . | ☎ (516) 239-2513
MR John E—W&M'92.Vt'96—at | "Bentley Corners"
☎ (410) 602-8149 . . 6625 Bonnie Ridge Dv, | 298 Tanglewood
Apt T2, Baltimore, MD *21209* . . . . | Crossing, Lawrence, NY *11559-2019*

Talmage MR Kenneth K—Cyb.Rv.Clare'68 . . . . . | ☎ (303) 322-2288
JUNIORS MISS Julie H—at Madeira . . . . | 458 High St, Denver, CO *80218-4024*

Talmage MR & MRS Prentice JR (Sylvia G Woolworth) Eh.Pn.P'50
☎ (908) 234-2454 . . Spook Hollow Rd, Box 245, Far Hills, NJ *07931*

Tamplin MRS Joanna T (Joanna L Tilghman) Chath'68.Md.Mv.Cda.Ncd.
☎ (410) 228-7551 . . "Monsieur's Folly" 5841 Castle Haven Rd, Cambridge, MD *21613*

Taney MR & MRS J Charles 2d (Amie R Hollingsworth) Pa'46 . . . . | ☎ (914) 235-4197
MISS M Brooke . . . . | 125 Sutton Manor Rd, New Rochelle, NY *10805*

Taney MR & MRS J Charles 3d (Carol J Diamond) NRoch'68.Hob'69 . . . . | ☎ (203) 637-8411
MISS Megan A . . . . | 9 Hillcrest Lane, Old Greenwich, CT *06870*

Tanis MR & MRS Stephen G (Cronin—Alida L Fish) Sth'67 . . . . | ☎ (302) 475-0537
JUNIORS MR Michael D . . . . | 1816 Millers Rd, Wilmington, DE *19810*

Tankersley MR & MRS Garvin E (Miller—Ruth E McCormick)
3591 N Bear Canyon Rd, Tucson, AZ *85749*

Tankersley GEN & MRS Will Hill (Theda C Ball) USA'50
☎ (334) 279-9663 . . 1830 Croom Dv, Montgomery, AL *36106*

Tankoos MR Bradley J—Pr.DU'74
☎ (303) 722-2334 . . 5 Polo Place, 3000 E Cedar Av, Denver, CO *80209*

Tannatt MR & MRS G Darrell (Vicki A Bell) NCol'60.Ariz'61.ArizSt'60
☎ (602) 257-1772 . . 12 E San Miguel Av, Phoenix, AZ *85012*

Tanner MRS Edward E 3d (Louise F Stickney)
201 E 17 St, New York, NY *10003*

Tanner MR & MRS Frederick C (Andrus—Dorelle Moulton) Cw.Cc.Y'39
☎ (203) 869-4487 . . 15 Dairy Rd, Greenwich, CT *06830*

Tanner DR & MRS Michael (Mary A Pritting) Ant'76.Cl'80.GeoW'89
316 W 79 St, New York, NY *10024*

Tanner MR & MRS Thomas J (Barbara J Woodworth) ☎ (617) 891-6717
MISS Sara E—at Trinity . . . . 412 Highland St,
MR Pratt M . . . . Weston, MA
02193-2628

Tansill MR & MRS Robert W (Margielou A Meinig)
☎ (805) 646-4647 . . 105 Layton Dv, Ojai, CA *93023*

Tappan MISS Alice M . . see P von S Jones

Tappan MR David L . . see P von S Jones

Tappan MR Michael A JR . . see P von S Jones

Taquey MR Antony—NEng'76
☎ (202) 333-5395 . . 1681–31 St NW, Washington, DC *20007-2968*

Taquey MR Charles H
☎ (202) 333-5971 . . 1681–31 St NW, Washington, DC *20007-2968*

Tarbox MR & MRS Thomas R (Rosa Scharz) ☎ (787) 722-7020
Wms'64 . . . . Candina Reef,
MISS Sonia M . . . . 2 Calle Candina,
Apt 1802, Condado,
Puerto Rico *00907*

Tarkington MR & MRS J Fred JR (Lila Jane ☎ (615) 356-3745
Anderson) Van'55.Ncd.Van'51 . . . . 614 Enquirer Av,
MISS Jane McF—Van'85—at ☎ (212) 831-3399 Nashville, TN *37205*
22 E 89 St, New York, NY *10128* . . . .

Tasman MRS Earl F (Goodwin—Josephine L K Reeve)
☎ (860) 354-6236 . . 2 Meadow Lane, Sherman, CT *06784*

Tasman MR & MRS W Graham (Amy L Thomas)
MmtVa'91.Pc.Rv.Ht.Duke'89
☎ (215) 886-6557 . . 702 Winding Way, Glenside, PA *19038*

Tasman DR & MRS William (Alice Lea Mast) ☎ (215) 247-3055
Bnd'55.Pc.Rv.Ht.Ac.Ncd.Dar.Dcw.Hav'51 . . . . 550 E Gravers Lane,
MISS Alice L M—Br'89.Pc.Ncd.—at Wyndmoor, PA
☎ (212) 780-9473 . . 140 W 4 St, Apt 10, *19038*
New York, NY *10012* . . . .
MR James B—Pc.Rv.Ht.Penn'87—
☎ (215) 233-3080 . . . .

Tate MR & MRS John H 2d (Priscilla T McClelland)
Tex'72.A.USA'64.Tex'72
☎ (210) 824-6224 . . 603 Olmos Dv E, San Antonio, TX *78212*

Tatham MRS Charles (Julie de F Campbell)
☎ (703) 548-7825 . . 1202 S Washington St, Apt 814C, Alexandria,
VA *22314*

Tatnall MRS Francis G (Amélie d'A Vauclain) . . . . ☎ (610) 828-0706
MR Francis JR—Pa'52 . . . . PO Box 289,
Plymouth Meeting,
PA *19462-0289*

Tatnall MR Henry C JR—Rcp.Pn.P'52.LIU'68
☎ (609) 924-1412 . . 801 Mt Lucas Rd, Princeton, NJ *08540*

Tatnall MR & MRS Samuel M V (Field—Pearson—Joan B Connelly)
Hav'60.H'63 . . of
☎ (212) 831-4621 . . 114 E 90 St, New York, NY *10128*
☎ (914) 234-7696 . . "Deerwood" PO Box 536, Bedford, NY *10506*

Tattersall MR & MRS Stowe H (Margaret D Carroll) Pa'78.Eyc.Yn.Br'72
☎ (609) 844-0423 . . 6 Green Av, Lawrenceville, NJ *08648*

Tatum MR & MRS John C JR (Mary Ann Little) Sth'74.Stan'72
☎ (214) 521-0444 . . 4243 Beverly Dv, Dallas, TX *75205*

Taussig MISS Ellen M
☎ (609) 898-1648 . . "Parsley Hall" 110 York Av, West Cape May,
NJ *08204*

Taussig MR & MRS Frederick (Browne—Ferriss— of ☎ (314)361-4191
Jean A Overstreet) Nf.H'36 ⚓ . . . . 5290 Waterman Av,
MISS Susan C—at ☎ (314) 367-8372 Apt 3E, St Louis,
5142 Westminster Place, St Louis, MO *63108* . . MO *63108*
☎ (314) 239-1955
"Bluff House"
St John's Rd,
Washington, MO
63090

Taussig MRS J Thomas (Jane G Cummings) Fy. . . . . ☎ (773) 281-2365
MISS Meredith J—at ☎ (312) 337-0963 2960 N Lake Shore
1350 N Lake Shore Dv, Chicago, IL *60610* . . . . Dv, Chicago, IL
MRS Annie T McAdoo (Annie C Taussig)—at *60657*
☎ (312) 787-9228 . . 1150 N Lake Shore Dv,
Chicago, IL *60611* . . . .

Taussig MR & MRS Thomas K (Evelyn C Thayer) CarnM'56.W&J'56
☎ (619) 599-4171 . . 1636 Olympus Loop Dv, Vista, CA *92083*

Taves DR Ernest H—Sb.Cl'38.Nu'45
☎ (617) 876-1730 . . 12 Hubbard Park Rd, Cambridge, MA *02138*

Tayloe MR & MRS William (Janet D Roszel) Cda.Ncd.
☎ (540) 687-3721 . . "Seldom Seen" 35165 Training Center Lane,
Middleburg, VA *20117*

Taylor MR A Thomas—Cho.Sr.On.Y'32 . . of
☎ (408) 624-7998 . . 1548 Cypress Dv, Pebble Beach, CA *93953*
☎ (847) 234-0170 . . 435 N Thorne Lane, Lake Forest, IL *60045*

Taylor MRS Abby P (Abby D Paine) Bnd'66 . . . . . . ☎ (215) 247-9459
MR Nathaniel A—Br'93 . . . . 203 E Evergreen
MR Peter L—Mid'94 . . . . Av, Philadelphia,
JUNIORS MISS Elizabeth E . . . . PA *19118*

Taylor DR & MRS Alexander H (Dale McCreedy)
Laf'78.Pa'85.Mont'78.Pa'90
☎ (610) 296-4116 . . 978 Delchester Rd, Newtown Square, PA *19073*

Taylor MR & MRS Alexander S 2d (Alexandra ☎ (216) 831-8276
Ryburn) Kt.Un.Tv.Y'56 31010 Edgewood
MR V Corydon 2d—at Exton, PA *19341* . . . . . . Rd, Pepper Pike, OH
44124

Taylor MISS Ashley C . . see H D McIntire

Taylor JUNIORS MR Ashton K . . see H D McIntire

Taylor MR Augustus (Isobel McCreery)
☎ (415) 343-0210 . . 950 W Santa Inez Av, Hillsborough, CA *94010*

Taylor MR & MRS Austin G E (Strong—M Elizabeth ☎ (519) 927-5228
Newbold) Cly. . . . . Briont Farm,
MISS Michelle C—at 5626 Dunbar St, Apt 301, 17401 Winston
Vancouver, BC V6N 1W7, Canada . . . . Churchill Blvd,
Belfountain, Ontario
L0N 1B0, Canada

Taylor MR & MRS B Loyall (Beverly J Booth) NCar'44
☎ (803) 681-2322 . . 1 Outerbridge Circle, Hilton Head, SC *29923*

Taylor MR & MRS B Loyall JR (Nancy S Harkins) ☎ (610) 725-1122
DeP'72.Cwr'74.Me.NCar'69 . . . . 600 Cedar Hollow
MISS Brooke S . . . . Rd, Paoli, PA *19301*
JUNIORS MR B Loyall 3d . . . .

Taylor MR Benjamin R . . see MRS R E Gregg

Taylor MRS C Harold (Juliet C Baldwin) Nyc.Cly.Yn.
☎ (508) 228-0991 . . 8 Walnut Lane, Nantucket, MA *02554*

Taylor MR & MRS Carroll S (Nancy S Tyson)
Cal'66.Y'65.Boalt'68 . . . . | ☎ (808) 235-1736
MISS Heather L—at U of Va . . . . | 46-429 Hololio St,
MISS Kimberly L—at Yale . . . . | Kaneohe, HI *96744*
MISS Tori N . . . . |
JUNIORS MISS Tiffany B . . . . |
JUNIORS MISS Tacy B . . . . |

Taylor MISS Caryl P . . see MISS J P Lovejoy

Taylor MRS Charles H (Dorothy F Ayer) D.Ncd.
☎ (617) 891-1198 . . 99 Norumbega Rd, Apt 108, Weston, MA *02193*

Taylor MR & MRS Charles M (Linda J Wilson) | ☎ (610) 642-1751
Me.Rc.H'59.Cl'63 . . . . | 248 Kent Rd,
MISS Alexandra A—at U of Pa Med . . . . | Wynnewood, PA
MR Andrew—at Harvard . . . . | *19096*

Taylor MISS Constance M . . see MISS (REV CANON) N A Roosevelt

Taylor MRS Cook (Jane T Cook) . . . . | ☎ (609) 924-0226
MR John B—at ☎ (212) 274-0306 | 60 Harrison St,
561 Broadway, New York, NY *10012* . . . . | Princeton, NJ *08540*
MR Joseph McC JR—at ☎ (609) 921-6864 |
30 Green St, Princeton, NJ *08540* |

Taylor MR & MRS David H JR (Milbrey T Rennie) | of ☎ (212)861-7129
V'68.Pr.Ri.Cly.H'68 . . . . | 53 E 66 St,
JUNIORS MISS Rennie M . . . . | New York, NY
| *10021*
| ☎ (516) 626-5531
| 1053 Friendly Rd,
| Upper Brookville,
| NY *11771*

Taylor MRS David S (Nancy Bryan) Pr.Y. . . . . | ☎ (516) 676-1932
MISS (REV) Nancy S—Macalester'78.Y'81—at | 227 Piping Rock Rd,
5800 Cobbler Lane, Boise, ID *83703* . . . . | Locust Valley, NY
| *11560*

Taylor MR & MRS David W (Jeanne L Dell) San.Ds.Mit'47
☎ (610) 935-9623 . . Triple T Farms, 128 Hares Hill Rd, Phoenixville,
PA *19460*

Taylor MR & MRS Donald B (Kristin A Chase) ColbyS'78.RI'80.Denis'81
''Heatherfield Cottage'' Queens Rd, Weybridge, Surrey KT13 0AH,
England

Taylor MR Douglas C—GeoW'73
☎ (212) 472-2153 . . 860 Park Av, New York, NY *10021*

Taylor MR & MRS Duncan R (Deeds—E Kathleen | ☎ (520) 529-6671
Brewer) Van'70.PacRel'74.Ariz'85.Ariz'66. | 3575 N Calle
Bost'69 . . . . | Rosario, Tucson, AZ
MR Duncan R JR—at 1505 Virginia St, Berkeley, | *85750*
CA *94703* . . . . |
MR Nathaniel B—at 2639 E 9 St, Apt 7, Oakland, |
CA *94601* . . . . |
  JUNIORS MR Blake Deeds . . . . |

Taylor MRS E Drayton (Rea—Elizabeth Drayton) Sth'42.Cvc.Sl.
☎ (202) 337-7154 . . 4000 Cathedral Av NW, Apt 144B, Washington,
DC *20016*

Taylor MRS E Hope (Thompson—E Hope Palmer) . | ☎ (603) 924-9258
JUNIORS MR Robert S JR . . . . | 53 Grove St,
| Peterborough, NH
| *03458*

Taylor MRS Earnshaw (M Rosalind Earnshaw)
☎ (212) 838-4452 . . 166 E 61 St, New York, NY *10021*

Taylor MR & MRS Edmund C (Emily T Pope) Cy.CtCol'84
11 Valley Rd, Wellesley, MA *02181-1456*

Taylor MRS Elizabeth Eyre (Elizabeth H Eyre) Csn . . .of
☎ (413) 229-8418 . . ''On the Rocks'' Southfield, MA *01259*
☎ (242) 332-2539 . . ''Little Friendship House'' Governor's Harbour,
Eleuthera, Bahamas

Taylor MRS Elspeth E (Elspeth H Eustis) | ☎ (617) 244-1322
Br'67.H'75 . . . . | 57 Grove Hill Av,
MISS Mary A—at 1400 N State P'kway, Chicago, | Newton, MA *02160*
IL *60610* . . . . |
MR William H . . . . |

Taylor MR & MRS Frank H 2d (Eve L Hebbard) USN'46 . . of
☎ (215) MA7-1694 . . 309 Spruce St, Philadelphia, PA *19106*
☎ (802) 464-5664 . . ''Negus Place'' HCR 63, Box 59, West Dover,
VT *05356*

Taylor MR & MRS Franklin J (Mary Elizabeth Rees)
SCal'39.Stan'37.Stan'39
☎ (310) 454-7381 . . 1040 Corsica Dv, Pacific Palisades, CA *90272*

Taylor MR & MRS Franklin P JR (Mary C Doolittle) St.G.
☎ (716) 881-4431 . . 1141 Delaware Av, Buffalo, NY *14209*

Taylor MR & MRS Frederic F (Blodgett—Judith T | ''Dorset Hollow''
McCormick) . . . . | Hollow Rd,
MISS Suzanne H—Vt'91 . . . . | RD 2, Box 1650,
MR Charles M—Vt'90 . . . . | Dorset, VT *05251*

Taylor MR & MRS H Furness 3d (Fantauzzi—Sheila | ☎ (610) 566-4705
W Reath) Pa'66.F&M'60 . . . . | 221 Martroy Lane,
MISS Samantha F Fantauzzi—at Simmons . . . | Wallingford, PA
| *19086*

Taylor MRS H Stillman (Taliaferro—Carolina C Denham) Pr.
☎ (516) 674-3153 . . ''Bagatelle'' 24 Underhill Rd, Locust Valley,
NY *11560*

Taylor MR & MRS H Tyler JR (Lillian S Fowlkes)
Swb'41.Cy.Rv.Dar.HampSydney'41
☎ (205) 871-3713 . . 7 Pine Ridge Lane, Birmingham, AL *35213*

Taylor MRS Henry J (Olander—Mercer—Taylor—Brownell—
Marion J E Richardson) Ri.Cly.
☎ (212) 744-7187 . . 2 E 70 St, New York, NY *10021*

Taylor MR & MRS Henry W JR (Sekula—Ann L Dayton) Leh'56.Nu'61 . . of
☎ (561) 575-5667 . . 953 Dolphin Court, Jupiter, FL *33458-4343*
☎ (208) 726-5498 . . 12694 H'way 75 S, Ketchum, ID *83340-2247*

Taylor MISS Hilary . . see MISS J P Lovejoy

Taylor MRS Holly (Bowles—Outten—Vogler—Holly Taylor) SFrSt'73
☎ (415) 435-1164 . . PO Box 208, Belvedere Tiburon, CA *94920-0208*

Taylor MRS Howard W JR (Elizabeth H Avery) Ac.Me.Ncd.
☎ (610) 527-0168 . . 424 Fisher's Rd, Bryn Mawr, PA *19010*

Taylor MR & MRS Hugh G JR (Carolyn W Eaton)
Br'82.Cl'85.Rc.Conn'82.Nu'88
☎ (212) 769-4135 . . 255 W 90 St, New York, NY *10024*

Taylor MISS Irene K
☎ (513) 791-0840 . . 10820 Deerfield Rd, Montgomery, OH *45242*

Taylor MR J Arthur . . . . Married
Hargroves MISS Jeannette . . . . Sep 25'93

Taylor MR & MRS J Arthur (Jeannette Hargroves)
Br'60.H'72.Ub.Earl'54 . . of
☎ (508) 371-0867 . . 44 Martin Rd, Concord, MA *01742*
Carney Farm, Woodstock, VT *05091*

Taylor MR James B 4th—NCar'71
☎ (203) 377-1770 . . 1751 N Peters Lane, Stratford, CT *06497*

Taylor MRS James C (Cecilia A Baldner) Miami'40
576 Sutton Place, Longboat Key, FL *34228*

Taylor MRS James Spear (Helen L MacG Strauss) Sl.Cly.Cvc.Cos.
☎ (202) 483-2323 . . 2325 S St NW, Washington, DC *20008*

Taylor MISS Jane F—Mls'35.H'39
☎ (415) 344-7315 . . 501 Edgewood Rd, San Mateo, CA *94402*

Taylor DR & MRS Jeffrey S (Sarah Mabrey) | ☎ (919) 782-8439
Wheat'69.Cyb.Br'68 . . . . | 3220 Millstream
MR Jeffrey S JR . . . . | Place, Raleigh, NC
JUNIORS MISS Sarah G . . . . | *27609*
JUNIORS MR Robert H . . . . |

Taylor MISS Jennifer H . . see MISS (REV CANON) N A Roosevelt

Taylor MR & MRS John David (Harris—Elizabeth C Cowles)
Nu'60.Cl'62.Cal'54.Cal'59
☎ (818) 792-8097 . . 1075 Pine Oak Lane, Pasadena, CA *91105-1138*

Taylor MR & MRS John I JR (E Carson Custer) Gchr'68.H'62
☎ (303) 444-0993 . . Sugarloaf Star Rte, 35 Owl Creek Rd, Boulder,
CO *80302*

Taylor MR & MRS John K (Delle Ernst)
☎ (513) 533-0162 . . 3580 Shaw Av, Apt 412, Cincinnati, OH *45208*

Taylor MR John M JR—Me.Rc.Gm.Cts.H. . . . . | ☎ (610) MI9-4111
MR Edward M . . . . | 37 Old Gulph Rd,
| Gladwyne, PA
| *19035*

Taylor DR & MRS John Martin (Billie Minx) LSU'46
☎ (601) 442-0201 . . 311 Jefferson St, Natchez, MS *39120*

Taylor MR & MRS John Read (Patricia L'amoureux | ☎ (516) MA6-0806
Green) . . . . | 19 Piping Rock Rd,
MR Kneeland L—Pa'70.DU'75—at | Upper Brookville,
☎ (907) 276-1003 . . 237 Fire Weed Lane E, | Glen Head, NY
Anchorage, AK *99503* . . . . | *11545*

Taylor MR John W—Srr.Cl'29
☎ (773) 935-1388 . . 2960 N Lake Shore Dv, Apt 2706, Chicago,
IL *60657-5600*

Taylor MR & MRS Jonathan T (Helen E Hurley) | ☎ (508) 475-1463
M'mack'70.Hart'67 . . . . | 4 Elysian Dv,
MISS Amy E—at 2704 Pillsbury Av S, | Andover, MA
Minneapolis, MN *55404* . . . . | *01810-1608*
MISS Betsy E—Mass'95 . . . . |
MR Jonathan T JR—at Boston Coll . . . . |
JUNIORS MISS Emily C . . . . |
JUNIORS MR Daniel C . . . . |
JUNIORS MR Richard R . . . . |

Taylor MR & MRS Jonathan V (Marjorie P Williams) | ☎ (617) 326-1516
Col'72.D.Cw.Bost'71 . . . . | 4 Newcourt Lane,
JUNIORS MISS Rebecca P . . . . | Dedham, MA *02026*
JUNIORS MISS Holly F . . . . |

Taylor MISS Katherine Potter (Colfelt—Katherine | ☎ (617) 277-1076
Potter Taylor) PhilaArt'66.H.'77 . . . . | 125 Middlesex Rd,
MISS E Avery Colfelt—Col'92 . . . . | Chestnut Hill, MA
MR Andrew B W Colfelt—Col'92 . . . . | *02167*

Taylor MRS Laighton (Caroline S Laighton) . . . . . . | ☎ (954) 564-6372
MISS Elizabeth L . . . . | PO Box 13051,
MRS Virginia B (Hertzler—Virginia B Taylor) . . | Ft Lauderdale, FL
| *33316*

Taylor MRS Lane (Elizabeth P Townsend) Rc.Sg.Rb.Ph.Ac.
Waverly Heights Villa 36, 1400 Waverly Rd, Gladwyne, PA *19035*

Taylor CAPT (RET) & MRS Le Roy T (Floride H Hewitt) Br'64.Ncd.USN'35
☎ (401) 846-2911 . . 170 Paradise Av, Middletown, RI *02842*

Taylor MRS Lesley E (McFadden—Lesley E Taylor) | ☎ (212) 249-5292
Ng.Mb. . . . . | 912 Fifth Av,
MISS Elizabeth C McFadden—Br'93 . . . . | New York, NY
| *10021*

Taylor MR M Darwood—Mich'47.Stan'55
☎ (610) MI9-4742 . . 115 W Montgomery Av, Ardmore, PA *19003*

Taylor MR & MRS Marshall M (Judith A Ferber) | ☎ (818) 799-7318
Cal'70.Vh.Y'69.Cal'74 . . . . | 285 Bellefontaine St,
JUNIORS MR Bryan D . . . . | Pasadena, CA *91105*

Taylor MRS Maxwell D (Lydia G Happer) An.Cvc.Sl.
☎ (202) 541-0306 . . 6200 Oregon Av NW, Washington, DC *20015*

Taylor MR & MRS (DR) Michael R (Theresa A Goularte)
Ne'79.Bost'84.Tufts'90.Me.Cr'79.Va'83
☎ (508) 359-7621 . . "Metcalfe Homestead" 589 Main St, Medfield,
MA *02052*

Taylor MR & MRS Nicholas C (Catherine H Blaffer) | ☎ (915) 683-7195
Cr'68.Unn.Au.Cly.H'59 . . . . | 1203 Country Club
MISS Katherine C—at Dartmouth . . . . | Dv, Midland, TX
LT Nicholas Van C—USMC.—at | *79701*
Camp Pendleton, CA *92055* . . . . |
JUNIORS MISS Christie H V—at St Paul's . . . . . . |

Taylor MR P Randolph—Pa'80
☎ (404) 875-9382 . . 37 S Prado St NE, Apt 1, Atlanta, GA *30309*

Taylor MRS Pamela A (Psoroyannis—Pamela A | ☎ (011-30-289)
Taylor) . . . . | 25469
MISS Ioanna R Psoroyannis—at | "L'Hameau"
☎ (718) 721-5138 . . 32-80—30 St, Astoria, | PO Box 606,
NY *11106* . . . . | 84 600 Mykonos,
| Greece

Taylor MRS R Stockton (Elizabeth F Griffith) . . . . . | ☎ (610) 867-7031
MR R Stockton JR—Leh'68 . . . . | 144 Moreland Av,
| Bethlehem, PA
| *18017*

Taylor MR & MRS Reuben Chapman JR (Bauchens—Goddard—
Jane Carpenter) BMr'38.Sim'39.Wash'36
☎ (561) 231-1792 . . 177 Island Creek Dv, John's Island, Vero Beach,
FL *32963*

Taylor MR & MRS Richard S (Waterman—Belle S | of ☎ (415)344-3577
Kilborne) Sfg.Sfy.Bur.Pcu.Cc.Myf.Cly.Ariz'64 | 1855 Willow Rd,
⚓ | Hillsborough, CA
MR Richard S . . . . | *94010-6356*
| ☎ (508) 428-2276
| 713 Sea View Av,
| PO Box 117,
| Osterville, MA
| *02655-0117*

Taylor MR & MRS Richard Sward (Sally M Sherman) ☎ (415) 388-2369
Scripps'50.BrigY'40. . . . . "Chamizal"
MR William R . . . . 80 Lee St,
Mill Valley, CA
94941

Taylor MR & MRS Robert C (Barbara W Tietzel) NMex'47.Pa'55
☎ (512) 329-8134 . . 3600 Flamevine Cove, Austin, TX *78735*

Taylor MR & MRS Robert C JR (Deborah A Beveridge)
Miami'84.Loy'89.DU'85.Ch'90
☎ (630) 790-2203 . . 905 Winslow Circle, Glen Ellyn, IL *60137*

Taylor MR Robert E L—Gm.Me.Rb.Yh.Cc.P'35 . . of
☎ (610) 526-9636 . . 33 Pond Lane, Bryn Mawr, PA *19010*
☎ (803) 747-2746 . . Yeamans Hall Club, PO Box 9455, Charleston,
SC *29410*

Taylor MR & MRS Robert E L 3d (Antoinette D Egger) Ph.P'69
☎ (206) 562-1769 . . 18719 SE 58 St, Issaquah, WA *98027*

Taylor MRS Robert G (Gates—Phyllis C Lueders) Dar.
☎ (941) 923-3693 . . Lake Point Woods Apt 253, 7979 S Tamiami Trail,
Sarasota, FL *34231*

Taylor MR Robert S . . . . ☎ (603) 924-7027
MISS Lisa K—at ☎ (207) 799-7657 Old Town Farm,
7 Orchid Rd, Cape Elizabeth, ME *04107* . . . . . . Peterborough, NH
MR William C *03458*

Taylor MR S B Richards—Rv.Y.'29
☎ (215) KI5-7363 . . Casa Fermi Apt 101, 1300 Lombard St,
Philadelphia, PA *19147*

Taylor DR & MRS Samuel G 3d (Kennedy—Jocelyn Pierson)
On.Cw.Cnt.Ncd.Y'27.Rush'32
☎ (715) 856-5908 . . Wausaukee Club, Athelstane, WI *54104*

Taylor DR & MRS (DR) Samuel G 4th (Morrin—Bonnie M McMahon)
StFran'80.Loy'94.Y'63.Saskatoon'69
☎ (773) 935-9740 . . 3024 N Kenmore Av, Chicago, IL *60657*

Taylor MRS Sandra B (Sandra S Brown) Mds.Cly. . ☎ (212) 734-9008
MISS Louise T . . . . 103 E 84 St,
New York, NY
10028

Taylor MISS Sara D—Skd'84
☎ (212) 722-3934 . . 320 E 91 St, Apt 2FC, New York, NY *10128*

Taylor MR & MRS Stephen H (Benjamin—Beatrix C Hoyt) S.Colg'53
☎ (516) 922-9537 . . 129 Cove Rd, Oyster Bay, NY *11771*

Taylor MR & MRS Stewart F (Josephine F Barroll) Rc.An.Yn.Y'51.H'56
☎ (610) 436-6520 . . Arborlea Farm, 450 Northbrook Rd,
West Chester, PA *19382*

Taylor MR Stuart S—Va'35
☎ (805) 969-8831 . . 300 Hot Springs Rd, Apt B57, Santa Barbara,
CA *93108*

Taylor MISS Susan—Mid'53
☎ (217) 344-4726 . . 606 W Michigan Av, Urbana, IL *61801-4840*

Taylor MR & MRS T Ryburn (Laura C Piper) Ty'83.Kt.Ty'84
☎ (916) 686-6968 . . 9930 Pleasant Grove School Rd, Elk Grove,
CA *95624*

Taylor MRS Thomas (Charlotte G Valentine) Rdc'38.Sbc.
☎ (508) 526-1016 . . "Sea Ledge" 29 Old Neck Rd,
Manchester-By-The-Sea, MA *01944*

Taylor MR & MRS Thomas P 3d (Anne L Johnston) ☎ (314) 994-1655
Rc.NCar'64 . . . . 6 Wickersham Lane,
MISS Lisa . . . . St Louis, MO *63124*
MR Phillip D . . . .

Taylor MISS Valerie (Burr—Spencer—Valerie Taylor) SCtSt'68.SCtSt'73
☎ (410) 822-2491 . . 401 S 2 St, Denton, MD *21629*

Taylor MR & MRS Vernon F JR (Cooke—Francis A Bonfoey)
Ln.B.Bhm.Dth'37
☎ (303) 985-0797 . . 6900 W Lakeridge Rd, Denver, CO *80227*

Taylor MRS W Waverly (BRNSS Edmée R M G ☎ (202) 333-5005
Snoy) Cvc. . . . . 3974 Georgetown
MR Gerald A W—at ☎ (805) 966-6860 Court NW,
2121 Stanwood Dv, Santa Barbara, CA *93103* . . Washington, DC
20007

Taylor MR & MRS Walter J (Shirley A Hopkins) . . . . of ☎ (970)920-4777
MISS Margaret J—at ☎ (406) 256-7855 777 Ute Av, 6,
119 W Yellowstone St, Billings, MT *59101* . . . . PO Box 1228,
Aspen, CO *81612*
☎ (406) 757-2235
W Lazy T Ranch,
PO Box 595, Busby,
MT *59016*

Taylor MRS Warren O (Katharine S Coe)
Brookhaven 207A, 1010 Waltham St, Lexington, MA *02173*

Taylor MRS William Davis (Ann C Macy) Tv.D.Cy.Chi.
☎ (617) 329-2621 . . 10 Longwood Dv, Apt 241, Westwood, MA *02090*

Taylor MR William Davis—Tv.D.Cy.Cw.H.'31
Burrage House, 314 Commonwealth Av, Boston, MA *02116*

Taylor MR & MRS William E (Mary A Pohren) ☎ (513) 321-3700
Pars'67.Pars'67 . . . . 1 Elmhurst Place,
MISS Whitney S . . . . Cincinnati, OH
MR David H *45208*

Taylor MRS William H JR (Anna P Stribling) Mls'34.Vh.
☎ (818) 794-0074 . . 1188 N Hill Av, Pasadena, CA *91104*

Taylor MRS William Nelson 2d (Lucy Ellen Gibson) ☎ (214) 696-0714
Tex'44 . . . . 5214 Lobello Dv,
MR Stephen C—Tex'91—at ☎ (214) 521-5936 Dallas, TX *75229*
4554 Glenwick Lane, Apt 1302, Dallas, TX
75225 . . . .

Taylor MR & MRS William O (Sally P Coxe) Cy.Sm.Tv.Chi.H'54
☎ (617) 262-4473 . . 2 Commonwealth Av, Apt 16F, Boston MA *02116*

Taylor MR & MRS William R (Victoria Tudor) ☎ (713) 937-6268
TexA&M'64 . . . . 15818 Tenbury St,
MISS Natasha T . . . . Houston, TX *77040*
JUNIORS MISS Megan H . . . .

Taylor MRS William R K (Elsie G Lathrop) Myf.
☎ (520) 529-4732 . . 1550 E River Rd, Apt 109, Tucson, AZ *85718*

Taylor MRS William Shipley (Margaret A Watson)
☎ (360) 479-2837 . . Canterbury Manor 103, 703 Callahan Dv,
Bremerton, WA *98310-3356*

Taylor MR & MRS William T (Elizabeth N Todd) Ncd.Laf'43
☎ (860) 658-5891 . . 52 West St, Simsbury, CT *06070*

Taylor MR & MRS Wilson H (Gaumer—Barbara A Bacon) Ty'64
1980 Rochambeau Dv, Malvern, PA *19355-9723*

Teagle MR & MRS Walter C 3d (Janet Dixon) ☎ (516) 922-3529
Rc.Lic.Ln.S.Ri.Pr.Cly.Md'72.Pa'76 . . . . "Dam House"
JUNIORS MISS Janet W . . . . Cleft Rd,
JUNIORS MR W Clark 4th . . . . Mill Neck, NY
JUNIORS MR Clifton D *11765*

Tearse MR & MRS David B (C Selden Wells) Ty'85.Chi.Cda.Dc.StLaw'87
☎ (617) 934-5452 . . 119 Oak St, Duxbury, MA *02332*

Teasdale MR & MRS David G (Judith C Ruble)
☎ (941) 598-1866 . . 1812 Princess Court, Naples, FL *34110*

Teasdale MR & MRS Kenneth F (Elizabeth D ☎ (314) 367-7316
Langdon) AmU'64.Nd.Rc.Aht'56.Wash'61 . . . . 33 Kingsbury Place,
MISS Caroline C . . . . St Louis, MO *63116*
MISS Cindy F . . . .
MR Douglas S . . . .

Techentin MISS Kristin E (Thomas A) . . . . Married at Pasadena, CA
Harrison MR Berkeley G (Carter H JR) . . . . Apr 20'96

Techentin MR & MRS Thomas A (Elayne R Griffin) ☎ (818) 578-1766
Stan'62.SCal'58 . . . . 640 Magnolia Av,
MR Warren A . . . . Pasadena, CA *91106*
MR Nicholas W . . . .

Teel MRS Rolland M JR (Beatrice H James) Mv. . . . . ☎ (410) 377-8308
MISS Mary Marshall . . . . 6132 Allwood
Court, Baltimore,
MD *21210*

Teetzel MR & MRS Roger S (Holly O Davidson) Wis'69.Wis'69
☎ (619) 481-0172 . . 14261 Minorca Cove, Del Mar, CA *92014*

Tegtmeyer MISS Elise D—Wash'70
☎ (314) 961-9946 . . 7876 Chatwell Dv, St Louis, MO *63119*

Teillon MR & MRS L Pierre JR (Margaret B ☎ (610) 687-1466
McCawley) Pa'70.Y'65.Cl'68 . . . . 472 Nob Hill Lane,
MISS Nicole S . . . . Devon, PA *19333*
MISS Sarah McK . . . .
MR Geoffrey P . . . .

Teller MR & MRS Andrew JR (Carrie Christine Chapman) Smu'86
☎ (214) 369-8584 . . 6630 Stefani Dv, Dallas, TX *75225*

Templeton MR James S (Elizabeth Thompson)
☎ (941) 366-0656 . . 1255 N Gulfstream Av, Apt 701A, Sarasota,
FL *34236*

Templeton MRS Rebecca P (Rebecca D Perkins)
45 Elm Lane, Rochester, NY *14610-3423*

Tener MISS Constance T—E&H'70
☎ (609) 465-4691 . . 207 Garden Lake Park, Cape May Court House,
NJ *08210*

Tener MR & MRS George Evans (Faber—Anne P ☎ (202) 338-2931
Potts) Ct.Mt.Sl.Ncd.Y'40 . . . . 3202 Scott Place
MISS Jenifer E—at ☎ (213) 650-9718 NW, Washington,
8939 Appian Way, Los Angeles, CA *90046* . . . . DC *20007-2946*

Tener MR Hampden E 3d—Aht'54
☎ (415) 567-1582 . . 2898 Jackson St, Apt 101, San Francisco,
CA *94115*

Tener MRS Hampden F (Virginia L Letson)
Shell Point Village, Pavillion Rm 312, Ft Myers, FL *33908*

TenEyck MRS Barent (Ford—Leslie Van Ness)
Meadow Lakes 30-07, Hightstown, NJ *08520*

Tenge MR John J JR—NotreD'56.Stan'61.Stan'65
☎ (916) 652-3200 . . 4980 Lexington Circle, Placer Canyon Estates,
Loomis, CA *95650*

TenHoopen MR & MRS Carl A JR (Nash—Ann D ☎ (410) 269-6783
Blackstone) Cy.Mv.Ayc.Geo'51 . . . . 2 Southgate Av,
MISS Diane E . . . . Annapolis, MD
MISS Gail M *21401*
MISS Katherine B . . . .
MR Carl A 3d . . . .

Tennant MR & MRS David A (M Frances Goddard) Camb'48
☎ (011-44-1244) 570405 . . "Stone House" Rossett, Clwyd,
North Wales LL12 0HS, UK

Tenney MISS Anne G
☎ (212) 472-6507 . . 200 E 82 St, Apt 25C, New York, NY *10028*

Tenney MRS Charles H (Joan P Lusk) . . . . Died at
Islip, NY Sep 1'96

Tenney MRS Charles I (Frances N Flack)
☎ (610) LA5-4633 . . 509 Spruce Lane, Villanova, PA *19085*

Tenney MR & MRS Daniel G JR (Constance L Franchot) Pr.Cly.Y'35 . . of
☎ (516) 671-0642 . . 250 Piping Rock Rd, Locust Valley,
NY *11560-2506*
☎ (518) 327-3187 . . "Wanakiwin" PO Box 268, Paul Smiths,
NY *12970*

Tenney MRS J Baker (Janet W Baker) ☎ (610) 688-5189
CtCol'50.Dar.Ncd. . . . . 784 Holly Rd,
MISS Elizabeth I—Susq'87 . . . . Wayne, PA
19087-2751

Tennyson MR & MRS Leonard B (Witherspoon—Anne E Rodgers)
Stan'60.Cos.Tcy.Ncd.Bow'42 . . of
☎ (415) 669-7173 . . 15 Kehoe Way, Box 206, Inverness, CA *94937*
☎ (202) 333-4416 . . 1517—30 St NW, Apt C21, Washington,
DC *20007*

Terbell MRS Thomas G (Gerli—Margaret E Nicoll)
☎ (203) 531-4565 . . 505 W Lyon Farm, Greenwich, CT *06831*

Terbell MR & MRS Thomas G JR (Hershey—Yolanda ☎ (970) 926-2793
I Mezey) V'66.Cl'68.Vh.Stan'60.H'62 . . . . PO Box 1598, Vail,
MISS Heather I . . . . CO *81658-1598*
JUNIORS MR Thomas G 3d . . . .

Terhune MRS Everit B JR (Irene Memery) . . . . Died at
Dayton, OH Jun 12'96

Terhune MR Everit B JR . . . . Died at
Richmond, VA Jan 22'96

Terhune MR Everit B 3d—Mvh.Hl.Wms'63
☎ (513) 297-0797 . . 301 Harman Blvd, Dayton, OH *45419*

Terhune MR & MRS Harry M (Talia B Soper) ☎ (609) 448-2664
RMWmn'60.JCitySt'53 . . . . 16 Exeter Rd,
MISS Leslie E . . . . Hightstown, NJ
MR William F *08520*

Terrel des Chênes MRS Guy (Benjamin—Odette de Brunière) Pars'45
☎ (912) 234-2222 . . 107 W Perry St, Savannah, GA *31401*

Terrell MR & MRS Allen M (Josephine H Peters)
Swth'39.Me.Rv.Wilm'31.Hav'32 . . of
☎ (610) 645-8868 . . Waverly Heights Blair 218, 1400 Waverly Rd,
Gladwyne, PA *19035-1254*
"Hemlock Woods" La Anna Rd, RD 2, Cresco, PA *18326*

Terry MR & MRS Anthony Denison (Dorsey— ☎ (520) 721-8788
Cecelia L Sullivant) Houst'68.Ariz'53 . . . . 7021 E Calle
MISS Elizabeth C Dorsey—Gonzaga'96—at Tolosa, Tucson, AZ
☎ (509) 325-2791 . . 224 E Sinto Av, Spokane, *85750*
WA *99202* . . . .

Terry MISS Elizabeth—Sl.
☎ (202) 659-3721 . . 500—23 St NW, Apt 607, Washington, DC *20037-2819*

Terry MRS H P Baldwin (Merrill—Suzanne Strauss) . . . Died in Jun 1995

Terry MR & MRS James L (Maude F Davis) | ☎ (617) 484-1567
Tv.H'53.H'58 . . . . | 75 Cedar Rd,
MISS Elizabeth G—Ty'88 . . . . | Belmont, MA *02178*
MR Mark T—Geo'86 . . . . |

Terry MRS Kathryn Pender (Kathryn J Pender)
☎ (212) 876-7025 . . 114 E 90 St, New York, NY *10128*

Terry MRS N Maxson (Rebecca D Wolcott) V'38.Ncd.
☎ (302) 734-2663 . . 36 The Green, Dover, DE *19901*

Terry MR & MRS Robert L (Ellen McH Bruce) BtP.Evg.Au.P'41
☎ (561) 832-0670 . . 137 Kings Rd, Palm Beach, FL *33480*

Terry DR & MRS Stephen (Barbara A Brown) | ☎ (520) 296-3455
Ariz'57.Cl'61 . . . . | 6121 E San Marino
MISS Sarah E—at U of Ariz . . . . | Dv, Tucson, AZ
MR Andrew B—at ☎ (520) 327-1631 | *85715*
1321 E Elm St, Tucson, AZ *85719* . . . . |

Terry MR & MRS Stephen W (Pamela Simmons) Pom'85.Nw'94
☎ (847) 475-5317 . . 1014 Main St, Apt 3, Evanston, IL *60202*

Terry MR Walter B JR—Rcn.Pr.LakeF'72.Cl'77
☎ (310) 275-2834 . . 1033 N Carol Dv, T5, Los Angeles, CA *90069*

Terry MRS Walter Bliss (Grace N Heiskell) Shcc.Cly.Ncd.
☎ (908) 234-0379 . . PO Box 147, Peapack, NJ *07977*

Terry MRS Whitelaw T (Julia Wells) Cy.
☎ (314) 725-9848 . . 710 S Hanley Rd, Clayton, MO *63105*

Terry MR & MRS Whitelaw T JR (Valerie E | ☎ (314) 997-0309
Pantaleoni) Nd.Cy.P'55 . . . . | 9 St Andrews Dv,
MISS Elizabeth Jane—MtVern'90—at | St Louis, MO *63124*
☎ (202) 342-3981 . . 2914 Q St NW, Apt B1,
Washington, DC *20007* . . . . |
MR Michael Whitelaw—Va'86.W&L'89—at |
☎ (202) 342-2144 . . 1632—30 St NW, Apt 13,
Washington, DC *20007* . . . . |

Terry MRS Wyllys (Elena Howell) Ac.Cc.
☎ (610) 388-7427 . . 204 Kendal Dv, Kennett Square, PA *19348*

Test MR & MRS Alfred L JR (Geneva C Porter) Pc.Yp.Y'49
☎ (941) 639-4243 . . 1373 San Mateo Dv, Punta Gorda, FL *33950*

Test MR & MRS Alfred L 3d (Linda G George)
Wes'78.Mid'83.Pc.P.'77.Temp'93
☎ (215) 542-8315 . . 512 Ironwood Way, Dresher, PA *19025*

Test MISS Bettina P (Shillig—Bettina P Test) P'80
☎ (216) 331-6047 . . 20843 Morewood P'kway, Rocky River, OH *44116*

Test MR & MRS Preston P (Kimberly A Dash) ChHill'88.Del'84
☎ (412) 264-2936 . . 114 S Jamestown St, Coraopolis, PA *15108*

Tetzeli MR Frederick E—Geo'52 ⛵ . . . . | ☎ (609) 921-8609
MR William G—at ☎ (804) 296-3841 | 336 Rosedale Rd,
912B Coleman St, Charlottesville, VA *22901* . . | Princeton, NJ *08540*
MR Christopher W—at ☎ (804) 295-9973 |
Rte 2, Box 308, Charlottesville, VA *22901* . . . . |

Tew MR & MRS James D 3d (Eleanor W Baldwin) | ☎ (508) 546-1024
H'66 . . . . | 33 Atlantic Av,
MISS Abigail H . . . . | Rockport, MA
MR Jonathan B . . . . | *01966*
MR James D JR . . . . |

Thacher MR & MRS Anthony (Barrett L Van Dyke) | of ☎ (617)329-9141
Sm.H'56 . . . . | 149 Common St,
MISS Antonia M . . . . | Dedham, MA *02026*
MISS Jennifer W . . . . | ☎ (207) 867-4749
| Crabtree Point,
| North Haven, ME
| *04853*

Thacher MR & MRS Hamilton JR (Dorothy M Edwards) H'33
☎ (619) 728-7360 . . 3909 Reche Rd, Apt 158, Fallbrook, CA *92028*

Thacher MRS Isabel F (Isabel J Firuski)
☎ (207) 774-4197 . . 340 Promenade E, Portland, ME *04101*

Thacher MR & MRS John H (Carol A Saam) | ☎ (610) 687-6591
Wheat'67.Me.Cry.P'66.Pa'72 . . . . | 154 Beaumont Rd,
MISS Ashley B—at St Lawrence U . . . . | Devon, PA *19333*
MISS Kimberly B—at U of Ariz . . . . |

Thacher MR & MRS Peter S (Mary C McGrath) | of ☎ (860)535-0888
BMr'54.C.Yn.Y'47 . . . . | 54 Gold St,
MISS Linda S—at ☎ (212) 534-2028 | Stonington, CT
55 E 93 St, New York, NY *10128* . . . . | *06378*
MR Peter Shaw JR—Cl'91—at | ☎ (202) 342-0885
☎ (202) 686-5637 . . 2801 Quebec St NW, | 1077—30 St NW,
Apt 475, Washington, DC *20008* . . . . | Washington, DC
| *20007*

Thacher MR & MRS Thomas (Barbara Auchincloss) | ☎ (203) 972-3193
BMr'40.C.Csn.Yn.Y'38 . . . . | 125 West Rd,
MR Peter A—in Saudi Arabia . . . . | New Canaan, CT
| *06840*

Thackara MR & MRS James J (Shirley Ingalls) H'36
☎ (408) 626-4839 . . 8545 Carmel Valley Rd, Carmel, CA *93923*

Thalman MR John R—Cy.Rv.Myf.Sar.Colg'68. | ☎ (216) 921-4476
Cwr'72.Pa'74 . . . . | 2919 Huntington Rd,
MISS Anne E—FP'77.H'88—at Harvard . . . . . . | Shaker Heights, OH
MR Robert W—Colg'76 . . . . | *44120*

Thatcher MR E Fusz—Str.Mo'28
☎ (941) 778-5013 . . 611 Gulf Dv N, Apt C26, Bradenton, FL *34217*

Thatcher MR & MRS John M P JR (Dorothy Riddell) Yn.Y'40
☎ (912) 638-2755 . . Cottage 275, Sea Island, GA *31561*

Thatcher MR & MRS John M P 3d (Marguerite S | ☎ (203) 869-2646
Funston) Sth'64.Ihy.Ny.Eyc.Ne.Y'65 ⛵ . . . . . | 14 Chateau Ridge
MISS Peggy . . . . | Dv, Greenwich, CT
MISS Katherine E—at Pomona . . . . | *06831-2940*
JUNIORS MISS Christina F . . . . |
JUNIORS MR John M P 4th . . . . |

Thatcher MRS Joseph O M (Anna L Stuart) Ncd.
☎ (757) 425-0763 . . 1117 Abingdon Rd, Virginia Beach, VA *23451*

Thaw MRS Lawrence Copley (Lotteringhi della Stufa—
Elizabeth D Francis)
☎ (212) 744-6355 . . 765 Park Av, New York, NY *10021*

Thaxter MR Edward H—DU'69
☎ (516) 324-7400 . . PO Box 194, Wainscott, NY *11975*

Thayer MR & MRS A Bronson (Stella L Ferguson) | ☎ (813) 986-2201
Hlns'62.Cl'65.H'61.Nu'67 . . . . | PO Box 429,
MISS Susannah—at Harvard . . . . | Thonotosassa, FL
| *33592*

Thayer MR & MRS Abbot A (Josephine H Graf) Denis'75.H'75.Cin'80
4825 Drake Rd, Cincinnati, OH *45243*

Thayer MR & MRS Edmund JR (Hayward—Therman—Anne L Grant) Me.Cts.Ph.Pa'42
☎ (610) 688-2246 . . 28 Sugar Knoll Dv, Devon, PA *19333*

Thayer MRS Edward Carrington (Margaret C Bullock) . . . . | 2101 Washington St, Lowell 112,
MR Edward C JR—at 40 Goodwin House, | Newton, MA *02162*
N Main St, Wolfeboro, NH *03894* . . . . |

Thayer MRS Frederick M JR (Barbara Russell) Ws'49.Yn.
☎ (610) 691-0691 . . ''Millhaus'' W Macada Rd, Bethlehem, PA *18017*

Thayer MRS Gordon B (Lydia C Prescott) Btn.
☎ (617) 876-6579 . . 16 Craigie St, Cambridge, MA *02138*

Thayer MR & MRS Isabel M (Isabel C Merrill) Wheat'61 . | ☎ (617) 235-8587
MR Henry H . . . . | 9 Sunset Rd,
MR Joshua Merrill—H'87.BostColl'93—at | Wellesley, MA
1443 Beacon St, Apt 109, Boston, MA *02146* . . | *02181*

Thayer MR & MRS James L (Harriette A Peper) | ☎ (516) 239-5547
H.'66.Nu'73 . . . . | 304 Ocean Av,
JUNIORS MR Thomas R—at Hotchkiss . . . . | Lawrence, NY
| *11559*

Thayer MRS John B JR (Charlotte R Toland) Pkg.
☎ (610) 692-0258 . . 258 Chatham Way, West Chester, PA *19380*

Thayer MRS John O (Imogen D Cathcart-Jones) . . . | ☎ (508) 356-5432
MISS Diana C—at 40 Dartmouth St, Somerville, | ''Holiday Hill''
MA *02145* . . . . | 44 Mill Rd, Ipswich,
MR David A . . . . | MA *01938*

Thayer MISS Katherine W . . . . Married at Kennebunkport, ME
McCammond MR James A . . . . Jun 1'96

Thayer MISS Margaret P . . see I Leclerc

Thayer MRS Margaretta (Hirsh—Margaretta Thayer) | ☎ (719) 473-2426
MISS Margaretta H Hirsh—at | 2501 Sycamore St,
☎ (719) 475-1455 . . 1907 W Platte Av, | Colorado Springs,
Colorado Springs, CO *80906* . . . . | CO *80906-3325*

Thayer MR Meade B—Me.LakeF'74.VillaN'83
☎ (202) 234-0673 . . 1431 Swann St NW, Washington, DC *20009*

Thayer MRS Nelson S T (Yuk—Mai Leung) . . . . . . | ☎ (201) 822-2293
MISS Mai-Ning—Sth'87 . . . . | 29 Fairview Av,
| Madison, NJ *07940*

Thayer MR Nelson S T JR—Y'87
☎ (202) 328-8143 . . 2314—19 St NW, Apt 3, Washington, DC *20009*

Thayer MR & MRS Philip K (Lauren G Meier) Pom'79.H'83.Bost'79.H'83
☎ (617) 491-7450 . . 39 Oak Av, Belmont, MA *02178*

Thayer MR & MRS R Dixon (Gail R Breslow) Pa'77.Rd.Me.Ph.Nyc.Pa'73
☎ (610) 696-1118 . . ''Merefield'' PO Box 706, Unionville, PA *19375*

Thayer MRS R Thruston H (R Leigh Moeser) . . . . . | ☎ (508) 468-1800
MR Frederick M 2d . . . . | 49 Walnut Rd,
| South Hamilton, MA
| *01982*

Thayer MRS Richard (Phyllis M Hock) Cin'47
☎ (513) 561-7548 . . 8420 Old Stable Rd, Cincinnati, OH *45243*

Thayer MR Robert H JR—Y'52
☎ (703) 339-6603 . . Holly Hills Farm, 6709 Springfield Dv, Lorton, VA *22079*

Thayer MR Russell—Ph.Sap.Fw.P'49 . . . . | ☎ (609) 924-2634
MR David A—at ☎ (206) 582-8129 | 21 Lilac Lane,
3012—81 St, Courtsouth, Tacoma, WA *98408* . . | Princeton, NJ *08540*

Thayer MAJ Samuel M—USA.Alaska'82
☎ (410) 969-0199 . . 8143 Turn Loop Rd, Glen Burnie, MD *21061*

Thayer MR & MRS Seth A (Frances F Macy) | of ☎ (941)966-2676
Nw'56.Ny.Ck.W&L'53 . . . . | 1808 Casey Key Rd,
MISS Jennifer M—Colby'83—*see* | Nokomis, FL *34275*
Dilatory Domiciles . . . . | ☎ (516) 626-0844
MISS Ann W—Colby'86—at ☎ (207) 846-5383 | 897 Remsens Lane,
Alpine Little, JH, Yarmouth, ME *04096* . . . . . | Oyster Bay, NY
MR Seth A JR—Colby'89—at ☎ (773) 327-4377 | *11771*
1325 W Newport Av, Chicago, IL *60657* . . . . . |

Thayer MR & MRS Stephen Cook (Jane Bierley) Fla'71.Wms'61
☎ (214) 521-0563 . . 4333 Westside Dv, Dallas, TX *75209*

Thayer MRS Sydney 3d (Drayton—Edith M Bettle) . . . . Married at
Little Compton, RI
Gardner MR Stephen V (late Colin) . . . . Jun 15'96

Thayer MRS William F (Neville—Sheila Ryan) BtP.Evg.Srb.Cda.
☎ (561) 655-8203 . . 170 Chilean Av, Palm Beach, FL *33480*

Thébaud MR & MRS Charles G (Sharon G Hall) | ☎ (508) 228-0626
Neb'58.Nyc.Snc.Cw.Ncd.Yn.Y'59 . . . . | ''Peace and Quiet''
MISS Charlotte G—Bow'93 . . . . | 140 Miacomet Rd,
MR Paul R—Bost'95 . . . . | PO Box 2162,
| Nantucket, MA
| *02554*

Thébaud MR & MRS Reynal de St M (Sally L | ☎ (203) 661-7008
Corlette) Sth'54.Nyc.Cw.Rv.Lm.Y'55 . . . . | 44 Howard Rd,
MISS Elizabeth R—ColC'86 . . . . | Greenwich, CT
MISS Andrea M—Bates'88 . . . . | *06831-3104*
MISS (LT CDR) Cynthia McC (Moser—Cynthia |
McC Thébaud) USN'85.GeoW'92 . . . . |

Theis MR & MRS Stuart H (Penelope D Writer) Swb'64.Kt.Tv.Rut'64
☎ (216) 255-4838 . . 9286 Creekwood Dv, Mentor, OH *44060*

Therman MRS Harrison (Talbot—Dorothy Harrison)
☎ (610) 688-4501 . . PO Box 7356, 752 Brooke Rd, St Davids, PA *19087-7356*

Thibault MR & MRS Carrow JR (Margaret H Donoho) Sfh.
☎ (610) 688-8493 . . 31 Sugar Knoll Dv, Devon, PA *19333*

Thibault MR Robert G—Vt'93 . . see H D Tiffany 3d

Thibault MRS Roberta L (Roberta L Walbridge) | 500 Newcastle Rd,
Syr'62.Buf'66.Syr'78 . . . . | Syracuse, NY *13219*
MISS Corinne L . . . . |
MR Robert E—SUNY'96 . . . . |

Thibault MISS Tammy M . . see H D Tiffany 3d

Thiele MR Kenneth W—Bz.Mor.Miami'37
☎ (561) 231-1687 . . 300 Ocean Rd, Apt 2E, John's Island, Vero Beach, FL *32963*

Thieriot MR & MRS Charles H (Carpenter—Edna H | ☎ (516) OR6-0506
Taylor) Rc.Srr.BtP.Evg.Pr.H'37 . . . . | Chicken Valley Rd,
MR Charles H JR—at 2500 Roscomare Rd, | PO Box 385,
Los Angeles, CA *90077* . . . . | Locust Valley, NY
| *11560*

Thieriot MR & MRS Juan Pablo (Leslie C Brady) Cal'88.Bur.Y'91
☎ (415) 441-6691 . . 3655 Clay St, San Francisco, CA *94118*

Thieriot MR & MRS Richard T (Withers—Angelica | ☎ (415) 921-1111
Reynal) Bur.Pcu.Sfg.Y'63 . . . . | 2829 Pacific Av,
MR Simon F . . . . | San Francisco, CA
JUNIORS MR Charles de Y . . . . | *94115*
JUNIORS MR Richard R . . . . |

Thierry MR & MRS Charles A (Diana R Laing)
H'80.Y'85.Myf.Hb.H'77.H'81
☎ (203) 637-9654 . . 26 Heusted Dv, Old Greenwich, CT *06870*

Thom MR & MRS Peter R 3d (Kinney—Laurelle A Hartley)
Cal'73.Hast'76.Sfy.Mich'69
☎ (510) 946-1418 . . "Hilltop" 1237 Laurel Lane, Lafayette, CA *94549*

Thoma DR & MRS George E JR (Neuhoff—M
Eugenia B Bryan) Cos.Rc.Day'43.StL'47 . . . . . .
MR Mark A—StL'82.StL'88 . . . .
☎ (314) 991-3841 | 5 Georgian Acres, | St Louis, MO *63131*

Thomas MRS Alexandra Stokes (Wheeler—Lloyd—
Alexandra C Stokes) . . . .
JUNIORS MR John A . . . .
    MISS Frances P Wheeler—at
        ☎ (610) 964-9294 . . 1050 King of Prussia Rd,
Radnor, PA *19087* . . . .
☎ (803) 648-1944 | 816 S Boundary Av, | Aiken, SC *29801*

Thomas MRS Alfred (Frances Flood)
1010 Waltham St, Apt D328, Lexington, MA *02173*

Thomas MR & MRS Andrew H (Nathalie A Wendell) Dth'58.Bab'73
☎ (508) 655-4373 . . 24 Marshall Rd, Natick, MA *01760*

Thomas MRS Anne M (Anne W Macdonald)
☎ (516) 676-3961 . . 7 Wood Lane, Locust Valley, NY *11560*

Thomas MR B Brooks—C.Me.Exy.Ny.Cc.Y.'53.Y'56 ⚓
☎ (212) 255-4084 . . 37 W 12 St, New York, NY *10011*

Thomas MR Benjamin M—Gc.Cybl.Yn.Y'17
☎ (561) 844-4403 . . 227 Miraflores Dv, Palm Beach, FL *33480*

Thomas MASTER Blakely Schmidlapp (Charles L 3d) . . . . Born at
                                                Cincinnati, OH May 25'96

Thomas MRS Charles A (Porter—Margaret S Chandler) Cysl.
☎ (508) 240-1566 . . Orleans Center, Apt 4, Daley Terr, Orleans,
MA *02653*

Thomas MRS Charles D (Nancy Kenney) Cl'43 . . . .
MR G Brinton—at ☎ (610) 649-8815
Old Lancaster Rd, Haverford, PA *19041* . . . . . .
☎ (610) 642-3297 | Old Buck & Buck | Lanes, Haverford, | PA *19041*

Thomas MR & MRS Charles L 3d (Elizabeth H Muhlhofer)
Cin'87.Van'84.Cin'90
1623 Bloomingdale Av, Cincinnati, OH *45230*

Thomas MR Christopher M—NHCol'86
☎ (609) 466-2783 . . 24 W Broad St, Apt 3, Hopewell, NJ *08525*

Thomas MR Colin M—Skd'94 . . see D D Gries

Thomas MR Cruger
☎ (208) 788-4270 . . PO Box 1221, Sun Valley, ID *83353*

Thomas MRS David 2d (Bullard—Jane L Longnecker)
☎ (610) 645-8817 . . 1400 Waverly Rd, Muirfield 201, Gladwyne,
PA *19035*

Thomas MR & MRS Donald W (Diana Hunt)
Sth'56.Sim'58.P'55.H'68 ⚓ . . . .
MR Mark E—RogerW'91 . . . .
☎ (617) 275-8789 | 231 Dudley Rd, | Bedford, MA *01730*

Thomas MR & MRS Douglas McM (Cora C Michalis) Cly.
☎ (203) 869-7458 . . 2 Stanwich Lane, Greenwich, CT *06830*

Thomas COL & MRS Dudley E JR (Susan A Horne)
USMC.Miss'59.Wash'76 . . . .
MISS Dorothy D E . . . .
MISS Sarah-Grace H . . . .
☎ (707) 252-8057 | 1038 Round Hill | Circle, Napa, CA | *94558*

Thomas MR & MRS E Robert (Dabrowska—Zofia
Tabecka) Me.Fst.Ac. . . . .
MR Christopher T—Me.—at ☎ (310) 454-2245
407 Beirut St, Pacific Palisades, CA *90272* . . . .
☎ (610) 649-2744 | 233 Winsor Lane, | Haverford, PA | *19041*

Thomas MR & MRS Edmond G (Sigler—Sarah O
Tracy) V'52.Y'33 . . . .
    MISS Gretchen C Sigler—at Camden, ME
    04843 . . . .
    MR Frederick G Sigler 4th . . . .
☎ (305) 294-5364 | 1207 Pine St, | Key West, FL *33040*

Thomas MR & MRS Edward C P (Marjorie M Prince) Rdc'42.Cs.H.'41 . . of
☎ (610) 525-0976 . . 16 Aldwyn Lane, Villanova, PA *19085*
☎ (508) 356-3867 . . PO Box 705, 190 Argilla Rd, Ipswich, MA *01938*

Thomas MR & MRS Frederick H (Suzanne Claypoole) OState'63.OState'63
☎ (716) 872-1718 . . 1200 Fox Hollow, Webster, NY *14580*

Thomas MR & MRS G Woodford (Dorothea E Humphreys) Cda.Mit'39
☎ (704) 662-9216 . . "Bodee Cove" 504 Beaten Path Rd, Mooresville,
NC *28115*

Thomas MR George C—Gc.Shcc.Lm.Pa'72
☎ (610) 525-4704 . . 115 Pennsylvania Av, Bryn Mawr, PA *19010*

Thomas MRS Gladys R (Gladys V Roberts) BMr'56
MISS Stephanie B . . . .
MR Landon JR . . . .
MR Frederic W . . . .
☎ (212) 722-0663 | 17 E 96 St, | New York, NY | *10128*

Thomas MR & MRS Henry B (Christina C Poole)
☎ (410) 323-1563 . . 5514 Roland Av, Baltimore, MD *21210*

Thomas MRS Henry M JR (Caroline C Bedell)
Sth'25 . . . .
MISS Eleanor C—at 2401 Calvert St NW,
Washington, DC *20008* . . . .
☎ (410) 243-6621 | Roland Park Place, | Apt 259, 830 W 40 | St, Baltimore, MD | *21211*

Thomas DR & MRS Henry M 3d (Karen A Purin)
Hav'57 . . . .
MR Richard H—Hav'91 . . . .
☎ (914) 478-3575 | 48 Lefurgy Av, | Hastings-on-Hudson, | NY *10706*

Thomas MRS Hilda E (Kimmet—Hilda E Thomas)
☎ (307) 645-3231 . . Bar X Ranch, 109 Rd 8WC, Powell, WY *82435*

Thomas MISS Hilleary T . . see H H Chappell

Thomas MR & MRS James A JR (Stewart—Susan G
Norton) LIU'84.Lx.Cly.Y'45 . . . .
MISS Augusta R—Nw'87—at ☎ (716) 473-0582
4 Strathallen Park, Rochester, NY *14607* . . . . . .
MR Skeffington N—L&C'86—at
☎ (303) 458-8409 . . 4110 Winona Court,
Denver, CO *80212* . . . .
☎ (413) 623-5094 | Beech Tree Lane, | PO Box 143, Lee, | MA *01238*

Thomas MR & MRS James A 3d—Cal'76
☎ (212) 966-3401 . . 280 Mott St, Apt 4R, New York, NY *10012*

Thomas MR & MRS James C (Susanna J Massie) P'80
☎ (606) 748-5848 . . Barter Farm, 465 Balden Lane, Harrodsburg,
KY *40330*

Thomas DR & MRS James Henry (Fitts—Fitts—Cynthia I Ford)
Ala'46.Ncd.H'47 . . of
☎ (205) 553-3824 . . 1 Fairmont Woods, Tuscaloosa, AL *35405-1711*
☎ (205) 758-2664 . . "Fordland" Fosters, AL *35463*

Thomas MR & MRS James W (Eleanora R Post) Shcc.Lm.Va'29
PO Box 1320, Bryn Mawr, PA *19010*

Thomas MR & MRS Jared E 2d (Vikianna Van Voorhis) Ariz'68.Ariz'67 . . . . MR Jared E 3d . . . . ☎ (602) 264-4330 1325 E Earll Dv, Phoenix, AZ *85014*

Thomas MR & MRS Jeffrey F (Evelyne Champin) Rcn.Y'60 . . . . MISS Fiona de F—at Hamilton . . . . MR Patrick J—at 19 rue Jean Giradoux, 75116 Paris, France . . . . ☎ (415) 567-2110 2425 Filbert St, San Francisco, CA *94123*

Thomas MR & MRS Jeremiah L 3d (Clara E Ruthrauff) AmU'71.Va'68 . . of
☎ (212) 861-1425 . . 530 E 86 St, New York, NY *10028*
☎ (914) 855-5957 . . 282 Quaker Hill Rd, Pawling, NY *12564*

Thomas MISS Katrina—BMr'49 . . of
☎ (212) 348-7765 . . 17 E 96 St, New York, NY *10128-0783*
☎ (914) 877-9775 . . "Mutton Hollow" RR 1, Box 63AB, Dover Plains, NY *12522*

Thomas MR & MRS Kyle W (Eliza L Karlson) Nu'85
☎ (011-65) 733-8087 . . Regency Apts, 9 Nathan Rd, 21-04, Singapore 1024

Thomas MR Landon—K.Rc.H'56
35 Sutton Place, New York, NY *10022*

Thomas MRS Lowell S (Josephine O McVey) Pc.
☎ (215) AD3-0112 . . 514 Auburn Av, Wyndmoor, PA *19038*

Thomas MR & MRS Lowell S JR (Judith K Evans) Sth'55.Ll.Cs.Sdg.Dth'53.Pa'60 ⚓ . . . . MR Lowell S 3d—Pc.Tufts'82—at
☎ (212) 925-9418 . . 1 Worth St, Apt 5R, New York, NY *10013* . . . . MR Taylor G—Pc.Dth'88—at ☎ (212) 787-0428 489 West End Av, Apt G, New York, NY *10024* ☎ (215) 248-5004 8012 Crefeld St, Philadelphia, PA *19118*

Thomas MR & MRS Norman M 3d (Susan M Allen) Elmira'64.P'63 . . . . MISS Constance C—at Carnegie Mellon . . . . ☎ (203) 268-5208 "Devil's Run" 159 Church St, Monroe, CT *06468-1818*

Thomas MISS Olivia Tucker—Cvc.
☎ (609) 924-4877 . . 41 Park Place, Princeton, NJ *08540*

Thomas MR & MRS R Griffith (B Page B Robinson) Va'86.Ct.Va'81.Rich'85
☎ (202) 244-3711 . . 4830 Tilden St NW, Washington, DC *20016*

Thomas MRS Raymond (Eells—Elizabeth H Raymond)
☎ (860) 236-4931 . . 61 Scarborough St, Hartford, CT *06105*

Thomas MR & MRS Robert L (Rosalie G Phelps) Cr'58.P'59 . . . . MR Bradford G—*see Dilatory Domiciles* . . . . . . MR James W—at Boston, MA . . . . ☎ (617) 934-5829 311 Powder Point Av, Duxbury, MA *02332*

Thomas MRS Roberta S (Roberta Shaw) . . . . MRS Anne A (McClelland—Anne A Thomas)—at ☎ (703) 370-1464 . . 1228 Prince St, Alexandria, VA *22314* . . . . ☎ (703) 370-1933 402 Cloverway Dv, Alexandria, VA *22314*

Thomas MR & MRS Samuel P (Lindsay C Richardson) Wh'lck'79.Md'78 . . . . JUNIORS MISS Ashley A . . . . ☎ (508) 526-9648 103 Summer St, Blueberry Hill, Manchester-By-The-Sea, MA *01944*

Thomas MR Samuel W—Louis'60.Louis'64
☎ (502) 895-5810 . . 122 Crescent Av, Louisville, KY *40206*

Thomas MRS Sherry L (Woodson—Sherry L Thomas) . . . . MISS Christina Woodson . . . . MR Mark N Woodson . . . . ☎ (407) 872-1211 PO Box 568795, Orlando, FL *32856*

Thomas MR & MRS Stephen D (Pleasant—Linda D Birch) Trans'64.OState'67 . . . . MISS Alison N—at Va Tech . . . . MR Whitney B—at Va Tech . . . . ☎ (704) 366-7544 4421 Town & Country Dv, Charlotte, NC *28226*

Thomas MR Stephen L JR . . see H H Chappell

Thomas MISS Susan G—Cl'91 . . see D D Gries

Thomas MR & MRS T Lewis 2d (Blake—Lois A Chamberlain) Pc.
☎ (215) 646-0459 . . 133 Culpepper Dv, Penllyn, PA *19422-1126*

Thomas MR & MRS Thomas R (Mary-Powel Jabaley) NotreD'83.W&L'83
☎ (718) 858-5375 . . 230 Wyckoff St, Brooklyn, NY *11217-2229*

Thomas MISS Virginia S (Norman M 3d) . . . . Married at Monroe, CT Talbot MR Fraser H (Fraser A H) . . . . Jun 1'96

Thomas MR & MRS W G Brooks (Constance Beels) Mv.Y'48
☎ (401) 423-0098 . . 320 Beavertail Rd, Jamestown, RI *02835-2718*

Thomas MR & MRS Weston L (Kaemmerer—Weston S Linn) . . of
☎ (212) 758-1317 . . 45 Sutton Place S, Apt 19D, New York, NY *10022*
☎ (860) 739-2538 . . 22 Hemingway Rd, Old Black Point, Niantic, CT *06357*

Thomas MR & MRS William P (Joan T Settle) Bnd'67.Pa'88.Co.Cry.Shcc.Lm.Y'66.Pa'74 ⚓ . . MISS Katharine C—Colby'93—at Georgetown . . MR Ashley A—Dth'91—at Hanover, NH . . . . . . ☎ (610) 668-1177 200 Conshohocken State Rd, Bala-Cynwyd, PA *19004*

Thomas MRS Williamson (May Duane Jones) Rm. . MISS Lucy W . . . . ☎ (908) 842-0114 1 S Rohallion Dv, Rumson, NJ *07760*

Thomas MR & MRS Wilmer J JR (Porteous—K Douglas Dockery) Swb'62.Evg.Ncd.Tul'47. Tul'50.H'53 . . . . MISS Alexandra K Porteous . . . . MR William D Porteous . . . . of ☎ (860)435-2546 Hope Hill Farm, 272 Undermountain Rd, Salisbury, CT *06068-1510*
☎ (212) 744-5322 1020 Fifth Av, New York, NY *10028*

Thomasson MR Nelson 3d—Cw.Ll.Pn.P'35 . . . . MR Nelson 4th . . . . of ☎ (847)381-1306 323 W Russell St, Barrington, IL *60010*
☎ (941) 349-5820 4420 Ocean Blvd, Sarasota, FL *33581*

Thompson MRS Albert E (Pattison—Marie Schoener) 3550 Shaw Av, Cincinnati, OH *45208*

Thompson MR & MRS Anthony de V (Lay—Elizabeth L Nager) MtVern'86.Pr.Ct.Emory'87
☎ (212) 772-7648 . . 125 E 74 St, New York, NY *10021*

Thompson MR Arthur R—Rr . . . see MRS J C McKay

Thompson MISS Beatrix H . . see MRS R Brock

Thompson MR & MRS Bob F (Mary B Higgins) StAndr'69.P'69 . . . . ☎ (615) 385-4374
MR Paul F . . . . 4430 Sheppard
JUNIORS MISS Catherine B . . . . Place, Nashville, TN
JUNIORS MR Walter B 37205

Thompson MR & MRS Bogart F (Elizabeth H ☎ (516) 537-0805
Higgins) Y.'39 . . . . "Southerlea"
MISS Pamela H—at ☎ (212) 683-5776 Ocean Rd,
350 E 30 St, New York, NY 10016 . . . . PO Box 986,
MISS Sarah B—at ☎ (516) 537-0385 Bridgehampton, NY
PO Box 1935, Bridgehampton, NY 11932 11932

Thompson MR & MRS Bruce R (Eleanor E Southworth) Ws'83.Del'85.Cly.Wes'83.Pa'87
☎ (713) 666-4461 . . 4146 Swarthmore St, Houston, TX 77005

Thompson MR & MRS C Haynes (Eva E Södergren) Ala'40.Ala'41
☎ (334) 281-0847 . . 3432 Bankhead Av, Montgomery, AL 36111

Thompson MRS Carolyn C (Morrison—Carolyn C Thompson)
☎ (713) 789-1806 . . 1806D Potomac Dv, Houston, TX 77057

Thompson MR Charles D W—H.'54.Cl'57
☎ (516) OR6-7077 . . Chagechagan Farm, 173 Buckram Rd, Locust Valley, NY 11560

Thompson MR & MRS Charles I (Woods—Judith ☎ (215) CH7-5179
Johnson) Wis'55.Sg.Pa'48 . . . . 330 W Mermaid
MR Rogers H W—at ☎ (305) 387-4725 Lane, Philadelphia,
10240 SW 154 Circle Court, Apt 106, Miami, FL PA 19118
33196 . . . .

Thompson MR & MRS Charles L 2d (Winifred C Duncan) Bv.P'29
☎ (314) 721-4343 . . 710 S Hanley Rd, St Louis, MO 63105

Thompson MR & MRS Charles O (Gibbons—Meyer—Jean H Garrison) Pr.Cly.H'52 . . of
☎ (516) 624-3848 . . 747 Remsens Lane, Oyster Bay, NY 11771
☎ (561) 734-9222 . . 6880 N Ocean Blvd, Apt 22, Ocean Ridge, FL 33435

Thompson MR Charles W JR—Del'66.Va'68 . . of
☎ (212) 879-8198 . . 12 E 72 St, Apt 2A, New York, NY 10021
☎ (301) 229-2094 . . 7906 Riverside Dv, Cabin John, MD 20818

Thompson MR & MRS Christopher (Margaret B ☎ (707) 965-1531
Meyer) Pitzer'74 . . . . PO Box 166,
MISS Felicity B—at Geo Wash'n U . . . . Pope Valley, CA
MR Noel B—at "Wit's End" Old Turnpike, 94567
Fareham, Hampshire PO16 7HA, England . . . . .

Thompson MR & MRS Christopher A (Sandra P Hitschler) Nw'85.Nw'82.Nw'87
☎ (847) 266-8503 . . 1200 St Johns Av, Highland Park, IL 60035

Thompson MISS Clare de K—BMr'41
☎ (508) 546-3057 . . 13R Pleasant St, Rockport, MA 01966

Thompson MRS D G Brinton (Anne H Bigelow) Sap.Ph.Cc.Ll.Snc.Myf.Cda.
☎ (860) 726-2183 . . Duncaster 304, 20 Loeffler Rd, Bloomfield, CT 06002

Thompson MR & MRS David C (Brown—Joan M ☎ (508) 627-5081
Palma) Stan'57.Eyc.Err.Dth'57 . . . . 33 Fuller St,
MISS Tracy J Brown—Geo'86 . . . . Box 5097,
Edgartown, MA
02539-5097

Thompson MR & MRS (DR) David H (Amy M Daniels) H'91.SUNY'95.H'91.H'94
☎ (202) 244-0408 . . 4000 Massachusetts Av NW, Apt 427, Washington, DC 20016

Thompson MR & MRS David R (Bernadette M O'Brien) M'mack'79.Cyb.Bates'81.Nw'88
☎ (516) 689-2753 . . 15 Mills Lane, East Setauket, NY 11733

Thompson MISS Deborah H—ColbyS'74
☎ (617) 740-4719 . . 24 Governor Andrew Rd, Hingham, MA 02043

Thompson MR & MRS Donald G (Miller—Ella Mae ☎ (561) 567-9790
Mathis) O'46.Y'45 . . . . 7405 Cypress Bend
MISS F Dana—at Denver, CO . . . . Manor, Vero Beach,
FL 32966-5172

Thompson MR & MRS Douglas A (Sarah A Chopping) Sar.Va'77.Pitt'83
☎ (412) 967-0402 . . 618 Glengary Dv, Pittsburgh, PA 15215

Thompson MR & MRS Edmonstone F (Garesché—La May H Capen) Cy.Nd.Y'34.H'37
☎ (314) 997-5409 . . 10140 Conway Rd, St Louis, MO 63124

Thompson MR & MRS Edward P (Margot R Levis) Woos'78 . . of
☎ (603) 431-4994 . . 55-37 Salter St, Portsmouth, NH 03801
☎ (207) 529-5675 . . "Cedar Oaks" Shore Rd, Round Pond, ME 04564

Thompson MR & MRS Fairman R (McNeal— ☎ (502) 987-0834
Crutcher—Pamela J Padwick) Louis'93. 3720 Crocus Lane,
Trans'66 . . . . Louisville, KY
MISS Darby E McNeal—at ☎ (502) 429-4907 40207-1413
8806 Furlong Dv, Apt 7, Louisville, KY 40222

Thompson MR Frank L JR . . . . ☎ 235 W 70 St, Apt
MR David H—at 24 Church St, Watertown, MA 4C, New York, NY
02172 10023

Thompson MISS Gale E—Ws'82.JHop'87.Pa'89
☎ (703) 242-9692 . . 2872 Sutton Oaks Lane, Vienna, VA 22181

Thompson MRS George W (Mary E Thomas) Cda.
☎ (334) 288-7690 . . 1243 Augusta St, Montgomery, AL 36111

Thompson MR & MRS George W (Margaret H Cooper) Snc.Rv.Cw.Dar.Cda.Pa'50
☎ (201) 543-4463 . . 27 Hilltop Rd, Mendham, NJ 07945

Thompson MR & MRS Gerard M JR (Barbara A Wilcox) Col'70.Yn.Y'67
☎ (561) 845-9416 . . 148 Seagate Rd, Palm Beach, FL 33480

Thompson MR & MRS Grant McM (Helen E Morrison) Wms'38
☎ (561) 231-4783 . . 2190 Mangrove Dv, Vero Beach, FL 32963

Thompson MR Guy Bryan—Sar.Tex'62.Cl'70 . . . . . ☎ (713) 977-4440
MISS Kathryn C—at SMU . . . . 5828 Valley Forge
Dv, Houston, TX
77057-2241

Thompson MR & MRS H David 3d (Suzanne C Zug) ☎ (607) 273-2966
Hawaii'72.Dick'68.H'78 . . . . 209 Iradell Rd,
MR David Z . . . . Ithaca, NY 14850
MR Tyler . . . .
JUNIORS MISS Lenore F . . . .
JUNIORS MR H Scott . . . .

Thompson MR & MRS Harry A 2d (Jane Arensberg) of ☎ (412)683-5250
Rr.Pg.Va'57.Pitt'64 . . . . 419 Devonshire St,
MISS Diana S—at ☎ (206) 545-9526 Pittsburgh, PA
1707 N 45 St, Apt 5, Seattle, WA 98103 15213
MR Andrew T—at ☎ (510) 653-5178 ☎ (412) 238-9225
6480 Benvenue Av, Apt 4, Oakland, CA 94618 . "Wonderwood"
Rector, PA 15677

Thompson MRS Henrietta W (Henrietta Wise) Rol'87.Me'92
☎ (207) 374-5770 . . Parker Ridge, HC 64, Box 270-208, Blue Hill, ME *04614*

Thompson MR & MRS Henry F (Elizabeth M Cross) Sa.Pa'53 . . . . | ☎ (610) 257-6191
MISS Grace B . . . . | 360 N Main St,
MISS Elizabeth C. . . . . | Sellersville, PA
MR Berkeley F . . . . | *18960*
MR Henry F JR . . . . |
MR John M D . . . . |

Thompson MR & MRS Henry L JR (Mary Elizabeth Willington) Ws'57.Cly.Cda.Br'57.H'59
☎ (212) 535-7619 . . 160 E 84 St, New York, NY *10028*

Thompson MR & MRS Henry S JR (Catharine J Ward) S'HmptonU'72.Edin'74.Cal'68.Cal'74.Cal'76.Cal'80
☎ (011-44-131) 337-6818 . . 11 Douglas Crescent, Edinburgh EH12 5BB, Scotland

Thompson MR Hugh S—Y.'50
☎ (516) 725-1790 . . "Boxwood" Main St, Sag Harbor, NY *11963*

Thompson MR & MRS J Lamar JR (Ada Rush) Brenau'74.Aub'72
☎ (344) 271-2779 . . 3826 Llyde Lane, Montgomery, AL *36106*

Thompson MR & MRS Jack E (Maria del C Larrea) ColM'47
☎ (520) 577-2036 . . 3200 E Crest Shadows Dv, Tucson, AZ *85718*

Thompson MRS James E (Ethel H Bartlett)
☎ (941) 349-0928 . . 5858 Midnight Pass Rd, Apt 25, Siesta Key, Sarasota, FL *33242*

Thompson MR James E JR—Y.'64 . . of
☎ (212) 289-6127 . . 1601 Third Av, New York, NY *10128*
☎ (860) 567-8910 . . 19 Blakeslee Rd, Litchfield, CT *06759*

Thompson MR & MRS John E JR (Julia A Forster) Hartw'82.Mid'72
☎ (212) 874-0669 . . 33 Riverside Dv, Apt 3E, New York, NY *10023*

Thompson MR & MRS John Miles JR (Williams— | ☎ (612) 473-7064
Wanda I Rolston) Rv. | 1194 Weston Lane
MR John Miles 3d—Chr.Rv.V'82—at | N, Plymouth, MN
☎ (212) 979-1689 . . 625 E 14 St, Apt 1C, | *55447*
New York, NY *10009* |

Thompson MRS Josephine M (Josephine U Merwin) On.
☎ (301) 986-0845 . . Somerset House, Apt 403, 5600 Wisconsin Av, Chevy Chase, MD *20815*

Thompson MRS Josiah Van K (Thompson—Rosalie | ☎ (410) 939-3020
C Hunter) Rcp.Cry.L.Ac.Cda. . . . . | New Wood Farm,
MISS Lida E—Pa'71 . . . . | 118 Foxridge Dv,
MR Daniel G—at Edmonton, Alberta, Canada . . | Havre De Grace,
MR Samuel R . . . . | MD *21078*
JUNIORS MISS Madeline G . . . . |
JUNIORS MR Samuel R JR . . . . |

Thompson MISS Laura Lee . . see O H Bullitt JR

Thompson MR & MRS Lawrence B (Louise M Blanchard) Un.Y'58.H'62
☎ (212) 749-4487 . . 322 Central Park W, New York, NY *10025*

Thompson MRS LeRoy (Alice B Painter)
☎ (412) 741-6694 . . Fox Hill Farm, Blackburn Rd, Sewickley, PA *15143*

Thompson MRS Lyman F (Hope Salisbury) Rol'45
☎ (407) 695-2447 . . 1221 Queen Elaine Dv, Casselberry, FL *32707*

Thompson MISS Maris Wistar—Rose'81.Ariz'85.Me.Ncd . . .of
☎ (610) 644-1827 . . 21 Oak Knoll Dv, Daylesford, Berwyn, PA *19312*
☎ (518) 286-2833 . . "Windward" Thompson Hill, Old Troy Rd, Rensselaer, NY *12144*

Thompson MR & MRS Mark J (Alison Mary Wilbur) Rich'90.GuildLond'89
Tucks Close, Thornham, Norfolk PE36 6LX, England

Thompson MR & MRS McKean (Barbara O Benkhart) Y'51
☎ (516) 569-1568 . . "Bubbling Spring" 81 Park Row, Lawrence, NY *11559*

Thompson MR & MRS Michael G T (Margaret L Kuhn) Cal'74.Wes'71.Stan'75
☎ (408) 274-4916 . . Rancho Yerba Buena, 3745 Old Yerba Buena Rd, San Jose, CA *95135*

Thompson MR & MRS Neil L (Kathleen Cox) | ☎ (617) 232-2757
Ws'80.Cy.Sm.Tvcl.Uncl.Yn.Y'64.H'66 . . . . | 155 Chestnut Hill
JUNIORS MISS Caroline R . . . . | Rd, Chestnut Hill,
| MA *02167*

Thompson MR & MRS O David (Nancy L Hooper) . . | 2953 Montavesta
MISS Jennifer L—at Dayton, OH. . . . . | Rd, Lexington, KY
MISS Kate G—at Denison . . . . | *40502*
JUNIORS MISS Sarah B . . . . |

Thompson MRS Parker (Cassie Parker) Cvc.Sl.
☎ (301) 229-0680 . . 4508 Tournay Rd, Bethesda, MD *20816-1843*

Thompson MR & MRS Paul 3d (Judith A Williams) Cl'86.Sg.T.Nf.Pa'73
☎ (610) 642-1624 . . 667 Dodds Lane, Gladwyne, PA *19035-1514*

Thompson REV & MRS Paul M (Sallie H | ☎ (802) 254-9619
McClenahan) Sw'58.EpiscTheo'62. . . . . | 3 Bradley Av,
MR Ian A . . . . | Brattleboro, VT
MISS Sallie H (Moore—Sallie H Thompson)—at | *05301*
67 Sea St, H-6, Hyannis, MA *02601* . . . . |

Thompson MRS Peter Hunter (Alice M Kreps) Cy. . | ☎ (617) 277-5531
MR Peter H 3d—Bab'76 . . . . | 394 Hammond St,
| Chestnut Hill, MA
| *02167*

Thompson MR Peter S—Ln.Md.H'40
see Dilatory Domiciles

Thompson MRS Phyllis A (Phyllis A Nitze) | ☎ (617) 566-0522
Ws'69.Tufts'86.Bost'94.Chi.Cy. . . . . | 214 Heath St,
MISS Phyllis E P—Y'96 . . . . | Chestnut Hill, MA
MISS Heidi A N—at Hotchkiss . . . . | *02167*
MR Nicholas E S—at Stanford . . . . |

Thompson MRS R Ellison (Helen Harte) Ac.
☎ (610) 644-0167 . . Barberry Hill Farm, Devon, PA *19333*

Thompson MR & MRS Radclyffe F (Maria T Mullen) | ☎ (610) 527-6286
Ty'69.Bost'71.Pa'67. . . . . | 1509 Montgomery
MISS Anne R—at Yale . . . . | Av, Rosemont, PA
| *19010*

Thompson MRS Ralph E (Rosamond R Higgins)
☎ (617) 934-2446 . . 151 King Caesar Rd, Duxbury, MA *02332*

Thompson MR & MRS Ralph F JR (Ailsa A | ☎ (412) 781-0824
McCouch) Ws'51.An.Ncd.Va'44.H'48 ⚓ . . . . | 8 Fieldvue Lane,
MR Eric A—WashColl'89 . . . . | Pittsburgh, PA
| *15215*

Thompson MR & MRS Richard H (Victoria P Cowperthwaite) Rd.Wcc.
☎ (610) 296-7020 . . Sea Horse Farm, 231 Spring Rd, RD 2, Malvern, PA *19355*

Thompson MR Richard H P—Unn.Snc.Rv.LakeF'80
☎ (617) 236-8188 . . 255 Marlborough St, Boston, MA *02116*

Thompson MRS Robert E S (Margaret C Miller) SL'36
☎ (203) 453-5841 . . 210 Uncas Point Rd, Guilford, CT *06437*

Thompson MR & MRS Robert T (Frances Bush-Brown)
Br'77.Cyb.H'76.Stan'83
☎ (203) 972-1668 . . 2 Wahackme Lane, New Canaan, CT *06840*

Thompson MR & MRS Rodman E JR (Ana C
Davidson) Cr'52.P'46. . . . .
MISS Ana A—at 1430 Eighth Av, San Francisco,
CA *94122*. . . . .
MISS Susan S H—at 55 Bethune St, New York,
NY *10014*. . . . .
MISS Julia O—at U of Rochester. . . . .
    ☎ (610) 644-2009
    S Leopard Rd,
    Berwyn, PA *19312*

Thompson MRS Rosemary (Franciscus—Rosemary Thompson) Rdc'55
☎ (011-41-30) 4-51-42 . . Box 62, CH 3780 Gstaad, BE, Switzerland

Thompson MISS Sara C (Kell—Sara C Thompson) Pa'70.Nu'73
☎ (610) 566-5005 . . 670 Ridley Creek Rd, Media, PA *19063*

Thompson MR & MRS Stephen E (Helen L Malarkey) An.Cly.Cda.
☎ (503) 223-3409 . . 2562 SW Hillcrest Dv, Portland, OR *97201*

Thompson MR & MRS Stuart D (Anne K Wetzel) Duke'87.Duke'87
☎ (905) 337-1753 . . 87 Chartwell Rd, Oakville, Ontario L6J 3Z3,
Canada

Thompson MRS Tandy C (Smith—Tandy C Thompson)
Mo'73.SIll'77.Cy . . .of
PO Box 31786, St Louis, MO *63131*
☎ (314) 966-0818 . . 12804 Pelham Estates Dv, St Louis, MO *63131*

Thompson MRS W Bryce 4th (Frances B Lippincott) Cr'80
see Dilatory Domiciles

Thompson MR W Bryce 4th
Sourland Farm, 33 Lindberg Rd, Ringoes, NJ *08551*

Thompson MR & MRS W Byrd (Helen McCloskey)
MaryMt'73.Pa'84.Md'63 . . . .
MISS Penelope M—Curry'92. . . . .
    ☎ (610) 388-7030
    1401 Stockford Rd,
    Chadds Ford, PA
    19317

Thompson MR & MRS W McIlwaine JR (Elsie D
Wilson) Rdc'72.Va'75.A.Cly.Yn.Y'69.Va'72. . .
JUNIORS MISS Alice H . . . .
JUNIORS MR William McI 3d—at Groton . . . .
    of ☎ (804)295-3535
    1 Apple Tree Lane,
    Charlottesville, VA
    22901
    ☎ (540) 839-2671
    ''Rosemary
    Cottage'' PO Box
    957, Hot Springs,
    VA *24445*

Thompson DR W Scott—Cv.Mt.Ri.Stan'63.Ox'67 . . of
☎ (202) 364-3039 . . 4650 Broad Branch Rd NW, Washington,
DC *20008*
☎ (540) 937-5189 . . Storybook Farm, 14398 Storybook Lane,
Amissville, VA *20106*

Thompson MR & MRS William (Potter—Thieriot—Julia K Macy)
☎ (520) 297-1904 . . 8050 N Casas Cameo, Tucson, AZ *85741*

Thompson MR & MRS William M (Mary N Lamb) P'31
☎ (203) 245-4585 . . 31 Canborne Way, Madison, CT *06443-3446*

Thompson MR & MRS Wirt L JR (Sara C Wood) Au.Cts.Y'34
☎ (610) 566-0679 . . ''Upper Bank House'' PO Box 486, Media,
PA *19063*

Thompson MR & MRS Wirt L 3d (Nan A Hunter) Hob'69
☎ (309) 449-6501 . . 3 Doctor's Court, PO Box 467, Hopedale, IL *61747*

Thomsen MR & MRS Stewart G (Rosemary B Harris) H'83.H'83.Suff'88
☎ (617) 244-8916 . . 200 Upland Rd, Newtonville, MA *02160*

Thomson MR & MRS A Lindsay (Emily A Bannard) Cc.Wms'37.Mit'39 . . of
☎ (860) 232-2129 . . 18 Ironwood Rd, West Hartford, CT *06117*
☎ (802) 824-6070 . . South Londonderry, VT *05155*

Thomson MR & MRS Archibald G (Griswold—Louisa J Whitney)
Ph.Rc.Me.Ssk.Rb.
☎ (610) MU8-6050 . . 938 Brower Rd, Radnor, PA *19087*

Thomson MR Archibald G JR—Rc.Me.Sa.San.Ty'61
☎ (610) 896-5566 . . 1132 Youngsford Rd, Gladwyne, PA *19035*

Thomson MR & MRS Chilton (Janet French) Y'42
☎ (216) 421-4015 . . ''The New House'' 12309 Fairhill Rd, Cleveland,
OH *44120*

Thomson MR & MRS George G (Sylvia
Grove-Palmer) H'41 . . . .
MISS Sandra J—at ☎ (718) 797-0155
200 Clinton St, Brooklyn, NY *11201* . . . .
    ☎ (603) 487-5206
    57 Meetinghouse
    Hill Rd,
    New Boston, NH
    03070

Thomson DR & MRS George G 3d (Rose Xenia Francklin)
Hn.H'76.CUNY'84
Butterfield Mill Farm, PO Box 433, New Boston, NH *03070*

Thomson SIR John A & LADY (Cabot—Bullitt—O Judith Ogden)
Rdc'62.C.Cly.Chi.Hn . . .of
☎ (908) 359-6434 . . ''Oak Hill'' RD 1, Princeton, NJ *08540*
☎ (011-44-171) 221-1848 . . 77 Palace Court, London W2, England

Thomson MR & MRS John C (Mary B Coker)
☎ (904) 426-6505 . . 202 N Peninsula Av, New Smyrna Beach,
FL *32169*

Thomson MR John S—Y'49 . . . .
MISS Melissa P . . . .
    ☎ (203) 264-6088
    636 S Britain Rd,
    PO Box 122,
    South Britain, CT
    06487-0122

Thomson MR & MRS Leon T (Eleanor A Hay) Pitt'55.Grove'51.CTech'61
☎ (412) 741-5144 . . 312 Maple Lane, Sewickley, PA *15143*

Thomson MR Richard S—Van'53
☎ (601) 264-2653 . . 1 Quail Hollow Rd, Hattiesburg, MS *39402*

Thomson MR & MRS Richard S JR (Deborah K Lightsey) Ala'81
☎ (601) 264-1133 . . 3 Quail Hollow Rd, Hattiesburg, MS *39402*

Thomson MR & MRS Robert G (Reinhard—Marjorie
L Pew) Ala'64 . . . .
MISS Courtney L . . . .
JUNIORS MR R Zachary . . . .
    ☎ (215) 643-2462
    205 Skippack Pike,
    Ambler, PA *19002*

Thomson MR & MRS Schuyler W (Heather S Neal)
Wms'76.Conn'85.Conn'69
☎ (860) 542-5081 . . 15 Pine Ledge Way, Norfolk, CT *06058*

Thomson MR & MRS Woodward (Eleanor C Wayland) Ncd.
☎ (203) 263-3404 . . 343 Weekeepeemee Rd, Woodbury, CT *06798*

Thomure MR & MRS Randall O (Michele J Dana) Mo'72
☎ (415) 579-4582 . . 563 Alhambra Rd, San Mateo, CA *94402*

Thorington MRS A French (A Anne G French) Rd.Ncd.
☎ (610) 644-4117 . . Maple Leaf Farm, 209 Spring Rd, Malvern,
PA *19355-3415*

Thorington MR & MRS James 2d (Whitman—Frances Armitage)
Cry.Rv.Pa'51 ⚓
☎ (410) 822-5936 . . 6942 Travelers Rest Circle, Easton, MD *21601*

Thorington MASTER James Roussel (Milby B) . . . . Born at
West Chester, PA Mch 12'96

Thorington MR & MRS Milby B (Susan M Petersen) WChesU'87
☎ (610) 269-4237 . . 14 Blakely Rd, Downingtown, PA *19335*

Thorington MRS Richard W (K Louise Moffat) Ws'24
☎ (610) 645-8990 . . 1400 Waverly Rd, Muirfield, Gladwyne,
PA *19035*

Thorington MR & MRS Richard W JR (M Caroline | ☎ (301) 320-3667
Miller) KasSt'65.GeoW'75.P'59.H'64 . . . . | 7714 Old Chester
MISS Ellen M . . . . | Rd, Bethesda, MD
     | *20817*

Thornburgh MASTER Bradford Scott (John K) . . . . Born at
Pittsburgh, PA Jun 5'96

Thornburgh MR & MRS David B (Rebecca McKillip)
BMr'80.Pa'87.Hav'81.H'85
☎ (215) 242-9683 . . 216 Nippon St, Philadelphia, PA *19119*

Thornburgh MR & MRS John K (Sharon L Kratz) Ri.Buck'79 . . of
☎ (412) 934-1172 . . 2538 Lindenwood Dv, Wexford, PA *15090*
Rainbow Farms, Eagles Mere, PA *17731*

Thornburgh MR & MRS Richard L (Virginia W | ☎ (202) 462-8693
Judson) Wheat'61.H'62.Y'54.Pitt'57 . . . . | 2540 Massachusetts
MR Peter L—at Governour's Place, Apt C106, | Av NW, Apt 405,
3300 Union Deposit Rd, Harrisburg, PA *17109* . | Washington, DC
MR William F . . . . | *20008*

Thorndike MRS A Frye (Amy F Frye)
Wh'lck'56.Wh'lck'63.SalemSt'76.Chi.Myf.
☎ (207) 643-2424 . . ''Panacea'' Embden-Concord Rd, PO Box 55,
Solon, ME *04979*

Thorndike MRS Benjamin A G (Elizabeth Gardiner) Cy.Chi.
☎ (617) 326-0577 . . 10 Longwood Dv, Dana 537, Westwood,
MA *02090*

Thorndike MR & MRS David N (Karin E Lunde) RogerW'88.J&W'91
☎ (540) 955-4288 . . Andley Farm, PO Box 510, Berryville, VA *22611*

Thorndike MISS Eliza W (Richard K 3d) . . . . Married at
Manchester-By-The-Sea, MA
Thissell MR John A (Ronald K) . . . . Aug 3'96

Thorndike MRS Gurnee (Phelps—Phillips—Isabel Gurnee Thorndike)
Evg.Cda.
☎ (561) 243-0000 . . Abbey Delray Apt 126, 2150 SW 10 Court,
Delray Beach, FL *33445-6011*

Thorndike MR & MRS John (Suzanne R Nicholls) | ☎ (203) 622-9190
GeoW'72.Rcn.Ln.H'64.Camb'65 . . . . | 12 Pheasant Lane,
MISS Anne Soline—at ☎ (011-33-1) 47-54-00-35 | Greenwich, CT
108 rue Cardinet, 75017 Paris, France . . . . | *06830*
JUNIORS MISS Hilary S . . . . |

Thorndike MR & MRS John L (Dorothy W Dudley) Ws'75.Un.D.Cw.H.'49
☎ (508) 785-0682 . . 10 Main St, Dover, MA *02030*

Thorndike MR & MRS Richard K (Archibald—M Mercy Bours)
Sbc.Lx.My.Cw.Ncd.H'35
☎ (904) 285-8322 . . 1000 Vicar's Landing Way, Apt F206,
Ponte Vedra Beach, FL *32082*

Thorndike MR & MRS Richard K 3d (Myers—Margaret J Eyre)
Drex'62.Lx.Sar.Dar.Burd'59
☎ (508) 922-3618 . . Box 189, 71 Paine Av, Prides Crossing, MA *01965*

Thorndike MASTER Samuel Augustus (David N) . . . . Born at
Winchester, VA Aug 25'95

Thorndike MR & MRS W Nicholas (Joan Ingram) | ☎ (617) 734-3693
Tv.Cy.K.Chi.H.'55 . . . . | 150 Dudley St,
MR William N . . . . | Brookline, MA
MR Alexander L . . . . | *02146*

Thorndike MR & MRS William A (Elizabeth M Lloyd)
Bost'69.Cy.Cw.Cc.Ind'53
☎ (617) 242-7351 . . 46 Shipway Place, Charlestown, MA *02129*

Thorne MRS Boston (Suzanne G Boston)
☎ (561) 225-2307 . . 202A Hutchinson House W, 1550 NE Ocean Blvd,
Stuart, FL *34996*

Thorne, Brinkley S & Cox, Mazie L—Sth'67. | ☎ (413) 584-5988
Y'71.Cly.Cda.Dc.Y'67.Y'72 . . . . | 48 Ward Av,
MISS Dune D—at Dartmouth . . . . | Northampton, MA
JUNIORS MR Yarrow M L . . . . | *01060*

Thorne MR & MRS Bruce (Marianne S Stevenson) On.Fy.Y'28
☎ (847) 234-0189 . . 1150 N Sheridan Rd, Lake Forest, IL *60045*

Thorne MR & MRS Daniel K (Hornblower— | of ☎ (603)763-5809
Alexandra C Tower) Ny.Srb.Stan'71 ⚓ . . . . | Star Lake Farm,
MR Josiah C Hornblower—at Trinity . . . . | Georges Mills, NH
JUNIORS MR Alexander W Hornblower—at | *03751-0308*
Groton . . . . | ☎ (212) 586-9469
   | 146 W 57 St,
   | Apt 68B,
   | New York, NY
   | *10019*

Thorne MR & MRS David H (Rose O'N Geer) Bost'77.Y'66.Cl'71
☎ (617) 734-3350 . . 56 Walnut Place, Brookline, MA *02146*

Thorne MR & MRS Francis B (Ann C Cobb) C.Rv.Cly.Y'43
☎ (212) RE7-3710 . . 116 E 66 St, New York, NY *10021*

Thorne MR & MRS Harold F JR (Sally Crimmins) | ☎ (515) 274-5489
JHop'69 . . . . | 5105 Waterbury Rd,
MR Gregory—Mich'96—at ☎ (773) 388-9250 | Des Moines, IA
425 W St James Place, Chicago, IL *60614* . . . . | *50312*
MR Jeffrey—at Ore State U . . . . |

Thorne MR John N (Niblack) . . . . Married at Mesa, AZ
Scheerle MISS Cheryl . . . . Jun 8'96

Thorne MRS Jorgi R (Jorgi Rasmusen)
☎ (212) 254-6938 . . 2 Stuyvesant Oval, New York, NY *10009*

Thorne MR & MRS Margaret Y (Margaret A Yates) Y'77.Cly.
139 E 79 St, New York, NY *10021*

Thorne MR & MRS Niblack (Wood—Suzanne Maurer) Nw'41
☎ (602) 840-8058 . . 5822 N 44 Place, Phoenix, AZ *85018*

Thorne MRS Nicholas G W (Fay A Stevens)
5330 Amorsolo St, Dasmarinas Village, 1200 Makati, Philippines

Thorne DR Oakleigh 2d—Yn.Y'51.Y'53.Col'58 . . . | ☎ (303) 447-1769
MR Jonathan O—at 1075—10 St, Boulder, CO | 2119 Spruce St, 5,
80302 . . . . | Boulder, CO *80302*
MR David R—at U of Wyoming . . . . |
JUNIORS MR Schuyler F . . . . |

Thorne MR & MRS Oakleigh B (Forg—Felicitas | ☎ (914) 677-3153
Selter) Rc.B.H'54 . . . . | ''Thorndale''
MISS Eliza—at Millbrook . . . . | Millbrook, NY
MR Jonathan—at Trinity . . . . | *12545*

Thorne MRS Oakleigh Lewis (Akin—Dorothy M Forbes). . . . . ☎ (561) 546-4919
    MISS Gwendolyn Akin—at ☎ (212) 431-3896   192 Gomez Rd,
55 Prince St, New York, NY *10012* . . . .   Hobe Sound, FL *33455*

Thorne MRS Samuel (Dabrowsky—Vera Sokolova) Cly.Dll.
  ☎ (860) 434-2116 . . ''Little House'' 3 Ferry Rd, Old Lyme, CT *06371*

Thorne MR & MRS Samuel JR (See—Elizabeth B Jones) Sth'55.Ec.My.Myc.Sm.Snc.Cw.Chi.Y'50
  ☎ (617) 742-0138 . . 42 Beacon St, Boston, MA *02108*

Thorne MR & MRS William T (Kathleen J Hammond)
  ☎ (518) 327-3676 . . HCR 1, Box 7A, Paul Smiths, NY *12970-9701*

Thornhill MR & MRS Arthur H JR (Dorothy M Matheis) Unn.Err.Unb.C.Sb.Eyc.P'48
  ☎ (603) 431-9914 . . 50 S School St, Portsmouth, NH *03801*

Thornhill MR & MRS Van Noy (Jane L Lucas) Char'ton'46.Cw.Ne.Cda.Clem'48
  ☎ (803) 723-4402 . . 24 Legare St, Charleston, SC *29401*

Thornton MRS Daphne S (R Daphne Sellar) Srb.
  ☎ (401) 849-3162 . . ''Sea View'' 37 Ledge Rd, Newport, RI *02840-4257*

Thornton MR & MRS Henry H M (Deborah A Speno) Rcn.Cl'54
  ☎ (413) 229-8463 . . ''Orchard Shade'' Maple Av, Sheffield, MA *01257*

Thornton MR John M—Y'43. . . . . ☎ (412) 741-8136
  MISS Liza T. . . . .   Box 15, RD 4,
  MR John R—NCar'74 . . . .   Sewickley, PA *15143*

Thornton MR & MRS William L (Anne H Rightor) H'67 . . of
  ☎ (415) 563-0113 . . 2101 Divisadero St, San Francisco, CA *94115*
  ☎ (707) 996-3962 . . Casa Rosa, 17850 Carriger Rd, Sonoma, CA *95476*

Thoron MRS Benjamin Warder (Violet Spencer) Sl.Ncd.
  ☎ (202) 234-5135 . . 3019 P St NW, Washington, DC *20007*

Thoron MRS J Lloyd (Janeth Lloyd) V'53.Chr.Cs. . . ☎ (212) 535-9527
  MISS Elise—Y'84—at ☎ (203) 393-0654   535 E 86 St,
49 Anella Dv, Bethany, CT *06524-3239* . . . . . .   New York, NY *10028-7533*

Thors MRS Denyse D (Mary Denyse Duval) Csh. . . ☎ (516) MY2-5753
  MR Geoffrey D—Box 3125, Edgartown, MA   33 Titus Lane,
02539 . . . .   Cold Spring Harbor,
  MR Tyler E—Y.Ty'89—at ☎ (212) 255-9701   NY *11724*
333 W 22 St, Apt 2A, New York, NY *10011* . . .

Thors MR & MRS Reginald F (Elizabeth T Cluett) Y'87.H'96.Ub.H'87.Duke'91
  ☎ (617) 266-1908 . . 176 Marlborough St, Boston, MA *02116*

Thors MR & MRS Thor JR (Virginia A Fincke)   of ☎ (212)288-9821
Bnd'59.Cl'86.Rc.Bgt.Fic.Cly.H'56 . . . .   215 E 72 St,
  MISS Virginia A—Cl'90—at ☎ (212) 786-3284   New York, NY *10021*
333 Rector Place, Apt 7B, New York, NY *10280*   ☎ (914) 241-4425
  MR Thor P—P'84.Pa'92—at ☎ (516) 725-7799   22 Bisbee Lane,
PO Box 198, Sag Harbor, NY *11963* . . . .   Bedford Hills, NY *10507*

Thorsen MR & MRS J Gwynne (Frances G Woods) Nyc. ⚓ . . of
  ☎ (561) 546-2094 . . on board Private Lives'' PO Box 307, Hobe Sound, FL *33475*
  ☎ (508) 257-4424 . . 32 Beach Club Rd, Siasconset, MA *02564*

Thorson MR Robert D JR—Bgt.Vt'88 . . see A Claude JR

Thouron MR George G 3d . . see C R Diffenderffer

Thouron SIR John R H—Wil.B.
  ☎ (561) 546-3577 . . 416 S Beach Rd, Hobe Sound, FL *33455*

Thrasher MRS Thomas R (Cameron—Harriet Connor) Chr.Ncd.
  ☎ (770) 804-0723 . . 10108 Ashford Gables Dv, Dunwoody, GA *30338*

Throdahl MR & MRS Monte C (Josephine Crandall) IaState'41
  ☎ (314) 993-4765 . . 36 Briarcliff, St Louis, MO *63124*

Throop MRS Enos T 4th (Barbara Williams) Mv.
  ☎ (410) 745-5352 . . ''Heatherington'' 1018 S Talbot St, PO Box 916, St Michaels, MD *21663*

Throop MR & MRS Enos T 5th (Muriel Bradshaw) NCarSt'69.Md.Hof'66.Hof'68 . . of
  ☎ (410) 727-1629 . . 10 E Lee St, Apt 2603, Baltimore, MD *21202*
  ☎ (410) 745-3169 . . 7480 Ryders Rest, Box 369, Royal Oak, MD *21662*

Thruston MRS Gates P (Joann Cope)
  ☎ (513) 299-3080 . . 502 Volusia Av, Dayton, OH *45409*

Thurber MRS A Edward JR (M Jane Bush)   ☎ (516) 671-8833
Ws'47.S.Cda.Dh.Ht.Ncd. . . . .   ''Thorland''
  MR A Edward 3d—Ne.Snc.Cw.Ht.Leh'86.Leh'90   Valley Rd, Locust Valley, NY *11560*

Thurber MR & MRS Alfred E JR (Sallyann M Harris)   ☎ (914) 762-0890
Marsh'56.K. . . . .   108 Birch Rd,
  MISS Elizabeth B—Mmt'89 . . . .   Briarcliff Manor,
  MISS Leigh B—Mmt'89 . . . .   NY *10510*

Thurber MR & MRS Gerrish (Webster—Jeanette E Scott) Ws'29.Cw.P'28.Cl'37
  ☎ (609) 426-6223 . . Meadow Lakes 3-11, Hightstown, NJ *08520*

Thurston MRS E Ladd JR (Hulley—Laura F   ☎ (202) EM2-3798
Broeksmit) V'49. . . . .   3507 Macomb St
  MR Elliott S—Swth'82—at ☎ (510) 845-1908   NW, Washington,
1407 Ward St, Berkeley, CA *94702* . . . .   DC *20016*
  MR David L—Wes'82. . . . .
  MR Zachary J—Denis'92—at ☎ (415) 864-5503
1355 Oak St, San Francisco, CA *94117* . . . . . .

Thys MISS Anne C—Col'82.Va'88
  ☎ (510) 339-2674 . . 6854 Ridgewood Dv, Oakland, CA *94611*

Thys MR E Barry (Edouard C) . . . . Married at Homewood, CA
  Bailie MISS Suzanne (David) . . . . Sep 16'95

Thys MR & MRS E Barry (Suzanne Bailie) Han'89.GoldG'89
1262 Sandy Way, PO Box 3672, Olympic Valley, CA *96146*

Thys MR Edouard (Beatrice P Horst)
  ☎ (916) GL6-6019 . . 1441—40 St, Sacramento, CA *95819*

Thys MR & MRS Edouard C (Christina Chute)   ☎ (510) 483-1669
Sth'55.Mit'51 . . . .   1679 Graff Av,
  MISS Edith O . . . .   San Leandro, CA *94577*

Thys MR Thierry N—Mit'53 ⚓ . . . .   ☎ (510) 569-8672
  MISS Lucienne M—Br'83—at U of Pa Grad . . . .   11765 Cranford
  MISS Danielle C—at 34 Pacheco St, Fairfax, CA   Way, Oakland, CA
94930 . . . .   *94605*
  MISS Tierney M—at Larkspur, CA *94939* . . . . . .

Tice MR & MRS Richard C (Harding—Muriel M C Kanahele) Whit'48.OWes'53
  ☎ (614) 876-4776 . . 4500 Dublin Rd, Columbus, OH *43221*

Ticknor REV & MRS William E (Correa—Elizabeth S Fleming) Ncd.Ga'30
  ☎ (904) 284-8608 . . PO Box 757, Penney Farms, FL *32079*

Tiedemann MR & MRS H Keith (Emily Le C Rogers)
Stan'75.Ht.Fr.Dar.Ncd.Wis'37
☎ (415) 346-2259 . . 2858 Vallejo St, San Francisco, CA *94123*

Tieken MISS Nancy B (Wheelock—Weber—Nancy
B Tieken) Rdc'63.Bost'88.Chi. . . . . | 1133 Race St,
　MR Joseph A Wheelock 3d—at Cambridge, | Apt 12N, Denver,
MA. . . . . | CO *80206*

Tieken MRS Theodore D (Elizabeth S Babson) Cho.Sr.Rc.Cas.Fy.
☎ (312) SU7-1169 . . 1500 N Lake Shore Dv, Chicago, IL *60610*

Tieken MR & MRS Theodore D JR (Charlotte H Goodwin)
Rc.Cho.Cas.On.Sr.K.P'66 . . of
☎ (773) 477-9785 . . 2430 N Lakeview Av, Chicago, IL *60614*
"Waverley" Somerset, VA *22972*

Tiemeyer MR & MRS Robert E (Condit—Carole Hickey) Cin'56
☎ (561) 234-4785 . . 10605 Wittington Av, Vero Beach, FL *32963*

Tiernan MR & MRS Bartholomew T 3d (Louise C | ☎ (516) 367-4813
Giffuni) Newt'69.Un.Rc.Csh.Mto.NotreD'65. | 1276 Ridge Rd,
Y'68. . . . . | Syosset, NY *11791*
　JUNIORS MISS Olivia A—at Milton |
　JUNIORS MISS Julia B—at Philips Andover . . . . . |

Tiernan MR & MRS Charles W JR (Carol H Stark)
Nu'82.Cardozo'86.Cs.Vt'67.Rut'70 . . .of
☎ (212) 255-0510 . . 575 Hudson St, New York, NY *10014*
☎ (516) 749-1485 . . 12 Burro Hall Lane, Shelter Island, NY *11964*

Tierney MR & MRS Hugh J JR (Baldwin—Virginia P Retting) Minn'60
☎ (602) 840-5281 . . 4905 E White Gates Dv, Phoenix, AZ *85018*

Tiffany MR & MRS Edwin P (Joan Thacher) | ☎ (617) 267-8612
DU'68.Btn.Bvl.Ub.NH'68 ⚓ . . . . | 19 Braddock Park,
　JUNIORS MISS Kathrene B . . . . | Boston, MA *02116*
　JUNIORS MR Thacher B . . . . |

Tiffany MR & MRS Gordon MacL (Ellen Auchincloss) Y'35.Cl'42
☎ (603) 228-3294 . . South Concord Meadows E2, 99 Clinton St,
Concord, NH *03301*
☎ (603) 529-2812 . . Tiffany Hill Farm, 197 Tiffany Hill Rd, Weare,
NH *03281*

Tiffany MR & MRS Henry D 3d (Thibault—Mary E | of ☎ (907)586-2180
Keegan) Sth'82.Mid'63 . . . . | PO Box 21049,
　MR Henry D 4th—at U of Alaska . . . . | Juneau, AK *99802*
　MR Edwin F . . . . | ☎ (941) 472-6883
　MISS Tammy M Thibault . . . . | "Worthington
　MR Robert G Thibault—Vt'93 . . . . | South" 1146
　　　　　　　　　　　　　　　　　　　　　　　　　　　　　　　| Buttonwood Lane,
　　　　　　　　　　　　　　　　　　　　　　　　　　　　　　　| Sanibel Island, FL
　　　　　　　　　　　　　　　　　　　　　　　　　　　　　　　| *33957*

Tiffany MRS Henry Dyer (Cleone D Place)
☎ (603) 529-2811 . . "Tiffany Hill" Weare, NH *03281*

Tiffin MR & MRS John A G (Elaine S Ewer) BMr'55 | of ☎ (011-44-171)
　MISS Martha . . . . | 720-1889
　MR Edward J S . . . . | 52 Lansdowne
　　　　　　　　　　　　　　　　　　　　　　　　　　　　　　　| Gardens, London
　　　　　　　　　　　　　　　　　　　　　　　　　　　　　　　| SW8 2EF, England
　　　　　　　　　　　　　　　　　　　　　　　　　　　　　　　| ☎ (011-44-1293)
　　　　　　　　　　　　　　　　　　　　　　　　　　　　　　　| 871-485
　　　　　　　　　　　　　　　　　　　　　　　　　　　　　　　| "Chowles Barn"
　　　　　　　　　　　　　　　　　　　　　　　　　　　　　　　| Rusper, Sussex
　　　　　　　　　　　　　　　　　　　　　　　　　　　　　　　| RH12 4RH, England

Tifft MR & MRS Henry N (Suzanne N McCarter) | ☎ (561) 234-5994
Bvl.Snc.P'49 . . . . | 745 Riomar Dv,
　MR Philip McC—CtCol'79—at | Vero Beach, FL
☎ (212) 246-7933 . . 322 W 55 St, Apt 3D, | *32963*
New York, NY *10019* |

Tifft MR & MRS William N (Ellen M Bruzelius) Ws'81.Rc.Bvl.Br'77.Cl'85
☎ (914) 738-2567 . . 127 Elderwood Av, Pelham, NY *10803-2011*

Tilden MR & MRS Victor M (Isabelle F C Tamalet) | of ☎ (011-44-171)
Wms'72.Ox'74.H'78 . . . . | 435-1278
　JUNIORS MISS Melanie T . . . . | "The White House"
　JUNIORS MR Graham T . . . . | Arkwright Rd,
　　　　　　　　　　　　　　　　　　　　　　　　　　　　　　　| London NW3 6AA,
　　　　　　　　　　　　　　　　　　　　　　　　　　　　　　　| England
　　　　　　　　　　　　　　　　　　　　　　　　　　　　　　　| ☎ (011-33)
　　　　　　　　　　　　　　　　　　　　　　　　　　　　　　　| 50-93-18-20
　　　　　　　　　　　　　　　　　　　　　　　　　　　　　　　| "Blueberry Châlet"
　　　　　　　　　　　　　　　　　　　　　　　　　　　　　　　| 380 rte du Taquy,
　　　　　　　　　　　　　　　　　　　　　　　　　　　　　　　| 74170 St-Gervais-
　　　　　　　　　　　　　　　　　　　　　　　　　　　　　　　| les-Bains, France

Tilden MRS William T 3d (Marjorie G Marquissee) . | ☎ (610) 297-5515
　MR William T 4th—P'65—at 6750 E Kiami St, | 6083 Carversville
Tucson, AZ *85716* . . . . | Rd, Doylestown, PA
　　　　　　　　　　　　　　　　　　　　　　　　　　　　　　　| *18901-9802*

Tilghman MR & MRS Benjamin C (Whitcomb—Anna Danzer)
Sth'43.Ws'54.Sm.Tvb.Y'41
☎ (410) 758-1324 . . "The Hermitage" 120 Hermitage Farm Lane,
Centreville, MD *21617*

Tilghman MR & MRS Benjamin C JR (Margo R | ☎ (508) 456-4170
Taggart) Lawr'65.Lawr'65 . . . . | 9 Elm St, Harvard,
　MISS Emily DeY . . . . | MA *01451*
　MISS Eliza C . . . . |
　JUNIORS MR Benjamin C 3d . . . . |

Tilghman MR & MRS George H (Elizabeth B Easton)
Pr.Mb.B.Cly.H'48 . . of
☎ (516) 671-1920 . . 14 Morgan Lane, Locust Valley, NY *11560*
☎ (561) 546-0104 . . 4 Bassett Creek N, Hobe Sound, FL *33455*

Tilghman MR & MRS George H JR (Nancy C Hoguet)
Bnd'83.Rc.Ri.Pr.Ty'81
☎ (516) 674-0601 . . 33 Valentine's Lane, Old Brookville, NY *11545*

Tilghman MR & MRS Henry R (Cordelia R Hodges)
Ken'86.L&C'92.Eyc.Geo'88.L&C'93
☎ (503) 236-3424 . . 2130 SE Tenino St, Portland, OR *97202*

Tilghman MR James W (Benjamin C) . . . . . . Married at Bennington, VT
Bucher MISS Anne E (John M) . . . . Jun 1'96

Tilghman MR & MRS Joseph F (McKoy—Lashley—Mary S Blabon)
BMr'48.Gm.Me.Y'44.Pa'48
☎ (610) 525-0478 . . 515 Lynmere Rd, Bryn Mawr, PA *19010*

Tilghman MRS M Wright (Schneidman—Margaret C Wright) Ac.Gm.Me.
☎ (610) 525-5090 . . 602 Woodleave Rd, Bryn Mawr, PA *19010*

Tilghman DR & MRS R Carmichael (Mary D Singer)
Elk.Cw.Rv.Lm.Cc.Mv.Ncd.JHop'25 . . of
☎ (410) 823-2963 . . 308 North Wind Rd, Baltimore, MD *21204*
☎ (410) 822-0236 . . "Wye House" 26080 Bruffs Island Rd, Easton,
MD *21601*

Tilghman MR & MRS Richard A (Diana Disston) Co.Gm.Ssk.P'43
☎ (610) 525-7674 . . 406 Gatcombe Lane, Bryn Mawr, PA *19010*

Tilghman MR & MRS Richard A (Joan McA Shiland) B.Cly.Yn.Y'51 .. of
☎ (203) 259-9854 .. 842 Redding Rd, Fairfield, CT *06430*
☎ (561) 546-6856 .. "La Joya" 7315 SE Golfhouse Dv, Hobe Sound, FL *33455*

Tilghman MR & MRS Richard A JR (Brooks—Mary L Strong) Me.Yn.Y'67 . . . . | ☎ (203) 972-1107
MISS Lindley R . . . . | 587 Carter St,
MR Richard A 3d . . . . | New Canaan, CT
   MR James B Brooks JR—at 168 Allston St, | *06840*
   Allston, MA *02134* . . . . |

Tilghman MR & MRS William F (Juliette Deleuze-Dordron) Ind'68.Y'66.Nu'71 . . . . | ☎ (770) 399-5057
MISS Isabelle F . . . . | 4978 Oak Trail Dv,
MR Christian D—at U of Georgia . . . . | Dunwoody, GA
   | *30338*

Tillman DR & MRS C Randolph (L Ann Combs) Van'72.Van'76 . . . . | ☎ (601) 446-8335
MISS Catherine E . . . . | 816 Main St,
MISS Margaret A . . . . | Natchez, MS *39120*
MR Clifford R JR . . . . |
JUNIORS MISS Rebecca C . . . . |

Tillman MR & MRS Eric W (Ann F Bates) OWes'78.OWes'77 . . . . | ☎ (203) 661-6259
JUNIORS MISS Abigail P . . . . | 57 Northfield St,
   | Greenwich, CT
   | *06830*

Tillson CAPT & MRS John G (Dana B Lamb) Del'54.USN'51 . . . . | ☎ (619) 481-3263
MISS Dana H—at 1631 Belvedere Av, Berkeley, | 13078 Survey Point,
CA *94702* . . . . | San Diego, CA
   | *92130*

Tilney MISS (DR) Augusta M—P'84.Cl'93
☎ (212) 874-3407 .. 200 W 86 St, Apt 17F, New York, NY *10024*

Tilney MR & MRS David W (Mary T Malone) DU'74.DU'73 . . . . | ☎ (719) 576-7097
MISS Elisabeth M—at Willamette . . . . | 3024 E Springlake
MISS Erin C—at Pacific Lutheran U . . . . | Circle,
JUNIORS MISS Megan W . . . . | Colorado Springs,
   | CO *80906*

Tilney MR & MRS Hugh J (Cavanagh—Wainwright—Helene E Henning) Plg.Mds.Cly.Grenoble'62 .. of
☎ (212) 644-6528 .. 439 E 51 St, New York, NY *10022*
☎ (516) 537-3505 .. Main St, Box 1413, Wainscott, NY *11975*

Tilney MR & MRS James W (Margaret H Herlihy) Y'65.H'69 . . . . | ☎ (860) 678-1907
MISS Elizabeth W—Y'93—at ☎ (212) 529-8522 | 21 Gibralter Lane,
194 Bleecker St, Apt 1A, New York, NY *10012* | Avon, CT *06001*
MISS Anne M—Y'95—at ☎ (415) 776-0610 |
1457 Chestnut St, Apt 2, San Francisco, CA |
94123 . . . . |
JUNIORS MR Alexander . . . . |

Tilney MRS John S (Cynthia Haskell) BtP.Cly.Cda.
☎ (561) 655-2565 .. 259 Pendleton Av, Palm Beach, FL *33480*

Tilney MR & MRS John S JR (Cathleen Reusch) Bnd'72.Cl'72 . . . . | 612 Lexington Rd,
JUNIORS MISS Melissa V . . . . | Concord, MA
JUNIORS MR John S 3d . . . . | *01742-3715*

Tilney MISS Mary A (Cords—Mary A Tilney) Bnd'70
☎ (212) 288-4132 .. 170 E 77 St, New York, NY *10021*

Tilney DR & MRS Nicholas L (Mary Graves) Ub.Cy.Tv.H'58.Cr'62 . . . . | ☎ (617) 742-1296
MISS Rebecca S—H'82—at ☎ (212) 633-1047 | 68 Beacon St,
54 Jane St, New York, NY *10014* . . . . | Boston, MA *02108*
MISS Victoria L—Bates'87—at ☎ (213) 848-8446 |
1008 N Sweetzer Av, Los Angeles, CA *90069* .. |
JUNIORS MISS Frances I . . . . |

Tilney MRS Norcross S (C Kane Merritt) V'49.BtP.Evg.Cly . . . of
☎ (561) 659-1248 .. 245 Pendleton Av, Palm Beach, FL *33480*
☎ (802) 867-4135 .. PO Box 924, Danby Mountain Rd, Dorset, VT *05251-0924*

Tilney MR & MRS Philip V R (Ellen R Gleason) H'63.H'63 . . . . | ☎ (207) 967-4436
MISS Katherine R—at 903 Goodrich Av, Apt A, | PO Box 841,
St Paul, MN *55105* . . . . | 15 S Maine St,
MR Peter V R—at Bates . . . . | Kennebunkport, ME
   | *04046*

Tilney DR & MRS Robert W JR (Peyton—Olney—Joan Paton) Mo.Cly.H'39.Pa'43 .. of
☎ (908) 234-2224 .. "White Oak" 36 Fowler Rd, Far Hills, NJ *07931*
☎ (212) 570-0429 .. 3 E 77 St, New York, NY *10021*

Tilney DR & MRS Robert W 3d (Lorraine M Greubel) Thiel'70.Guadal'74 . . . . | ☎ (603) 383-6153
JUNIORS MISS Kirsten C—at Holderness . . . . | "Peacefields"
JUNIORS MISS Heather W—at Riverview . . . . | Carter Notch Rd,
   | Box 476, Jackson,
   | NH *03846*

Tilney MR & MRS Schuyler M (Elizabeth C Arendall) Va'78.Dth'83.Unn.Va'79.Dth'83
☎ (713) 524-5818 .. 2910 Del Monte Dv, Houston, TX *77019*

Tilney MR & MRS Sheldon (Gail M Harrity) Bost'73.Y'82.Ty'68.Cl'70.Nu'74
☎ (212) 860-0694 .. 141 E 88 St, New York, NY *10128*

Tilson DR & MRS Hugh H (Judith Scullin) Wash'62.Reed'60.Wash'64.H'69 . . . . | ☎ (919) 832-8980
MISS Alice H—Colby'95 . . . . | 1116 Cowper Dv,
MR Hugh H JR—NCar'86.NCar'92.H'93—*see* | Raleigh, NC *27608*
Dilatory Domiciles |
DR Richard S—NCar'96—at Georgetown Med . |

Tilt MR Albert JR—Cc.Lm.Sar.Rv.H'26
☎ (860) 435-9243 .. Salmon Kill Farm, 317 Salmon Kill Rd, Salisbury, CT *06068*

Tilt MR & MRS Albert 3d (Clawson—Christina D Petrow) Rr.Cc.Sar.Hn . . . of
☎ (208) 456-2896 .. "Grouse Run" 150 Grouse Run Rd, Tetonia, ID *83452*
☎ (803) 844-2060 .. "Cuckholds Crossing" White Hall, Green Pond, SC *29446*

Tilt MR Albert 4th .. see J R Busk JR

Tilt MR & MRS Alexander C (Ellen L Weld) Swb'77.H'77.Nu'87
62 Strawberry Hill St, Dover, MA *02030*

Tilt MRS Jean P (Jean Preston) StJ . . .of
☎ (914) 234-7242 .. 403 Harris Rd, Bedford Hills, NY *10507*
☎ (212) TR9-3900 .. 1 E 66 St, New York, NY *10021*

Tilt MR & MRS Rodman K JR (Marilen L Grosjean) Ws'64.Bgt.StLaw'60 . . . . | ☎ (914) 232-5586
MISS Emlen K . . . . | 80 Upper Hook Rd,
MISS Elizabeth P . . . . | Katonah, NY *10536*
MISS Mary K . . . . |

Tilt MR Rodman King . . . . Died May 31'96
Tilt MRS Rodman King (Putnam—Frances Catlin) Bgt.Cly.
  ☎ (914) 234-7133 . . 33 The Hook Rd, Bedford, NY *10506*
Tilt MR & MRS Whitney C (M Stuart Crane) Duke'78.Hampshire'78
  ☎ (202) 363-0884 . . 4935 Eskridge Terr NW, Washington, DC *20016*
Tilton MR & MRS Webster JR (Nancy McB Payne)
  ☎ (607) 264-8100 . . Briar Hill Farm, RD 2, Box 634, Cooperstown, NY *13326-9305*

Tilton MR & MRS Webster 3d (Ellen Kay Witter)   ☎ (520) 742-9357
Ariz'74.Ariz'76 . . . . 1291 W Golden
JUNIORS MISS Kindall D Witter . . . . Gem Dv,
JUNIORS MR Webster 4th . . . . Oro Valley, AZ *85737*

Timberlake MR & MRS Marshall (Rebecca A Griffin)   ☎ (205) 969-2333
Ala'69.W&L'61 . . . . 3349 Brookwood
MISS Sumner . . . . Rd, Birmingham,
MISS Jane E. . . . . AL *35223*

Timbers MR & MRS Stephen B (Elaine C Mack)   ☎ (847) 234-3134
DU'72.Cho.Rc.Yn.Y'66.H'68 . . . . 210 S Green Bay
JUNIORS MR Alexander C A . . . . Rd, Lake Forest, IL *60045*

Timchak MR & MRS Louis J JR (Susan T Mueller)   ☎ (561) 626-7646
GeoW'70.Ct.Geo'62 . . . . 12079 Lost Tree
MR Louis J 3d. . . . . Way, North Palm
JUNIORS MR Alexander M . . . . Beach, FL *33408*
JUNIORS MR Christopher T . . . .

Timolat MR & MRS Louis K (Marie L Fuller) Rm.Cly.
  ☎ (908) 741-1374 . . ''Riverside'' 776 Navesink River Rd, Red Bank, NJ *07701*
Timpson MRS Carl W (Marcelle Vallon) Cly.
  ☎ (516) 569-0702 . . 7 Albro Lane, Cedarhurst, NY *11516*
Timpson MR & MRS Carl W JR (Patricia White) Rcn.Pr.Ln.Ng.H'52 ⚓
  ☎ (561) 243-1835 . . 725 Palm Trail, Apt 13, Delray Beach, FL *33483*
Timpson MR & MRS Carl W 3d (Phoebe Doubleday) Pr.Ng.Mb.
  ☎ (516) 759-0817 . . 10 Cherrywood Rd, Locust Valley, NY *11560*

Timpson MR & MRS James (Barnard—Rea—M   of ☎ (212)535-4665
Priscilla Goodrich) DU'76.DU'81.Pqt.Ny.Ncd.   960 Fifth Av,
Rens'47 ⚓ . . . . New York, NY
    MISS Anne Barnard—at 3 rue de la Pierre   *10021*
    Leveé, 75011 Paris, France . . . . ☎ (203) 254-1004
    MISS Phoebe Barnard—at ☎ (202) 237-0125   48 Harbor Rd,
    4226 River Rd NW, Apt 1, Washington, DC   Southport, CT *06490*
    20016 . . . .

Timpson MR James JR—Wes'82
26 Crescent Park Rd, Westport, CT *06880*
Timpson MR & MRS Lawrence L (Patricia B Grew) Lund'69
  ☎ (011-44-181) 942-5827 . . 17 Burghley Av, New Malden, Surrey KT3 4SW, England
Timpson MR & MRS Robert C L JR (Candace F Byers)
B'gton'72.Ln.Lm.H'66
  ☎ (203) 869-9132 . . 44 Harbor Dv, Greenwich, CT *06830*
Tindle MR James K . . . . Died at
Bryn Mawr, PA Nov 20'95
Tindle MRS James K (Eleanor V Morris)
  ☎ (610) 525-1277 . . 74 Pasture Lane, Apt 310, Bryn Mawr, PA *19010*

Tindle MR & MRS Robert McG (Elizabeth S Ott)   ☎ (610) 869-9245
Pa'39 . . . . Ryan Rd,
MISS Polly D . . . . Unionville, PA *19375*

Tiné MR & MRS Harold L (Louisa Rawle)   ☎ (914) 763-5854
Wheat'64.Ac.CarnM'67 . . . . 97 Spring St,
MR Christopher R—Bates'96 . . . . South Salem, NY
MR Matthew D'O—at Colo Coll *10590*

Tingley MR & MRS C Nicholas (Cary C MacFadden)   ☎ (203) 622-6672
Y'57.Ch'60 . . . . 30 Evergreen Rd,
MR Andrew M . . . . Greenwich, CT *06830*

Tingley MISS Priscilla A (Nogaim—Priscilla A Tingley)
  ☎ (702) 456-1210 . . 3671 Rosecrest Circle N, Las Vegas, NV *89121*
Tingue MR & MRS David M (Robin L Sundy) Buck'87.Br'87.Cr'92
1604 Lincoln St, Evanston, IL *60201*
Tingue MR & MRS Howard B (Mary M Morrison) Va'40
  ☎ (860) 739-7150 . . 9 Mosle Lane, Niantic, CT *06357*

Tingue MR & MRS William J (Diane E Crater)   ☎ (914) 234-3871
Bgt.Br'62 . . . . 475 Harris Rd,
. MR Christopher S—Br'91 . . . . Bedford Hills, NY *10507*

Tingue MRS William M (Marjorie C Stewart) Ncd.
  ☎ (860) 767-7337 . . 252 Essex Meadows, Essex, CT *06426*
Tipler MRS W Jackson (Elizabeth L Kilgore)
  ☎ (334) 438-2952 . . 509 Monroe St, Mobile, AL *36602*

Tippens MRS Mabel Raworth (Mabel C Raworth)   ☎ (601) 445-8228
Ncd.Dar. . . . . 500 Orleans St,
MISS Jessica D . . . . Natchez, MS *39120*
MR Adrian L . . . .
JUNIORS MISS Barbara B . . . .

Tippet MR Jerome—Woos'55
  ☎ (773) 239-6708 . . 10762 S Prospect St, Chicago, IL *60643*

Tippett MR & MRS J Royall (Susan R Pincoffs)   ☎ (410) 889-9491
V'43.JHop'32.Md'36 . . . . 4801 Keswick Rd,
MISS Susan R—at 47 Butter Hill Rd, Pelham, MA   Baltimore, MD
01002 . . . . *21210*
MR J Royall 3d . . . .

Tippett MR & MRS Joseph L (Keturah R Faurot) NCar'77.NCar'78
  ☎ (803) 957-7856 . . 125 Deerglade Run, Lexington, SC *29072*
Tippit MR & MRS C Carlisle (Margaret Mayo)
Sth'48.Cv.May.Pk.Uncl.Wms'42
  ☎ (407) 876-3622 . . 6242 Masters Blvd, Orlando, FL *32819*
Tippit MR Carl J—Kt.Wms'80.Ch'86
  ☎ (216) 247-2885 . . 616 Falls Rd, Chagrin Falls, OH *44022*
Tippitt MR & MRS Jerry L (Anna B McCullough) Houst'93.TexA&M'88
  ☎ (713) 961-4476 . . 4036 Branard St, Houston, TX *77027*
Tirana MISS Elizabeth E . . see MISS P M Auchincloss
Tirana MR Peter S—Stan'92
  ☎ (310) 376-0447 . . 117—1 St, Manhattan Beach, CA *90266*
Tirrell MISS Angela
  ☎ (707) 963-2040 . . 1415 Hudson Av, St Helena, CA *94574*
Tirrell MR David J—H'49
  ☎ (415) 346-7743 . . 2210 Broderick St, San Francisco, CA *94115*

Tittmann MR & MRS Barclay (Lucy Keith)
Sth'53.Durham'55.Tv.Y'53.Alb'62.Liège'68 . . .
MISS Sally—Y'86—at ☎ (212) 473-0390
269 E 10 St, Apt 6, New York, NY *10009* . . . . .
MISS Anna L—Y'89—at 93 Main St, Worcester,
MA *01609* . . . .
MR Edward—Hav'91—at 235 E 22 St, Apt 5R,
New York, NY *10010* . . . .
☎ (617) 491-7442
12 Gerry St,
Cambridge, MA
02138

Tittmann MRS Eugene C JR (Elizabeth H Rowley) Sth'47.Cysl.
☎ (203) 655-9377 . . 20 Fox Hill Lane, Darien, CT *06820*

Tittmann MR & MRS John B (Mary R Clifford) CtCol'80.Y'81.Y'86
☎ (617) 868-9479 . . 18 Fenno St, Cambridge, MA *02138*

Titus MR & MRS Daniel (Mary I Law) Me. . . . .
MISS Mary E . . . .
☎ (610) 527-3044
119 Morlyn Av,
Bryn Mawr, PA
19010

Titus MR David C—Unn.S.M.Me.Nyc.Yh.Lm.Rv.W&M'58
☎ (912) 638-1203 . . "Windrush" 149 Linkside Dv, St Simons Island,
GA *31522*

Titus MRS David L (D'Oench—Ackerman—Sarnoff—Magill—
A Faith Donaldson) Sl.
☎ (202) 244-0562 . . 4101 Cathedral Av NW, Apt 1004, Washington,
DC *20016-3585*

Titus MRS James G (Alice M Stevens)
☎ (212) 876-7160 . . 14 E 90 St, New York, NY *10128*

Titus MISS Phebe K—Vt'84
☎ (520) 327-9594 . . PO Box 44140, Tucson, AZ *85733*

Toberman MRS Beatrice B (Beatrice C Butler)
☎ (602) 956-8398 . . 3112 E Vermont Av, Phoenix, AZ *85016*

Tobey MRS Barbara E (Barbara W Eddy) Vt'68 . . . .
MISS Celine E . . . .
☎ (617) 237-6067
16 Upland Rd,
Wellesley, MA
02181

Tobias MR & MRS Terrence A (Cynthia du Pont)
Mit'72.Sb.Ober'66.NECons'72
☎ (610) 388-1201 . . 136 Ridge Rd, Chadds Ford, PA *19317*

Tobin MR Daniel C (Mark C) . . . . Married at Key West, FL
Kemezys MISS Deanna M (Algis) . . . . May 11'96

Tobin MR & MRS Daniel C (Deanna M Kemezys) Ken'88
☎ (305) 293-8071 . . 3075 Flagler Av, 19, Key West, FL *33040*

Tobin MR & MRS James E (A Laura Dalley) Wheat'74.NIa'74
☎ (609) 924-5581 . . 133 Mansgrove Rd, Princeton, NJ *08540*

Tobin MR & MRS Joseph O 2d (Dant—Edith T Andrews)
Br'76.Bhm.Bur.Pcu.Ore'76
☎ (415) 931-2863 . . 2108 Washington St, San Francisco, CA *94109*

Tobin MR & MRS Joshua (Medina—Janet B Williams)
☎ (561) 732-5307 . . 4 Country Club Circle, Village of Golf, FL *33436*

Tobin MISS Katherine O (Whipple—Katherine O Tobin)
☎ (415) 775-0676 . . 2480 Filbert St, San Francisco, CA *94123*

Tobin MR & MRS Mark C (Lois E Lindbloom)
Pe.Rv.Cw.Cspa.Wt.Dth'56 . . . .
MISS Alison P—Ken'86—at 288 Iven Av,
Apt 2B, St Davids, PA *19087* . . . .
☎ (508) 257-4052
35 Low Beach Rd,
PO Box 491,
Siasconset, MA
02564

Tobin MR & MRS Maurice B (Joan K Fleischmann)
Srb.Rr.Cos.Cly.Sl.Ben'57.Kas'61.GeoW'70
☎ (202) 232-0220 . . 2434 Belmont Rd NW, Washington, DC *20008*

Tobin MRS Michael H de Y (Sarah Fay) . . . . Died at
Hillsborough, CA Jly 21'96

Tobin MR Michael H de Y—Bur.Pcu.
☎ (415) 344-8079 . . 888 Irwin Dv, Hillsborough, CA *94010*

Tobin MR Michael H de Y 2d—Bur.
☎ (415) 441-7805 . . 1401 Jones St, San Francisco, CA *94109*

Tobin MRS Richard L (Weatherby—Sylvia B Cleveland) Plg.
☎ (203) 264-7824 . . 935A Heritage Village, Southbury, CT *06488*

Tobin MR Robert L B
☎ (210) 826-6263 . . 40 Oakwell Farms P'kway, San Antonio, TX *78218*

Toby MRS Thomas (Eleanor N Smith)
☎ (203) 531-7078 . . 10 E Lyon Farm Dv, Greenwich, CT *06831*

Todd MRS Alison S (Alison M Stuart)
☎ (802) 533-2346 . . "Baker Hill" PO Box 113, Greensboro, VT *05841*

Todd MR & MRS Anderson (Lawrence—Iris B Gracey)
Rice'49.Rice'59.Dar.Pn.P'43.P'49
☎ (713) 529-1932 . . 1932 Bolsover Rd, Houston, TX *77005-1614*

Todd MRS Anne P (Anne G Perry) SL'66.Cda. . . . . .
MISS Kathryn S—Wheat'92.Cda. . . . .
MR Richard P—at U of Conn . . . .
☎ (860) 927-4034
97 Kent Cornwall
Rd, Kent, CT *06757*

Todd MR & MRS Burt K (Frances Hays) Pg.Rr.Ox'49 . . of
☎ (412) 238-9821 . . Foxley Farm, RD 2, Ligonier, PA *15658*
☎ (242) 437-0738 . . "Kopje" Nassau, Bahamas

Todd MR & MRS David A (Wendy Price)
Nu'84.Rice'88.P'82.Rice'84.Emory'91
☎ (512) 442-3130 . . 709 E Monroe St, Austin, TX *78704-3131*

Todd MISS Elizabeth K . . see R E Vaughan

Todd MRS Emily L—P'79.Rice'88
☎ (713) 528-6673 . . 401 Anita St, Apt 32, Houston, TX *77006*

Todd MR & MRS Frederic A de P (Laura F Knox-Dick)
Rut'82.Pn.P'67.Nu'70
☎ (609) 924-7536 . . "Stuart Hall" 20 Boudinot St, Princeton, NJ *08540*

Todd MR James—Plg.P'27.Cl'53
☎ (914) BE4-3382 . . "High Tor" 80 Mianus River Rd, Bedford,
NY *10506*

Todd MR & MRS James de P (Margaret N Stage)
Ws'66.P'61.Stan'65 . . . .
MISS Margaret Van C—at Princeton . . . .
of ☎ (203)661-0456
Parsonage Rd,
Greenwich, CT
06830
☎ (802) 297-1554
Cole Pond Rd,
Jamaica, VT *05343*

Todd MR & MRS John Barnes (Victoria P MacNair)
Cw.Ncd.Pa'50 . . . .
MISS Sarah B . . . .
MR J Harrison—Cw.—at ☎ (610) 941-9699
602 Ford St, West Conshohocken, PA
19428-2926
☎ (610) MU8-5363
"Spring House"
658 Brooke Rd,
Wayne, PA
19087-4707

Todd MR & MRS John K (Downes—Charlotte Golden) . . of
☎ (410) 822-9439 . . 4565 World Farm Rd, Oxford, MD *21654*
☎ (561) 744-1417 . . 300 Beach Rd, Apt 201, Tequesta, FL *33469*

Todd MRS John R 2d (Frances A Starr) . . . .
MISS Mary S . . . .
MR Christopher B . . . .
☎ (908) 234-1569
121 Liberty Corner
Rd, Far Hills, NJ
07931

Todd MRS Joseph Z (Bliss—Hatherly Brittain) Tcy.
☎ (510) 547-4956 . . 95 Sea View Av, Piedmont, CA *94611*

Todd DR & MRS Kirkland W JR (Adrienne W Hill) V'43.Cr'44
2146 Golf Club Lane, Nashville, TN *37215*
Todd MRS Lucie Wray (Lucie H Wray).. of
☎ (713) 522-0070.. 9 Shadowlawn Circle, Houston, TX *77005*
☎ (409) 732-3416.. Wray Ranch, Armadillo Villa, RR 3596, Columbus, TX *78934*
Todd MR & MRS Samuel P JR (Emily L Gest) Cin'51.Ken'47.Cin'50.. of
☎ (513) 321-8658.. 670 Reisling Knolls, Cincinnati, OH *45226*
"Somerset" 940 Neahtawanta Rd, Traverse City, MI *49684*
Todd MRS Verser (Chase—Sally L Dickinson) Csn.Cda.
☎ (804) 288-6787.. 6207 Three Chopt Rd, Richmond, VA *23226*
Toerge MRS Falk (Weed—Symmes—Dixon—Tompkins—Mary E Falk)..
Died Apr 28'96
Toerge MR Nicholas 2d
87 St Mark's Place, Apt 2A, New York, NY *10009*
Tolan MR & MRS Henry L (Anita M Carroll) Pa'40
☎ (410) 653-1605.. 725 Mt Wilson Lane, Apt 231, Baltimore, MD *21208*

Toland MR & MRS Asheton C (Judith E Beckanstin) Wheat'57.Sr.Nrr.Br'77 .... | of ☎ (809)497-6627 PO Box 287, The Valley, Anguilla
MISS Lisa G—Mid'80—at Middletown, RI *02842* |
MISS J Jessie—at Hamilton .... | ☎ (401) 847-5595
MR M Maximillian—at 419 S 48 St, Apt 208, Philadelphia, PA *19143* .... | 441 Tuckerman Av, Middletown, RI
MR Samuel C—at Middletown, RI *02842* ...... | *02842*

Toland MR & MRS David A (Lou Ann Jackson) Ty'74
☎ (505) 982-2914.. 1116 N Plata Circle, Santa Fe, NM *87501*
Toland MR & MRS John G (Lita B Wickser) Skd'83.Wes'80
☎ (203) 966-9494.. "Point of View" 33 Turtle Back Rd S, New Canaan, CT *06840*
Toland MR & MRS M Keith (Lisa G Wedwick) WChesU'80.Me.VillaN'86
☎ (610) 687-3829.. 911 Newtown Rd, Devon, PA *19333*
Toland MRS Owen J (Pauline Talbott)
☎ (610) MI9-2573.. 309 Fairhill Rd, Wynnewood, PA *19096*
Toland MR & MRS Richard H R (Betty Jane Pepper) San.Pa'47
☎ (610) NI4-2625.. "Shelsley" 1200 N Valley Rd, Malvern, PA *19355*
Toland MR & MRS Richard H R JR (Diane L Adams) V'76.. of
☎ (212) 832-9428.. 200 E 66 St, Apt B205, New York, NY *10021*
☎ (914) 677-3565.. PO Box 1536, Millbrook, NY *12545*
Toland MR & MRS Robert JR (Marian M Thayer) Sth'48.Rb.Sa.Ty'47.H'49
☎ (610) 647-9960.. 1333 Wisteria Dv, Malvern, PA *19355*
Told MR William H JR—BtP.Evg.Chr.Sar.Fla'52.Cl'58.. of
☎ (212) 751-5311.. 434 E 52 St, New York, NY *10022*
☎ (561) 844-0424.. 201 Bermuda Lane, Palm Beach, FL *33480*
Toller-Bond MRS Dudley H (Allyn—Nancy J Ebert) Mo'41.Chr.Mto.Cly.
☎ (212) 535-8621.. 3 E 71 St, New York, NY *10021*

Tolles MR & MRS Bryant F JR (Carolyn C Kimball) Wheat'62.Y'61 .... | ☎ (302) 984-0244 1002 Kent Rd,
MR Bryant F 3d—Hav'90 .... | Wilmington, DE *19807-2820*

Tolles MRS V Jean (Casper—V Jean Binks)
☎ (216) 561-9002.. Moreland Courts Apt 6B, 13705 Shaker Blvd, Cleveland, OH *44120*

Tomerlin MR & MRS Monte Durham (Jacqueline Beretta) Ty'74.A.Cda.Ty'75 .... | ☎ (210) 828-2465 215 Parklane Dv,
MISS Emily A .... | San Antonio, TX
JUNIORS MISS Alice M .... | *78212*
JUNIORS MR John B .... |

Tomes MR Alexander H JR—Rc.T.Tr.StA.Hb.H'54.H'59
☎ (914) 351-2297.. W Lake Rd, Tuxedo Park, NY *10987*
Tomlin MR John F (Henry B JR) .... Married at Livingston, MT
Briet MISS Marcela (Christian) .... Nov 18'95

Tomlinson MR & MRS Henry P (Anne J Clapp) P'41 | ☎ (561) 231-0057
MRS Anne J (Gilvarg—Anne J Tomlinson)—at | The Moorings,
☎ (301) 972-7586.. Sugarloaf Equestrian | 159 Anchor Dv,
Center, PO Box 352, Barnesville, MD *20838*... | Vero Beach, FL
 | *32963*

Tomlinson MRS Richard F (Gay B Frey) Mg.
☎ (201) 540-8307.. Orchard Dv, Box 206, New Vernon, NJ *07976*
Tompkins MR & MRS Christopher P (Catherine de C Little) Sa.Cly.Cl'78
☎ (212) 752-7024.. 200 E 66 St, New York, NY *10021*

Tompkins MR & MRS Frederick K (Odile H Delente) Nu'75 .... | ☎ (314) 361-4157 70 Waterman Place,
MISS Anne-Cecile—at Art Inst Chicago ...... | St Louis, MO *63112*

Tompkins MRS Howard (Bishop—Eleanor S Mills) ..... Died May 6'96
Tompkins MRS Laurence (Van Norden—Eddison—Rebecca F Crane)
☎ (207) 734-2204.. Dark Harbor, Islesboro, ME *04848*

Toms MRS Charles C (Kathryn Murray) .... | ☎ (415) 346-2288
MR C Erik .... | 2541 Washington St, San Francisco, CA *94115*

Toms MRS Emily F (Kingston—Emily R Fuller) .... name changed to Kingston
Toms MRS Evangeline (Evangeline Gianoulis) Ri.
☎ (212) 249-3105.. 155 E 72 St, New York, NY *10021*
Toms MR Newby—Unn.Ri.Rv.Cw.P'65.Ox'67.H'70
see Dilatory Domiciles

Toms MR & MRS Robert F (Martha Saidy) .... | ☎ (415) 342-6937
MR William R .... | 731 Newhall St, Hillsborough, CA *94010*

Tonissi MR & MRS M Pierre (Bucklin—Deborah W Moses)
Gchr'73.Bab'76.Bvl.D.Tr.Un.Chi.Bost'71.Suff'75 ⚓
☎ (617) 731-0940.. 74 Clyde St, Chestnut Hill, MA *02167*

Toogood MISS Anna Coxe (Harvey—Anna Coxe Toogood) Pa'67 .... | ☎ (215) 836-5621 814 Southampton
JUNIORS MR Nathan A Harvey .... | Av, Wyndmoor, PA *19038*

Toogood MR & MRS Granville N (Patricia A Dale) Pa'66 .... | of ☎ (203)655-8207 5 Salem Straits,
MISS Heather D .... | Darien, CT *06820*
MR Chase—at Trinity .... | ☎ (207) 276-5695 "Ebbtide" Northeast Harbor, ME *04662*

Tooker MISS Tracey
☎ (212) 966-6695.. 18 Mercer St, New York, NY *10013*

Toole MR & MRS William F (Battey—Bertha B Lee)
Swb'46.Y'50.Y'52 . . . .
☎ (706) 733-5619
2644 Henry St,
Augusta, GA *30904*
    MR Thomas B Battey—at 187 Breckenridge
Dv, Augusta, GA *30907* . . . .

Topping MR & MRS Henry J JR (Rochelle Levinson)
Roch'77.Un.Stan'63.Va'65 . . of
☎ (914) 478-0734 . . 2 Hastings Landing, Hastings-on-Hudson,
NY *10706*
☎ (212) 929-4224 . . 140 Seventh Av, New York, NY *10011*

Topping MR Henry J 4th—Smu'91 . . see J V Missett 3d

Topping MISS Samantha S . . see J V Missett 3d

Topping MRS Sandra E (Sack—Sandra E Topping)
PO Box 2377, Georgetown, SC *29442*

Topping MR & MRS Thomas S R (Josephine H
Atkinson) AmU'71.Wes'69.Geo'72.Lond'73 . . .
☎ (011-41-22)
776-54-53
6 rte de Genève,
1291 Commugny,
Switzerland
    MISS Jennifer R . . . .
    MISS Christina H . . . .
    JUNIORS MISS Carolyn W . . . .
    JUNIORS MR Stephen G . . . .

Toralballa MR & MRS Leopoldo C (Goodbody—Betsy B Erskine)
V'68.Cl'76.P'68.Warwick'71
2260 Harcourt Dv, Cleveland Heights, OH *44106*

Torbert MR & MRS Clement C JR (Gene D Hurt) Aub'50.Aub'51.Ala'54
☎ (334) 745-4177 . . 611 Terracewood Dv, Opelika, AL *36801*

Tornga MR & MRS Thomas H (Nancy B Thomas)
Tcy.Hope'62 . . . .
☎ (415) 459-7774
Shady Lane,
PO Box 59, Ross,
CA *94957*
    MR Todd A . . . .
    MR Scott T . . . .
    JUNIORS MR Andrew J . . . .

Torno MR & MRS Laurent J JR (Elizabeth W
Garesché) Mar'vil'59.Wash'60 . . . .
☎ (314) 726-0407
7111 Waterman Av,
St Louis, MO *63130*
    MISS Elizabeth G—Wash'84 . . . .
    MISS Martha J . . . .
    MR Laurent J 3d . . . .

Torosian MRS Peter G (Titus—Lacey—Gardner—Elena E Pfeil)
Sc.Wa.Cas.
☎ (312) 944-4041 . . 179 E Lake Shore Dv, Apt 19W, Chicago,
IL *60611*

Torp MR & MRS Jonathan W (Mary S Stevens) UWash'74.SCal'76
818 Gretna Green Way, Apt 304, Los Angeles, CA *90049*

Torrance MRS Doreen M (Doreen J Morris) F&M'79
☎ (610) 688-7277 . . 418 N Bellevue Av, Wayne, PA *19087*

Torras MISS Mollie M—MtH'55
☎ (212) 228-1472 . . 115 E 9 St, New York, NY *10003*

Torrence MR Robert G—Elk.Cc.Yn.Y'45 . . . .
☎ (802) 649-1111
27 Beaver Meadow
Rd, Norwich, VT
05055-9455
    MR Grier de L—Cc.RISD'77.Y'81—at
☎ (914) 679-7437 . . PO Box 1204, Woodstock,
NY *12498* . . . .
    MR Corbett McP—Vt'83—at ☎ (352) 378-8890
2417 NW 47 Lane, The Lakes, Gainesville, FL
32605 . . . .

Torrey MR & MRS Carl G (Ella K Russell) B'gton'47.Pc.Y'45.H'55
☎ (215) CH8-2590 . . 134 W Highland Av, Philadelphia,
PA *19118-3818*

Torrey MR & MRS Donald F (Louise L Chidsey) B'gton'39.NCar'41
☎ (203) 227-3518 . . 157 Hillspoint Rd, Westport, CT *06880*

Torrey MR & MRS Donald F JR (Susan D Myers) Nw'82.Conn'80
see Dilatory Domiciles

Torrey MISS Ella King—Y'80.Miss'84
☎ (415) 771-9107 . . 950 Lombard St, San Francisco, CA *94133*

Torrey MISS Emily S . . see J T Barber

Torrey MR & MRS James A (Milhaupt—Rose P
Lynch) P'71.H'82.Rc.Eyc.K. . . . .
of ☎ (212)410-2134
1155 Park Av,
New York, NY
10128
☎ (614) 939-2134
4633 Yantis Dv,
New Albany, OH
43054
    MISS Serena C—at Brown . . . .
    JUNIORS MISS Anna H—at Nightingale-Bamford .

Torrey MR & MRS L Russell (Marie McGranaghan) MtStMary'84.Alf'81
☎ (610) 520-1502 . . 36 Aldwyn Lane, Villanova, PA *19085-1421*

Torrey MASTER Matthew Welsh (L Russell) . . . . Born at
Bryn Mawr, PA May 19'94

Torrey MR Owen C 3d . . see J T Barber

Torrey MR & MRS Philip C (Blake—Margaret M Kingsley) McG'49
☎ (215) 233-1126 . . 506 Wyndmoor Av, Wyndmoor, PA *19038*

Torrey MRS Robert D (Ligget—Amy J Cramp) Sa. .
☎ (215) 233-5540
7806 Linden Rd,
Wyndmoor, PA
19038
    MR Robert D JR—NCar'72 . . . .
    MISS Frances C Ligget—VPI'76 . . . .

Torti MR & MRS Maurice L JR (Nancy H Morse) Gchr'64.Mit'53
☎ (617) 259-0218 . . Weston Rd, Lincoln, MA *01773*

Totten MISS Cecily P . . see MRS M L Vaughan

Totten MR & MRS Charles A L (Alison H Goodyear) HWSth'90.HWSth'92
☎ (406) 582-9607 . . 318 S Tracy Av, Bozeman, MT *59715*

Totten MR & MRS Michael W (Alexandra C Train)
An.Ct.Sl.Wms'63.Beirut'74 . . . .
☎ (410) 639-2848
''Rosedale''
6800 Tolchester Rd,
Rock Hall, MD
21661
    JUNIORS MISS Ellen A C . . . .

Tottenham MRS Dinah T L (Groves—Orr—Dinah T Loftus-Tottenham)
☎ (011-44-171) 823-9760 . . 33 Sumner Place, London SW7 3NT,
England

Toulmin MISS Harrie
749 Elkcam Blvd NW, Port Charlotte, FL *33952*

Toulmin MR Henry C—Vt'88 . . see R D Langmann

Toulmin MR Hugh H JR—Au.NEng'84
☎ (617) 731-4841 . . 39 Prince St, Apt 3, Brookline, MA *02146*

Toulmin MR & MRS John H (Anne M Jones) Va'80.Dth'80.Pa'85
☎ (508) 369-9928 . . 861 Barretts Mill Rd, Concord, MA *01742*

Toulmin MR & MRS Peter N (Olga Sturtevant)
Sth'54.Ncd.H'50 . . . .
☎ (401) 421-8164
309 Olney St,
Providence, RI
02906
    MR Charles N—H'84.Mich'90—at
☎ (608) 250-9441 . . 451 W Wilson St, Apt 3,
Madison, WI *53703* . . . .
    MR Steven W—AmU'92 . . . .

Tourais MR & MRS Patrick R (J Zelie Calvocoressi)
Dc.FIU'79 . . . .
☎ (713) 359-5977
3311 Fawn Creek
Dv, Kingwood, TX
77339
    JUNIORS MISS Valerie F . . . .
    JUNIORS MR John N . . . .

Tourison MR & MRS Dudley Miles (Ann McDowell) Pc.USMMA'45
☎ (609) 884-7451 . . 901 Benton Av, Cape May, NJ *08204*

Toussaint MR L Townsend
☎ (860) 354-6608 . . 197 Keeler Rd, Bridgewater, CT *06752*

Towell MRS Timothy L (Dane A Nichols) | ☎ (202) 337-3410
Sth'68.Cvc.Msq.Mt.Tvcl. . . . . | 4821 W St NW,
MISS Dane Billings—ColC'94 . . . . | Washington, DC
MR Timothy Nichols—at U of Ariz . . . . | *20007*

Towell MR Timothy L—Cvc.Mt.Tvcl.Y'57.Cwr'62
1528—33 St NW, Washington, DC *20007*

Tower MISS Caroline H—CtCol'95 . . see E M Strauss

Tower MR & MRS James W (Dorothy P Moore) Sth'38.Csn.Hn.H'35
☎ (207) 721-9742 . . 65 Matthew Dv, Brunswick, ME *04011-3273*

Tower MR & MRS Jonathan R (Glickler—Cabell D | ☎ (310) 573-9295
Smith) CtCol'65.Bel'72 . . . . | 1167 Fiske St,
JUNIORS MISS Katharine V C . . . . | Pacific Palisades,
 | CA *90272*

Tower MISS (REV) Laurel P (Akers—Nichols— | ☎ (805) 963-0252
Laurel P Tower) . . . . | 550 Miramonte Dv,
MR Christopher G Akers . . . . | Santa Barbara, CA
 | *93109*

Tower MISS Lydia M . . see E M Strauss

Tower MR & MRS Whitney (Lucy N Lyle) | ☎ (518) 584-0538
K.Ri.Srr.H'45 . . . . | 249 Clinton St,
JUNIORS MISS Aurora de S . . . . | Saratoga Springs,
 | NY *12866*

Towers MR & MRS Charles S (Lois W Mason)
☎ (803) 838-5558 . . 747 N Reeve Rd, Dataw Island, SC *29920*

Towle MR Charles C JR . . . . Died at
San Francisco, CA Aug 20'95

Towle MRS Charles C JR (Sally Griffith) Cal'60.Tcy.
☎ (415) 931-2798 . . 2850 Broderick St, San Francisco, CA *94123*

Towle MR Charles G (late Charles C JR) . . . Married at San Francisco, CA
Woods MISS Dorine (Frank) . . . . May 31'94

Towle MASTER Charles Spencer (g—MRS Charles C Towle JR) . . . Born at
San Francisco, CA Aug 17'96

Towle MR James P (late Charles C JR) . . . . Married at Woodside, CA
Friedley MISS Melanie L (George) . . . . Sep 18'93

Towle MR Peter R (late Charles C JR) . . . . Married at
Puuwaawaa Ranch, HI
Lathan MISS Mimi (Robert) . . . . Jun 1'96

Towles MR & MRS Stokley P (Eddy—Jeanne H Glass) Sm.Cy.P'57
☎ (617) 329-9012 . . 67 Thatcher St, Westwood, MA *02090*

Towne MR Augur—Y'37
☎ (401) 596-7499 . . 74 East Av, Westerly, RI *02891*

Towne MRS John D C (Dorothy Vilas)
☎ (910) 292-4657 . . Meadowbrook Terrace, 1915 Boulevard St,
Greensboro, NC *27407*

Townes MR & MRS Charles H (Frances H Brown)
Bhm.Fur'35.Duke'37.CalTech'39
☎ (510) 527-4860 . . 1988 San Antonio Av, Berkeley, CA *94707*

Townsend MRS Barnard (Marjorie Bradley) Cly.
☎ (212) 737-4687 . . 40 E 78 St, Apt 10H, New York, NY *10021*

Townsend MR & MRS Bowman (Elizabeth L Adair)
Tenn'83.Tenn'86.Tenn'79
☎ (423) 673-0252 . . 1129 Southgate Rd, Knoxville, TN *37919*

Townsend MRS Charles C (Ames—Ewing—Charlotte Schoonmaker)
☎ (610) 296-0648 . . 44 Manchester Court, Berwyn, PA *19312*

Townsend MRS Charles Coe (von Wiesenthal—Ruth E Scott)
Un.Cly.Srr.Snc . . .of
☎ (212) 722-1718 . . 17 E 89 St, New York, NY *10128*
☎ (518) 851-9151 . . ''Pict Bush'' Snowberry Farm, 33 Scott Rd,
Hudson, NY *12534*

Townsend MR & MRS Charles Coe 3d (Alison D Keller)
RMWmn'75.Va'71.H'75
☎ (401) 247-1946 . . 63 Alfred Drowne Rd, Barrington, RI *02806*

Townsend MR & MRS Christopher B (Johannah Van V Dunham)
Wes'91.Bgt.Wes'89
☎ (214) 304-8406 . . 112 Dickens Dv, Coppell, TX *75019*

Townsend MR & MRS David D (Nancy H Lenz) Pa'49
☎ (704) 375-4701 . . 2331 Mecklenburg Av, Charlotte, NC *28205*

Townsend MR & MRS David D JR (Anne McP Edwards) Conv'79.Rm'80
☎ (804) 288-9175 . . 5906 York Rd, Richmond, VA *23226*

Townsend MR & MRS David G (Helen I Gaylord) | ☎ (860) 824-5653
Stan'52.L. . . . . | ''River House''
MISS Sheila C—at 4795 Easley Rd, Golden, CO | River Rd, Box 257,
80403 . . . . | Falls Village, CT
MISS Lila G—at ☎ (207) 775-0758 | *06031*
42 Alton St, Portland, ME *04102* . . . . |

Townsend MRS Edward (Andrade—Felicia C Thomas) Cly.
☎ (212) 879-3900 . . 1 E 66 St, New York, NY *10021*

Townsend MR Edward L—VaCmth'86
☎ (804) 573-5763 . . Maserville Farm, 3435 Musket Dv, Midlothian,
VA *23113*

Townsend MR & MRS Frederic (Olivia E Evans) L&C'80.DU'73.Cr'76
☎ (847) 615-1817 . . 65 Wimbledon Rd, Lake Bluff, IL *60044*

Townsend MR Henry C 3d
☎ (303) 530-4377 . . 6922 Frying Pan Rd, Boulder, CO *80301*

Townsend MR & MRS Howard (Tatistcheff—Catherine Van C
Van Rensselaer) H'53
☎ (518) 785-4181 . . 301 Old Loudon Rd, Latham, NY *12110*

Townsend MR & MRS Joseph B (Annis L Furness) Ac.Myf.
☎ (610) 459-2998 . . ''Bucklebury'' 301 W Baltimore Pike, Wawa,
PA *19063*

Townsend MR & MRS Kiliaen Van R (Robin Howe) Mid'80.Wms'80
1607 Anderson Pike, Signal Mountain, TN *37377*

Townsend MR & MRS Lewis R (Van Devanter—Ann P Cutler)
Br'58.GeoW'74.Mt.Cvc.Sl.Cl'47.Y'50
☎ (202) 342-0190 . . 2801 New Mexico Av NW, Washington, DC *20007*

Townsend MR & MRS Lyman B JR (Deborah A Schutzendorf) PineM'85
☎ (607) 547-6031 . . Lower Toddsville Rd, Box 951, Cooperstown,
NY *13326*

Townsend MR & MRS P Coleman JR (Susan | of ☎ (212)772-2248
Marshall) Wil.K.Del'69 . . . . | 955 Lexington Av,
MR John M—at ☎ (773) 667-2064 | New York, NY
5704 S Harper Av, Chicago, IL *60637* . . . . | *10021*
 | ☎ (302) 227-9377
 | 7 Dodds Lane,
 | Rehoboth, DE *19971*

Townsend MR & MRS R Hewitt (Louise R Bruce) Louis'46.Ncd.Mit'45
☎ (302) 762-7511 . . 1808 Shipley Rd, Wilmington, DE *19803*

Townsend MRS Rodman (Elizabeth A Bowman)
☎ (423) 523-2677 . . 3400 Lake View Dv, Knoxville, TN *37919*

Townsend MR & MRS Rodman JR (Katheryne L Smith) Tenn'82.Tenn'76
☎ (423) 573-7394 . . 3628 Maloney Rd, Knoxville, TN *37920*

Townsend MRS Samuel J C (Sarah Slawson) . . . . . . | ☎ (860) 726-2162
MISS (DR) Sallie S—Sth'67.NH'70.NH'77—at | Duncaster T208,
☎ (860) 647-0548 . . 119 Coleman Rd, | 20 Loeffler Rd,
Manchester, CT *06040* . . . . | Bloomfield, CT
| *06002-2273*

Townsend MR & MRS Stephen S JR (Jones—Baxter | ☎ (415) 668-1148
—Lucia P Whitman) Cal'68.H'75 . . . . | 136 Third Av,
JUNIORS MR John L—at St George's . . . . | San Francisco, CA
| *94118*

Townsend MR & MRS Thomas H (Mary F | ☎ (617) 227-5007
Friedmann) Sth'57.Bost'70.Myc.Ub.Ec.Cc.Cw. | 48 Chestnut St,
H'57 ⛵ . . . . | Boston, MA *02108*
MISS Katharine C—Bow'90 . . . . |
MISS Elizabeth P—Ty'91 . . . . |
MISS Caroline H . . . . |

Townsend MR William H (Howard) . . . . Married at Albany, NY
Sheehan MISS Mary E (late Robert) . . . . Apr 13'96

Townsend MR & MRS William H (Mary E Sheehan)
Bnd'87.Cl'91.Tufts'88.U'96
☎ (718) 274-6981 . . 31-14—35 St, Apt 3E, Astoria, NY *11106*

Townsend MRS Wisner H (Edith W Richard) Cly.Ncd.
☎ (561) 274-3940 . . 220 MacFarlane Dv, Delray Beach, FL *33483*

Townshend MRS Raynham (Robertson—Barbara Lomas) Why.Ncd.
☎ (203) 776-0106 . . 126 Hartford Tpke, Hamden, CT *06517*

Townzen MRS Muriel P (Muriel P Brady) . . see MRS S S Brady

Tozer MR & MRS W James JR (Elizabeth Farran) | ☎ (212) 534-7438
Ri.Ty'63.H'65 . . . . | 1112 Park Av, Apt
MISS Farran V—Wes'89.H'94—at 31 E 12 St, | 6A, New York, NY
New York, NY *10003* . . . . | *10128*
MISS Katharine C—Ty'90—at 240 E 55 St, |
New York, NY *10022* . . . . |

Trabbold MR David K . . see MRS M B von Czoernig

Trabka MRS Barbara S (Barbara M Shelnutt) . . . Married at Olympia, WA
Bolender MR Ben H . . . . Jan 1'93

Tracy MR & MRS Ernest B JR (Hazel R Bryan) | ☎ (802) 824-6531
Cl'61.Yn.Y'54 . . . . | PO Box 78,
MISS Virginia S—Van'90—at 62 W 62 St, | Londonderry, VT
New York, NY *10023* . . . . | *05148*
MR D Scott—Ty'92—at ☎ (415) 440-4323 |
2530 Fillmore St, San Francisco, CA *94115* . . . . |

Tracy MISS Nina T (Ernest B JR) . . . . Married at Old Lyme, CT
Jaeger MR Albers J (late Albert) . . . . Sep 16'95

Tracy MR Phelps K—Aht'31
☎ (508) 543-5913 . . 50 Granite St, Foxboro, MA *02035*

Tracy MRS William T (Marylin R Noble) Ne. . . . . . | ☎ (212) 980-8330
MR Paul W—Geo'82.Ford'86—at | 200 E 66 St,
☎ (914) 799-1066 . . 3 Midland Gardens, | New York, NY
Bronxville, NY *10708* . . . . | *10021*

Tracy MR William T—Geo'53
☎ (212) 535-1468 . . 35 E 84 St, New York, NY *10028*

Traer MRS Milton McN (Anne W Smith)
☎ (715) 588-3216 . . ''Cedar House'' PO Box 452, Woodruff,
WI *54568*

Trafford MR Perry—Pc.Pa'69
☎ (215) 248-4796 . . 123 W Springfield Av, Philadelphia, PA *19118*

Trafford MRS Perry D JR (Polly Potts) C.Sg.H.
☎ (215) 836-2109 . . 551 E Evergreen Av, Wyndmoor, PA *19038*

Trafford MRS William Bradford (Yates—Champollion—Stella Mallett)
☎ (617) 267-6837 . . 380 Marlborough St, Boston, MA *02115-1502*

Trafton LT & MRS Stephen D (Melissa F Geisler) USMC.H'92.H'92
☎ (619) 366-8995 . . 62294 Verbena Rd, Joshua Tree, CA *92252*

Train MR & MRS C Bowdoin (Marjory L Hardy) Hlns'79.Ct.Cvc.Mt.Ty'77
☎ (202) 337-2847 . . 2556—36 St NW, Washington, DC *20007*

Train MRS Cuthbert R (Clark—Noël Hall) Cvc.
☎ (202) 337-2656 . . 2804 R St NW, Washington, DC *20007*

Train MR Cuthbert R—P'64 | ☎ (207) 244-3295
MISS Elizabeth K—H'95 . . . . | Hodgdon Pond
MR Michael C—H'93 . . . . | Farm, Seal Cove,
| Mt Desert Island,
| ME *04674*

Train MR & MRS John (Tower—Fosburgh—Frances | of ☎ (914)234-7397
D Cheston) Rc.C.Bgt.Mt.Plg.Lm.H'50 ⛵ . . . . | 135 Mianus River
MISS Lisa . . . . | Rd, Bedford, NY
| *10506*
| ☎ (212) 535-5678
| 11 E 73 St,
| New York, NY
| *10021*

Train MRS Middleton G C (Audry N Campbell) Cvc.Mt.Ec.Rcch.Sl.
☎ (202) 333-7772 . . 700 New Hampshire Av NW, Apt 306,
Washington, DC *20037*

Train MR & MRS Russell E (Travers—Aileen L Bowdoin)
Cvc.Mt.C.Cly.Sl.P'41.Cl'48 . . of
☎ (202) 332-5800 . . 1801 Kalorama Square NW, Washington,
DC *20008*
☎ (410) 745-9217 . . Grace Creek Farm, 23470 Berry Rd, Bozman,
MD *21612*

Traina MR & MRS Albert S (C Vail Devereux) | ☎ (207) 846-4462
V'55.Gchr'56.Set'50.Nu'54 . . . . | ''Sunset Hill''
MR R Brooks—Bost'89—at 27 Georgetown Dv, | RR 1, Box 201,
Apt 12, Framingham, MA *01701* . . . . | Chebeague Island,
| ME *04017*

Traina MR Todd B . . see A S Wilsey

Traina MR Trevor D . . see A S Wilsey

Trainer MR David P JR—Loy'90
see Dilatory Domiciles

Trainer MR & MRS Edward S (Leslie A Falke) | ☎ (847) 475-6388
NCar'70.H'61 . . . . | 1426 Chicago Av,
MISS Kirsten B—at Harvard . . . . | Evanston, IL *60201*
MR John B—H'95—at ☎ (202) 466-7556 |
1511—22 St NW, Washington, DC *20036* . . . . . |

Trainer MR & MRS John N (Alice T Stone) V'33.Rcn.Hn.H'31
☎ (203) 264-5988 . . 35B Heritage Circle, Southbury, CT *06488-1429*

Trapnell MR Baylor H—Cw.Va'69.Cal'73
☎ (505) 983-7097 . . 212 Hyde Park Estates, Santa Fe, NM *87501*

Trapnell MR David S—Cal'94
☎ (310) 657-8283 . . PO Box 691475, West Hollywood, CA *90069*

Trapnell MISS E Marilla (Horris—E Marilla | ☎ (410) 457-4257
Trapnell). . . . . | 3203 Sandy Hook
JUNIORS MISS Alexa M J Horris . . . . | Rd, Street, MD
| *21154*

Trapnell COL (RET) & MRS Franklin W JR (Flannery—Elizabeth F Rich)
USA.NCarSt'68.NCar'70
☎ (703) 791-5902 . . 13368 Marie Dv, Manassas, VA *20112*

Trapnell MRS John M JR (Davison—Prudence K Johnson)
☎ (805) 969-8825 . . 300 Hot Springs Rd, Apt 126, Montecito, CA *93108*
Trask MRS Eleanor M (Connole—Richards—Eleanor M Trask) Cly.Cda.
☎ (206) 462-9374 . . 9631 Hilltop Rd, Bellevue, WA *98004*
Trask MR & MRS Frederick K (Samuelson—Sarah A Whittinghill) Ln.Unn.Plg.Hn.H'30
☎ (408) 626-4829 . . 8545 Carmel Valley Rd, Carmel, CA *93923*
Trask MRS John Jacquelin (Elsie Y Barber) Cs.Cda.
☎ (212) 371-4097 . . 200 E 66 St, New York, NY *10021*
Trautman MR Courtney L—LakeF'86
☎ (617) 247-2724 . . 58 W Rutland Square, Boston, MA *02118*
Trautman MRS Mary Lee (Mary Lee Love)
☎ (508) 748-2480 . . 555 Delano Rd, Marion, MA *02738*
Travell MR Clark—P'45
☎ (904) 285-9839 . . 2412 Brittany Court, Ponte Vedra Beach, FL *32082-2902*

Travell MRS Philippa W (Harlan—Breckenfeld—Philippa L Walter) . . . . | ☎ (860) 767-3307
MR William G Breckenfeld—at Villanova Law | Heritage Cove C6, 85 River Rd, Essex, CT *06426*

Travers MRS Mary Ann (Dam—Sodborg—Mary Ann Travers)
☎ (516) 671-9489 . . ''The Courtyard'' 8 Ash St, PO Box 194, Locust Valley, NY *11560*
Travis MR & MRS Albert H (Bettingen—Barbara E Brown) SCal'36.H'40
☎ (818) 793-5472 . . 1166 Mill Lane, San Marino, CA *91108*
Travis MR & MRS Lyn (Naomi W Wadsworth) NCol'81.MmtVa'87
☎ (716) 243-5266 . . 26 Crossett Rd, Geneseo, NY *14454*

Travis MR & MRS Martin B (Olivia B Taylor) | ☎ (516) 692-6767
BMr'38.Ncd.Aht'39 . . . . | ''Homestead''
MISS Helen W—Swb'74 . . . . | 533 Cold Spring Rd, Syosset, NY *11791*

Traxel MR & MRS David S (McIlvain—Rosemary Ranck) Cal'74 | ☎ (215) 242-6557
MR Samuel S McIlvain . . . . | 323 W Mermaid Lane, Philadelphia, PA *19118*
MR Joshua M McIlvain . . . . |

Treadway MR & MRS James Curran (Susan P Davis) | ☎ (914) 241-8602
Hlns'67.AmU'71.Bgt.Ct.Cvc.Mt.Ga'64. W&L'67 . . . . | ''Laurel Ledge Farm'' RD 4,
MISS Elizabeth P H—W&L'95 . . . . | 591 Croton Lake Rd, Bedford
MISS Caroline W H—at U of Vt . . . . | Corners, NY *10549*

Treadway MR & MRS Richard F (Simmons—Margaret S Hardwick) Sb.Btn.Chi.Dth'36
☎ (561) 231-1965 . . 251 Sabal Palm Lane, John's Island, Vero Beach, FL *32963*
Treadway MR & MRS William L (Anderson—Elizabeth G M Coale) V'57.GaTech'48
☎ (910) 724-5882 . . 18 Kent Park Circle, Winston-Salem, NC *27106*
Treadwell MRS George H JR (Winifred Allwork) Bnd'61
☎ (520) 749-9323 . . 8611 E Tourmaline Dv, Tucson, AZ *85750*
Treadwell MR & MRS Louis Mead 2d (Carol A Walsh) SUNY'80.Y'78.H'82
☎ (907) 258-7764 . . 528 N St, Anchorage, AK *99501*
Treadwell MASTER William Walsh (Louis Mead 2d) . . . . Born Jan 20'95
Treat MISS Beatrice C
☎ (212) PL2-1079 . . 440 E 56 St, New York, NY *10022*

Treat MRS L Smith (Lucinda Luce Smith) Cvc. . . . . | ☎ (202) 337-1718
MISS Lucinda K . . . . | 3851 Newark St
MR Charles E . . . . | NW, Apt 457,
MR John T E . . . . | Washington, DC *20016*

Treco MR & MRS Frank S JR (Diana G Dempsey) Hlns'49.Kt.Un.Mo.Y'48 . . of
☎ (216) 423-4755 . . 1190 Fox Hill Dv, Box 312, Gates Mills, OH *44040*
☎ (941) 649-1493 . . 1960A Bald Eagle Dv, Naples, FL *34105-2458*
Treco MR & MRS James D (Sarah H Bucknell) H'77.H'82.Yn.Y'77.Stan'84
☎ (908) 273-0238 . . 28 Windsor Rd, Summit, NJ *07901-3053*
Treffer MISS Christine E . . see A S Gruber
Treffer JUNIORS MISS Kimberly A . . see A S Gruber
Trefts MR Park E . . see MRS A P Ryan
Tregellas MRS S Staley (Green—Anne G Smith) Dar.
☎ (516) 324-7878 . . PO Box 406, Wainscott, NY *11975*
Tregellas MR S Staley—Mds.Cyb.
☎ (908) 219-0427 . . 114 Hillside St, Middletown, NJ *07701*
Treherne-Thomas MISS (REV) Rhoda M—Sth'48.Cl'51.UnTheo'80
☎ (718) 351-2791 . . 1055 Richmond Rd, Staten Island, NY *10304*

Treherne-Thomas MRS V Osborn (Hunt—Virginia B Osborn) . . . . | ☎ (401) 846-9553
JUNIORS MR Samuel A . . . . | ''Sea Meadow'' 527 Tuckerman Av, Newport, RI *02840*

Tremblay MR & MRS Donald P (Jean R Gilpin) MtH'79.Bost'80
☎ (610) 644-7559 . . 126 Lenape Dv, Berwyn, PA *19312*
Trench MR & MRS Archer W P (Hope T Humphreys) Hn.H'37
☎ (203) 966-3389 . . 47 Apple Tree Lane, New Canaan, CT *06840*
Trenholm MRS Elena de S (Bullock—Bowyer—Elena de Struve)
☎ (305) 868-9230 . . 9133 Collins Av, Surfside, FL *33154*

Trent MR & MRS Edmund K (Helen Read) | ☎ (412) 741-4496
Sth'37.Rr.Csn.P'36.H'39 . . . . | 121 Centennial Av,
MRS Stephane (Sen—Stephane Trent) . . . . | Sewickley, PA
JUNIORS MISS Nilani . . . . | *15143*

Trent MR & MRS John B JR (Nancy F Palmer) Skd'75.Rv.Cw.Pa'75
☎ (818) 366-7677 . . 10911 Sylvia Av, Northridge, CA *91326*
Trentman MRS Stephen A (Steel—Emalea Warner) B'gton'36.Sl.Ncd.Myf.
☎ (302) 656-4041 . . Stonegates Box 29, 4031 Kennett Pike, Greenville, DE *19807-2032*
Trescher MR & MRS Robert L (Glendora E Rollins) V'41.Gm.Me.Ac.Pa'34.Pa'37.Pa'82
☎ (610) 896-0561 . . Thacher Court 5, 251 Montgomery Av, Haverford, PA *19041*

Trevor MR & MRS Alexander B (Ellen R Armstrong) Un.Sar.Y'67 . . . . | ☎ (614) 846-8713
MISS Anne W—at Yale . . . . | 910 Clayton Dv, Worthington, OH *43085-3301*

Trevor MR & MRS Bronson (Eleanor D Fisher) Un.Rc.K.BtP.Pr.Cw.Sar.Cly.Dc.Ht.Cl'31
☎ (516) 759-1264 . . 125 Shu Swamp Rd, Locust Valley, NY *11560*

Trevor MR & MRS Bronson JR (Nancy C Fritz) | ☎ (516) 692-4812
MtH'75.Un.Pr.Cly.Okla'74 . . . . | 1306 Ridge Rd,
JUNIORS MR Bronson 3d—at Hotchkiss . . . . . . | Laurel Hollow, Syosset, NY *11791*

Trevor MISS Evelyn J B . . see J E Quinn
Trevor MISS Irene S . . see J E Quinn

Trevor MR & MRS John B JR (Evelyn L Bruen)
Unn.K.BtP.Evg.Plg.Snc.Lm.Sar.Cly.Cda.Cl'31
☎ (561) 655-5648 . . The Villas 5F, 425 Worth Av, Palm Beach,
FL *33480*

Trevor MR & MRS John B 4th (Eugenie C McPherson) Col'89.Col'89
☎ (401) 331-1125 . . 37 Hart St, Providence, RI *02906*

Trevor MASTER John Bond 5th (John B 4th) . . . . Born at
Providence, RI Dec 8'95

Trevor MASTER Kyle Colgate (Thomas W) . . . . Born Mch 14'95

Trevor MRS Michele (Simpson—Michele M Safley) | ☎ (602) 948-9680
Ariz'75 . . . . | 5029 Roadrunner
   JUNIORS MISS Melanie S Simpson—at | Rd, Paradise Valley,
   Choate Rosemary . . . . | AZ *85253*

Trevor MISS Sophia A B . . see J E Quinn

Trevor MR & MRS Thomas W (Sylvia H Schmokel) Vt'81.Dowling'80
☎ (802) 482-3948 . . RR 1, Box 447, Hinesburg, VT *05461*

Triant MR & MRS Thanos M (Deborah H Diller) SL'72.Ham'68.Cl'71
165 Canyon Dv, Portola Valley, CA *94028*

Triest MRS Willard G (Laura W Tuckerman) | ☎ (410) 268-2889
Ayc.Cvc.Sl.Cda. . . . . | 220 Norwood Rd,
MISS Laura W . . . . | Annapolis, MD
                                    | *21401*

Trigg MRS R C Ballard 3d (Helen B Milman) Ky'46
☎ (512) 258-3751 . . 7105 Danwood Dv, Austin, TX *78759*

Trimble MR & MRS Francis Elliott (Elizabeth H Rudolph) Van'38.Van'40
☎ (601) 442-7529 . . 24 Homochitto St, Natchez, MS *39120*

Trimble MRS I Ridgeway (Frances H Smith) Mv. . . | ☎ (410) 235-2564
MISS Elizabeth H—Ws'70.Va'73—at | 8 Bishop's Rd,
5601 Woodlawn Rd, Baltimore, MD *21210* . . . . | Baltimore, MD
                                    | *21218*

Trimble MRS John T (Marie E Gibbon) Evg.
☎ (561) 833-9681 . . 1 Royal Palm Way, Apt G4, Palm Beach,
FL *33480*

Trimble MRS Richard (Irene Jerkovitz) . . . . | ☎ (860) 536-6176
MISS Irene E—Pa'84—at ☎ (212) 685-3462 | Mason's Island,
240 E 35 St, New York, NY *10016* . . . . | Mystic, CT *06355*
MISS Cora—End'86—at ☎ (303) 534-5816 |
1020—15 St, Denver, CO *80202* . . . . |

Trimble MR William C . . . . Died at
Brooklandville, MD Jun 24'96

Trimble MRS William C (Nancy G Carroll) Md.Cc.Ncd.
☎ (410) 823-1714 . . 1021 Green Spring Valley Rd, Brooklandville,
MD *21022*

Trimble MR & MRS William C JR (Barbara Janney)
BMr'60.Md.Gv.Cc.Csn.P'58.Md'64
☎ (410) 363-0386 . . 409 Chattolanee Hill, Owings Mills, MD *21117*

Trimble MR & MRS William C 3d (Perry P Miller)
Denis'86.B.Nf.Gv.Md.Duke'84.Duke'87
☎ (202) 625-6518 . . 1406—30 St NW, Washington, DC *20007*

Trimingham MR & MRS de Forest W (Hamilton—Dorothy W King) Ny.Csn.
☎ (441) 236-2727 . . ''Woodstock Cove'' 10 Woodstock Hill,
Paget PG BX22, Bermuda

Trimingham MRS K Fenton (Jane O Tanner) S.Chi.
☎ (441) 236-1513 . . ''Ingate'' 2 Inglewood Lane, Paget PG 06,
Bermuda

Trimmier MR & MRS C Stephen (Rae E Wade) | of ☎ (205)967-4859
Ala'66.Ala'65.Ala'68 . . . . | 3819 River View
MR C Stephen 3d . . . . | Circle, Birmingham,
   | AL *35243*
   | ☎ (334) 928-4893
   | 9 Point Clear
   | Landing,
   | Point Clear, AL
   | *36532*

Trincal MR & MRS Alain J (Vivian B Vose) Cal'85.EcoleArt'85
☎ (011-33-1) 45-44-81-95 . . 30 rue des Sts Peres, 75007 Paris, France

Trinkle MR & MRS Peter B (Benita P Bryant) | ☎ (214) 522-3079
Sth'60.Csn.Lond'55.Dth'57 . . . . | 4548 Bordeaux Av,
MR Peter D—Skd'94 . . . . | Dallas, TX *75205*
JUNIORS MISS Elizabeth A—at Hockaday . . . . . . |

Tripp MRS A Wardwell (Alice C Wardwell)
☎ (603) 878-3630 . . ''Rosebrook'' King Rd, New Ipswich, NH *03071*

Tripp MRS Robert J (Audrey D Shortlidge) . . . . | ☎ (415) 324-7487
MR Stephen R 3d—at ☎ (408) 476-0795 | 850 Webster St,
4780 Porter Gulch Rd, Aptos, CA *95003* . . . . . . | Palo Alto, CA
   | *94301*

Trippe MR & MRS Charles W (Pamela J Reid) Ny.Ln.Yn.Y'57.H'59
☎ (561) 388-9822 . . 12376 N A1A, Vero Beach, FL *32963*

Trippe MISS Mary R
☎ (410) 235-7799 . . 100 W University P'kway, Baltimore, MD *21210*

Trkla MASTER Jackson Dexter (g—K Dexter Miller JR) . . . . Born at
Boston, MA Jun 6'96

Trommald MRS John P (Gretchen Corbett)
☎ (503) 636-4232 . . 11665 SW Military Rd, Portland, OR *97219*

Trostle MR & MRS Robert R (Ann H McCauley) | ☎ (518) 523-8161
Hlns'64.BaldW'92.Ch'63.Ch'65 . . . . | ''The Pumpkin
JUNIORS MISS Lauren H . . . . | Patch''
JUNIORS MR Michael McC . . . . | 2 Whiteface Inn Rd,
   | Lake Placid, NY
   | *12946*

Troth MR & MRS J Shipley (Anne S Waterman) | ☎ (610) 696-5841
Pn.P'33 . . . . | 894 Jefferson Way,
MR Peter R—Del'70 . . . . | West Chester, PA
   | *19380*

Trotman MR & MRS Arthur E 2d (Katharine H | ☎ (203) 972-3392
Richmond) Sth'64.Y'62.H'64 . . . . | 82 Shagbark Dv,
MISS Eleanor W—at Georgetown | New Canaan, CT
MR Philip T—Y'91—at Mexico City, Mexico . . | *06840*

Trotman MR & MRS Charles R (Whitney J Hibbett)
☎ (334) 262-7172 . . 3340 Montezuma Rd, Montgomery, AL *36106*

Trotman MR John McN SR—Aub'48
☎ (334) 288-4121 . . Rte 4, Box 223, Montgomery, AL *36116*

Trotman MR & MRS Robert T (Christine Pappas) Aub'86.Aub'85
☎ (770) 667-3745 . . 12125 Arnold Mill Rd, Roswell, GA *30075*

Trotman MR & MRS Stanley S JR (Susan C Page) | ☎ (516) 367-3238
Sth'65.Mb.Y.'65.Cl'67 . . . . | 1222 Moores Hill
MR Nicholas G—Tufts'94—at ☎ (508) 526-1132 | Rd, Laurel Hollow,
598 Summer St, Manchester, MA *01944* . . . . . . | Syosset, NY *11791*

Trott MR & MRS Elliott C (Gertrude M Singer) Rby.Ridley'62
☎ (268) 460-4165 . . ''Trott House'' Mill Reef Club, Antigua

Trott MRS & MRS Nicholas P (Arja R M Arola) | ☎ (610) 520-1196
Cry.Rby.Rc.Pa'71.Nu'77 . . . . | 67 Rosemont Av,
  JUNIORS MISS Anne A . . . . | Rosemont, PA
  JUNIORS MISS Christine A . . . . | 19010
  JUNIORS MISS Eugenie F . . . . |
Trotter MR & MRS Andrew F (Daphne W Gardiner)
Geo'84.AmU'91.W&L'82
  ☎ (202) 328-7869 . . 1904—17 St NW, Washington, DC 20009
Trotter MRS E Sterling (Maxwell—Eugénie Sterling Trotter) Cly.
  ☎ (202) 234-1777 . . 2029 Connecticut Av NW, Washington, DC 20008
Trotter MR & MRS Gordon Trumbull (Jean M | ☎ (410) 730-7936
Oberg) Md'73.Md'78.Md'56.JHop'72 . . . . | 10626 Fable Row,
  MISS Laura J . . . . | Columbia, MD
  MISS Linda M . . . . | 21044
Troussoff MRS George B (Kingsford—Marion E Jones) Shcc.Cly.
  ☎ (201) 543-9793 . . 8 Glen Gary Dv, Mendham, NJ 07945
Trova MR & MRS Ernest T (Weber—Carla C Rand)
  ☎ (314) WY4-7184 . . 6 Layton Terr, St Louis, MO 63124
Trowbridge MR & MRS Calvin D JR (Lee C Doran) | PO Box 527,
Bgt.Y'56.H'59 . . . . | Schoolhouse Rd,
  MISS Nina R—Bnd'91 . . . . | Cross River, NY
  MR David K W—Y'87 . . . . | 10518
Trowbridge MR & MRS James W (Susan M Bell) | ☎ (609) 921-2428
Newt'63.Pn.Y'60 . . . . | 225 Hun Rd,
  MR James S—Geo'91 . . . . | Princeton, NJ 08540
  MR Joseph B—Y'93 . . . . |
  MR Mark W—at Boston Coll . . . . |
  JUNIORS MR Matthew D—at Groton . . . . |
Trowbridge MR Thomas R JR . . . . Died at
  Bloomfield, CT May 31'96
Trowbridge MRS Thomas R JR (Eunice W Herrick) . | of ☎ (860)242-9011
  MR William W H—Bost'69.Mich'72—at | 400 Seabury Dv,
  ☎ (860) 364-5973 . . Lucas Rd, Sharon, CT | Apt 4158,
  06069 . . . . | Bloomfield, CT
  MR David P—Hart'73—at ☎ (205) 554-7353 | 06002
  40 Cherokee Hills, Tuscaloosa, AL 35404 . . . . . | ☎ (860) 364-5464
   | "Nequitamauk"
   | S Main St, Sharon,
   | CT 06069
Trowbridge MRS & MRS Thomas R 3d (Nancy J | ☎ (212) 988-6540
Wichman) Y'64 . . . . | 139 E 79 St,
  MISS Caroline W—at Yale . . . . | New York, NY
  MR Thomas R 4th—at Yale . . . . | 10021
  JUNIORS MISS Anne O . . . . |
Troy MR & MRS Joseph F (Brigitta A Balos) | ☎ (310) 472-4331
Rdc'61.Y'60 . . . . | 350 S Bristol Av,
  MISS Darcy K . . . . | Los Angeles, CA
  MR Austin R . . . . | 90049
Troy MR & MRS Richard H (Elizabeth J Nichols) | ☎ (203) 972-0634
Sth'65.Cly.Ds.Ncd.Geo'59.H'63 . . . . | 428 Laurel Rd,
  MISS Elizabeth D—H'96 . . . . | New Canaan, CT
   | 06840
Truax MRS Shaffer (Elizabeth H MacRossie) . . . . . . | ☎ (714) 640-8489
  MISS Lysbeth C . . . . | 3 Twin Lakes
  MISS Susanna F . . . . | Circle,
   | Corona Del Mar,
   | CA 92625

True MISS Amy Ballantine (Jeffrey R) . . . . Born Nov 20'95
True MR Edward Russell JR—Cvc.Mt.Ny.Aht'27 . . of
  ☎ (202) 387-4266 . . 2450 Belmont Rd NW, Washington, DC 20008
  ☎ (561) 546-5224 . . "Sunset Ridge" 106 South Trail, Hobe Sound,
  FL 33455
True MISS Gabriella M . . see MISS K T Emmet
True MR & MRS Jeffrey R (Carolyn D Ballantine) Hood'83
  ☎ (301) 682-4249 . . 8411 Rocky Springs Rd, Frederick, MD 21702
Trueblood MRS Edward Gatewood (Ella M Lyon) Cos.
  ☎ (520) 722-5515 . . Balmoral, 5830 E Pima St, Tucson, AZ 85712
Trueblood MRS Wilbur T (Anne C Taussig)
  28 Daisy Meadow Terr, Henderson, NV 89014
Truesdale MR & MRS Joseph R 3d (Pamela R | ☎ (603) 746-4797
McDonald) . . . . | Gage Hill Rd,
  MISS Katharine C . . . . | Hopkinton, NH
  MR Joseph R 4th . . . . | 03229
  JUNIORS MR Benjamin L . . . . |
Truesdale MRS Mary S (Mary R Skidmore) V'42.Cly.H.
  ☎ (212) 832-1595 . . 200 E 66 St, New York, NY 10021
Truesdale MISS Suzanne C . . see G D Jackson 3d
Truitt MRS Alexandra (Kusack—Remez— | ☎ (914) 533-2997
  Alexandra Truitt) . . . . | Box 320,
  JUNIORS MR Samuel D Kusack . . . . | Boutonville Rd,
  JUNIORS MR Alastair G Kusack . . . . | South Salem, NY
   | 10590
Truitt MRS Charles S (Henrietta S Gould) Ac.Gm.
  ☎ (610) 645-8667 . . 1400 Waverly Rd, Villa 18, Gladwyne, PA 19035
Truitt MRS James McC (Prescott—Evelyn Patterson)
  ☎ (011-52-415) 20419 . . Chiquitos 3, San Miguel de Allende,
  GTO 37700, Mexico
Truitt MR & MRS Peter G (Susan DeF Shattuck) Mid'69.Pa'72.Pa'69.Pa'72
  ☎ (410) 296-2927 . . 148 Stanmore Rd, Baltimore, MD 21212
Truitt MRS S Stokes (Allen—Louise B Grayson) Ac.Me.M.
  ☎ (610) 525-5906 . . 74 Pasture Lane, Apt 338, Bryn Mawr, PA 19010
Trumbull MRS Philip W (Pauline P Fraser-Campbell) . . . . Died at
  Weston, MA Jun 29'96
Trumbull MR Philip W—H'42
  ☎ (617) 893-4575 . . 4 Robin Rd, Weston, MA 02193
Trump MR & MRS Robert Townshend (Sandra F | ☎ (215) 233-1707
  Snowden) Cda. . . . . | 668 Bethlehem Pike,
  MISS Lillie F—Ithaca'90—at ☎ (770) 449-7509 | Whitemarsh,
  Peachtree Corners Circle, Norcross, GA 30092 . | Flourtown, PA
  MR Michael—Syr'93—at ☎ (818) 797-9896 | 19031
  280½ E Mendocino St, Altadena, CA 91001 . . . |
Trundle MRS Sidney A JR (MacDonald—Charmian | ☎ (212) 472-1821
  Campbell) Cda. . . . . | 311 E 72 St,
  MISS Catherine MacDonald—at Tory Hill Rd, | New York, NY
  Alstead, NH 03602 . . . . | 10021
  MR Joseph MacDonald . . . . |
Truscott MR & MRS George B (Edith R Howe) Ts.St.Ty'59
  ☎ (716) 885-6170 . . 32 Argyle Park, Buffalo, NY 14222
Truscott MR & MRS J Lovering (Varney Porter)
  Sth'51.BMr'78.Cts.Me.Cs.Dth'50.Cr'53
  ☎ (610) 896-6766 . . 1101 Rose Glen Rd, Gladwyne, PA 19035
Truslow MR & MRS Charles H (Mary Byers) Vt'82.Tex'82
  ☎ (617) 696-6050 . . 76 Canton Av, Milton, MA 02186

Truslow MR & MRS Frederic J (Aura M Garcia) Y'61.H'64 . . . . | of ☎ (202)333-8609 "The Bus Stop" 3009 Q St NW, Washington, DC 20007
MISS Aura M—B'gton'93—at Hunter . . . .
MISS Elizabeth J—at Cornell . . . .
MR Frederic J—at McGill . . . . | Tupac Farm, Rte 688, Delaplane, VA 20144

Truslow MR & MRS Godfrey G (Olivia H Van Norden) Csh.H.'56 . . . . | ☎ (516) 692-5639 428 Harbor Rd, Cold Spring Harbor, NY 11724
MR Edward D—StAndr'90—at U of Tex . . . . .

Truslow MR & MRS James L (Pauline C Hibbard) NCar'54 . . . . | ☎ (401) 635-4887 36 Sakonnet Point Rd, Little Compton, RI 02837
MR James L 5th—Tex'80.Tex'85 . . . .

Truslow MR & MRS Peter C (Andrea K Schaefer) Tufts'87.Ny.Tufts'86
☎ (904) 428-4103 . . 111 Cunningham Dv, New Smyrna Beach, FL 32168

Truslow MR & MRS William A (Miriam P Kellogg) Rdc'62.Sim'82.C.Sb.Tv.Y'58.H'64 . . . . | of ☎ (617)864-1327 4 Hawthorne St, Cambridge, MA 02138
MR Hugh K—Vt'91—at ☎ (212) 229-9240 120 Christopher St, Apt 16, New York, NY 10014 . . . . | ☎ (802) 234-9000 PO Box 104, Barnard, VT 05031
MR Samuel B—H'94—at ☎ (617) 742-2312 144 Chestnut St, Boston, MA 02108 . . . . . .

Tryon MR & MRS Philip T (Scheie—Mary Ann Tallman) Drex'45.M.Me.Pe.Sdg.Ac.Cs.Ncd. Manitoba'36.H'38 . . . . | ☎ (610) 645-0594 225 Cheswold Lane, Haverford, PA 19041
MISS Nancy Ware Scheie—at ☎ (908) 218-9055 . . 6 W Main St, Apt D, Somerville, NJ 08876 . . . .
MR Eric Glendon Scheie—Cal'78.SFr'82—at ☎ (510) 527-0169 . . 1024 Keith Av, Berkeley, CA 94708 . . . .

Tubbs MRS William R (Watson—Marion W Payne) Wilkes'54.Me.Dc.Ncd.
☎ (610) 649-3383 . . The Quadrangle 1308, 3300 Darby Rd, Haverford, PA 19041

Tubman MR & MRS Joseph R B (Kathryn D Geraghty) Ty'55.Ste.Pa'50.Md'56 . . . . | ☎ (410) 252-6414 11431 Mays Chapel Rd, Timonium, MD 21093
MISS Kathryn R—Denis'88 . . . .
MR John B—P'87.Nw'92 . . . .

Tubman MR & MRS S Alexander IV (Jean R Myer) Ncd.Dar.Va'51 . . . . | ☎ (410) 758-6843 307 S Commerce St, Centreville, MD 21617
MISS (DR) Eugenia R B—Ky'83.Pa'87 . . . .

Tubman MR & MRS Samuel A 5th (Rebecca A Elliott) Ky'91
1520 Chadwick Dv, Lexington, KY 40515

Tucker MISS Anne P . . see A L Donovan

Tucker MRS Cary S (Elizabeth T Becker) Sth'27
☎ (540) 463-2267 . . "Tulipwood" PO Box 1427, Lexington, VA 24450-1427

Tucker MRS Chester E (M Elizabeth Hopper) Cda.
☎ (215) 233-3044 . . 551 E Evergreen Av, Apt B114, Wyndmoor, PA 19038

Tucker MR Christopher S—Syr'84
☎ (817) 460-3016 . . 2030 Misty Glen Trail, Apt 2012, Arlington, TX 76011

Tucker MR & MRS D Stewart (Cécile L Ulbrich) H'91.Hb.H'92
☎ (215) 235-7132 . . 1609 Green St, Apt A, Philadelphia, PA 19130-3909

Tucker MR & MRS Daniel J (Lucy Thornton Lennon) Colby'87
☎ (207) 772-7127 . . 9 Wellstone Dv, Portland, ME 04103

Tucker MISS Frances M
☎ (314) 862-3363 . . 7388 Stratford Av, University City, MO 63130

Tucker MR & MRS Frederick A JR (Mary A Hutchinson) Nw'60.R.Me.Sdg.Pa'55 . . . . | ☎ (610) 527-1735 795 Darby-Paoli Rd, Bryn Mawr, PA 19010
MR William L—Me.Ithaca'94 . . . .
MR Matthew H—at U of Wisc Madison . . . .

Tucker MR & MRS Harry K (Payson—Sheila W Bullock) Cly. . . . . | ☎ (561) 770-1884 127 Prestwick Circle, Vero Beach, FL 32967
MR Bryan R—at ☎ (301) 684-0164 402 Hillsboro Dv, Silver Spring, MD 20902 . . .

Tucker MR James W—VPI'40
☎ (703) 820-1565 . . 6112 Beachway Dv, Falls Church, VA 22041

Tucker JUNIORS MR John M . . see A L Donovan

Tucker MRS Joseph W (Katherine E Tiers) Pc. . . . . | ☎ (401) 466-5994 PO Box 968, Harbor Pond Lane, Apt G, Block Island, RI 02807
MISS Mary E—at Stamford, CT . . . .
MR Michael J—at Berkeley, CA . . . .

Tucker MISS Katherine Adele (g—Randolph Catlin) . . . . Born at Boston, MA Apr 11'94

Tucker REV & MRS Luther (Josephine L Pullman) V'33.Ln.Qc.Csn.Yn.Y'31
☎ (513) 561-7167 . . 4535 Drake Rd, Cincinnati, OH 45243-4115

Tucker MR Marshall O—Cvc.Vt'84.Cl'91
☎ (212) 242-4118 . . 351 W 22 St, New York, NY 10011-2601

Tucker MRS Martha M (Martha L Metzger) Srb. . . . | ☎ (401) 847-9755 40 School St, Newport, RI 02840
MISS Alden S—Nu'88—at ☎ (212) 865-2581 251 W 95 St, New York, NY 10025 . . . .
DR Robertson B—Pa'90.Pa'94—at ☎ (215) 922-3704 . . 929 S 10 St, Philadelphia, PA 19147 . . . .

Tucker MR & MRS N Beverley JR (Constance H Kane) Chap'64.Unn.Csn.P'62.H'67 . . . . | ☎ (513) 771-6271 815 Woodbine Av, Cincinnati, OH 45246
MISS Sarah G—Macalester'88—at Maximo San Juan 10, 4F, 28017 Madrid, Spain .
MR Nathaniel B 3d—Drew'95 . . . .

Tucker MR & MRS Peter J (Sara A Glover) Geo'82.Cl'89.Geo'82
☎ (203) 222-7625 . . 151 Imperial Av, Westport, CT 06880

Tucker MR & MRS Richard B (Alice H Reed) Va'35
☎ (412) 421-2996 . . 5458 Aylesboro Av, Pittsburgh, PA 15217

Tucker DR Samuel H—Pc.Pn.P'52.Pa'56 ⚓
☎ (215) 848-9362 . . 4113 Apalogen Rd, Philadelphia, PA 19144

Tucker MR & MRS Spencer C (Barcus—Blount—Beverly R Blount) TexWmn'60.TexWmn'90.Vmi'59.NCar'62.NCar'66
☎ (817) 924-9050 . . 3200 Wabash Av, Ft Worth, TX 76109

Tucker MASTER Sterling Woodward 3d (g—Sterling Woodward Tucker 3d)
Born at Little Rock, AR Jan 16'96

Tucker MR & MRS Sterling Woodward 3d (Ann Hancock) NCar'46.Duke'43
☎ (501) 663-4051 . . 6 Armistead Rd, Little Rock, AR 72207

Tucker MRS Toinette (Randell—King—Toinette Tucker)
MmtMhn'80.Ri.Ds...of
☎ (860) 364-0004 . . Rosewood Farm, 6 Herb Rd, Sharon, CT *06069*
☎ (802) 297-9358 . . Piper Ridge, Bondville, VT *05340*
Tucker MASTER Tristan James (Daniel J) . . . . Born at
Portland, ME Jun 30'95
Tucker MR William B J—Me.Syr'92
☎ (215) 828-7901 . . 9307 Ridge Pike, Philadelphia, PA *19128*
Tucker MR & MRS William D JR (Mary E Hayes) | ☎ (914) 738-1499
HolyC'39.H.'42 . . . . | 133 Cliff Av,
MISS Elizabeth R—Ne'81 . . . . | Pelham, NY *10803*
MR W Duane 3d—Cl'71 . . . . |
Tucker MR & MRS William Hollingsworth (Nute—Sandra J Bernard)
WChesSt'62.Myf.Mit'44
☎ (410) 418-5121 . . 3357 N Chatham Rd, Apt K, Ellicott City,
MD *21042-2732*
Tucker MR & MRS William R (Carol M O Exnicios) | ☎ (813) 286-1621
Cvc.Y'50 . . . . | 5218 Neptune Way,
MISS Elinor D W—Tampa'88—at | Tampa, FL *33609*
☎ (813) 286-1326 . . 4350 W Kennedy Blvd,
Tampa, FL *33609* . . . . |
MR Michael W—Y'82—at ☎ (203) 772-2297
1172 Chapel St, New Haven, CT *06511* . . . . |
Tuckerman MRS Bayard (Whittall—Milicent Ewell) Sm.Chi.Ncd.
☎ (508) 636-4371 . . 743 Horseneck Rd, Westport, MA *02790*
Tuckerman MR & MRS Charles S (Marja-Liisa Lehto) H.'44
☎ (518) 766-5542 . . ''Nutshell'' RD 3, Averill Park, NY *12018*
Tuckerman MR & MRS Edward M (Grace L Russell) H'43
☎ (617) 383-0769 . . 393 S Main St, Cohasset, MA *02025*
Tuckerman MR & MRS Herbert S (Sarah P Cole) My.H'43
☎ (508) 927-0168 . . 413 Hale St, Prides Crossing, MA *01965*
Tuckerman MR & MRS Roger W (Edith D Fenton) | of ☎ (212)289-5474
Rc.Bgt.Cly.H'59 . . . . | 1112 Park Av,
JUNIORS MISS Katharine F . . . . | New York, NY
JUNIORS MR Oliver W . . . . | *10128*
| ☎ (914) 234-7886
| PO Box 174,
| Bedford Hills, NY
| *10507*
Tudor MR & MRS Daniel H (Jeanice Eddy) . . . . | ☎ (360) 683-7323
MR Geoffrey W . . . . | 352 S Solmar Dv,
| Sequim, WA *98382*
Tudor MR John H—SanJ'66
☎ (206) 643-3409 . . 4432—132 Av SE, Bellevue, WA *98006*
Tudor MISS Mary A (Holloway—Mary A Tudor) | ☎ (206) 364-5643
Wells'61 . . . . | 4739 NE 178 St,
MISS Mara Holloway . . . . | Seattle, WA *98155*
MR Brett Holloway . . . . |
Tudor MR Robert C—IIT'74
☎ (773) 472-2671 . . 748 W Buena Av, Chicago, IL *60613*
Tufari JUNIORS MISS Ilaria . . see W H Peace 3d
Tufari JUNIORS MISS Letizia . . see W H Peace 3d
Tullis MR Paul R—Cal'92 . . see T C Clarke

Tullis MISS Tracy—Br'86 . . see T C Clarke
Tulloch MRS John JR (Eleanor Cline) . . . . Died at
Needham, MA Jly 30'92
Tulloch MR & MRS Marshall E (Marilyn W Holmes) | ☎ (302) 658-6440
SL'66.Myf.Dth'62 . . . . | 918 Blackshire Rd,
MISS Margaret B—at Vassar . . . . | Wawaset Park,
JUNIORS MISS Hilary E . . . . | Wilmington, DE
| *19805*
Tully MR & MRS Richard G (Marie F Towne) V'37.Tcy.Ncd.Rol'37
☎ (415) 453-4999 . . 34 Allen Av, Box 52, Ross, CA *94957*
Tunis MISS M Patricia
☎ (610) MU8-0525 . . 510 Fletcher Rd, Wayne, PA *19087-2215*
Tunnell MR Bertram A 3d—Ken'95 . . see W B Hewson JR
Tunnell MR & MRS Kenneth W (Joanne Huntington) | ☎ (610) 692-2519
Cr'51.Cr'52 . . . . | 307 Devon Lane,
MISS Pamela W—at ☎ (203) 453-5351 | West Chester, PA
73 New England Rd, Guilford, CT *06437* . . . . . | *19380*
MISS Jean M—Rich'86.Roch'90—at |
☎ (201) 798-4532 . . 158—8 St, Hoboken, NJ |
07030 . . . . |
Tunnell MISS Tory L . . see W B Hewson JR
Tunner DR & MRS William S (Sallie B Woodul) | ☎ (804) 784-3256
W&L'55.Va'60 . . . . | Braedon Farm,
MR William W . . . . | 1240 Shallow Well
MR Jonathan S . . . . | Rd, Manakin-Sabot,
| VA *23103*
Tunney MR & MRS Peter W (Anian R Pettit) | ☎ (510) 653-7115
SCal'70.Vh.Occ'60 . . . . | 28 Bellevue Av,
MISS Adrienne R . . . . | Piedmont, CA *94611*
JUNIORS MISS Catherine S . . . . |
Turben MR & MRS David C (Lisa A Miller) StLaw'88.Kt.Cr'88.Cwr'93
☎ (216) 338-4814 . . 12 Chelsea Court, South Russell, OH *44022*
Turben MASTER Jacob Codman (David C) . . . . Born at
Cleveland, OH Apr 30'96
Turchi MR & MRS P Arthur (Elizabeth W Wright)
☎ (011-33-1) 44-09-03-85 . . 11 rue Labie, 75017 Paris, France
Turman MRS Christopher M JR (Elisabeth F Morris)
☎ (215) 643-1162 . . Spring House Estates F122, 728 Norristown Rd,
Lower Gwynedd, PA *19002*
Turman MR & MRS Christopher M 3d (Molly O | ☎ (215) CH7-3097
Cornelius) Sth'63.Sg.Pc.Ncd.Va'57 | 8315 St Martin's
MR Timothy M—at U of Montana . . . . | Lane, Philadelphia,
MR Christopher M 4th—at Geo Wash'n . . . . | PA *19118*
Turnbull MISS Connor E—Br'94 . . see W H Luers
Turnbull MISS Ramsay F—Geo'92 . . see W H Luers
Turnbull MRS Thomas 3d (Clara Howard) Cr'14
☎ (941) 687-0744 . . 16 Lake Hunter Dv, Lakeland, FL *33803*
Turnbull MR & MRS Thomas R (Rosamond U Perry) ColC'64.P'59
☎ (970) 963-2888 . . Four Bar Ranch, PO Box 686, Carbondale,
CO *81623*
Turnbull MR & MRS William (Elizabeth T Howe) StA.Cly.P'30
☎ (908) 234-0174 . . Teviot Farm, 485 Lake Rd, Far Hills, NJ *07931*

Turner MR & MRS Arthur N (Anne L Grove) Chi.Ncd.H.Y'43.Cr'56 . . . .
MR Arthur N JR . . . .

of ☎ (617)354-6414
1010 Memorial Dv, Cambridge, MA *02138*
☎ (207) 389-2586 "Hidden Ledge" Small Point Rd, Phippsburg, ME *04562*

Turner MRS Burton B (Hale—Jean N Gilbert)
☎ (415) 931-9034 . . 3311 Jackson St, San Francisco, CA *94118*

Turner MR & MRS Carson P (Nicole M Rana) CalSt'91
9612 Twelve Pins Dv, Las Vegas, NV *89129*

Turner MR & MRS Charles T (Margaret P Belt) Elk.Md.Cda.Pn.P'40
☎ (410) 323-3320 . . 4 Beechdale Rd, Baltimore, MD *21210*

Turner MR & MRS Clifford O (Louise B Evans) StLaw'81.Sl.PhilaArt'73
☎ (540) 687-5309 . . "Gritton Mills" 37247 Mountville Rd, Middleburg, VA *20117*

Turner MR Edward Clarence (Alice Louise Boone) Md'51.Md'66.Lm.Ncd.
☎ (301) 934-9203 . . 109 Wiltshire Court, PO Box 292, La Plata, MD *20646*

Turner MR & MRS Evan H (Brenda W Bowman) BMr'49.Fi.Cv.Tv.C.Csp.Csn.H'49 . . . .
MR John W—Hampshire'84 . . . .

☎ (216) 371-3707 3071 N Park Blvd, Cleveland Heights, OH *44118*

Turner MR & MRS Howard M JR (Josephine DeC Ross) Tv.Ub.Chi.H.'40
☎ (617) 523-1392 . . 72 Mt Vernon St, Boston, MA *02108*

Turner MR & MRS J V Peter (Marybelle Zearfaus) WLib'63 . . . .
MR Daniel N . . . .
MR William Z . . . .

☎ (717) 898-8935 3348 Stillwell Dv, Lancaster, PA *17601*

Turner MR & MRS Jackson (Mary J Pentecost) . . . . .
MR Thomas J . . . .
MR Richard P—at ☎ (401) 846-8414 953 Wapping Rd, Middletown, RI *02842* . . . . . .

☎ (508) 358-2401 7 Nob Hill Rd, Wayland, MA *01778*

Turner MRS James F (Mary M Chilcoat) Cy.
☎ (410) 472-9009 . . "Champ de Bataille" 1418 Corbett Rd, Monkton, MD *21111*

Turner MR & MRS James J 3d (Anica B Walker) Pg.CarnM'48 . . . .
MR David H . . . .

☎ (412) 422-1323 1533 Valmont St, Pittsburgh, PA *15217*

Turner MR & MRS James Sinclair (Harris—Alexandra Waring) A.Aht'39
☎ (310) 271-8796 . . 1626 Gilcrest Dv, Beverly Hills, CA *90210*

Turner MRS John F (Margaret P Buckley)
177—19 St, Oakland, CA *94612*

Turner MR & MRS Le Baron (Bradford—Katharine S Makepeace) MaryB'49
☎ (401) 738-5807 . . "The Cottage" 12 Windward Circle, Warwick Neck, RI *02889*

Turner MR Le Baron—H'50
☎ (508) 526-1545 . . 9 Highwood Rd, Manchester, MA *01944*

Turner LT COL (RET) & MRS Robert F 3d (Patricia B Rhein) USA.JMU'74.JMU'77.Va'81
☎ (540) 253-5158 . . "Edge Hill" 6186 Herringdon Rd, The Plains, VA *20198*

Turner MR & MRS Scott W (Marin C Eustis) LakeF'76.On.LakeF'76 . . of
☎ (847) 295-3949 . . 58 E Marion Av, Lake Forest, IL *60045*
Huron Mountain Club, Big Bay, MI *49808*

Turner MRS T Arnold JR (Lillie J Trimble) Ark'46
☎ (601) 366-3450 . . 4121 Crane Blvd, Jackson, MS *39216*

Turner MRS Theodore Francis (de Rham—Ruxton—Jackson—Ruth E Ledyard) . . . . Died Mch 10'96

Turner MRS Thomas (Caroline Embry) GeoW'46.CtCol'59 . . of
☎ (757) 565-1133 . . 5315 Patriots Colony Dv, Williamsburg, VA *23185*
☎ (011-33-1) 44-09-98-84 . . 8 rue Vernier, 75017 Paris, France

Turner DR Thomas B—Mv.Gi.StJColl'21.Md'25
☎ (410) 669-1021 . . 1426 Park Av, Baltimore, MD *21217*

Turner MR & MRS Thomas W (Elisabeth R Gebhardt) Hlns'83.VPI'81
2828 Titleist Dv, Salem, VA *24153*

Turner MR William G . . . .
MISS Katherine S . . . .
MR John B . . . .
MR William M . . . .

☎ (412) 371-7679 418 W Swissvale Av, Pittsburgh, PA *15218*

Turnure MISS Barbara F—Hartw'84
☎ (310) 399-8566 . . 245 Main St, Apt 108, Venice, CA *90291*

Turnure MRS David A (Marian V Wilson)
☎ (941) 966-2035 . . PO Box 176, 4015 Casey Key Rd, Osprey, FL *34229-0176*

Turnure MR & MRS Michael de B (Friend—Joan H Anderson) V'55.P'57
☎ (860) 435-2928 . . Lakeville, CT *06039*

Turnure MR Richard L—Cl'90.Cl'95
☎ (212) 932-1362 . . 434 Riverside Dv, New York, NY *10025*

Turpin MRS Carter M (Joane Barroll) . . . .
MISS Brett R—*see Dilatory Domiciles* . . . .
MR Carter M JR—at ☎ (757) 422-3180 604 Mediterranean Av, Virginia Beach, VA *23451* . . . .
MR Traynter B—🦀—at ☎ (561) 848-0110 4906D Poinsettia Av, West Palm Beach, FL *33407* . . . .
MR Coalter C—at 13 S 17 St, Apt B, Richmond, VA *23219* . . . .

☎ (804) 282-5388 6506 Edgehill Rd, Richmond, VA *23226*

Turpin MR & MRS John K (Bigio—Margery S Dillon) Nyc.Eh.Shcc.Md'67 . . . .
MR John D . . . .

☎ (908) 766-6363 Lake Rd, PO Box 98, Far Hills, NJ *07931*

Turullols MR & MRS José L A (Natalie M Burke) . . .
JUNIORS MR Alejandro D . . . .

☎ (203) 966-4870 355 Jelliff Mill Rd, New Canaan, CT *06840*

Tustian MR Alexander K—Del'88
☎ (302) 984-1302 . . 1601 N Broom St, Wilmington, DE *19806*

Tustian MISS Elizabeth E—Bost'86
☎ (617) 924-4764 . . 17 Fairview Av, Watertown, MA *02172*

Tustian MR & MRS Richard E (Jeanne B Borie) Pa'62.Tor'55.Pa'62
☎ (301) 469-6088 . . 9408 Seddon Rd, Bethesda, MD *20817*

Tuten MR & MRS John C JR (Margaret G Evans) Me.Ph.Rc.Rr.Pg.Cc.Myf.Y'66.Pa'69 . . . .
MISS Virginia E. . . . .
JUNIORS MR John C III . . . .

☎ (610) LA7-1609 128 Ashwood Rd, Villanova, PA *19085*

Tuthill MR & MRS John B (Hillis—Elizabeth A Rice) ☎ (214) 363-5752
Ind'39.Ind'39.H'43 . . . . 11745 Valleydale
MR Paul A . . . . Dv, Dallas, TX
MR David W *75230*
Tuthill MR & MRS John B JR (Carol J Weakley) ☎ (214) 369-4893
Cal'67 . . . . 7230 N Jan Mar Dv,
MISS Wells Lauren . . . . Dallas, TX
JUNIORS MR John B 3d *75230-3117*
Tutt MRS Charles L JR (LeMieux—Mildred Dailey)
☎ (719) 473-6418 . . 20 Loma Linda Dv, Colorado Springs, CO *80906*
Tutt MR & MRS R Thayer JR (Melani L Middleton)
BrooksInst'83.Rcn.Coa.P'77.Duke'79
☎ (719) 635-7219 . . 8 Broadmoor Av, Colorado Springs, CO *80906*
Tutt MR & MRS William Bullard (Frances Campbell) | ☎ (719) 473-0788
MR William Benjamin . . . . 51A Marland Rd,
Colorado Springs,
CO *80906*
Tuttle MISS Christeen C—Conn'73
☎ (216) 321-4628 . . 2290 N St James P'kway, Cleveland, OH *44106*
Tuttle MR Howard McD . . . . Died at
Boca Raton, FL Apr 25'96
Tuttle MISS Jane L—Cr'82
☎ (206) 775-5628 . . 7723—209 St SW, Edmonds, WA *98020*
Twede MR & MRS Charles R (Pollock—Elizabeth A Kerwin)
On.Wa.UWash'47.UWash'50 . . of
☎ (847) 234-3827 . . 77 Pembroke Dv, Lake Forest, IL *60045*
☎ (808) 667-7113 . . ''Puamana'' 136-1 Pualei Dv, Lahaina, Maui,
HI *96761*
Tweed MR & MRS Bruce P (Haan—Barbara J Olson) Nw'49.NCar'43
☎ (602) 954-6626 . . 83 Biltmore Estates, Phoenix, AZ *85016*
Tweedy MISS Margot M—Y'77
☎ (212) 722-3977 . . 114 E 90 St, New York, NY *10128*
Twerdahl MR Timothy D—Rc.Ham'91
☎ (212) 876-4765 . . 27 E 94 St, New York, NY *10128*
Twichell MR & MRS Jonathan E (Sophia L Brown) Pa'89.Dar.Ncd.Br'88
☎ (773) 528-8408 . . 3844 N Sheffield Av, Apt 204, Chicago, IL *60613*
Twining MR & MRS Alexander C (Nell M Willis)
Bost'74.Y'83.Y.'75.Y'77 . . of
☎ (914) 337-3121 . . 50 Highland Circle, Bronxville, NY *10708*
☎ (860) 434-2844 . . ''Toad Hall'' Sill Lane, Old Lyme, CT *06371*
Twining MR Edmund S 4th . . see M D Wheelock JR
Twining MR & MRS Kinsley (Cynthia C Thébaud) Yn.Y'41
☎ (860) 434-2844 . . Box 277, Sill Lane, Old Lyme, CT *06371*
Twining CAPT Robert B—USN. . . . . Died at
Wayne, PA Aug 21'95
Twining MR & MRS Robert C (Barbara C Chiampi) . | ☎ (609) 653-0895
MR Robert C . . . . 210 Joanne Dv, Egg
Harbor Township,
NJ *08234-7516*
Twining MR Taylor P . . see M D Wheelock JR
Twiss MR Donald L—Un.Bm.Cw.Ll.Lm.Vca.Wt. | ☎ (914) 591-8992
Coa.Va'65 . . . . 5 Hillside Terr,
MISS Louise E—at Princeton . . . . Irvington-on-
JUNIORS MR Russell W . . . . Hudson, NY *10533*

Twiss MR & MRS John R JR (Mary H Sheldon) | ☎ (703) 790-9449
Rcp.An.Mt.Y'61 . . . . 901 Turkey Run Rd,
MISS Alison M—at Kenyon . . . . McLean, VA *22101*
MISS Emily E . . . .
MR John S—at Middlebury . . . .
Twitmyer MR & MRS Robert Y (J Elise Tucker) | ☎ (610) 687-3677
Sa.Me.Pa'58.Pa'96 . . . . 502 Brookside Av,
MISS Julie E—Laf'92.Me . . . . St Davids, PA
MR Robert T—Me.Pa'90.Pa'96 . . . . | *19087*
Tye MR & MRS Robert D (Cynthia S Faville) V'76.Ky'74.Pa'77
☎ (212) 207-8396 . . 320 E 57 St, New York, NY *10022*
Tyler MR B Langdon (Louise B Gay)
☎ (617) 275-5954 . . 402 Winthrop Terr, Bedford, MA *01730*
Tyler MRS C Perin (Burling—Carnealia A Perin) Msq.Sl.
☎ (202) 333-8727 . . 2812 R St NW, Washington, DC *20007*
Tyler MISS Cecily W . . see A T Ogden 2d
Tyler MR & MRS George F JR (Josephine B Doughten)
Pc.Sg.Rb.Ph.H'38.Pa'54
☎ (215) CH8-0941 . . 600 W Hartwell Lane, Philadelphia, PA *19118*
Tyler MR & MRS Harold R JR (Barbara L Eaton) C.Csn.P'43.Cl'49
☎ (860) 435-8053 . . 14 Tokone Hills Rd, Lakeville, CT *06039*
Tyler MR & MRS Henry M (Susan J Janis) SUNY'79
☎ (207) 685-4422 . . Thunder Castle Rd, Box 116, Readfield, ME *04355*
Tyler MR & MRS John G (Mary Remick) . . of
☎ (508) 627-9595 . . SR 149A, Edgartown, MA *02539*
☎ (207) 685-4430 . . PO Box 351, Readfield, ME *04355*
Tyler MR John R—P'74.Vt'79
☎ (703) 548-5447 . . 304 Prince St, Alexandria, VA *22314*
Tyler DR & MRS Jonathan M (Wilhelmina R M Kearns)
BMr'77.Bost'80.Swth'76.H'80
☎ (403) 433-7723 . . 11704—91 Av, Edmonton, Alberta T6G 1A9,
Canada
Tyler MISS Mary T—Ty'94 . . see A T Ogden 2d
Tyler MR & MRS Sidney F JR (Betsy F Whitin) Vh.Cc.H'54
☎ (818) 793-4751 . . 969 S Madison Av, Pasadena, CA *91106*
Tyler MRS Thomas S (Douglass—Marian Phelps) . . . . Married at
Lake Forest, IL
Pawlick MR Albert (late Otto A) . . . . Apr 20'96
Tyler JUNIORS MR Wat H . . see A T Ogden 2d
Tyner MRS John H (Joan K Martin) Cly. . . . . of ☎ (508)945-0445
MR Christopher M—at ☎ (310) 457-7653 ''Turtle Bay''
4355 Ocean View, Malibu, CA *90265* . . . . 248 Old Harbor Rd,
Chatham, MA *02633*
☎ (212) UN1-4093
300 E 71 St,
New York, NY
10021
Tyng MRS Lila (Luce—Lila R Hotz) Cly.Cda.Ncd.
☎ (908) 234-0462 . . ''Lu Shan'' Rte 206, Gladstone, NJ *07934*
Tysen MRS John C (Manny—Constance L Lazo) BMr'44.Cly.
☎ (212) 472-1782 . . 157 E 75 St, New York, NY *10021*

Tyson MRS Anna Starr (Anna N Starr) Ws'59.Pc.Msq. . . . . of ☎ (215)233-9358 8530 Ardmore Av, Wyndmoor, PA *19038*
  MISS Anna B—at ☎ (617) 489-5546 25 Gale Rd, Belmont, MA *02178* . . . .
  ☎ (860) 767-3187 30 Hemlock Dv, Essex, CT *06426*

Tyson MR & MRS Anthony N (Lori J Marsden) Bnd'82.CUNY'86
  ☎ (516) 329-2350 . . PO Box 1381, 55 Osborne Lane, East Hampton, NY *11937*

Tyson MR & MRS Charles R (Barbara Kurtz) Ph.Sg.Ac.Ncd.
  ☎ (215) 628-2468 . . 225 Mathers Rd, Ambler, PA *19002-4109*

Tyson MRS Charles W (Frances M Kinney) V'34
  ☎ (505) 425-6369 . . Rte 1, Box 373, Las Vegas, NM *87701*

Tyson MRS Christopher G (Christiane J E Muller) V'54.Godd'77.Y'52.Y'57 . . . . ☎ (305) 446-1695 1498 Sevilla Av, Coral Gables, FL *33134*
  MR Edward S—at 6226 Miller Rd, South Miami, FL *33155* . . . .
  MR Alexander L . . . .

Tyson MISS Helen R (Shettle—Buchheit—Helen R Tyson) . . . . ☎ (207) 244-5481 ''Cove House'' PO Box 628, Somesville, Mt Desert, ME *04660*
  MISS Ann B Shettle—at Boston, MA . . . . . .
  MR Arthur F Shettle 2d—at Salisbury, MD *21801* . . . .

Tyson MR & MRS John 2d (Holly O Hoch) Bost'85.Duke'81
  ☎ (610) 688-6473 . . 241 Atlee Rd, Wayne, PA *19087*

Tyson MASTER John 3d (John 2d) . . . . Born at Bryn Mawr, PA Feb 18'96

Tyson MISS Julia Jane (Anthony N) . . . . Born at Southampton, NY May 27'96

U

Ufford MR & MRS Charles W JR (I Letitia Wheeler) Rdc'58.Hn.H'53
  ☎ (609) 921-8085 . . 150 Mercer St, Princeton, NJ *08540*

Ughetta MR & MRS William C JR (Margaret C Cist) Ncd.P.'82.Cl'84
  ☎ (212) 879-7360 . . 55 E 72 St, New York, NY *10021*

Uhle MRS Charles A W (Janet G Patterson) Cda.
  ☎ (302) 239-6472 . . Cokesbury Village, Box 81, 726 Loveville Rd, Hockessin, DE *19707*

Uihlein MR & MRS Edgar J (Lucia L Ellis) Btn.On.Cas.Wa. . . . . ☎ (847) 234-0198 1001 Sheridan Rd, Lake Bluff, IL *60044*
  MR Edgar J 3d—at 2407 Whitehall Manor, Lawrence, KS *66049* . . . .

Uihlein MISS Linda R—Swb'77
  ☎ (804) 973-6015 . . Little Owl Farm, 1842 Davis Shop Rd, Earlysville, VA *22936*

Uihlein MISS Lucia L (Higgins—Rio—Lucia L Uihlein) . . . . ☎ (941) 383-7245 715 Land's End Dv, Longboat Key, FL *34228*
  MISS Maura E Higgins—at 2000 N Lincoln Park W, Chicago, IL *60614* . . . .

Ulam MR Adam B—Br'42.H'47
148A Coolidge Hill, Cambridge, MA *02138*

Ulam MRS Burgwin (Mary H Burgwin) Rdc'52 . . . . ☎ (804) 979-7344 530 Kellogg Dv, Charlottesville, VA *22903-4642*
  MR Alexander—at New York, NY . . . .
  MR Joseph H—at 380 Riverside Dv, New York, NY *10025* . . . .

Ulman MR & MRS Cornelius M (Barbara W Hajek) Rdc'62.Lm.Ds.P'60 . . . . ☎ (516) 423-4436 16 Forest Dv, Lloyd Neck, Huntington, NY *11743*
  MISS Katharine Van R—H'92—at 440 S Chauncey Av, Apt 3, West Lafayette, IN *47906* . . . .
  DR Morrison—P'88.Mit'94—at
  ☎ (415) 965-9771 . . 400 Ortega Av, Apt 101, Mountain View, CA *94040* . . . .

Ulman MR & MRS Stephen Van R (Martha C Heck) Wheat'59.S.Lm.P'54.H'59
  ☎ (516) 922-5919 . . 10 Tennis Court Rd, Oyster Bay, NY *11771*

Umberger MR & MRS Max J (Julia S Johnston) Penn'92
  ☎ (610) 695-8972 . . 207 Charleston Greene, Malvern, PA *19355*

Umstattd MR & MRS James M (Elizabeth M Coles) Au.Myf.Dar.P'51
  ☎ (610) 525-7589 . . 733 Stoke Rd, Villanova, PA *19085*

Underhill MR Charles S—Wms'34 . . . . S7491 Center St, West Falls, NY *14170*
  MR James R—at 152 Willow Breeze Rd, Buffalo, NY *14223* . . . .

Underhill MRS Irving S (Elizabeth B King) . . see J R Fegela

Underhill MR R Kirk—Pcu.Sfy.Plg.StJ.Cp.Cal'28
  ☎ (415) 461-1566 . . The Tamalpais, 501 Via Casitas, Greenbrae, CA *94904*

Underwood MRS Agnes C (Agnes W Cochran) CtCol'63.Cl'76.Mt.Csn. . . . . of 3601 Lowell St NW, Washington, DC *20016*
  JUNIORS MR Frederic G W . . . .
  ☎ (802) 462-3686 PO Box 694, Middlebury, VT *05753*

Underwood MR & MRS Frederic B (Martin—Alison R Cady) Mid'71.Gv.Md.H'63.Cl'66.Cl'73
  ☎ (540) 955-1452 . . ''Ware's Mill'' Rte 2, Box 3865, Berryville, VA *22611*

Unger MR & MRS Peter J (Monica L Smith) Ws'63.Cda.Dar.Y . . .of
  ☎ (212) 753-4414 . . 200 E 66 St, New York, NY *10021*
  ☎ (516) 283-5745 . . Hill St, PO Box 732, Southampton, NY *11969*

Unruh MR & MRS Charles L (Mary L Sexton) NH'92.NH'91
  ☎ (011-49-6221) 351236 . . 10-1 Botheplatz, 69126 Heidelberg, Germany

Unterman JUNIORS MR Ian H . . see MRS T H Drew

Unterman JUNIORS MISS Megan D . . see MRS T H Drew

Untermeyer MR & MRS Charles G (Diana C Kendrick) Va'84.Sl.H'68
  ☎ (713) 840-0146 . . 3608 Locke Lane, Houston, TX *77027-4004*

Untermeyer MRS Milton F (Hill—Karel A Fry)
  ☎ (561) 659-3787 . . 525 S Flagler Dv, PH-3C, West Palm Beach, FL *33401*

Upchurch MR & MRS Samuel E JR (Cheryl J Viar) Swb'74.Cy.David'74 . . . . ☎ (205) 879-8478 3828 Forest Glen Dv, Birmingham, AL *35213*
  MISS Shannon V . . . .
  MISS Katherine V . . . .
  JUNIORS MISS Jeanne A . . . .

Upham MR & MRS Charles E (Frances Johnson) Stan'48
  ☎ (415) 928-6031 . . 945 Green St, San Francisco, CA *94133*

Upson MR & MRS Christopher L (Dana J French) Rob'tM'84.ONorth'83
  ☎ (540) 869-3659 . . 5086 Laura Dv, Stephens City, VA *22655*

Upson MR & MRS David R (Clara C Tracy)　　　　☎ (216) 991-9646
CtCol'45.Cwr'53.P'36.H'38 . . . . 3220 Green Rd,
MISS Florence T—Aht'77.Cwr'83—at　　　　　　Beachwood, OH
  ☎ (703) 243-6434 . . 2000 N Adams St,　　　　*44122*
Arlington, VA *22201* . . . .

Upson MR & MRS David R JR (Charlene Volpe) Nova'89.Se'93
  ☎ (954) 922-1289 . . 1426 Van Buren St, Hollywood, FL *33020*

Upson MRS J Warren (Grace S Fisher) Ncd.
  ☎ (203) 264-8496 . . East Hill Woods, 216 Birchwood, Southbury,
CT *06488*

Upson MRS K Darrow (Katherine C Darrow)　　　37 Forest Ridge Rd,
Stph'62.York'80 . . . . Weston, MA *02193*
MISS Mary Carter . . . .
MISS Martha T . . . . |

Upson MR Thomas F—Sar.Cw.W&J'63.Conn'68 . .　☎ (203) 753-1193
MR Secor . . . . 827 Oronoke Rd,
MR Chauncey J . . . . Apt 10-1,
　　　　　　　　　　　　　　　　　　　　　　Waterbury, CT
　　　　　　　　　　　　　　　　　　　　　　06708

Upson MR W Terrell—Y'60.Nu'68
  ☎ (941) 649-0256 . . 4055 Crayton Rd, Naples, FL *34103*

Upthegrove MRS C Gatch (Caroline O'F Gatch) Cy.　☎ (314) WY7-1594
MR William JR . . . . 9240 Clayton Rd,
MR Daniel 4th . . . . St Louis, MO *63124*

Upthegrove MRS Caroline O'F (Harrington—Caroline O'F Upthegrove)
  ☎ (314) 968-4850 . . 1453 Thrush Place, St Louis, MO *63144*

Upton MR & MRS J Gordon (Barbara Allen) V'43.Chi.Myf.Dar.Hn.P'44
  ☎ (603) 472-3433 . . "The Farm" PO Box 10397, Bedford,
NH *03110-0397*

Upton MR John D—Y'32 . . . . 185 Southport
MISS Mary D—at ☎ (213) 932-1160　　　　　　Woods Dv,
354 S Orange Grove Av, Los Angeles, CA *90036*　Southport, CT *06490*

Upton MRS John R (Anna L Sloan) Bur.Tcy.
  ☎ (415) 921-8927 . . 2440 Pacific Av, San Francisco, CA *94115*

Upton MR & MRS John R JR (Hall—Janet Sassoon) . . of
  ☎ (415) 775-8789 . . 2260 Pacific Av, San Francisco, CA *94115-1435*
  ☎ (707) 942-6553 . . 1112 Pine St, Calistoga, CA *94515-1734*

Upton MR & MRS King (Letitia Brown) H'33
  ☎ (617) 864-1663 . . 73 Francis Av, Cambridge, MA *02138*

Upton MR Richard W—Colby'69 . . of
  ☎ (212) 988-9619 . . 512 E 83 St, New York, NY *10028*
  ☎ (860) 567-9272 . . "Doll House" 153 Norfolk Rd, PO Box 372,
Litchfield, CT *06759*

Upton MR & MRS W Sloan (Priscilla Belmont)　　☎ (707) 963-4688
StJ.Pcu.Fr.SFr'66 . . . . 1533 Kearney St,
MISS Caroline P . . . . St Helena, CA
MISS Cecily A S *94574*

Upton MR & MRS W Vincent (Imogen R Richards)　of ☎ (908)756-4398
BMr'30.Mon'32.Ill'37 . . . . 955 Kensington Av,
MISS Emily F—MtH'71.Ill'74 . . . . Plainfield, NJ *07060*
　　　　　　　　　　　　　　　　　　　　　　☎ (860) 567-9272
　　　　　　　　　　　　　　　　　　　　　　"Doll House"
　　　　　　　　　　　　　　　　　　　　　　153 Norfolk Rd,
　　　　　　　　　　　　　　　　　　　　　　Litchfield, CT *06759*

Urbahn MR & MRS Eric M (Briggs—Clara O　　☎ (508) 257-4385
Rosengarten) Mt.Nyc.Ny.Ariz'73 ⚓ . . . . "South-by-East"
MR Jason R Briggs—Cl'94 . . . . 101 Low Beach Rd,
　　　　　　　　　　　　　　　　　　　　　　Siasconset, MA
　　　　　　　　　　　　　　　　　　　　　　02564

Urbahn MR & MRS John A (Deyanne F Miller) OWes'79.Myf.Ht.Conn'83
  ☎ (617) 489-0380 . . 69 Drew Rd, Belmont, MA *02178*

Urbahn MR & MRS Maximilian O 3d (Jennifer A Keith)
Wheat'81.Myf.Y'80.H'84
  ☎ (703) 556-0487 . . 8198 Hunting Hill Lane, McLean, VA *22102*

Urban MR & MRS George P 3d (Jean T Enos)　　☎ (508) 785-1126
D.Miami'66.Pa'69.Canisius'71 . . . . 2 Southfield Dv,
MISS Christy T—at Noble & Greenough . . . . Dover, MA *02030*
JUNIORS MR David P—at Noble & Greenough . . .

Urban MR & MRS Henry Z (Ruth de M Wickwire) Cy.St.Bf.Ts.Nyc.G.Y'43
  ☎ (716) 885-5630 . . 57 Tudor Place, Buffalo, NY *14222*

Urban MR & MRS Henry Z JR (Margaret A Kroth)
SUNY'83.St.Cy.Ham'77.Suff'80
95 Wagon Wheel Dv, East Amherst, NY *14051*

Urban MR & MRS Ward A W (Lisa M Lausier) AmU'81.Yn.Ham'82.Dth'88
  ☎ (914) 921-0156 . . 20 Ellsworth St, Rye, NY *10580*

Urban MASTER Ward Wickwire (Ward A W) . . . . Born at
　　　　　　　　　　　　　　　　　　　　　Rye, NY Dec 27'95

Urfer MR & MRS Richard P (Cynthia L Vaughan)　☎ (201) 538-1966
Swb'62.Unn.Mg.Wis'58.H'64 . . . . Willowbrook Farm,
MISS Jocelyn L . . . . Blue Mill Rd,
MISS Courtney V . . . . Morristown, NJ
MR Gilbert C F *07960*

Urmston MR Raymond J JR
  ☎ (201) 838-2474 . . 244 North Rd, Kinnelon, NJ *07405*

Urmston MRS Thomas H (Maude S Williams) Wil.Ncd.
  ☎ (302) 652-4775 . . Stonegates 72, 4031 Kennett Pike, Greenville,
DE *19807*

Urquhart MASTER Ian Robert (g—Kenneth T Urquhart of Urquhart) . . . . .
　　　　　　　　　　　　　　　　　　　　Born at Akron, OH Jun 20'95

Urquhart MAJ & MRS L Lionel B (Elisa A Longville)
USMC.Akron'89.Cc.Vmi'84
  ☎ (330) 773-9055 . . 303 N Firestone Blvd, Akron, OH *44301*

Urquhart of Urquhart MR & MRS Kenneth T (Mary Virginia Berdou)
StMarysDom'59.NOlns'74.Cc.Loy'56.Tul'58
  ☎ (504) 835-1343 . . 507 Jefferson Park Av, Jefferson, LA *70121*

Urry MR & MRS James A (Nathalie P Comfort)
PineM'87.BankSt'89.Rc.B.Pr.Cly.Br'76.Pa'81
  ☎ (516) 676-3751 . . 19 Meudon Dv, PO Box 242, Locust Valley,
NY *11560*

Urschel MR & MRS William P JR (Alexandra S Halsey) P'78.P'78
  ☎ (805) 969-6468 . . 226 E Mountain Dv, Santa Barbara,
CA *93108-1028*

Urstadt MR & MRS James Jeffrey (Susan H Powers)　☎ (203) 966-6111
Wheat'64.Ds.Dth'62 . . . . 103 Brushy Ridge
MR Bryant E . . . . Rd, New Canaan,
MR Jeffrey J . . . . CT *06840*
JUNIORS MISS Elizabeth C . . . .

Ursul MR & MRS George R (Ruth H Baker)　　　☎ (617) 738-5656
Sb.H.McM'60 . . . . 212 Dean Rd,
MISS Christina E . . . . Brookline, MA
　　　　　　　　　　　　　　　　　　　　　　02146

Utgoff CAPT & MRS Vadym V (Miriam D Scott)
An.Ct.Sl.Dc.Ncd.USN'39 ⚓
  ☎ (410) 268-8840 . . 2 Ridge Rd, Wardour, Annapolis, MD *21401-1201*
Uzielli MRS Barbara B (Achenbach—Barbara L Borkland) Ncd.
  ☎ (212) 472-7744 . . 66 E 79 St, New York, NY *10021-0233*
Uzielli MISS Caroline P—Rol'83
  ☎ (212) 274-9076 . . 105 Sullivan St, New York, NY *10012*

V

Vagliano MR & MRS Alexander M (Via—Pais—Sara E Ector) AScott'63.Va'71.B.H'49 . . . .
  MR Justin C—at U of Vt . . . . | of ☎ (860)542-5539 Sunset Ridge Farm, Norfolk, CT *06058* 25 Central Park W, New York, NY *10023*
Vagliano MRS Shirley L (Shirley T Lynch) . . of
  ☎ (212) 288-6973 . . 3 E 77 St, New York, NY *10021*
  ☎ (011-41-30) 4-36-73 . . Huus Am Bach, 3780 Gstaad, Switzerland
Vail MR & MRS Donald (Priscilla A Luke)
Man'vl'73.Rc.Chr.Ny.Bgt.Cly.P'42.H'48 . . . . . . | ☎ (914) 234-7423 760 Guard Hill Rd, Bedford, NY *10506*
  MR D Angus—at 90 Park Av, New York, NY *10016* . . . . |
Vail MR & MRS Gregory H (L Adalyn Esler)
  ☎ (714) 499-1075 . . 32006 Sunset Av, Laguna Beach, CA *92677*
Vail MRS Herman Lansing (Gleason—Mary L Frackelton)
Ws'24.ClevArt'27.Un.It.
  ☎ (216) 752-1455 . . 13901 Shaker Blvd, Cleveland, OH *44120*
Vail MISS Siri J (Lacey—Siri J Vail) Skd'75.Cly.Mds.Ne.
  ☎ (212) 685-1364 . . 77 Park Av, Apt 6C, New York, NY *10016*
Vail MR & MRS Thomas Van H (Iris W Jennings)
Bhm.Ln.Kt.Cv.Cly.P'48 . . of
  ☎ (216) 247-7066 . . ''L'Ecurie'' 14950 County Line Rd, Hunting Valley, OH *44022*
  ☎ (912) 435-6955 . . Wiregrass Plantation, 6113 Jenkins Rd, Albany, GA *31705*
Vail MR & MRS Thomas Van H JR (Julia P Barlow)
Br'81.Va'84.Kt.Geo'78.Va'84
  22775 Douglas Rd, Shaker Heights, OH *44122*
Vaill MR John A—Rut'41
  ☎ (212) 535-2864 . . 108 E 81 St, New York, NY *10028*
Vaillant DR & MRS George E (Caroline O Brown)
Melb'61.H'55 . . . . | ☎ (802) 785-4909 Box 170, East Thetford, VT *05043*
  MISS C Joanna . . . . |
Vaino MR & MRS Jaan E (Sharon L Worthing)
Bnd'75.Ford'78.Y.Cl'83.Nu'89
  ☎ (212) 316-9053 . . 510 Cathedral P'kway, New York, NY *10025*
Valdes MISS F Kelly . . see MRS D Mackie
Valdes MR John Terhune—BtP.Evg.P'45
  ☎ (561) 833-6544 . . 1515 S Flagler Dv, West Palm Beach, FL *33401*
Valentine MR & MRS Bruce (Virginia P Gray) Y'54 . | ☎ (303) 377-3249 1110 Race St, Denver, CO *80206*
  MISS Elizabeth (Gerber—Elizabeth Valentine) Roch'81—at ☎ (716) 244-4085 265 Milburn St, Rochester, NY *14607* . . . . |

Valentine MR & MRS E Massie (Van Alen—Virginia Guest) Srr.BtP.Va'56
  ☎ (804) 353-1579 . . 204 Lockgreen Court, Richmond, VA *23226*
Valentine MRS E Miles (Landreth—Joy Drew-Bear) Rr.Ac.
  ☎ (610) 869-8149 . . ''Knockmuira'' PO Box 397, Unionville, PA *19375*
Valentine MRS Edward R (Ophuls—Carol Lapham)
  ☎ (805) 969-4627 . . 1522 E Mountain Dv, Santa Barbara, CA *93108*
Valentine DR Edward S—Geo'72.NYMed'78
  ☎ (212) 627-0042 . . 51 Charles St, New York, NY *10014-2656*
Valentine MR & MRS Garrison L (Rosslyn M Rutter) WWAust'67.A.Tex'59
  ☎ (970) 476-0158 . . 278 E Hanson Ranch Rd, Vail, CO *81657*
Valentine MR & MRS Garrison N (Read—Inge C Froelich) Munich'62.Y'50.Y'64 . . . . | 17 Deer Meadow Rd, Durham, NH *03824*
  MISS Carolyn A Read—Colby'94—in US Peace Corps, Madagascar . . . . |
Valentine MISS Glynn—Vt'88 . . see R M Gardiner
Valentine MR & MRS H Stuart 4th (Kara K Mulcahy)
VillaN'92.Shcc.Yn.Y'86
  ☎ (908) 234-1388 . . 47 E Fox Chase Rd, Chester, NJ *07930*
Valentine MR & MRS John H (Elizabeth H Hiam) Un.Chi.Mid'49
  ☎ (508) 369-4860 . . 566 Acton St, Carlisle, MA *01741*
Valentine MR M Pratt . . see E T Boyd JR
Valentine MISS Sarah McK—Sth'58
  ☎ (512) 472-2803 . . 1707 W 29 St, Austin, TX *78703*
Valenzuela-Bock MR & MRS Alejandro (Anne A Du Bois) Sg.Wes'70.Pa'79 . . . . | ☎ (914) 967-9362 32 Cayuga St, Rye, NY *10580*
  MR Carroll A . . . . |
  JUNIORS MR Andres—at Kent . . . . |
Valeur MRS Robert (Lois Perkins)
  ☎ (202) 234-3203 . . 2737 Devonshire Place NW, Apt 122, Washington, DC *20008-3479*
Valiunas, Dominicus R & Lynn, Letitia C—Sth'71.Aht'71
  ☎ (803) 577-9216 . . 18 Queen St, Charleston, SC *29401*
Vallender MR Charles F 3d—Cvc.C.Mt.Sl.Y'61. Y'64 . . . . | ☎ (202) 966-1194 4000 Massachusetts Av NW, Apt 1514, Washington, DC *20016*
  MISS Prentiss W—NCar'92—at
  ☎ (202) 965-0922 . . 4564 MacArthur Blvd NW, Apt 103, Washington, DC *20007* . . . . |
  MISS Perrin K—NCar'94—at ☎ (970) 845-9081 PO Box 21-722, Avon, CO *81620* . . . . |
Van Alen MRS James H (Vanderlip—Candace B Alig)
Pr.K.Srb.Cvc.BtP.Evg.Cly.Ne.Dll . . .of
  ☎ (809) 773-7833 . . PO Box 1575, Christiansted, St Croix, VI *00821*
  ☎ (516) 621-6466 . . ''Penny Pond'' Greenvale, NY *11548*
  ☎ (401) 846-6564 . . ''Avalon'' Ocean Av, Newport, RI *02840*
Van Alen MR & MRS James L (Maris I Macleod)
Au.Un.Y'58.H'60 . . . . | ☎ (914) 677-9569 Rte 343, Box 668, Millbrook, NY *12545*
  MR James G—at Coll of Charleston . . . . |
Van Alen MR & MRS James L 2d (Jeanne de B Bartholomew) Cts.Gm.Rc.Rd.Y'57 . . . . | ☎ (610) 353-3417 Indian Run Farm, 936 Plumsock Rd, Newtown Square, PA *19073*
  MR James L JR . . . . |
  MR Alexander S—at 426 La Porte Av, Ft Collins, CO *80520* . . . . |
  MR Robert B . . . . |

Van Alen MR & MRS William L (Elizabeth B Kent)
Rcn.Rd.Ph.Rcp.Me.Gm.Ssk.Rb.B.Ac.Cly.Myf.Cam'29. Pa'37 . . of
☎ (561) 626-1134 . . 11701 Lost Tree Way, North Palm Beach,
FL *33408*
☎ (610) 353-7010 . . Dunwoody Village CH25, 3500 West Chester Pike,
Newtown Square, PA *19073*
☎ (207) 276-3213 . . ''Clifton Cottage'' Clifton Dock Rd,
Northeast Harbor, ME *04662*

Van Alen MR & MRS William L JR (Kanzler—Judith A Frost)
Srr.Ph.Gm.Rc.Ssk.Pa'57.VillaN'62
☎ (610) 644-9090 . . 975 Delchester Rd, Newtown Square, PA *19073*

Van Alstyne MRS Margaret H (Margaret R Hudson) | ☎ (608) 238-1562
V'49 . . . . | 3423 Sunset Dv,
MISS Gretchen A . . . . | Madison, WI *53705*

Van Alstyne MR & MRS W Scott JR (Marion G Walker)
Fla'58.Fla'70.Rv.Hl.Buf'48.Wis'50.Wis'53.Wis'54
☎ (352) 378-5039 . . 2726 SW 5 Place, Gainesville, FL *32607-3144*

Vanaman MISS Patricia A . . see W G Saunders

van Amerongen MR & MRS Jan A T (Patricia A Sager) Pa'60
☎ (201) 335-5824 . . 97 Kenilworth Rd, Mountain Lakes, NJ *07046*

Van Antwerp MR Theodore C—St.Cybf.
☎ (941) 365-6449 . . 988 Blvd of the Arts, Apt 510, Sarasota, FL *34236*

Van Antwerp MR & MRS Thomas B (Gypsie B Bear) | ☎ (770) 352-0470
Swb'73.Va'72 | PO Box 941010,
MISS Virginia O . . . . | Atlanta, GA *31141*
JUNIORS MR T Bragg JR . . . . |

Van Arsdale MRS Barbara B (Barbara Baker) . . . . . | ☎ (908) 449-6828
MR John H . . . . | 912 Sea Girt Av,
| Sea Girt, NJ *08750*

Van Arsdall MR & MRS Michael G (Alicia H Clark) David'90.RI'92.RI'92
☎ (310) 820-1466 . . 11954 Mayfield Av, Apt 5, Los Angeles, CA *90049*

van Beuren MR & MRS John A (Hope Hill) | ☎ (401) 847-3691
Unn.Y'54 . . . . | ''Sonnenhof''
MISS Andrea—Vt'88—at ☎ (212) 996-2454 | 15 Indian Av,
23 E 94 St, Apt 5B, New York, NY *10128* . . . . | Middletown, RI
| *02842*

van Beuren MR Michael M . . see MRS P W Archbold

Van Bibber MISS Katherine—BMr'24
☎ (410) 549-7452 . . Fairhaven, 7200 Third Av, Sykesville, MD *21784*

van Buren MRS Elizabeth P (Elizabeth P Prince) Chi.Myf.
☎ (617) 876-9625 . . 19 Coolidge Hill Rd, Cambridge, MA *02138*

van Buren MR & MRS Harold S JR (Buffington—Alice H Hall)
V'46.Nu'68.Tufts'74.H'45 ⚓
☎ (508) 432-0051 . . ''Moorings'' 22 Harbor Rd, Harwich Port,
MA *02646*

Vance MRS C Albert (Dominga E Macondray)
☎ (415) 461-2487 . . 501 Via Casitas, Apt 817, Greenbrae, CA *94904*

Vance MR & MRS Cyrus R (Grace E Sloane) | 2 E 93 St,
C.Mt.Y'39 | New York, NY
MISS Elsie N—at ☎ (212) 228-3768 | *10128*
60 Gramercy Park N, New York, NY *10010* . . . |
MISS Amy S—at ☎ (212) 369-0822 |
115 E 92 St, New York, NY *10128* . . . . |

Vance MR & MRS Lee G (Cynthia B King) P'80.H'85.Stan'80.H'85
☎ (011-44-171) 727-3218 . . 13 Brunswick Gardens, London W8 4AS,
England

Van Cleave MR & MRS John P (Margaret M | ☎ (423) 821-5662
Prigmore) Hlns'75.Tenn'73 . . . . | 202 W Brow Oval,
JUNIORS MISS Margaret G . . . . | Lookout Mountain,
| TN *37350*

van Daalen MR & MRS M Anthony E (Amy B Crocker) Wes'82.Wes'81
☎ (203) 454-1045 . . 43 River Rd, Weston, CT *06883*

Vandam MRS Albert R (Carolyn T Laughlin) Br'67 | ☎ (617) 749-1474
MISS Hilary R—Br'96 | 33 Fearing Rd,
LT Todd P—USA.Ub.Br'92—at | Hingham, MA
☎ (617) 424-1210 . . 124 Beacon St, Boston, MA | *02043*
02116 . . . . |

Vandam MR Albert R—Ub.Br'64
☎ (617) 545-1153 . . 63 Tilden Rd, Scituate, MA *02066*

VandenBerg MR & MRS Peter H (Nancy G Todd) Ken'81.Ken'80 . . of
☎ (414) 964-4514 . . 5835 N Shore Dv, Whitefish Bay, WI *53217*
''Waterfront Haven'' Treasure Cay, Bahamas

van den Bergh MR & MRS Adriaan M (Anne H Casey)
☎ (908) 781-6311 . . PO Box 426, Peapack, NJ *07977*

Vanderbeck MR & MRS Samuel R 3d (Eleanor K | ☎ (610) 286-5428
Wiederseim) . . . . | PO Box 76,
JUNIORS MISS Abigail . . . . | Geigertown, PA
JUNIORS MISS Sarah . . . . | *19523*
JUNIORS MISS Ruth . . . . |

Vanderbilt MRS Katharine S (Katharine F Spahr) . . | ☎ (415) 322-9080
MR William S—at 1834½ Selby Av, Los Angeles, | 1319 Hopkins Av,
CA *90025* . . . . | Palo Alto, CA
MR O De Gray 3d—Box 3233, Yountville, CA | *94301*
94599 . . . . |

Vanderbilt MR & MRS O De Gray (Frances M Philips) Mds.P'37 . . of
☎ (561) 546-7111 . . 111 Gomez Rd, Hobe Sound, FL *33455*
☎ (516) 324-8314 . . PO Box 1251, East Hampton, NY *11937*

Vanderbilt MRS William H (Cook—Helen | of PO Box 1506,
Cummings) B'gton'41.Cs. | Englewood, FL
MR Averill H Cook . . . . | *34295*
MR Willard P Cook . . . . | ☎ (212) 289-8525
| 1192 Park Av,
| New York, NY
| *10128*

van der Burgh MR & MRS Charles E 3d (Marielle M Nijdam)
Ct.Wms'63.H'66
☎ (703) 450-7099 . . 11317 Beach Mill Rd, Great Falls, VA *22066*

Van Deren MISS Nancy . . see MRS C MacCracken

van der Hoeven MR & MRS Bernard J C JR | 24 Tano Vida,
(Josephine W Lane) P'59 . . . . | Santa Fe, NM *87501*
MISS Annette W . . . . |
MISS Katrien J . . . . |

van der Hoeven DR & MRS Ludolph H (Francine C T Adèr)
Leyden'45.Utrecht'42
☎ (513) 298-2472 . . 255 Park Rd, Dayton, OH *45419*

Vander Horst MRS Elias (Blanche Manheimer)
☎ (215) 886-9902 . . 709 Custis Rd, Glenside, PA *19038*

Vander Horst MRS John (Helen G Lawrence) Swb'31.Ncd.
☎ (770) 428-6166 . . 267 Whitlock Av SW, Marietta, GA *30064*

Vander Horst MRS John JR (Kathleen A Purcell)
☎ (410) 366-7146 . . 4907 Roland Av, Baltimore, MD *21210*

Vander Horst MR John JR—Cc.
☎ (212) 426-0906 . . 7 E 95 St, New York, NY *10128-0796*

van der Kieft MRS John W 2d (Patricia Eakin)
☎ (207) 563-8377 . . 202 Schooner Cove, Damariscotta, ME *04543*

van der Kieft MR & MRS John W 3d (Michele T
Montgelas) Bost'61 . . . . | ☎ (203) 655-8372
MISS Barbara E—BostColl'92.Les'93—at | 6 Woods End Rd,
363 Beacon St, Apt 3R, Boston, MA *02116* . . . . | Darien, CT *06820*
MISS Daphne deG—at Kent . . . . |
MR John W 4th—Bost'91 . . . . |

Van der Leur MISS Suzanne . . see MRS G R Meneely

Vanderlip MR & MRS Henrik N (Christina J Hoyt)
LIU'74.P'74.Cl'76 ⚓ . . of
☎ (203) 622-0102 . . 70 Midwood Rd, Deer Park, Greenwich, CT *06830*
☎ (860) 542-5523 . . Loon Meadow Dv, Norfolk, CT *06058*
☎ (970) 925-2515 . . 35 Ute Place, Aspen, CO *81611*

Van der Mije MR Albert W J—Dijon'70.Geo'72 . . | of ☎ (212)838-3000
JUNIORS MISS Alexis—at Westminster Sch . . . . . | 680 Madison Av,
JUNIORS MR Alberto—at Hobart-Wm Smith . . . . | New York, NY
JUNIORS MR Peter—at Taft . . . . | *10021*
| ☎ (941) 923-6200
| Chelsea Farms,
| 5910 Dove St,
| Sarasota, FL *34241*

Vander Poel MRS Benjamin F (Beverly Sartorius) Pr.Cly.
☎ (516) 676-1242 . . 15 Rabbit Run, Glen Cove, NY *11542*

Vanderpoel CAPT (RET) & MRS Eric 2d (Marian B | ☎ (703) 941-4008
Livingston) USN.Hlns'76.ClarkTech'66 . . . . | 6109 Berlee Dv,
JUNIORS MR Eric 3d . . . . | Alexandria, VA
| *22312*

Vander Poel MR & MRS Halsted B (Reid—Dorothy Marlatt)
V'37.Rcn.K.Gr.C.Mt.Cvc.Sl.Y'35
☎ (011-39-6) 884-0049 . . via G Aldega, 2, 00198 Rome, Italy

Vander Poel MR Halsted B 2d
☎ (303) 979-6365 . . 8660 W Ken Caryl Av, Littleton, CO *80123*

Vanderpoel MR & MRS John A (Joan Waterhouse) | ☎ (508) 369-7237
Mit'40 | 119 Crescent Rd,
MR John A JR . . . . | Concord, MA *01742*
MISS Ellen Kate—at ☎ (508) 263-0327 |
5 Lothrop Rd, Acton, MA *01720* . . . . |
JUNIORS MR Aaron W—at ☎ (508) 263-0327 |
5 Lothrop Rd, Acton, MA *01720* . . . . |

Vanderpoel MR & MRS Wynant D 3d (Bishop—S Barrie Osborn)
Rc.Au.BtP.Shcc.Cly.P'53
☎ (212) 472-0405 . . 79 E 79 St, New York, NY *10021*

Vanderpool MRS Wynant D JR (Johnson—Ann W | ☎ (202) 338-6947
Wheeler) V'49.Cvc.Mt.Sl. . . . . | 1330—30 St NW,
MISS Wilhelmina C Johnson—Roch'82.Sl.—at | Washington, DC
☎ (212) 831-8761 . . 6 E 97 St, New York, NY | *20007*
10029 . . . . |

van der Straeten MR & MRS Vincent R (Myriam Y Loumaye)
☎ (011-32-2) 343-12-89 . . 21 Av Brg Herinckx, Box 27,
B1180 Brussels, Belgium

van der Stricht MR & MRS Paul R (E E Nora Eaton) Unn.Ghent'30
☎ (203) 869-4563 . . Mead Point, Greenwich, CT *06830*

Van Der Toorn MRS Marie C (Marie C Seabaugh) | ☎ (602) 998-8753
Dar. . . . . | 8226 E Rovey Av,
MISS Elizabeth M—Ariz'95.Dar. . . . . | Scottsdale, AZ
MR Eric W—at N Ariz U . . . . | *85250*
JUNIORS MR Andrew K . . . . |

Vandervoorn MR & MRS Richard M (Marianne K Tracy) Skd'84.Bab'84
☎ (510) 482-0325 . . 4101 Greenwood Av, Oakland, CA *94602*

van der Voort MR & MRS Michael V M (Helen E Crane)
Ws'84.Cl'90.Nijenrode'82 . . of
☎ (212) 473-7172 . . 45 Gramercy Park N, New York, NY *10010*
☎ (516) 286-4884 . . 18 Academy Lane, Bellport, NY *11713*

Vanderwarker MR & MRS Richard D (Patricia A | ☎ (203) 966-2980
Reese) Hl.Ncd. . . . . | 694 Weed St,
MR R Dean 3d . . . . | New Canaan, CT
MR Derek R . . . . | *06840*
JUNIORS MISS Meredith A . . . . |

VanDerzee MRS Leslie M (Leslie P Morgan) | ☎ (212) 289-4132
Ws'65.Syr'67.Cl'78 . . . . | 1192 Park Av, Apt
MISS Anne S—Rol'91 . . . . | 5A, New York, NY
MR Jefferson M—Rol'96 . . . . | *10128*

Vander Zwaag MR & MRS John B (Emmeline S Hunter)
MtH'79.Cl'84.Aht'79.Cl'82
☎ (610) 525-3006 . . 317 S Bryn Mawr Av, Bryn Mawr, PA *19010*

Vander Zwaag MASTER John Hunter (John B) . . . . Born at
Wynnewood, PA Jly 15'96

Van Deusen MISS Kathleen E
160 Harbor St, Glencoe, IL *60022*

Vandeveer MR & MRS Jay W (Jeanette A Jenkins) | ☎ (402) 393-4630
Ws'76.DU'73 . . . . | 1415 S 84 St,
JUNIORS MISS Elizabeth C . . . . | Omaha, NE *68124*
JUNIORS MR William W . . . . |
JUNIORS MR Austin C . . . . |

Van Devender MR & MRS William Jarvis (Mollie Magee)
SoMiss'77.Miss'71
☎ (601) 353-2080 . . 1040 Carlisle St, Jackson, MS *39202*

Van Deventer MR & MRS Francis H (Thaxter—Audrie S Hobbs) Ihy . . .of
☎ (203) 531-4663 . . 502 W Lyon Farm Dv, Greenwich, CT *06831*
☎ (520) 398-2596 . . PO Box 2611, Tubac, AZ *85646*

Van De Water MR Joseph C 2d—Stan'90.Stan'91
☎ (916) 985-2755 . . 231 Briggs Ranch Dv, Folsom, CA *95630-5269*

Van De Water MR & MRS Joseph M (Nancy E | ☎ (912) 474-5398
Noyes) Ws'62.Stan'56.Stan'60 . . . . | 416 Lamar Dv,
MISS Margaret S—at Stanford . . . . | Macon, GA *31210*
MR Eric N—Van'93 . . . . |

Van Dine MR & MRS Vance (Isabel E Brewster)
Un.Pr.S.Mto.Ny.Plg.Myf.Cly.Cs.Ncd.Y'49 ⚓
☎ (212) 831-6818 . . 1165 Park Av, New York, NY *10128*

Van Dusen MRS Francis L (Goodenough—Margaret E Brooks)
SL'35.Me.Ac.Ncd.
☎ (610) 527-5733 . . 74 Pasture Lane, Apt 239, Bryn Mawr, PA *19010*

Van Dusen MR & MRS Lewis H JR (Hodge—Ruth Patrick)
Coker'29.Va'34.Me.Ph.Gm.Rb.Cts.Pc.Ac.Ncd.P'32. Ox'35 . . of
☎ (215) 233-0941 . . ''Viburnum Ridge'' 750 Thomas Rd, Philadelphia,
PA *19118*
☎ (610) 754-7271 . . ''Glenn Mill'' Little Rd, PO Box 104,
Sassamansville, PA *19472*

Van Dusen MRS Lewis H 3d (Curtiss W Richardson) Rb.Ssk.Me.Ph.P.
☎ (610) 896-8548 . . "Glenview" 22 Conshohocken State Rd,
Gladwyne, PA *19035*

Van Dusen MR Robert La B—Hn.H'51
☎ (905) 639-2683 . . 1512-20 North Shore Blvd W, Burlington,
Ontario L7T 1A1, Canada

Van Dyke MRS Dorothy T (Dorothy R Tunis)
☎ (610) 642-2199 . . 429 Montgomery Av, Apt B504, Haverford,
PA *19041*

van Eck MR & MRS John C (Sigrid M G Sabottge) Plg.Wms'36.H'38 . . of
☎ (914) 762-2375 . . 270 River Rd, Scarborough, NY *10510-2416*
☎ (212) 753-5872 . . 575 Park Av, New York NY *10021*

Van Fleet MR & MRS Alan C (Janine M P Pellerin)   ☎ (415) 552-8468
Stan'58 . .   319 Haight St,
   MISS Josette P—at 295 Buchanan St, Apt 106,   San Francisco, CA
San Francisco, CA *94102* *94102*
   MISS Vicki F—at 440 Davis Court, Apt 312,
San Francisco, CA *94111* . . . .
   MISS Michele A—at 45 San Pablo Av,
San Francisco, CA *94127* . . . .

van Gerbig MISS Dorothy F . . see M S O'Brien

Van Gulick MRS Robert R (Gloria L Rogach) Pa'50.Sdg.Dll.
☎ (215) 968-6108 . . 19 Court St, Newtown, PA *18940-1909*

Van Gulick MR & MRS Robert R JR (Amy V Jennewine)
Del'86.Pe.Rv.Ht.Ll.Snc.Dll.Del'84
☎ (215) 997-2122 . . 108 Swan Court, North Wales, PA *19454*

van Heerden MR & MRS Christiaan I (J Cody Harper)
Colby'81.Br'84.Me'90.Nf. ⚓
PO Box 532, Northeast Harbor, ME *04662*

van Heerden MISS (DR) Gita S (Jan H) . . . . Married at New York, NY
Förster DR Eckart H (Heribert) . . . . Apr 27'96

van Heerden MR & MRS Jan H (Sandra S Ingalls)   ☎ (212) 628-2994
Ri.Cs.Stellen'42.Cr'54 . . . .   129 E 69 St,
   MISS Alida P—Mass'87 . . . .   New York, NY
   10021

Van Husan MRS Harold Mitchell (Cynthia Whitlock) BtP.Cda.
☎ (561) 833-6340 . . 350 Coconut Row, Palm Beach, FL *33480*

Van Ingen MISS Anne H—Mid'77.Cl'80
☎ (212) 866-9821 . . 285 Riverside Dv, Apt 4F, New York, NY *10025*

Van Ingen MR & MRS Lawrence B (Evelyn G Harris)
Au.B.Pr.Wk.Lic.Mit'45 . . of
☎ (516) OR6-0993 . . 67 High Farms Rd, Glen Head, NY *11545*
☎ (561) 546-7159 . . 8060 SE Little Harbour Dv, Hobe Sound,
FL *33455*

Van Ingen MRS P Davis (Pamela E Davis) Geo'84.Msq.Cly . . .of
☎ (212) 535-6796 . . 192 E 75 St, Apt 4D, New York, NY *10021*
☎ (860) 535-0420 . . "The Farmhouse" 67 Tipping Rock Rd,
Stonington, CT *06378*

Van Ingen MR William B—Rcn.Rr.Geo'84
☎ (415) 346-2995 . . 2400 Pacific Av, Apt 706, San Francisco,
CA *94115*

Van Kleeck MRS Richard R (Marion P Barker) Ws'49
☎ (410) 323-3659 . . 1105 Bryn Mawr Rd, Baltimore, MD *21210*

Van Lennep MRS Frederick Leas (Sprow—Mary E Hazen) Evg . . .of
☎ (561) 272-7800 . . 3377 N Ocean Blvd, Gulf Stream, FL *33483*
☎ (606) 231-6333 . . "Castleton House" 2469 Iron Works Pike,
Lexington, KY *40511*

Van Lennep MRS Gustave A JR (Vida H Stockwell)
502 E Oak Av, Easton, MD *21601*

Van Liew MR & MRS Alfred B (Frances A Hopper) Il.Ny.Srb.Cw.Br'57
☎ (401) 849-4850 . . "The Barn" 306 Indian Av, Middletown,
RI *02842-5767*

Van Liew MRS Harry Richards (Barbara Reynolds Ferris) Dh.Cda.
☎ (516) 584-5600 . . "Timothy House" PO Box 416, St James,
NY *11780*

Van Liew MR & MRS Jeffere F (Marcia W Nugent)   ☎ (516) 584-5933
SCal'63.Hl.Myf.SCal'65 . . . .   PO Box 570,
   MISS Camilla H—ColC'93 . . . .   481 N Country Rd,
   MR Bradford R—Hl.SCal'92 . . . .   St James, NY *11780*

van Limburg Stirum CT Wigbold A W & CTSS (Lucy M Caldwell) Cly.
☎ (914) 677-3604 . . "Si Bon" 184 Barmore Rd, Lagrangeville,
NY *12540*

van Maasdijk MISS Diana . . see B S Kernan

van Maasdijk MR Eric . . see B S Kernan

van Maasdijk JUNIORS MR Willem . . see B S Kernan

van Marken MR & MRS Bernard (Tuck—M Chase   ☎ (011-31-70)
Nicholson) V'51.Amster'55   3651442
   MISS Alexandra D—Gen'90.Gen'93—at   Mauritskade 41D,
133 rue St Dominique, Paris, France . . . .   2514 HE
   The Hague,
   The Netherlands

Van Metre MRS Charlotte C (Coyer—Charlotte   ☎ (202) 333-3307
Crofford) . . . .   3900 Cathedral Av
   MISS Charis M . . . .   NW, Washington,
   DC *20016*

Van Metre DR & MRS Thomas E JR (Winand—Adela B Hurst)
Gchr'50.Md.Cc.H'44
☎ (410) 825-6834 . . 1902A Indian Head Rd, Ruxton, MD *21204*

Van Mourik MRS Mary Dennis (Gurney—Mary D   ☎ (508) 263-9686
Mann) Wheat'61 . . . .   538 Old Stone
   MISS Kimberly Kellogg—at Colo Coll . . . .   Brook Rd,
   Nagog Woods, MA
   01718

van Nagell MRS John R (Rosamond P Musgrave)
☎ (502) 241-8743 . . Eden Hall Farm, 3700 W H'way 22, Crestwood,
KY *40014*

Van Natta MR Jason . . see MRS K H Buchanan

Vanneck MR & MRS William P (Scroggins—Margaret R Heffington)
AthSt'72.BtP.Evg.U'62
☎ (561) 833-5018 . . 315 S Lake Dv, Palm Beach, FL *33480*

Van Ness MRS Carroll (Helen G H Lyon) Gv.Ncd.
☎ (410) 363-0484 . . 10809 Hudson Rd, Owings Mills, MD *21117*

Van Ness MRS Cheatham (H Virginia Cheatham) V'32
☎ (206) 382-3277 . . 900 University St, Apt 12H, Seattle, WA *98101*

Van Ness MR & MRS Gardiner B 3d (Jessie T   ☎ (847) 234-5527
Steiner) On.LakeF'64 . . . .   133 Pembroke Dv,
   MR Gardiner B 4th—LakeF'93 . . . .   Lake Forest, IL
   MR Bradley McI *60045*
   JUNIORS MR Chapin R . . . .

Van Ness MRS J Merryman (S Josephine Merryman)   ☎ (805) 969-1362
   MR David P JR . . . .   595 Hot Springs Rd,
   MISS Rosalie M (Froelich—Rosalie M Van Ness)   PO Box 50021,
   Santa Barbara, CA
   93150

Van Ness MR & MRS Lewis W (Janis S Wren) Ark'78.Ark'78
☎ (501) 227-4711 . . 28 Huntington Rd, Little Rock, AR *72207*

Van Nest MR & MRS Dean G (Reigeluth—Joan A Houlihan) Chi.Snc.Hl.Hb.Hn.Nw'44.H'48 . . . . .
MISS Kathleen F . . . .
| ☎ (941) 263-7614
| 2900 Ft Charles Dv,
| Port Royal, Naples,
| FL *34102*

Van Nest MR & MRS Dean G JR (Virginia K Kegg) SL'80.Bost'77.Nu'82
☎ (203) 966-6297 . . 62C Heritage Hill Rd, New Canaan, CT *06840*

Van Nest MR & MRS Jeffrey C (Anne T W Forbes) Pa'74.Cr'81.Wes'75
☎ (617) 893-7016 . . 174 Conant Rd, Weston, MA *02193*

Van Nice DR & MRS Paul S (Susan E Scott) Cvc.Rcch.Nw'71.NMex'77.GeoW'83 . . . .
MR Cole S—at Wash'n & Lee . . . .
JUNIORS MR Scott A . . . .
| ☎ (301) 951-6199
| 7101 Meadow Lane,
| Chevy Chase, MD
| *20815*

Van Nice MR & MRS Peter E (Jeanette Hunt) Rc.Sc.Wa.Nw'64.Ch'66 . . . .
MR P Errett JR—Ariz'93—at 1723 W Honore Av, Apt 2R, Chicago, IL *60622* . . . .
MR Anthony H . . . .
| of ☎ (312)266-1120
| 1209 N Astor St,
| Chicago, IL *60610*
| ☎ (616) 469-0029
| 14340 Lake Shore
| Rd, Lakeside, MI
| *49116*

van Nierop MR & MRS Jan H (Martha P Enos) Col'67.Amster'64 . . . .
MISS Emily C . . . .
MR Daniel S . . . .
| ☎ (203) 655-2423
| 38 Pasture Lane,
| Darien, CT *06820*

Van Norden MRS Duncan (Cowles—Elizabeth C Rumbough) Evg.BtP.Cly.Cda.Ncd.
☎ (561) 842-3393 . . 1284 N Lake Way, Palm Beach, FL *33480*

Van Norden MISS Jeanie—Cly.Cda.
☎ (212) 838-0800 . . 825 Fifth Av, New York, NY *10021*

Van Norden MRS Langdon (Gloria I Barnes) Cda.
☎ (203) 869-5324 . . 91 Cherry Valley Rd, Greenwich, CT *06831*

Van Norden MR & MRS Montagnie (Gwendolyn Olson) Hl.P'45 . . . .
MR Adam . . . .
| ☎ (212) 832-8298
| 200 E 66 St,
| New York, NY
| *10021*

van Oosten MISS Elinor
☎ (805) 565-0353 . . 63 Eucalyptus Lane, Montecito, CA *93108*

van Oosten MISS Helene E—Sth'58.SCal'61
☎ (516) 788-7274 . . PO Box 503, Fishers Island, NY *06390*

Van Oot MISS Betsy (Ruppel—Betsy Van Oot) Y'85
☎ (410) 758-0433 . . Fairview Farm, 220 Fairview Farm Rd, Centreville, MD *21617*

Van Oot MR & MRS Peter D (Susan W Troy) Skd'81.Wms'78 . . of
☎ (802) 258-3067 . . 28 Hillwinds Rd, RR 1, Brattleboro, VT *05301*
☎ (603) 569-1481 . . "Buttonwood" Sewall Rd, Wolfeboro, NH *03894*

van Orman MR & MRS Chandler L (Kendall Wheeler) Cvc.Mt.Cc.Sl.NCar'63.Va'66 . . . .
MISS Robin—Mid'92—at ☎ (415) 327-1862 1106 Bryant St, Palo Alto, CA *94301* . . . .
MR Cameron—at Dartmouth . . . .
| ☎ (301) 951-0037
| 5201 Norway Dv,
| Chevy Chase, MD
| *20815* . . MR absent

Van Pelt MR & MRS Charles B P (Jane E Eger) Nw'64.Ph.BtP.Gm.Ssk.Rb.Ste.B.H'44.Pa'49 . . .
JUNIORS MISS Juliet E E . . . .
| ☎ (610) 525-7465
| "Wilton"
| PO Box 8199,
| 1260 County Line
| Rd, Radnor, PA
| *19087-8199*

Van Pelt MRS Elizabeth W (Royer—S Elizabeth Wickwire) . . . .
MR Theodore W Royer—Me. . . . .
| ☎ (610) 688-8414
| "Mallards Cottage"
| 316 Beaumont Rd,
| Devon, PA *19333*

Van Pelt MR Guy F C—Srb.Bost'80
☎ (401) 849-4856 . . "The Stable" 315 Bellevue Av, Newport, RI *02840*

Van Pelt MR William G—P'54
MISS Alida M—at 44 Greentree Lane, Malvern, PA *19555* . . . .
MR William G JR—at 857 Mt Moro Rd, Villanova, PA *19085* . . . .
| ☎ (610) 520-1758
| 423 S Ithan Av,
| Bryn Mawr, PA
| *19010*

Van Praagh DR & MRS Ian (Felicia Delafield) V'56.Cl'58.Cly.Tor'55 . . . .
MISS Cecily M—David'89—at ☎ (703) 243-6556 1210 N Taft St, Arlington, VA *22201* . . . .
MR Ian R—Drew'91—at ☎ (202) 546-7739 430 New Jersey Av SE, Washington, DC *20003*
MR Giles D—Rol'92—at ☎ (212) 288-7084 300 E 83 St, New York, NY *10028* . . . .
| ☎ (212) 662-6090
| 425 Riverside Dv,
| New York, NY
| *10025*

Van Rensselaer MR & MRS Alexander T (Sallie B Drackett) Cin'62.Ny.Pqt.Cc.Hl.Leh'58 ⚓ . . . .
MR Alexander R—at ☎ (212) 254-9846 1 Astor Place, New York, NY *10003* . . . .
MR Kiliaen D—Rc.Hl.Ty'92—at ☎ (212) 369-0362 . . 55 E 87 St, Apt 4A, New York, NY *10128* . . . .
| ☎ (203) 226-9285
| 12 Pier Way
| Landing, Westport,
| CT *06880*

Van Rensselaer MR Charles A—Lm.Snc.
☎ (561) 833-3596 . . 300 S Ocean Blvd, Palm Beach, FL *33480*

Van Rensselaer MRS Cortlandt S (Georgina L Wells) Bgt.Cly.Cda.
☎ (914) 234-3395 . . 10 Clinton Rd, Bedford Hills, NY *10507*

Van Rensselaer MRS Hilary P (Hilary J Prouty) Chath'66 . . . .
MISS Serena . . . .
MR R Miles . . . .
| ☎ (908) 439-3168
| 11 Church St,
| PO Box 563,
| Oldwick, NJ *08858*

Van Rensselaer MRS Knauth (Botsford—Anne W Knauth) . . . .
MR Blake Botsford—Rol'88—at 482½ Clarendon Av, Winter Park, FL *32789* .
| ☎ (212) 371-2655
| 1173A Second Av,
| Apt 311, New York,
| NY *10021*

Van Rensselaer MRS Nina M (Elliott—Kelly—Nina M Van Rensselaer) Stan'50.Cal'68.Tcy.
☎ (415) 346-4113 . . 130 Laurel St, San Francisco, CA *94118*

Van Rensselaer MRS Stephen (Mygatt—Lillie Langstroth) Cal'34.Paris'35.Pr.Cly.
☎ (516) 676-8864 . . 840 Chicken Valley Rd, Locust Valley, NY *11560*

Van Riper MRS Susan Evans (Susan F Evans) Br'63.Ncd. . . . .
MR Ransom E—at 4101 Randolph Av, Oakland, CA *94602* . . . .
| ☎ (615) 297-5711
| 5025 Hillsboro Rd,
| Apt 23D, Nashville,
| TN *37215*

van Roijen MR Christopher T . . of
☎ (202) 337-0919 . . "The Studio" 2911 M St NW, Washington, DC *20007*
☎ (561) 582-1209 . . La Coquille Club, Villa 105C, 450 S Ocean Blvd, Manalapan, FL *33462*

van Roijen MISS Laura W (de Vogel—Laura W van Roijen)
Va'74.Y'76.Cl'82.Cvc . . .of
☎ (307) 733-2913 . . PO Box 148, Teton Village, WY *83025*
☎ (540) 347-6476 . . St Leonard's Farm, Rte 211, PO Box 814,
Warrenton, VA *20188*

van Roijen MR & MRS Peter P (Beatrice S	☎ (202) 333-2570
Frelinghuysen) Cvc.Mt.McG'67	1327—33 St NW,
MISS Theodora	Washington, DC
MISS Linden	*20007*
JUNIORS MR P Matthew	

van Roijen MR & MRS Robert D JR (Susan E	☎ (407) 423-0199
Frelinghuysen) B.Mt.H'61	1700 W Ivanhoe
JUNIORS MISS Victoria F—at St Paul's	Blvd, Orlando, FL
JUNIORS MISS Valaer M	*32804*

van Rooten MR Courtlandt H K—Pl.Mid'65
☎ (215) 242-4214 . . 8811 Towanda St, Philadelphia, PA *19118*

Van Sant MR & MRS John F JR (Elizabeth R Brown) Va'79.Pg.Va'82
☎ (301) 657-3424 . . 3406 Leland St, Chevy Chase, MD *20815*

Van Schoonhoven MR William L—Bf.Rens'50
☎ (716) 885-7453 . . 84 Windsor Av, Buffalo, NY *14209*

Van Sciver MR & MRS Joseph B 3d (Carol M	☎ (215) CH8-1138
McLuckie) Pc.Leh'57	195 Bethlehem Pike,
MISS Carolyn L—Ithaca'92	Philadelphia, PA
MISS Julie M—Leh'96	*19118*
JUNIORS MR Joseph B 4th—at Yale	

Van Sciver MR Wesley J—Co.Mit'40.Stan'54 ⚓
☎ (904) 926-8011 . . 47 West Point Dv, Crawfordville, FL *32327*

Van Slyck MR & MRS Peter (Lyman—Rosemary A	☎ (860) 739-7916
O'Brien) Cc.Cly.Y'49	34 Great Wight
MISS Katharine C—Wheat'85—at	Way, Old Black
☎ (703) 812-8430 . . 600 N Vermont St, Apt 2,	Point, Niantic, CT
Arlington, VA *22203*	*06357*
MISS S Ashley—Syr'86—at ☎ (212) 794-3308	
406 E 83 St, New York, NY *10028*	
MR Nicholas H—Bost'88—at ☎ (803) 256-1715	
2312 Preston St, Columbia, SC *29250*	
MISS Charlotte P Lyman—Y'82—at	
☎ (212) 988-8684 . . 520 E 72 St,	
New York, NY *10021*	

Van Strum MRS Kenneth S (Anna Cecilia	☎ (415) 342-4222
Zimmermann) Bur.Pcu.Tcy.S.K.	2241 Forest View
MISS Clarissa	Dv, Hillsborough,
	CA *94010*

Van Tassel MR Peter B—Y'50.Y'55
☎ (508) 627-4410 . . 119 S Water St, PO Box 5172, Edgartown,
MA *02539*

van Tets MRS Willem (Dorothy Collins)
☎ (415) 346-6373 . . 1400 Geary Blvd, Apt 4P, San Francisco,
CA *94109*

Van Tuyl MR & MRS Harry E (Alice C Hawkins)	☎ (802) 759-2678
V'56.Kas'52	Box 1365, Rte 1,
MISS Elizabeth G—at ☎ (203) 334-2159	Vergennes, VT
69 Harbor Av, Apt C3, Bridgeport, CT *06605* . .	*05491*

Van Vleck MR & MRS Roy T (Emily N Trevor)	☎ (603) 795-4078
Ws'69.Cly.NH'72	Pinnacle Rd, Lyme,
JUNIORS MISS Harriet E	NH *03768*
JUNIORS MR Tielman T	

van Vliet MR & MRS John C (Karen Melling) Van'83.WmMitch'86.Minn'85
☎ (612) 926-0516 . . 4624 York Av S, Minneapolis, MN *55410*

van Vliet MASTER Paul Melling (John C) . . . . Born at
Minneapolis, MN Aug 8'94

van Vliet MR Willem F . . . . Died at
St Paul, MN Jun 17'96

van Vliet MRS Willem F (Grace S Carter)
☎ (612) 457-9007 . . 1012 Downing St, Mendota Heights, MN *55118*

van Voorhees MR & MRS Clifford I III (Kathryn A	☎ (011-44-171)
Mercer) Bcs.Rut'68.Cl'70	937-2384
MISS Kathryn M—St Mark's	64 Scarsdale Villas,
JUNIORS MISS Christiana M—at Amer Sch London	London W8 6PP,
JUNIORS MR Alexander P—at Trinity	England

Van Voorhis MRS Standish (Jane Whitney)
☎ (415) 254-2004 . . 23500 Cristo Rey Dv, Apt 404G, Cupertino,
CA *95014*

Van Voorhis MR Wesley C
☎ (206) 361-0149 . . 12316 NE 25 Av, Seattle, WA *98125*

Van Vranken MR & MRS J Frederick JR (Nancy J Sharp)
MHBaylor'60.Ri.Mb.Mid'57
☎ (516) 681-4077 . . Black Walnut Farm, PO Box 264, Cedar Swamp
Rd, Jericho, NY *11753*

van Wagenberg MR & MRS Hannes F (Susan T Long) W&L'74
☎ (410) 366-0320 . . 109 Overhill Rd, Baltimore, MD *21210-2917*

Van Wagner MR & MRS James R JR (Alyce E Kilpatrick)
Rm.Stc.Hl.Marq'70
☎ (908) 872-9311 . . ''Saewic'' PO Box 426, Locust, NJ *07760*

Van Winkle MR E Beach 3d—Bab'61
☎ (203) 655-8068 . . 29 Brush Island Rd, PO Box 3068, Darien,
CT *06820*

Van Winkle MR & MRS Edgar B 2d (Staempfli—E Fordyce Ewing) Hn.H'38
☎ (803) 681-5619 . . 20 Foxbriar, Hilton Head, SC *29928*

Van Winkle MR Edgar B IV—Conn'92
☎ (860) 229-3699 . . 1475 Stanley St, New Britain, CT *06053*

Van Winkle MRS Kingsland (Kate L Vondermuhll) V'36.Cda.
☎ (860) 726-2039 . . Duncaster, Prospect 203, 60 Loeffler Rd,
Bloomfield, CT *06002-2275*

Van Winkle MRS McLoughlin (Cornelia Whitehouse McLoughlin)
☎ (914) 234-7262 . . RD Box 115, Pine Brook Rd, Bedford, NY *10506*

Van Winkle MR & MRS Peter K (Prudence A	☎ (617) 244-9787
Bridges) Mls'64.BankSt'86.DelB.Hl.Denis'64.	41 Edge Hill Rd,
Cl'68.Va'79	Chestnut Hill, MA
MISS Trintje A—Ore'95	*02167*
MISS Elizabeth P—Ken'96	

Van Winkle MRS William Mitchell (Marjorie A Boesel) . . . . Died at
Litchfield, CT Jly 3'96

Van Winkle MR William Mitchell—Ll.H'35.Cl'39
☎ (860) 567-5600 . . ''Hillhome'' 293 N Lake St, PO Box 1089,
Litchfield, CT *06759*

Van Wyck MR & MRS E Hawley 3d (Susan L	☎ (540) 554-2235
Hammond) Hl.Ncd.AmU'69	17842 Raven Rocks
JUNIORS MR W Hawley—at St James	Rd, Bluemont, VA
	20135

Van Wyck MR & MRS F Bronson (Mary L Thomas)
GeoW'70.Hl.NCar'67.H'73 . . . . | ☎ (501) 349-5562
  MISS Mary Lynn—at U of NCar Chapel Hill . . . | Arrowhead Farms,
  MR F Bronson JR—Y'95—at ☎ (213) 650-1467 | 2141 H'way 224 E,
  8207 Mulholland Dv, Los Angeles, CA 90046 . . | Tuckerman, AR 72473

Varlay MR & MRS René G (Diana H Austin) | of ☎ (703)922-3974
Cw.Ht.Yn.Y'50 . . . . | 6102A Essex House
  MISS Alexandra R—Bnd'91 . . . . | Square, Alexandria,
  MISS Elizabeth S—Bnd'91 . . . . | VA 22310
  | ☎ (804) 493-9858
  | ''Panorama''
  | Rte 622, Montross,
  | VA 22520

Varner MRS David E (Mary F Rowe) Cvc.Sl.
  ☎ (301) 229-7042 . . 4936 Sentinel Dv, Apt 103, Bethesda, MD 20816

Vartanian MR & MRS Paul D (Christabel Kelly) | of ☎ (908)234-2798
Rol'68.Eh.Fic.Fiy.Dar.Rol'68 . . . . | Pin Oaks Farm,
  MISS Annabel K . . . . | 401 Fowler Rd,
  MR Nishan P . . . . | Far Hills, NJ 07931
  | ☎ (305) 367-4367
  | Key Largo Anglers
  | Club, 50 Clubhouse
  | Rd, Key Largo, FL
  | 33037

Vasquez MISS Alexandra Razzili Behice (Michael E) . . . . . . Born Sep 5'95
Vasquez MR & MRS Michael E (Maria del Carmen J Meyer)
BostColl'88.Tex'93.Colby'87
  ☎ (512) 472-8781 . . 708 Landon Lane, Austin, TX 78705

Vastine MRS Jacob H 3d (Mary A Brey) Me.Sdg.W.Ncd.
  ☎ (610) 889-2459 . . 408 Waynesbrooke Rd, Berwyn, PA 19312

Vauclain MR & MRS André C (Faris—Sabine de C de Canisy)
Algiers'51.Pa'30
  8080 SW Canyon Dv, Portland, OR 97225

Vauclain MR Samuel M 3d—Me.Pn.P'38 . . . . | ☎ (610) 645-8963
  MISS Edwina F—Me.Ncd.—at ☎ (610) 664-0486 | Waverly Heights
  212 Lantwyn Lane, Narberth, PA 19072 . . . . . . | A211, 1400 Waverly
  | Rd, Gladwyne, PA
  | 19035-1254

Vauclain MRS William E (Isabelle G Taylor) . . . . . . | of ☎ (610)525-2330
  MISS Lesley K—David'92.Me.—at | ''The Beech House''
  ☎ (910) 659-6157 . . 690 Rock Garden Circle, | 2109 County Line
  Winston-Salem, NC 27104 . . . . | Rd, Villanova, PA
  MR Jacques L 3d—Me.David'91—see | 19085
  Dilatory Domiciles . . . . | ☎ (941) 395-1446
  | PO Box 848,
  | Captiva, FL 33924

Vaughan MR & MRS Alan C (Patricia A Peterson) . . | ☎ (914) 967-1547
  MR Brian C—at Cornell . . . . | 30 Park Dv S, Rye,
  | NY 10580

Vaughan MR & MRS C Wheaton (Beverley Bromley)
Rcn.Me.Pqt.Mit'51.Cal'54
  ☎ (203) 259-1403 . . 66 Turkey Hill Rd S, PO Box 323, Greens Farms,
  CT 06436

Vaughan MR & MRS Curtis T 3d (Karen L McHugh) Tex'76.A.H'73
  ☎ (210) 826-6939 . . 324 Elizabeth Rd, San Antonio, TX 78209

Vaughan REV & MRS Forrest E (Marguerite Vliet) Mar'36.Ken'39.PhilaD'54
  ☎ (561) 770-3321 . . Countryside 118N, 8775—20 St, Vero Beach,
  FL 32966

Vaughan MR Henry N—Pc.
  ☎ (610) 525-1775 . . 74 Pasture Lane, Apt 104, Bryn Mawr, PA 19010

Vaughan MRS May L (Totten—May L Vaughan) | ☎ (202) 333-1280
CathU'83 . . . . | 1936—38 St NW,
  MISS Cecily P Totten . . . . | Washington, DC
  | 20007

Vaughan MISS Natalie W—Gchr'59.Myf.
  ☎ (609) 924-1801 . . 44 Princeton Av, Princeton, NJ 08540

Vaughan MR Reginald B—H'60.Leeds'72
  ☎ (011-44-171) 629-7200 . . The Lansdowne Club, Berkeley Square,
  London W1X 6JD, England

Vaughan MR & MRS Robert L (Melissa Tillotson) Tex'78.A.H'76.H'80
  ☎ (210) 820-3230 . . 364 Terrell Rd, San Antonio, TX 78209

Vaughan MR & MRS Roger E (Todd—Kathryn Kip | ☎ (410) 822-3946
Requardt) Br'59 | 4480 Bachelors
  MISS Elizabeth K Todd . . . . | Point, PO Box 298,
  | Oxford, MD 21654

Vaughan MR Todd K—Rcp.B.Nyc.Ste.Md'66.Pa'71
  ☎ (410) 820-6033 . . PO Box 1326, Easton, MD 21601

Vaughan MRS William L (Margaret Driggs) Sm.Ncd.
  ☎ (207) 623-4706 . . Elm Hill Farm, Hallowell, ME 04347

Vaughan DR & MRS William P (Esther F Drury) | ☎ (205) 822-3966
SUNY'68.Rice'68.Conn'72 | 2480 Altadena Rd,
  MISS Frances E—at Emory . . . . | Birmingham, AL
  JUNIORS MISS Hannah B . . . . | 35243
  JUNIORS MR Joseph D . . . . |

Vaughan Williams MR & MRS Rupert (Catherine C McCulloch)
Y'84.Mds.Buck'ham'83
  ☎ (011-65) 735-44-19 . . 10 Cuscaden Walk, 06-01 Four Seasons Park,
  Singapore 249693

Vaughn MR & MRS James H (Charlotte W Blaine) Sth'49.Bur.Pcu.Csn.Cr'49
  ☎ (408) 626-4325 . . PO Box 1218, Pebble Beach, CA 93953

Vaughn MR & MRS James M JR (Salle A Werner) TexWmn'61.Tex'61 . . of
  ☎ (713) 524-6574 . . 2235 Brentwood Dv, Houston, TX 77019
  ☎ (212) 879-9786 . . 9 E 82 St, Apt 5A, New York, NY 10028

Vaux MR George—Ph.Mt.W.Cspa.Cw.Hav'30.Lond'37
  ☎ (610) 525-4517 . . 320 Caversham Rd, Bryn Mawr, PA 19010-2928

Vaux MR & MRS Roberts (Mary Audrey Bolen) | ☎ (803) 757-2666
Lime'71.SCar'68.SCar'72 . . . . | ''Vaux Hall''
  JUNIORS MISS Mary G . . . . | Bluffton, SC 29910
  JUNIORS MISS Emily C . . . . |

Veale JUNIORS MR Lucius C . . see J A Donahue
Veale MR & MRS Tinkham 2d (Harriett Ernst)
CtCol'39.Un.Cv.May.It.Cwr'37
  ☎ (216) 423-4644 . . 1700 Epping Rd, Gates Mills, OH 44040

Veale MR & MRS Tinkham 3d (Lois E Black) | ☎ (610) 687-3258
Cwr'71.Cv.Uncl.W&L'69 . . . . | 422 S Waterloo Rd,
  JUNIORS MR Tinkham 4th . . . . | Box 134, Devon, PA
  JUNIORS MR Geoffrey B . . . . | 19333

Veeder MRS Nicholas P (Vardi H Marshall) Cy.
  ☎ (314) 993-0057 . . Gatesworth Apt 353, 1 McKnight Place, St Louis,
  MO 63124

Veeder MR & MRS Peter G (Sybil A Pickett)
CtCol'65.Pitt'91.Pg.Fcg.Hl.P'63.Pitt'66 . . . . | ☎ (412) 441-9774
  MISS Sybil G—at ☎ (401) 521-3904
181 Irving Av, Apt 2, Providence, RI *02906* . . . | 1221 Shady Av,
  MISS Hillary W—StLaw'91.Nu'93—at | Pittsburgh, PA
  ☎ (203) 226-7205 . . 6 Terhune Dv, Westport, | *15232*
CT *06880* . . . .
  MR Gerrit M—at Ohio Wesleyan . . . .

Vehslage MR & MRS Ramsay W (Ann W Bradley) | ☎ (609) 921-1175
P'59 . . . . | 206 Russell Rd,
  MISS M Murray—Colg'96 . . . . | Princeton, NJ *08540*
  MR Ramsay W JR—CtCol'94

Vehslage MR & MRS Stephen T (April Olmsted) Sth'61.Rcn.P'61
  ☎ (203) 661-4696 . . 40 S Stanwich Rd, Greenwich, CT *06830*

Vehslage MR & MRS Stephen T JR (Emily T Starr)
  ☎ (212) 533-9588 . . 12 E 11 St, New York, NY *10003*

Veit MR & MRS E Alexander (Ann C L Purves) P'49
  ☎ (011-33-93) 36-24-05 . . Paradis-Roc, Corniche St Christophe,
  06130 Grasse, France

Veit MR Henri C—P'46.NCar'69
  ☎ (860) 526-5067 . . PO Box 692, Old Lyme, CT *06371*

Veitch MRS William J A (Barker—Priscilla Curtis) | ☎ (514) 935-1084
Fy. . . . . | 3940 Côte des
  MR Jonathan C Barker . . . . | Neiges, Montreal,
                                                        | Quebec H3H 1W2,
                                                        | Canada

Velge MR & MRS Bertrand (Catherine C Wright) Namur'88
  ☎ (011-44-1233) 620-386 . . Ripple Court, Station Rd, Westwell,
  Ashford, Kent TN25 4NT, England

Velge MISS Philippine (Bertrand) . . . . Born at
                                                        Brussels, Belgium Feb 28'96

Venizelos MRS Nikitas (Katharine H Adams) . . . . . . | ☎ (212) 362-4881
  MISS Anna . . . . | 20 W 75 St, Apt 1,
  MISS Emily . . . . | New York, NY
  MR Kyriaco . . . . | *10023*
  MR John . . . .

Venizelos MR Nikitas
  ☎ (011-30-1) 922-7934 . . Ardittou 28, 11636 Athens, Greece

Vent MRS Thomas G (Mary Scull)
  ☎ (210) 677-8949 . . Air Force Village II, Apt 107,
  5100 John D Ryan Blvd, San Antonio, TX *78245*

Ventress MR & MRS James Alexander (E Ann Catchings)
  Miss'54.Dar.Miss'58
  ☎ (601) 888-4259 . . PO Box 23, Woodville, MS *39669*

Verbeck MRS Guido F JR (MacLeod—Butler—Reed—
  Carolyn R Waring) Eyc.Chi.
  ☎ (508) 693-0772 . . Seven Gates Farm, RFD, Vineyard Haven,
  MA *02568*

Verge MR William G—Cw.Ht.UMiami'64
  ☎ (305) 296-8469 . . 329 Peacon Lane, Key West, FL *33040*

Verkamp MR Joseph P—OState'50.SanJ'78 . . . . . . | ☎ (415) 327-6086
  MISS Mary G—Cal'90—at ☎ (408) 425-1817 | 1201 Cowper St,
318D Soquel Av, Santa Cruz, CA *95062* . . . . . . | Palo Alto, CA
                                                        | *94301*

Verkuil MRS Frances G (Frances H Gibson) | ☎ (407) 647-5674
W&M'66 . . . . | 1017 Temple Grove,
  JUNIORS MR J Gibson . . . . | Winter Park, FL
                                                        | *32789*

Verkuil MR & MRS (DR) Paul R (Rodin—Niejelow—Judith Seitz)
  Pa'66.Cos.An.Mt.Y.W&M'61
  ☎ (215) 898-3080 . . 3812 Walnut St, Philadelphia, PA *19104*

Vermeule MR & MRS Cornelius C 3d (Emily D | ☎ (617) 864-1879
  Townsend) BMr'50.Rcd'54.BMr'56.Tv.Hl.Lm. | 47 Coolidge Hill Rd,
  Csn.H'47.H'51.Lond'53 . . . . | Cambridge, MA
  MISS Emily D B—Y'88.Cal'93 . . . . | *02138*
  MR C Adrian C—H'90.H'93

Vermilye MR & MRS H Rowland 3d (Suzanne L Rea) Ala'81.Hl.Wms'58
  ☎ (803) 342-3548 . . 25 Royal James Dv, Hilton Head Island, SC *29926*

Verner MR & MRS Elliott K (Joan S Howard) Elk.JHop'52
  ☎ (518) 891-2266 . . HCR 1, Box 11C, Bloomingdale, NY *12913*

Verner MISS Victoria S (late William K) . . . . Married at
                                                        Blue Mountain Lake, NY
Sandiford MR William S (late George) . . . . Jun 29'96

Verner MRS William K (Abbie L Sunde) Sth'59
  ☎ (518) 372-8158 . . 855 Union St, Schenectady, NY *12308*

Vest MR & MRS Charles T (Andrea C Sierck) | ☎ (804) 295-4343
  Finch'66.VaCmth'69 . . . . | 11 Farmington Dv,
  MISS Sarah T—Scripps'94—at U of Va . . . . . . | Charlottesville, VA
                                                        | *22901*

Vest MR Michael E . . see R H Carpenter

Vest MISS Phebe Alexandra—Va'91.Cly.
  ☎ (212) 988-5696 . . 157 E 72 St, Apt 8J, New York, NY *10021*

Vestal MR Paul W—Bhm.Col'53
  ☎ (415) 921-2566 . . 710 Steiner St, San Francisco, CA *94117*

Vestal MR Peter L (Paul W) . . . . Married at Monte Rio, CA
  Alex MISS Judith L (Jack) . . . . Apr 27'96

Vestner MR & MRS Eliot N (Cutler—Louisa R | ☎ (617) 523-5074
  Baptiste) Aht'57 . . . . | 1 Devonshire Place,
    MR Donald F Cutler 4th—at 138 Lerner Rd, | Apt 2605, Boston,
    Huntington, VT *05462* . . . . | MA *02109*
    MR Q A Shaw Cutler—at 308 Sagamore Rd,
    PO Box 2176, South Hamilton, MA *01982* . .

Vetterlein MR & MRS Frederick S (Julia C | ☎ (717) 761-1276
  Droescher) . . . . | 247 N 17 St,
  MR Frederick S JR—Tufts'77—at | Camp Hill, PA
  ☎ (617) 522-4284 . . 96 Rossmore Rd, | *17011*
  Jamaica Plain, MA *02130* . . . .
  MR David S—Penn'84—at ☎ (352) 338-0526
  434 SW 2 St, Gainesville, FL *32601* . . . .
  MR Roy D—at ☎ (207) 236-4420
  PO Box 1027, Rockport, ME *04856* . . . .
  MR James S—Bloom'88—at ☎ (717) 529-2774
  RD 1, Box 59, Cochranville, PA *19330* . . . . . .

Vetterlein MR J Rodney—Me.Roan'65 . . of
  1041 N Jamestown Rd, Decatur, GA *30033*
  837 Youngsford Rd, Gladwyne, PA *19035*

Vetterlein MRS Millicent L (Washburn—Millicent Lell) Pa'61
  ☎ (207) 767-2120 . . 29 Westminster Terr, Cape Elizabeth, ME *04107*

Viall MR Richmond . . . . Died at
                                                        Saunderstown, RI May 4'96

Viall MRS Richmond (Elizabeth I Roberts) Ncd.
☎ (401) 294-3847 . . 145 Gilbert Stuart Rd, PO Box 235, Saunderstown, RI *02874*

Viault MR & MRS George B (Anne Albert)
Ncmb'64.Tul'64 . . . .
MISS Laurie R—Tex'92—at 901 Lismore, Smyrna, GA *30080* . . . .
MR John B—Smu'89.AGSIM'92—at 2824 Briarhurst Dv, Apt 8, Houston, TX *77057* .
| ☎ (713) 358-6545
2419 Pine Bend, Kingwood, TX *77339*

Viault MRS George F (Dorothy R Bartlett)
15133 Vantage Hill Rd, Silver Spring, MD *20906*

Viaux MR & MRS Frederic Ballou (Margarita Samayoa y Lerma)
NCar'38.H.'40.H'57
☎ (617) 433-0125 . . 865 Central Av, Apt L504, Needham, MA *02192*

Vickery DR & MRS Austin L JR (Amelia F Wheelwright) D.H.Nebr'44
☎ (508) 785-0648 . . 139 Walpole St, Dover, MA *02030*

Vickery MR Ethan S . . see J R Wierdsma

Vickery MR & MRS Howard L 2d (Mary C Wells)
Ws'77.S.Swth'70 . . . .
JUNIORS MISS Patricia W . . . .
| ☎ (203) 259-5838
295 Greens Farms Rd, Westport, CT *06880*

Vickery CDR (RET) & MRS Hugh B (Dorothy A Borden)
Sth'40.Cvc.Ny.USN'40
☎ (301) 925-7250 . . Collington 2001, 10450 Lottsford Rd, Mitchellville, MD *20721*

Victor MRS Alice S (Alice D Smith) V'62
☎ (203) 869-9789 . . 27 Alpine Rd, Greenwich, CT *06830*

Victor MR & MRS David (Copeland—Judith M James) Ariz'70.H'64.Va'68 . . . .
MISS Laurie—at Sydney, Australia . . . .
MR David—at Vienna, Austria . . . .
MR Andrew—at Boston, MA . . . .
| of ☎ (602)867-1335
8907 N Arroyo Grande Dv, Phoenix, AZ *85028*
☎ (520) 735-7252
PO Box 232, Greer, AZ *85927*

Victor MRS Martin (Helene L Peters) V'40.Pr.Cly . . .of
☎ (516) 676-1935 . . 15 Quail Ridge Rd, Glen Cove, NY *11542*
☎ (561) 231-0302 . . 450 Beach Rd, Apt 122, John's Island, Vero Beach, FL *32963*

Victor MR & MRS Royall 3d (Waldorf—Findlay—Wendy Farrell) Rcn.Yn.Y'64 . . . .
MISS Laura D Waldorf . . . .
| ☎ (203) 622-8826
610 Round Hill Rd, Greenwich, CT *06831*

Vidinghoff MISS Alison C . . see MRS A M Campbell 3d
Vidinghoff MR J David . . see MRS A M Campbell 3d
Vidron MR & MRS Jean-François (Marie-Hélène Verrecchia) Bab'85
☎ (011-33-1) 46-40-74-22 . . 22 blvd Jean Mermoz, 92200 Neuilly-sur-Seine, France

Viek DR & MRS Nicholas F (Smith—Jeanne S Barrett) WChesU'64.WChesU'68.WChesU'77. H'47.Temp'48 . . . .
MISS Cornelia C—Y'84—at ☎ (207) 443-2867 RFD 1, Box 426, King's Point Rd, West Bath, ME *04530* . . . .
MR Bernhard L—at Strasburg Rd, Coatesville, PA *19320* . . . .
| Box 208, Lilongwe, Malawi

Viele MR Chase—St.Rv.Sar.Ll.Hl.Ht.Buf'51
☎ (716) 884-6113 . . 338 Summer St, Buffalo, NY *14222*

Vieta MRS John O (Henrietta E Countiss) . . of
☎ (212) 838-7048 . . 200 E 66 St, New York, NY *10021*
☎ (203) 259-4436 . . ''Mine Acres'' 2300 Bronson Rd, Fairfield, CT *06430*

Vieta DR & MRS Paul A (Leila A May)
Sth'64.Cl'62.NJMed'66 . . . .
MISS Kathryn M—Sth'93—at Bowman Gray Sch of Med . . . .
MISS Amy E—Duke'95 . . . .
MISS Laura L—at Wake Forest . . . .
MR Paul A JR—at Notre Dame . . . .
| ☎ (910) 484-1329
2906 Skye Dv, Fayetteville, NC *28303*

Vietor MRS Alexander O (Anna G Butler)
Cly.Eyc.Ny.StJ.Ht.Lm.Cda.Dc.Ncd.Dh.Y.
MR Andreas H—Ny.Y.CtCol'91—see *Dilatory Domiciles* . . . .
JUNIORS MR Edward M . . . .
| of ☎ (212)249-4949
620 Park Av, New York, NY *10021*
☎ (508) 627-4654
''Grandma's House''
31 S Water St, Edgartown, MA *02539*

Vietor MR & MRS Alexander W (Carol L Bancker)
Eyc.Ny.Cda.Dh.Tufts'72.Nu'75 . . . .
MISS Cornelia O—at Coll of Charleston . . . .
MISS Lindsay J—at Taft . . . .
JUNIORS MISS Anna B . . . .
| ☎ (914) 967-3934
301 Purchase St, Rye, NY *10580*

Vietor MR & MRS David B (Williams—Megan L Williams)
Sim'74.Eyc.Ny.Sfy.Rcn.Snc.Cw.Y'63
☎ (508) 627-3483 . . 29 S Water St, Edgartown, MA *02539-2105*

Vietor MR & MRS G F Trevor (Paige B Jones) Y'77
☎ (301) 229-1884 . . 6312 Winston Dv, Bethesda, MD *20817*

Vietor MR & MRS George F (Helen S Trevor) Bnd'47.Y'40
☎ (713) 524-6417 . . 1817 Sharp Place, Houston, TX *77019*

Vietor MRS Julia B (Julia G Bastedo) Br'70.Cl'78 . .
MISS Barbara G—SCal'90—at ☎ (510) 820-6855 1306 Dawn Court, San Ramon, CA *94583* . . . . .
MR John R—CalSt'95—at ☎ (818) 705-2204 5688 Etiwanda St, Apt 208, Tarzana, CA *91356*
| ☎ (916) 587-8409
''On Top of the World'' 12676 Pinnacle Loop, PO Box 10178, Truckee, CA *96162*

Vietor MR & MRS Oliver R (Ashley E Waring) StJColl'94.Eyc.USN'93
570 Whitney Av, New Haven, CT *06511*

Vietor MR & MRS Richard R (Nicholls—Rosemary Schmitt) Un.Ny.Plg.Cly.Cda.Y'64.Cl'66 . . . . . .
MISS Abigail F—at Sarah Lawrence . . . .
| of ☎ (212)879-0420
149 E 73 St, New York, NY *10021*
☎ (860) 364-0643
''Tazewell Hall''
Amenia Union Rd, Sharon, CT *06069*
☎ (561) 795-3499
2220 Las Casitas Dv, Wellington, FL *33414*

Vietor MRS Thomas F (Carolyn Raymond) . . . . Died Aug 24'96
Vietor MR Thomas F—P'38
☎ (212) AT9-8263 . . 21 E 90 St, New York, NY *10128*

Viguers MRS Charles L 3d (Wheeler—Winifred D Smith) Pa'45
☎ (610) MU8-5073 . . 614 Brookside Av, St Davids, PA *19087*

Vilas MISS Elizabeth
☎ (216) 795-5820 . . 2469 E 124 St, Cleveland, OH *44120*

Vilas REV & MRS Franklin E JR (Joyce B Hoinacki)
Y'56.VaTheo'59.ANewton'70.NYTheo'79
☎ (201) 635-8211 . . 94 Chatham St, Chatham, NJ *07928*

Vilas MR & MRS Malcolm B JR (Kathleen Landerfin) Un.May.Cv.Y'40
☎ (216) 423-4563 . . Box 95, 1650 County Line Rd, Gates Mills,
OH *44040*

Villa MR & MRS Anthony G (Ann M Herkness) Pratt'79.B.Rcn.Eh.H'72
☎ (908) 234-1968 . . PO Box 396, Peapack, NJ *07977*

Villa MR Anthony L—Rcn.B.Eh.Shcc.H'42 . . . . | ☎ (908) 234-0464
MISS Diana B—at ☎ (213) 936-2266 | ''Minnow Manor''
367 N Sierra Bonita Av, Los Angeles, CA *90036* | Peapack, NJ *07977*
MR Nicholas G—Ne'84—☎ (908) 234-1260 . . . |

Villa MR & MRS L Blair (Sarah A Potter) LakeF'79
☎ (508) 468-1307 . . ''The Pebble'' 118 Grapevine Rd, Wenham,
MA *01984*

Villa MR & MRS Peter L (Alison A Read) Sth'76.B.Eh.DU'75
☎ (908) 781-1908 . . 15 Willow Av, Peapack, NJ *07977*

Villalba MISS Sonia M—Nu'78 . . see MRS S H Grimm

Villard MR Dimitri S—Rcn.Mt.Hn.H'64
☎ (310) 659-7016 . . 1542 Blue Jay Way, Los Angeles, CA *90069*

Villard MR & MRS Vincent S (Katharine A Tomkins) BMr'26.Cs.
☎ (212) 734-6473 . . 115 E 67 St, New York, NY *10021*

Villard MRS Vincent S JR (Judith M Mann) V'62.Cal'67.Cs.Ncd.Ne.
☎ (212) 628-6475 . . 945 Fifth Av, New York, NY *10021*

Villasenor MRS Andrew J (Cynthia A B Hart)
☎ (702) 265-4311 . . 1044 Riverview Dv, Apt H, Gardnerville,
NV *89410*

Villeré MR & MRS St Denis J (Margie S Hillery) | of ☎ (504)895-0578
Ncmb'60 | 1443 Eleonore St,
MISS Elizabeth D . . . . | New Orleans, LA
MISS Margaret T . . . . | *70115*
MISS Sidonie S . . . . | ☎ (601) 467-9564
MR St Denis J JR . . . . | ''Villeré Place''
| 625 N Beach St,
| Waveland, MS
| *39576*

Villmoare MR & MRS Edwin S 3d (Wrapp—Paula H | ☎ (415) 383-9436
Bowlin) Lindenwd'66.Smu'71.H'63.Va'69 . . . . | 828 Autumn Lane,
MR Brian A . . . . | Mill Valley, CA
MR Paul A . . . . | *94941*
MR Paul R Wrapp . . . . |

Vilter MRS Carl F (Elder—Barbara H Wood) . . . . . . | ☎ (513) 271-0770
MISS Alice L Elder . . . . | 7717 Ahwenasa
| Lane, Cincinnati,
| OH *45243*

Vincel MISS Carolyn A . . see A Fletcher JR

Vincent MR & MRS A W Bourn (Banet—Rivet—Delbos—
Elisabeth Tourne) Pcu.Bur.Camb'39
☎ (415) 921-2461 . . 1055 California St, Apt 11, San Francisco,
CA *94108*

Vincent MR Anthony T—Sfh.M.Me.StA.Pa'62
see Dilatory Domiciles

Vincent MRS Charles R (Charlotte J McCarroll) Denis'40
☎ (408) 625-1431 . . 91 Del Mesa Carmel, Carmel, CA *93923*

Vincent MR & MRS Gilbert T (Smith—Elinor | ☎ (607) 547-5577
Johnston) H'67.Camb'69.Del'72.Del'82 . . . . . . | ''Benjamin North
MR J Quincy Smith—Y'93—at 8 Palm Court, | House''
857 Partridge St, Menlo Park, CA *94025* . . . . | PO Box 525,
MR Nicholas O Smith—HWSth'95—at | Cooperstown, NY
☎ (208) 726-1024 . . PO Box 6695, Ketchum, | *13326*
ID *83340* . . . . |

Vincent MRS Linn Rumsey (M Linn C Rumsey) | ☎ (713) 973-7010
Tex'67 | 12644 Huntingwick
JUNIORS MR Kenneth R . . . . | Dv, Houston, TX
| *77024*

Vincent MR & MRS Peter C (Maureen A Reynolds) | ☎ (914) 234-9358
Bgt. . . . . | 5 Millbrook Rd,
MISS Catharine W—at St Lawrence U . . . . | Bedford, NY *10506*
MISS Allison E—at U of Hartford . . . . |
MISS S Kerby . . . . |
JUNIORS MISS Maureen E . . . . |

Vincent MR & MRS Robert C (Carlson—Karin | of ☎ (914)234-9697
Rahm) Rc.Bgt.Chr.Dth'61.Cl'65 . . . . | 197 Stone Hill Rd,
MISS Caroline T—Duke'88.Bgt.—*see* | Pound Ridge, NY
Dilatory Domiciles . . . . | *10576*
| ☎ (410) 778-0825
| ''Comegys Choice''
| PO Box 297,
| Chestertown, MD
| *21620*

Vincent MR Robert C 3d (Robert C) . . . . Married at Bedford, NY
Miller MISS Elise A (Charles G JR) . . . . Jly 27'96

Vincent MR & MRS Roger B (Nancy L Mosenson) | ☎ (914) 241-2468
V'67.Bgt.Y.'67.H'70 | Broad Brook Rd,
MR Roger B JR—at 110 W 96 St, Apt 6B, | Bedford Hills, NY
New York, NY *10025* . . . . | *10507-2235*
MR Andrew M—at Carleton . . . . |

Vincent MR & MRS Tiffany (Sandra Lachman) Cal'74.Alaska'84
☎ (907) 488-9765 . . 1966 Camomile Lane, Fairbanks, AK *99712*

Vinci MR & MRS Gerald F (Elizabeth E Connell) Me.VillaN'87.Temp'90
413 Brookwood Rd, Wayne, PA *19087*

Vineyard DR & MRS John Pendleton JR (Kolander—
Mary A Broussard) LSU'62.So'52
☎ (512) 452-5665 . . 3232 Tarry Hollow Dv, Austin, TX *78703*

Violich MR & MRS Thomas J (B Deanne Gillette) Sth'66.Cal'61
2295 Bella Vista Dv, Santa Barbara, CA *93108*

Virgin MR & MRS William P (Hester M Stickley) Mit'47.Dick'48
☎ (614) 267-9654 . . 200 Fallis Rd, Columbus, OH *43214-3726*

Vitagliano MRS Giuseppe (Kathryn E Ness) Sth'30 . . of
☎ (203) 661-2722 . . ''Villa Vitagliano'' 52 Upland Dv, Greenwich,
CT *06831-4451*
☎ (561) 659-6123 . . 3800 Washington Rd, West Palm Beach, FL *33405*

Vitagliano MISS Maria T (Pape—Skillin—Maria T Vitagliano) Bnd'69.Mid'71.Pace'79 . . . . | of ☎ (212)371-6330 403 E 58 St, New York, NY 10022
JUNIORS MISS Katrina V Pape . . . . |
JUNIORS MISS Adele E Skillin . . . . |

☎ (203) 661-2722 "Villa Vitagliano" 52 Upland Dv, Greenwich, CT 06831-4451

Vlcek MRS Jan Benes (Ann E Lewis) Stan'79.Geo'81.Cvc.Sl. . . . . | ☎ (301) 657-2035 30 Quincy St, Chevy Chase, MD 20815
MISS Elizabeth Ann—at Princeton . . . . |
JUNIORS MISS Katharine Benes—at Nat'l Cath Sch |

Vlietstra MR & MRS Klaas F (Dorothy T Royce) 14601 Bestor Blvd, Pacific Palisades, CA 90272

Voehl MISS Allison H—Duke'91 . . see MRS L R Palmer

Voevodsky MR & MRS John (Jennifer L Bain) Stan'64.Ariz'60.Stan'61 . . . . | ☎ (415) 854-3019 177 Goya Rd, Portola Valley, CA 94025
MR Greg . . . . |

Voevodsky MR & MRS Peter (Josephine R Spalding Reeve) Stan'59.Ariz'57.Ariz'67 ⚓
☎ (520) 298-3898 . . 10603 E Speedway Blvd, Tucson, AZ 85748

Vogel MR & MRS Ralph B (Mabel H Harris) My.Chi.Ncd.H.'56 . . . . | ☎ (508) 927-3759 675 Hale St, Beverly Farms, MA 01915
MR Ralph B 2d—H'91—at ☎ (773) 871-1828 2626 N Lakeview Av, Apt 1304, Chicago, IL 60614 . . . . |

Vogel MRS William D (Virginia K Booth) ☎ (414) 962-0689 . . 3704 N Lake Dv, Milwaukee, WI 53211

Vogel MR William D 2d—My.Rc.H.'84 ☎ (212) 288-8886 . . 45 East End Av, Apt 10F, New York, NY 10028-7982

Voges MRS Shelton C (Gaye Carroll) V'47 ☎ (314) 993-9450 . . 9450 Ladue Rd, St Louis, MO 63124

Voges MR & MRS Shelton C JR (Elizabeth E Pulitzer) Nu'83.Nd.ColC'73 ☎ (914) 223-5511 . . PO Box 30, Billings, NY 12510

Vogt MR & MRS Peter A (Nancy R Scharff) Tex'80.Me.Gm.Rc.Msq.P'78 ☎ (610) 649-5392 . . 824 Buck Lane, Haverford, PA 19041

Vogt MR Thomas Bulman . . . . | 5900 Old Ocean Blvd, Apt B7, Ocean Ridge, FL 33435
MISS Newell W . . . . |

Vogt MR & MRS William T (Lorine J Eshleman) Me.A.Gm.Rc.Fst.B.Msq.Ac.Ncd.P'45 ☎ (610) 649-2906 . . 437 College Av, Haverford, PA 19041

Vogt MR William T JR—Rcp.Me.Msq.A.Tufts'74 ☎ (512) 527-4118 . . Balderas Ranch, PO Box 477, Hebbronville, TX 78361

Vohr MISS Caroline Sheldon (Neal P) . . . . Born at Laurel Hollow, NY Sep 1'95

Vohr MR & MRS Neal P (Caroline C Jansing) LakeF'89.Ck.SUNY'82 ☎ (516) 692-9544 . . 592 Cold Spring Rd, Laurel Hollow, NY 11791

Volberding DR & MRS (DR) Paul A (McDonald—Mary M Cooke) Stan'73.Stan'77.Ch'71.Minn'75 | ☎ (415) 661-2361 112 Upper Terr, San Francisco, CA 94117
JUNIORS MR Alexander C . . . . |

Volk MRS Harold Francis (Dorothy L Hill) ☎ (214) 352-4277 . . 4928 Briarwood Place, Dallas, TX 75209

Volkman MRS Chester H (Amberg—Janet K Law) M&H'36 ☎ (314) 993-6514 . . 33 Woodcliffe Rd, St Louis, MO 63124-1336

Volkmann MRS William G JR (Smith—Orabelle S Carter) ☎ (209) 255-0266 . . 945 S Clovis Av, E, Fresno, CA 93727-4530

Volmert, Craig A & Buell, N Catherine—Wash'87 ☎ (314) 862-4649 . . 85 Greendale Dv, St Louis, MO 63121

von Arnim CT & CTSS Joachim (Camille R Campbell) Denis'84.Unn.Bab'86 ☎ (011-49-89) 98-51-05 . . Pienzenauerstrasse 9, 81679 Munich, Germany

von Bachmayr MRS Georg (Shirley G Collins) ☎ (505) 983-8319 . . Rte 4, Box 18, Santa Fe, NM 87501

von Braun MASTER Alexander Stewart Jansen (Peter C M S) . . . . Born Apr 5'94

von Braun MR & MRS Peter C M S (Denene G Jensen) Skd'72.Ny.Ihy.StJ.Yn.Y'64.Colog'66 "Athelcroft" 36 Zaccheus Mead Lane, Greenwich, CT 06831

von Briesen MR & MRS Edward F (Alice R Marvin) Tufts'70.Plg.Pr.Snc.Tufts'70 ☎ (516) 922-1052 . . 133 Horseshoe Rd, Mill Neck, NY 11765

von Czoernig MR & MRS Eric W (Alison A Miller) CedarC'87.M'vian'87 ☎ (610) 971-9139 . . 6 Hopeton Lane, Villanova, PA 19085

von Czoernig MR & MRS Frederick H JR (Jill S Skiem) Aug'80.ManMus'84.Lynch'84 3 Hopeton Lane, Villanova, PA 19085

von Czoernig MRS Mary B (von Czoernig—Trabbold—Mary B M Wheeler) Ac . . . . | ☎ (610) 687-2817 219 S Aberdeen Av, Wayne, PA 19087
MR John P . . . . |
MR David K Trabbold . . . . |

vonder Heyden MISS Erika . . see MRS R T Abbott

Vondermuhll MR & MRS George A JR (Rosamond Lombard) Rdc'32.P'35 ☎ (860) 726-2058 . . Duncaster P222, 60 Loeffler Rd, Bloomfield, CT 06002-2275

von Estorff MRS Fritz E (Erdmuthe F E von Lindeiner) ☎ (914) 725-2743 . . 241 Old Army Rd, Scarsdale, NY 10583

von Estorff MISS (DR) Irene—Ws'62.Mayo'80 ☎ (914) 534-2878 . . PO Box 505, Deer Hill Rd, Cornwall-on-Hudson, NY 12520

von Goeben MISS Hedda Windisch—Hart'66 ☎ (860) 868-9904 . . 23 Juniper Meadow Rd, Washington Depot, CT 06794

von Gontard MR & MRS Adalbert JR (Marie E W Williams) Wash'51 . . of ☎ (203) 869-3238 . . 530 Round Hill Rd, Greenwich, CT 06831 ☎ (401) 348-8944 . . "Sunnyledge Cottage" Ridge Rd, Watch Hill, RI 02891

von Gontard MR & MRS Adalbert 3d (Heath—Beatrice A Busch) GeoW'76 ☎ (540) 636-7118 . . Oxbow Farm, 1042 Milldale Rd, Front Royal, VA 22630

von Grchich . . see Grchich von Cvetkovacz

von Grosse MR & MRS Aristid V (Veronica J S Jack) P'56.Stan'59 . . . . | ☎ (714) 830-7671 25361 Champlain Rd, Laguna Hills, CA 92653
MISS Shane L—at U of Cal Irvine . . . . |
MR Kimbray V—SanDiegoSt'94 . . . . |

von Guggenberg MR & MRS Nicholas M (Martha M Butler) Flor'38 . . . .
MR Eric J—CathU'79—at ☎ (703) 548-1355 1707 Price St, Alexandria, VA 22301 . . . .
MR Christopher S—VPI'84—at
☎ (703) 683-6649 . . 316 E Bellefonte Av, Alexandria, VA 22301 . . . .
☎ (703) 683-5389
640 Oakland Terr, Alexandria, VA 22302

von Hafften MR & MRS Alexander H (E Sebelle Harden) Stan'44.Sfg.Pcu.Tcy.Ncd.Stan'34.Stan'39
☎ (415) 386-1895 . . 3898 Washington St, San Francisco, CA 94118

von Hafften DR & MRS (DR) Alexander H JR (Kerstin M Miller) Stan'81.Stan'82.GeoW'86.Stan'80.Stan'83.GeoW'87
☎ (907) 346-3477 . . 11540 Trails End Rd, Anchorage, AK 99516

von Heisermann MRS Julian H (Marion A Blunt) GeoW'65.Dar.Cda.
☎ (914) 533-6516 . . 165 Laurel Ridge Rd, South Salem, NY 10590-9544

von Heisermann MR Julian H—Vca.Witw'59
☎ (212) 348-5727 . . 1150 Fifth Av, Apt 3E, New York, NY 10128

von Hemert MR & MRS C A Philippe (Edith C Bancroft) Cc.Ac.Pn.P'44
☎ (215) CH8-3342 . . 8111 St Martin's Lane, Philadelphia, PA 19118-4102

von Hess MR Richard C—Evg.BtP.
"Tinsley Cottage" 300 E Main St, Lititz, PA 17543

von Lunz MR & MRS Robert C (Anna H Reese) Md'72.Cnt.UWash'61.UWash'62 . . . .
MISS Anne-Elizabeth B . . . .
MR Robert A H . . . .
JUNIORS MISS Sarah K L . . . .
☎ (410) 823-2926
"Belford"
524 E Seminary Av, Towson, MD 21286

von Mecklenburg MR Frederick H—Mt.Cvc.
RD 1, Box 55C, Fly Creek, NY 13337

von Meister MR & MRS Rudolph W (Chou Yen-ling) TaiwN'78.Pa'80.Cl'85
☎ (011-86-10) 6456-7551 . . GM Beijing, China, GM Bldg 3-220, Detroit, MI 48202

von Moltke MISS Annabel (g—Arthur A Houghton 3d) . . . . Born at Berlin, Germany May 22'96

von Moschzisker MR Felix—Y'65
☎ (802) 496-2059 . . Fish Haul Farm, Warren, VT 05674

von Moschzisker MR Michael . . . . Died at Sarasota, FL Dec 29'95

von Moschzisker MRS Michael (Marjorie E Drayton)
☎ (215) 242-3992 . . 1005 Hill House, 201 W Evergreen Av, Philadelphia, PA 19118

von Mueffling MR Charles F—Duke'92 . . see G Crawford
von Mueffling MR William A—Cl'90 . . see G Crawford

von Nirschl MR David A—Ct.Plg.Snc.Cc.Cp.Cw.Rv.Wt.Ill'85.Smu'91
☎ (703) 525-4070 . . 1050 N Stuart St, Apt 228, Arlington, VA 22201

von Oehsen MR & MRS (REV) William Henry Early (Nancy D Early) Vt'82.H'86.P'81.H'84.Geo'88
☎ (301) 774-3905 . . 1905 Brighton Dam Rd, PO Box 90, Brookeville, MD 20833

von Raab MISS Alexandra L—Denis'95 . . see C E Baskett

von Raab MR William—Rcn.B.Y'63.Va'66 . . of
☎ (540) 672-3493 . . Oldford Farm, Rochelle, VA 22738
☎ (703) KI8-7327 . . 215 Prince St, Alexandria, VA 22314

von Raits MR & MRS Eric A (Hollister—Heaton—Kathleen C Tripp)
☎ (904) 285-8244 . . Box A204, Vicar's Landing Way, Ponte Vedra Beach, FL 32082-3114

von Raits MR Peter de P—Cl'62
☎ (805) 969-0742 . . 122 Hermosillo Dv, Santa Barbara, CA 93108

von Russow MR & MRS Wolfgang L (Janet M Heckmann) Rol'76
☎ (516) 941-4145 . . 177 Old Field Rd, Setauket, NY 11733

von Stade MISS Caroline L—NCar'76
☎ (215) 247-3122 . . 7120 McCallum St, Philadelphia, PA 19119

von Stade MR & MRS Charles S (Eleanor F Trevor) Unn.Cly.Dc.Ht.Y'67 . . . .
MISS Eleanor F—Y'96—at Columbia Phys & Surg . . . .
JUNIORS MR Charles S 3d—at Tabor Acad . . . . .
☎ (970) 926-4700
2121 N Frontage Rd W, Apt 194, Vail, CO 81657

von Stade MRS F Skiddy JR (Susan Russell) Tvb.Chi. . . . .
MISS Susan . . . .
MR Christopher R . . . .
MR William F . . . .
☎ (603) 563-8184
PO Box 268, Dublin, NH 03444

von Stade MR & MRS Frederick H (Carolyn L Carrier) Sth'50.Ncd.
☎ (561) 243-8826 . . 1171 N Ocean Blvd, Apt 4NB, Gulf Stream, FL 33483

von Stade MR & MRS John T (Sandra K Carnahan) Rcn.Srr.Shcc.Eh.H'60
☎ (908) 234-0430 . . 54 Fowler Rd, Peapack, NJ 07977

von Stade MR & MRS John T JR (Ann G Crisp) StLaw'88
☎ (212) 348-6354 . . 200 E 90 St, New York, NY 10128

von Thelen MR & MRS Alexander C (Kristin G Rambusch) Bel'82.Va'76
☎ (540) 456-8243 . . "Mill Hill" Rte 1, Box 145, Greenwood, VA 22943

von Thelen MR & MRS Alexander J (Pamela J Macy) Va'37 . . . .
MR Christopher M—Va'86 . . . .
☎ (804) 293-3647
"Chathill"
675 Bloomfield Rd, Charlottesville, VA 22903

von Waldow MR & MRS Bernd (Maria Theresia Shrady) Kiel'66 . . . .
MISS Maria Donata
JUNIORS MISS Maria Christina
JUNIORS MISS Maria Benedicta . . . .
☎ (011-49-228) 35-21-92
Augusta Strasse 56, 53173 Bonn, Germany

von Weise MR & MRS W Gage JR (McCay—Meyer —June C Oltmans) Ariz'63.Str.Wash'62 . . . . . .
MISS Eliza F Meyer—at Stephens Coll . . . . .
MR Andrew T McCay—at 2883 Golden Gate Av, San Francisco, CA 94118 . . . .
☎ (314) 968-4570
370 Gray Av, Webster Groves, MO 63119-3608

von Wentzel MRS Elizabeth Cabot (Elizabeth T Cabot) V'64.Wes'65.Myc.Chi. ⚓ . . . .
MISS Severa—at Middlebury . . . .
MR John A—at Linde Jingumae 301, Jingumae 2 22 10, Shibuya-ku, Tokyo 150, Japan
MR Constantin—at 219 Broadway, Arlington, MA 02174 . . . .
☎ (207) 833-6724
Fire Lane 544, Rte 123, PO Box 313, South Harpswell, ME 04079-0313

von Werssowetz MR & MRS Richard O (Margaret R McLeod) Cyb.Sm.Ncd.GaTech'68.H'73
☎ (803) 723-6418 . . 8 Rutledge Av, Charleston, SC 29401

von Wettberg MR & MRS Eduard F 3d (Ella G Lewis) Y'61.Pa'64 . . . .
MR Eduard F 4th . . . .
MR Nicholas P . . . .
☎ (302) 655-4865
718 Greenhill Av, Wilmington, DE 19805

von Wiesenthal MISS Andrea S (late Peter G) . . . . Married at
Rancho Santa Fe, CA

Blanc MR Soren W (William R) . . . . Sep 16'95

von Wiesenthal MR & MRS Peter Christian (Linda J Hiatt)
IaState'80.Srr.ClarkU'79
☎ (414) 722-3813 . . 1385 Whipple Tree Lane, Neenah, WI *54956*

von Zweck MR & MRS Heimart (Laura B Pollock)
Wheat'77.Bvl.Graz'58 ⚓
☎ (617) 354-3385 . . 221 Mt Auburn St, Cambridge, MA *02138*

Voorham MR & MRS Markus A B (Vanessa H Hicks) Cr'91.Cl'94
☎ (212) 579-9145 . . 322 W 80 St, Apt 2, New York, NY *10024*

Voorham MASTER Timothy Paul Anthonius (Markus A B) . . . . . . Born at
Port Chester, NY Apr 1'96

Voorhees MR & MRS Clifford I Van (Nancy W Washburn)
Hl.Cr'44.Rut'51 . . of
☎ (561) 659-0921 . . 1200 S Flagler Dv, West Palm Beach, FL *33401*
☎ (516) 283-0781 . . "Hidden Treasure" PO Box 974, Southampton,
NY *11969*

Voorhees MR & MRS Donald A (Freeman—Jane E Pedley) SCal'42
☎ (707) 255-1756 . . Black Oak Ranch, 2846 Monticello Rd, Napa,
CA *94558*

Voorhees MR Roland—Ny.Hl.Pn.P'35
☎ (203) 655-6101 . . 72 Peach Hill Rd, Darien, CT *06820*

Voorhees MRS Theodore (Dora M Johnson)
☎ (202) 333-3786 . . 1731 Hoban Rd NW, Washington, DC *20007*

Voorhees MR & MRS Willard P (Natalie V C Ross) | ☎ (802) 457-1442
Hl. . . . . | Hartland Hill Rd,
MR Roland P—Vt'74—at West Woodstock, | Box 306,
VT *05091* . . . . | Woodstock, VT
| *05091*

Voorhies MRS Charles H (Doris Danenhower)
☎ (360) 693-8659 . . 8815 SE Hillcrest Dv, Vancouver, WA *98664*

Vosburgh MR & MRS Peter G (Scofield—Robinson | ☎ (860) 542-5788
—Edwina C Schock) Sth'53.Rdc'55.Hl.Sb.Snc. | 21 Litchfield Rd,
Y'52 . . . . | Norfolk, CT *06058*
MISS Caroline C—RISD'93—*see*
Dilatory Domiciles . . . .

Vose MR & MRS Elliott E (Murphy—Ann Cogswell) | of ☎ (212)744-4553
Bcs.Cly.Y'45w.Y'50 | 150 E 73 St,
MISS Esmé C Murphy—H'81—at Minneapolis, | New York, NY
MN . . . . | *10021*
| ☎ (516) 653-4574
| Old Point Rd,
| Box 442, Quogue,
| NY *11959*

Vose MRS Frederic H E (Vivian I Shelton) . . . . | ☎ (757) 380-0822
MR Frederic E—at Gainesville, FL . . . . | 7505 River Rd, Apt
| G6, Newport News,
| VA *23607-1772*

Vose MRS Pamela D (Law—Pamela Daly) Sth'51.Cal'85
☎ (619) 459-9011 . . 400 Prospect St, La Jolla, CA *92037*

Vose MR & MRS S Morton 2d (Ruth Denny) H.'31 . . | ☎ (617) 277-5630
MISS Virginia W—at 12049 Lakeside Place NE, | 111 High St,
Seattle, WA *98125* . . . . | Brookline, MA
MR Seth M 3d—CulverStock'74 . . . . | *02146*

Voss MR & MRS Edwin A P (Mary O Holmes) Sar.Dar.Cda.Van'58
1836 Old Natchez Trace, Franklin, TN *37064-4785*

Vowell MR & MRS J Scott (M Cameron McDonald)
Hlns'68.Ala'74.Tex'78.Aub'59.Va'61
☎ (205) 939-1166 . . 2625 Crest Rd, Birmingham, AL *35223*

Vreeland MRS Alexander (Sandra C Isham) . . . . Died at
Bridgehampton, NY Aug 5'96

Vulté MRS Richard T (Imogene C Price)
☎ (415) 388-3129 . . 113 Hillside Av, Mill Valley, CA *94941*

W

Wack MRS John T de Blois (Carolyn P Hoefer)
☎ (805) 969-4833 . . PO Box 5069, 105 Coronada Circle, Santa Barbara,
CA *93150*

Wack MR & MRS Patrick J JR (Laura H Sculley) SCal'89.Ihy.P'89
☎ (203) 869-5004 . . 21 John St, Greenwich, CT *06831-2608*

Wacker MR & MRS Frederick G JR (Ursula | ☎ (619) 568-4967
Comandatore) Sr.On.Rc.Y'40 . . . . | 74-105 Quail Lakes
MISS Wendy—at (847) 289-6546 | Dv, Indian Wells,
542 Michigan Av, Apt 3, Evanston, IL *60202* . . | CA *92210*
MR Joseph C . . . . | May 1 . .
| ☎ (847) 234-2833
| 1600 Green Bay Rd,
| Lake Bluff, IL
| *60044*

Wacker MR & MRS Frederick G 3d (Patricia S Sebesta)
Rc.Sr.P'81.LakeF'85.Nw'88
☎ (847) 234-5698 . . 569 Maple Av, Lake Bluff, IL *60044*

Waddell MR & MRS Frederick H (Catherine B Marlette) Dth'75.Dth'75
☎ (847) 256-3502 . . 1111 Ashland Av, Wilmette, IL *60091*

Wade MR & MRS Festus J (Gear—Elizabeth Dorsey | ☎ (601) 366-4552
Nicholson) RMWmn'65.Y'49 | 1848 E Northside
MISS Susan B . . . . | Dv, Jackson, MS
| *39211*

Wade MR & MRS George J (Gwendolen B | ☎ (212) 249-0537
Livermore) Cl'63.Un.Plg.StJ.Cly.Ford'59.H'62 . | 1 East End Av,
MISS Barbara C . . . . | New York, NY
MR George J—at Syracuse U . . . . | *10021*

Wade DR George R—Gm.Rc.Aht'40.Pa'43
☎ (610) 644-5098 . . Box 358, 1570 Le Boutillier Rd, Paoli, PA *19301*

Wade MR & MRS Jeptha H (Emily Vanderbilt) Mit'45.Sm.Tv.Mit'45
☎ (617) 275-6838 . . 251 Old Billerica Rd, Bedford, MA *01730-1275*

Wadhams MRS Barbara P (Barbara Perry) Rdc'47.Me.
☎ (610) 649-4762 . . 120 Buck Lane, Haverford, PA *19041*

Wadhams MR Edmund L—Y'69
☎ (757) 787-8626 . . 2 Lee St, Onancock, VA *23417*

Wadhams MR William H . . . . Died at
Edgartown, MA Apr 25'96

Wadhams MRS William H (Street—Margaret Sillcocks) Eyc.
☎ (508) 627-4298 . . "The Quiver" PO Box 954, Edgartown, MA *02539*

Wadick MISS Ashley K . . see A R Cooper 2d

Wadmond MRS Lowell (M Elita Cason) BtP.Evg.Mto.Cly . . .of
☎ (212) 289-5144 . . 1192 Park Av, New York, NY *10128*
425 Worth Av, Palm Beach, FL *33480*

Wadsworth, A William & McCulloch, Jeanne R (Taylor—Jeanne R McCulloch) Br'79.Cl'83.Wis'72.Cl'74
☎ (212) 529-9311 . . 24 W 11 St, Apt 4, New York, NY *10011*

Wadsworth MRS Augustus B (Grace M Putnam) Pg.Ncd.
☎ (518) 854-3300 . . ''Timberkill Meadows'' PO Box 6, Arlington, VT *05250*

Wadsworth MRS Burton G (Ordway Whitford)
☎ (603) 224-7884 . . Heritage Heights 300, 149 E Side Dv, Concord, NH *03301*

Wadsworth MRS Charles C (Virginia S Higginson)   ☎ (617) 864-3576
Bost'72.Les'73.Chi. . . . .   31 Hawthorn St,
MR Charles M—at ☎ (617) 864-7812   Cambridge, MA
205 Walden St, Apt 6F, Cambridge, MA *02140* .   *02138*

Wadsworth MR & MRS Dyer S (Beverley A D   ☎ (212) 688-8962
Barringer) Rdc'63.Cl'73.Un.Plg.Y'59.H'62 . . . .   215 E 48 St,
MISS Sophia B—Ty'90   New York, NY
MISS Jennifer S—Dth'90. . . . .   *10017*

Wadsworth MR & MRS Eugene D (Elizabeth E Frothingham) Pr.Cly.Cda.Y.'35 . . of
☎ (516) WA1-2476 . . RD Box 1858, Muttontown Rd, Syosset, NY *11791*
☎ (802) 362-3326 . . Box 641, River Rd, Manchester, VT *05254*

Wadsworth MR George—Mt.Cvc.P'44 . . . .   ☎ (011-52-5)
MR George C   520-7189
    Av Palmas 885,
    5-16-2, Mexico City,
    11000 DF, Mexico

Wadsworth DR & MRS John M (Nichols—Linda Kittinger) Ts.P'59
☎ (716) 886-1919 . . 313 Summer St, Buffalo, NY *14222*

Wadsworth MR & MRS Julius (Miner—Cleome Carroll) Mt.K.Cc.Cly.Sl.H'25 . . of
2304 Massachusetts Av NW, Washington, DC *20008*
Denis Bay Plantation, Box 40, Cruz Bay, St John, VI *00830*

Wadsworth MRS Oliver F (Barbara L Aldrich) Cly.Ncd.
☎ (212) BU8-3011 . . 7 Gracie Square, New York, NY *10028*

Wadsworth MR & MRS Oliver F JR (Ellen C   ☎ (508) 922-9068
Glessner) Bost'56.H'55 . . . .   Paine Av,
MISS Eliza A   Prides Crossing, MA
MR Oliver F III—at 510 E 13 St, Apt 3,   *01965*
New York, NY *10009* . . . .
MR John G . . . .

Wadsworth MR W Austin—Cr'59 . . . .   ☎ (716) 243-1413
MISS (LT) Martha C—USAF.ArizSt'93—at   ''The Homestead''
☎ (518) 381-9456 . . 417—11 St, Schenectady,   PO Box 5, Geneseo,
NY *12302* . . . .   NY *14454*
MR Craig P—at ☎ (716) 658-3364
PO Box 159, Geneseo, NY *14454* . . . .

Wagenlander MR Robert L—Cy.
☎ (216) 751-1100 . . Moreland Courts, 13415 Shaker Blvd, Cleveland, OH *44120*

Wagenlander MR & MRS William A (Susan A   ☎ (216) 834-1935
McAdams) Cy.Pars'67 . . . .   17444 Ravenna Rd,
MISS Katherine C . . . .   Burton, OH *44021*
MR William D. . . . .
MR John S. . . . .

Waggaman MRS Robert M (Welles—Le Breton—Adèle Harman) Cvc.Eyc.Sl.
☎ (301) 320-2363 . . 5209 Cammack Dv, Bethesda, MD *20816*

Waggaman MR & MRS William (Daphne H Geary) Colby'81.Eyc.Br'80
☎ (203) 853-7551 . . 17 Sasqua Rd, Norwalk, CT *06855*

Wagner MR & MRS Barry G (Rosekrans—Volk—Rosemarie Rousseau) Stan'51.Pcu.Stan'41
☎ (415) 751-5674 . . 3701 Washington St, San Francisco, CA *94118*

Wagner MR Charles H—Pr.S.Lic.H'74.Cr'78
☎ (212) 860-8479 . . 300 E 93 St, Apt 40C, New York, NY *10128*

Wagner MR & MRS Colton P (Carley Havemeyer) Rdc'48.Plg.Csh.B.Cly.H'41.H'48
☎ (516) 626-1369 . . 4 Remsen's Lane, East Norwich, NY *11732*

Wagner MISS Elisabeth Anstey (Jeffrey W) . . . . Born at
Bryn Mawr, PA May 2'96

Wagner MR & MRS H Whitney (Helen B Potter) Nat'lCollEd'79.Unn.Shcc.Cly.Ncd.Vt'78
☎ (908) 439-2311 . . PO Box 342, Lamington Rd, Oldwick, NJ *08858*

Wagner MR & MRS Jeffrey W (Catherine McL Vaughan) Buck'82.Me.Ty'79.Dick'82
☎ (610) 889-9747 . . 317 Lenape Dv, Berwyn, PA *19312*

Wagner MR & MRS John (Evelyn Schradiek) Pa'50
☎ (610) 353-5758 . . 102 Martins Run Rd, Media, PA *19063*

Wagner DR & MRS Joseph A (A Bernice Larsen) Cy.F&M'34.Pa'38
☎ (610) 525-4760 . . 201 Highland Lane, Bryn Mawr, PA *19010*

Wagner MR & MRS Richard E (Lucy E Brown) Cm.Qc.Cin'35 . . of
☎ (513) 871-5923 . . 3623 Traskwood Circle, Cincinnati, OH *45208*
☎ (561) 231-1195 . . 5680 N A1A, Apt 314, Vero Beach, FL *32963*

Wagner MRS Robert F (Cerf—Phyllis Fraser)   132 E 62 St,
Bgt.C.Cly.Km.   New York, NY
MR Duncan E—S'Hmptn'70—at 325 E 41 St,   *10021*
New York, NY *10017* . . . .

Wagner MR & MRS Samuel (Mary Ann G G Baker)   ☎ (610) 692-2736
Wh'lck'62.Ac.Ty'61.Temp'64.Pa'71 . . . .   Deborah's Rock
MR Michael C—F&M'92—at U of Pitt Law . . .   Farm, 1090 W
    Strasburg Rd,
    West Chester, PA
    19382

Wagner MR & MRS Stephen P (Carol A Ziemer) RI'72.FlaIT'76
☎ (508) 548-0971 . . 526 Woods Hole Rd, Woods Hole, MA *02543*

Wagner DR & MRS Theodore A (Iris Reid)   ☎ (206) 322-7565
UWash'73.Ty'64.Temp'68 . . . .   216 Fortieth Av E,
MISS Lara R   Seattle, WA *98112*
MR Thor A

Wagnière MR & MRS Daniel C (Anne-Marie   Kirchweg 17,
Perrenoud) SwissTech'61.H'63 . . . .   4102 Binningen,
MR Jean C .   Switzerland

Wagstaff MRS Alfred 3d (Julia A C Frederick)
☎ (011-44-1924) 253130 . . 3 Woodfield Park, Walton, Wakefield, Yorkshire WF2 6PL, England

Wagstaff MR & MRS David 3d (Suse Dignus)   ☎ (504) 524-2471
Ck.Ln.Plg.P'60 . . . .   1436 Jackson Av,
MR David 4th—Ck.Mid'84—at   Apt 4D,
☎ (310) 395-4191 . . 1007—5 St, Apt D,   New Orleans, LA
Santa Monica, CA *90403* *70130*

Wagstaff MR & MRS Richard B (Hope O Brady) Cp.Fr.Dar.Ncd.SFrSt'70
☎ (619) 727-9336 . . 850-155 Brooktree Lane, Vista, CA *92083*

Wainwright MR Alexander D—Gr.Pn.P'39.Cl'41
☎ (609) 924-3999 . . 89 Hartley Av, Princeton, NJ *08540-7209*

Wainwright MR & MRS Carroll L (Nina Walker)
Un.Mds.Cly.Y'49.H'52 . . of
☎ (212) 838-0800 . . 825 Fifth Av, New York, NY *10021*
☎ (516) 324-0312 . . 57 Dunemere Lane, East Hampton, NY *11937*

Wainwright MR & MRS D Walker (Alice E | ☎ (212) 249-3092
Baldridge) Ws'71.Mds.Un.Cly.Stan'72.Cl'74 . . . | 108 E 82 St,
JUNIORS MISS Nina W . . . . | New York, NY
JUNIORS MR Robert B . . . . | *10028*

Wainwright MR & MRS Jonathan M (Olmsted— | of ☎ (212)427-6740
Candace F Drake) Sth'66.Un.Mds.Y'65.Nu'68 . . | 1111 Park Av,
MR Jonathan M JR—Ham'93 . . . . | New York, NY
MR Andrew S—Ham'95 . . . . | *10128*
| ☎ (516) 537-0808
| "Goose Creek"
| Wainscott Rd,
| Wainscott, NY
| *11975*

Wainwright MR & MRS Mark L (Mary La B Stockman) Ws'77.Y'77.Dth'82
☎ (408) 395-5460 . . 32 Peralta Av, Los Gatos, CA *95030*

Wainwright MRS Nicholas B (Daffron—Christine Henry)
☎ (610) 645-8675 . . Waverly Heights, 1400 Waverly Rd, Gladwyne,
PA *19035*

Wainwright MRS Parsons (Janet I Parsons) | ☎ (202) 337-3443
Mds.Cda. . . . . | 3316 Reservoir Rd
MISS Belle B Waring—at U of Cal Berkeley | NW, Washington,
Grad . . . . | DC *20007*
MR Benjamin A Waring—at U of SCar
Columbia . . . .

Wainwright MR & MRS Peter S (Gerri F Jordan) Cl'48 . . of
☎ (602) 948-6935 . . 5039 E Doubletree Rd, Paradise Valley, AZ *85253*
☎ (520) 526-9344 . . "Duckwood" 4849 E Hightimber Lane, Flagstaff,
AZ *86004*

Wainwright MR & MRS Roger S (Deborah Wagstaff)
USwansea'71.L'chester'72
☎ (011-44-1924) 251820 . . 56 The Balk, Walton, Wakefield,
Yorkshire WF2 6JU, England

Wainwright MR Stuyvesant 2d—Un.Mds.Snc.Y'43 ⚓
☎ (516) 537-1122 . . Wainscott Rd, Wainscott, NY *11975*

Wainwright MR & MRS Stuyvesant 3d (Marcella C Mittendorf)
Godd'75.Un.Mds.AmU'65 . . of
☎ (212) 876-0139 . . 65 E 96 St, New York, NY *10128*
☎ (516) 324-0139 . . 16 Fithian Lane, East Hampton, NY *11937*

Wainwright MR Stuyvesant 4th—Cal'87
☎ (415) 752-5202 . . 322 Twentieth Av, San Francisco, CA *94121*

Wainwright MR T F Dixon (Wildman—Sharp—Frances M B Small)
☎ (610) 429-9777 . . 879 Jefferson Way, West Chester, PA *19380*

Wainwright MR Wainwright J—Hb.Sorb'37
☎ (011-33-93) 50-62-08 . . "Le Trocadèro" 43 av de Grande Bretagne,
Monte Carlo, MC 98000, Monaco

Wait MRS William G (Ann B Frothingham) . . . . . . | of ☎ (617)235-3693
MR William G JR—at Camphill Village, Copake, | 9 Marvin Rd,
NY *12516* . . . . | Wellesley, MA
| *02181*
| ☎ (518) 644-9674
| "Eagle's Nest"
| Bolton Landing, NY
| *12814*

Waite MR & MRS Parker R (M Florence Wardwell) Me.Myf.
☎ (610) 525-3947 . . 74 Pasture Lane, Apt 236, Bryn Mawr, PA *19010*

Wakefield MRS G Kennard (Mary M Binney) D.Chi.Ncd.
☎ (617) 333-0324 . . 1465 Brush Hill Rd, Milton, MA *02186*

Wakelin MRS James H JR (Holman—Carol R Ackiss) Cvc.Cos.Sl.
☎ (202) 338-3984 . . 1809—45 St NW, Washington, DC *20007*

Wakeman MR & MRS G Wiley (Michele Hallett) BostColl'86.Bvl.
☎ (207) 967-5803 . . 78R Beachwood Rd, Kennebunkport, ME *04046*

Wakeman MR Richard V JR—Bvl.Cy.Cr'73 . . . . . . | ☎ (508) 748-2860
MISS Wiley M . . . . | PO Box 825,
JUNIORS MR Richard V 3d . . . . | 7 Fraser Way,
| Marion, MA *02738*

Wakeman MRS Samuel (Frances McElwain) | ☎ (617) 383-6514
B'gton'36.Cy. . . . . | 257 Atlantic Av,
MISS Nancy—at ☎ (415) 821-4594 | Cohasset, MA *02025*
1183 Delores St, San Francisco, CA *94114* . . . .

Wakeman MASTER Samuel Hallett (G Wiley) . . . . Born Jan 18'96

Walbridge MISS W Snow . . see E J Doering 2d

Walbridge MR & MRS Cope B (Elizabeth H Mason) | ☎ (212) 744-3170
Un.Sg.Cly.Ncd.Y'35 . . . . | 164 E 66 St,
MISS Margaret B—Cr'74—at ☎ (607) 539-7264 | New York, NY
123 Hunt Hill Rd, Ithaca, NY *14850* . . . . | *10021-6643*

Walbridge MISS Elizabeth C (Leach—Elizabeth C Walbridge) Swb'72.H'88
☎ (520) 527-3726 . . 6550 Hutton Ranch Rd, Flagstaff, AZ *86004*

Walbridge MR & MRS Kenneth M (Jean Palmer) Sth'35.Aht'37
☎ (561) 732-0400 . . 4564 S Lake Dv, Boynton Beach, FL *33436*

Walbridge MR Robert P—Aht'36
☎ (207) 633-3846 . . Landing Rd, Southport, ME *04576*

Walbridge MR & MRS Ryckman R (Karen R | ☎ (610) 326-9280
Monaghan) NH'78.LakeF'70 . . . . | The Hill School,
MISS Kimberly W—at Westover . . . . | Pottstown, PA
| *19464*

Walcott MISS Alexandra (Wahl—Alexandra Walcott)
Br'63.RochTech'65.C.
☎ (212) 228-6892 . . 222 Park Av S, New York, NY *10003*

Walcott MR & MRS Eustis JR (Dickenson—Jenny B | ☎ (413) 567-8881
Jerome) Cy.H.'60 . . . . | 297 Ardsley Rd,
MISS Elisabeth—H'88 . . . . | Longmeadow, MA
MISS Diana P—Denis'92 . . . . | *01106-2505*

Walcott DR & MRS George (Elizabeth Wister) | ☎ (414) 354-3556
Rdc'62.H'54 . . . . | 8365 N Pelican
MISS Isabel—H'91—at ☎ (212) 593-3328 | Lane, Milwaukee,
308 E 53 St, Apt 3B, New York, NY *10022* . . . | WI *53209*
MR Roger—at Harvard . . . .

Walcott MR Richard—Cy.H'34
☎ (617) 232-0054 . . 33 Fairgreen Place, Chestnut Hill, MA *02167*

Walcott MR Wister—H'88.H'93
☎ (415) 566-0224 . . 1096 Ashbury St, Apt 1, San Francisco,
CA *94117-4411*

Walden MRS Charles C 3d (Freisenbruch—Emily A W Darrow)
☎ (914) 687-7332 . . 241 Buck Rd, Stone Ridge, NY *12484*

Walden MR & MRS Russell T (Natalie L Campbell) ColC'72.Conn'70
☎ (513) 561-1071 . . 8675 Camargo Club Dv, Cincinnati, OH *45243*

Waldorf MISS Laura D . . see R Victor 3d

Waldron MR & MRS Adam A (Susan M Wenzell)
Geo'85.Pa'89.HampSydney'84
☎ (610) 388-3472 . . 212 Fairville Rd, Chadds Ford, PA *19317*

Waldron MR & MRS Arthur N (Stones—Xiaowei E Yu)
Peking'81.P'87.Cl'92.Sm.Pn.Hb.Hn.H'71.H'81
☎ (401) 831-5835 . . 74 Humboldt Av, Providence, RI *02906-4533*

Waldron MISS Caroline W (Frederick C) . . . . . Married at Greenwich, CT
Brown MR Brian A H (C Thomas) . . . . Aug 24'96

Waldron MISS Dorothy W—V'75.Bab'78.Cy.
☎ (617) 235-5220 . . 26 Cleveland Rd, Wellesley, MA *02181*

Waldron MR & MRS Frederick C (Giard—Mary W | ☎ (203) 629-4423
Schager) Sth'63.Cl'81.Cly.Y'60.Cl'63 . . . . | 5 Hawkwood Lane,
MISS Allison W—Tufts'95—at New York, NY . | Greenwich, CT
| *06830*

Waldron MRS Sherwood (Norwood—Bolich—Snethen—Mary B Mixsell)
Pr.Ny.Cly.Ncd.Hl.
☎ (516) 671-0100 . . ''Maginot'' Piping Rock Rd, PO Box 433,
Locust Valley, NY *11560*

Waldron MR & MRS William A (Kinnicutt—Sybil K Jay) U'35.H'41
☎ (617) 876-1096 . . 15 Larch Rd, Cambridge, MA *02138*

Waldrop MR Andrew C—Cvc.H'61
☎ (202) 363-7255 . . 5120 Loughboro Rd NW, Washington, DC *20016*

Walk MR & MRS Everett G (Sybil A Prichard) Rc.Dh.OWes'32.Pa'36
☎ (610) 373-2670 . . 1309 Orchard Rd, Reading, PA *19611*

Walk MR Stephen G W—Ny.Snc.Ken'73.Cl'79
☎ (401) 849-0668 . . 18 Thames St, Newport, RI *02840*

Walker MR & MRS A David (Richards—Madeleine J Bittel) Yn.Y'41
☎ (203) 869-5877 . . 475 Field Point Rd, Greenwich, CT *06830*

Walker MR & MRS Alexander D 3d (Alyson B Henning)
Ty'77.Unn.Fic.Fiy.Vt'77
☎ (203) 869-0353 . . 58 Fairfield Rd, Greenwich, CT *06830*

Walker MRS Bayard (Maud Tilghman) Mds.Cly.Cda.
☎ (212) 744-6060 . . 66 E 79 St, New York, NY *10021*

Walker MR Bayard JR—Laf'71
☎ (215) 928-8979 . . 220 Locust St, Apt 23B, Philadelphia, PA *19106*

Walker MR & MRS Benjamin H (Elizabeth Sillcocks) Fw.Ll.Ds.Cw.Ncd.
☎ (401) 847-0677 . . Blenheim, 303 Valley Rd, Middletown, RI *02842*

Walker DR & MRS (DR) Benjamin Harrison JR (Susan M Wuthrich)
Tex'82.Tex'90.An.Il.Bow'80.Cl'85
☎ (401) 848-5994 . . 297 Black Point Lane, Portsmouth, RI *02871*

Walker MASTER Benjamin Harrison 3d (Benjamin Harrison JR) . . . . Born at
Newport, RI Apr 4'96

Walker MR & MRS Benjamin Watson 3d (Beth Carr) | ☎ (334) 264-2028
Ala'73.Ala'72 . . . . | 604 Thorn Place,
MISS April . . . . | Montgomery, AL
MISS Frances F . . . . | *36106*
MR Benjamin Watson 4th . . . . |

Walker MR & MRS Bradford H (Nancy A Alterman) Un.H'63 . . of
☎ (803) 649-4936 . . 523 Colleton Av SE, Aiken, SC *29801*
☎ (212) 888-2340 . . 1 Sutton Place S, New York, NY *10022*
☎ (803) 577-6188 . . 6 Longitude Lane, Charleston, SC *29401*

Walker MR & MRS Brian D (Abby M Gross) SL'77.Tufts'74
☎ (203) 966-6066 . . 34 Old Forge Rd, Wilton, CT *06897*

Walker MRS Brooks (Marjory E Walker) Tcy.
☎ (415) 474-8487 . . 807 Francisco St, San Francisco, CA *94109*

Walker MR & MRS C Carter JR (Julia B Armour) | ☎ (860) 868-0105
B.P'56.Cl'62 . . . . | ''Roughlands''
MISS Julia B—Vt'90 . . . . | 36 Hinkle Rd,
| PO Box 1271,
| Washington, CT
| *06793*

Walker MR & MRS Christopher B (Helen M McDill) | ☎ (617) 862-6943
Stan'55.Mit'51 . . . . | 22 Baskin Rd,
DR Christopher B JR—Carl'84.Col'89—at | Lexington, MA
☎ (612) 733-6968 . . 2158 Grand St, St Paul, MN | *02173*
55105 . . . . |
MR Alexander M—Mid'86—at |
☎ (307) 733-7154 . . PO Box 370, Wilson, WY |
83014 . . . . |
MR Bruce W—ColC'92 . . . . |

Walker MR & MRS Christopher R (Kathleen A Blakeslee) TCU'93.TCU'93
☎ (617) 740-0646 . . 3 Shute Av, Hingham, MA *02043*

Walker MR Daniel A—Y'59 | ☎ (617) 585-6772
MISS Paget H—Hampshire'93 . . . . | 12 Pembroke St,
MISS Eliza W—Ober'94 . . . . | Kingston, MA
| *02364*

Walker MR & MRS David A (Penelope Graham) | Kathmandu, USEF
V'66.H'67.Y'64.H'67 . . . . | DOS, Washington,
MISS Elizabeth McN . . . . | DC *20521-6190*
JUNIORS MR Graham A |
JUNIORS MR Evan M . . . . |

Walker MR & MRS David E (Lisa J Amoroso)
PineM'85.Cyb.Mds.B.Sm.Cly.Ty'83
☎ (203) 869-2988 . . 11 Greenbriar Lane, Greenwich, CT *06831*

Walker MR & MRS David M (Catherine H Bull) Cal'88.StAndr'90
☎ (011-44-171) 602-8443 . . 162 Blythe Rd, London W14 0HD, England

Walker MR Douglass E—Tr.Fic.Fiy.Tufts'86
☎ (617) 899-9482 . . 293 Bishops Forest, Waltham, MA *02154*

Walker MRS E Evans (Elizabeth B A Evans) Ncd.
☎ (803) 723-5339 . . 67 Legare St, Apt 107, Charleston, SC *29401-2447*

Walker MR & MRS E Perot (Elizabeth M Colt) Ph.Sa.Cw.Ac.Pa'38
☎ (610) 828-2442 . . 3009 Park Av, Lafayette Hill, PA *19444*

Walker MISS Electra Adele (David E) . . . . Born Mch 30'96

Walker MRS Frances S (Frances R Stewart) Ck.
☎ (516) 671-5036 . . 7 Coot Rd, Locust Valley, NY *11560*

Walker MRS George G (Lee—Emily D Schniewind) Pr.
☎ (516) 674-3212 . . ''Meadow Hill'' 7 Sheep Lane, PO Box 429,
Locust Valley, NY *11560-0429*

Walker MR & MRS George G JR (Teresa E Blatz) | ☎ (612) 473-6653
Rv.H'51.H'53 . . . . | 3000 Walnut Grove,
MRS Elizabeth S (Elizabeth Schroeder) . . . . | Plymouth, MN
| *55447*

Walker MRS George H (Mary Carter)
☎ (203) 869-1044 . . 5 Perkins Rd, Greenwich, CT *06830*

Walker MR & MRS George H 3d (Martin—Carol Banta)
DU'70.Cy.Lc.Ln.Y'53
☎ (314) 993-6948 . . 136 S Price Rd, St Louis, MO *63124*

Walker MR & MRS Graham McK (Anne Wigglesworth) Kas'65 . . . . ☎ (717) 992-3960 RD 4, Box 4407, Stroudsburg, PA 18360
  MR Thomas W—at ☎ (773) 929-4132 621 W Surf St, Apt 1E, Chicago, IL 60657 . . . .
  MR Lockhart McK—at ☎ (913) 432-3375 5100 Foxridge Dv, Mission, KS 66202 . . . .
  JUNIORS MISS Katherine . . . .

Walker MR & MRS Harry M (L Deery Mott) NCar'74.SoMiss'72 . . . . ☎ (601) 956-9687 148 St Andrews Dv, Jackson, MS 39211
  JUNIORS MISS Anna D . . . .

Walker MRS Helen P (Walker—Tucker—Helen C Prettyman) Pc. . . . . ☎ (215) 336-7709 314 Queen St, Philadelphia, PA 19147
  MISS Ann R—at 200 E 75 St, New York, NY 10021 . . . .
  MISS Sally C . . . .
  MR Webster U 3d . . . .

Walker MR & MRS J Ewing (Alston Barroll) Ph.Chi.Ncd.H'42
  ☎ (207) 563-3420 . . ''Barroll's Point'' Newcastle, ME 04553

Walker MR & MRS James A S (Alexandra R Forbes) Tv.H'50.H'54
  ☎ (508) 785-0679 . . Merrywind Farm, 125 Centre St, Dover, MA 02030

Walker DR & MRS James E C (Audrey C Wakeman) Wms'49 . . . . ☎ (860) 521-3575 111 Westmont Dv, West Hartford, CT 06117
  MR James E C JR—at 700 Lansdowne Way, Apt 208, Norwood, MA 02622 . . . .

Walker MR James G . . see F M Ridley

Walker MR & MRS James H (Elizabeth M Sherman) Mid'76.Hl.Cda.SUNY'79
  ☎ (401) 847-2347 . . 9 Baldwin Rd, Middletown, RI 02842

Walker MR & MRS James Leslie 3d (Elena A Madison) Stan'42 . . of
  ☎ (415) 921-5007 . . 2030 Vallejo St, Apt 204, San Francisco, CA 94123
  ☎ (415) 924-8550 . . ''Casa en Pais'' 36 Tamal Vista, Corte Madera, CA 94925

Walker MR & MRS James W (O'Keefe—Sara A Mitchell) Mb.Pr.Y'30 . . . . . . of ☎ (561)546-6020 104 Rabbit Run Rd, Hobe Sound, FL 33455
  MR John E O'Keefe—Y'60—at 10 Farm Rd, Dover, MA 02030 . . . . ☎ (516) 676-8494 2 Overlook Rd, Matinecock Farms, Glen Cove, NY 11542-3332

Walker MRS John B (Adèle Van A Frank) V'35.Cda. . . . . of ☎ (203)966-9704 643 Oenoke Ridge, New Canaan, CT 06840
  MISS Gwyneth V A (Burton—Gwyneth V A Walker) . . . . ☎ (561) 655-8624 232 Seabreeze Av, Palm Beach, FL 33480

Walker MR & MRS John B H (Frances McL Merryman) Ariz'87.Ariz'88.Ariz'71 . . . . ☎ (520) 325-0606 321 El Camino Del Norte, Tucson, AZ 85716
  JUNIORS MR Benjamin . . . .

Walker MR & MRS John D (Roskam—Schaedtler—Helen Hoogerwerff) Cvc.Plg.Cc.StJ.StA.NCar'44
  ☎ (202) 337-5696 . . 3271 P St NW, Washington, DC 20007

Walker MR & MRS John H (Colette J Hall) Bow'48
  ☎ (703) 356-0198 . . 6515 Ridge St, McLean, VA 22101

Walker MRS John M (E Louise Mead) SL'39 . . of
  ☎ (202) 966-0930 . . 2801 New Mexico Av NW, 724, Washington, DC 20007
  ☎ (561) 546-8622 . . 224 S Beach Rd, Hobe Sound, FL 33455

Walker MR & MRS John M JR (Bingham—Katharine Kirkland) Y'62.Mich'66 . . of
  ☎ (212) 637-0256 . . 500 Pearl St, New York, NY 10007
  ☎ (914) 439-3469 . . Highmeadow Rd, Lew Beach, NY 12753

Walker MRS John S (Katharine D Davidson) V'42.Cvc.
  ☎ (301) 654-3572 . . 7101 Glenbrook Rd, Bethesda, MD 20814

Walker MR John Y G (Mary L Riter)
  ☎ (201) 633-7420 . . 9 Christopher Court, Lincoln Park, NJ 07035

Walker MR Jonathan S . . see F M Ridley

Walker MR & MRS Kenneth B (Susan H MacColl) Wheat'81.OWes'78
  ☎ (860) 521-3039 . . 115 Westland Av, West Hartford, CT 06107

Walker MRS L Gordon 3d (Cara C Smith) . . . . ☎ (610) 935-2454 S Whitehorse Rd, Phoenixville, PA 19460
  MISS Page E—at ☎ (860) 435-4602 Indian Mountain School, 211 Indian Mountain Rd, Lakeville, CT 06037 . . . .
  MR L Gordon 4th—at ☎ (773) 248-0433 665 W Diversey P'kway, Chicago, IL 60614 . . .

Walker MR L Gordon 3d—Wms'62 329 Clothier Springs Rd, Malvern, PA 19355

Walker MRS Lee Telford (Griebel—Lee Telford Walker) . . . . ☎ (707) 833-2160 1693 Warm Springs Rd, Glen Ellen, CA 95442
  MR Webster A Griebel—at 29 White Clay Dv, Newark, DE 19711 . . . . .
  MR Evan W Griebel—at ☎ (410) 745-9125 1 Harrison St, Claiborne, MD 21624 . . . .

Walker MR & MRS Louis (Grace B White) Ln.Y'36
  ☎ (561) 546-6333 . . ''Waterlou'' PO Box 1255, Hobe Sound, FL 33475

Walker MRS Lucinda S (Niehoff—Lucinda K Schaefer) Briar'67 . . . . ☎ (617) 566-9868 128 Middlesex Rd, Chestnut Hill, MA 02167
  MISS Kelly B Niehoff . . . .
  MR K Richard B Niehoff JR . . . .

Walker MR & MRS Malcolm M (Allison Dean) On.Y'44
  ☎ (847) 234-0332 . . 598 Golf Lane, Lake Forest, IL 60045

Walker MR & MRS Mallory (Diana Hardin) Cvc.Mt. . . of ☎ (202)244-8094 3414 Lowell St NW, Washington, DC 20016-5023
  MR Taylor S—H'95—at ☎ (909) 625-6705 Webb School, 1175 W Baseline Rd, Claremont, CA 91711-2199 . . . .
  MR William M—H'95—at 25 de Mayo 299, 3500 Resistencia, Argentina . . . . ☎ (208) 726-8095 140 River Rock Rd, Ketchum, ID 83340-1206

Walker MRS Margo G (Margo K Geer) SL'73.Pr. . . . ☎ (516) 759-0070 ''Wing House'' West Island, Glen Cove, NY 11542
  MISS Sacha K—☎ (516) 759-0094 . . . .
  MR David H—☎ (516) 759-6889 . . . .

Walker MRS Marjorie (Coppin—Kennedy—Marjorie L Walker)
  ☎ (213) 937-5704 . . 117½ N Sycamore Av, Los Angeles, CA 90036

Walker DR Mark C—FlaAtl'82.AmUC'90 . . see MRS W D Findley

Walker DR & MRS Michael D (E Katherine Law) Yn.Y'54.Bost'60
☎ (301) 469-7866 . . 9305 Burning Tree Rd, Bethesda, MD *20817*
Walker MISS Michelle McC . . see F M Ridley
Walker MR & MRS Nicholas M (Cynthia Hyatt) | ☎ (215) 947-2459
NCar'41.Temp'55 . . . . | PO Box 707,
MISS Margaret M—at Villanova Law . . . . | Bryn Athyn, PA
             | *19009*
Walker MRS Norman S (Hélène A Sullivan) . . . . . . | ☎ (413) 628-3901
MR Bryce S—at ☎ (212) 868-0802 . . 17 E 95 St, | ''Little Switzerland''
New York, NY *10128* . . . . | Ashfield, MA *01330*
Walker MR & MRS Norman S (Marie Eve Cournand) | of ☎ (212)535-5689
Bnd'55.Cc.H'46 . . . . | 535 E 86 St,
MISS Anne—at Middlebury . . . . | New York, NY
MR Norman S JR—Ken'82.Nu'91—at | *10028*
307 E 70 St, New York, NY *10021* . . . . | ☎ (413) 628-3387
MR Alan S—Cl'86—at 523 E 85 St, New York, | ''Farmhouse''
NY *10028* . . . . | Hawley Rd,
             | Ashfield, MA *01330*
Walker MISS Pamela Buchanan (Potts—Pamela Buchanan Walker) Bcs.
☎ (212) 288-0370 . . 242 E 72 St, Apt 17B, New York, NY *10021*
Walker MISS Pamela D (Pamela N Drexel) SL'64 . . | ☎ (202) 363-8166
MR Andrew B H . . . . | 3685 Upton St NW,
MR James D—Box 14691, Minneapolis, MN | Washington, DC
55414 . . . . | *20008-3126*
Walker DR & MRS Peter F R (Susan P Locke) | ☎ (516) 673-1080
H'65.Bost'69 . . . . | 342 Woodbury Rd,
MISS Ariadna E M . . . . | Cold Spring Harbor,
MISS Taury S M . . . . | NY *11724-2231*
MR Peter P—at U of Vt |
Walker MR & MRS Philip D (Corlette Rossiter) Stan'46.Y'47
☎ (805) 969-1337 . . 1344 School House Rd, Santa Barbara, CA *93108*
Walker MR Raymond R . . see F M Ridley
Walker MRS Richard C (Clark—Dorothea Williamson) Pcu.Bur.Cly . . .of
☎ (415) 673-7094 . . 890 Chestnut St, San Francisco, CA *94133*
☎ (916) 426-3576 . . ''Sugar Bowl'' PO Box 5, Norden, CA *95724*
Walker MR Richard H—USN'43.Temp'56
☎ (203) 853-8382 . . 100 Gillies Lane, Norwalk, CT *06854*
Walker MR & MRS Richard W (Christine M | of ☎ (011-44-171)
Krumpholz) B.Pcu.Cly. . . . . | 589-2318
JUNIORS MR Marco C—at Brighton U . . . . | 39 Egerton Crescent,
             | London SW3 2EB,
             | England
             | ☎ (011-43-1)
             | 869-0654
             | Rudolfgasse 9,
             | A2380
             | Perchtoldsdorf,
             | Austria
Walker MR & MRS Robert A JR (Monique M Briend) | ☎ (301) 230-9809
Rennes'70.Rennes'71.Godd'74.Vt'83.Bost'86 . . | 10818 Brewer
JUNIORS MISS Charlotte M E . . . . | House Rd,
             | North Bethesda, MD
             | *20852*
Walker MRS Robert C JR (Bettina J Proske) MtH'67.Ariz'81
☎ (520) 744-8647 . . 7629 N Sonoma Way, Tucson, AZ *85743-9489*
Walker MR Robert L . . see F M Ridley

Walker MRS Robert W (Elizabeth Hobbs)
☎ (617) 484-5202 . . 75 Kilburn Rd, Belmont, MA *02178*
Walker MISS Sally B—Cly.
☎ (212) 628-0494 . . 116 E 66 St, New York, NY *10021*
Walker REV & MRS Samuel C (Alice E Rowswell) | ☎ (301) 884-3749
BowlG'68.M.Yn.Urs'65.Y'77 . . . . | Zach Fowler Rd,
MISS Jennifer S . . . . | PO Box 8, Chaptico,
MR Samuel C JR . . . . | MD *20621*
Walker MISS Sarah L (Peter F R) . . . Married at Cold Spring Harbor, NY
Popko MR Bruce G JR (Bruce G) . . . . Aug 3'96
Walker MR Stewart S (Steven S) . . . . Married at Barrington, RI
Gray MISS Andrea R (Dana) . . . . Aug 24'96
Walker MRS Talbott H (Patricia F Holt) Pom'41
☎ (970) 963-5911 . . 0583 Holland Hills Rd, Basalt, CO *81621*
Walker MR & MRS Thomas D (Page P Vincent)
Duke'85.Bgt.Ny.Cly.Bates'85
☎ (914) 234-0513 . . 43 Long Ridge Rd, Bedford, NY *10506*
Walker MR & MRS Thomas G JR (Diana A Lea) Shcc.LakeF'67
☎ (201) 538-0144 . . ''Glynden'' Van Beuren Rd, Morristown, NJ *07960*
Walker MRS W Addison (Judith J Boddie)
☎ (615) 684-9966 . . 363 Riverbend Rd, Shelbyville, TN *37160*
Walker MR & MRS W Wyatt JR (Wood—Hunter— | of ☎ (941)365-3561
Daphne Dodge) W&L'45 . . . . | 888 Blvd of the
  MISS Amanda Wood—Syr'91—at | Arts, Sarasota, FL
☎ (207) 874-9743 . . 32 Deering St, Portland, | *34236*
ME *04101* . . . . | ☎ (508) 257-6354
             | ''Sea Wing''
             | 17 Low Beach Rd,
             | Box 222, Siasconset,
             | MA *02564*
Walker MISS Whitney H—Duke'95 . . see MRS L H Newman
Walker MR & MRS William B (Wanda Wolff) Wash'26.H'28
5602 Williamsburg Landing Dv, Williamsburg, VA *23185*
Walker MR & MRS William B (Ruth E Lennard) Sm.Ri.H'44.JHop'51
☎ (011-41-29) 6-31-89 . . ''Ancien Prieuré'' Box 52, 1636 Broc,
Switzerland
Walker MR & MRS William H (Robin L Thompson) VaCmth'85.Duke'79
6511 Ridge St, McLean, VA *22101*
Walker MR William Henry 2d—St.Hob'33 . . . . | ☎ (716) 885-6725
MR J Thomas . . . . | 1088 Delaware Av,
             | Apt 14A, Buffalo,
             | NY *14209*
Walker MR & MRS William M II (Margaret B | ☎ (610) 687-3271
Bright) Yh.Ph.Fst.Gm.Pn.P.'64 . . . . | 332 Exeter Rd,
MISS Emily B—at Colo Coll . . . . | Devon, PA
MR William M 3d—at 100 Jane St, Apt 7N, | *19333-1710*
New York, NY *10014* . . . . |
Walker MR & MRS Wirt D (Margaret Ross) Wms'42
8360 Greensboro Dv, Apt 508, McLean, VA *22102*
Walker MR & MRS Wirt D 3d (Sally G White) | ☎ (703) 356-5052
CtCol'70.Cvc.Sl.Laf'68 . . . . | 1237 Meyer Court,
JUNIORS MR Wirt A . . . . | McLean, VA *22101*
Walkup MR & MRS Richard L (Jean L Gilbert) Bost'80.Cry . . of
☎ (610) 793-2095 . . ''Silverwood'' 878 Silverwood Dv, West Chester,
PA *19382*
☎ (717) 525-3246 . . ''Eagles Edge Roadhouse'' Allegheny Av,
Eagles Mere, PA *17731*

Walkup MR & MRS Ward G (Madeira—Nancy P Soulé) Cal'50.Myf.Stan'47
☎ (408) 389-4521 . . Rancho Gabilan, PO Box 35, Paicines,
CA *95043*

Wall MRS Albert Carey (Fincke—Virginia D Gardner) K.Fic.Cly.Chi.Ncd.
☎ (212) 535-1777 . . 136 E 79 St, New York, NY *10021*

Wall MRS Anne F (Otero—Anne F Wall) Pp . . .of
☎ (561) 276-3175 . . 2155 NW 14 St, Delray Beach, FL *33445*
☎ (609) 924-2850 . . 130 Westcott Rd, Princeton, NJ *08540*

Wall MR Ashbel T (late Ashbel T) . . . . Married at Newport, RI
Burdick MRS Ralph (Nancy J Lewis) . . . . Jun 21'96

Wall MR & MRS Ashbel T (Burdick—Nancy J Lewis) Nrr.Cda.Pn.P'37
☎ (401) 423-1448 . . 284 E Shore Rd, PO Box 55, Jamestown,
RI *02835-0055*

Wall MR & MRS F William (Mary T Livingston)
Y.'43 . . . .
MISS Hélène M—at ☎ (212) 496-2293
333 W 86 St, New York, NY *10024* . . . .
☎ (516) WA2-6648
Remsens Lane,
Oyster Bay, NY
11771

Wall MR & MRS H Peter (Patricia Allen) Fic.P'44 . . .
MR Alexander M—at U of Pa . . . .
☎ (609) 924-2850
130 Westcott Rd,
Princeton, NJ *08540*
Dec 7 . .
☎ (803) 524-7805
306 King St,
Beaufort, SC *29902*

Wall MR & MRS Michael A M (Neilson—Susanna S
M Mitchell) Rd.Cts.Mit'50 . . . .
MISS Ruth W Neilson—Ken'79—at
3024—31 Av W, Seattle, WA *98199* . . . .
MR Silas W M Neilson—Br'91.Cal'95—at
79 Sullivan St, Apt 1B, New York, NY *10012*
☎ (610) NI4-4125
808 Warren Av,
Malvern, PA *19355*

Wall MR Michael A P—Col'90 . . see J D Peabody JR

Wall MR & MRS R Michael (Sarah T Stevens)
Ec.Geo'70 . . . .
MISS Meghan MacL—Rich'95 . . . .
MISS Kily B—at Roanoke Coll . . . .
☎ (508) 283-0589
650 Washington St,
Gloucester, MA
01930

Wall MR & MRS Wayne W (S Margaret Bayne) Yn.Y'47
☎ (941) 383-8764 . . 1922 Harbourside Dv, Apt 1104, Longboat Key,
FL *34228*

Wallace MISS Anne S (David W) . . . . Married at Greenwich, CT
Juge MR David A (Peter E) . . . . May 18'96

Wallace MRS B Gring (Helen Barnet Gring) Cy.Chi.Ncd.
☎ (617) 547-3016 . . 15 Hubbard Park, Cambridge, MA *02138*

Wallace MR & MRS Christopher G (Margaret F Tucker)
Lynch'86.Me.Cda.Pa'74
☎ (215) 233-8027 . . 208 Yeakel Av, Erdenheim, PA *19038*

Wallace MRS Constance H (Rockefeller—Constance V Hamilton) Wil . . .of
☎ (941) 964-2275 . . 260 Gilchrist, Box 474, Boca Grande, FL *33921*
☎ (302) 658-4096 . . PO Box 4451, 122 Brook Valley Rd, Greenville,
DE *19807*

Wallace MISS Cornelia S—FIT'86.CalSC'92.Cly.
☎ (310) 472-4886 . . 555 S Barrington Av, Brentwood, CA *90049*

Wallace MISS (DR) Dale H—Buck'84.GeoW'89.GeoW'92
☎ (610) 254-0968 . . 282 Drummers Lane, Wayne, PA *19087*

Wallace DR & MRS David A (Cunningham—Joan H Dulles)
V'45-4.Pc.Pa'40.Pa'41.H'50.H'53
☎ (215) CH7-6083 . . 6 Moreland Circle, Philadelphia, PA *19118*

Wallace MR & MRS David W (Jean I McLean)
B.StA.Dar.Y.'48.H'51 . . . .
MISS Mary H—Sth'82 . . . .
of ☎ (203)869-3370
33 Midwood Rd,
Deer Park,
Greenwich, CT
06830
☎ (212) 472-2996
785 Park Av,
New York, NY
10021
☎ (602) 948-2100
John Gardiner's
Tennis Ranch,
Scottsdale, AZ
85253

Wallace DR & MRS Earl K JR (Jean A Luke)
Ncd.CTech'43.Pitt'47 . . . .
MISS Jean A L—at ☎ (404) 262-1420
2141 Virginia Place NE, Atlanta, GA *30305* . . .
MR Andrew M—at ☎ (803) 559-2179
1282 New Cut Rd, Wadmalaw Island, SC *29487*
☎ (803) 722-8945
8 Ford St,
Charleston, SC
29401

Wallace MR & MRS Frank Rich (Wister—Bright—Cynthia Wetherill)
Ph.Sg.Wms'39 . . of
☎ (609) 298-0614 . . Brookdale Farm, 68B Old York Rd, Bordentown,
NJ *08505-2914*
☎ (610) 896-8398 . . The Quadrangle 3110, 3300 Darby Rd, Haverford,
PA *19041*

Wallace MR Frederick R JR—Pa'50
☎ (610) 264-7222 . . 244 Prospect St, Catasauqua, PA *18032*

Wallace MISS Helen W—Lm. . . . .
MR Peter de L—Lm.Mit'52 . . . .
☎ (212) 876-4170
12 E 97 St,
New York, NY
10029

Wallace MR Hugh C
903 N French St, Wilmington, DE *19801*

Wallace MR & MRS Hugh C JR (Elise S Knight) Csh.
☎ (516) 367-1612 . . 459 Woodbury Rd, Cold Spring Harbor, NY *11724*

Wallace MRS Hugh Campbell (Gertrude de L Watts)
Cly.Chr.Cda.Lm.Dc.StJ.
☎ (212) AT9-4221 . . 16 E 98 St, New York, NY *10029*

Wallace MR & MRS J Berry (McAdam—Anne C Harrison)
Cvc.Mt.Myc.Ny.My.Sl.Geo'48
☎ (202) 667-3636 . . 2101 Connecticut Av NW, Apt 68, Washington,
DC *20008*

Wallace MR & MRS John A (Laura E Sauls)
Ga'63.P'60.H'63 . . . .
MISS Laura E . . . .
MR John A JR . . . .
MR Michael T . . . .
☎ (404) 351-2243
2551 Woodward
Way NW, Atlanta,
GA *30305*

Wallace MR & MRS John C (Mary O Willson) Ws'49.Y'42
☎ (814) 723-4514 . . 500 Third Av W, Warren, PA *16365*

Wallace MRS Kelleher (Mary L Kelleher) Sth'55 . . .
MR Peter Warren—Mit'83.Stan'86—at
2261 Market St, Apt 624, San Francisco, CA
94114 . . . .
☎ (415) 851-1426
PO Box 620285,
Woodside, CA
94062

Wallace MR & MRS Neil W (Elise Raymond)
MtH'55.Sim'57.Sm.D.Nh.P'55.H'58
☎ (508) 655-1061 . . "Little Pond" 23 South St, Sherborn,
MA *01770*

Wallace MRS Revett B (Katharine van D Shaw)
Tcy.Ncd. . . . . | ☎ (415) 851-1241
MISS Sarah R—Cal'76—at 425 West End Av, | 2885 Woodside Rd,
New York, NY *10024* . . . . | Woodside, CA
| *94062*

Wallace MR Richard S—Va'69
☎ (804) 277-5282 . . Southgate Farm, Roseland, VA *22967*

Wallace MR Richard W JR—Me.
1000 Conestoga Rd, Apt B129, Rosemont, PA *19010*

Wallace MRS Robert B (Gordon Grosvenor) . . . . Died Mch 17'94

Wallace MR Robert B—Cvc.IaState'40 . . . . | of ☎ (215)794-7746
JUNIORS MR Tyson W Fitzmorris—at | "Brooklea"
☎ (303) 781-9111 . . 1721 E Stanford Av, | 2943 Mill Rd,
Englewood, CO *80110* . . . . | RD 4, Doylestown,
JUNIORS MR Scott W Fitzmorris—at | PA *18901*
☎ (303) 781-9111 . . 1721 E Stanford Av, | ☎ (202) 965-0394
Englewood, CO *80110* . . . . | 1342—28 St NW,
| Washington, DC
| *20007*

Wallace MR & MRS Roger W (Mary R Griffith) | of ☎ (210)824-0127
RMWmn'68.A.B.Fst.W&L'67.Tufts'70 . . . . . . | 791 Grandview
MISS Fay Randolph . . . . | Place, San Antonio,
JUNIORS MR Windham S . . . . | TX *78209*
| ☎ (210) 833-4112
| Little Blanco Farm,
| Rte 4, Box 391,
| Blanco, TX *78606*

Wallace MR & MRS W Leland H (Elsa J Barclay) SUNY'77.Br'77
☎ (508) 526-8187 . . 4 Boardman Av, Manchester, MA *01944*

Wallace MR & MRS Wallace H (Helen K Justi)
M.Me.Myf.Ncd.P'50.Pa'52
☎ (610) 642-1181 . . 1119 Waverly Rd, Gladwyne, PA *19035*

Wallace MRS William Byron (Josephine J Player)
The Tamalpais 317, 501 Via Casitas, Greenbrae, CA *94904*

Waller MR F Ford—Ky'49.Ky'67 . . . . | of ☎ (606)263-3258
MISS Lillian W T—at ☎ (606) 276-3904 | Agincourt Farms,
1028 Cross Keys Rd, Lexington, KY *40504* . . . . | 8673 Adams Lane,
| Lexington, KY
| *40515-9306*
| "Agincourt" Oxford
| & Newtown Rds,
| Georgetown, KY
| *40324*

Waller MR & MRS Harold E JR (M Lisa Bowen) ColC'58.Ariz'60
☎ (011-51-14) 426007 . . Jorge Basadre 396, San Isidro, Lima 27, Peru

Waller MR & MRS John W 3d (Alexis P Robinson) MtVern'88.Va'71
☎ (212) 534-3242 . . 1112 Park Av, New York, NY *10128*

Waller MASTER John Wickliffe 4th (John W 3d) . . . . Born at
New York, NY Jun 22'95

Waller MR & MRS Thatcher (Lois Allan) | ☎ (312) 787-6884
Nw'45.Rc.Sc.Cnt.Va'40 . . . . | 1430 N Lake Shore
MISS Amy—Stan'75 . . . . | Dv, Chicago, IL
MR Thatcher JR . . . . | *60610*

Waller MRS Thomas M (Wilhelmine S Kirby) Srr.Bgt.Cly.Ht.Ncd.Dc . . .of
☎ (914) 666-5965 . . Tanrackin Farm, PO Box 457, Bedford Hills,
NY *10507*
☎ (803) 432-9969 . . 2256 Carter St, Camden, SC *29020*

Walley MR Matthew B—Ox'87 . . see W F Neville

Walley MR Noah J—Ox'84.Stan'90 . . see W F Neville

Wallick MR & MRS Philip M (Joan A M Carnevali)
Pa'54.Pa'56.Ant'51.Pa'56
☎ (718) 625-4824 . . 286 Hicks St, Brooklyn, NY *11201*

Walling MR & MRS Richard C JR (Alexandra K Van Alen)
Pa'82.Gm.Cry.Denis'80
☎ (610) 525-1821 . . 900 Old Gulph Rd, Bryn Mawr, PA *19010*

Walling MR Stephen P—Cw.Ofp.Rv.Vca.Ne.Coa.Ind'71
5713 Monroe Av, Evansville, IN *47715*

Walling MR & MRS Willoughby G 2d (Susan M | 20 Hawthorn Rd,
Leavitt) Cy.Stan'65.P'66.H.'75 . . . . | Brookline, MA
MISS Jessica L—H'94 . . . . | *02146*
JUNIORS MR W Hayden—at Boston U . . . . |

Wallis MR & MRS Bruce E (Righter—Kate R Butler) Cy.St.G.Ox'48 . . of
☎ (212) 838-0800 . . 825 Fifth Av, New York, NY *10021*
☎ (941) 966-5024 . . 101 Osprey Point Dv, Osprey, FL *34229*

Wallis MR Charles M
☎ (415) 546-7641 . . 461—2 St, Apt 560, San Francisco,
CA *94107-1416*

Wallis MR & MRS George R (Alice B Potts) Rdc'55.Bgt.CTech'53
☎ (207) 865-0556 . . 68 Old County Rd, Freeport, ME *04032*

Wallis MR James T 2d—P'51
☎ (212) 861-5288 . . 162 E 80 St, New York, NY *10021*

Wallis MR & MRS John (Charlotte Beddington) P'57 . | ☎ (011-44-1273)
MISS Sarah L. . . . . | 400-255
MR William A. . . . . | "The Old Post"
| South Chailey,
| East Sussex
| BN8 4AT, England

Wallis MR Nathaniel T (Robert C) . . . . Married at Perry, NY
Baumer MISS Katie L (Howard) . . . . May 11'96

Wallis MR & MRS Robert C (James—Margaret P | ☎ (215) 646-8601
Bodine) Sth'62.Sg.Rb.Ac.Ty'65 . . . . | 301 Willowmere
MR William D James—Sg.LakeF'91—at | Lane, Ambler, PA
☎ (617) 536-0628 . . 77 Park Dv, Apt 7, | *19002*
Boston, MA *02215* . . . . |

Wallop MR & MRS Malcolm (Goodwyn—French C | of ☎ (703)528-0081
Gamble) Mt.Mv.Y'54. . . . . | 1557 N 22 St,
MR Scott M Goodwyn—at Boston U . . . . | Arlington, VA
| *22209*
| ☎ (307) 674-6086
| Canyon Ranch,
| Big Horn, WY
| *82833*

Wallop MRS Victoria S (Victoria N Stebbins) | ☎ (617) 723-4952
Sorb'58 . . . . | 21 Joy St, Apt 4,
MISS Alexandra M—at ☎ (406) 222-3943 | Boston, MA *02114*
1313 Geyser St, Livington, MT *59047* . . . . |
MR Sam H—at U of Mass . . . . |

Walls MISS Lisbeth Lister (Stanek—Lisbeth Lister Walls) Col'63.St.
☎ (905) 894-2969 . . 2129 MacDonald Dv, Ridgeway, Ontario L0S 1N0,
Canada

Walmsley MRS Robert M (Virginia Johnston) V'38.Cda.
☎ (504) 524-8222 . . 2100 St Charles Av, Apt 12C, New Orleans, LA *70140*

Walmsley MR & MRS Robert M JR (Anne Wharton McIlvaine) P'68.Va'74 . . . . | ☎ (504) 865-9985
MR Peter S—at Swarthmore . . . . | 1 Dunleith Court,
JUNIORS MISS Anne B . . . . | New Orleans, LA
JUNIORS MR Lloyd W—at U of Va . . . . | *70118*

Walrath DR & MRS Martin H 3d (Hoopes—Judith E Turben) Fcg.Rr.Jef'49 . . . . | ☎ (412) 781-0371
MISS Pamela E Hoopes . . . . | 25 Windsor Circle,
MR James E Hoopes . . . . | Pittsburgh, PA
| *15215*

Walser MISS Karin D—Va'88
☎ (202) 232-6550 . . 2144 California St NW, Apt 304, Washington, DC *20008-1820*

Walser DR & MRS Mackenzie (Gleason—Elizabeth C A Gearon) C.Y'44.Cl'48 . . . . | ☎ (410) 337-7351
MISS Jennifer McK—H'90—at 162 Coolidge St, | 7513 Club Rd,
Brookline, MA *02146* . . . . | Ruxton, MD *21204*
MR Cameron MacK—Br'93 . . . . |
MR Eric H—at U of Colo Boulder . . . . |

Walsh MR & MRS Alexander de Witt (Marion J Walton) . . . . | ☎ (860) 974-1469
MR Nicholas W—at ☎ (617) 354-1033 | "New Stelling"
68 Wendell St, Cambridge, MA *02138* . . . . | PO Box 334,
| South Woodstock,
| CT *06267*

Walsh MR & MRS Basil S 3d (Marria L K O'Malley) M'wd'68.Adelphi'70.Me.Sa.Dar.Pa'61.VillaN'65
☎ (717) 622-3334 . . 411 Garfield Square, Pottsville, PA *17901*

Walsh MR & MRS Brian R (Davis—Daphne Gray) Un.Y'57.H'66
☎ (212) 628-8540 . . 320 E 72 St, New York, NY *10021*

Walsh MISS Catherine Jean (g—Kenneth T Urquhart of Urquhart) . . . Born at Akron, OH Sep 20'94

Walsh MR & MRS Edward F (Grace H Salt) St.Ts.G.Buf'48
☎ (716) 873-3119 . . 291 Lincoln P'kway, Buffalo, NY *14216*

Walsh MRS Edward J (Katherine McB Mahaffey) Str.Cy.
☎ (314) 361-7223 . . 30 Westmoreland Place, St Louis, MO *63108*

Walsh CAPT & MRS Eric F (Caroline E McK Earle) USMC.H'88.Ham'89
☎ (401) 273-9288 . . 20 Cooke St, Providence, RI *02906*

Walsh MR & MRS F Howard (Mary D Fleming) Smu'34.TCU'33
☎ (817) 924-3483 . . 2425 Stadium Dv, Ft Worth, TX *76109*

Walsh MR & MRS Frederick R JR (Hope I Mauran) NH'80.Aga.Ncd.Br'77.H'81
☎ (914) 967-2571 . . 665 Milton Rd, Rye, NY *10580-3239*

Walsh MR Hughes de W (late Thomas de W) . . . . Married at Bedford, NY
Barrett MISS K Dawn (Brian W) . . . . Aug 10'96

Walsh CAPT & MRS (CAPT) Ian K (Charlotte V Firth) USMC.Va'89.Ham'89
☎ (919) 354-6062 . . 7028 N Archer's Creek Dv, Emerald Isle, NC *28594*

Walsh MR & MRS John J JR (Virginia A Galston) Wheat'60.C.Y'61.Cl'65.Cl'71 . . . . | 37 Haldeman Rd,
MISS Anne G . . . . | Santa Monica, CA
MR Peter W . . . . | *90402*
MR Frederick M . . . . |

Walsh MR & MRS Laurence S (Ellen Scott) Nu'63.Br'66.Nyc.RISD'69 . . . . | ☎ (401) 273-9288
MISS Margaret L—at 147 Sterling Place, | 20 Cooke St,
Brooklyn, NY *11217* . . . . | Providence, RI
MR James H—at Hamilton . . . . | *02906*

Walsh MR & MRS Margaret F (Margaret S Fearey) Me . . . . | ☎ (415) 461-6257
MISS Samantha A—at 240 W Evergreen Av, | 644 Via Casitas,
Philadelphia, PA *19118* . . . . | Greenbrae, CA
| *94904*

Walsh MR & MRS Mark L (Mary B Vail) Skd'76.Hn.U'76.H'80
☎ (301) 657-3620 . . 5212 Dorset Av, Chevy Chase, MD *20815*

Walsh MISS Mary Ellen (g—Kenneth T Urquhart of Urquhart) . . . . Born at Akron, OH Jun 30'96

Walsh MR & MRS Nelson Salt (Victoria W Smith) Wms'84.Rc.Pr.Cly.Wms'84.Cl'90
☎ (212) 534-3732 . . 14 E 90 St, New York, NY *10128*

Walsh MISS Oona H . . see J F Meigs 2d

Walsh MRS Owen R (Olga Griscom) Rr. . . . . | ☎ (610) 688-6574
MISS Helyn B . . . . | 20 Crestline Rd,
| Strafford, PA *19087*

Walsh MR Philip C—Rcn.Eyc.Err.Km.Y'44
☎ (508) 627-8071 . . Caleb Pond Rd, SR 25, Edgartown, MA *02539*

Walsh MRS Richard J (Patricia V Stewart) R.Nyc.Pc.Sg.Ac . . . . | ☎ (215) 247-6533
MISS Valentine—Pa'75—at | 8870 Towanda St,
☎ (011-44-171) 602-5183 . . 8 Pembroke Rd, | Philadelphia, PA
London W8, England . . . . | *19118*

Walsh MR & MRS Robert L JR (Virlinda McC Gibson) Mt.Cvc.Sl. . . . . | ☎ (301) 229-8517
MR Nathaniel C T . . . . | 5111 Cammack Dv,
| Bethesda, MD
| *20816*

Walsh MRS Thomas de W (Ann Watson) Sth'53 . . . | ☎ (212) 838-0823
MISS Brooke M . . . . | 825 Fifth Av,
MR Thomas de W JR . . . . | New York, NY
| *10021*

Walsham DR & MRS John G (Sandra G M Gary) MtH'69.Csn.Birm'ham'62.Birm'ham'63.Birm'ham'66
☎ (415) 332-9581 . . 14 Arana Circle, Sausalito, CA *94965*

Walter MR & MRS Philipp J JR (Sandra L Clarke) Cts.Me.Cl'62
☎ (610) 525-8854 . . 461 S Roberts Rd, Bryn Mawr, PA *19010*

Walter MRS Robert H (Suzanne Iselin)
☎ (203) 762-3154 . . 688 Ridgefield Rd, Wilton, CT *06897-1627*

Walter MR & MRS William Todd (Eleanor M Ode) Mid'87.Me.Mid'87.Va'92
☎ (201) 509-9731 . . 215 Inwood Av, Upper Montclair, NJ *07043*

Walters MR & MRS David L S (Edith A Newhall) MooreArt'73.ChiArt'79
☎ (212) 627-5609 . . 217 W 13 St, New York, NY *10011*

Walters MR & MRS Everett (Jane C Schrader) Cos.Cin'36.Cl'47 . . . . | 2869 N Star Rd,
MR Everett G—at 1339 London Dv, Columbus, | Columbus, OH
OH *43221* . . . . | *43221*

Walters MR Frederick L—Laf'75.Cr'78.Pa'84
☎ (508) 362-6409 . . Box 317, Indian Hill Rd, Cummaquid, MA *02637*

Walters MR & MRS Seymour G (Phillips—Raker—Marcia Clinton) G.
☎ (716) 992-2256 . . 4394 Haag Rd, Eden, NY *14057*

Walther JUNIORS MISS Amanda L . . see J P Austin 3d

Walther MRS Elizabeth E (Elizabeth O Ellis) CedarC'70 . . . . ☎ (201) 428-0016
MISS Sarah A—at Syracuse U . . . . 83 Camelot Rd,
JUNIORS MR Paul D—at U of Mass . . . . Parsippany, NJ
07054

Walther MRS Frank O (Louise L Smith) Ac.Ncd. . . ☎ (610) 642-2368
MR Livingston S—ClarkU'70 . . . . 454 Moreno Rd,
Wynnewood, PA
19096

Walther MR Frank O 3d—Denis'68 . . . . ☎ (603) 436-2370
MISS Heather E—NH'92 . . . . "Eventide"
JUNIORS MR Peter deL . . . . RR 1, 3 Wentworth
Rd, Portsmouth, NH
03801

Walther DR & MRS Raymond J (Joan Thompson) SL'58 . . . . ☎ (617) 864-7372
MISS Robin Anne—at Winchester St, Brookline, 15 Park Av,
MA 02146 . . . . Cambridge, MA
MISS Sarah P 02138

Walthew MR Gerald F . . . . ☎ (212) 705-2340
MISS C Cary—at Denison . . . . 1641 First Av,
JUNIORS MISS Conway F—at W'minster . . . . New York, NY
10028

Walthew MRS K Conway (Bier—Karen M Conway) . . . . Married at
Palm Beach, FL
Morrish MR David H (late Frederick D) . . . . Jun 22'96

Walthour MISS L Courtney—Vt'88.Rr.Ncd.
☎ (802) 655-5679 . . 42 Oak Circle, Apt 3, Colchester, VT 05446

Walthour MRS Marshall B (Louise F Macfarlane) ☎ (412) 837-1749
Rr.Ncd. . . . . 216 Underwood Av,
MR Marshall B JR—Rr.StM'95 . . . . Greensburg, PA
15601

Walthuis MRS V Harloff (Veda W Harloff) . . . . name changed to Harloff

Walton MR & MRS Augustus B JR (M Ellis Bullion) MaryB'64.Ark'67.W&L'64.Ark'67
☎ (501) 225-0202 . . 48 Overlook Dv, Little Rock, AR 72207

Walton MRS Ellen R (Ellen F Rowland)
☎ (617) 237-2767 . . 34 Earle Rd, Wellesley, MA 02181

Walton MISS Florence—Myf.
431 Aster Trace, Canton, GA 30115-8428

Walton MR Geoffrey L B—Cc.Ht.Ty'66.Hav'71.Pa'82
☎ (610) 527-1494 . . 1030 E Lancaster Av, Rosemont, PA 19010-1444

Walton MR & MRS George B (Babette Jennings ☎ (803) 521-1419
Newton) Cspa.Y'36 . . . . 931 Oyster Cove
MR A Edward—at ☎ (803) 842-4898 Dv, Beaufort, SC
14 Sea Olive Rd, Hilton Head Island, SC 29928 29902
MR John B . . . .

Walton MR & MRS Henry Foster 3d (Jessie M Delp) EStroud'42
☎ (717) 897-5467 . . 3018 N Delaware Dv, PO Box 385, Portland, PA 18351

Walton MR & MRS J Hunter JR (Hovey—Carolyn F of ☎ (617)734-1141
Keel) Ln.Cy.Sm.Vt'62 . . . . 161 Clyde St,
MISS Frances B—H'94 . . . . Chestnut Hill, MA
MISS Jennifer B—at Middlebury 02167
JUNIORS MISS Amanda D—at St Paul's . . . . ☎ (207) 883-6033
JUNIORS MISS Hilary S—at St Paul's . . . . Massacre Lane,
JUNIORS MR David B—at St Paul's Prouts Neck, ME
MR William C Hovey—Mid'91—at 04074
☎ (212) 628-9782 . . 370 Park Av, New York,
NY 10022 . . . .

Walton MR & MRS James M (Ellen M Carroll) ☎ (412) 238-2956
Ln.Rr.Fcg.Pg.Y'53.H'58 . . . . Star Rte S,
MISS Rachel M—Y'80.MassGen'85—at Laughlintown, PA
778 Wagon Wheel Gap Rd, Boulder, CO 80302 15655
MISS Mary T—Conn'83—at Rte 1, Box 406,
Glorieta, NM 87535 . . . .

Walton MR & MRS James M JR (Elizabeth A Orr) Denis'88.Eh.Rr.Shcc.Cl'82
☎ (908) 953-0974 . . 271A Mt Harmony Rd, Bernardsville, NJ 07924

Walton MRS John F (Rachel L Mellon) Pg.Rr.
☎ (412) 621-4646 . . 3955 Bigelow Blvd, Pittsburgh, PA 15213

Walton MR & MRS John M 3d (Cornelia P Parsly) ☎ (215) 646-9320
Rc.Sg. . . . . 5 Fox Pond,
MISS Elfrida E—HWSth'84—at Spring House, PA
☎ (215) 233-8924 . . 6280 Henry Lane, 19477
Flourtown, PA 19031 . . . .

Walton MR & MRS Joseph C (Molly Erwin) Tex'81.Fcg.Pg.Rr.Wms'79.Tex'83
☎ (412) 421-7258 . . 1449 Wightman St, Pittsburgh, PA 15217

Walton MR Richard C—Bvl.Sm.Ty'77.H'79 . . of
☎ (617) 523-3868 . . 10 W Hill Place, Boston, MA 02114
☎ (508) 255-2959 . . off Barley Neck Rd, East Orleans, MA 02643

Walton MR & MRS Robert E (Mary K Heyl) Br'50.Gi.Cspa.Rv.W.Pa'43
☎ (410) 255-5765 . . St Giles Rd, Gibson Island, MD 21056

Walton MR & MRS Robert P (Rosalie T Slack) ☎ (516) 549-0562
Y'.59.Va'62 . . . . 69 Midland St,
MISS Jenifer S . . . . Cold Spring Harbor,
MR Robert D . . . . NY 11724

Walton MR William E—W&M'41 . . . . ☎ (404) 252-7713
MISS Ellen C—Ga'85 . . . . 4717 Roswell Rd
NE, Apt 01, Atlanta,
GA 30342

Walworth MR & MRS Edward H JR (Nancy Zinsser) Sth'38.Rdc'40.Roch'37.Mich'40
☎ (203) 966-1820 . . 25 Lambert Rd, New Canaan, CT 06840

Walz MR & MRS Carl (Anna Bliss McConnell) ☎ (413) 527-0885
Aht'31 . . . . 99 Mt Tom Av,
MISS Susanna . . . . Easthampton, MA
01027

Wampler MR F Hoopes—Me.Rich'91
☎ (202) 686-4732 . . 4324 Van Ness St NW, Washington, DC 20016

Wampler MR & MRS Fredrick D (Lura Ann ☎ (610) 688-6049
Coleman) Swb'60.Me.Rv.Wab'57 . . . . Little Place Farm,
MISS Eliza L—Buck'94 . . . . 1406 Thomas Rd,
Wayne, PA 19087

Wanamaker MR & MRS J Rodman JR (Daisy C Forbes) . . . . | ☎ (610) 431-3858
MISS Barbara W . . . . | ''Entropy''
MISS Catharine de K . . . . | 1133 Pottstown
| Pike, West Chester,
| PA 19380
| . . MR absent

Wanamaker MR & MRS John R (Louise de K Bowen)
Pe.Cry.Sg.Fw.Dc . . .of
☎ (215) 628-2888 . . 3 Bridle Lane, Blue Bell, PA 19422
☎ (941) 964-2549 . . 280 Harbor Dv, Boca Grande, FL 33921

Wanamaker MRS Rodman (Virginia Thaw) So.
☎ (516) 283-0230 . . 695 Hill St, PO Box 5046, Southampton,
NY 11969

Wang DR & MRS Jon B (Noreen S Hils) | ☎ (520) 299-8452
Buf'70.Pn.P'62 . . . . | 4960 Circulo Sobrio,
JUNIORS MR Davin . . . . | Tucson, AZ 85718

Wanstall MRS Robert E (Corinth E Commons) Wheat'50.SUNY'76 . . of
6752—41 Av SW, Seattle, WA 98136
''Birds' Nest'' Friends Point, Hague, NY 12836

Wantz DR & MRS George E (Hoguet—Diana W | ☎ (212) 879-5665
Dilworth) L.C.Cly.Mich'46 . . . . | 950 Park Av,
MISS Diana L Hoguet—at 464 Morrison Alley, | New York, NY
Boulder, CO 80302 . . . . | 10028

Wanzer, Charles T & Faesy, Lydia—Vt'86.Bastyr'94.Mid'85.H'92
☎ (802) 229-0901 . . 5 Edwards St, Montpelier, VT 05602

Waram MRS J Thomas C (L Louise Steffens)
☎ (510) 930-6088 . . 1132 Running Springs Rd, Apt 3, Walnut Creek,
CA 94595

Warburg MR & MRS Jonathan F (Highberg—Stephanie N Wenner)
Mich'63.Cl'65.Bvl.Sb.Cy.H.'63.H'68 . . of
☎ (617) 247-3208 . . 358 Beacon St, Boston, MA 02116
☎ (508) 748-2515 . . 9 Pie Alley, Marion, MA 02738

Ward MRS A Gordon (Amelia C Gordon) V'61.GeoW'75
☎ (410) 466-7277 . . 2201 Angelica Terr, Baltimore, MD 21209

Ward MRS A Reginald (Sage—Chryssicopoulos—Constance T Cluett)
Cly . . .of
☎ (011-44-171) 352-3743 . . 116 Swan Court, Chelsea Manor St,
London SW3, England
☎ (011-44-1796) 482-254 . . ''Balmacneil House'' Kinnaird Estate,
by Dunkeld, Perthshire PH8 0LB, Scotland

Ward MR & MRS Charles L (Katherine N Rowe) Bur.Vt'90
☎ (415) 474-4828 . . 1101 Green St, Apt 1303, San Francisco, CA 94109

Ward MRS Charles W (Priscilla Cuthell) . . . . | ☎ (212) 427-9870
MISS Barbara C . . . . | 46 E 91 St,
| New York, NY
| 10128

Ward MR & MRS Christopher L (Julia C Myer) BMr'80.Pc.Cr'78
☎ (215) 248-0550 . . 109 W Mermaid Lane, Chestnut Hill, PA 19118

Ward MR & MRS E Smedley JR (Alice L Murray) Sth'44.Fw.Ncd.Dth'43
☎ (561) 231-4952 . . 8830 Sea Oaks Way S, Apt 301, Vero Beach,
FL 32963

Ward MR E Smedley 3d—Me.Dth'71.Dth'73.Temp'86
☎ (610) 688-1510 . . 119 Eaton Dv, Wayne, PA 19087

Ward CDR (RET) & MRS Edward d'I M (Marilyn Hesser) USN . . .of
☎ (941) 923-7402 . . 6533 Bowline Dv, Sarasota, FL 34231
☎ (609) 399-1526 . . ''Homeport'' 400 St Davids Place, Ocean City,
NJ 08226

Ward MR & MRS Elmer L JR (Susan Clark) | ☎ (908) 439-3085
Sth'60.Rcn.Bg.B.Shcc.Cyb.Cda.H'47.H'50 . . . . | ''Potters Perch''
MR James W C . . . . | PO Box 157,
| Far Hills, NJ 07931

Ward MR & MRS Evans S (Patricia A Eldredge) | ☎ (508) 785-1811
Pa'68 . . . . | 168 Centre St,
JUNIORS MISS Haven G—at Noble & Greenough . | Dover, MA 02030
JUNIORS MISS Lilla N . . . . |

Ward MRS Forbes (Higley—C Hansell Forbes) | ☎ (561) 276-7923
Rose'83 . . . . | 821A NE Eighth
MISS Catharine H—at Tulane . . . . | Av, Delray Beach,
| FL 33483

Ward MRS George E (Frances S Worrall) S.
☎ (516) 676-3092 . . 457 Oyster Bay Rd, Locust Valley, NY 11560

Ward MRS Hawley W (Eleanor C Mastin)
☎ (716) 381-1221 . . 980 Allens Creek Rd, Rochester, NY 14618-3416

Ward MISS Hilary H . . see J F Murphy 3d

Ward MR & MRS Hugh C JR (Diana Goss) BMr'51.Ncd. . . | ☎ (508) 468-2009
MR Hugh C 3d—Pa'77 . . . . | PO Box 2028,
| South Hamilton, MA
| 01982

Ward JUNIORS MR James A . . see MISS C Armour

Ward MR James C—Geo'91
☎ (212) 861-0422 . . 125 E 83 St, Apt 2, New York, NY 10028

Ward MR & MRS Jeffrey C (Julia B Isham) | ☎ (205) 879-1397
Nw'72.Pr.Rr.LakeF'71 . . . . | 2840 Mountain
JUNIORS MISS Bleecker B . . . . | Brook P'kway,
| Birmingham, AL
| 35223

Ward MRS John (Ann H Browne) Cc.
☎ (201) 567-2192 . . 181 Jones Rd, Englewood, NJ 07631

Ward MR & MRS John G (Somes—Dubois—Joan Dunham) Rc.Pr.H'54
☎ (516) 922-4158 . . 6 Redmond Lane, Oyster Bay, NY 11771-3109

Ward MR & MRS John L (Ruth Page) H'34
7500 N Calle Sin Envidia, Apt 7201, Tucson, AZ 85718-7305

Ward MR & MRS Michael E A (Alexandra C Van Schaick) V'64.Cda.P'62
☎ (505) 820-2524 . . 425 Camino De Las Animas, Santa Fe, NM 87501

Ward MR Nicholas D—Mt.Cos.Ct.Cvc.Unn.Nrr.Cspa.Lm.Cw.Ht.Ne.Rv.
Wt.Snc.Vca.Ll.Myf.Cc.StJ.Ofp.Fw.Coa.Cl'63.Geo'66
☎ (202) 337-1653 . . 1690—32 St NW, Washington, DC 20007-2969

Ward MR & MRS Philip H 3d (Margaretta Dodge) Pc.P'42.H'48
☎ (215) CH8-0880 . . ''Wolfden'' 8605 Seminole Av, Philadelphia,
PA 19118

Ward MR & MRS Rodman JR (Susan S Hill) Wil.Wms'56.H'59
☎ (302) 655-5268 . . 52 Selborne Dv, Wilmington, DE 19807

Ward MR & MRS Seth C (Anne P Bowers) Va'83.My.Y'83.H'88
☎ (617) 723-5460 . . 17 Joy St, Boston, MA 02114

Ward MR & MRS T Johnson JR (Elizabeth Lodge Wright)
Rc.Me.Fw.Ac.Ncd.Y'36
☎ (610) LA5-3463 . . ''Homeward'' 114 N Roberts Rd, Rosemont,
PA 19010

Ward MR & MRS Thomas E JR (Margaret S Sater) | ☎ (802) 545-2367
Sth'47.Cw.Rv.Myf.Plg.Yn.Y'50 . . . . | RD 1, Box 86B,
MR Scott D—Colg'81—at Boston, MA . . . . | Middlebury, VT
| 05753

Wardell MRS Cathie B (Cathie G Bush) Wells'68.Csh. . . . . | ☎ (516) 673-5490
JUNIORS MISS Diana D . . . . | 212 Southdown Rd,
JUNIORS MR Charles W B 4th . . . . | Lloyd Harbor, NY
| *11743*

Wardell MR & MRS Charles W B JR (Elsa T Adam) V'35.Csh.Pr.P.'35.. of
☎ (516) 692-6313 . . 26 Springhill Rd, Cold Spring Harbor, NY *11724*
☎ (941) 261-2788 . . 3300 Gulf Shore Blvd N, Naples, FL *34103*

Wardell MR Charles W B 3d—Ln.Csh.H'73
see Dilatory Domiciles

Warden MRS Clarence A JR (Thompson—Anna M Farnum)
☎ (610) 642-0447 . . "Cottesmore" PO Box 66, Haverford, PA *19041*

Warden MRS David E (Alice Heard) Csh.
☎ (516) 692-6734 . . Box 1670, Moore's Hill Rd, Syosset, NY *11791*

Warden MR & MRS Derek P B (Margaret J Laudise) Geo'82.Pa'87.Pa'83
414 E Waverly Rd, Wyncote, PA *19095*

Warden MR & MRS Herbert W 3d (Post—Maulsby—Ann LaF Stanton)
Un.Yh.Cly.Cda.P'46.. of
☎ (203) 966-4766 . . 33 Bank St, New Canaan, CT *06840*
☎ (212) 249-6238 . . 116 E 66 St, New York, NY *10021*

Warden MR Herbert W 4th
H2 Ashby Place, Bedford, MA *01730*

Warden MR & MRS James Bryce (Sallie E McKee) | ☎ (011-44-171)
V'58.Ph.Pc.Fst.Yn.Y'59 . . . . | 351-1030
MR James McK—Ch'90—at ☎ (773) 404-0693 | 2 Tennyson
2107 W Fletcher Av, Chicago, IL *60618* . . . . . . | Mansions, Lordship
MR Andrew B—V'90—at ☎ (617) 648-1946 | Place, London
11 Lakeview, Arlington, MA *02174* . . . . | SW3 5HT, England

Warden MRS M Franca (M Franca Catelani) . . . . . . | ☎ (215) 297-5088
MR William B JR—☎ (215) 297-5052 . . . . | "Ash Brook"
| 3550 Aquetong Rd,
| New Hope, PA
| *18938*

Warden MISS Nancy A
☎ (805) 565-3401 . . 677A El Bosque Rd, Montecito, CA *93108*

Warden MR & MRS Stephen A (Amy Robbins)
☎ (011-61-67) 66-2375 . . 142 Carthage St, Box 523, Tamworth, NSW 2340, Australia

Warder MR & MRS William W (Wolf—Hallquist— | ☎ (610) 889-1640
Eleanor T Borton) MtH'58.Pc.Ty'58 . . . . | 53 Darby Rd, Paoli,
MISS Catherine E—Roan'92 . . . . | PA *19301*
MR W Scott Wolf—Tul'84—at | . . MRS absent
642 Sand Pine Circle, Apt 2811,
Deerfield Beach, FL *33341*

Wardman MR & MRS George A (Mason—Claudia M Radigan)
Syr'71.Unn.Wms'69
☎ (441) 236-1765 . . Peppercorn Farm, 3 Hallelu Lane, Paget, Bermuda

Wardman MR George S—Me'92 . . see J J Stockbridge

Wardman MISS Tiffany A—Cal'95 . . see J J Stockbridge

Wardrop MR James R—BrooksInst'72
☎ (412) 741-6060 . . Pink House Rd, Sewickley, PA *15143*

Wardrop MR & MRS Robert 2d (Ann Power) P'35 . . | ☎ (412) 681-7855
MISS Alison N. . . . . | 3955 Bigelow Blvd,
| Pittsburgh, PA
| *15213*

Wardwell MRS Edward R (Lelia A P Morgan) Cs . . .of
☎ (212) 744-0006 . . 911 Park Av, New York, NY *10021*
☎ (516) 374-6892 . . 11 Albro Lane, Lawrence, NY *11559*

Ware MRS A Gilkey (Ann S Gilkey) Cwr'53
☎ (718) 624-4799 . . 161 Henry St, Brooklyn, NY *11201*

Ware MR Charles E . . . . Died at Peterborough, NH May 10'96

Ware MRS Charles E (Sample—Kathleen B Calkins)
☎ (603) 924-0902 . . 15 River Mead Rd, Peterborough, NH *03458*

Ware MRS Charles P (Dorothy M Preston) Chi. . . . . | ☎ (011-33-1)
MR Andrew C—Paris'72. . . . . | 45-04-87-80
| 37 rue Decamps,
| 75116 Paris, France

Ware MR & MRS Gordon K (Ethlyn Dulin)
☎ (630) 584-4671 . . 1515 Shoreline Dv, St Charles, IL *60174*

Ware MRS J Boyd (Emma Coulter) Bnd'38.Str. . . . . | ☎ (314) 993-3915
MISS Nina C . . . . | 34 Clermont Lane,
| St Louis, MO *63124*

Ware MR J Lindsay—Ub.H'30.H'33
☎ (508) 548-0690 . . PO Box 711, Gansett Point, Woods Hole, MA *02543*

Ware MRS John JR (Walcott—Penelope H Perry) Sth'33.Ncd.
☎ (508) 785-0098 . . 131 Farm St, Box 537, Dover, MA *02030*

Ware MRS John D (Barbara Black)
☎ (802) 985-2925 . . 4308 Wake Robin Dv, Shelburne, VT *05482*

Ware MR & MRS Lawrence P (Martine O M Collas) | ☎ (011-41-25)
Grenoble'69 . . . . | 34-22-73
MISS Caroline L—at U of Fribourg . . . . | "Chalet Lamarica"
MR Eric P—Gen'95 . . . . | 1854 Leysin,
| Switzerland

Ware MR & MRS Thomas E JR (Andrea R Holmes) Ws'84.Dth'80.H'84
☎ (703) 425-4502 . . 6324 Blackburn Ford Dv, Fairfax Station, VA *22039*

Ware MASTER Thomas Holmes (Thomas E JR) . . . . Born Dec 9'94

Ware MR W Barlow—Cr'47
☎ (607) 257-6764 . . 55 Brown Rd, Ithaca, NY *14850*

Ware MR & MRS William (Susan L Fullerton) | ☎ (508) 563-5202
H.'59.H'64 . . . . | 270 Old Main Rd,
MISS (DR) Elisabeth P—Carl'87.Mass'95—at | North Falmouth,
☎ (513) 731-0250 . . 3501 Bellewood Av, | MA *02556-2402*
Cincinnati, OH *45213*. . . . . |
MISS Anne C—Wes'87 . . . . |
MISS Mary L—Amer'90—at ☎ (916) 642-2737
5821 Farish Rd, Placerville, CA *95667* . . . . |

Ware MR William JR—Mid'91.Dth'94
☎ (415) 368-9024 . . 660 Bair Island Rd, Apt 40, Redwood City, CA *94063*

Wareham MR John D—Cr'42
100 Norway St, Apt 804, Boston, MA *02115*

Warfield MAJ GEN (RET) & MRS Edwin 3d (Selby—Ellen R Owens)
USAF.Md.Md'50
☎ (941) 262-0075 . . 1910 Gulf Shore Blvd N, Apt 109, Naples, FL *34102*
Apr 1 . . ☎ (410) 442-2486 . . "Acorn" 16185 Ed Warfield Rd, Woodbine, MD *21797*

Warfield MR Peter F—Ham'40.Ill'44. . . . . | ☎ (908) 233-4698
MR Frederic P 2d—Clem'67—at | 508 Birch Av,
☎ (602) 840-2505 . . 5518 E Cambridge Av, | Westfield, NJ *07090*
Phoenix, AZ *85008* . . . . |

Wargo MR & MRS Charles F (Emily Gibbons-Neff)
TJef'76.Ford'72.Temp'75.Temp'85
☎ (610) 525-7228 . . 138 Barcladen Rd, Rosemont, PA *19010*
Waring MISS Belle B . . see MRS P Wainwright
Waring MR Benjamin A . . see MRS P Wainwright
Waring MR & MRS Bradish J (Amelia B Solomon) | of ☎ (803)577-4166
SCar'75.Ht.SCar'75.SCar'77 ⚓ . . . . | 47 King St,
JUNIORS MISS Amelia S . . . . | Charleston, SC
JUNIORS MISS Mary B R . . . . | *29401*
| ☎ (803) 559-5448
| ''Brambleberry''
| 6022 Maybank
| H'way, Wadmalaw
| Island, SC *29487*
Waring MR & MRS Richard B (Cornelia B Sise) Gchr'82.H'86.Drew'77
☎ (617) 489-1630 . . 33 Chandler St, Belmont, MA *02178-1326*
Waring MR & MRS Thomas R (Wehman—Ortmann—
Hermine L Cart) So'27
☎ (803) 722-8932 . . 10 Atlantic St, Charleston, SC *29401*
Warlow-Harry MRS Richard C (Mary I Hine)
☎ (011-44-1208) 850256 . . The Old Rectory, Michaelstow, Bodmin,
Cornwall, England
Warnecke MR John C—Pcu.Stan'41.H'42 . . . . | of ☎ (212)486-1555
MR Rodger C . . . . | 525 Park Av,
| New York, NY
| *10021*
| ☎ (707) 433-3300
| 13125 Chalk Hill
| Rd, Healdsburg, CA
| *95448*
Warner MRS Bradford A (Nancy Hill) S.Cly.Dh.Ncd.
☎ (212) BU8-9398 . . 116 E 68 St, New York, NY *10021*
Warner MR & MRS Brainard H 3d (Mildred K Jonathan)
BMr'45.Mt.Cvc.Sl.Y'46.GeoW'50
☎ (301) 656-3906 . . 6814 Connecticut Av, Chevy Chase, MD *20815*
Warner MR & MRS Brainard H 4th (Karen G Kelly)
☎ (301) 320-3361 . . 6726 Wilson Lane, Bethesda, MD *20817*
Warner MR & MRS Caleb (Alice F Sizer) Rdc'50.Sim'72.Mich'44
☎ (617) 862-9278 . . PO Box 254, Lexington, MA *02173*
Warner MISS Claire T—Myf.
☎ (718) 625-1330 . . 150 Joralemon St, Brooklyn, NY *11201*
Warner MR & MRS Douglas JR (Nancy H Atkinson) | ☎ (410) 366-3724
Hlns'50.Mv.Br'46.Mit'48.JHop'62 . . . . | 4908 Wilmslow Rd,
MISS Frances H—at ☎ (410) 821-6396 | Baltimore, MD
7928 Ruxway Rd, Baltimore, MD *21204* . . . . . . | *21210*
CAPT Douglas 3d—USMC.U'74 . . . . |
Warner MR & MRS Douglas A 3d (Patricia A Grant) | ☎ (516) 676-1113
Ck.Ln.Mb.Ng.Pr.Ri.Y'68 . . . . | 520 Chicken Valley
JUNIORS MISS Katherine A . . . . | Rd, Locust Valley,
JUNIORS MR Alexander G . . . . | NY *11560*
Warner MISS Elizabeth T
☎ (213) 850-7417 . . 1866 El Cerrito Place, Los Angeles, CA *90068*
Warner MR Everett F—Leh'42
☎ (505) 867-0137 . . 2102 Rivers Edge Dv, Rio Rancho, NM *87124*
Warner MR & MRS Frantz L (Eleanor Harding) | ☎ (508) 748-2562
Ch'40 . . . . | 33 Cove Circle,
MISS Pamela B . . . . | Marion, MA *02738*

Warner MR & MRS Frederick T (Louise B McKinney) V'40.P'37
☎ (910) 940-2651 . . 5122 Bermuda Village, Advance, NC *27006*
Warner MR Irving JR—Wil.P'35 ⚓ . . . . | ☎ (508) 693-0899
MR Nicholas H—at ☎ (908) 735-5356 | PO Box 607,
PO Box 67, Pittstown, NJ *08867* . . . . | Vineyard Haven,
| MA *02568*
Warner MR John C—Marq'68
☎ (941) 261-7036 . . 1930 Gulf Shore Blvd N, Apt 203C, Naples,
FL *34102*
Warner MR John M JR—Rc.Me.So.B.Sa.Pa'63
☎ (610) 645-0900 . . PO Box 716, Devon, PA *19333*
Warner MR & MRS Jonathan W (Elizabeth S Butler) Ala'41.W&L'40
☎ (205) 345-0801 . . 2731 Battlement Dv, Tuscaloosa, AL *35406*
Warner MR Mallory Reynolds—Y'81.Y'83
☎ (703) 548-4176 . . 1125 Prince St, Alexandria, VA *22314*
Warner MISS Margot
☎ (508) 768-6853 . . 177 John Wise Av, Essex, MA *01929*
Warner MR & MRS Miner H (Ellen C Murphy) | ☎ (212) 628-6070
Wheat'69.Ln.B.Ri.Fic.Mt.Plg.StJ.Myf.Cly.Cs. | 148 East End Av,
H'64.Lond'68.Pa'68 . . . . | New York, NY
MISS Alix M-P . . . . | *10028*
JUNIORS MISS Lily W . . . . |
Warner MISS Nina E . . see MRS J D Macneil
Warner MR & MRS Philip W (Susan Handal) | of ☎ (212)772-3224
Rcp.B.Bgt.So.Ri.Myf.Ac.Yp.Y.'64.H'66 . . . . . . | 755 Park Av,
MR Philip W JR . . . . | New York, NY
JUNIORS MISS Christina A . . . . | *10021*
| ☎ (914) 241-4546
| 83 Springhurst Rd,
| Bedford Hills, NY
| *10507*
Warner MR & MRS Rawleigh JR (Mary A de Clairmont)
V'45.Ln.Ri.Cly.P'44
☎ (561) 546-6543 . . 24 Riverview Rd, Hobe Sound, FL *33455*
Warner MR & MRS Rollin Miles JR—Gr.Y'53.Stan'60
☎ (209) 824-2862 . . 1164 Marion St, Manteca, CA *95337*
Warner MRS Silas L (Dingle—Elizabeth M | ☎ (508) 420-3986
Severinghaus) Cr'50.Me.Gm. . . . . | 24 Indigo Lane,
MISS Elizabeth L—Cr'87 . . . . | Osterville, MA
MR Michael H Dingle—Cr'74 . . . . | *02655*
Warner MRS Virginia McK (Virginia F McKeever) Me.Gm.
☎ (610) 293-9585 . . 216 Sinkler Dv, Radnor, PA *19087*
Warner MR & MRS William W (Kathleen B | ☎ (202) 333-4739
McMahon) K.Cda.P'43 . . . . | 2243—47 St NW,
MISS Alletta B—at ☎ (213) 852-1876 | Washington, DC
400 N Stanley Av, Apt 7, Los Angeles, CA | *20007-1034*
90036 . . . . |
MR John B—at ☎ (212) 691-9216 |
803 Greenwich St, New York, NY *10014* . . . . . |
MR William Andrew H . . . . |
Warnock MRS A Degrauw (Nancy W B Gatewood) | ☎ (610) 642-4672
Swb'41.Ncd. . . . . | ''Chipmunk Run''
MR Stockton B G . . . . | 146 Little Lane,
| Haverford, PA
| *19041*
Warnock MR & MRS Harold C (Mary L Phelps) Ariz'33.Ariz'35
☎ (520) 721-8848 . . 7255 E Camino Vecino, Tucson, AZ *85715*

Warnock MR & MRS William A 2d (Sidney S Sharp)
☎ (610) 644-0427 . . 314 Leopard Rd, Berwyn, PA *19312*

Warren MR & MRS Andrew C (Joan Claire Davis)
Swb'51.M.Sfh.Va'50 . . . .
MISS Greer T—Va'79 . . . .
MISS Polly C—Va'81 . . . .
MR Andrew C JR—Lynch'79 . . . .
MR Michael D . . . .
☎ (610) 525-3739
713 Woodfield Rd,
Villanova, PA *19085*

Warren MRS Bayard (Margaret Thomas) Sm. . . . . . .
MISS Mary A—at ☎ (508) 927-5441
657 Hale St, Prides Crossing, MA *01965* . . . . . .
☎ (011-353-28)
36173
''East House''
Castletownshend,
Skibbereen,
Co Cork, Ireland

Warren MR & MRS Benjamin S 3d (Margaret C
Pirie) Va'60.Va'63 . . . .
MISS Alison A—Va'86 . . . .
MISS Leslie P—Md'89—*see Dilatory Domiciles*.
☎ (301) 948-5524
10 Esworthy Terr,
Travilah, MD *20878*

Warren MRS Caroline W (Caroline B Whiteside)
Sth'54 . . . .
MISS Amy T—Y'80 . . . .
MR Henry P 4th—Cal'84—at U of Cal Berkeley
☎ (203) 264-1404
147B Heritage
Village, Southbury,
CT *06488*

Warren MISS Catharine K (Bernstein—Catharine K Warren) SL'69 . . .of
☎ (212) 288-9228 . . 145 E 74 St, New York, NY *10021*
☎ (011-33-90) 92-51-13 . . Mas de Mérmbeau, Chemin de Calanquet,
13210 St Rémy-de-Provence, France

Warren MRS Charles E JR (M Florence Rodgers)
☎ (212) RE4-0869 . . 25 E 67 St, New York, NY *10021-5804*

Warren MR Chester I 3d—Fst.Sg.WakeF'76
☎ (215) 699-7215 . . 132 Gwynedd Manor Rd, North Wales, PA *19454*

Warren MR & MRS Christopher D (Dotti—Jennifer L Baker)
Mid'83.SacredH'90.Duke'75
☎ (602) 840-9197 . . 2440 N 56 St, Phoenix, AZ *85008*

Warren DR & MRS Claude M JR (Esther Regan) Louis'38
☎ (334) 473-5824 . . 1916 Springhill Av, Mobile, AL *36607*

Warren MR & MRS David U (Lynne Foster)
Wh'lck'63.H'54 . . . .
MISS Lisl—at Colby . . . .
MR Tristan U—at Colby . . . .
☎ (508) 927-2975
431 Hale St,
Prides Crossing, MA
01965

Warren MR & MRS Geoffrey S (Elizabeth A Curran) BMr'49.P'47
☎ (847) 835-3375 . . 900 Valley Rd, Glencoe, IL *60022*

Warren MR & MRS H Robert (Diana Macurda)
Ariz'60.AGSIM'63.Ncd.GrandC'62.AGSIM'63 .
MISS Wendy C . . . .
☎ (520) 299-6645
5555 N Via Alcalde,
Tucson, AZ *85718*

Warren DR & MRS Henry B (Cornelia W Brown) Rdc'71.Pa'75.H'72.Pa'80
☎ (617) 232-1095 . . 50 Gorham Av, Brookline, MA *02146*

Warren MR & MRS Howland S (Margaret H Turner) Tv.H'32
☎ (617) 581-0656 . . 409 Nahant Rd, Nahant, MA *01908*

Warren MR Hugh L—Sm.H'74
☎ (617) 492-3636 . . 145 Prospect St, Cambridge, MA *02139*

Warren MR James C JR—P'49 . . . .
MISSES Alexandra B & Catherine L—at
''Mount Kemble'' Bailey Hollow Rd,
Morristown, NJ *07960* . . . .
MR James F M—at ''Mount Kemble''
Bailey Hollow Rd, Morristown, NJ *07960* . . . . .
319—4 St SE,
Washington, DC
20003

Warren MR & MRS James F JR (Lillian M Givens) Me.
☎ (803) 689-2595 . . 18 Wild Laurel Lane, Hilton Head Island,
SC *29926*

Warren MR & MRS John B JR (Platt—Anna W Dickinson) Sth'70
☎ (313) 882-8674 . . 50 Renaud Rd, Grosse Pointe Shores, MI *48236*

Warren MR & MRS John C (Laura P Appell) Ws'83.Stan'78
☎ (617) 696-1929 . . 170 Centre St, Milton, MA *02186*

Warren MRS John D (Helen G Lynch) Exy.
☎ (860) 767-1180 . . 134 Essex Meadows, Essex, CT *06426*

Warren MISS Leslie . . see MRS C J La Roche

Warren MRS Lynne A (Cunningham—Lucie E Bedford) Ncd.
☎ (203) 259-0140 . . 93 Beachside Av, Greens Farms, CT *06436*

Warren MR & MRS Paul S (Ashley Janeway)
☎ (215) 248-1823 . . 322 W Moreland Av, Philadelphia, PA *19118*

Warren MASTER Peter Milliken (Peter W) . . . . Born at
New York, NY Jun 22'95

Warren MR & MRS Peter W (Harriette M Moore) RISD'85.Rc.Srb.Nrr.H'82
☎ (212) 288-8335 . . 106 E 85 St, Apt 8S, New York, NY *10028*

Warren MRS Samuel D (Jessica Van R Despard) SL'46.Rdc'71.Sbc.
☎ (508) 768-6851 . . Harlow St, Essex, MA *01929*

Warren MRS Simonds (Carla G Simonds)
☎ (401) 351-0162 . . 51 Blackstone Blvd, Providence, RI *02906*

Warren DR & MRS W Stuart (Jane M Clark)
Dth'56.GeoW'60 . . . .
MISS Anne B—at New York, NY . . . .
MR Thomas W—at Washington, DC . . . .
MR John A F—at Washington, DC . . . .
☎ (717) 432-9445
1215 Old Gettysburg
Pike, Dillsburg, PA
17019

Warren MR & MRS William B (Arete B Swartz)
Nw'68.NCar'70.K.Gr.C.Plg.Myf.Cly.H.'56.H'59 . . of
☎ (212) 734-2779 . . 520 E 86 St, New York, NY *10028*
☎ (860) 364-0574 . . ''Ulubrae'' 8 Mudgetown Rd, Sharon, CT *06069*

Warren MR William S—Franklin'72 ⛵
☎ (360) 837-3198 . . ''Three Tree Point'' Milepost 1.03R, Riverside Dv,
Washougal, WA *98671*

Warren MRS Winslow (Jessamine Gordon)
☎ (508) 668-2703 . . 962 North St, Walpole, MA *02081*

Warrick MR & MRS Alexander B (Frances W Stone) Cly.Y'42
☎ (561) 234-8490 . . 1250 W Southwinds Blvd, Apt 113, Vero Beach,
FL *32963*

Warrick MR & MRS William H JR (Elizabeth A
Werner) Cly.Dth'62.Cl'66 . . . .
MISS Samantha S—at 105 Roberts Lane,
Alexandria, VA *22314* . . . .
MR William H 3d—at U of NCar . . . .
☎ (603) 964-8367
430 Central Rd,
Rye, NH *03870*

Warriner MISS Blair—Stan'94 . . see W W Blunt JR

Warriner MRS John D (Putnam—Jane D Hamilton) Me.Cts. . . . . of ☎ (215)592-9795 531 Pine St, Philadelphia, PA *19106*
MISS Sarah S D—HWSth'88—at ☎ (719) 632-5374 . . 815 Pleasant St, Colorado Springs, CO *80904* . . . . ☎ (717) 278-2317 Elk Lake, RR 4, Box 240, Montrose, PA *18801* ☎ (011-44-1241) 871506 24 Auchmithie by Arbroath, Angus DD11 5SQ, Scotland

Warriner MR & MRS Lendall P (Ruth Rutter) Sth'37.P'34 ☎ (410) 745-9668 . . 24382 Oakwood Park Rd, St Michaels, MD *21663*

Warriner MR Reuel E JR—Y'60 ☎ (714) 494-7955 . . 710 Summit Dv, Laguna Beach, CA *92651*

Warriner MR & MRS Samuel D 2d (J Linda Trimingham) Eyc. ☎ (508) 627-8059 PO Box 407, 49 Hamblen Way, Edgartown, MA *02539*
MISS Alexandra . . . .
MR Stephen—at 17 Renshaw Rd, Darien, CT *06820* . . . .

Warrington MRS Elsie H (Bailey—Reed—Elsie H Warrington) Gm.Ac.Eyc . . .of ☎ (513) 561-7444 . . 4705 Burley Hills Dv, Cincinnati, OH *45243* ☎ (410) 758-1518 . . Spring Cove Farm, Centreville, MD *21617*

Warrington MR & MRS George H (H Drewry Gores) Cr'77.Cin'77 ☎ (513) 751-7174 . . 3125 Wold Av, Cincinnati, OH *45207*

Warrington MR John W . . . . Died at Cincinnati, OH Apr 12'96

Warrington MRS John W (Suzanne Mooney) Cm.Qc. ☎ (513) 561-7013 . . 8625 Camargo Club Dv, Cincinnati, OH *45243*

Warrington MR & MRS John W JR (Mary C Gosiger) Denis'83.Law'79 ☎ (513) 321-7166 . . 3433 Berry Av, Cincinnati, OH *45208*

Warth MR & MRS Robert S (Patricia H Lawson) Rb.Rc.Sg.Pa'57 . . . . ☎ (215) AD3-5231 657 Bethlehem Pike, Flourtown, PA *19031*
MR Robert S JR—USN. . . . .

Warwick MR & MRS Edward W (M Virginia Pennypacker) PhilaArt'43.Pc.Ac.PhilaArt'43 ☎ (215) CH7-1477 . . 101 W Springfield Av, Philadelphia, PA *19118*

Warwick MR & MRS Nelson D JR (Barbara S Moffly) Pc.W&L'63.Pa'69 . . . . ☎ (215) 233-3119 6151 Parkside Rd, Flourtown, PA *19031*
MISS Katharine S—at Wash'n Coll . . . .
MR Samuel F . . . .

Warwick MRS Nelson Dudley (Elizabeth G Brown) MISS Mary M . . . . ☎ (215) 248-4635 235 Rex Av, Philadelphia, PA *19118*

Warwick MR W Laird . . . . ☎ (703) 549-4087 114 Cameron Mews, Alexandria, VA *22314*
MISS Natalie S. . . . .

Washburn MR & MRS Alexander D (Sherry J Blackwell) Cy.Cw.Aht'65.Cl'71 . . . . ☎ (617) 235-7137 9 Elm St, Wellesley Hills, MA *02181*
JUNIORS MISS Lisa D . . . .
JUNIORS MR William B . . . .

Washburn MISS Alexandra L (Fanjul—Alexandra L Washburn) . . of ☎ (561) 588-3309 . . 112 Gregory Place, West Palm Beach, FL *33405* ☎ (561) 287-4152 . . 13184 Gilson Rd, Palm City, FL *34990*

Washburn MRS Amanda F (Amanda B Foster) ☎ (703) 683-4424 . . 217 S Columbus St, Alexandria, VA *22314*

Washburn MR Charles G III ☎ (612) 290-7772 . . 339 Summit Av, St Paul, MN *55102*

Washburn MR & MRS George (Anne G Clark) McG'42.Y'45.BtP.Mds.Nu'36 . . of ☎ (212) 288-6986 . . 20 E 74 St, New York, NY *10021* ☎ (561) 844-3261 . . Placido Mar Apt 2201, 5200 N Dixie H'way, West Palm Beach, FL *33407*

Washburn MRS Harold C (Jeannette M Adenaw) ☎ (860) 567-9080 . . 134 Whiskers Lane, Litchfield, CT *06759*

Washburn MR & MRS J Murray 3d (Karen E Wagner) Thiel'66.Purd'62.Cal'69. . . . . ☎ (603) 643-2829 Dogford Rd, Etna, NH *03750*
MISS Wynne C—at 4117 N Albina Av, Portland, OR *97217*. . . . .
MISS Anne K. . . . .
MR Peter C—Hampshire'95—at 51 Bay Rd, Hadley, MA *01035* . . . .

Washburn MR J Murray 4th—ColC'93 ☎ (719) 578-5816 . . 2126 W Kiowa Av, Colorado Springs, CO *80904*

Washburn MR & MRS Louis C (Barbara I Russell) Sg.Rd.P.'52 . . . . ☎ (610) 644-9372 310 Boot Rd, Malvern, PA *19355*
MR Mark D . . . .

Washburn MISS Sandra L—H'78.Nu'83 ☎ (214) 358-3806 . . 5112 Horseshoe Trail, Dallas, TX *75209*

Washburn MR & MRS Stanley JR (Anna B Leinbach) Pa'48.Cl'49.Eyc.Y.'31 . . of ☎ (212) 355-5791 . . 860 United Nations Plaza, New York, NY *10017* ☎ (508) 627-5873 . . ''Mara'' 101 S Water St, Edgartown, MA *02539*

Washburn MR & MRS William T (Elvira Alfageme) H'41.NCar'52 ☎ (011-34-1) 630-04-91 . . Cabo de Azohia 13, Club de Golf, Las Matas, 28290 Madrid, Spain

Washburne MR & MRS Elihu B (Mary E Willets) Wms'41 ☎ (214) 361-6967 . . 4110 Lovers Lane, Dallas, TX *75225*

Washburne MRS John C (Nancy de La T Howland) Oakland'71 ☎ (908) 647-9411 . . 180 Jamestown Rd, Basking Ridge, NJ *07920-3048*

Washburne MR Ray W—Smu'84 ☎ (214) 528-0205 . . 4155 Herschel Av, Dallas, TX *75219-3014*

Washburne MR & MRS Richards P (Lucy A S Hunter) Van'76.Tex'72 ☎ (214) 526-7718 . . 4323 Potomac Av, Dallas, TX *75205*

Washburne MR Seth P—Mich'81.Wash'84.Ch'87 ☎ (212) 289-1506 . . 241 E 86 St, Apt 17B, New York, NY *10028*

Washburne MR & MRS Stephen H (Amanda Ellis) WmSth'80.D.Hob'76 ☎ (508) 359-6561 . . 17 School St, Medfield, MA *02052*

Washburne MR & MRS Thomas D (Katharine S Marshall) Adelphi'50.Loy'70.Gv.P'49.Va'53 . . . ☎ (410) 363-1371 ''Green Spring'' 112 Green Spring Valley Rd, Owings Mills, MD *21117*
MISS (DR) Mary D—Swth'84.Temp'91 . . . .

Washington MR & MRS John A (Alice C Lacey) | ☎ (301) 652-3334
Cvc.Mt.Cc.Hn.H'42 . . . . | 4208 Rosemary St,
  MISS (DR) Lacey—Pa'93—at ☎ (215) 735-8845 | Chevy Chase, MD
  1512 Spruce St, Philadelphia, PA *19104* . . . . . . | *20815*
  MR John A 5th—at ☎ (213) 969-1696
  Malibu Canyon Apt 544, 5902 Las Virgines Rd,
  Calabasas, CA *91302* . . . .

Wasley MRS John S W (Margaret G McCall) . . . . . . | ☎ (860) 739-2027
  MISS Timmy—Bost'83—at ☎ (212) 772-8945 | 246 Old Black Point
  151 E 83 St, New York, NY *10028* . . . . | Rd, Niantic, CT
  | *06357*

Wasley MR & MRS John S W JR (M Elizabeth Savage)
Wheat'78.Bost'80 . . of
  ☎ (212) 674-7986 . . 1 Stuyvesant Oval, New York, NY *10009*
  ☎ (516) 788-7936 . . PO Box 674, Fishers Island, NY *06390*

Wastcoat MR & MRS John W (Jenkins—Mary S | of ☎ (603)526-4993
Pynchon) Chi.Aht'34 . . . . | PO Box 1453,
  MISS Alexandra Jenkins—HRdc'94—at | 88 Main St,
  405—33 Av, Apt 205, San Francisco, CA | New London, NH
  94121 . . . . | *03257*
    MSRS William P JR & Jonathan W Jenkins—at | ☎ (602) 488-9585
    ☎ (802) 446-2455 . . "Spring Meadow" RD 1, | PO Box 1235,
    Box 538, Wallingford, VT *05773* . . . . | Carefree, AZ *85377*

Waste MR & MRS William H 2d (Lisa M Saveri)
Stan'78.SFr'83.Bhm.Fr.Ore'73
  ☎ (415) 221-9492 . . 2925 Lake St, San Francisco, CA *94121*

Waterbury MRS Bayard H (Paternotte—Mary M Harris)
  ☎ (410) 377-4580 . . 7 Over Ridge Court, Baltimore, MD *21210-1109*

Waterbury MR & MRS Jackson D (Carolyn A | ☎ (314) 862-2424
Jenkins) Kas'79.Br'59 . . . . | 118 N Bemiston Av,
  MR Arthur B—Mo'91—at U of Mo Grad . . . . . . | St Louis, MO *63105*
  LT Timothy B—USMC.Va'95—at Quantico, VA
  22134 . . . .

Waterbury MR & MRS Jackson D 3d (Margaret P Trigg) OWes'83.Mo'85
  ☎ (314) 822-0024 . . 602 Bambury Way, St Louis, MO *63122*

Waterbury MR & MRS James M (Kay J Simonson) | ☎ (516) 324-3196
Man'vl'49.Mds.Y.'50 . . . . | 96 Egypt Lane,
  MISS Hope . . . . | East Hampton, NY
  MISS Christine . . . . | *11937*
  MISS Susan . . . .

Waterman MR Frederick W 4th—Cy.JHop'75
  ☎ (617) 545-3588 . . 233 Beaver Dam Rd, Box 61, Scituate, MA *02066*

Waterman MISS Jorie M—H'95 . . see MRS G F Dunaway

Waters MR & MRS Bertram G 3d (Hall—Elizabeth B | ☎ (617) 326-8076
Reece) Flor'60.H'60 . . . . | 8 Rodman Place,
  MISS Elizabeth B Hall—SL'88—at Islesford, | Dedham, MA *02026*
  ME *04646* . . . . | . . MR absent
    MR Winthrop T Hall—Emer'92—at
    ☎ (310) 581-9700 . . 257 Hampton Dv,
    Venice, CA *90291* . . . .

Waters MRS Henry Harcourt (Patricia W Brown)
  ☎ (504) 525-8334 . . 2315 Chestnut St, New Orleans, LA *70130*

Waters MR Mark C—Mass'89.Ford'93
  ☎ (212) 581-8211 . . 120 Central Park S, New York, NY *10019*

Waters MR & MRS Somerset R (Jane Fuller) JHop'35
  ☎ (914) 967-1716 . . 3 Hunter Lane, Rye, NY *10580-1615*

Waters MR & MRS Somerset R 3d (Wieslawa Brenk) | ☎ (203) 938-5633
Finch'74.Sar.Pa'70.Camb'72 . . . . | 14 Black Rock
  JUNIORS MISS Marianna F . . . . | Tpke, Redding, CT
  JUNIORS MR Somerset R . . . . | *06896*

Waters MR & MRS Thomas J (Elizabeth Day Parker)
Duke'87.Fiy.SUNY'86.Cal'93
  ☎ (214) 521-6761 . . 3910 Hawthorne Av, Dallas, TX *75219*

Waterston MR George C JR
  ☎ (860) 672-6906 . . 92 Great Hollow Rd, West Cornwall, CT *06796*

Watkins DR & MRS George M (Alison S Hall) Van'57.Van'60
  ☎ (309) 673-9242 . . 223 W Hollyridge Circle, Peoria, IL *61614*

Watkins MR Lowry Rush II—Louis'68 ⚓
  3630A Brownsboro Rd, Louisville, KY *40207-1861*

Watkins MR Marshall Bullitt . . . . Died at
  Norton, OH Jly 22'96

Watkins MRS Peter M (Meyns—Elizabeth G Ellis) SL'50
  ☎ (804) 355-6014 . . 3803 Dover Rd, Richmond, VA *23221*

Watkins MR Robert O—Aht'49.Cl'51 . . . . | ☎ (212) EN9-2478
MR Richard S—at ☎ (617) 277-9097 | 520 E 90 St,
5 Gorham Av, Brookline, MA *02146* . . . . | New York, NY
  | *10128*

Watkins MR & MRS W Bell (Anne I Presnikoff) An.Me'38
  ☎ (540) 955-2659 . . Kittery Point Farm, Rte 3, Box 6008, Berryville,
  VA *22611*

Watriss MRS Denckla (Biddle—Paula B Denckla) . . | ☎ (410) 771-4509
MR Patrick A . . . . | 15710 Falls Rd,
MR Michael B . . . . | Sparks, MD *21152*

Watriss MR & MRS James B (Hopkins—Fenwick—Mary L W Wanamaker)
Gv.
  ☎ (410) 771-4493 . . "Warburton" 2601 Butler Rd, Glyndon, MD *21071*

Watrous MR & MRS Philip M (Stevens—Dorothy A Poole)
Rd.Cw.Fw.Ht.Ll.Myf.Ofp.Rv.Ac.Dll.Ncd.Ch'27
  ☎ (610) 642-2382 . . 449 Montgomery Av, Apt 301, Haverford,
  PA *19041*

Watson MR & MRS Charles G (Nancy E McCall) | of ☎ (203)966-1955
NCar'62.Ln.Plg.Y.'54 . . . . | 566 Weed St,
  MISS Wendy F—Woos'89 . . . . | New Canaan, CT
  MR Charles E—Mid'92 . . . . | *06840*
  | ☎ (212) 935-0618
  | 435 E 57 St,
  | New York, NY
  | *10022*

Watson MISS D Anne
  ☎ (212) 688-3495 . . 30 Beekman Place, New York, NY *10022*

Watson MR & MRS Donald C (Priscilla B Hirons) | ☎ (908) 273-9407
Myf.Dc.Y'35 . . . . | 18 Pine Ridge Dv,
  MISS Susan H . . . . | Summit, NJ *07901*
  MISS Ann B . . . .

Watson MR & MRS Donald C (Rosita L Richmond) D.H'40
  ☎ (617) 326-7873 . . 33 Woods End Rd, Dedham, MA *02026*

Watson DR & MRS (DR) Donald C JR (Susan R | ☎ (901) 761-9076
Prince) Leh'68.Stan'69.Duke'72.Van'92 . . . . . . | 6367 River Tide Dv,
  MISS Kea H . . . . | Memphis, TN *38120*
  JUNIORS MISS Katherine A . . . .
  JUNIORS MISS Kirsten P . . . .

Watson MR & MRS Douglas (Marie K Latshaw) Stan'39.Stan'38
☎ (707) 963-7219 . . 225 Knoll Place, PO Box 441, St Helena, CA *94574-0441*

Watson MRS Electa H (Electa M Huber) . . . . | ☎ (610) 644-0605
MISS Linn P—at Westtown . . . . | 308 Sidley Rd,
MR James W—at Widener Law . . . . | Malvern, PA *19355*
MR David R—at Brown . . . . |

Watson MR & MRS Gavin W (Alice W Marbach)
MtH'77.Cl'79.Wms'78.Dth'82
☎ (203) 655-3044 . . 58 Horseshoe Rd, Darien, CT *06820*

Watson MR & MRS George E 3d (Louisa Carter | ☎ (202) 244-7033
Johnson) Wheat'62.Cos.Y'53.Y'61.Y'64 . . . . . . | 4323 Cathedral Av
MISS Elisabeth Carter—Ws'91—at | NW, Washington,
☎ (202) 237-7113 . . 3516—34 St NW, | DC *20016*
Washington, DC *20008* . . . . |
MR George E IV—Duke'94—at |
☎ (704) 342-5756 . . 2108 Park Rd, Apt 1, |
Charlotte, NC *28203* . . . . |

Watson MR & MRS H Ross JR (Ann P Hart)
☎ (610) 353-5190 . . ''Frog Hollow'' Langdale Rd, Newtown Square, PA *19073*

Watson MRS Katrine (Wilson—Katrine Watson) Cal'56
☎ (916) 582-0979 . . PO Box 2539, Truckee, CA *96160*

Watson MR & MRS Louis Hanner (Frances Egger)
Ncmb'60.Miss'87.Tul'60.H'68
☎ (601) 981-7413 . . 1936 Petit Bois St, Jackson, MS *39211-6707*

Watson MISS Lucinda B (Kew—Mehran—Lucinda | of ☎ (415)435-5923
B Watson) SL'77 . . . . | 10 Crest Rd,
MISS Christina E Kew . . . . | Belvedere, CA
MISS Annabel M Mehran . . . . | *94920*
JUNIORS MR Alexander R Mehran JR . . . . | ☎ (415) 868-2028
| 29 Dipsea Rd,
| Stinson Beach, CA
| *94970*

Watson MRS Margaret P (Margaret T Pattison) | of ☎ (617)876-8274
Cal'65.Chi.Ncd. . . . . | 27 Reservoir St,
MISS Katherine K—Br'91—at ☎ (415) 752-1090 | Cambridge, MA
1350 Lake St, San Francisco, CA *94118* . . . . . | *02138*
MISS Bonnie F—at Brown . . . . | ☎ (207) 789-5312
MR T William—Y'94—at 338 W 14 St, Apt 2C, | ''Faraway''
New York, NY *10014* . . . . | PO Box 6,
| Lincolnville, ME
| *04849*

Watson MRS Nina V M (Robertson—Nina V | ☎ (416) 482-5571
Manganaro) Alberta'80.Ds.W. . . . . | 81 Chaplin Crescent,
JUNIORS MISS Celeste A . . . . | Toronto, Ontario
JUNIORS MR Warwick G . . . . | M5P 1A4, Canada

Watson MISS Olive F—Mid'70 🔱 . . of
150 W 56 St, Apt 6902, New York, NY *10019*
☎ (516) 726-6694 . . ''Land of Oz'' Rose Hill Rd, Water Mill, NY *11976*

Watson MR & MRS Peter A (Jeremy L Thompson) | ☎ (203) 245-4290
Y'58 . . . . | 26 Grove Av,
MISS Sara E . . . . | Madison, CT *06443*

Watson MR & MRS Ralph E (McCleary—Deirdre S | ☎ (401) 621-3272
Marsters) Br'62 . . . . | 102 Williams St,
MISS Nicole V—at 418 N Dotger Av, Charlotte, | Providence, RI
NC *28204* . . . . | *02906*
MR Lucas E—Ham'94—at 2 Stillman Place, |
Boston, MA *02113* . . . . |
MISS Katherine C McCleary—Br'95—at |
282 Highland Av, Providence, RI *02906* . . . . |
MR Benjamin P McCleary—F&M'94—at |
5855 Tomahawk Dv, Winston-Salem, NC |
27106 |

Watson MR & MRS Robert B (Pauline Blodgett) | of ☎ (617)367-8447
Cy.Chi.Hn.H'37 . . . . | 29 Branch St,
MISS Jeannie—Bost'68—at 526 North Av, | Boston, MA *02108*
Weston, MA *02193* . . . . | ☎ (508) 563-6187
| ''Hill Brow''
| Scraggy Neck Rd,
| Cataumet, MA
| *02534*

Watson MR & MRS Robert C (Dorothy Clay) Mit'32
☎ (804) 435-3684 . . ''Watson's Landing'' White Stone, VA *22578*

Watson MR Ross—Camb'56
☎ (202) 965-2262 . . 1605—32 St NW, Washington, DC *20007*

Watson MR & MRS Simon C H (Madeleine S Dickerson) Hlns'65
☎ (011-44-171) 978-2471 . . 51 Clapham Manor St, London SW4 6DT, England

Watson MR T Stanley—Evg.P'34
☎ (561) 844-0394 . . 225 Arabian Rd, Palm Beach, FL *33480*

Watson MR & MRS Theodore S JR (Margaret R Creed) Y'50
☎ (520) 398-9372 . . 845 Calle de Anza, Box 4050, Tubac, AZ *85646*

Watson MR & MRS Thomas A D (P Frances Randolph)
H'87.H'96.Sb.RISD'88
21 Chauncy St, Apt 42, Cambridge, MA *02138*

Watson MRS Thomas J JR (Olive F Cawley) Ihy.Cly.
☎ (203) 629-2923 . . 100 Field Point Park, Greenwich, CT *06830*

Watson MR & MRS Thomas J 3d (Starbuck—Karen A Drobeck)
Wit'74.Sm.Colby'69.Bost'72
☎ (203) 761-1029 . . 3 Musket Ridge Rd, Wilton, CT *06897*

Watson MR Thomas S—SanJ'73
☎ (408) 374-0378 . . 2331 Valerie Court, Campbell, CA *95008*

Watson MR & MRS Walter 2d (Mary Watts) Rcn.Sm.Cy.Snc.Cw.Chi.Va'50
☎ (617) 227-4353 . . 132 Chestnut St, Boston, MA *02108*

Watson MR & MRS Walter 3d (Ann C Bailey) Va'73
☎ (504) 751-7192 . . 1623 Michel Delving Rd, Baton Rouge, LA *70810*

Watson MRS Walter J (Murchison—Leard | ☎ (619) 346-0225
Andrews) . . . . | 47-102 El Menara
MISS Anne A Murchison—Box 8968, Aspen, | Circle, Palm Desert,
CO *81611* . . . . | CA *92260*

Watt MISS Ashley M . . see MRS A M Campbell 3d

Watt JUNIORS MR John H . . see MRS A M Campbell 3d

Watt MRS Thomas McC (Haywood—Shennan—A Elizabeth Wood)
Cho.Cas.
PO Box 492, Pebble Beach, CA *93953*

Watters MRS Edward McL JR (Lucy F Disston) Dar.
☎ (610) 692-6234 . . 717 Inverness Dv, West Chester, PA *19380*

Watters MR & MRS Edward McL 3d (Susan E Secor) | ☎ (610) 647-1331
Miami'77.M.Pe.Y.'65.Pa'70 . . . . | 458 Green Hill
JUNIORS MISS Jennifer S . . . . | Lane, Berwyn, PA
JUNIORS MISS Ann E . . . . | *19312*

Watters MRS Gustav F (Marie L Schmidt)
35 Baynard Park Rd, Villa 406, Hilton Head Island, SC *29928*

Watterson MRS David G (Jane Van Gorder) Ws'31.May.
☎ (216) 231-8414 . . 2181 Ambleside Dv, Apt 802, Cleveland, OH *44106*

Wattis MRS Paul L (Phyllis Cannon) Bur.
☎ (415) 441-8444 . . 2006 Washington St, San Francisco, CA *94109*

Watts MRS David M (Anne T Day) Pa'49 . . . . | ☎ (610) 446-5897
MISS Elizabeth A D—WChesU'76—at | 160 Charles Dv,
☎ (302) 478-9179 . . 3102 Ruby Dv, Wilmington, | Havertown, PA
DE *19810* . . . . | *19083*

Watts MR & MRS Edward E 3d (Elise M Phillips) | ☎ (617) 326-1045
P'65.Va'73 . . . . | 311 West St,
MISS Hilary H . . . . | Dedham, MA *02026*
MR Hardy G—at Princeton . . . . |
JUNIORS MR Christopher P—at Groton . . . . |

Watts MRS Edward Everett JR (Isabella R Hardy)
☎ (508) 758-3363 . . 11 Shipyard Lane, Mattapoisett, MA *02739*

Watts MRS Henry M JR (Pepper—Anna B Harris) | ☎ (215) 925-5459
Rb.Ac.Fw.Cc.Ncd. . . . . | 219 Spruce St,
MR Henry M 3d . . . . | Philadelphia, PA
MR David P—at Denison . . . . | *19106*

Watts MR & MRS James Harrison (Janice Fahey)
RISD'74.Sdy.RISD'74 ⚓
☎ (619) 298-0404 . . 3619 Front St, San Diego, CA *92103*

Watts MRS Robert H (Mathes—Mary C Chapman) Cy.Chi.Ncd.
☎ (617) 566-7258 . . 60 Fairgreen Place, Chestnut Hill, MA *02167*

Waud MR & MRS Cornelius Byron (Corinna Roosevelt Reeve)
Glc.Nf.On.Cw.Cnt.StLaw'62 ⚓
☎ (847) 234-9080 . . 1050 E Illinois Rd, Lake Forest, IL *60045*

Waud MR Ernest P 3d—On.Rc.Cw.P'60
☎ (847) 234-0439 . . 126 Pembroke, Lake Forest, IL *60045*

Waud MR & MRS Morrison (Anne B Smith) On.P'32
☎ (941) 262-5562 . . 4051 Gulf Shore Blvd N, Apt 102, Naples, FL *34103*

Waud MR & MRS Reeve B (Melissa Ann Wheeler)
Mid'85.On.Rc.Cw.Mid'85.Nw'89
☎ (847) 234-1738 . . 455 Oakwood Av, Lake Forest, IL *60045*

Waud MR & MRS Sydney P (Nancy C Stanley) Tex'75.Rc.Rm.Pa'63 . . of
☎ (212) 288-5925 . . 181 E 73 St, New York, NY *10021*
☎ (970) 925-4636 . . 1046 Vine St, Aspen, CO *81611*
☎ (213) 654-3875 . . 950 N Kings Rd, Apt 120, Los Angeles, CA *90069*

Waugh MRS Welby A (Welby A O'Brien) Biola'78
☎ (503) 254-8721 . . 8721 NE Beech St, Portland, OR *97220*

Waxter MR & MRS Arthur L S (Nancy Daniels) Md.Y'48 . . of
☎ (410) 822-6504 . . 8845 Teal Point Rd, Easton, MD *21601*
☎ (410) 235-5997 . . 4401 Roland Av, Apt 1A, Baltimore, MD *21210*

Waxter MR Arthur L S JR—MdArt'77
5542 Suffield Court, Columbia, MD *21044*

Waxter MRS Thomas J S SR (Margaret H Ewing) Elk.
☎ (410) 467-4644 . . 4721 East Lane, Baltimore, MD *21210*

Way MRS Channing JR (Hermione Barret)
Beaumont, 601 N Ithan Av, Bryn Mawr, PA *19010*

Wear MR & MRS Joseph W (Gowen—Katharine S | ☎ (610) 430-3388
Hare) Sg. . . . . | Carousel Farm, 920
MISS Jennifer W—at Brown . . . . | Hillsdale Rd, West
| Chester, PA *19382*

Wear MISS Katherine S . . see T P Wright

Wear MRS William Potter (Doris L Stewart) Cry.Ac.
☎ (410) 275-2040 . . ''Enterprise'' Cecilton, MD *21913*

Weary MR & MRS Rollin D JR (Joan C Butler). Ih.
☎ (561) 231-2546 . . 297 Island Creek Dv, John's Island, Vero Beach, FL *32963*

Weary MR & MRS Rollin D 3d (Julie A Bidinger) | ☎ (847) 441-5032
Wis'70.Menlo'68 . . . . | 15 Bristol Rd,
JUNIORS MR Rollin D 4th . . . . | Northfield, IL *60093*
JUNIORS MR Charles F . . . . |

Weary MR & MRS Thomas S (Helen G Stephenson) Me.Rc.Cs.H.'47.H'50
☎ (610) 527-1056 . . 210 Curwen Rd, Rosemont, PA *19010-1617*

Weatherley MR & MRS Kent W (Rosemary R | ☎ (410) 821-6551
Carusi) Va'71 . . . . | 577 Woodbine Av,
JUNIORS MR Ian W . . . . | Towson, MD *21204*
JUNIORS MR Devin K . . . . |

Weatherley-White MR & MRS Carl C (Carley C Rand)
CtCol'84.Rc.Pr.Cly.Br'86
☎ (212) 996-8123 . . 49 E 96 St, Apt 12E, New York, NY *10128*

Weatherly MR & MRS Robert S JR (Mary Anne Burr) Ala'54.Cy.P'50.H'53
☎ (205) 967-7308 . . 4608 Old Leeds Rd, Birmingham, AL *35213*

Weathers MRS Suzanne J (Kenefick—Suzanne Jerauld) G.
☎ (716) 876-1108 . . 77 Nottingham Terr, Buffalo, NY *14216*

Weaver MRS Elizabeth L (Smithers—Elizabeth A Luther) WmSth'78
☎ (203) 255-7606 . . 120 Taintor Dv, Southport, CT *06490*

Weaver MRS M Parker (Mary S Parker) . . . . | ☎ (805) 898-1256
MISS M Seabury . . . . | 229 W Isley St, Apt
MR John F JR . . . . | 2, Santa Barbara,
| CA *93101*

Weaver DR Robert P—Penn'49 . . . . | ☎ (814) 237-3368
MISS Debra L . . . . | 601 W Park Av,
MISS Donna L . . . . | State College, PA
MISS Diana P . . . . | *16803*
MISS Dana T . . . . |

Weaver MR William V—Cl'77
350 Central Park W, Apt 15A, New York, NY *10025*

Webb MR & MRS Alexander D (Mary R D'Adamo) . | ☎ (410) 876-1920
MISS Melissa M—at Md Inst of Art . . . . | 106 Winchester
| Court, Westminster,
| MD *21157*

Webb MR & MRS Benjamin P (Gardiner—Catherine | ☎ (415) 461-5072
O Mather) Sfg.Tcy.Cly.Dth'40 . . . . | 8 Laurel Way,
MR Timothy M Gardiner—Box 1040, | Kentfield, CA
Sun Valley, ID *83353* . . . . | *94904-2618*

Webb MR & MRS Benjamin P JR (Marsha Compton) Sw'73
☎ (415) 454-4406 . . 5 Lilac Av, Kentfield, CA *94904*

Webb MRS Charles JR (Lucy E Hoffman) | ☎ (202) 745-7749
BMr'48.Cvc.Eyc.Mt.Cly.Sl.Cda. . . . . | 2910 Woodland Dv
MR Charles H—Md'84 . . . . | NW, Washington,
MR Livingston R . . . . | DC *20008*

Webb DR & MRS Charles A (Ann C Heroy) V'60.Cl'64.JHop'71.Ty'60.Cl'64.JHop'69 ⚓ .
MR William H—Emory'91 . . . .
☎ (410) 226-5554
4504 World Farm Rd, Oxford, MD *21654*

Webb MR Charles A 3d—Rens'86
☎ (908) 741-3651 . . 62 Waterman Av, Rumson, NJ *07760*

Webb MR & MRS Charles J 2d (Elizabeth H Holmes) Sg.Nyc.Ac.Dth'43
☎ (215) CH7-4347 . . 434 W Chestnut Hill Av, Philadelphia, PA *19118*

Webb MR & MRS Elmon D (Virginia F Dancy) V'62.Y'65.Tul'58
☎ (212) 595-9138 . . 105 W 72 St, New York, NY *10023*

Webb MRS H St John 3d (Marie B Whittle) Ga'62.Me . . . .
MR H St John 4th—Col'92—at
☎ (303) 449-4704 . . 636 Spruce St, Boulder, CO *80302* . . . .
MR Lucian A . . . .
JUNIORS MR William B—at U of Ore Eugene . . .
PO Box 336, Bryn Mawr, PA *19010*

Webb MR H St John 3d—Me.Y'60
☎ (610) 527-4563 . . 624 Black Rock Rd, Bryn Mawr, PA *19010*

Webb MR J Watson JR—Y'38
☎ (310) 472-3537 . . 11740 Crescenda St, Los Angeles, CA *90049*

Webb MR & MRS James A JR (Caroline Bartlett) Ala'44.Van'44.Van'46
☎ (615) 292-1709 . . 615 Belle Meade Blvd, Apt 110, Nashville, TN *37205-3851*

Webb MR & MRS James C (Clare M Blossom) Pars'70.Pars'70 . . . .
MISS Jennifer B . . . .
MISS Susan J . . . .
MISS Cynthia C . . . .
☎ (310) 395-0302
253—20 St, Santa Monica, CA *90402*

Webb MRS Jesse L (Elizabeth L Protzman) Gchr'25
☎ (410) 795-4242 . . Fairhaven, 7200 Third Av, Sykesville, MD *21784*

Webb MRS Nola P (Foreman—Nola Poynton) Me.Dar.Ht.
☎ (610) 896-8259 . . 1153 Maplecrest Circle, Gladwyne, PA *19035*

Webb MR & MRS Richard N (Sjostrom—Herbert—Joan Frazier) Br'53
☎ (203) 227-3493 . . 24 Sterling Dv, Westport, CT *06880*

Webb MR & MRS Samuel B JR (Weir—Marshall M Brown) SFr'75.Cl'86.Rcn.B.Pr.BtP.So.Cly.Y'61. Y'63.Cal'70 . . . .
MR Edward W—Vt'92—at ☎ (617) 964-5337 31 Highland Av, Apt 1, Newton, MA *02160* . . .
MR William V—at ☎ (802) 865-3801 7 Bradley St, Burlington, VT *05401* . . . .
☎ (802) 985-4151 "Deerhill" Southern Acres Farm, Harbor Rd, PO Box 216, Shelburne, VT *05482*

Webb MR & MRS T Ladson (Charlotte Ann Moore) Char'ton'39.StA.Ne.Ht.Ncd.Cit'32
☎ (803) 577-4766 . . 48 Church St, Charleston, SC *29401-2557*

Webb CAPT & MRS T Ladson JR (Kristin B Dillon) USN.Tex'72.An.Tul'72.Chap'78 . . . .
MISS Katherine D—at Wm & Mary . . . .
JUNIORS MR T Ladson 3d—at Episcopal . . . .
☎ (703) 750-3512
680 N Armistead St, Alexandria, VA *22312*

Webb MR & MRS William J G (Carolyn R Ordway) Yn.Y'52
☎ (561) 234-3547 . . 911 Ladybug Lane, Vero Beach, FL *32963*

Webb MR & MRS William M (Bottomley—Patricia Diamond) Me.Hav'38.Pa'48
☎ (610) 687-3309 . . 111 Woods Lane, Radnor, PA *19087*

Webbe MR Richard W—My.Mid'66 . . . .
MISS Emily S . . . .
MR Andrew L—at U of Vt . . . .
☎ (508) 526-4993
44 Proctor St, Manchester, MA *01944*

Webbe MR & MRS Robert M (Melinda L Lewis) Ill'76.Barcelona'78.Rcch.Red'76
☎ (617) 834-3272 . . 378 Congress St, Duxbury, MA *02332*

Webel MR & MRS Richard C (Sandra D Lawrance) Pa'74.Pa'78.Ln.Pr.Csh.Pa'74.Pa'78 . . . .
JUNIORS MR Peter C . . . .
☎ (516) 671-0999
Linden Farms Rd, Locust Valley, NY *11560*

Webel MR & MRS Richard K (Pratt—Pauline D Dodge) C.Pr.H'23
☎ (516) 626-0676 . . 1089 Cedar Swamp Rd, Brookville, Glen Head, NY *11545*

Weber DR & MRS Barrett H (Elise B Broun) Bhm.Sfg.Fr.Stan'46.Stan'49 . . . .
MR Barrett F . . . .
MR David H . . . .
MR Robert W . . . .
☎ (415) 567-7706
3491 Pacific Av, San Francisco, CA *94118*

Weber MR & MRS Douglas J (Carey U Mack) Conn'83.Conn'81
☎ (203) 226-3222 . . 16 Bridge St, Westport, CT *06880*

Weber MRS John C (Charlotte D Colket) Rd.Ri.Srr.Ac.Cly. . . . .
MISS Christina C . . . .
MR John C JR—Srr . . . .
MR Chester C . . . .
of ☎ (352)854-6776 "Live Oak" 9275 SW 9 Street Rd, Ocala, FL *34481*
☎ (212) 517-8833 3 E 77 St, Apt 4B, New York, NY *10021*

Weber DR John C—Rd.Ri.Srr.Colg'61.Cl'65
☎ (212) 249-5433 . . 960 Fifth Av, New York, NY *10021*

Weber MRS John J (Levenson—Helen B Freeman) Ws'52.Cly.Myf.Cda . . .of
☎ (212) 360-5560 . . 50 E 89 St, New York, NY *10128-1225*
☎ (860) 399-5264 . . "Witch Wood" 489 Stevenstown Rd, Westbrook, CT *06498*

Weber MRS Mary-Evan (Mary-Evan Keenan) Ithaca'68 . . . .
MISS Carrie G—at Cal Poly San Luis Obispo . . .
MR Mark C—at U of Cal Berkeley . . . .
☎ (352) 380-0023
PO Box 15205, Gainesville, FL *32604*

Weber DR & MRS Peter B (Karen E Duffy) Cal'82.Rice'90.Duke'82.Emory'86
☎ (415) 567-7706 . . 3491 Pacific Av, San Francisco, CA *94118*

Weber MR & MRS Robert E E (Barbara Brassell) Skd'53.Cy.St.G.Cr'53
☎ (716) 689-4188 . . 115 Briarhill, Williamsville, NY *14221*

Weber MR Robin M—Ithaca'69.Conn'72
20672 Gardenside, Cupertino, CA *95014*

Webster MR & MRS Andrew F (Murza—Deborah L Smith) Ph.Pc.W.Cspa.Pa'83
☎ (609) 722-9813 . . 257 E 3 St, Moorestown, NJ *08057*

Webster MRS Bethuel M (Case—M Elizabeth Wylie) V'30.Csn . . .of
☎ (609) 426-6268 . . Meadow Lakes 13-04U, Hightstown, NJ *08520*
☎ (860) 379-2946 . . "Windrush" RR 1, 152 Grantville Rd, Winsted, CT *06098*

Webster MR Charles D—K.Rc.Gr.Wk.Dth'26
☎ (516) 581-0965 . . "Twyford" St Marks Lane, PO Box 196, Islip, NY *11751*

Webster MASTER Danforth Minton (James G 4th) . . . . Born at
Bozeman, MT Jun 28'96

Webster MR & MRS Daniel E (Mollie E K Cooper) ☎ (212) 861-5852
Cly.Wis'61.H.'64.Cl'91 . . . . 29 E 64 St,
MISS Camilla E—StAndr'95 . . . . New York, NY
10021

Webster MR & MRS David Z (Janie S Huntley) ☎ (617) 449-1824
Bow'57.GeoW'64.Bab'73 . . . . 58 Avon Circle,
MR C Scott—U'86 . . . . Needham, MA
02194

Webster MR & MRS Edward S (Patricia J Scott) ☎ (215) 233-5299
Ty'73.Ty'74 . . . . 8211 Ardmore Av,
JUNIORS MISS Alexandra L . . . . Wyndmoor, PA
19038

Webster MR & MRS G Hartley D (Karen G Smith) ☎ (508) 456-3942
Dth'61 . . . . 14 Whitney Lane
MR Daniel A—at ☎ (307) 739-2406 Farms, Harvard, MA
PO Box 7178, Jackson, WY *83001* *01451*

Webster MR & MRS Geoffrey L (Lucy R Anthony) MtVern'87.Cly.Cda.
☎ (212) 772-9919 . . 314 E 83 St, New York, NY *10028*

Webster MR & MRS Geoffrey R (Deborah Daniels) CarnM'67.Ofp.Cly.Ch'78
☎ (203) 629-4999 . . 361 N Maple Av, Greenwich, CT *06830-4710*

Webster MR & MRS Henry C (Elizabeth Slater) Sg.W.Ac.Pa'49
☎ (215) 646-0925 . . Greystone Farm, 543 W Butler Pike, Box 413,
Ambler, PA *19002*

Webster DR & MRS Henry de F (Marion Havas) ☎ (301) 654-3324
Au.Aht'48.H'52 . . . . 4515 Willard Av,
MR Christopher W—at Washington, DC . . . . . . Apt 2303S,
MR Steven G—at Cedar Rapids, IA . . . . Chevy Chase, MD
20815

Webster MR & MRS Hugh K (K deLancey Joyce)
Duke'80.Cvc.Mt.Sl.Mid'83
☎ (301) 657-4790 . . 5106 Westport Rd, Chevy Chase, MD *20815*

Webster MR & MRS James G 4th (Valerie H Minton) Mid'80.Srb.StLaw'80
☎ (406) 587-7202 . . 311 S Third Av, Bozeman, MT *59715*

Webster MR & MRS Jerome P JR (Patterson— of ☎ (970)925-8161
Rockefeller—Anne C Sammis) Ny.Pn.P'61 . . . . "Bas Alpan"
MISS Marcella D—Cal'96 . . . . PO Box 7936,
MISS Brooke E . . . . 574 Johnson Dv,
MR Hunter McA—ColC'96 . . . . Aspen, CO
81612-7936
☎ (809) 693-8613
"Southern Cruz
Plantation" Great
Cruz Bay, Box 37,
St John, VI *00831*

Webster DR & MRS (DR) John C (Jancar—Barbara Wolfe)
Sth'56.Cl'65.Ia'41.Ia'43.Ia'53
☎ (716) 352-8333 . . 4733 Lyell Rd, Spencerport, NY *14559*

Webster MRS John R (Adams—Mary R Naylor) ☎ (301) 299-9109
Cvc. . . . . 12100 Piney
MR Hughlett M Adams . . . . Meetinghouse Rd,
Potomac, MD *20854*

Webster MR & MRS Maurice A JR (Nancy Landenberger)
Me.M.W.Ac.Hav'39 . . of
☎ (904) 285-3258 . . 1000 Vicar's Landing Way, B102,
Ponte Vedra Beach, FL *32082*
☎ (610) 520-0589 . . 28 Pond Lane, Bryn Mawr, PA *19010*

Webster MRS Priscilla L (Priscilla A Little) Bost'71
☎ (617) 449-5190 . . North Hill J401, 865 Central Av, Needham,
MA *02192*

Webster MR & MRS Richard G (Marguerite A Brush) Me.Fw.Pa'58
☎ (610) 527-1557 . . "Colony Cottage" 324 Avon Rd, Bryn Mawr,
PA *19010*

Webster MR & MRS Robert D (Elizabeth Weld Brett) | of ☎ (212)722-2362
Cly.Colg'59.H'62 . . . . 1088 Park Av,
MISS Hope B—at ☎ (212) 472-3967 New York, NY
131 E 80 St, New York, NY *10021* *10128*
JUNIORS MR Christopher W . . . . ☎ (860) 434-9457
158 Joshuatown Rd,
Lyme, CT *06371*

Weed MR & MRS Arthur H (Karoleonko—Natalia S Akulinichev)
Col'64.Col'67
☎ (805) 683-4910 . . 1250 N San Marcos Rd, Santa Barbara, CA *93111*

Weed MRS Barbara L (Barbara McD Lewis) Swb'59 | ☎ (914) 834-1352
MR Joseph J 2d—StLaw'87—at 63 Iselin Terr,
☎ (801) 521-9024 . . 1274 E South Temple St, Larchmont, NY
Salt Lake City, UT *84102* *10538*
MR Edward L . . . .

Weed MRS Roger H (Hilary T Lunt) Ncd.
2 Penrose Blvd, Colorado Springs, CO *80906-4214*

Weed DR & MRS Timothy (Lucinda Nalle) Ty'87.W&L'83.Aub'94
☎ (803) 642-0368 . . 321 Orangeburg St, Aiken, SC *29801*

Weedon MR & MRS Alexander R (Elizabeth L Warner) WmSth'77.Cy.Ty'77
☎ (617) 237-5292 . . 6 Woodlawn Av, Wellesley Hills, MA *02181*

Weedon MRS William Stone (Elizabeth du P Bayard) Nyc.
☎ (804) 293-7886 . . PO Box 3492, University Station, Charlottesville,
VA *22903*

Weekes MR & MRS Arthur D 3d (Constantine—Margery B Schwab)
Rcn.My.Cc.H'62
☎ (508) 468-3051 . . Box 172, 25 Meyer Lane, Hamilton, MA *01936*

Weekes MRS Bradford G (Rita Ravenel) Pr.S.
☎ (516) 922-6313 . . 92 Cove Rd, Oyster Bay, NY *11771*

Weekes MR & MRS Bradford G III (Phyllis M | ☎ (516) 624-7693
Reynolds) Au.Ng.Pr.Mb. . . . . 357 Ridge Lane,
MR Bradford G IV Mill Neck, NY
JUNIORS MR Christopher R *11765*

Weekes MR & MRS James T (Jane M Benziger) . . . . | ☎ (904) 285-3672
MISS Jeannine M—at 336 Bellemeade St, 129 N Roscoe Blvd,
Apt 206, Greensboro, NC *27401* . . . . Ponte Vedra Beach,
MISS Katharine S—at Goddard FL *32082*
MR James T JR—at Grunbergerstrasse 65,
Hinterhaus, 10245 Berlin, Germany . . . .

Weekes MR & MRS John M (Tamsen A Rideout) | ☎ (208) 788-3833
Chico'70.Mid'63 . . . . PO Box 3784,
MISS Elizabeth S—at ☎ (208) 622-6528 Hailey, ID *83333*
PO Box 2974, Ketchum, ID *83340* . . . .
MR Henry deF—at ☎ (208) 726-5597
PO Box 4774, Ketchum, ID *83340* . . . .

Weekes MR John M JR—SanDiego'90
☎ (208) 726-9135 . . PO Box 1150, Ketchum, ID *83340*

Weekes MISS Nancy G
☎ (208) 788-1680 . . PO Box 4554, Ketchum, ID *83340*

Weekley MR & MRS Richard W (Margaret E Neuhaus) Ws'72.Smu'67
☎ (713) 552-9744 . . 3708 Inverness Dv, Houston, TX *77019*

Weeks MR & MRS Albert H (M Christine Herlihy) Man'vl'69.P'70.CathU'82
☎ (603) 357-0589 . . 16 Portland St, Keene, NH *03431*

Weeks MISS Ann S
☎ (707) 833-1111 . . 10867 Slattery Rd, Glen Ellen, CA *95442*

Weeks MRS Annabel C (Annabel Caner) Rdc'54 . . . | ☎ (516) 367-4659
MISS Isabel C . . . . | 1592 Laurel Hollow
| Rd, Syosset, NY
| *11791*

Weeks MISS Carly Allyn (Gerald C) . . . . Born Jun 29'95

Weeks MRS Edward A (Phoebe-Lou Adams) C.Yh.
☎ (860) 923-2320 . . PO Box 2, Thompson, CT *06277*

Weeks MR & MRS Gerald C (Nancy K Allen) StL'84.StL'85
☎ (802) 885-9306 . . 831 Randall Hill Rd, Springfield, VT *05156*

Weeks MR Howard C
Hill Rd, Alstead, NH *03602*

Weeks MR & MRS John T (Jeanne M Thiery) Ws'44.Dth'44
☎ (603) 643-3091 . . Kendal at Hanover 165, 80 Lyme Rd, Hanover,
NH *03755*

Weeks MR & MRS Louis S JR (Teresa R Herring) Bnd'76.Cly.Pn.P'40.Cl'46
☎ (860) 535-3747 . . Main St, Stonington, CT *06378*

Weeks MR & MRS Louis S 3d (Marjorie M Wilcox) Skd'76.Pratt'84.Skd'75
☎ (410) 664-6434 . . 1602 The Terraces, Baltimore, MD *21209*

Weems MR & MRS F Carrington 2d (Mary Ann | ☎ (713) 522-2935
Sledge) Ala'57.Sar.Myf.Col'52 . . . . | 919 Kirby Dv,
MISS (DR) Mathilde S—Tex'95—at Stanford . . . . | Houston, TX *77019*
MISS Alexandra L—at ☎ (212) 369-6907
200 E 94 St, Apt 3, New York, NY *10128* . . .

Weems MR & MRS Tommy Lewis (Knowlton—Miriam O Wilson)
Miss'63.MissSt'63
☎ (601) 353-0101 . . 1809 Peachtree St, Jackson, MS *39202*

Wees MR & MRS Charles A (Mary L Kinsella) | ☎ (314) 994-1684
Mo'42 . . . . | 8227 Delmar Blvd,
MISS Pamela A—Fontb'96 . . . . | St Louis, MO *63124*

Wehle MISS Edith M P
☎ (212) 777-3842 . . 30 W 9 St, New York, NY *10011*

Wehr MRS Frederick L (Nancy de W Theobald) | ☎ (410) 823-1111
Mv.Ncd.Myf. . . . . | 1209 Berwick Rd,
MISS Nancy de W Smith . . . . | Ruxton, MD *21204*
MISS Wendell C Smith . . . . |
MR Peter de W Smith . . . . |

Wehrle MR & MRS John S (Jennifer L Gregory)
Skd'77.Unn.Rc.T.Cly.Wash'74.StL'77
☎ (314) 991-6851 . . 8 Briarcliff, St Louis, MO *63124*

Weicker MISS Alexa Gray (Gray G) . . . . Born at
Greenwich, CT Sep 2'94

Weicker MR & MRS Gray G (Penne L Brooks) StLaw'85.StLaw'84
☎ (203) 655-9432 . . 120 Five Mile River Rd, Darien, CT *06820*

Weicker MRS Marie Godfrey (Marie Louise | ☎ (203) 869-3291
Godfrey) CtCol'52 . . . . | 6 Deer Lane,
MR Brian B—at 110 Country Club Park, | Greenwich, CT
Grand Junction, CO *81503* . . . . | *06830*

Weicker MR & MRS Scot B (Lisa M Hull) Rich'81.Rich'80
☎ (203) 622-6091 . . 475 North St, Greenwich, CT *06830*

Weidenkopf CAPT & MRS David W (Joyce V Brenholts) USN'51
☎ (216) 221-7360 . . 17891 Captain's Cove, Lakewood, Cleveland,
OH *44107*

Weidlein MR & MRS Edward R JR (Mary C Rea) Temp'42.Rr.C.Pg.Cs.P'40
☎ (412) 238-2203 . . Bakobils Farm, PO Box 45, Rector, PA *15677*

Weil MR & MRS Adolph I JR (Jean R Kaufman) Dth'35
☎ (334) 263-6068 . . 2100 Allendale Rd, Montgomery, AL *36111*

Weil MR & MRS Andrew L (Margaret G Thompson) Chath'49.P'43
☎ (412) 828-9345 . . 108 White Gate Rd, Pittsburgh, PA *15238*

Weil MR & MRS David S (Hope B Wickser) Skd'86.Cly.Skd'84
☎ (914) 232-1707 . . PO Box 152, Cross River, NY *10518-0152*

Weil MR & MRS Frank A (Denie P Sandison) | of ☎ (202)338-6007
Rdc'54.C.Mt.Cs.H.'53 . . . . | 1516—28 St NW,
MISS Amanda E—at 123 Prince St, New York, | Washington, DC
NY *10012* . . . . | *20007*
MR Sandison E—at 324 E 41 St, New York, NY | ☎ (212) 472-4677
10017 . . . . | 10 E 68 St,
MR William S . . . . | New York, NY
| *10021*

Weil MRS Peter (Susan S F Cooper) Ncd. . . . . | ☎ (914) 666-8582
MISS Sara S—Wes'84 . . . . | Baldwin Rd, RD 2,
MR Henry F C—Cl'86 . . . . | Mt Kisco, NY
| *10549*

Weil DR & MRS Richard 3d (Polly W Edgar) Sth'59.Csn.P'57.Cl'61
☎ (401) 274-0049 . . 540 Cole Av, Providence, RI *02906*

Weil MR Richard MacC—Duke'85.Ch'89
☎ (714) 675-9099 . . 433 Begonia Av, Corona Del Mar, CA *92625*

Weil MR & MRS Robert S (Virginia Loeb) Wheat'42.Dth'40
☎ (334) 281-5050 . . 3608 Thomas Av, Montgomery, AL *36111*

Weiler MR & MRS Joseph F JR (Allison—Joan C Glover)
☎ (813) 596-5259 . . 11375 Shipwatch Lane, Apt 1836, Largo, FL *33774*

Weille MRS Eleanor W (Eleanor P Walker)
166 E 96 St, New York, NY *10128*

Weille MR & MRS F Blair (Martha G Tanner) | ☎ (212) 831-1167
Rdc'53.Ne.H'53 . . . . | 166 E 96 St,
MISS Lee H—Wes'86 . . . . | New York, NY
| *10128*

Weinberger MR & MRS Caspar W (Jane Dalton) Bhm.C.Tcy.H'38
700 New Hampshire Av NW, Apt 1221, Washington, DC *20037*

Weinig MR & MRS Robert F (Mackerer—Putnam—
Nancy L Anderson) Dth'25
☎ (941) 261-7349 . . 122 Moorings Park Dv, Apt G611, Naples,
FL *34105*

Weinman MR Michael L de R—Adelphi'90 . . see MRS Z Van W de Ropp

Weinmann MR & MRS Eric W (Carothers—Mary E de Limur)
Ct.Mt.Sl.Cl'47.Cl'57.Geo'61
☎ (202) 363-3244 . . 3244 Nebraska Av NW, Washington,
DC *20016-2704*

Weintz MR & MRS J Frederick JR (Elisabeth H Brewer) Ne.Hn.Stan'48.H'51 . . . . | of ☎ (203)637-3577 "Harbor Lights" 43 Jones Park Dv, Riverside, CT *06878*
MR Eric C—Stan'85—at Portola Valley, CA . . . | ☎ (415) 851-1443 16 Franciscan Ridge, Portola Valley, CA *94025*

Weintz MISS Polly W (J Frederick JR) . . . . Married at Greenwich, CT
Sanna MR John A 3d (John A JR) . . . . Jun 22'96

Weir VCTSS (Metzger—Hutton—Dorothy B Dear) Ri.Cly.
☎ (908) 766-4428 . . Pennbrook Farm, 144 Lake Rd, Far Hills, NJ *07931*

Weir MRS Ann H (Derr—Clement—Ann H Weir) Sth'63.Edg. . . . . | ☎ (412) 741-6957 715 Beaver St, Sewickley, PA *15143*
MISS Helen D H Derr . . . .
JUNIORS MR Andrew L Derr . . . .

Weir MRS David R (Arria Morison)
239 River Mead Rd, Peterborough, NH *03458*

Weir MR & MRS Michael B (McConoughey—Deborah N Jaynes) Miami'64.Nu'78.Plg.Yn. Y'47.Pa'50 . . . . | ☎ (203) 869-0427 18 Dempsey Lane, Greenwich, CT *06830*
MISS M Michaela—Md'77 . . . .
MR Mark A—SConn'82 . . . .
MISS Caitlin H McConoughey—Hlns'91 . . . .

Weir MR & MRS Richard 3d (Paula C Youngs) Vt'72.S.Dar.Cr'68 . . . . | ☎ (516) WA2-1956 174 Cove Rd, Oyster Bay, NY *11771*
JUNIORS MISS Abby Y . . . .
JUNIORS MR Richard 4th—at W'minster . . . .

Weir MRS William C (Cynthia E Elmslie) V'36
☎ (617) 876-4623 . . 5 Malcolm Rd, Cambridge, MA *02138*

Weiser REV & MRS Ivan (Antoinette Graham) Col'62.BankSt'75.Ch'57.Tor'60.Ox'62 . . . | ☎ (505) 820-6567 848 Camino de Levante, Santa Fe, NM *87501*
MISS Katharine C—Ken'94 . . . .
MR Thomas G—Geo'93 . . . .
MR Daniel—at U of Ariz . . . .

Weiss MR & MRS John R (Camille H McDonald) Sth'48.Sc.Cnt.Ncd.Han'50
☎ (773) LA5-8355 . . 504 W Barry Av, Chicago, IL *60657*

Weiss MR & MRS John Ward (K Menelle Head) Conv'75.Presby'77.Ala'80.Nu'85
☎ (334) 834-9596 . . 2147 Allendale Rd, Montgomery, AL *36111*

Weiss LT & MRS William B (Kathleen A Lapey) USA.Wms'90.Va'94.Wms'91
☎ (540) 829-4991 . . 600B Southview Court, Culpeper, VA *22701*

Weiss MR & MRS William D (Robin B Martin) Rr.B.Cly.Pars'68 . . . . | ☎ (307) 733-0221 7555 Moose Wilson Rd, PO Box 1108, Jackson, WY *83001*
JUNIORS MISS Katrina D . . . .

Weiss MR William U (William D) . . . . Married at Jackson, WY
Peters MISS May W (Hagen) . . . . Jly 6'96

Weist MRS Edward C (J Louise Stursberg)
☎ (561) 231-1869 . . PO Box 3208, Vero Beach, FL *32964*

Weitman MISS Catherine S . . see MRS C B Beyer
Weitman JUNIORS MR Michael B . . see MRS C B Beyer

Welborne MR & MRS John Howard (Martha Lampkin) NotreD'75.Mit'81.Bhm.Cal'69.Cal'74.Cal'77
☎ (213) 935-1918 . . 434 S Plymouth Blvd, Los Angeles, CA *90020-4708*

Welch MR & MRS E Sohier (Mary C Eddison) B'gton'40.Chi.H'39
☎ (508) 456-8091 . . PO Box B, Harvard, MA *01451-0371*

Welch MR & MRS Francis C (Ellen Cushing) Bost'62.H'33.H'36
☎ (508) 526-1037 . . 23 Harbor St, Manchester, MA *01944*

Welch MRS Francis W JR (Emily L Travers) . . . . . . | ☎ (410) 822-1275 16 N Aurora St, Easton, MD *21601*
MR Francis W 3d—Md'73.Ariz'78 . . . .
MR John H 2d . . . .

Welch MR & MRS James O JR (Virginia Bridge) V'55.Cyb.Ec.Bg.Chi.H'52 . . . . | ☎ (201) 376-2324 165 Old Short Hills Rd, Short Hills, NJ *07078*
MR Miles P—at New York, NY . . . .
MR Christopher W—at New York, NY . . . .
MR Gardiner B—at New York, NY . . . .
MR Samuel P—at New York, NY . . . .

Welch MR & MRS James S JR (Marianne Cabot) P'81
☎ (502) 228-2899 . . "Wissahickon" 11811 Covered Bridge Rd, Prospect, KY *40059-9509*

Welch MRS John H (Martha McKeen)
☎ (914) 234-3308 . . 188 Baldwin Rd, RD 2, Mt Kisco, NY *10549*

Welch MR & MRS Leighton B (Beatrice W Bast) Wms'85.Cyb.Ac.H'83
☎ (914) 779-8648 . . 83 Warwick Rd, Bronxville, NY *10708*

Welch MISS (DR) Martha G (Horan—Martha G Welch) Nu'66.Cl'71 . . . . | of ☎ (212)861-6816 952 Fifth Av, New York, NY *10021*
JUNIORS MR T Bramwell Welch Horan . . . . . . | ☎ (203) 661-1413 235 Cognewaugh Rd, Cos Cob, CT *06807*

Welch MISS Natalie K (W Perry) . . . . Married at Westbury, NY
Gilmore MR John J JR (John J) . . . . Jly 13'96

Welch MR Noble—Ihy.Y'53 ⚓
☎ (203) 637-2055 . . 1465 E Putnam Av, Apt 106, Old Greenwich, CT *06870*

Welch MR & MRS Stuart C (Edith I Gilbert) Rdc'54.K.Cly.Cda.H'50 . . . . | 868 Rte 103 E, Warner, NH *03278*
MISS Lucia C . . . .

Welch MR & MRS Thomas C (Liane P E Luke) HRdc'79.H'83.Hn.H'79.Cal'86
☎ (617) 666-9527 . . 58 Francesca Av, Somerville, MA *02144*

Welch MR & MRS Thomas D (Pyle—Jeannette Brewer) Chi.Ncd.H'35 . . . . | ☎ (561) 231-2165 2721 Ocean Dv, Vero Beach, FL *32963*
MISS Frances E—at 191 Beacon St, Marblehead, MA *01945* . . . . |

Welch MR & MRS W Perry (Catherine K Knott) Pr.Cw.Y'58 ⚓
☎ (516) 922-3808 . . 6120 Rte 25A, East Norwich, NY *11732*

Weld MRS A Matthew (Jacqueline Bograd) SL'68.Cl'71.Cly.Ri.
☎ (212) 755-1005 . . 485 Park Av, New York, NY *10022*

Weld MR A Matthew—Ri.H'64.Cl'71
"Bocaditos" 2305 Ponce De Leon Blvd, Coral Gables, FL *33134*

Weld MISS Ashley N . . see W V Pietsch

Weld MISS Caroline R—Bost'88
☎ (212) 427-6025 . . 1150 Fifth Av, Apt 4A, New York, NY *10128*

Weld MR & MRS Christopher (Mary E D'Aprix) Syr'67.Ub.Ec.Dth'52
☎ (619) 320-5043 . . 380 Crestview Dv, Palm Springs, CA *92264*

Weld MR & MRS Christopher M (Susanna R ┊ ☎ (508) 768-7673
Boocock) Rdc'55.Sbc.B.Nrr.Sm.Mt.H'54 . . . . . . ┊ John Wise Lane,
MISS Kate W . . . . ┊ Essex, MA *01929*

Weld MR & MRS Christopher P (Tyler Ingham) Skd'89.Skd'87
☎ (415) 380-8212 . . 700 View Point Rd, Mill Valley, CA *94941*

Weld MR David L JR—Au.Dth'85.Dth'90
☎ (206) 323-2577 . . 615 Bellevue Av E, Seattle, WA *98102*

Weld DR & MRS Francis M (Helene S Mueller) ┊ ☎ (212) 288-6438
Au.C.Cs.H.'61.Cl'65 . . . . ┊ 1 East End Av,
MISS Alexandra S . . . . ┊ New York, NY
MR Francis M JR . . . . ┊ *10021*
JUNIORS MISS Margaret D . . . . ┊

Weld REV & MRS George F 2d (Louise D ┊ ☎ (803) 559-1057
Gwathmey) Conv'66.VaTheo'76 ⚓ . . . . ┊ "Weldweel"
MISS Elizabeth A . . . . ┊ 1624 Clark Hill
MR George F 3d—David'95 . . . . ┊ Circle, PO Box 272,
MR Richard G—at U of Vt . . . . ┊ Johns Island, SC
JUNIORS MR William N 2d . . . . ┊ *29457*

Weld MRS Hope (Adamson—Hope Weld) Sth'66.Roch'68.Bost'76.Bost'82
70 Willow St, Dover, MA *02030*

Weld MR J Garneau 3d—Cysl.Nyc.
☎ (714) 649-2138 . . PO Box 37, Silverado Canyon, CA *92676*

Weld MR & MRS Lothrop M JR (Loberg—Priscilla Q ┊ ☎ (617) 934-7318
Peters) Chi.Cda.H'50 . . . . ┊ 34 Lovers Lane,
MR Thomas L 2d—Box 106, Orland, ME *04472* ┊ Duxbury, MA *02332*
MR John S—at Great Wood Island,
PO Box 1998, Duxbury, MA *02331* . . . .
MISS Ingrid A Loberg—Ore'82—at
25 Colonial Terr, Plymouth, MA *02360* . . . . .
MISS Karen Q Loberg—ArtCtr'83—
☎ (617) 934-0968 . . . .

Weld MR & MRS William F (Susan Roosevelt) ┊ ☎ (617) 864-5743
Rdc'70.Yen'71.H'74.Au.Mt.H'66.Ox'67.H'70 . . ┊ 28 Fayerweather St,
MISS Ethel D—at NYU . . . . ┊ Cambridge, MA
MISS Mary B—at Milton . . . . ┊ *02138*
MR David M—at Harvard . . . . ┊
JUNIORS MISS Frances W—at Shady Hill Sch . . . ┊
JUNIORS MR Quentin R—at Milton . . . . ┊

Weld MR & MRS William G JR (Ellen L Carleton) ┊ ☎ (203) 869-9611
StL'54 . . . . ┊ 120 Zaccheus Mead
MR William G 3d—Wit'84 . . . . ┊ Lane, Greenwich,
MR Edward K—Tufts'86.Mit'91 . . . . ┊ CT *06831*

Weld MR & MRS William N (Carol I O'Grady) ┊ ☎ (914) 234-3287
StMarys'66.H.'66 . . . . ┊ 463 Pound Ridge
MISS Jennifer H—H.'91.Pa'95 . . . . ┊ Rd, Bedford, NY
MISS Victoria A—H.'92 . . . . ┊ *10506-9618*
MR William C—H'94 . . . . ┊

Welden MRS Richard C (Mary C Thenebe) . . . . . . ┊ ☎ (508) 627-7060
MR Trafford T—Reed'80.Ox'82—at ┊ "Thornwyck Hall"
☎ (603) 643-9470 . . 19 S Park St, Hanover, NH ┊ PO Box 2907,
03755 . . . . ┊ Mill Hill Rd,
┊ Edgartown, MA
┊ *02539*

Welden MR Richard C—Y'48.H'51 . . . . ┊ ☎ (212) 472-5151
MR Wickford W—Cw.Rv.Rol'77 . . . . ┊ 305 E 72 St,
┊ New York, NY
┊ *10021*

Weldon JUNIORS MR Henry L 3d . . see J C Plowden-Wardlaw

Wellborn MR & MRS John Bennett (Kelly G Dunnam) Tex'88.Okla'90 . . of
☎ (214) 350-9615 . . 5433 Druid Lane, Dallas, TX *75209*
☎ (616) 256-9619 . . "Wildwood" PO Box 13, Leland, MI *49654*

Wellborn MR & MRS Robert H (Sylvia A Palmer) StJ.Smu'59 . . of
☎ (214) 526-9847 . . 4500 Roland Av, Apt 101, Dallas, TX *75219-1629*
☎ (616) 256-9619 . . "Wildwood" PO Box 13, Leland, MI *49654*

Wellborn MR & MRS Robert H JR (Kathryn S Brockett)
Austin'90.HampSydney'87.Van'89
☎ (214) 348-8575 . . 9507 Millridge Dv, Dallas, TX *75243*

Weller MR & MRS Frank H JR (Keyser—Eleanor J ┊ ☎ (410) 771-4239
Constable) Elk.Md.Nyc.Mv.Y'62.Va'65 . . . . . . ┊ "Foxgloves"
MISS Eleanor W . . . . ┊ 16135 Old York Rd,
┊ Monkton, MD
┊ *21111*

Welles MR & MRS Arnold (Dana E Ogden) Wheat'77.Y'69
☎ (203) 661-4684 . . 16 Kenilworth Terr, Greenwich, CT *06830*

Welles MR Caldwell Mead—Bates'90
☎ (612) 474-8671 . . 20690 Linwood Rd, Excelsior, MN *55331*

Welles MR Christopher S—H'80
☎ (617) 894-8048 . . 45 Willard Rd, Weston, MA *02193*

Welles MR & MRS David W (Marcia L Andersen) ┊ ☎ (212) TR6-5042
Y'61.Va'64 . . . . ┊ 55 E 76 St,
MISS Dede W—Y'92 . . . . ┊ New York, NY
MISS Margaret D—at Yale . . . . ┊ *10021*
MR Michael L—Ch'94 . . . . ┊

Welles MRS Edward R 2d (Malcolm—Ferne Bingham)
☎ (816) 756-0880 . . Parkway Towers Apt 1002, 4545 Wornall Rd,
Kansas City, MO *64111*

Welles MR & MRS Edward R 3d (Anne E La Hines) ┊ ☎ (207) 244-5015
⚓ ┊ Learning Place,
MISS Laura . . . . ┊ Manset, ME *04656*
MR William B v A . . . . ┊

Welles MR & MRS James B JR (Ann B Thom) V'45.Cl'39
☎ (914) 666-3497 . . 25 Ivy Hill Rd, Chappaqua, NY *10514*

Welles MR & MRS Jeffrey F (Maud D Iselin)
Dth'77.Nu'91.Rc.Ck.Dth'77.Cl'85
☎ (212) 369-4958 . . 1220 Park Av, New York, NY *10128*

Welles MR & MRS Peter de L (Anna Roberts) ┊ ☎ (404) 250-9101
LSU'68.LIU'66 ⚓ . . . . ┊ 320 Sea Marsh
MISS Suzanne R . . . . ┊ Court NW, Atlanta,
JUNIORS MR Peter de L JR . . . . ┊ GA *30328*

Welles MRS Sherrerd Belin (Welles—Edmonds—Georgia F Mast)
☎ (617) 894-7132 . . "Ledgehill" 103 Rolling Lane, PO Box 367,
Weston, MA *02193*

Wellesley MR Gerald G—Wms'80
☎ (011-44-171) 603-8930 . . 47 Milson Rd, London W14 0LH, England

Wellesley MR & MRS Robin A (Marianne McDonald) . . of
☎ (011-44-171) 727-4503 . . 36 Edge St, London W8 7PN, England
☎ (011-44-1732) 86-2251 . . "Shingle Barn" Dwelly Lane, Edenbridge,
Kent, England

Wellford MR & MRS R Carter 4th (Priscilla A Morris) Pa'72 . . . . | of ☎ (302)655-2930 10 Dickinson Lane, Westhaven, Wilmington, DE *19807*
JUNIORS MISS E Landon . . . . |
JUNIORS MR R Carter 5th . . . . |
| ☎ (804) 333-3931 Sabine Hall Farm, Warsaw, VA *22572*

Wellin MRS Ariane Y (Reed—Ariane Yassukovich)
☎ (516) 676-5116 . . 118 Piping Rock Rd, Locust Valley, NY *11560*

Wellin MR & MRS Keith S (Negley—Nancy N Brown)
K.A.Ri.Cs.Ham'50.H'52
☎ (212) 319-7290 . . 435 E 52 St, New York, NY *10022*

Welling MR & MRS W Lambert (Louise A Partridge) | ☎ (508) 785-1313 9 Sherbrooke Dv, Dover, MA *02030*
Mid'54.Cl'58 . . . . |
MR Andrew L—at Hartwick Coll . . . . |
MR C David—at Middlebury . . . . |

Wellington MR & MRS Benjamin B (Colette A Gratz) | of ☎ (617)232-7307 57 Rangeley Rd, Chestnut Hill, MA *02167*
Curry'88.Les'90.BtP.Cy.Curry'73 . . . . |
MISS Alexandra S—at Guilford . . . . |
MISS Victoria A—at Lawrence Acad . . . . |
MR William S 2d—at Curry . . . . |
| ☎ (561) 655-4071 226 Brazilian Av, Palm Beach, FL *33480*

Wellington MR & MRS David H (Carol T Strong)
LakeF'69.Sim'73.Ham'67.Cl'69
28 Oxford Rd, Wellesley, MA *02181*

Wellington MR & MRS Herbert G JR (Patricia Bull) | ☎ (516) 676-1468 94 Piping Rock Rd, PO Box 512, Locust Valley, NY *11560-0512*
Rc.Pr.Cly.P'43 . . . . |
MR Charles H—Pr.LakeF'70—☎ (516) 759-6275 |

Wellington MR & MRS Roger U JR (Elise C Braestrup) Ws'64.Cy.H'64 . . . . | ☎ (508) 835-2065 66 Malden St, West Boylston, MA *01583*
MISS E Christina—Bates'94 . . . . |
MR Roger U 3d—Ty'89—at 10 Emerson Place, Boston, MA *02114* . . . . |

Wellman MRS Elizabeth D (Elizabeth Davis)
☎ (216) 381-4626 . . 1587 Sheridan Rd, South Euclid, OH *44121*

Wells MISS A Merry (Warren M JR) . . . . Married
Logan MR Steven D . . . . Jun 1'96

Wells MISS Alexandra—Pa'80.Pa'85
☎ (215) 248-9696 . . 438 W Durham St, Philadelphia, PA *19119*

Wells MR & MRS C McGregory 3d (Mary Mattison) | ☎ (508) 428-4363 312 Smoke Valley Rd, PO Box 487, Osterville, MA *02655*
Ey.Chi. . . . . |
MISS Leslie D—Denis'94 . . . . |
MR Channing M 4th—Ty'93 . . . . |

Wells MR & MRS Christopher B (Janet C Morris) Vt'88.Tr.Colg'84
PO Box 7487, Breckenridge, CO *80424*

Wells MR Christopher J—Ht.Lm.Cl'72
☎ (011-44-171) 584-7533 . . 21 Sumner Place, London SW7 3EG, England

Wells MR & MRS David H (Stahl—Rebecca W Reynolds) Scripps'65.H'55
700 Bay Rd, PO Box 1975, Duxbury, MA *02331*

Wells MRS David Q (Jean Kiley) Bv.Cw.
☎ (314) 727-2616 . . 900 S Hanley Rd, St Louis, MO *63105*

Wells MR & MRS David Q JR (Virginia L Upthegrove) Cy.Cw.Mit'69
☎ (314) 993-4265 . . 901 S Price Rd, St Louis, MO *63124*

Wells MAJ & MRS Edward F (Dorothea Hamlin) USMC.Ub.An.Chi.Ncd.H'68 . . . . | ☎ (703) 532-8758 4734 N 40 St, Arlington, VA *22207*
JUNIORS MR Edward H . . . . |

Wells MR & MRS Francis D (Mary Anne Harrison)
Dom'56.Ford'65.Cl'71.Laf'56.Nw'58
☎ (202) 686-0206 . . 4000 Massachusetts Av NW, Washington, DC *20016*

Wells MRS Frederic Jay (Ilona A Terins) . . . . | ☎ (860) 388-5278 44 Otter Cove Dv, Old Saybrook, CT *06475*
MISS Ilona S—at ☎ (212) PL8-3159 455 E 51 St, New York, NY *10022* . . . . |

Wells MR Geoffrey S (L Dana) . . . . Married at Rutherford, CA
Lee MISS Serena R (Fred A) . . . . May 11'96

Wells MASTER George Breckinridge (Mason B 2d) . . . . Born at Norwalk, CT Jun 19'95

Wells MR & MRS Gordon Menard (Maxine Richbourg)
☎ (601) 373-4407 . . 1564 Wood Glen Dv, Jackson, MS *39204*

Wells MRS James L 3d (Ann V P Radcliff) . . . . | ☎ (215) 348-2419 220 Cherry Lane, Doylestown, PA *18901-3100*
MISS Lee R . . . . |

Wells JUNIORS MR James P . . see J O Minott

Wells MR & MRS Jonathan G 3d (H Wayne Caner) SL'57.P'54.H'60
☎ (508) 465-5618 . . 184 Middle Rd, Newbury, MA *01922*

Wells MR & MRS Jonathon H (Lucretia M Osborne)
Bost'85.PortSt'96.Mass'88.Bost'95
☎ (215) 860-6168 . . George School, PO Box 4631, Newtown, PA *18940*

Wells MR & MRS L Dana (Regina M Witt) Va'58 . . . | of ☎ (540)348-5453 Cloverdale Farm, 4216 Brownsburg Tpke, Raphine, VA *24472*
MR Michael D—at ☎ (818) 584-9451 425 Waldo Av, Apt 306, Pasadena, CA *91101* . . |
| ☎ (941) 475-7618 7365 Manasota Key Rd, Englewood, FL *34223*

Wells MR & MRS Lloyd P (Newbold—Ellen Van Pelt)
Pa'50.Cry.Fw.Cspa.Ac.Pa'47
☎ (207) 781-2604 . . 35 Old Powerhouse Rd, Falmouth, ME *04105*

Wells MR & MRS M Henry (Patricia P Brown) | ☎ (215) CH7-7084 8022 Roanoke St, Philadelphia, PA *19118*
BMr'44.Ox'49.Pc.Ill'37.Y'47 . . . . |
MISS Emily H—Earl'86.BMr'93—at ☎ (610) 239-0415 . . 1220 Skippack Pike, Blue Bell, PA *19422* . . . . |

Wells MR & MRS Mason B 2d (Kathryn Breslin) Ham'85.Rcn.Mid'84
☎ (203) 656-0535 . . 7 Old Stone Rd, Darien, CT *06820*

Wells MR & MRS Michael H (M Phyllis Polk) | ☎ (802) 492-3348 Spring Lake Ranch, Cuttingsville, VT *05738*
CasSt'67 . . . . |
MR A Geoffrey—Hartw'88 . . . . |

Wells MR & MRS Peter Scoville (Patricia A Trent) Rv.Vca.Ll.Cl'61 . . of
☎ (212) 535-6859 . . 449 E 78 St, New York, NY *10021*
☎ (610) 388-6286 . . ''Firefly'' PO Box 244, Chadds Ford, PA *19317*

Wells MR & MRS Roger K (Susan Shaffer) | ☎ (401) 846-9537
Hlns'66.Mit'67 . . . . | 229 Gibbs Av,
  MISS Kiley A—at Boulder, CO . . . . | Newport, RI *02840*
  MISS Louise L . . . . |

Wells MISS Susan W—Hlns'83.Myf.
1530 N State P'kway, Chicago, IL *60610*

Wells MR & MRS Thomas E JR (Carolyn S Chapman) Cho.On.
☎ (954) 462-4489 . . 633 Solar Isle Dv, Ft Lauderdale, FL *33301*

Wells MR & MRS Warren M JR (Diana Warren) | ☎ (617) 235-1246
D.Gm.Ll.H.Pa'52 . . . . | 723 Charles River
  MISS Isabel L—Colby'86 . . . . | St, Needham, MA
  MISS Elizabeth W—Pa'94 . . . . | *02192*

Wells MRS William H S (Marcy C Browne) Ac.
☎ (610) 645-6630 . . 1400 Waverly Rd, M230, Gladwyne, PA *19035*

Welsh MR Charles N—Me.Hav'51
100 Grays Lane, Apt 104, Haverford, PA *19041*

Welsh MRS Charles Wesley 2d (Frazier—H Moffat | ☎ (610) 268-0588
Collingwood) . . . . | 253A Church Hill
  MISS Moffat Canby Frazier . . . . | Rd, Landenberg, PA
  MR Christopher S Frazier JR—Sg. . . . . | *19350*

Welsh MR & MRS Donald E (Elizabeth B Floyd) Rc.C.Cl'65 . . of
☎ (212) 988-8921 . . 501 E 79 St, New York, NY *10021*
☎ (518) 329-4832 . . Boston Corners, Millerton, NY *12546*

Welsh MR & MRS John E 3d (Dreyfous—Andrée E Devendorf)
Geo'78.Ln.Pr.Leh'73.Pa'78 . . of
☎ (516) 367-2343 . . 3 Fox Hunt Lane, Cold Spring Harbor, NY *11724*
☎ (212) 734-4938 . . 265 E 66 St, New York, NY *10021*
☎ (516) 537-5456 . . Wheaton Way, Water Mill, NY *11976*

Welsh MR & MRS John L JR (Phoebe Cook) Sth'48.Pn.P'46 ⚓
☎ (713) 622-8816 . . 1 Briar Trail, Houston, TX *77056*

Welsh MR & MRS Joseph Wickes (de Uribe—Mary Ellen Restrepo)
Cw.Y'34 . . of
☎ (561) 231-6082 . . 1303 Spyglass Lane, Vero Beach, FL *32963*
☎ (413) 229-2719 . . PO Box 52, Southfield, MA *01259*

Welsh MISS Leah B (Donald E) . . . . Married at Millerton, NY
Kass MR Douglas A (Joseph) . . . . May 26'96

Welton MRS Arthur D (Juliet Earle) Md.Ncd.
☎ (410) 820-5925 . . 501 Dutchmans Lane, Apt 108, Easton, MD *21601*

Weltz MR & MRS S Robert JR (Fleming— | ☎ (805) 565-1419
Cushman—Gloria Fay Reeder) Stan'55.Cvc. | 415 Hot Springs Rd,
Cly.Dc.Cda.Nu'51.Ford'55 . . . . | Montecito, CA
  MISS Catherine C Cushman—Smu'91—at | *93108*
  ☎ (214) 559-0463 . . 3405 Binkley Av, Apt F, |
Dallas, TX *75205* . . . . |

Wemple MR & MRS Francis H (Virginia H Waller) | ☎ (516) MA7-0483
H'35 . . . . | 21 Heights Rd,
  MR Francis H JR—at ☎ (860) 742-6292 | Plandome, NY
Pine Ridge Dv, Andover, CT *06232* . . . . | *11030*

Wenaas DR & MRS John E J (Sally W Schafer)
Denis'56.Louis'57.NDak'54.Young'55.Louis'60. Wash'61
☎ (520) 298-8777 . . 5910 E West Miramar Dv, Tucson, AZ *85715*

Wende MR Albert B—St.Dth'59.Cr'62
☎ (716) 886-0969 . . 78 Oakland Place, Buffalo, NY *14222*

Wendell MRS Carol O'Neill (Carol B O'Neill) Sth'72.Hast'79
☎ (510) 254-2573 . . 125 Meadow View Rd, Orinda, CA *94563*

Wendell MR David R—Bur.Dth'75.Stan'79
☎ (415) 493-1643 . . 2102 Old Page Mill Rd, Palo Alto, CA *94304*

Wendell MRS F Lee H (Armour—Joan E Monroe) On.
☎ (847) 234-0274 . . 1002 Woodbine Place, Lake Forest, IL *60045*

Wendell MR & MRS Harlan L P (Dorothea Richardson)
Sth'47.Bur.Ec.Ncd.Y'45.H'48
☎ (415) 854-9282 . . 1250 Trinity Dv, Menlo Park, CA *94025*

Wendell DR & MRS (DR) James I JR (Kathleen E | ☎ (610) 326-6797
Kirk) BMr'41.Cl'44.Ac.P'39.Pa'43 . . . . | 327 N Roland Av,
  MR James F—Leh'77.JHop'83—at | Pottstown, PA
☎ (410) 461-7278 . . 8390 Park Dv, | *19464*
Ellicott City, MD *21043* . . . . |

Wendell MRS John W (Nancy W Crompton) V'43.Ncd.
☎ (617) 235-0760 . . 37 Garden Rd, Wellesley Hills, MA *02181*

Wendt MR & MRS Albert G (Margaret M Macomber) Ia'45.Cal'47
☎ (602) 945-9630 . . 4020 N 16 St, Phoenix, AZ *85016*

Wendt MR E Allan—Y'57.H'67
☎ (202) 965-2124 . . 3234 Volta Place NW, Washington,
DC *20007-2731*

Wenklar MR & MRS Walter M (Courtney Henderlite) Penn'83.LochH'88
☎ (717) 540-0869 . . 106 Huntley Dv, Harrisburg, PA *17112*

Wenman MRS Byrd W (Rhoda T Buchanan) . . . . . . | ☎ (619) 945-7437
  MISS Diana B . . . . | 4816 Marathon
   | Way, Oceanside, CA
   | *92056*

Wennberg MR & MRS Benkt (Dorothy H Guenther) | ☎ (215) 886-5061
Pa'47.Drex'50.Upsala'50.Pa'56 . . . . | 328 Greenwood Av,
  MISS Louise—at 77 S Valley Rd, Paoli, PA *19301* | Wyncote, PA *19095*
  MR John C . . . . |

Wenninger MISS Margaret E . . see T C Coleman

Wenninger MR Theodore B—StLaw'95 . . see T C Coleman

Wentz DR & MRS Clarkson (Eleanor D Booth)
Wells'38.Pa'68.Me.Cs.Y.'37.Dick'38.Temp'43
☎ (610) 933-9552 . . Box 151, Pikeland Rd, RD 1, Malvern, PA *19355*

Wenzell MR & MRS Alan T (Susan M Cutler)
Rdc'53.K.C.Cs.H'45.H'49 . . of
☎ (518) 589-6596 . . Valley Farm, East Jewett, NY *12424*
☎ (212) 289-0772 . . 1170 Fifth Av, New York, NY *10029*

Werle MRS Raymond M (Charlotte M Jones) Wash'41
☎ (314) 725-5088 . . 453 N Hanley Rd, St Louis, MO *63130*

Werlein MR & MRS J Parham (Ehlinger—Lise Anne Hartson) Tul'48
☎ (504) 891-1488 . . 5510 St Charles Av, New Orleans, LA *70115-5048*

Werlich MRS Robert O'D (Nancy V Shanklin) An.Ct.
☎ (202) 338-3391 . . 3218 O St NW, Washington, DC *20007*

Wermuth MRS Alice L (Alice H Leas) . . . . | ☎ (610) 525-2054
  JUNIORS MR William C 5th—at Lafayette . . . . . . | 1525 County Line
  MISS Ann P Leas . . . . | Rd, Rosemont, PA
   | *19010*

Werner MISS Anne K F D—Cal'76
☎ (307) 543-2939 . . PO Box 124, Moran, WY *83013*

Werner MR & MRS Charles P (Shelby I Schoonmaker) Laf'62.Toul'63 . . . . JUNIORS MR Nicholas B . . . . of ☎ (212)831-1456 65 E 96 St, New York, NY *10128* ☎ (914) 855-9080 Blue Heron Farm, 111 N Quaker Hill Rd, Pawling, NY *12564*

Werner MRS Charles S (Mary E Portfolio) Cly.So. ☎ (212) 861-6082 . . 945 Fifth Av, New York, NY *10021*

Werner MR & MRS David A (Susan M Sheaffer) Cent'y'72.Me.Rut'71 . . . . MISS Elizabeth C . . . . JUNIORS MR Christopher C . . . . ☎ (610) 688-0611 976 Ivycroft Rd, Wayne, PA *19087*

Werner MR & MRS Joseph L 2d (Susan W Kobusch) ☎ (312) 944-0440 . . 1867 N Bissell St, Chicago, IL *60614*

Werner MRS L Matthews (Margaret Steele) Wash'24 ☎ (305) 854-7716 . . 1855 S Bayshore Dv, Miami, FL *33133*

Werner MR & MRS Peter G D (Susan K Besser) Stan'79.Y'86.Stan'79.Cl'85 ☎ (406) 587-4436 . . 8898 Sandy Creek Lane, Bozeman, MT *59715*

Wertenbaker MRS George L (A Elizabeth Lyon) ☎ (540) 338-4496 . . 35960 Paxson Rd, Purcellville, VA *20132*

Werwaiss MR & MRS John A (Beth Nielsen) Un.Pr.Mds.Cly.Geo'64 . . . . MISS Gretchen N—Geo'92.Geo'95—at ☎ (212) 755-3912 . . 433 E 31 St, New York, NY *10022* . . . . MR John A JR—at Williams . . . . JUNIORS MR Christian W—at Riverdale Country Sch . . . . of ☎ (212)722-2551 1107 Fifth Av, New York, NY *10128* ☎ (516) 671-5105 Peacock Point, Lattingtown, NY *11560*

Wesley MR & MRS Timothy A (Susan G Tobin) ArizSt'77 ⚓ ☎ (602) 954-9480 . . 3601 E Pasadena Av, Phoenix, AZ *85018*

Wessells MR & MRS Daniel B (Deborah L Dunn) Sfh.Ds.P'50 . . . . MISS Alexandra B—Syr'90—at ☎ (415) 892-3774 . . 27 Hillside Terr, Novato, CA *94947* ☎ (610) 942-4383 781 Fairview Rd, Glenmoore, PA *19343*

West MISS Anne N ☎ (215) 283-7171 . . 116 Foulkeways, Sumneytown Pike, Gwynedd, PA *19436*

West MR & MRS C David (Julia T MacLaren) Skd'61.Pom'59 . . . . MISS Elizabeth N . . . . MR C Denison—at 505 Western Skies Dv SE, Albuquerque, NM *87123* . . . . ☎ (310) 696-7009 2910 Descending Dv, Hacienda Heights, CA *91745*

West MR Edward P—Occ'87 ☎ (818) 285-8249 . . 6118 Ivar Av, Temple City, CA *91780*

West MR & MRS Eric F (Eugenia Lovett) Wk.H'46 . MISS Eugenia . . . . ☎ (860) 434-9134 12 Sterling City Rd, Lyme, CT *06371*

West MR & MRS Frank A (Gene MacDonald) Ws'40.Pcu.P'32 ☎ (408) 625-1544 . . 8545 Carmel Valley Rd, Carmel, CA *93923*

West MR & MRS George P (Susan B Kemble) BMr'68.Cal'71.Bost'78.Snc.Penn'49.Utah'59 ☎ (914) 762-4132 . . Whitson Farm, 229 Pines Bridge Rd, Ossining, NY *10562*

West MR & MRS George S (Mildred S Stuart) Me.Rv.Y'63.H'67 . . . . MR George S JR—StLaw'91 . . . . MR Nicholas Stuart—StLaw'94 . . . . MR Alexander S—Vt'95 . . . . JUNIORS MISS Christine G . . . . ☎ (714) 248-2927 21 Emerald Glen, Laguna Niguel, CA *92677*

West MISS Geraldine W . . see MRS W Greenough 2d

West MRS Harry F (Pitts—Saulsbury—Mai G N Dick) Ph.Rc.Sg.Ac.Ncd. . . . . MISS Isabel D—at 700 New Hampshire Av NW, Apt 502, Washington, DC *20037* . . . . ☎ (410) 832-8344 Blakehurst 234, 1055 W Joppa Rd, Towson, MD *21204*

West MR & MRS Harry I JR (Ann K Watson) Ncd.AlaPoly'47.Stan'55 . . . . MISS Elizabeth J—Cal'83 . . . . MR David L—Cal'83 . . . . MR Leonard K—Cal'89 . . . . ☎ (510) 447-4639 1126 Tulane Court, Livermore, CA *94550*

West MRS James W (Hewitt—Mary Louise Stillman) ☎ (212) 472-9565 . . 165 E 66 St, Apt 18B, New York, NY *10021-6132*

West MRS John C (M Barbara Robinson) . . of "Charlotte's Web" PO Box 1122, Boca Grande, FL *33921* ☎ (610) 869-2009 . . PO Box 501, Unionville, PA *19375*

West DR & MRS John C (Amory—Mary A Gillespie) Me.Rv.Y'66.Pa'70 ☎ (717) 275-1165 . . "Elska Farm" 2719 River Dv, Danville, PA *17821*

West MR & MRS Millard F (Bomar—Doris Thomas) Mt.Cvc.P'32 ☎ (301) 654-3950 . . 18 W Kirke St, Chevy Chase, MD *20815*

West MR & MRS R Angus (Elizabeth Conway) Ws'78.H'83.My.Sm.Hn.H'77.H'82 ☎ (508) 468-1906 . . 7 Walnut Rd, Wenham, MA *01984*

West MR & MRS Ralph E JR (Karen E Kivic) MtH'66.Pc.Rv.Pa'63.Va'65 . . . . MISS Elizabeth T—at U of Va . . . . MR Jacob—at U of Va . . . . ☎ (215) CH8-3613 233 Rex Av, Philadelphia, PA *19118*

West MR & MRS Ralph O'Neal (Mary D Anthony) Rdc'46.H'46.H'51 ☎ (617) 237-0940 . . 8 Ingraham Rd, Wellesley, MA *02181*

West MR & MRS Richard S (Ruth Simonds) Sbc.Sm.My.Chi.Ncd.H'47 . . . . MISS Ruth—at 66 Dudleyville Rd, Leverett, MA *01054* . . . . MISS Emily—at 39 Revere St, Boston, MA *02108* ☎ (508) 468-2818 79 Dodges Row, Wenham, MA *01984*

West MR & MRS Stephen K (Ann L Wick) V'52.Eh.Ri.Ln.Y'50.H'53 . . . . MR Timothy W—Box 209, Gladstone, NJ *07934* MR Todd K—Y'83—at 2 Charlton St, New York, NY *10014* MR Daniel W—at ☎ (508) 257-4549 PO Box 56, Siasconset, MA *02564* . . . . ☎ (908) 766-1492 42 Old Wood Rd, Bernardsville, NJ *07924*

West MRS Susan W (Susan S White) . . . . MISS Amber B—Ariz'94—at St Lawrence Grad . MISS Laurel T . . . . ☎ (610) 896-7313 910 Nicholson Rd, Wynnewood, PA *19096*

West MR & MRS Thomas H JR (Macy—Dorothy Gannett) Cy.Chi.H'50 . . . . MR Richmond—Cy.—at Cincinnati, OH . . . . MR Christopher—Mid'82—at 300 Commercial St, Boston, MA *02109* . . . . ☎ (617) 329-9666 304 Clapboardtree St, Westwood, MA *02090*

West MR & MRS Travis T (Gwendolyn D Waterman)
H'93.Hb.USMMA'90.Ch'95
see Dilatory Domiciles
West MRS William Nelson (Edith T Harris) BMr'26
☎ (610) 746-1125 . . Moravian Hall Square, 175 W North St, Nazareth, PA *18064*
Westcott MR & MRS John A JR (Betty Lane) Smu'51.Dar.Aub'50
☎ (334) 279-9311 . . 1612 Croom Dv, Montgomery, AL *36106*

Westcott MR & MRS John McM JR (Suzanne H Laporte) Sth'69.Cy.Sm.Ub.Chi.Ncd.Y'66.H'69 .
MISS Valerie L—Y'94.Ncd.—at
☎ (212) 586-4819 . . 200 W 58 St, Apt 9C, New York, NY *10019* . . . .
JUNIORS MR John McM 3d—at Bowdoin . . . .
JUNIORS MR Jeffrey H . . . .
☎ (617) 738-4443
21 Essex Rd,
Chestnut Hill, MA
02167

Westdahl MRS Anne M (Smith—E Anne Merrill) . .
MR Lawrence M—L&C'90—at 6120 SW 18 Dv, Apt 35, Portland, OR *97201* . . . .
☎ (415) 925-8987
526 Old Quarry Rd
N, Larkspur, CA
94939

Westerfield MR F Bradford—Msq.H.'78
☎ (212) 744-5093 . . 300 E 75 St, Apt 30J, New York, NY *10021*
Westerfield MR & MRS Putney (Anne Montgomery) Stan'52.Pcu.Bur.Y'51
☎ (415) 348-5179 . . 10 Green View Lane, Hillsborough, CA *94010*
Westerfield MRS Robert H (Portia C Patterson) V'53
☎ (941) 425-3968 . . 4115 Creek Woods Lane, Mulberry, FL *33860*

Westervelt MR & MRS Peter J (Alice F Brown) Wells'51.Mit'42
MR Dirck E—Wes'82—at 8 Newtown St, Middletown, CT *06457* . . . .
☎ (401) 751-8286
16 John St,
Providence, RI
02906

Westfeldt MR & MRS Thomas D 2d (Linda S Hawthorne) LSU'74.LSU'75
☎ (504) 522-1680 . . 2340 Prytania St, New Orleans, LA *70130*
Westmoreland GEN & MRS William C (Katherine S Van Deusen) Cr'49.Cvc.B.Yh.Cc.USA'36 . . of
☎ (803) 577-3156 . . 107 Tradd St, Charleston, SC *29401*
☎ (704) 733-2912 . . "Caisson" PO Box 1168, Linville, NC *28646*
Yeamans Hall Club, PO Box 9455, Charleston, SC *29410*

Weston MR & MRS Theodore 2d (Phoebe R Scull) Y'39 . . . .
MISS Mary S . . . .
☎ (610) 688-2614
461 Devon State Rd,
Devon, PA *19333*

Westwater MR & MRS William King (Shirle J Nesbitt) OState'35
☎ (614) 253-5559 . . 2371 Commonwealth Park S, Columbus, OH *43209*

Wetherbee MRS Winthrop (Carolyn Hall) . . . .
MISS Helen—at 2228 Southwood Rd, Jackson, MS *39211* . . . .
Brookhaven 362C,
1010 Waltham St,
Lexington, MA
02173

Wetherell MR & MRS D Bradford JR (Frances A Smith) Rdc'55.H.'54
☎ (617) 354-7257 . . 221 Mt Auburn St, Apt 506, Cambridge, MA *02138*
Wetherill MR & MRS A Frederic M (Rosemary Howe)
☎ (919) 928-4603 . . PO Box 297, Ocracoke, NC *27960*
Wetherill MISS Ashley F . . see H A A Sargent

Wetherill MR & MRS Cortright JR (Janice S Nestle) Rd.Cry.Sg.Ph. . . . .
MISS Amanda W . . . .
☎ (610) 647-7973
Wide Rill Farm,
129 Davis Rd,
Malvern, PA *19355*

Wetherill MR & MRS David C (Pamela H Byecroft) CtCol'65.Me.Nyc.P.'64 . . . .
MR Douglas P—Ty'92 . . . .
MR Daniel B—P'95 . . . .
☎ (914) 591-6808
9 Bertha Place,
Ardsley-on-Hudson,
NY *10503*

Wetherill MR Elkins—Ph.Rc.Sg.Pa'48
☎ (610) 828-3680 . . Ardfuar Farm, 2642 Butler Pike, Plymouth Meeting, PA *19462*
Wetherill MR F Dring JR—Sg.
☎ (215) 540-9388 . . 565 Beale Rd, Blue Bell, PA *19422*
Wetherill MR & MRS Francis D (Wickes—Aimée du Pont) Sg.Ph.Gm.Ny.Ac.Pa'39
☎ (215) 247-5234 . . 154 Hillcrest Av, Philadelphia, PA *19118*

Wetherill MR & MRS John P 4th (Diane R McMeel) Gi.HampSydney'57 . . . .
MR John P 5th . . . .
☎ (301) 654-3280
7110 Georgia St,
Chevy Chase, MD
20815

Wetherill JUNIORS MISS Leason R . . see H A A Sargent
Wetherill MRS Leonore S (Smith—Gibson—Leonore Smart) Rd.Ncd.
☎ (610) 692-7028 . . 1056 Kennett Way, West Chester, PA *19380-5732*
Wetherill MR Peter W—Srr.
☎ (610) 356-1805 . . Happy Hill Farm, 912 N Providence Rd, Newtown Square, PA *19073*
Dec 1 . . ☎ (561) 795-0411 . . 3689 Jappeloup Lane, West Palm Beach, FL *33414*
Wetherill MR Ramsay—Me.Pe.Rv.Cspa.Ll . . .of
☎ (610) MI2-3892 . . 200 N Wynnewood Rd, Wynnewood, PA *19096*
☎ (954) 941-2220 . . Hillsboro Club, Pompano Beach, FL *33062*
Wetherill MRS Samuel P (Jewett—Alice Groom Constable) Me.Nyc.Ncd.
☎ (813) 545-9728 . . 6260 Sixtieth Av N, St Petersburg, FL *33709*
Wetherill MR & MRS Stephen H (Hatter—Susan Sallada) W&M'73.Sg.Nasson'74
☎ (215) 643-5576 . . 85 Hogan Lane, Broad Axe, Ambler, PA *19002*
Wetherill MRS W Chattin (Mary S Townsend)
☎ (860) 868-7132 . . Nettleton Hollow Rd, Washington, CT *06793*

Wetmore MRS Andrew C (Mona A Waters) Cly. . . .
MISS Alexandra C—Denis'89—at
☎ (212) 717-4524 . . 213 E 66 St, New York, NY *10021* . . . .
☎ (212) 832-6836
200 E 66 St,
New York, NY
10021

Wetmore MISS Virginia L—Hlns'80
☎ (212) 988-0781 . . 225 E 66 St, New York, NY *10021*

Wetmore MR & MRS William T JR (Margaret F Kiser) Rdc'54.H'53 . . . .
MR Michael. . . . .
☎ (914) 373-9435
Flint Hill Rd,
Amenia, NY *12501*

Wettlaufer MR & MRS (DR) C Penn (Margaret H McAloon) Ty'67.PaMed'71.St.P.'58.Dth'60 . . . .
MISS Elizabeth P—at 277½ Linwood Av, Buffalo, NY *14209* . . . .
MISS Talley D . . . .
JUNIORS MISS Virginia S . . . .
☎ (716) 881-6462
20 Mayfair Lane,
Buffalo, NY
14201-1522

Wettlaufer MISS Susan—Syr'71
☎ (716) 836-5313 . . 270 Berryman Dv, Amherst, NY *14226*

Wetzel MR & MRS Carroll R (Phoebe M Francine) Ph.Wes'27 . . . .
MISS Anne F . . . .
☎ (215) MI6-1104
353 Lewis Lane,
Ambler, PA *19002*

Wetzel MR & MRS Robert B (Kerri J Hamilton)
Pitt'88.Pitt'90.Van'86.CarnM'88
☎ (011-81-3) 719-8487 . . Miyake Homes 102, 10-6 Ebisu-Minami,
3 Chome Shibuya-ku, Tokyo 150, Japan
Wetzel MR & MRS Rolla K (M Anne Baldwin) | ☎ (314) 966-2277
Nd.Cy.Ncd.Wash'56 . . . . | 439 Steeplechase
MISS Caroline B . . . . | Lane, St Louis, MO
| *63131*
Weyburn MISS Elizabeth L—Syr'81
☎ (770) 333-9354 . . 1414 Vinings P'kway, Smyrna, GA *30080*
Weyburn MRS Reed A (Elsa C Mohr)
☎ (203) 263-2052 . . 19 Washington Rd, Woodbury, CT *06798*
Weyer MR & MRS Thomas E (Andrea D Morgan) | ☎ (540) 687-6877
W&J'67.H'74 . . . . | Quiet Lyme Farm,
MISS Wilhelmina S . . . . | PO Box 978,
MISS Susanna W . . . . | Middleburg, VA
| *20118*
Weyher MR Harry F—Rc.Cc.Cw.NCar'46.H'49
☎ (212) 879-3031 . . 211 E 70 St, New York, NY *10021*
Weyher MR & MRS Harry F 3d (Anda Gailitis) Mid'77.Mid'78.Rcn.Mid'77
☎ (203) 761-9433 . . 215 Ridgefield Rd, Wilton, CT *06897*
Weymouth MR & MRS A Kent JR (Callaghan—Sara | ☎ (610) 687-9692
P Crozer) Cent'y'68.Myf.Md'65.Md'71 . . . . | 256 W Valley Rd,
MSRS A Kent 3d & Mark C—at Ocean City, MD | Strafford, PA *19087*
21842 . . . . |
    MISS Sara G Callaghan—at Trinity . . . . |
    MISS Elisabeth P Callaghan—at Amherst . . . . |
Weymouth MRS George T (du Pont—Katharine P Lewars)
Wh'lck'42.Wil.Ny.Csn.Csp.
802 Hillside Rd, Greenville, DE *19807*
Whann MR & MRS Richard A (Suzanne B Maginnis) | ☎ (504) 891-1362
Ncmb'66.Tul'62.Tul'63.Tul'68 . . . . | 1030 State St,
MR Richard T—Smu'93—at 3021 Fairmount St, | New Orleans, LA
Dallas, TX *75201* . . . . | *70118*
Wharton MR & MRS C William JR (Hoyt—Emily Nichols) W.Myf.
☎ (860) 535-1068 . . PO Box 349, 20 Denison Av, Stonington,
CT *06378*
Wharton MRS Charles W 3d (Nancy E Reynolds)
☎ (510) 524-6481 . . 1032 Oxford St, Berkeley, CA *94707*
Wharton MR Charles W 3d—Bost'74
☎ (415) 461-1224 . . 333 Old Quarry Rd, Larkspur, CA *94939*
Wharton MR & MRS Henry R 3d (Marilyn Marshall) . . . . | ☎ (703) 836-5576
MR Thomas M—Va'73—at ☎ (703) 548-1954 | 413 Tyler Place,
801 Hilltop Terr, Alexandria, VA *22301* . . . . . . | Alexandria, VA
| *22302*
Wharton MR Heyward M—P'43.Cl'55
☎ (610) 688-5244 . . 294-3D Iven Av, St Davids, PA *19087*
Wharton MR James M—Nrr.F&M'73
☎ (401) 423-3841 . . 21 Hamilton Av, Jamestown, RI *02835*
Wharton DR & MRS Lawrence R JR (Alison A de Ropp)
Elk.Cw.Cda.P'45.JHop'47
☎ (410) 825-2028 . . 1307 Berwick Rd, Ruxton, MD *21204*
Wheary MRS Eugene C (Cynthia Towne) SL'37.Sfg.
☎ (408) 626-4853 . . 8545 Carmel Valley Rd, Carmel, CA *93923*
Wheat MRS Beverly L (Meinfelder—Jane Jameson) | ☎ (561) 744-3597
MR Edmond L Meinfelder 3d . . . . | 139 Beacon Lane,
MR Jason J Meinfelder . . . . | Jupiter, FL *33469*

Wheat MR & MRS Clayton C C (Melissa Palmer) Tul'79
☎ (203) 380-9045 . . 559 Hawley Lane, Stratford, CT *06497-1514*
Wheat MR & MRS Clayton E (Mary Chappell) Y'40 . | ☎ (203) 655-3428
MISS Jennifer C—Ws'74—at 25183 Malumalu, | 22 Searles Rd,
Hilo, HI *96720* . . . . | Darien, CT *06820*
Wheatland MR & MRS Richard (Cynthia N McAdoo)
Bnd'46.Tv.Sm.K.Hn.H'45.Cl'49
☎ (617) 523-1324 . . 33 Branch St, Boston, MA *02108*
Wheaton MRS George S (Virginia R Murphy) Vh.Tcy.Ncd.
☎ (805) 969-8097 . . 300 Hot Springs Rd, Apt J199, Montecito,
CA *93108*
Wheaton MRS Margery J (Saunders—Margery J Wheaton) Vh.
☎ (408) 625-5547 . . PO Box 6326, Carmel, CA *93921*
Wheaton MRS Polly J (Lewis—Rutt—Polly J | ☎ (818) 441-3473
Wheaton) Vh. . . . . | 1003 Hillside Terr,
  MISS Diana J Lewis—*see Dilatory Domiciles* | Pasadena, CA *91105*
  MR Christopher F Lewis . . . . |
Wheaton MR Silas P—Cp. . . . . | PO Box 961,
MISS Victoria A . . . . | Millbrae, CA *94030*
MISS Caroline E . . . . |
Wheaton MR & MRS William C (Elizabeth C | ☎ (508) 468-7944
Briscoe) My.P'68.Pa'72 . . . . | 180 Bridge St,
MISS Courtney B—at Princeton . . . . | PO Box 166,
JUNIORS MISS Elizabeth B . . . . | Hamilton, MA
JUNIORS MR Philip C . . . . | *01936*
Wheaton-Smith MR & MRS Craig (Marshall—Elizabeth Cryan) Ox'39
☎ (802) 867-2242 . . RR 2, Box 1800, Dorset, VT *05251*
Wheeler MR A Jackson—Ey.Cw.Hawaii'73 . . of
☎ (302) 654-0184 . . 215 E 2 St, New Castle, DE *19720*
☎ (508) 526-7839 . . "The Nest" 31 Briggs St, Salem, MA *01970*
Wheeler MRS Alexander (Agnes H Grew) Chi.Ncd. . | ☎ (508) 526-1703
MISS Agnes—Ncd.—☎ (508) 526-4603 . . . . | PO Box 374,
| Manchester, MA
| *01944*
Wheeler MR Alexander JR—H.'45
☎ (508) 653-3895 . . 3 Parks Dv, Sherborn, MA *01770*
Wheeler MRS Alexander B (Sharples—Grace F Russell)
B'gton'48.Temp'68.Me.Ac.
☎ (610) 525-4179 . . 3824 Darby Rd, Bryn Mawr, PA *19010*
Wheeler MR & MRS Alexander B JR (Parry—Deborah N Trench) Pa'70.Me.
☎ (202) 362-4949 . . 5425 Galena Place NW, Washington, DC *20016*
Wheeler MISS Alexandra—Br'82
☎ (212) 679-3702 . . 235 E 22 St, Apt 12C, New York, NY *10010*
Wheeler MR & MRS Arthur L (Carolyn B Leisenring) Gm.Ssk.Me.P'44
☎ (610) 526-9494 . . 15 Pond Lane, Bryn Mawr, PA *19010*
Wheeler MRS Benjamin Webb (Edith E Milnes)
☎ (602) 972-7953 . . 10010 Shasta Dv, Sun City, AZ *85351*
Wheeler MRS C Julian (Doanda R Putnam) Cvc.Ncd.
☎ (415) 325-1109 . . 1850 Oakdell Dv, Menlo Park, CA *94025*
Wheeler MR & MRS Charles B 2d (Eleanor Bissell) Lm.Buf'48
☎ (301) 320-3755 . . 7710 Maryknoll Av, Bethesda, MD *20817*
Wheeler MRS Charles S 3d (Kathryn I Lillard) Fr.
☎ (714) 673-4269 . . 401 Avocado Av, Corona Del Mar, CA *92625*
Wheeler MR & MRS David P (Lee C Montross)
Wheat'78.Rcn.Nyc.L.Cly.Bow'74.Pa'76
☎ (011-44-171) 589-6353 . . 26 Pelham Crescent, London SW7 2NR,
England

Wheeler MR & MRS David W (Mary M Harrison) ☎ (508) 655-7068
Me'68.Me'66 . . . . "Sabiar House"
MISS Marjory B . . . . 45 High St, Natick,
MR Paul H . . . . | MA *01760*

Wheeler MISS Deirdre W—Hampshire'71
☎ (412) 441-8831 . . 309 S Linden Av, Pittsburgh, PA *15208*

Wheeler MISS Frances P . . see MRS A S Thomas

Wheeler MR Frederic C 3d—Ithaca'80 . . . . | ☎ (610) 574-0707
JUNIORS MISS Kerry W . . . . 605 W Market St,
Apt 38,
West Chester, PA
19380

Wheeler MR & MRS George Y 2d (Orthwein—Katherine B Gatch)
Msq.P'37.GeoW'53
☎ (561) 546-3250 . . "Cottontail Cottage" 101 Rabbit Run,
Hobe Sound, FL *33455*

Wheeler MR & MRS George Y 3d (Frances Culp) ☎ (202) 223-1011
Mich'64.Cvc.Mt.Sl.P'63 . . . . 2019 N St NW,
MISS Genevieve E . . . . Washington, DC
MR George Y 4th . . . . | *20036*

Wheeler MR & MRS Halsted W (Elsie Y Trask) ☎ (203) 655-9512
Sth'54.Csn.Y'49 . . . . 23 Tokeneke Trail,
MISS Elsie C—at Brown . . . . Darien, CT *06820*
MR Richard R—at U of RI . . . . |

Wheeler MR & MRS Henry P (Florence J Forgan)
SL'46.On.Sr.Cas.Fy.Y'42 . . of
☎ (847) 234-0893 . . 10 N Mayflower Rd, Lake Forest, IL *60045*
☎ (561) 736-8815 . . 6830 N Ocean Blvd, Ocean Ridge, FL *33435*

Wheeler MISS Isabelle Hopkins (Mark M) . . . . Born Sep 28'94

Wheeler MR & MRS James G (Mary E Lowell) ☎ (617) 329-0643
Tv.Ncd.H'46 . . . . 552 Gay St,
MR William H . . . . Westwood, MA
MR Jonathan L . . . . | *02090*

Wheeler MRS John P (Mary Binney Montgomery) . . . . Died at
Philadelphia, PA Apr 23'95

Wheeler MRS Leonard (Cornelia Balch) Sb.
☎ (617) 876-6787 . . 123 Coolidge Hill, Cambridge, MA *02138*

Wheeler MRS Leslie (Clare H Rolph)
☎ (415) 461-4060 . . 58 Elizabeth Circle, Greenbrae, CA *94904*

Wheeler DR & MRS Mark M (Elizabeth M Hopkins)
Denis'80.P'76.WakeF'86
☎ (410) 472-0170 . . 14936A Carroll Rd, Sparks, MD *21152*

Wheeler MR Murray JR—Y'62
☎ (617) 661-3669 . . 20 Maple Av, Cambridge, MA *02139*

Wheeler DR & MRS Paul S (Barbara J Bradley) ☎ (410) 467-6143
H'57.H'61 . . . . 302 Somerset Rd,
MR Bradley E—H'90 . . . . Baltimore, MD
21210

Wheeler MR & MRS Richard C (Robbins—Cook— ☎ (508) 291-1319
Sandra Stuart Smith) NECons'62.H'52.H'55. PO Box 3176,
H'69 . . . . Salt Marsh Lane,
MISS Jennifer G—Cr'92—at ☎ (206) 528-2969 off Great Neck Rd,
7826 Lake City Way NE, Seattle, WA *98115* . . Wareham, MA
MISS Letitia M Robbins—OWes'83—at *02571*
☎ (617) 277-8860 . . 27 Osborne Rd,
Brookline, MA *02146* . . . .
MISS Helen A R Robbins—Pom'85.Ariz'91—
at ☎ (520) 322-9638 . . 1931 E Silver St,
Tucson, AZ *85719* . . . .

Wheeler MR & MRS Samuel B 4th (Ellen C Porterfield)
RMWmn'76.Me.GeoW'76
☎ (610) 293-1749 . . 693 Timber Lane, Devon, PA *19333*

Wheeler MR & MRS Thomas B (Anne T Robertson) | of 288 Park Dv,
Sth'61.Ln.Cly.Yn.Y'58 ⚑ . . . . Springfield, MA
MISS Wendy B—Cr'90—at 17 Gloucester St, *01106*
Boston, MA *02115* . . . . ☎ (508) 540-2244
"Snug Harbor
House"
22 Nashawena St,
PO Box 33,
West Falmouth, MA
02574

Wheeler DR & MRS W Mark 3d (Katherine M ☎ (207) 443-5712
Norcross) P'60.Wash'64 . . . . Harndon Farm,
MISS Elizabeth F . . . . RR 3, Box 828,
MR Timothy N . . . . Montsweag Rd,
MR Andrew C . . . . Woolwich, ME
MR Geoffrey H . . . . | *04579*

Wheeler MR & MRS Warwick S (Mollie McNickle) Y'76.Me.Ph.Ssk.Pa'71
☎ (610) 526-2297 . . 700 Sproul Rd, Bryn Mawr, PA *19010-1115*

Wheeler DR & MRS William M (Beatrice B Nickerson) H.'54
☎ (617) 566-2028 . . 174 Laurel Rd, Chestnut Hill, MA *02167*

Wheeler MR & MRS Wilmot F JR (Post—Nonnye ☎ (203) 259-0468
Landers) Ln.Yn.Y'45 . . . . PO Box 429,
MISS Susan C—at Boston, MA . . . . 28 Center St,
MISS Alexa M—at Fairfield, CT . . . . Southport, CT *06490*

Wheeler MR & MRS Winslow (Harriet A Winslow) ☎ (914) 291-3932
Ncd.Myf. . . . . Glen Arden,
MR Charles H 3d—Pa'66—at ☎ (914) 878-3864 Apt 1018,
Byron Court, 316 Cornwall Meadows, Patterson, 214 Harriman Dv,
NY *12563* . . . . | Goshen, NY *10924*

Wheelis MRS Reuben E (Jo Ann Scott)
☎ (334) 478-4369 . . 272 Park Terr, Mobile, AL *36604-1625*

Wheelock MRS A Bassett (Ann W Bassett) Pars'70 . | ☎ (415) 381-2176
JUNIORS MISS Katherine B . . . . 46 Claire Way,
JUNIORS MR Graham B . . . . | Tiburon, CA *94920*

Wheelock MR & MRS Arthur K JR (Swain—Perry ☎ (202) 244-8967
Newbold Carpenter) Pa'72.GeoW'88.Wms'65. 3418 Rodman St
H'73 . . . . NW, Washington,
MISS Laura H—at 129 Eleventh Av, DC *20008*
San Francisco CA *94118* . . . .
MR Matthew H . . . .
JUNIORS MISS Sarah E Swain . . . . |

Wheelock MISS Cynthia A—RISD'84
☎ (313) 761-9239 . . 315 Mulholland Av, Ann Arbor, MI *48103*

Wheelock DR & MRS E Frederick (M Jean Lowery)
Ala'51.Mit'50.Cl'55.Rock'61 . . . . | ☎ (610) 525-5270
MR Scott F—PAFA'88 . . . . | 315 Baintree Rd,
Rosemont, PA
19010

Wheelock MR & MRS George F (Elisabeth A Martin) | ☎ (301) 416-8235
NCar'66.NCar'72 . . . . | 29 W Baltimore St,
MR Austin W . . . . | Box 807,
MR Philippe M—at U of South . . . . | Funkstown, MD
21734-0807

Wheelock MASTER Hawxhurst Daedalus (William H JR) . . . . Born at
Randolph, VT Mch 29'96

Wheelock MR Joseph A 3d . . see MISS N B Tieken

Wheelock MRS Mary Jane V (Olason—Mary Jane Victor) Houst'66.Cly.
☎ (212) 249-2195 . . 301 E 66 St, Apt 7M, New York, NY *10021*

Wheelock MRS Morgan Dix (Bowers—Stabler—Elizabeth G Thompson)
☎ (203) 966-4104 . . 729 Weed St, New Canaan, CT *06840-4017*

Wheelock MR & MRS Morgan Dix JR (Twining— | of ☎ (617)868-2371
Judith K Taylor) Nf.Cy.H'60 . . . . | 33 Fresh Pond
MR Edmund S Twining 4th . . . . | P'kway, Cambridge,
MR Taylor P Twining . . . . | MA *02138*
☎ (505) 989-7009
''Cloudstone''
Rte 7, Box 129M,
Cloudstone Dv,
Santa Fe, NM *87505*

Wheelock MR Stephen B—Mto . . .of
☎ (305) 672-5406 . . 1050 Washington Av, Miami Beach, FL *33139*
☎ (268) 460-4154 . . ''Tamarind'' Mill Reef Club, Antigua

Wheelock MRS Thomas G (Janet B Buchanan) V'36.Cly . . .of
☎ (954) 970-3750 . . 2701 N Course Dv, Pompano Beach, FL *33069*
☎ (268) 460-4145 . . ''J'ouvert'' Mill Reef Club, Antigua

Wheelock MR Thomas G B—Un.Mto.Pr.Clark'65.Wyo'72
☎ (212) 794-4720 . . 7 E 84 St, New York, NY *10028*

Wheelock MR & MRS William H JR (Charity R Appell) RISD'91.RISD'91
☎ (802) 276-3042 . . RR 1, Box 100, Brookfield, VT *05036*

Wheelwright MISS Elizabeth B—Bost'47
☎ (206) 322-3230 . . 508 Lakeside Av S, Seattle, WA *98144*

Wheelwright MR & MRS George W 4th (Budd—Maureen R Lyle-Purdy)
Ox'58.Ariz'56
see Dilatory Domiciles

Wheelwright MR George W 5th—AmU'84
see Dilatory Domiciles

Wheelwright MRS (DR) Gretchen (Gretchen Gross) | ☎ (510) 865-1662
Br'56.Minn'60.Cal'77 . . . . | 2925 Northwood
MISS Alice—Br'81—at ☎ (612) 377-0036 | Dv, Alameda, CA
1623 Cedar Lake P'kway, Minneapolis, MN | *94501*
55416 . . . . |
MR Nathaniel C—at ☎ (770) 381-1638
5566 Wylake Dv, Norcross, GA *30093* . . . . |

Wheelwright MR & MRS Henry C (Celeste M Adams)
Hlns'77.Ct.B.Cc.Cda.Va'65
☎ (540) 253-5057 . . 6644 John Marshall H'way, The Plains, VA *20198*

Wheelwright DR & MRS Henry J (Mary S Matthiessen) V'46.Chi.Y'44.Cl'47
☎ (207) 236-4840 . . 4 Wilson Av, Camden, ME *04843*

Whelan MR & MRS Richard Q (Virginia M Jarvis) Pa'78.Pa'78.Tul'81
☎ (610) 664-0927 . . 740 Hazelhurst Av, Merion, PA *19066*

Whelan MR Robert W
☎ (410) 247-3462 . . 717 Maiden Choice Lane, Apt 123, Catonsville,
MD *21228*

Whelan MR & MRS Sidney S JR (Anne S McCook)
Wheat'69.NCar'73.Bost'82.Rc.Ty'51.Ford'59 . . of
☎ (212) 831-0177 . . 125 E 93 St, New York, NY *10128*
☎ (802) 293-5704 . . PO Box 40, Danby, VT *05739*

Whelan MR & MRS William V (Ellen E Hollister)
Cal'81.Stan'84.Pom'81.Cal'84
☎ (619) 298-1745 . . 1076 Myrtle Way, San Diego, CA *92103*

Whelpley MRS Lamberton (Anna B Lamberton) . . . | ☎ (910) 763-3739
MISS Mary B B . . . . | 2311 Gillette Dv,
Wilmington, NC
28403

Whidden MR Peter A—MacM'76
☎ (910) 692-9550 . . 1067 Ft Bragg Rd, Southern Pines, NC *28387*

Whiddon DR & MRS Frederick P (June M Ledyard) Emory'63
☎ (334) 460-6111 . . 2157 Venetia Rd, Mobile, AL *36605*

Whipple MR & MRS George S (Sescilla—Lydia A Buckley) H'74
☎ (970) 925-2295 . . 121 S Galena St, 203, Aspen, CO *81611*

Whipple MRS Hope A (Hope Auchincloss) Ri.Cly.T.
☎ (212) BU8-5225 . . 720 Park Av, New York, NY *10021*

Whipple MR & MRS Hugh W (Margaret E Wiff) Ripon'76.Ripon'76
☎ (630) 584-1778 . . 465 Persimmon Dv, St Charles, IL *60174*

Whipple MR & MRS Jack V H 2d (Victoria P Eyre) Rcn.
☎ (770) 409-0750 . . 3783 Club Forest Dv, Norcross, GA *30092*

Whipple MRS Taggart (Katharine G Brewster)
☎ (516) 922-1284 . . 177 Cove Rd, Box 457, Oyster Bay, NY *11771*

Whipple MRS Truxal (MacGeorge—Moffett— | ☎ (847) 498-0641
Margaret A Truxal) . . . . | 1445 Cedar Lane,
MISS Margaret Elizabeth Moffett—at | Northbrook, IL
150 W 87 St, New York, NY *10024* . . . . | *60062*

Whisnand MR & MRS R Van Arsdel JR (E Campbell | of ☎ (908)842-9242
Baker) Unn.Ln.Rm.Stc.Br'66.Va'68 . . . . | 973 River Rd,
MR Tyler S—Va'90 | Fair Haven, NJ
MR Carter Van A—Va'94 . . . . | *07704-3317*
☎ (941) 591-8653
6131 Pelican Bay
Blvd, Naples, FL
34108

Whistler MRS Ross (Ayer—Anne Phillips)
☎ (561) 546-4201 . . PO Box 217, Jupiter Island, Hobe Sound, FL *33475*

Whiston MRS Eleanor B (Eleanor C Blakeslee) Sth'37
☎ (703) 824-1145 . . 4800 Fillmore Av, Apt 545, Alexandria, VA *22311*

Whitaker MR Andrew B R—Ht.Ds.Syr'84
☎ (203) 856-1338 . . 10 St John Place, Westport, CT *06880*

Whitaker MR & MRS Caleb C III (Price—Dorothy | of ☎ (561)655-3020
Ann Wood) CtCol'52.Rcn.BtP.Evg.Cc.P'49 . . . . | PO Box 2966,
MR Caleb C IV—at ☎ (602) 460-2241 | Palm Beach, FL
110 E Mountain Sky Av, Phoenix, AZ *85048* . . | *33480*
MISS Elizabeth W Price—at ☎ (312) 654-8070 | ☎ (513) 871-5333
1445 N State P'kway, Apt 2702, Chicago, IL | 24 Elmhurst Place,
60610 . . . . | Cincinnati, OH
45208

Whitaker MR Clement S—Bur. . . . . | ☎ (415) 931-5944
MISS Isabella A . . . . | 2040 Broadway St,
Apt 301,
San Francisco, CA
94115
Whitaker MR Edward R B—Col'85
☎ (212) 535-3944 . . 532 E 83 St, New York, NY *10028*
Whitaker MR John T (Patricia C Pettengill) . . . . . . | ☎ (561) 225-8889
MR Jeffrey T—at 215 Dorland St, San Francisco, | 6980 SE Harbor
CA *94114* . . . . | Circle, Stuart, FL
34996
Whitaker MRS Patricia W (Patricia Wing) Bnd'55
☎ (941) 794-6266 . . 1122 Mallorca Dv, Bradenton, FL *34209*
Whitbeck MR & MRS B Hunt JR (S Katherine | of ☎ (212)472-0990
Oechler) Ws'71.Plg.Cly.Ncd.H'65.H'67 . . . . . . | 53 E 66 St,
JUNIORS MISS Caroline N—at Phillips Andover . . | New York, NY
JUNIORS MR Brainerd H 3d—at Phillips Exeter . . | *10021*
☎ (516) 653-4625
''Far East''
PO Box 672,
Quogue, NY *11959*
Whitbeck MRS Brainerd H (Mary V Ranck) V'33.Cly.
☎ (212) 737-8710 . . 1 E 66 St, New York, NY *10021*
Whitbeck MR Franklin P . . . . Died Jun 24'96
Whitbeck MRS Franklin P (Lila B Rand)
☎ (203) 264-2162 . . 643B Heritage Village, Southbury, CT *06488*
Whitbeck MR & MRS John V (Tara M M Beauregard) H'68.H'73
☎ (011-33-1) 45-55-06-58 . . 150 rue de l'Université, 75007 Paris,
France
Whitcraft MR & MRS Edward C R (Dubois—Andrea Dowd)
Pr.BtP.Cly.Y'36
☎ (516) 671-9860 . . PO Box 486, Locust Valley, NY *11560*
Whitcraft MR & MRS Edward T (Susan K Runyon) | ☎ (516) 549-0095
Y'63 . . . . | Smugglers Cove
MISS Samantha R . . . . | Path, Lloyd Harbor,
Huntington, NY
11743
White MRS A Duritz (Anne L Duritz) . . . . | ☎ (610) LA5-8222
MISS Nicole S . . . . | 25 Meadows Lane,
MISS Nathalie A . . . . | Haverford, PA
19041
White MR & MRS A Ridgely (Mary W Davy)
☎ (540) 687-8741 . . Chilton Farm, 23028 St Louis Rd, PO Box 54,
Middleburg, VA *20117*
White MR & MRS Alexander W (Anne H Meissner) | ☎ (508) 462-8753
NCar'65.Bost'70.H'93.Ty'67.Nu'72 . . . . | 167 Elm St, Byfield,
MISS Cynthia N—at Colo Coll . . . . | MA *01922*
JUNIORS MR Alexander W JR—at Cambridge Sch
White MRS Anne Burpee (Anne C A Burpee) | ☎ (904) 249-8380
BMr'54 . . . . | 1729 Seminole
MISS Lee B—at 88A N Bedford St, Arlington, VA | Beach Rd,
22201 . . . . | Atlantic Beach, FL
MR Loomis L 3d—at 4520 Chestnut St, | *32233*
New Orleans, LA *70115* . . . . |
MR Thomas D—at U of Fla . . . . |

White MR & MRS Anthony W (Katherine P Isham) | ☎ (301) 229-1641
Sth'61.Rcch.P'58 . . . . | 5872 Marbury Rd,
MR Walker G—at Jackson Hole, WY . . . . | Bethesda, MD
MR Nelson I . . . . | *20817*
White MR & MRS Augustus Barnes (Gale L Thorne) Belh'67
☎ (601) 981-3224 . . 305 Glenway Dv, Jackson, MS *39216*
White DR & MRS Benjamin Winthrop (Tuttle—Janet | ☎ (617) 864-3028
C Soltis) Bates'65.Cl'67.H.'67.ClP&S'71. | 77 Francis Av,
H'90 . . . . | Cambridge, MA
MISS Genevieve d'I . . . . | *02138-1911*
MR Tobias S . . . . |
White MR & MRS C Stuart JR (Matilda B Romaine) | of ☎ (802)649-1654
P'59.Cl'63 . . . . | Happy Hill Rd,
MISS Laura B—at 206 Lakeshore Rd, Grand Isle, | PO Box 40,
VT *05458* . . . . | Norwich, VT *05055*
MR Cleveland S 3d—at 44 Pleasant St, Ludlow, | ☎ (508) 548-1081
VT *05149* . . . . | ''Windymoor''
34 Chapoquoit Rd,
PO Box 35,
West Falmouth, MA
02574
White MISS Caroline J—P'87
☎ (212) 362-5128 . . 250 W 75 St, Apt 1B, New York, NY *10023*
White MRS Charles B (Anne S G Holmes) Cly. . . . . | ☎ (401) 348-8108
MR W King . . . . | Longshore II, 11
Oceanview H'way,
Watch Hill, RI
02891
White DR & MRS Charles S 3d (Patricia A Thorstens) | ☎ (214) 352-7872
Mt.Cvc.H'65.Pitt'69 . . . . | 4714 Wildwood Rd,
JUNIORS MISS Sarah V . . . . | Dallas, TX *75209*
JUNIORS MR Charles S 4th . . . . |
White MISS Charlotte C—Dunb'68
☎ (202) 363-4185 . . 3951 Langley Court NW, Apt C585, Washington,
DC *20016*
White MR & MRS Christopher M (Cornish—Alice L | ☎ (617) 424-1081
Johnson) Wash'73.Mass'79.Cl'89 ⚓ . . . . . . | 390 Commonwealth
MR Nathaniel T—at U of Chicago . . . . | Av, Apt 610,
JUNIORS MR Gavin W—at Buxton . . . . | Boston, MA *02215*
White MR Christopher W—Wms'53
☎ (508) 645-3659 . . Great White Way, Menemsha, MA *02552*
White MRS Constance V R (Constance V R Dexter) | ☎ (617) 523-0479
Chi. . . . . | 68 Beacon St,
MISS Isabella . . . . | Boston, MA *02108*
White MR Daniel W—V'78
☎ (212) 734-7494 . . 151 E 81 St, Apt 2F, New York, NY *10028*
White MR Dixon B—Cw.Myf.Sar.Wms'50 . . . . | ☎ (603) 428-3330
MR Bradford P—H'83 . . . . | ''Pa'tridgeberry
Lodge'' 55 Quaker
Hill, Henniker, NH
03242-3319
White MR & MRS E Laurence 3d (Jane S Giammattei)
PineM'81.Rcn.NEng'73.Mid'75
☎ (201) 379-1740 . . 58 Merrywood Lane, Short Hills, NJ *07078*
White MISS E Leonore
☎ (518) 374-5444 . . 1046 Parkwood Blvd, Schenectady, NY *12308*

White MR & MRS Edgar P E (Dorothy Jeanne Fuhrer) Un.H'52 . . . . | of ☎ (212)744-1470 901 Lexington Av, New York, NY 10021-5902
  MISS Daphne—at ☎ (212) 410-7388
  315 E 86 St, New York, NY 10028 . . . .
  ☎ (908) 295-1836 "Overflow" 1225 Bay Av, Mantoloking, NJ 08738

White MR & MRS Edward A (Wetmore—Nancy A Rhodes) Ariz'63.Tufts'47
  ☎ (602) 840-0704 . . 5786 N Echo Canyon Circle, Phoenix, AZ 85018-1242

White MR & MRS Edward P (Katherine E Wilson) Wells'42.Cr'41
  ☎ (919) 933-0738 . . 379 Carolina Meadows Villa, Chapel Hill, NC 27514-7521

White MR & MRS F L Peter (Jehanne H Price) Man'vl'41.H'38 . . . . | ☎ (516) 584-6651 "Box Hill" PO Box 341, St James, NY 11780
  MR Christopher F—at 54 Horseblock Rd, Centereach, NY 11720 . . . .
  MR Peter R C

White MRS Francis D (Cynthia A Terry) CtCol'46.Dar.
  ☎ (803) 681-5514 . . 5 Anglers Pond Lane, Hilton Head Island, SC 29926

White MR & MRS Frank E JR (Susan B R Greenlee)
  ☎ (803) 787-5424 . . 4832 Forest Ridge Lane, Columbia, SC 29206

White MRS Fred Rollin JR (Emma G Raymond) Kt.Un.It.
  ☎ (216) 321-4506 . . 18900 Shelburne Rd, Cleveland, OH 44118

White MR & MRS Galen J JR (Ethel S Wright) V'58.P'56.Pa'62 . . . . | ☎ (502) 894-9579 600 Sunset Rd, Louisville, KY 40206
  MR Galen J 3d

White MR Gilbert F—Cos.Ch'32
  ☎ (303) 444-0169 . . 624 Pearl St, Apt 302, Boulder, CO 80302

White MR & MRS Harold T (Penelope Weld) Sth'39.H'37 ⚓
  ☎ (203) 966-9605 . . 111 Parish Lane, New Canaan, CT 06840

White MRS James N (Picton—Frances A Richardson)
  ☎ (904) 285-6104 . . 1000 Vicar's Landing Way, E208, Ponte Vedra Beach, FL 32082

White MR & MRS John H (Mary T Schwarz) Ny.Yn.Y'36
  47 S Meadow Lane, Barrington, RI 02806

White MR & MRS John H (Eleanor A Ring) . . . . | ☎ (203) 869-1856 101 Maple Av, Greenwich, CT 06830
  MISS Elizabeth H
  MR Paul R

White MR John T JR . . see MRS L A Chilcote

White MR & MRS Lawrence P (Helen L Dinkey) Pc.Sg.Fw.Yn.Y'38
  ☎ (215) 247-5160 . . "Anchor Down" 424 W Springfield Av, Philadelphia, PA 19118-4138

White MR & MRS Lawrence P JR (Sandra W Allen) Swb'65.Cvc.Y'65 . . . . | ☎ (301) 229-7892 5910 Welborn Dv, Bethesda, MD 20816
  MISS Elizabeth P
  MR Nicholas A

White MR & MRS Lawrence Wheeler (Jane Thompson) Myc.My.Chi.H'46
  ☎ (508) 526-7554 . . Boardman Av, Manchester, MA 01944

White MRS M Brannan (Mary W Brannan) . . . . | ☎ (504) 892-0223 227 Robinhood Rd, Covington, LA 70433
  MISS Jessica W

White MRS (DR) Mary Alice (Kimball—Mary A White) V'41 . . . . | ☎ (860) 435-9121 PO Box 426, Salisbury, CT 06068
  MISS Katharine W Kimball

White MISS Mary B—CalArts'69.CalArts'82
  ☎ (510) 848-3932 . . 2327—5 St, Berkeley, CA 94710

White DR & MRS Matthew M (Claire M Meyer) StL'80.Tufts'75.StL'81.VPI'83
  ☎ (614) 594-2219 . . 154 Morris Av, Athens, OH 45701

White MR & MRS Michael B (Virginia G Burke) Hlns'86.Va'80 . . of
  ☎ (504) 835-8510 . . 18 Englewood P'kway, Metairie, LA 70005
  ☎ (601) 467-4130 . . Royal Oaks Farm, Rte 2, Box 507, Bay St Louis, MS 39520

White MR & MRS Michael M (Vignes—Nadège de Brantes) Hn.H'49
  ☎ (011-33-93) 58-00-06 . . L'Oustaroune, Chemin des Salles, 06140 Vence, France

White MRS Milbank (Daphne Milbank) Sth'48.AmU'79.Myf.
  ☎ (408) 372-8824 . . 313 Bishop Av, Pacific Grove, CA 93950

White MR & MRS Ogden JR (Bonnie Donnell Richardson) Rdc'59.Cyb.Chi.H'60 . . . . | of ☎ (561)546-5611 128 S Beach Rd, PO Box 1669, Hobe Sound, FL 33475
  MR Ogden 3d—at ☎ (617) 267-3144
  9 Holyoke St, Apt 4, Boston, MA 02116 . . . . . .
  ☎ (207) 883-7020 "Eastern Point" 26 Jocelyn Rd, Prouts Neck, ME 04074

White MRS Paton Rauch (Paton S Rauch) . . . . | ☎ (561) 795-3427 341 Mozart Rd, West Palm Beach, FL 33411
  MR Andrew H
  MR S Taylor
  MR Thomas B

White MASTER Patrick McManus (Richard L) . . . . Born at Alexandria, VA Jun 26'95

White MR & MRS Paul D (Rowlands—Gibson—Arden K duB James) . . . . | ☎ (212) TR6-9208 65 E 96 St, New York, NY 10128
  MR P Desmond JR—LakeF'72—at
  ☎ (408) 438-2654 . . 2000 Glenwood Dv, Scotts Valley, CA 95060 . . . .
  MISS Penelope I Rowlands—Bard'73.Stan'85 —at 950 Via Casitas, Greenbrae, CA 94904 . .

White MR & MRS Pendleton P (Julia S Clarke) Wheat'56.Eyc.Err.Sm.H'53 . . . . | ☎ (912) 598-8522 6 Breckenridge Lane, Savannah, GA 31411
  MISS Anne C

White MR & MRS R Quincy JR (D Joyce Caldwell) NCar'55.Rc.Fy.Wa.Y'54.H'60 . . . . | ☎ (312) 337-5356 1310 N Ritchie Court, Apt 20B, Chicago, IL 60610
  MISS Annelia E

White MR & MRS Randolph Stockton (Nancy L Robertson) WashColl'72 . . . . ☎ (406) 587-7176 Pheasant Run Ranch,
MISS Carey A . . . .
MISS Sarah L . . . . 1320 Manley Rd, Bozeman, MT *59715*

White MR & MRS Richard D (Marjorie V Kelsey) Ty'73.Ty'72.JHop'75 . . . . ☎ (703) 642-0749 4007 Whispering
JUNIORS MR Charles M . . . . Lane, Annandale, VA *22003*

White DR & MRS Richard L JR (Mary A McManus) Geo'79.Cr'82.Cl'86
☎ (704) 543-4714 . . 4608 Morrowick Rd, Charlotte, NC *28226*

White MR & MRS Richardson JR (Margaret M Rodes) Sl.P'52.H'54
''Stillhouse Hollow'' PO Box 279, Sperryville, VA *22740*

White MR & MRS Robert D (Jeanne A Shipper) Me.Penn'72.Penn'74
☎ (610) 644-5104 . . 1763 Thistle Way, Malvern, PA *19355*

White MRS Robert E (Marion Jewett) Ws'41 . . . . . . ☎ (617) 259-8433
MR Bruce B—at 4 Trowbridge Place, Cambridge, 153 S Great Rd,
MA *02138* . . . . Lincoln, MA *01773*

White MR & MRS Robert H 2d (Katherine S West) P'80.Colg'77
☎ (609) 466-4927 . . 57 N Greenwood Av, Hopewell, NJ *08525*

White MR & MRS Robert K (Ellen Virden) Fiy.Y.'50 of ☎ (516)788-7439
MISS Katherine S . . . . PO Box 331,
MR Andrew S . . . . Fishers Island, NY
MR David D *06390*
PO Box 993, Old Lyme, CT *06371*

White MR & MRS Rollin H 3d (Ann L Harriman) ☎ (561) 545-9810
LErie'88.Cw.Myf.Ncd.P'51 . . . . 7775 SE Loblolly
MISS Wende E—at ☎ (011-61-89) 397-260 Bay Dv,
Batchelor, Northern Territory 0845, Australia . . Hobe Sound, FL *33455*

White MR & MRS S Bonsal (Hague—Britt—Constance M O'Neil)
SUNY'67.Md.Elk.B.P'48
☎ (410) 557-7830 . . Fox Fire Farm, 3311 Jarrettsville Pike, Monkton, MD *21111*

White MR S Stockton 4th—Myf.
☎ (406) 222-6497 . . Lazy Heart Ranch, Rte 38, Box 2060, Livingston, MT *59047*

White MR & MRS Samuel G (Landreth—Elizabeth P ☎ (212) 831-7280
Jones) Sth'69.C.H'68.Pa'74 . . . . 16 E 95 St,
MISS Sarah P Landreth—at Harvard . . . . New York, NY
MR David C Landreth—Cl'95—at Rome, Italy *10128*

White MISS Sandra Macleod
☎ (415) 332-3379 . . PO Box 202, Sausalito, CA *94965*

White MR & MRS Somers H (Susan K Hoff) Aht'53.H'59
☎ (602) 952-0025 . . 4432 E Camelback Rd, Apt 121, Phoenix, AZ *85018*

White MRS Sowers (Ruth F Sowers) Cvc.Ncd.
☎ (202) 338-0784 . . 3900 Watson Place NW, Washington, DC *20016*

White MR & MRS Stephen B 3d (Carolyn A Cooke) VaCmth'84
1 East Av, Norwalk, CT *06851*

White MR & MRS Stephen H (Virginia T Simonds) ☎ (508) 785-0375
Cy.Ncd.Lawr'65.Dth'67 . . . . 30 Dover Rd, Dover,
MISS Hilary B—at Colby . . . . MA *02030*
MR Christopher L—at Dartmouth . . . .

White MR & MRS Stephen H (Ann R Kelly) ☎ (203) 761-8550
Col'71.Col'68 . . . . 35 Branch Brook
MISS Hillary Ann . . . . Rd, Wilton, CT
MISS Jessica R *06897*
JUNIORS MISS Emily H . . . .

White MR & MRS Steven J (Susan G Curran) ☎ (206) 453-9026
PugetS'69.PugetS'68 . . . . 3326—78 Place NE,
MR Christopher T . . . . Bellevue, WA *98004*
JUNIORS MR Tyler O . . . .

White MRS Sumner W JR (Virginia Earle) . . . . Died at New York, NY May 1'96

White MRS Sumner W 3d (Eleanor C Phillips) . . . . . ☎ (201) 701-0994
MR Timothy P . . . . 215 River Edge Dv, Chatham, NJ *07928*

White MISS Susan F . . see W S Coates JR

White MRS Thomas Raeburn JR (Charlotte Gerhard) Sg.Ac.
☎ (610) 645-8905 . . 1400 Waverly Rd, Blair 314, Gladwyne, PA *19035*

White MR & MRS Thomas W 4th (Joan W Woods)
Cy.Nyc.Cw.Rv.Cc.Ncd.Aht'41
☎ (314) 726-6329 . . 6326 Alexander Dv, Clayton, MO *63105*

White MR & MRS V Gerald (Virginia Elliot) . . . . ☎ (415) 323-3356
MISS Tamzen B . . . . 1890 Oak Knoll
MR Victor G 3d . . . . Lane, Menlo Park,
MR Ross E . . . . CA *94025*

White MR & MRS W Winchester JR (Maryanne Lohrfink) JHop'38
☎ (910) 455-8015 . . 3102 Northwoods Dv, Jacksonville, NC *28540*

White MR & MRS Walter H (M Jane Davenport) Metro'82.P'50
☎ (715) 798-2408 . . ''The Cove'' HC 60, Box 309, Cable, WI *54821-9543*

White MRS Wilbert W (Nancy Freund)
☎ (303) 733-5404 . . 3333 E Florida Av, Apt 1, Denver, CO *80210*

White MRS Willard A (Washburn—Barbara Poole)
231 Dogford Rd, Etna, NH *03750*

White MR & MRS William B (Virginia L Rutter) . . . . ☎ (904) 278-8155
MISS Mary A—at ☎ (404) 262-2835 2643 Whipple Av,
999 Northrope Dv NE, Atlanta, GA *30324* . . . . . Orange Park, FL *32073*

White MR & MRS William D (Olivia P Murray) Rc.Cc.Hn.Hav'67.H'75
☎ (773) HY3-1641 . . 5607 S Dorchester Av, Chicago, IL *60637*

White MR & MRS William I (Elizabeth H Barton) Cda.
☎ (410) 795-5105 . . Fairhaven G11, 7200 Third Av, Sykesville, MD *21784*

White MRS William MacI JR (Matilda O Brown) . . . . Died Feb 17'95

White MRS William Poe (Elizabeth M Baum) . . . . . ☎ (610) MU8-3847
MR William P JR . . . . 511 Woodland Court, Wayne, PA *19087*

White MR & MRS William T 3d (Heather W Murray) Pr.Dth'82
☎ (847) 735-1246 . . 129 Ravine Forest Dv, Lake Bluff, IL *60044*

Whitehead MR & MRS Charles E 2d (Lydia M ☎ (301) 656-3823
Thompson) SL'71.P'69.H'72 . . . . 4824 Chevy Chase
MISS Amanda P . . . . Blvd, Chevy Chase,
MISS Molly T . . . . MD *20815*
JUNIORS MISS Anna M M . . . .

Whitehead MISS Patricia T—Br'78
☎ (212) 570-5677 . . 345 E 80 St, New York, NY *10021*

Whitehead MR & MRS Thomas F (Patricia W Merrill).................................. | 295 Old Limekiln Rd, Chalfont, PA *18914*
MISS Elizabeth E—Geo'81—at ☎ (212) 472-3880
1680 York Av, New York, NY *10128* ....

Whitehill MRS Walter Muir (Jane R Coolidge) V'23
☎ (508) 686-4838 . . 44 Andover St, North Andover, MA *01845*

Whitehouse MR & MRS Charles S (Grayson—Janet Ketchum) V'46.Mt.Cvc.Y'44 | ☎ (540) 364-2595 "Orion House"
MR Charles R—at 769 Greenwich St, New York, NY *10014*............................ | Box 176, Rte 2, Marshall, VA *20115*

Whitehouse MRS G Meredith (Genevieve S Philips)
☎ (802) 457-1216 . . Rose Hill, Woodstock, VT *05091*

Whitehouse MR Robert F (Senseney—Carleton—Florence Keats Noyes)
☎ (520) 881-1757 . . 2272 E Drachman St, Tucson, AZ *85719*

Whitehouse MR & MRS Sheldon (Sandra C Thornton) Y'81.Y'78.Va'82 . . of
☎ (401) 421-7341 . . 32 Elmgrove Av, Providence, RI *02906*
☎ (401) 849-2621 . . "Lily Pond House" 175 Carroll Av, Newport, RI *02840*

Whitehouse MR & MRS William F (McCracken—Margaret A Van Vliet) Nrr.Srb.Br'38
☎ (561) 848-0721 . . 268 Jamaica Lane, Palm Beach, FL *33480*

Whitehurst DR Walter R 3d—StJ.Vmi'49.Va'53
☎ (205) 879-0075 . . 3532 Victoria Rd, Birmingham, AL *35223*

Whitelaw MR & MRS Charles M (Maury B Gatch) Rich'80.Mo'77
☎ (314) 991-2630 . . 2 Bon Aire Dv, St Louis, MO *63132*

Whitelaw MR & MRS George P JR (Nancy F O'Donnell) Cysl.Aht'43
6 Kingston Manor, St Louis, MO *63124-1913*

Whitelaw MR & MRS George P 3d (Linda A Peters) AmU'76.Cy.StLaw'72
☎ (314) 994-1609 . . 65 Briarcliff, Ladue, MO *63124-1765*

Whiteley MISS Anne F—VtLaw'80
RR 2, Box 1812, Stowe, VT *05672*

Whiteley MR & MRS George C 3d (Hamilton—Jeanne E Stockman) Bnd'73.H.'62.Nu'65
☎ (212) 724-8366 . . 210 W 90 St, New York, NY *10024*

Whiteley MR & MRS Richard Peyton (Kathryn A Halvorson) Va'72
☎ (703) 631-8394 . . 5820 Deer Pond Rd, Centreville, VA *20120*

Whiteley MRS Robert F S (Audrey H Bathke) Cvc.
☎ (804) 438-6323 . . PO Box 418, York Rd, Irvington, VA *22480*

Whiteley MISS Susan H—AmU'70
☎ (415) 337-8277 . . 163 Mangels Av, San Francisco, CA *94131*

Whiteman MR & MRS Daniel S JR (Dorothy H Ritterbush) Pc.Ncd.
☎ (215) 628-4618 . . Pheasant Run Farm, Box 3067, Maple Glen, PA *19002*

Whiteman MR & MRS David B (Marilyn A Hurley) Rose'80.Ithaca'80
☎ (610) 793-0496 . . 1156 Lake Dv, West Chester, PA *19382*

Whiteman MR & MRS George M (Stasia S Hamilton) W&M'82.Pc.Bur'83
☎ (610) 687-9420 . . 882 Box Hill Lane, Wayne, PA *19087*

Whiteman MR & MRS H Clifton (Leib—Joan E Coffin) Pr.Cly.Dth'50
☎ (212) 758-6235 . . 136 E 64 St, New York, NY *10021*

Whiteside MR Alexander—Sm.H'66 .... | ☎ (617) 696-0183
JUNIORS MISS Margaret M—at Cambridge Sch . . | 79 Hillside St, Milton, MA *02186*

Whiteside MRS Christiana B (Christiana Bartlett) D.
☎ (617) 326-6826 . . Fox Hill Village D443, 10 Longwood Dv, Westwood, MA *02090*

Whiteside MISS Elizabeth S
22 Ridge Av, Newton Center, MA *02159*

Whiteside MRS Frederick S (Caroline F Lawrence)
☎ (804) 980-9133 . . 250 Pantops Mountain Dv, WCBR 133, Charlottesville, VA *22901*

Whiteside MR George A 3d—H'87 . . see T M H Nimick JR

Whiteside MR Thomas—H'32
☎ (617) 320-8423 . . Fox Hill Village, Clark House, 30 Longwood Dv, Westwood, MA *02090*

Whiting MISS Betty W—JHop'54.Gi.Cy.Mv.Cda.
4221 Greenway, Baltimore, MD *21218*

Whiting MRS J Marshall T (J Noel Hopkins)
☎ (410) 377-0928 . . 6003 Lakehurst Dv, Apt 5, Baltimore, MD *21210-1031*

Whiting MR & MRS John K 3d (Marian M Crawford) Ind'53.Myc.H'53
☎ (508) 356-0998 . . 39 Country Club Way, Ipswich, MA *01938*

Whiting MRS Richard G (Rosemary Menzies-Wilson) Bost'69
☎ (617) 227-7192 . . 14 Brimmer St, Boston, MA *02108*

Whitlock MR & MRS Bache McE (Jean C Murphy) H'38.............................. | ☎ (601) 875-7998 "Doon Dock"
MR Gavin S .... | 1322 Helmers Lane, Ocean Springs, MS *39564*
MR Christopher E ....

Whitlock MR & MRS Emmet (Case—Gloria Welch) SL'50.Evg.Mb.Pr.B.H'41
☎ (561) 863-4110 . . 249 Via Linda, Palm Beach, FL *33480*

Whitlock DR Prentice E—USA'46.Woff'50.Cl'51. Cl'65.Ford'73.PTheo'80.Drew'83.Nu'85.Drew'92
☎ (516) 931-7205 . . 97 W Cherry St, Hicksville, NY *11801-3856*

Whitlock MISS Suzanne de L (Kostmayer—Suzanne de L Whitlock) LSU'75 | ☎ (504) 863-2188 11 Log Cabin Lane, Pearl River, LA *70452*
MISS Ashley A Kostmayer ....
MISS Virginia K Kostmayer ....
JUNIORS MISS Mary Kostmayer............

Whitman MR & MRS Alexander H (Sylvia Choate) B.Ne.H.'41
☎ (516) 569-0519 . . 200 Burton Lane, Lawrence, NY *11559*

Whitman MR & MRS Charles S JR (Janet Russell) BMr'40.Plg.Msq.Why.Coa.Snc.StJ.Rv.Cc.Cw. Cly.Dc.Cda.Dar.Aht'37.H'40 | of ☎ (212)289-4586 70 E 96 St, New York, NY *10128-0752*
MISS Janet—Ws'69.Cl'75.Msq.Dc.—at ☎ (212) 628-4150 . . 231 E 76 St, New York, NY *10021*............................ | ☎ (401) 348-8750 "Snug Harbor" 15 Breen Rd, Watch Hill, RI *02891*

Whitman MR & MRS Charles S 3d (Christina L Madden) V'67.Cl'76.Un.B.Ln.Msq.Plg.Snc.Cc. Cly.H'64.H'67.Camb'68................... | of ☎ (011-44-171) 938-1821 78 Campden Hill Rd, London W8 7AA, England
JUNIORS MISS Elizabeth R—at St Paul's .... | ☎ (914) 232-9417 114 Todd Rd, Katonah, NY *10536*

Whitman MR Ezra B JR—Me.Cr'31
☎ (610) 645-8681 . . 1400 Waverly Rd, Blair 110, Gladwyne, PA *19035*

Whitman MRS H Motley (Henriette L Tjaarda)
☎ (707) 935-1456 . . 1367 Avenida Sebastiani, Sonoma, CA *95476*

Whitman MR & MRS Harold C 3d (Aimee B
Du Puy) Wheat'58.Bgt.Cly.Geo'53 . . . . | ☎ (914) 666-8181
MR H Cutler 4th—Emer'86 . . . . | 28 Wood Rd,
| Mt Kisco, NY
| *10549*

Whitman MRS Hendricks H (Margaret C Goodhue)
☎ (516) 922-6938 . . 3 Adams Court, Oyster Bay, NY *11771*

Whitman MR & MRS Ian M (Marie P de Valois | of ☎ (011-33-1)
de St Aymour) Geo'70.Hart'89 . . . . | 47-05-74-86
MR Edouard . . . . | 3 rue Ernest
JUNIORS MR Alfred . . . . | Psichari, 75007
| Paris, France
| ☎ (011-33)
| 21-85-70-32
| ''Château de la
| Palme'' 62370
| Nortkerque, France

Whitman MR & MRS J Glenn (Fanny N Lyon) | ☎ (410) 356-7094
Mv.Cda.Cr'36 . . . . | 11534 Garrison
MISS Fanny N L—at St Thomas, VI *00801* . . . . . | Forest Rd,
MR Marcus E—Md'82—at 1425 Green Spring | Owings Mills, MD
Valley Rd, Stevenson, MD *21153* . . . . | *21117*

Whitman MR & MRS John R (Christine T Todd) | ☎ (908) 234-0255
Wheat'68.Y'66.H'71 . . . . | PO Box 146,
MISS Kate R . . . . | Oldwick, NJ *08858*
JUNIORS MR Taylor P . . . . |

Whitman MR & MRS Johnston de F (Christina B | ☎ (516) 367-4761
Rand) Colby'59.Csh.Colby'59 . . . . | 1638 Moore's Hill
MISS Susan D—Ithaca'86—at ☎ (770) 516-1861 | Rd, Laurel Hollow,
934 Woodridge Dv NW, Atlanta, GA *30339* . . . | Syosset, NY *11791*
MR Johnston de F JR—Colg'89—at |
Fordham Law . . . . |

Whitman MR Lawrence B . . of
☎ (941) 394-3232 . . 940 Swallow Av, Apt 9, Marco Island, FL *33969*
☎ (516) 584-5508 . . Driftwood Lane, RR 1, Box 110-3, St James,
NY *11780*

Whitman MR & MRS M Hamilton (Josephine Lee Chatard) Mv.Cda.P'36
see Dilatory Domiciles

Whitman MRS Malone (Ruth B Malone) Cly.
☎ (212) 734-1466 . . 155 E 73 St, New York, NY *10021*

Whitman MRS Peter M (F Elizabeth Blodget) Nyc.Cly.
☎ (610) 321-7221 . . 506 Brightwood Club Dv, Lutherville, MD *21093*

Whitman MR & MRS Peter M JR (Winifred D Tilney) | ☎ (508) 468-1490
Wh'lck'90.My.H'66.Nu'68 . . . . | 292 Bridge St,
MR Peter T . . . . | South Hamilton, MA
MR Nicholas L . . . . | *01982*

Whitman MR & MRS R Eugene (Daphne Tewksbury) | ☎ (617) 237-7175
Un.Me.Cw.Rv.Snc.Br'58 . . . . | 74 Carisbrooke Rd,
MR Ralph E JR—at New York, NY . . . . | Wellesley Hills, MA
| *02181*

Whitman MR & MRS Robert F (Marina von Neumann)
Rdc'56.Cl'62.Pg.Cr'49.H'56
2101 Belmont Rd, Ann Arbor, MI *48104*

Whitman REV CANON & MRS Robert S Sturgis (Eleanor English)
Lx.StJ.YDiv'61
☎ (413) 637-0001 . . Pinnacle Farm, 115 Hubbard St, Lenox, MA *01240*

Whitman MRS Royal (Mary Buck) . . . . | ☎ (203) 762-7946
MR Robert Sturgis—Un.—at ☎ (212) 249-3788 | 941 Ridgefield Rd,
192 E 75 St, New York, NY *10021* . . . . | Wilton, CT *06897*

Whitman MR & MRS Stephen L (Susan C Watson) NH'74.Ey.H'74
206 Grove St, Westwood, MA *02090*

Whitmarsh MR & MRS Francis L JR (Nesta Stephens) | ☎ (011-33-1)
H'48 . . . . | 47-83-78-12
MISS Sarah . . . . | 7 rue Alexandre
MISS Mary . . . . | Cabanel, 75015
| Paris, France

Whitmarsh MR & MRS Theodore F (Mary L Ward)
Un.Chr.Ri.Pr.Plg.Ht.Cly.Cda.H'41 . . of
☎ (212) 879-8053 . . 333 E 68 St, New York, NY *10021*
☎ (516) 626-1285 . . Linden Lane, Glen Head, NY *11545*

Whitmer MR & MRS Robert F 3d (Mary Leigh Pell) | ☎ (203) 255-6140
StJ.Y'51.H'56 . . . . | 99 Old Barn Rd,
MR Robert F 4th . . . . | Fairfield, CT *06430*
MR Walden P—Duke'86 . . . . |
MR John L—RogerW'87 . . . . |

Whitmore MR & MRS John R (Suzanne Smith) | of ☎ (203)661-5980
Hlns'60.B.Cvc.Mt.Mo'54.Mo'58 ⚓ . . . . | 50 Fox Run Lane,
MISS Elizabeth A—Dth'89—at Harvard Business | Greenwich, CT
| *06831*
| ☎ (212) 879-1244
| 115 E 67 St,
| New York, NY
| *10021*
| ☎ (410) 745-6382
| Langdon Farm,
| PO Box 18,
| Sherwood, MD
| *21665*

Whitney MRS Alexandra E (Alexandra Ewing)
☎ (212) 289-7140 . . 1158 Fifth Av, New York, NY *10029-6917*

Whitney MISS Anita C . . see J D Young

Whitney MRS Arthur T (Sack—Mary K Pape) Cly.Mds.
☎ (516) 537-0963 . . ''Pine Oaks'' PO Box 139, Wainscott, NY *11975*

Whitney MRS Barbara E (Barbara I Elvin) . . . . | 4361 Westover
MISS Patricia C—Ty'86 . . . . | Place NW,
MISS Wendy P—Br'88 . . . . | Washington, DC
MISS Meredith A—Br'92 . . . . | *20016*

Whitney MR C Searle—Y'70
2131 University Av, Apt 402, San Francisco, CA *94704*

Whitney MRS Caroline H B (Caroline H Blake) | ☎ (617) 354-9073
SL'59.Cy. . . . . | 31 Linnaean St,
MISS Vanessa C . . . . | Apt 3, Cambridge,
| MA *02138-1530*

Whitney MRS Cornelius Vanderbilt (Hosford—Marie L Schroeder)
B.Ri.Mb.Pr . . .of
☎ (518) 584-2166 . . ''Cady Hill House'' 40 Geyser Rd,
Saratoga Springs, NY *12866*
☎ (212) 838-0800 . . 825 Fifth Av, New York, NY *10021*
284 Bal Bay Dv, Bal Harbour, FL *33154*

Whitney MRS Craig W (Bross—Priscilla B Prince)
☎ (603) 954-3907 . . ''Summerhill'' 83 Old Dublin Rd, Peterborough,
NH *03458*

Whitney MISS Cynthia F (Lawton—Cynthia F Whitney) Col'64.NH'93 . . . .
  MR Robert E Lawton . . . .
  JUNIORS MISS Whitney A Lawton . . . .
☎ (603) 659-8281 Connemara Farm, 291 Wadleigh Falls Rd, Lee, NH 03824

Whitney MR & MRS Edward B (Stover—Martha C Howell) Geo'66.Cl'79.H'66.H'69 . . . .
  JUNIORS MR William H . . . .
  JUNIORS MR John H . . . .
of ☎ (212)662-5124 307 W 102 St, New York, NY 10025
☎ (914) 424-4772 Cat Rock Rd, Garrison, NY 10524

Whitney MR Edward F—H'38
  ☎ (603) 563-8415 . . PO Box 134, Main St, Dublin, NH 03444

Whitney MRS Frances J (Frances J Lannon) C.Cs.
  ☎ (212) 226-6495 . . 537 Broadway, New York, NY 10012

Whitney MRS George F (Caroline B Huston) Sg.
  ☎ (215) 628-3844 . . 5 Equestrian Lane, Blue Bell, PA 19422

Whitney MR George H 3d . . see J D Young

Whitney MR & MRS Gifford C (Francine C Douwes) Cl'89 . . of
  ☎ (212) 749-7664 . . 415 Central Park W, Apt 11E, New York, NY 10025
  ☎ (215) 242-9717 . . 323 W Springfield Av, Philadelphia, PA 19118

Whitney MR & MRS John R JR (Martinez—Katharine MacDuffie)
  ☎ (617) 326-1696 . . 58 Village Av, Dedham, MA 02026

Whitney MR & MRS Jonathan B (Janine A Safer) Swth'75.H.'84.T.Skd'77.Ford'81
  ☎ (914) 351-5626 . . Tower Hill Rd, Tuxedo Park, NY 10987

Whitney MR & MRS Mark H (Claudia L Tufts) SFrSt'73.Cy.Nass'75
  ☎ (508) 758-4770 . . 27 Pine Island Rd, Mattapoisett, MA 02739

Whitney MISS Nancy M
  ☎ (860) 868-9598 . . ''Hightops'' 106 Church Hill Rd, Washington, CT 06794

Whitney MR P Gordon—Ty'57 . . . .
  MR Francis H—Ty'87 . . . .
  MR Patricio A J—Ty'91 . . . .
of ☎ (011-54-1) 802-9490 Av del Libertador 2621, 14C, 1425 Buenos Aires, Argentina
☎ (011-598-5842) 70582 ''La Casona'' La Barra, Uruguay

Whitney MRS Patricia T (Lovejoy—Patricia W Tailer)
  ☎ (212) 758-2228 . . 200 E 66 St, New York, NY 10021

Whitney MR Richard B (Hage—Margaret Porter) .
  MR David P—Snc.Rv.Occ'70—at
  ☎ (202) 625-7065 . . 4013 Davis Place NW, Washington, DC 20007 . . . .
☎ (941) 484-2137 250 Santa Maria St, Apt 120C, Venice, FL 34285

Whitney MR & MRS Richard P (Patton—Carlene A Filkins) Mt.L.Br'59
  ☎ (410) 280-2056 . . 3441 Hidden River View, Annapolis, MD 21403

Whitney MR Robert B—H'65.Stan'76 . . . .
  MR Stephen W . . . .
  MR Jason—at U of Colo . . . .
☎ (970) 487-3277 PO Box 268, 204 Plateau Av, Collbran, CO 81624

Whitney MRS Roger de M (L Alexandra Clarke) . . . . Died at Harrison, NY Apr 8'96

Whitney MR & MRS Thomas H P (Horst—Remick—Margaret Boney) Bnd'34.Sm.Cy.Chi.H'35
  ☎ (617) 266-4190 . . 180 Beacon St, Boston, MA 02116-1401

Whitney MR & MRS Thomas H P JR (Doelger—Victoria Milbank) SL'72.Cy.Sm.Chi.V'73. Bost'78 . . . .
  JUNIORS MISS Sarah B . . . .
  MISS Emily M Doelger—at Georgetown . . . .
  MR Matthew M Doelger—at Wheaton . . . . .
☎ (617) 734-0486 47 Sargent Rd, Brookline, MA 02146

Whitney MRS W Beaumont 2d (Louisa V Newlin)
  ☎ (610) 353-5894 . . Dunwoody Village D105, 3500 West Chester Pike, Newtown Square, PA 19073

Whitney MR & MRS W Beaumont 3d (Mary T Brock) Ph.Sg.P'44
  ☎ (215) 247-4973 . . 8013 Crefeld St, Philadelphia, PA 19118

Whitney MR & MRS William T JR (Sonja E Friberg) Bost'74
  ☎ (617) 696-1366 . . 59 Highland St, Milton, MA 02186

Whiton MRS A Sherrill (Garcia—Jean Overman) Cal'39 . . . .
  MISS Barbara C—Bnd'70 . . . .
☎ (203) 453-9110 51 Long Hill Farm, Guilford, CT 06437

Whiton MR Herman F JR—ColC'66 . . . .
  MR Henry D . . . .
  MR Christian P . . . .
☎ (208) 720-2824 PO Box 1341, Sun Valley, ID 83353

Whiton MRS Herman Frasch (Katherine M O'Brien) Cly . . .of
  ☎ (212) 838-3000 . . 680 Madison Av, New York, NY 10021
  ☎ (603) 823-5264 . . 440 Bickford Hill Rd, Franconia, NH 03580

Whitridge MR & MRS David P (Torrance—Barbara A Pettit) Wash'70.Y'70.Hast'74 . . . .
  MISS Abby . . . .
  JUNIORS MR Sam . . . .
☎ (209) 462-6840 1109 Elmwood Av, Stockton, CA 95204

Whitridge MRS Horatio Hall (Gracia Grieb) Mv.Elk.
  ☎ (410) 243-4018 . . Roland Park Place, Apt 303, 830 W 40 St, Baltimore, MD 21211

Whitridge MR & MRS Roland W (Sarah E Lincoln) Fran'67.Cy.Wes'59.Pa'65 . . . .
  MR Bradford S . . . .
  JUNIORS MR Stoddard L . . . .
☎ (617) 894-3353 52 Arrowhead Rd, Weston, MA 02193

Whitridge MRS William C (Emmy L Phillips)
  ☎ (713) 861-8662 . . 12 Crestwood Dv, Houston, TX 77007

Whitson MR & MRS Albert P JR (Alice R Swords) Ala'77.Va'76.Va'80
  ☎ (615) 356-3543 . . 508 Park Hill, Nashville, TN 37205

Whitson MR & MRS Christopher C (Julia C Higdon) Fla'84.Van'87.NCar'83.Van'87
  ☎ (615) 386-9372 . . 4300 Sneed Rd, Nashville, TN 37215

Whittaker MR & MRS Laurence H (Maura L Parrish) MeMarit'78
  ☎ (207) 846-5418 . . 4 Meadow Way, Yarmouth, ME 04096

Whittaker MR & MRS Philip H P (Elizabeth R Stevenson) San.Pa'40 ⚓
  ☎ (508) 563-6720 . . ''Home Port'' 2 Ironwood Lane, PO Box 1408, North Falmouth, MA 02556

Whittall MR & MRS Ian Q (Lisa G Leighton)
  ☎ (203) 869-7783 . . 20 Park Av, Greenwich, CT 06830

Whittall MR & MRS James P JR (Constance A Farley) H'56 . . . .
  MR Rean J . . . .
  JUNIORS MISS Heather P . . . .
☎ (508) 948-2410 ''Long Hill'' 885 Haverhill St, Rowley, MA 01969

Whittell MISS Mary K
  ☎ (212) 757-6787 . . 240 Central Park S, New York, NY 10019

Whittelsey MR & MRS Frank C 3d (Margaret A Gerli)
Unn.Plg.Bow'58.Cl'60 . . of
☎ (802) 496-2088 . . PO Box 419, Waitsfield, VT *05673*
☎ (208) 622-4444 . . PO Box 5686, Ketchum, ID *83340*
Whittemore MR & MRS Allen W (Terry A McIlvaney) Cysl.Dar.Br'56
☎ (561) 731-1759 . . 4773 S Lake Dv, Boynton Beach, FL *33436*
Whittemore MR & MRS Edward B (Brooke E Sterne)
Cr'90.Msq.Dth'90.GeoW'95
☎ (202) 363-4257 . . 4620—47 St NW, Washington, DC *20016*
Whittemore MR & MRS Frederick B (Marion Willi)
Wheat'57.Un.B.Msq.Mto.Plg.Why.Ne.Cly.Dth'53.Dth'54 . . of
☎ (212) 288-6964 . . 925 Park Av, New York, NY *10028*
☎ (401) 322-7595 . . 29 Knowles Av, Weekapaug, RI *02891*
☎ (401) 348-8392 . . 72 Ocean View H'way, Watch Hill, RI *02891*

Whittemore VERY REV & MRS H Lawrence JR | ☎ (802) 388-1349
(Elizabeth Eschmann) Dar.Cda.Wms'39 . . . . . . | 14 Nedde Lane,
MISS Elizabeth B—Sth'77.Sth'81—at | Middlebury, VT
☎ (617) 646-1196 . . 37 Hamlet St, Arlington, | *05753-2107*
MA *02174* . . . . |

Whittemore MRS J Howard (Priscilla Stimson)
☎ (203) 758-9419 . . 317 Tranquility Rd, Middlebury, CT *06762*
Whittemore MR & MRS Laurence F 3d (Kathleen A Mackay)
VillaN'86.Un.Why.Msq.Dth'88.Dth'93 . . of
☎ (212) 744-3100 . . 136 E 79 St, New York, NY *10021*
☎ (401) 322-7595 . . 29 Knowles Av, Weekapaug, RI *02891*
Whittemore MR & MRS Lawrason L (Jocelyn Meacham)
☎ (619) 443-8741 . . 10880 H'way 67, Apt 99, Lakeside, CA *92040*

Whittemore CAPT (RET) & MRS Robert M (Margaret | ☎ (617) 566-2030
A Burrows) USN.Cy.Chi.Ncd.H'38 . . . . | 203 Heath St,
MISS Nancy A . . . . | Chestnut Hill, MA
| *02167-2806*

Whittier MRS Ross (Katharine B Hamlin)
☎ (508) 922-0011 . . 875 Hale St, Beverly Farms, MA *01915-2215*
Whittlesey MRS Julian H (Eunice S Smith)
☎ (203) 762-7081 . . 29 Chicken St, Wilton, CT *06897*
Whyte MR & MRS Robert (Katharine L Souder) T.Pa'48
☎ (508) 255-7280 . . RR 1, Box 173, 15 Charlie Noble Way, Eastham,
MA *02642*

Whyte MR & MRS Ronald M (Ann L von Weise) | ☎ (408) 395-9284
Sth'66.Wes'64 . . . . | 220 Prospect Av,
MISS Susan P . . . . | Los Gatos, CA
MR Kevin M . . . . | *95032*

Whyte MR & MRS W Hollingsworth (Jenny Bell Bechtel) C.Cc.Cs.P'39
☎ (212) 369-0014 . . 175 E 94 St, New York, NY *10128*
Wichman MR & MRS Herman L 3d (Cook—Wichman—Betty J Morse)
Wash'46.Wash'42
☎ (619) 341-9519 . . 75114 Concho Dv, Indian Wells, CA *92210*

Wick MR & MRS (DR) Christopher M (Smith— | ☎ (860) 536-1840
Shirley W Holbrook) Bost'71.Vt'73.Tufts'79.Yn. | 6 Skiff Lane,
Y'67.Stan'73 | Mystic, CT *06355*
JUNIORS MISS Kathleen C . . . . |
JUNIORS MISS Heather M . . . . |

Wick MR & MRS David (Helen L Moore) Ariz'46.Ariz'48.ArizSt'53
☎ (520) 282-4420 . . PO Box NN, West Sedona, AZ *86340*
Wick MR Douglas—Kt.Un.Cv.Tv.Y'39.Cwr'46
☎ (216) 423-4545 . . 7581 Chelsea Lane, Box 148, Gates Mills,
OH *44040*

Wick MR & MRS Henry C 3d (Hart—Barbara A | ☎ (602) 948-7731
Ireland) Y'34 . . . . | Judson School,
MISS Virginia Chandler . . . . | 6601 E Indian Bend
MISS Alyssa . . . . | Rd, Paradise Valley,
MR Alexander Henry . . . . | AZ *85253*

Wick MR & MRS K Bryant JR (Churchill—Emily S Roberts) OWes'85
☎ (617) 527-2687 . . 1175 Chestnut St, Apt 2, Newton, MA *02164*
Wick MR & MRS Kent D (Jerre L Barber)
ArizSt'78.ArizSt'89.Dar.Cda.ArizSt'77
☎ (602) 948-3170 . . 6414 E Maverick, Paradise Valley, AZ *85253*
Wick MRS Myron A JR (Elizabeth L Dillingham)
☎ (561) 546-7033 . . 444 S Beach Rd, Hobe Sound, FL *33455*
Wick MR & MRS Peter A (Kathleen Lord) Sm.Y'43
☎ (617) 523-4748 . . 41 W Cedar St, Boston, MA *02114*
Wick MRS Philip JR (Marguerite Merrick) SL'39 . . of
☎ (561) 231-5699 . . The Moorings Apt 105, 1903 Bay Rd, Vero Beach,
FL *32963*
☎ (860) 767-2341 . . 123 Essex Meadows, Essex, CT *06426*
Wick MISS Sumner Chapman (g—MRS John Hildt) . . . . . . Born May 3'96
Wick MISS Tallulah Dillingham (Walter D) . . . . Born at
Boston, MA Jly 7'96

Wick MR & MRS Walter D (Donna L Leahy)
WmSth'79.H'95.Cy.Unn.Ri.Van'77.Cl'83
☎ (617) 547-8026 . . 9 Follen St, Cambridge, MA *02138*
Wick MR & MRS William O JR (Carolyn M Brown)
Wms'80.Lond'84.Stan'76.Nw'96
8722 Olentangy River Rd, Delaware, OH *43015*

Wickersham MRS A A Tilney (Joan Ryder) | ☎ (508) 548-0863
Rdc'57.Ncd . . . . | ''Nobska West''
MR F Clark . . . . | PO Box 62,
| Woods Hole, MA
| *02543-0062*

Wickersham DR & MRS C Wendell 3d (Virginia | ☎ (860) 646-8224
Marth) Hob'60.Alb'64 . . . . | 4 Dimock Lane,
MISS Elizabeth J—at Hartwick Coll . . . . | Bolton, CT *06043*
MR William W—Skd'94 . . . . |
MR Andrew K—at Lafayette Coll . . . . |

Wickersham REV & MRS George W 2d (Elizabeth W Craighill) H'35
☎ (540) 348-5847 . . McCurdy Lane, Rockbridge Baths, VA *24473*
Wickersham MR & MRS James E (Mildred Turnbow) Bhm.Fr.Ncd.Stan'43
☎ (510) 547-4594 . . 15 Glen Alpine Rd, Piedmont, CA *94611*

Wickersham MR & MRS James H JR—Ny.Y'51 | ☎ (203) 255-1793
MR Peter M—CarnM'92—at ☎ (505) 345-3626 | 200 Daybreak Rd,
2425 Teodoro Rd NW, Albuquerque, NM *87107* | Southport, CT *06490*

Wickersham MR & MRS Theodore S (Glazier—Norma J Spruell)
Un.Chr.Plg.Snc.Cly.H.'61.Cal'64
☎ (212) 534-4939 . . 250 E 87 St, New York, NY *10128*
Wickersham MR & MRS Walter M (Allison M Mills) Ne'93.Bost'91.Bost'95
☎ (617) 927-8154 . . 15 Chauncey St, Watertown, MA *02172*
Wickes MR Christopher P—Me . . . see MRS M Scott
Wickes MR Nicholas du P . . see D R Carse JR
Wickes MR Schuyler C—Del'92
☎ (914) 699-2218 . . 60 W Broad St, Apt 4H, Mt Vernon, NY *10552*
Wickes MR & MRS W Forman 4th (Nicola L Le Clair) Mid'87
☎ (011-44-181) 946-1240 . . 47 Pepys Rd, London SW20 8NL, England
Wickes MR William L
☎ (610) 272-6722 . . 551 Plymouth Rd, Plymouth Meeting, PA *19462*

Wickett MR & MRS James F (Magdalena Yesil) Stan'80.Stan'81 . . of
☎ (415) 322-8407 . . 325 Kipling St, Palo Alto, CA *94301*
☎ (415) 851-8407 . . Star Hill Ranch, 1492 Star Hill Rd, Woodside, CA *94062*

Wickett MR & MRS John D (Nancy W Read) Stan'76.Stan'78.Stan'71
2411 Bryant St, Palo Alto, CA *94301*

Wickham MRS Brodhead (Sarah S Brodhead) Ds. . . | ☎ (610) 688-4043
 MR John Channing 2d—Carl'79.JHop'83—at | 348 Harbison Rd,
☎ (202) 333-7788 . . 1540—44 St NW, | St Davids, PA
Washington, DC 20007 . . . . | *19087*

Wickham MRS Thomas K (Kirchen—Mary E | ☎ (610) 640-4178
Norman). . . . . | 505 Foxwood Lane,
 MISS Leslie K . . . . | Paoli, PA
 | *19301-2010*

Wicks MRS David O (Elizabeth Leonard)
☎ (617) 320-9359 . . 10 Longwood Dv, Apt 420, Westwood, MA *02090*

Wickser MR & MRS Gaius H (Jacqueline Jones) NTexSt'80.Syr'78
☎ (818) 500-8327 . . 1139 N Geneva St, Glendale, CA *91207*

Wickser MR & MRS John P (Frances M Halsey) St.Cy.Rv.G.Y.'45.Cl'49
☎ (716) 884-2115 . . 22 Oakland Place, Buffalo, NY *14222*

Wickser MISS M Melissa—Vt'73.Pace'85.Nyc. ⚓
☎ (508) 228-3693 . . 12 Roberts Lane, Nantucket, MA *02554*

Wickser MR Philip J 2d—St.Pa'76.Cl'81
☎ (310) 476-4586 . . 338 S Anita Dv, Los Angeles, CA *90049*

Widdoes MR & MRS W Peirce (Barbara R Landauer) | ☎ (412) 361-7862
Pg.Rr.Wes'49. . . . . | 5705 Dunmoyle
 MR William P JR . . . . | Place, Pittsburgh,
 | PA *15217*

Widing MR & MRS Eric P (Laura K Todd)
Ox'78.Un.Rr.Ln.Plg.Snc.Cly.Wms'81 . . of
☎ (914) 669-8242 . . Hattersbrook Farm, RR 1, Titicus Rd,
North Salem, NY *10560*
☎ (412) 238-7784 . . Log Cabin Farm, PO Box 720, Ligonier, PA *15658*

Widing MR & MRS J William JR (Helen C Judson) Ncd.Wms'52.Pa'57
PO Box 757, Williamstown, MA *01267*

Widing MR & MRS J William 3d (Mary J McManus)
Duke'78.Rc.Rv.Cw.Wms'76.Duke'79
☎ (610) 678-0201 . . 81 Downing Dv, Wyomissing, PA *19610*

Widmer MRS Harriet S (Stephens—Terhune— | ☎ (914) 887-6502
Harriet S Widmer) NewSchSR'90 . . . . | ''School House''
 MR John K Stephens—Wright'89—at | PO Box 44,
☎ (513) 296-0751 . . 1713 Shroyer Rd, | Long Eddy, NY
Dayton, OH *45419* . . . . | *12760*

Wiedel DR & MRS Philip D (Monique H Watson) C.Cly.Cs.Cl'37 . . of
☎ (212) 410-5512 . . 40 E 94 St, Apt 20D, New York, NY *10128*
☎ (203) 743-0092 . . ''Ridge House'' 125 Long Ridge Rd, Danbury, CT *06810*

Wiedemann MISS Anne S . . see T M Bancroft JR

Wiedemann MR Christopher B—Ty'93 . . see T M Bancroft JR

Wiedemann MR & MRS (DR) Frederic Franklin (Florence Leachman)
RMWmn'47.USN'45
☎ (214) 528-5630 . . 4939 Crooked Lane, Dallas, TX *75229*

Wiederhold MR & MRS Michael L (Margaret F | ☎ (210) 271-7555
Sayre) Mit'61. . . . . | 203 King William
 JUNIORS MR Theodore L—at MIT . . . . | St, San Antonio, TX
 | *78204-1315*

Wiederseim MR & MRS Theodore E 3d (Gillian T Brogan) Rv.Cw.Ll.
☎ (610) 363-1213 . . 1102 St Michaels Court, Chester Springs, PA *19425*

Wiederseim MR & MRS William B (Margaret R | ☎ (610) 971-0314
Richards) Houst'84.M.Ll.Swb'78 . . . . | 186 Steeplechase
 JUNIORS MISS Elizabeth R . . . . | Rd, Devon, PA
 | *19333-1229*

Wiegand MR & MRS Michael D (Valerie J Doran) Wheat'75.Nu'80.S.
☎ (516) 624-8714 . . 418 Centre Island Rd, Oyster Bay, NY *11771*

Wiehl MR & MRS Ernest A JR (Mary Lee Hewitt) | ☎ (203) 227-7818
Pqt.Ny.Cly.Y'45 ⚓. | 303 Harvest
 MR E Peter—at ☎ (860) 355-3815 | Commons, Westport,
2 Squash Hollow Rd, New Milford, CT *06776* . . | CT *06880*

Wiehl MR & MRS Richard V (Dana D Murphy) | ☎ (203) 255-2900
PineM'77.Pa'75 . . . . | 370 Sturges Rd,
 JUNIORS MR James D . . . . | Fairfield, CT *06430*

Wieler MR & MRS Scott A (Mary M Baily) Geo'79.BostColl'81.Pa'87
☎ (410) 323-6417 . . 811 St George's Rd, Baltimore, MD *21210*

Wiener MR Alexander L—W.Rv.Cw.Wt.Y'31
☎ (313) 886-7875 . . 17111 E Jefferson Av, Grosse Pointe, MI *48230*

Wierdsma MR Clark R . . see N N Solley

Wierdsma MISS Emily F . . see N N Solley

Wierdsma MR & MRS John R (Strandberg—Susan B | ☎ (516) 624-0160
Salant) Pr.Cly.Wms'55 . . . . | 23 Fieldstone Lane,
 MR A David Strandberg 3d—Duke'84. | Oyster Bay, NY
Mich'88—at ☎ (202) 462-1609 | *11771*
1824 California St NW, Washington, DC
20009 . . . . |
 MR Ethan S Vickery—at ☎ (714) 360-8031 |
33 Rambling Lane, Aliso Viejo, CA *92656* . . |

Wierzel MR & MRS Robert M (P Michele Sugg)
FlaSt'77.Bost'86.SoFla'79.Y'84
☎ (203) 481-3728 . . 14 Goodsell Point Rd, Branford, CT *06405*

Wiese MR & MRS William E (Mary L Chambers) | ☎ (314) 965-2310
Sth'35.Wis'38 . . . . | 711 N Taylor,
 MR William R—at 9520 Old Bonhomme Rd, | Kirkwood, MO
St Louis, MO *63132*. . . . . | *63122*

Wiesen MR Gavin B . . see MRS B A Brackenridge

Wietlisbach MR & MRS Bruce D (Binney H Connell) Penn'85.Gm.Xav'81
☎ (610) 688-3103 . . 730 Laurel Lane, Strafford, PA *19087*

Wietlisbach MISS Larissa Ester (Bruce D) . . . . Born at
Bryn Mawr, PA Jly 16'96

Wiggers MRS Thomas C (Helen Baker) . . of
☎ (513) 321-3698 . . 3536 Bayard Dv, Cincinnati, OH *45208*
☎ (941) 262-5024 . . 1466 Galleon Dv, Naples, FL *34102*

Wiggin MRS Morrill (Margaret Patterson) V'24.Cy.
865 Central Av, Needham, MA *02192*

Wiggin MR & MRS Rollin H JR (Whelpley—Emilie O'D Iselin)
Csn.Cly.H'45
☎ (203) 655-2106 . . 106 Pear Tree Point Rd, Darien, CT *06820*

Wiggins MR & MRS Charles (Janet Stone) H'36
☎ (508) 875-7249 . . 10 Auburn St, Framingham Center, MA *01701*

Wiggins MRS Grafton (Natalie Janvrin) . . . . | ☎ (860) 434-2587
 MISS Mary Janvrin . . . . | Homestead Circle,
 | Old Lyme, CT
 | *06371*

Wiggins MRS John (Jeanne Lee Sargeant)
☎ (207) 359-2283 . . Cold Brook Farm, Sargentville, ME *04673*

Wight MR & MRS Crocker (Frederica Sargent) Cy.Un.H'38
☎ (617) 277-9318 . . 415 Warren St, Brookline, MA *02146*

Wight MR Devereux Pinkus—Y.
☎ (212) 777-2526 . . 34 E 4 St, New York, NY *10003*

Wight MR & MRS Richard M (Mary H Wise) OState'52
☎ (904) 285-4238 . . 2745 Biarritz Court, Ponte Vedra Beach, FL *32082*

Wightman MR & MRS Orrin S 3d (Letitia A Stephens) Cy.Lc.B.Wms'63 . . . .
MR Orrin S 4th . . . .
☎ (314) 991-2031
32 Glen Eagles Dv,
St Louis, MO *63124*

Wigton MISS Barbara F—W'minster'81
205 Woodcrest Dv, Sewickley, PA *15143*

Wigton MR & MRS Robert W JR (Dixie J Good) Stan'45.Me.Pn.P'45
☎ (610) 525-2685 . . 911 Sorrel Lane, Box 831, Bryn Mawr, PA *19010*

Wikander MR & MRS Lawrence E (Ethel M Whitlow) AmU'37.Wms'37.Cl'39.Pa'49
☎ (413) 458-3888 . . 21 Cluett Dv, Williamstown, MA *01267*

Wike MR & MRS J Roffe 2d (Penelope Pryor) Ph.Me.Rd.Ac.P'48.Pa'50.Pa'55 . . . .
MISS Zara P . . . .
MR Timothy A . . . .
MR David A . . . .
MR Mark A P . . . .
of ☎ (610)647-1397
Toad Hall,
Twinbrook Rd,
Berwyn, PA *19312*
☎ (809)590-277209
"La Corniche"
Pointe Milou, 97098
St Barthélemy

Wikstrom MR & MRS Gresham (Stuart—Katherine F Burks)
☎ (334) 660-0263 . . 6025 Cedar Knot Court, Mobile, AL *36609*

Wilbanks MR & MRS Thomas A (Sandra G McKay) DU'76.Okla'73
☎ (303) 744-2580 . . 370 Humboldt St, Denver, CO *80218*

Wilberding MR & MRS Joseph C (Katherine Van Cortlandt) Bgt.Cda.Y.'34
☎ (914) 666-4947 . . 108 Guard Hill Rd, Mt Kisco, NY *10549*

Wilberding MR & MRS Stephen Van C (Ann S Spaulding) FlaSo'65.Au.Plg.Csn.Yn.Y'63.Cl'71
MISS Ashley McL-B . . . .
MR Augustus Van C—USA . . . .
MR Robert R . . . .
of ☎ (011-91-22)
493-6785
Ghia Mansion,
18 Carmichael Rd,
Bombay 400 026,
India
☎ (011-44-171)
730-0514
13 Sloane Court W,
London SW3 4TD,
England

Wilbor MR A Wells—H'30
☎ (612) 473-6862 . . 15225 Gleason Lake Dv, Plymouth, MN *55447*

Wilbur DR Andrew C—Stan'74.GeoW'78
☎ (312) 902-3226 . . 605 W Madison St, Tower 3, Apt 4403, Chicago, IL *60606*

Wilbur MRS Blake C (Mary C Sloan) Stan'22
☎ (415) 327-7779 . . 490 Kingsley Av, Palo Alto, CA *94301*

Wilbur MRS Brayton (Matilda G Baker) Bur.Fr. . . . .
MISS Lola J . . . .
☎ (415) 343-7558
809 Irwin Court,
Hillsborough, CA
94010

Wilbur MR & MRS Brayton JR (Judith Flood) Cal'63.Bhm.Pcu.Bur.Y'57.Stan'61 . . . .
MISS Claire B . . . .
MR Edward F . . . .
MR Michael D . . . .
of ☎ (415)579-1747
821 Irwin Dv,
Hillsborough, CA
94010
☎ (408) 624-2278
Camino & 13 Sts,
Carmel, CA *93921*

Wilbur MR & MRS Colburn S (Mary G Verburg) Cal'62.Stan'56.Stan'60
☎ (415) 327-6799 . . 571 Jefferson Dv, Palo Alto, CA *94303*

Wilbur MR & MRS E Packer 4th (Laura M Ferrier) Y'59.H'65 . . . .
MISS Gillian Elizabeth—Leh'94 . . . .
MR Andrew Packer—Leh'93 . . . .
☎ (203) 255-3318
648 Harbor Rd,
Southport, CT *06490*

Wilbur MR & MRS J Benjamin 4th (Cynthia A Cunning) Man'vl'81.U'77.Ford'82.Nu'89
157 Prospect Park W, Brooklyn, NY *11215*

Wilbur MR & MRS James B 3d (Margie A Mattmiller) Ky'47.Cl'54.Hn.Ky'48.Cl'51.Cl'54
☎ (802) 362-1525 . . "Gardener's Cottage" PO Box 376, Manchester, VT *05254*

Wilbur MR & MRS LeRoy A JR (Anne E Rogers) Gi.Cw.Rv.Ncd.JHop'53
☎ (410) 255-3757 . . Broadwater Way, Gibson Island, MD *21056*

Wilbur MR & MRS Peter D (Mary E Eastman) Pac'71.Stan'75.Ch'78
☎ (216) 765-8024 . . 29049 Harvard Rd, Orange, OH *44122*

Wilbur MRS Peter I S (Dole—Wickett—Jean E Dodge) Ncd.
☎ (415) 854-6549 . . 2140 Santa Cruz Av, Apt E204, Menlo Park, CA *94025*

Wilbur DR & MRS Richard S (Betty L Fannin) Stan'50.Stan'43.Stan'47.JM'90
MR Thomas S—Stan'79.Ch'84 . . . .
☎ (847) 234-1353
985 N Hawthorne
Place, Lake Forest,
IL *60045*

Wilcox MR & MRS Benjamin D W (Marion S Wallace) Yn.Y'67 . . . .
MR McClelland W—Van'94 . . . .
JUNIORS MR Benjamin G—at Harvard . . . .
2904 Ferndale Place,
Houston, TX *77098*

Wilcox DR & MRS Donald F (Sharon L King) Stan'59.Tcy.Y'53
☎ (415) 454-5540 . . PO Box 67, 3 Woodside Way, Ross, CA *94957*

Wilcox MRS F Samuel JR (Mary E Stine) Wil.Ncd. Stonegates 60, 4031 Kennett Pike, Greenville, DE *19807* Dec 30 . . ☎ (561) 278-3104 . . 3300 Polo Dv, Gulf Stream, FL *33483*

Wilcox MR G Jarvis G JR—Y'64 . . . .
MR Charles R—at 1555 Stewarts Corner Rd, Genoa, NY *13071* . . . .
☎ (516) 725-4012
334 Brickiln Rd,
PO Box 1388,
Bridgehampton, NY
11932

Wilcox MR Gordon Cumnock—Cw.Snc.Ne.Myf.
☎ (212) 348-0820 . . 400 E 88 St, New York, NY *10128*

Wilcox MR & MRS Herbert E (Elizabeth E Wilson) Csn.Y'30.Cl'34
☎ (203) 483-0777 . . 88 Notch Hill Rd, Apt 207, North Branford, CT *06471*

Wilcox MR & MRS Herbert B 3d (Catherine E Du Pasquier) U'62.H'69 . . . .
MISS Tanya E—at U of Toronto . . . .
MR Alexander D—Vt'94 . . . .
☎ (802) 372-5049
E Shore Ridge,
PO Box 66,
North Hero, VT
05474

Wilcox MISS Lisa A—Br'86
☎ (415) 885-2909 . . 2542 Polk St, San Francisco, CA *94109*

Wilcox MISS Lynn P—Cal'83
☎ (415) 583-3835 . . 2155 Buchanan St, Apt 9, San Francisco, CA *94115*

Wilcox MRS Ormonde B M (Smith—Barbara Cabell) Cly.Ncd.Cda.
☎ (804) 263-5877 . . ''Bon Aire'' 1843 Cabell Rd, Wingina, VA *24599*

Wilcox MR & MRS Ronald L (Jane W Stoddart) SUNY'77.DU'83
5100 S Franklin St, Littleton, CO *80121*

Wild MR & MRS Henry S (Anne O Russell) Y.'63 . . . | ☎ (212) 744-8884
MISS Anna . . . . | 444 E 82 St,
MR Wellesley . . . . | New York, NY *10028*

Wilde MRS Bertram M (Florence L Deal) Me.
Waverly Heights, 1400 Waverly Rd, Gladwyne, PA *19035*

Wilde MR & MRS H George (Marjorie L Field) | ☎ (413) 243-2676
Lx.USA'29.H'34 . . . . | ''High Lawn''
MR G William—at Residencias Tequendama, | Lenox, MA *01240*
Bogotá, DE, Colombia . . . . |

Wildenthal DR & MRS Kern (Margaret Dehlinger)
Rice'62.Ch'64.Tex'64.Camb'70
☎ (214) 648-2508 . . 4001 Hanover Av, Dallas, TX *75225*

Wilder MR Charlton M—W&L'58 . . . . | 535 Manhattan Dv,
MISS Katherine McK—at Duke . . . . | Apt 103, Boulder, CO *80303-4052*

Wilder MRS David (Coleman—Nancy Nye)
☎ (617) 267-0117 . . 790 Boylston St, Apt 20B, Boston, MA *02199*

Wilder MR Harris E . . . . Died Apr 4'94

Wilding-White MR Charles F B—Pn.Mit'42.Rens'59
☎ (202) 337-1004 . . 2801 New Mexico Av NW, Apt 521, Washington, DC *20007*

Wildman MR Peter L
☎ (310) 540-3478 . . 513 Av G, Apt A, Redondo Beach, CA *90277*

Wilds MR & MRS Charles M (Elizabeth Newman) | ☎ (203) 869-6981
Ws'41.Wms'40 . . . . | Belle Haven,
MISS Adrienne A (Kirkpatrick—Griffith— | 50 Byram Dv,
Adrienne A Wilds) Bost'73.Hawaii'77—at | Greenwich, CT
☎ (410) 719-0567 . . 31 Shady Nook Av, | *06830*
Catonsville, MD *21228* . . . . |

Wilds MR & MRS Peter G (Sara R Wetherill) Me.M. . | ☎ (561) 388-2514
MISS Jennifer K—DU'91.Me.—at | 10635 Fife Av,
☎ (201) 792-0154 . . 214 Park Av, Apt 5R, | Vero Beach, FL
Hoboken, NJ *07030* . . . . | *32963*
MISS Grayson W—Rol'94.Me.—at |
☎ (404) 875-1056 . . 794 Frederica St NE, Apt 3, |
Atlanta, GA *30306* . . . . |

Wilds MR Walter . . . . Died at
New York, NY Jun 14'96

Wilds MRS Walter (Bonnie Farber) Un.Ln.Rr.B.Plg.Cly.
☎ (212) 249-8383 . . 20 E 68 St, New York, NY *10021*

Wiles MR & MRS Christopher C (Elizabeth Lisa Gilman)
Mont'79.SFrSt'80.CalCoast'91 . . of
☎ (818) 888-5055 . . 23535 Windom St, West Hills, CA *91304-5359*
296 Seadrift Rd, Stinson Beach, CA *94970*

Wiles MR & MRS Ellis W (Natalie W Huston) | ☎ (011-49-711)
Pa'75.NMMI'70.ClCol'89 . . . . | 85-33-88
JUNIORS MR Geoffrey H . . . . | Heidlochstrasse 159, B4, 70376 Stuttgart, Germany

Wiles MR & MRS Stephen C (Judith S Holmes) . . . . | ☎ (818) 445-1168
JUNIORS MR John S . . . . | 1001 Monte Verde
JUNIORS MR Brian E . . . . | St, Arcadia, CA *91007*

Wiley MR & MRS George S (Sally Pattishall) Y'57 . . | ☎ (847) 432-1350
MR Michael G—Nw'84 . . . . | 175 Linden Park Place, Highland Park, IL *60035*

Wiley MR & MRS Hugh (LADY Serena Lumley) . . . . . | ☎ (804) 589-3475
MR Justin H . . . . | ''Oak Hill''
MR Marcus T . . . . | Palmyra, VA *22963*
MR Peter A . . . . |

Wiley MR & MRS Hugh C (Judith C Riker) Bow'84.Bow'82
☎ (203) 966-6496 . . 173 Soundview Rd, New Canaan, CT *06840*

Wiley MR & MRS Laurence D (Douthit—Susan H | ☎ (609) 921-1960
Weist) Dc.Cda.Knox'63.Nw'65.Cl'78 . . . . | 65 Farrand Rd,
JUNIORS MISS Laura H . . . . | Princeton, NJ
JUNIORS MR Christopher W . . . . | *08540-6770*

Wiley MR & MRS Richard M (Zimmerman— | ☎ (909) 676-8292
Margaret A Palmer) Col'73.ArizSt'67 . . . . | 31430 Corte
MISS Abigail P Zimmerman . . . . | Montiel, Temecula,
JUNIORS MR Casey K Zimmerman . . . . | CA *92592*

Wilgis MR & MRS Herbert E JR (Jane W VandeGrift) GeoW'59.P'57 . . of
☎ (410) 433-7329 . . 1106 Bellemore Rd, Baltimore, MD *21210*
☎ (302) 227-2479 . . 35 Pine Reach, Henlopen Acres, DE *19971*

Wilgis MR & MRS Herbert E 3d (Linda J Mason) Skd'81.P'83
☎ (206) 524-6817 . . 326 NE 59 St, Seattle, WA *98105*

Wilgis MASTER Herbert Elijah 4th (Herbert E 3d) . . . . Born at
Seattle, WA Apr 11'95

Wilhelm MR & MRS Frederick C S JR (Norma A Carlson) Hob'56
☎ (904) 437-6688 . . 62 Villa Lago Lane, Ormond Beach, FL *32174*

Wilhelm MR & MRS J Robert (Laura M Elmer) Rdc'34.Me.Rc.Aht'34
☎ (610) MU8-8149 . . 37 Ridgewood Rd, Radnor, PA *19087*

Wilhelm MR Mark R—LoyMmt'90
☎ (310) 796-6977 . . 2912 Manhattan Av, Manhattan Beach, CA *90266*

Wilich MR & MRS Frank J JR (Clare A Steers) | ☎ (603) 436-2842
NH'76.Dth'75 . . . . | 107 Piscataqua St,
JUNIORS MISS Alexandra C . . . . | PO Box 710, New Castle, NH *03854*

Wilkens MR & MRS Robert G JR (Esther McC | ☎ (203) 656-0687
Boynton) Va'65.Rcn.Pn.Rut'66 . . . . | 6 Wilson Ridge Rd,
MR Robert T . . . . | Darien, CT *06820*

Wilkes MR & MRS E Harry (Elizabeth S Lippincott)
☎ (310) 544-0358 . . 30124 Avenida de Calma, Rancho Palos Verdes, CA *90275*

Wilkey MR & MRS Richard L (Susan H Locke) Wis'59 . . . . | of ☎ (414)367-3348 5112 N H'way 83, Hartland, WI *53029*
MR Richard E . . . . | ☎ (414) 434-3623
MR David A . . . . | "The Farm" 2096 Riverside Dv, Green Bay, WI *54303*
MR Daniel S—at U of Wisc . . . . |

Wilkie MR Angus McN—Y.'80 . . of
☎ (212) 988-4412 . . 66 E 83 St, New York, NY *10028*
☎ (860) 526-1202 . . "Bentwood" 2 Selden Rd, Hadlyme, CT *06439*
Wilkie MR Austin T—H.'84
☎ (212) 737-6917 . . 151 E 80 St, New York, NY *10021*
Wilkie MRS D Jones (Dorothea W Jones) V'32
☎ (212) 535-7426 . . 120 E 79 St, New York, NY *10021*
Wilkie DR George H—Ri.Wms'53.H'57
☎ (212) 861-1010 . . 40 E 62 St, New York, NY *10021*
Wilkie MRS John (Morrow—Margot Loines) Rdc'34.Eyc.Cs.H.
☎ (212) 288-0912 . . 50 E 77 St, Apt 15B, New York, NY *10021*
Wilkie MR & MRS John McN (Grover—Eugenia M Van Horn) Hn.H'60 . . . . | ☎ (970) 728-0139 126 W Colorado Av, PO Box 1723, Telluride, CO *81435*
MISS Allison Van H . . . . |
JUNIORS MISS Christina W—at Groton . . . . |
JUNIORS MISS Jennifer R—at Cate . . . . |
Wilkie MR John McN JR—V'90.Tul'94
☎ (212) 628-1624 . . 35 E 85 St, Apt 11AN, New York, NY *10028*
Wilkie MR & MRS Peter L (Elizabeth McK Smith) Pa'69.Cl'68.Wis'69
☎ (914) 473-0624 . . 75 S Randolph Av, Poughkeepsie, NY *12601*
Wilking DR & MRS Leo F J (Virginia C Nichols) Csn.H'41.Cl'44
☎ (302) 378-9286 . . Box 508, 109 High St, Odessa, DE *19730*
Wilking MR & MRS Leo F J 3d (Martha K Leclerc) Geo'82.H'74.Ford'78
☎ (701) 293-7026 . . 1115 S 8 St, Fargo, ND *58103*
Wilking REV DR & MRS Spencer Van B (Louisa Dennis) DU'71.Cl'70.CDSP'73 . . . . | ☎ (508) 369-6064 35 Robin Wood Rd, Concord, MA *01742*
MISS Nina D . . . . |
MISS Anna V W . . . . |
JUNIORS MR Spencer Van B JR . . . . |
Wilkins MR & MRS Fraser Bryan (Katherine M Grayson) Y'77.Cvc.Mt.Pa'73 . . of
☎ (202) 966-5789 . . 4332 Garfield St NW, Washington, DC *20007*
☎ (540) 592-3608 . . Blue Ridge Farm, 1858 Blue Ridge Farm Rd, Upperville, VA *20185*
Wilkins MR Henry Hepburn—Bhm.Ore'35
☎ (415) 453-8267 . . PO Box 1084, 110 Winding Way, Ross, CA *94957*
Wilkinson MR Duncan B E—Br'91
6 Columbus Square, Boston, MA *02116*
Wilkinson MR & MRS George A (Marisue Fairchild) Miss'60.Miss'59
☎ (601) 956-1534 . . 210 Brae Burn Dv, Jackson, MS *39211*
Wilkinson MR & MRS Gordon C (Bette McCrum) Mich'67.Pep'77 . . . . | ☎ (770) 434-4403 3890 Brandy Station Court NW, Atlanta, GA *30339*
MISS Rica K—at ☎ (714) 770-8860 24535 Los Alisos St, Apt 299, Laguna Hills, CA *92653* . . . . |
MISS Holly D—Ga'85—at 589 E Northridge Rd, Dunwoody, GA *30338* . . . . |
MISS Vallé A . . . . |
Wilkinson MR Kent K JR—Tufts'89 . . see MRS N B Ponvert

Wilkinson MR & MRS Kirk C (Fyler—Carolyn R Gunzer) C.Csn.Pars'31
☎ (508) 349-3682 . . "Oakwood" PO Box 1405, Wellfleet, MA *02667*
Wilkinson MRS Lawrence (Josephine Colgate)
☎ (609) 426-6260 . . Meadow Lakes 7-07U, Hightstown, NJ *08520*
Wilkinson MR & MRS Leland (Ruth E VanDemark) V'66.H'69.Conn'76.C.Csn.H'66.H'69.Y'75 . . . . | ☎ (847) 869-7282 1127 Asbury Av, Evanston, IL *60202*
MISS Anne M—H'89.Cal'95—at Harvard . . . . . . |
MISS Caroline C—V'92—at Albany, NY . . . . . . |
Wilkinson MRS Robert A (Spangler—Sandra H Dodd) . . . . | ☎ (704) 556-0185 2916 Heathstead Place, Charlotte, NC *28210*
JUNIORS MISS Nancy H . . . . |
Wilkinson MR Robert A—My.Bab'64
☎ (617) 246-0662 . . Oakfield Farm, PO Box 36, Hamilton, MA *01936*
Wilkinson MR & MRS Warren S (Mireille N De Bary) H'41
☎ (313) 882-8530 . . 2 Woodland Place, Grosse Pointe, MI *48230*
Wilkinson-Gould MRS Josephine (Gould—Josephine Diana Wilkinson)
☎ (441) 293-7536 . . "Coral Ledge" 10 Cedarberry Dv, Bailey's Bay CR 04, Bermuda
Will MR & MRS Jeffrey Scott (Colleen E Gorman)
☎ (602) 998-2374 . . 9322 N Ironwood Dv, Paradise Valley, AZ *85253*
Willard MR & MRS Daniel 3d (Linda R Zeller) Swth'58.Okla'83.Y'49.Y'50.Mit'54 . . of
☎ (301) 530-0408 . . 9401 Rockville Pike, Bethesda, MD *20814*
"Arbacia" 45 Forest Lane, Mollusk, VA *22517*
Willard MRS De Voe H (Martha L Daniels)
☎ (301) 587-5538 . . 1515 Red Oak Dv, Silver Spring, MD *20910*
Willard MRS Elizabeth Chew (Richardson—Elizabeth M Chew) Cly.
☎ (212) 861-3405 . . 254 E 68 St, New York, NY *10021*
Willard MR John O—Pitt'66
☎ (215) 732-8814 . . 326 S 19 St, Apt 5A, Philadelphia, PA *19103*
Willard MR & MRS Le Baron S JR (Lawson—Alice Kistler) Gv.BtP.So.Evg.Elk.Md.Plg.Mv.Myf.Dar.Cda . . of
☎ (410) 532-7490 . . 404 Brightwood Club Dv, Lutherville, MD *21093*
☎ (561) 835-0293 . . 129 Woodbridge Rd, Palm Beach, FL *33480*
Willard MISS Sarah (Devens—Sarah McK Willard)
18 Peatfield St, Ipswich, MA *01938*
Willard MR & MRS Thomson C (Gillian M York) Elk.Mt.Md.Md'67 . . . . | ☎ (410) 377-2697 6502 Montrose Av, Baltimore, MD *21212*
MISS Gillian G . . . . |
JUNIORS MR LeBaron S . . . . |
Willard LT COL (RET) William B JR—USA.Cvc.Vmi'60. TennTech'70.Utah'75 . . of
☎ (011-599-4) 62498 . . Willard's of Saba, Windwardside, Saba, Netherlands Antilles
Box R23, Garmisch, Unit 24514, APO AE, *09053*
Willard MR William Bradley (Florence Fatio Keys) Cvc.Mt.Ct.Sl.Ncd.Cda.
☎ (202) 333-5774 . . 2700 Virginia Av NW, Washington, DC *20037*
Willauer MR Whiting R—Cvc.P'53
☎ (202) 686-7118 . . 4201 Cathedral Av NW, Apt 701W, Washington, DC *20016*
Willauer MR & MRS Whiting R JR (Marjorie S Arundel)
31 North St, Katonah, NY *10536*
Willauer MR William A . . see MRS J M Arnold
Willcox CAPT F Havemeyer—USAF.Miss'77
☎ (607) 627-6247 . . "Aquidneck House" Willcox Hill Rd, Smyrna, NY *13464*

Willcox MR & MRS J Keating (Robin T Kneeland) ☎ (508) 468-3869
Cal'83.My.Bost'79.Bost'83.Bost'91 ⚓ . . . . . . 3 Longmeadow
MISS Barbara G—at RI Sch of Design . . . . Way, Hamilton, MA
01936

Willcox MR & MRS J Taney JR (Catherine E ☎ (610) 525-5613
Goldschmidt) StJos'50.Temp'58. . . . . 800 Harriton Rd,
MISS Catherine E—at 232 Dudley Av, Narberth, Bryn Mawr, PA
PA *19072* *19010*
MR Bryan C—at ''Ivy Mills'' 109 Ivy Mills Rd,
Glen Mills, PA *19342* . . . .

Willcox MISS Louisa L . . see MRS F A Lewis
Willcox MR & MRS Mark JR (Jill St C Forbes) ☎ (610) GL9-3165
Ph.Pa'34 . . . . 226 Ivy Mills Rd,
MR William F . . . . Glen Mills, PA
19342

Willcox MR & MRS Mark 3d (Anne M Moore)
☎ (610) 358-5369 . . Wynd Blough Farm, 266 Ivy Mills Rd, Glen Mills,
PA *19342*

Willcox MR & MRS Thomas O (Therese F of ☎ (610)644-7454
Cavanaugh) Pa'51 . . . . Box 505,
MISS Leslie A—VillaN'89 . . . . 4 Old Barn Lane,
Malvern, PA *19355*
☎ (609) 967-3739
74 E 12 St,
Avalon, NJ *08202*

Willcox DR & MRS Thomas O JR (M Courtenay Smith)
Grove'81.Pa'81.Duke'83.Pa'87
☎ (610) 964-7642 . . 364 Sentry Lane, Wayne, PA *19087*

Willcox MR & MRS Wayne C (Cintra E Eglin) P'80.P'75.Pa'82
☎ (504) 393-7356 . . 22 English Turn Dv, New Orleans, LA *70131*

Willett MRS Cleveland (Victoria T Cleveland) . . . . . ☎ (212) 873-3855
MR Scott V—Denis'91—at ☎ (212) 744-1004 100 W 87 St,
215 E 81 St, New York, NY *10028* . . . . New York, NY
10024

Willett MR Herbert L III—P'41
☎ (508) 548-2404 . . 399 Quissett Av, Falmouth, MA *02540-1307*

Willett MR & MRS J Jackson 3d (Ryan—Elizabeth ☎ (410) 832-0078
Van N Willard) Unn.Plg.Mv.Y'53 . . . . 906 E Wind Rd,
JUNIORS MISS Elizabeth Le B . . . . Baltimore, MD
21204

Willett MR J Jackson 4th—W&L'86.Nu'94
☎ (212) 535-8617 . . 114 E 84 St, New York, NY *10028*

Willett MR Thornton W—H'50.NYTech'78 . . . . ☎ (718) 855-6460
MISS Georgia R—at ☎ (718) 237-1585 206 Kane St,
142 Hoyt St, Brooklyn, NY *11217* . . . . Brooklyn, NY *11231*
MISS Tamosin R—SUNY'88.CUNY'95 . . . .
MR Benjamin C . . . .

Willetts MR & MRS (HON) David L (HON Sarah Butterfield) Ox'78
21 Ashchurch Grove, London W12, England

Williams COL (RET) & MRS A Sidney JR (B Louise Felton)
USA.Me.Rc.Ph.Fw.Cw.Cc.Rv.Cda.Pa'42.Wis'49
Dunwoody Village CH107, 3500 West Chester Pike, Newtown Square,
PA *19073*

Williams MR & MRS Alan D (Rosina F Rue) Br'74.C.Yn.Y'49
☎ (201) 963-3408 . . 560 Palisade Av, Jersey City, NJ *07307*

Williams MR & MRS Albert D JR (Gary—Joyce McC ☎ (847) 234-5127
Hadley) On.Rc.Cho.Sr.Wa.Cnt.Y'55 . . . . 120 Alden Lane,
MISS Leslie L—LakeF'91—at ☎ (503) 452-7670 Lake Forest, IL
6902 W 52 Av, Portland, OR *97219* *60045*
Jan 1 . .
☎ (561) 790-6946
Polo Club Rd,
Apt A101,
West Palm Beach,
FL *33414*

Williams MR Alexander H 4th . . see P S Ness
Williams MR & MRS Alexander J (Sue Seifert) ☎ (513) 294-2516
Han'65.Mvh.Bz.Mor.Mariet'66 . . . . 1800 Ridgeway Rd,
JUNIORS MR Alexander J JR . . . . Dayton, OH *45419*
JUNIORS MR Daniel V . . . .
JUNIORS MR Robert S . . . .

Williams MR & MRS Alexander Scott (Katherine C Kennedy) Me.
see Dilatory Domiciles

Williams MR & MRS Andrew M (Edith R Derby) Ncd.P'38.H'41
☎ (206) 463-2702 . . Mileta Farm, 24349 Dockton Rd SW, Vashon,
WA *98070-7905*

Williams MISS Anne A—Carl'78
48 Saddle Shop Rd, Ringoes, NJ *08551*

Williams MISS Ashley . . see P S Ness
Williams MR & MRS Ben A JR (Jessie A Marshall) Cy.Sm.Dth'38
☎ (617) 524-3234 . . 98 Rockwood St, Jamaica Plain, MA *02130*

Williams MR & MRS Benjamin J—Ec.Myc.Ty'58 . . . . ☎ (508) 922-4398
MISS Hope A—Ty'87 52 Valley St,
MR Ralph B 2d—Ty'90 . . . . Beverly Farms, MA
01915

Williams MR & MRS Benjamin J JR (Elizabeth W Pierce)
Colby'82.Un.Bow'82
☎ (617) 259-0277 . . 32 Beaver Pond Rd, Lincoln, MA *01773*

Williams MRS Burdick F (Barbara M Taylor) Stan'42
☎ (213) 851-8108 . . 2033 Hercules Dv, Los Angeles, CA *90046*

Williams MR C Dickerman—C.Csn.Yn.Y'22
☎ (203) 248-7414 . . 200 Leeder Hill Dv, Hamden, CT *06517*

Williams MR & MRS Carter D (Virginia F Sharp)
☎ (410) 252-6874 . . 15 Castlebar Court, Timonium, MD *21093*

Williams MR Charles J 4th—David'73
☎ (904) 384-8620 . . 4661 Ortega Island Dv, Jacksonville, FL *32210*

Williams MR & MRS Charles R (Amy L Atwell) ☎ (203) 656-1001
Sth'76.Rcn.Msq.Va'74 . . . . 201 Leroy Av,
JUNIORS MISS Christina A . . . . Darien, CT *06820*

Williams MR & MRS Christopher Sewall (Sarah C Cecil) Br'77.Vt'78
☎ (207) 761-0458 . . 28 Winter St, Portland, ME *04102*

Williams MR & MRS Claude K (Rouse—Mary Elting Church) P'45
☎ (805) 969-0233 . . 640 Ashley Rd, Montecito, CA *93108*

Williams MR & MRS Daniel H III (Sue B McGrattan) ☎ (716) 873-5441
Wh'lck'65.Cr'70.Cy.St.Bf.Dth'66.Cr'69 . . . . . . 175 Middlesex Rd,
MISS Jennifer B . . . . Buffalo, NY *14216*
MR Daniel H IV . . . .

Williams MR & MRS Daniel S (Deborah O Owen) Hob'64
☎ (802) 525-4532 . . RR 1, Box 159A, Barton, VT *05822*

Williams MR & MRS Dave H (Reba J White)
StMarys'54.Duke'58.H.'70.CUNY'88.K.Ct.Cos.Dar. Tex'56.H.'61
☎ (212) 969-1177 . . 510 Park Av, New York, NY *10022*

Williams MRS David B (Edith C Huntington) Sth'44.Un.Cs.
☏ (212) 249-4580 . . 1035 Fifth Av, New York, NY *10028*
Jan 1 . . ☏ (246) 423-5063 . . ''Williams Cottage'' Castle Close,
St Philip, Barbados

Williams DR & MRS David E (Martha R Royster) | 1528 Garrison Place,
Colby'63.Jef'67 . . . . | San Diego, CA
MISS Holly B—Cal'92 . . . . | *92106*
MR David A—Cal'94 . . . . |

Williams MRS David E 3d (Jane Torchiana) . . . . . . | 18 Bennett St,
MISS Marion C—at ☏ (617) 924-4517 | Manchester, MA
68 Spring St, Watertown, MA *02172* . . . . | *01944*

Williams MR & MRS David H (Elizabeth Steinert) BMr'47.Cr'49
☏ (301) 585-9558 . . 9 Devon Rd, Silver Spring, MD *20910*

Williams MR & MRS David R JR (Baxter—Kerr—Anne Wright)
Rc.Cv.Uncl.Rr.Mds.Ri.Y.'43 . . of
☏ (520) 287-8995 . . Oak Bar Ranch, Rte 82, HCR 22, Nogales,
AZ *85621*
☏ (212) PL1-0100 . . 447 E 52 St, New York, NY *10022*

Williams MR & MRS Davidson D (Barbara M Raymond) Ihy.JHop'76.Vt'80
☏ (203) 367-5576 . . 140 Grovers Av, Black Rock, CT *06605*

Williams MRS Donald R (Elizabeth P Winston)
☏ (508) 228-4670 . . 86 N Liberty St, Nantucket, MA *02554*

Williams MR & MRS Douglas (Priscilla M de Forest)
Un.C.Lm.Snc.Cly.Dc.Cda.Y.'40 . . of
☏ (516) 692-7462 . . PO Box 242, Cold Spring Harbor, NY *11724*
☏ (212) 288-4712 . . 116 E 66 St, New York, NY *10021*

Williams MR & MRS Duane N (Ellen McL Scull) Muhl'50
☏ (941) 454-7283 . . 3408 Sundial Court, Ft Myers, FL *33908*

Williams MRS Edward W (E Priscilla Hakes) Myf.
☏ (716) 672-8030 . . Birchwood Dv, Apt E2, Fredonia, NY *14063*

Williams MRS Ellis T (Daphne Reynolds) Stph'39.Md'41
☏ (610) 388-1602 . . 214 Crosslands Dv, Kennett Square,
PA *19348-2021*

Williams MR & MRS Ernest G (Cecil L Butler) Swb'47.Ala'38
☏ (205) 553-8740 . . 156 The Highlands, Tuscaloosa, AL *35404*

Williams MR & MRS Eugene F (Evelyn D | ☏ (314) 993-1551
Niedringhaus) Cy.Lc.Nd.Mds.Y'45 . . . . | 701 Barnes Rd,
MR Edward W—at 2450 Union St, Apt 301, | St Louis, MO *63124*
San Francisco, CA *94123* . . . . |

Williams MR & MRS Eugene F 3d (Jacqueline D Russell)
Un.Ln.Mb.Mds.Cly.
☏ (212) 570-2272 . . 66 E 79 St, New York, NY *10021*

Williams MR & MRS Francis H (Susan B Martin) | ☏ (212) 737-9206
Cyb. . . . . | 175 E 70 St,
MR Francis H JR—StLaw'93—at | New York, NY
☏ (212) 717-4046 . . 326 E 65 St, New York, NY | *10021-5109*
10021 . . . . |

Williams MR & MRS Franklin H (Emily D Wallace) Pc.Cda.
☏ (215) 283-7375 . . 1407 Foulkeways, Sumneytown Pike, Gwynedd,
PA *19436*

Williams MRS George P 3d (Mary G Humphreys) | ☏ (215) 247-1967
Pc.Ac. . . . . | 539 W Moreland
MISS Elizabeth G—Pa'88.Pc.Ac.—at | Av, Philadelphia,
2031 Locust St, Philadelphia, PA *19103* . . . . . . | PA *19118*

Williams MR & MRS George W (Katherine W | ☏ (816) 361-0691
Kennedy) Wheat'43.Br'40 . . . . | 6417 Jefferson St,
MISS Leslie H . . . . | Kansas City, MO
MR Winthrop S . . . . | *64113*
MR George W JR . . . . |

Williams MR Gordon Page—C.Cos.Y'31.Camb'33
☏ (301) 925-7386 . . 10450 Lottsford Rd, Apt 105, Mitchellville,
MD *20721-2734*

Williams MR & MRS Hanson L (Alison T Forrest) Colg'89.Colg'90
☏ (847) 853-8174 . . 135 Prairie Av, Wilmette, IL *60091*

Williams MR Henry C—Y'40 . . . . | ☏ (914) 234-6931
MR H Martyn—Geo'73 . . . . | RFD 1, PO Box
| 622, Guard Hill Rd,
| Bedford, NY *10506*

Williams MR & MRS Holden B (Fordyce L Staempfli) Vt'73.Myf.Br'64
☏ (508) 852-0476 . . 68 Clark St, Worcester, MA *01606*

Williams DR & MRS Howard C (Marian L Vejvoda)
Bost'76.H'76.Nu'80 ⍜
☏ (516) 669-1103 . . PO Box 406, West Islip, NY *11795*

Williams MR & MRS Hoyt H (Judith A George)
☏ (716) 634-5238 . . 1332 Cleveland Dv, Cheektowaga, NY *14225*

Williams MRS Hoyt I (Mildred H Harris) . . . . | ☏ (518) 459-4985
MISS Bonnie H . . . . | 4 Marriner Av,
| Albany, NY *12205*

Williams MR & MRS Hugo A Y (Natalie Wolcott) H'85.Cly.CourtArt'87
☏ (011-44-171) 727-5817 . . 24 E Westbourne Gardens, London
W2 5PU, England

Williams MR & MRS Ian R D (Debora A Wornom) | ☏ (540) 837-1192
Rich'73.Mt.Cc.Roan'69.Rich'74. . . . . | ''Priskilly''
JUNIORS MISS Anne McC—at Kent . . . . | Rte 1, Box 28A,
JUNIORS MR Ashton B D—at Kent. . . . . | White Post, VA
| *22663*

Williams MRS Ichabod Thomas (Eda M Dunstan) V'29.Cly.Ncd . . .of
☏ (941) 676-2286 . . Mountain Lake, Lake Wales, FL *33859-0832*
☏ (518) 325-3846 . . PO Box 245, Texas Hill Rd, Hillsdale, NY *12529*

Williams MR J Harlan JR—Md.Gv. | ☏ (410) 584-2833
MISS Lela Ingram . . . . | Old Orchard Farm,
| Falls Rd, Butler,
| MD *21023-0086*

Williams VERY REV (DR) J Lawrence B—Chi.Unn.Mt.An.
Cc.Cw.Va'36 . . of
☏ (540) 687-8090 . . ''Huntland'' 35955 Huntland Farm Rd, Middleburg,
VA *20117*
☏ (561) 659-2257 . . 334 Chilean Av, Palm Beach, FL *33480*

Williams MR & MRS J Peter 3d (Laura W Oliver) Ph.Rb.P.'35.H'40
☏ (610) 356-1901 . . 6041 Goshen Rd, Newtown Square, PA *19073*

Williams MR & MRS J Randall (Elizabeth Z Kirkbride) Wms'34
☏ (508) 896-5450 . . West Way, Box 127, Brewster, MA *02631*

Williams MISS Joanne B . . see B T Gosling JR

Williams MR & MRS John C (Helen G Gilbert) | ☏ (847) 835-0216
V'55.Wes'51.Y'54 . . . . | 486 Greenleaf Av,
MISS Sarah M—Y'88 . . . . | Glencoe, IL *60022*

Williams MR & MRS John C (Patricia O'Connell) Fr.Col'57 . . . . ☎ (415) 751-7272
MISS Lorna . . . . 17 Seventeenth Av,
MISS Samantha—at ☎ (707) 938-9278 San Francisco, CA
19205—7 St E, Sonoma, CA 95476 94121
MR Douglas P—Ariz'85

Williams MRS John G (Phyllis A Gerry) Rdc'39.Gm.Me.
☎ (610) 642-9074 . . 831 Black Rock Rd, Gladwyne, PA 19035

Williams DR & MRS John G JR (Lucille A Allen) H'63
☎ (207) 236-8118 . . 9 Arey Av, Box 771, Camden, ME 04843

Williams MR & MRS John M (Joan Freeman)
Pr.S.P'48 ⚓ . . . . ☎ (516) 922-4472
MISS Maris S—Colg'82—at ☎ (212) 935-3167 "South Slope"
301 E 62 St, New York, NY 10021 . . . . . . 515 Centre Island
MR Roderick C—B'gton'81—at RR 1, Box 543, Rd, Oyster Bay, NY
Woodstock, VT 05091 11771

Williams MR & MRS John P (Margaret A Agamenoni) Cal'77.Clare'78
☎ (818) 309-1391 . . 416 Alabama St, San Gabriel, CA 91775

Williams MR John P JR—Bz.Qc.Bhm.Tcy.P'63.Cin'66
229 Hastings St, Cincinnati, OH 45219

Williams MR & MRS John W (Holly A Flickinger) Bow'87.Purd'87.Cr'81
☎ (704) 274-9159 . . 8 White Oak Rd, Asheville, NC 28803

Williams MR & MRS Keith H (Connie B Urbaniak)
☎ (716) 837-2715 . . 67 Kendale Rd, Buffalo, NY 14215

Williams MRS Lewis C (Lydia F Emmet) Kt.Un.Cv.Csn.
☎ (216) 449-5087 . . 5150 Three Village Dv, Lyndhurst, OH 44124

Williams MR & MRS Lloyd E JR (M Anne Miller) Ill'56.Ih.Y'56
☎ (847) 251-5803 . . 714 Forest, Wilmette, IL 60091

Williams MISS Louise B . . see F F Staniford JR

Williams DR & MRS M Lee (Brune—Katherine H see
Ryland) Elk.Mv.Cc.Cw.Rv.Va'47 . . . . Dilatory Domiciles
MR Phillip L—HampSydney'89 . . . .

Williams MISS Marie F—Stan'78
☎ (310) 474-4360 . . 7816 Oceanus Dv, Los Angeles, CA 90046

Williams MISS Marion
☎ (617) 449-7966 . . 865 Central Av, Apt E405, Needham, MA 02192

Williams MISS Martha W—Sth'76
☎ (818) 796-4614 . . 27 Oak Knoll Gardens Dv, Pasadena, CA 91106

Williams MR & MRS Matthews (Camilla F Thompson) Cts.Me.
☎ (803) 525-1424 . . 400 Craven St, Beaufort, SC 29902

Williams MISS Maude A—Rich'69.Cda.
☎ (703) 527-6166 . . 121 N Columbus St, Arlington, VA 22203

Williams DR & MRS McKim (F Jane Dildy)
Cs.H'55.Duke'59 . . . . ☎ (757) 595-6962
MR McKim JR—W&M'88 . . . . 201 Riverside Dv,
Newport News, VA
23606

Williams MRS Moses (Mary B Holden) . . . . Died at
Boca Grande, FL Jun 9'96

Williams MRS Murat Willis (Joan Cunningham) Mt.Sl.
☎ (804) 980-9365 . . 250 Pantops Mountain Rd, Charlottesville,
VA 22901

Williams JUNIORS MR Nicholas C . . see R D Melen

Williams MR & MRS Pat T (Olivia A Atwood) Ala'59.Dar.Aub'57
☎ (334) 263-2863 . . 1442 Midlane Court, Montgomery, AL 36106

Williams MR Paul W—B.Lic.BtP.So.Evg.Plg.
Coa.Cc.Fw.Cw.Rv.Myf.Hn.H'25
☎ (561) 622-8234 . . 12445 Plantation Lane, North Palm Beach,
FL 33408

Williams MASTER Peter Forrest (Hanson L) . . . . Born Jun 16'96

Williams MR & MRS Quincy N (Nancy A Gillen)
MtH'54.Au.Me.Ds.H'53.Pa'57 . . . . ☎ (610) 896-5966
MR Quincy G—WashColl'84 . . . . 240 Booth Lane,
Haverford, PA
19041-1717

Williams MRS R Norris 2d (Frances Sue W Gillmore) Au.Me.Ac.
☎ (610) 353-3967 . . Dunwoody Village CH8, 3500 West Chester Pike,
Newtown Square, PA 19073

Williams MRS Ralph B (Margaret Creighton) Cy.Chi.Ncd.
☎ (617) 275-1560 . . 302 Winthrop Terr, Bedford, MA 01730-1281

Williams MR & MRS Richard D (Mary H Kongsgaard) Col'72.H'69
☎ (707) 257-0438 . . 4345 E Third Av, Napa, CA 94559

Williams MR Richard H 3d . . . . Died at
Ossining, NY Jly 8'96

Williams MRS Richard H 3d (Dorothy D Downes) Cc.
☎ (212) YU8-5659 . . 157 E 81 St, New York, NY 10028

Williams MR & MRS Richard N 3d (Suzanne de Z ☎ (610) MU8-5314
Moffly) Me.Ds. . . . . 337 Oak Terr,
MR Richard N 4th—at ☎ (610) 539-3547 St Davids, PA
721 N Ridge Dv, Norristown, PA 19403 19087

Williams MR Richard P JR—H'77 . . of
☎ (202) 483-7558 . . 2220—20 St NW, Apt 46, Washington, DC 20009
☎ (703) 777-1353 . . "Little Oatlands" Rte 2, Box 365, Leesburg,
VA 20176

Williams MRS Robert Hugh (Alice N Tuckerman) Sl.Cda.
☎ (202) 337-1230 . . 3900 Watson Place NW, Apt 7HB, Washington,
DC 20016

Williams MR Robert W—Va'81 . . see H Loomis

Williams MR & MRS Robert W JR (Rosetta M Adams)
MichSt'48.NewarkSt'59.Y'47.Nu'58 ⚓
☎ (941) 482-8255 . . 14708 Triple Eagle Court, Ft Myers, FL 33912

Williams MR & MRS Roderick O (M Dorothea Culver) Ncd.Y'34
☎ (203) 966-3769 . . 125A Heritage Hill Rd, New Canaan, CT 06840

Williams MR & MRS Roger JR (Carolyn J Pierce) Y'31
☎ (860) 535-1070 . . 19 L'Hirondelle Lane, PO Box 31, Stonington,
CT 06378

Williams MRS Rosamond K (Rosamond R Kuehn)
V'57.Cy. . . . . ☎ (617) 891-4847
MISS Katherine W—Colby'84—at 111 Merriam St,
173 Bay State Rd, Apt 4, Boston, MA 02215 . . . Weston, MA 02193
MR Charles D—Skd'86 . . . .

Williams MR & MRS Rufus M G (Sheila Janney)
Gchr'86.Elk.Md.Va'55 . . of
☎ (410) 526-4880 . . Locust Hill Farm, 3012 Butler Rd, Glyndon,
MD 21071
☎ (941) 676-3184 . . Mountain Lake, Lake Wales, FL 33853

Williams JUNIORS MR Samuel A F . . see R D Melen

Williams MR & MRS Samuel D (Susan D Welch) Un.B.Plg.Snc.Cly.Dar.H'59
☎ (212) 570-6860 . . 160 E 65 St, New York, NY 10021

Williams MR & MRS Samuel M Felton (Sienna— ☎ (520) 577-0763
Cheryl E Collins) SanJ'78.Cc.Stan'74.Stan'76 . . 2915 E Cerrada Los
JUNIORS MR Samuel A F . . . . Palitos, Tucson, AZ
85718

Williams MR Samuel P—San.Y'35
☎ (203) 264-9088 . . 576 Main St N, Southbury, CT *06488*

Williams MR & MRS Sean O'C (Bari A Kelleher) Col'85.Col'86
☎ (415) 457-5973 . . 58 Winship Av, Ross, CA *94957-0374*

Williams MR & MRS Staunton JR (Barbara R Sayres)	☎ (203) TO9-9198
Sth'60.Cl'78.Yn.Y'58.Cl'62	184 Parsonage Rd,
MISS Jennifer H	Greenwich, CT
MR Timothy W C	*06830*

Williams MR & MRS Stephen M (Charlotte T McLaughlin) P'84.P.'81
☎ (212) 874-3108 . . 15 W 75 St, Apt 9B, New York, NY *10023*

Williams MR Stuart H
☎ (603) 878-1218 . . RFD 1, Box 34, Wilton, NH *03086*

Williams MR & MRS Sydney M 3d (Caroline D	☎ (860) 434-0781
Elliott) NH'63	15 Smith Neck Rd,
MISS Caroline C—WashColl'90	Old Lyme, CT
MR Sydney M 4th—Dth'89	*06371*
MR Edward S—Buck'93	

Williams MRS Thomas (Nadia Iungerich) Pitt'34
☎ (617) 546-2166 . . ''Old Garrison House'' 188 Granite St, Box 2337, Pigeon Cove, MA *01966*

Williams MR & MRS Thomas A (Anne L Bell)	of ☎ (914)967-2470
Ny.Y'59.Y'62 ⛵	20 Ridgewood Dv,
MR David D—Cr'93—*see Dilatory Domiciles* . .	Rye, NY *10580*
	☎ (802) 297-1693
	108 W Round Rd,
	Stratton Mountain,
	VT *05155*

Williams MR & MRS Thomas J C (Maude B Anderson)
JHop'35.Cda.Dar.JHop'34
4800 Fillmore Av, Apt 919, Alexandria, VA *22311*

Williams MR & MRS Thomas L (Jennifer L Greiwe) Regis'77.Geo'79
☎ (513) 871-6368 . . 20 Grandin Lane, Cincinnati, OH *45208*

Williams MR & MRS W Grant (Betty J Tarlton) Sth'45.Cy.Lc.Ariz'45 . . of
☎ (314) 993-0723 . . 9465 Clayton Rd, St Louis, MO *63124*
3145 Polo Dv, Gulf Stream, FL *33483*
☎ (970) 476-3555 . . 302 Mill Creek Circle, Vail, CO *81657*

Williams MR & MRS Walworth B (Mary Louise French) V'42.Y'41 . . of
☎ (617) 729-4291 . . 15 Ledgewood Rd, Winchester, MA *01890*
☎ (603) 329-5078 . . ''Tall Timbers'' Governors Island, PO Box 97, Hampstead, NH *03841*

Williams MR & MRS Wilbur F (Janis Nott)
☎ (602) 955-6952 . . 2260 E Bethany Home Rd, Phoenix, AZ *85016*

Williams MRS William D (Andrews—Henrietta Towers)
☎ (805) 969-8079 . . Casa Dorinda 65, 300 Hot Springs Rd, Montecito, CA *93108*

Williams MRS William George JR (Doris Ann Witter)	Married at
	Montecito, CA
Everett MR Hulbert H	Apr 13'96

Williams MR & MRS William L (H Dana Linn)	☎ (610) 688-2804
V'49.Me.M.P'48	410 Fox Chapel
MR Peter D—P'82.Ore'88—at ☎ (303) 455-2987	Lane, Radnor, PA
4941 Newton St, Denver, CO *80221*	*19087*

Williams-Ness MR James D . . see P S Ness

Williamson MR Alexander F C—Sfg.CalPoly'85
☎ (206) 324-8312 . . 917 Lake Washington Blvd S, Seattle, WA *98144*

Williamson DR Brandt H—Mid'88.Va'92 . . see MRS E F McSweeney

Williamson MRS Burke (Elise H Clow) Cho.Cnt.Fy.Cda.Ncd.
☎ (704) 274-2642 . . 18 Cedarcliff Rd, Biltmore Forest, Asheville, NC *28803*

Williamson MISS Charlotte M—WmSth'78
☎ (415) 621-7293 . . 24 Danvers St, San Francisco, CA *94144*

Williamson MR & MRS Craig R (Helen W Johnson) P'77.P'76
☎ (203) 655-8646 . . 15 Red Rose Circle, Darien, CT *06820*

Williamson MR & MRS D Stephen C (Hanley—Alexandra Bowes)
Cal'81.Tex'87.Cal'80
☎ (415) 776-6647 . . 3662 Clay St, San Francisco, CA *94115*

Williamson MR & MRS Edwin D (M Kathe Gates)	☎ (202) 337-1717
Duke'69.Rcn.Mt.Csn.So'61.Nu'64	2805 P St NW,
MISS Sara E.	Washington, DC
LT Samuel G—USMCR.Duke'93	*20007*
MR Edwin D JR	

Williamson MISS Eleanor H . . see MRS E F McSweeney

Williamson MR & MRS Frederick B 3d (Katherine Stryker) P'41
☎ (215) 598-3367 . . 1265 Eagle Rd, New Hope, PA *18938*

Williamson MRS Harold L JR (Jacqueline L Lanérès)	☎ (212) 535-3833
Un.Fic.Cly.	150 E 73 St,
MR Peter L—Ty'78	New York, NY
	10021

Williamson MR & MRS James G JR (Carole R McCann) Emory'66
☎ (501) 474-0511 . . 1009 Azure Hills W, Van Buren, AR *72956*

Williamson MR & MRS John F (Emily G Damon)
☎ (610) 644-4729 . . 465 Darby-Paoli Rd, Paoli, PA *19301*

Williamson MISS Julia N—LakeF'84
☎ (847) 735-1876 . . 1510 N Green Bay Rd, Lake Forest, IL *60045*

Williamson MRS Maclean (Marion M Colt) B'gton'42
☎ (802) 457-1185 . . ''Sunny Side Up'' RD 1, Box 546, Woodstock, VT *05091*

Williamson MR & MRS Norman B (Victoria W Andrew)
Scripps'58.Vh.Clare'59 ⛵
1550 Orlando Rd, Pasadena, CA *91106*

Williamson MR & MRS Peter (Sandra E Shupp) BMr'54.P'57
☎ (301) 791-6506 . . 25 Laurel St, Hagerstown, MD *21742*

Williamson MR & MRS Samuel H (Janet M Macomber)
Wes'85.Bost'90.Les'93.Ore'82.H'89
☎ (503) 222-0053 . . 2134 SW Edgewood Rd, Portland, OR *97201*

Williamson MISS Susan G . . see C du F Ravenel

Williamson MR Thomas B JR . . see C du F Ravenel

Williamson MR & MRS William J JR (Ewart—Evelyn F Brennan)
D'ville'56.SUNY'65.St.G.Pa'58
☎ (716) 881-5780 . . 130 Oakland Place, Buffalo, NY *14222*

Willim MR & MRS John S JR (Eva L Carlson)	☎ (352) 429-2575
MR John S 3d—at 5834 E Anderson Rd,	''Fox Point''
Groveland, FL *34736*	5832 E Anderson
	Rd, Groveland, FL
	34736

Willis MISS Amanda Janet (Richard S) . . . . Born at
Willow Grove, PA Dec 21'95

Willis MRS B Murray (Bilodeau—Beatrice L Murray) Chi.
☎ (617) 934-5074 . . Crescent St, Box 1252, Duxbury, MA *02331*

Willis MR & MRS Christopher H (Sara N Bobbitt) Char'ton'81.Drew'82
☎ (212) 722-1461 . . 115 E 86 St, New York, NY *10028*

Willis JUDGE David J—JHop'73.SCal'76.Houst'92
☎ (713) 621-3100 . . 3110 Stoney Brook Dv, Houston, TX *77063*

Willis MRS Emily K (Emily H Knapp) . . . .
MR Edward S 2d . . . .
☎ (718) 789-8041
925 Union St,
Brooklyn, NY *11215*

Willis MR & MRS Gregory T (Lois M Cross) Denis'86.Bost'83
☎ (203) 324-1446 . . 1 Devon Rd, Darien, CT *06820*

Willis MRS Gwendolyn H (Gwendolyn Handy) Chr.Dc.Cda.Ht.
☎ (212) 722-5539 . . 25 E 86 St, New York, NY *10028*

Willis MRS Harold B JR (Artemis G Pazianos)
Ws'51.Btn.Sb.Hn.H.
MISS Artemis B—Ws'88 . . . .
MR Gardiner F—HWSth'92 . . . .
☎ (617) 899-5919
Box 226,
39 Concord Rd,
Weston, MA *02193*

Willis MR & MRS Philip L (Beatrice M C Neuman de Vegvar) Drew'76
☎ (718) 549-6523 . . 5275 Sycamore Av, Bronx, NY *10471*

Willis MR & MRS Rhett N (Elizabeth W Mercer) Ga'78.Cc.Ncd.WashColl'78
☎ (912) 927-6973 . . 32 Rockwell Av S, Savannah, GA *31419*

Willis MR & MRS Richard S (Bowers—Cynthia Gardner) Ne'82.Bost'78
☎ (215) 657-4725 . . "Squirrel Run" 1636 Twining Rd, Willow Grove, PA *19090-4229*

Willis MR & MRS William H JR (Pauline S Smith) Rcn.Yn.Y'49 . . of
☎ (203) 869-3778 . . 55 Zaccheus Mead Lane, Greenwich, CT *06831*
☎ (207) 276-3682 . . "Edgecliff" Seal Harbor, ME *04675*

Willits MR & MRS Christopher N (Sarah E Edwards)
Pa'69.Cry.Nich'68 ⚓
MISS Alexandra C—at ☎ (803) 577-7442
2½ Gibbes St, Charleston, SC *29401* . . . .
MISS Amanda B—at Episcopal . . . .
"Oaklands Cottage"
28271 Widgeon
Terr, Easton, MD
21601

Willits MR & MRS W Cooper (Marjorie D Huber) Cry.Bab'37
☎ (610) 644-2680 . . "Spring Bank" 179 Grubb Rd, PO Box 971, Paoli, PA *19301*

Willkie MRS Alléon de Varcourt (CTSSE Michèle Alléon de Varcourt)
ArtetMetier'72 . . of
☎ (404) 351-1772 . . 30 Collier Rd NW, Apt 7, Atlanta, GA *30309*
☎ (011-33-99) 89-11-79 . . "Le Vieux Vaulerault"
35350 St Méloir-des-Ondes, France

Willkie MRS H Frederick (Helen Fowler Hall) . . . . Died Mch 5'96

Willkie MR Hall Francis—Ind'74 . . of
☎ (212) 362-7643 . . 525 West End Av, Apt 12C, New York, NY *10024*
☎ (607) 832-4330 . . Chestnut Hill Farm, Pink St Rd, Bovina, NY *13740*

Willkie MISS Julia F—SL'70.Ind'74.Cly.
☎ (212) 472-2679 . . 179 E 79 St, New York, NY *10021*

Willmann MISS Lyndell S—Nw'68.Tufts'69.Suff'78
☎ (617) 484-1273 . . 165 Clifton St, Belmont, MA *02178*

Willock MR & MRS George J 3d (Katharine H Young) Fcg. . . . .
MISS Kimberly K—at ☎ (212) 595-7333
124 W 80 St, New York, NY *10024* . . . .
☎ (412) 963-8145
105 Millstone Dv,
Pittsburgh, PA
15238

Willoughby MR & MRS Alan T (Roberta W Milne) Me.Ncd.Hav'51.Pa'65 . . . .
MR Alan T JR—at ☎ (503) 331-1377
2843 NE 13 St, Portland, OR *97212* . . . .
☎ (610) 527-0924
"Owl's Nest"
1626 Spring Mill
Rd, Gladwyne, PA
19035

Willoughby MR & MRS David W (Lucile C Gildersleeve) Denis'90.Denis'90
☎ (617) 739-6386 . . 22 Perry St, Apt 3, Brookline, MA *02146*

Willoughby MR & MRS Rodney E (Marie Jo Johnston) Rice'44.Bur.Pcu.Tcy.Tul'45.H'47 . . .
DR Rodney E JR—JHop'81 . . . .
☎ (415) 348-1132
55 New Place Rd,
Hillsborough, CA
94010

Wills MRS Elizabeth G S (Shaw—Trott—Elizabeth S Gilmor) Ri.Pr.Cly.Ht.
MISS Elizabeth R Shaw—Pa'92 . . . .
☎ (212) 355-7214
470 Park Av,
New York, NY
10022

Wills MR & MRS William Ridley 2d (Irene W Jackson) CtCol'60.Van'56 . . . .
DR Morgan J—Van'96 . . . .
MR Thomas W
☎ (615) 791-4955
3200 Del Rio Pike,
Franklin, TN *37069*

Wills MASTER William Ridley 4th (g—William Ridley Wills 2d) . . . . . Born at Nashville, TN Aug 31'95

Willson MR Stuart van V JR—Yn.Y'53.H'55
☎ (609) 896-3329 . . 50 Carter Rd, Box 2020, Princeton, NJ *08543*

Wilmanns MRS Frederick A (Berne—Martha L Hauck) . . . . Died at Milwaukee, WI Aug 11'91

Wilmer MR & MRS John Whittingham (Jean R Smith) V'41.P'38
☎ (561) 278-1961 . . 1115 NW Fifth Av, Delray Beach, FL *33444*

Wilmer REV DR & MRS Richard H JR (Sarah King) Pg.Cvc.Cc.Y'39.Ox'48
☎ (412) 682-5901 . . 5023 Frew St, Apt 5C, Pittsburgh, PA *15213*

Wilmer MR & MRS Richard H 4th (Wendy Norris) Cc.Y'65 . . . .
MR R Derenne . . . .
JUNIORS MR Christopher K . . . .
☎ (703) 533-9675
2218 N Kensington
St, Arlington, VA
22205

Wilmer MR & MRS William Holland 2d (Lucy W Parrish) Md.Cw.Cc.StJ.Mv.Y'52.H'55 . . . .
MISS Lucy W P—Ncd.Dc. . . . .
MR William Holland 3d—Cw.Cc.WashColl'89 . .
☎ (410) 329-6286
"Little Oxmead"
White Hall, MD
21161

Wilmerding MRS Helen C (Heap—Abeel—Helen C Wilmerding) Rut'90
MISS Angela D Heap—HWSth'93 . . . .
MISS Jane A Heap—Skd'93.LondEc'95—at
6 Carlisle Mansion, Carlisle Place, London SW1, England
☎ (908) 359-2571
"John Honeyman
House" 1008 Canal
Rd, RD 1, Princeton,
NJ *08540*

Wilmerding MR Henry A JR—Rc.Pr.Ln.Ng.Mb.
Colby'61.Cl'63 . . . .
MISS Kathryn H . . . .
MISS Patsy R . . . .
MISS Daphne H . . . .
☎ (516) 671-8107
Piping Rock Rd,
Locust Valley, NY
11560

Wilmerding MR & MRS Henry A 3d (Christina L Horn)
see Dilatory Domiciles

Wilmerding MR & MRS James W W (Marsha A Mullikin) Rcn.Nf.LIU'69 . . . .
MR Andrew C—at U of Portland . . . .
MR Alexander W—at Tulane . . . .
JUNIORS MR Nicholas H . . . .
☎ (207) 276-5345
"Cove Cottage"
PO Box 534,
Cove End Rd,
Northeast Harbor,
ME *04662*

Wilmerding MR John—C.Pn.H'60
☎ (609) 497-1968 . . 154 Library Place, Princeton, NJ *08540-3018*

Wilmerding MRS John C (Polk—Katharine H Salvage)
☎ (516) 922-7294 . . 168 Cove Rd, Oyster Bay, NY *11771*

Wilmerding MR Lucius JR—Rcn.C.Ri.Cos.P'27.Ox'29
☎ (609) 924-0925 . . 27 Rosedale Rd, Princeton, NJ *08540*

Wilmerding MR & MRS Lucius 3d (Adela S Bartholomew) Sth'55.K.P'52 . . . . | ☎ (609) 921-8266 / 9 Russell Rd, Princeton, NJ *08540-6729*
MISS Gay—Sth'79 . . . .
MR Murray—Leh'80 . . . .
MR Austin—Ty'83 . . . .
Wilmerding MRS M Hodges (Marilyn C Hodges) Pr.Ln.Ng.Mb.Cly.
see Dilatory Domiciles
Wilmerding MR & MRS Patrick R (Elsie Storm) Nf. ⚓ . . . . | ☎ (617) 232-4555 / 35 Crafts Rd, Chestnut Hill, MA *02167-1823*
MISS Eliza R—at Bowdoin . . . .
MR Patrick S . . . .
MR Michael R . . . .
Wilmsen MRS Joseph L (Wood—J Virginia Coleman) Ac.Sg.
☎ (215) CH7-4130 . . ''Pheasant Hill'' 8848 Montgomery Av, Philadelphia, PA *19118*
Wilsey MR & MRS Alfred S (Traina—Diane D Buchanan) Pcu. . . . . | of ☎ (415)922-2875 / 2590 Jackson St, San Francisco, CA *94115*
MR Trevor D Traina—at ☎ (415) 563-3027 / 2938 Clay St, San Francisco, CA *94115* . . . . .
MR Todd B Traina . . . . | ☎ (707) 963-9407 / Rutherford River Ranch, 999 Rutherford Rd, Rutherford, CA *94573*
Wilshire MR & MRS W Murray (Beresford—Kingsbury—Charlotte E Meyer) Err.Eyc.Cly.P'22 . . of
☎ (941) 924-7593 . . Lake Pointe Woods 153, 7979 S Tamiami Trail, Sarasota, FL *34231*
☎ (508) 627-4670 . . ''Compass House'' 115 Pease's Point Way, Box 803, Edgartown, MA *02539*
Wilson MISS Abigail Noelle (g—Frederick E Wilson) . . . . Born at Red Bank, NJ Dec 11'95
Wilson MRS Albert S JR (Polly Lord Galey) SL'41.Yn. . . . . | of ☎ (908)899-3270 / 754 Clayton Av, Bay Head, NJ *08742*
MISS Mary Blair—at 2240 Church Rd, Toms River, NJ *08753* . . . . | ☎ (809) 469-2848 / ''Windfall'' Golden Rock Estate, Nevis
Wilson MR & MRS Alec MacLaine (Gilmour—Helen R Tower) MaryMt'77
14 Independence Av, Lake Oswego, OR *97035*
Wilson MISS Amy . . see B W Drew JR
Wilson MR & MRS Andrew B (Beth A Boundy) Stan'68 . . . . | ☎ (314) 821-0719 / 445 N Taylor Av, St Louis, MO *63122*
MISS Curtis Elizabeth
Wilson MR & MRS Andrew Bruce (Marion P Ferriss) Bost'69.WatLuth'72.Tor'73 . . . . | ☎ (847) 441-7335 / 1155 Chatfield Rd, Winnetka, IL *60093*
MISS Kathryn B . . . .
MR Andrew P . . . .
MR Clifford C . . . .
JUNIORS MISS Rosalie P . . . .
Wilson MISS Ann M—Wheat'53.Mds.
☎ (212) BU8-2208 . . 151 E 83 St, New York, NY *10028*

Wilson MRS Anna O'D (Harvey—Anna S O'Donovan) NotreD'78.MdArt'81.Nyc. . . . . | ☎ (410) 821-8944 / 2004 Ridgecrest Court, Baltimore, MD *21204*
MISS Louisa R—HWSth'89.NCar'96 . . . .
MISS Emily O'D—Skd'91 . . . .
MRS A Charlotte Harvey (Rienhoff—A Charlotte Harvey) . . . .
Wilson MRS Anne Sears (Anne Ware Sears) Rdc'53 . . . . | ☎ (508) 371-0047 / 100 Newbury Court, Apt 202, Concord, MA *01742*
MISS Erica Sears—at 504 Nashua St, Box 717, Milford, NH *03055* . . . .
Wilson MR & MRS Anthony M W (Dolly L Smith) Ne'92.Ne'92
☎ (617) 279-7738 . . 181 Central St, Stoneham, MA *02180*
Wilson MR Benjamin V M . . . . | ☎ (610) 688-4133 / 309 Orchard Way, St Davids, PA *19087*
MISS Tyler V—at Travianna Farm, Box 217, Rte 1, Check, VA *24072* . . . .
Wilson MR & MRS Charles F JR (Winifred H Horn) Cvc.Va'39
601 Laurel Av, Apt 804, San Mateo, CA *94401*
Wilson MR Charles H (Tolles—Ysabel Angulo) Cly.
4521 PGA Blvd, Apt 109, Palm Beach Gardens, FL *33418*
Wilson MR Charles S . . see B W Drew JR
Wilson MR Charles W—Ober'59.H'67
☎ (717) 766-1876 . . 400 Park Hills Dv, Mechanicsburg, PA *17055*
Wilson MR & MRS Claude A JR (Brown—Janet M Bowden) Man'vl'84.NCar'50.Nu'57 . . . . | ☎ (912) 598-0657 / 15 Shellworth Crossing, Savannah, GA *31411*
MISS Elizabeth B—Ken'89—at ☎ (718) 834-6068 . . 141 Smith St, Brooklyn, NY *11201* . . . .
MR Marshall C—Roch'92—at New York, NY . .
Wilson MR & MRS David K (Bell—Pauline F Ridley) Van'54.Ln.Mt.Van'41
☎ (615) 383-4183 . . 4343 Glen Eden Dv, Nashville, TN *37205*
Wilson MR & MRS David S (Elizabeth Burden) VillaN'67 . . . . | 802 Mayflower Court, Middletown, NJ *07748*
MISS Meredith B . . . .
JUNIORS MISS Dana E . . . .
Wilson CDR (RET) & MRS Dennis K (Barbara D Downey) Wells'59.USN'58
☎ (703) 522-7753 . . 4141 Henderson Rd N, Apt 1211, Arlington, VA *22203-2424*
Wilson MISS Dorothy
1028 Fairway Rd, Santa Barbara, CA *93108*
Wilson MISS Dorothy D—Pg. . . . . | ☎ (412) 621-0650 / 700 S Aiken Av, Pittsburgh, PA *15232-1409*
MISS Dorothy V—Ty'89.Pg. . . . .
Wilson MR & MRS Edward Beale (Barbara C Ladd) Mit'49 . . . . | ☎ (603) 383-9441 / Thorn Mountain Rd, Jackson, NH *03846*
MR Thomas T—Syr'80—at 38 Harvard Av, Apt 2, Brookline, MA *02146* . . . .
Wilson MR Edward C—JHop'76.JHop'78
☎ (202) 337-4065 . . 4501 MacArthur Blvd NW, Washington, DC *20007*
Wilson MRS Edward G (Jane H Johnson) Chr.Mt.Csn.
Noble Horizons, 17 Cobble Rd, Salisbury, CT *06068*
Wilson MR & MRS Edward Hamilton JR (Cynthia G Smith) Ala'73.Ala'73.Cumb'77 . . . . | ☎ (334) 263-1447 / 2228 Country Club Dv, Montgomery, AL *36106*
JUNIORS MISS Louise B . . . .
JUNIORS MISS Cynthia H . . . .

Wilson MR Eric L—Y'55.Pa'60
☎ (803) 642-2852 . . 554 Banks Mill Rd, Aiken, SC *29801*

Wilson MRS Francis W (Elizabeth T Horrocks)
Sth'58.Chi.Ncd. . . . . | ☎ (508) 369-1810
MISS Elizabeth Janney—Y'87.H'92—at | 422 Elm St,
239 Commonwealth Av, Apt 63, Boston, MA | Concord, MA *01742*
02116 . . . .
MR John T—Ty'85.Duke'90—at
810 Farmington Av, West Hartford, CT *06119* .

Wilson MR & MRS Frederick E (Nancy L Caulton)
Co.Myf.Ds. ⚓ . . . . | ☎ (610) 644-0649
MR Richard C—Co.Myf.Ds.Dick'90—at | 745 Conestoga Rd,
☎ (540) 280-0747 . . 9101 Barrick St, Fairfax, | Berwyn, PA *19312*
VA *22031* . . . .

Wilson MR & MRS G Ross (Mary Jane L Browne)
MooreArt'73.Tor'67.Pa'73
☎ (215) 625-8601 . . 508 Delancey St, Philadelphia, PA *19106*

Wilson MR & MRS (REV) Gene M (Anne McG Warrington) Ty'75.Cin'67
☎ (513) 561-5641 . . 7730 Tecumseh Trail, Cincinnati, OH *45243*

Wilson MR & MRS Gordon (April Donald) Cvc.Mt.P'56
☎ (202) 363-1862 . . 2913 Glover Dv NW, Washington, DC *20016*

Wilson MR & MRS Gordon F JR (Peggy Henican) Barat'59.Tul'54
☎ (504) 891-2953 . . 2415 Coliseum St, New Orleans, LA *20130*

Wilson MR & MRS (DR) Grover Gray (Marguerite H Trover)
Duke'76.David'73
☎ (910) 721-2519 . . 2816 Fieldwood Court, Winston-Salem, NC *27106*

Wilson MR & MRS Harvard E (Lawson—Elida Debevoise) Sth'57.Dth'58
☎ (360) 943-3071 . . 6330 Northill Dv SW, Olympia, WA *98512-2037*

Wilson MR & MRS Henry T (Alison G Griscom)
H.'89.Cl'95.Rc.Srb.Cly.Va'81.Va'86
☎ (212) 861-6794 . . 151 E 83 St, Apt 8A, New York, NY *10028*

Wilson MR & MRS Holden JR (Sally E Sampson) | of ☎ (513)961-1939
Yh.Cw.Miami'52 | 1901 Madison Rd,
MISS Caroline P—at 1236 Eads Rd, Crittenden, | Cincinnati, OH
KY *41030* . . . . | *45206*
MISS Laura W—at 3521 Pembroke Av, | "Seven Oaks"
Cincinnati, OH *45226* . . . . | Yeamans Hall Club,
MR Holden 3d . . . . | PO Box 9455,
| Charleston, SC
| *29410*

Wilson MRS J Brayton (Jeremy C Brayton) Ws'57 . . | ☎ (216) 932-5383
MR Charles B—USMC.Ken'90 . . . . | 2188 Coventry Rd,
MISS Clarke C (Pierce—Clarke C Wilson) | Cleveland Heights,
Wheat'84 . . . . | OH *44118*

Wilson MRS J M Putnam (Putnam—Jean Merrill | ☎ (561) 659-6931
Flint) Cda. | 326 Australian Av,
MISS Carley P Putnam . . . . | Palm Beach, FL
MR James E Putnam . . . . | *33480*

Wilson MR James A
Box 4516, RFD, Long Grove, IL *60047*

Wilson MR & MRS James Lawrence JR (M Margaret Klingman)
Conv'26.V'26
☎ (601) 759-3376 . . Terrene Rd, Rosedale, MS *38769*

Wilson MRS James Stevens (Alexandra E Collie) | ☎ (410) 560-0834
Swb'76 . . . . | 1520 Applecroft
JUNIORS MISS Jennifer W . . . . | Lane, Hunt Valley,
| MD *21030*

Wilson MR John A—Pn.P'50 . . . . | ☎ (602) 483-8617
MISS Heather C—Wheat'84 . . . . | 7604 E Clinton St,
MR Bradley A—Van'88 . . . . | Scottsdale, AZ
MR John J—Van'90 . . . . | *85260*

Wilson MRS John B (Rose W Page)
☎ (919) 489-8222 . . 2527 Sevier St, Durham, NC *27705*

Wilson MR & MRS John C (Mona B Dick) | ☎ (415) 771-3863
BMr'70.StJos'68 | 2368 Broadway St,
JUNIORS MR Angus M B—at Princeton . . . . | San Francisco, CA
JUNIORS MR Joshua E B—at Berkshire . . . . | *94115*

Wilson MR & MRS John C JR (Kristin M Buck) | ☎ (415) 668-1074
Sfg.Cal'59 | 156 Commonwealth
MISS Mary K . . . . | Av, San Francisco,
MR John C 3d . . . . | CA *94118*
MR Christian C . . . .

Wilson MR John R—Cv.Pn.P'49.Md'54
☎ (216) 442-5810 . . 6800 Mayfield Rd, Apt 709, Cleveland, OH *44124*

Wilson MRS John R M (Lucy W Dominick) Ncd.
Villa Campana Apt 203, 6653 Carondelet Dv E, Tucson, AZ *85710*

Wilson MRS Judith G (Hinckley—Judith C Gonczo) Man'vl'59
☎ (505) 660-2295 . . 509 Webber St, Santa Fe, NM *87501*

Wilson MR & MRS Justin P (Barbara Engelhardt) Heid'76.Stan'67
see Dilatory Domiciles

Wilson MRS Kathryn L (Cuevas—Kathryn T Loud) Nu'68.Rby.
☎ (212) 421-7050 . . 340 E 57 St, New York, NY *10022*

Wilson MR & MRS Kendrick R (Van Cott—Katharine F Gordon)
Ln.Ny.Cda.Dth'36
☎ (561) 231-4945 . . 1925 S Ocean Dv, Vero Beach, FL *32963*

Wilson MR & MRS Kendrick R 3d (Linda K | ☎ (914) 234-3628
Babcock) Pars'72.Bgt.Ny.Ln.Dth'72 . . . . | 161 Cantitoe Rd,
JUNIORS MISS Jane D . . . . | Katonah, NY *10536*
JUNIORS MISS Olivia T . . . .

Wilson MR & MRS L Raycroft (Kitchens—M Leah | ☎ (847) 234-2038
Hume) Tex'75.San.Ty'58 | 140 W Old Elm Rd,
MISS Beth A—Miami'86—at U of Ore . . . . | Box 335,
MISS Deborah L—Wis'87 . . . . | Lake Forest, IL
MISS Deanna L—Wis'87 . . . . | *60045*

Wilson MR & MRS Laurence P (Maureen T | ☎ (415) 347-8454
Nicodemus) P'75.Lawr'66.Nw'75 | 63 De Sabla Rd,
JUNIORS MISS Catherine F—at Phillips Exeter . . . | San Mateo, CA
JUNIORS MR Blake T—at Phillips Exeter . . . . | *94402*

Wilson MRS Lois S (Lois H Shelton)
☎ (610) 527-2261 . . 539 Maison Place, Bryn Mawr, PA *19010*

Wilson MR & MRS Marvel JR (Sara J Bingham) | ☎ (610) 566-1222
Syr'53.Rv.Sar.StA.Ac.Ncd.Dar. . . . . | 212 Hempstead
MISS Elizabeth J . . . . | Lane, Wallingford,
MISS Sara Jane G . . . . | PA *19086*
MR Garrett M . . . .

Wilson MISS Mary Faith
☎ (202) 342-3685 . . 2512 Q St NW, Washington, DC *20007*

Wilson MR & MRS Michael S (Anna C Burack)
Dth'79.NH'83.Wms'75.Calgary'78
☎ (303) 674-1271 . . 6361 Arapahoe Dv, Evergreen, CO *80439*

Wilson MR & MRS Milton JR (Barbara Hixon) Bur.Pcu.Fr . . .of
☎ (415) 921-6031 . . 2540 Green St, San Francisco, CA *94123*
☎ (916) 645-3644 . . PO Box 157, Lincoln, CA *95648*

Wilson MR & MRS Milton 3d (Margaret M Cimino)
SFrColl'71.Bhm.Bur.Stan'66.SCal'72 ⚓
  ☎ (415) 456-8622 . . 5 Morrison Rd, PO Box 1451, Ross, CA *94957*

Wilson MISS Nancy H—Wells'68 . . see G P Bassett 4th

Wilson JUNIORS MR Nathaniel L . . see R H Stone

Wilson MRS Orme JR (Mildred E Dunn) Cvc.Cly.Sl.
  ☎ (540) 837-1127 . . Westfield Farm, White Post, VA *22663*

Wilson MR & MRS Orme 3d (Mary G Hilliard) Ws'75.Rcn.H'75
  ☎ (502) 897-6267 . . 2600 Top Hill Rd, Louisville, KY *40206*

Wilson MRS P Perkins (Penelope Perkins) Rd.Ph.Cs.
  ☎ (610) 644-9070 . . ''The Wolery'' 1371 N Valley Rd, Malvern, PA *19355*

Wilson MR & MRS Page (Bacon—Marjorie K Goodyear) Stan'43
  ☎ (805) 969-1006 . . 545 Valley Club Rd, Santa Barbara, CA *93108*

Wilson MISS Pamela S—Les'66
  ☎ (787) 887-8250 . . HCI Buzon 13055, Rio Grande, Puerto Rico *00745*

Wilson MR & MRS Percy H JR (Virginia Raycroft) Sap.Pa'22.Y'28
  ☎ (941) 966-2336 . . 4004 Casey Key Rd, Nokomis, FL *34275*

Wilson MRS Perkins (Mary E Mackall) BMr'55 . . . . | ☎ (804) 288-7353
MR William M—W&L'84 . . . . | 204 Tuckahoe Blvd, Richmond, VA *23226-2227*

Wilson MR Peter H (Milton JR) . . . . Married at Lincoln, CA
Sanborn MISS Loren . . . . Jly 1'95

Wilson MR Philip D . . see B W Drew JR

Wilson MR & MRS R Clifford 3d (Stacy C McCrocklin)
Geo'81.Un.P.'80.Cl'86
  ☎ (212) 861-0052 . . 935 Park Av, New York, NY *10028*

Wilson MR R Thornton . . . . Died at
Newport, RI Jun 5'96

Wilson MRS R Thornton (Durot—Sonia Lowis) K.Srb.B.Nrr.Plg.
  ☎ (401) 846-1404 . . ''South Wind'' Jeffrey Rd, Newport, RI *02840*

Wilson MR Ramsay (Renée G Thébaud) Ny.Y'45
  ☎ (860) 434-9447 . . 18 Riverview Dv, Box 409, Old Lyme, CT *06371*

Wilson MR & MRS Ransom C (Stephanie Young) Stan'78.Un.Cly.P'78.Cl'81
  ☎ (212) 722-0656 . . 1050 Park Av, New York, NY *10028-1031*

Wilson MRS Robert C (Bessie A Larkin) Chr.Cly.
  ☎ (212) 861-7012 . . 876 Park Av, New York, NY *10021*

Wilson MR & MRS Robert Letchworth (Comstock—Sarah Y Buck)
St.G.Ham'31.Buf'34 . . of
  ☎ (716) 885-4545 . . 1088 Delaware Av, Apt 11-I, Buffalo, NY *14209*
  ☎ (716) 941-3536 . . ''Lintemar-Ho'' 10001 Emerling Rd, Boston, NY *14025*

Wilson MR & MRS Russell P (Marcy E Anthony) Rich'82.P'82.Va'88
  ☎ (301) 654-7711 . . 4114 Aspen St, Chevy Chase, MD *20815*

Wilson MR Scott C . . see B W Drew JR

Wilson MR Stephen A . . . . Died at
Manchester, VT May 28'96

Wilson MRS Stephen A (Smith—Campbell—Elizabeth C de Cravioto) Dar.Yn.
  ☎ (802) 362-2684 . . ''Point O'View'' PO Box 454, Manchester, VT *05254*

Wilson MISS Susan P . . see H W Harrison

Wilson MR & MRS Terrence G (Virginia C Belcher) . | of ☎ (707)252-0778
MISS Lily E—Cal'95 . . . . | 1360 Wooden Valley Rd, Napa, CA *94558*
MISS Erin B—at U of Cal Santa Cruz . . . . |
JUNIORS MISS Silvie W . . . . | ☎ (808) 248-8640
JUNIORS MR David H . . . . | 1550 Uakea Rd, Hana, Maui, HI *96713*

Wilson DR & MRS Thomas A S (Mary K Quinn)
RMWmn'56.W&L'56.Ala'60
  ☎ (205) 871-4524 . . 2860 Southwood Rd, Birmingham, AL *35223*

Wilson MR & MRS V Mellor (Allen—Virginia H Mellor)
  ☎ (803) 796-2633 . . 4305 Exum Dv, West Columbia, SC *29169*

Wilson MRS W Wesley (Anita G Brown) Ac.
  ☎ (310) 832-3122 . . 4345 Via Frascati, Rancho Palos Verdes, CA *90275*

Wilson MRS William A (Stewart—Joan Merritt)
  ☎ (352) 735-0867 . . 715 N Helen St, Mt Dora, FL *32757*

Wilson MR & MRS William B (Weitzman—Cramer—Joan M Erickson)
Stan'64.Me.Rd.Wms'43 . . of
  ☎ (610) 525-0777 . . 812 Potts Lane, Bryn Mawr, PA *19010*
  ☎ (212) 838-0510 . . 140 E 56 St, New York, NY *10022*

Wilson MR William B—Syr'83.Duke'85
1918 W Greenleaf St, Allentown, PA *18104*

Wilson MR & MRS William F (Nancy G Parker) Wes'81.Sm.Srb.H.'68 . . of
  ☎ (617) 423-6673 . . 7 Union Park, Boston, MA *02118*
  ☎ (401) 847-3268 . . Greenvale Farm, 582 Wapping Rd, Portsmouth, RI *02871*

Wilson MR William H—San.Wms'56 . . . . | ☎ (954) 524-3832
MISS Kimberly—at U of Wash'n . . . . | 2420 SE 17 St, Apt 405C, Ft Lauderdale, FL *33316*

Wilson MR & MRS William N (Barbara M Lane) | ☎ (201) 635-5096
Sth'62.Colg'54 . . . . | 230 Washington Av, Chatham, NJ *07928*
MISS Katherine N—Ty'90—at ☎ (212) 348-9619 |
1755 York Av, New York, NY *10128* . . . . |
MISS Margaret L—Colg'92—at |
☎ (212) 534-6882 . . 120 E 89 St, New York, NY |
10128 . . . . |
JUNIORS MR Samuel W |

Wilson LT William W—USN.ECar'85
2283 London Bridge Rd, Virginia Beach, VA *23456*

Wilson MR Winn Cameron . . . . | ☎ (860) 450-0784
MR Lee M—at ☎ (860) 456-2144 | 81 Main St, Willimantic, CT
255 Pleasant St, Willimantic, CT *06226* . . . . | *06226*

Wiltberger MRS Constant F (Rosalind W Dubell) Sdg.Ncd.Dar.
  ☎ (215) 563-1800 . . 2415 Logan Square E, 2 Franklin Town Blvd, Philadelphia, PA *19103*

Wilton MR & MRS Frank P (Annette J Stevens) ☎ (716) 874-4441
Wh'lck'56.St.G.Y.'52.H'54 . . . . 38 Middlesex Rd,
MISS Annette P—Sth'88.NCar'93—at Buffalo, NY *14216*
☎ (716) 631-3362 . . 15 Spindrift Court, 3,
Williamsville, NY *14221* . . . .
MISS Lucy B—StLaw'90.Roch'93—at
☎ (716) 874-2542 . . 27 N End Av, Kenmore,
NY *14217* . . . .
MISS Katherine P—Wit'93—at
☎ (614) 529-4399 . . 3885 Habitat Dv,
Columbus, OH *43228* . . . .
MR Benjamin W . . . .

Wimpress DR & MRS G Duncan JR (Jean Margaret Skerry)
Ore'46.A.Ore'46.Ore'50.DU'58
☎ (210) 492-2956 . . 11102 Whisper Ridge, San Antonio, TX *78230*

Winans MR & MRS Thomas J (Jane M Stubenbord) ☎ (703) 356-1448
V'61.P'55.Y'58 . . . . 1206 Perry William
MISS Susan M—Gchr'90.Bost'94—at Dv, McLean, VA
☎ (617) 266-0075 . . 451 Park Av, Boston, MA *22101*
02215 . . . .
MR Thomas W—DavEl'92 . . . .

Winans MR & MRS Walter E (Pauline L Harrison) ☎ (914) 234-7090
Bgt.Wms'40 . . . . Box 572, Middle
MISS Pauline C—at ☎ (212) 348-3573 Patent Rd, Bedford,
188 E 93 St, New York, NY *10128* . . . . NY *10506*
Jan 1 . .
☎ (941) 472-1051
1004 Spanish Laurel
Lane, Sanibel, FL
33957

Winant MRS John G (Janine L Perret)
☎ (609) 924-2626 . . Coventry Farm, 549 The Great Rd, Princeton,
NJ *08540*

Winant DR & MRS John G JR (Kathleen A ☎ (609) 924-7643
Schardong) Kent'73.P'71.Cin'75 . . . . 590 The Great Rd,
JUNIORS MISS Janine C . . . . Princeton, NJ *08540*
JUNIORS MISS Constance T . . . .

Winburn MR & MRS William A 3d (Emily W Coxe) Swb'55.Cda.NCar'48
☎ (912) 232-8228 . . 2601 Atlantic Av, Savannah, GA *31405*

Wincenc DR & MRS Joseph (Killeen—Ruth Dold)
Bf.G.Ober'37.StCons'38.Cl'42.Canis'62 . . of
☎ (716) 885-4915 . . 1088 Delaware Av, Apt 7F, Buffalo, NY *14209*
☎ (716) 941-9312 . . 8211 Lower E Hill Rd, Colden, NY *14033*

Winchell MR & MRS Albert B (Johnson—Lida F Wilson) Bost'58
☎ (941) 433-0549 . . 1519 Reynard Dv, Ft Myers, FL *33919*

Winchester MR & MRS Gordon (Ann C Pascault) ☎ (202) 547-6108
H'52 . . . . 513—7 St NE,
MISS Maud T . . . . Washington, DC
MR J Slade *20002*

Winchester MR & MRS John F (Susan L Lawrence) ☎ (508) 927-0446
H'58 . . . . 64 Paine Av,
MISS Shiela B—at 142-11—248 St, Rosedale, NY PO Box 95,
11422 . . . . Prides Crossing, MA
MR Robert L *01965*

Winchester MR John G 2d—Y.V'83
1435 Lexington Av, Apt 2B, New York, NY *10128*

Windebank MR & MRS Charles S (Towle—Robinson—Esther L O'Brian)
Swb'36.Lond'33.Mit'37.H'53
☎ (716) 649-1788 . . 145 Charlotte Av, Hamburg, NY *14075*

Windle MR & MRS William W (Closson—Fabia ☎ (617) 731-5462
Frenning) Rdc'55.Cy.Wms'51 . . . . 19 Fairgreen Place,
MISS Hope H . . . . Chestnut Hill, MA
MISS Sarah P *02167*
MISS Lilly F D . . . .
MISS Fabia B Closson . . . .
MR Lawrence F Closson . . . .

Winfield MRS M Lee (Martha S Lee) Cl'67
☎ (401) 245-8256 . . 7 Virginia Rd, Barrington, RI *02806*

Wing MRS Henry Van D (Clarke—Baruch—Davis—Tolly English) Cly.
☎ (212) 988-3891 . . 120 E 81 St, New York, NY *10028*

Wing MRS S Bryce (Parr—M Lawrason Riggs)
☎ (410) 494-4579 . . 307 Brightwood Club Dv, Lutherville, MD *21093*

Wing MRS Winthrop B (Cabot—Genevieve M Winslow) Chi.
☎ (508) 359-4451 . . 23 Prentiss Place, Medfield, MA *02052*

Winkelman MR & MRS Mark O (Dorinda J P of ☎ (212)677-0672
Cruickshank) . . . . 22 E 11 St,
JUNIORS MISS Victoria P . . . . New York, NY
10003
☎ (860) 767-7903
''Hayden's Point''
PO Box 362, Essex,
CT *06426*

Winmill MR & MRS Bassett S (Sarah P Jones) Unn.Ny.Rm.Stc.Cly.
☎ (908) 530-7044 . . 5 Sailers Way, Box 362, Rumson, NJ *07760*

Winmill MR Mark C—Rc.Ny.Sa.Va'80.Duke'87 . . of
☎ (212) 375-1232 . . 370 Park Av, New York, NY *10022*
☎ (914) 677-5187 . . Trotwood Farm, Tower Hill Rd, Millbrook,
NY *12545*

Winmill MISS S Starr—Va'78.Nu'88.Nyc.
☎ (513) 583-0477 . . 6802 Sand Harbor Court, Maineville, OH *45039*

Winmill MR & MRS Thomas B (Mary C Wilkin)
Y'81.UWash'88.Rc.Ny.Y'81.UWash'85
☎ (212) 876-3375 . . 300 E 93 St, New York, NY *10128*

Winn MR Charles M A—David'89
☎ (704) 372-4332 . . 2201 Cumberland Av, Charlotte, NC *28203*

Winn MR & MRS James J JR (Elizabeth K Lacy) ☎ (410) 833-0099
Hlns'69.Gv.Md.Mv.Pn.P'64.W&L'70 . . . . ''Gwydir''
MISS Mary Ann K—W&L'94 . . . . 14606 Dover Rd,
MISS E Lacy—at Trinity . . . . Glyndon, MD *21071*

Winn MR & MRS Michael P A (Caroline K Lipscomb)
Chr.StJ.Ncd.Bard'59 . . of
☎ (212) UN1-7318 . . 301 E 69 St, Apt 9D, New York, NY *10021*
☎ (803) 577-9793 . . 4 Battery Place, Charleston, SC *29401*

Winnacker DR & MRS John L (Elizabeth W ☎ (573) 442-4448
Fulbright) BMr'58.Cvc.Wms'57 . . . . 609 Thilly Av,
MR Matthew F—at 7860 Southern Dv, Columbia, Columbia, MO
MO *65201* *65203*

Winpenny MISS Julia J—Cly.Cda. . . . . ☎ (212) 794-0146
MR Bruce W . . . . 25 E 67 St,
New York, NY
10021

Winship MR & MRS Frederick M (Thompson—Joanne Tree)
Cc.Cw.Snc.Myf.Ofp.Rv.Sar.Cl'46
☎ (212) TE8-3095 . . 417 Park Av, New York, NY *10022*

Winslow MRS Albert F (Katherine P Larned)
T.Ne.Snc.Ht.Ll.Cw.Wt.Fw.Cda.Dar.
☎ (914) 351-2623 . . Pine Hill Rd, PO Box 444, Tuxedo Park, NY *10987-0444*

Winslow MRS Cameron McR (Natalie Hamilton Hess) GeoW'42.Srb.
☎ (401) 847-4693 . . "Camenat Cairns" Coggeshall Av, Newport, RI *02840*

Winslow MR & MRS Christopher W (Ann P Cunningham)
Dom'81.Ofp.Sar.Ht.
☎ (914) 986-8896 . . 35 Kenilworth Lane, Warwick, NY *10990*

Winslow MR Hamilton—Bard'48 . . . . | ☎ (717) 563-1263
MR Christopher H . . . . | Liaison Farm, 1351 Northup Hill, Clarks Summit, PA *18411*

Winslow MRS John C (Mary A Amory) . . . . | ☎ (941) 966-3112
MR John C JR—at 127 Putman Circle NE, Atlanta, GA *30342* . . . . | 420 N Casey Key Rd, Osprey, FL *34229*

Winslow MR & MRS John G (Baldwin—Helen L Michalis)
B.Nrr.Srb.Plg.Snc.Cly.StJ.Dc.Cda.
☎ (212) 759-6516 . . 200 E 66 St, Apt D1902, New York, NY *10021*

Winslow MISS Laura—BMr'50.Cvc . . .of
☎ (301) 652-3050 . . 15 E Lenox St, Chevy Chase, MD *20815*
☎ (302) 227-7859 . . 4 Pennsylvania Av, Rehoboth Beach, DE *19971*

Winslow MR & MRS Richard K (Marjorie Shreeve) DeP'45.Hn.H'43 . . of
☎ (602) 396-4032 . . 6616 E Sugarloaf St, Mesa, AZ *85205*
☎ (617) 934-7333 . . 44 Marshall St, Box 2247, Duxbury, MA *02331*

Winslow MISS Susan H—B'gton'73
☎ (703) 556-0233 . . 908 Lawton St, McLean, VA *22101*

Winslow MRS T Scudder (Campbell—Eunice Coit Johnson) Cly.Pr.Myf.
☎ (516) 676-8175 . . "Kaintuck Cottage" PO Box 593, Locust Valley, NY *11560*

Winsor MR & MRS Curtin (Eleanor M Webster) | ☎ (610) 642-5598
Hlns'63.Pa'66.Rc.P'27.Pa'30 . . . . | 101 Cherry Lane,
MISS Ellen W . . . . | PO Box 671, Ardmore, PA *19003*

Winsor MR & MRS Henry (Lander—Josephine L Reeves) Ssk.Gm.P'60
☎ (610) 649-5797 . . "Hedgeley" 101 Cherry Lane, Wynnewood, PA *19096*

Winsor MR & MRS James D 3d (Sally Wistar Waterman) Gm.Fst.Ncd.P'29
☎ (610) MI2-0326 . . "Forebay House" Cherry Lane, Ardmore, PA *19003*

Winsor MISS Jessica (g—MRS Julian H Richardson) . . . . Born at Stamford, CT May 19'95

Winsor MR & MRS Philip (Marion Steyn) | ☎ (814) 234-6943
H'50.Col'55 . . . . | 507 Crickwood Dv,
MISS Marina . . . . | State College, PA *16803*

Winsor MR R H Bancroft JR—WIT'78
☎ (508) 255-7914 . . 310 Windjammer Lane, RR 1, Eastham, MA *02642*

Winstead MR & MRS David L (Louise T Vietor) | ☎ (301) 951-6353
Bost'73.Cvc.Mt.Md.Elk.Rr.Denis'69.Cl'71. | 5505 Kirkside Dv,
CathU'83 ⚓ . . . . | Chevy Chase, MD
JUNIORS MR Trevor V . . . . | *20815*

Winter MR & MRS Andrew B (Rebecca L Roebuck)
Laf'86.Suff'94.Ub.Bow'89.Nw'96
☎ (617) 720-7823 . . 127 Pinckney St, Boston, MA *02114*

Winter MR Anthony R (Donald F) . . . . Married at Woodstock, VT
Bent MISS Courtney A (C Frederick 3d) . . . . Jun 29'96

Winter MRS Edwin W 2d (West—Ruth Elting) . . . . Died at Lake Forest, IL Mch 3'96

Winter MR & MRS John W (Jeanne A Rozier)
☎ (813) 254-2877 . . 84 Davis Blvd, Apt 700, Tampa, FL *33606*

Winter MRS Katherine B (Katherine C Blodgett) | ☎ (617) 262-6182
Rdc'63 . . . . | 10 Marlborough St,
MR Matthew F—GeoW'92—at ☎ (415) 681-0474 | Boston, MA *02116*
399 Upper Terr, San Francisco, CA *94117* . . . . . |

Winter MR & MRS Munroe A (Virginia Linville) H'42.LakeF'47
☎ (847) 234-5333 . . 333 Crescent Dv, Lake Bluff, IL *60044*

Winter MR & MRS Thomas G (Josephine E Grasselli) | ☎ (918) 742-8912
V'53.Stan'47 . . . . | 1819 E 27 St,
MISS Clare McG—at U of Ore . . . . | Tulsa, OK *74114*
MR Thomas A—ColC'84.AGSIM'88 . . . . |
MR Frank C—Cal'86 . . . . |
MR William H—Br'89 . . . . |

Winter MR & MRS William F (Elise Varner) Miss'48.Miss'49
☎ (601) 366-1741 . . 4205 Crane Blvd, Jackson, MS *39216*

Winterbotham MR John R JR . . . . Died at Lake Forest, IL Jly 17'95

Winterbotham MRS John R JR (Chloe Tyler French) | of ☎ (847)234-4419
BMr'44.Cas.Sc.On. | PO Box 374,
MRS (DR) Chloe Tyler (Cheston—Chloe Tyler | Lake Forest, IL
Winterbotham) BMr'74.Ill'82.Cas. . . . . | *60045*
| ☎ (801) 649-4687
| 207 Woodside,
| Box 4162,
| Park City, UT *84060*

Winterhoff DR & MRS Walter J (Lyall—Kathryn M Merikle) Wash'31
☎ (520) 881-3546 . . 2500 N Rosemont Blvd, Tucson, AZ *85712*

Winters MR & MRS J Samuel (Dorothy J Rushing) Tex'48.Tex'44.Tex'48
3504 Mt Bonnell Rd, Austin, TX *78731*

Wintersteen MR & MRS George F (Gretchen L | ☎ (610) 869-2225
Miller) Srr. . . . . | "Fairyhouse"
MISS Laura McI . . . . | 221 Ryan Rd, West Grove, PA *19390*

Wintersteen REV DR & MRS Prescott B (Storey—Sheila Mills)
StMarg'38.Sb.Cw.H'34.H'54
☎ (508) 744-6336 . . Essex Apt 103, 11 Church St, Salem, MA *01970*

Winthrop MISS Cornelia T
☎ (212) 255-2887 . . 708 Greenwich St, New York, NY *10014-2585*

Winthrop MRS Deborah H (Deborah Holbrook) Wheat'60
☎ (203) 622-8959 . . 11 River Rd, Apt 101, Cos Cob, CT *06807*

Winthrop MISS E Amory (Baker—Snead—Ripley—Shatz—
E Amory Winthrop) Ri.Cly.
☎ (914) 677-8181 . . "Winley" RR 1, Box 40, Millbrook, NY *12545*

Winthrop MR & MRS Grant F (Hope H Brock) Rdc'71.K.H'71
☎ (212) 348-3356 . . 1115 Fifth Av, New York, NY *10128*

Winthrop MR H Grenville—NEng'89
☎ (803) 406-8831 . . PO Box 80551, Charleston, SC *29416*

Winthrop MR & MRS John (Elizabeth Goltra) | ☎ (803) 722-8480
K.Hn.H'58 . . . . | 9 Ladson St,
MR Bayard—at ☎ (415) 928-4713 | Charleston, SC
2428A California St, San Francisco, CA *94115* . | *29401*

Winthrop MR & MRS John JR (Louisa L Daley) Duke'87.H'86.H'92
☎ (212) 988-4885 . . 527 E 72 St, Apt 5A, New York, NY *10021*

Winthrop MR & MRS Jonathan (Sydney Cheston) Sm.K.My.H'75.Pa'82
☎ (617) 367-1904 . . 68 Beacon St, Boston, MA *02108*

Winthrop MR Matthew B
☎ (617) 437-1694 . . 790 Boylston St, Apt 26F, Boston, MA *02199*

Winthrop MRS Nathaniel T (Eleanor R Beane) Ws'40.Cs.
☎ (212) 879-9567 . . 770 Park Av, New York, NY *10021*

Winthrop MR & MRS Robert (Haas—Hailparn—Wilkes—
Floreine J Nelson) Rc.Pr.B.Mb.Ri.Sm.Msq.H'26
☎ (516) 626-3942 . . 40 Piping Rock Rd, Upper Brookville,
PO Box 306, Glen Head, NY *11545*

Winthrop MR & MRS Robert 2d (Carol A Veatch)
Wes'72.Mo'74.Ga'83.K.Stan'89
☎ (706) 546-1341 . . 633 Milledge Circle, Athens, GA *30606*

Winthrop MRS Serita (Barzun—Serita Winthrop) | 151 E 83 St,
Cl'69 . . . . | New York, NY
MISS Mariana Barzun . . . . | *10028*
MISS Lucy Barzun . . . . |
MR Matthew Barzun . . . . |
MR Charles Barzun . . . . |

Winton MR & MRS David H (Haebler—Suzanne Talcott Curry) Myf.Pn.
☎ (802) 457-1931 . . Merrily Farm, South Woodstock, VT *05071*

Wirts DR & MRS Steven B (Mary Ann L Bridger) | ☎ (215) 248-4585
Pc.Ac.Ncd.NCar'70.Jef'74 . . . . | 8008 Lincoln Dv,
MISS Jennifer B . . . . | Philadelphia, PA
JUNIORS MISS Julia C . . . . | *19118*
JUNIORS MR Christopher N . . . . |

Wirtz MR & MRS Arthur M JR (Sunny A Soldwedel) Pa'58
☎ (847) 729-8730 . . 730 Glendale Dv, Glenview, IL *60025-4415*

Wirtz MR & MRS W Rockwell (Kathleen M | ☎ (847) 446-0026
Whiston) Nw'75 . . . . | 90 Locust Rd,
JUNIORS MISS Hillary W . . . . | Winnetka, IL *60093*
JUNIORS MR Daniel R . . . . |

Wirtz MR Willem K
☎ (561) 655-1088 . . 228 Phipps Plaza, Palm Beach, FL *33480*

Wirtz MR & MRS William W (Hargrave—Alice L | ☎ (847) 446-6626
Pirie) Cyc.Rc.Sc.Cas.Cnt.Br'50 ⚓ . . . . . . | 181 De Windt Rd,
MISS Alison M . . . . | Winnetka, IL *60093*
MR Peter R—at 926 Edgemere Court, Evanston, |
IL *60202* . . . . |
MR William A Hargrave—at |
☎ (312) 944-3972 . . 1555 N Astor St, |
Chicago, IL *60610* . . . . |

Wisdom JUDGE & MRS John Minor (Bonnie Mathews)
Swb'27.Mt.W&L'25.Tul'29
☎ (504) 866-2632 . . 1732 Palmer Av, New Orleans, LA *70118*

Wise MR & MRS Christopher T (Boit—Marka Spalding) H'70
☎ (508) 636-2266 . . 514 Old Country Rd, Westport, MA *02790-1105*

Wise MR & MRS D Scott (Linden Havemeyer) K.C.Y.'74
☎ (212) 249-9203 . . 133 E 80 St, New York, NY *10021*

Wise MR & MRS Daniel P (Susan F Kingery) H'52
☎ (508) 922-1835 . . 11 Grove St, Box 5505, Beverly Farms, MA *01915*

Wise MR Henry A JR—An.Gi.Vmi'31.Y'34 . . . . . . | ☎ (941) 775-3027
MISS Diana A . . . . | Glades Country
MISS Susan Robertson . . . . | Club, Apt A,
| 175 Palm Dv,
| Naples, FL *34112*

Wise DR & MRS Henry A 2d (Joshan R Backus) | ☎ (941) 591-1399
Hlns'65.Va'59.Va'64 . . . . | Le Dauphin,
MISS J Ridgely—Syr'94 . . . . | 9811 Gulfshore Dv,
| Naples, FL *34108*

Wise MRS James A (Drum—Isabel Davis) BallSt'64.BallSt'66
☎ (941) 482-2630 . . The Forest, 16000 Forest Oaks Dv, Ft Myers,
FL *33908*

Wise MR & MRS John H JR (Margaret R Hinckley) B.Chi.Ncd.Stan'43
☎ (540) 364-3532 . . "Tasmania" PO Box 239, Orlean,
VA *20128-0239*

Wise MR John S JR—Va'60.Ga'66.Ga'67 . . . . | ☎ (334) 687-6747
MR Henry A—at ☎ (334) 687-3057 | 200 W Chewalla
101 Chocktaw Dv, Eufaula, AL *36027* . . . . | Creek Dv, Eufaula,
| AL *36027*

Wise MRS Parker S (Nancy S Register) . . . . | ☎ (914) 533-6050
LT Parker S 3d—USMC.Wis'94 | 107 Oakridge Dv,
MR Ashley R—at U of Ariz . . . . | South Salem, NY
JUNIORS MISS Kathryn P . . . . | *10590*

Wise MR Parker S—H.'69.W&L'72
☎ (914) 277-7943 . . PO Box 216, Waccabuc, NY *10597*

Wise CAPT & MRS Peyton R 2d (Charlas E Williams) | ☎ (410) 833-9363
Md.Mv.USN'53.JHop'61 | 2909 Butler Rd,
MISS Elizabeth D . . . . | Butler, MD
MR Peyton R 3d . . . . | *21023-0105*
MR John H . . . . |
MR Charles W W . . . . |

Wise MR & MRS Richard H (Sharon M Malone) | ☎ (415) 921-0104
CalSt'62.Cc.P'59.Cal'63.Cal'66 . . . . | 3500 Baker St,
MISS Catherine R . . . . | San Francisco, CA
MR William M . . . . | *94123*
JUNIORS MISS Elizabeth H . . . . |

Wise MR & MRS William A (Marie C Figge) | of ☎ (915)581-4903
NYSID'69.Van'67.Col'70 . . . . | 5605 Westside Dv,
MISS Vivian M—*see Dilatory Domiciles* . . . . . . | El Paso, TX *79932*
MISS Genevieve M . . . . | 0269 N Starwood
MISS Mary E . . . . | Dv, Aspen, CO
| *81611*

Wiseman MR & MRS William F (Linda F White) | ☎ (617) 235-6232
Wells'61.Cl'62.Ub.Myf.Cr'61.Bab'77 . . . . | 48 Oxbow Rd,
LT Christopher S—USN.P'91—at Norfolk, VA . | Weston, MA *02193*

Wisner MR & MRS Charles M (L Catherine A Hull)
5 Pleasant Place, Cambridge, MA *02139*

Wissa MR & MRS Nuri A E Z (Cornelia V R Streeter) H.'85.My.Sm.Skd'86
☎ (508) 887-7909 . . Copper Beech Farm, 83 Asbury St, Topsfield,
MA *01983*

Wissa MISS Victoria Van Rensselaer (Nuri A E Z) . . . . Born at
Beverly, MA Jly 6'95

Wist MR & MRS Andrew L (Susan F Nolte) SUNY'72.NH'72
☎ (804) 978-7985 . . 3303 Meadowfield Lane, Charlottesville, VA *22911*

Wistar MR & MRS C Cresson (Ailsa F Freeman) Pa'49.Cda.Pa'43
☎ (215) 646-4026 . . 527 Stenton Av, Blue Bell, PA *19422-2126*

Wistar MISS Caroline P
☎ (215) 247-6782 . . 8027 Roanoke St, Philadelphia, PA *19118*

Wistar MR & MRS James B (Elaine D Flanagan) P.'82.Dth'86.P'82.Pa'87
249 Batleson Rd, Ambler, PA *19002*

Wistar MR Stephen M—Ant'77
☎ (818) 398-7800 . . 742 N Mentor Av, Pasadena, CA *91104-4623*

Wistar MR & MRS Thomas JR (Elizabeth Beall) W.Hav'30.Pa'34
☎ (603) 526-4351 . . ''Merryfield'' 84 Knights Hill Rd, New London, NH *03257*

Wister MR & MRS Caspar (Cass—Uta G Schlegel) P'32
☎ (619) 753-0589 . . PO Box 232082, Leucadia, CA *92023-2082*

Wister MRS E P Benson (Ethel Pew Benson)
Stan'63.Me.Rd.Rc.Cts.Ac. . . . .
MISS Ethel. . . . .
MISS Sabina . . . .
MISS Noelle. . . . .
JUNIORS MR William R 3d . . . .
☎ (610) 647-7315
2175 Buttonwood
Rd, Berwyn, PA
19312

Wister MR & MRS L Wynne (Joan G Harris) Me.P'36
RD 2, Bethel, VT *05032*

Wister MR & MRS Malcolm L (Rosato—Lillian A Hirschbeck) SacredH'54.Me.Gm.P'34
☎ (610) 525-9837 . . 1135 Brynllawn Rd, Villanova, PA *19085*

Wister MRS William R (Jenkins—Gibb—Hannah E Willets)
☎ (908) 439-2142 . . PO Box 151, Oldwick, NJ *08858*

Wister MR & MRS William R JR (Crompton—Norris —Diana D Strawbridge) K.Rc.Cts.BtP.Evg. Cly.H'55.Pa'61 . . . .
MISS Margaret D Norris . . . .
MR John S Crompton—at ☎ (561) 840-4097
1558 N Ocean Way, Palm Beach, FL *33480* .
of ☎ (561)655-0547
335 El Vedado,
Palm Beach, FL
33480
☎ (610) 383-4034
''Runnymede''
RD 3, Coatesville,
PA *19320*

Wister MR & MRS William W (Reichner—E Jane Kuhlman) Pa'46.Pc.Ll.Dll . . .of
☎ (215) 836-5731 . . 604 Pleasant Av, Wyndmoor, PA *19038-8531*
☎ (561) 622-3729 . . 115 Club Dv, Palm Beach Gardens, FL *33418*

Wiswall MR & MRS Frank L (Elizabeth C Nelson) Wells'63.C.Cos.Colby'62.Cr'65.Camb'67 . . . . .
MR Frank L 3d—at ☎ (216) 650-9772
Western Reserve Academy, 115 College St, Hudson, OH *44236*. . . . .
☎ (207) 326-4243
Meadow Farm,
PO Box 201,
Castine, ME
04421-0201

Witesman MRS Arthur F JR (Harriet A Heenan) Minn'40
☎ (520) 745-2578 . . 5450 E 7 St, Tucson, AZ *85711*

Witherbee MR & MRS John Hemenway (Downing—Beckwith— Mary I Osborne) Cl'57 . . of
☎ (609) 921-2427 . . 45 Carson Rd, Princeton, NJ *08540*
☎ (802) 533-2971 . . ''Partridge Hill'' Greensboro, VT *05841*

Witherby MR & MRS Frederick R H (Anne B Reed) Rdc'47.Sm.Btn.Chi.Cly.H'40.H'47
☎ (617) 426-3366 . . Four Seasons Place, 220 Boylston St, Boston, MA *02116*

Witherby MR & MRS Frederick R H JR (Margaret C Pratt) BostColl'95.Hn.H.'65.Cl'71.Bost'92 . . . .
MR Frederick R H 3d—at U of Colo Boulder . . .
☎ (617) 277-0870
46 Woodman Rd,
Chestnut Hill, MA
02167
see
Dilatory Domiciles

Withers MR & MRS Carl R (Jenny C Cory) C.Ncd.Dar.Witt'50.Mich'53 . . . .
MISS Wren A—Sth'77
MR Bradford J—Wit'83.ClevSt'88 . . . .

Withers MR & MRS John P JR (Dorothy S Dent) Fmy.Cda.P'65.Stan'70 . . . .
MR John P 3d—at San Luis Obispo, CA. . . . . . .
JUNIORS MISS Charlotte S . . . .
JUNIORS MR Charles L—at U of Va. . . . .
☎ (415) 948-8231
26353 Esperanza
Dv, Los Altos Hills,
CA *94022*

Withers MR & MRS Paul M (G Sheldon Gerry) . . . . .
JUNIORS MR H Averell—at Eton Coll . . . .
☎ (011-44-1420)
538-215
Reeds Farm,
Empshott, Liss,
Hampshire
GU33 6HT, England

Withers MRS Polk (Alicia C Polk)
☎ (314) 725-5766 . . 7732 Delmar Blvd, St Louis, MO *63130*

Withers MR & MRS Wendt L (Christine T Favre) MissSt'85.Skd'85.Dth'87
☎ (318) 988-4669 . . 303 Champs Elysee, Maurice, LA *70555*

Withers MR & MRS William Z (Sarah M Latimer) USN'58 . . . .
MISS Wendy A—Cal'89 . . . .
MISS Emily M—ColSt'91 . . . .
☎ (815) 942-6758
1209C Lakewood
Dv, Morris, IL
60450

Witherspoon MR & MRS Andrew J (Katherine V Randolph) Duke'89.Nu'94.Cp.Duke'87
☎ (610) 388-3945 . . 344 Kennett Pike, Chadds Ford, PA *19317*

Witherspoon MR & MRS James T (Loughlin— Dorothy Mudd) Rose'69.Denis'63.Wash'72 . . . .
MISS Anna M Loughlin . . . .
MISS Clare M Loughlin . . . .
MR John J Loughlin JR . . . .
☎ (314) 726-5674
57 Ridgemoor Dv,
St Louis, MO *63105*

Withington MR & MRS Lothrop JR (Millican—Dorothy Shedd) Myf.H'42
☎ (941) 433-5633 . . 804 Cape View Dv, Ft Myers, FL *33919*

Withington MR & MRS Nathan N (June E Hamilton) Ken'62 . . . .
MR Nathan N 3d . . . .
JUNIORS MISS Meghan E . . . .
☎ (508) 746-2468
188 Old Sandwich
Rd, Plymouth, MA
02360

Withington MRS Paul R (Lucy A Chipley) . . . .
MISS Ann F—Rdc'66—at ☎ (518) 462-5152
Dutch Village Apt 8-1R, Menands, NY *12204* . .
☎ (804) 846-1059
2940 Rivermont Av,
Apt 23D,
Lynchburg, VA
24503

Withington MR & MRS Richard F (Katharine Driscoll) H'46 . . . .
MR Richard F JR . . . .
MR Sean W . . . .
☎ (508) 746-0946
165 Sandwich St,
Plymouth, MA
02360

Withington MISS Sara G—CtCol'59.Myf.Cda.
☎ (617) 574-9449 . . 35 Fayette St, Boston, MA *02116*

Withrow MR John A JR—Cal'68.H'70
☎ (415) 324-3273 . . PO Box 1315, Menlo Park, CA *94026*

Witker MR & MRS James B (McKenna—Christine M Sullivan) Ford'87.H'58 . . . .
MR James B 3d—at N'western . . . .
JUNIORS MISS Pauline A—at Taft . . . .
☎ (413) 637-4620 110 Old Stockbridge Rd, Lenox, MA 01240-2810

Witmer MR & MRS Richard H JR (Jean C Hudson) Wes'77.L.Cly.Br'74.H'76 . . of
☎ (203) 862-9708 . . 16 Ft Hills Lane, Greenwich, CT 06831
☎ (717) 775-7371 . . Blooming Grove Hunt & Fish Club, Hawley, PA 18428

Witsell MR & MRS Frederick C JR (Daphne V Towne) Pr.Ln.Va'56
☎ (561) 546-0207 . . 7029 SE Golfhouse Dv, Hobe Sound, FL 33455

Witte MR & MRS Nicholas M (Louisa R Coffin) Hn.H'47
☎ (207) 865-3646 . . 77 South St, Porter's Landing, Freeport, ME 04032

Witten MR & MRS Arthur L (Sherwood—Virginia Lawson) Ncmb'50.Cal'41
☎ (805) 967-9577 . . 521 Carriage Hill Court, Santa Barbara, CA 93110

Witter MRS Susan R (Susan H Rentschler) V'55.Cly . . . .
MISS Sidney W—at 960 Park Av, New York, NY 10028 . . . .
MR William P—at ☎ (303) 473-9907 1205 Mariposa Av, Boulder, CO 80302 . . . .
☎ (212) 249-0772 1040 Fifth Av, New York, NY 10028

Witter MR & MRS Wendell W (Harkins—Gooding—Evelyn Grinter) Bhm.Pcu.Sfg.Sfy.Fr.Cal'32 . . of
☎ (415) 776-4052 . . 1400 Geary Blvd, Apt 2109, San Francisco, CA 94109-6572
☎ (707) 224-9027 . . 303 Deer Hollow, Napa, CA 94558

Witter MR & MRS William D (Inger K Kullberg) Bhm.Ln.Pcu.Y'51
☎ (212) 758-2226 . . 870 United Nations Plaza, New York, NY 10017

Witter-Gillette MRS Ann (Gillette—H Ann Witter) Bur.Fr.Ncd. 2615 Larkin St, San Francisco, CA 94109

Wittmann MR & MRS J vanBeuren JR (Barbara C Swaim) Bgt.Cw.Snc.Lm.Nu'57 . . . .
MISS Rachel DeWitt—Buck'89.Lm.Dh.Ncd.—at
☎ (212) 288-7446 . . 925 Park Av, New York, NY 10028 . . . .
MR J vanBeuren 3d—Lm.Snc.Cw.Quinn'89. NewHaven'93—☎ (914) 232-4816 . . . .
☎ (914) 232-5968 "Rensselaerwyck" RFD 6, Dr Tony's Rd, Katonah, NY 10536

Wixom MR & MRS William D (Nancy Coe) Skd'49.Ober'56.Hav'51.Nu'63 . . . .
MISS Rachel de W . . . .
MR Llewelyn C . . . .
MR Andrew H . . . .
☎ (914) 793-6684 61 Ridge St, Eastchester, NY 10707

Wladyka MR & MRS William J (Hejja—Cynthia Bogart) Rose'75.LIU'77.S.RyTech'67 ⚓
☎ (516) 624-6979 . . 48 Harbor Rd, Oyster Bay, NY 11771

Wodell MR W Page—Fic.Y'44 . . . .
MR Willis C Arndt JR—Fic.Yn.Y'90 . . . .
☎ (860) 434-0263 "Meadow House" 6 Academy Lane, Old Lyme, CT 06371

Wolbach MRS Josephine H (Josephine N Harmar) Sth'44.Cy.Ec.Ncd.
☎ (617) 232-4732 . . 185 Sargent Rd, Brookline, MA 02146

Wolbach MR & MRS William W (Emma D Crispin) Cyb.Ec.My.Hb.
☎ (242) 334-6073 . . "Sea Wind" Cotton Bay Club, Eleuthera, Bahamas

Wolcott MR & MRS Charles S (Elisabeth J Lamont) My.Bost'79
☎ (508) 468-3624 . . 900 Bay Rd, Hamilton, MA 01936

Wolcott MR & MRS Frank E III (Linda H Low) Exy.Ny.Sap.Pa'61 ⚓
☎ (860) 767-2491 . . 4 Crosstrees Hill Rd, Essex, CT 06426

Wolcott MR & MRS Oliver JR (Carolyn S Kinney) Chi.H'52
☎ (508) 468-1565 . . 918 Bay Rd, Box 155, Hamilton, MA 01936

Wolcott MR Oliver III—My.OWes'75
☎ (508) 468-2001 . . 18 Lake Av, Wenham, MA 01984

Wolcott MR & MRS Randolph A (Georgianna C Conger)
☎ (803) 649-6276 . . 222 Florence St, Aiken, SC 29801

Wolcott MRS Robert S (Blaine—Ruth W Robb) My.
☎ (508) 526-8141 . . 11 Lincoln St, Manchester, MA 01944

Wolcott MRS Robert W (Molthan—Caroline Reed) . . . . Died at Bryn Mawr, PA Nov 9'95

Wolcott MR & MRS Robert W JR (Margaret W Hoopes) M.Gm.Ph.Me.Myf.Ncd.P'48
☎ (610) 688-5768 . . 236 Atlee Rd, Wayne, PA 19087

Wolcott MR & MRS Samuel H JR—Cy.Sm.My.Cc.H'33
☎ (617) 329-1933 . . Fox Hill Village 157, 10 Longwood Dv, Westwood, MA 02090

Wolcott MR & MRS Samuel H 3d (Nora Bradley) Sth'59.Ln.Pr.Bur.Cly.H'57
☎ (516) 676-2915 . . 384 Duck Pond Rd, Locust Valley, NY 11560

Wolf MR Christopher R—K.Ri.OWes'78.Y'83 . . of
☎ (212) 807-8775 . . 233 W 26 St, New York, NY 10001
☎ (011-52) 376-60278 . . "Villa Los Suenos" Apdo Postal 604, Ajijic, 45920 Jalisco, Mexico

Wolf MRS Dwight E (Elizabeth W Dandridge) Dar.
☎ (803) 785-7841 . . 300 Woodhaven Dv, Apt 2403, Hilton Head Island, SC 29928

Wolf MR & MRS George D (Martin—Messa—Elinor N Kraft) . . . .
MR Dennis K . . . .
☎ (610) 449-4827 3200 Township Line Rd, Apt 215E, Drexel Hill, PA 19026-1943

Wolf MR & MRS John F JR (Jeanne M Jordan) Bethany'48.SUNY'79.Bf.G.Cr'49 . . . .
MISS April Harding—Br'82—at
☎ (401) 467-0179 . . 78 Stanwood St, Providence, RI 02907 . . . .
MR & MRS John F 3d (Norma M Quesada) MtH'82.SUNY'84—at ☎ (413) 586-6288 77 Prospect St, Northampton, MA 01060 . . . . . .
☎ (716) 992-4289 "treehouse" 8880 Sisson Rd, Eden, NY 14057

Wolf MR & MRS Richard A (Christine Marburg) Msq.Pa'69
JUNIORS MISS Olivia I . . . .
of ☎ (805) 565-1555 1481 E Mountain Dv, Montecito, CA 93108
☎ (212) 772-2955 12 E 86 St, New York, NY 10028

Wolf MR & MRS S George 3d (Maggy J Sawin) Ws'77.Cl'72.Cl'73.Ox'80.Ox'86
☎ (504) 866-6023 . . 440 Fern St, New Orleans, LA 70118

Wolf DR Stewart G JR—Y'35.JHop'38
☎ (610) 588-5817 . . "Monseybrook" RD 1, Box 1120G, Bangor, PA 18013

Wolf MR W Scott—Tul'84 . . see W W Warder

Wolfe MR Albert B—Cw.Hb.P'31.H'34
☎ (603) 924-0854 . . 133 Rivermead Rd, Peterborough, NH 03458

Wolfe MRS C Sibley (Carolyn C Sibley) Sth'45.Cly. | ☎ (716) 442-8328
MISS Amy W . . . . | 39 Babcock Dv,
Rochester, NY
14610

Wolfe MR & MRS Charles Holmes (Suzanne M Offill)
Nw'45.Pitt'72.Pg.H'42.Pitt'48
☎ (412) 361-4422 . . 1172 Murray Hill Av, Pittsburgh, PA *15217*

Wolfe MR & MRS John J JR (Elizabeth L Moser) | ☎ (314) 991-1171
Wash'50. . . . . | 28 Black Creek
MISS Elizabeth . . . . | Lane, St Louis, MO
MR John J 3d . . . . | *63124*
MR Mathew S . . . . |

Wolfe MRS John W (Lovelace—Norina Vannucci)
☎ (614) 231-2952 . . 485 Columbia Place, Columbus, OH *43209*

Wolfe DR Peter R—Pg.H'75.Pitt'79
8840 Appian Way, Los Angeles, CA *90046*

Wolfe MR & MRS Richard P (Ann P Terrell)
Ncmb'59.Wt.Myf.Dc.Hn.P'59.H'62
☎ (504) 861-0149 . . 7916 Plum St, New Orleans, LA *70118*

Wolfe MR & MRS Townsend D 3d (Jane R Lee) | of ☎ (501)372-4567
Nu'62.Nu'64.AtlArt'58.Cranbr'59.H'70 . . . . | 2102 Louisiana St,
MISS Zibilla L—at ☎ (212) 982-3467 | Little Rock, AR
341 E 10 St, Apt 5E, New York, NY *10009*. . . . | *72206*
☎ (802) 457-1608
Upper Line Farm,
PO Box 11,
Woodstock, VT
05091

Wolfenden MR & MRS John T (Lois Clark) Cy.Un.Tv.Dar.Purd'50 . . of
☎ (216) 371-1973 . . 20200 N Park Blvd, Shaker Heights, OH *44118*
☎ (602) 990-7977 . . ''L'Oasis'' 7296 E San Miguel Rd, Scottsdale,
AZ *85253*

Wolff MR & MRS George JR (Joy Petersmeyer) Cal'43
☎ (707) 433-8566 . . PO Box 607, Healdsburg, CA *95448*

Wolff MISS Gerry P—Cal'56.Stan'75
☎ (415) 854-2245 . . 151 Stanford Av, Menlo Park, CA *94025-6325*

Wolff MR John B JR—Sar.Dth'32
☎ (860) 526-1009 . . 317 W Main St, Chester, CT *06412-1057*

Wolfner MR & MRS Thomas P (Caro H S Schneithorst) Smu'87.Rc.StL'78
☎ (314) 993-3337 . . 2 Warson Hills, St Louis, MO *63124*

Wolfsberger MR & MRS Donald L (Joyce E Reith) Stph'59.Wash'55 . . of
☎ (314) 725-9506 . . 211 N Bemiston Av, St Louis, MO *63105*
☎ (305) 367-2568 . . Ocean Reef Club, 35 Card Sound Rd,
North Key Largo, FL *33037*

Wolkenberg MISS Abigail Janine Gordon (g—Spencer Gordon JR) . . . .
Born May 3'94

Wolkonsky DR & MRS Peter (Ward—Mary G Van Etten)
V'29.Cas.On.Cho.Fy.Ch'48.Ch'50.Ch'52 . . of
☎ (312) 787-9567 . . 1040 N Lake Shore Dv, Chicago, IL *60611*
☎ (847) 234-2269 . . 1596 N Green Bay Rd, Lake Forest, IL *60045*

Wolkonsky MRS Walls (Lamb—Mary L Walls) Rcch.
☎ (316) 223-5550 . . Ft Scott Presbyterian Village, Apt 132,
2400 S Horton St, Ft Scott, KS *66701*

Wollenberg MR & MRS David A (Katrina Moulton) | ☎ (415) 326-4400
Bost'75.Br'69.Stan'73 . . . . | 85 Michaels Way,
JUNIORS MR Andrew R . . . . | Atherton, CA *94027*
JUNIORS MR Blake E . . . . |

Woltz MRS A Ervin (Anne S Ervin) Va'70
☎ (910) 768-6842 . . 2794 Clayburne Court, Williamsburg Square,
Winston-Salem, NC *27103*

Womble MR & MRS William F (Jane P Gilbert) Cc.Duke'37
☎ (910) 722-9970 . . 2027 Virginia Rd, Winston-Salem, NC *27104*

Wommack MR & MRS William W (Jean M Emery) Ws'48.NCarSt'43.H'48
☎ (513) 561-4595 . . 7310 Sanderson Place, Cincinnati, OH *45243*

Womrath MRS Robert S (Dorothy S Goadby) Cda.Dc.
☎ (860) 767-0646 . . 145 Essex Meadows, Essex, CT *06426*

Wonham MR & MRS Frederick S (Ann H Brunie) Au.P'53
☎ (561) 231-9452 . . 501 River Dv, Vero Beach, FL *32963*

Wonham MR & MRS Henry B (Cornelia G Quarles) P'83.Au.P'83.Va'86
☎ (541) 344-4244 . . 3145 Whitten Dv, Eugene, OR *97405*

Wonham MASTER Henry Grant (Henry B) . . . . Born Oct 14'94

Wonham MASTER Jack Henry (g—Frederick S Wonham) . . . . Born
Oct 21'95

Wood MR Alan 4th. | ☎ (610) 658-0706
MR Richard H M—at ☎ (201) 433-6071 | 188 River Rd,
341 Monmouth St, Apt 306D, Jersey City, NJ | Gladwyne, PA
07302. . . . . | *19035*
JUNIORS MISS Canby B |
JUNIORS MR Crosby—at Kenyon . . . . |

Wood MISS Alden R . . see W F Harrity JR

Wood MISS Amanda—Syr'91 . . see W W Walker JR

Wood MRS Arnold (Cornelia A Ely) Rm.Snc.
Tryon Estates, Apt A102, Columbus, NC *28722*

Wood MR Arthur M—Cho.On.P'34.H'37
☎ (941) 966-6540 . . 1400 N Casey Key Rd, Osprey, FL *34229*

Wood MRS B Lindner (Barbara A Lindner) | ☎ (904) 273-8250
MR Ramsay—at 182 Fordwych Rd, London NW2, | Vicar's Landing
England . . . . | Inverness 101, 1000
Vicar's Landing
Way, Ponte Vedra
Beach, FL
32082-1251

Wood DR & MRS Benjamin S JR (June C Greene) | ☎ (303) 757-3037
Cr'54.Ant'54.Pa'58 . . . . | 3133 S Milwaukee
MISS Robyn L—at ☎ (415) 488-9001 | St, Denver, CO
PO Box 772, Forest Knolls, CA *94933*. . . . . . . | *80210*
MR Gregory R—at ☎ (303) 329-8059 |
8335 Fairmont Dv, Apt 1-202, Denver, CO *80231* |

Wood MR & MRS C Clark (Katherine Goltra)
☎ (202) 966-1268 . . 4507 Van Ness St NW, Washington, DC *20016*

Wood MRS C Martin JR (Veva P Miller) V'40.Ncd.
☎ (203) 531-4167 . . 303 W Lyon Farm Dv, Greenwich, CT *06831*

Wood MRS Carolyn E (Moorhead—Carolyn F | ☎ (206) 454-4641
Wood) CtCol'64. | 2719—93 Av NE,
MISS Ariel K (Tomeny—Ariel K Wood) | Clyde Hill, WA
Syr'93.Syr'94—at 6522 Ambrosia Dv, Apt 5314, | *98004*
San Diego, CA *92124* . . . . |
MISS Allison F Moorhead—SCal'93—at
1860 McGilvra Blvd, Seattle, WA *98112* . . . .
MR Dudley T Moorhead 3d—at U of Mont . .

Wood MRS Chalmers B (Patricia Houghton) . . . . . . | ☎ (609) 924-4490
MISS Felicity T . . . . | 45 Cleveland Lane,
MISS Penelope B . . . . | Princeton, NJ *08540*

Wood MR Charles H 3d
☎ (716) 992-3578 . . 4283 Haag Rd, Eden, NY *14057*

Wood MR Charles N . . of
☎ (908) 879-6521 . . Millhouse Farm, 31 N Four Bridges Rd,
Long Valley, NJ *07853*
☎ (540) 837-2459 . . Edgewood Farm, PO Box 962, Middleburg,
VA *20118*

Wood MR & MRS Charles R (Anna S Farnum) | ☎ (610) 649-3590
BMr'58.Sg.Me.Rc.Yn.Y'53 . . . . | 229 Rose Lane,
MISS Sarah S—Y.'93.Me.—at ☎ (212) 787-9142 | Haverford, PA
200 W 79 St, Apt 17M, New York, NY *10024* . | *19041*
MISS Hannah D—at Davidson . . . . |

Wood MISS Charlotte Lee (W Kip) . . . . Born at
Falls Church, VA Aug 6'95

Wood MR & MRS Christopher W (Mignone A Allen)
Cal'76.H'82.Sap.Dar.Pa'75.FP'78
☎ (415) 364-1852 . . 140 Brecon Court, Redwood City, CA *94062*

Wood REV & MRS Cornelius Ayer (Coward— | ☎ (508) 475-1213
Rosalyn Kempton) Mt.Cvc.Hn.H.'42 . . . . | ''Arden''
MISS Claire Frances Coward—Bnd'89—at | PO Box 367,
☎ (212) 496-9409 . . 325 W 87 St, Apt 3, | Andover, MA *01810*
New York, NY *10024* . . . . |

Wood MRS David E (M Ellen Halstead) | ☎ (808) 732-3414
MR David E JR—at ☎ (805) 388-7199 | 4826 Matsonia Dv,
120 San Miguel, Camarillo, CA *93010* . . . . | Honolulu, HI *96816*
MR Thomas R—at Portland, OR . . . . |
MISS (DR) Sarah E (Kline—Sarah E Wood)— |
CalPsych'87—at ☎ (510) 945-6939 |
150 Heritage Court, Walnut Creek, CA *94596* . . |

Wood DR & MRS (DR) David W (Browning— | ☎ (610) MU8-3757
Elizabeth L McGee) PaMed'49.Me.R.Sa.Pa'50 . | 640 N Valley Forge
MR Henry D—at ☎ (610) 286-0179 | Rd, Devon, PA
PO Box 494, Elverson, PA *19520* . . . . | *19333*
MISS Margaretta W Browning—at |
☎ (520) 474-7592 . . PO Box 247, Young, AZ |
85554 . . . . |

Wood MR & MRS David W JR (Marianne Stewart)
Wagner'76.Wid'86.Sa.Pa'70.NCar'73
☎ (610) 399-0221 . . 633 James Dv, West Chester, PA *19382-7410*

Wood MRS Dorothea S (Moore—Dorothea S Wood) . . . . Married at
Lake Tahoe, CA
Wittrich MR Jon R (Ralph) . . . . Jun 5'93

Wood MRS Dudley P K (Montgomery—McVickar—de Sales—
Ruth C Wilmerding) K.Cly.
☎ (212) TR9-3859 . . 115 E 67 St, New York, NY *10021*

Wood MR Edward F R JR—Sg.Ph.Pa'44
☎ (215) 233-0487 . . 235 Northwestern Av, Philadelphia,
PA *19128-1808*

Wood MISS Elizabeth N (Robert E 2d) . . . . Married at New York, NY
Hull MR Larry D JR (Larry D) . . . . May 18'96

Wood MRS Emily C (Andrews—Wadsworth—Emily C Wood) Pa'81.Ac.
☎ (215) 829-9065 . . 322 Lombard St, Philadelphia, PA *19147*

Wood MISS F Parnell—CtCol'89 . . see D M Hinckley

Wood MR & MRS Francis C (Lorton—Collins—Beverley B Rogers) Cl'30
☎ (561) 231-1783 . . 389 Island Creek Dv, John's Island, Vero Beach,
FL *32963-3306*

Wood MRS Francis Clark (Mary Louise Woods) Me. | ☎ (610) MI2-1434
MISS Elizabeth V . . . . | 212 Laurel Lane,
| Haverford, PA
| *19041*

Wood MR Frederic D . . see D M Hinckley

Wood MR & MRS Frederick L (Debra L Gentile) SL'85.Penn'77.Wid'78
☎ (610) 459-2358 . . ''Blossom Hill'' 240 Wawa Rd, Wawa, PA *19063*

Wood MR & MRS Frederick William 2d (Elaine | ☎ (410) 823-2578
Fennell) WestMd'37.JHop'41 . . . . | 512 Epsom Rd,
MR Frederick William 3d—Md'68 . . . . | Towson, MD *21286*
MR Wesley F—Ogle'74 . . . . |

Wood MR & MRS George M JR (Powell—Marguerite | ☎ (334) 281-9574
H McDaniel) Swb'57.Tex'47 . . . . | 3425 Thomas Av,
MISS Marguerite McD Powell . . . . | Montgomery, AL
| *36111*

Wood MRS Harleston R (Emily N Campbell) Ds. . . . | ☎ (561) 286-5630
MR Ross G . . . . | 4149 Old St Lucie
MR M Campbell . . . . | Blvd, Stuart, FL
| *34996*

Wood MR & MRS Harrison Wilson JR (Sabina S Adamson) Gm.Br'78.Cl'80
☎ (610) 649-3318 . . 448 Sabine Av, Wynnewood, PA *19096*

Wood MR & MRS Henry C (Fall—Sara R Bull) | ☎ (847) 251-2529
Ih.Sr.Cnt.Y'40 . . . . | 1420 Sheridan Rd,
MR David A—Y'74.Cl'77—at 911 Dorset St, | Apt 8G, Wilmette,
Apt 5, South Burlington, VT *05403* . . . . | IL *60091*
| Jan 1 . .
| ☎ (941) 598-2449
| 634 Bridgeway
| Lane, Naples, FL
| *34108*

Wood MR Henry N
☎ (619) 452-1904 . . 8370 Via Sonoma, Apt B, La Jolla, CA *92037*

Wood MR J Austen F—K.
☎ (704) 859-5223 . . 200 Warrior Dv, Tryon, NC *28782*

Wood MRS J Frank (Ann Budd) Br'37.Cl'39.Csp.Dar.Ncd.
☎ (813) 633-3237 . . 601 Nutmeg Place, Sun City Center,
FL *33573-5711*

Wood MR & MRS James (Frances J Randall) Hav'50
☎ (914) 666-8602 . . ''Braewold'' 153 Wood Rd, Mt Kisco, NY *10549*

Wood MR & MRS John Cotton (Denise Hyde) V'39.H'38
☎ (610) 388-2653 . . 29 Lonsdale Lane, Kennett Square, PA *19348*

Wood MRS John Walter (Suzanne J Cort) Chr.H.
☎ (212) 988-0487 . . 340 E 74 St, New York, NY *10021*

Wood MR & MRS John Walter JR (Charlotte M | of ☎ (011-44-171)
Cusack-Jobson) Lond'72.Unn.Plg.Ty'62. | 581-5274
SCal'77.Ox'79 . . . . | 35 Brompton
MR W Duncan—Cr'86—at Oxford . . . . | Square, London
| SW3 2AE, England
| ☎ (011-44-1333)
| 330-228
| Wynd House, Elie,
| Fife, Scotland

Wood MR & MRS Leighton C JR (Sarah L Hall) Lm.Dar.U'70 . . of
☎ (408) 972-4219 . . 17420 Lakeview Dv, Morgan Hill, CA *95037*
☎ (401) 423-2006 . . ''Tiffany Cottage'' 22 Old Walcott Av, Jamestown,
RI *02835*

Wood MRS Lindsay W (Linda L Jones)
Rich'65.NCar'68.Dar.....................
MISS Heather L—at 4511 Taney Av, Apt 201,
Alexandria, VA 22304 ....
MISS Tracy A—at Colgate ....
☎ (804) 233-2727
5817 Forest Hill Av,
Richmond, VA
23225

Wood MR & MRS Malbon R (Anne R Slingluff) Cda.
MISS Cynthia B—at ☎ (504) 943-4659
4019 Royal St, New Orleans, LA *70117* ......
☎ (504) 945-8630
4219 Burgundy St,
New Orleans, LA
70117

Wood MISS Margot W
☎ (617) 547-5899 . . 54 Lexington Av, Cambridge, MA *02138*

Wood MISS Nancy C
1525 Elliott Place NW, Washington, DC *20007*

Wood MR & MRS Peter H (Nina K Stuart) K.Hav'53.
MISS Daphne F ....
MR David P ....
MR Michael H H......................
☎ (914) 763-3614
Spring Hill Farm,
Cross River, NY
10518

Wood MR & MRS R Lyman JR (Hamilton—M
Meredith Young) H'59.H'61 ....
MISS (DR) Emilia F—Ws'90.Tufts'94—at
☎ (608) 278-8523 . . 805 Harbor House Dv,
Apt 8, Madison, WI *53719* ....
MR Henry W Hamilton—Ty'89—at
☎ (718) 871-5368 . . 71 Ocean P'kway,
Apt 6M, Brooklyn, NY *11218* ....
☎ (413) 566-3231
95 Mountain Rd,
Hampden, MA
01036

Wood MR & MRS Rawson L (Elizabeth F Ford) Sb.Csn.Chi.Hn.H'30 . . of
☎ (603) 253-4479 . . High Haith, PO Box 502, Center Harbor,
NH *03226*
☎ (617) 236-1571 . . 330 Beacon St, Boston, MA *02116*

Wood MR & MRS Richard D JR (Jeanette Andrews)
Ph.Gm.Va'60.Pa'64 ....
MISS Lisa A—Ham'88 ....
MR Richard D 3d—WashColl'91 ....
☎ (610) 459-5130
"Treetops"
501 Station Rd,
Wawa, PA
19063-5699

Wood MRS Richard Gilpin 3d (Martha W Thayer)
Ph........................
MISS Margaretta D—at ☎ (610) 935-3673
"Penllyn Cottage" Phoenixville, PA *19460* ....
☎ (610) 935-1776
Penllyn Farm,
PO Box 707,
Phoenixville, PA
19460

Wood MR & MRS Robert E 2d (Susan Mayer) Rc.Sc.On.Sr.Cos.Fy.P'60 . . of
☎ (312) 944-4475 . . 1430 N Lake Shore Dv, Chicago, IL *60610*
☎ (212) 486-9325 . . 136 E 64 St, Apt 3A, New York, NY *10021*

Wood MRS Robert L (Barbara Pulitzer) ....
MR Nicholas W—Alf'77—at ☎ (817) 277-9629
510 Lynda Lane, Arlington, TX *76010*........
☎ (415) 474-7246
1889 Broadway,
Apt 103,
San Francisco, CA
94109

Wood MISS Rowena A F—FIT'79 . . of
☎ (212) 988-7363 . . 167 E 82 St, New York, NY *10028*
☎ (513) 281-2681 . . 2706 Cleinview Av, Cincinnati, OH *45206*

Wood MR & MRS Stephen H (Chirlian—Jennifer A Lloyd)
☎ (406) 842-5722 . . 2997 H'way 287, Sheridan, WY *59749*

Wood MR & MRS Stephen J (Emily L Trautman) RI'85
☎ (508) 992-2504 . . 302 Nasketucket Way, Fairhaven, MA *02719*

Wood MR & MRS Theodore V JR (Betty S Deming)
Sg.Rc.Y'57.H'62 ⚓ ....
MISS Betty-Schuyler ....
MR Theodore V 3d ....
☎ (215) 247-2341
8765 Montgomery
Av, Wyndmoor, PA
19038

Wood MR & MRS Thomas W (Martha McA Borie) Pars'80.Dth'75 . . of
☎ (847) 234-5915 . . 1078 Edgewood Rd, Lake Forest, IL *60045*
☎ (616) 348-1902 . . 58 L'Arbre Croche, Harbor Springs, MI *49740*

Wood MRS Valentine (Vera Van B Richard) Aga.Cly.Sl.
☎ (561) 231-2691 . . 130 Island Creek Dv, John's Island, Vero Beach,
FL *32963-3301*

Wood MR & MRS W Godfrey (Deborah C Gray)
Conn'80.Cyb.Hb.H'63 ....
MISS Whitney B ....
see
Dilatory Domiciles

Wood MR & MRS W Kip (Rebecca L Cox) SCar'79.P'81
☎ (703) 698-7537 . . 2631 Woodley Place, Falls Church, VA *22046*

Wood MRS Walter Abbott (Van Alen—Renée Menassa) Cairo'45.Ri.
☎ (561) 833-4215 . . 161 Woodbridge Rd, Palm Beach, FL *33480*

Wood MR Wilfrid P—Mo.StL'58.H'60
☎ (864) 225-7442 . . 425 Green Pond Rd, Rte 7, Anderson,
SC *29624*

Wood MR & MRS William A JR (Gertrude Le Boutillier)
☎ (910) 692-7781 . . "Woodbin" PO Box 1257, Pinehurst, NC *28374*

Wood MR & MRS William H (Rebecca D Wentz)
Buck'77.Ds.H.'78.VillaN'82
☎ (610) 688-3468 . . 212 Midland Av, Wayne, PA *19087*

Wood MR & MRS William L (Marion F Geer) Csh.H.'40
☎ (516) 922-3013 . . 62 Ivy St, Oyster Bay, NY *11771*

Wood MR & MRS William P (Grace—Sara E Wadsworth)
Ph.Ssk.K.
MR Jeremy B Grace ....
MR Eric W Grace ....
☎ (716) 243-3862
"Swann Manor"
4060 Roots Tavern
Rd, Geneseo, NY
14454

Wood MR & MRS William R (Kay J von Hausswolff) Gm.Me.Penn'51
☎ (610) 688-5866 . . 8 Fenimore Lane, St Davids, PA *19087*

Woodbridge MRS M Brooks (Mary C Brooks)
Sth'60.Ncd.
MISS Calista H ....
MISS Amelia N ....
MR Harold R Brooks—Edg..............
see
Dilatory Domiciles

Woodbury MRS Perry S (Kane—Marjorie R Saisselin) Skd'35
☎ (904) 285-0680 . . Vicar's Landing Way, Box F208,
Ponte Vedra Beach, FL *32082*

Woodcock MRS Betty S B (Trent—Hussey—Betty S Barnes)
Cl'72.Dar.Ncd.Dc.Lm.
☎ (561) 832-8793 . . 308 Cocoanut Row, Apt 3, Palm Beach, FL *33480*

Woodd-Cahusac REV CANON & MRS Sydney A (Jean E Fleming) P'40.Y'47
☎ (203) 869-1060 . . 121 Clapboard Ridge Rd, Greenwich, CT *06830*

Woodger MR & MRS Bruce A (Lake—Cynthia R
Bullock) V'53.UnTheo'55.Eyc.Bost'58 ....
MISS Amanda R Lake—Ham'91.StJ'95—at
Portland, ME ....
MR Whitney B Lake—at Los Angeles, CA . .
of ☎ (609)924-6657
43 Cleveland Lane,
Princeton, NJ *08540*
☎ (508) 627-4089
"The Lighthouse"
Star Rte 52,
Edgartown, MA
02539

Woodhouse MR & MRS Henry Macauley (Joan K Neuberger) SL'53.Y'52
☎ (561) 234-8206 . . 341 Sabal Palm Lane, Vero Beach, FL *32963*

Woodhouse MRS James M (Gifford—Helen G MacLeod)
  ☎ (212) 744-8883 . . 101 E 75 St, New York, NY *10021*
Woodhull MR & MRS Timothy C (Deirdre K Guernsey) Bgt.Bost'80
  ☎ (914) 234-7630 . . The Farms Rd, Bedford, NY *10506*
Woodhull MRS William T (Harriet B Hubbard) Ncd.
  ☎ (401) 635-4537 . . "Top O'The Lane" 2 Taylor's Lane,
  Little Compton, Ri *02837-1111*
Woodhull MR & MRS William T JR (Clark—A Eve | ☎ (401) 849-3149
Bradnick) Nu'70.Park'65 . . . . | 27 Kay St, Newport,
  MISS A Kiersted C Clark—at Trinity . . . . | RI *02840*
Woodland MR Henry T JR—Eyc.Ny. ⚓
  ☎ (401) 846-7873 . . 35 Corne St, PO Box 1199, Newport, RI *02840*
Woodman MRS Herbert B (Jean F Maw) Csn.
  ☎ (802) 375-2766 . . River Rd, Rte 1, Box 3520, Arlington, VT *05250*
Woodrow MR & MRS William T JR (Mack— | ☎ (401) 849-9579
Catherine M Booth) Cw.Y'48 . . . . | "Highstairs"
  MISS Cornelia T—Ws'81 . . . . | 64 Prospect Hill St,
                                     | Newport, RI *02840*
Woodruff MRS Allen M (Emily M Hitch) Ant'75 . . | 350 W Allen Lane,
  MR John M—Earl'81.Duke'84 . . . . | Philadelphia, PA
  MR Matthew M—Mid'84.Cr'93 . . . . | *19119*
Woods MR Anthony H—Ham'94
  ☎ (310) 826-5093 . . 11966 Dorothy St, Brentwood, CA *90049*
Woods MRS Charles A JR (Elisabeth Gilbert) CtCol'38.An.
  ☎ (717) 232-2235 . . 1750 Mountainview Rd, Apt A21, Harrisburg,
  PA *17110*
Woods MR & MRS David P (Marjorie H Leech) Chi.
  ☎ (508) 771-0036 . . PO Box 355, Centerville, MA *02632*
Woods MISS Diantha L . . see MRS D M Long
Woods MR Douglas R . . see MRS D M Long
Woods MR & MRS Edward F (Lucia R Hedge) | ☎ (617) 383-1555
BMr'44.Stan'50.Ub.Cc.Bow'43.Tufts'50 . . . . . . | 231 Jerusalem Rd,
  MR William H—at Stanford . . . . | Cohasset, MA *02025*
Woods MR & MRS Edward L A (Virginia D Simpson) Y'20.Va'21
  ☎ (513) 321-1355 . . 3580 Shaw Av, Apt 509, Cincinnati, OH *45208*
Woods MISS Frances S (Etcheverry—Raffo— | ☎ (802) 684-3437
Frances S Woods) Ihy. . . . . | Heavensent Farm,
  MR John A—at N'eastern . . . . | PO Box 201,
                                       | Peacham, VT *05862*
Woods MRS Frank H (Louise H Brewer) On.Fy.Ncd.
  ☎ (847) 234-0550 . . 105 E Laurel Av, Apt 207, Lake Forest, IL *60045*
Woods MR & MRS Henry C JR (Jane Cheney) Y'44
  ☎ (609) 466-0497 . . 170 Rolling Hill Rd, Skillman, NJ *08558*
Woods MR & MRS James A (Elisabeth L Raymond) Csh.Y.Va'56 ⚓
  ☎ (516) 624-7653 . . 2 Fieldstone Lane, Oyster Bay, NY *11771*
Woods MISS Louisa V M (late Brewer C) . . . . Married at Aspen, CO
  Boudreau MR David K . . . . Jly 13'96
Woods MRS Patricia Fay (Woods—Guiberson—Patricia O Fay) Bur.
  ☎ (415) 931-7975 . . 145 Laurel St, Apt 5, San Francisco, CA *94118*
Woods MR & MRS Richard M (Robin E Brown) | ☎ (203) 655-2381
Man'vl'92.Bhm.Co.Cp.Cly.P'59 ⚓ . . . . | 174 Mansfield Av,
  MISS Whitney S . . . . | Darien, CT *06820*
  MISS Ashley E. . . . . |
  MR Richard S . . . . |

Woods MR & MRS Ward W JR (Priscilla Bacon) | of ☎ (212)722-5372
Rdc'64.Rc.Pr.Ln.Ri.B.Stan'64 . . . . | 1133 Fifth Av,
  MISS Katharine . . . . | New York, NY
  MISS Alexandra. . . . . | *10128*
                                       | ☎ (516) 759-1930
                                       | Old Tappan Rd,
                                       | Locust Valley, NY
                                       | *11560*
Woods MR William R (James A) . . . . . Married at Cold Spring Harbor, NY
  Wygand MISS Suzanne E (Allan R) . . . . Jun 29'96
Woodson MISS Christina . . see MRS S L Thomas
Woodson MR Mark N . . see MRS S L Thomas
Woodville MRS Louisa (Sweatt—Louisa Woodville) Bost'76.Va'79.Nu'85
  ☎ (540) 364-4435 . . 7025 Owl Road, Marshall, VA *20115*
Woodville MR & MRS Richard W (Faézé Talieh) Pa'70.H'75
  ☎ (610) 687-1031 . . 116 Windermere Av, Apt E2, Wayne,
  PA *19087-4132*
Woodward MR Bruce A—H'53
  ☎ (516) 747-5827 . . 109—14 St, Garden City, NY *11530*
Woodward MRS Charles H (Elizabeth P Gadsden) Yh.Pc.Sg.Ac.
  ☎ (215) 247-1149 . . 8000 Seminole Av, Philadelphia, PA *19118*
Woodward MR Charles W . . see MRS W Horan
Woodward MR George 3d
  ☎ (215) CH2-2034 . . 255 W Hartwell Lane, Philadelphia, PA *19118*
Woodward MR & MRS George S 4th (Hope T Potter)
  ☎ (508) 681-9056 . . 56 Stagecoach Rd, North Andover, MA *01845*
Woodward MR & MRS Gordon H (Ann E Bakewell) Y'91.Rut'92.H'92
  ☎ (914) 273-4788 . . 20 Old Mt Kisco Rd, Armonk, NY *10504*
Woodward MR Herbert N—Cw.Cr'33.Ch'36
  ☎ (508) 222-6242 . . 80 Ridgewood Rd, Attleboro, MA *02703*
Woodward MRS Hiram W (Letitia R McKenrick) . . . . Died at
                                       Deer Isle, ME Jun 23'96
Woodward MR & MRS Hiram W JR (Ann L | ☎ (410) 323-2135
Detwiler) CtCol'71.Mich'78.Mv.H'62.Y'75 . . . . | 908 W Northern
  JUNIORS MR Andrew H W . . . . | P'kway, Baltimore,
                                       | MD *21210*
Woodward MR James S JR. . . . . | ☎ (717) 359-4961
  MR David F . . . . | 1946 Fish & Game
                                       | Rd, Littlestown, PA
                                       | *17340*
Woodward MISS (DR) Kate S—Towson'66.SUNY'69.Cr'86 . . of
  ☎ (315) 364-7057 . . PO Box 88, Aurora, NY *13026*
  ☎ (803) 671-2648 . . 8 Gull Point Rd, Sea Pines, Hilton Head Island,
  SC *29928*
Woodward MR Matthew (W Philip) . . . . Married at Houston, TX
  Montague MISS Michelle (late Jon W) . . . . Apr 16'94
Woodward MISS Nancy Hyden
  ☎ (516) 324-5977 . . 54 Glade Rd, East Hampton, NY *11937*
Woodward MR & MRS Robert F JR (Mary J Reilly) | ☎ (301) 229-6376
Geo'67 . . . . | 17 Ericsson Rd,
  MR Jonathan F—at 62020 E Cottonwood, | Cabin John, MD
  Brightwood, OR *97011-0024* . . . . | *20818*
Woodward MR & MRS Robert S (Brenda Brady) | ☎ (805) 969-6349
Cal'51 . . . . | 1147 High Rd,
  MR Brendan B . . . . | Montecito, CA
                                       | *93108*

Woodward MR & MRS W Philip (Diane McQuown)   ☎ (415) 435-0540
Col'62.Nw'64. . . . . | 19 Oak Av,
MISS Anne. . . . . | Belvedere, CA
MISS Karen . . . . | *94920*

Woodward MRS William H (Phyllis McDougall)   ☎ (415) 492-2592
Sth'37.Dar. . . . . | 100 Thorndale Dv,
MISS P Lynn—Ore'73—at ☎ (707) 996-5216 | Apt 410,
1340 Lubeck, Sonoma, CA *95476* . . . . | San Rafael, CA
| *94903*

Woodwell MR & MRS J Knowles JR (Martha L Reed)   ☎ (561) 231-9678
Pg.Fcg.Rr. . . . . | 8367 Baytree Dv,
MR J Knowles 3d—at ☎ (541) 276-7862 | Vero Beach, FL
908 SE Byers Av, Pendleton, OR *97818* . . . . . . | *32963*

Woodwell MISS Pamela R (J Knowles JR) . . . . Married at Ligonier, PA
Geerdes MR Gregg P (late John E) . . . . Jly 8'95

Woodwell MR & MRS Richard H (Linda M Preston)
☎ (201) 444-7627 . . 36 Wyncote Rd, Ho Ho Kus, NJ *07423*

Woodworth MR & MRS A Vernon (Mary B Ringwalt) Tv.D.H'33
☎ (508) 785-1665 . . 67 Wilsondale St, Dover, MA *02030*

Woodworth MR & MRS J Gordon (Sally R Coleman) . . of
☎ (904) 277-4512 . . 3047 Sea Marsh Rd, Amelia Island Plantation,
Amelia Island, FL *32034*
☎ (207) 846-3255 . . 64 Blueberry Cove, Yarmouth, ME *04096*

Woodworth MR & MRS Robert S (Hillary F Hensel)
☎ (612) 473-1513 . . 15705 Second Av N, Plymouth, MN *55447*

Woody MR & MRS Bernard L (Cécile M Bakewell)   ☎ (303) 322-0024
Stan'48. . . . . | 25 Elm St, Denver,
MR Brian N—Col'87 . . . . | CO *80220*
MR Cary T—Col'89—at ☎ (303) 771-5147
4500 S Monaco St, Apt 1726, Denver, CO *80237* |

Woody MR Eric L—ColSt'80
☎ (303) 320-4387 . . 327 Dahlia St, Denver, CO *80220*

Wooldridge MRS William P (Van Stralen—C Elizabeth Tubby)
100 Thorndale Rd, Apt 426, San Rafael, CA *94903*

Woollam MR & MRS Philip M (Anacker—Tina L Freeman)
ArtColl'72.Exet'70 ⚓
☎ (504) 865-9344 . . 1640 State St, New Orleans, LA *70118*

Woolman MR Henry N JR—Cc.Aht'25.Mit'29 . . . . . | ☎ (717) 646-3649
MRS Joan W Glenn (Joan L Woolman) . . . . . | Pocono Lake
MISS Holly T Glenn . . . . | Preserve, PA *18348*
MR George S Glenn JR . . . . |

Woolsey MISS R Audrey (Dvorak—R Audrey Woolsey) Va'75.UMiami'91
☎ (703) 413-3619 . . 1505 Crystal Dv, Apt 613, Arlington, VA *22202*

Woolverton MRS Ethel M (Handy—Ethel L Manville)
☎ (516) 624-8878 . . 78 Harbor Rd, Oyster Bay, NY *11771-1702*

Woolverton MR William H JR—Y'41
☎ (615) 356-7488 . . 6666 Brookmont Terr, Apt 1205, Nashville,
TN *37205*

Woolverton MR & MRS William H 3d (Theresa L Mara)
Bnd'79.Nu'86.Cy.Sar.Aht'73.Camb'75.Cl'79
☎ (617) 235-8341 . . 56 Westcliff Rd, Weston, MA *02193*

Woolwine MR & MRS Woodrum E (Susanne B Phillips) GaTech'39
☎ (714) 640-1146 . . 212 Morning Canyon Rd, Corona Del Mar,
CA *92625*

Wooten MRS Harry C JR (Dorothy M Caroé) . . . . . . | ☎ (919) 527-0581
MR T Sheffield . . . . | 2114 Hardee Rd,
| Kinston, NC *28501*

Wooten MAJ GEN & MRS Sidney C (Mary W Gibson)
McG'36.An.Cvc.Cc.USA'30
☎ (301) 656-4519 . . 8101 Connecticut Av, S509, Chevy Chase,
MD *20815*

Worcester MR Dean K JR—Y'44.Camb'50
☎ (212) 794-2198 . . 506 E 88 St, New York, NY *10128*

Worcester MR & MRS R O Colt (Anastasia I   ☎ (410) 472-2153
Epsilantis) JHop'75.JHop'72 . . . . | 1904 Corbridge
MISS Anastasia C . . . . | Lane, Monkton, MD
MR Sothoron K . . . . | *21111*
JUNIORS MR Gordon B 2d . . . . |

Worcester MRS Sothoron (Elizabeth K Sothoron) Cda.
☎ (410) 532-7003 . . 5203 Falls Rd, Baltimore, MD *21210*

Worcester MR & MRS William W (Constance V   ☎ (860) 868-7013
Tenney) V'52.Y'50 . . . . | 6 Four Steeples Rd
MR Benjamin T—at 2799 Rustic Place, Apt 221, | S, Box 358,
Little Canada, MN *55117* . . . . | Washington Depot,
| CT *06794-0358*

Worden MR James A—Ll.P'35
PO Box 245, Princeton, NJ *08540*

Worden MISS Pamela—Ws'66
☎ (508) 433-9793 . . PO Box 20, Groton, MA *01450*

Worman MR & MRS Horace D 2d (Sarah Armstrong)
MaryW'48.Nu'49.Va'49.Va'52
☎ (213) 464-7077 . . 569 N Wilcox Av, Los Angeles, CA *90004-1110*

Worman MISS Mignon D (Roark—Mignon D Worman)
Va'84.Coro'85.SCal'90
☎ (513) 871-6957 . . 1245 Halpin Av, Hyde Park, Cincinnati, OH *45208*

Worman MISS Sally Hopson—SCal'80.Day'87
☎ (213) 464-7077 . . 569 N Wilcox Av, Los Angeles, CA *90004*

Worman MISS Sarah W (Pretzinger—Sarah W Worman) Day'76
7860 Stonegate Dv, Cincinnati, OH *45255*

Worm de Geldern MR & MRS Vagn (Sarah Barrows)   ☎ (860) 395-0939
Rdc'56.Ny.Co.Exy.StLaw'61 ⚓ . . . . | ''Toad Hall''
MISS Erika A . . . . | 9 Mill Rock Rd W,
MR Barrows . . . . | Old Saybrook, CT
MR Andrew. . . . . | *06475*

Worrall MISS Catherine A—Sim'77
☎ (215) 233-1305 . . 211 Glendalough Rd, Erdenheim, PA *19038*

Worrell MR Granville 3d—Pa'50 . . . . | ☎ (301) 598-6786
MISS Carolyn E . . . . | 3406 Chiswick
| Court, Apt 1B,
| Silver Spring, MD
| *20906*

Worsham MR & MRS David D (Alexandria Wall)
☎ (808) 324-0676 . . PO Box 390866, Kailua Kona, HI *96739*

Worsley MR & MRS James R JR (Cornelia Cheston)
V'46.Mt.Cvc.ECar'44.H'49
☎ (301) 656-3961 . . 11 Quincy St, Chevy Chase, MD *20815*

Worsley MR & MRS Peter F (Lila G Purinton) Y'65.SFrArt'67
☎ (415) 669-1381 . . PO Box 319, Inverness, CA *94937*

Worth MR & MRS David McAlister (Laurenze Jones)   ☎ (910) 273-5414
Stph'76.NCar'72 . . . . | 1604 Granville Rd,
JUNIORS MR Alexander McA 3d . . . . | Greensboro, NC
| *27408*

Worth MR James H
☎ (212) 861-1256 . . 237 E 81 St, New York, NY *10028*

Worth MISS Jaqueline M—BMr'86.Nu'91.Cly.Ds.
☎ (212) 595-5996 . . 205 W 89 St, New York, NY *10024*

Worth MR & MRS Theron O JR (Merwin C Braxton) | ☎ (212) 838-6288
Sth'61.Cl'64.CUNY'94.Cly.Ds.Myf.Ncd.P'60. | 200 E 66 St,
Nu'67 . . . . | New York, NY
MR Carter Braxton—Ds.Bost'89— | *10021*
☎ (212) 826-9676 . . . . |
MR Spencer E—Ds.JHop'92 . . . . |
MR Blaine Huntting—Ds.—at NYU . . . . |
JUNIORS MISS Laura Marshall—Ds.—at Groton . . |

Worth MR William A JR—Wil.
☎ (212) 874-4243 . . 40 W 67 St, Apt 10A, New York, NY *10023*

Worthing MR & MRS Clifford A (Louise W Pugh) Sar.Cw.Ofp.Ncd.Me'48
☎ (513) 871-2085 . . 802 Wakefield Dv, Cincinnati, OH *45226*

Worthington MRS Arthur L (Burdeene Irvin)
☎ (603) 772-1494 . . Dixville Village 207, 7 Riverwoods Dv, Exeter, NH *03833*

Worthington MRS Edward E (Maryann Wright) . . . | ☎ (216) 256-1133
MISS Ann R—at ☎ (813) 343-0472 | "Thrushwood"
1219—80 St S, St Petersburg, FL *33707* . . . . . . | 7980 Eagles Rd W,
MR Edward E JR . . . . | Kirtland, OH *44094*

Worthington MR & MRS Edward H 3d (Josephine S E George)
Wheat'82.Gv.P'82
☎ (410) 363-7010 . . 102 Garrison Forest Rd, Owings Mills, MD *21117*

Worthington MR George M G—Geo'86.LondEc'93
☎ (011-61-41) 220-1777 . . PO Box 1131, Bondi Junction, NSW 2022, Australia

Worthington MR George W
☎ (301) 934-9235 . . "Gilbert Hill" Box 323, Charlotte Hall, MD *20622*

Worthington MR & MRS Henry M (Sallie G W Hurst) Gv.P'52
☎ (410) 363-0579 . . 106 Garrison Forest Rd, Garrison, MD *21117-9999*

Worthington MR & MRS Ralph 4th (Lucinda K Morrisey) Rc.Lic . . .of
☎ (212) 744-3252 . . 196 E 75 St, New York, NY *10021-3261*
☎ (516) 653-6614 . . 25 Edgewood Rd, Box 1399, Quogue, NY *11959*
☎ (305) 367-4945 . . Ocean Reef Club, 408 Carysfort Rd, Key Largo, FL *33037*

Worthington MRS Sarah G (Price—Sarah Gilmer)
☎ (804) 977-6695 . . Box 274, 977 Seminole Trail, Charlottesville, VA *22901*

Wrangham MRS Josefa M (Josefa M Wilson) SL'60.Cl'63.Sim'80
☎ (617) 396-9169 . . 69 Sturges St, Medford, MA *02155*

Wrapp MR Paul R . . see E S Villmoare 3d

Wray MR & MRS David B (Patty H Bundy)
Cy.K.Sm.Chi.Ht.Cda.Aht'52.H'55
☎ (617) 731-8863 . . 37 Woodman Rd, Chestnut Hill, MA *02167*

Wray MRS Gay F (Gay I Firestone) . . . . | ☎ (602) 948-8270
MR Timothy F—P'88 . . . . | 7308 N Red Ledge
MISS Maryanne H (Aeed—Maryanne H Wray) . . | Dv, Paradise Valley,
MISS Laurie D (Thaxter—Laurie D Wray) . . . . | AZ *85253*

Wray MR & MRS Michael B (Reid—Mary Denny Scott)
Swb'61.K.Fic.Rv.Ht.Ll.Aht'57.Cl'60
☎ (804) 359-3052 . . 6 John Christopher Court, Richmond, VA *23226*

Wray MR & MRS Michael B (Charlotte B Daniel)
SL'88.BostColl'92.Fic.Fiy.Bow'83.Me'87
☎ (212) 772-9533 . . 500 E 85 St, Apt 6L, New York, NY *10028*

Wrenn MR George L—H'50
☎ (603) 539-7265 . . Maple St, Box 247, Freedom, NH *03836*

Wrenn MR & MRS Robert D (Patricia Spinning) | ☎ (617) 326-1707
D.Chi.H'48 . . . . | 725 High St,
MR George L 2d . . . . | Dedham, MA *02026*

Wright MR & MRS Albert J 3d (Jane S Morgan)
MtH'48.Cy.St.Sar.Ham'49.Buf'53
☎ (716) 839-2776 . . 252 Burroughs Dv, Amherst, NY *14226-3907*

Wright MRS Barbara Brush (Barbara A Brush) | of ☎ (212)663-3703
CtCol'67.Nu'81 | 336 Central Park W,
MISS Christina P—at Georgetown . . . . | New York, NY
| *10025*
| ☎ (516) 749-1496
| 74 N Ferry Rd,
| Shelter Island, NY
| *11964*

Wright MRS Bartlett B (H Jean Croy)
234 Beaupre Av, Grosse Pointe Farms, MI *48236*

Wright MRS Beaumont W (Sarah K C Griest) | ☎ (215) MI6-6555
Sg.Ac.Cda. . . . . | "The Orchards"
MR William B . . . . | 617 Plymouth Rd,
| Gwynedd Valley,
| PA *19437*

Wright CAPT Benjamin T—USMC.An.USN'85
☎ (617) 942-2720 . . 129 Woburn St, Apt 2, Reading, MA *01867*

Wright MR & MRS Burdette S JR (King—Suzanne W | ☎ (703) 777-1169
Walker) Cvc.Geo'54 | Locust Hill Farm,
MR Andrew W . . . . | Rte 4, Box 48,
MISS Rahel O'F Crowley . . . . | Leesburg, VA *20176*

Wright MR & MRS Carroll A (Bisharat—Janet E Schweifler) Cal'56.SFr'51
☎ (916) 265-0707 . . "Tamerlane" 14765 Banner Lava Cap, Nevada City, CA *95959*

Wright MR & MRS Charles A (Clarke—Eleanor | ☎ (512) 453-4855
Custis Broyles) V'45.C.Yn.Wes'48.Y'49 . . . . . . | 5304 Western Hills
MISS Margot Clarke . . . . | Dv, Austin, TX
| *78731*

Wright MR & MRS Charles P JR (Holly McIntire) | ☎ (804) 979-2373
Cal'66.Dav'57 . . . . | 940 Locust Av,
MR Luke S H—So'92.Va'94—at New Coll | Charlottesville, VA
Oxford . . . . | *22901*

Wright MR & MRS Christopher Q (Nancy G DuBois) | ☎ (860) 242-5436
BMr'60.Ty'59.Cl'62 . . . . | Guilmartin Rd,
MISS Elizabeth D—Br'86—at ☎ (801) 539-8138 | Bloomfield, CT
702 Eleventh Av, Salt Lake City, UT *84103* . . . | *06002*

Wright MR & MRS Clifford R JR (Eleanor B White) B'gton'46.Y'49
☎ (805) 969-5024 . . 848 Picacho Lane, Santa Barbara, CA *93108*

Wright MR Dudley H A 2d (Vernon H C) . . . . . Married at Granville, OH
Forbes MISS Bronwyn . . . . Nov 25'95

Wright MRS Dudley Hugh (Helen M Carroll)
"New Old House" 20500 Gunpowder Rd, Millers, MD *21107-1524*

Wright MRS Edward B JR (Bruch—Marguerite Copper)
2218 Dogwood Circle, Mt Dora, FL *32757*

Wright MR & MRS George I 3d (M Ann Kyle) | ☎ (610) 524-9463
Bvr'66.StA.Rv.VillaN'66 . . . . | 408 Balderston Dv,
MISS Jessica M—at ☎ (704) 822-6531 | Exton, PA *19341*
2428 Belsite Dv, Belmont, NC *28012* . . . . |

Wright MR & MRS Gordon R (Swift—Margaret C Whipple) Cas.On. . . . . ☎ (805) 969-8843
MR Gordon W. . . . . 300 Hot Springs Rd,
MISS Lindsay C Swift . . . . Apt 158, Montecito,
MISS Helen S Brown . . . . CA *93108*

Wright MISS Henrietta (Hinson—Henrietta Wright) . . . . Married at
Lake Tahoe, CA
Stead MR Edward B (Charles E) . . . . Mch 16'96

Wright MRS Ian Michael (Catherine A Skelly) . . . . ☎ (301) 652-4308
MR John Story—Conn'84—at 91 Spring St, 7209 Lenhart Dv,
Hartford, CT *06105* . . . . Chevy Chase, MD
20815

Wright DR Irving S—Bgt.Snc.Cr'23.Cr'26
☎ (212) 288-5342 . . 25 East End Av, New York, NY *10028*

Wright MR & MRS Jefferson C (Sara C ☎ (011-33-42)
Breckenridge) V'54.B.Pn.P'52 66-97-99
MR Jefferson C JR . . . . Grand Côté Nord,
F13100
Le Tholonet,
Aix-en-Provence,
France

Wright MRS Jerauld (Phyllis Blagden Thompson) ☎ (202) 363-5402
Cvc.Sl. . . . . 4101 Cathedral Av
MR William M 3d . . . . NW, Apt 1001,
Washington, DC
20016

Wright MR John B 2d—P'76
☎ (215) 248-4429 . . 702 W Mt Airy Av, Philadelphia, PA *19119*

Wright MR & MRS John M (Jeanne W Lewis) Me.Rv.Ncd.Pitt'31
☎ (610) 527-0568 . . 1314 Old Gulph Rd, PO Box 719, Bryn Mawr,
PA *19010*

Wright MR & MRS Kenneth T (Judith B Atwood) ☎ (847) 251-9262
Sr.Cw.Aht'52.Stan'54. 626 Warwick Rd,
MISS Kimberly T. . . . . Kenilworth, IL
MISS Cameron M *60043*
MR Kenneth T JR—StLaw'91 . . . .

Wright MISS Louise V W (Schmucki—McHaffie—Louise V W Wright)
Swb'79.Dar.Ncd.
535 Baeder Rd, Jenkintown, PA *19046*

Wright MRS Lydia W (Shearer—Lydia R Woolman) Me.Cs.Ncd.
☎ (610) 827-7246 . . 3639 Conestoga Rd, Glenmoore, PA *19343*

Wright MRS Margaret Z (Margaret H Zook) Ncd. . . ☎ (610) 964-1322
MR Robert T—Rv. . . . . 1477 Lexington
Lane, Wayne, PA
19087

Wright MR & MRS Minturn T 3d (Nonya R Stevens) ☎ (610) 647-0492
V'55.Ph.Y.'49.Pa'52 . . . . 1200 Sugartown Rd,
MISS Marianne F H—Cl'90—at Berwyn, PA *19312*
☎ (212) 541-8829 . . 301 W 53 St, Apt 19K,
New York, NY *10019* . . . .
MR Richard S—Br'82—at 2552 Dearborn Dv,
Hollywood, CA *90068* . . . .
MR Robert M—Rich'87—at ☎ (508) 433-8814
9 River Rd, Pepperell, MA *01463* . . . .

Wright MR Minturn T 4th (Minturn T 3d) . . . . . . Married at Berwyn, PA
Marcus MISS Gwen L (Samuel C) . . . . Jun 29'96

Wright MR & MRS Minturn T 4th (Gwen L Marcus)
Y'79.Y'81.Y'80.Cal'82.Cal'86
☎ (202) 462-8741 . . 1726 S St NW, Apt 1, Washington, DC *20009*

Wright SIR Paul H G & LADY (Rathbone—Beatrice F Clough)
☎ (011-44-171) 828-7633 . . 62 Westminster Gardens, Marsham St,
London SW1P 4JG, England

Wright MR & MRS Peter (Mary S Roberts) Rc.Gm.Ac.Y'41
☎ (610) 687-1024 . . 155 Beaumont Rd, Devon, PA *19333*

Wright MRS Preston L JR (Dyett—Irene G Soyka) G.St.
☎ (716) 885-3563 . . 731 W Ferry St, Apt 9W, Buffalo, NY *14222*

Wright MR & MRS R Denny (Anne C Griffin) Col'43
☎ (334) 342-6133 . . 70 Croydon Rd, Mobile, AL *36608*

Wright MR Ralph W JR
1040 Jasmine Court, Vista, CA *92083*

Wright CAPT (RET) & MRS (DR) Richard T (Pierson— ☎ (860) 434-7495
Anne Bingham) V'51.Cl'55.Cl'72.An.Cw.Csn. Griswold Point,
Cda.USN'53. . . . . Old Lyme, CT
MISS Christian L—Bard'85—at *06371*
☎ (212) 988-3915 . . 201 E 66 St, Apt 10H,
New York, NY *10021* . . . .
MISS Elizabeth T—Ken'90—at
☎ (617) 942-2720 . . 129 Woburn St, Reading,
MA *01867* . . . .

Wright MRS Sandra S (Tower—Ohrstrom— ☎ (212) 541-9005
Houghton—Sandra S Wright) Cly. . . . . 146 W 57 St,
MISS Winifred E A Ohrstrom . . . . New York, NY
MR Wright R S Ohrstrom—Ken'93 . . . . *10019*

Wright MR & MRS Spencer D 3d (Marie L W Oller)
R.Pc.Pe.Ph.Wms'43 . . of
☎ (215) 984-8385 . . Cathedral Village K106, 600 E Cathedral Rd,
Philadelphia, PA *19128*
☎ (011-33) 33-07-53-11 . . ''Alouette'' 50590 Regneville-sur-Mer,
France

Wright MR & MRS Stevens T M (Rosamond W Hall) Sb.Cy.H.'33
Fox Hill Village 114, 10 Longwood Dv, Westwood, MA *02090*

Wright MRS Sylvia A (Van Sloun—Sylvia A Almy) MontSt'57.MontSt'59
☎ (602) 991-1578 . . 6863 E Kelton Lane, Scottsdale, AZ *85254*

Wright MRS Thomas A (Alice D McAllister) ☎ (415) 986-6646
Cal'53.Fr. . . . . 352 Chestnut St,
MISS Peggy M . . . . San Francisco, CA
MISS Kathy B *94133*

Wright MR & MRS Thomas Henry JR (Elizabeth D Labouisse)
Sth'55.NCar'41
☎ (910) 762-0224 . . 2232 Acacia Dv, Wilmington, NC *28403*

Wright MR & MRS Thomas P (Wear—Elizabeth S ☎ (603) 563-8435
Smith) Ty'55 . . . . W Lake Rd,
MISS Georgia B . . . . PO Box 100,
MR Thomas S—at 4 Derne St, Apt 3, Boston, MA Dublin, NH *03444*
02114 . . . .
MR James A—at 54 Marshall St, Brookline, MA
02116 . . . .
MISS Katherine S Wear . . . .

Wright MRS Thruston JR (Patricia M Bahen) SHill'43
☎ (941) 953-3692 . . 336 Bob White Way, Sarasota, FL *34236*

Wright MR & MRS Vernon H C (Lucy H Babb) NotreDMd'66.Balt'69 . . . . ☎ (410) 239-2224
MISS Katherine B—at 1210 W 10 St, Apt 1, 21619 Gunpowder
Wilmington, DE *19806* . . . . Rd, Lineboro, MD
21102-2415

Wright MR & MRS Whitney (Anne Wigglesworth) of ☎ (617)326-3595
Cy.H.'39 . . . . 10 Longwood Dv,
MISS Elisabeth—at ☎ (415) 927-7091 Apt 457, Westwood,
116 Crescent Rd, Corte Madera, CA *94925* . . . . MA *02090*
☎ (508) 775-0484
PO Box 185,
Hyannis Port, MA
02647

Wright MRS William Quinby JR (Eleanor Wurtsbaugh) Cal'26
☎ (415) 892-9941 . . 11 Celeste Court, Novato, CA *94947*

Wrinkle MISS Anne Blair—Va'83.CUNY'91
☎ (212) 979-6056 . . 83 E 7 St, Apt 2B, New York, NY *10003*

Wrinkle MR & MRS John N (Louise R Agee) ☎ (205) 871-6767
Conv'52.Va'56.K.Cy.Chi.Ncd.Yn.Van'51.Y'55 . 2 Beechwood Rd,
MISS Margaret R—Y'85.Y'92.Ala'92 . . . . Birmingham, AL
35213

Wriston MR & MRS Walter B (Kathryn A Dineen) Ri.Ln.Mt.Cly.Cs.Wes'41
870 United Nations Plaza, New York, NY *10017*

Wulfing MR & MRS Charles 4th (A Barbara Fritze) ☎ (314) 863-5454
Rc.P'51 . . . . 168 N Central Av,
MISS Andrea G . . . . St Louis, MO *63105*

Wulfing MR & MRS Frederick W (Shirley A Thomas) ☎ (770) 396-3445
Colg'55.Wash'59 . . . . 7609 Auden Trail,
MISS Kathryn W . . . . Dunwoody, GA
MR John T *30338*

Wulsin DR & MRS John H (Rosamond F Reed) ☎ (513) 791-1720
H'42.Roch'44 . . . . 8405 Spooky
MISS Rosamond R . . . . Hollow Rd,
Cincinnati, OH
45242

Wulsin MR Lucien—Qc.H'39.Va'47
☎ (303) 444-9035 . . 2250 Mariposa Av, Boulder, CO *80302*

Wulsin MRS Pamela P (Macdonald—Pamela Pardee)
☎ (303) 759-8813 . . 2305 S Fillmore St, Denver, CO *80210*

Wunder DR Richard P—C.Chr.Mto.StJ.H'46.H'52.H'55 . . of
☎ (212) 586-5287 . . 24 W 55 St, New York, NY *10019*
☎ (619) 454-5301 . . ''Villa San Maurizio'' 7280 Carrizo Dv, La Jolla,
CA *92037*

Wuorinen MR Charles P—C.Cl'61
☎ (212) 666-6068 . . 870 West End Av, New York, NY *10025*

Wurlitzer MRS Rembert (Roth—Anna L Little) Cly. | ☎ (212) 861-8195
MR Rudolph . . . . 920 Park Av, Apt
15B, New York, NY
10028-0208

Wurts MR Christopher C J—Me.Rc.
☎ (610) 827-1585 . . 1620 Conestoga Rd, Chester Springs, PA *19425*

Wurts MR & MRS Clarence Z (Patricia E Weaver) ☎ (215) 643-1731
Rc.Rb.Ph.Pc.B.P.'62 ⚓ . . . . Plymouth Rd,
MR Charles S—Rc.Conn'86 . . . . Box 297, Blue Bell,
MR Benjamin W—Rc.Ny.HWSth'87 . . . . PA *19422*

Wurts MR & MRS John S (Roberta P Ray) Sth'46
☎ (941) 484-7471 . . 146 Inlets Blvd, Nokomis, FL *34275*

Wurts MR & MRS John W JR (Tracy T Johnson) ☎ (610) 644-6938
V'64.Me.Pa'61 . . . . 831 Forest Lane,
MISS M Wister . . . . Malvern, PA *19355*

Wurts MRS Molthan (Neilson—Caroline R ☎ (610) 687-2593
Molthan) . . . . 400 S Wayne Av,
MR Reed M W . . . . Wayne, PA
MR Henry C—BrigY'88—at 9417 Great Hills *19087-4017*
Trail, Apt 2051, Austin, TX *78759* . . . .
MISS Caroline M (Smith—Caroline M Wurts)
Boise'86 . . . .
MISS (DR) Marian E Molthan—Cl'52—at Rte 1,
Box 346, Laveen, AZ *85339* . . . .

Wyatt MR & MRS Felton Mark (Ann A Storrow) of ☎ (202)965-3054
BMr'48.Cos.Ncd.Cal'43 . . . . 3310 P St NW,
MISS Susan A—at ☎ (212) 254-8310 . . 35 E 9 St, Washington, DC
New York, NY *10003* *20007*
☎ (916) 583-3157
''Dolce Far Niente''
PO Box 176,
Carnelian Bay, CA
96140

Wyatt MRS Joseph W (Dorothy Georgens)
☎ (703) 329-1572 . . 2101 Belle Haven Rd, Alexandria, VA *22307*

Wyatt-Brown MR & MRS Bertram (Anne J Marbury)
Rdc'61.JHop'62.Cwr'72.So'53.Camb'57.Camb'61. JHop'63
☎ (352) 377-2189 . . 3201 NW Eighteenth Av, Gainesville, FL *32605*

Wyckoff MR Andrew P . . see C W Banta

Wyckoff MR & MRS Clinton R JR (Dorothy K Goodyear) St.
☎ (716) 655-0065 . . 61 Troon Rd, East Aurora, NY *14052*

Wyckoff MR & MRS Clinton R 3d (Shelby S of ☎ (716)873-7672
de Peyster) Fic . . . . 51 Nottingham Terr,
MR Ashton G—Vt'92 . . . . Buffalo, NY *14216*
☎ (561) 655-2725
315 Pendleton Lane,
Palm Beach, FL
33480

Wyckoff MR & MRS Ferdinand L JR (Mary L Bayles)
Mid'54.Un.Hl.Mid'54.CarnM'57
☎ (914) 241-3728 . . 19 Crow Hill Rd, Mt Kisco, NY *10549*

Wyckoff MR Kevin B (Kevin M) . . . . Married at Buffalo, NY
O'Connor MISS Emily K (Daniel F) . . . . Aug 24'96

Wyckoff MR Stephen S—Hl.F&M'82.Nu'88
☎ (212) 410-7111 . . 160 E 89 St, Apt 4B, New York, NY *10128*

Wyeth MISS Carolyn L—Denis'78.Me.
☎ (610) 520-0357 . . 220 Rodney Circle, Bryn Mawr, PA *19010*

Wyeth MISS Christina L (Manice—Christina L Wyeth)
☎ (212) 861-1883 . . 410 E 74 St, Apt 1B, New York, NY *10021*

Wyeth MR & MRS Leonard J (Pamela I Evans)
☎ (860) 435-2358 . . ''Gander Run'' 417 Salmon Kill Rd, Lakeville,
CT *06039-0393*

Wyeth MR & MRS Leonard J JR (Susan Edler) RISD'77.Syr'75.Va'77
☎ (860) 767-2346 . . 9 Summit St, Box 427, Ivoryton, CT *06442*

Wyeth MR & MRS Marion S JR (Nancy Coffin) P'48
☎ (914) 232-7986 . . 257 Mt Holly Rd, Katonah, NY *10536*

Wyeth MRS Stuart Mac R (Cresap—Madeleine C Reed) Me.Gm.Ac. . . . .
   MR Mark W Cresap 3d—Wms'74 . . . . | ☎ (610) LA7-2190 945 Crestmont Rd, Bryn Mawr, PA *19010*

Wylie DR & MRS Harold W JR (Mavis J Leavitt) Ws'54.GeoW'88.Cos.Park'53.H'57
  ☎ (202) 546-1452 . . 11—7 St NE, Washington, DC *20002-6021*

Wylie MRS Shelby S (Shelby Crawford Simon) SL'77.Myf.
  ☎ (212) 799-2258 . . 275 Central Park W, New York, NY *10024*

Wyman MISS Anne C . . . .
  MR Jeffries JR—at ☎ (617) 784-3692
  9 Jefferson Lane, Sharon, MA *02067* . . . . | ☎ (617) 354-6029 72 Raymond St, Cambridge, MA *02140*

Wyman MR & MRS Franklin JR (Ruth Cheney) V'46.Cy.Cw.Ds.Chi.Ncd.H'43 . . . .
  MR Franklin 3d—Cyb.H'70—at
  ☎ (212) 685-3948 . . 415 E 37 St, Apt 14A, New York, NY *10016* . . . .
  MR Charles C—H'75—at ☎ (914) 739-6864
  6 Chester Court, Peekskill, NY *10566* . . . . | ☎ (617) 566-0120 83 Lee St, Brookline, MA *02146-5912*

Wyman MR & MRS Joseph C (Anne H Joyce) Un.Cly.Dc.Dh.Ncd.Delft'50.Cl'59
  MISS Anne B—Y'90.INSEAD'93.Cly.Yn.—at
  ☎ (011-44-171) 351-0716 . . 60 Redcliffe Rd, London SW10 9NQ, England . . . . | of ☎ (212)838-7942 570 Park Av, New York, NY *10021*
☎ (516) 653-4029 "The Loj" 14 Shinnecock Rd, PO Box 337, Quogue, NY *11959*

Wyman MR & MRS Parker D (Patricia C Howland) Gi.Cvc.Myf.Sl.Cda.H'44 ⚓
  ☎ (301) 654-1463 . . 3806 Raymond St, Chevy Chase, MD *20815*

Wynne MISS Mildred E—Me.Dar.W.
  ☎ (610) 896-7068 . . 25 N Buck Lane, Apt 7, Haverford, PA *19041*

Wynne-Willson MR & MRS Michael F (Anne W Patterson) Cy.Chi.
  MR Mark L—at 2918 Mountain Springs Rd, Reno, NV *89509* . . . . | ☎ (617) 329-4680 29 Orchard Circle, Westwood, MA *02090*

Wyper MISS Florence A—RISD'75
  ☎ (212) 744-5152 . . 311 E 72 St, New York, NY *10021*

Wyrough MR & MRS Alexander P H (Kathryn M Brown) Ty'82.Mt.W&M'80.JHop'87.Pa'87
  ☎ (914) 478-5184 . . 4 Pond Lane, Hastings-on-Hudson, NY *10706-3639*

Wyrough MR & MRS (DR) Peter S (Misty L Wray) Ga'83.Ga'88.StV'83
  ☎ (301) 982-0070 . . PO Box 268, Greenbelt, MD *20768*

Wyrough COL & MRS Richard R (Frances M Smith) Mt.Sl.Cda.USA'50.Geo'55.GeoW'67
  ☎ (301) 694-0856 . . 101 Record St, Frederick, MD *21701-5417*

Wyrough MR & MRS Richard R P (Mary Elizabeth Glascock) WashColl'82.Cc.W&L'78.W&L'85
  ☎ (410) 257-3357 . . 533 Herring Av, Dunkirk, MD *20754*

Y

Yacubian MR & MRS Lawrence M (Susan G Almy) .
  MR Job A . . . .
  MR Lawrence G . . . . | ☎ (508) 636-2431 Quansett Farm, 1194 Horseneck Rd, South Westport, MA *02790*

Yahn MR & MRS William B (Nancy S Stiles) Tex'90.Ty'59.Pa'64.Ga'65 . . . .
  JUNIORS MISS Elizabeth S . . . . | ☎ (512) 263-2331 1101 Crystal Creek Dv, Austin, TX *78746*

Yancey MR C Stephen JR—Ty'71
  ☎ (214) 522-4985 . . 4703 Travis St, Dallas, TX *75205*

Yancey MRS Charles S (Anne Richardson) V'36.Ncd. . . . .
  MISS Sherod A—V'68.Ncd. . . . . | ☎ (207) 833-2951 Merriconeag Rd, South Harpswell, ME *04079*
Feb 1 . .
4242 Lomo Alto Dv, Dallas, TX *75219*

Yandell MRS David W (Catherine S Colt) . . . .
  MISS Hope . . . .
  MISS Robin—at 2710 S Lafayette St, Denver, CO *80210* . . . . | ☎ (802) 878-3742 Oak Hill, RR 1, Williston, VT *05495*

Yandell MR Lunsford P—Rcn.P'24 . . . .
  MR Alexander V N Barney—at 1015—1 St, Manhattan Beach, CA *90266* . . . . | ☎ (602) 948-4848 6114 N Invergordon Rd, Scottsdale, AZ *85253*

Yandell MR & MRS Lunsford P JR (Barlow—Cynthia A Pierson) . . . .
  MR Lunsford P 6th—at ☎ (817) 377-2704 5035 Birchman Av, Ft Worth, TX *76107* . . . . . . | ☎ (214) 528-7695 4433 Stanhope Av, Dallas, TX *75205*

Yarbrough MR & MRS David Coleman (May H Taylor) Ala'61.Ala'60.Ala'63 . . . .
  MR David C JR . . . .
  MR George T . . . . | ☎ (334) 834-2793 3344 Boxwood Dv, Montgomery, AL *36111*

Yardley MRS Alfred J (Augusta H L Du Val) Cly.Ncd.
  ☎ (203) 655-1137 . . PO Box 1071, Darien, CT *06820*

Yardley MR & MRS John L McK (Mikkelsen—Leaf V Heathcote) Plg.Cw.P'50.Pa'56 . . . .
  MR Michael A . . . . | ☎ (011-44-171) 235-1442 31 Pont St, Apt 10, London SW1X 0BB, England

Yardley MRS Ralph B (Seely—Anne C Smith) . . . .
  MR Ralph B JR—Godd'81 . . . . | ☎ (215) HY3-2171 136 N Main St, Yardley, PA *19067*

Yarington DR & MRS Charles T JR (Barbara T Johnson) Roch'60.Cos.P'56.H'mannMed'60 ⚓
  MISS Leslie A—Scripps'86—at Los Angeles, CA
  MISS Barbara J—Gchr'91.Vt'94 . . . . | ☎ (206) 720-0779 1840 E Hamlin St, Seattle, WA *98112*

Yarnall MR Alexander C (late Alexander C) . . . . . | Married at Radnor, PA
  Frost MRS Deborah A (Deborah A Gluck) . . . . Dec 14'94

Yarnall MR & MRS Charlton 2d (Jean A Scullion) Me.Gm.Ph.Rc.Sa.Pa'55 . . . . | ☎ (610) LA5-5836
MISS Mary E—at 4150 Apple St, Philadelphia, PA 19122 . . . . | 319 Caversham Rd, Bryn Mawr, PA
MR Alexander B . . . . | 19010

Yarnall MR & MRS Richard A (Dolan—Margaret M Knight) Ac.Colg'45.Pa'48
☎ (215) 862-2558 . . Ely Rd, Box 255, Solebury, PA 18963-0255

Yassukovich MRS Dimitri M (Denise Henry) Pr.Cly.
☎ (561) 546-5226 . . PO Box 731, Hobe Sound, FL 33475

Yassukovich MR Nicholas A
☎ (011-44-181) 675-1350 . . Ducane Court Apt B76, Balham High Rd, London, England

Yassukovich MR & MRS Stanislas M (Diana V O Townsend) B.Pr.H'57 . . . . | ☎ (011-44-171) 229-5103
MR Michael . . . . | 13 Hillgate Place,
  MRS Tatyana Y Dubow (Tatyana Yassukovich) | London W8 7SL, England

Yates DR & MRS C Michael (Katherine R Babcock) Camb'50.StThos'53 | ☎ (011-44-171) 730-5908
MR Henry P—Edin'91—at ☎ (011-44-171) 351-2110 . . 6 Ifield Rd, London SW10 9AA, England . . . . | 25 Bloomfield Terr, London SW1W 8PQ, England

Yates MRS Dallas Pell (N Dallas Pell) Bost'78.Srb.Cly.
☎ (914) 398-0714 . . 12 Woods Rd, Palisades, NY 10964

Yates MR & MRS Douglas T (Margaret L Titus) Chr.Rc.Fw.StJ.Cly.Wms'38
☎ (212) 879-5721 . . 150 E 73 St, New York, NY 10021

Yates MR Eames H—Nrr.Lm.Wy'74
242 E 72 St, New York, NY 10021

Yates MRS John Sellers (Marguerite K Tabor) V'46. | of ☎ (212)874-6285
MR Christopher M R . . . . | 239 Central Park W, New York, NY 10024
 | ☎ (717) 646-3268
 | Yates Camp, Pocono Lake Preserve, PA 18348

Yates MR & MRS L Randall (Hope S Lloyd) Sg.Myf.Cly.Y'73.Cl'75
☎ (212) 722-0616 . . 1105 Park Av, New York, NY 10128

Yatsevitch COL (RET) & MRS Gratian M (Raff—Barbara S Franks) USA.Mt.Hb.H'33
☎ (207) 236-3033 . . "Easterly" Shermans Point, Camden, ME 04843

Yeager MR & MRS John G (Arthur—Jean E McConkey) Rdc'49.A.Rice'36 . . of
☎ (713) 683-1655 . . 121 N Post Oak Lane, Apt 2503, Houston, TX 77024
☎ (210) 896-0614 . . 304 Lakewood Dv, Kerrville, TX 78028

Yeager MR & MRS Raymond H JR (Cathleen B Benedict)
☎ (602) 930-1814 . . 8219 W Tuckey Lane, Glendale, AZ 85303

Yellott MRS Anne J (Anne S James) Ncd. . . . . | ☎ (717) 236-1056
MR John B JR—Ken'77.W&L'80—at 311 E Market St, Charlottesville, VA 22901 . . . | 110 Locust St, Harrisburg, PA 17101

Yellott MRS Richard E (Barbara D Hoffhines) JHop'76
☎ (410) 823-8639 . . 1500 Dunlora Rd, Ruxton, MD 21204

Yeoman MR & MRS John W (Lynn Lancaster) LakeF'80.Ch'85.S.Denis'67.Ch'73
☎ (415) 435-0442 . . 2260 Centro E, Tiburon, CA 94920

Yeomans MR & MRS Clinton B (Joan G Barrows) Cw.Myf.Ncd.Wes'43
☎ (603) 924-0891 . . 4 Rivermead Rd, Peterborough, NH 03458

Yeomans MRS Grace A—Sth'77.Ncd.
☎ (617) 247-3102 . . 357 Beacon St, Boston, MA 02116

Yerdon MR & MRS Gerald G (Moss—Nancy F Lancaster) . . . . | ☎ (804) 580-7181
MR Steven R—at Hayward, CA . . . . | "Bayberry"
MR Peter S—at Virginia Beach, VA . . . . | Rte 2, Box 298P, Heathsville, VA 22473

Yerkes MRS Catharine M (Frantzman—Graham—Bande—Catharine M Yerkes) Ct.
☎ (540) 364-4600 . . PO Box 69, Orlean, VA 20128

Yerkes MR & MRS Harry Estile 3d (Nancy Spofford) V'52.Un.Fic.P.'48 ⚓ . . . . | ☎ (212) 876-1353
MISS Nathalie S—Conn'88—at 1192 Park Av, ☎ (212) 427-8754 . . 245 E 93 St, New York, NY 10128 . . . . | New York, NY 10128
MR J Nicholas—Fic.Rol'92—see
Dilatory Domiciles . . . .

Yerkes MISS Hope R (Bodan—Hope R Yerkes) . . . . | ☎ (302) 998-1508
MISS Susan R Bodan . . . . | 2602 Frederick Av, Wilmington, DE 19805

Yerkes MR & MRS William H J (Elizabeth B Lassiter) Msq.Y'64
☎ (908) 277-3215 . . 65 Edgewood Rd, Summit, NJ 07901

Yiameos MISS Rosemary C . . see MRS C C Hill

Ylvisaker MRS Jane P M (Jane P Mitchell) Cho.Rcch.BtP . . .of
☎ (011-44-171) 727-1589 . . 5A Lansdowne Rd, London W11 3AL, England
☎ (561) 795-4892 . . 2601 Sheltingham Dv, Wellington, FL 33414

Ylvisaker MR William T—Srr.Cho.Ln.BtP.Rcn. Y'48 . . . . | ☎ (561) 793-2236
MR Jon A . . . . | 2329 Golf Brook Dv, West Palm
MISS Laurie E (Koehler—Laurie E Ylvisaker) . . | Beach, FL 33414

Yntema MR & MRS Douwe B (Esther P Shiverick) V'47.Swth'49.H'55 . . . . | ☎ (617) KI7-2854
MISS Mary P—H'87.JHop'94.Cl'96 . . . . | 92 Brattle St, Cambridge, MA 02138

Yoder MR & MRS Glenn III (Victoria W Darlington) Cda.Ht.NCar'78.GeoW'80
☎ (704) 375-6323 . . 1800 E 8 St, Charlotte, NC 28204

Yoder MRS Lloyd E (Bailey—Alma Cella)
☎ (415) 771-2842 . . 1170 Sacramento St, San Francisco, CA 94108

Yoh MRS Harold L (Pickering—M Catherine O'Hey) BtP.Evg.Mt.
☎ (561) 655-0533 . . "Villa Giardina" 341 Peruvian Av, Palm Beach, FL 33480

Yokana MR & MRS Lucien D (Anne D Guthrie) Pn.P'48
☎ (609) 924-4255 . . 87 Battle Rd, Princeton, NJ 08540

Yonce MR & MRS S McClay JR (Virginia H Vogel) Ty'87.Fic.Cda.Hb.Y'86
☎ (612) 476-1326 . . 18202 Shavers Lake Dv, Wayzata, MN 55391

Yonce MR & MRS Samuel McC (Lizora S Miller) Swb'59.Rr.Fic.Ncd.Yn.Y'54 . . . . of ☎ (941)964-1729 Box 372, Boca Grande, FL *33921*
MR Logan H—Fic.LakeF'89 . . . .
MR Clifford M—Rr.Fic.Cw.Yn.Va'91 . . . .
☎ (203) 869-7297 34 Evergreen Rd, Greenwich, CT *06830*

York MR & MRS B Hamlin 3d (Pamela M Demus)⚓
8 Hitching Post Circle, Tequesta, FL *33469*

York MRS Barney H (Newell—Mary S Foster) Cv.
☎ (941) 488-6121 . . PO Box 1605, Nokomis, FL *34274*

York MR & MRS Clifton Gaston (Louise B Whitton) Mid'88.Rc.Va'87.Nu'95
☎ (212) 988-8775 . . 155 E 72 St, Apt 5D, New York, NY *10021-4371*

York MASTER Clifton Gaston JR (Clifton Gaston) . . . . Born at New York, NY Aug 26'96

York MR & MRS E Howard (Huston—Evelyn Q Cox) Me.Sa.Cts.Fw.Pa'40
☎ (610) LA5-3715 . . 26 Pond Lane, Bryn Mawr, PA *19010*

York MR & MRS Gordon B (Harriet I Glover) Cda.Dth'35 . . . .
MISS Pamela G . . . .
☎ (520) 625-6054 1467 W Via De Roma, Green Valley, AZ *85614*

York MRS Janet B (Janet L Brewster) MmtMhn'75.Nu'77 . . . .
MISS Torrance Brewster—Y'88 . . . .
☎ (212) 249-0676 155 E 72 St, New York, NY *10021*

York MR & MRS John C (Judith A Carmack) Van'67.Rc.Cho.Cas.Cnt.Wa.Van'68.H'71 . . . . .
MISS Charlotte B—at Georgetown . . . .
MR George E C—Br'95 . . . .
JUNIORS MISS Alice M . . . .
of ☎ (312)642-7434 1242 N Lake Shore Dv, Chicago, IL *60610*
☎ (616) 429-1664 "Watermelon House" 3965 Lake Forest Path, Stevensville, MI *49127*

York MR & MRS John W (Eleanor Rulon-Miller) P'46 . . . .
MR John W JR—at ☎ (207) 799-0843 18 Ocean St, South Portland, ME *04106* . . . . . .
☎ (207) 883-2440 3 Acorn Lane, Scarborough, ME *04074*

Yort MR & MRS Albert Arthur JR (Lockhart—Johns—Sarah M Wainwright) Rr.P'55 . . . .
MISS Emily R Lockhart—at ☎ (202) 362-6518 . . 4200 Massachusetts Av NW, Washington, DC *20016* . . . .
☎ (213) 654-4003 1495 Queens Rd, Los Angeles, CA *90069*

Yoskin MRS D James (Dorothea P James) . . . .
MISS Dorothea D . . . .
MR Nickolaus D . . . .
☎ (215) 233-5854 "Mill House" 6013 W Valley Green Rd, Flourtown, PA *19031*

Yoskin MR & MRS Jon W 2d (Elizabeth A Groves) Rc.Md.Ll.Sar . . .of
☎ (215) 735-2751 . . 1606 Pine St, Philadelphia, PA *19103*
☎ (561) 225-7207 . . Dune Apts, 4651 NE Ocean Blvd, Jensen Beach, FL *33457*

Yoskin DR Maurice P—Temp'91.Pitt'95
☎ (310) 478-5070 . . 11669 Rochester Av, Apt 104, Los Angeles, CA *90025*

Yost MR & MRS Dudley D (Sally V Belden) Sth'54.It.P'54 . . . .
MR David H . . . .
☎ (216) 321-0550 2500 Guilford Rd, Cleveland Heights, OH *44118*

Youmans MR & MRS Scott A (Valerie C Faure) Unn.
MR Craig C—at ☎ (011-41-29) 4-79-75 La Craitsette, 1837 Château-d'Oex, Switzerland .
☎ (011-41-29) 4-82-20 "La Cour de Ferme" Rougemont, 1839 Flendruz, Switzerland

Younes MR & MRS Mohamed S (Evelyn T Bossange) K.Srb.Cly.Cairo'60.H'63 . . . .
MR Saleh Tarek—Duke'92 . . . .
MR Khaled M—☎ (212) 517-6754 . . . .
☎ (212) 988-3862 130 E 75 St, New York, NY *10021*

Young MISS Alison L . . see M D Morehouse JR

Young MR & MRS Andrew B (Olive C Sherley) Sg.Ph.Ac.P'28.H'31
☎ (215) 283-7253 . . 613 Foulkeways, Sumneytown, Pike, Gwynedd, PA *19436*

Young MR & MRS Andrew J 3d (Gordon—D'Arcy Hilles) Md.Elk.Cw.Cc.Rv.Mv.Cda.JHop'39 . . . .
MISS Linn J . . . .
☎ (410) 377-7924 101 Estes Rd, Baltimore, MD *21212*

Young MR Andrew P—Cal'87.ChArt'89
☎ (773) 549-2560 . . 1117 W Oakdale Av, Apt 3A, Chicago, IL *60657*

Young MRS Ann Booth (Doak—Ann B Young) NH'82
☎ (757) 220-1572 . . 140 Hunting Cove, Williamsburg, VA *23185*

Young MISS Anne N (Model—Anne N Young) . . see J E Nielson

Young MRS Arthur M (Paine—Thomas—Ruth Forbes) Ph.
☎ (510) 848-8385 . . 2924 Benvenue Av, Berkeley, CA *94705*

Young MRS Brinton Coxe (Hilda M Osterhout) V'46.Geneva'68.PAFA'72.Sfh . . .of
☎ (610) 688-9352 . . "Willow Brook" 695 Walker Rd, Wayne, PA *19087*
☎ (508) 325-5094 . . "House of the Three Lights" 7 Eat Fire Spring Rd, Nantucket, MA *02554*

Young MR & MRS Brinton O C (Catherine J Wong) HRdc'85.H'88.Y'74.H'79
☎ (617) 367-2653 . . 44 Chestnut St, Apt 5, Boston, MA *02108*

Young DR & MRS Charles C (Patricia P Frech) Sar.Ht.Emp'72.Nu'74.LSU'80
☎ (860) 767-3005 . . PO Box 694, Essex, CT *06426*

Young MRS Charles D (Verdi—Hope Aspell) Ox'40
☎ (212) 755-2828 . . 30 Sutton Place, New York, NY *10022*

Young MR & MRS Charles T 3d (Milliken—Nancy H Cooper) Ny.Wms'39
The Moorings, 1916 Mooring Line Dv, Vero Beach, FL *32963*

Young MR Christopher (Messler—Mary E Bird)
☎ (860) 364-5695 . . 25 Bowne Rd, Sharon, CT *06069*

Young MR Edward H—An.Rc.Wash'32 . . . .
MISS Rosemary—at ☎ (314) 821-2792 10341 Manchester Rd, St Louis, MO *63122* . . . .
☎ (314) 361-0346 5394 Pershing Av, St Louis, MO *63112-1708*

Young MRS Edward L (Mary Ellen Anderson)
☎ (314) 962-1773 . . 25 W Rose Av, Webster Groves, MO *63119*

Young MR Eric C—Cal'84.Nw'87
375 Bonair St, Apt 1, La Jolla, CA *92037*
Young DR & MRS Frank Coleman JR (Jo Ann M Addy)
MedSC'60.MedSC'60
☎ (334) 834-4145 . . 3165 Rolling Rd, Montgomery, AL *36111*
Young MR & MRS G Stewart (Dorothy M Rackemann)
Bost'77.Cy.Pa'73.JHop'76
☎ (617) 259-0698 . . 55 Oxbow Rd, Lincoln, MA *01773*
Young MR George A—Ty'80
☎ (860) 688-8948 . . 460 Park Av, Windsor, CT *06095*
Young MRS George B (Mary S Adams) On.Sr.Fy.Cas . . .of
☎ (773) 281-9117 . . 2430 N Lakeview Av, Chicago, IL *60614*
☎ (847) 234-0509 . . 130 E Onwentsia Rd, Lake Forest, IL *60045*
Young MR & MRS H Peyton (Fernanda F Toueg) Gren'71.Cos.H'66
☎ (202) 333-9367 . . 2711—34 Place NW, Washington, DC *20007*
Young MR Henry Knowlton—DelB.Hn.
☎ (561) 276-3552 . . PO Box 8, Delray Beach, FL *33447*

Young MR Hillyer McD—P'64.Van'68 . . . . ☎ (404) 350-8327
MR Jonathan C . . . . 103 Verlaine Place
MR Geoffrey P . . . . NW, Atlanta, GA
                                     30327

Young MR & MRS Hobart P (Louise Buchwalter) V'40.St.60.Ih.H'37
☎ (847) 251-5424 . . 1420 Sheridan Rd, Wilmette, IL *60091*

Young DR & MRS Hugh H 2d (C Joyce Lenz) . . . . . . ☎ (617) 899-6830
Swb'56.Cy.Y'57.Va'61 . . . . 12 Robin Rd,
MISS Martha H—Y'92 . . . . Weston, MA *02193*
MR Hugh H 3d . . . .
MR Mark E—Va'87 . . . .

Young MR & MRS (DR) J Kent H (Patricia A Britten) . . ☎ (410) 758-1713
Pa'63.P'50.Cl'55 . . . . ''Windward''
MR J David F . . . . 211 Easy Lane,
JUNIORS MISS Honore Childs . . . . Centreville, MD
                                     21617

Young MRS James N (Elisabeth R Proudfit) . . . . Died Apr 22'96
Young MR James N—Y'40
☎ (212) MU8-3997 . . 455 E 51 St, New York, NY *10022*

Young MRS Jane S (Toland—McDermott—Jane . . . . . ☎ (603) 924-0979
Stewart) Chi. . . . . 207 Rivermead Rd,
MR John D JR—at ☎ (212) 229-9034 . . . . Peterborough, NH
100 W 12 St, New York, NY *10011* *03458*

Young MR & MRS John C (Nancy Cutting) . . . . ☎ (216) 321-2690
Skd'52.It.Ken'50 . . . . 2683 Leighton Rd,
MISS Heather H—at 3125 Holmes Av S, ... Shaker Heights, OH
Minneapolis, MN *55408* *44120*
MR MacKenzie C—at 2685 W County Rd,
Apt H2, Mounds View, MN *55112* . . . .

Young MR & MRS John D (Whitney—Elizabeth C . . . ☎ (912) 638-9448
Stettinius) Cyb.Cw.H'47 . . . . 187 Merion St,
  MISS Anita C Whitney—at New York, NY . . St Simons Island,
  MR George H Whitney 3d—at Brookline, MA GA *31522*

Young MR & MRS John M (Marian Hillyer Wolff) Hlns'29.Cly.Ncd.Dc.
☎ (404) 264-3310 . . Lenbrook Square 1818, 3747 Peachtree Rd NE,
Atlanta, GA *30319*

Young MR & MRS John R (Mary K Armbrister) . . . . . ☎ (203) 637-4957
Wells'61.Gr.Ch'53 . . . . 11 Ledge Rd,
MISS Anne H . . . . Old Greenwich, CT
MISS Mary K *06870*

Young MRS John Randolph (MacLeod—Elizabeth T McMullin) Gm.Me.
☎ (610) 525-4018 . . 19 Pond Lane, Bryn Mawr, PA *19010*
Jan 1 . . ☎ (787) 741-0412 . . Box 1404, Vieques, Puerto Rico *00765*

Young MR & MRS Joseph R JR (Kathleen B Kimmel) | ☎ (803) 577-9355
Yh.Va'65.Va'68 . . . . 70 Tradd St,
MR Joseph R 3d—Va'94—U of SCar Law . . . . . Charleston, SC
JUNIORS MR Simons W—at U of Va *29401*

Young MR & MRS Ledlie W JR (Edson—Joan McKay) Pg.
☎ (412) 362-5814 . . 1101 S Negley Av, Pittsburgh, PA *15217-1047*
Young MR Mahonri S . . . . Died at
                                       Bridgehampton, NY Jun 16'96
Young MISS Margaret A Chisholm—LakeF'89
☎ (617) 266-1106 . . 16 Concord Square, Boston, MA *02118*
Young MR Philip F . . of
''Windy Hill'' Box 97, Drifton, PA *18221*
☎ (610) 525-0729 . . Radnor House 720, 1030 E Lancaster Av,
Rosemont, PA *19010*
Young MRS Richard N SR (Edith W Warner)
☎ (610) 688-3997 . . 318 Chester Rd, Devon, PA *19333*

Young MR & MRS Richard N JR (Mary M Simpson) | of ☎ (610)296-3260
Gm.Pa'68 . . . . 326 Waterloo Av,
MR Richard N 3d—Colg'94—at Baltimore, MD. . Berwyn, PA *19312*
MR Alexander S—at Ohio Wesleyan . . . . ☎ (941) 676-3425
                                       Mountain Lake
                                       Club, Lake Wales,
                                       FL *33859*

Young MR & MRS Robert W JR (Ryan—Margot E Airey) H'45
☎ (516) 759-2396 . . 39 Overlook Rd, Locust Valley, NY *11560*
Young MR & MRS Ronald J—VillaN'85
☎ (610) 284-3218 . . 260 N Wycombe Av, Apt 209, Lansdowne,
PA *19050*
Young MR & MRS Roslyn D JR (Long—Julia A Jackson)
Cvc.Sl.Ncd.Va'51 . . of
☎ (301) 654-3345 . . 3544 Hamlet Place, Chevy Chase, MD *20815*
☎ (410) 745-5712 . . ''Heron Cove'' PO Box 90, Bozman, MD *21663*
Young MR & MRS Stuart A JR (Elizabeth H Ilsley) Rm.Cw.P'41.Y'47
☎ (908) 842-1130 . . 6 Conover Lane, Rumson, NJ *07760*

Young MRS Susan B (Victor—Susan S Beaty) Gv. . | ☎ (212) 826-2811
MISS Stephanie Morgan—Ox'91 . . . . 245 E 60 St,
MR Alexander Morgan . . . . New York, NY
                                      10022

Young MR & MRS Thomas G 3d (K Beverley . . . . . . of ☎ (410)323-5403
Whiting) Wells'73.Md.Mv.Cw.Cda.Y'62.Va'65 . . 200 Cedarcroft Rd,
JUNIORS MISS Brooke W . . . . Baltimore, MD
                                      21212
                                      ☎ (410) 833-2218
                                       Huntly Farm,
                                       3940 Butler Rd,
                                       Glyndon, MD *21071*

Young MRS William B (Margaret L Canfield) Ihy.
☎ (203) 531-7559 . . 528 W Lyon Farm Dv, Greenwich, CT *06831-4362*
Young MR & MRS William B JR (Katherine P Kelly) Ihy.
12 Lockwood Av, New Canaan, CT *06840*
Young MASTER William Beekman 3d (William B JR) . . . . Born at
                                       Stamford, CT Mch 20'96

Youngman MISS Helen I—P'93 . . see T L Pulling

Youngman MR & MRS Robert P (Barbara G Pollock)
Ny.Cly.Mid'64 . . . . | ☎ (212) 369-2024
MISS Eloise P . . . . | 1130 Park Av,
                                   | New York, NY
                                   | *10128*
Youngman MR & MRS Thomas M (Robin W Crawford)
NH'82.BostColl'88.NH'79.WakeF'81
  ☎ (508) 470-0551 . . 18 Tiffany Lane, Andover, MA *01810*
Youtsey MR & MRS Thomas H (Kathryn M Lyons) PortSt'88.UWash'86
  ☎ (206) 820-3562 . . 8228 NE 115 Way, Kirkland, WA *98034*

Z

Zabriskie MR & MRS Charles JR (Star P Myles)
Bab'79.Bab'85.Un.Ncd.Vt'53
  ☎ (617) 235-2228 . . 22 Salem Rd, Wellesley Hills, MA *02181*
Zacharias MR & MRS David L (Sandra Latin) | ☎ (602) 265-2031
BowlG'65 . . . . | 126 E Country Club
MISS Stephanie L . . . . | Dv, Phoenix, AZ
MISS Christine M . . . . | *85014*
JUNIORS MISS Elizabeth A . . . . |
Zacharias MR & MRS Thomas E (Clelia LeBoutillier)
Pa'72.Cly.P'76.Y.'79 . . of
  ☎ (212) 534-8542 . . 1215 Fifth Av, Apt 4B, New York, NY *10029*
  ☎ (516) 283-1136 . . 65 Post Crossing, Southampton, NY *11968*
Zacher JUNIORS MR Edward G . . see MRS N Nicolaus-Zacher
Zacher MISS Katherine A—Geo'91.Cal'96 . . see MRS N Nicolaus-Zacher
Zacher MRS N Nicolaus (Nancy H Nicolaus) . . . . name changed to
                                      Nicolaus-Zacher
Zacher MR Peter A—Col'90 . . see MRS N Nicolaus-Zacher
Zachrisson MR & MRS Carl U (Adele L Hall) | of ☎ (415)221-8164
SL'65.Bhm.Csn.Ncd.Stan'62.Gen'65.Ox'67 . . . . | 45—25 Av,
MR Carl F . . . . | San Francisco, CA
JUNIORS MR Christopher D . . . . | *94121*
                                     | ☎ (415) 879-0790
                                     | ''Sans Souci''
                                     | Butano Canyon,
                                     | Pescadero, CA
                                     | *94060*
Zaldastani MR & MRS Othar (Elizabeth R Bailey) | of ☎ (617)739-1756
BMr'54.Bost'62.Sm.Cy.Rr.Paris'46.H'50 . . . . . . | 70 Suffolk Rd,
MR Alexander G B—at ☎ (617) 262-7817 | Chestnut Hill, MA
160 Commonwealth Av, Boston, MA *02146* . . . | *02167*
                                     | ☎ (717) 525-3402
                                     | ''Bailiwick''
                                     | Eagles Mere, PA
                                     | *17731*
Zane MR & MRS Anthony M (Mary E Thayer) Tv.Va'52.Camb'58
  ☎ (508) 999-0186 . . 202 Bedford St, New Bedford, MA *02740*
Zangrillo MISS Alexandra Barlow (g—Fred C Larkin) . . . . Born at
                                    Aspen, CO Dec 9'95
Zantzinger MR Alfred G—Pa'61.Pa'67
  ☎ (610) 933-0662 . . PO Box 2, Devault, PA *19432*
Zantzinger MRS C Clark (Mary A Cook) Cs.
  ☎ (610) 645-8985 . . 1400 Waverly Rd, Andrews 322, Gladwyne,
PA *19035*

Zanze MR & MRS Anthony O (Denise M Ward)
SFr'93.Bhm.Mt.Dth'82.Wis'88
  ☎ (415) 668-6111 . . 35 Parker Av, San Francisco, CA *94118*
Zanze MR James F—Mid'89
  ☎ (415) 986-2595 . . 285 Chestnut St, San Francisco, CA *94133*
Zanze MR William I . . see H Ritchie
Zapffe MRS Carl A (A C Denise du Pont) Cy.
  ☎ (410) 377-7294 . . 6410 Murray Hill Rd, Baltimore, MD *21212*
Zara MR & MRS George A (Kand—Patricia A | ☎ (602) 451-6041
Teeter) Kas'73.DU'71.Pitt'77 . . . . | 10115 E Paradise
JUNIORS MISS Elizabeth A . . . . | Dv, Scottsdale, AZ
JUNIORS MISS Kellie M . . . . | *85260*
JUNIORS MR Michael T . . . . |
Zara MR & MRS Michael (Mathilde Alexandre) H'42
  ☎ (803) 838-4580 . . PO Box 399, Frogmore, SC *29920*
Zara MR & MRS Thomas D (Mary W Borie) | ☎ (203) 966-4040
Wheat'75.Br'74 . . . . | 134 Marshall Ridge
JUNIORS MISS Eliza S . . . . | Rd, New Canaan,
JUNIORS MR Cameron B . . . . | CT *06840*
Zbinden MASTER James Pearson (Louis H 3d) . . . . Born at
                                   Charlotte, NC Jly 18'96
Zbinden REV & MRS Louis H JR (Katherine S Shoaf) | ☎ (210) 826-7575
Sw'58.A.Sw'58.UnTheo'63.PTheo'64 . . . . | 135 Oakhurst Place,
MISS Anne S—at 7815 Broadway St, Apt 306, | San Antonio, TX
San Antonio, TX *78209* . . . . | *78209*
MISS Elizabeth M . . . . |
Zbinden DR & MRS Louis H 3d (Jodi Lynn Pearson) David'86.David'86
  ☎ (704) 525-4532 . . 3124 Willow Oak Rd, Charlotte, NC *28209*
Zeisler MR Richard S—C.Gr.Aht'37
  ☎ (212) 737-7882 . . 980 Fifth Av, New York, NY *10021-0126*
Zellerbach MR & MRS Stephen A (Beaumont—Cecile M Nervo)
Sfy.Cp.Cal'51 . . of
  ☎ (415) 922-1422 . . 3235 Clay St, San Francisco, CA *94115*
  ☎ (707) 431-2249 . . 14625 McDonough Heights Rd, Healdsburg,
CA *95448*
Zelov MR Peter E—Me.DavEl'81
  ☎ (610) 896-7064 . . 237 W Montgomery Av, 2H, Haverford, PA *19041*
Zelov MR & MRS Randolph D (Josephine E Frank)
Gm.Me.Rv.Ac.Myf.Ncd.USN'48.Mit'56
  ☎ (610) 525-6505 . . 716 Old Gulph Rd, Bryn Mawr, PA *19010*
Zembrzuski MAJ & MRS Michael A (Wendy L Phillips)
USA.Ariz'90.An.Ty'84
2154 Commissary Circle, Odenton, MD *21113*
Zetterberg MR & MRS Martin C (Rita Pantsar)
  ☎ (609) 252-0759 . . 99 Ridgeview Rd, Princeton, NJ *08540*
Zick MR & MRS John W (Mary A Sutter) Rcn.Tvb.Ih.Sr.Nw'48 . . of
  ☎ (305) 367-2893 . . Ocean Reef Club, 9 Harbor Lane, Key Largo,
FL *33037*
  ☎ (203) 531-0569 . . 621 W Lyon Farm Dv, Greenwich, CT *06831*
Ziegler MRS Carter C (Carter Carroll) Cly . . . . | ☎ (804) 978-1558
MISS Sophie—at 178 Hancock St, San Francisco, | PO Box 146,
CA *94114* . . . . | Free Union, VA
                                     | *22940*
Ziegler MR Frederick S—Harvey'91
  ☎ (408) 746-2971 . . 979 Pinto Palm Terr, Apt 21, Sunnyvale,
CA *94087-3740*

Ziegler MR & MRS Henry S (Hoffman—Jourdan Arpelle)
Houst'68.Rc.K.C.StJ.H'55.Cl'58 . . of
☎ (212) 758-4745 . . 230 E 50 St, Apt 2D, New York, NY *10022*
☎ (860) 491-3456 . . Box 140, Thompson Rd, Goshen, CT *06756*

Ziegler MRS Jessica M (Cardew—Jessica M Ziegler) . . . . Married at
 New York, NY
Lucey MR James X (Robert F) . . . . Mch 30'96

Ziegler MR & MRS John C (Montanari—Marie-Claire Fougoux) H'53.Cl'61
☎ (212) 473-5044 . . 111 Fourth Av, New York, NY *10003*

Ziegler MR Timothy O . . see MISS P Blackmore

Ziel MISS Cynthia J (John G M) . . . . Married at Lake Oswego, OR
Robert MR Douglas B (Richard) . . . . Jly 8'95

Ziel MRS John G (Elizabeth McC Merrill) Ncd.
☎ (707) 538-4871 . . Oakmont, 6480 Meadowridge Dv, Santa Rosa,
CA *95405*

Ziel MR & MRS John G M (Diane E Clymer) | ☎ (503) 638-4562
Cp.Menlo'64 | 2880 SW Turner Rd,
MR J David—at 948 Fillmore St, Eugene, OR | West Linn, OR
97402 . . . . | *97068*

Zieman MR & MRS Thomas T JR (Linyer B Ward) | ☎ (334) 479-3075
Salem'71.At.Va'66.Va'69 . . . . | 311 McDonald Av,
JUNIORS MISS Linyer B | Mobile, AL *36604*

Ziener MR & MRS George H (Diana Dial) StP'66 . . . | ☎ (301) 656-4193
MR Christopher D—Dick'94 . . . . | 5506 Center St,
JUNIORS MR Nathaniel K—at Boston U . . . . | Chevy Chase, MD
 | *20815* . . MR absent

Ziesing MISS Heather W . . see MRS J W Eckman

Ziesing MR & MRS Hunter S (Marcy A Engler) Cal'84.Cal'89.DU'82
☎ (415) 435-7025 . . 107 Reed Ranch Rd, Tiburon, CA *94920*

Ziesing MISS Jane D . . see MRS J W Eckman

Ziesing MISS Janet E
☎ (802) 899-4303 . . RD 1, Box 314B, Jericho, VT *05465*

Ziesing MR & MRS Richard D JR (Leslie D Kedash) Del'77.Rol'73
☎ (302) 652-0222 . . 1112 Blackshire Rd, Wilmington, DE *19805*

Ziesing MR & MRS Robert A (M Sinclair Adams) | ☎ (610) 688-2424
Me.Gm.Ac.Ncd.Yn.Y'44 | 481 St Davids Av,
MR Robert A JR—at ☎ (802) 862-0149 | St Davids, PA
469 St Paul St, Apt 1, Burlington, VT *05401* . . . | *19087-4204*

Zilkha MISS Bettina L (Trink—Bettina L Zilkha) P'82
☎ (011-33-1) 47-27-33-54 . . 80 av Victor Hugo, 75116 Paris, France

Zilkha MR & MRS Daniel A (Frances P Rogers) | ☎ (207) 879-0190
SL'69.K.Sm.Csn.P'64.H'69 . . . . | 150 Vaughan St,
MISS Leonora R—at Princeton . . . . | Portland, ME *04102*
JUNIORS MISS Rebecca R—at Tabor Acad . . . . . |
JUNIORS MR Nathaniel M—at Princeton . . . . |

Zilkha MR & MRS Ezra K (Cecile Iny) Rc.K.Wes'47 | of ☎ (212)879-1497
MR Donald—at 993 Fifth Av, New York, | 4 E 66 St,
NY *10021* . . . . | New York, NY
 | *10021*
 | ☎ (011-33-1)
 | 42-65-53-25
 | 24 av Gabriel,
 | 75008 Paris, France

Zimmerman MISS Abigail P . . see R M Wiley

Zimmerman JUNIORS MR Casey K . . see R M Wiley

Zimmerman MR & MRS Christian B (Garroway—Sarah Lee Lippincott)
Pa'42.Penn'43
☎ (609) 829-2099 . . 306 Bell Rd, Cinnaminson, NJ *08077*

Zimmerman MRS John G (Jane C Slaymaker) Fcg.Ncd.
153 North Dv, Pittsburgh, PA *15238*

Zimmerman MR & MRS John G JR (M Fraser | ☎ (412) 741-7647
Ratcliffe) Ac.Y'58.Pa'60 . . . . | 305 Shady Lane,
MISS Margaret F—CtCol'92—at 6621 Fairfax Rd, | Sewickley, PA
Chevy Chase, MD *20815* . . . . | *15143*
MR John G 3d—Gettys'89 . . . . |

Zimmerman MR & MRS Landis P (Abigail S Marshall)
Bnd'83.Bost'86.Pa'81.Pa'85
☎ (203) 622-0313 . . 27 Perry Ridge Rd, Greenwich, CT *06830*

Zimmerman MR & MRS Paul M (Gwen H Drum) BallSt'73
☎ (941) 489-1483 . . 16016 Forest Oaks Dv, Ft Myers, FL *33908*

Zimmerman MR & MRS Peter H (Elizabeth P Montgomery)
Wh'lck'80.Rd.Colg'78.H'82
☎ (610) 827-1362 . . 2363 Chester Springs Rd, Chester Springs,
PA *19425*

Zimmerman MR & MRS Robert W JR (Dodd—Jeanne Bowlan) An.Rv.Va'35
☎ (516) 728-8621 . . 42 Lovell Rd, Hampton Bays, NY *11946*

Zimmermann MR & MRS John E 3d (Suzanne S | ☎ (215) CH2-6344
Shippen) Cry.Tufts'66 . . . . | 135 W Highland Av,
MISS Phoebe S | Philadelphia, PA
MR Edward J—at Temple . . . . | *19118*

Zimmermann MR & MRS Peter J (Leigh Morel) Cda.Dar.Tenn'74
☎ (615) 833-4101 . . 600 Jackson Blvd, Nashville, TN *37205*

Zimmermann MR & MRS Richard Z (Helen W Brown) V'43.Nrr.Drex'57
☎ (401) 294-2631 . . 54 Willett Rd, Box 312, Saunderstown, RI *02874*

Zimmermann MR & MRS T C Price (Margaret U Ferris)
Rdc'67.Cda.Wms'56.Ox'58
☎ (704) 892-3050 . . PO Box 58, Davidson, NC *28036*

Zingg MISS Emma McWilliams (g—Richard G Kehoe) . . . . Born at
 Providence, RI Mch 9'96

Zingg MR J Drew—V'81 . . see R G Kehoe

Zink MISS Julianna Colton (g—MRS Joseph D Croll) . . . . Born at
 Princeton, NJ Mch 1'96

Zinsser MRS Hans H (Armstrong—Barbara Lewis) C.Cly.StJ.
☎ (212) 288-9222 . . 120 E 80 St, New York, NY *10021*

Zirinis MR & MRS Basil (Jessica D Cates) K.Bow'84.Cl'85
☎ (212) 319-9656 . . 45 E 62 St, New York, NY *10021*

Zoch MR & MRS Frank Peter III (Shafer—Marion | ☎ (210) 866-3540
Lee Chandler) TexA&I'68.Rcn.A.Tex'66 . . . . . . | Cedar Lake Ranch,
MISS Laura F . . . . | PO Box 252,
MISS Rhonda L . . . . | Mountain Home, TX
MISS Patricia F . . . . | *78058-0252*
MISS Elizabeth C . . . . |
MR Frank P 4th . . . . |
JUNIORS MR F Morgan . . . . |

Zogbaum MR & MRS Ferdinand 3d (Anne deW Galpin)
☎ (304) 497-3317 . . Spring Creek Station Rd, PO Box 126, Renick,
WV *24966*

Zook MR & MRS Dunwoody (Susanna Crew) | ☎ (610) 469-9007
Rc.Pkg.Rv. . . . . | Pheasant Hill Farm,
JUNIORS MISS Melissa D . . . . | RD 1, Glenmoore,
 | PA *19343*

Zouck MR & MRS Peter G (Katharine Symington) Elk.Md.Ncd.H'41 . . of
☎ (941) 261-7044 . . 421 Bow Line Dv, Naples, FL *34103*
☎ (410) 377-0869 . . 6100 Bellinham Court, Apt 1022, Baltimore,
MD *21210*

Zoullas MRS Mariana S (Mariana S Souyoutzoglou)
☎ (212) 980-1479 . . 580 Park Av, New York, NY *10021*

Zoullas MR Nicholas S—Ri.Un.So.BtP.H'59 . . . . . . | of ☎ (212)249-1719
MR Alexis P—H'93—at Fordham Law . . . . | 350 E 72 St,
| New York, NY
| *10021*
| ☎ (516) 283-0706
| ''Fairwinds''
| 145 Ox Pasture Rd,
| PO Box 2454,
| Southampton, NY
| *11969*

Zoullas MR & MRS Sophocles N (Louiza P Roussopoulos) K.So.Cly.
☎ (011-41-21) 312-79-24 . . 5 Av Eglantine, 1006 Lausanne, Switzerland

Zoullas MR & MRS Sophocles N (Silvia Cruz Suarez) Web'93.H'89.IMD'93
710 Park Av, New York, NY *10021*

Zuber MR & MRS Jean P (Diane E de T | of ☎ (011-33-1)
de Villefranche) . . . . | 45-25-41-43
MISS Camille . . . . | 68 quai Louis
MISS Pauline . . . . | Bleriot, 75016 Paris,
JUNIORS MISS Eleonore . . . . | France
| ☎ (011-33)
| 86-32-11-25
| Montréal, 89420
| Guillon, France

Zuber MR Maurice P . . of
☎ (011-33) 86-32-11-25 . . Montréal, 89420 Guillon, France
☎ (011-33-1) 40-20-93-50 . . 23 rue de Lille, 75007 Paris, France

Zug REV & MRS Albert E R (Suzanne Verner) Smu'85.Me.Ty'82
☎ (610) 356-4521 . . 46 Old Covered Bridge Rd, Newtown Square,
PA *19073*

Zug MR & MRS Graham F (Elizabeth A Kendall)
SCal'76.Pa'78.Me.Dick'74.Pa'78
☎ (610) 896-8455 . . 127 Rose Lane, Haverford, PA *19041*

Zug MR & MRS Harry Coover (Anne W Mayer)
Me.Rc.Pe.M.Rv.Dick'34.H'36
☎ (610) 645-8958 . . Waverly Heights A121, 1400 Waverly Rd,
Gladwyne, PA *19035*

Zug MR & MRS James W (Debora W Collier) | ☎ (610) 525-9633
Wheat'63.Me.M.Rv.P.'62.H'64 . . . . | 1164 St Andrew's
MR James W JR—Me.Dth'91 . . . . | Rd, Bryn Mawr, PA
| *19010*

Zug MR & MRS Richard V (Margaret P Pollock) Ws'31.Dick'28.Pa'32
☎ (610) 388-7768 . . 63 Kendal Dv, Kennett Square, PA *19348-2325*

Zug MRS Sara Griswold (Sara P Griswold) Col'64 . . | of ☎ (610)649-5284
MISS Eliza W—Mid'96 . . . . | Gladwyne Apt A,
MR Charles G 4th—Pa'92 . . . . | 341 Conshohocken
| State Rd, Gladwyne,
| PA *19035*
| ☎ (441) 293-0812
| ''Fair Winds''
| 20 South Rd,
| Hamilton Parish HS
| 02, Bermuda
| ☎ (011-44-1304)
| 853-408
| ''The Old
| Vicarage'' East
| Langdon, nr Dover,
| Kent CT1S 5JF,
| England

Zug MR & MRS Thomas V (Lenore R French) Me.Ncd.W.Dick'33
☎ (610) 645-8690 . . Waverly Heights Villa 41, 1400 Waverly Rd,
Gladwyne, PA *19035*

Zug MR & MRS Thomas V JR (Patricia L Spencer) | ☎ (610) 896-5727
Penn'75.Penn'77.Me.Dick'68.H'74 . . . . | 1331 Monk Rd,
JUNIORS MISS Holly E . . . . | Gladwyne, PA
| *19035*

Zwack de Wahl MISS Iris M . . see MRS H F Argento
Zwack de Wahl MR John R—NH'89 . . see MRS H F Argento

MARRIED MAIDENS

The following maiden names taken from the present number of the Social Register
are arranged alphabetically for the purpose of convenient reference to the married name.

Abbett Margery P ....Bartlett
Abbot Brenda L ....Anderson
Abbot Judith G ....Easterby
Abbott Elisabeth D ....Schoettle
Abbott Lynette J ....MacLeod
Abbott Nancy V.......................Ballard
Abeel Daphne ....Abeel
Abeille-Demay Stéfane...............Bartlett
Abell Caroline S ....Coleman
Abell E Andreé ....Petticrew
Abell Eleanor S.........................Owen
Abell Elizabeth A ....Harrington
Abell Helene P............................Loring
Abell Ishtar J..............................Abell
Abendroth Lucy W ....Lee
Abendroth Susan W...............Mulligan
Abler Katherine E.......................Harvey
Abrahamson Loise ....Morgan
Achelis Audrey ....Platt
Acher Elizabeth B..................Gillespie
Acheson Jane S...........................Brown
Achilles Marian S ....O'Brien
Achorn Jeanne E.........................Irving
Ackerly Margaret......................Hubbard
Ackerman Ellen J ....Eyre
Ackerman Jean C..................Robinson
Ackiss Carol R......................Wakelin
Adair Elizabeth L ....Townsend
Adair Marianna ....Rees
Adam Elizabeth H ....Smithers
Adam Elsa T ....Wardell
Adam Margaret E ....Halaby
Adam Trudy S ....Mollenberg
Adams Abigail.............................King
Adams Abigail..........................Manny
Adams Agnes C......................Robinson
Adams Ann B ....Pritchard
Adams Anne C ....Laumont
Adams Arabella Peyton.......Duncanson
Adams Barbara.............................Butler
Adams Barbara B ....Stewart
Adams Cameron C ....Soroko
Adams Carol L ....Sculley
Adams Caroline S.......................Muller
Adams Celeste M ....Wheelwright
Adams Cornelia M ....Foster
Adams Diane L........................Toland
Adams Harriette H.......................Palen

Adams Helen C...........................Isaacs
Adams Irma ....Bonner
Adams Jane G...............................Bunn
Adams Janet S...........................Jacobs
Adams Joan...........................Mondale
Adams Judith ....Smith
Adams Judith H......................Clifford
Adams June M ....Disston
Adams Karen E........................Howard
Adams Katharine H ....Venizelos
Adams Katharine W ....Bouras
Adams Kyle ....Carney
Adams M Sinclair........................Ziesing
Adams Margaret J.....................Nichols
Adams Margaret R.........................Peltz
Adams Marie L......................Olhausen
Adams Marjorie P.......................Cooke
Adams Mary S ....Young
Adams Maryan O.........................Lewis
Adams Mervyn W ....Seldon
Adams Nancy J.........................Downey
Adams Patricia M ....Story
Adams Phoebe-Lou ....Weeks
Adams Rosamond ....Chadwick
Adams Rosetta M ....Williams
Adams Stella C.........................Cochran
Adams Sybil E.............................Herron
Adams Wende S ....Alford
Adams Wendell ....Giard
Adamson Evelyn A......................Baird
Adamson Helen M.................Adamson
Adamson Sabina S.......................Wood
Addington Helen V....................Passano
Addison Caroline C.......................Clark
Addison Josephine B ....Gamble
Addison Margaret L ....Shepard
Addison Mary G ....Fenwick
Addy Jo Ann M ....Young
Adelizzi Mary Lee.................Brendsel
Adenaw Jeannette M ....Washburn
Adèr Francine C T........van der Hoeven
Adreon Margaret McP........McWilliams
Adrian Josephine T......................Keyes
Adrian Thérèse M ....Harding
Afshar Shala..............................Powell
Agajanian Joan..........................Quinn
Agamenoni Margaret A..........Williams
Agardy Adrienne ....Miller

Agayoff Kathleen B...................Barzun
Agee Louise R ....Wrinkle
Agnew Beatrice M....................Adams
Agnew Drika N.........................Purves
Agnew Lydia M........................Speller
Agnew Rosanna E ....La Bonte
Agnew Suzanne K ....Buffum
Ahern Nancy A.......................Haywood
Ahlberg Gail ....Brown
Aiello Alexandria A ....Hundt
Aiguier Antoinette ....Pearman
Aiguier Eugénie ....Havemeyer
Ainsworth Eleanor ....Forbes
Airey Dolores N ....Gillmore
Airey Margot E..........................Young
Aitcheson Mary E.........................Gore
Ake Nancy C................................Cecil
Akerlund Agneta.......................Currey
Akeroyd Edith......................Purviance
Akeroyd Helen..........................Curtis
Akin Jane ....Melville
Akoyunoglou Aleka A...........Blackwell
Akulinichev Natalia S...............Weed
Albert Anne ....Viault
Albert Phoebe P........................Driscoll
Albert Sarah M ....Eisenhart
Albert Virginia...........................Adams
Albertson Shirley B ....Burley
Albertsson Susanne ....Davis
Alcebo Maria L...........................Duke
Aldcroftt Elena de R....................Macy
Alden Susan W ....Frelinghuysen
Alderson Dorothy L ....Starkey
Aldrich Barbara L...............Wadsworth
Aldrich Elizabeth B ....Redmond
Aldrich Frances G......................Llopis
Aldrich Harriet C.......................Bering
Aldrich Lucy T ....Burr
Aldrich Mary ....Homans
Aldrich Virginia D...................Munson
Aldridge Mary C.......................Harris
Alesbury Nancy H.....................Bradley
Alesci F P Lia.............................Carter
Alexander Anne ....Lathrop
Alexander Beatrice D ....Rothermel
Alexander Constance ....McCarrens
Alexander Dorothy ....Moore
Alexander Elizabeth F ....Richards

Alexander Emory Graham...... Hamilton
Alexander Janet ....Pell
Alexander Judith T ....Seawell
Alexander Katharine M ....Fletcher
Alexander Katherine C ....Field
Alexander Margaret C ....Parker
Alexander Mary A...................d'Arnoux
Alexander Phebe P ....Bowditch
Alexander Ruth...........................Smith
Alexander Shara...........................Green
Alexander Susan M ....Bogart
Alexander Thanis G.......................Field
Alexandre Anne L........................Brett
Alexandre Denise E....................LeComte
Alexandre Mathilde ....Zara
Alexandre Patricia ....Claiborne
Alfageme Elvira....................Washburn
Alfaro Yolanda M......................Maddux
Alford Doris.................................Fort
Alford Mary L ....Ames
Alger Anne..............................Rollins
Alger Suzette.............................Howard
Algren Joanne M ....Bowles
Alig Anita E.............................Saman
Alig Candace B...................Van Alen
Alker Joan M ....Arbon
Alker Nancy K......................Craigmyle
Allan D M June ....Carter
Allan Isabel M ....Coxe
Allan Jocelyn B ....Linke
Allan Lois...................................Waller
Allan Rebecca L S..............Freisenbruch
Allen A Christine ....Allen
Allen Adrienne B.......................Du Bois
Allen Alice...................................Allen
Allen Ann R.............................Flanigan
Allen Anne ....Symonds
Allen Anne L...........................Chapin
Allen Barbara..............................Short
Allen Barbara...............................Upton
Allen Bonnie J.........................Martin
Allen Caroline..............................Talbot
Allen Christine L ....Lawrence
Allen Cornelia W......................Ireland
Allen Dana E............................Sands
Allen Diana H..........................Metcalf
Allen Eleanor L.............................Allen
Allen Elisabeth W....................Lapey

Allen Elizabeth T B .... Shertenlieb
Allen Ellen ....Martin
Allen Evelyn S............................ Eberts
Allen Florence M.......................Schade
Allen Harriette B .... Mellen
Allen Helen................................Green
Allen Helen M ....Jones
Allen Ione .... Itgen
Allen Jane C ....Dohan
Allen Julia G. .... Armstrong
Allen Justine C ....Eaton
Allen Kathleen B ....Forbes
Allen L Louise ....Grout
Allen Lilly ....Papin
Allen Linda L .... Burkhart
Allen Louise D .... Armstrong
Allen Louise E...........................Purves
Allen Lucille A .... Williams
Allen M Frances .... Rossiter
Allen M Lathrop ....La Farge
Allen Margaret........................ Palmer
Allen Margaret........................ Potter
Allen Margaret.......................Sedgwick
Allen Margaret S ....Hoffberger
Allen Mary E..........................de Lyrot
Allen Mary M .... Newman
Allen Mary Virginia ....Geyelin
Allen Mignone A ....Wood
Allen Nancy K...........................Weeks
Allen Pamela D..............DeBardeleben
Allen Patricia ....Carpenter
Allen Patricia ....Wall
Allen Patricia S..........................Ross
Allen Priscilla A ....Hallowell
Allen Renée de R.........................Rand
Allen Sandra W ....White
Allen Sharon M ....Lord
Allen Sunshine H

    Ferrante di Ruffano

Allen Susan M.........................Thomas
Allen Suzanne H........................Frantz
Alléon de Varcourt Michèle.......Willkie
Alley Kirstie L...........................Parker
Allin Kelly A ....Butler
Allison H Elizabeth ....Blacker
Allison Mary............................Millett
Allison Virginia ....Clark
Allnutt Veirs C ....Browne
Allwork Winifred.................. Treadwell
Allyn Diana............................ Granbery
Allyn Elizabeth C .....Lowsley-Williams
Allyn Mary L........................ Sunderland
Allyn Sarah N ....Bahlman
Almansa Ana M L ....Hyde
Almy Carolyn ....Gerry
Almy Mary L............................Dabney
Almy Susan G.........................Yacubian
Almy Sylvia A .... Wright
Alonso Helen E......................Applegate
Alphin Mary...........................Coward
Alsop Corinne R..........................Chubb
Alsop Emily H..........................Moody
Alsop Kelso ....Everett

Alt Leslie ....Mott
Altegoer Gertrud M F................Mellon
Alterman Nancy A....................Walker
Althans Mary L.......................... Abbott
Altmaier Priscilla H..................du Pont
Alvarez Jeanne T ....LeBlanc
Alverson Nancy R .... Fick
Amberg Agnes..........................Fiedler
Amberg Frances A...................... Spence
Amberg Marie I .... Tallmadge
Amberg Pamela B.............Loewenstein
Amberger Barbara H ....Brackett
Ambler Mary Cary .... Ambler
Ambrose Elizabeth.....................Madeira
Ambrose Letitia .... Gates
Ambrose Mary K ......Paston-Bedingfeld
Ambrosius Renate E E .... Nash
Amburn Martha R.................Chapman
Amerman Lucy S L ....Bullock
Ames Elizabeth L ....Edwards
Ames Emily A .... Simmons
Ames Frances W........................Stark
Ames Georgia M ....Fulstone
Ames Jennifer D .... Ames
Ames Joan .... Burr
Ames Knowlton ....Reynders
Ames Mary H ....Miller
Ames Millicent W .... Adamson
Ames Olivia ....Manice
Ames Phyllis..............................Cox
Ames Sally J .... Robinette
Amidon Charlene .... Simpson
Ammidon Eliot H ....Jacobs
Amoroso Lisa J.......................Walker
Amory Kimberly E ....Alessio
Amory Margaret.......................Storer
Amory Mary ....Baker
Amory Mary A .... Winslow
Amory Violet............................Eaton
Amos Carolyn ....Mason
Andersen Marcia L .... Welles
Anderson Annie W ....Anderson
Anderson Barbara A ....Carruthers
Anderson Barbara A ....Fraker
Anderson Blayney .... Hull
Anderson Camille McL ....Jensen
Anderson Florence C ....Gibson
Anderson Jane G......................Dudley
Anderson Jean M .... Johnson
Anderson Joan ....Russell
Anderson Joan H ....Turnure
Anderson Kathleen L...................Parry
Anderson Kathryn A....................Miller
Anderson Lea E .... Smith
Anderson Lila Jane ....Tarkington
Anderson Lorna M .... Reimers
Anderson Lynn A .... Poole
Anderson M Helen ....Fisher
Anderson M Lee........................Carty
Anderson Marcella C................Distad
Anderson Margaret M ....Clough
Anderson Margaret R .... Cleavenger
Anderson Marguerite S.................. Buff

Anderson Marjorie.................Matheson
Anderson Mary Ainslie .... Gardner
Anderson Mary C .... Blake
Anderson Mary Ellen ....Young
Anderson Mary F....................Sheehan
Anderson Mary K......................Coy
Anderson Maude B ....Williams
Anderson Merry...................... Harsch
Anderson Nadya V ....Anderson
Anderson Nancy L.....................Weinig
Anderson Phyllis J ....Callaway
Anderson Rachel L .... Roberts
Anderson Shirley A ....Gaither
Anderson Sidney W .... Kenyon
Anderson Susan M .... Johnston
Anderson Sylvia..........................Kallio
Anderson Virginia....................Merriman
Anderson Vivian A .... Smith
Anderson-Talmage Carey E .... Davis
Anderton Helen E .... Reed
Andrade Lydia E................... de Sanctis
André Danielle P .... Crawford
André Rosane B.........................Hayes
Andresen Daphne K ....Corcoran
Andresen Judy E..........................Paige
Andresen Karen E................... Kennedy
Andretta Karen C.......................Green
Andrew Dorothy C ....McCandless
Andrew Victoria W ....Williamson
Andrews Doris I ....Crofut
Andrews Edith T ....Tobin
Andrews Ellen D .... Andrews
Andrews Frances .... Dillingham
Andrews Isabel ....Burgess
Andrews Jane C .... Pohl
Andrews Jeanette ....Wood
Andrews Leard........................ Watson
Andrews Lilian F B .... Beck
Andrews Lois E ....Bragdon
Andrews Lucetta R ....Clifford
Andrews Nancy K ....Stetson
Andrews Patricia V ....Steffan
Andrews Penelope .... Sprague
Andrews Shelley K .... Johnson
Andrews Susan ....Farr
Andrews Susan B ....Mace
Andrews Susan T.....................Carlson
Andrews Tabitha R.....................Huber
Andrews Toni Marie.......... Muckerman
Andreyev Olga.........................Carlisle
Andrus Carol J.....................Cavanagh
Andrus Julia D .... Aubry
Andvord Ingegjerd....................Stuart
Angel Nona M ....Butterworth
Angell Marjorie .... Hamilton
Angell Nancy E ....Streeter
Angelozzi Lisa P........................Barnhill
Angermeier Joie ....Anderson
Angier Helen H........................ Adamson
Angle Eleanor ....Richmond
Angulo Ysabel ....Wilson
Annan M Barbara ....Annan
Annenberg Evelyn ....Hall

Annibali Sophie C ....Mellon
Anson Dorothy R......................Metcalf
Anstine Lucille A ....Currier
Antell Patricia ....Andrews
Antell Ruth..............................McGehee
Anthon Margaret Primm.............Bundy
Anthon Victoria V ....Keefer
Anthony Aileen F........................Henry
Anthony Helen B.......................James
Anthony Judith H ....McLane
Anthony Lucy R ....Webster
Anthony Marcy E ....Wilson
Anthony Mary D........................West
Anthony Virginia L .... Soule
Anthony Winifred C ....Stearns
Antoine Kathleen........................Lloyd
Antuña Sofia I...........................Owen
Appel Elizabeth M.......................Brown
Appel Jacqueline ....Anderson
Appel Lydia S...........................Forbes
Appel Patricia ....Malloy
Appell Charity R .... Wheelock
Appell Laura P...........................Warren
Appleby Elizabeth T ....Gezelschap
Applegate Mary C ....Reigeluth
Appleton Anne S .... Park
Appleton Barbara R ....Blaxter
Appleton Diana G.................. McKnight
Appleton Frances B ....Jewett
Aquino Catherine S .... Gregory
Aquirre-Aquisto Alejandra ..... McClintic
Arcand Denise L......................McClintic
Archbald Marion....................de Forest
Archbold E Anne.......................Collins
Archbold Frances.......................Hufty
Archer Caroline H ....Kearney
Archer E Thayer ....Dewey
Archer Elizabeth C ....Guthrie
Archer Elizabeth H...................McLean
Archer Jane ....Buchanan
Archer Yvonne G ....Pons
Archibald Margaret E ....Ratcliffe
Archibald Mary Katherine......Blount
Ardlie Margot .... Neff
Arend Carolyn R......................Coleman
Arendall Elizabeth C .... Tilney
Arensberg Jane.....................Thompson
Arey Mary E.............................Freeman
Arguimbau Mariette S ....Badger
Arguimbau Suzanne.................. Davis
Arias Gladys E..........................Sohier
Armat Virginia A........................Hurt
Armbrister Mary K....................Young
Armesto M Norita.................Frenning
Armitage Frances...................Thorington
Armour Courtney K .... Regan
Armour Cynthia.........................Armour
Armour Elizabeth.....................Hollins
Armour Julia B ....Walker
Armour Laura S..........................Cook
Armour Leola.........................Macdonald
Armour M Brooks ....Diesel
Armstrong Ann M ....Baines

Baker Cornelia L	Baxter
Baker Dorothea C	Stockwell
Baker E Campbell	Whisnand
Baker Elisabeth S	Johnstone
Baker Elizabeth A	Scott-Paine
Baker Elizabeth R	Atwood
Baker Elizabeth S	Mathews
Baker Geraldine H	Masters
Baker Helen	Wiggers
Baker Hope L	Burley
Baker Janet W	Tenney
Baker Jennifer L	Warren
Baker Julia M	Menzies
Baker Katherine A	du Pont
Baker Katherine H	Spring
Baker Lucy	Dickey
Baker Lucy B	Patricola
Baker Margaret M	Chrisman
Baker Marie C	Simonds
Baker Marion D	Sloan
Baker Mary Ann G G	Wagner
Baker Mary C	Moulding
Baker Mary Caroline	Hunt
Baker Mary O	Supplee
Baker Matilda G	Wilbur
Baker Pauline M	Boardman
Baker Phyllis M	Tabler
Baker Priscilla F	Hill
Baker Roberta L	Cropsey
Baker Robin K	Barrell
Baker Roxana E	Pinkerton
Baker Ruth H	Ursul
Baker Ruth S	Gamble
Baker Sarah A	Bell
Baker Susan E	Fritz
Baker Susan V	Powell
Baker Sybil K K	Carton
Baker Victoria M	Masters
Baketel Barbara	Leonards
Bakewell Ann E	Woodward
Bakewell Cécile M	Woody
Bakewell Dorothy J	Bakewell
Bakewell G Elizabeth	Alexander
Bakewell Hester L	Bakewell
Bakewell Joan	Chouteau
Bakewell Margaret J	Rather
Bakewell Mildred C	Muckerman
Bakewell Polly C	Nichols
Bakewell Sarah	Bakewell
Balazs-Tagle L Patricia	Hume
Balboni Christina F	Patterson
Balboni Laura L	Merriman
Balch Cornelia	Wheeler
Balch Elizabeth	Hobson
Balderston Eleanore	Hoeffel
Balding F Bettina	Blackford
Balding Linda	Shearer
Balding Sheila F	Jewell
Baldini Julia C	Baldini
Baldner Cecilia A	Taylor
Baldra Becky S	Sandman
Baldridge Alice E	Wainwright
Baldridge Brooke B	Baldridge
Baldridge Christina Branson	Baldridge
Baldwin Alice	Kamm
Baldwin Almira S	Sant
Baldwin Barbara S	Miller
Baldwin Eleanor W	Tew
Baldwin Emily A	McKay
Baldwin Frances	Bitting
Baldwin Jane	Gillespie
Baldwin Jean W	Ritchie
Baldwin Joan	Cartwright
Baldwin Joyce B	Fahnestock
Baldwin Judith A	Lefferts
Baldwin Juliet C	Taylor
Baldwin Lee	Dalzell
Baldwin M Anne	Wetzel
Baldwin Margaret S	Dozier
Baldwin Martha B	Reilly
Baldwin Martha R	Guy
Baldwin Nona P	Brown
Baldwin Rosemary H	Coffin
Baldwin Ruth	Sharp
Baldwin Tracey E	Newhall
Balfour Clara E	George
Balis Eliza S	Chrystie
Balis Elizabeth W	Goodyear
Balis Nancy M	Morse
Balkwill Susanne	Cass
Ball Barbara	Cosden
Ball Betty L	Newhall
Ball Christine B	Fearey
Ball Helen	Schniewind
Ball Kate E	Davis
Ball Kathleen E	Crane
Ball Linda A	Paige
Ball Linda M	Smith
Ball Marie P	Meier
Ball Martha J	Heppenheimer
Ball Monica Van D	Colvin
Ball Nancy A	Roudebush
Ball Penelope S	Rutter
Ball Theda C	Tankersley
Ball Tracy J	Greer
Ballantine Carolyn D	True
Ballantine Elizabeth E	Gardner
Ballantine Elizabeth K	Spencer
Ballantine Elizabeth P	Overholser
Ballantine Elodie S	Emig
Ballantine Katherine	Badman
Ballantine Marguerite	Putnam
Ballard Ann S	Hallowell
Ballard Jean T	Hebard
Ballard Jennifer E	Ballard
Ballard Jill E	Hamilton
Ballard Kathleen R	Cabot
Ballard Susan R	Boal
Ballard Wendy F R	Ballard
Ballentine Jeanne A	Riegel
Ballin Diana A	Abbott
Ballin Marion	Spiro
Ballinger Jean	Rauch
Balmer Cynthia B	Coleman
Balos Brigitta A	Troy
Bancker Carol L	Vietor
Bancroft Edith C	von Hemert
Bancroft Jane	Cook
Bancroft Mary Jane	Bancroft
Bancroft Muffie W S	Murray
Bandanza Deborah C	Crawford
Bandeira de Mello Angela O	Keesee
Bandler Patricia R	Hornblower
Bane Janet	Richardson
Bane Patricia H	Long
Banes Frances D	Rentschler
Banfield Laura	Hoguet
Bangs Diana O	Garmey
Banks Bonica	Earle
Banks Charlotte A	Brown
Banks Elspeth H	Furlaud
Banks Emilie K	Dague
Banks Honor L	MacLean
Banks Lucy H	McBee
Banks Marjory A	Grannis
Banks Maud B	Duke
Banks Vieva F	Halsey
Bannard Emily A	Thomson
Banning Barbara	Estill
Baños Catherine L	Eustis
Baños Julia D	Poitevent
Banszky Catherine M	Alsop
Banta Carol	Walker
Banta Clara W	Kennedy
Baptiste Elizabeth	Cooper
Baptiste Louisa R	Vestner
Baram Evelyn	Clothier
Barba Joan S	Merrill
Barba Phyllis	Gibbons-Neff
Barber Elsie Y	Trask
Barber Jerre L	Wick
Barber Julia S	Benedict
Barbey Anita M	Redway
Barbey Anne	Hartt
Barbey Constance	Bowditch
Barbour Alicia	Megowen
Barbour Alison	Fox
Barbour Dorothy H	Hayes
Barbour Elysabeth C	Higgins
Barbour Joanne	Hines
Barbour Katharine S	Sutro
Barbour Louisa B	Parker
Barbour Susanne	Bullock
Barclay Barbara T	Ritter
Barclay Elizabeth M	Pennink
Barclay Elsa J	Wallace
Barclay Hilary W	Cooke
Barclay Margaret M	Chambers
Barclay Susan Le F	Ely
Barczyk Margaretha E	Alexander
Bardenheier Joan Marie Rose	Bardenheier
Bardes Brittain	Cudlip
Bardin Linda D	Adleta
Barela Rita	Seligman
Barili Mary C	Griffin
Baring-Gould A Merriol	Almond
Baring-Gould Judith A	Orthwein
Barkan Constance J	Kerr
Barkan Phoebe S	Gilpin
Barker Elizabeth M	Ring
Barker Frances M	Harde
Barker Helen	Martin
Barker Jean-Lamont	Fiske
Barker Marion P	Van Kleeck
Barker Maud Dulany	Jones
Barker Priscilla C	Miller
Barlerin Patricia P	Farman-Framaian
Barletta Nelia F	Cates
Barloga Cindy Cay	Barloga
Barlow Julia P	Vail
Barlow M Elizabeth	Emmons
Barlow Sarah J	Ittmann
Barnard Daphne D	Davis
Barnard Pamela	Ruzicka
Barnard Sylvia L	Brown
Barnes Amanda E	Mucklé
Barnes Angelina	Jackson
Barnes Barbara L	Singmaster
Barnes Bertha Lea	Stone
Barnes Betty S	Woodcock
Barnes Cecily W	Geyelin
Barnes Charlton L	Corson
Barnes Dolores K	Cassidy
Barnes Gloria I	Van Norden
Barnes Gloria M	Harper
Barnes J Lea	Iselin
Barnes Jennifer	Griffin
Barnes Joan H	Pool
Barnes Joyce	Farmer
Barnes Julia W	May
Barnes Marion R	Babcock
Barnes Phoebe	Caner
Barnes Sandra H	Gillespie
Barnes Sara E	Sonne
Barnett Anne A	Merrill
Barnett Caroline E	Bryan
Barnett Elizabeth A	Schmidt
Barnett Helen L	Diserens
Barnett Katharine K	Grantham
Barnett M Cecilia	Meers
Barnett Taylor S	Slaughter
Barney Alexandra W	Cowley
Barney Amanda La M	Layng
Barney Harriet L	Lidgerwood
Barney Margaret	Shields
Barney Marie L	Perrin
Barngrove Sally Ann	Barngrove
Barnhart Helen E	Henderson
Barr Carrie S	Miller
Barr Elizabeth H	Barr
Barr Katherine C	Norling
Barr Katherine V	Sherwin
Barr Lucy A	Fowler
Barr Sandra M	Boyd
Barratt Edith L	Lenssen
Barrena Denise J	McLaughlin
Barret Hermione	Way
Barrett Barbara A	Heekin
Barrett Beatrice A	Deacon
Barrett Beatrice H	Barrett

Beckwith A Kennedy .... Nelson
Beckwith Doris L .... Crans
Beckwith Dorothy Q .... Nelson
Beckwith Elizabeth P .... Dickey
Beckwith Gloria .... Blaine
Beckwith Kathryn P .... Gaier
Beckwith Rosa H L .... Sands
Beddington Charlotte .... Wallis
Bedell Caroline C .... Thomas
Bedell Virginia .... Nunan
Bedford Barbara .... Mathieu
Bedford Dorothy L .... Taggart
Bedford Lily L C .... Raines
Bedford Lucie E .... Warren
Bee M Susan .... Stine
Beebe Diana .... Richardson
Beebe Janet .... Taber
Beebe Judith M .... Gummere
Beebe June D .... Atwood
Beebe Lois W .... Shantz
Beech Anne C .... Lewis
Beech Linda A .... Cutler
Beech Sandra A .... Lane
Beecher Harriet .... Field
Beecher Mary K .... Price
Beede Kimberly Anne .... Soule
Beedy Mary E .... Murphy
Beekman Isabelle S .... Fergus
Beekman Sabina C .... Forbes
Beeler Betty .... Churchman
Beels Constance .... Thomas
Beer Grace L .... Martin
Beer Marguerite L E .... Platt
Beers Elizabeth N .... Hoguet
Beers Mary B .... Dillard
Beers Mary E .... Conrad
Beers Victoria A .... Knox
Beersman Diane L .... MacFadyen
Beesley Terry R A .... Phipps
Befani Gabriella .... O'Donnell
Befanis Carol .... O'Donnell
Beggs Bonnie J .... Lincoln
Beggs Deborah .... Moncrief
Béguelin Virginia .... Clarke
Beha Ann M .... Radloff
Behn Aphra .... Behn
Behn Margaret C .... Ertman
Behn Monica .... Le Pelletier
Behn Sharon Maria .... Guinan
Behneman Marjorie S .... Newsom
Behr Ann C .... Baldwin
Behre Gretchen .... Street
Beidler A Virginia .... Neff
Belcher Mary W .... Pemberton
Belcher Virginia C .... Wilson
Belden Sally V .... Yost
Belden Tacey .... Hole
Belew Alice W .... Lonsdorf
Belfield Barbara E .... Keenan
Belk Sarah W .... Gambrell
Belknap Louise .... Carter
Bell Amy .... Gatchell
Bell Anne L .... Williams

Bell Barbara A .... Leith
Bell Connie M .... Mason
Bell Deborah E .... Spoehel
Bell Elizabeth S .... Corser
Bell Jane A .... Coddington
Bell Jeanne .... Hero
Bell Mignon A .... Cameron
Bell Nancy .... Driscoll
Bell Nancy Loomis .... Chandlee
Bell Phyllis K .... Bell
Bell Roxanne F .... Casscells
Bell Ruth J .... McEwan
Bell Sarah A .... Bullard
Bell Sophie S .... Donaghy
Bell Susan M .... Trowbridge
Bell Susan R .... McIntosh
Bell Vicki A .... Tannatt
Bellah Ann P .... Copeland
Bellamy Lillian M .... Boney
Bellan Mary .... Eidt
Bellardini Eileen .... Leith
Bellé Cécile .... Carson
Bellinger Patricia .... Kauffmann
Bellins Elaine .... Lane
Bellis Blair B .... Judson
Bellis Catherine C .... Brown
Bellis Martha H .... Gregg
Belmont Priscilla .... Upton
Belson Marie T .... Hoeffner
Belt Margaret P .... Strelinger
Belt Margaret P .... Turner
Belz Caroline .... Belz
Bemis Barbara T .... Bartlett
Bemis Esther .... Goodwin
Benacerraf Claire S .... Pereira
Benedict Adrienne P .... Brough
Benedict Alice D .... Dunn
Benedict Anna C .... Millar
Benedict Anne .... Swain
Benedict Barbara A .... Price
Benedict Carol .... Hall
Benedict Cathleen R .... Yeager
Benedict Gail C .... Miller
Benedict Laura A .... Jones
Benedict Mildred D .... Cook
Benjamin A Leith .... Hill
Benjamin Anne R .... Barry
Benjamin Beverley C .... Goodwin
Benjamin Charlotte P .... Carver
Benjamin Mary .... Herring
Benjamin Mary A .... Henderson
Benjamin Sarah M .... Prentice
Benkard Joan D .... Jackson
Benkhart Barbara O .... Thompson
Benkhart Nancy H .... Borner
Bennett Barbara .... Fearing
Bennett Barbara V V .... Bradford
Bennett Beatrice Gay .... Stoltz
Bennett Diana M F .... Benjamin
Bennett Eunice .... Stauffer
Bennett Josephine .... Musgrave
Bennett Julester J .... Bennett
Bennett Lindalyn .... Adams

Bennett Madeleine E .... Schreiber
Bennett Mary A .... Aiken
Bennett Mary Alice .... Baumberger
Bennett Nancy C .... Haynes
Bennett Rhonda R .... Fournier
Bennett Ruth A .... Jordan
Benoist G G Courtney .... Fish
Benoist Marie Elizabeth .... Igleheart
Benoist Tam .... Barry
Bensinger Suzanne V .... Orrick
Benson Anne H .... Poor
Benson Christine .... Pell
Benson Ethel .... Nalle
Benson Ethel Pew .... Wister
Benson Frieda S .... Grimball
Benson Jennifer .... Kelly
Benson Lisa J .... Burns
Benson Marion F .... Miller
Benson Sheryl L .... Acheson
Bent Margaret S .... Patterson
Bentley Alice Wrenn .... Rinaker
Bentley Joan S .... Lippincott
Bentley Josephine .... Offutt
Bentley Patricia .... Hooper
Bentley Ruth .... Parker
Bentley Zara .... Roberts
Benton Deborah E .... Motley
Bentsen Pamela L .... Havens
Bentz Jean M .... Burnham
Benziger Jane M .... Weekes
Béra Emilie .... Smith
Beranger Barbara F .... Miller
Bérard Monique O H .... Kinsolving
Berdou Mary Virginia
     Urquhart of Urquhart
Berean Barbara .... Alfriend
Berenson Elizabeth .... Gates
Beresford-Owen Catherine J ... Coolidge
Beretta Jacqueline .... Tomerlin
Berg C Christina .... Sailer
Berg Hildegard .... Richardson
Berg Joan K .... Mullen
Bergasse Betty M .... Bitting
Berger Ann H .... Berger
Berger Elizabeth S .... Eberhart
Berger Margaret B .... Miller
Berger Marilyn .... Engman
Berger Rebecca B .... Wells
Bergland Jean E .... Robins
Bergman Debra .... Haywood
Bergman Jettie L .... Johnston
Bergner Louise W .... Cope
Bergsten Sandra A .... Shiverick
Bergstrom Nancy V .... Havens
Berguido Jill .... Gill
Berkey June .... D'Arcy
Berkfield Dorothy H .... Stahr
Berkley Cynthia .... Kirkland
Berl Alexandra S .... Flour
Berl Marie W .... Brodhead
Berlin Elizabeth I .... Peters
Berlin Linda L .... Emmet
Bermejillo Beatriz B .... Moore

Bernard April A .... Robinson
Bernard Rita .... Cooke
Bernard S Julia .... O'Malley
Bernard Sandra J .... Tucker
Bernau Phyllis D .... Macomber
Bernhardt Brigitte .... Royce
Berns Deborah .... McGovern
Berns Lolita .... Renshaw
Berrien Stephanie .... Ragan
Berry Alice .... Hoguet
Berry Frances S .... Spradley
Berry Jean S .... Howard
Berry Jeanette M .... Houghton
Berry Margaret .... Lowder
Berry Rosina O .... Dixon
Berry Violetta L .... Otis
Berth Francine P .... Myles
Berthe Brigitte M .... Emory
Bertozzi Alessandra .... Billingslea
Bertrand Cara M .... Niles
Bertschmann Shelagh B .... Richards
Berwind Kathleen .... Flannery
Berwind Margaret .... Schiffer
Besch Lorraine W .... Gibson
Beshar Cornelia A .... Spring
Besozzi Karla L .... King
Bessellieu Eleanor B .... Horton
Besser Susan K .... Werner
Bessire Paulette .... Cushman
Best Virginia .... Adams
Bethea Laura T .... King
Bethge Sabine R .... Moffett
Bettle Edith M .... Gardner
Bettle Sarah .... Bettle
Betts Phyllys C .... Fleming
Betz Elizabeth W .... Kneen
Betz Phyllis J .... Rhein
Bever Carroll .... English
Bever Sarah G .... Henderson
Beveridge Deborah A .... Taylor
Bevill Susan B .... Livingston
Beyea Marianne M .... Ellis
Beyer Charlotte B .... Beyer
Beyer Deming P
    de Hemricourt de Grunne
Bickel Minnette C .... Boesel
Bickford Emily A .... Lansbury
Bickford Leila V .... Sawyer
Bickford Ruth H .... Brainard
Bickham Maria E .... Bender
Bickley Louise W .... Farnum
Bicknell Frances W .... Page
Bicknell Kate H .... Kirkham
Bicknell Martha Henry .... Kellner
Bidart Cynthia A .... Harris
Biddle Adele .... Schoettle
Biddle Anne G .... Biddle
Biddle Ann-Patton .... Matthews
Biddle Catherine P .... Dunning
Biddle Charlotte H .... Biddle
Biddle Constance M .... Biddle
Biddle Daisy L .... Eiman
Biddle Elizabeth E .... Barrett

Biddle Helene ....Dick
Biddle Julia C ....Biddle
Biddle Letitia C ....Blitzer
Biddle Mary A.........................Scheetz
Biddle Mary D.......................Semans
Biddle Mathilde M .... Hilton
Biddle N Pandora Duke...............Hentic
Biddle Priscilla Ann ....Hepburn
Biddle Sarah Lee ....Stokes
Biddle Tamia J.......................Patterson
Bidinger Julie A.........................Weary
Bidlack Amanda S ....Strand
Bidwell Hillary D ....Mackay
Bidwill Nicole L.......................Bidwell
Bielaski Jennifer Townsend
                                              Lawrence
Bierau Beatricia ....Herrick
Bierley Jane ....Thayer
Bierwirth Nancy E ....Baldridge
Biette Suzanne M ....McCance
Bigelow Anne C .... MacFarlane
Bigelow Anne H .... Thompson
Bigelow Florence ....Schaff
Bigelow Kate ....Benton
Bigelow Louise .... Parsons
Bigelow Mary C ....Soutter
Bigelow Natalie S.....................Gates
Biggar Anne McM....................Neville
Biggar Elizabeth S .... Hellmuth
Biggs Allegra G.....................Lubrano
Biggs Fiona K........... Druckenmiller
Biggs Jane F ....Sanger
Biggs Melissa E.....................Bradley
Biggs Robin B ....Noble
Bigham Anne S......................Hutchins
Bigham Hildreth J.....................Massey
Bikle Bettine S...........................Boyd
Bilkey Laura B ....Barclay
Bill Catherine A.........................Osborn
Bill Sonia A ....Robertson
Billings Lucretia ....Fisher
Billings Martha B ....Binney
Billings Mary F P .... Hummeler
Billups Marcella...................Symington
Binding Martha ....Frothingham
Binger Charlotte H ....Hasen
Binger Frances S......................Mitchell
Bingham Anne .... Wright
Bingham Anne D........................Lord
Bingham Barbara ....Moore
Bingham Burks Y ....Lapham
Bingham Eleanor Berry ....Mallory
Bingham Emily S ....Reily
Bingham Ferne.........................Welles
Bingham Heidi M ....Stott
Bingham Marian ....Bingham
Bingham Sara J........................Wilson
Binkerd Patricia ....Jeanrenaud
Binks V Jean..............................Tolles
Binney Caroline Thorn ....Binney
Binney Constance ....Harris
Binney Edith A ....Metcalf
Binney Mary M ....Wakefield

Binney Susan A ....Flake
Binnié D Dené A ....Ballantine
Bintz Barbara C ....Gray
Birch Linda D ....Thomas
Bird Helen L...........................Rasmussen
Bird Mary E.............................Young
Bird Marys ....Hoagland
Bird Nancy C ....McKown
Bird Peyton W ....Sise
Bird Sarah-Braeme..................Congdon
Birney Agnes M ....Hood
Bischoff Marion L ....Ketcham
Bischoff Marion M ....Black
Biscoe Sally ....Palache
Bishop Barbara S ....Bartle
Bishop Cynthia C ....Dickey
Bishop Elizabeth F ....Coburn
Bishop Gerry L ....Hibbard
Bishop Jane H ....Putnam
Bishop Kathleen A ....Cannon
Bishop Mary F...................Millspaugh
Bishop Melinda.......................MacColl
Bishop P Brooks ....Gernerd
Bishop Susan M.....................Hartwell
Bishop Wilder O ....Regalbuto
Bisig Mary P...............................Boyce
Bissell Antonia V ....Laird
Bissell Beverly S ....Sullivan
Bissell Eleanor ....Wheeler
Bissell Joan ....Lucas
Bissell Julia du P ....Leisenring
Bissell Lesley W ....Hoopes
Bissell Susan P ....Parker
Bisso Elizabeth A ....Morris
Bitner Martha B ....Strain
Bitner Susan A..............................Cobb
Bittel Madeleine J....................Walker
Bitting Barbara.........................Frazer
Bixby Patricia ....Hoopes
Bixby Sarah T............................Defty
Blabon Diana M ....Holt
Blabon Mary S ....Tilghman
Blachly Patricia A...................Meadows
Black Barbara ....Ware
Black Barbara A ....Lowry
Black Elizabeth L ....Atlee
Black Lois E ....Veale
Black Marcia S ....Holder
Black Margaretta B.....................Huber
Black Margo Duer ....Carlisle
Black Mary Grace........................Leas
Black Maureen M ....Ogden
Black Ruth ....Henchey
Black Suzanne ....O'Toole
Black Sylvia ....Black
Black Viola M J ....Bement
Blackburn Nancy L....................Hamon
Blackett Priscilla.....................Houghton
Blackford Elizabeth ....Middleton
Blackinton Ann M ....Davis
Blackistone Jane S ....Hughes
Blackley Margo M...................Sullivan
Blackman Madeline .... Parker

Blackmore Druanne .... Sweetser
Blackmore Patricia................Blackmore
Blackstone Ann D...............TenHoopen
Blackwell Eileen ....Bane
Blackwell Eleanor E .... Churchill
Blackwell Elizabeth R ....Drake
Blackwell Sherry J.................Washburn
Blaffer Catherine H ....Taylor
Blagden Anne W.....................Blodgett
Blagden Carol V ....Allen
Blagden Elise G..........................Lufkin
Blagden Elizabeth H...........Strawbridge
Blagden Mary K ....Kinsolving
Blagden Sarita S ....Choate
Blaine Cecelia M ....Littlefield
Blaine Charlotte W ....Vaughn
Blair Carolyn C.........................Sheffield
Blair Dorothy A...........................Sage
Blair Frances M ....Steele
Blair Joan ....Overton
Blair Joan G ....Sullivan
Blair Kathleen ....Leisure
Blair Laura L ....Marvel
Blair Margaretta P ....Mueller
Blair Mary O..........................Simmons
Blair Sara M .... Dougherty
Blaisdell Susan C ....Blaisdell
Blake Anna J..............................Pier
Blake Barbara ....Putnam
Blake Caroline H ....Whitney
Blake Diana M......................Hayward
Blake Edith S ....Meinfelder
Blake Elisabeth J ....Loring
Blake Julia O ....Beals
Blake M Catharine ....Currier
Blake Mary A ....Holmes
Blake Ruth ....Oliver
Blake Ruth F ....Munson
Blake Sallie C ....Sullivan
Blakeslee Eleanor C ....Whiston
Blakeslee Kathleen A ....Walker
Blakney Barbara ....Brumder
Blanchard Ann E .... Richardson
Blanchard Louise M ....Thompson
Bland Elizabeth N......................Nesbit
Blankarn Marcia T ....Chorley
Blankarn Martha T ....Halsey
Blankenship E Faye ....Fowle
Blatchford Barbara...................Fowler
Blatchford Lucy M ....Pinkerton
Blatchford Sarah H ....Ijams
Blatz Teresa E...........................Walker
Blaurock Ingeborg E.............Seggerman
Blaxter Anne P ....Page
Bleecker Mary De W............. Simmons
Bleecker Patricia H......................Jones
Blenheim Vera G...................Brigham
Blettner Margaret J ....Angell
Blind Anne C ....Cook
Blinov Natasha M....................Randolph
Bliss Barbara...........................Moore
Bliss Elinor ....Malcom
Bliss Elizabeth A ....Cobb

Bliss Elizabeth G ....Divine
Bloch Anne-Marie ....Bullen
Bloch Martha M ....McLanahan
Blodget F Elizabeth ....Whitman
Blodgett Cynthia.......................Martin
Blodgett Esther P ....Meyer
Blodgett Jayne A ....Murray
Blodgett Julia R ....Curtis
Blodgett Katherine C .... Winter
Blodgett Kendra R...............Schechter
Blodgett Pauline.......................Watson
Blomquist Amelia P ....Buckley
Blondet Isabel ....Armour
Blood Margaret L ....Collins
Bloomer Elizabeth ....Ford
Blossom Clare M ....Webb
Blount Beverly R ....Tucker
Blount Mary A........................Penton
Blue Alice T G ....Irving
Blue E Stuart................................Blue
Blue S Katharine.........................Roper
Blum Anne B ....Brengle
Blumberg Beverly H.................Erdreich
Blumer Phoebe M ....Hornblower
Blunt Marion A........... von Heisermann
Blyth Cynthia N M.................Limbocker
Blyth Marjorie R...........................Bell
Boal Mathilde ....Lee
Boardman Agnes D ....Church
Boardman Alexandra R .... Reynolds
Boardman Christina W ....Buckley
Boardman Dorothy P.................Dewart
Boardman Elisabeth...................Lloyd
Boardman Elizabeth H ....Ross
Boardman Jane B....................La Besse
Boardman Virginia J....................Baker
Boas Deborah M.......................Mitchell
Boatman Bettie J.......................Ripley
Boatwright Ann B......................... Igoe
Boaz Susan Tucker.......................Low
Bobbitt Sara N ....Willis
Bobrowicz Elaine J....................Mason
Bockius Anna W ....Sasso
Bockius Margaret S ....Devereux
Boddie Judith J ....Walker
Bodell Robin A.........................Fisher
Bodman Nancy A ....Mantz
Bodman Violet...........................Coffin
Bodnar Beverly J.....................Rodiger
Bodrero Lydia P ....Redmond
Bodtke Barbara A ....Simpson
Boeger Barbara B ....Mason
Boers Shirley J...........................Fowler
Boersma Mary D L......................Leeds
Boeschenstein Isabelle H...........Storey
Boethelt Elizabeth I ....Stockly
Boettger Charlotte.........................Ryan
Bogart Cynthia ....Wladyka
Bogert Katrina V N O .... Hart
Boggs Augusta H...................Radcliffe
Boggs Mary G ....Doub
Bogner Erika ....Reichner

Braddon Joan I	Means
Braden Elizabeth	Foster
Braden Nancy L	Stevens
Bradfield Barbara H	Taft
Bradford Angela	Freeman
Bradford Ann Hickling	Mathias
Bradford Cynthia A	Skvarch
Bradford Frances K	Meigs
Bradford Gertrude E	Peake
Bradford J Lee	Daley
Bradford Louise H	Clayton
Bradford Melinda A	Lyons
Bradford Pamela W	Andrews
Bradford Priscilla W	Ripley
Bradford Rebecca C	Chase
Bradford Susan	Roberts
Bradlee Adeline L	Polese
Bradlee Constance	Devens
Bradlee Elizabeth	Perry
Bradley Ann W	Vehslage
Bradley Anne	Donahoe
Bradley Anne C	Hancock
Bradley Anne W	Brucker
Bradley Barbara J	Wheeler
Bradley Carol	Davis
Bradley Carolyn F	Caswell
Bradley Deborah	Latta
Bradley Deborah	Oberholtzer
Bradley Edith M	Perkins
Bradley Elise B	Mackay
Bradley Elizabeth C	Sluder
Bradley Elizabeth S	Brookfield
Bradley Hannah L	Henderson
Bradley Jane D	Blau
Bradley Jennifer T	Cannell
Bradley Josephine C	Bush
Bradley Josephine W	De Young
Bradley Marian A	Morehouse
Bradley Marian D	Crawford
Bradley Marjorie	Townsend
Bradley Nora	Wolcott
Bradley Sally P	Elsey
Bradley Virginia C	Clark
Bradnick A Eve	Woodhull
Bradshaw Constance	Morrill
Bradshaw Elizabeth C	Magee
Bradshaw Muriel	Throop
Bradshaw Priscilla W	Page
Brady Alice L	Gordon
Brady Anna E C	Evans
Brady Barbara	Miller
Brady Barrett	Frelinghuysen
Brady Beverly	Roche
Brady Brenda	Woodward
Brady Elizabeth H	Richards
Brady Hope O	Wagstaff
Brady Jennifer C	Coley
Brady Katherine C	Cutler
Brady Leslie C	Thieriot
Brady Mary Beth	Bright
Brady Muriel P	Townzen
Brady Robin E	Mead
Brady Winifred	Noble
Braestrup Elise C	Wellington
Braff Jane S	Paquet
Braga Allegra	Figg
Bragdon Margaret	Shepley
Bragg Catherine H	Lanier
Bragg Jan E	Marshall
Bragg Paulette	Fownes
Braggiotti Gloria	Etting
Braid Alexandra E	Graham
Brainard Jennifer C	Philip
Brainard Mary E	Grant
Braislin Elizabeth C	Powers
Braley Karen A	Potts
Bramwell Heidi E	Humes
Branciforte Deborah A	Fowler
Brand Beverly C	Strong
Brand Margaret A	Bafford
Brandon Barbara G	Kaiser
Brandon Elaine	Morshead
Brandon Kate D	Adams
Brandon Louisa P	Barker
Brandon Lucy M	Parlange
Brandt Helen N	Moore
Brandt Tatiana	Copeland
Brannan Mary W	White
Brannon Isabel C	Spencer
Branson Jennifer L	Fowler
Brashares Merry J	Parker
Brassard Jane A	Metcalf
Brassell Barbara	Weber
Bratcher Kenna M	Lewis
Brauer Amy	Hoyt
Braun Sarah A	Bushing
Brawley Jane H	Nigra
Brawner Elisabeth P	Bingham
Braxton Merwin C	Worth
Bray Angeline Mary	Hamilton
Bray Barbara	Richey
Bray Carole A	Sheffield
Bray Dorothy A	Hartenstein
Bray Pauline H	Nutting
Brayer Mary A	Doty
Brayton Elizabeth	Dawson
Brayton Jeremy C	Wilson
Brayton Marsha Crandall	Everett
Brazill Kelly A	MacKay
Bready Anna Garey	Sterling
Breckenridge Carolyn H	Gregg
Breckenridge Sara C	Wright
Breckenridge Wilder	Selman
Breckinridge Gertrude B	Peyton
Breckinridge Isabella G	Breckinridge
Breckinridge Lila R	Field
Breckinridge M Marvin	Patterson
Brede Ann H	Swint
Bredt Prudence	Gamble
Breed Ellen W	Staniford
Breed Jilda K	Barker
Breed Lynden R	Miller
Breed M Elizabeth	Haneman
Breed Nell I	Lutken
Brégy Phyllis F	Flail
Breitzke Madalyn T	Dortch
Bremer Barbara	Kinne
Bremer Grace	Gallaway
Bremner Alice	Drake
Brenchley Marguerite Cammack	Baldwin
Breneman Betty C	Ames
Breneman Charlee	Blaine
Brengle Millicent A	Gates
Brenholts Joyce V	Weidenkopf
Brenizer Nancy K	Benedict
Brenk Wieslawa	Waters
Brennan Cynthia H	Annibali
Brennan Evelyn F	Williamson
Brennan Lucie E	Holmes
Brennan Mary E	Gerster
Brennan Mora	Clark
Brenner Mary J	Gay
Brennig Margaret M	Sheets
Brent Harriet C	Dame
Brentlinger Judith A	Caner
Brereton Mary	Frost
Brereton Nancy M	Robinson
Brereton Sara B	Cutler
Breslin Ellen P	Davidson
Breslin Kathryn	Wells
Breslow Edith L	Munroe
Breslow Gail R	Thayer
Brett Dorothy A	Stone
Brett Elizabeth Weld	Webster
Brett Katryna R	Carothers
Brewer Anne	Stone
Brewer Daryln U T	Hoffstot
Brewer E Kathleen	Taylor
Brewer Effie L	Kimball
Brewer Elisabeth H	Weintz
Brewer Elizabeth L	Noble
Brewer Jeannette	Welch
Brewer Judith A	Campbell
Brewer Louise H	Woods
Brewer Pamela	Molyneux
Brewer Wendy E	Paddock
Brewer Wendy H A	Daras
Brewington H Gail	O'Donovan
Brewster Anne	Brittain
Brewster Carryl B	Mare
Brewster Diana K	Doswell
Brewster Frances S	Rauch
Brewster Isabel E	Van Dine
Brewster Janet L	York
Brewster Katharine G	Whipple
Brewster Nancy D	Paternotte
Brewster Sheila J	Hill
Brewster Sydney R	Spofford
Brewster V Whitney	Armstrong
Brey Dorothy M	Anderson
Brey Mary A	Vastine
Brian Jane	Engelhard
Briant Elisabeth G	McCullough
Briceño Rosélène	Robinson
Brick Anne Coles	Creep
Brick Clementine B C	Miller
Bricker Kathryn M	Jenks
Bridge Anne M	Baddour
Bridge Virginia	Welch
Bridger Mary Ann L	Wirts
Bridges Prudence A	Van Winkle
Bridgett Cecile B	Stewart
Bridgman Marion	Slusser
Bried Eleanor	Kingsbury
Briend Monique M	Walker
Brier Mary E	Goodhue
Brigg Pamela H	McKown
Briggs Ashley C	Bernhard
Briggs Katherine M	Goldberg
Briggs Nancy G	Fell
Brigham Beryl H	Cox
Bright Anita Le R	Curran
Bright Elinor	Richardson
Bright Fanny	Goodhue
Bright Margaret B	Walker
Bright Margaret M	Harding
Bright Maria	Church
Brinckerhoff Carol B	Henderson
Brine Beverly A	Blagden
Brink Susanne J	Bomeisler
Brinkema Bernice A	Ennis
Brinkman Janet B	Day
Brinley Dorothy R	Manou
Brinn Gail M	Putnam
Brinser Barbara	Maniha
Brinton Joan F	Johnson
Brisbane Elinor	Philbin
Briscoe Elizabeth C	Wheaton
Briscoe Serena B	Montague
Bristol Joan A	Henderson
Bristow Romaine	Adams
Brittain Hatherly	Todd
Britten Patricia A	Young
Brittingham Carol A	Meyer
Britton Barbara T	Reque
Britton Miriam M	Spiller
Broadbent Marion F	Philbrick
Broaddus Katherine G	Blue
Broadley Lee P	Greenwood
Brock Mary T	Whitney
Brock Rebecca G	Richardson
Brock Susan M	Saltonstall
Brock Virginia L	Moorhead
Brockenbrough Henrietta Q	Frost
Brockett Kathryn S	Wellborn
Broderick Sherri A	Lex
Brodhead Janet F	Brodhead
Brodhead Josephine C	Moore
Brodhead Sarah S	Wickham
Brodhead Virginia S	Clemmer
Brodie Diana M	Grafmueller
Brodie Marta	Greene
Brodie P June	Finlayson
Broeksmit Laura F	Thurston
Brogan Gillian T	Wiederseim
Brokaw Carolyn	Delanoy
Brokaw Edna	Morris
Brokaw Elizabeth C	Metcalfe
Brokaw Julia E	Statter
Bromberg Deborah A	Ely
Bromeyer Beebe Eileen	Roberts

Bromley Beverley	Vaughan
Bromley Binney B	Miller
Bromley Ellen R	McFarland
Bromley Nancy C	Kirkland
Bromley Sandra	Morris
Bromley Sheila	Kellogg
Bronaugh Elinor R	Pagel
Bronkie Gina B	Hammond
Bronson Beatrice W	Garvan
Bronson Jean W W	Kilborne
Bronson Madeleine	Dugan
Brooke Anita B	Beck
Brooke Cornelia E	Gilder
Brooke Elizabeth M	Blake
Brooke Hallie M	Slidell
Brooke Mary A	Rice
Brookfield Nancy B	Burke
Brookhart Suzanne	Harrison
Brooks Ann H	Carter
Brooks Barbara	Kroos
Brooks Bertha B	McCormick
Brooks Carolyn J S	Morrin
Brooks Charlotte	Korth
Brooks Edith W	Forrester
Brooks Eleanor	Brown
Brooks Elizabeth C	Currier
Brooks Elizabeth D	Stull
Brooks Elizabeth L	Ford
Brooks Gwendolyn	Bass
Brooks Joy B	Greenway
Brooks Katharine	Pennebaker
Brooks Lucretia G	Matheson
Brooks Marana L	Morosani
Brooks Margaret E	Van Dusen
Brooks Mary	Robbins
Brooks Mary C	Woodbridge
Brooks Mary M	Griswold
Brooks Nancy	Hale
Brooks Nevada L	Cook
Brooks Penne L	Weicker
Brooks Rachel W	Evans
Brooks Rosamond	McDowell
Brooks Ruth K	Chapin
Brooks Susan	Morris
Broome Elizabeth T	Miller
Broome Karin S J	Ohrstrom
Broome Ynez C	Jones
Broomhead Barbara V	Bromley
Broun Elise B	Weber
Broussard Mary A	Vineyard
Brouwier France A	Beekman
Brower Caroline W	Cuthbert
Brower Karen M	Goehring
Brown A Cary	Epstein
Brown Abigail O	Crittenden
Brown Aimee E	DuPre
Brown Alice C	Mack
Brown Alice D	Graves
Brown Alice E	Pullman
Brown Alice F	Westervelt
Brown Amy	Polk
Brown Angela B	Fischer
Brown Anita G	Wilson

Brown Ann E	Newbold
Brown Ann H	Bell
Brown Anne T	Colgan
Brown Ardon B	Armstrong
Brown Barbara	McClenahan
Brown Barbara	Parrott
Brown Barbara	Stetson
Brown Barbara A	Dennett
Brown Barbara A	Terry
Brown Barbara E	Travis
Brown Beatrice R	Guthrie
Brown Betsey S	Steeger
Brown Betsy J	Baker
Brown Bettina S	Irvine
Brown Blair T	Hoyt
Brown Cameron E	Peter
Brown Caroline O	Vaillant
Brown Carolyn M	Wick
Brown Catharine M	Ebling
Brown Catherine Duer	Stanton
Brown Charlotte A	Richardson
Brown Charlotte Houston	Dallett
Brown Christine P	Goozée
Brown Constance	Berkley
Brown Cornelia W	Warren
Brown Deborah A	Lynch
Brown Deborah S	Berger
Brown Drusilla	Grubb
Brown Elizabeth	Ketner
Brown Elizabeth A	Martinet
Brown Elizabeth D	Dickerson
Brown Elizabeth G	Warwick
Brown Elizabeth L	Carson
Brown Elizabeth R	Van Sant
Brown Elizabeth S	Phillips
Brown Elizabeth W	Bradley
Brown Ellen V	Lapham
Brown Frances H	Townes
Brown Greta B	Schutt
Brown Helen W	Zimmermann
Brown Hope	Canfield
Brown Hope	Perlberg
Brown Janet F	Allen
Brown Janet H	Brewer
Brown Jean I J	Gross
Brown Jean T T	Lewin
Brown Juanita H	Groton
Brown Judith	Chew
Brown Karen L	Kelly
Brown Katharine C	Brown
Brown Kathryn M	Wyrough
Brown Kimberly A	Ferguson
Brown Laura H	Montant
Brown Letitia	Upton
Brown Louise G	Risk
Brown Lucy E	Wagner
Brown Lucy Manning	Barry
Brown M Harriett	Dalton
Brown M Winifred	Foss
Brown Madeline H	Mortimer
Brown Margaret	Marting
Brown Margaret R	Shiverick
Brown Marion H	Simpson

Brown Marjorie A	Lawrence
Brown Marshall M	Webb
Brown Mary B	Kreger
Brown Mary E	Bauer
Brown Mary E	Bigelow
Brown Mary I S	Stiles
Brown Mildred H	Hyde
Brown Nancy A	Smith
Brown Nancy C	Mercer
Brown Nancy C P	Buck
Brown Nancy N	Wellin
Brown Nathalie	Lawrence
Brown Nina	Brown
Brown Pamela W	Kloman
Brown Patricia P	Wells
Brown Patricia W	Waters
Brown Pauline S	Baugh
Brown Rachel	Fowler
Brown Robin E	Woods
Brown Rosalie L	Maury
Brown Ruby	Neville
Brown Sandra S	Taylor
Brown Sara E	Morgan
Brown Sara W	Gilliam
Brown Sarah L	Smith
Brown Sarah M	Smallhouse
Brown Sheila T	LeBrecht
Brown Shirley	Haselton
Brown Sophia L	Twichell
Brown Stella W	Kenly
Brown Susan Coe	Brown
Brown Tracy M	Pearson
Brown Valerie V	Stauffer
Brown Violetta T	Dodge
Brown Virginia B	Clarke
Brown Virginia F	Sudler
Brown Vivian G	Smith
Brownback Mary V	Swain
Browne Ann H	Ward
Browne Cecilia	Kuhn
Browne Julia B	Sause
Browne Kathleen	Moss
Browne Lucy O	Browne
Browne Marcy C	Wells
Browne Marguerite La B	Houston
Browne Marion La B	Dickerman
Browne Mary Jane L	Wilson
Browne Nancy A	Leeson
Browne Susan C	Pfeiffer
Browning Dominique	Lemann
Browning Elizabeth W	Gerard
Browning Josephine Wells	Pierce
Brownley Nancy de F	Holt
Broyles Eleanor Custis	Wright
Brubaker Judith	Martinez
Bruce Ellen McH	Terry
Bruce Emily K	Chapman
Bruce Louise R	Townsend
Bruch Aileen L	Ayers
Bruder Marilynn	Alsdorf
Bruen Constance L J	Barrow
Bruen Evelyn L	Trevor
Bruen Marian A	Marrin

Bruening Elizabeth	Lewis
Bruère Alison T	Carnahan
Bruff Nancy	Gardner
Bruford F Jane	de Haven
Brumback Helen C	Leonard
Brumbaugh Joanne M	Archer
Brunar Erika M	Hills
Brundred Elizabeth Dilworth	Glore
Brundred Jean M	Murray
Brunell Luise	Fryer
Brunhoff Marjorie	Lutz
Brunie Ann H	Wonham
Brunker Barbara	Martin
Brunner Connie R	Strong
Brunner Joy E	Frye
Brunovskis Katrina	Coxe
Bruns Mary Ellen H	Webster
Brunson Cordelia O	Grosvenor
Brush Barbara A	Wright
Brush Joan de F	Parish
Brush Marguerite A	Webster
Bruun Margaret	Lippincott
Bruzelius Ellen M	Tifft
Bryan Beverly	Sibley
Bryan Hazel R	Tracy
Bryan Joan	Gates
Bryan Karen A	Clement
Bryan Kathryn M	Hampton
Bryan M Eugenia B	Thoma
Bryan Marie L B	Blair
Bryan Mary Anne T	Hoffmann
Bryan Mary I	Leib
Bryan Mary T	Perkins
Bryan Nancy	Taylor
Bryant Benita P	Trinkle
Bryant Leslie P	Hume
Bryant M Anne	Ross
Bryant Margaret C	Everett
Bryant Patricia L	Rode
Bryce Ariel	Appleton
Bryce Sylvie	Bryce
Brydon Margaret S	Hills
Bryer Victoria A	Abeel
Buccierelli Ann	Hopper
Buchanan Ann G	Regan
Buchanan Barbara	Eldridge
Buchanan Barbara A	Seed
Buchanan Betty R	Elmore
Buchanan Bonnie R	Matheson
Buchanan Diane D	Wilsey
Buchanan Elizabeth B	Lawrence
Buchanan Ellen G	Heberton
Buchanan Janet B	Wheelock
Buchanan Lucia B	Livingston
Buchanan Mary G	Buchanan
Buchanan Rhoda T	Wenman
Bucher Pamela Van D	Loree
Buchwalter Louise	Young
Buck Beverly R	Brunker
Buck Catherine	Fessenden
Buck Dorothy Weekes	McAuliffe
Buck Elizabeth R	King
Buck Ellen E	Browning

Buck G Marsland....................Moncrief
Buck Georgia G ....Ridder
Buck Janet R..........................Carpenter
Buck Joan H ....Menken
Buck Josephine M ....Bartlett
Buck Kristin M ....Wilson
Buck Laura K .... Marshall
Buck Mary............................Whitman
Buck Mary Richardson................Miller
Buck Sarah Y ....Wilson
Buck Wendy E.........................Brown
Buckingham Nancy C............ Snowdon
Buckley Barbara M....................Schulze
Buckley Christina W ....Hoff
Buckley Elizabeth C .... Blake
Buckley Elizabeth M ....Morris
Buckley Joan............................Cox
Buckley Lucie A L ....Filmer
Buckley Lydia A....................Whipple
Buckley Margaret P ....Turner
Buckley Mary G ....Sethness
Bucklin Susanne M....................Henze
Buckman Jane ....Aylward
Bucknall Elizabeth M .... Petty
Bucknell Sarah H........................Treco
Buckner Sophie H........................Bell
Budd Ann ....Wood
Budd Frances E.........................Eddy
Budd Martha L ....Shelnutt
Buddington Barbara....................Angle
Budge Jennifer W ....Shattuck
Budik Mary L ....Gorham
Buel Anne C ....Clelland
Buell Elizabeth J ....Labrot
Buell Karen M ....Gale
Buell Lucette..........................Dennis
Buell Nancy Dickinson.................Ellis
Buenzle Holly V ....Fergusson
Buer Age............................Diedrick
Buescher Cynthia W ....Merrill
Bugbee Dorothy........................Kelsey
Buggie Mary Blair ....Garvey
Bughman Stephenie G.............Clement
Buhse Joan D ....Bose
Buker Doris L ....Smith
Bulas Margaret E.......................Flood
Bulkley Rebecca J ....Saunders
Bulkley Wynanda ....Clifford
Bull Agnes D ....Sherman
Bull Barbara R..........................Peake
Bull Catherine H......................Walker
Bull Elizabeth ....Noyes
Bull Francine N ....Hallowell
Bull H Amy ....Brigham
Bull Patricia ....Wellington
Bull Romia ....Kimball
Bull Sara R ....Wood
Bullard Ann ....Allen
Bullard Antonia R.....................Clarke
Bullard Esther ....Griffith
Bullard Linda ....Bastedo
Bullard Mary.........................Rousseau
Bullion M Ellis ....Walton

Bullitt Eve S ....Pierce
Bullitt Evelyn B ....Hausslein
Bullitt Janet L ....Smith
Bullitt Virginia G........................Leith
Bullivant Anne MacC S ....Steere
Bullman M Jeanette ....Saylor
Bullock Cynthia R ....Woodger
Bullock Fair Alice S ....McCormick
Bullock Madeleine B ....Livingston
Bullock Margaret C .... Thayer
Bullock Nancy L..................... Henkels
Bullock Sheila W....................... Tucker
Bullock Sylvia M....................Clarkson
Bumgarner Barbara N...........Robertson
Bumstead Ida R ....Spilman
Bunce G Cristen .... Barnes
Bundgaard Pia.......................Neilson
Bundy Harriet L........................Belin
Bundy Katharine Lawrence
....Auchincloss
Bundy Patty H ....Wray
Bunker Elizabeth F ....Bunker
Bunker Ellen M ....Bunker
Bunker Emma C ....Bunker
Bunker Sheila.......................Nickerson
Bunker Suzanne ....Hopkins
Bunn Alexandra A ....Ijams
Bunn Mildred ....Hailand
Bunnell Lee A ....Pickering
Buntin Elizabeth S ....Finucane
Buntin Rachel D .... Armstrong
Bunting Sandra P.......................Arnold
Bunting Susan H.......................Larson
Bunyan Janet P ....Kramer
Burack Anna C ....Wilson
Burbank Cynthia K ....Godfrey
Burch Barbara J ....Melhado
Burch Katharine M ....Brey
Burchenal Allie ....Ault
Burchenal Joan L ....Nycum
Burchenal Mary H ....Nottebohn
Burchfield Mary P .... Pivirotto
Burck M Borden ....Stevens
Burde Tracey M........................Horner
Burden Elizabeth ....Wilson
Burden Frances D ....Burden
Burden Pamela M ....Milholland
Burden Winifred E ....Collins
Burdett Martha......................Billings
Burdick Barbara A........................Ford
Burdick Elizabeth E A.................Jones
Burdick Julia T ....Monge
Burdick Martha A ....Fisher
Burding Barbara J....................Kemp
Burford Ann S ....Fletcher
Burge Frances E ....Shepard
Burger Beverly.....................Alexandre
Burgess Carolyn...............Featheringill
Burgevin Julia D ....Egan
Burghard Dorothy K...............Munger
Burgher Joan D ....Flynn
Burgin Jane S....................Lawrence
Burgwin Mary H.........................Ulam

Burk Janet ....Ross
Burk Julie M ....Dent
Burke Anne S .... de Fontnouvelle
Burke Arleen N.....................Lovering
Burke Elizabeth A .... Drum
Burke Joan E........................Kennedy
Burke Marney A ....Cooney
Burke Mary E ....Strawbridge
Burke Natalie M ....Turullols
Burke Patricia ....Phelps
Burke Patricia A ....Savage
Burke Sheela G........................ Plater
Burke Suzanne H....................Biddle
Burke Virginia N........................White
Burkett Juliet A.......................Hooker
Burkett Katherine C..............Congdon
Burkham Barbara D..................Borders
Burkham Sarah G ....Rorem
Burks Katherine F..................Wikstrom
Burks Rose B ....Emery
Burling Lucinda ....Doubleday
Burlingham Betty....................Andrews
Burnam S Randolph ....Land
Burnap Naneen ....Bunnell
Burnet Mary Rutledge ....Cox
Burnett Bleecker S ....Isham
Burnett Calvine S ....Bowen
Burnett Dorothy H ....Huddleston
Burnett Eugenia G .... Affel
Burnett H Hildreth ....Potts
Burnett Joan ....Jenney
Burnett Sally D ....Searle
Burnham Dorothy B ....Bartlett
Burnham Louise C....................Packard
Burns Carolyn S ....Foxworth
Burns Kathleen F...................Lowther
Burns Kathleen I.............Buddenhagen
Burns M Bridget ....Bucknall
Burns Madeleine D ....Jones
Burns Mary C ....Cunningham
Buros Juliana ....Smith
Burpee Anne C A ....White
Burpee Blanche E ....Dohan
Burpee Jeannetta M ....Richards
Burr Mary Anne ....Weatherly
Burr Susan C.............................Hall
Burr Susan L ....Clifford
Burrage Anne-Douglas .... Atherton
Burrage Feroline P..............Higginson
Burrall Elizabeth L ....Medearis
Burroughes Barbara ....Lloyd
Burroughs Anita C......................Fahy
Burroughs Maria M ....Livingston
Burrowes Mariby ....Johns
Burrows Laura F......................Keller
Burrows Margaret A..........Whittemore
Burrows Nancy ....Putnam
Burry Betsy G........................Cunneen
Burstenbinder Uta M E .... Melone
Burt Susan J ....Collins
Burt Virginia A ....Gunnell
Burton Betty L ....Sheerin
Burton J Leslie...................McPhillips

Burton Jenepher L ....Parr
Burton Leila Eliott......................Luce
Burton Linda E ....Mungall
Burton Marguerite R .... Humphrey
Burton Nancy L ....Honan
Burton Nancy L ....Kinerk
Burton Naomi C .... Stone
Burwick Laura S.......................Brandt
Busbee Lessie H L..................Davison
Busch Beatrice A .... von Gontard
Busch Emilie S ....de Hellebranth
Busch Gertrude M ....Junod
Busch Paula ....Luppen
Bush Caroline G ....Emeny
Bush Caroline P ....Cole
Bush Cathie G..........................Wardell
Bush Cora D ....Michalis
Bush Flora S ....Jansing
Bush Gage ....Englund
Bush Gretchen ....Bates
Bush M Jane ....Thurber
Bush Mary C..........................Digges
Bush Michaelyn A ....Mitchell
Bush Pamela C ....Astigueta
Bush-Brown Frances .... Thompson
Bush-Brown Nancy ....Gimbel
Bush-Brown Martha ....Risom
Bushkin Christina O ....Merrill
Bushnell Mary ....Colhoun
Buss Philippa D ....Roosevelt
Bussang Marion G..................Harfield
Busse Ann W ....Sutro
Busselle Katherine Scott............... Scott
Bussema Donna J ....Storer
Busser Virginia L ....Rynning
Buswell Anne E ....Bingham
Butcher Constance A ....Heckscher
Butcher Elizabeth A ....Baird
Butcher Florence.......................Harris
Butcher Leslie W ....Littlejohn
Butcher Noël S ....Nettl
Butkowsky Joan A....................Storey
Butler Anna G..........................Vietor
Butler Anne............................Dunn
Butler Anne...........................Leonard
Butler Anne J .... Muckerman
Butler Barbara ....Lounsbery
Butler Beatrice C ....Toberman
Butler Beth H...........................May
Butler Blair ....Bellis
Butler Carole...........................Hall
Butler Cecil L ....Williams
Butler Deborah.........................Balis
Butler Diane L ....Lloyd-Butler
Butler Dorothy D ....Harder
Butler Elizabeth S ....Warner
Butler Frances M ....Devlin
Butler Garnett ....Stackelberg
Butler Hannah D........................Steel
Butler Harriet I ....Stevenson
Butler Jane U ....Robinette
Butler Jean L...........................Dean
Butler Joan C ....Weary

Butler Jorie F ....Kent
Butler Julia M ....Stenson
Butler Kate R ....Wallis
Butler Kathleen A ....Phelan
Butler Marcella ....O'Malley
Butler Margaret S ....Gardner
Butler Marian...............................Hooker
Butler Marnette ....Stone
Butler Martha M ....Von Guggenberg
Butler Mary E S ....Gordon
Butler Mary Judith...................Pohlers
Butler Mary M ....Nichols
Butler Ruth T ....Harper
Butt Barbara E ....Gill
Butt Lucy J ....Butsch
Butterfield Sarah ....Willetts
Butterworth Cynthia A ....Burns
Butterworth Janet M ....Balaguer
Button Judith S ....Keyes
Buttrick Charlotte D ....Reback
Butvay Lee ....Childs
Butzer M Betty ....Brown
Buzby Camille H ....Lamont
Buzby Ellenor Colgate ....Jarrett
Byam Audrey.............................Pierce
Byard Margaret.......................Stearns
Bye Deborah E ....Kean
Bye Sara A ....Clyde
Byecroft Pamela H .... Wetherill
Byerly Carolyn J ....Birge
Byerly Roxana ....Brakeley
Byers Alison G ....Norton
Byers Candace F ....Timpson
Byers Marie M ....Reed
Byers Mary ....Truslow
Byers Virginia D..................Churchill
Byford Patricia.........................Goodale
Byrd Diana L ....Stevens
Byrd E Bolling.........................Clarke
Byrd Evelyn H....................Blackmon
Byrne Elizabeth A ....Byrne
Byrne Phyllis M..............................Cox
Byrnes Dorothy D....................Bowles
Byron Emily D ....Sturtevant
Cabané Marta...........................Navarro
Cabeen M Lea..........................Cabeen
Cabell Barbara ....Wilcox
Cabell Catharine DeW............Bennett
Cabell Margaret ....Gunter
Cable Susan ....Herter
Cabot Elizabeth M......................Minot
Cabot Elizabeth T ..... von Wentzel
Cabot Judith ....Marriner
Cabot Linda ....Clapp
Cabot Lucy C ....Smethurst
Cabot Marianne ....Welch
Cabot Melanie H........................de Jong
Cadilhac Eliane ....O'Murray
Cadoret Julie A.....................McMillen
Cadwalader Amanda C ....Burton
Cadwalader Caroline C............Leland
Cadwalader Emma L.................Bunker
Cadwalader M Nicoll ....Brinley

Cadwalader Mae G ....Hollenback
Cadwalader Sandra L ....Schroeder
Cadwalader Sophia F.................Hayes
Cady Alison R ....Underwood
Cady Ann R ....Scott
Cady Clarissa ....Leslie
Caffery Hannah M S ....Cox
Cahill Joan ....Mittendorf
Cahill Louise M........................Carter
Cahoon Margery D ....Parker
Cailliau-de Gaulle Sabine...........Haythe
Cain Candace ....Reese
Cain Marcia A ....Crone
Caldwell Barbara C ....Korosi
Caldwell D Joyce.......................White
Caldwell Julia W ....Morris
Caldwell Lucile ....Sims
Caldwell Lucy M
van Limburg Stirum
Caldwell Marjorie H.............Anderson
Caldwell Mary A ....McLanahan
Caldwell Peggy B ....McComas
Caldwell Sara A ....Junkin
Cale Rachel A............................Claflin
Calella Maryanne ....Sullivan
Calkins Anne S ....Grady
Calkins Kathleen B ....Ware
Calkins Patricia C ....Schoellkopf
Callaghan M Kathryn ....Miller
Callahan Anne M ....Keech
Callahan Katherine N ....Forrestal
Callan Virginia J ....Baxter
Callander Sara K ....Stephens
Callard Elizabeth H ....Olson
Callaway Beth V ....Alexander
Callaway Dorothy ....Belknap
Callaway Mary I ....Gores
Callen Lindsey M ....Strong
Callender M Virginia.................Hiland
Callery Roberdeau ....Du Bois
Callies Jennifer A ....Ferrarini
Calligar Catherine D................Marron
Callister Barbara .... Hamachek
Calmer Alden H ....Read
Calvé Catherine ....Pierce
Calvert Elizabeth B S ....Bodman
Calvert Mary M ....Conger
Cálves Jean C ....Hemphill
Calvin C Elizabeth....................Bonner
Calvocoressi J Zelie.................Tourais
Cameron Flora ....Crichton
Cameron Jane A ....Manoogian
Cameron Jean.........................Phleger
Camm Arlene H ....Melen
Cammann Elizabeth S ....Holcombe
Cammann Jean T ....Dana
Cammann Katharine S...............Lipson
Camp E Rosemary ....Lizars
Camp Elizabeth McK.................Driscoll
Camp Madeleine L'Engle.........Franklin
Camp Mary E ....Boulware
Campbell Alison ....de Frise
Campbell Anne J ....Clay

Campbell Annette ....Lauck
Campbell Audrey L .... Bird
Campbell Audry N ....Train
Campbell Camille R ....von Arnim
Campbell Charmian ....Trundle
Campbell Dorothy M..................Keefer
Campbell Elizabeth S ....Ashby
Campbell Emily N......................Wood
Campbell Eunice G....................Campbell
Campbell Frances .... Fennebresque
Campbell Frances ....Tutt
Campbell Jennette H.................Herbert
Campbell Joanna L....Dellenbaugh
Campbell Julie de F.................Tatham
Campbell Juliet ....Folger
Campbell Katherine C ....Campbell
Campbell Lucinda J ....Crocker
Campbell M Camilla B ....Platt
Campbell Margaret P...............Aertsen
Campbell Margot B ....Bogert
Campbell Marjorie K................Campbell
Campbell Mary L ....Henderson
Campbell Mary M ....Humphreys
Campbell Mary M ....Minnis
Campbell Mary Schuyler.........Campbell
Campbell Nancy D ....Shober
Campbell Natalie L.................Walden
Campbell Sharon P ....Stewart
Campbell Susan ....Downe
Campbell Susan B ....Meyer
Campbell Susan M ....Lloyd
Campbell Virginia H ....Fox
Campbell Virginia L ....Clinch
Camper Louise P ....Booth
Campiglia Jane H ....Ames
Campodonico Lisa M ....James
Campos Elba V ....Regan
Canby Elizabeth F ....Semple
Canby Leila ....Frazier
Canby Sarah A F ....Stewart
Candlin Rosalind .... Benedict
Caner Annabel............................Weeks
Caner H Wayne ....Wells
Caner Joan ....Goodfellow
Caner Mary A ....Mehlman
Caner Sarah Ann......................Schofield
Canfield Frances M..................Bonsal
Canfield Margaret L ....Young
Canham Eleanor S ....Shanley
Cann Stefanie C ....Marsh
Cannell Cynthia ....Gross
Cannon Cynthia ....Cogswell
Cannon Cynthia L...................Naughton
Cannon Eleanor F ....Pfingst
Cannon Marie ....Notebaert
Cannon Phyllis ....Wattis
Canrobert Élene ....de Saint Phalle
Cantrell Maryanne ....Colas
Cantwell Ann L...........................Penrose
Cantwell Carolyn.......................Lewis
Cantwell June...........................Hodges
Cantwell Louise ....Connell
Cao Jie ....McKinney

Capen Audrey ....Plumer
Capen La May H ....Thompson
Capen Marjorie ....Sheldon
Cappuyns Martine F................Smith
Caracciolo di Brienza Anna Marie
Palmer
Card Helen L ....Hay
Card Jean ....Brown
Card Margaret B ....Suydam
Carden Constance P..................Carden
Cardoff Corinne C ....Dailey
Carega M Cristina.......................King
Carell Julia A ....Stadler
Carey Audrey T ....Koehler
Carey Elizabeth P ....Boden
Carey Emily ....Cronin
Carey Frances W .... MacMaster
Carey Lorna U .... Mack
Carey M Millicent ....McIntosh
Carey Margaret E ....DeMichelis
Carhart Marion.......................Marsh
Carico Betty L ....Ludington
Carleton Elizabeth H ....Righter
Carleton Ellen L ....Weld
Carleton Mary C ....Lejeune
Carlile E Anita ....Hackett
Carlisle Katherine ....Ourusoff
Carlisle Mary D ....Hamilton
Carll Mary S ....Kopper
Carlson Donna R ....Pflieger
Carlson Ellen L ....Snodgrass
Carlson Eva L ....Willim
Carlson Jocelyn..........................Baltzell
Carlson Nancy B ....du Pont
Carlson Norma A ....Wilhelm
Carlson Patricia A ....Mapes
Carlton Mary G.........................Swope
Carlton Rhona N...........Carlton-Foss
Carlyon-Evans Susan ....Cook
Carmack Judith A ....York
Carmichael Marion E .... Scott
Carmichael Martha ....Oliphant
Carmichael Mary E................Rohrbach
Carmody Elizabeth D .... Berens
Carnahan Alison A .... Michael
Carnahan Sandra K ....von Stade
Carnathan Melinda...................Bowron
Carnes Susan B ....Reeder
Carnese Margaret M .... Stuurman
Carnett Alice G ....Hall
Carnett Susan H ....Carnett
Carnevali Joan A M ....Wallick
Carnevali Rose E ....Gunson
Carney Carol J ....Murphy
Carney Lisa ....Stebbins
Caroé Dorothy M......................Wooten
Caroe Mimi R ....Inmam
Carothers Sara T ....Hatab
Carpenter Ann.....................Chamberlin
Carpenter Anne S .... Dillon
Carpenter Elaine C ....Doddridge
Carpenter Eleanor T ....Peters
Carpenter Jane ....Taylor

Carpenter Jane D ....Bradley
Carpenter Jean .... Miles
Carpenter Jean E......................Chronis
Carpenter Karen L .... Althaus
Carpenter Katherine E .... McCallum
Carpenter Louise......................Russell
Carpenter Manette L.................Goodman
Carpenter Margaret R ....Staples
Carpenter Perry Newbold ...... Wheelock
Carpenter Sallie B.....................Brooke
Carpenter Sophie C....................Speidel
Carr Amy B .... Klinefelter
Carr Anne Fairfax...................Bingham
Carr Anne P .... Bethea
Carr Barbara F ....Fritz
Carr Beth..................................Walker
Carr Gretchen N ....Grice
Carr J Josephine...................Brodhead
Carr Janet C .... Bayley
Carr K Searcy ....Schwarz
Carr Leslie W .... Cox
Carr Louise L........................... Paul
Carr Margaret N ....Daniel
Carr P Joan .... Kirk
Carr Patricia B ....Morris
Carr Susan O...........................Chalfant
Carras Eugenie M ....Radziwill
Carrick Mary C......................Mitchell
Carrier Carolyn L .... von Stade
Carrier Chelsey A ....Remington
Carrigan Anne F ....Dearden
Carrillo Elena A.....................Patterson
Carrillo de Albornoz Dolores
                                                Marshall
Carrington Delia D .... Blake
Carrington Elizabeth ....Bierman
Carrington Judith ....Green
Carrizo Escudero Enelia del C
                                                Bidwill
Carroll Anita M .... Tolan
Carroll Anne B L ....Bruch
Carroll Carter ....Ziegler
Carroll Cleome.....................Wadsworth
Carroll Elizabeth H....................Carroll
Carroll Ellen M.......................Walton
Carroll Gaye.............................Voges
Carroll Helen M...................... Wright
Carroll Joan Estelle....................Evans
Carroll Judith I.......................Patterson
Carroll L Norton .... McDonough
Carroll Margaret D .... Tattersall
Carroll Mary E......................Grambs
Carroll Nancy G ....Trimble
Carroll Nancy M......................Donan
Carrott Jane ....Boardman
Carruthers Elizabeth P .... Larson
Carruthers Reba R ....Lawrence
Carry June..............................Seaman
Carse Anne W...........................Paul
Carse Shirley D......................Ollivier
Carskadon Kathleen G...............Graves
Carson Barbara A E...................Snyder
Carson Deborah ....Davis

Carson Dorothy I ....Rhett
Carson Joan...............................Havens
Carson Lea................................Sherk
Carson Sarah W..........................Robb
Carstensen Judson S ....Green
Cart Barbara J ....Macauley
Cart Hermine L.........................Waring
Carter Amy L...........................Carter
Carter Anna S .... Snyder
Carter Barbara G...................Clements
Carter Candace.........................Crosby
Carter Cherry J ....Bianchi
Carter Cintra H ....Sander
Carter Constance T ....Lawson
Carter Cynthia D.....................Roenisch
Carter Dona M.............................Irwin
Carter Enriqueta P ....Bond
Carter Frances ....Sturtevant
Carter Grace S ....van Vliet
Carter Guanda M ....Reynolds
Carter Jane Levis.......................Carter
Carter Joy..................................Luke
Carter Judy............................Cormier
Carter Julia D............................Hoar
Carter Louisa B.....................Cunningham
Carter M Ann...............................Lee
Carter Margaret L ....Heckman
Carter Mary...............................Jones
Carter Mary...............................Walker
Carter Mary F ....Smith
Carter Mary Jane ....Fenner
Carter Orabelle S ....Volkmann
Carter Ruth...........................Stevenson
Carter Sarah A ....Grey
Carter Susan..............................Harris
Cartmell M Paige ....Alford
Carton Catharine ....Smith
Carton Frances ....Pauley
Carton Katherine L ....Hammer
Carton Margaret K...................Stanley
Cartwright Mariella R....................Coe
Cartwright Stella R ....Pettus
Carty Barbara C ....Bodine
Carusi Lalitte ....Scott
Carusi Rosemary R ....Weatherley
Caruthers Alice E ....Middlebrook
Carver Eugenia C
                                Espinosa de los Monteros
Carver Pauline E...................Duxbury
Carver Susan T ....Buchanan
Carver Victoria L......................Newton
Cary Cynthia.............................Russell
Cary Elizabeth B.....................Harrison
Cary Linn F C ....Mehta
Cary Mary C...............................Rea
Casadesus Therese G ....Rawson
Case Ann................................ Hunter
Case Constance H B ....Hallowell
Case Elinor N ....Nadherny
Case Elizabeth ....Kenady
Case Genet T .... May
Case Jerri L...............................Jensen
Case Penelope ....Davis

Case Penelope J ....Henneman
Casey Anne H.................van den Bergh
Casey Bettie J ....Heppe
Casey Caroline Y ....McGehee
Casey E Catherine ....Nottingham
Casey Elizabeth W ....Cullen
Casey Jane D ....Hughes
Casey Joan..............................Leisure
Casey Katherine A ....Richards
Casey Mary M ....Harp
Casey Rosemary C ....Carter
Cashman Elizabeth ....Stephenson
Caskey Frances G ....Calkins
Casler Charlotte R ....Carroll
Cason M Elita......................Wadmond
Cass Cynthia W...................Skowronek
Cassard Karen D........................Dreher
Cassatt Minnie Fell...............Hickman
Cassella Virginia M...................Metcalf
Casserly Mariana ....Smith
Cassidy Beverley A ....Brooke
Cassidy C Stirling.......................Smith
Cassidy Kathleen ....Heersema
Cassinari Anne Marie L ....Davis
Cassinerio Edna ....Ott
Castadot Muriel A ....Palmer
Castle Ann O B ....Boswell
Castle Leslie L.........................de Noüe
Castle Mary K.......................Steinway
Castles Patricia J....................Acheson
Castor Rose............................Baird
Casuso-Dons Annette M...........Baddour
Caswell Virginia L ....Pingree
Catchings E Ann.....................Ventress
Catelani M Franca ....Warden
Cater Kristin.............................Biddle
Cates Barbara...........................Bogdan
Cates Jessica D ....Zirinis
Cathcart Martha P......................Lavine
Cathcart-Jones Imogen C .... Thayer
Catherwood V Tucker ....Gresh
Catlin Elisabeth....................Fergusson
Catlin Frances ....Tilt
Catlin Leigh ....French
Catling Sheila O S ....Conroy
Catron H Elizabeth ....Meyer
Catron Marjorie F.................Sherwood
Cattell Alice M ....Caperton
Cattell Jeanne E ....Rhinelander
Catterton Ann C.........................Brown
Cauffman Ann P ....Snyder
Cauffman Barbara C.................Hartman
Cauffman Mary H...................Hastings
Cauffman Patricia E ....Brush
Cauffman Susan V................Butterworth
Caughey Beatrice.........................Hale
Caulkins Bliss ....Clark
Caulton Nancy L ....Wilson
Causey Nancy Scott....................Dawson
Cavanagh Cora........................Cushny
Cavanagh Elise F......................Bradley
Cavanagh Mae A ....Slagsvol
Cavanagh Nanette C .... Herrick

Cavanaugh Louise ....Griffith
Cavanaugh Margaret A...............Baugh
Cavanaugh Therese F ....Willcox
Cave F Virginia ....Pettus
Cave Marjorie ....Dodge
Cave Nancy................................Howard
Cave Nina W ....Devine
Cawley Margaret L ....Dewar
Cawley Olive F..........................Watson
Cay Elizabeth M ....Hines
Cecil Amanda A ....Schuster
Cecil Caroline ....Adams
Cecil Dianne E............................Cash
Cecil Mary R ....Cutler
Cecil Patricia C...........................Hass
Cecil Roberta A .... English
Cecil Sarah C ....Williams
Cella Alma.................................Yoder
Center Marie A ....Mecaskey
Ceresole Patricia L ....Dunnell
Chabrier Yvonne....................Chabrier
Chace Cynthia F ....Gray
Chace Diana L ....Hoyt
Chace Eliot................................Nolen
Chace Elizabeth ....Emmet
Chace Jane C ....Carroll
Chace Kathleen F ....Larzelere
Chadbourne Leila...........................Pile
Chadbourne Mary J ....Scott
Chadeayne Marilee de B ....Martin
Chadwick Barbara ....McPherson
Chadwick Katherine B ....Edlin
Chadwick Maryan F ....Floyd
Challinor Mary............................Ewing
Chalmers Jacqueline A ....Loomis
Chamberlain Brooke H..................Cook
Chamberlain Denise E...........Buchanan
Chamberlain Elizabeth D ....Leonard
Chamberlain Lois A ....Thomas
Chamberlain Lucia...................Pomeroy
Chamberlain Peggy B ....McComas
Chamberlain Wendy ....Navarro
Chamberland Eileen W..................Gill
Chamberlin Judith M..................Stroud
Chamberlin Kate de F ....Johnson
Chamberlin Patricia A ....Saunders
Chamberlin Talbot.......................Harris
Chambers Anne de la M...........Crudge
Chambers Catherine S ....Boericke
Chambers Constance ....Clement
Chambers Grace S ....Busk
Chambers Katherine S ....Faunce
Chambers Laurette W....................Duke
Chambers Martha B ....Rice
Chambers Mary L.......................Wiese
Chambers Noel L ....Brinton
Chambers Penelope ....Percy
Champe Jane..............................Payne
Champe Nancy..........................Peters
Champin Evelyne.....................Thomas
Champion de Crespigny Nancy
                                                Movius
Champlin Brenda K .... Sizemore

Champlin Jo......................Casey	Chapuis Evelyn......................Marshall	Chieppo Julia L................McConnell	Church Helen D......................Minton
Chance Florence M......................Neff	Chaqueneau Adelaide R.......Donaldson	Chilcoat Mary M......................Turner	Church Joan L......................Roberts
Chance Helen S......................Morgan	Charbonneau Suzanne................Mack	Child Linda H......................Clark	Church Josephine E......................Ames
Chance Suzanne......................Schenkel	Charles Carolyn......................Morss	Child Marion......................Sanger	Church Mary Elting................Williams
Chandlee Josephine P..................Fitts	Charles Jean......................Gansa	Childers Diana......................Stewart	Church Patricia S......................Ernst
Chandlee Mae K......................Foss	Charleston Alice E................Anderson	Childress Charlot R................Foster	Churchill Anne M......................Jones
Chandler Abigail B..................Norling	Charlton Mary J......................Alcott	Childs Barbara B......................Off	Churchman A Beatrice............du Pont
Chandler Amy......................Krulak	Charzuk Janet L......................Gilmor	Childs Barbara R......................Lawrence	Churchman Anne W......................Johns
Chandler Caroline......................Murray	Chase Abigail B......................Miller	Childs Catherine......................Bentley	Churchman Cynthia G............Marshall
Chandler Dian C......................Schock	Chase Alison R......................Moore	Childs Christine B......................Palmer	Churchman Eleanor N......................Smyth
Chandler Dorothy......................Reigart	Chase Anne H......................Miller	Childs Eleanor Stuart................Sackett	Churchman Emily W......................Starr
Chandler Fanny Bemis..........Raymond	Chase C Arria D......................Bilodeau	Childs Elizabeth B................Johnson	Churchman Penelope L....Bartholomew
Chandler Gail......................Gaston	Chase Elisabeth................Geissbühler	Childs Ellen W......................Lovejoy	Chute Christina......................Thys
Chandler Harriet A......................Hill	Chase Kristin A......................Taylor	Childs Julia A......................Augur	Chute Judith C......................Chute
Chandler Jane......................Saltonstall	Chase Lucy C......................Goodhue	Childs June P......................Richardson	Chute Ruth W......................Knapp
Chandler Laura G..................Marshall	Chase Margaret D......................Hager	Childs Laura M......................Saverin	Cigole Francine S......................Hall
Chandler Margaret S................Thomas	Chase Rebecca E......................Hughes	Childs Lisa H......................Laskow	Cimino Margaret M......................Wilson
Chandler Marion Lee................Zoch	Chase Sally L......................Chase	Chiles Virginia......................Bruch	Cist Margaret C......................Ughetta
Chang Katherine Y................Schiffeler	Chase Susan A......................Culver	Chinn Ellen D......................Curtis	Citron Christine H......................Moore
Chanler Elizabeth......................Chatwin	Chasens Jill L......................Moss	Chinn Louise S......................Ducas	Ciullo Barbara A......................Fuller
Chanler F Randall......................Hunt	Chatard Josephine Lee............Whitman	Chinn Sally D......................Pew	Cizek Helen P......................Niedringhaus
Chanler Leslie M......................Brooks	Chatard Octavia W......................Dugan	Chipley Lucy A................Withington	Cizek Marjorie A......................Eddy
Chanler Rosanna......................Harris	Chatfield Helen H......................Black	Chisholm Barbara......................Cole	Clagett Juliette N......................McLennan
Chanler Shiela L......................Swett	Chatfield-Taylor Joan	Chisholm C Muriel..........Le Bourgeois	Claghorn Anne S................Longstreth
Channing Elizabeth H................Meyer	Henry de Tessan	Chisholm Cynthia W.......Saint-Amand	Claghorn Elizabeth L................McIlvain
Channing Katherine B..........Raymond	Chatham Jeanne W......................Bemis	Chisholm Jean G......................Lindsey	Clancy Correll......................Galatti
Chantler Barbara A.........Shellenberger	Chave Victoria A......................Clement	Chisholm Katharine S................Almy	Clanton Helen L......................Morrin
Chapin Alma F......................Owen	Cheatham H Virginia............Van Ness	Chisholm Maude B......................Grenfell	Clapp Anne J......................Tomlinson
Chapin Betty......................Husting	Cheek Amelia......................Gordon	Chisolm Frances B......................Land	Clapp Barbara......................Miller
Chapin Caroline......................Clephane	Cheek Evelyn V......................Stevenson	Chisolm Page A......................Hughes	Clare Christina P......................Evans
Chapin Elise M......................Arnone	Cheek Huldah W......................Sharp	Choate Anne H......................Patterson	Clare Marcia H......................Lucas
Chapin Elizabeth M................Grummon	Cheek Katharine DeW................Mast	Choate Cynthia P......................Bjorlie	Clark A Valer......................Austin
Chapin Helen......................Metz	Cheek Sally......................Mee	Choate Elizabeth R......................Morrill	Clark Alicia H......................Van Arsdall
Chapin Joan K......................Hutton	Cheever Jane H......................Lyman	Choate Priscilla......................Hallowell	Clark Alix......................Diana
Chapin Marian......................Higbie	Cheney Constance L......................Larsen	Choate Sylvia......................Whitman	Clark Anne B......................Martindell
Chapin Michelle F......................Hunter	Cheney Deidre A......................McGurk	Cholmeley-Jones Grace G.........Gilbert	Clark Anne G......................Brooks
Chapin Sally M......................Levin	Cheney Elizabeth S................Buckley	Chopping Sarah A.............Thompson	Clark Anne G......................Washburn
Chapin Samantha G..................Scully	Cheney Jane......................Woods	Choremi Jane H......................Roll	Clark Anne P......................Haffner
Chapin Susan R......................Edgerly	Cheney Maribel......................Humpstone	Chou Yen-ling......von Meister	Clark Barbara A......................Bering
Chapin Vera K......................de Rham	Cheney Marjory B......................Shaw	Chouteau Jeanne C......................Murphy	Clark Bethine......................Church
Chapleau Elaine K D......................Lee	Cheney Rosalie A......................Fiske	Chow Elizabeth Pingchang	Clark Betty S......................Rafferty
Chaplin Alice T................Langenberg	Cheney Ruth......................Wyman	Nicodemus	Clark Bonnie-Jean................Fetridge
Chapman Aldys B......................Davis	Chenoweth Margaret I............Oehmig	Christ Geraldine P......................Cooper	Clark C Jay......................Cooper
Chapman Alison C......................Moore	Cherbonnier Laurie G................Nielsen	Christal Mary Lee B..............Anderson	Clark Cornelia T......................Paine
Chapman Carolyn S......................Wells	Cheremeteff Catherine............Davison	Christensen Erika......................Scully	Clark Cornelia Van R..............Roberts
Chapman Carrie Christine..........Teller	Cherrington Joanne H............Buchanan	Christensen Lucy Ann................Davis	Clark Deborah H......................Robbins
Chapman Diana F......................Kamilli	Chesbro G Alanna................Rathbone	Christian Marjorie D................Schley	Clark Diane C......................Chapman
Chapman Eleanor S................Beidler	Cheston Caroline M................Shipley	Christiansen Evelyn B................Odell	Clark Dorothy......................Ramer
Chapman Henrietta P................Judson	Cheston Charlotte M................Betancourt	Christiansen Maxine D................Finch	Clark Dorothy E......................Blackmun
Chapman Jacqueline A..........Guernsey	Cheston Cornelia................Worsley	Christie Rosalie A......................Ramsey	Clark Edith E......................Bouscaren
Chapman Jane H......................Huber	Cheston Elizabeth M................Forster	Christie-Miller Maralyn.........Rittenour	Clark Edith L......................Klick
Chapman Josephine C..........Borthwick	Cheston Frances D......................Train	Christlieb Yvonne......................McAdoo	Clark Eleanor......................Purnell
Chapman Judith J................Steinmetz	Cheston Mary L......................McAdoo	Christman Marion A................Beyea	Clark Eugenia......................Boies
Chapman Mary C......................Watts	Cheston Sydney......................Winthrop	Christopher Lori A......................Post	Clark Evelyn B......................Clarkson
Chapman Nancy D..............Sherwood	Chevreux Claude......................Heckscher	Christy Anne M......................Franchot	Clark Evelyn Q......................Gregory
Chapman Nancy V......................Ewell	Chew Elizabeth M................Willard	Christy Barbara L................Kimberly	Clark Frances D......................Braxton
Chapman Rebecca P......................Booth	Chew Elizabeth O......................Bennett	Christy Vieva F......................Grenier	Clark Frances E......................Paul
Chapman Sally L......................Goodyear	Chiampi Barbara C................Twining	Chrones Cassandra......................Moore	Clark Georgia A......................Flood
Chapman Sara M......................Ledes	Chichester Suzanne......................Fischer	Chu Julie F......................Low	Clark Geraldine......................Sylvester
Chapman Theodosia......................Bowie	Chick Chaunci G......................Aeed	Chubb Sarah C......................Sauvayre	Clark Helen R......................Clark
Chapman Virginia......................Hopkins	Chick Elizabeth......................Parker	Church Caroline W......................Church	Clark Hope M......................Jackson
Chappell Judith......................Mallery	Chick Jeanne H......................Rose	Church Chara D......................Phillips	Clark Huguette M......................Clark
Chappell Mary......................Wheat	Chidsey Louise L......................Torrey	Church Charlotte D......................Collins	Clark Jane M......................Warren

Clark Janice E......................Roosevelt
Clark Jean E...........................Marlow
Clark Jean Q ....Clark
Clark Joan A.....................Kegelman
Clark Jody L.................................Jones
Clark Judith C.............................Kyser
Clark Julia I.................................Boak
Clark K Leslie.......................Stedman
Clark Katharine H..............Pillsbury
Clark Katharine R............De Long
Clark Linda G.........................Gooder
Clark Lisa W.......................... Godfrey
Clark Lois ....Wolfenden
Clark Louisa P..............................Old
Clark Louise F..........................Smith
Clark Majella K .... Fenton
Clark Margaret.................MacDonald
Clark Margaret C .... Speese
Clark Mariette R ....Orth
Clark Mary Alice ....Peddle
Clark Mary H......................... Talbot
Clark Mary N...................Swinerton
Clark Mary T.....................Rockefeller
Clark Nancy ....Smith
Clark Nancy J ....Adler
Clark Nancy R ....Russell
Clark Noël C..............................Miller
Clark Pamela D......................Solley
Clark Robin J..............................Clark
Clark Sarah A ....Hawley
Clark Stephanie M....................Abel
Clark Susan ....Ward
Clark Susan C............................Cann
Clark Susan R ....Ogden
Clark Trinkett...........................Clark
Clark Virginia ....Darneille
Clark Virginia L ....Clarkson
Clarke Ann........................... Morgan
Clarke Ann A ....Spivy
Clarke Anna P...................... Rogers
Clarke Anne H ....Logan
Clarke Eleanor S........................Byrd
Clarke Elizabeth.......................Ames
Clarke Elizabeth M...............Newell
Clarke Jane G ....Fowkes
Clarke Janet B..............................Irwin
Clarke Jean M.....................Caldwell
Clarke Julia S..............................White
Clarke Margaret C ....Howland
Clarke Martha O ....Miller
Clarke Mary D.............................Miles
Clarke Mary-Elizabeth L.............Beane
Clarke Patricia A ....Flynn
Clarke Sally D.............................Hall
Clarke Sandra L.......................Walter
Clarkson Alison H ....Goodenough
Clarkson Frances L...............Breckner
Clarkson Ruth T ....Costello
Clary Ann M...............................Judy
Clary Doris A ....Lesesne
Claska Susan L.......................Burnett
Class Katherine J ....Pancoast
Classen Dorothy.....................Cumming

Clattenburg Margaret F ....Sabo
Clawson Cleo...........................Lambert
Clay Dorothy .... Watson
Clay Elizabeth R.......................Lange
Clay Joy ....Plauché
Clay Mary C .... Disston
Clay Mary F..............................Muller
Clay Patricia..................... Hancock
Clay Susan L............................Smith
Clayburgh Alma.........................Grew
Claypoole Suzanne ....Thomas
Clayton Diana J ....Peters
Clayton Jane E...........................Boyd
Clayton Julia S.........................Baker
Clayton Lella H ....Bromberg
Clayton Sarah H ....Lawson
Clayton Thomasene McC ....Collins
Claytor Mary I ....Smith
Cleave Mary...............................Barker
Cleaves Leila D ....Safford
Clegg Ann S ....Holloway
Clegg Cynthia C ....Gerdsen
Clegg Donna J .... Moffly
Clegg Helen G ....Moss
Clegg Phyllis J .... Cadwalader
Clemens Eleanor............................Dix
Clemens Karen..........................Kernan
Clement Alice K ....Carrington
Clement Beatrice ....Bardin
Clement Frances ....Earle
Clement Ida L ....Steen
Clement Joan H .... Stevenson
Clement L Catherine A .... Hull
Clement Leslie L ....Finger
Clement Margaret F.................Conrad
Clement Pamela A ....Butt
Clements Laura C ....Robinson
Clemm Charlotte H von ....Iselin
Cleveland Charlotte G ....Look
Cleveland Cynthia ....Doughty
Cleveland Sylvia B ....Tobin
Cleveland Victoria T ....Lindgren
Cleveland Victoria T ....Willett
Cliffe Virginia H...........................Ely
Clifford Ann M...................Newhall
Clifford Carol A ....Mitchell
Clifford Florence E...............Boothby
Clifford Margery M ....Henneman
Clifford Marjorie D ....Denton
Clifford Mary R ....Tittmann
Clifton Caroline .... Drewes
Clifton Margaret V ....Boyd
Cline Charlene .... Marsh
Cline H Catharine .... Hamilton
Cline Laura J...........................Sadtler
Cline Marguerite P B..................Almy
Clingman Penelope A...........Auchincloss
Clinton Audrey G ....Oswald
Clinton Marcia ....Walters
Clinton Margaret K......................Burt
Clinton Margaret W.............Richardson
Close Luette R ....Bourne
Closson Isabel D.....................Shattuck

Clothier Ann H .... Clothier
Clothier Anne H ....Haydon
Clothier Carolyn ....Killefer
Clothier Catharine B.............. Rumsey
Clothier Christina W...................Moses
Clothier Dorothy ....Kellett
Clothier Emily E................Strawbridge
Clothier Helen ....Ballard
Clothier Lydia M ....Seeley
Clothier Mary C........................Brown
Clothier Melinda A...................Biddle
Clothier Sandra L .... Singer
Cloud Jane S ....Kennedy
Clough Beatrice F......................Wright
Clouser Beth G ....Hare
Clow Elise H.......................Williamson
Clow Emily D.............................Condo
Clow Frances R ....Bowers
Clow Nancy N ....Odén
Clucas Frances P......................Paddock
Cluett Constance T ....Ward
Cluett Elizabeth T...................Thors
Cluett Mary M ....Belden
Clymer Diane E............................Ziel
Clymer M Rose......................Rumford
Clymer Miriam R ....Brooke
Coady Carolyn M ....Lea
Coakley Lisa F........................Coakley
Coakley Patricia H.................Oppmann
Coale Elizabeth G M...........Treadway
Coale Ellen J ....Foley
Coates Cynthia M.......................Miller
Coates Elise .... Alsop
Coats Sandra V .... Morrel
Cobb Alison Gallatin .... Herber
Cobb Ann C.............................Thorne
Cobb Barbara A .... Boyce
Cobb Beatrice C ....Stebbins
Cobb Deborah de Land ....Sendax
Cobb Jane T .... Langhorne
Cobb Jean Gallatin ....Crocker
Cobb Lydia B ....Perkins
Cobb V Reiland ....Hendrickson
Cobbs F Jayne.............................Davis
Coble Carolyn I ....Lewis
Coburn Joan S.............................Casini
Coburn Mary C.......................Hazard
Coccitto Giovanna
                                Giacomuzzi-Moore
Cochran Agnes W..........Underwood
Cochran Annabel ....Moore
Cochran Beverly ....Fleming
Cochran Donna ....McLarty
Cochran Donna-Lindsey..........Bowman
Cochran Gwendolyn G.............Brown
Cochran Jane............................Peck
Cochran Marion R ....Gillette
Cochran Patricia G ....Lau
Cochrane Diana A ....Prince
Cochrane Elizabeth J.................Davis
Cochrane Eugénie H.................Fenton
Cochrane Joyce L.......................Lewis
Cochrane Ramelle F ....Adams

Cocke Alice ....Goodwin
Codman Hester S ....Smith
Codoner Emilie ....Stetson
Coe Cynthia W ....Devine
Coe Katharine S.........................Taylor
Coe Marguerite H .... Neilson
Coe Mariella C .... Morrin
Coe Nancy ....Wixom
Coe Nancy-Bell ....Coe
Coe Ruth H ....Fergusson
Coerper Lois P ....Randall
Coffell Elizabeth A....................Morton
Coffey Carol M..........................Swift
Coffey Cynthia K ....Patterson
Coffey H Shirley.....................Robinson
Coffin Esther..............................Perrin
Coffin Joan E ....Whiteman
Coffin Louisa R ....Witte
Coffin Nancy ....Wyeth
Coffin Ruth P ....Nash
Coffin Sarah D.....................Klebnikov
Coffman Mildred K ....Flowers
Coggeshall Patricia ....Dominick
Coghlan Jean S ....Griswold
Cogswell Ann ....Vose
Cogswell Ann E....................McMullen
Cogswell Cornelia L...................Rossi
Cogswell Cynthia.....................Johnston
Cohen Roberta A ....Holden
Coifman Eva A ....Sommaripa
Coisne Loicka ....Hodges
Coke Kathryn L ....Rienhoff
Coker Mary B ....Thomson
Colahan Elizabeth P ....Phillips
Colburn Clarissa H ....Hunnewell
Colby Jane A .... Emerson
Colby Mary E ....Reakirt
Cole Adelaide ....Griswold
Cole Alice L S ....Jones
Cole Camilla R ....Smidt
Cole Carla M ....Stebbins
Cole Carol.................................. Herrera
Cole Carol N...............................Pelzer
Cole Caroline W ....Seymour
Cole Eleanor ....Coolidge
Cole Emilie M ....Stoddart
Cole Iris ....Clark
Cole Janette W ....Stetson
Cole Kathryn W ....Manace
Cole Mary ....Kinsolving
Cole Mary C ....Gryska
Cole Mary H ....Childs
Cole Patricia I .... Langenberg
Cole Sarah F...............................Hirsh
Cole Sarah P ....Tuckerman
Cole Susan S ....Gildersleeve
Colella Cathleen A ....Graham
Coleman Audrey F .... Nichols
Coleman Barbara ....Donnelley
Coleman Carolyn P..................Callen
Coleman Catharine B ....Alexander
Coleman Dorothy J.................Roudebush
Coleman E Ann ....Carmack

Copeman Sarah C ....Gould
Copper Marguerite.....................Wright
Coppersmith Ruth E ....Anderson
Coquillette Anna R ....Caspersen
Corballis Camilla ....McFadden
Corbet Gwynn......................Hanchett
Corbet Sharon J ....Dunham
Corbett Gretchen.................Trommald
Corbett Virginia N ....Marshall
Corbin Clementine S ....Day
Corbin Dolly O'Neile .... Stone
Corbin Elizabeth E ....Kingsland
Corbin Elizabeth M ....Rexford
Corbin Margaret T ....McNally
Corbin Mary W.......................Stewart
Corby Kathleen E ....Clark
Corcoran Lucinda E ....Childs
Cordts Doris ....Peake
Corell Barbara J ....Havighurst
Corey Patricia ....Montgomery
Corigliano Letizia A L ....Bogart
Corkran Anne S ....Nimick
Corlette Sally L.....................Thébaud
Corley Carol............................Nelson
Cornelius Molly O ....Turman
Cornell Elizabeth W ....Cochran
Cornell Katharine E ....Gorka
Cornell M Lynn ....Bodenstab
Corning Margaret...................Boldrick
Coronel Juliette ....Cobian
Corpening Virginia C ....Ijams
Correale Susan M ....Aberg
Correll Gay ....Brown
Corrigan Joan M ....Merryman
Corris Jean ....Phyfe
Corroon Helen Van V ....Robinson
Corscaden Helen Wolcott.........Higgins
Corscaden Julia........................Beaty
Corscaden Patricia ....ReQua
Corsini Immacolata B ....Bland
Corsini Ruth A ....Sharon
Corsini di Laiatico Allegra......Poccianti
Cort Suzanne J ....Wood
Cortellini Margaret J.................Bartlett
Cortesi Katharine P ....Armstrong
Cory Caroline T ....Affoumado
Cory Jenny C ....Withers
Coryllos Elizabeth ....Lardi
Cosby Carolyn Du B ....Dorsey
Cosgriff Barbara Lucia ....Overland
Cosnard des Closets Elisa J ....Colas
Cosner Claire F ....Leggett
Costa Susan J ....Smith
Costantino Helen E ....Fioratti
Coste Betsey .... Outerbridge
Coste Judith R....................Chapman
Costello Christine ....Pernoud
Coster Josephine ....McLean
Costikyan Rosemary ....Knight
Cotsworth Alice B ....Goltra
Cotter Cathleen B ....Nowland
Cotter Maureen E ....Potter
Cottereau Françoise ....Little

Cotton Cynthia S ....Orrick
Cotton Jane ....Fletcher
Cotton Nancy D ....Swindell
Cottrell A Joyce.......................Perkins
Cottrill Jean ....Farrelly
Couch Nancy S ....Stent
Coudert Marie ....Curry
Coudert Paula M ....Rand
Coues Pamela D ....Dimond
Coues Phoebe A ....Houghton
Coulborn Joan H ....Stevens
Coulson Mary A ....Phillips
Coulter Emma ....Ware
Coulter Jean M ....Crane
Coulter Wendy ....Goodrich
Coumantaros Aglaia ....Choremi
Countiss Henrietta E.................Vieta
Couper Virginia H ....Johnson
Courchene Andrea G ....Ross
Cournand Marie Eve.................Walker
Coursen Kathleen Howell

                        Buttenheim
Courtney Mary E ....Gardiner
Cousturier Michelle ....Bigelow
Covel Dennis ....Dickson
Cover Olivia von S ....Beattie
Covey Ann B ....Reese
Covington Eleanor W ....Devens
Covington Elizabeth ....Smith
Covington Lynn ....Davies
Cowan Arlis B ....Morton
Cowan Barbara A ....Hyde
Cowan Barbara W ....Peebles
Cowan Eugenie C ....Havemeyer
Cowan Jennifer A ....Schabacker
Cowan Quinette ....Jens
Coward Deborah Allen..............Damon
Coward Jenifer G.........................Sims
Cowden Christy Ann ....Brown
Cowdrey Elinor Q ....Rust
Cowgill Mildred A ....de Surian
Cowles Edith F ....Poor
Cowles Elizabeth C ....Taylor
Cowles Jane C ....Horton
Cowles Mary E ....Moore
Cowperthwaite Victoria P ....Thompson
Cox A Chandler ....Mashek
Cox Ann W ....Bartram
Cox Anne T ....Riker
Cox Audrey M ....Moncrieff
Cox Avril H ....Mills
Cox Barbara ....Diller
Cox Barbara ....Emeny
Cox Carol J ....Madeira
Cox Christina G ....Davison
Cox Evelyn Q ....York
Cox F Diane.........................Harrison
Cox Harriet ....Hansen
Cox Jane............................MacElree
Cox Jane A ....Hettrick
Cox Judith A ....Bundy
Cox June O ....Cullen
Cox Kathleen ....Thompson

Cox Marianna C ....Hirons
Cox Martha B ....Farrell
Cox Mary Cooper...............Heiserman
Cox Mary Lyman ....Cammann
Cox Nomina N.......................Horton
Cox Priscilla L ....Richardson
Cox Rachel M.........................Grove
Cox Rebecca L ....Wood
Cox Ruth E ....Crocker
Coxe Elizabeth G ....Kysely
Coxe Emily W ....Winburn
Coxe Jane G............................Fletcher
Coxe Jane R.........................Lippincott
Coxe Louisa W ....Finch
Coxe Sally P ....Taylor
Coy Sheila M ....Secor
Coyne Margaret A ....Lloyd
Coyro Gillian ....Oppedahl
Cozad Cynthia A ....Shafer
Crabbe Idoline W ....Scheerer
Crabtree Mary A ....Hare
Craemer Virginia C ....Oler
Cragg Emily M ....Stoughton
Craig Elizabeth M...................Miller
Craig Gertrude R ....Reese
Craig Jean F ....Howe
Craig Kathleen C ....Knight
Craig Sara M ....Ballantine
Craig Susan J ....Guernsey
Craighill Elizabeth W ....Wickersham
Cram M Jane....................Strekalovsky
Cramer Katharine C................De Witt
Cramp Amy J..........................Torrey
Crandall Carolyn.....................Preston
Crandall Josephine ....Throdahl
Crandell Helen J M ....Duer
Crandon Anne T ....Heiner
Crane Dorothy J.......................Lewis
Crane Elizabeth L ....Royer
Crane Helen E................van der Voort
Crane M Stuart ....Tilt
Crane Marilyn C ....Low
Crane Nancy B ....Heller
Crane Rebecca F ....Tompkins
Crane Sara S ....Foss
Cranfill Helen M ....Elliott
Cranston Eleanor ....Cameron
Cranstoun Priscilla ....Cammann
Crapo Mary Morley ....Eccles
Crary Caroline S ....Nordmann
Crary Sharon ....Griffin
Crass Barbara...............de San Damián
Crater Diane E ....Tingue
Craven Averyl Vaux ....O'Brien
Crawford Allyson B ....Louthan
Crawford B Adele..................Grimball
Crawford Barbara W ....Gardner
Crawford Dianne M ....Anderson
Crawford Elizabeth J ....Fee
Crawford Elizabeth O'N...........Powell
Crawford Janet A ....Master
Crawford Judith A ....Stanton
Crawford Lynn E....................Johnson

Crawford Marian M.................Whiting
Crawford Mary N....................Cummin
Crawford Robin W ....Youngman
Crawford Shirley ....Dorrough
Crawford Susan H ....Stevens
Crawford Virginia L.............Pierrepont
Creamer Cordelia G...............Richards
Crean Helen N ....Smith
Crecca Nancy V ....Schaefer
Creed Margaret R ....Watson
Creel Alexandra G ....Goelet
Creel Elizabeth C ....Moore
Creely Jean M ....Kipp
Creese Elizabeth K ....Davis
Creighton Elizabeth L.............Harwell
Creighton Margaret................Williams
Crellin Anne P ....Seggerman
Cremer Thelma T ....Sherrer
Cremin Genevieve A ....Hambleton
Cresap Madeleine R ....Bartow
Cresson Emily Vaux ....Satterthwaite
Cresswell Audrey S ....Kellison
Creviston C Lynn ....Shiverick
Crew Marsha E ....Price
Crew Susanna ....Zook
Crews Vicki J ....Crews
Crichton Anne B ....Clark
Crichton Kate C ....Gubelmann
Crichton Lili...........................Monell
Crimmins Jennifer M.............Crimmins
Crimmins Margaret C ....Kuhns
Crimmins Sally ....Thorne
Crimmins Sheila ....Parsons
Crisp Ann G..........................von Stade
Crisp Lucetta G..........................Knox
Crisp Wendy P.....................Henderson
Crispin Emma D ....Wolbach
Crittenden Caroline J ....Adams
Crittendon Sally C ....Baldwin
Crivelli Gioconda M K.............Crivelli
Crocker Abigail E.....................Reagan
Crocker Agnes C ....Brengle
Crocker Amy B ....van Daalen
Crocker Anne H.......................Hefter
Crocker Deborah H...................Deering
Crocker Diana H.......................Nouri
Crocker Gladys ....Dana
Crocker Lispenard S ....Conger
Crocker Marianne ....Montoro
Crockett Anne H.......................Pepper
Crockett Nancy L ....Morris
Crofford Charlotte ....Van Metre
Crofton Margaret ....Balbach
Crofton Marita ....Rappleye
Crofts Patricia ....Saunders
Crofut Elizabeth G......................Day
Crofut Irène E ....Roberts
Croker Jean E ....McMillan
Cromelin Alexandra.....................Earle
Cromer Marjorie A.....................Minot
Crompton Marie S ....Robinson
Crompton Nancy W ....Wendell
Cromwell Elizabeth M ....Speers

Cromwell Gertrude W .... Levy
Cromwell Mollie W................. Baldwin
Cromwell Patricia M ....Miller
Cromwell Rebecca H.............. Levering
Cronan Shannon E..................... Alford
Crone Cameron ....Bilger
Cronin Camilla M......................Dinan
Cronin Theodora H P .... Morse
Cronk Jean D .... Andrews
Cronkhite Cynthia Gordon ....Jones
Cronkhite Helen .... Chester
Crook Jeanne C........................Classen
Crook Margaret E ....Donnelley
Crooks Elizabeth......................Cramer
Crooks Gail A ....Currie
Cropley Louise W .... Eaton
Cropper Errol ....Lovering
Cropper Pauline ....Mallory
Crosby Arvia B ....Morris
Crosby Eleanor L............................Hall
Crosby Letitia E........................Haynes
Crosby Rosalie de F .... Gevers
Crosby Rubie S............................Bell
Crosman Elisabeth C .... Frederick
Cross Elizabeth M .... Thompson
Cross Emily .... Reigate
Cross I Balene................... McCormick
Cross Lois M ....Willis
Cross Mary N ....Spence
Cross Rosalind M .... Dujardin
Cross Sarah .... Klinefelter
Crossan Aimée H.............de Cordova
Crosset Carolyn C .... Rowland
Crossett Jean M ....Crew
Crossette Barbara..................McGaughy
Crosson Caroline .... Gilpin
Crouse H Isabel .... Litchfield
Crow Carol G ....Gray
Crow Nancy R ....Allen
Crowder Emma Atkyns ....Brown
Crowder Sally .... Doering
Crowe C Leigh ....Bolton
Crowe Kelly A..........................Horne
Crowell Catharine .... Cagle
Crowell Emma P .... Carmichael
Crowell Mary G....................... Devaney
Crowl Cathy A.......................... Kraft
Crowley Constance E ....Peabody
Crowley E Susan .... Black
Crowley Janet C ....Cowles
Crowley Jeanne........................ Prentice
Crowley Margaret E .... Chapin
Crowninshield Katharine ....Ferguson
Crowninshield Louise ....Riemer
Crowther Deborah B................. Cooke
Croy H Jean .... Wright
Crozer Betsy Carlyle ....Crozer
Crozer H Allaire ....du Pont
Crozer Sara P ....Weymouth
Crozier Nesta I...........................Parry
Cruger Mary Van R .... Pendl
Cruice Cynthia L .... Peterson
Cruice Kathryn W ....Francis

Cruice Sydney F ....Dixon
Cruickshank Blair F.......... Cruickshank
Cruickshank Dorinda J P..... Winkleman
Cruickshank Joy............................Hall
Cruikshank Janet F .... McCawley
Crump Cynthia B......................Crimmins
Crumpler Olivia Lindsay .... Nolting
Cruso M Thalassa A .... Hencken
Crutcher Katherine................Chisholm
Cruz Suarez Silvia ....Zoullas
Cryan Elizabeth .... Wheaton-Smith
Cudahy Sheila ....Pellegrini
Cudahy Tamsen T...................... Resor
Cuddihy Harriet DeH .... Butz
Cuddy Elizabeth C....................Moore
Cuendet Elizabeth ....Meigs
Cuendet Rachel L .... Drummond
Cugeber Shirley T...........................Ohl
Ćuković Lilliana .... Sinclair
Culbertson Nancy C .... Eddy
Culbertson Stephanie E .... Kerns
Culbertson Viola T ....Geer
Cullen Lindsay S .... Scott
Cullum Lee B ....Cullum
Culp Anne R R ....Farran
Culp Frances ....Wheeler
Culver Jane K ....Sargent
Culver M Dorothea.................Williams
Cumby Dana D .... Hurt
Cumings Eleanor G .... Hackett
Cumings Sarah M.................... Morse
Cummin Ellen C .... Cousins
Cummin M Starr .... Bright
Cumming Dorothy C .... Scott
Cummings Dorcas O ....Cochran
Cummings Helen .... Vanderbilt
Cummings Hollyday ....Cummings
Cummings Jane G.................... Taussig
Cummings Joyce D.................... Hobbs
Cummings Lila Douw ....Cummings
Cummings Molly ....Cook
Cummings Nancy Hoyt ....Henry
Cummings Philomena B .... Mahony
Cummings Ruth D .... Mead
Cummings Sandra........................Lee
Cummins Cornelia A .... Blake
Cuningham Anne ....Goodwin
Cunning Cynthia A ....Wilbur
Cunningham Ann P .... Winslow
Cunningham Anna G .... McClure
Cunningham Cynthia B .... Coulson
Cunningham Cythlen..............Maddock
Cunningham Diana M ....Bunting
Cunningham Edith P...............Crocker
Cunningham Elizabeth B.............. Hurd
Cunningham Gail P.................Supplee
Cunningham Helen ....Crocker
Cunningham Jane....................Legier
Cunningham Jane B............... Robinson
Cunningham Joan ....Williams
Cunningham Johanne.................Miller
Cunningham Katherine R .... Minevitz
Cunningham Kristina................. Rogers

Cunningham Madalyn ....Hindman
Cunningham Marie ....Jones
Cunningham Melissa M ....Dugan
Cunningham Pamela..............Copeland
Cunningham Priscilla..............LickDyke
Cuno Angela M ....Dusenbury
Curby Sally F........................ Johnston
Curd Joyce L............................ Curry
Cureton Margaret V .... Straehley
Curie Eve D .... Labouisse
Curran Alexandra J ....Jennison
Curran Elizabeth A .... Warren
Curran Helen............................Nield
Curran Susan G........................White
Curran Teresa M ....Clarkson
Currens Genya M ....Hopkins
Currey Stephanie C..................Ingram
Currie Anne .... Butcher
Currie Jane W .... Smith
Currier Theodosia H .... Easter
Curry Ann E .... Haux
Curry Elizabeth H .... Kingsley
Curry Jill L .... Roberts
Curry Susan H .... Cadwalader
Curry Suzanne Talcott...............Winton
Curtis Anne L ....Curtis
Curtis Caroline C ....Bramhall
Curtis Caroline C .... Rounds
Curtis Catherine C ....Allard
Curtis Clare H .... Rimmer
Curtis Ellen W ....Boiselle
Curtis Fanny R...........................Luke
Curtis Hilary W ....Hartman
Curtis Irene W .... Davis
Curtis Isabel S....................Baldridge
Curtis Kristin L......................Lothrop
Curtis Laura E.........................Curtis
Curtis Laura G ....Cutler
Curtis Lettys E ....Hallock
Curtis Mary C ....Burrus
Curtis Mary T .... Fair
Curtis Pauline................. Hollingsworth
Curtis Priscilla .... Veitch
Curtis Sarah C.........................Iselin
Curtis Sarah M.......................Hetfield
Curtis Virginia A .... Badger
Curtiss Constance ....Manuel
Curtiss Harriet S ....Coughlin
Curtis-Setchell Elizabeth A .... Paul
Cusack-Jobson Charlotte M ....Wood
Cushing Alexandra C ....Howard
Cushing Alyce C....................... Stick
Cushing Elizabeth McK .... Dilworth
Cushing Ellen...........................Welch
Cushing Florence B ....Perkins
Cushing Nancy J ....Ostheimer
Cushing Pamela ....Donner
Cushman Clare H ....Prouvost
Cushman Eleanor ....Dixon
Cushman Elizabeth S................ Putnam
Custer E Carson ....Taylor
Custis Elizabeth W .... Robbins
Cutchins Barbara W .... Reed

Cuthbert Lynn C .... Kimball
Cuthell Priscilla ....Ward
Cutler Ann P ....Townsend
Cutler Carolyn V ....Goodman
Cutler Diana V ....Rowe
Cutler Judith B ....Shinkle
Cutler Margaret A..............Humphreys
Cutler Mary W............................Buell
Cutler Naneen S......................Ijams
Cutler Susan K.........................Aldrich
Cutler Susan M ....Wenzell
Cutter Caroline.......................Stevens
Cutter Helen ....Maclennan
Cutting Grace M ....McGrath
Cutting Helen S ....Pilkington
Cutting Justine B .... Cushing
Cutting Nancy.............................Young
Cuyler Juliana S.....................McIntyre
Cuypers Engelina E .... Dickerson
Czarick Lisa A .... Sibley
Dabney Beatrice........................ Adams
D'Adamo Joan A .... Peyton
D'Adamo Mary R ....Webb
Daggett Frances .... Aldrich
Daher Rachel M....................Stephaich
Daigle Susan B .... Davis
Dailey Mildred.............................Tutt
Dain Sandia E ....Lambert
Dale Patricia A ....Toogood
Daley Alexa C .... Kroeger
Daley Cornelia ....Mettler
Daley L Lansdale ....Gardiner
Daley Louisa L ....Winthrop
Daley M Dolores .... Field
Dall Katharine G.......................Bolton
Dall Mary B ....Dunham
Dallas Constance H ....Millet
Dallas Mary W .... Hetherington
Dallett Estelina L ....Dallett
Dalley A Laura ....Tobin
Dalley Nancy A ....Lindsay
Dalley Rives G ....Hewitt
Dalton Elizabeth A ....Emes
Dalton Elizabeth D ....Chickering
Dalton Jane ....Weinberger
Dalton Susan B ....Boyden
Daly Alison .... Gerard
Daly Bevin ....Patterson
Daly Joan ....Murphy
Daly Josette de G .... Károlyi
Daly Mercedes.....................Littlejohn
Daly Pamela .... Vose
Daly Rosemarie H ....King
Dalzell Mary M .... Leonard
Dambrie Joan M .... Fleming
Dame Harriet Carrington ....Hooper
Dame Josephine P...................de Butts
Dame Lenora ....Dolan
Damgard Barbara O....................Cates
Damon Diane G.......................Morang
Damon Emily G.................Williamson
Damours Carolyn A ....Commons
Dana Anstiss ....Jones

Dana Barbara .... Greppin
Dana Elizabeth M .... Ford
Dana Marion T ....Curtis
Dana Michele J .... Thomure
Dancy Marsha W .... Ambler
Dancy Virginia F ....Webb
Dandridge Elizabeth W .... Wolf
Dane Barbara P...........................Harris
Danenhower Doris .... Voorhies
Danforth Laura T .... Barnes
Dangerfield Carol..................McGregor
Danglade June P .... Speight
Dangler Margaret..................Fernandez
Daniel Charlotte B ....Wray
Daniel Deborah L ....Long
Daniel H Hampton R ....Carey
Daniel Mary H...........................Cay
Daniel Mason .... Barrett
Daniel-Dreyfus Suzanne M
                         Fitzgerald
Daniels Amy M .... Thompson
Daniels Deborah .... Webster
Daniels Dorothy M ....Pattishall
Daniels Frances S ....Cobb
Daniels Katharine F.................... Kane
Daniels Martha L .... Willard
Daniels Nancy .... Waxter
Danielson Marion ....Campbell
Danielson Pamela S ....Sharples
Dankmeyer Anne E .... Hopkins
d'Antona Maria....................... Melano
Danzer Anna .... Tilghman
Danzig Evelyn ....Haas
Danziger Anne K ....King
Daoust Susan B...........................Miller
D'Aprix Mary E ....Weld
Darby Diane Scott .... Quillman
Darby Kortny S. .... Johnson
D'Arcy Frances..................Auchincloss
Darling Eleanore H................Everdell
Darling Jean J ....Peale
Darling Julia W .... Spahr
Darling Mary C.......................Hewes
Darling Vena H...................... Darling
Darlington Ann N.................Edwards
Darlington Caroline S...............Perkins
Darlington Cynthia S ....Beyer
Darlington Elaine .... Fowler
Darlington Jane R ....Irwin
Darlington Victoria W ....Yoder
Darmanin Katharine V ....Smith
Darnall Rebecca P ....Morris
Darneille Anne L .... Snodgrass
Darneille Eda W ....Doyle
Darneille Virginia C .... Estes
Darnell Marguerite J...............Hamrick
Darrah Jane E ....Claflin
Darrah Marion M...................Brewster
Darrell Nancy S .... Baldwin
Darrell Patricia E .... Gunther
Darrow Emily A W .... Walden
Darrow Jean J W ....Nugent
Darrow Katharine C .... Upson

Darsie Nancy A .... Putnam
Darst Anne Volger....................Perkins
Dart Susan M....................McCutcheon
Dash Kimberly A ....Test
Date Winifred H ....Hayes
Daughaday Anne C .... Adams
Daughdrill Elizabeth G.................Boyd
Daugherty Lisa....................Daugherty
Daumen Paulette......................Henry
Dauphinot Sheila R....................Cole
Davendorf Andrée E................Dreyfous
Davenny Diane D ....Darneille
Davenport Amy M.................Durrance
Davenport Ann Van V..................Dixon
Davenport Caroline H............ Johnson
Davenport Carolyn W...........Davenport
Davenport Cynthia M ....Sweeny
Davenport G Louise .... Smyth
Davenport M Ann ....Geer
Davenport M Jane....................White
Davenport Nancy Lu ....Missett
Daves Deborah L .... Richards
Davey Anne H ....Hahn
Davidson Alice H ....Outwater
Davidson Ana C .... Thompson
Davidson Anne T.......................Hardy
Davidson Elizabeth B ....Sloane
Davidson Elizabeth H.............. McCulloh
Davidson Holly O....................Teetzel
Davidson Katharine D .... Walker
Davidson Lee H........................Leach
Davidson Mildred C ....Coues
Davidson Olga M ....Nagy
Davidson Susan H ....Ravenscroft
Davidson Teresa A .... Daniels
Davies Alexandra O'N .... Dewey
Davies Annette..................Monmonier
Davies Diane..............................Page
Davies Eleanor .... Ditzen
Davies Emlen K........................Evers
Davies Faith R .... Le Sauvage
Davies Gail B ....Irwin
Davies Maryon L ....Lewis
Davies N Allison .... Talbot
Davies Robin ....Hubbard
Dávila Isabel ....Hammond
Davin Patricia R .... Robinson
Davin Sharon L .... Skinner
Davis A Meredith ....Lamberton
Davis A Pickett.....................Randolph
Davis Alexandra M...................Cummin
Davis Alexandra R .... Carell
Davis Alice B ....Hulme
Davis Alice R .... Gunter
Davis Alison B ....See
Davis Betsey W ....Davis
Davis Carol .... Johnson
Davis Carolyn R .... Corson
Davis Catherine S .... Ledyard
Davis Cornelia V ....Heddens
Davis Diana C.........................Spencer
Davis Diana E.......................Kingman
Davis Diana P .... Ferris

Davis Dola S .... Stemberg
Davis Edith C .... Park
Davis Elizabeth....................Wellman
Davis Elizabeth F ....Crossman
Davis Elizabeth J .... Holt
Davis Elliot ....Paolella
Davis Emily C .... Croll
Davis Emily C .... Record
Davis Flora............................... Maull
Davis Gabriella P.....................Pennock
Davis Grace T.......................Mitchell
Davis Harriet M .... Parham
Davis Helen C.........................Preston
Davis Helga ....Moore
Davis Isabel ....Wise
Davis Isabelle S .... McBride
Davis Jane ....Rees
Davis Jean H ....Brown
Davis Joan Claire ....Warren
Davis Katharine V ....Côté
Davis Kathleen..........................Lindh
Davis Kathleen S ....Darlington
Davis Leise ....Kehl
Davis Leslie A .... Herrick
Davis Lisa D .... Porter
Davis Louise R .... Morse
Davis Lucy .... Donovan
Davis Lydia R ....Goodhue
Davis Marcey C .... Mills
Davis Marcia O.....................Hammond
Davis Margaret ....Arrott
Davis Marian L .... Pearson
Davis Marjorie A .... Merwin
Davis Martha K .... Soper
Davis Mary A .... Booth
Davis Mary G .... Cooke
Davis Mary Jane....................Hartwell
Davis Mary P .... Potter
Davis Maude F.........................Terry
Davis Nancy .... Reagan
Davis Pamela .... Prentice
Davis Pamela E.................Van Ingen
Davis Phoebe Ann ....Freeman
Davis Phoebe E.....................Eshleman
Davis Robin L .... Cushman
Davis Rodney M ....Dowdall
Davis Sally A .... Holbrook
Davis Sally L .... Pratt
Davis Sandra A .... Blake
Davis Sarah W ....Geer
Davis Shirley B .... Gross
Davis Slocumb .... Hollis
Davis Susan P .... Treadway
Davis Sydney A .... Stevens
Davis Virginia...................... Boyce
Davis Virginia N...................... Loomis
Davis Wendy C.................... Cartwright
Davison Constance La M .... Mail
Davison E Ellida .... Rea
Davison Lilla T ....Knox
Davison Margaret O ....Freeman
Davisson Ira C .... Ketcham
Davol Gaynor........................... Casner

Davy Mary W ....White
Dawes E Hutchinson ....Cummin
Dawes Josephine B ....Hall
Dawkins Jo Cille........................ Hafter
Dawson Ann C .... Stanton
Dawson Deborah J .... Beman
Dawson Elizabeth V .... Blackwood
Dawson Martha L .... Blake
Dawson Mary E.......................Gullen
Dawson Pamela M .... Moffat
Dawson Susan G.........................Gries
Day Allison B .... Lanni
Day Ann W .... Becker
Day Anne T .... Watts
Day B Billings ....Smith
Day Deborah A .... Elledge
Day Diane A ....Morris
Day Elizabeth H .... Forster
Day Elizabeth L.........................Bolton
Day Elizabeth W......................Moulton
Day Estella P ....Parsons
Day Evelyn M..........................Lasry
Day Hélène C ....Day
Day Joanne S ....Grymes
Day Jule M ....Sloane
Day Katherine E ....Bourne
Day Lydia Melville....................Hart
Day Madge S ....Monck
Day Margaret D ....Dilks
Day Mary W ....Garrison
Day Nancy C .... Sharp
Day Nancy Lee .... Gillespie
Day Pauline P .... French
Day Sara A .... Poole
Day Vivian Weyerhaeuser........Stroh
Dayton Alice S ....Dayton
Dayton Ann L ....Taylor
Dayton Sally B .... Clement
Dea Lorna A .... Nelson
Deacon Mary E.......................Rowland
Deacon Sara A ....Powell
Deal Florence L ....Wilde
Dean Allison ....Walker
Dean Carla L...............................Day
Dean Dianne M........................Ripley
Dean Dorothy M .... Nelson
Dean Elizabeth F ....Greeff
Dean Emilie E.........................McBride
Dean Laura .... Kaltenbach
Dean Leatrice L ....Elliman
Dean Nancy C.........................Felch
Dean Patricia C .... Day
Deane Eleanor D........................Bierbower
Dear Dorothy B ....Weir
Dear Frances B .... Dewey
de Araujo Anésia C ....Holland
Dearman Jean S .... Anderson
Dearth Margaret D...................Dearth
Deasy Barbara A......................Dennis
Deatly Cinthia C........................Ross
de Bagneux Marie Blanche
                         de Broglie
de Barany Judith ....Prout

de Barros Gomes Rosina M .....Hastings
De Bary Mireille N...............Wilkinson
de Baubigny Faith D ....Denton
de Baubigny Hélène ....Madeira
de Berry Erica L ....Forbes
Debevoise Elida ....Wilson
Debevoise Elizabeth A ....Healy
Debnam Laurette W .... Chambers
De Boer E Constance ....Hatch
de Boisblanc Danielle M ....Boone
De Bord Margaret R ....Stent
de Bottari Cynthia.........................Colt
de Bottari Olga ....Osborne
de Bourbon de Parme Françoise
                              Lobkowicz
de Bragança Anita S .... Stockbridge
de Brantes Nadège ....White
de Bravura Catherine A H C A
                              Knerly
de Bretteville Frances ....Blair
de Bretteville Leslie..........de Bretteville
de Brouchoven de Bergeyck Ghislaine
                              Iliff
de Brunière Odette.... Terrel des Chênes
de Bullet Elizabeth W ....Hall
De Bus Mary E ....Knauft
De Camp Julia R ....Hobart
DeCamp Nancy W ....Bahlman
de Canisy Sabine de C ....Vauclain
De Cardona Lisa A J ....Nimick
de Carvalho Dias Genoveva ....Knapp
deCernea Grace ....Reiniger
de Chadenédes Marie L...........Murdock
De Chant Joan P ....Sterrett
Dechert Frances E....................Ricketson
Dechert H Hope ....Mitchell
Decker Jerilyn J ....Coates
Decker Mary F............................Dent
Decker Susan G W ....Keith
Decker Sylvia G ....Kendrick
de Clairmont Mary A ....Warner
de Clairville Gwendolyn...........Kemper
de Colommès Claude Rivière...... Lippe
de Coninck Nadine ....Bigbie
de Cosson Euretta ....Rathbone
de Cravioto Elizabeth C ....Wilson
Decroix Marguerite..................... Gales
de Croy Marie Louise...............Adams
de Daubek Jarmila....................Packard
Dee Mary H ....Claude
Deeds Suzanne B ....McShane
Deely Ann P ....Bradley
Deering Alexandra K................Haigney
Deering Anne L ....DeLoskey
Deering Katherine F ....Grieves
Deering Keith R........................Morgan
Deering Margaret S L ....Carlson
Deering Nancy..........................Chinn
de Erney Alexandra W ....Rudman
de Fontaine de Logeres M A Guyonne
                              Cates
de Forest Priscilla M ....Williams
De Friest Mary............................Clary

Defty Sarah S ....McCutcheon
Degener Eleanor B ....Brown
Degener Lois A..........................Brown
de Gersdorff Celia C .... Kittredge
de Give Ghislaine ....de Give
de Give M Dominique.... Benvenuto
DeGraff Pamela J ....Porter
de Greeff Marjorie ....Litchfield
de Gruchy M Susan ....Robinson
deHaven Dorothy........................Lovett
Dehlinger Margaret..............Wildenthal
Deibel Ruth ....Mathews
Deisroth Amy P ....Coxe
Deitz Paula ....Morgan
Dekle Elizabeth C....................... Riggs
de Koranyi Patricia D'A.......... Slingluff
de Kwiatkowski Michelle M
                    Corsini di Laiatico
de Labar Margot Adams Hoagland
                              de Labar
de la Borbolla M Luisa.........Hunnewell
de la Croix Janice C ....Sessions
Delafield Caroline M ....Cox
Delafield Clelia ....Carey
Delafield Diana F.........................Muir
Delafield Eleanor ....Everett
Delafield Felicia...............Van Praagh
Delafield Julia L ....Sutro
Delafield Margaret ....Brandt
Delafield Penelope L .... Johnson
de la Houssaye Courtney A........Freeman
Delamater Laurel L ....Sévigny
De Laney Alison A.................. Granger
DeLaney Barbara J ....Smith
Delaney Mary Frances.............Austin
De Laney Susan L ....Morgan
Delano Elisabeth B .... Shotzberger
Delano Jane W ....Ridder
Delano Leila ....Patterson
Delano Margaret ....Paul
de Lapeyrouse Anne M ....Singer
de La Prée Catherine ....Lincoln
de Lara Angela D ....de Lara
de La Rochefoucauld Anne P.....Manice
De Lavallade Carmen P...............Holder
Delécraz Suzanne.......................Stewart
deLedesma Jane F.....................Packard
de Lenclos Suzanne ....Eyre
Delente Odile H ....Tompkins
de Léon y Zayas Irma.....................Hall
de Lesseps Tauni ....de Lesseps
de Leusse Pauline......................Carter
Deleuze-Dordron Juliette........Tilghman
Delgado Ana Maria ....Keene
de Lidertejed Marianne H K ....Perkin
de Limur Mary E......................Weinmann
Dell Jeanne L...........................Taylor
Dellard Christine.......................Gamble
Delmás Rosa E ....Menocal
DeLong Elizabeth ....Kuhl
De Long Mary Bell ....Case
de Lorimier Hélène A..............Bossange
Delp Jessie M ....Walton

Del Piano Patricia A ....Downing
De Mallie Clara C .... Sherwin
de Marcellus Hélène............Cummings
De Marco Karen D .... Converse
Demarest Nancy.........................Miller
de Marneffe Daphne E .... Becker
De Martini Elena ....Sharp
Demas Esther ....Johnson
De Matteo Kendall A ....Berkey
de Menocal Esmée.....................Brooks
Deming Betty S ....Wood
Deming Catherine H................Pierson
Deming Celia B ....Munson
Deming Jeanne C.........................Harris
Demmer Claire...........................Cutler
de Módolo Sacon Carla J G.......Brunet
deMohrenschildt Fernanda ....Hastie
Demonchaux Dominique S M
                              Gardiner
de Montel Annie J .... Kilgore
de Montmollin Edmée C ....Firth
De Mott Harriet C ....Betner
DeMoville Margaret Jock..... DeMoville
Dempsey Diana G.......................Treco
Dempsey Elizabeth T ....Hewitt
Dempsey Julia B ....Cox
Dempsey Marie J.......................Carter
Dempsey Melissa H.....................Gerrity
Dempwolf Mary S ....Roberts
Dempwolf S Helen....................Goodhue
Demus Pamela M ....York
de Nagy Thérèse L ....Lea
Denby Allison ....Hand
Denckla Paula B .... Watriss
Denebeim Nancy A ....Mitchell
de Neuflize Jacqueline P .... Simpkins
Dengler Christine.................. La Valley
Denham Carolina C ....Taylor
Denham Cynthia.........................Smith
de Nicolay Alix ....Mohl
Denious Susan C.......................Pflager
Denison Evelyn E
                    Carrillo de Albornoz
Denison Mary A ....Connell
Denman M Jane......................Hamric
Denney Mary E...........................Rogers
Dennig Corinne L.......................Jones
Dennin Mary Lou A ....Galston
Dennis Louisa .... Wilking
Dennis Nancy N ....Burrows
Dennis Patricia M ....Carruthers
Dennis Terry E.......................Passano
Dennis Winifred M....................Drake
Dennison Anne P .... Fleming
Dennison Diana M........................Smith
Dennison Laura H....................Leeson
Dennistoun Vivian M ....Boulos
Denny Amey D.............................Hoag
Denny Ruth ....Vose
Dent Charlotte C.......................Ashton
Dent Dorothy S........................Withers
Dent Edith B ....Moore
Dent Maida W ....Dent

Dent Mildred H............................Stuart
Denton Elizabeth ....Blake
Denvir Ellen ....Costello
De Patie Linda A ....Buffum
DePew Hope V ....Jones
de Peyster Shelby S ....Wyckoff
dePins Dagmar...........................Sullivan
de Poblet y Vinadé Elena V.......Ronan
Depping Janet M........................Resnik
d'Eprémesnil Nadine Marie
                              d'Eprémesnil
de Quesada Teresa.......................Kuser
de Quevedo Pessanha Merces S
                              Freemon
de Rancougne Isabel...................Smith
Derby Edith R ....Williams
Derdeyn Catherine A..................Little
DeRenne Eudora N J ....Roebling
de Rham Elizabeth.....................Leonard
de Ridder Solange ....Baumann
De Riemer Jan G ....Cauffman
Dermody Patricia ....Leonard
Dern Caroline E........................Johnston
de Rochefort Ghislaine Anne ..... Shrady
De Roeck Linette..........................Good
de Ropp Alison A ....Wharton
de Ropp Georgiana ....Ducas
de Ropp Margaret E .... Du Vivier
de Ropp Zoé Van W ....de Ropp
de Ropp-Weinman Zoé................ Hart
De Rosis Heloise E ....Morgan
de Rosty-Forgach Ilona ....Harrison
de Rothschild Bettina ....Looram
Derr Patricia..............................March
Derrick Alice D ....Reynolds
Derrick Gloria S ....Rawlings
de Ru Jacomina M ....Nicholas
de St Aymour Marie P de Valois
                              Whitman
de Sa Sottomaior Aimée.......de Heeren
de Schauensee Maxine M...........Lewis
de Schirding E Christine ....Dauch
de Sibour Jacqueline.............de Sibour
de Sibour Stephanie S ....de Sibour
Desloge Anne K F ....Bates
Desloge Zoé ....Lippman
Des Mare Kinta ....di Carpegna
de Sola Leonora ....Saurel
Despard Jessica Van R............Warren
Despard Katharine G ....Page
de Sparré Olga ....Rowland
d'Esse I Fay de Danek ....Prince
Dest Janet M............................Dodge
de Struve Elena ....Trenholm
de Sugny France M ....Bark
de Sugny Nicole M............MacDonald
de Surville Mary S leBrun.....McDuffie
deTarr Claire V A ....Smith
Detay Dominique........................Milbank
Detchon Deborah N ....Dodds
Deters Lee A ....Melville
Detert Marie-Louise K ....Garrett
Detert Sandra L.............................Cover

Donald April .... Wilson
Donald Margot R .... Leonard
Donald Marian .... Means
Donald Mary M ....Miller
Donald Virginia .... Prentice
Donaldson A Faith .... Titus
Donaldson Barbara H .... Stout
Donaldson Beirne .... Donaldson
Donaldson Georgia A .... Cummings
Donaldson Nancy B ....Starring
Donaldson Susan .... Romaine
Donaldson Virginia...................Carter
Donalson Loulie G ....Hirst
Donavin Patricia S .... Owens
Dondero Marion...................... Pressley
Donelson Virginia D .... Collins
Donnell Ruth .... Rogers
Donnell Susan W ....Donnell
Donnelley Diana K .... Smith
Donnelley Naoma .... Haggin
Donnem Elizabeth P .... Sigety
Donner Dora B .... Ide
Donoghue Deborah .... Sanders
Donoho Margaret H................. Thibault
Donohoe Katherine D ....Peña
Donohue Nancy C .... Rees
Donovan Ann S .... Marshall
Donovan Julie R ....Jensen
Donovan Mary E ....Nolen
Doody Juanita .... Blundon
Dooley Cornelia H...................... Frank
Doolittle Abby A L ....Ross
Doolittle Esther W .... Ames
Doolittle Julia T...................... Putnam
Doolittle Mary C...................... Taylor
Doom Patricia C .... Pell
Doran Lee C ....Trowbridge
Doran Valerie J...................... Wiegand
Dorchester Craig.......................Morris
Dordai Gabriela ....Morris
Doretti M Elizabeth .... Shober
Dorflinger June ....Hardy
Dormer Adrianne P L .... Foshay
d'Ormesson Olivia.................. Hudson
Dorn Thérèse A .... Bernbach
Dornin Marcia......................Schoettle
Dorr Katherine E ....Gregg
Dorrance Mary A.................... Malone
Dorris Janis R ....Kientz
Dorsaneo Wendy E.................. Mackey
Dort Anne V .... Moffett
Dortch Louisa Bethune..............Bartlett
Dortch Margaret A .... Brooks
Dotrice Karen............................Nalle
Doty Elsie B .... Prentice
Doty George Ann H .... Ryland
Doub Anne A...........................Marzin
Doubleday Dorothy T.............. Massey
Doubleday Marguerite A............. Buck
Doubleday Patricia .... Irons
Doubleday Phoebe .... Timpson
Doubleday Wendy B .... Havens
Dougherty Alice E..................Chaplin

Dougherty Brian B .... Draper
Dougherty Elizabeth S ....Halle
Dougherty Linda E .... Borland
Dougherty Lydia S .... Cockman
Dougherty Nancy B .... Grace
Dougherty Sheila V .... Newman
Dougherty Virginia .... Glover
Doughten Josephine B .... Tyler
Doughten M Dixon .... Brinton
Doughty Helen S .... Lester
Doughty Tatyana ....Olyphant
Douglas Barbara B .... Dixon
Douglas Barbara J ....Lamberton
Douglas Carolyn S .... Kilbourne
Douglas Diane M.................. Goodrich
Douglas Ellen H .... Snow
Douglas Hope .... Hope
Douglas Isabelle F ....Seggerman
Douglas June G.................. Diffenbach
Douglas Katharine E .... Fenton
Douglas Katherine L .... Brady
Douglas Katherine S .... Douglas
Douglas Louise .... Morrison
Douglas Margaret G .... Frank
Douglas Naomi M .... Kitchel
Douglas Sandra L ....Parker
Douglass Jane C ....Carter
Douglass Louise J ....Douglass
Douglass Trent .... Caddis
Douwes Francine C .... Whitney
Dow Barbara S .... Chenoweth
Dow Eleanor L ....Farnam
Dow Nancy F............................ Grover
Dowd Andrea...................... Whitcraft
Dowd Mary Jane .... Hammett
Dowdle Frances E ....Lyon
Downard Martha L .... Fusz
Downe Hilary V .... Hayes
Downes Dorothy D .... Williams
Downes Elizabeth .... McDevitt
Downey Barbara D .... Wilson
Downey Joan F .... Humphrey
Downey Katherine Van I........... Goddard
Downey Margaret .... Chew
Downey Marjorie A...............Knowlton
Downs Nancy I S............... Stephenson
Dows Evelyn L .... Gates
Dowse Rispah A .... Schwering
Dowson Mary Gayle..................... Kalt
Doykos Catherine .... Oliver
Doyle Cynthia ....MacColl
Doyle Ellen B .... Dimond
Doyle Karen F .... Bradbury
Doyle Noreen E .... Prindle
Doyle Sheila G ....O'Day
Drackett Sallie B .... Van Rensselaer
Dragan Carla R .... Olinger
Drake Barbara L .... Daspit
Drake Candace F .... Wainwright
Drake Chloé A .... Martin
Drake Elizabeth .... Harvey
Drake Susan .... Dick
Drane Barbara C .... Roberson

Dranow Patricia ....Beard
Draper Anna B........................Shaw
Draper Ellen McK .... Pendergast
Draper Harriette C .... Downer
Draper Joan K .... Bishop
Draper Katharine R.................... Schutt
Draper Mary P .... Lord
Drashpil Debra A.................... O'Neill
Draughn Sandra ....Freeman
Drayton Elizabeth ....Taylor
Drayton Elizabeth W .... Hopkins
Drayton Margaret A .... Reventlow
Drayton Marjorie E

        von Moschzisker

Drayton Mary......................... Grant
Drayton Phebe ....Strong
Drayton Ruth P .... Dodge
Drescher Ann H .... Desloge
Drescher Edda ....Hare
Dresselhuys Lorraine M ....Amato
Dresser Elizabeth .... Flood
Drew Adelaide A .... Masterson
Drew Deirdre E........................DuBose
Drew Diana L .... Harbison
Drew Gloria Willard....................Starr
Drew Marie J .... Powers
Drew-Bear Joy .... Valentine
Drewry Virginia W ....Martin
Drexel Diana ....Raibourn
Drexel E M Noreen .... O'Farrell
Drexel Jane B ....Porteous
Drexel Nancy Lois F .... Bissinger
Drexel Pamela N...................... Walker
Driggs Diane M .... Mallory
Driggs Kate T......................... Perry
Driggs Margaret .... Vaughan
Drinker Ernesta .... Ballard
Drinker Mary E........................ Elek
Drinkwater Nancy M .... O'Brien
Dripps Elizabeth J.................... Royer
Dripps Susan A ....Stauffer
Driscoll Diane .... MacDonald
Driscoll Katharine .... Withington
Driscoll Phoebe P ....Fisher
Driver Ann D .... Chapman
Driver Ruth ....Lowry
Drobeck Karen A .... Watson
Droescher Julia C ....Vetterlein
Droescher Kathleen .... Buffum
Drossel Cordula E A .... Brown
Drowne Kelsey K .... Leachman
Drum Diana .... Platt
Drum Gwen H .... Zimmerman
Drummer Dorothy J....................Morton
Drummond Irene M .... Casner
Drummond Jean ....Crane
Drummond R Lee .... Macneil
Drury Clifton .... Andrews
Drury Esther F .... Vaughan
Drury Heath ....Boote
Drury Hope L ....Goddard
Drury Innes Kane .... Hollos
Drury Katherine R .... Dibblee

Drury Sallie C B ....Iselin
Drury Sarah A .... Howe
Dry Nancy .... Sumner
Dryden Leila M .... Drury
Dryer Geraldine G .... Morgan
Dryselius Anita B .... Lamb
Duane Catharine F ....Stryker
Duane Mai .... Harper
Duane Margaret F .... Lunt
Duane Margaretta S L ....Iselin
Duane Marguerite C ....Ellis
DuBarry Barbara.....................Erdman
DuBarry Elizabeth .... Ernst
DuBarry Suzanne .... Sellers
Dubben Elizabeth................. Livingston
Dubben Judith Y ....Ryland
Dubbs Jane M .... McPherson
Dubé Nancy A .... Hand
Dubell Rosalind W .... Wiltberger
Du Bois Anne A .... Valenzuela-Bock
DuBois Caroline D .... Hutton
DuBois Louise D .... Perkins
Dubois Michele D .... Neff
DuBois Nancy G...................... Wright
DuBois Rebeckah .... Glazebrook
Du Bois Sarah F .... Kingsley
Du Bose Harriet .... Gray
Duca Pamela J .... Marshall
Ducey Ethel B................... Coggeshall
Ducey Katharine T ....Hardy
Ducey Maria B .... Ryerson
Duchaine Barbara .... Foster
Ducommun Electra B ....de Peyster
Dudley Cécile M.................. Amesbury
Dudley Dorothy W .... Thorndike
Dudley Lillian M .... Owen
Dudley Rebecca L .... Smid
Dudley Sarah W .... Plimpton
Duel Virginia W .... Crosby
Duer Charlotte A .... Brice
Duer Josephine P .... Gilkyson
Duer Mary...............................Brown
Duer Mary G..........................Colen
Duff Barbara D ....Miller
Duff Diana J ....Carter
Duff Marion Robinson .... Filley
Duffey Mary E................... Huddleston
Dufficy Kirsten E .... Henderson
Duffus Deborah L.................... Cozens
Duffy Karen E .... Weber
Duffy Katherine H .... Clarke
Duffy Minnette C .... Bickel
Dufort Sandra E ....Glendinning
Dugall Patricia A .... Stone
Dugan Catherine Van S.............Swift
Dugan Cathleen P ....Riley
Dugan Helen C....................... Morgan
Duhé Dawn C .... Ballenger
Duhon Marlene L .... Dodge
Duke Lois C .... Niles
Duke Maria-Luisa B .... Cluett
Duke Renée........................ Eckelberry

Edwards Anne McP ....Townsend
Edwards Barbara H......................Hicks
Edwards Dorothy L ....Horne
Edwards Dorothy M .... Thacher
Edwards Eleanor .... Prince
Edwards Elizabeth Anne .... Hord
Edwards Harriet V ....Spencer
Edwards Helen B ....Fosburgh
Edwards Isabella M ....Martin
Edwards Jayne A ....Cox
Edwards Jo Anne ....Miller
Edwards Laura L .... Rulon-Miller
Edwards Lee R .... Peace
Edwards Lucy B ....Despard
Edwards M Page ....Peyton
Edwards Margaret.....................Francis
Edwards Margaret H.................Perkins
Edwards Nancy ....Barker
Edwards Patricia M ....Carpenter
Edwards Sarah F..................... Norfleet
Edwards Sarah H .... Baltzell
Edwards Sarah L......................Rueter
Eells Adèle C ....Pierce
Eells Sarah L......................Hoagland
Egan Eleanor............................Everett
Egan Eleanor M ....Murdoch
Egan Kerry C ....Darby
Egbert Allison Huntting ....Brokaw
Egbert Anne Merrill ....Grape
Egbert Jane K ....Brown
Eger Jane E .... Van Pelt
Egeressy Jane E ....Cannon
Egerton Martha S...................Atkinson
Egger Antoinette D...................Taylor
Egger Frances .... Watson
Eggert Mary W ....Hotchkiss
Eggins Estelle T............................Burr
Eggleston A Louise ....Averill
Eggleston Helen A......................Bellas
Eglin Cintra E.........................Willcox
Ehrenclou Alice C .... Poole
Ehrenclou Alice M ....Cole
Ehrenclou Jessie H ....Browne
Ehrhard Jennifer W..................Nichols
Ehrhorn Elisabeth A A ....Pumphrey
Ehrman Joan ....Avenali
Ehrmann-Egry Marie Louise
                                    McKinney
Eichenholtz Carol A ....Schabacker
Eichhorn Rita W.........................Hall
Eide Rachel N.......................Baumann
Eidell Victoria ....Johnston
Eifert Laura Lee....................Montross
Eighmy Elizabeth A ....Applegate
Eilers Veva M.........................McKee
Eiman Laura Y ....Brooks
Eimicke Alicia K .... Barbieri
Eimicke Laura S ....Klimley
Eisenbeis Christina H ....Eisenbeis
Eisenbrey J Kendall ....Chew
Eisenhauer Alta D.................McNeely
Eisenhower B Anne.....................Flöttl
Eisenmayer Anne...........................Ross

Ekberg Karen S.........................Carhart
Ekengren Christina ....Hawkins
Ekengren Elsie W ....O'Dunne
Elavsky Anne J.......................Redfield
Elder Margaret L ....Neuhaus
Elder Mary ....Schaff
Eldredge Carley ....Smith
Eldredge Elaine ....Brown
Eldredge Helen L....................Bradley
Eldredge Joan P ....Schmitt
Eldredge Patricia A....................Ward
Eldridge Anne W ....Kane
Elek Frances B Wharton .... McComb
Eliason M Thayer ....Roberts
Eliot Evelyn B ....Hawkins
Eliot Mary A................................Fay
Elkins Carole A ....Large
Elkins Elizabeth D.......................Gray
Elkins Katherine F.......................Boyd
Elkins Linda T ....Bohlen
Eller Anita C...............................Hunt
Ellett Joan ....Benjamin
Ellice Anne P.............................Adam
Ellicott Ann M ....Madeira
Ellicott Grace J ....Jones
Elliman Claudia L.......................Jenks
Elliman Julia S.........................Crout
Elliman Patricia Y ....Leo
Elliot Eleanor G......................Mulder
Elliot Frances M ....Storey
Elliot H Gay..............................Scott
Elliot Hope.............................Carter
Elliot Louise E R .... Halsey
Elliot Merlin.....................Nuti-de Biasi
Elliot Virginia ....White
Elliott Ann S ....Blanchard
Elliott Anne L ....Gruen
Elliott Barbara H........................Niles
Elliott Caroline D ....Williams
Elliott Caryl M.......................Osborn
Elliott Edith J......................Hunnewell
Elliott Glenaan M ....Robbins
Elliott Jacquelyn D ....Crocker
Elliott Katharine H ....Baker
Elliott Kathryn R ....Benedict
Elliott Lydia H ....Schweppe
Elliott M Lee.................MacWilliams
Elliott Mary S.........................Fogarty
Elliott Rebecca A ....Tubman
Elliott Ruth S ....Holmes
Ellis Amanda ....Washburne
Ellis Ann C ....Powel
Ellis Anne H ....Glaccum
Ellis Dorry ....Hellman
Ellis Elizabeth C.........................Ellis
Ellis Elizabeth G...................Watkins
Ellis Elizabeth O....................Walther
Ellis Ellen Buntzie ....Churchill
Ellis Helen P ....Prouty
Ellis Lee C ....Horne
Ellis Lucia L ....Uihlein
Ellis Marie-Armide L ....Storey
Ellis Marjorie H.......................Preston

Ellis Mildred ....Reynolds
Ellis Nancy...............................Cooke
Ellis Patricia............................Corey
Ellis Ruth D ....Layton
Ellis Willoughby K ....Royce
Ellison Elizabeth F ....Borie
Ellison Mary ....Hastings
Ellsworth Alice C ....Sturges
Ellsworth Dale N ....Longmaid
Ellsworth Jane H...................Hotchkiss
Elmendorf Joan L ....Flood
Elmer Laura M ....Wilhelm
Elmer Victoria H ....Kanaga
Elmes Cecily ....Kayes
Elmore Lucia L...........................Santy
Elmore Maralyn A ....Marsteller
Elmquist Roxanne M ....Almond
Elms Teresa T ....Lindsay
Elmslie Cynthia E.......................Weir
Elsom Harriet......................Rothstein
Elting Helen M ....Boom
Elting Sarah S ....Finocchio
Elvin Barbara I.......................Whitney
Elwes Aline M M .... McDonnell
Ely Adrienne H.......................Grannis
Ely Angela A ....Matthias
Ely C Day .... Ravenscroft
Ely Cornelia A ....Wood
Ely Elizabeth W ....Haff
Ely Esther S ....Bowen
Ely Gertrude B ....Bullock
Ely J Carolyn .... Pyle
Ely Jane S ....Pearce
Ely Jessica W ....Hart
Ely Kathryn C ....Ely
Ely Katrina B.............................Carter
Ely Margaret R ....Pringle
Ely Marion C ....Johnston
Ely Martha R ....Fuller
Ely Melinda ....Dubow
Ely Nancy B ....Kales
Ely Virginia E.......................Paterson
Embree Susan N ....Parker
Embry Caroline.........................Turner
Emerich Susan L..................Henderson
Emerick Elizabeth L ....Dethleps
Emerson Mary C........................Macy
Emerson Susan H ....Cooke
Emery Elizabeth P ....Kelley
Emery Irene ....Goodale
Emery Jean M....................Wommack
Emery Josephine.........................Harris
Emery M Charlotte ....Russell
Emery Mary ....Bird
Emery Susan B ....Dumaine
Emlen Frances S ....Cullen
Emley Susan L ....Luebbermann
Emling Audrey P ....Saer
Emmet Anne ....McLucas
Emmet Daphne ....Hallowell
Emmet Helen D ....Emmet
Emmet Katharine H ....Gardiner
Emmet Katharine Temple...........Emmet

Emmet Kathleen ....Darman
Emmet Lydia F......................Williams
Emmet Margaret F
                          Alvarez de Toledo
Emmons Frances McL................ Rogers
Emmons Lisa A..........................Pyne
Emory Elizabeth K M ....Gatchell
Emory Katherine E ....Stookey
Emory Lucy D ....Ambach
Empringham Mary-Elizabeth ......Atkins
Endicott Beatrice ....Macleod
Engel Barbara ....Dixon
Engel Rúna L.........................Magowan
Engelhard Anne F..............de la Renta
Engelhard Sally.......................Pingree
Engelhardt Barbara ....Wilson
Engelhorn Tamra ....Raven
Engelsman Elizabeth R.............Flanigan
Engett Eileen A ....Chambers
England Keo ....Jordan
England Nancy D ....Siedlarz
Engler Gail E..............................Day
Engler Marcy A ....Ziesing
English Ann C ....Randt
English Betsy J ....Leiper
English Carolyn ....Rosengarten
English Drue M..........................Heinz
English Eleanor.......................Whitman
English Elizabeth Patricia.............. Saul
English Jhan C ....Choate
English Marjorie ....Little
English Suzanne..........................Jones
Engs Christianne E ....Carty
Engs Eleanor ....Hilken
Ennis Blanid M..........................Scott
Ennis Nancy P ....Follett
Enos Alice H...........................Stokes
Enos Jean T.............................Urban
Enos Martha P ....van Nierop
Epes Isota T.............................Potter
Eppinger Catherine C ....Ball
Epsilantis Anastasia I ....Worcester
Ercklentz Hildegarde M W ... Mahoney
Erdman Caroline B ....Hare
Erdmann Judith A ....Makrianes
Erhard Joan F.............................Hough
Erickson Alexandra W ....Golinkin
Erickson Betty A ....Ludington
Erickson J Lee ....Ingram
Erickson Joan M........................Wilson
Erickson Virginia G ....Pinkham
Ericsson Rebecca W ....Hunter
Erikson Margareta B.................Colmore
Erler Letitia L M ....Michotte
Erminger Bertha ....Browne
Ernst Delle ....Taylor
Ernst Dorothy J.........................Foster
Ernst Harriett ....Veale
Ernst Juliana...............................Geer
Ernst Sarah Ellen ....Christensen
Ernst Susanne............................Geier
Erskine Alison R.........................Farrar
Erskine Betsy B ....Toralballa

Erskine Florence W	Sinton
Erskine Karen M	Biddle
Ervin Anne S	Woltz
Ervin Katharine M	Baker
Ervin Louise S	Dick
Ervin Mary E	Potts
Ervin Miriam	Caskey
Erwin Hope	Goodwin
Erwin Maureen M	Motley
Erwin Molly	Walton
Escamilla Elisa K	Schwartz
Escamilla Victoria J	Fleishhacker
Escartin Katia L	De Jarnette
Eschmann Elizabeth	Whittemore
Eshleman Amabel K	Barrows
Eshleman Eileen	Stewart
Eshleman Elizabeth B	Brooks
Eshleman Lorine J	Vogt
Eshleman Lucy P	Sprayregen
Esler L Adalyn	Vail
Esmerian Jacqueline P	King
Espy Delphine S	Eberhart
Espy Mary Burwell	Schorr
Espy S Carlotta	Ford
Essock Margaret	Lovell
Estabrook Laura	Romine
Estelle Barbara R	Glore
Estes Genevieve L	du Pont
Estin Lee L	Cauro
Estrada Annette	Kellogg
Esty Mary G	Sanderson
Etienne Marjorie C	Benedict
Ettelt Louise E	Hunter
Ettl Cordelia	Clement
Etz Constance T	Logan
Eugene Jean A	Leber
Eustis Elspeth H	Taylor
Eustis Jane G	Suydam
Eustis Leslie	Hill
Eustis Leslie Pomeroy	Hallowell
Eustis Margaret H	Curtis
Eustis Margaret S	Richardson
Eustis Marin C	Turner
Eustis Peggy B	Keating
Evans Alexa L	Marvin
Evans Alexandra D	Guild
Evans Alice A	Nahigian
Evans Alma F	Munroe
Evans Barbara	Ferris
Evans Berrell	Street
Evans Betty Lou	Streett
Evans Catharine C	Grigsby
Evans Claire L	Fair
Evans Dorothy E	Pattee
Evans Eleanor F	Grose
Evans Eleanor P	Hamel
Evans Elizabeth B A	Walker
Evans Elizabeth V	Morton
Evans Florence P	Jordan
Evans Gayle F	Brookfield
Evans Jane S	Hamilton
Evans Janet	Dunn
Evans Jean A	Penton
Evans Judith K	Thomas
Evans Julia	Detmer
Evans Julia E	Passano
Evans K Serena	Carson
Evans Katharine F	Jackson
Evans Katharine L	May
Evans Kathleen M	Conklin
Evans Loraine H	Pollak
Evans Louise B	Turner
Evans Margaret G	Tuten
Evans Nancy V	Gruner
Evans Olivia E	Townsend
Evans Pamela I	Wyeth
Evans Patricia	Humphreys
Evans Phyllis S	Swindells
Evans Susan F	Van Riper
Evans Suzanne	Reeves
Evans Suzanne W	Andrews
Evans Virginia J	Noell
Evarts Alice C	Schipper
Evarts Elizabeth M	de Rham
Evarts Katharine M	Merck
Everdell Rosalind	Havemeyer
Everett Clara B	Low
Everett Gwendolen N	Perkins
Everett Jane C	Kehl
Everett Laura L	Stowe
Everett Marion L	Gallagher
Evers Sally	Everett
Eversman Jane H	Smithers
Eversole Kimberly A	Koch
Ewart Eleanor W	Southworth
Ewart Katherine W	McKnight
Ewell Milicent	Tuckerman
Ewer Elaine S	Tiffin
Ewer Emelyn S	Kirkland
Ewing Alexandra	Whitney
Ewing Anne E	La Motte
Ewing Caroline B	Michahelles
Ewing E Fordyce	Van Winkle
Ewing Grace V	Huffman
Ewing Jacklyn B	Rush
Ewing Jessie V	Phillips
Ewing Margaret A	Lloyd
Ewing Margaret H	Waxter
Ewing Mary L	Krone
Ewing Nancy	Ruthrauff
Ewing Rosalie McR	Engler
Exnicios Carol M O	Tucker
Exum Ellen M	Raoul
Eyre E Jane	Rives
Eyre Eileen	Manuel
Eyre Elizabeth H	Taylor
Eyre Florence A	Bryan
Eyre Janet V S	Eyre
Eyre Margaret J	Thorndike
Eyre Martha K	McDaniel
Eyre Victoria P	Whipple
Eysmans Mary-Emory	Haberstam
Fabbri M Germana D	Day
Fabe Ellen E	Russell
Fabyan Frances	Davis
Faesy Margaret	MacKenzie
Faesy Marian N	Hupper
Fagen Polly P	McConney
Fageol Sally J	Morris
Fagerstrom Grace	McKittrick
Fahey Janice	Watts
Fahey Lee A	MacDonald
Fahle Amanda S	Ellis
Fahnestock Clare H	Moorhead
Fahnestock M Lee	Leggett
Fahnestock Mary C	Clark
Fahrner Mary	Sethness
Fahy Laura L P	Robertson
Fail Kathryn A	Smith
Fail Marcia	Boykin
Faile Sarah J	Fogarty
Fairbairne Lisa C	Houston
Fairbank Elizabeth	Cameron
Fairbank Laura	Sudler
Fairbank Wendy	Fairbank
Fairbanks H Virginia	Neale
Fairbanks Margarita L	Fairbanks
Fairchild Marisue	Wilkinson
Fairchild Stephanie B	Griswold
Faircloth Jean	MacArthur
Fairfax Sarah Louise	Harris
Fairlie Katherine A	Ebright
Fairman Elaine E	Lincoln
Fairman Gail B	Cook
Fairman Joan D	Gummey
Fairman Josephine F	Elting
Fairman Leilani J	McCall
Fales Angelica Van R	Bentley
Fales Barbara H	de Bragança
Fales Ellen D	Hewitt
Fales Sandra	Hillman
Fales Willia F	Eckerberg
Falise Carol A	Owens
Falk Jeanne V	Adams
Falke Leslie A	Trainer
Fallert Ann M	Knapp
Falley Katharine	Bennett
Falvey Alice J	Greif
Falvey Joan	Parker
Fancher Robin L	Strandberg
Fanjul Maria C	Ryan
Fankhauser Elizabeth R	Lewis
Fannin Betty L	Wilbur
Farber Bonnie	Wilds
Farber Deborah B	Kallop
Fargas Francisca	Brady
Fargo Clotilde A	Merle
Farhad Mina	Burger
Farinholt Ilse Ann	Stein
Farish Martha B	Gerry
Farley Constance A	Whittall
Farley Elise M	Higgins
Farley Elizabeth E	Berdell
Farley Florence	Peet
Farley Maria M	Gerrity
Farlow Catherine H	Hitchings
Farmer Alice Cary	Brown
Farmer Elizabeth J	Jarvis
Farmer Patricia A	Randolph
Farmer Suzanne	Farmer
Farnam Nancy Y	Gannett
Farnham Louise	Buchanan
Farnsworth Alice	Andresen
Farnsworth Ann	Mestres
Farnsworth Barbara L	Fairburn
Farnsworth Margaret K	Lawson
Farnsworth Mary M	Marsh
Farnum Anna M	Warden
Farnum Anna S	Wood
Farquharson Denise F F	Bryan
Farr Adelaide	Cohû
Farr Hazel S	Freeman
Farr Nancy D	Solley
Farr Virginia P	Ramsey
Farran Elizabeth	Tozer
Farrar Isabel	de Szinay
Farrar Mary	Hatchette
Farrar Maud Ellen	Farrar
Farrel Marian	McAleenan
Farrell Eileen Joan	Kasten
Farrell Eileen M	Edson
Farrell Erin H	Loud
Farrell H Caroline	Pereira
Farrell Ritchey C	LaRoche
Farrell Wendy	Victor
Farrelly Anne C	Locher
Farrelly Elizabeth C	O'Brien
Farrelly Patricia	Richards
Farrelly Patricia B	Murphy
Farrington Anita R	Earl
Farrington Jennifer S	Jhaveri
Farrington Judith K	Swartwood
Farris Maria L	Smythe
Farwell Elizabeth	Swanson
Fates Janet MacL	Scovil
Faulconer Anne M	Hurley
Faulconer Katharine	Kenniston
Faulkner Jill	Summers
Faulkner Joan	Cutting
Fauls Georgia B	Stilson
Faunce Elizabeth A	Andrews
Fauntleroy Elizabeth P	Glasgow
Fauquet-Lemaitre Nicole E	Stroh
Faure Valerie C	Youmans
Faurot Keturah R	Tippett
Favill Cynthia S	Tye
Favre Christine T	Withers
Favrot Michelle St C	Heidelberg
Faxon Sarah	Johnson
Fay Alice A	Hutton
Fay Dorothy	Robinson
Fay Elise H	Hawtin
Fay Frances	Bowes
Fay Hope	Cobb
Fay Jessie	Sargent
Fay Katherine Ann	Barry
Fay Katherine F	Hammonds
Fay Marion B	Henny
Fay Patricia O	Woods
Fay Sarah B	Baird
Fay Sarah S	Cottingham
Fay Victoria A	Leonard

Fearey Margaret S .... Walsh
Fearey Mary K E ....Fearey
Fearing Gwendolen W .... Hosken
Fearing Hesterly......................... Black
Fearn Irwin................................Cortelyou
Featherstone Alice E................ Caldwell
Febiger Ethel S ....Hall
Febiger Lindsay C .... Scott
Feddery Billie E........................... Smith
Fedor Susan J ....Parry
Feeley Kathleen M ....Schwab
Fehr Elizabeth T ....Peters
Feick Nancy N ....Kendall
Feijóo Sonia A ....Littlejohn
Felix Elizabeth R ....Parrack
Felix Gene L ....Dilks
Fell Dorothy M ....Farrelly
Fell Elisabeth H ....Allen
Fell Natalie L ....Spencer
Feller Janice M .... Bowen
Fellner Anita M ....Swetland
Fellows Jeanne E .... Smith
Felton B Louise .... Williams
Felton Janet G ....Cooper
Felton Jennifer B .... Cabot
Felton Mary Copley...................Loring
Fenger Rebecca S ....Doub
Fenic Karen J ....Parker
Fenimore Margaret J.................Morris
Fenn Judith S .... Duncan
Fenn Margaret H P .... Hilles
Fenn Mary C ....Raley
Fenn Patricia L .... McGeorge
Fennell Elaine ....Wood
Fennell Rosemary S R ....Feick
Fennelly Carol P ....Hutchins
Fennelly Marcia A ....Gowen
Fenner Flora.............................. French
Fennimore Beth .... Hill
Fenton Diane S ....Russell
Fenton Edith D .... Tuckerman
Fenton Elinor S.......................Marshall
Fenton Jennifer A ....Jones
Fenton Melinda E .... Henderson
Fenton Nancy B ....Perkins
Fenton Pamela T .... Henderson
Fentress Elizabeth L ....Goodwin
Fentress Juliette W .... Bacon
Fenwick Frances A ....Edelen
Fenwick Gillian C .... Earle
Feola Stephanie A ....Coppins
Ferber Cornelia V H ....Potter
Ferber Judith A ....Taylor
Fergus Nellie M .... Smith
Ferguson Adeline A......................Gay
Ferguson Allene P.......................Perry
Ferguson Carroll H .... Chapman
Ferguson Dorothy ....Brown
Ferguson Elizabeth Y A ....Mills
Ferguson Helen C.........................Kay
Ferguson Jane D ....Codman
Ferguson Joan ....Ellis
Ferguson Joan P........................Cooley

Ferguson Joan S........................ Marsh
Ferguson Mary...........................Russell
Ferguson Mary F .... Sullivan
Ferguson Rosamond A ....Brown
Ferguson Stella L.......................Thayer
Ferguson Virginia C ....Leach
Fergusson Laura H ....Plumb
Fergusson Sarah A.....................Brown
Fernegg Joan ....Ledoux
Fernley Joan A....................McCracken
Fernley Lois A .... McNeil
Ferrall Michelle A .... Flickinger
Ferrante di Ruffano Virginia
                                        MacVeagh
Ferrara Alison A ....Chase
Ferrari Ellen D ....Morrison
Ferrarini Lynn E .... Pitts
Ferrell Lilly S .... Rex
Ferrell Patricia P ....Kendrick
Ferrier Laura M .... Wilbur
Ferris Alwilda J .... de Matteo
Ferris Barbara Reynolds .... Van Liew
Ferris Carole D .... Kroeger
Ferris Jean D .... Anderson
Ferris Margaret U ....Zimmermann
Ferriss Marion P .... Wilson
Ferroggiaro Jill A .... Ames
Ferry Frances I...................... Dennison
Ferté Isabelle...........................Armour
Ferwerda Lisa .... Johnston
Fessenden Enid ....Gifford
Fessenden Gay Mesta................. Macy
Fetridge Blakely.........................Bundy
Fetter Jennifer A .... Isler
Fetter Margaret M ....Graham
Fetterman Katharine B ....Moran
Fetterolf Shirley E .... Mackenzie
Fetzer Monica ....Clark
Few Elizabeth V ....Penfield
Few Ellen H .... Anderson
ffolliott Sheila ....Krech
Fiaux Annelyse M ....Allen
Fick Grace L ....Ghiselli
Fick Heather B .... Paull
Fickes Sarah E ....Drymalski
Ficklen E Kay ....Neuhaus
Fiedler Deborah ....Stiles
Fiedler Mary B ....Larkin
Field Alexandra ....Lackey
Field Bettie R .... Farber
Field Deirdre D .... Field
Field Dorothy S .... Edmonds
Field Gail C ....Hayne
Field Joy T .... Herrick
Field Lisa ....Eustis
Field Mariana ....Hoppin
Field Marjorie L .... Wilde
Field Mary A ....Jackson
Field Nancy De V ....Mullan
Field Pauline ....Cummings
Fielding Mathilde E................... Cruice
Fields Luanne............................Miller
Fields Mary G.............................. Off

Fields Nancy W ....Sellers
Figge Marie C .... Wise
Filkins Carlene A....................Whitney
Filley K Haven ....Cutler
Filley Mary G ....McVickar
Finch Anne C Delafield................Cox
Finch Christine D ....Bullock
Finch M Noelle Delafield .... Haskell
Finch Margaret R........................Nicol
Finch Sandra L ....Parnell
Fincke Virginia A .... Thors
Findlay Joan S ....Dunham
Fine Amy M ....Collins
Fine Shayla Spencer ....Spencer
Finkbeiner Elizabeth A.......Crumpacker
Finlay Alexis E ....Eliott
Finlay Ann .... Pyle
Finlay Virginia B .... Dillon
Finlayson Elizabeth C............... Gregory
Finley C Gwathmey H...............Gomila
Finley Kathryn A .... Greaves
Finn Anna ....Pressly
Finn Barbara .... Bentley
Finn Denyse R .... Clancy
Finnell Gabriella A .... Eggers
Finnell Lesley H ....Blanchard
Finnell Patricia ....Colket
Finney Mary V ....Beach
Finney Maryett K .... Cale
Finney Rosemary .... Edmonston
Finney Susan H...................McNeely
Finnie Elizabeth S.................. Stabler
Fioramonti Alice A....................Hall
Firestone Gay I ....Wray
Firestone Lendy S....................Brown
Firth Charlotte V...................... Walsh
Firth Elizabeth Morgan................ Love
Firuski Isabel J.......................Thacher
Fischbeck Grace H ....Riker
Fischer Alison A .... Ellison
Fischer Debra J ....French
Fischer M Joan .... Meyer
Fischer Rosmarie G ....Paris
Fischer Sara H ....Betekhtin
Fischer Susan J ....Spencer
Fish Alida L ....Tanis
Fish Elizabeth ....Stoddard
Fish Elizabeth L.........................Atalay
Fishback Martha .... Robinson
Fisher Alice S ....Blood
Fisher Ann G ....Schellenberg
Fisher Christine C....................Allen
Fisher Claudette M .... Johnson
Fisher Eleanor D .... Trevor
Fisher Elizabeth H ....Ray
Fisher Elizabeth L..................Hasley
Fisher F Alexandra ....Mitch
Fisher Frances O.....................Collins
Fisher Genevieve C .... Stanton
Fisher Grace S ....Upson
Fisher Helen E ....Fisher
Fisher Jean ....Gibbs
Fisher Josephine C................de Give

Fisher Marcella ....Anderson
Fisher Margaret A ....McKean
Fisher Margaret N.......................Knox
Fisher Margaret W.....................James
Fisher Marilyn T ....Hanford
Fisher Mary E ....Klein
Fisher Mary M ....Coleman
Fisher Melinda G ....Callaway
Fisher Nancy H ....Reeder
Fisher Ninna T ....Denny
Fisher Rebecca D ....Dunn
Fisher Sally R ....Carpenter
Fisher Sarah A ....McCawley
Fisher Sheryl A ....McCready
Fisher Susan S ....Purdy
Fisher Zarada ....Gowenlock
Fishwick Ellen B ....Martin
Fisk Gwendolyn ....Halleran
Fiske Dorothea ....Darlington
Fiske Dorothy B ....Claxton
Fiske Gail...............................Holloway
Fiske June W ....McHugh
Fiske Phyllis G .... Smith
Fiske Virginia ....Childs
Fitch Helen J ....Emery
Fitch Rosamound T .... Richardson
Fitchett Kathleen W .... Dinning
Fite Dorothy F ....Bonsack
Fite Minnie W ....Mattes
Fite Whitney A .... Clay
Fitler Lydia C ....Kimball
Fitler Margaret H ....Anderson
Fitler Margaretta L ....Rockefeller
Fitzgerald Gail H ....Serfaty
Fitz-Gerald Helen Savery ......Rorimer
FitzGerald Kelley J..................Reuben
Fitzgerald Louisa G ....Huber
Fitzgerald Nancy C ....Smith
Fitzgerald Nellie I....................Miller
FitzGibbon Sabina ....Philip
Fitz-Hugh Claudia T ....Kelleher
Fitzhugh Louise C ....Hickox
Fitzhugh Portia L .... Karol
Fitzpatrick Mary H ....Gwynn
FitzPatrick Patricia M ....Selden
Fiuza Deborah.......................de Mello
Flack Frances N ....Tenney
Flagg Carol K ....Stevens
Flagg Marjorie S ....Strawbridge
Flagg Mary........................Campbell
Flail Leslie A ....Lewis
Flament Diane M ....Dautel
Flanagan Cecily W ....Loizeaux
Flanagan Elaine D ....Wistar
Flanagan Jean P ....Banks
Flanagan Sharon M................Buchanan
Flander Christina ....Holbrook
Flanders Mary S ....Boline
Flanders Sarah E......................Dietz
Flanders Virginia L..................Gurnee
Flaschen Sheryl........................Talbot
Flatau Sybilla G......................Freeman
Flautt Emma............................Crisler

Fleischmann Dorette L ...... Fleischmann
Fleischmann Joan K .... Tobin
Fleischmann Melanie H............. Garnett
Fleishhacker Delia .... Ehrlich
Fleitas Lucretia G .... Irwin
Fleming Alice M................... Renchard
Fleming Angeline E................... Austin
Fleming Dorothy S .... French
Fleming Elizabeth S .... Ticknor
Fleming Frances F .... Barnard
Fleming Jean .... Goodwyn
Fleming Jean E .... Woodd-Cahusac
Fleming Martha R .... McNally
Fleming Mary D .... Walsh
Flershem Ann D .... Gaylord
Fleschler Lenore .... Davis
Fletcher Ann D .... Robinson
Fletcher Anne....................... Nixon
Fletcher Helen L....................Stanley
Fletcher Jane G .... Higgins
Fletcher Joan C ....Hopkins
Fletcher Marjorie C .... Balboni
Fletcher Mary H .... Colket
Fletcher Mary M....................... Baker
Fletcher Rhodabel S ....Morton-Smith
Fletcher Sara E F .... Hanson
Fletcher Susan A......................... Eddy
Flickinger Holly A...............Williams
Flickinger Wendy W .... Ross
Flint Anne R .... Ogilvy
Flint Elizabeth W.....................Steel
Flint Jean Merrill .... Wilson
Flint Katharine .... Joyce
Flippin Lucy A .... Buford
Flocco Debra Ann.................Gnichtel
Flockhart Mary Louise .... Persse
Flood Frances.......................Thomas
Flood Judith .... Wilbur
Floquet Danielle A M........... Haskell
Florian Constance L .... McVoy
Flothow A Elizabeth.............Goddard
Flournoy Mildred C ....de Marcellus
Flowers C Leigh .... Gannaway
Flowers Maury deG.................Shields
Flowers T Taliaferro................Crozer
Floyd Elizabeth B ....Welsh
Floyd Martha W ....Selke
Floyd Mary C ....King
Floyd Patricia S .... Charman
Flynn Barbara .... Argenti
Flynn Cheryl V .... Baruch
Flynn Collette .... De Silver
Flynn Elisabeth A C ....Glass
Flynn Patricia T .... Spurgeon
Flynt Marjorie ....Muir
Foedisch Joan....................... Adibi
Foerderer Mignon E .... Davis
Foerderer Shirley A .... Murray
Fogarty Mary .... Berne
Fogo Annette E..................... Harper
Folds Suzanne D.............. McCullagh
Foley Kay..............................Hauer
Foley Marie Thérèse................ Parsons

Foley Martha E .... Nype
Foley Mildred L H...................Deering
Foley Susan M .... Larson
Foley Suzanne K................Strawbridge
Folinsbee Joan B........................ Cook
Follen Mary Catherine...............Hawley
Follin Katherine C .... Maxwell
Folliss Ann V............................ Jeffery
Folsom Mary....................... Champe
Folts Jeanne E .... Leo
Folwell D Buvel ....Miller
Fontaine A Elizabeth ....Harrison
Foote Barbara........................... Fales
Foote Doris .... Jackson
Foote Helen M......................Knowlton
Foote Sarah P........................Hubby
Foraker Pauline S .... Marshall
Forani Ludmilla ....Rhein
Forbes Alexandra R .... Walker
Forbes Alice T .... Bowie
Forbes Brenda .... Shepard
Forbes C Hansell .... Ward
Forbes Cynthia .... Lyman
Forbes Daisy C .... Wanamaker
Forbes Diana............................Forbes
Forbes Diana S .... Olney
Forbes Dorothy M .... Thorne
Forbes Eleanor H .... Slater
Forbes Elizabeth D .... Morison
Forbes Felicity I......................Barber
Forbes Jill St C ....Willcox
Forbes Moira H....................Mumma
Forbes Pamela ....Forbes
Forbes Pauline .... Hutchinson
Forbes Phyllis .... Leland
Forbes Ruth .... Young
Forbes Shirley A .... Brock
Forbes Suzannah P .... Bigham
Forbes-Johnson Polly.................Storey
Forbush Sarah D .... Lee
Ford Cornelia D .... Sise
Ford Cynthia I........................Thomas
Ford Elizabeth F .... Wood
Ford Ellen .... Nichols
Ford Emily Van O ....Cox
Ford Faith........................... McLean
Ford Felia........................Le Boutillier
Ford Hilarie B .... Arguimbau
Ford Jean S .... Smith
Ford Jill B ....Murray
Ford Margaret T .... Francis
Ford Mara H..........................Ferriss
Ford Patricia .... Smith
Ford Rosemary.........................Gault
Forderer Elizabeth .... Charleston
Fordyce Katherine B...................Peake
Fordyce Susan G .... Dunaway
Forgan Florence J .... Wheeler
Forman Carol A .... Tabler
Forman Diana M.................... Colgate
Forman Lucile ....Scherbatow
Forman Mary B........................Guy
Forman Melissa K ....Bomeisler

Formanek Kamila M............. Remington
Forney Pauline P.................. O'Connell
Forney Priscilla J .... Gates
Forrest Alison T.....................Williams
Forrester Marion W .... Jarrett
Forrester Therese B .... Pindar
Forson Helen H............................Pratt
Forster Alice B ....Russell
Forster Julia A .... Thompson
Forster Phyllis ....McGusty
Forsyth Hope G .... Platt
Fort Chloe F............................Fort
Forte Emilie P................... Stephanoff
Fortenbaugh Jennifer .... Post
Fortner Nancy E ....Conrad
Foshay Barbara B .... Duke
Foshay Katharine F...................... Plum
Foshay Laura E...................... Conklin
Fosher Karen S .... Illoway
Foss Constance ....Anthony
Foss Dora S .... Mann
Foss Nancy............................ Heath
Foss Nannette B........................... Orr
Fosset Marie-France .... Schaefer
Foster Amanda B .... Washburn
Foster Carolyn V N .... Morris
Foster Eleanor .... Kinnaird
Foster Eleanor A .... Scully
Foster Elizabeth A .... Egerton
Foster Elizabeth B .... Schoyer
Foster Elizabeth V .... Blair
Foster Ellen A .... Stirling
Foster Frances H........................Foster
Foster Helen ....Morgan
Foster Jane A ....Lapham
Foster Jane A .... Rhein
Foster Jane de M ....Foster
Foster L Clare ....Marlowe
Foster Louisiana S .... Spurzem
Foster Lynne ....Warren
Foster M Virginia .... Belknap
Foster Mary R .... Kock
Foster Mary S .... York
Foster Maureen ....Lyons
Foster Melissa .... Fetter
Foster Nancy.........................Perkins
Foster Sarah H .... Soule
Foster Susan McC.................. Haigler
Fotouhi Rebecca J......................Bent
Fotterall Carolyn L .... Robinson
Fotterall Suzanne E .... Seeley
Fougoux Marie-Claire .... Ziegler
Fouke Claude V .... Benoist
Fouke Susan S .... Pettus
Foulis Sally L .... Davidson
Foulk Elizabeth C ....Kehoe
Foulk Mary Louise .... Clarke
Foulke Louisa Lawrence ....Newlin
Fowle Jane ....Hewes
Fowler Amanda S .... Stimson
Fowler Catherine Anne.............. Fowler
Fowler Cecily W.......................Grand
Fowler Charlotte M .... Bentley

Fowler Deborah J .... Rollins
Fowler Elaine F ....Pierce
Fowler Elizabeth M .... Azoy
Fowler Emily A .... Ennis
Fowler Mary D .... Kinney
Fowler Mary Louise ....Dunn
Fowler Nathalie .... Alberts
Fowler Robin .... Hemphill
Fowler Susan .... Boies
Fowlkes Jennie R.......................Hyatt
Fowlkes Lillian S......................Taylor
Fowlkes Lucy B ....Breed
Fowlkes Mary B ....Espy
Fox Alice V .... Campbell
Fox Ann S...........................Roome
Fox Anne W ....Cutler
Fox Cary R ....Fisher
Fox Diane B C .... Downs
Fox Dorothy C .... Osborne
Fox E Elizabeth .... Shonnard
Fox Elizabeth M .... Fox
Fox Emily R ....Conant
Fox Helen W .... Delafield
Fox Honor M .... Sage
Fox Hope Alden ....Coates
Fox Lydia K .... Humphreys
Fox Marianne C .... Barriger
Fox Marion R .... Henderson
Fox Mary A .... Baurmeister
Fox Mary K .... Cullumbine
Fox Maryan G...................... Chapin
Fox Patricia .... Haig
Fox Priscilla V .... Etherington
Fox Susan S .... Castellini
Foxen Ellen M .... Duke
Foy Cynthia C........................... Rupp
Foy Joan C .... French
Frackelton Mary L .... Vail
Frail Joan C .... Lonergan
Fraley Josephine .... Getze
Fraley Karen W .... Scott
Fraley Marie B .... Fairman
Frampton Bette .... Miller
France Catherine H.................. Harrison
France Pembroke T.....................Noble
Francese Vanda .... Baker
Franchot Christy L....................James
Franchot Constance L .... Tenney
Francine Emilie E....................Francine
Francine Phoebe M .... Wetzel
Francis Elizabeth D .... Thaw
Francis Mary ....Etzold
Francis Mary D......Plowden-Wardlaw
Francis Mary P.......................Brower
Francke Ada...........................Whitaker
Francke Nora F .... Cammann
Francklin Rose Xenia .... Thomson
Frank Adèle Van A.................. Walker
Frank Elizabeth L .... McGraw
Frank Gretchen R ....Carey
Frank Josephine E....................... Zelov
Franklin A Remsen ....Lyon
Franklin Barbara J .... Stevenson

Franklin Cassandra S ....Drake
Franklin Deborah S......................Light
Franklin Emily A .... Harmar
Franklin Emily S...................Fairchild
Franklin Jane.....................MacMillan
Franklin Jeanne K.....................Ferrer
Franklin Laura M........................Dunn
Franklin Nancy W .... Price
Franks Barbara S .... Yatsevitch
Franks Jacqueline L...........McGoodwin
Franks Margery W ....Hensel
Franz Mary L .... Knight
Franzen Elizabeth ....Lefkowitz
Fraser Ann ....Brewer
Fraser Bess A.............................Enloe
Fraser Caroline W....................Brower
Fraser Phyllis ....Wagner
Fraser Sarah ....Robbins
Fraser Susan L ....Bruner
Frasher Ann ....Hudson
Frazer Aeriel ....Eweson
Frazer Alice ....Pickhardt
Frazer Barbara R.....................Franks
Frazer Eliza H............................Hood
Frazer Frida .... Burling
Frazer Helen H ....Jeanes
Frazer Jean E .... Simmons
Frazier Elizabeth....................Peabody
Frazier Jean ....Evans
Frazier Joan ....Webb
Frazier Sandra L ....Connelly
Frech Carole D ....Crabbe
Frech Helen F ....Kippax
Frech Irma Claire....................St John
Frech Linda C H ....Taft
Frech Patricia P........................Young
Frederick Alexandra C M.......Frederick
Frederick Barbara L.................Forbes
Frederick Danah C.................Stimpson
Frederick Helen T.....................Gray
Frederick Joan M.....................Clancy
Frederick Julia A C ....Wagstaff
Frederick Mary P......................Smith
Frederick Nancy........................Sweet
Frederick Sarah A ....Frederick
Free Karen P........................Royce
Freedman Louise ....Eiseman
Freeland Nancy .... Richardson
Freeman Adair D ....Parr
Freeman Ailsa F ....Wistar
Freeman Ann M....................Schoder
Freeman Ann Rebecca.......McClenahan
Freeman Anne C.....................Clothier
Freeman Barbara L.................du Pont
Freeman Cameron M.................Napier
Freeman E Condict.....................Hyde
Freeman G Dabney......................Reed
Freeman H Sims....................Freeman
Freeman Helen B....................Weber
Freeman Joan ....Williams
Freeman Kristin J.....................Lowry
Freeman Margaret N..................Cabot
Freeman Marian L ....Niles

Freeman Marion F ....Ellis
Freeman Mary S ....Lyman
Freeman Mary Tyler.........McClenahan
Freeman Ruth W......................Swain
Freeman Sarah G ....McCord
Freeman Sarah H ....Roloson
Freeman Shirley A ... McCullough
Freeman Suzanne T ....Minturn
Freeman Tina L ....Woollam
Freeman Virginia Scott................Rowan
Freemon Lisa K......................Lowell
Freer Patricia M......................Cushing
Freiberg Susan L....................Coolidge
Freie Katharine J......................Gaillard
Frelinghuysen Adaline H
                                    Ogilvie-Laing
Frelinghuysen Barbara.................Israel
Frelinghuysen Beatrice S......van Roijen
Frelinghuysen Susan E ....van Roijen
Frelinghuysen Victoria ....Bates
Fremont Jean H........................Gillette
French A Anne G ....Thorington
French Barbara.......................Koehler
French Barbara R .... French
French Carey B......................Millard
French Chloe Tyler......... Winterbotham
French Christina C......................Porter
French Cynthia B....................Schoen
French Dana J ....Upson
French Elsie P...........................Hall
French Ethel .... Black
French Frederica P................McFerran
French Jane M ....Dill
French Janet ....Thomson
French Julianna....................Pinckney
French Lenore R ....Zug
French Louise R ....Blodget
French Marion ....Hammond
French Mary.....................Rockefeller
French Mary Louise ....Williams
French Mimi T....................Hartmeyer
French Patricia N......................Shaw
French Shirley A....................Baldwin
French Virginia M ....Pool
French Wendy......................Carver
Frenning Blanche ....Strater
Frenning Fabia ....Windle
Freudenberg Sigrid K ....Lott
Freund Nancy........................White
Frew Emily B ....Oliver
Frey Barbara R ....Graves
Frey Dorothy...................... Montague
Frey Elizabeth S ....Clark
Frey Gay B ....Tomlinson
Frey Suzanne ....Luetkemeyer
Freyhof Betty K .... Johnson
Freytag Joanne ....Bradley
Friberg Sonja E......................Whitney
Frick Martha H ....Symington
Frick Olivia E ....Robinson
Frick Ruth S...........................Cox
Friedmann Mary F.................Townsend
Friedrichs Virginia G.................Burke

Friend Catherine H ....Ireland
Friend Lillian McC....................Bassett
Frieze Charlotte M......................Jones
Frieze Pamela J ....Cobb
Frigo Carol S ....Morgan
Frisby Maree L ....Rambo
Fritchman Anne H ....Hamilton
Fritschi Jill ....Reese
Fritts Anne L .... Stewart
Fritz E Leslie ....Moss
Fritz Margaret P.................Schneider
Fritz Nancy C ....Trevor
Fritze A Barbara ....Wulfing
Fritze Mary E.........................Pollard
Froeb Constance Linington ....Fischer
Froehlich Inge C ....Valentine
Froehlich Mary L ....Meyer
Froelicher Madeleine ....Stebbins
Frohan Nancy A ....Hinckley
Frohlich Ingrid L ....Burns
Frost Alice M........................Kennedy
Frost Alison J ....Gildred
Frost Carolann ....Marshall
Frost Elizabeth P.....................Davidson
Frost Helen H ....Hale
Frost Judith A ....Van Alen
Frost Laura G.......................Crabtree
Frost Margaret ....Rogers
Frost Martha L ....Keating
Frost Peri M...........................Clark
Frothingham Ann B ....Wait
Frothingham Elizabeth E .....Wadsworth
Frothingham Ellen ....Dunnell
Frothingham Mary E ....Jackson
Fry Evelyn C........................Peterson
Fry Julia N ....Landstreet
Fry Karel A ....Untermeyer
Fry Louise B ....Scudder
Fry Margaret S....................Letchworth
Fry Mary J ....Brodie
Fry MinnieBelle.....................Sellers
Frye Amy F.........................Thorndike
Fugazzi Jeanne...........................Bull
Fuguet L Gurney.....................Stokes
Fuguet Stephanie B.....................Arndt
Fuguet Suzanne W ...... Steigerwalt
Fuhrer Dorothy Jeanne ....White
Fulbright Elizabeth W ....Winnacker
Fulbright Roberta W ....Foote
Fulenwider Cynthia ....Denham
Fulenwider Katherine J..........Strickland
Fulle Mareon L ....Dunlap
Fuller Catherine ....Payne
Fuller Charlotte I ....Sinkler
Fuller Claire ....Emlen
Fuller Elizabeth Wiley.............Cooper
Fuller Emily R ....Kingston
Fuller Helen ....Miller
Fuller Jane ....Waters
Fuller Lisa A ....Taft
Fuller Marcia M......................French
Fuller Margarita ....Lillard
Fuller Marie L ....Timolat

Fuller Marilyn Anne ....Casey
Fuller Martha M.......................Clark
Fuller Marye Y ....Jones
Fuller Nancy L...........................Cone
Fuller Phoebe W ....Branson
Fuller Sandra L ....Randol
Fuller Virginia ....Fish
Fullerton Daphne M ....Churbuck
Fullerton Elizabeth..............Manchester
Fullerton Eloise R....................Hynson
Fullerton Mary W ....Fullerton
Fullerton Susan L ....Ware
Fulton Helene...........................Belz
Fulton Lauran A ....Corson
Fulton Leslie ....Flemer
Fulton Miriam ....Block
Fulton Nancy Bruce....................Storer
Fulweiler Lydia M ....Pyne
Fulweiler Marie-Louise ....Allen
Fulweiler Rebecca D ....Duschatko
Funk Sarah T ....Ringe
Funston Marguerite S ....Thatcher
Furlaud Eleanor J.....................Adam
Furlong Heather A ....Dunlap
Furlong Nancy W ....Salisbury
Furlong Silvina M.......Choumenkovitch
Furlow Susan ....Child
Furness Annis L......................Townsend
Furness Mary Radclyffe ....Savage
Furse Diana P ....Fiske
Furst Linda ....Mayne
Furstenberg Lucie A ....Huger
Fusz Anne ....Grace
Fusz Josephine D ....Connett
Fyke Helen E ....Montgomery
Gableman Joyce A ....Engs
Gaddis Elizabeth P ....Hitchcock
Gade R Allyne ....Barnes
Gaderick Joanne M..................Reynolds
Gadsby Virginia E ....Fuller
Gadsden Elizabeth P..............Woodward
Gaebelein Gretchen E..................Hull
Gaffney Amy E.......................Saunders
Gaffney Mary L......................Cullen
Gafford Peggy A ....Balliet
Gafke Joyce E...........................Noble
Gagarin Evgenia ....Pujol
Gage Heidi L..........................Jenkins
Gahan Ursula M ....Boyle
Gaidzik Beatrice ....Perry
Gailitis Anda ....Weyher
Gaillard Monica B ....Peck
Gaillard Virginia T ....Chew
Gaines Julia K.....................Claypoole
Gaines Katherine B................Bolman
Gaither Anne M ....Rivinus
Galbreath Mary A ....Jabaley
Gale Geri L ....Cavanagh
Gale Grace L...........................Paris
Gale Louise O ....Runnells
Gale Martha L..........................Lyle
Gales Helene S ....Hoge
Gales Holly C ....Holbrook

Galey Marion A .... Ingersoll
Galey Polly Lord .... Wilson
Galitzine Alexandra .... Armour
Gall Carolyn J .... Reisinger
Gallagher Anne R .... Putnam
Gallagher Jane N ....Hall
Gallagher Joan Killian ....Gallagher
Gallagher Marilee Lucas ....Gallagher
Gallagher Susan E .... Goodall
Gallardo Rosa S ....Cabot
Gallatin Edith P ....Egan
Gallatin Margaret H ....Cobb
Gallatin Mary B .... Stobaugh
Gallaudet Suzanne M .... Engel
Gallion Mallory ....Bear
Galloway Elizabeth G................. Smith
Galloway Jean E ....Crocker
Gallup Julia E .... Sadtler
Galpin Anne deW .... Zogbaum
Galpin Lucy K E .... Moorhead
Galston Virginia A .... Walsh
Galt Harriet T .... Robbins
Galuppo Fredericka A .... Mabon
Gamage Pamela ....Kent
Gamble Anne C ....Peterson
Gamble Eleanor R ....Funkhouser
Gamble French C......................Wallop
Gamble Joan M...........................Hering
Gamble Maria S.......................Lederer
Gammino Grace E .... Noyes
Gammon Rella M ....MacDougall
Gamwell Mary E .... Reed
Gamwell Sarah......................Cochrane
Ganelin Vera E ....Honey
Ganis Joan C............................Dollard
Ganne Joan E...........................Strader
Gannett Dorothy .... West
Gannett Mary.........................Crowell
Gannon Elizabeth M.................Gannon
Gannon M Cynthia .... MacLean
Ganson Georgia E.................Engelbert
Gant Elisabeth L ....Reich
Garbisch Gwynne C .... McDevitt
Garcés-Echavarria Maria E
....Campagna
Garcia Aura M........................Truslow
Garcia Elizabeth L....................Boyd
Gardella Joanne .... Gardiner
Gardiner Claire J G ....Burke
Gardiner Daphne W................. Trotter
Gardiner Elizabeth ....Thorndike
Gardiner Patricia T .... Hill
Gardiner R Caroline ....Russell
Gardiner Sally T ....Murray
Gardner Alexandra.........Papanicolaou
Gardner Cynthia.........................Willis
Gardner Elizabeth ....DuBarry
Gardner Elizabeth ....Norweb
Gardner H Penn ....Rand
Gardner J Blake ....Cook
Gardner Joan S ....Buchanan
Gardner Laura M .... Stoddart
Gardner Leslie O .... Hankey

Gardner Mary J .... Fenton
Gardner Mary L .... Pooley
Gardner Nancy E ....Galt
Gardner Phyllis .... Sunderland
Gardner Rebecca B .... Campbell
Gardner Rose P........................Cutler
Gardner Sarah P.................Cunningham
Gardner Susan D.....................Donovan
Gardner Suzanne G .... MacLear
Gardner Virginia D....................Wall
Gareschè Dorothy ....Holland
Gareschè E Lee ....Collins
Gareschè Elizabeth W ....Torno
Gareschè Inez H .... Bender
Gareschè Jane T....................McMullen
Gareschè Laura H ....Haffenreffer
Gareschè Mimika L ....Nusrala
Gareschè Virginia McB .... Ballantine
Gareschè Virginia McB .... Gareschè
Garfield Hester .... Schepens
Garfield Jane .... Cheever
Garfield Janet D........................Brown
Gargaro Mary D ....Pirrung
Garland Courtney...................Iglehart
Garmer Patricia E ....McComas
Garner A Laurie..........................Ford
Garnett Anne Wister.............. Boenning
Garnett Shirley..........................Hardin
Garnette Michelle ....Swetland
Garnsey Louisa B ....Lambert
Garrabrant E Elaine ....Stulb
Garretson Juliet........................Hollister
Garrett Elizabeth B .... Holt
Garrett Julia .... Fox
Garrett Juliet .... Munroe
Garrett Martha A .... Breed
Garrett Ruth B ....Preucel
Garrett Tamara K .... Black
Garrison Jean H .... Thompson
Garrison Lydia K ....Auchincloss
Garrison Margaret S ....Murphy
Garrison Patricia L ....Boorman
Garrison Vivian .... Arensberg
Garrity Eileen........................ Robinson
Garrity Sheila T .... Frantz
Garrott Cornelia ....Seat
Garside Helen ....Randolph
Garside Sheila A ....Jordan
Garth Elizabeth B .... Franke
Garth Florence .... Lamblé
Gartner M Wendy................. Rowland
Garver Allison ....Caesar
Garver Edith P ....Larkin
Garvie Margaret E .... Gleason
Garvin Frances C ....Britton
Garvin Gloria ....Christy
Garvin Linda P ....Austin
Garvy Elizabeth A ....Doyle
Garwood Andrea N................Littleton
Gary Helen ....Moran
Gary Laura B ....Butler
Gary Mary L ....Harrison
Gary Sandra G M .... Walsham

Gascoigne Nancy J .... Richards
Gaskell M Elaine ....de Spoelberch
Gaskill Evelyn W ....Howard
Gaspar Suzanne M .... Shrady
Gasque Ann F .... McKown
Gass Mary H......................... Robinson
Gaston Diana B........................Lindon
Gatch Caroline O'F ....Upthegrove
Gatch Katherine B ....Hellmuth
Gatch Katherine B .... Law
Gatch Katherine B ....Wheeler
Gatch Maury B ....Whitelaw
Gatch Sarah C ....Fehlig
Gates Elena A ....Motlow
Gates Ellen D......................D'Oench
Gates M Anne ....Ponce
Gates M Kathe ....Williamson
Gates Mary A ....Rainer
Gates Natalie P ....Morrison
Gates Patricia S........................Norris
Gates Sarah L ....Colley
Gates Susan H.........................Cooper
Gates Virginia ....Atterbury
Gates Virginia O......................Lewis
Gatewood Nancy W B............Warnock
Gatins Barbara H ....Simpson
Gatins Dorothy W .... Brewster
Gatterburg Elisabeth .... Palmer
Gaty Allene P ....Hatch
Gaunt Anne E ....Cassatt
Gavin Geales............................Sands
Gavin Kelly F ....Brooks
Gavin Marjorie A ....Lewis
Gaw Janet E ....Bailey
Gawthrop G Gail ....Lumpkin
Gay Colette D............................Irving
Gay Edith W ....Crozer
Gay Elizabeth A ....Doughdrill
Gay Elizabeth N ....Pierce
Gay Elizabeth S .... Pfisterer
Gay Gladys L......................Le Breton
Gay Louise B .... Tyler
Gay Lucia C ....Burks
Gay Nancy ....See
Gay Rebecca P....................... Mahoney
Gay Shirley H .... Cleveland
Gayer Kathleen ....Nichols
Gayley Mary B ....Gnichtel
Gaylord Helen I ....Townsend
Gaylord Mary E ....Stanley
Gear Jean G ....Lamont
Gearon Elizabeth C A ....Walser
Geary Charlotte......................Gilmore
Geary Daphne H ....Waggaman
Gebelein Louisa A....................Jones
Gebhardt Elisabeth R.................Turner
Gebhart Gail P ....Shelby
Gebhart Karen R.........................Flint
Geer M Amy...........................Stewart
Geer Margo K.........................Walker
Geer Marion F ....Wood
Geer Marrian L ....Johnson
Geer Rose O'N ....Thorne

Gehman Susan E...................McCawley
Gehres Leslie V ....Girard
Geiger Carol A ....Stewart
Geiger Eva A ....Sellers
Geisler Melissa F......................Trafton
Geissbühler Christine................Dupuy
Geissenhainer Lisa A..................Shaw
Geissinger Edythe M ....Storrow
Gelinas Margaret ....Dalva
Gemberling Grace T ....Keast
Gemberling Josephine ....Cochran
Gengler Marion ....Pearce
Genske Jane A .... Briggs
Gensler Frances E....................Morrisey
Gentile Debra L.........................Wood
Gentry Elizabeth F E ....Sayad
Gentry Patricia A ....Edington
Geoghegan Gertrude ....Chamberlain
Geoghegan Lucile ....Cheshire
Geoghegan Patricia A ....Munn
Georgantas Susan N ....Britton
George Elizabeth L.....................Baker
George Josephine S E........Worthington
George Judith A ....Williams
George Julie G ....Colt
George Linda G ....Test
Georgens Dorothy.......................Wyatt
Gere Grace B ....Eddison
Gerhard Anna R.........................Ames
Gerhard Charlotte.......................White
Gerlach Catherine ....Blair
Gerli Margaret A .... Whittelsey
Gerli Muriel ....Jenkins
Gerli Pauline ....Orr
Gerlinger Jean H ....Doyle
German Jane ....Irwin
Gerrish Anne M ....Law
Gerrity Margot M ....Finley
Gerrity Nancy S ....Achilles
Gerry Angelica L.................. Dearborn
Gerry E Bowen ....Bauer
Gerry G Sheldon ....Withers
Gerry Marjorie K ....Ryland
Gerry Nancy L ....Bedford
Gerry Phyllis A ....Williams
Gerst Jeanie P ....McAlpin
Gerstberger Hildegarde...............Baird
Gerstell Marguerite F ....Gerstell
Gerstenberg Mary P..................Hulitar
Gerster Alice F ....Breed
Gervais Marie-Claude.................Butler
Gest Emily L..............................Todd
Geyelin Antoinette R....................Hoar
Geyelin Cecily ....Clark
Geyelin Eleanor ....Casey

Geyelin Patricia A	Drexel
Gherardi Lilia R	Nash
Ghirardelli Polly	Lawrence
Giammattei Jane S	White
Giannini Anne M	McWilliams
Gianoulis Evangeline	Toms
Gibb Jean R	Lee
Gibb Martha C	Bayne
Gibb Mary V	Pascoe
Gibbon Marie E	Trimble
Gibbon Marjorie Y	Battles
Gibboney Constance F	Bailey
Gibbons Barbara W	Peabody
Gibbons Carolyn	Abernethy
Gibbons Christine E	Roberts
Gibbons Joanella R	Cannell
Gibbons Margaret	Fish
Gibbons-Neff Emily	Wargo
Gibbons-Neff Julie	Cox
Gibbons-Neff Sewall	Hornsey
Gibbs Christine C	Leness
Gibbs Colleen F	Howland
Gibbs Ellen B	Lewis
Gibbs Harriet C	Gardiner
Gibbs Jean S	Hare
Gibbs Margaret G	Moore
Gibbs Sarah S	McClure
Gibby Frances H	Roberts
Gibby Margery E	Paige
Gibney Mary B	Bodel
Gibson Alexandra McC	Moses
Gibson Bridgette S	Goodman
Gibson Deborah Wylie	Raab
Gibson Eleanor	Hollingsworth
Gibson Eleanor A	Hale
Gibson Elizabeth B	Ferry
Gibson Elizabeth J	Hoffman
Gibson Elizabeth McC	Du Bois
Gibson Frances H	Bayard
Gibson Frances H	Verkuil
Gibson Irene D	Darrell
Gibson Louisa B	Martineau
Gibson Lucy Ellen	Taylor
Gibson Marjorie L	Daniel
Gibson Mary P	McLean
Gibson Mary W	Wooten
Gibson Nancy M	Russell
Gibson R Fraser	Davis
Gibson Ruth	Morris
Gibson Ruth P	Shore
Gibson Virlinda McC	Walsh
Gicker Gloria A	Kendall
Giese Ann M	Porter
Giese Clara L	Cist
Giesler M Christine	Barth
Giesser Arlene	Inch
Giffuni Louise C	Tiernan
Gignoux Jeanne	Hatch
Gigstad Jordice H	Browning
Gilady Sally G	Chubb
Gilbert Adèle L	Painter
Gilbert Ann	Getty
Gilbert Ann C	Christ

Gilbert Cornelia D	Harris
Gilbert Cynthia	Allen
Gilbert Debora D	Ryan
Gilbert Edith I	Welch
Gilbert Elisabeth	Woods
Gilbert Elizabeth H	Blumeyer
Gilbert Emily T	Pribble
Gilbert Helen	Fowler
Gilbert Helen G	Williams
Gilbert Jane P	Womble
Gilbert Jarvis	Nichols
Gilbert Jean L	Walkup
Gilbert Jean N	Turner
Gilbert Joan	Starr
Gilbert Madeleine M	Geoghegan
Gilbert Mary F	Conner
Gilchrist Janet R	Dickey
Gilchrist Patsy	Howard
Gildersleeve Lucile C	Willoughby
Gilfillan Edna L	Bradley
Gilkey Ann S	Ware
Gill E Anne	Locke
Gill Juliet P	Davis
Gill Kathleen L	Miller
Gill Roberta A	de Kay
Gill Susan B	Dunn
Gillen Mary T	Crozer
Gillen Nancy A	Williams
Gilles Marji O	Morosi
Gillespie Alberta E M	Porter
Gillespie Eileen S S	Slocum
Gillespie Eleanor	Dyett
Gillespie Elizabeth P	Billings
Gillespie Emma	Miller
Gillespie Grace J	McClendon
Gillespie Jane F	Robbins
Gillespie Joan O'N	Swift
Gillespie Julia H	Sanders
Gillespie Mary A	West
Gillespie Mary S	Monroe
Gillespie R Patricia	Cook
Gillespie Sarah E	Fairbarns
Gillett Elizabeth W	Berry
Gillett Mary D	Rockefeller
Gillette B Deanne	Violich
Gillette Helen	Chapin
Gillette Paige R	Louthan
Gillette Tatiana	Infante
Gilliam Olivia L	Randolph
Gilliam Priscilla J	Moore
Gillies Jeannette W	Cross
Gillies Margaret M	Carlton
Gillig Carol	Coblentz
Gillig Gladys	Moore
Gillinder Emma	Masland
Gillis Carol R	Manning
Gillis Patricia	Sheppard
Gillis Sibley	Classen
Gillmore Frances H	Pratt
Gillmore Frances Sue W	Williams
Gillmore Lyn C	Cook
Gilman Alison	Howe
Gilman Andrea R	Marr

Gilman Anne McI	Pickard
Gilman Elizabeth Lisa	Wiles
Gilman Kathleen H	Hibbard
Gilman Susan	Hanson
Gilmer Belinda S	Bender
Gilmer Sarah	Worthington
Gilmor Elizabeth A	Conlin
Gilmor Elizabeth S	Wills
Gilmore C Tobey	Shaw
Gilmore Frances L	Scaife
Gilmore Grace E	Knoop
Gilmore Joan S	Patton
Gilmour Anne	Grant
Gilmour Jennifer B	Deleplanque
Gilmour Julie T	Bowen
Gilpin Jean R	Tremblay
Gilsey Mary H	Parmley
Giltinan Ethelind A	Eddy
Gimbel Robin S	Senior
Gimbernat Camilla M	Ridley
Gindhart Mary E	Hodge
Ginn Barbara	Reece
Ginn Marian R	Jones
Ginn Nancy S	Poole
Ginther Anne C	Keating
Giovíné Mary Jo	McKleroy
Girgus Signe L	Rhea
Girling Nancy J	Peterkin
Girvin Helen E	Bates
Gisel Barbara	Robinson
Givens Lillian M	Warren
Gladden Nancy D	Dorr
Glascock Mary Elizabeth	Wyrough
Glasgow Stefani	Santy
Glass Angeline J W	Coffin
Glass Jeanne H	Towles
Glass Katherine H	Parker
Glass Saragene	Boericke
Glauser Fritzi T	Story
Glavin Melissa	Huffman
Glazier Jane E	Board
Gleason Eleanor	Bleakie
Gleason Ellen R	Tilney
Gleason Persis E	Laverack
Gleaves Carolyn I	Lightfoot
Glendinning Ellen	Mikell
Glenn Hope I	Athearn
Glenn Sarah F	Meyer
Glenn Virginia W	Darlington
Gleske Nancy M	Helme
Glessner Ellen C	Wadsworth
Glidden A Verlinda	Marrack
Glogau July C	Drury
Glover Harriet I	York
Glover Jean M	Hodges
Glover Joan C	Weiler
Glover Nancy E	Symington
Glover Sara A	Tucker
Gnagy Polly	Seymour
Goadby Dorothy S	Womrath
Goddard Ann B	Corrigan
Goddard Anne H	Leschen
Goddard Carol J	De Chard

Goddard Jennifer	Goddard
Goddard M Frances	Tennant
Goddard Margaret G	Ittner
Goddard Margaret H	Leeson
Godfrey Ann F	Ogilvie
Godfrey Emily S	Bowring
Godfrey Marie Louise	Weicker
Godfrey Sandra R	Daly
Godfrey Sibyl V	Geiger
Godley Anne F	St Goar
Godley Elizabeth McM	Sargent
Godshalk Elizabeth L	Burger
Godwin Mae	Bancroft
Godwin Mildred M	MacLennan
Goebel Cornelia V R	Bronson
Goelet Beatrice	Manice
Goessling Lauren N	Selkirk
Goff E Ann	Alexander
Goff Tanya S	Richmond
Goffre Katy M	de Lyrot
Goggin Lilla D	Goggin
Golaszewski Joan M	Lenssen
Golberg Jane L	Blair
Gold Caroline H	Hart
Gold Katharine K	Sommerfield
Gold Marjorie T	Angelo
Golden Carolyn J	Bayne
Golden Charlotte	Todd
Golden Meredith M	Hiatt
Golden Virginia G	Steffens
Goldman Olexa Celine	Farrell
Goldsborough Eleanor L	May
Goldschmidt Catherine E	Willcox
Goldsmith Betty A	Forbes
Goldsmith Constance E	Addington
Goldsmith Jennifer L	Adams
Goldsmith Marion	Cholmeley-Jones
Goldsmith Nancy H	Coolidge
Goldwater Carolyn	Goldwater
Goltra Elizabeth	Winthrop
Goltra Katherine	Wood
Gonczo Judith C	Wilson
Gontier Eleanor	Major
Gonzalez Amalia	Buxton
Gooch Gay	Estes
Gooch Mary A	Armour
Gooch Sally	Paynter
Good Dixie J	Wigton
Good Margaret L	Kippax
Good Margaret S	Stockwell
Goodale Susan Cabot	Smith
Goodall Patricia	Mason
Goodall Virginia J	Johnson
Goodbody Helen H	Bancroft
Goode Catherine V	Link
Goodfellow Eleanor P	Ames
Goodfellow Emily C	Goodfellow
Goodhue Jill P	Hoeksma
Goodhue Margaret C	Whitman
Goodhue Phoebe T	Milliken
Goodin Joan E	Day
Gooding Marie C	Eaton
Goodlett Charlotte	Frey

Goodlett Virginia O'N..............Goodlett
Goodman Christine C..................Price
Goodman Elizabeth ....Aberg
Goodman Nancy L .... Brinker
Goodman Patricia A ....Ammons
Goodman Prudence A................Simson
Goodman Susan M ....Rossbach
Goodnow Lois T............................Jay
Goodrich Elsie Ives ....Bakewell
Goodrich M Priscilla .... Timpson
Goodrich Mary......................Johnson
Goodridge Paula F ....Armentrout
Goodwin Charlotte H .... Tieken
Goodwin Ellen T ....Schmitz
Goodwin Mathilde .... Bird
Goodwin Nancy ....Cobb
Goodwyn Lydia H ....Lorentzen
Goodyear Alison H....................Totten
Goodyear Bradley ....Smith
Goodyear Dorothy K ....Wyckoff
Goodyear Marjorie K ....Wilson
Goodyear Martha A ....Mason
Goodyear Mary C....................Dossett
Gopcevic Tania P ....Biddle
Gordan Lucy L ....Jeffers
Gordan Marjorie W ....Bowden
Gordan Susan F ....Knott
Gordon Agnes A..........................Stark
Gordon Alice B........................Abbett
Gordon Amelia C ....Ward
Gordon Bonnie G ....Flickinger
Gordon Caroline L................Rutherfurd
Gordon Iris Fitzhugh ....McClintock
Gordon Jessamine....................Warren
Gordon Katharine F ....Wilson
Gordon Kathleen A..................Putnam
Gordon Laurie W......................Carney
Gordon M Elizabeth B ....Kirk
Gordon Mary A ....Roberts
Gordon Mary S ....Kraft
Gordon Mary S ....Platt
Gordon Ruth H ....Noone
Gordon Sally W ....Roberts
Gordon Sandra S...................Starkey
Gordon Sarah S....................Edwards
Gordy Carolyn .... Swett
Gore D Anne......................Hostetler
Gores H Drewry ....Warrington
Gores Mary I...........................Peters
Gorham Ellen M ....Motter
Gorman Colleen E .... Will
Gorman Gwendolen N.................Bond
Gorman Joan M..................Carpenter
Gorman Kathleen S ....Colket
Gorman Leslie R......................DeRosa
Gorman Sallie O ....Smith
Gornto Catherine T ....Freeman
Gosiger Mary C ....Warrington
Goss Cassandra....................Simonds
Goss Diana ....Ward
Goss Garril C...........................Page
Goss Harriet W ....Madeira
Goss Tania ....Evans

Goss Wayne V ....Douglas
Gotcher Sara C .... Greer
Gotham Sandra ....Meehan
Gotthelf Florence M ....Axton
Goularte Theresa A..................Taylor
Gould Anna E ....Lenos
Gould Catharine McK ....Smith
Gould Edith K.........................Martin
Gould Elizabeth L..................Reeves
Gould Frances D .... Fox
Gould Harriet L ....Rogers
Gould Henrietta S .... Truitt
Gould Janet C ....Greene
Gould Mary P....................Ellicott
Gould May .... English
Gould Nancy H........................Ripley
Gould Sesaly ....Krafft
Gould Susan C ....McLean
Gould Winifred Dana ....Coddington
Goulian Elizabeth J...................Kahle
Gow Heather H ....Firestone
Gowen Cynthia H ....Crawford
Gowen Elizabeth C...............Kuensell
Gowen Lee C ....Marine
Gowen Sally M ....Francis
Gower Caroline C.....................Harris
Grabfield Audrey M ....Hicks
Grace Evelyn M ....Mehurin
Grace Geraldine C ....Benoist
Grace Jocelyn..........................Howe
Grace Karen A ....Smith
Grace Natalie R L............Brinckerhoff
Grace Patricia..........................Corey
Grace Roxie C ....Lancaster
Grace Susan B ....Glass
Grace Suzanne ....Pemberton
Grace Theresa ....Sears
Gracey Iris B..........................Todd
Graddy Cheryl A ....Miltenberger
Graeve Mary A ....Frantz
Graf Josephine H ....Thayer
Graf Myra Ann ....Pearson
Graff Kimberley W .... Johnson
Graff Sara M ....Cooke
Grafmueller Patricia R......Buddenhagen
Graham Antoinette....................Weiser
Graham Constance...................Bischof
Graham Edith S ....Blake
Graham Gail L ....Church
Graham Hilary L L...................Ponti
Graham Jennifer S ....Brunson
Graham Joyce A ....Bullen
Graham Karen C......................Harrison
Graham Kathleen M ....Hutchinson
Graham Linda A ....Fuller
Graham Margaret H...................Lord
Graham Marie-Louise B ...... Ingersoll
Graham Mary F ....Miles
Graham Moira O'C....................Ryan
Graham Molly..........................Bond
Graham Patricia ....Arrott
Graham Penelope....................Walker
Graham Valerie ....Schweppe

Graham Wendy E ....Mathews
Grahame Margaret E ....Haight
Gram Margaret..........................King
Gramberg Valerie J..............Middleton
Granbery Barbara K ....Hall
Granbery Elise B ....Becket
Granbery Joya Weld ....Hoyt
Granbery Pamela ....Granbery
Grand Minette D...................Krech
Grandis Susan B ....Brander
Granger Beverly J ....Kramer
Grannis Hilary E ....Grannis
Grannis Jane G ....Grannis
Grant Anne D .... Hollingsworth
Grant Anne D ....Metzger
Grant Anne L ....Thayer
Grant Carole F ....Clarkson
Grant Carolyn H ....Fay
Grant Constance M ....Meyers
Grant Elizabeth A ....Hand
Grant Elizabeth C ....Clark
Grant Elizabeth E ....Lasell
Grant Gail K ....Slingluff
Grant Lisa J ....Clough
Grant Lucille L...................Sellers
Grant Mary E ....Burrows
Grant Mary P ....Lynch
Grant Patricia ....Scull
Grant Patricia A ....Warner
Grant Suzanne P ....MacKenzie
Grantham Eve ....Kingsland
Grantham Sue McQ ....Chisholm
Grason Mary E ....Christmas
Grasselli Elaine ....Hadden
Grasselli Grace O ....Bowman
Grasselli Josephine E................Winter
Grassi Barbara A ....Preston
Grasty Susanne C ....Marty
Gratwick Lisa ....Nagel
Gratwick Martha ....Knapp
Gratz Colette A ....Wellington
Grau Alice L ....Smith
Grau Antoinette M.....................Sims
Grau Suzanna K.........................Haas
Grauer Frances ....Kirkpatrick
Grauer Phebe ....Appleton
Graupner Eleanor L ....Mosden
Gravatt Cary P ....Mason
Gravatt Elizabeth ....Ferrer
Gravel Marie T ....Dempsey
Graves Alice ....Dejonge
Graves Eugenia F ....Carter
Graves June H.......................Enos
Graves Lorraine ....Grace
Graves Martha L...........Mallinckrodt
Graves Mary ....Tilney
Gray Anne.............................Harrison
Gray Beatrice Milo ....Gray
Gray Daphne G .... Walsh
Gray Deborah C ....Wood
Gray Diana ....Bostwick
Gray Elise C ....Magnuson
Gray Elizabeth C ....Brokaw

Gray Elizabeth C ....Buck
Gray Elizabeth Noble ....Sackett
Gray Helen................................Rom
Gray Katharine N ....Currier
Gray Kathleen M ....MacArthur
Gray Linda L ....Fischer
Gray Lucinda H ....Carey
Gray Margaret........................Howell
Gray Margaret Anne ....Kincaid
Gray Margaret B ....Conklin
Gray Marian S ....Bruen
Gray Mary.............................Ehrhorn
Gray Pauline .... Briger
Gray Penelope....................Conderman
Gray Sara D ....Barroll
Gray Shawn L ....Butterworth
Gray Sheila A ....Jordan
Gray Virginia P....................Valentine
Graydon Lucy L ....Ratliff
Grayson Katherine M ....Wilkins
Grayson Louise B .... Truitt
Greabell Noelle L ....MacMahon
Greacen Edith L P ....Joy
Greaves Laurie G ....Landreth
Greaves Mary McG ....Hodge
Greeff Diana S ....MacVeagh
Greeff Evangeline C ....Michell
Greeff Stevens .... de Vargas Machuca
Green Anne M Hart ....Smithers
Green Arden..........................Moulton
Green Barton ....Gubelmann
Green Carol C ....Jellinghaus
Green Elisabeth F ....Blua
Green Ellen E ....Miller
Green Ethel B ....Banta
Green Evelyn M ....Haynes
Green Gertrude ....Hammond
Green Jacqueline E...................Harcum
Green Kathryn L ....Peabody
Green Maxine M ....Fox
Green Patricia C ....Prioleau
Green Patricia L'amoureux ....Taylor
Green R Lindsay ....Carroll
Green Sandra A H ....Blaine
Green Virginia I ....Legaré
Greenan Marjorie ....Marks
Greene Elizabeth S ....Herrick
Greene Helen W ....Perry
Greene June C..........................Wood
Greene Marilyn.........................Rork
Greene Tobey J ....Chappell
Greene Una C ....Kernan
Greenewalt Nancy C............. Frederick
Greenfield A Glyde.................Cooper
Greenfield Annette L ....Strauss
Greenfield Faith ....Lewis
Greenlee Isabel ....Farrar
Greenlee Susan B R..................White
Greenslade Rosemary P............. Belson
Greenwell Deirdre D ....Blain
Greenwood Josephine Q...........Killhour
Greer E Florianne ....Meldrum
Greer Elizabeth ....Edwards

Haigler Sara ....Babcock
Hailand Leslie M ....Newman
Haile A Frances ....Kelleher
Haile Mary E ....Noble
Haines Carlotta ....Talbot
Haines I Ann ....Braham
Haines Irene J ....Leet
Haines Janet ....McMeen
Haines Laura T ....Belman
Haines Lottie Lee ....Radsch
Haines Marian H......................Minton
Hajek Barbara W ....Ulman
Hajek Olga J ....Cassard
Hakes E Priscilla....................Williams
Halbach Mary E....................Kemmerer
Haldane Elisabeth P......................Pell
Halden Abbie D............................Fick
Hale Anna M ....Bowditch
Hale Barbara H ....Clark
Hale Barbara J ....Hawley
Hale E Patricia ....Swoyer
Hale Ellen ....Few
Hale Eunice ....Smith
Hale Helen E................................Mead
Hale Julie C ....Rhinelander
Hale Linda ....Bucklin
Hale Linda ....Makiver
Hale Mary S.............................Gillette
Hale Nancy P...............................Hoyt
Hale Ruth E...........................Buchanan
Hale Vianda P................................Hill
Hall Adele L ....Zachrisson
Hall Alice H.........................van Buren
Hall Alison S ....Watkins
Hall Anne L ....Flaccus
Hall Barbara..............................Banks
Hall Barbara K...........................Austin
Hall Beth W...............................Porter
Hall Carolyn..........................Wetherbee
Hall Carolyn A ....Eager
Hall Catherine S ....Jensen
Hall Colette J ....Walker
Hall Constance P M...................Safelle
Hall Deborah M ....Duffee
Hall Edith C............................Bancroft
Hall Edith C...............................Fisher
Hall Edith M............................Carlisle
Hall Eleanor C ....Painter
Hall Eleanor F........................Saunders
Hall Elizabeth F ....Talbot
Hall Elizabeth M..........................Hutz
Hall Elizabeth M.................McDonnell
Hall Elizabeth S ....Hidalgo
Hall Eloise Holly ....Hall
Hall Emlen F...............................Ehrlich
Hall Faith G...............................Harvie
Hall Frances L ....Atkinson
Hall Gail T ....Swearinger
Hall Georgine........................Du Vivier
Hall Helen I.................................Hoyt
Hall Jean H...............................Shoop
Hall Joan K...........................McEwen
Hall Joannah C ....Glass

Hall Julie C ....Livingston
Hall Lara M ....Oliphant
Hall Lilian C...............................Fisher
Hall Llewellyn P........................Alden
Hall Lloyd A.............................Brown
Hall Louise S ....Hall
Hall Mary A............................Howland
Hall Millicent E ....Gaudieri
Hall Nancy E ....Rutgers
Hall Noël....................................Train
Hall Pamela M ....Derringer
Hall Rosamond W ....Wright
Hall Ruth A. ....Smithers
Hall S Joy ....Cully
Hall Sadie R H..........................Howe
Hall Sarah E.............................Hansel
Hall Sarah L................................Wood
Hall Sharon G.........................Thébaud
Hall Susan H...........................Andrews
Hall Susanne S ....Alford
Hall Tamara L.............................Lloyd
Hall Vicki G ....Daughdrill
Hallanger Joan E...................Menocal
Hallberg Allene ....Dabney
Hallenborg Jane S........................Peters
Haller Gerda..............................Morris
Hallerman Judith A.......................Borie
Hallett Michele ....Wakeman
Hallock Avery K.....................Dickson
Hallock Helena P........................Pless
Hallock Mary P.........................Fields
Hallock Mary S.....................Edwards
Halloran Marita B...................Duryea
Halloran Valerie J...............Barneson
Hallowell Adèle L ....de Vries
Hallowell Beatrice W ....Edgar
Hallowell Bertinia......................Bailey
Hallowell Dorothy S..............Clapham
Hallowell Eleanor H...........Lippincott
Hallowell Ellen R ....Pratt
Hallowell Jean Hunter ....Draper
Hallowell Josselyn ....Bliss
Hallowell Nancy ....Apgar
Hallowell Patricia ....Stedman
Halpern Hilary ....Cecil
Halsey Alexandra S ....Urschel
Halsey Frances M ....Wickser
Halsey M Catesby ....Kilmer
Halsey Sarah E ....Hazard
Halstead M Ellen ....Wood
Halsted Joan ....Holmes
Halvorson Kathryn A ....Whiteley
Ham Catherine C ....Denckla
Hambrick C Jan ....Hodgson
Hamill Agnes B ....Ashbridge
Hamill Amelia R......................Hopkins
Hamill Jane M ....Sommer
Hamill Joan..............................Porter
Hamill Marjorie S ....Darrell
Hamilton Ann Hollister ....Moore
Hamilton Ann Louise H ....Brown
Hamilton Ann M.....................Bucknall
Hamilton Barbara.......................Almy

Hamilton Barbara Y ....Johnson
Hamilton Betty Mae ....Madden
Hamilton Christy ....McGraw
Hamilton Constance V ....Wallace
Hamilton Darsie..........................Gregg
Hamilton Elizabeth J ....Foy
Hamilton Elsie C ....Connors
Hamilton Jane D....................Warriner
Hamilton Jean ....Malone
Hamilton Jean McW................Pearman
Hamilton Josephine S ....Fischer
Hamilton June E ....Withington
Hamilton Katharine H ....Brinkley
Hamilton Katherine L...........Buchanan
Hamilton Kerri J ....Wetzel
Hamilton M Helen ....Bixby
Hamilton Margaret E...................Howe
Hamilton Margaret L...................Steers
Hamilton Maribeth R...................Moore
Hamilton Martha F ....Morris
Hamilton Mary Cloud........Hollingshead
Hamilton Mary P ....Sprague
Hamilton Nancy A ....Abbott
Hamilton Rachel M ....Chapman
Hamilton Stasia S ....Whiteman
Hamlen Catherine R ....Motley
Hamlin Dorothea ....Wells
Hamlin Elizabeth ....Chamberlain
Hamlin Katharine B..................Whittier
Hamm Alexandra H...................Pickett
Hamm Julie F ....Finley
Hamm Martha J ....Spencer
Hamm Nancy C ....Fournier
Hammer Judith A ....Hammer
Hammett Ann L ....Gant
Hammett Barbara D..................Bigelow
Hammett Carter...........................Irwin
Hammond Adèle S ....Emery
Hammond Allison L...............Murdoch
Hammond Ann P.........................Dure
Hammond Barbara S ....Schoenly
Hammond Dorothy S

Lawson-Johnston
Hammond Elizabeth ....Llewellyn
Hammond Grace P........................Boss
Hammond Kathleen J ....Thorne
Hammond Madeleine DeG Livingston
Alatas
Hammond Mary C ....Norton
Hammond Mary Stewart ....Allen
Hammond Rachel ....Breck
Hammond Susan L ....Van Wyck
Hammond Wendy.........................Evarts
Hampton Kim ....Gay
Hampton M Daniele ....Foote
Hamrick M Elaine ....Shields
Hamrick Pamela W....................Huber
Hanahan Frances G..................Middleton
Hanavan Virginia M...................Brown
Hanbury-Williams Elizabeth ......Husted
Hance Helen O ....Rathbun
Hanckel Judith ....Middleton
Hanckel Suzanne ....Ranlet

Hancock Ann .... Tucker
Hancock Edwina.............................Cox
Hancock Katharine L............Francis
Hancock Laura M ....Flint
Hancock Mary L.........................Rippel
Hancock Patricia C ....Miller
Hancock Ruth B ....Bromley
Hancock Suzanne F ....Ross
Hand Barbara G...........................Clow
Hand Margaret C ....Anderson
Hand Mary D............................Darrell
Hand Sarah H ....Pope
Handal Susan ....Warner
Handy Elizabeth P ....de Buys
Handy Evelyn B ....Hilgenberg
Handy Evelyne R ....Ryan
Handy Gwendolyn ....Willis
Handy H Bredt............................Reynolds
Handy Marjorie S ....Nichols
Handy Mary Ballou ....Ballentine
Haneman Elizabeth P ....Stinchcomb
Hanes Agnes ....McKnight
Hanes Elizabeth L...................Strubing
Hanewald Rae E ....Harsch
Haney Esther...............................Fleming
Hanford Helen C.......................Johnson
Hanger Elizabeth W ....Lippincott
Hankey Caroline C A ....Huntington
Hankey Patricia B ....Alsop
Hankey Stephanie Anne ....Griswold
Hanks Karen ....Bray
Hanley Allison C ....Frantz
Hanley Kathleen ....Keith
Hanlon Elizabeth A ....Seherr-Thoss
Hanlon Margaret J ....Clark
Hanly Dean ....Overall
Hanna Mary C ....Pulsifer
Hanna Rebecca S ....Spicer
Hannaford Caroline E.............Pillsbury
Hannaford Charlotte S ....Drake
Hannaford Tayloe ....Churchill
Hannah Katharine M ....Servick
Hannan Cherry...........................Johnson
Hannon Catherine M ....Auchincloss
Hannon Dorothy S ....Gardner
Hannon Mary Lou ....Ochsner
Hanrahan Julia S.....................Greenlee
Hansell Wayne.........................Steeper
Hansen Barbara J......................Magee
Hansen Carol R ....Gilmour
Hansen Gillette K ....Pool
Hansen Judith F ....Somers
Hansen Julia L ....Hilton
Hansen Kirsten M ....Gildersleeve
Hansen Kirsten N ....Lewis
Hansen Leanne.............................Taft
Hansen Mary J ....Clark
Hansen Patricia E ....Bridge
Hanson Barbara G.......................Pierce
Hanson Judith D.........................Hume
Hanson Laura J ....Carey
Hanson Nicola D ....Amey
Hanssen Jennifer B ....Peabody

Hanto Kari ....Hagar
Happer Lydia G ....Taylor
Harbage Diana E........................Baker
Harbaugh Elise...........................Mejia
Harcourt Holly A ....Riley
Harcourt Jennifer S ....Buchanan
Hard Florence ....Hughes
Hardcastle Ruth ....Barngrove
Hardee Pamela G.....................Jackson
Hardeman Betty K......................Haas
Harden E Sebelle .... von Hafften
Harden Mary L ....Littlefield
Hardenbergh Adelaide C ....Knight
Hardenbergh Caroline W ....Ohler
Hardenbergh Elizabeth K ....Dillon
Harder Deirdre B ....Laveran-Stiebar
Harder G Avery ....Kennedy
Hardie Marian E S ....Blackman
Hardigg Jeanet E........................Irwin
Hardin Carol D ....Henderson
Hardin Diana............................Walker
Hardin Dorothy D ....Dillon
Hardin Edith D ....Seymour
Harding Anita N ....Kistler
Harding D Ann ....Robinson
Harding Dorothy........................Callaway
Harding Eleanor........................Warner
Harding Joan............................Lewis
Harding Joan M ....Bartlett
Harding Margaret K ....Owen
Harding Marie..........................Harding
Harding May P ....Pierce
Harding Phoebe ....Davis
Harding Susan S ....Colby
Hardwich Frances J ....Jones
Hardwick Margaret S ....Treadway
Hardwick Maud ....Littleton
Hardy Isabella R ....Watts
Hardy Jean E.............................Little
Hardy Katharine M ....Erskine
Hardy Marjory L........................Train
Hare Harriett B ....Shanahan
Hare Katharine S ....Wear
Harfield Susan B ....Peck
Hargrave Judith L ....Coleman
Hargrave Noeline.......................Baruch
Hargroves Jeannette....................Taylor
Harken Anne L ....Hall
Harkins Nancy S ....Taylor
Harkins Rita M ....Dickinson
Harkness Cynthia K ....Hallahan
Harl Suzanne ....Stockmar
Harlan Anne B ....Edgar
Harlan Edith B ....Powell
Harloff Veda W ....Harloff
Harlow Mary C ....Lees
Harman Adéle ....Waggaman
Harmar Josephine N ....Wolbach
Harmon Denise H................Hinchman
Harmon Heather R ....Dane
Harmon Katherine ....Emmerich
Harmon Welthyan....................Brydon
Harms Marie J ....Simmons

Harnischfeger Elizabeth............Ogden
Harper Charlotte C ....Stone
Harper Felicity ....Letsou
Harper J Cody..................van Heerden
Harper Jane ....Kennedy
Harper Mary A ....Preston
Harrah Lorna C ....Bruen
Harrigan Elizabeth C ....Jenks
Harriman Ann L ....White
Harriman Joan B ....Dann
Harriman Kathleen L .... Mortimer
Harrington Adeline M ....Garvy
Harrington Elizabeth S ....Cole
Harrington Gwendolyn L ....Fisher
Harrington Mary B ....Harrington
Harrington Sophia W ....Bischof
Harrington Virginia K ....Minot
Harris Aileen H.........................Conkey
Harris Ann C ....Mohun
Harris Anna B .... Watts
Harris Anna S ....Heckscher
Harris Barbara.........................Pearson
Harris Barbara.........................Shreve
Harris Betty L.........................Barrow
Harris Carol U ....Bradley
Harris Dorothy J ....Osborn
Harris Edith T ....West
Harris Eleanor S ....Howard
Harris Elizabeth D ....Kennedy
Harris Elizabeth H ....Holmes
Harris Elizabeth M ....Coggill
Harris Evelyn G ....Van Ingen
Harris Florence D ....Koontz
Harris Frances B ....Streett
Harris Georgiana F ....Shober
Harris H Keyser ....Glancy
Harris Jill ....Luckie
Harris Jo Ann...........................Harris
Harris Joan ....Hawkey
Harris Joan G ....Wister
Harris Kathleen A T ....Stevens
Harris Lavinia S ....Pigford
Harris Linda ....Gibbons
Harris M Ellen ....Liggett
Harris Mabel H ....Vogel
Harris Marcia L .... Scott
Harris Margherita G ....Sinkler
Harris Martha M ....Fuhrmann
Harris Mary Ann ....Livens
Harris Mary G ....Knipe
Harris Mary M ....Waterbury
Harris Mildred H ....Williams
Harris Nancy U ....Biddle
Harris Natalie ....Neagle
Harris Pamela P ....Moore
Harris Patricia M ....Nevill
Harris Rosemary B ....Thomsen
Harris Sallyann M....................Thurber
Harris Sarah F..........................Burton
Harris Valeria M ....Symington
Harrison Ann ....Casto
Harrison Ann ....Offutt
Harrison Anne C .... Wallace

Harrison Anne S ....Forbes
Harrison Dorothea M............de Milhau
Harrison Dorothy ....Therman
Harrison Edna ....Murray
Harrison Elise L ....Lemmon
Harrison Elizabeth H ....Austin
Harrison Frances T ....Howland
Harrison G Floyd-Jones........Parkman
Harrison Henrietta A ....Marshall
Harrison Holly E ....Johnson
Harrison Jean R ....Hyland
Harrison Joanne H ....Stevenson
Harrison Josephine C ....Evarts
Harrison Josephine Lea ....Bolling
Harrison Juliet W ....Messimer
Harrison Lalla F........................Dodge
Harrison Louise H ....Bullitt
Harrison Lucy D ....Campbell
Harrison Mary A ....Lindsay
Harrison Mary Anne..................Wells
Harrison Mary M ....Wheeler
Harrison Mary S ....Lansing
Harrison Mildred C ....Dent
Harrison Patricia P....................Jacobs
Harrison Pauline L ....Winans
Harrison Penelope A ....Dixon
Harrison Phyllis D ....Dennis
Harrison Phyllis E ....Ballantine
Harrison R Lorraine ....Steele
Harrison Sally D ....Foster
Harrison Sarah M ....Price
Harrity Gail M ....Tilney
Harron Renée J ....Monell
Harrower H Struthers ....Gignoux
Harshbarger L Eugenie.............Lewis
Harshman Patricia.....................Clement
Hart Ann P ....Watson
Hart Cynthia A ....Baise
Hart Cynthia A B ....Villasenor
Hart Donna.............................Pollock
Hart Eileen ....Hinkson
Hart Eleanor ....Robbins
Hart Elizabeth L ....Poor
Hart Genevieve P................Pennington
Hart Martha A...........................Kent
Hart Nancy E ....Glanville
Hart Sarah P............................Hansen
Harte Helen ....Thompson
Harte Jane ....Choate
Hartenstein Helene H ....Hesser
Hartford Patricia ....Keesee
Hartiala Mimmu M A ....Sloan
Hartig Susan L ....Marovic
Hartley Barbara S ....Lord
Hartley Elizabeth Fletcher.........Hartley
Hartley Laurelle A ....Thom
Hartman Elisabeth W ....Cannell
Hartman Katharine L ....Macy
Hartman Martha J ....Anderson
Hartmann Elizabeth L................Rand
Hartmann Mary E ....Myer
Hartmeyer Gloria B ....Howard
Harts Deanne D ....Mallory

Hartsell F Madeline ...... Lamb
Hartsell Jean G ....McNulty
Hartshorne Emily B ....Gloeckner
Hartson Lise Anne ....Werlein
Hartwell Emily.........................Mueller
Hartwell Janet D ....Eyre
Harty Althea T.........................Corsini
Hartz Elizabeth ....Forster
Harvey A Charlotte...................Harvey
Harvey Adèle M A ....McKeever
Harvey Alice H .... Swett
Harvey Anne W .... Gerli
Harvey Dorothy ....Davis
Harvey Eleanor ....Egerton
Harvey Helen D ....Mills
Harvey Jean G ....Hooker
Harvey Judith...........................Steers
Harvey Lane ....Montgomery
Harvey Marian E ....Edelen
Harvey Marjorie M....................Swift
Harvey Stephanie C ....Lukacs
Harwood Ellen G............Bennet-Alder
Hasek Eliska........................Coolidge
Haselton Eleanor D...................Barrett
Hasen Louisa B ....Mattson
Haskell Anne T ....Ellis
Haskell Cynthia ....Tilney
Haskell Elizabeth D ....Fleitas
Haskell Hope............................Jones
Haskell Janet F ....Spalding
Haskell Julia K ....Paine
Haskell Margaret R......................Ross
Haskins Margaret E ....Beales
Haslam Deborah P..................Peniston
Hasler Audrey.........................Chesney
Hasler Constance ....Ames
Hasler Shirley ....Bird
Hastie Sara C .... Low
Hastings Ada E ....Duncan
Hastings Gail T....................Macdonald
Hastings Mary........................Bainbridge
Hastings Susan S ....Lohmann
Haswell Fredericka.................Hunter
Hatch Evelyn O ....Holmes
Hatch Georgia B ....Bemberg
Hatch Marjorie Jane ....Coverley
Hatch Nancy F ....Mortimer
Hately Eleanor M H ....Prugh
Hater Suzanne L ....Meyer
Hatfield Catherine L ....Shafer
Hatfield Gretchen G............Eggleston
Hatfield Helen ....Campbell
Hatfield Isabel McN ....Gaskill
Hatfield Ola M ....Blodgett
Hatfield Patricia ....Benedict
Hathaway B Sealy ....Hopkinson
Hathaway Gail A ....Herrlinger
Hathaway Mallory ....Hathaway
Hathaway Mary L ....Carver
Hathaway Rebecca P ....Lynch
Hattauer Elizabeth G ....Holden
Hattersley Julie ....Righter
Hatton Jean ....Fangboner

Haug Doris E ....Ogden
Hauprich Mary W ....Levering
Haussman Jane........................ Eckman
Haux Jane C........................Darovskikh
Havas Marion.......................... Webster
Havemeyer Adaline ....Rand
Havemeyer Carley ....Wagner
Havemeyer Linden..................... Wise
Havemeyer Priscilla...................Huston
Havemeyer Rosalind.............Roosevelt
Haven Jocelyn A........................Mickle
Havens Angela C .... Finch
Havens Ann ....McIlvain
Havens Suzanne C ....Jackson
Haverson Shelby L ....Fullerton
Havre Felecia ....Pierce
Hawes Harriet B .... Savage
Hawkes Jane Hawley.................Liddell
Hawkes Jean B ....Gray
Hawkey Sandra G......................Peck
Hawkings Parish H .... Hawkings
Hawkins Agnes E ....Potter
Hawkins Alice C .... Van Tuyl
Hawkins Elisabeth .... Hawkins
Hawkins Elizabeth ....Custer
Hawkins Helen B.....................Storrs
Hawkins Karen D ....Sharples
Hawkins Kyra .... Le Roy
Hawkins Lysbeth B ....Kent
Hawkins Trudy ....O'Reilly
Hawkins Virginia ....Andrews
Hawley Alethea S .... Elkins
Hawley Patricia A ....Riefler
Haworth Paula D .... Curran
Hawthorne Linda S ....Westfeldt
Hay Eleanor A ....Thomson
Hay Elinor R ....Martin
Hay Lisa Lowell ....Morrin
Hay Suzin V ....Rutter
Hayden Joan L ....Cadwalader
Hayden JoAnn P ....Rand
Haydock Ann ....Schwarz
Haydock Anne S ....Heald
Haydock Olivia L ....Kistner
Hayes Anna S ....Connard
Hayes Barbara J ....Henward
Hayes M Helen .... Attride
Hayes Margaret C....................Colwell
Hayes Marie Van V ....Davenport
Hayes Mary E .... Tucker
Hayes Mary S .... Stewart
Hayes Mildred B......................Cross
Hayes R Eaddy W ....Kiernan
Hayes Sally C .... Dorn
Hayman Gale ....Hoffman
Hayne Amanda C ....Kirkwood
Hayne Martha W ....Talbot
Hayne Susan W .... Read
Haynes Amanda.................Haynes-Dale
Haynes Fairlie G....................Rinehart
Haynes Frances G ....Hilgartner
Haynes Helen S ....Fries
Haynes Virginia E ....Montgomery

Hays Catharine H .... Curry
Hays Frances...............................Todd
Hays Gertrude H ....Arensberg
Hays Janet L ....Austin
Hays Laura P ....Barr
Hays Marjorie T ....McFarland
Hays Mary D ....Off
Hayward Amy B ....Sawers
Hayward Anna H ....Lisle
Hayward Barbara ....Carpenter
Hayward Christine ....Sherrill
Hayward Cynthia P.....................Allen
Hayward Nancy L ....Hayward
Hayward Sarah H .... Draper
Haywood-Reuben J Hope............. Paul
Hazan Elizabeth .... Hicks
Hazard Adeline ....Perkins
Hazeltine Susan L ....Connell
Hazen Mary E ....Van Lennep
Hazzard Julia P .... Merck
Hazzard Mary J ....Farrington
Hazzard Sarah E ....Slaymaker
Head Charlotte B .... Simmons
Head K Menelle........................Weiss
Headley Edna J ....Offield
Headley Frances L ....Hundt
Heald L Dabney......................Dupuy
Healey Elizabeth A..................Baldini
Healy Dorothy W ....Hupper
Healy Ellen P .... Cross
Healy Patricia M ....Howells
Healy Virginia M ....Studwell
Heard Alice ....Warden
Heard Elizabeth ....Farr
Heard Elizabeth C...................Donald
Heard Elizabeth G ....Gambee
Heard Elizabeth S ....Laffey
Heard Elsie............................McAdoo
Heard Frances ....Billups
Heard Helen H ....Hetherington
Heard Marileeds..................Chamberlain
Heare Helen G ....McKinley
Hearne Cynthia A .... Darling
Hearne Linda S ....Daniel
Hearst Deborah ....Gay
Hearst Lisa T ....Espy
Heath Cynthia .... Sunderland
Heath Jean............................Lytle
Heath Laura K ....Reboul
Heath Mary ....Keesling
Heath Susan H ....Everett
Heathcote Leaf V ....Yardley
Heatley Lori ....Draper
Heaton Elizabeth A ....Bicknell
Heaton Florence T .... Clementson
Heavey Rosemarie......................Daly
Hebard Helen E ....Lee
Hebard Margaret C P ....Lloyd
Hebbard Eve L ....Taylor
Heberton Frances S...................Hannafin
Hebrank Betty J ....Evans
Hecht Lynne P ....Farwell
Heck Margaret Elise .... Knight

Heck Martha C ....Ulman
Heckelmann Marlis..................Harris
Heckman Rebecca L....................Clark
Heckmann Janet M ....von Russow
Heckscher Angela................Lippincott
Heckscher Madeline .... de Lone
Heckscher Nancy A .... Price
Hedblom Carol W ....Currie
Hedén Monica E ....Fowler
Hedge Lucia R ....Woods
Hedger Katherine P ....Bicket
Hedges Ann E ....Kellett
Hedlund Gay M ....Carnahan
Hedrick Virginia ....Biddle
Heed Elizabeth ....McLane
Heenan Harriet A ....Witesman
Heenan Ingrid A ....Hammond
Heffelfinger Lucia B ....de Grazia
Hefferan Julia P ....Rollinson
Heffington Margaret R ....Vanneck
Heffron Cynthia S...................McAdoo
Hefford Sarah A ....Claytor
Hegamaster Tracy A .... Bieser
Hehr Elizabeth J ....Berg
Heilman Elizabeth A ....Brooke
Heinzerling Margaret A............Kelsey
Heiskell Grace N ....Terry
Heiss Mary E ....Boynton
Heist Susan B ....Plumer
Heizer Elizabeth L ....Palmer
Hekma Jacqueline B ....Stone
Heller Diana L ....Dalton
Heller Mary P ....Pool
Hellier Carlotta M..................Hartmann
Hellier Corinne .... Buck
Hellman Nancy ....Bechtle
Hellum Madeline H .... Hamersley
Hellyer Edith G.........................Felker
Hellyer Elizabeth C ....King
Hellyer Eloise Le G ....Hellyer
Hellyer Elsie M.........................Page
Hellyer Lynn ....Mathias
Helm Margaret S ....Bonney
Helme Suzanne J ....Bowden
Helmer Mary Jo ....Huber
Helms Carol H ....Lippincott
Helsing Donna J ....Henderson
Hemenway Phoebe S ....Armstrong
Hemenway Prudence ....Hodge
Hemingway Ann C ....Symington
Hemingway Madeleine C.............Ryan
Hemmerly Joan.......................Grove
Hempel Geraldine A ....Davis
Hemphill Anne P ....Hanna
Hemphill Anne T ....Fischer
Hemphill Hope C.......................Carter
Hemphill Nan.............................Cook
Hemphill Rebecca M ....Firth
Hempstead Katherine R............. Humm
Hempstone Eleanor Noyes ...... Bowman
Hemry Mary A ....Sheridan
Henchey Hope G ....Scully
Hencken Ala M O'N ....Reid

Hendee Mary L...........................Furrh
Henderlite Courtney.................Wenklar
Henderson Amanda J...............Cannell
Henderson Andrea .... Fahnestock
Henderson Anne V ....Bauer
Henderson Catherine E.............Berwind
Henderson Cecily.....................Pennoyer
Henderson Cynthia T E ....Mortimer
Henderson Elizabeth M ....Hoagland
Henderson Ethel M.....................Jones
Henderson Isabel van S ....Brooks
Henderson Jane F ....Maynard
Henderson Judith B ....Adda
Henderson Julie S ....Low
Henderson Martha T ....Coolidge
Henderson Mary E.......................Hale
Henderson Mary F ....Riggs
Henderson Natalie B........................Lee
Hendren Joyce H ....Rogers
Hendrick Alice L ....Hardigg
Hendricks Ann H ....Bass
Hendricks M Cantey ....Ferchill
Hendrickson A Jane.............. Reynolds
Hendrix Georgia ....Grey
Hendy Carole St C...............Schabacker
Henican Peggy .... Wilson
Henkel Eloise R........................ Gates
Henkle Margaret G ....Goddard
Hennecart Patricia....................Roberts
Hennessy Elizabeth A................Sawyer
Henney Kathleen ....Lacey
Henning Alison Morgan ....Stebbins
Henning Alyson B......................Walker
Henning Helene E........................Tilney
Henning Janet R ....Miller
Henning Martha J ....Cockcroft
Henning Mildred L ....Hellmuth
Henninger Jean ....Srodes
Henrichs Maud...........................Cabot
Henriques Christine Fuller ....Dodge
Henry A Christine............:......Hoffmann
Henry Alice J .... Barnes
Henry Annie M......................McLucas
Henry Caroline M....................Royster
Henry Christine .... Wainwright
Henry Denise ....Yassukovich
Henry Eleanor B ....Coates
Henry Hope P ....Hill
Henry Julia R B ....Armour
Henry Louise F ....Clark
Henry Louise L ....Kamihachi
Henry Margaret R ....Smith
Henry Mary.......................Hubbard
Henry Mary J ....Rubin
Henry Nancy C ....McKelvy
Henry Patricia M .... Fox
Henry Paula F P ....Straube
Henry Sarah S ....Lupfer
Henry Suzanne B ....Kraft
Henry Wendy C ....Lane
Hensel Hillary F ....Woodworth
Henshaw Hope ....Owen
Henshaw Mary-tom ....Leefeldt

Hudson M Kathleen....................Rivers
Hudson Margaret R ....Van Alstyne
Hudson Meriwether W ....Morris
Hudson Sarah G......................Krueger
Hudson Virginia.........................Hyde
Huebner Jean H ....Fetridge
Huey Sydney M.....................Lowndes
Huff Genevieve M....................Cook
Huffman Ada McI ....Hall
Huffman Brenda C ....Floyd
Huffman Jeannette L ....Clegg
Huffman Maria Ewing ....Huffman
Huffman Melissa H ....DeGraw
Huffman Nancy T ....Benedict
Hufstader Lucy B ....Sharp
Hufty Frances A ....Leidy
Hufty Page L...........................Hufty
Huger Caroline M......................Boone
Huggins Helen F....................Henshaw
Huggins Marguerite V ....Clayton
Huggler Shirley J...................Da Costa
Hughes Alexandra W ....Curran
Hughes Alexandria M...............Cannell
Hughes Carol T.....................Lindburg
Hughes Carolyn H ....Powelson
Hughes Charlotte E...............Bateman
Hughes Charlotte F................Combs
Hughes Eleanor......................Barber
Hughes Elizabeth A ....Baker
Hughes Elvira W ....Brigg
Hughes Enid C.......................Munroe
Hughes Helen.....................Campbell
Hughes Holly ....Griffin
Hughes Leslie W ....Pierpont
Hughes Marjory Bruce ....Johnson
Hughes Patricia.......................Clark
Hughes Veronica M................Salsbury
Hughson Ann ....de Bragança
Huhn Marcia ....Lane
Huick Katherine L ....Hubner
Huidekoper Ann du P ....Brown
Hulbert Catherine ....Harts
Hulbert Ethel P ....Renwick
Hulbert Helen.......................Bowring
Hulburd Marie L ....Dalton
Hulings Isabel S.......................Klots
Hull Catharine P ....Fleming
Hull Diane D.......................Hammond
Hull Dorcas F ....Hardin
Hull Dorothy B ....Osgood
Hull Elisabeth W ....Hume
Hull Eunice L ....Drewsen
Hull Gail F.............................Healy
Hull L Catherine A ....Wisner
Hull Lisa M...........................Weicker
Hull Meredyth M ....Smith
Hull Shirley T ....Huntington
Hulme Joan W ....Perera
Hulse Anna M.....................Charrington
Hulsey Mary Ellen.....................Brown
Hult Elinor ....Scott
Hults Anna P...........................Harmar
Humason Jean G.............McCullough

Humberstone Gayle A ....Swift
Hume Barbara F ....Bartlett
Hume Elizabeth R ....Hill
Hume Jean M...........................Hamill
Hume Jeanette T ....Sprague
Hume M Leah.........................Wilson
Humes Janice A ....Merrill
Humes Mary S ....Quillen
Hummel Ann E...........................Hoag
Hummel Dorothy M ....Leonard
Hummel Elizabeth ....Kinney
Hummel Margaret E ....Miller
Hummer Brooke ....Mower
Hummer Helen H ....Feid
Humphrey Diana E....................Halsey
Humphrey Florence P...............Gardner
Humphrey Laurie A...................Drake
Humphrey Pamela ....Duncan
Humphrey Pamela ....Firman
Humphrey Susan H.....................Keller
Humphreys Andrea B B .....La Cava
Humphreys Dorothea E............Thomas
Humphreys Frances G...........Roosevelt
Humphreys Hope T ....Trench
Humphreys Inness ....Humphreys
Humphreys Judith J ....Meagher
Humphreys Mary G................Williams
Humphreys Sandra...............Stemmler
Humpton Joan S ....Murdoch
Hundley Charlotte R ....Nelsen
Hundley Sara T ....Bartlett
Hundt Elizabeth S.................Moorhead
Hungerford Katharine C ......Hungerford
Hungerford Sally-Byrd.........Hungerford
Hunkin Patricia ....Lineberger
Hunner Katherine....................Lewis
Hunnewell Caroline A ....Blake
Hunnewell Gertrude.................Donald
Hunnewell Louisa B ....Clemm
Hunsicker Louisa W ....Pierson
Hunsicker Nina S ....Lockwood
Hunsiker Melissa L.................Driscoll
Hunsiker Minnette L............Cummings
Hunsiker Susan W ....Howard
Hunt Alice St J ....Sokoloff
Hunt Barbara H.....................Campbell
Hunt Cynthia A.........................Gray
Hunt Diana ....Edgerton
Hunt Diana...........................Thomas
Hunt Elizabeth ....Blanc
Hunt Jeanette ....Van Nice
Hunt Julia B ....Bogardus
Hunt Leslie K ....Palumbo
Hunt Mary L...........................Petty
Hunt Sara A ....Boenning
Hunt Tawni...........................Ferrarini
Hunter Adele.......................Hepburn
Hunter Barbara.......................Foster
Hunter Bonnie ....Hunter
Hunter Constance L.................Dupuy
Hunter Elisabeth O ....Brooks
Hunter Elizabeth ....Moore
Hunter Elizabeth ....Morrill

Hunter Elizabeth Bond ....Scott
Hunter Elizabeth D ....Lang
Hunter Elizabeth P S ....Lorenzen
Hunter Emmeline S ....Vander Zwaag
Hunter Florence ....Ault
Hunter Frances A.....................Fowler
Hunter Frances E ....Green
Hunter G Devereux ....Andrews
Hunter Lindley L ....Scarff
Hunter Lucy A S ....Washburne
Hunter Marguerita S ....Page
Hunter Mary Buff ....Penrose
Hunter Nan A ....Thompson
Hunter Nancy.........................Keefe
Hunter Patricia W ....Gregory
Hunter Rosalie C ....Thompson
Hunter Rosalie L.......................Ferry
Hunter Sarah E ....Abel
Hunter Susan W ....Purser
Hunter Virginia.......................Miller
Huntington Claire Swain ......McCloud
Huntington Clarinda B ....Pettengill
Huntington Claudia P ....Miller
Huntington Constance W ....Barrett
Huntington Edith C...............Williams
Huntington Elizabeth ....Dyer
Huntington Joanne ....Tunnell
Huntington Madeleine D ....Murdock
Huntington Sarah ....Fisher
Huntington Sarah P.................Fletcher
Huntington Susan B ....Fisher
Huntley Elodie B ....Smith
Huntley Janie S ....Webster
Huntoon Carolyn G ....Allen
Huntting H Louise ....Johnson
Huppman Mary L ....Nesbitt
Hurd Anne ....Samuel
Hurd Elise ....Switz
Hurd Victoria E ....Shurtleff
Hurd Victoria M ....Campbell
Hurlbut Elsa ....Cole
Hurlbut Patricia A...................Jenkins
Hurley Helen E ....Taylor
Hurley Jeannette ....Reuben
Hurley Margaret Lee ....Keating
Hurley Marilyn A ....Whiteman
Hurley Martha.......................Cravens
Hurley Patricia A ....Dillon
Hurlock Elizabeth C ....Augustus
Hurlock Helen L ....Schildhauer
Hurry Emily Clarkson ....Fuller
Hurst Adela B ....Van Metre
Hurst Eunice A ....Cooper
Hurst Frances L ....Ballman
Hurst Sallie G W ....Worthington
Hurt Beverly J........................Kaiser
Hurt Dorothy...........................Price
Hurt Gene D ....Torbert
Huse M Beverley ....Ryburn
Huser Eleanor L ....Kirk
Hussey Elizabeth H ....Burlingame
Hussey Faith ....Staub
Husson Joëlle M T N ....Jennison

Husted Priscilla A....................Griscom
Huston Caroline B ....Whitney
Huston Elinor A.......................Lashley
Huston Margaret E ....Coleman
Huston Marjorie C ....Shields
Huston Natalie W ....Wiles
Hutcheson Louise W ....Ainsworth
Hutchins Anne L.....................Rivinus
Hutchins Diana de B ....Angulo
Hutchins Ernestine H...............Evans
Hutchins Jania J ....Peter
Hutchins Margaret ....Ryerson
Hutchins Olivia Endicott ....Dunn
Hutchinson Anne ....Hutchinson
Hutchinson Audrey P S ....Swain
Hutchinson Christiana D ....Anderson
Hutchinson Diana D ....Sodi
Hutchinson Edith ....Page
Hutchinson Florence M ....Myers
Hutchinson Mary A ....Tucker
Hutchinson Nancy ....Johnson
Hutchison Betty Lloyd ....Boland
Hutnik Pauline C ....Pharr
Hutson Rosa T ....Blankin
Hutt Sally L ....Nelson
Hutton Carlotta P.......................Irving
Hutton Consuelo V ....Seherr-Thoss
Hutton Inez C ....Hutton
Hutton Joann L ....Borie
Hutton Marianne D......................Felch
Hutton Muriel V .....de Chabert-Ostland
Hutz Diane M ....Hoscheit
Huxley Angela M B ....Darwin
Huxley Frederica L..................Huxley
Hyatt Cynthia.........................Walker
Hyde Barbara I ....Ryerson
Hyde Denise.............................Wood
Hyde Elizabeth P ....Littlefield
Hyde Florence F ....Ayers
Hyde Hester ....Griffin
Hyde Jean R.........................Hitchcock
Hyde Lorna ....de Wangen
Hyde Loulie G ....Sutro
Hyde Mary P............................Millard
Hyde Natalie ....Sherman
Hyland Cassandra F.............Henderson
Hyland Elizabeth P ....Lee
Hyland Jill T ....Frankenhoff
Ibbitson Helen........................Jessup
Ibey Judith A ....Harjes
Ibrahim D Sophia ....Johnston
Ide Susan ....Symington
Igert Mary L ....Buell
Iglehart Elizabeth G..................Blair
Iglehart Jane M C ....Purinton
Iglehart Katharine C ....French
Igleheart Cary S ....Grady
Igoe Ann Bacot C ....McGehee
Igoe Eileen E ....Day
Ijams Allison D.......................Sargent
Ijams Margaret D..................Josephson
Ijams Rachel L......................Schmader
Ill Frances G ....Dalzell

Illoway Katherine ....Schoettle
Ilsley Ann B ....Johnson
Ilsley Elizabeth H ....Young
Ilsley J Lloyd ....Cutler
Indjayan Rosemarie ....Politzer
Ingalls Anne T ....Lawrence
Ingalls Elesabeth Ridgely ....Gillet
Ingalls Sandra S ....van Heerden
Ingalls Shirley ....Thackara
Ingersoll Anna W ....Roberts
Ingersoll Elizabeth V ....Bartow
Ingersoll Emily N ....Large
Ingersoll Gainor B ....Miller
Ingersoll Lauren R ....Murray
Ingersoll Sarah B ....Mestres
Ingham Lucile H ....Dickey
Ingham Phyllis ....Baker
Ingham Tyler ....Weld
Inglis Sheila E S ....Milliken
Ingraham Alice G ....Davies
Ingraham Alice W ....Loomis
Ingram Alice L ....Hooker
Ingram Barbara P ....Hart
Ingram E Virginia....................Dugaw
Ingram Hellen ....Plummer
Ingram Joan ....Thorndike
Ingram Mary F..........................Grant
Ingram Robin B ....Patton
Ingrum Ann B ....Fawcett
Inkley J Christian.....................Manuel
Innes Mary T ....Bowman
Innes Tracy E ....Stephenson
Iny Cecile................................Zilkha
Ireland Barbara A ....Wick
Ireland Louise ....Humphrey
Ireland Louise D ....Ireland
Ireland Nancy...........................Stahl
Irey Annabelle V ....Forrestel
Irons Louise D ....Jonas
Irvin Burdeene ....Worthington
Irving Alexandra D.............Fessenden
Irving Antoinette V du P ....Beck
Irving Beatrice ....Beals
Irving C Fay ....Squibb
Irving Evelyn du P ....Leonard
Irving Katherine D...................Baxter
Irving Tanya............................McCormick
Irwin Edith ....Blodgett
Irwin Joan ....Green
Irwin Keturah G........................Gray
Irwin Yukiko...........................Irwin
Isaacson Dodie M ....Londen
Isacks Lucile G ....Andrus
Iselin Audrey A ....Clark
Iselin Barbara..........................Sears
Iselin Emilie O'D ....Rollin
Iselin Joan L ....Hyde
Iselin Maud D ....Welles
Iselin Nancy............................Marburg
Iselin Suzanne.........................Walter
Iselin Urling S..........................Searle
Isenbruck Jacqueline H.........Ellinwood
Isham Eleanor D ....Dunne

Isham Janet M..............................Field
Isham Julia B ....Ward
Isham Katherine P ....White
Isham Pamela T ....Clute
Ituarte Maria Teresa Ortiz de Barron
Caldwell
Iturralde Edna Maria..................Kernan
Iungerich Nadia ....Williams
Iversen Lydia A ....Hutton-Miller
Iverson Alicia L ....Floyd
Ives Barbara C ....Riegel
Ives Cynthia L ....Cauffman
Ives Elizabeth H ....Clark
Ives Mary ....Greely
Ives Sarah..............................Howland
Ivey E Dorsey ....Seed
Ivins Elizabeth ....Haskins
Jabaley Mary-Powel ....Thomas
Jack Barbara J ....Pfingst
Jack Elizabeth M ....Ghriskey
Jack Jennifer J............................Blake
Jack Veronica J S ....von Grosse
Jackson Aileen C ....Hoguet
Jackson Caroline D..................Preston
Jackson Clara S...................McCracken
Jackson Constance C ....Darrell
Jackson Denise S ....Sutherland
Jackson Elinor S ....Lloyd
Jackson Elisabeth A..................Amory
Jackson Eliza G ....Ewing
Jackson Elizabeth.......................Buck
Jackson Ella S ....Nuckols
Jackson F Irene ....Rebmann
Jackson Frances M ....Adams
Jackson Hope ....Garvan
Jackson Irene W ....Wills
Jackson Jane E ....Breeden
Jackson Jaquith ....Rhodes
Jackson Jean T ....Scully
Jackson Jeannette L ....Bradford
Jackson Jennifer T ....Davies
Jackson Joan ....Forté
Jackson Julia A ....Young
Jackson Lou Ann ....Toland
Jackson Madeline.....................Emery
Jackson Margaret G ....Clowes
Jackson Marian Q ....Davidson
Jackson Martha S.....................Bucklin
Jackson Mary B ....Phillips
Jackson Mary Katherine ....Hays
Jackson Mary Rose Hamilton
Stevens
Jackson Melissa C ....Morgan
Jackson Miranda D....................Hook
Jackson P Gail ....Clark
Jackson Priscilla E ....Ruegg
Jackson Rebecca P ....Sargent
Jackson Rose D......................Milbank
Jackson Sara W ....Rasmussen
Jackson Sarah B ....Doyle
Jackson Sheila W ....Leach
Jackson Sibyl K ....Brown
Jackson Susan P........................Garrett

Jackson Susanne ....Miller
Jackson Suzanne ....Cartier
Jackson Suzanne B ....McDevitt
Jackson Virginia R ....Jackson
Jacobs Ann L ....Pakradooni
Jacobs Barbara.........................Baxter
Jacobs Charlton Y...................Phelps
Jacobs Jamee B ....Field
Jacobs Nancy P ....Haneman
Jacobs Phebe A ....Baum
Jacobs Vera J ....Speakes
Jacobsen Betty ....Guilfoil
Jacobson Carole ....Smith
Jacoby Joan ....Byrd
Jacoby Mary S ....Brown
Jaeckel Audrey.........................Lake
Jaeckel Dorothy ....Hamlin
Jaeger Natalie..........................Keys
Jaekle Angela M ....Rapalyea
Jaharis Kathryn M ....Ledes
James Alexandra L ....Gray
James Anne S ....Yellott
James Arabella A.....................Eldredge
James Arden K duB.....................White
James Beatrice H ....Teel
James C Elizabeth ....Claude
James Dorothea P ....Yoskin
James Eleanor G ....Perkins
James Elizabeth M.............Fulenwider
James Innes G........................Chanler
James Jennifer.........................McHugh
James Judith M ....Victor
James Katherine H......................Hall
James Kathryn ....Clark
James Mabel F ....Resor
James Margaret Alice ....James
James Monique ....Prince
James Sheilah L ....Doble
James Winifred A......................Dick
Jameson Jane ....Wheat
Jameson Jennifer J ....Snow
Jameson Lois ....Eliot
Jameson Margaret D..............Littlefield
Jamieson Anne L ....Flues
Jamison Constance A ....Pierce
Jamison Jeanne L......................Cahill
Jamison Sarah P........................Mohr
Janeway Ashley ....Warren
Janeway Augustine W ....Rhodes
Janien Linda L ....Hickox
Janis Susan L ....Tyler
Janney Barbara........................Trimble
Janney Sheila ....Williams
Janoska Joanna M ....Peterkin
Janowski Carole M D von T
Cushman
Jansing Caroline C ....Vohr
Janson Anne E ....Hasen
Janusz Judith A ....Fielding
Janvier Meredith T ....Labouisse
Janvrin Natalie ....Wiggins
Jaques Alice ....Roberts
Jaques Francine ....McCance

Jaques Lorna T...........................Lind
Jaramillo Delia...........................Scott
Jarratt Mary C M ....Groff
Jarrett Janet F...........................Pigott
Jarrett Laurie C ....Rogers
Jarvis Anne R ....Gerbner
Jarvis Virginia M.....................Whelan
Jay Augusta............................Huffman
Jay Sally..................................Steward
Jay Sarah L ....Hughes
Jay Susan M.............................Alsop
Jay Sybil K ....Waldron
Jayasuriya Anula K................Gilmour
Jayne Pamela S ....Miller
Jayne Sarah K ....Everdell
Jaynes Deborah N......................Weir
Jeanes Caroline ....Hollingsworth
Jeffcott Lucy B ....Pell
Jeffers Anne S ....Robinson
Jeffers Mary N ....Lovett
Jefferson Elizabeth...............Ackerman
Jefferson Joan K ....Reynolds
Jeffery Anne R.............Fremont-Smith
Jeffery Frances C ....Fahnestock
Jeffery Janet B ....Harris
Jefferys Adelaide McC..............Garrett
Jeffords Sarah D F ....Radcliffe
Jeffress Elise E H ....Ryan
Jehle Jane J ....Letchworth
Jelke Janet MacLeod ....Kenworthy
Jelke Victoria J ....Avery
Jellett Josephine Heron............Marston
Jemison Dorothy S ....Day
Jena Irène ....Kinnicutt
Jenkin Edith S ....Spink
Jenkins Ann ....Prouty
Jenkins Carolyn A ....Waterbury
Jenkins Dorothy C ....Pearre
Jenkins Jane ....Schmidlapp
Jenkins Jeanette A ....Vandeveer
Jenkins June A ....Hodges
Jenkins Louisa Bradbury ....Jenkins
Jenkins Madeline Denison.........Rohlfs
Jenkins Margaret.......................Loose
Jenkins Marguerite M.................Clark
Jenkins Nina M....................Bondurant
Jenkins Phyllis.........................Biddle
Jenkins Ruth A ....Ford
Jenkins Ruth I ....Rich
Jenks Margaret I ....Heckman
Jenks Priscilla ....Newhall
Jennewine Amy V ....Van Gulick
Jenney Betty..........................Richards
Jennings Candice L...............Benjamin
Jennings Constance M ....Bowen
Jennings Debra P ....Gillette
Jennings Elizabeth A................Howell
Jennings Iris W ....Vail
Jennings Laura H ....Ingraham
Jennings Margaret E ....Saunders
Jensen Alexandra ....Dame
Jensen Betty A ....Hall
Jensen Camille M ....Douglas

Kendall Helen L .... Kenney
Kendall Kim........................... Campbell
Kendall Mary L .... Robinson
Kendall Rebecca S................ Simmons
Kendall Rosa Lee .... Sinnott
Kendall Susan C .... Marsh
Kendig Agnes E........................... Rolin
Kendrick Barbara J .... Callander
Kendrick Christine M .... Mucklé
Kendrick Diana................ Untermeyer
Kendrick Margaret L .... Crawford
Kendrick Marie........................... Otto
Kenefick Angeline D .... Fryer
Kenefick Sallie G........................ Otto
Kenefick Sheila....................... Bertozzi
Kenly Miriam B........................ Earle
Kenna Nancy M......................... Ivison
Kennard Elizabeth D .... Neal
Kennard H Louise................ Broderick
Kennard Lucy K........................... Bell
Kennard Mary E G .... Perry
Kennedy Ann Carter............ Stonesifer
Kennedy Anne....................... O'Neil
Kennedy Anne F..................... Ehrbar
Kennedy Carmita.............. Schildhauer
Kennedy Caroline B .... Schlossberg
Kennedy Dolores M .... Barnes
Kennedy Donna L..................... Sones
Kennedy E Ann .... Brown
Kennedy Eleanore A............... Plunkett
Kennedy Elizabeth .... Funston
Kennedy Elizabeth L .... McFarland
Kennedy Eunice M .... Shriver
Kennedy Frances McC .... Heller
Kennedy Frances R.................... Graff
Kennedy Helen W .... Cahill
Kennedy Isabel A .... Butterfield
Kennedy Jane....................... Strange
Kennedy Jane McL.................. Doherty
Kennedy Jean C....................... Laney
Kennedy Jean I .... Innes
Kennedy Joan S........................ Ottman
Kennedy Karen E .... Esty
Kennedy Katherine C .... Williams
Kennedy Katherine L .... Barney
Kennedy Katherine W .... Williams
Kennedy Laura T................. de Blank
Kennedy M Locke P.................. Brown
Kennedy Margaret L................. Murray
Kennedy Mary S .... Adamson
Kennedy Moira .... O'Malley
Kennedy Moira B................... Holden
Kennedy Patricia............... Schmidlapp
Kennedy Patricia..................... Scott
Kennedy Patricia J .... Begley
Kennedy Sandra L....................... Pew
Kennedy Susan C .... Brooke
Kennelly Ellen L................... Kennelly
Kennerly Noël...................... Le Blanc
Kenney Nancy .... Thomas
Kenney Robyn Place .... Ross
Kenny Bonaventura .... Cooper
Kenny Helen......................... Flowers

Kent Eleanor .... Kent
Kent Elizabeth B...................... Reeve
Kent Elizabeth B................... Van Alen
Kent Joan A .... Dillon
Kent Katherine A .... De Buys
Kent Lilias M...................... Moseley
Kent Linda D .... Boothby
Kent Lucinda .... Maushardt
Kent Martha C .... Denniston
Kent Pamela A...................... Cornell
Kent Ruthann........................ Grace
Kent Suzanne A .... Hitchcock
Kenworthy Christine P .... Scarlett
Kenworthy H Lydia .... Clay
Kenworthy Sherryn E............. Stauffer
Keogh Katherine A.................. Gulden
Keon Susan T .... DeWyngaert
Kephart Susan H................... Simpson
Kepler Barbara A....................... Clare
Kepler Nancy L .... Hallowell
Keppel E Tracy .... Drury
Ker Susanna W .... Allen
Kerensky Diana....................... Hopper
Kermode Karen D.............. de Peyster
Kern Mary F M .... Brown
Kernan C Anita...................... Halton
Kernan Corinne A R............... Sévigny
Kernan Emily H................... Rafferty
Kernan Isabel .... Livermore
Kernan Mary...................... Butler
Kernan Mary S .... Rutherford
Kernan Rosemary D .... Hill
Kernan Sheilah E.................... Kernan
Kernott Catherine C .... Shields
Kerr Alice B .... Moorhead
Kerr Ann .... Franklin
Kerr Frances E .... Roesler
Kerr Ida M E .... Lofting
Kerr Jane L .... Prime
Kerr Margaret .... Goodyear
Kerr Margaret H .... Parker
Kerr R Keith .... Loud
Kerrigan Laura A.................... Appel
Kershaw Cicely L .... Rosenberry
Kerstein Barbara P.................. Biddle
Kerwin Elizabeth A .... Twede
Kerwin Margaret A.................. Crane
Kesmodel Karen A .... Brown
Ketcham Marsha .... Bozarth
Ketcham Janet .... Whitehouse
Ketchum Rebekah............... Richardson
Ketting Julie B .... Baker
Kettlety Janice A .... Macy
Key Ann T .... Lucas
Key Elizabeth D .... Reid
Key Marjorie .... Andrews
Keyes Elizabeth H .... Cook
Keyes Frances Parkinson............ Keidel
Keyes Janet B .... O'Connell
Keyes Margaretta M .... Orbegoso
Keys Florence Fatio................ Willard
Keys Karen L .... DuVal
Keys Laura E .... Dunlap

Keyser H Leigh........................ Phillips
Keyser Susanna H................... Borghese
Kidd Elizabeth LeD.................... Sachs
Kidd Jane de D...................... Eichorn
Kidder Anne......................... Beatty
Kiely Marie S..................... Snowden
Kiendl Helen V.................... Lindsay
Kier Frances M....................... Pellenc
Kiernan Anne M.................... Lewis
Kieser Ruth .... Austin
Kiesewetter Constance A .... Elliott
Kiessling Muriel Gurdon............ Cooper
Kilborne Belle S .... Taylor
Kilborne Elizabeth A .... Hudnut
Kilborne Nancy T .... Fox
Kilbourn Constance M .... Clarke
Kilbourn Helen A........................ Ball
Kilbourn Victoria T .... Munson
Kilbourne Rachael W .... Gould
Kilburn Katharine .... Bullard
Kilcullen M Elizabeth .... Lanier
Kildea Sarah E...................... Gentry
Kiley Jean .... Wells
Kilgen Marie M .... Drain
Kilgore Elizabeth L .... Tipler
Kilgore Nell .... Stires
Killery Marina E...................... Reese
Killgallon Katherine .... Michelsen
Killiam Mary Elizabeth .... Pilcher
Killion Sandra L .... Hamlin
Kilner Joan .... Hunt
Kilpatrick Alyce E............ Van Wagner
Kilroy Mari A .... Moorhead
Kilvert Madeleine A .... Butcher
Kim Hollis R........................ Bowles
Kim Mimi .... Plum
Kimball Carolyn C .... Tolles
Kimball Catherine A.............. Kimball
Kimball Cynthia.................... Hoagland
Kimball Cynthia F.................. Kimball
Kimball E Lee........................ Byron
Kimball Helen Chase............... Brooke
Kimball Maie B .... Schlafly
Kimball Mary Eliza .... Kimball
Kimball Nancy B .... Baumgarten
Kimbark Helen G .... Boocock
Kimberly Nina A .... Ives
Kimmel Dorothy K.................... Newlin
Kimmell Kathleen B .... Young
Kincaid Helen W .... Bryan
Kincaid Margaret .... Bird
Kincaid Nancy .... Breslin
Kinczel Ann S......................... Clapp
Kindleberger Elizabeth R .... Stone
Kindred Kathleen.................... Connor
King Anne C......................... Costin
King Ashley W .... Goddard
King Coralie S .... Key
King Cynthia B .... Vance
King D Barrington .... Fuchs
King Delphis B .... Leith
King Dorothy W .... Trimingham
King Elizabeth B .... Underhill

King Elizabeth D .... Rodiger
King Elizabeth M................... Elliman
King Emmie K........................ Stroh
King F Kathryn........................ Eddy
King Frances....................... Schafer
King Frances H .... Field
King Gertrude E .... Bédard
King Helene W .... Perot
King Jan A........................... Evans
King Katharine .... Johnson
King Katherine..................... Baccile
King Lee Ann S .... Eustis
King Margaret C..................... Moore
King Margaret Eakins............. Campbell
King Marian S .... Barbour
King Marie L .... Beale
King Mary..................... Frothingham
King Mary C .... Palmer
King Mary E .... Swayzee
King Mary J......................... Bullock
King Nancy K...................... Mettler
King Nancy P .... Putnam
King Noëlle W .... O'Connor
King Patricia G .... Kinkade
King Patricia J .... Cantlay
King Sarah .... Wilmer
King Sarah S .... Neumann
King Saranne .... Neumann
King Sharon L .... Wilcox
King Susan K....................... Stickney
King Susanne E .... Morrison
King Ursula G...................... Middleton
King Virginia F..................... Nicholson
Kingery Susan F .... Wise
Kingman Eugenia .... Palmer
Kingsbury Hope M .... Register
Kingsbury-Smith Eileen .... Pulling
Kingsford Frances H.................. Clark
Kingsland Marian C .... Frelinghuysen
Kingsland Mary E................ Kingsland
Kingsland Nancy B.................. Maebius
Kingsland Pauline T .... Dall
Kingsley Elizabeth C.............. Stanley
Kingsley Margaret M .... Torrey
Kinkade Patricia H .... Kinkade
Kinloch Julia P .... Hays
Kinnard Judith McD................. Cabot
Kinnear Polly .... Lincoln
Kinnear Susan E .... Ness
Kinney Anne .... Duffy
Kinney Carolyn S .... Wolcott
Kinney Donna E .... Speers
Kinney Frances M .... Tyson
Kinney Mary L....................... Porter
Kinney Sarah H .... Contomichalos
Kinnicutt Lois L .... Lockwood
Kinnicutt Pamela M................ Motley
Kinsella Judith R .... Clifford
Kinsella Mary L...................... Wees
Kinsella Patricia B .... Farrelly
Kinsman Alice .... Brodhead
Kinsolving Katharine C......... Baumann
Kinsolving Lucie Lee .... McElhiney

Law E Katherine	Walker
Law Janet K	Volkman
Law Joan	Gamble
Law Mary I	Titus
Lawler Ann C	Brockway
Lawler Ann R	Dewey
Lawler Margery E	Newbold
Lawler Martha E	Schiff
Lawless Suzanne	Johnson
Lawley Carolyn S	Bowman
Lawrance Emily	Frelinghuysen
Lawrance Margaret L	Frost
Lawrance Sandra D	Webel
Lawrence Andrea B	Dodds
Lawrence Barbara K	Lawrence
Lawrence Barbara W	Garside
Lawrence Caroline F	Whiteside
Lawrence Diantha	Nype
Lawrence Doris L	Roberts
Lawrence Helen G	Vander Horst
Lawrence Helen Lee	Pierce
Lawrence Janet	Adams
Lawrence Judith J	Carmany
Lawrence Linda O	Dwinell
Lawrence M Lee	Albright
Lawrence Marie D	Rollow
Lawrence Mary	Robertson
Lawrence May G	Strange
Lawrence Nancy B	Sargent
Lawrence Rosalind R	Hunnewell
Lawrence Rosemary McV	Seggerman
Lawrence Susan L	Winchester
Lawrence Susanna	Colloredo-Mansfeld
Lawrence Valerie F	Donham
Lawrence Virginia	Parker
Laws Stephanie A	Barrell
Lawson Caroline T	Lee
Lawson Elsie H	Fisher
Lawson Jeanne	Prince
Lawson Margaret de V	Steere
Lawson Patricia H	Warth
Lawson Virginia	Witten
Lawson-Johnston Denise	Fitch
Lawton Vanessa J	Peirce
Lay Susan	Atwell
Layman Sara E	Morris
Layne Rosemary	Khan
Layton Ann S	Scott
Layton Judy C	Duggar
Lazenby Catherine H	Davis
Lazo Constance L	Tysen
Lazo Meleanor	Deming
Lea Diana A	Walker
Lea Elizabeth G	Oliver
Lea Ellen C	Paine
Lea Ellen E	Disston
Lea Helen S	Humphrey
Lea Hilary M	Bernard
Lea Louise C	McGlinn
Lea Mary N	Page
Leach Mary V	Heppner
Leach Sanda C	Cooper
Leachman Florence	Wiedemann
Leahey D Elizabeth	Johnson
Leahy Anita J	Engs
Leahy Barbara	Regan
Leahy Donna L	Wick
Leahy Pamela M	Shands
Leahy Patricia A	Cahill
Leake Elizabeth H	Burden
Leake M Susanne	Stevens
Leake Nina M	Richardson
Leake Nora	Cameron
Lear Cynthia J	Stauffer
Learmont Diana C H	Mitchell
Learned Hope C	Colt
Leas Alice H	Wermuth
Leas D Scarlett	Robertson
Leas Katharine M	Dall
Leatherbury Lucille	Grant
Leavenworth Phyllis	Rianhard
Leavitt Martha E	Nelson
Leavitt Mavis J	Wylie
Leavitt Susan M	Walling
Le Blond Mildred L	Liggett
Le Boutillier Clelia	Zacharias
Le Boutillier Cornelia	Eyre
Le Boutillier Daisy	Bishop
Le Boutillier Elizabeth N	Barnett
Le Boutillier Gertrude	Wood
Le Boutillier Marjorie	McElroy
LeBreton G F Gay	Farwell
Le Clair Nicola L	Wickes
Leclerc Martha K	Wilking
LeCocq Lucille M	Robins
Lederman Erika Holly	Kremer
Ledes Sara J	Aiken
Ledford Margaret H	Hadden
Ledoux Jeanne-Nicole	Ledoux
Ledyard June M	Whiddon
Lee Agnes L	Ballenger
Lee Barbara J	Morrison
Lee Bertha B	Toole
Lee Charlotte F	Miller
Lee Christina S	Brown
Lee Cynthia	Dow
Lee Cynthia	Russell
Lee Deborah S	Symonds
Lee Dulcinea H	Green
Lee Eleanora O'D	Marshall
Lee Elizabeth	Cutler
Lee Esther S	Sallee
Lee Evalyn B	Bacon
Lee Felicia J	Istel
Lee Frances C	Pilling
Lee Hannah A T	Spradling
Lee Isabella M	Elsey
Lee Jacqueline	Lee
Lee Jane	Wolfe
Lee Janis L	Du Val
Lee Jennifer E	McDougal
Lee Joan F	Kremer
Lee Judith L	Flynn
Lee June	de Tristan
Lee Karen L	Spaulding
Lee Latané Lisle	Lee
Lee Laura W	Bullitt
Lee Lucy O	LaCasse
Lee M Nicole	Campbell
Lee Marie C	McAshan
Lee Martha S	Winfield
Lee Mary	Lambert
Lee Mary H	Horsey
Lee Mary W	Bowman
Lee Peggie Louise	Craig
Lee Ruth S	Smith
Leech Barbara E	Childs
Leech Barbara F	Jacquette
Leech Barbara S	Neilson
Leech Marjorie H	Woods
Leeds Gretchen A	Smith
Lees Aubrey	Lees
Lees Brenda A	Ott
Leetch Louise P	Speer
LeFeaver Daphne B	Ball
LeFevre Sarah M	Swain
Lefferts Elizabeth	Longcope
Lefferts Lysbet W	Bartlett
Le Fort Marie E	Cullen
Legato Marianne	Killian
Legendre Anne A	Armstrong
Legendre Bokara	Legendre
Legendre Janet N	McClelland
Legendre Landine S	Manigault
Legg Clara	Scherer
Legg F Barbara	Gardner
Legg M Elizabeth	Dinsmore
Leggett Betty L	Patterson
Leggett Nancy H	Pitarys
Le Grand Joan G	Nash
Lehideux Hélène	David-Weill
Lehto Marja-Liisa	Tuckerman
Leib Marian B	Adams
Leichtle Adrienne d'A	Maxwell
Leidy Phyllis R	Palsgrove
Leigh Carolyn S	Patterson
Leigh Jane R	Bodell
Leighton Constance E	Marshall
Leighton Janet G	Maechling
Leighton Jeanne F	Hackman
Leighton Lisa G	Whittall
Leighton Nancy E	Calfee
Leighton Patricia	Mann
Leinbach Anna B	Washburn
Leininger Marguerite	Augustine
Leiper Mary F	Denckla
Leisenring Carolyn B	Wheeler
Leisenring Erica B	Sears
Leisk Elizabeth D	Mills
Leiter M Victoria	Mele
Leitzow Nancy A	Brown
Le Jacq Sarah T	Howell
LeJeune Ann	Schneider
Leland Betsy	Link
LeLand Daphne	Borden
Leland Jane	Pedley
Lell Millicent	Vetterlein
Lemann Nancy E	Clein
LeMay Patricia A	Burr
Lembcke Consuelo M	Peck
Lembo Mary E	Horne
Lemkuil Sharilyn L	Gallison
Lemmon Elizabeth Minor	Brinkley
Lenahan Grace E	Rich
Leness Christine R	Boudreau
Lenfest Marie	Schmitz
Lengfeld Frances H	Meyer
Lenher Ann	Robinson
Lenihan Mary J	Bacon
Lenkiewicz Isabel	Fowlkes
Lennard Ruth E	Walker
Lennig Louise G	Henry
Lennig Mary F	Perot
Lennig Millicent J	Snyder
Lennig Nancy W F	Bayard
Lennig Patricia F	Peterson
Lennon Lucy Thornton	Tucker
Lenssen Isabel B	Shinn
Lentz Barbara L	Lentz
Lenz C Joyce	Young
Lenz Nancy H	Townsend
Leonard Carole S	Parks
Leonard Elizabeth	Wicks
Leonard Elizabeth S	Goodale
Leonard I Jane	Swing
Leonard Jessie H	Hill
Leonard Jessie H	Reid
Leonard Jonna R	Chewning
Leonard Joyce K	Moss
Leonard Laura H	Ault
Leonard Lisa	Baldwin
Leonard Lynda K	Claytor
Leonard Margaret	Proctor
Leonard Margaret P	Brown
Leonard Mary P	Robinson
Leonard Sara	Taft
Leonard Stephanie	Mixter
Leovy Barbara C	Miller
Le Pere Frances B	Ball
Lerch Alberta L	Brooks
Lerner Julie B	Perry
Lerner Margaret A	Eyre
Leroux Antoinette J	Jewell
Le Roux Francine G	Haskell
Leroux Susan S	Butler
Leroy Chantal	Hodges
Le Roy Jane Gates	Greene
Le Roy Joan M	Clarkson
LeRoy Nina	Hunnewell
Le Sage Judith H	Grassi
Le Sage Nancy R	Hellmuth
Leslie Georgianna S	Middlebrook
Leslie Tucker C	Mitchell
Lesser Susan K	Kirkland
Lester Mary E	Donaldson
Lester Virginia B	Melvin
Letchworth Ann J	Huntington
Letchworth Caroline	Kimber
Letchworth Diane M	Burgess
Letchworth Nathalie	Smith
Lethbridge Ann	Platt

Locke Sarah A W ....Clark
Locke Susan H.........................Wilkey
Locke Susan P ....Walker
Locker Em Bowles ....Alsop
Lockett Kathryn L ....Hard
Lockhart Cynthia H ....Bolton
Locklin Susan V ....Grau
Lockman Mary E.................Denkinger
Lockton Judith H ....Jones
Lockwood Anne A ....Benjamin
Lockwood Dorothy ....Forbes
Lockwood Helen J ....Hewson
Lockwood Susan E...................Hansen
Loder Alexandra S ....Punnett
Lodge Emily S ....Pingeon
Loeb Virginia.............................Weil
Loeffler Carolyn H ....Coyle
Loew Deirdre G....................Guenther
Loew Jane C ....Sharples
Lofting Penelope A................Sheppard
Loftis Charlotte S ....Carmichael
Loftus-Tottenham Dinah T ... Tottenham
Logan Bailey..............................Meyer
Logan Carolyn G ....Rupp
Logan Henrietta B ....Kust
Logan Joanna G ....Register
Logan Josephine S ....Merrill
Logan Peggy M ....Howcott
Logan Sally ....Hunter
Logan Susie N ....Gribbel
Logan V Hollister ....Clark
Logan Virginia A ....Rockafellow
Logan-Jones Jacqueline ....McMahon
Logsdon Georgann.....................Mastin
Logue Margaret C ....Bunting
Lohman Marion C ....Schieffelin
Lohmann Ann N ....Mateer
Lohmeyer Madge B ....Stout
Lohmeyer Mary Anne P.............Cover
Lohrfink Maryanne ....White
Loines Margot..........................Wilkie
Loizeaux Juliette C ....Rose
Loker Ruth A ....Ingham
Lollar Jerauld............................Hill
Lomas Barbara ....Townshend
Lombana-Cadavid Lucia del C .....Abell
Lombard Cornelia McL................Cook
Lombard Rosamond.........Vondermuhll
Lombardi Gabriela A...................Doyle
London Barbara ....Lemann
Lonergan Helen ....Clark
Loney Susan A ....Oestreich
Long A Elizabeth ....Anderson
Long C Virginia...................Linthicum
Long Carol R ....Ogelsby
Long Constance M ....Spalding
Long Elizabeth J ....Burr
Long Karen ....Long
Long Linda C.............................Day
Long Margaret A ....Macauley
Long Mary ....Sutro
Long Mary B ....Pritchard
Long Ruth A ....Karpeles

Long Sara H...........................Buck
Long Susan T............. van Wagenberg
Long Suzanne H ....Rogers
Longcope Barbara ....Keyser
Longcope Mary L ....Johansen
Longley Nancy ....Agnew
Longnecker Jane L ....Thomas
Longnecker Jean H ....Grady
Longnecker Ruth B..............Pemberton
Longnon Annette L.....................Geddes
Longridge Katharine R ....Barnes
Longstreth Priscilla C ....Roche
Longville Elisa A ....Urquhart
Lonsdale Susan ....Iglehart
Look Barbara A ....Edgar
Loomis Dawn.........................Coleman
Loomis Elizabeth Jacqueline......Quillen
Loomis Lucy W ....Creighton
Loomis Mary K ....Straub
Loomis Nancy L ....Chance
Loomis Sarah W ....Campbell
Loomis Sarah W ....Grew
Loose Dean J ....Pendleton
Lord Anne K ....Andrews
Lord Barbara H.......................Edwards
Lord Barbara L ....Gow
Lord Carol V ....Means
Lord Elizabeth A .... Peyton
Lord Elizabeth C......................Gray
Lord Elizabeth W .... Bonsal
Lord Kathleen ....Wick
Lord Kathleen E ....McKnight
Lord Rebekah L ....Gardiner
Lord Susan E ....Peace
Lord Suzanne ....Folds
Lorenzen Lisbeth A ....Heisinger
Lorillard Edith P ....Cowley
Lorillard M Elizabeth ....Halsted
Lorimer Sarah L ....Morris
Loring Alice P ....Pickman
Loring Mary B ....Clapp
LoRusso Stephanie E...............Pearson
Losee Kendall L ....Graebner
Lothrop Jane T ....Gardiner
Lothrop Mary B ....Bundy
Lott Deborah M ....Davidge
Lottes Elizabeth M ....Barry
Loucks Karen B ....Klein
Loud Annabelle ....Redway
Loudon Constance ....Mellen
Louer La Verne ....Pruyn
Loughead M Margaret............Brenizer
Louis Michelle A ....Bauch
Loumaye Myriam Y ... van der Straeten
Lounder Gertrude E...................Haskins
Lounsbery Abigail ....Hemphill
Lounsbery Barbara....................Johnson
Love Anne T...........................Marso
Love Carolyn G ....Longmire
Love Eleanor J ....Love
Love Jane V ....McGraw
Love Margaret McC ....Stevens
Love Mary K ....Love

Love Mary Lee ....Trautman
Love Mary P ....Lehmann
Love Moss L.........................Compton
Love Suzanna P ....Love
Love Victoria A ....Greenlee
Lovegrove Marcia E...............Moseley
Lovejoy Barbara R ....Spring
Lovejoy Helen M .... Gardner
Lovejoy Janet P ....Lovejoy
Lovelace Laura S A ....Guernsey
Lovell Carol A ....Carmody
Lovell Caroline ....Johnson
Lovering Alis H ....Fern
Lovering Elsie B ....Cheston
Lovering Ruth ....Almy
Lovett Barbara ....Sheble
Lovett Eugenia ....West
Lovett Evelyn de H ....Shumlin
Lovett Julia E S ....Ashbey
Low Faith.............................Humann
Low Jonne E S C ....de Lara
Low Linda H.........................Wolcott
Low Lynda C ....Reynolds
Low Marli ....Hinckley
Low Sallie R ....Beckner
Low Suzanne M ....Clarke
Lowdon Patty K ....Mason
Lowe Caroline T.....................Brown
Lowe Jane ....Edgerton
Lowe Laura ....Harmon
Lowe Margaret P ....Etherington
Lowe Martha H ....Goodale
Lowe Susan B ....Kilbourne
Lowell Frances B ....Hunsaker
Lowell Mary E ....Wheeler
Lowery M Jean ....Wheelock
Lowery Margaret L .... Hart
Lowis Sonia ....Wilson
Lowrey H Virginia ....Brown
Lowrey Jill P............................Dowd
Lowrey Mary C ....Gregory
Lowrey Patricia R ....Hooper
Lowrie Ann W ....Arnold
Lowry Constance C ....Cartier
Lowry Harriet R ....King
Lowry I Eustis ....Cluett
Lowry Jacquelyn R ....Berkey
Lowry Linda ....Pearson
Lowry Marion H ....Pennell
Lowry Mary T ....Strawbridge
Lowry Ruth E ....Arnold
Lubecka M Dorota Drucka ....de Wolf
Lubini Silvana R A....................Safrin
Lucas Ann ....Garrett
Lucas Ann W ....Mesnard
Lucas Carol C ....Elsaesser
Lucas Elizabeth A....................Gilbert
Lucas Jane L ....Thornhill
Lucas Linda M.........................Steele
Lucas Margaret B ....Page
Lucas Peggy ....Plimpton
Lucas Priscilla G.....................Stevens
Lucas Roberta C ....Harris

Luce Caroline A ....Phillips
Luce Christena C ....McNicol
Luce Clare M ....Abbey
Luce Elisabeth M.......................Moore
Luce Elisabeth R........................Luce
Lucey Eileen M ....Hoffman
Luchsinger Polly R ....Clark
Lucius Anne T ....Davis
Luck Betty T...........................Fewell
Lucyk Mary Ann ....Millar
Ludes Eleanor M ....Rogers
Ludgate Verity M ....Ludgate-Fraser
Ludington Fytie ....Drayton
Ludington Mary F B ....Henningsen
Ludington Nancy ....Brash
Ludlow Louisa G ....Brooke
Ludzinski Elizabeth J ....Pilling
Lueders Phyllis C ....Taylor
Lukacs Annemarie G.............Cochrane
Luke Beverly June.................Dempsey
Luke Hope S ....Hetherington
Luke Jane T ....Murphy
Luke Jean A ....Wallace
Luke Joan B ....Hills
Luke Liane P E ....Welch
Luke Nancy K ....Griffen
Luke Priscilla K ....Vail
Luke Virginia.......................Hattersley
Lukens Ann E ....Chaffe
Lukens Anne B ....Edgar
Lukens Anne B ....Saunders
Lukens Eleanor L ....Blanchard
Lukens Elizabeth B.......................Day
Lukens Isabella R B ....Higginson
Lukens Lorraine D......................Minott
Lukens Margaret A...................Lukens
Lumaghi Katherine O'N............Clifford
Lumley Serena ....Wiley
Lummis Elizabeth M ....Orcutt
Lummus Mary W ....Douglas
Lund Carole E.........................Benning
Lund Erle T........................Lionberger
Lund Lydia M ....Kennard
Lund Sarah Brandon ....Donnem
Lundbeck Clare C ....Fraser
Lunde Karin S ....Thorndike
Lundeen Sarah J ....Leo
Lundgren Roberta L ....Mohlman
Lunding Virginia ....Coulter
Lundy Gabrielle ....Boucher
Lunny Liane......................Neuhauser
Lunsford Sara J ....Cantey
Lunt Hilary T ....Weed
Lupfer Mary Hope ....Brooks
Luppen Kate R..........................Rose
Lupton Sara E ....Jennings
Luquer Grace T.....................Madeira
Luscia Mary N ....Inches
Luther Brenda ....Slater
Luther Elizabeth A ....Weaver
Lutkins Wendy S ....Nagy
Luttrell Nancy L ....Orme
Lutz Adelaide L ....Ladd

Lutz Barbara Y ....Rinehart
Luxem Katherine G ....Countiss
Lwowski Ulrike H ....McConnell
Lyde Alexandra J....................Adriance
Lydon Alicia L ....Crawford
Lydon Dorothy H ....Bigelow
Lyeth Charlotte D .... Burton
Lyle Léontine.......................Harrower
Lyle Lucy N............................Tower
Lyman Anne ....Powers
Lyman Charlotte C ....Clark
Lyman Cynthia F ....Freeman
Lyman Dorothy M ....Hewitt
Lyman Edith F ....Kuhn
Lyman Edmona.......................Mansell
Lyman Eleanor Lee ....Dober
Lyman Eleanor M ....Hodges
Lyman Elizabeth A ....Potter
Lyman Elizabeth A ....Riegel
Lyman Géneviève B ..... di San Faustino
Lyman Margot A .... Sprague
Lyman Mary C ....Archer
Lyman Mary M ....Goodale
Lyman Ruth B ....Rigg
Lynah Louise ....Harrison
Lynch Ann F...........................Heuer
Lynch Caroline D .... Brackenridge
Lynch Helen B..........................Dickey
Lynch Helen G ....Warren
Lynch Louise T D ....Gaston
Lynch Madelaine L....Anagnostopoulos
Lynch Michelle G ....Lynch
Lynch Nancy H.........................Handy
Lynch Nancy V.......................Boericke
Lynch Rose P...........................Torrey
Lynch Shirley T ....Vagliano
Lynch Signa J ....Mills
Lynch Sylvia Leland...................Lynch
Lynch Vernon ....Merrill
Lynch Virginia D........................Dean
Lyne Frances C........................Heiner
Lyne Virginia B .... Sloan
Lyon A Elizabeth............Wertenbaker
Lyon Alice E.............................Lyon
Lyon Charlotte M ....Bradbury
Lyon Constance B ....Chatard
Lyon Dorothy E ....Bishop
Lyon Elizabeth F ....Jones
Lyon Fanny N........................Whitman
Lyon Helen G H ....Van Ness
Lyon Hilda L ....Austin
Lyon Laura A ....Slaymaker
Lyon Sarah S ....de Menocal
Lyon Susan P...........................Singer
Lyons Bonnie S ....Richards
Lyons Harriet B ....MacCracken
Lyons Julia M ....McCulloch
Lyons Kathryn M ....Youtsey
Lyons Virginia D..............de Neufville
Lyth Eunice C........................Davis
Lytle Rebecca B ....Everett
McAdams Barbara J....................Hoyt
McAdams Juliet G.....................Carey

McAdams Susan A .... Wagenlander
McAdoo Anne B.....................Mingoli
McAdoo Bettina C.................Pedersen
McAdoo Cynthia N .... Wheatland
McAdoo Dorothy B ....MacColl
McAdoo Jean M ....Miler
McAdoo Sally...........................Coy
McAfee Frederica .... Richardson
McAfee Mary Ann .... McAfee
McAlister M Cayce ....Joyce
McAllen Gordon......................Baker
McAllister Alice D ....Wright
McAllister Holly B .... Swett
McAloon Margaret H .... Wettlaufer
McAlpin Alice ....Cryan
McAlpin Esther M ....Brownell
McAlpin Lorna U ....Hauslohner
McAlvin Betsy C......................Farwell
McAndrews Adrienne A ......Schiffner
McAnulty Ruth E ....Moody
McArthur Lorraine..................... Love
McAshan Mary Celeste .... Scott
McAvity Nancy A .... Mackenzie
McBean Edith ....Newberry
McBride A Tudor ....Austin
McBride Anne W ....Simons
McBride Edith ....Bass
McBride Jeane ....Sterrett
McCabe Lee S ....de Rham
McCabe Mary Jane ....Belt
McCabe Susan S ....Gillotti
McCaffery Priscilla B ....Constable
McCaffrey Rosanne ....Mackie
McCagg Katharine H............. Robinson
McCagg Mary W ....Perkins
McCain J Alexandra ....Morgan
McCain Linda Jo ....Burrows
McCain Pamela M ....Miller
McCall Alison G ....McCall
McCall Jane M ....Barry
McCall Leslie A ....Shoemaker
McCall Margaret G....................Wasley
McCall Margaret V ....Engelhardt
McCall Melanie J .... Pyle
McCall Nancy E ....Watson
McCammon Susan..............Gubelmann
McCampbell Katherine..........Hardiman
McCance Ellen M ....Parker
McCance Suzanne V ....Huguely
McCandless Rosemary Van L
.....................................McCandless
McCann Carole R ....Williamson
McCann Margaret E .... Du Bois
McCann Mary E .... Karrick
McCarrens Constance...........McCarrens
McCarroll Charlotte J ....Vincent
McCarter Suzanne N ....Tifft
McCarthy Carol L.....................Duhme
McCarthy Frances E .... Rulon-Miller
McCarthy Francis M...............Hinckley
McCarthy Karen A ....Cady
McCarthy M Anne ....Jensen
McCarthy Sarah A ....Bryan

McCartin Ann ....Patterson
McCartney Jennifer S ....Rumbough
McCary Mary L .... Schlumberger
McCauley Ann H......................Trostle
McCauley J Virginia....................Byrne
McCauley Ruth ....Clyde
McCauley Sully R ....Bogardus
McCawley Eliza.........................Parkin
McCawley Heath B ....Porter
McCawley Margaret B ....Teillon
McCawley Mary Y ....Haskins
McCawley Sally..........................Fridy
McCeney Susan L ....Anderson
McChesney Kerry Ann ....Campbell
McChord Anne G ....Hutcheson
McChristian Anne.......................Blake
McChristie Elizabeth J ....Pettit
McChristie Helen L ....Hine
McClain Mary E ....Meehan
McClamroch Virginia...............Barber
McClary Susanna A ....Smith
McClellan Lucy A ....Barrett
McClellan Melanie L.............Hiemenz
McClellan Nancy A ....Sewall
McClellan Philippa H ....Bainbridge
McClelland Marion C ....Peters
McClelland Priscilla T ....Tate
McClenahan Alida B ....Geoffroy
McClenahan Ann B ....McClenahan
McClenahan Lorna ....Anderson
McClenahan Patricia L.............Neiley
McClenahan Sallie H..........Thompson
McClenahan Wynn E ....Burkett
McClendon Vicki A ....Schwab
McClintic Miranda P M ....Smith
McClintock Andrea E.............McClintock
McClintock Elizabeth S... McClintock
McClintock Lucy V ....Calhoun
McCloskey Helen ....Thompson
McClune Kathleen ....Senseman
McCluney Carolyn W ....Buford
McClung Judith P ....McClung
McClure Letitia D.....................Potter
McClure Margaret ....Platt
McClure Marilyn E....................Plumb
McClurg Barbara O ....Potter
McClurg Eleanor W ....Hunnewell
McColl Karen ....Barney
McCollum Hollis A ....Schenck
McComas Rhonda ....Jacob
McComb Averyl B ....Phipps
McConihe Alexandra D........Delapalme
McConkey Jean E ....Yeager
McConnell Anna Bliss ....Walz
McConnell Elizabeth H ....Eells
McConnell Kathleen M ....Anderson
McConnell Marion duP ....Lassen
McConnell Patrice C C ....Cromwell
McConnell Sally .... Marks
McCook Anne S ....Whelan
McCook Marie T ....Cooper
McCord Elizabeth ....Perry
McCorkle Mary J ....Rauscher

McCormac Lynn E .... Schuyler
McCormack Louise M..............Condie
McCormack Mary P ....Keasbey
McCormick Anna B ....Hallowell
McCormick Christina D ....Merrill
McCormick Debra M ....Ostheimer
McCormick Eleanor M ....Collier
McCormick Ella L ....Brittingham
McCormick Jacqueline ....Heyward
McCormick Jennifer S...............Hall
McCormick Joanne .... Reynolds
McCormick Judith T...............Taylor
McCormick Mary P S .... Hustead
McCormick Roxanna B ....Leighton
McCormick Ruth E.............Tankersley
McCormick-Goodhart Anstiss H
....Smithers
McCormick-Goodhart Henrietta V
....Burke
McCouch Ailsa A .... Thompson
McCoun Barbara R ....Bradley
McCoun Mary E ....Monroe
McCourt Marjorie F .... Clement
McCown Lindsay W.................DuBarry
McCoy Joyce S ....Hupper
McCoy Katharine R ....Bassett
McCoy Louisa S ....Brown
McCoy Lucy B ....Sayre
McCoy Margaret E ....Flickinger
McCoy Marlene M ....Alcott
McCoy Mary K........................Robertson
McCoy Rebecca D.......................Blind
McCrea Mary P ....Fant
McCready Theresa M ....Amos
McCreary Kate H ....Buffinton
McCreary Phoebe S .... Hemenway
McCreedy Dale ....Taylor
McCreery Isobel ....Taylor
McCreery Joan.......................Gerster
McCreery Renée ....Moore
McCrocklin Stacy C ....Wilson
McCrory Angela ....Kilroy
McCrum Bette ....Wilkinson
McCulloch Catherine C
.....................................Vaughan Williams
McCulloch Hope H....................Martin
McCulloch Jeanne R.............McCulloch
McCulloch Mary Sue .... Linden
McCullough Anna B.................Tippitt
McCullough Elizabeth ....Knowles
McCune Elizabeth C................Murphy
McCune Irene B ....Detweiler
McCune M Lynn ....Hagin
McCurdy Ellen S ....Burchenal
McCurdy Hope T ....Olmsted
McCurrach Jane C ....Talcott
McCusker Heather A ....Putnam
McCutcheon Anne ....Lewis
McDaniel Elizabeth C .... Sutherland
McDaniel Elizabeth W ....Moss
McDaniel Linda ....Darrow
McDaniel Marguerite H ....Wood
McDaniel Montine ....Freeman

McDaniel Nancy ....Miller
McDermott Caroline .... Kennedy
McDermott Catherine ....McLaury
McDevitt Margaret J................Biddle
McDill Helen M ....Walker
McDill Jane S ....Smith
McDill Laura ....McDill
McDonald Camille H ....Weiss
McDonald Helen J ....Exum
McDonald Irene C .... Kilborne
McDonald Julia F .... Stephens
McDonald M Cameron.............Vowell
McDonald Margaret B................ Priest
McDonald Marianne................Wellesley
McDonald Mary R..................Chandor
McDonald Nancy M .... McDonald
McDonald Pamela R.............Truesdale
McDonnell Barbara ....Blair
McDonnell M Claire ....Purnell
McDonnell Mary Kathryn
        Brackenridge
McDonnell Sheila ....Collins
McDougal Lucretia A .... Scudder
McDougal Madeleine Le M
        Leinberger
McDougal Sarah A ....Brooke
McDougall Jean ....Scott
McDougall Phyllis ....Woodward
McDougall Sarah A ....Saltus
McDowell Ann ....Tourison
McDowell Barbara....................Nelson
McDowell Barbara J...................Kyle
McDowell Margaret P ....Löfberg
McDuffie Edwina A .... Goodman
McEldowney Laura .... Bishop
McElroy Cornelia S..................Leach
McElroy Jean A .... Converse
McElroy Margaret C..............Arundel
McElroy Ruth B E.................Childress
McElvain Catherine F..............Harvey
McElwain Frances .... Wakeman
McEneaney Cornelia M
        Rulon-Miller
McEnerney Kathleen C .... Harper
McEnerney Martha ....Brigham
McEuen Andrea R ....Reid
McEwen Alexandra ....Casey
McFarlan Ethel L B ....Hamann
McFarland Margaret J ....Symington
McGan Tracey E .... Hamill
McGann Margaret...................McNally
McGary Mary ....Driscoll
McGaughy Frances N ....Edwards
McGee Elizabeth L.....................Wood
McGehee Laura H .... McCloy
McGeoch Joan ....Perry
McGhee Kasi ....Parsons
McGill Barbara J ....Childs
McGinley Elizabeth Bulkeley ....Borden
McGinness Margaret M.............Liggett
McGinnis Claire ....Stephenson
McGinty Tami .... Collier
McGlennon Caroline B...............Stride

McGlinchey Karen A .... Foss
McGlinn Ann C ....McGlinn
McGlinn Marion L .... Lockwood
McGlothlin Susan L ....Detchon
McGlynn Caroline M ....Killhour
McGoodwin Whitney L.............Fulmer
McGovern Elizabeth L ....Johnstone
McGovern Lynn A ....Moore
McGovern Mary L........................Ford
McGowan Mary V ....Davis
McGowin Katherine ....Mitchell
McGrail Augusta D ....Keevil
McGrail Mary M .... Capen
McGranaghan Marie ....Torrey
McGrath Anne D ....Lederer
McGrath Elizabeth C ....Brown
McGrath Kathleen M...............Nickel
McGrath Lisa N ....Evans
McGrath Mary C ....Thacher
McGrath Mary P ....Cabot
McGrath Patricia K....................Steers
McGrattan Sue B .... Williams
McGraw Barbara W ....Sweet
McGraw Jean N .... Brookfield
McGraw Kathryn .... Berry
McGraw Laura M .... Hutchinson
McGraw Marban E ....Sparkman
McGraw Mary L ....Piccoli
McGregor Carol E .... Grant
McGregor Jennie F ....Bernard
McGrew Jean ....Brown
McGuckin Mary-Jane ....Emmet
McGuinn Patricia M ....Ringe
McGuinness Louise H ....Ludlow
McGuinness Margaret A ....Denny
McGuire Catharine B ....Lombardo
McGuire Esther.............................. Hill
McGuire Mavis ....Bunker
McGuire Sara A ....Muspratt
McGuire Susanne T .... Curry
McGurrin Alexa M P.............McGurrin
McGusty Kathleen ....Agate
McHale Linda B .... Smith
McHugh Ernestine L ....McHugh
McHugh Karen L .... Vaughan
McHugh Kathryn C .... O'Brien
McHugh Patricia H...................Swift
McIlhattan Jo ....Ballengee
McIlhenny M Louise .... Roberts
McIlvain Alida B .... Haslett
McIlvain Beatrice G ....Harkins
McIlvain Emilie H ....Barber
McIlvain Isabel ....Shedd
McIlvain Janet L.........................O'Hara
McIlvain Mary L ....Begg
McIlvain Patricia ....St Georges
McIlvain Sandra H ....Slaymaker
McIlvaine Anne Wharton ...... Walmsley
McIlvaine H Heathcote..............Lamb
McIlvaine Joan H ....Schenkel
McIlvaine K Lee....................Churchman
McIlvaine Priscilla C ....Fleitas
McIlvaine Sarah Ellmaker .... Muench

McIlvaney Terry A .... Whittemore
McIlwain Elizabeth S ....Cummin
McInnes Susan ....Howard
McInnis Jennifer D ....Ehrhard
McInnis Margaret R ....Coudert
McIntire Catherine M ....Leslie
McIntire Holly .... Wright
McIntosh June.............................Maus
McIntosh Molly ....Nicoll
McIntyre Carol ....Mills
McIntyre Felicia D .... Johnson
McIntyre Juliana S C ....Sowles
McIntyre Lucille W .... Jewett
McIntyre Rita R
    Bourbon del Monte di San Faustino
McIver Anne S ....Dunn
McIver Nancy R ....Chaffe
McKaig Annah Colket ....Sellers
McKaig Muriel ....Miller
McKain Linda G ....Collins
McKay Amy ....Biddle
McKay Carla H ....Lucey
McKay Catherine P .... Shelton
McKay Cynthia B ....Meeker
McKay Frances .... Armstrong
McKay Joan ....Young
McKay Mary E ....Mitchell
McKay Sandra G .... Wilbanks
McKean Abigale H....................Peck
McKean Judith ....Parker
McKecknie Catherine B .... Sherman
McKee Catherine B ....Donovan
McKee Elizabeth B......................Lewis
McKee Frances Dunn ....O'Brien
McKee Lloyd ....Minton
McKee Margaret ....Breyer
McKee Mary M ....Maxwell
McKee Sallie E .... Warden
McKee Virginia .... Roberts
McKeen Martha .... Welch
McKeever Chauncie .... Rodzianko
McKeever Virginia F..................Warner
McKelvy Joan ....Taft
McKelvy Margaret.........................Bird
McKenna Heather Q..........Glendinning
McKennan Alexandrine................Rust
McKenzie Elizabeth F ....Bailey
McKeon Louise H ....Belt
McKeon Mary Ellen ....Harvey
McKeon Mary J.....Cosnard des Closets
McKeon Patricia ....Supper
McKernan Nancy A ....Lavin
McKey Mary F ....Hallowell
McKie Marjorie ....Neely
McKillip Rebecca .... Thornburgh
McKim Florence F ....Chase
McKinlay Judith L....................Prosser
McKinley Deborah F .... Bright
McKinley Ellen G....................McKinley
McKinley Kimberly D ....Potter
McKinney Cynthia D ....Drayton
McKinney Elizabeth S................Brien
McKinney Heather L...............Rodiger

McKinney Katherine .... Phillips
McKinney Louise B ....Warner
McKinney Lucy ....Parsons
McKinney Marion ....Ramstad
McKinney Mary L.......................Cope
McKinney Nancy M ....McNeil
McKinney Sarah ....Bastick
McKinnie Moira J.......................Hoyt
McKisick Evelyn ....Kleinsorge
McKissick Jacqueline ....Cowell
McKissock Barbara .... Schmidlapp
McKisson Camilla S ....Marvel
McKittrick Victoria ....Oliva
McKnew Patricia ....Nielsen
McKnew Susan ....Caskin
McKnight Alice G ....Mackroth
McKnight Ann .... de Rham
McKnight Edith ....Moore
McKown Martha F .... Spofford
McKoy Linda C .... Maruca
McLachlan Darlene ....Auerbach
McLain Mary C ....Smith
McLain Mary M ....Carter
McLanahan Louise S ....Noble
McLane Cornelia G ....Burchfield
McLane Elizabeth F ....McKinney
McLane Julia T.............................Hall
McLane Shirley J .... Putnam
McLaren Eluned A ....Demarest
McLaren Genevieve P
        Prideaux-Brune
McLaughlin Beverly E ....Nunan
McLaughlin Corinne A..............Mullins
McLaughlin Edith R ....Ouwerkerk
McLaughlin Hollis L ....Shank
McLaughlin Jane E.....................Foster
McLaughlin Janet ....Stockton
McLaughlin Kathleen ....Jeffords
McLaughlin Lys.............................Pike
McLaughlin Mary J ....Ely
McLaughlin Patricia M.............Jackson
McLean Arleen ....Hesse
McLean Clare ....Cross
McLean E Swan ....Grant
McLean Elizabeth I .... Reynolds
McLean H Brooke.............Katzenbach
McLean Jacqueline C L......... Severson
McLean Jean I .... Wallace
McLean Jenepher......................Kelly
McLean Katherine M ....Constable
McLean Leith..............................Adams
McLean Lisa ....Fellowes-Gordon
McLean Mary B ....Markle
McLean Phyllis P .... French
McLean Ray.............................Gordon
McLean Samantha ....Spruance
McLendon Melanie E .... Johnson
McLeod Margaret R ....von Werssowetz
McLeod Marian L.....................Lauck
McLeod Patricia L.................. de Witt
McLeod Sue H............................Carter
McLoughlin Cornelia Whitehouse
        Van Winkle

Macy Pamela J .... von Thelen
Maczko Marilyn J .... Bundy
Madara Ann H .... Kraftson
Madara Marion S .... MacNeish
Madarang Antonia .... Farrington
Madarkova Maria .... Morgan
Madden Christina L .... Whitman
Madden Lynne .... McDonough
Madden Mardie .... Gorman
Madden Myra .... Hughes
Madden Sally A .... Hayward
Maddock P Mimi .... McMakin
Maddox Evelyn H .... Pope
Maddux Jeanette .... Dunckel
Maddux Polly A .... Harlow
Madeira Alexandra C .... Harrison
Madeira Carolyn C .... Brauer
Madeira Elizabeth .... Loring
Madeira Leslie P ....Quist
Madeira Marion .... Gogolak
Madeira Mary V .... Madeira
Madeira Susanne C .... Coffin
Madigan Janet A .... Harrity
Madigan Patricia A .... Henshaw
Madison Elena A .... Walker
Maduro Glenna L .... de Rham
Maffitt Katherine C .... O'Connor
Maganini Margaretta Mason ...... Clulow
Magavern Jane C .... Beebe
Magavern Margaret E .... Hargraves
Magee Elizabeth S .... Ely
Magee Mary M .... Oshei
Magee Mollie .... Van Devender
Magee T Jane .... Murkland
Magi Kersti E .... Crawford
Magie Emily Elizabeth .... Coffin
Magie Margaret E .... Dunham
Maginnes Nancy .... Kissinger
Maginnis Ruth .... Blum
Maginnis Suzanne B .... Whann
Magner Katherine I .... James
Magnus Norma W .... Bartol
Magnuson Alicia R .... Hendrix
Magnuson Laura S .... Siemon
Magro Susan .... Pfeil
Magruder Anne M .... Cole
Magruder Catherine G .... Armour
Magruder Charlotte E .... Buttrick
Magruder Eleanor M .... Harris
Maguire Elizabeth J .... Maguire
Maguire Katherine H .... Oliphant
Maguire Mary Anne M .... Stetzer
Maguire Mary Helen .... Hildebrandt
Maguire Nancy .... Pyne
Maguire Patricia .... Semple
Mahaffey Adelaide .... Schlafly
Mahaffey Dorothy J .... Moore
Mahaffey Elizabeth C .... Mullins
Mahaffey Katherine McB ...... Walsh
Mahana Dorothy S .... Macauley
Mahany Ghia .... Papy
Maher Carolyn J .... Bell
Maher Janet .... Beech

Maher Katherine H .... Landreth
Mahler Margaret A .... Dean
Mahon Marinna .... Mahon
Mahone Mary A .... Grannis
Mahoney Ellen J .... McLanahan
Mahoney M Susan .... Lambert
Mahoney Mary Louise .... Cox
Mahoney Rebecca L .... Burnham
Mahony Katharine L .... Church
Mahony Mary M .... Brown
Mahony Moira .... Atterbury
Mailliard Kathleen .... Rende
Mailliard Nancy L .... Peck
Main Janette ....Hellmann
Mair Susan A .... Gray
Mairs Wendy W .... Cameron
Maitland Andrée B .... Dean
Maitland Helen V .... Corroon
Maitland Sylvia W .... Lynch
Major Teresa L .... Caldwell
Makepeace Katharine S .... Turner
Makepeace Lucetta D .... Larkin
Makino Kyoko .... Pendleton
Makins Carolyn Diana Mary ..... Morgan
Makrianes Mary G .... McLaughlin
Makrianes Susan .... Bacon
Malarkey Helen L .... Thompson
Malcomson Jean F ....Owen
Maldonado Violeta .... Putnam
Mali Carol J .... Du Bois
Mallam Mary E .... Armistead
Mallan Dorothy H .... Fullerton
Mallan Mary Stuart .... McInerney
Mallan Patricia A .... Penhallow
Mallett Stella .... Trafford
Malley Kathleen A .... Skinner
Mallinckrodt Catherine S .... Reese
Mallinger Joyce E .... King
Mallon M Elise .... Ford
Mallory Barbara S .... Hathaway
Mallory Diana W .... Hawes
Mallory Joan U .... Reeves
Mallory Veronica S .... Stubbs
Malloy Barbara C .... Glaze
Malm Billie J .... Stubbins
Malone Caroline W .... Pratt
Malone Mary T .... Tilney
Malone Ruth B .... Whitman
Malone Sharon M .... Wise
Maloney Bronwyn T .... Quillen
Maloney Gae E .... Brown
Maloney Joan .... Rodgers
Maloney Mary J .... Andrews
Maloney Virginia M .... Lawrence
Maloon Anne W .... Kingery
Malpass Rosina D .... Schwartz
Maltby Phoebe .... Dohrmann
Mamulski Mary L .... MacColl
Manchee Cynthia W .... Brown
Mander Fabienne H B .... Edmeades
Mander Melanie R .... Mander
Manegold Alice .... Osborne
Manewal Dorothy .... Stephens

Maney Kathryn C .... Cowles
Maney M Ruth .... Stout
Mangan Barbara A .... Pitocchelli
Mangan Joanna E .... Kennard
Mangan Nancy G .... Le Roy
Manganaro Ellen W .... Gray
Manganaro Nina V .... Watson
Manger Isabelle P .... Beuttell
Manger Lilian W .... Fleming
Manger Lillian J .... Barbey
Mangus Gladys A .... Cramer
Manheimer Blanche .... Vander Horst
Manice Amelia F .... Berkowitz
Manice Anne G .... La Haye Sousselin
Manimon Susan E .... Morgan
Manley H Langdon .... Mannion
Manly Georgiana W .... Abreu
Mann D Faye .... Marvin
Mann Earline .... Gould
Mann Elizabeth .... Miller
Mann Frances M .... Franns
Mann Isabel .... Lenssen
Mann Jennifer .... Landon
Mann Judith M .... Villard
Mann Judith S .... Chapman
Mann Marguerite .... Reed
Mann Mariana V .... de Saint Phalle
Mann Martha H .... Bethea
Mann Mary B .... Ernst
Mann Mary D .... Van Mourik
Mann Nancy .... Murray
Mann Suzanne .... Papin
Mann Violette R .... Koons
Mannal Janice H .... Mannal
Manning Elizabeth D .... Russell
Manning Ellen W .... Keefer
Manning Florence T H .... Manning
Manning Margery .... Cole
Manning Mary A .... Cleveland
Manning Susan L .... Kundtz
Mannion Mary E .... Stern
Manopoli Jane E .... Patterson
Manos Santhea .... Ogden
Manowitz Dale .... Coudert
Mansur Doris .... Ames
Manternach Josie C .... Manternach
Manthorpe Jennifer L .... Mackey
Manton Diana H .... Morton
Manuel Cornelia A .... Ford
Manuel Florence .... Colgate
Manville Ethel L .... Woolverton
Manville Maria-Helene .... de Laire
Manwaring Dorothy M .... Huber
Manzo Ellen M Ill
Mapes Kristie W .... Rutter
Mapes Priscilla H .... Maresi
Mara Theresa L .... Woolverton
Marbach Alice W .... Watson
Marble Mary Ellen .... Medearis
Marburg Christine .... Wolf
Marburg Mary Lynn H .... Brett
Marbury Anne J .... Wyatt-Brown
Marbury Lucy M .... Blundon

Marchant Jill E .... Gaston
Marchant Mary Ann .... Gilman
Marchet Elisabeth .... Nicodemus
Marcin Kristin L .... Conlan
Marckwald Isabelle K .... Bushnell
Marckwald Jean T .... Chapin
Marckwald Susan .... Mackay
Marconnet Andrée de L .... Clarke
Marcotte Joan E .... Fuller
Marculescu Karen .... Hammond
Marcus Gwen L .... Wright
Marcy Martha L .... Richards
Marden Mary T .... Dean
Marean Pauline P .... Evans
Maresca Mary Frances .... Blynn
Margey Sheila M .... Post
Marical Ingrid .... McCall
Marikle Helen C .... Passano
Markell Marion .... McAdoo
Markey Joan .... Steele
Markham Elizabeth A .... McLanahan
Markle Margaretta J .... Lovell
Markley Mary .... Marshall
Markoe Annette .... Schieffelin
Markoe Ritchie H .... Scribner
Markus Linda M .... Doyle
Marlas Jacqueline E .... Garrett
Marlatt Dorothy .... Vander Poel
Marlette Catherine B .... Waddell
Marlette Mary C .... Smith
Marlette Patricia S .... Nalle
Marlette Suzanne H .... Sears
Marley Rebecca B .... O'Rear
Marlinière Charlotte E .... Redhead
Marquez Anita R .... Fay
Marquissee Marjorie G .... Tilden
Marr Pamela B .... More
Marroquin Aida .... Gardner
Marrow Ann M .... McKinney
Marsden Lori J .... Tyson
Marseilles Marley .... Katzenbach
Marsh Adrienne A .... Marsh
Marsh Beatrice H .... Spencer
Marsh C Melissa .... Sands
Marsh Elizabeth C .... Saint
Marsh Genevieve W .... Fisher
Marsh Isabel S .... Mundy
Marsh Jeannette .... Larkin
Marsh Louise D .... Boesel
Marsh Mary .... Hill
Marshall Abigail S .... Zimmerman
Marshall Alice A .... Nichols
Marshall Anne .... Oliver
Marshall Anne E .... Henry
Marshall Carol .... Paumgarten
Marshall Deborah P .... Gates
Marshall Dorothy A .... Rhodes
Marshall Elizabeth LeB .... Games
Marshall Elizabeth R .... Snyder
Marshall Esther D .... Pappas
Marshall Florence B .... Mallory
Marshall Ida .... Kershaw
Marshall Jane I .... Fisher

Marshall Jessie A.................Williams
Marshall Joan N.........................Losee
Marshall Julia Bundy................Purnell
Marshall June.............................Smith
Marshall Katharine S.........Washburne
Marshall Margaret E..........Strawbridge
Marshall Marianna C.............Heyward
Marshall Marilyn...................Wharton
Marshall Marion D..................Hooper
Marshall Mary M.....................Bowen
Marshall Nancy.......................Forcier
Marshall Nancy E...................Pollard
Marshall Nancy G................Strebeigh
Marshall Nancy H.....................Athey
Marshall Patti L......................Collins
Marshall Pauline F.............San Román
Marshall Roberta R C...............Irving
Marshall S Olivia....................Nields
Marshall Sara A.....................Knight
Marshall Sophie S..............Nicholson
Marshall Susan....................Townsend
Marshall Trina C.....................Norton
Marshall Vardi H.....................Veeder
Marsigli Annalita.................Alexander
Marsters Deirdre S..................Watson
Marsters Katherine V...............Hurd
Marston Diana A...................Oliphant
Marston Dorothy........................Haas
Martel Lorinda B....................Proctor
Marth Virginia..................Wickersham
Marthinson Sherrard C...........Addison
Martin Agnes W.......................Booher
Martin Amy P..........................Chapin
Martin Ann E............................Calder
Martin Barry............................Osborn
Martin Caroline........................Larsen
Martin Carolyn L...................Corrigan
Martin Constance..................Goodyear
Martin Cynthia A.......................Meek
Martin Cynthia R....................Hellyer
Martin Deborah K...................Simons
Martin Doré M..........................Morse
Martin Dorothy B.....................Moore
Martin Eda A............................Joyce
Martin Edith C............................Cox
Martin Eleanor T..................Hoagland
Martin Elisabeth A...............Wheelock
Martin Elizabeth A..................Merrill
Martin Elvia...........................Penrose
Martin Fanny A....................Cracknell
Martin Fay M...........................Franck
Martin Frances H.............Bellingrath
Martin Frances L.....................Malone
Martin Harriet...........................Ruffin
Martin Harriet A..................Saunders
Martin Helen B.........................Bryan
Martin Hélène............................Lynn
Martin Isabel W........................Jones
Martin Jane L............................Pyne
Martin Jeanne F..........................Ross
Martin Joan K............................Tyner
Martin Kathleen C.........Goldsborough
Martin Laura A.......................Lambert

Martin Leanice.......................Devens
Martin M Sabina.....................Milbank
Martin Martha.......................Houston
Martin Martha E.......................Jones
Martin Mary F....................Craigmyle
Martin Mary Vincent................Martin
Martin Mayer W.......................Baker
Martin Meredith V..................Gardner
Martin Myra T.......................Mathers
Martin Patricia A...............Montgomery
Martin Patricia C...................Seidler
Martin Patricia L......................Frazer
Martin Rebecca D..................Connard
Martin Rebecca S.....................Evarts
Martin Roberta M.......................Odell
Martin Robin B..........................Weiss
Martin Sandra L........................Fisher
Martin Susan B....................Williams
Martin Sylvia V........................Talbot
Martin Vera B.......................Crawford
Martin Virginia V.............de Margitay
Martin Vivian........................Bunting
Martindale Helen I.................Roberts
Martineau Jeanne L...............Landreth
Martinelli Louisa B................Newcomb
Martinez Anita G...............Clattenburg
Martinez Maria..........................Mead
Martinez Melinda M.................Arndt
Martinez Patricia...................Martinez
Martinez de Eguiluz Marianela
....Morgan
Martinovic Andrea A...........Newcomer
Marti-Ventosa Lieta Elena........Glidden
Martucci Lia A.......................Skillern
Marty Madonna.....................Lawton
Martyn Jill C.........................Kreimer
Marvel Mary.........................Donohue
Marvin Alexandra E.................Harris
Marvin Alice R.................von Briesen
Marvin Bryanne B..............Applegate
Marvin Camilla.......................Marvin
Marvin Diana.........................Gibson
Marvin Melinda........................Kittell
Marvin-Smith Marguerite........Mitchell
Marwedel Katherine McC.........Nutting
Más Elba L...........................Hadden
Maserang Deborah D...................Carr
Mason Adelaide H................Comstock
Mason Amelia E...................Coombs
Mason Ann Goodyear..................Sears
Mason Elizabeth H.............Walbridge
Mason Elizabeth P.................Orlandini
Mason Emily W...........................Rose
Mason Frances M......................Miller
Mason Hope...........................Pracht
Mason Jane M.........................Flicker
Mason Junia T.......................Bradley
Mason Laura M........................Putney
Mason Linda J.........................Wilgis
Mason Lois W..........................Towers
Mason Louise C..........................Allen
Mason M Lee.........................Granger
Mason Marjorie....................Robinson

Mason Mary J.........................Johnson
Mason Persis W........................Morris
Massey Barbara K.................Clothier
Massey Erveane D....................Portner
Massie Olive M........................Gowen
Massie Susanna J....................Thomas
Masson Marie-Caroline M........Russell
Mast Alice Lea........................Tasman
Mast Georgia F........................Welles
Masters Christina.......................Jones
Masters Merle F..................Henderson
Masters Patricia F.............Schoelkopf
Mastin Eleanor C.......................Ward
Mastin Rebecca D...................Perkins
Mater Beverly..........................Folger
Matheis Dorothy M..............Thornhill
Mather Catharine A...............Nassau
Mather Catherine O..................Webb
Mather Constance.......................Price
Mather Dorothy MacG....................Ix
Mather Elizabeth H..............McMillan
Mather Jane...........................Sullivan
Mather Laurie........................Edinger
Mather Margaret L....................Byard
Mather Mary R............................Cox
Mather Sally D.........................Gibson
Mathes Mary F.......................Jackson
Mathes Ruth............................Gerrity
Matheson Heather G................Shiland
Matheson Helen D...................Hilliard
Matheson Julia T..........................Guy
Matheson Lilla Y...................Ohrstrom
Mathews Anne V..........................Farr
Mathews Bonnie....................Wisdom
Mathews Elizabeth H..............Prezioso
Mathews Julia I...................Meneghin
Mathews Louise C...................Bozorth
Mathews M Alice..................Bohannon
Mathews Margaret D.................Jenks
Mathieson Joan..........................Platt
Mathieu Elizabeth M..........McFarland
Mathis Ella Mae..................Thompson
Mathis Lillian A...................Faulconer
Matranga Marie A..................Ashdown
Matson Sally A.....................Edwards
Matter Marilyn......................Marshall
Matthews A Rachel.................Prioleau
Matthews Ann S...................Hemphill
Matthews Consuelo................Steadman
Matthews Gertrude...................Jaques
Matthews Jeanine de Croze S......Miller
Matthews Kathryn I....................Greer
Matthews Marylee................Bacharach
Matthews Priscilla S.................Hanley
Matthews Susan T....................Regan
Matthiessen Mary S..........Wheelwright
Mattison Anna C.....................Murray
Mattison Mary.........................Wells
Mattlage L Valerie..................Mattlage
Mattmiller Margie A.................Wilbur
Matushak Dolores A...................Moran
Matz Alexandra..........................Horn
Matz Claire H......................Anderson

Matz Frances..........................Kayser
Matzinger Hazel R.......................Moot
Maughan Mary M....................Patton
Maultsby Kimberly A...............Liggett
Maupin Gabrielle C............Bielenstein
Mauran Alice F...........................Freed
Mauran Harriette A..................Merrill
Mauran Hope I..........................Walsh
Mauran Louise K.....................Nadler
Mauran Marion H....................Mariner
Maurer Jane D.......................Reiniger
Maurer Jill S...............................Tait
Maurer Suzanne......................Thorne
Maury Barbara M..................Ballenger
Maury Daniéle M..................Beekman
Maury Rosalie G.....................Chanler
Maw Jean F.........................Woodman
Maxam Lydia C..........................Breck
Maxon M Elaine....................Burnham
Maxson Letitia C........................Almy
Maxted Marillyn M..............Olmstead
Maxwell Eleanor McC..............Oliver
Maxwell Jean.......................St Claire
Maxwell M Noreen.................Newbold
Maxwell Marcella H..........Chamberlain
Maxwell Marie R.....................Humes
Maxwell Sydney A.................Crimmins
Maxwell-Bresler Felicity A........Rodner
May Alice..............................Gardiner
May Emilia S............................Fanjul
May Katherine H.....................Bickford
May Leila A...............................Vieta
May Leslie H..........................Rundlett
May Nancy A..............................Field
May Nancy L..............................Pratt
Maybank Roberta M...............Prioleau
Mayberry Lotta H........................Hunt
Mayeda Joyce M...................Randolph
Mayer Anne W.............................Zug
Mayer Elizabeth A..............Boeckman
Mayer Margaret A....................Condie
Mayer Marguerite B................Browne
Mayer Pauline A........................Fallon
Mayer Renate I.........................Motley
Mayer Susan...............................Wood
Mayes Susan.....................d'Eprémesnil
Mayfield Heather G......................Kelly
Mayfield Karen A....................Seymour
Mayhew Anne E..........................Pfau
Maynard Audrey................Auchincloss
Maynard Audrey.......................Smith
Maynard Katherine A...........Armstrong
Maynard Kathleen E....................Page
Maynard Sarah deF....................Davis
Maynard Sheila...........................Platt
Maynard Susan R...................Haydock
Mayne Christine M................Crawford
Mayne Margaret M...................Kridel
Mayo Barbara L....................Llewellyn
Mayo Margaret........................Tippit
Mayo Nancy C P....................Dunham
Mayock Mary E.....................Flanagan
Mazaheri Melinda S......................Justi

Meacham Catherine V	Durgin
Meacham Jocelyn	Whittemore
Meacham Marjorie	Meek
Mead Darcy A	Leeds
Mead E Louise	Walker
Mead Elizabeth A	Merck
Mead Marianna H	O'Brien
Mead Mary	Flanagin
Mead Mary A	Lake
Mead Mary G	Hagen
Mead Nora	Brownell
Meade E Stokes	Bingenheimer
Meade Hope Alden	Fox
Meade Kristin A	Robinson
Meaders Phyliss P	Hurley
Meagher Deborah L	Stanley
Means Cynthia A	Steinbreder
Means Martha A	Coburn
Means Susan	Noble
Means Virginia B	Giddens
Mechling Mary A W	Bridger
Medin Barbro A	Hardy
Medina Meredith H	Murray
Medley Joy L	Park
Medlin Elizabeth W	Hale
Meehan Marcia A	Schaeffer
Meehan Mary Ellen	Meehan
Meek Elizabeth P	Faber
Meek Jacklyn O	Potter
Meeker Mary	Cramer
Meeker Sidney P	Keith
Meeks Natalie B	Meeks
Meentemeier Diane C	Hird
Megear Leslie R	Connors
Mehan Anne	Swain
Mehlinger Doris L	Hallanan
Mehnert Susan A	Closson
Meier Lauren G	Thayer
Meière Louise H	Dunn
Meigs Anne L	Campbell
Meigs Anne R	Larkin
Meigs Jane P	Barton
Meigs Margaret M	Cabral
Meigs Sarah P	Cody
Mein Frances W	de Bretteville
Mein Katherine E	Stewart
Meinig Margielou A	Tansill
Meirs Ellen W	Conlan
Meirs Mary A W	Hutchinson
Meissner Anne H	White
Meister Gretchen E	Gorog
Meister Margaret K	Godfrey
Melano Laura	Flanagan
Melcher Cynthia R	Ackerman
Melcher Deborah D	Stout
Melcher Marian K	Hanson
Melcher Sarah P	Jarvis
Melcher Ursula W	Melcher
Mele Samantha A	Hepting
Melemai Eyvonne K	Brown
Mellander Ragna	Caron
Mellen Abigail	Mellen
Mellen Nancy	Ijams
Melling Karen	van Vliet
Mellon Cassandra K	Milbury
Mellon Eliza	Gowen
Mellon Helen S	Schmidt
Mellon Jane C	Simonds
Mellon Katherine H	Jones
Mellon M Carroll	Mellon
Mellon Margaret	Hitchcock
Mellon Mary C	Jenney
Mellon Rachel L	Walton
Mellor Enid C A	Channing
Mellor Virginia H	Wilson
Melloy Anne Marie	Gould
Melonakis Mary	Pennington
Melville Margaret	Blackwell
Melville Mary E	Richards
Melville Mary M	Pratt
Melvin Anna M	Penrose
Menadier Mary M	Cromwell
Menassa Renée	Wood
Mendle Mary E	Bird
Menefee Betty A	Cavender
Menefee Marianne	Byrd
Meneghini Gloria	Browne
Menge Ann	Loomis
Menocal Elisa D	Barton
Menocal Suzanne	Rhea
Mentz Susan B R	Donnell
Mentzer Lesley A	Findlay
Menzel Helen E	Mantius
Menzies Mary	Page
Menzies-Wilson Rosemary	Whiting
Méquet Jeannik M C	Littlefield
Mercer Christie	Platt
Mercer Elizabeth	Nason
Mercer Elizabeth W	Willis
Mercer Kathryn A	van Voorhees
Mercer Lucy C	Dabney
Mercer Maryann T	Street
Mercer Natalie A	Latimer
Merchant Mary F	Stokes
Merckens Alice C	Chappell
Mercury Jeanne A	Ewing
Meredith Curry C	Darlington
Meredith Margaret E	Brown
Meredith Paula	Mosle
Mericle Dana L	Gardner
Merikle Kathryn M	Winterhoff
Merkel Becky	Babson
Merker Margaret H	Pinkham
Merle Mary Jane	O'Connor
Merriam Laura E	Fay
Merrick Anne M	Pinkard
Merrick Deborah H	Brisbane
Merrick Eleanor R	Bissell
Merrick Marguerite	Wick
Merrick Nellie M	Semans
Merrill Alice R	Hyland
Merrill Barbara L	Huggins
Merrill Doris	Magowan
Merrill E Ann C	Westdahl
Merrill Edith M	Smart
Merrill Elizabeth McC	Ziel
Merrill Eugenia A	Seamans
Merrill H Penelope	Brouder
Merrill Helen	Buckingham
Merrill Isabel C	Thayer
Merrill Janet G	Merrill
Merrill Josephine L	Eastman
Merrill Katharine P	Lambert
Merrill Lynn	Gray
Merrill Margery P	Lewis
Merrill Mary E	Snow
Merrill Nina K	Ogan
Merrill P Pepperell	Crofoot
Merrill Page B	Brady
Merrill Patricia W	Whitehead
Merrill Signa V	Hermann
Merrill Susan LeR	Sprague
Merriman H Anne	Krout
Merriman Helen	Fernald
Merriman Katharine F	Nichols
Merriman Mallory B	Constantine
Merritt Ann	Rudd
Merritt Ann E	Hunter
Merritt C Kane	Tilney
Merritt Camilla	McLane
Merritt Catherine	Stokes
Merritt Harriet P	Garde
Merritt Jane B	El-Yacoubi
Merritt Joan	Wilson
Merritt Marjorie F	Robinson
Merritt Saraellen	Langmann
Merritt Susan	McIlvaine
Merritt Tessa H	Le Baron
Merryman Eleanor W	Hardy
Merryman Emily McL	Hackett
Merryman Frances McL	Walker
Merryman Frances N	Rollman
Merryman S Josephine	Van Ness
Merryweather Anne	Close
Merryweather Juliet I	Evans
Mersereau Lynda A	Elliott
Mersfelder Nancy L	Mann
Mersich Mildred D	Plate
Merwin Josephine U	Thompson
Mesa Maria Hortencia	Gilpin
Meserve Anne	Davis
Meserve Marcia	Poutiatine
Messimer Anita G	Silva-Sadder
Messimer Juliet G	Gede
Mester Marianne S	Allen
Meston Susan	McGovern
Metcalf Barbara E	Metcalf
Metcalf Caroline W	Saylor
Metcalf Esther E	Mauran
Metcalf Joan C	Lee
Metcalf Katherine R	Nelson
Metcalf M Eleanor	Childs
Metcalf Sandra	Shober
Metcalfe Jane	Culver
Metcalfe Linda M	Mortimer
Metz Helen W	Ketchum
Metz M Charlotte	Hanes
Metz Mary Selden	Evans
Metzger Gloria J	Gilbert
Metzger Martha L	Tucker
Meuller Elizabeth E	Sheehan
Meuth Marilyn B	Johnson
Meyer Anne	Cross
Meyer Anne C	Manuel
Meyer Averil C	Haydock
Meyer Berry P	Stuart
Meyer Beverly V	Meyer
Meyer Carolyn O	Grace
Meyer Catherine H	Lange
Meyer Charlotte E	Wilshire
Meyer Claire M	White
Meyer Claresa F	Brown
Meyer Doris I	Cort
Meyer Elizabeth T	Eaton
Meyer Florence C	Hoffman
Meyer Harriet W	Quarré
Meyer Katherine L	Merritt
Meyer Lucie W	Meyer
Meyer Margaret B	Thompson
Meyer Margaret McC	Seybolt
Meyer Maria del Carmen J	Vasquez
Meyer Marjorie A	Kyte
Meyer Molly	O'Connor
Meyer Nancy	Cheston
Meyer Nancy S	Hovey
Meyer R Jan	Diesel
Meyer Véronique	McKeon
Meyerkort Margaret	Dall
Meyers Catherine A	Randolph
Meyle Colleen B	Chance
Meyler Jacqueline deF	Mackay
Meyns Willoughby G E	Adams
Mezey Yolanda I	Terbell
Michael Amanda B	Gamble
Michael Dorothea F	Michael
Michael Frances H	Burnam
Michalis Cora C	Thomas
Michalis Helen F	Bonebrake
Michalis Helen L	Winslow
Michalis Martha M	Hare
Michel Barbara L	Fountain
Michel Celeste N	Drain
Michellod Janet M	Ashford
Michenfelder Caryl J	Baetjer
Michie Anne H	Lamberton
Micka Janice J	Scullin
Middendorf Jean R	Rasmussen
Middleton C Carter	Sollers
Middleton Caroline Yates	Amason
Middleton Elizabeth W	Parker
Middleton Ellen Alice	Middleton
Middleton Grace T	Neumann
Middleton Kathleen E	McAlpin
Middleton Laurinda P	Oswald
Middleton Melani L	Tutt
Middleton Ruth	Cheney
Middleton Sylvia E	Seymour
Mifflin Mary D	Griffin
Mihalea Rodica I	Liggett
Mikkelson Helen A	Casey
Milam Diane J	Dennis
Milam Margaret	McDermott

Milam Martha G....Jones
Milani Liliana....Baehr
Milask Laurette B....Marshall
Milbank Daphne....White
Milbank Edith D....Corbin
Milbank Elenita....Drumwright
Milbank Margaret....Bogert
Milbank Victoria....Whitney
Milburn Ann....Beal
Milburn Eleanor....Connelly
Miles Anne B....Ludlum
Miles Serena W....Miles
Milholland Mary A....Dick
Milks M Kathryn....Lenahan
Millar Adele G....Pulitzer
Millard Elizabeth C....Hanes
Millard Marsha....Crawford
Millard Mary R....Redmond
Miller Adair H....Curtiss
Miller Alexandra C....Howard
Miller Alexandra M....Cooper
Miller Alison A....von Czoernig
Miller Alison B....Estes
Miller Anne....Mason
Miller Anne C....Arensberg
Miller Avery S....Mocek
Miller Barbara B....Eversole
Miller Beverly....Orthwein
Miller Blossom L....Boles
Miller Bright....Judson
Miller Carley A....Sullivan
Miller Carol A....Guernsey
Miller Carolyn T E....Holmes
Miller Caryl L....Roach
Miller Catherine A....Dixon
Miller Catherine H....Sokoloff
Miller Charlotte B....McCarthy
Miller Christina L....Cocroft
Miller Christine S....High
Miller Claire....Gummere
Miller Claire J B....Proffitt
Miller Claire M....McGowan
Miller Constance D....Anderson
Miller Constance L....Bergh
Miller Cynthia....Akabane
Miller Deborah B....Lalor
Miller Deyanne....Urbahn
Miller Diane T....Poole
Miller Donna....Straat
Miller Donna E....Casey
Miller Dorothy....Ostrom
Miller Eleanor A....Norris
Miller Elena....Shoch
Miller Elena F....Caruso
Miller Elise B....Barnett
Miller Elizabeth G....Pierpont
Miller Elizabeth H....Campbell
Miller Elizabeth K....Sayler
Miller Estelle....Cashman
Miller Evelyn D....Peale
Miller Evelyn G....Sultan
Miller F Holliday....Pulsifer
Miller Frederica M....Davis
Miller Georgina T....Bissell
Miller Gretchen B....Elkus
Miller Gretchen L....Wintersteen
Miller Guenn S....Miller
Miller Hope H....Horn
Miller Jacqueline d'Oggier....Dunnington
Miller Jamie....Kozumbo
Miller Jean S....Davis
Miller Jean W....Biddle
Miller Jeanine S....Abrahams
Miller Jerilyn K....Lowe
Miller Julie F....Clay
Miller Kelly L....Bridges
Miller Kerstin M....von Hafften
Miller Kristine E....McGehee
Miller Laura G....Duncan
Miller Laura S....Bland
Miller Leslie S....Chrismen
Miller Lindsay M....Ambler
Miller Lisa A....Turben
Miller Lizora S....Yonce
Miller Lucie L....Carroll
Miller M Anne....Williams
Miller M Caroline....Thorington
Miller Margaret C....Thompson
Miller Margaret L....Douglas
Miller Margery K....Miller
Miller Margo L....King
Miller Marila M....Beatty
Miller Marion....Lindley
Miller Marnie A....Nicholson
Miller Martha C....Massey
Miller Martha W....Bolling
Miller Mary C....Gonzalez
Miller Mary Coxe....Smith
Miller Mary E....Newton
Miller Mary G....Sharp
Miller Maureen....Grace
Miller Nancy C....Siedler
Miller Nancy G....Adler
Miller Nancy M....Cavanagh
Miller Nancy S....Gale
Miller Nancy S....Redpath
Miller Nina J....Griggs
Miller Nina LeR....Lyon
Miller Patricia H....Bane
Miller Patricia M....Place
Miller Perry P....Trimble
Miller Phyllis A....Lee
Miller Rebecca P....Harvey
Miller Rosa C....Persons
Miller Sarah R....Hart
Miller Susan B....Reuben
Miller Susan G....Jackson
Miller Susan W....Knott
Miller Sybil K....Hebb
Miller Veva P....Wood
Miller Virginia....Ellis
Miller Wendell E....Steavenson
Miller Wendy....Johnson
Miller Winifred E....Davidson
Milligan Nancy L....Miller
Milliken Alida D....Camp
Milliken Jane P....Hague
Milliken Judith E....Holden
Milliken Ruth B....Murphy
Milling Mary....Brick
Millon Jo Jeanne....Barton
Mills A Louise....Cunningham
Mills Allison M....Wickersham
Mills Barbara L....Henagan
Mills Dorothy Telfair....Parker
Mills H Lee....Petty
Mills Helen F....Allen
Mills Henrietta W....Mead
Mills Julia H....Levine
Mills Lucy....Doxford
Mills Marcia L....Bogert
Mills Nancy A....Lee
Mills Natalie S....Bontumasi
Mills Pauline I....Low
Millspaugh Amanda C....Ford
Millspaugh Ann E....Huff
Millspaugh Elisabeth G....Schroeder
Millspaugh M Josephine....Drayton
Millspaugh Virginia....Parker
Milman Helen B....Trigg
Milne Helen B....Justi
Milne Roberta W....Willoughby
Milne Sheila N....Ferguson
Milne Varya V....Anderson
Milner Gwendolyn L....Cheesewright
Milner M Margaret....Richardson
Milnes Caroline....Cronson
Milnes Edith E....Wheeler
Milota Elsa A....Shackleton
Miltimore Cynthia S....Chapman
Milton Abby R....O'Neill
Milton Elizabeth G....Hunnewell
Milton Patricia A....Morgan
Mingea E Gillette....Brown
Minich Elizabeth G....Husted
Minkin Annellen....Simpkins
Minnick Catherine....Rezny
Minnick Renee W....Smith
Minnigerode Helen L G....Hume
Minot Abby M....Gross
Minot Anna Lodge....Biddle
Minot Caroline M....Bell
Minot Marian L....Cheever
Minskoff Jean B....Grant
Minster Carol Y....Pendergrass
Minton Carole O F....Nelson
Minton Helen D....Farley
Minton Marian....Ballard
Minton Valerie H....Webster
Minx Billie....Taylor
Mirc Joan de B....Aalde
Mirick Heath....Kennedy
Miro Maria-Luz....Mallace
Mitchel Kathleen M....Lyon
Mitchel Priscilla....Meek
Mitchell Alice Plunkett....Richey
Mitchell Angela....Campbell
Mitchell Ann F....Brasfield
Mitchell Augusta W....Besse
Mitchell Barbara A....Perry
Mitchell Beatrice H....Sperry
Mitchell Betty....Ames
Mitchell Caroline P....Simons
Mitchell Caroline T....Clark
Mitchell Cynthia W....Cheston
Mitchell Elizabeth J....Dugan
Mitchell Ethel C....Cates
Mitchell Ginevra F....Hunter
Mitchell Irene W....Moore
Mitchell Jane P....Ylvisaker
Mitchell June....La Motte
Mitchell Kathryn W....Pettengill
Mitchell Laura....Eaton
Mitchell Marjorie G....Maguire
Mitchell Mary B....McClintock
Mitchell Mary E....Conaway
Mitchell Mary Elizabeth B....Reeve
Mitchell Nancy....Neill
Mitchell Nannie P....Koppelman
Mitchell Ruth I....Freeman
Mitchell Ruth W....Cogan
Mitchell Sally....Dorr
Mitchell Sara A....Walker
Mitchell Sarah A....Reath
Mitchell Susanna S M....Wall
Mitchell Suzanne S....Davis
Mitchell Virginia....Dimsey
Mitchiner Barry....Caldwell
Mittendorf Marcella C....Wainwright
Mittnacht Barbara K....Daly
Mitton Tara C....Catáo
Mix Helen B....Casey
Mix Madeline V....Hunter
Mix Mary B....McDonald
Mixsell Mary B....Waldron
Mixter Dorothy Fay....Crabb
Mixter Elizabeth E....Ballantine
Mixter Valerie....Dove
Mize Anne E....Barnett
Mize Elizabeth D....Currie
Mjornell Ingrid A....Hinckley
Model Jeannette....Ogilvy
Moecke Walthraut G....Marshall
Moerdyke Priscilla E....Austin
Moeser R Leigh....Thayer
Moest Mary E....Highmore
Moffat Alice D....Randolph
Moffat Frances W....Sargent
Moffat Grace....Davidson
Moffat K Louise....Thorington
Moffat Leslie F....Little
Moffat Marilyn....Salant
Moffat Patricia....Pope
Moffat Virginia....Nickerson
Moffett Helen W....Brooks
Moffett Martha....Forbes
Moffett Melissa....Rumbough
Moffitt Anne P....Moffitt
Moffitt M Meredith....Osterhus
Moffly Barbara S....Warwick
Moffly Suzanne de Z....Williams

Mohn Anne Mercier M .... Mohn
Mohn Sally Parker .... Kneen
Mohr Elsa C .... Weyburn
Mohr Helen L .... Montross
Mohrman Jean M .... Springer
Mohun Bronwyn P .... Brunner
Mohun Patricia B .... Smith
Moir Elizabeth .... Cunningham
Moir Elizabeth .... Mattison
Moise Marion G .... Bierwirth
Molden Alexandra P .... Deniau
Mole Ruth L .... Hoagland
Mollenhauer Mary E .... Lugar
Möller Katharina deF .... Merrell
Moller Nancy .... Howland
Molthan Caroline R .... Wurts
Moltke Alette .... Ahlefeldt
Moltke Alexandra .... Isles
Monachino Jennifer L .... Labey
Monaghan Karen R .... Walbridge
Monahan Annamary P .... Coyle
Monahan Jane .... Driscoll
Monahan Norma R .... Reals
Monahan Susan L .... Parkinson
Moncrieff Lucinda B .... Buttrick
Mondschein Faye V .... Sarkowsky
Monek Carol .... Sweet
Monek Dorothy L .... Davis
Moneta Judith A .... Moneta
Monier Martha E .... Steves
Monks Edith A .... Stark
Monks Ellen E .... Higgins
Monks Mary C .... Cowell
Monks Virginia .... Burr
Monnette Helen H .... Amestoy
Monroe Elizabeth .... Stanton
Monroe Jeanne E .... Stockman
Monroe Joan E .... Wendell
Monroe Mary Lee .... Birmingham
Monroe Patricia C .... Emery
Montague Constance A .... Baldwin
Montant Alice .... McGuigan
Montgelas Michele T .... van der Kieft
Montgomery Alexandra .... Estey
Montgomery Anne .... Westerfield
Montgomery Brynne A .... Staley
Montgomery Catharine E .... Hunt
Montgomery Claudine .... Brown
Montgomery Elizabeth P
        Zimmerman
Montgomery Ella S .... Flower
Montgomery Emily S .... Lynch
Montgomery Grace .... Fowler
Montgomery Julia C .... Coleman
Montgomery Justine B .... Corbin
Montgomery M Louise .... Snyder
Montgomery Margery P .... Pope
Montgomery Mary C .... Beecheno
Montgomery Maurine W .... Gibbs
Montgomery Nancy E .... Deshler
Montgomery Phoebe Sands .... Moeller
Montgomery Ruth C .... Murphy
Montgomery Sally B .... Jones

Montgomery Sylvia M .... Erhart
Montgomery Virginia L .... Baily
Montross Barbara .... Magee
Montross Lee C .... Wheeler
Moody Anne .... Ayer
Moody Caroline P .... Roberts
Moody R Elizabeth .... Kemp
Moon A Bodine .... Lamont
Moon Barbara F .... Perry
Moon Carol B .... Cardon
Moon Katherine E .... Sargeant
Moon Linda L .... Newcomer
Moon Melinda M .... Kiefer
Mooney Ethel M .... Bayard
Mooney Marjorie B .... Hodges
Mooney Ruth E .... Smith
Mooney Suzanne .... Warrington
Moor Betty L .... MacGuire
Moore Alma O .... Bauch
Moore Anne M .... Willcox
Moore Ashley .... Ammidon
Moore Barbara M .... Childs
Moore Barbara M .... Ingalls
Moore Beatrice V .... Forsberg
Moore Bettine .... Close
Moore Carin E .... Laughlin
Moore Catherine B .... Barrett
Moore Cecelia B .... Maas
Moore Charlotte Ann .... Webb
Moore Christina W .... Millet
Moore Claire A .... Dickerson
Moore Dorothy P .... Tower
Moore E Adele
        Czoernig von Czernhausen
Moore Edith B .... Blair
Moore Edith B .... Carhart
Moore Eleanor M .... Sterne
Moore Elizabeth B .... Moriarty
Moore Elizabeth H .... Collier
Moore Elizabeth S .... Lamdin
Moore Elizabeth W .... Barclay
Moore Elizabeth W .... Dickinson
Moore Evelyn B .... McGee
Moore Frances W .... Gagarin
Moore Gillian A .... Crawford
Moore Gwendolyn E .... Owings
Moore Gwendolyn M .... Gilbert
Moore Harriette M .... Warren
Moore Helen L .... Wick
Moore Henrietta Ayres .... Moore
Moore Jane R .... Banks
Moore Jean D .... Amory
Moore Joan A .... Biddle
Moore Joan B .... Hammer
Moore Joyce .... Maclay
Moore Julia S .... Jones
Moore Kathleen F .... Parrish
Moore Kay D .... Bowles
Moore Linda .... Post
Moore Louisa J .... Consagra
Moore M Elizabeth .... Summers
Moore Margaret G .... Clucas
Moore Maria C .... Mack

Moore Marianna .... Butler
Moore Marilyn .... Boring
Moore Marion R .... Cope
Moore Mary E .... Kenney
Moore Mary J .... Heyl
Moore Mary L .... Bates
Moore Melinda M .... Cropsey
Moore Natalie M .... Montgomery
Moore Nina .... Galston
Moore Olive Gale .... Mullet
Moore Pamela M .... Bushing
Moore Patricia A .... Patterson
Moore Pauline H .... Nickerson
Moore Sallie B .... Johnson
Moore Sarah M .... Barron
Moore Sheila A .... Nields
Moore Sophia .... Godfrey
Moore Susan C .... Grady
Moore Virginia A .... Niles
Moore Virginia C .... Briggs
Moores Lauren S .... Auchincloss
Moorhead Suzanne C .... Spencer
Moorhouse Laura A .... Kenna
Moot Suzanne .... Strother
Mora M Victoria .... Heaney
Morales Thelma E .... Pope
Moran Bettina de B .... Anthony
Moran Conchessa M .... Brownell
Moran Leslie A .... Drew
Moran Mariana C .... Grove
Mordecai Linda A .... Benkwith
More Alison M .... Davies
More Anne G .... Kirkpatrick
More Robin M .... Eddy
Morehead Nancy S .... Stone
Morehouse Jill W .... Lum
Morehouse Merry E .... Chellas
Morel Leigh .... Zimmermann
Moreland Nancy G .... Bomonti
Morell Irma .... Chamberlin
Morey Ada D .... Draesel
Morey Loraine L .... Rust
Morey Marion D .... Meenan
Morey Mary P .... Bradley
Morey Patricia C .... Pratt
Morey S May .... Leonard
Morfit Leigh E K .... Pannell
Morgan Andrea D .... Weyer
Morgan Caroline .... Macomber
Morgan Catherine A .... Peltier
Morgan Catherine C .... Stockwell
Morgan Cintra .... Badenhausen
Morgan Deborah B .... Luquer
Morgan Diana M .... Olcott
Morgan Diana T .... Senior
Morgan Diana V .... Grove
Morgan Eleanor .... Patterson
Morgan Eleanora Carroll .... Block
Morgan Elisabeth A .... Pendleton
Morgan Elizabeth B .... Pack
Morgan Frances C B .... Carpenter
Morgan Frances P .... Hartigan
Morgan H Suzette .... Alsop

Morgan Jane P .... Mosle
Morgan Jane S .... Wright
Morgan Joan .... Baldwin
Morgan K Jane .... Dommerich
Morgan Lelia A P .... Wardwell
Morgan Leslie P .... VanDerzee
Morgan Linda P .... Bridges
Morgan Louise C .... Rankin
Morgan Margaret C .... Morgan
Morgan Margaret E .... Pepper
Morgan Margaret G .... Harbison
Morgan Margaret H .... Archambault
Morgan Margaret T .... Stewart
Morgan Marianna C .... Morgan
Morgan Marilyn W .... Hitchcock
Morgan Mary E .... Burry
Morgan Meredith A .... Dale
Morgan Nancy J .... Runnells
Morgan Natalie .... Macy
Morgan Norma .... Cooke
Morgan Rosalind H .... Rockwell
Morgan Susan L .... Phillips
Morgan Teresa Adelaide
        Lineaweaver
Morgan Wendy C .... Richardson
Morian Isabel H .... Lamb
Morian Mary J .... Bell
Moriarty Lilias S S .... Johnson
Morison Arria .... Weir
Morison Emily M .... Beck
Morley Rikki D .... Saunders
Mormino di San Vincenzo Ferreri M
        Raffaela .... Schirmer
Morones Dosamantes Victoria
        Barkan
Morot-Sir Catherine H .... Gordan
Morphy Sallie E .... Colmery
Morrell Diane D .... Marshall
Morrell Isabel P .... Beadleston
Morrell Judith B .... Devitt
Morrill Ann R .... Schmid
Morrill Elizabeth L .... Pearson
Morrill Nancy E .... Cooper
Morrill Nancy L .... Smith
Morrill Patricia .... Starr
Morrill Priscilla .... Revell
Morrin Sheila C .... Humphreys
Morris A Elizabeth .... Bair
Morris Alice .... Heyl
Morris Ann E .... Blaisdell
Morris Anne D .... Macdonald
Morris Barbara W .... Caspersen
Morris Carolyn H .... Farrell
Morris Christina A .... Raymond
Morris Corinne DeL .... Bartolec
Morris Diana .... Saviano
Morris Doreen J .... Torrance
Morris E K Alexandra G .... Robson
Morris Eleanor .... Illoway
Morris Eleanor B .... Morrison
Morris Eleanor V .... Tindle
Morris Elisabeth F .... Turman
Morris Ellen N W .... Manganaro

Morris Eloise D ....Clark
Morris Gerd K ....Grace
Morris Helen de Russy ....Minich
Morris Isabelle T ....Roman
Morris Jane ....Stewart-Clark
Morris Jane Grubb...............Bissell
Morris Joy T ....Ligget
Morris Julia P ....Disston
Morris Katharine S ....Fisher
Morris Linda L ....Jenne
Morris Lydia L ....Reeves
Morris Margaret G...............Powell
Morris Margaret G...............Stineman
Morris Mary Wistar ....O'Connor
Morris Meredith D...............Newton
Morris Myra P ....Fuguet
Morris Priscilla A ....Wellford
Morris Susan B ....Carter
Morris Theodora W ....Marran
Morrisey Lucinda E...............Worthington
Morrison Elizabeth J...............Baker
Morrison Helen E ....Thompson
Morrison Joan ....Comstock
Morrison Linda H ....Robbins
Morrison Mary F ....Shaffer
Morrison Mary M ....Tingue
Morrison Sarah ....Kerlin
Morrison-Bell Shelagh J........Campbell
Morriss Annette W ....Clow
Morrissey Kathleen M...............Browne
Morrissey Tracie Anne ....Lee
Morrow Barbara...............Julian
Morrow Carolyn N ....Bowen
Morrow Constance C...........Fulenwider
Morrow Katherine M...............Jefferson
Morrow Marion ....Stott
Morrow Mary A ....Melvin
Morse Betty J...............Wichman
Morse Carol M ....Perkins
Morse Dorothy R ....Mudd
Morse Georgia R ....Heitner
Morse Jean F...............Berwind
Morse Jenny L ....Bradley
Morse Marilynn ....Marston
Morse Mary ....Shaw
Morse Nancy...............Borland
Morse Nancy H...............Torti
Morse Priscilla G...............McWilliams
Morse Priscilla R ....Allyn
Morse Susan T ....Hilles
Morshead Marilynne M...........Rohrer
Morsman Margaret H ....Page
Morss Anne...............Combs
Morss Barbara...............Marshall
Morss Sylvia W ....Page
Morten Sarah H ....Fisher
Mortensen Marcia G...............Cluxton
Mortimer Eve ....Ledyard
Mortimer Katharine ....Blaine
Morton Elizabeth G ....Stehlin
Morton Frances H...............Froelicher
Morton Josephine J...............Bever
Morton Judith...............Ottley

Morton M Blair...............Armstrong
Morton Margaret V...............Creese
Morton Marian R...............Brown
Morton Nancy M ....Dawson
Morton Pamela A ....Dowler
Morton Sylvia C ....Kingsley
Morton-Smith Adrienne...........Gignoux
Moseley Ailsa ....Crawford
Moseley Ardelle S ....Fullerton
Moseley Ellen P...............Ames
Moseley Mary L ....Schwartz
Mosenson Nancy L...............Vincent
Moser Elizabeth L ....Wolfe
Moser Emily F...............Sharpe
Moser M deLancey...............Converse
Moses Deborah W ....Tonissi
Moses Marianne M ....Smith
Moss Anna H...............Spiller
Moss Constance E C...............Skeele
Moss Elizabeth D ....Phillips
Moss Nancy B ....Rick
Moss Nancy L...............McDaniel
Mosser Patricia L...............Crolius
Motley Eleanor ....Richardson
Motley Elizabeth...............Ames
Motley Nancy ....Adams
Mott Anne C...............Booth
Mott L Deery ....Walker
Mott Marcie L...............Slaughter
Mottice Linda K ....Sayler
Mouchett Virginia R...............Poillon
Moulder Kathleen C...............Dibble
Moulton Alexandra C...............Cutler
Moulton Dorelle...............Tanner
Moulton Francesca...............Miller
Moulton Katrina...............Wollenberg
Mountain Beverley C ....Galban
Mountcastle Anne C...............Bainbridge
Movius Rose S...............Palmer
Mower Dorothy H ....Anderson
Mower Mary K...............Mitchell
Moyer Alice E ....Stewardson
Moyer Katharine D...............Kissel
Moyer Loma ....Allen
Moyle Joyce N...............Dickey
Moynihan Elaine K...............Lisle
Mucci Tina M ....Simonin
Muchmore Jean L...............McCleary
Muckerman Barbara L...............Fisher
Muckerman Lucy A...............Lamb
Muckerman Margaret...............Swift
Muckerman Margo C ....Hields
Muckerman Martha M...........Champlin
Muckle Christine M...........Rosengarten
Mudd Dorothy M...............Witherspoon
Mudd Frances Dail ....Loyd
Mudd Margaret E ....Fletcher
Muehlen Erika O ....Slack
Mueller Christine E B...............Northrop
Mueller Helene S ....Weld
Mueller Lois E ....Roulston
Mueller Margaret S...............Rundlöf
Mueller Patricia H ....Dary

Mueller Ruth M ....Colket
Mueller Sandra F ....Dick
Mueller Susan T ....Timchak
Muelling Bettina E ....Barnes
Muetze Edith W...............Bell
Muggleton Betty ....Patterson
Mugler Molly S ....Sullivan
Muguiro Mercedes...............Sargent
Muhlfeld Louise...............Patterson
Muhlhofer Clarinda S...............Harris
Muhlhofer Elizabeth H...............Thomas
Muhlstein Anne ....Begley
Muir Eleanor W ....Johnson
Muirhead C Marie ....Escher
Muirhead Susan P...............Bates
Mulcahy Kara K...............Valentine
Mulford Barbara G...............Karr
Mulford Nancy M...............Burrill
Mulford Patricia A...............Livermore
Mulgrew Ann S...............Goldsmith
Mulhall Marie M ....Roome
Mullally Amanda M ....Drake
Mullally Eleanor H ....Snyder
Mullen Charlotte V...............Sullivan
Mullen Elizabeth A...............Samuel
Mullen Jeanine E ....Steele
Mullen Julia R ....Hart
Mullen Maria T...............Thompson
Mullen Mary E ....Gribbel
Mullen Mary Lou ....Hall
Mullen Renée M...............Brown
Muller Christiane J E...............Tyson
Mulliken Sherrill...............Houghton
Mullikin Marsha A ....Wilmerding
Mullin Tracy ....Moroney
Mullins C Brewer ....Schoeller
Mullins Dorothy P...............Holland
Mullins Elizabeth A...............Findley
Mullins Laura E M ....McMullin
Mulvane Katherine ....Straus
Mulvey Mary B ....Buck
Mulville Ann H...............Geupel
Mumford Barbara ....Hand
Mundy Judith L ....Knapp
Mundy Marion P...............Cooke
Munighan Virene A ....Dewhurst
Munn Linda A ....McConnaughey
Munnell Catherine C...............Smith
Munro Carol...............Barker
Munro Margaret A...............Dayton
Munroe Charlotte...............Hoover
Munroe Dorothy F...............Munroe
Munroe Maria C ....Browne
Munson Catherine M...............Rogerson
Munson Jane R ....Harrison
Munson Kate R ....Rowe
Munson Laura A...............Kobelt
Munson Louise F ....Herring
Munson Marjorie S...............Munson
Munson Natalie...............Brengle
Münter Eirin T...............Muenter
Munthe de Morgenstierne Marjorie B
...............Dahlgren

Murchison Ann ....Reeves
Murchison Jane...............Hamilton
Murchison Katherine ....Browning
Murdoch Jane R ....Howland
Murdoch M Stevenson...............Knox
Murdoch Susan H ....Gilbert
Murdock Katharine L ....Bakker
Murdock Patricia G ....Davis
Murkland Lindsey A...............Hoffman
Murnane Marianna McD ....Smith
Murphey Antoinette...............Harkness
Murphey Katharine Ludington........Pell
Murphy Abigail R...............Kean
Murphy Aleta N ....Gleason
Murphy Anita W...............Fritze
Murphy Antoinette C...............Johnson
Murphy Carol S ....Lyden
Murphy Constance M...............Paine
Murphy Courtney...............Benoist
Murphy Dana D...............Wiehl
Murphy Eleanor P...............Lentz
Murphy Elizabeth A ....Lowe
Murphy Ellen C ....Warner
Murphy Honoria A ....Donnelly
Murphy Jean C ....Whitlock
Murphy Jeanne-Cerre C ....Fox
Murphy Katherine A A ....McClintic
Murphy Kathryn L...............Oram
Murphy Leslie R...............Jones
Murphy Linda M ....Churchman
Murphy M Jane C...............Samuel
Murphy Margaretta H...............Bickford
Murphy Mary W...............Davies
Murphy Michele C ....Francis
Murphy Nona K...............Collin
Murphy Renée C...............Backerman
Murphy Virginia R...............Wheaton
Murphy Wilma A ....Gardner
Murray A Margaret...............Lovering
Murray Adrienne I...............Dyett
Murray Alice L ....Ward
Murray Anne M...............Smith
Murray B Evelyn ....Johnson
Murray Beatrice L ....Willis
Murray Carolyn M...............Barrett
Murray Heather W...............White
Murray Jane D...............Broeksmit
Murray Janet S...............Fiske
Murray Kathryn ....Toms
Murray Kelly A ....Kole
Murray Llew Ann ....King
Murray Louisa G ....Crissman
Murray M Alden...............Lederer
Murray Margot...............O'Mara
Murray Mary G L...............Keech
Murray Olivia C...............White
Murray Rosita N...............Caulfield
Murray S Ramsey...............Alexander
Murray Susanne W ....Low
Murray Suzanne S ....Murray
Murray-Jacoby Beatrice F...............Cayzer
Murrill Patricia E...............de Bary
Murtagh Jane ....McCain

Murugesan Shyamala.............. Parmley
Musche Geraldine M .... Diefenbach
Muse Margaret V................... Angevine
Musgrave Olive A ....Kleberg
Musgrave Rosamond P........van Nagell
Muskat Jane B .... Copeland
Mussat Catherine A .... Chappell
Musser Eleanor C .... Rodgers
Musser Ellis .... Kirkham
Musto Elena .... Forrester
Musto Judith K .... Hachman
Musto Marie L .... Mugnaini
Muth Frances H ....Snedeker
Muth Nancy B .... Clements
Muzzey Martha M .... Ballard
Muzzy Mary Jane S ....Holden
Myer Carol C .... Gibson
Myer Jean R .... Tubman
Myer Julia C ....Ward
Myer M Cassandra ....Surer
Myer M Elizabeth.................McMillan
Myers Alice W .... Rogers
Myers Anne W ....Churchman
Myers Carol L.........................Bissell
Myers Doris E..........................Pew
Myers Dorothy A................... Hildreth
Myers Elisabeth L....................Baer
Myers Eliza S ....Miller
Myers Elizabeth B .... Christhilf
Myers Julia J............................Clay
Myers Katharine W .... Huston
Myers Marion S ....Johannsen
Myers Phyllis P........................Kipp
Myers Sarah E .... McGinty
Myers Susan D ....Dush
Myers Susan D .... Torrey
Myers Winifred R......................Booth
Myles Edith B .... de Montebello
Myles Emily.......................de Nemethy
Myles Sarah Lindsay ....Myles
Myles Star P .... Zabriskie
Myrin Elin C .... Phinizy
Nace Jane .... Hopkinson
Nafzger Betty J .... Gordon
Nagel Marta D ....Burroughs
Nager Elizabeth L................ Thompson
Nager Geraldine M .... Griffin
Nagle Francesca ....Parkinson
Nahas Maureen ....Donnell
Naify Georgette ....Rosekrans
Naile Mary G .... Ashbridge
Nairn Anne W .... Spellman
Nalle Edith T .... Schafer
Nalle Ellen R ....Hass
Nalle Jean T ....Peck
Nalle Lucinda .... Weed
Narizzano Eileen.................... Baldwin
Nash Eleanor .... Starkey
Nash Elizabeth S................... Nicholson
Nash Isabel J .... Eberstadt
Nash Katharine C .... Caldwell
Nash Linell C...........................Smith
Nash Louise S .... Robbins

Nash Lucinda V ....Dudley
Nashashibi Lola A .... Grace
Nason Carolyn ....King
Nason Kathryn T .... Burchenal
Nastase Karen J .... Hamilton
Nathan Ann M .... Simpson
Naudin Elizabeth G ....Snedeker
Naunheim Carolyn......................Hager
Navarro Carmen E .... Pelaez
Nawojchik Christina ....Dubois
Naylor Mary R .... Webster
Neal Diane E D .... Emmons
Neal Heather S...................... Thomson
Neal Marcia E........................Rowley
Neal Rebekah MacL G .... Kennedy
Neall Marian E ....Brown
Neave Sandra P...................... Brauns
Needham Betsy ....Getz
Needham Kathryn E .... Hodges
Needham Virginia W .... Judson
Neel Alice N .... Hagan
Neely Virginia .... Berry
Neely Yvonne .... Dunning
Neese Marianna .... Robertson
Neff Carole W .... Michael
Neff Laura D........................ Reaper
Neff Louise A .... Collins
Neff Sally I .... Bennett
Neidhart Sybille U ....Crafts
Neiley Carol B .... Baxter
Neiley Ellen R .... Ritter
Neill Anne S .... Peck
Neill Diana L ....Beardsley
Neill Elysbeth A .... Piersol
Neill N Lee ....MacCallum
Neilson Katherine B .... Kurtz
Neilson Madeline B .... Rockwell
Neilson Margaret J .... Neilson
Neilson Nina L ....Christiansen
Neilson Susan .... Neilson
Neithercut Harriet S..................Jones
Nellen Lillian A ....Conklin
Nelligan Ann F ....Ross
Nelson Alice E...................... Furlaud
Nelson Anne C .... Pate
Nelson Anne D .... Apgar
Nelson Dorothy Q..................Kellogg
Nelson Dyane R...................... Person
Nelson Eda C ....Halberstadt
Nelson Edith E .... Milbury
Nelson Eleanor R......................Lewis
Nelson Elizabeth C ....Wiswall
Nelson Emily M ....Baxter
Nelson Floreine J .... Winthrop
Nelson Helen S .... Bosland
Nelson Jane S .... Keyes
Nelson Jennifer L .... Fain
Nelson Joan A .... Norfleet
Nelson Judith A .... Dohan
Nelson Julie .... Firestone
Nelson Krista L..................... Osborn
Nelson Margaret E...................Moore
Nelson Marilyn J .... Bassett

Nelson Marion A ....Scharffenberger
Nelson Nancy.........................Lewis
Nelson Rhonda K .... Fowler
Nelson Susan L...................... Marshall
Nelson Wendy ....Florance
Nenner Sally A .... Neville
Neri Carole R...........................Lembo
Nervo Cecile M .... Zellerbach
Nes Catherine M.................... Gatchell
Nesbit Hope C ....Brown
Nesbitt Elizabeth L....................Lane
Nesbitt Lynne......................Mitchell
Nesbitt Shirle J .... Westwater
Nespoulos-Neuville Nathalie
                             de Fontouvelle
Ness Kathryn E....................Vitagliano
Nestle Janice S....................... Wetherill
Nestor Nancy J .... Bakewell
Nestrud Margaret M ....Dickinson
Neth Catherine .... Church
Nettell Hazel .... Hacker
Netter Patricia J ....Shiland
Netterville Mary L.................Shields
Nettleton Greta S ....Lalire
Neubauer Brenda V ....Straus
Neuberg Janet D .... Richey
Neuberger Joan K .... Woodhouse
Neufeld Tamara J ....Lott
Neugebauer Gael A ....Parks
Neuhaus Margaret E .... Weekley
Neuhaus Sarah G................... Hastings
Neuhaus Stephanie A .... Loomis
Neukermans Els M ....Paine
Neuman Mary ....Bartow
Neuman de Vegvar Beatrice M C
                                      Willis
Neumann Victoria K.............. Maddock
Neven Mary F......................Reynders
Neville Betsey B.....................Neville
Neville Betsy .... Anderson
Neville C Page .... Pyle
Nevills Dorothy V .... Abels
New Ann........................... Kendall
New Nancy A .... Finch
Newall Virginia L................... Armat
Newbaker Margery ....Keen
Newbold Anne T ....Clark
Newbold Elizabeth Ann ...Le Boutillier
Newbold Katherine ....Lowe
Newbold M Elizabeth.................Taylor
Newbold Madeleine F ....Fleitas
Newbold Margaret Y ....Pearson
Newbold Marie H ....Hart
Newbury Sylvia ....Merwin
Newcomb Grace C ....Cochran
Newcomb Simone....................Clark
Newcomer Josephine .... Inkley
Newell Ellen H ....Bryan
Newell Mary E ....Broadhurst
Newell Nancy ....Holloway
Newell Paula P ....Doty
Newell Tamara L B ....Leddy
Newell Yvonne M .... Hoelscher

Newell-Price Sarah R .... Groman
Newhall Barbara C ....Newlin
Newhall Carol H....................... Neilson
Newhall Edith A .... Walters
Newhall Jenifer .... Saliba
Newhall Marjorie M ....Heckscher
Newhard Anne K ....Martin
Newhard Frances .... Hensley
Newhard Jean H .... Mortimer
Newhouse Louise M .... Igoe
Newkirk Mary E ....Martin
Newland Nanette .... Newland
Newlin Louisa V ....Whitney
Newman A Carol .... Biegler
Newman Eleanor Walton
                                  McSweeney
Newman Elizabeth.................... Wilds
Newman Nancy M.................McIlvaine
Newman Rosemary....................Moroney
Newsom Nancy.....................Browning
Newsome Dorothy L .... McGeorge
Newton Babette Jennings ....Walton
Newton Barbara L ....Newton
Newton Carol L .... Boone
Newton Carrie G........................Gunn
Newton Joan L........................Calder
Newton Sylvia B ....Cotton
Newton Sylvia S .... Summers
Newton Virginia P..................... Jacobi
Neylan Jane F .... Childs
Ng Maie-Lee..............................Chen
Nguyen Ngoc Chât ....Boardman
Nguyen Theresa T H ....Brinckerhoff
Nicely Judith A........................Doman
Nicely Katharine P T ....Emsden
Nichol Vivian........................... Norden
Nicholas Nancy....................Hatfield
Nicholas Virginia E ....Byram
Nicholls Suzanne R ....Thorndike
Nichols Betty .... Knutsen
Nichols Dane A .... Towell
Nichols Elizabeth ....Forker
Nichols Elizabeth .... Sargent
Nichols Elizabeth J ....Troy
Nichols Elizabeth M ....Nichols
Nichols Emily ....Wharton
Nichols Helen Lucy .... Baker
Nichols Hope S .... Prockop
Nichols Jane N..........................Page
Nichols Jane T .... Fogg
Nichols Joan...........................Rizzo
Nichols Lee ....Bliss
Nichols M Carolyn ....Morgan
Nichols Margaret R ....Jewett
Nichols Martha H ....Brown
Nichols Mary E.........................Fahs
Nichols Melinda A .... Donovan
Nichols Minerva C ....Canavan
Nichols S Blair ....Chandler
Nichols Sandra B ....Nash
Nichols Sharon E ....Grindinger
Nichols Virginia C .... Wilking
Nicholson Elisabeth B .... Holmes

Pantaleoni Lucinda M............. Hamilton
Panteleoni Valerie E ....Terry
Pantsar Rita..........................Zetterberg
Pape Mary K..........................Whitney
Papillon Elizabeth A....................... Hill
Pappas Christine ....Trotman
Pappas Kathryn ....Petsas
Paquot Claire C........................Barney
Pardee Margaret S ....Bates
Pardee Pamela..........................Wulsin
Pardue Sarah B .... Hart
Parham Frances W....................Jeanes
Paris Nancy ....Pruden
Paris Star..............................Myles
Parish A Meredith......................Parish
Parish Eliza S....................Chauncey
Parish May A ....Bartlett
Park Anne T.............................. Ryan
Park Edith ....Coogan
Park Helen B...........................Haskell
Park Jolene E ....Eyre
Park Martha D ....Koekkoek
Parke Margaret W....................Gober
Parke Martha H........................Gibian
Parke Mary B......................Ostheimer
Parker Alice J ....Ober
Parker Caroline S........................Andrus
Parker Cassie ....Thompson
Parker Catherine R ....Lynch
Parker Cécile..........................Carver
Parker Christine .... McAfee
Parker Comfort T........................Parker
Parker Cynthia A.........................Cook
Parker Daphne W....................Hawkes
Parker Diane R ....Palmer
Parker Elizabeth A....................Chapin
Parker Elizabeth C....................Hollister
Parker Elizabeth D...................Sanders
Parker Elizabeth Day ....Waters
Parker Elizabeth J........................Kase
Parker Elizabeth R....................Driscoll
Parker Emily Le C ....Morris
Parker Jean C............................Phifer
Parker Margaret ....Mason
Parker Marion ....Myers
Parker Martha A ....Allison
Parker Mary S.........................Weaver
Parker Mimi ....Amos
Parker Nancy G ....Wilson
Parker Patricia........................Gadsden
Parker Sally............................Barton
Parker Sarah M ....Rawlings
Parker Virginia L......................Murray
Parkhurst Anglesea A ....Newman
Parkhurst Hope H ....Annan
Parkinson M Elizabeth ....Gourlay
Parkman Mary R.......................French
Parks Melinda B ....Conrad
Parlin Margaret L ....Parlin
Parmely Elizabeth ....Hobbs
Parriott Lisa L...........................Imbs
Parrish Elizabeth................Glendinning

Parrish Joanne ....Knight
Parrish Lucy W ....Wilmer
Parrish Maura L ....Whittaker
Parrish Stephanie W
              La Rochefoucauld
Parrish Susan T........................Carter
Parrott Cynthia H ....MacNair
Parrott Erwin W.......................Brown
Parry Frances M ....Burnham
Parry Louise L ....McShane
Parry Valerie T.....................Campbell
Parsly Cornelia P ....Walton
Parson Arrel ....Linderman
Parsons A J Penelope ....Harris
Parsons Anne ....Frame
Parsons Denyse A ....Browne
Parsons Diana deB...................Scholle
Parsons Edythe A ....Austin
Parsons Emily F....................Ridgway
Parsons Frances D ....Pingeon
Parsons Isabelle C....................Loring
Parsons Janet I .... Wainwright
Parsons Leonora H ....Paxton
Parsons Llewellyn S ....Smith
Parsons Louise ....Ott
Parsons Louise ....Pietsch
Parsons Margaret B ....Stout
Parsons Margaret S ....Bowditch
Parsons Marion S ....De Groff
Parsons Martha L ....Paine
Parsons Mary C .... Liversidge
Parsons Mary C ....Long
Parsons Pauline ....Bodine
Parsons Rose P ....Lynch
Parsons Sarah L ....Oriel
Parsons Victoria L ....Pennoyer
Parsons Virginia H ....Raymond
Parten Morene ....Cutler
Partridge Beryl M D..................Sexton
Partridge Louise A.....................Welling
Pascault Ann C ....Winchester
Pasch Leslie J ....Rogers
Paschal Eleanor M ....Reich
Paschall Maria C....................... Hill
Paschall Virginia......................Moorhead
Pasework Brigitte E ....Pettit
Pasquini Amelia di C...............Stillman
Pass Dorothée Ann .... Houdry
Passano H Kemp........................Hill
Patalak Mary ....Lenssen
Patch H Grier ....Bowditch
Patch Saralee O....................Haskins
Patchin Elizabeth M ....Greene
Patchin Mary H........................Hopper
Patecell Sherrylyn ....Lovejoy
Patenaude Janet L ....Shattuck
Paterno Carla ....Darlington
Paterson A Diana ....Fischer
Paterson Judith.......................Gordan
Paterson Martha R ....Holbrook
Pathy Nicolette S ....Bingham
Patiño Marita C........................Rosen
Paton Joan ....Tilney

Patrick Catherine ....Hazlett
Patrick Roberta A ....Corse
Patrick Ruth .... Van Dusen
Pattee Anne L ....Hale
Patten Brita ....Gwinn
Patten Florence ....Howell
Patterson Abby Ann N ....Patterson
Patterson Alice R ....Slade
Patterson Anne W........ Wynne-Willson
Patterson Bettina B ....Murray
Patterson Catharine H................Forbes
Patterson Eleanor L ....Nichols
Patterson Elisabeth L ....Smith
Patterson Elise P ....Gelpi-Toro
Patterson Emily A................Pantaleoni
Patterson Evelyn ....Truitt
Patterson Fay M .... Bullitt
Patterson Gail C .... Shafer
Patterson Janet G ....Uhle
Patterson Julia K ....Hansen
Patterson Katharine ....Halsted
Patterson Knight .... Meem
Patterson Leila C ....Peck
Patterson Lenore B ....Hall
Patterson Leslie L ....Buck
Patterson Lucy S ....Cox
Patterson Margaret ....Wiggin
Patterson Mary W.................Maclean
Patterson Mary W ....Southam
Patterson Michelle B ....Flaherty
Patterson Nancy ....Sevcenko
Patterson Pamela S ....Roach
Patterson Patricia C ....Kean
Patterson Patricia M ....Patterson
Patterson Portia C ....Westerfield
Patterson Roberta......................Grady
Patterson Susan H....................Patterson
Patterson Tamia J ....Karlinski
Patterson Virginia F ....Potter
Pattishall Sally ....Wiley
Pattison Julia L ....Farrell
Pattison Margaret T ....Watson
Patton Nancy R ....Osgood
Patton Virginia.........................Keith
Patzner Rita E S ....Michaelsen
Paul Anne ....Owsley
Paul Cheryl O ....Drake
Paul Deborah M ....Clemo
Paul Linda ....Olney
Paul Miriam U ....Leslie
Paul Monika C ....Betts
Paul Patricia L ....Olive
Paul Rebecca R.......................Harris
Paul Susan C.........................Firestone
Paul Virginia A ....Dickenson
Paul Wendy D..........................Paul
Pauley Julia Sanford.........Montgomery
Pauley Patricia Aileen ....Cappel
Paull Hettie J.............................Lisle
Pauly Elizabeth C ....Donnan
Pawlenka Franziska ....Janes
Paxson Sally C ....Davis
Paxton Elizabeth .... Gardner

Paxton Lois A ....Kling
Payne Barbara D...................Doughten
Payne Helen ....Clarke
Payne Helen A ....Ray
Payne Margaret A...............Lannamann
Payne Margaret E ....Collins
Payne Marion W ....Tubbs
Payne Miriam W ....Prioleau
Payne Nancy McB.....................Tilton
Payne Pamela B ....Patterson
Payne Victoria M.......................Payne
Payson Deborah S...................Churchman
Payson Lorinda ....de Roulet
Payson Payne W ....Middleton
Payson Sandra M.......................Payson
Pazianos Artemis G ....Willis
Peabody Cora W ....Emlen
Peabody Eugenia ....Slaughter
Peabody Gertrude L...................McCue
Peabody Harriet J ....Laveran-Stiebar
Peabody Julia B ....Potter
Peabody Katharine ....Brewster
Peabody Leslie M ....Gore
Peabody Nancy G ....Lee
Peabody Teresa D ....Metcalf
Peace Lenora............................Brown
Peach Anne C ....Biddle
Peacock Betty Jo.........................Hay
Peake Alison C ....Henning
Peake Ann R ....Stuart
Peake Barbara A ....Frazier
Peake Miraed M ....Smith
Peale Patricia ....Peale
Peaquin Claudia A ....Steers
Pearce Elizabeth...................McKnight
Pearce Elizabeth F ....Cronin
Pearce M Tracy....................Rutherford
Pearce Mary Ann ....Shaw
Pearce Nina............................Erensel
Peard Sidney A ....Brown
Pearman Nancy T ....Ferguson
Pearsall Marcia Van E................Rorick
Pearson Charlotte E ....Park
Pearson Edith F...................Darlington
Pearson Isabella T.......................Ryan
Pearson Jodi Lynn ....Zbinden
Pearson June .... Halsted
Pearson Mary G ....Park
Pearson Olive C ....Sheppard
Pearson Penni C ....Beuf
Pearson Victoria E.....................Miller
Pearson Virginia L ....Smithers
Pease Marjorie B ....Applegate
Pease Martha C ....Babcock
Pease Veronica M...................Farrington
Peaslee Daphne L ....Hollingshead
Pechin Annis L ....Blyth
Peck Allison L ....Hughes
Peck Carolyn E ....Farris
Peck Dorothy R ....Hallenborg
Peck Evelyn B ....McCall
Peck Kim Ely ....Stanelius
Peck Lee C............................Gifford

Peck Louise G.............................Safrin
Peck Lucie W ....Moffett
Peck Mary L............................Schwartz
Peckinpaugh Patricia ....Hubbard
Pecor Patricia A.........................Motch
Pécot Kathryn H .... Swartwood
Pedley Jane E........................ Voorhees
Peebles Irene M .... Field
Peebles Susan V ....Pillsbury
Peerson Patricia .... Corbin
Peet Marguerite.........................Foster
Peglau Pamela J............................Root
Pehrson Barbara A..................Carroll
Peightal Mary Jane ....Haight
Peirce Ann ....Morris
Peirce Helen E A .... Prince
Peklo Jill A ....Lawrence
Pell Alison C..............................Helms
Pell Anne DeW...........................Osborn
Pell Dorinda T .... Cruickshank
Pell Mary Leigh .... Whitmer
Pell N Dallas .... Yates
Pelland Susan L .... Sullivan
Pellegrini-Quarantotti Elisabetta
                                        Binstock
Pellegrini-Quarantotti Sophy ......Haynes
Pellerin Janine M P .... Van Fleet
Peloubet A Lynn.........................Potter
Peltz Mary E ....Nevius
Peltz Mary L ....Perry
Pemberton Nancy....................Hopkins
Pemberton Pamela K ....Green
Peña Mayra ....Lindsay
Pender Kathryn J ....Terry
Pendergast C Le Vaun...................Bell
Pendergast Helen L .... Halsey
Pendergast Norma A...................Jones
Pendergrass Elizabeth M .... Scott
Pendergrast Mary P ....Boykin
Pendleton Helen M .... McKown
Pendleton Lucille C ....Seaton
Pendleton Marjorie A A ....Clark
Pendleton Mary L ....Parvis
Penfield Mary.............................Allen
Penfield Virginia B .... Barr
Penhallow Sarah D .... Jeffery
Penn Nancy E ....Penson
Penney Virginia .... Lane
Penniman Christine S ....Strawbridge
Penniman Leila T ....Hardy
Penniman Virginia D...............Bowden
Pennock Elizabeth C................Sawyer
Pennock Helen C ....Collings
Pennock Léonie .... Huntington
Pennoyer Deirdre E ....Nadai
Pennoyer Jennifer E...............Emerson
Pennoyer Virginia M ....Livermore
Pennybaker Anabelle L ....Bennett
Pennypacker Charlotte E H ....Pearson
Pennypacker M Virginia.........Warwick
Penovich Katherine Redwood ....Clark
Penrose Frances D ....Haythe
Pentecost Mary J ....Turner

Peper Anne M ....Kniffin
Peper Harriette A ....Thayer
Pepper Betty Jane ....Toland
Pepper Josephine W .... Scully
Pepper Marion T....................Bromley
Pepper Rebecca W ....Sinkler
Pepper Virginia.....................Purviance
Peppin Marjorie R ....Hayhurst
Percival Penelope W.................Moore
Perera Caroline F .... Barry
Perez Marjorie ....Scribner
Pérez-Porro Irene ....Stillman
Perin Carnealia A ....Tyler
Perkin Kristina T ....Davison
Perkins Anne...............................Cabot
Perkins Anne B .... McDowell
Perkins Carol ....Oelsner
Perkins Cornelia N ....Johnston
Perkins Dorothy F...................... Gilbert
Perkins Elizabeth ....Nickerson
Perkins Elizabeth H ....Moseley
Perkins Evelyn M ....Perkins
Perkins Frances S ....Kellogg
Perkins Grete L.......................Perkins
Perkins Isabel C ....Perkins
Perkins Karen G ....Connell
Perkins Lois ....Valeur
Perkins Louisa C ....Porter
Perkins M Louise ....Hoblitzell
Perkins Margaret.....................Manlove
Perkins Margaret S ....Skallerup
Perkins Marguerite C................Perkins
Perkins Nancy R ....Andrews
Perkins Nancy W ....Shutt
Perkins Natalie B ....Bartlett
Perkins Paige S ....Dugdale
Perkins Penelope.......................Wilson
Perkins Priscilla C ....Grew
Perkins Rebecca D ....Templeton
Perkins Sallie ....Sullivan
Perkins Sarah H ....Perkins
Perkins Suzanne........................ Gordon
Perman Karin E ....Roosevelt
Perrenoud Anne-Marie ....Wagnière
Perret Janine L.........................Winant
Perrin Cynthia......................Schneider
Perrin Patricia ....Lawrence
Perrin Suzanne ....Kloman
Perris Kathryn R ....Heberton
Perry Adèle Augustine .... Rex
Perry Anne .... Talbot
Perry Anne G ....Todd
Perry Anne S ....Henson
Perry Ashley B ....Kineon
Perry Barbara ....Wadhams
Perry Constance A ....Genrich
Perry Elizabeth L ....Chick
Perry Jan MacC ....Mayer
Perry Jane B ....Hollyday
Perry Linda S ....Petty
Perry Margaret G .... Garvin
Perry Nancy L ....Cooke
Perry Pauline ....Kestler

Perry Penelope H ....Ware
Perry Phoebe M ....Griffin
Perry Priscilla P ....Morris
Perry Rebecca...........................Lewis
Perry Rosamond U ....Turnbull
Perry Sarah B ....Limberg
Perry Suzanne De G .... O'Connor
Perry Yvonne de C .... Segerstrom
Perryman Gretchen.............Lahourcade
Persse-Sealy Daphne.....................Rose
Pertzoff Tatiana C.....................Fischer
Peruzzi Paula M......................Slingluff
Pervan Jasna........................Heurtley
Peskay Joy .... Melone
Pesnell Carolyn M ....Amory
Peter Anne R ....Hahn
Peter Phyllis E ....Shrock
Peter Sylvia ....Preston
Peterkin Clare ....McDermott
Peterkin Joy ....Rasin
Peters Anne B ....Brooks
Peters Antoinette........................Day
Peters Edwina A........................Riblet
Peters Eleanor L ....Morse
Peters Elisabeth W.................O'Malley
Peters Elizabeth B ....Schiff
Peters Elizabeth D ....Dudley
Peters Helene L ....Victor
Peters Janice L..........................Hughes
Peters Josephine H ....Terrell
Peters Linda A ....Whitelaw
Peters Marian A ....Peters
Peters Marion A ....Stine
Peters Mary B ....Hunton
Peters Mary I ....Bolton
Peters Olivia A..........................Henry
Peters Priscilla Q ....Weld
Peters Sandra C......................Hutchings
Peters Sarah R......................DuBose
Peters Virginia T.....................Hagner
Petersen Alice F....................Stringham
Petersen Elizabeth A..................Clark
Petersen Phyllis J....................Adams
Petersen Susan M ....Thorington
Petersmeyer Joy ....Wolff
Peterson Barbara J ....Hackett
Peterson Carrie L ....Beresford
Peterson Diane M ....Edwards
Peterson Elise J...................Lonsdale
Peterson Elizabeth A ....Prien
Peterson Elizabeth D ....McLean
Peterson June.......................Blanchard
Peterson Kristen B ....Krag
Peterson Lynne ....Picard
Peterson Margery B ....Lee
Peterson Mary T...................Colhoun
Peterson Nancy A ....Clough
Peterson Patricia A ....Vaughan
Peterson Patricia F ....Skelly
Peterson Patricia J.................McCurdy
Peterson Patricia L......................Colt
Peterson Valerie L ....Fick
Petite Anna T ....Lee

Petrasch Linda ....Denison
Petrossian Elaine T ....Rauch
Petrow Christina D ....Tilt
Pettengill Mary E........Smith-Petersen
Pettengill Patricia C................Whitaker
Petti Lisa C ....Calvocoressi
Pettis Jean ....McDonald
Pettit Anian R ....Tunney
Pettit Barbara A ....Whitridge
Pettit Barbara P ....Finch
Pettit Helen ....Hinckley
Pettit Hildagarde M ....Dugan
Pettit Lindsay F....................Fullerton
Pettus Rosalie...........................Price
Petty Gail N ....Riepe
Petty Sarah K ....Dagenhart
Petzhold Joan ....Baily
Pew Ann S ....Curran
Pew H Marim .... Hamilton
Pew Margaret C ....Moorhouse
Pew Marjorie L ....Thomson
Peyton Bayne...........................Russell
Peyton Josephine G ....Flood
Peyton Linda ....Hancock
Peyton Pamela............................Post
Pezon Solange M F ....Brown
Pfaff Ingeborg T ....Coleman
Pfaff Martha Gretchen.................Riley
Pfeifer Carol A .... Stewart
Pfeifer Carolyn........................Horchow
Pfeil Elena E ....Torosian
Pfile Mary J...........................Currier
Pfingst Mary A ....Stulb
Pfisterer Kendra J ....Grannis
Pflieger Monique A ....Leaman
Pflug Elizabeth A...................McMahon
Pflug Helen ....MacKay
Pfohl Dale Porter ....Matthews
Phair Sharon L ....Fortenbaugh
Phelan Marilyn R ....Beaver
Phelan Mary S ....Bowles
Phelps Barbara H ....Anderson
Phelps Dorothea-Louise.............Cooper
Phelps Elizabeth A ....Abell
Phelps Ellen S...........................Schell
Phelps Isabel T ....Furland
Phelps Marian ....Pawlick
Phelps Mary C ....Mellen
Phelps Mary L ....Warnock
Phelps Mary V ....Hampton
Phelps Meredith C ....Rugg
Phelps Page T ....Pelliconi
Phelps Patricia P ....Cisneros
Phelps Rosalie G ....Thomas
Phemister Martha C ....Forbes
Philbin Carolyn W ....Duane
Philbrick Ann H.........................Knight
Philen Barbara M.......................Chase
Philips Frances M .... Vanderbilt
Philips Genevieve S ....Whitehouse
Phillips Adelaide N....................Bernard
Phillips Amy L ....Ashbridge
Phillips Anna Wharton ....Anderson

Phillips Anne C.........................Bryant
Phillips Anne C.............................Nott
Phillips Anne C........................Ogilby
Phillips Beatrice S ....Strauss
Phillips Bertha Jane ....Brown
Phillips Beverly ....Jenkins
Phillips Bonnie M .... Stewart
Phillips Brenda.............de Garbolewski
Phillips Brooke Byrd ....Carhartt
Phillips C Penelope....................Dexter
Phillips Caroline A ....Phillips
Phillips Eleanor C.......................White
Phillips Elise M ....Watts
Phillips Elizabeth F.................Marshall
Phillips Emmy L......................Whitridge
Phillips Emory B .... Stein
Phillips Katherine A ....Labouisse
Phillips Lisa W ....Phillips
Phillips Lorraine A .... Ambler
Phillips Louisa B ....MacLaren
Phillips Marion ....Pogue
Phillips Mary A T T ....Harrison
Phillips Millie J...........................Heine
Phillips Patrice E ....Gillespie
Phillips Sandra L H .... Phillips
Phillips Shirley I ....Liggett
Phillips Sidney H......................Morse
Phillips Susanne B ....Woolwine
Phillips Victoria A ....Corbett
Phillips Wendy L............. Zembrzuski
Phillips Winn ....Dean
Philson Carmel A ....Beale
Phinney Harriet G ....Cook
Phinney Louise S ....Caldwell
Phippen Lydia R ....Ogilby
Phipps Anne........Sidamon-Eristoff
Phipps Averyl S ....de Dominicis
Phipps Martha S ....Maguire
Phleger Mary E.........................Goodan
Piattelli Barbara ....Phillips
Pick Erika E M ....Hall
Pickands Seville J ....Dautel
Pickard Ann E.....................McDermott
Pickering Catherine M............De Vault
Pickering Dorothy C...............Bossidy
Pickering Marie-Louise ....Grose
Pickering Mary B ....Lauricella
Pickering Natalie ....Béguelin
Pickett Sybil A..........................Veeder
Pickles Betty W ....Cox
Pickman Deborah...................Clifford
Pickman Martha....................Baltzell
Pickrell C Edwina ....Oliver
Pickrell Sally D........................Jones
Pickup Jean ....Eakins
Pidgeon Helen............................Ford
Pienaar Danielle E ....Kuper
Pier Phoebe G ....Fairburn
Pierce Barbara...........................Bush
Pierce Barbara ....Clement
Pierce Carolyn J ....Williams
Pierce Cynthia E ....Belak
Pierce Dorothy W .... McKellar

Pierce Elizabeth G ....Fuchs
Pierce Elizabeth W ....Williams
Pierce Emily D ....Crouter
Pierce Esther G ....Brown
Pierce Frances .... Field
Pierce Grace W ....Forbes
Pierce Janet B ....Hunsicker
Pierce Jessie B ....Rousmaniere
Pierce Mary M ....Adams
Pierce Priscilla B ....Cochran
Pierce Roberta W ....Mendle
Pierce Sarah S ....Béguelin
Pierpoint Harriet W .... Bos
Pierpont Georgia W ....Foster
Pierpont Lulie S ....Eide
Pierpont Virginia L ....Pierpont
Pierrepont Louise R ....Muir
Pierrepont Nathalie ....Comfort
Piersol Helen ....Price
Piersol Jean McK.......................Miller
Pierson Annabelle V ....Irey
Pierson Cordelia S C ....Smela
Pierson Cynthia A....................Yandell
Pierson Elizabeth ....Friend
Pierson Florence H ....Hammond
Pierson Jocelyn ....Taylor
Pierson Julia B ....Gavin
Pierson Margaret W ....Mallory
Pierson Olivia T.......................Jacobs
Pierson Sandra E...........................Prior
Pietrasanta Alexandra ....Rose
Pietropaoli Theresa M ....Alexander
Pifer Grace E ....Sellers
Pigott Cynthia I............................Bacon
Pike A Claire ....Smith
Pike Diana .... Harding
Pike Patricia C ....Larsen
Pile Carolyn A..............................Allen
Pile Laurie C..............................Barrett
Pile Leila H.............................de Bruyne
Pile Marjorie C ....Mountain
Pilling Catharine R ....Lennon
Pilling Mary E ....Lewis
Pillow Virginia ....Porter
Pillsbury Cynthia G ....Smith
Pillsbury Joan K ....DePree
Pillsbury Marietta B ....Dewey
Pilson Anne W ....Smyth
Pilson Nancy L .... Hawkins
Pinckney Betsey G ....Apple
Pinckney Janet D ....Gawthrop
Pinckney Julia D ....Frenzel
Pincoffs Susan R ....Tippett
Pine Sandra ....Doubleday
Pinger Carol C ....Buck
Pingitore Diane ....Elliott
Pink Lucia ....Ames
Pinkley Clara J ....Huser
Pinks Nancy Taylor ....Nichols
Pinneo Elizabeth C ....Ogden
Pinson Andrea W................Hanhausen
Pinson Kathryn C ....Davison

Pintler Polly P...........................Digges
Pioda M Virginia ....Ruth
Piper Anne .... Harty
Piper Eleanore L ....De La Cour
Piper Helen E.........................Cresswell
Piper Jane L ....Bond
Piper Laura C............................Taylor
Piper Lauren S .... Franco
Piper Margaret ....Nelson
Pipes Alice Pickslay ....Jahncke
Pipes Margaret G ....Peabody
Pirie Alice L ....Wirtz
Pirie Dale D ....Cabot
Pirie Heather A ....Arenchild
Pirie Joan ....Leclerc
Pirie Margaret C ....Warren
Pirie Suzanne ....Pattou
Pironti Franca M ....Lally
Pitcairn Patricia H ....Edgar
Pitigliani Letizia....................Benenson
Pitman Betsy J ....Savage
Pitman Rose M ....Hughes
Pitney Mary F ....Parrott
Pitney Sarah R ....Fiske
Pittman Marie D ....Pickrell
Pitts Fitje L .... Pitts
Pitts Linda ....Custard
Pitts Mai Garesché....................Carter
Pitts Marion E ....Becker
Pivirotto Mary B ....Murley
Place Angela T ....Supplee
Place Cleone D ....Tiffany
Place Judith G....................McMillan
Plant Amy C ....Clarke
Plant Sandra L ....Gilmor
Platt Caroline A ....Leff
Platt Deborah ....Sterling
Platt Dorothy S ....Schellenbach
Platt Eleanor...........................Caldwell
Platt Eleanor W ....Erisman
Platt Emily K ....McDaniel
Platt Helen H ....du Pont
Platt Mary C

Grchich von Cvetkovacz

Platt Mary Clay...........................Lee
Platt Patricia L ....Fulweiler
Platt Rita N ....Coney
Player Josephine J....................Wallace
Plimpton Alice H........................Enos
Plimpton Gabriella....................Ressler
Plimpton Priscilla W................Morphy
Plimpton Reinette ....Phillips
Plimpton Victoria M................Babcock
Plowden Perdita R T ....Burlingame
Plowman Suzanne C....................Auten
Plumb Diana C ....Cashman
Plumb Joyce C ....Smith
Plumb Mary D ....Kemper
Plummer Alice M ....Davis
Plummer Nancy V ....Robertson
Plummer Susan L ....Smith
Plunkett Lyda F ....Robbins
Plunkett Margaret A ....Lord

Poag Barbara L ....Dantzler
Pochon Catherine M du B ....Dike
Podesta Mary Ann ....Burch
Podliessnie Marili ....Boyd
Podmaniczky Katinka............Coleman
Poe Augusta M ....Maynard
Poe Eleanor Livingston ....Barlow
Poe Ella K .... Burling
Poe Grace M ....Brawner
Poe Katherine Bancroft ....Duer
Poerstel Nancy J ....Goddard
Poett Carolan .... Knott
Poett Jeanne G .... Leonard
Poffenberger Mary J ....Collens
Poggi-Cavalletti Maria Antonietta
                                                        Penna
Pogue H Celeste ....Sanders
Pogue Stephanie W ....Crawford
Pohl Jane ....Moore
Pohlers Paige Catherine............Pohlers
Pohren Mary A ....Taylor
Poindexter Polly ....Lumbard
Polacek Jill M ....Aulisi
Polcini Pamela G ....Reimers
Polese Lucy A...........................Rohner
Polese Sarah B ....Reineman
Polhemus Ann G....................Ferrarini
Polhemus Lisa S .... St John
Polinger Karen J ....Foster
Politzer Mary C ....Pradier
Polk Alice ....Rutherfurd
Polk Alicia C ....Withers
Polk Cynthia A ....Bonnie
Polk Julia ....Clarkson
Polk M Delphine ....Gatch
Polk M Phyllis ....Wells
Polk Paula L ....Lillard
Pollack Rebecca J ....Parker
Pollard Jeannette A .... Kurtz
Pollard Judith C ....Danforth
Pollard Mary L ....Lay
Pollard Wendy J ....Metzger
Polley Thelka W ....Putnam
Pollitz Diane ....Austin
Pollock Barbara G ....Youngman
Pollock Katherine G ....Pollock
Pollock Laura B .... von Zweck
Pollock Margaret P ....Zug
Pollock Nancy T ....Patterson
Pomeroy Catherine L ....Collins
Pomeroy Laura C....................Anderson
Pomeroy Lindsay A ....Jones
Pomeroy Louise A ....Dempsey
Pomeroy Margaret C C C.......Anderson
Pomeroy Nancy H ....Foster
Poniatowska Elizabeth A.............Kiendl
Ponsold Renate ....Motherwell
Ponvert E Terry ....Hanson
Pool Barbara L ....Fenzl
Pool Diana B.............................Delano
Pool Katharine B ....Schmidt
Pool Nancy E..........................Hewson
Poole Barbara.............................White

Pool Nancy E .... Hewson
Poole Barbara .... White
Poole Christina C .... Thomas
Poole Dorothy A .... Watrous
Poole Elizabeth R .... Dominick
Poole Evelyn R .... Smith
Poole Lauren J .... Dixon
Poole Mary A .... Sudderth
Poor Ann E .... Litsas
Poor Avery .... Maher
Poor Deborah .... Poor
Poor Frances M .... Gaines
Poor Jean E .... Burden
Poor Penelope .... Poor
Poor Susan A .... Dingle
Pope Carol L .... Halstead
Pope Elvira D .... McKone
Pope Emily T .... Taylor
Pope Geraldine .... Pope
Pope Katherine B .... Duer
Pope Margaret .... McLemore
Pope Maria Cristina .... Rowley
Porcher Mary F W .... Bond
Porter Barbara F .... Schofield
Porter Cynthia McL .... Ogden
Porter Devon T .... Fleming
Porter Edith L .... Hickox
Porter Gail .... Porter
Porter Geneva C .... Test
Porter Jamie .... Gagarin
Porter Jane A .... Burpee
Porter Jean R .... Rogerson
Porter Jess .... Cooley
Porter Lachlan M .... Braden
Porter Lee .... Page
Porter Margaret .... Whitney
Porter Margaret H .... Miller
Porter Margaret T .... Davis
Porter Nancy .... Rothwell
Porter Peggy .... Poole
Porter Susan .... Rose
Porter Susan T .... Mann
Porter Terrell .... Cooper
Porter Varney .... Truscott
Porter Virginia A .... Beckwith
Porterfield Ellen C .... Wheeler
Portfolio Mary E .... Werner
Portner Margaret E M .... Johnston
Portner Mary Anna .... Brown
Portner Shelly E M .... Murray
Posey Ruth L .... DeMent
Post Alice M .... Howells
Post Eleanora R .... Thomas
Post Helen S .... Curry
Post Joy A R .... Bennett
Post Julester L .... Balch
Post Julia G .... Bastedo
Post Juliana .... Pfeil
Post Katharine H .... Mason
Post Mary H .... Armstrong
Post Nancy L .... Magro
Post Priscilla E .... Howland
Postenrieder Marie .... Dohan

Potter Agnes F .... Chouteau
Potter Deborah J .... Hoffmann
Potter Eleanor M .... Harris
Potter Elizabeth N .... Kruesi
Potter Eugenie M B .... de Rham
Potter Frances .... Lochridge
Potter H Virginia .... Bingham
Potter Helen B .... Wagner
Potter Hope T .... Woodward
Potter Isabel F .... Olney
Potter Linda .... Shriver
Potter Lisa M .... Roberts
Potter Louise R .... Ross
Potter Margot T .... Denny
Potter Martha J .... Phillips
Potter Natalie .... Davenport
Potter Nora .... Krech
Potter Patricia L L .... Chapman
Potter Pengwynne E C .... Blevins
Potter Polly .... Balding
Potter Roslyn M .... Jarratt
Potter Sarah A .... Villa
Potter Victoria .... Lewis
Potts Alice B .... Wallis
Potts Anne P .... Tener
Potts Elisabeth B .... Potts
Potts Georgie F .... Dwight
Potts Helen C .... Palmer
Potts Jacquelin .... England
Potts Marjorie L .... Spencer
Potts Polly .... Trafford
Poulin Terry A .... Gruener
Pow Angela R .... Koenig
Powell Anne P .... Mathews
Powell Elizabeth P .... Lohmann
Powell Hallie N .... Horton
Powell Helen C .... Gregory
Powell Helen M .... O'Brien
Powell Jane .... Goings
Powell Mary H .... Byers
Powell Mary L .... Churchill
Powell Pamela E .... McMullin
Powell Patricia B .... Gordon
Powell V Lois .... Cheston
Power Ann .... Wardrop
Power Patricia I .... Marston
Powers Barbara B .... Brenard
Powers Barsha .... Grace
Powers Carol Joan .... Blomquist
Powers Cynthia L .... Chamness
Powers Elizabeth B .... Conze
Powers Joan W .... Harwood
Powers Kathleen I .... Pflueger
Powers L Lindley .... Fosbroke
Powers Marie E .... Cummings
Powers Patricia H .... Frech
Powers Susan H .... Urstadt
Powning J Jane .... Gates
Poynton Nola I .... Webb
Prager Denny .... Sullivan
Pragoff Olivia R .... Kloman
Pranger Martha J .... Gardner
Prant Nancy E .... Hooker

Prather Helen A .... Mason
Prator Pamela M .... Dean
Pratt Anne Biddle .... Pratt
Pratt Caroline .... Cavanagh
Pratt Deming .... Holleran
Pratt Dorothy D .... Barrett
Pratt Elisabeth S .... Livingston
Pratt Frances W .... Gray
Pratt Imogene R .... Luther
Pratt Lydia M .... Speir
Pratt Margaret C .... Witherby
Pratt Mary .... Boyd
Pratt Mary L .... Montgomery
Pratt Mary M .... Barringer
Pratt Mary T .... Mullally
Pratt Pauline D .... Brown
Pratt Virginia C .... Agar
Pray Dorothy A .... Barringer
Pray Natasha Justina .... Grayson
Pray Patricia B .... Bradley
Pray Sandra F .... Culbert
Prebensen Evelyn .... Harrison
Prentice Clare E .... Potter
Prentice Margaret E S .... Kilmer
Prentice Phoebe O .... Dewing
Prentice Susan S .... Cochran
Prescott Lydia C .... Thayer
Prescott Micaela .... Obregón-Peña
Prescott Phebe A .... Greenwood
Presley Cheryl A .... Becker
Presnell Polly A .... Herron
Presnikoff Anne I .... Watkins
Pressley Page P .... Solomon
Pressprich Alyce .... Brookfield
Pressprich Joan .... Metcalf
Preston Diana M .... Gonzalez
Preston Dorothy M .... Ware
Preston Eleanor C .... Ritchie
Preston Elizabeth .... Hutchings
Preston Jane C .... Evans
Preston Jean .... Tilt
Preston Linda M .... Woodwell
Preston Margaret .... Palmer
Preston Margaret .... Symonds
Preston Marion M .... Cecil
Preston Mary Ord .... Massey
Preston Susan M .... Resnik
Prettyman Helen C .... Walker
Preuit Dorothy J .... Naughton
Prewer Marguerite G .... Martin
Prezzano Katherine A .... Durfee
Price Alexandra Montague .... Hogan
Price Andrea H .... Pryal
Price Barbara S .... McDougal
Price C Blair .... Iodice
Price Clarissa T .... Marckwald
Price Dale M .... Miller
Price Diana M .... Hill
Price Eleanor R .... Lloyd
Price Evelyn T .... Scott
Price Helen H .... Ballantine
Price Imogene C .... Vulte
Price Jehanne H .... White

Price Joy T .... Barrows
Price Keith McC .... McKenrick
Price Martha A .... Price
Price Mary-Stuart Montague
 .... Diefenbach
Price N Gail .... Messiqua
Price Nancy M .... Hiestand
Price Rew .... Carne
Price Sarah M .... Chittenden
Price V Jane .... Hall
Price Virginia E .... Damon
Price Wendy .... Todd
Prichard Anne P .... Miller
Prichard Helen L .... King
Prichard Sybil A .... Walk
Prichitt Margaret H .... MacNair
Prickett Elisabeth De B .... Deans
Prideaux-Brune Cynthia M D .... Gray
Priest Susan C .... Mesker
Prigmore Margaret M .... Van Cleave
Prillaman J Leanne .... Harrison
Prime Charlotte L .... Bonds
Prime Mary G .... Peet
Primm Louise G .... Samuel
Prince Elizabeth P .... van Buren
Prince Justine .... Elliott
Prince Lawson .... Allen
Prince Marjorie M .... Thomas
Prince Priscilla B .... Whitney
Prince Susan R .... Watson
Prince Winifred C .... Hyson
Prindle Margaret B .... Mathews
Pringle Isabel A .... Clark
Pringle Louisa Huger .... Cameron
Priory Jane E .... Gummere
Pritchard Barbara L .... Hope
Pritchard Mary E .... Dallett
Pritting Mary A .... Tanner
Pritzlaff Ann O .... Symington
Privett Allison .... Robbins
Probasco Alice M .... Lupton
Prochnik Valerie S .... Ragland
Procter Hope .... Stokes
Proctor Barbara .... Richardson
Proctor Dell W .... Hollstein
Proctor Hannah D .... McInnis
Proctor Jean-Lamont .... Dane
Proctor Joy W .... Schieffelin
Prokoff Elizabeth .... Hyde
Proper Margaret L .... Powell
Prophet Annette J .... McCabe
Proske Bettina J .... Walker
Prosser Elizabeth W .... Richards
Prosser Ethel .... Baker
Prothero Elizabeth A .... Slaymaker
Prothro Nita C .... Clark
Protzman Elizabeth L .... Webb
Prout Claudia .... Casey
Prout Pamela B .... Odgers
Prouty Hilary J .... Van Rensselaer
Provosty Jacqueline .... Avegno
Prowell Leonora P .... Paxton
Pruett Sharon K .... Adams

Pruit Helen ....Matthews
Prus Lucille J ....Lamy
Pruyn Patricia V S ....Storey
Pryor Janice A ....Noble
Pryor Penelope...........................Wike
Ptak Leslie A ....Baker
Pugh Elizabeth W ....Pugh
Pugh Louise W .... Worthing
Pukkila Marja T ....Emmett
Pulitzer Barbara ....Wood
Pulitzer Elizabeth E .... Voges
Pulitzer Gladys M...................Preston
Pulitzer Liza D...........................Leidy
Pullen Harriet S ....Phillips
Pulleyn Pamela W ....Machold
Pulling E Joan.......................Shepard
Pulling Lucy...........................Cutting
Pulling Patricia ....Sands
Pulling Victoria S ....Allen
Pullman Josephine L.................Tucker
Pund Susan C...........................Park
Purcell Kathleen A ....Vander Horst
Purdon Pamela B ....Link
Purin Karen A........................Thomas
Purinton Jane M C ....Donahue
Purinton Lila G ....Worsley
Purnell Elizabeth D...............Raffetto
Purry Daphne E S ....Button
Purves Ann C L ....Veit
Purves Margaretta F G ....Johnston
Purviance Eleanor.................Bostwick
Purviance Sydney ....Blynn
Purvine Helen ....Burnett
Purvis Clover D.....................Roulette
Purvis Roberta E.....................Murray
Purvis Sara L ....Connolly
Pusateri Nancy F........................Davis
Putman Sheridan L ....Conway
Putnam Anne E........................Canby
Putnam Barbara ....Graham
Putnam Barbara L....................Lyman
Putnam Charlotte M ....Bagley
Putnam Doanda R................Wheeler
Putnam E Louise C..................Stoner
Putnam Gail ....Emmet
Putnam Grace M.................Wadsworth
Putnam Kate D ....Baxter
Putnam Katherine E.................Delaney
Putnam Kimberly H..................Lanier
Putnam Macy B ....Janney
Putnam Mary C.....................Chatfield
Putnam Nancy H....................Schwartz
Putnam Sally ....Chapman
Putnam Shirley G ....Grange
Puttkammer Helen L.................Straus
Pyke Patricia M ....Munn
Pyle Anne T ....Dennis
Pyle Diana M ....Rowan
Pyle Elizabeth C ....Handler
Pyles Courtney L........................Kahn
Pyles Elizabeth A ....Nelson
Pyles Kathryn B......................Hubby
Pynchon June H...........................Binz

Pynchon Mary S ....Wastcoat
Pynchon Michelle ....Osborn
Pyne Alison...............................Ewing
Pyne Leta W ....Kniffin
Pyne Lillian S ....Corbin
Pyne M Alison ...... McNaughton
Quale Marcia ....Kay
Qualey Regina ....Keating
Quarles Barbara J .... Harper
Quarles Cornelia G ....Wonham
Quay Elizabeth M ....Andrews
Quealy Susie J ....Dwyer
Queener Alyne .... Massey
Queripel Yvonne......................Schley
Quesada Norma M.....................Wolf
Quick Mary A ....Flinn
Quigley Meggan C ....Mackay
Quigley Ruth M.......................Fleitas
Quinlan Elizabeth .... Ingersoll
Quinn Barbara......................Seymour
Quinn Constance C................... Holth
Quinn Lee E........................Fischbach
Quinn Mary K........................Wilson
Quinn Patricia A....................Connolly
Quinn Virginia ....Stiger
Quinsler Elizabeth B................. Frost
Quintal Barbara M................Berglund
Quintana Carmen ....Reynal
Quirk Betty ....Bryan
Quirk M E Louise ....Holmes
Quirk Nancy..........................Potter
Rabenberg Kimberly M.............Barnes
Rabon Jill............................Davidge
Rackemann Dorothy M ....Young
Radcliff Ann V P.......................Wells
Radigan Claudia M...............Wardman
Radoonsoff Natasha.............Hopkinson
Radosavljevic Denise....................Hale
Rae Helen.............................Stebbins
Rae Kristin A ....Allen
Rafferty L Anne....................Carpenter
Rahm Karin...........................Vincent
Rainey Gloria A ....Renwick
Rainold Cynthia W ....Hammond
Rainsford Rita ....Rouner
Raisin Suzanne.......................Ritchie
Raisor Lynn K ....Kelley
Raith C Diane ....Garesché
Rajacich Lynn.........................Osborn
Rake Georgine L...................Goodman
Rake Susannah E ....Butash
Rakestraw M Thérèse ....Pew
Ralph Patricia L ....Fowler
Ralston Joan G....................Cochran
Ralston Joanne E ....Brown
Ralston Lucile R.....................Northrop
Rambo Louise B ....King
Rambo Louise de C ....Adams
Rambusch Kirstin G ....von Thelen
Ramirez M Antonia R ....Hudson
Ramm Tanja.........................McKee
Ramsay E Joan ....Palmer
Ramsay Jane G A .... Pomeroy

Ramsay Jean C ....Bower
Ramsdell Helen ....Bingham
Ramsey Olivia ....Brown
Rana Nicole M........................Turner
Rancic Marina ....Maybank
Ranck Mary V ....Whitbeck
Ranck Rosemary ....Traxel
Rand Alicia ....Möller
Rand Carla C ....Trova
Rand Carley C .... Weatherley-White
Rand Christina B ....Whitman
Rand Elizabeth A ....Alexander
Rand Jennifer S.......................Bodoia
Rand Lila B ....Whitbeck
Rand Mary F............................Rand
Randall Carroll D ....Harris
Randall Frances J.......................Wood
Randall Joanne M.................Dunlaevy
Randall Mary W ....Alford
Randall Susan D..........................Lee
Randel Catherine ....Kilduff
Randel Claudia A ....Little
Randle Barbara A ....Robins
Randolph Bruce D....................Murray
Randolph Hannah Hope ....Shipley
Randolph Irene N ....Morrill
Randolph Jean W....................Houston
Randolph Katharine G ....Stovell
Randolph Katherine V .... Witherspoon
Randolph P Frances ....Watson
Randolph Pickett D..................Randolph
Randolph Rosalie F ....Dickson
Raney Elizabeth ....Harvey
Ranken Mary A ....Reese
Rankin Anne W ....Nelson
Rankin Joyce A ....Cumings
Ranney Dorothy W ....Donnelley
Ransom Eleanor B ....Swift
Rantoul Edith F....................Greenwood
Raoul-Duval Diane ....King
Rapalus Diane E ....Beir
Rapp Joan..............................Mayhew
Rapp M Estelle ....Sarran
Rasch Elizabeth W ....Morehouse
Rasinski Patricia B ....Locke
Rask Berit E ....Stanton
Rasmusen Jorgi ....Thorne
Rasmussen Ann B....................Kinney
Rasmussen Janet K ....Cox
Rasmussen Sara A ....Fraser
Rast Martha E .... De Buys
Rastetter Margaret E.................George
Ratcliff Susan M.................Symington
Ratcliffe M Fraser.............Zimmerman
Rath Jean S ....Kopp
Rath Nancy P ....Nigro
Rathbone Eliza E ....Hamilton
Rathbone Ernestine N

          DeNormandie
Rathbone Nancy W ....Rathbone
Ratko Lisa J ....Roome
Ratliff Deborah G ....Miller
Rau Frances M.......................Phillips

Rauch Eleanor G.......................Crosby
Rauch Katrina ....Byers
Rauch Paton ....Roberts
Rauch Paton S..........................White
Rauch Sheila B ....Kennedy
Rauh Emily S........................Pulitzer
Rauh Virginia A ....Gallagher
Raushenbush Lisa K ....Pettengill
Ravenel Julia V ....Dougherty
Ravenel Margaret Benoist ....Elliott
Ravenel Rita...........................Weekes
Rawle Harriet C ....Hemenway
Rawle Judith ....Neilson
Rawle Louisa ....Tiné
Rawle Mary Elizabeth M .... Slattery
Rawlings Jean ....Chickering
Rawn Jessie L ....Cale
Raworth Mabel C ....Tippens
Raworth Roberta G......................Page
Raworth Roberta G...............Scarbrough
Rawson Elizabeth ....Macgill
Rawson Linda K ....Harrison
Ray Abby ....Catledge
Ray Beverly V ....Coope
Ray Katharine A ....Sturgis
Ray Kathryna H ....Stetson
Ray M Joanna ....Inches
Ray Monica A ....Key
Ray Roberta P...........................Wurts
Raycroft Virginia ....Wilson
Raymond Ann..............................Luce
Raymond Barbara J ....Hickox
Raymond Barbara M ....Williams
Raymond Elisabeth L .... Woods
Raymond Elise ....Wallace
Raymond Elizabeth H ....Thomas
Raymond Emma G ....White
Raymond Marion W ....Bestani
Raymond Nancy J......................McCune
Raymond Phoebe A ....Flickinger
Raymont Pamela A................. Simpson
Raynor-Smith Gertrude L M

          Notman
Rea Mary C...........................Weidlein
Rea Shelley S ....Gilbert
Rea Suzanne L ....Vermilye
Read Alison A ....Villa
Read Ann E.............................Jones
Read Anne E..........................Rogers
Read Anne E..........................Sayen
Read Caroline G ....Harding
Read Cornelia L F.....................Eggert
Read Elizabeth........................Foster
Read Helen............................Trent
Read Jean ....Knox
Read Judith A ....Danenhower
Read Linda B ....Hobbs
Read Melissa W ....Jackson
Read Nancy W ....Wickett
Read Pamela A ....Peck
Read Rachel B ....Hillman
Read Rachel W ....Hopkinson
Read Sandra L ....Read

Reade Nancy H.........................Everett
Reading Eleanor L.....................Finley
Ready Beverly A.................Crawford
Reagan Keturah MacArthur........Faurot
Reagan Mary E............................Dick
Reagan Nora ....Etheridge
Reakirt Nancy E........................Martin
Ream Carolyn T......................Lincoln
Ream Elizabeth A....................Noble
Reams Lea K...........................Emery
Reardon Kathleen C....................Earl
Reardon Lucy C......................Eustis
Reardon Maura L...................Reardon
Reasor Laura...........................Allis
Reath Alberta P........................Reath
Reath Mary ....Funk
Reath Robin ....Graves
Reath Sheila W.........................Taylor
Reaves Ouida L....................Goehring
Reavis Berry ....Eitel
Reay Miriam S.............................Bell
Reber Ann C............................Brown
Rebmann Ann ....Daudon
Red Margaret T........................Evans
Reddick Rosemary......................Clark
Reddy Jean ....Armour
Redenius Josephine Louise.........Baker
Redfield Elizabeth C.............Redfield
Redfield Margaret ....Mayfield
Redfield Nicole Von G..............Fanjul
Rediker Diana B ....Slaughter
Redlich Philipa A ....Caldwell
Redman Janet ....Hill
Redman Kathleen.......................Colket
Redmon Skipwith C W ....Banker
Redmond Cynthia ....Mead
Redmond Marylouise E.........Coolidge
Redmond Moira L ....Filley
Redmond Nancy E.................Maniere
Redpath Jean C ....Becton
Redway Dora M ....Pierce
Redwood Eleanor T...............Penovich
Reece Charlotte Cameron.........Disston
Reece Elizabeth B....................Waters
Reed Alice B.........................McGuire
Reed Alice H ....Tucker
Reed Alixe C.............................Glen
Reed Anne B......................Witherby
Reed Barbara de S ....Delafield
Reed Beatrice A.....................Morrison
Reed Carol L...........................Ewart
Reed Charlotte C ....Pugh
Reed Cynthia ....Beachboard
Reed Edith J............................Catlin
Reed Eleanore M.......................Coffin
Reed Elizabeth W..................Eiseman
Reed Gwynne.........................Moffitt
Reed Harriet B.........................Harris
Reed Julia C...........................Palmer
Reed Katherine N ....Humphrey
Reed Laura L G ....Bell
Reed Louise M ....Rhinelander
Reed Madeleine C ....Wyeth

Reed Martha L.....................Woodwell
Reed Mary R..............................Fisher
Reed Polly G..............................Daniel
Reed R Lindley.........................Hunter
Reed Rosamond F....................Wulsin
Reed Ruth ....Gillespie
Reed Serena ....Kusserow
Reed Thyra Elizabeth ....Bramwell
Reed Virginia B ....Gaffney
Reeder Diana A ....Schley
Reeder Gloria Fay......................Weltz
Reeder Nancy F ....El Bouhali
Rees Mary Elizabeth...................Taylor
Reese Anna H........................von Lunz
Reese Elisabeth ....Chance
Reese Patricia A ....Vanderwarker
Reese Victoria S ....Kennedy
Reeve Anne W.........................Childs
Reeve Cassandra S ....Stone
Reeve Cintra L.............................Reeve
Reeve Corinna Roosevelt ....Waud
Reeve Eleanor F W ....Peterson
Reeve Elizabeth N....................Bright
Reeve Josephine L K ....Tasman
Reeve Josephine R Spalding
                              Voevodsky
Reeve Katharine R....................Reeve
Reeve Victoria R ....Spaulding
Reeves Beverly J ....Politzer
Reeves E Jane ....McKay
Reeves E Lovejoy....................Duryea
Reeves Joan B........................Lapham
Reeves Josephine L ....Winsor
Reeves Margaret M ....Drury
Reeves Marguerite S..................Joseph
Reeves Mary F.........................Packard
Reeves Sally L.......................Edmonds
Reeves Stella E...........................Hall
Reeves Susan R ....Deland
Regan Ellen F...........................Brown
Regan Esther.............................Warren
Regan Nancy W....................Lombard
Register Candace B ....Langan
Register Cornelia E................Hoagland
Register Nancy S ....Wise
Reich Lucille E ....Hurd
Reichart Lynne E.....................Graves
Reichenbach Virginia ....Mallery
Reichmann Elizabeth A.............Crowell
Reichmuth Barbara A ....Geisler
Reichner Barbara F..............Middleton
Reichner Sally K......................Mayor
Reid Alice F............................Abbott
Reid Cordelia D.....................McCuaig
Reid Cynthia A.....................Anderson
Reid Iris ....Semple
Reid Katherine B ....Frick
Reid Margaret B ....North
Reid Margaret C ....Mueller
Reid Margaret P........................Ogden
Reid Mary Armour......................Miller
Reid Pamela J............................Trippe
Reid Sarah R..............................Absher

Reid Winthrop ....Burns
Reifsnider Eleanor A ....Riggs
Reigle Patricia L.....................Benoist
Reijmers Joan H ....Parish
Reilly Josephine E ....Stevenson
Reilly Macy Ann ....Beha
Reilly Madeleine H....................Bailey
Reilly Marjorie.......................Bromley
Reilly Martha E ....Smith
Reilly Mary J ....Woodward
Reilly Nancy M ....Prentice
Reimers Doris E ....O'Brien
Reimers Virginia.........................Perry
Reinicke Ann C....................Peabody
Reinke Ann E...........................Strong
Reisinger Mary H ....Stevens
Reiss Lucy M...........................Mullen
Reiss Rita K............................Gorman
Reist Dorothy E ....McCombs
Reith Joyce E ....Wolfsberger
Reksten Astrid ....Reksten
Remick Eleanor H ....Seaman
Remick Joan F ....McNee
Remick Mary ....Tyler
Remington Elizabeth R.............McKay
Remington Georgia W................Martin
Remington Margaret P ....Smith
Remke Katherine J ....Blagden
Renchard Christine F..............Huffman
Renchard Cynthia W ....French
Renchard Jeanie A ....Adcock
Renchard Roberta S ....Freer
Renchard Stella M ....Seamans
Renfert Melita B ....Lane
Renfro Amy R ....May
Renner Judith H ....Bullitt
Rennie Milbrey T ....Taylor
Rennolds Caroline K ....Milbank
Rentschler Mary C...................Lowrey
Rentschler Phoebe ....Stanton
Rentschler Susan H..................Witter
Renwick Beatrice L.................Jordan
Reny Jane F ....Frank
Renzy Caroline D ....Bellinger
Repp Cheryl ....Sargent
Reppert Ann B ....MacDonald
ReQua A Suzanne.......................Feurich
ReQua Catharine H......................Cluett
ReQua K Marka.........................Burnett
Reque Susan B.........................Reque
Requardt Chesley Fenton ....Harrison
Requardt Kathryn Kip ....Vaughan
Retting Virginia P...................Tierney
Retz Grace M...........................Donald
Reusch Cathleen ....Tilney
Reuther Anne ....Harris
Revilla Elena Socorro...................Craig
Revis Anne E......................Grosvenor
Rex Diane J.................................Kelly
Rex Sandra H.........................McCall
Rexford Susan E ....Livingston
Reynal Angelica M....................Thieriot
Reynolds Alice K ....Reynolds

Reynolds Annette H ....Ramsing
Reynolds Carol M.....................Dunham
Reynolds D Chase ....Ewald
Reynolds Daphne....................Williams
Reynolds Deborah ....Harrington
Reynolds Dorothy ....Breck
Reynolds Elizabeth S..................Colt
Reynolds Elizabeth T E........Henderson
Reynolds Jeanne S ....Stallings
Reynolds Judith Ann ....Newell
Reynolds Karen E........................Hires
Reynolds Katharine L.............Chandler
Reynolds Laura W ....Appell
Reynolds Margaret P ....Leavens
Reynolds Mary G ....Middendorf
Reynolds Maureen A ....Vincent
Reynolds Mildred A ....Orme
Reynolds Nancy...........................Day
Reynolds Nancy E ....Wharton
Reynolds Phyllis M ....Weekes
Reynolds Rebecca W ....Wells
Reynolds Ruth ....Baxter
Reynolds Susan F ....Reynolds
Reynolds Virginia W ....Parker
Rhame Ann B ....Coffin
Rhame Lucy S ....Rhame
Rhea Margaret Ritchie...................Scaife
Rhein Elizabeth K...................Collins
Rhein Patricia B........................Turner
Rhinelander Clare H ....Rhinelander
Rhinelander Elizabeth T ....MacEwen
Rhinelander Jeannine B ....Schoeffer
Rhinelander Le Brun C ......McKnight
Rhinelander Louise duP ....Doyle
Rhines Sandra ....Smith
Rhoades Dorothy I..................Herrick
Rhoads Margaret G.....................Evans
Rhodes Anne H........................Amos
Rhodes Colley ....Griffin
Rhodes Mary...........................Lowery
Rhodes Mary A.........................Hicks
Rhodes Nancy A.......................White
Rhodes Nancy B....................Burrows
Rial Bruce ....Hennessy
Rial Sally W ....French
Rianhard Elizabeth L...........Hilgenberg
Ribbel Ann H.........................Seymour
Ricci Melissa McL ....Stewart
Rice Barbara.............................Allen
Rice Barbara J........................Bracken
Rice Barbara L......................Dempsey
Rice Eleanor ....Morse
Rice Elizabeth ....Felder
Rice Elizabeth A ....Tuthill
Rice Helen J............................Magee
Rice Janet C............................French
Rice M Melinda.........................Potter
Rice Margaret A ....Stout
Rice Martha ....Crocker
Rice Mary A.............................Potter
Rice Mary M............................King
Rice Natalie C..........................Rafferty

Rice Roselle M .... Eldredge
Rice Suzanne .... Morse
Rice Virginia B .... Johnson
Rich Elizabeth F .... Trapnell
Rich Elizabeth K .... Reardon
Rich Frances L .... Donohue
Rich Louise C .... Means
Rich Margaret E .... Carr
Rich Nancy W .... Coolidge
Rich Priscilla .... Ritter
Richard Edith W .... Townsend
Richard Katharine T .... Marcy
Richard Phyllis Van B .... Fritts
Richard Vera Van B .... Wood
Richards Ann K .... Nitze
Richards Carlissa K .... Hughes
Richards Catherine.................. Register
Richards Catherine J .... Froeb
Richards Elizabeth B .... Houghton
Richards Emily L...................... Haines
Richards Frederica G K ....Struse
Richards Imogen R .... Upton
Richards Jane K ....Roth
Richards Jeannetta Murray .... Richey
Richards June B ....Flake
Richards Katherine ....Pleasants
Richards Lindy S ....Carmalt
Richards Lydia A......................Boyer
Richards Margaret R .... Wiederseim
Richards Margaret W .... Coogan
Richards Mary T .... Bartlett
Richards Mary van C .... Sloan
Richards Muriel G .... Holzman
Richards Nancy A..................... McCabe
Richards Pamela .... Brooks
Richards Sarah D .... Frost
Richards Susan......................... Little
Richards Toni............................ King
Richardson Anita .... Gildersleeve
Richardson Anne .... Yancey
Richardson Anne P .... Howland
Richardson Anne S .... Hoversten
Richardson Beth M................. Clements
Richardson Bonnie Donnell .... White
Richardson Carolyn L................. Aller
Richardson Curtiss W .... Van Dusen
Richardson Dorothea .... Wendell
Richardson Evelyn S .... Groome
Richardson F Elizabeth .... Simmons
Richardson Faith...................... Barnett
Richardson Florence M .... Groman
Richardson Frances A................. White
Richardson Grace S .... Stetson
Richardson Hildegard ....Dyett
Richardson Juliet .... French
Richardson Laura..................Houghton
Richardson Laura .... Payson
Richardson Lily .... Leonard
Richardson Lindsay C .... Thomas
Richardson Mandy-Jayne ....Fischer
Richardson Margery E...........Claghorn
Richardson Marion J E.............Taylor
Richardson Martha....................Moore

Richardson Meryl E....................Nolan
Richardson Prudence L.............Beidler
Richardson R Melody Sawyer
.... Richardson
Richardson Sarah A ....Litchfield
Richardson Susan B .... Patton
Richardson Susan E .... Duncan
Richardson Wendy L................. Ardrey
Richbourg Maxine .... Wells
Richmond Ann....................... Jennings
Richmond Jane B....................Crocker
Richmond Janet V V M ....Richmond
Richmond Julia M .... Pomeroy
Richmond Katharine H............. Trotman
Richmond Marjorie N.............Lambert
Richmond Mary-Louise...........Annibali
Richmond Nancy .... Blackett
Richmond Rosita L .... Watson
Richoz Dianne E .... Barclay
Rickards F Murrell ....Chadsey
Ricketson Margaret C .... Sprague
Ricks Ann E...............................Case
Riddell Dorothy .... Thatcher
Riddell Lucy E.........................Jones
Ridder Barbara..........................Irwin
Ridder Gretchen..................... Nicholas
Ridder Katherine L .... Pennoyer
Riddle Nancy A .... Mann
Riddle Virginia B .... Pearson
Rideout Tamsen A ....Weekes
Ridgely Julia M ....Howe
Ridgley Marilyn Lea...................Fuller
Ridgway Emily S......................Crisp
Ridgway Geraldine ....Mason
Ridgway Sara P .... McLean
Ridley Pauline F .... Wilson
Ridoux Francois T ....Gooding
Riegel Anne M ....Parrish
Riegel Ashley P .... Harrington
Riegel Edith duP......................Miller
Riegel Jennifer N ....Elmlinger
Riegel Katherine E .... Emory
Riegel Laura Cushing .... Curry
Rielly Barbara E ....Hubbard
Riemer Elizabeth L..................Reece
Riess Katherine E .... Irving
Riggins Anne K ....Ponti
Riggio Flavia A .... Hackett
Riggio Nina E .... Hay
Riggs Alethea N .... Michie
Riggs Camilla K ....Meigs
Riggs Elizabeth L ....Brandon
Riggs F Blair .... Boone
Riggs Jane C ....Garcia-Mansilla
Riggs M Lawrason ....Wing
Riggs Susan D .... McIntosh
Righter Elinor .... Oakes
Righter Tracey D .... Mulligan
Rightor Anne H .... Thornton
Rightor Jane Pillow ....Lee
Rigor Lydia V .... Barringer
Riker Alison C .... Friedel
Riker Anne T .... Buttrick
Riker Cornelia......................... Chéhab

Riker Judith C .... Wiley
Riker Margaret....................... Harding
Riley Cynthia .... Parsons
Riley Dorothy A ....O'Reilly
Riley Elizabeth H ....Shaw
Riley Eugenie W................... Anderson
Riley Joan B .... Burchenal
Riley Linda K .... Parrish
Riley Margaret D .... Stillman
Riley Nancy .... Carson
Rinehart Rebecca S ....Taft
Ring Eleanor A ....White
Ringe Barbara G .... Ritter
Ringer Arlene M........................Lattu
Ringle Leslie A .... Kellogg
Ringwalt Mary B .... Woodworth
Riordan Eugenia M.................... Callan
Ripley Annabel F...................Ebersole
Ripley Frederica P .... French
Ripley Julie D S.......................Miller
Ripley Priscilla B........................Lichty
Ripley Rosalie W .... Furniss
Ripley Rosemary L ....Ripley
Ripley Sylvia McN.................. Addison
Rippin Ann S ....Rae
Risien Diana R .... Jannetta
Ristine Dorothy S .... Althouse
Ritch Barbara E ....Jackson
Ritchey Ann McD....................Baruch
Ritchie Charlotte S .... Ritchie
Ritchie Louise L .... Beale
Riter Mary L .... Walker
Riter Mary V.......................Pancoast
Riter Patricia B .... Lander
Rittenhouse Jane .... Wright
Rittenour Carolyn C ....Lind
Ritter Eleanor F .... Dulles
Ritter Elizabeth J .... Pugh
Ritter Lucinda U.....................Jackman
Ritter Marie S .... Potter
Ritter Patricia E .... Tait
Ritter Serena T..................... Livingston
Ritterbush Dorthy H ....Whiteman
Rittershofer Anne F .... Neumann
Rittmueller Jean .... Dohan
Ritz Caroleigh .... Evarts
Rivera M Mayela.................. Chapman
Rivers L Marion .... Ravenel
Rivinus Emilie M ....Brégy
Rivinus Martha ....Page
Rivinus Mary H .... Madeira
Rivkin Judith F .... Davison
Rizzo Andrea N .... Cuvelier
Roach Ann C ....Hoover
Roach Cecile H ....Delafield
Roach Edith M......................Bissell
Roach Mary S .... Sawyer
Roach Susan W........................Duer
Robb Adelaide S .... Gaillard
Robb Ann G .... Smith
Robb Cornelia T .... Brock
Robb Edith B ....Dixon
Robb Gale A .... Guild

Robb Janice........................... Anderson
Robb Roberta H .... Bratenahl
Robb Ruth W.........................Wolcott
Robbins Amy .... Warden
Robbins Barbara .... Anderson
Robbins Barbara .... Armstrong
Robbins Carolyn .... Laflin
Robbins Celina........................Kellogg
Robbins I Helen.......................Forbes
Robbins Joan M .... Barkan
Robbins Katherine .... Met
Robbins Laura......................... Lyman
Robbins Margaret P ....Charpentier
Robbins Marie A .... Barlow
Robbins Martha D ....Macdonald
Robbins Mary ....Runyon
Robbins Nancy B ....Rea
Robbins Pamela A .... Fahnestock
Robbins Sarah F .... Bradshaw
Robbins Sarah L .... Carmalt
Robbins Virginia............. Raynor-Smith
Robbins Wendy H .... Foulke
Roberg M Carolyn..................Moseley
Roberson Elizabeth de V ....Gibson
Roberts Alice .... Connolly
Roberts Alice W ....Pierson
Roberts Amy W .... Lee
Roberts Anna .... Welles
Roberts Anne .... Duff
Roberts Annette C .... Slowinski
Roberts Antoinette L .... Brewster
Roberts Catherine G .... Benedict
Roberts Diana B ....McCarley
Roberts Diana H .... Slocum
Roberts E Page .... Gowen
Roberts Elizabeth I ....Viall
Roberts Elizabeth J .... Richardson
Roberts Ellanor T .... Notides
Roberts Emily S ....Wick
Roberts Flora ....Ghriskey
Roberts Frances P .... Davies
Roberts Gail L ....Evans
Roberts Gladys V ....Thomas
Roberts Harriet E ....Painter
Roberts Janae........................Harris
Roberts Jane F .... Sloat
Roberts June......................... Lilienthal
Roberts Katharine E .... Mack
Roberts Letitia S ....Lee
Roberts Louise McI .... Johnston
Roberts M Louise ....Stengel
Roberts M Megan ....Gabriel
Roberts M Patricia ....Shriver
Roberts Margaret D .... Stevenson
Roberts Margaret R ....Culp
Roberts Mary E........................Farr
Roberts Mary E...................... Morgan
Roberts Mary S .... Wright
Roberts Noma Ann ....Roberts
Roberts Octavia ....Allis
Roberts Pauline S .... Anderson
Roberts Rosalinda B ....Madara
Roberts Rosamond G..................Dean

Roberts Susan .... Bean
Roberts Sydney M .... Shuman
Roberts Virginia L .... Flaccus
Robertson Anne B .... Spencer
Robertson Anne T .... Wheeler
Robertson Elizabeth T ....Fondaras
Robertson Frances ....Chandler
Robertson Gertrude T ....Dodson
Robertson Gratia L .... McLane
Robertson Janis .... Penton
Robertson Laura Lea .... Hatch
Robertson Lillian F................Bradford
Robertson Margaret A ....Clark
Robertson Mary D .... Barron
Robertson Mary L .... Abbott
Robertson Nancy L....................White
Robertson Nancy M .... Jewett
Robey Harriet L....................... Myers
Robineau Patricia ....McCulloch
Robinett Suzanne P C ....Brown
Robins Barbara .... Anderson
Robins Gloria J .... Guarino
Robins Lisa .... MacKay
Robins Mary Van R .... McKee
Robins Susannah F .... Albright
Robinson Alexis P ....Waller
Robinson Alice A ....Righter
Robinson Althea D .... Gorman
Robinson Andrea C ....Ross
Robinson Ann C ....Clay
Robinson Augusta McL.............Alsop
Robinson B Page B .... Griffith
Robinson Chata..........................Smith
Robinson Christine L .... Secor
Robinson Cynthia .... Kirby
Robinson Elinor C ....Greene
Robinson Elizabeth C ....O'Connell
Robinson Elizabeth W ....Page
Robinson Frances I ....Baker
Robinson Hannele.................Lawrence
Robinson Jane P .... Chester
Robinson Jean F ....Burke
Robinson Jessica B .... Cochran
Robinson Lauretta D.............. Robinson
Robinson Lois A .... Russell
Robinson Louisa L ....Brown
Robinson Lucy Grosvenor.........Cooley
Robinson Lynne .... Brookfield
Robinson M Ann C ....Kelly
Robinson M Barbara..................... West
Robinson Martha M .... Higgins
Robinson Mary A .... Clarkson
Robinson Mary S .... Grote
Robinson Nora .... Stark
Robinson Pamela Q .... Plater
Robinson Rhea A ....Claggett
Robinson Sarah M ....Blair
Robinson Susan ....Lammert
Robinson Virginia C ....Bogert
Robinson Virginia C ....Munn
Robinson Virginia O ....Downey
Robinson Virginia T ....Frelinghuysen
Robinsson Constance A H...........Pigott

Robison Gail ....Brodie
Roblin Carolyn...........................Chew
Roche Hilary S ....Geary
Roche Janice E ....Bull
Roche Kathleen E ....Horne
Roche L Coverly............................Rees
Rochester Betsey ....Spragins
Rochfort Mary I .... Harville
Rock Adele D .... Nickel
Rockage Anne T .... Sanger
Rockefeller Almira G .... Scott
Rockefeller Ann......................Elliman
Rockefeller Edith McK...............Laird
Rockefeller Georgia S ....Rose
Rockefeller Mary C .... Callard
Rockefeller Nancy C S ....Copp
Rockefeller Victoria S ....Philip
Rockhill Erdice ....Pardee
Rockwell Alix H......................Jacobs
Rockwell Brenda K .... Reed
Rockwell Elizabeth .... Marshall
Rockwell Marie H .... Galbraith
Rockwood Charlotte L ....Irvin
Rodale Nina ....Houghton
Roden Melanie W ....Bartlett
Roden Valerie-Clark ....Roden
Rodenbaugh Caroline C ....Nassau
Rodenhauser Mary E ....Moore
Rodes Janet .... Hester
Rodes Margaret M ....White
Rodewald Glorvina H.............Schwartz
Rodgers Anne E ....Tennyson
Rodgers E Anne ....Harvey
Rodgers Katherine N ....Denckla
Rodgers M Florence ....Warren
Rodgers M Katharine T ....Ellicott
Rodgers Nancy L ....Knipe
Rodgers Suzanne ....Nelms
Rodham Hillary ....Clinton
Rodman Eunice R ....Packer
Rodolph Helen .... Ames
Rodriguez Susan T .... Lowrey
Roe Eleanor B.............................Clark
Roe Emily B ....Rotch
Roe Genevieve ....Flickinger
Roe Martha G ....Lancaster
Roe Page K ....Barroll
Roebuck Rebecca L .... Winter
Roeding Dorothea .... Bishop
Roeding Margaret ....Chickering
Roelker Katrina T .... Stokes
Roesler Anne M ....Roesler
Roesler Charlotte ....Lindsey
Roesler Jane L ....Corcoran
Roesler Lucile A H.................Bollman
Roeth Janine A ....Hooker
Rogach Gloria L .... Van Gulick
Rogalla von Bieberstein Elisabeth
.... Childs
Rogers Alice L ....Sadtler
Rogers Alison W .... Knight
Rogers Ann C ....Rooth
Rogers Anne C ....Leslie

Rogers Anne E..........................Wilbur
Rogers Beverley B ....Wood
Rogers Camille C ....Campbell
Rogers Constance L ....Roosevelt
Rogers Deborah D .... Butler
Rogers Deborah E .... Bowers
Rogers Elizabeth ....Strough
Rogers Elizabeth E ....Rathborne
Rogers Elizabeth S .... Brokaw
Rogers Emily Le C .... Tiedemann
Rogers Evelyn W ....Chanler
Rogers Frances P ....Zilkha
Rogers Gladys A...........................Buck
Rogers Gladys L .... Brooks
Rogers Gretchen H ....Colby
Rogers Iris G.......................... Argento
Rogers Jane C ....Foster
Rogers Judy A .... Boring
Rogers Louise W ....Kniffin
Rogers Marian P ....Bowditch
Rogers Mary B .... Rhoades
Rogers Mary J.............................Clay
Rogers Mary M.................Auchincloss
Rogers Mary W ....Soule
Rogers Nancy B .... Bowen
Rogers Nancy H .... Baker
Rogers Susan G .... Iliff
Rogers Susan L ....Barnard
Rogers Susanna P B ....Kelham
Rogerson Helen C ....Haddad
Rogerson Martha ....Estabrook
Rohde Betty L...............................Hall
Rohrbach Augusta ....Rohrbach
Rohrbacher Judith A ....McAlpin
Roitsch Karen A ....Norman
Rolfe Barbara ....Prettyman
Rolfe Joan ....Donohoe
Rolfes G Paige .... Horine
Rolin Edith P ....Roach
Rolla Anne K .... Thompson
Rollins Elizabeth...................Creelman
Rollins Elizabeth......................Greene
Rollins Glendora E ....Trescher
Rollins Joan P ....Frazier
Rollins Louise ....Pillsbury
Rollinson Judith S .... Rulon-Miller
Rolph Catherine J ....Metcalf
Rolph Clare H.........................Wheeler
Rolston Ellen E ....Cabell
Rolston Wanda I .... Thompson
Romaine Eva Jane ....Coombe
Romaine Matilda B ....White
Romaneck Cynthia...........McCormick
Romano Carmelita .... Mattei
Romanoff Stephena A ....Boggess
Romanov Marina ....Beadleston
Romeyn Rosemary....................Dent
Romig Corinne T ....Roxby
Romney Jille..............................Jones
Ronalds F Lorillard...........Kulikowski
Ronan Diana V ....Quasha
Ronan Martha A ....Kuehn
Ronan Monica V ....Ronan

Ronan Patricia M ....Hosch
Rood Mary Patience ....Sanford
Rood Rebecca M ....Atwood
Roodhouse Ashley A ....Parriott
Roome Barbara S ....Roome
Roome Barbara V .... Stagg
Rooney Jean M ....Johnson
Roosen Dorothy O ....Diebold
Roosevelt Alexandra ....Dworkin
Roosevelt Anne S ....Gibson
Roosevelt D Virginia..........Armentrout
Roosevelt Fay S ....Fisher
Roosevelt Jane G ....Roosevelt
Roosevelt Lucy M ....Sewall
Roosevelt Margot...............Hornblower
Roosevelt Nancy A ....Roosevelt
Roosevelt Nancy D ....Jackson
Roosevelt Nancy S ....Ireland
Roosevelt Susan ....Weld
Root Louise A ....Melby
Roozen Mary K ....Hass
Ropes Harriet ....Cabot
Rorer E Whitney ....Chandor
Rorer Faith ....Sloan
Rosales Rosalinda A ....Morgan
Rosati Carlyne R ....Benkhart
Rose Anne F .... Hilliard
Rose Anne Lee .... Stewart
Rose Barbara B ....Callaway
Rose Candace ....Olds
Rose Claudia B ....Fielding
Rose Diana St John ....Sanden
Rose Edith.............................Nicholson
Rose Edith A ....Hopkins
Rose Elizabeth R .... Stanton
Rose Georganne R ....Cunningham
Rose Georgia R .... Crompton
Rose Gwendolyn ....Mackay
Rose Jean E .... Gilpin
Rose Jean E..............................Snyder
Rose Jean G ....Gould
Rose Karin M ....McIlvaine
Rose Keithley............................Miller
Rose Mary L ....Silverthorne
Rose Miriam A ....Gilpatric
Rose Nancy ....Jones
Rose Shirley N..............................Ely
Roselli Francine ....Rowley
Rosen Felice H ....Francis
Rosen Helen.................................Bern
Rosenauer Kathleen V ....Henriques
Rosenfeld Megan D ....Spencer
Rosengarten Clara O...............Urbahn
Rosengarten M Suydam ....Lansing
Rosenthal Louise D ....Glasser
Rosenthal Susan................Oppenheimer
Rosicki Patricia M ....Greenough
Ross Abigail H ....Sioussat
Ross Alice R ....Dewey
Ross Anne L ....Dechert
Ross Carolyn A ....Smith
Ross Charlotte G.........................Hyde
Ross Eve L ....Roberts

Ross Isabel F..........................Lincoln
Ross Jane R.........................Orthwein
Ross Joan ....Bolling
Ross Josephine DeC ....Turner
Ross Katherine C...................Sharkey
Ross Margaret ....Walker
Ross Mildred O....................Eckfeldt
Ross Natalie V C ....Voorhees
Ross Parthenia ....Kiersted
Ross Parthenia B.....................Gibson
Ross Sara C........................Cleveland
Ross Sarah B.............................Blake
Ross Sarah J..........................Fernley
Ross Sheilah B.......................Gignoux
Rossbach Anne C ....Munch
Rossbach Cynthia R ....Stebbins
Rossell Betty D....................McGowin
Rossiter Barbara L...................Agnew
Rossiter Corlette ....Walker
Roszel Janet D ....Tayloe
Rotch Ann S ....Magendantz
Rote Clarice M C.......................Starr
Roth Joan ....Herschede
Roth Lurline..........................Coonan
Roth Marilyn C.....................Sumner
Roth Mary E.......................Kendrick
Rothbart Marion E...............Newbold
Rothe Christine G......................Cole
Rothe Lillian A ....Dick
Rothermel Josephine B.................Bull
Rothermel Louise E................Allinson
Rothermel Rosalean.............McNeely
Rothman Nancy J ....Symington
Rothschild Phyllis......................Farley
Rothstein Sarah E ....Eustis
Rothwell Violet H................Crimmins
Rott Gesine ....deWolf
Roudebush Lailey H...............Jenkins
Roudebush Mary C.................Nowotny
Roudebush Susan D'A ....Rava
Rouillion Jane D ....Boyer
Rouillion Winifred..................Seibert
Roulhac Deborah ....Poitevent
Rounds Elizabeth ....Lawton
Rouse Ellen B ....Conrad
Rouse Susan L............................Hall
Rousmaniere Frances ....Storrs
Rousseau Maria A ....Boalt
Rousseau Olive Y ....Burt
Rousseau Rosemarie ....Wagner
Rousseau Sandra J ....Boykin
Roussopoulos Louiza P ....Zoullas
Rowan Robin S.........................Clarke
Rowbotham E Sara ....Cornell
Rowbotham Marcia T.............Simonds
Rowe Abigail F........................Oswald
Rowe Barbara C ....de Marneffe
Rowe Betty ....Bowdoin
Rowe Julie Jane ....Dougherty
Rowe Katherine N......................Ward
Rowe M Whitney ....Long
Rowe Margaret A ....Chatfield
Rowe Mary F ....Varner

Rowe Nancy S ....Conner
Rowe Pamela O ....Peabody
Rowe Pamela R ....Neville
Rowe Ruth A ....Philbrick
Rowinska Barbara
Paumgarten-Hohenschwangau-Erbach
Rowland Cornelia ....Levering
Rowland Ellen F ....Walton
Rowley Andria F ....Lawson
Rowley Billie S...................MacArthur
Rowley Elizabeth A.....................Jones
Rowley Elizabeth H...............Tittmann
Rowley Mary F..........................Colt
Rowswell Alice E ....Walker
Roy Mary E ....Almy
Roy Suzanne ....Morrow
Royce Dorothy T ....Vlietstra
Royce Mary ....Baker
Royce Patricia S ....Ingersoll
Royce Rosemary ....Dunlop
Royer Emily E L ....Haskell
Royer Harriet K ....Beegle
Royer Margaret ....Pepper
Royes Katherine D ....Boyd
Royse Nancy A ....Crossman
Royster Elspeth M ....Holch
Royster Martha R ....Williams
Rozier Jeanne A ....Winter
Rübel Judith S......................Bradford
Rubicam Ann W ....Lilly
Rubidge Meredyth N ....Armitage
Rubin Jane E ....Hoffman
Rubin Kate M ....Springs
Ruble Judith C ....Teasdale
Rucker Saundra J ....Steele
Ruckert Jane J ....McLean
Rudd Mary D ....Dreyer
Rudd Susan E ....Swain
Rudderow Anne W ....Dudley
Rudigier Mary F ....Lambert
Rudisill Carolyn C ....Swiggart
Rudkin M Mercedes ....Gotwald
Rudolph Alice ....Goodman
Rudolph Elizabeth H ....Trimble
Rudolph Josephine ....Sloan
Rue Rosina F ....Williams
Ruehrwein Andrea L ....Raynor
Ruff Cynthia L....................O'Connor
Ruffin Virginia C ....Richardson
Ruffner Genevieve ....Stirling
Ruggles Eleanor M ....O'Leary
Ruhl Patricia ....Rath
Rule Jane ....Davis
Rulon-Miller Eleanor ....York
Rulon-Miller Elizabeth ....Burton
Rulon-Miller Mary ....Fowler
Rumbough Elizabeth C.......Van Norden
Rumbough Suzanne D ....Sallee
Rump Claire L Wentworth.......Graham
Rumpf Dorothy M ....Sheaffer
Rumsey Allison B....................Emery
Rumsey M Linn C ....Vincent
Runk M Amélie ....Rorer

Runnells Helen R.....................DuBois
Runnells Mary W ....Glanz
Runton Winifred ....Lyons
Runyon Nathalie F..................Seltman
Runyon Susan K ....Whitcraft
Ruple Claire E ....McAllister
Rupp Susan S ....La Forte
Rusen Bettyanne ....Barringer
Rush Ada ....Thompson
Rush Alexandra H ....Domínguez
Rush Anne H ....Cook
Rush Louise K ....Bamberger
Rushing Dorothy J ....Winters
Rushton Edith E ....Johnston
Ruskin Julie L..........................Schurz
Russe Ann H ....Prewitt
Russe Elizabeth D...................Fordyce
Russe Susan B.............Daniel-Dreyfus
Russel Elizabeth C....................Craig
Russel M Augusta.............Scattergood
Russell Aimée G......Corsini di Laiatico
Russell Alexandra.......................Rich
Russell Allene G....................Pierson
Russell Anne F ....Heck
Russell Anne O...........................Wild
Russell Antoinette E ....Bailey
Russell Barbara......................Thayer
Russell Barbara F ....Flight
Russell Barbara I ....Washburn
Russell Barbara J ....Rockwell
Russell Brooke..........................Astor
Russell Charlotte ....Ham
Russell Elaine A ....Cooke
Russell Ella K ....Torrey
Russell Grace F ....Wheeler
Russell Grace L ....Tuckerman
Russell Isabel D.........................Potter
Russell Jacqueline D...............Williams
Russell Jane D ....Dennison
Russell Janet ....Whitman
Russell Jennie ....Darlington
Russell Joan E ....Neff
Russell Joan R ....Low
Russell Lillian H....................Carter
Russell Lisa A ....Stockman
Russell Louise K ....Jackson
Russell Louise R ....Irving
Russell Margaret ....Gordon
Russell Margaret F ....Hollister
Russell Martha L ....Davis
Russell Mary E ....Russell
Russell Nancy ....Primm
Russell Phebe ....Gregg
Russell Phyllis A ....Chandler
Russell Sally B ....Dyett
Russell Sarah M ....Hadden
Russell Susan ....von Stade
Russenberger Anne ....Keefe
Russert Jean ....Davidson
Rust Alexandrine G....................Rose
Rust Alice C ....Scheetz
Rust Katharine A....................Donery
Rust Katherine ....Kuehn

Rutan Eleanor H ....Rutan
Rutan Elizabeth.......................Royster
Rutherfurd Barbara M ....Knowles
Rutherfurd Freda........................Brehm
Rutherfurd Leith W ....Talamo
Rutherfurd Robin W ....Grace
Rutherfurd Sally C ....Roberts
Ruthrauff Clara E ....Thomas
Ruthrauff Florence B ....Goodrich
Rutledge Ann.........................Freeman
Rutledge Elise ....Swan
Rutter Mary E ....Smith
Rutter Nancy A...........................Green
Rutter Olivia H ....Petrasch
Rutter Rosslyn M ....Valentine
Rutter Ruth.............................Warriner
Rutter Virginia L ....White
Ruwe Bettyjane ....Halsey
Ruxton Cass L ....Shaw
Ryan Cynthia F ....Lambros
Ryan Dionne K ....Slater
Ryan Dolores E...........................Dana
Ryan Irene M ....Shaw
Ryan Jennifer M ....Rutherfurd
Ryan Josephine L ....Hopkins
Ryan Katharine D ....Aldrich
Ryan Katherine P.....................French
Ryan Kathleen A ....Gerard
Ryan Lillie B ....DeBevoise
Ryan Linda C..............................Jones
Ryan Lynn ....Hummer
Ryan Michelle M..................Hubbard
Ryan Nancy ....Beha
Ryan R Therese ....Julien
Ryan Sally N............................Shaw
Ryan Sheila ....Thayer
Ryan Tookie.........................Appelbe
Ryburn Alexandra......................Taylor
Ryburn Marie duP ....Foster
Ryckman Robin L ....Graziano
Ryden Cecile E ....Pierson
Ryder Joan ....Wickersham
Rydlo Magda A ....Jones
Ryerson Annie L......................Harris
Ryerson Ellen L ....Conant
Ryerson Mary McB...................Brown
Ryerson Nancy........................Milliken
Ryland Katharine H...............Williams
Rymer C Marcy ....Bevan
Rymer Emma H ....Roberts
Rynne Susan E ....Field
Rynne Virginia A ....Richard
Saam Carol A ....Thacher
Sabatier Bernadette ....Lirakis
Sabey Charlotte E ....Greenwood
Sabottge Sigrid M G............ van Eck
Sachs Margaret N ....Bissell
Sack Alexandra-Louise Emerson
                                             Cogswell
Sacré Jacqueline M G..................Earle
Sadtler Alice L R ....Davis
Sadtler Frances M.......................Coles
Sadtler Joanna ....Day

Sadtler Marian .... Carson
Safe Edith Shaw ....Loebs
Safe Elizabeth S...................... Bitting
Safe Louise K S .... Mauran
Safer Janine A........................Whitney
Safley Michele M ....Trevor
Sagar Margaret S ....Pierpoint
Sage Deborah C ....Rockefeller
Sage Julie ....Day
Sage Nancy W ....Shea
Sage Sarah .... McAlpin
Sager Patricia A...........van Ameringen
Sager Silvia M ....Baer
Saidy Martha....................... Toms
Sailer Alice W ....Lingelbach
Sailer Marie ....Altemus
St Aubyn Gail M ....Hickman
St Clair Archer.......................Harvey
St Clair Janet E ....Dicke
St Claire Alice P .... Long
St George Madeline ....Carroll
St Goar Elizabeth.................... Putnam
St John Amy R .... Hamilton
St John Cora A ....Gebhardt
Saint-Léger Christine .... Knight
Saisselin Marjorie R .... Woodbury
Saladine Andrea....................... Knight
Salant Susan B ....Wierdsma
Sales Mary E.............................Cruger
Salisbury Betsy A ....Creekmore
Salisbury Hope.................... Thompson
Sallada Susan ....Wetherill
Sallé Katharine B.........................Peltz
Sallee Anne D............................ Slater
Sallom A Aileen ....Freeman
Salm Margaret D ....Melone
Salmon Elizabeth A .... Simons
Salmond Wendy .... Oler
Salomon Alice-Ann .... Bast
Salt Grace H .... Walsh
Salter Patricia J ....Bradshaw
Salteri Katerina .... Gates
Saltonstall Emily B ....Byrd
Saltonstall Natalie ....Forbes
Saltonstall Priscilla ....Catlin
Saltus Katherine E .... Painter
Saltus Lydia L.......................Menendez
Salvage Katharine H...........Wilmerding
Salvage Magdelaine R ....Anthony
Salvage Margaret S ....Taliaferro
Salvatore Elena R ....Raymond
Salvatore Gina M........................Miller
Samayoa y Lerma Margarita ....Viaux
Sammis Anne C .... Webster
Sample Rebecca A ....Habenicht
Sample Sally ....Aall
Samples Mary S ....Stuckey
Sampsell Anne C ....Anthony
Sampsell Miranda C ....Donnelley
Sampson Clara L .... Shinn
Sampson Jean A ....Mormoris
Sampson Lorraine ....McCreery
Sampson Sally E .... Wilson

Sampson Susan J ....Sampson
Samuel Mary Jane ....Haffner
Samuel Victoria L...................Anthon
Sanchez-Elia Maria V ....Piñon
Sande Ellen Marie H ....O'Dowd
Sanders Blanton ....Parks
Sanders Hebe ....Dowling
Sanders Helen I..........................Gray
Sanders Mary E ....Phelps
Sanders Sarah..........................Dees
Sanderson Beatrice M............. Alexander
Sanderson Sandra B ....Wood
Sanderson Tanya.......................Marks
Sanderson Victoria L..............Sieglaff
Sandison Denie P.........................Weil
Sands Blair L ....Sands
Sands Elizabeth D....................... Petty
Sands Esther W.........................Hocker
Sands Hope ....Blakeley
Sands Mary H .... Arnot
Sands Nancy L........................... Geist
Sands Renée L ....Sterling
Sandys Evangela L................... Burton
Sanford Barbara J ....Atlee
Sanford Barbara Le R................Donohue
Sanford Gertrude .... Legendre
Sanford Jeannette C ....Fowlkes
Sanford Mary E ....Atwood
Sanger Anne..............................Feld
Sanger Joan R .... Griffith
Sanpaolesi Cristina ....Grassi
Sanson Kate van D ....Hill
Sanson M Gale ....Gillespie
Sansoucie Ruth ....Burke
Santa Maria Joanne M................Dhody
Santa Maria Maquita E...............Driscoll
Santa Maria Patricia E..............Roberts
Santora Barbara ....McDaniel
Santos Katharine D.................Harrison
Santos de Garza Yolanda

                    Garza-Laguera
Santry M Louise ....Emmet
Sanzone Marian A ....Rowe
Saranec Cynthia R ....Livermore
Sarantos Valeria A...................Cruice
Sargeant Jane Byrd .... McCurdy
Sargeant Jeanne Lee ....Wiggins
Sargeant Virginia ....Reynolds
Sargent Felicity H...................Blundon
Sargent Frederica ....Wight
Sargent Jessie........................... Sargent
Sargent Phebe McK .... Harding
Sargent Ruth V ....Sargent
Sartorius Beverly .... Vander Poel
Sartorius Ruth M ....Doyle
Sass Elizabeth E .... Phillips
Sass Kathryn L ....Pool
Sasscer Anne Lansdale ....Newman
Sassoon Janet ....Upton
Sater Margaret S ....Ward
Satolias Ecaterini .... Sturgis
Satterlee Barbara W ....Blackburn
Satterlee Millicent W ....Mali

Satterthwaite Anne W........Montgomery
Satterthwaite Sarah D ....Gibson
Sattley Pamela H ....Morris
Sauer Mary W .... Sloneker
Sauerbrun Virginia M.................Everett
Saulnier Amy H...........................Scott
Sauls Laura E........................Wallace
Saunders Elizabeth L..................Hornor
Saunders Hope B .... Robbins
Saunders M Calvert C .... Griffin
Saunders Marjorie E ....Magruder
Saunders Martha R ....Ferguson
Saunders Mary D ....Edgar
Saunders Mary T ....Ashmead
Saunders Phyllis M...................Barton
Saunders Sally L....................Saunders
Saunders Suzanne E ....Donlan
Savage Anne L ....Barnum
Savage Caroline W ....Langan
Savage Catherine E...................Roberts
Savage Fredericka A....................Shaw
Savage Jane B ....Roberts
Savage M Elizabeth ....Wasley
Savage Margaret ....Alexander
Savage Mary L............................Huber
Savage Susan ....Speers
Saville Charlotte L....................Metcalf
Saville Patricia A......................Palmer
Saville Susanna ....Grinnan
Sawhill Sarah E ....Supplee
Sawin Edith M ....Keppel
Sawin Maggy J ....Wolf
Sawtelle Frances M ....Cowenhoven
Sawtell Katharine ....Plimpton
Sawyer Anne J ....Greene
Sawyer Barbara H ....Lowry
Sawyer Carol A ....McCall
Sawyer Helen ....Jones
Sawyer Helengrace ....Poynter
Sawyer Janet B ....Merrill
Sawyer Jo Ann M ....Delafield
Sawyer Mary Ann ....Meyer
Saxe Mary Van R ....Littell
Saxer Jeane B ....Eddy
Saxer Ruth .... Potter
Saxon Mary M ....Apostol
Sayen Sandra J ....Rosenblad
Sayen Susan H ....Pierce
Sayman Dojean.......................Smithers
Sayre Margaret F ....Wiederhold
Sayres Barbara R ....Williams
Sbarboro Yvonne M ....Schneider
Scadding Marguerite A.............. Norris
Scafe Florence ....Seymour
Scally Mary J...............................Rose
Scarbrough Sherry D ....Jones
Scarlett Heather A ....Lee
Scarlett Kathleen B D................Burnett
Scarlett Mary B....................DeMott
Scattergood Evelyn M ....Day
Scattergood Marion C.................Ballard
Scattergood Mary M .... Norris
Schaaf Susan E ....Bonesteel

Schabacker Kirsten J .... Aldrich
Schade Sarah B .... Bowman
Schaefer Andrea K ....Truslow
Schaefer Annelore J....................Hansen
Schaefer Betty A....................Appleton
Schaefer Christine L .... Gates
Schaefer Gretchen L ....Jackson
Schaefer Katharine B ....Foy
Schaefer Lucinda K ....Walker
Schaefer Margaret M ....Lamberton
Schaefer Marion L ....McCurdy
Schaefer Mary H N ....Cist
Schaeffer Lois J .... Boericke
Schaenen Beatrice........................Sherman
Schafer Nola ....Boomer
Schafer Sally W ....Wenaas
Schaff Isabel H ....Cabanne
Schaff Jane A ....Odell
Schager Francesca F W ....Anderson
Schager Mary W ....Waldron
Schalck Eleanor ....Keil
Schallert Nancy.......................Burkett
Schallon Melody M ....Butterworth
Schantz Margaret F...................Roosevelt
Schardong Kathleen A..............Winant
Schardt Elizebeth ....O'Gara
Scharff Nancy R ....Vogt
Scharin Jean U ....Spalding
Scharman Ann K ....Rutter
Scharz Rosa ....Tarbox
Schaus Lela R ....Philip
Schecter Elizabeth J...............Mayhew
Scheerer Idoline A.......................Duke
Scheerer Lynda ....Stokes
Scheerer Mary L D ....Babcock
Scheetz Alice L ....Longman
Scheetz Mary A H ....Hunt
Scheffler Mary D ....de Windt
Schefler Lara Brook........... McLanahan
Scheid Diane ....Hedges
Scheidt Nina C ....Klapp
Schenck Florence A.................. Neilson
Schepens Bernadette..................Butler
Schepens Claire ....Delori
Scherer Elaine ....Romaine
Schieren Julie S ....Duff
Schierenberg Dorothy ....Alexander
Schierloh Janet A ....Howard
Schiffer Susan Berwind ....Stautberg
Schiller Caroline C ....Bartol
Schilling Mary L........................Macon
Schimenz Rosanna ....Clarke
Schimpf Joan L............................Root
Schipfer Odessa R ....Miller
Schirrman Eunice..................... Gardiner
Schiverick Mary A ....Morss
Schlaff Frederica P ....Rentschler
Schlafly Ellen A.........................Shafer
Schlapp Sylvia C ....Symington
Schlegel Uta G...........................Wister
Schleiter Malabar ....Brewster
Schlesinger Lucille ....Lockwood

Sellar Alexandra .... Sadron
Sellar R Daphne .... Thornton
Sellar Rosalie D .... Brainard
Sellers Amy L .... Glascock
Sellers Edith C .... Farnum
Sellers Marion K .... Hepburn
Sellers Therese P .... Parrish
Selman Mary W .... Le Bourgeois
Selman Sara StJ .... Lowrance
Selter Felicitas .... Thorne
Seltzer Isabelle M .... Fleck
Seltzer Lydia .... Barry
Semenenko Christine .... Clark
Seminara R Anne .... Auchincloss
Semler Hope .... Berg
Semlow Virginia G .... Park
Semones Katherine M .... Reuben
Semple Anne T F .... Ness
Semple Constance .... Brown
Semple Heather H .... Semple
Sen-Gupta Shyamoli .... Pyne
Senior Mary C .... Fearey
Sentman Joyce L .... Richardson
Seredynski Martha A .... Desloge
Sergeant Alva .... Flanagan
Serra-Garibaldi Laura .... Roberts
Serrell Katherine N .... Rorimer
Sessions Gertrude S G .... Slingluff
Sethness Mary B .... Arnold
Seton Janneke .... Neilson
Seton Mary L .... Abele
Settle Joan T .... Thomas
Severance Faith D .... Stewart
Severin Marion .... Despard
Severinghaus Elizabeth M .... Warner
Severn M Bain .... Moore
Severson Kirsten C McL .... Moore
Sewall Margaret H R .... Boogaard
Sewell Anna Belle .... Sise
Sewell Ethel H .... Driggs
Sexton Barbara .... Pratt
Sexton Ellen S .... Grubb
Sexton Felicity J .... Bowditch
Sexton Mary L .... Unruh
Seybolt Edwina P .... Seybolt
Seybolt Reva B .... Seybolt
Seyburn Suzanne .... Meyer
Seyburn Winifred D .... Cheston
Seyler Catherine A .... Armitage
Seymour Gertrude .... Hornung
Seymour Jennifer A .... Foley
Seymour Lenore E .... Cavallero
Seymour Mary C .... Garfield
Shadle Bette J .... Hamilton
Shafer Charlotte .... Dunbar
Shafer Priscilla H .... Dana
Shaffer Susan .... Wells
Shahin Barbara A .... Kennedy
Shallcross Elizabeth .... Pool
Shallcross Nan B .... Clemens
Shallenberger Marion B .... Bryan
Shanahan Harriett D .... Coleman
Shand Mary B .... de Fremery

Shanklin Nancy V .... Werlich
Shanks C Meteer .... Schwab
Shanks Margaret J .... Moore
Shanley Brigid .... Lamb
Shanley Elizabeth .... Ferguson
Shanley Maureen V .... Kirk
Shannon Eleanor B .... Salem
Shapleigh Suzanne .... Limberg
Sharbrough Amanda R .... Bryan
Sharon Jane .... Bolling
Sharp Anne S .... Nichols
Sharp Cherie J .... Smith
Sharp Cornelia D .... Claiborne
Sharp Enid .... Ford
Sharp Helen L .... Anderson
Sharp Lillian A .... Hoag
Sharp Lynda S .... Paine
Sharp Mary .... Cronson
Sharp Mary C .... Howard
Sharp Nancy B .... Greiner
Sharp Nancy J .... Van Vranken
Sharp Ruth Sloane .... Keilty
Sharp Sidney S .... Warnock
Sharp Virginia Beverly .... Amberg
Sharp Virginia F .... Williams
Sharpe Barbara L .... Harris
Sharples Grace E .... Cooke
Sharples Martha B .... Daniels
Sharples Mary Franklin .... Allison
Sharples Wynne .... Ballinger
Sharrett Ruth A .... Payne
Shattuck Isabel M .... Plimpton
Shattuck Patricia C .... Gallagher
Shattuck Stefanie R .... Hufnagel
Shaw Cherry .... Swords
Shaw Deborah S .... Shaw
Shaw Dora D .... Neidecker
Shaw Eleanor S .... Mittendorf
Shaw Elizabeth A .... Perry
Shaw F Theodora .... King
Shaw Gayle P .... Camden
Shaw Gertrude B .... Crittenden
Shaw Joan S .... Coburn
Shaw Katharine van D .... Wallace
Shaw Margaret L .... Coe
Shaw Margaret L .... Maycock
Shaw Phyllis E .... Shaw
Shaw Roberta .... Thomas
Shaw Rosemary .... Blake
Shaw Susanne .... Hooe
Shea Alicia N .... Kilpatrick
Shea Barbara C .... Bispham
Shea Elizabeth M .... Clement
Shea Norma J .... Langworthy
Shea Susan H .... McPherson
Sheafe Mary A .... Jewett
Sheaffer Eloise Joy .... Hall
Sheaffer Susan M .... Werner
Shearer Louise M .... Brock
Shearer Margaret J .... Baker
Shearer Pamela D .... Eberhart
Sheble Martha W .... Agate
Shedd Dorothy .... Withington

Shedd E Hartley .... Mannion
Shedd Elizabeth M .... Murphy
Shedden Barbara A .... Peaslee
Sheehan Mary E .... Townsend
Sheehan Rita C .... Devens
Sheerar Alexandra P .... Dewey
Sheerin Edith B .... Patterson
Sheerin Maria W .... Harrison
Sheffield Anne .... Sheffield
Sheffield Katherine S .... Kernan
Sheffield Wende L .... McIlwain
Shelburne Marjorie .... Carmichael
Shelburne Sarah S .... Newhall
Shelby Bobbie L .... Green
Shelby Lydia H .... Coyle
Sheldon Kathleen .... Parker
Sheldon Mary H .... Twiss
Shellabarger Elizabeth B .... Bayne
Shellenback Christine A R ...... McElroy
Shelly Ann .... Schafer
Shelly Elizabeth Van D .... Barker
Shelly J Sue .... Jewell
Shelnutt Barbara M .... Trabka
Shelnutt L Ann .... Barry
Shelton Helen A .... Duytschaever
Shelton Lois H .... Wilson
Shelton Vivian I .... Vose
Shelvey Sandra W .... Sheffield
Shennan Elizabeth E .... Loring
Shepard Deborah S .... Petri
Shepard Francine J .... McKelvy
Shepard Helen R .... Scott
Shepard Judith G .... Long
Shepard Kate P .... Busby
Shepard Polly .... Stevenson
Sheperd Jean E .... Putnam
Shephard Patricia .... Patterson
Shepherd Elizabeth T .... Scott
Shepherd Gloria J .... McCoy
Shepherd Kathryn F .... Le Roy
Shepherd Mary Briscoe .... Gardner
Shepherd Sally .... Herrlinger
Shepherd Stephanie D .... Pearce
Shepherd Susan W .... Ittner
Shepley Clare F .... Conzelman
Sheppard Gail G .... Moloney
Sheppard Isobel Y .... Haines
Sheppard Jane S .... Harper
Sheppard Lynn S .... Manger
Sheppard Mary S .... Bartram
Sheppard Mary-Helen C .... Boothby
Sheppard Susan C .... Arrison
Shepperd Joan D .... Keenan
Sheridan Jane M A .... Murray
Sheridan Marguerette S .... Smylie
Sheridan Mary K .... Hayes
Sherley Olive C .... Young
Sherman Elizabeth M .... Walker
Sherman Frances C .... McCloskey
Sherman Hannah Lee .... Stokes
Sherman Katherine F J .... Lodge
Sherman Katherine L .... Hastings
Sherman Mary-Hoyt .... Joyce

Sherman Melinda A .... Swift
Sherman Sally M .... Taylor
Sherrer Alexandra Baylor .... Diffee
Sherrerd Lisa B .... Barker
Sherrill Ann Wilkinson .... Pyne
Sherrill Rebecca W .... More
Sherry Kathleen .... Strang
Sherston-Baker Margaret E .... Kirkbride
Shertz Carol A .... Lennig
Sherwood Barbara D .... Rolph
Sherwood Caryn .... Cutler
Sherwood Jan .... Cavanagh
Sherwood Katherine M .... Roberts
Shethar Gwendolen .... McKinnie
Shethar Lois .... Smith
Shevers Nancy H .... Loney
Shewan Patricia .... de Sibour
Shields Caroline C .... Clifford
Shields Cinthia S .... Dalziel
Shields Moya B .... King
Shields Pamela .... Smith
Shikamura Marion T .... Osborne
Shiland Dianne P .... Smith
Shiland Joan McA .... Tilghman
Shiland Tracy H .... Kemper
Shin Catalina I .... Hatch
Shine Kathleen .... Purdon
Shink Susan E .... Hatch
Shippee Joan B .... Oram
Shippen Suzanne S .... Zimmermann
Shipper Jeanne A .... White
Shirk Anne B .... Burrage
Shirley Betsy .... Michel
Shiverick Esther P .... Yntema
Shiverick Jane B .... Hall
Shoaf Katherine S .... Zbinden
Shober Agnes H .... Stroud
Shober Catharine E .... Ross
Shober Elizabeth W .... Hooper
Shober Jane H .... Fox
Shober Josephine M .... Borie
Shockley Stephanie J .... Armistead
Shoemaker Claire W .... Smith
Shoemaker Jane R .... Storm
Shoemaker Mary Elizabeth .... Miner
Shoener Judith L .... Semple
Shoninger Gloria R .... Mooney
Shonk Sally .... Smith
Shontz Elizabeth N .... Strong
Shook Adele W .... Merck
Shook Kathryn .... Bates
Shoop Donabeth .... Jensen
Shore Barbara G .... Shore
Shore Barbara N .... Hastings
Shore Sally .... Payne
Shore Susanna .... Le Boutillier
Short Caroline N .... Beebe
Short Caroline T .... Beisswanger
Short Julie S .... Rinaldini
Short Pamela A .... Rogers
Shortlidge Audrey D .... Tripp
Shortman M Claudia .... Franklin
Shortt Norma F .... Rantoul

Shotton Margaret A .... Meynell
Showalter Claudia R .... Reynders
Showell Clara A .... Murray
Shrady Maria Theresia ...... von Waldow
Shrady Marie L .... Smith
Shreeve Marjorie .... Winslow
Shrigley Elisabeth J .... Bundy
Shriver Harriet Van B .... FauntLeRoy
Shriver Mary O .... Pierrepont
Shropshire Lynn M .... Pearson
Shryock Anne E. .... La Motte
Shryock Elizabeth S .... Butcher
Shryock Kimberley A .... Cooke
Shuey Sevilla H .... Shinn
Shuler Janalin M .... Gorham
Shulman Molly .... Kellogg
Shultz Barbara R .... Arthur
Shultz Marianne .... Galt
Shumaker Karen L .... Register
Shumaker Margaret B .... Nalle
Shumaker Penelope J .... Longmaid
Shumate Christine S .... Capers
Shumway Grace L .... Adair
Shumway Helen E .... Mayer
Shupp Sandra E .... Williamson
Sibley Anne D .... Cannon
Sibley Carolyn C .... Wolfe
Sibley Jane H .... Auchincloss
Sibley Marie Louise .... Scudder
Sickels Mary S .... Seelye
Sidamon-Eristoff Elizabeth .... Lewis
Side Karina .... McIntosh
Sidford Sandra C .... Cornelius
Sidway Edith .... Stevens
Sidway Margaret StJ .... McCaffree
Siedenburg L Kathryn .... Starr
Siedlarz Nancy C .... Bruechert
Siegel Susan K .... Henshaw
Siegel Toni Jo .... Perkins
Siegler Lucinda .... Brown
Siems Dorothy S .... de Peyster
Siems Vernon M R .... Smith
Sierck Andrea C .... Vest
Sierck Carsten W .... Sierck
Siewers Lucy G .... Damgard
Sigafoos Florence .... Corson
Sigler Elizabeth .... Mather
Sigmon Angela G .... Gale
Sigmond Sylvia S .... Birckhead
Sigourney Amélie .... Scott
Sigourney Hélène .... Knowlton
Sigourney Louise .... Kauders
Siker Elaine C .... Burden
Silberberg Mary P .... Gilbreath
Silcox Joann .... Farley
Sillcocks Elizabeth .... Walker
Sillcocks Margaret .... Wadhams
Sillcocks Sarah J .... Graham
Sillcox Enid B .... Brown
Silliman Doris du P .... Stockly
Sills Beverly .... Greenough
Sills Dorothy G .... Lindsley
Silver Joan .... Ewing

Silverio Luz M .... Kean
Silverthorne Jaquelin .... Reed
Simard Rita .... Jacob
Simes Rosamond .... Richardson
Simes Victoria .... Poole
Simkins Roberta A .... Rose
Simkus B Natasha .... Ehrenclou
Simmelink Barbara L .... McChord
Simmers Hillary R .... Kennedy
Simmons Allison L .... Prouty
Simmons Carol .... Rathborne
Simmons Dorothy M .... Ehrhard
Simmons Georgia W .... Pierpont
Simmons Lucretia .... Mali
Simmons Mary C .... Howell
Simmons Mary Kay .... Newbld
Simmons Pamela .... Terry
Simon Shelby Crawford .... Wylie
Simonds Amy C .... Naimi
Simonds Carla G .... Warren
Simonds Elizabeth S .... Maynard
Simonds Ethel D .... Bowditch
Simonds Harriet K .... Carr
Simonds Holly S .... Callery
Simonds Janet .... Short
Simonds Lansing .... Moran
Simonds Margaret M .... Lincoln
Simonds Mary K .... Parkman
Simonds Ruth .... West
Simonds Susan C .... Page
Simonds Virginia T .... White
Simonin Suzanne .... Murphy
Simons Annie B .... Hasell
Simons Caroline .... Kent
Simons Caroline P .... Finnerty
Simons Katherine Bailey .... Egan
Simons Linda K .... de Menocal
Simons Marjorie J .... Harvey
Simonson Kay J .... Waterbury
Simpkins Jane W .... Rush
Simpson Gwendolyn .... Chabrier
Simpson Irving R .... Benoist
Simpson Jane .... Bemis
Simpson Karen N .... Harvey
Simpson Lucy S .... Douglas
Simpson Mary E .... Hanahan
Simpson Mary L .... Roberts
Simpson Mary M .... Young
Simpson Nancy C .... Noel
Simpson Virginia D .... Woods
Simrall Louise C .... Hall
Sims Georgia A .... Carson
Sims Joan L .... Faville
Sims Margaret H .... Hopkins
Sims Monica L .... Lott
Sims Pauline W .... Medlin
Sinclair J Candace .... Hamm
Sinclair Jean .... Tailer
Sinclair Judith .... Perry
Sinclair Murr D .... Murdoch-Muirhead
Sinclair Sandra .... Pershing
Sinclair Suzanne .... Shinkle
Singer Carole .... Detweiler

Singer Gertrude M .... Trott
Singer Marlene L .... Stone
Singer Mary D .... Tilghman
Singleton Martha J .... Ferris
Sinkler Alida D .... Barnwell
Sinkler Diana W .... Clagett
Sinkler Ella B .... Jackson
Sinkler Louise E .... Hoffman
Sinkler Mildred P .... Stuart
Sinkler Nina .... Talbot
Sinkler Robin N .... Burch
Sinko Laurie A .... Barrows
Sinnott Jean S .... Drew
Sinon Kelly A .... Manly-Power
Sinwell Marion B .... Smith
Siple Linda S .... Callard
Sippel Irene F .... Brophy
Sipple Mary L .... Lambert
Siragusa Irene D .... Phelps
Sise C Frances .... Humphrey
Sise Cornelia B .... Waring
Siska Rosalia M .... Castleton
Sisson Emilie H .... Osborn
Sisson Gail P .... Shields
Sivage Suzanne R .... Borland
Sizemore Rebecca .... Henderson
Sizer Alice F .... Warner
Sizer Caroline .... Cochran
Sizer Ruth R .... Marshall
Sizer Sandra .... Moore
Sizer Wendy R .... Sizer
Skacel Anna D .... Gilhuley
Skakel Ethel .... Kennedy
Skeats Mavis .... Atwood
Skeele Sarah H .... Post
Skelly Ann L .... Skelly
Skelly Catherine A .... Wright
Skerrett Anna P .... Kirkpatrick
Skerry Jean Margaret .... Wimpress
Skidmore Mary R .... Truesdale
Skidmore Shelby S .... Woodard
Skiem Jill S .... von Czoernig
Skiff Virginia L .... Brutschy
Skillen Lisa P .... Gresh
Skillern Sarah A .... Jarrett
Skinker Sandra Isabella .... Bruno
Skinner Carol H .... Lawson
Skinner Cynthia P P .... Cromie
Skinner Henrietta D .... Raymond
Skinner Janice D .... Noojin
Skinner Jeanne L C .... Niven
Skinner Mary Lee C .... Bayne
Skinner Mary Oakes .... Smith
Skinner Patricia F .... Huntington
Skinner Sandra M .... Ely
Skipwith Emma W .... Hopkins
Skjöldebrand Catharina .... Ford
Skluth Barbara A .... Hale
Skouras Daphne D .... Root
Slack Rosalie H .... Seely-Brown
Slack Rosalie T .... Walton
Slade Georgiana J .... Mellgard
Slade Katharine .... Newbegin

Sladen Kathleen M L .... Drake
Slater Elizabeth .... Webster
Slater Joy L .... Carrier
Slater Stella N .... Russell
Slater Susan .... Dillon
Slaughter Janey .... Briscoe
Slaughter Sandra .... Dent
Slauson Sue Ann .... Houser
Slawson Sarah .... Townsend
Slaymaker Jane C .... Zimmerman
Sledge Mary Ann .... Weems
Slidell Marie Louise .... Leahy
Slingluff Anne R .... Wood
Slingluff Frances D .... Clotworthy
Slingluff Jennifer G .... Robinson
Slingluff Mary H Ill
Slingluff Mary Le G .... Fisher
Slingluff Melissa K .... Morley
Slingluff Suzanne .... Holcomb
Sloan Anna L .... Upton
Sloan Anne .... Morrison
Sloan Delphine M .... Damon
Sloan Elisabeth P .... Riddle
Sloan Ethel D .... Allen
Sloan Florence L .... Schoyer
Sloan Lidie L .... McBurney
Sloan Margaret E .... Mapes
Sloan Margaret W .... Runnette
Sloan Mary C .... Orr
Sloan Mary C .... Wilbur
Sloan Mary J .... Belknap
Sloane Cornelia B .... McConnell
Sloane Evelyn .... Pyne
Sloane Grace E .... Vance
Sloane Margaret D .... Patterson
Sloane Nancy .... Coates
Sloat Camilla A .... Adams
Slocum Elizabeth A .... McKay
Slocum I Marguerite .... Quinn
Slocum Louise .... Abbott
Slocum Marie L .... Roberts
Slosar Nadine M .... Brunner
Sloss Margaret .... Lowe
Slough Susan C .... Pratt
Slowik Maureen A .... Hallowell
Slusser Caroline E .... Converse
Slusser Kathleen E .... Mullen
Slutter Caroline K .... O'Neill
Small Frances M B .... Wainwright
Small G Susanna .... Sutro
Small Josephine F .... Stebbins
Small Louise J .... Griffen
Smallidge Melissa L .... Harris
Smallwood Jane .... Montant
Smart Katharine .... Place
Smart Leonore .... Wetherill
Smiley Mary R .... Murray
Smissaert Natalie E .... De Voe
Smit Elizabeth I .... Chamberlain
Smith A Claiborne .... Jones
Smith Abigail Alden .... Shriver
Smith Adelaide B .... McClung
Smith Adele C .... Pittman

Smith Adeline E ....Boyd
Smith Agnes W.......................Harrison
Smith Alice D .... Victor
Smith Alice P...........................Cornish
Smith Allyn D......................... Simmons
Smith Anita L ....Hilbert
Smith Ann T ....Seabright
Smith Anne ....Duncan
Smith Anne B ....Waud
Smith Anne C .... Feld
Smith Anne C ....Yardley
Smith Anne E ....du Pont
Smith Anne G ....Tregellas
Smith Anne W ....Traer
Smith Anne W C ....Jones
Smith Audrey L........................Fowle
Smith Audrey L ....Nichols
Smith Barbara A ....Masoner
Smith Barbara F..........................Peck
Smith Barbara P.......................Metcalf
Smith Bernice M....................Hinckley
Smith Betty ....Jones
Smith Betty ....Josey
Smith Betty A .... Hetherington
Smith Beverly A.....................Patterson
Smith Bonnie M ....Girvin
Smith C Fay...........................Heilman
Smith Cabell D .... Tower
Smith Cara C ....Walker
Smith Caro N....................Schneithorst
Smith Carol MacD........... Hafkenschiel
Smith Carol S ....Lewis
Smith Caroline B ....Chappell
Smith Celeste O'D.....................Penney
Smith Cendy M........................Cooper
Smith Charlotte A....................Quinn
Smith Constance G ....Plimpton
Smith Cynthia G ....Wilson
Smith Cynthia J ....Bartol
Smith Damaris S S ....Horan
Smith Deborah.......................Lewallen
Smith Deborah D ....Haight
Smith Deborah L ....Webster
Smith Deborah N....................McKechnie
Smith Devon M ....Menges
Smith Diana L....................Frothingham
Smith Dolly L..........................Wilson
Smith Dora P.............................Haas
Smith Dorothea S ....Mathews
Smith Dorothy ....Catherwood
Smith Dorothy S ....Rudkin
Smith E Marion ....Dyett
Smith Edith D ....Mungall
Smith Eleanor C ....Johnston
Smith Eleanor K.......................Morris
Smith Eleanor M P .... Millspaugh
Smith Eleanor N.........................Toby
Smith Eleuthèra B...................... Grassi
Smith Eliza F............................Brown
Smith Elizabeth B..................Lawrence
Smith Elizabeth B ....McGowin
Smith Elizabeth F .... Rumsey
Smith Elizabeth M .... McCreary

Smith Elizabeth McK ....Wilkie
Smith Elizabeth S .... Wright
Smith Elke U .... Fox
Smith Ellen D .... Buchen
Smith Ellen F .... de Rham
Smith Emilie de Mun .... Kilgore
Smith Emily J M ....Cain
Smith Emily M .... Henderson
Smith Emma D ....Johnston
Smith Eunice S .... Whittlesey
Smith Evelyn C..........................Rogers
Smith Flora J............................Bartlett
Smith Florence D.....................Morton
Smith Florence O..................... Stone
Smith Frances A ....Wetherell
Smith Frances H ....Trimble
Smith Frances Moran .... Wyrough
Smith G G Meredith ....Smith
Smith Gale ....Mayfield
Smith Grace H ....McNeal
Smith Gwendolyn ....Bleakley
Smith H Ashley .... Frank
Smith Harriet M........................Riegel
Smith Heather Lee....................Kleiner
Smith Heidi J ....Parker
Smith Helen LeR .... Clay
Smith Iris V ....Christ
Smith Jacqueline A.................Littlejohn
Smith Jane G............................. Rush
Smith Jane T ....Moore
Smith Jean R ....Wilmer
Smith Jean W............................Kipp
Smith Jeanne M ....Browning
Smith Jeanne M ....McCracken
Smith Jennifer W ....Lohmann
Smith Joan .... ReQua
Smith Joan E .... Haskell
Smith Joan H .... Blair
Smith Johanna V......................Clark
Smith Josephine Y ....Masterson
Smith Judith W .... Fairbank
Smith Julie A ....Lowry
Smith Julie L..............................Hoyt
Smith Karen G...................... Webster
Smith Karin M.........................Seeley
Smith Katherine M ....Bayne
Smith Katherine P N .... Merle-Smith
Smith Katheryne L ....Townsend
Smith Kirby E.........................Graham
Smith Laura E..........................Fisher
Smith Laura H ....Bissell
Smith Leslie A B ....Dorsey
Smith Lois................................Clover
Smith Lois L ....Schieffelin
Smith Louise deM .... Bross
Smith Louise L ....Walther
Smith Lu Ann ....Polk
Smith Lucile R.......................McGehee
Smith Lucile E.........................Morgan
Smith Lucinda A...........................Hay
Smith Lucinda L ....Seale
Smith Lucinda Luce ....Treat
Smith Lydia L.........................Perkins

Smith Lynda D ....Atterbury
Smith Lynne............................Rhett
Smith M Courtenay ....Willcox
Smith M Elizabeth ....Hubbard
Smith M Hope ....Pollard
Smith Madeleine M ....Almirall
Smith Madeline M...................Carver
Smith Margaret L ....Paul
Smith Margot C ....Cramer
Smith Margret R ....Reusch
Smith Marie A ....Chabrier
Smith Martha C .... Bishop
Smith Mary Alyce ....Merow
Smith Mary Ann ....Barbier-Mueller
Smith Mary E A ....Podles
Smith Maud W ....Daudon
Smith Melinda A ....Jerauld
Smith Meryl C .... Renwick
Smith Miranda Griscom ....Prezioso
Smith Monica L......................Unger
Smith Muriel F....................Quintal
Smith Natalie B ....Smith
Smith Nathalie L ....Bonistall
Smith Olivia M ....Leale
Smith Pauline S ....Willis
Smith Phyllis...........................Swayze
Smith Rosalie L.........................Clark
Smith Rosalynn......................Carter
Smith Rosemary H ....Marlette
Smith Ruby N ....Gardner
Smith Sally B.............................Miller
Smith Sally B..............................Swift
Smith Sally C ....Cross
Smith Sandra C....................Griswold
Smith Sandra P ....Mongendre
Smith Sandra Stuart ....Wheeler
Smith Sarah L O .... Kise
Smith Sarah M ....Price
Smith Sarajane P...................Alexander
Smith Selene R ....Obolensky
Smith Sharon A ....Doyle
Smith Sharon C.......................Bullard
Smith Sharon L.........................Keller
Smith Sheila C........................Shuford
Smith Sheila K...................Huidekoper
Smith Sheila M......................Cochran
Smith Shirley K.....................Bubendey
Smith Simone M .... Stephens
Smith Stephanie C ....Breed
Smith Stephanie V ....Evans
Smith Susan D ....Hawkings
Smith Susan R ....Talbot
Smith Suzanne ....Whitmore
Smith Suzette de M ....Smith
Smith Valerie S....................Holberton
Smith Victoria W .... Walsh
Smith Virginia C........................Burke
Smith Virginia C.......................Snider
Smith Virginia F..................Rosengarten
Smith Wenche ....Hemphill
Smith Wendy Morgan ....Brainerd
Smith Whitney C ....Sutton
Smith Winifred D ....Viguers

Smither Charlotte S ....Haygood
Smithers Bonnie L......................Falla
Smithers Elizabeth....................Klose
Smithers Marian B....................Moore
Smith-Hutton Cynthia............ Bowers
Smitter Caroline A................ Nicholson
Smolianinoff Anya..................... Bagley
Smoot Sarah M .... Ingraham
Smotherman Anne E............... Haskell
Smull Katharine ....Smoot
Smyth Barbara S ....Edgar
Smyth Elizabeth B ....Garlich
Smyth Jane B ....Schroeder
Smyth Noël H ....Jackson
Smythe A Virginia.................. Spofford
Smythe Bertha F ....Graham
Smythe Christine L .... Smythe
Smythe Clarissa ....Melcher
Smythe Mary A ....Sheppard
Smythe Patricia S ....Leach
Smythe Sue M ....Joyce
Snader Martha J ....Funk
Sneath Cyrena K........................Gouge
Snodgrass Alice W ....Beckwith
Snodgrass Dorothy B.......Goldsborough
Snodgrass Jean ....Chambers
Snodgrass Karen A ....Lammert
Snodgrass Mary L...................Raymer
Snorf Susan A .... Lansbury
Snow Enid C..............................Ives
Snow Julia M ....Neagle
Snow Kathleen.......................Kendrick
Snow Mary V ....Austin
Snow Nancy S ....Bailey
Snow Nancy W........................Carter
Snow Sara R E ....Cabot
Snowden Amanda A.................. Bulazel
Snowden Ann F ....Johnson
Snowden Elizabeth A ....Griscom
Snowden Imogen R ....Augsbury
Snowden Julia B ....Neumeyer
Snowden Sandra F....................Trump
Snowden Suzanne S ...... Rentschler
Snowdon Elizabeth R ....Hoopes
Snoy Edmée R M G ....Taylor
Snyder Ann E ....Allport
Snyder E Nivin ....Stott
Snyder Elizabeth G.....................Miller
Snyder Elizabeth P ....Goodby
Snyder Hannah L .... Hollingshead
Snyder Johanna C ....Shaw
Snyder Judith F......................Kaufman
Snyder M Anne L...................Pritchard
Snyder Marjorie ....Roosevelt
Snyder Melanie ....Gill
Snyder Pamela S ....Borman
Soares Sonia L.......................Freiberg
Sobek Monica U ....Proctor
Södergen Eva E .... Thompson
Sodi Giovanna M ....Phillips
Sokolova Vera ....Thorne
Solbert Leslie K ....Fogg
Solby Myra ....Sutro

Soldwedel Sunny A .... Wirtz
Soles Adelaide D .... Kirkbride
Soles Cynthia C .... Schwabacher
Soliday Carol L.....................Cameron
Sollers Dorothy ....Fraser
Sollitto Rossana M .... Leeper
Solomon Amelia B ....Waring
Soltau Hannelore ....Brown
Soltis Janet C ....White
Somers Hilary L ....Deely
Somers Katherine L .... Hawkins
Somers Susan .... Hanson
Somervell Susan B ....Griswold
Somerville Marion ....Babcock
Sommer Astrid E .... Flood
Sommer Jane B.....................Millard
Sonne Sheila B A .... Pulling
Soper Martha P .... Koekkoek
Soper Talia B ....Terhune
Soppas Despina.....................Clement
Sorensen Paula D .... Merrifield
Sorensen Sandra ....Henning
Sothoron Elizabeth K .... Worcester
Soubiran Virginie T ....Niedermayer
Souchon Dolly Ann ....Johnsen
Souder Katharine L.....................Whyte
Souder Susan M .... Black
Soule Alice M.................... McDonald
Soule Ann M .... Reed
Soule Evelyn M .... Cunningham
Soule Jane ....Engert
Soulé Jeanne ....Dickey
Soule Marjorie H ....Orrick
Soulé Nancy P ....Walkup
Southerland Katharine .... Johnson
Southgate Frances ....Gibson
Southwell Priscilla L .... Southwell
Southwell Victoria C .... Ellis
Southworth Dorothy P.............Bromley
Southworth Eleanor E.......... Thompson
Southworth Elizabeth.................Sutton
Southworth Jean R .... Leness
Southworth Katharine D............. Smith
Southworth Mayotta ....Kendrick
Soutter Lindsay ....Boyer
Soutter Susanna .... Livingston
Souyoutzoglou Mariana S ....Zoullas
Sowers Dorothea H...................Agnew
Sowers Ruth F ....White
Soyka Irene G.......................Wright
Spahr Katharine F..............Vanderbilt
Spalding Camilla H ....Prosser
Spalding Caroline H .... Bulkeley
Spalding Jean M .... Sterling
Spalding Marka......................Wise
Spalding Mary E.....................Garrison
Spalding Susan H ....Munroe
Spalding Susan J.........................Bull
Spangler Barbara H ....Porter
Spangler M Elizabeth ....Edgell
Spangler M Jane ....Frank
Sparre Teresita ....Currie
Sparrow Helen C ....Roosevelt

Sparry Ellen K ....Brush
Spaulding Alice ....Paolozzi
Spaulding Ann S .... Wilberding
Spaulding Isabel M .... Roberts
Spaulding Joan S ....Cobb
Spaulding Marion ....Goodyear
Spaulding Shirley D ....Gary
Spaulding Suzanne ....Rockwell
Speakman Marion W .... Mathews
Spear Eleanor H......................Cálves
Spear Elizabeth A ....Brewer
Spear Suzanne ....Lawrence
Specker Lynn A ....Martin
Speed May Mason .... Sexton
Speer Eleanore T .... Leigh
Speer Margaret T ....Classen
Speer Mary W ....Marr
Speers Susan A .... Herrmann
Speir Betty Ruth ....Speir
Speller Roberta T .... Reuter
Spence Anne T ....Seidlitz
Spence Frances A .... de Ganay
Spence Mae M ....Krulak
Spence Sallie B ....Smith
Spencer Abby A .... Moffat
Spencer Agnes A ....Burke
Spencer Cornelia C ....Ives
Spencer Cynthia Mary...........Cockcroft
Spencer Elizabeth L ....Pfau
Spencer Evelyn ....Gay
Spencer Janet I .... Dougherty
Spencer Jean R ....Lemaitre
Spencer Julia A ....Reichner
Spencer M Anne ....Gaudreau
Spencer Nancy W ....Smith
Spencer Patricia L ....Zug
Spencer Patricia T..................Simonds
Spencer Penelope A .... Pulver
Spencer Susan ....Begien
Spencer Violet ....Thoron
Spencer Virginia C ....Shaw
Spencer Vivian M ....Ahern
Spenker Elizabeth A ....Harris
Speno Deborah A ....Thornton
Sperow Jacqueline B ....Jacobs
Sperry Dale ....Mudge
Sperry Elisabeth C ....Smith
Sperry Judith G ....MacEwan
Spicer Claudia J ....Alexander
Spicer Colleen I ....Harrity
Spiegelhauer Jeanie .... Kilroy
Spielberger Candace A ....Haydock
Spier Carol P...........................Riley
Spier Rosemary.......................French
Spika Susan E.................. Higinbotham
Spinning Patricia ....Wrenn
Spiro Laura M........................Forbes
Spivey Alice............................Doran
Spivy Mary Plant............Dangremond
Spoehrer Susan J...................... Elliott
Spoerer Jeanne R ....Cornell
Spofford Alexandra G .... Johnston
Spofford Helen W ....Bell

Spofford Margaret W .... Benkard
Spofford Nancy......................... Yerkes
Sponberg Phyllis C ....Montgomery
Spong Rosalind B ....Payson
Spöngberg S Lyerly ....Peniston
Sponsler A Rebecca...................Hanna
Spooner Eleanor G .... Crawford
Spottiswoode Jean Marianne.... McLane
Sprague Anne H ....Sclufer
Sprague Christina R ....Rihm
Sprague Eliza H .... Rowe
Sprague Elizabeth S ....Stout
Sprague Jean K ....Fisher
Sprague Julie H ....Sprague
Sprague Lucy C ....Foster
Sprague Victoria C ....Auchincloss
Spratt Rebecca J ....Justi
Spreckels Dorothy C...................Munn
Spreckels Geraldine ....Fuller
Sprigg Julia D ....Cameron
Springer Carole J ....Schoettle
Springer Lynn E .... Roberts
Springer Margaret S ....Denham
Springer Sandra J.....................Mellon
Sproul Janet E .... Robinson
Spruance Alice L ....Talbot
Spruell Norma J .... Wickersham
Spruill Fay ....Davidson
Spurgeon Elizabeth D............. Spurgeon
Squire Aldys ....Chapman
Squires Alice T ....Martin
Stachnik Elizabeth H ....Norfleet
Stackpole Abigail F ....McCall
Stackpole Amy F ....Brigham
Stackpole Susan M ....Lord
Stacom Tara I ....Diedrick
Staeble Anna M ....Barker
Staempfli Fordyce L ....Williams
Stafford Ann L..................... Anderson
Stafford Cora Edith ....Bruce
Stafford Mary........................Page
Stafford Sara H ....Barloga
Stafford Virginia H ....Ray
Stage Margaret C ....Salter
Stage Margaret N.......................Todd
Stahl Annette M ....McClughan
Staley Sally C ....Scott
Stalker Deborah M .... Ambler
Stallard Jean M ....Hardie
Stallard Marion S ....Myer
Stallcup Elizabeth ....Hennings
Stallworth Sanford P....................Kay
Stalter Mary Louise G ....Radsch
Stambaugh Anne W .... Satterthwaite
Stamm Lisa ....Booher
Stammers Katherine Esther ....Bullitt
Stamos Suzanne K ....Carter
Stamp Lynne S ....Merrell
Stampley Susan E.....................Seden
Standish Barbara S ....Matthews
Standish Margaret R ....Bickham
Stanger Jean H .... Stanger
Stanger Susan V ....Mitchell

Staniford Gloria .... Hamilton
Stanley Barbara............................Behr
Stanley Jane E............................ Inch
Stanley Janet Van W ....Hoffmann
Stanley Josephine......................Gourd
Stanley L Courtney......................Brady
Stanley Melinda F..................... Douglas
Stanley Nancy C......................Waud
Stanley Nancy P....................Brickley
Stanley-Brown Katharine O ...... Abbott
Stanton Ann LaF....................Warden
Stanton Delores.....................Francine
Stanton Susan H ....Benedict
Stanton Susan L ....Francis
Staples Emily H ....Hearin
Stark Carol H ....Tiernan
Stark Katherine L.........................Bull
Stark Mollie McM ....Eckelberry
Starkey Joan M ....Palmer
Starkloff Ardath ....Cole
Starnes Phyllis A ....Little
Starr Anna N...........................Tyson
Starr Anne............................Lyons
Starr Anne T ....Cunningham
Starr Eleanor H ....Darcy
Starr Elizabeth N ....Gephart
Starr Emily T ....Vehslage
Starr Frances A ....Todd
Starr Hope.............................Lloyd
Starr Marjorie M ....Frazier
Starr Mary A ....Ritchie
Starr Mary W ....Carstensen
Starr May ....Emerson
Starr Patricia ....Jones
Starr Sheila H ....Armstrong
Starr Susan ....Burchenal
Starr Tallmadge ....Renault
Starr Veronica M ....Batzer
Starring Carolyn.......................Meyer
Starry Pamela S ....Sheffield
Stary Ruth E ....Bole
Stats Jennifer......................... Phillips
Staub Harriet B ....Huston
Staub Sharon H..........................Doty
Stauder Meta M ....Casey
Staudt Constance D .... de Ropp
Stauffer Cynthia W ....Spurdle
Stauffer Jill..............................Cobbs
Stead Nancy S.........................Duble
Stearns Annabel W ....Stehli
Stearns Dorothy C ....Mortensen
Stebbins Helen Y ....Sutter
Stebbins Jane E........................Sykes
Stebbins Marion ....Heydt
Stebbins Victoria N ....Wallop
Steck Anna K............................Carey
Steck Margaret R ....Carpenter
Stedman Helen M ....Cluett
Steege Merrilee J ....Ribbel
Steel Arlette B ....Swift
Steel Elizabeth E.................. Longstreth
Steel Nancy McL ....Sinkler
Steele Elizabeth ....Skinner

Steele Jeanette...........................Muller
Steele Linda F........................Hastings
Steele Margaret.....................Werner
Steele Sandra C...................Greenfield
Steele Virginia.........................Felch
Steers Clare A...........................Wilich
Steers Claudia M......................Cutter
Stefan Lorene C.....................Gevalt
Stefan Patricia K....................Moore
Steffan Carol J G ....Griffis
Steffan I G Brigitte.................. Barrell
Steffens L Louise....................Waram
Steffens Pamela W ....Sailer
Stefik Mary Anne ....Henderson
Stehli Marguerite ....Kelly
Stehlin Helene N.......................Lortz
Stein Alexandra .... Kouwenhoven
Stein Virginia G.....................Pitcher
Steinacker Elaine R .... Scott
Steine Peggy W ....Richter
Steiner Dorothy F ....Henry
Steiner Jean E...........................Frye
Steiner Jessie T ....Van Ness
Steiner Marie-Louise ....Nickerson
Steinert Anne C ....Anable
Steinert Elizabeth ....Williams
Steinman Caroline M H...............Nunan
Steinmetz Brooke M..............MacLeod
Steinmetz Deborah J............Koppelman
Steinschneider Barbara ....Newington
Steinthal Sandra ....Ames
Steinwedell Ann.......................Hardy
Steinwedell Jane ....Russell
Steketee Marie ....Landreth
Stell J Cecille ....Pulitzer
Steman Susan Morris................Laffoon
Stenborg Elizabeth L ....Burnham
Stengel Martha O.....................Miller
Stenhouse Edith W ....Bingham
Stent Katherine R ....Somers
Stepanova Tatiana...................Gardner
Stephanoff Nika G.....................Ashey
Stephens Dorothy C...................Gray
Stephens Helen H ....Storey
Stephens Letitia A ....Wightman
Stephens Nesta ....Whitmarsh
Stephens Sally J.......................Logan
Stephens Virginia F ....Sloan
Stephenson Ellen P ....Porteous
Stephenson Helen G ....Weary
Stephenson Louisa T ....Myrin
Stephenson Mary W ....Osborn
Sterling Isla C.....................Masterson
Sterling Judith R ....Morse
Sterling Sara E........................Rubin
Sterling Susan H ....Monjauze
Stern Ann B........................Kloman
Sterne Brooke E....................Whittemore
Sterner Cheryl L ....Straub
Sterner Elizabeth S ....Johnson
Sterrett Adlumia D ....Hagner
Sterrett Edith............................Hornor
Sterrett Mary F ....Anderson

Stetson Elizabeth J...................Kratovil
Stetson G Stuart.........................Daly
Stetson Iola W ....Haverstick
Stettinius Achsah C ....O'Donovan
Stettinius Elizabeth C ....Young
Stevens Alice M ....Titus
Stevens Annette J ....Wilton
Stevens Avice M...........................Lea
Stevens Betty L........................Sherrill
Stevens Catherine M...................Greeff
Stevens Edwene ....McCollum
Stevens Elisabeth G ....Schleussner
Stevens Elizabeth ....Bakewell
Stevens Elizabeth.................Ballantine
Stevens Elizabeth.....................Landen
Stevens Elizabeth P ....Sanders
Stevens Fay A........................Thorne
Stevens Frances G ....Reese
Stevens Frederica.....................Berard
Stevens Grace B ....Sutton
Stevens Helen ....Bell
Stevens Helen E......................Jackson
Stevens Jane P ....Alloo
Stevens Marian B.....................Powers
Stevens Martha S.......................Daly
Stevens Mary Ann ....Hamilton
Stevens Mary Ruth ....Sevier
Stevens Mary S.........................Torp
Stevens Nancy M........................Mix
Stevens Nancy W ....Purdy
Stevens Natalie ....Parker
Stevens Nonya R ....Wright
Stevens Priscilla C....................Rhoads
Stevens Sara ....McKnight
Stevens Sarah L.........................Jones
Stevens Sarah T ....Wall
Stevens Sarah W...................Heckscher
Stevens Sheelagh G T ....Carr
Stevens Susan D.....................Bartlett
Stevens Susan F ....Fremantle
Stevens Viola Y ....Eustis
Stevenson Ann de D................Dewart
Stevenson Burd B ....Fleischmann
Stevenson Catherine Van A ....Glines
Stevenson Charlotte P..................Hood
Stevenson Elizabeth R ....Whittaker
Stevenson Emilie R ....McClellan
Stevenson Gertrude Gouverneur
                                    Stevenson
Stevenson Hildegarde ....Hard
Stevenson Jane ....Potter
Stevenson Linda McK ....Roosevelt
Stevenson Marianne S ....Thorne
Stevenson Nancy ....Baker
Stevenson Patience F ....Scott
Stevenson Roberta ....Plummer
Stevenson Sally B ....Hughes
Stevenson Sharon H ....Caldwell
Stevenson Virginia J..............Stevenson
Steves Gale C ....Steves
Steward Cynthia K ....Ringe
Stewart Ann D ....Fenwick
Stewart Anne T ....Satterthwaite

Stewart Barry M ....Grace
Stewart Beatrice L........................Smith
Stewart Doris L.........................Wear
Stewart Elizabeth B ....Stewart
Stewart Ewell B ....du Pont
Stewart Frances G.....................Logan
Stewart Frances R....................Walker
Stewart Jane ....Young
Stewart Jenny M ....Chandler
Stewart Judy P ....Merrill
Stewart Julia D ....Neill
Stewart Katharine K ....de Spoelberch
Stewart Katherine S..................Ingalls
Stewart Linda C ....Dickason
Stewart M Leslie....................Meneely
Stewart Margaret.......................Moss
Stewart Margaret J.................Hedberg
Stewart Marianne......................Wood
Stewart Marion K ....Lins
Stewart Marjorie C ....Tingue
Stewart Mary L......................Baldwin
Stewart Mary L.........................Reid
Stewart Mary W ....Borie
Stewart Nina G ....Strawbridge
Stewart Patricia V ....Walsh
Stewart Roxanna ....Dennis
Stewart Sara R ....Robertson
Stewart Sarah P.........................Ruth
Stewart Victoria A ....Downey
Steyn Marion ....Winsor
Stiassni Helen ....Benedict
Stiassni Sylvia M............Frelinghuysen
Stick Anne H ....Mackenzie
Stickel Helen A.........................Hyde
Stickley Hester M ....Virgin
Stickley Janet V ....Brady
Stickney Louise F....................Tanner
Stidger Elizabeth G.............Hemenway
Stieren Betty Ann ....Kelso
Stierhem Eleanor ....Rawson
Stiles Jean R ....Snyder
Stiles Mary E...........................Borie
Stiles Mary J.........................Marvel
Stiles Mary S S ....Howard
Stiles Nancy S...........................Yahn
Stillman Anne W ....Nordeman
Stillman Helen B ....Coolidge
Stillman Helen Lee ....Maher
Stillman Katherine C ....Marsters
Stillman Louise L ....Lehrman
Stillman Lyle D ....Carter
Stillman Mary Louise ....West
Stillman Nancy B ....Pearson
Stilson Barbara W....................Myers
Stimmel Nancy V....................Herpin
Stimmel Susan ....Metcalf
Stimson Ann F ....Kennedy
Stimson Priscilla ....Whittemore
Stinchfield Berta C ....Hees
Stine Barbara A ....Cruice
Stine Mary E.........................Wilcox
Stineman Eleanor ....Skinner
Stingily Sandra.......................Simpson

Stinson Catherine M ....Carleton
Stires Anne H ....Blackwell
Stirling Elizabeth L..................Stirling
Stith Susan D W ....Price
Stith V Elizabeth.......................Peters
Stitt Joan B ....McMenamin
Stivers Louise ....Davies
Stoakes Diane G ....Mackey
Stockdale Margaret J ....Havens
Stocker Gayle..........................Denègre
Stockfish Virginia A..................Borland
Stockman Helen P ....Stovell
Stockman Jeanne E..................Whiteley
Stockman Mary La B .... Wainwright
Stockman Mina M ....Pell
Stockton Lynne M ....Mutart
Stockton Sandra J....................Kokesh
Stockwell Julie A......................Leland
Stockwell Vida H ....Van Lennep
Stoddard F Jeanne.......................Pidot
Stoddard Frances Le B ....Dunn
Stoddard Fredrica B....................Smith
Stoddart Jane W ....Wilcox
Stoddart Penelope ....Potter
Stoepel Helen R ....McGraw
Stokely Devereux.......................Carter
Stokes Alexandra C ....Thomas
Stokes Anne S..........................Bright
Stokes Diana ....Callaway
Stokes H Carol ....Fremont-Smith
Stokes Marsyl ....Hammond
Stokes Martha E ....Price
Stokes P Stephanie ....Shea
Stokes Sarah Lee ....Stokes
Stokes Sylvia ....Perry
Stolba Elizabeth A......................Reese
Stone Alice T ....Trainer
Stone Alyce McC ....Stevens
Stone Anne E........................McIlvain
Stone Aroline F.....................Gallagher
Stone Barbara.............................Chase
Stone Catherine D.....................Diebold
Stone Elizabeth F.......................Potter
Stone Frances W .... Warrick
Stone Francine L.....................Bakewell
Stone Herberta ....Eustis
Stone Jane S..............................Pratt
Stone Janet ....Wiggins
Stone Katherine S ....Fedor
Stone Lucy B..........................Keyes
Stone Mary N ....Phipps
Stone Olivia R ....Arnold
Stone Patricia L ....Battram
Stone Patricia S.........................Smith
Stone Pauline P.........................Rowe
Stone Polly C.........................Hanson
Stone Ruth D ....Dwinell
Stone Susanna A ....Doyle
Stoneham Catherine ....Carr
Stoner Aurelia........................Garland
Stonesifer A Landon................Johnson
Stonor Julia M C M...................Stonor
Stonor M S Noreen......................Drexel

Stoop Pieternel..................Knollenberg
Storck Louise..........................Laidlaw
Storck Susan.............................Binger
Storer Adelaide E ....Rowley
Storer Elizabeth ....Paynter
Storey Gertrude C..................Bancroft
Storey Jill P....................Cunningham
Storey Patricia....................De Camp
Storey Ruth B ....Felton
Storey Susan J..........................Lyman
Storey Susan V ....Aspinwall
Storm Elsie.......................Wilmerding
Storm Sandra L................Greenwood
Storm Sarah D.........................Lockee
Storrow Ann A ....Wyatt
Story Alexandra.....................Scarlett
Story Jessica..........................Doehring
Story Vera F........................Roosevelt
Stott Julia.................................Reber
Stottlemyer Laura L.................Felder
Stout Ann V ....Smythe
Stout Barbara J ....Crocker
Stout D Hope ....Connors
Stout Deborah D ....Nutt
Stout Ethel D ....Chapin
Stout Lydia H ....Dane
Stout Mary R ....Lawrence
Stovall Elizabeth E ....King
Stovall Meriwether L........McGettigan
Stovell Ann P...........................Moyer
Stovell Penrose.......................Laffon
Stover Ellen B............................Eddy
Stowe Mary E ....Chamberlin
Straat S Hilary..........................Rath
Strachan Elizabeth G ....Carpenter
Stradella Marjorie ....Hodgman
Straessley Margaret ....Isler
Strahorn Janet B ....Powell
Strain Karen A ....Smythe
Straker Dorothy A ....Sawyer
Strange Nancy W ....Maitland
Strangfeld Edna ....Larocque
Strangfeld May Katharine ....Lee
Strannigan Martha ....Coe
Strater Sarah Morgan..............Gregory
Stratford Margo ....Russell
Straton Carol C..................LeBrecht
Stratton A Cary...........................Boyd
Strauch Alice C......................Gerdine
Straumann Kathrin ....Platt
Strauss Helen L MacG ....Taylor
Strauss Jane A........................Palmer
Strauss Jane E........................McGarr
Strauss Nancy B..................Halbreich
Strawbridge Alexandra W ....Maurer
Strawbridge Anita B ....Pellet
Strawbridge Diana D ....Wister
Strawbridge Elizabeth A............Nord
Strawbridge Florence T .....McDonough
Strawbridge Heather T ....Platt
Strawbridge Margaret ....Clews
Strawn Margaret S ....Cathcart
Street Amanda V ....Palmer

Street Claudia A H ....Smith
Street Katharine W ....Shannon
Street Lori Lee ....Ames
Street Marjorie R ....Macomb
Street Martha ....Nachman
Streeter Cornelia V R ....Wissa
Streeter Josephine E ....Harrison
Streeter Lilian C ....Chance
Streeter Mildred C ....Buffum
Streeter Ruth C ....Brimelow
Stribling Anna P ....Taylor
Stribling Anne C ....Klenk
Strickland Gloria E ....Batten
Stringfield Janet M ....Biddle
Strobel Sally P ....Diggs
Strohmeier Judith D..................Reece
Strong Barbara P....................Lorenz
Strong Carol T ....Wellington
Strong Mabel A ....Lord
Strong Mary L ....Tilghman
Strong Selina ....Hobart
Strong Susan S....................Godfrey
Strong Susan T ....Kelley
Strong Virginia N....................Newlin
Stroud Anne ....Hannum
Strubing Stephanie H..................Flinn
Struthers Mary G ....Pinkham
Struthers Sara....................Frothingham
Stryker Catharine D...........Strawbridge
Stryker Katherine ....Williamson
Stuart Alison M ....Todd
Stuart Anna L ....Thatcher
Stuart Anne ....Batchelder
Stuart Dianne ....Humes
Stuart Elizabeth....................Gowing
Stuart Elizabeth M ....Hallowell
Stuart Ellen ....Poole
Stuart Helen C ....Sloane
Stuart L Lynn.........................Merrell
Stuart Leslie A ....Rogers
Stuart Margaret ....Graupner
Stuart Margaret ....Hart
Stuart Martha J ....Jewett
Stuart Mary ....Ogden
Stuart Mildred S ....West
Stuart Nina K ....Wood
Stuart Ruth ....Bell
Stubbs Eleanor G....................Haight
Stubbs Lilian R ....Adams
Stubbs Sue G ....Cutler
Stubenbord Jane M ....Winans
Stuckey Eva M ....Stuart
Stuckey Idelle M...................Barnhart
Studt Jane ....Symington
Stulb Elizabeth H......................Scull
Stull Kathleen E.........................Smith
Stumb Florence P ....Davis
Stupin Susan L.......................Gamble
Stupp Anne M.......................McAlpin
Sturges A Mary.........................King
Sturges Elizabeth W ....Browne
Sturges Marie H...................Houston
Sturges Sarah ....Bancroft

Sturgis Linda...........................Ribeiro
Sturgis Suzanne ....Miller
Stursberg J Louise ....Weist
Sturtevant Olga ....Toulmin
Suarez Helen M ....Rockwell
Subers Mary H..........................Lee
Succop Mary Louise..................Bell
Sudler Patricia R ....Stimpson
Sugalski Julie Ann ....Andrews
Sugg P Michele....................Wierzel
Suleri Sara..........................Goodyear
Sulger Jennifer R ....Blanchard
Sullivan Anne E.........................Gray
Sullivan Barbara A ....Birney
Sullivan Barbara A ....Coudert
Sullivan Carlisle...................Blodgett
Sullivan Cathleen H..............Applegate
Sullivan Christine M..............Witker
Sullivan Dorothy.......................Scott
Sullivan Elizabeth T ....Davis
Sullivan Erica G ....Fuller
Sullivan Florence D ....Lynch
Sullivan Genevieve B ....Robertson
Sullivan Hannah W.............Randolph
Sullivan Hélène A..................Walker
Sullivan Jennifer ....Dewar
Sullivan Joan ....Shaw
Sullivan Katherine R ....Scovil
Sullivan Kathryn A ....Biddle
Sullivan Leslie A ....Horn
Sullivan Lois A ....Rand
Sullivan Margot K K ....Grosvenor
Sullivan Maureen.....................Kelley
Sullivan Melissa P ....de Castro
Sullivan Nancy R...................Reynolds
Sullivan Pamela G ....Banker
Sullivan Paula ....Escher
Sullivan Roma M....................Hodges
Sullivan Rosalie K......................Ross
Sullivan Rosemary F ....Poole
Sullivant Cecelia L.....................Terry
Sultana Anna R ....Crompton
Sulzby Martha Hilton.................Clark
Summerell Lynne H ....Grant
Summerfield Gail S ....Ker
Summers Mary Jean ....Gulden
Summers Pamela A ....Kean
Sumner Suzanne S ....Miller
Sumwalt Nancy.........................Ayer
Sunde Abbie L ....Verner
Sunderland Joan.....................Scribner
Sundy Robin L ....Tingue
Suppes Jill M ....Bowers
Suppes Martha J ....Battin
Supplee Angela T ....Chesser
Suran Marlene F ....Davis
Surdam Susan Fiske ....Johnston
Susman Katherine B ....Howe
Susman Nancy J ....Gulick
Sutch Nancy ....Arndt
Suter Margaret ....Rood
Sutherland Mary J......................Strong
Sutherland Natalie ....Carney

Sutherland Pamela ....King
Sutherland Sandra L ....Holman
Sutherland Sarah H.................Stoner
Sutphen Marion H ....Fessenden
Sutphin Katharine B ....Ficks
Sutro Katharine N................Dougherty
Sutter Mary A ....Zick
Sutton Caroline M ....Dumaine
Sutton Kay F..........................Lowney
Sutton Margaret P...............McConnel
Sutton Mary O ....Moore
Suyat Cecilia A....................Marshall
Suzedell Gail ....Saxton
Svensson A Brita I.....................Smith
Sverbeyeff Elizabeth
                    Byron-Patrikiades
Swackhamer Grace V N.........Jennings
Swaim Barbara C.................Wittmann
Swaim Olivia Bradley ....LeFeaver
Swain Elizabeth K.................de Luca
Swain Helen..........................Burgin
Swan Helen B R ....Merrill
Swan Joan ....Branch
Swan Josephine C S ....Blagden
Swann Rosaly ....Bass
Swanson Audrey H.................Hardy
Swanson Christina M ....Montgomery
Swanson Cynthia E....................Miller
Swanson Dorothy J.................Brooke
Swanson Gail K ....Rees
Swanson Lorraine H ....Calhoun
Swanson Patricia C ....Carlson
Swarts Mary S ....Singer
Swartwood Heather W ....Dazet
Swartz Arete B ....Warren
Swartz M Killeen.....................Durand
Swartz Marie L ....Gerard
Swartz Susan P ....Gurin
Swasey Gladys Lovering...........Perkins
Swatling Barbara ....Griswold
Sweatt Martha W ....Reed
Sweeney Annabell E...................Ames
Sweeney Anne H ....Shuman
Sweeney Diana M ....Helie
Sweeney Dorothy...................Beckwith
Sweeney Patricia A...................Laflin
Sweet Brenda ....Parker
Sweet Nancy A ....Master
Sweet Sandra H.........................Sweet
Sweet Susan ....Lombard
Sweetland Elizabeth R..........Musgrave
Sweetman Sally J..................Prioleau
Sweetser Anne C ....Ireland
Sweetser Julianna................Bullerjahn
Sweetser Nancy J...................Flather
Swem Leslie R ....Fuller
Sweney Patricia ....du Pont
Sweney-Borden Beatrice
                    Knox-Johnston
Swenson Louise W................Downer
Swenson Marjorie J...............Lamport
Swenson Sylva........................Shores
Swetenburg Johnnie B ....Frazer

Swett Evelyn R ....Miller
Swift Alice ....Riginos
Swift Ann H........................Robinson
Swift Catherine Van S ....Swift
Swift E Ann ....Cronin
Swift Eleanor ....Reeve
Swift Elizabeth H ....Morris
Swift Laura L......................Burbank
Swift Margaret W ....Seaman
Swift Mildred M.....................Crispin
Swift Nina E .... Farley
Swift Sharon C .... Batterworth
Swift Shelia K..............................Keil
Swift Suzanne P...................Cummings
Swinerton Susan ....McBaine
Swing Elizabeth ....Robertson
Swing Mary C..................Rittershofer
Swissler Mary E ....Oldberg
Switzer Grace E ....Sloan
Switzler Jane ....Macrae
Swope Gloria A ....Marron
Swope Josephine A.............Santa Maria
Swords Alice R......................Whitson
Swords May W ....Hoppin
Swoyer Susan E.......................McAtee
Swoyer Winifred ....Phyfe
Sykes Cordelia ....Menges
Sykes Marguerite P.................Nichols
Symes Virginia B ....McMurtry
Symington A Byrd........................Platt
Symington A Leith ....Griswold
Symington Anne W ....Rhodes
Symington Arabella H..................Dane
Symington Helen C ....Chace
Symington Katharine ....Zouck
Symington Mabelle.....................Moore
Symington Maud L..............Symington
Symington Pattie...................Penniman
Symmers Barbara H ....Bancroft
Symmons Janet C ....Hollyday
Symons Ivy E ....Howells
Syms Alexandra E .... Pagenstecher
Synek Yveta............................Graff
Sysak Marianne ....French
Tabb Margot W ....Miller
Tabbert Jerilyn.............................Kelly
Tabecka Zofia ....Thomas
Tabler Judith A...........................Tabler
Tabor Marguerite K ....Yates
Tackett Margaret A......................Carr
Taft Clara F.............................Nixon
Taft Elizabeth W....................Johnson
Taft Lucie C.................................Bard
Taft Phyllis..................................Study
Taggart Margo R ....Tilghman
Taggart Patricia A......................Bellis
Tailer Fern ....de Narvaez
Tailer Patricia W....................Whitney
Tait Margaret Fullbrook ....Hand
Talbot A Tracy ....Spencer
Talbot Evelyn O ....Leeson
Talbot Lane H ....Sparkman
Talbot Laura A ....Noyes

Talbot Lorna .... Talbot
Talbot M Elizabeth .... Johnston
Talbot Mary Wallace ....Havens
Talbot Nannie W ....Brown
Talbot Prudence .... Esberg
Talbot Ruth ....Plimpton
Talbott Elizabeth N.......................Lake
Talbott Margaret T ....Noyes
Talbott Pauline.........................Toland
Talcott Judith L .... McCormick
Talcott Julia M...........................Meigs
Talcott Katharine T...............Atterbury
Talcott M Hope.......................Goodwin
Taliaferro Ann H ....Bailey
Taliaferro Cassandra L ....Hiland
Talieh Faézé..........................Woodville
Tallmadge Andrea F............Merryman
Tallman Mary Ann ....Tryon
Talmage Caroline L ....Sloan
Talmage Marion..........................Boyer
Talmage Sylvia B ....Kissel
Tamalet Isabelle F ....Tilden
Tamborrel Maria L ....Montgomery
Tanburn Jean L ....Delafield
Tanenbaum Ellen L ....Arthur
Tankoos Dianne C ....Montague
Tanner Jane O ....Trimingham
Tanner Kathryn M ....Pocock
Tanner Martha G ....Weille
Tansey Kathleen ....Gawthrop
Tansill Bonnie L ....Holmes
Tansill Doris ....Anderson
Tapia Teresa M...............................Day
Tappan Catherine H......................Farlow
Tappen Elisabeth C.................Ketcham
Tarasi Elizabeth M ....Stevenson
Tarlton Betty J ....Williams
Tarpey Hope C V ....Brady
Tarrant Cornelia L ....Bailey
Tarride Carolyn F ....Hudson
Tarto Malle ....Andrade
Tarver Pauline............................. Scott
Tatnall Rachel B ....Cox
Tattersall D Susan....................Francis
Tattersall M Nancy ....Roberts
Taulane Judith A.........................Lame
Taunton Sarah A ....Sessions
Taussig Anne B .... Bush
Taussig Anne C ....Trueblood
Taussig Annie C ....McAdoo
Taussig Elizabeth B ....Flersham
Taussig J Ellis...........................Phyfe
Taussig Jean ....Robertson
Taussig Mary B ....Hall
Taussig Patricia A...................Marshall
Tavares M Purita ....Cummings
Taws Katharine ....Claghorn
Tayloe Elizabeth ....Courts
Tayloe Roberta L ....Fuller
Taylor Aileen S.........................Butler
Taylor Alice L ....Stengel
Taylor Ann.........................Debevoise
Taylor Ann C ....Hines

Taylor Anne G.........................Meyer
Taylor Anne G.........................Mount
Taylor Anne W ....Richardson
Taylor Barbara A ....Guthans
Taylor Barbara J ....Honeyman
Taylor Barbara M ....Williams
Taylor Catherine E .... Kidder
Taylor Charlotte P ....Miller
Taylor Claudia A ....Johnson
Taylor Constance W .... Blackwell
Taylor Edna H ....O'Hara
Taylor Edna H ....Thieriot
Taylor Edna K ....Hopkins
Taylor Elisebeth ....Grenata
Taylor Elizabeth J......................Frank
Taylor Elizabeth S....................Lukens
Taylor Emily P ....Andrews
Taylor Eva L ....Holt
Taylor F Margaret......................Jones
Taylor Felicia R S ....Schuster
Taylor H Adèle ....Byford-Brown
Taylor H Suzanne ....Millard
Taylor Helen L ....Fitz-Gerald
Taylor Hilda A.......................Deupree
Taylor Holly...............................Taylor
Taylor Isabelle G ....Vauclain
Taylor Jean ....Johnson
Taylor Judith K ....Wheelock
Taylor June E.............................Norris
Taylor Katherine ....Hutchinson
Taylor Katherine Potter ....Taylor
Taylor Lelia S ....Stege
Taylor Lesley E ....Taylor
Taylor Lisa S ....Jones
Taylor Lucinda ....Hoffman
Taylor Margaret ....Leonard
Taylor Margaret ....Nelson
Taylor Marjorie C ....Barba
Taylor Mary E............................Hall
Taylor Mary I.............................Duke
Taylor May H ....Yarbrough
Taylor Michael E.................McGreevy
Taylor Miriam S ....Barnett
Taylor Nancy M ....Dougherty
Taylor Nina S ....Marden
Taylor Norma.............................Clark
Taylor Olivia B ....Travis
Taylor Pamela A ....Taylor
Taylor Pamela I ....Clyne
Taylor Pamela T ....Pendleton
Taylor Pamela W ....Norweb
Taylor Patricia A ....Buckley
Taylor Phoebe E ....Biddle
Taylor Priscilla T ....Kennedy
Taylor Sally P ....Abeles
Taylor Sandra E....................Goodwin
Taylor Sara H ....Swift
Taylor Sarah H ....Payson
Taylor Sarah H ....Stephenson
Taylor Tracy L.........................Callard
Taylor Valerie ....Taylor
Taylor Virginia ....Klose
Taylor Virginia A ....Simonin

Taylor Virginia B ....Taylor
Taylor Wendy S ....Foulke
Tchoukaleff Katherine ....Kean
Teagle Brenda L ....Callaway
Teagle Helen ....Clements
Teagle Jayne W............................Keith
Teague Cecily F.......................Bentley
Teasdale Lois C ....Poole
Teasley Martha M....................Deméré
Techentin Kristin E..................Harrison
Teckemeyer Helen.....................Allison
Tedeschi Mary C ....Eberstadt
Teel Betty ....Bivins
Teel Beverly J ....Dest
Teeple Susan ....Auler
Teeter Patricia A ....Zara
Teller Marcia E....................Feinstein
Tellier Sheila A....................Nottebohm
Temple Judy E...........................Carter
Temple Mary F ....Melone
Templeton J Lynne ....Brickley
Tenaglia Marian P ....Lynch
ten Broeke Laura J...............Rumbough
Tener Kathleen W........................Smith
Ten Eyck Catryna ....Seymour
Tennant Barbara G ....Jaicks
Tenney Constance V ....Worcester
Tenney Joan L ....Howard
Tenney Marguerite....................Embry
Tenney Nancy C ....Coleman
Tenney Patricia L ....Ruggieri
Tenney Rebecca W ....Agnew
Tenney Sara T.........................Osborne
Tenny Ula H ....Cole
Tenny Dixie ....Lehmann
Teodecki Jennifer C....................Ponce
Terbell Jennifer L ....Wisdom
Terhune Jane E ....Hall
Terins Ilona A..............................Wells
Te Roller Suzanne ....Busch
Terrell Ann P............................Wolfe
Terrell Susanna K ....Saunders
Terry Celeste S ....Forbes
Terry Cynthia A ....White
Terry Emily R ....Kates
Terry Georgia R ....Schley
Terry Josephine T ....Brune
Terry Julia ....Barnes
Terry Linda ....Sturgis
Terry Martha E ....Stewart
Terry Mary E ....Mason
Terry Sara Grey ....Graves
Terzian Nellie ....Morris
Tessman Susan Lee ....Alexander
Test Bettina P ....Test
Teti Phyllis.................................Lapin
Tetreault Josephine E ....Allen
Tetreault Kathleen ....Robb
Tew Hathaway ....Brewster
Tewksbury Daphne ....Whitman
Tewksbury Patricia ....Eide
Teyssandier Marguerite A ....Pough
Thacher Catharine W...............Barnett

Thacher Frances	Grauer
Thacher Helen	Brown
Thacher Joan	Tiffany
Thaler Victoria L J	Cabot
Thamm Susanne	Crooker
Thatcher Joe Ann C	Gerrity
Thatcher Katherine	Leach
Thaw Virginia	Wanamaker
Thaxter Harriette H	Irvine
Thaxton Anne C	Bass
Thayer Barbara S	Sibley
Thayer Carol	Schroeder
Thayer Cornelia Van R	Adams
Thayer Elizabeth P	Dixon
Thayer Evelyn	Chace
Thayer Evelyn C	Taussig
Thayer Jane	MacGaffin
Thayer Joan	Nalle
Thayer Lois	Frazier
Thayer Margaret C	Hollingsworth
Thayer Margaretta	Thayer
Thayer Marian B	Gemes
Thayer Marian M	Toland
Thayer Martha W	Wood
Thayer Mary E	Zane
Thayer Pauline	Maguire
Thayer Pauline R	Duke
Thayer Polly R	Starr
Thayer Sally S	Sears
Thayer Susan R	Wilmerding
Theakstone Sally E L	McGleughlin
Thébaud Cynthia C	Twining
Thébaud Cynthia McC	Thébaud
Thébaud Marie Eugenie	Compton
Thébaud Mathilde E	Allen
Thébaud Paula de B	Breeding
Thébaud Renée G	Wilson
Thenebe Mary C	Welden
Theobald Nancy de W	Wehr
Theopold Ann H	Chaplin
Theopold Freda	Swan
Thibault Ruth M	D'Ambly
Thibaut Eleanor V	Smithers
Thiebaut Elena	Biddle
Thiele Barbara	Carr
Thiele Jane W	Higgins
Thieriot Frances T	Bourgeix
Thieriot Julia D	Cain
Thiermann Heidi D	Hole
Thiery Jeanne M	Weeks
Thigpen Elizabeth L	Emmet
Thirkell Valerie F	Schmidt
Thom Ann B	Welles
Thom Elizabeth K	Graham
Thoma Diana	Knox
Thomas Aljean	Scudder
Thomas Amelia B	Morsell
Thomas Amy L	Tasman
Thomas Anne A	Thomas
Thomas Anne M	Gibbons
Thomas Anne P	Conklin
Thomas Anne R	Clayton
Thomas Annette B	Kaier

Thomas Carey M	Maloumiam
Thomas Carolyn P	Lawson
Thomas Cornelia A	Carroll
Thomas Cynthia J	Miller
Thomas Doris	West
Thomas Eleanor	Nelson
Thomas Eleanor L	Elliott
Thomas Elisabeth McC	Peterson
Thomas Elizabeth B	Greene
Thomas Emily K	Reed
Thomas Felicia C	Townsend
Thomas Frances C	Martin
Thomas Frances Gurney	Hamilton
Thomas Geraldine B	Carroll
Thomas Harriett R	Barton
Thomas Hilda E	Thomas
Thomas Jane E	Acton
Thomas Jennie R	Inch
Thomas Joan	Darlington
Thomas Jocelyn	Shaw
Thomas Josephine F R	Reeve
Thomas Joyanne B	Sundlun
Thomas Judith A	Patton
Thomas Juliet M	Beckett
Thomas Katharine B	Nyce
Thomas Katharine T	Bidwell
Thomas Laura E	Buck
Thomas Lenore M	Stoddart
Thomas Lillian S	Taylor
Thomas Louisa V	Hargrave
Thomas Margaret	Warren
Thomas Margaret W	de Neufville
Thomas Mary Alice	Nichols
Thomas Mary E	Thompson
Thomas Mary Jo	Campbell
Thomas Mary L	Sprague
Thomas Mary L	Van Wyck
Thomas Mary V N	Colmore
Thomas Mary W	Clevenger
Thomas Maryanne	Pratt
Thomas Matilda L	Oehmig
Thomas Maude A	Katzenbach
Thomas Megan E	Olson
Thomas Megan L	Hollister
Thomas Nancy B	Tornga
Thomas Peggy L	McKnight
Thomas Sally L	Milbank
Thomas Sherry L	Thomas
Thomas Shirley A	Wulfing
Thomas Virginia S	Baldwin
Thomas Virginia S	Talbot
Thomasson Indie S G	Cather
Thompson Amanda J	Riegel
Thompson Barbara J	Davis
Thompson Camilla C	Brauer
Thompson Camilla F	Williams
Thompson Carol	Hemingway
Thompson Caroline H	Simmons
Thompson Carolyn C	Thompson
Thompson Diana	Oldham
Thompson Dixie	Caulkins
Thompson Eleanor L	Penniman
Thompson Elizabeth	Templeton

Thompson Elizabeth B	Daly
Thompson Elizabeth G	Wheelock
Thompson Emily B	Gable
Thompson H Lee	Berger
Thompson Henrietta B	Clews
Thompson Ingrid A	Morsman
Thompson Isabelle	Farrington
Thompson J Nancy	Godfrey
Thompson Jacqueline D	Thompson
Thompson Jane	White
Thompson Jean	Makepeace
Thompson Jeremy L	Watson
Thompson Joan	Walther
Thompson Joan P	Gilmour
Thompson Judith A	Bradley
Thompson Katharine R	Hanser
Thompson Kathleen H	May
Thompson Lida L	Lloyd
Thompson Lois H	Davis
Thompson Lois L	Bromley
Thompson Lydia	Leavitt
Thompson Lydia M	Whitehead
Thompson M Avery	Funkhouser
Thompson M Bayard	Larson
Thompson Margaret G	Weir
Thompson Marian G	Carew
Thompson Marion E	Murfey
Thompson Marion McL	Greene
Thompson Marion R	Brown
Thompson Martha E	Becker
Thompson Nancy A	Fowler
Thompson Nancy A	Jubitz
Thompson Nancy W	Isham
Thompson Patricia A	Metcalf
Thompson Phyllis Blagden	Wright
Thompson Pollie A P	Frothingham
Thompson Rachael K	de Rham
Thompson Robin L	Walker
Thompson Rosemary	Thompson
Thompson Sallie H	Thompson
Thompson Sara C	Thompson
Thompson Susan C	Lynd
Thompson Suzanne C	Strasenburgh
Thompson Suzanne E	Davies
Thompson Suzanne E	Richards
Thompson Tandy C	Thompson
Thompson Virginia E M	Merryman
Thomson Anne	Smith
Thomson Carolyn D	Baldwin
Thomson Dianne	Embree
Thomson Elizabeth L	Park
Thomson Faith S	Chandler
Thomson Martha P	Crimmins
Thomson Susan H	Rutland
Thorn Landon R	Storrs
Thorn Sheilah L	Smith
Thorndike Isabel Gurnee	Thorndike
Thorndike R Lee	Sprague
Thorndike Sarah E	Haydock
Thorndike Sylvia M	Pope
Thorndike Winifred	Hare
Thorne Ann Boughton	Niles
Thorne Candace K	Canton

Thorne Elizabeth S	Pyott
Thorne Emeline L	Brawley
Thorne Gale L	White
Thorne Leslie	Kountze
Thorne Phebe E	Marrin
Thornley Ann P	Metcalfe
Thornton Barbara	Oyler
Thornton Carroll H	Chapin
Thornton Cynthia C	Mitchell
Thornton Elena M	Kissel
Thornton Emilie H	Forte
Thornton Mildred F	Johnson
Thornton Sandra C	Whitehouse
Thoron Ann A	Hale
Thoron Claire	Pyle
Thoron Ellen W	MacVeagh
Thoron Faith	Knapp
Thorsen Wendy J	Pearre
Thorsey Karen A	Reisky de Dubnic
Thorson Karen L	Colesberry
Thorson Martha A	Gould
Thorstens Patricia A	White
Thouron Anne L	Ryle
Thouron Margaret P	Harrell
Thouron Nancy A	Nash
Thrall Kathryn Anne	Porter
Thrasher Audrey	de Russow
Thresher Sylvia	Grebe
Throckmorton Katherine	Parisot
Thune-Ellefsen Gerd	Perkins
Thurber Katharine B	O'Boyle
Thurlow Tania	Chandler
Thurman Mary L	Martin
Thurston Barbara	Guernsey
Thurston Elizabeth C	Miller
Thurston Patricia B	Schwab
Thys Beatrice C	Moe
Thys Diane H	Prioleau
Tibbals Rosanne W	Allen
Tibbetts Zoë	Bartlett
Tieken Elizabeth C	Kirkpatrick
Tierney Eleanor C	Johnston
Tiers Gertrude R	Stevens
Tiers Helen W	Houghton
Tiers Katherine E	Tucker
Tiers Madeleine M	Parry
Tietzel Barbara W	Taylor
Tiffany Christine S	Prado
Tiffany Cleone G	Graham
Tiffany Diane T	Reilly
Tiffany Lyn P	Edmonston
Tilden Callie B	McLellan
Tilden Elmina R	Edmonston
Tilford Joan J	Larson
Tilford Martha F	Green
Tilghman Ann A	Lyman
Tilghman Helen G	Gordon
Tilghman Jamie B	Deming
Tilghman Joanna L	Tamplin
Tilghman Maud	Walker
Tillier Claudine M	Knight
Tillman Elizabeth C	Middleton
Tillman Mildred F	Camp

Tillotson Cheryl A ....Purdon
Tillotson Melissa ....Vaughan
Tilney Anne C ....Brune
Tilney Anne M ....Holmes
Tilney Mary A ....Tilney
Tilney Susanne G .... Peyton
Tilney Victoria M ....Bevan
Tilney Winifred D ....Whitman
Tilson Ann C ....Janvier
Tilt Jean McA ....Sammis
Tilt Priscilla P ....Pochna
Tilton Ann de K.......................... Milroy
Tilton Elizabeth La M ....Seeley
Tilton Maud T ....Kernan
Timanus Mary R .... Black
Timbal Christiane ....Rowley
Timbal Monique B ....Ridruejo
Timberlake Camille A .... Reich
Timberman Jane S ....Into
Timmerman Diana ....Hitschler
Timpson Brenda A ....Koëhn
Timpson Joan H.......................de Kay
Tindle Randall ....Smith
Tingley Priscilla A...................Tingley
Tingue Margret S....................Shuford
Tippett Robin C ....Duke
Tirrell Constance ....McEvoy
Tirrell Dorothy Q......................Clagett
Tischer Annelies B M .... Reed
Tison Shelby P...................Cromwell
Titcomb Joan ....Perkins
Titford Mary .... Burlingham
Tittmann Eleanor .... Andrews
Tittmann Louise A...................Mitchell
Tittmann Vesta B....................McLean
Titus Cynthia F.........................Powers
Titus Margaret L ....Yates
Titus Stephanie A ....Schley
Titzell Joan W.........................Frentzel
Tjaarda Henriette L.................Whitman
Tjäder Mona H ....Slack
Tjarda van Starkenborgh-Stachouwer
   Christine J ....Cheston
Toberman Lucy A Q ....McBain
Tobey Ida Louise.........................Pate
Tobey Mary H ....Cook
Tobey Pauline L ....Mercer
Tobey Suzanne...........................Smart
Tobian Susan ....Palmer
Tobin Consuelo........................Martin
Tobin Elaine.........................Bovaird
Tobin Katherine O ....Tobin
Tobin Muriel St J.........................Farr
Tobin Patricia C.........................Kubal
Tobin Susan G ....Wesley
Todd Alexandra ....Holmyard
Todd Alice de P.........................Biays
Todd Anne H de P....................Osborn
Todd Christine T.....................Whitman
Todd Dorothy M ....Newhall
Todd Elizabeth N.......................Taylor
Todd Emily E ....Stefani
Todd Emily H...........................Lynch

Todd F Jane .... Soper
Todd Frances H .... Stewart
Todd Joan.............................Robinette
Todd Kate P.............................Beach
Todd Laura K ....Widing
Todd Louise L .... Ambler
Todd Lynne H.........................Edgerton
Todd Margaret ....Dunham
Todd Margery W ....Bell
Todd Mary L.........................Maguire
Todd Nancy G .... VandenBerg
Todd Priscilla S ....Coords
Tognazzini Valerie J ....Kieser
Toland Charlotte R .... Thayer
Toland Lilah T ....Goodman
Toland Roselle L .... Chambers
Toland Susan H ....LeFevre
Toll Deborah A .... Reynolds
Tolles Thayer C ....Mickel
Tomacelli-Filomarino Eleonora
                                  Meier
Tomasco Jean A ....Schloss
Tomick Joan F ....Harnes
Tomita Tomiyo ....Prout
Tomkins Katharine A .... Villard
Tomlin C Joyce.........................Griffith
Tompkins Eliza Ann ....Gustavson
Tompkins Leslie B .... Hancock
Tompkins Mary W ....Houghton
Tompkins Suzanne H .... Ramseur
Toms Barbara ....Mills
Tonner Marjorie F ....Gold
Toogood Anna Coxe...............Toogood
Toohey Rita R..........................Murrie
Toomey Virginia E ....Morgan
Tootle Lillian L ....Reinhardt
Topping Sandra E ....Topping
Torchiana Jane.......................Williams
Torney Jane K.........................Menefee
Torrance Mary M ....Abbott
Torrey Katharine.....................Cameron
Torrey Louise..............................Gray
Torrillo Rosalind M ....Pendergast
Torrvella Carmen B ....Slade
Tortorelli Silvia E ....Ogilvie
Totten Virginia.........................Dodds
Toueg Fernanda F ....Young
Toulmin Elizabeth B ....Parson
Toulmin Frances B .... Griffith
Toulson Helen I ....Johnston
Tourison Linda McD .... Simpson
Tourne Elisabeth ....Vincent
Tourville Gabrielle M .... Hill
Tous Ninive .... Dohrmann
Toussel Judy A ....Moore
Tower Alexandra C .... Thorne
Tower Helen R ....Wilson
Tower Helen S ....Brunet
Tower Jean ....Rennie
Tower Laurel P ....Tower
Tower Pamela ....LeBoutillier
Towers Henrietta ....Williams
Towle Alleen .... Bullitt

Towles Louise L ....Obermeyer
Towne Cynthia.........................Wheary
Towne Daphne V ....Witsell
Towne Marie F ....Tully
Townes Charlie L ....Carter
Townsend Ann I ....Simpson
Townsend Barbara................. Crawford
Townsend Carroll R ....Miller
Townsend Diana B .... Butterworth
Townsend Diana V O ....Yassukovich
Townsend Edith H.....................Boyce
Townsend Elisabeth G................Bridge
Townsend Elise P ....Chisolm
Townsend Elizabeth ....Donaldson
Townsend Elizabeth I.............Hardwick
Townsend Elizabeth P .... Hutchinson
Townsend Elizabeth P ....Taylor
Townsend Emilie K......................Riley
Townsend Emily D...............Vermeule
Townsend Frances .... Marshall
Townsend Mary R ....Hamill
Townsend Mary S .... Wetherill
Townsend Meredith ....Jenney
Townsend Mona ....McLean
Townsend Nancy T..............Townsend
Townsend Rosalind V ....Hodgkins
Townsend Rose J ....Balis
Townsend Vassar M ....Conkling
Townsend Wendy .... Stocker
Townshend Juliet......................Newton
Towson Ann M.........................Brown
Toy Léontine Marié.................Audrain
Tozzer Joan..............................Cave
Tracy Alison B ....Nalle
Tracy Ann ....Carvell
Tracy Anne M.........................Bricker
Tracy Clara C ....Upson
Tracy Emily P ....Gilbert
Tracy Marianne K............. Vandervoorn
Tracy Sarah O.........................Thomas
Trafford Ada B ....Mason
Trafton Mary F ....Simonds
Train Alexandra C ....Totten
Train Errol C..........................Giordano
Train Helen ....Klebnikov
Train Lucinda E ....Longstreth
Train Nina T ....Choa
Trainer Martha D ....Dingman
Trainer Nancy B ....Muse
Tramelli Marie A....................Morrison
Trammell Grace H....................Murphy
Trapnell Emily Marilla .... Horris
Trapp Ashley A ....Currey
Trasel Martha P ....Fava
Trask Eleanor M ....Trask
Trask Elsie Y ....Wheeler
Trask Penelope M....................Curtis
Traub E Florianne......................Greer
Trautman Emily L ....Wood
Travell Janet G ....Powell
Travers Emily L.........................Welch
Travers Mary Ann .... Travers
Traynor Elizabeth A .... Fowler

Traynor Kathleen S....................Millard
Treadway Margaret M................. Sloan
Treat Anne McP ....Francis
Treat Cynthia L.....................Hollister
Treat Mary Esther C ....Treat
Tree Joanne ....Winship
Trefz Emily.............................Newbold
Tregler Annette ....Sterrett
Treibick Alice ....Lynch
Tremaine Dorothy C .... Hildt
Tremaine Mary M ....Soutendijk
Treman Jane S ....Gilbert
Trench Deborah N ....Wheeler
Trenholm Eleanor S.................Bandler
Trent Elizabeth M.................Heberling
Trent Patricia A .... Wells
Trent Stephane ....Trent
Trevor Caroline W ....Salas
Trevor Eleanor F.................. von Stade
Trevor Emily N..................... Van Vleck
Trevor Genevieve L................... Nomer
Trevor Helen S ....Vietor
Trevor Jane S ....Fetter
Trevor Phyllis R G ....Higgerson
Triant Catherine A....................Buxton
Tribble Marthe W ....McKinnon
Trigg Margaret P ....Waterbury
Triller Hollace E ....Page
Trimble Carroll Lloyd ....Cabot
Trimble Helen G ....Nauman
Trimble Lillie J ....Turner
Trimble Margery M ....Kennelly
Trimble Winifred.........................Carter
Trimingham J Linda ....Warriner
Trimm N Suzanne ....Payne
Trimmer Jean A ....Astrop
Trimmier Hallie W ....Gibbs
Trimper Letitia F ....Hurst
Tripi Gloria P..........................Banning
Tripp Kathleen C ....von Raits
Tripp Sharon A F.......................Griffis
Tripp Virginia H...........................Gray
Trippe Betsy S .... De Vecchi
Trishman Betty ....Lowry
Troia Kathleen M ....McFarland
Trombley Marianne R ....Endicott
Troth Emily G..............................Frick
Trotman Julia L...........................Brady
Trotter Eugénie Sterling .... Trotter
Trotter Mary L ....Armat
Troudner Helen L.....................Corbyn
Trover Marguerite H....................Wilson
Trowbridge Barbara J...........Montgelas
Trowbridge Barbara W .... Barnes
Trowbridge Janet S..................Bohlen
Trowbridge K Nancy ....Holmes
Trowbridge Sarah F.................Savage
Trowbridge V Elvira..................Sibley
Troxell Jean F......................Chandor
Troy Susan W ....Van Oot
Trudeau Elizabeth B ....Morgan
Trudeau Jeanne D ....Fenn
True Alice W ....Gasch

Voorhees Lenore M ....Jefferson
Voorhees Mary Isabel...............Hickok
Vos Monique J.........................Merrill
Vose A Virginia.........................Nicoll
Vose Vivian B ....Trincal
Voth Suzanne G..................Dillenbeck
Votoras Sonia F...........................Ives
Vought Elizabeth D ....Henshaw
Vowels Marianne P ....Cattier
Voyatzis Mary E...........Frelinghuysen
Vrignon Josée.........................Reboul
Wacker Ellen J......................Johnston
Wadbrook Winifred M ....Megear
Waddell Eleanor I......................Libby
Wade Alice E.....................Milinowski
Wade Rae E ....Trimmier
Wadhams Katherine S ....Cox
Wadick Miriam W ....Kersey
Wadsworth Alice T....................Strong
Wadsworth Anne D ....Markle
Wadsworth Caroline F..............Hudson
Wadsworth Nancy E..................Larson
Wadsworth Naomi W ....Travis
Wadsworth Sara E ....Wood
Wadsworth Susan ....Plimpton
Wadsworth Susan M...........Bourdelais
Wagg Elizabeth M.......................Gray
Waggaman Frances V..............Tallman
Wagley Mary E.......................Danforth
Wagner Dorothy S ....Bemis
Wagner Karen E ....Washburn
Wagner Lelia A ....Devereux
Wagner Maria T ....Fox
Wagner Martha J ....Farr
Wagner Mary A .... Gordon
Wagner Mary Jane ....Elliott
Wagner Nancy Van H ....Mixter
Wagner Patricia C..................Bahlman
Wagner Renate.....................Chapman
Wagner Sarah J ....Longnecker
Wagner Vivian A A.....................Gast
Wagnière Anne H ....Spiess
Wagnon Nathalie P ....Madeira
Wagoner Prudence.................Hotchkiss
Wagstaff Audrey C.......................Robb
Wagstaff Deborah ....Wainwright
Wagstrom Margaretha ....Rumbough
Wailes Ann E........................Buchanan
Wainwright Christine............Sowanick
Wainwright Mary K ....Auchincloss
Wainwright Sarah M ....Yort
Waite Ann F ....Howard
Waite Judith.........................Freeman
Wakefield Elisabeth A ....Doermann
Wakefield Joan F ....Millspaugh
Wakefield Sarah D..............Carmichael
Wakeman Audrey C ....Walker
Walbridge Ann A ....Holmes
Walbridge Elizabeth C ....Walbridge
Walbridge Roberta L ....Thibault
Walcott Alexandra ....Walcott
Walcott Anna ....Likins
Walcott Diana ....Phillips

Walcott Sophie L ....Kolachov
Waldhauser Roxanne.....................Bliss
Waldo Ruth ....Newhall
Wales Ellen M ....Kingsbury
Wales Louise C .... Field
Wales Natalie S ....Douglas-Hamilton
Walgren Karen ....Milne
Walker Alice P ....Conley
Walker Anica B ....Turner
Walker Annabelle L B...............Ranck
Walker Audrey T ....Perkins
Walker Bailey ....Symington
Walker Barbara L ....Rollhaus
Walker Caroline A........................ Hill
Walker Carolyn ....Powning
Walker Christine ....Maier
Walker Cynthia T

Diacre de Liancourt
Walker Diana S.......................Steers
Walker Doris E ....Bauer
Walker Dorothy J ....Collins
Walker Elaine ....Fiske
Walker Eleanor P......................Weille
Walker Elizabeth D ....Edgeworth
Walker Elizabeth E....................Boncella
Walker Elizabeth G ....Gardiner
Walker Elizabeth P.....................Crofts
Walker Emily ....Drew
Walker Frances D ....Patterson
Walker Gloria ....Milliken
Walker Grace ....Locke
Walker Gwyneth V A................Walker
Walker Harriet E...................Henderson
Walker Helen ....Snodgrass
Walker Helen M ....Spencer
Walker Helen P.....................Kenefick
Walker Helen P.........................Parker
Walker Holly B.........................Nixon
Walker Jacqueline......................Smith
Walker Jacqueline E ....Ernst
Walker Jane A ....McCall
Walker Jane B ....Morgan
Walker Janet S ....Sarran
Walker Jo ....Seaton
Walker Judith......................Laughlin
Walker Kate Ewing ....Curran
Walker Laura B ....Danforth
Walker Lee Telford ....Walker
Walker Louise W ....Houdry
Walker Lucile T........................Hays
Walker Margaret M ....Spofford
Walker Marion G.............Van Alstyne
Walker Marjorie L ....Walker
Walker Marjory E ....Walker
Walker Maud T.........................Pratt
Walker Melissa L ....O'Shaughnessy
Walker Mollie C ....Cox
Walker Muriel-Anne................Chadsey
Walker Nina ....Wainwright
Walker Olivia K ....Hamilton
Walker Pamela Buchanan..........Walker
Walker Patricia H ....Plumb
Walker Phyllis C.......................Ewing

Walker Polly R ....Beal
Walker Suzanne ....Robinson
Walker Suzanne W ....Wright
Walker Wendy ....Glen
Wall Alexandria...................Worsham
Wall Anne F ....Wall
Wall Camilla ....Lee
Wall Joan C ....Potter
Wall Linda L....................Schieffelin
Wall Lyde H .... Carr
Wall M Virginia ....de St Phalle
Wall Maria C ....Patterson
Wall Marilyn F ....Obolensky
Wall Mary Anne.........................Hyde
Wall Sheila M........................Hundt
Wallace Angela ....Augur
Wallace Antonia ....Leidy
Wallace Derith R ....MacBride
Wallace Douglass A ....Newbold
Wallace Elise N ....Carr
Wallace Elizabeth ....Muller
Wallace Elizabeth P..............Edmunds
Wallace Emily D ....Williams
Wallace Grace S ....Cochran
Wallace Helen H ....Kiesel
Wallace Helene D ....Garnett
Wallace Janet B ....Jones
Wallace Janet C ....Huff
Wallace Joan B ....MacPherson
Wallace Judy M ....Cook
Wallace Julia.........................Bennett
Wallace Julia H..........................Boyd
Wallace Katharine van D ....O'Reilly
Wallace Katherine ....Stevenson
Wallace Lucy H ....Rankin
Wallace Marion S ....Wilcox
Wallace Mary F ....Bance
Wallace Nancy M ....McKinley
Wallace Winifred S ....Kelsey
Wallach Hope ....Porter
Waller Agnes ....Loring
Waller Katherine ....Barnes
Waller M Trigg ....Lentz
Waller Mary Alice ....Stoddard
Waller Mary R ....Pinnell
Waller Milbrey W ....Andrews
Waller Virginia H ....Wemple
Walling Janet B ....Lawrence
Wallingford Kay ....Hepp
Wallis Eleanor O ....Herkness
Wallis Joanna J ....Rees
Walls Lisbeth Lister ....Walls
Walls Mary L...................Wolkonsky
Walsh Alma de B ....Kirkland
Walsh Annette T ....Bergsma
Walsh Carol A ....Treadwell
Walsh Eleanor S ....de Limur
Walsh Frances C................Cummings
Walsh Jane J ....Glidden
Walsh Joan M ....Brandt
Walsh Judith C ....Malcom
Walsh Kathleen A ....Carr
Walsh Mary J...............................Ellis

Walsh Meghan M ....Knight
Walsh Sarah E ....Rose
Walsh Walburga ....Maxwell
Walter Diane.............................Hester
Walter Hannah S.........................Edens
Walter Janet ....Pringle
Walter Philippa L ....Travell
Walters Eleanor M....................Beaton
Walther Amy L..................La Marche
Walthour Susan R......................Coyne
Walton C Jean P ....Clemmer
Walton Elizabeth B.......................Koob
Walton Joly ....Stewart
Walton Marion J ....Walsh
Walton Martha K S ....Coonley
Walton Mary T.........................Curley
Walton Nancy McM ....Follansbee
Wanamaker Lynn W....................Rice
Wanamaker Mary L W ....Watriss
Wang Agnes L......................Atterbury
Wang Amy ....de Rham
Wangenheim Anne ....Cronin
Warburg Jeremy.........................Russo
Ward Alison.........................Burdick
Ward Amy N ....Beir
Ward Anne E ....Guinan
Ward April A ....Bodman
Ward Catharine J ....Thompson
Ward Denise M........................Zanze
Ward Eileen M ....Barrett
Ward Eleanor Harner...............Altemus
Ward Elinor ....Francis
Ward Elizabeth ....Pearce
Ward Elizabeth H ....Robbins
Ward Elizabeth L ....Preble
Ward Emily A.........................Nixon
Ward Frana L ....Coates
Ward Jane C ....Newhall
Ward Linyer B ....Zieman
Ward Louise B..........................Harris
Ward Marianna ....Haydock
Ward Mary L ....Whitmarsh
Ward Mary Louise ....Ryus
Ward Mollie A ....Brown
Ward Nancy Lee ....Berry
Ward Pansy B............................Jones
Ward Sylvia ....Sawyer
Ward Virginia C ....Brophy
Ward Wendelyn A ....Campbell
Ward Winifred A ....Keith
Ward Winifred S..........................Irish
Wardell Wendy T ....Chamberlin
Warden Adèle ....Paxson
Warden Alice E ....Guida
Warden Anne H ....Sinkinson
Warden E Hazel.......................Roberts
Warden Sally M.........................Stone
Wardenburg E Blair................Fosburgh
Wardlaw Kelly A.........................Hawes
Wardle Ruth E ....Scott
Wardrop Constance W ....Combes
Wardrop Stacy N ....Roe
Wardropper Mary P ....Malabre

Wardwell Alice C ....Tripp
Wardwell Clarissa........................... Pell
Wardwell Helen R .... Du Bois
Wardwell Jayne ....Christy
Wardwell M Florence.................. Waite
Wardwell Polly G .... Hutchins
Ware Alice de V ....Perry
Ware Nancy ....Cutler
Ware Susan C ....Huber
Warfield Judith Marie................... Price
Warick Stephany...................... Haines
Waring Alexandra......................Turner
Waring Ashley E ....Vietor
Waring Beverly.........................Cutler
Waring Carolyn R.....................Verbeck
Waring Patricia C ....Swift
Warnecke Margaret E...............Merck
Warner Alice P .... McLennan
Warner Alison H.........................Pyne
Warner Barbara E.....................Hallowell
Warner Barbara L....................Kammer
Warner Carol R......................... Cooke
Warner Dorothy A ....Evans
Warner Edith W..........................Young
Warner Emalea ....Trentman
Warner Helen S .... Pepper
Warner Jane ....Dick
Warner Janet K....................Miller
Warner Judith M................... McCarthy
Warner Katharine S ....Cook
Warner Lorraine.......................Bulkley
Warner Marion........................Hodgkins
Warner Marjorie W ....Off
Warner Melissa S .... Norton
Warner Rosalind B ....Lewis
Warner Sherrill H ....Scullin
Warner Suzanne........................Kenly
Warner Suzanne de C .... Parsons
Warnhammar M Birgitta ....Davis
Warnock Eugenia M C .... Siedlarz
Warnock Sheila M G...................Seus
Warren Caroline S .... Black
Warren Catharine K..................Warren
Warren Cheryl L............ Sensenbrenner
Warren Diana ....Wells
Warren Dorothy Bell ....Littlehales
Warren Dorothy Q..................... Arnold
Warren Jessica V R ....Bennett
Warren Josephine.....................Doelger
Warren Lily................................Russell
Warren Mary E.........................Fagan
Warren Mary E......................Murphy
Warren Mary G.........................Foster
Warren Norma L.......................Hansen
Warren Ola.................................Heath
Warren Penny S ....Chester
Warren Virginia S....................Shriver
Warren Whitney........................Agnew
Warrick Tara L ....Cameron
Warrington Anne McG.............Wilson
Warrington Elsie H............. Warrington
Warrington Mary H.................Cassidy
Warrington Sarah H...................Selnick

Warrington Virginia............... Morosani
Warth Stacy H .... Fiechter
Wasem Mary L........................ Putnam
Washburn Alexandra L..... Washburn
Washburn Diana J................ Slaymaker
Washburn Elizabeth ....Delano
Washburn Lynn S .... Hanke
Washburn Mary D ....Gray
Washburn Nancy W .... Voorhees
Washburn Phoebe .... Driver
Washburne Caroline ....Heyer
Washburne Eleanor P .... Dickey
Wasley Bruce.............................Atkins
Wasley M Gordon .... Austin
Wasserman Barbara J .... Bonoff
Waterbury Lois A .... French
Waterfall Mary F .... May
Waterhouse Ane Louise ....Royall
Waterhouse Joan ....Vanderpoel
Waterman Anne B ....Bingham
Waterman Anne S......................Troth
Waterman Barbara B .... Folger
Waterman Gwendolyn D............... West
Waterman Jane S .... Bedford
Waterman Kathryn E.................. Davis
Waterman Marcena P ....Love
Waterman Sally ....Owen
Waterman Sally Wistar...............Winsor
Waterman Shirley G .... Amory
Waters Elizabeth A...................Cooper
Waters Janet S ....Flagle
Waters M Beirne.....................Richmond
Waters Mona A......................Wetmore
Waters Suzette H ....Connard
Waterworth Elisabeth A ....Russell
Watjen Catherine .... Pemberton
Watjen Paula.......................Rockefeller
Watkin A Ray ....Hoagland
Watkins Betty ....Blair
Watkins Fanchon M ....Burnham
Watkins Martha S .... Steiger
Watkins Virginia H..................... Kress
Watkins Virginia S ....Mitchell
Watson Alice B...................Faulkner
Watson Alice D .... Houston
Watson Ann .... Walsh
Watson Ann K ....West
Watson B Burrill....................Haskell
Watson Eleanor L .... Kinsella
Watson Elizabeth D............. Blanchard
Watson Ellen B .... Eager
Watson Faith C........................Meigs
Watson Forsyth ....Kineon
Watson Franchelle H ....Link
Watson Gail ....Barber
Watson Helen M................Blodgett
Watson Jane W .... Stetson
Watson Jeannette W ....Brewer
Watson Katharine C ....Hiam
Watson Katrine ....Watson
Watson Kyri ....Claflin
Watson Laurie McL..................Moss
Watson Lucinda B .... Watson

Watson Margaret A ....Taylor
Watson Margaret E................. Hartnett
Watson Monique H................... Wiedel
Watson Olive L...........................Cobb
Watson Priscilla W ....Liggett
Watson Sheila ....Babcock
Watson Susan B ....Crosland
Watson Susan C ....Whitman
Watson Virginia.........................Logan
Watt Elizabeth C..................... Smith
Watters Christine ....Moore
Watters Eugenia.....................Stillman
Watters Mary C ....Reichner
Watters Valeska A ....Grubstein
Watterson Sarah V G............ Mortimer
Wattles Peggy .... Pulleyn
Watts Elizabeth A ....Petersen
Watts Elizabeth B
                Bromley-Davenport
Watts Elizabeth H..................Boileau
Watts Gertrude de L .... Wallace
Watts Isabella K .... Cunynghame
Watts Jennifer H......................Rodiger
Watts Julia C........................Buchanan
Watts Laura B...........................Pearson
Watts Mary ....Watson
Watts Natalie O ....Grace
Watts Wendy M........................Pierson
Wauchope Caroline W M...........Martin
Waud Beverley M............. Sutherland
Waud Eleanor M........................Dorr
Waud Isabel P..........................Hertz
Way Edith ....Curtis
Way Elizabeth A.....................Franklin
Wayland Eleanor C.............. Thomson
Wayland Lucy E........................Hall
Waylett Anna P...................... Shackford
Weakley Carol J ....Tuthill
Weakley Janet.......................Haskins
Weaks Mariana C .... Richardson
Wear Barbara ....Burkham
Wear Nancy H ....Polk
Wearn Susan L ....Drew
Weatherby Christie ....Hastings
Weatherman Julia M........... Stephenson
Weathers Barbara A .... MacLean
Weaver Alita D..........................Reed
Weaver Barbara L........................Ferrin
Weaver Hannah A .... Batchelder
Weaver J Marcia ....Campbell
Weaver Margaret C .... Crawford
Weaver Patricia E.....................Wurts
Weaver Rachel G...................Danforth
Webb Ann M .... Stafford
Webb Betty J ....Clark
Webb Cassandra ....Gerez
Webb Charlotte A....................Kendall
Webb Elizabeth St J .... Baldwin
Webb Frederica V....................Gamble
Webb Karyn R.......................Campbell
Webb Kate B ....Harris
Webb Laura H ....Brown
Webb Margaret O .... Hart

Webb Nancy B ....Martin
Webb Nancy S ....Stroud
Webb Pamela .... Dawson
Webb Rebecca Peyton ....Easterby
Webb Sarah C..........................Brown
Webber Jean C ....Sutphin
Webber Julie ....Bowring
Webber Linda L .... Sturtevant
Weber Catherine A .... Saxton
Weber Juliet C ....Reid
Webster Ann D L .... Johnson
Webster Diana W ....Lynch
Webster Donna V ....Reimer
Webster Eleanor M...................Winsor
Webster Elizabeth L .... Purvis
Webster Geraldine McA...... Dellenback
Webster H Elizabeth......................Dean
Webster Helen F .... Badger
Webster Jane C.............................Gray
Webster Julie H ....Barclay
Webster Mary E..........................Levit
Webster Mary L.......................Kellogg
Webster Norma A ....Read
Webster Rebecca .... McKinnon
Webster Wendy K .... Keleher
Wechsler Eileen ....Finletter
Wedelstaedt Barbara L .... Mark
Wedemeyer Isabelle D .... Carse
Wedwick Lisa G .... Toland
Weed Judith A ....Perera
Weed Margaret B ....Jacobs
Weeden Mary C.......................Pollock
Weeder Dorothy C....................Simpson
Weedon Anne J.............................Petri
Weekes Clarissa Crawford ......Burgevin
Weekes Elizabeth B ....Burden
Weekes Sarita ....Gates
Weeks Barbara A ....Kellar
Weeks Beatrice .... Bast
Weeks Frances L ....Lawrence
Weeks Leonie B ....Cole
Weeks Martha S ....Sherrill
Weeks Mary Q ....Peck
Weeks Sara T.........................Peabody
Wegg Dorothy S ....Morgan
Weibel Klara ....Nicholson
Weichel Alma U ....Anderson
Weicker Mary-Audrey...............Mellor
Weidemann Marie L E .... Knapp
Weidemueller Virginia ....Lortz
Weidenkopf Susan J ....Livingston
Weidlein Joan K .... Mudge
Weil Wendy H ....Rush
Weiland Lilian ....Glascock
Weinberg Nancy L ....Auersperg
Weiner Martha G .... Burger
Weingarten Joan ....Levy
Weinig Rita P ....Cheyney
Weins Helen L ....Korrick
Weir Ann H ....Rush
Weir Virginia Lee ....Colladay
Weis Virginia A.......................Harrity
Weisbrodt Laura L....................Nimick

Weisenbach Ann L .... Gerhard
Weisenstein Kristina E .... Stillman
Weissinger Jill L ....Northrop
Weist Helen L.............................Karl
Weist Susan H ....Wiley
Weizer Patricia M........................Long
Welborn Sandra J .... Renzy
Welch Anne W .... De Bardeleben
Welch Barbara G ....Cook
Welch Barbara H .... Sturtevant
Welch Edith ....Potter
Welch Gloria..........................Whitlock
Welch Kathy G ....Rolfe
Welch Marriott L ....Moszka
Welch Martha G ....Welch
Welch Mary Elizabeth............Coolidge
Welch Phyllis.......................MacDonald
Welch Rhoda.........................Schultz
Welch Ruth .... Laidlaw
Welch Susan D ....Williams
Weld Ada R ....Osborn
Weld Adelaide ....Knott
Weld Anne F............................Collins
Weld Ellen L................................Tilt
Weld Eloise............... Hodges
Weld Eloise R..........................Choate
Weld Florence L......................Hawes
Weld Helen M ....Paschal
Weld Hope ....Weld
Weld Jane L...........................Brown
Weld Katharine ....Bacon
Weld Penelope ....White
Weld Rose............................Baldwin
Welden Thorn T ....Ivanoff
Weldon Elizabeth L ....Smith
Welfley Mae.................................Esty
Welldon Janet ....Graham
Weller Emily...............................Jay
Weller Nancy ....Pierrepont
Welles Paula G ....Orr
Welles Serena ....Moss
Wellford Renée M .... Shettle
Wellin Janis L...........................Notz
Welling Harriet ....Richards
Wellington Linda ....Perkins
Wellington Nancy...................Lee
Wellington Ruth B ....Shaw
Wellington Virginia ....Cabot
Wellman Helen C .... Stickle
Wells A Shannon...................Atkeson
Wells Anne ....Branscomb
Wells C Selden ....Tearse
Wells Carolee J......................Henney
Wells Elizabeth ....Bunten
Wells Elizabeth .... Fox
Wells Florence H......................Fox
Wells Frances B.....................Johnson
Wells Georgina L .... Van Rensselaer
Wells Gray ....Josephs
Wells Harriet B.......................Bailey
Wells Jane ....Alt
Wells Jane ....Holt
Wells Jane E ....Sadtler

Wells Jean L ....Bealke
Wells Judy A C ....Hoffman
Wells Julia................................Terry
Wells Katharine L..............Hoblitzelle
Wells Kathryn M ....Rose
Wells L Hope...........................Reese
Wells Mary C ....Vickery
Wells Mary E........................Reiner
Wells Mary G ....Ogden
Wells Rebecca ....Jones
Wells Rebecca G ....Mattison
Wells Sarah O......................Robertson
Wells Sophia D.......................Pfeiffer
Wells Suzanne E ....Bergmann
Wells Virginia........................ Simonds
Welman Mary .... Snow
Welsch Sandra L........................Spahr
Welsh Phoebe LeM .... Muzzy
Welsh Susan H .... Darlington
Welton Juliet S ....Guimont
Welwood Diana N ....Caron
Welwood Helen T...................Gavales
Wende Carolyn M ....Niles
Wendelius Lisa W ....Choate
Wendell Barbara ....Kerr
Wendell Caroline ....Abdulrazak
Wendell Gwendolen C ....Klaus
Wendell Nancy H ....Evans
Wendell Nathalie A ....Thomas
Wendler Cathryn A......... Mecaskey
Wendt Margaret F.........................Akin
Wendt Phyllis E...........................Pierce
Wenner Stephanie N................ Warburg
Wenning Eleanor L...................Atwell
Wente Carolyn ....Layton
Wentling Sally L..........................Rial
Wentworth Anne.......................Morss
Wentworth Elizabeth A ....Perera
Wentworth Margaret..................Owings
Wentz Jeannette A.............Lingelbach
Wentz Rebecca D ....Wood
Wentzel Jennifer L...................Gulden
Wenzell F Tracy ....Davlin
Wenzell Susan M..................Waldron
Were Suzanne ....Lawrence
Werenfels Martha L......... Satterthwaite
Werlein Betty...........................Carter
Werlein Elizabeth Lorraine ....Moore
Werlein Leila .... Adamoski
Werlemann Marie T .... Pero
Werner Barbara .... Kratovil
Werner Claire A .... Henriques
Werner Conchita G....................Stuhl
Werner Elise G ....Crosby
Werner Elizabeth A .... Warrick
Werner Jane B ....Aye
Werner Salle A ....Vaughn
Wesbrook Janet ....Davis
Wesley Carol J.......................Schrauff
Wesselhoeft Frances ....Bush-Brown
Wessells D Reed ....Nichols
Wesselman Linda J.................Jackson
Wesson Nancy B ....Coe

West Cynthia H ....Benney
West Deborah M.....................Eldridge
West Dorothy.............................Butler
West Dorothy K.........................North
West Edith T..............................Daub
West Elisabeth J .... Fell
West Isabel D ....Reath
West Janet..................................Lloyd
West Janet M ....Garrett
West Jeanne H ....Riggs
West Margot S ....Anderson
West Mary ....Barnes
West Mary H G ....Neblett
West Mary J ....Kraft
West Maxine ....Gaither
West Priscilla W ....Ballou
West Ruth ....Houghton
West Shelley A ....Adams
West Susan S ....Ross
West Victoria ....Lee
Westberg Mary M....................Francis
Westerfield Clare ....Evans
Westervelt G Maxine ....Darby
Westlake Mary E ....Davant
Wetherald Ann-Elisa .... Black
Wetherald Winifred J ....McGennis
Wetherbee Alice ....Badger
Wetherill Alexandra....................Gerry
Wetherill Anne.........................Parker
Wetherill Cynthia ....Wallace
Wetherill Edith B ....Ellis
Wetherill Elizabeth C ....McMeel
Wetherill Fernanda Wanamaker
                                          Niven
Wetherill Georgena ....Stanger
Wetherill Georgiana C ....Lewis
Wetherill Marita W......................Muir
Wetherill Sara R ....Wilds
Wetmore Marian L ....Milbank
Wetten Eleanor .... Pennington
Wetten Mildred B ....McDermott
Wettlaufer Alexandra K ....Carpenter
Wettlaufer Jennifer S.............Sednaoui
Wetzel Phoebe ....Griswold
Weyburn Ruth..........................Parker
Weyerhaeuser Lynn O ....Day
Weyerhaeuser Vivian O .... Piasecki
Weyher Laura G ....Hall
Weymouth Sara E S ....Russell
Whalen Jessica S .... Haverstick
Whann Charlotte M .... Adams
Wharton Aileen E ....Price
Wharton Elizabeth S ....Beeler
Wharton Louise H ....Pistell
Wharton Stephanie H ....Holbrook
Wheat Sally B.......................Stevenson
Wheatland Anna ....Ordway
Wheatland Nancy......................Biglow
Wheatland Sarah McA ....Fisher
Wheatley Wendy T..................Riefler
Wheaton Margaret L.................Tuttle
Wheaton Margery J ....Wheaton
Wheaton Polly J ....Wheaton

Whedbee Elizabeth M ....Constable
Wheeler Ann B ....McNealy
Wheeler Ann W ....Vanderpool
Wheeler Barbara J ....Coit
Wheeler Brook R ....Berlind
Wheeler Carol R ....Stevenson
Wheeler Catherine A ....Pillsbury
Wheeler Eleanor P ....Bogert
Wheeler Elisabeth T ....Damon
Wheeler Elizabeth C ....Soule
Wheeler Elizabeth P ....Dunn
Wheeler I Letitia.........................Ufford
Wheeler Jacqueline ....Milstead
Wheeler Joan .... du Pont
Wheeler Joan T M ....Mackie
Wheeler Kathryn E ....Markle
Wheeler Kendall .... van Orman
Wheeler Laura B ....Golding
Wheeler Louise B ....Grosvenor
Wheeler Martha A ....Donner
Wheeler Martha H ....Burke
Wheeler Mary B M ....von Czoernig
Wheeler Melissa Ann ....Waud
Wheeler Nancy L ....Speed
Wheeler Olivia D....................Alexandre
Wheeler Patricia F.....................Schotz
Wheeler Patricia N ....Fox
Wheeler Penelope I....................Locke
Wheeler Polly ....Guth
Wheeler Sue E ....Mason
Wheeler Sylvia I ....Clement
Wheeler Winifred ....McIntyre
Wheeler Winifred B ....Devereux
Wheelwright A Elizabeth ....Leckie
Wheelwright Amelia E ....Vickery
Wheelwright Eleanor R ....Crunden
Wheelwright Martha H ....Galleher
Whelahan Katherine E.............Schwab
Whelan Eleanor ....Ewart
Whelan Georgette ....Rutherfurd
Whelen Alexandra P.....................Sears
Whelen Violet ....Bowling
Whetstone Edith B........................Page
Whetstone M Virginia ....Lucas
Whetstone Maribell R..............Maschal
Whidden Teresa A M .... St Claire
Whipple Elizabeth C.............McKenna
Whipple Louise B......................Gillock
Whipple Margaret C ....Wright
Whipple Margaret R ....Finch
Whippo Georgia E........................Fuller
Whiston Kathleen M .... Wirtz
Whitaker Amanda W ....Lough
Whitaker Ellen M ....Curtis
Whitaker Helen J ....Meyer
Whitaker Katharine R...................Dyer
Whitaker Margaret E ....Garrett
Whitall Frances S ....Calvocoressi
Whitall Gertrude L ....Martin
Whitall Sarah O M ....Sullivan
Whitcomb Marjorie L.................Hucks
Whitcraft Alexandra C ....Pennisi
White Alexandra.........................Smith

White Barbara R .... Morse
White Bertrude B ....Catterfeld
White Betty J .... Bohlen
White Camden G .... Percival
White Cary R .... Schaperkotter
White Cecelia R....................... Abbott
White Claire N...........................Knox
White Cleaver L .... Knapp
White Cynthia A .... Halle
White Cynthia M .... Jay
White Cynthia Saunders ..... Cadwalader
White Deborah K .... Reynolds
White Doris B ....Clarke
White Eleanor B .... Wright
White Eleanor H .... Durling
White Elinor...........................Janeway
White Elizabeth B ....Glascock
White Elizabeth E ....Fenwick
White Elsie...............................Miller
White Elsie M ....Parsons
White Ethel W ....McFarlan
White Frances E ....Gale
White Grace B ....Walker
White Harriet H ....Jones
White Jacquelyn V .... Parmele
White Janet ....Lawrence
White Jeanne L ....Miller
White JoAnne ....Blair
White Joanne P ....Kille
White Jocelyn C ....Rose
White Judith C ....Gray
White Katherine A..................Drescher
White Linda F........................Wiseman
White Louise D.....................Marburg
White Louise G........................Carter
White M Christine .... Man
White M Clarissa.......................Brown
White Margaret E R .... Plum
White Margaret R .... Bennett
White Margery .... McGovern
White Marjorie V .... Sinnott
White Mary A...........................White
White Mary G......................Anderson
White Mary Lee.......................Galvis
White Patricia ....Farrar
White Patricia ....Lovell
White Patricia .... Timpson
White Phyllis ....Cherbonnier
White Placidia........................Carter
White Prudence S ....Martin
White Reba J........................Williams
White Rita M ....Mathews
White Sally G........................Walker
White Sally S..............................Lee
White Susan F................. Allenburger
White Susan S .... West
White Susan T .... Redfield
White Susannah ....Rhinelander
White Suzannah C .... Fischer
White Suzanne..........................Frank
White Suzanne E ....Humphreys
White Suzanne W .... McKown
White Virginia .... Sigety

White Wanda M .... Blanchard
Whitehead A Blair ....Blunt
Whitehead Frances.................Remington
Whitehead Marguerite ....Edwards
Whitehill Diana...........................Laing
Whitehill Jane C ....Rotch
Whitehouse Alice V ....Harjes
Whitehouse Joan D..................McLeod
Whitehouse Louise B ....Sides
Whitehouse Sylvia.................... Blake
Whitelaw Corinne E ....Fusz
Whiteley Eleanor ....Foster
Whiteley Mary N S ....Denault
Whiteley Susan ....Quinby
Whiteman Elizabeth U ....Mueller
Whiteman Margaret G ....Snyder
Whitener Croft ....Lane
Whitesell Susan L ....Hillman
Whiteside Caroline B ....Warren
Whiteside Deirdre M ....McFadden
Whitesides Elizabeth L........Holdsworth
Whitfield Alice ....Howell
Whitford Ordway................ Wadsworth
Whitham Margaret H R ......Manchester
Whitin Betsey F ....Tyler
Whitin Sarah M ....Brownell
Whitin Sophie C .... Draper
Whiting Barbara E ....Lee
Whiting Carol ....Ratchuk
Whiting Elizabeth St J ....Hays
Whiting K Beverley...................Young
Whiting Margaret Le M .... Redding
Whiting Marilyn J.....................Andrew
Whiting Martha A.........................Cox
Whiting Sara A .... Coxhead
Whiting Suzanne L ....Gallavan
Whitlock Cynthia .... Van Alen
Whitlock Suzanne de L ....Whitlock
Whitlock Veronica P ....Laughlin
Whitlow Ethel M ....Wikander
Whitman Ann Hamilton .... Hurd
Whitman Ann S ....Hackl
Whitman Claire S .... Marshall
Whitman Cynthia G...................Swank
Whitman Elizabeth T.............Ricketson
Whitman Josephine......................Gray
Whitman Lucia P.....................Townsend
Whitman M Josefa C ....Myer
Whitman N Peace ....Baxter
Whitman Olive.........................Parsons
Whitman Suzanne de S ....Smithwick
Whitmarsh Dorothy S............. Sprague
Whitmarsh Linda L.................Hawkins
Whitmarsh Pamela ....Gores
Whitney Alice.........................Lorillard
Whitney Anne B ....Chatfield
Whitney Anne L .... Clements
Whitney Aurelia M...................Lowry
Whitney Barbara .... Balding
Whitney Barbara .... Rogers
Whitney Carol H....................Cudahy
Whitney Cynthia .... Drayton
Whitney Cynthia F ....Whitney

Whitney Eleanor ....Montgomery
Whitney Elizabeth R...................Evans
Whitney Florence B ....Clark
Whitney H Eugenia L.............Hotchkiss
Whitney Hope ....Lapsley
Whitney Jane .... Van Voorhis
Whitney Jane Dumaresq.......... Marshall
Whitney Joan H ....Schaupp
Whitney Louisa J .... Thomson
Whitney Martha A......................Steers
Whitney Martha P........................Rowe
Whitney Mary B ....Haussermann
Whitney Mary Jane.................. Sprague
Whitney Mary L .... Stevens
Whitney Nancy ....Gerry
Whitney Pamela A.......................Swift
Whitney Patricia E......................Butler
Whitney Rosamond .... Carr
Whitney Rosamond .... Kelsey
Whitney Virginia H ....Bradley
Whiton Emelyn L ....Patterson
Whiton Romalda B ....Clark
Whitridge Jane ....Leake
Whitridge Julia.......................Bergland
Whitridge Nan W .... Hamilton
Whitsitt M Ashley ....Conner
Whittaker Dorothy .... Reed
Whittell Marie-Louise ....Detert
Whittemore Dorothy E .... Schafer
Whittemore Elizabeth H .... Stewart
Whittemore Kathryn C .... Knight
Whittemore Rayma L ....Murray
Whittemore Virginia C ....Packer
Whittinghill Sarah A .... Trask
Whittle Gladys C ....Jones
Whittle Marie B ....Webb
Whittlesey Amy E ....O'Neill
Whittlesey Julia R....................Feeley
Whittlesey Marietta H .... Berkey
Whittlesey Peregrine W............Freund
Whitton Louise B .... York
Whyte Penelope L ....Bianchi
Wiberg Margaret.........................Pew
Wichite Cynthia L ....Niedringhaus
Wichman Nancy J..............Trowbridge
Wichman Susan ....Pendleton
Wick Ann L .... West
Wick Constance ....Stobs
Wick Helen Underhill................ Sloan
Wick Kathleen ....Galacar
Wick Mary C ....Bole
Wick Pamela..............................Lincoln
Wick Penelope ....De Young
Wickenberg Elizabeth C..................Ely
Wickenden Sandra H .... Ewing
Wickersham Barbara D .... Follett
Wickersham Hilary J....................Clark
Wickes Ann A ....Brewer
Wickes Carole du P................Marani
Wickett Caroline E .... Oliver
Wickham Anne M M................Brazer
Wickham Mary E ....Harrison
Wickham Susan Read.......................Ross

Wickser Alexandra .... Ballantine
Wickser Hope B ....Weil
Wickser Lita B .... Toland
Wickser Melissa P .... Banta
Wickwire Roma L .... Knight
Wickwire Ruth de M ....Urban
Wickwire S Elizabeth .... Van Pelt
Widmaier Helen E ....McCulloch
Widmer Harriet S .... Widmer
Widrin Tanya L .... Brooks
Wieboldt P Anne .... Seipp
Wiebusch Margaret B................Milner
Wiederseim Eleanor K .... Vanderbeck
Wiedersheim Katherine E............ Petrie
Wiedersheim M Elizabeth ....Carter
Wiehl Margaret F ....Gilfoy
Wiel Elizabeth J.......................McCabe
Wieland Alice M ....Harrison
Wieland Ann D.........................Spaeth
Wieland Jennifer M ....Peterkin
Wieland Kay A ....Brown
Wiener Katherine .... Du Bois
Wiener Liane R............................ Atlas
Wiener Mary L .... Marsh
Wier E March ....Pepper
Wier Virginia C ....Crosby
Wierman Emilie D.................Carpenter
Wiese Gerd K ....Lorentzen
Wiesmann Linda E ....Clark
Wiff Margaret E ....Whipple
Wiggin Nancy .... McVickar
Wiggin Polly B .... Hamilton
Wigglesworth Anne ....Walker
Wigglesworth Anne .... Wright
Wigglesworth Mary ....McAdoo
Wigglesworth Mary D .... Cawley
Wigglesworth Philio E ....Cushing
Wight Anne.........................Phillips
Wight Brooke C............................Cabot
Wight Cornelia E .... Mann
Wight Elizabeth B .... Herring
Wight Esther C L ....Keeney
Wight Jeanne .... Bostwick
Wight Julia R.......................Schniewind
Wight Mary...............................Lakin
Wight Ottilie A ....Conway
Wight Susan R........................Bostwick
Wightman Margaret M .... Kobusch
Wigor Lori J ....McElroy
Wigton Elizabeth G ....Brewer
Wigton Louise .... Davison
Wike Betty M ....Shields
Wilbanks Barbara .... Roberts
Wilbourn Jo Ellen........................Ford
Wilbur Alison Mary .... Thompson
Wilbur Ann N ....Morrison
Wilbur Elizabeth N .... Hodges
Wilbur Theodora B ....Simons
Wilcox Barbara A .... Thompson
Wilcox Betty ....Schaefer
Wilcox Marjorie M ....Weeks
Wilde Louise P ....Miller
Wilder Ann B ....Boyd

Wilder Candace	Heaphy
Wilder Deborah	Cooke
Wilder Dorothea F	Smith
Wilder Sarah F	Fuller
Wildman Lynne N	Chapman
Wildman Phoebe R	Archbold
Wildman Tonya C	Mailliard
Wildrick Belle O'D	Robbins
Wilds Adrienne A	Wilds
Wilds Pamela	Cole
Wilds Stephanie	Shea
Wiles Catherine C	Pickering
Wiley Elizabeth A	Laplante
Wiley Margaret M	Carr
Wiley Mary Anna	Ross
Wilfley Rosamond G	Neilson
Wilford Marguerite E	Labrot
Wilkin Mary C	Winmill
Wilking Elionora van T	Silbersack
Wilkins Roeann P	Linzee
Wilkinson Elizabeth	Rast
Wilkinson Evelyn M	Cudahy
Wilkinson Jean K	MacDermid
Wilkinson Josephine Diana	Wilkinson-Gould
Wilkinson Susan	Stith
Will Eleanor C	Kuser
Will Jane	Smith
Will Kay	Livingstone
Willard Alice H	Johnson
Willard Elizabeth Van N	Willett
Willard Nancy G	Holliday
Willard Sarah McK	Willard
Willcox Elizabeth P	Milliken
Willcox Esther McK	Putnam
Willens Ann F	Gorham
Willet Ann L	Kellogg
Willets H Ann	Boyd
Willets Hannah E	Wister
Willets Mary E	Washburne
Willets Sarah A	Nichols
Willi Marion	Whittemore
Williams Alison H	Lambart
Williams Ann H	Schroeder
Williams Anne L	Goff
Williams Barbara	Throop
Williams Beatrice C	Ake
Williams C Bliss	Browne
Williams Carol D	Brown
Williams Carol L	du Pont
Williams Caroline F	Gay
Williams Catharine D	Keatley
Williams Charlas E	Wise
Williams Charlotte R	McClain
Williams Christina	Davis
Williams Cynthia M	Collins
Williams Daphne S S	Johnson
Williams Deborah W	MacKenzie
Williams Dorothy L	Smith
Williams E F Maida	La Farge
Williams Edith	Dunham
Williams Eleanor Addison	Miles
Williams Eleanor S	Benziger

Williams Elisabeth T	Ireland
Williams Elizabeth B	Price
Williams Elizabeth M	Clark
Williams F Randall	Chanler
Williams Frances M	Rusch
Williams Frances Sue	Ganoe
Williams Gael	Gardner
Williams Georgie	Lewis
Williams Helen B	Montague
Williams Helen D	Marston
Williams Jacquelynn B	Dorrance
Williams Jane W	Runyeon
Williams Janet B	Tobin
Williams Janet L	Bransome
Williams Jennifer A	Pulitzer
Williams Jessie M	Howland
Williams Joan	Farr
Williams Joan	Rhame
Williams Joan C	Cox
Williams Joan F	Erhard
Williams Judith A	Thompson
Williams Judith H	Gibbons
Williams Katrina W	Lester
Williams Kerbey	Clark
Williams Laura L	Jodice
Williams Laura P	Ivey
Williams Linda H	Dale
Williams Louise A	Brown
Williams Louise C	Devine
Williams Lucy G	Burton
Williams Lynn N	Ruthrauff
Williams M Susan	Pile
Williams Margaret	Casey
Williams Margaret E	Braff
Williams Margaret E	Spears
Williams Marie E W	von Gontard
Williams Marjorie P	Taylor
Williams Mary E	Kyte
Williams Mary H	Herrick
Williams Mary Hathaway	Cortesi
Williams Mary J	Arnold
Williams Mary J	Mulford
Williams Mary L	Avery
Williams Mary W	Gregg
Williams Maude S	Urmston
Williams Megan L	Vietor
Williams Merrill E	Noble
Williams Nell A	Merryman
Williams P Page	Dwyer
Williams Patricia A	Hamlen
Williams Patricia K	MacVeagh
Williams Pauline B	Lampshire
Williams Rebecca D	de Kertanguy
Williams Rosa D C	Miller
Williams Ruth Mary	Sutterley
Williams Sarah E	Righter
Williams Sarah Fenno	Lord
Williams Sheila	Fisher
Williams Sheila	Scott
Williams Susan	Miller
Williams Susan D	Catherwood
Williams Sybil K	Dukehart
Williams Tamara J	Hutchinson

Williams Virginia D	Reeve
Williams Whitney M	Jones
Williamson Ann C	Stubblefield
Williamson Barbara	Haines
Williamson Dorothea	Walker
Williamson Edith M	Kean
Williamson Lillian E	Dennis
Williamson Luanne R	Williamson
Williamson Mary E	Gross
Williamson Phyllis	Aldrich
Williamson R Lee	Hitchcock
Williamson Ursula	Bergin
Willim Sarah E	Hutchings
Willing Margaret	Farwell
Willingham Susan	Simons
Willington Mary Elizabeth	Thompson
Willis Cordelia A	Jennings
Willis Elizabeth A	Fischer
Willis Elizabeth T	Reid
Willis Hannah B	Chadwick
Willis Mary B	Sprague
Willis Mary Fleming H	Finlay
Willis Nell M	Twining
Willis Sara L	Meigs
Willis Vallory	Clark
Willkie Arlinda F	Miranda
Willoughby Allison A	Hosbein
Willoughby Cynthia A	Haueter
Willoughby Marilyn J	Santry
Willoughby Suzanna M	Killea
Wills Ellen M	Martin
Willson Mary O	Wallace
Wilmarth Kathryn J	Cruice
Wilmer Christine G	Barkus
Wilmer Elizabeth	Sexson
Wilmer Margaret Van D	Bartlett
Wilmer Natalie E	Blenk
Wilmerding Barbara B	Macleod
Wilmerding Helen C	Bastedo
Wilmerding Helen C	Wilmerding
Wilmerding Jane A	Binger
Wilmerding Lila	Kirkland
Wilmerding Ruth C	Wood
Wilmot Carolyn	Gray
Wilmot Jane B	Field
Wilms Paula E	McCutcheon
Wilshire Renze	Johnston
Wilson A Beverley B	Parry
Wilson Adèle R	Sanger
Wilson Alice B	Stovell
Wilson Andrea	Green
Wilson Anne A	Evans
Wilson Audrey F	Taliaferro
Wilson Barbara F	Marshall
Wilson Carmel S	Fromson
Wilson Caroline G	McLean
Wilson Carolyn F	Long
Wilson Catherine T	Smith
Wilson Clarke C	Wilson
Wilson Consuelo D	Pierrepont
Wilson Donna M	Long
Wilson Dorothy	Briscoe

Wilson Dorothy E	Osmond
Wilson Dorothy M	Ashton
Wilson Edna	Macomb
Wilson Eleanor C	Staniford
Wilson Elizabeth	Gonzalez
Wilson Elizabeth D	Parrish
Wilson Elizabeth E	Wilcox
Wilson Elizabeth L	Taliaferro
Wilson Elsie D	Thompson
Wilson Ethel M	McBryde
Wilson Grace D	Martin
Wilson H Octavia	Maginnis
Wilson Jane Fraser	Armstrong
Wilson Joan	Stephenson
Wilson Josefa M	Wrangham
Wilson Josephine L	Hammer
Wilson Katherine E	White
Wilson Lee	Lockwood
Wilson Leslie A	Bennett
Wilson Lida F	Winchell
Wilson Linda J	Taylor
Wilson Louise B	Austin
Wilson M Kenneth	Donald
Wilson Marcia E	Smith
Wilson Margaret C	Kerr
Wilson Margaret L	Dodd
Wilson Marian V	Turnure
Wilson Martha A	MacLaren
Wilson Mary	Neel
Wilson Mary C	Supplee
Wilson Mary E	Leys
Wilson Mary John	Siphron
Wilson Mary R	Kelsey
Wilson Miriam O	Weeks
Wilson Natalie T	Beese
Wilson Patricia	Hanna
Wilson Prudence	Crone
Wilson Rebecca A	Armstrong
Wilson Rosemary	Jacobs
Wilson Rosemary H	Johnson
Wilson Schuyler V C	Field
Wilson Sharon	Bates
Wilson Susanne P	Grandin
Wilson Suzanne	Rogers
Wilson Wendy	O'Brien
Wiltshire Paula J	Perkins
Wiman Katherine D	Findlay
Wimpenny Joyce	Bennett
Winant Holly L	Scudder
Winchester Anne	Penniman
Winchester Elizabeth	Huntington
Winckelmann Ruth L	Fiske
Winder Joy	Ford
Windfohr Anne B	Marion
Windisch Gay B	Baer
Windle Susan P	Rogers
Wing Amy W	Quigley
Wing Diana M	Davie
Wing Elizabeth E	Byram
Wing Patricia	Whitaker
Wing Whitney C	Oppersdorff
Wingerd A Elizabeth S	Morris
Wingfield Julia	Pizzinat

Winkenwerder Joanne .... Rienhoff
Winkhaus Kathryn A .... Maxwell
Winkler Gretchen A .... Sinclair
Winner Geralyn .... Roden
Winner Taryn E .... Sprague
Winnett Glenn H..................... Boocock
Winslow Eleanor D ....Brown
Winslow Elizabeth L................Cutler
Winslow Gale O ....Minot
Winslow Genevieve M .... Wing
Winslow Harriet A .... Wheeler
Winslow Mary O .... Mygatt
Winslow Mary-Chilton.............. Mead
Winslow Mildred V ....Ashcraft
Winslow Rose O'N......................Geer
Winslow Sylvia C.................Burnham
Winslow Theodora M...................Noël
Winslow Wendy R ....Lofting
Winsor Adelaide ....Gifford
Winsor Diana...........................Chase
Winsor Elizabeth W ....Coolidge
Winsor Margaret McD ....Stubbs
Winsor Sally Wistar ....Miller
Winston Carolina M...................Barrie
Winston Caroline J ....Cochran
Winston Diane H ....Crocker
Winston Dudley ....Baker
Winston Elizabeth P ....Williams
Winston Mary ....Daly
Winston Virginia ....De Young
Winter C Alix ....Hardie
Winter Mary A ....Driver
Winterbotham Chloe Tyler
                           Winterbotham
Winthrop Angela ....Getchell
Winthrop Cornelia B .... Bonnie
Winthrop E Amory .... Winthrop
Winthrop Katharine ....McKean
Winthrop Serita.....................Winthrop
Winthrop Theodora....................Hooton
Wiper Sibyl A .... Otter
Wire Rosemary .... Anderson
Wirth Dorothea F...................Carpenter
Wirtz Cynthia W.................MacArthur
Wisdom Adelaide ....Benjamin
Wisdom Kathleen M................Scribner
Wise Barbara D .... Macsherry
Wise Elizabeth A .... Copeland
Wise Hannah L ....Orlowski
Wise Henrietta .... Thompson
Wise Jean G...........................Lincoln
Wise Katherine P....................Hannan
Wise Linda J ....Campbell
Wise Margaret M .... Benham
Wise Mary H ....Wight
Wisner Winifred ....Pinson
Wistar Eleanor S..................Crampton
Wister Elizabeth.....................Walcott
Wiswall Elaine J ....Betts
Wiswall M Hope ....Griffin
Witherspoon Anne ....Kuhn
Withington Virginia C...........Neubauer
Witsell Elizabeth W ....Eaton

Witt Harriet A......................Claiborne
Witt Regina M .... Wells
Witte Elisabeth......................McIntire
Witte Susan J .... Andrews
Wittenberg Angela A..............Kinsella
Witter Doris Ann ....Everett
Witter Ellen Kay......................Tilton
Witter H Ann .... Witter-Gillette
Witter Nancy...........................Bates
Wodell Lois P ....Poinier
Wofford Florence J ....Liddell
Wolcott Allyn M....................Greeney
Wolcott Brent ....Roehrs
Wolcott Edith P ....Devens
Wolcott Helen ....Parson
Wolcott Martha A .... Davis
Wolcott Natalie.....................Williams
Wolcott Pamela.....................Fingleton
Wolcott Rebecca D ....Terry
Wolcott Susan ....Dexter
Wolf Charlotte L.......................Mark
Wolf Charlotte M ....Hewson
Wolf Janine A ....Hill
Wolf Louise S .... Arnold
Wolfe Barbara .... Webster
Wolfe Helena A .... Potter
Wolfe Susan T ....Huppman
Wolferth Caroline G .... Amidon
Wolferth Catherine F.............. Piasecki
Wolff Elizabeth J ....Côté
Wolff Ella W ....Brucker
Wolff Margarethe V ....Hopkins
Wolff Marian Hillyer................Young
Wolff Wanda .... Walker
Wolffe Alexandra H .... O'Grady
Wolkonsky Maria W ....de Peyster
Wolverton Lynn....................Kilbourne
Womelsdorf Lyda M....................Hall
Womrath D Selden .... Sutton
Womrath Mary K .... Olson
Wong Catherine J ....Young
Wonham Stapley...................Emberling
Wonkka Debra L ....Palfrey
Wood A Elizabeth ....Watt
Wood Anita K ....Kneass
Wood Anne E .... Harsch
Wood Ariel K ....Wood
Wood Barbara H...................... Vilter
Wood Caroline E ....Guthrie
Wood Carolyn F ....Wood
Wood Cecile T.......................Beacham
Wood Christina.........................Swain
Wood Daphne N ....Gawthrop
Wood Dorothea S ....Wood
Wood Dorothy Ann ....Whitaker
Wood Eleanor P......................Potter
Wood Eleanor S....................McFarland
Wood Elise Ravenel .... du Pont
Wood Elizabeth B....................Wood
Wood Ellen R..........................Barth
Wood Ellen S........................Freeman
Wood Emilie M ....Corbin
Wood Emily C ....Wood

Wood Florence L ....Hacker
Wood Grace M ....Keppel
Wood Hannah C ....Hepburn
Wood Hope C ....Patterson
Wood Hope van B .... Price
Wood Jane ....Harvey
Wood Joan Alice .... Kimball
Wood Julia D...........................Sellers
Wood Katherine K...................McIver
Wood Katherine M ....Colwell
Wood Leslie ....Cameron
Wood Louisa L ....Foulke
Wood Margaret ....Schroeder
Wood Margaret A ....Birgbauer
Wood Margaret D .... Stiff
Wood Margaret V .... Fleming
Wood Margaret W .... Robinson
Wood Mary C ....Kanovsky
Wood Mary W ....Lewis
Wood Meri ....Moody
Wood Patricia ....Harrison
Wood S Wendell.......................Collins
Wood Sandra J W ....Johnston
Wood Sara C ....Thompson
Wood Sarah E ....Wood
Wood Sarah M......................Lewis
Wood Sarah M.........................Post
Wood Sarah S ....Armour
Wood Selina R ....Hewlett
Wood Shirley C ....Dubell
Wood Wendy D ....Chapple
Wood Zoë N ....Dodge
Woodall Gretchen ....Dixon
Woodard Susan H...................Crawford
Woodbury Sally ....Handy
Woodbury Susan C..................Lombardi
Woodcock Cynthia A ....Pierce
Woodcock Frances E .... Saulnier
Woodhead Judith F.................Bonnet
Woodhouse Alexandra............. Drayton
Woodhouse Hope B.................. Canty
Woodhouse Jane ....McLaughlin
Woodin Elizabeth F..................Rowe
Woodrow Nancy G .... McKelvy
Woodrow Ruth A ....Bancroft
Woodruff Anne C .... Stout
Woodruff Edith L ....Kunhardt
Woodruff Sally L....................Ingold
Woods Andrea L ....Gauvreau
Woods Carolie F ....Noble
Woods Dale C.......................Dingledine
Woods Dorothy.......................McLeod
Woods Dorothy M .... Le Roy
Woods Frances G ....Thorsen
Woods Frances S ....Woods
Woods Harriet C...................Campbell
Woods Joan W ....White
Woods Louise H ....Benkert
Woods Lucia W ....Lindley
Woods Mary Louise ....Wood
Woods Nancy H .... French
Woods Sigourney...................Cheek
Woods Wendy W .... Luers

Woodul Sallie B ....Tunner
Woodville Louisa...................Woodville
Woodville Mary C....................Snyder
Woodward Christina M ....Strong
Woodward Colegate N ....Nuttle
Woodward Cynthia S ....Rawle
Woodward Deborah N...............Leach
Woodward Elise W................Hopkins
Woodward Kathryn V ....Patch
Woodward M Hooker ....Judson
Woodward Matilda H ....Dorsey
Woodward Quita.......................Horan
Woodward Ruth E ....Finch
Woodward Susan G ....Ravenel
Woodwell Inga J...........................Ball
Woodworth Barbara J...............Tanner
Woodworth Sarah C ....Gallagher
Woolfe Ruth H ....Bunn
Woolhiser Britt F................Pendergast
Woolman Joan L...........................Glenn
Woolman Lydia R .... Wright
Woolsey Anne S ....La Farge
Woolsey Mary Lee .... Springs
Woolsey R Audrey ....Woolsey
Woolston Beulah J..................... Durfee
Woolston Jeannie H................ Fenton
Woolston Marian ....Catlin
Woolworth Georgina B ....Carter
Woolworth Sally K .... Lynch
Woolworth Sylvia G................Talmage
Wooten Jewelle A.................Bickford
Wooten Mary V .... Dancy
Worcester Josephine B ....MacMillan
Work Cecily S ....Slade
Worley S Jane.....................Pantaleoni
Worman Mignon D....................Worman
Worman Sarah W ....Worman
Wornom Debora A ....Williams
Worrall Ellen H ....Greenleaf
Worrall Fanny Cox ....Dale
Worrall Frances S ....Ward
Worrall Martha ....Mitchell
Worrall Virginia F ....Jenkins
Worrell Sonia M ....Griffin
Worsley Cornelia S................Newell
Worth Rosemary.......................Collins
Worthen Charlotte ....de Pedroso
Worthing Sharon L...................Vaino
Worthington Anne ....Symonds
Worthington Ethel ....Riley
Worthington Jean M ....Cross
Wotherspoon Anne P..................Ross
Wotton Mary ....Frenning
Wottrich Felicity .... Foote
Woźniacka Elzbieta ....Hyde
Wraith Jane ....Holbrook
Wray Laurie D...........................Wray
Wray Lucie H ....Todd
Wray Maryanne H ....Wray
Wray Misty L ....Wyrough
Wren Janis S ....Van Ness
Wrenn Margot L ....Beckett
Wrenn Nancy ....Ogburn

CLUBS AND THEIR OFFICERS

Acorn Club
☎ (215) 735-2040
1519 Locust St
Philadelphia, PA 19102
President .... MRS Robert S Hines
Vice President.......... MRS Alfred W Putnam JR
Rec'g Sec'y .... MRS Robert F Irwin IV
Cor Sec'y .... MRS Brooke Roberts
Treasurer .... MRS Frank K Tarbox

Agamenticus Yacht Club
☎ (207) 363-9814
York Harbor, ME 03911

see Summer Social Register

Algonquin Club of Boston
☎ (617) 266-2400
217 Commonwealth Av
Boston, MA 02116
President ....Lawrence Thornton Shields
Vice Presidents .... James H Barnhart
Richard C Ockerbloom
Chester R Frost
Secretary .... James M Paulsen
Treasurer ....Kenneth I Watchmaker

American Association of the Sovereign Military Order of Malta
☎ (212) 371-1522
1011 First Av
Room 1500
New York, NY 10022
President .... William J Flynn
Vice President.............. MRS James B Peabody
Vice Pres-Exec Dir...........Henry J Humphreys
Treasurer .... Paul B Murray

The American Society of the Most Venerable Order of the Hospital of St John of Jerusalem
☎ (212) 316-7497
1047 Amsterdam Av
New York, NY 10025
Chancellor...........................G William Haas
Vice Chancellors ....Alton E Peters
Christopher C Forbes
Theodore R Gamble JR
Prelate .... REV Richard F Grein
Secretary .... Don W Lundquist
Treasurer .... Corbin R Miller

Annapolis Yacht Club
☎ (410) 263-9279
PO Box 908
Annapolis, MD 21404-0908

see Summer Social Register

The Argyle
☎ (210) 824-1496
934 Patterson Av
San Antonio, TX 78209
President ....Clyde C Crews
Vice Presidents .... R H Tibaut Bowman
MRS Diana Morehouse
Secretary .... Edward F Feith
Treasurer ....William Scanlan

The Army and Navy Club
☎ (202) 628-8400
Farragut Square
901--17 St NW
Washington, DC 20006
President .... BRIG GEN William L McCulloch
Vice Pres...................... MAJ GEN Bruce Jacobs
Secretary .... CAPT Thomas F Pike JR
Treasurer .... MAJ William J Lang
Gen'l Manager ....Bruce H Klappa

Athelstan Club
☎ (334) 432-8604
170 St Francis St
Mobile, AL 36601
President .... Thomas M Roberts
Vice President........................Marion B Lyons
Sec'y-Treas ....Thomas Clark

Ausable Club
☎ (518) 576-4411
St Huberts, NY 12943
President ....Morgan K Smith JR
Vice President...............Edward L Hoffman JR
Secretary ....John G Fritzinger JR
Treasurer ....Frederick S Wonham

The Badminton Club of the City of New York
President .... Frank E Johnson
Vice President.......................Charles Crawford
Secretary .... Thomas J Morrissey
☎ (212) 753-6833
865 United Nations Plaza
New York, NY 10017
Treasurer .... MISS Karen Giannelli

Badminton & Tennis Club
☎ (617) 536-1870
52 Hemenway St
Boston, MA 02115
President ....T Edward Bynum
Vice Presidents ....John T Hemenway
Herbert W Vaughan
Secretary .... MRS Barbara Applegate
Treasurer ....Samuel Leland

Baltimore Country Club
☎ (410) 889-4400
4712 Club Rd
Baltimore, MD 21210
President ....Edward A Johnston
Vice President..............................Harry Ratrie
Secretary ....Paul F Obrecht JR
Treasurer ....Joseph W Mosmiller

Baltusrol Golf Club
☎ (201) 376-1900
Shunpike Rd
Springfield, NJ 07081
President ....F Duffield Meyercord
Vice Presidents .... Edward G Beimfohr
L Randy Riley
Vice Pres & Sec'y ....Kenneth L Estabrook
Treasurer ....Hilton M Jervey

Bar Harbor Yacht Club
☎ (207) 288-3275
5 Stephens Lane
Bar Harbor, ME 04609-1807

see Summer Social Register

Bath & Tennis Club
☎ (561) 832-4271
1170 S Ocean Blvd
Palm Beach, FL 33480
President ....Fitz Eugene Dixon JR
Vice Pres & Treas ....William C Lickle
Secretary ....William K Norris

Bath & Tennis Club
☎ (847) 234-5001
105 N Green Bay Rd
Lake Bluff, IL 60044
President ....Edmund R McGlynn JR
Vice President...............................Peter Reisner
Secretary .... J William Gimbel III
Treasurer .... Dennis Hurst

Bathing Corporation of Southampton
☎ (516) 283-0545
14 Gin Lane
Southampton, NY *11968*
President ....Montague H Hackett JR
Vice President......................Richard Mortimer
Secretary ....Craigh Leonard
Treasurer ....John W Geary II

Bedford Golf & Tennis Club
☎ (914) 234-7275
Bedford, NY *10506*
President ....John P Renwick III
Vice President.............. MRS Phillips Lounsbery
Secretary .... MRS Joseph L Mankiewicz
Treasurer ....William M Waterman

Bellerive Country Club
☎ (314) 434-4400
12925 Ladue Rd
St Louis, MO *63141*
President ....John S Ross
Vice President........................Ernest C Behnke
Secretary ....Joseph J Gazzoli
Treasurer ....Robert B Karn III

Beverly Yacht Club
☎ (508) 748-0540
99 Water St
PO Box 181
Marion, MA *02738-0181*

see Summer Social Register

Birmingham Country Club
☎ (205) 879-4611
PO Box 130280
New Country Club Rd
Mountain Brook, AL *35213*
President ....James F Hughey JR
Vice President....................James E Popwell JR
Secretary ....Robert A Carr
Treasurer ....Bill Reed

Bogey Club
☎ (314) 993-0161
9266 Clayton Rd
St Louis, MO *63124*
President .... Andrew B Craig III
Vice President........................Richard A Liddy
Secretary ....Andrew Taylor
Treasurer ....John Jordan

Bohemian Club
☎ (415) 885-2440
624 Taylor St
San Francisco, CA *94102-1075*
President ....Paul L Davies JR
Vice President...........................Eric A Pedley
Secretary ....Henry M Duque
Treasurer ....Peter H Zischke
Directors ....Kurt Hauser
Robert D Rossi
Geoffrey T Tayler

The Brook
☎ (212) 753-7020
111 E 54 St
New York, NY *10022*
President ....Michael J Meehan II
Vice President..............William T Ketcham JR
Secretary .... Miner H Warner
Treasurer .... Alexander M Laughlin JR
Ass't Treas...........................John D T Gerber

The Buffalo Club
☎ (716) 886-6400
388 Delaware Av
Buffalo, NY *14202*
President ....Paul E Ruch
Vice Presidents .... DR W Merrick Hayes JR
Edward T Hunt JR
DR Pasquale A Greco
Secretary .... John P Robshaw JR
Treasurer ....Richard O Hopkins

Buffalo Tennis & Squash Club
☎ (716) 884-6048
314 Elmwood Av
Buffalo, NY *14222*
President ....Charles L Yeager
Vice President..........................Philip Celniker
Secretary ....Nelson T Montgomery II
Treasurer ....H George Kreiner II

Buffalo Yacht Club
☎ (716) 883-5900
One Porter Av
Buffalo, NY *14201-1097*

see Summer Social Register

Burlingame Country Club
☎ (415) 696-8100
80 New Place Rd
Hillsborough, CA *94010*
President .... Henry N Kuechler III
Vice Presidents ....James T Curry JR
Rupert H Johnson JR
Secretary .... Robert E Henderson
Treasurer ....James T Curry JR

The Casino
☎ (312) 787-2100
195 E Delaware Place
Chicago, IL *60611*
President .... MRS William W Wirtz
1st Vice President............ Richard H Needham
2d Vice President .... MRS Arthur L Kelly
Secretary .... MRS Barry G Hoyt
Treasurer ....Richard J L Senior

Century Association
☎ (212) 944-0090
7 W 43 St
New York, NY *10036*
President ....Haliburton Fales II
Vice Presidents ....Matt Clark
Elizabeth Barlow Rogers
Sec'y ....Henry Spotswood Fenimore Cooper
Treasurer ....R Dyke Benjamin

Chagrin Valley Hunt Club
☎ (216) 423-4414
Old Mill Rd
Gates Mills, OH *44040*
President ....Courtenay O Taplin
Vice President....................Robert W Gelbach
Secretary ....Robert G Markey
Treasurer ....Walter P Ginn

Chevy Chase Club
☎ (301) 652-4100
6100 Connecticut Av
Chevy Chase, MD *20815*
President .... Henry A Dudley JR
Vice Presidents ....John L Bowles
Daniel J Callahan III
Secretary ....Paul B Cromelin III
Treasurer ....James G Dougherty JR

Chicago Club
☎ (312) 427-1825
81 E Van Buren St
Chicago, IL *60605*
President .... David W Fox
Vice President..................Charles T Brumback
Secretary ....Howard J Trienens
Treasurer ....Thomas P Flanagan

Chicago Yacht Club
☎ (312) 861-7777
Foot of Monroe St
Chicago, IL *60603*

see Summer Social Register

Chilton Club
☎ (617) 266-4860
152 Commonwealth Av
Boston, MA *02116*
President .... MRS Frank O'Brien JR
1st Vice President....... MRS James F Gerrity III
2d Vice President .... MRS Herbert P Dane
Secretary .... MRS Gordon Abbott JR
Treasurer .... MRS M Pierre Tonissi

The Church Club
☎ (212) 988-5452
35 E 72 St
New York, NY *10021*
President ....A Walker Bingham III
Vice Presidents .... MRS C Robert Allen III
Alan F Blanchard
Chauncey G Olinger JR
Secretary .... MISS Adelaide Perry Farah
Treasurer ....Robert D Schumacher

City Tavern Club
☎ (202) 337-8770
3206 M St NW
Washington, DC *20007*
President ....Nicholas D Ward
Vice President.......................... Phillip M Grier
Secretary .... MRS Marie Gilson
Treasurer ....Daniel R Heller

Cold Spring Harbor Beach Club
☎ (516) 692-6540
101 Shore Rd
Cold Spring Harbor, NY *11724*
President ....Ray Schuville
Secretary .... MRS John W Galston
Treasurer .... Rod Thaler

Colonial Dames of America
☎ (212) 838-5489
421 E 61 St
New York, NY *10021*
President .... MRS David A Bird
Vice Presidents .... MRS Robert C Evans JR
MRS Franklin B Tuttle
Rec'g Sec'y .... MRS Robert F Lynch III
Cor Sec'y .... MRS Charles F Morgan
Treasurer .... MRS John H Schlesinger
Ass't Treas.......................... MRS James L Neff

Colonial Dames of America (Chap I--Baltimore, MD)
President .... MRS David B Baker JR
☎ (410) 823-5737
6601 Darnall Rd
Baltimore, MD *21204*
Vice President...... MRS A Rutherfoord Holmes
Cor Sec'y .... MISS Anne R Holmes
Treasurer .... MISS Hyatt H Young

Colonial Dames of America (Chap II--Philadelphia, PA)
President .... MRS C Cresson Wistar
☎ (215) 646-4026
527 Stenton Av
Blue Bell, PA *19422-2126*
1st Vice President........ MRS John L Crittenden
2d Vice President .... MRS J Albury Fleitas
Rec'g Sec'y .... MRS Alfred P Simon
Cor Sec'y .... MRS E Norton Hunt
Treasurer .... MRS John Cadwalader
Registrar................. MRS H Dawson Penniman

Colonial Dames of America (Chap III--Washington, DC)
☎ (202) 244-0199
PO Box 40153
Washington, DC *20016*
President .... MRS Francis J Hughes
Vice Presidents .... MRS Frank M Carter
MRS Robert B Hughes
Rec'g Sec'y .... MRS Gregg E Dougherty
Cor Sec'y .... MISS Christine V Emery
Treasurer .... MRS John J Wilson

Colonial Dames of America (Chap V--San Francisco, CA)
President .... MRS Floyd Stanley Hicks
☎ (415) 583-5603
64 Escanyo Dv
South San Francisco, CA *94080*
Vice President.............. MRS Daniel E Bertram
Rec'g Sec'y .... MRS James E Hults
Treasurer .... MRS Donald L Kleyensteuber

Colonial Dames of America (Chap XII--St Louis, MO)
President .... MRS William Bedford Ford
1209 Belleville
Lebanon, IL *62254*
Vice President........... MRS Bobby L Valentine
Rec'g Sec'y .... MRS Sterling H Schoen
Cor Sec'y .... MRS Paul Mayer
Treasurer .... MRS John V Kelly
Registrar.......................... MRS Joseph Preston

Colonial Dames of America (Chap XIV--Chicago, IL)
☎ (847) 446-7468
509 Elder Lane
Winnetka, IL *60093*
President .... MRS Virgil Vincent Clary
Vice Presidents .... MRS Arthur S Rakestraw JR
MRS Lee Houts
Secretary .... MRS Dennis Pryor JR
Treasurer .... MRS William L Harwood

Colonial Dames of America (Chap XVII--Palm Beach, FL)
President .... MRS Caroline C Seymour
☎ (561) 659-5904
PO Box 2801
Palm Beach, FL *33480*
Vice President......... MRS Louis A Dommerich
Rec'g Sec'y .... MRS Stanley F Reed
Cor Sec'y............... MRS Michael T B Dennis
Treasurer .... MRS David Crichton

Colonial Lords of Manors in America
☎ (212) 289-8471
5 E 93 St
New York, NY *10128*
President ....Timothy Field Beard
1st Vice President.............Henry H Livingston
2d Vice President .... MRS Charles L Fleming
Secretary ....Roger M L Schmitt
Treasurer ....William Willis Reese

Colonial Order of the Acorn
Chancellor................................Sidney Hughes
☎ (212) 838-5632
200 E 66 St, Apt E507
New York, NY *10021-6728*
Treasurer ....John Campbell Henry

Colonial Society of Pennsylvania
215 S 16 St
Philadelphia, PA *19102*
Governor............................John A Baird JR
Deputy Governors .... George C Shafer
Lewis L Neilson JR
Secretary ....J Baldwin Siedlarz III
Treasurer ....Douglass W Hocker

Colony Club
☎ (212) 838-4200
564 Park Av
New York, NY *10021*
President .... MRS Robert E Carroll
Vice Presidents .... MRS David W Peck JR
MRS James B Hurlock
Secretary .... MRS B Hunt Whitbeck JR
Treasurer .... MRS Stephen C Kratovil

Commercial Club
☎ (513) 621-2708
331 E 4 St
Cincinnati, OH *45202*
President ....William A Friedlander
Vice President................... William R Burleigh
Secretary .... Charles D Lindberg
Treasurer .... Eugene P Ruehlmann

Contemporary Club
☎ (312) 944-1330
120 E Bellevue Place
Chicago, IL *60611*
President .... MRS Frank A Priebe JR
1st Vice President...... MRS Jackson W Smart JR
2d Vice President .... MRS Thomas W Heenan
Rec'g Sec'y .... MRS Edward C McNally
Treasurer .... MRS Henry T Chandler

Corinthian Yacht Club
☎ (610) 521-4705
2d & Taylor Sts
Essington, PA *19029*

see Summer Social Register

The Corinthians
☎ (203) 836-1311
PO Box 1623
Darien, CT *06820*

see Summer Social Register

Cosmopolitan Club
☎ (212) 734-5950
122 E 66 St
New York, NY *10021*
President .... MRS John A Millard
Vice Presidents .... MRS Allan J Robbins
MRS Edgar G Lansbury
Secretary .... MRS Allen E Compagno
Treasurer .... MISS Alice C Brown

Cosmopolitan Club
☎ (215) 735-1057
1616 Latimer St
Philadelphia, PA *19103*
President .... MRS Carolyn P Langfitt
Vice Presidents .... MRS McBee Butcher
MISS Carol H Parlett
Secretary .... MISS Dorothy A Hoffman
Treasurer .... MRS Patricia M Morley

Cosmos Club
☎ (202) 387-7783
2121 Massachusetts Av NW
Washington, DC *20008*
President .... MRS Janet L Norwood
Vice President...................... Daniel B Krinsley
Secretary .... Michael Michaelis
Treasurer.................................... Gerald F Tape

The Country Club
☎ (617) 566-0240
191 Clyde St
Brookline, MA *02147*
President ....Noah T Herndon
Secretary .... John M Cornish
Treasurer.............................Frank E Ellsworth

Country Club
☎ (216) 831-9200
2825 Lander Rd
Cleveland, OH *44124-4899*
President ....Lucien B Karlovec JR
Vice President..........................Forrest D Hayes
Secretary ....George R Barry
Treasurer .... Paul E Altig

Country Club of Buffalo
☎ (716) 632-1100
250 N Youngs Rd
Williamsville, NY *14221-5889*
President ....Albert J Wright III
Vice President.................Gregory C Yungbluth
Secretary .... Alexander C Meyer JR
Treasurer ....Peter C Hitchcock

The Courts
☎ (610) 642-0510
101 Old Gulph Rd
Wynnewood, PA *19096*
President .... James O Hubbard
Vice President............. Erik Tank-Nielsen
Secretary .... W Gresham O'Malley III
Treasurer .... Philipp J Walter JR

The Creek
☎ (516) 676-1405
Horse Hollow Rd
Locust Valley, NY *11560*
President .... William F Kenny III
Vice President.........................Robert Gardner
Vice Pres & Sec'y ....John C Thomas JR
Treasurer.............................James B Patterson

**Dames of the Loyal Legion of the
United States of America
(State of New York)**
President .... MISS Helen Leale Harper
Vice Presidents .... MRS Louis F Bishop III
MRS Robert A Gale
Secretary .... MRS Jerome J Caulfield
☎ (203) 869-7780
35 Stanwich Rd
Greenwich, CT *06830*
Treasurer .... MRS Edgar W Hatfield

Daughters of the Cincinnati
☎ (212) 319-6915
122 E 58 St
New York, NY *10022*
President .... MRS Thomas B Hynson Brown JR
Vice President....... MRS Charles S Whitman JR
Secretary .... MRS William M Manger
Treasurer .... MRS Cordelia C Richards

Dedham Country and Polo Club
☎ (617) 326-6210
124 Country Club Rd
PO Box 430
Dedham, MA *02027-0430*
President .... Arthur W Gregory III
Vice President.................. Thomas D Bushman
Secretary ....J Lincoln Passmore
Treasurer ....John B Gray

Delray Beach Yacht Club
☎ (561) 272-2700
110 MacFarlane Dv
Delray Beach, FL *33483*

see Summer Social Register

**Descendants of the Signers of the
Declaration of Independence, Inc**
President-General .... Allan McA Heyward
☎ (804) 740-8352
202 N Mooreland Rd
Richmond, VA *23229-7102*
1st Vice Pres-Gen'l .... Philip S Pyne
2d Vice Pres-Gen'l....................F Nelson Light
Sec'y-Gen'l........ MRS William D Gottwald JR
Treas-Gen'l............................William Ward IV

Devon Yacht Club
☎ (516) 267-6340
Devon Rd
Amagansett, NY *11930*

see Summer Social Register

Dillon Yacht Club
PO Box 4308
Dillon, CO *80435-4308*

see Summer Social Register

Eastern Yacht Club
☎ (617) 631-1400
Foster St
Marblehead, MA *01945*

see Summer Social Register

Edgartown Reading Room, Inc
☎ (508) 627-4466
PO Box 1393
Edgartown, MA *02539*
President ....Peter E Guernsey
Vice President.....................John E MacKenty
Treasurer ....Arthur Yorke Allen
Clerk ....Robert J Whipple

Edgartown Yacht Club
☎ (508) 627-4361
PO Box 1309
One Dock St
Edgartown, MA *02539*

see Summer Social Register

The Edgeworth Club
☎ (412) 741-8500
511 East Dv
Edgeworth, Sewickley, PA *15143*
President ....Arthur L Coburn III
Vice President..........................Robert W Gray
Sec'y-Treas ....D Edward Stouffer

Elkridge Club
☎ (410) 377-9200
6100 N Charles St
Baltimore, MD *21212*
President ....Charles W Cole JR
Vice President..........................Ralph N Willis
Secretary ....Thomas Schweizer
Treasurer ....John A Luetkemeyer JR

Essex County Club
☎ (508) 526-7311
School St
Manchester, MA *01944*
President .... Denison M Hall
Secretary .... MRS Jane McConnell
Treasurer ....R Douglas Hall III

Essex Hunt Club
☎ (908) 234-0062
Holland Rd
Peapack, NJ *07977*
President ....Philip J Bowers III
Secretary .... MRS James R Lamb
Treasurer ....James G Hall II

Essex Yacht Club
☎ (860) 767-8121
19 Novelty Lane
Essex, CT *06426*

see Summer Social Register

The Everglades Club, Inc
☎ (561) 655-7810
356 Worth Av
Palm Beach, FL *33480*
President ....John M Reynolds III
Vice President.....................James C Alban JR
Secretary ....Robert L Terry
Treasurer ....Richard P Scott

The Family
☎ (415) 781-0800
545 Powell St
San Francisco, CA *94108*
President ....O Greg Linde
Secretary ....Edmund Bartlett
Treasurer ....William J Griffin

Fishers Island Club
☎ (516) 788-7225
Fishers Island, NY *06390*
President ....Richard W Goss II
Vice Presidents ....Harris B Parsons
                                            Charles G Arnold
Secretary ....Robert White Parsons
Treasurer ....W Page Wodell

Fishers Island Yacht Club
☎ (516) 788-7036
PO Box 141
Fishers Island, NY *06390*

see Summer Social Register

Fishing Bay Yacht Club
☎ (804) 740-0597
PO Box 7327
Richmond, VA *23221*

see Summer Social Register

Fourth Street Club
☎ (215) 545-6597
1519 Locust St
Philadelphia, PA *19102*
President ....Robert Glendinning II
Vice President.........................James M Smartt
Secretary ....Radcliffe Cheston
Treasurer ....Frank E Rutan IV

Fox Chapel Golf Club
☎ (412) 967-9081
426 Fox Chapel Rd
Pittsburgh, PA *15238*
President ....W Duff McCrady
Vice President........... G Nicholas Beckwith III
Secretary ....Edward W Seifert
Treasurer ....F Gordon Kraft

The Francisca Club
☎ (415) 781-1200
595 Sutter St
San Francisco, CA *94102*
President .... MRS Kenneth G Berry
1st Vice Pres.......... MRS Michael A O'Hanlon
2d Vice Pres .... MRS Thomas B Malarkey JR
Rec'g Sec'y .... MRS Geoffrey T Tayler
Cor Sec'y...................... MRS Daniel B Gale II
Treasurer .... MRS Thomas Klitgaard

Franklin Inn Club
☎ (215) 732-0334
205 S Camac St
Philadelphia, PA *19107*
President ....Nathan Sivin
Vice President................. MRS Milton Rothman
Secretary ....Milton Rothman
Treasurer ....Samuel Feinberg

The Friday Club
President .... MRS John W Cameron
1st Vice Pres................. MRS Leslie DeGroot
2d Vice Pres .... MRS Lawrence Howe
Rec'g Sec'y .... MRS Joseph Beale
Cor Sec'y..................... MRS Morris S Weeden
                                            111 E Ridge Lane
                                            Lake Forest, IL *60045*
Treasurer .... MRS F Conrad Fischer

The Garret Club
☎ (716) 885-6010
91 Cleveland Av
Buffalo, NY *14222*
President .... MRS John F Cant
Vice Presidents .... MRS Charles F Kreiner
                                 MRS Theodore R Sanders
Rec'g Sec'y .... MRS William E Francisco JR
Cor Sec'y........................ MRS Paul J Koessler
Treasurer .... MRS Reginald V Williams JR

The Germantown Cricket Club
☎ (215) 438-9900
411 Manheim St
Philadelphia, PA *19144*
President ....Sheldon Goldberg
Vice President.......................... MRS Jean Park
Secretary .... MISS Karen Du Brul
Treasurer ....Harvey Kolodner

Gibson Island Club
☎ (410) 255-1414
Gibson Island, MD *21056*
President ....David B Baker III
Vice President............................. James S Farr
Secretary .... MRS William J Launder
Treasurer .... John B Richardson III

Great Lakes Cruising Club
☎ (312) 372-2344
20 N Wacker Dv, Suite 1540
Chicago, IL 60606

see Summer Social Register

Green Spring Valley Hunt Club
☎ (410) 363-0433
30 Green Spring Valley Rd
Owings Mills, MD 21117
President .... Francis Graham Riggs
Secretary .... Richard O Beall
Treasurer .... Thomas F Obrecht

Grolier Club
☎ (212) 838-6690
47 E 60 St
New York, NY 10022
President .... William B Warren
Vice President.................. William T Buice III
Secretary .... MISS Caroline L Smith
Treasurer .... R Dyke Benjamin

Gulph Mills Golf Club
☎ (610) 828-0717
200 Swedeland Rd
King of Prussia, PA 19406
President .... David Wilmerding
Vice President.................. Edward T Goodman
Secretary .... Albert C Oehrle
Treasurer .... John C van Roden

Harvard Club of Boston
☎ (617) 536-1260
374 Commonwealth Av
Boston, MA 02215
President .... Glenn M Johnson
Vice Presidents .... James H Anderson
MISS Karen M Van Winkle
Secretary .... William Shaw McDermott
Treasurer .... James V Young

Harvard Club of New York City
☎ (212) 840-6600
27 W 44 St
New York, NY 10036
President .... Peter S Heller
Vice Presidents .... MRS J Sinclair Armstrong
Michael G Yamin
Kenneth G Standard
Secretary .... Charles T Lee
Treasurer .... Richard M Broad

Harvard-Radcliffe Club of Philadelphia
☎ (610) 649-8894
425 Glyn Wynne Rd
Haverford, PA 19041
President .... Michael Cullina
Vice President....................... Alfred W Putnam
Secretary .... Edward J Kaier
Treasurer .... Charles Dunne

The Holland Society of New York
☎ (212) 758-1675
122 E 58 St
New York, NY 10022
President .... Roland H Bogardus
Secretary .... REV Louis O Springsteen
Treasurer .... Peter Van Dyke

The Huguenot Society of America
☎ (212) 755-0592
122 E 58 St
New York, NY 10022
President .... William Willis Reese
Vice Presidents .... Harlan B Hamilton
MRS Dennis D McCrary
Secretary .... MRS John K Armstrong
Treasurer .... Courtney A Haff

Ida Lewis Yacht Club
☎ (401) 846-1969
Box 479, Wellington Av
Newport, RI 02840

see Summer Social Register

Indian Harbor Yacht Club, Inc
☎ (203) 869-2484
710 Steamboat Rd
Greenwich, CT 06830

see Summer Social Register

Indian Hill Club
☎ (847) 251-1711
1 Indian Hill Rd
Winnetka, IL 60093
President .... John M Dixon
Vice President....................... Allan E Bulley JR
Secretary ....John B Snyder
Treasurer .... Peter B McNitt

Intown Club
☎ (216) 621-0422
1375 Euclid Av
Cleveland, OH 44115
President .... MRS Osman K Mawardi
Vice President...................... MRS Ridley Watts
Secretary .... MRS William C Daley JR
Treasurer .... MRS John Sherwin JR

The Kirtland Country Club
☎ (216) 942-4400
39438 Kirtland Rd
PO Box 966
Willoughby, OH 44094-0966
President .... Arthur D Baldwin II
Vice President........................... John F Herrick
Secretary .... William R Stewart
Treasurer .... Donald J Dailey

Knickerbocker Club
☎ (212) 838-6700
807 Fifth Av
New York, NY 10021
President ....John Pierrepont
Vice President...................... Grant F Winthrop
Secretary .... Marco Grassi
Treasurer .... Michael Hamilton Davis

The Leash
☎ (212) 838-0114
41 E 63 St
New York, NY 10021
President .... Nathaniel B Day
Vice President........................... Howard S Buck
Secretary .... John H Flahive
Treasurer .... Michael R Bruce

The Lenox Club
☎ (413) 637-0030
111 Yokun Av
Lenox, MA 01240
President .... B Carter White
Vice President...................... Richard S Jackson
Secretary .... MRS Bayard Kellam
Treasurer .... Jonas Dovydenas

The Links
☎ (212) 838-8181
36 E 62 St
New York, NY 10021
President .... Peter L Shea
Vice President................... Stephen M McPherson
Vice Pres & Sec'y .... Whitney D Pidot
Treasurer .... John T Fogarty

Log Cabin Club
☎ (314) 993-0154
1140 Log Cabin Lane
St Louis, MO 63124
President .... James L Hoagland
Vice Presidents .... Andrew N Baur
Orrin S Wightman III
Secretary .... Hugh Scott III
Treasurer .... Patrick J Behan

The Long Island Wyandanch Club
☎ (516) 325-0580
PO Box 63
Eastport, NY *11941*
President .... Victor C McCuaig JR
Vice President.............Lawrence B Van Ingen
Secretary ....Peter L Shea
Treasurer .... Alexander B Slater

Longue Vue Club
☎ (412) 793-2232
400 Longue Vue Dv
Verona, PA *15147*
President ....Guy L Warman
Vice President....................Thomas A Gaitens
Secretary .... Donald G Lauck
Treasurer .... John Dickinson

Maidstone Club
☎ (516) 324-0510
PO Box 5110
East Hampton, NY *11937*
President ....Richard W Smith JR
Vice President............. CTE Loic de Kertanguy
Secretary .... MRS Robert B Kyle JR
Treasurer ....Peter L Smith

Manchester Yacht Club
☎ (508) 526-4595
Tuck's Point Rd
Manchester, MA *01944*

see Summer Social Register

Maryland Club
☎ (410) 727-2323
1 E Eager St
Baltimore, MD *21202*
President .... Richard C Riggs JR
Vice President..............................Allan J Mead
Secretary ....George Beall
Treasurer ....Mark R Fischer

**Massachusetts Society of Mayflower
Descendants**
☎ (617) 266-1624
376 Boylston St
Boston, MA *02116*
Governor................................Robert W Parker
Deputy Governor........ MISS Linda W Siciliano
Secretary .... MRS Annette P Sechen
Treasurer ....C Whitney Clayton JR

**The Massachusetts Society of the Order of
the Founders and Patriots of America, Inc**
☎ (617) 367-0998
60 State Street, Ste 2200
Boston, MA *02109-1803*
Governor ....Charles A Hubbard II
Deputy Governor................. Richard C Wright
Secretary ....Rush B Lincoln JR
Treasurer ....Thaddeus F Bell

Mayfield Country Club
☎ (216) 381-0826
1545 Sheridan Rd
South Euclid, OH *44121*
President .... William E MacDonald III
Vice President.............................. H Gene Nau
Secretary ....Ronald H Neill
Treasurer.......................................Dale B King

Meadow Brook Club
☎ (516) 935-6500
PO Box 58, Cedar Swamp Rd
Jericho, NY *11753*
President ....Elbridge T Gerry JR
Vice Presidents ....C Nicholas Potter
Robert A Geddes
Secretary ....Belden Frease
Treasurer ....Charles R Thompson

Merion Cricket Club
☎ (610) 642-5800
Montgomery Av
Haverford, PA *19041*
President ....Paul B Bartle
Vice Presidents .... MRS Constance Satterfield
John H Thacher JR
Thomas A Williams
Secretary .... MRS Claudia C McIlvain
Treasurer .... Andrew R Nehrbas

Merion Golf Club
☎ (610) 642-5600
450 Ardmore Av
Ardmore, PA *19003*
President ....M Rust Sharp
Vice Presidents .... J Thomas Ligget JR
Alexander Ewing
Secretary ....Thomas W Murrell III
Treasurer .... William Bates JR

The Metropolitan Club
☎ (202) 835-2500
1700 H St NW
Washington, DC *20006*
President ....W Reid Thompson
Vice President................Charles G Mackall JR
Secretary ....Frederick P Hitz
Treasurer ....Thomas U Dudley II

Metropolitan Opera Club
☎ (212) 799-3552
Lincoln Center
New York, NY *10023*
President ....Garrison W Brinton
Vice President.....................Edward A Hansen
Secretary .... MRS Elizabeth L Battle
Treasurer .... G William Haas

Miami Valley Hunt & Polo Club
☎ (513) 293-2311
5152 Lamme Rd
Dayton, OH *45439*
President ....Bruce Benedict
Vice President........................... Tyler Messick
Secretary ....Charles Shook
Treasurer ....J Ramsey McGregor

**Military Order of Foreign Wars
(New York Commandery)**
☎ (212) 751-5168
122 E 58 St
New York, NY *10022*
Commander....................William Willis Reese
Vice Commanders .... Thomas J Morrissey
Frederick A Parker JR
Austin N Volk
Secretary .... William A Winant III
Treasurer .... John C Straton JR

**Military Order of Foreign Wars
(Pennsylvania Commandery)**
Commander.................Jack Thomas Tomarchio
Vice Commanders .... Andrew R Sullivan
Henry R Bilhuber
David J Urban
O Daniel Ansa
Secretary ....James F Mitchell III
☎ (610) 525-8890
726 Waverly Rd
Bryn Mawr, PA *19010*
Treasurer ....Douglass W Hocker

**Military Order Loyal Legion of the US
(Maryland Commandery)**
Commander..........................Nathan J Winslow
9703 Oak Summit Av
Baltimore, MD *21234*
Vice Cdr................. COL Samuel A Rittenhouse
Recorder.......................... DR Edward F Cooper
Treasurer .... Bernard J Sweeney

Military Order Loyal Legion of the US (New York Commandery)
☎ (212) 758-2297
44 E 57 St
New York, NY 10022
Commander........................... David L Dalva II
Sr Vice Commander.......... John E Connelly III
Jr Vice Commander................John W Pershing
Recorder.................................... Malcolm Smith
Treasurer.................................. Gerald F Fisher

Military Order Loyal Legion of the US (Pennsylvania Commandery)
☎ (215) 546-2425
1805 Pine St
Philadelphia, PA 19103
Commander....................... Lewis L Neilson JR
Sr Vice Cdr.................... Benjamin C Frick JR
Jr Vice Cdr .... Herbert K Zearfoss
Recorder .... John J W F McFadden
Treasurer .... Thomas F Adams III

The Misquamicut Club
☎ (401) 348-8577
PO Box 2086
Westerly, RI 02891
President ....William T Vogt
Vice Presidents .... Thomas D O'Connor
Thomas W Smith
Daniel P Nugent
Secretary ....Chaplin Bradford Barnes
Treasurer .... Francis P Jenkins JR

Moraine Country Club
☎ (513) 294-6200
4075 Southern Blvd
Dayton, OH 45429
President ....Hugh E Wall III
Vice President...................... Joseph R Lehman
Secretary ....W Anthony Huffman
Treasurer ....Robert S Laing JR

Morris County Golf Club
☎ (201) 539-7200
Punchbowl Rd
Convent Station, NJ 07961
President ....Thompson H McDaniel
Vice President........................Robert C Smith
Secretary .... Richard E Doremus
Treasurer ....William P Henry

The Morristown Club
☎ (201) 539-0116
27 Elm St
Morristown, NJ 07960
President ....Harry G Carpenter
Vice President........................Anthony G Wahl
Secretary ....Gordon A Millspaugh JR
Treasurer ....James C Collins

Mount Vernon Club
☎ (410) 837-3240
8 W Mt Vernon Place
Baltimore, MD 21201
President .... MRS Frank B Ober JR
Vice President............. MRS James D Hardesty
Cor Sec'y..................... MRS Ogden C Gorman
Treasurer .... MRS Edward W Campbell JR

Myopia Hunt Club
☎ (508) 468-4433
435 Bay Rd
South Hamilton, MA 01982
President ....John W McKean
Secretary ....Benjamin H Moore
Treasurer ....Brehon S Griswold

Nantucket Yacht Club
☎ (508) 228-1400
S Beach St
PO Box 667
Nantucket, MA 02554

see Summer Social Register

National Golf Links of America
☎ (516) 283-0410
Sebonac Inlet Rd
Southampton, NY 11968
President ....S Parker Gilbert
Vice Pres & Ass't Treas.........John F Horn
William H Black
Secretary ....T David Mullen
Treasurer ....R Peter Sullivan III

National Society of Colonial Dames in the State of New York
☎ (212) 744-3572
215 E 71 St
New York, NY 10021-4501
President .... MRS David C Fuchs
Vice Presidents .... MRS Roland J Hawkins
MRS Thomas B Hynson Brown JR
Rec'g Sec'y .... MRS Blair W Smith
Cor Sec'y .... MRS Zissimos A Frangopoulos
Treasurer .... MRS Joseph J Steuert

National Society of Colonial Dames of America in California
☎ (415) 441-7512
2645 Gough St
San Francisco, CA 94123
President .... MISS Margaret T McCaul
Vice President.............. MRS Craig A Stephens
Secretary .... MRS Gilman Haynes JR
Treasurer .... MRS Rolf Scherman

National Society of Colonial Dames of America in the Commonwealth of Massachusetts
☎ (617) 742-3190
55 Beacon St
Boston, MA 02108
President .... MRS Burgess P Standley
Vice Presidents ...... MRS Hollis W Plimpton JR
MRS Richard E Gustavson
Rec'g Sec'y .... MRS Robert G Crocker
Treasurer .... MRS Frederick W Martin

National Society of Colonial Dames of America in the Commonwealth of Pennsylvania
☎ (215) 735-6737
1630 Latimer St
Philadelphia, PA 19103
President .... MRS Putnam T Stowe
Vice Presidents .... MRS Richard W Billings
MRS Richard M Armstrong JR
MRS Edmund H Robinson
MRS Edgar R Taylor JR
Cor Sec'y .... MRS Edmund B Spaeth JR
Treasurer .... MRS Henry H Kohl

National Society of Colonial Dames of America in the District of Columbia
☎ (202) 337-2288
2715 Que St NW
Washington, DC 20007
President .... MISS Joan C Stansbury
Vice Presidents .... MRS Thomas J Comp JR
MRS George A Caldwell JR
MRS Peter T Russell
Cor Sec'y .... MRS Barbara M Burns
Treasurer .... MISS Martha C Peter

National Society of Colonial Dames of America in the State of Illinois
☎ (312) 944-1330
120 E Bellevue Place
Chicago, IL 60611-1112
President .... MISS Diane Curtis
Vice President............. MRS Clyde W Reighard
Cor Sec'y .... MRS J Jay Nichols
Treasurer .... MRS Rudolf E Knepper

National Society of Colonial Dames of America in the State of Maryland
☎ (410) 837-3267
Mount Clare Museum House
Carroll Park
Baltimore, MD 21230
President .... MRS James W Wilson
Vice Presidents .... MRS George A Hughes
MRS Philip H Grantham
MRS Cornelia Peyton Fowler
Secretary .... MRS S Alexander Tubman IV
Treasurer .... MRS William O Doub

National Society of Colonial Dames of America in the State of Missouri
President .... MRS Francis C Corley
☎ (314) 991-5680
51 Magnolia Dv
St Louis, MO *63124-1554*
Vice Presidents ...... MRS Shadrach F Morris JR
MRS Pierce W Powers
Rec'g Sec'y .... MISS Jeannette C Rodemyer
Cor Sec'y .... MRS Edward L O'Neill JR
Treasurer .... MRS J John Brouk

National Society of Daughters of the American Revolution
☎ (202) 628-1776
1776 D St NW
Washington, DC *20006*
President General........ MRS Charles K Kemper
1st Vice Pres General .... MRS Dale K Love

New England Society in the City of New York
☎ (212) 752-1938
122 E 58 St
New York, NY *10022*
President .... Frederick A Parker JR
Vice Presidents ....George A Doyle JR
MRS Cornelia Hamilton Greenspan
William Willis Reese
Secretary .... Clarence Harvey Kelley
Treasurer .... S Scott Nicholls JR

New York Society of the Order of Founders and Patriots of America
PO Box 6158, FDR Station
New York, NY *10150*
Governor ....Noble Gregory Pettit
Deputy Governor ....Frederick F Kellogg JR
Secretary .... Ernst Rothe
Cor Sec'y ....Nelson V Harper JR
Treasurer ....Noble Gregory Pettit

New York State Society Descendants of the Signers of the Declaration of Independence
President .... Carter B Worth
1st Vice Pres .... MRS James A Harper
163 E 81 St
New York, NY *10028*
2d Vice Pres .... MISS Elisabeth H O'Connor
Treasurer .... MRS Hunter Brown

New York Yacht Club
☎ (212) 382-1000
37 W 44 St
New York, NY *10036*

see Summer Social Register

Newport Reading Room
☎ (401) 846-0480
29 Bellevue Av
Newport, RI *02840*
President .... Tylor Field II
Secretary .... James B Callahan
Treasurer ....Brian G Bardorf
House Chairman ....E MacGregor Strauss

Noonday Club
☎ (314) 231-8452
1 Metropolitan Square, Ste 4000
St Louis, MO *63102*
President .... Alfred H Kerth III
Vice President....................... Robert B Karn III
Secretary ....John K Pruellage
Treasurer .... Michael H Lane

Norfolk Hunt
☎ (508) 785-1206
PO Box 242, Centre St
Dover, MA *02030*
President ....James E Loer JR
Joint Masters.................. MRS Albert Andersen
MRS John E Sheldon
Secretary .... MRS William E Ternes
Treasurer .... Nicholas LaVerghetta

The Northeast Harbor Fleet
☎ (207) 276-5101
South Shore Rd
Northeast Harbor, ME *04662*

see Summer Social Register

Onwentsia Club
☎ (847) 234-0120
300 N Green Bay Rd
Lake Forest, IL *60045*
President .... C H Randolph Lyon
Vice Presidents .... Thomas B Hunter III
Lawrence C Ross
Secretary .... Timothy C Coleman
Treasurer .... Thomas C O'Neil

The Pacific-Union Club
☎ (415) 775-1234
1000 California St
San Francisco, CA *94108-2204*
President ....John A Sproul
Vice President.......................Richard F Shelton
Secretary ....William H Banker
Treasurer .... Brayton Wilbur JR

The Penn Club
☎ (215) 743-4070
1522 Overington St
Philadelphia, PA *19124-5808*
President .... Anthony H Murray JR
Vice President................... Charles D Shields JR
Sec'y-Treas .... George Chimples

The Pennsylvania Society of the Order of the Founders and Patriots of America
Governor .... Richard A Scudder
Deputy Governor ....Truman H Newberry
Secretary ....Thomas R Kellogg
☎ (610) 644-6152
2248 Yellow Springs Rd
Malvern, PA *19355*
Treasurer ....Ward S Curtiss

The Pepper Pike Club
☎ (216) 831-9400
2800 SOM Center Rd
Cleveland, OH *44124*
President ....A William Reynolds
Vice President.......................James M Biggar
Secretary ....Fred D Kidder
Treasurer .... Earl F Molloy

Pequot Yacht Club
☎ (203) 255-5749
669 Harbor Rd
Southport, CT *06490*

see Summer Social Register

The Philadelphia Club
☎ (215) 735-5924
1301 Walnut St
Philadelphia, PA *19107*
President ....Alfred W Putnam JR
Secretary .... Alexander Kerr
Treasurer ....Harry R Madeira JR
House Chairman ....William R Klaus

Philadelphia Cricket Club
☎ (215) 247-6001
415 W Willow Grove St
Philadelphia, PA *19118*
President .... James S Walker
Vice Presidents .... MRS Allen Harberg
John E Jennings
Secretary .... William S Colehower
Treasurer ....Richard E DeGennaro

Pickering Hunt
President .... DR Henry Snedden
Vice President .... Benjamin F Leaman
Secretary .... Barry N Snader
☎ (610) 827-7742
Conestoga Pike, Rte 401
Chester Springs, PA *19425*
Treasurer .... Frederick H von Czoernig

The Pilgrims of the United States
☎ (212) 943-0635
80 Broadway
New York, NY *10005*
President .... Hugh Bullock
Vice Presidents .... Grayson L Kirk
Paul Moore JR
Elliot L Richardson
Secretary .... Herbert Brownell
Treasurer .... John R Drexel III

Piping Rock Club
☎ (516) 676-2332
150 Piping Rock Rd
Locust Valley, NY *11560*
President .... Thomas M Bancroft JR
Vice Presidents .... Henry P U Harris JR
Randolph Harrison
Secretary .... J Hamilton Crawford JR
Ass't Sec'y .... MRS James M Duryea
Treasurer .... Gilbert W Chapman JR
Ass't Treas .... Philip B Pool JR

The Pittsburgh Golf Club
☎ (412) 621-4530
5280 Northumberland St
Pittsburgh, PA *15217*
President .... MRS Henry H Armstrong
Vice Pres & Treas .... David McL Hillman
Secretary .... MRS John C Unkovic

The Players
☎ (212) 475-6116
16 Gramercy Park
New York, NY *10003*
President .... Michael Allinson
Vice Presidents .... Aaron Frankel
Herbert Blodgett
Secretary .... William Thom
Treasurer .... Theodore L Manekin

Princeton Club
☎ (212) 596-1200
15 W 43 St
New York, NY *10036-7497*
President .... Daniel P Lieblich
Vice Presidents .... Wayne A Comer
MRS Kathleen L Strother
George F Schmucki
Secretary .... Clyde E Rankin III
Treasurer .... Alexander Farman-Farmaian

Princeton Club
☎ (215) 896-0138
701 Hunt Lane
Flourtown, PA *19031*
President .... Donald H Roberts JR
Vice President .... James A Bennett
Secretary .... Richard K Stevens JR
Treasurer .... Stephen E Stambaugh

Queen City Club
☎ (513) 621-2708
331 E 4 St
Cincinnati, OH *45202*
President .... John J Schiff SR
Vice President .... Oliver W Waddell
Secretary .... William R Burleigh
Treasurer .... Lyle J Everingham

The Rabbit
☎ (215) 473-0875
Belmont Av & Christ Church Lane
Philadelphia, PA *19131*
President .... Richard T Nalle JR
Sec'y-Treas .... Henry E Crouter

Racquet Club
☎ (312) 787-3200
1365 N Dearborn P'kway
Chicago, IL *60610*
President .... Richard M Norton
Vice President .... John J Borland JR
Secretary .... Ronald F Young
Treasurer .... Christopher K Hehmeyer

Racquet Club
☎ (314) 361-2100
476 N Kingshighway Blvd
St Louis, MO *63108*
President .... John R Fox
Vice Presidents .... J Curtis Engler
Robert E Sherwood
Secretary .... Frederick J Oertli
Treasurer .... Michael R Liesmann

Racquet Club
☎ (215) 735-1525
215 S 16 St
Philadelphia, PA *19102*
President .... John W McNamara
Vice Presidents .... Walter L Foulke
Stephen G Park
Secretary .... Harry T Hare
Treasurer .... Edward J Reitmeyer

Racquet & Tennis Club
☎ (212) 753-9700
370 Park Av
New York, NY *10022*
President .... John D Soutter
Vice President .... Richard Mortimer
Secretary .... Winthrop Rutherfurd JR
Treasurer .... John W Mettler III

Radnor Hunt
☎ (610) 644-4439
826 Providence Rd
Malvern, PA *19355*
President .... Samuel W M Griffin
Vice President .... Thomas J Gorman
Secretary .... Donald B Wilkins JR
Treasurer .... MRS Arthur C Olsen

Rappahannock River Yacht Club
☎ (804) 438-6650
PO Box 55
Irvington, VA *22480*

see Summer Social Register

Rittenhouse Club
☎ (215) 563-1771
1811 Walnut St
PO Box 15906
Philadelphia, PA *19103*
President .... N Ramsay Pennypacker
Vice Presidents .... Boyd Lee Spahr
Charles J McManus JR
Secretary .... Alvan Markle III
Treasurer .... Christian Hueber II

River Club
☎ (212) 751-0100
447 E 52 St
New York, NY *10022*
President .... William E Jackson
Vice Presidents .... MRS John M Stewart
Jonathan J Bush
Secretary .... MRS Thomas J Devine
Treasurer .... Thomas N McCarter III

Rolling Rock Club
☎ (412) 238-9501
Ligonier, PA *15658*
President .... Albert H Burchfield III
Vice Presidents .... Andrew W Mathieson
Edwin F Scheetz JR
Sec'y-Treas .... John W Douglas JR

Royal Bermuda Yacht Club
☎ (441) 295-2214
Albouys Point
PO Box HM 894
Hamilton, Bermuda HM DX

see Summer Social Register

Rumson Country Club
☎ (908) 842-3333
163 Rumson Rd
Rumson, NJ *07760*
President .... Niels M Johnsen
Vice Pres & Sec'y .... Rodney N Houghton
Treasurer .... Joseph J Fahey

Saddle & Cycle Club
☎ (773) 275-6600
900 W Foster Av
Chicago, IL *60640*
President .... Robert W Thomas
Vice President .... Ronald J Allen
Secretary .... MRS Peter Elliott
Treasurer .... John D Stanhaus

**St Andrew's Society
of the State of New York**
☎ (212) 397-4849
3 W 51 St
New York, NY *10019-6909*
President .... Victor E Stewart
Vice Presidents .... Roderick E Kerr JR
Sean S Macpherson
Secretary .... Francis F Bodkin JR
Treasurer .... David S Andrews

St Anthony Club
☎ (607) 272-3344
PO Box 876
Ithaca, NY *14851*
Administrator .... Peter McChesney

St Anthony Club
215 S 16 St
Philadelphia, PA *19102*
President .... David V Peake
Vice President .... Alexander T Cook
Secretary .... David W Wood
Treasurer .... Charlton Yarnall II

St Botolph Club
☎ (617) 536-7570
199 Commonwealth Av
Boston, MA *02116*
President .... Donald D Babcock
Vice Presidents .... William H Berman
MRS Patricia L Chute
Vice Pres & Treas .... Ronald G Sampson
Secretary .... James H Crissman

St Elmo Club
☎ (215) 222-9876
3627 Locust Walk
Philadelphia, PA *19104*
President .... Christian Hueber II
Vice President .... John P H Holton
Secretary .... MISS Mary Ann McClatchy
Treasurer .... David S J Smith

St Francis Yacht Club
☎ (415) 563-6363
On the Marina
San Francisco, CA *94123*

see Summer Social Register

St Louis Country Club
☎ (314) 994-0011
400 Barnes Rd
St Louis, MO *63124*
President .... John E Mackey
Vice Presidents .... Donald Danforth JR
Orrin S Wightman III
Secretary .... Stephen C Jones
Treasurer .... James M Snowden JR

St Nicholas Society
☎ (212) 753-7175
122 E 58 St
New York, NY *10022*
President .... William R Miller
Vice Presidents .... Lansing R Palmer
John Milnes Baker
Samuel D Williams
William Willis Reese
Secretary .... Norman F Nelson
Treasurer .... Donald G Allison

San Diego Yacht Club
☎ (619) 221-8400
1011 Anchorage Lane
San Diego, CA *92106-3005*

see Summer Social Register

San Francisco Golf Club
☎ (415) 469-4100
Junipero Serra & Brotherhood Way
San Francisco, CA *94132*
President .... Charles R Schwab
Vice President .... J Robert Lehman
Secretary .... Brooks Walker JR
Treasurer .... Thomas A Morton

Saratoga Reading Rooms
☎ (518) 584-1539
PO Box 1452
Saratoga Springs, NY *12866-0885*
President .... G Watts Humphrey JR
Vice President .... Daniel G Van Clief JR
Secretary .... Joseph E Aulisi
Treasurer .... John T von Stade

Saturn Club
☎ (716) 884-8800
977 Delaware Av
Buffalo, NY *14209*
Dean .... George F Phillips JR
Vice Dean .... Thomas C Bailey
Registrar .... Peter M Stevens
Bursar .... Charles J Hahn
House Chairman .... Robert Lang Miller

Seabright Lawn Tennis & Cricket Club
☎ (908) 842-0624
PO Box 233
Shrewsbury, NJ *07701*
President .... Herwig W Kogelnik
Vice Presidents .... Harkness G De Voe
MRS Mary Lou Strong
Membership Sec'y .... MRS Mary Lou Strong
Rec'g Sec'y .... Richard M Eittreim
Treasurer .... Christopher Henderson

Seawanhaka Corinthian Yacht Club
☎ (516) 922-6200
314 Yacht Club Rd
Centre Island
Oyster Bay, NY *11771*

see Summer Social Register

Sedgeley Club
☎ (215) 765-3585
15 Kelly Dv
Philadelphia, PA *19130*
President .... MRS Francis W De Serio
Vice President .... MRS A Richard Bell JR
Rec'g Sec'y .... MRS Jacob H Vastine III
Cor Sec'y .... MRS Harold L Johnson
Treasurer .... MRS Gary A Horn

Shoreacres
☎ (847) 234-1470
PO Box 246
Lake Bluff, IL 60044
President .... Donald B Davidson
Vice Pres & Treas ....Christopher Burke
Secretary ....Mark M Heatwole

Singing Beach Club
☎ (508) 526-4965
117 Beach St
PO Box 44
Manchester, MA 01944
President .... Charles S Bird III
Secretary .... Steven R Holt
Treasurer ....Mark K Brislin

Skycastle French Hounds
Chairman.......................................Stephen Hoyt
Vice Chairman.................. R Barrie Slaymaker
Secretary .... MRS Daniel B Wessells
☎ (610) 942-4383
781 Fairview Rd
Glenmoore, PA 19343
Treasurer .... Murray Halton
Master .... James Fagan Scharnberg

Society of California Pioneers
☎ (415) 957-1849
PO Box 191850
San Francisco, CA 94119-1850
President .... Gerald C Davalos
Vice President..........................James C Flood
Secretary .... David Cebalo
Treasurer .... Robert H Goldsmith

Society of the Cincinnati
☎ (202) 785-2040
2118 Massachusetts Av NW
Washington, DC 20008
President-General ....William McG Matthew
Vice Pres-Gen'l .... William R Raiford
Sec'y-Gen'l...........................Andrew P Miller
Treas-Gen'l................................ Jay W Jackson

Society of the Cincinnati--California
☎ (707) 538-4171
6293 Meadowridge Dv
Santa Rosa, CA 95409
President .... Peter S Wheeler
Vice President............Richard H Breithaupt JR
Secretary ....John R Justice
Treasurer ....Horace R Boynton III
Chaplain..........................Benjamin C Allin IV

Society of the Cincinnati--Connecticut
President .... Peter W North
Vice President..................... DR David F Musto
Secretary ....George D Selden
☎ (860) 536-0563
14 Brandon Lane
Mystic, CT 06355
Treasurer .... COL Harold G Holcombe JR

Society of the Cincinnati--Delaware State
President ....Charles S Maddock
Vice President................... Herbert K Zearfoss
Secretary ....G Forrest Pragoff
414 Burnt Mill Rd
Chadds Ford, PA 19317
Treasurer ....E Morris Davis IV

Society of the Cincinnati--Maryland
☎ (410) 339-7270
7800 York Rd, Ste 370
Towson, MD 21204
President ....Leslie E Goldsborough JR
Vice President.........................Brian W Brooke
Secretary ....Frank K Turner JR
Treasurer ....William A Fisher III

Society of the Cincinnati--Massachusetts
President ....Warren M Little
Vice President....................Christopher Hussey
Secretary ....J Archer O'Reilly III
☎ (617) 738-9640
160 Thorndike St
Brookline, MA 02146
Treasurer .... Kenneth S Safe JR

Society of the Cincinnati--New York State
Mount Gulian
145 Sterling St
Beacon, NY 12508
President ....George Boyd V
Vice President..........................Kent M Brown
Secretary .... Benjamin B McAlpin III
Treasurer ....Eugene W Potter JR

Society of the Cincinnati--Pennsylvania
President ....H Bartholomew Cox
Vice President........................Robert H Sproat
Secretary ....Lewis S Graham JR
5016 Gayman Rd, RD 7
Doylestown, PA 18901
Treasurer ....John C Tuten JR

Society of Colonial Wars in the Commonwealth of Massachusetts
☎ (617) 357-1776
101 Tremont St, Ste 608
Boston, MA 02108-5004
Governor...............................Kenneth M Hills
Deputy Governor ....Robert P Clark
Secretary ....Donald C Carleton JR
Treasurer .... E Russell Peach JR

Society of Colonial Wars in the Commonwealth of Pennsylvania
☎ (215) 836-7738
The Union League of Philadelphia
140 S Broad St
Philadelphia, PA 19102-3083
Governor.............................. William J Clothier
Deputy Governor ....William L Hires
Secretary ....James W Johnstone
Treasurer ....Charles J Ingersoll II

The Society of Colonial Wars in the State of Florida
PO Box 3097
Palm Beach, FL 33480
Governor.....................................Allan W Ferrin
Deputy Governor ....Joseph A Atkinson
Secretary ....David H Morrish
Treasurer ....Hewitt A Conway

Society of Colonial Wars in the State of Illinois
☎ (847) 657-4011
3600 W Lake Av
Glenview, IL 60025-5811
Governor.................................Donald R Weber
Deputy Governor .... Albert H Tippens JR
Secretary .... Howell E Browne
Treasurer ....Barry J Carroll

Society of Colonial Wars in the State of Missouri
Governor............................... David Q Wells JR
Secretary ....Clarkson Carpenter III
4646 Pershing Place
St Louis, MO 63108
Treasurer .... David C Wisland

Society of Colonial Wars in the State of New York
☎ (212) 755-7082
122 E 58 St
New York, NY 10022
Governor...................................John Badman III
Deputy Governor ....William T Ketcham JR
Secretary ....James B Gardiner II
Treasurer ....Horace B B Robinson

Society of Colonial Wars in the State of Texas

☎ (210) 349-9896
7500 Callaghan Rd, No 234
San Antonio, TX 78229
Governor .... Paul Woolman Adams
Deputy Governor .... Frank Sutherland-Hall
Lt Governor .... David H Peterson
Sec'y-Treas .... Thomas F Bresnehen JR

Society of Daughters of Colonial Wars in the Commonwealth of Massachusetts, Inc

President .... MRS Henry P Mucciaccio
Vice President................... MRS Oscar W Harp
Cor Sec'y .... MRS Daniel Ledegang
14 Thompson St
Dedham, MA 02026-4911
Treasurer .... MRS Alexander J Smith JR

Society of Daughters of Holland Dames

Directress Gen'l........ MRS Alexander O Vietor
Cor Sec'y .... MRS John B Glass JR
1158 Fifth Av
New York, NY 10029
Treasurer .... MRS Ernest P Brinkley JR

Society of Mayflower Descendants in the Commonwealth of Pennsylvania

280 Upper Gulph Rd
Wayne, PA 19087-2416
Governor .... Frederick T J Clement JR
Ass't Governor .... Stacy B C Wood JR
Secretary .... MISS Janet A Springer
Treasurer .... Norman P Robinson

Society of Mayflower Descendants in the State of Illinois

☎ (847) 255-5219
115 N Forest Av
Mt Prospect, IL 60056
Governor .... MRS Charles O'Keefe
Deputy Governor .... David Hall
Cor Sec'y .... Jon N Austin
Treasurer .... MRS Jan A Stortz

Society of Mayflower Descendants in the State of New York

☎ (212) 759-1620
122 E 58 St
New York, NY 10022
Governor .... Robert P Morse
Deputy Governor .... William Willis Reese
Secretary .... MRS Daniel T Le V Coleman
Treasurer .... Walter R Brewster JR

Society of the War of 1812 in the Commonwealth of Pennsylvania

President .... Forrest R Schaeffer
Vice Presidents .... Herbert K Zearfoss
David H Kollock JR
William H Cowper
Secretary .... Richard R Di Stefano
☎ (610) 896-9229
425 Haverford Rd
Wynnewood, PA 19096
Treasurer .... Richard A Weller

Society of the War of 1812 in the State of Maryland

☎ (410) 666-9097
905 Saxon Hill Dv
Cockeysville, MD 21030
President .... Lawrence B Chambers
Vice Presidents .... Eugene N Moore JR
Willis C Tull JR
Nathan J Winslow
Cor Sec'y .... LT COL Stanley L Howard
Treasurer ...... BRIG GEN M Hall Worthington JR

Society of the War of 1812 New York Division

President .... Thomas E Bird
PO Box 630189
Little Neck Hills, NY 11363-0189
Sec'y-Registrar .... John Mauk Hilliard
Treasurer .... William Willis Reese

Somerset Club

☎ (617) 227-1731
42 Beacon St
Boston, MA 02108
President .... Richard L Tucker
Secretary .... Francis L Coolidge
Treasurer .... Richard B Boardman

Somerset Hills Country Club

☎ (908) 766-0043
Box 180, Mine Mount Rd
Bernardsville, NJ 07924
President .... John A Scully
Vice President.............................. John C Hartz
Secretary .... MRS James R Lamb
Treasurer .... Robert D Johnson

Sons of the American Revolution New York Chapter

☎ (212) 206-1776
47 Fifth Av
New York, NY 10003
President .... Robert J Stackpole
1st Vice President........... COL David J Ramsay
2d Vice President .... James C Jaegers
3d Vice President .... Thomas D Lovely
Secretary .... P Layton Sanders JR
Treasurer .... Christian S Johnson

Sons of the American Revolution Philadelphia-Continental Chapter

President .... F Russell Greenspan
Vice Presidents .... Winchell S Carroll
William J Yearsley
Secretary .... George F Mohr
☎ (610) 688-3886
217 Gulf Creek Rd
Radnor, PA 19087-3719
Treasurer .... Richard J Randolph

Sons of the American Revolution San Francisco Chapter

President .... Clarence E Lucas
Vice Presidents .... Robert D Ebert
Philip H Speck
DR Vernon C Harp JR
Secretary .... James O Schuyler
898 Cordilleras Av
San Carlos, CA 94070
Treasurer .... Richard N Andriano-Moore
Registrar.................................... Robert D Ebert

Sons of the Revolution in the Commonwealth of Massachusetts

President .... André R Sigourney
Vice President....................... Asa E Phillips III
Secretary .... Charles A Hubbard II
☎ (617) 444-2231
4 Colonial Rd
Dover, MA 02030
Treasurer ....David J Gray

Sons of the Revolution in the State of Maryland

☎ (410) 560-1853
8 Sawgrass Court
Lutherville, MD 21093-7000
President .... Kendall S Young
Vice President................ Frank P L Somerville
Secretary .... William F Yonkers
Treasurer ....John H Highby

Sons of the Revolution in the State of New York

☎ (212) 425-1776
54 Pearl St
New York, NY 10004
President .... William T Livingston III
Vice President..................... Warren J McEntee
Secretary ....Michael P Coneys
Treasurer .... Richard L N Weaver

Sons of the Revolution
(Pennsylvania Society)
☎ (215) 545-1888
215 S 16 St
Philadelphia, PA *19102*
President .... Walter J Maiden
Secretary .... Richard R Di Stefano
Treasurer .... Benjamin C Frick

Southampton Club
☎ (516) 283-0500
PO Box 1247
Southampton, NY *11969-1247*
President .... G Bruce Leib
Vice President............... Edward P Sharretts JR
Sec'y-Treas .... Arthur B Schoen JR

Southampton Yacht Club
☎ (516) 283-9888
Little Neck Rd, PO Box 833
Southampton, NY *11969*

see Summer Social Register

Spouting Rock Beach Association
☎ (401) 847-1900
Ocean Av
Newport, RI *02840*
President .... John G Winslow
Secretary .... Charles B Grosvenor
Treasurer .... Kenneth W Washburn

State in Schuylkill
Governor .... G Morris Dorrance JR
Secretary ....Charles H Davis
☎ (610) 688-9085
150 Biddulph Rd
Radnor, PA *19087*
Treasurer ....T Sergeant Pepper

Strathalbyn Farms Club
☎ (314) 441-1281
552 Old Wolfrum Rd
Weldon Spring, MO *63303*
President .... David M Woods
Vice President.................... Hiram S Liggett JR
Secretary ....William T Crowell
Treasurer ....George P Dorris III

Sulgrave Club
☎ (202) 462-5800
1801 Massachusetts Av NW
Washington, DC *20036*
President .... MRS Richard G Brown
1st Vice Pres .... MRS John Edgar Chapoton
2d Vice Pres .... MRS Robert B Smith JR
Rec'g Sec'y .... MISS M Jan Clark Holderness
Cor Sec'y .... MRS Peter T Russell
Treasurers .... MRS John A Shaw
MRS Ardon B Judd

Sunnybrook Golf Club
☎ (610) 828-9617
398 Stenton Av
Plymouth Meeting, PA *19462*
President ....Gordon W Gerber
Vice Presidents ....John Bromley JR
Ross L Campbell
Secretary .... G Daniel O'Donnell
Treasurer ....John P Gallagher

Tavern Club
☎ (617) 338-9682
4 Boylston Place
Boston, MA *02116*
President ....Francis W Hatch JR
Vice President...........................James L Terry
Secretary .... Charles W Hare
Treasurer ....John L Gardner

Tavern Club
☎ (216) 431-3220
3522 Prospect Av
Cleveland, OH *44115*
President ....Ralph B Webster
Vice President......................Henry Ott-Hansen
Sec'y-Treas ....Robert Y White JR

Tennis & Racquet Club
☎ (617) 536-4630
939 Boylston St
Boston, MA *02115*
President ....Devens H Hamlen
Secretary .... Richard L Brickley JR
Treasurer ....Francis J Hughes JR

Town & Country Club
☎ (415) 362-4951
218 Stockton St
San Francisco, CA *94108*
President .... MRS Edward J Taaffe
Vice President............ MRS Terence J O'Reilly
Secretary .... MRS Stacy R Mettier JR
Treasurer .... MRS Robert Tuller

Tuxedo Club, Inc
☎ (914) 351-4791
West Lake Rd
Tuxedo Park, NY *10987*
Chairman...........................Jonathan E Romero
Secretary ....Edwin J Wheeler
Treasurer ....James F Smith

The Twentieth Century Club
☎ (412) 621-2353
4201 Bigelow Blvd
Pittsburgh, PA *15213*
President .... MRS Frank L Wiegand
Vice Presidents .... MRS David M Curry
MRS Peter Stipanovich
Cor Sec'y .... MRS Douglas P Dick
Treasurer .... MRS Curtiss F Berry

Union Boat Club
☎ (617) 742-1520
144 Chestnut St
Boston, MA *02108*
President .... David E Winship
Vice President.....................Charles F Kane JR
Secretary ....Samuel D Perry
Treasurer .... Eugene H Clapp III

Union Club
☎ (617) 227-0589
8 Park St
Boston, MA *02108*
President ....Buckman McPeek
Vice Presidents ....Peter G Fallon JR
Richard M Harter
Gordon Smith
Secretary ....Harold I Pratt
Treasurer ....Carl F Jenkins

Union Club
☎ (212) 734-5400
101 E 69 St
New York, NY *10021*
President ....John A Millard
Vice President.............Richard W Pendleton JR
Secretary ....Bryan Webb
Treasurer ....Wilmot H Kidd III

The Union Club Company
☎ (216) 621-4230
1211 Euclid Av
Cleveland, OH *44115*
President ....George M Humphrey II
Vice Presidents ....George J Dunn
Henry Ott-Hansen
Secretary ....William L Ziegler
Treasurer ....Alexander S Taylor II

The Valley Hunt Club
☎ (818) 793-7134
520 S Orange Grove Blvd
Pasadena, CA *91105*
President .... Thomas S Jones
Vice President........................ Sidney F Tyler JR
Secretary .... MRS William K Doyle
Treasurer .... MRS Philip J Koen

Veteran Corps of Artillery Constituting the Military Society of the War of 1812
☎ (212) 249-3919
643 Park Av
New York, NY *10021*
Commandant....... MAJ GEN John E Connelly III
Vice Commandant..... BRIG GEN Ralph A Olson
Chief of Staff................. COL Henry J Bedlivy
Adjutant .... MAJ Arnold Albert

Watch Hill Yacht Club
☎ (401) 596-4986
Watch Hill, RI *02891*

see Summer Social Register

Waynesborough Country Club
☎ (610) 296-2122
440 Darby-Paoli Rd
Paoli, PA *19301*
President .... MISS Helen B Leaman
Vice President........................Richard I Greene
Secretary .... Philip C Burtoft
Treasurer .... William G McDowell

The Welcome Society of Pennsylvania
President ....Andrew F Webster
Vice Presidents .... MRS Joseph B Siedlarz JR
MRS H Fairfax Leary
Richard Jenkins
Secretary .... MRS Sara Lees March
☎ (215) 732-2322
415 S Croskey St
Philadelphia, PA *19146*
Treasurer .... William N Potts

Westminster Kennel Club
☎ (212) 682-6852
230 Park Av, Ste 644
New York, NY *10017*
President ....Chester F Collier
Vice President......................Robert V Lindsay
Secretary ....Thomas J Hubbard
Treasurer .... Peter R Van Brunt

Wilmington Club
☎ (302) 658-4287
1103 N Market St
Wilmington, DE *19801*
President .... Willard A Speakman III
Vice President........................Walter J Laird JR
Secretary ....John E Riegel
Treasurer ....Wendell Fenton

Woman's Athletic Club
☎ (312) 944-6123
626 N Michigan Av
Chicago, IL *60611*
President .... MRS Helen D Miller
Vice Presidents .... MRS Thomas E Cronin
MRS George A Bay
MRS Ronald Wolff
MRS John P McGowan
Rec'g Sec'y .... MRS John K Notz JR
Cor Sec'y .... MRS John A Daniels
Treasurer .... MRS Jeffry J Knuckles

Yale Club
☎ (212) 661-2070
50 Vanderbilt Av
New York, NY *10017*
President ....Frederick A Leone
Vice President.................. Henry de F Baldwin
Secretary ....Charles S Guggenheimer
Treasurer .... Kurt C Jomo

Yale Club
PO Box 28513
Philadelphia, PA *19149*
President ....Jeffrey L Pettit
Vice President..........................Neil P Hoffman
Secretary .... MISS Elizabeth M Ahrens
Treasurer ....Rafael A Porrata-Doria JR

Yeamans Hall Club
☎ (803) 744-3351
PO Box 9455
Charleston, SC *29410*
President ....Samuel W Fleming III
Vice President.............................James J Ford
Secretary ....Henry L Terrie JR
Treasurer ....John W Noble JR

Ye Buz Fuz Club
☎ (513) 223-6612
2860 Kettering Tower
Dayton, OH *45423*
Sergeant .... Thomas I Stephens
Benchers .... Irvin G Bieser JR
Robert M Connelly
Allan L Johnston JR
Joseph M Williams